ENCYCLOPÆDIA
BRITANNICA

MACROPÆDIA

The Encyclopædia Britannica
is published with the editorial advice
of the faculties of the University of Chicago;
a committee of persons holding
academic appointments at the universities
of Oxford, Cambridge, London, and Edinburgh;
a committee at the University of Toronto;
and committees drawn from members of the faculties
of the University of Tokyo
and the Australian National University.

THE UNIVERSITY OF CHICAGO

"Let knowledge grow from more to more
and thus be human life enriched."

The New
Encyclopædia
Britannica

in 30 Volumes

MACROPÆDIA
Volume 18

Knowledge in Depth

FOUNDED 1768
15TH EDITION

Encyclopædia Britannica, Inc.
William Benton, Publisher, 1943–1973
Helen Hemingway Benton, Publisher, 1973–1974
Chicago/London/Toronto/Geneva/Sydney/Tokyo/Manila/Seoul

Taylor, Frederick Winslow

The inscription "Frederick W. Taylor, Father of Scientific Management" appears on the grave marker of the U.S. inventor and engineer who introduced fundamental reforms in management practices. At a time when power-driven machines were beginning to have revolutionary effects in the countries of the West, he developed a means of improving the quality of industrial management by viewing it as an art based upon scientific principles. Universal in concept, his system, called scientific management, has influenced the development of virtually every country enjoying the benefits of modern industry.

Taylor.

Taylor was born in Philadelphia on March 20, 1856, the son of a lawyer. His early education included study at Germantown Academy and a European trip with his mother. Intending to follow his father's profession, he entered Phillips Exeter Academy in New Hampshire in 1872; he led his class scholastically and excelled in baseball as pitcher and team captain. After passing the entrance examination for Harvard, he was forced to abandon plans for matriculation, as his eyesight had deteriorated from night study. With sight restored in 1875, he was apprenticed to learn the trades of patternmaker and machinist at the Enterprise Hydraulic Works in Philadelphia.

Three years later he went to the Midvale Steel Company, where, starting as a machine shop labourer, he became successively shop clerk, machinist, gang boss, foreman, maintenance foreman, head of the drawing office, and chief engineer.

In 1881, at 25, he and a tennis partner won the National Doubles Championship; the same year he introduced time study at the Midvale plant. The profession of time study was founded on the success of this project, which also formed the basis for Taylor's subsequent theories of management science. Essentially, Taylor suggested that production efficiency in a shop or factory could be greatly enhanced by close observation of the individual worker and elimination of waste time and motion in his operation. Though the Taylor system provoked resentment and opposition from labour when carried to extremes, its value in rationalizing production was indisputable and its

Time and motion study

impact on the development of mass-production techniques immense.

Studying at night, Taylor earned a degree in mechanical engineering from Stevens Institute of Technology in 1883. The following year he became chief engineer at Midvale and completed the design and construction of a novel machine shop. In 1884 he also married Louise Spooner. Taylor might have enjoyed a brilliant fulltime career as an inventor—he had more than 40 patents to his credit—but his interest in what was soon called scientific management led him to resign his post at Midvale and to become general manager of the Manufacturing Investment Company (1890–93), which in turn led him to develop a "new profession, that of consulting engineer in management." He served a long list of prominent firms ending with the Bethlehem Steel Corporation; while at Bethlehem, he developed high-speed steel and performed notable experiments in shoveling and pig-iron handling.

At 45 Taylor declared that he could no longer afford to work for money, and he retired, partly also for reasons of health. He continued, however, to devote time and money to promote the principles of scientific management through lectures at universities and professional societies. From 1904 to 1914, with his wife and three adopted children, Taylor lived in Philadelphia. For recreation, he grew roses, transplanted huge box trees in his garden, and, developing an enthusiasm for golf, built one of the first putting greens with natural ground contours. (His innovative putter with the shape of a capital Y was, however, banned by the U.S. Golf Association.)

The American Society of Mechanical Engineers elected him president in 1906, the same year that he was awarded an honorary doctor of science degree by the University of Pennsylvania. Many of his influential publications first appeared in the *Transactions* of that society, namely, "Notes on Belting" (1894); "A Piece-rate System" (1895); "Shop Management" (1903); and "On the Art of Cutting Metals" (1906). *The Principles of Scientific Management* was published commercially in 1911.

Taylor's fame increased after his testimony in 1912 at the Hearings Before a Special Committee of the House of Representatives to Investigate the Taylor and Other Systems of Shop Management. Considering himself a reformer, he continued expounding the ideals and principles of his system of management until his death from pneumonia on March 21, 1915, in Philadelphia, 18 days after his last lecture in Cleveland, Ohio.

BIBLIOGRAPHY. FRANK BARKLEY COPLEY, *Frederick W. Taylor: Father of Scientific Management*, 2 vol. (1923), is a comprehensive and historical portrayal of the ancestry, boyhood, education, career, and contributions to scientific management of Frederick Winslow Taylor.

(J.F.Me.)

Tchaikovsky, Peter Ilich

Among the most subjective of composers, Peter Ilich Tchaikovsky and his music are inseparable. His work is a manifestation, sometimes charming, often showy, and occasionally vulgar, of repressed feelings that became more and more despairing in later years and culminated in the composition of the *Sixth Symphony*, one of the greatest symphonic works of its time. Though unequal, his music shows a wealth of melodic inspiration and imagination and a flair for orchestration. Its lapses of taste are partly redeemed by enormous technical efficiency. Though his later work rejected conscious Russian nationalism, its underlying sentiment and character are as distinctively

Tchaikovsky, 1888.
Novosti Press Agency

Russian as that of the Russian nationalist composers. Tchaikovsky's success in bridging the gulf between the musician and the general public partly accounts for the exalted position he enjoys in the U.S.S.R.

Early life and education. Tchaikovsky was born on May 7 (April 25, old style), 1840, in Russia at Votkinsk (now in the Udmurt A.S.S.R), where his father was superintendent of government-owned mines. Because his mother was half French, and it was a customary practice among upper-class Russians of the period, he had a French governess. Tchaikovsky was musically precocious, but his interest in the subject was not actively encouraged because his parents considered that it had an unhealthy effect on an already neurotically excitable child. He adored his governess, but she was dismissed in 1848 when his father changed his post and moved to Moscow and then to St. Petersburg (Leningrad), where the boy entered the preparatory department of the School of Jurisprudence in 1850. There he was obviously disturbed by being treated as a "country bumpkin," but soon settled down happily.

His state of mind was more seriously affected in 1854 when he was 14 and his mother, whom he loved with all the ardour of an acutely introspective child, died of cholera. To alleviate the distress caused to him both by her death and by his easygoing father's comparative indifference to it, he composed a short waltz for piano and even thought of composing an opera. His abnormal love for his now-deceased mother and the ineffectualness of his father did nothing to hinder his latent homosexuality, and the disciplinary regime of the all-male School of Jurisprudence cannot have helped. There is, however, no evidence of his having given any active outlet to his secret desires. During these school days, desultory singing, piano and harmony lessons were all the musical education he received, complemented by increasingly numerous visits to the opera, which had a lasting influence on his musical taste.

Entry into the St. Petersburg Conservatory

He entered the newly founded St. Petersburg Conservatory of Music in 1862. His job as a clerk in the Ministry of Justice was hardly interesting enough to prevent his increasing absorption with music. A tale is told of his absentmindedly tearing pieces from an official document, munching at them steadily, and recovering his senses only to find that he had consumed them altogether. He soon left the government service and became a music student. His first orchestral score (composed, 1864), an overture based on Aleksandr Ostrovsky's play The Storm, is remarkable in showing many of the stylistic features later to be associated with his music and a youthful vulgarity that was not the only constituent in it to appal his primly Mendelssohnian teacher, Anton Rubinstein. Even so, he was offered in late 1865 a post as professor of harmony by Rubinstein's brother at the Moscow Conservatory.

Career. Tchaikovsky settled down comfortably in Moscow in January 1866, although he underwent a mental crisis as a consequence of overwork on his Symphony No. 1 in G Minor (Winter Daydreams), Opus 13 (1866). His compositions of the late 1860s and early 1870s reveal a distinct affinity with the music of the nationalist group of composers in St. Petersburg, both in their treatment of folk song and in their harmonies deriving from a common link with Mikhail Glinka, the "father" of a Russian nationalist style. He corresponded with the leader of the group, Mily Balakirev, at whose suggestion he wrote a fantasy overture, Romeo and Juliet (1869). Tchaikovsky's intrinsic charm, testified to by many who knew him, is nowhere more apparent than in the nationalist comic opera Vakula the Smith (1874; first performed, 1876), which in its revised form, Cherevichki (The Little Shoes), is of similar merit to another opera, Sorochintsy Fair (also based on one of Nikolay Gogol's Ukrainian tales), by the most original composer in the Petersburg group, Modest Mussorgsky. Tchaikovsky's opera, however, is much closer to Balakirev's own folkloric idiom than anything Mussorgsky ever wrote.

After a fleeting, but unsuccessful, love affair with Désirée Artôt, the prima donna of a visiting Italian opera company, he had only one further romantic relationship with a woman. In the mid-1870s, he had another nervous breakdown. One of the symptoms of this nadir in his life was almost hysterical activity in composition culminating in the Symphony No. 4 in F Minor, Opus 36 (1877), and the opera Eugene Onegin (1877–78) based on a poem by Pushkin, with whose heroine Tatyana he felt in such sympathy that when a former music student, Antonina Milyukova, became infatuated with him, threatening suicide should he reject her, he identified her in his mind with the cruelly spurned Tatyana and consented to marry her. He must have subconsciously known all along that an unconsummated marriage was hardly likely to be successful, but it was doubly unfortunate that his wife should have been a nymphomaniac who repelled him to such an extent that he made an abortive attempt at suicide. He now fully realized that in the eyes of society he was permanently to be a sexual outcast. He loved children but would never have any of his own. He was to live the rest of his life in frustration and loneliness alleviated only by occasional heavy drinking and by composition. Even the happy summers spent at his sister's house at Kamenka in the Ukraine were later spoiled by an overwhelming sense of guilt when he fell in love with her son, his young nephew "Bob" (Vladimir) Davydov.

Marriage

Meanwhile, he had begun late in 1876 an extraordinary correspondence with an admirer of his compositions, Nadezhda von Meck, a wealthy widow, who settled upon him an annuity sufficient to allow Tchaikovsky to give up his teaching post and devote himself entirely to composition. By her wish, the two never met. Their intimate correspondence was more revealing of her than of Tchaikovsky. Compelled by a necessity to be liked, he was always apt to write what he thought people wanted to read rather than what he really thought. The detailed program of his Fourth Symphony, which he made up especially for her, for example, is generally regarded with circumspection. He later averred that replying to her frequently effusive letters had become "irksome." All the same, this curious relationship apparently fulfilled a deeply felt psychological need for both, particularly for Tchaikovsky, whose wife, proving importunate even after a separation had been arranged, had to be bought off. The platonic relationship with Mme von Meck was much more to his taste.

Correspondence with Nadezhda von Meck

His attempts to justify to himself her generous annuity were the cause of his overproduction of the next few years, which included some of his drier compositions— the Piano Sonata in G Major, Opus 37 (1878), the orchestral Suite No. 1 in D Minor, Opus 43 (1878–79), music for the coronation of his patron the emperor Alexander III, and the first of his mature attempts to write a commercially successful opera, The Maid of Orleans (1878–79), for he never imagined that Eugene Onegin was dramatic enough in the "theatrical" sense to be a popular success. The years 1878 to 1881 also included several major achievements: the sparkling *Violin Concerto in D Major*, Opus 35 (1878), and the popular *Serenade for Strings in C Major*, Opus 48 (1880); *Capriccio italien*, Opus 45 (1880), and the *1812 Overture*, Opus 49 (1880). *Onegin*, which was only a token success at its Moscow première, enjoyed great popularity in St. Petersburg because of the tsar's admiration. The *Manfred Symphony*, Opus 58, composed in 1885, not only called forth unstinted praise but showed in some of its histrionically despairing episodes the path that Tchaikovsky's life and music were to follow in the last years.

In 1885 he bought a house of his own at Maidanovo in the vicinity of Moscow, where he lived until the year before his death, when he moved into the house that is now the Tchaikovsky House Museum in the nearby town of Klin. He began to travel more in Russia, spending two particularly delightful vacations in the Caucasus, where he was enthusiastically feted at Tbilisi. He overcame an aversion to conducting, with successful performances of the newly revised *Vakula*, and in 1888 he undertook an important foreign tour, directing his own works in Leipzig (where he met the composers Johannes Brahms and Edvard Grieg), Hamburg, Berlin, Prague, Paris, and London. His music was well received everywhere.

The great foreign tour

This tour was the apex of Tchaikovsky's later life. From then on, in spite of the continuing success of many of his former compositions and the acclamation of new ones, including his second Pushkin opera, *The Queen of Spades*, and his favourite ballet, *The Sleeping Beauty* (first received coolly; both performed 1890), he was working his way toward another nervous breakdown. His major compositions, starting with *Symphony No. 5 in E Minor*, Opus 64 (1888), became more and more intense and emotional, filled with hysterical exaltation and neurotic despair.

Tchaikovsky went on further tours, including the United States and England, where he conducted his popular *Piano Concerto No. 1 in B Flat Minor*, Opus 23 (composed, 1874–75), in 1889 and his *Fourth Symphony* in 1893. In 1893 he was also awarded at Cambridge an honorary degree of doctor of music. These and other successes, including the tumultuous reception accorded to the suite he hastily made for concert performance from his *Nutcracker* ballet music (1892), did not alter the inexorable decline in his mental condition, which was aggravated in 1890 when Nadezhda von Meck suddenly ended both their correspondence and the annuity. From a financial standpoint, however, this hardly mattered because the royalties from *The Queen of Spades* covered the loss without difficulty, and he was by this time a recipient of a state pension. Tchaikovsky never forgave her for her behaviour, and the nature of the psychological wound it inflicted upon him can be judged by the fact that in the delirium of his last illness he repeated her name again and again in indignant tones.

His last work

Tchaikovsky completed his *Symphony No. 6 in B Minor*, Opus 74, which was his last and which he rightly regarded as a masterpiece, in August 1893. In October he conducted its first performance in St. Petersburg but was disappointed with its reception. Its novel slow finale could hardly have been expected to induce such applause as had greeted, only 1½ years before, the première of the lighter *Nutcracker* suite. Yet perversely, Tchaikovsky did expect it and was determined to make an issue of it with himself. Into this work, with its "secret" program, he had put his whole soul, and the public did not appreciate it. In spite of an epidemic of cholera in St. Petersburg and although he complained of feeling unwell, he drank a glass of unboiled water. He died of the disease on November 6. Whether or not he had already contracted the disease before he drank the water, the rumour was soon rife that he had really committed suicide as a result of the failure of his last symphony, whose very title, *Pathétique*, if nothing else, was enough to ensure instant notoriety in the context of the composer's mysterious death.

Assessment. No composer since Tchaikovsky has suffered more from changes of fashion or from the extremes of over- and undervaluation. On the one hand, he achieved an enormous popularity with a very wide audience, largely through his more emotional works; on the other, the almost hypnotic effect that he was able to induce led to serious questioning of his true musical quality. It appears plausible that time will add to, rather than diminish, his stature, if only because performances, recordings, and publications have disclosed that there are fine works of Tchaikovsky still to be discovered. He is certainly the greatest master of the classical ballet, demonstrated by *Swan Lake* (1877) and the symphonically conceived *Sleeping Beauty* (1890). The six symphonies may be variable in quality but all contain important music. The last three are deservedly famous, though to these should be added the neglected *Manfred Symphony*. The *First Piano Concerto* and the *Violin Concerto*, on the other hand, deserve a higher reputation than vehicles for virtuosity. Notable among his other orchestral works are the early *Romeo and Juliet Overture* and the exquisite *Serenade for Strings*. Of the operas, *Eugene Onegin* is a masterpiece and *The Queen of Spades* dramatically effective. His string quartets are excellent but his piano music is largely undistinguished. His numerous songs include several fine examples.

MAJOR WORKS
Theatre music

OPERAS: *Voyevoda* (first performed 1869); *Undine* (1869); *Oprichnik* (1874); *Vakula the Smith* (1876); *Eugene Onegin* (1879); *The Maid of Orleans* (1881); *Mazepa* (1884); *Cherevichki* (*The Little Shoes*, 1887; revised version of *Vakula the Smith*); *The Sorceress* (1887); *The Queen of Spades* (1890); *Iolanta* (1892).

BALLETS: *Swan Lake* (1877); *The Sleeping Beauty* (1890); *The Nutcracker* (1892).

Instrumental music

SYMPHONIES: Seven symphonies, including *No. 2 in C Minor* (*Little Russian*), op. 17 (composed 1872, revised 1879); *No. 3 in D Major*, op. 29 (1875); *No. 5 in E Minor*, op. 64 (1888); *No. 6 in B Minor* (*Pathétique*), op. 74 (1893); and the *Manfred*, op. 58, based on Byron's drama and unnumbered (1885).

SOLO AND ORCHESTRA (PIANO): Three concertos—*No. 1 in B Flat Minor*, op. 23 (1874–75); *No. 2 in G Major*, op. 44 (1879–80); and *No. 3 in E Flat Major*, op. 75 (1893; one movement only). (VIOLIN): *Concerto in D Major*, op. 35 (1878). (CELLO): *Variations on a Rococo Theme*, op. 33 (1876); *Pezzo capricioso*, op. 62 (1887).

OTHER ORCHESTRAL WORKS: Overture to Ostrovsky's play *The Storm*, op. 76 (1864); symphonic poem, *Fate*, op. 77 (1868); fantasy-overture, *Romeo and Juliet*, 3 versions (1869, 1870, and 1880); fantasy, *Francesca da Rimini*, op. 32 (1876); *Marche slave*, op. 31 (1876); *Serenade for Strings in C Major*, op. 48 (1880); *Capriccio italien*, op. 45 (1880); *1812 Overture*, op. 49 (1880); overture-fantasy, *Hamlet*, op. 67a (1888); suite from *The Nutcracker* ballet, op. 71a (1892); 3 orchestral suites.

Chamber music

Three string quartets; one trio; one sextet (*Souvenir de Florence*, op. 70; composed 1890–92); various pieces for violin and piano; various sets with the title "Pieces"; two sonatas.

Vocal music

SONGS: About 100 songs, including "Don Juan's Serenade," op. 38, no. 1 (1878); "Mid the Din of the Ball," op. 38, no. 3 (1878); "None but the Lonely Heart," op. 6, no. 6 (1869); "Why Did I Dream of You?" op. 28, no. 3 (1875). VOCAL DUETS: Six duets (1880).

BIBLIOGRAPHY. Major catalogs of Tchaikovsky's compositions may be found in GERALD ABRAHAM, *Tchaikovsky* (1944); and (ed.), *Tchaikovsky: A Symposium* (1945); EDWIN EVANS, *Tchaikovsky*, rev. ed. (1966), shortly to be replaced by EDWARD GARDEN, *Tchaikovsky* (in prep.), with a select Russian bibliography. All Tchaikovsky's memorabilia, together with collections of correspondence and sketchbooks, may be found in the Tchaikovsky museum at Klin near Moscow. His complete correspondence is now in the process of being published. See *The Diaries of Tchaikovsky*, trans. with notes by WLADIMIR LAKOND (1945); ROSA NEWMARCH, *Tchaikovsky: His Life and Works*, rev. ed. (1908); and MODEST TCHAIKOVSKY, *The Life and Letters of Peter Ilich Tchaikovsky* (1905), an abbreviated and severely edited English version by ROSA NEWMARCH from the definitive Russian volume of 1900–02. A definitive modern biography is HERBERT WEINSTOCK, *Tchaikovsky* (1943).

(E.J.C.G.)

Teacher Education

While arrangements of one kind or another for the education of the young have existed at all times and in all societies, it is only recently that schools have emerged as distinctive institutions for this purpose on a mass scale, and teachers as a distinctive occupational category. Parents, elders, priests, and wise men have traditionally seen it as their duty to pass on their knowledge and skills to the next generation. As Aristotle put it, the surest sign of wisdom is a man's ability to teach what he knows. Knowing, doing, teaching, and learning were for many centuries, and in some societies are still today, indistinguishable from one another. For the most part the induction of the young into the ways of acting, feeling, thinking, and believing that are characteristic of their society has been an informal—if serious and important—process, accomplished chiefly by means of personal contact with full-fledged adults, by sharing in common activities, and by acquiring the myths, legends, and folk beliefs of the culture. Formal ceremonies, such as the puberty rite, marked the point at which it was assumed that a certain range of knowledge and skill had been mastered and that the individual could be admitted to full participation in tribal life. (Residual elements of such ceremonies remain in some modern arrangements; it has been seriously contended that the study of the Latin language in the Renaissance and post-Renaissance school can be interpreted as a form of puberty rite.) Even in the formally established schools of the Greek city-states and of the medieval world there was little separation between, on the one hand, the processes of organizing and setting down knowledge and, on the other, those of teaching this knowledge to others.

This does not mean that prior to the 19th century little attention was given to a training in teaching methods as distinct from "subjects." The great works of medieval scholasticism were essentially textbooks, designed to be used for the purpose of teaching. Today, as in the medieval world, methods of teaching and the organization of knowledge continue to be reciprocally influential. Nor are the problems that today surround the qualifications and certification of teachers wholly new. State, church, and local authorities everywhere have long recognized the importance of the teacher's work in maintaining or establishing particular patterns of social organization and systems of belief, just as radical and reformist politicians and thinkers have looked to the schools to disseminate their particular brands of truth. In medieval and post-Reformation Europe, for example, there was considerable concern with the qualifications and background of teachers, mainly but not entirely with reference to their religious beliefs. In 1559 Queen Elizabeth I of England issued an injunction that prohibited anyone from teaching without a license from his bishop, which was granted only after an examination of the applicant's "learning and dexterity in teaching," "sober and honest conversation," and "right understanding of God's true religion." Thus the certification of teachers and concern for their character and personal qualities are by no means new issues.

What is new for most societies—European, American, African, and Asian—is the attempt to provide a substantial period of formal education for everyone and not just for the small proportion of the population who will become political, social, and religious leaders or for those few who possess surplus time and money for the purpose. Universal literacy, already achieved in most European and American and many Asian societies, has become the goal of all. In an increasing proportion of countries every child now proceeds automatically to secondary education; many remain at school until 16 or 18 years of age, and large numbers go on to some form of postsecondary education and training. The scale and variety of educational provision that all this requires makes the supply, education, training, and certification of an adequate number of teachers a worldwide issue of education policy and practice. In developed and developing countries alike, no factor is of greater importance in relation to the quantity and quality of education; it is significant that a substantial

The importance of teacher education

proportion of the budget of the United Nations Educational, Scientific and Cultural Organization (UNESCO) is devoted to the improvement of teacher preparation.

The term "teacher" in this article is used to mean those who work in schools providing education for pupils up to the age of 18. Thus, "teacher education" refers to the structures, institutions, and processes by means of which men and women are prepared for work in elementary and secondary schools. This includes preschool, kindergarten, elementary, and secondary institutions for children from the age of 2 or 3 to 18. (The education and training of lecturers and other staff members of technical colleges, polytechnics, universities, and other institutions of postsecondary education, both general and specialized, are treated in HIGHER EDUCATION.)

THE EVOLUTION OF TEACHER EDUCATION

Teacher education, as it exists today, can be divided into two stages, preservice and in-service. Preservice education includes all the stages of education and training that precede the teacher's entry to paid employment in a school. In-service training is the education and training that the teacher receives after the beginning of his career.

Early development. The earliest formal arrangements for teacher preparation, introduced in some of the German states during the early part of the 18th century, included both preservice and in-service training. A seminary or normal school for "young men who had already passed through an elementary, or even a superior school, and who were preparing to be teachers, by making additional attainments, and acquiring a knowledge of the human mind, and the principles of education as a science, and of its methods as an art" was set up in Halle in 1706. By the end of the century there were 30 such institutions in operation in Germany. Systematic training was linked to an equally systematic process of certification, control of teaching conditions, and in-service study. All public teachers were required to attend a series of meetings to extend their practical knowledge. Parochial conferences took place monthly in the winter, district conferences bimonthly in the summer, a circle conference twice a year, and a departmental conference annually. Each seminary was responsible for maintaining contact with all the teachers working within a six-mile radius, and some established "repetition courses" for experienced teachers who wanted to refresh and add to their knowledge.

The German normal school

Nineteenth-century developments in the United States, Britain, France, Belgium, and Japan owed much to the pattern that had been established in Germany. In France efforts were made after 1792 to set up a system of normal schools, and in 1808 Napoleon established the École Normale (later the École Normale Supérieure) to train teachers for the *lycées*. But it was not until after 1833 that a uniform system of *écoles normales* (initially only for male students) was created, and the normal-school systems of several countries date from the third decade of the century.

During the first 30 years of the 19th century, teacher preparation in the United States, Britain, and elsewhere was dominated by the monitorial methods introduced by Andrew Bell and Joseph Lancaster. In the simplest terms, the method involved a master instructing a number of senior pupils or "monitors," who then passed on their newly acquired knowledge to a larger number of pupils. Such methods were cheap, simple, and, it was widely believed, effective. They required a necessary emphasis upon facts, drill, repetition, mechanical learning, and ease of teaching. By 1820 there were 20 Lancastrian schools in the state of New York, where the system had official status until the middle of the century. With hindsight it is easy to condemn the monitorial system. At the time, when the supply of educated persons available and willing to teach in the elementary schools was severely limited, and when the public funds to employ them were in short supply, the system enabled a large number of children to achieve the minimum level of literacy on which future development could build. Just as the organization of knowledge characteristic of medieval times im-

Lancastrian schools

plied its own pattern of pedagogy, so the Lancastrian system embodied a distinctive approach to the process of teaching; one of the attractions of such systems is that they offer a built-in solution to the problem of reconciling what the teacher needs to know and the methods he should learn.

Among those who were unimpressed by the claims of the Lancastrian system was David Stow, who in 1834 founded the Glasgow Normal Seminary from which "trainers," as his graduates came to be called, went to schools in Scotland and many of the British colonial territories. In the United States, after an uncertain start, the Massachusetts Normal Schools founded by Horace Mann in the 1830s became a model for similar developments in Connecticut, Michigan, Rhode Island, Iowa, New Jersey, and Illinois. In England, churches and voluntary foundations were in process of establishing the first of the teacher training colleges. Australia began the organized preparation of teachers in the early 1850s. At this early stage certain issues were already emerging that were to remain alive for the next hundred years and that are to some extent still relevant today.

The needs of pupils and schools were beginning to advance beyond basic literacy. Human knowledge was becoming more diverse and scientific and was being organized into new disciplinary systems. Secondary education was expanding. The early inclusive pedagogic systems were falling into disfavour. The problem arose of reconciling the teacher's personal need for education with his professional need for classroom technique. There were other than purely pedagogic considerations involved; the inhibitions of class society in England, the demand for practicality in the United States, a fear of liberal agitation in France, the patriotic missionary role of the teacher in Japan—all tended to maintain an emphasis upon the practical techniques of school management and to limit the range and level of the elementary teacher's intellectual accomplishments to mastery of only such subject knowledge as was needed at the school level.

General education versus professional training

Some educators asserted that the curriculum of the normal school should be academic, on the ground that the future teacher needed nothing more than experience of conventional subjects soundly taught. Others argued that training should have a purely professional function, including only such subject knowledge as the teacher would need in his classroom work. Some advocates claimed that the liberal and professional elements could readily be harmonized or integrated. The work of Derwent Coleridge, principal of St. Mark's College, London, who admitted that he took his models not from the pedagogical seminaries of Germany but from the universities of Oxford and Cambridge, exemplified the attempt to introduce a larger element of general education into teacher preparation. Sir James Kay-Shuttleworth, founder of another London college, emphasized basic subject matter; he held that

not merely the subjects of instruction, but also the methods of teaching the candidates, should be so ordered as to be in itself a preparation for their future vocation as teachers. On this account the oral instruction of classes in a Normal school is greatly to be preferred to any other mode.

In the United States, Horace Mann supported the value of a training in the "common branches" of knowledge, as a means of mental discipline. But the views of Derwent Coleridge, Kay-Shuttleworth, and Horace Mann, in common with those of many other educators of the time, reflected social as well as pedagogical considerations. Mann, it has been suggested, failed to recognize that the Prussian system that so impressed him was one that took lower class pupils and trained them as teachers of the lower classes—a system already under fire from German educators at the time that it was being used as a model for developments abroad.

Between 1870 and 1890, legislation was enacted in a number of countries to systematize and broaden the work of the normal schools. In Japan an ordinance of 1886 established higher normal schools providing a four-year course for boys and girls who had completed eight years of elementary education. A French law of 1879 estab-

lished a nationwide system of colleges for training women primary teachers (écoles normales d'institutrices). In Russia a statute on teachers' seminaries was promulgated in 1870; within five years there were 34 such institutions, with nearly 2,000 students. A further statute in 1872 provided for institutes to train teachers for the new higher grade schools that were beginning to appear in the larger towns. In Scotland, the universities of Edinburgh and St. Andrews established chairs in education in 1876. In the United States a large number of universities had by 1895 set up education departments, and in some of them the preparation of teachers for work in the schools was beginning to be combined with systematic study and research in education processes.

Developments in American universities owed a great deal to the efforts of men such as Henry Barnard, who, as schools commissioner in Rhode Island from 1845 to 1849, stimulated a local interest in education that led to the creation of a department of education at Brown University. Barnard wrote an influential series of books on pedagogy and teacher education and later, as president of Columbia University, inspired Nicholas Murray Butler and others to found Teachers College in 1888. This soon became the foremost university school of education in the United States. It incorporated two schools as teaching laboratories, enrolling children from kindergarten to college age. As its "Announcement" of 1901 made clear, it was not restricted to any one level of professional preparation:

The purpose of Teachers College is to afford opportunity, both theoretical and practical, for the training of teachers of both sexes for kindergartens and elementary and secondary schools, of principals, supervisors and superintendents of schools, and of specialists in various branches of school work, including normal schools and colleges.

Late 19th- and early 20th-century developments. Until about 1890 the "theoretical" elements in teacher preparation were of two kinds: the study of certain principles of teaching and school management, exemplified in the textbooks written by experienced schoolmen that were published in many countries during the second half of the 19th century; and instruction in "mental and moral philosophy," history of education, psychology, and pedagogics. Some of the most popular and influential works, such as Rosencrantz' *Philosophy of Education*, which was translated into English in the 1870s, made little distinction between philosophical and psychological data. But after 1890 psychology and sociology began to crystallize as more or less distinctive areas of study; students of education had a wider and more clearly structured range of disciplines to draw upon for their data and perspectives and to provide a "scientific" basis for their pedagogic principles.

Evolution of educational theory

In the middle years of the 19th century the ideas of the Swiss educator J.H. Pestalozzi and of the German Friedrich Froebel inspired the use of object teaching, defined in 1878 by Alexander Bain in his widely studied *Education as a Science* as the attempt

to range over all the utilities of life, and all the processes of nature. It begins upon things familiar to the pupils, and enlarges the conceptions of these, by filling in unnoticed qualities. It proceeds to things that have to be learnt even in their primary aspect by description or diagram; and ends with the more abstruse operations of natural forces.

The work of these pioneers also led to a clearer recognition of the developmental needs and character of childhood. Later contributors to the corpus of ideas that underlie the processes of teacher education continued to provide philosophical, sociological, and psychological justification for particular views of the nature of education and of teaching, and also had a greater or lesser influence on the methods to be employed in classroom and school.

The work of the German philosopher Johann Friedrich Herbart (1776–1841) was of particular importance in this latter respect. Herbart wrote a number of pedagogical works during his teaching career at the universities of Göttingen and Königsberg. In the latter part of the 19th century, the study of education along Herbartian lines became established in every European country, in America, and in Japan. Herbartianism offered a complete system—a philosophical theory, a set of educational aims, a rational psychology, and a pedagogy. Teaching, it held, should build on what the child already knows and should seek to inculcate, by the choice of appropriate materials, the highest moral character. It should be organized in accordance with the "five formal steps" of preparation, presentation, comparison, generalization, and application. The Herbartian doctrine rested as much upon the interpretation of his followers as upon the master's own works, and its influence was of relatively limited duration. Other ideas were coming to the fore, less direct and comprehensive than Herbart's but having greater impact upon the educational consciousness of the next half-century.

The influence of Darwinian evolutionary ideas upon pedagogy was very marked. To the extent that the evolutionary viewpoint emphasized the processes by which individuals become adapted to their environment, as in the teachings of the English philosopher Herbert Spencer, their influence was profoundly conservative. But evolutionary ideas were also embodied within the child development theories of the American psychologist G. Stanley Hall, who argued that the stages of individual growth recapitulated those of social evolution and therefore that the distinctive character and status of childhood must be respected. The American philosopher William James also included evolutionary notions in his psychology. James's emphasis, however, was not so much upon the processes by which individuals adapt as upon those through which they react creatively and positively with their circumstances, helping to shape and change these to meet their needs. James's formulation of associationism, the building up of useful habit systems, had implications for the study of learning that teacher educators were quick to recognize and that were made more significant by the later experiments of the American psychologist Edward L. Thorndike (1874–1949). Thorndike's work with animals stands at the beginning of a tradition that continues to the present day. The laws of learning that he formulated have for long been a staple of teacher training courses in many countries. Thorndike saw psychology as the basis of a genuinely scientific pedagogy, and claimed that "Just as the science and art of agriculture depend upon chemistry and botany, so the art of education depends upon physiology and psychology." He went on to argue, with a degree of confidence that rings strangely today, that

A complete science of psychology would tell every fact about everyone's intellect and character and behavior, would tell the cause of every change in human nature, would tell the result which every educational force—every act of every person that changed any other or the agent himself—would have.

The greatest influence on teacher-training curricula in the United States and many other countries was exercised not by the experimental psychologists but by the pragmatist philosopher John Dewey. Dewey began with a conception of the nature of scientific method that he generalized into a specific pedagogical approach (popularized by others as the "project" method and, more recently, as inquiry-based learning). This he combined with a consideration of the nature of the child's interests and capacities for learning and life experience, the nature and claims of different types of subject matter, and the importance of democratic values in the social context of the school. Just as James's psychology gave back to the teacher and the school some of the influence on individual development that the interpreters of evolutionary adaptation had seemed to deny, so Dewey's notion of the school as the embodiment of community ideals and the spearhead of social reform lent a new importance to the processes of teacher education.

Conservative and progressive views

It is tempting to categorize these various perspectives as "conservative" or "progressive." The former stress the importance of subject matter and of standard methods of effective instruction: the need for regularity and order in the classroom and for means that will encourage children to apply themselves diligently to learning; the importance of the teacher as a subject-matter expert and as an exemplar of accepted morality; and the existence of objective standards of scholarship and achievement to which teachers and students alike should aspire. The progressives, on the other hand, emphasize a more child-centred approach, designed to build upon the natural interests and curiosity of the child: a flexible pattern of teaching and classroom organization recognizing individual differences in motivation, capacity, and learning style; a conception of the teacher as an organizer of children's learning rather than as an instructor; and the need to integrate the subject matter of different disciplines into topics and projects that have meaning in terms of the pupil's own experience.

Such conservative and progressive ideas have their roots in differing conceptions of the nature of man and society, of knowledge, and of the learning process. The differences are not new. The fortunes of the two perspectives tend to wax and wane in accordance with the times. Thus in the United States, fears of a loss of technological supremacy in the late 1950s encouraged conservative critics to point to the weaknesses of "child-centred" education. In the same way, anxieties about the meaninglessness of the education experienced by the poor, coupled with evidences of widespread alienation among the young, encouraged a revival of interest in progressive ideas in the early 1970s. Many educators, of course, do not fall into either the conservative or the progressive category but draw their ideas from various sources. There has been a tendency in many countries, however, for the curricula of teacher-preparing institutions to be identified with progressive educational ideas.

Many other ideas also influenced the curriculum and organization of teacher preparation during the last decade of the 19th and the first half of the 20th centuries. The dynamic psychology of Sigmund Freud and his early associates, the work of the Gestalt psychologists, the methods of measuring human abilities that were being developed in France, Great Britain, and the United States, the development of religious ideas in the Roman Catholic countries, the imposition of Marxist and Leninist ideologies in the Soviet Union—all of these in varying measure affected the normal schools, teachers' colleges and seminaries, and university departments of education. Such new ideas and systems of thought had their impact at three main levels.

The use of education in promotion of values

First, they influenced the nature of the social commitment that teacher-preparing institutions strove to instill in their students: commitment to the values of democracy and of opportunity in the United States, as exemplified in the writings of Dewey; to a sense of national purpose or patriotism, as in France, Germany, and Japan; to the pursuit of the socialist revolution, as in the post-tsarist Soviet Union; or to a religious outlook as manifested by Catholic doctrine in Italy, Spain, and Latin America.

Second, the philosophers, psychologists, and sociologists helped to redefine the teacher–pupil relationship. Whatever their differences of view, clear continuities are visible among them on such issues as the significance of the child's needs and interests, the weaknesses of the formal academic curriculum, and the nature of individual development.

Third, the new contributions affected the organization of learning through the measurement and assessment of abilities; the diagnosis of special learning problems; the placing of children in homogeneous age and ability groups by means of "tracking" and "streaming"; the emphasis on problem solving; and the project method. These changes, reflected both in the way in which teachers were trained and in the architecture and equipment of schools, transformed education for younger children in many countries during the first half of the 20th century.

Organization of teacher education in the 20th century. The educational doctrines that inspired, conceptualized, and legitimated this transformation themselves reflected other social, political, economic, demographic, and technological changes. Urbanization, the reduction of infant mortality, improvements in child health, the fact that families, individuals, and whole societies could afford longer and better schooling, growth in the size of populations, greater capacity for control by central and local government, the availability of new kinds of educational apparatus and teaching aids—all these did much to shape the progress of teacher education during the decades after 1900.

<table>
<tr><td>Levels of
teacher
prepara-
tion</td><td></td></tr>
</table>

Among the countries of the world the arrangements for the preparation of teachers vary widely. In some countries "monitors" still receive short courses of training as their preparation to teach large classes of young children. In North America, and to an increasing extent in other developed countries, most teachers are university graduates who begin their teacher preparation after completing four to six years of secondary education. Between these extremes many other arrangements exist. At one level, which for present purposes might be called Normal School A, entry is prior to the usual age of completion of secondary education. Training is limited to the achievement of competence in teaching a range of the subjects taught at the primary level and does not last more than five years.

The second level, which may be called Normal School B, also begins prior to the age of completing secondary education, but usually after the "first certificate" at approximately age 16 or at the end of the period of compulsory schooling. This level provides combined courses of education and professional training, the former not necessarily limited to subjects taught at the primary level and extending beyond the usual age of completion of secondary education.

A third level, the college level, requires a full secondary education, usually ending at 18 but not necessarily with the same qualifications as are demanded of university entrants. Two- or three-year concurrent courses of general and professional education lead to the award of a teaching certificate, often valid for work in primary, intermediate, and lower secondary schools.

Finally, there is the university level, in which, after completing a full period of secondary education, the future teacher enters a multipurpose institution of higher education to follow three- to five-year courses of combined general education and professional training, the latter being either concurrent or consecutive, that lead to the award of a university degree and teaching qualification. Such qualification is considered valid for work at primary or secondary levels, or at both, according to the nature of the course followed.

Until the middle 1960s the normal-school pattern applied to students preparing for primary work in many European countries (Austria, Belgium, Spain, France, Italy, Iceland, The Netherlands, Switzerland, and Turkey), in Latin America, and in a number of Asian countries, although in many places there was more than one route to the attainment of qualified teacher status. The education and training of secondary school teachers was complicated by the general growth of secondary education for all. This encouraged the tendency to educate and train both primary and secondary teachers alongside one another in postsecondary colleges or in multipurpose universities. More recently there has been a widespread movement away from the types of training described here as Normal School A and B to the college and university patterns. But the fact that a country has adopted what has been called here the university pattern of training should not be taken to mean that all the institutions in which teachers are prepared are comparable to the pre-existing universities; some are devoted mainly to teacher preparation.

ISSUES AND PROBLEMS IN TEACHER EDUCATION

<table>
<tr><td>Elements
of
teacher
education</td><td></td></tr>
</table>

In nearly all countries, courses of the Normal School B, college, and university categories contain three main elements. The first element is the study of one or more academic, cultural, or aesthetic subjects for the purpose both of continuing the student's own education and of providing him with knowledge to use in his subsequent teaching career. A second element is the study of educational principles, increasingly organized in terms of social science disciplines such as psychology, sociology, philosophy, and history. A third element consists of professional courses and school experience. Primary teachers may also receive instruction in the content and methods of subjects other than their own specialties that figure in the primary curriculum. In normal schools and colleges, and some universities, the three elements run parallel to one another, and the student is professionally committed from the outset of his course. Elsewhere, the study of educational processes and professional work (including school experience) may follow the completion of a period of academic study that the student has begun without any prior commitment to teaching as a career. There are still advanced countries where the possession of a university degree, without any qualification in education as such, is sufficient basis for the award of qualified teacher status. In England and Wales, for example, compulsory training for graduates, generally comprising two terms (six months) of professional and theoretical studies and a further three-month period of school experience, was scheduled to come into effect only in 1973.

General education. The sequencing, balance, content, and organization of general and specialist academic work, courses in education, and professional studies and teaching experience has been a subject of discussion since the earliest days of organized teacher education. The importance of the element of general education has been defended on various grounds. Sometimes such academic work may be highly specialized. Students in many colleges of education in England study only one principal subject, to which they devote about one-third of their total time, and teachers who graduate from universities have often pursued three-year courses for single-subject honours degrees. In the United States and elsewhere the academic element is broader, and the first two years of college or university work may embody a wide range of elective subjects from diverse disciplinary fields. Both patterns have their critics, the first because it produces narrow intellectual specialists, the second because it encourages dilettantism and inadequate depth. Where a pattern of electives is combined with a units/credits system, as in some universities in Japan and the United States, it is claimed that one result is an undesirable fragmentation of study and effort. In his influential *Education of American Teachers* (1963), James B. Conant recommended that half the course requirements of the four-year program of preparation for elementary teachers should be given over to general courses, a further quarter to an "area of concentration," and the remaining quarter to professional studies, including school experience. Prospective secondary teachers would spend still more time on the subjects they were preparing to teach, with less than 10 percent of their time devoted to practice teaching and special methods. Such a subject emphasis for secondary teachers can be found in many countries. In France the École Normale Supérieure still places freedom of study and the nurture of intellectual curiosity above questions of professional teacher training. Generally speaking, wherever there is a stress upon academic excellence and the achievement of high standards of scholarship, there is likely to be skepticism as to the claims of professional training for teaching. Oxford University had still not appointed a professor of education by the beginning of the 1970s.

In countries where technical or vocational education forms an important part of secondary school provision, there have sometimes been specialist institutions for the training of teachers for this work. Such teachers tend to have lower status than the secondary school staff who teach academic subjects, and efforts have been made to upgrade the position of the teacher of agricultural and industrial arts, home economics, and handicrafts. Nearly all the universities in England and Wales that now offer the bachelor of education degree for college of education students include technical subjects within their list of approved options.

The element of educational courses in the teacher preparation program has been the object of criticism from academic specialists, defenders of liberal culture, and practical-minded professional educators. The growing range of speculation and empirical data generated by the burgeoning social sciences, philosophy, and history, have provided a rich ore from which those responsible for teacher preparation mined the materials they needed for the construction and legitimation of their pedagogic systems and principles. But such borrowing has done little to establish any very coherent system of educational ideas, or to provide the basis for a systematic theory of teaching adequate to sustain the variety and complexity of teacher preparation programs. In his *Evolution of American Educational Theory* (1964), C.J. Brauner was forced to conclude that

> middleman theorists, inexpert as scholars, had naïvely striven for some impossible synthesis that would be at once faithful to scholarship, useful to the practitioner, intelligible to the populace and thus comprehensive as a discipline, workable as a general method, and defensible as a social institution.

The study of educational principles. There has been much dispute as to whether the study of educational principles is to be seen as part of the liberal element in the course, contributing to the teacher's general education and personal development, or whether it is properly an adjunct to the professional sequence, serving to illuminate and enrich students' method courses and practical work. Where it was well done, the study of the philosophy, sociology, and history of education and of educational psychology clearly served both ends and also provided an introduction to a systematic exploration of human conduct and affairs that was both educationally defensible and important in its own right. But all too often it was not well done. As the field of the social sciences grew, it became increasingly difficult for those employed in teacher-preparing institutions to keep pace. In some places, student teachers could follow courses in psychology, sociology, and so on given by recognized authorities in their respective disciplines, and in all countries there were some prominent social scientists who themselves took a close and direct interest in educational matters. But, given the large number of institutions responsible for teacher preparation and the fact that the majority of their staff were necessarily recruited for their teaching competence rather than for their high academic qualifications, much of the teaching of educational principles tended to become out-of-date and secondhand.

In recent years there has been a revival of interest in the social sciences as an integral feature of teacher-education programs. This is partly a recognition of the popularity of studies of this kind among students, partly a reflection of their relevance in a time of rapid social and educational change, and partly a function of the larger supply of qualified social scientists available to teach them. There is now also becoming available a substantial volume of research material on problems such as the dynamics and correlates of children's learning, language development, differences in individual educability and response to teaching, and social class and educational opportunity. In his 1929 lecture, "The Sources of a Science of Education," John Dewey saw the elements of such a science being drawn out of other natural and social sciences, organized in relation to problems defined by the educational process. These hopes are now closer to realization.

Practical training. Professional and practical studies constitute the third major element in the teacher-preparation program. "Teaching practice" has always been important, initially carried out in the model or demonstration school attached to the normal school or college, later in the schools of the neighbourhood, and more recently in a variety of school, college, and community settings. The model and demonstration school was frequently criticized for the unreality of its teaching settings; some model schools attached to universities tended to become academically oriented and ceased to play an experimental role. But if there are advantages in practicing in more typical schools, there are also difficulties in relating the variety of experience thus attained to the purpose and content of the college course, particularly when there are discrepancies between the methods and approaches taught in the colleges and those that the student encoun-

ters in the school. In some countries, experienced teachers view the work of teacher-preparing institutions with a certain amount of disdain. It is sometimes claimed that college and university staff lack the recent, firsthand experience of schools that is needed if training is to be fully effective. Efforts have been made to reduce the separation between school and college; these include the transfer of college staff to periods of classroom teaching and of experienced teachers to college work, dual appointment to a college and to a school where the "teacher-tutor" assumes responsibility for supervision of the student's school-based work, the involvement of teachers' organizations in the determination of national policy on teacher education, the involvement of individual teachers in the government and committee work of teacher-preparing institutions, and the use of periods of school-based teacher education in which a tutor and group of student teachers are attached to a school or a number of schools for an extended period of observation, practical teaching, and theoretical study. Courses are also being devised in which periods of education, training, and paid employment in schools alternate with one another to make up a four- or five-year program.

APPOINTMENT PROCEDURES
AND PROBATIONARY REQUIREMENTS

Generally speaking, in federal countries such as the United States, Canada, and Australia, each state or province sets its own requirements for certification, which inevitably do much to shape the content and organization of the teacher-education programs. The variety of such regulations often means that teachers who have received their education and training in one province or state are not qualified to teach in schools elsewhere without satisfying additional requirements. In other countries, such as England and France, requirements are determined on a national basis. Responsibility for recommending the granting of qualified teacher status may, however, be delegated. In England this responsibility is exercised by regional consortia of colleges, local educational authorities, universities, and teacher interests known as area training organizations that were established after 1944.

There are likewise considerable variations among countries in the way in which teachers are appointed to their first posts after graduation from college or university. In a small number of countries, students have a completely free choice among all the schools of the type in which their training qualifies them to teach, and they make their applications directly to the school in which they wish to serve. A more common pattern is that of appointment to the service of a local, state, or provincial authority, which then places the teacher in a school where a suitable vacancy exists. In some places there is a tendency for beginning teachers to be placed in schools in more remote or less desirable areas. In countries that have universal military service, such as Israel, it is sometimes possible for trained teachers to satisfy military requirements by being drafted to a school of the government's choice.

Another aspect of the diversity of certification requirements is the extent to which teachers are permitted to undertake work in subjects other than those they specialized in at college or university. Generally speaking, where national and state rules exist they tend to be interpreted liberally during periods of teacher shortage and more stringently as the supply of teachers improves; it is often possible for a teacher to secure the additional qualifications required to undertake a greater variety of work by taking university summer sessions or other kinds of in-service courses.

IN-SERVICE TRAINING

Training on the job involves more than courses, conferences, and other organized study programs. Such efforts belong to a much broader system of communication whereby all those who are involved in the educational enterprise—teachers, administrators, research workers, curriculum-development specialists, teacher trainers—keep in touch with one another and with developments in their respective fields. One must therefore consider the

Model schools

Certification

media that are available for in-service education as well as institutional arrangements by means of which such training is provided.

Learning materials

Printed matter forms the most obvious kind of communication medium among teachers. In all countries there are both general and specialist educational journals and newspapers; educational bodies of various kinds issue their own newsletters, broadsheets, and bulletins. The volume of material published in this form has increased enormously. In some countries books, journal articles, and research reports are systematically abstracted and distributed, and some schools have their own library and information services.

A second group of media for in-service training includes lectures and related types of face-to-face instruction and discussion. Greater use is now being made of seminars, working parties, discussions, and other group activities that require a higher level of individual participation. Alongside these methods, a beginning has been made with the use of case studies and simulation materials. Among the advantages of such techniques are the high degree of personal involvement they encourage, the "realism" of the problems dealt with, a reduction in the didactic element (especially important in work with senior staff), and the opportunities for questions of theory and principle to arise in the discussion of actual teaching and administrative incidents.

Multimedia approaches to in-service studies are encouraged by closed-circuit and broadcast television facilities within individual school systems and local areas. The work that professional and specialist associations have long performed in bringing teachers together for the discussion of issues of mutual concern is now being extended by such developments as the establishment of teachers' centres in Britain. These help to disseminate a wide range of new educational practices and ideas, including those that derive from the teacher-controlled Schools Council for Curriculum and Examinations. In North America, Australia, the United Kingdom, Germany, and some other European countries, credit-bearing courses are now available for teachers through broadcast television, radio, and correspondence tuition.

The use of a wider range of media has diversified the institutional settings in which in-service teacher education is provided. Universities, colleges, teachers' centres, and teachers' homes are now among the places where the teacher can pursue his education and seek to improve his qualifications. Given the larger number of teachers on the staffs of many schools, there is also scope for school-based in-service education. A new idea or principle may find more ready acceptance within a group of like-minded people than when it must make its way against the organizational conservatism of a particular school. Department discussions, staff working parties, and other forms of school-based meetings enable matters of curriculum and organization to be discussed in depth, facilitate the induction of younger members of the profession, and help to limit the isolation of the teacher within the classroom. School-based in-service education has the important merit of recognizing that there is a gap between the ideas, techniques, and approaches that teachers acquire as a result of their training and the application of these ideas and approaches within the social system of the school. With the growth of team teaching and interdisciplinary work, and the reinterpretation of the teacher's role as an organizer and manager of learning resources rather than a solo performer on the classroom stage, the importance of bridging this gap will become increasingly important.

FUTURE DEVELOPMENTS IN TEACHER EDUCATION

Coming decades are likely to see continuing development and change in teacher education. Postsecondary and higher education may soon reach between a third and a half of the population in many advanced countries. The teacher must adjust to new developments in educational technology, the growth of human knowledge, and the problem of creating a relevant and appropriate curriculum from the enormous range of material available. There will be new understanding of how children develop and learn. The patterns of authority in society will continue to change, and it is likely that there will be a greater recognition of the importance of moral and personal education in a world of pluralistic values and goals. All these factors will affect the ways in which teachers are educated and trained.

In all countries, whether or not any fundamental institutional changes are contemplated, there are evidences of radical change in the structure of ideas and assumptions that underlie the preparation of teachers. But it is unlikely that coming decades will see the introduction of any comprehensive pedagogical system resembling those of the 19th century. No single theory of learning or teaching is likely to satisfy the diversity of individual needs and societal arrangements.

BIBLIOGRAPHY. A useful recent review, on a comparative and international scale, is EDMUND J. KING, *The Education of Teachers* (1970). More detailed comparative perspectives are provided in GEORGE Z.F. BEREDAY and JOSEPH A. LAUWERYS (eds.), *The Education and Training of Teachers, The Yearbook of Education* (1963). J.B. CONANT, *The Education of American Teachers* (1963); and J.D. KOERNER, *The Miseducation of American Teachers* (1963), provide contrasting mid-century perspectives on teacher education in the United States. Similar contrasts for Great Britain may be found in contributions to W. TAYLOR (ed.), *Towards a Policy for the Education of Teachers* (1969). Historical developments for the U.S. are surveyed in W.S. MONROE, *Teaching Learning Theory and Teacher Education, 1890 to 1950* (1952); M.L. BORROWMAN, *The Liberal and the Technical in Teacher Education* (1956); and L.A. CREMIN, *The Transformation of the School: Progressivism in American Education, 1876–1956* (1961); and for England in R.W. RICH, *The Training of Teachers in England and Wales During the Nineteenth Century* (1933); and W. TAYLOR, *Society and the Education of Teachers* (1969). European provision for teacher education is reviewed in J. MAJAULT, *Teacher Training* (1965), in the Council of Europe series "Education in Europe." The Organization for Economic Cooperation and Development (OECD) issued between 1968 and 1970 a series of "Studies on Teachers," which cover all the western European countries, the United States, Canada, and Japan. Recommendations for the reform of teacher education in England and Wales are embodied in the *Report of the Committee of Inquiry on the Training of Teachers* (1972). Teacher education in developing countries is discussed in C. BEEBY, *The Quality of Education in Developing Countries* (1966); and PHILIP H. COOMBES, *The World Educational Crisis* (1967).

(W.Ta.)

Teaching Profession

Measured in terms of its members, teaching is the world's biggest profession. There are said to be about 20,000,000 teachers throughout the world. Though their roles and functions vary from country to country, the variations are generally greater within a country than they are between countries.

Because the nature of the activities that constitute teaching depends more on the age of the persons being taught than on any other one thing, it is useful to recognize three subgroups of teachers: primary-school, or elementary-school, teachers; secondary-school teachers; and university teachers—for whom UNESCO in 1967 estimated an approximate worldwide ratio of 62 percent, 30 percent, and 8 percent, respectively (the figures exclude China). The proportions differ by country and continents; in North America, for instance, they are 53, 29, and 18; in the Soviet Union, 71, 19, and 10; and in Africa, 77, 20, and 3.

Characteristics of the profession

The entire teaching corps, wherever its members may be located, shares most of the criteria of a profession, namely (1) a process of formal training; (2) a body of specialized knowledge; (3) a procedure for certifying, or validating, membership in the profession; and (4) a set of standards of performance—intellectual, practical, and ethical—that are defined and enforced by members of the profession. Teaching young children and even adolescents could hardly have been called a profession anywhere in the world before the 20th century. It was, instead, an art or a craft in which the relatively young and untrained women and men who held most of the positions "kept school" or "heard lessons" because they had been better than average pupils themselves. They had learned the art solely by observing and imitating their own teachers. Only university professors and possibly a few teachers of elite secondary schools would have merited being called members of a profession in the sense that medical doctors, lawyers, or priests were professionals, and in some countries even today the primary school teacher may fairly be seen as a semiprofessional. The dividing line is unprecise. It is useful, therefore, to consider the following questions: (1) What is the status of the profession? (2) What kinds of work are done? (3) How is the profession organized?

THE STATUS OF TEACHERS

Teaching enjoys average to high status, depending in part on the amount of study required to prepare for employment. Since this ranges from a relatively brief time to many years, the levels of social and economic status span a wide range.

The economic status. *Salaries.* The salaries of elementary- and secondary-school teachers have generally been relatively low, at least in all the years before 1955, when in some countries they increased sharply. In industrialized nations at the beginning of the 20th century, teachers in this group were paid hardly more than semiskilled labourers. In Europe during these years they were relatively better off than they were in America, in part because many primary-school teachers in Europe were men, with families to support. In general, primary-school teachers who are women and have relatively little academic training for their jobs receive low salaries. In Brazil in 1957, for instance, the average annual salary of a teacher—usually a woman—in the official state primary-school system was the equivalent of about $850. It was even less, only $231, in the locally financed municipal schools. Since the school day in primary schools in Brazil is only three to five hours, teachers may, and generally must, take other jobs or look after their families and homes concurrently. The poorest countries, in any case, have continued with relatively low primary teachers' salaries down to the present time. In India, for example, poorly trained teachers in village schools are paid only one-tenth as much as teachers in select city schools; and even in commercially prosperous Japan, primary-school teachers are paid only about as much as a bank clerk, an office worker, or a salesperson in a department store.

The history of teachers' salaries in a developed country like the United States reflects two factors: (1) the effects of a rising level of training and (2) the effects of a teacher shortage and the impact of collective bargaining. Studies made by the National Education Association reveal that the average salary of elementary- and secondary-school teachers in American public schools was $3,010 in 1949–50, $4,350 in 1956–57, and $7,129 in 1966–67. The average salary of such teachers increased 57 percent between 1955 and 1964, while the average pay of factory employees was increasing only 40 percent in the same period. Interestingly, though, it was an increase in birthrates for the period 1946 to 1960 that crowded the schools and put the teachers in a good bargaining position for an escalation in salaries.

When salaries are too low for what teachers regard as necessities, they add other jobs. Men are more likely to do this than women. In 1965-66, male municipal schoolteachers in the United States derived 84 percent of their total income from their salaries as teachers; 7 percent from summer employment; and 6 percent from "moonlighting," or working at a second job, during the school year. Working at a second job is much more frequent in countries in which the school day is less than seven hours or the teaching load (for secondary-school teachers) less than about 25 classes a week. In Brazil and other Latin American countries, for example, where the average teaching load of a secondary-school teacher is about 12 classes a week, many teachers take two full teaching jobs, and some go beyond that to earn a living.

University salaries

The salaries of university teachers and others who teach in postsecondary institutions have traditionally been substantially higher than those of secondary-school teachers.

This reflects the fact that university professors generally have spent more years in preparation for their work and are more highly selected. But in recent years university salaries have not increased as much as those of schoolteachers. Thus, again in the United States, the 1965-66 median salary of full-time teachers in four-year higher institutions was $9,081, only about 40 percent higher than the comparable figure for primary- and secondary-school teachers. Though these North American university salaries are the highest of their kind in the world, they fall below the average incomes of medical doctors, dentists, lawyers, and engineers. Salaries in higher education in Russia are higher, in relation to other comparable occupations, than American salaries. A teacher in a Russian pedagogical institute (which trains schoolteachers), for example, is paid slightly more than an engineer who has completed a university course.

Fringe benefits and other advantages. Vacations and leaves give a prized flexibility to teaching careers. One of the attractive things about teaching, for instance, may be the long annual vacation, usually in summer, which can be used for recreation, for further study or training, or for earning more money.

Leaves of absence are also more frequent than in other occupations. The sabbatical leave is a widespread practice among universities and is even available in some school systems. Formerly a fully paid leave for study or research every seventh year, it is now often reduced to a fully paid leave for a half year or half-salary for a full year. Maternity leave (without pay) is generally available to women teachers. Sick leave and short-term leave for personal needs are also often provided—with continuing salary for the teacher validly absent for a few days.

Other benefits are becoming quite common; some of them, such as pensions, have been in practice in Europe for many decades. Life-and-health insurance, another fringe benefit, is usually paid partly or wholly by the school system or the university.

Seniority rights, enjoyed by teachers in many school systems, give them preferential treatment in transfers to other schools and class assignments within their system.

Social and occupational status. According to a number of sociological surveys, university professors generally rank high in public estimation, comparable to medical doctors, lawyers, owners of large business and industrial establishments, bankers, and officials of national government. On a status scale ranging from 1 (high) to 7 (low), a university professor would be ranked 1 in most countries and 2 in some countries. A secondary-school teacher is generally ranked 2 or 3 on the same scale, sharing the level with journalists, clergymen, business managers, accountants, insurance agents, real-estate or land agents, and substantial landowners. A primary school teacher is generally ranked 3 or 4 on the seven-point scale, on the same level occupied by social workers, office managers, bank clerks, small independent farmers, and foremen.

Occupational status in the teaching profession is roughly related to the degree of selection involved in obtaining the teaching post and to the amount of training necessary to qualify for it. In a country with a selective university-preparatory secondary school, such as, for instance, the *lycée* in France, the grammar school in England, and the *Gymnasium* in Germany, the teacher must have the equivalent of a university education and must pass rigorous examinations or selective screening. This teacher has a higher occupational status than teachers in other branches of secondary education, such as industrial or commercial schools, which are less selective and require less training and accept lower examination standards of their teachers. Whenever a secondary-school system is divided into a number of branches or types of schools, the teachers and the public both make status distinctions among them.

Throughout the period from about 1850 to 1925, when schooling was becoming universal in the more developed countries, the elementary-school, or primary school, teacher had lower status than the teachers of the more advanced schools. Still, there was a good deal of variation between countries. In Germany, for example, the primary-school teachers were more frequently men than women, and the male *Volksschullehrer* had relatively high status. If he taught in a rural school, he usually had a comfortable house adjoining his school and was above peasant landowners in social status. If he taught in a city, he could look forward to becoming the head teacher or school director. The German schoolteachers had a series of about seven status positions, from the classroom teacher in the primary school to the department chairman in the *Gymnasium,* or academic secondary school. The four to six year primary school was followed by a set of middle schools that were related to the occupational destiny of the student, and the middle schools were followed by a variety of higher secondary schools, some leading to employment and some leading to the university. Teachers were ranked in this sequence. Many *Gymnasium* teachers —that is, teachers of college-preparatory schools—were scholars of some distinction, almost on the same status level as a university teacher. Oswald Spengler, for instance, with his broad-gauged historical writing (*The Decline of the West*) was a history teacher in a Hamburg *Gymnasium* and never a university professor.

In Japan, the evolution of the teaching profession has been somewhat similar to that in Germany. Both countries have more men than women teaching in elementary schools, and as late as 1964, only 22 percent of Japan's secondary-school teachers were women. Women were not encouraged to become teachers in Japan until after 1874, when the first Women's Normal School was founded. Both countries had several clearly marked status positions within a school level, depending on amount of training and on seniority. The moral stature of the Japanese teacher was regarded as an extremely important part of his qualification.

Status distinctions

Distinctions between primary- and secondary-school teaching die hard. In Europe and South America, for example, adolescent students training in normal schools to become primary-school teachers are generally addressed, referred to, and treated as children, while their counterparts in university preparatory schools are addressed as adults. Prospective primary-school teachers are normally called pupils and not students and are often addressed in the familiar forms of speech (*tu* or *Du* instead of *vous, usted,* or *Sie*) in contrast to university students.

In most modern countries, however, where the goal of universal schooling has been extended to the secondary level, distinctions in status between primary- and secondary-school teachers have been moderating. In such situations, secondary-school teaching becomes relatively less selective as additional teachers are sought for, at the same time that primary-school teachers are increasing their training level and, therefore, their salary and status levels. In a growing number of countries, including Germany, England, and the United States, primary-school teachers must now have as much university-level training as secondary-school teachers, and a single salary scale has been established, based on amount of training and years of experience. In 1964, for example, the average annual salary of primary-school teachers in the public schools of the United States was about 93 percent of that of secondary school teachers, indicating that the occupational status differential is being eliminated. France, on the other hand, still maintains two different systems of training and has different names for the primary-school teacher (*instituteur*) and the secondary-school teacher (*professeur*).

Whatever the status distinctions may be, the teaching profession in general is an important avenue of upward social mobility. Because teaching does not require capital, property, or family connection, it provides a good opportunity for the economic and social advancement of able and ambitious young people. A study of Chicago public-school teachers in 1964 indicated that approximately half of them had come from families of skilled, semiskilled, or unskilled workers (Robert J. Havighurst, *The Public Schools of Chicago: A Survey Report,* ch. 16, 1964). A study of the social origins of middle-school teachers in Brazil in 1963 showed that approximately half of them

had moved up in social class as a result of becoming teachers (Robert J. Havighurst and Aparecida J. Gouveia, *Brazilian Secondary Education and Socio-Economic Development,* ch. 9, 1969).

Within the profession, the degree of status mobility is not great, at least in the primary and secondary schools. A classroom teacher is likely to remain a classroom teacher, unless he or she seeks out an administrative post or follows some specialty, such as curriculum work, counselling, or the teaching of handicapped pupils. In university teaching, on the other hand, there is a hierarchy of three or four steps within any institution and of prestige and salary among institutions. Thus a university teaching career in the United States normally leads from the rank of instructor or assistant professor to associate professor and to full professor; in Britain the titles are assistant lecturer, lecturer, senior lecturer or reader, and professor; similar rankings occur in other countries.

Geographical mobility of teachers. The high mobility of university teachers within their country has been noted. They also move from one country to another with relative ease, so that the profession of university teaching has a cosmopolitan character unique among the professions. Educators at this level belong to international professional organizations and tend to think of themselves as members of a worldwide profession.

For several reasons, there is less geographical mobility among primary- and secondary-school teachers. Because schoolteachers are licensed (whereas university teachers usually are not) they usually cannot secure a teaching job outside their own country, unless the receiving country has such a severe shortage of teachers that it seeks out immigrant teachers and gives them licenses to teach. Many African nations and India have, for this reason, a relatively large number of North American and European teachers. The language factor also interferes with geographical mobility.

Where there is a national system of state schools, as in France and England, teachers are licensed for the entire system and are able to move around from one locality to another more easily than they can in countries in which there are multiple school systems organized on state or provincial lines. In the United States, where each of the 50 states has its own licensing laws and standards, teachers tend to be held within the state (though some states do have "reciprocity" with each other).

Stereotype of the teacher. The aphorism attributed to George Bernard Shaw, "He who can, does; he who cannot, teaches," appears to have wide credence among intellectuals and educated groups. Schoolteaching is often seen as a refuge for mediocre people who are industrious but unimaginative and uncreative. Writing in the *Profession of Teaching* in 1901, a Boston educator, James P. Monroe, said:

It is, indeed, the exceptional teacher—outside the faculties of colleges—who seriously looks upon himself as a professional man. The ordinary schoolmaster has little of the personal weight, of the sense of professional responsibility, of what may be called the corporate self-respect of the lawyer, the physician, or the engineer. The traditions of the teaching guild do not yet demand a wide education, a slow and laborious preparation, a careful and humble apprenticeship, such as are required for entrance into the really learned professions. A broad education and the poise of mind which follows it are the vital needs of a great majority of the public school teachers of today. They are ceaselessly complaining of a condition of things which is indeed grievous, but which is largely of their own creation. They demand high place without qualifying themselves to hold high place; they rebel at a not uncommon attitude of contempt or of contemptuous toleration on the part of the public, but do not purge themselves of the elements which excite that contempt; they accuse the parents and the public of indifference toward their work, but do little to render that work of such quality as to forbid indifference.

Over 60 years later a professor of education at Utrecht in The Netherlands, Martinus J. Langeveld, taking a rather ambivalent position, quoted the director of a Swiss teacher-training college, as saying, "The teaching profession is permeated with individuals who from youth upwards reveal the following characteristics: average drive for power, average ambition, and escapism [*Lebensscheu*]." Langeveld discerned an occupational type, or stereotype, characterized by lack of independence, social courage, limited social horizon, on the one hand, and industriousness, intellectual interest, achievement motivation, and love for teaching children, on the other.

Whether or not this has to be given credence, it hardly applies to university teachers; and the events of the 1960s seemed to be moving teachers toward much more social and political action as a group and toward greater personal initiative.

One stereotyped characteristic that does seem to be true for most, though not all, countries in the contemporary world is that it is a woman's profession. There is a preponderance of woman teachers, particularly on the elementary level. Of the 20,000,000 teachers in the world, a rough estimate is that two-thirds are women. Incomplete estimates for several countries and areas give the following percentages of woman teachers for the year 1965 or nearby years.

Percentage of Woman Teachers			
	elementary level	secondary level	higher education
United States	87	51	22
Soviet Union	81	68	44
Japan	48	22	24
Australia-New Zealand	63	46	31
Western Europe	58	41	low*
Brazil	93	45	low*

*Official data are not available but it is known that the percentages are lower than other countries with the possible exception of the United States.

There is a good deal of variation in the sex ratio among teachers in European countries. In 1965 the percentage of primary-school teachers who were women in the United Kingdom, France, The Netherlands, and West Germany was 76, 66, 52, and 52, respectively. These percentages reflect the Central European tradition of male teachers in the rural village schools.

Building the profession in a new country. Since World War II it has been necessary to create or to rebuild the teaching profession in a new country, under varying conditions. Sometimes it was an old country becoming modern, such as India and China; sometimes it was a tribal society becoming a nation, as in central Africa; and in one case it was a religious society becoming a modern nation, as in Israel. In all such cases, the pattern of schools has been copied from older countries, but the teaching personnel have to be drawn from the human material available, and thus a wide variety of solutions to the problem of building the profession have been worked out.

In the case of Israel, there were 6,500 teachers in the school system in 1948 and 31,700 in 1963, while the school enrollment increased from 160,000 to 700,000. Since the nation was building a modern economy from a very small beginning, manpower was scarce, and especially educated manpower. This made it difficult for the state to secure male teachers, since educated men were in high demand for other more prestigious work. Consequently, the great majority of new teachers were women. The proportion of male teachers in the elementary and secondary schools was 49 percent in 1948 and 41 percent in 1963. The government has established a generous scholarship and loan program for prospective teachers and requires students who accept these stipends to teach at least five years. The Teachers' Association is the country's oldest trade union.

The evolution of the teaching profession in Hungary illustrates the problems of the teaching profession and their solution in a society that moves from capitalist to communist rule after war and revolution. In the period from 1945 to 1950, there was a serious shortage of teachers at all levels, due to wartime loss of life and to flight of teachers and professors to the West. Before World War II, most teachers were trained in institutions operated by the Catholic Church. For the first five years after 1945, there were strenuous attempts to recruit new teachers and to re-train experienced teachers so that they could serve the purposes of the new society. The retraining program consisted of a two-year part-time course of lectures that stressed a "progressive-Marxist" political and economic ideology. There were 10,000 elementary and secondary school teachers enrolled in this program in 1950.

The period from 1955 to 1967 saw a systematic upgrading of the training of elementary and secondary school teachers in Hungary, similar to what was being done in most countries. More university-level work was required. At the same time, recruiting was aimed at young people from the working class (50 percent of all university students were from peasant or working-class families during the decade of the 1950s). Secondary school entrance became more popular during the 1960s, and the numbers of secondary school teachers increased from 8,800 in 1960 to 12,300 in 1967, with a corresponding increase of school enrollment. By 1967 the supply of secondary school teachers exceeded demand. In that year, 614 positions were advertised, and 1,268 secondary school teachers were graduated from the universities. Salaries, however, are relatively low (in 1965 a rural teacher earned slightly less than an industrial or construction worker).

The teaching profession in the Soviet Union. As in all other modern countries, the length of preparation for elementary school and secondary school teaching in the Soviet Union has expanded since 1920. Most new teachers have had four years of work in a university or pedagogical institute after completing the basic ten-year school of general education. Competition is intense for places in the universities and pedagogical institutes. About 80 percent of teachers in elementary and secondary schools are women, the highest proportion in any major country.

Teachers are paid for a 20-hour week of actual teaching time in elementary schools, and 18 hours in secondary schools. They are paid extra for overtime work, which includes correcting papers in some subjects, holding conferences, and visiting parents. Many teachers earn up to twice the basic salary by extra hours of teaching. In rural areas, housing is furnished, including heating and lighting. After the age of 55, teachers may retire on a pension of 40 percent of the last salary received. They may draw the pension and continue to earn a regular salary if they wish to continue teaching.

University faculty members have a high status, comparable to that of other professional groups. Their salaries place them among the highest paid workers and they receive, in addition, payment for lectures, articles, and books.

FUNCTIONS AND ROLES OF TEACHERS

Broadly speaking, the function of a teacher is to help a client learn things, by imparting knowledge to him and by setting up a situation in which the client can and will learn effectively. But the teacher fills a complex set of roles, which vary from one society to another and from one educational level to another. Some of these roles are performed in the school or university, and some are performed in the community.

Roles in the school or university
Mediator of learning
Disciplinarian or controller of student behaviour
Parent substitute
Confidant to students
Judge of achievement
Organizer of curriculum
Bureaucrat
Scholar and research specialist
Member of teachers' organization
Roles in the community
Public servant
Surrogate of middle class morality
Expert in some area of knowledge or skills
Community leader
Agent of social change
In those areas in which teaching has not yet become a profession, the teacher may fill fewer of these roles. The

primary-school teacher in a simple agricultural society, for example, will fill only the first five of the school roles and the first and possibly the second of the community roles.

Some of the roles conflict; that is, the performance of one, that of disciplinarian, for example, tends to conflict with another, such as that of confidant to students, or the role of independent and creative scholar will tend to conflict with that of the bureaucrat. In the community, the role of surrogate of middle class morality tends to conflict with the role of agent of social change. In the presence of these role conflicts, the teacher must learn to balance, to know when and how vigorously to act in a particular role, and when to shift to another in a flexible way.

Role in curricular design. The family, the government, the church or religious authority, and the economic or business-industrial authority all have an interest in the development of children and youth, and all play a part, therefore, in setting up and controlling formal and many informal means of education. In the more developed societies, they employ teachers to do the work of education, and they work out with the teacher an understanding of what the teacher is expected to do. The more "professional" the teacher is, the more autonomy he demands and is given to teach within the concept of understood and mutually accepted goals and methods.

Teaching of skills, information, and attitudes

The elementary-school teacher must teach the basic mental skills—reading, writing, and arithmetic. Beyond this, the elementary-school teacher must teach facts and attitudes favourable to the nation or the church or any other institution supporting the school. Thus he must teach in a way that is favourable to Communism in the Soviet Union, to a mixed capitalist-socialist economy in Britain or the United States, to the French or Brazilian systems in France or Brazil, and so forth. In a society in which schools are directed by churches or religious groups, as in Spain, he must teach the relevant religious beliefs and attitudes.

In national and state systems of education, the legislature generally requires that certain subjects be taught so as to "improve" the citizenship or the morality or the health of the students. Many systems, for instance, require secondary schools to teach about the pitfalls of alcohol, drugs, and tobacco. A growing number of nations require teaching in favour of conservation of natural resources and protection of the physical environment against air and water pollution. Before World War II a central course required in the Japanese schools was "moral education." After the war, this was abolished by the American occupation forces on the grounds that it tended to inculcate a kind of authoritarianism and nationalistic ideology. With the ending of the military occupation, however, the Japanese government reintroduced a compulsory course in moral education, which became a source of major controversy between conservatives and progressives within the Japanese educational profession. The French school system also has a compulsory course in "civic morality."

Teaching freedom

Matters of curriculum and choice of textbooks and materials of instruction are determined in some countries with little or no participation of the individual teacher. Thus, in France, with a highly centralized national educational system, the course of instruction in the elementary schools is fixed by the Ministry of Education. In the United States, where each of the 50 states is its own authority, there is much more curricular variation. Some states require statewide adoption of textbooks, whereas others leave such matters to local decision. Many large city school systems have a curriculum department to set policy in such matters, and the individual teacher in a city school system or in certain state systems thus has relatively little power to decide what to teach. There is more flexibility at the secondary-school level than in the primary-school level. As for methods of teaching within the classroom, the individual teacher probably has more autonomy in the United States than in most European school systems.

The university teacher almost anywhere in the world has substantial autonomy in his choice of textbooks, of content to be covered in a particular course, and of methods of teaching. In general the only limits on the university teacher are set by the nature of his teaching assignment. If he is one of a number of teachers who teach a popular course, such as general chemistry or physics or history, which is taken by several hundred students and offered by several different instructors, he may have to use the same textbooks as those used by other instructors, and he may have to prepare his students for common examinations. On the other hand, in those courses that he alone gives, he has wide freedom to choose the content and methods of instruction.

In terms of the professional responsibility of teachers for what they teach, there is a major distinction between the university and elementary-secondary school systems. At the level of higher education, teachers have the power and the responsibility of defining the curriculum—its contents and its methods. This is the essence of academic freedom in higher education. The governing board of the university, whether it be a government or independent university, does not tell teachers what to teach or how to teach. There are, nevertheless, some external requirements operative on the university teacher. If he is preparing his students for examinations not under university control (civil service examinations, state bar and medical examinations, examinations for a certificate as a public accountant, or the like), his autonomy is limited by the necessity that his students be well prepared for these external examinations.

In contrast to the power of the university governing board, the board of an elementary- or secondary-school system has, but generally delegates to the school administration, the power to determine what is taught. The school administration, consisting of the superintendent, school directors, inspectors, and curriculum specialists, has effective power over the curriculum and brings the classroom teacher into the process as much or as little as it chooses. With the growth of teachers' unions and organizations, however, it appears that collective action by teachers is tending to increase the effective autonomy of the classroom teacher. Administrative and legislative prescriptions for the school curriculum are generally resisted in *principle* by the teaching profession; the profession presumes itself better able to decide what to teach and how to teach it.

The doctrine of in loco parentis. When minor children are entrusted by parents to a school, the parents delegate to the school certain responsibilities for their children, and the school has certain liabilities. In effect, the school and the teachers take some of the responsibility and some of the authority of the parents. The exact extent and nature of this responsibility and power vary from one society to another and from one school system to another. This is spelled out to some extent in the law, but much of it is determined by local custom and practice.

There is, of course, a relation between the age of the child on the one hand and the teacher's responsibility and liability for it on the other. The young child *must* obey the teacher, and the teacher may use the methods expected and tolerated in the community to control the child's behaviour. Furthermore, the child's physical safety is entrusted to the school and to the teacher, who thus become legally liable for the child's safety, insofar as negligence can be proved against them.

In the matter of corporal or physical punishment, local attitudes establish a wide range of expected and permissible behaviour on the part of the teacher. In most parts of the world, young children may be punished by a limited infliction of physical pain at the hands of the teacher or school principal, using a wooden ruler or a whip of one kind or another. But there are some systems and cities that explicitly bar a teacher from using corporal punishment. This seems most common in large cities; the teacher in a rural or small-city school is more apt to be expected to use physical measures for controlling pupil behaviour. As students become older, their behaviour is less apt to be controlled by physical measures, and they are more likely to be suspended from classes or expelled from school. This is the common last resort in the upper years of the secondary school and in the university.

Another facet of the doctrine of *in loco parentis* is seen

in the relation between parents and teachers with respect to the promotion of pupils and to their counselling or guidance. Parent and teacher may be in conflict about the best procedures to use with a pupil. Shall this pupil be promoted from a fifth to a sixth year class or be "kept back" to repeat the year's work? This decision is generally seen as the responsibility of the school, though the parents may be brought in for consultation. If the parents object to the school's decision, what rights and powers do they have? May they see the school's records on their child? May they examine the pupil's examination papers or other school work? The answers to these questions are more fixed in some countries than in others, but in general, the school's authority is supported in these matters.

A more difficult problem is presented by a student, generally an adolescent, who is having serious problems with his school performance or with his school behaviour. He is sent to the school counsellor, who finds him in need of therapeutic counselling and proceeds to counsel him. Must the counsellor secure prior consent from the parents? Must the counsellor disclose to the parents what he learns about or from the student in confidence? Perhaps the counsellor concludes that a part of the student's difficulty is caused by his parents. Must the counsellor tell this to the parents? Is the counsellor intruding on the *privacy* of the parents by asking the student about his relations with them or by listening if the student volunteers such information? This is *terra incognita* for the teaching profession, and has become something of an issue in the places where personal counselling is regarded as part of the school's responsibility.

At the level of higher education, the doctrine of *in loco parentis* does not present as much of a problem for the teacher, since the student, even though he may be legally a minor, is presumed to be a more responsible person. But the university may have a problem in relation to the local police or city government. May university property—including classrooms in which teachers are trying to teach —be regarded as private property, with police and other outside persons barred unless they are explicitly asked for their help? The question (and others like it) has no clear and unequivocal answer.

Extramural activities of teachers. Traditionally, the schoolteacher has been a surrogate of middle class morality who serves the local community in various clerical or secretarial capacities because he or she can write legibly and spell accurately. Furthermore, the schoolteacher has often been expected to support the local religious group, if there is one, by teaching children, singing in the choir, and so forth. In other words, the teacher is seen as a useful minor civil servant, without deviant political or economic attitudes.

Though this may be true of most teachers in most countries, there are exceptions. In places where the community is polarized along religious or political lines, for instance, teachers generally have to take sides in local politics and cannot easily serve the whole community. Thus, in the small towns of France, the stereotype of schoolteacher is traditionally that of a man with leftist political leanings, always at war with the village priest. In the cities, schoolteachers are needed less to perform local community services and tend as teachers to be politically neutral or invisible.

University teachers are more likely to be leaders in local politics and local civic affairs. Since the university is expected to be a source of ideas as well as of information in controversial areas, university professors may perform this function by taking sides on political and economic issues. Also their expertness in the natural sciences makes them influential advisors on local and state problems of health, water supply, transportation, and the use and conservation of natural resources. When the university teacher does take sides on controversial economic or political issues, he may expect counterpressures to have him discharged, and his institution may or may not support him in the name of academic freedom.

As elementary- and secondary-school teachers have organized themselves for collective action, they have succeeded increasingly in protecting those of their group who do take unpopular positions on political and economic matters. In countries with two-party or multiparty political systems, teachers may now run for elective offices, and they and their organizations are likely to take sides on political issues. Thus the teacher at any educational level is increasingly free to take part in promoting social changes, and at least a few teachers are generally found in leadership roles in local and national politics.

Scholarship and the profession. Within the profession, prestige has traditionally gone to the productive scholar, the one who contributes to the growth of knowledge, literature, or art. Promotion in the university and fame in the world outside the university have gone to the person who does research or scholarly work—and publishes. The university is seen as an institution to discover new knowledge, as well as to pass on what is known, and these two functions are not necessarily tied together. The teacher of adolescents and of university undergraduates does not find that research or scholarly work makes him a better teacher. Only when he is teaching graduate students who themselves are being trained for scholarship does the university professor find himself working at the frontier of knowledge, with his students as apprentices.

The universities of the world have adapted to this situation in two ways. One is to assign some teachers a teaching role, with a heavy teaching load and recognition when they do a good job of teaching; the other is to give teachers a reduced teaching load and expect them to do research or writing. A second adaptation is to assign some staff members to full-time research with a few graduate students associated with them as apprentices and research assistants. In any case, it is the fact that the universities of the world, which claim the responsibility of advancing knowledge, do continue to judge their teachers more by their research and writing than by their teaching.

University teachers are also much in demand for consultation and advice to industry, business, government, and school systems. The best experts on problems of innovative development and on the conduct of industrial research and development are generally found in universities, and many teachers find as much as a quarter to a half of their time taken with consultation.

THE CAREER OF THE TEACHER

The professionalization of teaching. In the 19th century, systems of public education developed in order to meet the recognized need for universal literacy in an industrializing society. Teaching at this primary level was at first no more than a high-level domestic service, in which the teacher took over some of the child-rearing responsibility of the family. In some parts of the world, a year as a cadet teacher working under a more experienced teacher became the model for teacher training. Frequently, courses were added to the secondary school in the largest town of the county or province, for training classroom teachers. Even today in many countries, notably in Latin America, the training of teachers is still carried on largely in certain types of secondary schools, called "normal schools," which take students (mainly girls) at about age 15 or 16 for a two- or three-year course of study. In Europe and North America, the earlier normal schools or teachers colleges have since moved up to the postsecondary level of higher education. In any event, by the turn of the 20th century some rudiments of a teaching profession had begun to evolve. There was the beginning of a program of formal training; the emergence of a body of specialized knowledge called pedagogy; the imposition of an inchoate system of licensing or certification; and the recognition of a few minimal standards of performance to be defined, expanded, and enforced by the corps of teachers.

The combined efforts of educational reformers and teachers' organizations were required to fashion the beginnings of a profession. Men and women saw themselves becoming committed to a career in teaching and therefore sought to make this career more personally and socially satisfying. The Chicago Teachers' Federation, founded in 1897, for example, comprised a group of female primary-school teachers who were faced by an experimental pension system that was actuarially unsound and by salaries that were very low. Margaret Haley, a dynamic 36-year-old Irish woman, was their leader, and in the 15 years after she helped found the Teachers' Federation, it brought a successful suit against the public utilities, forcing them to pay more taxes; forced the board of education to use the added tax income to increase teachers' salaries; affiliated with the Chicago Federation of Labor; sued the *Chicago Tribune* for revising its lease of school-owned land; and engineered the election of Chicago's woman superintendent of schools to the presidency of the National Education Association. Writing in 1915 in his publication, *The Daybook,* Carl Sandburg referred to her latest victory:

> Margaret Haley wins again! . . . For fifteen years, this one little woman has flung her clenched fists into the faces of contractors, school land leaseholders, tax dodgers and their politicians, fixers, go-betweens and stool pigeons. . . . Over the years the *Tribune,* the *News* and the ramified gang of manipulators who hate Margaret Haley have not been able to smutch her in the eyes of the decent men and women of this town who do their own thinking.

Tenure   Gradually, throughout the world, classroom teachers won "tenure" of their positions. In the early days, they were employed by the governing body of the school system on annual contracts; under such a system no teacher was assured of his job for the ensuing school year until he had received formal notice of his reappointment for the year. There then developed the practice of automatic renewal of the contract unless the teacher was notified by a certain date (usually three or four months before the beginning of the school year) that his services would *not* be needed. Finally, as school systems—local, state or provincial, and national—became more stabilized and organized, the rule of life tenure or tenure up to the age of retirement was adopted. Generally, under such a system, after two or three years of satisfactory service, a teacher achieves tenure and cannot be removed from his position except for specific reasons of incompetence or moral turpitude, and, even then, he has the right to a formal hearing on such charges.

This history of public-school teachers, involving a slow upgrading of teacher education combined with a struggle for professional recognition, has not been experienced by university teachers. Because higher education throughout the world has been limited to a selected few, it has correspondingly required relatively few teachers, and they seem to have emerged within the universities and to have been selected by the university authorities themselves. They frequently have constituted an inner circle or closed clique. There have, however, been a few instances of pressure by students and by civil government for improved professional standards. The South American University Reform of 1918, for instance, was started by students at the University of Córdoba in Argentina and was aimed at improving the low professional standards of teachers in Latin American universities.

The status and prestige of the university professor has been relatively high in most countries, and he has needed no politico-economic organization to fight for his professional status. Only in the late 20th century has there been a strong movement organized and led by university teachers to further upgrade or reform their profession. This movement has been particularly apparent in the United States, where the enormous extension of higher education has led to a growing teaching force and a consequent problem of maintaining professional standards. Since the 1950s the American Association of University Professors (AAUP) has pressed for higher salaries, by publishing various studies of salary levels that have singled out universities paying relatively low salaries. At the same time the AAUP has continued an aggressive campaign for academic freedom of the professor, by defining a code of professional ethics for the teacher and a procedure through which an institution must go if it proposes to discharge a professor.

Educational associations and teachers' unions. Professional groups all over the world have organized for collective action to do two quite different things. One objective of a professional organization is to improve the economic status and the working conditions of its members. A second broad objective is to improve the service that the profession performs for society. These two objectives may best be viewed separately, and it is not clear, a priori, to what extent they are mutually conflicting or mutually supportive.

Commencing in the latter half of the 19th century, elementary- and secondary-school teachers banded together to form societies of teachers in the various types of schools and in the various school subjects. Thus Germany and France with their stratified school systems had as many as five teachers' organizations that operated more or less independently of each other. By the middle of the 20th century, however, such organizations in European countries tended to coalesce into strong national organizations.

Professional associations. University teachers have generally organized themselves into associations for the improvement of scholarship and higher education. As a rule they have operated on the assumption that society will support them financially and morally if they do a good job of scholarly research, writing, and teaching. They accept as members scholars who are not actually teaching in higher institutions but are engaged in industrial, artistic, literary, or other work.

Every country has its national learned societies, which hold annual meetings, publish journals, and generally work for the improvement of scholarship. There are national organizations of classicists, foreign-language teachers, biologists, physical scientists, sociologists, psychologists, anthropologists, literature students, historians, and so forth. In addition there are interdisciplinary organizations, such as the Tavistock Institute of Human Relations (Britain) and the Social Science Research Council (U.S.). Selective prestige associations also exist to further the cause of the professions and to honour individual leaders. Some famous examples are the Académie Française, the Royal Academy (Britain), the National Academy of Sciences (U.S.), the Academy of Sciences of the U.S.S.R., and the Nippon Gakushiin (Japan).

International associations make the university teaching profession a worldwide force. There are international associations of scholars in chemistry, psychology, sociology, human development, gerontology, and other branches of scholarship. Special attempts have been made in recent years to bridge the gap separating the Communist bloc of nations from the European-North American bloc. International meetings have been held in Yugoslavia, Bulgaria, and Russia, and scholars from the Communist countries have been encouraged to attend conferences in non-Communist countries.

Teachers' unions and teachers' associations. In most countries there is one major teachers' organization to which all or nearly all teachers belong and pay dues. Sometimes membership is obligatory, sometimes voluntary. Thus there is the National Union of Teachers in England, the Japanese Teachers Union, the relatively young Fédération Générale d'Enseignement in France, and the Australian Teachers Union. In the Soviet Union, where much of the political and social life of the people is organized around unions, there are three teachers' unions —for preschool teachers, primary- and secondary-school teachers, and teachers in higher education. These unions in the U.S.S.R. provide pensions, vacation pay, and sick-leave pay and thus touch the welfare of teachers at many points. There are also professional societies for subject-matter specialists within the unions and subordinate to them.

The organizational complex is stable in some countries and changing in others. England, for example, has two different associations for male and female secondary-school teachers, two different associations for male and female headmasters of secondary schools, and a separate Association of Teachers in Technical Institutions. These associations are parallel to the National Union of Teachers, which is open to any qualified teacher from nursery school to university level. The National Union has no political affiliation but is politically powerful in its own right. France, in contrast, has a wide variety of teachers' organizations, with various political leanings, but they do not get on well together and are politically less effective.

In the United States, there is a basic rivalry between the National Education Association, which includes teachers of various levels as well as administrators, and the American Federation of Teachers, a trade union that excludes administrators. Since about 1960 the NEA, a loose federation of local, state, and national organizations, has become more militant in working for the economic improvement of teachers and has tolerated strikes. This policy has resulted in a reorganization of the NEA into a looser federation, with classroom teachers operating quite separately from the associations of administrators. It has also brought the NEA into direct competition with the AFT, which is relatively strong in several large cities.

Although the classroom teachers' organizations began as agents for obtaining better salaries and working conditions, wherever they have succeeded substantially in this effort they have turned to the other activity—setting standards of performance and attempting to improve educational policy and practice. Faced with great difficulties in educating children in the slums and ghettoes of the big cities, the teachers' union in the U.S., for instance, has put into its collective bargaining agreements a statement of interest in, and responsibility for, educational policy and for the development of teaching methods and the training of teachers for those difficult positions.

The various national primary- and secondary-school teachers' associations have moved toward the formation of two loose international federations. One includes the national associations from the Communist bloc of countries—the World Federation of Teachers' Unions. The other, the World Confederation of Organizations of the Teaching Profession, was founded in 1952 and includes most of the national associations from the non-Communist bloc. They both compete for the allegiance of teachers' organizations in the uncommitted countries.

THE TEACHING PROFESSION
AND CONTEMPORARY SOCIAL REVOLUTIONS

In almost every country with a free public voice, there are found today new militants urging professional associations to take sides in political controversies over problems that do not lie in their fields of professional competence. The argument in favour of militancy is that modern societies are engaged in a social revolution that is changing profoundly the nature of contemporary society, that this revolution will have profound effects on the teaching profession, and that teachers should assume responsibility for directing education toward constructive participation in the social revolution.

At the same time, the militants foresee a drastic change in the teaching profession. They see it as: (1) more critical of itself—new members are skeptical of many of what were once supposed to be established propositions of pedagogy and of science; (2) impatient for rapid change—the rate of social change of the past 50 years is presumed to be too slow; (3) adopting human welfare—the well-being of all people and especially of disadvantaged people—as the crowning objective of the profession; (4) looking to the consumer for guidance in the work of the profession —they believe in sharing power with students or clients in the shaping of education; and (5) becoming less concerned with formal professional standards, such as diplomas, licenses, and university degrees and turning more teaching responsibility over to teacher aides, using pupils as tutors, or admitting students to the university with little or no examination of their formal knowledge.

BIBLIOGRAPHY. UNESCO, *Statistical Yearbook* (1952–), an annual report giving the latest available data on teachers throughout the world; A.M. CARR-SAUNDERS and P.A. WILSON, *The Professions* (1933), a standard work; R.L. EBEL (ed.), *Encyclopedia of Educational Research*, 4th ed. (1969), summary articles on teachers in America, under various headings; NATIONAL EDUCATION ASSOCIATION, *NEA Research Bulletin* (quarterly), a periodical on the status of public-school teachers; AMERICAN ASSOCIATION OF UNIVERSITY PROFESSORS, *AAUP Bulletin* (quarterly), a publication analyzing salaries and academic freedom of teachers in higher education.

(R.J.H.)

Tea Production

Tea is made from the young leaves and leaf buds of the tea plant, a species of evergreen (*Camellia sinensis*). Ancient Chinese and Japanese legends refer to a beverage made from an infusion of dried tea leaves, the introduction of tea sometimes being attributed to the emperor Shen Nung about 2737 BC. Existing records credit the Chinese with originating tea cultivation, although it is possible that some tribes in Shan States in Burma, China, and Siam (Thailand) have used tea in some form as long as the Chinese. Lu Yu, writing in about AD 780, said that there were "a thousand and ten thousand" teas. He described the tea leaf, specifying that it must be plucked only during certain moons and in clear weather, and he explained how the leaf is manipulated in the hands, dried, and sealed. The China tea plant, brought to Japan about AD 800, was regarded as a medicine for 500 years, until green tea was developed and became a popular Japanese beverage.

China introduced tea to the world. The word tea comes from a Chinese ideogram pronounced "tay" in the Amoy dialect and came into English with that pronunciation, changing to its present form in the 18th century. Tea was introduced into Europe in the early 17th century, with the beginning of trade between Europe and the Far East. By 1715 the British East India Company, with a monopoly on overseas trade held over those British companies that were operating in Asia, was firmly established in Canton. The tea trade increased so rapidly that in 1805 England imported 7,500,000 pounds. In 1833, the Company, losing its legal monopoly, began to look for other sources of supply. The cultivation of tea in India began in 1834, with the planting of wild tea found growing in Assam in 1823. The tea produced was sold in London in 1839 and, with its acceptance, the modern tea industry began.

In the late 19th century China still supplied the bulk of the tea exported, with a peak figure in 1886 of 300,-000,000 pounds, of which 170,000,000 were exported to Britain. India, which that year produced 90,000,000 pounds, soon moved into the lead of exporting countries. Ceylon followed India as a tea producer in 1867, after leaf disease caused the failure of its coffee plantations. Tea production began in Java in 1878. Tea is currently produced in about 30 countries, ranging from Soviet Georgia, latitude 42° N, to South Africa, latitude 29° S. The greatest producers are India, Sri Lanka (formerly Ceylon), and China, with Japan, eight African countries, Caucasia (Soviet Georgia, Turkey, and Iran), and South America responsible for the remaining production.

The table shows the distribution of tea planting, the amount produced in each area, and 1967 exports.

Tea Areas, Production and Export			
country	area (000 ac)	production (000,000 lb)	export (000,000 lb)
China	...	600	70
Japan	121	187	4
India	868	672	471
Pakistan	100	65	0
Sri Lanka	599	496	477
Indonesia	164	89	59
Taiwan	88	54	42
Malaya and Vietnam	26	16	10
Africa	267	211	164
Caucasia	297	211	20
South America	89	45	39
Total	2,619	2,646	1,356

Habitat of the tea plant

The natural habitat of the tea plant is considered to be within the fan-shaped area between the Nāgāland, Manipur, and Lushai hills along the Assam-Burma frontier in the west; through to China, probably as far as Chekiang province in the east; and from this line south through the hills of Burma and Thailand into Vietnam. The east-west axis extends about 1,500 miles (2,400 kilometres) from longitude 95° to 120° E, and the north-south axis covers about 1,200 miles (1,920 kilometres), from the northern part of Burma, latitude 29° N, passing through Yunnan and Indochina, reaching latitude 11° N.

Tea growing. *Tea plant varieties.* The three main varieties of the tea plant, China, Assam, and Cambodia, each occur in their most distinct form at the extremes of the fan-shaped area. There are an infinite number of hybrids between the varieties; such crosses can be seen in almost any tea field.

The China variety, a multistemmed bush growing as high as 9 feet (2.75 metres), is a hardy plant able to withstand cold winters and has an economic life of at least 100 years. When grown at an altitude near that of Darjeeling and Ceylon, it produces teas with valuable flavour during the season's second flush or growth of new shoots.

The Assam variety, a single-stem tree ranging from 20 to 60 feet (6 to 18 metres) in height and including several subvarieties, has an economic life of 40 years with regular pruning and plucking. The tea planter recognizes five main subvarieties: the tender light-leaved Assam, the less tender dark-leaved Assam, the hardy Manipuri and Burma types, and the very large-leaved Lushai. In Upper Assam, the dark-leaved Assam plant, when its leaves are highly pubescent, produces very fine quality "golden tip" teas during its second flush. (The Chinese word *pek-ho*, meaning "white hair" or "down," refers to the "tip" in tea, which is correlated with quality.)

The Cambodia variety, a single-stem tree growing to about 16 feet (5 metres) in height, is not cultivated but has been naturally crossed with other varieties.

The mature leaves of the tea plant, differing in form according to variety, range from 1½ to 10 inches (3.80 to 25 centimetres) in length, the smallest being the China variety and the largest the Lushai subvariety. In harvesting, or plucking, the shoot removed usually includes the

By courtesy of the Ceylon Tea Centre, London

A tea shoot comprising a bud and two leaves being plucked by hand in Sri Lanka (Ceylon).

bud and the two youngest leaves. The weight of 2,000 freshly plucked China bush shoots may be one pound (454 grams); the same number of Assam shoots may weigh two pounds (908 grams). Tea leaves may be serrated, bullate, or smooth; stiff or flabby; the leaf pose ranges from erect to pendant; and the degree of pubescence varies widely from plant to plant.

Cultivation. Three basic requirements must be considered in planning a tea estate: climate, soil acidity, and labour availability.

A suitable climate has a minimum annual rainfall of 45 to 50 inches (1,140 to 1,270 millimetres), with proper distribution. If there is a cool season, with average temperatures 20° F (11° C) or more below those of the warm season, the growth rate will decrease and a dormant period will follow, even when the cool season is the wetter one.

Tea soils must be acid; tea cannot be grown in alkaline

soils. A desirable pH value is 5.8 to 5.4 or less. A crop of 1,500 pounds of tea per acre (1,650 kg/ha) requires 1.5 to 2 workers per acre (3.7 to 4.9/ha) to pluck the tea shoots and perform other fieldwork. Mechanical plucking has been tried, but because of its lack of selectivity, cannot replace hand plucking.

Scientific study of tea production began about 1890. Most tea-producing countries maintain scientific research stations to study every aspect of the subject, including seed production, clonal selection (for the propagation of single leaf cuttings), tea nursery management, transplanting, de-

By courtesy of Brooke Bond Oxo Ltd.

Single node cuttings growing in a tea vegetative propagation nursery, Kenya. The cuttings or clones are taken from a bush carefully selected for productivity, hardiness, and quality.

velopment of the bush and subsequent pruning and plucking, soil management and fertilizer use, and the ultimate replanting of the stand. Although procedures in all countries are related, appropriate details must be determined for each area. Since 1900, advancements in tea cultivation have increased the average yield per acre in Assam from 400 to 1,000 pounds, with many estates producing over 1,500 pounds.

The scientific study of tea

Pests and diseases. The tea plant is subject to attack from at least 150 insect species and 380 fungus diseases. In northeast India, where 125 pests and 190 fungi have been detected, losses from pests and diseases were recently estimated at 67,000,000 pounds (30,000,000 kilograms) of tea per annum. More than 100 pests and 40 diseases occur in the tea fields of Japan. Sri Lanka, where estates are close together or contiguous, has recorded many blights and suffered serious losses. Africa has little trouble with blights; the tea mosquito (*Helopeltis theivora*) is the only serious pest. Caucasia, with a climate similar to that of Japan, grows the China variety of plant and has no serious pests or blights.

Blight control has become highly developed. Northeast Indian scientists have issued a list of 40 approved proprietary pesticides. Some of these pesticides cannot be applied during the plucking season; others require that the two subsequent rounds of weekly pluckings be discarded.

Tea preparation. Hand methods for the preparation of tea shoots, consisting of the young leaves and terminal leaf bud, have their origin in antiquity. Tea is designated as black (fermented), green (unfermented), or oolong (semifermented), depending upon the process applied. Green tea is produced mainly in China, Japan, and Taiwan, but 98 percent of the international trade is in black tea.

When black tea is made by the small producer, the leaf is plucked on a clear day after the dew is gone, exposed to the sun and air for at least an hour, then lightly rolled on a table to develop a red colour and an aroma. The leaves are heated in a hot iron pan, rolled, heated several additional times, and finally dried in a basket over a charcoal fire. With China mechanizing its industry, China teas may retrieve their importance in the world markets.

In China, green tea is made by heating the freshly plucked leaf in an iron pan for a few minutes, causing the leaf to turn yellow, inactivating the enzymes, and killing the leaf. It is then hand rolled and given further roastings,

Chinese and Japanese green tea

which turn it to olive green and then to a bluish tint. In Japan, where most of the crop is made into green tea, the leaf is heated by steam, and modern machines perform the rolling and drying.

Oolong, semifermented tea, is prepared in South China and Taiwan from a special form of China plant, *chesima*, that gives this tea unique flavour. Preparation is similar to that followed in making China black tea. Both China and oolong teas are sometimes scented with flowers, such as jasmine.

Brick tea, made in China for export to inner Asia, is of little importance in world trade. It may consist of leaf, stalk, and even twigs, or mainly of tea dust and fannings (coarse tea dust). The bulk is softened with steam and then compressed into blocks or bricks.

In Burma, Thailand, and China, the tea leaf may be pickled and the product, which is called *leppet-so*, eaten as a vegetable.

Modern processing. When tea cultivation began in Assam, Chinese growers came to instruct the planters in leaf preparation. It was soon apparent that village hand methods were not suited to plantation work, and new processing methods were developed. In the new withering process, the leaves were spread on trays and left overnight, then rolled only once, and spread on the floor to ferment. Drying began in a hot iron pan and was finished on trays placed over a charcoal fire. Hand-rolling required the greatest amount of labour. The modern mechanical roller was developed in Assam in 1887. In the same year drying machines were produced in which the rolled, fermented leaf, spread on moving metal trays, was subjected to hot air currents. By 1890 the tea factory had replaced the tea house. The leaf, withered, or dehydrated, on racks for 18 hours, was then machine rolled for about an hour, fermented in a cool, humid room for three to four hours (including the rolling period); then dried by machine firing. Mechanical sorting or grading was carried out on wire mesh trays, ranging from 8- to 30-mesh. Six or more grades were produced, ranging in size from the unbroken orange pekoe to the smaller broken grades, fannings, and dust.

Tea leaf withering or wilting has always presented difficulties. Controlled loft withering was studied in Ceylon, but it was not until 1958 that trough withering was invented in the Congo. In the trough method conditioned air is forced through an 8-inch (20-centimetre) layer of leaf, producing an even wither. In the loft method the leaf is spread thinly, producing a wither that varies widely from rack to rack. In Assam 100 parts of fresh leaf may lose 30 parts of water during the wither, whereas in Sri Lanka the loss may be as much as 45 parts.

In Assam, where natural conditions often discourage withering, the loft is impractical; rolling frequently had to be performed on unwithered leaf prior to the invention of the trough. Unwithered leaf does not roll well, and in 1925 the "unorthodox" procedure was instituted, in which a Legg tobacco cutter was used to shred fresh leaf. This method makes a cut about 1/32 inch (0.08 centimetre) wide, distorting most of the leaf cells, and is followed by a short roll, a brief fermentation period, and firing.

The shredding and rolling process

A CTC (crushing, tearing, and curling) machine was invented in Assam in 1930. Normally withered leaf is given a short, light roll, then put through the machine. Two engraved metal rollers, one making 70 revolutions per minute (rpm) and the other, 700, distort the leaf in a fraction of a second. Other machines producing rapid and full leaf distortion have also been perfected. The unorthodox method is currently applied to 70 percent of the tea manufactured in northeast India, and the method is also prevalent in several other countries. The grades of tea produced are mainly dust and fannings, with some brokens.

The tea is machine fired, and on the following day it is sorted into grades. It is then stored in bins until a sufficient amount accumulates to make up an invoice of about 60 to 240 chests. Tea chests, made of three-ply wood and lined with aluminum foil and rice paper, hold 80 to 120 pounds (36 to 50 kilograms) of tea.

Tea bags. The tea bag, or tea ball, originally used over a century ago, regained its popularity in the 1950s. It is made of special paper and filled with the smaller sized grades of teas.

Instant or soluble teas. Green tea powders or soluble tea extracts have been used in Japan for many years. The tea industry is now developing and producing instant or powdered black teas. Instant teas offer greater convenience than ordinary leaf tea; they are easy and quick to infuse, leave no grouts for disposal, and can be used in vending machines. Instant tea powder may be produced by evaporating an ordinary infusion to dryness, but a more satisfactory and economical method is to distort and ferment tea leaf and then extract it, unfired. The resulting extract is evaporated to dryness at a low temperature, so that the resultant powder will produce an infusion with a bright, brisk liquor and the tea aroma. The evaporation may be carried out at a low temperature under reduced pressure, or the liquor may be spray-dried or freeze-dried. Infusions from the instant teas now available usually lack the character of a normal tea infusion but are improving as study continues.

Chemistry of tea. A freshly plucked tea shoot, consisting of two leaves and a bud, contains about 77 percent water and 23 percent solid matter. Half of the solid matter is insoluble in water; it is made up of crude fibre, cellulose, starches, proteins, etc. The remaining soluble half includes over 20 amino acids, about 30 polyphenolic bodies, 12 sugars, and 6 organic acids. The Assam variety of plant is richer in caffeine and polyphenolic bodies than the China plant.

The caffeine content of the tea shoot is highest in the terminal bud, where it may be 4 to 5 percent of the dry matter, and lowest in the stalk, where it may be 1.5 percent. Although caffeine does not play an active part in changes occurring during processing, it is one of the constituents, with theaflavins and thearubigins, that forms the "cream" or precipitate when a tea infusion cools.

The role of caffeine in tea

Two polyphenols of the flavanol group, *l*-epi gallo catechin and its gallate, are mainly involved in the changes that take place during fermentation. After the leaf is distorted, the tea leaf enzyme, a copper-protein compound, acts on these two substances, oxidizing them to orthoquinones. When the enzyme action ceases, the orthoquinones dimerize to form bis-flavanols and rapidly condense to theaflavins (yellow bodies) and then still further to thearubigins (red and brown bodies). Some of the last have strong tanning properties and precipitate leaf proteins that are lost to the tea infusion. Correct manufacture aims at getting a suitable ratio of theaflavins to thearubigins. In a good tea the ratio may be 1 to 12, in a poor tea, lacking briskness and brightness, it may be 1 to 20, and in a commercial blend it may be 1 to 16.

In orthodox teas as much as a quarter of the oxidizable polyphenols may remain unchanged, but in unorthodox teas practically all of them are changed.

The various aromas of tea are developed in the field and during each stage of manufacture. The 14 volatile compounds found in tea include methyl and ethyl alcohol, several aldehydes, and sulfur compounds.

Pharmacology of tea. Although tea is consumed primarily for its caffeine content, the action of the caffeine is not apparent for some minutes, and the immediate comforting effect of the liquor is due to its warmth. A tea infusion provides only about 4 calories per cup but, with the addition of a tablespoon of milk (10 calories) and a lump of sugar (25 calories), it provides about 40 calories. In Great Britain, where six cups a day are average, tea may contribute 240 calories to the daily adult diet. Tea contains several of the B-complex vitamins, and six cups provide about 10 percent of the average daily adult requirement.

One pound of good tea (0.45 kilogram) may contain up to 245 grains (15.9 grams) of caffeine and is sufficient to make 200 cups of the beverage.

When an infusion is kept hot, changes in the thearubigins take place with a deterioration in quality. A tea infusion made with distilled water has a pH value of about 5. In areas where tap water is hard because of high lime content, a tea infusion made with the local water will have a high pH value (*e.g.*, 6.6 in London), producing changes in some of the constituents responsible for the bright orange colour and causing the liquor to look dull.

The tea trade. Although there has always been correlation between the planting and trading sections of the industry, a balance of supply and demand has never been achieved for long. Tea deteriorates and cannot be stockpiled for more than a few months. Because of these difficulties, many price slumps have occurred over the years, with serious slumps in 1866, 1879, 1896, 1920, and 1932, following which the International Tea Committee was formed by India, Ceylon, and the Dutch East Indies (Indonesia) to stabilize the market. In 1952, however, another slump developed, and by 1970 the expanding production in 30 leading tea-producing countries had brought another.

Public auctions. The first London public tea auctions were held in 1834; current London auctions deal with teas from about 25 countries. Public auctions opened in Calcutta in 1861, in Colombo in 1883, in Cochin in 1947, in Chittagong in 1949, and in Nairobi in 1956. These centres deal with teas produced in their own countries or areas. There are also some local tea marts, and considerable amounts of tea are traded privately.

Tea tasting. Teas bought at auction are blended and packaged by the traders to suit their own markets. Each firm bases its bidding on information provided by a tea taster, who notes the appearance of the dry tea, the infused leaf, and the infusion; the aroma of both the dry tea and the infused leaf; and the taste and flavour of the infusion.

The tea taster's infusion is made from a weight of tea equal to that of a silver sixpence (1/10 ounce; 2.83 grams), which is infused in a China mug having ¼ pint capacity (0.12 litre) and fitted with a lid. Boiling water is poured on the tea and allowed to stand for five or six minutes; the resulting liquor is poured into a handleless cup, and the infused leaf is shaken from the mug onto the lid. The liquor, without additives, is tasted at a temperature of about 110° F (43° C), usually from a spoon, after which it is spat out. The special vocabulary of the tea taster includes about 120 terms.

Fox Photos Ltd.

London tea brokers tasting tea.

Tea blending. Teas to be used for a blend are selected for the quality, flavour, strength, and body of the liquors and the size, style, and density of the leaf. A proportion of neutral teas or "fillers" may be used to round off a blend and balance the price, and the blend may include four or five Assam teas, the same number of Ceylons, and a few Africans. China teas usually blend well only with Darjeelings and fine Ceylons.

Teas are blended by mixing the leaf in a machine consisting of a revolving drum fitted with veins. Satisfactory

The world market and the International Tea Committee

blending requires about 16 revolutions. The drum is half-filled with leaf, the charge ranging from 300 pounds (136 kilograms) to 5,000 pounds (2,265 kilograms) according to the size of the machine. The smallest drum may revolve at 20 revolutions per minute and the largest at three revolutions per minute.

BIBLIOGRAPHY. J.R. SEALY, *A Revision of the Genus Camellia*, sect. 6, designated "Thea" (1958), comprises five species, but only three of these are connected with the tea plant of commerce. INTERNATIONAL TEA COMMITTEE, *Bulletin of Statistics* (annual), gives current figures on production, export, consumption, tea stocks, and auction prices. E.A.H. ROBERTS, "Economic Significance of Flavonoid Compounds: Tea Fermentation," in T.A. GEISSMAN (ed.), *The Chemistry of Flavonoid Compounds*, ch. 16 (1962), discusses the properties of a tea infusion, which are based largely on flavonoid compounds. W.H. UKERS, *All About Tea*, 2 vol. (1935), deals with the historical, technological, scientific, commercial, social, and artistic aspects of tea production and includes extensive bibliographies. C.R. HARLER, *The Culture and Marketing of Tea*, 3rd ed. (1964), *Tea Growing* (1966), and *Tea Manufacture* (1963), are works discussing methods and current problems of the tea industry. C.J. HARRISON, *Indian Tea* (1953), deals with the development of tea production in India, where the modern tea industry originated. T. EDEN, *Tea* (1958), discusses tea production in Sri Lanka and in the newly developing African tea industry.

(C.R.H.)

Technological Sciences

The technological sciences are a range of disciplines embracing the traditional engineering branches, the agricultural sciences, the modern disciplines relating to space, computers, and automation. From man's earliest emergence, technology has been one of the four environments within which he has lived—the others being the cosmic, the natural, and the social.

Technology has changed radically in quantity and quality over the millennia. For thousands of years science and technology constituted distinct traditions. Beginning sometime in the 19th century, they entered into a new and much closer relationship (see also TECHNOLOGY, HISTORY OF and TECHNOLOGY, CONCEPTIONS OF).

Emergence of the technological sciences. During the Renaissance in Europe, men of learning took new notice of the ancient crafts and advocated a closer relationship with them. The arts, it was suggested, could provide problems for science to solve, and the latter might provide laws and rules that would allow the former to progress more rapidly. Something of the sort began to happen in the 19th century, and a number of technological sciences —analogous to the physical sciences—began to appear and to develop competence; finally, they became indispensable for most progress in engineering.

The engineering disciplines. The rise of the technological sciences came only with the creation of a community of practitioners separate from either the body of inventors or that of scientists. The new group of specialists, who came to be called engineers, had, on the one hand, scientific training and a grasp of mathematics and, on the other, a commitment to and intimate knowledge of technology.

In some areas, such as strength of materials and hydraulics, engineering sciences evolved out of theoretical and experimental physics. In other cases, such as kinematics of mechanisms, the new science grew directly from traditional engineering practice. Either way, such fields were distinct from their antecedents and by the end of the 19th century formed a separate body of knowledge that allowed technological problems to be treated scientifically.

The problem of the strength of materials provides an example of this development. During the first decades of the 19th century, iron became a common material in the construction of buildings, bridges, and other structures. Its users accumulated practical experience, but scientifically collected data and theory were conspicuously lacking. Until rule of thumb was replaced by reliable formulas, material was wasted in overbuilding or lives were lost through underbuilding. Some development of this science was begun in the 18th century, but systematic experimentation only began with Eaton Hodgkinson and Sir William Fairbairn of Great Britain in 1826. Fairbairn's *On the Application of Cast and Wrought Iron to Building Purposes* (1854) immediately became a classic among builders. In France such investigators as Emiland-Marie Gauthey and Claude-Louis-Marie Navier worked on similar problems. Their efforts were extended by mathematicians at the École Polytechnique in Paris (see below). In the United States, the strength of materials was scientifically investigated in 1830 by Alexander D. Bache, working for the Franklin Institute of Philadelphia on the causes of steam-boiler explosions. During the next half century there was a concerted effort to extend the competence and variety of such scientific investigations into practical engineering problems. In 1872, for example, the American Society of Civil Engineers successfully asked the U.S. Congress to appropriate funds for a testing machine to discover the properties of iron and steel. Such knowledge was increasingly necessary for the safe and efficient use of materials in the burgeoning economy of the late 19th century.

Neither individual scientists nor government agencies had the long-term commitment necessary to continue progress in the technological sciences. It was the engineering schools and their faculties that made the primary contributions to this task. Engineering education received its initial impetus in France. During the French Revolution the School of Bridges and Highways and the School of Mines were supplemented by the excellent and broader Polytechnic School (École Polytechnique; 1794), which had wide influence outside France, for example, on the new United States Military Academy at West Point (1802).

Engineering education (margin)

A new development was the founding, in 1824, of the Rensselaer Polytechnic Institute in Troy, New York, the first private engineering school. After the passage of the Morrill Land-Grant College Act (1862), by which the United States government granted land to state colleges to aid engineering and agricultural education, such schools as the Massachusetts Institute of Technology (1861) became prominent in the engineering sciences and the training of engineers. In Great Britain the universities of London and Glasgow began instruction in engineering in the 1840s, with other universities following.

Agricultural engineering. Agricultural engineering also had its origins in the 19th century. Here, too, it was hoped that the application of mathematics, the scientific method, and known scientific laws would produce improved implements. Thomas Jefferson, for example, tried to redesign the moldboard of the plow with the aid of mathematics. The difficulty of producing machines that would perform adequately under the wide range of conditions found on farms retarded machine development, however, as did the lack of a cheap, adequate, and flexible source of power. Mechanization was most advanced in the United States, where during the first decade of the 20th century, gasoline tractors began to break the power bottleneck. At this same time, in 1907, the American Society of Agricultural Engineers was founded by farm mechanics teachers. In 1909 the first department of agricultural engineering was established at the Iowa State College. By midcentury, 44 such departments were operating in the United States, and 40 additional institutions around the world granted degrees in agricultural engineering.

Agricultural science was not neglected. By the middle of the 19th century, soil chemistry, botany, genetics, and physiology were all being tried in an effort to improve agricultural practice. The leading scientist in this area was a German organic chemist, Justus von Liebig, who, after training in France, operated a famous laboratory at the University of Giessen. His classic work *Chemistry in its Applications to Agriculture and Physiology* (London, 1842) stirred wide response, and he trained students from many countries who then returned to their homes to apply the science. Many of them pressed for government support of agricultural education and agricultural experiment stations. When such institutional support was grant-

ed, agricultural science began to flourish. By the mid-20th century, agricultural innovation involved the efforts of both engineers and scientists, the former designing machines to handle particular crops and the latter redesigning the crops themselves to make them more amenable to machine culture.

The study of the history of technology. The history of technology, while only recently defined as a separate professional discipline, has roots in several older traditions, such as the search for priority of invention. Since patents are awarded only to the first inventor of a device, patent searches and court litigation necessarily include a historical survey of previous work in the field.

Patent searches (margin)

General historians have also given consideration to the history of technology. Especially since the 19th century, the progress of invention and industry has been considered a key index to the progress of civilization. Another scholarly source of writing has been the economic historians, especially those studying the Industrial Revolution, in which new devices obviously played an important role in economic change. Marxist scholars have had a special concern for the history of technology, concentrating on the development of implements of labour within the social structure of production. Finally, the history of technology has long been considered a branch of the history of science and has been cultivated along with that discipline.

Historians of technology continue to draw heavily upon other special and more general disciplines for data, insight, and techniques, especially on the discipline of history itself. Many important studies can only be undertaken by specialists in the physical, biological, or engineering sciences. Since technology is a social activity, all the social sciences—sociology, economics, psychology, political science, anthropology—are also pertinent to studies of its social origins and influence.

In several countries, especially the United States and Great Britain, industrial archaeology has developed as an important tool for discovering and recording technological remains—*e.g.*, dams, mill sites, quarries, and foundries, long buried or otherwise forgotten. The importance of this technique was perhaps first realized in 1962 by historians in Northern Ireland. In 1963 the British Ministry of Public Buildings and Works began an Industrial Monuments Survey, and in 1964 the British quarterly the *Journal of Industrial Archaeology* was established. Although such physical sites and the tools and machines associated with them are of critical importance in researching and writing the history of technology, the traditional narrative sources of social history (*e.g.*, the written word in the form of correspondence, diaries, and reports) remain the indispensable basis for most significant work in this field.

The history of technology is currently in a very flourishing condition. Either combined with the history of science or in separate courses, it is being taught at an increasing number of colleges both in Europe and the United States. The centre of professional training in the United States is Case Western Reserve University in Cleveland, Ohio. The Centre for the Study of the History of Technology, Bath University of Technology, Bath, England, was created in 1964. The previous year a department of history of science and technology was established at Imperial College of Science and Technology, London.

The major international organization in the field is the International Cooperation in History of Technology Committee (ICOHTEC), organized in 1965. In the United States the major organization is the Society for the History of Technology, incorporated in 1958. During the winter of 1959 the society began publication of *Technology and Culture*, an international quarterly devoted to the history of technology. Other national organizations include the Institute of History of Science and Technology, established within the framework of the Academy of Sciences of the Soviet Union and an outgrowth of the original Commission on the History of Science, Philosophy and Technology set up in 1921.

Organizations for historical studies (margin)

Outstanding among private institutions is the British organization the Newcomen Society for the Study of the

History of Engineering and Technology, which began publication of its *Transactions* in 1920. Other important serials include the German *Technik Geschichte*, begun in 1909, discontinued in 1941, and revived in 1965.

The study of the history of technology is facilitated by the existence of a number of excellent museums of science and technology. Major repositories include the Museo di Storia della Scienza in Florence, the Tekniska Museet in Stockholm, the Science Museum in London, the Conservatoire des Arts et Métiers in Paris, the Deutsches Museum in Munich, the Politekhnichesky Musey (Russian Polytechnic Museum) in Moscow, and the Smithsonian Institution in Washington, D.C.

BIBLIOGRAPHY. For general reference in this field, see MELVIN KRANZBERG and CARROLL W. PURSELL (eds.), *Technology in Western Civilization*, 2 vol. (1967). A longer work that gives relatively more emphasis to British achievements and less to the 20th century is CHARLES SINGER *et al.* (eds.), *A History of Technology*, 5 vol. (1954–58). Both of these contain extensive bibliographies, which should be supplemented by EUGENE S. FERGUSON, *Bibliography of the History of Technology* (1968). A very important effort to trace the rise of the engineering sciences is EDWIN LAYTON, "Mirror-Image Twins: The Communities of Science and Technology in 19th-Century America," *Technology and Culture*, 12:562–580 (1971). Histories of particular sciences include HUNTER ROUSE and SIMON INCE, *History of Hydraulics* (1957); EUGENE S. FERGUSON, "Kinematics of Mechanism from the Time of Watt" *Bull. U.S. Natn. Mus.*, no. 228 (1962); ISAAC TODHUNTER, *A History of the Theory of Elasticity*, 3 vol. (1893, reprinted 1960); STEPHEN P. TIMOSHENKO, *History of Strength of Materials* (1953); CYRIL STANLEY SMITH, *A History of Metallography* (1960); and FOREST R. MOULTON (ed.), *Liebig and After Liebig: An Analysis of the Progress in Agriculture Chemistry* (1942). Two yearbooks of the United States Department of Agriculture, both ed. by ALFRED STEFFERUD, survey American developments: *Power to Produce* (1960) and *After a Hundred Years* (1962).

(C.W.Pu.)

Technology, Conceptions of

The systematic study of technology as a special branch of human activity is an essentially modern phenomenon, despite roots extending back to classical Greece. The term itself, a combination of the Greek *techne*, "art, craft," with *logos*, "word, speech," meant in Greece a discourse on the arts, both fine and applied. When it first appeared in English in the 17th century, it was used to mean a discussion of the applied arts only, and gradually these "arts" themselves came to be the object of the designation. By the early 20th century, the term was coming into general usage and embraced a growing range of means, processes, and ideas in addition to tools and machines. By the second half of the century, technology was defined by such phrases as "the means or activity by which man seeks to change or manipulate his environment." Even such broad definitions have been criticized by observers who point out the blurring line between scientific inquiry and technological activity.

More significant than the problem of definition has been the debate over the value of technology, a debate in which radically differing conceptions have been developed. To perceive the roots of these conflicting conceptions, a historical perspective is indispensable.

THE CHANGING VIEW OF TECHNOLOGY

Origins and nature of technology. "Man," said Benjamin Franklin, "is a tool-making animal." Franklin might have substituted "the" for "a"; man is man precisely because he makes tools. Animals occasionally use natural tools such as sticks or stones, and the creature that became man doubtless did the same for hundreds of millennia before the first giant step of fashioning his own tool. Even then it was an interminable time before he put such toolmaking on a regular basis, and still more aeons passed as he arrived at the successive stages of standardizing his simple stone choppers and pounders and of manufacturing them—that is, providing sites and assigning specialists to the work. A degree of specialization in toolmaking was achieved by the time of Neanderthal man (70,000 BC); more advanced tools, requiring assemblage

Man, the toolmaker

of head and haft, were produced by Cro-Magnon *Homo sapiens* (40,000 BC), while the application of mechanical principles was achieved by pottery-making Neolithic man (20,000 BC) and by Metal Age man (10,000 BC).

Science and technology. With that step it might be said that the toolmaking animal introduced the great characteristic of modern technology, its relationship to science. This would be an exaggeration, however, for, until quite recently, science has remained largely divorced from technology, with each pursuing its separate path and maintaining its separate identity. Science in the classical world, East and West, belonged to the aristocratic philosophers and embodied all of knowledge, while technology was the possession of the working craftsmen. The separation was probably due less to the class division than to the fact that the speculative science of Aristotle and Ptolemy had little relevance for the technological problems of tanners, millers, silversmiths, and coopers. It was not until the lively social–economic interchange provoked by the commercial revolution of the Middle Ages that science and technology began to draw closer together. Roger Bacon, English savant of the 13th century, predicted mechanically powered ships and flying machines and was credited with the invention of gunpowder. The robust growth of technology, involving improvements in sailing ships, waterwheels, windmills, and firearms, could not fail to attract the interest of educated men. By the 16th century, Roger Bacon's namesake, Francis Bacon, was advocating experimental science, further suggesting that scientists study the methods of craftsmen and that craftsmen acquire more knowledge of science. Bacon organized a group whose purpose he described as "the knowledge of causes and the secret of things, and the enlarging of the bounds of human empire to the effecting of all things possible." Bacon, with Descartes and other contemporaries, for the first time saw man becoming the master of nature.

Yet the wedding of science and technology proposed by Francis Bacon was only slowly consummated. Over the next 200 years, carpenters and mechanics built iron bridges, steam engines, and textile machinery, but only during the course of the 19th century did technology gradually become based on science. The first scientist to become a major figure in technology emerged: Justus von Liebig, the German father of organic chemistry and inventor of synthetic fertilizer. More typically, the great 19th-century inventors built on the work of scientists: Edison, inventor of the first practical system of electrical lighting, on that of Faraday and Henry, early experimenters in electricity; Bell, inventor of the telephone, on that of Helmholtz; Marconi, inventor of radiotelegraphy, on that of Hertz and Maxwell. In the case of Edison, a significant further development took place: the union of science and technology was institutionalized. Scarcely anyone, even Edison, noticed the fact at the time, but the massive trial and error process by which he found the carbon filament for his electric light bulb resulted in the creation at Menlo Park, New Jersey, of the world's first research laboratory. Thus, the date of Edison's demonstration of the electric light, October 21, 1879, may also be taken as the birthday of modern technological research.

The first research laboratory

From this point forward the application not only of scientific knowledge but of scientific principles to technology grew. The engineering rationalism that Frederick W. Taylor applied to the organization of workers in mass production and the time and motion studies of Frank and Lillian Gilbreth were logically followed later in the 20th century by the invention of systems engineering, operations research, simulation studies, and mathematical models. These developments, added to the increased specialization and professionalization of technological work, brought technology to its highly efficient modern state.

Judged entirely on its own traditional grounds of evaluation—that is, in terms of efficiency—the result was admirable. Voices from other fields, however, were raising questions grounded in other modes of evaluation.

19th-century optimism: faith in progress. In the mid-19th century the non-technologists were almost unanimously enchanted by the wonders of the new man-made environment growing up around them. The London Exposition of 1851, with its arrays of machinery housed in the dazzling and truly innovative Crystal Palace, seemed the culmination of Francis Bacon's prophecy of "the effecting of all things possible" and the justification of Bacon's comfortably materialistic view that "Works themselves are of greater value than Assurances of the Truthfulness (of Theories) because they add to the Pleasures of Life." The new technology seemed to fit the new laissez-faire economics like a glove and to guarantee the rapid realization of the Utilitarian philosophers' ideal of "the greatest good for the greatest number." Even Marx and Engels, approaching from a radically different political orientation, saw in technology nothing but good, for in their eyes it produced an imperative toward socialist ownership and control of the means of production. Similarly, the American utopian Edward Bellamy, in his novel *Looking Backward*, foresaw a planned society in the year 2000 in which technology would play a conspicuously beneficent role.

The anti-technology trend. Yet, even in the midst of Victorian optimism, a few voices of dissent were heard, such as Emerson's ominous warning, "Things are in the saddle and ride mankind." Henry Adams, the introspective scion of one of America's most distinguished families, visiting the Paris Exhibition of 1900, experienced sensations very different from those of the admirers of the Crystal Palace. Describing his reactions in the third person in *The Education of Henry Adams*, he recorded that, to him:

the dynamo became a symbol of infinity . . . As he grew accustomed to the great gallery of machines, he began to feel the forty-foot dynamos as a moral force, much as the early Christians felt the Cross . . . He could see only an absolute *fiat* in electricity, as in faith.

His companion Samuel P. Langley, secretary of the Smithsonian Institution and a noted experimenter in flight, could give him no comfort and in fact added a new and disturbing thought. The Curies' discovery of radioactivity had shown that physical matter could actually disintegrate, something theretofore unthinkable. As Adams put it, radium "denied its God, or, what was to Langley the same thing, denied the truth of his Science . . . The force was wholly new."

Adams had another thought, less mystically profound but extraordinarily perceptive for his time:

The automobile, which since 1893 had become a nightmare at a hundred kilometres an hour, (was) almost as destructive as the electric tram which was only ten years older; and threatening to become as terrible as the locomotive steam engine . . . .

It was half a century before other intellectuals began to take up the anti-automobile theme.

Aldous Huxley's anti-utopia

Disenchantment with technology was first expressed in a dramatic and generalized way in a remarkable novel. *Brave New World*, by the British author Aldous Huxley, appearing in the midst of the Great Depression in 1932, contrasted sharply with Edward Bellamy's *Looking Backward*. Huxley pictured a society of the near future in which technology was entirely enthroned, keeping mankind in bodily comfort without knowledge of want or pain, but also without freedom, beauty, or creativity, and robbed at every turn of a unique personal existence. An echo of Huxley's viewpoint found unexpected artistic expression in the film *Modern Times*, in which Charlie Chaplin depicted the depersonalizing effect of the mass-production assembly line.

After World War II, technology came increasingly under fire for its specific wrongdoings. The outstanding contribution to this branch of anti-technology literature was *Silent Spring*, a magazine series and book by the American science writer Rachel Carson that had tremendous impact in the 1950s and 1960s, revealing the harmful effects on plant and animal life of the unrestricted use of pesticides such as DDT. Writers and politicians both in Europe and the United States joined in an anti-technology chorus that seemed to be reaching a crescendo at the very time that technology was achieving its most remark-

able results in the purely technical sense, thus realizing the aphorism of the English essayist G.K. Chesterton that "Nothing fails like success."

The two thrusts of the anti-technology literature of the second half of the 20th century remained those of Henry Adams. On one level, the immediately discernible social defects of technological progress, such as automobile fatalities, air and water pollution, urban overcrowding, and excessive noise, were roundly assailed in the press and the political forum. On a deeper level, the theme of technological tyranny over man's individuality and traditional patterns of life was refined and broadened. Perhaps the outstanding contribution to the literature of this theme was *La Technique*, published in 1954 by Jacques Ellul, a professor at the University of Bordeaux. Defining technology as "the ensemble of practices by which one uses available resources in order to achieve certain valued ends," Ellul asserted that it had become so pervasive that man now lived in a milieu of technology rather than in his old milieu, nature. The new milieu he characterized as artificial, autonomous, self-determining, nihilistic (that is, not directed to ends, though proceeding by cause and effect), and, in fact, with means enjoying primacy over ends.

Technology, Ellul held, has become so powerful and ubiquitous that other social phenomena such as politics and economics are situated "in it" rather than influenced "by it." "Modern man's state of mind is completely dominated by technical values," Ellul wrote, "and his goals are represented only by such progress and happiness as is to be achieved through techniques." The individual, in other words, had come to be adapted to the technical milieu rather than the other way around.

While Ellul broadened and deepened the thrust of the more sophisticated anti-technology criticism, he dismissed the much talked-about immediate social problems created by technology. In this he followed Huxley, whose *Brave New World* was untroubled by air and water pollution. Ellul dismissed the social problems created by technology as fake, saying,

We make too much of the disagreeable features of technical development . . . I am convinced that all such inconveniences will be done away with by the ongoing evolution of Technique itself and indeed, that it is only by means of such evolution that this can happen.

But the solution of such fake problems, he maintained, could do nothing to solve the basic problem he was describing, which he summarized in two questions:

First, is man able to remain master in a world of means —that is, a world in which technology's own imperatives determine social directions?

Second, can a new civilization appear that will encompass technology and still permit man to be free? Anticipating one line of response, he observed that technology has indeed freed man from many restrictions of time and space, but he added a searching question, "Is this what it means to be free?"

Accelerated rate of change. One of the principal elements of the context in which such critics as Ellul appeared in the last half of the 20th century was the rate of acceleration of technological advance. Illustrations abound, of which perhaps the most dramatic was the six and one-half years that passed between the disclosure of the fission of uranium in January 1939 and the detonation of the first atomic bomb at Alamogordo in July 1945. A distinctive feature of the progress from laboratory experiment to awesome realization was that scientists as well as laymen were unprepared for the result; in the words of the British scholar Ritchie Calder, "The safebreakers had forced the nuclear lock before the locksmiths knew how it worked."

Many of the "safebreakers" were profoundly troubled by the fact. J. Robert Oppenheimer, who directed the work of the assembly of the bomb at Los Alamos, later opposed the decision to build the thermonuclear (fusion) bomb; but inevitably the decision was made and the more powerful bomb built, in the Soviet Union as well as the United States. In a lecture, Oppenheimer described the new accelerated pace of technology in these words:

The beginning of the atomic age

One thing that is new is the prevalence of newness, the changing scale and scope of change itself, so that the world alters as we walk in it, so that the years of man's life measure not some small growth or rearrangement or moderation of what he learned in childhood, but a great upheaval.

The information revolution, centring on the computer, for a time appeared almost more alarming than the bomb; the "electronic brain" seemed capable of replacing the human brain. Many computer limitations have since become obvious, though an entirely new type of computer, built as an analogue to the human nervous system, may presently raise new spectres along this line.

Yet, despite the admittedly headlong pace of modern technology, some qualification is in order on historical grounds. There have been times in man's past history in which technological innovation swept all or part of the world with extraordinary force; for example, the windmill in medieval Europe, the firearm in 16th-century Japan, and electric communication in the 19th century. Even granting technological acceleration, the present is not the first age to face the problem of rapid change.

A WORLD VIEW OF TECHNOLOGY'S PROMISE AND THREAT

One of the most striking aspects of modern conceptions of technology is the continuing deep division between the views of the developed and the underdeveloped nations. Broadly speaking, the anti-technology criticism on both the sophisticated and the popular level has come from the developed countries, while the underdeveloped and semi-developed nations have generally taken a favourable, often even an aggressively favourable, view.

Past and present benefits. That technology has produced incalculable material benefits for the developed nations is hardly in dispute, and that it has the potential for producing similar benefits for the underdeveloped nations may certainly be assumed. Even though Gandhi opposed the industrialization of India up to his death in 1948, his hope for a return to the pre-industrialized economy symbolized by the hand spinning wheel was so little shared by his countrymen that his successors have embraced modern technology as eagerly as all the other leaders of the underdeveloped world. Of all technology's successes, the outstanding one is probably the increase and stabilization of the food supply through the application of machinery and power, fertilizers and pesticides, hybridization, and processing techniques. These, reinforced by the medical–pharmaceutical–sanitation revolution, have brought rapid decreases in mortality rates and increases in life-spans. It is highly characteristic of the opposing world views that such obvious material benefits, longed for by humanity through the ages, have stimulated in the developed countries a considerable alarm over the resulting population increase. Among the many secondary but still important benefits much desired in the underdeveloped countries are the freeing of labour from the drudgery of the old-fashioned farm, the dramatic reduction in cost of manufactured commodities through mass-production techniques (sometimes to a tenth or twentieth of their former cost), the enormous improvement in literacy and educational levels, and the increased convenience and enrichment of life by the transportation–communications revolution.

Promise for underdeveloped regions. The fact that the underdeveloped countries want to import technology from the developed countries and the fact that the developed countries see the export of their technology as in their own self-interest would seem to provide a congenial base for collaboration. Many problems have become obvious, several of which have to do with differing conceptions of technology's role. Two important principles have emerged: first, that the technology of the developed nations is not automatically ideal, or even always suitable, for the underdeveloped nations, and, second, that the underdeveloped nations need not necessarily pass through the same succession of stages that the vanguard of developed nations has undergone. The first principle is illustrated by the Malayan observer at a World Power Conference who passed by the giant atomic power station exhibit, explaining that he was looking for a little floating

Development of food supply

generator that could be used to harness a stream to provide light for illumination—"then we could read and learn about all these wonderful things they are talking about here." Largeness and complexity, the basic characteristics of so much of modern technology, are unsuited to most underdeveloped countries because the national markets are small, skilled labour is scarce, and the cost in foreign exchange is high. Simple, inexpensive machinery that can be operated and maintained by persons of little education is far more appropriate to these agrarian nations than computers and automated devices. A unit for producing methane gas from cow dung may be better, at least in the short run, than an atomic-power installation.

Yet the second principle, that the new nations should be assisted to avoid the hardships undergone by the old, is equally important in meeting what Adlai E. Stevenson called "the revolution of rising expectations." A Southeast Asian diplomat used this metaphor: while the developing nations must carry their own cross of technology, it need not be of the same weight as that borne by Europe and the United States in the 19th century; it can be of aluminum (a 20th-century material). Part of this conception, in the view of many, is the effort to export not the technology of the European–American past or even present but, rather, that of the future—that is, the newest ideas now emerging, such as emission-free engines.

Dependence of new nations on the old

Role of the scientist. The problem of the developing nations has had a stimulating effect on certain already apparent educational tendencies within the developed nations that have large implications for the problem of control of technology. Partly in response to a widely voiced criticism of the "two cultures" that seemed to separate educated Westerners into two intellectual classes, two broad, complementary trends had appeared by the 1970s: an added emphasis in the science and engineering curricula on humanities and social science and the education of humanities students in the history and philosophy of science and technology. A revealing study showed that the creative scientist knows more about the history of science than does his more routine-minded colleague; a reasonable inference is that the creative man knows better, from his study of history, what is truly novel and, therefore, worth pursuing.

The autonomy of technology. Such better educated scientists, engineers, and laymen are needed both to operate and to criticize the increasingly complex technological apparatus. In the past the technologist has not been expected to police his own technology, because he could control, and indeed could envision, only a small part of it. As a whole, the monster remained out of reach. In itself technology is fundamentally neutral, and even passive; in Lynn White's phrase, "Technology opens doors; it does not compel men to enter." Yet, from the beginning, the fact that technology exists in a social medium has imposed certain constraints. These were more affirmative than negative; that is, the social medium tended to push technology in certain directions rather than to keep it from going in certain others. Technology has never been wholly autonomous in the sense of being out of reach of the control of its human creators and operators. If there have been few important instances of moral constraints hampering technology, there have been many of technology itself creating a potential for moral decisions; for example, in the case of aid to the underdeveloped nations. It is also evident that technology's direction is itself often determined by political considerations with moral (or immoral) overtones.

It can be demonstrated that man exhibits resistance to inexorable changes in the milieu; for example, as Lynn White, an authority on medieval technology, has pointed out, the crank, which is used to convert reciprocal motion into rotary motion and vice versa, was slow to be invented and slow to disseminate. The reason seems to be that reciprocal motion is natural to living things, while rotary motion never occurs in them. Yet the crank became a universal part of man's technical apparatus. There is perhaps an important insight for the future here. "To use a crank," in White's words, "our tendons and muscles must relate themselves to the motion of galaxies and electrons. From this inhuman adventure our race long recoiled."

The history of the crank may have significance for the future of 20th-century man. The distinguished German physicist Werner Heisenberg has made this prediction:

Many of our technical apparatuses will perhaps in the future belong as inescapably to man as the snail's shell does to the snail or the spider's web to the spider . . . the apparatus would then be rather a part of our human organism.

An idea from which men at first tend to recoil may come to be accepted and even embraced. Humans may acquire, for example, through implanted electrodes, access to vast memory storage banks, enormously increasing their intellectual powers. Thus, a changing concept of technology may involve a changing concept of man himself. Yet even in Heisenberg's forecast, man remains the master.

Technology's continuing presence. Whatever justice lies in the views of Ellul, his predecessors, and his successors to come, no actual repudiation of technology appears to be possible. Technology seems destined to grow, in accordance with laws that man can in all likelihood discover only in retrospect. The need to exercise control over technology at once raises the question of who or what is to control the controllers. Yet some critics feel that this question may not be as formidable as Huxley and others have made out, because a planned technological society in which the planning would be limited to producing abundance and eliminating the need for drudgery might leave great scope for freedom and democracy. At least in a relatively short run, it would be fair to say that the momentous political–philosophical questions with which the world will grapple in the closing decades of the 20th century and the first decades of the 21st may be influenced by technology in a favourable as well as unfavourable sense. A few general principles in respect to technology's future have won broad acceptance: that the problem is global and cannot be adequately dealt with inside national borders; that institutions are needed to study technological problems, both technical and social; that both technologists and non-technologists must be given appropriate educational formulas; and that, by these means and whatever others are discovered, technology must be made man's servant. "In the final analysis," as Peter Drucker says, "this surely means mastery by man over himself, for if anyone is to blame, it is not the tool but the human maker and user." It is a poor carpenter, according to the adage, who blames his tools, and, just as it was naïve for the 19th-century Victorians to imagine that technology would bring paradise, it seems equally so for the 20th-century pessimists to make technology itself a scapegoat for man's shortcomings.

One of man's shortcomings may be a common failure to appreciate the charm of technology. Novelist and social critic Arthur Koestler has pointed out that the traditionally humanities-educated Western man is reluctant to admit that a work of art is beyond his comprehension but will cheerfully confess that he does not understand how his radio or heating system works. Koestler characterizes such a modern man, isolated from a technological environment that he possesses without understanding, as "an urban barbarian." Despite its publicized shortcomings and its sometimes sinister hint of autonomy, technology is after all a human product, growing not only out of man's need to improve his material condition but out of his love of play and adventure. It is capable of furnishing a distinctively human pleasure at its workings and a human excitement at its unfolding. Man orbits the Earth and visits the Moon because, among other reasons, he finds the experiences thrilling.

The spirit of adventure that has been associated throughout history with man's association with technology will certainly be of value in confronting the massive challenges of the future. "The day before yesterday," wrote Gaston Berger, president of the *Encyclopédie Française,*

we followed unconsciously what was called Nature; yesterday we tried conscientiously to conform to "nature," but today, our power having grown considerably, it behooves us sometimes to protect nature and sometimes to arrange it

in ways which seem favourable. We have somehow become responsible for evolution . . . a reality is to be constructed and events awaited.

BIBLIOGRAPHY. CARL F. STOVER (ed.), *The Technological Order* (1963), proceedings of an Encyclopædia Britannica conference on this subject; MELVIN KRANZBERG and CARROLL W. PURSELL, JR. (eds.), *Technology in Western Civilization*, 2 vol. (1967), a compact history of technology with chapters on implications; *Britannica Perspectives* (1968) contains several essays touching on the subject, especially R.J. FORBES, "The Conquest of Nature and Its Consequences"; JACQUES ELLUL, *La Technique* (1954; Eng. trans., *The Technological Society*, rev. ed., 1967), the author's basic critical work; LYNN T. WHITE, JR., *Medieval Technology and Social Change* (1962), a penetrating study of an important aspect of this subject.

Technology, History of

If technology may be defined as the systematic study of techniques for making and doing things, then the history of technology is, in a sense, the history of man. Essentially, techniques are methods of creating new tools and products of tools, and the capacity for constructing such artifacts is a determining characteristic of manlike species. Other species make artifacts: bees build elaborate hives to deposit their honey, birds make nests, and beavers build dams. But these attributes are the result of patterns of instinctive behaviour and cannot be varied to suit rapidly changing circumstances. Man, in contrast with other species, does not possess highly developed instinctive reactions but does have the capacity to think systematically and creatively about techniques. He can, thus, innovate and consciously modify his environment in a way no other terrestrial species has achieved. An ape may on occasion use a stick to beat bananas from a tree: a man can fashion the stick into a cutting tool and remove a whole bunch of bananas. Somewhere at the point of transition between the two, the hominid, or the first manlike species, emerges. By virtue of his nature as a toolmaker, man is therefore a technologist from the beginning, and the history of technology encompasses the whole evolution of man.

In the process of using his rational faculties to devise techniques and modify his environment, man has attacked problems other than those of survival and the production of wealth with which the term technology is usually associated today. The technique of language, for example, involves the manipulation of sounds and symbols in a meaningful way, and similarly the techniques of artistic and ritual creativity represent other aspects of the technological incentive. This article does not include detailed consideration of these cultural and religious techniques, but it is valuable to establish their relationship at the outset because the history of technology reveals a profound interaction between the incentives and opportunities of technological innovation on the one hand and the sociocultural conditions of the human group within which they occur on the other.

Social involvement in technological advances. An awareness of this interaction is important in surveying the development of technology through successive civilizations. To simplify the relationship as much as possible, there are three points at which there must be some social involvement in technological innovation: social need, social resources, and a sympathetic social ethos. In default of any of these factors it is unlikely that a technological innovation will be widely adopted or be successful.

The sense of social need must be strongly felt, or people will not be prepared to devote resources to a technological innovation. The need may be for a more efficient cutting tool, a more powerful lifting device, a labour-saving machine, a means of utilizing new fuels, or a new source of energy. Or, military needs having always provided a stimulus to technological innovation, it may take the form of a requirement for better weapons. In modern societies, needs have been generated by advertising. Whatever the source of social need, it is essential that enough people be conscious of it to provide a market for an artifact or commodity that can meet the need.

Social resources are similarly an indispensable prerequisite to a successful innovation. Many inventions have foundered because the social resources vital for their realization—the capital, materials, and skilled personnel— were not available. The notebooks of Leonardo da Vinci are full of ideas for helicopters, submarines, and airplanes, but few of these reached even the model stage because of deficient resources of one sort or the other. The resource of capital involves the existence of surplus productivity and an organization capable of directing the available wealth into channels in which the inventor can use it. The resource of materials involves the availability of appropriate metallurgical, ceramic, plastic, or textile substances that can perform whatever functions a new invention requires of them. The resource of skilled personnel implies the presence of technical skill capable of constructing new artifacts and devising novel processes. A society, in short, has to be well primed with suitable resources in order to sustain technological innovation.

A sympathetic social ethos implies an environment receptive to new ideas, one in which the dominant social groups are prepared to consider innovation seriously. Such receptivity may be limited to specific fields of innovation concerned—for example, with improvements in weapons or in navigational techniques—or it may take the form of a more generalized attitude of inquiry, as was the case among the industrial middle classes in Britain during the 18th century, who were willing to cultivate new ideas, and inventors, the breeders of such ideas. Whatever the psychological basis of inventive genius, there can be no doubt that the existence of socially important groups willing to encourage inventors and to use their ideas has been a crucial factor in the history of technology.

Social conditions are, thus, of the utmost importance in the development of new techniques, some of which will be considered below in more detail. It is worthwhile, however, to register another explanatory note. This concerns the rationality of technology. It has already been observed that technology involves the application of reason to techniques, and in the 20th century it has come to be regarded as almost axiomatic that technology is a rational activity stemming from the traditions of modern science. Nevertheless, it should be observed that technology, in the sense in which it is being used here, is much older than science, and also that techniques have tended to ossify over centuries of practice or to become diverted into such pararational exercises as alchemy. Some techniques became so complex, often depending upon processes of chemical change which were not understood even when they were widely practiced, that technology sometimes became itself a "mystery" or cult into which an apprentice had to be initiated like a priest into Holy Orders, and in which it was more important to copy an ancient formula than to innovate. The modern philosophy of progress cannot be read back into the history of technology; for most of its long existence technology has been virtually stagnant, mysterious, and even irrational. It is not fanciful to see some lingering fragments of this powerful technological tradition in the modern world, and there is more than an element of irrationality in the contemporary dilemma of a highly technological society contemplating the likelihood that it will use its sophisticated techniques in order to accomplish its own destruction. It is thus necessary to beware of overfacile identification of technology with the "progressive" forces in contemporary civilization.

On the other hand it is impossible to deny that there is a progressive element in technology, as it is clear from the most elementary survey that the acquisition of techniques is a cumulative matter in which each generation inherits a stock of techniques on which it can build if it chooses, and if social conditions permit. Over a long period of time the history of technology inevitably highlights the moments of innovation which show this cumulative quality as some societies advance, stage by stage, from comparatively primitive to more sophisticated techniques. But although this development has occurred and is still going on, it is not intrinsic to the nature of technology that such

a process of accumulation should occur, and it has certainly not been an inevitable development. The fact that many societies have remained stagnant for long periods of time, even at quite developed stages of technological evolution, and that some have actually regressed and lost the accumulated techniques passed on to them, demonstrates the ambiguous nature of technology and the critical importance of its relationship with other social factors.

Modes of technological transmission. Another aspect of the cumulative character of technology which will require further investigation is the manner of transmission of technological innovations. This is an elusive problem, and it is necessary to accept the phenomenon of simultaneous or parallel invention in cases in which there is insufficient evidence to show the transmission of ideas in one direction or the other. The mechanics of technological transmission have been enormously improved in recent centuries by the printing press and other means of communication and also by the increased facility with which travellers have been able to visit the sources of innovation and to carry the ideas back to their own homes. Traditionally, however, the major mode of transmission has been through the movement of artifacts and craftsmen. Trade in artifacts has ensured their widespread distribution and encouraged imitation. Even more important, the migration of craftsmen—whether it be the itinerant metalworkers of early civilizations or the German rocket engineers whose expert knowledge was acquired by both the Soviet Union and the United States after World War II—has promoted the spread of new technologies.

The evidence for such processes of technological transmission is a reminder that the material for the study of the history of technology comes from a variety of sources. Much of it relies, like any historical examination, on documentary matter, although this is sparse for the early civilizations because of the general lack of interest in technology on the part of scribes and chroniclers. For these societies, therefore, and for the many millennia of earlier unrecorded history in which slow but substantial technological advances were made, it is necessary to rely heavily upon archaeological evidence. Even in connection with the recent past, the historical understanding of the processes of rapid industrialization can be made deeper and more vivid by the study of "industrial archaeology." Much valuable material of this nature has been accumulated in museums in the last few decades, and even more remains in the place of its use for the observation of the field worker. The historian of technology must be prepared to use all these sources, and to call upon the skills of the archaeologist, the engineer, the architect, and other specialists as appropriate.

A highly compressed account of the history of technology such as this must adopt a rigorous methodological pattern if it is to do justice to the subject without grossly distorting it one way or another. The plan followed in the present article is primarily chronological, tracing the development of technology through phases which succeed each other in time. Obviously, the division between phases is to a large extent arbitrary. One factor in the weighting has been the enormous acceleration of Western technological development in recent centuries; Eastern technology is considered in this article in the main only as it relates to the development of modern technology.

Within each chronological phase a standard method has been adopted for surveying the technological experience and innovations. This begins with a brief review of the general social conditions of the period, and then goes on to consider the dominant materials and sources of power of the period, and their application to food production, manufacturing industry, building construction, transport and communications, military technology, and medical technology. In a final section the sociocultural consequences of technological change in the period are examined. This framework is modified according to the particular requirements of every period; new materials, for instance, occupy a substantial place in the earlier phases when new metals were being introduced but are compar-

Why
some
inventions
fail

The
rationality
of
technology

Historical
method-
ology

atively unimportant in some of the later phases. But the general pattern, with a review of the primary materials and power sources followed by their application, sandwiched between a survey of social conditions and social consequences, is retained throughout. One key factor which does not fit easily into this pattern is that of the development of tools. It has seemed most convenient to relate these to the study of materials, rather than to any particular application, but it has not been possible to be completely consistent in this treatment.

The article follows this outline:

I. Technology in the ancient world

THE BEGINNINGS—STONE AGE
TECHNOLOGY (TO C. 3000 BC)

The identification of the history of technology with the history of manlike species does not help in fixing a precise point for its origin, because the estimates of prehistorians and anthropologists concerning the emergence of human species vary so widely. The tendency has been for this time period to become increasingly extended as new excavations, especially in Central Africa, reveal evidence of progressively earlier human habitation. Suffice it to say here that over the long period of time before the dawn of recorded history there were few human beings on the face of the planet; that they did not, by reason of their simple way of life, leave many monuments or artifacts by which they might be recognized; and that there is not much chance of adding significantly to knowledge of human existence in this period, although assiduous excavation and new archaeological techniques may yet fill in some useful details.

Earliest communities.   What is known, therefore, may be summarized fairly briefly. For all except approximately the last 10,000 years, man has lived almost entirely in small nomadic communities, dependent for survival on his skill in gathering food by hunting and fishing and in avoiding predators. It is reasonable to suppose that most of these communities developed in tropical latitudes, especially in Africa, where climatic conditions are most favourable to a creature with such poor bodily protection as man. It is also reasonable to suppose that tribes of men moved out thence into the subtropical regions and eventually into the landmass of Eurasia, although their colonization of this region must have been severely limited by the successive periods of glaciation which rendered large parts of it inhospitable and even uninhabitable, even though man has shown remarkable versatility in adapting to such unfavourable conditions.

The Neolithic Revolution.   Toward the end of the last Ice Age, some 15,000 to 20,000 years ago, a few of the

From C. Singer (ed.), A History of Technology

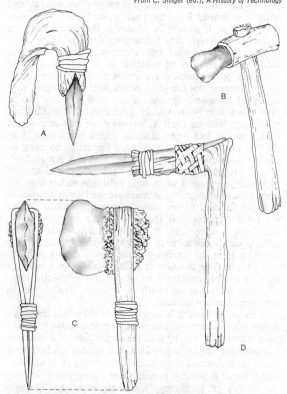

Methods of hafting axes and adzes with stone blades.
(A) Adz with blade bound in split of shouldered haft. (B) Ax with blade inserted in socket of deer antler which is perforated for the haft. (C) Side and front views of ax with blade gripped in bend of withy, with attachment strengthened with hardened gum and lashing. (D) Adz with blade lashed in wooden sleeve which is attached to shouldered haft by band of plaited cane.

human communities which were most favoured by geography and climate began to make the transition from the long period of Paleolithic, or Old Stone Age, savagery to a more settled way of life depending on animal husbandry and agriculture. This period of transition, the Neolithic Period, or New Stone Age, led eventually to a marked rise in population, to a growth in the size of communities, and to the beginnings of town life. It is sometimes referred to as the Neolithic Revolution because the speed of technological innovation increased so greatly and the social and political organization of human groups underwent a corresponding increase in complexity. To understand the beginnings of human technology it is thus necessary to survey developments from the Old Stone Age through the New Stone Age down to the emergence of the first urban civilizations about 3000 BC.

Stone. The material that gives its name and a technological unity to these periods of prehistory is stone. Though it may be assumed that primitive man used other materials such as wood, bone, fur, leaves, and grasses before he mastered the use of stone, apart from bone antlers, presumably used as picks in flint mines and elsewhere, and other fragments of bone implements, none of these has survived. The stone tools of early man, on the other hand, have survived in surprising abundance, and over the many millennia of prehistory important advances in technique were made in the use of stone. Stones

The earliest tools

became tools only when they were shaped deliberately for specific purposes, and, for this to be done efficiently, suitable hard and fine-grained stones had to be found and means devised for shaping them and particularly for putting a cutting edge on them. Flint became a very popular stone for this purpose, although fine sandstones and certain volcanic rocks were also widely used. There is plenty of Paleolithic evidence of skill in flaking and polishing stones to make scraping and cutting tools. These early tools were held in the hand, but gradually ways of protecting the hand from sharp edges on the stone, at first by wrapping one end in fur or grass or setting it in a wooden handle, were devised. Much later, the technique of fixing the stone head to a haft converted these hand tools into more versatile tools and weapons.

With the widening mastery of the material world in the Neolithic Period, other substances were brought into the service of man, such as clay for pottery and brick; and increasing competence in handling textile raw materials led to the creation of the first man-made fabrics to take the place of animal skins. About the same time, curiosity about the behaviour of metallic oxides in the presence of fire promoted one of the most significant technological innovations of all time and marked the succession from the Stone Age to the Metal Age.

Power. The use of fire was another basic technique mastered at some unknown time in the Old Stone Age. The discovery that the natural calamity of a forest fire could be tamed and controlled and the further discovery that a fire could be generated by persistent friction between two dry wooden surfaces were momentous. Fire was the most important contribution of prehistory to power technology, although little power was obtained directly from fire except as defense against wild animals. For the most part, prehistoric communities remained completely dependent upon manpower but, as part of the transition to a more settled pattern of life in the New Stone Age, man began to derive some power from animals that had been domesticated. It also seems likely that by the end of prehistoric times the sail had emerged as a means of harnessing the wind for small boats, beginning a long sequence of developments in marine transport.

Tools and weapons. The basic tools of prehistoric man were determined by the materials at his disposal. But once the techniques of working stone had been acquired, he was resourceful in devising tools and weapons with points and barbs of flaked stone. Thus the stone-headed spear, the harpoon, and the arrow all came into widespread use. The spear was given increased impetus by the spear thrower, a notched pole that gave a sling effect. The

The bow and arrow

bow and arrow were an even more effective combination, the use of which is clearly demonstrated in the earliest "documentary" evidence in the history of technology, the cave paintings of southern France and northern Spain which depict the bow being used in hunting. The ingenuity of these primitive hunters is shown also in their slings, throwing sticks (the boomerang of the Australian aborigines is a remarkable surviving example), blowguns, bird snares, fish and animal traps, and nets. These tools did not evolve uniformly as every primitive community developed only those instruments that were most suitable for its own specialized purposes, but all were in use by the end of Stone Age. In addition, the Neolithic Revolution had contributed some important new tools that were not primarily concerned with hunting. These were the first mechanical applications of rotary action in the shape of the potter's wheel, the bow drill, the pole lathe, and the wheel itself. It is not possible to be sure when these significant devices were invented, but their presence in the early urban civilizations suggests some continuity with the Late Neolithic Period. The potter's wheel, driven by kicks from the operator, and the wheels of early vehicles both gave continuous rotary movement in one direction. The drill and the lathe, on the other hand, were derived from the bow and had the effect of spinning the drill piece or the workpiece first in one direction and then in the other.

Developments in food production brought further refinements in tools. The processes of food production in Paleolithic times were simple, consisting of gathering, hunting, and fishing. If these methods proved inadequate to sustain a community, it moved to better hunting grounds or perished. With the onset of the Neolithic Revolution, new food-producing skills were devised to serve the needs of agriculture and animal husbandry. Digging sticks and the first crude plows, stone sickles, querns that ground grain by friction between two stones and, most complicated of all, irrigation techniques for keeping the ground watered and fertile; all these became well established in the great subtropical river valleys of Egypt and Mesopotamia in the millennia before 3000 BC.

Food production

Building techniques. Prehistoric building techniques also underwent significant developments in the Neolithic Revolution. Nothing is known of the building ability of Paleolithic man beyond a few fragments of stone shelters, but in the New Stone Age some impressive structures were erected, primarily tombs and burial mounds and other religious edifices, but also, towards the end of the period, showing a beginning in the use of sun-dried brick for domestic housing. In northern Europe, where the Neolithic transformation of primitive society began later than in the eastern Mediterranean societies and lasted longer, the huge stone monuments, of which Stonehenge in England is the outstanding example, still bear eloquent testimony to the technical skill, not to mention the imagination and mathematical competence, of the later Stone Age societies.

Manufacturing. Manufacturing industry had its origin in the New Stone Age, with the application of techniques for grinding corn (the quern), baking clay (pottery), spinning and weaving textiles, and also, it seems likely, in dyeing, fermenting, and distilling. Some evidence for all these processes can be derived from archaeological findings, and some of them at least were developing into specialized crafts by the time that the first urban civilizations appeared. In the same way, the early metalworkers were beginning to acquire the techniques of extracting and working the softer metals, gold, silver, copper and tin, which were to make their successors a select class of craftsmen. All these incipient fields of specialization, moreover, implied developing trade between different communities and regions, and again the archaeological evidence of the transfer of manufactured products in the later Stone Age is impressive. Flint arrowheads of particular types, for example, can be found widely dispersed over Europe, and the implication of a common source of manufacture for each is strong.

Such transmission suggests improving facilities for transport and communication. Paleolithic man presumably depended entirely on his own feet, and this remained the normal mode of transport throughout the Stone Age.

Domestication of animals undoubtedly brought some help here, however, with the ox, the donkey, and the camel, although difficulties in harnessing the horse long delayed its effective use. On water, the dugout canoe and the birch-bark canoe had demonstrated the potential of this means of transport, and, again, there is some evidence that the sail had already appeared by the end of the New Stone Age.

It is notable that the developments so far described in human prehistory took place over a long period of time, compared with the 5,000 years of recorded "history," and that they took place first in very small areas of the earth's surface and involved populations minute by modern standards. The Neolithic Revolution occurred first in those parts of the world with an unusual combination of qualities: a warm climate, encouraging rapid crop growth, and an annual cycle of flooding that made the fertility of the land in part at least naturally regenerative. On the Eurasian–African landmass such conditions occur only in Egypt, Mesopotamia, northern India, and some of the great river valleys of China. It was here, then, that men and women of the New Stone Age were stimulated to develop and apply new techniques of agriculture, animal husbandry, irrigation, and manufacture; and it was here that their enterprise was rewarded by increasing productivity, which encouraged the growth of population and triggered a succession of sociopolitical changes that converted the settled Neolithic communities into the first civilizations. Elsewhere, the stimulus to technological innovation was lacking or was unrewarded, so that these areas had to await the transmission of technical expertise from the more highly favoured areas. Herein is rooted the separation of the great world civilizations, for while the Egyptian and Mesopotamian civilizations spread their influence westward through the Mediterranean and Europe, those of India and China were limited by geographical barriers to their own hinterlands, which, although vast, were largely isolated from the mainstream of Western technological progress.

THE URBAN REVOLUTION (C. 3000–500 BC)

The technological change so far described took place very slowly over a long period of time, in response to only the most basic social needs, the search for food and shelter, and with few social resources available for any activity other than the fulfillment of these needs. About 5,000 years ago, however, a momentous cultural transition began to take place in a few well-favoured geographical situations. It generated new needs and resources and was accompanied by a significant increase in technological innovation. It was the beginning of the invention of the city.

Craftsmen and scientists. The accumulated agricultural skill of the New Stone Age had made possible a growth in population, and the larger population in turn created a need for the products of specialized craftsmen in a wide range of commodities. These craftsmen included a number of metalworkers, first those treating metals that could be easily obtained in metallic form and particularly the soft metals, such as gold and copper, which could be fashioned by beating. Then came the discovery of the possibility of extracting certain metals from the ores in which they generally occur. Probably the first such material to be used was the carbonate of copper known as malachite, then already in use as a cosmetic and easily reduced to copper in a strong fire. It is impossible to be precise about the time and place of this discovery, but its consequences were tremendous. It led to the search for other metallic ores, to the development of metallurgy, to the encouragement of trade in order to secure specific metals, and to the further development of specialist skills. It contributed substantially to the emergence of urban societies, relying heavily upon trade and manufacturing industries and thus to the rise of the first civilizations. The Stone Age gave way to the early Metal Age, and a new epoch in the story of mankind had begun.

By fairly general consent, civilization consists of a large society with a common culture, settled communities, and sophisticated institutions, all of which presupposes a mas-

tery of elementary literacy and numeration. Mastery of the civilized arts was a minority pursuit in the early civilizations, in all probability the carefully guarded possession of a priestly caste. But the existence of the skills, even in the hands of a small minority of the population, is significant because it made available a facility for recording and transmitting information that greatly enlarged the scope for innovation and speculative thought.

Hitherto, technology had existed without the benefit of science, but, by the time of the first Sumerian astronomers, who plotted the motion of the heavenly bodies with remarkable accuracy and based calculations about the calendar and irrigation systems upon their observations, the possibility of a creative relationship between science and technology had appeared. The first fruits of this relationship appeared in greatly improved abilities to measure land, weigh, and keep time, all practical techniques, essential to any complex society, and inconceivable without the literate skills and the beginnings of scientific observation. With the emergence of these skills in the 3rd millennium before Christ, the first civilizations arose in the valleys of the Nile and of the Tigris–Euphrates.

Copper and bronze. The fact that the era of the early civilizations coincides with the technological classification of the Copper and Bronze ages is a clue to the technological basis of these societies. The comparative softness of copper, gold, and silver made it inevitable that they should be the first to be worked, but archaeologists now seem to agree that there was no true "Copper Age," except perhaps for a short period at the beginning of Egyptian civilization, because the very softness of these metals limited their utility for everything except a decorative purpose or for use in coinage. Attention was thus given early to means of hardening copper in order to make satisfactory tools and weapons. The reduction of mixed metallic ores probably led to the discovery of alloying, whereby copper was fused with other metals to make bronze. Several bronzes were made, including some with proportions of lead, antimony, and arsenic, but by far the most popular and widespread was that created by copper with tin in proportions of about ten to one. This was a hard yellowish metal that, when molten, could be cast into the shape required. The bronzesmiths took over from the coppersmiths and goldsmiths the technique of heating the metal in a crucible over a strong fire and casting it into simple clay or stone molds to make ax or spear heads or other solid shapes. For more complicated shapes, such as hollow vessels or sculpture, they devised the so-called cire perdue technique in which the shape to be molded is formed in wax and set in clay, the wax then being melted and drained out to leave a cavity into which the molten metal is poured.

Bronze became the most important material of the early civilizations, and elaborate arrangements were made to ensure a continuous supply of it. Metals were scarce in the alluvial river valleys where civilization developed and therefore had to be imported, involving complicated trading relationships and mining operations at great distances from the homeland. Tin presented a particularly severe problem, as it was in short supply throughout the Middle East. The Bronze Age civilizations were compelled to search far beyond their own frontiers for sources of the metal, and in the process knowledge of the civilized arts was gradually transmitted westwards along the developing Mediterranean trade routes.

In most aspects other than the use of metals, the transition from the technology of the New Stone Age to that of early civilizations was fairly gradual, although there was a general increase in competence as specialized skills became more clearly defined, and in techniques of building there were enormous increases in the scale of enterprises. There were no great innovations in power technology, but important improvements were made in the construction of furnaces and kilns in response to the requirements of the metalworkers and potters and of new craftsmen such as glassworkers. Also, the sailing ship assumed a definitive shape, progressing from a vessel with a small sail rigged in its bows and suitable only for sailing before the prevailing wind up the Nile River, into the substantial

Effect of climatic conditions

Early extraction of metals

Discovery of alloying

The sailing ship

Drawing of an Egyptian seagoing ship, *c.* 2600 BC, based on vessels depicted in the bas-relief discovered in the pyramid of King Sahure at Abū Sīr, Cairo.
By courtesy of the Science Museum, London

oceangoing ship of the later Egyptian dynasties, with a large rectangular sail rigged amidships. Egyptian and Phoenician ships of this type could sail before the wind and across the wind, but for making headway into the wind they had to resort to manpower. Nevertheless, they accomplished remarkable feats of navigation, sailing the length of the Mediterranean and even passing through the Pillars of Hercules into the Atlantic.

Irrigation. Techniques of food production also showed many improvements over Neolithic methods, including one outstanding innovation in the shape of systematic irrigation. The civilizations of Egypt and Mesopotamia depended heavily upon the two great river systems, the Nile and the Tigris–Euphrates, which both watered the ground with their annual floods and rejuvenated it with the rich alluvium they deposited. The Nile flooded with regularity each summer, and the civilizations building in its valley early learned the technique of basin irrigation, ponding back the floodwater for as long as possible after the river had receded, so that enriched soil could bring forth a harvest before the floods of the following season. In the Tigris–Euphrates Valley the irrigation problem was more complex, because the floods were less predictable, more fierce, and came earlier than those of the northward-flowing Nile. They also carried more alluvium, which tended to choke irrigation channels. The task of the Sumerian irrigation engineers was that of channelling water from the rivers during the summer months, impounding it, and distributing it to the fields in small installments. The Sumerian system eventually broke down because it led to an accumulation of salt in the soil, with a consequent loss of fertility. Both systems, however, depended on a high degree of social control, requiring skill in measuring and marking out the land and an intricate legal code to ensure justice in the distribution of precious water. Both systems, moreover, depended on intricate engineering in building dikes and embankments, canals and aqueducts (with lengthy stretches underground to prevent loss by evaporation),

and the use of water-raising devices such as the shadoof, a balanced beam with a counterweight on one end and a bucket to lift the water on the other.

Urban manufacturing. Manufacturing industry in the early civilizations concentrated on such products as pottery, wines, oils, and cosmetics, which had begun to circulate along the incipient trade routes before the introduction of metals; these became the commodities traded for the metals. In pottery, the potter's wheel became widely used for spinning the clay into the desired shape, but the older technique of building it up by hand from rolls of clay remained in use for some purposes. In the production of wines and oils various forms of press were developed, while the development of cooking, brewing, and preservatives justified the assertion that the science of chemistry began in the kitchen. Cosmetics too were an offshoot of culinary art.

Transport was still primarily by animal, with the wheeled vehicle developing slowly to meet the divergent needs of agriculture, trade, and war. In the latter category, the chariot appeared as a weapon, even though its use was limited by the continuing difficulty of harnessing a horse. Military technology brought the development of metal plates for armour.

Wheeled vehicles

Building. In building technology there were developments comparable in importance to those in the field of metalworking, but their significance was in the scale of operations rather than in any particular innovation. The late Stone Age communities of Mesopotamia had already built extensively in sun-dried brick. Their successors continued the technique but extended it in scale to construct the massive brick temples called ziggurats. These were built on a square plan, with a core and facing of sun-dried mud bricks, the facing walls tapering slightly inward and broken by regular pilasters built into the brickwork, the whole structure ascending in two or three stages to a temple on the summit. Sumerians were also the first to build columns with brick, and this material from local clay provided the writing material for the scribes.

In Egypt, where clay was scarce but good building stone was plentiful, builders turned emphatically to stone, constructing the pyramids and temples which remain today as the outstanding monuments of Egyptian civilization. Stones were pulled on rollers and raised up the successive stages of the structure by ramps and by balanced levers adapted from the water-raising shadoof. The shaping of the stones was performed by skilled masons, and they were placed in position under the careful supervision of priest-architects who were clearly competent mathematicians and astronomers, as is evident from the precise astronomical alignments. It seems certain that the heavy labour of construction fell upon armies of slaves, which helps to explain both the achievements and limitations of early civilizations. Slaves were usually one of the fruits of military conquest, which presupposes a period of successful territorial expansion, although their status as a subject race could be perpetuated indefinitely. Slave populations provided a good and docile labour force for the major constructional works that have been described. On the other hand, the availability of slave labour discouraged technological innovation, a social fact that goes far toward explaining the comparative stagnation of mechanical invention in the ancient world.

Slave labour in building

Transmitting knowledge. In the ancient world, technological knowledge was transmitted by traders, who went out in search of tin and other commodities, and by craftsmen in metal, stone, leather, and the other media, who passed their skills to others by direct instruction or by providing models that challenged other craftsmen to copy them. This process of transmission by intermediary contact was occurring between the ancient civilizations and their neighbours to north and west during the 2nd millennium before Christ. The pace quickened in the subsequent millennium, distinct new civilizations arising in the Mediterranean, in Crete and Mycenae, in Troy and Carthage. Finally, the introduction of the technique of working iron caused another profound change in the capabilities and resources of human societies and ushered in the classical civilizations of Greece and Rome.

By courtesy of the Metropolitan Museum of Art, New York

Egyptian shadoof, "Apuy's House and Garden," tempera reproduction of a wall painting, *c.* 1250 BC, from the tomb of Apuy, Thebes. In the Metropolitan Museum of Art, New York.

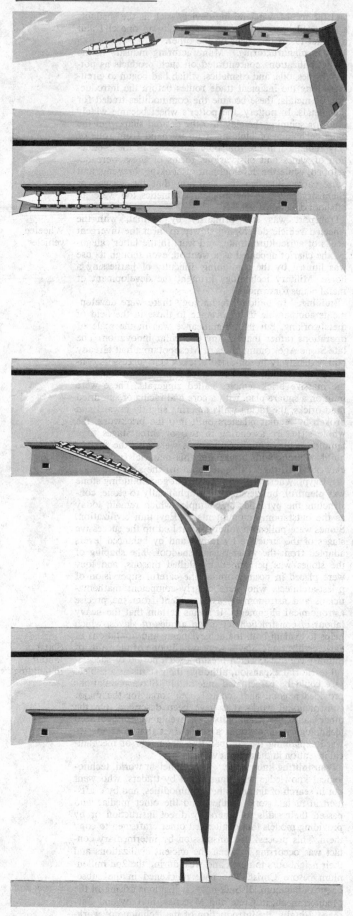

Erection of an obelisk; (top to bottom) obelisk hauled up ramp by sledge; partial removal of sledge; with all lashings removed, obelisk eased into surrounding sand; obelisk drawn upright on its pedestal.

TECHNOLOGICAL ACHIEVEMENTS
OF GREECE AND ROME (500 BC–AD 500)

The contributions of Greece and Rome in philosophy and religion, political and legal institutions, poetry and drama, and in the realm of scientific speculations were in spectacular contrast with their relatively limited contributions in technology. Their mechanical innovation was not distinguished, and, even in the realms of military and construction engineering, in which they showed great ingenuity and aesthetic sensibility, their work represented more a consummation of earlier lines of development than a dramatic innovation. This apparent paradox of the classical period of the ancient world requires explanation, and the history of technology can provide some clues to the solution of the problem.

The mastery of iron. The outstanding technological factor of the Greco-Roman world was the mastery of iron, a technique derived from unknown metallurgists, probably in Asia Minor, about 1000 BC, and which spread far beyond the provincial frontiers of the Roman Empire. The use of the metal had become general in Greece and the Aegean islands by the dawn of the classical period about 500 BC, and it appears to have spread quickly westward thereafter. Iron ore, long a familiar material, had defied reduction into metallic form because of the great heat required in the furnace to perform the chemical transformation (about 1,535° C [2,795° F] compared with the 1,083° C [1,981° F] necessary for the reduction of copper from its ores). To reach this temperature, furnace construction had to be improved and ways devised to maintain the heat for several hours. Throughout the classical period, these conditions were achieved only on a small scale, in furnaces burning charcoal and using foot-bellows to intensify the heat, and even in these furnaces the heat was not sufficient to reduce the ore completely to molten metal. Instead, a small spongy ball of iron—called a bloom—was produced in the bottom of the furnace. This was extracted by breaking open the furnace and then consolidated by being hammered into bars of wrought iron, which could be shaped as required by further heating and hammering. Apart from its greater abundance, iron for most purposes provided a harder and stronger material than the earlier metals, although the inability to cast it into molds like bronze was an inconvenience. At an early date some smiths devised the cementation process for re-heating bars of iron between layers of charcoal to carburize the surface of the iron and thus to produce a coat of steel. Such case-hardened iron could be further heated, hammered, and tempered to make knife and sword blades of high quality. The very best steel in Roman times was Seric steel, brought into the Western world from India where it was produced in blocks a few inches in diameter by a crucible process; i.e., melting the ingredients in an enclosed vessel to achieve purity and consistency in the chemical combination. *(Improvements in metal furnaces)*

Mechanical contrivances. Though slight, the mechanical achievements of the Greco-Roman centuries were not without significance. In Archimedes the world had one of its great mechanical geniuses, who devised remarkable weapons to protect his native Syracuse from Roman invasion and applied his powerful mind to such basic mechanical contrivances as the screw, the pulley, and the lever. Alexandrian engineers, such as Ctesibius and Hero, were responsible for a wealth of ingenious mechanical contrivances including pumps, wind and hydraulic organs, compressed-air engines and screw-cutting machines. They also devised toys and automata such as the *aeolipile*, which may be regarded as the first successful steam turbine. Little practical use was found for these inventions, but the Alexandrian school marks an important transition from very simple mechanisms to the more complex devices that properly deserve to be considered as "machines." In a sense it provided a starting point for modern mechanical practice.

Although they contributed few significant innovations, the Romans were responsible, through the application and development of available machines, for an important technological transformation involved in the widespread introduction of rotary motion. This was exemplified in the *(Introduction of rotary motion)* use of the treadmill for powering cranes and other heavy lifting operations, the introduction of rotary water-raising devices for irrigation works (a scoop wheel powered by a treadmill), and the development of the waterwheel as a prime mover. The 1st-century Roman engineer Vitruvius gave an account of watermills, and by the end of the Roman era many were in operation.

Agriculture. Iron Age technology was applied to agriculture in the form of the iron (or iron-tipped) plowshare, which opened up the possibility of deeper plowing and of cultivating heavier soils than those normally worked in the Greco-Roman period. The construction of plows improved slowly during these centuries, but the moldboard for turning over the earth did not appear until the 11th century AD, so that the capacity of turning the sod depended more on the wrists of the plowman than on the strength of his draft team; this discouraged tackling heavy ground. The potentialities of the heavy plow were thus not fully exploited in the temperate areas of Europe until after the Roman period. Elsewhere, in the drier climates of North Africa and Spain, the Romans were responsible for extensive irrigation systems, using the Archimedean screw and the noria (an animal- or water-powered scoop wheel) to raise water.

A network of Roman aqueducts showing a section undergoing repairs, painting by Michael Zeno Diemer (born 1867). In the Deutsches Museum, Munich.
By courtesy of the Deutsches Museum, Munich

Transport. Transport, again, followed earlier precedents, the sailing ship emerging as a seagoing vessel with a carvel-built hull (that is, with planks meeting edge-to-edge rather than overlapping as in clinker-built designs), and a fully developed keel with stempost and sternpost. The Greek sailing ship was equipped with a square or rectangular sail to receive a following wind and one or more banks of oarsmen to propel the ship when the wind was contrary. The Greeks began to develop a specialized fighting ship, provided with a ram in the prows, and the cargo ship, dispensing with oarsmen and relying entirely upon the wind, was also well established by the early years of classical Greece. The Romans took over both forms, but without significant innovation. They gave much more attention to inland transport than to the sea, and constructed a remarkable network of carefully aligned and well-laid roads, often paved over long stretches, throughout the provinces of the empire. Along these strategic highways the legions marched rapidly to any crisis at which their presence was required. The roads also served for the development of trade, but their primary function was always military, as a vital means of keeping a vast empire in subjection.

Greek sailing ships

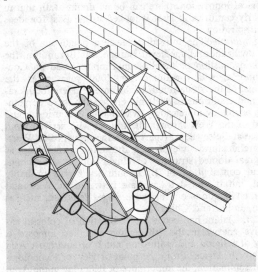

The noria, used to raise water to a higher level. Arrow indicates direction of rotation of the wheel.

Building. Though many buildings of the Greeks survive as splendid monuments to the civilized communities that built them, as technological monuments they are of less significance. The Greeks adopted a form of column and lintel construction that had been used in Egypt for centuries and was derived from experience of timber construction. In no major sense did Greek building constitute a technological innovation. The Romans copied the Greek style for most ceremonial purposes, but in other respects they were important innovators in building technology. They made extensive use of fired brick and tile as well as stone, they developed a powerful cement that would set under water, and they explored the architectural possibilities of the arch, the vault, and the dome. They then applied these techniques in amphitheatres, aqueducts, tunnels, bridges, walls, lighthouses, and roads. Taken together, these constructional works may fairly be regarded as the primary technological achievement of the Romans.

Other fields of technology. In manufacturing, transport, and military technology, the achievements of the Greco-Roman period are not remarkable. The major manufacturing crafts—pottery, glass, textiles, leather working, fine-metalworking, and so on—followed the lines of previous societies, albeit with important developments in style. Superbly decorated Athenian pottery, for example, was widely dispersed along the trade routes of the Mediterranean, and the Romans made good quality pottery available throughout their empire through the manufacture and trade of the standardized red Samian ware, originally from Greek Samos.

Roman innovations

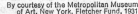
By courtesy of the Metropolitan Museum
of Art, New York, Fletcher Fund, 1931

Weaving of wool on a vertical loom, detail of a painting on an Athenian scent bottle, c. 560 BC. In the Metropolitan Museum of Art, New York.

Military technology. Roman military technology was inventive on occasion, as in the great siege catapults, depending on both torsion and tension power. But the standard equipment of the legionary was simple and conservative, consisting of an iron helmet and breastplate, with a short sword and an iron-tipped spear. As most of their opponents were also equipped with iron weapons and sometimes with superior devices, such as the Celtic chariots, the Roman military achievements depended more on organization and discipline than on technological superiority.

The Greco-Roman era was distinguished for the scientific activity of some of its greatest philosophers. In keeping with Greek speculative thought, however, this tended to be strongly conceptual so that it was in mathematics, geometry, and other abstract studies that the main scientific achievements are to be found. Occasionally these had some practical significance, as in the study of perspective effects in building construction. Aristotle in many ways expressed the inquiring empiricism which has caused scientists to seek an explanation for their physical environment. In at least one field, that of medicine and its related subjects, Greek inquiry assumed a highly practical form, Hippocrates and Galen laying the foundations of modern medical science. But this was exceptional, and the normal Hellenic attitude was to pursue scientific enquiry in the realm of ideas without much thought of the possible technological consequences.

II. From the Middle Ages to 1750

MEDIEVAL ADVANCE (AD 500–1500)

The millennium between the collapse of the Western Roman Empire in the 5th century AD and the beginning of the colonial expansion of western Europe in the late 15th century has been known traditionally as the Middle Ages, and the first half of this period consists of the five centuries of the Dark Ages. We now know that the period was not as socially stagnant as this title suggests. In the first place, many of the institutions of the later empire survived the collapse and profoundly influenced the formation of the new civilization that developed in western Europe. The Christian Church was the outstanding institution of this type, but Roman conceptions of law and administration also continued to exert an influence long after the departure of the legions from the western provinces. Second, and more important, the Teutonic tribes who moved into a large part of western Europe did not come empty-handed, and in some respects their technology was superior to that of the Romans. It has already been observed that they were people of the Iron Age, and although much about the origins of the heavy plow remains obscure these tribes appear to have been the first people with sufficiently strong iron plowshares to undertake the systematic settlement of the forested lowlands of northern and western Europe, the heavy soils of which had frustrated the agricultural techniques of their predecessors.

The invaders came thus as colonizers. They may have been regarded as "barbarians" by the Romanized inhabitants of western Europe who naturally resented their intrusion, and the effect of their invasion was certainly to disrupt trade, industry, and town life. But the newcomers also provided an element of innovation and vitality. About AD 1000 the conditions of comparative political stability necessary for the re-establishment of a vigorous commercial and urban life had been secured by the success of the kingdoms of the region in either absorbing or keeping out the last of the invaders from the East, and thereafter for 500 years the new civilization grew in strength and began to experiment in all aspects of human endeavour. Much of this process consisted of recovering the knowledge and achievements of the ancient world. The history of technology in the Middle Ages is thus largely the story of the preservation, recovery, and modification of earlier achievements. But by the end of the period the new Western civilization had begun to produce some remarkable technological innovations which were to be of the utmost significance.

Innovation. The word innovation raises a problem of great importance in the history of technology. Strictly, an innovation is something entirely new, but there is no such thing as an unprecedented technological innovation because it is impossible for an inventor to work in a vacuum and, however ingenious his invention, it must arise out of his own previous experience. The task of distinguishing an element of novelty in an invention remains a problem of patent law down to the present day, but the problem is made relatively easy by the possession of full documentary records covering previous inventions in many countries. In the millennium of the Middle Ages, however, few such records exist, and it is frequently difficult to explain how particular innovations were introduced to western Europe. The problem is especially perplexing because it is known that many inventions of the period had been de-

Effect of the barbarian invasions

veloped independently and previously in other civilizations, and it is sometimes difficult if not impossible to know whether something is spontaneous innovation or an invention that had been transmitted by some as yet undiscovered route from those who had originated it in other societies.

The problem is important because it generates a conflict of interpretations about the transmission of technology. On the one hand there is the theory of the diffusionists, according to which all innovation has moved westward from the long-established civilizations of the ancient world, with Egypt and Mesopotamia as the two favourite candidates for the ultimate source of the process. On the other hand is the theory of spontaneous innovation, according to which the primary determinant of technological innovation is social need. Scholarship is as yet unable to solve the problem so far as technological advances of the Middle Ages are concerned because much information is missing. But it does seem likely that at least some of the key inventions of the period—the windmill and gunpowder are good examples—were developed spontaneously. It is quite certain, however, that others such as silk working were transmitted to the West, and, however original the contribution of Western civilization to technological innovation, there can be no doubt at all that in its early centuries at least it looked to the East for ideas and inspiration.

Byzantium. The immediate eastern neighbour of the new civilization of medieval Europe was Byzantium, the surviving bastion of the Roman Empire based on Constantinople, which endured for 1000 years after the collapse of the western half of the empire. Here the literature and traditions of Hellenic civilization were perpetuated, becoming increasingly available to the curiosity and greed of the West through the traders who arrived from Venice and elsewhere. Apart from the influence on Western architectural style of such Byzantine masterpieces as the great domed structure of Hagia Sophia, the technological contribution of Byzantium itself was probably slight, but it served to mediate between the West and other civilizations one or more stages removed, such as Islām, India, and China.

Islām. Islām had become a civilization of colossal expansive energy in the 7th century and had imposed a unity of religion and culture on much of southwest Asia and North Africa. From the point of view of technological dissemination, the importance of Islām lay in the Arab assimilation of the scientific and technological achievements of Hellenic civilization, to which it made significant additions, and the whole became available to the West through the Moors in Spain, the Arabs in Sicily and the Holy Land, and through commercial contacts with the Levant and North Africa.

Islām also provided a transmission belt for some of the technology of the ancient civilizations of East and South Asia, especially those of India and China. Chinese civilization had already developed a host of crafts and techniques which were still unknown in the West by AD 1000. Such techniques included silk working, gunpowder, iron casting, papermaking, the junk and dhow, kites, windmills, and porcelain. The fact that several of these techniques had become well established in the West by 1500 suggests that they were transmitted.

Yet despite the acquisition of many techniques from the East, the Western world of 500–1500 was forced to solve most of its problems with little interference from outside. In doing so it transformed an agrarian society based upon a subsistence economy into a dynamic society with increased productivity sustaining trade, industry, and town life on a steadily growing scale. This was primarily a technological achievement, and one of considerable magnitude.

Power sources. The outstanding feature of this achievement was a revolution in the sources of power. With no large slave labour force to draw on, Europe experienced a labour shortage which stimulated a search for alternative sources of power and the introduction of labour-saving machinery. The first instrument of this power revolution was the horse. By the invention of the horseshoe,

Theory of spontaneous innovation

Chinese technology

the padded, rigid horsecollar, and the stirrup, all of which first appear in the West in the centuries of the Dark Ages, the horse was transformed from an ancillary beast of burden useful only for light duties into a highly versatile source of energy in peace and war. Once the horse could be harnessed to the heavy plow by means of the horsecollar, it became a more efficient beast of burden than the ox, and the introduction of the stirrup made the mounted warrior supreme in medieval warfare and initiated complex social changes to sustain the great expense of the knight, his armour, and his steed, in a society close to the subsistence line.

Water-power and wind power

Even more significant was the success of medieval technology in harnessing water and wind power. The Romans had pioneered the use of water power in the later empire, and some of their techniques probably survived. The type of watermill which flourished first in northern Europe, however, appears to have been the Norse mill, using a horizontally mounted waterwheel driving to a pair of grindstones directly without the intervention of gearing. Examples of this simple type of mill survive in Scandinavia and in the Shetlands; it also occurred in southern Europe where it was known as the Greek mill. It is possible that a proportion of the 5,624 mills recorded in the Domesday Book of England in 1086 were of this type, although it is probable that by this date the vertically mounted undershot wheel had established itself as more appropriate to the gentle landscape of England; the Norse mill requires a good head of water to turn the wheel at high speed in order to maintain an adequate grinding speed without gearing for the upper millstone (the practice of rotating the upper stone above a stationary bedstone became universal at an early date). Most of the Domesday watermills were used for grinding grain, but in the following centuries other important uses were devised in fulling cloth (shrinking and felting woollen fabrics), sawing wood, and crushing vegetable seeds for oil. Overshot wheels were also introduced where there was sufficient head of water, and the competence of the medieval millwrights in building mills and earthworks and in constructing increasingly elaborate trains of gearing grew correspondingly.

Post windmill with grinding machinery in mill housing, engraving from Agostino Ramelli's *Li diverse et artificiose macchine*, 1588.

Wind power in the shape of the sail had been harnessed from the dawn of civilization, but it was unknown in the form of the windmill in the West until the end of the 12th century. Present evidence suggests that the windmill developed spontaneously in the West despite precedents in Persia, but the question remains open. What is certain is that the windmill became widely used in Europe in the Middle Ages. Wind power is generally less reliable than waterpower, but where the latter is deficient wind power is an attractive substitute. Such conditions are found in areas that suffer from drought or from a shortage of surface water and also in low-lying areas where rivers offer little energy. Windmills have thus flourished in places such as Spain or the downlands of England on the one hand, and in the fenlands and polders of The Netherlands on the other hand. The first type of windmill to be widely adopted was the post-mill, in which the whole body of the mill pivots on a post and can be turned to face the sails into the wind. By the 15th century, however, many were adopting the tower-mill type of construction, in which the body of the mill remains stationary with only the cap moving to turn the sails into the wind. As with the watermill, the development of the windmill brought not only greater mechanical power but also greater knowledge of mechanical contrivances, which was applied in making clocks and other devices.

Origin of the windmill

Agriculture and crafts. With new sources of power at its disposal, medieval Europe was able greatly to increase productivity. This is abundantly apparent in agriculture, where the replacement of the ox by the faster-gaited horse and the introduction of new crops brought about a distinct improvement in the quantity and variety of food, with a consequent improvement in the diet and energy of the population. It was also apparent in the developing industries of the period, especially the woollen cloth industry in which the spinning wheel was introduced, partially mechanizing this important process, and the practice of using waterpower to drive fulling stocks (wooden hammers raised by cams on a driving shaft) had a profound effect on the location of the industry in England in the later centuries of the Middle Ages. The same principle was adapted to the paper industry late in the Middle Ages, the rag from which paper was derived being pulverized by hammers similar to fulling stocks.

Meanwhile, the traditional crafts flourished within the expanding towns where there was a growing market for the products of the rope makers, barrel makers (coopers), leatherworkers (curriers), and metalworkers (goldsmiths and silversmiths), to mention only a few of the more important crafts. New crafts such as that of the soapmakers developed in the towns. The technique of making soap appears to have been a Teutonic innovation of the Dark Ages, being unknown in the ancient civilizations. The process consists of decomposing animal or vegetable fats by boiling them with a strong alkali. Long before it became popular for personal cleansing, soap was a valuable industrial commodity for scouring textile fabrics. Its manufacture was one of the first industrial processes to make extensive use of coal as a fuel, and the development of the coal industry in northern Europe constitutes another important medieval innovation, no previous civilization having made any systematic attempt to exploit coal. The mining techniques remained primitive as long as coal was obtainable near the surface, but as the search for the mineral led to greater and greater depths the industry copied methods that had already evolved in the metallic mining industries of north and central Europe. The extent of this evolution was brilliantly summarized by Georgius Agricola in his *De re metallica*, published in 1556. This large, abundantly illustrated book shows techniques of shafting, pumping (by treadmill, animal power, and waterpower), and of conveying the ore won from the mines in trucks, which anticipated the development of the railways. It is impossible to date precisely the emergence of these important techniques, but the fact that they were well established when Agricola observed them suggests that they had a long ancestry.

Soap-making

Architecture. Relatively few structures survive from the Dark Ages, but the later centuries of the medieval period were a great age of building. The Romanesque and Gothic architecture that produced the outstanding aesthetic contribution of the Middle Ages embodied significant technological innovations. The architect-engineers who had clearly studied classical building techniques, showed a readiness to depart from their models and thus to devise a style that was distinctively their own. Their solutions to the problems of constructing very tall masonry buildings while preserving as much natural light as possible were the cross-rib vault, the flying buttress, and the great window panels providing scope for the new craft of the glazier using coloured glass with startling effect.

Military technology. The same period saw the evolution of the fortified stronghold from the Anglo-Saxon motte-and-bailey, a timber tower encircled by a timber-and-earth wall, to the formidable, fully developed masonry castle that had become an anachronism by the end of the Middle Ages because of the development of artillery. Intrinsic to this innovation were the invention of gunpowder and the development of techniques for casting metals, especially iron. Gunpowder appeared in western Europe in the mid-13th century, although its formula had been known in the Far East long before that date. It consists of a mixture of carbon, sulfur, and saltpetre, of which the first two were available from charcoal and deposits of volcanic sulfur in Europe, whereas saltpetre had to be crystallized by a noxious process of boiling stable sweepings and other decaying refuse. The consolidation of these ingredients into an explosive powder had become an established yet hazardous industry by the close of the Middle Ages.

Gun-powder

The first effective cannon appear to have been made of wrought-iron bars strapped together, but although barrels continued to be made in this way for some purposes, the practice of casting cannon in bronze became widespread. The technique of casting in bronze had been known for several millennia, but the casting of cannon presented problems of size and reliability. It is likely that the bronzesmiths were able to draw on the experience of techniques devised by the bellfounders as an important adjunct to medieval church building, as the casting of a large bell posed similar problems of heating a substantial amount of metal and of pouring it into a suitable mold. Bronze, however, was an expensive metal to manufacture in bulk, so that the widespread use of cannon in war had to depend upon improvements in iron-casting techniques.

The manufacture of cast iron is the great metallurgical innovation of the Middle Ages. It must be remembered that from the beginning of the Iron Age until late in the Middle Ages the iron ore smelted in the available furnaces had not been completely reduced to its liquid form. In the 15th century, however, the development of the blast furnace achieved such a reduction, with the result that the molten metal could be poured directly into molds ready to receive it. The emergence of the blast furnace was the result of attempts to increase the size of the traditional blooms. Greater size made necessary the provision of a continuous blast of air, usually from bellows driven by a waterwheel, and the combination increased the internal temperature of the furnace so that the iron became molten. At first, the disk of cast iron left in the bottom of his furnace was regarded as undesirable waste by the iron manufacturer; it possessed properties completely unlike those of the wrought iron with which he was more familiar, being crystalline and brittle and thus of no use in the traditional iron forge. But the casting property of the new iron was soon discovered and turned to profit, particularly in the manufacture of cannon.

Transport. Medieval technology made few contributions to inland transport, though there was some experimentation in bridge building and in the construction of canals; lock gates were developed as early as 1180, when they were employed on the canal between Bruges (now in Belgium) and the sea. Roads remained indifferent where they existed at all, and vehicles were clumsy throughout the period. Wayfarers like Chaucer's pilgrims travelled on horseback, and this was to remain the best mode of inland transport for centuries to come.

Sea transport was a different story. Here the Middle Ages produced a decisive technological achievement: the creation of a reliable oceangoing ship depending entirely on wind power instead of a combination of wind and muscle. The vital steps in this evolution were, first, the combination of the traditional square sail, used with little modification from Egyptian times through the Roman Empire to the Viking long boats, with the triangular lateen sail developed in the Arab dhow and adopted in the Mediterranean, which gave it the "lateen" (Latin) association attributed to it by the northern seafarers. This combination allowed ships so equipped to sail close to the wind and thus to escape from dependence upon a following wind. Second, the adoption of the sternpost rudder gave greatly increased manoeuvrability, allowing ships to take full advantage of their improved sail power in tacking into a contrary wind. Third, the introduction of the magnetic compass provided a means of checking navigation on the open seas in any weather. The convergence of these improvements in the ships of the later Middle Ages, together with other improvements in construction and equipment—such as better barrels for carrying water, more reliable ropes, sails, and anchors, the availability of navigational charts (first recorded in use on board ship in 1270), and the astrolabe (for measuring the angle of the sun or a star above the horizon)—enabled mariners to become progressively more adventurous and thus led directly to the voyages of discovery that marked the end of the Middle Ages and the beginning of the expansion of Europe that has characterized modern times.

The lateen sail

Communications. While transport technology was preparing for these revolutionary developments, techniques of recording and communication were making no less momentous advances. The medieval interest in mechanical contrivances is well illustrated by the development of the mechanical clock, the oldest of which, driven by weights and controlled by a verge, an oscillating arm engaging with a gear wheel, and dated 1386, survives in Salisbury Cathedral, England. Clocks driven by springs had appeared by the mid-15th century, making it possible to construct more compact mechanisms and preparing the way for the portable clock. The problem of overcoming the diminishing power of the spring as it unwound was solved by the simple compensating mechanism of the fusee—a conical drum on the shaft that permitted the spring to exert an increasing moment, or tendency to increase motion, as its power declined. It has been argued that the medieval fascination with clocks reflects an increased sense of the importance of timekeeping in business and elsewhere, but it can be seen with equal justice as representing a new sense of inquiry into the possibilities and practical uses of mechanical devices.

Even more significant than the invention of the mechanical clock was the 15th-century invention of printing with movable metal type. The details of this epochal invention are disappointingly obscure, but there is general agreement that the first large-scale printing workshop was that established at Mainz by Johannes Gutenberg, which was producing a sufficient quantity of accurate type to print a Vulgate Bible in 1448. It is clear, however, that this invention drew heavily upon long previous experience with block printing—using a single block to print a design or picture—and on developments in typecasting and ink making. It also made heavy demands on the paper industry, which had been established in Europe since the 12th century but which developed slowly until the invention of printing and the subsequent vogue for the printed word. The printing press itself, vital for securing a firm and even print over the whole page, was an adaptation of the screw press already familiar in the winepress and other applications. The printers found an enormous demand for their product, so that the technique spread rapidly and the printed word became an essential medium of political, social, religious, and scientific communication as well as a convenient means for the dissemination of news and information. By 1500 there were already almost 40,000 recorded editions of books printed in 14 European countries, with Germany and Italy accounting for two-thirds. Few single inventions have had such far-reaching consequences.

Printing with movable type

For all its isolation and intellectual deprivation, the new civilization that took shape in western Europe in the millennium 500 to 1500 achieved some astonishing feats of technological innovation. The intellectual curiosity which led to the foundation of the first universities in the 12th century and applied itself to the recovery of the ancient learning from whatever source it could be obtained was the mainspring also of the technological resourcefulness which encouraged the introduction of the windmill, the improvement and wider application of waterpower, the development of new industrial techniques, the invention of the mechanical clock and gunpowder, the evolution of the sailing ship, and the invention of large-scale printing. Such achievements could not have taken place within a static society. Technological innovation was both the cause and the effect of dynamic development. It is no coincidence that these achievements occurred within the context of a European society which was increasing in population and productivity, stimulating industrial and commercial activity, and expressing itself in the life of new towns and striking cultural activity. Medieval technology mirrored the aspiration of a new and dynamic civilization.

THE EMERGENCE OF WESTERN TECHNOLOGY (1500–1750)

The technological history of the Middle Ages was one of slow but substantial development. In the succeeding period the tempo of change increased markedly and was associated with profound social, political, religious, and intellectual upheavals in western Europe.

The emergence of the nation-state, the cleavage of the Christian Church by the Protestant Reformation, the Renaissance and its accompanying scientific revolution, and the overseas expansion of European states all had interactions with developing technology. The overseas expansion was made possible by the advance in naval technology which had opened up the ocean routes to Western navigators. The conversion of voyages of discovery into imperialism and colonization was made possible by the new firepower. The combination of light, manoeuvrable ships with the firepower of iron cannon gave European adventurers a decisive advantage, enhanced by other technological assets.

Effect of the Protestant Reformation

The Reformation, not itself a factor of major significance to the history of technology, nevertheless had interactions with it; the capacity of the new printing presses to disseminate all points of view contributed to the religious upheavals, while the intellectual ferment provoked by the Reformation resulted in a rigorous assertion of the vocational character of work and thus stimulated industrial and commercial activity and technological innovation. It is an indication of the nature of this encouragement that so many of the inventors and scientists of the period were Calvinists, Puritans, and—in England—Dissenters.

The Renaissance. The Renaissance had more obviously technological content than the Reformation. The concept of "renaissance" is, however, elusive. As a "rebirth" of classical knowledge, since the scholars of the Middle Ages had already achieved a very full recovery of the literary legacy of the ancient world, the Renaissance marked rather a point of transition after which the posture of deference to the ancients began to be replaced by a consciously dynamic, progressive attitude. Even while they looked back to classical models, Renaissance men looked for ways of improving upon them. This attitude is outstandingly represented in the genius of Leonardo da Vinci. As an artist of original perception he was recognized by his contemporaries, but some of his most novel work is recorded in his notebooks and was virtually unknown in his own time. This included ingenious designs for submarines, airplanes, and helicopters and drawings of elaborate trains of gears and of the patterns of flow in liquids. The early 16th century was not yet ready for these novelties: they met no specific social need, and the resources necessary for their development were not available.

An often overlooked aspect of the Renaissance is the scientific revolution that accompanied it. As with the term Renaissance itself, the concept is complex, having to

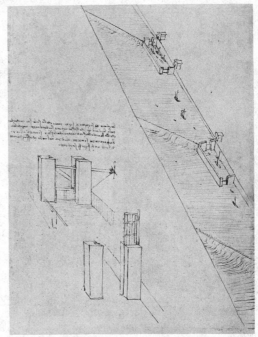

Canal and lock system, sketch by Leonardo da Vinci, *c.* 1500.
In the Biblioteca Ambrosiana, Milan.
By courtesy of the Biblioteca Ambrosiana, Milan

do with intellectual liberation from the ancient world. For centuries the authority of Aristotle in dynamics, of Ptolemy in astronomy, and of Galen in medicine had been taken for granted. Beginning in the 16th century their authority was challenged and overthrown, and scientists set out by observation and experiment to establish new explanatory models of the natural world. One distinctive characteristic of these models was that they were tentative, never receiving the authoritarian prestige long accorded to the ancient masters. Since this fundamental shift of emphasis, science has been committed to a progressive, forward-looking attitude and has come increasingly to seek practical applications for scientific research.

Technology performed science a service in this revolution by providing it with instruments which greatly enhanced its powers. The use of the telescope by Galileo to observe the moons of Jupiter was a dramatic example of this service, but the telescope was only one of many tools and instruments which proved valuable in navigation, map making, and laboratory experiments. More significant, however, were the services of the new sciences to technology, and by far the most important of these was the theoretical preparation for the invention of the steam engine.

The steam engine. The researches of a number of scientists, especially those of Robert Boyle of England with atmospheric pressure, of Otto von Guericke of Germany with a vacuum, and of the French Huguenot Denis Papin with pressure vessels, helped to equip practical technologists with the theoretical basis of steam power. Distressingly little is known about the manner in which this knowledge was assimilated by pioneers such as Thomas Savery and Thomas Newcomen, but it is inconceivable that they could have been ignorant of it. Savery took out a patent for a "new Invention for Raiseing of Water and occasioning Motion to all Sorts of Mill Work by the Impellent Force of Fire" in 1698 (No. 356). His apparatus depended on the condensation of steam in a vessel, creating a partial vacuum into which water was forced by atmospheric pressure.

Credit for the first commercially successful steam engine, however, must go to Newcomen, who erected his first machine near Dudley Castle in Staffordshire in 1712. It operated by atmospheric pressure on the top face of a piston in a cylinder, in the lower part of which steam was condensed to create a partial vacuum. The piston was connected to one end of a rocking beam, the other end of which carried the pumping rod in the mine shaft. New-

The Newcomen engine

The atmospheric engine of Thomas Newcomen.
Culver Pictures

comen was a blacksmith in Dartmouth, Devon, and his engines were robust but unsophisticated. Their heavy fuel consumption made them uneconomical when used where coal was expensive, but in the British coal fields they performed an essential service by keeping deep mines clear of water and were extensively adopted for this purpose. In this way the early steam engines fulfilled one of the most pressing needs of British industry in the 18th century. Although waterpower and wind power remained the basic sources of power for industry, a new prime mover had thus appeared in the shape of the steam engine, with tremendous potential for further development as and when new applications could be found for it.

Metallurgy and mining. One cause of the rising demand for coal in Britain was the depletion of the woodland and supplies of charcoal, making manufacturers anxious to find a new source of fuel. Of particular importance were experiments of the iron industry in using coal instead of charcoal to smelt iron ore and to process cast iron into wrought iron and steel. The first success in these attempts came in 1709, when Abraham Darby, a Quaker ironfounder in Shropshire, used coke to reduce iron ore in his enlarged and improved blast furnace. Other processes, such as glass making, brick making, and the manufacture of pottery had already adopted coal as their staple fuel. Great technical improvements had taken place in all these processes. In ceramics, for instance, the long efforts of European manufacturers to imitate the hard, translucent quality of Chinese porcelain culminated in Meissen at the beginning of the 18th century and was subsequently discovered independently in Britain in the middle of the century. Stoneware, requiring a lower firing temperature than porcelain, had achieved great decorative distinction in the 17th century as a result of the Dutch success with opaque white tin glazes at their Delft potteries, and the process had been widely imitated.

In addition to mining for coal and iron, the period from 1500 to 1750 witnessed a steady expansion in other mining activities. The gold and silver mines of Saxony and Bohemia provided the inspiration for the treatise by Agricola, *De re metallica*, mentioned above, which distilled the cumulative experience of several centuries in mining and metalworking and became, with the help of some brilliant woodcuts and the printing press, a worldwide manual on mining practice. Queen Elizabeth I introduced German miners to England in order to develop the mineral resources of the country, and one result of this was the establishment of brass manufacture. This metal, an alloy of copper and zinc, had been known in the ancient world and in Eastern civilizations, but was not developed

Brass manu-facture

commercially in western Europe until the 17th century. Metallic zinc had still not been isolated, but brass was made successfully by alloying copper with calamine, an oxide of zinc mined in England in the Mendip Hills and elsewhere, and was worked up by hammering, annealing (a slow-cooling process to toughen the material), and wiredrawing into a wide range of household and industrial commodities. Other nonferrous metals such as tin and lead were sought out and exploited with increasing enterprise in this period, but as these frequently occurred at some distance from sources of coal, as in the case of the Cornish tin mines, the employment of Newcomen engines to assist in drainage was rarely economic, and this restricted the extent of the mining operations.

New commodities. Following the dramatic expansion of the European nations into the Indian Ocean and the New World, the commodities of these parts of the world found their way back into Europe in increasing volume. These commodities created new social habits and fashions and called for new techniques of manufacture. Tea became an important trade commodity but was soon replaced in volume and importance by the products of specially designed plantations such as sugar, tobacco, cotton, and cocoa. Sugar refining, depending on the crystallization of sugar from the syrupy molasses derived from the cane, became an important industry. So did tobacco processing, for smoking in clay pipes (produced in bulk at Delft and elsewhere) or for taking as snuff. Cotton had been known before as an Eastern plant, but its successful transplantation to the New World made much greater quantities available and stimulated the emergence of an important new textile industry.

The woollen cloth industry in Britain provided a model and precedent upon which the new cotton industry could build. Already in the Middle Ages, the processes of cloth manufacture had been partially mechanized with the introduction of fulling mills and the use of spinning wheels. But in the 18th century the industry remained almost entirely a domestic or cottage one, with most of the processing being performed in the homes of the workers, using comparatively simple tools that could be operated by hand or foot. The most complicated apparatus was the loom, but this could usually be worked by a single

The textile industry

Historical Pictures Service, Chicago

Drawloom, engraving from Diderot's *Encyclopédie*, 18th century.

weaver although the wider cloths required an assistant. It was a general practice to install the loom in an upstairs room with a long window giving maximum natural light. Weaving was regarded as a man's work, the women of the family being responsible for spinning. The weaver could use the yarn provided by up to a dozen "spinsters," and the balanced division of labour was preserved by the weaver assuming responsibility for supervising the cloth through the other processes, such as fulling. Pressures to increase the productivity of various operations had already produced some technical innovations by the first half of the 18th century. The first attempts at devising a spinning machine, however, were not successful; and without this, John Kay's technically successful flying shuttle (a device for hitting the shuttle from one side of the loom to the other, dispensing with the need to pass it through by hand) did not fulfill an obvious need. It was not until the rapid rise of the cotton cloth industry that the old, balanced industrial system was seriously upset and that a new, mechanized system, organized on the basis of factory production, began to emerge.

Agriculture. Another major area that began to show signs of profound change in the 18th century was agriculture. Stimulated by greater commercial activity, the rising market for food caused by an increasing population aspiring to a higher standard of living and by the British aristocratic taste for improving estates to provide affluent and decorative country houses, the traditional agricultural system of Britain was transformed. It is important to note that this was a British development, as it is one of the indications of the increasing pressures of industrialization there even before the Industrial Revolution, while other European countries, with the exception of The Netherlands, from which several of the agricultural innovations in Britain were acquired, did little to encourage agricultural productivity. The nature of the transformation was complex, and it was not completed until well into the 19th century. It consisted partly of a legal re-allocation of land ownership, the "enclosure" movement, to make farms more compact and economical to operate. In part also it was brought about by the increased investment in farming improvements, because the landowners felt encouraged to invest money in their estates instead of merely drawing rents from them. Again, it consisted of using this money for technical improvements, taking the form of machinery—such as Jethro Tull's mechanical sower—of better drainage, of scientific methods of breeding to raise the quality of livestock, and of experimenting with new crops and systems of crop rotation. The process has often been described as an agricultural revolution, but it is preferable to regard it as an essential prelude to and part of the Industrial Revolution.

Construction. Construction techniques did not undergo any great change in the period 1500–1750. The practice of building in stone and brick became general, although timber remained an important building material for roofs and floors, and, in areas in which stone was in short supply, the half-timbered type of construction retained its popularity into the 17th century. Thereafter, however, the spread of brick and tile manufacturing provided a cheap and readily available subsititute, although it suffered an eclipse on aesthetic grounds in the 18th century when classical styles enjoyed a vogue and brick came to be regarded as inappropriate for facing such buildings. Brick making, however, had become an important industry for ordinary domestic building by then and, indeed, entered into the export trade as Dutch and Swedish ships regularly carried brick as ballast to the New World, providing a valuable building material for the early American settlements. Cast iron was beginning to be used in buildings, but only for decorative purposes. Glass was also beginning to become an important feature of buildings of all sorts, encouraging the development of an industry that still relied largely on ancient skills of fusing sand to make glass and blowing, molding, and cutting it into the shapes required.

Land reclamation. More substantial constructional techniques were required in land drainage and military fortification, although again their importance is shown rather in their scale and complexity than in any novel features. The Dutch, wrestling with the sea for centuries, had devised extensive dikes; their techniques were borrowed by English land owners in the 17th century in an attempt to reclaim tracts of fenlands.

Military fortifications. In military fortification, the French strongholds designed by Sébastien de Vauban in the late 17th century demonstrated how warfare had adapted to the new weapons and, in particular, to heavy artillery. With earthen embankments to protect their salients, these star-shaped fortresses were virtually impreg-

nable to the assault weapons of the day. Firearms remained cumbersome, with awkward firing devices and slow reloading. The quality of weapons improved somewhat with increasing skill by the gunsmiths.

Transport and communications. Like constructional techniques, transport and communications made substantial progress without any great technical innovations. Road building was greatly improved in France, and, with the completion of the Languedoc Canal between the Mediterranean and the Bay of Biscay in 1692, large-scale civil engineering achieved an oustanding success. The canal is 500 miles (240 kilometres) long, with a hundred locks, a tunnel, three major aqueducts, many culverts, and a large summit reservoir.

The sea remained the greatest highway of commerce, stimulating innovation in the sailing ship. The Elizabethan galleon with its great manoeuvrability and firepower, the Dutch herring *busses* and *fluitschips* with their commodious hulls and shallow draft, the versatile East Indiamen of both the Dutch and the British East India companies, and the mighty ships of the line produced for the French and British navies in the 18th century, indicate some of the main directions of evolution.

The needs of reliable navigation created a demand for better instruments. The quadrant was improved by conversion to the octant, using mirrors to align a star with the horizon and to measure its angle more accurately: with further refinements this evolved as the modern sextant. Even more significant was the ingenuity shown by scientists and instrument makers in the construction of a clock that would keep accurate time at sea: such a clock, by showing the time in Greenwich when it was noon aboard ship would show how far east or west of Greenwich the ship lay (longitude). A prize of £20,000 was offered by the British Board of Longitude for this purpose in 1714, but it was not awarded until 1762 when John Harrison's so-called No. 4 chronometer fulfilled all the requirements.

Chemistry. Robert Boyle's contribution to the theory of steam power has been mentioned, but Boyle's main claim to fame is as the "father of chemistry," in which field he was responsible for the recognition of an element as a material that cannot be resolved into other substances. It was not until the end of the 18th and the beginning of the 19th century, however, that the work of Antoine Lavoisier and John Dalton put modern chemical science on a firm theoretical basis. Chemistry was still struggling to free itself from the traditions of alchemy. Even alchemy was not without practical applications, for it promoted experiments with materials and led to the development of specialized laboratory equipment that was used in the manufacture of dyes, cosmetics, and certain pharmaceutical products. For the most part, pharmacy still relied upon recipes based on herbs and other natural products, but the systematic preparation of these eventually led to the discovery of useful new drugs.

The period from 1500 to 1750 witnessed the emergence of Western technology in the sense that the superior techniques of Western civilization enabled the nations that comprised it to expand their influence over the whole known world. Yet, with the exception of the steam engine, this was not an outstanding period of technological innovation. What was, perhaps, more important than any particular innovation was the evolution, however faltering and partial and limited to Britain in the first place, of a technique of innovation, or what has been called "the invention of invention." The creation of a political and social environment conducive to invention, the building up of vast commercial resources to support inventions likely to produce profitable results, the exploitation of mineral, agricultural, and raw material resources for industrial purposes, and, above all, the recognition of specific needs for invention and an unwillingness to be defeated by them, together produced a society ripe for an industrial revolution based on technological innovation. The technological achievements of the period 1500–1750, therefore, must be judged in part by their substantial contribution to the spectacular innovations of the following period.

margin notes:

Brick and tile manufacture

The Languedoc Canal

Emergence of Western technology

III. The Industrial Revolution (1750–1900)

The term Industrial Revolution, like similar historical concepts, is more convenient than precise. It is convenient because history requires division into periods for purposes of understanding and instruction and because there were sufficient innovations at the turn of the 18th and 19th centuries to justify the choice of this as one of the periods. The term is imprecise, however, because the Industrial Revolution has no clearly defined beginning or end. Moreover, it is misleading if it carries the implication of a once-for-all change from a "pre-industrial" to a "post-industrial" society, because, as has been seen, the events of the traditional Industrial Revolution had been well prepared in a mounting tempo of industrial, commercial, and technological activity from about AD 1000 and led into a continuing acceleration of the processes of industrialization that is still proceeding in our own time. The term Industrial Revolution must thus be employed with some care. It is used below to describe an extraordinary quickening in the rate of growth and change, and more particularly, to describe the first 150 years of this period of time, as it will be convenient to pursue the developments of the present century separately.

The Industrial Revolution, in this sense, has been a worldwide phenomenon, at least in so far as it has occurred in all those parts of the world, of which there are very few exceptions, where the influence of Western civilization has been felt. Beyond any doubt it occurred first in Britain, and its effects spread only gradually to continental Europe and North America. Equally clearly, the Industrial Revolution that eventually transformed these parts of the Western world surpassed in magnitude the achievements of Britain, and the process was carried further to change radically the socio-economic life of the Far East, Africa, Latin America, and Australasia. The reasons for this succession of events are complex, but they were implicit in the earlier account of the buildup toward rapid industrialization. Partly through good fortune and partly through conscious effort, Britain by the early 18th century came to possess the combination of social needs and social resources that provided the necessary preconditions of commercially successful innovation and a social system capable of sustaining and institutionalizing the processes of rapid technological change once they had started. This section will thus be concerned, in the first place, with events in Britain, although as the period develops it will be necessary to trace the way in which British technical achievements were diffused and superseded in other parts of the Western world.

Spread of the Industrial Revolution

POWER TECHNOLOGY

An outstanding feature of the Industrial Revolution has been the advance in power technology. At the beginning of this period, the major sources of power available to industry and any other potential consumer were animate energy and the power of wind and water, the only exception of any significance being the atmospheric steam engines which had been installed for pumping purposes, mainly in coal mines. It is to be emphasized that this use of steam power was exceptional and remained so for most industrial purposes until well into the 19th century. Steam did not simply replace other sources of power: it transformed them. The same sort of scientific inquiry that led to the development of the steam engine was also applied to the traditional sources of inanimate energy, with the result that both waterwheels and windmills improved in design and efficiency. A number of engineers contributed to the refinement of waterwheel construction, and by the middle of the 19th century new designs made possible increases in the speed of revolution of the waterwheel and thus prepared the way for the emergence of the water turbine, which is still an extremely efficient method of producing power.

Windmills. Meanwhile, British windmill construction was improved considerably by the refinements of sails and by the self-correcting device of the fantail, which kept the sails pointed into the wind. Spring sails replaced the traditional canvas rig of the windmill with the equivalent of a modern venetian blind, the shutters of which

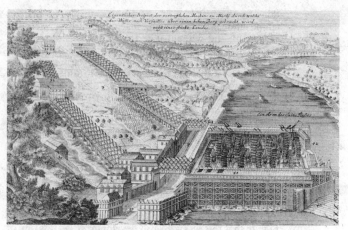

Waterwheels driven by the force of the river current activate a system of pumps to provide an inland water supply. Engraving from Jakob Leupold's *Theatrum Machinarum*, 1724–39.

could be opened or closed, to let the wind pass through or to provide a surface for its pressure. Sail design was further improved with the "patent" sail in 1807. In mills equipped with these sails, the shutters were controlled on all the sails simultaneously by a lever inside the mill connected by rod linkages through the windshaft with the bar operating the movement of the shutters on each sweep. The control could be made more fully automatic by hanging weights on the lever in the mill to determine the maximum wind pressure beyond which the shutters would open and spill the wind. Conversely, counterweights could be attached to keep the shutters in the open position. With these and other modifications, British windmills adapted to the increasing demands on power technology. But the use of wind power declined sharply in the 19th century with the spread of steam and the increasing scale of power utilization. Windmills that had satisfactorily provided power for small-scale industrial processes were unable to compete with the production of large-scale steam-powered mills.

Steam engines. Although the qualification regarding older sources of power is important, steam became the characteristic and ubiquitous power source of the British Industrial Revolution. Little development took place in the Newcomen atmospheric engine until James Watt patented a separate condenser in 1769, but from that point

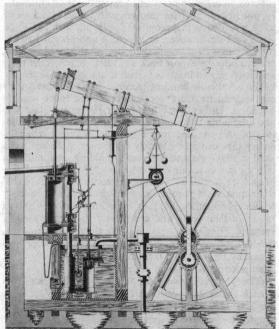

James Watt's rotative steam engine with sun-and-planet gear, original drawing, 1788. In the Science Museum, London.

Watt's
separate
condenser

onward the steam engine underwent almost continuous improvements for over a century. Watt's separate condenser was the outcome of his work on a model of a Newcomen engine which was being used in a University of Glasgow laboratory. Watt's inspiration was to separate the two actions of heating the cylinder with hot steam and cooling it to condense the steam for every stroke of the engine. By keeping the cylinder permanently hot and the condenser permanently cold, a great economy on energy used could be effected. This brilliantly simple idea could not be immediately incorporated in a full-scale engine because the engineering of such machines had hitherto been crude and defective. It needed the backing of a Birmingham industrialist, Matthew Boulton, with his resources of capital and technical competence, to convert the idea into a commercial success. Between 1775 and 1800, the period over which Watt's patents were extended, the Boulton and Watt partnership produced some 500 engines, which despite their high cost in relation to a Newcomen engine were eagerly acquired by the tin-mining industrialists of Cornwall and other power users who badly needed a more economic and reliable source of energy.

During the quarter of a century in which Boulton and Watt exercised their virtual monopoly over the manufacture of improved steam engines, they introduced many important refinements. Basically they converted the engine from a single-acting (*i.e.*, applying power only on the downward stroke of the piston) atmospheric pumping machine into a versatile prime mover that was double acting and could be applied to rotary motion, thus driving the wheels of industry. The rotary action engine was quickly adopted by British textile manufacturer Sir Richard Arkwright for use in a cotton mill, and although the ill-fated Albion Mill, at the southern end of Blackfriars Bridge in London, was burned down in 1791 when it had only been in use for five years and was still incomplete, it demonstrated the feasibility of applying steam power to large-scale grain milling. Many other industries followed in exploring the possibilities of steam power, and it soon became widely used.

Watt's patents had the temporary effect of restricting the development of high-pressure steam, necessary in such major power applications as the locomotive. This development came quickly once his patents lapsed in 1800. The Cornish engineer Richard Trevithick introduced higher steam pressures, achieving an unprecedented pressure of 145 pounds per square inch (ten kilograms per square centimetre) in 1802 with an experimental engine at Coalbrookdale, which worked safely and efficiently. Almost

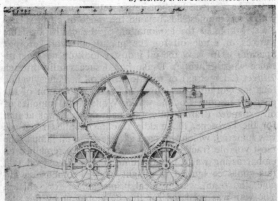

Trevithick steam locomotive, drawing by an unknown artist.
In the Science Museum, London.

First
steam
locomotive

simultaneously, the versatile American engineer Oliver Evans built the first high-pressure steam engine in the United States, using, like Trevithick, a cylindrical boiler with an internal fire plate and flue. High-pressure steam engines rapidly became popular in America, partly as a result of Evans' initiative and partly because very few Watt-type low-pressure engines crossed the Atlantic. Trevithick quickly applied his engine to a locomotive vehicle,

making the first successful steam locomotive for the Penydarren tramroad in South Wales in 1804. The success, however, was technological rather than commercial because the locomotive fractured the cast iron track of the tramway: the age of the railroad had to await further development both of the permanent way and of the locomotive.

Meanwhile, the stationary steam engine advanced steadily to meet an ever-widening market of industrial requirements. High-pressure steam led to the development of the large beam pumping engines with a complex sequence of valve actions, which became universally known as Cornish engines; their distinctive characteristic was the cutoff of steam injection before the stroke was complete in order to allow the steam to do work by expanding. These engines were used all over the world for heavy pumping duties, often being shipped out and installed by Cornish engineers. Trevithick himself spent many years improving pumping engines in Latin America. Cornish engines, however, were probably thickest on the ground in Cornwall itself, where they were used in large numbers in the tin and copper mining industries.

Another consequence of high-pressure steam was the practice of compounding, of using the steam twice or more at descending pressures before it was finally condensed or exhausted. The technique was first applied by Arthur Woolf, a Cornish mining engineer, who by 1811 had produced a very satisfactory and efficient compound beam engine with a high-pressure cylinder placed alongside the low-pressure cylinder, with both piston rods attached to the same pin of the parallel motion, which was a parallelogram of rods connecting the piston to the beam, patented by Watt in 1784. In 1845 John McNaught introduced an alternative form of compound beam engine, with the high-pressure cylinder on the opposite end of the beam from the low-pressure cylinder, and working with a shorter stroke. This became a very popular design. Various other methods of compounding steam engines were adopted and the practice became increasingly widespread, until in the second half of the 19th century triple- or quadruple-expansion engines were being used in industry and marine propulsion. By this time also the conventional beam-type vertical engine adopted by Newcomen and retained by Watt began to be replaced by horizontal-cylinder designs. Beam engines remained in use for some purposes until the eclipse of the reciprocating steam engine in the 20th century, and other types of vertical engine remained popular, but for both large and small duties the engine designs with horizontal cylinders became by far the most common.

A demand for power to generate electricity stimulated new thinking about the steam engine in the 1880s. The problem was that of achieving a sufficiently high speed of revolutions to make the dynamos function efficiently. Such speeds were beyond the range of the normal reciprocating engine (*i.e.*, with a piston moving backward and forward in a cylinder). Designers began to investigate the possibilities of radical modifications to the reciprocating engine to achieve the speeds desired, or of devising a steam engine working on a completely different principle. In the first category, one solution was to enclose the working parts of the engine and force a lubricant around them under pressure. The Willans engine design, for instance, was of this type and was widely adopted in early British power stations. Another important modification in the reciprocating design was the uniflow engine, which increased efficiency by exhausting steam from ports in the centre of the cylinder instead of requiring it to change its direction of flow in the cylinder with every movement of the piston. Full success in achieving a high-speed steam engine, however, depended on the steam turbine, a design of such novelty that it constituted a major technological innovation. This was invented by Sir Charles Parsons in 1884. By passing steam through the blades of a series of rotors of gradually increasing size (to allow for the expansion of the steam) the energy of the steam was converted to very rapid circular motion, which was ideal for generating electricity. Many refinements have since been made in turbine construction and the size of turbines has

Invention
of the
steam
turbine

been vastly increased, but the basic principles remain the same and this method still provides the main source of electric power except in those areas in which the mountainous terrain permits the economic generation of hydroelectric power from water turbines. Even the most modern nuclear power plants use steam turbines because technology has not yet solved the problem of transforming nuclear energy directly into electricity. In marine propulsion, too, the steam turbine remains an important source of power despite competition from the internal-combustion engine.

Electricity. The development of electricity as a source of power preceded this conjunction with steam power late in the 19th century. The pioneering work had been done by an international collection of scientists including Benjamin Franklin of the U.S., Alessandro Volta of the University of Bologna, Italy, and Michael Faraday of Britain. It was the latter who had demonstrated the nature of the elusive relationship between electricity and magnetism in 1831, and his experiments provided the point of departure for both the mechanical generation of electric current, previously available only from chemical reactions within voltaic piles or batteries, and the utilization of such current in electric motors. Both the mechanical generator and the motor depend on the rotation of a continuous coil of conducting wire between the poles of a strong magnet: turning the coil produces a current in it, while passing a current through the coil causes it to turn. Both generators and motors underwent substantial development in the middle decades of the 19th century. In particular, French, German, Belgian, and Swiss engineers evolved the most satisfactory forms of armature (the coil of wire) and produced the dynamo which made the large-scale generation of electricity commercially feasible.

The next problem was that of finding a market. In Britain, with its now well-established tradition of steam power, coal, and coal gas, such a market was not immediately obvious. But in continental Europe and North America there was more scope for experiment. In the United States the inventive genius of Thomas Edison was applied to finding fresh uses for electricity, and his invention of the carbon-filament lamp showed how this form of energy could rival gas as a domestic illuminant. The problem here had been that electricity had been used successfully for large installations such as lighthouses in which arc lamps had been powered by generators on the premises, but no way of subdividing the electric light into many small units had been devised. The principle of the filament lamp was that a thin conductor could be made incandescent by an electric current provided that it was sealed in a vacuum which prevented it from burning out. The U.S. inventor Thomas A. Edison and the English chemist Sir Joseph Swan experimented with various materials for the filament and both chose a carbon substance. The result was a highly successful small lamp, which could be varied in size for any sort of requirement. It is relevant that the success of the carbon-filament lamp did not immediately mean the supersession of gas lighting. Coal gas had first been used for lighting by William Murdock at his home in Redruth, Cornwall, where he was the agent for the Boulton and Watt company, in 1792. When he moved to the headquarters of the firm at Soho in Birmingham in 1798, Matthew Boulton authorized him to experiment in lighting the buildings there by gas, and gas lighting was subsequently adopted by firms and towns all over Britain in the first half of the 19th century. Lighting was normally by a fishtail jet of burning gas, but under the stimulus of competition from electric lighting the quality of gas lighting was greatly improved by the invention of the gas mantle. Thus improved, gas lighting remained popular for some forms of street lighting until the middle of the present century.

Lighting alone could not provide an economical market for electricity because its use was confined to the hours of darkness. Successful commercial generation depended upon the development of other uses for electricity, and particularly on electric traction. The popularity of urban electric tramways and the adoption of electric traction on subway systems such as the London Underground thus

Development of the electric light

coincided with the widespread construction of generating equipment in the late 1880s and 1890s. The subsequent spread of this form of energy is one of the most remarkable technological success stories of the 20th century, but most of the basic techniques of generation, distribution, and utilization had been mastered by the end of the 19th century.

Internal-combustion engine. Electricity does not constitute a prime mover, for however important it may be as a form of energy it has to be derived from a mechanical generator powered by water, steam, or internal combustion. The internal-combustion engine is a prime mover, and it emerged in the 19th century as a result both of greater scientific understanding of the principles of thermodynamics and a search by engineers for a substitute for steam power in certain circumstances. In an internal-combustion engine the fuel is burned in the engine: the cannon provided an early model of a single-stroke engine; and several persons had experimented with gunpowder as a means of driving a piston in a cylinder. The major problem was that of finding a suitable fuel, and the secondary problem was that of igniting the fuel in an enclosed space to produce an action that could be easily and quickly repeated. The first problem was solved in the mid-19th century by the availability of town gas supplies, but the second problem proved more intractable as it was difficult to maintain ignition evenly. The first successful gas engine was made by Étienne Lenoir in Paris in 1859. It was modelled closely on a horizontal steam engine, with an explosive mixture of gas and air ignited by an electric spark on alternate sides of the piston when it was in midstroke position. Although technically operational, the running costs of the engine were high, and it was not until the refinement introduced by the German inventor Nikolaus Otto in 1878 that the gas engine became a commercial success. Otto adopted the four-stroke cycle of induction–compression–firing–exhaust that has been known by his name ever since. Gas engines became extensively used for small industrial establishments which could thus dispense with the upkeep of a boiler necessary in any steam plant, however small.

The Otto cycle

Petroleum. The economic potential for the internal-combustion engine lay in the need for a light locomotive engine. This could not be provided by the gas engine, depending on a piped supply of town gas, any more than by the steam engine, with its need for a cumbersome boiler; but, by using alternative fuels derived from oil, the internal-combustion engine took to wheels, with momentous consequences. Bituminous deposits had been known in Southwest Asia from antiquity and had been worked as building material, illuminants, and for medicinal products. The westward expansion of settlement in America, with many homesteads beyond the range of city gas supplies, promoted the exploitation of the easily available sources of crude oil for the manufacture of kerosene (paraffin). In 1859 the oil industry took on new significance when Edwin L. Drake bored successfully through 70 feet (21 metres) of rock to strike oil in Pennsylvania, thus inaugurating the search for and exploitation of the deep oil resources of the world. While world supplies of oil expanded dramatically, the main demand was at first for the kerosene, the middle fraction distilled from the raw material, which was used as the fuel in oil lamps. The most volatile fraction of the oil, petroleum, remained an embarrassing waste product until it was discovered that this could be burned in a light internal-combustion engine; the result was an ideal prime mover for vehicles. The way was prepared for this development by the success of oil engines burning cruder fractions of oil. Kerosene-burning oil engines, modelled closely on existing gas engines, had emerged in the 1870s, and by the late 1880s engines using the vapour of heavy oil in a jet of compressed air and working on the Otto cycle had become an attractive proposition for light duties in places too isolated to use town gas.

The greatest refinements in the heavy-oil engine are associated with the work of Rudolf Diesel of Germany, who took out his first English patent in 1892. Working from thermodynamic principles of avoiding heat losses as

The diesel engine

much as possible, Diesel devised an engine in which the very high compression of the air in the cylinder secured the spontaneous ignition of the oil when it was injected in a carefully determined quantity. This ensured high thermal efficiency, but it also made necessary a heavy structure because of the high compression maintained, and also a rather rough performance at low speeds compared with other oil engines. It was therefore not immediately suitable for locomotive purposes, but Diesel went on improving his engine and in the 20th century it became an important form of vehicular propulsion.

Meantime the light high-speed gasoline (petrol) engine predominated. The first applications of the new engine to locomotion were made in Germany, where Gottlieb Daimler and Carl Benz equipped the first motorcycle and the first motorcar respectively with engines of their own design in 1885. Benz's "horseless carriage" became the prototype of the modern automobile, the development and consequences of which can be more conveniently considered in relation to the revolution in transport.

By the end of the 19th century, the internal-combustion engine was challenging the steam engine in many industrial and transport applications. It is notable that, whereas the pioneers of the steam engine had been almost all Britons, most of the innovators in internal combustion were continental Europeans and Americans. The transition, indeed, reflects the general change in international leadership in the Industrial Revolution, with Britain being gradually displaced from its position of unchallenged superiority in industrialization and technological innovation. A similar transition occurred in the theoretical understanding of heat engines: it was the work of the Frenchman Sadi Carnot and other scientific investigators which led to the new science of thermodynamics, rather than that of the British engineers who had most practical experience of the engines on which the science was based.

It should not be concluded, however, that British innovation in prime movers was confined to the steam engine, or even that steam and internal combustion represent the only significant developments in this field during the Industrial Revolution. Rather, the success of these machines stimulated speculation about alternative sources of power, and in at least one case achieved a success the full consequences of which were not fully developed. This was the hot-air engine, for which a Scotsman, Robert Stirling, took out a patent in 1817. The hot-air engine depends for its power on the expansion and displacement of air inside a cylinder, heated by the external and continuous combustion of the fuel. Even before the exposition of the laws of thermodynamics, Stirling had devised a cycle of heat transfer that was ingenious and economical. Various constructional problems limited the size of hot-air engines to very small units, so that although they were widely used for driving fans and similar light duties before the availability of the electric motor, they did not assume great technological significance. But the economy and comparative cleanness of the hot-air engine were making it once more the subject of intensive research in the early 1970s.

The transformation of power technology in the Industrial Revolution had repercussions throughout industry and society. In the first place, the demand for fuel stimulated the coal industry, which had already grown rapidly by the beginning of the 18th century, into continuing expansion and innovation. The steam engine, which enormously increased the need for coal, contributed significantly toward obtaining it by providing more efficient mine pumps and, eventually, improved ventilating equipment. Other inventions such as that of the miners' safety lamp helped to improve working conditions, although the immediate consequence of its introduction in 1816 was to persuade mine owners to work dangerous seams, which had hitherto been regarded as inaccessible. The principle of the lamp was that the flame from the wick of an oil lamp was enclosed within a cylinder of wire gauze through which insufficient heat passed to ignite the explosive gas (firedamp) outside. It was subsequently improved, but remained a vital source of light in coal mines

until the advent of electric battery lamps. With these improvements, together with the simultaneous revolution in the transport system, British coal production increased steadily throughout the 19th century. The other important fuel for the new prime movers was oil, and the rapid expansion of oil production has already been mentioned. In the hands of John D. Rockefeller and his Standard Oil organization it grew into a vast undertaking in the United States after the end of the Civil War, but the oil-extraction industry was not so well organized elsewhere until the 20th century.

DEVELOPMENT OF INDUSTRIES

Metallurgy. Another industry that interacted intimately with the power revolution was that concerned with metallurgy and the metal trades. The development of iron and steel techniques was one of the outstanding British achievements of the Industrial Revolution. The essential characteristic of this achievement was that by converting the iron and steel industry from dependence upon charcoal to coal as a fuel it enormously increased the production of these metals. It also provided another incentive to coal production and made available the materials that were indispensable for the construction of steam engines and every other sophisticated form of machine. The transformation that began with a coke-smelting process in 1709 was carried further by the development of crucible steel in 1744 and by the puddling and rolling process to produce wrought iron in 1784. The first development led to high quality cast steel by fusion of the ingredients (wrought iron and charcoal, in carefully measured proportions) in sealed ceramic crucibles that could be heated in a coal-fired furnace. The second applied the principle of the reverberatory furnace, whereby the hot gases passed over the surface of the metal being heated rather than through it, thus greatly reducing the risk of contamination by impurities in the coal fuels, and the discovery that by puddling, or stirring, the molten metal and by passing it hot from the furnace to be hammered and rolled, the metal could be consolidated and the conversion of cast iron to wrought iron made completely effective.

Iron and steel. The result of this series of innovations was that the British iron and steel industry was freed from its reliance upon the forests as a source of charcoal and was encouraged to move toward the major coal fields. Abundant cheap iron thus became an outstanding feature of the early stages of the Industrial Revolution in Britain. Cast iron was available for bridge construction, for the framework of fireproof factories, and for other civil-engineering purposes such as Thomas Telford's dramatic cast-iron aqueducts. Wrought iron was available for all manner of mechanical devices requiring strength and precision. Steel remained a comparatively rare metal until the second half of the 19th century, when the situation was transformed by the Bessemer and Siemens processes for manufacturing steel in bulk. Henry Bessemer

The Bettmann Archive

Manufacture of steel using Bessemer converters, engraving by C. Laplante, 1875.

The hot-air engine

Use of coal in iron and steel industry

took out the patent for his converter in 1856. It consisted of a large vessel charged with molten iron, through which cold air was blown. There was a spectacular reaction resulting from the combination of impurities in the iron with oxygen in the air, and when this subsided it left mild steel in the converter. Bessemer was virtually a professional inventor with little previous knowledge of the iron and steel industry; his process was closely paralleled by that of the American iron manufacturer William Kelly, who was prevented by bankruptcy from taking advantage of his invention. Meanwhile, the Siemens–Martin open-hearth process was introduced in 1863, utilizing the hot waste gases of cheap fuel to heat a regenerative furnace, with the initial heat transferred to the gases circulating round the large hearth in which the reactions within the molten metal could be carefully controlled to produce steel of the quality required. The open-hearth process was gradually refined and by the end of the 19th century had overtaken the Bessemer process in the amount of steel produced. The effect of both these processes was to make steel available in bulk instead of small-scale ingots of cast crucible steel, and henceforward steel steadily replaced wrought iron as the major commodity of the iron and steel industry.

Low-grade ores. The transition to cheap steel did not take place without technical problems, one of the most difficult of which was the fact that most of the easily available low-grade iron ores in the world contain a proportion of phosphorus, which proved difficult to eliminate but which ruined any steel produced from it. The problem was solved by the British scientists S.G. Thomas and Percy Gilchrist, who invented the basic slag process, the principle of which was that by lining the furnace or converter with an alkaline material the phosphorus could be made to combine with it to produce a basic slag, which turned out to be an important by-product in the nascent artificial-fertilizer industry. The most important effect of this innovation was to make the extensive phosphoric ores of Lorraine and elsewhere available for exploitation. Among other things, therefore, it contributed significantly to the rise of the German heavy iron and steel industry in the Ruhr. Other improvements were made in British steel production in the late 19th century, particulary in the discovery of alloys for specialized purposes, but these contributed more to the quality than the quantity of steel and did not affect the shift away from Britain to continental Europe and North America of dominance in this industry. British production continued to increase, but by 1900 it had been overtaken by that of the United States and Germany.

Mechanical engineering. Closely linked with the iron and steel industry was the rise of mechanical engineering, brought about by the demand for steam engines and other large machines, and taking shape for the first time in the Soho workshop of Boulton and Watt in Birmingham, where the skills of the precision engineer, developed in manufacturing scientific instruments and small arms, were first applied to the construction of large industrial machinery. The engineering workshops that matured in the 19th century played a vital part in the increasing mechanization of industry and transport. Not only did they deliver the looms, locomotives, and other hardware in steadily growing quantities, but they also transformed the machine tools on which these machines were made. The lathe became an all-metal, power-driven machine with a completely rigid base and a slide-rest to hold the cutting tool, capable of more sustained and vastly more accurate work than the hand or foot operated wooden-framed lathes which preceded it. Drilling and slotting machines, milling and planing machines, and a steam hammer invented by James Nasmyth, an inverted vertical steam engine with the hammer on the lower end of the piston rod, were among the machines devised or improved from earlier woodworking models by the new mechanical engineering industry. After the middle of the 19th century, specialization within the industry became more pronounced, as some manufacturers concentrated on vehicle production while others devoted themselves to the particular needs of industries such as coal mining,

paper-making, and sugar refining. This movement toward greater specialization was accelerated by the establishment of mechanical engineering in the other industrial nations, especially in Germany, where electrical engineering and other new skills made rapid progress, and in the United States, where labour shortages encouraged the development of standardization and mass-production techniques in fields as widely separated as agricultural machinery, small arms, typewriters, and sewing machines. Even before the coming of the bicycle, the automobile, and the airplane, therefore, the pattern of the modern engineering industry had been clearly established. The dramatic increases in engineering precision, represented by the machine designed by British mechanical engineer Sir Joseph Whitworth in 1856 for measuring to an accuracy of 0.00001 of an inch (even though such refinement was not necessary in everyday workshop practice), and the corresponding increase in the productive capacity of the engineering industry, acted as a continuing encouragement to further mechanical innovation.

Textiles. The industry that, probably more than any other, gave its character to the British Industrial Revolution was the cotton-textile industry. The traditional dates of the Industrial Revolution bracket the period in which the processes of cotton manufacture in Britain were transformed from those of a small-scale domestic industry scattered over the towns and villages of the South Pennines into those of a large-scale, concentrated, power-driven, mechanized, factory-organized, urban industry. The transformation was undoubtedly dramatic both to contemporaries and to posterity, and there is no doubting its immense significance in the overall pattern of British industrialization. But its importance in the history of technology should not be exaggerated. Certainly there were many interesting mechanical improvements, at least at the beginning of the transformation. The development of the spinning wheel into the spinning jenny, and the use of rollers and moving trolleys to mechanize spinning in the shape of the frame and the mule, respectively, initiated a drastic rise in the productivity of the industry. But it could be maintained that these were secondary innovations in the sense that there were precedents for them in the experiments of the previous generation; that in any case the first British textile factory was the Derby silk mill built by the Lombe brothers in 1719; and that the most far-reaching innovation in cotton manufacture was the introduction of steam power to drive carding machines, spinning machines, power looms, and printing machines. This, however, is probably to overstate the case, and the cotton innovators should not be deprived of credit for their enterprise and ingenuity in transforming the British cotton industry and making it the model for subsequent exercises in industrialization. Not only was it copied, belatedly and slowly, by the woollen-cloth industry in Britain, but wherever other nations sought to industrialize they tried to acquire the expertise of British cotton industrialists and artisans and British cotton machinery.

One of the important consequences of the rapid rise of the British cotton industry was the dynamic stimulus which it gave to other processes and industries. The rising demand for raw cotton, for example, encouraged the plantation economy of the Southern states of the U.S. and the introduction of the cotton gin, an important contrivance for separating mechanically the cotton wool from the seeds and stem of the plant.

Chemicals. In Britain, it brought a sudden increase of interest in the chemical industry, because one formidable bottleneck in the production of textiles was the long time taken by natural bleaching techniques, relying on sunlight, rain, sour milk, and urine. The modern chemical industry was virtually called into being to develop more rapid bleaching techniques for the British cotton industry. Its first success came in the middle of the 18th century, when John Roebuck invented the method of mass producing sulfuric acid in lead chambers. The acid was used directly in bleaching, but it was also used in the production of more effective chlorine bleaches, and in the manufacture of bleaching powder, a process perfected by Charles Tennant at his St. Rollox factory in

Glasgow in 1799. This effectively met the requirements of the cotton-textile industry, and thereafter the chemical industry turned its attention to the needs of other industries, and particularly to the increasing demand for alkali in soap, glass, and a range of other manufacturing processes. The result was the successful establishment of the Leblanc soda process, invented by Nicolas Leblanc in France in 1791, for manufacturing sodium carbonate (soda) on a large scale; this remained the main alkali process in Britain until the end of the 19th century, even though the Belgian Solvay process, considerably more economical, was replacing it elsewhere.

Innovation in the chemical industry shifted, in the middle of the 19th century, from the heavy chemical processes to organic chemistry. The stimulus here was less a specific industrial demand than the pioneering work of a group of German scientists on the nature of coal and its derivatives. Following their work, W.H. Perkin, at the Royal College of Chemistry in London, produced the first artificial dye from aniline in 1856. In the same period, the middle third of the 19th century, work on the qualities of cellulosic materials was leading to the development of high explosives such as nitrocellulose, nitroglycerine, and dynamite, while experiments with the solidification and extrusion of cellulosic liquids were producing the first plastics, such as celluloid, and the first artificial fibres, so-called artificial silk, or rayon. By the end of the century all these processes had become the bases for large chemical industries.

An important by-product of the expanding chemical industry was the manufacture of a widening range of medicinal and pharmaceutical materials as medical knowledge increased and drugs began to play a constructive part in therapy. The period of the Industrial Revolution witnessed the first real progress in medical services since the ancient civilizations. Great advances in the sciences of anatomy and physiology had had remarkably little impact on medical practice. In 18th-century Britain, however, hospital provision increased in quantity although not invariably in quality, while a significant start was made in immunizing people against smallpox culmi-
Improve-
ments in
control of
disease nating in Edward Jenner's vaccination process of 1796, by which protection from the disease was provided by administering a dose of the much less virulent but related disease of cowpox. But it took many decades of use and further smallpox epidemics to secure its widespread adoption and thus to make it effective in controlling the disease. By this time Louis Pasteur and others had established the bacteriological origin of many common diseases and thereby helped to promote movements for better public health and immunization against many virulent diseases such as typhoid fever and diphtheria. Parallel improvements in anesthetics (beginning with Sir Humphry Davy's discovery of nitrous oxide, or "laughing gas," in 1799) and antiseptics were making possible elaborate surgery, and by the end of the century X-rays and radiology were placing powerful new tools at the disposal of medical technology, while the use of synthetic drugs such as barbitone, cocaine, quinine, and aspirin (acetylsalicylic acid) had become established.

Agriculture. The agricultural improvements of the 18th century had been promoted by people whose industrial and commercial interests made them willing to experiment with new machines and processes to improve the productivity of their estates. Under the same sort of stimuli, agricultural improvement continued into the 19th century and was extended to food processing in Britain and elsewhere. The steam engine was not readily adapted for agricultural purposes, yet ways were found of harnessing it to threshing machines and even to plowing by means of a cable pulling the plow across a field between powerful traction engines. In the United States mechanization of agriculture began later than in Britain, but because of the comparative labour shortage it proceeded more quickly and more thoroughly. The McCormick reaper and the combine harvester were both developed in the United States, as were barbed wire and the food-packing and canning industries, Chicago becoming the world-famous centre for these processes. The introduc-

tion of refrigeration techniques in the second half of the 19th century made it possible to convey meat from Australia and Argentina to European markets, and the same markets encouraged the growth of dairy farming and market gardening, with distant producers such as New Zealand able to send their butter in refrigerated ships to wherever in the world it could be sold.

Civil engineering. As far as large civil-engineering works were concerned, the heavy work of moving earth continued to depend throughout this period on human labour organized by building contractors. But the use of gunpowder, dynamite, and steam diggers helped to reduce this dependence increasingly toward the end of the 19th century, and the introduction of compressed air and hydraulic tools also contributed to the lightening of drudgery. The latter two inventions were important in other respects, such as in mining engineering and in the operation of lifts, lock gates, and cranes. The use of a tunnelling shield, to allow a tunnel to be driven through soft or uncertain rock strata, was pioneered by the French émigré engineer Marc Brunel in the construction of the first tunnel underneath the Thames River in London, (1826–42), and the technique was adopted elsewhere. The iron bell or caisson was introduced for working below water level in order to lay foundations for bridges or other structures, and bridge building made great advances with the perfecting of the suspension bridge by the British engineers Thomas Telford and Isambard Kingdom Brunel and the German-American engineer John Roebling and the development of the truss bridge, first in timber, then in iron. Wrought iron gradually replaced cast iron as a bridge-building material, although several distinguished cast-iron bridges survive, such as that erected at Ironbridge in Shropshire between 1776 and 1779, which has been fittingly described as the "Stonehenge of the Industrial Revolution." The sections were cast at the Coalbrookdale furnace nearby and assembled by mortising and wedging on the model of a timber construction, without the use of bolts or rivets. The design was quickly superseded in other cast-iron bridges, but the bridge still stands as the first important structural use of cast iron. Cast iron became very important in the framing of large buildings, the elegant Crystal Palace of 1851 being an outstanding example. This was designed by the ingenious gardener-turned-architect Sir Joseph Paxton on the model of a greenhouse that he had built on the Chatsworth estate of the Duke of Devonshire. Its cast-iron beams were manufactured by three different firms and tested for size and strength on the site. By the end of the 19th century, however, steel was beginning to replace cast iron as well as wrought iron, and the new technique of reinforced concrete was being introduced. In water-supply and sewage-disposal works, civil engineering achieved some monumental successes, especially in the design of dams, which improved considerably in the period, and in long-distance piping and pumping. Advances
in bridge
construc-
tion

Transport and communications. Transport and communications provide an example of a revolution within the Industrial Revolution, so completely were the modes transformed in the period 1750–1900. The first improvements in Britain came in roads and canals in the second half of the 18th century. Although of great economic importance, these were not of much significance in the history of technology, as good roads and canals had existed in continental Europe for at least a century before their adoption in Britain. A network of hard-surfaced roads was built in France in the 17th and early 18th centuries and copied in Germany. A notable improvement was introduced in road construction by Pierre Trésaguet of France in the later 18th century, in separating the hard-stone wearing surface from the rubble substrata and taking care to provide ample drainage. Nevertheless, by the beginning of the 19th century British engineers were beginning to innovate in both road- and canal-building techniques, with J.L. McAdam's cheap and long-wearing road surface of compacted stones and Thomas Telford's well-engineered canals. The outstanding innovation in transport, however, was the application of steam power, which occurred in three forms.

Steam locomotive. First was the evolution of the railroad: the combination of the steam locomotive and a permanent travel way of metal rails. Experiments in this conjunction in the first quarter of the 19th century culminated in the Stockton and Darlington Railway, opened in 1825, and a further five years of experience with steam locomotives led to the Liverpool and Manchester Railway, which, when it opened in 1830, constituted the first fully timetabled railway service with scheduled freight and passenger traffic relying entirely on the steam locomotive for traction. This railway was designed by George Stephenson, and the locomotives were the work of Stephenson and his son Robert, the first being the famous "Rocket," which won a competition held by the proprietors of the railway at Rainhill, outside Liverpool, in 1829. The opening of the Liverpool and Manchester line may fairly be regarded as the inauguration of the Railway Era, which continued until World War I. During this time railways were built across all the countries and continents of the world, opening up vast areas to the markets of industrial society. Locomotives increased rapidly in size and power, but the essential principles remained the same as those established by the Stephensons in the early 1830s: horizontal cylinders mounted beneath a multitubular boiler with a firebox at the rear and a tender carrying supplies of water and fuel. This was the form developed from the "Rocket," which had diagonal cylinders, being itself a stage in the transition from the vertical cylinders, often encased by the boiler, which had been typical of the earliest locomotives (except Trevithick's Penydarren engine, which had a horizontal cylinder). Meanwhile, the construction of the permanent way underwent a corresponding improvement on that which had been common on the preceding tramroads: wrought iron, and eventually steel, rails replaced the cast-iron rails which cracked easily under a steam locomotive, and well-aligned track with easy gradients and substantial supporting civil-engineering works became a commonplace of the railroads of the world.

Beginning of the Railway Era

Road locomotive. The second form in which steam power was applied to transport was that of the road locomotive. There is no technical reason why this should not have enjoyed a success equal to that of the railway engine, but its development was so constricted by the unsuitability of most roads and by the jealousy of other road users that it only achieved general utility for heavy traction work and such duties as road rolling. The steam traction engine, which could be readily adapted from road haulage to power farm machines, was nevertheless a distinguished product of 19th-century steam technology.

Steamboats and ships. The third application was much more important, for it transformed marine transport. The first attempts to use a steam engine to power a boat were made on the Seine in France in 1775, and several experimental steamships were built by William Symington in Britain at the turn of the 19th century. The first commercial success in steam propulsion for a ship, however, was that of the American Robert Fulton, whose paddle steamer "Clermont" plied between New York and Albany in 1807, equipped with a Boulton and Watt engine of the modified beam or side-lever type, with two beams placed alongside the base of the engine in order to lower the centre of gravity. A similar engine was installed in the Glasgow-built "Comet," which was put in service on the Clyde in 1812 and was the first successful steamship in Europe. All the early steamships were paddle-driven, and all were small vessels suitable only for ferry and packet duties because it was long thought that the fuel requirements of a steamship would be so large as to preclude long-distance cargo carrying. The further development of the steamship was thus delayed until the 1830s, when I.K. Brunel began to apply his ingenious and innovating mind to the problems of steamship construction. His three great steamships each marked a leap forward in technique. The "Great Western" (launched 1837), the first built specifically for oceanic service in the North Atlantic, demonstrated that the proportion of space required for fuel decreased as the total volume of the ship increased. The "Great Britain" (launched 1843)

Robert Fulton's "Clermont"

was the first large iron ship in the world and the first to be screw propelled; its miraculous return to the port of Bristol in 1970, after a long working life and abandonment to the elements, is a remarkable testimony to the strength of its construction. The "Great Eastern" (launched 1858), with its total of 18,918 tons (17,162,400 kilograms), was by far the largest ship built in the 19th century. With a double iron hull and two sets of engines driving both a screw and paddles, this leviathan was never an economic success, but it admirably demonstrated the technical possibilities of the large iron steamship. By the end of the century, steam was well on the way to displacing the sailing ship on all the main trade routes of the world.

Printing and photography. Communications were equally transformed in the 19th century. The steam engine helped to mechanize and thus to speed up the processes of papermaking and of printing, the latter being achieved by the introduction of the high-speed rotary press and the Linotype machine for casting type and setting it in justified lines (*i.e.*, with even right-hand margins). Printing, indeed, had to undergo a technological revolution comparable to the 15th-century invention of movable type to be able to supply the greatly increasing market for the printed word. Another important process which was to make a vital contribution to modern printing was discovered and developed in the 19th century: photography. The first photograph was taken in 1826 by the French physicist J.-N. Niepce, using a pewter plate coated with a form of bitumen that hardened on exposure. His partner L.-J.-M. Daguerre and the Englishman W.H. Fox Talbot adopted silver compounds to give light sensitivity, and the technique developed rapidly in the middle decades of the century. By the 1890s George Eastman in the United States was manufacturing cameras and celluloid photographic film for a popular market, and the first experiments with the cinema were beginning to attract attention.

Telegraphs and telephones. The great innovations in communications technology, however, derived from electricity. The first was the electric telegraph, invented or at least made into a practical proposition for use on the developing British railway system by two British inventors, Sir William Cooke and Sir Charles Wheatstone, who collaborated on the work and took out a joint patent in 1837. Almost simultaneously, the American inventor Samuel F.B. Morse devised the signalling code that was subsequently adopted all over the world. In the next quarter of a century the continents of the world were linked telegraphically by transoceanic cables, and the main political and commercial centres were brought into instantaneous communication. The telegraph system also played an important part in the opening up of the American West by providing rapid aid in the maintenance of law and order. The electric telegraph was followed by the telephone, invented by Alexander Graham Bell in 1876 and quickly adopted for short-range oral communication in the cities of America, and at a somewhat more leisurely pace by those of Europe. About the same time, theoretical work on the electromagnetic properties of light and other radiation was beginning to produce astonishing experimental results, and the possibilities of wireless telegraphy began to be explored. By the end of the century, Guglielmo Marconi had transmitted messages over many miles in Britain and was preparing the apparatus with which he made the first transatlantic radio communication on December 12, 1901. The world was thus being drawn inexorably into a closer community by the spread of instantaneous communication.

Morse Code

Military technology. One area of technology was not dramatically influenced by the application of steam or electricity by the end of the 19th century: military technology. Although the size of armies increased between 1750 and 1900, there were few major innovations in techniques, except at sea where naval architecture rather reluctantly accepted the advent of the iron steamship and devoted itself to matching ever-increasing firepower with the strength of the armour plating on the hulls. The quality of artillery and of firearms improved with the new high explosives which became available in the middle of the 19th century, but experiments such as the three-wheeled iron gun carriage, invented by the French army engineer Nicolas Cugnot in 1769, which counts as the

By courtesy of the Science Museum, London

Nicolas Cugnot's steam carriage, showing (left) the boiler and (right of boiler) the vertical cylinders, 1770. In the Science Museum, London.

first steam-powered road vehicle, did not give rise to any confidence that steam could be profitably used in battle. Railroads and the electric telegraph were put to effective military use, but in general it is fair to say that the 19th century put remarkably little of its tremendous and innovative technological effort into devices for war.

In the course of its dynamic development between 1750 and 1900 important things happened to technology itself. In the first place, it became self-conscious. This change is sometimes characterized as one from a craft-based technology to one based on science, but this is an oversimpli-

Increasing awareness of technology fication. What occurred was rather an increasing awareness of technology as a socially important function. It is apparent in the growing volume of treatises on technological subjects from the 16th century onward, and in the rapid development of patent legislation to protect the interests of technological innovators. It is apparent also in the development of technical education, uneven at first, being confined to the French polytechnics and spreading thence to Germany and North America, but reaching even Britain, which had been most opposed to its formal recognition as part of the structure of education, by the end of the 19th century. Again, it is apparent in the growth of professional associations for engineers and for other specialized groups of technologists.

Second, by becoming self-conscious, technology attracted attention in a way it had never done before, and vociferous factions grew up to praise it as the mainspring of social progress and the development of democracy, or to criticize it as the bane of modern man, responsible for the harsh discipline of the "dark Satanic mills" and the tyranny of the machine and the squalor of urban life. It was clear by the end of the 19th century that technology was an important feature in industrial society and that it was likely to become more so. Whatever was to happen in the future, technology had come of age and had to be taken seriously as a formative factor of the utmost significance in the continuing development of civilization.

IV. The 20th century

TECHNOLOGY FROM 1900 TO 1945

Recent history is notoriously difficult to write, because of the mass of material and the problem of distinguishing the significant from the insignificant among events that have virtually the quality of contemporary experience. In respect to the recent history of technology, however, one fact stands out clearly: despite the immense achievements of technology by 1900, the following seven decades witnessed more advance over a wide range of activities than the whole of previously recorded history. The airplane, the rocket and interplanetary probes, electronics, atomic power, antibiotics, insecticides, and a host of new materials have all been invented and developed to create an unparalleled social situation, full of possibilities and dangers, which would have been virtually unimaginable before the present century.

In venturing to interpret the events of the present century it will be convenient to separate the years before 1945 from those which have followed. The years 1900 to 1945

were dominated by the two world wars, while those since 1945 have been preoccupied by the need to avoid another major war. The dividing point is one of outstanding social and technological significance: the detonation of the first atomic bomb at Alamogordo, New Mexico, in July 1945.

There have been profound political changes in the 20th century related to technological capacity and leadership. It may be an exaggeration to regard the 20th century as "the American century," but the rise of the United States as a superstate has been sufficiently rapid and dramatic to excuse the hyperbole. It has been a rise based upon tremendous natural resources exploited to secure increased productivity through widespread industrialization, and the success of the United States in achieving this objective has been tested and demonstrated in the two world wars. Technological leadership passed from Britain and the European nations to the United States in the course of these wars. This is not to say that the springs of innovation went dry in Europe: many important inventions of the 20th century originated there. But it has been the United States that has had the capacity to assimilate innovations and to take full advantage from them at times when other nations have been deficient in one or other of the vital social resources without which a brilliant invention cannot be converted into a commercial success. As with Britain in the Industrial Revolution, the technological vitality of the United States in the 20th century has been demonstrated less by any particular innovations than by its ability to adopt new ideas from whatever source they come.

The two world wars were themselves the most important instruments of technological as well as political change in the 20th century. The rapid evolution of the airplane is a striking illustration of this process, while the appearance of the tank in the first conflict and of the atomic bomb in the second show the same signs of response to an urgent military stimulus. It has been said that World War I was a chemists' war, on the basis of the immense importance of high explosives and poison gas. In other respects the two wars hastened the development of technology by extending the institutional apparatus for the encouragement of innovation by both the state and private industry. This process went further in some countries than in others, but there were no major belligerent nations which could resist entirely the need to support and coordinate their scientific–technological effort. The wars were thus responsible for speeding the transformation from "little science," with research still largely restricted to small-scale efforts by a few isolated scientists, to "big science," with the emphasis on large research teams sponsored by governments and corporations, working collectively on the development and application of new techniques. While the extent of this transformation must not be overstated, and recent research has tended to stress the continuing need for the independent inventor at least in the stimulation of innovation, there can be little doubt that the change in the scale of technological enterprises has had far-reaching consequences. It has been one of the most momentous transformations of the 20th century, for it has altered the quality of industrial and social organization. In the process it has assured technology, for the first time in its long history, a position of importance and even honour in social esteem. The world wars and their effect

Fuel and power. There were no fundamental innovations in fuel and power before the breakthrough of 1945, but there were several significant developments in techniques that had originated in the previous century. An outstanding development of this type was the internal-combustion engine, which was continuously improved to meet the needs of road vehicles and airplanes. The high-compression engine burning heavy-oil fuels, invented by Rudolf Diesel in the 1890s, was developed to serve as a submarine power unit in World War I and was subsequently adapted to heavy road haulage duties and to agricultural tractors. Moreover, the sort of development that had transformed the reciprocating steam engine into the steam turbine occurred with the internal-combustion engine, the gas turbine replacing the reciprocating engine Developments in engine design for specialized purposes such as aero-engines, in which a high power-to-weight ratio is important. Admittedly, this adaptation had not proceeded very far by 1945, although the first jet-powered aircraft were in service by the end of the war. The theory of the gas turbine, however, had been understood since the 1920s at least, and in 1929 Sir Frank Whittle, then taking a flying instructor's course with the Royal Air Force, combined it with the principle of jet propulsion in the engine for which he took out a patent in the following year. But the construction of a satisfactory gas-turbine engine was delayed for a decade by the lack of resources, and particularly by the need to develop new metal alloys which could withstand the high temperatures generated in the engine. This problem was solved by the development of a nickel-chromium alloy, and with the gradual solution of the other problems work went on in both Germany and Britain to seize a military advantage by applying the jet engine to combat aircraft.

Gas-turbine engine. The principle of the gas turbine is that of compressing and burning air and fuel in a combustion chamber and using the exhaust jet from this process to provide the reaction which propels the engine forward. In its turbopropellor form, which developed only after World War II, the exhaust drives a shaft carrying a normal airscrew (propeller). Compression is achieved in a gas-turbine engine by admitting air through a turbine rotor. In the so-called ramjet engine, intended to operate at high speeds, the momentum of the engine through the air achieves adequate compression, but this form of the engine is still in its experimental stages. The gas turbine has been the subject of experiments in road, rail, and marine transport, but for all purposes except that of air transport its advantages have not so far been such as to make it a viable rival to traditional reciprocating engines.

Petroleum. As far as fuel is concerned, the gas turbine burns mainly the middle fractions (kerosene, or paraffin) of refined oil, but the general tendency of its widespread application has been to increase still further the dependence of the industrialized nations on the producers of crude oil, which has become a raw material of immense economic value and international political significance. The refining of this material has itself undergone important technological development. Until the present century, it consisted of a fairly simple batch process whereby oil was heated until it vaporized, when the various fractions were distilled separately. Apart from improvements in the design of the stills and the introduction of continuous-flow production, the first big advance came in 1913

Petroleum cracking

with the introduction of thermal cracking. This process took the lower fractions after distillation and subjected them to heat under pressure, thus cracking the heavy molecules into lighter molecules and so increasing the yield of the most valuable fuel, petrol or gasoline. The discovery of this ability to tailor the products of crude oil to suit the market marks the true beginning of the petrochemical industry. It received a further boost in 1937, with the introduction of catalytic cracking. By the use of various catalysts in the process means were devised for still further manipulating the molecules of the hydrocarbon raw material. The development of modern plastics has followed directly on this (see below *Plastics*). So efficient had the processes of utilization become that by the end of World War II the petrochemical industry had virtually eliminated all waste materials.

Electricity. All the principles of generating electricity had been worked out in the 19th century, but by the end of that century these had only just begun to produce electricity on a large scale. The 20th century has witnessed a colossal expansion of electrical power generation and distribution. The general pattern has been toward ever-larger units of production, using steam from coal- or oil-fired boilers. Economies of scale and the greater physical efficiency achieved as higher steam temperatures and pressures were attained both reinforced this tendency. United States experience indicates the trend: in the first decade of the century a generating unit with a capacity of 25,000 kilowatts with pressures up to 200–300 pounds per square inch at 400°–500° F

(about 200°–265° C) was considered large, but by 1930 the largest unit was 208,000 kilowatts, with pressures of 1,200 pounds per square inch at a temperature of 725° F, while the amount of fuel necessary to produce a kilowatt-hour of electricity and the price to the consumer had fallen dramatically. As the market for electricity increased, so did the distance over which it was transmitted, and the efficiency of transmission required higher and higher voltages. The small direct-current generators of early urban power systems were abandoned in favour of alternating-current systems, which could be adapted more readily to high voltages. Transmission over a line of 155 miles (250 kilometres) was established in California in 1908 at 110,000 volts; Hoover Dam in the 1930s used a line of 300 miles (480 kilometres) at 287,000 volts. The latter case may serve as a reminder that hydroelectric power, using a fall of water to drive water turbines, has been developed to generate electricity where the climate and topography make it possible to combine production with convenient transmission to a market. Remarkable levels of efficiency have been achieved in modern plants. One important consequence of the ever-expanding consumption of electricity in the industrialized countries has been the linking of local systems to provide vast power grids, or pools, within which power can be shifted easily to meet changing local needs for current.

Alternating current

Atomic power. Until 1945, electricity and the internal-combustion engine were the dominant sources of power for industry and transport in the 20th century, although in some parts of the industrialized world steam power and even older prime movers remained important. Early research in nuclear physics was more scientific than technological, stirring little general interest. In fact, from the work of Ernest Rutherford, Albert Einstein, and others to the first successful experiments in splitting heavy atoms in Germany in 1938, no particular thought was given to engineering potential. The war led to the Manhattan Project to produce the fission bomb that was first exploded at Alamogordo. Only in its final stages did even this program become a matter of technology, when the problems of building large reactors and handling radioactive materials had to be solved; and at this point it also became an economic and political matter, because very heavy capital expenditure was involved. Thus, in this crucial event of the mid-20th century, the convergence of science, technology, economics, and politics finally took place.

Industry and innovation. There have been technological innovations of great significance in many aspects of industrial production during the 20th century. It is worth observing, in the first place, that the basic matter of industrial organization has become one of self-conscious innovation, with organizations setting out to increase their productivity by improved techniques. Methods of work study, first systematically examined in the United States at the end of the 19th century, were widely applied in United States and European industrial organizations in the first half of the 20th century, evolving rapidly into scientific management and the modern studies of industrial administration, organization and method, and particular managerial techniques. The object of these exercises has been to make industry more efficient and thus to increase productivity and profits, and there can be no doubt that they have been remarkably successful, if not quite as successful as some of their advocates have maintained. Without this superior industrial organization it would not have been possible to convert the comparatively small workshops of the 19th century into the giant engineering establishments of the 20th with their mass-production and assembly-line techniques. The rationalization of production, so characteristic of industry in the present century, may thus be legitimately regarded as the result of the application of new techniques which form part of the history of technology since 1900.

Studies of work and industrial organization

Improvements in iron and steel. Another field of industrial innovation in the present century has been the production of new materials. As far as volume of consumption goes, man still lives in the Iron Age, with the utilization of iron exceeding that of any other material.

But this dominance of iron has been modified in three ways: by the skill of metallurgists in alloying iron with other metals; by the spread of materials such as glass and concrete in building; and by the appearance and widespread use of entirely new materials, particularly plastics. Alloys had already begun to become important in the iron and steel industry in the 19th century (apart from steel itself, which is an alloy of iron and carbon); self-hardening tungsten steel had been first produced in 1868, and manganese steel, possessing toughness rather than hardness, in 1887. Manganese steel is also non-magnetic, which suggests great possibilities for its use in the electric-power industry. In the 20th century steel alloys multiplied. Silicon steel was found to be useful because, unlike manganese steel, it is highly magnetic. In 1913 the first stainless steels were made in England by alloying steel with chromium, and the Krupp works in Germany produced stainless steel in 1914 with 18 percent chromium and 8 percent nickel. The importance of a nickel–chromium alloy in the development of the gas-turbine engine in the 1930s has already been noted. Many other alloys also came into widespread use for specialized purposes.

Building materials. Methods of producing traditional materials like glass and concrete on a larger scale have also supplied alternatives to iron, especially in building; in the form of reinforced concrete they have supplemented structural iron. Most of the entirely new materials have been nonmetallic, although at least one new metal, aluminum, has reached proportions of large-scale industrial significance in the 20th century. The ores of this metal are among the most abundant in the crust of the Earth, but before the provision of plentiful cheap electricity made it feasible to use an electrolytic process on an industrial scale, the metal was extracted only with great difficulty. The strength of aluminum, compared weight for weight with steel, has made it a valuable material in aircraft construction, and many other industrial and domestic uses have been found for it. In 1900 world production of aluminum was 3,000 tons, about half of which was made using cheap electric power from Niagara Falls. Production has since risen rapidly.

Electrolytic processes had already been used in the preparation of other metals. At the beginning of the 19th century, Davy had pioneered the process by isolating potassium, sodium, barium, calcium, and strontium, although there was little commercial exploitation of these processes. By the beginning of the 20th century, significant amounts of magnesium were being prepared electrolytically at high temperatures, and the electric furnace made possible the production of calcium carbide by the reaction of calcium and carbon. This material provided a useful step in the processing of synthetic resins and thus of plastics.

Plastics. The quality of plasticity is one that had been used to great effect in the crafts of metallurgy and ceramics. The use of the word plastics as a collective noun, however, refers not so much to the traditional materials employed in these crafts as to new substances produced by chemical reactions and molded or pressed to take a permanent rigid shape. The first material to be manufactured artificially in this way was Parkesine, developed by the British inventor Alexander Parkes from a mixture of chloroform and castor oil which produced "a substance hard as horn, but as flexible as leather, capable of being cast or stamped, painted, dyed or carved . . ." The words are from a guide to the Great Exhibition of 1862 in London, at which Parkesine won a bronze medal for its inventor. It was soon followed by other plastics, but apart from Celluloid, a cellulose nitrate composition using camphor as a solvent and produced in solid form (as imitation horn for billiard balls) and in sheets (for men's collars and photographic film), these had little commercial success until the 20th century.

The early plastics had relied upon the large molecules in cellulose, usually derived from wood pulp. However, Leo H. Baekeland, a Belgian-U.S. inventor, took out his patent for Bakelite in 1909, based on the reaction between formaldehyde and phenolic materials, and by fusing these in powder form at high temperatures he was able to produce a plastic that was hard, infusible, and chemically resistant (the type known as thermosetting plastic). As a nonconductor of electricity it proved to be exceptionally useful for all sorts of electrical appliances. The success of Bakelite gave a great impetus to the plastics industry, to the study of coal-tar derivatives and other hydrocarbon compounds, and to the theoretical understanding of the structure of complex molecules. This activity led to new dyestuffs and detergents, but it also led to the successful manipulation of molecules to produce materials with particular qualities such as hardness and flexibility. Techniques were devised, often requiring catalysts and elaborate equipment, to secure these polymers—that is, complex molecules produced by the aggregation of simpler structures. Linear polymers give strong fibres, surface polymers have been useful in paints, and mass polymers have formed solid plastics.

Synthetic fibres. The possibility of creating artificial fibres was another 19th-century discovery which did not become commercially significant until the 20th century, when it developed alongside the solid plastics with which it was closely related. The first artificial textiles had been made from rayon, a silklike material produced by extruding a solution of nitrocellulose dissolved in acetic acid into a coagulating bath of alcohol, and various other cellulosic materials were used in this way. But later research exploited the polymerization techniques being used in solid plastics, and culminated in the production of nylon just before the outbreak of World War II. Nylon consists of long chains of carbon-based molecules, giving fibres of unprecedented strength and flexibility. It is formed by melting the component materials and extruding them, the strength of the fibre being greatly increased by stretching it when cold. Nylon was developed with the women's stocking market in mind, but the conditions of war gave it an opportunity to demonstrate its versatility and reliability in such things as parachute cord. This and other synthetic fibres became generally available only after the war.

Synthetic rubber. The chemical industry in the 20th century has thus put a wide range of new materials at the disposal of society. It has also succeeded in replacing natural sources of some materials: an important example of this has been the manufacture of artificial rubber to meet a world demand far in excess of that which could be met by the existing rubber plantations. This technique was pioneered in Germany during World War I. Here, as in other materials such as high explosives and dyestuffs, the consistent German investment in scientific and technical education paid dividends, for advances in all these fields of chemical manufacturing were prepared by careful research in the laboratory.

Pharmaceuticals and medical technology. An even more dramatic result of the growth in chemical knowledge has been the expansion of the modern pharmaceutical industry. The science of pharmacy emerged slowly from the traditional empiricism of the herbalist, but by the end of the 19th century there had been some solid achievements in the analysis of existing drugs and in the preparation of new ones. The discovery in 1856 of the first aniline dye had been occasioned by a vain attempt to synthesize quinine from coal-tar derivatives. Greater success came in the following decades with the production of the first synthetic antifever drugs and pain-killing compounds, culminating in 1899 in the development of salicylic acid into acetylsalicylic acid, which as aspirin is still the most widely used drug. Progress was being made simultaneously with the sulfonal hypnotics and the barbiturate group of drugs, and early in the 20th century Paul Ehrlich of Germany successfully developed an organic compound containing arsenic (No. 606, denoting how many tests he had made, but better known as Salvarsan) which was effective against syphilis. The significance of this discovery, in 1910, was that it was the first drug devised to overwhelm an invading micro-organism without offending the host. In 1932 the discovery that Prontosil, a red dye developed by the German synthetic-dyestuff industry, was an effective drug against streptococcal infections (leading to blood poisoning) introduced the

Importance of aluminum (margin note)

Chemical advances in plastics (margin note)

important sulfa drugs. Alexander Fleming's discovery of penicillin in 1928 was not immediately followed up, because it proved very difficult to isolate the drug in a stable form from the mold in which it was formed. But the stimulus of World War II gave a fresh urgency to research in this field, and successful production of the first of the antibiotics began in 1943. These drugs work by preventing the growth of pathogenic organisms. All these pharmaceutical advances demonstrate an intimate relationship with chemical technology.

Other branches of medical technology made significant progress. Anesthetics and antiseptics had been developed in the 19th century, opening up new possibilities for complex surgery; techniques of blood transfusion, examination by X-rays (discovered in 1895), radio therapy (following demonstration of the therapeutic effects of ultraviolet light in 1893), the discovery of radium in 1898, and orthopedic surgery for bone disorders all developed rapidly. The techniques of immunology similarly advanced, with the development of vaccines effective against typhoid and the other fever diseases.

Food and agriculture. The increasing chemical understanding of drugs and micro-organisms was applied with outstanding success to the study of food. The analysis of the relationship between certain types of food and human physical performance led to the definition of vitamins ("vital amino acids") in 1911 and to their classification into three types in 1919, with subsequent additions and subdivisions. It was realized that the presence of these materials was necessary for a healthy diet, and eating habits and public-health programs were adjusted accordingly. The importance of trace elements, very minor constituents, was also discovered and investigated, beginning in 1895 with the realization that goitre was caused by a deficiency of iodine.

As well as improving in quality, the quantity of food produced in the 20th century increased rapidly as a result of the intensive application of modern technology. The greater scale and complexity of urban life created a pressure for increased production and a greater variety of foodstuffs, and the resources of the internal-combustion engine, electricity, and chemical technology were called upon to achieve these objectives. The main service of the internal-combustion engine was in the shape of the tractor, which became the almost universal agent of mobile power on the farm in the industrialized countries. The same engines powered other machines such as combine harvesters, which became common in the United States in the early 20th century, although their use was less widespread in the more labour-intensive farms of Europe, especially before World War II. Synthetic fertilizers, an important product of the chemical industry, became popular in most types of arable farming, and other chemicals appeared toward the end of the period that performed something of an agrarian revolution as pesticides and herbicides. Once again, it was World War II which gave a powerful boost to this development. Despite problems of pollution by residue that developed later, the marketing of DDT as a highly effective insecticide in 1944 was a particularly significant achievement of chemical technology. Food processing and packaging also made advances, with the introduction of dehydration techniques such as vacuum-contact drying in the 1930s, but the 19th-century innovations of canning and refrigeration remained the dominant techniques of preservation.

Civil engineering. Important development occurred in civil engineering in the first half of the 20th century, although there were few striking innovations. Advancing techniques for massive construction, such as skyscrapers, bridges, and dams, produced many spectacular achievements all over the world, but especially in the United States. The city of New York acquired its characteristic skyline, built upon the exploitation of steel frames and reinforced-concrete techniques. Conventional methods of building in brick and masonry had reached the limits of feasibility in the 1800s with office blocks up to 16 stories high, and the future lay with the skeleton frame or cage construction pioneered in the 1880s in Chicago. The vital ingredients for the new tall buildings or skyscrapers that

followed were abundant cheap steel for columns, beams, and trusses, and efficient passenger elevators. The availability of these and the demand for more and more office space in the thriving cities of Chicago and New York caused the boom in skyscraper building that continued until 1932, when the Empire State Building, with its total height of 1,250 feet (378 metres) and 102 stories, achieved a limit only recently exceeded and demonstrated the strength of its structure by sustaining the crash impact of a B-25 bomber in July 1945 with only minor damage to the building. The Depression brought a halt to skyscraper building from 1932 until after the war.

Concrete, and more especially reinforced concrete (that is, concrete set around a framework or mesh of steel), played an important part in the construction of the later skyscrapers, and this material also led to the introduction of more imaginative structural forms in buildings and to the development of prefabrication techniques. The use of large concrete members in bridges and other structures has been made possible by the technique of prestressing: by stretching the reinforcing material, often in the form of high-tension piano wire, it has been possible to introduce tensions into the concrete opposite to those of the external loading, and in this way the members can be made stronger and lighter. The technique was particularly applicable in bridge building. The construction of large-span bridges received a setback, however, with the dramatic collapse of the Tacoma Narrows (Washington) Suspension Bridge in the United States in 1940, four months after it was completed. This led to a reassessment of wind effects on the loading of large suspension bridges and to significant improvements in subsequent designs. Massive use of concrete has produced spectacular high arch dams, in which the weight of water is transmitted in part to the abutments by the curve of the concrete wall, rather than depending upon the sheer bulk of impervious material as in a conventional gravity or embankment dam.

Transportation. Some of the outstanding achievements of the 20th century are provided by transportation history. In most fields there was a switch from steam power, supreme in the previous century, to internal combustion and electricity. Steam, however, retained its superiority in marine transport, with the steam turbine providing power for a new generation of large ocean liners beginning with the Cunard "Mauretania," developing 70,000 horsepower and a speed of 27 knots (27 nautical miles, or 50 kilometres, per hour) in 1906, and continuing throughout the period, culminating in the "Queen Elizabeth," launched in 1938, with about 200,000 horsepower and a speed of 28.5 knots. Even here, however, there was increasing competition from large diesel-powered motor vessels. Most smaller ships adopted this form of propulsion and even the steamships accepted the convenience of oil-burning boilers in place of the cumbersome coal burners with their large bunkers.

On land, steam fought a long rear-guard action, but the enormous popularity of the automobile deprived the railways of much of their most lucrative traffic and forced them to seek economies in conversion to diesel engines or electric traction, although these developments had not spread widely in Europe by the outbreak of World War II. Meanwhile, the automobile stimulated prodigious feats of production. Henry Ford led the way in the adoption of assembly-line mass production; his spectacularly successful Model T, the "Tin Lizzie," was manufactured in this way first in 1913, and by 1923 production had risen to nearly 2,000,000 a year. Despite this and similar successes in other countries, the first half of the 20th century was not a period of great technological innovation in the motorcar, which retained the main design features given to it in the last decade of the 19th century. For all the refinements (for example, the self-starter) and multitudinous varieties, the major fact of the automobile in this period was its quantity.

Unlike the automobile, to which its development was intimately related, the airplane is entirely a product of the 20th century. This is not to say that experiments with flying machines had not taken place earlier. Throughout the 19th century, to go back no further, investigations into aerodynamic effects were carried out by inventors such as Sir George Cayley in England, leading to the successful glider flights of Otto Lilienthal and others. Several designers perceived that the internal-combustion engine promised to provide the light, compact power unit that was a prerequisite of powered flight, and on December 17, 1903, Wilbur and Orville Wright in their "Flyer I" at the Kill Devil Hills in North Carolina achieved sustained, controlled, powered flight, one of the great "firsts" in the history of technology. The "Flyer I" was a propeller-driven adaptation of the biplane gliders that the Wright brothers had built and learned to fly in the previous years. They had devised a system of three-dimension control through elevator, rudder, and a wing-warping technique that served until the introduction of ailerons. Within a few years the brothers were flying with complete confidence, astonishing the European pioneers of flight when they crossed the Atlantic to give demonstrations in 1908. Within a matter of months of this revelation, however, the European designers had assimilated the lesson and were pushing ahead the principles of aircraft construction. World War I gave a great impetus to this technological development, transforming small-scale scattered aircraft manufacture into a major industry in all the main belligerent nations, and transforming the airplane itself from a fragile construction in wood and glue into a robust machine capable of startling aerobatic feats.

The end of the war brought a setback to this new industry, but the airplane had evolved sufficiently to reveal its potential as a medium of civil transport, and during the interwar years the transcontinental air routes were established and provided a market for large, comfortable, and safe aircraft. By the outbreak of World War II, metal-framed-and-skinned aircraft had become general, and the cantilevered monoplane structure had replaced the biplane for most purposes. War again provided a powerful stimulus to aircraft designers; engine performance was especially improved. The gas turbine received its first practical application. Other novel features of these years included the helicopter, deriving lift from its rotating wings, or rotors, and the German V-1 flying bomb, a pilotless aircraft.

The war also stimulated the use of gliders for the transport of troops, the use of parachutes for escape from aircraft and for attack by paratroops, and the use of gas-filled balloons for anti-aircraft barrages. The balloon had been used for pioneer aeronautical experiments in the 19th century, but its practical uses had been hampered by the lack of control over its movements. The application of the internal-combustion engine to a rigid-frame balloon airship by Ferdinand von Zeppelin had temporarily made a weapon of war in 1915, although experience soon proved that it could not survive in competition with the airplane. The apparently promising prospects of the dirigible (that is, manoeuvrable) airship in civil transport between the wars were ended by a series of disasters, the worst of which was the destruction of the "Hindenburg" in New Jersey in 1937. Since then the airplane has been unchallenged in the field of air transport.

Communications. The spectacular transport revolution of the 20th century has been accompanied by a communications revolution quite as dramatic, although technologically springing from different roots. In part, well established media of communication like printing have participated in this revolution, although most of the significant changes here such as the typewriter, the Linotype for casting and setting complete lines of print, and the high-speed power-driven rotary press were achievements of the 19th century. Photography was also a proved and familiar technique by the end of the 19th century, but cinematography was new and did not become generally available until after World War I, when it became enormously popular.

The real novelties in communications in the 20th century came in electronics. The scientific examination of the relationship between light waves and electromagnetic

The
Wright
brothers'
flight

The
rise of
electronics

waves had already revealed the possibility of transmitting electromagnetic signals between widely separated points, and on December 12, 1901, Guglielmo Marconi succeeded in transmitting the first wireless message across the Atlantic. Early equipment was crude, but within a few years striking progress was made in improving the means of transmitting and receiving coded messages. Particularly important was the development of the thermionic valve, a device for rectifying (that is, converting a high-frequency oscillating signal into a unidirectional current capable of registering as a sound) and amplifying an electromagnetic impulse. This was essentially a development from the carbon-filament electric light bulb. It had been observed that an ordinary vacuum bulb with a carbon filament with use acquired a black coating on the inside (the Edison effect, after Edison's observation of 1883), and this was correctly attributed to a stream of electrons radiated by the hot filament. In 1904, Sir John Ambrose Fleming of Britain discovered that by placing a metal cylinder around the filament in the bulb and by connecting the cylinder (the plate) to a third terminal, a current could be rectified so that it could be detected by a telephone receiver. This was known as the diode, and two years later, in 1906, Lee De Forest of the United States made the significant improvement which became known as the triode by introducing a third electrode (the grid) between the filament and the plate. The outstanding feature of this refinement was its ability to amplify a signal. Its application made possible by the 1920s the widespread introduction of live-voice broadcasting in Europe and America, with a consequent boom in the production of wirelesses and other equipment.

This, however, was only one of the results derived from the application of the thermionic valve. The idea of harnessing the flow of electrons was applied in the electron microscope, radar (a detection device depending on the capacity of some radio waves to be reflected by solid objects), the electronic computer, and in the cathode-ray tube of the television set. The first experiments in the transmission of pictures had been greeted with ridicule. Working on his own in Britain, John Logie Baird in the 1920s demonstrated a mechanical scanner able to convert an image into a series of electronic impulses that could then be reassembled on a viewing screen as a pattern of light and shade. Baird's system, however, was rejected in favour of a method of electronic scanning developed in the United States by Philo Farnsworth and Vladimir Zworykin with the powerful backing of the Radio Corporation of America, which operated much more rapidly and gave a more satisfactory image. By the outbreak of World War II, television services were being introduced in several nations, although the war suspended their extension for a decade. The emergence of television as a universal medium of mass communication is thus a phenomenon of the postwar years. But already by 1945 the cinema and the radio had demonstrated the power of the mass media in communicating news, propaganda, commercial advertisements, and entertainment.

Military technology. It has been necessary to refer repeatedly to the effects of the two world wars in promoting all kinds of innovation. It should be observed also that technological innovations have transformed the character of war itself by the introduction of new mechanical and chemical devices. One weapon developed during World War II deserves a special mention. The principle of rocket propulsion was well known earlier, and its possibilities as a means of achieving speeds sufficient to escape from the earth's gravitational pull had been pointed out by such pioneers as the Russian Konstantin Tsiolkovsky and the American Robert H. Goddard. The latter built experimental liquid-fuelled rockets in 1926. Simultaneously, a group of German and Romanian pioneers, including Hermann Oberth, was working along the same lines, and it was this team that was taken over by the German war effort in the 1930s and given the resources to develop a rocket capable of delivering a warhead hundreds of miles away. At the Peenemünde base on the island of Usedom in the Baltic, Wernher von Braun and his team created the V-2. Fully fuelled, it weighed 14 tons; it was 40

Development of rockets

German V-2 rocket on its launch vehicle.
Bilderdienst im Suddeutschen Verlag

feet (12 metres) long and was propelled by burning a mixture of alcohol and liquid oxygen. Reaching a height of over 100 miles (160 kilometres), the V-2 marked the beginning of the Space Age, and members of its design team were instrumental in both the Soviet and United States space programs after the war.

Technology had a tremendous social impact in the period 1900–45. The automobile and electric power, for instance, radically changed both the scale and the quality of 20th-century life, promoting a process of rapid urbanization and a virtual revolution in living through mass production of household goods and appliances. The rapid development of the airplane, the cinema, and radio made the world seem suddenly smaller and more accessible. The development of modern pharmaceutics, medicine, antibiotics, pesticides, and the many products of the chemical industry further transformed the life of most people. In the years following 1945 the constructive and creative opportunities of modern technology could be exploited, although the process has not been without its problems.

SPACE AGE TECHNOLOGY (1945–70)

The years since the end of World War II have been spent under the shadow of the atomic bomb, even though this weapon has not been used in war since August 1945. Nuclear weapons have undergone momentous development, first with the achievement of the technique of hydrogen fusion (1950), and second with their combination with long-range rockets. This new military technology has had an incalculable effect on international relations, for it has contributed to the polarization of world power blocs while enforcing a caution, if not discipline, in the conduct of international affairs which was sadly absent earlier in the 20th century.

The fact of nuclear power is by no means the only technological novelty of the post-1945 years. So striking, indeed, have been the advances in engineering, chemicals, medical technology, transport and communications, that some commentators have written, somewhat misleadingly, of the "second Industrial Revolution" to describe the changes in these years. The rapid development of electronic engineering has created a new world of computer technology, remote control, miniaturization, and instant communication, which has transformed almost every department of industry and administration and reached into every household. Even more expressive of the character of the period has been the leap over the threshold of extraterrestrial exploration. The techniques of rocketry, first applied in weapons, were developed to provide launch vehicles for satellites, lunar and planetary probes, and eventually, in 1969, to set the first men on the Moon and to bring them home safely again. This astonishing technological achievement was stimulated in part by the international ideological rivalry already mentioned, as only the Soviet Union and the United States had both the

resources and the will to support the huge programs of expenditure that the achievement required. It justifies the description of this period, however, as that of "Space Age technology."

Power.   The great power innovation of this period has been the harnessing of nuclear energy. The first atomic bombs represented only a comparatively crude form of nuclear fission, releasing all the energy of the radioactive material immediately and explosively. But it was quickly appreciated that the energy released within a critical atomic pile, a mass of graphite absorbing the neutrons released from radioactive material inserted into it, could generate heat which in turn could create steam to drive turbines and thus convert the nuclear energy into usable electricity. Atomic power stations have been built on this principle in the advanced industrial nations, and the system is still undergoing refinement, although so far atomic energy has not vindicated the high hopes placed in it as an economic source of electricity and presents formidable problems of waste disposal and maintenance. Nevertheless, it seems probable that the effort devoted to experiments on more direct ways of controlling nuclear fission will eventually produce results in power engineering. Meanwhile, nuclear physics has been probing the even more promising possibilities of harnessing the power of nuclear fusion, of creating the conditions in which simple atoms of hydrogen combine, with a vast release of energy, to form heavier atoms. This is the process that occurs in the stars, but so far it has only been created artificially by triggering off a fusion reaction with the intense heat generated momentarily by an atomic-fission explosion. This is the mechanism of the hydrogen bomb. So far scientists have devised no way of harnessing this process so that continuous, controlled energy can be obtained from it, although researches into plasma physics, generating a point of intense heat within a stream of electrons imprisoned in a strong magnetic field, hold out some hopes that such means will be discovered in the not-too-distant future.

Alternatives to fossil fuels.   It may well become a matter of urgency, before the end of the present century, that some means of extracting usable power from nuclear fusion be acquired. At the present rate of consumption, the world's resources of mineral fuels, and of the available radioactive materials used in the present nuclear-power stations, will be exhausted within a period of perhaps a few decades. While pressure on coal reserves has slackened slightly, demands for fuel oil and natural gas have increased at a prodigious rate and the exhaustion of these reserves cannot be long delayed. The most attractive alternative is thus a form of energy derived from a controlled fusion reaction that would use hydrogen from seawater, a virtually limitless source, and that would not create a significant problem of waste disposal. Other sources of energy that may provide alternatives to mineral fuels include various forms of solar cell, deriving power from the sun by a chemical or physical reaction such as that of photosynthesis. Solar cells of this kind are already in regular use on satellites and space probes, where the flow of energy out from the sun (the solar wind) can be harnessed without interference from the atmosphere or the rotation of the earth. Unless such alternative sources fulfill their promise of more general application, industrial civilization will face a major crisis of energy starvation within the 21st century.

Wankel engine.   While new sources of energy hold out some hope for the future, the heavy consumption of oil fuels has been steadily increasing in the last quarter century as oil-burning engines and boilers have become ever more widespread. The conventional internal-combustion engine is still the reciprocating engine used in most automobiles, although the more efficient Wankel rotary engine is beginning to displace it. In this engine, a three-sided inner rotor moves within an outer rotor or casing, forming chambers within which the four-stroke cycle can be performed without conventional valves. Although there had been many previous ideas for rotary-piston engines, the first to work satisfactorily as a light internal-combustion engine was that invented in 1954 by Felix

The harnessing of nuclear energy

Solar cells

Wankel of West Germany. This was introduced as a gasoline engine for automobiles in 1968, and its advantages regarding weight, economy, compactness, and smooth running make it very attractive, especially to manufacturers not too heavily committed to the traditional reciprocating engine.

Gas turbine. The gas turbine has undergone substantial development since its first successful operational use at the end of World War II. The high power-to-weight ratio of this type of engine made it ideal for aircraft propulsion, so that in either the pure jet or turboprop form it was generally adopted for all large aircraft, both military and civil, by the 1960s. The immediate effect of the adoption of jet propulsion was a spectacular increase in aircraft speeds, the first piloted airplane exceeding the speed of sound in level flight being the American Bell X-1 in 1947, and by the late 1960s supersonic flight was becoming a practicable, though controversial, proposition for civil-airline users. Ever-larger and more powerful gas turbines have been designed to meet the requirements of airlines and military strategy, and increasing attention has been given to refinements to reduce the noise and increase the efficiency of this type of engine. Meanwhile, the gas turbine has been installed as a power unit in ships, railroad engines, and automobiles, but in none of these uses has it proceeded far beyond the experimental stage.

Materials. The Space Age has spawned important new materials, and uncovered new uses for old materials. A vast range of applications has been found for plastics that have been manufactured in many different forms with widely varied characteristics. Glass fibre has been molded in rigid shapes to provide motor-car bodies and hulls for small ships. Carbon fibre has demonstrated remarkable properties that promise to provide an alternative to metals for high-temperature turbine blades. Research on ceramics has produced materials resistant to high temperatures suitable for heat shields on spacecraft. The demand for iron and its alloys and for the nonferrous metals has remained high. The modern world has found extensive new uses for the latter, copper for electricity conductors, tin for protecting less resistant metals in the form of tinplate, lead as a shield in nuclear-power installations, and silver in photography. In most of these cases the development began before the 20th century, but the continuing increase in demand for these metals is affecting their prices in the world commodity markets.

Automation and the computer. Both old and new materials are used increasingly in the engineering industry, which has been transformed since the end of World War II by the introduction of control engineering with automation and computerized techniques. The vital piece of equipment has been the computer, and especially the electronic digital computer, a 20th-century invention the theory of which was expounded by the English mathematician and inventor Charles Babbage in the 1830s. The essence of this machine is the use of electronic devices to record electric impulses coded in the very simple binary system, using only two symbols, but other devices such as punched cards and tape for storing and feeding information have been important supplementary features. By virtue of the very high speeds at which such equipment can operate, even the most complicated calculations can be converted into the binary system and performed in a very short space of time.

The Mark I digital computer was at work at Harvard University in 1944, and after the war the possibility of using it for a wide range of industrial, administrative, and scientific applications was quickly realized. The early computers, however, were large and expensive machines, and their general application was delayed until the invention of the transistor revolutionized computer technology. The transistor is another of the key inventions of the Space Age. The product of research on the physics of solids, and particularly of those materials such as germanium and silicon known as semiconductors, the transistor was invented at Bell Telephone Laboratories in the United States in 1948. It was discovered that crystals of semiconductors, which have the capacity to conduct electricity in some conditions and not in others, could be

made to perform the functions of a thermionic valve but in a shape that was much smaller, more reliable, and more versatile. The result has been the replacement of the cumbersome and fragile heat-producing thermionic valve by the small and strong transistor in a wide range of electronic equipment. Most especially, this conversion has made possible the construction of much more powerful computers while making them more compact and less expensive. Indeed, so small can effective transistors be that they have made possible the new skills of miniaturization and microminiaturization, whereby complicated electronic circuits can be printed on minute pieces of metal and incorporated in large numbers in computers. By the late 1950s the computer was in office use in industries and other organizations.

These techniques have seemed to hold out the prospect of completely automated factories, with computer-controlled machines performing every stage in the production process. The fact that this consummation was not rapidly achieved on a large scale may be an indication of the power of social factors rather than of the inadequacy of the technology, for there is no reason to doubt that the computer is capable of very much greater development in the future. So powerful, it seems, can this instrument become, that some commentators have likened it to the human brain, and there is no doubt that human analogies have been important in its development.

The chemical industry provides some of the most striking examples of fully automated, computer-controlled manufacture. The characteristics of flow production, in contrast to the unit production of most engineering establishments, lend themselves ideally to automatic control from a central computer monitoring the information fed back to it and making adjustments accordingly. Many large petrochemical plants producing fuel and raw materials for manufacturing industries are now run in this way, with the residual human function that of maintaining the machines and of providing the initial instructions. The same sort of influences can be seen even in the old established chemical processes, although not to the same extent: in the ceramics industry, in which continuous firing has replaced the traditional batch-production kilns; in the paper industry, in which mounting demand for paper and board has encouraged the installation of larger and faster machines; and in the glass industry, in which the float-glass process for making large sheets of glass on a surface of molten tin requires close mechanical control.

Even in medicine and the life sciences the computer has provided a powerful tool of research and supervision. It is now possible to monitor complicated operations and treatment. Surgery has made great advances in the Space Age. The introduction of transplant techniques has attracted worldwide publicity and interest, but perhaps of greater long-term significance has been the research in microbiology, with the aid of modern techniques and instruments, that has begun to unlock the mysteries of cell formation and reproduction through the self-replicating properties of the DNA molecules present in all living substances, and thus to explore the nature of life itself.

Food production. Food production has also been subject to technological innovation, such as accelerated freeze-drying and irradiation as methods of preservation, as well as the increasing mechanization of farming throughout the world. The widespread use of new pesticides and herbicides has in some cases reached the point of abuse, causing worldwide concern. Despite such problems, farming has been transformed in response to the demand for more food; scientific farming, with its careful breeding, controlled feeding, and mechanized handling, has become commonplace. New food-producing techniques such as aquiculture and hydroponics, for farming the sea and the seabed and for creating self-contained cycles of food production without soil respectively, are being explored, either to increase the world supply of food or to devise ways of sustaining closed communities such as may one day venture forth from the earth on the adventure of interplanetary exploration.

Civil engineering. One industry which has not been deeply influenced by new control-engineering techniques

Use of the gas turbine in aircraft

Semiconductor devices

Automated chemical production

is civil engineering, in which the nature of the tasks involved makes dependence on a large labour force still essential, whether it be in constructing a skyscraper, a new highway, or a tunnel. Nevertheless, some important new techniques have appeared since 1945, notably the use of heavy earth-moving and excavating machines such as the bulldozer and the tower crane. The use of prefabricat-

Pre-
fabricated
buildings

ed parts according to a predetermined system of construction has become widespread. In the construction of housing units, often in large blocks of apartments or flats, such systems are particularly relevant because they make for standardization and economy in plumbing, heating, and kitchen equipment. The revolution in home equipment that had begun before World War II has continued apace since, with a proliferation of electrical equipment.

Transport and communications. Many of these changes have been facilitated by improvements in transport and communications. The transport developments have, for the most part, continued those well established in the earlier part of the century. The automobile has proceeded in its phenomenal growth in popularity, causing radical changes in many of the patterns of life, although the basic design of the motorcar has remained unchanged. The airplane, benefitting from jet propulsion and a number of lesser technical advances, has made spectacular gains at the expense of both the ocean liner and the railroad. The growing popularity of air transport, however, has brought problems of crowded airspace, noise, and airfield siting.

World War II helped bring about a shift to air transport, with direct passenger flights across the Atlantic introduced immediately after the war. The first generation of transatlantic airliners were the aircraft developed by war experience from the Douglas DC-3 and the pioneering types of the 1930s incorporating all-metal construction with stressed skin, wing flaps and slots, retractable landing gear, and other advances. The coming of the big jet-powered civil transport in the 1950s kept pace with the rising demand for air services, but accentuated the social problems of air transport. The solution to these problems may lie partly in the development of vertical takeoff and landing techniques, a concept successfully pioneered by the British military aircraft, the Hawker Siddeley Harrier. Longer term solutions may be provided by the development of air-cushion vehicles derived from the Hovercraft, in use in the English Channel and elsewhere, and

The
Hovercraft

one of the outstanding technological innovations of the period since 1945. The central feature of this machine is a down-blast of air which creates an air cushion on which the craft rides without direct contact with the sea or ground below it. The remarkable versatility of the air-cushion machine is beyond doubt, but it has proved difficult to find very many transportation needs that it can fulfill better than any craft already available. Despite these difficulties, it seems likely that this type of vehicle will have an important future. It should be remembered, however, that all the machines mentioned so far, automobiles, airplanes, and Hovercraft, use oil fuels, and it is possible that the exhaustion of these will turn attention increasingly to alternative sources of power, and particularly to electric traction (electric railroads and autos), in which field there have been promising developments such as the linear-induction motor.

In communications, also, the dominant lines of development continue those which were established before or during World War II. In particular, the rapid growth of television services, with their immense impact as media of mass communication, has built on foundations laid in the 1920s and 1930s, while the universal adoption of radar on ships and airplanes has followed the invention of a device to give early warning of aerial attack. But in certain features the development of communications in the Space Age has produced important innovations. The transistor, so significant for computers and control engineering, has also made a large contribution to communications technology. Second, the establishment of space satellites, considered to be a remote theoretical possibility in the 1940s, had become part of the accepted technological scene in the 1960s, and these have played a dramatic

part in telephone and television communication as well as in relaying meteorological pictures and information. Third, the development of magnetic tape as a means of recording sound and, more recently, vision, has provided a highly flexible and useful mode of communication. Fourth, new printing techniques have developed. In phototypesetting, a photographic image is substituted for the conventional metal type. In xerography, a dry copying process, an ink powder is attracted to the image to be copied by static electricity and then fused by heating. Fifth, new optical devices such as zoom lenses have increased the power of cameras and correspondingly improved the quality of film available to the cinema and television. Sixth, new physical techniques such as those which produced the laser (light amplification by stimulated emission of radiation) are making available an immensely powerful means of communication over long distances, although these are still in their experimental stages. The seventh and final communications innovation is the use of radio waves to explore the structure of the universe by means of the radio telescope and its derivative, the X-ray telescope. This technique was pioneered after World War II and has since become a vital instrument of satellite control and space research. Radio telescopes have also been directed toward the Sun's closest neighbours in space in the hope of detecting electromagnetic signals from other intelligent species in the universe.

New uses
of radio
waves

Military technology. Military technology in the Space Age has been concerned with the radical restructuring of strategy caused by the invention of nuclear weapons and the means of delivering them by intercontinental ballistic missiles. Apart from these major features and the elaborate electronic systems which purport to give an early warning of missile attack, the main emphasis of military reorganization has been on high manoeuvrability through helicopter transport and a variety of armed vehicles. Such forces have been deployed in wars in Korea and Vietnam, and the latter has also seen the widespread use of napalm bombs and chemical defoliants to remove the cover provided by jungle foliage. At sea, World War II marked the demise of the heavily armoured battleship. The only large ships to survive in the navies of the world are aircraft carriers. The emphasis now is on electronic detection and the support of nuclear-powered submarines equipped with missiles carrying nuclear warheads. The only major use of nuclear power since 1945, other than generating large-scale electric energy, has been in the power plants of ships, and particularly the breed of missile-carrying submarines capable of cruising for extended periods below sea level.

Space exploration. The rocket, which has played a crucial part in the revolution of military technology since the end of World War II, has acquired a more constructive significance in the space programs of the Soviet Union and the United States. The first spectacular step was Sputnik 1, a sphere with an instrument package of 184 pounds (83 kilograms), launched into space by the Soviet Union on October 4, 1957, to become the first artificial satellite. The feat precipitated the so-called space race, in which achievements soon followed each other in rapid succession. They may be conveniently grouped in four chronological although overlapping stages. In the first stage, the emphasis was on increasing the thrust of rockets capable of putting satellites into orbit and on exploring the possible uses of satellites in communications, in weather observation, in monitoring military information, and in topographical and geological surveying. The second stage was that of the manned space program. This began with the successful orbit of the Earth by the Soviet cosmonaut Yury Gagarin on April 12, 1961, in the space vehicle Vostok 1. This flight demonstrated mastery of the complex problems of weightlessness and of safe re-entry into the atmosphere of the Earth. It was followed by a series of Soviet and United States space flights in which the techniques of space rendezvous and docking were acquired, flights up to a fortnight were achieved, and men "walked" in space outside their craft. The third stage of space exploration was the lunar program, beginning with approaches to the Moon and going

Manned
space
flights

228 days and sent back photographs which showed with startling clarity that the surface of Mars closely resembles that of the Moon. Further photographs were taken from space probes in 1969 and 1971, but the frequency of these attempts is limited to the few weeks every two years or so when the two planets are in a favourable relationship to each other. Serious thought is now being given to the possibility of extending space exploration beyond the orbits of the nearest planets to the giant planets of Jupiter and beyond. With existing technology much useful information could be gathered, but the cost is extraordinarily high, especially in the launching stages when an enormous amount of fuel and equipment is consumed without any attempt at recovering the launch vehicle.

At the dawn of the Space Age it is possible to perceive only dimly its scope and possibilities. But it is relevant to observe that the history of technology has brought the world to a point in time at which man, equipped with unprecedented powers of self-destruction, stands on the threshold of extraterrestrial exploration. Only the gradual accumulation of skills over many millennia, the acceleration in the processes of industrialization in the last 200 years, the diffusion of these processes over the whole earth, and the vast increase in investment in technology, both in hardware and in social forms of investment such as technical education, could have created the situation which modern civilization reached in the 1970s. Many problems attended the rush of technological advance, and it is appropriate to conclude with a brief survey of these problems.

TECHNOLOGY AND THE ENVIRONMENT

Technology confronts modern civilization with a challenge to make a decision, or rather, a series of decisions, about how the enormous power now available to society will be used. The need to control the development of technology by regulating its application to creative social objectives makes it ever more necessary to define these objectives while the problems presented by rapid technological growth can still be solved.

These problems, and the social objectives related to them, may be considered under four broad headings. First is the nuclear problem, of controlling the application of nuclear technology. Second is the population problem, arising out of the population explosion to which 20th-century medical technology has made such a momentous contribution. A third is the complex of social difficulties created by the impact of technology on life in town and countryside, bringing about an upheaval of traditional social and educational systems. Finally, there is the ecological problem, brought on by advanced technology causing the pollution of the environment and disturbing the balance of natural forces of regeneration.

Nuclear technology. The solution to the first problem, of controlling nuclear technology, is generally thought to be political in essence. Its root is the anarchy of national self-government, for as long as the world remains divided into a multiplicity of nation-states, or even into two power blocs, each committed to the defense of its own sovereign power to do what it chooses, nuclear weapons merely replace older weapons by which such nation-states have been maintained. The availability of a nuclear armoury, indeed, has brought home the weaknesses of a world political system based upon independent nation-states, though it has not made it any easier to overcome them. Here, as elsewhere, technology is a tool which can be used creatively or destructively. But the manner of its use depends utterly on human decisions, and in this matter of nuclear self-control the decisions are those of governments.

Nuclear weapons and international politics

Population problem. Assuming that the nuclear threat can be averted, world civilization will have to come to grips with the population problem long before the end of the present century if life is to be tolerable on the planet Earth in the next century. The problem can be tackled in two ways, both drawing on the resources of modern technology. On the one hand, efforts may be made to limit the rate of population increase. Medical technology, which, through new drugs and other techniques, has provided a

U.S. weather satellite orbiting the Earth.
By courtesy of National Aeronautics and Space Administration

on through automatic surveys of its surface to manned landings. Again, the first achievement was Soviet: Lunik 1, launched on January 2, 1959, became the first artificial body to escape the gravitational field of the Earth, fly past the Moon, and enter an orbit around the Sun as an artificial planet. Lunik 2 impacted on the Moon on September 13, 1959, to be followed by Lunik 3, launched on October 4, 1959, which went round the Moon and sent back the first photographs of the side turned permanently away from the Earth. The first soft landing on the Moon was made by Lunik 9 on February 3, 1966; this craft carried cameras which transmitted the first photographs taken on the surface of the Moon. By this time, however, excellent close-range photographs had been secured by the United States Ranger 7, 8, and 9, which crashed into the Moon in the second half of 1964 and the first part of 1965; and between 1966 and 1967 the series of five Lunar Orbiters photographed almost the entire surface of the Moon from a low orbit in a search for suitable landing places. The United States Surveyor 1 soft-landed on the Moon on June 2, 1966, and this and following Surveyors acquired much useful information about the lunar surface. Meanwhile, the size and power of launching rockets climbed steadily, and by the late 1960s the enormous Saturn V rocket, standing 353 feet (108 metres) high and weighing 2,725 tons (92,472,000 kilograms) at lift-off, made possible the United States three-man Apollo series which climaxed on July 20, 1969, when Neil Armstrong and Edwin Aldrin clambered out of the Lunar Module of their Apollo 11 spacecraft onto the surface of the Moon. The manned lunar exploration begun thus continued with a widening range of experiments and achievements.

Space probes

The fourth stage of space exploration has been that which has looked out beyond the Earth and its immediate satellite, the Moon, to the possibilities of planetary exploration. The two closest planetary neighbours of the Earth, Venus and Mars, were the first to receive attention. The United States space probe Mariner 2 was launched on August 27, 1962, and passed by Venus the following December, relaying back information about that planet which indicated that it was hotter and less hospitable than had been expected. These findings were confirmed by the Soviet Venera 3 which crash-landed on the planet on March 1, 1966, and by Venera 4, which made the first soft-landing on October 18, 1967. Meanwhile, Mariner 4, launched on November 28, 1964, passed within about 6,000 miles (9,700 kilometres) of Mars after a journey of

powerful impulse to the increase of population, also offers means of controlling this increase through contraceptive devices and through painless sterilization procedures. Again, technology is a tool that is neutral in respect to moral issues about its own use, but it would be futile to deny that artificial population control is inhibited by powerful moral constraints and taboos. Some reconciliation of these conflicts is essential, however, if stability in world population is to be satisfactorily achieved. On the other hand, even the most optimistic program of population control can only hope to achieve a slight reduction in the rate of increase by the end of the 20th century, so that a second approach to the population problem must be made simultaneously in the shape of an enormous effort to increase the world's production of food. Technology has much to contribute here, both in raising the productivity of existing sources of food supply and in creating new sources by making the deserts fertile and by farming systematically the riches of the oceans. There is enough work here to keep engineers and food technologists busy for many generations.

Social difficulties. An operative solution to these first two problems will bring to the fore secondary social problems associated with a way of life based upon large-scale technology. These are already clearly visible in the advanced industrial countries, but they are likely to become more widespread. The cities of many industrial nations are already afflicted by urban blight, as the traditional centres are deserted by the middle class and left to socially disfavoured and impoverished groups, with a consequent loss of social order.

Urban decay

This decay of megalopolis has been caused largely by the automobile and electricity, which made possible the rapid expansion of towns and then contributed to their depopulation. Another consequence has been the increase of urban sprawl around cities, and the spoiling of the neighbouring countryside as traditional rural communities have been overwhelmed. At another level, social dislocation has been prompted by technology through the pressure for education. Technical education has long been recognized as an essential feature of any advanced industrial nation. Such education, however, requires a high level of literacy and numeracy, so that industrial survival has come to be equated with an elaborate system of national education.

Ecological problems. The fourth and final problem area of modern technological society is the ecological problem of preserving a healthy environmental balance. Though man has been damaging the environment for centuries by overcutting trees and farming too intensively, and though some protective measures, such as the establishment of national forests and wildlife sanctuaries, were taken decades ago, great increases in population and in the level of industrialization have caused a public crisis. Thus the great public concern with pollution in the advanced nations is both overdue and welcome. Once more, however, it needs to be said that the fault for this waste-making abuse of technology lies with man himself rather than with the tools he uses. For all his intelligence, man behaves in communities with a thoughtlessness for his environment that is potentially suicidal. It is debatable, then, whether technology is a blessing or a bane. The history of technology has led from the earliest technological achievements of man the toolmaker to the crossroads at which the species now stands, in the last third of the 20th century, confronted by a choice, that of self-destruction or a millennium of adventurous growth and expansion, reaching out to colonize the universe, unlocking the secrets of controlled nuclear fusion as a source of power, exploiting exotic sources of food, and creating a healthy and well-regulated environment.

BIBLIOGRAPHY. The best general work is still CHARLES SINGER et al., A History of Technology, 5 vol. (1954–58); the single-volume companion study, T.K. DERRY and T.I. WILLIAMS, A Short History of Technology (1960), is a valuable summary. Both are confined to western technology and its antecedents, and both stop at the year 1900. M. KRANZBERG and CARROLL W. PURSELL, JR., Technology in Western Civilization, 2 vol. (1967), brings the story into the mid-20th century. Good specialized works include: V.G. CHILDE, What Happened in History (1942), a classic study of man's mastery of his environment in prehistory; H. HODGES, Technology in the Ancient World (1970); L.T. WHITE, JR., Medieval Technology and Social Change (1962); A.P. USHER, A History of Mechanical Inventions, 2nd ed. (1954); and J. JEWKES, D. SAWERS, and R. STILLERMAN, The Sources of Invention, 2nd ed. (1969). F. KLEMM, Technik: Eine Geschichte ihrer Probleme (1954; Eng. trans., A History of Western Technology, 1959), is a useful selection of documents. The economic and social implications of technological development are explored in W.H.G. ARMYTAGE, A Social History of Engineering, 2nd ed. (1970); DAVID S. LANDES, The Unbound Prometheus (1970); and S. LILLEY, Men, Machines and History (1948). LEWIS MUMFORD, Technics and Civilization (1934), remains a very stimulating essay on this theme. R.J. FORBES, Man, the Maker (1958), is a good general review of the history of technology; and R.A. BUCHANAN, Technology and Social Progress (1965), may also be found useful as an introductory text. EUGENE S. FERGUSON, Bibliography of the History of Technology (1968), is a comprehensive and thorough study. The two outstanding sources of periodical literature are: Technology and Culture, the quarterly journal of the Society for the History of Technology, published since 1959; and the Transactions of the Newcomen Society for the Study of the History of Engineering and Technology, published annually since 1920 except for some irregular volumes during and immediately after World War II.

(R.A.Bu.)

Tecumseh

Tecumseh, chief of the North American Indian tribe of the Shawnees, a gifted orator and magnanimous military leader and the determined advocate of an Indian confederation, has been regarded as an outstanding representative of his people. He urged the Indians to substitute intertribal alliance for intertribal warfare and to restore the integrity of their own culture by freeing themselves from the alien influence of the white man's culture. He tried to save for his people their ancient lands, which at that time—the late 18th and early 19th centuries—were being seized with impunity by whites or bartered off by chiefs for petty annuities that provided for their own comfort but left only meagre amounts for the tribesmen. Tecumseh's cause failed, but his vision and zeal put him among the great leaders of primitive peoples who have tried to protect their homelands and their culture against the inexorable advance of civilization.

In appearance Tecumseh was straight, slim, and muscular; he stood about five feet, 10 inches, with proud bearing and intent hazel eyes. Of light, copper colouring, as were most Shawnees, he has been described erroneously at times as part white. He was capable of withstanding long, exhausting journeys on foot, by canoe, and by pony. Fierce in battle, he was suave and urbane in conversation. He shunned the garments of the whites, dressing in unadorned buckskin, with a tomahawk and silver-hilted hunting knife thrust through his belt.

Tecumseh was born in 1768 in the Indian village of Old Piqua, near present-day Springfield, Ohio. His father was killed by whites in 1774. His mother, a Muskogee (Creek Confederacy), instilled in the boy a spirit of vengeance and bitter hatred of the whites. When he was seven years old, she left him to accompany part of the tribe to Missouri and then passed into obscurity. Tecumseh was reared by an elder sister, Tecumapease, who trained him in the strict Shawnee code of honesty; an elder brother Cheeseekau taught him woodcraft and hunting. He was adopted by the Shawnee chief Blackfish and grew to young manhood with several white foster brothers whom Blackfish had captured. Among them was the famous frontiersman Daniel Boone, who was captured in Kentucky but who escaped after a short time.

Early life and training

Murder, massacre, and invasion of Shawnee land and the destruction of their crops deepened the hatred for whites instilled in Tecumseh by his mother. When he was about 14 years old, during the U.S. War of Independence, he accompanied Blackfish in combined British and Indian attacks on Americans. As hostile as he was toward whites, however, about a year later Tecumseh rebuked his fellow Shawnees for the cruelty they themselves practiced, and it was then that he discovered that words could be as powerful as weapons. He had accompanied one of the predatory Shawnee raids on the flatboats that were bringing encroaching white settlers down the Ohio River; he had seen a white man tied to a stake and burned. Horrified, he had showered his fellow tribesmen with such abuse that they never tortured a prisoner in his presence again. On a later occasion, he denounced and personally subdued his warriors when he found them beginning to slaughter captured prisoners, risking his life by hurling the attackers to the ground.

After the war Tecumseh for a number of years was a marauder, fighting small actions against the whites in the Northwest and assisting the Cherokees in the South. He saw his brother Cheeseekau killed in an unsuccessful raid near Nashville, Tennessee, in September 1792. Though he was the youngest of the Shawnee band, he was chosen leader, fought a number of small actions in the South, and made an acquaintance with the Creeks that helped him later to form an alliance with them. At the call of Bluejacket, the Shawnee chief who was collecting a force to meet a U.S. army under Maj. Gen. Anthony Wayne, he returned to Ohio, where he directed the unsuccessful attack on Ft. Recovery in June 1794. On August 20, he led part of Bluejacket's force when it was decisively defeated by Wayne at Fallen Timbers. There he saw another older brother, Sauwaseekau, killed.

When the leading chiefs of the Old Northwest gathered at Wayne's call at Greenville, in Ohio, Tecumseh held aloof; and when the Treaty of Greenville was negotiated in August 1795, he refused to recognize it and roundly attacked the "peace" chiefs who signed away land that he contended they did not own. Land, he said, was like the air and water, the common possession of all Indians. This doctrine of communal ownership of the land became the cornerstone of his policy.

Break with the "peace" chiefs

Partly because of his superb oratory, which the whites compared with that of the young Henry Clay, the rising political leader in Kentucky, Tecumseh became the spokesman for the Indians in great councils at Urbana (1799) and Chillicothe (1804) in Ohio that undertook to settle grievances. For a time he studied treaties, spoke at councils, and lived peacefully in Ohio and Indiana.

About 1808 Tecumseh settled in Indiana with his brother Tenskwatawa, called "the Prophet" because he claimed to have had a revelation from the "Master of Life." There the brothers sought to induce the Indians to discard white customs and goods (particularly whiskey, which was making drunkards of many Indians and destroying entire tribes) and to abjure intertribal wars for unity against the white invader. The code of the Prophet had a mysticism that appealed to the Indians, and many became converts.

Organizer of Indian confederation

With inexhaustible energy, Tecumseh began to form an Indian confederation to resist white pressure. He made long journeys in a vast territory, from the Ozarks to New York and from Iowa to Florida, gaining recruits (particularly among the tribes of the Creek Confederacy, to which his mother's tribe belonged). The tide of settlers had pushed game from the Indians' hunting grounds, and, as a result, the Indian economy had broken down.

In 1811, while Tecumseh was in the South, William Henry Harrison, governor of the Indiana Territory, marched up the Wabash River and camped near the brothers' settlement. The Prophet unwisely attacked Harrison's camp and was so decisively defeated in the ensuing Battle of Tippecanoe that his followers dispersed, and he, having lost his prestige, fled to Canada and ceased to be a factor in Tecumseh's plans.

Seeing the approach of war (the War of 1812) between the Americans and British, Tecumseh assembled his followers and joined the British forces at Ft. Malden on the Canadian side of the Detroit River. There he brought together perhaps the most formidable force ever commanded by a North American Indian, an accomplishment that was a decisive factor in the capture of Detroit and of 2,500 United States soldiers (1812).

Fired with the promise of triumph after the fall of Detroit, Tecumseh departed on another long journey to arouse the tribes, which resulted in the uprising of the Alabama Creeks in response to his oratory, though the Chickasaws, Choctaws, and Cherokees rebuffed him. He returned north and joined the British Gen. Henry A. Procter in his invasion of Ohio. Together they besieged Ft. Meigs, held by William Henry Harrison, on the Maumee River above Toledo, where by a stratagem Tecumseh intercepted and destroyed a brigade of Kentuckians under Col. William Dudley, coming to Harrison's relief. He and Procter failed to capture the fort, however, and were put on the defensive by Oliver Hazard Perry's decisive victory over the British fleet on Lake Erie (September 10, 1813). Harrison thereupon invaded Canada. Tecumseh with his Indians reluctantly accompanied the retiring British, whom Harrison pursued to the Thames River, in present-day southern Ontario. There, on October 5, 1813, the British and Indians were routed and Harrison won control of the Northwest. Tecumseh, directing most of the fighting, was killed. His body was carried from the field and buried secretly in a grave that has never been discovered. Nor has it ever been determined who killed Tecumseh. Tecumseh's death marked the end of Indian resistance in the Ohio Valley and in most of the lower Midwest and South, and soon thereafter the depleted tribes were transported beyond the Mississippi.

BIBLIOGRAPHY. BENJAMIN DRAKE, *The Life of Tecumseh and His Brother the Prophet* (1841), the best of the early biographies, based on Ohio archival sources and a memorandum from one of Tecumseh's foster brothers; WILLIAM A. GALLOWAY, *Old Chillicothe, Shawnee and Pioneer History* (1934), a good account of Shawnee customs that contains the story of Tecumseh's suit of Rebecca Galloway, and of Rebecca's instruction of Tecumseh; NORMAN S. GURD, *The Story of Tecumseh* (1912), a relatively brief but interesting account of Tecumseh from a Canadian viewpoint; E.O. RANDALL, "Tecumseh, the Shawnee Chief," a series in the *Ohio Archeological and Historical Society Proceedings* (1906), an interesting story of the chief by a competent Ohio historian; *Lyman C. Draper Manuscript Collection of the State Historical Society of Wisconsin* (microfilm at Library of Congress), the best source of material about Tecumseh; GLENN TUCKER, *Tecumseh: Vision of Glory* (1956), a thorough biography with a full bibliography, that exonerates the British government from the charge of inciting the Indians to warfare against the Americans prior to the War of 1812.

(G.Tu.)

Teeth and Gums, Human

In man there are two dentitions, or sets of teeth. The first of these, the primary, or deciduous, dentition, is functional from shortly after birth to about the time of puberty, by which time it has been entirely replaced by the permanent dentition. The process of replacement takes place in an orderly progression between the ages of seven and 12 years, so that the permanent dentition is completed between 18–20 years, with the appearance of the third permanent molars, the so-called wisdom teeth.

Each tooth has three parts, the root, the neck, and the crown. The root is the part of the tooth that is attached to the tooth-bearing bone—the alveolar processes—of the jaws by a fibrous ligament called the periodontal ligament or membrane. The crown is that portion of the tooth that projects into the mouth. Between the root and the crown is the neck, the portion of the tooth that is embraced by the fleshy gum tissue, a specialized area of mucous membrane that lines the mouth cavity.

Tooth form and function. Man has 20 deciduous and 32 permanent teeth. In each jaw there are four incisors, two canines, and four molars belonging to the deciduous dentition. The permanent dentition is made up of four incisors, two canines, four premolars, and six molars in each jaw. The deciduous molars are succeeded by premolars; the permanent molars have no deciduous predecessors.

Incisors and canines are used for cutting (incising), while premolars and molars are used for crushing and grinding food. The forms of the teeth reflect their functions: the incisor crowns having cutting edges, and premolars and molars a series of elevations, or cusps, used for breaking up particles of food. Human dentition is unique in the relatively small size of the canines. The number of roots (fangs) for each tooth varies from one for incisors and canines to three for upper molars.

The development of teeth. Each tooth is the product of a tooth germ, or bud, which grows out of the lining of the developing oral cavity. The tooth germ is a cap, called an enamel organ, over a collection of cells called the dental papilla or primary pulp. Both enamel organ and papilla are surrounded by a fibrous tissue sac, the dental follicle, attaching each germ to the overlying gum.

Origin of enamel, dentin, and cement

From the enamel organ there develops the specialized hard enamel that covers the crown of the tooth; from the dental papilla develops another hard tissue, dentin, that surrounds the pulp of the tooth. From the follicle originate both cement (or cementum), another calcified tissue covering the root area of each tooth, and the periodontal membrane.

Around each developing tooth the alveolar bone forms a bony socket to which the tooth becomes attached by the periodontal membrane. As each tooth develops and its hard tissue elements, enamel, dentin, and cement, commence to calcify, the tooth erupts towards and into the mouth cavity. During eruption the remains of the enamel organ unite with the outer layer or epithelium of the overlying gum to form an attachment between the gum and the surface of the tooth.

There is still uncertainty regarding all the factors involved in tooth eruption.

During replacement of deciduous teeth by permanent teeth, the overlying bone and the greater part of the root area of each deciduous tooth is resorbed and a fresh socket is produced for the succeeding permanent tooth.

The structure of teeth. Enamel, the hardest tissue produced by the body, is the product of a special layer of cells, the ameloblasts, situated at the inner surface of the enamel organ adjacent to the dental papilla. The ameloblasts produce a substance filled with tiny fibres, or fibrils; inorganic salts derived from the blood are deposited in this matrix as minute crystals. Enamel is formed as a series of adjacent prisms or rods, each growing toward the outer surface of the tooth. After each prism is fully formed, there is no further deposition. If enamel is destroyed or worn away with use, it cannot be replaced or repaired. Enamel formation depends on an adequate supply of inorganic substances in the diet and on certain hormones and vitamins. Starvation or severe malnutrition and certain diseases interfere with its formation. Poorly calcified teeth are more liable to decay.

Dentin is the product of special cells, odontoblasts, derived from the tooth pulp. As dentin develops at the expense of the pulp, projections of odontoblasts come to occupy narrow tubes (dentinal tubules) in the dentin. Unlike enamel, dentin is capable of continuous formation (secondary dentin), especially in response to stimulation after loss of enamel or decay, and the tubules may become closed by further calcification. Dentin is less highly mineralized and more elastic than enamel.

Cement is formed by specialized cells of the dental follicle, cementoblasts, in layers upon the surface of the roots of teeth. It provides anchorage for the fibre bundles of the periodontal membrane. It is similar in its composition

From *Cunningham's Textbook of Anatomy* edited by G.J. Romanes and published by Oxford University Press as an Oxford Medical Publication

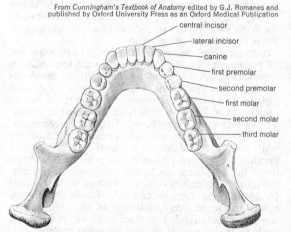

central incisor
lateral incisor
canine
first premolar
second premolar
first molar
second molar
third molar

Figure 1: Lower jaw and its permanent teeth.

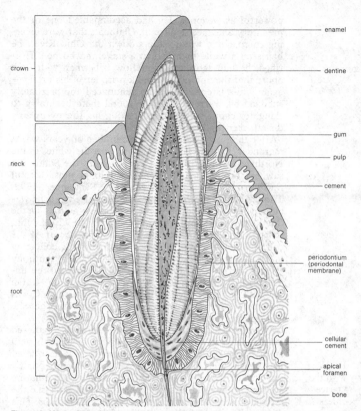

enamel
crown
dentine
gum
pulp
neck
cement
periodontium (periodontal membrane)
root
cellular cement
apical foramen
bone

Figure 2: Vertical section through a tooth showing its parts and surrounding tissues.
Adapted from *Cunningham's Textbook of Anatomy* edited by G.J. Romanes and published by Oxford University Press as an Oxford Medical Publication

and structure to bone and is more capable of repair than any other calcified dental tissue.

The pulp of a tooth occupies a central pulp cavity connecting through root canals with the tooth surface at the apex of each root. Pulp cavities decrease with age because of the deposition of secondary dentin. Pulp consists of cells, a delicate framework of fibres, blood vessels, and nerves that respond with toothache to damage to pulp and dentin. With age, the pulp becomes more fibrous and less cellular, vascular, and sensitive. It provides nutrition for the adjacent dentin, but a fully formed tooth can remain functional when its pulp is removed.

Peri-odontal membrane

The periodontal membrane consists of bundles of fibrous tissue that hold each tooth in its socket. Other fibre bundles attach the gum tissue to the tooth and adjacent teeth to one another. The periodontal membrane contains blood vessels and sensory nerve endings for pain, touch, and proprioceptive sensation (sensation arising from stimuli within rather than outside the body), the latter providing the central nervous system with the feedback information necessary for coordinated muscle activity in complex activities such as mastication and swallowing. The ability of the periodontal membrane to repair itself is an essential factor in tooth transplantation.

Development and structure of gum tissue. Before the erupting teeth enter the mouth cavity, gum pads develop (slight elevations of the overlying oral mucous membrane). When tooth eruption is complete the gum embraces the neck region of each tooth. Gum is attached to the adjacent alveolar bone and to the cement of each tooth by fibre bundles. It is also attached to the tooth enamel.

Diseases of teeth and gums. *Variations in number and shape of teeth.* Complete congenital absence of teeth (anodontia) is a rare condition. Congenital absence of individual teeth is uncommon in the deciduous dentition and more frequent in the permanent dentition. The teeth most often absent (as confirmed by X-ray examination) are upper lateral incisors, lower premolars, and third permanent molars.

Teeth over and above the normal number (supernumerary teeth) are also more common in the permanent dentition. They are most often found in the upper incisor region, the premolar region, and the permanent molar series. In some cases they resemble normal teeth; more often they are abnormal in form, usually peg shaped.

Variations in the shape of teeth may be the result of genetic abnormalities, often associated with some degree of mental disturbance, or of abnormal development due to malnutrition or disease.

Irregularity of the teeth resulting in deformed dental arches (the curves formed by the upper and lower rows of teeth) and abnormality of relationship between the teeth in opposing jaws (malocclusion) is frequent in modern civilized societies. In the less severe forms one or more teeth may be out of alignment though the jaws are in normal relation to one another. In more serious forms the jaws are themselves out of alignment. Treatment consists of moving the teeth by the use of special fixed or removable appliances. Sometimes teeth are extracted to provide space for the remaining teeth. In more serious cases surgery may be necessary.

Pulp abscesses and gumboils

Infection of pulp. Infection of the pulp of a tooth usually results from rapidly penetrating and neglected dental caries (see below) or wear of tooth substance (attrition) leading to exposure of dentin or even of the pulp cavity. Inflammation of the pulp, owing to the rigidity of its limiting walls and the resultant strangulation of blood vessels, is liable to produce abscess formation or death of pulp tissue. Pulp abscesses tend to spread to the tissues around the root tips and from these spread through the alveolar bone, opening into the mouth cavity (gumboil) or into the deeper regions of the mouth and face. Such infection may enter the bloodstream and set up secondary abscesses or destruction of tissue in various body organs including the valves of the heart.

Tumours. Tumours of dental tissues vary from extra cusps or roots to complex growths involving a multiplicity of dental tissues (odontomas), which may on rare occasions become malignant.

Dental decay. Dental decay (caries), along with gum infection (gingivitis), is by far the most frequent of dental diseases; perhaps, apart from the common cold, the most frequent disease in contemporary society.

It is generally accepted that tooth decay is due to the destruction of the dental calcified tissues, especially enamel or dentin, by acids produced locally in the mouth by bacterial fermentation of sugar and starchy food debris. Caries usually commences on surface enamel, especially in pits and fissures and between adjacent teeth. From enamel the process of decay spreads to the underlying dentin, and may finally involve the tooth pulp. Dentin may respond by the formation of secondary dentin in the pulp chamber and by the obliteration of its tubule.

Poorly calcified teeth are more vulnerable to caries. It has been demonstrated that dental decay, especially in deciduous teeth, can be greatly reduced by the addition of fluorides to drinking water.

Although the above outline of caries causation is generally accepted, there remain unexplained features and alternative theories, as would be expected in a disease that does not easily fit into any particular pathological classification. Treatment is by removal of decayed tissue and replacement by inert filling substances.

Diseases of gums. The most frequent of gum diseases is gingivitis. Gingivitis, or inflammation of the gum, usually commences at or close to the gum margins, often between adjacent teeth. Pockets form between the gum and the adjacent teeth, sometimes penetrating deeply into the tissues. This leads to further infection, with inflammation and bleeding from the ulcerated gums. Deeper penetration produces destruction of alveolar bone and involvement of the periodontal membrane, leading to loosening and loss of teeth. When the teeth are lost or extracted the condition clears up.

Predisposing factors are poor oral hygiene, some abnormal relationship of gum to underlying bone, excessive masticatory load on individual teeth, badly fitting partial dentures or corrective appliances, obscure hormonal conditions, and lack of certain vitamins, especially vitamin C (lack of this vitamin results in scurvy).

The most common forms of gingivitis are not related to any particular group of micro-organisms, but some more severe types are due to specific infection (*e.g.,* Vincent's gingivitis, or trench mouth), producing marked ulceration of the gums. Certain poisons, including lead, bismuth, and mercury, are excreted in the oral cavity and especially in relation to the gums, leading to a special form of gingivitis.

Effective treatment of gum infection once it becomes established may involve surgery followed by strict oral hygiene.

Treatment of gingivitis

Other gum conditions include atrophy (lack of gum substance), hyperplasia (excess of gum tissue), and local overgrowth of tissue (epulis). Malignant tumours arising directly from gum tissue are rare, although deeply seated malignant tumours may involve the gums and adjacent structures, with resultant loosening of teeth.

Research. Recently there has been considerable addition to existing knowledge of the structure of dental tissues, especially of enamel and dentin. In this process use of the electron microscope has made a useful contribution. There has also been a steady accumulation of information regarding the development of teeth and growth of the skull. Much work remains to be done regarding the causation of dental abnormalities and of the two major diseases of the oral cavity, dental caries and gingivitis.

Another stimulating field of research is that of oral neurophysiology, the functional relationship between the processes that take place in the mouth and the nervous system.

BIBLIOGRAPHY. Additional information on this subject may be found in the following texts: B.S. KRAUS, R.E. JORDAN, and L. ABRAMS, *Dental Anatomy and Occlusion* (1969); J.H. SCOTT and N.B.B. SYMONS, *Introduction to Dental Anatomy*, 6th ed. (1971); and H.H. STONES, *Oral and Dental Diseases*, 5th ed. by E.D. FARMER and F.E. LAWTON (1966).

(J.H.S.)

Tehrān

Tehrān (Teheran) is the capital city of both the country and the Central *ostān* (province) of Iran. It is situated on the southern slopes of the Elburz Mountains, which separate it from the Caspian Sea 62 miles (100 kilometres) to the north. The city lies at an altitude of about 3,800 feet (1,200 metres) above sea level between the Jājrūd and the Karaj rivers, which flow down from the mountains. To the south extends the Central Plateau of Iran.

The name Tehrān is derived from the Old Persian words *teh*, "warm," and *ran*, "place." In order to escape the heat, many of the city's inhabitants go to summer resorts, such as Shemiran, in the mountains ten miles to the north. About 44 miles to the northeast rises the snow-covered peak of Mt. Dāmavēnd, which figures in Persian legends; the mountain is an inactive volcano 18,624 feet (5,678 metres) high. Tehrān has a metropolitan area of 109 square miles (282 square kilometres) and a population in the early 1970s of over 3,000,000. It is the residence of the *shāh* of Iran. (For an associated physical feature, see ELBURZ MOUNTAINS.)

History. Tehrān is the successor to the ancient Iranian capital of Rey, which was destroyed by the Mongols in AD 1220; traces of Rey—where the conqueror Alexander the Great (*q.v.*) halted while pursuing Darius III, king of Persia, in 330 BC—are still to be found almost four miles south of Tehrān.

The village of Tehrān is believed to have been a suburb of Rey in the 4th century. An observer who visited it at the beginning of the 13th century, just before the destruction of Rey, described it as a considerable town with 12 districts; all dwellings were then built underground, and there were many gardens. The town was then reported to be in a state of civil discord, although the government of the day chose to be lenient in dealing with the inhabitants. After the fall of Rey, many of the inhabitants who escaped the massacre took refuge in Tehrān. The first European to mention Tehrān was Don Ruy Gonzales de Clavijo, ambassador of the King of Castile to the court of Timur (Tamerlane), who visited the town in 1404.

In 1553 and 1554, Shāh Ṭahmāsp I of the Safavīd dy-

Modern business section and northern suburbs of Tehrān at Takhat-Jamsheed Avenue. The rectangular building (centre left) houses the National Iranian Oil Company offices. In the background are the Elburz Mountains.
Gerry Cranham—Rapho Guillumette

The rise of the city

nasty of Persia provided Tehrān with a bazaar and built a wall around it; the wall had four gates and 114 towers.

An English writer, Thomas Herbert, author of "Travels in Persia" (published in 1634), visited Tehrān in 1628–29 and estimated the number of houses at 3,000; he described the city as being very hot, with many orchards and "lovely women." The *shāh* Ḥoseyn, of the Safavīd dynasty, held court in Tehrān in 1720, a short while before his defeat by invading Afghans. Karīm Khān Zand, who ruled Iran from 1758 to 1779, considered making Tehrān his capital but instead chose Shīrāz, in southern Iran.

Tehrān became prominent after its capture (1785) by Āghā Moḥammad Khān, the founder of the Qājār dynasty (1779 to 1925), who made the city his capital in 1788 because the tribe to which he belonged lived in the vicinity. Since that date Tehrān has been uninterruptedly the capital of Iran. After the deposition of the last of the Qājārs in 1925, the city experienced a period of great expansion under Reza Shah Pahlavi (1925 to 1941). In 1943 the World War II leaders of the Allies, representing the United States, the United Kingdom, and the Soviet Union, met at the Teheran Conference, at which, among other decisions, they guaranteed the independence of Iran. The reign of the *shāhanshāh* ("king of kings") Mohammad Reza Pahlavi (since 1941) has been marked by a rapid and increasing modernization of the city; his queen, Farah, with her interest in architecture, has been entrusted by the *shāhanshāh* with the formulation of plans for a greater Tehrān to house more than 5,000,000 people.

The city. The city, as mentioned, stands at a mean altitude of 3,800 feet on ground that rises gently northward toward Shemiran. Shemiran itself is inhabited by many wealthy people; surrounded by magnificent mountain scenery, it attracts thousands of city dwellers during the hot summer months.

In contrast to the fashionable districts in the northern part of the city, the old town and the bazaar are to the south. Firdowsī Square, at the junction of Shah Reza Avenue and Firdowsī Street, forms the city's centre, which was formerly Sepah Square (Maidan-e Sepah), but the population centre is still Sepah Square with the bazaar located on its southern side.

The centre of Tehrān's modern district lies to the north of Shah Reza Street. The growth of the city can also be observed along the two roads connecting it with Shemiran. Modern villas, attractive buildings, and the private houses

along the highways in the suburbs of Tajrīsh, Darband, Qolhak, and Niavaran, surrounded by ancient trees, complete the scene.

Area and population. Tehrān—which in the early 19th century had a municipal area of two square miles and a population of 120,000—in 1970 had a municipal area of 83 square miles and a population of over 3,-300,000. The population has grown rapidly in recent years. Numbering only 540,000 in 1939, it increased to 2,000,000 in 1960. Planners estimate that the municipal area will have increased to 250 square miles and the population to 5,000,000 before the end of the 20th century. In 1970 the rate of population growth was 26 per thousand per year, and the population density was 39,759 per square mile. About half of the population lives in about one-third of the city's area in the south and southeast.

Population growth

The main factor causing population increase has been the expansion of Iran's economy, partly the result of the exploitation of oil. Tehrān, as the capital city, has attracted industry, commerce, and banking, as well as hundreds of thousands of workers who have flocked there, especially from the northern and northwestern provinces.

Climate. Tehrān experiences warm summers and relatively cool winters. High and low mean monthly temperatures are 84° F (29° C) in July and 39° F (4° C) in January. The average annual rainfall is about eight inches; rain usually falls from November to the end of May, and snow also occurs from December to the end of February. Air pollution is worsening each year as a result of the increase in motor traffic and the increased use of oil fuel by industry.

Transport. Tehrān is a focus for road, rail, and air transport. Three paved roads run northward, one runs to the west, two to the south, and one to the east. The Iranian state railway has lines running north, northwest, south, and east from Tehrān; Tehrān is also linked to the trans-Europe railway system via Turkey.

Tehrān is linked by air to major cities in Europe and Asia and to states in the Persian Gulf. Domestic air services also link the capital to major Iranian towns. There is an international airport at Mehrābād, six miles west of Firdowsī Square; two smaller airports—at Qalʿeh Morghī and Daushan-Tapeh—are used by small aircraft. A second international airport, capable of handling giant aircraft, is due to be completed by 1976.

The people. The ethnic composition of Tehrān is similar to that of Iran in general. The majority of the inhabitants are Muslim, a Christian minority includes Armenians and Assyrians, and there are also small numbers of Jews and Zoroastrians. Persian is the language in general use, with about a quarter of the population using the Azari dialect. The Armenian and Assyrian minorities speak their own languages. Colleges and universities use many textbooks in English or French.

Housing. There are about 370,000 dwelling units in the city; about 40 percent of the population live in one-room units, about 30 percent in two rooms, and the remaining 30 percent in houses with three or more rooms. Almost 85 percent of the houses have piped water and electricity.

Architecture. Because it has grown rapidly since 1925, Tehrān, of all Iranian towns, has the least Oriental aspect. Since the 1950s a number of buildings with from ten to 18 stories have been constructed.

As it is a comparatively young city, Tehrān lacks the historical and architectural heritage of towns such as Isfahan. Among the significant buildings constructed since 1800 are the Sepāh-sālār Mosque, the Baharstān Palace (which now seats the *majles*, or parliamentary deputies), the Shams ol-Emāreh, the Golestān Palace (one of the world's most celebrated palaces; used as a museum, it contains the famous peacock throne as well as the jewel-studded Nāderī throne), the Niavaran Palace, and the Masjed-e Shāh (another beautiful mosque, located in the bazaar quarter). Since 1925 a number of other important buildings have been added, including various ministries, the police headquarters, and the Senate, in addition to the Saʿadābād Palace, the Reza Shāh Mausoleum, and—most significant of all—the Marmar, or Marble Palace.

Economic life. There are about 2,000 industrial establishments of varying size in the city and its immediate environs. These are engaged in the manufacture of such items as textiles, cement, sugar, tobacco, footwear, chinaware and pottery, household utilities, glass and glass products, electrical equipment, pharmaceuticals, and furniture. There is also a car-assembly industry, and an oil refinery is in operation at Rey.

The nation's chief city, Tehrān produces 51 percent of all Iran's manufactured goods and accounts for 33 percent of its total investment and for 60 percent of all of its wages and salaries. About 30 percent of Iran's enterprises are located in the city, and there are numerous government and private banks and insurance companies, as well as a stock exchange.

Government. As the capital city, Tehrān is administered by the national government. There is also a municipal council, composed of 30 members, all of whom are elected every four years by the Iranian residents of the city who are over 18 years of age. The council elects a mayor (as distinct from the governor), who, together with his staff, is responsible for the provision of municipal services.

Public utilities. Public utilities, including the water supply, electricity supply, and telephone service, are government owned and operated. Water is obtained from the Amīr Kabīr Dam, at Karaj, and from the Latyan (or Farahnāz Pahlavī) Dam. Electrical power is obtained from various sources, including the Amīr Kabīr and Latyan dams and the Mohammad Reza Shāh Dam, about 500 miles to the southwest.

Health and safety. The city has about 100 hospitals, and there are about 40 hospital beds available for every 10,000 people. The health standards of Tehrān hospitals are among the highest in Asia. There are about 1,700 doctors and about 800 dentists in the city.

Fire protection is provided by one main fire station and five substations. In addition, well-equipped fire stations are maintained by the army, the state railway, and the National Iranian Oil Co. There is one main police headquarters, 18 major police stations, and five substations.

Education. Kindergartens—of which there are about 175, with an enrollment of 10,000 children—are privately operated. There are about 1,200 public and private primary schools, with more than 500,000 pupils, and 500 public and private high schools, with about 230,000 pupils. There are also a number of vocational schools, teacher-training centres, schools for nurses, and business schools.

Tehrān has three universities, all public—the University of Tehrān and the National University of Iran and Āryamehr Industrial University. Together they have more than 30 faculties and 25,000 students.

Cultural life. The National Academy of Literature is located in Tehrān, where there are also about 12 cultural societies and councils sponsored by foreign countries. The city has a modern opera house, opened in 1967, nine theatres, and more than 100 cinemas.

There are 11 museums, of which four are of international repute and are noted tourist attractions. One of these, the Archaeological Museum, has on display the most precious art objects discovered at the excavations of Susa, Persepolis, and other sites in Iran. The Treasury Building, where the crown jewels are kept, houses a dazzling and priceless collection of jewels.

Among the dozens of libraries, the more important are the Mellī (national), the Malek, the Majles (parliament), and the library of the University of Tehrān.

The media. At the beginning of the 1970s there were about a dozen daily and about 40 weekly publications, all in Persian, as well as a number of monthlies. There were also a number of foreign-language publications. Tehrān had three radio transmitters and four television stations. Tehrān broadcasts television programs to the west and south of the country and was planning to extend its television broadcasting to the whole of Iran later in the 1970s.

Recreational facilities. There are a number of attractive parks and squares in the city, as well as a zoo. There are about 30 sports centres, some of which have stadiums. In 1971 a stadium for 100,000 spectators was inaugurated in preparation for the 1974 Asiatic Olympics.

BIBLIOGRAPHY

General: LAURENCE LOCKHART, *Persian Cities* (1960); D.N. WILBER, *Iran, Past and Present*, 6th ed. (1967), with map; and *Contemporary Iran* (1963); VINCENT MONTEIL, *Iran* (1957; Eng. trans., 1965).

Historical background: LORD CURZON OF KEDLESTON, "Teheran," in *Persia and the Persian Question*, vol. 1 (1892); W.B. FISHER (ed.), *The Cambridge History of Iran* (1968), references in vol. 1.

Photographic views: ROGER WOOD, "Tehran and Modern Persia," in *Persia* (1969).

(Z.R.)

Tektite

Tektites (from the Greek *tektos*, "molten") are glassy objects found in limited areas on the earth, and most probably formed on the moon or the earth. In diameter tektites range from a few tens of microns to about ten centimetres. Those larger than a few millimetres are all rich in silica;

By courtesy of B.P. Glass

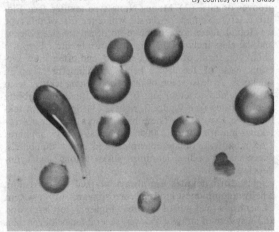

Figure 1: Microtektites from the Australasian strewn-field (magnified 35 ×).

Margin notes:
Religious groups
Manufacturing
The universities

 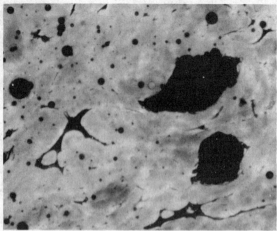

Figure 2: *Muong-Nong tektites.*
(Left) Specimen with soil retained on the surface to illustrate layering (magnified 2 ×).
(Right) Interior of a tektite showing the composite structure (magnified 220 ×).
By courtesy of D. Reidel Publishing Co.

Location and characteristics

they are somewhat like terrestrial obsidians (black volcanic glasses), but are distinguished from them and from other terrestrial volcanic glasses by their lower water content. An obsidian heated by a blowtorch will foam; a tektite will melt with the formation of only a few bubbles. Chemically, tektites are further distinguished from acid igneous (granitic) rocks by their lower content of soda and potash, and their higher content of lime, magnesia, and iron (Table 2). Under the microscope, tektites are seen to lack the small crystals (microlites) characteristic of terrestrial volcanic glasses.

Some terrestrial glasses produced by meteorite impact have approximately the same composition as tektites, but these impact glasses always contain some unmelted or partially melted material from the parent rock. Thus far, these inclusions have not been found in tektites.

Microtektites, of millimetre and smaller size, first discovered in 1968, have a wider range in composition than the large tektites; their silica content, for example, can be as low as 50 percent, similar to that of terrestrial basalts. Microtektites have been found so far only in deep-sea sediments, probably because of the difficulty of distinguishing them in the more abundant and coarser land sediments. They are distinguished from volcanic ash by their rounded shapes and by their chemical constitution, which, for the more silicic microtektites, is identical with that of the large tektites.

Tektite types

Form and markings. Four principal tektite types can be distinguished: (1) Microtektites (see Figure 1). These have diameters less than two millimetres. Their form is most often nearly spherical, although a few are oblate spheroids, and some are shaped like rods, teardrops, and dumbbells. These forms can be collectively described as those typically taken up by rotating liquid drops. Some microtektites also appear to be corroded, having deep grooves or pits. (2) Muong-Nong type tektites (see Figure 2, left). Named for the site where the first of this type was found, these are centimetre- to decimetre-size objects, and the class includes the largest known tektites. They are chunky in form, often tablet-shaped, and often show layering, each of the layers being a millimetre or so in thickness. At least some of the Muong-Nong tektites seem to be welded together out of fine particles resembling microtektites (see Figure 2, right). (3) Splash-form tektites (see Figure 3). These have shapes like the microtektites but are about 1,000,000 times as massive. Spheres (the majority), oblate spheroids, and a few dumbbells, canoe-shaped bodies, teardrops, disks, batons, and cylinders are found.

Splash-form tektites are always marked by corrosion. The two commonest kinds of corrosion are: (1) a system of hemispherical pits of all sizes (Figure 3, top left); and (2) a system of straight grooves, several times longer than they are wide, and of uniform width on a given specimen (Figure 3, top right). On oblate spheroids, the grooves

tend to be perpendicular to the equator of the specimen (Figure 3, bottom left).

Some tektites also show long furrows that meander over the surface like worm tracks (Figure 3, bottom right). Others show narrow cuts, or sawtooth notches at the edges.

By courtesy of (top left) the U.S. National Museum, Washington, D.C., (top right) Museum National d'Histoire Naturelle, Paris

Figure 3: *Splash-form tektites.*
(Top left) Philippine tektite showing hemispherical pits.
(Top right) Indochinite, after Alfred Lacroix, showing grooves. (Bottom left) Moldavite, after F.E. Suess, showing radial arrangement of grooves on a flattened ellipsoidal body (weight 56.4 g.). (Bottom right) Billitonite, after Suess, showing worm-track grooves (weight 40.3 g.).

Many specimens show a set of fine lines, somewhat like the grooves on a phonograph record, not usually parallel to the coarser grooves and furrows. These are the surface exposures of a system of contorted layers (schlieren) extending through the tektite and corresponding to variations in the silica content. They grade into the layering of the Muong-Nong tektites. (4) Australites and related forms. About 10 percent of the tektites found in Australia (australites) show a characteristic lenslike form, with an attached flange around the edge (Figure 4), the whole having the shape of a saucer of ice cream. The underside of the saucer is called the anterior side; the surface of the ice cream is the posterior side; and the edge of the saucer is the flange.

On the anterior side are found low circular or spiral ridges, concentric with the overall outline of the specimen. A set of fine ridges radiates from the centre. When a flanged australite is sectioned, the schlieren form reveals that molten glass has been drawn backward from the anterior side and coiled in the flanges.

Flanged australites have clearly been formed out of

bodies that are much like the splash-form tektites, by heating and melting at the anterior surface. Transition forms between the splash-form tektites and the australites have been found, some ("cores") in which part or all of the flange has dropped off, and others having only a clearly defined lens shape with a sharp keel.

Some tektites have interior voids with smooth, shining surfaces. These voids sometimes contain helium and neon at pressures of more than a few millionths of an atmosphere; others contain atmospheric gases at pressures of a little under one atmosphere.

By courtesy of Dean Chapman and the National Aeronautics and Space Administration, Ames Research Center, Moffett Field, California

Figure 4: (Top) Three Australian button tektites and (bottom) three glass models ablated by aerodynamic heating. Actual size ranges from 16 to 25 mm. In the British Museum.

Distribution. Tektites are found only within definite areas, called strewn-fields (see Figure 5 and Table 1). The North American strewn-field, dated at 33,000,000 years ago, has yielded a few tens of thousands of tektites, mostly splash-form, but with a few Muong-Nong type tektites and a few corelike specimens. The Czechoslovakian strewn-field, dated at 15,000,000 years ago, has yielded a few tens of thousands, mostly splash-form but with a few of the Muong-Nong type and at least one core-type specimen. These tektites are rich in silica and potash. The Ivory Coast strewn-field has yielded a few hundred specimens; it is dated about 1,000,000 years ago. Most of its specimens are of the splash-form type, but there are a few that suggest a trend toward the core type. In the Ivory Coast region, microtektites had been found up to 1970 only off the Liberian coast. Most of these match the larger Ivory Coast tektites in composition, but about 5 percent have a much more basic composition (the "bottle-green microtektites"). The Australasian strewn-field extends from South China over the Malay Archipelago to Australia and Tasmania.

Microtektite finds, including a few percent of the bottle-green type, indicate that the strewn-field also covers most

Location and dating of strewn-fields

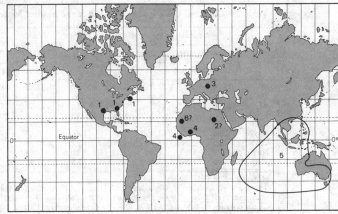

1. North American tektites (Texas, Georgia, Massachusetts)—33,000,000 years
2. Libyan Desert glass—26,000,000 years. Tektite?
3. Moldavites (Czechoslovakia)—15,000,000 years
4. Ivory Coast tektites (land and sea)—1,000,000 years
5. Australasian tektites (land and sea)—750,000 years
6. Aouelloul Crater (Mauritania) glass—300,000 years. Tektite?

Figure 5: Global distribution of tektites.
By courtesy of the National Aeronautics and Space Administration

of the Indian Ocean to points nearly as far away as Madagascar. Millions of specimens have been recovered; most are splash-form, but a considerable amount of Muong-Nong material has been found in Laos, Thailand, and South Vietnam.

Chemistry and petrography of tektites. If the microtektites are included, the compositional range in tektites extends from glasses that in some respects resemble terrestrial ultrabasic rocks all the way to rocks that are more acid than any terrestrial igneous rock. Typical compositions are shown in Table 2. These compositions should be thought of as points on continuous curves rather than as discrete classes.

Silica, SiO_2, is a convenient parameter against which to plot the other oxides. With silica content from 58–85 percent, almost all oxides show a steady upward trend with decreasing silica content. The exception is the potassium oxide, K_2O, content which is positively correlated with silica content. With a silica content of from 50–58 percent, new trends show themselves: the alumina, Al_2O_3, content levels off and the magnesium oxide, MgO, content climbs more rapidly (toward values of 25 percent) than for higher silica values.

Ordinary tektites (typically with about 70 percent SiO_2) are much like granites in composition, though deficient in sodium monoxide, Na_2O, and K_2O and enriched in MgO and ferrous oxide, FeO. These trends are similar to those found in rocks intermediate between the shales and sandstones. No parallel is found in a terrestrial igneous rock; it is, thus, generally considered that if tektites are terrestrial

chart no. (see Figure 5)	names	date (000,000 years)	microtektites	Muong-Nong	splash-form	australite	remarks
			\multicolumn{4}{types}		
1	North American tektites, viz., bediasites (Texas), georgiaites	−33	—	X	X	—	very low in magnesium, calcium
2	Libyan Desert glass	−26	—	X	—	—	may be unrelated; found in Egypt, not Libya; almost pure silicon dioxide
3	Moldavites	−15	?	X	X	X	found in Czechoslovakia, not Moldavia; rich in silicon, potassium
4	Ivory Coast tektites	−1.0	X	—	X	?	sodium more abundant than potassium
5	Australasian tektites, viz., australites, billitonites, Darwin glass, indochinites, javanites, lei-gong-mo (China), philippinites (=rizalites), thailandites	−0.75	X	X	X	X	Darwin glass may be unrelated; it strongly resembles Aouelloul
6	Aouelloul Crater glass	−0.3	—	X	—	—	may be unrelated; silicon dioxide around 85%

Table 1: Strewn-Fields of Tektites and Glasses That May Be Related to Tektites

Table 2: Chemical Composition of Tektites and Similar Materials

	Australasian strewn-field				Europe moldavite	North America bediasite	Ivory Coast tektite	Libyan Desert glass	Henbury subgraywacke	average granite
	microtektites		austra-lite	Muong-Nong						
	basic	regular								
SiO₂	56.8	64.2	73.45	81.36	80.07	76.37	68.02	98.20	77.40	74.22
TiO₂	0.6	0.6	0.69	0.47	0.80	0.76	—	0.23	0.77	0.20
Al₂O₃	8.0	11.0	11.53	8.87	10.56	13.78	16.39	0.70	10.92	13.61
Fe₂O₃	8.4*	9.6*	0.58	0.39	0.15	0.19	0.57	0.53	3.01	1.83*
FeO			4.05	2.81	2.29	3.81	5.99	0.24	1.28	
MgO	20.6	7.2	2.05	1.14	1.46	0.63	3.32	0.01	2.07	0.27
CaO	2.9	3.3	3.50	1.00	1.87	0.65	1.12	0.30	0.65	0.71
Na₂O	0.8	1.8	1.28	1.17	0.51	1.54	2.06	0.33	0.91	3.48
K₂O	0.3	1.5	2.28	2.26	2.95	2.08	1.88	0.02	2.86	5.06

*Calculated as FeO.
Source: W.A. Cassidy, B. Glass, and B.C. Heezen, "Physical and Chemical Properties of Australasian Microtektites," *Journal of Geophysical Research* (1969); E.C.T. Chao, "The Petrographic and Chemical Characteristics of Tektites," in J.A. O'Keefe (ed.), *Tektites* (1963); V.E. Barnes, "Variation of Petrographic and Chemical Characteristics of Indochinite Tektites within their Strewn-Field," *Geochimica et Cosmochimica Acta* (1964); F. Cuttitta and M.K. Carron, unpublished; G. Baker, *Tektites, Memoir of the Natural Museum of Victoria*, no. 23 (1959); S.R. Taylor, *Australites, Henbury Impact Glass, and Subgraywacke: A Comparison of the Abundances of 51 Elements;* C.C. Schnetzler and W.H. Pinson, Jr., "The Chemical Composition of Tektites," in J.A. O'Keefe (ed.), *Tektites* (1963).

in origin then they must have been derived from sedimentary rather than igneous rocks.

Refined analyses have shown that water is present only to the extent of about 100 parts per million (ppm) in tektites, far below the value for terrestrial igneous or sedimentary rocks. Relative to the most nearly similar terrestrial rocks, tektites are depleted in other volatile (relatively low-melting) elements, particularly including copper, lead, tin, thallium, indium, and bismuth. Like terrestrial rocks, and to much the same extent, tektites are depleted in nickel, cobalt, and the precious metals, including gold, platinum, osmium and iridium, etc.

Isotopes in tektites. Considerable information about tektite history can be obtained by a study of the radioactive isotopes (see DATING, RELATIVE AND ABSOLUTE). The most important of these in the present context is potassium with atomic weight 40 (^{40}K), which decays into argon, ^{40}Ar, with a half-life of approximately 900,000,000 years. The ^{40}Ar is expelled when the material is strongly heated. Thus by comparing the amount of ^{40}K with the amount of ^{40}Ar found in a tektite, it is possible to determine how long ago the material was last thoroughly melted. The ages cited above for the tektite strewn-fields were found by potassium–argon dating.

The isotope of uranium, ^{238}U, which is the parent of one of the principal radioactive-decay series of elements, may also decay by spontaneous fission. The tracks of the particles produced through fission are left in the glass and can be traced millions of years later by etching a polished surface. By comparing the number of tracks with the amount of uranium, it is possible to find the age of the glass since it was last melted.

Bodies that pass through space outside the earth's atmosphere are subjected to the action of primary cosmic rays that produce a number of radioactive isotopes including especially aluminum, ^{26}Al. This has been sought in tektites several times without success and its nonappearance, in all probability, means that tektites spent much less than 1,000,000 years as isolated objects in space. It is also possible to examine tektites for tracks due to fission fragments resulting from collisions of primary cosmic rays with atomic nuclei in tektites. Tracks produced this way can be distinguished from those due to ^{238}U. Their complete absence from tektites sets an upper limit of about 1,000 years to the sojourn of tektites in space.

The time elapsed since tektites received their present chemical constitution can be measured by isotope pairs appearing in radioactive-decay chains: rubidium, ^{87}Rb, and strontium, ^{87}Sr, into which it decays; ^{238}U and lead, ^{206}Pb; ^{235}U and ^{207}Pb; thorium, ^{232}Th, and ^{208}Pb. The point is that rubidium, uranium, and thorium are concentrated in volcanic rocks by the process that leads to the formation of lavas. Thus the rate of production of the radioactive end product, namely strontium or lead, is greatly enhanced. Because there is a spread in the ratio of rubidium to strontium in the tektites, it is possible to work

out both the initial value of the ratio of the strontium isotopes $^{87}Sr/^{86}Sr$ (^{86}Sr is used because it is a nonradiogenic isotope that takes no part in the radioactivity) and the length of time since the lava was produced. A straightforward application of this method gives ages that tend to be lower than 100,000,000 years and, thus, too small to be measured accurately. When, however, the possible effects of volatilization are included, and when the assumption is made that the initial value of $^{87}Sr/^{86}Sr$ can be known in advance, then most tektites appear to be some 300,000,000 years old and those from the Ivory Coast are interpreted as having an age of 2,000,000,000 (2×10^9) years.

The problem of tektite origin. *Evidence on an origin beyond the moon.* Meteorites, which appear to arrive from beyond the moon, typically contain accumulations of isotopes and fission tracks corresponding to a sojourn in space of millions of years. For tektites the upper limit is around 1,000 years, so that it would appear that they cannot have come from beyond the moon.

The limited distribution of tektites on the earth also suggests a localized origin because there has clearly been little dispersion of the tektite showers. A cluster of objects travelling through space near the earth's orbit will be torn apart and dispersed by the differential gravitational attraction of the sun unless the average density is more than about a millionth of that of water. A cloud of tektites of this density and with a diameter equal to the size of the Australasian strewn-field would blanket the area to a depth of several metres and this is not observed; this again points to an origin within the earth-moon system.

Evidence for and against lunar origin. One of the specimens brought back from the Apollo 12 lunar flight bears a remarkable resemblance in major element composition to some tektites from Java. There are, however, serious discrepancies in the rare-earth elements, and in barium, uranium, and thorium; for these reasons it is disputed whether the specimen is really tektite material or not.

An important argument in favour of an extraterrestrial and probably lunar origin of tektites comes from aerodynamic studies of the australites. D.R. Chapman took lenses of tektite glass and subjected them to a heated air stream in an arc jet. The glass flowed backward and formed flanges similar to those observed in australites as shown in Figure 4. The similarity is not only external; thin sections show that a peculiar kind of folding is exhibited by both the natural and artificial glass of the flanges.

These studies leave little doubt that the flanged australites were shaped by aerodynamic ablation (erosion due to air-friction melting). Numerical analysis of the relevant conditions, which cannot be entirely duplicated in the wind tunnel, shows that velocities on the order of 11 kilometres per second are required to produce this ablation if the body enters at a steep angle to the horizontal. For very flat trajectories, the observed ablation can be produced by velocities in the neighbourhood of the earth satellite velocity of 8 kilometres per second.

Reduced volatile constituents

Tektite ages

Aerodynamic studies

Chapman and others have also drawn attention to the fact that the escape of tektites from the ground surface through the atmosphere is physically impossible unless the atmosphere is bodily removed in some manner or unless the air moves along with the tektite. Tektites cannot pass through more than about 1 percent of the normal atmosphere without having their velocity reduced to approximate equality with that of the air.

A second point that seems to favour a nonterrestrial origin is the fact that many tektites are composed of a homogeneous glass of low water content with less than 1 percent bubbles (vesicles). Typical terrestrial rocks or soils contain more than 5,000 parts per million of water. When heated, this amount of water is enough to form bubbles whose total volume at atmospheric pressure would be 30 or more times that of the glass. If tektites are terrestrial in origin, such bubbles must have formed and escaped. For typical bubbles, some 100 microns in radius, and for a viscosity of 10^2 poises, corresponding to about $1,800°$ C, approximately 15 minutes would be required to move the bubble one centimetre under a gravitational attraction like that at the earth's surface; but in flight the tektite would experience no gravitational force and would cool within a few seconds to temperatures below $1,800°$ C, so that bubbles, if they had been formed, would have remained.

Similarly the homogenization of glass demands complete diffusion of the components into one another. It has been shown that for diffusion distances of the order of 100 microns, minutes would be required for diffusion at a temperature of $1,800°$ C. Actual sandstones have grain sizes considerably larger than 100 microns; it would actually require the mixing of several hundred grains to reduce the sampling errors to the level of the observed inhomogeneities.

Comparison with other natural glasses

These arguments based on glass technology apply with particular force to three remarkable glasses whose silica content is higher than that generally accepted for tektites: Darwin glass, found in Tasmania; Aouelloul Crater glass, found around and to the east of a 250-metre crater near Atar in Mauritania; and Libyan Desert glass, found in western Egypt. These glasses range from 85 percent to 98 percent silicon dioxide, SiO_2. Darwin glass has the same date, according to fission track methods, as the Australasian strewn-field. Some workers associate these glasses, especially Aouelloul, with local sandy materials, but the above arguments from the field of glass technology seem to imply that they are extraterrestrial.

There are serious arguments against a lunar origin for tektites. Most importantly, up to the early 1970s, analysis of the lunar surface had not disclosed any regions of tektite composition. If they exist, such areas are restricted. Hence the suggestion that tektites are ejected from the moon by meteorite impact also requires a mechanism responsible for destroying a great part of the tektites produced and permitting only those of acid composition to survive. Another possibility is that (as Verbeek suggested in 1897) tektites are ejected not by impact but by volcanism; explosive volcanoes on the earth are always acid, but it has not been shown that acidic volcanism of a similar kind could have occurred on the moon.

The second important argument against the lunar origin is the localized distribution of tektites on the earth. Detailed mechanisms have been worked out by which a jet of material from some lunar crater might be distributed over a local area on the earth, such as a tektite strewn-field. But what of those tektites that have missed the earth on the first pass and have gone into orbit around the sun? Calculations show that these should eventually be captured by the earth but that their distribution over the earth's surface should be completely uniform, and this is certainly contrary to the facts. If tektites come from the moon, there must exist a mechanism in space that destroys them in a relatively short time so that they cannot come back from orbit around the sun. A suggested mechanism is the spin-up of the tektites, caused by asymmetrical radiation pressure and resulting in rotational bursting.

Evidence for and against terrestrial origin. The chemical constitution of tektites strongly resembles that of the earth's crust. Petrological analyses of lunar material show that the moon produces basaltic rocks with a broad resemblance to terrestrial basalts; but a lunar origin of tektites would imply the existence of rocks resembling terrestrial granites on the moon.

Analyses of the gases in tektite vesicles show that some vesicles are nearly empty, but that others are filled with oxygen, nitrogen, and argon in the same proportions as in the earth's atmosphere. These vesicles do not appear to have leaks. If these gases had been trapped while the tektite was liquid, their presence would imply a terrestrial origin.

Presence of atmospheric gases in vesicles

Correlations between tektite strewn-fields and terrestrial impact craters have been cited in support of a terrestrial origin for tektites. The moldavites in southern Bohemia, for example, occur some 200 to 300 kilometres from a large crater, the Ries Kessel, in southern Germany; tektites and crater are dated at 15,000,000 years ago. But, since there are differences in chemical composition, water content, oxygen-isotope ratios, and Rb/Sr ratios between the crater glass and the moldavites, there is probably no real relationship between them. Ivory Coast tektites occur 300–1,600 kilometres from the Bosumtwi Crater in Ghana; tektites and crater are dated at 1,000,000 years ago. Resemblances have been traced between the crater glass of Bosumtwi and the Ivory Coast tektites in chemical composition, Rb/Sr ratios, K-Ar dating, Pb/U ratios, and oxygen-isotope ratios. Though for any one criterion alone the relationship is weak, the cumulative effect is impressive and therefore a generic connection between crater and tektites is claimed by most authorities.

Since many tektites contain nickel-iron spherules, it is possible that if tektites were formed on the earth, the impact of a comet or a meteorite might have been associated with the event. Their chemical composition suggests that the impacts must have occurred in material with the composition of sandstone. In the cases of the Australasian and Ivory Coast groups the region also should contain a few percent of an unusual pyroxenite (to explain the bottle-green microtektites). The velocities to which the particles were accelerated must have been as much as six kilometres per second to cover the Australasian strewn-field, but higher velocities must have been very rare, in view of the lack of a worldwide distribution. The temperatures reached in the region where tektites were formed must have been $2,000°$ C or higher in order to explain the formation of relatively homogeneous glass and the loss of water in a very short time. The atmosphere must have been removed from the site by the impact or else must have moved outward with the tektites, having a velocity relative to them of a few tens of metres per second.

There are thus difficulties in assigning the origin of tektites unambiguously to either the earth or the moon, and even more to a site in space beyond the moon. Until enough of the negative evidence can be satisfactorily explained, the question of tektite origin must remain open.

BIBLIOGRAPHY. F.E. SUESS, "Die Herkunft der Moldavite und verwandter Gläser," *Jb. k. k. Geol. Reichsanst.,* 50:193–382 (1900), classical monograph reviewing the 19th-century literature, and establishing the notion of tektites as a separate class; G. BAKER, "Tektites," *Mem. Natu. Mus. Vict.,* no. 23 (1959), a complete review of the then existing tektite literature, especially for the period 1900–55; J.A. O'KEEFE (ed.), *Tektites* (1963), a comprehensive account of recent work by many authors on the tektite problem, and "The Origin of Tektites," *Space Sci. Rev.,* 6:174–221 (1966), an account of recent tektite research, 1962–66; D.R. CHAPMAN and H.K. LARSON, "On the Lunar Origin of Tektites," *J. Geophys. Res.,* 68:4305–4358 (1963), the aerodynamic evidence on the probable origin of tektites; reports from the Third International Tektite Symposium, *Geochim. Cosmochim. Acta,* 33:1013–1147 (1969), and *J. Geophys. Res.,* 74:6722–6852 (1969), two series that review the problem up to 1969. Popular accounts of the subject are given by V.E. BARNES, "Tektites," *Scient. Am.,* 205:36, 58–65 (1961); and by B.P. GLASS and B.C. HEEZEN, "Tektites and Geomagnetic Reversals," *Scient. Am.,* 217:32–38 (1967).

(J.A.O'K).

Tel Aviv-Yafo

Combining the characteristics of an entirely new planned modern city with those of an ancient Mediterranean port, a duality reflected in its hyphenated name, the Tel Aviv-Yafo of the 1970s is one of the more unique of the great Middle Eastern cities. Yafo (Arabic Yāfa, formerly called Jaffa), the ancient Joppa, had been an important city and port almost continuously since the beginning of the 2nd millennium BC. Tel Aviv, however, was named after Theodor Herzl's novel *Altneuland* (1902, translated into Hebrew as *Tel Aviv* [*tel*, "hill"; *aviv*, "spring"; hence "Hill of Spring"]), in which the founder of modern political Zionism laid down his ideas for a new Jewish state; the name also has a biblical association, being mentioned in Ezekiel as a settlement of exiled Jews in Babylon. Tel Aviv was founded by pioneer Zionist settlers in 1909 as a Jewish garden suburb of Arab Jaffa. Since the union of the two settlements in 1950 and the associated departure of the original Arab inhabitants, Tel Aviv-Yafo, a long, narrow city fronting the Mediterranean for about six miles along the southern portion of the Israeli coastline, has become the nation's largest urban centre and its main business, communications, and cultural centre. By 1970 the 20-square-mile municipality was the home of more than 380,000 people, all but 2 percent of whom were Jews; the metropolitan area, or conurbation, of which it was the centre, covered more than 115 square miles (300 square kilometres) and contained a little more than 1,000,000 people, or fully a third of the entire Israeli population. All local port operations ceased in 1965, with the opening of the port of Ashdod, 19 miles south of the city.

Tel Aviv from old Yafo, with a minaret in foreground and modern Shalom Tower in the background.

History. *Foundation and early growth.* Although Jaffa (Yafo) had been an ancient port and commercial centre, Tel Aviv is a new city, the foundations of which were laid in 1909, when the Jewish quarter of Jaffa had become overcrowded from the influx of immigrants. The Zionist founders of Tel Aviv set out to build a European-style suburb, with straight, wide streets, parks, and modern urban facilities and services. The suburb was to be run by an elected autonomous local council, although nominally it was part of Jaffa. Initially, an area of 27 acres of completely barren sand dunes, northeast of the Jewish quarter, was acquired. By the end of 1914 Tel Aviv had become a purely residential suburb of 245 acres, with 140 houses and 1,500 inhabitants. At its heart stood the Herzliyya Secondary School (now the site of Shalom Tower,

Zionist origins

the city's tallest skyscraper), on which the cultural and social life centred.

During World War I the entire population of Tel Aviv, as well as the Jewish population of Jaffa, was expelled northward by the Turkish military authorities on suspicion of sympathy with the advancing British Army, and the settlements remained completely deserted for nearly a year. Only several months after Jaffa and Tel Aviv were taken by the British, on November 10, 1917, did many of the residents return to their homes.

The Balfour Declaration and the British mandate. Renewed growth began in 1920, with the wave of Jewish immigration that followed the Balfour Declaration and the establishment of the British mandate over Palestine (1923–48). Tel Aviv was separated from Jaffa and granted the status of a town in 1921, following anti-Jewish riots in Jaffa. By the end of 1926 the population had reached 38,000; central Tel Aviv, the area built up before World War I, became a thriving business centre, and a number of industries were established.

Urban growth gathered momentum in the early 1930s, after the Nazis rose to power in Germany. A substantial part of the flood of immigrants that subsequently sought refuge in what was to become Israel settled in and around Tel Aviv. By the end of 1933 the population of Tel Aviv had reached 72,000 and exceeded that of Jaffa, while by the end of 1936 it had risen to 130,000: Tel Aviv became Palestine's largest and most important city.

Nationhood and after. The birth of the State of Israel, in 1948, initiated a dynamic, if turbulent, stage in the development of Tel Aviv. The influx of immigrants caused the population to swell by no less than 60 percent within four years, reaching 350,000 toward the end of 1952. With the incorporation of Jaffa in 1950, the united city became known officially as Tel Aviv-Yafo. When Jaffa surrendered to Jewish military forces in 1948, almost the entire Arab population of 65,000 fled, and Jewish immigrants soon took over a virtually empty city. In the process of its expansion, Tel Aviv-Yafo also swallowed up six villages: five Arab and one (Sarona) German. The Arab villages were abandoned during the bitter 1948 war, while the German inhabitants of Sarona—founded in 1871 by members of a small Protestant sect known as the Tempelgesellschaft ("Temple Society")—had been deported by the British authorities during World War II.

During the 1950s and 1960s the steep rise in land prices in Tel Aviv-Yafo and the expansion of the central business, administration, communication, and entertainment centres brought about a sharp slowdown in the overall outward expansion of the city. A small but continuous decline in the population of the central city set in as inhabitants began an outward movement to homes in towns and suburbs outside the municipal area.

The environment. *The site.* The natural advantages of the site of Jaffa attracted settlement early in the ancient history of the region. The old part of Jaffa is situated on a 2,000-foot-long promontory on the otherwise straight coastline of southern and central Israel. A 100-foot-high hill is bounded by cliffs on the west and the north, while sand dunes and marshy areas made access difficult from the south and southeast. A row of reefs, running close inshore parallel to the coast, forms a natural breakwater for the small bight, or inlet, just north of the promontory. In addition to defensive advantages, the hill has easily accessible small springs and groundwater supplies, as well as an agricultural hinterland that extends almost to the eastern outskirts of the city.

The climate. Tel Aviv has a typical Mediterranean climate. Winter and spring are mild and pleasant, the summer hot and humid. Rainfall is confined to winter months, mainly November–March. The mean daily temperature of the coldest month, January, is about 56° F (13° C) with an average minimum, for the same month, of 47° F (8° C). Temperatures seldom fall below 41° F (5° C), and frost is almost unknown. The mean daily temperature for the hottest month, August, is 80° F (26° C), with a mean daily maximum of almost 89° F (31° C). The hottest days of the year generally occur in

Urban growth and the incorporation of Jaffa

Natural advantages

May or in September, when easterly desert winds bring heat waves; temperatures exceeding 95° F (35° C), however, are rare. The mean annual precipitation amounts to 22 inches (559 millimetres), but there is considerable variation from year to year.

Contemporary city layout. *The heart of the city.* Modern Tel Aviv-Yafo is built over three low ridges of soft sandstone hills that run almost parallel to the coastline. A narrow belt of small sand dunes covering the westernmost of these ridges expands inland where gaps in the relief occur. More sandstone ridges lie to the east, and the built-up area has now spread beyond them into the rich agricultural land of the undulating coastal plain. The ridges have influenced decisively the layout of the modern city and its street pattern. The long main arteries run north–south in the shallow troughs between ridges, with short east–west streets crossing gaps in the ridges.

There is a narrow, flat sand beach fronting the entire coast. The inhabitants of Tel Aviv and its suburbs are able to swim, or simply bask in the Mediterranean sunlight, along large sections of this beach. The first hilly ridge then rises steeply behind the beach in a series of cliffs, and the city's striking modern hotels line its crest. This impressive strip is cut in two places: the city's main east–west artery, Allenby Street, follows a gap one-half mile north of the Jaffa promontory, itself a spur of the coastal ridge; and the Yarqon River Valley cuts a wide gap across the entire belt of coastal hills and dunes.

The city's two main north–south streets, Ben-Yehuda and Dizengoff, follow the trough between the first and second ridge, as does Jaffa's main thoroughfare, Jerusalem Boulevard (previously King George V Boulevard). The main roads leading out of Tel Aviv to the north and northeast, Petah Tiqwa and Haifa roads, run similarly between the second and third line of hills, while the city's most easterly quarters straddle the third ridge, though much of this ridge is outside the municipal area.

The suburbs. To the east and south, Tel Aviv-Yafo proper blends into a continuous built-up area including the substantial settlements of Ramat Gan, Givʿatayim, Bat Yam, and Holon. The suburbs of Bene Beraq, Petah Tiqwa, Qiryat Ono, and Or Yehuda lie farther east. To the north some open space and agricultural land, mainly given over to citrus groves and market gardening, lies between Tel Aviv and the towns of Herzliyya and Ramat ha-Sharon.

City regions. A rapidly growing central business district, the economic heart of Israel, occupies the older part of Tel Aviv and expands northward and eastward into the residential areas built during the 1920s and early 1930s. To the south and east lies the main manufacturing district, with numerous small industrial plants and workshops. Most big industries moved out to outlying areas during the 1940s and 1950s, and the main industrial belt of the whole region centres on the major northeast highway running through Ramat Gan, Bene Beraq, and Petah Tiqwa. Most government offices are concentrated in the district known as ha-Qirya (the former German village of Sarona), northeast of the business centre.

Transportation. Road transport is dominant in Israel, and Tel Aviv is the main national route focus and the headquarters of all major bus and truck companies. Co-operative societies operate the nearly 100 bus lines within the region and also the network of lines serving cities, towns, and rural areas throughout the country. There are two small railway stations, in the north for Haifa-bound trains and in the southeast for Jerusalem and Beersheba. Lod (Lydda) airport, nine miles to the southeast, serves the city's international air traffic.

The port of Jaffa was the country's second largest before it was shut down in 1965, on the inauguration of the modern port at Ashdod. Tel Aviv's small port also was closed in 1965, except for fishing boats.

The people. Tel Aviv's population has been declining from a 1963 peak of 394,000 and had fallen to 382,000 at the beginning of 1970, a drop due to a growing movement of residents, mainly young people, to outlying suburbs. The population of the whole region has continued to grow at an average rate of about 20,000 per year.

Composition. By 1970 the non-Jewish population of Tel Aviv-Yafo numbered about 7,100, nine-tenths of them Arabs, of whom nearly two-thirds were Muslims, and one-third Christians, mostly Greek Orthodox and Roman Catholic. The remaining tenth included Druzes, Armenians, and European Christians of various nationalities. Non-Jews in the whole metropolitan area barely numbered 1 percent of the total population.

Of the Jewish population of the city proper, 41 percent was born in Israel; 13 percent of the rest came from Asian countries, 5 percent from African—mostly North African—countries, and 41 percent from Europe and America. The region as a whole had an Israeli-born population of 42 percent, while 33 percent came from Europe and 25 percent from Asia and Africa.

Density. The mean density of population for the municipal area of Tel Aviv is 20,200 persons per square mile —reaching 64,500 per square mile in the northern part of the city—but less than one-half of this figure for the whole urban region. The average number of persons per room, however, indicates that the highest density is found in the slum areas in the southeastern part of Tel Aviv and in central Jaffa (see below *Housing*).

Housing. Most of Tel Aviv's buildings consist of three- and four-story concrete and cement brick homes, their height restricted by building laws. Only since the early 1960s have much taller buildings been allowed in some residential areas. Districts with small one- and two-story houses and villas take up only a small part of the municipality but occupy substantial parts of outlying regions.

The main slum areas of Tel Aviv-Yafo—still housing some 45,000 people by the early 1970s, in spite of an intensive slum-clearance program—have developed in the southeastern part of the city: ha-Tiqwa Quarter, ʿEzra Quarter, Shapira Quarter, Kefar Shalem (the former Arab village of Salamah), and parts of formerly Arab Jaffa. These slums are almost entirely inhabited by Jews who originate from Arab-speaking countries, mainly Yemen, Iraq, and Morocco, but also some from Iran and Turkey. They are mainly unskilled workers, peddlers, petty traders, and owners of small workshops.

There are no buildings of outstanding architectural beauty in the city proper or the surrounding region. The massive building of the Federation of Trade Unions (known popularly as the "Kremlin") was Tel Aviv's most conspicuous building until the early 1960s, when the urban skyline became studded with a growing number of tall buildings, mainly rather undistinguished office buildings. The Palace of Culture (Mann Auditorium; a concert hall), the Habima Theatre, the university library, the new municipal museum, and the law courts are, nevertheless, fine buildings.

Economic life. Tel Aviv's dominance in the economic life of Israel is clearly evinced by the fact that 25 percent of all the employed persons in the country work in the city, including almost 40 percent of Israel's employees in banking and commerce, 26 percent of those employed in manufacturing, and 30 percent of those engaged in transport work. Almost one-half of the workers resided outside of Tel Aviv municipality by the early 1970s.

More than one-half of Israel's industrial plants are found in the Tel Aviv metropolitan area. The main industries are: textile and clothing, food and tobacco, metal and engineering, vehicles and transport equipment, diamond polishing, furniture and wood products, printing and publishing, and electric and electronic instruments and equipment.

Israel's only stock exchange is located in Tel Aviv, and virtually all the banks, insurance companies, and other enterprises operating in Israel locate their main offices in the city. Some 70 percent of Israel's wholesale trade is channelled through Tel Aviv firms, and its retail firms constitute one-quarter of the national total. The city is also the main centre of Israel's important tourist industry. The city has about 70 hotels, of which more than a dozen are in the luxury (five star) and first-class (four star) category. Herzliyya, a seaside resort just north of Tel Aviv, is the only other tourist centre of the region: it also boasts several large luxury and first-class hotels.

Governmental institutions and services. *Structure of government.* The city is governed by a 31-member council, elected for a four-year period by direct proportional elections. Every adult (above the age of 18) who has been residing in the city for at least one year has the right to vote. Administration is by the mayor and six deputy mayors elected by the city council.

The Labour Front (Hamaarakh) and the union of the Liberal and Freedom parties (the right-wing Gaḥal) are the largest political parties. The National Religious Party and several smaller parties also are active. A coalition headed by the Labour Front, in which the National Religious Party and two of the smaller parties are included, took control of the city in 1959, ending a period of right-wing rule that had been almost continuous since 1921.

Each of the peripheral towns has a similarly elected council (with fewer members) and mayor. All are governed by coalitions, mostly headed by the Labour Party.

Public utilities. Tel Aviv's water supply comes from two sources: wells sunk predominantly in the eastern municipal area and utilizing available groundwater supplies, and the national main, carrying water from the Jordan (via the Sea of Galilee) and the sources of the Yarqon (a dozen miles east of Tel Aviv) to the southern and drier parts of the country. The region's water supply, like that of the nation as a whole, is rationed as a result of the general water scarcity.

A modern sewage system with purification and disposal plants serves the entire municipal area, as well as about three-fourths of the metropolitan region. There is also a drainage system, connected with the sewage system, designed to prevent flooding of low areas during rainstorms. Parts of the sewage system that still empty into the sea cause some pollution.

Educational institutions. By far the greatest part of the educational institutions of Tel Aviv, ranging from kindergarten to university, are financed and run by the national Ministry of Education or by the city's department of education. Private institutions are comparatively few and are mostly kindergartens and institutions for professional training. Elementary education (ages six to 14) is almost entirely confined to state schools. About 30 of the 130 elementary schools are state religious schools. In addition to secondary schools, there are vocational schools and teacher-training colleges. Extramural studies are provided by the city authorities and the Federation of Trade Unions, and various voluntary organizations are active in the field of adult education.

Tel Aviv University—incorporating the three leading regional hospitals for teaching purposes—was founded in 1953 and inaugurated in 1956.

The Bar-Ilan University, a religious university in Ramat Gan, was founded in 1955. Tel Aviv also has 12 rabbinical and theological institutes (yeshivas), but the main concentration of such schools is in Bene Beraq, to which students are drawn from Jewish communities in all parts of the world.

Cultural life. The Israel Philharmonic Orchestra, the only one of its kind in the Middle East, has its home in Tel Aviv, as do the Chamber Ensemble, Israel's two leading choirs (Rinat and Zadikov), the Israeli Opera, and nearly all of Israel's dozen or so theatres, including the Habima National Theatre and the Chamber Theatre, the country's most popular. Ten of Tel Aviv's 13 museums are municipal, and there are 40 private art galleries.

Tel Aviv has a municipal library with 15 branches, and each of the other local authorities has its own public library, generally with a number of branches.

The media. Most of Israel's newspapers and periodicals—including dailies in Hebrew, German, French, Polish, Hungarian, Romanian, Bulgarian, and Yiddish—are published in Tel Aviv, as well as more than 80 percent of the books and pamphlets that appear in the country.

The Israeli Broadcasting Authority has radio and television studios in Tel Aviv, although the central studios and offices are in Jerusalem. Armed forces broadcasting facilities are also housed in the city.

Recreation. Tel Aviv is poor in parks and public gardens, which cover only 5 percent of the municipal area.

The main park areas are being developed along, and to the north of, the Yarqon River (including a 250-acre park) and in the northern part of the city's beach.

The smaller peripheral towns are much better provided with parks than the municipality itself. The region's largest park—the National Park— is situated within Ramat Gan, as is Israel's largest stadium (50,000 seats). Tel Aviv has two stadiums, one used for football matches and athletics and the other mainly for basketball, but most of the city's sporting activities are carried out on sport grounds and facilities outside the city.

Tel Aviv has a small zoo (which is, nevertheless, Israel's largest), extending over seven acres in the densely built-up area north of the central part of the city.

BIBLIOGRAPHY. There is much literature on all aspects of Tel Aviv in Hebrew but very little in European languages, most of it in English. Of the Hebrew publications, the most authoritative work is the detailed *Sefer Tel Aviv* (1936), prepared for the 25th anniversary of the city's founding, and containing chapters on the history, environment, and social life of the city. It contains seven coloured maps. A municipal bulletin (in Hebrew, some with English résumés), which appeared regularly several times per year between 1932 and 1956, contains much valuable data on the growth of the city. The *Tel Aviv-Yafo Municipal Yearbook* (annual) is the best source of information in English on the city. The detailed volumes from 1961 onward have a good summary in English of the annual report in Hebrew that forms the main part of the yearbook, and all statistical tables are given in both Hebrew and English. The 1969 volume of this yearbook has a good historical survey written on the occasion of the city's 60th anniversary. Each of the numerous books in many languages on the history and achievements of Zionist settlement in Israel deals with the founding, growth, and importance of Tel Aviv as an economic and cultural centre. DAVID BEN GURION, *The Jews in Their Land* (1966), is the best of recent books on this subject. A. BEIN, *The Return to the Soil: A History of Jewish Settlement in Israel* (1952; orig. pub. in Hebrew, 1945), is another good work of this kind. Tel Aviv's dominance among the urban centres of Israel is well portrayed in D.H.K. AMIRAN and A. SHAHAR, "The Towns of Israel," *Geogr. Rev.*, 51:348–369 (1961).

(M.Br.)

Telegraph

The telegraph was the first, for many years the most important, and even into the 1970s still a principal system of telecommunication, or communication at a distance. In common with other electrical communications media, such as the telephone, the purpose of the telegraph is the instantaneous transfer, by electrical means, of intelligence over distance. Telegraphy differs, however, from other electrical systems because, first, it transmits dispatches or messages as a sequence of codified alphabetic letters, numerals, punctuation, and symbols; and, second, it records them on paper as telegrams at a distant office for delivery to addressees not only as information but for subsequent reference.

The word telegraph was coined in France around 1792 to describe a pioneer optical-relay semaphore system invented by a French physician and inventor, Claude Chappe. Its literal derivation from the Greek *tele*, "far," *graphein*, "to write"—describes teleprinter telegraphy of the 1970s even more accurately than it did any of the systems from Chappe's through the electric telegraphs of the English inventor W.F. Cooke, the English scientist and inventor Sir Charles Wheatstone, and the United States inventor Samuel F.B. Morse. In a typical modern form, a business-office typist, with a few hours' adaptive practice, manipulates a typewriter-like keyboard literally "to write far" in a correspondent's distant office, upon a typewriter-like platen, as though the typing mechanism, platen, and paper were physically present and mechanically linked with the keyboard.

Prior to the general introduction of simple teleprinters in the 1930s, writing far, on the part of senders of messages, was accomplished chiefly through the intermediary of telegraph operators, who had laboriously mastered one of the dot-and-dash codes by which alphanumeric characters were translated into electrical signals that could be transmitted and at the reception point deciphered and written down.

Applications of telegraphy techniques

The techniques of telegraphy are now widely used in nonalphabetic, nonmessage systems including radar and telemetry, used to measure or transfer measurement data to a distance, either for record purposes or control of machines, weapons, or processes. Another example of increasing utility is the joining together, by means of the telegraph, of geographically separated computers either for storage of information or for processing; *e.g.*, in the control of space-flight vehicles by microwave radiotelegraph.

HISTORY

The history of telegraphy embraces four stages: nonliteral or nonalphabetic message transmission—*i.e.*, drums; visual telegraphy or semaphore; wire telegraphy; and wireless telegraphy, or radio. The term telegraph is reserved primarily for the third stage, wire telegraphy, which is emphasized in the following summation.

Pre-electric telegraphy. *Nonalphabetic signalling.* Prehistoric man learned to beat on resonant logs and tree trunks with a stick, then to make more effective drums of stretched membranes, and finally to use the knowledge to extend the range of his voice; rhythms and intonations applied to drum beats could be made to express emotions and ideas. The next step in communicating by means of the drum, the reed pipe, bone whistle, or ram's horn was to prearrange a set of meanings for certain sounds and sequences. The counting of beats led to the development of codes. Smoke signals by day and fires by night were also used by the ancient people of China, Egypt, Assyria, and Greece. Beacon fires, established on line-of-sight locations, brought to Queen Clytemnestra, at her palace at Argos, Greece, the news of the fall of Troy and her husband's imminent homecoming, in 1084 BC. As recounted by the poet Aeschylus nine relay points on natural prominences covered a total distance of some 500 miles (800 kilometres). Signal fires are also recorded as having been used by the Picts against the Roman invaders of Britain in the 1st century AD and by American Indians in Ohio in early colonial times.

Alphabetic signalling. According to the Greek historian Polybius a method of signalling the 24-letter Greek alphabet was devised by about 300 BC. The code was formed by placing the letters on a grid of five horizontal rows and five vertical columns, so that the first letter, alpha, fell on the first row of the first column and the last, omega, on the fifth row of the fourth column. To signal all 24 positions, ten vases were held in reserve behind two low walls, in a row, but separated by a few feet. In signalling omega, the sender would place five vases on the left wall and four on the right.

Essentially the same method was used by medieval prisoners to communicate through the wall of adjoining cells. Today's 26-letter Roman alphabet was contained within the five-by-five pattern because I and J were combined as one letter. The numbers were tapped out in series of pairs, 1-1 indicating A. This idea transferred the code from a purely spatial configuration to one involving time. In 1551 an Italian mathematician, Gerolamo Cardano, suggested that five torches on five towers could be used to spell out letters, with all five beacons figuring in the code as "light" or "dark." The invention of the telescope in the 17th century stimulated interest in visual signalling, and several fresh proposals were put forward by such men as the English physicist Robert Hooke, though none was immediately developed.

Optical telegraphs. Two optical telegraphs, built by and for government, were of particular importance: the semaphore of the First Republic, France, 1794; and the shutter telegraph of the Admiralty, England, 1795.

As to the first, Claude Chappe and his older brother invented in 1791 and applied the name telegraph to their system of two-arm semaphores (from the Greek: "bearing a sign"; see Figure 1A). In 1793 Claude Chappe was given the title "ingénieur-télégraphe." A relay station was a hilltop tower sheltering the operators and equipped with telescopes directed up-line and down-line. At the top of the tower a vertical timber supported a beam (the regulator). At each end of the beam an arm (indicator)

could be made to assume seven angular positions 45 degrees apart. The 49 positions accommodated alphabetic letters and symbols.

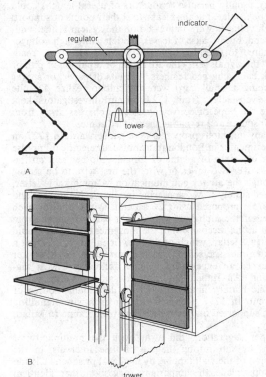

Figure 1: *Optical telegraphs.*
(A) Chappe semaphore. The heavy black lines indicate six of the many possible arm and indicator configurations, representing six hieroglyphs, or coded characters.
(B) Murray six-shutter semaphore.

The horizontal beam could be tilted 45 degrees clockwise or counterclockwise, or held in a vertical position. Signals associated with the positions of the beam provided communication in cipher or code. Towers were spaced three to six miles (five to ten kilometres) apart. At a rate of three signals a minute for each relay under conditions of good visibility, transit time from Toulon to Paris, through 120 towers, was 40 minutes, or, roughly, an hour for a message of 50 signals. This performance was more than 90 times as fast as mounted couriers.

The value of the semaphore telegraph was established when it was used to relay news of French victories over the Austrians at Quesnoy and Condé-sur-Escaut in August 1794. Within the decade, variations of Chappe's semaphore appeared in Russia, Sweden, and Denmark and eventually in Prussia, India, and Egypt.

Only slightly later, in 1795, George Murray (1761–1803), an English bishop credited with many improvements in the telegraph, established for the British Admiralty another successful visual system called a shutter telegraph, consisting of six solid shutters (see Figure 1B), each independently rotatable 90 degrees on a centred horizontal axis, arranged in the three-by-two pattern shown. The code that governed how many and which shutters to open simultaneously was similar to that of Cardano's five light and dark torches except that a larger number of combinations was possible (64 as compared to 32). The shutter telegraph

Various forms of the Murray shutter rapidly appeared in England and spread to the United States, where a number of vantage points bearing the name Telegraph Hill and Signal Hill still dot maps. A Murray line, used principally by merchants, connected New York and Philadelphia until 1846.

It was while the United States Congress in 1837 was considering a petition to authorize a New York–New Orleans Chappe-semaphore line that Samuel F. B. Morse first argued for government support of his electric telegraph.

Telegraphs using electricity. Prior to the invention of the primary battery in 1800, attempts to communicate alphabetically by electricity had failed as operable systems, usually because conductors of useful lengths could not be insulated against leakage at their points of support. High voltages were impressed on the system at the sending end, but because of losses, the relatively high voltages required to energize the then-known devices for "reading" the signals sent (the attraction or repulsion of pith or cork balls, charged feathers, and bits of paper; or sparks jumping a small gap) were difficult to realize. Despite these obstacles, from 1727 onward investigators kept alive the hope of conveying electric charges away from their source and revealing them at a distance.

Early experiments

Many ingenious proposals were put forward. In 1727 an experimenter in London transmitted an electrical impulse over one-sixth of a mile of thread. Another sent an impulse over two miles of wire, the first wire to be strung through the air for communication. A remarkable letter, signed simply C.M., appearing in a magazine in Scotland in 1753, proposed using 26 separate wires, one for each letter of the alphabet, with a light ball suspended from each at the receiving end; the movement of a ball would signify a letter, which could be written down, creating a written message sent by electric current. A Swiss worker produced an experimental model following C.M.'s suggestion. An Italian physicist, Alessandro Volta, whose voltaic battery finally provided a dependable source of current, in 1777 proposed that an iron-wire signalling line, supported on posts, be strung from Como to Milan, Italy.

Other suggestions did away with the multiplicity of wires by substituting the use of time intervals, in the fashion of the wall tapping by medieval prisoners. Claude Chappe made the important suggestion that identical clockworks at either end of a communication wire could be made to indicate numbers which would be translated into words by a codebook. But Chappe abandoned his electrostatic experiments in favour of his optical semaphore; and in 1816 a synchronized-clock telegraph was produced in Hammersmith, England, with a dial rotated at one revolution per minute to permit reading of letters and numerals through an aperture in a fixed disk hiding the dial. The scheme, which was not pursued, was the precursor of stock tickers and printing telegraphs of a later era.

Electrolytic telegraphs. Other researchers explored another possibility. Noting that when certain liquids were decomposed by an electric current the current could be detected by the formation of bubbles, experimenters in Germany sent current impulses over wires by means of voltaic batteries; the impulses released bubbles in a trough at the receiving end. The scheme proved too slow to be useful.

Needle-telegraph pioneers. The observation of the deflection of a pivoted, magnetized needle by an electric current, reported by Hans Christian Ørsted of Denmark in 1819, pointed the way to the true future telegraph. André-Marie Ampère of France and others predicted the communications applicability of the idea, and as early as 1832 a Russian established a needle-telegraph circuit between the tsar's winter and summer palaces at St. Petersburg.

Carl Friedrich Gauss and Wilhelm Eduard Weber (Göttingen, Ger., 1833) constructed a two-wire telegraph line of copper, carried 1.4 miles (2.3 kilometres) over housetops. The receiver was a heavily constructed bar galvanoscope (a compass-like device for detecting the flow of current) on which was mounted a tiny mirror. A few feet away, a telescope-and-scale arrangement made it possible to observe and record slight movements of the bar. The galvanoscope-mirror device became the forerunner of the mirror galvanometer used on the first transatlantic cables. The code consisted of five successive deflections of the bar, right or left, for each character, again, after the manner of Cardano. It was the forerunner of the modern start–stop teleprinter code. Other researchers developed a two-wire, single-needle telegraph employing a uniform-length, five-unit code and erected a single-wire line nearly

six miles (ten kilometres) long, on poles with crossarms, between Munich and Bogenhausen, with an earth (ground) return.

William Fothergill Cooke, an Englishman, devised (at Heidelberg, Ger., in 1836) a three-needle telegraph of six wires and, in 1837, formed a partnership with Charles Wheatstone in London to introduce electric telegraphy as an adjunct to visual signals on railways. Together they patented and, in July 1837, demonstrated for railway use a six-wire, five-needle apparatus that could be read visually (see Figure 2). At the receiver, five external pointers

Five-needle telegraph

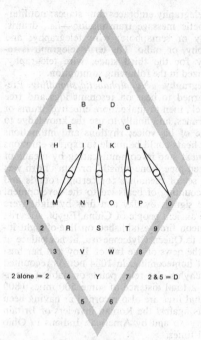

Figure 2: The Cooke and Wheatstone five-needle telegraph (see text).

were mounted on horizontal shafts that also held the needles of five galvanoscopes mounted behind the scribed panel. The needles moved clockwise or counterclockwise against stops as currents were fed through the respective wires by switches that applied voltage from a sending battery. The sixth wire served as the common return. To send a numeral, only one needle was moved at a time—the receiving operator's eye followed the line of axis of the deflected pointer diagonally toward a selected numeral on the lower edge of the display grid. To send a letter, two switches were moved at the same time; two pointers took diagonal positions and the proper letter was found at the intersection produced by their axes, whether in the upper half or the lower half of the grid. A codebook based on 20 letters and ten numerals handled the railway's requirements. The system was in use on the railway between Paddington (London) and West Drayton in July 1839 and was extended to Slough (18 miles [29 kilometres]) in 1843. Because six-wire construction was costly, Cooke and Wheatstone, in 1845, patented a successful single-needle instrument, but it required skilled operators. In 1846 several telegraph companies adopted it in England for public use; on the Continent it competed for favour with Morse's register (1844); it employed equal-duration, left and right deflections of a needle to denote characters, in a code resembling Morse.

Electromagnets applied to telegraphy. In 1825, it was learned that it is possible to increase the intensity of magnetic fields many times by introducing soft-iron cores into coils carrying current. The cores were shaped into horseshoe form to attract iron-bar armatures more effectively. Joseph Henry (Albany, N.Y., 1829) discovered laws governing the design of coils of electromagnets and of applied voltages to produce maximal effects. In 1831 he signalled over a one-mile (1.6-kilometre) circuit by causing a horseshoe electromagnet to swing a pivoted, permanent-magnet armature and strike a bell; he predicted in the same year that his method would be used to communicate other intelligence electrically.

In the United States, Samuel F.B. Morse, in 1832, made sketchbook entries of ideas that involved the electromagnet in telegraphy. In general they called for rows of marks of different lengths on moving tape in response to signals of shorter or longer time duration applied by battery to denote the ten numerals. Use of a codebook was contemplated to include words, names, dates, and sentences. To gain transmitting speed, lead types for the numerals, individually cast, were to be assembled in a long composing stick called a port-rule; this was to be drawn rapidly under contacts that would apply battery to a two-wire circuit. Morse cast such types in brass molds in 1832. By 1835 he had abandoned his codebook idea and had drawn up the Morse Code of dots and dashes representing letters, numerals, and punctuation (see Figure 3, column A). His handmade model of 1835 contained type cast in Morse Code. Later he concluded that setting type was too slow and substituted a simple key to

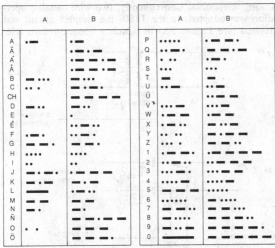

Figure 3: (Column A) American Morse Code. (Column B) Continental, or International, Morse Code.

open and close the circuit by hand movement as on a piano key. After incorporating these improvements in the model, Morse demonstrated it to friends in his quarters in 1837, filed a patent caveat, and formed a partnership with Alfred Vail (as Cooke and Wheatstone were doing in England in the same year).

Vail and Morse quickly made drastic changes in the aspect of the receiver, or register, making the leverage compact and forming a message consisting of dots and dashes in a straight line, embossed on an unwinding band of paper. Public demonstrations of the new equipment were made in 1838 at Vail's shop in Morristown, N.J.; at New York University; before the Franklin Institute in Philadelphia; and United States government officials in Washington. A government appropriation became available to Morse early in 1843. He built his first line between Baltimore and Washington, 37 miles (60 kilometres), abandoning underground construction in favour of a pole line. Public use between cities was inaugurated on May 24, 1844, with the message: "What hath God wrought?" The registers were actuated by terminal relays.

Morse's first line

Early problems of growth. Open-wire pole lines, erected by separate private enterprises under Morse licenses, spread rapidly in the United States and Canada. Because messages had to be transferred between companies for forward handling, mergers were formed, beginning on a grand scale with the formation in 1851 of the Mississippi Valley Printing Telegraph Company, changed in 1856 to Western Union Telegraph Company. Though Morse was barred from obtaining British patents, he succeeded in introducing his register, as a competitor to Wheatstone's needle, to the various governments of Europe in rapid succession, beginning with France in 1845. Since it lacked letters with diacritical marks, the signalling code drawn

up by Morse was not wholly satisfactory for use on the Continent. By agreement, a variant called Continental Morse (Figure 3, column B) was adopted by European countries in 1851. Morse's spaced letters (C, O, etc.) were replaced with unspaced letters. When demonstrated, Morse's 1844 line between Baltimore and Washington was operated as a complete metallic loop but before being extended to New York and Boston in 1845 the wire loop was replaced by a single wire with current return through the ground. The technical disadvantage of this more economical mode of operation was current leakage from wire to ground at every pole, especially in wet or foggy weather. Morse's register was modified from an embosser to an inker, using inked felt to moisten a tiny recording wheel affixed to the moving armature. The inker, in turn, was replaced by the exceedingly simple sounder (c. 1856) after operators (beginning with Vail) had developed the skill to write down what they heard the register "say" as accurately and even more quickly than they could transcribe on a blank what the register "wrote." Operating speed, acquired through practice, was limited by the sender. Normal operating speeds were 20 to 25 words a minute; only exceptional operators maintained speeds of 30 to 35. Railroad operators were often required to transcribe manifold copies by stylus rather than pen. The typewriter was adapted to telegraph office use soon after the introduction in 1878 of key-shift, type-bar models.

Operating speeds

Lines and wires. Ezra Cornell, who erected Morse's first line, used glass doorknobs as insulators. Improved insulators of glass and porcelain were soon designed. Initially, wires were of iron; not until about 1900 was strong copper wire available. Lightning arresters and fuses were concomitant developments of the telegraph, anticipating use in power distribution.

Wheatstone and Morse experienced difficulty with insulation in underground installations, but the need was great for such installations. While pole lines were used on railroad rights-of-way in both the United States and Great Britain, practice differed as to city terminations, partly because cities in England were too congested to admit railways above ground. Consequently, underground wires laid in pipe, following gas- and water-mains practice, joined central telegraph offices with pole lines on the outskirts. Electrical failure due to moisture was common; tarred cotton, silk insulation, and gutta-percha proved ineffective. In 1860 aerial cables, consisting of 30 to 100 ground-return copper wires insulated with India rubber and overlaid with narrow tape to prevent abrasion, were being used successfully in construction over housetops in London. When introduced to underground practice, India rubber satisfied rubber requirements.

District telegraphs. Though present-day readers may think of the telegraph in terms of distant-city or global interconnections, for the 35 years from 1845 until telephones became generally available in 1880, the telegraph was the standard metropolitan means of communication. The telegraph ended the isolation of police precincts and fire brigades. District telegraph systems with branch offices and wire networks were established in London (1859), Paris (1864), and in Germany and the United States at about the same time. They consisted of: (1) telegraph offices (in London there were 84), with wires converging at manual-relaying central offices that catered to businesses and the public; (2) a system of instruments and intracity wires offered for lease to business houses that employed their own operators; (3) general messenger services; and (4) burglar-alarm services. Among the messenger services was the pickup and delivery of domestic and foreign intercity messages. The district telegraphs maintained call boxes to summon messengers and for the filing of messages.

A need for a private wire system that required no knowledge of code was met by Wheatstone's direct-reading system, the so-called *A-B-C* system. Similar versions in France were known as Breguet and in Germany as Siemens-Halske. In these systems a step-by-step, ratchet-driven receiving indicator progressed around a clock face displaying all the letters and numerals. A character was

A-B-C system

read and recorded by the operator each time the pointer stopped. The sending communicator was another dial similarly arranged. When buttons around a circle were depressed they arrested all motion of the communicator and distant indicator. The rotating member inside the communicator was driven by a tiny crank that was turned by the operator. On its shaft was a magnetogenerator that made one-half of a turn per letter traversed, sending to the line one-half cycle of alternating current per letter. Cranking with one hand, the operator could push buttons with the other and continue to crank until inhibited by the depressed character. A speed of eight to 15 words a minute was possible. Wheatstone's magnetogenerator, which was the precursor of both the dynamo and alternator, had avoided the need for a battery.

The advantages of private wires, otherwise called leased or dedicated circuits, spread from the districts to intercity use in the United States in 1869. Among earliest users were newspaper publishers, quickly followed by stockbrokers.

Telegraphs and the press.   In the United States the telegraph and the railroad mail (1834) became catalysts for an evolving journalism. The "penny press," with the aid of the telegraph, was able to feature domestic "spot news" in place of journalism's traditional editorial comments in support of political parties and commentary on intelligence received by mail. After 1866 this transformation carried over into news received by cable.

The concept of a press wire service originated in England with the telegraphic activity of Paul Julius Reuter, who supplemented incomplete line construction on the Continent by using pigeons to bridge gaps (1849). In the 1860s he was operating submarine cables wholly or partly owned by Reuters Limited as a news agency. In the United States the first intercity, leased wire service was the Associated Press' New York–Philadelphia–Baltimore–Washington service of 1875. The Associated Press had previously been established (1848) to pool telegraphic expenses.

Increasing the efficiency of wires.   Much ingenuity was expended in devising direct-current repeaters so contrived that an operator receiving on line B could interrupt the operator sending on A, and in turn send to him. Also important to the efficient utilization of lines was the so-called duplex, perfected in Germany, which made it possible for one wire to provide separate eastbound and westbound paths for simultaneous transmissions. The schematic wiring of the (later) bridge polar duplex (Figure 4) shows the variable resistances and capacitances

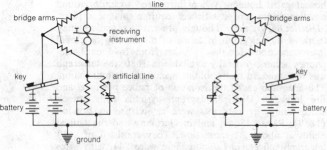

Figure 4: Bridge polar duplex circuit.

used in both artificial lines. These are carefully adjusted to balance (*i.e.*, to match) those of the main line and distant terminal. Balance is achieved when the key at the west terminal, for example, is moved up and down and the west receiving instrument is completely unresponsive to it. The east terminal is balanced similarly. On this facility four operators can handle two telegrams at the same time.

Thomas A. Edison, in 1874, designed a double duplex, called the quadruplex, requiring the services of eight operators who handled four messages at one time, two in each direction. It filled a need for about 35 years and was confined to hand Morse sending.

A high-speed automatic Morse system (1858), the achievement for which Wheatstone was knighted, was

The quadruplex

used throughout the world until around 1910 on landlines, and in the early 1970s it was still being used in radiotelegraphy. An inker—a greatly improved Morse register which could run at 70 to 300 words a minute—was the receiver.

The transmitter, first driven by clockwork then by motor, was the first to use holes punched in tape as the control for keying. While sitting in front of a mallet punch, the operator struck anvils with two mallets, one for dots and the other for dashes, with middle feed holes. A third anvil punched feed holes only to separate letters and words. When the tape was passed through the transmitter, sensing pins, called pecker rods, came up through the holes to establish keying contacts. The mechanism was so designed that the contact would lock up on the top hole for the duration of a dash, then be unlatched by the bottom hole following. In time, the slow preparation of tape by mallets was superseded by faster, typewriter-like keyboards.

Using the telephone.   During the early days of the telephone, it was found that ground-return circuits on intercity open-wire lines caused intolerable levels of cross talk among telephones. Consequently, two-wire metallic operation was adopted. In the 1880s the simplex circuit was devised (see Figure 5A) in which a ground-return tele-

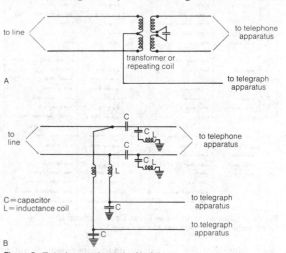

Figure 5: *Telephone-telegraph circuits.*
(A) Simplex circuit; (B) composite circuit.

graph could be derived from a working metallic telephone pair without interference. Later, a composite set (see Figure 5B) permitted the derivation of two grounded telegraphs. Composite sets were still to be found occasionally in 1970 in use on intercity trunk circuits.

Submarine cables.   The first underwater conductors were laid by Morse in New York Harbor (1842) and by Cornell across the Hudson River (1845). Both were constructed of copper, insulated in part with India rubber, and both were short-lived. Three Mississippi River cables (1853) were successful. Machines to apply gutta-percha as insulation were devised by Werner (Sir William) Siemens (London, 1847); submarine cables so insulated were laid from Dover to Calais, 1850–51. The next cables were laid across the Irish and North seas. A cable crossed the Mediterranean in 1855. Two were laid in 1856 from Newfoundland to Canada to meet anticipated transatlantic cables. Before 1866, the year that the first two successful Ireland–Newfoundland cables were completed, there were 51 cables elsewhere. Transatlantic attempts in 1857, 1858, and 1865 were unsuccessful. The 1858 cable worked 27 days before it failed, and the 1865 cable was pieced out and completed in 1866. Cyrus West Field, a United States financier, and William Thomson, Lord Kelvin, British physicist and inventor, are famed for their skill and persistence in seeing the transatlantic projects through.

In 1865 a New York–Paris landline telegraph route was surveyed through British Columbia, Alaska, Bering Strait, and Siberia. Actual construction began northwestward

The first transatlantic cable

from British Columbia and eastward from St. Petersburg. Completion of the first two entirely successful transatlantic cables in 1866 ended the project, but public and governmental interest in it was a factor in the purchase of Alaska from Russia by the United States in 1867.

After 1866 nearly a score of transatlantic cables were laid by the British, French, and Americans. Cables laid by Americans in 1924, 1926, and 1928 were inductively loaded with helical tapes of a magnetic alloy (Permalloy or mu-metal) wound around the conductor and under the insulation. By equalizing the arrival time of the high- and low-frequency components of the transmitted signal, the transmitting speed—hence, traffic capacity—of these newer cables was raised. Coupled with the use of vacuum-tube amplifiers that were made available in the early 1920s, the fastest of these cables worked in printer-multiplex of eight channels instead of one. By the 1940s, there were 20 transatlantic cables. In the 1950s, some of the cables failed and could not be repaired economically. Telephone cables were laid, beginning in 1956; cable and radio companies alike leased telegraph bands of frequencies in the new cables with the result that the last of the exclusively telegraph transatlantic cables was abandoned in 1966, after a century of cable-system service. In oceans other than the North Atlantic, telegraph cables still operated because alternative facilities obtainable from some telephone cables or satellite-relay services were economically unfeasible.

The original mirror galvanometer (Kelvin, 1858) required two receiving operators, one to watch and call out the signals, the second to transcribe. The method was replaced by Kelvin's delicate ink-siphon recorder (1867), which marked a wavy line on a strip of paper drawn in front of one operator. The dots and dashes of Continental Morse were of equal length, but the dots were transmitted as one polarity and the dashes as the opposite polarity (about 24 volts). The cable was grounded between letters. This was the shortest of all codes used in telegraphy. In the mid-1920s, rotary repeaters and code converters precisely controlled by tuning forks or pendulums made it possible to repeat cable signals on landline or radiotelegraph circuits and vice versa. A submerged vacuum-tube amplifier, powered from shore, was first inserted in an Anglesey–Isle of Man cable in 1943, and in a transatlantic cable for the first time in 1950.

Military uses of the telegraph. The telegraph was first employed militarily by the Allied Army in the Crimean War, at Varna, Bulgaria (1854), where lines were erected to connect command headquarters with troop units. In the same war a submarine cable was laid (1855) across the Black Sea. In the United States a transcontinental telegraph was built in the 1850s. From the Mississippi westward a solitary wire at first ran through a string of forts along the route of the pony express and of ox-drawn Conestoga wagons. The wire reached the Pacific in 1861, just as the Civil War began.

Use in the U.S. Civil War

The American Civil War made enormous use of the telegraph. Telegraph operators enlisted in large numbers; the president of the merged telegraph companies was made a general and put in charge of all the telegraphs in the North. Lines already installed were placed at the disposal of the army; others were constructed to follow the armies. New techniques suitable for army field use were developed to unreel and reuse wire strung between command posts. Batteries, keys, relays, and sounders became essential war materiel.

In the Spanish–American War (1898), landline and cable telegraphs were geared for the first time to meet the needs of newspaper war correspondents. The war also marked the first time in which cables were cut at sea as an act of belligerency (at Cienfuegos, Cuba, and at Manila), resulting in new provisions in international law to protect such installations. In the Russo-Japanese War (1904–05) radiotelegraphy was used for the first time, both in tactical deployment and in news coverage by civilians. World War I brought the first use of teleprinter encryption, in which two identically prepared, but meaningless, key tapes are used. One is passed through the transmitter to garble the intelligence tape, while the other, passed

through the receiving teleprinter, restores the original message.

The outstanding electric-signalling innovation of World War II was radar, a form of radiotelegraphic direction finder. Radar techniques have been integrated with those of telegraphy to produce some modern forms of the latter.

Early printing telegraphs. In 1846, only two years after Morse, Royal E. House of the United States invented a printing telegraph. The transmitter had a keyboard of 28 keys, each assigned a character. Behind the keyboard was a cylinder on the surface of which projected short pegs aligned on a one-turn helix. The cylinder was turned with a crank; its motion was arrested when a peg was blocked by a depressed key. Contacts that closed and opened the line, once for each letter, were positioned at the end of the cylinder. The impulses through an electromagnet stepped a ratchet and printing wheel to corresponding positions at the receiver. When rotation stopped, a miniature press forced a blackened silk ribbon against an endless paper strip, backed by the embossed letter on a wheel, to make a printing impression. Motive power was treadle-compressed air. The system was crude and required two men to send and two men to receive. Its speed was described as "twice as fast as Morse." It lasted only a few years, but is remarkable for its anticipation of the typewriter ribbon, the simplex tape printer of the 1930s, the so-called Hughes printer, and the stock ticker.

House's printing telegraph

David Edward Hughes (Kentucky, 1855) patented a system which became standard in Europe. His chief point of departure from House was to regulate the transmitting cylinder and the receiving typewheel by tuning forks and to keep both rotating without stopping; the only signals sent over the line were one dash per revolution for synchronization and one dot for each letter pressed against paper tape. The tape was gummed and was attached to a blank sheet of paper for delivery. The equipment, antedating electric motors, was driven by weights raised by a treadle and was handled by one operator at each station.

Stock tickers, step-by-step tape printers, operating at 40 words a minute, mounted on pedestals and under bell jars, had a long life (1867–1932). Generically, the piano-keyboard, pegged-cylinder transmitter of House and Hughes was combined with the one-alternation-per-character scheme of Wheatstone's *A-B-C*. In the receiver an electrically polarized relay actuated a weight-driven escapement (a ratchet device that permits motion in one direction only and in equal steps) on the printing wheel to move the various letters into position at high speed. Printing was accomplished by impact from an arm actuated by an electromagnet too sluggish to be moved by the rapid reversals of letter-selecting currents but responsive to the steady application of either pole of the battery, applied when the transmitting cylinder's rotation was arrested by a peg-striking key. Two printing wheels, rotating as a unit, were used, one to print letters, the other numbers and fractions. A unison signal brought all tickers on the line into initial register and made the tickers self-winding. By 1933 the market had outgrown step-by-step tickers. They were replaced by 500-characters-per-minute teleprinters. In 1964 these, in turn, were replaced by 900-characters-per-minute, six-level code teleprinters (see below). The use of transparent tape and narrow screens for the projection of quotations for general viewing dates from 1924; the automatic quotation boards for brokerage office data display, from about 1927.

Time-division multiplex. Jean-Maurice-Émile Baudot (France, 1845–1903), in 1872, invented a time-division multiplex-printing telegraph system containing elements from which modern equipment has evolved. The idea of synchronized rotary motion at both circuit ends (which Chappe had proposed in 1790) led, in 1853, to a proposal that in sweeping a full circle, the first half of the synchronized rotating arms' revolution could put the line at the disposal of one pair of operators, while the second half could be used by a second pair. A further proposal, that a uniform five-unit code be utilized, was made in 1860. Nothing came of either idea at the time. Baudot thought in terms of multiplexing the line, time-dividing its capaci-

Baudot's system

ty among not two but several pairs of operators. By 1877 the French Administration of Posts and Telegraphs had officially adopted Baudot's working system, the heart of which was a distributor consisting of a stationary faceplate of concentric copper rings swept by brushes mounted on a rotating assembly (see Figure 6). Depending

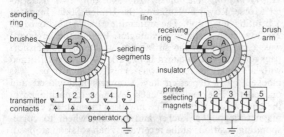

Figure 6: *Baudot time-division multiplex system.*
(Left) Sending ring of one distributor and (right) companion receiving ring (see text).

upon traffic-load capacity and requirements of the line, the faceplate was divided first into sectors: if they were 90° quadrants, as shown, the multiplex became known as a quad; if 120°, a triple; if 180°, a double. A quad would keep four operators busy at each end, interweaving the characters, one at a time, from four telegrams. Each faceplate sector, whatever its arc, was further subdivided into segments representing code pulses of equal length, corresponding to the five levels of the Baudot code. For simplicity Figure 6 shows only the sending ring of one distributor and its companion receiving ring at the far end of the line. There were auxiliary rings, not shown, and brush mounts on the rotating brush arm which paced the transmitting operation and the printing. On the receiving side, each of Baudot's quad printers had the time of three-quarters of a revolution to print and clear out the character that had been set up in its five selecting bars during the initial one-quarter turn. There was therefore no line time lost in separating a character from its follower—a clear gain over Morse Code in any of its forms.

Baudot went further in loading his time-division multiplexed line by duplexing it in the manner described earlier. Baudot adopted the corrected-synchronism method of Hughes but added necessary adaptations to avoid mixing up the channels.

Baudot's inventions of the 1870s were contemporary with the typewriter and although his machines printed on tape some of his patents were used in page-writing typewriters. He was sole originator of the idea of using five sliding, notched, selecting code bars, or disks, as a means of permuting 32 printer controls, as called for by his code. Generically, his method, which was still being used in the early 1970s, was to block the downward movement of the keys of a typewriter-like mechanism by placing a bundle of thin code bars (numbered one to five) on edge, transversely under the keybars. These bars were then slotted in such a manner that the proper key would be actuated upon receipt of the proper code signal.

The paging function. In the late 1890s attention was directed to transmitting telegrams in page form, dispensing with gumming wheels and similar expedients to affix narrow tape to paper blanks at the receiver.

Donald Murray (England, 1903), taking much from Baudot, devised a time-division multiplex system used by the British Post Office. For receiving, his page printers used cut blanks; for transmitting, he used a typewriter-like keyboard after Rowland (U.S., 1899); but, in five-level configuration, he punched tape with it, like Wheatstone. Murray designed a transmitter to accept such tape and also permuted Baudot's 32 code combinations, assigning those with fewest punched holes scientifically to letters and functions most frequently encountered in telegrams: what is today loosely and not undeservedly called Baudot is in fact Murray's code, revised in minor respects by later American practice and European agreements.

Murray sold his American rights to Western Union and Western Electric in 1912. To American variants of Murray apparatus was added the auto control—a device like

a telephone dial, which was probably the first to interpolate extraneous control signals into language transmission without harm. The auto control dialed control-bell signals, one to five, in the printer's uppercase *J*, printing nothing. Single open wires with ground-return were assigned two, three, or four duplexed channels, each handling 40 to 66 words a minute eastward and westward.

Regeneration of signals. Signals in transit through a succession of repeaters suffer cumulative deterioration from their original timing of transitions between the instant the electrical circuit is closed and when the circuit is opened, due partly to extraneous interference the signals pick up enroute and partly to variations in the value of circuit constants. On wires of transcontinental length and on ocean cables, rejuvenation is required. The principles of a rotary repeater, which completely regenerated signals to their pristine timing, was comprehended among the inventions Murray sold overseas. The principles were not put to work until some returning World War I veterans, who saw telegraph service in Europe, installed a rotary repeater in the United States in 1919. Signal regeneration is of great modern importance in feeding error-free input to computers.

Start–stop printer systems. Though well suited to intercity trunk lines, the multiplex was not adapted to the need for a simple, one-channel, back-and-forth or two-way printer system. To fill the need the simplex printer (later called teleprinter generically, and often, in the United States, by its tradename, Teletype) was developed and applied widely between 1924 and 1928. The simplex at first reverted to the tape-printing method of Baudot and his predecessors for reasons of cost, ruggedness, efficiency, and ease of making paste-over corrections. The tape was manufactured with adhesive on the back and passed through a hand-held wick-moistener before being affixed to the blank and severed, line by line, with a cutting thimble worn on a finger. Since this process was not popular among untrained operators, page-printing machines were furnished for private-wire use.

The electricity source by that time was being kept so close to 60 hertz (cycles a second) that small synchronous motors in printers could sweep brushes of small distributors over five commutator segments in perfect step. The brushes stopped by being declutched after sweeping the fifth-level pulse in each revolution and then restarted on the next character by a clutching signal received over the line. The start pulse was of the same duration as each of the five signalling pulses; the stop, or rest, pulse was about 1.5 times as long. In modern parlance, the five-level code was transmitted as 7.5 units, pulses, or bits. Start–stop transmission lent itself readily to being repeated by simple forms of start–stop regenerators. Today there is nothing so ubiquitous in telegraphy as the self-synchronizing, start–stop teleprinter, or teletypewriter—in five- to eight-level codes and seven to 11 units.

A 1930 model Teletype was basic to a manually-switched teletypewriter exchange service (TWX), started by American Telephone & Telegraph Company in the United States in 1931. Within 15 years, 65,000 Teletypes had been manufactured, and the name had entered the language through the press in connection with police networks. TWX service in the United States was converted to automatic switching in 1962 and extended to Canada in 1963; at the same time a speed option of 100 words per minute was offered to supplement and possibly to eventually replace the 75 word-per-minute machines. Telex, an automatic-switching service in Europe and elsewhere, originated in Germany and rapidly expanded to other countries after World War II.

Frequency-division multiplex. Though carrier telegraphy (superposition of several telegraph signals on a single carrier) had been anticipated by Bell in his quest for a harmonic telegraph in 1875, practical systems had awaited the development of components such as band-separation filters and vacuum-tube circuitry. Techniques for carrier telephony and telegraphy were perfected at the same time in 1918.

The centres of voice-frequency bands are spaced 4,000

Simplex printer

hertz apart for telephony (3,000 hertz on submarine cable). In 1940 frequency-modulated (FM) carrier in preference to amplitude modulation (AM) was adopted in the United States and later became the international standard in Europe.

Facsimile telegraph systems. In 1850 F.C. Bakewell, in London, invented a "copying telegraph," consisting of tinfoil wrapped around a rotating cylinder, upon which writing, added by a pen dipped in varnish, could be scanned by a contact carried by an endless screw. The receiver was similar, except for the substitution of paper wet with a chemical. Successful manipulation of the scanning process in telegraph offices had to wait for the discovery of substances and methods (1934) leading to a dry-process recording paper not affected by long exposures to light. By 1964 over 40,000 simple drum scanner-recorders, known as Desk-Fax, were handling over 50,000,000 messages annually. Operation required no skill, yet insured error-free copy.

The TelAutograph is a short-line telegraph invented by Elisha Gray of the United States and A.C. Cowper of England about 1895. The transmitter has two rheostats (variable resistors) varied through mechanical linkages by the motion of a stylus held in the hand and moved as in ordinary writing. It leaves a sending record, if desired, by pen on a wide band of paper beneath. Each rheostat is connected to a separate line transmitting a varying current to a coil at the receiving end. The armatures of these coils are correspondingly linked to a recording pen resting on paper. The pen thus reproduces roughly the original stylus writing in facsimile. Refinements were made possible by servomechanisms developed during World War II.

Telegraphic radio-beam circuits. Expansion and improvements have made microwaves a mainstay of telegraphy in many countries in the early 1970s. By combining wideband telephone and telegraph dependably on a single telecommunication facility, radio consigned the open-wire plant of the late 1940s to early obsolescence. Telegraph contracts with the railroads were not renewed in the 1950s, and pole lines, except on some multiconductor-cable routes, were abandoned.

Reperforators. A useful means of transmission is to duplicate at the receiver of station B a counterpart of a tape used to transmit at station A. This was done by Murray with five-level code and by F.G. Creed (England, 1902) with three-level cable code. Reperforators and transmitters in the early 1940s were placed in juxtaposition and operated as a unit. For the benefit of switching operators and as an aid in reading the holes in tape, a combined printer reperforator printed a translation either on the edge of a slightly wider tape or directly on the perforations. In the latter the tape was cut chadless; *i.e.*, the holes were not punched all the way through, producing small bits of paper (chads) to be discarded, but were punched as hinged lids. They did not impede penetration by the sensing pins but did permit overtyping.

Beginning in 1934 reperforator offices were installed in the United States, based on the switching from circuit to circuit of start–stop printer-reperforator transmitters. In the early 1940s the telephone and telegraph companies started to apply similar equipment on a wide scale to large leased teletypewriter networks. This system is described as store and forward. In both applications mentioned there is a momentary storage at the receiving reperforator from line A, cross-office transmission at high speed, and an orderly accumulation of tape at the sending reperforator on line B to queue up with other messages awaiting transmission in turn.

Two-letter indicators, otherwise called director signals, punched ahead of all other elements of message transmissions automatically to switch messages through reperforators, were in private-wire networks in 1943 and in public-message switching in 1947. Automatic switching may be said to mark the beginning of modern telegraphy.

MODERN TELEGRAPHY

Large business and governmental users of telegraph services began to demand facilities compatible with the computer and its associated machinery, coupled with the need for language and nonlanguage systems on a worldwide basis. As a result wire and radio-telegraph companies broadened their bandwidth offerings, redesigned terminal equipment for greater speed and versatility, and designed switched communication paths through a maze of facilities. New developments include coaxial cables; microwave radio; waveguides; satellite links; and, experimentally, beams of coherent light (laser).

High-speed data transmission. Analogue (continuous) signals can be converted to digital (discrete) signals by pulse-code modulation techniques in which information is transmitted as a series of pulses (see TELEPHONE AND TELECOMMUNICATIONS SYSTEMS). Digital signals are desirable because they degenerate far less than analogue signals when passed through repeaters enroute to their destination, and because they can be electronically regenerated and freed from noise picked up along the way. Pulse-code modulated signals are equally amenable to complete electronic regeneration at every repeater; so are teleprinter and data signals traversing a pulse-code modulated circuit.

Telegraph and telephone companies in Canada and the U.S., and government telecommunication administrations elsewhere, offer combination telephone-data services under trade names like Datel, Data-Phone, and Broadband Exchange, whereby patrons dial voice-frequency connections as they would long distance. By mutual agreement buttons are then operated, activating apparatus for sending data telegraphically at high speeds. Digital facilities for handling the entire call were being installed on a wide scale in the early 1970s.

Like most telegraphic make-and-break contact signals, the wave form of the electrical pulse generated by a dot is square topped, and each transition from the 0-to-1 and the 1-to-0 conditions is abrupt. A curve having such an abrupt rise time becomes sloped and rounded off as it travels along a transmission line. The more sloped the curve, the more it is susceptible to further degradation by the addition of impulse noise picked up enroute from various sources. Devices are installed at various points along the transmission line to counteract some of the adverse effects of the line. These are called equalizers, and they serve to prevent excessive sloping or rounding off of the curve.

The same type of transformation in the arrival curve occurs when a square-top pulse modulates a carrier frequency. In carrier practice the phenomenon is called envelope-delay distortion. It has a minor effect on voice reproduction in a voice-frequency band assigned to telephony but has to be carefully equalized in telegraph channels assigned to high-speed data handling. The time required for a pulse to reach its full amplitude (rise time) determines the capability of a circuit to handle traffic. A circuit is pushed to its traffic capacity when a succession of bits like 01010101 is speeded up to the point that it can no longer be properly detected and reshaped at the first repeater. One expedient for increasing operating speed is to move repeaters closer together. Some representative repeater spacings are: open-wire line, 250 miles (400 kilometres); open-wire carrier, 100–150 miles (160–240 kilometres); loaded multipair cable, 50 miles (80 kilometres); repeatered submarine cable, 45 miles (72 kilometres); broadband-microwave carrier, 15–30 miles (24–48 kilometres), determined by line-of-sight, not transmission; underground telephone carrier, 6–17 miles (10–27 kilometres); coaxial cable, 4–8 miles (6–13 kilometres); pulse-code modulated cable pair, 1.2 miles (1.9 kilometres).

Signals and noise. Pulses are also deformed by extraneous electrical disturbances collectively called noise. Lightning may induce into wire and radio facilities alike enough energy to obliterate signals. Interference in telegraph lines from paralleling power lines may occur when circuit breakers trip or insulators fail. Sparking motors, commutators, and contacts near line wires or in telegraph switching centres cause a buildup of noise. Crosstalk (interference to adjacent circuits) among telecommunication circuits, caused by proximity of conductors, can be a

marginalia: "Copying telegraph"; Automatic switching; Envelope-delay distortion

major source of noise. This effect can be minimized by transposing open-wire pairs at intervals so that one wire lies first on the left and then on the right side or by interweaving twisted pairs in multipair cable. In both cases the objective is to prevent two pairs from being contiguous for more than a fraction of their length. Wherever possible, opposite-bound transmissions are assigned to different multipair or coaxial cables.

Signal-to-noise ratio

The general level of noise may be measured and compared with the strength of signal to give a factor known as the signal-to-noise ratio. Additive bursts of noise in a circuit cannot be entirely avoided; in practice they are continuously counted during prescribed units of time, and when the count is excessive an alarm is sounded for attention.

Telegraph lines, by type. Telegraph lines are basically similar to telephone lines, and almost invariably the same facilities are used for both. The construction of new open-wire lines is being avoided because of mechanical and electrical vulnerability, but continued operation of many older lines is economically justified. Buried multipair cable is widely used on long and short hauls and is pulled through underground ducts for local runs in municipalities. River and swamp subfluvial crossings are ordinarily protected by burying. Manholes not only facilitate repairs and provide points on the lines a mile or so apart for inserting devices to improve transmission but often contain repeaters that are fed electrical power over the signal conductors. The number of pairs in a cable may run from 25 to 900 or more. Insulation is paper pulp or, more recently, the plastic polyethylene. Lead sheaths have been replaced by polyvinyl chloride plastic with an underlay of steel and aluminum sheathing. Aerial cable is made similarly; in place of manholes, junction boxes and other equipment are installed on or near poles. A typical pair in cable will accommodate 24 voice-frequency channels in one direction. Coaxial cables transmitting video signals and wideband carriers up to the 12-megahertz (12,000,000 cycles per second) range are in common use. Eight such cables may surround a bundle of standard pairs and be laid underground as a unit. A coaxial cable is made up of a central conductor separated from a flexible, cylindrical, outer conductor by low-loss insulation, often consisting of ceramic wafers and air. When used as a transoceanic submarine cable, sea-bottom hydrostatic pressures encountered make it necessary to replace the ceramic with polyethylene, which is less efficient and lowers the traffic capacity to 720 voice channels or less.

Line-of-sight microwave radio is a backbone element in the present-day, high-speed, telegraphic data transmission plant. Traffic capacity of a single microwave circuit may be 1,800 voice-frequency channels. In one application in the late 1960s a 1,200-voice-channel telegraph microwave carried teleprinter pulses, signals for facsimile transmission, broadband (high-speed) data, and special time-division-multiplexed video at rates up to 40,000,000 bits a second. Frequency modulation was used throughout to reduce susceptibility to circuit and extraneous noise. In the early 1970s satellite circuits were in daily international broadband telegraph use. Synchronous satellites, maintaining fixed positions 22,300 miles (35,880 kilometres) above the Atlantic, Pacific, and Indian oceans and earth stations dotting the globe constituted the system (see SATELLITE COMMUNICATION). Consideration was being given to eventual substitution of digital for analogue transmission, and for expansion of satellite repeaters to provide intracontinental and domestic telegraph and data links.

Satellite transmission

High-frequency bands in the radio spectrum carry major international telegraph loads overseas. Frequency-shift keying shares acceptance with time-division multiplexing of single-sideband systems with subcarriers for high-speed Morse, teleprinter (the prevailing mode), and radiophoto transmissions. Tropospheric (over-the-horizon) circuits are used in special situations. The telegraph frequency-modulated carrier is used extensively for remote control of switching, telemetering, and teleprinter communication over high-voltage power lines. Modern

submarine cables, developed primarily for transoceanic telephony, share the overseas-telegraph data-traffic loads with satellites.

Direct-current keyed facilities. The rate at which direct currents are interrupted, or keyed, for signalling purposes is measured in bauds. Steady reversals could be described, for example, as taking place at 50 bauds, 50 bits per second, 25 cycles per second, or at 25 hertz. All mean the same; bauds and hertz are speed terms.

A pair of wires connecting a customer with a telegraph office or a subscriber with a telephone exchange is called a loop; often the loop is divided into sending and receiving legs. Such legs have to operate at the baud or bit rate called for by the service. On–off keying is usually accomplished by closing and opening the circuit, whether the circuit is powered by dc or ac. Circuit loops from the central office to the subscriber and return are usually supplied with a battery voltage or an alternating current (audio frequency) from the central office. If these loops are unusually long and are operated on direct current, the telegraph code may be transmitted by reversing the polarity of the dc power, instead of closing and opening the circuit. Teleprinters and data sets are designed to be versatile in initiating suitable signals on loops. An important condition to be signalled is whether the circuit is idle and, hence, available or busy and not available.

Pulse-code modulation. Pulse-code modulation has been briefly mentioned earlier in the contexts of its digital generation and its adaptability to regeneration and repeater spacing; it is discussed at greater length in the article TELEPHONE AND TELECOMMUNICATIONS SYSTEMS. Pulse-code modulation techniques in the early 1970s were rapidly being adapted to the interweaving of multiple streams of data going directly into data-processing inputs at rates up to 50 kilobits (50,000 bits) a second and bypassing the digital-to-analogue conversion necessary to transmit digits over frequency-division telephone carriers. The growth of pulse-code modulation networks has been rapid in Japan, the United Kingdom, France, and the United States.

Equipment refinements. Most of the elaborate relays and mechanical switches formerly used in direct-current telegraphy were made obsolete by the substitution of ferrite magnetic cores, arranged in arrays, or grids. Magnetization of a core will temporarily store pulses until called upon by a computer control to transfer them to an ongoing circuit or logic operation. Such cores or magnetized areas on memory tapes, drums, or disks, with no contacts mounted on parts having mechanical inertia, overcome the drawbacks of the fastest of relays. The techniques and hardware of digital-logic circuit design which evolved in the computer field in the 1960s were being applied widely in the telegraph field in the early 1970s.

Ferrite magnetic cores

Multichannel carrier facilities. By means of frequency-division multiplex, 4,000-hertz voice-frequency bands can be utilized for teleprinter and data facilities. Guard bands between channels prevent overlap and reduce the usable band to about 3,000 hertz. For 75-words-per-minute printers, where the operating rate is 57 bauds, as many as 26 channels may be spaced 120 cycles apart in a voice band. For 100-words-per-minute eight-level printers operating at 110 bauds, 18 channels may be spaced 170 cycles apart.

Some digital transmissions (for example, high-speed data) need bands in excess of voice-band widths. Broadband facilities are available for such applications in steps from 48 kilohertz to eight megahertz wide. The latter figure has been used for digital signals in missile tracking; the former for frequently-used systems of alternate voice and data.

The terminal–facility interface. Simple relays, contact rectifiers, or modulators and demodulators (often built as a unit called a modem) are inserted between customers' or branch-office loops and the multiplexed carrier channels. Modems convert binary bits at the telegraph office into a suitable form to modulate the telegraph carrier. The digital-analogue modems designed to couple business machines located on business premises with intercity voice-carrier or broadband facilities are usually called data sets.

Baudot-Code teleprinters. Teleprinter codes have been standardized for circuits that cross international borders. They are adopted by government telegraph administrations or representatives in the International Telecommunications Union headquarters in Geneva, usually upon recommendation of the International Consultative Committee on Telegraphs and Telephones. Its International Alphabet No. 2, as amended, usually called the Baudot Code, permits countries to assign certain code combinations to nationally-used symbols and letters (such as $, £); it merely prohibits their use in international telegrams.

The Baudot Code

Domestic manufacturers produce conforming teleprinters for use domestically, others internationally for sale abroad.

All makers have produced several types. The one selected for brief description here is the 75-words-per-minute Teletype model 28 of 1953, still in wide use in the early 1970s. Its keyboard is shown in Figure 7A and the layout of its printing typebox, viewed from the front of the printer, in Figure 7B. The typebox is a lightweight member moved in steps by a carriage along the line being typed and carrying horizontal, spring-mounted type pallets, in holes arranged as shown. Any one of these, bearing raised type on its end next to the paper platen, may be tapped on the near end by a carriage-borne hammer and driven against the ribbon and paper. In its function of aligning pallets under the hammer, the typebox has two "home" column positions, shown as vertical blank spaces; the typebox is positioned at one or the other by receipt of the figures (FIGS) or letters (LTRS) signals, controlled by keyboard keys so marked. Assuming the LTRS-mode to have been selected, the mechanism that moves the typebox up and down (four positions, from the top) and left and right (four positions left, four right) will take its direction, in order, from the five pulses which arrive in succession to represent any letter transmitted.

The shaded squares represent nonprint code characters. The pallets bear no type; the hammer does no work. In the back of the printer is a function box containing coded levers and contacts, responsive to incoming characters at the same time the typebox is responsive. These levers and contacts do such things as space the typebox carriage between words; bring the carriage back to the beginning of a line (carriage return—C.R.); feed the paper up one line on the platen (line feed—L.F.); and ring a supervisory bell. The function-box mechanism can be arranged at will to carry out the valuable attribute of reading signals—*i.e.*, watching for sequences of two, three, or even more characters and acting upon them. For instance, a FIGS-shift followed by ?/ might constitute a sequence which, upon receipt of the stroke, would throw a switch, starting up tape reperforators to interweave information

From *Technical Review* ®; (top) January 1956 and (bottom) July 1955

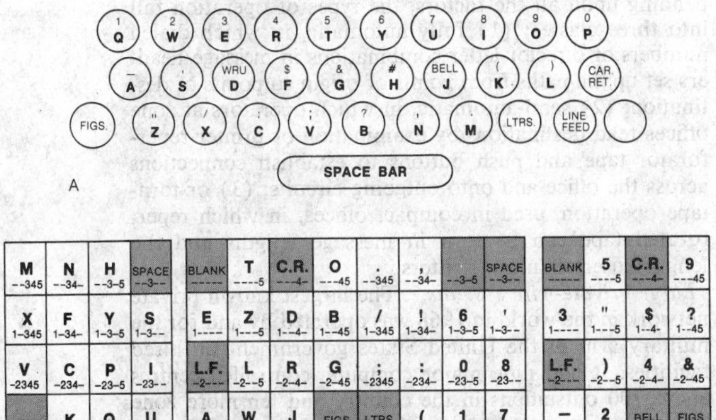

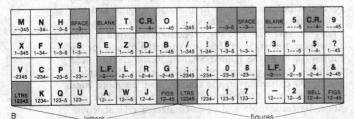

Figure 7: *Baudot-Code teleprinter.*
(A) The five-level, three-row keyboard and (B) the layout of the printing typebox.

into the traffic stream. FIGS H is often used to shut down connected teleprinters by switching off their motors. Alternatively, a two-character combination might be selected to disable the machine as a printer but enable it to exercise control and switching functions, thus giving it great versatility in programming the interpolation of constant information stored in tape or devices awaiting release. Examples are telegram serial numbers, place of origin of message, time of day, date. The function box is also a means for controlling printer operations such as tabulating, backspacing for underlining, and automatically measuring paper feedout.

An advantage of typeboxes over the typebars of older teleprinters is that special applications of any code, such as Baudot, can be made simply by changing the typeboxes and key-caps.

ASCII-*type printer systems.* The inadequacy of Baudot five-level code in meeting all practical communicating and switching needs first became apparent when computers achieved a high degree of acceptance in the early 1960s, at which time a competitive effort was made by communication carriers, supported by teleprinter manufacturers, to transmit data economically in the high volumes generated by business machines. Independent system designs found a common denominator in 1966, at least temporarily, in the seven-level American Standard Code for Information Interchange (ASCII). As embodied in the Teletype model 37 of 1968, to which reference will be made, the seven-level code is signalled at 150 words a minute (15 characters a second) from an eight-level tape shown in Figure 8. Circles represent holes punched in the tape by depressing control keys (top line), such as carriage return (CR) and line feed (LF), no

American Standard Code for Information Interchange

From *Technical Review* ® (November 1967)

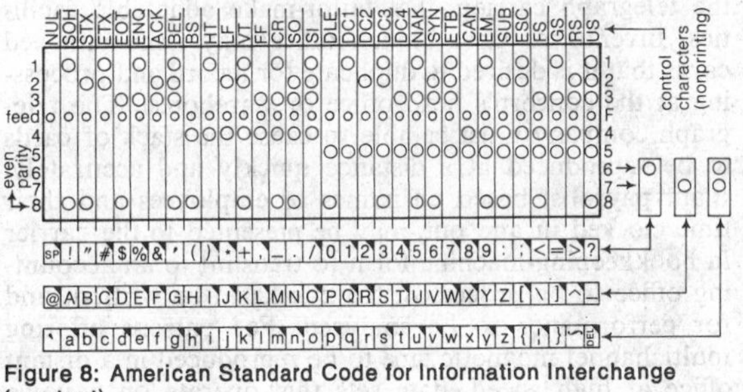

Figure 8: American Standard Code for Information Interchange (see text).

holes being punched in levels 6 and 7. For alphanumeric symbols (three lines at bottom), depressing a key, with shifts, will punch levels 1 to 5 as shown above it; levels 6 and 7 as indicated at right; and level 8 (parity check for errors) only if needed to make the hole count even. Seven levels accommodate 2^7, or 128, different alphanumeric and control signals. The typist has a four-row keyboard and typebox which print normally lowercase alphabetic letters (new in general telegraphy and shown on the bottom line of the code). A shift to uppercase (capital letters) is made by depressing a shift key and holding it there so long as uppercase is being used, then releasing it to revert to lowercase, the same as on an office typewriter. The number of units, or bits, per eight-level character is ten: seven for intelligence, one for parity check, one for start, and one for stop.

Other modern teleprinters. Several other proprietary codes and systems are in common use over leased telegraph facilities. Computer manufacturers offer telegraphic peripheral units and transceivers that produce readouts at prodigious speeds. Some that print a whole line at a time consist of 80 to 120 wafer-like typewheels—essentially 80 to 120 separate, ganged printers—lined up across the paper band. Each one is independently controlled, not bit after bit, as on a wire, but all bits in each character thrown in at the same instant. In some models the wheels do not stop—a throwback to the Hughes printer of 1855. Outputs are of the order of 1,000 lines a minute, or at the rate of 333 words a second if the lines were filled. Other systems produce copies from cathode-ray tubes, electrostatic, photographic, and electrother-

mally produced chemical papers, with speeds in the range of 5,000 to 11,000 words a second.

Error detection and correction. There are two classes of protection: one in which errors in transmission are detected and flagged in some way at the receiver for correction, the other in which errors are detected and automatically corrected before being printed or entering a computer. Complete redundancy in transmission; *i.e.,* sending everything twice and making an automatic check for identity, is simple but would be wasteful of long-distance facilities. Expedients are used to avoid it yet retain the advantages of moderate redundancy. For extreme accuracy (probability being one in 100,000,000 for undetected errors in words of 23 bits each), a code is used that involves a set of several nonprinted characters following each computer word. For many years automatic error-correction has been applied to transoceanic radiotelegraphy in the form of the independently invented J.B. Moore (U.S.) and H.C.A. van Duuren (The Netherlands) uniform codes. The Moore time-division-multiplex printer code consists of seven-level characters, each of which contains three 1s and four 0s. Upon receipt, each character is measured instantaneously for that three to four ratio and rejected by nonprinting if any other ratio is measured. On a fully operative duplex circuit, the receiver at B automatically interpolates an unprinted signal in B's transmission back to A, signifying that a mutilation has occurred; takes over control of A's transmitter; backs A's transmitter a measured number of characters to compensate for the interruption; and triggers resumption of movement of A's tape, beginning with the errored character.

Digital computers and peripheral units. What telegraph customers do with data processors is a concern of the telegraph carriers that tailor-make adaptable facilities. Inventories of a branch office may issue punched cards that it is desired to duplicate for record and processing at the concern's head office or warehouse. The telegraph company must be able to cause the stack of cards to be reproduced at a distance quickly and accurately. Plant payrolls, based on names of employees and their time clocked in and out, may be presented to the carrier in bookkeeping-machine form to transmit to an accounting office to be processed, for checks to be written, and for performance to be analyzed. For patrons offering multichannel magnetic tape to be reproduced in a distant office at high speed, data sets that operate on a voice bandwidth are furnished by telegraph carriers. There is a growing field of shared computers and contract processing, both kinds involving occasional interrogation by wire of specialized data banks and obtaining teleprinter responses. An example is stored library-book listings and current-literature abstracts, retrieved by computers upon presentation of descriptors or names of authors.

In addition to these tasks performed for customers, telegraph companies use computers and associated equipment to conduct their own technical functions. In these operations the logic and memory units of computers are employed far more often than the arithmetic unit. To telegraphy, the whole assemblage is less a computer than a complex switch. The control unit, in accordance with stored programs, moves about among the interoffice lines connected with the input, conducting a rollcall to uncover messages bidding for connections; probing the message headers for entitlement to priority service; determining traffic destinations; calling the roll of facility outlets and alternative routes toward destination; assigning, from apparatus held in stock reserve, the necessary interface units; and accomplishing memory storage, access, and transfer. All this complementary equipment may be, as required, independently programmed.

A most important component of the control unit of computers, particularly those operating in tandem as in telegraph practice, is the timing control; the techniques for maintaining synchronism between transmitter and receiver are an integral part of this control.

One purpose of installing computers in place of store-and-forward relay systems has been to eliminate that component of total origin-to-destination delay caused by

message handling within the office. Computers, by reviewing the status of all messages in storage as frequently as once a second, have cut to one or two seconds cross-office transmissions which formerly took a minute or more.

Carriers and administrations that offer public message service through computers are obligated to provide memory units—random-access magnetic drums, disks, tapes, and matrices—of adequate size to accept all traffic and to guard its integrity. The computer has no control of destination equipment, which may be busy; nor of lines from computer to destination, which may be inadequate at a given moment to handle all loads offered, even though many alternate routes have been engineered into the switching plan. Communication computers are different from others in the comparatively huge amounts of material offered memories for brief retention, from a few seconds to several minutes. For safety, communication computers are often installed as dual-input pairs—one on line, the other for standby protection against catastrophic failure.

Computers used by the several international carriers at the United States gateway connecting points with the landline telegraph companies have the versatility of computers described later under large private-wire systems. In addition they transform Canadian and United States message formats into others conforming to requirements for delivery in various parts of the world, and vice versa. They act as a buffer against slight speed differences between American and European teleprinters, and they supply serial numbers to messages so that messages may be billed to customers and connecting carriers and taken into account for international settlements in foreign currencies.

Telegraph networks. A description of the public system for the handling of telegrams is best approached through consideration of the simpler private-wire systems, both small and large.

Small private-wire systems. A simple two-way duplexed circuit joining two teleprinters can be extended in usefulness by providing for extra drops or stations en route; each drop can remain silent until activated by local initiative or from a distance. In the case of some press associations more than 200 newspapers are so connected to a duplexed round robin 4,300 miles (6,920 kilometres) long; dispatched from a head office, each newspaper can send in response to query and command and continuously copy all transmissions in both directions around the loop.

Within an industrial organization a traffic study is commonly made of loads among all offices; the busy hours and busy half hours during representative days are determined; and costs of alternative patterns of lines and operations are estimated. Out of these studies come least-cost figures for a hierarchy of branch, group, area, and zone offices; their location; an estimation of speed of service to be expected; a circuit layout; and the specification and cost estimates for the rental of lines and equipment. Depending upon all the factors, the types of operation fall into three classes: (1) fully automatic, in which dialed numbers or director letter combinations in message headers set up the paths from points of origin to points of destination; (2) semi-automatic, in which operators at zone offices read destinations by examination of printer-reperforator tape and push buttons to establish connections across the office and onto outgoing circuits; (3) or torn-tape operation, used in compact offices, in which reperforated tape can be torn in message lengths and the lengths inserted in transmitters.

Large private-wire systems. The largest known private network in the world in 1968 was operated by and for the military arm of the United States government on hired facilities. It had nine major computer-controlled centres and 2,700 outstations in the country and ten more zone centres to serve 1,600 transatlantic and transpacific stations. Its compatible and cross-connected civilian counterpart is a fully automatic hybrid network of three zone centres; an average of eight district offices subsidiary to and connected with the zone centres; finally, more than

1,600 subscribers' teleprinters and data sets in 600 cities —a hierarchy of three echelons. It is called hybrid because the zones and districts each carry on simultaneously both alternative functions of private and public networks: (1) a circuit-switching function to join facilities together end to end, point to point, to extend from a dialing subscriber all the way through to his called party, to use ad lib after the connection has been completed; (2) a message-switching function for accepting messages, one at a time, into temporary storage, dismissing the subscriber, then discharging a responsibility to establish a route (thus, store and forward) which the message is to follow to reach its destination.

In sending single, off-network messages, the subscriber dials his zone centre by number. There his equipment is put through to a store-and-forward processing computer, which has many capabilities besides switching calls through. In its memory are stored all alternate routes that messages can take. It makes interconnections with "outside" networks. It can convert one keyboard code, like Baudot or ASCII, to another. It can render compatible the unmatched speeds of teleprinters. It makes message-format conversions. It can provide teleprinter or wideband data channels. It recognizes and appropriately schedules several classes of transmission priorities, and it distinguishes between full-rate and overnight messages. It has a store-and-forward memory. It can accept and switch multiple-address messages; i.e., messages having one text but deliverable to any number of addresses. In its memory it can retrieve lists of such multiple addresses, identified as frequently used groups. It performs message accounting and makes statistical analyses.

The user of this store-and-forward private service must present messages to the computer in a fixed format, subject to the computer's rejection if incorrect. For this reason, off-line preparation of correct tape is preferred over on-line keyboard manipulation.

In a store-and-forward system it is inevitable that queues of messages should be formed in the computer's memory, each awaiting its turn for transmission to addressees whose teletypewriters are in use. The computer supervises this queue and constantly makes attempts to find the terminal available, following a mathematically determined pattern of intervals between attempts and maintaining an orderly, first-come-first-serve lineup in queue.

Teleprinter-subscribers' exchanges. Intermediate between private-wire leased systems and the public telegram service are the public teletypewriter exchanges, interconnected throughout the world. These systems are much larger than any private-wire system, but basically their operation differs only in detail from circuit switching in the large private-wire systems just described. The exchanges do not incorporate store-and-forward features. In 1969 the largest such system had 43,000 subscribers, using 75-word Baudot and 100-word ASCII-keyboard printers.

In 1970 the Western Union Telegraph Company acquired TWX from the American Telephone & Telegraph Company and amalgamated it with Telex in the continental U.S. The resulting four-echelon hierarchy of switching points consisted of nine zonal junction points, an average of ten districts per zone and eight subdistricts per district.

Directories supplied to customers differ from the usual telephone directories by embracing continental U.S. and Canada. Busy conditions en route and at the called terminal are fully exposed to the calling subscriber; hence, the number of facilities and pieces of switchable equipment placed for prompt completion of on-demand calls have reached a high mark in telegraphy through Telex and TWX. On the receiving side a Telex will operate unattended. The calling subscriber may ring a bell in the printer to attract attention of anyone present.

Characteristic of Telex calls in Europe and America has been the employment of a time-and-zone meter and clock-driven counter that is associated with the subscriber's loop and registers cumulative bulk-charge usage by the month; the clock rate in beats a minute is greater or less in proportion to the mileage zone determined by the

number called. Most Telex and TWX connections are half duplex; i.e., they will work alternately, back and forth. Ordinarily the printer associated with a keyboard records faithfully what is sent, but if for some reason the receiving operator wishes to interrupt, he may do so by striking keys at random. This will break up the copy at both ends of the wire to signify an interruption.

Three landline-system telegraph computers went on line in New York, Chicago, and San Francisco in 1969; their versatility was initially applied to Telex calls in the same way that computers had hitherto been applied to large private-wire installations described earlier. A subscriber dials the computer by number for Telex computer communications service beyond that afforded by his ordinary directory calls. If he encounters a busy condition in making a regular call, for instance, and does not wish to wait to redial, the computer, on signal, will store his message immediately and will transmit it to destination as soon as the called party's machine is free. Or the subscriber may offer a collect message; not only will the computer handle it but will bill the addressee also. The computer will relay Telex messages to TWX subscribers. The Telex subscriber may file public telegrams with the computer, addressed to nonnetwork addressees—also multiple-address messages with identical texts, whether for Telex or off-network addressees. It is estimated that in 1969 there were 200,000 Telex subscribers in 154 countries.

Public telegram service. The acceptance and delivery of regular and overnight telegrams requires the functioning of telegraph offices and agencies connected electromechanically, in one way or another, with reperforator centres—area-relaying offices—so located that each acts as the focal point for traffic originating in or destined to most localities in the area. Each reperforator office is tied in with every other by direct teleprinter channels. With a few exceptions, full duplex operation of 75-words-a-minute Baudot tape printers was characteristic of operation.

In addition to the network of facilities interconnecting area-switching centres, there was a separate network of multiple-trunk duplexed printer channels between pairs of the dozen largest terminal cities and even between a few pairs of city branch offices, like commodity exchanges. The area and terminal networks were mutually supporting as alternate, automatically switchable routes in the event of interruptions to portions of either network.

Gentex and Telex. In telegraphically compact countries like Belgium and The Netherlands, Telex lines and equipment are furnished to each post office so that separate connections may be established from post office of origin to post office of destination for each telegram as it is filed. The service is called Gentex. The economics justifying this is favourable where lines are short and cheap and the facility-utilization factor of no moment.

Operations in large cities. In the early 1970s within a large city there was often a complex of branch offices, and in such cases the hierarchy of facilities appeared on a third level, tributary to the main, or central, office. The central office had pneumatic tubes radiating underground through ducts to the branches for transporting telegrams physically in both directions. Its other ties with a branch were mainly by teleprinters and facsimile-telegram Desk-Fax machines; the telephone was used to a lesser extent. Major business customers of the public message service frequently bypassed the branch offices in one direction or both; some of them manned teleprinter or Desk-Fax tie lines with the main office; some preferred the telephone for sending, others for receiving telegrams. Uniformed messenger boys and call boxes in business offices, once mainstays of message pickup and delivery from main and branch offices, had virtually disappeared.

Special arrangements in routing reperforated traffic between main and branch offices were found necessary in large terminal cities. Not only were there complications due to house numbers on one street being assigned to different branches, but many telegrams bore no addresses other than a firm's name. Also the delivery preferences of patrons had to be consulted—whether service was to be by messenger, telephone, Desk-Fax, or teleprinter tie line.

Margin notes: Capabilities of the processing computer; Telex and TWX; Desk-Fax

The use of facsimile enjoyed popularity among customers until Telex offered advantages as a substitute. The Desk-Fax telegram had merely to be wrapped around a cylinder and in two minutes it could be transmitted or received by a scanning process. In large cities all inbound city tape telegrams were converted to page form: it was done (without computers) by a translator which could count text characters. On the first word space after the 58th character it would automatically insert carriage return and line feed; and so on, from line to line. Additionally, it would count lines from prefix to signature. If there were fewer than 16, it would insert the remainder up to 16 to feed the page blank as a standard-size telegram out of the burster printer. The burster was a device that tore the blank loose from its roll and deposited the completed telegram on a conveyor belt, to be assembled with others for delivery by facsimile or pneumatic tube and messenger. At the same time, punched tape in page mode would be created for semi-automatic switching. An operator, with an explicit route chart to memorize or consult, would push one button in a raster of buttons to transmit the telegram to a branch office by wire, or to a tie-line operator, or telephone delivery department. Complexities of this kind are within the scope of a programmed switching and translating computer; in the early 1970s plans were being formulated to incorporate them into a redesigned public telegram system.

Telegraph offices and agencies. Between 1945 and 1970, the physical character of telegraph service changed considerably. Individual customers were less frequent users, except for the purpose of sending money. For other services the customer usually used the telephone rather than going to the telegraph office to place his message. A number of conveniences, such as special holiday-greeting messages and congratulatory telegrams, were offered.

Successful experiments were carried out with equipment by means of which telegram-recording operators could send dictated messages directly into the public-message system. The message, as it was built up, was displayed on a TV-like screen under electronic control of associated apparatus. If the patron wished to change a phrase or strike a sentence or insert a word, what had appeared on the screen could be obliterated at once and the new material substituted. When dictation was finished, the operator would add (using the proper keyboard controls) the route to be followed and billing information. Meanwhile the equipment had been converting the message format to one required for switching through the network. No other work remained to be done in the office or elsewhere except automatic switching.

Other pilot tests in the 1970s were being made to link this type of operation with centralized, single-number telephone bureaus, at the disposal, toll free, of anybody, anywhere, to dial for filing telegrams by telephone as input into the rapidly evolving nationwide computer network.

Imminent developments. Modernization of the present reperforator system for handling public telegrams will involve replacing it with a complex of computer centres in all the large cities of the world. To these computers, all telegraph offices and agencies, area telephone-recording centres, and the rapidly growing, specialized, industry-oriented series of teleprinter-data networks will be tributary, ultimately creating a worldwide electronic-communication system with universal automated connections.

BIBLIOGRAPHY

Historical: H.R. POPHAM, *Telegraphic Signals* (1803); I.U.G. CHAPPE, *Histoire de la télégraphie* (1824); J.R. PARKER, *Semaphoric System of Telegraphs* (1838); E. HIGHTON, *The Electric Telegraph* (1852); T.P. SHAFFNER, *Telegraph Manual* (1859); G.B. PRESCOTT, *History, Theory, and Practice of the Electric Telegraph* (1860); W.H. RUSSELL, *The Atlantic Telegraph* (1865); R. SABINE, *The Electric Telegraph* (1867); G. SAUER, *The Telegraph in Europe* (1869); T.A.L. DU MONCEL, *Exposé des applications de l'électricité*, vol. 3, *Télégraphie électrique* (1874); J.D. REID, *Telegraph in America* (1879); J.J. FAHIE, *A History of Electric Telegraphy to the Year 1837* (1884); H.M. FIELD, *Story of the Atlantic Telegraph* (1893); I.F. JUDSON (ed.), *Cyrus W. Field: His Life and Work* (1896); C. BRIGHT, *Story of the Atlantic Cable* (1903); J.C.

HEMMEON, *History of the British Post Office* (1912); E.L. MORSE (ed.), *Samuel F.B. Morse: His Letters and Journals*, 2 vol. (1914); G.A. SCHREINER, *Cables and Wireless and Their Role in the Foreign Relations of the United States* (1924); H.G. SELLERS, *A Brief Chronology of Telegraphs, Telephones, and Posts* (1927); R. APPLEYARD, *Pioneers of Electrical Communication* (1930); A.F. HARLOW, *Old Wires and New Waves* (1936); J.M. HERRING and G.C. GROSS, *Telecommunications* (1936); F.C. MABEE, *The American Leonardo: A Life of Samuel F.B. Morse* (1943); I.S. COGGESHALL (ed.), *American Telegraphy After 100 Years* (1944); A. STILL, *Communication Through the Ages* (1946); R.L. THOMPSON, *Wiring a Continent* (1947); E.A.B.J. TEN BRINK, *De Optische Telegraaf* (1957); B. DIBNER, *The Atlantic Cable* (1959); J.C. DURHAM, *Telegraphs in Victorian London* (1959); INTERNATIONAL TELECOMMUNICATIONS UNION, GENEVA (ed.), *From Semaphore to Satellite* (1965); H. GACHOT, *Le Télégraphe optique de Claude Chappe* (1967).

Handbooks: K. HENNEY (ed.), *Radio Engineering Handbook*, 5th ed. (1959); D.H. HAMSHER (ed.), *Communication System Engineering Handbook* (1967); H.P. WESTMAN (ed.), *Reference Data for Radio Engineers*, 5th ed. (1968); the first two have extensive bibliographies.

Technical: H.W. MALCOLM, *Theory of the Submarine Telegraph and Telephone Cable* (1917); H.W. PENDRY, *Baudôt Printing Telegraph System*, 2nd ed. (1920); H.H. HARRISON, *Printing Telegraph Systems and Mechanisms* (1923); J.A. FLEMING, *Propagation of Electric Currents in Telephone and Telegraph Conductors*, 4th ed. (1927); F.J. BROWN, *Cable and Wireless Communications of the World*, 2nd ed. (1930); T.E. HERBERT, *Telegraphy*, 5th ed. (1930); F. SCHIWECK, *Fernschreib-Technik*, 2nd ed. (1943); W.T. PERKINS, *Modern Telegraph Systems and Equipment* (1946); R. ROQUET, *Théorie et technique de la transmission télégraphique* (1954); D. FAUGERAS, *Appareils et installations télégraphiques* (1955); H. FULLING, *Fernschreib-Übertragungstechnik* (1967); J.W. FREEBODY, *Telegraphy* (1959); E. ROSSBERG and H. KORTA, *Fernschreib-Vermittlungstechnik* (1959); N.N. BISWAS, *Principles of Telegraphy* (1964); F. BOXALL, *Pulse Code Modulation* (1930); U.S. NAVY, Navpers 10088, *Digital Computer Basics* (1969); E.H. JOLLEY, *Introduction to Telephony and Telegraphy* (1970).

(I.S.C.)

Telemann, Georg Philipp

In the eyes of his 18th-century contemporaries, Georg Philipp Telemann was the greatest living composer. The dreaded critic Johann Mattheson wrote of him that "Corelli and Lully may be justly honoured but Telemann is above all praise." Through his public concerts Telemann introduced to the general public music previously reserved for the court, the aristocracy, or a limited number of burghers. His enormous output of publications provided instrumental and vocal material for Protestant churches throughout Germany, for orchestras, and for a great variety of amateur and professional musicians.

The son of a Protestant minister, Telemann was born at Magdeburg, Germany, on March 14, 1681. He was given

By courtesy of the Kunsthalle, Hamburg

Telemann, engraving by Georg Lichtensteger (1700–81).

a good general education but never actually received music lessons. Though he showed great musical gifts at an early age, he was discouraged by his family from becoming a professional musician, at that time neither an attractive nor a remunerative occupation. By self-teaching, however, he acquired great facility in composing and in playing such diverse musical instruments as the violin, recorder, oboe, viola da gamba, chalumeau, and clavier. In 1701 he enrolled at the University of Leipzig as a law student, but musical activities soon prevailed and were to engross him for the rest of his life.

Early career at Leipzig

Leipzig became the stepping-stone for Telemann's musical career. The municipal authorities there realized that, apart from his musical gifts, the young firebrand possessed extraordinary energy, diligence, and a talent for organization. They commissioned him to assist the organist of the Thomaskirche, Johann Kuhnau, by composing church cantatas for alternate Sundays, and also gave him a position as organist at the university chapel, Neuenkirche. Telemann reorganized the collegium musicum, the student musical society, into an efficient amateur orchestra that gave public concerts (then a novelty) and became director of the Leipzig Opera, for which he also composed. Telemann's next positions were at two princely courts: first as *kapellmeister* (conductor of the court orchestra) in Sorau (now Żary, Poland: 1704–08), then as *konzertmeister* (first violinist) and later *kapellmeister* in Eisenach (1708–12). By playing, conducting, studying, and composing he gained the musical knowledge, practical experience, and facility in composing that were to be vital when he assumed the musical directorship of Frankfurt am Main (1712–21) and Hamburg (1721–67). In Frankfurt he was musical director of two churches and in charge of the town's official music. As in Leipzig, he reorganized the students' collegium musicum and gave public concerts with the group. In Frankfurt Telemann started publishing music that made him famous not only in Germany but also abroad. As musical director of Hamburg, one of the outstanding musical positions of the time, he supplied the five main churches with music, was in charge of the Hamburg Opera, and served as cantor at Hamburg's renowned humanistic school, the Johanneum, where he also was an instructor in music. In Hamburg, too, he directed a collegium musicum and presented public concerts. In 1729 he refused a call to organize a German orchestra at the Russian court. He had also declined an offer in 1722 from municipal authorities in Leipzig to succeed Kuhnau as organist of the Thomaskirche. This proffered position, which had been promised him 17 years earlier by authorities in the event of Kuhnau's death, manifested the high esteem in which even the young Telemann was held. (Following Telemann's refusal, the position fell to Johann Sebastian Bach.) In addition to all his activities in Hamburg, he also supplied (by contract) the courts of Eisenach and Bayreuth, as well as the town of Frankfurt, with music and continued to publish his compositions.

Musical director of Hamburg

Qualities and style of Telemann's music

A master of the principal styles of his time—German, Italian, and French—he could write with ease and fluency in any of them and often absorbed influences of Polish and English music. He composed equally well for the church as for opera and concerts. His music was natural in melody, bold in harmonies, buoyant in rhythm, and beautifully instrumentated. Profound or witty, serious or light, it never lacked quality or variety. Telemann's printed compositions number more than 50 opuses, among them (counting each as one item) the famous collection *Musique de table* (published in 1733; containing 3 orchestral suites, 3 concerti, 3 quartets, 3 trios, and 3 sonatas); the first music periodical, *Der getreue Music-Meister* (1728–29; containing 70 compositions); *Der harmonische Gottesdienst* (1725–26; 72 church cantatas); and 36 fantasias for harpsichord.

Except for a brief journey to France (1737–38), where he was enthusiastically received, Telemann never left Germany. He married twice and had eight sons and three daughters. His first wife died young in childbirth; his second wife absconded with a Swedish officer, leaving Telemann with a debt of 3,000 taler. Apart from being a prolific composer, he was also a keen writer; his two autobiographies of 1718 and 1739 are comparatively well documented. He published a long poem after his first wife's death, and many words in his vocal compositions came from his own pen. Especially noteworthy came Telemann's many prefaces to collections of his music, which contain a great amount of practical advice on how his compositions (as well as those of his contemporaries) should be performed. A friend of Bach and Handel, he was godfather to Bach's son Carl Philipp Emanuel, who succeeded as musical director of Hamburg after Telemann's death on June 25, 1767, at the age of 86.

The multiplicity of Telemann's activities and the great number of his compositions are remarkable, indeed. In his lifetime he was most admired for his church compositions. These vary from small cantatas, suitable for domestic use or for use in churches with limited means, to large-scale works for soloists, chorus, and orchestra. His secular vocal music also has a wide range, from simple strophic songs to the dramatic cantata *Ino*, written at the age of 84. Of his operas the comic ones were the most successful, particularly *Pimpinone*. His orchestral works consist of suites (called *ouvertures*), concerti grossi, and concerti. His chamber works are remarkable for their quantity, the great variety of instrumental combinations, and the expert writing for each instrument.

After Telemann's death, the new music styles of Haydn and Mozart obliterated the older ones. And in the 19th century, when the works of Bach and Handel were reappraised, Telemann's reputation was reduced to that of prolific but superficial scribbler. In the 20th century, however, a historically and aesthetically more correct opinion has been formed, largely through studies by Max Schneider and Romain Rolland. New editions of his work have appeared, especially since the 1930s, and the interest of players, conductors, and publishers has increased.

MAJOR WORKS

OPERAS: More than 50, including *Der gedultige Socrates* (first performed 1721); *Der neu-modische Liebhaber Damon* (1724); *Pimpinone* (1725).

ORATORIOS AND CANTATAS: *Der Tag des Gerichts* (1762); *Ino* (1766); *Die Tageszeiten; Der Tod Jesu; Die Auferstehung Christi; Seliges Erwägen*, 46 Passions.

INSTRUMENTAL: *Musique de table*, productions 1–3 (published 1733); innumerable concerti, suites, quartets, and sonatas, for varying instrumental combinations.

BIBLIOGRAPHY. MARTIN RUHNKE, "G.P. Telemann," in *Die Musik in Geschichte und Gegenwart* (1966), a condensed, but the best informed report on Telemann's life and works (in German); WOLF HOBOHM, "Verzeichnis des Telemann-Schrifttums," in *Beiträge zu einem neuen Telemannbild*, pp. 83–95 (1963), a good compilation of the major books and articles on Telemann; WERNER MENKE, *Das Vokalwerk Georg Philipp Telemann's Überlieferung und Zeitfolge* (1942), a survey of Telemann's vocal compositions; MAX SCHNEIDER, preface to vol. 28 of *Denkmäler Deutscher Tonkunst* (1907), the first Telemann biography of the 20th century, also containing Telemann's autobiographies of 1718 and 1739; ROMAIN ROLLAND, *Voyage musical aux pays du passé*, 2nd ed. (1920; Eng. trans., *A Musical Tour Through the Land of the Past*, 1922); ERICH VALENTIN, *Georg Philipp Telemann* (1952), a revised version of the author's biography of 1931 (in German); RICHARD PETZOLDT, *Georg Philipp Telemann: Leben und Werk* (1967), so far the most extensive Telemann biography (in German); MARTIN RUHNKE, "Relationships Between the Life and the Works of Georg Philipp Telemann," *The Consort*, 24:271–279 (1967); ALAN THALER, "Der Getreue Music-Meister: A 'Forgotten' Periodical," *ibid.*, pp. 280–293.

(W.G.B.)

Telemetry

Telemetry, as a name, designates a highly automated communications process by which measurements are made and other data connected at remote or inaccessible points and transmitted to receiving equipment for monitoring, display, and recording. Originally the information was sent over wires; modern telemetry more commonly uses radio transmission. Basically, the process is the same in either case. Among the major applications are monitoring electric-power plants, gathering meteorological data, and monitoring manned and unmanned space flights.

History. The original telemetry systems were termed supervisory because they were used to monitor electric-power distribution. In the first such system, installed in Chicago in 1912, telephone lines were used for transmitting data on the operation of a number of electric-power plants to a central office. Such systems spread to other fields besides power networks and underwent extensive improvements, culminating in the introduction in 1960 of the so-called interrogation–reply principle, a highly automated arrangement in which the transmitter–receiver facility at the measuring point automatically transmits needed data only on being signalled to do so. The technique is applied extensively throughout the world in such fields as oil-pipeline monitor-control systems and oceanography, in which a network of buoys transmits information on demand to a master station (see illustration).

By courtesy of Serck Controls

Master station control position and mimic diagram for pipeline supervisory telemetry scheme. Two logging typewriters are on the desk.

Aerospace telemetry

Aerospace telemetry dates from the 1930s, with the development of the balloon-borne radiosonde, a device that automatically measures such meteorological data as temperature, barometric pressure, and humidity and that sends the information to an earth station by radio.

Aerospace telemetry for rockets and satellites was inaugurated with the Soviet satellite Sputnik, launched in 1957, and systems have grown in size and complexity since then. Observatory satellites have performed as many as 50 different experiments and observations, with all data telemetered back to a ground station. The techniques developed in aerospace have been successfully applied to many industrial operations, including the transmission of data from inside internal-combustion engines during tests, from steam turbines in operation, and from conveyor belts inside mass-production ovens.

Telemetering systems and components. A telemetering system consists of an input device called a transducer, a medium of transmission (usually radio waves), equipment for receiving and processing the signal, and recording or display equipment.

The transducer. The transducer converts the physical stimulus to be measured, such as temperature, vibration, or pressure, into an electrical signal and, thus, operates as the actual measuring instrument. A fuller discussion of transducers is included in the article ELECTRONICS.

Transducers can take many forms. They can be either self-generating or externally energized. An example of the self-generating type is a vibration sensor based on the use of a piezoelectric material—that is, one that produces an electrical signal when it is mechanically deformed (see also PIEZOELECTRIC DEVICES).

One class of transducer, which includes radiation detectors, produces a pulsed or numerical type of digital output, as distinct from an encoded digital output. This is also provided by rotary flowmeters, the output of which is generated when a magnet on a turbine rotor moves close to a stationary coil.

Many externally energized transducers operate by producing an electrical signal in response to mechanical deformation. Typical physical inputs producing such deformations are pressure, mechanical stress, and acceleration.

A simple mechanical transducer-sensing device is a strain gauge based on the change in electrical resistance of a wire or a semiconductor material under strain.

Another externally energized transducer, called the variable-reluctance type, is one in which the magnetic circuit is broken by an air gap. The mechanical movement to be measured is used to change this air gap, thus changing the reluctance, or opposition, to the production of a magnetic field in the circuit. The change in reluctance is then translated into an electrical signal. A somewhat similar device is the variable-capacitance transducer, in which mechanical motion is converted to a change in capacitance in an electronic circuit.

Temperature sensors can be divided into two classifications: temperature-dependent resistance elements and self-generating thermocouples. Thermistors are of the first type; they have a high negative temperature coefficient—that is, their resistance drops very rapidly as the temperature increases. The thermistor is small and provides rapid response to changes in temperature. Thermocouples are wire junctions of dissimilar metals that produce an electrical current when heated; they have a very low output, and each must be used with a second thermocouple held at a constant cold temperature for a reference point.

Temperature sensors

There are many types of specialized sensors and transducer systems. One is the previously mentioned radiosonde system, designed specifically to radio weather information from a balloon to a ground station. Weather-sensing and transmitting elements usually measure temperature, pressure, and humidity. In manned space probes, sensors for measuring such factors as the astronaut's blood pressure, heartbeat, and breathing rate are employed. Sensors have also been developed to indicate the rate of flow of a fluid through a pipe.

Communications links. In the early 1970s, communications facilities for telemetry still consisted of either radio or wire links. Alternatives such as light beams or sonic signals were under investigation, but environmental factors such as atmospheric obstructions and local masking noises made them impractical except for specialized applications.

Radio communication is used for aerospace work and for supervisory systems in which it is impractical to provide wire line links. For public utility installations in built-up areas, radio communication is usually ruled out by the difficulty of finding antenna sites and unobstructed line-of-sight radio paths. In such cases, cables and line links are used.

An important consideration in radio links is the choice of operating frequency, a choice limited to bands allocated by international agreement. Propagation varies enormously over the range of frequencies involved. For aerospace applications in which transmissions must penetrate the atmosphere, the frequency range is 100 megahertz (100,000,000 cycles per second) to 10,000 megahertz, or a wavelength of from three metres to three centimetres.

Line links for supervisory applications usually employ a comparatively narrow band. They may utilize the whole or only a section of a conventional voice channel with a bandwidth of 3,000 hertz (cycles per second). The link may be either a direct wire circuit or one of the channels in a carrier communications system.

The performance of radio and line links for telemetry depends on two basic system characteristics: the amount of power lost over the radio propagation path or on the transmission line, and system noise, which may either be inherent or a function of engineering design.

Multiplexing and sampling. A telemetry system ordinarily must handle more than one channel of information (*e.g.*, routine measurements from an orbiting satellite, or flow rate and reservoir levels in a water-distribution network). These data-measurement channels are brought together by a process known as multiplexing, which combines the channels into one composite signal for transmission over the communication link. (An explanation of multiplexing is contained in the article TELEPHONE AND TELECOMMUNICATIONS SYSTEMS.)

Multiplexing may be based on either a time division or a

frequency division. In time division, channels are combined one after another in time sequence; in frequency division, each channel is assigned on an individually allocated, discrete frequency band, and these bands are then combined for simultaneous transmission. Finally, data may be handled within the telemetry system in a continuous (analogue) or discrete (digital) way. The latter systems are relatively more complex because it is necessary to convert analogue signals to digital form, a process known as encoding, for a purely digital arrangement.

Time-division multiplexing involves a sequential action in which samples are selected in turn from a number of different measurement channels for transmission to the receiving point. In fixed cycle selection, a switching device connects a particular channel to the outgoing communication link in accordance with a pre-arranged sequence.

With a so-called address–reply system, data are sent only as a result of a command signal: sampling is in accordance with a predetermined scanning program. The program is flexible because it can be arranged to meet priority requirements for information, as, for instance, when an alarm condition develops.

Transmission. A process called modulation is used to impress the information on the carrier frequency. Of the many design choices that must be made, that of the modulation method is among the most important. Not only does it have a direct influence on system performance but it also tends to define areas of design in both the sender and receiver (see also RADIO).

Modulation methods fall into two divisions. The first includes amplitude and frequency modulation (as in commercial amplitude-modulation and frequency-modulation broadcasting) and related types. These related types include two pulse-based methods in which several pulses are spaced out in time, each pulse representing one information channel. The two types are pulse-width (or pulse-duration) modulation and pulse-position modulation. In the first, the information produces variations in the width (or duration) of the pulse; in the second, the variation is in the position of the pulse with respect to time. In the second main class, pulse-code modulation, the information is coded digitally into groups of pulses and then transmitted.

Pulse-based methods

In most telemetering systems, modulation is carried out in two stages. First, the signal modulates a subcarrier (a radio-frequency wave the frequency of which is below that of the final carrier), and then the modulated subcarrier in turn modulates the output carrier. Frequency modulation is used in many of these systems to impress the telemetry information on the subcarrier. If frequency-division multiplexing is used to combine a group of these frequency-modulated (FM) subcarrier channels, the system is known as an FM/FM system.

Processing the received signal. At the receiving end of the telemetry chain, two tasks must be performed: the original measurement data must be extracted from the received signal, and it must be presented or displayed in intelligible form.

The extraction of the data takes place in two stages and is the reverse of the steps taken in producing the modulated composite transmitting signal. Initial demodulation produces the modulated subcarrier; this subcarrier is then split up into its original measurement channels by demultiplexing (the reverse of multiplexing). The separated signals are fed individually to their respective points in the presentation system.

Data is presented in "real time"—that is, at the instant the variable is being measured—and in one or more recorded forms. Magnetic tape is the most widely used recording medium.

The presentation of aerospace data differs from that of supervisory data. For the routine requirements of the latter, formal diagram displays normally are provided, together with printout of the data by electric typewriter. Aerospace systems, on the other hand, being experimental in nature, generally display a wide range of measurements. Almost without exception, data are recorded in a form suitable for processing by computers.

Special applications and techniques. New applications of telemetry are constantly appearing, particularly in the fields of research and scientific investigation. An important area is biomedical research, in which biological information is telemetered from inside patients by means of microminiature transmitters that are either swallowed or surgically implanted. External monitoring of body conditions can be carried out with surface transducers, as is done with astronauts.

Biomedical telemetry

Another scientific area in which telemetry is applied is oceanography. In this case, unmanned instrumented buoys are interrogated by a central master station at appropriate intervals. Both oceanographic data (*e.g.*, water temperature and salinity) and surface meteorological information are recorded, ready to be transmitted to the master station in response to interrogation.

In mechanical engineering, information is transmitted from inside prime movers (electric, gas, steam, and diesel engines) over various types of radio links to an external receiver. Information normally includes temperature and pressure.

Telemetry is frequently provided by television-like facilities usually employing a low bandwidth communication link. Such a facility is advantageous when a visual indication is desired of a process inaccessible to humans. Applications include rocket-motor testing and remote observation of operations with highly radioactive material.

BIBLIOGRAPHY. R.E. YOUNG, *Telemetry Engineering* (1968), a general text covering both aerospace telemetry in which measurement data is transmitted from an aerospace vehicle, such as a manned capsule, over a one-way radio path, and supervisory telemetry, which is characterized by address–reply–interrogation of outstations by a central master station over a two-way communication system; *International Telemetering Conference Proceedings* (1963), a unique conference that was the first of its kind to review the whole of the formative period in the field of telemetry, with its *Proceedings* covering both aerospace and supervisory telemetry; H.L. STILTZ (ed.), *Aerospace Telemetry* (1961), a text giving detailed information on aerospace telemetry; G.E. MUELLER and E.R. SPANGLER, *Communication Satellites* (1964), a work covering the use of artificial space satellites in communication.

(R.E.Y.)

Teleostei

The name teleost is applied to members of the Teleostei, a diverse group (infraclass) that includes virtually all of the world's important sport and commercial fishes, as well as a much larger number of lesser known species. The infraclass is distinguished primarily by the presence of a homocercal tail; *i.e.*, one in which the upper and lower halves are about equal. The teleosts, sometimes called "advanced bony fishes," comprise some 20,000 species (about equal to all other vertebrate groups combined), with new species being discovered each year.

General characteristics of teleosts

The great abundance of some large species, such as the tunas and halibuts, and of smaller species, such as the various herrings, have made teleost fishes extremely important to mankind as a food supply. In almost every part of the world local fishes are used as food by men at all stages of economic development. In addition to being a commercial food resource, teleost fishes provide enjoyment to millions of people and in many countries of the world support a large sport fishing industry. As aquarium subjects both marine and, especially, small freshwater teleosts provide esthetic beauty for millions of aquarists, supporting a multimillion dollar industry. Part of the interest in teleosts as aquarium subjects is derived from the great diversity of their anatomical structures, functions, and colour. Indeed, these fishes vary more in structure and behaviour than do all the mammals, birds, reptiles, and amphibians combined. Teleosts range in size from tiny gobies less than an inch long when fully adult to large marlins exceeding 11 feet in length and 1,200 pounds in weight. Another large fish, the ocean sunfish (*Mola*), reaches at least 10 feet and may weigh more than a ton.

Natural history. Different species and groups have widely varying life cycles and behaviours. Teleost fishes are adapted to widely varied habitats from cold Arctic and Antarctic oceans that remain colder than the freezing point of fresh water to desert hot springs that reach temperatures over 100° F. Usually a particular species will have a restricted temperature tolerance, often between 10° to 20° F above and below the mean temperature of its environment. In terms of physical habitat, the advanced bony fishes are adapted to a wide and interesting variety of conditions, from fast, rock-laden torrential streams in the Himalaya Mountains to the lightless depths of ocean trenches 35,000 feet below the surface, where many species manufacture their own light.

A species of teleost fish is usually restricted to one kind of habitat at any given stage of its life cycle. It may occupy this habitat throughout its life, or it may change habitats as it grows older. The various species living in rocky marine shores, mud flats, sandy shores, and coral reefs are usually all different, a diversity of habitat adaptation reflected in the life cycle, behaviour, locomotion, anatomy, and reproduction. Some cyprinodonts or killifishes, for example, confined to annual ponds in Africa and South America, live only the few months during the rainy season that their ponds retain water. They hatch from eggs buried in the mud, grow up, lay their own eggs in the mud in the short space of four to eight months. Such fishes are known as annuals. Others, such as the Pacific salmon, hatch from eggs laid in the gravel of cool, temperate zone streams, spend their first year growing in the streams, then enter the sea to grow and migrate for two, three, or four years, finally returning to the streams where they first grew up. There they lay their eggs and die. Such fishes, spawning in fresh water and living most of their lives in the ocean, are called anadromous.

Reproductive behaviour

Many freshwater and marine teleosts lay eggs on rocks or aquatic plants, the male and sometimes the female defending the eggs and even the young against predators. Many of these fishes will live two, three, or four years or more, usually spawning in the spring in temperate regions and in the rainy season in the tropics. There are large numbers of teleosts, especially those in the ocean, whose breeding habits are unknown. Most fishes lay numerous eggs, often simply scattering them over plants or in the open ocean, where they provide food for many organisms, only a few young surviving to adulthood. Most offshore marine teleosts lay planktonic (free-floating) eggs, whereas most freshwater fishes lay demersal eggs; i.e., eggs that sink to the bottom. Some teleosts, such as certain of the perchlike African cichlids, some catfishes, and some marine fishes (e.g., cardinal fishes) are oral brooders, the male or female incubating the eggs in its mouth.

Some fishes, for example, some of the sea perches (Serranidae), are functional hermaphrodites, one individual producing both sperm and eggs. Self-fertilization is evidently possible in some cases, but more often the fish plays the male and female roles alternately. In some species an individual is a male during the early part of its adult life and a female later.

About a dozen families of teleosts produce living young. In some the eggs are abundantly supplied with yolk and merely hatch in the ovary (ovoviviparous), in others the eggs have little yolk, the young hatch at a relatively undeveloped state and are nourished by a placenta-like structure of the ovary (viviparous).

The behaviour of teleosts is as varied as their other attributes. Some oceanic fishes travel in close-ordered schools, seemingly responding to predation from larger fishes almost as a single organism. Larger, predatory fishes are usually solitary and hunt or wait for prey alone. Many marine shore and freshwater fishes establish territories during the breeding season, and some may travel in relatively loose schools or shoals when not breeding. Many kinds of teleosts enter into symbiotic relationships with other species of fishes and organisms, for example, a small, blind goby along the California coast lives together with a shrimp in the shrimp's cavelike tubular dwelling. The shrimp carries food to the goby while the goby keeps the shrimp's burrow clean. Many species of wrasse pick parasites from larger fishes, even entering the mouths of these fishes to clean the gill chambers. On the other hand, in South America some small catfishes, one to four inches

long, appear to be parasitic on certain other species of catfishes that reach lengths of over eight feet. The smaller fishes enter the mouths of the larger catfishes and feed on gill tissue. Unfortunately, little is known about the behaviour of most teleosts, but study of the details of their behaviour has been greatly increased in the last several decades.

Form and function. Defining teleost fishes by functional morphology is hard, for they have evolved into many diverse shapes; but if a relatively simple teleost, a trout, is examined, its basic swimming motion can be determined. Forward motion is provided by bending of the body and caudal fin; waves of muscular action pass from the head to the tail, pushing the sides of the body and tail against the water and forcing the fish forward. The structure of the tail and the efficiency of the swimming mechanism is the prime character that distinguishes teleosts from other, "lower," fishes. The dorsal fin and the anal fin (a ventral median fin) are used partly to aid in stability and in turning, and partly in forward locomotion. The paired pelvic or ventral fins and the paired pectoral fins behind the head are used to help stabilize the body and to turn the fish. The fusiform shape of the trout reduces the turbulence and drag of water flowing over the fish's body, offering least resistance to the water.

Locomotion

The head of the fish must be adapted for feeding, breathing, and detecting prey and enemies. At the same time it must be relatively streamlined, offering as little resistance to the water as possible. The head of a trout is well formed for these functions by being fusiform but expandable, where necessary, to take in food and water. The fish forces the water in one direction, into the mouth, over the gills, and out the gill slits. Back flow is prevented by valves at the mouth and by the gill covers. The fish, however, can eject undesirable particles and water out the mouth by special action. The teleost head is efficient in having eyes and organs for the sense of smell located in optimum spots for seeing and smelling food. At the same time these organs offer little resistance to water flowing over the head.

For a classification of teleosts see the article FISH.

BIBLIOGRAPHY. For references to the literature on teleostei, see the bibliographies for the article FISH and for the articles on the individual teleost orders.

(S.H.W.)

Telephone and Telecommunications Systems

The term telephone (from the Greek roots *tēle*, "far," and *phonē*, "sound") was first used to describe any apparatus for conveying sound to a distant point. Specifically, the word was applied as early as 1796 to a megaphone, and not long afterward to a speaking tube. The name string telephone was given some years after its invention (1667) to a device in which vibrations in a diaphragm caused by voice or sound waves are transmitted mechanically along a string or wire to a similar diaphragm that reproduces the sound. Still later, devices employing electric currents to reproduce at a distance the mere pitch of musical sounds were called telephones. Nowadays, the name is assigned almost exclusively to apparatus for reproducing articulate speech and other sounds at a distance through the medium of electric waves. The term telephony covers the entire art and practice of electrical speech transmission, including the many systems, accessories, and operating methods used for this purpose. Telecommunications broadens the concept still further to cover all types of communication, including television data, teletypewriter, and facsimile.

This article is divided into the following sections:

III. Telecommunications networks
    Telephone networks
    Data-message networks
IV. Future trends in communications

I. History

The essential elements necessary for the telephone were available at least a third of a century before Alexander Graham Bell's patent was granted in March 1876. The concept of sound as a vibration was understood at the beginning of the 19th century, as was the fact that the vibration could be transferred to solid bodies. Michael Faraday in 1831 showed how the vibrations of a piece of iron or steel could be converted into electrical pulses. Though science and technology by that time had reached the point that all that needed to be known for the invention of the telephone was known, more than 40 years were to pass before the telephone was actually to appear.

What was needed was an entrepreneur who could foresee the applications for such a device. Why it took so long for such a person to appear is a question that can be only partially answered by suggesting that it may have been because the social need was not great enough. Though it could be expected that a few persons were experimenting with the idea in the intervening period, in fact there were very few. In the 1820s an English scientist, Charles Wheatstone, demonstrated that musical sounds could be transmitted through metallic and glass rods. By the time he had become involved with the telegraph in the late 1830s, however, he had abandoned the earlier line of investigation and apparently never attempted to connect the two fields. Charles Bourseul of France seems to have been the first to suggest a means for transmitting sounds electrically by means of a diaphragm making and breaking contact with an electrode. There is, however, no evidence that he ever did more than contemplate its possibilities. Other inventors similarly failed to appreciate the potential of instruments they had designed, and Bell, in 1875, appears to have been the first to understand not only that the electrical transmission of voice was possible but that it was commercially practical as well.

DEVELOPMENT OF THE TELEPHONE

Operating principles. The principles of the telephone are the same today as they were in the 19th century. The voice vibrates the air, which in turn vibrates a diaphragm. The motion of the diaphragm produces a corresponding vibration in an electric current. In the ordinary modern telephone, the diaphragm presses against an assembly of carbon particles and causes their electrical resistance to vary, so that an electric current flowing through the particles is altered and fluctuates in accord with the pressure on the particles. At the receiver, the current flows through an electromagnet. As the power of this magnet fluctuates, so does its attraction for an adjacent steel diaphragm. The diaphragm vibrates, moving the air and producing sound.

Other methods of telephone construction are possible, and several were actually considered in the 19th century.

In 1861 Philipp Reis, a German schoolteacher, designed several instruments for the transmission of sound. In them, a contact in an electrical circuit was established between a metal point and a metal strip resting on a membrane in the transmitter (Figure 1). It was Reis's theory that as the membrane vibrated the metal point would bounce up and down, producing intermittent contact and intermittent current, synchronous with the vibrations, and that, furthermore, the height of the bounce, the force of its return, and the size of the current pulse would vary with the intensity of the sound. Thus, he expected that something of the quality as well as the intensity of the sound would be conveyed. Reis's receiver consisted of an iron needle surrounded by a coil and resting on a sounding box. It was designed to operate on the principle of magnetostriction (a phenomenon in which the length of a metal rod varies as the magnetic field through it varies). It had been known since 1837 that an interrupted current would produce corresponding "ticks" in such a device. Reis believed that simple musical tones could be transmitted by the apparatus—which he called a tele-

Work of Philipp Reis

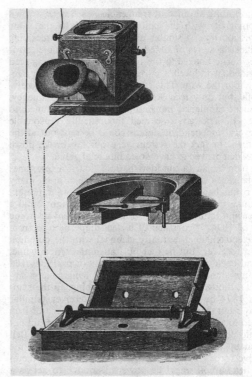

Figure 1: Contemporary sketch of early Philipp Reis telephone transmitter (top) and magnetostriction receiver (bottom). Cut-away view of transmitter in centre shows electrical contact points (see text).
By courtesy of the Smithsonian Institution

phone—and such demonstrations with his instruments were common. In addition, however, there were several reports of successful speech transmission. These reports were subsequently discounted in court cases upholding the Bell patent, largely because it was recognized that speech transmission would be impossible if the instruments operated as Reis believed they did. It is a fact, however, that if the sound entering a Reis transmitter is not too strong, contact between the metal point and the metal strip will not be broken. Instead, the pressure of the former on the latter will fluctuate with the sound, causing fluctuations in the electrical resistance and therefore in the current. Similarly, the receiver will respond to continuously fluctuating as well as to intermittent currents (but not by magnetostriction). The sensitivity, however, is extremely low, so low that it is not unreasonable to question the validity of the limited testimony regarding successful voice transmission in the 1860s.

There is no evidence that Reis himself thought of his devices as more than "philosophical toys," good for lecture demonstrations to illustrate the nature of sound. He authorized their reproduction, and numerous copies were sold for this purpose. No one apparently tried to coax any more out of them.

In the period 1872–75 inventors Elisha Gray and Alexander Graham Bell, both working in the United States, developed a number of ideas and instruments that were strikingly similar. Gray, who had been placed at an early age on his own resources, worked his way through three years at Oberlin College and by 1870 was fairly well-known and moderately successful as an electrical inventor, primarily in the field of telegraphy. Bell's education stopped after one year at the University of Edinburgh. Although he was well-read in many subjects, his knowledge of electricity was virtually nonexistent at the time his family emigrated to Canada, in 1870, for his health.

Interested in telegraphy, Bell attempted to solve a problem that had attracted many inventors: that of sending several telegraph messages over the same wire at the same time. He approached the problem through acoustics, and Gray approached the same problem through electricity. Each arrived at the concept of a harmonic telegraph, the transmitter of which consisted of a series of metallic

Early instruments of Gray and Bell

reeds, vibrating at different frequencies, each near its own electromagnet, with the coils all attached to the same transmission line. A similar arrangement at the receiving end placed a series of tuned reeds near a set of electromagnets, each hooked to the line. When transmitting reed A vibrated, it induced a current of a corresponding frequency into the wire. This current went to all the receiving coils, but only reed A, tuned to the same frequency, responded. Similarly, transmitting reed B was tuned to receiver B. Though it seemed theoretically reasonable that several independent signals could be sent out at the same time, in fact the system very quickly broke down and the idea proved to have no commercial value.

Both men began to consider the fact that if a few tones could be sent over a wire at the same time, a great many tones could be transmitted, enough indeed to represent the human voice. Gray understood how he might build a receiver and immediately constructed such a device in the spring of 1874. It consisted of a steel diaphragm in front of an electromagnet, virtually identical with the common modern receiver. But he had no transmitter. Meanwhile, Bell had been considering the possibility of multiple-reed transmitters and receivers (many tuned reeds near a single coil), though he had constructed nothing. In the summer of 1874 he conceived a membrane receiver (similar to Gray's but using a skin membrane with a piece of iron attached to the centre). Having no transmitter, he did not construct the device. In the spring of 1875, however, Bell was led by his telegraph experiments to believe that the inductive force from a piece of iron on a vibrating membrane near a coil might be powerful enough to act as a transmitter, and that his receiver might be sensitive enough to produce the desired effect. In June his assistant, Thomas Watson, constructed two identical instruments, one to be used as a transmitter, one as a receiver. The experiment was performed but failed (it probably would have worked if Bell's surroundings had been quieter). Bell temporarily abandoned the telephone to attend to his financial needs, but he remained convinced he was on the right track. By the end of the year he was writing patent specifications.

That same autumn Gray developed a transmitter in which a moving membrane caused one rod to move near another in water to which a small amount of acid had been added to make it electrically conducting (Figure 2).

By courtesy of the Smithsonian Institution

Figure 2: Photograph of Elisha Gray's telephone receiver (left) and transmitter (right). The container for acidulated water and the vertical rod connected to the diaphragm are visible in the transmitter photograph (see text).

As the distance between the rods changed, so did the electrical resistance, and thus the current in the circuit. Apparently Gray did not attempt to test his device. He did prepare a description to be filed at the Patent Office as a caveat, or "notice of invention." The caveat was filed on February 14, 1876. Bell, meanwhile, had completed his specifications and had them notarized in Boston on January 20. They were filed, as a patent application, on February 14.

At this point, neither man had successfully transmitted speech. In some ways Gray was closer to a solution: he used a metal diaphragm that was considerably more efficient than Bell's skin membrane, and he had designed a variable-resistance transmitter. Seemingly as an afterthought Bell had inserted a variable-resistance clause in his patent application; his main emphasis, however, was on the induction device. Gray apparently lost confidence. Perhaps he was convinced that Bell had beaten him; or perhaps he was still unable to see the potential of the idea. In any case, he did virtually nothing to develop his work further in the next critical years.

Bell, on the other hand, clearly felt the goal was at hand. On March 10, 1876 (three days after the patent was issued), he successfully transmitted words using a variable-resistance transmitter formed by a metal rod attached to a membrane, the top of the rod dipped into acidified water. The receiver was a damped reed (damped by holding it against the ear) of one of his telegraphic tuned membranes. Experiments using other variable-resistance transmitters followed, without success. By April he had reverted to his old induction transmitter and found that with some modifications it worked well enough to be demonstrated, most noticeably at the Centennial celebration in Philadelphia in June (Figure 3).

By courtesy of the Smithsonian Institution

Figure 3: An early Bell induction instrument, successfully demonstrated in June 1876. The instrument could be used either as a transmitter or as a receiver. Voice currents flow through the cylindrical coil (centre).

The device was still not efficient enough for public use, and it took Bell and Watson the remainder of the year to make it so. The major improvement during that time was substitution of a steel diaphragm for the skin membrane. Commercialization began early in 1877.

Bell's patent claims were granted by the U.S. courts in the broadest possible manner to cover the principle of speech transmission by electricity. Elsewhere they were restricted to the special devices.

There were, of course, other claimants, such as Elisha Gray. But regardless of the merits of particular claims, it is clear that as an innovator and entrepreneur Bell was virtually alone in recognizing the commercial potential of the telephone.

Immediately after the introduction of the commercial telephone, two things became obvious: that the transmitter was its weakest link and that it would be profitable to develop a better one. Apparently it was also obvious that a variable-resistance device, preferably using some form of carbon, represented the best direction in which to go. Carbon-resistance transmitters were soon developed by several inventors, with Thomas Edison eventually winning the basic patent rights. By 1878, Edison transmitters, essentially the same as modern devices, were being used commercially.

Other methods. A new type of receiver was invented by Edison in 1878 to avoid interference with the Bell patent in England. In his device a metal stylus rested lightly on a chalk drum, and the transmitted current flowed from stylus to drum as the drum was rotated by hand. Fluctuation in the current caused variations in the frictional resistance between the two components, resulting in corresponding variations in sound that could be heard distinctly. This receiver, in combination with Edison's carbon transmitter, was called his "loud speaking" telephone. Its use was short-lived, however, since the Edison and Bell interests in England soon joined forces, henceforth relying on the Bell induction receiver and the Edison carbon transmitter.

Still another method of transmitting sound electrically was developed in 1878 when A.E. Dolbear, a professor of physics, devised a transmitter in which the diaphragm was one plate of a small battery. When it vibrated, so did the voltage of the battery and the current in the circuit. In a separate arrangement Dolbear designed a receiver with metal plates in the form of a capacitor. The fluctuating current caused one plate to vibrate, producing sound. Dolbear's devices were not competitive as telephone instruments, though the capacitor principle proved valuable in some microphone designs in the 20th century.

Patents. Since the Bell patent, No. 174,465, is often called the most valuable ever issued in the U.S., a brief look at its history is appropriate. In 1877 Bell offered to sell it to Western Union for $100,000; Western Union instead bought the Gray, Edison, and other patents and moved to develop its own telephone network. Suit for infringement was brought by the Bell Company in 1878. In due course Western Union decided to capitulate, obtaining 20 percent of the profit made by the Bell Company on the rental of telephone instruments and relinquishing their own patents. Subsequent court cases in the United States pitted Bell against claims made for several other inventors. A number of these cases were joined together in an appeal to the Supreme Court. In a 4–3 decision in 1893, the Court upheld Bell's claims in the very broad scope mentioned earlier.

Networks. Although to some extent the commercial development of the telegraph could serve as a guide, there were many special problems in the path of the telephone. One of the most formidable arose from the fact that instead of a single terminal in each town, there were many, and each had to be connected to any of the others at a moment's notice. Obviously, the lines had to be brought together at one or more common points where connections could be made. The first commercial telephone switchboard was placed in service in New Haven, Connecticut, in January 1878. It served 21 telephones and consisted of a series of switches so mounted that the various lines could be interconnected. There now existed microphone and receiver, and the wires and switching mechanism necessary to hook them together. There also existed a large number of people who were ready to accept the idea that these new devices were useful to them.

First commercial switchboard

19th-century telephony. Within a very short time after its introduction, telephony was a sophisticated system, capable of connecting moderately large numbers of users over relatively short distances. As a result it is perhaps not surprising that expansion of its uses should have been so rapid, though this is as much a testimony to the energy of the system's promoters as it is to its mechanical and electrical completeness. By March 1880, there were 138 exchanges in operation in the United States, with 30,000 subscribers. By 1887, only a decade after the commercial introduction of the telephone, there were 743 main and 444 branch exchanges connecting over 150,000 subscribers with about 146,000 miles (235,000 kilometres) of wire. Developments in other countries were also rapid, and by 1887 the number of subscribers in Canada was over 12,000, in the United Kingdom 26,000, in Germany 22,000, Sweden 12,000, France 9,000, Italy 9,000, and Russia 7,000.

Some attempts were made to expand the telephone to other uses. Most notable were systems of wired broadcasting, introduced experimentally as early as 1881 and commercially in the 1890s. In the experimental arrangement, microphones were placed on a concert stage in Paris, while in a nearby room receivers (the transmission was stereophonic, consisting of two channels) were provided for listening. Commercially wired broadcasting was most highly developed in Budapest, starting in 1893. By the turn of the century there were 6,500 subscribers in that city. Music, news, stock market reports, and even dramatic presentations were transmitted over the wires on a schedule of up to 14 hours a day. This system continued until supplanted by radio in the 20th century. Similar systems were developed in London and Paris.

LONG-DISTANCE TELEPHONY

As soon as distances of more than local extension were attempted, problems arose and produced a variety of ingenious products and procedures.

Hard-drawn copper wire, the first of these innovations, was stronger than ordinary copper wire and was a better conductor of electricity than the steel wire commonly in use. After a long-distance test between Boston and New York in 1883 proved its worth, hard-drawn copper became the standard material for overhead wire lines.

Development of strong copper wire

Underground cables, important in the cities where mazes of telephone poles and wires were becoming a hazard, were also essential in crossing rivers, lakes, and oceans. Experiments performed in the 1880s led to the widespread use of dry-core cable in the 1890s. The value of the dry core (in which each wire conductor was surrounded by paper and air and the bundle of wires enclosed in a watertight cover) was that it improved the transmission properties of the cable.

It was soon found that reliance on a ground return (having a circuit formed by a wire in one direction and a conducting path through the earth in the other) produced severe problems when two or more wires were routed close to each other. The signals in one wire would get mixed up with the signals in the others in a phenomenon called cross talk. The first public demonstration of an all-metal (two-wire) circuit was made between Boston and Providence in 1881, but general commercial adoption did not take place until the 1890s.

The loading coil. Over the years the length of transmission had increased as various improvements were made. But about 1,200 miles (1,900 kilometres), the distance achieved when Boston and Chicago were connected successfully in 1893, seemed to be a practical maximum. The basic problem was one of distortion introduced into the signal by the electrical characteristics of the circuit. A British theorist, Oliver Heaviside, in 1887 showed the conditions under which distortion could be minimized and suggested that this be done by increasing the inductance of the circuit or line. In 1893 Heaviside suggested further that this might be done by introducing coils along the cable at periodic intervals, but he went no further in calculating precise values or in performing tests. American engineers attempted to apply the theory by using a bimetallic wire of copper and iron to increase the inductance. Work was later shifted to the use of discrete coils located at regular intervals along a line, a technique called loading. The first loaded circuits were opened to public use in May 1900. These applications were completely successful, and the principle was rapidly applied elsewhere. Line lengths doubled; in addition the coil made possible a reduction in the size of wire used on short lines, with consequent valuable savings.

The repeater. Once the distortion problem was mastered, another need became apparent: that of a means for boosting, or amplifying, the signal. Early efforts attempted to combine the telephone receiver and microphone into something analogous to the telegraph repeater. Though a successful instrument, called a mechanical repeater, was designed in 1904, it was insensitive to low input energy, and the amplification varied somewhat with the frequency of the input signal. It served, however, for a number of years, until replaced by the superior vacuum tube.

Signal boosters

Although the three-element vacuum tube was invented by Lee De Forest in 1906, its usefulness as an amplifier in a telephone repeater was not immediately realized; the first commercial demonstrations were made in 1915, when it was shown that three repeaters, or relays, were sufficient to carry voice signals across the United States.

De Forest's vacuum tube consisted of a filament (source of electrons), a plate (collector of electrons), and a wire mesh in between for controlling the flow of electrons. A small signal impressed on the grid could result in a greatly amplified signal at the plate.

Getting a signal across the ocean proved more difficult. Repeaters were short-lived, and there was no way to replace them in a submarine cable. Furthermore, many would be needed because of the distortion imposed on the signal. A submarine telegraph cable involves two conductors—one the wire, the other the water—and the effect is to blur the input signal. Commercial transatlantic telephony, therefore, had to rely upon shortwave radio at first; this service was available starting in 1926.

Radio techniques were useful on land also. High-frequency microwave radio links have been commonplace since 1946, when they were first used experimentally. The bandwidth of such a facility is broad enough to handle large numbers of telephone conversations. Even before this, however, the principle of superimposing a number of voice signals on a carrier wave was employed on a coaxial cable, a tubular conductor with another conductor concentric with it. The first commercial messages using the carrier technique were sent in 1937 between New York and Philadelphia.

Transatlantic cable telephony was made possible by the development of a vacuum-tube amplifier with a life expectancy of 20 years, long enough to make the cable laying economical. The development of the plastic polyethylene, which has exceptionally good insulating properties, also contributed to making the project practical.

A coaxial cable with submerged repeaters was laid as a test between Miami and Havana in 1950. When it proved successful, two transatlantic cables were laid in 1956; there were 51 one-way repeaters in each line between Scotland and Newfoundland. Sixteen larger two-way repeaters were used in a single line from Newfoundland to Nova Scotia. The system was capable of handling 60 telephone conversations at a time. Other cables have subsequently been laid in the Atlantic and elsewhere.

Satellite repeaters   Another means of spanning long distances became possible with the advent of satellites. The possibilities were first demonstrated in 1962 by the satellite Telstar, a low-orbit nonsynchronous relay station. Regular commercial service was made possible when the synchronous satellite Syncom II was positioned over the Atlantic in 1963. A synchronous satellite is one whose period of rotation is the same as that of the Earth; if positioned above the equator, it thus appears to be stationary, whereas a nonsynchronous satellite moves with respect to the Earth's surface. Radio signals are sent up to the satellite from one point on Earth, are amplified, and are retransmitted back to another point on Earth (see also SATELLITE COMMUNICATION).

Multiplexing. In view of the fact that the telephone was created out of attempts to develop a multiplex telegraphy system—that is, a system for sending several telegraph messages over the same wire at the same time—it is not surprising that efforts should have been made at an early date to multiplex telephone signals. In 1883 an arrangement was patented that produced what is known as a "phantom" circuit. If one pair of wires carried one conversation and a second pair of wires another, then by proper electrical balancing the two pairs could be used to constitute a third, or "phantom," circuit. Maintaining a balance, however, proved difficult, and it was not until 1910 that a successful practical method was found.

More recently, attention has been paid to utilizing the waste time that occurs in any telephone conversation. One method, called time assignment speech interpolation, was especially well suited to the first two Atlantic cables since they had been laid in pairs, with each cable carrying channels in only one direction. Each cable was only being used, on the average, less than 50 percent of the time. Circuitry installed in 1960 was able to detect the instant that each new speech element commenced and assign it to a vacant channel. The effect was to double the capacity of these cables. Recent improvements in the technique have led to an even larger capacity.

Another method of increasing the capacity of existing channels is by taking only periodic samples of the wave to be transmitted. This technique, which has long been used for multiplex telegraphy, involves a brush rotating rapidly around a segmented disk so as to make successive contact with each of the several segments. In order to convey the more subtle complexities of voice communication, however, the frequency of sampling must be much more rapid and therefore must be done electronically. Experiments in recent years have shown that high quality reproduction can be achieved, with the result that as many as 12 conversations can be carried over a channel formerly reserved for one. The technique, known as pulse code modulation, is discussed in more detail later in this article.

Switching. As the volume of telephone usage has increased, the problems of joining transmitter and receiver have become more complex. By the mid-1880s the switchboard had evolved to a point where hundreds and even thousands of subscribers could be handled. Special switches and flexible cords were devised. Switchboards were produced in multiple units with identical parts so that more than one operator could service the same telephones, and methods were devised whereby each operator could determine which lines were "busy" without listening in.

Originally, individual telephones had been equipped with their own batteries. The first central office with a common battery for talking and signalling was installed in Lexington, Massachusetts, in 1893. Among other things, the development meant that the subscriber could signal the operator merely by lifting the receiver from its hook. Beginning in 1894 this signalling could be done by miniature light bulbs on the switchboard.

Automatic switching systems were contemplated as early as 1881, when an automatic system was shown at the Paris Electrical Exposition. That system proved impractical, but a workable arrangement was patented in 1889. Important modifications were made over the next few years. The essentials of the system consisted of a mechanism that could send out a series of pulses that would first raise, then rotate a shaft through a corresponding number of steps to make the appropriate contact. Thus for the number 295, the shaft would be raised two steps, then revolved through nine large steps, then through five intermediate contact points.

The original patent specifications required the caller to press a different button the required number of times for each number, and separate lines to the central station were necessary for each button. Improvements eliminated the need for extra lines, and in 1898 a dial mechanism was patented, eliminating the buttons. *First dial mechanism*

The first large test installation of automatic equipment was made in Newark, New Jersey, in 1914; actually the system should be termed semi-automatic, since an operator was still used to accept the incoming calls. The first fully automatic system was installed in Omaha in 1921.

OTHER USES FOR TELEPHONE CIRCUITS

Networks of telephone wires were necessary to provide connections among individual telephone instruments. But once created they were then available for a variety of other purposes, all of them concerned with the transfer of information over distance. Thus lines that may have been developed primarily for telephone service now carry telegraph, telephoto, and television signals and data in a form that can be fed directly into processing devices (that is, computers can "talk" to each other over these lines). As a consequence it has become impossible to discuss modern telephone systems apart from telecommunications systems in general. (B.S.F.)

II. Principles and problems of telecommunications

Telecommunications in the 1970s centres on the problems involved in transmitting large volumes of messages over long distances without damaging loss due to noise and interference. Such problems with short-distance messages are not as severe; the signal travels over two-wire lines as described earlier without additional processing.

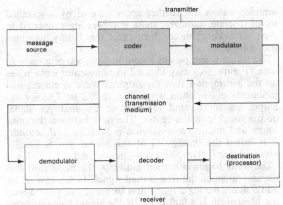

Figure 4: Simplified block diagram of a typical long-distance telecommunications system.

Figure 4 shows the basic components of a typical long-distance telecommunications system capable of transmitting voice, teletypewriter, facsimile, data, or television signals. If digital transmission is employed, signals are first processed in a coder that completely transforms their character. Typically the coder includes filtering and coding circuits that convert the signal into digital form; in data transmission this step is bypassed because the signals are already in digital form.

For analogue transmission, that is, transmission of voice and other signals without converting them to digital form, the coding stage may be omitted. Most modern TV and voice communication use the analogue system; data, teletypewriter, and many other forms of telecommunications use digital techniques.

After coding, the signal is further processed in a so-called modulator, a device for impressing the intelligence signal onto a radio-frequency signal of the proper frequency for the form of transmission to be used. High-frequency signals are usually used for radio transmission; low-frequency signals are used in coaxial cables and other wire lines (described later). The combination of coder and modulator is called the transmitter.

A receiver picks up the transmitted signal at the destination. A demodulator eliminates the carrier wave, and a decoder transforms the message signal into usable form. In many systems the decoder and demodulator are not physically distinguishable but are simply parts of a subsystem that combines both. In two-way communications systems, with a transmitter and receiver at either end, a modulator–demodulator combination, called modem for short, is employed.

In transmission of speech, music, or picture information, the object is high fidelity—that is, the best possible reproduction of the original message. In some cases, however, other pertinent information may have to be extracted from the received signal. Examples include processing of seismic signals (natural or man-made Earth vibrations) to obtain information about the medium through which they are transmitted and the processing of sonar and radar signals. Signal processing that involves the interpretation of data includes such medical data as electrocardiograms and X-rays and environmental data such as air-pollution measurements.

THE DIGITAL COMMUNICATIONS SYSTEM

Binary system. The basis of relatively noise-free and interference-free telecommunication is the so-called binary signal. The simplest possible signal of any kind that can be employed to transmit messages, the binary signal consists of two states only: the dot–dash of Morse code, an on–off signal in teletype, a 0 or 1 in binary arithmetic, and a punch or no-punch command of computer cards. Practically all voice, picture, instrumentation, and other data can be coded in binary form. Figure 5 illustrates two kinds of binary signal. Both signal sequences carry the same information; *i.e.*, the binary sequence 101,100, or on–off–on–on–off–off. Once a particular pair of signals has been selected, the presence of one or the other is de-

termined by the binary symbol, 1 or 0, to be transmitted. These signals are called binary digits, or bits. The transmission rate is described as one bit per time unit. In practice, on–off (Figure 5A) or bipolar (Figure 5B) signals or variations thereof are used.

The simplest form of modulator transmits bursts of a radio-frequency signal when a 1 appears and nothing when the 0 appears. This is the binary version of amplitude modulation, or AM (described later). This binary AM system contains a radio-frequency oscillator, designed to transmit a particular frequency only when a 1 appears and to stop transmitting when the 0 appears.

Other forms of modulation used for binary signalling include frequency-shift keying, in which a binary 1 or 0 causes the frequency to shift to either one of two predetermined frequencies (representing either 1 or 0); and phase-shift keying, in which the sign, or polarity, of a high-frequency carrier shifts between positive and negative when the binary input shifts from 0 to 1. The first method is the binary version of FM, or frequency modulation (explained later); the second is an example of phase modulation (PM).

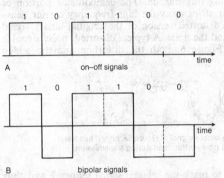

Figure 5: Representation of the binary number (101100) as (A) on–off signals and (B) as bipolar signals.

Distortion and noise. As a high-frequency radio signal travels through the transmitting path, noise and interference are encountered. Some of this comes from switching circuits and antennas; most is encountered in the atmosphere, or the space between the transmitting and receiving antennas. In addition, the message may be distorted during transmission.

One common type of distortion is called alternate path propagation, in which a signal traverses two or more different paths, usually because of reflections, and the split signals arrive at the receiver at slightly different times, causing echoes, or in the case of television transmission, ghosts. This is called multipath effect. If the separate paths are of identical length, the individual signals are in effect added together; if the path lengths differ so that they are exactly out of step, they are said to be out of phase with each other, and the result will be to subtract one from the other and reduce the strength of the total received signal. If they are in phase, they add, strengthening the signal, but the overall result of several signal paths, leading to signals that are in phase and out of phase by varying amounts, is fluctuation. Shortwave broadcasts, in which signals are directed into space and reflected back by the Earth's ionosphere, typically show fading characteristics, characterized by fluctuating amplitude.

There are many other sources of signal distortion and attenuation:

Noise added during transmission can include interfering signals in the same frequency range, interference from nearby electrical sources, the effects of electrical storms in the atmosphere, and spurious effects introduced by malfunctioning circuits. The effect of these noise sources often can be minimized or eliminated by appropriate equipment design. In addition to these noise disturbances, there is a type due to "spontaneous fluctuations" that can never be eliminated. The Sun and the Earth's atmosphere continually generate electrical energy at all frequencies. All sources of heat emit so-called thermal noise. Such

Function of the modulator

Frequency-shift keying

Thermal noise

noise can also arise within the communications system itself.

Systems design involves predicting the average effect of distortion and noise and providing maximum protection against them. Various modulation and coding schemes have been devised for this purpose, and one of the reasons for using binary signal transmission is in fact to benefit from the improved noise immunity that such transmission offers.

Although signal distortion and noise introduced by the transmission medium are common to all forms of communication, the relative effects differ in various systems. In telephony, signal distortion is a much more serious problem than noise. In space communications, however, in which signals are transmitted over extremely long distances, the desired signal energy received may be only as strong as, or even considerably less than, the noise and it then becomes a major task to sort out the signal from the noise.

Receiving the digital signal. The binary amplitude-modulated signal (explained later) arriving at the receiver (Figure 4) contains whatever noise and distortion was added during transmission. The demodulator portion of the receiver strips away the high-frequency carrier, leaving only a distorted version of the original binary signal sequence and the noise. A typical distorted, noisy signal is shown in Figure 6. Both the distortion and the added

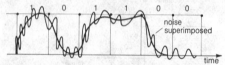

Figure 6: The binary signal of Figure 5A after it has been distorted and noise introduced during transmission.

noise tend to mask the original signal sequence and thus introduce errors in deciphering. One of the major tasks in communications technology is to develop techniques for reducing errors in decoding the message signal. Because of the presence of spontaneously occurring noise whose effects are random and unpredictable, some errors will always be made. A typical design criterion is to limit the average number of errors to no more than one for every 100,000 bits transmitted.

Methods for minimizing errors include appropriate processing of the signals at the transmitter, coding at the transmitter to make the signals and noise as distinguishable as possible, insertion of filters at the receiver to decrease the noise energy without destroying too much of the signal characteristics, and appropriate signal processing at the receiver. For systems in which fading and multipath predominate, diversity techniques have been developed: several replicas of the signal are transmitted, either in time (time diversity) or using different antennas, receivers, and transmitters (space diversity). By appropriate combination of the separate versions of the received signals, the fading effects may be overcome to some extent.

ANALOGUE-TO-DIGITAL CONVERSION

Thus far the transmission of binary signals has been stressed. If the signal to be transmitted is already binary in form (teletypewriter, computer output), there is no problem. But ordinary voice communications via telephone are not in binary form; neither is the temperature, pressure, solar-flare data, or other data that might be gathered for transmission back to Earth as a part of a space-probe mission. Such forms of data are said to be analogue, or continuously time varying, in contrast to digital (discrete number) data transmission, of which binary transmission is the most important case. In digital communications systems, analogue signals must first be converted to digital form. The process of making this signal conversion is called analogue-to-digital (A/D) conversion.

The sampling process. The basis of the process is sampling, or measuring the analogue wave shape to be transmitted at equally spaced discrete instants of time. The

sampled values are further approximated by a specified set of discrete numbers; these numbers are converted to their equivalent binary form and the binary numbers transmitted.

The fact that samples of a continuously varying wave in time (Figure 7A) may be used to represent a wave relies on the assumption that the original wave is constrained in its rate of variation with time. In Figure 7A, for example, the most rapid variation of the analogue signal occurs roughly in the centre. The time between the minimum and maximum excursion is labelled $1/B$ seconds. B is called the bandwidth of this signal and is usually given in hertz (Hz), or cycles per second.

The term bandwidth then indicates the maximum frequency range of the transmitted signal. In the case of an audio signal having a maximum frequency of 4,000 hertz, the bandwidth is 4,000 hertz. If the signal contains components at a frequency higher than the bandwidth, distortion may occur or the high-frequency components may be filtered out. In general, the higher the bandwidth, the less the distortion. The concept of bandwidth is central to all telecommunications.

In terms of this concept of bandwidth, there is a fundamental theorem that states that the signal may be uniquely represented by discrete samples spaced no more than one over twice the bandwidth ($1/2B$) apart. This theorem is commonly referred to as the sampling theorem, and the sampling interval ($1/2B$ seconds) is referred to as the Nyquist interval (after the American scientist Harry Nyquist).

As an example, in telephone practice the bandwidth is commonly fixed at 3,300 hertz. Filters are actually inserted to prevent higher frequencies from coming through. Samples therefore should be taken every $1/6,600$ second. In practice somewhat more samples are used, 8,000 per second, with a spacing or interval of $1/8,000$ second (125 microseconds).

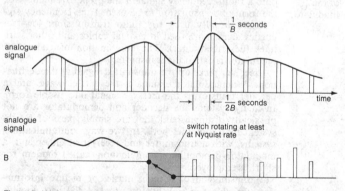

Figure 7: (A) Continuously varying sound wave sampled at intervals of $1/2B$ seconds (B is the bandwidth). (B) Conceptual form of the sampling process (see text).

Figure 7B shows the sampling process carried out conceptually. The analogue signal is shown being sampled periodically by a switch rotating at least at the Nyquist rate, $2B$ times a second. A mechanical switch is shown for clarity, but in practice high-speed electronic switches are used. The switch essentially allows a small portion of the analogue wave to go through, repeating this process at least $2B$ times each second.

Conversion to binary form. Not only voice signals but other analogue signals require conversion into binary form for pulse transmission; in each case an arbitrary scale of numbers is chosen to represent varying amplitude. For ease in conversion to binary form, the scale is usually a multiple of 2; that is, 8, 16, 32, 64, 128, and so on, depending on the degree of precision required. For example, if the problem is transmitting the temperature inside a space vehicle back to an Earth station, the potential variation is only between 9° and 25° C, and the precision required is not high, a scale of 16 might be used. This would permit using one scale number to represent each degree C between 9° and 25°, and readings would omit fractions. If, on the other hand, in the same circumstances a higher degree of precision were required, a scale of 256 might be employed, permitting the division of the 16 degrees into decimal fractions to record such readings as 15.2° or 21.6°.

In digital transmission of voice, 128 levels are commonly used because tests have shown that this provides adequate fidelity for the average telephone listener. An unnecessarily large scale is not desirable, because larger scales require more transmitted bits per number. That this is so may be seen from an examination of the encoding process. A portion of an encoding table is shown below:

binary equivalent	decimal number (or signal level)
000	0
001	1
010	2
011	3
100	4
101	5
110	6
111	7

It is apparent that eight levels require three binary digits, or bits; 16 levels require four bits; and 128 levels require seven bits. In general 2^n levels require n bits. A binary encoder performs this conversion.

If 128-level transmission is used, each quantized signal sample must be represented by a sequence of seven bits. All of these bits must be transmitted before the next sample appears. To use more levels, more binary samples would have to be squeezed into the allotted time slot between successive signal samples. The circuitry becomes more costly, and the bandwidth of the system following the binary encoder becomes correspondingly greater, requiring an increased bandwidth for the transmission medium, or channel. Some channels (telephone wires are one example) may not have the bandwidth capability required for the increased number of binary samples and would distort the binary signals. Others are limited by law to a specific bandwidth. Although the accuracy required determines the number of quantization levels used, the resultant binary sequence must still be within the bandwidth tolerance allowed.

An example of a sequence of quantized samples and its

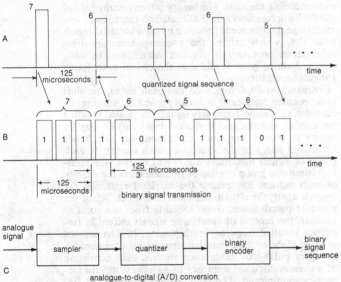

Figure 8: (A) Quantized samples of an analogue signal and (B) the conversion of these samples to equivalent binary pulses. (C) Simplified block diagram of the analogue-to-digital conversion process.

binary equivalent is shown in Figure 8A and 8B, respectively. The numbers 7, 6, 5, 6, 5 have been selected arbitrarily. Eight-level (three-bit) samples are shown for simplicity. The entire analogue–digital processing—sampling, quantizing, binary encoding—is shown in block-diagram form in Figure 8C.

The binary signals of Figure 8B provide superior noise immunity to the equivalent quantized sequence of Figure

8A. The receiver has merely to recognize either one of two states in the binary case—the presence or absence of a signal in the on–off sequence shown or a positive or negative signal in a bipolar sequence—an easier task than recognizing one of many possible amplitude levels. More importantly, the maximum signal amplitude that may be used is determined by the transmitter power. In Figure 8A the number 7 uses the maximum power available, while lower numbers use less power. For a given average noise added during transmission, the lower amplitude signals are more readily affected by the noise. In binary signal transmission the signal level is always the same, and all signals are transmitted at the maximum amplitude. The coding into binary form thus provides considerably enhanced noise immunity.

One of the major aims of communications system design has been to find other forms of coded communications signals that provide still better noise immunity. Some of these techniques will be considered later in this article.

MODULATION TECHNIQUES

Pulse code modulation. Communications systems that use digitized and coded signals are commonly called pulse-code-modulation (PCM) systems. Binary digital systems constitute the most frequently encountered form of PCM systems.

The basic characteristic of the PCM system is that it transmits signals in a form that largely overcomes the problems of noise, interference, and other distortion. In addition, the system has other advantages: (1) The signals may be reshaped and strengthened en route, since the information is no longer carried by continuously varying pulse amplitudes but by discrete symbols. The reshaping is carried out by specially designed circuits called repeaters that perform two functions: amplification and reshaping. The signals, having been attenuated (lost power) during transmission, are amplified and reshaped to their original power level and form to combat noise. (2) All-digital circuitry can be used throughout the system. With the advent of integrated circuits this has become economically desirable, and pulse-code-modulation communication of all forms—telephony, telemetering, pure data transmission—is under rapid development throughout the world. (3) Digital signals are in the appropriate form for computer processing. Sophisticated computer techniques may thus be used to carry out signal processing if needed.

A typical pulse-code-modulation system consists of an analogue–digital converter, an appropriate form of modulator at the transmitter to raise the binary signals to the desired frequency range for transmission, and a receiver.

Multiplexing. *Time multiplexing.* An additional process carried out at the transmitter is of utmost importance in the value of pulse code modulation. A multitude of independent signal messages may be sequentially combined for transmission over a common channel. In telephony, for example, a telephone signal (group of pulses) must be sent every $\frac{1}{8,000}$ of a second; yet the transmission of the signal takes so little time that a large part of the $\frac{1}{8,000}$ of a second is not used. By a process called time multiplexing, a number of signals, representing sequential parts of different telephone messages, can all be sent one after the other and sorted out again at the receiver. The process is diagrammed in Figure 9. Each of the four signal lines shown is successively (sequentially) sampled, the successive samples appearing on the common line following the sampler. In this example each signal line is assumed to be of the same bandwidth, so that the minimum sampling rate required is the same for each.

A single pulse-code-modulation system may carry several other kinds of signals besides voice. These other signals may not require a sampling frequency of $\frac{1}{8,000}$ of a second; some data transmissions may have very slow fluctuations, requiring sampling only once an hour; a great number of such signals can be accommodated along with one or more voice transmissions. In such mixed transmissions, signals with the same bandwidth are first multiplexed into a single stream of samples; different band-

Amplitude level requirements

Minimization of noise and interference

Versatility of PCM system

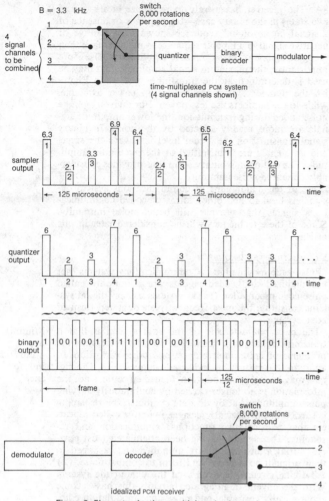

Figure 9: *Elements of a time-multiplexed pulse-code-modulation (PCM) system.*
At the top is a simplified block diagram of the sampler, quantizer, encoder, and modulator for a four-channel system. The analogue signal for each channel is successively sampled, quantized, and then converted to a binary output. At the bottom is a simplified block diagram of an idealized PCM receiver, consisting of a demodulator, decoder, and channel-switching arrangement synchronized with the transmitter sampling switch.

width samples are then interleaved. The sequence of binary signals that represents one sample of each of the signals multiplexed is said to constitute a frame.

The number of signals time multiplexed into one stream varies from application to application. In one telemetering system used aboard a meteorological spacecraft, 544 inputs are multiplexed, of which 32 are sampled once every second, and 512 are sampled once every 16 seconds. Two levels of multiplexing are thus used. In a pulse-code-modulation system used for short-range telephone communication, 24 speech signals are time multiplexed for transmission over the same line. In PCM telegraph systems 660 telegraph channels are multiplexed. In many of these applications seven-bit analogue-to-digital conversion is used; that is, a group of seven bits represents a single sample of the transmitted information.

As more signal channels are multiplexed, the number of bits per second required to represent the composite data stream increases. The bandwidth required of the transmission medium goes up correspondingly, and the high-speed circuitry required to handle the flow ultimately limits the number of channels that may be multiplexed. The circuitry limitation has been changing rapidly, however, due to advances in digital technology. Integrated circuits and smaller electronic components and spacings have been bringing about a revolution in the speed or bandwidth of operation of these circuits.

In one type of telephone system 24 subscribers are time

multiplexed into a single circuit. With an eight-kilohertz (thousands of cycles per second) sampling rate and seven-bit binary transmission, $24 \times 8,000 \times 7$ bits of information are transmitted every second. In practice an additional bit time interval is inserted after each seven-bit sequence, so that 1,536,000 ($24 \times 8,000 \times 8$) bits per second are actually transmitted. Laboratory demonstrations of systems carrying over 500,000,000 bits per second have been successfully carried out, and such systems may become commercially practicable in the near future. A system of this type could carry hundreds of simultaneous telephone conversations or six simultaneous television broadcasts. Television bandwidths are typically six megahertz (6,000,000 hertz). To sample six signals at twice this rate, using seven-bit analogue-to-digital conversion, would require over 500,000,000 bits per second. The bandwidth required is also of the order of 500 megahertz or more, thus bandwidth considerations play a key role in engineering a system. Coaxial cables, millimetre wave guides, and optical tubes are being considered as transmission media for such high-bandwidth systems.

The reception of time-multiplexed signals requires precise synchronization with the transmitter (Figure 9). After demodulation (removing the carrier frequency), the binary signals are decoded back into quantized signal form. Each signal is then sent to its appropriate destination (in the case of telephony the appropriate telephone line). Electronic switches precisely synchronized with those at the transmitter are used.

The synchronization problem is commonly handled by inserting in every frame a particular symbol or sequence of symbols that is readily recognized at the receiver. The receiver timing information necessary for synchronized switching is then derived from these synchronization pulses.

For telephone communication over short distances of ten to 50 miles (16 to 80 kilometres), a system has been tested in which a network of 24 telephone subscriber lines are time multiplexed, sampled, and coded into pulse code modulation for carrier transmission. Each voice channel is first filtered to a bandwidth of 4,000 hertz, which determines the signal bandwidth, sampled and multiplexed at the 8,000-per-second rate. Seven-bit quantization and binary encoding are used. The binary pulses occupy half of the 0.65 microsecond's time allocated to them. Each seven-bit signal sequence is followed by an additional eighth time slot, which carries the exchange-area signalling information necessary to connect subscribers. In addition, a framing pulse is added at the end of each frame for synchronization.

Frequency multiplexing. As has been noted, the shift to a specified frequency is accomplished by varying, or modulating, a radio-frequency signal. This signal is called the carrier, and the resultant modulated carrier may be shown to possess frequency components or side bands (described later) in the vicinity of each carrier. If each group of signals modulates a different carrier, the resultant composite group consists of frequencies in the vicinity of each carrier. By spacing the carrier frequencies far enough apart, the signals can be kept distinct. When the group of signals is sent simultaneously from one point to another, the process of combining signals shifted in frequency is called frequency multiplexing. It is sometimes used in place of time multiplexing. More commonly a group of pulse-code-modulation signals, each consisting of a time-multiplexed sequence of signals, is in turn frequency multiplexed. The combination of time and frequency multiplexing thus results in the simultaneous transmission of many individual signals.

The use of frequency multiplexing is particularly common in telephone transmission. Each of the base band signals in a given set, whether time-multiplexed pulse code modulation or the original analogue telephone message, is first raised in frequency to an appropriate carrier, with the carriers spaced apart by at least twice the bandwidth so that the amplitude-modulated signal may be separately recovered. The frequency-multiplexed set, consisting of the sum of all of these signals, may then in turn modulate another, much higher frequency carrier

Insertion
of
synchro-
nization
processes

for final transmission over the appropriate transmission medium.

Amplitude modulation. The simplest form of modulation is amplitude modulation (AM), in which the modulating signal slowly varies the amplitude of a carrier. The on–off binary signal sequence switches the carrier on and off.

Physically, an amplitude-modulated signal consists of the carrier frequency plus two side bands separated from the carrier frequency by an amount equal to the frequency of the modulating (voice) signal. Each of these side bands, one above and one below the carrier frequency, carries all of the modulating information. The signal as a whole, therefore, carries with it superfluous information. It is possible to transmit one side band only, eliminating the carrier and the other side band, and still retrieve the modulating information intact.

Systems are in use in which the carrier is taken out before transmission; in systems of this type (suppressed carrier) the carrier is restored at the receiver. Special circuitry and techniques are required at the receiver in such systems. Since the economics involved make it impractical to build such receivers for widespread use, suppressed-carrier transmission is not used for normal radio broadcasting but is reserved for point-to-point communications and other shortwave radio applications, in which it achieves a substantial saving in transmitted power.

Suppressed-carrier systems with both side bands transmitted are commonly called double-side-band AM systems. Systems with one of the two side bands removed (filtered out) are called single-side-band systems and are in common use for all forms of point-to-point communications (radio and wire transmission, data, telephony, telegraphy). Since they too require insertion of a carrier at the receiver, they are not used in conjunction with home receivers. These systems provide still further power reduction and a reduction by one-half in bandwidth.

Frequency-multiplexed single-side-band systems are common in commercial practice. These systems range from those multiplexing simultaneously a few telegraph circuits to those combining many hundreds of telephone circuits.

Frequency modulation. In amplitude modulation, the amplitude of the carrier varies in accordance with the information-bearing, or modulating, signal. In frequency modulation (FM), on the other hand, the frequency of the carrier varies in accordance with the modulating signal. The resultant modulated carrier has a frequency spectrum centred about the unmodulated carrier frequency, again with upper and lower side bands, but the spectrum bears no simple resemblance to the spectrum of the modulating signal.

A simple form of frequency modulation occurs when the modulating signal is a pulse-code-modulation output. In this case the frequency of the carrier shifts between two values, one when a binary pulse is present in the modulating signal and the other when no pulse is present. As an example, in a typical telephone data set using frequency modulation, the two frequencies are 1,200 hertz and 2,200 hertz. At much higher radio frequencies, they could be any pair of frequencies in the desired band. Such a binary FM system is called a frequency-shift-keying (FSK) system. As the spacing between the two frequencies (or frequency deviation) is increased, the FM bandwidth increases accordingly. For small frequency deviations, however, the FM bandwidth corresponds to the AM bandwidth.

If a continuously varying (analogue) signal rather than the binary data signal is used as the modulating signal, the overall bandwidth of the modulated signal is approximately twice the frequency deviation plus twice the modulating signal frequency. The bandwidth is thus greater than for an AM system. An FM system in which the frequency shift is much greater than the modulating signal frequency is called a wide-band FM system. If the frequency shift is less, it is called a narrow-band FM system.

Even though frequency modulation requires wider bandwidths than the corresponding AM systems, it is

employed as a modulation technique because wide-band FM signals are more effective than the equivalent AM signals in combatting noise and interference. The larger the modulation index (and hence the wider the bandwidth required for transmission), the more effectively FM performs.

EXAMPLES OF COMMUNICATIONS SYSTEMS

All telecommunications systems in use throughout the world follow some or all of the basic principles outlined above. They differ principally in the specific types of messages handled and the channels or media over which they are transmitted. When digital techniques are employed, once the various types of signals have been encoded into digital form and combined, they cannot be identified as to original source until they are decoded at their destination. The modulation technique (AM, FM) is selected after cost, power, bandwidth requirements, the availability of the proper transmitters and receivers, and the way the particular modulation technique is matched to the channel to introduce a minimum of distortion have been carefully considered. All possible combinations of the various techniques discussed are in fact in use in actual systems.

The two major communications media—wire and radio—are discussed below, with examples of systems drawn from each. Wire transmission commonly refers to the transmission of electrical signals over various types of wire lines including open wire, multipair cable (twisted pairs), and coaxial cable. These lines are used to transmit voice frequencies, telegraph, low-speed data, signalling for carrier systems (combining many voice or data signals by multiplex techniques), and television. Radio transmission commonly refers to the transmission, through the air or space, of electrical signals in relatively narrow frequency bands.

Radio communications. Because radio space is potentially available to any user, international and national regulations have evolved to limit usage, frequency bands available, and geographical limits of transmission. International radio regulations have been developed by the International Telecommunication Union in Geneva.

Two committees of the International Telecommunication Union are charged with studying technical and operating questions relating to telecommunications and issuing recommendations. These are the International Radio Consultative Committee (CCIR), dealing with radio communications, and the International Telegraph and Telephone Consultative Committee (CCITT), dealing with problems in telegraphy and telephony.

Among the regulations developed by the International Telecommunication Union are those pertaining to radio spectrum utilization, or allocations within particular frequency bands of the radio spectrum. The allocations are generally made on the basis of service type, or usage. The types of services include fixed service, involving radio communication between specified fixed points (point-to-point high-frequency communication and shortwave and microwave links are examples); mobile radio (aeronautical mobile, maritime, land mobile); radio navigation (aeronautical and maritime); broadcasting (AM, FM, and TV broadcasting intended for general public usage); amateur radio; space communications (telemetry, tracking, Earth–space communications as in satellite communications, and communications between space stations); radio astronomy; and standard frequency (radio transmission of specified frequencies of high precision for scientific and technical purposes).

These services are in general distributed in specific bands throughout the radio spectrum, from a few kilohertz to 40 gigahertz (40,000 megahertz). Each service in turn uses several of the modulation techniques mentioned.

In the U.S., for example, AM broadcasting is allocated the 535–1,605 kilohertz band, FM is allocated the 88–108 megahertz band, and television broadcasting is allotted four bands, 54–72 megahertz, 76–88 megahertz, 174–216 megahertz, and 470–890 megahertz (the ultrahigh frequency [UHF] band).

Carrier and side bands

Frequency-shift keying

International Telecommunication Union

International point-to-point communications

Fixed, point-to-point communication, commonly used for international radiotelegraphy and radiotelephony, is allotted about 60 percent of the spectrum in the so-called HF (high-frequency) band from three to 30 megahertz. Transmission in this range depends on reflection from the ionosphere, a series of ionized layers of the atmosphere ranging in height from 50 to 300 kilometres (30 to 200 miles) above the Earth. Ionization is caused primarily by radiation from the Sun and so varies with height and in time. Transmission conditions thus change with time, resulting in received signals that fluctuate in amplitude. Special procedures are required for shifting frequencies within the high-frequency band as certain frequencies become unusable due to the changing conditions of the ionosphere. Diversity techniques (multiple frequencies, multiple transmitters and receivers, and multiple antennas) are used to combat fading.

High-frequency radiotelegraph systems commonly use either frequency-shift keying or single-side-band transmission with subcarriers. The data transmitted includes Morse, teletypewriter, and other signals. The international standard of signal transmission is 50 signal intervals per second (or 50 baud). With binary data transmission one baud is one bit per second. If one of four possible signals is transmitted every interval, as would be the case with four-frequency FSK, one baud would correspond to two bits in that interval. Automatic error-correction equipment keeps the number of errors in data transmission to less than one in 10,000 bits. Time-division multiplexing is extensively used, with either two or four 50-baud signals being multiplexed to form 100- or 200-baud channels respectively.

Single-side-band systems are employed for high-frequency radiotelephony. These systems use from three- to 12-kilohertz bandwidths, accommodating one to four voice channels respectively. In the four-voice-channel system, two channels are transmitted above and two below the carrier frequency. These voice channels can be used alternately to accommodate a group of frequency-division-multiplexed telegraph channels. In one technique, three single-side-band telegraph subcarriers (channels), each carrying 200 baud and requiring 340 hertz bandwidths, are spaced 340 hertz apart to cover a portion of the voice 2,465 hertz band. Each telegraph channel is in turn capable of accommodating four 50-baud teleprinter channels in time-multiplexed form. Facsimile and radiophoto transmission is also carried out with high-frequency communications channels (see also RADIO; TELEGRAPH).

Wire transmission. Wire lines transmit communications signals ranging from relatively narrow bandwidth telegraph and telephone (voice and data) to wide bandwidth, multiplexed signals and television. The major wire lines employed are open wire (bare-line conductors mounted on poles), multipair cables (aerial cables on poles, cables buried in the ground, underground cables in conduits, and submarine cables for water crossings), and coaxial cables. Each type provides progressively greater bandwidth and hence allows more signal channels to be transmitted (multiplexed).

Major wire lines

A single open-wire pair may be used for carrier telephony up to a frequency of 150 kilohertz. In one typical carrier system, 12 voice channels, each requiring nominally four kilohertz, are frequency multiplexed using single-side-band techniques. Transmission in one direction is by means of the 40–88 kilohertz range, while transmission in the other direction uses the 100–148 kilohertz range.

Typical multiplexing arrangement

Cable systems provide wider bandwidths than the open-wire systems (up to 500 kilohertz) and hence can accommodate more voice or telegraph channels. In one typical case, 24 voice channels are combined to form a composite single-side-band signal covering the range 40–140 kilohertz. Transmission in the reverse direction in this case is handled by using another pair of wires in the 164–264 kilohertz range.

Coaxial cables allow considerably more bandwidth, ranging into the megahertz range. As many as 600 voice channels may be combined by successive multiplexing to attain a final composite single-side-band signal with the 600 channels stacked side by side in frequency.

Any voice channel or group of channels could be used to accommodate a group of narrower bandwidth telegraph channels. Up to 24 telegraph channels may be multiplexed into one voice channel. Generally this is accomplished by frequency-shift-keying techniques. The spacing between signals in the final multiplexed group is 120 hertz for 60-word-per-minute telegraphy systems and 170 hertz for 100-word-per-minute systems.

III. Telecommunications networks

Where communication between a large number of information sources is desired, the sources must be organized into some form of network, as direct connections between any two among a large number would obviously be uneconomical and technically difficult. Generally there are two aspects to the problem of network organization in a geographically distributed communications system. Since most sources (such as an individual telephone subscriber) are idle a good portion of the time, it is possible first to combine or concentrate communications traffic in a localized area. Interconnections are then provided between the various concentration points to effect the appropriate distribution of the signals. Network organization involves the design of systems to carry out the concentration and distribution of traffic in an economical manner, with a minimum of time delay.

The time-multiplexing and frequency-multiplexing techniques discussed earlier are schemes for combining signals from various sources. There is no concentration involved, however, since a channel (whether in time or in frequency) is always allotted to each source.

Telephone and telegraph networks are prime examples of well-established communications networks. They consist of both public and private systems. There exist as well many other types of data-gathering and distribution networks—telemetry networks used in the remote control and operation of geographically distributed industrial processes, communications networks for railroads, and automobile traffic control in large cities. Airline reservation systems, bank and stock transaction systems, time-shared computer systems, community antenna, or cable television (CATV): these are all examples of modern data-gathering and distribution networks.

A multitude of data-concentration techniques and various types of network distribution systems are in existence or in the process of being developed. Two major classes, the telephone network and message (digital-data) networks, will be described.

TELEPHONE NETWORKS

A telephone subscriber is usually connected by way of a loop (two- or four-wire line) to a local telephone exchange or end (central) office. End offices are in turn interconnected via a hierarchy of switching centres. The connection medium between centres is called a trunk, which consists physically of cable, coaxial cable, or microwave-radio links.

A typical incoming telephone call is routed at its end office into an appropriate outgoing trunk. With the message destination known, various alternative routes are available. Under the modern direct-distance-dialing system, five classes of switching centres (see Figure 10) come into play. The class 5, or end, offices are the lowest in the hierarchy. They interconnect customers' lines directly and are connected to other end offices and, by trunk, to a higher office in the hierarchy. Class 4 switching centres, called toll centres, lead to the higher centres.

A typical set of possibilities for routing a call between an end office in one city and the destination end office in another city is shown in Figure 10. The order of choice in leaving a particular centre is indicated by number. Thus, primary centre 1 is connected directly, via a high-usage trunk, to toll centre 2, which in turn connects to the destination end office. This would be the first choice in routing to end office 2. If this trunk is fully occupied, the route via regional centre 2 is used. If this in turn is unavailable, the route via sectional centre 1 is used. In prac-

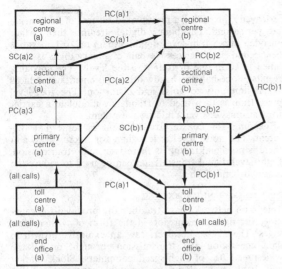

Figure 10: Simplified block diagram of a typical telephone circuit with five classes of switching centres, showing possible alternate routings of a call from end office (a) to end office (b). The order of preference for routing from a given office is indicated by number (see text).
From *Transmission Systems for Communications;* Bell Telephone Labs

Automatic switching

tice, a maximum of seven different links may be allowed.

Automatic switching using alternate routes provides large economies in connection. High-usage groups are provided between any two offices that carry a sufficiently high mutual traffic.

Figure 11 is an example of a simplified telephone system connecting a group of cities. Various types of channels

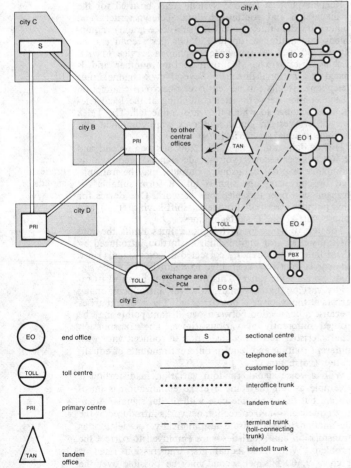

From *Transmission Systems for Communications;* Bell Telephone Labs

EO	end office		S	sectional centre
TOLL	toll centre	o	telephone set
PRI	primary centre	————	customer loop
TAN	tandem office	••••••••••	interoffice trunk
		————	tandem trunk
		– – – –	terminal trunk (toll-connecting trunk)
		═══════	intertoll trunk

Figure 11: Simplified telephone system for interconnecting a block of cities. The intertoll trunks may be microwave radio, coaxial cable, multipair cable, or open-wire lines and may utilize various types of multiplexing. The exchange area trunk may utilize a pulse-code-modulation (PCM)system.

are used for the interconnecting trunks: coaxial cable, microwave radio, multipair cable, and open-wire line. Each of these carrier systems in turn uses various types of frequency-division-multiplexed schemes to combine many message channels. In the figure, PCM indicates pulse code modulation and PBX a private branch exchange.

Various hierarchies of frequency-division multiplexing, combining individual message channels into groups, then further into mastergroups and supergroups, have been developed following recommendations of the International Telegraph and Telephone Consultative Committee and other organizations.

Microwave-radio communications account for about one-half the trunk mileage in the U.S. In these systems the groups of frequency-multiplexed messages treated earlier are most commonly used to frequency modulate carriers in the microwave range. The most common carrier frequencies used are 6,000 and 11,000 megahertz for short-haul transmission (up to 250 miles) and 4,000 and 6,000 megahertz for long-haul transmission (up to 4,000 miles). Overall bandwidths available in these bands are 500 megahertz for the four- and six-gigahertz bands (one gigahertz equals 1,000 megahertz) and 1,000 megahertz for the 11-gigahertz band. Only a fraction of this bandwidth is actually used. For a microwave system, three mastergroups and one supergroup, with a total of 1,860 message channels, are combined to form the modulating signals. The bandwidth of this overall group is on the order of eight megahertz.

Common carrier frequencies

The extremely high frequencies used in microwave transmission enable relatively small antennas to be employed for focussing the energy. Signals are transmitted line of sight between relay stations located 20–30 miles (30–50 kilometres) apart. These repeaters serve to repower the signal periodically. In long-distance transmission the receiver at a relay station converts the microwave FM signal to 70 megahertz. It is then amplified, as much as possible of the noise and interference are removed, and the signal is converted back to the desired microwave frequency for retransmission. Four antennas are commonly used at any one station: two for reception (one for each direction) and two for retransmission.

Switching and dialing. The procedure that enables telephone messages to be placed into a system and switched into a trunk is called switching. As noted earlier, a loop commonly connects the subscriber to a telephone exchange (end office). This loop (using two-wire transmission) provides a path for the two-way speech signals as well as the signals used for ringing, switching, and supervisory functions. The telephone set on the customer's premises consists of a transmitter for converting voice energy into electrical energy, a receiver for performing the reverse process, and appropriate circuitry for carrying out the necessary additional functions.

The conversion from acoustic to electrical energy is accomplished by varying the resistance of carbon granules held between a cup and a diaphragm. Lifting the telephone headset off its hook connects a battery current from the central office to the subscriber's set. This current, flowing through the granules, is varied, or modulated, in accordance with varying pressure on the diaphragm. The telephone receiver is similar in function to a loudspeaker: the varying portion of the loop current passes through a winding on a permanent magnet, causing the magnetic field to vary accordingly, and this in turn changes the force on a diaphragm, causing it to vibrate in accordance with the current fluctuations. The diaphragm moves the air in front and the vibrations are picked up by the ear as a sound wave.

The local exchange office to which a telephone is connected must make the connection between the telephone and an appropriate outgoing trunk. The connection is made by a switching system located at the exchange office. Switching systems have been classified according to the type of switches used (stepping switches, rotary, panel, crossbar); or whether they are electromechanical, electronic, or combinations. A connection must be made at the intersection of an incoming wire and an appropriate outgoing wire.

Since the number of trunks is typically much smaller than the number of subscriber lines, there is a great deal of line concentration, which in turn is possible because an individual customer uses his phone only a small portion of the time.

The appropriate connection is obtained from the number dialed in by the subscriber. A typical seven-digit code allocates four digits (for a maximum of 10,000 possibilities) to a subscriber loop in any one exchange. The exchange itself is identified by the first three digits. The seven numbers are transmitted to the exchange via the subscriber loop by appropriate dialing. In the common dial system each digit dialed sends a different number of pulses to the office. These address digits either control the settings of switches or, in more modern systems, are stored and then used to set up a circuit. In push-button dialing now being introduced, as each button is pushed a two-frequency tone is generated and sent to the central office. The resultant train of tones is interpreted as equivalent dial pulses at the central office and used to set the appropriate switches.

Push-button dialing

The seven digits allow 9,000,000 telephone numbers to be assigned. Where needed, additional "area code" digits can be assigned; at present three such additional digits are in use in the United States and Canada and two in the U.K.; for international dialing, two international code digits precede the country number and an additional digit to show the language of the party calling.

Typical automatic switching systems in operation include the step-by-step system, used throughout the world for local exchanges and private branch exchanges, accommodating up to 10,000 lines; various crossbar systems for local offices, with up to 30,000 lines; and a computer-controlled electronic switching system capable of handling up to 60,000 lines, employed for both local and toll service exchanges.

Video-telephone service. Early in the 1970s the Bell System introduced video-telephone service. The equipment consists of a 12-button push-button telephone; a display unit with picture (viewing) tube, camera tube, and loudspeaker; a control unit with a microphone; and associated circuitry. The picture signal consists of 250 lines, displayed 30 times per second on a 5½-inch by five-inch screen. The bandwidth required to transmit the signal is one megahertz. The voice-only portion of the telephone call and the voice portion of the video service use normal two-wire subscriber loops. Two more pairs of wires are needed in a telephone cable, however, for the picture signals, one pair for each direction of transmission. Picture (video) signals are switched separately at the central office to which they are connected. Because of this additional switching requirement, not all switching systems can accommodate the system.

For transmission beyond six miles, the picture, voice, and interoffice information are all encoded at a local office into a 6.3-megabit-per-second digital pulse-code-modulation signal. To accomplish this the signal is sampled some 2,000,000 times per second. Three binary digits per sample are then used to produce a six-megabit rate. Voice and data signals of much lower bandwidth are also digitized and then intermixed with the video bits.

Three bits per sample provide representation of the signal by eight amplitude levels, resulting in a coarse and grainy picture. A modified form of pulse code modulation called differential PCM is used to improve picture quality. In this system, the difference between successive amplitude samples is encoded and sent. If the signal is changing slowly, as is normally the case in a picture signal, the encoder signal is often close to zero. More of the eight quantization levels can thus be allocated to this region and fewer to the higher amplitude region, which occurs less often and only when rapid motion is taking place on the screen.

Most 6.3-megabit-per-second encoded video-phone signals are transmitted over microwave radio or coaxial cable trunks. With microwave, up to three such digital signals plus necessary synchronizing signals are sent over one channel. For this purpose, the three signals plus synchronizing signals are sequentially time multiplexed (in-

terleaved), providing a multiplexed bit rate of 20.2 megabits per second. This binary digital stream is then further encoded into a four-level digital stream of 10.1 megabits per second. Each successive pair of binary digits is combined to form one of four possible levels. The encoding results in one-half the bandwidth requirement but reduces signal immunity to noise and distortion. The four-level pulse train is then used to frequency modulate a carrier for transmission over a microwave system.

Encoding for coaxial transmission is somewhat different. The noise level is less than for microwaves, and there is no signal fading as there is in radio transmission. Eight-level digital transmission can be used to reduce the required bandwidth.

Encoding for coaxial transmission

DATA-MESSAGE NETWORKS

Telegraph networks have traditionally provided the capability for data transmission in the form of written messages. The 1960s, however, saw an explosive growth in data generation and transmission, brought on by the widespread use of high-speed computers. Stock market and bank transactions are rapidly consummated via data-transmission facilities, airline reservations are routinely processed via geographically widespread data networks, and large companies carry out business and bookkeeping transactions via high-speed data networks.

Techniques for efficiently processing, transmitting, and routing these data messages are still undergoing development. Much of the data is currently transmitted over the public telephone networks or private, leased voice-quality lines. More engineering effort, however, is going into the development of high-speed data-transmission and switching facilities.

In the early 1970s, data-transmission facilities are conveniently classified into categories of public switched networks or private (leased) lines or networks.

Regular public telephone systems may be used for the transmission and routing of data. Teletypewriters and other low-data-rate (so-called sub-voice-grade) equipment transmitting at up to 150 bits per second can be connected to a teletypewriter exchange service (TWX). Each subscriber has his own dial-up number and is listed in a national directory. Several TWX channels plus telephone circuits can be sent over one voice channel on the telephone network after combining at the local telephone exchange to which they are connected. The Telex service of Western Union and TWX were combined into a single national service in 1970.

Higher data rate signals, at 1,200 bits per second and 2,400 bits per second (voice-grade signals), representing computer or other data-source outputs, may be transmitted by converting the signals into a form suitable for transmission over the telephone network. One device for this purpose uses both frequency-shift-keying (FSK) and phase-shift-keying (PSK) techniques.

Voice-grade signals

The use of voice-grade telephone lines limits the rate of transmission of digital data. Distortion introduced by these lines may be readily corrected in voice signals since the ear is relatively insensitive to distortion of voice signals over a wide range. This distortion is harmful to rapidly varying digital signals, however, introducing many errors at the receiver if not corrected. The problem arises because a connection between two distant points may be routed differently at various times. The transmission characteristics and hence distortion introduced vary with different routing and require different amounts of equalization (correction).

With a voice signal, random variation in distortion is tolerable as long as some average equalization is introduced, but this is not the case with digital signals. Adaptive equalizers—i.e., correction networks introduced at the destination to compensate automatically for deleterious transmission characteristics—are employed to correct the problem. With these equalizers, transmission rates as high as 9,600 bits per second may be possible over the telephone network. The higher transmission rates are accomplished by combining several successive binary digits in a binary data stream and transmitting one of a multiple set of amplitudes or phases of a pulsed carrier. This reduces the required bandwidth, enabling the signal to be transmitted over a three-kilohertz bandwidth line.

Worldwide public teletypewriter service is available through an automatic teletypewriter exchange service called Telex. This was first set up in Europe after World War II by the various European telecommunications utilities. It was introduced in Canada in 1956 and in the U.S. in 1957 and is now combined with the Bell System TWX. The system operates at 66 words per minute (50 baud, or 50 bits per second). Each subscriber has his own number and may dial any other number in his own country, just as with the telephone system.

Private-line data communications

Private-line systems for data communications have come into widespread use in the past decade. These may provide point-to-point communications or, in the case of large systems, network switching as well. They provide an advantage over public systems in that they are assigned (dedicated) to a specific purpose or customer and hence may be specially conditioned to provide superior performance. Voice-grade private lines transmit 2,400 and 4,800 bits per second with conditioning, and adaptive equalization features allowing up to 9,600 bits per second are available.

Private wide-band data channels allowing up to 500,000-bits-per-second transmission are also currently available.

When many message sources are to be interconnected in one common private network, switching and routing techniques must be incorporated. Standardized procedures had not been adopted by the early 1970s. Unlike telephone (voice) data, different message sources to be interconnected may have vastly different data rates, data statistics, and data-transmission requirements. The data sources to be switched into the same network may include a telemetry signal that is transmitted continuously at a few bits per second, a teletypewriter producing 50 bits per second intermittently, and a satellite computer communicating at a high data rate with a master computer. Unlike the telephone network, in which direct transmission is required and a busy signal is given when the destination or trunks are all occupied, many data messages may be stored until transmission becomes possible. Priority classifications may be set up, with certain messages allowed to go through and others temporarily held up. Some sources may be regularly queried as to whether immediate transmission is required or can come through as facilities become available.

The strategies of combining or concentrating sources with different data rates, of temporarily storing certain messages, and of determining how to connect the sources and how to route them can all be accomplished by computer, and the trend is in the direction of completely automatic computer-message switching.

Several methods are available for connecting many data terminals to one central point or computer. The methods include connection of the terminals to a computer in a time-shared mode or to a local exchange before retransmission elsewhere. In the so-called roll-call polling technique, a computer successively asks, or polls, each terminal in prearranged order whether a message is to be transmitted. If the answer is yes, polling stops and the message is transmitted. Polling then continues with the next terminal. If the answer is no, the computer goes on to the next terminal. Some terminals may be interrogated more than once in a particular sequence, and priorities are often introduced. In the hub polling technique, the terminals are all connected in a line. The first terminal is polled by the computer. If it has nothing to send, the polling message is forwarded down the line to the next terminal. The computer resumes control only when a particular terminal down the line has something to transmit. At the end of the transmission, the computer resumes the polling at the next terminal, which in turn forwards the message down the line. In the contention, or asynchronous, technique, an individual terminal requests transmission when needed. If a transmission channel is available, transmission proceeds. If not, the channel waits its turn in line.

In these techniques, as in the method of concentrating low-speed data for retransmission at a higher rate, data storage becomes significant. Devices, called buffers, used to provide this function include magnetic tape, disc, and other kinds of memory devices. Paper tape has long played the same role in teletypewriter systems.

Roll-call polling

Error control. It has been noted that errors occur in data transmission. More specifically, in binary transmission a 1 may be received as a 0 or vice versa or two adjacent levels may be confused in multilevel phase or amplitude pulse transmission, because of noise added during transmission or on reception of a pulse signal, signal distortion during transmission, signal fading during transmission, and other effects. Much of modern communications research involves the search for new communications systems and techniques that will provide improved error performance. Appropriate signal design and encoding at the transmitter and unique modulation techniques all play a role. Different receiver configurations and processing techniques are also compared on the basis of their error performance.

If noise is the predominant perturbing effect of the transmission medium, frequency modulation provides improvement over amplitude modulation. If fading plays a significant role, single-side-band transmission is usually preferred. Errors may occur in fading when the signal level drops to a level comparable to that of the noise. At this point an FM system deteriorates rapidly compared to an AM system. The FM improvement is possible only when the signal level is high compared to the noise. If noise is the limiting factor in systems performance, the receiver incorporates a matched filter, whose frequency response is just that of the binary signal pulses received.

Noise appearing at the receiver antenna is the predominant deteriorating effect in space communications. In telephone data transmission, however, it is the signal distortion introduced during transmission that plays the major role. Particular types of pulse shapes at the transmitter are used to minimize the distortion. Repeaters spaced at relatively short distances along the transmission path prevent distortion from building up. Equalizers, both of the fixed type and the adaptive type mentioned earlier, reduce the distortion as well.

Signal distortion

With all of these improved techniques, errors still occur, and error-detection and correction techniques are necessary. By appropriately coding a binary pulse-code-modulation sequence, for example, it is possible to detect errors and even to correct them. In such a scheme additional binary digits (redundant bits) are added at the transmitter to the binary message stream in a controlled manner. There are many techniques for adding the redundant bits and determining the optimum number to use, and significant improvements in performance can be realized by their use.

It is possible, by inserting a large number of redundant bits, actually to locate the error in question and correct it. With still more redundant bits two or more errors may be corrected. The disadvantage is that as more redundant bits are added the transmission rate is reduced accordingly. Thus if five redundant bits are added to ten message bits, there is a one-third reduction in the data rate.

Coded binary transmission has been used in recent space probes. At the large distances involved, the signal power returned is so small compared to the noise received at the Earth receiving-station antennas that the binary pulses must be stretched out over a relatively long time to provide enough signal energy to overcome the noise. The use of coded transmission reduces the errors or allows a faster rate of transmission for the same error rate.

As an example, the signal received from a space vehicle 1,000,000 miles out in space may be on the order of 10^{-16} watt. If the distance is increased by 10,000,000 miles, the received power is about 10^{-18} watt. To keep the average number of errors to less than one in 100,000 binary digits—a common design figure—the maximum data rate is 1,000 bits per second. At 1,000,000 miles each bit must last at least 0.001 second to ensure enough signal energy. If the distance is increased to 10,000,000 miles, the maximum data rate is only ten bits per second. Thus, normal voice communication with existing techniques is not possible at these distances.

Increasing data rate. A theorem from information theory, developed in 1948 by U.S. scientist Claude Shannon, is invoked to increase the data rate. Dr. Shannon proved that for a communications channel with white noise added (random noise the intensity of which is constant at all frequencies), there exists an upper limit to the information rate in bits per second that may be transmitted over the channel. This he called the capacity of the channel. Packing more bits per second into the channel than this theorem allows increases the probability of an error being introduced. By using a data rate less than the allowed upper limit of capacity, however, the error rate can be made to approach zero with appropriate encoding. The theorem does not tell how this encoding may be carried out, and much of the error-correction encoding effort has gone into this question of finding good codes.

The capacity of the channel depends on three parameters: the bandwidth of the channel (the maximum frequency component it can transmit), the signal power received, and the noise power measured at the same point as the signal. In particular, as the bandwidth gets larger, the capacity increases to a maximum value directly proportional to the ratio of signal power to noise intensity. For instance, in the specific space communications example, maximum capacity is 14,500 bits per second at the 1,000,000-mile range (compared to 1,000 bits per second without coding) and 145 bits per second at the 10,000,000-mile range (compared to ten bits per second). The figures indicate the possible advantage in coding for space communications and indicates why coded systems are used.

Similar considerations may be applied to the three-kilohertz voice channel used with the public telephone network. Although distortion plays a greater role than noise in this case, a channel capacity may be found for it as well. Typically, it is on the order of 20,000 bits per second. Since 9,600 bits per second may be possible with multilevel transmission and adaptive equalizers, the theoretical limit of channel capacity has been much more closely approached than in the space communications example. In data networks of the future, with the individual links especially devised for data rather than voice, these numbers may be expected to increase considerably. Coding techniques have been investigated for a different type of noise than that which appears in space channels. In the telephone channel, noise bursts tend to occur because of faulty switches in exchanges and lightning bursts. These bursts may last for many bits, wiping out all signal pulses while they last. Various error-control techniques and codes have been developed to handle the problem.

IV. Future trends in communications
Some examples of future systems have already been noted in passing: public switched networks especially designed for high-speed data transmission, extremely wide band data transmission (systems allowing 500 megabits per second transmission), and the widespread use of computers in all these systems.

With the increased concentration of population in large metropolitan regions, more efficient means are being sought to provide the data requirements envisioned in the future. One result could be a computer terminal in each home, with shopping, banking, and other services carried out routinely. Widespread use of cable television would provide an alternate, wide-band communications system in each home, parallel with the telephone system. All kinds of data and picture services could be provided via such a system. Professional, social, shopping, business, and educational activities could all be conducted inside the home.

Public-service communications of various types—fire, police, education, health, transportation—are commonly carried out separately in urban areas. These communications could perhaps be more effectively conducted via one flexible computer-controlled system, adjusting the capacity to each service as required. To this must be added the communications requirements within cities of business data sources, computer networks of the future, radio

Cable television (margin note)

operated taxicabs, traffic-control systems, information-retrieval systems, and others, complicating the task of allocating communications resources effectively.

Synchronous communications satellites, already extensively used for international voice and TV communications, can be readily adapted to provide worldwide data coverage. They are also being considered as an alternate means of communications coverage within a nation or continent. Trunk connections between distant switching centres might be made via satellite. Educational TV broadcasts, covering an entire region, might also be transmitted this way (see SATELLITE COMMUNICATION).

The current communications capabilities could be increased in a dramatic way by broadening the radio spectrum into the millimetre (100,000 megahertz and higher) and optical-frequency (1,000,000 gigahertz and above) ranges. These extremely high frequencies allow proportionately wider bandwidth signals to be transmitted. It has been suggested, for example, that a single millimetre channel could provide the capacity of a quarter of a million voice channels. Still higher frequency optical communications could provide the possibility of at least 1,500 colour TV channels on one optical-frequency carrier. There are major technical problems in the transmission of these extremely high frequency signals, however. The development of the optical laser has provided a coherent carrier source needed for optical-frequency communications (see also LASER AND MASER). Millimetre wave-guide transmission systems, millimetre pipes, are under intensive developement in that range of frequencies (see also ANTENNAS AND WAVE GUIDES). Manufacturing tolerances are strict; discontinuities, bends, and imperfections must be kept to within a fraction of a millimetre for long sections of pipes. The problems are even more difficult in the optical range; the atmosphere tends to scatter the coherent light rays, while fog and rain absorb them. Point-to-point communications over long distances might be possible in space. But there the narrow beams involved mean highly sophisticated tracking systems in which the highly directional transmitting and receiving antennas must be kept constantly lined up with one another. In the case of terrestrial communications over long distances, scattering and absorption probably preclude transmission through the air. Optical pipes, lens systems, and fibre optics have been suggested as alternate transmission approaches and are under intensive investigation. These may materialize as economic and reliable competitors or adjuncts to existing communications facilities.   (M.Sch.)

Use of extremely high frequencies (margin note)

BIBLIOGRAPHY
Telephone: FREDERICK L. RHODES, *Beginnings of Telephony* (1929), a good general account from a Bell System point of view with excerpts from several of Bell's patent cases; J.E. KINGSBURY, *The Telephone and Telephone Exchanges* (1915), the best account available of the development of telephone apparatus in the early period; A.G. BELL, *The Bell Telephone: The Deposition of Alexander Graham Bell in the Suit Brought by the United States to Annul the Bell Patents* (1908), a prime source for Bell's own account of his work that must be used critically since it was given as court testimony in a case involving large amounts of money and prestige.

Telecommunications: MISCHA SCHWARTZ, *Information Transmission, Modulation, and Noise*, 2nd ed. (1970), a basic undergraduate textbook in telecommunications; JAMES MARTIN, *Telecommunications and the Computer* (1969), and *Teleprocessing Network Organization* (1970), two books for a person with some technical background but with no particular experience in telecommunications; DONALD H. HAMSHER (ed.), *Communication System Engineering Handbook* (1967), a highly technical encyclopaedic volume; *Reference Data for Radio Engineers*, 5th ed. (1968), a handbook for practicing electronic engineers; *Computer Processing in Communications*, vol. 19 (1970), proceedings of a symposium at Polytechnic Institute of Brooklyn emphasizing the impact of computers and digital processing in the communications field.

Useful periodicals on telephone and telecommunications include: *Bell Laboratories Record* (monthly); *Bell System Technical Journal* (10/yr); *Telecommunications* (monthly); *Bell Telephone Magazine* (bimonthly); the IEEE *Transactions on Communication Technology*; and the IEE *Transactions*.
(B.S.F./M.Sch.)

Telescope

A telescope is an instrument used to view distant objects. The word is derived from the Greek *tēle*, "far," and *skopein*, "to see." Modern telescopes are of two types, optical and radio. In optical telescopes light is collected and focussed so that it can be magnified and either examined through an eyepiece or photographed. The light may also be directed into an auxiliary device, such as a spectrograph (see also OPTICS, PRINCIPLES OF; OPTICAL ENGINEERING). A radio telescope may consist of a single wire, a pattern of wires, a spherical or parabolic dish, or a number of dishes arranged in a pattern. Very sensitive electronic detectors and amplifiers have been developed for radio telescopes, which are usually much larger and more complex than optical telescopes. In one such telescope, the long-baseline radio interferometer, the two elements may be separated by hundreds or even thousands of miles.

EARLY HISTORY

The effects achieved by looking through a magnifying lens, and especially by looking through two lenses in alignment, are so startling that it is likely that the telescope was "invented" independently and accidentally many times before Galileo turned it on the heavens in 1609. Glass was made in Egypt as early as 3500 BC, and crude lenses have been unearthed in Crete and Asia Minor believed to date from 2000 BC. Euclid wrote about the reflection and refraction of light in the 3rd century BC, and in the 1st century AD the Roman writer Seneca noted that the glass globe filled with water referred to by the Greek dramatist Aristophanes could be used as a magnifying glass. The 11th-century Arab scientist Alhazen (al-Ḥansan ibn al-Haythan) published the results of his experiments with parabolic mirrors and the magnifying power of lenses. Alhazen's works were translated into Latin in 1572, but much earlier Roger Bacon (c. 1220–c. 1292) had recognized the usefulness of lenses, writing:

> ... thus from an incredible distance we may read the smallest letters ... the Sun, Moon, and stars may be made to descend hither in appearance ... which persons unacquainted with such things would refuse to believe.

The invention of the printing press in the 15th century, followed by the ever-increasing need for spectacle lenses by scholars, probably made inevitable the final invention of the telescope and its widespread use. It is clear that the oft-repeated statement that the telescope was first invented in 1608 by Hans Lippershey in Middelburg, the United Netherlands, is incorrect. Lippershey made a number of telescopes in 1608 and sold them to the government of the United Netherlands, which was particularly interested in their military applications. His request for a 30-year privilege or patent was denied on the grounds that "many other persons had a knowledge of the invention." Telescopes were on sale in Paris early in 1609 and in that same year appeared in Germany, in various cities in Italy, and in London.

Galileo heard of Lippershey's invention, and reinvented the telescope, using basic optical principles. His first telescope, constructed in a day, magnified three diameters and consisted of a convex lens (curving outward) and a concave lens (curving inward) fitted into opposite ends of a tiny lead tube. The results were so gratifying that Galileo made several larger telescopes, grinding his own lenses. His largest telescope was 1¾ inches (about 4.4 centimetres) in diameter and had a magnifying power of 33 diameters. With these simple instruments he discovered the mountains and craters of the Moon's surface, the satellites of Jupiter, the starry nature of the Milky Way, and the fact that Venus undergoes phases like those of the Moon. His observations showed that Venus shines by reflected sunlight, is spherical, and goes around the Sun, contrary to Ptolemaic theory. These discoveries of Galileo's resulted from two distinct characteristics of a telescope, its magnifying power and its light-gathering power. The magnifying power made it possible for him to see the changes of phase in Venus, while the light-gathering power permitted him to detect Jupiter's faint satellites and the countless dim stars of the Milky Way. The light-gathering

power is proportional to the square of the diameter (or aperture) of the lens, while the magnifying power depends on the relative focal lengths of the object glass and eyepiece, which in turn depends on the curvature and composition of these lenses.

Rarely has a new scientific instrument had a more dramatic impact than that of Galileo's telescope, which not only advanced scientific knowledge by enormous strides but stirred vast waves in philosophy and religion by upsetting the traditional picture of a universe centred on a stationary Earth.

From the 17th century on, telescopes grew steadily in size and power. The cost of construction naturally increased as well, often in a way difficult to justify at the time of construction because no one can predict what a new, more powerful telescope will discover. For example, the 200-inch Hale reflector on Mt. Palomar has been used to make a series of important discoveries that lay entirely beyond the conceptions of professional astronomers in 1928, the year of the telescope's funding.

OPTICAL TELESCOPES

Optical telescopes are of two basic types, refracting and reflecting. In recent times a combination of the two has been devised.

Refracting telescopes. The term refracting refers to the bending of light by a lens. The large lens, called the object glass, of a Galilean telescope is convex; the eyepiece, placed in front of the focus of the object glass, is concave. The image formed by this combination of lenses is enlarged and erect (Figure 1). The instrument is short and light, and its principle is used in present-day opera

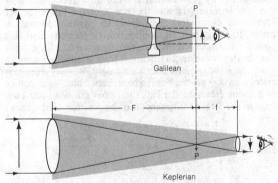

Figure 1: Galilean and Keplerian telescopes (see text).

glasses. Both the magnification and field of view are limited. The modern visual refracting telescope is based on the Galilean telescope as modified in accordance with the suggestion of Galileo's contemporary, Johannes Kepler, who pointed out the advantages of using a convex eyepiece placed in back of the focus (see Figure 1), greatly enlarging the field of view. The image produced by this eyepiece is inverted, because it is a magnification of the small, inverted image formed by the objective at the point P. It is possible to reinvert the image by adding additional lenses, as is done in telescopic gun sights and in the telescopes used in engineer's transits. The loss of light through absorption by these additional lenses is sufficiently severe, however, so that an erecting eyepiece is not used by astronomers, who publish photographs "upside down" in order to correspond to the orientation seen at the telescope.

Other advantages of the Keplerian telescope, generally adopted by astronomers about the middle of the 17th century, are its increased possibilities for magnification (up to 1,000 times or more) and the fact that a small object—such as a thin wire or wires—can be placed at the common focus, P, of the two lenses. By bringing the image of a star as seen in the eyepiece exactly into coincidence with the intersection of two crosswires, which are also seen in focus, the astronomer can determine the position of the telescope—and the star—with great accuracy. This advantage was first pointed out by the English astronomer William Gascoigne, who developed the microm-

Alhazen's experiments

Use of the
micrometer
for
astronomical
measure-
ment

eter, based on this principle, and who used this device before 1640 for measuring planetary diameters. The micrometer revolutionized astronomical measurement and made it possible to measure positions much more accurately than was possible with the open sights used earlier. The micrometer is still used effectively today in the precise measurement of the positions of the stars, planets, Moon, and Sun; in the measurement of differential positions of comets, asteroids, and close double stars; and in measuring the diameters of planets and satellites. Telescopic sights eventually led, in the 1890s, to a revolution in naval gunnery.

The magnifying power, M, of an astronomical telescope is defined as the ratio of the focal length, F, of the objective to the focal length, f, of the eyepiece: $M=F/f$ (Figure 1). The focal length of a lens is approximately the distance from the principal focus to the midpoint of the lens. Increasing the magnification can be accomplished by using an eyepiece of shorter focal length. The astronomer usually has a collection of eyepieces of different focal lengths to meet his varying needs; higher magnification corresponds to a reduced field of view. A practical limit to the magnifying power that can be usefully used with a large telescope is normally set by the quality of the astronomical viewing. It is of little value to magnify an image that is greatly diffused and distorted by the atmospheric irregularities in the light path. Other optical effects also play a role, especially for the smaller telescopes, and magnifications of 50 or 60 for each inch of aperture (diameter of the objective lens) is about the useful limit.

The early astronomers, using refractors, soon discovered that the stellar images were defective in a degree not accounted for by poor optical glass or imperfect shaping of the lens surfaces. It was the result of an image defect known as chromatic aberration. In passing through a prism, light is changed in direction (refracted) and this change in angle varies with the wavelength, blue light (of shorter wavelength) being refracted somewhat more than red light. A lens may be thought of, very approximately, as two prisms base to base, hence blue light comes to a focus closer to the lens than does the red light (see Figure 2). Similar differences in the position of the focal

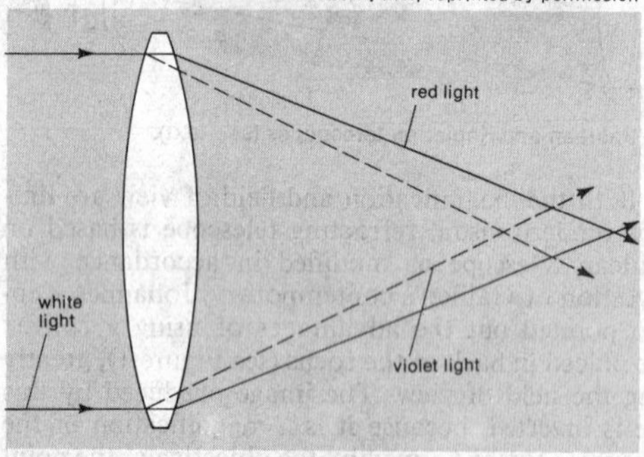

Figure 2: Chromatic aberration (see text).

point exist for other colours. A stellar image inspected at the red focus would show an out-of-focus blue halo, and vice versa. A compromise focus in the green-yellow would show a smaller purple halo—a combination of the out-of-focus blue and red light. Chromatic aberration can be minimized by using very thin lenses, which are necessarily of very long focal length. Incredibly long and unwieldy telescopes were thus constructed that had focal lengths of over 200 feet (60 metres); for example, the English astronomer James Bradley used a telescope of 212-foot (65-metre) focal length in measuring the diameter of Venus in 1722.

Following his discovery in 1666 that light of different colours is refracted in different amounts, Isaac Newton erroneously concluded from some hasty optical experiments that all refracting substances disperse the colours in constant proportion to their average refraction; and this being true, no combination of lenses could eliminate these colour effects and hence no further improvement in

the refracting telescope could be expected. About 70 years later, Chester Moor Hall of Essex, England, concluded otherwise, arguing correctly that the human eye is a complex lens showing no chromatic aberration, and, therefore, it should be possible to combine lenses of different kinds of glass to eliminate this aberration. He successfully constructed the first achromatic telescope in 1733 by combining lenses composed of different kinds of glass. Unfortunately he did not publicize his accomplishment. John Dollond of London independently invented the achromatic telescope in 1758, and modern refractors are based on his use of a combination of a convex lens or lenses of a type of glass known as crown glass, combined with a concave lens of a type of glass known as flint glass. This correction of chromatic aberration is possible because the refractive characteristics of flint glass lens are such as to counteract the refractive characteristics of the crown glass lens, thus correcting the aberration. The correction is complete at only two widely separated wavelengths, however, and other wavelengths show a residual chromatic aberration. The variation of focus setting with wavelength is usually evaluated for a large refractor so that the astronomer can make the best compromise setting for the particular colour region within which he is working.

First
achro-
matic
telescope

Dollond's telescopes were immediately successful but were limited in size to three or four inches in diameter because at that time it was not known how to cast larger flint glass disks. This limitation was overcome in time, and a century later, spurred on by the desire for greater and greater light-gathering power, ever-larger refractors were constructed, culminating near the end of the 19th century in the 36-inch telescope at the Lick Observatory and the 40-inch telescope at the Yerkes Observatory. The lenses for these giant telescopes, still the largest refractors in the world, were made by the U.S. firm of Alvan Clark and Sons. Their optical work was superb, the secret of their success being their remarkable patience in the use of local correction (figuring) to obtain the sharpest possible focus. This technique was better than striving for mathematically true curves, because of the inhomogeneities in the glass. These opticians stimulated the expansion of astronomy in the U.S. in the period 1850–1900.

Reflecting telescopes. A reflecting telescope is a device in which the light is gathered and focussed by a mirror. In his *Optica Promota*, James Gregory, a Scottish mathematician, suggested the reflecting telescope in 1663 but the opticians of the day were not able to grind good mirrors for him. In Gregory's design the light reflected from the primary concave mirror was reflected again by a smaller concave mirror, reaching the observer's eye by passing through a circular hole in the primary. Isaac Newton turned his attention to the problem and successfully devised methods of grinding and polishing an alloy of tin and copper known as speculum metal. His mirror was spherical, rather than paraboloidal, and the image was viewed horizontally at the side of the tube by means of a flat mirror inclined at an angle of 45° at the upper end of the tube. His second telescope, presented to the Royal Society on January 11, 1672, had a magnifying power of 38 diameters. The speculum metal mirror had a focal length of 6⅓ inches (16 centimetres) and a diameter of about two inches (five centimetres). Because the light rays in such a telescope are only reflected and not refracted, chromatic aberration is nonexistent and this is an inherent advantage of all reflectors. Nevertheless, the invention was not of practical value until about 1740, when James Short of Edinburgh succeeded in routinely grinding concave mirrors; he sold reflecting telescopes as an ordinary workshop product. These reflectors became favourites with astronomers and amateurs, who found them preferable to the longer, thinner refractors with their pale and blurred images. It was not easy, however, to attach these mirrors to measuring instruments, so refractors were still used in this most important type of professional work.

The reflecting telescope was greatly advanced by William Herschel of England, often called the father of stellar astronomy, who made his own mirrors because they were too expensive to buy. Herschel's sensational discovery of the planet Uranus in 1781 was made with a seven-inch (18-centimetre) reflector, which was large enough to show the disk. His two most famous telescopes (1789) were of 19-inch (48-centimetre) and 48-inch (122-centimetre) aperture. Herschel developed the art of making and figuring his mirrors of speculum. This alloy reflects only about 60 percent of the light that falls on it, even when freshly polished. It tarnishes rather quickly to a much lower reflectivity, and the removal of this tarnish requires a long and tedious job of refiguring. The largest speculum mirror ever made was a 72-inch (183-centimetre) reflector (first used in 1845), constructed by Lord Rosse, an Irish amateur astronomer, who discovered the spiral structure of nebulae with it.

The development of the silver-on-glass mirror in the 1850s and '60s overcame the difficulties inherent in the use of speculum mirrors. A fresh coating of silver has a reflectivity greater than 90 percent throughout the visible spectrum, and a tarnished mirror can be easily resilvered without refiguring. The reflectivity starts falling at a wavelength of 4500 angstroms (one angstrom is 10^{-10} metre) and is so low at 3300 angstroms as to be essentially useless in this important region of the ultraviolet. A method of depositing aluminum on an astronomical mirror in a vacuum was developed by John Strong in California in 1931. Aluminum has a high reflectivity in the ultraviolet, scatters relatively little light, and a coating, when properly protected, is extraordinarily tough and will last many years.

Relative advantages of refractors and reflectors. Both types of telescope have been brought to a high state of perfection, but each type has its own special advantages, disadvantages, and purposes. Since light must pass through a lens, the glass from which it is made must be optically homogeneous and free of bubbles. The glass of a mirror need only be mechanically homogeneous, a less severe requirement. There are four surfaces to figure on the two lenses of a refractor and only one surface for a reflector. Reflectors are therefore less expensive to build than refractors of the same aperture, and their complete lack of chromatic aberration is an advantage in spectrographic and photographic work. Small differences in temperature between different parts of a large mirror can often seriously distort the shape of the mirror, but this disadvantage has been largely overcome by the use of low-expansion glasses. Because of chromatic aberration, refractors are normally built with longer focal lengths than reflectors of the same aperture. A large refractor is somewhat more unwieldy in use and requires a much larger and more expensive dome than a reflector of the same light-gathering power. The flint lens of a refractor becomes increasingly opaque to wavelengths shorter than 4000 angstroms and the refractor is relatively useless in this spectral region. If refractors larger than 40 inches (100 centimetres) in diameter were built they would require larger and hence thicker lenses, which would absorb more light, thus tending to offset the increased light-gathering power. For this reason alone, the largest optical telescopes must be reflectors. The largest optical telescope, with a 236-inch (six-metre) diameter reflector, was under construction in the early 1970s near Zelenchukskaya, in the Caucasus, 1.3 miles above sea level. The 850-ton telescope, built and test assembled in Leningrad, has an 82-foot (25-metre) tube and a mirror almost 20 feet (6½ metres) in diameter. A special furnace was needed to melt the glass, which took two years to cool. The heavy mirror is kept from deflecting under its own weight by a support system attached to the rear surface by means of drilled cavities. Because of mechanical problems involved in mounting the large machine, the Soviet instrument has an altazimuth mount, with horizontal and vertical axes, instead of an equatorial mount as do other large optical telescopes. The 700-ton movable section of the telescope may easily be turned, because of hydraulic oil-pressure bearings on both axes. Reflectors possess great advantages in spectroscopic work and excel especially in the observation of faint objects such as nebulae and galaxies.

Refractors usually have much wider fields of good def-

inition than reflectors. In current practice, refractors are used almost exclusively in visual observations and astrometric measurements of stellar parallax and binary stars and in the overall visual and photographic determination of stellar positions. Observations of annual stellar parallax (the apparent shifting of the image of a nearby star with respect to the images of more distant background stars caused by the orbital motion of the Earth about the Sun) are particularly important. Such observations of parallax are fundamental to the knowledge not only of stellar distances but also to the knowledge of stellar luminosities and velocities.

A large reflector is more flexible than a refractor in that a choice of usually three focal lengths (and three f-numbers) are available. These are known as the prime, Cassegrain and coudé focuses. For example, the 200-inch Hale telescope has a focal length of 660 inches (1,680 centimetres), giving it an f-number (focal length divided by diameter) of 3.3 at the prime focus. To make use of this focal length and f-number the observer sits in a cage directly in the beam of starlight. The consequent percentage loss of starlight is small, and with only one reflection loss—from the main mirror—loss of light is kept to a minimum. In the Cassegrain arrangement, the light is reflected by a hyperbolic mirror inserted in front of the prime focus, passes through a hole in the large mirror, and comes to a new focus in back of the mirror. The Cassegrain focal length is 3,000 inches, giving an f-number of 15. In the coudé arrangement the light is reflected by other auxiliary mirrors (by two alternate paths, depending on the declination setting) down the polar axis of the telescope. The coudé focal length is 6,000 inches, giving an f-number of 30. The great advantage of the coudé focus is that it does not move as the telescope follows the star in its diurnal motion. At this point a fixed, large, and efficient coudé spectrograph has been built that would be difficult to attach to any moving part of the telescope.

The Schmidt telescope. A continuing and highly important observational problem is to determine the contents of the universe. For this purpose it is necessary to photograph the entire sky, including as faint objects as possible, with as large a scale as possible, and to photograph in many wavelength (colour) regions. The requirement in the normal optical regions (wavelengths of 3000–10,000 angstroms) is a very large achromatic telescope with a wide field of good definition (of the order of five degrees square), which is also fast enough (with a small enough f-number) that the limit imposed by the light of the night sky background can be reached in reasonably short exposure times. Parenthetically it should be stated that two such telescopes would be necessary, one in each hemisphere. The large parabolic reflector is not the answer—its field of good definition is much too small. The refracting telescope is too small, too slow, and not sufficiently achromatic but does have the necessary wide-angle characteristics. A telescope combining the best features of both refractor and reflector has been found to be the solution, and such an instrument is the Schmidt telescope.

The primary image defect in a parabolic reflector is coma—star images off axis are not round but look like tiny comets with their tails pointed away from the plate centre. This effect increases linearly with distance from the optical axis, and for different objectives and for a given angle off axis, coma worsens rapidly as the diameter of the objective is increased, varying as the square of the aperture.

A spherical mirror has no unique axis of symmetry and therefore should exhibit no coma. But on axis (off axis also) the rays reflected from the outer region of the mirror converge to a focus that is closer to the mirror than the focus of the rays coming from the inner regions of the mirror. This image defect, also present in refractors, is called spherical aberration, and a spherical mirror generates poor images for light coming in from all angles. All rays of light that pass through an aperture located at the centre of curvature of the mirror strike the mirror surface perpendicularly, hence there is no off-axis aberration. If a thin, weak lens (called a correcting plate) is placed at this point, it can be shaped so as to correct completely for spherical aberration, at the expense of introducing a small but tolerable amount of chromatic aberration. This ingenious optical system was invented in 1930 by Bernhard Schmidt, an optician at the Bergedorf Observatory, Hamburg, who also made the first such telescope. The main disadvantages of such a telescope are (1) the difficulty in making the correcting plate, which has a complex curvature; (2) the curvature of the focal plane, which requires curved photographic plates or films; and (3) the increased (doubled) length of the telescope tube. The telescope is achromatic over a wide colour range, can be made in large size with a very wide useful field, and is fast (has a small f-number). The mirror is normally made substantially larger than the correcting plate so that off-axis rays will not miss the mirror (see Figure 3).

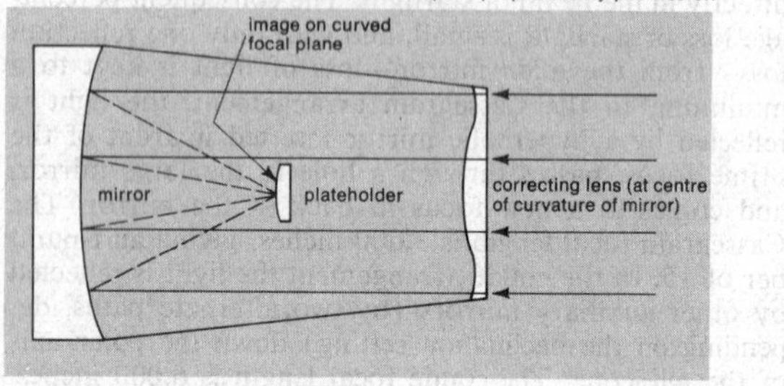

Figure 3: The Schmidt telescope.

The largest Schmidt telescope is the 52.8-inch-aperture instrument at the Karl Schwarzschild Observatory in Jena, East Germany. Its primary mirror has a diameter of 79 inches. Even larger Schmidt telescopes should be possible, but other things being equal, the focal length of a Schmidt must be increased more rapidly than the aperture in order to keep critical chromatic aberrations to tolerable levels. Schmidt telescopes have been used effectively in relatively poor climates because so much information can be acquired in a short time. They are also used extensively as cameras in astronomical spectrographs, in the photography of meteors, and in tracking artificial satellites. Schmidt cameras, with their wide-angle properties and their bright images, are widely used in science and industry.

Special types. *Solar telescopes and instruments.* The Sun is an object of special interest to astronomers and many unusual and different telescopes and instruments have evolved specifically for solar astronomy. A few will be described.

The size of the Sun's image in a telescope is $\frac{1}{108}$ of the focal length. In the popular 35-millimetre camera of 50-millimetre focal length, the solar image is only one-half millimetre across (one-fiftieth inch), while the Mc-Math solar telescope at Kitt Peak National Observatory near Tucson, Arizona, with a focal length of 300 feet (90 metres) yields an image three feet (0.9 metre) in diameter. Like most large solar telescopes it is fixed in direction. Sunlight is reflected, from an 80-inch (200-centimetre) fused silica flat mirror, 500 feet (150 metres) obliquely down the south polar axis at an angle of 32° —the latitude of Kitt Peak. This beam, focussed by a 60-inch (150-centimetre) concave mirror, is returned up the axis slightly below the incoming beam to a 48-inch (122-centimetre) flat mirror that directs the image vertically downward to spectrographs and other instrumentation.

Because solar radiation is intense and hot, special precautions must be taken in regard to the effect of the heat in solar telescopes. The entire McMath telescope, which is two-thirds underground, is cooled to the temperature of its surroundings. The 80-inch mirror is located 100 feet above the terrain to minimize ground effects. The bold step of evacuating the air from the entire telescope was taken in the 30-inch-diameter, 180-foot-focal-length, pyramidal tower telescope dedicated in 1969 at Sacra-

mento Peak Observatory, Sunspot, New Mexico. A lengthy solar site survey made in Southern California by the Hale Observatories showed that the best solar seeing occurred at sizable lakes, mountain lakes combining good seeing with good transparency of the atmosphere. As a result, the Big Bear Solar Observatory is located on an artificial island in Big Bear Lake at a 6,735-foot altitude in the San Bernardino Mountains.

The solar corona has a brightness only one-millionth that of the Sun and prior to 1931 could only be observed at the time of a total solar eclipse. It was only by going to a high mountain peak and by building a "perfect" telescope, free of all scattered light, that the French astronomer, Bernard Lyot, first succeeded in photographing the corona on a daily basis. The largest coronagraph, at Sacramento Peak (a duplicate is at the High Altitude Observatory in Boulder, Colorado), uses a 16-inch-diameter single lens completely free of bubbles, scratches, dust, and other defects. Elaborate precautions, involving sophisticated instrumentation, are taken to prevent the light of the solar disk from reaching the photographic plate. Because of the chromatic aberration introduced by the single lens, this is possible only over a narrow range of wavelengths, which can be varied. For this reason, a narrow-band filter is used that transmits the light in just the desired band. A green emission line of iron is strong in the corona, and direct photographs and motion pictures of the corona can be made in the light of this and other strong coronal emission lines. The chief application of the coronagraph, however, is in the spectroscopy of the corona.

The spectroheliograph is an instrument used to photograph the Sun in the light of a "single" wavelength—typically a narrow band of wavelengths centred on either 6563 angstroms or 3933 angstroms, emission lines of hydrogen and ionized calcium. An exit slit is placed in the focal plane of a solar spectrograph to isolate this narrow band of wavelengths. That slice of the solar image that falls on the entrance slit of the spectrograph appears as a monochromatic image at the exit slit. If the two slits are synchronously moved perpendicular to their length, the entire solar image may be scanned and recorded on a photographic plate or film. If this is done repeatedly, time-lapse motion pictures can be made. Daily photographs are taken with the spectroheliograph at many solar observatories throughout the world.

It is also possible to construct narrow-band filters that essentially do the same thing. Such filters with a pass band at 6563 angstroms of from one-eighth to 20 angstroms have been constructed; those used in coronal work have bandwidths of about two angstroms. By these techniques, activity on the solar disk, and in the chromosphere (prominences) and corona, can be repeatedly and routinely photographed.

The solar magnetograph, a device for measuring the magnetic field at a point on the solar disk, was developed (1952) at Mt. Wilson Observatory (now part of Hale Observatories) near Pasadena, California, by Horace W. and Harold D. Babcock. It is used daily at the 150-foot tower on Mt. Wilson to map the changing magnetic field over the solar disk precisely and in detail.

Meteor cameras. Bright meteor fireballs are rare at any one spot and astronomers have great difficulty in analyzing their paths through the atmosphere and their point of impact (if any), especially when the sources of information are the scattered and unreliable observations of laymen. The paths and solar system orbits of many faint meteors have been routinely derived from photographs obtained by using two widely separated wide-angle meteor cameras to photograph an overlapping region of the sky. By using a rotating shutter, the simultaneously photographed meteor trails appear as a series of dashes. The derived distances, velocities, and decelerations also give information about physical conditions in the upper atmosphere. A Super-Schmidt camera, developed for meteor photography, has a 12-inch (30-centimetre) aperture and a focal length of only eight inches (20 centimetres). A field of 55° is covered and exposure times, with fast films, are limited to only ten minutes by the sky

McMath solar telescope (left margin)

Spectro-heliograph (right margin)

background. The focal surface in such a camera is highly curved, with a radius of curvature of only eight inches, and the film must be heated and molded to conform to this surface.

Meteors have been detected by radio and radar as well. A meteoroid leaves a trail of ionized air that reflects radar signals, thus making it possible to measure both range (distance) and direction out to the trail. Velocities can be derived from the rate at which these factors change. Simultaneous observations from two radar stations give the altitude, velocity, and direction of fall of the meteoroid. This technique is especially useful in that it permits daylight meteors and meteor showers to be observed.

Transit circle (meridian circle). The observational problem that dominated the thoughts of the majority of the astronomers during the 18th and 19th centuries was to establish a network of positions and proper motions of many thousands of stars with the highest possible precision and as free as possible from systematic errors, and to observe the changing positions of the Sun, Moon, and planets with respect to this fundamental network.

The basic instrument that was developed to accomplish this was the transit (or meridian) circle. This instrument consists of a refractor that may be moved only in the plane of the meridian by rotation about a horizontal axis fixed in the east–west direction. The meridian is that imaginary great circle on the celestial sphere that passes through the celestial poles, zenith, nadir (direction vertically downward), and the north and south points on the horizon. Stars are accurately timed as they cross the meridian and differences in time are differences in right ascension. A large vertical circle, precisely graduated and fixed to the telescope tube, can be read through microscopes. The position of the nadir can be fixed on this circle by observations of reflections of the cross wires from a mercury surface directly under the telescope. The location of the celestial pole, and thus the latitude of the observer, is determined from observations of stars above and below the pole from which the declination of any other observed star may be derived. Modern transit circles use sophisticated instrumentation often involving photographic and photoelectric recording, with positional errors of the order of 0.25 second of arc. Observations are normally limited to relatively bright stars that are visible in a low-power telescope.

Double telescopes. As will be noted below, radio telescopes have been usefully operated in pairs as an interferometer. An optical interferometer, serving as an intensity interferometer, was built in Australia by R.H. Brown and R.Q. Twiss. It is used to measure the angular diameters of a few of the brightest stars. Two optically crude 264-inch reflectors, each a mosaic of many small mirrors, are mounted on rails and can be separated up to an eighth of a mile. Starlight is focussed on the sensitive surface of a phototube in each telescope, and by correlating the outputs of the two phototubes it is possible to derive angular diameters as small as 0.0007 second of arc.

Examples of more conventional double telescopes are the 18-inch photovisual and 24-inch photographic refractors fixed side by side on the same mounting at the Royal Cape Observatory, near Cape Town, South Africa, and the double 16-inch Edinburgh reflectors in which one telescope is continuously monitoring a bright star in a cluster and the other is offset differentially by known amounts to observe photoelectrically the other cluster members.

Future of the optical telescope. In spite of the many advantages of radio telescopes (see below), the future of optical telescopes seems assured, since there will be a continuing need for new and highly specialized small instruments. Both visual and photographic astrometry (positional measurements) of the brightest half-million stars can be carried out most effectively with 6- to 8-inch refractors. The radial velocities, spectral types, colours, magnitudes, and polarizations of these brighter stars are incompletely known, even though they could be observed with high precision, using reflectors or Schmidt telescopes, or both, in the 24- to 36-inch range. The big, important

problems in astronomy and cosmology seem to be the province of the larger reflectors and it is here that the greatest progress in optical astronomy may be expected. The useful life of a large reflector—unlike that of many radio telescopes—is certainly more than half a century, since this instrument can be continually modernized and improved by new auxiliary instrumentation, such as spectrographs and photoelectric photometers. As a result of improvements of this kind, the 20-inch telescope of today can make a variety of observations that would have been impossible with a 200-inch telescope as recently as the 1940s.

RADIO TELESCOPES

The Earth's atmosphere (including the ionosphere, the region of ionized air high above the Earth) is transparent to incoming electromagnetic radiation in two great wavelength windows. One, the optical window, which includes visible light, is from 3000 to about 140,000 angstroms; the other, the radio window, extends from a few millimetres to about 30-metres wavelength. Up until the 1930s only the optical window was used, with special emphasis on the photographic region from 3500 to 5000 angstroms and the partially overlapping visual region from about 4500 to 7000 angstroms.

In 1931 Karl Jansky, a U.S. engineer, was studying radio noise in the 15-metre range with a directional antenna. He received the first known extraterrestrial radio noise signals, which he correctly concluded came from the general direction of the galactic centre in the constellation Sagittarius. In 1937, also in the U.S., Grote Reber constructed a parabolic reflector antenna (dish) in his backyard in Wheaton, Illinois, and used it to scan the sky for radio noise. In 1940 he published the first radio map of the Milky Way; it was made at a wavelength of 1.9 metres. The directional properties of Reber's dish were such that he could receive signals in a conical beam about 12° wide. A lack of resolving power or the ability to distinguish between two closely spaced sources, inherent in the use of radio wavelengths, and the consequent inability to determine positions accurately, has plagued radio astronomy since its inception, especially in the crucially important matter of trying to identify radio sources with optical telescopes. Radio sources are extraordinarily weak and, with few exceptions, are very much weaker at centimetre wavelengths than at metre wavelengths. As with optical telescopes, the resolving power of a radio telescope increases linearly with its aperture, with the result that very large steerable dishes have been built, up to 20 times larger than their optical counterparts. The first of these was the Mark I 250-foot (76-metre) dish (paraboloid) at Jodrell Bank, Cheshire, near Manchester. Building this experimental telescope was a remarkable engineering achievement.

Another result has been that very large directional antennas called arrays have been constructed that look entirely different from any optical telescope (see ANTENNAS AND WAVE GUIDES). These antennas may be fixed or partially fixed (mounted on rails) to the Earth's surface and have large collecting areas measured in acres. Finally, a wide variety of very large unfilled aperture radio telescopes (telescopes in which portions of the aperture do not have signal-collecting equipment) have been built, which in an extreme form become very long base-line interferometers with the two elements (radio telescopes) observing the same object simultaneously, separated by an ocean at a distance of a few hundred million wavelengths. The resolving power of such a device is measured in thousandths of a second of arc, which is very much better than is possible with any optical telescope.

Dish antennas. Radio telescopes vary so greatly in design that none can be called truly typical, but one widely used type consists of a large metal parabolic dish reflector mounted on a support tower (see Figure 4). This dish can be rotated in azimuth (horizontal direction) about a vertical axis and (independently) in altitude (vertical direction) about a horizontal axis; this is called an altazimuth mounting. The drive system is controlled by a high-speed computer so that the telescope can be pointed

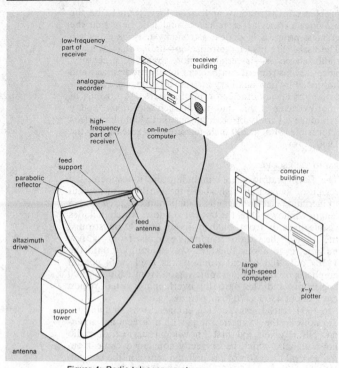

Figure 4: Radio telescope system.
From J.D. Kraus, *Radio Astronomy* (1966); McGraw-Hill Book Co.

accurately to any designated celestial position (right ascension and declination) and kept on that point as the Earth rotates. The drive may also be so controlled as to permit scanning in either right ascension or declination, or in other coordinates. The dish's surface reflects and focusses the incoming radiation to a small pickup device called a feed antenna. After preamplification at this point the amplified radio power is conveyed by cable to an adjacent building where it is further amplified, detected, and perhaps integrated over long periods of time. This may be done over a single band of frequencies, or simultaneously and independently over dozens of adjoining narrow bands of frequencies. The signals may be displayed on a moving chart or recorded in digital form on tapes for further processing by a high-speed computer. This entire system, not just the antenna, is called a radio telescope.

The largest fully steerable dish in the world is the Bonn 328-foot (100-metre) radio telescope located at Max Planck Institute for Radio Astronomy near Bonn, West Germany, and dedicated in 1970. The largest one in the Southern Hemisphere is the 210-foot (64-metre) dish located at Parkes, Australia. It is difficult to build such dishes rigidly enough so that they preserve their parabolic figure sufficiently well at all orientations, and the larger the dish the more it will deform under its own weight. If a surface deviates more than about a tenth of a wavelength from the ideal parabolic curve it will begin to lose efficiency; this deformation problem is therefore 100 times more severe at centimetre wavelengths than at metre wavelengths. The surface of the Jodrell Bank Mark I dish was renovated (1970–71) so that full operating efficiency could be achieved in the 21-centimetre region, a region that is important for observations of interstellar hydrogen. Recent theoretical studies have shown how a 100-metre dish may be constructed so that when shifted from one orientation to another gravitational forces will cause the surface to deform continuously from one paraboloid to another; this can be done down to wavelengths as short as one centimetre. Such dishes are called homologous reflectors; the Bonn dish is the first such and can be used effectively at one-centimetre wavelengths.

An important modification of the fully steerable dish is the large meridian-transit dish, a design first used by Reber. Such a device is first pointed in the desired direction along the meridian and then locked in place. It thus scans a specific strip in the sky as the Earth rotates. Observa-

tions on any given source with devices of this kind are limited to a few seconds or minutes as the source crosses or transits the meridian, but they are much less expensive to build, are much less complex, and can be designed and built quickly. The largest unit of this type in the world is the 300-foot- (90-metre-) diameter dish at Green Bank, West Virginia; it can be used at wavelengths as short as 20 centimetres. Another basic modification is the fixed spherical dish, the largest of which is the 1,000-foot (300-metre) spherical reflector at Arecibo, Puerto Rico, operated by Cornell University. The surface of this antenna is constructed of wire mesh anchored in a large natural depression in the ground. The radio waves are reflected from this surface to the focal point of the sphere, where a pickup arrangement or feed is located that is specially constructed to correct for spherical aberration. This feed swings from a truss that can be controlled to steer the beam anywhere within 20° of the zenith.

A modification of the fixed spherical dish is the fixed parabolic cylinder. An example is the 400-foot by 600-foot cylindrical reflector at the University of Illinois. The focal "point," or feed, of this survey-type telescope is the focal line of the parabolic cylinder and is some 600 feet (180 metres) long. Beam steering (adjusting the direction for maximum signal pickup) is in declination only and is controlled by adjustments of the pickup or feed arrangement.

Arrays. The work of English astronomers shortly after World War II clearly pointed to the need to survey the entire sky for radio sources with the highest possible positional accuracy, and shortly thereafter a wide variety of most ingenious antenna arrays were constructed, notably in Cambridge, England, and Sydney, Australia. In the metre-wavelength region receiver sensitivities and radio-source intensities are such that, with quite small antennas, more objects can be detected than can be resolved (separated) by the instrument. As the area of the antenna is increased the situation becomes worse, since the number of sources increases faster than the number that can be resolved. The emphasis then and into the 1970s has been on the construction of antenna arrangements that have a higher resolving power than their physical area would suggest. One such arrangement is the Mills Cross, developed in Australia by B.Y. Mills; at Cambridge University, a phase-switching interferometer has been used.

The original Mills Cross consists of two 1,500-foot- (460-metre-) long arms crossing at 90°, and containing 500 suitably designed antenna elements located above a wire mesh reflector (see Figure 5). The beam width is

The Mills Cross

From G.R. Miczaika and W.M. Sinton, *Tools of the Astronomer*, copyright 1961 by the President and Fellows of Harvard College

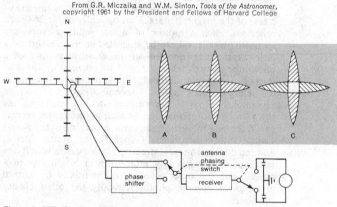

Figure 5: *Mills Cross radio telescope.*
(Left) Relationship of arms to receiver and phase shifter and (right) receiving pattern of (A) one arm, (B) two arms connected out of phase.

0.08° at a wavelength of about 3.5 metres. The north–south arm has a fan-shaped beam pattern 0.6° wide in the east–west direction, and the east–west arm has a similar pattern in the north–south direction (along the meridian). If the two arms are connected in phase (Figure 5b) a source at the intersection of the two beams will be strongly received. If the two arms are connected out of phase (Figure 5c) the signals from this same source will completely cancel one another. A source located in a region of only one of the lobes will be picked up regardless of the phase relationships, but if the connections to the recorder are switched synchronously and rapidly with an antenna phasing switch, the signals from such a source will cancel out. A source at the intersection of the two lobe patterns will not. The result is a narrow pencil-like beam with the resolving power equivalent to a dish having a diameter equal to the extent of the arms. In practice, the beam can be shifted in declination by proper phasing of the dipoles in the north–south arm. The cross has the disadvantages that it operates satisfactorily only at the wavelength for which it was designed, it does not have the energy-collecting ability of a dish of the same size, and it cannot track a source. But these disadvantages do not impair its primary function as a high-resolution survey instrument.

A newer University of Sydney cross at Molonglo, Australia, has arms nearly one mile (1,600 metres) in length. Both arms consist of cylindrical parabolic reflectors about 40 feet (12 metres) wide. The beam is steered in declination along the meridian by tilting the east–west arm about its long axis and phase shifting the feeds of the stationary north–south element. The feed is arranged to provide simultaneous beams at a number of adjacent declinations. This makes it possible to survey the sky strip by strip in a reasonable length of time. The beam width is 3′ of arc at 408 megahertz (0.74 metre), a considerable improvement over the original Mills Cross. The new cross has distinguished itself in the discovery of more than half of the known pulsars, rotating neutron stars whose pulses provide extraterrestrial clocks accurate to one part in 100,000,000. Such objects were unknown and undreamed of at the time of its construction.

Phase-switching radio interferometer

The phase-switching radio interferometer is the basis for a wide variety of radio telescopes, including arrays used for surveys. To understand its operating principles, consider two antennas located on an east–west line and connected to the same receiver. Radiation from a point source will reach one antenna before the other, unless the source is on the meridian. If the path difference is an integral number of wavelengths (or zero), the signals will be in phase and the receiver output will be a maximum; if 180° out of phase the signals will cancel and there will be no output. As the source moves across the sky in its diurnal motion, the path difference will change continuously, causing variations in the receiver output. The result will then be variations of signal intensity on the recording chart, called interference fringes. The spacing of these fringes will depend on the declination of the source, the spacing being least for a source on the celestial equator (east–west plane perpendicular to a line between the celestial north and south poles). The fringes will be superimposed on the signals caused by background radiation. If, however, the phase of one of the antennas with respect to the other is periodically and rapidly reversed, and the output of the receiver is reversed in synchronism, a phase-switched interferometer results. Only the fringes are seen; the background radiation and the receiver noise are cancelled out. The right ascension of the source may be obtained by identifying and timing the central fringe maximum; the declination may be obtained from the spacing of the fringes. The amplitude of the fringe pattern is proportional to the intensity of the source.

If the source is not a true point source but is somewhat extended, part of it may be producing a maximum at the same time that another part is producing a minimum, and there will be a partial cancellation with consequent reduced amplitude of the fringe patterns. The larger the source with respect to the fringe pattern, the more complete this cancellation will be. The spacing of the fringes, however, is inversely proportional to the separation of the antennas; as the separation is increased, a point will eventually be reached—for an extended source—where the fringes will disappear. This principle is used to measure angular diameters of radio sources. The spacing of the fringes can also be changed by varying the wavelength at which observations are made.

The two antennas do not have to be on an east–west line nor do they have to be of the same size or type. One antenna may be large dish or array, while its much smaller companion is movable, perhaps on rails. For antenna separations of a few miles or more the transmission line to the common receiver may become too long and a radio link may be used. For a very long base-line interferometer the path length of radio waves through the Earth's changing ionosphere varies so much as to make it impractical to use a radio link. In such cases the signals are recorded separately on magnetic tapes at each station, timed with extreme precision by atomic clocks and brought together later for correlation and analysis.

More than two antennas may be used as an interferometer. If a number of equally spaced antennas are used the system is called a grating interferometer. If a sky survey is repeatedly made in which one (or both) of the arrays or dishes is shifted on rails day by day to a new location so as to eventually "fill in" a very large area, the resulting magnetic tape recordings may all be synthesized in a computer so as to simulate what would have been observed by a radio telescope with this very large area. This is called aperture synthesis. There is a second way in which a large aperture may be synthesized. If a line aperture is rotated, a two-dimensional aperture may be generated. It is possible to use the Earth's rotation to perform this type of synthesis. A single area of the sky may be observed continuously for many hours with a number of in-line dishes, and from the synthesis, made possible by high-speed computers, may be derived a detailed, high-resolution contour pattern of a relatively small area of the sky.

Radio-heliograph

The Culgoora (Australia) radioheliograph is a remarkable solar telescope that provides nearly instantaneous moving pictures of the activity in the Sun's atmosphere as exhibited at a frequency of 80 megahertz (3.75 metres). Ninety-six 45-foot (14-metre) dishes are equally spaced in a circle of 1.86-miles (3 kilometres) diameter. The signals received by each dish are brought to a central receiving station and processed electronically to form the final image; this image is displayed on a cathode-ray tube and photographed on motion picture film. This telescope has a total receiving area equivalent to a 400-foot (120-metre) dish but has the resolving power of a 9,800-foot (3,000-metre) dish. The field of view is about 2°—four solar diameters. Observations are made daily, even through clouds, and active regions on the Sun can be easily detected, kept under watch, and compared with photographic observations made with conventional optical telescopes.

AUXILIARY INSTRUMENTS

Almost all astronomical research is done photographically or photoelectrically, rather than visually. If a photographic plate is placed in the focal plane, a telescope becomes a large camera. A photograph provides a permanent record that can be measured and studied in detail at any convenient later date under optimum conditions. Astronomical exposure times are often measured in hours rather than in fractions of a second. Special guiding techniques must be used to keep the telescope centred on the object being photographed. A star image outside the field being photographed may be kept accurately centred on illuminated cross hairs; sometimes an auxiliary guiding telescope is used, firmly attached to the main telescope tube. Objects can be photographed that are many times fainter than can be seen by looking through the eyepiece. One photographic plate may contain a vast amount of information. For example, a plate from a large Schmidt telescope could easily have 1,000,000 star images and 100,000 galaxian images on it. In principle it is possible to derive not only the relative positions of all these objects but also their magnitudes. A more rewarding activity is to make a second plate at a later date—sometimes years later—and compare it with the first. This comparison will disclose those few very interesting stars that have moved, or have varied in brightness.

Exposure times

Spectroscopic instruments. The most commonly used photographic emulsion is insensitive to wavelengths longer than 5000 angstroms and is useful in ground-based research down to 3000 angstroms, the limit imposed by the atmosphere. There are a wide variety of other emulsions that can be used, usually with colour filters, in the visual, red, and infrared regions out to a limit of about 12,500 angstroms. These different emulsions also find their uses in spectroscopy, which occupies at least half of the available observing time of large reflectors (see also ASTRONOMICAL SPECTROSCOPY, PRINCIPLES OF; SPECTROSCOPY, PRINCIPLES OF).

Grating spectrograph

In a prism spectrograph, the light of a star first passes through a slit located in the focal plane. The diverging beam is then collimated (made parallel) by a collimating lens. It then passes through a prism, or series of prisms, which disperses the light into a spectrum. Finally, the spectrum is brought to a focus on the photographic plate by a camera lens, the violet rays being bent more by the prism than the red rays. A grating spectrograph uses a reflection grating as the dispersing device. The grating is a glass plate coated with aluminum on which many parallel lines have been closely ruled. All of the parts of the astronomical spectrograph—slit, the two lenses, the prism or grating, and the photographic plate—must be attached to a rigid framework so that they do not shift during a long exposure. The interior of a spectrograph is often kept at a constant temperature. A comparison spectrum provides standards of known wavelength against which the stellar spectrum may be compared and measured. To preserve spectral purity, the width of the slit must be such that its monochromatic image on the plate is 0.015 to 0.020 millimetre—of the order of the resolving power of the emulsion. When high dispersion is desired it is necessary to use a long focal length camera lens, necessitating in turn a very narrow slit and loss of starlight. This can be overcome in part by using a very large collimated beam, hence a very large spectrograph. Such an instrument must, of necessity, remain stationary. It is placed at the coudé focus, since in this arrangement the focus does not move with the telescope.

Spectroscopy is the observational basis of much of the astrophysics and stellar astronomy of today. The spectrograph can be used to determine the masses and radii of stars, as well as their distances and velocities. It can also be used to determine stellar rotations, temperatures, magnetic fields, chemical compositions, and other properties. The spectrograph has been used to establish the expanding nature of the universe and its approximate age; the radial velocities of galaxies have been measured spectroscopically at distances of several billion (thousand million) light-years.

Instruments for photoelectric photometry. The photoelectric cell is now of basic importance in another fundamental field in observational astronomy, photometry. Light striking certain alkali surfaces causes electrons to be emitted from that surface, the number of electrons emitted being strictly proportional to the intensity of the light. Light, in itself, is difficult to measure with high precision, especially in all of the various colours; an electric current can be precisely measured and the colour regions standardized by the use of appropriate filters. Photoelectric photometry came of age in 1946 with the introduction of the 1P21 photomultiplier tube, developed during World War II. This tube not only converts a beam of light into a beam of electrons but, through a process of secondary emission, it multiplies the original phototelectrons by factors of the order of a million within the small vacuum tube (see also ELECTRON TUBE). Photomultiplier tubes have been especially effective in the observations of tens of thousands of stars for their ultraviolet, blue, and "visual" magnitudes. Observations of the magnitudes and colours of the faintest photographable stars and galaxies are also possible. Red and infrared photocells have also found their uses, and very sensitive photoconductive (lead sulfide) cells have been successfully employed, especially at the University of Arizona, in connection with wavelengths up to and beyond 36,000 angstroms. A number of large observatories have developed photoelectric scanners that combine the spectroscope and the phototube. With such a device, the energy distribution of very

Photomultiplier tube

faint objects, as well as the bright stars, can be obtained. A multichannel spectrometer that has been in operation at Mt. Palomar Observatory (now part of Hale Observatories) since 1969 allows simultaneous observations with 32 photomultipliers in 32 wavelength bands. A technique of this sort permits collection of data far more rapidly than if the channels were observed one at a time. Furthermore, simultaneous observations may be substantially more accurate, because of changing sky conditions.

OTHER DEVELOPMENTS

Telescopes above the Earth. The atmosphere influences astronomical observations in many undesirable ways. It enlarges the stellar images. It causes the intensity of the image, especially in a smaller telescope, to fluctuate rapidly (scintillate) and causes the image to change rapidly in its apparent position. The atmosphere completely absorbs the incoming radiation, hence the information it contains, in the wavelengths outside the optical and radio regions; within these regions the absorption may be so great, as in the case of overcast skies, or may vary so rapidly as to make useful observations impractical or impossible.

The optical region is chopped up in the infrared by strong absorbing bands of water vapour that mask, partially or completely, spectroscopic features of the planets and the Sun in this region. Sensitive infrared spectrographs have been operated successfully in aircraft at altitudes of 40,000 feet or higher, where this water-vapour absorption becomes negligible. Using airborne spectrographs, astronomers have scanned the solar spectrum out to 51,000 angstroms with high resolving power. Balloons have carried instruments and telescopes to altitudes up to 120,000 feet where the seeing is so good that the theoretical resolving power of the telescope has been reached. An unmanned balloon, Stratoscope II, launched in March 1970 by Princeton University astronomers, reached 80,000 feet. Direct photographs with a 36-inch reflecting telescope of the planet Uranus at a resolving power of 0″.1 of arc showed for the first time the conspicuous limb (outer edge) darkening and a slight oblateness (flattening) of the disk. Earlier stratoscope flights had resulted in excellent photographs of the Sun.

Infrared spectrographs

Rocket observations made from just above the Earth's atmosphere, notably by astronomers at the U.S. Naval Research Laboratory, have extended the solar spectrum in detail to the one-angstrom X-ray region. Over a hundred X-ray sources have been discovered. Of the few that have been optically identified, the most exciting is the pulsating radio star, called a pulsar, in the Crab Nebula. This X-ray source pulsates 30 times a second, as in the optical and radio regions, but with much greater energy (see also X-RAY SOURCES, ASTRONOMICAL; PULSARS).

Although it is still in its infancy, space astronomy has already had spectacular successes. Instruments have been landed on the Moon and Venus. There have been a number of flights close to Venus and Mars. A Mars flyby provided the first direct photography and knowledge of the Martian craters. The side of the Moon facing away from the Earth has been thoroughly photographed and mapped. By the early 1970s there were a number of orbiting solar and astronomical observatories in operation and more were to come. Planning the instrumentation for these expensive "sites" must be based almost entirely on knowledge garnered by ground-based astronomy. Each new space observatory requires years of thoughtful preparation in order to make the most useful types of observations, particularly since observations involve new types of telescopes and instrumentation for previously little-used wavelengths. The instruments must be remote-controlled from distances of a few hundred miles to 100,000,000 miles. Amazingly detailed information—such as that obtained by a direct photograph—must be sent back to Earth over these same enormous distances. Telescopes and cameras must be protected from the intense unfiltered radiation of the Sun and from erosion by micrometeorites. A very high level of reliability must be built into their operation. Observations of the stars in the far ultraviolet have just begun, and if the

Remote-controlled instrumentation

history of radio astronomy is a guide, important discoveries can be expected with the opening up of this previously inaccessible wavelength region.

International cooperation. A number of telescopes and observatories have been built and operated on an international basis. Harvard University, Ireland, and North Ireland jointly financed the 32-inch Schmidt telescope located near Bloemfontein, South Africa; this observatory is operated by this group and other European countries. An Anglo-Australian 150-inch reflector will be erected in the early 1970s at Siding Springs, Australia. The Carnegie Institution of Washington, D.C., and radio astronomers of the Argentine jointly built twin 100-foot dishes near Buenos Aires. Six European countries are jointly building and operating the very large European Southern Observatory north of La Serena, Chile, and the nearby Cerro Tololo Inter-American Observatory is used by visiting U.S. astronomers, as well as by Chilean and other South American astronomers. There is still a great need for more radio telescopes in South America and South Africa, particularly to carry out very long base-line interferometry of southern sources jointly with Australia.

BIBLIOGRAPHY. The early history of the telescope is discussed in H.C. KING, *The History of the Telescope* (1955); and A. PANNEKOEK, *De Groei van ons Wereldbeeld* (1951; Eng. trans., *A History of Astronomy*, 1961). Modern instruments are treated in G.P. KUIPER and B.M. MIDDLEHURST (eds.), *Telescopes* (1960); G.R. MICZAIKA and W.M. SINTON, *Tools of the Astronomer* (1961); G.O. ABELL, *Exploration of the Universe* (1969); and J.D. KRAUS, *Radio Astronomy* (1966). Specific telescopes are described in the publications of the observatories operating them. See also current issues of the monthly periodical *Sky and Telescope.*

(J.B.I.)

Television

Television is the electrical transmission of pictures in motion and the simultaneous electrical transmission of the accompanying sounds. Additional discussion of the principles upon which such transmission is based will be found in the articles RADIO and ELECTRONICS; programming aspects are covered in the article BROADCASTING.

This article is outlined as follows:

The purpose of a television system is to extend the senses of vision and hearing beyond their natural limits. Television systems are designed, therefore, to embrace the essential capabilities of these senses, with appropriate compromises between the quality of the reproduction and the costs involved. The aspects of natural vision that must be considered in a television system include the ability of the human eye to distinguish the brightness, colours, details, sizes, shapes, and positions of the objects in the scene before it. The aspects of hearing include the ability of the ear to distinguish the pitch, loudness, and distribution of sounds. The television system must also be designed to override, within reasonable limits, the effects of interference and to minimize visual and aural distortions in the transmission and reproduction processes. The particular compromises adopted for public television service (*i.e.*, by broadcast means) are embodied in the television standards adopted and enforced by the responsible government agency in each country.

Television technology deals with the fact that human vision employs many hundreds of thousands of separate electrical circuits, in the optic nerve from the retina to the brain, to convey simultaneously in two dimensions the whole content of the scene on which the eye is focussed, whereas in electrical communications it is feasible to employ only one such circuit (*i.e.*, the broadcast channel) to connect the transmitter and the receiver. This fundamental disparity is overcome in television by a process of image analysis and synthesis, whereby the scene to be televised is first translated into an electrical image, and the latter is then broken up into an orderly sequence of electrical impulses that are sent over the channel one after the other. At the receiver the impulses are translated back into a corresponding sequence of lights and shadows, and these are reassembled in their correct positions on the viewing screen.

How television differs from the human eye

This sequential reproduction of visual images is feasible only because the visual sense displays persistence; that is, the brain retains the impression of illumination for about 0.1 second after the source of light is removed from the eye. If, therefore, the process of image synthesis occurs within less than 0.1 second, the eye is unaware that the picture is being reassembled piecemeal, and it appears as if the whole surface of the viewing screen were continuously illuminated. By the same token, it is then possible to re-create more than ten complete pictures per second and to simulate thereby the motion of the scene so that it appears to be continuous.

In practice, to depict rapid motion smoothly, it is customary to transmit from 25 to 30 complete pictures per second. To provide detail sufficient to accommodate a wide range of subject matter, each picture is analyzed into 300,000 or more elementary details. This analysis implies that the rate at which these details are transmitted over the television system exceeds 4,000,000 per second. To provide a system suitable for public use and also capable of such speed has required the full resources of modern electronic technology.

I. History

MECHANICAL SYSTEMS

Early ideas for the realization of television assumed the transmission of every picture element simultaneously, each over a separate circuit (as, for example, a system suggested by George Carey of Boston in 1875); but in about 1880 the important principle—subsequently adopted in all forms of television—of rapidly scanning each element in the picture in succession, line by line and frame by frame, with reliance on persistence of human vision, was proposed, notably by W.E. Sawyer in the United States and Maurice Leblanc in France. This established the possibility of using only a single wire or channel for transmission.

In 1873 the photoconductive properties of selenium were discovered; that is, the fact that its electrical conduction varied with the amount of illumination. This appeared to provide an important clue to the secret of practical television and led in 1884 to a patent by Paul Nipkow in Germany of a complete television system. The distinctive feature of Nipkow's system was the spirally apertured rotating disk that provided, at both sending and receiving ends, a simple and effective method of image scanning. Until the advent of electronic scanning, all workable television systems depended on some form or variation (*e.g.*, mirror drums, lensed disks, etc.) of the mechanical sequential scanning method exemplified by the Nipkow disk.

Nipkow system

As illustrated in Figure 1, the image to be televised is focussed on a rotating disk having square apertures arranged in a spiral. As the disk rotates, the outermost aperture traces out a line across the top of the image, and the light passing through the aperture varies in direct proportion to the light and shade (*i.e.*, brightness values) of that line of the image as it is traversed by the aperture. When the outermost aperture has passed over the image, the next inner aperture traces out another line, parallel to and immediately below the line just traced. The changes in the light passing through the second aperture represent, in sequence, the brightness values present in the image along this second line. As the disk continues to rotate, successive lines are traced out, one beneath the other, until the whole area of the image has been explored, one line at a time. The process is repeated with each rotation of the disk; the more apertures, and hence lines, the greater the detail that can be analyzed.

In this way the detail of the whole image is sequentially explored in an orderly manner. The light passing through the apertures enters a photoelectric cell that translates the sequence of light values into a corresponding sequence of electric values. These are transmitted over a single circuit to the receiver, where the electrical impulses cause light to be produced by a lamp (such as a gas-discharge lamp) capable of reproducing the sequence of light values. The light from the lamp is projected onto the surface of a disk similar to that at the transmitter. This disk must rotate in precise synchronism, and, by a scanning process the reverse of that already described, the brightness values are reassembled in their proper positions and the original image is reproduced. Provided the rotation is at sufficient speed, persistence of vision enables the eye to see the image as a whole rather than as a series of moving points. The need for exact synchronism between camera and receiver scanning speeds is fundamental not only to the mechanical system that has been described above but to every television system.

Selenium, when used as the photosensitive material for the photoelectric cell, had a serious handicap; its response to changes of light was very slow. Researches in Germany resulted (1913) in a potassium hydride-coated cell with both an improved sensitivity and the ability to follow rapid changes of light. This made possible for the first time a practical working system.

In 1897 K.F. Braun of Germany had introduced a cathode-ray screen with a fluorescent screen; that is, a screen that produced visible light when struck by a beam of electrons. The Russian scientist Boris Rosing in 1907 suggested its use in the receiver of a television system that, at the camera end, made use of mirror-drum scanning. Rosing succeeded in transmitting and reproducing some crude geometrical patterns and so ranks as an important pioneer.

In 1904 the English physicist J.A. Fleming invented the two-electrode valve; the American inventor Lee De Forest added the grid in 1906 and made amplification possible, another essential step toward practical television.

In 1908 came a most remarkable contribution by the Scottish electrical engineer A.A. Campbell Swinton, who outlined a method that, in all essentials, is the basis of modern television. Lack of amplifiers and other difficulties confined this to what Swinton called "an idea only," but he clarified and elaborated it in an address to the Röntgen Society of London in 1911. He proposed, in essence, the use of cathode-ray tubes, magnetically deflected, at both camera and receiver. In the former was a mosaic screen of photoelectric elements; the image of the scene to be transmitted was focussed onto this screen, the back of which was then discharged by a cathode-ray beam tracing out a line-by-line scanning sequence. Swinton's brilliant ideas were too advanced for early application, and it was left to others to put them into practice many years later.

Meanwhile, experimenters in Europe and the United States were trying to make a less ambitious beginning. The neon gas-discharge lamp, produced by D.M. Moore of the U.S. in 1917, made it possible to vary the light intensity at the receiver by varying the electrical input to

Swinton's proposals

the neon lamp, thus in effect producing modulated light. It was adopted by J.L. Baird in England and C.F. Jenkins in the United States, both of whom in 1923 began experimenting with mechanical methods using the Nipkow principle. In 1926 Baird gave the first demonstration of true television by electrically transmitting moving pictures in halftones. These pictures were formed of only 30 lines, repeating approximately ten times per second. The results, though inevitably crude—flickering badly and with a dim receiver screen a few inches high—nevertheless became the start of television as a practical technology and did much to stimulate further research, while also forming the basis of some experimental broadcasting in England between 1929 and 1935.

ELECTRONIC SYSTEMS

Mechanical systems lacked sensitivity, as became progressively manifest with attempts to increase the number of lines and thus the degree of definition of the pictures. Swinton and others had pointed out that television pictures, for good quality and definition on a screen of reasonable size, would need to be analyzed into at least 100,000 and preferably 200,000 elements. Since the number of elements is approximately equal to the square of the number of lines, it can be seen that any system using 30 or even 100 lines would be inadequate—300 being more nearly the minimum. Although mechanical systems were with difficulty made to operate on 200 and more lines, thought increasingly turned toward the greater potential of electronic methods. A most important landmark was V.K. Zworykin's patent, first filed in 1923, for the iconoscope camera tube. Later, he constructed such a tube; and by 1932 the Radio Corporation of America (RCA), with an improved cathode-ray tube for the receiver, demonstrated all-electronic television (initially on 120 lines), so proving the soundness of Swinton's theoretical ideas. The compactness and convenience of the electronic camera were remarkable, and its sensitivity, greatly aided by the unique "storage" feature of the iconoscope, was comparable with motion-picture cameras of the time.

Continuing work on electronic systems was greatly stimulated. In the United States the development was mainly carried out in the RCA laboratories; very soon the number of scanning lines was increased to 343, and other improvements followed rapidly. German investigators also were active, especially in the development of high-vacuum cathode-ray tubes. By 1935 a regular broadcasting service had begun in Germany, though with medium definition only—180 lines. In The Netherlands, too, the Philips Laboratories took up television research.

In Great Britain, Electric and Musical Industries (EMI) set up in 1931 a television research group under Isaac (later Sir Isaac) Shoenberg, a dynamic and far-sighted man of long experience in the field of radio transmission in both the Soviet Union and England. He fostered the evolution of a complete and practical system based on: (1) a camera tube known as the Emitron—an advanced version of the iconoscope—and (2) an improved high-vacuum cathode-ray tube for the receiver. The team produced by 1935 a complete and practical system, including all of the complex electronics surrounding the camera and receiver tubes, as well as the intervening control and amplifying circuits. Shoenberg saw the need to establish a system that would endure for many years, since any subsequent changes in basic standards—particularly the number of scanning lines and their repetition rate—could give rise to severe technical or economic problems. He therefore proposed the use of 405 lines with 50 frames per second, and interlaced scanning (see below) to give 25 pictures per second without flicker—ambitious for those days, but fully justified by events. The government authorized the British Broadcasting Corporation to adopt these standards, as well as the complete EMI system, from the outset of the world's first public high-definition service, which was launched in London in 1936. Until 1964 they formed the sole basis of the British service, later being gradually superseded by the international 625-line standard. Initially, and for a short time only, the system was under comparison with alternate broadcasts from a 240-line, 25-picture system developed by the Baird company. The latter employed mechanical scanning methods in the camera and suffered from lack of sensitivity as well as other limitations.

By the mid-1930s electronic television was fast advancing in all its aspects. Important questions were the settling of basic standards (number of lines and frames per second) before the introduction of public broadcasting services in the United States and elsewhere, though these questions were not everywhere fully resolved until about 1951. The United States soon adopted a picture repetition rate of 30 per second, while in Europe it became 25. These two standards have been perpetuated, and all the countries of the world use one or the other, though technical advances have now obviated the original need for disparity. The arguments in relation to the number of lines were based on the need for an effective compromise between, on the one hand, adequate picture definition, and, on the other, a frequency bandwidth that could be technically and economically acceptable. World standardization has never been achieved, though for new television services all countries are adopting one of only two standards, namely, 525 lines per picture at 30 pictures per second—the United States standard—and 625 lines at 25 pictures per second, usually known as the European standard. Complications arise when programs are transmitted between countries using different standards.

United States and European standards

Regular television broadcasting began in the United States in 1941, but most other countries, apart from Great Britain, were not ready to begin services until the 1950s, when television was widely introduced throughout the world. When wartime restrictions governing the manufacture of receivers were removed in 1946, the stage was set in the United States for a rapid growth of the television broadcasting industry. By 1949 there were 1,000,000 receivers in use; the 10,000,000 mark was passed in 1951 and the 50,000,000 mark eight years later. About half of that number were in use in the 50 other nations that by then had established regular program services.

By the early 1970s, receivers in use throughout the world totalled about 275,000,000; about 93,000,000 were in the United States, 18,000,000 in the United Kingdom, 8,000,000 in Canada, 25,000,000 in Japan, 28,000,000 in the Soviet Union, 12,000,000 in France, 17,000,000 in West Germany, and 10,000,000 in Italy.

Technical advances have been continuous, particularly the great improvements in camera tubes (*e.g.*, the image orthicon and the Vidicon, the latter of which was at last able effectively to exploit the photoconductivity principle) that were made from 1945 onward (see below *Television camera tubes*). By the early 1950s technology had progressed so far, and television had become so widely established, that the time was ripe to tackle in earnest the problem of creating television images in natural colours.

THE DEVELOPMENT OF COLOUR

Colour television was by no means a new idea, since its attraction and possibility early engaged the imaginations of inventors. A German patent in 1904 contained the earliest proposal, while in 1925 Zworykin filed a patent disclosure for an all-electronic colour television system. The first practical demonstration of television in colour was given by Baird in 1928; he used mechanical scanning with a Nipkow disk having three spirals of 30 apertures, one spiral for each primary colour in sequence. The light source at the receiver comprised two gas-discharge tubes, one of mercury vapour and helium for the green and blue colours, and a neon tube for red. In 1929 H.E. Ives and colleagues at Bell Telephone Laboratories transmitted 50-line colour television images between New York City and Washington, D.C.; this also was a mechanical method, but one that sent simultaneously the three primary colour signals over three separate circuits. In the same year Frank Gray, also of Bell Laboratories, applied for a patent that described a method of transmitting two or more signals over a single channel; this introduced important new principles that were to be the foundation of modern (compatible) colour television as it was developed about 20 years later.

It soon became apparent that two basic approaches to colour television were possible. One was the frame-by-frame sequential transmission of signals corresponding to each of the three primary colours. This method was in most respects relatively simple to achieve but involved an increased rate of scanning in order to avoid colour flicker, with resulting transmission difficulties from both the higher bandwidth and the inability to use existing black-and-white receivers to reproduce any pictures originated in colour. This kind of system is therefore usually described as noncompatible. The alternative approach—practically much more difficult, even daunting at first—recognized the advantage to be derived from a colour transmission system in which signals representing the three primary colours were transmitted simultaneously and which could also be compatible with existing black-and-white transmissions. Such a system would mean that any pictures originated in colour could still be receivable (in black and white) on a black-and-white receiver.

Compatible and non-compatible colour television

In 1938 Georg Valensi of France pioneered the path to compatible colour television when he patented a method that enabled

the output from a single transmitter to be received not only by television receivers provided with the necessary equipment but also by the ordinary type of receiver which is more numerous and less expensive and which reproduces the pictures in black and white.

Although Valensi's proposals have not been precisely adopted in practice, they were influential in later approaches to the problem of compatibility.

Experimental work on colour (on high-definition standards) was taken up in both Great Britain and the United States during the late 1930s. Similar methods were explored by Baird in Great Britain and Peter Goldmark of the Columbia Broadcasting System (CBS) in the United States, both of whom demonstrated sequential systems using rotating colour filters on the cameras and the receivers. The CBS method was used for some experimental broadcasts before World War II, and these were resumed in 1951 as a service authorized by the Federal Communications Commission (FCC). Public interest was small, however, and after only a few months the broadcasts were abandoned.

Serious attention was then given by the National Television Systems Committee (NTSC) in the United States to the development of a fully compatible simultaneous system. The committee's work led in 1953 to a system capable of operating within the current black-and-white standards and was accepted by the FCC. The essentials of this system, known as the NTSC system, have formed the basis of colour systems throughout the world. The basic principle is the combination of two image transmissions: one carrying information about the brightness, including the finest details of the televised scene, to which black-and-white receivers respond; the other, of coarser structure, carrying the colour information. This second component has no appreciable effect on black-and-white sets, while colour receivers use a combination of the two image transmissions. Since the ability of the human eye to perceive detail is most acute when viewing white light, the brightness component of the colour images carries the impression of fine detail, and the superimposed coarse colour information does not substantially alter the sharpness of the resulting colour picture.

In the United States, public broadcasting using the NTSC system began in 1954. The same system was adopted by Japan, where it came into service in 1960. Other countries favoured modifications of the NTSC system. One such was devised by W. Bruch of the German Telefunken Company; known as PAL (phase alternation line), this comprised a small but subtle variant of the NTSC method. The other, SECAM (*système électronique couleur avec mémoire*), differing rather more radically, had been put forward earlier by Henri de France in Paris. Both alternatives aimed at reducing the sensitivity of the colour system to certain forms of distortion encountered in transmission and broadcasting, and had special application to European conditions. Countries were divided in their preferences: in 1967 Great Britain and the Federal Republic of

The SECAM system

Germany began colour broadcasting using the PAL system, while in the same year France and the Soviet Union also introduced colour, adopting the SECAM system. One or the other of these three systems was being adopted by all countries in the 1970's.

Colour television is technically much more complex than black and white. In the early 1970s most cameras embodied either three or four pickup tubes, while in the receiver a shadow-mask, three-gun, cathode-ray tube, first demonstrated in 1950, formed a successful and widely adopted type of display device for domestic purposes. Widespread purchase of colour receivers began in the United States in 1964. By the early 1970s, more than 40,000,000 colour sets were in use throughout the world; about 31,000,000 were in the United States, 5,000,000 in Japan, 1,300,000 in West Germany, 1,000,000 in Canada, and 750,000 in the United Kingdom. Beginning in 1971, purchases of colour receivers in the United States exceeded sales of domestically manufactured black-and-white sets. (T.H.B.)

II. Principles of picture transmission and reception

BASIC CONSIDERATIONS

The quality and quantity of television service are limited fundamentally by the rate at which it is feasible to transmit the picture information over the television channel. As noted above, in modern practice the televised image must be capable of being dissected, within a few hundredths of a second, into more than 100,000 picture elements. This implies that the electrical impulses corresponding to the picture elements must pass through the channel at a rate as high as several million per second. Moreover, since the picture content may vary from simple close-up shots having little fine detail to comprehensive distant scenes in which the limiting detail of the system comes into play, the actual rate of transmitting the picture information varies from time to time, from a few impulses per second to several million per second. The television channel must be capable, therefore, of handling information over a continuous band of frequencies several million cycles wide. This is testimony to the extraordinary comprehension of the sense of sight. Hearing is comparatively crude. The ear is satisfied by impulses that can be carried over a channel only 10,000 cycles wide.

In the United States, the television channel occupies a width of six megacycles (6,000,000 hertz, or cycles per second) in the radio spectrum. This is 600 times as wide as the channel used by each standard sound broadcasting station. In fact, each television station uses nearly six times as much spectrum space as all the commercial amplitude-modulation (AM) sound broadcasting channels combined. Since each television station must occupy so much spectrum space, few channels are available in a given locality. Moreover, the quantity of service is in conflict with the quality of reproduction. If the detail of the television image is to be increased, other parameters of the transmission being unchanged, the channel width must be increased proportionally, and this decreases the number of channels that can be accommodated in the spectrum. This fundamental conflict between quality of transmission and number of available channels dictates that the quality of reproduction shall just satisfy the typical viewer under normal viewing conditions. Any excess of performance beyond this ultimately would result in a restriction of program choice.

Flicker. The first requirement to be met in image analysis is that the reproduced picture shall not flicker, since flicker induces severe visual fatigue. Flicker becomes more evident as the brightness of the picture increases. If flicker is to be unobjectionable at brightness suitable for home viewing during daylight as well as evening hours (25 to 100 footlamberts), the successive illuminations of the picture screen should occur no fewer than 50 times per second. This is approximately twice the rate of picture repetition needed for smooth reproduction of motion. To avoid flicker, therefore, twice as much channel space is needed as would suffice to depict motion. The same disparity occurs in motion-picture practice, in which satisfactory performance with respect to flicker

requires twice as much film as is necessary for smooth simulation of motion.

A way around this difficulty has been found, in motion pictures as well as in television, by projecting each picture twice. In motion pictures, the projector interposes a shutter briefly between film and lens while a single frame of the film is being projected. In television, each image is analyzed and synthesized in two sets of spaced lines, one of which fits successively within the spaces of the other (Figure 2). Thus the picture area is illuminated twice during each complete picture transmission, although each line in the image is present only once during that time. This technique is feasible because the eye is comparatively insensitive to flicker when the variation of light is confined to a small part of the field of view. Hence flicker of the individual lines is not evident. If the eye did not have this fortunate property, a television channel would have to occupy about twice as much spectrum space as it now does.

Projecting each picture twice

It is thus possible to avoid flicker and simulate rapid motion by a picture rate of about 25 per second, with two screen illuminations per picture. The precise value of the picture-repetition rate used in a given region has been chosen by reference to the electric power frequency that predominates in that region. In Europe, where 50-hertz power is the rule, the television picture rate is 25 per second (50 screen illuminations per second). In North America the picture rate is 30 per second (60 screen illuminations per second) to match the 60-hertz power that predominates there.

The higher picture-transmission rate of North America allows the pictures there to be about five times as bright as those in Europe for the same susceptibility to flicker, but this advantage is offset by a 20 percent reduction in picture detail for equal utilization of the channel.

Image structure. The second aspect of performance to be met in a television system is the detailed structure of the image. A printed halftone engraving may possess several million halftone dots per square foot of area. Such reproductions are intended for minute inspection, and the dot structure must not be apparent to the unaided eye even at close range. Such fine detail would be a costly waste in television, since the television picture is viewed at comparatively long range (five to 15 feet, or 1.5 to 4.5 metres, in the typical home setting) and the picture area is not greater than about two square feet (1,800 square centimetres). Under these conditions, a picture structure of about 200,000 halftone elements is a suitable compromise. This detail is about equal to that provided by 16-millimetre home motion pictures and substantially exceeds that of the eight-millimetre film widely used for amateur cinematography.

Picture shape. The third item to be selected in image analysis is the shape of the picture. This has been standardized universally as a rectangle the width of which is one-third longer than its height. This 4:3 ratio (aspect ratio) was originally chosen to match the dimensions of standard 35-millimetre motion-picture film (prior to the advent of the wide-screen cinema) in the interest of televising film without waste of frame area. The width of the screen rectangle is greater than its height, as in the proscenium of a theatre, to accommodate the horizontal motion that predominates in virtually all televised events.

Scanning. The fourth determination in image analysis is the path over which the image structure is explored at the camera and reconstructed on the receiver screen. In the original Nipkow disk, this path was a series of arcs of circles (Figure 1). In modern television, the pattern is a series of parallel straight lines, each progressing from left to right, the lines following in sequence from top to bottom of the picture frame. The exploration of the image structure proceeds at a constant speed along each line, since this provides uniform loading of the transmission channel under the demands of a given structural detail, no matter where in the frame the detail lies. The line-by-line, left-to-right, top-to-bottom dissection and reconstitution of television images is known as scanning, from its similarity to the progression of the line of vision in reading a page of printed matter. The agent that disassembles

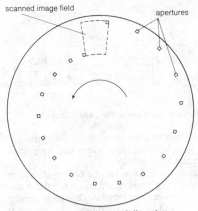

Figure 1: Nipkow disk for an 18-line picture (see text).

region or country	number of lines per frame	number of pictures per second	maximum detail (picture elements per frame)	available picture band-width (MHz)	channel band-width (MHz)
Television Systems of the World					
United Kingdom	405–625	25	130,000–210,000	3–6	5–8
North America, South America, Japan	525	30	130,000	4	6
Europe, Australia, Africa, Eurasia	625	25	210,000	6	8
France and French dependencies	625–819	25	210,000–440,000	6–10.4	8–14

the light values along each line is called the scanning spot, and the path it follows is the scanning pattern, or raster.

The geometry of the modern scanning pattern is shown in Figure 2. It consists of two sets of lines. One set, marked A, is scanned first, and the lines are so laid down

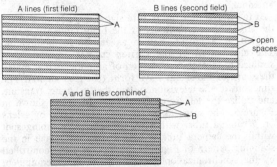

Figure 2: Interlaced scanning, combining two separate scanning cycles (fields) to form a complete picture (see text).

Interlaced scanning

that an equal empty space is maintained between lines. The second set, marked B, is laid down after the first and is so positioned that its lines fall precisely in the empty spaces of set A. The area of the image is thus scanned twice, but each point in the area is passed over once. This is known as interlaced scanning, and it is used in all the television broadcast services of the world. Each set of alternate lines is known as a scanning field; the two sets together, comprising the whole scanning pattern, are known as a scanning frame. The repetition rate of field scanning is standardized in accordance with the frequency of electric power, as noted above, at either 50 or 60 fields per second. Corresponding rates of frame scanning are 25 and 30 frames per second. The localities for various scanning standards are listed in the Table.

The total number of lines in the scanning pattern has been set to provide a maximum pictorial detail of the order of 200,000 picture elements. Since the frame area is four units wide by three units high, this figure implies a pattern of about 520 picture elements in its width (along each line) and 390 elements in its height (across the lines). This latter figure would imply a scanning pattern of about 400 lines, were it not for the fact that many of the picture details, falling in random positions on the scanning pattern, lie partly on two lines and hence require two lines for accurate reproduction. Scanning patterns are designed, therefore, to possess about 40 percent more lines than the number of picture elements to be reproduced on the vertical direction. Actual values in use in television broadcasting in various regions are 405 lines, 525 lines, 625 lines, and 819 lines per frame, as listed in the Table. These values have been chosen to suit the frequency band of the channel actually assigned in the respective geographical regions.

The scanning spot is made to follow the paths shown in Figure 2 by imparting two repetitive motions to the spot simultaneously (Figure 3). One is a horizontally direct-

ed back-and-forth motion. The spot is moved at constant speed from left to right and then returned as rapidly as possible, while extinguished and inactive, from right to left.

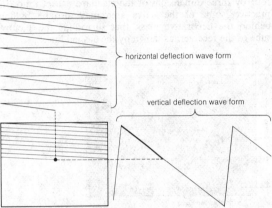

Figure 3: Scanning pattern and wave forms for horizontal and vertical deflection in sequential parallel-line scanning.

Simultaneously, a vertical motion is imparted to the spot, moving it comparatively slowly from the top to the bottom of the frame. This motion spreads out the more rapid left-to-right scans, forming the first field scan of alternate lines and empty spaces. When the bottom of the frame is reached, the spot moves vertically upward as rapidly as possible, while extinguished and inactive. The next top-to-bottom motion then spreads out the horizontal line scans so that they fall in the empty spaces of the previously scanned field. Precise interlacing of the successive field scans is facilitated if the total number of lines in the frame is an odd number. All the numbers of lines used in ordinary transmissions (see the Table) were so chosen.

The return of the scanning spot from right to left and from bottom to top of the frame, during which it is inactive, consumes time that cannot be devoted to transmitting picture information. This time is used to transmit synchronizing control signals that keep the scanning process at the receiver in step with that at the transmitter. The time lost during retracing of the spot proportionately reduces the actual number of picture elements that can be reproduced. In the 525-line scanning pattern used in the United States, about 15 percent of each line is lost in the return motion, and about 35 out of the 525 lines are blanked out while the spot returns from bottom to top of two successive fields. The scanning area actually in use for reproduction of the picture contains a maximum of about 435 picture elements along each line and has 490 active lines, capable of reproducing 350 picture elements in the vertical direction. The frame can accommodate at maximum, therefore, about 350×435 or 152,000 picture elements. The detail-transmission capacity of the scanning patterns of other systems is listed in the Table.

The time taken by the scanning spot to move over the active portion of each scanning line is of the order of 0.00005 second (50 microseconds). In the United States system, 525 lines are transmitted in one-thirtieth of a second, which is equivalent to about 64 microseconds per line. Up to 15 percent of this time is consumed in the

Time needed for scanning

horizontal retrace motion of the spot, leaving 54 microseconds (54×10^{-6} seconds) for active reproduction of as many as 435 picture elements in each line. This represents a maximum rate of $435 \div 54 \times 10^{-6} \cong 8,000,000$ picture elements per second.

Two picture elements can be approximately represented by one cycle of the transmission signal wave. The signal must therefore be capable of carrying components as high as 4,000,000 hertz (four megahertz, MHz). The United States six-megahertz television channel provides a sufficient band of frequencies for this (plus an additional two megahertz for transmission of the sound program, to protect against interference, and to meet the requirements of vestigial side-band transmission [see below *The television channel*]).

The relationship between the ideal and actual scanning patterns is shown in Figure 4. The part shown as darker is lost as the spot retraces. The remaining area of the pattern is actively employed in analyzing and synthesizing the picture information and is adjusted to have the four by three dimensions of the standard aspect ratio. In practice, some of the active area may also be hidden behind the decorative mask that surrounds the picture tube of the receiver, as shown by the dashed line.

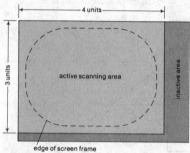

Figure 4: Active and inactive portions of scanning pattern.

THE TELEVISION PICTURE SIGNAL

The signal wave form (the sequence of electrical impulses that makes up a television picture signal) embodies all the picture information to be transmitted from camera to receiver screen as well as the synchronizing information required to keep the receiver and transmitter scanning operations in exact step with each other. The television system, therefore, must deliver the wave form to each receiver as accurately and as free from blemishes as possible. Unfortunately, almost every item of equipment in the system (amplifiers, cables, transmitter, the transmitting antenna, the radio wave in space, the receiving antenna, and the receiver circuits) conspires to distort the wave form or permits it to be contaminated by "noise" or interference.

Distortion and interference

Among the possible distortions in the signal producing the picture are: (1) failure to maintain the rapidity with which the wave form rises or falls as the scanning spot crosses a sharp boundary between light and dark areas of the image, producing a loss of detail or smear in the reproduced image; (2) the introduction of overshoots, which cause excessively harsh outlines; and (3) failure to maintain the average value of the wave form over extended periods, which causes the image as a whole to be too bright or too dark.

Throughout the system, amplifiers must be used to keep the television signal strong relative to the random electrical currents (noise) that are everywhere present. These random currents, caused by thermally induced motions of electrons in the circuits, cause interference having a speckled appearance, known as "snow." Pictures received from distant stations are subject to this form of interference, since the radio wave is then so weak that it cannot override the random currents in the receiving antenna. Interference of a striated type may be caused by the signals of stations other than that to which the receiver is tuned. Care in the design of the receiver tuner and amplifier circuits is necessary to minimize such interference,

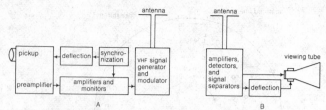

Figure 5: Essential elements of (A) transmitter, and (B) receiver.

and channels must be allocated to neighbouring communities at sufficient geographical separations and frequency intervals to protect the local service.

The television signal wave form can be conveyed within transmitting and receiving apparatus, and over short distances, by wires and cables. For transmission over greater distances, however, as in network connections and over the air, the signal wave form must be imposed on a high-frequency carrier wave. The broadcast transmitter, for example, is actually a generator of very-high-frequency or ultrahigh-frequency radio waves. When such a current (known as the carrier current) is passed through the transmitting antenna, it produces a radio wave of the same frequency that travels through space and induces a weaker, but otherwise identical, current in the receiving antenna.

At the transmitter the picture signal wave form changes the strength, or amplitude, of the high-frequency carrier current by a process known as amplitude modulation. The alternations of the carrier current are thus constrained to take on a succession of amplitudes that match the shape of the signal wave form (see also RADIO). The functions of the television system that generate, transmit, and utilize the television signal wave form are shown in Figure 5. The scene to be televised is focussed by a lens on a camera tube, within the camera. A scanning spot within the camera tube is passed over the image in the scanning pattern of Figure 3, its motion being controlled by the synchronization generator. The latter equipment also renders the scanning spot inactive during its retrace motions and generates the necessary synchronization signals. The camera produces the signal wave form; the synchronizing signals are then added, and the complete signal wave form is established. The signal is then amplified as required, by amplifiers capable of operating over the wide band of frequencies (from a few hertz to 4,000,000 or 5,000,000 hertz) necessary to preserve the precise shape of the wave form. In a transcontinental network, the signal may pass through more than 100 such amplifiers in tandem before it finally reaches the transmitter. There the wave form is amplified to a high power level. Concurrently, the carrier current is generated by other circuits of the transmitter. The signal wave form and carrier current are then combined in the modulator, which imposes the wave form on the carrier. The modulated carrier current may then be further amplified (typically to 10,000 watts or more) and finally passed through the transmitter antenna, which radiates the television radio wave. A similar but enormously weaker current is induced in any receiving antenna within the service area. Reception of excellent quality is possible when the power picked up by the receiving antenna is as low as 0.00000001 (10^{-8}) watt. The power picked up from a distant station may be as low as 10^{-11} watt; but even this low power is capable of producing reception of acceptable quality.

Amplifying the wave form

The transmitter antenna must be as high and in as exposed a location as possible, since the radio waves tend to be intercepted by solid objects, including the Earth's surface at the horizon. Reception beyond the horizon is possible, but the signal at such distances becomes rapidly weaker as it passes to the limit of the service area.

In the receiver, the current from the antenna is passed through a tuner that separates it from other currents of different carrier frequencies that may be present from other stations. The desired current is then amplified in several successive amplifier stages, while still in the amplitude-modulated form. Passage through a detector follows. The picture signal wave form is thereby recovered and is passed through still another amplifier before passing to the picture tube. The picture screen displays a scanning spot the brightness of which is controlled by the picture signal. Simultaneously, the signal is applied to synchronizing circuits, which abstract from it the synchronizing signals. These are used to control the motion of the scanning spot so that it traces out the scanning pattern in precise synchronism with the motion of the scanning spot in the camera.

Transmission and reception of the accompanying sound program are accomplished by apparatus similar to that used for frequency-modulated (FM) radio broadcasting. The carrier frequency for this sound channel is usually spaced 4.5 megahertz from the picture carrier and is separated from the picture carrier in the receiver by appropriate circuitry.

The amount of amplification conferred on the picture and sound currents by a typical television receiver is extremely large. When tuned to a station at a distance of 50 miles (about 80 kilometres), the power picked up by the antenna is typically 10^{-11} watt, as noted above, whereas the signals fed to picture tube and loudspeaker, after amplification, are of the order of one watt; that is, the receiver produces a faithful amplification of the order of 100,000,000,000 times.

TELEVISION CAMERA TUBES

The television camera tube is an electronic device that converts an optical image into a sequence of electrical impulses; *i.e.*, it produces the television picture signal. Three types of television camera tube are in wide use: the image orthicon, the orthicon, and the Vidicon. These devices differ in detail but have in common the following elements: (1) a photosensitive surface (on which the scene is focussed) that converts each light value into a corresponding value of electric charge and forms thereby an electrical image; (2) a means of storing the electrical image—that is, a way of causing the charge to accumulate during the interval of several hundredths of a second between successive scannings of each line in the image; (3) an electron beam, formed in an electron gun and deflected over the electrical image, following the scanning pattern of Figure 2; and (4) a mechanism for producing an electrical current or voltage that is proportional at every instant to the electric charge accumulated at the point passed over by the electron beam at that instant.

Means are also provided for extinguishing the scanning beam during its retrace motions, so that no television signal is then generated. A television pickup device that does not store the electrical image is the flying spot scanner.

Iconoscope. The iconoscope is no longer used, since it is not as sensitive as the image orthicon and its images are subject to uneven shading and flare. But it is well suited to introduce the concepts of electron image storage and scanning in simple form. The iconoscope is housed in a dipper-shaped, vacuum-tight glass envelope, as shown in Figure 6. Within the wide end is a flat sheet of mica. A uniform metallic coating (the signal plate) is placed on the rear surface of this sheet, away from the image. The front surface of the mica is covered with a mosaic comprised of many hundreds of thousands of tiny globules of silver.

During the manufacture of the tube the mosaic is treated with cesium vapour and oxygen, so that each globule has a surface of the oxides of silver and cesium. This combination of elements provides a surface from which electrons are readily liberated, by the photoelectric effect, when light falls on it. Since the globules are insulated from each other and from the signal plate by the mica, the loss of electrons under illumination causes the globules to assume and hold a positive charge, the charge on each globule being proportional to the strength of the illumination falling on it and to the time it has been illuminated.

When an optical image is focussed on the mosaic, the whole surface assumes a distribution of positive charge that matches the distribution of light in the image, and

Common elements of television camera tubes

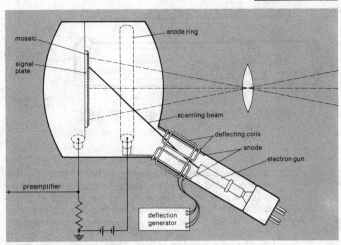

Figure 6: Iconoscope camera tube.

the amount of charge at each point steadily increases, if the optical image is maintained, until the scanning spot passes over the globule at that point.

The scanning spot of the iconoscope is formed by a narrow beam of electrons, shot out of an electron gun in the side arm of the tube. On its way to the mosaic, this beam passes within two sets of electromagnet coils. Currents like those of Figure 3 are passed through these coils, causing the beam to be deflected horizontally at a rapid rate and vertically at a slower rate. The extent of the horizontal motion is adjusted from top to bottom of the mosaic, so that the pattern traced out by the electron beam on the mosaic is a rectangular pattern like that in Figure 2.

Iconoscope scanning spot

As each globule is passed over by the beam, it undergoes a sudden change in electrical potential, the amount of the change being proportional to the light falling on it. The change in potential of the globule is transferred through the mica support to the signal plate behind it, the globule and plate forming in effect the plates of an electrical capacitor. Thus, as the beam passes in succession over the globules lying along a given scanning line, the signal plate assumes a succession of voltages (the picture signal) that match the corresponding succession of light values along that line. The signal plate is connected to an amplifier, external to the iconoscope, that increases the strength of the picture signal.

The phenomenon of charge storage, by which the magnitude of the electrical image is continually increased between successive scannings of each line, is of the utmost significance in television technology. The Nipkow disk (and other non-storage television pickup devices) employs only the light that is present at a given point in the image at the instant the scanning spot passes over that point. Since in modern television the area of the scanning spot is only about one two-hundred-thousandth of the area of the scanning pattern, only this small fraction of the light of the image can be used. But when the image charge is stored in increasing amount for the full interval between successive scannings of a given point, the accumulated charge is then theoretically about 200,000 times the single charge that can be accumulated during the time the beam moves through its own width.

Orthicon. The orthicon camera tube was the first successor to the iconoscope. This tube (Figure 7) is housed in a cylindrical glass structure, on one end of which the optical image is focussed on a mosaic. This mosaic is similar to that of the iconoscope but is made up of a precise array of squares of photosensitive material, formed by evaporation of the material onto a transparent support. A transparent metal coating on the reverse side serves as the signal plate.

The optical image is focussed on the signal plate, passing through it and the support to the mosaic, where it creates and stores a positive electrical charge image, in the manner of the iconoscope. The electron beam is directed toward the mosaic and deflected by electromagnet coils

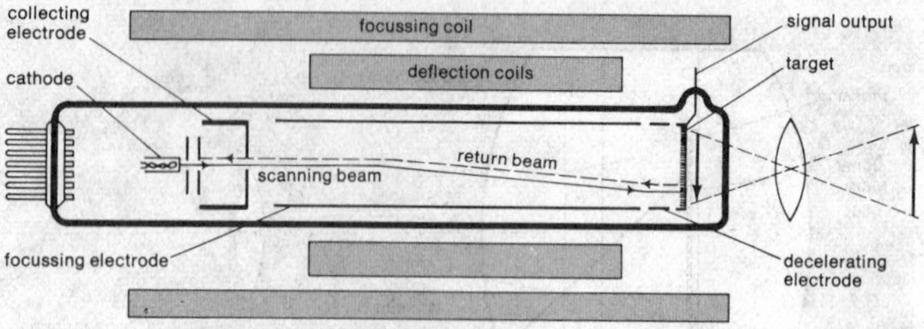

collecting electrode
focussing coil
signal output
cathode
deflection coils
target
return beam
scanning beam
focussing electrode
decelerating electrode

Figure 7: Orthicon camera tube.
By courtesy of RCA

surrounding the tube, so that it passes over the mosaic in the standard interlaced scanning pattern. The electrons are accelerated by a low voltage, so that they strike the mosaic with a low velocity and do not liberate any substantial number of secondary electrons. Instead, the negative electrons in the beam land on the mosaic squares, neutralizing the stored positive charge and ultimately building up a negative charge. The electrons in the beam are then repelled and return to the opposite end of the tube, where they are removed by a positive collecting electrode that surrounds the electron gun. The change in electrical potential, undergone by each mosaic element as its charge is neutralized, is transferred by capacitive action, as in the iconoscope, to the signal plate. The latter thereby undergoes a succession of voltage changes that constitute the picture signal and that are passed to amplifier stages external to the tube.

Image orthicon. The image orthicon is the most highly developed of the television camera tubes and is perhaps the most remarkable electronic device in existence. In its most refined form, its sensitivity to light is phenomenally great. It can respond to light levels far below those capable of exposing motion-picture film or affecting the eye itself. Less sensitive image orthicon tubes are used in broadcasting practice; they serve to produce satisfactory image quality under any light levels likely to be encountered in studio and outdoor scenes.

The image orthicon (Figure 8) is similar to the orthicon but includes an additional electrical-imaging process and contains a high-gain amplifier based on the phenomenon of electron multiplication. It is housed in a cylindrical glass envelope having an enlarged section on one end, which is closed by an optically flat glass plate on the inside of which is deposited a continuous photosensitive coating (photocathode). The optical image is focussed through the glass support onto the coating, where it liberates electrons by photoelectric emission, the emission at each point matching the amount of light in the image at that point.

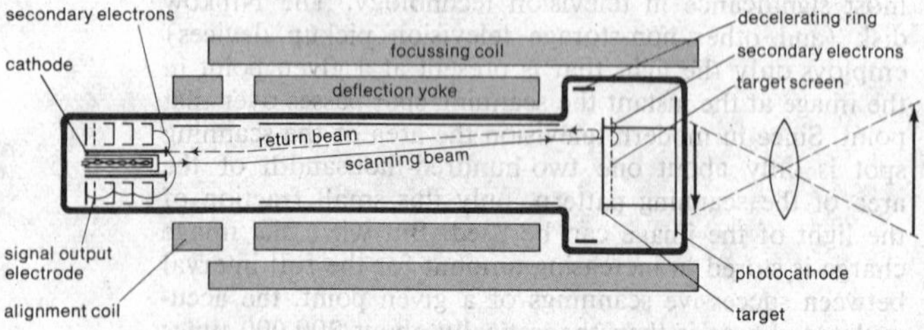

Sensitivity of the image orthicon

secondary electrons
cathode
focussing coil
deflection yoke
return beam
scanning beam
signal output electrode
alignment coil
decelerating ring
secondary electrons
target screen
photocathode
target

Figure 8: Image orthicon camera tube.

The liberated electrons stream away from the photosensitive surface, through the enlarged cylindrical portion of the tube, until they encounter the target electrode, a piece of very thin glass of uniform thickness. The streams of electrons induce secondary emission of electrons from the surface of the glass, and the latter are collected by a fine-mesh screen that lies parallel and close to the glass target; the streams of image electrons pass through it on their way to the target.

The changes in electrical potential induced by secondary emission are transferred to the opposite face of the target, where they are scanned by the electron beam. Because of the characteristics of the glass target, the fine structure of the electrical image is preserved throughout the scanning interval. Moreover, as the streams of electrons from the

photocathode continue to fall on the target glass, the intensity of the electrical image continually increases; that is, storage of charge occurs.

Both the photocathode and the target are continuous surfaces and in themselves contribute no structural limit to the detail of the image. The fine-mesh screen that collects the secondary electrons from the target could, however, impose a limit on detail, and consequently the holes in the screen must be substantially smaller than the scanning spot. Actually, the screen possesses nearly 1,000,000 holes in an area of 1.5 square inches (about ten square centimetres), compared with the roughly 200,000 picture elements into which the image is dissected.

The stored charge image on the reverse side of the target is scanned by an electron beam that, like that of the orthicon, is accelerated at lower voltage and is actually slowed down before hitting the target, so that the scanning electrons have a very low velocity when they strike the target. Consequently, the secondary emission caused by scanning is negligible.

In the standard interlaced scanning pattern the electron beam is magnetically deflected over the electrical image by coils external to the tube. When the beam electrons hit the target, they neutralize the stored positive charge, as in the orthicon, and when equilibrium is reached, further electrons may not land on that spot. Thereafter, the electrons in the beam are turned around at the target and return to the vicinity of the electron gun at the other end of the tube. At this juncture the action differs from that of the orthicon. Instead of taking the picture signal from a signal plate at the target, the return beam of electrons is used. The number of electrons returning from each point in the scanning pattern is conditioned by the prior positive charge neutralization occurring at that point. Consequently, the return beam constitutes a picture signal current.

When the return beam reaches the opposite end of the tube, it is passed through an amplifier structure that contributes greatly to the sensitivity of the tube. This structure, known as an electron multiplier, comprises several metal pinwheels. The surfaces of the pinwheel vanes are treated to emit secondary electrons copiously when the return-beam electrons hit them; more electrons are emitted than strike the surface. The pinwheel shape causes the secondary electrons liberated at the first vane to be deflected to the next vane in the same structure, where still further emission of secondary electrons occurs. The magnified stream then passes to the next pinwheel structure to the rear, where the process repeats and the electron stream is cumulatively multiplied. The amplified current at the final stage of the electron multiplier is passed out of the tube to a conventional vacuum-tube or transistor amplifier.

The return beam

Vidicon. The Vidicon camera tube, first used in the early 1950s, was the first camera device to employ the phenomenon of photoconductivity. In its early form it was sluggish (objects in motion were reproduced with noticeable smear), and hence it was limited to industrial applications. Later versions were free of this defect, and the Vidicon now enjoys wide use in broadcasting, in monochrome and colour service. The tube elements (Figure 9) are contained in a cylindrical glass envelope, substantially smaller than the image orthicon and hence more adaptable to portable cameras. At one end, a transparent

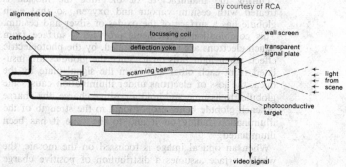

By courtesy of RCA

alignment coil
cathode
focussing coil
deflection yoke
scanning beam
wall screen
transparent signal plate
light from scene
photoconductive target
video signal

Figure 9: Vidicon camera tube.

metallic coating serves as a signal plate. Deposited directly on the signal plate is a photoconductive material (*e.g.*, a compound of selenium or lead) the electrical resistance of which is high in the dark but becomes progressively less as the amount of light increases.

The optical image is focussed on the end of the tube and passes through the signal plate to the photoconductive layer, where the light induces a pattern of varying conductivity that matches the distribution of brightness in the optical image. The conduction paths through the layer allow positive charge from the signal plate (which is maintained at a positive voltage) to pass through the layer, and this current continues to flow during the interval between scans. Charge storage thus occurs, and an electrical charge image is built up on the rear surface of the photoconductor.

An electron beam, deflected in the standard interlaced scanning pattern, scans the rear surface of the photoconducting layer. The beam electrons neutralize the positive charge on each point in the electrical image, and the resulting change in potential is transferred by capacitive action to the signal plate, from which the television signal is derived.

The electron beam scanning spot size imposes the only limit on the image detail. It is possible, therefore, to derive an image of broadcast quality (200,000 or more picture elements) from a photosensitive area no larger than 0.2 square inch (1.3 square centimetres). This permits the use of small and comparatively inexpensive lenses, with correspondingly large depth of focus for a given lens opening. The internal structure of the tube is very simple, and this, with its small size, makes it adaptable to a wide range of camera arrangements in broadcasting, industrial, and military applications.

Flying spot scanner. Another form of television pick-up device, used to transmit images from film transparencies, either still or motion pictures, is the flying spot scanner (Figure 10). The light source is a cathode-ray

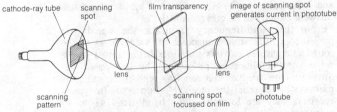

Figure 10: Flying spot camera system.

tube in which a beam of electrons, deflected in the standard scanning pattern, impinges on a fluorescent phosphor surface. The beam produces thereby a spot of light that moves in the scanning pattern on the face of the tube. The light from this spot is focussed optically on the surface of the photographic film transparency to be televised. As the image of the spot moves, it traces out a scanning line across the film, and the amount of light emerging from the other side of the film at each point is determined by the transparency of the film at that point. The emerging light is collected and caused to enter a photoelectric cell, which produces a current proportional to the light entering it.

This current thus takes on a succession of values proportional to the successive values of film density along each line in the scanning pattern; that is, it is the picture signal current. No storage action occurs, so the light from the cathode-ray tube must be very intense and the optical design very efficient to secure noise-free reproduction. The flying spot system may be used with motion-picture film if an optical immobilizer is used (see below *Television recording*).

VIDEO AMPLIFICATION

The picture signal wave form produced by the television camera is initially very weak, of the order of a few hundredths of a volt, and is therefore vulnerable to the random currents (noise) present in the succeeding transmission circuits. Immediately upon leaving the camera,

therefore, the signal must be strengthened, and this process must be repeated at intervals throughout the transmission to the picture tube at the receiver. The strengthening process, known as video amplification, occurs in electron tubes or transistors (see ELECTRONICS).

Video amplifiers, of both the tube and transistor varieties, can be designed to cover a remarkably comprehensive range, amplifying a picture signal comprising any combination of frequency components lying from ten hertz to as high as 10,000,000 hertz. This implies not merely that the amplitudes of all such components are uniformly increased but that their relative times of occurrence are strictly preserved. Only if these requirements are met can the fine structure, as well as the gross outline, of the picture signal wave form be preserved from the camera to the receiver picture tube.

THE TELEVISION CHANNEL

When the band of frequencies in the picture signal is imposed on the high-frequency broadcast carrier current in the modulator of the transmitter, two bands of frequencies are produced, above and below the carrier frequency (as described in the article RADIO). The side bands are identical in frequency content; that is, both carry the complete picture signal information. One of the side bands is superfluous and, if transmitted, would wastefully consume space in the broadcast spectrum. Therefore, the major portion of one of the side bands is removed, and the other is transmitted in full. Complete removal of the superfluous side band is possible, but this would complicate receiver design. Hence, a vestige of the unwanted side band is retained to serve the overall economy of the system. This technique is known as vestigial side-band transmission. It is now universally employed in all of the television broadcasting systems of the world.

The television channel for a black-and-white picture (monochrome) contains the picture carrier frequency, one complete picture side band, and a vestigial portion of the other picture side band. In addition, the carrier for the sound transmission and its side bands is included within the channel. Since the band of frequencies needed to convey the sound is very much narrower than that needed for the picture, it is feasible to include both sound-carrier side bands. Frequency modulation (see RADIO) is employed to transmit the sound information. To avoid mutual interference between sound and picture, the picture and sound side bands must not overlap. Moreover, some space must be allowed at the edge of the channel to avoid interference with the transmissions of stations occupying the adjacent channels.

These requirements are met in the television channel shown in Figure 11. Each contains the following bands: 4.5 megahertz for the fully transmitted picture side band, 1.25 megahertz for the vestige of the other picture side band, 0.15 megahertz for the sound carrier and its two side bands, and the remaining 0.1 megahertz to guard against overlap between picture and sound and between channels. In compatible colour transmissions an additional colour-information signal, shown as the chrominance subcarrier, is included within the fully transmitted picture side band (see below).

The television channels of the United States are assigned 6 megahertz each in the following segments of the spectrum: VHF (very-high-frequency) channels 2, 3, and 4,

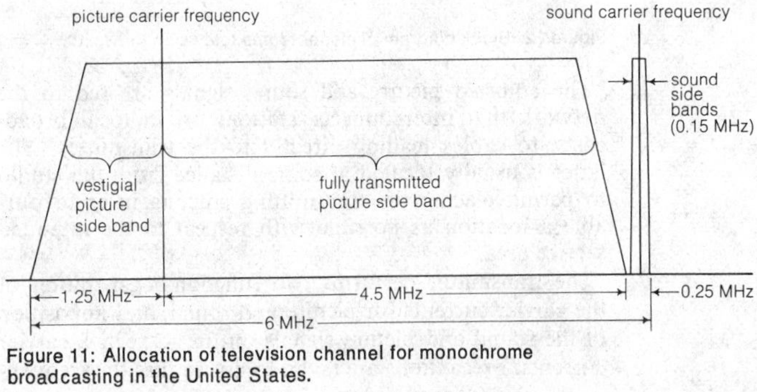

Figure 11: Allocation of television channel for monochrome broadcasting in the United States.

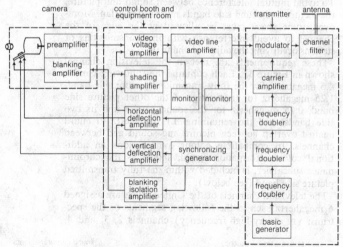

Figure 12: Block diagram of monochrome television transmitter.

At this point the picture and sound signals are separated. Another video amplifier passes the picture signal to the picture tube, where it controls the brightness of the scanning spot. Simultaneously, the picture signal wave form is passed to a circuit (the synchronizing signal separator) that selects the blank periods in the wave form containing the superimposed synchronizing signals.

Finally, the sound signal is passed through a sound intermediate amplifier and frequency detector (discriminator, or ratio detector) that converts the frequency modulation back to an audio signal current. This current is passed through one or two additional audio-frequency amplifier stages to the loudspeaker.

Meanwhile, at the synchronizing signal separator the synchronizing signals are passed through circuits that separate the horizontal and vertical synchronizing impulses. They are then passed, respectively, to the horizontal and vertical deflection generators, which produce the currents that flow through the electromagnet deflection coils, causing the scanning spot of the picture tube to be deflected across the viewing screen in the standard scanning pattern.

The synchronizing signals control the timing of these currents, causing the scanning spot of the receiver to move synchronously with that of the camera. Pains are taken in the synchronizing action of the receiver to prevent the scanning motion from being disturbed by interference, since such disturbances would displace the picture elements from their correct positions in the pattern. It is one of the achievements of the modern television system that the scanning pattern is stably reproduced even when the picture signal is so weak and infested with noise that the picture elements themselves are barely recognizable. This fact is of particular significance in colour transmissions.

In addition to the amplifiers, detectors, and deflection generators described above, the receiver contains two power-converting circuits. One of these (the low-voltage power supply) converts the alternating current from the power line into the direct current needed for the tube or transistor circuits; the other (high-voltage power supply) produces the high voltage, typically 15,000 to 20,000 volts, needed to create the scanning spot in the picture tube.

Viewer's receiver controls   The receiver controls commonly provided for adjustment by the viewer are: (1) the channel switch, which connects the required circuits to the radio-frequency amplifier and superheterodyne mixer to amplify and convert the sound and picture carriers of the desired channel; (2) a fine-tuning control, which precisely adjusts the superheterodyne mixer so that the response of the tuner is exactly centred on the channel in use; (3) a contrast control, which adjusts the voltage level reached by the picture signal in the video amplifiers, producing a picture having more or less contrast (greater or less range between the blacks and whites of the image); (4) a brightness control, which adjusts the average amount of current taken by the picture tube from the high-voltage power supply, thus varying the overall brightness of the picture; (5) a horizontal-hold control, which adjusts the horizontal deflection generator so that it conforms exactly to the control of the horizontal synchronizing impulses; and (6) a vertical-hold control, which performs the same function for the vertical deflection generator. Additional adjustments provided for the serviceman include adjustments for the height and width of the picture (magnitudes of the deflection currents) and adjustments (linearity controls) to secure precisely uniform rates of horizontal and vertical scanning to avoid distortion of the shapes of the objects in the picture. Colour receivers have additional controls for hue (tint) and intensity (vivid versus pastel), as described below.

TELEVISION PICTURE TUBES

A typical television picture tube is illustrated in Figure 13. The tube is a highly evacuated, funnel-shaped structure. The viewing screen is located inside the tube face, a slightly curved glass plate that closes the wide end of the funnel. The screen itself, in monochrome receivers, is

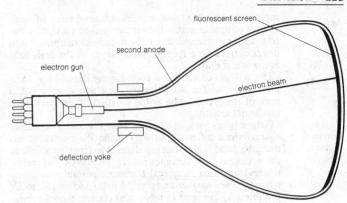

Figure 13: Basic elements of monochrome picture tube.

typically composed of two fluorescent materials, such as silver-activated zinc sulfide and silver-activated zinc cadmium sulfide. These materials, known as phosphors, glow with blue and yellow light, respectively, under the impact of high-speed electrons. The phosphors are mixed, in a fine dispersion, in such proportion that the combination of yellow and blue light produces white light of slightly bluish cast. A water suspension of these materials is settled on the inside of the face plate of the tube during manufacture, and this coating is overlaid with a film of aluminum sufficiently thin to permit the bombarding electrons to pass without hindrance. The aluminum provides a mirror surface that prevents the backward-emitted light from being lost in the interior of the tube and reflects it forward to the viewer.

At the opposite end of the tube is the electron gun, a cylindrical metal structure that generates and directs a stream of free electrons, the electron beam.   *The electron gun*

A part of this gun is a cylindrical sleeve made electrically positive with respect to the cathode (the element that emits the electrons). The positively charged sleeve (first anode) draws the negative electrons away from the cathode, and they move down the sleeve toward the viewing screen at the opposite end of the tube. They are intercepted, however, by a flat disk (the control electrode) having a small circular aperture at its centre. Some of the moving electrons pass through the aperture; others are held back.

The television picture signal is applied between the control electrode and the cathode. During those portions of the picture signal wave form that make the potential of the control electrode less negative, more electrons are permitted to pass through the control aperture, whereas during the more negative portions of the wave, fewer electrons pass. The brightness control applies a steady (but adjustable) voltage between control electrode and cathode. This voltage determines the average number of electrons passing through the aperture, whereas the picture signal causes the number of electrons passing through the aperture to vary from the average and thus controls the brightness of the spot produced on the fluorescent screen.

As the electrons emerge from the sleeve, each electron experiences a force that directs it toward the centre of the viewing screen. The electron beam is thus brought to focus on the screen, and the light there produced is the scanning spot. Additional focussing may be provided by an adjustable permanent magnet surrounding the neck of the tube. The scanning spot must be intrinsically very brilliant, since (by virtue of the integrating property of the eye) the light in the spot is effectively spread out over the whole area of the screen during scanning.

Scanning is accomplished, as outlined above, by two sets of electromagnet coils. These coils must be precisely designed to preserve the focus of the scanning spot no matter where it falls on the screen, and the magnetic fields they produce must be so distributed that deflections occur at uniform velocities.

The current in the horizontal deflection coil must change very rapidly in order to provide a rapid retrace of the scanning spot on the face of the picture tube. This rapid rate of change of current causes pulses of high voltage to appear across the circuit feeding current to the coil, and the succession of these pulses, smoothed into direct current by a rectifier tube, serves as the high-voltage power supply.

The two sets of deflection coils are combined in a structure known as the deflection yoke, which surrounds the neck of the picture tube at the junction of the neck with the funnel section.

Picture tubes vary widely in screen size and are usually characterized by measurements made diagonally across the tube face. Tubes having diagonals from as small as three inches (7.5 centimetres) to 18 inches (46 centimetres) are used in typical transistor portable receivers, whereas tubes measuring from 23 to 27 inches (58 to 69 centimetres) are used in table- and console-model receivers. The design trend has called for greater angles of deflection, with correspondingly wider funnel sections and shallower overall depth from electron gun to viewing screen. The increase in deflection angle from 55° in the first (1946) models to 114° in models produced in the 1970s required corresponding refinement of the deflection system because of the higher deflection currents required and the greater tendency of the scanning spot to go out of focus at the edges of the screen.

III. Compatible colour television

BASIC PRINCIPLES—UNITED STATES SYSTEM

The technique of compatible colour television comprises two transmissions. One of these, the luminance (brightness) transmission, employs methods essentially identical to those of the monochrome television system. The second, the chrominance (colour) transmission, has virtually no effect on monochrome receivers. When used with the luminance transmission in a colour receiver, however, it produces an image in full colour.

The luminance–chrominance method of representing colour values is one of several alternative ways in which coloured light may be analyzed and synthesized. This method is particularly appropriate in a television system since it produces a compatible signal that can serve both black-and-white and colour receivers by the same broadcast.

Historically, compatibility was of great importance because it allowed colour transmissions to be introduced without obsolescence of the many millions of monochrome receivers in use. In a larger sense, the luminance–chrominance method of colour transmission is advantageous because it utilizes the limited channels of the radio spectrum more efficiently than other colour transmission methods.

To create the luminance-chrominance values, it is necessary (in the present state of technology) first to analyze each colour in the scene into primary colours. Coloured light may thus be analyzed by passing the light through three coloured filters, typically red, green, and blue. The amounts of light passing through each filter, plus a description of the colour transmission properties of the filters, serve uniquely to characterize the coloured light.

The fact that virtually the whole range of colours may be synthesized from only three primary colours is essentially a description of the process by which the eye and mind of the observer recognize and distinguish colours. Like visual persistence, this is a fortunate property of vision, since it permits a simple three-part specification to represent any of the 10,000 or more colours and brightnesses that may be distinguished by human vision. If vision were dependent on the energy versus wavelength relationship (the physical method of specification), it is doubtful if colour reproduction could be incorporated in any mass-communication system.

By transforming the primary-colour values, it is possible to specify any coloured light by three other numbers: (1) its luminance (brightness or "brilliance"); (2) its hue (the redness, orangeness, blueness, or greenness, etc., of the light); and (3) its saturation (its vivid versus pastel quality). If the intended luminance value of each point in the scanning pattern is transmitted by the methods of the monochrome television system, it is only

necessary to transmit, via an additional two-valued signal, supplementary information giving the hue and saturation of the intended colour at the respective points in the scanning pattern.

Chrominance, defined as that part of the colour specification remaining when the luminance is removed, represents two independent quantities, hue and saturation.

In the colour television system of the United States, the chrominance signal is an alternating current of precisely specified frequency (3.579545 ± 0.000010 megahertz), the precision permitting its accurate recovery at the receiver even in the presence of severe noise or interference. Any change in the amplitude of its alternations at any instant corresponds to a change in the saturation of the colours being passed over by the scanning spot at that instant, whereas a shift in time of its alternations (a change in the "phase angle" of the alternations) similarly corresponds to a shift in the hue. The colour information in the European (PAL and SECAM) systems described below is carried on a chrominance signal frequency of 4.43+ megahertz. In the United States system, as the different saturations and hues along each scanning line are successively uncovered by scanning in the camera, the amplitude and phase, respectively, of the chrominance signal change accordingly. The chrominance signal is thereby simultaneously modulated in amplitude and in phase. This doubly modulated signal is imposed on the picture signal carrier current, along with the luminance signal.

The television channel, when occupied by such a compatible colour transmission, appears as shown in Figure 14 (compare this with the channel when occupied by a black-and-white transmission, Figure 11). The chrominance signal takes the form of a subcarrier located precisely 3.579545 megahertz from the picture carrier frequency.

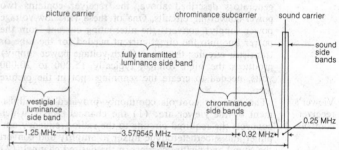

Figure 14: Allocation channel for compatible colour transmission in the United States.

The picture carrier is thus simultaneously amplitude-modulated by the luminance signal to represent changes in the intended luminance, and by the chrominance subcarrier that, in turn, is amplitude-modulated to represent changes in the intended saturation and phase-modulated to represent changes in the intended hue.

When compatible colour transmissions are received on a monochrome receiver, the receiver treats the chrominance subcarrier as though it were a part of the intended monochrome transmission. If steps were not taken to prevent it, the subcarrier would produce interference in the form of a fine dot pattern. The dot pattern, fortunately, can be rendered almost invisible in monochrome reception by deriving the timing of the scanning motions directly from the source that establishes the chrominance subcarrier itself. The dot pattern of interference from the chrominance signal, therefore, can be made to have opposite effects on successive scannings of the pattern; that is, a point brightened by the dot interference on one line scan is darkened an equal amount on the next scan of that line, and the net effect of the interference, integrated in the eye over successive scans, is virtually zero. Thus, the monochrome receiver, in effect, ignores the chrominance component of the transmission. It deals with the luminance signal in the conventional manner, producing from it a monochrome image. This monochrome rendition, incidentally, is not a compromise; it is essentially identical to the image that would be produced by a monochrome television system viewing the same scene.

The channel for colour transmissions, when used by colour receivers, would appear to be affected by mutual interference between the luminance and chrominance components, since these occupy a portion of the channel in common. Such interference is avoided by the fact that the chrominance subcarrier component is rigidly timed to the scanning motions. The luminance signal, as it occupies the channel, is actually concentrated in a multitude of small spectrum segments, by virtue of the periodicities associated with the scanning process. Between these segments are empty channel spaces of approximately equal size. The chrominance signal, arising from the same scanning process, is similarly concentrated. Hence it is possible to place the chrominance channel segments within the empty spaces between the luminance segments, provided that the two sets of segments have a precisely fixed frequency relationship. The necessary relationship is provided by the direct control by the subcarrier of the timing of the scanning motions. This intersegmentation is known as frequency interlacing. It is one of the fundamentals of the compatible colour system, and without it the superposition of colour information on a channel originally devised for monochrome transmissions would not be feasible.

Frequency interlacing

When a colour receiver is tuned to the transmission represented in Figure 14, the picture signal is recovered in a video detector in the usual manner. An amplifier stage, tuned to the 3.58-megahertz chrominance frequency, then selects the chrominance from the picture signal and passes it to a detector that recovers independently the amplitude-modulated and phase-modulated components.

EUROPEAN COLOUR SYSTEMS

The United States colour system has been adopted by Canada, Mexico, Japan, and several other countries. In Europe, two alternative systems have been developed and introduced. The PAL (phase alternation line) system has been adopted in the United Kingdom and most of the countries on the Continent. France, the Soviet Union, and their allied countries and dependencies have adopted the SECAM (*système électronique couleur avec mémoire*) system.

The PAL and SECAM systems embody the same principles as the United States system, including matters affecting compatibility and the use of a separate signal to carry the colour information at low detail superimposed on the high-detail luminance signal. The European systems were developed, in fact, to improve on the performance of the United States system in only one area, the constancy of the hue (tint) of the reproduced images.

It has been pointed out that the hue information in the U.S. system is carried by changes in the phase angle of the chrominance signal, and that these phase changes are recovered in the receiver by synchronous detection. The transmission of the phase information, particularly in the early stages of colour broadcasting in the United States, was subject to incidental errors arising in broadcasting stations and network connections. Errors are also caused by reflections of the broadcast signals by buildings and other structures in the vicinity of the receiving antenna. In recent years, transmission and reception of hue information has become substantially more accurate in the U.S. through care in broadcasting and networking, as well as by automatic hue-control circuits in receivers. The PAL and SECAM systems are inherently less affected by phase errors.

In the PAL and SECAM systems, the nominal value of the chrominance signal is 4.43+ megahertz, a frequency that is derived from and hence more accurately synchronized with the frame-scanning and line-scanning rates. This chrominance signal is accommodated within the six-megahertz range of the fully transmitted side band. By virtue of its synchronism with the line and frame scanning rates, its frequency components are interleaved with those of the luminance signal, so that the chrominance information does not affect reception of colour broadcasts by black-and-white receivers.

PAL system. The PAL system resembles the United States system in that the chrominance signal is simultaneously modulated in amplitude to carry the saturation (pastel versus vivid) aspect of the colours and in phase to carry the hue (tint) aspect. In the PAL system, the phase information is reversed during the scanning of successive lines. Thus if a phase error is present during the scanning of one line, a compensating error (of equal amount but in the opposite direction) is introduced during the next line. Thus the average phase information, presented by the two successive lines taken together, is free of error.

Two lines are thus required to depict the corrected hue information, and the vertical detail of the hue information is correspondingly lessened. This produces no serious degradation of the picture when the phase errors are not too great, since, as noted above, the eye does not require fine detail in the hues of colour reproduction, and the mind of the observer averages out the two compensating errors. If the phase errors are more than about 20°, visible degradation does occur. This effect can be corrected by introducing in the receiver (as in the SECAM system described below) a delay line and electronic switch.

SECAM system. In the SECAM system, the luminance information is transmitted in the usual manner, and the chrominance signal is interleaved with it. But the chrominance signal is modulated in only one way. The two types of information required to encompass the colour values do not occur concurrently, and the errors associated with simultaneous amplitude and phase modulation do not occur. Rather, in the SECAM system (SECAM III), alternate line scans carry information on luminance and red, while the intervening line scans contain luminance and blue. The green information is derived within the receiver by subtracting the red and blue information from the luminance signal. Since individual line scans carry only half the colour information, two successive line scans are required to obtain the complete colour information, and this halves the colour detail, measured in the vertical dimension. But, as noted above, the eye is not sensitive to the hue and saturation of small details, so no adverse effect is introduced.

To subtract the red and blue information from the luminance information to obtain the green information, the red and blue signals must be available in the receiver simultaneously, whereas they are transmitted in time sequence. This requirement is met by holding the signal content of each line scan in storage (or "memorizing" it, hence the name *système électronique couleur avec mémoire*). The storage device is known as a delay line; it holds the information of each line scan for 0.000064 second. To match successive pairs of lines, an electronic switch is also needed. When the use of delay lines was first proposed, such lines were expensive devices. Recent advances have reduced the cost, and the fact that receivers must incorporate these components is no longer viewed as decisive.

Since the SECAM system reproduces the colour information with a minimum of error, it has been argued that SECAM receivers do not require receiver controls for hue and saturation. Such adjustments, however, are usually provided to permit the viewer to adjust the picture to his individual taste and to correct for signals that are in error as broadcast, due to such factors as faulty use of cameras, lighting, and networking.

COLOUR CAMERA AND PICTURE TUBE

The terminals of the colour television system, the camera and picture tube, analyze and synthesize, respectively, the colour quantities present at each point in the scanning pattern. The television camera in its current state of development does not produce the luminance, hue, and saturation values directly. Rather it produces three picture signals, representative of the amounts of three primary colours present at each point in the image pattern. From these signals the luminance and chrominance components are then derived by manipulation in electronic circuits.

The typical colour television camera (Figure 15) contains three image orthicon tubes, with an optical system that casts an identical image on the sensitive surface of

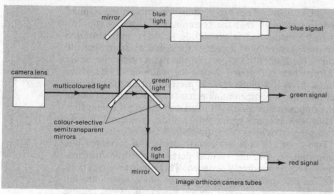

Figure 15: Diagram showing selective separation of light in colour camera.

Optical system of a colour television camera

each tube. The optics comprise a lens and four mirrors that reflect the image rays from the lens onto the three camera tubes, as shown. Two of the mirrors are of a colour-selective type (dichroic mirror) that reflects the light of one colour and transmits the remaining colours. The mirrors, plus colour filters that perfect their colour-selective action, direct a blue image to the first tube, a green image to the second tube, and a red image to the third tube.

The deflection systems of the three camera tubes are arranged to produce identical scanning patterns in each tube, so the picture signals developed by the respective tubes represent images of the same geometrical shape, differing only in colour. The respective primary-colour signals are passed through video preamplifiers associated with each camera tube and emerge from the camera as separate entities. If compatibility were not required, and if sufficient space were available in the radio spectrum, the three signals might be transmitted to the receiver over separate channels. Actually, as mentioned above, the primary-colour signals are recast into luminance and chrominance components; at the receiver the latter are converted back into primary-colour signals before application to the colour picture tube. In the mid-1960s, colour cameras employing four camera tubes were introduced, particularly for studio work. The fourth tube is exposed directly to the scene without an intervening mirror or filter and thus produces a luminance signal of high quality. The three remaining tubes are then confined to the less demanding functions of producing the primary-colour signals. Three-tube cameras based on this principle have also been developed.

Much attention has been paid to the design of camera tubes for colour service, and greatly improved colour rendition, particularly of subtle variations in skin tone, has resulted. The Plumbicon version of the Vidicon, developed in The Netherlands, is particularly noteworthy in this respect.

The colour picture tube (Figure 16) contains three electron guns, which produce three separate electron beams. These are deflected simultaneously in the standard scanning pattern over the viewing screen. One of the beams is controlled by the red primary-colour signal and produces a red image. The second beam produces a blue image and the third a green image.

Colour picture tube screen

To permit three primary-colour images to be formed simultaneously, the screen is composed of three sets of individual phosphor dots, which glow respectively in the three different colours and which are uniformly interspersed over the screen (Figure 16). The "red" beam impinges only on the red-glowing phosphor dots, being prevented from hitting the other two colours, with similar restriction of the other two beams to the blue and green dots, respectively.

The sorting out of the three beams so that they produce images of only the intended primary colour is performed by a mask that lies directly behind the phosphor screen. This mask contains about 200,000 precisely located holes, each accurately aligned with three different coloured phosphor dots on the screen in front of it. Electrons from

the three guns pass together through each hole, but at slightly different angles. The angles are such that the electrons arising from the gun controlled by the red primary-colour signal fall only on the red dots, being prevented from hitting the blue and green dots by the shadowing action of the mask. Similarly, the "blue" and "green" electrons fall only on the blue and green dots, respectively. A major improvement consists in surrounding each colour dot with an opaque black material, so that no light can emerge from the portions of the screen between dots. This permits the screen to produce a brighter image while maintaining the purity of the colours. This type of screen (black matrix screen) is more expensive to produce, but in the early 1970s it was widely used in the larger colour tubes.

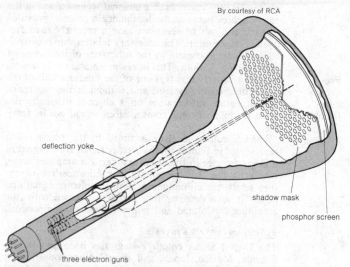

By courtesy of RCA

Figure 16: Colour picture tube employing the shadow-mask technique.

Thus three separate primary-colour images are formed simultaneously, as the scanning proceeds. The colour dots of which each image is formed are so small and so uniformly dispersed that the eye does not detect their separate presence, although they are readily visible through a magnifying glass. The primary colours in the three images thereby mix in the mind of the viewer and a full-colour rendition of the image results.

The shadow-mask tube

This type of colour tube is known as the shadow-mask tube. It has several shortcomings: (1) the electrons intercepted by the mask cannot produce light, and the image brightness is thereby limited; (2) great precision is needed to achieve correct alignment of the electron beams, the mask holes, and the phosphor dots at all points in the scanning pattern; and (3) precisely congruent scanning patterns, as among the three beams, must be produced. In the late 1960s a different type of colour tube, the Trinitron, was introduced in Japan. In this tube the shadow-mask is replaced by a metal grille having vertical slits extending from the top to the bottom of the screen. The three electron beams pass through the slits to the coloured phosphors, which are in the form of vertical stripes aligned with the slits. The grille directs the majority of the electrons through the slits, few of the electrons are intercepted by the grille, and a brighter picture results. The electron gun of the Trinitron tube remains in fine focus throughout the scanning of the image, since a major portion of the focus mechanism is common to all three beams.

COLOUR TRANSMITTER AND RECEIVER

Figure 17 shows the essential elements of the colour transmitter, as they differ from the monochrome transmitter shown in Figure 12. Immediately following the colour camera is the colour coder, which converts the primary-colour signals into the luminance and chrominance signals. The luminance signal is formed simply by applying the primary-colour signals to an electronic addi-

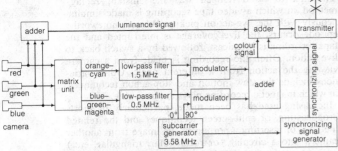

Figure 17: Block diagram of colour transmitter.
By courtesy of RCA

tion circuit that adds the values of the three signals at each point along the respective picture signal wave form. Since white light results from the addition, in appropriate proportions, of the primary colours, the resulting sum signal represents the black-and-white (luminance) version of the colour image. The luminance signal thus formed is subtracted individually, in three electronic subtraction circuits, from the original primary-colour signals, and the colour-difference signals are then further combined to produce two signals, which are then applied simultaneously to a modulator, where they are mixed with the chrominance subcarrier signal. The latter is thereby amplitude-modulated in accordance with the saturation values and phase-modulated in accordance with the hues. The luminance and chrominance components are then combined to form the overall colour picture signal, which is then carried to the transmitter over the network or studio–transmitter link.

The chrominance subcarrier is generated in a precise electronic oscillator at the standard value of 3.579545 megahertz. Samples of this subcarrier are injected into the signal wave form during the blank period between line scans just after the horizontal synchronizing pulses. These samples are employed in the receiver to control the synchronous detector, mentioned above. Finally, the horizontal and vertical deflection currents, which produce the scanning in the three camera tubes, are formed in a scanning generator, the timing of which is controlled by the chrominance subcarrier. This common timing of deflection and chrominance transmission produces the dot-interference cancellation in monochrome reception and frequency interlacing in colour transmission, noted above.

At this stage, the colour picture signal can be handled in the same manner as the monochrome signal, except that throughout the network and in the transmitter special precautions must be taken to transmit the chrominance subcarrier at its correct amplitude, with its amplitude and phase modulations preserved against incidental distortions.

Colour receiver components
The colour receiver contains a tuner and intermediate-frequency amplifiers similar to those used in monochrome receivers, but especially designed to preserve the chrominance subcarrier during its passage through these stages. The colour receiver also has power supplies, sound reception circuits, and synchronization and deflection current generators similar to those used in monochrome reception.

The colour reproduction processes are divided into the luminance and chrominance functions. A video detector develops the luminance component and applies it through video amplifiers simultaneously to all three electron guns of the picture tube. This part of the signal thereby activates all three primary-colour images, simultaneously and identically, in the fixed proportion needed to produce white light. When tuned to monochrome broadcasts, the colour receiver produces a monochrome image by means of this mechanism, the chrominance component then being absent.

When the receiver is tuned to a colour broadcast, the chrominance subcarrier component appears in the output of the video detector and it is thereupon operated on in circuits that ultimately recover the primary-colour signals originally produced by the colour camera.

The three colour-difference signals are applied separately to the respective electron guns, where each reduces the strength of the corresponding electron beam to change the white light, which would otherwise be produced, to the intended colour for each point in the scanning line. The net control signal applied to each electron gun bears a direct correspondence to the primary colour signal derived from the respective camera tube at the studio. In this manner, the three primary-colour signals are transmitted as though three separate channels had been used.

The colour receiver controls to be adjusted by the viewer (in addition to the tuning, brightness, contrast, and synchronizing controls present in monochrome receivers) are the hue control and the saturation control. The hue control shifts all the hues in the reproduced image. It is usually adjusted by reference to the colour of the flesh of the performers, since unnatural flesh tone is readily recognized even if the viewer has no knowledge of the intended hues in other parts of the scene. The saturation control adjusts the magnitudes of the colour-difference signals applied to the electron guns of the picture tube. If these magnitudes are reduced to zero, by turning the saturation control to the "off" position, no colour difference action occurs and the reproduction occurs in monochrome. As the saturation control is advanced, the colour differences become more accentuated, and the colours become progressively more vivid. In the late 1960s, the more elaborate colour television receivers began to employ a system known as "automatic hue control." In this system, the viewer makes an initial manual adjustment of the hue control to produce a rendition of flesh tones to suit his preference. Thereafter, the hue control circuit automatically maintains the preselected ratio of the primary colours corresponding to the viewer's choice. Thus the most critical aspect of the colour rendition, the appearance of the faces of the performers, is prevented from changing when cameras are switched from scene to scene or when tuning from one broadcast to another.

Automatic hue control

Since care in tuning is essential in colour receivers to assure correct reception of the chrominance signal, automatic circuits to set the fine-tuning adjustment are provided in the more expensive receivers. A recent development is a single touch-button control that sets the fine tuning and adjusts the hue, tint, contrast, and brightness to preset ranges. These automatic adjustments override the settings of the corresponding knobs, which then function over narrow ranges only. Such refinements permit reception of acceptable quality by viewers who might otherwise be confused by the many misadjustments possible when ordinary manual controls are used.

IV. Applications of television

TELEVISION RECORDING

Commercial systems. Recording of television programs on photographic film or magnetic tape is an important technique, not only to preserve a permanent record of a live-scene program for subsequent rebroadcast but also to perfect a performance prior to its initial presentation. Recorded segments are often used in a "live" studio program when it is impractical to set up the desired scene in the studio. Transmission of films originally produced for motion-picture theatres is also a major activity in broadcasting.

Television film projectors fall into two classes, continuous and intermittent, according to the type of film motion. In the continuous projector, a scanning spot from a flying spot camera tube is passed through a rotating optical system, known as an immobilizer, which focusses the scanning spot on the motion-picture film. As the film moves continuously through the projector, the immobilizer causes the scanning pattern as a whole to follow the motion of the film frame, so that there is no relative motion between pattern and frame. The light passes through the film to a phototube where the light, modified by the transmissibility of the film at each point, produces the picture signal. As one film frame moves out of the range of the immobilizer, the next moves into range and there is a condition of overlap between successive scanning patterns.

The optics are so arranged that the amount of light in the spot focussed on the film is constant at all times and in all positions. This constancy permits the film to be moved at any desired speed, while the pattern scans at the standard rate of 25 or 30 pictures per second. The film is actually moved at the standard rate for motion pictures, 24 frames per second, so the speed of objects and pitch of the accompanying sounds (picked up from the sound track by conventional methods) are reproduced at the intended values.

The intermittent projector

In the intermittent projector, which more nearly resembles the type used in theatre projection, each frame of film is momentarily held stationary in the projector while a brief flash of light is passed through it. The light (which passes simultaneously through all parts of the film frame) is focussed on the sensitive surface of a storage-type camera, such as the Vidicon. The light flashes are timed to occur during the intervals between successive field scans—that is, while the extinguished scanning spot is moving from bottom to top of the frame. The light is strong enough to produce an intense electrical image in the tube during this brief period. The electrical image is stored and is scanned during the next scanning field, producing the picture signal for that field. Light is again admitted between fields and the stored image scanned thereupon by the second field. When one film frame has been thus scanned, it is pulled down by a claw mechanism and the next frame takes its place.

In Europe and other areas where the television scanning rate is 25 picture scans per second, it has been the custom to operate intermittent projectors also at 25 frames per second, or about 4 percent faster than the intended film projection rate of 24 frames per second. The corresponding increases in speed of motion and sound pitch were not so great as to introduce unacceptable degradations of the performance. In the United States and other areas where television scanning occurs at 30 frames per second, it is not feasible to run the film projector at 30 film frames per second, since this would introduce speed and pitch errors of 25 percent. Fortunately, a small common factor, 6, relates the scan rate of 30 and the film projection rate of 24 frames per second. That is, four film frames consume the same time as five scanning frames. Thus, if four film frames pass through the projector while five complete picture scans (ten fields) are completed, both the film motion and the scanning proceed at the standard rates. The two functions are kept in step by holding one film frame for three scanning fields, the next frame for two scans, the next for three scans, and so on.

Television recording tape

Television program recording for rebroadcast is done on magnetic tape, although film is used for longer storage purposes. The tape technique permits prompt rebroadcast of programs the quality of which, when the tape equipment is in good adjustment, is virtually indistinguishable from the original broadcast. The magnetic tape, two inches (five centimetres) wide, is moved at 15 inches (38 centimetres) per second past a magnetic recording head that rotates across the width of the tape, imposing on it a series of crosswise magnetic line patterns that correspond to the lines of the scanning pattern. To keep the pickup and tape motions identical during recording and playback, index signals are imposed during recording, and these are used to control the drive motors during playback. The television signal is recorded by frequency modulation on a carrier signal, thus avoiding the difficult problem of direct recording at the extremely low frequencies present in the picture signal itself.

Magnetic video recording is widely used in broadcast operations, in colour as well as monochrome, not only because of its high quality but because it is immediately available (without subsequent processing) for playback. In the United States, many of the network programs broadcast in and west of Chicago are derived from magnetic recordings, stored for an hour or more after their release along the eastern seaboard to allow for the difference in time in western cities.

Many variations of the basic techniques of recording television program material were introduced in the late 1960s and early 1970s, especially in sports telecasting.

The first to be developed was the "instant replay" method, in which a video tape recording is made simultaneously with the live-action pickup. When a noteworthy episode occurs, the live coverage is interrupted and the tape recording is broadcast, followed by a switch back to live action. Often the recording is made from a camera viewing the action from a different angle. Other variations include the slow-motion and stop-action techniques, in which magnetic recording plays the basic role.

Increasing used has been made, particularly in sports broadcasting, of split-screen techniques and the related methods of inserting a portion of the image from another camera into a circular (or rectangular, triangular, etc.) area cut out from the main image. These techniques employ an electronic switching circuit that turns off the signal circuit of one camera for a portion of several line scans, while simultaneously turning on the signal circuit of another camera, the outputs of the two cameras being combined before the signal is broadcast. The timing of the electronic switch is adjusted to blank out, on successive line scans of the first camera, an area of the desired size and shape. The timing may be shifted during the performance and the area changed accordingly. One example of this technique is the wipe, which removes the image from one camera while inserting the image from another, with a sharp, moving boundary between them.

Home recording and playback systems. In the early 1970s several auxiliary systems of television reproduction were under development as adjuncts to the home receiver. These are of two general types, using the "record-plus-playback" and the "playback-only" techniques.

The record-plus-playback systems employ video recording on magnetic tape, including the accompanying sound. They are intended to make a permanent sight-and-sound record of programs, either as broadcast (off-the-air recording) or by using a simple television camera and microphone in the home, as in amateur sound motion pictures. The use of prerecorded programs on tapes purchased or rented was also intended in these systems.

The playback-only systems are analogous to the phonograph record system of sound reproduction. The program material is prerecorded on a disk or on nonmagnetic film and is played back through the home receiver by means of an attachment similar in principle to the phonograph record player. No facilities for the recording are provided, the recording methods being too specialized for use in the home.

Video-cassette systems

By 1971 some 20 different "video-cassette" systems (as they had come to be known by analogy to the cassette sound recorders) were under development. While some were in small-scale production, few were available for use in the home. One of the initial drawbacks was the high cost of the recording material, estimated at from $10 to $35 per hour for the magnetic or nonmagnetic films employed. The video disk was an exception, with a material cost for a one-hour program estimated at $3 or less.

The initial demonstrations were largely confined to black-and-white programs, although all the developers planned the eventual introduction of colour. The high cost led to suggestions that a rental system, similar to the lending-library concept of distributing books, would be essential if widespread public use were to be achieved. The market for such recorded programs was confined in the early 1970s to educational institutions and industrial uses.

The record-plus-playback systems of the early 1970s employed half-inch magnetic tape housed in a cartridge similar to the sound tape cartridge, but larger. These systems, some eight in number, were under development in the United States, Japan, and The Netherlands. The approach of each system was sufficiently different that complete interchangeability of cartridges was not feasible, and the need for standardization was evident. The earliest estimated prices of the recorder-playback units ranged substantially above the cost of the home receiver to which they were attached. The quality of reproduction was highly acceptable, although somewhat poorer than that possible under ideal broadcasting conditions. The video bandwidth employed in playback ranged from two to three megahertz.

Among the playback-only systems, one exciting particular interest because of its low cost-per-hour of recording was a video disk system that originated in Germany. Since the rate of transmitting picture information (three megahertz) is about 400 times greater than that required for sound, the video disk must rotate much faster and possess many more grooves than a phonograph record. In the German system, the disk rotates at 1,500 revolutions per minute (to be increased to 1,800 revolutions per minute for colour), and the grooves are packed on it to the extent of 3,300 per inch. The disk is made of plastic, covered with a thin embossed metal foil. The pickup cartridge does not make physical contact with the grooves, but rides on a thin cushion of air, the information in the groove being transferred to the cartridge by variations in air pressure.

Three different playback-only systems using nonmagnetic film were in evidence; the electronic video recording (EVR) method, the Holotape (Selectavision) system, and systems using conventional eight-millimetre colour motion-picture film (Super-8 techniques).

In the EVR system, the image is prerecorded by electrophotographic means on silver halide emulsion or diazo photosensitive film. Each frame is imposed in two paired images: the luminance (black-and-white) image, used alone for black-and-white material, and a coded image that is decoded by the playback unit to supply the low-detail chrominance information. These are combined into a standard colour-television signal before being fed to the colour receiver. Both images are picked up, in the playback unit, by a flying spot scanner.

The Holotape system makes use of the principles of holography (q.v.) to emboss on plastic tape the luminance and chrominance information of each frame. In the playback unit, coherent light produced by a laser picks up the embossed information and directs the visual content of the luminance and chrominance signal to a Vidicon, which translates the light into an electrical signal that is fed to the conventional colour receiver. The anticipated cost of prerecorded programs in this system is reduced, relative to photographic or magnetic means, by the use of the embossing technique, similar in principle to that used for making phonograph records.

The Super-8 systems use conventional eight-millimetre motion-picture film as the source of the prerecorded images, combined with magnetic recording for the accompanying sound. The frames are scanned by a Vidicon or a flying spot scanner, in a simplified version of the film-scanning techniques employed in broadcasting (see also SOUND RECORDING AND REPRODUCING).

TELEVISION BROADCASTING

Transoceanic broadcasts. The initial attempt to interconnect the television networks of Europe and North America came in 1962, when the American Telephone and Telegraph Company used its artificial satellite, Telstar, to relay television signals between Andover, Maine; Goonhilly Downs, Cornwall; and Pleumeur-Bodou, Brittany. The first transmission, of a purely experimental nature, originated in the United States on July 10, 1962, and this was followed the next day by transmissions to the U.S. from France and England; the first colour transmission occurred on July 16. Reception was limited to about 15 minutes, the period during which the satellite was within sight of the sending and receiving stations. To maintain continuous transmissions, the planners of the system proposed using a series of satellites, so that at least one would always be in position to relay signals. In the mid-1960s, however, an alternative technique came to the fore: a single relay satellite in a "stationary" orbit, so adjusted that it would remain always above the same point on the surface of the earth. The first public demonstration of this system was on October 10, 1964, when television coverage of the opening ceremonies of the Olympic Games was relayed from Tokyo to North America via a Syncom satellite positioned above the Pacific Ocean. The so-called "synchronous" communications satellite maintained an altitude of about 23,000 miles (37,000 kilometres), its position fixed with respect

Broad-casting the Olympic games

to the Earth, their periods of rotation being identical. In the early 1970s, such satellites were so placed that virtually any area of the Earth was within reach of any other by space-relay circuits. The transmitters and receivers used in space are capable of carrying many television channels simultaneously, in addition to telephone and other communications. The landing on the moon by the American astronauts in 1969 was carried by satellite to an estimated audience of more than 100,000,000 viewers (see also BROADCASTING; SATELLITE COMMUNICATIONS).

Community antenna television (CATV) systems. In 1950 a new method of providing television service to the home was introduced and rapidly gained acceptance in many communities. This involved setting up a "community antenna" in a high and exposed location, where excellent reception is obtainable, and re-transmitting the signals via a local coaxial cable system to homes in the vicinity. The CATV system is particularly advantageous in towns surrounded by hills or other obstructions that prevent high-quality reception by individual antennas at each home. Another, later, application occurred in major metropolitan areas where local reception is degraded by the reflection of signals from tall buildings ("multipath interference"), which produce one or more "ghost" images displaced on the screen from the desired picture. The CATV service is provided, after an initial installation charge of $15–$35, at a monthly charge of about $5. By the early 1970s there were more than 5,400,000 subscribers served by some 2,600 CATV systems in the United States. Similar growth has occurred in Canada and in several other countries.

The plans of the CATV industry have shifted from merely delivering available programs to a more ambitious outlook for services to the home other than from distant broadcast stations. Moreover, under active development in the early 1970s was a system of two-way cable television, which would permit the householder to "call back" over the cable connection to secure all manner of visual and audible information on demand, participate in polls, have access to a computer, etc. The advent of Picturephone (video telephone) service in the United States (described below) has lent impetus to the two-way cable concept. A movement has developed for action by regulatory agencies and the Congress to protect the public interest as the two-way system evolves.

Typical future plans envisage some 20 television channels being available to the home through a single cable connection, far more than existing broadcast programs would require. The additional channels would supply program material produced by community groups and local governments, educational institutions, libraries, and the like. One study estimated that, by 1975, 25 percent of the homes in the United States would be wired for 20 or more channels, and that by 1980 the percentage might rise to 60 percent. Such universal acceptance has suggested the prospect of sending first-class mail visually through the cable network, with delivery time reduced to minutes.

CLOSED-CIRCUIT TELEVISION

The term closed-circuit television, which originally meant a local system consisting of a camera and several monitor receivers connected by a coaxial cable, came to refer to any system, however extensive, in which the televised subject matter is intended for the organization that owns or has hired the system for its exclusive use, as against broadcasting or other general use by the public. Such systems are widely used in industry and commerce and for educational purposes. They range from a single camera and monitor installed in a steam plant to monitor flame condition or water level to a nationwide network hired on a single-occasion basis (e.g., by an automobile manufacturer to present information on new models to dealers assembled in theatres having projection television equipment). Coaxial cable is used in local installations, but microwave relay systems identical to those used in broadcasting may be employed for large closed-circuit hookups.

Since a closed-circuit system is entirely under the control of its proprietor and is not intended to serve the

Slow-scan
system

general public, it is possible to employ scanning standards that differ from those used in broadcasting. Advantage of this freedom in system design is taken in the so-called slow-scan closed-circuit system, which is used to transmit signature records and balances in banks, for example.

In the typical slow-scan system, the pictures may be scanned at a rate as slow as one picture every three seconds with a scanning pattern of 180 lines per picture. The maximum frequency in the picture signal then reaches only 8,000 hertz, which can be transmitted inexpensively; i.e., over ordinary telephone lines. In the majority of closed-circuit systems for industry, education, and theatre projection, however, the image-quality requirements are essentially identical to those of broadcasting.

Equipment. Equipment for closed-circuit television is similar to, but generally less elaborate than, that used for broadcast purposes. The Vidicon camera tube is used in industrial television almost to the exclusion of other types, since it is less expensive than the other types and more suitable for compact cameras. In educational television, however, image orthicon tubes and associated equipment very similar to broadcast-station units are widely used. Since closed-circuit installations in industry are seldom operated by television specialists, care must be taken in equipment design to make operation and maintenance simple. An important industrial use is in viewing remote or hazardous events. For such purposes, controls for remote operation of the camera, including adjustment of lens aperture and focus, are provided.

Applications in education. Educational television is often conducted on a public-broadcast basis in cities in which a channel is available for this purpose and in which the expense of the transmitting station can be borne. The simpler and less costly closed-circuit system found increasing favour with educators, however, particularly in larger institutions and in medical schools.

In education, television's most impressive use is extending the range of a gifted teacher beyond a single classroom. When a broadcast system is available, pupils in many schools may be taught simultaneously by a particularly able teacher prior to a more personal instruction and discussion of the subject matter in individual classes with a local teacher in attendance. While motion pictures may also be used in this way, the televised image commands the pupils' attention to a far greater extent. Even when film is used as a program source, the psychological impression on the student is heightened.

Television is also an important teaching aid in bringing to a number of students simultaneously the details of an experiment or operation that otherwise could be viewed only by a single person or small group. Examples include viewing through a microscope and bringing medical students directly into visual contact with operating procedures without interfering with those performing the operation. Use of closed-circuit television for instruction in surgical procedures is widespread; elaborate colour television installations have been made in medical schools and hospitals, colour being an important adjunct in delineating diagnosis and procedure. An important advantage of television in such instruction is that the final outcome is not known as the demonstration proceeds.

Closed-
circuit
television
in
medicine

Video telephone. The use of television as an adjunct to telephone service has been planned since the earliest demonstrations of television itself. In 1927, in the first public showing of television in the United States, the pictures were sent in connection with a telephone conversation between Secretary of Commerce (later president) Herbert Hoover and Walter Sherman Gifford, president of the American Telephone and Telegraph Company. In the mid-1930s, a television-telephone service was operated by the German Post Office over coaxial cables between Berlin, Leipzig, Nürnburg, and Hamburg. By the 1960s, slow-scan experimental video-telephone experiments were reported in Italy and Japan. The Soviet Union used the broadcast network for telephone connections outside broadcast hours, and a commercial video telephone was exhibited in London.

The Picturephone system, which became available to subscribers of the American Telephone and Telegraph Company in 1971 in Chicago and Pittsburgh, was first demonstrated at the New York World's Fair in 1964. From 1965 to 1970, tests of the Picturephone system were conducted in large corporation headquarters in New York, Chicago, and Pittsburgh. By the early 1970s, the techniques for local and long-distance service had been established, but acceptance by the public was disappointing. By the end of 1972, only about 100 Picturephone units were in regular use by subscribers. One of the difficulties was the expense of long-distance connections and routing, requiring a bandwidth equivalent to the demands of more than 300 long-distance telephone connections. Research was under way to reduce the required bandwidth for the video service (currently one megahertz) by sophisticated digital-coding techniques.

The Model II Picturephone subscriber set, used in the early 1970s, has a viewing screen 5 by 5.5 inches (13 by 14 centimetres), displaying a 250-line picture at 30 frames per second, with interlaced scanning. The camera tube is of new design, employing a mosaic of tiny photosensitive semiconductor elements. Focus for normal use by the subscriber is set at approximately three feet. The focus can be reset to one foot for viewing graphic materials, which are laid flat on the desk in front of the subscriber set, being reflected into the camera by a 45° mirror.

For the video connection from the subscriber's location to the central office, two conventional wire telephone circuits (pairs) are used in connection with equalizing networks that arrange for the one-megahertz channel to be divided equally between the two circuits. A third circuit is used for the voice connection. The equalization scheme is not adequate for distances beyond six miles (ten kilometres). For long-distance transmission between central offices, wide-band circuits (coaxial cable or microwave relay) were being used in the early 1970s. A future prospect is the use of wire pair circuits at distances of several hundred miles by transforming the video signal into digital form and regenerating it at intervals.

The Picturephone may be used for communication with computers and other sources of digital data. The subscriber uses the 12 keys of a Touch-Tone telephone set to feed data into the system, and receives data visually over the Picturephone screen (see also TELEPHONE AND TELE-COMMUNICATIONS SYSTEMS).

Industrial applications. One of the first uses of closed-circuit television in industry was an installation of boiler water-level monitors at the Hell Gate electric generating station in New York, made directly after World War II. This application later was extended to the monitoring of flames in burners and smoke issuing from stacks. Here the justification for television, as against photographic methods, is the need for immediate information without the delay of film processing. Other applications involve the safe handling of nuclear materials, jet fuels, and other hazardous substances. A stereoscopic form of television, comprising two complete systems that present two images separately to the two eyes of the operator, has been used in conjunction with precise remote-handling equipment for packing radioactive substances, disposing of radioactive wastes, and the like. The ability of the television camera to operate in situations hostile to human observers (as outside the fuselage of an airplane in flight, to observe operation of landing gear during engineering tests) also accounts for increasing usage in industry.

The radiation hazard brought industrial television into play in X-ray technology. A fluoroscope or other device for translating X-ray intensities into visible light is viewed by a sensitive television camera and the image brought out at a safe distance from the exposure site. Motion-picture photography might be used, but the television system permits immediate observation without processing delays and avoids the cost of film and processing.

Television systems may also be used for surveillance, particularly to assist guards in patrolling restricted areas. Another surveillance application is in reading numbers on freight cars in railway switchyards to aid the yardmaster in making up trains.

Surveil-
lance
applica-
tions

Commercial applications. The primary application of closed-circuit television in commerce, as contrasted with industry, is remote inspection of records in banks and other institutions. In one installation, four branches of a bank were connected with 12 miles (19 kilometres) of coaxial cable to permit any teller to call for the signature card or the current balance of any depositor from a central bookkeeping department. Although the initial and maintenance costs of such a system are substantial, the speed and accuracy with which doubtful accounts may be checked justifies the use of the system. Extension of this technique to remote reading of blueprints and other records depends upon lowering the cost of interconnecting cables and increasing the detail of images so that, for example, a full 8½-by-11-inch page of typewritten material could be read on a monitor without error.

The cathode-ray tube is finding wide use as a display device in applications other than television, particularly in connection with electronic computers. Display of information stored in computer memory, or resulting from calculations, is now widely offered to bank tellers, reservation clerks, inventory managers, and others.

Techniques akin to those of television are finding increased use in other commercial and industrial fields. One application is a scanning technique whereby printed characters are "read" and identified by comparing the character with each of a series of standard templates or matrices. This may be done by storing the video signal arising from scanning in a memory array in the form of voltages that may be compared with a similar array of voltages in a matrix corresponding to each letter or number to be recognized. Either mechanical or electronic scanning may be used in this technique.   (D.G.F.)

BIBLIOGRAPHY. D.G. FINK and D.M. LUTYENS, *The Physics of Television* (1960), nontechnical treatment of television principles in paperback form, written for high school physics students; G.M. GLASFORD, *Fundamentals of Television Engineering* (1955), definitive textbook and reference work for the college student; D.G. FINK (ed.), *Television Engineering Handbook* (1957), standard reference work on all technical aspects of monochrome and colour television; B. GROB, *Basic Television*, 3rd ed. (1964), a comprehensive treatment of monochrome and colour television, particularly from the standpoint of receiver maintenance and service requirements; J.W. WENTWORTH, *Color Television Engineering* (1955), standard text and reference work on the USA (NTSC) compatible colour television system that covers the basic principles of colour vision, as well as equipment and system aspects; H.A. CHINN, *Television Broadcasting* (1953), covers equipment, facilities, and techniques of broadcasting practice; P. LEWIS, *Educational Television Guidebook* (1961), information on instructional television from the educational and technical points of view; R. BRETZ, *Techniques of Television Production*, 2nd ed. (1962), on the creative and technical aspects of producing television programs; K. SIMONS, *Technical Handbook for CATV Systems*, 3rd ed. (1968), standard reference work on cable television systems; EDITORS OF TELEVISION DIGEST, *Videocassette Sourcebook* (1971), a collection of short reports on home television recording and playback systems.

(T.H.B./D.G.F.)

Television and Radio, Arts of

Radio and television, though they are primarily means of communication, have early made specific contributions to the arts. Through them music, drama, poetry, ballet, and spectacle have all become universally available, reaching audiences that number in the millions. Radio and television have also engendered new art works conceived specifically for them.

By the time radio broadcasting became established in the 1920s, the motion picture had already won recognition as an art form. Sound broadcasting, on the other hand, was recognized only as a potentially powerful uncomplicated medium for the transmission of information, and for relaying certain established art forms such as music. The artistic potential of radio was not explored until the 1930s, that of television not until the 1950s.

BROADCASTING AS A MEDIUM OF ART

Its nature as an art form

The artistic potential of any medium is determined by the unique form it offers and forces on the artist, and its capacity as an effective vehicle of communication in its own right. The form of any art includes the circumstance through which it reaches its public. Shakespeare's stage was little more than an open platform on which any action he cared to represent could be compassed provided he gave his actors the necessary words to indicate the place, circumstance, and atmosphere of the action. But his plays would have been null as practical drama without the circumscribing enclosure of the Elizabethan circular theatre auditorium—the "wooden O"—which gathered the audience around the platform, sealing them off from the outside world and concentrating their attention on the performance. As active auditors they became an integral part of the drama, and one must be constantly aware of them in the very writing, structure, and timing of the plays. Shakespeare's art was born of the discovery of the potentialities of the actor–audience relationship.

The art of radio. In a similar way the art of radio began to be discovered when those engaged in broadcasting became aware of the nature of the medium in which they were working, and of their special relationship to their audience. The discovery took time. Radio was the only medium in which performers were invisible to their audience. Broadcasters tended at first to adopt the manner of the stage or the pulpit: thinking in terms of a mass audience, the inexperienced broadcaster gave his voice and style an artificial inflation totally unsuited to the new medium. His actual audience was composed of small groups and individuals, usually at home or in informal circumstances, often doing other things at the same time. The basic art of radio consisted in adapting manner and style to these new circumstances. Few programs could expect to take their audiences for granted.

News broadcasts were among the exceptions, and news broadcasts in most countries came to be delivered in a fixed, impersonal manner, the newsreader suppressing his personality as far as possible and adopting a "team" voice. Most other spoken radio required using the voice in such a way as to hold the attention of the listener, and this in turn meant recognizing the nature of the microphone as a medium. The public's span of attention was found to be limited. The news summary was allotted five or ten minutes, while a talk might last 15 minutes, or in special instances up to 30 minutes. Much consideration was also given to the appropriate styles for various audiences, depending on the classes of listeners to whom broadcasts were addressed.

The art of radio emerged in Britain—and in certain other countries adopting the same "public service" approach—as a medium nominally addressed to everyone but actually resembling a kind of broad-based national journal with special sections addressed to specific interests and tastes, some more demanding on the intelligence than others. The popular radio talk (a form of spoken journalism, or essay, often excellently composed and delivered) was shorter and more informal in style than that of the "serious" or purely educational talk. Broadcasting offered unique opportunities for bringing the nation's highest intelligences into the living rooms of so-called minority audiences (often amounting to millions) who were prepared to listen to concentrated exposition and argument. From this developed, particularly in Europe, channels specializing for part or all of the day in minority interests. The listeners supported the service by paying an annual license fee. In the United States, on the other hand, privately owned broadcasting companies got their revenues from advertising, and tied their programming to the advertiser's desire to reach the widest possible public. In Japan there were both public and commercial broadcasting services, the former being financed, as in Europe, by license fees from owners of receiving sets. In the Soviet Union broadcasting was recognized, in the words of *Pravda*, as "one of the most powerful weapons of the cultural revolution." Under Stalin virtually all receivers were wired to local exchanges so that the listener could choose only among approved programs. The service had to be regionalized since the U.S.S.R. includes populations speaking some 80 principal languages. Aside from news and commentary, the broadcasts were generally cultural rather than directly propagandistic.

The development of radio as an art form was thus dependent on the way it was organized and financed. There were rich new fields to be opened up in drama, light entertainment, and documentary programming, conceived specifically for the medium, while at the same time some traditional art forms (notably stage drama and music) were transmitted with success. Fiction and poetry reading also became a staple part of sound broadcasting.

The art of television.   In the 1950s and 1960s radio was overtaken by television. At first television was considered to be little different as a medium from the film. But although television was a hungry user of film, it needed film in forms that differed from those required by the theatres.

The difference between film and television as art forms stemmed from the physical and financial conditions governing production, distribution, and exhibition. The relationships between the media and their publics were also quite different. The initial difference lies in the cameras and their function in production. The film camera supplies a record on celluloid in the form of a two-dimensional image, which, suitably edited, can be subsequently projected onto a screen. The television camera accepts and makes available for immediate transmission a two-dimensional image that remains unrecorded and passes with the event, like the image in a mirror (though this image can, by using additional equipment, be recorded on film or videotape). The film camera is associated with a lengthy effort of photographing, cutting, editing, and dubbing—an elaborate process of selection and assembly that may involve months of work. Although television images may also be stored and edited through videotape, the essential television form is the immediate transmission to the public of events occurring at the moment—political and social events, news summaries, commentary, and discussion.

The basic art of television is the control of this immediate flow of images. They can be preselected insofar as the cameras may be set up at chosen vantage points; after that, however, the director must select among the images they give him. The director-editor uses his skill to secure an immediately effective flow of images from the multiple viewpoints his cameras and their lenses collectively represent. In the film the same end is achieved by the quite different process of fragmenting and recording the action piecemeal, thus creating a succession of images that can be subsequently put together by editing and dubbing.

Those who first struggled with the practical aesthetics of television attempted to see the medium on one hand as a kind of visual radio, and on the other as a form of "diluted cinema," a rather poor cousin of the theatrical film. This was in part because they came either from radio or from film making, and saw the medium in relation to their previous occupations. Writers, directors, and performers from radio tended at first to reduce the television image to a "talking head," with the addition of occasional still pictures, film clips, or cut-ins from other broadcasting stations. This was especially the case in countries in which television initially lacked adequate financing (such as France) and directors could not afford costly pictorialization. On the other hand, personnel coming from film making were appalled at the speed with which they were required to prepare and mount their television programs.

Television differs most from film in its relationship to the audience. The film is an event designed for a theatre with an audience specially assembled for the performance. Television, on the other hand, resembles a private performance in the home. The attitude of a person sitting perhaps alone and often for hours on end before a comparatively small picture screened in the familiar surroundings of his living room is quite different from that of a person who has gone out to share the special audience experience of a theatre. The tension is more slack; concentration is constantly threatened by irrelevant interruption. Whereas one is absorbed by a good film in a theatre to the exclusion of all else, one merely "watches" television. The television audience is preoccupied not so much with an individual item as with the free

flow of item after item. Television is like a talking picture magazine, going on daily and nightly, asking little, giving out along with its entertainment a quantity of easily assimilated information ranging from formal news coverage to informal, gossipy discussions of the lighter affairs of the day.

Television also differs from film with respect to its visual impact. In the movie theatre a highly magnified image fills the central part of the field of vision in an otherwise darkened hall, exciting curiosity and response to a degree far beyond that obtained by the very small television screen in a relatively undarkened living room. The great, fully loaded images of the big screen, from Griffith's *Intolerance* of 1916 to the Russian *War and Peace* of 1968, have involved the investment of large sums of money in what is called "production value"—the accumulated content of those images with their crowds of people and their elaborate sets. Skilled viewers in the movie theatre perceive and appreciate an astonishing amount of detail. In television, however, one has only to watch a film produced for big-screen theatre to realize the limitations of the small TV screen, in which the actors, speakers, or commentators must occupy most of the visual field.

TECHNIQUES AND BORROWINGS

It is useful to view all of the media together, ranging from the individual performer appearing in the flesh before his audience to the complex presentations of the electronic and allied media. They may be compared in terms of the relationship of the performer to his audience as shown in Table 1. The media also vary in the kind of performance on which they can draw, either derivatively or creatively, as shown in Table 2.

Table 1: Relationship of a Performer to His Audience

performer	audience	relationship
individual speaker, storyteller, or singer	assembled group or audience in any place	direct; performer to audience
company of players, singers, dancers, or musicians	assembled audience in a theatre or concert hall	direct; in an enclosed area
performance by an actor or performer recorded on film; factual film with commentator	assembled audience in a motion-picture theatre, hall, classroom, or other formal place	remote; through a photographed and projected two-dimensional image on either a large or small screen, with recorded sound
radio broadcast by an actor, aural performer, newsreader, or commentator	dispersed audience, located mainly in their own homes	remote; through a signal broadcast in sound only
televised presentation by an actor, singer, dancer, performer, or commentator	dispersed audience, located mainly in their own homes	remote; through a two-dimensional image on a small screen, accompanied by sound

The tables make clear the extent to which the various media borrow from each other. Just as the Greek drama drew on ancient myths and legends, and the Renaissance drama on classical and contemporary material alike, so the voracious demands of the new 20th-century media have driven producers and scriptwriters to acquire the rights to existent material in other media, particularly the novel and the drama. Radio and television have overlapped increasingly with journalism, many journalists becoming broadcasters and commentators.

But much of the borrowing has been mechanical and technical rather than artistic in nature. Radio broadcasting exploited the phonograph record as a means of preserving sound; in a similar way, television drew upon the film. The invention of magnetic tape for recording both sound and video signals has now linked together all of the mechanized media—phonograph, telephone, radio, sound film, and television—and made available a virtually complete record of the sights, sounds, arts, and culture of modern society.

Preservation by recording is in itself not a creative art, but a service to art created elsewhere. A principal func-

Table 2: Relationship of the Medium to the Performance

medium	nature of presentation	type of material
rostrum	visible, audible performance by a single person	oratory, preaching, recital; the speech, sermon, song, reading, monologue, monodrama
live theatre; concert hall	visible, audible performance by a group or company	drama, opera, ballet, revue, circus, *etc.*, with or without music; the concert
motion pictures (silent)	visible, but not audible performance presented by means of cinematograph projection	mimed drama with titles, documentary presentation, news record, or animated film; presented with "live" sound (music, commentator)
motion pictures (sound)	visible, audible performance presented by means of a cinematograph projection	original screenplays or material adapted from theatrical, fictional, or other sources; according to degree of adaptation, the sound film supervenes on the form of its source, making something new; also news, factual, and documentary material
sound radio	audible but not visible broadcast performance	the whole range of human activity, from the news bulletin, report, commentary, discussion, talk, or actuality recording to the complete cycle of the audible arts—story and poetry reading, drama and documentary, music and opera, including material specially created for the medium
television	visible and audible broadcast performance	includes all of the above, but seen as well as heard

tion of radio and television broadcasting has been the dissemination of works of art created for other media. This is particularly true of radio; in television these works are more often transformed to meet the requirements of the medium, and become different art forms. When an opera is performed in a television studio in a way that meets the potentialities of the electronic cameras, the result is television opera—a different form from stage opera. When an opera is commissioned and composed specifically for television (as was Benjamin Britten's *Owen Wingrave*) the television becomes an artistic medium in its own right.

Story-telling

Dramatic techniques. Radio began by restoring the ancient art of the storyteller. Writers for radio next learned how to suggest place and time by word of mouth, accompanied by the impressionistic use of sound and music. Thus was born radio drama. The radio dramatist must address himself to the imagination of listeners who, like blind men, are unable to see what they are experiencing. This limitation carries with it a certain freedom. Just as Shakespeare's independence from stage decor left him free to move his action widely in time and space (*Antony and Cleopatra* has 42 wide-ranging changes of scene), so radio has been free to create its own plastic continuities of action and time-space reference. Radio has been highly creative in the fields of drama and documentary, and also in quite new forms of imaginative light entertainment.

Television, on the other hand, adapted techniques already established by the sound film of the 1930s and 1940s. In the initial rivalry between film and television, economic and technical factors both played a part. The first television plays were like the simplest kind of film dialogues; they avoided elaborate sets or large casts, because the screen was not large enough and because they cost too much. Television material was most expendable, like newspapers and journals that are discarded after a single use. Only gradually did the international distribution of selected television programs, particularly within the large Anglo-American market, permit more money to be spent on "production value" in television.

Television drama came into its own during the 1950s with the emergence of writers and directors who shook

themselves free from the old models and began to develop their own techniques—an extension of the two-dimensional image with sound into fields that the cinema could not or would not enter. The creativity of television in the purely artistic sense lies in the unique opportunities it offers the maker. These opportunities were beyond the reach of the film maker, who had no way of impelling his sponsor to finance him in such ventures. Here art and the nature of sponsorship can be said to overlap, as is so often the case in the history of art.

Film techniques. The basic principles that the television image shares with the film image are, of course, its freedom to select the compass of each individual shot and its freedom to determine the nature of the movement within it. The form of presentation depends in both cases on a continuity of such shots in order to build up a narrative flow. Film and television narrative are based on the same principles of mobile composition—the selective (or edited) flow of selective shots of the action. Despite their technological differences they are aesthetically very closely linked and will continue to have a close relationship with each other. This relationship naturally extends into the technical field. Television adopted videotape in order to achieve an immediate high-quality record of the electronic image. This seemed at first a threat to the use of film in television, but that has not proved to be so; the film camera is indispensable in many branches of television production. On the other hand, film makers have found videotape useful in cinema production, since it provides a way of checking the shot before the film is processed.

Use of videotape

The development of television as an art form has not excluded its use as a channel for works produced in other media. On the contrary, production in other media increasingly has been financed out of revenues from its subsequent transmission on television. Since the earliest years of its existence, television has depended on the regular screening of a vast backlog of movie films. The high rentals paid on old films have induced television interests themselves to undertake the production of new films to be shown in theatres and subsequently on the television channels they operate. The feature films they produce often have relatively small casts and a higher ratio of in-close shooting, making them suitable for the smaller TV screen, just as most films now shot for wide screens keep the essential action in the centre so that they can later be shown on television.

FORMS OF RADIO AND TELEVISION BROADCASTING

Drama. Radio and television have provided an entirely new field for the dramatist. The recurrent nature of broadcasting, both radio and television, led to an early adoption of serial forms. The series represents a regular spot in the week filled by standardized blocks of 13, 26, or even 52 successive weekly episodes (covering a quarter, half, or full year). For the writer, director, or actor the series means prolonged employment, though in the actor's case it is also attended by the danger of overidentification with one character. Some of the characters in radio and television serials develop with time, living almost natural life-spans over the years and becoming familiar to a public numbered in millions. An outstanding example is the British television serial *Coronation Street*, which by 1971 had been playing twice weekly for ten years to an average audience large enough to keep a theatre filled for 130 years. To many of its followers, the characters in *Coronation Street* are as real as their friends next door.

The dramatic series

But it is with the nonserial play that the dramatist comes into his own, in both radio and television. In radio, for all but a very few writers of distinction, the nature of the medium (and the comparatively low fees it commands) acts as a deterrent, though some radio plays of high quality have been written, including Dorothy Sayer's *The Man Born to Be King* and Eric Linklater's conversation pieces *The Cornerstone, The Raft,* and *Socrates Asks Why*. In particular, the plays by Louis MacNeice—*Christopher Columbus* and *The Dark Tower*—set to evocative music by William Walton and Benjamin Brit-

Tele-
vision
plays

ten, respectively, and Dylan Thomas' *Under Milk Wood*, showed how the heightened speech of poetic drama could conjure up a whole world in the imagination of the listener. But radio for the most part has offered only efficient, run-of-the-mill writing by professional radiowriters, or, in a higher level, adaptations of stage plays and classical novels.

In television the performance has been more impressive. American writers of the calibre of Paddy Chayefsky (*Marty*) or Reginald Rose (*Twelve Angry Men*) wrote creatively for television as early as the 1950s. But American television turned increasingly to the formula series (though sometimes of high quality, as in *The Defenders*). In Britain the nonserial drama, or the short series by a single writer (such as John Hopkins' four-part series *Quartet*), or the short series by different writers (such as those based on the lives of Henry VIII and Queen Elizabeth I) have provided more opportunity for distinguished writing. Drama is unfortunately the most expensive item in the television repertory (with the exception of light entertainment personalities), and it has constantly to be fought for by its supporters in order to survive in competition with old films and packaged series. Television plays must also be able to hold their own against the competition of news, documentaries, and light entertainment. Television drama has nevertheless proved one of the great creative enterprises of the 20th century. Like the public theatres of Shakespeare's time, television has provided a platform for a whole school of dramatists. It has led to a new kind of dramatic writing, new concepts of character and play structure, new psychological approaches, and new themes. In some instances these have been taken up by the live theatre and the film.

Documentary. Another creative form originating in radio and television is the documentary. Originally a development of the film, it became established on radio in the 1930s. It took many forms, the simplest being a news commentator's presentation backed by selective "on-the-spot" interviewing. This form of broadcasting led to dramatized documentary, with sophisticated scripting and special sound effects, analogous to the newspaper feature story. In the United States it included series such as *March of Time; We, the People;* and *CBS Workshop;* or Norman Corwin's wartime series *This Is War*. Advanced forms of radio documentary were developed during World War II, using radio's full armoury of narrator, scripted dialogue, sound effects, and music to present complex actions—notably in Cecil McGivern's *The Harbour Called Mulberry,* a documentary of the Normandy landings.

Television in its turn offered the documentary film maker an opportunity to develop his art along new and creative lines suitable for the wide-ranging needs of the medium. Documentary, or factual, television can be classified as follows.

The news broadcast. The regular news broadcast in television is supported by illustrations from studio files, videotape recordings, and direct on-the-spot transmissions from the location where events are taking place. The impersonal newscaster eventually gave way to the friendly personality whose warmth makes him a household intimate. An extension of the newscaster is the man in the field, who interprets what is happening, and beyond him the distinguished commentator.

News and
current
affairs

The news magazine. The effort to provide background to the news led to what may be called the television news magazine. Examples of this format are, in the U.S., *CBS Reports;* in Britain, *Panorama, This Week,* and *World in Action;* and in France, *Cinq colonnes à la une.* The essence of a news magazine is that it should have facilities to send film units and reporters to any part of the world at a moment's notice, as well as to handle home stories as they occur. Coverage can then become fully creative, with the degree of objectivity that may be expected of trusted reporters and commentators.

The documentary of current affairs. Normally filmed rather than videotaped, the current affairs documentary is an investigation in depth of a single subject at home or abroad. Outstanding examples include *See It Now*, which

began in the U.S. in 1951, the National Broadcasting system's *White Paper* series of the 1960s, and the British Broadcasting Corporation's *Special Enquiry*. Such documentaries can be highly controversial, as a *See It Now* confrontation with Sen. Joseph McCarthy in 1954 or a Columbia Broadcasting System's *Selling of the Pentagon* of 1971. Made with more leisure than the news magazine, the current affairs documentary shares its techniques with that of the nontheatrical film documentary. More recently, light-weight portable equipment has made possible an intimate, fluid, and mobile technique known as "tele-vérité."

The documentary of general knowledge. Television moved early into the field of general knowledge documentaries, among the first being *Victory at Sea* (NBC), *Air Power* (CBS), and *War in the Air* (BBC). The historical documentary is now used regularly on television, as in NBC's *Project XX*, CBS's *20th Century* series (begun in 1957), and ABC's series *Winston Churchill: The Valiant Years* (1960–61), and the BBC's series *The Great War* and *The Lost Peace*. Some documentaries have been devoted to the sciences, medicine, and the arts—notably in British and Soviet television. Biography is another field. In Britain, Ken Russell's idiosyncratic biographical studies of composers (Debussy, Elgar, Delius, Strauss) caused controversy with their experimental, impressionistic approach, a technique Russell later developed in his feature film *The Music Lovers*.

The personal essay. Some television directors, especially in Britain, have been able to establish highly individual styles. They have used camera and tape on live, unrehearsed subjects in ways that take advantage of new technical developments. Videotape offers more freedom than film, since tape can be erased and reused; tape also can operate with less light than film (to make night shots possible) and can combine coverage from a number of cameras operating in turn on a single, immediate recording.

Educational radio and television. The application of documentary techniques to educational material directed to schools, colleges, and individual students of every kind has become a special field of broadcasting. These services are provided through the public broadcasting networks and through closed-circuit transmissions within school systems.

Other forms. *Music.* Most musical forms may be better suited for radio than for television, since they offer little to the small-screen viewer. Popular singers, however, have become a regular feature on television where they often receive elaborate or fanciful visual presentation—particularly effective on colour television. Opera and ballet are difficult to present effectively on the small screen, though techniques of multicamera coverage have been developed, fragmenting the performance to allow the camera to work more closely with part of the scene at a time.

Popular
singers
and stars

Comedy and satire. A feature of both radio and television is the comedy series; either the half-hour sketch featuring a well-known star or the wholly idiosyncratic show in which burlesque and the verbal or visual gag can be carried to the point of surrealism. In this field radio and television have been strongly creative. Television, notably in Britain, has carried satire to the point of national controversy, as happened with *That Was the Week That Was*.

The television commercial. The television commercial has, at its best, become an art form in its own right. The purest example is the animated commercial, combining its own succinct, witty style and lightning continuity, an art born entirely of television.

THE PROSPECT

The creative use of television in the United States has depended largely on the enlightened sponsor, as in the cases of *Omnibus, Kraft Television Theatre,* and *Playhouse 90*. In Britain the charter of incorporation of the BBC enjoins it to enlighten as well as to entertain, while the Independent Television Authority has the duty to supervise the program content of the commercial television companies. But the main hope for more creative television lies in the adoption of new techniques such as the video cassette and cable TV, which will cater to minority interests that cannot be adequately represented in network programming.

BIBLIOGRAPHY. RUDOLF ARNHEIM, *Radio* (1936), was an early evaluation of the broadcast medium; and MARSHALL MCLUHAN, *Understanding Media* (1964), one of the more recent. A definitive history of the BBC appears in ASA BRIGGS, *The History of Broadcasting in the United Kingdom*, 3 vol. (1961–70). In the United States the art of television has generally been discussed in terms of documentary programs, most notably in A. WILLIAM BLUEM, *Documentary in American Television* (1965); a survey of both American and British documentary work occurs in NORMAN SWALLOW, *Factual Television* (1966). The whole field of television art in Britain was covered in PAUL ROTHA (ed.), *Television in the Making* (1956). ROGER MANVELL, *On The Air* (1953), has sections on the arts of radio and television. Among the pioneer manuals on television drama, ARTHUR SWINSON, *Writing for Television* (1955), is among the best. RICHARD LEVIN, *Television by Design* (1961); and WALTER HERDIG and JOHN HALAS, *Film and TV Graphics* (1967), deal respectively with decor and graphics, including animation for titling, commercials, and so forth. A stock-taking of the achievements and limitations of television in Britain is JOAN BAKEWELL and NICHOLAS GARNHAM (eds.), *The New Priesthood* (1970). A. WILLIAM BLUEM and ROGER MANVELL, *Progress in Television* (U.S. title, *TV: The Creative Experience*, 1967), assesses television's development in both the United States and Britain with a selection of articles from the *Journal of the Society of Film and Television Arts* and from the *Television Quarterly*.

(R.M.)

Teller, Edward

The development in 1952 of the world's first thermonuclear weapon, the hydrogen bomb, is generally credited to Edward Teller, who became known in America as "the father of the H-bomb." Although other physicists and mathematicians contributed enormously to the project, his stubborn perseverance in the face of skepticism, and even hostility, from many of his peers played the major role. Teller's work was officially recognized in 1962 when the U.S. Atomic Energy Commission bestowed on him the Enrico Fermi Award.

By courtesy of the University of California Lawrence Radiation Laboratory, Berkeley

Teller.

Born of prosperous Jewish parents in Budapest, Hungary, on January 15, 1908, Edward Teller was encouraged in intellectual pursuits at an early age. A precocious gift for mathematics and curiosity about the natural world characterized his formative years. After attending the Institute of Technology in Budapest, Teller earned a degree in chemical engineering at the Institute of Technology in Karlsruhe, Germany. He then went to Munich and Leipzig to earn a Ph.D. in physical chemistry. While a student in Munich he fell under a moving streetcar and lost his right foot. Despite this tragedy, Teller's robust spirit and sense of fun, as well as his brilliant mind and

arresting appearance—an angular face under a shock of unruly black hair and massive eyebrows—have made him a striking figure throughout his life.

During the years of the Weimar Republic, Teller was absorbed with atomic physics, first studying under Niels Bohr in Copenhagen and then teaching at the University of Göttingen. In 1935 Teller and his bride, the former Augusta Harkanyi, went to the United States, where he taught at George Washington University, Washington, D.C. Following Bohr's stunning report on atomic fission in 1939 and inspired by the words of President Roosevelt, who had called for scientists and statesmen to act together to defend "our science, our culture, our American freedom and our civilization," Teller resolved to devote his energies to developing nuclear weapons. *Studies in Germany*

By 1941 Teller had taken out U.S. citizenship and joined Enrico Fermi's team in the classic and successful experiment to produce the first nuclear chain reaction. Teller then accepted an invitation from the University of California at Berkeley to work on theoretical studies on the atomic bomb with J. Robert Oppenheimer; and when Oppenheimer set up the secret Los Alamos weapons laboratory in New Mexico in 1943, he was among the first men recruited. Although the Los Alamos assignment was to build a fission bomb, Teller digressed more and more from the main line of research to continue his own inquiries into a potentially much more powerful thermonuclear hydrogen fusion bomb. At war's end he wanted the priority moved to the H-bomb. Hiroshima, however, had had a profound effect on most of the Los Alamos men, and few had the desire to continue in weapons.

Teller accepted a position with the Institute for Nuclear Studies at the University of Chicago in 1946 but returned to Los Alamos as a consultant for extended periods. The Soviet explosion of an atomic bomb in 1949 made him more determined that the United States have a superbomb, but the Atomic Energy Commission's general advisory committee, headed by Oppenheimer, voted against a crash program. The debate was settled by the confession of the British atomic scientist Klaus Fuchs that he had been spying for the Soviet Union since 1942. Fuchs had known of the U.S. interest in a superbomb. President Truman ordered the go-ahead on the weapon, and Teller laboured on at Los Alamos to make it a reality. *Work after World War II*

At the Oppenheimer security hearings in 1954, Teller's evidence was decidedly unsympathetic to his former chief. "I would feel personally more secure," he told the inquiry board, "if public matters would rest in other hands." Teller became estranged from Oppenheimer and many other scientists after this.

Teller was instrumental in the creation of the United States' second weapons laboratory, at Livermore, California, concentrating on thermonuclear devices, and was its director for two years from 1958. At the same time he continued as professor of physics at the University of California in Berkeley. Teller resigned from Livermore in 1960 to devote more of his time to his crusade to keep the United States ahead in nuclear arms. He became an influential spokesman in atomic affairs and was a particular champion of Project Plowshare, the Atomic Energy Commission program to find peaceful uses for atomic explosives. He maintained that means could easily be found to guard against radiological pollution from atomic power plants and underground explosions. He advocated nuclear explosions to gain freer access to oil and gas and as a means to create harbours and ship canals.

In a major public statement in December 1970, Teller urged the lifting of secrecy surrounding much of the nation's scientific research, including work in nuclear science, in the interests of clarifying the national debate on the effects of science and technology on society.

BIBLIOGRAPHY. Two works by TELLER are *The Legacy of Hiroshima*, with ALLEN BROWN (1962), the story of the development of the hydrogen bomb; and *The Reluctant Revolutionary* (1964), a discussion of nuclear weaponry and the cold war. For information on Teller, see ROBERT JUNGK, *Heller als tausend Sonnen* (1956; Eng. trans., *Brighter Than a Thousand Suns: The Moral and Political History of the Atomic Scientists*, 1958).

(P.Mi.)

Tennessee

Though classified as an east south central state of the United States, Tennessee is best described as a state of the upper South in its traditions. It entered the Union in 1796 as the 16th member, and, with the disappearance of the Old Southwest in the early 1800s, it became a part of the Old South in spirit and way of life. Such native sons as the frontiersman-legislator Davy Crockett and the soldier-president Andrew Jackson symbolized the state's contribution of a populist political and social philosophy that broke the hold an educated Eastern-Seaboard gentry had maintained on the federal government during the first four decades of the American nation. Unlike the Deep South, in which huge plantations were the symbol of the cotton empire, Tennessee developed largely as an agglomeration of small farms, but most of its people enthusiastically followed the Confederacy into secession and the Civil War.

In the 20th century, however, Tennessee has adapted itself somewhat more readily than most of its sister states to national rather than regional patterns of life. From the beginning, a geography that divided it into three distinct regions tended to soften its Southern cast. East Tennessee always showed marked Northern attitudes, and the two-party political system, which had endured, however weakly, has returned to full flower. Though the state has suffered many of the conflicts of the civil rights struggles since the 1950s, leaders of both whites and blacks hope that an accommodation fully acceptable to both races can be effected.

Four of the state's major cities and their surrounding counties have attained metropolitan size, reflecting Tennessee's growth in population, industry, and urbanization at a generally more rapid pace than its neighbours. Knoxville, the site of the University of Tennessee, and Chattanooga, where in 1863 Confederate and Union soldiers clashed in the famous "Battle above the Clouds" on Lookout Mountain, are the major centres of east Tennessee. Nashville, the state capital and focus of middle Tennessee, is perhaps best known as the national capital of country–western music. Memphis is the hub of west Tennessee, and its history includes its major role in the Mississippi River steamboat traffic and its prominent and colourful position in the development of American jazz.

Tennessee's geography is unique, also, in its extreme breadth of 432 miles (695 kilometres), stretching from the Appalachian Mountain boundary with North Carolina in the east to the Mississippi River borders with Missouri and Arkansas in the west; and its narrow width, only 112 miles (180 kilometres) separating its northern neighbours, Kentucky and Virginia, from Georgia, Alabama, and Mississippi on the south. Its 42,244 square miles (109,411 square kilometres), according to the census of 1970, held a population of 3,923,687 persons, about 16 percent of whom were black. (For information on related topics, see the articles UNITED STATES; UNITED STATES, HISTORY OF THE; CIVIL WAR, U.S.; NORTH AMERICA; APPALACHIAN MOUNTAINS; and MISSISSIPPI RIVER.)

THE HISTORY OF TENNESSEE

From settlement to Civil War. Much of Tennessee's early history consisted of prototypal frontier dramas, for its patterns of exploration and settlement in the late 18th and early 19th centuries were to be repeated in all of the states west of the Appalachians. Tennessee became a sort of mother state for the entire Old Southwest. Its pioneer families fanned out into the newer regions of Alabama, Mississippi, Arkansas, north Louisiana, and east Texas. The bloody, destructive Civil War laid its scourge upon Tennessee, which became a major battleground of the war in the west. The battlegrounds, neatly kept and well-marked, can be found today, but for decades an abiding political and ideological scar kept company with the old fields of conflict.

The long aftermath. The war bound Tennessee closely to the "lost cause" of the Confederacy and to the New South, which became a regional attempt to graft the Old South to the modern trends of the nation. The roaring industrial prosperity of the Eastern and Great Lakes states left the devastated South largely untouched. Though decade by decade Tennessee became a wealthier and growing state, it, like other Southern states, had difficulty in catching up to the booming national standards, despite a diversifying economy and an energetic people. The Great Depression of the 1930s, which came early and ended late in Tennessee, staggered the internal rates of improvement and growth.

New directions. After World War II, Tennessee's history again took new directions. The technological revolutions of the 20th century loosened its traditional modes of life. The unities of thought and feeling that sprang from a well-remembered past splintered in the face of the excruciating changes of modern America. In the 1940s and 1950s, the state's economy changed from one dominated by agriculture to one based on manufacturing. Its leaders, with deep conviction, allied themselves with what one observer has called the emerging South, a South less isolated, less rural, less militant, and at the same time more prosperous and more a part of the national scene.

Postwar recovery

THE LANDSCAPE

The natural environment. East Tennessee comprises rugged mountains and broad valleys of great beauty that give way to the rolling hills and wide basins of middle Tennessee. West Tennessee, on the other hand, is a relatively undulating plain broken by deep gullies.

Geographical regions. Geographers divide the state more scientifically into six natural regions. Sixteen peaks in the Unaka Mountains—a section of which is popularly known as the Great Smoky Mountains—rise above 6,000 feet, the tallest of them, Clingmans Dome, at 6,642 feet (2,024 metres). The Great Appalachian Valley, varying from 30 to 60 miles in width, has within it a series of low ridges that rise 800 feet or more above the intervening valleys. The Cumberland Plateau has a generally flat, slightly undulating surface, but it has been cut by deep and sometimes wide river valleys. The Interior Low Plateau, the largest of the regions, is dominated by the Nashville Basin and its Highland Rim. About 60 miles wide and running roughly north to south across the state, the basin floor is a slightly rolling terrain punctuated by small hills known as knobs. To the west, the Eastern Gulf Coastal Plain undulates only slightly and is laced with meandering, low-banked streams. In the extreme west, the plain ends in the Mississippi Alluvial Plain, a narrow strip of swamp and floodplain alongside the river.

Peaks, plateaus, and plains

Rivers and soils. The land drains directly into three major rivers. The Tennessee River, which flows southward in the east and northward in the west, drains the east, the southern part of the middle region, and a major part of the west. The Cumberland River, dipping into the state from the north, drains the upper middle region, while the Mississippi River directly drains a small portion of the west. The damming of the Tennessee and, to a lesser extent, of the Cumberland has created an impressive chain of slack-water lakes, sometimes known as the Great Lakes of the South, many of which lie in Tennessee. In general, the valleys and upland basins of Tennessee have moderately fertile soil of limestone origins, and the streams have created rich alluvial lands along their beds. The soils of the ridges and the plateau, however, are thin, stony, and moderately acid, while the coastal plain has a sandy, thin soil that does not lend itself to agriculture. Thirty-five percent of the state's soils are unfit for any kind of cultivation.

Climate. Tennessee has a moderate climate featuring cool but not cold winters and warm but not hot summers. The drop in elevation causes temperatures to rise significantly from east to west. Mountain summers in the east are not unlike those of more northerly states. The growing season ranges from 160 days in the east to 260 days in the southwest. The state receives ample precipitation, about 50 inches (1,270 millimetres) a year, rather evenly distributed over the seasons and regions.

Vegetation and animal life. The state's central position in the eastern half of the United States and its diverse elevations have meant that many plants, animals, and fish identified more with the extremes of north and south can be found in the state. Tennessee is about 52 percent forested by more than 200 species of trees, of which 59 are commercially valuable. Found throughout the state are such common trees as locust, poplar, maple, oak, elm, beech, pine, spruce, walnut, hickory, and sycamore.

Human regionalism. The late settlement of west Tennessee, long an Indian reserve, combined with the obvious geographical separations to create a strong sectionalism within Tennessee. The Civil War further accentuated the differences, with most people in the east remaining Union and loyal, whereas the west and middle became a Confederate stronghold in ideology. The east thereby formed a traditional tie to the Republican Party, as opposed to the equally strong bonds with the southern wing of the Democratic Party that existed in the other regions. The east would also, in legend and partial fact, advertise itself as a fortress for "mountain culture"—independence, small farms, and underemployed mountaineers, poor but proud—whereas middle Tennessee, particularly in the Nashville Basin, allied closely with the New South of the late 19th and early 20th centuries, a South that embraced much of the new technological life but clung mightily to the romanticism of the Old South in its popular lore. The west emphasized a Jacksonian democracy of entrepreneurial yeomen and vigorous Democratic politics for its white majority. Even today, with superhighways and airlines spanning the state, the sense of three different Tennessees influences the politics and thinking of the state. In recent years Memphis and surrounding Shelby County, radically different from agricultural west Tennessee, has increasingly become a distinct section as well.

Sectional-
ism
and
sentiment

Small farms and small towns characterize most of the inhabited Tennessee landscape. Its average farm size, 114 acres (46 hectares), is only about one-third of the national size. In 1970 three of the 95 counties had fewer than 4,000 residents, and 57 had fewer than 25,000 people. The urbanization rate of 59 percent represented an increase of only 7 percent during the 1960s. Thus Tennessee continued to urbanize more slowly than the United States in general. The metropolitan areas of the four major cities, however, with their varied industrial bases, spreading suburbs, and urban opportunities and problems, resemble metropolitan areas across the nation. Tennessee's long and traditional rural character, though deeply embedded, is being eroded.

THE PEOPLE OF TENNESSEE

Ethnic and religious composition. At one time, uniformity and homogeneity aptly described Tennessee's white population, relatively untouched as it was by the waves of immigration into the United States. From its beginnings, Tennessee literature and folklore has stressed the Anglo-Saxon tradition celebrated by frontiersmen like Davy Crockett and Andrew Jackson, by such modern heroes as World War I army sergeant Alvin York, and by the entertainers at Nashville's country–western-music mecca known as the "Grand Ole Opry." The state's white population worshipped as Protestants—more than two-thirds of the church members belong to the Southern Baptist and Southern Methodist churches—and had a fundamentalist American approach to such values as patriotism, honesty, courage, work, duty, and personal morality.

Yet from the beginning, uniformity and homogeneity pertained only in part. Slavery entrapped more than 280,000 blacks in 1860, some 26 percent of the population. The black percentage has declined consistently since 1880. Black and white Tennesseans, though touching each other in many ways, have lived in most important ways apart and isolated from one another. Blacks grew up and died in a segregated world, separate but very much unequal. In their separate institutions—the church, the lodge, the schools, and other public places—they developed a significant subculture within the general American culture. Beginning in the 1950s, after decades of protest and the slow accumulation of power, many leaders of the black Tennesseans organized and worked for a

Segrega-
tion

new, integrated Tennessee: in schools, in factories, and in public places. Their demands for a fair and equal society reverberated across the state. The turns and twists of this black revolution have had a profound impact on the people of Tennessee, creating strains in the social and political life of whites and blacks alike as the legal structure of segregation and some of its habits were broken. The clashes of culture and power probably will continue, but a countertrend of black and white accommodation and understanding is also at work.

Demography. Tennessee's population grew much more slowly than the national rate from 1940 to 1970, but its 8 percent and 10 percent growth in the 1950s and 1960s, respectively, was a faster rate than those of other east south central states. The census of 1970 showed Tennessee with slightly lower percentages of persons in the younger and older age groups and a higher percentage between 18 and 44 years of age. During the 1960s, the birthrate declined well below 20 births per 1,000 of population, and by 1970 the death rate was 9.5 per 1,000 population. The death rate of black Tennesseans, however, was 58 percent higher than that of the white population. The decades-long trend of greater emigration than immigration was broken in the 1960s, when Tennessee became the only east south central state to have greater inflow than outflow of people. In the same decade, urbanization continued, and a slight movement of population from east to west could be detected. Blacks continued to migrate to the cities in large numbers: by 1970 more than 60 percent of the black population lived in the four metropolitan areas.

THE STATE'S ECONOMY

General economic picture. Tennessee's agricultural resources were always slim: almost 70 percent of the land is unfit or poor for cultivation, and less than 2 percent is classified as good. Until the state's agonizing shift from agriculture to manufacturing began in the 1940s, these weak resources made it appear statistically as an area of high underemployment, low income, low educational levels, substandard housing, and deficient health facilities. The shift to manufacturing has failed to improve Tennessee's position in national rankings, since the nation as a whole has boomed even more, but it has brought about vastly improved standards of living within the state. Regionally, Tennessee became a manufacturing state more quickly and more fully than any other east south central state, and its per capita income, about three-quarters of the national average, is the second highest among these states. It ranks among the top 20 states in value added by manufacture and in industrial employment.

Industry
and
standards
of
living

Components of the economy. Though the service industries employed somewhat more persons and provided slightly more personal income, Tennessee's manufacturing employment grew nearly 50 percent during the 1960s. This reflects in part the state government's aggressive policy, over several decades, of enticing industry from other states. The major industries in value added by manufacture were chemicals, food processing, apparel, electrical machinery, and textiles. Agriculture produced less than 4 percent of personal income. The state has moderate coal and stone deposits and is the nation's largest producer of zinc.

Tennessee Valley Authority. The creation of the Tennessee Valley Authority (TVA) in 1933 greatly enhanced a transition to industry in Tennessee as well as neighbouring states affected by it. The growing stock of electricity from the authority's dams, steam plants, and nuclear stations, which made the TVA the nation's largest producer of electricity, attracted such major industries as the Oak Ridge nuclear plant and the works of the Aluminum Company of America. It brought great changes also in rural life throughout much of the South, bringing the first electrification to many areas. The TVA often is looked upon as one of America's major achievements in regional economic development, upgrading the land, industry, and overall standards of living.

Transportation. In the last half of the 19th century, the railroads pushed through the valleys and across the ridges, but the peak mileage of 1920 had declined by the 1970s. By this time, the more than 70,000 miles of highway had lifted the state out of the mud to dependable all-weather travel. Major airline service to the metropolitan cities and the ever increasing use of barge tows along the Cumberland and Tennessee rivers supplement the transportation network. Tennessee's cities are traffic choked, however, because of their critical need for modern, urban mass transit.

ADMINISTRATION AND SOCIAL CONDITIONS

Structure of government. The constitution of 1870 differed little from the original document formulated in 1796. Reflecting the needs and points of view of an earlier America, it remained unaltered until, beginning in 1953, a series of amendments were passed that have helped to modernize state government.

Among the changes effected were clauses liberalizing the complicated amendment procedure, increasing the terms of the governor and state senators from two to four years (with the provision that the governor cannot succeed himself), increasing the pay of state legislators, providing for annual rather than biennial meetings of the state legislature, abolishing the poll tax, and increasing the power of cities to govern themselves independently of the state.

Today, the structure of the executive, legislative, and judicial branches of government in Tennessee resembles closely that of many other states. The governor is the only popularly elected executive official. The speaker of the state Senate serves as lieutenant governor. Other executive officeholders are elected by the entire legislature, while the attorney general is appointed by the Supreme Court. Executives of major departments and important state commissions are appointed by the governor. The bicameral General Assembly comprises a 33-member Senate and a 99-member House of Representatives. It can override a governor's veto by a simple majority. The legislature is not considered a full-time occupation, for its members receive only token remuneration.

The judicial system consists of a complex of inferior courts—chancery courts, circuit courts, and criminal courts—that try various types of cases. The Supreme Court and the lower Court of Appeals have their judges apportioned among the three traditional sections of the state.

Local government also clings to the national pattern. In some counties, a county court made up of elected trustees collects taxes and maintains most county services. Education and safety forces, however, are administered by an elected or appointed school board and the sheriff, respectively. In several counties, the county court is composed of an elected county judge together with justices of the peace elected by districts. City government includes city manager-council, mayor-council, and commissioners-council forms.

Experimentation in local government. Tennessee has under way a major experiment in local government. In 1962 Nashville and its county, Davidson, began a consolidation into a single governmental unit called Metropolitan Government, or "Metro." Metro has solved some old problems, left others untouched, and created some of its own. As this type of extended-area government frequently has been suggested as a step toward possible improvements in America's urban crises, urban planners across the country are studying Metro closely.

Politics. Tennessee never had the multifactional, one-party politics that characterized so many other Southern states. The Democratic domination was leavened always by the possibility of successful challenges from the Republicans, whose strength remained steady in east Tennessee. The result was a Democratic Party usually made up of two factions, not always ideologically differentiated, that fought in the primary elections and then united for the general election. Since Reconstruction, only four Republican governors have been elected, though two Republican congressmen have been traditional. At the end of the 1960s, this traditional arrangement was shattered badly by the replacement of the two Democratic senators by Republicans. Republicans, though still a minority, dramatically increased their representation in state and local government, and since 1948 Tennessee's presidential vote has gone to the Republicans, except in 1964. In 1970 the Republicans won the governor's chair for the first time in 50 years. With the state's election results no longer certain, they will most likely be disputed hotly by the parties and within the parties' councils as well.

Social services. Tennessee's social needs are many and its wealth slim; its showing in expenditures for public needs in relation to national figures is poor. By the early 1970s, Tennessee's annual budget of about $1,500,000,000 was financed principally by a general sales tax, license and privilege taxes, and several usage taxes, but the tax structures, both state and local, rank among the five lowest states in effort. By 1971 it was one of 12 states that did not have a general income tax. Tennessee's lower living costs are balanced by average weekly and hourly wage rates well below the national average. In 1969, even in the four east south central states, it ranked only third in these rates. Tennessee's population generally ranks very low in educational attainments. Its $560 per student expenditure for public schools in 1970 was 44th in the nation and its per capita expenditure for higher education ranked 50th. By 1970, one of every 16 Tennesseans received welfare funds of some sort, but its per capita payments under such aid programs as for dependent children and the blind or sick ranked in the lower third of the states. Federal and state activity to solve its economic and social problems in the 1960s was almost revolutionary in comparison to previous decades, but Tennessee, hampered by its Appalachian poverty, its low-wage industry, and its depressed west Tennessee agriculture, has not been a national leader in these trends.

CULTURAL LIFE AND INSTITUTIONS

The cultural milieu. Tennessee long has had a national image as the "hillbilly state." The mountaineer—a person of drawling speech dressed in blue-denim overalls, operating an illegal whiskey still—became a figure of national mythology. The image actually was nurtured and sustained by a remarkable institution, the "Grand Ole Opry," founded in Nashville in 1925. This radio broadcast of country-and-western music made Nashville the capital city of country America. Today, Nashville is a leading centre for the production and distribution of popular-music records, particularly country–western, but it is also the seat of Vanderbilt University, founded in 1873, and today one of the most highly regarded universities in the South.

As might be expected, however, Tennessee is in many ways a cultural carbon copy of the greater United States. It has nearly 60 institutions of higher education, both public and private, enrolling more than 130,000 students. More than 200 libraries and branches make books and learning materials available for Tennesseans. All four major cities have active professional symphonic orchestras, and each city supports several art galleries. Museums, such as the American Museum of Atomic Energy at Oak Ridge, help to create a significant educational environment. Sophisticated daily newspapers such as the *Chattanooga Times* (often considered among the finest in the South), the *Memphis Commercial-Appeal*, and the *Nashville Tennessean* circulate across the state. Network and educational television can be seen in every county. Nashville has major publishing houses for the Baptist and Methodist churches. Graceful antebellum architecture dots the landscape, in startling contrast to examples of strikingly modern architecture. The TVA dams and new steam- and nuclear-power plants, symbols of industrial Tennessee, modify considerably the old "hillbilly" image of Tennessee life. In short, Tennesseans participate fully in the great cultural and social movements of their times.

Prospects. Tennessee in the early 1970s offers, somewhat more sharply than some other states, the diversities that make up the United States. The state has a steady drive toward more factories and more people living in congested cities, but a continuing isolated and wooded countryside, a recent rural domination, and many small

Learning, communications, and the arts

towns still link it to an older America. Its political habits have developed a chronic uncertainty as the Republican Party enjoys unprecedented success at the polls. But the shifts in party allegiance over the past 25 years can be deceptive, for both parties tend to be more conservative than their national leadership.

For the most part, Tennessee has not been a leader in effecting change or experimenting with new ways for a new society. Rather, the history of the state shows a people and a set of institutions adjusting slowly to the changes that appear to be working within the nation.

BIBLIOGRAPHY. The most recent, usable history of the state is STANLEY FOLMSBE, ROBERT CORLEW, and ENOCH MITCHELL, *Tennessee: A Short History* (1969). The extensive bibliography on pp. 579–613 directs the reader to the richness of Tennessee's past. JOHN KNOX BALLINGER, *The People of Tennessee* (1949), examines the demography of Tennessee from the 1790s through the 1940s. The best sources of information about the contemporary state may be found in the occasional publications of the TENNESSEE STATE PLANNING COMMISSION, whose studies are directly concerned with the demography, economic and human resources, and social structure of the state, as well as leading problems of government. Information on recent and old publications may be obtained from the State Library and Archives, Nashville.

For the basic physical geography of the state, see HAROLD C. AMICK and L.C. ROLLINS, *The Geography of Tennessee* (1937). A good interpretative work on Tennessee politics in the 20th century may be found in V.O. KEY, *Southern Politics in State and Nation*, pp. 59–81 (1949). See also NORMAN PARKS, "Tennessee Politics Since Kefauver and Reece: A Generalist View," *Journal of Politics*, 28:144–168 (1966). HUGH DAVIS GRAHAM, *Crisis in Print: Desegregation and the Tennessee Press* (1969), gives great insight into racial conflict in the state. See also HARRY HOLLOWAY, *The Politics of the Southern Negro*, pp. 65–90, 272–309 (1969), on race relations in the state.

(J.A.Ho.)

Tennis and Allied Court Games

Games of the tennis family are played with racket and ball on various sorts of courts and trace their origin back to a 12th–13th century French game *jeu de paume* ("palm game") or, in England, "tennis." Its descendant, lawn tennis, was first played in the early 1870s and has become so popular that to most people tennis means lawn tennis, and throughout this article, unless qualified, tennis refers to lawn tennis. The more ancient game, for purposes of differentiation, is usually called real tennis in Great Britain, court tennis in the U.S., or royal tennis in Australia—much to the annoyance of purists.

The various forms of rackets (including squash rackets) and table tennis are covered in separate articles under those titles. Other modern variations include deck tennis, paddle (or padder) tennis, and platform tennis. This article deals with lawn tennis, real tennis, and badminton.

Lawn Tennis
ORIGINS AND EARLY HISTORY OF LAWN TENNIS
The old game of real tennis had been played in covered courts for many centuries and it is not surprising that from time to time efforts were made to play it in the open air. In the history of the game, various mention is made of such experiments, but none succeeded until the use of rubber resulted in a ball that was able to bounce on a grass surface. Rubber was known to the Aztecs and Columbus saw balls "made of the gum of a tree" being used by the Indians of Haiti. But not until the mid-19th century did Europe learn how to manipulate rubber successfully.

There has been much dispute over the invention of tennis, but certainly it was a Major Walter Wingfield of Nantclwyd in North Wales who first published a book of rules in 1873 and took out a patent on his game in 1874. Wingfield's court was of the "hourglass" shape that had become the rule in badminton (see below). But the publication of his version of "Sphairistikè, or Lawn Tennis" led to a spate of other claims to the invention of the game, most of which involved a rectangular court. R.A. Fitzgerald, secretary of the Marylebone Cricket Club (MCC), then the governing body of real tennis, pointed out that

First book of rules

the MCC had only recently revised the rules of real tennis and might be a suitable body to standardize the rules of tennis. Moreover, a distinguished real tennis player, J.M. Heathcote, had developed a better ball, made of rubber but covered with white flannel. And so it came about that the MCC first established the rules of tennis in 1875.

Meanwhile the game spread to the U.S. in 1874 when Miss Mary Outerbridge of New York saw it being played by the British garrison in Bermuda and brought a set of rackets and balls to her brother, a director of the Staten Island Cricket and Baseball Club. Soon afterward, tennis courts were established in Boston, Newport, R.I., Plainfield, N.J., New Orleans, and Philadelphia.

A significant milestone in the history of tennis was the decision of the All-England Croquet Club, in 1875, to set aside one of its lawns at Wimbledon for tennis, which soon proved so popular that the following year the club changed its title to the All-England Croquet and Lawn Tennis Club. In 1877 the club decided to hold a Tennis Championship, open to amateurs only, for a silver Challenge Cup presented by *The Field* magazine. A special championship subcommittee of three was appointed and, probably because two of them were distinguished players of real tennis, they decided on certain rules different from those of Sphairistikè. They decided on a rectangular court, 26 yards (24 metres) long by 9 yards (8 metres) wide; they adopted the real tennis method of scoring by 15s; and they allowed the server one fault (*i.e.*, two chances to deliver a correct service on each serve). These major decisions remain part of the rules today.

Twenty-two entries were received and the first winner of the Wimbledon Championship was Spencer W. Gore, an old Harrovian rackets player, renowned for a heavily cut underhand service and for his net-storming tactics. The scene was very different from that of today. There was no stand for spectators. Players wore white flannel shirts with a tie, long white trousers kept up by a schoolboy belt, and a white cap. Rackets bore traces of their real tennis forebears and were somewhat square-topped with a plain wooden handle. Balls were lighter, weighing 1¼ to 1½ oz (35.4 to 42.5 g), compared with the modern 2 to 2¹⁄₁₆ oz (56.7 to 58.5 g).

Two hundred spectators paid a shilling each to watch the final, after which nets, posts, and guy ropes were sold off at 30 shillings a set and the club made a net profit of £10.

The All-England Croquet Club was first in the championship field, but it was followed in 1878 by the Scottish Championship and in 1879 by the Irish Championship, which for many years rivalled Wimbledon in repute.

DEVELOPMENT OF THE SPORT
There were several alterations in some of the other rules (*e.g.*, governing the height of the net) until 1880 when the All-England Club and the MCC published revised rules that approximate very closely those in use today. In 1880, the first American championship of national interest was held at the Staten Island Cricket and Baseball Club. The victor was an Englishman, O.E. Woodhouse. The fast-growing popularity of the game in the U.S. and frequent doubts about rules led to the foundation of the U.S. National Lawn Tennis Association (later renamed the U.S. Lawn Tennis Association [USLTA]), following a meeting of 33 clubs held in New York in 1881.

Under the auspices of the USLTA, the first official U.S. National Championship was held in 1881 at the Newport Casino, R.I., next to the real tennis court, which provided a gallery for spectators. It was played under English rules. The winner, R.D. Sears, was U.S. Champion for seven consecutive years.

In the United Kingdom the All-England Club was dominant and the British Lawn Tennis Association (LTA) did not come into existence until 1888.

Meantime, lawn tennis had taken firm root in Australia. It started in Victoria in 1880 under the aegis of the Melbourne Cricket Club and in New South Wales in 1885, when the first interstate championships were played. The first New Zealand National Championship was held in 1886. The Lawn Tennis Association of Victoria took over

Founding of national associations and championships

control from the Melbourne Cricket Club in 1889, but not until 1904 was the Australasia Association founded, to include all the states of Australia and New Zealand.

The National Lawn Tennis Association of France instituted the French National (hard [clay] court) Championship in 1891, but it was not opened to players from other nations until 1925. The National Championship of Canada was instituted in 1890; others included Spain 1910, South Africa 1920, Denmark 1921, Egypt 1925, Italy 1930, and Sweden 1936.

The year 1884 was remarkable for the introduction of a Women's Championship at Wimbledon, as well as the transfer there of the Men's Doubles previously held at Oxford. The first Women's Champion was Maud Watson, who won it two years running. She was succeeded by Miss Blanche Bingley, later Mrs. Blanche Bingley Hillyard, who won the title six times between 1886 and 1900. Lottie Dod, a child prodigy, won her first championship in 1887 at the age of 15 and was victorious every year until 1893 except in 1889 and 1890, when she did not compete. In the U.S., the first Women's Tennis Championship, held in 1887, was won by Miss Ellen F. Hansell.

Ladies' tennis fashions of those early days look very strange to modern eyes. Long white dresses with voluminous skirts, black stockings, black sandshoes (gym shoes), and a white straw hat were considerable obstacles to overcome in order to play an active game.

The first Australian Women's Championship, in 1923, was won by Mrs. B.H. Molesworth. Miss Suzanne Lenglen won the first two French Women's Championships in 1925 and 1926.

Outstanding players

Tennis in the 1880s was dominated by the remarkable twin brothers William and Ernest Renshaw. William won the Wimbledon Championship seven times, on three occasions defeating his brother in the final. Ernest was victorious once, and in partnership they won the British Doubles Championship, first played at Oxford in 1879, seven times. In 1883 they played two exhibition matches at Wimbledon against the U.S. brothers C.M. and J.S. Clark, and defeated them decisively.

The Field

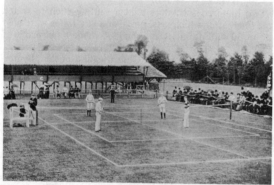

W. and E. Renshaw, England, and C.M. and J.S. Clark, U.S., in the first international match at Wimbledon, 1883.

After the popularity of the Renshaw twins, the 1890s came as an anticlimax and public interest began to wane. The craze for the bicycle was in full swing and some newspapers even predicted that tennis was dying. The Wimbledon Championships showed a financial loss in 1894 and 1895; the All-England Club committee turned back to croquet to revive its flagging fortunes. The situation was saved by the arrival of two more brothers: Reginald F. and H.L. (Hugh) Doherty. R.F. won the Wimbledon Championship in 1897, 1898, 1899, and 1900. H.L. won in 1902, 1903, 1904, 1905, and 1906. H.L. also won the U.S. Singles Championship in 1903 and a Gold Medal at the Olympic Games in Paris in 1900. In partnership they won the Wimbledon Doubles eight times between 1897 and 1905, won the U.S. Doubles in 1902 and 1903, won the Davis Cup in 1903, 1904, 1905, and 1906, and won the Gold Medal for doubles at the 1900 Olympic Games. The crowds flocked back to Wimbledon and the international popularity of the game made rapid progress.

Not only were the Dohertys masters of the game; they were also renowned for their charm of manner and good sportsmanship. Their travels abroad throughout Europe and to the U.S. laid the foundations of the worldwide popularity of the game.

The first international competition was the Davis Cup, donated by U.S. Doubles champion Dwight Davis, in 1900. Only Great Britain challenged the first year and was defeated by the U.S., Davis himself playing on the victorious team. There was no challenge in 1901, but in 1902 a strong British team that included the Doherty brothers went to America. For some strange reason, the non-playing captain omitted H.L. from the singles, although he was the Wimbledon Champion, and the U.S. retained the trophy. The following year the Doherty brothers swept all before them and won the Cup, which was retained by Great Britain for the next three years.

The Davis Cup

The Doherty reign ended in 1906. Although H.L. won the Wimbledon Singles, the brothers were defeated in the Doubles by S.H. Smith and F.L. Riseley, who had beaten them once before in 1902. R.F. died in 1910; H.L. retired to play golf and died in 1919. But tennis had become too well established for any falling off in popularity. A new star appeared on the scene, Norman Brookes, the first in a long line of outstanding Australian tennis players. He was vanquished in 1905 by H.L. Doherty, but became Wimbledon Champion in 1907 and again on his next visit in 1914—and was the first left-hander to reach the top. His great friend and doubles partner was Anthony F. Wilding from New Zealand, Wimbledon Champion from 1910 to 1913. In partnership they won the Wimbledon Doubles on both occasions that they entered the event—1907 and 1914. More important, they wrested the Davis Cup from Great Britain in 1907 and held it for the next four years. Their victory in this world-famous international competition and the fact that they defended their title with such success for several years in Australia began there a lively public interest that has never waned.

Of the lady champions of the early 20th century, Mrs. Lambert Chambers was outstanding. As Miss Dorothy K. Douglass, she won her first Wimbledon Championship in 1903 and again in 1904, 1906, 1910, 1911, 1913, and 1914, not competing in 1909 and 1912. She was undoubtedly the outstanding British player of the decade, but in 1905 she met her match in the first U.S. Women's Champion to win at Wimbledon, May Sutton, aged 18, who again defeated her for the Wimbledon Championship in 1907. Like many of her American successors, Miss Sutton possessed a powerful topped forehand drive, more usually associated with the men's game.

The outbreak of World War I in 1914 caused an interruption in tennis activities throughout most of the interested nations, but, with the exception of 1917, American championships continued to be played.

The early postwar years saw the triumph of two outstanding champions, whose prowess in the opinion of many people has never been surpassed—W.T. ("Big Bill") Tilden of the U.S. and Miss Suzanne Lenglen of France.

Tilden, U.S. Champion from 1920 to 1925 and again in 1929, won the Wimbledon Championship for the first time in 1920, defeating in the final of the all-comers competition Z. Shimizu, the first Japanese player to make a mark at Wimbledon. Tilden retained the title in 1921 and won it again in 1930. In the same period he won 15 Davis Cup singles and contributed largely to the American victories in this competition from 1920 to 1926.

All-time champions W.T. Tilden and Suzanne Lenglen

Miss Lenglen dominated the ladies' game from 1919 to 1925; but for the war years she might well have started her international career earlier, for she won the hardcourt championship of the world at Saint-Cloud (near Paris) in 1914 at age 15. She won the Wimbledon Championship at her first attempt, in 1919, after a memorable final against Mrs. L. Chambers. She won it again in 1920, 1921, 1922, 1923, and 1925, having retired in 1924 because of illness. In 1920 she won the Gold Medal at the Olympic Games in Antwerp. In 1913 two new championships had been introduced at Wimbledon, for Women's Doubles and Mixed Doubles. In partnership with Elizabeth Ryan of the U.S., Miss Lenglen won the Women's Dou-

William Tilden, U.S., who dominated world tennis from 1920 to 1925, completing an overhead smash.
Culver Pictures

bles six times between 1919 and 1925. Miss Ryan, who never won the Wimbledon Women's Singles, won 19 doubles events at Wimbledon between 1914 and 1934 despite the interruption of the war. Miss Lenglen also won the Mixed Doubles three times, in partnership with G.L. Patterson (1920), P. O'Hara Wood (1922), and Jean Borotra (1925). In 1920 she became the first woman to win all three Wimbledon Championships.

She had developed a powerful game by practicing with men and she needed far more freedom of movement than current fashion allowed. Her first appearance at Wimbledon in a calf-length white dress with short sleeves and without petticoat or suspender belt caused a sensation, but her success soon led to others copying her.

Her only failure was on an American visit in 1921, where she was scheduled to play a series of exhibition matches against Norwegian-born Mrs. M. Bjurstedt Mallory, the U.S. Women's Singles Champion in 1918, 1920, 1921, 1922, and 1926. Mrs. Mallory had won the first set 6–2 and the first game of the second set when Miss Lenglen retired, feeling ill, and cancelled the rest of the tour.

Central Press Photos

Suzanne Lenglen, France, outstanding player between 1919 and 1925, striding forward to complete a forehand return.

She turned professional in 1926 and made a successful tour of the U.S. before retiring altogether.

Miss Lenglen demonstrated that the English-speaking world had no monopoly of tennis champions and this point was emphasized by four brilliant Frenchmen, Jean Borotra, Henri Cochet, René Lacoste, and Jacques Brugnon. Between them they won the Wimbledon Singles Championship six times in a row from 1924 to 1929 and the Doubles five times; the U.S. Singles three times, and the French Singles 10 times and the Doubles 11 times. They wrested the Davis Cup from the U.S. in 1927 and held it until 1932.

Meanwhile, a new American star had dawned in the ladies' field—Miss Helen Wills, later Mrs. Wills Moody and later still Mrs. Roark. She won her first U.S. Championship in 1923 and won it seven times in all; she won at Wimbledon eight times between 1927 and 1938 and won the French Singles four times between 1928 and 1932. Only once, at the beginning of her career, did she play against Miss Lenglen, at Cannes, where she lost in two straight sets. Her great rival was another young American, Helen Jacobs, Wimbledon Champion in Mrs. Moody's absence in 1936 and U.S. Champion from 1932 to 1935.

With the advent of the 1930s, French predominance began to wane and American and British players came to the fore, along with one Australian, J.H. Crawford. For Great Britain, Fred Perry was the principal contender. He won the Wimbledon Championship for three years running (1934–36), the U.S. Championship three times in 1933, 1934, and 1936, the Australian Championship in 1934, and the French in 1935. Thanks to him and H.W. ("Bunny") Austin, the pioneer of short trousers, Great Britain won the Davis Cup from 1933 to 1936.

From America came such champions as S.B. Wood, H. Ellsworth Vines Jr., J. Donald Budge, and Robert L. Riggs. Budge was the first man to score a grand slam by winning all four major championships, the British, American, French, and Australian, in one year, 1938. American predominance regained the Davis Cup for them in 1937 and 1938, although surprisingly they lost it to Australia in 1939. And finally Alice Marble, U.S. Champion in 1936, and 1938–40, won all three championships at Wimbledon (Singles, Doubles, and Mixed) in 1939, a feat accomplished previously only by Miss Lenglen.

The development of the game was interrupted by World War II, although the U.S. Championships continued to be played. International tennis started up again in 1946 and once again U.S. players predominated, led by J.A. Kramer, U.S. Champion in 1946 and 1947 and Wimbledon Champion at Singles and Doubles in 1947.

American women, too, dominated the scene in the early postwar years—Miss P.M. Betz, Miss M.E. Osborne, and, in particular, Miss A. Louise Brough, who had an outstanding record at Wimbledon. She won the Women's Singles three years running, 1948–50, and again in 1955. She won the Women's Doubles from 1948 to 1950 and in 1954, and the Mixed Doubles from 1946 to 1948 and in 1950. At Forest Hills (N.Y.) she won the Women's Doubles with Mrs. du Pont (Miss Osborne) for the 12th time in 1957.

The hegemony of the Americans was soon challenged by their old Davis Cup rivals, the Australians, who regained the cup in 1950 and almost monopolized it for the next 17 years, winning every year except for three American victories in 1954, 1958, and 1963. This was accomplished by a steady stream of outstanding Australian players such as Frank Sedgman, Lew Hoad, Ken Rosewall, Roy Emerson, Rod Laver, and a brilliant doubles player, John Bromwich, who played a two-handed shot on his right, a left-handed forehand on his left, and served and smashed with his right hand. They were led by an outstanding non-playing captain, Harry Hopman.

As well as the names of these brilliant Australians the Wimbledon Championship roll of the 1950s and 1960s contains several outstanding American players and three victors for countries that had not hitherto featured. Jaroslav Drobny, who was born in Czechoslovakia, naturalized Egyptian and then a British subject, won in 1954 at age 32. Alex Olmedo from Peru won in 1959 and the popu-

Stars of the 1930s, 1940s, 1950s, and 1960s

lar Spaniard Manuel Santana in 1966. The Australians' dominance waned at the end of the 1960s as their best players became professionals.

But if Australia had dominated the field of men's tennis, the U.S. kept a firm hold on the ladies' championships. Not until 1959 did anyone except an American win the Women's Singles at Wimbledon. Among the outstanding players of those years were Doris Hart, Althea Gibson, and the greatest of them all, Maureen Connolly, familiarly known as "Little Mo." She won her first championship at Forest Hills in 1951 at the astonishing age of 16 and remained U.S. Champion in 1952 and 1953. She won the Wimbledon Championship every year she played from 1952 to 1954. In 1953 she achieved the distinction of winning all four major championships—Wimbledon, Forest Hills, Australian, and French—in the same year. It was a tragedy when a serious riding accident in 1954 ended her tennis career.

The first to break the American monopoly of ladies' tennis championships was Maria Bueno from Brazil, Wimbledon Champion in 1959, 1960, and 1964, but American dominance recurred with three consecutive victories by Billie Jean King from 1966 to 1968. There were some outstanding British and Australian players, however, who also won the Championship, such as Angela Mortimer (1961), Ann Jones, and Margaret Court (nee Smith), who won all four major championships in 1970.

PROFESSIONAL AND OPEN TENNIS

In both real tennis and lawn tennis, there had always been professionals. In real tennis they were in charge of the courts, made the rackets and balls, coached amateur players, and "marked" (kept the score). As early as the 15th century, there had been a guild of racket and brush makers in France. By 1571, when Charles IX granted them statutes, they had separated from the brush makers and become known as "Master Professionals."

When lawn tennis began there was an equal need for the professional to coach and organize, but his job remained relatively unknown and, unlike real tennis, there were no competitions in which he could play. All this changed in 1926 when Charles C. ("Cash and Carry") Pyle, a successful football promoter in the U.S., offered Suzanne Lenglen $50,000 to go on a professional tour of America.

Origins of professional circuit

As an opponent he provided Mary Browne, who had won the U.S. Women's Singles Championship from 1912 to 1914. To provide a male spectacle he contracted a Frenchman, Paul Feret, and three Americans, Harvey Snodgrass and Howard Kinsey from California, and Vincent Richards, then ranked third in the world after Tilden, and William "Little Bill" Johnston. The tour was a financial success and the professional tennis circuit was established. The professionals carried their own portable indoor courts with them, set them up in New York's Madison Square Garden or San Francisco's Cow Palace, and brought in large crowds. In the 1930s the professional game received a further significant boost when the greatest player of his day—and many consider of any day—Tilden, turned professional. From that day on Wimbledon champions, including, for example, Vines, Perry, Budge, and Riggs, almost automatically joined the professional ranks.

The pattern was re-established after the war, when in 1947, U.S. and Wimbledon Champion Kramer, then ranked the leading player in the world, turned professional. He took over Tilden's mantle and organized the professional circuit. One by one the leading amateur champions of their day joined the professional ranks. Pancho Gonzales, Frank Sedgman, Tony Trabert, Ken Rosewall, Lew Hoad, Rod Laver, Roy Emerson, and others all signed contracts with guaranteed minimum receipts to play in professional tournaments against one another all over the world.

It was obvious at the same time that even while playing as amateurs the leading players had been making their living from the game. Major championships could afford to follow the amateur (expenses-only) rules, but lesser tournaments, if they were to get the stars, who in turn attracted the crowds, had to hold out offers of pecuniary

reward. H.F. David, chairman of the All-England Club, said that the tennis amateur had become "a living lie."

The All-England Club was the first to take action. On November 3, 1959, a resolution was passed by 100 votes to 6 recommending that the Wimbledon Championships should be open to all players, amateurs and professionals alike. That recommendation was rejected by the British LTA. In 1960 a proposal to the International Lawn Tennis Federation (ILTF) that experimental open championships be held in 1961 failed by only 5 votes (134 to 75) to obtain the necessary two-thirds majority. In 1961 a simple majority of 133 to 101 agreed to the principle of experimenting with a limited number of open tournaments, but the resulting recommendations in 1962 failed to get the required majority. Further similar proposals were defeated in 1964 and 1967.

Finally, in December 1967, the British LTA announced that they had abolished the distinction between amateurs and professionals in Great Britain. This unilateral action led to a threat of suspension from the ILTF but it was averted by a decision of that group in March 1968 allowing each country to determine for itself the status of its own players. The ILTF reserved the right to sanction a limited number of open tournaments.

Thus the first Open Championships of tennis were played in Great Britain in 1968, the British Hard Court Championships at Bournemouth, and the first Open Champions there were Rosewall and Virginia Wade. They were followed by the first Wimbledon Open, won by Laver and Mrs. King. The total stake money at this first Wimbledon Open was £26,150, of which £2,000 went to the winner of the Men's Singles and £750 to the winner of the Women's Singles.

Laver successfully defended his Wimbledon title the following year and, duplicating his grand slam as an amateur in 1962 (a feat matched only by Budge, in 1938), became the first Open Champion to win all four major championships in one year—British, U.S., French, and Australian. Laver must be reckoned among the all-time great players and without doubt the best left-hander. The 1969 Wimbledon Championships were also remarkable for the longest match ever played there, in which Pancho Gonzales beat Charlie Pasarell in 5 hours and 20 minutes.

In the meantime, two professional circuits had come into existence in the U.S. in the 1960s: the National Tennis League (NTL) and World Championship Tennis (WCT). Between them they had the world's leading players under contract, all of whom became affiliated with WCT when it absorbed the NTL in 1970. This led to a confused situation in which the ILTF controlled the Open Championships with their historic stadia and their glamorous past, while the commercial sponsors controlled the leading players, whose interests were divided between the relative freedom of competition in Open Championships and the financial security of the professional circuit.

ORGANIZATION AND MAJOR CHAMPIONSHIPS OF TENNIS

The Governing Body of Tennis is the International Lawn Tennis Federation, founded 1912, headquarters at West Kensington, London, to which are affiliated national lawn tennis associations. In the 1970s there were about 65 full members, various members having a different number of votes, and about 25 associate members. The ILTF is responsible for the rules of lawn tennis, for upholding the regulations for the Davis Cup and Federation Cup, for the recognition of official championships, and for the general promotion of the game at the international level. It has been greatly preoccupied with the amateur versus professional controversy and the establishment of open championships.

As from January 1, 1970, the ILTF recognized three categories of players:

Categories of players

1. Amateurs who receive no pecuniary advantage for playing the game.

2. Players who derive material profit for the game but who accept the authority of their national associations and therefore the final authority of the ILTF; sometimes known as independent professionals.

3. Touring professionals under contract to an organiza-

tion other than a national association; the contract professionals.

Categories 1. and 2. may compete in the Davis Cup, Federation Cup, and competitions of all sorts. Category 3. could compete in open tournaments approved by the ILTF. In 1972 the ILTF and WCT announced agreement that all existing contracts would be allowed to expire and no new ones signed, thus eliminating Category 3.

For many years the four major tennis tournaments have been the All-England Championships at Wimbledon, the U.S. Championships at Forest Hills, the French Championships at the Stade Roland Garros (Auteuil), and the Australian Championships, which previously were played alternately in New South Wales, Victoria, South Australia, and Queensland, but since 1970 have been confined to Sydney and Melbourne.

The courts of the Stade Roland Garros on the outskirts of Paris are hard (*i.e.*, clay) courts and the French Championships played there are considered the world's premier hard-court events. Second only to the French Championships on hard courts are ranked the Italian Championships played at the Foro Italico in Rome and the German Championships at the Klub an der Alster in Hamburg.

Of indoor tennis courts, those of the King's Club in Stockholm, Sweden, are considered the most outstanding.

The ILTF recognizes the following major championships:

1. Those held at present in Australia, France, Great Britain, South Africa, and the U.S.
2. The Scandinavian Championships.
3. The South American Championships.
4. The Championships of Asia.

Any national association staging an official championship may make it an open event or hold an open event as well as the official championship. Other national associations may apply to the ILTF for permission to hold open tournaments.

International events The principal international tennis events are the Davis Cup (Men), the Federation Cup (Women), the King's Cup (European men on covered courts), and the Wightman Cup (Women—Great Britain versus the U.S.). The Davis Cup, as mentioned above, was established in 1900. Each team consists of two singles players, who play each of the two opponents, and a doubles pair, which may or may not include one or both of the singles players. There are thus five matches, four singles and one doubles. With growing interest in the Cup in the 1920s—the 4 nations that had challenged in 1919, increased to 14 in 1922 and to 24 by 1926—the competition was divided in 1923 into two zones, Europe and America, with an inter-zone final to determine who had the right to challenge the holders. At the same time Australasia split into its two constituent parts, Australia and New Zealand, and competed in the American zone. Since 1966 play has been in four zones: European zones A and B, an American zone, and an Eastern zone. Through 1971 the country that held the trophy did not play in the competition but defended its title against the winner of the four zones in the Challenge Round. Beginning in 1972 the holder of the trophy had to participate in the eliminations.

In ladies' tennis the Davis Cup equivalent is the Federation Cup, inaugurated in 1963 and played annually in the spring. Each match consists of two singles and a doubles.

Of longer standing is the annual Great Britain versus U.S. ladies' match for the Wightman Cup. In 1923, Mrs. H.V. Wightman, formerly Miss Hazel Hotchkiss, U.S. Women's Champion in 1909, 1910, 1911, and 1919, gave the cup for annual competition between the ladies of the U.S. and Great Britain to be played alternately in the U.S. and England. The competition consists of seven matches, five singles and two doubles.

The King's Cup dates from 1936 and was presented for competition between European nations on indoor, or covered, courts by King Gustav V of Sweden, himself a first-class player of the game. When Crown Prince, he was one of the first to play in Sweden and his enthusiasm, coupled with a northern climate, led to the building of indoor courts in Stockholm. It was most appropriate, therefore, that he should give a cup for international competition on indoor courts. The Scandinavian countries have been most successful in King's Cup play, Sweden and Denmark each having won it more times than any other country. Other countries that have won one or more times include Great Britain, France, Germany, Yugoslavia, and Czechoslovakia. The early stages of the competition are played as the Davis Cup; *i.e.*, four singles and a doubles, but the semifinals and final take place at a selected venue and each match consists of two singles and a doubles.

Other first-class tournaments within individual countries are too numerous to mention, but, in general, as well as the national championships, there are held indoor court championships and junior championships. In addition, in countries where the national championship is played on grass, there are often hard-court championships as well.

For winners of the major men's and women's championships and of the Davis Cup competition, see SPORTING RECORD in the *Ready Reference and Index*.

PLAYING THE GAME

The court and equipment. As is clear from its history and its name, lawn tennis was originally played on grass, and the world's major tournaments continue to be played on this natural surface. The popularity of the game led, however, to various experiments to produce playing surfaces for winter use for areas where grass did not grow.

Origins of hard (clay) courts The originator of the hard, or clay, court was Claude Brown, the manager of a brickworks in the English Midlands, a keen tennis player, and a friend of G.W. Hillyard, secretary of the All-England Lawn Tennis Club for 25 years, whose wife was five times Wimbledon champion. Brown had seen various attempts to construct a hard court, but all had failed to provide sufficiently good drainage to combat English climatic conditions. He was also aware of the fact that one of the clays he used for brickmaking was unsatisfactory because it was too porous.

In 1909 he laid down an experimental area 20 x 20 ft (6 x 6 m) with an ash foundation, covered with a 1-in.- (2.5-cm-) thick layer of the porous clay, burned and crushed to a maximum size of ¼ in. Tested by the leading players of the day, it proved a great success.

Since that date many other experiments have been made with different playing surfaces, especially with a view to finding a surface that not only drains well but also requires no upkeep. Asphalt and similar surfaces are widely used for recreational tennis but not for tournament competition. Considerable progress has been made in developing artificial surfaces.

As tennis grew in popularity, those who lived in countries where cold or inclement weather was liable to prevent play, as in Sweden, turned to covered courts. The wheel had turned full cycle and the game that had its origins in a desire to escape into the open air now was provided with indoor facilities. The natural surface for an indoor floor is wood, and indoor court championships throughout the world are played on wooden floors.

In recent years the development of the professional circuit has given rise to a need for a portable court. The most popular of these is a carpet of artificial grass, which can be laid on any smooth surface.

The dimensions of the tennis court are 78 x 27 ft (23.8 x 8.2 m) for singles and 78 x 36 ft (23.8 x 11 m) for doubles. The height of the net at the centre is 3 ft (0.9 m) and it is supported at each side of the court by posts 3 ft 6 in. high at 3 ft outside the court.

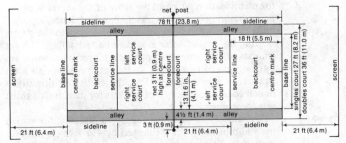

Playing area for lawn tennis. The alleys are used only in doubles play.

There is nothing in the rules of lawn tennis to specify the type of racket to be used, but in practice it has come to be of uniform shape and size, although various models differ marginally in weight and balance. Traditionally, the racket has consisted of a laminated wood frame, strung with sheep gut. The wood has been chosen from ash, beech, hickory, sycamore, mahogany, and West African obeche, using a combination of these according to the particular quality of each wood. One racket requires 33 ft (10 m) of gut to provide 18 main, or vertical, strings and 20 cross strings. There are also one or more coloured threads at the head and throat of each racket. Synthetic gut and nylon are extensively used. The handle is usually covered with a leather grip. Steel and other metallic-alloy frames have been developed and are used by many leading players.

A tennis ball consists of a pressurized rubber core covered with high-quality cloth, usually wool mixed with up to 35 percent of nylon. Gradual loss of inflation tends to make the ball go soft in the course of time and experiments have been carried out with an unpressurized core. The specific properties for a conventional ball are: diameter, $2^{37}/_{64}$ to $2^{43}/_{64}$ in. (6.55 to 6.8 cm); weight 2 to $2^{1}/_{16}$ oz. (56.7 to 58.47 g); bound when dropped from 100 in. (250 cm), 53 to 58 in. (135 to 147 cm); compression 0.265 to 0.29 in. (.673 to .737 cm), at 18 lb (8 kg) load. World usage of tennis balls is in excess of 25,000,000 per annum.

Principles of play. The following exposition is designed to help a spectator understand a game he may be watching. For information on specific rules or how to play the reader should consult the works listed in the bibliography.

In singles play, the players spin a racket to decide on side and service. One spins, the other calls "rough" or "smooth," referring to the threading of the small strings at the top and bottom of the racket face. The player who wins the toss may decide to serve or receive service first, in which case his opponent chooses the side, or he may decide on a choice of side, in which case his opponent may choose to serve or receive service first. The players serve alternate games and change sides after every "odd" number of games; *i.e.,* after the first, third, and each subsequent alternate game of each set.

Beginning each game from behind his right-hand court, the server has both feet behind the base line and strikes the ball diagonally across the net and into his opponent's right-hand service court. Should the ball on service strike the top of the net before falling in the correct service court, it is a "let" and does not count. The server is allowed one miss, or "fault." If he fails to deliver a correct service at two attempts, he loses the point.

To return service, the receiver strikes the ball back before it hits the ground a second time, over the net and within the boundaries of his opponent's court. After the service has been correctly returned, either player may volley the ball or hit it after its first bounce and the game continues until one player fails to make a correct return. This may occur either if he fails to hit the ball over the net or if he hits it outside his opponent's boundaries or if he fails to hit it before it strikes the ground a second time on his side of the net.

The winner of each exchange scores 15, the scoring going 15, 30, 40 (abbreviated for 45), game; this system, derived directly from real or court tennis, is medieval in origin and dates from a time when 60 was looked upon as a whole number, rather as 100 has been in modern times; for identification purposes the score of the server is called first. Should both players reach 40, called deuce, a player must then score two consecutive points to win the game. Scoring the first of these is said to be "advantage." A set consists of six games, except that a player must win a set by a margin of two games, so that at five-games-all a set cannot be won before 7–5 at the earliest. Normally a match consists of the best of five sets for men and of three sets for women.

The same basic principles apply to doubles, for which the width of the court is enlarged by 4½ feet (1.4 m) on each side. Service alternates between the two opposing teams, but each team must decide at the start of each set which of the two partners shall serve first. Equally the receiving team must decide at the start of each set which of them shall receive the first service and they will then receive service alternately for the rest of that set.

The indeterminate length of matches under the conventional system of scoring has always been inconvenient for those who have to organize tournaments, but recently the demands of television have resulted in some experiments in new methods. In essence these have relied on some form of tie-break system at five games all, usually the best of nine points.

The USLTA allows the use of a tie-break in certain approved tournaments. It has laid down strict rules governing the order of service in a tie-break in order to avoid as far as possible giving an advantage to either side. The 9-point system, in which the first player to score 5 points wins, was first used in the U.S. Open in 1970.

More radical changes in scoring are contained in the VASSS (Van Alen Simplified Scoring System, devised by U.S. tennis buff James H. Van Alen), which has been experimented with in the U.S. The VASSS No-Ad system consists of a 4-point game and a 6-game set. At 5 games all, a 9-point tie-break is played. The VASSS Single Point system is similar to table tennis. The game consists of 31 points, service changing after every 5 points. At 30 points all a tie-break of 9 points is played.

Strategy and technique. Throughout the history of tennis there have been two keys to tactical success. One has been the service, the other, effective play at forward position at the net. The server has a considerable advantage, as he is able to run up to the net immediately after serving. He is vulnerable to a passing shot (a return shot played by the receiver down the side of the court and passing out of his reach), but such a return is not easy from a powerful service, especially if it is also cleverly angled. An effective return is even more difficult in doubles when the server's partner is already at the net.

The result is that very often, particularly in doubles, games tend to be won by the side that serves. The faster the surface of the court, the more this is true. Some experiments have been tried to counteract the dominance of service by allowing one serve only, for example, or by reducing the size of the service court, but so far none have proved acceptable.

A powerful first service is, therefore, a very considerable asset. For best effect, the server should be able to vary the placing of the service so that his opponent cannot anticipate its direction with certainty. Equally important is the ability to deliver an aggressive second service, which is often the distinguishing mark of a first-class player. Often, in less than first-class tennis, the first service is struck with great ferocity and is usually a fault; there follows either a double fault or a lightly hit second service that gives the attack to the receiver. In first-class tennis, there is much less distinction between first and second service, although often the second service is more controlled, using top or side spin to make up for the slightly reduced speed.

For return of service and in the subsequent play, the ability to play a consistent drive shot on either forehand or backhand is essential. This so-called ground stroke is the foundation of a good player's game. It is a long, smooth stroke in which the racket starts from well behind the body, strikes the ball immediately in front of the body, with the racket at full arm's length, and ends with a long follow through. At the moment of impact, the face of the racket is moving parallel to the ground and this ensures that the ball is struck back with a flat trajectory low over the net and with no loss of speed on its first bounce. Both length and direction are important in the forehand and backhand drive. Ideally, the ball should bounce as near the opponent's base line as possible in order to keep him at the back of the court, and it should be placed down one or the other of his sidelines to pass him if he should attempt to play at the net.

There are of course several variations of the basic drive. Instead of striking the ball with a flat racket, it may be struck with cut to impart back spin to the ball to slow it up on its first bounce (useful for a drop shot) or with top spin to make the ball dip quickly over the net and bound high and fast (useful in returning a short ball).

Other return strokes are the volley, the half-volley, and the lob. The volley is normally played from the net position or by a player coming up to the net. It requires speed of eye and foot to intercept an opponent's drive and to return it with equal force and good placement or both. The volley is an attacking stroke and is of great significance, especially in men's doubles when both sides are attempting to establish a dominant position at the net.

When an opponent has established himself at the net, there are only two ways around him. One is to play a drive out of his reach down one or the other of his sidelines; the other is to play a lob over his head and deep. Should a lob fall short, it will allow an opponent a chance to execute an overhead volley, or smash, in which the ball is played from as high as possible, allowing it to be smashed down with great force. The smash, like the more usual volley, requires accurate placing to be really effective.

The half-volley is a defensive stroke in most cases. Normally a player will be driving the ball from the base line or volleying it at the net. But on occasions he may be caught between the two and there will be no alternative but to half-volley. This is a difficult stroke to make but doubly difficult to prevent it giving an easy smash to an opponent. Control is therefore most important to ensure that the ball is played as low as possible over the net and placed as far out of reach as possible.

Real tennis (court tennis or royal tennis)

HISTORY

The origins of real tennis lie in medieval France where the game has always been called *jeu de paume* ("palm game"; *i.e.*, the ball was struck with the palm of the hand). The curious layout of the court, with its sloping penthouse roof around three sides, pillared openings below, and wooden hatch (grille), suggests a cloister, and the fact that the earliest mention of the game is usually in ecclesiastical writings confirms the probability that tennis originated when young French priests started playing a form of handball in cathedral cloisters. It would seem to date from the 12th or 13th century.

Origins and early history in France   Its French origins are still apparent in the use of various French words to describe parts of the court; *e.g.*, dedans, grille, tambour, bandeau, and in scoring the use of the word deuce (a corruption of the French *à deux*).

How it came to be called tennis in English is not known for certain. The most likely theory is that the French players were in the habit of calling out "*tenez!*" ("attention!") before serving.

Certainly by the end of the 13th century the game was well established, for it is recorded that in 1292 there were 13 makers of tennis balls in Paris. There is no doubt that it was a popular game with king and court, and Shakespeare's reference to tennis balls sent by the French Dauphin to King Henry V of England was based on historical fact. But the 16th century was the golden age of tennis in

France. Francis I, Henry II, Charles IX, and Henry IV were all keen players.

Francis I built a court in his Louvre Palace in Paris in 1530, the plan of which was included in a contemporary Italian book by Antonio Scaino, entitled *Trattato del Giuoco della Palla*, published in 1555. The layout is identical to that of a modern real tennis court and the plan also shows a racket of the time, rather different from the more powerful instrument that is used today, but proving that at least by the middle 16th century the hand had given way to the racket as a means of propelling the ball.

The ball was originally made of hair or wool covered with sheepskin, but as rackets were developed the ball was made harder by using scraps of cloth, moistened, tightly wadded together, bound with string, and covered with white cloth—the same process used today.

Francis I also built a floating court on board the ship "La Grande-Françoise," which was intended to outdo Henry VIII of England's four-masted warship the "Great Harry," but which unfortunately grounded and sank at Le Havre.

François Gregory d'Ierni, who accompanied the Papal Legate to Paris in 1596, reported that there were 250 well-appointed tennis courts in the city and that the game gave employment to 7,000 people. But by 1657 the number of courts had shrunk to 114 according to the Dutch ambassador, who expressed his surprise that there were not more.

Tennis continued to be popular until the French Revolution. In defiance of King Louis XVI, the Third Estate had declared itself to be the National Assembly of France on June 17, 1789. The King retaliated by locking them out of the normal meeting place, but they found an alternative in the tennis court at Versailles, where they proclaimed the famous Tennis Court Oath of June 20th, swearing never to disperse until France had a constitution. The court still stands and is a museum dedicated to the Revolution.

From France tennis spread rapidly all over the continent of Europe and was well known in Italy, Germany, Austria, Sweden, Russia, and the Netherlands. It probably reached Scotland before England, for there were always close links between France and Scotland. In England the game was initially discouraged as it tended to distract men from sports of greater military value such as archery. In fact the earliest mention of the game is in connection with a prosecution in Canterbury about 1396.

The game in England   As in France, tennis flourished in England in the 16th century and it continued to be very popular in the 17th century. Henry VII set an example and he is known to have played on courts at Westminster, Windsor, Woodstock, Sheen, and Wycombe. Henry VIII was especially keen. Having dispossessed Cardinal Wolsey of his palace at Hampton Court, he built there in 1530 a tennis court that is still in use. He also built a tennis court at St. James's Palace and had four courts, two open and two covered, at his palace at Whitehall.

Queen Elizabeth was a keen spectator and planned a new court, which was never completed, at Windsor Castle. King James I recommended the game to his eldest son, Prince Henry. King Charles I was a frequent tennis player and continued to play whenever possible during the Civil War. Oliver Cromwell looked on the game as a frivolity, and, from the beginning of his protectorate in 1653, tennis courts were used for other purposes until the Restoration in 1660.

But then the game was resumed with increased vigour. Charles II was the most enthusiastic player since Henry VIII. He not only restored many of the existing courts but also built a new one at Whitehall, where Samuel Pepys watched him play, and one at Windsor.

Modern courts   The 18th century saw a general decline in tennis playing, and many courts were put to other uses; for example, as theatres, but Victorian England set in train a revival of the game, which spread throughout the English-speaking world. Many famous clubs built courts: the MCC, Queen's Club, and Prince's Club in London; the Manchester Tennis and Racquet Club; and the Leamington Tennis Club. Courts were built at the universities of Oxford and Cambridge; and many private houses could boast of their own courts. There remain 15 courts in use in England and

The Bettmann Archive

Copper engraving of a real tennis court, 1612, clearly showing its cloister origins. The net is a fringed cord, called the line, and the rackets are typical of the period. This court is a *jeu carré* without dedans. Winning openings, *la lune* and *le petit trou*, are on the far end wall.

Scotland. Once more, real tennis became a royal game when H.R.H. the Prince of Wales played at Cambridge in 1967–68.

Real tennis spread to the U.S. in 1876 when a court was built at Boston. Seven courts are in use: two at the New York Racquet and Tennis Club, and others at Boston, Philadelphia, Tuxedo Park, N.Y., Greentree (Manhasset, L.I.), and Aiken (S.C.). In Australia there are two courts, one at Hobart, Tasmania, built in 1874 and one at Melbourne, built in 1882. In France only two courts remain in play, one in Paris and one in Bordeaux.

Championship competition

The top honour at real tennis is to be Champion of the World. This title is held until the holder is successfully challenged by a worthy contender. A challenge match is normally the best of 13 sets, played over three days in the reigning champion's court; but when the championship is vacant, the two principal claimants normally play two best-of-13-set matches, one in each of their own home courts. The Championship dates back to 1816, since when the holders have been: 1816, Marchisio (Italy); 1819, Philip Cox (Great Britain); 1829, J.E. Barre (France); 1862, Edmund Tompkins (Great Britain); 1871, George Lambert (Great Britain); 1885, Tom Pettitt (United States); 1896, Peter Latham (Great Britain); 1905, Cecil Fairs (Great Britain); 1907, P. Latham (Great Britain); 1908, C. Fairs (Great Britain); 1912, G.F. Covey (Great Britain); 1914, Jay Gould (United States); 1922, G.F. Covey (Great Britain); 1928, Pierre Etchebaster (France); 1955, James Dear (Great Britain); 1957, Albert Johnson (Great Britain); 1959, Northrup R. Knox (United States); 1969, G.H. Bostwick (United States); 1972, James Bostwick (United States).

Peter Latham also had the distinction of being world champion of rackets. J. Gould, N.R. Knox, and G.H. and James Bostwick are the only amateurs ever to have won the world championship. Pierre Etchebaster, a French Basque and professional at the New York Racquet and Tennis Club, held the title for 27 years until he retired undefeated at the age of 60 and was undoubtedly the outstanding player of the modern era.

The Open Championship in Great Britain is held and challenged for in the same way. In the U.S. it is played for in ánnual competition. In both countries there are annual Amateur Championships, both singles and doubles, and additional Gold Racket competitions in London (MCC prizes at Lord's Cricket Ground), Tuxedo, and Manchester. The Bathurst Cup, an international competition originally (1922) competed for alternately in London and Paris, has been played also in the U.S. since 1969. Oxford and Cambridge play a university match that dates back to 1859, and since 1956 British and American university teams have competed for the Van Alen Trophy.

In France the Coupe de Paris (1910) and the Coupe de Bordeaux (1909) are amateur championships open to players of all nations. The Raquette d'Or (1899) and the Raquette d'Argent (1899), played alternately in Paris and Bordeaux, are open only to French nationals.

In Australia the principal competition, the Open Championship, is played annually in Hobart or Melbourne. The Royal Melbourne Tennis Club (RMTC) holds an annual championship for the Gold Racquet and the Hobart Tennis Club annual championships for the H.J. Hill Cup (singles), the Captain James Johnson Cup (doubles), and the Bendena Cup (women's singles). There is also an annual match between the two clubs for the Percy Finch Trophy (singles) and the RMTC Trophy (doubles).

There is no international authority and the game is controlled in each country by its own national association.

THE GAME OF REAL TENNIS

The court and equipment.   The real tennis court is an enclosed area with a paved or artificial stone floor measuring approximately 96 by 32 ft (29 by 10 m). Around three sides of the court is a sloping roof (penthouse) starting about 7 ft (2 m) from floor level. At certain points beneath the penthouse roof there are netted openings known as "galleries" (see diagram). Two of these galleries are winning openings and a ball entering them immediately wins a point. These are the dedans and the

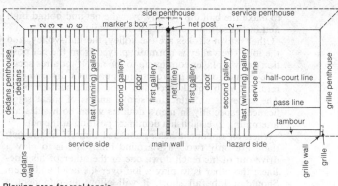

Playing area for real tennis.
Adapted from *The Lonsdale Book of Sporting Records;* Seeley, Service & Co.

winning gallery, where the ball rings a bell to mark a successful shot. Another winning opening is the grille.

There was a variation of this court, the *jeu carré*, of which the only remaining example is at Falkland Palace in Scotland. The *jeu carré* had no dedans, but instead two other winning openings, *la lune* and *le petit trou*.

The court is divided in two by a net, technically called the line, since originally it was only a piece of cord. Service is always delivered from the dedans side of the court; the other side is known as the hazard side. On the main wall on the hazard side is a projecting buttress, called the tambour, which, since it deflects balls that chance to hit it, adds to the difficulty of the game.

The earliest balls were stuffed with hair and in Shakespeare's *Much Ado About Nothing* occur these lines: ". . . the barber's man hath been seen with him; and the old ornament of his cheek hath already stuffed tennis-balls." But for very many years balls have been made of cloth. Around a small central cloth core are coiled further strips of cloth until the ball is about 2 in. (5 cm) in diameter. It is then placed in a special wooden "cup" and gently hammered until perfectly round. The subsequent tying of the ball is a work of great artistry; 16 turns of string are made round the ball to hold it securely in shape. It is then covered with two pieces of white cloth, firmly sewn together. The final ball must be not less than $2\frac{7}{16}$ in. (6.2 cm) and not more than $2\frac{9}{16}$ in. (6.5 cm) in diameter. It must weigh between $2\frac{1}{2}$ and $2\frac{3}{4}$ oz (71 and 78 g). A set of balls normally consists of nine dozen.

Early balls and rackets

The great skill required to make real tennis balls has led to a recent and not unsuccessful experiment to produce real tennis balls by a process similar to that used in the manufacture of lawn tennis balls.

The racket is made of ash, strung with sheep gut. It has 18 main (vertical) strings and 26 cross strings, of which the top 3 are usually of thinner gut. It has a characteristic lopsided head, designed to impart greater cut to the ball. The handle is usually bare wood, although it may be covered with a leather or towelling grip if desired.

Principles of play.   Scoring is as in lawn tennis. There are normally six games in a set, although in France there are sometimes eight. Play follows the same principles as in most other games except for the additional complication of "chases." In most other ball games a ball is dead when it bounces a second time on the ground. In tennis it makes a chase at the point where it strikes the floor on the second bounce and the floor is marked out with painted lines that enable the marker (scorer) accurately to describe the exact point (see diagram). Equally, a chase is made when the ball enters one of the galleries, other than a winning gallery or dedans.

When a chase is made, neither side scores and the chase is held in the marker's memory until either a second chase is made or one player comes within a point of winning a game. In either case the players then change sides and play off the one or two chases. The player who made the chase (*i.e.*, who would have won the point in most other games) now defends it and his opponent attacks it. To win the chase the attacker must make a better chase—and "better" in real tennis means nearer the back wall. In other words, the attacker must ensure that each stroke that he plays will cause the ball, if allowed to bounce twice, to hit the floor on its second bounce nearer the back wall than the line of the chase being played. If he fails, the defender will allow the ball to bounce a second time and thereby win the point. The defender may also win the chase by hitting the ball into any of his opponent's galleries.

Strategy and technique. The great merit of real tennis lies in the chase, explained above. This medieval device tends to favour skill rather than brute force. In very few other games is it possible for a player to allow the ball to hit the ground a second time without necessarily losing the point. The skill required, therefore, is to play a normal stroke that will always make a "short" chase, if allowed to bounce a second time. In other words, ideally every ball should strike the floor on its second bounce within half a yard of the opponent's back wall.

This is obviously impossible, but in order to make as short a chase as possible, it is important that on striking the opponent's back wall the ball should come down sharply toward the floor to strike it on second bounce as near the back wall as possible. This means that the best stroke is one that is heavily cut. The familiar top spin shot of lawn tennis would bound far out from the back wall of a real tennis court and make a very poor chase. The classic real tennis shot bounces first somewhere about chase 4, strikes low on the back wall and comes down sharply to strike the floor on its second bounce within a yard or two of the wall. The need for this heavily-cut stroke led to the curious design of the racket.

The server undoubtedly has an advantage, although not nearly so dominant a one as in lawn tennis. An unreturnable service is much more difficult in real tennis, but the server has the advantage of being able to play at two winning openings (the grille and the winning gallery), or at the tambour. Moreover, there are no chases at the back of the hazard side and the server can win a point outright in that area.

Real tennis is a complicated game to watch for the uninitiated, but its very complication is its attraction to those who play it.

Badminton

HISTORY

Badminton is descended from the old children's game of battledore and shuttlecock. Rackets of one sort or another developed over the centuries as a means of improving the striking power of the human hand, but the invention of the shuttlecock is less clear. This weird object is a variation on the more usual ball, consisting of a cork base fitted with a crown of feathers. The racket, or battledore, is a primitive form of racket, the head of which was normally covered with vellum or, latterly, strung like a racket.

One rainy day in the 1860s, so the story goes, a house party at Badminton in Gloucestershire, home of the Duke of Beaufort, got hold of the children's battledores and shuttlecocks, stretched a cord across the hall, and invented the game that has come to be called badminton. One member of the house party subsequently found himself in India, where he introduced the game to others and where the first attempt to formulate rules was made in 1877 at Karāchi. The hall at Karāchi where the game was played was not much wider than the court and access to it was gained from doors at the centre that opened inward. To

make allowance for this, the court was laid out in "hourglass" form, the width at the net being shorter than at the base line. This curious feature provided the reason why Major Wingfield adapted the "hourglass" shape for his first lawn tennis courts. Soon after badminton became popular, the primitive battledore was replaced by a lightweight racket.

Two Americans, Bayard Clark and E. Langdon Wilkes, were impressed by seeing badminton in England and formed The Badminton Club of the City of New York during the winter of 1878–79. There were about 40 members originally, limited to men and "good-looking" single girls.

In 1893 the Badminton Association was formed in England and the rules were codified—including the hourglass court, which was finally abolished in 1901. The All-

England Championships were instituted in 1899 and were soon followed by Irish Championships in 1902 and Scottish in 1907. The game gradually achieved worldwide popularity, and in 1925 and 1930 an English team visited Canada. In 1936 the American Badminton Association was formed.

The governing body of badminton is the International Badminton Federation (IBF), formed originally in 1934 by nine founder-members—Canada, Denmark, England, France, Ireland, The Netherlands, New Zealand, Scotland, and Wales. In the 1970s there were more than 50 affiliated "National" organizations, affiliated "International" organizations, and temporary "Associate Members." The IBF is responsible for the laws of badminton and for the organization of the International Badminton Championships, the Thomas Cup for men and the Uber Cup for women.

The Thomas Cup was presented in 1939 by the founder-president of the IBF, Sir George Thomas, Baronet, one of the most distinguished figures in the game. It is played on similar lines to the Davis Cup, zone winners meeting in interzone ties (competitions) and the final winner having the right to challenge the holder for the cup. The 1969–70 competition was organized in four zones—American, Australasian, Asian (east and west sections), and European, covering an entry of 25 nations. A change in the rules required the 1969–70 and subsequent holder nations to compete at the interzone stage.

Each tie consists of nine matches—five singles and four doubles—and the players must be selected from a nominated team of not less than four and not more than six bona fide amateurs.

The competition, which has been held every three years since 1948–49, has been dominated by Malaya and Indonesia.

The Uber Cup was presented by Mrs. H.S. Uber and first played for in 1956–57. It is organized on similar lines to the Thomas Cup, except that each tie consists of seven matches—three singles and four doubles. The U.S. and Japan have been predominant in Uber Cup competition. For listing of Thomas and Uber Cup winners, see SPORTING RECORD in the *Ready Reference and Index*.

Numerous national championships are held annually all over the world, some reserved for nationals, others open to any competitor, but all of them restricted to bona fide amateurs. The All-England Championships, held at the Empire Pool, Wembley, in March, are open to all amateurs and enjoy the highest prestige. These championships began in 1899 as the Badminton Association Tournament and the title of All-England was assumed in 1902. There was no competition in 1899 and the first winners in 1900 were S.H. Smith and Miss E. Thomson, both of England. The rules provide that three consecutive victories or four victories in all win the cup outright and this has been achieved in the singles by the following great players; the total number of their victories is shown in parentheses:

Sir G.A. Thomas, Baronet, England (4)	Miss E. Thomson, England (5)
J.F. Devlin, Ireland (6)	Miss M. Lucas, England (6)
R.C.F. Nichols, England (5)	Miss Kathleen McKane, England (4)
Wong Peng Soon, Malaya (4)	Mrs. F.G. Barrett, England (5)
Eddy B. Choong, Malaya (4)	Mrs. G.C.K. Hashman (*nee* Judy Devlin) U.S. (10)
Erland Kops, Denmark (7)	
R. Hartono, Indonesia (5)	

Although he visited Europe only once, winning the All-England Championship in 1949, David Freeman is generally regarded as the best-ever singles player of the game. He was singles champion of the U.S. from 1939 until American participation in World War II put an end to the championship in 1943. When it was resumed, he won it again in 1947 and 1948 before retiring from active competition. He returned, however, to win once again in 1953.

THE GAME OF BADMINTON

Since the slightest wind affects the flight of the shuttle, competitive badminton is played indoors, though the game is popular out-of-doors as a recreational pastime. It consists essentially of the striking of a shuttle over a 5-ft-

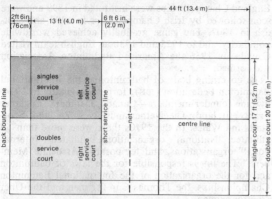

Badminton court.

General principles

(1.5-m-) high net and within the boundaries of the court (see diagram). The shuttle does not bounce and therefore has to be kept in play without touching the ground. A point is lost if it is allowed to strike the ground, provided it lands within the court or if it fails to cross the net. A doubles or men's singles game consists of 15 or 21 points with an option to play a further 5 points at 13-all or 19-all and a further 3 points at 14-all or 20-all. A ladies' single consists of 11 points with an option to play a further 3 points at 9-all or 2 points at 10-all. A match is the best of three games; players change ends after each game and in the middle of the third game, if there is one.

Before starting, the players toss for choice of service or side. Service is delivered from one service court diagonally across the net into the opponent's service court, starting from the right-hand court. In singles players serve from the right-hand court when their own score is 0 or an even number and from the left-hand court when it is an odd number. The shuttle when struck for service must be below the server's waist at the head of the racket below his hand; both the server's and receiver's feet must be on the ground and entirely within the lines of the service court.

Unlike tennis, only one service is allowed and a single fault loses a point. A service in which the shuttle hits the top of the net and still falls within the correct service court is "good"—not a "let" as in tennis.

After service a rally takes place until one side fails to return the shuttle within the bounds of his opponent's court. If the server wins the rally, a point is added to his score. If the receiver wins it, the service passes to him, but no point is scored. In doubles each partner serves in turn (except for the first service of a game when only one partner of the side that serves first has an inning), and the service passes to their opponents only when they have both been "put out" by the loss of two rallies.

Rackets and shuttles

As in tennis, there are no rules governing the racket. It is desirable that it should be as light as possible, consistent with the required strength, and it normally consists of a wooden head frame, made from hickory and strung with gut of nylon, and a metal handle; its weight is about 5 to 5½ oz (142 to 156 g). Experiments have been made with an all-metal racket.

The shuttlecock, shuttle, or bird weighs from 73 to 85 gr (5 to 6 g) and is made of 14 to 16 goose feathers fixed in a piece of cork. It is 3½ in. (9 cm) in length. Variations to the exact specifications are permitted when climatic or other conditions make this necessary. Plastic shuttles have come into use, but feathers are used in major tournaments.

The skill of badminton depends on four principal strokes, which bear some resemblance to tennis strokes but are different in effect with a shuttle. This is due to the fact that the speed of the shuttle declines very rapidly and it falls, therefore, much more steeply.

First, the high drop or "clear" is a shot struck hard and high into the air to clear any opponent at the net and to fall as near the back of the court as possible. Second, the smash is an overhead volley as in tennis, struck as hard as possible down into an opponent's court. Third, the drive, also as in tennis, is a hard-hit shot, passing as low as possible over the net and usually aimed along one or other of the sidelines. Fourth, the drop shot, as its name implies, is a gentle stroke, which just clears the net and falls almost vertically beyond it.

These four shots are played in an infinite variety of combinations and it is the skill and control required to vary them and to develop a suitable shot in reply that makes the game so fascinating to play and to watch. The ability to disguise the type of shot to be played until the very last moment is of great importance to the highly skilled player and it demands even greater finesse; for example, to shape up for a smash and finally to play a gentle drop shot requires complete control and masterful skill.

Ball badminton

An interesting variation of the game, known as ball badminton, is played in India and is particularly popular in the southern states there. Its name derives from the fact that a ball, made of wool and coloured yellow, is used instead of a shuttlecock. The racket is similar to a normal racket, but is heavier in the head and the frame is normally made of bamboo or steel. Ball badminton is played out-of-doors on a large court, 80 ft (24 m) long by 40 ft (12 m) wide, with five players on each side, two forward, two back, and one in the centre. Singles and doubles are also played on a smaller court 80 ft x 20 ft. The game consists of 21 points with a set of 7 points at 20-all, but on reaching 6-all in the set one player has to establish a lead of two points to win the game.

The open air and the woollen ball give great opportunity for high spinning shots, particularly in the service, and the wrist is used to a large extent.

BIBLIOGRAPHY

Lawn tennis: LORD ABERDARE, *The Story of Tennis* (1959), also includes information on real tennis; MYERS A. WALLIS, *Fifty Years of Wimbledon, 1877 to 1926* (1926); UNITED STATES LAWN TENNIS ASSOCIATION, *Fifty Years of Lawn Tennis in the United States* (1931) and the *Official Encyclopedia of Tennis* (1972); PARKE CUMMINGS, *American Tennis* (1957); MAURICE BRADY (comp.), *Lawn Tennis Encyclopaedia*, pt. 1, "Biographies," and pt. 2, "Facts and Figures" (1969); J.G. SMYTH, *Lawn Tennis* (1953).

Real tennis: ALBERT DE LUZE, *La Magnifique Histoire du jeu de paume* (1933); LORD ABERDARE, *Rackets, Squash Rackets, Tennis, Fives and Badminton* (1933); JULIAN MARSHALL, *The Annals of Tennis* (1878); E.B. NOEL and J.O.M. CLARK, *A History of Tennis* (1924).

Badminton: P.R. DAVIS, *Badminton Complete* (1967); SPORTS ILLUSTRATED, *Book of Badminton* (1967); the *International Badminton Federation Handbook* (annual).

The official rules of tennis may be obtained from the Tennis and Rackets Association (U.K.) and from the U.S. Court Tennis Association.

(A.)

Tennyson, Alfred, Lord

Alfred, Lord Tennyson, the leading poet of the Victorian Age in England, had come by the middle of the 19th century to occupy a position similar to that of Pope in the 18th. Tennyson was generally regarded by his contemporaries both as a consummate poetic artist, consolidating and refining the traditions bequeathed to him by his predecessors in the Romantic movement—especially Wordsworth, Byron, and Keats—and as the pre-eminent spokesman for the educated middle class Englishman, in moral and religious outlook and in political and social consciousness no less than in matters of taste and sentiment. His poetry dealt often with the doubts and difficulties of an age in which the old religious sanctions and the traditional assumptions about man's nature and destiny were increasingly called into question; it dealt with them, moreover, as the intimate personal problems of a sensitive and troubled individual inclined to melancholy. Yet through his poetic mastery—the spaciousness and nobility of his best work, its classical aptness of phrase, its distinctive harmony—he conveyed to sympathetic readers a feeling of implicit reassurance, even serenity. Tennyson may be seen as the first great English poet to be fully aware, and qualified to speak, of the new picture of man's place in the universe revealed by modern science. While the contemplation of this unprecedented human situation sometimes evoked his fears and forebodings, it also gave him a larger imaginative range than most of the poets of his time and added a greater depth and resonance to his art.

Early life and work.   Tennyson was born in England at Somersby rectory, Lincolnshire, on August 6, 1809, into an old Lincolnshire family. The fourth of 12 children, Alfred, with two of his brothers, Frederick and Charles, was sent in 1815 to Louth grammar school—where he was unhappy. He left in 1820, but, though home conditions were difficult, his father managed to give him a wide literary education. Alfred was precocious, and before his teens he had composed in the styles of Pope, Scott, and Milton. To his youth also belongs *The Devil and the Lady* (first published in 1930), which shows an astonishing understanding of Elizabethan dramatic verse. Byron was a dominant influence; at the news of his death (1824) Tennyson flung himself on the ground in a passion of grief and carved on sandstone, "Byron is dead."

Tennyson, oil painting by Samuel Laurence, *c.* 1840. In the National Portrait Gallery, London.

At the lonely rectory the children were thrown upon their own resources. All writers on Tennyson emphasize the influence of the Lincolnshire countryside on his poetry: the plain, the sea about his home, "the sand-built ridge of heaped hills that mound the sea," and "the waste enormous marsh."

In 1824 the health of Tennyson's father began to break down, and he took refuge in drink. Alfred, though depressed by unhappiness at home, continued to write, collaborating with Frederick and Charles in *Poems by Two Brothers* (1826; dated 1827). His contributions (more than half the volume) are mostly in fashionable styles of the day.

Early publications

In 1827 Alfred and Charles joined Frederick at Trinity College, Cambridge. There Alfred made friends with Arthur Hallam, the gifted son of the historian Henry Hallam. This was the deepest friendship of Tennyson's life. The friends became members of the "Apostles," an exclusive undergraduate club of earnest intellectual interests. Tennyson's reputation as a poet increased at Cambridge. In 1829 he won the Chancellor's gold medal with a poem called *Timbuctoo*. In 1830 *Poems, Chiefly Lyrical* was published; and in the same year Tennyson, Hallam, and other "Apostles" went to Spain to help in the unsuccessful revolution against Ferdinand VII. Tennyson took away many vivid memories, especially of the scenery of the Pyrenees. In the meantime, Hallam had become attached to Tennyson's sister Emily but was forbidden by her father to correspond with her for a year.

In 1831 Tennyson's father died. Alfred's misery was increased by his grandfather's discovery of his father's debts. He left Cambridge without taking a degree, and his grandfather made financial arrangements for the family. In the same year, Hallam published a eulogistic article on *Poems, Chiefly Lyrical* in *The Englishman's Magazine*. He went to Somersby in 1832 as the accepted suitor of Emily.

In 1832 Tennyson published another installment of his poems (dated 1833), including "The Lotos-Eaters," "The Palace of Art," and "The Lady of Shalott." Among them was a satirical epigram on the critic "Christopher North" (pseudonym of the Scottish writer John Wilson), who had attacked *Poems, Chiefly Lyrical* in *Blackwood's Magazine*. Tennyson's sally prompted a scathing attack on his new volume in the *Quarterly Review*. The attacks distressed Tennyson, but he continued to revise his old poems and compose new ones.

In 1833 Hallam's engagement was recognized by his family, but while on a visit to Vienna in September he died suddenly. The shock to Tennyson was severe. It came at a depressing time; three of his brothers, Edward, Charles, and Septimus, were suffering from mental illness, and the bad reception of his own work added to the gloom. Recent research has shown that his frustrated courtship of Rosa Baring and his attachment to Sophie Rawnsley increased his psychological difficulties. Yet it was in this period that he wrote some of his most characteristic work: "The Two Voices" (of which the original title, significantly, was "Thoughts of a Suicide"), "Ulysses," "St. Simeon Stylites," and, probably, the first draft of "Morte d'Arthur." To this period also belong some of the poems that became constituent parts of *In Memoriam* and lyrics later worked into *Maud*.

In May 1836 his brother Charles married Louisa Sellwood of Horncastle, and at the wedding Alfred fell in love with her sister Emily. For some years the lovers corresponded, but Emily's father disapproved of Tennyson because of his bohemianism, addiction to port and tobacco, and liberal religious views; and in 1840 he forbade the correspondence. Meanwhile the Tennysons had left Somersby and were living a rather wandering life nearer London. It was in this period that Tennyson made friends with many famous men, including Gladstone, Thomas Carlyle, and the poet Walter Savage Landor. Carlyle, writing to Ralph Waldo Emerson in 1842, described him as

Friendships with Gladstone and Carlyle

a man solitary and sad, dwelling in an element of gloom, carrying a bit of Chaos about him, which he is manufacturing into Cosmos . . . one of the finest-looking men in the world. A great shock of rough, dusky, dark hair; bright, laughing hazel eyes; massive aquiline face, most massive yet most delicate; of sallow brown complexion, almost Indian looking, clothes cynically loose, free-and-easy, smokes infinite tobacco. His voice is musically loose, fit for loud laughter and piercing wail, and all that may lie between; speech and speculation free and plenteous; I do not meet in these last decades such company over a pipe!

In 1840 Tennyson invested his patrimony in a project for wood carving by machinery. Its failure plunged him into financial difficulty; and family worries, besides his ill health and nervous instability, brought him near to a breakdown. But the then fashionable "water cure," which he took several times during the 1840s, seems to have done him good, for one hears of his resuming his port-and-tobacco regime.

Major literary work.   In 1842 he published *Poems*, in two volumes, one containing a revised selection from the volumes of 1830 and 1832, the other, new poems. The new poems included "Morte d'Arthur," "The Two Voices," "Locksley Hall," and "The Vision of Sin" and other poems that reveal a strange naïveté, such as "The May Queen," "Lady Clara Vere de Vere," and "The Lord of Burleigh." The new volume was not on the whole well received. But the grant to him at this time, by Sir Robert Peel, of a pension of £200 helped to alleviate his financial worries.

The year 1850 marked a turning point. Tennyson resumed his correspondence with Emily Sellwood, and their engagement was renewed and followed by marriage. Meanwhile, Edward Moxon offered to publish the elegies on Hallam that Tennyson had been composing over the years. They appeared, at first anonymously, as *In Memoriam*, which had a great success with both reviewers and the public, won him the friendship of Queen Victoria, and helped bring about, in the same year (1850), his appointment as poet laureate.

Appointment as laureate

After his marriage, which was happy, Tennyson's life

became more secure and outwardly uneventful. There were two sons: Hallam (1852–1928) and Lionel (1854–86). The times of wandering and unsettlement ended in 1853, when the Tennysons took a house, Farringford, in the Isle of Wight. Tennyson was to spend most of the rest of his life there and at Aldworth (near Haslemere, Surrey), which he built as a summer home in 1868.

His position as the national poet was confirmed by his ode on the death of Wellington (1852)—though some critics at first thought it disappointing—and the famous poem on the charge of the Light Brigade at Balaklava, published in 1855, first in the press and then in the *Maud* volume. *Maud* itself, a strange and turbulent "monodrama," provoked a storm of protest; many of the poet's admirers were shocked by the morbidity, hysteria, and bellicosity of the hero. Yet *Maud* was Tennyson's favourite among his poems.

The Arthurian project he had long considered at last issued in *Idylls of the King* (1859), which had an immediate success. Tennyson, who loathed publicity, had now acquired a sometimes embarrassing public fame. The *Enoch Arden* volume of 1864 perhaps represents the peak of his popularity. New Arthurian *Idylls* were published in *The Holy Grail, and Other Poems* in 1869 (dated 1870). These were again well received, though some readers were beginning to show discomfort at the "Victorian" moral feeling that Tennyson had imported into his source material from Sir Thomas Malory.

Poetic drama In 1874 Tennyson decided to try his hand at poetic drama. *Queen Mary* appeared in 1875, and an abridged version was produced at the Lyceum in 1876 with only moderate success. It was followed by *Harold* (1876; dated 1877), *Becket* (not published in full until 1884), and the "village tragedy" *The Promise of May*, which proved a failure at the Globe in November 1882. This play—his only prose work—shows Tennyson's growing despondency and resentment at the religious, moral, and political tendencies of the age. He had already caused some sensation by publishing a poem called "Despair" in *The Nineteenth Century* (November 1881). It evoked a parody by Swinburne and a stream of pamphlets, lectures, and sermons. A more positive indication of Tennyson's later beliefs appears in "The Ancient Sage," published in *Tiresias and Other Poems* (1885). Here the poet records his intimations of a life before and beyond this life.

Tennyson accepted a peerage (after some hesitation) in 1884. In 1886 he published a new volume containing "Locksley Hall Sixty Years After," consisting mainly of imprecations against modern decadence and retracting the earlier poem's belief in inevitable human progress. This challenge to the liberal thought of the day prompted Gladstone to write a protesting article in *The Nineteenth Century* for January 1887.

In 1889 Tennyson wrote the famous short poem "Crossing the Bar," during the crossing to the Isle of Wight. In the same year he published *Demeter and Other Poems*, which contains the charming retrospective "To Mary Boyle," introducing "The Progress of Spring," a fine lyric written much earlier and rediscovered, and "Merlin and the Gleam," an allegorical summing-up of his poetic career. In 1892 his play *The Foresters* was successfully produced in New York. Despite ill health, he was able to correct the proofs of his last volume, *The Death of Oenone, Akbar's Dream, and Other Poems*. He died at Aldworth on October 6, 1892.

Assessment. Tennyson's ascendancy among Victorian poets began to be questioned even during his lifetime, when Browning and Swinburne were serious rivals. And 20th-century criticism, influenced by the rise of a new school of poetry headed by T.S. Eliot (though Eliot himself was an admirer of Tennyson) has proposed some drastic devaluations of his work. Undoubtedly much in Tennyson that appealed to his contemporaries has ceased to appeal to many readers today. He can be mawkish and banal, pompous and orotund, offering little more than the mellifluous versifying of shallow or confused thoughts. The rediscovery of earlier poets like Donne or Hopkins (a poet of Tennyson's own time who was then

unknown to the public), together with the widespread acceptance of Eliot and Yeats as the leading modern poets, opened the ears of readers to a very different, and perhaps more varied, poetic music. A more balanced estimate of Tennyson has begun to prevail, however, with the recognition of the enduring greatness of "Ulysses," the unique poignancy of Tennyson's best lyrics, and, above all, the stature of *In Memoriam* as the great representative poem of the Victorian Age. It is now also recognized that the realistic and comic aspects of Tennyson's work are more important than they were thought to be during the period of the reaction against him. Finally, the perception of the poet's awed sense of the mystery of life, which lies at the heart of his greatness, as in "Crossing the Bar" or "Flower in the Crannied Wall," unites his admirers in this century with those in the last. Though less of Tennyson's work may survive than appeared likely during his Victorian heyday, what does remain—and it is by no means small in quantity—seems likely to be imperishable.

MAJOR WORKS

VERSE: *Poems, Chiefly Lyrical* (1830), includes "Mariana," "The Poet," "Love and Death," "Oriana," and "Claribel"; *Poems* (1832, dated 1833), includes "The Lady of Shalott," "The Dream of Fair Women," "Oenone," "The Lotos-Eaters," "The Palace of Art," and "The Miller's Daughter"; *Poems*, 2 vol. (1842), includes "Locksley Hall," "Ulysses," "Sir Galahad," "Morte d'Arthur," "The Two Voices," and "The Vision of Sin"; *The Princess* (1847); *In Memoriam* (1850); *Ode on the Death of the Duke of Wellington* (1852); *Maud and Other Poems* (1855), includes "The Charge of the Light Brigade"; *Idylls of the King* (1859); *Enoch Arden* (1864), includes "Sea Dreams," "Aylmer's Field," and "The Northern Farmer"; *The Holy Grail and Other Poems* (1869, dated 1870); *The Window, or the Song of the Wrens* (privately printed 1867, first published edition 1870, dated 1871), music by Arthur Sullivan; *Gareth and Lynette* and *The Last Tournament* (1872); *Ballads and Other Poems* (1880), includes "Rizpah," "The Revenge," and "The Defence of Lucknow"; *Tiresias and Other Poems* (1885), includes "To Virgil," "Balin and Balan," and "The Ancient Sage"; *Locksley Hall Sixty Years After* (1886); *Demeter and Other Poems* (1889), includes "To Mary Boyle," "The Progress of Spring," and "Merlin and the Gleam"; *The Death of Oenone, Akbar's Dream, and Other Poems* (1892).

DRAMA: *Queen Mary* (published 1875); *Harold* (1876, dated 1877); *The Promise of May* (1882); *The Cup* and *The Falcon* (1884); *Becket* (1884); *The Foresters* (1892).

BIBLIOGRAPHY. CHRISTOPHER RICKS (ed.), *The Poems of Tennyson* (1969), presents all the known poetry, published and unpublished, with full textual, bibliographical, and explanatory notes. *Alfred Tennyson*, by the poet's grandson, SIR CHARLES TENNYSON (1949, reprinted 1968), is the most authoritative modern biography, revealing much that was previously unknown about his early life. R.W. RADER, *Tennyson's Maud: The Biographical Genesis* (1963), explores the relationship between the poet's private life and his art. Victorian criticism of Tennyson is extensively represented in J.D. JUMP (ed.), *Tennyson: The Critical Heritage* (1967). Some of the best modern criticism is collected in JOHN KILLHAM (ed.), *Critical Essays on the Poetry of Tennyson* (1960).

(W.W.R.)

Terence

Distinguished primarily for the purity of his Latin and the urbane realism of his plays, Terence ranks as one of the two masters of classical Roman drama, along with the more boisterous and popular Plautus. Like the other comic dramatists of classical Rome, Terence based his plays on Greek originals: his skillful interrelation of character and plot, his subtle handling of situation, and the limpidity of his style are also seen in the Athenian playwright Menander, his main source. It is chiefly from Terence's application of these qualities, however, that the modern comedy of manners derives its essential character.

Terence—the anglicized form of the name of Publius Terentius Afer—wrote six verse comedies, all extant, for the Roman stage in the 2nd century BC. Reliable information about his life and dramatic career is defective. There are four sources of biographical information on him: a short, gossipy life by the Roman biographer Suetonius, written nearly three centuries later; a garbled version of a commentary on the plays by the 4th-century grammarian Aelius Donatus; production notices prefixed to the play texts recording details of first (and occasionally also of later) performances; and Terence's own prologues to the plays, which, despite polemic and distortion, reveal something of his literary career.

Terence was born, probably in 186/185 BC, in the North African town of Carthage. He was taken to Rome as a slave by Terentius Lucanus, an otherwise unknown Roman senator who was impressed by his ability and gave him a liberal education and, subsequently, his freedom.

The plays Most of the available information about Terence relates to his career as a dramatist. During his short life he produced six plays, to which the production notices assign the following dates: *Andria* (*The Andrian Girl*), 166 BC; *Hecyra* (*The Mother-in-Law*), 165 BC; *Heauton timoroumenos* (*The Self-Tormentor*), 163 BC; *Eunuchus* (*The Eunuch*), 161 BC; *Phormio*, 161 BC; *Adelphi* (or *Adelphoe*; *The Brothers*), 160 BC; *Hecyra*, second production, 160 BC; *Hecyra*, third production, 160 BC. These dates, however, pose several problems. The *Eunuchus*, for example, was so successful that it achieved a repeat performance and record earnings for Terence, but the prologue that Terence wrote, presumably a year later, for the *Hecyra*'s third production gives the impression that he had not yet achieved any major success. Yet alternative date schemes are even less satisfactory.

From the beginning of his career, Terence was lucky to have the services of Lucius Ambivius Turpio, a leading actor who had promoted the career of Caecilius, the major comic playwright of the preceding generation. Now in old age, the actor did the same for Terence. Yet not all of Terence's productions enjoyed success. The *Hecyra* failed twice: its first production broke up in an uproar when rumours were circulated among its audience of alternative entertainment by a tightrope walker and some boxers; and the audience deserted its second production for a gladiatorial performance nearby.

Attacks on his dramatic method Terence faced the hostility of jealous rivals, particularly one older playwright, Luscius Lanuvinus, who launched a series of accusations against the newcomer. The main source of contention was Terence's dramatic method. It was the custom for these Roman dramatists to draw their material from earlier Greek comedies about rich young men and the difficulties that attended their amours. The adaptations varied greatly in fidelity, ranging from the creative freedom of Plautus to the literal rendering of Luscius. Although Terence was apparently fairly faithful to his Greek models, Luscius alleged that Terence was guilty of "contamination"—*i.e.*, that he had incorporated material from secondary Greek sources into his plots, to their detriment. Terence sometimes did add extraneous material. In the *Andria*, which like the *Eunuchus*, *Heauton timoroumenos*, and *Adelphi* was adapted from a Greek play of the same title by Menander, he added material from another Menandrean play, the *Perinthia* (*The Perinthian Girl*). In the *Eunuchus* he added to Menander's *Eunouchos* two characters, a soldier and his "parasite"—a hanger-on whose flattery of and services to his patron were rewarded with free dinners—both of them from another play by Menander, *The Kolax* (*The Parasite*). In the *Adelphi*, he added an exciting scene from a play by Diphilus, a contemporary of Menander. Such conservative writers as Luscius objected to the freedom with which Terence used his models.

A further allegation was that Terence's plays were not his own work but were composed with the help of unnamed nobles. This malicious and implausible charge is left unanswered by Terence. Romans of a later period assumed that Terence must have collaborated with the Scipionic circle, a coterie of admirers of Greek literature, named after its guiding spirit, the military commander and politician Scipio Africanus the Younger. Though he may have been friendly with the Scipio household, Terence also may have died before this circle existed. The younger Scipio was about Terence's age, and intimacy with him could have led to the presentation of the *Adelphi* and the *Hecyra* for production at the funeral games of Lucius Aemilius Paulus, Scipio's father.

Terence died young. When he was 25, he visited Greece and never returned from the journey. He died either in Greece from illness or at sea by shipwreck on the return voyage. Of his family life, nothing is known, except that he left a daughter and a small but valuable estate just outside Rome on the Appian Way.

Modern scholarship Modern scholars have been preoccupied with the question of the extent to which Terence was an original writer, as opposed to a mere translator of his Greek models. Positions on both sides have been vigorously maintained, but recent critical opinion seems to accept that, in the main, Terence was faithful to the plots, ethos, and characterization of his originals: thus, his humanity, his individualized characters, and his sensitive approach to relationships and personal problems all may be traced to Menander, and his obsessive attention to detail in the plots of *Hecyra* and *Phormio* derives from the Greek models of those plays by Apollodorus of Carystus of the 3rd century BC. Nevertheless, in some important particulars he reveals himself as something more than a translator. First, he shows both originality and skill in the incorporation of material from secondary models, as well as occasionally perhaps in material of his own invention; he sews this material in with unobtrusive seams. Second, his Greek models probably had expository prologues, informing their audiences of vital facts, but Terence cut them out, leaving his audiences in the same ignorance as his characters. This omission increases the element of suspense, though the plot may become too difficult for an audience to follow, as in the *Hecyra*.

Striving for a refined but conventional realism, Terence eliminated or reduced such unrealistic devices as the actor's direct address to the audience. He preserved the atmosphere of his models with a nice appreciation of how much Greekness would be tolerated in Rome, omitting the unintelligible and clarifying the difficult. His language is a purer version of contemporary colloquial Latin, at times shaded subtly to emphasize a character's individual speech patterns. Because they are more realistic, his characters lack some of the vitality and panache of Plautus' adaptations (Phormio here is a notable exception); but they are often developed in depth and with subtle psychology. Individual scenes retain their power today, especially those presenting brilliant narratives (*e.g.*, Chaerea's report of his rape of the girl in the *Eunuchus*), civilized emotion (*e.g.*, Micio's forgiveness of Aeschinus in the *Adelphi*, Bacchis' renunciation of Pamphilus in the *Hecyra*), or clever theatrical strokes (*e.g.*, the double disclosure of Chremes' bigamy in the *Phormio*).

Influence The influence of Terence on Roman education and on the later European theatre was very great. His language was accepted as a norm of pure Latin, and his work was studied and discussed throughout antiquity.

MAJOR WORKS

VERSE COMEDIES (WITH PROLOGUES): Dating of first production follows the production notices, but is problematic. *Andria* (166 BC; *The Andrian Girl*; *The Lady of Andros*; *The Girl from Andros*); *Heauton timoroumenos* (163 BC; *The Self-Tormentor*; *The Self-Punisher*); *Eunuchus* (161 BC; *The Eunuch*); *Phormio* (161 BC); *Adelphi* (160 BC; *Adelphoe*; *The Brothers*); *Hecyra* (three productions, two unsuccessful in 165 and 160 BC, the third later in 160 BC; *The Mother-in-Law*).

BIBLIOGRAPHY. The best edition of the complete Latin text is that by R. KAUER and W.M. LINDSAY, Oxford Classical Texts (1926; reprinted with supplementary critical information, 1958). Notable English translations are those by LAURENCE ECHARD et al., *Terence's Comedies* (1689, reprinted 1963); GEORGE COLMAN THE ELDER, *The Comedies of Terence Translated into Familiar Blank Verse* (1765 and later editions); and BETTY RADICE, *The Brothers and Other Plays* (1965), and *Phormio and Other Plays* (1967), both Penguin Classics. For a survey of the extensive Terentian bibliography, see H. MARTI, "Terenz 1909–1959," *Lustrum*, 6:114–238 (1961) and 8:5–93 (1963). For general comment, see G.E. DUCKWORTH, *The Nature of Roman Comedy* (1952); H. HAFFTER, *Terenz und seine künstlerische Eigenart* (1967; reprinted from *Museum Helveticum*, vol. 10, 1953); W. BEARE, *The Roman Stage*, 3rd ed. rev. (1965). For comment on particular aspects, see O. RIETH, *Die Kunst Menanders in den Adelphen des Terenz* (1964); W. LUDWIG, "The Originality of Terence and His

Greek Models," *Greek, Roman and Byzantine Studies,* 9:169–192 (1968); and w.g. ARNOTT, "Phormio Parasitus: A Study in Dramatic Methods of Characterization," *Greece and Rome,* 17:32–57 (1970).

(W.G.A.)

Terrestrial Ecosystem

A terrestrial ecosystem basically is a landscape that supports life; its components include earth materials at least as deep as roots extend, boundary layers of air, films of water, and interacting organisms. It is not simply these components but the interactions and diverse relations among them that fulfill the concept of an ecological system. Facing the complexity of his environment, man seeks first to analyze the various components; later he attempts to synthesize a broader perspective to understand how the components relate functionally to each other. This synthesis implies, first, an understanding of processes and roles—hence also measures of performance and of subsystems within larger systems. The conceptual basis for ecological systems is dealt with in the article ECOSYSTEM; particular ecological systems in watery environments are considered in the article AQUATIC ECOSYSTEM.

Tables, which list major terrestrial ecosystems, also include preliminary estimates of area and of productivity in live organic carbon for areas of major terrestrial ecosystems. For a perspective on the functions that all ecosystems perform, terrestrial ecosystems are contrasted briefly with aquatic ecosystems. After this review of constraints of life on land, consideration is given to corresponding adjustments of life-forms and the kinds of ecological roles, or niches, that have become available in both natural and modified ecosystems.

THE LAND ENVIRONMENT

Land as a medium for life. The complexes of ecosystems in Table 1 may be compared with the temperature–moisture array of plant types in the article COMMUNITY, BIOLOGICAL to give an impression of the wide range of temperatures and precipitation encountered in different communities throughout the world. If monthly or hourly extremes of these and other climatic variables are considered, as well as the conditions at different levels (micro-environments) above or below the ground, some idea may be gained of the constraints that land organisms had to overcome, during their evolution, after leaving the confines of water. Organisms that are available to colonize a given area and the local physical factors of soil, topography, and moisture availability limit what can arrive, survive and thrive.

Pioneer organisms Pioneer organisms may change a bare land surface, thus making it suitable for other species, which, in turn, further modify the local ecosystem and prepare the way for still later generations of mutually compatible species. Some combinations of species persist for hundreds or thousands of years if average rates of change of soil and other internal system conditions are slow enough. For intervals of more than a few thousand years, however, gradual shifts in the boundary conditions are imposed from larger systems (*e.g.,* climatic changes bringing on glaciers and major relocation of populations and life zones; gradual shifts and extinctions of species available over wide regions. Undisturbed natural systems adjust accordingly on a time scale that is long by comparison with the recovery times of communities resulting from perturbations of both human and natural impacts. Organisms along the evaporating fringes of the ice cap creeping into Antarctica's dry valleys may encounter water during only a few days in summer when temperatures rise enough to melt ice. Mountains—from Antarctica, along many Andean summits, around the Tibetan Plateau, and locally elsewhere—reach altitudes above which only windborne, wind-nourished life (with few or no vascular plants) persists. These and other extreme outposts of Earth's life were colonized from places where the obstacles to survival were not so severe.

The use of studies of successively smaller ecosystems and subsystems—not in isolation from one another but as

nested in the progressively large systems—provides the breadth of data needed to comprehend fully the workings of the global ecosystem.

Smaller systems are dependent on larger ones in many ways. Like space vehicles or stations, some fascinating natural ecosystems depend on the importation of outside energy and some nutrients (see CAVES AND CAVE SYSTEMS; SPRINGS AND WELLS).

Land and water. Shore waters, especially, depend on materials flowing in from the land as well as solar energy penetrating the surface. Deep, dark waters depend on what is produced and transformed in the shallow, sunlit waters. Yet the local upwelling of deep waters, with mineral nutrients released by the decay of sinking organic debris, strongly influences the amounts and kinds of plankton and, hence, of fishes and birds, which return some small fraction of the continents' nutrient loss back to the streams or shore areas.

More or less natural ecosystems on land convert solar energy to organic material by incorporating the carbon of atmospheric carbon dioxide. Man's crops deflect an increasing fraction of this energy and carbon into foods and other products for society. Agriculture and industry, however, consume not only the human energy refueled by foods but also fossil fuels stored long ago in the coal beds and oils of sediments by ecosystems of past ages.

Land, sea, and boundary zones Fewer than 133,000,000 square kilometres (51,000,000 square miles) are accounted for by glacier-free land, compared with 362,000,000 square kilometres (140,000,000 square miles) by the oceans and adjacent waters. Small but important fractions of these areas lie in shifting boundary zones between land and water. Floodplain, swamp, and delta complexes include some of the world's most productive landscapes. Tides and currents, however, wash away some nutrients from these complexes—and from grassy salt marshes—fertilizing shallow marine waters and stimulating the aquatic food-chain growth.

Even regions so dry that they have no exterior outlets of water to the sea gather saline waters in some rare storms or during moist years. Adjacent flatlands of sodium chloride and even sodium carbonate may be mostly barren but yet support salt-tolerant plants at certain times and places after water flows in from surrounding highlands.

Such cases of shifting boundary conditions of land and water are of interest partly because special displays of clear-cut environmental control of life can be sorted out in the extremes. Similarly, bogs and mires receive widespread interest as wetlands dispersed widely, from the vast lowland Arctic tundras through boreal forest (taiga) belts to a few places further south.

The ancestors of present land life evolved in fresh and salt waters with the appropriate membranes and metabolic processes for selecting the scarce elements and compounds that each cell requires for survival, possible genetic change (mutation), and further evolution.

Adaptation to land living **Limiting factors to living on land.** Many adaptations were required before organisms could leave the seas and live on the land. Most green plants evolved from algae that had fluid sacs (vacuoles) inside cells that helped maintain water and chemical balances in the living cell substance. Vascular conducting systems help pipe water to all tissues. Impermeable outer coverings control outgoing water and incoming carbon dioxide through special openings called stomates, which are regulated by guard cells. Specialized adaptations have allowed desert succulents to take in carbon dioxide at night, when temperature and stress of moisture loss are low. Certain organisms have drought-resistant cytoplasm. Lichens, fungi that enclose algal cells in a biological partnership, survive far into the polar regions and into temperate and tropical deserts. The right species can photosynthesize for brief periods under favourable conditions of moisture or humidity, while resisting attrition of their accumulated assets of water and organic compounds during the long times of intervening aridity. In the dry as well as in fairly wet areas of tundra and taiga and especially in the rocky parts of mountain landscapes, other lichens and many mosses illustrate the patchwork patterns of coloni-

Table 1: Approximate Zonal Distribution of Major Pre-agricultural Ecosystems

major bioclimatic zones, temperature, relief	moisture	ecosystem type	area* (000,000 sq km)
Polar to subpolar area			
Polar	arid to humid	tundra, barren	7.86
Polar to boreal	wet peat	open bog and mire	1.30
Boreal alpine	mostly humid	"tundra" meadow	1.58
Subpolar	mostly humid	scrub, herb, bog–woods	2.80
Total			13.54
Boreal and semiboreal area			
Boreal	mostly humid	taiga	10.10
Semiboreal or montane	mostly humid	mostly coniferous	6.91
Total			17.01
Temperate forest complexes			
Cool or montane	mostly humid	mostly coniferous	3.77
Cool	humid	mostly deciduous	3.76
Warm	humid	evergreen, deciduous	5.76
Warm or montane	mostly semi-arid	woodland, scrub	3.83
Warm (moist site)	arid to semi-arid	herb–woods mix	1.07
Total			18.19
Grassland area			
Alpine	mostly humid	mountain meadow	1.81
Temperate	humid	tallgrass, marsh	1.05
Temperate or montane	semi-arid	grass, scrub, puna	9.43
Cold tropical montane	humid	paramo, scrub	0.94
Tropical, subtropical	mostly semi-arid	grassy savanna	9.73
Total			22.96
Desert and semidesert area			
Temperate and tropical	semi-arid to arid	sandscapes	5.77
Cold montane	semi-arid to arid	mountain desert	3.20
Other temperate	arid	desert	10.45
Tropical and subtropical	very arid to arid	desert	9.93
Total			29.35
Tropical forest complexes			
Hot (moist site)	humid	lowland rain forest	4.56
Hot	mostly humid	semi-evergreen	8.83
Hot to montane	humid–dry	monsoon deciduous	1.18
Warm to montane	humid	mostly evergreen	2.42
Total			16.99
Other tropical woodland– savanna complexes			
Hot (moist site)	arid to semi-arid	herb–woods mix	0.32
Hot	humid–dry	woodland, savanna	8.93
Hot	dry–humid	scrub, wood, savanna	5.12
Total			14.37

*Areas regrouped after N.I. Bazilevich, L.E. Rodin, and Rozov.

zation such as might have occurred as the continents first became populated by green plants. Microbes and animals were ready to follow, consuming dead or live organic matter, or both.

Major divisions of the land environment. *Polar regions and tundra.* The colder divisions of the land environment can be grouped broadly as tundra and polar barrens, which include cold "deserts" and spotty tundra (Table 1). Bogs and mires accumulate dead carbon wherever decomposition fails to match production over a long period. Altitudinal and local mixtures of tundra dwarf scrub and meadow extend to many boreal mountains (and also to Alpine temperate and tropical areas tabulated under grassland in Table 1). Sub-polar areas also include cold maritime herb meadow and scrub, bogs with dwarf woods, and open wooded or tall-shrub "tundra" (see POLAR BIOMES; TUNDRA).

Boreal forest (taiga). The boreal forest is here differentiated between northern (transitional to tundra), middle (open woodland to closed forest), and southern (denser forest). Estimates of typical forest area (and total carbon in living organisms) are separated from figures for unwooded and sparsely wooded bogs on peaty soils. Although "boreal" is frequently used in the general sense to refer to anything northern, it is best distinguished from several other predominantly coniferous zones here called semiboreal. These include the sub-alpine and montane zones of mountains, as in the western American Cordillera. A mixed forest zone in eastern and western Eurasia has some broad-leaved species besides the usual poplar and birch that are common in boreal and its grassland fringe zone of western Siberia and south central Canada. Except in these and a few other areas in which aridity and local relief complicate the pattern, a broad climatic outline around most boreal and semiboreal ecosystems is bounded on the north by the farthest extent of the 10° C

(50° F) July average temperature and on the south by areas with more than four months above this temperature.

Temperate areas. Temperate areas include some predominantly coniferous forests; *e.g.*, from the central British Columbian interior to lower elevations around alpine–sub-alpine–montane complexes farther inland in North America. Except in parts of a cool coastal belt and some other local rain forests, conifer growth is usually limited by droughts as well as by sporadic insect outbreaks. These repeated disturbances, plus sporadic lightning fires before man began burning and logging, have influenced the extent of most conifer stands. Giant evergreen forests locally attain much greater than average carbon mass. Evergreens of lesser stature, dwarfed in areas of salt–wind exposure, may line these and other vegetation belts in coastal strips too narrow to map on a global scale.

Temperate summer-green or cold-deciduous forest, in contrast to the drought-deciduous forest of tropical monsoon regions, prevailed originally in the now industrialized areas of northeastern United States, midlatitude Europe, central eastern Asia, and locally elsewhere. Conifers peculiar to special habitats, especially in mountains and sand plains, also may have been part of the original vegetation and certainly have been extended in plantings in much of the cool temperate zone. In North America, for example, below the latitudes or altitudes where spruce-fir was common, pines were important pioneer species on burned-over forest land and abandoned clearings; eastern hemlock, which is more shade-tolerant, persists or even expands in areas protected from fire, especially in the Great Lakes and Appalachian regions (see FORESTS).

The warm temperate zone, as generally understood in English, is referred to as subtropical in Soviet atlases and literature (which provided many of the preliminary esti-

The summer-green forest

mates in the tables accompanying this article). Broad-leaved forests are partly deciduous but increasingly evergreen near the southern coasts of the United States, Japan, and China. Only a few conifers are important. Forest and woodland areas include also maquis and garigue scrub in the Mediterranean area, chaparral in California, and similar vegetation capable of maintaining its leaves through dry summers or wet winters or spring seasons (see SCRUBLANDS).

Mostly evergreen broad-leaved forests prevailed in humid portions of the Southern Hemisphere areas: *Eucalyptus* in Australia, *Nothofagus* in New Zealand and the southern Andes. Here oceanic climates moderate winter cold. Wet hard-leaved (sclerophyll) forest and temperate rain-forest ecosystems are quite localized on favourable sites; dry sclerophyll communities of varied height and tree spacing are especially prominent in both temperate and subtropical parts of Australia. Monterrey pine outgrows other planted conifers and the several native evergreen genera.

Wetlands with mixtures of floodplain or swamp herbs are locally important in semi-arid to arid lands. They provide grazing and watering places for animals and invited man's early agriculture and irrigation.

Grasslands. In the same manner that the cool temperate forests interfinger with grassland in the Soviet Union and the northern United States, so the warm temperate forest alternates with grassland on different substrates west of 95° W longitude in the south central United States. As in tropical savannas, burned fringes of all the foregoing forests included open woodlands (*e.g.*, burr oak and post oak openings) and sparser groupings of trees. Semi-arid grassland is here typical throughout, but gradations to cold alpine vegetation and semidesert are also evident.

Tall grassland includes the belt of meadow steppe south of the Eurasian forest and the North American prairie. Short or mixed grassland prevails in the next drier belt. From Mongolia westward, barely interrupted by the mountain meadows and terraced conifer forests of the Altai and other mountains, the shortgrass steppes offered a corridor for Asian horsemen to the Caucasus, the Crimea, and central Europe.

In the Southern Hemisphere occur the pampas of Uruguay and Argentina and the grassy parts of the South African veld, which share the scattered parklike tree growth of the subtropical savannas. With woodland or scrub mixed in, these latter are marked by seasonal moisture and fire (see GRASSLANDS).

Arid regions. Arid lands, climatically defined, include mixtures of grassy and open scrub or special life forms. Cool semidesert steppes typically are marked in the north by silvery *Artemisia* species. Extremes of hot and cool temperatures, in addition to low moisture, further constrain plant growth in the warm semidesert. Saline deserts are interspersed among both of the above arid lands and even in some grasslands but occur in greatest extent in central Asia (see DESERTS).

In Table 1, sandy landscapes, especially those with dunes, are probably estimated conservatively, but biomass is not great even in semi-arid, grassy sand hills or in the *Haloxylon* sand woodlands actively cultivated in the Kara-Kum Desert. Almost 10,000,000 square kilometres (4,000,000 square miles), from semidesert savanna to absolute barren deserts of several kinds, are included as tropical desert.

Tropical forests. When these and transitional semideciduous and semi-evergreen forest or woodland are taken into account, the area of completely evergreen tropical forest is more limited than many maps suggest. Massive tropical or equatorial rain forests occupy only a fraction of this total area. Sites that are enriched by nutrients from upstream or upslope give the exceptionally high production noted on Table 3—but only over still more limited areas, which have long been the first to attract shifting cultivation (see JUNGLES AND RAIN FORESTS).

Woodlands. Below the highest snowfields are equatorial mountains that include treeless zones with temperatures near freezing on most days of the year. These areas,

with a peculiar combination of low and exceptionally tall cold-resistant herbs, are called paramo in Colombia and Ecuador. Far less localized are elfin woodlands and scrub vegetation, widespread near the summit of mountains in both the tropics and subtropics. Evergreen subtropical mountain forests are typical of monsoon regions that have drought-deciduous forests in the lowlands.

Natural deterioration by leaching of nutrients and by clearing and erosion have already created much savanna and scrub in the coastal rain forest belt of eastern Brazil and in many areas of the Amazon Basin. In West Africa, rain forest and moist evergreen forest appear to be more vulnerable to conversion to grassy savanna than are drier types of ecosystems because fire-resistant trees are not already present. Moist semideciduous forest, dry deciduous forest, and woodland are considered more likely for conversion to savanna woodlands through selection favouring resprouting of resistant trees already mixed in the vegetation or available for invasion from the vegetation of surrounding regions. Original savanna woodland maintains resistant trees but has opened up to allow more grass or scrub since burning has become an annual management tool—especially where fires are mostly started late in the dry season.

Development of savanna and scrub

MAJOR LIFE FORMS AND CLASSES

Growth habits and indicator organisms. A classic ecological approach to interpreting environmental constraints on regional plant formations or local community and site types within regions is based on the kind of plant group, or life-form, that predominates (see Table 2). Anglo-American and Soviet forestry traditions have tended to emphasize the indicator value of such life-forms and, where possible, the genus and species of the main community or perhaps each of several layers (strata) approximating a class. Preliminary indications of community change are based on the prevailing heights of plants constituting the class and include the appearance of very different species combinations in seedling or other young strata as compared with currently dominant vegetation.

In a complex ecosystem, however, the species of greatest abundance is frequently not such a sensitive indicator of habitat conditions as are others having lesser abundance but greater fidelity or differential occurrence. Several Eurasian schools of ecosystem classification and newer techniques of statistical analysis have introduced the relative importance of various combinations of factors distinguishing one ecosystem type from another.

Ecologically similar species within major genera are recognizable among quite distant areas—especially in the Northern Hemisphere. On the other hand, the physical constraints of water relations and energy balance have led to convergent evolution of similar life-forms from genetically distant stock. Notable examples among plants include the hard-leaved (sclerophyll), mostly evergreen scrub and woodland or forest in the winter-rain, summer-drought (Mediterranean-type) climates of Chile, Australia, and California, as well as southernmost Europe, northernmost and southwest (Cape) Africa, and areas of southwest Asia.

The evolution, successional change, and seasonal movements of animals are related directly to plants that provide them food and shelter. In the very cold or dry regions noted earlier, herbivorous and especially predatory and scavenging animals may have to range widely to survive and reproduce. Warmer, humid regions include migrants but also allow a wide variety of other organisms within almost any habitat.

Classification by habitat. The habitat—where an organism lives—is frequently used to categorize the living things in an ecosystem. The types of habitat may be divided broadly as soil organisms, rooted plants, organisms attached to plants, and free-moving animals.

Soil organisms include a size range from microbiota (micro-organisms and minute animals) through mesobiota (arthropods and smaller larvae) to macrobiota (roots of plants, larger invertebrates and burrowing vertebrates). Plants provide an aboveground layer consist-

Habitats and niches

Vegetation zonation (trees to stunted trees to alpine grasses) in the Colorado Rockies.

Mariposa grove of sequoias, Yosemite National Park, California.

Elfin woodland at an elevation of 10,000 feet in Celebes.

Boreal forest, or taiga, of Labrador.

Deciduous hardwood forest of northeastern United States.

Alaskan tundra in the summer.

Plate 1: (Top left) Grant Heilman—EB Inc., (top right) Gene Ahrens—Bruce Coleman Inc., (centre left) A.J. Jermy, (centre right) Tom Willock—Ardea Photographics, (bottom left) Walter Chandoha, (bottom right) Willis Peterson

Plate 2   Terrestrial Ecosystem

Chaparral in California showing (top) chaparral fire, necessary factor in the maintaining of the chaparral ecosystem and (bottom) denseness and extent of scrubland.

Savanna on the Serengeti Plain, Tanzania.

Tropical rainforest on western Madagascar.

Sub-alpine grassland, Yellowstone National Park.

Bamboo forest at Sagano, Kyōto, Japan.

Warm desert plant life on the Sonoran Desert ot southern California.

Sphagnum bog in northern Wisconsin.

Cold desert in the Pine Nut Mountains of Nevada.

Okefenokee Swamp of Georgia.

Sand dunes on the Atlantic coast of southern Spain.

Plate 3: (Top left) Dennis Brokaw, (top right) Harold Hungerford—Photo Researchers, (centre left) J.W. Wilburn, (bottom left) C. Hardin—Shostal, (bottom right) Alfonso Gutierrez Escera—Ostman Agency

Plate 4   Terrestrial Ecosystem

Oasis on the Sahara of Morocco.

Shepherds herding their sheep on the alpine tundra of the Austrian Alps.

Mosses, ferns, fungi, and other plant life that form the extremely dense undergrowth in the Olympic National Forest of Washington.

Lichen community thriving on a rocky cliff.

Spring wildflowers growing in the desert in Namaqualand, South Africa.

Plate 4: (Top left) A.J. Huxley—EB Inc., (top right, centre right, bottom left) Shostal, (top right) J. Turver, (centre right) B. Nelson, (bottom left) W. Wiley, (bottom right) Gerald Cubitt

Table 2: Life-Forms of Primary Producers

plant life-form group	height	Raunkaier categories*
Epiphytes (growing on plants of the following groups)		
Woody or evergreen perennials (bud-bearing shoots above ground)	buds more than 0.25 metre above ground	Phanerophytes
Trees (one to few stems; self-pruning)	taller than 30 metres	Megaphanerophytes
	10–30 metres	Mesophanerophytes
	less than 10 metres	Microphanerophytes
Shrubs (smaller woody plants, often with many stems and with shoot replacement)	taller than 0.5 metre	Microphanerophytes
	less than 0.5 metre	Nanophanerophytes
subshrubs	less than 0.25 metre	Chamaephytes
semishrubs	partly dying annually	Chamaephytes
Lichen-moss layer(s)	buds near ground surface	bryoid-chamaephyte
Perennial (or biennial) herbs		
Grass-like (including sedge, rush, etc.)	buds near ground surface	Hemicryptophytes
Forbs (including non-grassy herbaceous plants)	buds below ground	Geophytes
Water plants	buds or bulbs below water	Hydrophytes
Marsh plants	buds or bulbs in wet ground	Helophytes
Annuals		
Summer, winter, and facultative perennial	"buds" in seed	Therophytes
Special forms†		

*A traditional standard terminology for life-forms as devised about 1900 by C. Raunkaier, a Danish botanist. †Including: bamboos (woody grasses); tuft plants; climbers (lianas); succulents (stem and leafy).
Source: After H. Ellenberg, D. Mueller-Dombois, A. Kuchler, W. McGinnies, and others.

ing of prostrate herbaceous plants, shrubs, vines, and trees. The organisms that attach to such plants are called epiphytes; those that cling but can move are often called periphytes. The freely moving animals—both walking and flying—are referred to as permeants.

Classification by niche. Not only the habitats but the niches (operating roles of organisms throughout their life) are involved in a careful consideration of ecosystems and their evolving populations. Just as persons "find their own niches" in a complex society and adapt, through learning, to their own special vocations, an indefinitely large number of species possibilities have been narrowed down during the course of evolution to those especially adapted to definite and perhaps discrete "vocations" in a natural ecosystem.

Considering first the environment as conditioning a local ecosystem through climate, the presence of other organisms, pre-existing surface, surrounding relief, and related moisture factors, then within a specified local area, or volume, on the Earth's surface, the range of variables is seen to be much smaller than in the entire biosphere, or zone of life.

If each available species in neighbouring ecosystems is allotted a dimension, for example, those that never become established in a local ecosystem in question measure zero. Whatever the measure used, pioneer species are those scoring high soon after a bare or disturbed area has opportunity for recovery but declining—usually to zero —as waves of replacement species arrive. Self-perpetuating (climax) species may have more dimensions than the pioneer species or those that typically rise and disappear in stages of succession.

If the individual species and its niche be examined, the organisms with which a species coexists at one time or another (a kind of intersection set) constitute part of its niche. Microclimatic variables within the local habitat occupied by the species limit the range of favourable conditions. Soil conditions, microtopography, and moisture conditions, all of which change with the other variables, are additional ecosystem properties that influence most of its inhabitants directly or indirectly. Also upper

and lower limits of physiological tolerance influence where and how long a species can persist—either locally, on the time scale of a species life cycle, of succession, or globally, on the time scale of evolution.

Not only mere survival but the probable rates of intake of resources, of elimination, of growth and reproduction, and of death for each kind of organism are influenced by the other variables. An organism can fill any of three niches at any given time in its life: it can be a producer of goods, like green plants; a consumer of goods, like most animals; or a decomposer of goods, like many micro-organisms. The entire complex constitutes a food web or network. Energy passes along this net as in a power grid, and is dispersed as heat along the way.

The three types of niches

Producers. With minor exceptions (chemosynthetic bacteria) green plants fulfill the prime role of providing energy for all other organisms by means of the process of photosynthesis, the conversion of sunlight and raw materials to sugars and other foods. Roots and other underground parts of plants replenish water losses and also withdraw mineral nutrients from substrates. Both for plants with and plants without above-ground woody parts, storage of photosynthetic products underground may be very important. Above-ground stems provide the support for displaying the photosynthetic machinery through as great a vertical column of air as the habitat, life form, and stand age will permit.

Consumers. Under optimal conditions well over 10 percent of the net primary production may be channelled through various consumers, but a lower percentage is the usual case. Plant-eating animals (herbivores) are the primary consumers; they extract their varied food needs from the predominant carbohydrate storage of plants, accumulating large stores of protein. Predators consume other animals, thus taking advantage of the concentrations of protein already accumulated by the prey. Direct feeding on other animals is accomplished also in diverse ways by parasites. Disease organisms represent extreme cases, in which the host is not actually consumed but is debilitated or even killed by gradual depletion of its resources.

Table 3: Net Primary Production,* Carbon Pool, and Turnover

ecosystem complexes	production† (10⁹ metric tons of carbon per year)	live carbon pool (10⁹ tons)	turnover fraction‡ per year
Non-woodland			
Tundra and bog (treeless)	0.88	8.08	0.109
"Tundra" meadow and scrub	1.46	13.20	0.1
Grassland (sub-Alpine to tropical)	10.27	30.89	0.332
Deserts (excluding local moist sites)	3.37	8.58	0.394
Total non-woodland	15.98	60.75	0.26
Forest, woodland			
Boreal taiga	3.33	121.80	0.0275
Semiboreal forest, woodland	1.93	64.12	0.0301
Cool temperate, montane conifer	2.08	68.38	0.0304
Cool temperate, mostly deciduous	2.09	67.88	0.0308
Warm temperate, mostly broadleaf	4.05	97.76	0.0414
Warm temperate wetland	2.97	10.32	0.2878
Warm, montane woodland (semi-arid)	2.40	24.80	0.0968
Warm temperate wetland (arid to semi-arid)	3.14	12.82	0.2449
Tropical rich wetland (arid to semi-arid)	0.79	2.66	0.2970
Tropical scrub, woodland savanna	10.52	139.13	0.0756
Tropical montane forest	4.08	99.62	0.0410
Tropical lowland rainforest	11.17	83.86	0.1331
Other tropical forest	10.82	216.26	0.0500
Total forest, woodland	59.37	1,009.41	0.059
Total land	75.35	1,070.00	0.07

*Equivalent to the gross primary production less the respiration of all parts of green plants. †Includes carbon tied up in all living plants. ‡Annual loss of carbon from the live carbon pool to dead organic matter/live pool.

Omnivores have kept more feeding options open: they can consume both plants and animals. Certain birds and mammals switch readily between these foods according to season and abundance of food types.

Decomposers. Plant parts and animals die and pass on to organisms called decomposers, which break down organic structure—using and dispersing energy from the compounds left over by other organisms. This important functional role has the further consequence of releasing mineral nutrients for eventual recycling through succeeding generations of plants.

Various decomposers are adapted to diverse microhabitats within an ecosystem and create and modify new kinds of niches for other organisms as well.

PRODUCTIVITY IN TERRESTRIAL ECOSYSTEMS

Ecologists use the word production in a strict sense to mean the processes by which plants and animals convert nutrients to their own kind of body substance. Production can be carefully measured in terms of production rate per unit of time, or it can be expressed graphically as a generally rising curve of cumulative increase of input with time. Sometimes the word productivity is used specifically to indicate a short-term or instantaneous rate or derivative of change rather than a long-term average. Productivity of dry matter or economic products from a given ecosystem is frequently given as a prediction rather than a measurement, varying with the intensity and kind of management. Here the meaning is broad enough to cover the phenomena related to all the aspects of production.

Carbon as a measure of productivity

Net primary production. Relatively refined physiological studies are necessary for estimating what is termed gross primary production of an ecosystem. This measurement is usually expressed as the total amount of carbon absorbed by plants as carbon dioxide and converted to organic matter. Subtracting the compounds returned in any form of respiration by green plants gives net primary production. If expressed instead as the dry matter equivalent of carbon, this and the following terms must include an appropriate additional few percent for mineral elements (*e.g.*, nitrogen, sulfur) that accompany the carbon, hydrogen, and oxygen of all organic compounds. Energy equivalents are often preferred.

On the basis of the best data available in the early 1970s, Table 3 provides estimates of net primary production. Metric tons of organic carbon per square kilometre per year (which equals grams per square metre per year and 0.1 kilogram per hectare per year) is multiplied by the

areas from Table 1 to give the current approximation of the contribution of each ecosystem to worldwide net primary production (first column of Table 3).

Both the inventory, or "pool," of carbon in the biosphere and its distribution are judged according to pre-agricultural conditions; *i.e.*, before extensive forest clearing and widespread modification of natural vegetation.

If the annual income of carbon were approximately balanced by annual losses from all sources under natural conditions (*i.e.*, if the pool were neither increasing nor declining in comparison with the annual atmospheric exchange of photosynthesis), the following equation would hold true:

$$\frac{\text{production}}{\text{live pool}} = \frac{\text{sum of losses}}{\text{live pool}} = \text{turnover fraction per year.}$$

Among the groups of tundra-like ecosystem complexes in Table 3, about 11 percent of the vegetation is replaced each year. The production of about 170 grams of organic carbon per square metre per year averages over a wide variance between polar deserts (near zero) and mountain-meadow ecosystems, which approximate values for grasslands, noted below.

Grassy ecosystems turnover is about 30 percent of the plant life per year. Production rates average 450 grams of carbon per square metre per year—from about 60 percent or less for shortgrass prairies to 140 percent or more for wet prairies and marshes.

Desert-like ecosystems average consistently lower—about 100 grams of carbon per square metre per year—but this aveage obscures a wide variance from near zero to values approaching grassland production where moisture is frequently replenished. Turnover of plant material also varies widely, perhaps near 20 percent per year where woody or underground parts are prominent, to nearly 60 percent where short-lived vegetation is relatively more prominent.

Special moist sites having small area but high production per unit area have been purposely treated separately so as not to influence disproportionately the estimates for the surrounding widespread landscapes of arid, semi-arid, and temperate humid regions. These wetlands have high turnover (25–30 percent per year) because herb growth is prominent, and the ratio of shrub and tree growth to biomass is higher than in other woodlands and forests.

By contrast, true forests of the boreal and temperate zones have a consistently low annual turnover—averaging slightly over 3 percent per year if the data in Table 3 are widely representative. Primary production rates per unit area vary widely. Sub-alpine and other semiboreal coniferous ecosystems average only slightly higher than tundra margin or bog woodlands. Warm temperate forests, such as those in the southeastern United States, are only slightly more productive than tropical and subtropical woody savanna, thorn forest and scrub; 600–800 grams of carbon per square metre per year.

Production estimates for tropical forests are high relative to those for other forests. For the nutritionally enriched forests, estimates of roughly 2,500 grams of carbon per square metre per year production are given. The turnover rate of 13 percent per year is only half that attributed to wetlands of the cooler and drier areas, where more of the vegetation is killed and replaced each year.

While future research may modify the estimated areas and carbon pools of Table 1 and production rates of Table 3, the general trends of turnover fraction outlined above and the following interpretations of world totals are not expected to change too drastically.

Ecosystems of low productivity Tundra-like ecosystems and deserts must have contributed low production and live pool of organic carbon, although wetter parts of the tundra have stored much former live material as dead peat or meadow humus (not listed in Table 3). Grasslands and grassy savanna-like ecosystems probably had higher production rates and pools of live carbon than did tundra and deserts together, and they probably had accumulated deep humus in mineral soils.

The same table suggests that moist, cold, and seasonally dry categories of open or low woodland and scrub combined produce more carbon than either tundra or grasslands and several times as much stored carbon in live plants. It suggests further that denser forests (boreal, temperate, and tropical together) contributed more than half of the land's annual carbon fixation, and more than 75 percent of its carbon storage in live organisms—mostly plants and, more specifically, the woody parts of trees. Of course much of this wood is physiologically dead, but its entry into the decomposer food chains is mostly delayed while the outer trunk of the tree remains alive even if heartrot and cavities begin to break down the inner wood. As reflected also in the low turnover fractions for forest and some woodlands, these ecosystems evolved a life-form and structure that allows their photosynthetic machinery to operate through a considerable depth of atmosphere as compared with all the other kinds of ecosystems.

Secondary production and decomposition. Only a fraction of the plant material lost each year in the biosphere is consumed by animals; much of this vegetation falls to the decomposer organisms. Food that is consumed is only partly assimilated in the digestive tract and becomes part of the secondary production in an ecosystem; the remainder may be fairly promptly regurgitated, defecated, or excreted in other fluids.

Equations used for balancing incomes and losses for major decomposers as well as aboveground consumers help to identify the environmental control of each major transfer in the ecosystem. It is likely, however, that there is a significant remaining group of decomposers that cannot be analyzed independently of the surfaces in which they are inextricably dispersed. For this remaining group or for a summary equation expressing the joint action of all decomposers and the surfaces on which they act in a combined subsystem, the net change in mass can be summarized in a balance equation combining the terms for income of dead organic materials and respiration rates of the decomposers concerned.

If the last line of Table 3 fairly approximates the pre-agricultural annual income and inventory of live organic carbon on land, the long-lived and short-lived compounds together averaged about 7 percent replacement per year. Losses were less than income for the entire biosphere for certain long periods because there was a downhill washing from lands to waters and a net accumulation of dead organic materials in peat, coal, and petroleum. This represents a net storage of solar energy fixed ages ago, over geologically long periods, by the photosynthesis of past ecosystems.

Man-influenced ecosystems and their productivity. A growing international research effort is attempting to understand ecosystems well enough to improve upon estimates heretofore given and to predict the consequences of changes in income and loss rates. The uncertainty in present agricultural and man-modified landscape production rates is large, but several assessments made in 1968–70 added up to incomes around 56,000,000,000 metric tons of live carbon per year, compared with an inventory or live pool about ten times as large. It is clear that a real decrease has occurred in the inventory and that much of this is the result of forest clearing. Roughly 70 percent of the former forest–woodland area remains and about 70 percent of the mass per unit area on this remaining area is probably a generous estimate. Less than half as much organic carbon, mass, and energy is carried on remaining forests when compared to the natural ecosystems. These cleared areas were subsequently replaced by pastures and almost 15,000,000 square kilometres (6,000,000 square miles) of agricultural land.

Disruption of natural ecosystems Intense and efficient agricultural practices—constituting the "Green Revolution"—have drastically increased carbon fixation rates on some fairly small fraction of this land, but soil deterioration has probably decreased it on other cropland and on many semiwild ecosystems. Overgrazing and other misuse have diminished biological and economic productivity of large areas and have allowed the sand or dust in some desert fringe areas to encroach on formerly arable landscapes and, in Mediterranean areas, on cities that were formerly supported by better biological production.

Glowing hopes have been raised about optimizing the mixture of material and intangible values of the landscapes that are left, but it remains far from clear that constraints of the real world will permit a bare maintenance of present living standards as populations rise—much less the higher living standards to which much of the world aspires. The growth of industry and cities—and of mechanized agriculture to support both—has been tapping fossil fuel reserves (coal, oil, and gas) at rates that are still rising and measurably increasing the atmosphere's carbon dioxide faster than it is absorbed by vegetation. It will take much collective wisdom to foresee the consequences of all these changes and even more determination than man has yet shown for his environment in order to steer the Earth's future in the most beneficial manner (see AGRICULTURE, TECHNOLOGY OF; FORESTRY; and URBANIZATION).

BIBLIOGRAPHY. Information on terrestrial ecosystems can be found in the voluminous literature of biology and Earth sciences.

Methods and results of research are provided in *Ecological Studies*, the first volumes of which are: D.E. REICHLE (ed.), *Analysis of Temperate Forest Ecosystems* (1970), and HEINZ ELLENBERG (ed.), *Integrated Experimental Ecology* (1971).

Forest ecosystems are emphasized in the two volumes cited above and in V.N. SUKACHEV and N. DYLIS, *Fundamentals of Forest Biogeocoenology* (1968). This text–reference book and the following on a wider variety of world ecosystems are translations of major Russian sources: L.E. RODIN and N.I. BAZILEVICH, *Production and Mineral Cycling in Terrestrial Ecosystems* (1967); N.I. BAZILEVICH and L.E. RODIN, "Geographical Regularities in Productivity and the Circulation of Chemical Elements in the Earth's Main Vegetation Types," *Soviet Geography: Review and Translation*, 12:24–53 (1971), which includes maps derived from the foregoing data.

These and several other results from the two were incorporated in Reichle's book cited above, and in maps distributed by the organization, Students of Earth's Future, Oak Ridge, Tennessee.

The relation of terrestrial animal production to ecosystems is treated in diverse entomological and zoological as well as ecological literature, but the following highlight some important problems of integration: K. PETRUSEWICZ and A. MacFADYEN, *Productivity of Terrestrial Animals*, IBP Handbook No. 13 (1970); R.V. BELL, "A Grazing Ecosystem in the Serengeti," *Scient. Am.* 225:86–93 (1971), which together with G.M. VAN DYNE, *Analysis of Structure and Function of Grassland Ecosystems* (1970), offers a diverse sampling of studies or syntheses describing very different ecosystem groups, and their practical importance or unsolved questions.

(J.S.O.)

Terry, Ellen

For decades Ellen Terry's beauty, charm, vivacity, and immediate, sincere command of sentiment and pathos made her one of the most popular stage performers in both Britain and North America; an actress whose success was based essentially on her personality that imbued even the dullest part with a stirring vitality, she was most celebrated during her long partnership (1878–1902) with Sir Henry Irving. Although her career became desultory after his death, she never lost her hold on the public imagination and continued to be loved and admired, more for her great warmth of personality than for her infrequent theatrical performances after Irving's death.

Ellen Terry, c. 1878.

Alice Ellen Terry was born in Coventry, Warwickshire, on Feb. 27, 1847, the second surviving daughter in a large family of which several were to become well-known on the stage. She had no formal schooling, but trained by her parents, she rapidly developed into a celebrated child actress. At the age of nine she made her debut in the child's part of Mamillius in *The Winter's Tale*, which Charles Kean, son of the actor Edmund Kean, produced in London in April 1856. She remained in Kean's company until 1859 and later joined the stock company playing at the Theatre Royal, Bristol, where she played leading parts in Shakespeare and in repertory theatre.

In 1864, at the age of 16, she left the stage to marry the painter G.F. Watts, whose model she had been. Watts, a melancholic man almost three times her age, made many fine portraits and sketches of her, but the marriage survived a bare ten months; his rich patroness was determined that Ellen should go. In her despair, she could scarcely be induced to return to the stage but eventually did so, though playing with little of her former distinction. It was in 1867 that she first appeared, by chance, with Sir Henry Irving, playing Katherine in *The Taming of the Shrew*.

The following year she left the stage abruptly to live for six years in Hertfordshire with the architect and theatrical designer Edward Godwin (1833–86), whom she had met in Bristol and who became the father of her children, Edith and Edward Gordon Craig (1872–1966), who was to become a renowned actor, stage designer, and producer. When her association with Godwin began to fail, it was the author, dramatist, and producer Charles Reade who found her and brought her back to the stage. In the role of Portia she showed new maturity in a striking production of *The Merchant of Venice* (1875), designed by Godwin. On parting from Godwin (who married in 1876), she became responsible for maintaining their children. Before joining Irving at the Lyceum Theatre in 1878, she completed a successful season at the Court Theatre. In 1877 she received a divorce from Watts and married an actor, Charles Kelly, mainly to give her children a "name." They soon separated, and Kelly died in 1885.

When Ellen Terry joined Irving, she was 31 and he 40. It was the beginning of a close association with a man of genius whose life and resources were to be dedicated to the theatre and who was to make the Lyceum a centre for new, striking interpretations—of Shakespeare in particular. His approach to sponsorship of new plays was that of a great stage visualizer and star actor who required a scenarist to assemble a script that would give him a framework for compelling performance and spectacular stage effects. As part of his *mise-en-scène*, he needed a beautiful woman to lend her own glamour to his productions. Ellen Terry responded to his needs with selfless dedication, playing many great Shakespearean parts—Portia (1879), Juliet and Beatrice (1882), Lady Macbeth (1888), Queen Katharine (1892), Imogen (1896), Volumnia (1901), Ophelia (1878), Desdemona (1881), and Cordelia (1892). She willingly undertook such humble roles as Rosamund in Tennyson's *Becket* (1893), in which all the limelight shone upon the master.

Career with Irving

Whether in London or on arduous provincial tours, in New York or on exhausting excursions across North America, Ellen Terry acted as Irving's leading lady until she had grown too old for most of the parts in his repertory. They severed their partnership only in 1902, three years before his death. Their relationship was as close in private as in public life, and it was only when his affection began to wane in the 1890s that she entered into her famous "paper courtship" with Bernard Shaw. This correspondence is one of the most brilliant in the history of English letter writing. In 1907 she married the American actor James Carew, some 30 years her junior; although they soon parted, he remained her friend.

It was in comedy and in plays of tender sentiment, as well as in Shakespeare, that Ellen Terry's talent shone. When she left Irving it was to appear with Sir Herbert Beerbohm Tree in *The Merry Wives of Windsor* (1902), and Shaw eventually persuaded her to appear as Lady Cecily Wayneflete in *Captain Brassbound's Conversion* (1905), one of several parts he wrote with her in mind. When she celebrated her golden jubilee in 1906 at the Theatre Royal, Drury Lane, all the theatrical personalities of the day shared the stage with her.

Bernard Shaw saw Ellen Terry as a shining example of a modern, intelligent actress, capable alike of naturalistic and intellectual performance. During the 1890s he constantly urged her to leave Irving, whom he regarded as reactionary, and to dedicate herself to promoting the modern drama, represented in the work of Ibsen and himself. But unlike Sarah Siddons, her 18th-century predecessor as undisputed queen of the English theatre for a whole generation, Ellen Terry was ill suited by temperament to become a theatrical leader in her own right. Her particular, instinctual genius flowered only through her long service with Irving.

Although Irving had paid her £200 a working week for most of 20 years, she still had to earn a living in her later years. She worked in the theatre, last appearing on stage in 1925; in films; and as a Shakespearean lecturer-recitalist, reinterpreting her successes on tours in the U.S., Britain, and Australia. Her warm, generous personality made her a favourite wherever she went, but eyesight and memory began to fail. Belatedly, in 1925, she was made a Dame Grand Cross of the British Empire. She died on July 21, 1928, at her cottage, Small Hythe, Kent, which became the Ellen Terry Memorial Museum and in 1939 was given to the National Trust by her daughter Edith Craig.

BIBLIOGRAPHY. The principal biography is ROGER MANVELL, *Ellen Terry* (1968). See also her *Story of My Life* (1908; as *Ellen Terry's Memoirs*, with preface, notes, and additional biographical chapter by E. CRAIG and C. ST. JOHN, 1932); her *Four Lectures on Shakespeare* (1932); EDWARD GORDON CRAIG, *Ellen Terry and Her Secret Self* (1931); and EDWARD A. CRAIG, *Gordon Craig* (1968), in which the relationship between Ellen Terry and her son is developed by Gordon Craig's son, Ellen Terry's grandson. The correspondence with Shaw was edited by C. ST. JOHN (1931; 2nd ed. as *Ellen Terry and Bernard Shaw: A Correspondence*, 1949). Other important works are: LAURENCE IRVING, *Henry Irving, the Actor and His World* (1951), which gives a full account of Irving's and Ellen Terry's place in the Victorian theatre; GEORGE BERNARD SHAW, *Dramatic Opinions and Essays,* 2 vol. (1906), which contains the articles in which Shaw attacked Irving and praised Ellen Terry; and ROGER MANVELL, *Sarah Siddons, Portrait of an Actress* (1971), which provides insight into the theatrical tradition from which Ellen Terry emerged.

(R.M.)

Tertiary Period

The Tertiary Period is the geological time interval from 65,000,000 to about 2,500,000 years ago, after the Cretaceous Period and before the Quaternary Period. The name Tertiary was first used in 1760 for younger rocks that rest on the "Secondaries" or Mesozoic strata (from 225,000,000 to 65,000,000 years ago) in northern Italy. It is derived from the Latin *tertiarius,* meaning "belonging to the third part." In 1811 the deposits in the Paris Basin, and soon thereafter all the rocks younger than Mesozoic, were called Tertiary in western Europe.

Subdivision of Tertiary time The Tertiary faunas of western Europe that were known in the 19th century consisted mostly of mollusca of modern aspect. By 1830 those of the Paris Basin were being intensively studied and compared with those of other parts of Europe. Sir Charles Lyell proposed four subdivisions of the Tertiary. These were, from oldest to youngest: the Eocene, with its type deposits in the Paris Basin; the Miocene, with its type deposits, the "Faluns (shelly marls) of the Loire" of southwestern France; older Pliocene, with its type deposits, the "Subapennine formations" of northern Italy; and the newer Pliocene, with its type deposits, the strata in the Val di Noto of Sicily. The fauna of the Eocene was characterized by 3.5 percent of living species, the Miocene by slightly less than 18 percent, and the undifferentiated Pliocene (including both older and newer) by 49 percent. It also was noted that the fauna of the newer Pliocene included an immense preponderance of Recent (synonymous with Holocene Epoch—the last 10,000 years, approximately) species. The name Pleistocene was substituted for the newer Pliocene in 1839, and in 1846 it was applied to glacial deposits of post-Pliocene and pre-Recent age.

Lyell expressly provided for the recognition of intermediate divisions of Tertiary time. A study of the Tertiary deposits of the Mainz Basin of West Germany in 1854 led to the suggestion that the time interval between the Eocene and Miocene be termed the Oligocene. This was to include the Tongrian and Rupelian stages (Table 1) as well as strata that subsequently formed the basis of the Chattian Stage. In 1874 "Paleocene" was proposed for an interval characterized by a flora intermediate between that of the Cretaceous and that of the Eocene; the "Sands of Bracheux," "the Travertines of Sezanne," and the "Lignites and sandstones of Soissonais" (Suessonian) from the Paris Basin were cited as typical. The Paleocene as thus defined included strata now assigned to the Ypresian Stage, which is here accepted as basal Eocene. In 1846 the Danian Stage was proposed and was assigned to the Cretaceous on the basis of contained megafossils. In the last two decades, however, micropaleontologists have found that the planktonic foraminifera (floating, one-celled, marine organisms) of the Danian are more nearly related to those of the overlying Montian Stage of the Paleocene than to those of the underlying Maastrichtian; for this reason, the Danian is considered by some authorities as the earliest stage of the Tertiary.

The name Paleogene was proposed in 1856 for the three older Tertiary epochs, and Neogene for the two younger epochs, but this twofold division of the Tertiary has not been as widely used as the fivefold.

In 1948 the 18th International Geological Congress decided to place the base of the Pleistocene at the base of the marine strata of the Calabrian Stage of northern Italy, at the first appearance of northern or cool-water invertebrates. As thus defined, the base of the Pleistocene would fall within the Pliocene, according to original usage. There is much disagreement about the subdivisions and their time significance. Table 1 shows the most widely used subdivisions of the Tertiary Period and their diverse usage; recommended usages are starred.

This article treats Tertiary rock deposits, life-forms, and aspects of stratigraphic correlation of deposits. It also presents a synopsis of the paleogeography and paleoclimatology of Tertiary time. For information on previous and subsequent intervals of geological time, see CRETACEOUS PERIOD; PLEISTOCENE EPOCH; see also CENOZOIC ERA for an overview of Tertiary, Pleistocene, and Holocene events. Additional detail on relevant life-forms and stratigraphy is presented in the articles FOSSIL RECORD; STRATIGRAPHIC BOUNDARIES.

TERTIARY ROCK DEPOSITS

Distribution of deposits Within the continents Tertiary marine deposits are mostly found along continental margins (except in western Europe), along the Tethyan Seaway (see map), and in the Mississippi Valley of North America. Marine Tertiary deposits are known *in situ* in Antarctica only on Seymour Island in the Palmer Peninsula area, but marine fossils recently have been recorded from glacial erratics (ice-transported rocks) in the Ross Sea area.

In Europe, western Asia, and the Near East, the marginal seas and the various branches of Tethys expanded greatly at times during Early and Middle Tertiary time, and marine and brackish deposits are widespread in these regions. In most regions the Paleocene–Eocene seaways extended farther inland than they did later in the Tertiary. Deposits of Tertiary age also are widely exposed on the sea floor of all ocean basins. Nonmarine deposits of both sedimentary and volcanic origin are widespread in North America west of the Mississippi River, and in the Neogene extend westward almost to the coast. In South America, very thick nonmarine clastic sequences (conglomerates, sandstones, and shales) are known in the Andes Mountains and along their eastern front; these extend eastward for a considerable distance into the Amazon Basin. Nonmarine sediments are also widely distributed in the interior of Asia, and similar sequences are present in northeastern Africa.

Volcanism and orogenesis. Evidence of Tertiary volcanism is absent in western Europe and most of Africa, except in Northern Scotland and Ireland during the Early Tertiary; in central Germany and the Massif Central of France during the Oligocene; in Algeria during the Middle Tertiary; and in the rift zone of East Africa during the Middle and Upper Tertiary. It also is largely absent in Asia, except in the Caucasus during the Early and Middle Tertiary. The rim of the Pacific, from the Philippine Islands in the southwest to California in the southeast, except for a segment around the head of the Gulf of Alaska, was the site of much volcanism through the Tertiary. Extensive volcanism occurred, however, in the Outpourings of lava on land and beneath the sea Indonesian area after the middle Miocene. The Deccan Plateau of India was the site of extensive outpourings of lava at the onset of the Tertiary. In the Miocene, similar outpourings of basaltic rocks occurred over an extensive area of eastern Washington and Oregon, southern Idaho, and northeastern California. The northern Rocky Mountains of North America were the site of active volcanism during the Early Tertiary, but in the southern Rockies volcanism was more common during the Middle and Late Tertiary. In Central America, volcanic activity began near the end of the Oligocene and has continued to the present. In South America, volcanism is almost exclusively confined to the Andean Belt; most of it occurred during the Middle and Upper Tertiary. The North Island of New Zealand was also the site of much volcanic activity during the Middle and Upper Tertiary, but in Australia notable volcanic activity occurred only during the Early Tertiary, and was largely restricted to Queensland and adjacent areas of the continent. Within the Pacific Ocean Basin, the major island groups, such as the Hawaiian and Galápagos, basically are composed of volcanoes that rise from the sea floor. The ancestral Hawaiian Islands probably had their inception in Late Mesozoic time, whereas the Galápagos seem to date from the Miocene. The Caribbean area was the site of volcanism throughout the Tertiary, with the locus of activity shifting from time to time. Greenland and Iceland in the Atlantic Ocean were the site of much Cenozoic volcanism, whereas on

Table 1: Comparison of Some Tertiary Classification Schemes

										European stages
Pleistocene	original Pliocene of Lyell	Pleistocene	Pliocene	Pleistocene	Pleistocene	Pleistocene	Pleistocene*	Neogene	Pleist.	Calabrian
						Plio-Pleistocene				
Tertiary		Pliocene		Pliocene	Pliocene	Pliocene	Pliocene*		Neogene*	Plaisancian
						Mio-Pliocene				Tortonian
	Miocene of Lyell	Miocene	Miocene	Miocene	Miocene	Miocene	Miocene*			Langhian
			Miocene							Burdigalian
										Aquitanian
						Oligo-Miocene				Chattian
	Oligocene of Beyrich	Oligocene	Oligocene	Oligocene	Oligocene	Oligocene	Oligocene*	Paleogene	Paleogene*	Rupelian
						Eo-Oligocene				Lattorfian
	Eocene of Lyell	Eocene				Eocene	Eocene*			Bartonian
			Eocene	Eocene	Eocene					Lutetian
		Eocene				Paleocene-Eocene				Ypresian
	Paleocene of Schimper	Paleocene	Paleocene	Paleocene*	Paleocene	Paleocene	Paleocene			Thanetian
										Montian
Cretaceous						transition				Danian

*Indicates recommended usage.

Mountain building

the sea floor the Mid-Atlantic Ridge was the site of volcanic outpourings throughout the Tertiary.

In North America, the Laramide orogeny (mountain-building episode) that formed the Rocky Mountains began in the late Cretaceous and continued into the Eocene. Along the Pacific Coast, the Sierra Nevada and the Coast Ranges of British Columbia, which had been involved in a mid-Cretaceous orogeny, were the site of recurrent movement during Late Tertiary and Pleistocene time. The Andean Geosyncline (depositional trough) of South America was broken up by the late Cretaceous orogeny; activity was renewed near the end of the Miocene. Final uplift occurred during Pliocene and Pleistocene time.

Complex tectonic activity occurred in Asia and Europe in the Tethyan Sea area during the Tertiary. The main Alpine orogeny began in the Oligocene and continued throughout the Tertiary. The Apennines of Italy are the culmination of a series of movements that began in the Tyrrhenian Sea during the Oligocene and moved eastward until near the end of the Miocene. The last of the recurrent orogenies that affected the Pyrenees occurred in the late Eocene. On the south side of the Tethys, the coastal Atlas of North Africa underwent its major uplift in late Eocene time, but minor orogenic movements continued through most of the Tertiary. Along the Tethyan Belt in the Near East and India, tectonic activity began during the Eocene and continued recurrently throughout the Tertiary, with the seaway being disrupted at the end of the Oligocene. The most intensive Himalayan orogeny

occurred in the middle Miocene, but tectonic activity continued until the middle Pleistocene. In the Malaysian–Indonesian–Japanese region, major orogenic episodes occurred in the Miocene, and lesser episodes continued on into the Pleistocene. In New Zealand, the principal Cenozoic orogeny occurred during the Miocene and continued intermittently thereafter.

Sedimentary sequences. Compared to those of geosynclinal areas, the Tertiary rocks of the Paris Basin are relatively thin, are nearly horizontal, and often are highly fossiliferous. The sediments occur in a roughly oval area, about 125 by 225 kilometres (78 by 140 miles) in maximum dimensions, with Paris near the centre. They show marked lateral changes in facies (all aspects of a geological unit, including rock type and contained fauna), and, in consequence, the local stratigraphy is highly complex. The sequence has a maximum thickness of less than 300 metres (less than 1,000 feet) and is composed of sands, clays, marls, limestones, and gypsum, which reflect numerous alternations of marine, brackish, lacustrine, and terrestrial environments during their deposition. Approximately 50 stratigraphic units are commonly recognized in the interval from the beginning of the Paleocene through the Burdigalian, and about 25 of these comprise the restricted typical Eocene.

In contrast, the Tertiary deposits of the Gulf of Mexico embayment cover a much larger area, extending from Yucatan in the southwest to Florida in the southeast, a distance of around 3,000 kilometres (2,000 miles) along

Marine sediments of the Paris Basin and Gulf of Mexico

the present coastline. At its maximum, during the Paleocene, this embayment extended inland to southwestern North Dakota, a distance of about 2,000 kilometres (1,250 miles) from the present shoreline. In southwestern North Dakota the Cannonball Formation, with a maximum thickness of about 90 metres (300 feet), is marine, and although formerly referred to the Late Cretaceous, it is now known to correlate with part of the Midway Group of the Gulf Coast; it represents the maximum encroachment of the Tertiary seas in North America. Marine deposits of Tertiary age have been eroded from the intervening area between northwestern South Dakota and southern Illinois, but from this latter locality marine deposits continue southward and underlie the Gulf of Mexico. At the margin of the Gulf these sediments are estimated to be more than 12,000 metres (40,000 feet) thick and range in age from Paleocene to Pleistocene. Most of the exposed rocks are of Paleogene age, but as the present shoreline is approached, great thicknesses of Neogene sediments occur in deep wells and are suggested by geophysical data. The sediments vary from dominantly calcareous in the Florida area to arenaceous (sandy) in the west. Individual units may thin, pinch out, and disappear, and then recur; they are generally thin in the east and thick near the deltas of the Mississippi River and the Rio Grande. An immense number of local stratigraphic names are in use, but in the central region the outcropping Paleogene sediments are often assigned, in ascending order, to the Midway, Wilcox (or Sabine), Claiborne, Jackson, and Vicksburg stages. The overlying Neogene sediments, which are best known in the subsurface, may be assigned to the Chickasawhay, Anahuac, Napoleonville, Duck Lake, Clovelly, and Foley Stages.

In contrast to the preceding geosynclinal region, there was a series of local basins in the Utah–Colorado–Wyoming area of the Rocky Mountains in which nonmarine sediments were laid down. In northeastern Utah–southwestern Wyoming the Paleocene–Eocene is represented, from oldest to youngest, by: North Horn Formation, about 550 metres (1,800 feet) of sandstone, conglomerates, and shale of lacustrine and fluviatile origins; Flagstaff Limestone, 100 to 500 metres (330 to 1,600 feet) of limestone with minor thicknesses of sandstone and shale, of late Paleocene–lower Eocene age; the Colton Formation, 500 metres (1,600 feet) of sandstone, siltstone, and shale, of lower Eocene age; Green River Formation, 1,000 to 1,670 metres (3,300 to 5,480 feet) of lacustrine beds, mostly shales, of middle Eocene age; Uinta Formation, 500 to 600 metres of variegated shale with interbedded sandstone, of Upper Eocene Age; Duchesne River Formation, about 500 metres (1,600 feet) of fluvial sandstone, shale, and conglomerate, of latest Eocene or Oligocene age; Bishop Conglomerate, 30 metres (100 feet) of conglomerate that is unconformable on older formations (deposition was interrupted), of Oligocene or Miocene age. The North Horn, Flagstaff Limestone, and Colton Formations were formerly known as the Wasatch Formation or Group. The typical mammal-bearing beds of the North American Provincial Uintan and Duchesnean land mammal ages are in this sequence.

Deposits on seamounts   In the Pacific Ocean Basin numerous truncated seamounts known as guyots, now sunk below sea level, have been found. Guyots represent former volcanoes that rose or were built up from the sea floor, were truncated by wave action at sea level, and subsequently depressed below sea level. Marine sediments, representing various stages of the Tertiary, occur on the summits of many of the guyots. On some of these peaks, formation of coral limestones has kept pace with the sinking, and coral atolls have been formed. At Eniwetok Atoll in the Marshall Islands more than 1,400 metres (4,610 feet) of limestone was drilled before basalt was encountered. The sequence ranged in age from late Eocene to Recent (see CORAL ISLANDS, CORAL REEFS, AND ATOLLS).

In the last few years a number of wells have been drilled in the deep-sea floor. A well in the Equatorial Pacific at 0°28.9′ N and 133°13.7′ W penetrated 481 metres (1,578 feet) of calcareous ooze and chalk, eventually stopping in basalt. The oldest sediments were of late Eocene age.

TERTIARY LIFE

The biota of the Tertiary has a distinctly modern aspect. No major taxa except the belemnites and discoasters became extinct, although much evolution took place and minor lineages disappeared or evolved into others. Some early Tertiary species are closely similar to their living descendants, although because of modern refined taxonomic practices few if any Paleocene and Eocene organisms are now assigned to living species. In the sea, the "larger" foraminifera (nummulitids, discocyclinids, miogypsinids, lepidocyclinids, and so forth), the planktonic foraminifera, coccolithids, discoasterids, gastropods, and clypeastroid echinoids were evolving rapidly, but in other invertebrate groups evolution generally was not as marked. On land, the pulmonate gastropods and especially the mammals, underwent rapid evolution; some groups (pinnipeds and cetaceans) returned to the sea. Among the plants, the grasses appear in the Eocene, the Compositae in the Paleocene, and the Leguminosae are recorded in the early part of the late Cretaceous. All these plant families underwent rapid evolution, diversification, and dispersal during the Tertiary. Presumably the Orchidaceae (with no known fossil record), which are numerically one of the most diverse of living plant families, also arose in the Tertiary and had a similar history.

Evolution and distribution of foraminifera.   In the last two decades, detailed studies have shown that, during the Cenozoic, planktonic foraminifera (Superfamily Globigerinacea) evolved rapidly and were dispersed widely. As a result, they are excellent organisms to use for correlation of marine deposits. Data on the rate of evolution of Cenozoic planktonic foraminifera indicate that evolution does not proceed at a consistent rate, but that it may change markedly at any time during phyletic evolution. As a result, the duration of individual species may vary markedly. Conical members of the genus *Globorotalia* have stratigraphic ranges that vary from about 1,500,000 to 5,000,000 years per species. The average duration of species in different phyletic groups of this superfamily varies from 700,000 years in rapidly evolving lineages to 9,000,000 years in slowly evolving lineages.

Among the larger foraminifera, the genus *Nummulites* (which occurs in limestones used to build the Pyramids) presents a peculiar distribution pattern. In the Eurasian Tethyan Province it occurs throughout the middle and upper Paleocene, Eocene, and lower and middle Oligocene, but only a few nummulitids reached the New World. Their rarity in the Neotropical region is puzzling in view of current concepts of continental drift (*q.v.*). One of the notable trends in the nummulitids was an increase in size up to the middle Eocene, at which time individuals with a diameter of 150 millimetres (six inches) are known. In the Oligocene only small types are known. The Miogypsinids are an important group that range from the late Oligocene to the middle Miocene, generally showing an increase in complexity of the test (structural hard parts) by the addition of lateral chambers and changes in the arrangement of the embryonal apparatus and first subsequent chambers.

The extinct discoasters are minute (around ten microns) radiate skeletal remains of organisms that presumably were members of the oceanic nannoplankton. The skeletal unit is a single calcite crystal, in contrast to that of the coccoliths, which have a radiating fibrous structure. Discoasters appear in the Late Cretaceous and become extinct at about the Pliocene–Pleistocene boundary.

Other marine invertebrates.   Mollusca are the most conspicuous and diversified of Tertiary marine megafossils (in contrast to foraminifera and other microfossils). Among the various classes, the Gastropoda are the most diversified and evolved the most rapidly. Most of the early Tertiary genera are extinct, and most living species are assigned to genera that arose in the Middle Tertiary. Some genera, such as *Velates* and *Athleta*, are known only in the Paleocene and Eocene. The New World genus *Orthaulax* is found only in the late Oligocene and early Miocene. Others, such as *Pseudoliva* and *Rimella* (in a broad sense), are worldwide in distribution during the Pa-

Gastropods, pelecypods, and echinoderms

leocene–Eocene and later become restricted geographically. *Pseudoliva* lives only along the west coast of Africa, and *Rimella* lives only in the Indonesian area. It has been estimated that there are about 40,000 living species of gastropods in the marine environment. They were presumably as diverse throughout the Tertiary.

The Bivalvia (mollusca), or clams, are much less diversified than the gastropods, with only about 12,000 living marine species. Many of the Paleocene–Eocene species are assigned to extant genera, and relatively few new genera appeared during this interval. Some genera of the Pectinidae, such as *Lyropecten* and *Patinopecten*, evolved rapidly during the Tertiary and make good index fossils, particularly in the Neogene. In the Paleocene–Eocene, large-sized species of the genus *Venericardia* are common and evolved rapidly; they also make good index fossils.

Among the echinoderms, the order Clypeasteroida begins its rapid evolution and diversification in the middle Eocene. Two genera are known from the latest Cretaceous and 36 from the Miocene, but only 24 in the Recent fauna. About 75 genera are recognized in the Cenozoic, with a number of them, such as the sand dollars *Astrodapsis* and *Dendraster*, existing for periods of only 10,000,000 to 15,000,000 years, or less, during the Neogene, but yet undergoing much speciation. Five species in an evolutionary lineage can be recognized in the extinct genus *Scutellaster* during the Pliocene, spanning an interval of less than 5,000,000 years.

In the nonmarine environment, snails of the superorder Pulmonata diversified as much as all other gastropods. The first accepted records are of aquatic forms in the Middle Jurassic (about 170,000,000 years ago), whereas the purely terrestrial types appear in the Late Cretaceous (about 70,000,000 years ago). It is estimated that there are around 40,000 living species in the Recent fauna. It appears that most of this diversification followed the appearance of angiospermous plants in the mid-Cretaceous, and, by inference, largely within the Tertiary, even though their fossil record has not been well studied.

Vertebrates. In the terrestrial environment the most spectacular event of the Cenozoic has been the diversification and rise to dominance of the Mammalia. Nineteen families of marsupials are known in the Tertiary, with only one (Didelphidae) extending back into the Cretaceous. Among the placental mammals, 25 orders are recognized in the Tertiary, and only three originated in the Cretaceous. Inasmuch as there are about 4,400 living species, it is apparent that mammalian evolution has been very rapid. In many lineages there was a trend toward larger size. The early horse *Hyracotherium*, a browser, was about the size of a fox, but most of its descendants increased in size, leading up to horses the size of a mustang. While the legs were increasing in length, the ancestral four front toes and three hind toes were gradually being lost until only one remained, producing a more cursorial animal. Meanwhile, the cheek teeth were becoming higher crowned, giving a longer-lasting tooth, more suitable for grazing.

Among the carnivores, early members of the Felidae (cat family) are present in the lower Oligocene and lead up to the modern large cats. During this interval, marked enlargement of the upper canine tooth occurred at least three separate times, producing three unrelated groups of sabre-toothed cats, the last of which culminated in the Pleistocene *Smilodon*, well known from the tar pits of Rancho La Brea, California. In the Middle Tertiary one branch of the Carnivora adopted an aquatic habitat, producing the seals and sea lions. In the Early Tertiary one of the generalized creodonts entered the sea and gave rise to the whalelike zeuglodonts.

In contrast to the rapidly evolving groups of mammals, the Insectivora, which had appeared in the Cretaceous, were conservative and underwent little marked change during the Tertiary. A modern shrew resembles its Cretaceous ancestors.

The Primates diverged from the Insectivora during the latest Cretaceous and went on to give rise to such diverse types as the spider monkeys, the great apes, and man.

Recognizable early hominoids are known from sites in East Africa such as Rusinga Island, for which a radiometric (potassium–argon) date of 18,500,000 to 22,000,000 years has been established.

CORRELATION

The subdivisions of the Tertiary originally were based on percentages of living species in the different faunas (largely Mollusca) of western Europe. Early correlations were made by direct comparison with the faunas of the type areas in Europe, when in the same general faunal region, or by utilization of the percentage method when in different faunal regions. Because of the faunal isolation of the region, an independent set of percentages for the Indonesian region was proposed in 1919. In Europe, the need for improved means of correlation was recognized, and the concept of stages was introduced in 1842 for stratigraphic sequences recognized by a characteristic assemblage of fossils. The methodology was modified and improved, and it provides the basis for modern biostratigraphic correlation. Unfortunately, these methods did not come into extensive use on a worldwide basis until the last few decades.

Radiometric dating and foraminiferal zones. During the last three decades it has been widely recognized that the products of radioactive decay of the elements may be retained in certain minerals, and that by measurement of these products the age of formation of these minerals and the containing rocks may be calculated (see DATING, RELATIVE AND ABSOLUTE). The method utilizing the decay of potassium-40 to argon-40 has proved to be the most useful, and numerous dates are now available. During the same interval, it has been demonstrated that the Earth's magnetic field has undergone numerous reversals in the past, and that most rocks take on and retain the magnetic orientation of the Earth's field at the time of their formation (see ROCK MAGNETISM). With the development of techniques for measuring this original magnetization, a sequence (see Table 2) of geomagnetic reversals has been dated and built up for the later Mesozoic and Cenozoic. If an appropriate sequence of reversals is available, the age of the rock sequence can be determined.

In the last two decades it has been recognized that many marine planktonic organisms have evolved rapidly and are widely distributed geographically. In the late Mesozoic and Cenozoic eras the planktonic foraminifera, coccoliths, and discoasters are particularly useful, and a very refined worldwide zonation utilizing the foraminifera has been built up. For convenience the zones are numbered, from the oldest, P1, P2, and so forth, in the Paleogene and N1, N2, and so forth, in the Neogene. A chart comparing several different chronologies and possible correlations between them is shown in Table 2. Radiometric dates are used to control the vertical allocation of the units wherever possible. A considerable number of radiometric dates are tied into the planktonic foraminiferal zones. Other radiometric dates are tied into the sequence of North American land mammal ages. The planktonic foraminiferal zonation has been used as far as possible to establish equivalencies between the different schemes applicable to the marine environment.

Boundaries and chronologies. The base of the Saucesian Stage in California is about 22,500,000 years old. This horizon corresponds to the base of the planktonic foraminiferal zone N4 or the *Globigerinoides quadrilobatus primordius—Globorotalia kugleri* zone, which is also recognized at the base of the Aquitanian Stage in France. Inasmuch as the base of the Aquitanian Stage is currently accepted as the base of the Miocene, this also dates the Oligocene–Miocene boundary at 22,500,000 years before the present. The boundary between the Relizian and Saucesian stages is set at about 14,000,000 years ago. Because this horizon closely approximates the first appearance of the foraminiferan *Orbulina*, this gives a slightly younger age for this datum than previously accepted. The base of the Calabrian Stage in Northern Italy corresponds to the base of the planktonic foraminiferal zone N22, which has been determined by correlation with geomagnetic reversals to be about 1,860,000 years old.

Mammalian evolutionary change

Utility of planktonic foraminifera

The boundaries of the Tertiary

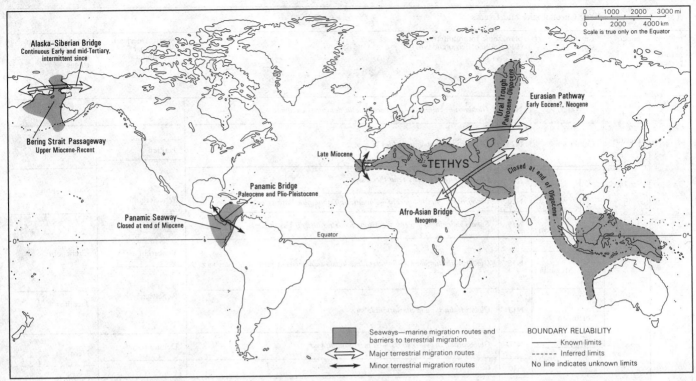

Principal Cenozoic migration routes and barriers.

By definition, this is the base of the Pleistocene. A radio-metric date of 64,800,000 years has been obtained for the base of the North American basal Paleocene land mammal age; this date is usually rounded out to 65,000,000 years and is used for the Cretaceous–Tertiary boundary.

Precise stratigraphic positions for the boundaries of the various Tertiary epochs were not specified by early workers, and as a result there has been much variation in usage (see Table 1). In recent years the International Geological Congress has specified that the base of the marine Calabrian Stage be taken as the Pliocene–Pleistocene boundary, and it has been recommended to them that the base of the Pliocene be accepted as the base of the Zanclian Stage in Italy, and that the base of the Miocene be placed at the base of the Aquitanian in southwestern France. The base of the Lattorfian is usually taken to mark the base of the Oligocene, as defined by Beyrich. Current usage usually places the base of the Eocene at the base of the Ypresian Stage of the Paris Basin, although the Ypresian was included in the original type Paleocene.

PALEOGEOGRAPHY AND PALEOCLIMATOLOGY

By the inception of the Tertiary, the continents had nearly attained their present positions, although current notions of continental drift and plate tectonics indicate that the Atlantic Ocean was still spreading, with the continents moving away from the Mid-Atlantic Ridge.

Land–sea distribution and continental movements. Some of the available data from the North Atlantic suggest that during the last 40,000,000 years the North American and African plates, two of the major segments of the Earth's crust that move above the mantle, have been rotating about a position south of Greenland near 52° N and 34° W, at a relatively uniform spreading rate of between one and 1.4 centimetres per year. A rate of 1.3 centimetres per year would result in 520 kilometres (325 miles) of opening between the two plates for this interval. If this rate prevailed throughout the Cenozoic, the total amount of Tertiary spreading would be about 845 kilometres (528 miles). Similar rates of spreading presumably prevailed between the North American and European plates. Northward movement of India is responsible for the closure of Tethys near the end of the Oligocene and the formation of the Himalayan Mountains. Australia and New Zealand were completing their northward movement during the Cenozoic. On the Pacific Coast of North

Rates of sea-floor spreading

America the formation of the Gulf of California is attributed by many to plate tectonics, as is the documented lateral displacement of 300 kilometres (189 miles) on the San Andreas Fault in the last 23,500,000 years.

The Mediterranean Sea is a remnant of the essentially east–west Tethyan Seaway (see map) that formerly separated Africa and India from the northern continents, and was broken up at the end of the Oligocene. An arm of it extended northward to the Arctic along the east side of the Ural Mountains throughout most of the Paleocene–Eocene–Oligocene, although there was a temporary retreat during the Eocene. This seaway effectively prevented migration of terrestrial mammals between Africa and Europe–Asia until the early Miocene. By Burdigalian time, proboscideans with an Early Tertiary African origin had migrated to Asia and western Europe. During the late Miocene the old portal to the Atlantic was closed and evaporites (mineral deposits formed by the evaporation of saline waters) were deposited throughout much of the Mediterranean. At the beginning of the Pliocene the present western portal opened.

In the North Pacific region there was no seaway through the Bering Strait region to the Arctic until near the end of the Miocene. This seaway was open for a short time and then closed again until near the end of the Pliocene. Thus, migration of terrestrial animals between Asia and America was possible throughout most of the Tertiary, and until late Pliocene marine organisms were not able to move from the Pacific to the Arctic to the North Atlantic or vice versa, except for a short interval in the late Miocene. In the Central American–northwest Colombian region there was a seaway, at times rather wide, that connected the Caribbean and Pacific oceans throughout the Tertiary until the end of the Miocene; one interval in the Paleocene is a possible exception. It was not until after this that a land bridge permitted free terrestrial migration between North and South America. As a result, the differences between the faunas of the Caribbean and Panamic (Central American) marine provinces did not arise until the Pliocene, and the pre-Pliocene marine faunas of these areas were part of a large unified biotic province that included the tropical Eastern Pacific and the tropical Western Atlantic–Caribbean regions.

Early Tertiary climates. Much evidence shows that during the Early Tertiary warm climates extended much farther poleward (see Table 2) than now. Reef corals

Table 2: Some Tertiary Chronologies and Events

million years before present	epochs	European stages		planktonic foraminiferal zones* (Blow, 1969; Berggren, 1969)		North American West Coast foraminiferal stages†	North American West Coast megafaunal stages
0	Holocene			N23	*Globigerina calida* ss—*Sphaeroidinella dehiscens excavata* ASZ		
	Pleistocene	Calabrian		N22	*Globorotalia truncatulinoides* ss PRZ	Hallian	
	Pliocene	Plaisancian	Astian	N21	*Globorotalia tosaensis tenuitheca* SRZ	Wheelerian	San Joaquin
				N20	*Globorotalia multicamerata*—*Pulleniatina obliquiloculata* ss PRZ		
			Zanclian	N19	*Sphaeroidinella dehiscens* ss—*Globoquadrina altispira* ss PRZ		
5			Messinian	N18	*Globorotalia tumida* ss—*Sphaeroidinellopsis subdehiscens paenedehiscens* PRZ	Venturian	Etchegoin
	Miocene	Tortonian		N17	*Globorotalia tumida plesiotumida* SRZ	Repettian	Jacalitos
10				N16	*Globorotalia acostaensis* ss—*G. merotumida* PRZ	Delmontian	Neroly
				N15	*Globorotalia continuosa* SRZ		Cierbo
		Langhian		N14	*Globigerina nepenthes*—*Globorotalia siakensis* CRZ	Mohnian	Briones
				N13	*Sphaeroidinellopsis subdehiscens* ss—*Globigerina druryi* PRZ		
				N12	*Globorotalia fohsi* PRZ	Luisian	
				N11	*Globorotalia praefohsi* SRZ		
				N10	*Globorotalia peripheroacuta* SRZ		
				N9	*Orbulina suturalis*—*Globorotalia peripheroronda* PRZ		
		Burdigalian		N8	*Globigerinoides sicanus*—*Globigerinatella insueta* PRZ	Relizian	
15				N7	*Globigerinatella insueta*—*Globigerinoides quadrilobatus trilobus* PRZ		Temblor
				N6	*Globigerinatella insueta*—*Globigerinita dissimilis* CRZ		
		Aquitanian		N5	*Globoquadrina dehiscens praedehiscens*—*G. dehiscens* ss PRZ	Saucesian	
20				N4	*Globigerinoides quadrilobatus primordius*—*Globorotalia kugleri* CRZ		
	Oligocene	Chattian		N3			Vaqueros
25				P22	*Globigerina angulisuturalis* PRZ		
				N2			
				P21	*Globigerina angulisuturalis*—*Globorotalia opima* ss CRZ	Zemorrian	
30				N1			Blakeley
				P20	*Globigerina ampliapertura* PRZ		
35		Rupelian		P19	*Globigerina sellii*—*Pseudohastigerina barbadoensis* CRZ		

Table 2: Some Tertiary Chronologies and Events (continued)

North American land mammal ages‡	New Zealand marine	Indonesia (letter stages)		South American land mammal stages	North American paleobotanical stages §	NW North American terrestrial climatic trend‖ sub-tropical ← cool temperate →	N American Pacific coast climatic trend¶ tropical ← temperate →	New Zealand marine climatic trend♀ Celsius 22° 20° 18° 16° 14° 12°	geomagnetic reversalsδ (black equals normal polarity)
									event number
Rancholabrean	Castlecliffian								1
Irvingtonian	Nukumaruan								2
Blancan	Waitotaran	h	2	Chapadmalalan	Clamgulchian				
	Opoitian		1	Montehermosan					3
Hemphillian	Kaipitean	g		Tunuyanian					4
									5
	Tongaporutuan			Huayquerian	Homerian				
Clarendonian	Waiauan	f	3						
	Lillburnian		2	Mesopotamian					
Barstovian	Clifdenian		1	Chasicoan					
	Altonian								
	Awamoan			Friasian					
	Hutchinsonian			Santacrucian					
Hemingfordian		e	5						
	Otaian			Colhuehuapian	Seldovian				6
Arikareean			4						
	Waitakian		3						
Whitneyan			2		unnamed				7
	Duntroonian		1						8
Orellan									9
		d		Deseadan					10
Chadronian	Whaingaroan				Kummerian				11
		c							12

Table 2: Some Tertiary Chronologies and Events (continued)

million years before present	epochs	European stages	planktonic foraminiferal zones* (Blow, 1969; Berggren, 1969)	North American West Coast foraminiferal stages†	North American West Coast megafaunal stages
35 —	Oligocene	Lattorfian	P18 *Globigerina tapuriensis* SRZ		
			P17 *Globigerina gortanii* ss—*Globorotalia centralis* PRZ	Zemorrian	Blakeley
	Eocene	Bartonian	P16 *Cribrohantkenina inflata* TRZ		Lincoln
40 —				Refugian	
			P15 *Globigerapsis mexicana* PRZ		Keasey
				Narizian	
45 —		Lutetian	P14 *Truncorotaloides rohri*—*Globigerinita howei* PRZ		Tejon
			P13 *Orbulinoides beckmanni* TRZ		
			P12 *Globorotalia lehneri* PRZ	Ulatisian	transition
			P11 *Globigerapsis kugleri* PRZ		- - - - -
			P10 *Hantkenina aragonensis* PRZ		Domengine
50 —		Ypresian	P9 *Acarinina densa* PRZ	Penutian	Capay
			P8 *Globorotalia aragonensis* PRZ		
			P7 *Globorotalia formosa* PRZ		
			P6 b *Globorotalia subbotinae*—*Pseudohastigerina wilcoxensis* CRZ	Bulitian	Meganos
			P6 a *Globorotalia velascoensis*—*G. subbotinae* CRZ		
55 —	Paleocene	Thanetian	P5 *Globorotalia velascoensis* PRZ		
			P4 *Globorotalia pseudomenardii* TRZ		
			P3 *Globorotalia pusilla*—*G. angulata* CRZ	Ynezian	Martinez
60 —		Montian	P2 *Globorotalia uncinata*—*G. spiralis* CRZ		
		Danian	P1 *Globoconusa daubjergensis*—*Globorotalia pseudobulloides* CRZ — c *Globorotalia compressa*—*G. inconstans*—*G. trinidadensis*		
			b *Globigerina triloculinoides*	Cheneyan ("Danian")	
			a *Globorotalia pseudobulloides*		
65 —	Cretaceous	Maestrichtian	*Globotruncanella mayaroensis* TRZ		
			- - - - -		
			Globotruncana gansseri PRZ		
70 —					

*ASZ = Assemblage Zone; CRZ = Concurrent Range Zone; PRZ = Partial Range Zone; SRZ = Consecutive Range Zone; TRZ = Total Range Zone. †K-A radiometric dates from Turner, 1970. ‡K-A radiometric dates from Evernden *et al.*, 1964. §Wolfe 1966, 1968. ‖Wolfe and Hopkins, 1967.

Table 2: Some Tertiary Chronologies and Events (continued)

North American land mammal ages[‡]	New Zealand marine	Indonesia (letter stages)	South American land mammal stages	North American paleobotanical stages[§]	NW North American terrestrial climatic trend[‖] sub-tropical ← cool temperate →	N American Pacific coast climatic trend[¶] tropical ← temperate →	New Zealand marine climatic trend[♀] Celsius 22° 20° 18° 16° 14° 12°	geomagnetic reversals[δ] (black equals normal polarity)
Chadronian	Whaingaroan	c	Deseadan					event number
Duchesnean		2	Divisaderan	Kummerian				13
	Runangan							14
								15
Uintan		b						16
								17
	Kaiatan	1	Mustersan	Ravenian				18
	Bortonian							19
Bridgerian	Porangan	2		Fultonian				20
	Heretaungan			Franklinian				
Wasatchian	Mangaorapan	a	Casamayoran					
	Waipawan	1						21
Tiffanian			Riochican					22
Torrejonian	Teurian							23
								24
Puercan								25
								26
								27

[¶]Modified from Durham, 1950; Addicott, 1969.   [♀]Devereaux, 1967.   [δ]Hairtzler *et al.*, 1968.
Compiled by J. W. Durham, January 1970.

and tropical molluscs occur at 48° N on the Pacific Coast of North America, and ecologically similar faunas occur in the correlative beds of the Paris Basin. On land, palms and similar warmth-requiring plants grew in southern Alaska, Washington, and western Europe during the Paleocene–Eocene. In the Northern Hemisphere there was a slow climatic deterioration until the middle Miocene, then a short interval of warming in middle latitudes, followed by a climatic deterioration until the onset of continental glaciation in middle latitudes in the Pleistocene. It is worth noting, however, that there is clear evidence of local glaciation at sea level in the Gulf of Alaska (60° N latitude) in the Miocene, and continental glaciation prevailed in Antarctica during much, if not all, of the Cenozoic. Oxygen isotope ratios from marine shells indicate that there was a general warming in southern Australia until the Oligocene, followed by a gradual cooling from the Miocene on. This Early Tertiary warming trend in Australia may be correlated with the northward drift of the continent into lower latitudes. Similar data for the oceans suggest that deep-sea temperatures in the Pacific were 8° to 10° C warmer in the Eocene–Oligocene than they are today.

Effect of climatic changes on faunas

The wider distribution of warm climates, combined with the existence of the Tethyan Seaway and the Panamic Passageway, resulted in much more cosmopolitan marine faunas during the Early Tertiary. Subsequent breakup of Tethys and closure of the Panamic Passageway, together with a more restricted tropical zone, combined to produce the Late Cenozoic provinciality of marine faunas. On land, the barriers presented by the Tethyan Sea produced largely endemic mammalian faunas in Africa, western Europe, and the Asia–North American area in the Early Tertiary. Once Tethys was broken up, the African–western Europe–Asian areas lost much of the faunal provinciality that had characterized them previously. Meanwhile, the isolation of South America and Australia permitted the development of their peculiar Tertiary mammal faunas, and it was not until the Pliocene that migration of North American mammals into South America caused the extinction of many of its endemic mammals.

BIBLIOGRAPHY. The literature on the Tertiary Period tends to be both diverse and specialized. For general coverage of geology, stratigraphy, and paleontology, the interested reader should consult the following works: B.M. FUNNEL, "The Tertiary Period," in W.B. HARLAND et al. (eds.), Phanerozoic Time Scale, pp. 179–191 (1964); MAURICE GIGNOUX, Géologie stratigraphique, 4th ed. (1950; Eng. trans., Stratigraphic Geology, 1955); and W.B. HARLAND et al (eds.), The Fossil Record (1967). Important papers on Tertiary climates and foraminiferal zonation include: W.O. ADDICOTT, "Tertiary Climatic Change in the Marginal Northeastern Pacific Ocean," Science, 165:583–586 (1969); W.A. BERGGREN, "Cenozoic Chronostratigraphy, Planktonic Foraminiferal Zonation and the Radiometric Time Scale," Nature, 224:1072–1075 (1969); W.H. BLOW, "Late Middle Eocene to Recent Planktonic Foraminiferal Biostratigraphy," Proceedings First International Conference on Planktonic Microfossils," 1:199–421 (1969); J.F. EVERNDEN et al., "Potassium-Argon Dates and Cenozoic Mammalian Chronology of North America," Am. J. Sci., 262:145–198 (1964); D.L. TURNER, "Potassium-Argon Dating of Pacific Coast Miocene Foraminiferal Stages," Spec. Pap. Geol. Soc. Am., 124:91–129 (1970); J.A. WOLFE and D.M. HOPKINS, "Climatic Changes Recorded by Tertiary Land Floras in Northwestern North America," in Tertiary Correlation and Climatic Changes in the Pacific (Eleventh Pacific Science Congress, Tokyo, 1966), pp. 67–76 (1967); and M.G. WILMARTH, "Geologic Time Classification of United States Geological Survey Compared with Other Classifications," Bull. U.S. Geol. Surv., no. 769 (1925).

(J.W.Du.)

Tertullian

Tertullian (Quintus Septimius Florens Tertullianus), an early Christian author and polemicist, helped to establish Latin—rather than Greek, which was the most widely used language at that time—as an ecclesiastical language and as a vehicle for Christian thought in the West. He coined many new theological words and phrases and gave currency to those already in use, thus becoming a signifi-

cant thinker in forging and fixing the vocabulary and thought structure of Western Christianity for the next 1,000 years. Because he was a moralist rather than a philosopher by temperament—which probably precipitated his famous question, "What has Athens to do with Jerusalem?"—Tertullian's practical and legal bent of mind expressed what would later be taken as the unique genius of Latin Christianity.

The life of Tertullian is based almost wholly on information written by men living over a century after him and from obscure references in his own works. On this basis a general outline of his life has been constructed, but most of the details have been continually disputed by modern scholars.

Education and conversion

Tertullian was born in Carthage in the Roman province of Africa, present Tunisia, a little over 100 years after the beginning of Christianity; i.e., approximately AD 155–160. Carthage at that time was second only to Rome as a cultural and educational centre in the West, and Tertullian received an exceptional education in grammar, rhetoric, literature, philosophy, and law. Little is known of his early life; in fact, most of the details of his life are unknown and disputed. His parents were pagan, and his father may have been a centurion (i.e., a noncommissioned officer) in an African-based legion assigned to the governor of the province. After completing his education in Carthage, he went to Rome, probably in his late teens or early 20s, to study further and perhaps begin work as a lawyer. He is most likely not the jurist Tertullian mentioned in the Digest, a collection of Roman legal opinion compiled under the aegis of the 6th-century Byzantine (Eastern Roman) emperor Justinian, though this is disputed.

While in Rome, he became interested in the Christian movement, but not until he returned to Carthage toward the end of the 2nd century was he converted to the Christian faith. He left no account of his conversion experience, but from his early works, Ad martyras ("To the Martyrs"), Ad nationes ("To the Nations"), and Apologeticum ("Defense"), he indicated that he was impressed by certain Christian attitudes and beliefs: the courage and determination of martyrs, moral rigourism, and an uncompromising belief in one God. By the end of the 2nd century the church in Carthage had become large, firmly established, and well organized and was rapidly becoming a powerful force in North Africa. By the year 225 there were approximately 70 bishops in Numidia and Proconsularis, the two provinces of Roman Africa. Tertullian emerged as a leading member of the African church, devoting his talents as a teacher in instructing the unbaptized seekers and the faithful and as a literary defender (apologist) of Christian beliefs and practices. According to Jerome, a 4th-century biblical scholar, Tertullian was ordained a priest. This view, however, has been challenged by some modern scholars.

Literary activities

During the next 20 to 25 years—i.e., from his early 40s to mid-60s—Tertullian devoted himself almost entirely to literary pursuits. Developing an original and unprecedented Latin style, the fiery and tempestuous Tertullian became a lively and pungent propagandist though not the most profound writer in Christian antiquity. His works abound with arresting and memorable phrases, ingenious aphorisms, bold and ironic puns, wit, sarcasm, countless words of his own coinage, and a constant stream of invectives against his opponents. Yet, he could be gentle and sensitive, as in a treatise to his wife (Ad uxorem), and he could be self-critical and reflective, as in his treatise on patience (De patientia), a virtue that he admitted was conspicuously absent in his life.

As a historical personage Tertullian is known less for what he did than for what he wrote. The range of his interests and the vigour with which he pursued them, however, encouraged other Christians to explore previously uninvestigated areas of life and thought. Like his contemporaries, he wrote works in defense of the faith (e.g., Apologeticum) and treatises on theological problems against specific opponents: Adversus Marcionem ("Against Marcion," an Anatolian heretic who believed that the world was created by the evil god of the Jews),

Adversus Hermogenem ("Against Hermogenes," a Carthaginian painter who claimed that God created the world out of pre-existing matter), *Adversus Valentinianos* ("Against Valentinus," an Alexandrian Gnostic, or religious dualist), and *De resurrectione carnis* ("Concerning the Resurrection of the Flesh"). He also wrote the first Christian book on Baptism (*De Baptismo*), a book on the Christian doctrine of man (*De anima* ["Concerning the Soul"]), essays on prayer and devotion (*De oratione* ["Concerning Prayer"]), and a treatise directed against all heresy (*De praescriptione Haereticorum* ["Concerning the Prescription of Heretics"]). In addition to apologetical and polemical works, he addressed himself to a whole range of moral and practical problems on issues facing Christians of his day: what is appropriate dress, the wearing of cosmetics (*De cultu feminarum* ["Concerning the Cult of Femininity"]), service in the military (*De corona* ["Concerning the Crown"—a military decoration]), whether one should flee under persecution (*De fuga in persecutione* ["Concerning Flight in Persecution"]), on marriage and remarriage (*De exhortatione castitatis* ["Concerning the Exhortation to Chastity"]; *De monogamia* ["Concerning Monogamy"]), on the arts, theatre, and civic festivals (*De spectaculis* ["Concerning Spectacles"]; *De idololatria* ["Concerning Idolatry"]), on repentance after Baptism (*De poenitentia* ["Concerning Repentance"]), and others.

Tertullian is usually considered the outstanding exponent of the outlook that Christianity must stand uncompromisingly against its surrounding culture. Recent scholarship has tended to qualify this interpretation, however. Like most educated Christians of his day, he recognized and appreciated the values of the Greco-Roman culture, discriminating between those he could accept and those he had to reject.

Tertullian as a Montanist Sometime before 210 Tertullian left the orthodox church to join a new prophetic sectarian movement known as Montanism (founded by the 2nd-century Phrygian prophet Montanus), which had spread from Asia Minor to Africa. His own dissatisfaction with the laxity of contemporary Christians was congenial with the Montanist message of the imminent end of the world combined with a stringent and demanding moralism. Montanism stood in judgment on any compromise with the ways of the world, and Tertullian gave himself fully to the defense of the new movement as its most articulate spokesman. Even the Montanists, however, were not rigorous enough for Tertullian. He eventually broke with them to found his own sect, a group that existed until the 5th century in Africa. According to tradition, he lived to be an old man. His last writings date from approximately 220, but the date of his death is unknown.

In antiquity most Christians never forgave him for his apostasy (rejection of his earlier faith) to Montanism. Later Christian writers mention him only infrequently, and then mostly unfavourably. Somewhat grudgingly, however, they acknowledged his literary gifts and acute intelligence. Modern scholars, however, do not share this earlier view. In the 19th and 20th centuries Tertullian has been widely read and studied and is considered one of the formative figures in the development of Christian life and thought in the West.

BIBLIOGRAPHY. For a complete listing of Tertullian's works, see JOHANNES QUASTEN, *Patrology*, vol. 2, pp. 246–319 (1953), with extensive bibliography. Editions of his work appear in *Corpus scriptorum ecclesiasticorum Latinorum*, vol. 20 (1890), and *Corpus Christianorum*, 2 vol. (1953–54), the latter with bibliography. English translations of all his works are in the "Ante-Nicene Fathers," vol. 3 and 4 (1869–70, reprinted 1957). Modern English translations of individual treatises are by ERNEST EVANS, WILLIAM P. LE SAINT, and others in the various series of translations of the Fathers. There is no modern critical biography. For continuing bibliography, see the annual listing in WILHELM SCHNEEMELCHER, *Bibliographia Patristica*. For a recent study with an up-to-date bibliography of Tertullian that considers anew the evidence of his life and the chronology of his writings, disputing the opinions of many modern scholars, see TIMOTHY D. BARNES, *Tertullian: A Historical and Literary Study* (1971).

(Ro.W.)

Tesla, Nikola

Nikola Tesla, who discovered the rotating magnetic field, which is the basis of practically all alternating-current machinery, has been called the genius who ushered in the power age.

Tesla was born on July 9/10, 1856, in Smiljan, Croatia (Yugoslavia), of a family of Serbian origin. His father was an Orthodox priest; his mother was unschooled but highly intelligent. A dreamer with a poetic touch, as he matured, Tesla added to these earlier qualities those of self-discipline and a desire for precision.

Culver Pictures

Tesla.

Training for an engineering career, he attended the Technical University at Graz, Austria, and the University of Prague. At Graz he first saw the Gramme dynamo, which operated as a generator and, when reversed, became an electric motor (see ELECTRIC MOTOR); and he conceived a way to use alternating current to advantage. Later, at Budapest, he visualized the principle of the rotating magnetic field and developed plans for an induction motor, that would become his first step toward the successful utilization of alternating current. In 1882 Tesla went to work in Paris for the Continental Edison Company, and while on assignment to Strassburg in 1883, he constructed, in after-work hours, his first induction motor. Tesla sailed for America in 1884, arriving in New York with four cents in his pocket, a few of his own poems, and calculations for a flying machine. He first found employment with Thomas Edison, but the two inventors were far apart in background and methods, and their separation was inevitable.

In May 1885, George Westinghouse, head of the Westinghouse Electric Company in Pittsburgh, bought the patent rights to Tesla's polyphase system of alternating-current dynamos, transformers, and motors. The transaction precipitated a titanic power struggle between Edison's direct-current systems and the Tesla-Westinghouse alternating-current approach, which eventually won out.

Tesla soon established his own laboratory, where his inventive mind could be given free rein. He experimented with shadowgraphs similar to those that later were to be used by Wilhelm Röntgen when he discovered X-rays in 1895. Tesla's countless experiments included work on a carbon button lamp, on the power of electrical resonance, and on various types of lighting. **Tesla's laboratory experiments**

Tesla gave exhibitions in his laboratory in which he lighted lamps without wires by allowing electricity to flow through his body, to allay fears of alternating current. He was often invited to lecture at home and abroad.

The Tesla coil, which he invented in 1891, is widely used today in radio and television sets and other electronic equipment. That year also marked the date of Tesla's United States citizenship.

Westinghouse used Tesla's system to light the World Columbian Exposition at Chicago in 1893. His success was a factor in winning him the contract to install the first power machinery at Niagara Falls, which bore Tesla's name and patent numbers. The project carried power to Buffalo by 1896.

In 1898 Tesla announced his invention of a teleautomatic boat guided by remote control. When skepticism was voiced, Tesla proved his claims for it before a crowd in Madison Square Garden.

In Colorado Springs, where he stayed from May 1899 until early 1900, Tesla made what he regarded as his most important discovery—terrestrial stationary waves. By this discovery he proved that the earth could be used as a conductor and would be as responsive as a tuning fork to electrical vibrations of a certain pitch. He also lighted 200 lamps without wires from a distance of 25 miles (40 kilometres) and created man-made lightning, producing flashes measuring 135 feet (41 metres). At one time he was certain he had received signals from another planet in his Colorado laboratory, a claim that was met with derision in some scientific journals.

Returning to New York in 1900, Tesla began construction on Long Island of a wireless world broadcasting tower, with $150,000 capital from the U.S. financier J. Pierpont Morgan. Tesla claimed he secured the loan by assigning 51 percent of his patent rights of telephony and telegraphy to Morgan. He expected to provide worldwide communication and to furnish facilities for sending pictures, messages, weather warnings, and stock reports. The project was abandoned because of a financial panic, labour troubles, and Morgan's withdrawal of support. It was Tesla's greatest defeat.

Tesla's work shifted to turbines and other projects. Because of a lack of funds, his ideas remained in his notebooks, which are still examined by engineers for unexploited clues. In 1915 he was severely disappointed when a report that he and Edison were to share the Nobel Prize proved erroneous. Tesla was the recipient of the Edison Medal in 1917, the highest honour that the American Institute of Electrical Engineers could bestow.

Tesla allowed himself only a few close friends. Among them were the writers Robert Underwood Johnson, Mark Twain, and Francis Marion Crawford. He was quite impractical in financial matters. An eccentric, driven by compulsions and a progressive germ phobia, Tesla had a way of intuitively sensing hidden scientific secrets and employing his inventive talent to prove his hypotheses. He was a godsend to reporters who sought sensational copy, but a problem to editors who were uncertain how seriously his futuristic prophecies should be regarded. Caustic criticism greeted his speculations concerning communication with other planets, his assertions that he could split the earth like an apple, and his claim to having invented a death ray capable of destroying 10,000 airplanes, 250 miles (400 kilometres) distant.

Criticism of Tesla's prophecies

Tesla demanded much of his employees but inspired their loyalty. Though he admired intellectual and beautiful women, he had no time to become involved.

Tesla died on January 7, 1943. The Custodian of Alien Property impounded his trunks, which held his papers, his diplomas and other honours, his letters, and his laboratory notes. These were eventually inherited by Tesla's nephew, Sava Kosanovich, and later housed in the Nikola Tesla Museum, Belgrade, Yugoslavia. Hundreds filed into New York City's Cathedral of St. John the Divine for his funeral services, and a flood of messages acknowledged the loss of a great genius. Three Nobel Prize recipients addressed their tribute to: ". . . one of the outstanding intellects of the world who paved the way for many of the technological developments of modern times."

BIBLIOGRAPHY. INEZ HUNT and WANETTA W. DRAPER, *Lightning in His Hand: The Life Story of Nikola Tesla* (1964), is a complete, authoritative, nontechnical biography. NIKOLA TESLA MUSEUM, *Nikola Tesla 1856–1943: Lectures, Patents, Articles* (1956), contains authentic reprints, diagrams, lectures, and considerable detailed information. NIKOLA TESLA, *Experiments with Alternate Currents of High Potential and High Frequency* (1904), furnishes Tesla's own story of his Colorado experiments.

(I.W.H.)

Tetraodontiformes

The order Tetraodontiformes is a group of primarily tropical marine fishes that evolved from the Perciformes (the typical advanced spiny-rayed fishes) during the Eocene Period of the Cenozoic Era, about 50,000,000 years ago. The approximately 320 species of modern tetraodontiforms are notable for a high degree of diversity in anatomical structure and way of life. The great diversity evident among the 11 families of the order is also seen within some families, but not in others. Members of the deepwater, bottom-dwelling Triacanthodidae, the most primitive family, for example, range from relatively normal configurations to weirdly specialized forms with extremely long tubular snouts; the shallow-water members of the Triacanthidae, closely related and derived from the Triacanthodidae, are of rather uniform configuration. Likewise, the balistids are rather uniform in body plan; but monacanthids, which evidently evolved from them, include a series of species ranging from the normal to the exceedingly elongated and highly specialized.

General features. The tetraodontiforms make up about 5 percent of the tropical marine fishes of the world. Most species range in size from about eight to 60 centimetres (three to 24 inches) in length, but one ocean sunfish reaches more than three metres (11 feet). They are often strikingly patterned or gaudily coloured. With the exception of the relatively deepwater Triacanthodidae and Triodontidae, the members of this order are usually found in waters less than about 65 metres (200 feet) in depth and are especially prominent around coral or rocky reefs and on open sand and grass flats.

Importance to man. Many species, especially of puffer fishes (Tetraodontidae), have poisonous flesh, at least during certain seasons of the year, but most of the highly poisonous substance (tetraodontoxin) responsible for the numerous annual fatalities in Indo-Pacific regions is contained in the viscera. The flesh of the poisonous species can be safely eaten only when the freshly caught specimen has been carefully cleaned and washed in the exacting manner of fugu (or puffer fish) chefs in Japan. But the majority of tetraodontiforms are palatable, and, in numerous tropical regions, the flesh of various triggerfishes and trunkfishes is highly esteemed. Other than as food in tropical coastal areas, man makes little direct use of tetraodontiforms, except for the dried bodies of the hard-cased boxfishes and the spine-studded, inflated puffers as curios. In fact, the order Tetraodontiformes contains so many strangely specialized species that the group has intrigued mankind from early times; a 1st-century Roman author, Pliny the Younger, for example, discussed puffer fishes and ocean sunfishes in his *Naturalis Historiae*. While most adult tetraodontiforms have thick, spiny skins or other defensive mechanisms that protect them from most predacious fishes, the young, relatively defenseless stages are eaten in great quantities by certain game fishes—dolphin, marlin and other billfishes, tunas, and various jacks.

Poisonous flesh

Natural history. *Feeding habits.* As one would suspect from their usually well-developed and massive dentition, often with the teeth fused together in a parrotlike beak, most tetraodontiforms feed on hard-shelled crustaceans, mollusks, and echinoderms. But some, with massive, crushing jaws and teeth, such as the ocean sunfishes, often feed extensively on such soft-bodied invertebrates as jellyfishes (medusae). Some, such as boxfishes, blow a jet of water out of their mouths onto sand bottoms to expose burrowing invertebrates; others (such as some triggerfishes) specialize in eating spiny sea urchins or even clams and oysters. A few species, especially the long-snouted Triacanthodidae, have reduced or even rudimentary teeth, some apparently feeding on the scales of other bottom fishes. Other species probably feed on soft-bodied invertebrates, probing with the snout into holes in the bottom or into recesses in outcroppings to obtain food unavailable to less specialized fishes. Although many species have specialized feeding habits, the order as a whole can be considered as comprised of opportunistic predators on invertebrates.

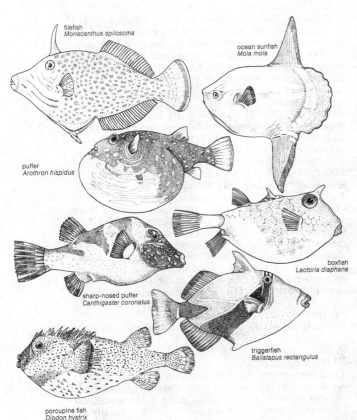

filefish
Monacanthus spilosoma

ocean sunfish
Mola mola

puffer
Arothron hispidus

boxfish
Lactoria diaphana

sharp-nosed puffer
Canthigaster coronatus

triggerfish
Balistapus rectangulus

porcupine fish
Diodon hystrix

Body plans of representative tetraodontiform fishes.
From Spencer W. Tinker, *Hawaiian Fishes* (1944)

Locomotion. Most tetraodontiforms swim by the rather unusual method of rapid undulations or complex scullings of the soft dorsal and anal fins (in the midline of the back and underside, respectively); the powerful caudal fin (except in the Molidae) is reserved for rapid bursts of speed. The paired pectoral fins (just behind the gills) are in an almost constant state of rapid vibration, which gives a delicacy of control to their movements that is unusual even among fishes.

Activity cycle. Those tetraodontiforms for which data are available are diurnal, feeding or otherwise active during daylight but quiescent at night, often retiring to holes or crevices in coral or rocky reefs to sleep. When disturbed during the day, as by a potential predator, some species take rapid flight; others dive into reef crevices. Other species avoid the attention of predators by remarkable colorations or patternings that permit them to blend into the environment, which may be anything from a coral reef to a bed of bottom sea grass. One relatively defenseless species (a filefish), moreover, is an excellent mimic in body form and bright coloration of a spiny-skinned, inflatable, and perhaps poisonous puffer.

Form and function. The Tetraodontiformes are distinguished externally by a small gill opening restricted to a relatively short slit on the side of the head and a small mouth, usually equipped with massive teeth. The scales of the body are typically highly modified into overlapping (in triacanthoids and balistoids) and even sutured (in ostraciontoids) plates, or into sharp, projecting spines (in tetraodontoids and diodontoids); in some cases, the skin itself may be thickened and hardened by deep layers of connective tissues (molids). There are no anal fin spines, and the dorsal fin spines are either absent or present only in reduced number (never more than six). The pelvic fin, which in the perciforms has one spine and five soft rays, in tetraodontiforms is either absent or reduced to no more than one spine and two small soft rays. The skeleton of tetraodontiforms is notable for a reduced number of bones, a number of the separate bony elements of the ancestral perciforms having been lost through the processes of reduction, consolidation, fusion, or failure to develop. The hallmark of the evolution and diversification of the

Fin and skeletal features

tetraodontiforms, in fact, has been the reductive tendencies in some parts—number of skeletal elements, number of fin spines, size of mouth and gill opening, and number of teeth—with the simultaneous elaborative tendencies in other systems—scale and skin development, inflation apparatus, size of teeth and fusion with jawbones, and poisonous flesh.

Classification. *Annotated classification.* The Tetraodontiformes are classified as follows, with only the most obvious external differences that distinguish the groups mentioned.

ORDER TETRAODONTIFORMES (PLECTOGNATHI)
Small mouth and gill openings; reduced dorsal and pelvic fin spines; no anal fin spines; skin usually tough or spiny.
Suborder Balistoidei (Sclerodermi)
Teeth separate, discrete, individual units.
Superfamily Triacanthoidea

Six dorsal spines and a large pelvic spine.

Family Triacanthodidae (spikefishes). The most primitive members of the order; deepwater species with a truncated or rounded tail; deep caudal peduncle; nonstreamlined body; soft dorsal and anal fins of about same length along their bases; Indo-Pacific and Caribbean.

Family Triacanthidae (triple spines). Shallow-water derivatives of the spikefishes; deeply forked caudal fin; slender caudal peduncle (the region between the end of the anal fin and the front of the tail); relatively streamlined body for rapid swimming; soft dorsal fin base much longer than anal fin base; Indo-Pacific.
Superfamily Balistoidea

Two or 3 dorsal spines, the 2nd spine serving to lock the 1st in an erected position; pelvic spine rudimentary or absent.
Family Balistidae (triggerfishes). Three dorsal spines; 8 outer teeth in each jaw; worldwide.
Family Monacanthidae (filefishes). Two dorsal spines; 6 or fewer outer teeth in each jaw; worldwide.
Superfamily Ostraciontoidea

No dorsal spines, body encased in a turtle-like cuirass (carapace) of sutured, platelike scales.

Family Aracanidae (keeled boxfishes). Carapace open behind the dorsal and anal fins and bearing a ventral keel; usually in deeper water than the ostraciontids; Indo-Pacific.

Family Ostraciontidae (boxfishes, trunkfishes, cowfishes). Carapace closed behind anal and usually behind dorsal fin, no ventral keel; worldwide.
Suborder Tetradontoidei (Gymnodontes)
Teeth more or less fused to the jawbones, forming a parrot-like beak.
Superfamily Triodontoidea

Three tooth plates, 2 in upper and 1 in lower jaw.

Family Triodontidae (pursefish). Most primitive member of the suborder, the only species to retain even the pelvic bone of the pelvic fin apparatus (completely lost by all other members of suborder); 1 species; deep water; Indo-Pacific.
Superfamily Tetraodontoidea

Four tooth plates, 2 in each jaw; the skin bearing small erectile spines.

Family Tetraodontidae (puffer fishes). A large number of species, differing from the sharp-nosed puffers mainly in osteological structure, but always having a prominent nasal apparatus; worldwide.

Family Canthigasteridae (sharp-nosed puffer fishes). Single, inconspicuous nostril on each side of head; snout more laterally compressed than in the tetraodontids; worldwide.
Superfamily Diodontoidea

Two tooth plates, 1 in each jaw; the skin bearing huge spines; caudal fin normal.

Family Diodontidae (porcupine fishes and burrfishes). Characteristics of superfamily. Spines erectile (porcupine fishes) or fixed (burrfishes); worldwide.
Superfamily Moloidea

Two tooth plates, 1 in each jaw. Skin relatively smooth but often exceptionally thick; caudal fin highly modified or absent.

Family Molidae (ocean sunfishes). Three species, 2 of which reach enormous size, 1 up to 3.3 metres (11 feet) in length and 1,900 kilograms (4,000 pounds) in weight; worldwide.

Critical appraisal. The classification of the order is still in a state of flux, and some authorities recognize as families only those listed above as superfamilies. More important, the ostraciontoids are often recognized as a third suborder of Tetraodontiformes rather than, as above, a superfamily of the suborder Balistoidei. Only recently has the ordinal term Tetraodontiformes come into use; the group still is often called the Plectognathi and its two suborders the Sclerodermi and Gymnodontes.

BIBLIOGRAPHY. JAMES E. BOLHKE and CHARLES C.G. CHAPLIN, *Fishes of the Bahamas and Adjacent Tropical Waters* (1968), includes an excellent combination of scientific and popular accounts of the Caribbean tetraodontiforms, with all species well illustrated. BRUCE W. HALSTEAD, *Poisonous and Venomous Marine Animals of the World,* vol. 2, *Vertebrates* (1967), contains a comprehensive review of the poisonous properties of the tetraodontiforms, with numerous illustrations of poisonous species. JAMES C. TYLER, *A Monograph on Plectognath Fishes of the Superfamily Triacanthoidea* (1968), is a technical monograph on the two most generalized families of tetraodontiforms but also includes general accounts of the way of life, distribution, and relationships of these families, as well as an extensive bibliography on related articles.

(J.C.T.)

Texas

The vastness and diversity of Texas, the largest of the 48 coterminous states of the United States, are evident in nearly all aspects of the state's physical character, of its history, and of the economic and social life of its people. As a classic example, January temperatures in the Rio Grande Valley have registered well over 90° F (32° C) while, at the same time, nearly halfway to Canada, blizzards were blocking highways in the Panhandle. The image of the state was of a raw and lawless frontier when, in 1845, it surrendered its status as an independent nation to become the 28th member of the Union. This picture has altered drastically to incorporate Texas' present-day combinations of agricultural wealth with high national rankings in industry and finance, of huge urban centres that foster a cosmopolitan cultural life with seemingly unending stretches of high prairie and range devoted to cattle and cotton.

Image and heritage of Texas

Texas, with the forth-longest seacoast among the coterminous states and a shipping industry to match, occupies the south central segment of the nation. Its 267,338 square miles (692,379 square kilometres) make it larger than any nation in Europe except the Soviet Union. Water delineates many of its borders: the Rio Grande carves a shallow channel separating Texas from Mexico on the southwest; the Gulf of Mexico laps its crescent-shaped coast on the southeast; the Sabine River forms most of the eastern boundary with Louisiana (where by land it bounds Arkansas as well); and the wriggling course of the Red River on the north makes up two-thirds of the boundary with Oklahoma. The Panhandle juts northward, forming a counterpart in western Oklahoma, and New Mexico lies to the west.

The Texan who talks endlessly about the marvels of his native state can be justified by many facts. To talk of Texas is to talk more of a region than of a state, and the articles of its admission to the Union allow it the option —unlikely to be taken up—of dividing itself into as many as four states. Texans are keenly conscious, also, of their land's unique location at the confluence of four deep and diverse streams of human development: the underlying influx of Indian culture from the northwest; the passionate involvement of Spanish patterns of life moving northward from Mexico; the pragmatic outlook brought by the Anglo-Saxon and later European immigrants; and the sensitive and brooding tide of black history that has flowed increasingly stronger out of the past of slavery. They will note proudly that, counter to the usual idea that all American history originated with the colonies of the Eastern seaboard, Texas looked southward as well for its beginnings and that the National Autonomous University of Mexico was awarding degrees almost 70 years before the Pilgrim Fathers set foot on Plymouth Rock in 1620.

Like other Southern states, however, Texas has been struggling in recent decades to right inequities in education, economic opportunity, and housing that have mitigated in particular against the personal advancement of Mexican-Americans—or Chicanos, as many of them prefer to call themselves—and of blacks, who made up about 15 and 13 percent, respectively, of the 11,196,730 Texans counted in the census of 1970. The economic expansion since World War II has spread its benefits unequally, widening the gap between the affluent and the marginal-income families. The sturdy concept that those who fail simply have not exerted the necessary will power or zeal for work long helped to keep Texas among the lowest ranking states in welfare and other social services, and the notion is fading only reluctantly. The Republican Party in Texas has gained unusual strength for a Southern state, perhaps through a recognition that its more conservative stance on the national level may provide a more appropriate voice for many Texans than does the national Democratic Party. Recognition has come, also, that the economic growth of the state to date has come primarily from the exploitation of its natural resources, an avenue that cannot continue to offer ever-increasing rates of expansion. (For information on related topics, see the articles UNITED STATES; UNITED STATES, HISTORY OF THE; MEXICO, HISTORY OF; CIVIL WAR, U.S.; NORTH AMERICA; RIO GRANDE; GREAT PLAINS; and MEXICO, GULF OF.)

THE HISTORY OF TEXAS

The forerunners of the west Texas Indians lived in camps whose remains indicate they were made perhaps as much as 37,000 years ago. Possessing only crude spears and flint-pointed darts, these hunters survived primarily on wild game. In the more fertile areas of east Texas, tribes established permanent villages and well-managed farms and evolved political and religious systems. Forming a loose federation to preserve peace and provide mutual protection, they came to be known as the Caddo confederacies. By 1528, when the first white man set foot on Texas soil, the area was sparsely settled, but Indian culture and habitation exerted measurable influence on the later history of the region.

Settlement. By the 1730s, the Spanish had sent more than 30 expeditions into Texas. San Antonio, which by 1718 housed a military post and one or more missions, had become the administrative centre. Missions, with military support, were established in Nacogdoches in east Texas, Goliad in the south, and near El Paso in the far west. The French poked their way briefly into Texas. The explorations of Robert Cavelier, sieur de La Salle, and his colony at Matagorda Bay were the bases of French claims to east Texas.

Anglo-American colonization gained impetus when the United States purchased the Louisiana Territory from France in 1803 and claimed title to lands as far as the Rio Grande. By 1819, however, the United States had accepted the Sabine River as the western boundary of the Louisiana Territory. Moses Austin secured permission from the Spanish government to colonize 300 families on a grant of 200,000 acres. When Mexico became an independent country in 1821, his son, Stephen F. Austin, received Mexican approval of the grant. He led his first band of settlers to a site named San Felipe de Austin near the Gulf Coast. By 1832, Austin's several colonies had about 8,000 inhabitants. Other impresarios with similar grants brought the territory's Anglo-American population to about 20,000.

Spanish-Anglo confrontations

Revolution and the republic. Unrest throughout Mexico, including Texas, resulted in a coup by Antonio López de Santa Anna, who assumed the presidency in 1833. Texans, hopeful for relief from restrictive governmental measures, supported Santa Anna. Austin expected a friendly hearing about these grievances but instead was imprisoned in Mexico City for encouragement of insurrection. Freed in 1835, he returned home to find that skirmishes had already developed between colonists and Mexican troops and that Santa Anna was preparing to send reinforcements. Texans formed a provisional government in 1835 and in 1836 issued a declaration of independence at Washington-on-the-Brazos. David G. Burnet was chosen provisional president of the Republic of Texas, Sam Houston was appointed military commander, and Austin became commissioner to the United States to secure strategic aid and enlist volunteers.

The famous siege of the Alamo in San Antonio lasted from February 23 to March 6, 1836. The strategic objective of the stand was to delay Mexican forces and thereby permit military organization of the Texas settlers. As the battle climaxed with a massive attack over the walls, the defenders (about 187) were all killed. Among the dead were the famous frontiersmen Jim Bowie and Davy Crockett. On April 21, Sam Houston led a surprise attack on the Mexican troops at San Jacinto, and he succeeded in capturing Santa Anna and also securing victory for the Texans.

The Texan revolution was not simply a fight between Anglo-American settlers and Mexican troops; it was a revolution of all people living in Texas against what was regarded as tyrannical rule from a distant source. Many of the leaders in the revolution and many of the armed settlers were Mexicans.

The Republic of Texas was officially established with Sam Houston as president and Stephen Austin as secretary of state. Cities already had been named in their honour: Houston was the capital until 1839, when Austin was approved as the permanent capital.

The republic led a difficult ten-year life. Financing proved critical, and efforts to secure loans from foreign countries were unsuccessful. Protection against raids from Mexico and occasional attacks by Indians required a mobile armed force. Before the revolution certain commissioned officers in the colonies had been called Rangers. During the republic a squad of armed men, the famous Texas Rangers, was maintained to ride long distances quickly to repel or punish raiding forces.

Annexation and statehood. As early as 1836, Texans had voted for annexation by the United States, but the proposition was rejected by the Van Buren administration. Great Britain favoured continued independence to block further westward expansion of the United States, but this attitude swung Americans toward annexation. A treaty of annexation was approved by the Texas and the U.S. congresses in 1845, and the transfer of authority from the republic to the state of Texas took place in 1846. A feature of the annexation agreements was a provision permitting Texas to retain title to public lands, a situation unique among the 50 states.

The U.S. Civil War brought intense disruption. Gov. Sam Houston strongly opposed secession, and, after refusing to take the oath of allegiance to the Confederacy, he was removed from office. During the war, Texans had to defend themselves from Indian attacks, from Mexican encroachments, and from Federal gunboats and invading soldiers. Federal forces ultimately gained control of much of the Gulf Coast but were unable to move far inland.

The last three decades of the 19th century saw rapid developments in population and economy. The state was readmitted to the Union under a new constitution in 1869. By 1874 the Comanches had been forced into a reservation in present-day Oklahoma. Under waves of immigration from North and South as well as from Europe, towns were established, farming spread throughout the central areas, and the cattle industry began to thrive on the plains of west Texas. Railroad building and increased shipping fashioned new links with the rest of the world. Manufacturing, forced into life by the isolation of Civil War years, continued to grow. The population had climbed to more than 3,000,000 by 1900.

The 20th century. In 1901 the oil well that blew in at Spindletop redirected the entire economy of the state. By the early 1970s Texas was the nation's major petroleum producer, but already the state had begun to diversify its economic base. In the same period population increased nearly fourfold, creating several metropolises, and the state system of education became one of the nation's largest.

Civil War and aftermath

THE NATURAL AND HUMAN LANDSCAPE

Physical regions and exploitation. Far from being merely wide, arid plains filled with cattle and cowboys, Texas comprises a series of gigantic steps, from the fertile and densely populated Coastal Plains in the southeast to the high plains and mountains on the west and northwest.

Coastal Plains. Stretching inland from the Gulf Coast, the Coastal Plains range from sea level to about 300 feet (90 metres). These flat, low prairies extend inland to form a fertile crescent, varying in width from 50 to 200 miles (80 to 320 kilometres), that is well adapted to farming and cattle raising. Near the coast much land is marshy, almost swamp, except where drained by man-made devices.

The western anchor of the Coastal Plains is the Rio Grande Valley, where a heavy investment in citrus farming was damaged by rare but disastrous freezes. It now features diversified farming, with vegetables intermingled with citrus. The low coastal lands between Port Lavaca and Port Arthur are ideal for rice cultivation. Inland from Houston the flatlands provide grazing for fine-breed cattle. Forests of pine and cypress grow extensively from Beaumont to the Red River and spill into Louisiana and Arkansas, making lumbering and paper mills important industries.

Access to water transportation, reservoirs of natural gas and oil, and availability of raw materials have made the coastal area the centre of industry in Texas. It is also the most densely populated part of the state. Houston, Texas' largest city, is a focal point, while Fort Worth, Dallas, Waco, Austin, and San Antonio form a line at the inner edges of the Coastal Plains. Corpus Christi, Galveston, and the Beaumont–Port Arthur–Orange complex augment the Port of Houston, one of the nation's largest.

The North Central Plains, the Hill Country, and the Edwards Plateau. The Coastal Plains, encompassing about one-third of the land area, break abruptly when they encounter the Balcones Escarpment, where in the distant geological past the surface of the earth cracked and slipped. Northwest of the fault, the land rears up into the Texas Hill Country and then into the tablelands of the Edwards Plateau to the south and the North Central Plains to the north. The last two regions generally are considered extensions of the Great Plains. The entire region varies from about 750 to 2,500 feet (230 to 760 metres) above sea level. Farming and cattle raising constitute the basic economy. The Hill Country mixes orchard crops with ranching, small industries, summer camps, and tourism.

The High Plains and the Trans-Pecos region. At the western edge of the North Central Plains lies the Cap Rock Escarpment, an outcropping of rock that stretches north and south for about 200 miles. Protruding above the plains like a huge barricade, it is starkly visible in some places in cliffs of 200 to 300 feet. Beyond that escarpment lies the third big step of Texas: the High Plains country and, to the south, the Trans-Pecos region.

From the High Plains country emerged many of the legends of Texas weather and of the Texas cowboy. In this region lies the flat, dry area known as the Staked Plains (Llano Estacado). Legend has it that, as it moved westward, the Coronado expedition laid down stakes to serve as guides for the return trip and that even Indian tribes hesitated to venture across these lands. On these plains, sandstorms can cut down vision in midday, filter tiny bullets of sand into the best-built homes, and scour the paint from exposed automobiles. Many wide, flat riverbeds remain dry most of the year, but they can become sluiceways for flash floods. Through the northern portal, beyond Amarillo, "blue northers" sweep out of the Rocky Mountains with a frenzy of freezing wind, ice, and snow. In the 19th century such famous ranches as the XIT, the Yellow Horse, and the Matador spread their cattle over these ranges.

The North Plains subdivision, centred around Amarillo, depends economically on grain farming, ranching, oil, and small industries. The South Plains subdivision, with Lubbock the principal city, has large underground water reservoirs that allow large-scale irrigated cotton farming.

Agriculture on the coast

The Staked Plains

The state's most rugged terrain lies west of the Pecos River. Trailing down from the Rockies, the Guadalupe Mountains lead into mountains of the Big Bend country, a name derived from a loop of the Rio Grande. The highest peak in Texas is Guadalupe Peak, at 8,751 feet (2,667 metres). Big Bend National Park preserves the native ruggedness of the region.

Climate. Generalizations about Texas weather on a statewide basis are almost meaningless. The Gulf Coast area around Houston has an average annual temperature of about 70° F (21° C) and rainfall of 45 inches (1,143 millimetres), whereas the Panhandle registers about 60° F (16° C) and less than 19 inches (483 millimetres) of rain. The driest region is the Trans-Pecos country, and the wettest is the northeast. Southern areas have freezing weather only rarely. In Brownsville, the southernmost city, no measurable snow has fallen in more than 70 years, but the northwest corner averages 23 inches (584 millimetres) annually.

THE TEXANS

Texas has been a huge reservoir for diverse streams of race and culture. For the bands of prehistoric hunters, for the waves of Indian tribes, for the Spanish and Mexicans pushing northward, for the Anglo-Americans from the North and East, and for colonizers direct from Europe, there was more than enough room for settlement and opportunity for their influence on the institutions of the state. Some churches still conduct services in Swedish, Czech, or Spanish, and, throughout the south and west, Spanish remains the family language of much of the populace.

The Indians. Census reports show only about 18,000 Indians living in Texas today, but this figure fails to account for the many families with some Indian blood. By contrast, more than 20 tribes existed when the first Europeans entered Texas. In following centuries other tribes, including Comanche and Kiowa, were driven into the area; and expanding American colonies pushed Choctaw, Chickashaw, and Alabama-Coushatta westward across the Mississippi. They remained an intermittent threat to white settlements, though many tribes sought peace with the settlers. Military campaigns often failed to distinguish between friend and foe.

Indian tribal diversity

In 1867 representatives of the federal government and of the Comanche, Kiowa, and Apache tribes signed a treaty restricting the Indians to a 3,000,000-acre reservation in Indian Territory (present-day eastern Oklahoma). Indian parties broke the treaty with fierce raids in the Panhandle, but in 1874–75 were pushed back to the reservation. Most present-day Indians are unobtrusive city dwellers, but two tribes remain cohesive units. The Alabama-Coushatta Indians occupy the only reservation in the state, in east Texas. About 300 Tiguas live in a site now enveloped by El Paso.

The Chicanos. Though subtle differences exist between such terms as Mexican-American and Chicano, popular usage has tended to fuse them, and the federal census distinguishes only a single group through the criterion of Spanish surnames. This measurement fails to account, however, for the intermingling of Spanish with Indian and European bloodlines, including families whose surnames have lost all Mexican-American flavour. Up to 20 percent of Texans probably are of Mexican-American descent.

Many communities along the American side of the southwestern border are almost totally Mexican-American, and larger cities such as Brownsville, Laredo, Corpus Christi, El Paso, and San Antonio carry the mark of Spain and Mexico in architecture, in names of streets and parks, in homes shaped around patios and flower gardens, and in the ever-present flow of the Spanish language on street corners. With the urbanization of the state and the decrease in demand for agricultural workers, large Chicano populations have converged on the major metropolitan centres farther from the border.

Many Mexican-Americans have won distinction as scholars, artists, writers, and business leaders—as well as active revolutionaries against Mexico in 1836. The lands north of the Rio Grande, however, have always attracted subsistence-level families fleeing the harshness of northern Mexico, and over many decades easy entry into the United States, both legal and illegal, provided a flow of Mexicans who served as poorly paid harvesters for landowners in Texas and other states. The Anglos owned the land and dominated political life, so the Mexican-Americans remained the tillers, the unskilled labourers, and the holders of jobs for which education was not an essential requirement.

In spite of improved conditions since World War II, Chicanos remain at the bottom of all ethnic groups in terms of education, income, and political power. To overcome these deficiencies has become an increasingly strong goal of the Chicanos. School systems that once barred Spanish and seemed in many ways to belittle the home life and cultural patterns of the Chicano have begun to adopt new approaches.

Community control by Anglo minorities has been challenged with considerable success by voter-registration drives and balloting. Occasional violence has erupted, and charges have been made that law-enforcement officers show favouritism for the Anglos, but Mexican-Americans have gained control of some local political offices. Some Chicano leaders have proved too inexperienced, and various factions have quarrelled among themselves, but further gains in municipal, county, and state elections are likely.

The blacks. From the earliest European penetration, the Southwest offered a haven for Negro slaves. When the United States purchased Louisiana in 1803, the Spanish rulers of Mexico declared that any slave who escaped into Texas would be a free man. Many sought this opportunity. Runaway slaves also intermarried with Indian populations, and many eventually established homes near the Rio Grande. The Civil War brought freedom for thousands of slaves within the state. In recent decades the black population has clustered in the central parts of the larger cities, and nearly 50 percent of the black Texans are concentrated in the urban areas of Dallas and Houston.

Despite the constant existence of racial discrimination, blacks have gained many positions of significance. Many black Texans have gained fame as athletes, while others have become educational leaders in both the black and larger communities.

The civil rights movements of recent years and the actions of federal courts have brought the black greater access to the ballot. Black candidates have been elected to some school boards, to a few city councils, and to the state legislature. In many ways, however, the position of the black in Texas resembles his position nationwide. Moving from rural communities and clustering in the central city, while whites move to suburbs in which mere lip service is paid to the open-housing principle, he is faced with subtle discrimination in education and employment.

The European-Americans in Texas. The 19th century witnessed streams of migration into Texas. Between 1821 and 1836 an estimated 38,000 settlers, on promises of 4,000 acres per family for small fees, trekked from the United States into the territory. In the 30 years before the Civil War came shiploads of Germans, Poles, Czechs, Swedes, Norwegians, and Irish, suffering many hardships but establishing footholds in the frontier land. By 1850, about 33,000 Germans, one-fifth of the state's population, had settled here.

Land ownership—difficult to acquire in Europe—provided an impelling motive for many immigrants. Many families fled Europe to seek personal and religious freedom, including many intellectuals, believers in suffrage, human rights, and education. Turning generally to farming, they were frugal, hardworking, and civic-minded, with a large reservoir of fortitude. Church-oriented, they brought with them a stern dedication to Catholic or Protestant faith.

Post-Civil War years brought numerous families from devastated southern plantations to farms and ranches of the Southwest. From the North Central states came communities of farming families with Swedish, Polish, and Irish backgrounds seeking relief from the tight economy. Others came from Europe, including Belgians, Danes, and Greeks, to become city dwellers, craftsmen, keepers of small shops.

THE STATE'S ECONOMY

Cotton, cattle, and oil—all based on land resources—dominated the successive stages in Texas' economic development until the mid-20th century, and they still undergird the state's basic wealth. Retailing and wholesaling, banking and insurance, and construction have been among activities reflecting a general affluence and urbanization and the semblance of a diversifying economy.

The unequal spread of affluence, however, has produced the phenomenon of a statewide per capita income further below the national average in the late 1960s than it was 20 years earlier. The legislature has paid scant attention to minimum-wage laws, and only federal standards have supported those jobs not subject to union–management bargaining.

Economic optimism

For the future, greater optimism is found in the moves to Texas by numerous national corporate headquarters and the exploration by petroleum companies for new sources of energy to continue their leadership in the fuelling of the nation. The National Aeronautics and Space Administration (NASA), headquartered in Houston, is among many federal air installations in Texas. In addition, tourism has become a major business, and Dallas is attracting worldwide attention as a fashion centre—generally a low-wage industry, however, for most employees. Texas also has become eminent in its oceanographic investigations into uses of the continental shelf and in the relatively unpublicized areas of medicine and surgery. The economic consequences of these activities cannot as yet be estimated fully.

Resources of the land. The fertile lands of east Texas attracted cotton farmers before the Civil War, and, following that struggle, cotton became the state's major crop. As mechanized farming developed, production shifted to the High Plains country of west Texas, where irrigation and fertilizer fostered bountiful crops and maintained Texas' national leadership in cotton production. Occasional crop failures due to drought led to crop diversification. In total value of farm crops, Texas consistently has ranked third or fourth among the states in recent years and has been the leading producer of grain sorghums, rice, grapefruit, peanuts, and watermelons.

Sixty percent of the world's mohair and 95 percent of the U.S. total comes from the Angora goats of Texas. The state leads all states in beef cattle and sheep. The vast cattle empires of the 19th century have tended to shift to coastal areas during the 20th century, reversing the path of cotton.

The average farm size has doubled since 1940, absentee ownership has increased, and the farmer has encountered increasing difficulty in surviving. Farm labourers dropped sharply in number during the 1960s, and migrant workers were left jobless for long periods, facing problems of education for their children, fair-employment treatment, and overall economic survival.

Mineral wealth

New uses for oil were being developed when in 1901 the Spindletop gusher blew in near Beaumont. Today, Texas leads all other states in oil and natural-gas production and oil-refining capacity, and it has more than 40 percent of the nation's proved reserves. Oil deposits have been found under more than two-thirds of the state's area, though many finds seem too light for commercial development. Sixty percent of the nation's sulfur comes from large primary deposits and as a by-product of oil and gas refining.

Manufacturing. Manufacturing began naturally with the processing of local raw materials: cotton gins and cotton-seed mills, meat-packing plants, flour mills, and fruit- and vegetable-canning plants. Food processing remains the largest manufacturing employer and ranks third in value added by manufacture.

Oil refining is a major processor of raw materials, though the manufacture of oil-field equipment has proved profitable. The Gulf Coast area is the centre for the petrochemical industrial complexes. About 40 percent of the basic petrochemicals that are produced in the United States come from plants ranging from Beaumont to Corpus Christi.

Reflecting a maturing economy, manufacturing has moved toward the fabrication of finished consumer products. In this category, the growth of the electronics industry has been outstanding. Other finished goods now manufactured in quantity include air conditioners, furniture, boats, household appliances, machinery, leather goods, and clothing.

Transportation. The vastness of Texas and its contrasts in terrain posed great difficulties for transportation yet greatly stimulated its development. The desire to develop inland areas was one factor leading to the establishment of Austin as the capital. In 1852 the legislature granted public lands to railroads for each mile of track constructed, and in 1883 it authorized a county road tax for farm-to-market dirt roads. By 1900 railroads crisscrossed the state, and dirt roads straggled between most communities.

Recent estimates indicate that automotive vehicles are driven more than 62,000,000,000 miles annually over Texas highways and roads. By 1970 the state had 66,970 miles of highways, and its annual expenditures for building and maintenance were more than $500,000,000. In addition, counties and cities maintained more than 164,-000 miles of public roads.

As in other states, the actual mileage of mainline railroads has diminished, and passenger transportation by the early 1970s had been discontinued over most lines. Operating freight revenues, however, have increased tremendously over recent decades.

Texas pioneered in the development of the airplane. In or near San Antonio alone were the first army flying schools, established at Ft. Sam Houston in 1910; Kelly Field, which became a training camp for pilots in 1917; and Randolph Field, which by 1931 was serving as "the West Point of the Air." The need for air power in World War II brought air training to more than 40 military bases in Texas.

Focal centres for civil air travel are Dallas–Fort Worth, Houston, and San Antonio. Intercity rivalries have been resolved, and by 1976 the Dallas–Fort Worth complex will be served by one of the nation's major airports. In 1969 Houston unveiled a new Intercontinental Airport, encompassing 7,300 acres and providing a computer-run train to carry passengers from each of four terminals to flight gates.

The discovery of oil and gas necessitated the cheaper avenue of water transportation to markets in the East and North. Federal aid permitted harbour improvements at Galveston, Sabine Pass (opening water routes to Port Arthur and Beaumont), Aransas Pass, and Corpus Christi. The opening of a 50-mile channel has made Houston an international port, the third-largest in the nation in tonnage moved in the early 1970s. In the 1930s an Intercoastal Canal was completed from New Orleans to Sabine Pass and from Galveston to Corpus Christi, and in 1946 the Gulf Intracoastal Canal was opened from Brownsville to Florida. Continuous dredging operations have opened lanes of ocean commerce to many smaller ports. Galveston, oldest among the major ports, is headquarters port for extensive commercial fishing enterprises.

In exports, agricultural products generally are first: in 1970, Texas ranked fourth nationally in this respect. Petroleum products, petrochemicals, sulfur, and basic chemicals were the second-largest category of export.

ADMINISTRATION AND SOCIAL CONDITIONS

Structure of government. The constitution of 1876 outlines the prevailing structure of Texas government. The governor, elected for a two-year term, may initiate legislation, call special legislative sessions, veto bills, and appoint boards and commissions. His power is limited, however, because numerous officials and executive boards are elected rather than appointed. The bicameral legislature comprises a Senate of 31 members who serve for four years and a House of Representatives with 150 members elected for two years. The top court for civil matters is the Supreme Court, with a chief justice and eight associate justices elected for six-year terms. The highest court for criminal matters is the Court of Criminal Appeals, with five justices elected for six-year terms. There are 14 courts of civil appeal and 183 state district courts, with judges elected for four-year terms. Lower courts comprise county courts, justice of peace courts, and corporation courts.

Texas comprises 254 counties ranging in size from Brewster County, with 6,208 square miles—equal to the combined areas of Connecticut and Rhode Island—to Rockwall County, with 147 square miles. Within constitutional limitations, the legislature may create new counties. Each county is administered by a commissioners' court, which is an administrative rather than a trial body. Cities of more than 5,000 population may adopt their own charters; by 1969 there were 188 such home-rule cities with varying forms of executive and legislative government.

The more critical problems of local government inevitably involve finances. The traditional source of local financing has been the property tax, but the movement of workers to suburbs and a hodgepodge of governmental agencies with taxing power has complicated the scene.

The functioning of government operates against a political backdrop at all levels.

Politics. Traditionally, the Democratic Party has dominated elections since the Reconstruction period. Except on rare occasions the Democratic primary, pitting the many splinters of the party against one another, has determined the eventual winners of state offices. Within the one party, the political philosophies of candidates have ranged from extreme liberalism to extreme conservatism.

Certain new trends have emerged. The influx of new businesses and industries has brought many Republicans into Texas. The conviction that a two-party system would allow elections based on issues rather than personalities has led some Democrats into the Republican camp, and strong support of civil rights by the national Democratic Party has caused widespread defections by ultraconservatives. In addition, many strong Texas liberals have begun subtly to lend influence to Republicans whom they consider more liberal than the old-time Democratic leaders. Thus, by the early 1970s, the Republican Party, gaining strength by playing upon the divisions within the Democratic Party, had its first senator since Reconstruction, several representatives, and numerous local officeholders.

Political campaigning also has changed. It was possible once for W. Lee "Pappy" O'Daniel, a little-known flour salesman, to burst upon the electorate in the late 1930s with a whirlwind of country music and a slogan of "pass the biscuits, Pappy!" and emerge as governor. The public-relations expert, however, has replaced the entertainer. Old-fashioned oratory has yielded to a soft-voiced message, loaded with sincerity, speaking personally and intimately from the television set.

Politics also is becoming more organized. Both Chicanos and blacks have discovered the power of the ballot to elect city officials, to influence state decisions, and to move upward in the power structure. The increasing tempo of party rivalry and the efforts of the minorities to gain power may stimulate a citizenry that often is apathetic at election time.

Education. Efforts to meet, understand, and solve educational problems arising from the multitudinous social, economic, and other changes since World War II have brought mixed results. An observer may visit a school in which an environment of library self-study and a building designed to accommodate innovation place the educational emphasis upon individual growth rather than grade classification. Conversely, he may sit in a formal classroom in which Mexican-American children are forbidden to utter a word in their family language, the teacher is an autocrat, and dogmatic instruction is regarded as the bridge to wisdom.

Historical factors have helped to shape Texas' present-day educational system. In the 19th century, Texas retained many vestiges of colonial culture. Many communities were colonized by European settlers who brought the concept that public education was only for orphans and children of indigents. In such localities parochial schools were common, and often English remained a second language. The Indians, the labourers from northern Mexico, and the freed slaves, however, had no family tradition of education. In the early years of the republic, leaders tried to reconcile private and free schools. Lacking adequate financial support, the concept of public education became blurred, and, for the populace at large, privately supported education remained the way to secure a sound education.

Another restraining factor has resulted from the divided responsibility between local and state authorities. Local school systems, despite minimum standards established by the state, vary greatly in accordance with local financial resources, prevailing adult educational levels, and demands for equal education for all segments of the population.

Public lands have been used to support education from the years of the Texas Republic. The Texas Congress in 1839 set aside lands in each county to support schools and a university. Railroad building was encouraged in 1854 by land grants for each mile of track—with the proviso that an equal amount be set aside for education. The constitution of 1876 affirmed the endowment of 52,000,000 acres for public schools, another 2,000,000 for a state university and agricultural college. Oil discoveries on these lands by the early 1970s had accumulated well over $1,000,000,000 in permanent endowment funds that can be used to swell legislative appropriations for public education at all levels.

Education of minorities. Most of the 58,000 freed slaves in 1865 were illiterate or barely able to read and write. Despite honest efforts in many communities, the separate but equal principle contained in the constitution of 1876 proved inadequate, though the number of black children enrolled in accredited schools continued to rise. In a test case in 1950 the U.S. Supreme Court ordered the admission of a black student to the University of Texas School of Law, a decision that opened the doors of public colleges and universities in the South to Negro enrollment. Following the Supreme Court's rejection of the separate but equal principle in 1954, public school systems prepared to integrate, but the legislature in 1957 made it illegal for school boards to abolish segregation without approval by local election. Nevertheless, the federal Civil Rights Act and the threat of withholding federal funds from schools that do not integrate adequately have conquered resistance in most areas.

In the early 1970s, the major obstacles to school integration resulted from discrimination in housing. In addition, black youths from segregated schools find it difficult to gain admission to better colleges or to survive if admitted. These problems are by no means peculiar to Texas, of course, nor to the South, but pervade all urban centres in the nation.

Some of the Mexican-American families have been Texans since the Spanish and Mexican regimes, and many of them are scholars of distinction or wealthy leaders in professional life. But the majority are not, and, hoping to break the barriers of language and culture, schools in heavily Mexican-American areas long forbade the use of any language but English in the classroom and pursued curricula oriented toward Anglo-Saxon social institutions. Recently, however, increased recognition of the cultural heritage has made the family language a springboard into learning experiences.

In spite of these brights spots, a far greater proportion of Mexican-Americans and blacks than Anglos remain outside the educational structure, fail to reach high school, or receive an inadequate education.

Higher education. In 1971–72 the University of Texas system enrolled nearly 70,000 students, more than half of them on the main campus in Austin. Among the 115 colleges and universities are 22 public senior institutions

Local government and taxation

Emergence of two-party political life

School integration

and 40 public junior colleges. Seven new institutions have been authorized for the state university system, with completion scheduled for 1975.

The University of Texas regularly confers more doctoral degrees than any other Southern university, and 13 of its Ph.D. programs are ranked among the nation's top 20. Rice University, a private institution, in Houston, long has been recognized for the scholarly excellence of its faculty and its high academic standards.

Texas has more than 50 private or church-supported colleges and universities. Baylor University, in Waco, founded in 1845, is the only remaining university of the five established during the republic. In 1970 the state legislature was approached by 50 private institutions with requests to provide financial support through contractual arrangements.

Health and welfare. Among the states Texas ranked 43rd in 1970 in average per capita aid from state and local funds for all categories. In that year voters defeated a measure that would have permitted raising the ceiling on state welfare spending. By the early 1970s, 23 percent of the individuals over 65 in the state were receiving old age assistance, one of the highest percentages in the nation; but the average monthly payment ranked 33rd among such averages in all states. The average payment of $67 monthly to persons totally or permanently disabled ranked 42nd among the states.

Programs for the mentally ill and mentally retarded have been slow to develop in Texas; but increasing public concern has been making itself felt in the legislature. There are six mental health hospitals within the state. Likewise, for aged senile patients there are two geriatric centres, and a neuropsychiatric institute. Increasing attention is being given to outpatient clinic services. Nine state schools care for the mentally retarded.

Annual family incomes demonstrate that the Mexican-American and black families suffer by comparison with Anglo families. The 1960 census figures revealed that over one-half of the Mexican-American and the nonwhite families, as compared with about one-fifth of the Anglo families, had an annual income of less than $3,000. Stimulated by federal antipoverty programs, efforts are increasing to provide adequate employment and equal salary treatment to all segments of the population.

In medical education, research, and preventive medicine the state ranks among national leaders. The University of Texas Southwestern Medical School, in Dallas, is typical of these vigorous programs. It planned to double enrollment by 1975 and to develop a Life Sciences Center emphasizing prevention, cure, and control through combining medicine with the social sciences.

CULTURAL LIFE AND INSTITUTIONS

Preservations. Entering the Institute of Texan Cultures in San Antonio is like walking back into history. The visitor is enveloped quickly in large panoramas of coastline and prairie and in sounds of wind and animal life that contribute to a sense of reality. Moving along, he stands before recreated scenes of Indian life, then of pioneer dwellings, with drawings, dioramas, and preserved objects. The emphasis is upon the various nationalities and cultures that converged to form the life of the Southwest.

Appreciation of cultural diversity

The sense of the past has traditionally been strong in born and bred Texans. The emphasis long was based upon the heroics of living in a frontier land, upon individuals and their deeds, but in recent decades an increasing appreciation of the diverse cultures that have enriched the life of Texas has helped to preserve and strengthen those customs. Throughout the state, regional historical associations quietly search out and help to restore striking examples of 19th-century homes. San Antonio has recreated the early-18th-century Mexican-Spanish flavour in both restoration and in public shopping and walking areas in the heart of the city. Fredericksburg, with its historic German background, preserves many 19th-century customs and continues to cling to German as a family tongue. Even a metropolitan city like Houston has found space adjacent to its downtown area for re-stored historic homes. Brownsville vividly dramatizes the marriage of Mexican and Anglo cultures with an annual Washington's birthday parade and fete. Particularly evident are influences from Mexican culture, from the deep-rooted impact of the cattle country, and from the newer yet vibrant life fashioned by oil booms, wildcatting, refineries, and pipelines.

The arts. Art, music, and literature occupy significant places in the lives of many communities in Texas. The Amon G. Carter Museum of Western Art in Fort Worth, dedicated to "the visual documentation of the culture of western North America," houses many paintings and bronzes of Western artists and maintains a microfilm collection of Western newspapers published before 1900. With the Fort Worth Art Center, the William Edrington Scott Theatre, the Kimbell Art Museum, and the Fort Worth Children's Theater, the Amon G. Carter Museum provides a cultural centre for study and appreciation of the arts.

The Civic Center nestles in 150 acres amid the tall buildings of downtown Houston. It serves as the home for the Houston Symphony Orchestra and the Grand Opera Association. The world-famous Alley Theater has moved into new quarters nearby. Dallas has developed diverse centres for cultural activities. The Margo Jones Theatre was opened in the 1960s, and the Dallas Theater Center provides an outlet for cultural and educational groups. The Dallas Symphony Orchestra is among the better known classical ensembles in the nation. Such interests, however, are not restricted to large metropolitan areas. Odessa, for example, with an area population of about 100,000, supports the unique Museum of the Presidents, showing extensive memorabilia of the American presidents, as well as an accurate replica of London's Globe Theatre, in which a summer program of Shakespearean and other Elizabethan plays is produced. Colleges and universities in the state are active in all areas of the arts.

Recreation. Water has added new dimensions to popular recreation. In 1913 there were only eight major lakes or reservoirs in Texas, but by the early 1970s there were 200 or more, many built to husband water against periodic droughts. Several national parks and some 70 state parks dot the state, many of them providing fishing, swimming, camping, and picnicking. An increasing tourist trade has turned sports fishing into a major recreation along the Gulf Coast.

Sports and amusements

Other dimensions of entertainment—for tourists and Texans alike—include Six Flags Over Texas, a Westernized amusement park halfway between Dallas and Fort Worth, and, near the Dallas suburb of Mesquite, a reservation into which motorists can drive, as on an African safari, and watch apparently free-roaming elephants, giraffes, and other African wildlife. In Houston the well-publicized Astrodome has become a centre of professional sports, rodeos, bullfights (with no killing), circuses, and other spectaculars.

Literary resources. Book publishing, though not as yet a big business within the state, has gained a strong foothold. The University of Texas Press has gained national acclaim through its scholarly and historical works, and the Southern Methodist University Press likewise has established discriminating standards. Several commercial publishing companies have concentrated on books and monographs related to the history of the Southwest.

The university libraries, art galleries, and special collections contain remarkable treasures. The Armstrong Browning Library at Baylor houses more than 5,000 books and manuscripts by and about Robert and Elizabeth Barrett Browning. At the University of Texas in Austin, the new Presidential Library, dedicated in 1971 and operated as a branch of the Library of Congress, will house about 34,000,000 documents on public affairs since the mid-1930s, related to the public career of former President Lyndon B. Johnson. At this university, also, the Latin-American collection, the Michener Collection of Art, and a number of other special collections are available to scholars, historians, and the public.

Press and broadcasting. From colonial days, the news media have played a special role in the development of

Texas. Gail Borden, Jr., founded the *Telegraph and Texas Register* in 1835 in San Felipe and used the newspaper to advocate the cause of Texas freedom and to strengthen support for the republic. In the years before the Civil War, Texas editors were combinations of educators, newsmongers, and chamber of commerce promoters for their communities, characteristics that persisted until modern times.

Interactions of newspapers and communities

In nearly every city or town a newspaper has grown up with the community, influencing decisions and promoting community virtues to outsiders. The *Fort Worth Star-Telegram* thus became a major force in stirring Fort Worth to leadership in the cattle business, in browbeating railroad officials into routing more trains through the town, and in attracting investment capital from the East. In a similar way, the *Dallas Morning News* and later the *Dallas Daily Times Herald*, the *Houston Post* and the *Houston Chronicle*, and the *San Antonio Express* and the *San Antonio Light* similarly shaped the destinies of their cities, until in many ways the cities and the newspapers came to reflect one another. Austin's *Texas Observer* has gained distinction through its dogged stabs at racial inequities, political dealings, and other injustices throughout the state. Newspapers in smaller communities—the *Victoria Advocate*, the Beeville *Bee-Picayune*, or the *Smithville Times*—are as deeply embedded as the county courthouse. In the early 1970s, the fastest growing segment of the press was in suburban communities.

The first radio station in Texas began operating in 1920 under the ownership of the city of Dallas. The first television station went on the air in 1947. In 1970 Texas had more than 400 AM and FM radio stations and about 70 television stations. By 1970, cable television had established itself firmly in most Texas cities and had reached out to some of the smaller communities. Educational television, or "public broadcasting," also reached a large audience in Texas.

Prospects. Certain trends that will continue into the future emerge logically from the developments of post-World War II Texas. In ensuing decades it seems likely that the population of the state will increase at a rate faster than that of the nation as a whole. Industry and business must certainly diversify, to place greater emphasis upon end products rather than natural resources. Mexican-American and black minorities will become more cohesive and more politically astute, thereby exerting greater influence upon government and politics. As a consequence, educational integration will progress with decreasing friction as new schools are built between neighbourhoods, rather than in the centre of homogeneous residential areas. In addition, integration will become more realistic and less token in public life, in churches, and eventually in housing. The struggle to establish additional bases for taxation will remain acute, as governmental bodies within the state assume greater burdens and voters become convinced of the necessity for increasing expenditures for the improvement of society. These upgraded programs inevitably will fall in such areas as public health and welfare, the salaries of public employees, education, mental-health programs, and law enforcement.

BIBLIOGRAPHY. The single most valuable volume of facts about various aspects of Texas life and industry is *The Texas Almanac*, ed. by WALTER B. MOORE and published every two years. The *Handbook of Texas*, ed. by WALTER PRESCOTT WEBB (1952), provides encyclopaedic information about individuals, ranches, Indians, colonizations, education, government, and other glimpses into Texas development. The comprehensive *Texas: A Guide to the Lone Star State*, rev. ed., ed. by HARRY HANSEN (1969), is particularly helpful in its guide to the large and middle-size cities of the state. CLIFTON MCCLESKEY, *The Government and Politics of Texas*, 3rd ed. (1969), is the most authoritative book on Texas government, emphasizing the social and economic contexts. Lively glimpses of 20th-century Texas, written with attention to human interest and colour, include STANLEY WALKER, *Texas* (1962); and GEORGE M. FUERMANN, *Reluctant Empire* (1957). Both authors examine the people and their doings with the eyes of an interpretative reporter. The student of the West, seeking authentic information of frontier days, will find information in such books as J. FRANK DOBIE, *The Mustangs* (1952), which recaptures the smells, sounds, and sights of the Western plains and the wild horses that once lived there. WALTER PRESCOTT WEBB, *The Texas Rangers*, rev. ed. (1965), is the best book about the subject. W.W. NEWCOMB, JR., *The Indians of Texas from Prehistoric to Modern Times* (1961), is a scholarly and lucid report. FRED B. GIPSON, *Cowhand: The Story of a Working Cowboy* (1953), is a day-by-day real-life story that has the movement and feeling of fiction. R. HENDERSON SHUFFLER *et al.*, *From Many Texans: A Gathering of Cultures* (1970), relating colourful stories of the mixture of cultures in the Southwest; and CURTIS and GRACE BISHOP, with C.I. MARTIN, *Trails to Texas* (1965), re-creating the cattle decades, are written for young people but appealing to adults as well. The INSTITUTE OF TEXAN CULTURES in San Antonio has begun the production of a series of monographs depicting the various ethnic or immigrant streams of life that have flowed into the Southwest, including *The Indian Texans* and *The Norwegian Texans* (both 1970).

(DeW.C.R.)

Textile Industry

The term textile, derived from the Latin *texere* ("to weave"), originally applied only to woven fabrics, is now a general term for fibres, yarns, and other materials that can be made into fabrics and for fabrics produced by interlacing or any other construction method. Thus threads, cords, ropes, braids, lace, embroidery, nets, and fabrics made by weaving, knitting, bonding, felting, or tufting are textiles. Some definitions would also include those products obtained by the paper-making principle that have many of the properties associated with conventional fabrics.

This article is concerned with the development of the textile industry, the conversion of fibres to yarn, fabric construction, finishing processes applied to textiles, end uses of textile materials, and the relationship between the producer and the consumer. Specific textile fibres are treated in the articles FIBRES, MAN-MADE; and FIBRES, NATURAL. Other related articles include FLOOR COVERINGS and DYES AND DYEING. Aesthetic aspects are discussed in the articles RUGS AND CARPETS and TAPESTRY. This article is divided into the following sections.

I. Development of the textile industry
- History to the 19th century
  - Early textile production
  - Effects of the Industrial Revolution
- From the 19th century to the present
  - Application of scientific methods
  - The modern industry

II. Production of yarn
- Textile fibres
- Conversion to yarn
  - Treatment of raw fibre
  - Spinning
  - Yarn packages
- Types of yarn
  - Classification based on number of strands
  - Novelty yarns
  - Classification based on use
  - Measurement systems

III. Production of fabric
- Woven fabrics
  - The weaving process
  - Development of the loom
  - Basic weaves
  - Complex weaves
- Knitted fabrics
  - Knitting machines
  - Weft knitting
  - Warp knitting
- Other interlaced fabrics
- Noninterlaced fabrics
  - Felt
  - Bonding
  - Laminating

IV. Textile finishing processes
- Basic methods and processes
  - Preparatory treatment
  - Finishes enhancing appearance
  - Finishes enhancing tactile qualities
  - Finishes improving performance
- Dyeing and printing
  - Dyeing
  - Printing

V. Textile consumption and trade

Changing uses of fabric in apparel
    Soft furnishings
    Industrial fabrics
    Fabrics for protective clothing
World production and trade

I. Development of the textile industry

HISTORY TO THE 19TH CENTURY

Early textile production. Textile structures derive from two sources, ancient handicrafts and modern scientific invention. The earliest were nets, produced from one thread and employing a single repeated movement to form loops, and basketry, the interlacing of flexible reeds, cane, or other suitable materials. The production of net, also called limited thread work, has been practiced by many peoples, particularly in Africa and Peru. Examples of prehistoric textiles are extremely rare because of the perishability of fabrics. The earliest evidence of weaving, closely related to basketry, dates from Neolithic cultures of about 5000 BC. Weaving apparently preceded spinning of yarn; woven fabrics probably originated from basket weaving. Cotton, silk, wool, and flax fibres were used as textile materials in ancient Egypt; cotton was used in India by 3000 BC; and silk production is mentioned in Chinese chronicles dating to about the same period. The history of spinning technology will be touched on below in the section *Production of yarn: Spinning* and that of weaving technology in the section *Production of fabric.*

Early fabrics. Many fabrics produced by the simple early weaving procedures are of striking beauty and sophistication. Design and art forms are of great interest, and the range of patterns and colours is wide, with patterns produced in different parts of the world showing distinctive local features.

Yarns and cloth were dyed and printed from very early times. Specimens of dyed fabrics have been found in Roman ruins of the 2nd century BC; tie-and-dye effects decorated the silks of China in the T'ang dynasty (AD 618–907); and there is evidence of production of printed textiles in India during the 4th century BC. Textiles found in Egypt also indicate a highly developed weaving craft by the 4th century AD, with many tapestries made from linen and wool. Persian textiles of very ancient origin include materials ranging from simple fabrics to luxurious carpets and tapestries.

Textiles in the Middle Ages. By the early Middle Ages certain Turkish tribes were skilled in the manufacture of carpets, felted cloths, towels, and rugs. In Mughal India (16th–18th centuries), and perhaps earlier, the fine muslins produced at Dacca in Bengal were sometimes printed or painted. Despite the Muslim prohibition against representation of living things, richly patterned fabrics were made in Islamic lands.

In Sicily, after the Arab conquest in AD 827, beautiful fabrics were produced in the palace workshops at Palermo. In about 1130, skilled weavers who came to Palermo from Greece and Turkey produced elaborate fabrics of silk interlaced with gold.

Growth of the textile industry in Italy

Following the conquest of Sicily in 1266 by the French, the weavers fled to Italy; many settled in Lucca, which soon became well-known for silk fabrics with patterns employing imaginative floral forms. In 1315, the Florentines captured Lucca, taking the Sicilian weavers to Florence, a centre for fine woven woollens from about 1100 AD, also believed to be producing velvet at this time. A high degree of artistic and technical skill was developed, with 16,000 workers employed in the silk industry and 30,000 in the wool industry at the close of the 15th century. By the middle of the 16th century a prosperous industry in velvets and brocades (see below *Production of fabric*) was also established in Genoa and Venice.

Textile industries of France and Germany. French manufacture of woven silks began in 1480, and in 1520 Francis I brought Italian and Flemish weavers to Fontainebleau to produce tapestry under the direction of the King's weaver. Others were brought to weave silk in Lyons, eventually the centre of European silk manufacture. Until 1589, most of the elaborate fabrics in France were of Italian origin, but in that year Henry IV founded the royal carpet and tapestry factory at Savonnières. Flem-

ish weavers were brought to France to produce tapestries in workshops set up by Jean Gobelin in the 16th century. By the time of Louis XIII (1610–43), French patterned fabrics showed a distinctive style based on symmetrical ornamental forms, lacelike in effect, perhaps derived from the highly regarded early Italian laces. In 1662, the French government, under Louis XIV, purchased the Gobelin factory in Paris. Rouen also became known for its textiles, with designs influenced by the work of Rouen potters. French textiles continued to advance in style and technique, and under Louis XVI (1774–93) design was refined, with classical elements intermingled with the earlier floral patterns. The outbreak of the French Revolution in the 1790s interrupted the work of the weavers of Lyons, but the industry soon recovered.

Flanders and its neighbour Artois were early centres of production for luxurious textiles: Arras for silks and velvets; Ghent, Ypres, and Courtrai for linen damasks; and Arras and Brussels for tapestries. The damasks, characterized by heraldic motifs, were especially well known, and linen damasks of very high quality were produced in the 18th century. In Germany, Cologne was an important medieval cloth centre, renowned for Orphrey webs (narrow cloths of gold bearing richly embroidered woven inscriptions and figures of saints).

Textile manufacture in England. English textiles of the 13th and 14th centuries were mainly of linen and wool, and the trade was influenced by Flemish fullers (finishers) and dyers. Silk was being woven in London and Norwich in 1455, and in 1564 Queen Elizabeth I granted a charter to Dutch and Flemish settlers in Norwich for production of damasks and flowered silks. The revocation of the Edict of Nantes in 1685, renewing persecution of French Protestants, caused many weavers to move to England, settling in Norwich, Braintree, and London. The most important group of refugees, some 3,500, lived in Spitalfields, a London settlement that became the chief centre for fine silk damasks and brocades. These weavers produced silk fabrics of high quality and were known for their subtle use of fancy weaves and textures. Norwich was also famous for figured shawls of silk or wool.

Textiles in the New World. Weaving and dyeing were established in the New World before arrival of the Europeans. Weaving was in an advanced state in North and South America during prehistoric times; both the Peruvians and Mexicans had fine woven fabrics. The Peruvian fabrics were much like those of ancient Egypt, although contact between the two civilizations is generally considered unlikely. Inca cotton and wool fabrics were brilliantly coloured, with patterns based on geometric and conventionalized human forms. Fabrics, especially blankets, made by the Navajos of Arizona and New Mexico had exceptionally close texture and brilliant colour.

American Indian textiles

English settlers established a cloth mill in Massachusetts in 1638. There Yorkshire weavers produced heavy cotton fustians; cotton-twill jeans; and linsey-woolsey, a coarse, loosely woven fabric of linen and wool. Fulling mills were operating in Massachusetts by 1654, freeing the community from dependence on England for fine linen and worsted. The industry developed steadily, and received a major impetus from Eli Whitney's invention of the cotton gin in 1793.

Effects of the Industrial Revolution. The textile industry, although highly developed as a craft, remained essentially a cottage industry until the 18th century. The advantages of cooperative operations were realized much earlier, and numbers of workers occasionally operated together under one roof, with one such group operating a mill in Zurich in 1568 and another in Derby, England, in 1717. Factory organization became most advanced in the north of England, and the Industrial Revolution, at its height between 1760 and 1815, greatly accelerated the growth of the mill system.

John Kay's flying shuttle, invented in 1733, increased the speed of the weaving operation, and its success created pressure for more rapid spinning of yarn to feed the faster looms. Mechanical spinners produced in 1769 and 1779 by Sir Richard Arkwright and Samuel Crompton encouraged development of mechanized processes of carding and combing wool for the spinning machines (see below *Production of yarn: Carding and combing*). Soon after the turn of the century the first power loom was developed. The replacement of water power by steam power increased the speed of power-driven machinery, and the factory system became firmly established, first in England, later in Europe and the United States.

FROM THE 19TH CENTURY TO THE PRESENT

Throughout the 19th century a succession of improvements in textile machinery steadily increased the volume of production, lowering prices of finished cloth and garments. The trend continued in the 20th century, with emphasis on fully automatic or nearly fully automatic systems of machinery.

Application of scientific methods. The mechanical developments in textile production associated with the Industrial Revolution resulted from the application of comparatively simple engineering and physical principles. Further progress required a clear understanding of the scientific principles of textile processing. Lack of basic information on the structure and properties of fibres limited understanding, delaying a scientific approach to textile processing. In the late 19th century, however, increasing knowledge of the physical and chemical properties of fibres led to application of scientific methods. Applications of chemistry originally attracted the greatest attention, largely because of the production of new compounds and the realization that fibres could be considered the result of chemical activity. In the 20th century, with the development of electronics and computers, new physical and engineering concepts were employed in textile research and development. An outstanding application of science to the textile industry was the development of man-made fibres, providing new textile materials and leading to the application of new processes to traditional fibres, thereby providing faster processing methods and introducing a wider variety of new techniques. The man-made fibre industry originally employed textile expertise developed through years of experience with natural fibres, but the excellent results obtained by the scientific approach encouraged increased industrial use of applied science, and information was soon accumulated on the behaviour of fibres under a variety of conditions.

The modern industry. Both industrialized and developing countries now have modern installations capable of highly efficient fabric production. In addition to mechanical improvements in yarn and fabric manufacture, there have been rapid advances in development of new fibres, processes to improve textile characteristics, and testing methods allowing greater quality control.

The modern textile industry is still closely related to the apparel industry, but production of fabrics for industrial use has gained in importance. The resulting wide range of end uses demands a high degree of specialization. In the most technically advanced communities, the industry employs technicians, engineers, and artists; and a high degree of consumer orientation leads to emphasis on marketing operations. Some manufacturing operations, usually serving specialized or local markets and dependent on a limited number of firms for product consumption, still employ many hand operations, however.

Modern fabrics. The many types of modern textile fabrics, produced from both traditional and man-made materials, are often classified according to structure. Fabrics made by interlacing include woven and knitted types, lace, nets, and braid; fabrics produced from fibre masses include bonded types, wool felt, and needle-woven types; composite fabrics are produced by uniting layers of various types. Conventional weaving and knitting methods are currently the major textile manufacturing techniques, but newer construction methods are achieving acceptance, and may replace certain long-established products as costs of conventional textiles continue to rise and rapid technological advances continually develop new materials.

Quality control. Textile fabrics are judged by many criteria. Flexibility and sufficient strength for the intend-

ed use are generally major requirements, and industrial fabrics must meet rigid specifications of width, weight per unit area, weave and yarn structure, strength and elongation, acidity or alkalinity, thickness, and porosity. In apparel fabrics design and colour are major considerations, and certain physical properties may be of secondary importance. In addition, the various tactile properties of a fabric, described as its "hand," "handle," or "feel," influence consumer acceptance.

The textile industry increasingly employs research and development in the area of quality control. Medieval craft guilds were concerned with maintaining high quality standards, and later textile mills established rigid systems of inspection, realizing that a reputation for supplying fault-free goods encouraged repeat orders. Modern quality control has been assisted by development of techniques and machines for assessing fibre, yarn, and fabric properties; by the introduction of legislation regarding misrepresentation in many industrialized countries; and by the establishment of rigid specifications by a growing number of buyers. Specifications have been established for the purchase of industrial fabrics, for textiles used by the military and other branches of governments, and for similar purchasing methods adopted by some retailers and other large buyers. In consumer-oriented areas, the public is becoming aware of product testing, and is beginning to require proof that products have met certain test standards.

Many modern textile organizations test product quality at every major stage of processing. Yarns are tested for uniform thickness and other characteristics; fabric pieces are checked for defects; and the fastness of finishes and colours to various conditions is determined. Although it would not be feasible to test each yarn or fabric piece produced, statistical techniques allow maintenance of quality within previously specified limits, and the introduction of automatic testing devices has greatly reduced testing time and cost. Methods for assessing such properties as dimensions, strength, and porosity have been established, and their validity is generally accepted within the industry. Standards are available for colour fastness, although such important properties as water-repellency, resistance to creasing, and flame resistance are presently more difficult to define, and various organizations have adopted their own test procedures. It is important, for example, that a fabric described as flame resistant should conform to some specification in which the meaning of flame resistance is clearly defined.

Some manufacturers attach trademarks and quality labels to tested goods, and licensed trademarks are often associated with particular processes for which the manufacturer has been granted a license. The terms of the license require the manufacturer to ensure that his products meet the standards laid down by the proprietors of the particular process.

II. Production of yarn

Yarn is a strand composed of fibres, filaments (individual fibres of extreme length), or other materials, either natural or man-made, suitable for use in the construction of interlaced fabrics, such as woven or knitted types. The strand may consist of a number of fibres twisted together; a number of filaments grouped together but not twisted; a number of filaments twisted together; a single filament, called a monofilament, either with or without twist; or one or more strips made by dividing a sheet of material, such as paper or metal foil, and either twisted or untwisted. The properties of the yarn employed greatly influence the appearance, texture, and performance of the completed fabric.

TEXTILE FIBRES

Raw materials. Fibres are units of matter having length at least 100 times their diameter or width. Fibres suitable for textile use possess adequate length, fineness, strength, and flexibility for yarn formation and fabric construction, and for withstanding the intended use of the completed fabric. Other properties affecting textile fibre performance include elasticity, crimp (waviness), moisture

(margin notes)

Effects of development of man-made fibres

Criteria for evaluating textile fabrics

Qualities required in textile fibres

absorption, reaction to heat and sunlight, reaction to the various chemicals applied during processing and in the dry cleaning or laundering of the completed fabric, and resistance to insects and micro-organisms. The wide variation of such properties among textile fibres determines their suitability for various uses.

The first fibres available for textile use were obtained from plant and animal sources. Over a long period of experimentation with the many natural fibres available, cotton, wool, jute, flax, and silk have become recognized as the most satisfactory. The commercial development of man-made fibres began late in the 19th century, experienced much growth during the 1940s, expanded rapidly after World War II, and in the 1970s was still the subject of extensive research and development. This group includes regenerated fibres, such as rayon, made from fibre-forming materials already existing in nature and manipulated into fibrous form, and synthetic fibres, with the fibre-forming substance produced from chemicals derived from such sources as coal and oil, and then made into such fibres as nylon and polyester.

Factors affecting cost. The cost of fibres is determined by availability, the kind and amount of processing required, and their versatility. Natural fibres usually require extensive land area for their production, are affected by climatic conditions, and must frequently be transported long distances to the point of manufacture. Because quantity and quality are not easily controlled, prices tend to fluctuate. Recent research has been directed toward improving various properties during the manufacturing processes.

Man-made fibres can usually be produced near the point of use; their production does not require large land areas; they can be manufactured quickly, in desired quantities, with specific built-in properties; and they require little advance preparation for conversion to yarn. Initial costs are high because of the production equipment employed, but prices tend to be stable and may be reduced as production expands. Recent research has been directed toward improving the properties of man-made fibres and developing types suitable for specific purposes.

Although the major natural fibres continue to dominate the textile industry, production and consumption of man-made fibres are growing.

CONVERSION TO YARN

Because filaments, such as silk and the man-made fibres, have extreme length, they can be made into yarn without the spinning operation necessary for the shorter staple fibres. When grouped together in a loose, continuous rope without twist, man-made filaments are called tow. Filaments may be loosely twisted together to form yarns of a specified thickness. Staple fibres, such as cotton, only a few inches long, must be tightly twisted together to produce satisfactory length.

Filament yarns are usually thin, smooth, and lustrous; staple yarns are usually thicker, fibrous, and without lustre. Man-made filaments cut to a predetermined short length become staple fibres, usually described by combining the fibre name with the term staple, as in rayon staple.

Treatment of raw fibre. In modern mills, most fibre-processing operations are performed by mechanical means. Such natural fibres as cotton, arriving in bales, and wool, arriving as fleece, are treated at the mill to remove various foreign materials, such as twigs and burrs. Wool must also be treated to remove suint, or wool grease; silk must be treated to remove sericin, a gum from the cocoon, and the very short silk fibres, or waste silk. Raw linen, the fibre of flax, is separated from most impurities before delivery. Man-made fibres, since they are produced by factory operations, rarely contain foreign materials. Blending, frequently employed for natural fibres, involves mixing fibres taken from different lots to obtain uniform length, diameter, density, and moisture content, thus assuring production of a uniform yarn. Blending is also employed when different fibres are combined to produce yarn. Man-made fibres, which can be cut into uniform tow, do not require blending unless they are to be mixed with other fibres.

Cotton, wool, waste silk, and man-made staple are subjected to carding, a process of separating individual fibres and causing many of them to lie parallel, and also removing most of the remaining impurities. Carding produces a thin sheet of uniform thickness that is then condensed to form a thick, continuous, untwisted strand called sliver.

When very fine yarns are desired, carding is followed by combing, a process that removes short fibres, leaving a sliver composed entirely of long fibres, all laid parallel, and both smoother and more lustrous than uncombed types. Slivers may be loosely twisted together, forming roving. Hackling, a process applied to straighten and separate flax, is similar to combing.

Spinning. *Early spinning methods.* Spinning is the process of drawing out and twisting fibres to join them firmly together in a continuous thread or yarn. Spinning is an indispensable preliminary to weaving cloth from those fibres that do not have extreme length. From early times through the Middle Ages spinning was accomplished with the use of two implements, the distaff and the spindle. The distaff was a stick on which the mass of fibres was held. The drawn-out length of fibre was fastened to the weighted spindle, which hung free. The spinner whirled the spindle, causing it to twist the fibre as it was drawn from the distaff. As a length was drawn out the operation was halted, the new yarn wound on the spindle and secured by a notch, and the operation repeated. The spinning wheel, invented in India and introduced to Europe in the Middle Ages, mechanized the process; the spinning of the wheel supplanted the whirl of the weighted spindle, and after each operation the spinner wound the new yarn on the spindle. This was accomplished simply and speedily by holding the yarn outstretched with the left hand and feeding it as the wheel was spun in the reverse direction.

An important advantage conferred by the spinning wheel was the fact that it tended to add more twist at thin places in the forming yarn and to draw out the thicker places, giving a more uniform yarn.

The spinning wheel continued in use into the 19th century, receiving an important improvement in the 16th century in the form of the Saxony wheel, which made possible continuous spinning of coarse wool and cotton yarn. With this improvement in speed, three to five spinning wheels could supply one loom with yarn, but Kay's flying shuttle (described below under *Woven fabrics*) greatly increased the output of the loom and created a demand for spinning machinery. James Hargreaves' spinning jenny (patented 1770) operated a number of spindles simultaneously, but was suitable only for making yarn used as filling. Sir Richard Arkwright, making use of earlier inventions, produced a better machine, capable of making stronger yarn than Hargreaves' jenny. Still a third machine, Samuel Crompton's "mule" (1779), vastly increased productivity, making it possible for a single operator to work more than 1,000 spindles simultaneously; and it was capable of spinning fine as well as coarse yarn. Several further modifications were introduced in Britain and the United States, but the Crompton mule effectively put yarn spinning on a mass production basis.

Modern spinning. In modern spinning, slivers or rovings are fed into machines having rollers that draw out the strands, making them longer and thinner, and that insert the amount of twist necessary to hold the fibres together. The tightness of the twist determines the strength of the yarn, although too much twist may eventually cause weakening and breakage. Yarns twisted to the right, or clockwise, are described as Z-twist; yarns twisted to the left, or counterclockwise, are described as S-twist. Crepe yarns, producing a crinkled effect in fabrics, are made with a very high degree of twist, producing a kink. Shadow effects can be produced in finished fabrics by the use of yarns combining opposing twists, producing differing light reflections. The spinning process is completed by winding the yarn on spools or bobbins.

Reeling and throwing. Reeling is the process of unwinding raw silk filament from the cocoon directly onto a holder. When several filament strands, either raw silk or man-made, are combined and twisted together, producing yarn of a specified thickness, it is called throwing.

Carding

Improvements on the spinning wheel

Tow

Yarn packages. The intended use of a yarn usually determines the packaging method employed. Bobbins are wood, cardboard, or plastic cores on which yarns are wound as they are spun, and have holes in their centres allowing them to fit on spindles or other holding devices. Spools are cylindrical, with end flanges. Cones, having a conical-shaped core, produce a package of conical shape; tubes, with cylindrical-shaped cores, produce cylindrical packages. Cheeses are cylindrical yarn packages wound on a tube, and unlike most other packages, they have greater diameter than height. Skeins are coils of yarn wound with no supporting core.

Pirns are large barrel-shaped packages used to hold the weft, or filling, yarn supply for the shuttle in weaving; quills are small tapered tubes holding the weft yarns for weaving. Beams are wood or metal cylinders, about five feet long and up to ten inches in diameter, on which yarns used as warp in weaving are wound.

For detailed information on individual fibres, including their production, processing, individual properties, and uses, see FIBRES, MAN-MADE and FIBRES, NATURAL.

TYPES OF YARN

Classification based on number of strands. Yarns can be described as single, or one-ply; ply, plied, or folded; or as cord, including cable and hawser types.

Single yarns. Single, or one-ply, yarns are single strands composed of fibres held together by at least a small amount of twist; or of filaments grouped together either with or without twist; or of narrow strips of material; or of single man-made filaments extruded in sufficient thickness for use alone as yarn (monofilaments). Single yarns of the spun type, composed of many short fibres, require twist to hold them together and may be made with either S-twist (clockwise) or Z-twist (counter-clockwise) (see Figure 1). Single yarns are used to make the greatest variety of fabrics.

From Evelyn E. Stout, *Introduction to Textiles*
(© 1970); John Wiley & Sons, Inc.

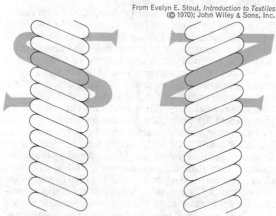

Figure 1: (Left) S- and (right) Z-twist yarns.

Ply yarns. Ply, plied, or folded, yarns are composed of two or more single yarns twisted together. Two-ply yarn, for example, is composed of two single strands; three-ply yarn is composed of three single strands. In making ply yarns from spun strands, the individual strands are usually each twisted in one direction and are then combined and twisted in the opposite direction. When both the single strands and the final ply yarns are twisted in the same direction, the fibre is firmer, producing harder texture and reducing flexibility. Ply yarns provide strength for heavy industrial fabrics and are also used for delicate-looking sheer fabrics.

Cord yarns. Cord yarns are produced by twisting ply yarns together, with the final twist usually applied in the opposite direction of the ply twist (see Figure 2). Cable cords may follow an SZS form, with S-twisted singles made into Z-twisted plies that are then combined with an S-twist, or may follow a ZSZ form. Hawser cord may follow an SSZ or a ZZS pattern. Cord yarns may be used as rope or twine, may be made into very heavy industrial fabrics, or may be composed of extremely fine fibres that are made up into sheer dress fabrics.

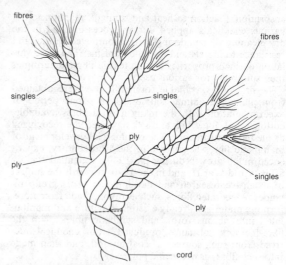

Figure 2: Single, ply, and cord yarns.
From Evelyn E. Stout, *Introduction to Textiles*
(© 1970); John Wiley & Sons, Inc.

Novelty yarns. Novelty yarns include a wide variety of yarns made with such special effects as slubs, produced by intentionally including small lumps in the yarn structure, and man-made yarns with varying thickness introduced during production. Natural fibres, including some linens, wools to be woven into tweed, and the uneven filaments of some types of silk cloth are allowed to retain their normal irregularities, producing the characteristic uneven surface of the finished fabric. Man-made fibres, which can be modified during production, are especially adaptable for special effects such as crimping and textures.

Textured yarns. Texturizing processes were originally applied to man-made fibres to reduce such characteristics as transparency, slipperiness, and the possibility of pilling (formation of small fibre tangles on a fabric surface). Texturizing processes make yarns more opaque, improve appearance and texture, and increase warmth and absorbency. Textured yarns are man-made continuous filaments, modified to impart special texture and appearance (see Figure 3). In the production of abraded yarns, the surfaces are roughened or cut at various intervals and given added twist, producing a hairy effect.

Bulking creates air spaces in the yarns, imparting absorbency and improving ventilation. Bulk is frequently introduced by crimping, imparting waviness similar to the natural crimp of wool fibre; by curling, producing curls or loops at various intervals; or by coiling, imparting stretch. Such changes are usually set by heat application, although chemical treatments are sometimes employed.

Bulking

From G.E. Linton, *Applied Basic Textiles*, 2nd ed. (1973)

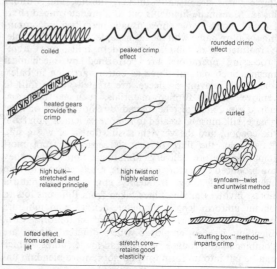

Figure 3: Examples of textured yarns.

In the early 1970s bulky yarns were most frequently produced by the "false twist" method, a continuous process in which the filament yarn is twisted and set, and then untwisted and heated again to either stabilize or destroy the twist. The "stuffing box" method is often applied to nylon, a process in which the filament yarn is compressed in a heated tube, imparting a zigzag crimp, then slowly withdrawn. In the knit de knit process, a synthetic yarn is knitted, heat is applied to set the loops formed by knitting, and the yarn is then unravelled and lightly twisted, producing the desired texture in the completed fabric.

Bulk may be introduced chemically by combining filaments of both high and low shrinkage potential in the same yarn, then subjecting the yarn to washing or steaming, causing the high shrinkage filaments to react, producing a bulked yarn without stretch. Such regenerated yarns as rayon and acetate, which are not made malleable by heat, may be air-bulked by enclosing the yarn in a chamber where it is subjected to a high-pressure jet of air, blowing the individual filaments into random loops that separate, increasing bulk.

Stretch yarns. Stretch yarns are frequently continuous-filament, man-made yarns that are very tightly twisted, heat-set, then untwisted, producing a spiral crimp giving a springy character. Although bulk is imparted in the process, a very high amount of twist is required to produce yarn that has not only bulk, but also stretch.

Elasto-meric fibres

Spandex is the generic term for a highly elastic synthetic fibre composed mainly of segmented polyurethane. Uncovered fibres may be used alone to produce fabrics, but they impart a rubbery feel. For this reason, elastomeric fibre is frequently used as the core of a yarn, and covered with a nonstretch fibre of either natural or man-made origin. Although stretch may be imparted to natural fibres, other properties may be impaired by the process, and the use of an elastic yarn for the core eliminates the need to process the covering fibre.

Metallic yarns. Metallic yarns are usually made from strips of a synthetic film, such as polyester, coated with metallic particles. In another method, aluminum foil strips are sandwiched between layers of film. Metallic yarns may also be made by twisting a strip of metal around a natural or man-made core yarn, producing a metal surface.

The article FIBRES, MAN-MADE provides more information about the production, characteristics, and uses of modern man-made novelty yarns.

Classification based on use. *Fabric construction yarns.* Almost any textile yarn can be used to produce such interlaced fabrics as woven and knitted types. In weaving, the warp, or lengthwise, yarns are subjected to greater stress, and are usually stronger, smoother, more even, and have tighter twist than the weft, or crosswise, yarns. A sizing (stiffening) material such as starch may be applied to warp yarns, increasing their strength to withstand the stresses of fabric construction operations. Weft yarns, subjected to little stress during weaving, may be quite fragile.

Warp and weft threads used in the same fabric may be of differing diameter, producing such special effects as ribbing or cording in the fabric. Special effects may also be obtained by combining warp and weft yarns of fibre from differing origin, or with different degrees of twist, or by introducing metallic threads into weaves composed of other fibres.

Yarns for machine knitting are usually loosely twisted because softness is desired in knit fabrics.

Yarns used in handwork. Yarns used in hand knitting are generally of two or more ply. They include such types as fingering yarns, usually of two or three plys, light to medium in weight and with even diameter, used for various types of apparel; Germantown yarns, soft and thick, usually four-ply and of medium weight, frequently used for sweaters and blankets; Shetland yarns, fine, soft, fluffy, and lightweight, frequently two-ply, used for infants' and children's sweaters and for shawls; worsted knitting yarn, highly twisted and heavy, differing from worsted fabric by being soft instead of crisp, and suitable for sweaters; and zephyr yarns, either all wool, or wool blended with other fibres, very fine and soft, with low twist, and used for lightweight garments.

Embroidery floss, used in hand embroidery, generally has low twist, is of the ply or cord type, and is made of such smooth filaments as silk and rayon. Yarn used for crocheting is frequently a loose cotton cord type; and darning yarns are usually loosely spun.

Sewing thread. Sewing threads are tightly twisted ply yarns made with strands having equally balanced twist, producing a circular cross section. Thread for use in commercial or home sewing machines and for hand sewing should allow easy movement when tension is applied and ease in needle threading; should be smooth, to resist friction during sewing; should have sufficient elasticity to avoid the breaking of stitches or puckering of seams; and should have sufficient strength to hold seams during laundering or dry cleaning and in use.

Threads for special uses may require appropriate treatment. Garments made of water-repellent fabrics, for example, may be sewn with thread that has also been made water-repellent. Thread is usually subjected to special treatment after spinning, and is then wound on spools. Thread size is frequently indicated on the spool end, and systems for indicating degree of fineness vary according to the textile measurement system used locally.

Silk, cotton, and nylon threads

Silk thread has great elasticity and strength combined with fine diameter. It can be permanently stretched in sewing, and is suitable for silks and wools. Buttonhole twist is a strong, lustrous silk about three times the diameter of normal sewing silk, and is used for hand-worked buttonholes, for sewing on buttons, and for various decorative effects.

Cotton thread is compatible with fabric made from yarn of plant origin, such as cotton and linen, and for rayon (made from a plant substance), because it has similar shrinkage characteristics. It is not suitable for most synthetics, which do not shrink, or for fabrics treated to reduce shrinkage. Its low stretch is useful for woven fabrics, but not for knits, which require more stretch.

Nylon thread is strong, with great stretch and recovery, does not shrink, and is suitable for sheers and for very stretchy knits. Polyester thread has similar characteristics, and is appropriate for various synthetic and preshrunk fabrics, and for knits made of synthetic yarns.

Measurement systems. Yarn measurements are expressed as yarn number, count, or size, and describe the relationship of length and weight (or approximate diameter). Because methods of measurement were developed in various areas of the world, there has been a lack of uniformity in such systems.

Indirect systems. Indirect measuring systems are those employing higher number to describe finer yarns, and are based on length per unit weight. Most countries measure yarns made from staple fibres according to the weight of a length of yarn. If one pound is used as a standard unit, for example, a very fine yarn will have to be much longer than a coarser yarn to weigh a pound, so higher counts indicate finer yarns. The size number is an indication of the length of yarn needed to reach a weight of one pound. In the United States, the system is based on the number of hanks per pound, with a hank of 840 yards for cotton and spun silk, 300 yards (a lea) for linen, 256 yards for woollen yarns, and 560 yards for worsted yarns. A widely used continental system is based on the number of hanks of 1,000 metres (one kilometre) required to reach a weight of one kilogram.

Denier system. The denier system is a direct-management type, employed internationally to measure the size of silk and man-made filaments and yarns, and derived from an earlier system for measuring silk filaments (based on the weight in drams of 1,000 yards). Denier number indicates the weight in grams of 9,000 metres of filament or filament yarn. For example, if 9,000 metres of a yarn weigh 15 grams, it is a 15-denier yarn; if 9,000 metres of a yarn weigh 100 grams, it is a 100-denier yarn, and much coarser than the 15-denier yarn. Thus a smaller number indicates a finer yarn. This system is not convenient for measurement of staple yarns because their greater weight would require the use of very large numbers.

Tex system. The tex system, originally devised in 1873, is a universal method developed for the measurement of staple fibre yarns, and is also applicable to the measurement of filament yarns. It is based on the weight in grams of one kilometre (3,300 feet) of yarn. Although representatives of ten nations voted to adopt the system in 1956, tex was still not widely used in the early 1970s.

III. Production of fabric

Fabric construction involves the conversion of yarns, and sometimes fibres, into a fabric having characteristics determined by the materials and methods employed. Most fabrics are presently produced by some method of interlacing, such as weaving or knitting. Weaving, currently the major method of fabric production, includes the basic weaves, plain or tabby, twill, and satin, and the fancy weaves, including pile, Jacquard, dobby, and gauze. Knitted fabrics are rapidly increasing in importance and include weft types and the warp types, raschel and tricot. Other interlaced fabrics include net, lace, and braid. Non-woven fabrics are gaining importance and include materials produced by felting and bonding. Laminating processes are also increasing in importance, and fairly recent developments include needle weaving and the sewing-knitting process.

WOVEN FABRICS

Woven fabrics are made of yarns interlaced in a regular order called a binding system, or weave. Weaving is the process of combining warp and weft components to make a woven structure. The components need neither be parallel to each other nor cross each other at right angles, but most woven structures are comprised of two sets of components, both flexible and crossing at right angles. Weaving is differentiated from warp and weft knitting, braiding, and net making in that these latter processes make use of only one set of elements. In addition, there are geometrical differences, one of the most significant being the small angles through which the components of a woven structure are, in general, bent, in contrast with the components of other structures.

Weaving is a widely used constructional method because it is cheap, basically simple, and adaptable. Woven fabrics have valuable characteristics resulting partly from the geometrical conformation of their components and partly from the fact that the components are held in position not by rigid bonding but by friction set up at the areas where they make contact. Woven fabrics are used in household, apparel, and industrial textiles.

Textile designers can produce a very large variety of cloths by their selection of yarns, finishing processes, and binding systems. Yarns vary in thickness, smoothness, fibre content, twist, and colour, all of which have a profound influence on the finished cloth. Finishing processes range from such simple treatment as brushing up the nap on a woven fabric to such a complicated chemical process as that employed to change opaque cotton fabric to transparent, permanently stiffened organdy.

The binding system, or weave, however, is the basic factor in determining the character of a woven fabric. The three basic systems are plain or tabby, twill, and satin. In complex binding systems, the basic weaves are combined or enriched by hand manipulation or mechanical loom attachments; these include multiple-plane, pile, inlaid, and gauze weaves. Regardless of the binding system, other devices—manipulation of warp spacing, beating in, or tension—can be used to alter the appearance of any weave, to make it looser or more compact, to make it more or less regular.

Weave drafts

As musical notation conveys a composer's ideas, so weave drafts or point paper plans communicate a textile designer's directions for constructing woven fabrics. The draft is a plan on graph paper showing at least one repeat or weave unit of the fabric to be woven. This information enables the weaver or mill specialist to plot the drawing in of the warp, tie up of harnesses to shedding mechanism, and shedding order.

The weaving process. Woven cloth is normally much longer in one direction than the other. The lengthwise threads are called the warp; the other threads, which are combined with the warp and lie widthwise, are called the weft (synonyms are "filling," "woof," and "shoot," or "shute"). An individual thread from the warp, of indefinite length, is called an end; each individual length of weft, extending from one edge of the cloth to the other, is called a pick, or shot. Consecutive picks are usually consecutive lengths of one piece of weft yarn that is repeatedly folded back on itself.

In all methods of weaving cloth (except the rudimentary form of darning), before a length of weft is inserted in the warp, the warp is separated, over a short length extending from the cloth already formed, into two sheets. The process is called shedding and the space between the sheets the shed (Figure 4A). A pick of weft is then laid between the two sheets of warp, in the operation known as picking (Figure 4B). A new shed is then formed in accordance with the desired weave structure, with some or all of the ends in each sheet moving over to the position previously occupied by the other sheet. In this way the weft is clasped between two layers of warp.

Since it is not possible to lay the weft close to the junction of the warp and the cloth already woven, a further operation called beating in, or beating up (Figure 4C), is necessary to push the pick to the desired distance away

Shedding, picking, and beating in

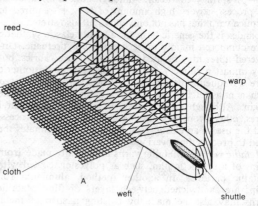

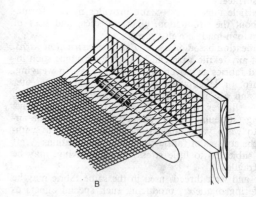

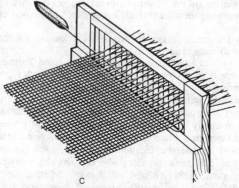

Figure 4: *The three basic motions of weaving:* (A) shedding, (B) picking, and (C) beating in.

from the last one inserted previously. Although beating in usually takes place while the shed is changing, it is normally completed before the new shed is fully formed.

The sequence of primary operations in one weaving cycle is thus shedding, picking, and beating in. At the end of the cycle the geometrical relation of the pick to the warp is the same as it would have been if the pick had been threaded through the spaces between alternate ends, first from one side of the cloth and then from the other, as in darning. This is the reason the weaving process is considered an interlacing method.

Development of the loom.   The word loom (from Middle English *lome*, "tool") is applied to any set of devices permitting a warp to be tensioned and a shed to be formed. Looms exist in great variety, from the bundles of cords and rods of primitive peoples to enormous machines of steel and cast iron.

Except on certain experimental looms, the warp shed is formed with the aid of heddles (or healds). Usually one heddle is provided for each end, or multiple end, of warp thread, but on some primitive looms simple cloths are produced with heddles provided only for each alternate end. A heddle (Figure 5A) consists of a short length of cord, wire, or flat steel strip, supported (in its operative position) roughly perpendicular to the unseparated sheet of warp threads and provided, in modern looms, with an eyelet at its midpoint, through which the warp end is threaded. By pulling one end of the heddle or the other, the warp end can be deflected to one side or the other of the main sheet of ends. The frame holding the heddles is called a harness.

In most looms, the weft is supplied from a shuttle, (Figure 5B), a hollow projectile inside which a weft package is mounted in such a way that the weft can be freely unwound through an eyelet leading from the inside to the outside. The shuttle enters the shed and traverses the warp, leaving a trail of weft behind.

Beating in is generally effected by means of a grating of uniformly spaced fine parallel wires, originally made of natural reeds and thus called a reed (Figure 5C), which, mounted at right angles to the warp, oscillates between the heddles and the junction of the warp and the cloth. The ends pass, one or more at a time, through the spaces between consecutive reed wires, so that the reed, in addition to beating in, controls the spacing of the ends in the cloth.

Early looms.   The earliest evidence of the use of the loom (4400 BC) is a representation of a horizontal two-bar (or two-beamed—*i.e.*, warp beam and cloth beam) loom pictured on a pottery dish found at al-Badārī, Egypt. The warp is stretched between two bars or beams, pegged to the ground at each of the four corners. Lease (or laze) rods are used to separate the warp yarns, forming a shed and aiding the hands in keeping the yarns separated and in order. Lease rods were found in some form on every later type of improved loom, and their use at this very early date indicates that the loom already had been in use long enough to have reached a stage of improvement by addition of devices to aid the hands.

Before lease rods were added, it would have been necessary for the fingers to separate each odd from each even warp thread to create the shed through which the weft yarn was passed. A third rod also seen in this early drawing may be a heddle rod. If so, this loom represents a still more advanced stage of development.

The heddle rod rests on top of the warps. To produce a plain weave, alternate warp yarns are tied to the rod, and when it is raised, the shed is formed quickly and accurately. Some authorities consider the heddle to be the most important step in the evolution of the loom. A shed stick is ordinarily used with the heddle, forming the second, or countershed, opening for the return of the weft.

In addition to the horizontal two-bar loom, there are two other primitive varieties, the warp-weighted and the vertical two-bar loom. The warp-weighted loom consists of a crossbar supported by two vertical posts. The warp threads hang from the crossbar and are held taut by weights of clay, ceramic, or chalk tied to their free ends. Loom weights have been found at archaeological sites

Lease
rods

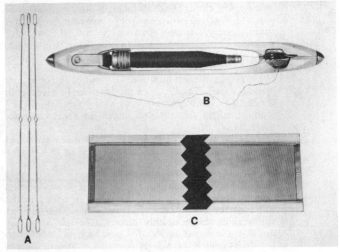

Figure 5: *Loom devices and their functions:* (A) heddles, used for shedding; (B) the shuttle, used for picking; (C) the reed, used for beating in (see text).
By courtesy of the University of Manchester
Institute of Science and Technology, England

dating from 3000 BC, but this type of loom may have originated even earlier. The earliest picture of a vertical two-bar loom is from the Egyptian 18th dynasty (1567–1320 BC). It coincides with the appearance of more intricate textile patterns, the earliest known tapestries (datable between 1483 and 1411 BC) having been found in the tomb of Thutmose IV at Thebes. (Even today the vertical loom is preferred for tapestry weaving.) In the vertical two-bar loom the ends of the warp yarns are attached to a second crossbar, thus combining features of both the horizontal two-bar and the warp-weighted looms.

The heddle rods and shed sticks are used in a similar way on all three types.

Counterparts of these very early looms have been used through the ages in many cultures. The Navajo Indians, probably the best known of the American Indian weavers, have used the simple two-bar vertical loom for several centuries to produce their beautiful rugs and blankets. A form of the horizontal two-bar loom was the backstrap loom, in which one bar was tied to a tree or other stationary device, the second being attached to the weaver's waist by a strap. The weaver could control the tension of the warp yarns by applying pressure as necessary. The backstrap loom was used in pre-Columbian Peru, in other cultures of Central and South America, in Asia, and elsewhere.

Horizontal frame looms.   By about 2500 BC a more advanced loom was apparently evolving in the Far East. Fragments of silk fabrics found adhering to bronzes of the Shang (or Yin) period (1766–1122 BC) in China, show traces of a twill damask pattern, suggesting an advanced weaving knowledge, since such fabrics could not practicably be woven on the looms described above. These fabrics were probably produced on a horizontal frame loom with treadles. The logical connecting link between the horizontal two-bar and the horizontal frame loom with treadles would have been a loom with a heddle rod that was controlled by one foot, for which no early illustrations have been found.

The earliest European pictorial record of the horizontal frame loom with a treadle dates from the 13th century, when it appears in a highly developed form, almost certainly introduced from the East. This two-bar loom was mounted in a frame; to this was connected a treadle operated by the feet, moving the heddles, an improvement of the heddle rod or cord controls now mounted between bars and called a shaft. The advantages of this type of loom were many. First, in the two-bar loom, though more than two heddle rods could be used, the number of groupings of warp threads was limited. Although highly complex patterns could be woven, it was not practical to do so in producing any but very small

Early
horizontal
two-bar
treadle
looms

quantities of cloth. The shaft loom allowed as many as 24 shafts to be set up easily, enabling the weaver to produce comparatively intricate patterns. Second, the weaver's sword or comb formerly used to beat the weft into place was replaced by the batten, supported in a heavy wooden frame from the main frame of the loom; its weight and free-swinging motion improved the beating-in action and made it easier. Third, use of the foot treadle freed both hands to throw the shuttle and swing the batten. The loom remained virtually unchanged for many centuries thereafter.

Drawlooms. The shaft loom was adequate for plain and for simply patterned fabrics, but a more complex loom was needed for the weaving of intricately figured fabrics, which might require 100 or more shafts. This kind of weaving was accomplished on the drawloom. Its origin is unknown, but it probably was first used in the Far East for silk weaving and was introduced into the silk-working centres of Italy during the Middle Ages. The drawloom had two devices for shedding: in addition to the shafts, which the weaver operated by treadles, cords were also used to raise the warp threads, gathered into groups as required by the pattern. The cords were worked by an operator (called a drawboy) seated on top of the loom.

The drawloom was improved in Italy and France in the early 17th century by the addition of a type of mechanical drawboy, allowing the assistant to stand on the floor at the side of the loom and increasing the control of the cords. The continued inconvenience of employing an assistant, however, who might also make errors, led to a search for an automatic mechanism that would perform all work of the drawboy. Most of the later developments in automatic mechanisms to control the shedding operation originated in France, which had become one of the leading countries in the weaving of figured silks.

In 1725 Basile Bouchon added to the mechanical drawboy a mechanism that selected the cords to be drawn to form the pattern. Selection was controlled by a roll of paper, perforated according to the pattern, which passed around a cylinder. The cylinder was pushed toward the selecting box and met with needles carrying the warp-controlling cords; the needles that met unperforated paper slid along, and the others passed through the holes and remained stationary. The selected cords were drawn down by a foot-operated treadle.

The mechanical drawboy made the proper selection of warp threads, eliminating errors, but still required an operator. The mechanism was improved in 1728 by increasing the number of needles and using a rectangular perforated card for each individual shedding motion, the cards being strung together in an endless chain. In 1745 Jacques de Vaucanson constructed a loom incorporating a number of improvements. He mounted the selecting box above the loom, where it acted directly on hooks fastened to the cords that controlled the warp yarns. The hooks passed through needles and were raised by a strong metal bar. The needles were selected by perforated cards passing around a sliding cylinder, without the aid of a second operator or assistant. The cylinder was very complex, and the mechanism is not known to have been adopted, but it served as the foundation for the successful Jacquard attachment.

The Jacquard attachment. The French inventor Joseph-Marie Jacquard, commissioned to overhaul Vaucanson's loom, did so without any of the directions, which were missing. In 1801, at the Paris Industrial Exhibition, he demonstrated an improved drawloom, and in 1805 he introduced the invention that ever since has caused the loom to which it is attached to be called the Jacquard loom.

The Jacquard attachment is an automatic, selective shedding device, mounted on top of the loom and operated by a treadle controlled by the weaver. As in the drawloom, every warp yarn runs through a loop in a controlling cord, held taut by a weight. Each cord is suspended from a wire ("hook") that is bent at the bottom to hold the cord and bent at the top in order to hook around the blades or bars of the griff, the lifting mechanism. To

allow only those warp threads that are needed to form the pattern to be raised, some hooks must be dislodged from the rising griff. This is accomplished by horizontally placed needles connected to the hooks. As the perforated pattern card moves into place on the cylinder (which is, in fact, a quadrangular block), the needles pass through the holes in the card, and the warps are raised; where there are no holes, the needles are pushed back (by a spring action on the opposite end of each), pulling the hooks away from the rising griff bar, and the warps are not raised.

Each card represents one throw of the shuttle, and the pattern is transferred to the cards from the designer's weave draft. Although each Jacquard attachment is limited in the number of hooks it can control and, therefore, in the size of the repeat pattern, by adding several Jacquard attachments to one loom, the weaver not only can produce intricately figured fabrics but also can weave pictures of considerable size.

The flying shuttle. The first decisive step toward automation of the loom was the invention of the flying shuttle patented in 1733 by the Englishman John Kay. Kay was a weaver of broadloom fabrics, which because of their width required two weavers to sit side by side, one throwing the shuttle from the right to the centre, the other reaching between the warps and sending it on its way to the left and then returning it to the centre. The stopping of the shuttle and the reaching between the warps caused imperfections in the cloth. Kay devised a mechanical attachment controlled by a cord jerked by the weaver that sent the shuttle flying through the shed. Jerking the cord in the opposite direction sent the shuttle on its return trip. Using the flying shuttle, one weaver could weave fabrics of any width more quickly than two could before. A more important virtue of Kay's invention, however, lay in its adaptability to automatic weaving.

Power-driven looms. The first power-driven machine for weaving fabric-width goods, patented in 1785 by Edmund Cartwright, an English clergyman, was inadequate because it considered only three motions: shedding, picking, and winding the woven cloth onto the cloth beam. Cartwright's second patent (1786) proved too ambitious, but his concept of a weaving machine became the basis for the successful power loom.

One of the great obstacles to the success of the power loom was the necessity to stop the loom frequently in order to dress (i.e., apply sizing to) the warp, an operation that, like many others, had been done in proportionately reasonable time when the weaving was done by hand. With the power loom a second man had to be employed continuously to do this work, so there was no saving of expense or time. In the early 19th century a dressing machine was developed that prepared the warp after it had been wound onto the warp beam and as it was passed to the cloth beam. Although later superseded by an improved sizing apparatus, this device made the power loom a practical tool.

Advances made by William Horrocks of Scotland between 1803 and 1813 included an improvement in the method of taking up the cloth (i.e., winding the woven fabric onto the cloth beam) and making a more compact machine of iron, requiring little space as compared with wooden handlooms.

Francis Cabot Lowell, of Boston, experimented with the power loom, adding improvements to increase the weaving speed, and also improved the dressing machine.

A valuable improvement was that of the let-off and take-up motions, to maintain uniform warp tension automatically. The principle of holding at the beat (i.e., not permitting the warp to be let off until the pick was beaten into place) first applied by Erastus Brigham Bigelow in the carpet loom, was successfully applied to all kinds of weaving. Another Bigelow invention, applicable to power looms in general, although first used on a carpet loom, was the friction-brake stop mechanism, allowing the loom to be stopped without a shock.

These developments were primarily concerned with the power loom used for weaving plain goods. William Crompton, an English machinist working in the machine

The mechanical drawboy

Early difficulties of the power loom

shop attached to a cotton factory in Massachusetts, undertook the development of a loom that could weave fancy goods, patented in both the U.S. and England in 1837. The loom was later much improved by his son George Crompton. Such 19th-century inventions made possible the production of textile goods for every use in great volume and variety, and at low cost.

Modern looms. Modern looms still weave by repeating in sequence the operations of shedding, picking, and beating in, but within that framework there has been considerable development during the 20th century. Several new types of loom have come into industrial use, whereas older types have been refined and their scope extended. Two main influences have been the rising cost of labour and the increasing use of man-made, continuous-filament yarns. The first has led to an increase in automatic control, in automatic handling of yarn packages, and in the use of larger packages; the second, to greater precision and finish in loom construction, because deficiency in these qualities is readily reflected in the quality of the cloth made from these yarns.

Modern looms can be grouped into two classes according to whether they produce cloth in plane or tubular form (see Figure 6). Looms of the first kind, comprising

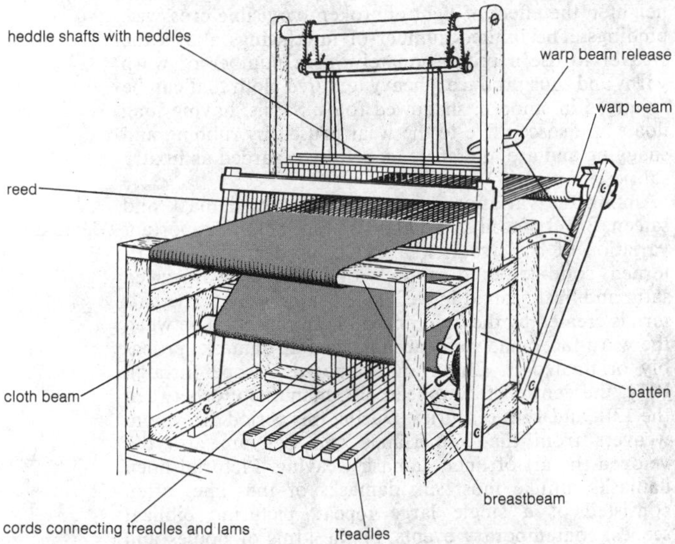

Figure 6: Principal parts of a modern handloom.

The two classes of modern looms

all but a few, are called flat looms; the others are described as circular. Since the majority are flat looms, the adjective is used only when a distinction has to be drawn. Flat looms fall into two categories: those that employ a shuttle and those that draw the weft from a stationary supply, usually called shuttleless looms. (This term is not entirely satisfactory, as some primitive looms make no use of a shuttle, merely passing through the shed a stick with weft wound on it.) Shuttle looms fall into two groups according to whether the shuttle is replenished by hand or automatically. The second kind is often described as an automatic loom, but, except for shuttle replenishment, it is no more automatic in its operation than the hand-replenished or so-called nonautomatic loom, which, like all modern looms, is power-operated by electric motor. With both types of loom the actual weaving operation is entirely automatic and is performed in exactly the same manner.

Hand replenished, or nonautomatic, looms are used only where particular circumstances—of yarns, fabrics, or use—make automatically replenished looms either technically unsuitable or uneconomic. Basically they differ little from the power looms of the latter half of the 19th century. They do not run appreciably faster but are better engineered, making use, for example, of machine-cut instead of cast gear wheels. Often there is no superstructure, which makes for cleanliness and improved illumination; frequently rigid heddle connectors are em-

ployed, leading to precise and stable setting of the shed; and usually the overpick mechanism has been replaced by the cleaner and safer underpick.

Automatically replenished flat, or automatic, looms are the most important class of modern loom, available for a very wide range of fabrics. In virtually all such looms, the shuttle is replenished by automatically replacing the exhausted bobbin with a full one. In principle they are thus the same as the automatic looms introduced at the end of the 19th century. Since that time, automatic shuttle-changing looms have also been introduced but have largely become obsolete, because bobbin-changing looms have been developed to a point where they can deal with most of the yarns for which it was once thought necessary to use shuttle-changing looms.

Apart from the general engineering refinements, automatic looms have advanced mainly in respect of the weft supply. Alternatives to the hand-replenished bobbin now exist in the form of the automatic bobbin loader, the loom being supplied with boxes of pirned (reeled) weft; and the automatic loom winder, the loom being fed with large cones of yarn, which is wound onto pirns at the loom. These alternatives are technically feasible and economic only with certain yarns. Therefore, all three types of weft supply continue to be used. An alternative to the rotary battery, when weft of more than one colour is used, is a series of vertical stacks.

The principle of shuttle replenishment is the same for all three systems. When the shuttle is stationary in the shuttle box, and the bar carrying the reed is farthest forward, a feeler enters the shuttle and senses whether the weft is on the point of exhaustion. Feelers may be mechanical or electrical, relying, respectively, on the change in friction or the change in electrical resistance brought about by the absence of weft. Alternatively, with delicate wefts, an optical feeler may be used that depends for its action on the change in the amount of light reflected when the bare pirn is revealed.

When the feeler has sensed that the bobbin is nearly empty, mechanical or electrical signals are transmitted to the transfer mechanism that, when the shuttle is appropriately positioned and momentarily at rest, both as regards warp-way and weft-way motion, hammers a new bobbin into position, simultaneously ejecting the empty one through the open base of the shuttle. The loom continues to run at its normal speed throughout.

In the course of this operation, there are created unwanted lengths of weft extending from the nearer selvage. These, if not controlled and disposed of, may find their way into the cloth and appear as defects. Modern looms supplement the earlier mechanical methods by pneumatic suction, with the result that the most delicate fabrics can be woven on automatic bobbin-changing looms without any loss of quality. To make certain of removal of the remnant of weft on the old bobbin, extending to the eye of the shuttle, a cutter moves forward into the shuttle box and cuts the weft close to the eye just before the bobbin is ejected.

High speed, often combined with the use of large and heavy shuttles, means that these modern looms are noisier than ever. The noise level in a typical textile mill is above the level at which deafness occurs following prolonged exposure.

Shuttleless looms are of three kinds, of which the first predominates: dummy shuttle, rapier, and fluid jet. The dummy-shuttle type, the most successful of the shuttleless looms, makes use of a dummy shuttle, a projectile that contains no weft but that passes through the shed in the manner of a shuttle and leaves a trail of yarn behind it.

The rapier type covers a pick of weft from a stationary package through the shed by means of either a single rapier or a pair of rapiers. Rapiers are either rigid rods or flexible steel tapes, which are straight when in the shed but on withdrawal are wound onto a wheel, in order to save floor space. Rapier looms are, on the whole, simpler and more versatile than dummy-shuttle looms, but they have failed to achieve such high rates of weft insertion, the maximum being not more than 400 yards (365 metres) per minute. They differ in respect of the number

Types of shuttleless looms

of rapiers employed and the type of selvage provided; some of them operate by gripping the free end of the weft and conveying that through the shed rather than by starting with a loop. Fluid-jet looms, most recently developed of the shuttleless types, are produced and used on a much smaller scale than the two other types described above. They are of two kinds, one employing a jet of air, the other a water jet, to propel a measured length of weft through the shed. The significance of this development is that for the first time nothing solid is passed into the shed other than the weft, which eliminates the difficulties normally associated with checking and warp protection, and reduces the noise to an acceptable level.

In addition to those looms that have established themselves industrially, there are looms still in the experimental stage. Loom development is always slow: some of the looms just gaining favour had their origins in inventions made 50 or even 100 years earlier. The most intense activity is in the field of shuttleless looms, because these offer the greatest prospect of achieving increased rates of weft insertion and of avoiding the drawbacks of noise, danger, vibration, high power consumption, and wear attendant on the use of a shuttle. The ultimate in direct projection is a method, still experimental, in which the weft is projected longitudinally at high speed and traverses the warp under its own momentum, nothing entering the shed but the pick of weft. The name inertial has been given to this method. Another experimental loom employs multiple rapiers for weft insertion and, in addition, eliminates the heddles and the reed.

Basic weaves. The basic weaves include plain (or tabby), twills, and satins (see Figure 7).

Figure 7: *Types of weaves:* (Left) plain, (centre) twill, (right) satin.

Plain weave. Plain, or tabby, weave, the simplest and most common of all weaves, requires only two harnesses and has two warp and weft yarns in each weave unit. To produce it, the warp yarns are held parallel under tension while a crosswise weft yarn is shot over and under alternate warps across the width of the web. The weave unit is completed at the end of the second row, when the weft has been inserted over and under the opposite set of warps, thus locking the previous weft in place. Fabric length is increased with the insertion of each succeeding weft yarn. When warp and weft yarns are approximately equal in size and quantity, the finished fabric is balanced and potentially stronger than cloth made of the same kind and number of warp and weft yarns in any other basic weave. Tabby woven with different-sized warp and weft yarns results in such fabrics as taffeta and poplin, in which many fine warps are interlaced with proportionately fewer thick weft yarns to form cloths with crosswise ridges or ribs.

The term extended tabby describes any weave in which two or more warps or wefts, or both, are interlaced as a unit. The group includes fabrics with basketry effects and fabrics with ribs formed by groups of warps or wefts in each shed.

Tapestry weave
Tapestry weave is a tabby in which a variety of coloured weft yarns is interlaced with the warp to form patterns. It is usually an unbalanced weave, with wefts completely covering a proportionately low number of warps. These cloths are sturdy and compact. Although they are flat and generally do not drape well, they have been used for centuries to make ceremonial and decorative dress and costumes.

Twill weave. Twill weave is distinguished by diagonal lines. The simplest twill is that created by the weft crossing over two warp yarns, then under one, the sequence being repeated in each succeeding shot (pick), but stepped over, one warp either to the left or right. Twills with more warps than wefts floating on the fabric's face

are called warp faced; those with wefts predominating, weft faced. The angle of the twill can also vary.

Twills can be varied by changing the relative number of warps and wefts in each repeat (2:1, 2:3, 3:1, 6:2, etc.); by stepping the repeat in one direction; by breaking the direction of the diagonals formed by the twill at regular intervals; by reversing the direction of the diagonal at regular intervals to form chevrons or lozenges; or by combining several twills or modifying them to create a pattern.

Twills drape better than plain weaves with the same yarn count because twills have fewer interlacings. Twill weaves have been used throughout history in many weights and textures, from wool serges mentioned in medieval French manuscripts to English diapered (diamond patterned) table linens, patterned bed coverlets, and Indian shawls.

Satin weave. Although satin-weave drafts superficially resemble those of twills, satin weave does not have the regular step in each successive weft that is characteristic of twills. Thus, there is no strong diagonal line, and the fabric is smooth faced, with an unbroken surface made up of long floating warp yarns. A true satin must have at least five warp and weft yarns in each complete weave repeat and thus requires at least five harnesses. Most satin fabrics are made of smooth, lightly twisted yarns that heighten the effect of light unbroken by visible crosswise bindings. The limited number of interlacings allows the weaver to use a proportionately large number of warp yarns and thus produce a heavy textured cloth that can be arranged in smooth, shadowed folds. Satins, having long floats, are susceptible to the wear caused by rubbing and snagging and are, therefore, generally regarded as luxury fabrics.

Among the variations of satin weave are damask and sateen, a weft-faced satin. Damask is the most important variation of basic satin weave. Classic damask is a patterned, solid-coloured fabric with figures in warp-faced satin and background in weft-faced satin weave. The pattern is created by the difference in light reflection between the warp-faced and weft-faced areas. Silk damasks probably originated in China and came to Europe through Italy, the centre of European silk manufacture between the 13th and 17th centuries. During this period drawloom weavers from the Netherlands and Belgium also developed the art of linen damask weaving. Pictorial linen damasks, unlike most silk damasks of the time, often consisted of a single large repeat, picturing biblical scenes, contemporary events, or the arms of nobles and kings.

Damask

Complex weaves. Complex weaves include multiple plane, pile, inlaid, Jacquard, dobby, and gauze (or leno) weaves.

Multiple plain weave. Reversible double-woven cloth is produced by multiple plain weaving. It is woven in two layers, which may be completely independent, may be joined at one or both selvages, may be held together along the edges of a pattern, or may be united by a separate binding weft. Though often tabby weave is employed on both surfaces, any of the basic weaves may be used, depending on the intended use of the fabric.

Double-woven cloths have been used for clothing, but, though warm, they tend to be heavy and to drape poorly. They are most often used as bedcovers or wall hangings. German 18th-century *Beiderwand* is an example of antique double-woven cloth consisting of two layers of tabby weave joined only along the edges of the pattern. A dark-coloured pattern in one layer is set against the light-coloured ground of the other layer; the pattern is seen in negative or the reverse side of the cloth.

Nonreversible cloth with two or more sets of warp and sometimes of weft can also be produced. These cloths have an intricately patterned face, and all warps and wefts that do not appear on the face are carried along and bound into the web on the reverse side. This class includes important historic textiles, such as early Persian and Byzantine figured fabrics, as well as more recent Jacquard-woven imitation tapestries and a wide range of imitation brocaded fabrics.

Pile weave. Pile weaves have a ground fabric plus an extra set of yarns woven or tied into the ground and projecting from it as cut ends or loops. A great range of textures is included in this binding system, from terry pile towelling and corduroy to silk velvets and Oriental rugs.

In warp-pile fabrics the pile is formed by an extra set of warp yarns. To create such a fabric, first one set (sheet) of ground warps is raised, and the weft makes its first interlacing with the ground warp. Next, pile warps are raised, and a rod is inserted through the entire width of the web. The remaining ground warps are raised to form the third shed; then the ground weft is shot across again. This sequence is repeated several times; then the rods are slipped out, leaving a warp pile. To form cut-pile velvet, a knife on the end of the rod cuts the pile warps it passes, creating two fine rows of cut pile. Although the system has many technical variations, the same basic process can be applied to most warp-pile weaving.

If the pile is not cut when the rod is removed, a loop pile fabric results. In weaving terry pile fabrics, the ground warp is under tension, and the pile warp stays slack. When wefts are beaten in, the slack yarns are pushed into loops on both sides of the cloth.

To make velvets by double-cloth construction, two layers of cloth are woven simultaneously face-to-face, with long pile warp yarns connecting the two layers. After the cloth is woven, a knife slices the two layers apart.

Corduroy and velveteen are weft-pile constructions. Weft yarns having long floats are inserted between ground-weave picks. The floats are slit longitudinally after the fabric is completed, thus forming a ribbed surface of cut pile. In manufacture of velveteen the floats are formed over the whole surface of the fabric and cut evenly to imitate velvet.

Hand-knotted Oriental and Scandinavian rugs are constructed on a tabby-weave ground, with each row of knots followed by tightly beaten-in wefts. The pile of fine Oriental rugs may contain 160 knots per inch, thus completely obscuring the knots in the rug's foundation.

Inlaid weave. In all of the fabrics of this class, designs are created by inserting pattern warp or weft yarns between ground warps or wefts.

Brocaded fabric Brocaded fabric has a pattern of coloured or metallic threads, or both, set in low relief against the ground weave. The ground weave can be any basic weave, since the brocaded pattern is merely inserted between ground wefts and is bound by ground warps. Until the advent of the Jacquard mechanism in the early 19th century, brocaded fabrics were woven by drawloom weavers who inserted the pattern wefts by hand. These weft yarns were wound on small brocading shuttles that travelled across the width of each pattern repeat, a separate shuttle being used for each colour in the repeat. Generally, these extra wefts were found only in the area in which the pattern was located and usually formed long floats on the reverse side of the fabric.

A mechanical process closely corresponding to hand brocading is called swivel, a system of figuring fabrics by using mechanically controlled pattern shuttles. The figures, inserted between ground-weft picks, interlace with the warp. The lappet system produces figured fabrics resembling those made by swivel figuring, but the pattern yarns are extra warps (rather than wefts) brought into play from separate warp beams. Lappet weaving is generally confined to coarse pattern yarns and can be distinguished from swivel by its interlacing with weft rather than with warp yarns.

Jacquard weave. The Jacquard weave, used to make allover figured fabrics such as brocades, tapestries, and damasks, is woven on a loom having a Jacquard attachment to control individual warps. Fabrics of this type are costly because of the time and skill involved in making the Jacquard cards, preparing the loom to produce a new pattern, and the slowness of the weaving operation. The Jacquard weave usually combines two or more basic weaves, with different weaves used for the design and the background.

Dobby weaves. Dobby weaves also produce allover figured fabrics. They are made on looms having a dobby attachment, with narrow strips of wood instead of Jacquard cards. Dobby weaves are limited to simple, small geometric figures, with the design repeated frequently, and are fairly inexpensive to produce.

Gauze or leno weave. Gauze weaving is an open weave made by twisting adjacent warps together. It is usually made by the leno or doup, weaving process, in which a doup attachment, a thin hairpin-like needle attached to two healds, is used, and the adjacent warp yarns cross each other between picks. Since the crossed warps firmly lock each weft in place, gauze weaves are often used for sheer fabrics made of smooth fine yarns. Although gauze weaving, with its multitude of variations, has been adapted to modern production, it is an ancient technique.

KNITTED FABRICS

Knitted fabrics are constructed by the interlocking of a series of loops made from one or more yarns, with each row of loops caught into the preceding row. Loops running lengthwise are called wales, those running crosswise courses. Hand knitting probably originated among the nomads of the Arabian Desert about 1000 BC and spread from Egypt to Spain, France, and Italy. Knitting guilds were established in Paris and Florence by the later Middle Ages. Austria and Germany produced heavily cabled and knotted fabrics, embroidered with brightly coloured patterns. In the Netherlands, naturalistic patterns were worked on fabric in reverse stocking stitch, and several Dutch knitters went to Denmark to teach Danish women the Dutch skills. The craft of hand knitting became less important with the invention of a frame knitting machine in 1589, although production of yarns for hand knitting remains an important branch of the textile industry.

The frame knitting machine allowed production of a complete row of loops at one time. The modern knitting industry, with its highly sophisticated machinery, has grown from this simple device.

Knitted fabrics were formerly described in terms of the number of courses and wales per unit length and the weight of the fabric per unit area. This system is limited, however, and there is a shift to use of the dimensions and configuration of the single loop, the repeating unit determining such fabric characteristics as area, knitting quality, and weight. The length of yarn knitted into a loop or stitch is termed the stitch length, and in a plain knitted structure this is related to the courses per inch, wales per inch, and stitch density. The two basic equilibrium states for knitted fabrics are the dry-relaxed state, attained by allowing the fabric to relax freely in the air, and the wet-relaxed state, reached after static relaxation of the fabric in water followed by drying. **Nomenclature of knitted fabrics**

Knitting machines. The needle is the basic element of all knitting machines. The two main needle types are the "bearded" spring needle, invented about 1589, and the more common latch needle, invented in 1847.

The bearded needle, made from thin wire, has one end bent, forming an operating handle; the other end is drawn out and bent over, forming a long flexible tipped hook resembling a beard. A smooth groove, or eye, is cut in the stem or shank of the needle just behind the tip. In use this needle requires two other units, a sinker to form a loop and a presser to close the needle beard, allowing the loop to pass over the beard when a new stitch is formed. Bearded needles can be made from very fine wire and are used to produce fine fabrics.

The latch needle is composed of a curved hook, a latch, or tumbler, that swings on a rivet just below the hook, and the stem, or butt. It is sometimes called the self-acting needle because no presser is needed; the hook is closed by the pressure of a completed loop on the latch as it rises on the shaft. Needles differ greatly in thickness, in gauge, and in length, and appropriate types must be selected for specific purposes. A 4-gauge needle, for example, is used for heavy sweaters, but an 80-gauge needle is required for fine hosiery.

Weft knitting. The type of stitch used in weft knitting affects both the appearance and properties of the knitted fabric. The basic stitches are plain, or jersey (see Figure

8) rib; and purl. In the plain stitch, each loop is drawn through others to the same side of the fabric. In the rib stitch, loops of the same course are drawn to both sides of the fabric. The web is formed by two sets of needles, arranged opposite to each other and fed by the same thread, with each needle in one circle taking up a position between its counterparts in the other. In a 2:2 rib, two needles on one set alternate with two of the other. The interlock structure is a variant of the rib form in which two threads are alternately knitted by the opposite needles so that interlocking occurs. In the purl stitch, loops are drawn to opposite sides of the fabric, which, on both sides, has the appearance of the back of a plain stitch fabric. Jacquard mechanisms can be attached to knitting machines, so that individual needles can be controlled for each course or for every two, and complicated patterns can be knitted. To form a tuck stitch, a completed loop is not discharged from some of the needles in each course, and loops accumulating on these needles are later discharged together. The plaited stitch is made by feeding two threads into the same hook, so that one thread shows on the one side of the fabric and the other on the opposite side. A float stitch is produced by missing interlooping over a series of needles so that the thread floats over a few loops in each course.

From Isabel B. Wingate, *Textile Fabrics and Their Selection*, 6th ed. (© 1970), Prentice-Hall, Inc.

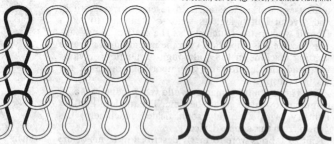

Figure 8: *Stitches in a plain weft-knitted fabric.*
(Left) A wale in a plain, circular-knit fabric. (Right) A course in a plain circular-knit fabric.

Types of knitting machines

Knitting machines can be flat or circular. Flat machines have their needles mounted in a flat plate or needle bed or in two beds at right angles to each other and each at a 45° angle to the horizontal. The knitted fabric passes downward through the space between the upper edges of the plates, called the throat. In the knitting process, the needles are pushed up and down by cams attached to a carriage with a yarn guide, which moves over the length of the machine. The width of the fabric can be altered by increasing or decreasing the number of active needles, allowing production of shaped fabrics, which when sewn together make fully fashioned garments. Although flat-bed machines are suited for hand operation, they are power driven in commercial use, and, by selection of colour, type of stitch, cam design, and Jacquard device, almost unlimited variety is possible. The cotton frame, designed to knit fine, fully fashioned goods, shaped for improved fit of such items as hosiery and sweaters, is fitted with automatic narrowing and widening devices.

Circular machine needles are carried in grooves cut in the wall of a cylinder, which may be as small as one centimetre (0.4 inch) in diameter and as large as 1.5 metres (five feet). Some circular machines have two sets of needles, carried in concentric cylinders, so that the needles interlock. During the knitting operation the butts of the needles move through cam tracks, the needles sliding up and down to pick up yarn, form a new loop, and cast off the previously formed loop. In the least complicated of these machines, yarn is supplied from one package, each needle picking up the yarn once per revolution of the cylinder. Modern machines may have as many as 100 feeders, allowing each needle to pick up 100 threads per revolution. Both latch and spring needles are used, with the former more common. Modern, large, circular, plain or jersey machines having 90–100 feeders are frequently used to produce medium-weight fabric. Small bladelike units, or sinkers, are inserted between every two needles to engage and hold the completed fabric, preventing it from riding up with the needles as they are lifted to form new stitches. Machines may be fitted with pattern wheels controlling needle action to produce tuck and float stitches, and a Jacquard mechanism may also be attached. Stop motions are essential to stop the machine when a thread breaks. Because yarn tension affects fabric uniformity, various tension controllers have been devised. An alternative method, positive feed, feeding precisely measured amounts of yarn into the machine, is now considered more satisfactory.

Circular rib machines consist of a vertical cylinder, with needle slots on the outside, and a horizontal bed in the form of a circular plate or dial with needle slots cut radially, so that the two sets of needles are arranged at right angles to each other.

Seamless hosiery, knitted in tubular form, is produced by circular knitting machines. Modern hosiery machines, such as the Komet machine employ double-hooked needles directly opposite each other in the same plane to knit the leg and foot portions, the heel and the toe. The toe is later closed in a separate operation. In the Getaz toe, the seam is placed under the toes instead of on top of them.

Underwear fabrics are usually knitted on circular machines, and—except for fully fashioned underwear, tights, and leotards, which are knitted to pattern and sewn together—underwear making is a cut, make, and trim operation. Tights or panty hose are a combination of hosiery and underwear and can be fully fashioned. Seamless panty hose are made on circular hose machines modified to make very long stockings with open tops, two of which are cut open at opposite sides and seamed together front and back. The wearing quality and fit of modern panty hose have been greatly improved with the development of stretch nylon and spandex, and greater variety has been introduced with the development of texturized yarn.

Much hosiery is finished by washing, drying, and a boarding process in which the hosiery is drawn over a thin metal or wooden form of appropriate shape and pressed between two heated surfaces. The introduction of nylon fibre led to the development of a preboarding process, setting the loops and the fabric in the required shape before dyeing and finishing. The article, fitted on a form of appropriate shape, is placed in an autoclave or passed through a high-temperature setting unit. Fabric treated in this way does not distort during dyeing.

Circular knitting machines can be adapted to make simulated furs. One type intermeshes plush loops with the plain-stitch base fabric then cuts the loops, producing a pile. A more common method forms the pile with a carded sliver. A plain-stitch fabric is used as the base and loose fibres from a sliver, fed from a brushing or carding device, are inserted by a V-shaped claw, forming the pile. Pile depth is determined by the length of the fibres in the sliver.

One of the most sophisticated knitting machines incorporates electronic selection of sinkers in a Jacquard circular knitting machine.

Warp knitting. The two types of warp knitting are raschel, made with latch needles, and tricot, using bearded needles.

Raschel. Coarser yarns are generally used for raschel knitting, and there has recently been interest in knitting staple yarns on these machines. In the Raschel machine, the needles move in a ground steel plate, called the trick plate. The top of this plate, the verge, defines the level of the completed loops on the needle shank. The loops are prevented from moving upward when the needle rises by the downward pull of the fabric and the sinkers between the needles. Guide bars feed the yarn to the needles. In a knitting cycle, the needles start at the lowest point, when the preceding loop has just been cast off, and the new loop joins the needle hook to the fabric. The needles rise, while the new loop opens the latches and ends up on the shank below the latch. The guide bars then swing through the needles, and the front bar moves one needle space sideways. When the guide bar swings back to the front of the machine, the front bar has laid the thread on the hooks. The needles fall, the earlier loops close the latch to trap the new loops, and the old loops are cast off. Raschels, made in a variety of forms, are usually more open in construction and coarser in texture than are other warp knits.

Tricot. Tricot, a warp knit made with two sets of threads, is characterized by fine ribs running vertically on the fabric face and horizontally on its back. The tricot knitting machine makes light fabrics, weighing less than four ounces per square yard. Its development was stimulated by the invention of the so-called FNF compound needle, a sturdy device that later fell into disuse but that made possible improved production speeds. Although approximately half of the tricot machines in current use make plain fabrics on two guide bars, there is increasing interest in pattern knitting. In this type of knitting, the warp-knitting cycle requires close control on the lateral bar motion, achieved by control chains made of chunky metal links.

Special effects in warp knits. The scope of warp knitting has been extended by the development of procedures for laying in nonknitted threads for colour, density, and texture effects (or inlaying), although such threads may also be an essential part of the structure. For example, in the form called "zigzagging across several pillars," the ground of most raschel fabrics, the front bar makes crochet chains, or "pillars," which are connected by zigzag inlays.

An extension of conventional warp knitting is the Co-We-Nit warp-knitting machine, producing fabrics with the properties of both woven and knitted fabrics. The machines need have only two warp-forming warps and provision for up to eight interlooped warp threads between each chain of loops. These warp threads are interlaced with a quasiweft, forming a fabric resembling woven cloth on one side.

<u>OTHER INTERLACED FABRICS</u>

Net and lace making. The popularity of handmade laces led to the invention of lace-making machines. The early models required intricate engineering mechanisms, and the development of the modern lace industry originated when a machine was designed to produce laces identical with Brussels lace. In the Heathcot, or bobbinet, machine, warp threads were arranged so that the threads moved downward as the beams unwound. Other threads were wound on thin, flat spools or bobbins held in narrow carriages that could move in a groove or comb in two rows. The carriages carrying the bobbins were placed on one side of the vertical warp threads and given a pendulum-like motion, causing them to pass between the warp threads. The warp threads were then moved sideways, so that on the return swing each bobbin thread passed around one of them. Then the warp threads moved sideways in the opposite direction, thus completing a wrapping movement. In addition, each row of bobbins was moved by a rack-and-pinion gearing, one row to the left and one to the right. As these movements continued, the threads were laid diagonally across the fabric as the warp was delivered. Improvements on the Heathcot machine followed through the 19th century: Nottingham-lace machines, used primarily for coarse-lace production, employ larger bobbins, and the pattern threads are wound independently on section spools; in another type, the Barmens machine, threads on king bobbins on carriers are plaited together, sometimes with warp threads.

Schiffli lace, a type of embroidery, is made by modern machines, evolved from a hand version, using needles with points at each end. Several hundred needles are placed horizontally, often in two rows, one above the other. The fabric to be embroidered is held vertically in a frame extending the full width of the machine, and the needles, supplied with yarn from individual spools, move backward and forward through the fabric. At each penetration a shuttle moves upward and interlaces yarn with the needle loop. Movement of both fabric and needles is controlled by Jacquard systems.

Many types of machine-made laces are made, frequently with geometrically shaped nets forming their back-

Early machine-made laces

grounds. Formerly made only of cotton, they are now frequently made from man-made fibre yarns. Bobbinet lace, essentially a hexagonal net, is used as a base for applique work for durable non-run net hosiery, and, when heavily sized, for such materials as millinery and veilings. Barmens lace has a fairly heavy texture and an angular pattern; flowing lines, heavy outline cords, and fine net backgrounds are not usually made on Barmens machines.

The introduction of light-resistant polyester yarns led to a revival of Nottingham machine-made curtains. Leavers lace is available in an infinite variety of patterns, since the manufacturing technique allows use of almost any type of yarn. The high strength and comparatively low cost of man-made fibre yarns has made sheer laces widely available.

Net, an open fabric having geometrically shaped, open meshes, is produced with meshes ranging from fine to large. Formerly made by hand, the various types are now made on knitting machines. Popular types include bobbinet, made with hexagonal-shaped mesh and used for formal gowns, veils, and curtains, and tulle, a closely constructed, fine net having similar uses. Fishnet, a course type with knots in four corners forming the mesh formerly made by fishermen, is now a popular machine-made curtain fabric.

Braiding or plaiting. Braid is made by interlacing three or more yarns or fabric strips forming a flat or tubular narrow fabric. It is used as trimming and for belts and is also sewn together to make hats and braided rugs. Plaiting, usually used synonymously with braiding, may be used in a more limited sense, applying only to a braid made from such materials as rope and straw.

<u>NONINTERLACED FABRICS</u>

With the exception of felt, nonwoven materials are in the early stages of development. There is controversy about the precise meaning of the term nonwoven, but one authority defines nonwoven fabrics as textile fabrics made of a fibrous layer having randomly laid or oriented fibres or threads.

Felt. Felts are a class of fabrics or fibrous structures obtained through the interlocking of wool, fur, or some hair fibres under conditions of heat, moisture, and pressure. Other fibres will not felt alone but can be mixed with wool, which acts as a carrier. Three separate industries manufacture goods through the use of these properties. The goods produced are wool felt, in rolls and sheets; hats, both fur and wool; and woven felts, ranging from thin billiard tablecloths to heavy industrial fabrics used for dewatering in the manufacture of paper. Felts of the nonwoven class are considered to be the first textile goods produced, and many references may be found to felts and their uses in the histories of ancient civilizations. The nomadic tribes of north central Asia still produce felts for clothing and shelter, utilizing the primitive methods handed down from antiquity.

Bonding. Several methods for making nonwoven materials are now firmly established, and others are being developed.

In adhesive bonding, fabrics are made by forming a web of fibres, applying an adhesive, then drying and curing the adhesive. The web can be produced by a garnetting machine or a conventional card, several layers being piled up to obtain the required thickness. Such webs are weak across the width, but this does not limit their use for certain end products. A more uniform product results from cross laying the web. Other machines, such as the Rando-Webber, lay down the fibres by an airstream.

The fibres in the web may be stuck together in various ways. The web may be sprayed with an emulsion of an adhesive—*e.g.*, a latex based on synthetic rubber, acrylic derivatives, or natural rubber—or, alternatively, may be carried on a mesh screen through a bath of latex, the excess being squeezed out by a pair of rollers. Adhesives may also be applied as a foam or a fine powder. Thermoplastic fibres can be incorporated in the blend and on heating will bond together, giving strength to the mass of fibres.

Mechanically bonded nonwoven products (or fibre-

Adhesive and mechanical bonding

bonded nonwovens) are webs strengthened by mechanical means. The web, sometimes reinforced by a thin cotton scrim in the middle or by texturized yarns distributed lengthwise through it, is punched by barbed needles mounted in a needle board. The fibres in the web are caught up by the needle barbs, and the resulting increased entanglement yields a compact product sufficiently strong for many purposes. Modern needle-felting or punching machines perform 900 punches per minute, and selection of appropriate needles is based on the fibre being processed and the desired product.

Stitch bonding

The Arachne machine, the best known unit for stitch bonding, operates much like a warp-knitting machine. Fibrous web is fed into the machine, and stitches are made by a series of needles placed about eight millimetres apart, giving the web longitudinal strength; lateral strength is provided by the fibre interactions. The products are attractive for many purposes and can be improved by treatment with polyester resins to increase their wear resistance and with thermosetting precondensates to reduce their tendency to pill (*e.g.*, to form small tangles). A new device attached to the Arachne machine permits introduction of weft ends at every single course, making colour effects possible. Araloop machines yield loop-pile fabric suitable for towels and floor coverings.

Three sewing-knitting machines were invented in East Germany in 1958. In the Malino machine process, warp yarns are placed on top of filling yarns and stitched together by a third yarn. The Maliwatt machine interlaces a web of fibres with a sewing thread, giving the effect of parallel seams. The Malipol machine produces a one-sided pile fabric by stitching loop pile through a backing fabric. A new British process makes double-sided terry fabric, called Terrytuft, by inserting pile yarn into a backing and knotting it into position.

Webs made of yarns having a core of one polymer and an outer sheath of another material having a lower softening point, may be lightly pressed and then heated to an appropriate temperature. The core yarn will "spot weld" together at the junction points, binding the mass of fibres together. Products made in this way find uses as industrial fabrics, coatings, and interlinings.

Laminating. The joining of one fabric to another by an adhesive such as natural rubber has long been practised in rainwear manufacture. Composite materials were later joined by bonding a layer of polyurethane or other foam to a conventional textile fabric. The two components were stuck together by flame bonding or by an adhesive in the form of a continuous coating, in spots, or as a powder. This laminating process has been extended to the joining of two layers of fabric. Each fabric layer can be quite thin, and the amount and type of adhesive are chosen to add only minimum stiffening. Such materials offer a variety of applications. A coating fabric, for example, may be joined to a lining; dimensionally stable composites can be made from cloth layers that are in themselves dimensionally unstable. Acetate knitted fabrics are frequently used as backing material in laminates.

IV. Textile finishing processes

BASIC METHODS AND PROCESSES

The term finishing includes all the mechanical and chemical processes employed commercially to improve the acceptability of the product, except those procedures directly concerned with colouring. The objective of the various finishing processes is to make fabric from the loom or knitting frame more acceptable to the consumer. Finishing processes include preparatory treatments used before additional treatment, such as bleaching prior to dyeing; treatments, such as glazing, to enhance appearance; sizing, affecting touch; and treatments adding properties to enhance performance, such as preshrinking. Newly formed cloth is generally dirty, harsh, and unattractive, requiring considerable skill for conversion into a desirable product. Before treatment, the unfinished fabrics are referred to as gray goods, or sometimes, in the case of silks, as greige goods.

Finishing formerly involved a limited number of comparatively simple operations evolved over the years from hand methods. The skill of English and Scottish finishers was widely recognized, and much British cloth owed its high reputation to the expertise of the finisher. More sophisticated modern finishing methods have been achieved through intense and imaginative research.

Preparatory treatments. It is frequently necessary to carry out some preparatory treatment before the application of other finishing processes to the newly constructed fabric. Any remaining impurities must be removed, and additives used to facilitate the manufacturing process must also be removed. Bleaching may be required to increase whiteness or to prepare for colour application. Some of the most frequently used preparatory processes are discussed below.

Burling and mending. Newly made goods, which frequently show imperfections, are carefully inspected, and defects are usually repaired by hand operations. The first inspection of woollen and worsted fabrics is called perching. Burling, mainly applied to woollen, worsted, spun rayon, and cotton fabrics, is the process of removing any remaining foreign matter, such as burrs and, also, any loose threads, knots, and undesired slubs. Mending, frequently necessary for woollens and worsteds, eliminates such defects as holes or tears, broken yarns, and missed warp or weft yarns.

Scouring. When applied to gray goods, scouring removes substances that have adhered to the fibres during production of the yarn or fabric, such as dirt, oils, and any sizing or lint applied to warp yarns to facilitate weaving.

Bleaching. Bleaching, a process of whitening fabric by removal of natural colour, such as the tan of linen, is usually carried out by means of chemicals selected according to the chemical composition of the fibre. Chemical bleaching is usually accomplished by oxidation, destroying colour by the application of oxygen, or by reduction, removing colour by hydrogenation. Cotton and other cellulosic fibres are usually treated with heated alkaline hydrogen peroxide; wool and other animal fibres are subjected to such acidic reducing agents as gaseous sulfur dioxide or to such mildly alkaline oxidizing agents as hydrogen peroxide. Synthetic fibres, when they require bleaching, may be treated with either oxidizing or reducing agents, depending upon their chemical composition. Cottons are frequently scoured and bleached by a continuous system.

Mercerization. Mercerization is a process applied to cotton and sometimes to cotton blends to increase lustre (thus also enhancing appearance), to improve strength, and to improve their affinity for dyes. The process, which may be applied at the yarn or fabric stage, involves immersion under tension in a caustic soda (sodium hydroxide) solution, which is later neutralized in acid. The treatment produces permanent swelling of the fibre.

Drying. Water, used in various phases of textile processing, accumulates in fabrics, and the excess moisture must eventually be removed. Because evaporative heating is costly, the first stage of drying uses mechanical methods to remove as much moisture as possible. Such methods include the use of centrifuges and a continuous method employing vacuum suction rolls. Any remaining moisture is then removed by evaporation in heated dryers. Various types of dryers operate by conveying the relaxed fabric through the chamber while festooned in loops, using a frame to hold the selvages taut while the fabric travels through the chamber, and passing the fabric over a series of hot cylinders. Because overdrying may produce a harsh hand, temperature, humidity, and drying time require careful control.

Finishes enhancing appearance. Treatments enhancing appearance include such processes as napping and shearing, brushing, singeing, beetling, decating, tentering, calendering or pressing, moiréing, embossing, creping, glazing, polishing, and optical brightening.

Napping and shearing. Napping is a process that may be applied to woollens, cottons, spun silks, and spun rayons, including both woven and knitted types, to raise a velvety, soft surface. The process involves passing the fabric over revolving cylinders covered with fine wires that lift the short, loose fibres, usually from the weft yarns, to the surface, forming a nap. The process, which increases warmth, is frequently applied to woollens and worsteds and also to blankets.

Shearing cuts the raised nap to a uniform height and is used for the same purpose on pile fabrics. Shearing machines operate much like rotary lawn mowers, and the amount of shearing depends upon the desired height of the nap or pile, with such fabrics as gabardine receiving very close shearing. Shearing may also be applied to create stripes and other patterns by varying surface height.

Brushing. This process, applied to a wide variety of fabrics, is usually accomplished by bristle-covered rollers. The process is used to remove loose threads and short fibre ends from smooth-surfaced fabrics and is also used to raise a nap on knits and woven fabrics. Brushing is frequently applied to fabrics after shearing, removing the cut fibres that have fallen into the nap.

Singeing. Also called gassing, singeing is a process applied to both yarns and fabrics to produce an even surface by burning off projecting fibres, yarn ends, and fuzz. This is accomplished by passing the fibre or yarn over a gas flame or heated copper plates at a speed sufficient to burn away the protruding material without scorching or burning the yarn or fabric. Singeing is usually followed by passing the treated material over a wet surface to assure that any smoldering is halted.

Beetling. Beetling is a process applied to linen fabrics and to cotton fabrics made to resemble linen to produce a hard, flat surface with high lustre and also to make texture less porous. In this process, the fabric, dampened and wound around an iron cylinder, is passed through a machine in which it is pounded with heavy wooden mallets.

Decating. Decating is a process applied to woollens and worsteds, man-made and blended fibre fabrics, and various types of knits. It involves the application of heat and pressure to set or develop lustre and softer hand and to even the set and grain of certain fabrics. When applied to double knits it imparts crisp hand and reduces shrinkage. In wet decating, which gives a subtle lustre, or bloom, fabric under tension is steamed by passing it over perforated cylinders.

Tentering, crabbing, and heat-setting. These are final processes applied to set the warp and weft of woven fabrics at right angles to each other, and to stretch and set the fabric to its final dimensions. Tentering stretches width under tension by the use of a tenter frame, consisting of chains fitted with pins or clips to hold the selvages of the fabric, and travelling on tracks. As the fabric passes through the heated chamber, creases and wrinkles are removed, the weave is straightened, and the fabric is dried to its final size. When the process is applied to wet wools it is called crabbing; when applied to synthetic fibres it is sometimes called heat-setting, a term also applied to the permanent setting of pleats, creases, and special surface effects.

Calendering. Calendering is a final process in which heat and pressure are applied to a fabric by passing it between heated rollers, imparting a flat, glossy, smooth surface. Lustre increases when the degree of heat and pressure is increased. Calendering is applied to fabrics in which a smooth, flat surface is desirable, such as most cottons, many linens and silks, and various man-made fabrics. In such fabrics as velveteen, flat surface is not desirable, and the cloth is steamed while in tension, without pressing. When applied to wool, the process is called pressing, and employs heavy, heated metal plates to steam and press the fabric. Calendering is not usually a permanent process.

Moiréing, embossing, glazing and ciréing, and polishing. These are all variations of the calendering process. Moiré is a wavy or "watered" effect imparted by engraved rollers that press the design into the fabric. The process, applied to cotton, acetate, rayon, and some ribbed synthetic fabrics, is only permanent for acetates and resin-treated rayons. Embossing imparts a raised design that stands out from the background and is achieved by passing the fabric through heated rollers engraved with a design. Although embossing was formerly temporary, processes have now been developed to make this effect permanent.

Glazing imparts a smooth, stiff, highly polished surface to such fabrics as chintz. It is achieved by applying such stiffeners as starch, glue, shellac, or resin to the fabric and then passing it through smooth, hot rollers that generate friction. Resins are now widely employed to impart permanent glaze. Ciré (from the French word for waxed) is a similar process applied to rayons and silks by the application of wax followed by hot calendering, producing a high, metallic gloss. Ciré finishes can be achieved without a sizing substance in acetates, which are thermoplastic (*e.g.*, can be softened by heat), by the application of heat.

Polishing, used to impart sheen to cottons without making them as stiff as glazed types, is usually achieved by mercerizing the fabric and then passing it through friction rollers.

Creping. A crepe effect may be achieved by finishing. In one method, which is not permanent, the cloth is passed, in the presence of steam, between hot rollers filled with indentations producing waved and puckered areas. In the more permanent caustic soda method, a caustic soda paste is rolled onto the fabric in a patterned form; or a resist paste may be applied to areas to remain unpuckered and the entire fabric then immersed in caustic soda. The treated areas shrink, and the untreated areas pucker. If the pattern is applied in the form of stripes, the effect is called plissé; an allover design produces blister crepe.

Optical brightening. Optical brightening, or optical bleaches, are finishes giving the effect of great whiteness and brightness because of the way in which they reflect light. These compounds contain fluorescent colourless dyes, causing more blue light to be reflected. Changes in colour may occur as the fluorescent material loses energy, but new optical whiteners can be applied during the laundering process.

Finishes enhancing tactile qualities. Finishes enhancing the feel and drape of fabrics involve the addition of sizing, weighting, fulling, and softening agents, which may be either temporary or permanent.

Sizing. Sizing, or dressing, agents are compounds that form a film around the yarn or individual fibres, increasing weight, crispness, and lustre. Sizing substances, including starches, gelatin, glue, casein, and clay, are frequently applied to cottons and are not permanent.

Weighting. Weighting, in the processing of silk, involves the application of metallic salts to add body and weight. The process is not permanent but can be repeated.

Fulling. Also called felting or milling, fulling is a process that increases the thickness and compactness of wool by subjecting it to moisture, heat, friction, and pressure until shrinkage of 10 to 25 percent is achieved. Shrinkage occurs in both the warp and weft, producing a smooth, tightly finished fabric that may be so compact that it resembles felt.

Softening. Making fabrics softer and sometimes also increasing absorbency involves the addition of such agents as dextrin, glycerin, sulfonated oils, sulfated tallow, and sulfated alcohol.

Finishes improving performance. The performance of fabrics in use has been greatly improved by the development of processes to control shrinkage, new resin finishes, and new heat-sensitive synthetic fibres.

Shrinkage control. Shrinkage control processes are applied by compressive shrinkage, resin treatment, or heat-setting. Compressive, or relaxation, shrinkage is applied to cotton and to certain cotton blends to reduce the stretching they experience during weaving and other processing. The fabric is dampened and dried in a relaxed state, eliminating tensions and distortions. The number of warp and weft yarns per square inch is increased, contributing greater durability, and fabrics treated by this method are usually smooth and have soft lustre. The process involves spraying the fabric with water, then pressing the fabric against a steam heated cylinder covered with a thick blanket of woollen felt or rubber. The manufacturer is often required to specify the residual shrinkage, or percentage of shrinkage, that may still occur after the preshrinking process.

Residual shrinkage

Rayons and rayon blends may be stabilized by the use of resins, which impregnate the fibre. Such fabrics may also be stabilized by employing acetals to produce cross-linking, a chemical reaction. Such synthetics as polyesters and nylons, which are heat sensitive, are usually permanently stabilized by heat-setting during finishing.

Shrinkage of wools is frequently controlled by treatment with chlorine, partially destroying the scales that occur on wool fibres, thus increasing resistance to the natural tendency of wool to felt. Other methods employ coating with resins or with enzymes that attach to the scales in order to discourage felting shrinkage.

Durable press. Durable press fabrics have such characteristics as shape retention, permanent pleating and creasing, permanently smooth seams, and the ability to shed wrinkles, and thus retain a fresh appearance without ironing. Such fabrics may be safely washed and dried by machine. These useful characteristics are imparted by a curing process. Depending upon composition and desired results, fabrics may be precured, a process in which a chemical resin is added, the fabric is dried and cured (baked), and heat is applied by pressing after garment construction; or fabrics may be postcured, a process in which resin is added, the fabric is dried, made into a garment, pressed, and then cured.

Wash and wear fabrics

Wash and wear was an early durable press process employing chemical treatment and curing of fabrics; at least light ironing was required to restore appearance. Later, however, processes were developed that allowed such fabrics to regain smoothness after home machine washing at moderate temperature, followed by tumble drying.

Crease resistance. Crease, or wrinkle, resistance is frequently achieved by application of a synthetic resin, such as melamine or epoxy.

Soil release. Soil release finishes facilitate removal of waterborne and oil stains from fabrics such as polyester and cotton blends and fabrics treated for durable press, which usually show some resistance to stain removal by normal cleaning processes. Other finishes have been developed that give fabrics resistance to water and oil stains.

Antistatic finishes. The accumulation of static electricity in such synthetic fibres as nylon, polyesters, and acrylics produces clinging, which may be reduced by application of permanent antistatic agents during processing. Consumers can partially reduce static electricity by adding commercial fabric softeners during laundering.

Antibacterial and antifungus finishes. Antibacterial finishes are germicides applied to fabrics to prevent odours produced by bacterial decomposition, such as perspiration odours, and also to reduce the possibility of infection by contact with contaminated textiles. Fabrics may also be treated with germicides to prevent mildew, a parasitic fungus that may grow on fabrics that are not thoroughly dried. Both mildew and rot, another form of decay, may also be controlled by treatment with resins.

Moth-repellent treatments. Wool and silk are subject to attack by moths but may be made moth repellent by the application of appropriate chemicals either added in the dye bath or applied to the finished fabric.

Waterproofing and water-repellence. Waterproofing is a process applied to such items as raincoats and umbrellas, closing the pores of the fabric by application of such substances as insoluble metallic compounds, paraffin, bituminous materials, and drying oils. Water-repellent finishes are surface finishes imparting some degree of resistance to water but are more comfortable to wear because the fabric pores remain open. Such finishes include wax and resin mixtures, aluminum salts, silicones, and fluorochemicals.

Flameproof, fireproof, and fire-resistant finishes. Flameproof fabrics are able to withstand exposure to flame or high temperature. This is achieved by application of various finishes, depending upon the fabric treated, that cause burning to stop as soon as the source of heat is removed. Fireproofing is achieved by the application of a finish that will cut off the oxygen supply around the flame. Fire-resistant finishes cause fabrics to resist the spread of flame.

DYEING AND PRINTING

Dyeing and printing are processes employed in the conversion of raw textile fibres into finished goods that add much to the appearance of textile fabrics.

Dyeing. Most forms of textile materials can be dyed at almost any stage. Quality woollen goods are frequently dyed in the form of loose fibre, but top dyeing or cheese dyeing is favoured in treating worsteds. Manufacturers prefer piece dyeing, which allows stocking of white goods, reducing the risk of being overstocked with cloth dyed in colours that have not been ordered.

The dye used depends on the type of material and the specific requirements to be met. For some purposes, high lightfastness is essential; but for others it may be inconsequential. Factors considered in dye selection include fastness to light, reaction to washing and rubbing (crooking), and the cost of the dyeing process. Effective preparation of the material for dyeing is essential.

Types of dyes

Basic dyes include acid dyes, used mainly for dyeing wool, silk, and nylon; and direct or substantive dyes, which have a strong affinity for cellulose fibres. Mordant dyes require the addition of chemical substances, such as salts, to give them an affinity for the material being dyed. They are applied to cellulosic fibres, wool, or silk after such materials have been treated with metal salts. Sulfur dyes, used to dye cellulose, are inexpensive, but produce colours lacking brilliance. Azoic dyes are insoluble pigments formed within the fibre by padding, first with a soluble coupling compound and then with a diazotized base. Vat dyes, insoluble in water, are converted into soluble colourless compounds by means of alkaline sodium hydrosulfite. Cellulose absorbs these colourless compounds, which are subsequently oxidized to an insoluble pigment. Such dyes are colourfast. Disperse dyes are suspensions of finely divided insoluble, organic pigments used to dye such hydrophobic fibres as polyesters, nylon, and cellulose acetates.

Reactive dyes combine directly with the fibre, resulting in excellent colourfastness. The first ranges of reactive dyes for cellulose fibres were introduced in the mid 1950s. A wide variety is now available (see also DYES AND DYEING).

Printing. Printing is a process of decorating textile fabrics by application of pigments, dyes, or other related materials in the form of patterns. Although apparently developed from the hand painting of fabrics, such methods are also of great antiquity. There is evidence of printing being carried out in India during the 4th century BC, and a printing block dated at about AD 300 has been unearthed in the burial grounds of Akhmin in Upper Egypt. Pre-Columbian printed textiles have been found in Peru and Mexico. Textile printing has become highly sophisticated and has involved the skills of many artists and designers.

Principal methods of textile printing

The four main methods of textile printing are block, roller, screen, and sublistatic printing. In each of these methods, the application of the colour, usually as a thickened paste, is followed by fixation, usually by steaming or heating, and then removal of excess colour by washing. Printing styles are classified as direct, discharge, or resist. In direct printing, coloured pastes are printed directly on the cloth. For discharge printing, the cloth is first dyed with a background colour, which is destroyed by reagents, or reducing agents, carried in a print paste. This action may leave the discharged design white on a coloured background, although print pastes may also contain colouring matters not destroyed by the discharging agent, producing a coloured design. In the resist process, the cloth is first printed with a substance called a resist, protecting these printed areas from accepting colour. When the cloth is dyed or pigment padded only those parts not printed with the resist are dyed. A special application of this technique, imparting plissé effects, is the printing of the fabric with a resist, followed by treatment with caustic soda.

Block printing. Wooden blocks, carved with a design standing out in relief, are made from solid pieces of wood or by bonding closely grained woods with cheaper ones. When designs include large areas, these are recessed and the space filled with hard wool felt. Fine lines are usually built up with copper strips, and other effects are obtained with copper strips interleaved with felt. To facilitate registration of successive prints, or lays, each block has several pitch pins arranged to coincide with well-defined points in the pattern. Cloth is printed on a table covered with several thicknesses of fabric or blanket, the whole covered with a thick sheet of tightly stretched synthetic rubber. The cloth to be printed is spread on the rubber, either gummed in position or pinned to a back cloth attached to the table. Colour is applied evenly to the block, and the pattern is stamped on the fabric to be printed, using the handle of a small heavy hammer, or maul, to aid penetration of the paste. More colour is then applied to the block and the process is repeated using the pitch pin to obtain true registration. After the fabric has been entirely printed with one colour, other colours are applied in the same way until the design is complete. Although block printing is becoming too laborious and costly for commercial use, some of the most beautiful prints have been made in this way.

Roller printing. This technique is used whenever long runs of fabric are to be printed with the same design. The modern machine, based on one originally devised in 1783, consists of a large central cast iron cylinder over which passes a thick endless blanket providing a resilient support for the fabric. Backing fabrics, called back grays, are placed between the blanket and the fabric to prevent undue staining of the blanket. Although formerly made of cotton fabric, most modern back grays are continuous belts of nylon. The blanket and back gray are appropriately tensioned, so that the fabric moves through the machine as the central cylinder rotates. Engraved printing rollers, one for each colour, press against the fabric and the central cylinder. The pattern on the roller is etched on the surface of a copper shell supported on a mandrel. High quality engraving is essential for good printing. Each printing roller is provided with a rotating colour-furnishing roller, partially immersed in a trough of printing paste. Finely ground blades (doctor blades) remove excess colour paste from the unengraved areas of these rollers, and each also has a lint blade. The printed fabric passes from the main cylinder and through a drying and steaming chamber to fix the colour. Although this machine prints only one side of the fabric, the Duplix roller machine, essentially a combination of two roller machines, prints both sides. Modern printing machines are smooth-running precision machines fitted with carefully designed roller bearings and hydraulic or pneumatic mechanisms to ensure uniform pressure and flexibility. Pressure is regulated from an instrument panel, and each roller is controlled independently. Automatic registration is effected by electromagnetic push-button control, and modern electric motors provide smooth-running, variable-speed drives. The washing of back grays and printer's blankets has also been automated.

Spray printing is the application of colour from spray guns through stencils and has limited but occasionally profitable use.

Screen printing. Screen printing may be a hand operation or an automatic machine process. The cloth is first laid on a printing table, gummed in position or pinned to a back gray, and then the design is applied through a screen made of silk or nylon gauze stretched over a wooden or metal frame, on which the design for one colour has been reproduced. This is usually a photographic process, although hand painting with a suitably resistant blocking paint is an alternative. A screen is placed over the fabric on the table against registration stops, ensuring accurate pattern fitting. Print paste is poured on to the screen edge nearest the operator and is spread with a squeegee over the surface of the screen so that colour is pushed through the open parts. The screen is moved until one colour has been applied to the cloth. For application of other colours, the process is repeated with different screens.

With the growing importance of screen printing, the hand operation has been largely replaced by mechanical methods. In some machines, the screens are flat, as in hand printing; others employ rotary screens.

Sublistatic printing. The popularity of polyester fabrics has led to the development of a completely new form of printing termed sublistatic printing, which prints the pattern on paper with carefully selected dyes. The paper is then applied to the fabric by passing the two together through a type of hot calender, and the pattern is transferred from one to the other. This method opens up new possibilities such as the production of half-tone effects.

In all textile printing, the nature and, particularly, the viscosity of the print paste is important, and the thickeners employed must be compatible with all the other components. For conventional methods the thickeners are such reagents as starch, gum tragacanth, alginates, methyl cellulose ethers, and sodium carboxymethyl cellulose. Many types of dye can be applied, including direct cotton, vat, mordant, and reactive dyes, as well as pigment colours. Most dyes are fixed by steaming or ageing, by a batch or continuous method, and more rapid fixation is effected by flash ageing—*e.g.*, allowing a shorter steaming period by employing smaller machines. After steaming, the fabric must be thoroughly washed to remove loose dye and thickener, ensuring fastness to rubbing.

Most textile materials can be printed without special pretreatment, but wool cloths are generally chlorinated before printing. Tops (long, parallel wool fibres), printed in stripes, are used for mixed effects, and printed warps produce shadowy effects. Tufted carpets are printed by a process designed to ensure good penetration.

V. Textile consumption and trade

CHANGING USES OF FABRIC IN APPAREL

Textiles are commonly associated with clothing and soft furnishings, an association that accounts for the great emphasis on style and design in textiles. These consume a large portion of total industry production. Great changes have occurred in the fabrics used for clothing, with heavy woollen and worsted suitings being replaced by lighter materials, often made from blends of natural and man-made fibres, possibly due to improved indoor heating. Warp-knitted fabrics made from bulked yarns are replacing woven fabrics, and there is a trend away from formality in both day and evening dress to more casual wear, for which knitted garments are especially appropriate. The use of man-made fibre fabrics has established the easy-care concept and made formerly fragile light and diaphanous fabrics more durable. The introduction of elastomeric fibres has revolutionized the foundation-garment trade, and the use of stretch yarns of all types has produced outerwear that is closely fitting but comfortable.

Manufacturers of tailored garments formerly used interlinings made of horsehair, which was later replaced by goat hair, and then by resin-treated viscose rayon. Now fusible interlinings and various washable synthetics are widely used. The performance of a garment is greatly influenced by such factors as the interlining used and the sewing threads employed.

The care required by a textile fabric depends upon both fibre content and the application of various finishing processes. In 1972 the United States Federal Trade Commission passed regulations requiring fabric manufacturers to provide the consumer with care labels to be sewn into homemade garments, and requiring ready-to-wear manufacturers to sew permanent care information labels into clothing (see also CLOTHING AND FOOTWEAR INDUSTRY).

Soft furnishings. Household textiles, frequently referred to as soft furnishings, are fabrics used in the home. They include items frequently classified as linens, such as bath and dish towels, table linens, shower curtains, and bathroom ensembles. Related items include sheets, pillowcases, mattresses, blankets, comforters, and bedspreads. In addition, textile products contributing to the atmosphere and comfort of the home include rugs and carpeting, draperies, curtains, and upholstery fabrics.

Most of these items are also used in hotels and motels, and many are used in offices, showrooms, retail stores, restaurants, recreational facilities, and various other commercial establishments.

Industrial fabrics. This class of fabrics includes composition products, processing fabrics, and direct use types.

Print paste viscosity

Interlinings

Composition products. In composition products, the fabrics are used as reinforcements in compositions with other materials, such as rubber and plastics. These products—prepared by such processes as coating, impregnating, and laminating—include tires, belting, hoses, inflatable items, and typewriter-ribbon fabrics.

Processing fabrics. Processing fabrics are used by various manufacturers for such purposes as filtration; for bolting cloths used for various types of sifting and screening; and in commercial laundering as press covers and as nets segregating lots during washing. In textile finishing back grays are used as backing for fabrics that are being printed.

Direct-use fabrics. Direct-use fabrics are manufactured or incorporated into finished products, such as awnings and canopies, tarpaulins, tents, outdoor furniture, luggage, and footwear.

Fabrics for protective clothing. Fabrics for military purposes must frequently withstand severe conditions. Among their uses are Arctic and cold-weather clothing, tropical wear, rot-resistant material, webbing, inflated life vests, tent fabrics, safety belts, and parachute cloth and harnesses. Parachute cloth, for example, must meet exacting specifications, air porosity being a vital factor. New fabrics are also being developed for garments used in space travel. In protective clothing a subtle balance between protection and comfort is required.

The many uses of textiles enter into almost every aspect of modern life. For some purposes, however, the role of textiles is being challenged by developments in plastic and paper products. Although many of these presently have certain limitations, it is likely that they will be improved, presenting a greater challenge to textile manufacturers, who must be concerned both with retaining present markets and expanding into completely new areas.

WORLD PRODUCTION AND TRADE

Table 1 shows the world's leading producers of woven

Table, therefore, gives only a rough estimate of the world production for the main fibres and the main producing countries for one year. Mixture cloths are included under the heading of the dominant fibre, and a special category is included for woven carpets because at least three different kinds of fibres are normally used in their construction.

A summary table of this kind is necessarily incomplete, and some relatively large producers in a particular field (*e.g.*, Bangladesh in jute—a very large producer) are inevitably omitted. The Table also excludes wire, flax, silk, sisal, asbestos, and other miscellaneous fibres. It seems probable, therefore, that world production of all kinds of woven cloth in 1969 approached 90,000,000,000 square yards, equivalent to nearly 30 square yards (25 square metres) per person. These figures indicate the importance of weaving as an industrial process. Table 2 provides the same information for knitted fabrics.

Table 2: Estimated World Production of Knitted Fabrics, 1969
(in metric tons)

Africa	13,982
South Africa	12,956
North America	338,415
U.S.	316,700
South America	9,234
Venezuela	2,122
Asia	186,306
Japan	175,029
Europe	290,822
Czechoslovakia	19,299
West Germany	66,785
U.K.	70,024
Oceania	8,857
Australia	7,109
U.S.S.R.	
Total	859,922

Source: *The Growth of World Industry*, 1969 edition, vol. 2, Commodity Production Data, 1960–1969, 1971.

Table 1: Estimated Production of Woven Cloth, 1969*
(in 000,000 of square yards)

	cotton	man-made† fibres	jute	wool	carpets
Africa	1,607	91	65	18	...
Egypt	782	91	65	9	...
North America	20,764	3,056	...	447	614
U.S.	9,116	2,661	...	412	586
South America	3,383	500	89	30	...
Venezuela	93	63	...	5	...
Asia	17,525	3,623	3,801	630	47
India	10,637	1,471	2,251	22	...
Japan	3,324	1,916	167	510	42
Europe	11,431	3,034	619	1,864	453
France	1,732	48	115	221	5
West Germany	1,170	762	49	170	128
Italy	1,520	164	53	377	...
Poland	970	146	72	166	8
U.K.	817	706	133	286	146
Oceania	56	36	...	36	23
Australia	56	36	...	32	16
U.S.S.R.	8,043	984	159	973	33
Total‡	62,809	11,324	4,733	3,998	1,399

*Continent totals represent only countries for which data was available. †Figures may exclude noncellulosic fabrics. ‡World totals represent only countries for which data was available.
Source: *The Growth of World Industry*, 1969 edition, vol. 2, Commodity Production Data, 1960–1969, New York, 1971.

International trade in textiles, as in other products, is subject to international agreements and restrictions. In the early 1970s many industrialized nations were members of the General Agreement on Tariffs and Trade (GATT) organization, concerned with regulating and promoting international trade. The Organization for Economic Cooperation and Development (OECD), under the sponsorship of the United Nations was mainly concerned with developing countries. Restrictive quotas, tariffs, and duties on textile raw materials, fabrics, and apparel, in effect or under consideration in various countries were the subject of much controversy.

BIBLIOGRAPHY. Works of general interest include: GEORGE E. LINTON, *Applied Basic Textiles* (1966); ISABEL B. WINGATE, *Textile Fabrics and Their Selection*, 6th ed. (1970); EVELYN E. STOUT, *Introduction to Textiles*, 3rd ed. (1970); and N. HOLLEN and J. SADDLER, *Textiles*, 2nd ed. (1964). Helpful dictionaries of the textile industry are: GEORGE E. LINTON (ed.), *The Modern Textile Dictionary*, 3rd ed. rev. (1963); ISABEL B. WINGATE (ed.), *Fairchild's Dictionary of Textiles*, 5th ed. (1967); and the TEXTILE INSTITUTE, *Textile Terms and Definitions*, 6th ed. (1970). The history and development of the textile industry is treated in ADELE C. WEIBEL, *Two Thousand Years of Textiles* (1952); and the TEXTILE INSTITUTE, *Review of Textile Progress*, 18 vol. (1949–67). Specific fibres, their processing, and their characteristics are surveyed in: J. GORDON COOK, *Handbook of Textile Fibres* (1968); H.R. MAUERSBERGER (ed.), *Matthews' Textile Fibres*, 6th ed. (1954); R.W. MONCRIEFF, *Man-Made Fibers*, 5th ed. (1970); J.J. PRESS (ed.), *Man-Made Textile Encyclopedia* (1959); and H.F. MARK, S.M. ATLAS, and E. ARNIA (eds.), *Man-Made Fibers: Science and Technology*, 3 vol. (1967–68). Yarn production is the subject of P.R. LORD, *Spinning in the Seventies* (1970); and G.R. WRAY (ed.), *Modern Yarn Production from Man-Made Fibres* (1960). Works treating fabric production include: A.T.C. ROBINSON and R. MARKS, *Woven Cloth Construction* (1967); D.G. THOMAS, *An Introduction to Warp Knitting* (1971); H. WIGNALL, *Knitting* (1964); V. DUXBURY and G.R. WRAY (eds.), *Modern Developments in Weaving Machinery* (1962); and R. KROMA, *Non-Woven Textiles* (1962). Textile finishing is the subject of A.J. HALL, *Handbook of Textile Finishers* (1952); and works

Difficulties in reporting production

fabrics, based on total yardage, for the year 1969. The statistics are fairly reliable, though by no means complete. Figures for handwoven fabrics are often excluded because of the difficulty of ascertaining them, although in some countries large amounts of such cloth are produced. In India, in particular, the annual production of handloomed cloth is roughly 2,000,000,000 square yards (1,700,000,000 square metres).

Another difficulty arises in attempting to analyze production in terms of type of fibre used, since a significant proportion may consist of cloths in which different fibres are combined, either in the component yarns or by using a different fibre in the weft from that in the warp. The

treating the dyeing and printing of textiles include A.J. HALL, *Handbook of Textile Dyeing and Printing* (1955); S.R. COCK-ETT, *Dyeing and Printing* (1964); L.W.C. MILES, *Textile Printing* (1971). Works concerned with textile quality control include: E.B. GROVER and D.S. HAMBY, *Handbook of Textile Testing and Quality Control* (1960); BRITISH STANDARDS INSTITUTION, *Methods of Test for Textiles, B.S. Handbook No. 11*, rev. ed. (1956); AMERICAN SOCIETY FOR TESTING AND MATERIALS, *1966 Book of A.S.T.M. Standards*, part 24–25 (1966); SOCIETY OF DYERS AND COLOURISTS, *Standard Methods for the Determination of the Colour Fastness of Textiles*, 3rd ed. (1962; suppl. 1966). Studies of the potential of textile industries in developing countries include the UNITED NATIONS INDUSTRIAL DEVELOPMENT ORGANIZATION, *Industrialization of Developing Countries: Problems and Prospects, Textile Industry* (1969); and the *ECAFE Seminar on the Man-Made Fiber Industry: Japan's Man-Made Fibers* (1966). Periodicals and trade papers concerned with the textile industry include: *Ciba Review* (quarterly); *American Fabrics* (quarterly); *Textile Institute Journal* (irregular); *Textile Organon* (monthly); and *Textile Progress* (quarterly).

(C.S.Wh.)

Textual Criticism

Textual criticism distinguished from related fields

Textual criticism is the technique of restoring texts as nearly as possible to their original form. Texts in this connection are defined as writings other than formal documents, inscribed or printed on paper, parchment, papyrus, or similar materials. The study of formal documents such as deeds and charters belongs to the science known as "diplomatic"; the study of writings on stone is part of epigraphy; while inscriptions on coins and seals are the province of numismatics and sigillography. Textual criticism, properly speaking, is an ancillary academic discipline designed to lay the foundations for the so-called higher criticism, which deals with questions of authenticity and attribution, of interpretation, and of literary and historical evaluation. This distinction between the lower and the higher branches of criticism was first made explicitly by the German biblical scholar J.G. Eichhorn; the first use of the term "textual criticism" in English dates from the middle of the 19th century. In practice the operations of textual and "higher" criticism cannot be rigidly differentiated: at the very outset of his work a critic, faced with variant forms of a text, inevitably employs stylistic and other criteria belonging to the "higher" branch. The methods of textual criticism, insofar as they are not codified common sense, are the methods of historical inquiry. Texts have been transmitted in an almost limitless variety of ways, and the criteria employed by the textual critic—technical, philological, literary, or aesthetic—are valid only if applied in awareness of the particular set of historical circumstances governing each case.

The value of textual criticism

An acquaintance with the history of texts and the principles of textual criticism is indispensable for the student of history, literature, or philosophy. Written texts supply the main foundation for these disciplines, and some knowledge of the processes of their transmission is necessary for understanding and control of the scholar's basic materials. For the advanced student the criticism and editing of texts offers an unrivalled philological training and a uniquely instructive avenue to the history of scholarship; it is broadly true that all advances in philology have been made in connection with the problems of editing texts. To say this is to recognize that the equipment needed by the critic for his task includes a mastery of the whole field of study within which his text lies; for the editing of Homer (to take an extreme case), a period of some 3,000 years. For the general reader the benefits of textual criticism are less apparent but are nevertheless real. Most men are apt to take texts on trust, even to prefer a familiar version, however debased or unauthentic, to the true one. The reader who resists all change is exemplified by Erasmus' story of the priest who preferred his nonsensical *mumpsimus* to the correct *sumpsimus*. Such people are saved from themselves by the activities of the textual critic.

The law of diminishing returns operates in the textual field as in others: improvements in the texts of the great writers cannot be made indefinitely. Yet a surprisingly large number of texts have not yet been edited satisfactorily. This is particularly true of medieval literature, but also of many modern novels. Indeed the basic materials of most textual investigation, the manuscripts themselves, have as yet not all been identified and catalogued, much less systematically exploited. The first edition of the works of Dickens to be founded on critical study of the textual evidence did not begin to appear until 1966, when K. Tillotson's edition of *Oliver Twist* was published. Reliable principles of Shakespearean editing have begun to emerge only with modern developments in the techniques of analytical bibliography. The Revised Standard Version of the Bible (1952) and the New English Bible (1970) both incorporate readings of the Old Testament unknown before 1947, the year in which early biblical manuscripts—the so-called Dead Sea Scrolls—were discovered in the caves of Qumrān.

THE MATERIALS OF THE INVESTIGATION

The premise of the textual critic's work is that whenever a text is transmitted, variation occurs. This is because human beings are careless, fallible, and occasionally perverse. Variation can occur in several ways: through mechanical damage or accidental omission; through misunderstanding due to changes in fashions of writing; through ignorance of language or subject matter; through inattention or stupidity; and through deliberate efforts at correction. The task of the textual critic is to detect and, so far as possible, undo these effects. His concern is with the reconstruction of what no longer exists. A text is not a concrete artifact, like a pot or a statue, but an abstract concept or idea. The original text of Aeschylus' *Agamemnon* or Horace's *Odes* has perished; what survives is a number of derived forms or states of the text, approximations of varying reliability preserved by tradition. The critic must reduce these approximations as nearly as possible to the first or original state that they imperfectly represent; or if, as sometimes happens for reasons that will be explained below, no single original can be reconstructed or postulated, he must reduce their number to the lowest possible figure. His methods and the degree of his success will be determined by the nature of the individual problem; *i.e.*, the text itself and the circumstances of its transmission. The range of possible situations is vast, as the following survey indicates. The types of text with which the critic is concerned may be classified broadly under three heads.

Books transmitted in print. For practical purposes it is often assumed that the latest edition of a modern book published during the author's lifetime may be treated as the original. This is a simplification. The actual author's original may have been a manuscript or a typescript or a recording; in the process of publication it has passed through several stages of transmission, including possibly storage in a computer, at any one of which errors have necessarily occurred. Experience teaches that some errors will survive uncorrected in the published version. Further errors are likely to occur if a book is reprinted. Even an edition revised by the author is not to be regarded as textually definitive. Errors committed and overlooked by the author himself may be corrected by the critic in appropriate cases. Special problems are posed by an author's second thoughts, whether preserved in his books and papers or incorporated in editions revised by him; recent research has shown that authorial revision in modern printed books has been underestimated. The extent to which a critic is free to choose between authorial variants on aesthetic grounds is a matter of debate.

Books published before the 19th century pose essentially similar problems in a more intractable form, as may be seen in the case of Shakespeare. No manuscript of any of Shakespeare's plays survives, and there were substantial intervals between the dates of composition and the first printed versions, in which unauthorized variation clearly occurred. For Shakespeare's plays, indeed, the very concept of an author's original may be misleading. Elizabethan printers clearly had little regard for strict textual accuracy, so that allowance must be made not only for error but for deliberate alteration by compositors; thus the textual criticism of 16th- and 17th-century books must include a study of the practices of early printers.

Books transmitted in manuscript. Nearly all classical and patristic texts, and a great many medieval texts, fall into this category. Every handwritten copy of a book is textually unique, and to that extent represents a separate edition of the text. Whereas the characteristic grouping of printed texts is "monogenous" (*i.e.*, in a straight line of descent), that of manuscript texts is "polygenous" or branched and interlocking. The critic is in principle obliged to establish the relationship of every surviving manuscript copy of a text to every other. The difficulty and indeed the feasibility of this undertaking varies enormously from case to case. The following extremes embrace a wide range of intermediate possibilities. (1) The authority for a text may be a single surviving copy (*e.g.*, Menander, *Dyscolus*) or a copy that can be shown to be the source of all other copies (*e.g.*, Varro, *De Lingua Latina*) or an edition printed directly from a copy now lost (*e.g.*, the work of the Roman historian Velleius Paterculus); or a text may be transmitted in scores of copies whose interrelationships cannot be exactly determined (*e.g.*, Claudian, *De raptu Proserpinae*). (2) The interval between the original and the earliest surviving copies may be very short (*e.g.*, the French medieval poet Chrétien de Troyes) or very long (*e.g.*, the Attic tragedians). (3) A tradition may be "dynamic"—*i.e.*, the text may have been copied and recopied many times even in a short time (*e.g.*, Dante's *La divina commedia*); or it may be "static"—*i.e.*, the number of transmissional stages even over a long period may have been few (e.g., *Epigrammata Bobiensia*, a Latin translation of Greek epigrams). (4) A text may be a religious or literary work that was respectfully treated by copyists and protected by an exegetical tradition (*e.g.*, the Bible, the Latin poet Virgil); or a popular book that was exposed to correction, glossing, and amplification by readers (*e.g.*, the *Regula magistri* ["Rule of the Master," a Latin work related to the Rule of St. Benedict] and much medieval vernacular literature). (5) A text may have been written and transmitted after the establishment of a scholarly tradition, or it may show signs of "wild" and arbitrary variation dating from an age in which standards of exact verbal accuracy were low. To this extent all Greek books written before the establishment of the Alexandrian library (see below) were exposed to the hazards associated with oral transmission.

Books transmitted orally. Many texts have been orally transmitted, sometimes for long periods, before being committed to writing, and much textual variation may be attributable to this stage of transmission. Often in such cases the critic cannot attempt to construct an "original" but must stop short at some intermediate stage: thus the edited text of Homer means in practice the closest possible approximation to the text as established by the scholars of Alexandria. The length, complexity, and fidelity of oral traditions varies enormously. The text of the old Indian Ṛgveda was transmitted orally almost without variation from very ancient to modern times, whereas much old French epic and Provençal lyric has descended in variant redactions for which a common source may be postulated but cannot be reconstructed. Sometimes this is attributable not to spontaneous variation but to deliberate reworking, whether by the author, as appears to be the case with the three versions of the English poem *Piers Plowman*, or by later revisers, as with the four versions of *Digenis Akritas* (a Greek epic). The distinction, however, is not always easy to draw. These considerations apply to a wide range of texts from ancient Hebrew through Old Norse to modern Russian, but they are especially important for medieval literature. In this field perhaps more than in any other the critic's aims and methods will be dictated by the character of the oral tradition, the stage at which it attained a more or less fixed form in writing, and the attitude of copyists in a particular genre to precise verbal accuracy. A problem of particular difficulty and importance is posed by the Greek New Testament. Though the text appears to have been transmitted from the first in writing, the textual variations are in many ways analogous to those of an oral tradition, and it is commonly held that the essential

task of the critic is not to try to reconstruct the "original" but to isolate those forms of the text that were current in particular centres in the ancient world.

CRITICAL METHODS

General principles. From the preceding discussion it is apparent that there is only one universally valid principle of textual criticism, the formulation of which can be traced back at least as far as the 18th-century German historian A.L. von Schlözer: that each case is special. The critic must begin by defining the problem presented by his particular material and the consequent limitations of his inquiry. Everything that is said below about "method" must be understood in the light of this general proviso. The celebrated dictum of the 18th-century English classical scholar Richard Bentley that "reason and the facts outweigh a hundred manuscripts" (*ratio et res ipsa centum codicibus potiores sunt*) is not a repudiation of science but a reminder that the critic is by definition one who discriminates (the word itself derives from the Greek word for "judge"), and that no amount of learning or mastery of method will compensate for a lack of common sense. To study the great critics in action is incomparably more instructive than to read theoretical manuals. As the English critic and poet A.E. Housman wrote,

> A man who possesses common sense and the use of reason must not expect to learn from treatises or lectures on textual criticism anything that he could not, with leisure and industry, find out for himself. What the lectures and treatises can do for him is to save him time and trouble by presenting to him immediately considerations which would in any case occur to him sooner or later.

Admittedly, the technical advances in textual bibliography mentioned below are not such as would sooner or later occur to any reflective and intelligent person; but bibliography, like paleography, is ancillary to textual criticism proper, and Housman's words are strictly true. What they imply is that good critics are born, not made.

The critical process can be resolved into three stages: (1) recension, (2) examination, and (3) emendation. Though these stages are logically distinct, (2) and (3) are in practice performed simultaneously, and even (1) entails the application of criteria theoretically appropriate to (2) and (3).

Recension. The operation of recension is the reconstructing of the earliest form or forms of the text that can be inferred from the surviving evidence. Such evidence may be internal or external. Internal evidence consists of all extant copies or editions of the text, together with versions in other languages, citations in other authors, and other sources not belonging to the main textual tradition. These witnesses (as they may be called) must be identified, dated, and described, using the appropriate paleographical and bibliographical techniques. They must then be collated; *i.e.*, the variant readings that they contain must be registered by comparison with some selected form of the text, often a standard printed edition. Where the number of witnesses is large, collation may have to be of selected passages. If there is only one witness to a text, collation and recension are synonymous, and the critic passes straight to examination and emendation. Generally, however, he will be faced with two or more witnesses offering variant forms or states of the text.

Collateral evidence as to the transmission of a text may be supplied from sources external to the direct or indirect textual tradition. Thus the ancient biographers throw light on the circumstances in which Virgil's *Aeneid* was published. Inferred textual stages may be dated on the evidence of copying practices at different periods, or by association with a particular scholar, or from entries in medieval library catalogues. Generally speaking, information of this sort will contribute more to the history than to the criticism of the text, but the two fields are intimately connected; and the better the textual history is known, the more reliable the control of the critic over conjectural solutions to specific problems. In the case of printed books, such external evidence is as a rule more plentiful; it is often essential, since so much may turn on

The importance of common sense

The search for the earliest transmitted form of the text

the accurate dating of editions. Relevant information must be sought in the published and unpublished records of stationers, printers, booksellers, and publishers and in other archival material.

Having assembled his evidence, the critic may proceed, broadly speaking, in one of two different ways, according as he decides to handle the problem of interrelationships "genealogically" or "textually."

The "genealogical," or "stemmatic," approach. The attempt to reconstruct an original text here relies on the witnesses themselves regarded as physical objects related to each other chronologically and genealogically; the text and the textual vehicle (the book itself) are treated as a single entity. On the basis of shared variants, chiefly errors and omissions, a family tree of the witnesses (*stemma codicum*) is drawn up. Those witnesses that repeat the testimony of other surviving witnesses are discarded, and from the agreements of the remainder the text is reconstructed as it existed in the lost copy from which they descend, the "archetype." Thus in the tradition of the 6th-century monk Cassiodorus' *Institutiones* the relationships of the manuscripts of the authentic version of the text of Book II may be represented by the accompanying diagram. The Roman letters represent extant manuscripts,

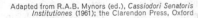

Adapted from R.A.B. Mynors (ed.), *Cassiodori Senatoris Institutiones* (1961); the Clarendon Press, Oxford

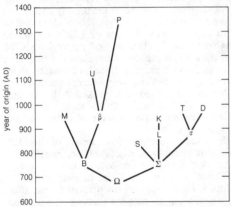

Manuscript genealogy, with Greek letters representing sources upon which known manuscripts (Roman letters) must have been based.

and the Greek letters represent the lost manuscripts from which they derive, here arbitrarily dated. The text of the archetype Ω is established by the agreement of B and Σ. Since B survives, the readings of MUP, which are derived from it, would be of value only where B had suffered damage after M and β were copied from it. In such cases the text of β could be inferred from the agreement of UP and the text of B from the agreement of Mβ (or MU or MP). The text of Σ can be inferred from the agreement of SLσ or SL or Sσ (or ST or SD) or Lσ (or LT or LD). K, being copied from L, would be of value only where L had suffered damage after K was copied from it. An important distinction is here exemplified between "trifid" and "bifid" *stemmata*. Where there are three independent witnesses to a source, as with Σ, its reading is certified by the agreement of all three or of any two; where there are only two witnesses, as with Ω, and they disagree, the reading of the source cannot be certified. Even in the latter situation, however, the number of possible variants existing in the source would have been reduced to two. Thus in theory the genealogical, or stemmatic, method allows the critic to eliminate from consideration all variants that cannot be traced back to the archetype or earliest inferable textual state.

While in principle this method is unassailable, it depends for its practical validity on the assumption that each copyist followed only one model or exemplar and generated only variants peculiar to himself. This is called "vertical" transmission, and a tradition of this kind is called "closed." Once the possibility is admitted that a copyist used more than one exemplar or (the more probable supposition) copied an exemplar in which variants from

another source or sources had been incorporated—*i.e.,* that more than one textual state may coexist in a single witness—the construction of a *stemma* becomes more complicated and may be impossible. This is called "horizontal" transmission, and a tradition of this kind is called "open" or "contaminated." The practice of critics faced with contamination tends to vary, for historical reasons, from field to field. Editors of classical texts generally adopt a controlled eclecticism, classifying the witnesses broadly by groups according to the general character of their texts and choosing between their readings largely on grounds of intrinsic excellence. Medievalists, following the French scholar Joseph Bédier (see below), sometimes revert to the traditional practice, to which their training may dispose, of selecting a single witness as the main basis of the text. For editors of printed books, contamination is not an important problem.

The "textual," or "distributional," approach. In the alternative method, the text and the textual vehicle are dissociated; the emphasis is on the analysis of the variants themselves and their distribution rather than on the character of the text as presented by individual witnesses. The techniques or models employed include those of statistics, symbolic logic, and biological taxonomy. Two theoretical advantages are suggested for this approach. First, objectivity: no judgments of value are entailed, whereas the genealogical method calls for decisions as to the correctness of readings or textual states. Second, the possibility of mechanization: long and elaborate calculations involving thousands of variants may be performed by a computer. This possibility is especially attractive to New Testament critics, who are confronted with about 5,000 manuscripts of the Greek text as well as versions in other languages and patristic citations. In practice, however, these advantages are to a large extent illusory. An "objective" (*i.e.,* undiscriminating) treatment of all variants in a literary text such as Ovid's *Metamorphoses* (of which more than 300 manuscripts exist) without regard to their metrical and stylistic quality would be a self-evident waste of time and produce merely confusion. The critic cannot abrogate his critical function, which implies discrimination, at the very beginning of the critical process. Moreover, the preparation or programming of a text for treatment in this way, whether mechanical aids are used or not, is long and laborious, and one must consider whether in a given case the results justify the expenditure of effort. Texts have been transmitted by a combination of purpose and accident that in any particular instance is both unique and unpredictable, and no machine or statistical model exhibits the versatility necessary to unravel the incomplete and tangled skein. Mechanical methods have been most successful in fields other than recension (see below).

Examination. The process of determining whether the transmitted text or any of the transmitted variants of it is "authentic"—*i.e.,* what the author intended—is known as examination. The prior process of recension has reduced the number of textual states having a claim to be considered "authoritative." Many different situations are possible. In a completely closed tradition it is theoretically feasible to reconstruct the archetype with such certainty that only a single form of the text without variants remains to be examined. In practice this is extremely unlikely to be the situation. Usually the critic is faced with pairs (sometimes triplets) of variants, all with a presumptive claim to be considered authoritative. In some traditions he will confront variant versions of the whole text. Where papyri or other early sources independent of the main tradition are available, he may have to reckon with "pretraditional" (*i.e.,* pre-archetypal) variants. The process of examination calls upon the critic's full range of knowledge as well as his innate powers of taste and discrimination. The criteria applied must be those appropriate to the particular author (supposing his identity to be known), the period, the genre, and the particular character of the work. The opposing demands of analogy and anomaly must be weighed according to the circumstances. Many of the older generation of critics based their decisions on aprioristic or rigidly analogical princi-

Analysis of variants

Authenticity of a text

ples of elegance and propriety, while the canons of modern criticism are based on historical studies of language and style. It is here that the circularity inherent in the whole operation is most evident, for the linguistic and stylistic criteria employed are themselves based on inductions from texts, probably including the one under examination. There is no escape from this difficulty; as the German philologist Karl Lachmann observed, it is precisely the task of the critic "to tread that circle deftly and warily."

Emendation. The attempt to restore the transmitted text to its authentic state is called emendation. There will usually be a chronological gap, sometimes of several centuries, between the archetype, or earliest inferable state of the text, and the original; nearly all manuscripts of classical authors date from the Middle Ages. The history of the text during the intervening period may be illustrated from external sources; but if examination has convinced the critic that the transmitted text (or its variants) are not authentic, he normally has no resource but to bridge the gap by conjecture. Conjectural emendation has been defined by the American scholar B.L. Gildersleeve as "the appeal from manuscripts we have to a manuscript that has been lost." Theoretically this definition is acceptable, if we interpret "manuscript" as "source," but in practice the making of conjectures, as distinct from testing them, is intelligent guesswork.

Conjectural emendation

No part of the theory of textual criticism has suffered more from misunderstanding than has conjectural emendation. Such conjectural, or divinatory, criticism has in the past enjoyed a traditional pre-eminence: Dr. Johnson observed that William Warburton's correction of "good" to "god" in the second act of *Hamlet* (scene 2, line 182) almost set the critic on a level with the author. That idea is as erroneous as the frame of mind in which the Italian scholar C. Pascal founded the Paravia series of editions in order to purge Latin texts of German conjectures. The best critic is he who discriminates best, whether between variants or between transmitted text and conjecture.

Conjectures as a rule occur to the mind spontaneously or not at all; diagnosis and prescription often present themselves at the same moment. This instinctive process is not under the critic's control, though he can sharpen and regulate it by constant study and observation. The outcome of the process, the emendation itself, can and must be controlled and tested by precisely the same criteria as are used in deciding between variants. This is essentially an exercise in balancing probabilities. These probabilities are historical. The conventional distinction between intrinsic and transcriptional (*i.e.,* paleographical or bibliographical) probability tends to obscure a fundamental historical point. If the transmitted form of the text lies at few removes or a short distance in time from the original, a conjectural solution which violates transcriptional probability is less likely to be correct than if the text has undergone a long and complex process of deterioration. In the latter case the critic may attach little or no importance to transcriptional probability. The critic cannot neglect the study of paleography or bibliography, but he must not give them more than their critical due. What that may be depends on the particular historical circumstances. He will study carefully the rationale of error in manuscripts and books themselves rather than in the schematic classifications of critical manuals; and he will learn from experience to distinguish between the types of error that may be called "psychological" (*i.e.,* those committed by a tired or inattentive copyist, whatever language or instruments he uses) and those contingent on the period and the medium of transmission, whether it be the mouth and the ear, the pen, the hand composing stick, the linotype or typewriter keyboard, the computer or photo-copying machine, or the printing press. Two complementary principles originated by the New Testament critics of the 18th century are often cited as aids to decision: *utrum in alterum abiturum erat?* ("which reading would be more likely to have given rise to the other?") and *difficilior lectio potior* ("the more difficult reading is to be preferred"). These are no more than useful rules of thumb; it has been suggested that in practice these and other such principles reduce themselves to the truism *melior lectio potior,* "the better reading is to be preferred."

From this discussion it is apparent that the traditional opposition between "conservative" and "radical" styles of criticism that has haunted textual criticism since St. Jerome has no meaning. The critic does not attack or defend the transmitted text; he asks himself whether it is authentic. How radically he treats it, and how many conjectural readings he substitutes for transmitted readings, depends not on his temperament but on the nature of the problem. If he has studied the history of textual criticism he will know that as a matter of demonstrable fact nearly all conjectures are wrong, and he will accept that many of his solutions are in the nature of things provisional.

Editorial technique. Critical texts are edited according to conventions that vary with the type of text (classical, medieval, modern) but follow certain general principles. In some cases, as with newly edited papyri and with palimpsests (writing materials re-used after erasure), the edition will take the form of a diplomatic transcript; *i.e.,* the most accurate possible representation of a particular textual form. Generally, however, the editor constitutes his text in accordance with his own judgment on principles explained in his introduction; and he indicates his sources in critical notes (*apparatus criticus*), preferably at the foot of the page. These notes are usually couched in a special terminology that relies heavily on abbreviation and the use of conventional signs or letters (*sigla*) to identify the witnesses. In classical and patristic texts the language of the notes is usually Latin. Editorial judgment will be influenced by the presumed needs of readers: in an edition intended for scholars, very corrupt passages are often printed as transmitted and marked with a dagger (†), whereas in an edition for the student or general reader some compromise may be accepted in the interests of readability.

A much-discussed problem is the treatment of "accidentals"—variations in spelling, capitalization, punctuation, and the like. Few if any ancient text traditions preserve reliable evidence of authorial practice in these matters, so that the editor is concerned only with variants that affect the sense; in preparing his text for printing he will adopt modern conventions of presentation and punctuation and a normalized orthography. The same holds good for the majority of medieval texts. Printed texts, however, were generally corrected or seen through the press by the author, or at all events by a contemporary, so that the editor may be reasonably confident of reproducing at least a decent approximation to authorial usage. Whether, or to what extent, he should do so is much debated; opinions differ sharply as to the usefulness of "old-spelling" editions of Shakespeare and other early writers.

ORIGINS AND DEVELOPMENT

From antiquity to the Renaissance. Until the 20th century the development of textual criticism was inevitably dominated by classical and biblical studies. The systematic study and practice of the subject originated in the 3rd century BC with the Greek scholars of Alexandria. Literary culture had before that time been predominantly oral, though books were in common use by the 5th century, and many texts had suffered damage because the idea of precise textual accuracy and reproduction was unfamiliar. The aim of the librarians of Alexandria was to collect and catalogue every extant Greek book and to produce critical editions of the most important together with textual and interpretative commentaries. Many such editions and commentaries did in fact appear. Alexandrian editing was distinguished above all by respect for the tradition; the text was constituted from the oldest and best copies available, and conjectural emendation was rigidly confined to the commentary, which was contained in a separate volume. An elaborate battery of critical signs was used to refer from text to commentary. These techniques were applied, though on a less ambitious scale, by Roman scholars to Latin texts. Fidelity to tradition was the chief legacy of ancient textual scholarship to later ages; the copyist was expected to reproduce his exemplar as exactly

The librarians of Alexandria

as he could, and correction was based on comparison with other copies, not on the unaided conjectural sagacity of the scribe. Such was the practice of the best monastic scriptoria such as that of Tours, or of the best scholars, such as Lupus of Ferrières (fl. 850). From about 1350, however, a change in attitude is evident, particularly in the West. What is often called the revival of learning was in reality a practical movement to enlist the heritage of classical antiquity in the service of the new Christian humanism. In order to make them usable (*i.e.*, readable), texts were corrected freely and often arbitrarily by scholars, copyists, and readers (the three categories being in fact hardly distinguishable). At its best, as seen in the activities of a scholar like Demetrius Triclinius, later medieval and early Renaissance criticism verges on scientific scholarship, but such cases are exceptional. For the most part the correction of texts was a purely subjective display of taste, sometimes right but much more often wrong, and resting as a rule on nothing more solid than a superficial sense of elegance. In consequence, by the 1470s, when the first printed editions (*editiones principes*) of classical texts began to appear, most Greek and Latin authors were circulating in a textually debased condition, and it was manuscripts of this character that almost always served as copy for the early printers. Very little editing in any real sense of the word was done; the scholars who saw the *editiones principes* through the press generally confined themselves to superficial improvements.

> **From Politian to Cobet.** This state of affairs entailed that down to the 19th century most critics were engaged not in establishing and emending texts on scientific principles but in correcting, in a necessarily unsystematic fashion, a vulgate or received text (*lectio recepta*) that was itself the product of an almost entirely haphazard process of variation and conjecture. The situation was aggravated by the fact that the manuscripts themselves, the basic materials of the investigation, were largely inaccessible to scholars. The Italian poet and scholar Politian, unlike most of his contemporaries, was aware that only through the identification and comparison of the best manuscripts could texts be improved; his notes and collations show that he understood the problem correctly as essentially one of control of the sources. What might have been done in this field is shown by his work, cut short by his early death, on the Florentine codex of Justinian's Pandects. Many manuscripts were still privately owned, their very existence unknown to scholars; public libraries were few and published catalogues fewer; travel was difficult, expensive, and often dangerous. It was not until the twin disciplines of diplomatic and paleography were founded by the great Benedictine monks Mabillon and Montfaucon, and developed by their successors, that a critical use of the evidence became possible; and much of the evidence itself did not become available until after the Napoleonic Wars, when most of the private stock of manuscripts passed finally into public collections.

Some advances were taking place, slowly and unsystematically, in both the theory and practice of textual criticism. The history of critical method in this period is most profitably studied in the best editions of the best editors. The accepted method was to correct the text (*i.e.*, the text of the last printed edition) *codicum et ingenii ope; i.e.*, with the aid of the manuscript and printed sources and the critic's own ingenuity. Divination was subordinated to authority, and any reading found in a manuscript or printed text was accounted superior to any conjecture, whatever its intrinsic merits. The first important departure from this pattern is seen in the edition of Catullus by J.J. Scaliger (1577), in which the possibilities of the genealogical method, already understood in principle by Politian and other Renaissance scholars, were exemplified by the demonstration that all the extant copies derived from a lost manuscript, whose orthography and provenance Scaliger was prepared to reconstruct. Almost equally significant was Richard Bentley's edition of Horace (1711), in which for the first time the role of conjecture in the critical and editorial process was recognized and the tradition of producing a corrected version of the

text of previous editors was decisively rejected. Bentley's scholarship was greatly admired in the Netherlands, and the editions of the great Dutch Latinists J.F. Gronovius and N. Heinsius were informed by Bentleian principles. Under his influence there grew up what may be called an Anglo-Dutch school of criticism, the two most typical representatives of which were Richard Porson and C.G. Cobet. Its strength lay in sound judgment and good taste rooted in minute linguistic and metrical study; its weaknesses were an excessive reliance on analogical criteria and an indifference for German science and method. Its influence may still be seen in the empiricism that characterizes much critical work by English scholars.

> **From Bentley to Lachmann.** The decisive influence on the editing of secular texts came from the New Testament critics of the 18th century. The printed text of the Greek New Testament in common use was still essentially that established in 1516 by Desiderius Erasmus. For his edition, produced in great haste, he had used such manuscripts, neither ancient nor good, as chanced to be accessible to him. Superficially revised, this was the text termed in the Elzevier edition of 1633 "now received by all," *nunc ab omnibus receptum*. Bentley proposed an edition on radical lines in which he engaged to give the text "exactly as it was in the best exemplars at the time of the Council of Nice. So that there shall not be twenty words, nor even particles, difference; . . ." This project never materialized, but editions of the Greek text that did not reproduce the *textus receptus* were published in England by Daniel Mace (1729), William Bowyer, the Younger (1763), and Edward Harwood (1776). On the Continent, meanwhile, New Testament criticism was being developed on scientific and historical lines by a succession of distinguished scholars, notably J.A. Bengel, J.J. Wettstein, J.S. Semler and J.J. Griesbach. They shaped the genealogical method that was later refined by editors of classical texts. Wettstein also deserves commemoration as the first New Testament critic to use *sigla* systematically. This was important, since some at least of the deficiencies of classical editions at this time are attributable to the lack of suitable conventions for the presentation of critical information, together with a conservative and belletristic attitude to technical jargon by publishers, scholars, and users of books in general. Though *sigla* occur sporadically in editions as early as the 16th century and were used by S. Haverkamp in his Lucretius (1725) in something like the modern style, they did not become normal until the second half of the 19th century.

The genealogical, or stemmatic, method of recension has already been described. It is usually associated with the name of the German Karl Lachmann, but it had its origins in the work of J.A. Bengel and his successors, and almost every essential feature of it was already present in the work of Lachmann's precursors such as J.A. Ernesti, F.A. Wolf, K.G. Zumpt, F.W. Ritschl, and J.N. Madvig. Nevertheless Lachmann occupies a central position in the development of textual criticism because of the unusual power and penetration of his scholarship, the range of textual material on which he worked, and his immense contemporary and posthumous influence. His edition of the Greek New Testament (1831; 2nd ed. 1842–50) was intended primarily as a vindication of the principles of Bentley and Bengel and a demonstration that the *textus receptus* must be finally rejected. Similarly his famous edition of Lucretius (1850) is important as an exemplification of the method in action, since the tradition of Lucretius is peculiarly suitable for the purpose. The demonstration fell short of completeness, for Lachmann had not fully grasped the problem and so failed to exploit the method fully. It has been suggested that Lachmann's best critical work was in his editions of medieval German texts; their influence will be considered below. The Lachmannian model of recension derived added authority from seemingly analogous models in other fields, especially that of comparative philology. As propagated by disciples, notably Moritz Haupt, it dominated textual studies for half a century.

> **Related developments in the late 19th century.** *Photography*. Possibly the most important technical advance

Debasement of texts during the Renaissance

Richard Bentley's influence

The genealogical method of Karl Lachmann

in the latter part of the 19th century was the perfection of photography. Instead of travelling in search of his material, the paleographer or critic could now assemble and study it at relatively little expense and without leaving his desk.

Papyri. During the last quarter of the 19th century the tempo of archaeological discovery in classical and biblical lands was vastly increased, and many new texts were unearthed. Some of these were in previously unknown languages, setting new problems of decipherment. Specifically relevant to textual studies are the many Greek papyri recovered from Egypt. These have thrown much light on the history and techniques of ancient book production and scholarship and hence, indirectly, on critical problems. Where the texts they contain are already known, their evidence has tended to emphasize our ignorance of the textual history of classical literature in antiquity itself. Being usually far older than the manuscripts already known, they often illuminate the "pretraditional" state of the text; by sometimes offering readings that agree with those of late and "inferior" medieval copies they justify editors in a policy of cautious eclecticism. Papyrus discoveries have been of particular moment for the text of the New Testament.

English studies. Editors of printed texts, having invariably received a classical education (no other being available), had naturally followed, with minor modifications, the methods of classical editing. They would reprint the text of the last edition with such improvements as editorial taste and learning suggested but with no attempt to investigate the sources of the text. Since Lachmann's method was inapplicable to printed texts, this procedure continued until, by the end of the 19th century, the text of Shakespeare, for example, was in a state somewhat analogous to that of most classical writers at the time of the *editiones principes.* Much of the work of modern Shakespearean editors has consisted of undoing the damage inflicted by their predecessors. The early 20th century saw the rise of a new school of "biblio-textual" criticism, most notably represented by A.W. Pollard, R.B. McKerrow, and W.W. Greg. Its object was to devise a style of recension appropriate to the special circumstances under which early printed texts were produced and propagated, and its methods were those of analytical bibliography. These developments are of direct importance for the criticism and editing of a large range of texts of the 16th, 17th, and 18th centuries, particularly those of the Elizabethan and Jacobean dramatists. They have also engendered a discussion of general methodological interest on the role of bibliographical as opposed to historical and literary criteria in the editorial process. This debate continues.

Medieval studies. Critics and editors of medieval texts had also inevitably been influenced by developments in the classical field. Before Lachmann it had been usual to choose a single manuscript as the main basis for an edition. Because of the circumstances in which much medieval literature was composed and transmitted this was not necessarily unscientific, and the surviving bulk of texts was so large as to dictate that approach in many cases if they were to be edited at all. This had been the style of editing followed by the Belgian Jesuits known as Bollandists, the French Benedictines called Maurists, and the Italian scholar L.A. Muratori, and perpetuated in the indispensable *Patrologiae Cursus Completus* (edition of the Church Fathers) of the French priest Jacques-Paul Migne. At its best it is seen in the editions of medieval Latin chronicles by the 18th-century Oxford antiquary Thomas Hearne, some of which are still standard works. A more scientific approach was adopted in the publications of the *Monumenta Germaniae Historica,* the later volumes of which (from about 1880) were produced by editors trained in the school of Lachmann. Similarly, editors of vernacular texts followed the lead that Lachmann had given in his editions of such early German poems as the *Nibelunge Not* (1826) and the *Iwein* (1827). An important development in the application of the method was due to the medievalists G. Gröber and G. Paris, who first emphasized the significance of common errors. But in the general uncritical enthusiasm for scientific method, the genealogical approach was too often used without regard for the special conditions under which medieval literature has been handed down.

Reaction against the genealogical method. Haupt had proclaimed in his lectures that his main object was to teach method. But confidence in method led to its misuse. The Lachmannian formula of recension was applied to texts, classical as well as medieval, for which it was unsuitable, often with grotesque results. Commonly this took the form of choosing on "scientific" (*i.e.*, stemmatic) grounds a "best manuscript" (*codex optimus*) and defending its readings as authoritative even where common sense showed that they could not be authentic. This was the type of editing satirized by A.E. Housman in the brilliant prefaces to his editions of Manilius (1903) and Juvenal (1905) and in many reviews and articles. It flourished chiefly between 1875 and 1900, but the dangers of excessive methodological rigidity had already been foreseen. In 1841 H. Sauppe in his *Epistola Critica ad G. Hermannum* had emphasized the diversity of transmissional situations and the difficulty or actual impossibility of classifying the manuscripts in all cases. In 1843 Lachmann's pupil O. Jahn, in his edition of Persius, had repudiated the strict application of the genealogical method as unsuitable to the tradition of that poet. The most extreme position was taken by E. Schwartz, who in his edition of Eusebius' *Historia ecclesiastica* (1909) denied that "vertically" transmitted texts of Greek books existed at all. The limitations of the stemmatic method have subsequently been stressed in a more temperate fashion by other writers. The modern tendency is to acknowledge the validity of the method in principle while recommending a cautious empiricism in its application. For the editor of a contaminated tradition—and most traditions are probably contaminated—the lesson of recent research is that authoritative evidence may survive even in late and generally corrupt or interpolated sources.

More radical criticism of the method has come from medievalists. In 1913 and again in 1928 the French scholar J. Bédier attacked the stemmatic method because the *stemmata* it produced for medieval texts almost invariably had only two branches. Subsequent investigation has shown that Bédier overrated the inherent improbability of this situation, and it is generally agreed that his criticisms had to do with improper application rather than with the method itself. The point taken by H. Quentin (1922) has already been mentioned: that the method entails argument in a circle, since it relies on the identification of errors at the beginning of a process designed to lead to that very end. This objection, more cogent in theory than in practice, applies with greater force to medieval than to classical texts. The linguistic and stylistic canons of classical Greek and Latin are relatively strict and well defined, whereas the vocabulary, grammar, and usage of many medieval authors (especially when an oral prehistory is in question) is often not certain enough to allow reliable discrimination between variant and error. Classical texts, moreover, have passed through a series of bottlenecks in their history, which have simplified editorial problems by eliminating a high proportion of the evidence (*cf.* the remarks on papyri above). With a few exceptions, such as the commentary of Servius, only one version of each text remains to be reconstructed, whereas many medieval texts are extant in several redactions that cannot be winnowed by the stemmatic method so as to leave only one. Quentin's own method, which depended on the comparison of variants in groups of three, without prejudice as to their correctness, has not been generally adopted. It is immensely laborious and does not in practice possess the objectivity that its inventor claimed for it. Bédier and Quentin have, however, done good service to textual criticism in enjoining caution. The best critics in all fields now agree in rejecting the "logical" (*i.e.*, the illogical) application of any method if the results conflict with common sense, and in stressing the necessity of judging variant readings and forms of a text on their intrinsic merits in the light of the information available.

Mechanical methods. Quentin also gave a lead to later investigators in calling attention to the possibility of bas-

Shakespeare texts

Bédier and Quentin

ing recension on the variants themselves, and the more sophisticated methods of Greg (1927), Archibald Hill (1950), Vinton Dearing (1959), and J. Froger (1968) may be seen as a continuation of his work. It has already been suggested that methods of this type, so far as recension is concerned, have been of primarily theoretical interest. But the use of mechanical and computing techniques in this field is in its infancy, and assessment must be provisional. Certain practical applications seem to have proved themselves. Mechanical aids to collation have been successfully used in editing Shakespeare and Dryden. Computer storage and analysis of texts can provide information about authorial usage, such as stylistic and metrical patterns, and facilitate the production of concordances. These aids are more relevant to conjectural emendation (as shown by their application to the Dead Sea Scrolls) and the "higher" criticism (*e.g.*, determination of authenticity) than to the recension of texts. The formula or machine that will do the critic's essential work for him still awaits discovery; the best texts are produced by the best scholars, whatever their method or lack of method. Lachmann observed that the establishment of a text according to its tradition is a strictly historical undertaking. Twentieth-century research into the composition and transmission of ancient, medieval, and modern texts has confirmed the truth of his pronouncement.

Use of the computer (margin)

BIBLIOGRAPHY

Transmission of texts: For oral transmission the fundamental work is H.M. and N.K. CHADWICK, *The Growth of Literature,* 3 vol. (1932–40, reprinted 1969). Classical, biblical, and medieval texts are all covered (but somewhat unevenly) by H. HUNGER et al., *Geschichte der Textüberlieferung der antiken und mittelalterlichen Literatur,* 2 vol. (1961–64). For classical texts in general the best introduction is L.D. REYNOLDS and N.G. WILSON, *Scribes and Scholars* (1968); more specialized are A.C. CLARK, *The Descent of Manuscripts* (1918); and A. DAIN, *Les manuscrits,* 2nd rev. ed. (1964). For special areas, see B.A. VAN GRONINGEN, *Traité d'histoire et de critique des textes grecs* (1963); R.D. DAWE, *The Collation and Investigation of Manuscripts of Aeschylus* (1964); R. RENEHAN, *Greek Textual Criticism: A Reader* (1969); L. HAVET, *Manuel de critique verbale appliquée aux textes latins* (1911), an exhaustive catalogue raisonné of scribal error; E.G. TURNER, *Greek Papyri: An Introduction* (1968), important for the history of Greek texts in antiquity. For biblical texts, in addition to Hunger (*op. cit.*), the standard work on the New Testament is B.M. METZGER, *The Text of the New Testament,* 2nd ed. (1968). For patristic texts an excellent case study raising important general issues is M. BEVENOT, *The Tradition of Manuscripts: A Study in the Transmission of St. Cyprion's Treatises* (1961). For medieval texts a good exposition of typical problems may be found in D'A.S. AVALLE, "Die Liederhandschriften und die Textkritik," in Hunger (*op. cit.*), 2:273–290; see also J.A. ASHER, "Truth and Fiction: The Text of Medieval Manuscripts," *Aumla,* 25:6–16 (1966). For printed books the standard work is F. BOWERS, *Bibliography and Textual Criticism* (1964); while a useful collection of essays may be found in O.M. BRACK and W. BARNES (eds.), *Bibliography and Textual Criticism: English and American Literature, 1700 to the Present* (1969).

Method (the stemmatic method): For its history and the contribution of Lachmann, S. TIMPANARO, *La genesi del metodo del Lachmann* (1963), is definitive. For its application, P. MAAS, *Textual Criticism* (Eng. trans. 1958), an austere theoretical exposition; and G. PASQUALI, *Storia della tradizione e critica del testo,* 2nd ed. (1952), brilliant but discursive, are complementary and fundamental. The reaction to the stemmatic method may be studied in H. QUENTIN, *Mémoire sur l'établissement du texte de la Vulgate* (1922), *Essais de critique textuelle—ecdotique* (1926); J. BURKE SEVERS, "Quentin's Theory of Textual Criticism," *English Inst. Annual 1941,* pp. 65–93 (1942); J. BEDIER, "La tradition manuscrite du Lai de L'Ombre: Réflexions sur l'art d'éditer les anciens textes," *Romania,* 54:161–96, 321–56 (1928). A. CASTELLANI, *Bédier avait-il raison?* (1957); W.W. GREG, *The Calculus of Variants* (1927); A.A. HILL, "Some Postulates for Distributional Study of Texts," *Stud. in Biblphy.,* 3:63–95 (1950). For further discussion of these developments, see W.P. SHEPARD, "Recent Theories of Textual Criticism," *Mod. Philol.,* 28:129–141 (1930); J. ANDRIEU, "Principes et recherches en critique textuelle," in *Mémorial des études latines . . . J. Marouzeau,* pp. 458–74 (1943); E.B. HAM, "Textual Criticism and Common Sense," *Romance Philol.,* 12:198–215 (1959). For mechanized techniques, see V.A. DEARING, *A Manual of Textual*

Analysis (1959); J. FROGER, *La critique des textes et son automatisation* (1968). For the taxonomic approach, see J.G. GRIFFITH, "A Taxonomic Study of the Manuscript Tradition of Juvenal," *Mus. Helv.,* 25:101–138 (1968); "Numerical Taxonomy and Some Primary Manuscripts of the Gospels," *J. Theol. Stud.,* 20:390–406 (1969).

Editorial technique: For classical texts the standard works are still: O. STAHLIN, *Editionstechnik,* 2nd ed. (1914); and A. DELATTE and A. SEVERYNS, *Emploi des signes critiques* (1938). For medieval texts, see A. DONDAINE, "Abbréviations latines et signes raccommandés pour l'apparat critique des éditions des textes médiévaux," *Bull. de la soc. int. pour l'étude de la philosophie méd.,* 2:142–149 (1960); and for papyri, see Turner (*op. cit.*); and H.C. YOUTIE, *The Textual Criticism of Documentary Papyri: Prolegomena* (1958).

General discussions: Many of the works cited above include discussion of general principles. In addition, the following works may be mentioned: H. KANTOROWICZ, *Einführung in die Textkritik* (1921), sound emphasis on the roles of probability and common sense; A.E. HOUSMAN, "The Application of Thought to Textual Criticism," *Proc. Class. Assoc.,* 18:67–84 (1922), a brilliant polemic against hard-and-fast "rules" of criticism; L. BIELER, "The Grammarian's Craft," *Folia,* 10:3–42 (1956), a useful summary discussion of modern developments; and A.H. MCDONALD, "Textual Criticism," in *Oxford Classical Dictionary,* 2nd ed. (1970), a sound and up-to-date exposition for classical students.

(E.J.Ke.)

Thackeray, William Makepeace

One of the great English Victorian novelists, William Makepeace Thackeray is chiefly celebrated as the author of *Vanity Fair* and *Henry Esmond,* though many critics also think highly of *Barry Lyndon* and *Pendennis.* His novels, teeming with innumerable personages (mostly of the upper and middle classes) and incidents, give the illusion of an actual world and reflect his belief in the conduct of the gentlemanly code of Victorian England. In the preface to the second edition (1848) of her novel, *Jane Eyre,* which she dedicated to Thackeray, Charlotte Brontë wrote that she regarded him as "the first social regenerator of the day." During his lifetime and for long afterward he was considered equal to or even superior to Charles Dickens, who was also his contemporary.

By courtesy of the National Portrait Gallery, London

Thackeray, oil painting by S. Laurence (1812–84). In the National Portrait Gallery, London.

Early life and career. Thackeray was born on July 18, 1811, in Calcutta, India, the only child of Richmond and Anne Thackeray. His father, an official of the British East India Company, died in 1815, and two years later Thackeray was sent to live with relatives in England. After attending schools in Southampton and in Chiswick, a suburb of London, he went in 1822 to Charterhouse, the London public school, where he led a rather miserable existence. His mother and her second husband, Major Carmichael-Smyth, whom she had married in 1817, had moved to England in 1819. Thackeray was on affectionate terms with them, although occasionally he chafed at his mother's domineering personality and strict religious views. In 1829 he entered Trinity College, Cambridge, but he left in the following year without taking a degree. He had already visited France, and now he went to Germany (July 1830–March 1831), staying for most of the time at Weimar, where he met Goethe, Germany's leading man of letters. Back in London, he studied law and engaged in bill discounting for brief periods. Although he led a desultory existence, he read widely and critically in English, French, and German, was an enthusiastic theatregoer, and cultivated stimulating friendships (with the poets Alfred Tennyson and Edward Fitzgerald at Cambridge, for example); he had a natural ability to write fluently and amusingly, and he was a skillful artist. Knowing that he was to inherit a considerable patrimony on his 21st birthday, he thought it unnecessary to apply himself seriously to a profession. Journalism, however, had long attracted him; and in May 1833 he became the owner of a weekly literary periodical, *The National Standard*. He was encouraged in this project by William Maginn, one of the leading journalists of the time. He wrote much for the periodical but was forced to close it in February 1834 for financial reasons. By that time, he had lost all his fortune, partly because it was invested in Indian banks that failed and partly because of his own improvidence. He took up the study of art in Paris, where he met Isabella Shawe, the daughter of an army officer. He married her on August 20, 1836, at the British Embassy in Paris; and in the following year they moved to London. Three daughters were born to them: Anne, Jane (who died in infancy), and Harriet.

Professional journalist

With a family to support and no private means, Thackeray began to work hard as a professional journalist, abandoning any thought of becoming a professional artist. In Paris, between September 1836 and February 1837, he had written articles on French politics for *The Constitutional*, a short-lived newspaper in which his stepfather, hoping to help Thackeray, had acquired a business interest. In London he wrote on a variety of topics for numerous periodicals. His work was unsigned, or written under such pen names as "Michael Angelo Titmarsh" and "George Fitz-Boodle." He contributed book reviews to *The Times*, *The Foreign Quarterly Review*, and *The Morning Chronicle*; but his most notable writing was done for *Fraser's Magazine* and *Punch*. His old friend Maginn, who was mainly responsible for editing *Fraser's Magazine* in the early 1830s, probably brought Thackeray on to its staff in 1834. Influenced by Maginn, the "Fraserians" were irreverent assailants of cant and pretension. Thackeray wrote scathing, witty articles about such subjects as Edward Bulwer-Lytton, a popular novelist (one of the magazine's chief butts), and the *Annuals*, elegantly produced volumes of insipid prose, verse, and pictures. Some of his best known contributions also arose from his scornful attitude to certain prevalent literary fashions: *The Yellowplush Correspondence* started as a review of a foolish book of etiquette; his short novel, *Catherine*, and his first full-length novel, *Barry Lyndon*, were intended as satires on the vogue for fiction with romanticized criminals as heroes. Other works serialized in *Fraser's Magazine* were *A Shabby Genteel Story* and *The History of Samuel Titmarsh and the Great Hoggarty Diamond*. He began writing and drawing for *Punch* in 1842, achieving his greatest success with *The Snobs of England*, later published as *The Book of Snobs*. His *Paris Sketch Book*, a collection of his writings about French matters, reprinted from various periodicals, appeared in 1840. *The Irish Sketch-Book* was a lively personal record of a stay in Ireland, and *Notes of a Journey from Cornhill to Grand Cairo* a similar account of a journey he took to the Mediterranean between August 1844 and February 1845.

This period was an unhappy one for him. He often found journalism irksome, had little money, and could not help feeling aggrieved that his great talents should go unrecognized for so long. He had, moreover, to bear a heavy personal sorrow, as his wife became insane in 1840; he was compelled to separate from her, and eventually to place her in the care of a friendly family living in the country. In 1846 Thackeray and his two daughters, to

whom he was a devoted father, settled in Kensington, the district of West London where he was to live for the rest of his life. A tall, heavily built man of striking appearance, with prematurely white hair and a nose that had been flattened in a schoolboy fight at Charterhouse, he was a convivial clubman, affectionate and sentimental toward those close to him. He fell in love with Jane Brookfield, the wife of a friend from Cambridge days, the Rev. William Henry Brookfield, and this passionate but platonic affair tormented him until it ended in 1851. Thackeray had always known it could have no happy outcome, and Brookfield was determined that it should stop.

Personal characteristics

Mature writings.   Under the influence of such anxieties and griefs, Thackeray's writing increasingly mellowed in the novels of his great period, which began with *Vanity Fair*. Although his early writing is amusing, acute, and full of vitality, it had remained unknown to the general public. *Vanity Fair*, however, first serialized in monthly shilling parts between 1847 and 1848, and illustrated by himself (as were many of his books), suddenly and belatedly brought Thackeray fame and prosperity. This "novel without a hero" (to use his own description), set in the second decade of the 19th century, the period of the Regency, deals mainly with the interwoven fortunes of two contrasting women, Amelia Sedley and Becky Sharp. The latter, an unprincipled adventuress, is the leading personage and is among the most memorable characters that Thackeray created. *Vanity Fair* was followed by *Pendennis*, which is partly fictionalized autobiography. In it, Thackeray traces the youthful career of Arthur Pendennis—his first love affair, his experiences at "Oxbridge University," his working as a London journalist, and so on—achieving a convincing portrait of a much-tempted young man. Thackeray was now a celebrated author, and in the summer of 1851 he set the seal on his fame by delivering a series of public lectures in London (subsequently repeated in other towns) on "The English Humourists of the 18th Century." He had always admired the authors of that time, and he chose the reign of Queen Anne for the period of his next novel, *Henry Esmond*. Some critics had thought that *Pendennis* was a formless, rambling book. Being highly sensitive to adverse criticism, Thackeray constructed *Henry Esmond* with great care, taking pains to get its historical detail correct. Unlike his other novels, it was published in book form without having been previously serialized. There is much of the author in its hero, Henry Esmond, a sensitive, brave, aristocratic soldier, whose love for two women, Beatrix and her mother, Lady Castlewood, is its main theme. Many admirers of Thackeray's work consider it to be his greatest novel. Throughout his works, he analyzed and deplored snobbery (but at the same time had some sympathy with it); he frequently gave his opinion on human behaviour and the shortcomings of society, though usually prompted by his narrative to do so. Subjects upon which he discoursed include hypocrisy, people's secret emotions, the sorrows sometimes attendant on love, remembrance of things past, and the vanity of much of life—such moralizing being, in his opinion, an important function of the novelist. He had little time for such favourite devices of Victorian novelists as exaggerated characterization and melodramatic plots, preferring in his own work to be more true to life, subtly depicting various moods and plunging the reader into a stream of entertaining narrative, description, dialogue, and comment, all flowing as one.

In October 1852, Thackeray went to the United States to deliver his lectures on the English humorists. After a highly successful tour, he travelled in Europe with his daughters, writing meanwhile *The Newcomes*. This novel is essentially a detailed study of prosperous middle class society, centred upon the family of the title; the love Clive Newcome and his cousin Ethel have for each other is unhappily thwarted for years because of worldly considerations. Like Dickens, Thackeray wrote "Christmas books," of which the best known, *The Rose and the Ring*, written mostly in Italy, appeared in 1854. He travelled to America again in October 1855, this time

Lecturer in the United States

to lecture on "The Four Georges" (the four Hanoverian kings of England of that name); he repeated the series of lectures in England and Scotland in 1856 and 1857. In July 1857, he unsuccessfully stood as an independent, reforming candidate for the city of Oxford constituency in a Parliamentary election. *The Virginians,* his next novel, is set partly in America and partly in England in the latter half of the 18th century and is concerned mostly with the vicissitudes in the lives of two brothers, George and Henry Warrington, the grandsons of Henry Esmond, the hero of his earlier novel. During its serialization, he became involved in a protracted quarrel with a young journalist and fellow member of the Garrick Club, Edmund Yates, who had written a satirical portrait of Thackeray in a periodical, *Town-Talk,* and who enlisted the support of Dickens in the dispute. Thackeray and Dickens were not reconciled until 1863.

The final years of Thackeray's life were dominated by *The Cornhill Magazine,* of which he became the first editor in January 1860. For this magazine he wrote two serial novels, the brief *Lovel the Widower* and the longer *Adventures of Philip,* and charming essays, *Roundabout Papers,* which, in the opinion of some critics, rank with the essays of Charles Lamb. He relinquished the editorship in March 1862, although he continued to write for the magazine. In May 1863 he began another historical novel set in the 18th century, *Denis Duval,* but did not live to complete it. He had been troubled by ill health for a number of years, suffering from digestive and urethral maladies, and died quite suddenly on December 24, 1863. He was buried in Kensal Green Cemetery in the suburbs of London, and a commemorative bust was placed in Westminster Abbey.

MAJOR WORKS

NOVELS: *Catherine* (serialized 1839–40; pub. 1869); *The Luck of Barry Lyndon* (serialized 1844; pub. 2 vol., 1852; rev. as *The Memoirs of Barry Lyndon, Esq.,* 1856); *Vanity Fair* (serialized 1847–48, pub. 1848); *The History of Pendennis* (serialized 1848–50; pub. 2 vol., 1849–50); *The History of Henry Esmond, Esq.,* 3 vol. (1852); *The Newcomes* (serialized 1853–55; pub. 2 vol., 1854–55); *The Virginians* (serialized 1857–59; pub. 2 vol., 1858–59); *Lovel the Widower* (serialized 1860, pub. 1861); *The Adventures of Philip on His Way Through the World* (serialized 1861–62; pub. 3 vol., 1862); *Denis Duval* (unfinished, serialized 1864; pub. 1864).

ESSAYS, SKETCHES, AND MISCELLANIES: *The Yellowplush Correspondence* (serialized 1837–38; pub. 1838, complete ed. 1852 as *The Yellowplush Papers*); *Some Passages in the Life of Major Gahagan* (serialized 1838–39, pub. in vol. 2 of *Comic Tales and Sketches*); *The Paris Sketch Book,* 2 vol. (1840); *Comic Tales and Sketches,* 2 vol. (1841); *The Irish Sketch-Book,* 2 vol. (1843); *Notes of a Journey from Cornhill to Grand Cairo* (1846); *The Snobs of England* (serialized 1846–47; pub. as *The Book of Snobs,* 1848); *The History of Samuel Titmarsh and the Great Hoggarty Diamond* (serialized 1841; pub. as *The Great Hoggarty Diamond,* 1848); *Miscellanies: Prose and Verse,* 2 vol. (1849–51); *The Kickleburys on the Rhine* (1850); *Rebecca and Rowena. A Romance upon Romance* (1850); *A Shabby Genteel Story, and Other Tales* (1852), includes "The Professor," "The Bedford Row Conspiracy," and "A Little Dinner at Timmins's"; *Men's Wives* (serialized 1843, pub. 1852); *Mr. Brown's Letters to a Young Man About Town; with The Proser, and Other Papers* (serialized 1845–50, pub. 1853); *Punch's Prize Novelists, The Fat Contributor, and Travels in London* (serialized 1844–50, pub. 1853); *The Confessions of Fitz-Boodle* (1852); *The Rose and the Ring* (1854, dated 1855); *Miscellanies: Prose and Verse,* 4 vol. (1855–57); *Christmas Books* (1857); *Roundabout Papers* (serialized 1860–63, pub. 1863); *Miscellanies,* 6 vol. (1864); *Early and Late Papers Hitherto Uncollected* (1867); *Miscellanies* (1870); *The Orphan of Pimlico, and Other Sketches, Fragments and Drawings* (1876); *Sultan Stork, and Other Stories and Sketches* (1829–44) (collected 1887).

LECTURES: *The English Humourists of the Eighteenth Century* (1853); *The Four Georges* (1860).

OTHER PROSE: *The Letters and Private Papers of William Makepeace Thackeray,* 4 vol. (1945–46); *Contributions to the Morning Chronicle* (1955).

BIBLIOGRAPHY. For a full description and assessment of writing on Thackeray, see LIONEL STEVENSON, "William Makepeace Thackeray," in *Victorian Fiction: A Guide to Research* (1964). The most comprehensive bibliography is HENRY S. VAN DUZER, *A Thackeray Library* (1919, reprinted 1971).

Important manuscripts of letters and literary works are held by the Henry E. Huntington Library, San Marino, California; the Pierpont Morgan Library, New York; and the Berg Collection of the New York Public Library. The *Oxford Thackeray,* ed. by GEORGE SAINTSBURY, 17 vol. (1908), is the standard collected edition of the works. *The Letters and Private Papers of William Makepeace Thackeray,* ed. by GORDON N. RAY, 4 vol. (1945–46), provides much biographical information, and the letters are of absorbing interest in themselves. Ray's two-volume biography, *Thackeray: The Uses of Adversity, 1811–1846* (1955) and *Thackeray: The Age of Wisdom, 1847–1863* (1958), is definitive and indispensable. DUDLEY FLAMM, *Thackeray's Critics* (1967), is an annotated bibliography of 19th-century criticism, some of the most important items of which are reproduced in *Thackeray: The Critical Heritage,* ed. by GEOFFREY TILLOTSON and DONALD HAWES (1968). An interesting critical estimate by a friend and fellow novelist is provided by ANTHONY TROLLOPE, *Thackeray* (1879, reprinted 1968). Saintsbury's acute and enthusiastic introductions to the volumes in the *Oxford Thackeray* were collected as *A Consideration of Thackeray* (1931). GEOFFREY TILLOTSON, *Thackeray the Novelist* (1954), is a subtle, persuasive exploration of his art. A variety of 20th-century opinions is assembled in *Thackeray: A Collection of Critical Essays,* ed. by ALEXANDER WELSH (1968).

(D.Ha.)

Thailand

A nation wedged like a keystone into the heart of Southeast Asia, Thailand in the last decades of the 20th century holds a critical position in the attempts of the countries of this area to achieve and maintain a political, economic, and social stability. Since 1932, when an absolutist monarchy was overthrown, the nation has been a constitutional monarchy with a representative legislature; in 1939 the official name was changed from Siam to Prathet Thai, or Thailand—literally, the "land of the free." The several ethnic and religious groups represented among Thailand's more than 34,000,000 people are characteristic of the cultural diversity that for centuries has spread across this portion of the continent, a mélange of influences from the two Asian giants, China and India.

Thailand's landscape is one of high mountains at the edge of the Himalayan chain, of fertile, alluvial plains dotted with rice paddies, and of sandy beaches and tropical forests set amid the latitudes of the Asian monsoons. The main body of the country is surrounded by Burma on the west and northwest, Laos on the northeast and east, Cambodia on the southeast, and the Gulf of Thailand (Gulf of Siam) on the south. From the southwest corner, part of Thailand stretches southward down the Malay Peninsula as far as Malaysia. This peninsula cuts off shipping using Thailand's capital and chief port, Bangkok, from points westward; Bangkok is, nevertheless, the international air hub of Southeast Asia.

Contacts of long standing between Thailand and the West have affected the forms if not the realities of Thailand's political and economic life. The relative political stability Thailand has maintained in the face of continual Communist guerrilla warfare inside its borders since World War II is largely the result of Western support. Thailand's free-enterprise economy participates vigorously in worldwide commerce yet remains based on primary products and relies on imports for manufactured goods. In addition, the nation's economic balance is maintained by aid from the United States and other nations. (For information on the nation's history, see the article SIAM AND THAILAND, HISTORY OF; for its linguistic background, TAI LANGUAGES; for its arts, SOUTHEAST ASIAN PEOPLES, ARTS OF; for an associated physical feature, MEKONG RIVER. See also the article BANGKOK.)

THE NATURAL AND HUMAN LANDSCAPE

The natural environment. Three main geological regions cover most of Thailand's 198,455 square miles (514,000 square kilometres)—the folded mountains in the north, the Khorat uplift in the east, and the Chao Phraya depression, comprising much of the central plains. In addition, the maritime southeast and the long, slender peninsula in the southwest constitute separate physical regions. The monsoon climate prevailing across most of the country has a distinct influence on the land-

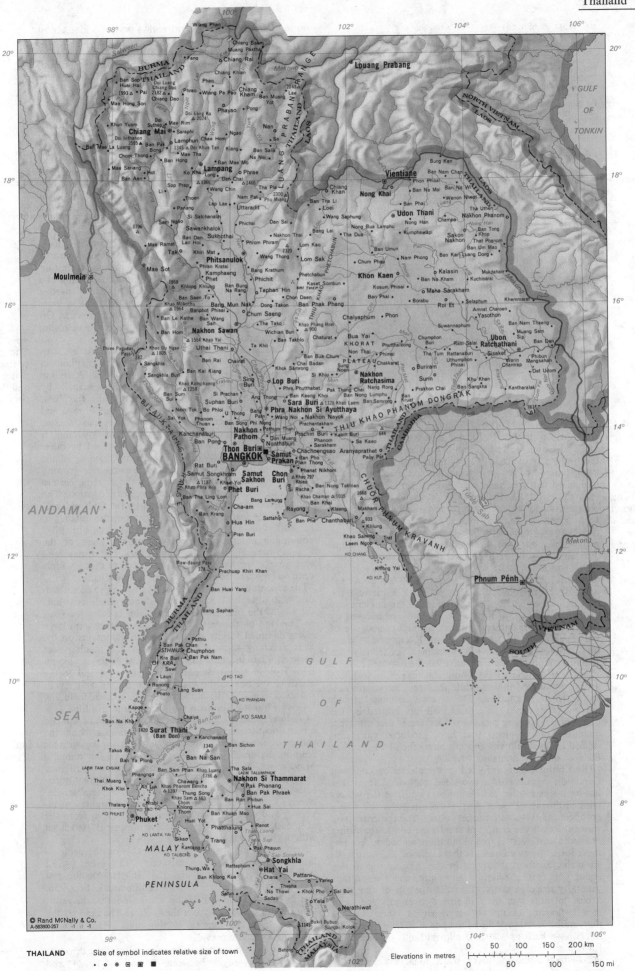

20°

98° 100° 102° 104° 106°

BURMA

GULF
OF
TONKIN

Wiang Phan

Chiang Saen
Muang Paktha

Salween

Ban Sop
Huai Hai
1993 △ Pai
THAILAND
Doi Luang
Chiang Dao
2182 △
1964

Fang Chiang Rai

Phan Chiang Khan

Mekong

Louang Prabang

NORTH VIETNAM

Khun Yuam
Mae Hong Son Chiang Dao
Doi Lang Ka
2024

Mae Rim
Saraphi

Chae Hom

Wiang Pa Pao
Chiang Dao

Pong

Nan

Ban Muang
Yot
Lae

2061

DANG PRABANG RANGE

LAOS

Chiang Mai
Doi Inthanon
2595 △
Ban Pak
Bong
1345 △ Doi Khun Tan

Lamphun Klang
Ban Saik

Ban Mae La Luang Mae Tha
Chom Thong
Ban Hong Ban Mae Mo
Ko Kha

LAOS

Vientiane

Bung Kan

Ban Nam Chan

THAILAND

Mae Sariang
Hot
Ban Aen

Lampang
Long

Na Noi
Den Chai

Phrae

1366
1466 Tha Pla

2300

Chiang
Khan

Nong Khai

Phon Phisai

Ban Na Mai Ban Na
Nakhon Phanom

Udon Thani

Ban Phai

Wanon Niwat
Tha Uthen

Sop Prap
Wang Chin

Phu Miang

Ban Tha Li
Loei

Nong Han
Kumphawapi

Champa

Sakon
Nakhon

That Phanom

Ban Tong
Khop

Sam Ngao
1796

Si Satchanalai
Sawankhalok

Ban Dan
Lan Hoi

Thoen
Lap Lae

Uttaradit

Nakhon Thai
Dan Sai Bang Lai

Wang Saphung Nong Bua Lamphu

Nam Phong

Ban Kan
Luang Dong

Ban Um Mao

Mae Ramat

Khiri Mat

Pichai

Phrom Phiram

Lom Kao

Chum Phae

Kalasin

Mukdahan

Tak Mae Sot

Phran Kratai

Phichit

Wang Thong
Phitsanulok
2320

Lom Sak

Ban Umon

PHETCHABUN

Khon Kaen

Maha Sarakham

Kuchinarai

Khemmarat

1868

Kamphaeng
Phet

Bang Krathum

Phetchabun

THIU KHAO

Koaum Phisai
Borabu

Roi Et

Selaphum

Amnat Charoen

Ban Saen To Na Rang

Ban Bung

Taphan Hin

Kaset Sombun

SRI THEP

Ban Phai

Yasothon

Khao Mokochu
1964

Dong Takon

Ban Phak Phang

Chon Daen

Ban Phai

Suwannaphum

Ban Nam Thaeng

Banphot Phisai

Khao Phang Hoei

Chaiyaphum Phon

Chumphon
Buri

Muang Sam
Sip

Three Pagodas
Pass

Khao Du Ngar
1805 △

Ban Le Kathe
Ban Kai Kiang
Khao Kamphaeng

Ban Wang
San

Ban Hom

1554 Khao Yai △
Nakhon Sawan
Uthai Thani

Ban Rai

Ta Khli

282 Ban Takhlo

Ban Bua Chum

Chaturat

KHORAT

PLATEAU

Rasi Salai

Ubon
Ratchathani

Ban Dan

1258

Khok Samrong

Si Khiu

Nang Rong

Surin

Phibun
Mangsahan

Det Udom

Sangkhla
Sangkhla Buri

Chai Badan

Sung
Noen

Nakhon
Ratchasima

Buriram

Prakhon Chai

Ban Sangkha

Kantharalak

Ban Sum
Sui

Chainat
Sing
Buri

Lop Buri

Pak Thong Chai

Phimai

Tha Tum Rattanaburi
Ulthumphon
Phisai

Khu Khan

Khao Kampheng

1328 Khao Laem

Phra Phutthabat

Ban Nong Lumphu

Warin
Chamrap

761

Nam Tok
Si Yok

Bo Phloi

Suphan Buri Ang Thong

Sara Buri

Ban Kaeng Khoi

Samrong

THIU KHAO PHANOM DONGRAK

Ban Song Phi Nong

U Thong
Pathum
Thuan

Phra Nakhon Si Ayutthaya

Wang Noi Nakhon Nayok

644

Kanchanaburi

Nakhon
Pathom

Pathum Thani

Prachin Buri Kabin Buri

Sa Kaeo

CAMBODIA

Ban Pong

Don Muang
Nonthaburi

Phanom
Sarakham

Aranyaprathet

Paôy Pêt

Thon Buri
BANGKOK

Samut
Prakan

Chachoengsao

Ban Pho
Phan Thong

Phanat Nikhom

Rat Buri

Samut Songkhram

1187 △
Khao Phra Roji

Samut
Sakhon

Chon
Buri

Khao 797
Khleo

Ban Nong Takhien

CHUOR PHNUM KRAVANH

Phnum Pénh

VIETNAM

ANDAMAN

Phet Buri
Khao Yoi

Si Racha

Khao Chamao △ 1035

1668

Makham

933

Cha-am

Bang Lamung

Rayong

Klaeng

Ban Phe Chanthaburi

Khlung

Tonle Sab

Mekong

Hua Hin

Sattahip

Khao Saming
Laem Ngop

Trat

KO CHANG

SEA

Pran Buri

Khlong Yai

KO KUT

SOUTH

Maw-daung Pass
374

Prachuap Khiri Khan

GULF

Ban Huai Yang

Bang Saphan

OF

BURMA
THAILAND

Pathiu

Ban Pak Chan
ISTHMUS
Chumphon

Kra Buri
OF KRA
Sawi

Ban Pak Nam

THAILAND

Laun

KO TAO

Ranong
Phato

Lang Suan

Kapoe

KO PHANGAN

Chaiya

KO SAMUI

Ban Na Kha

1420
Surat Thani
(Ban Don)

Ban Don

Kanchanadit

Takua Pa

Ban Ya Plong

1340
Ban Na San

Ban Sichon

LAEM TAM CHUAK

Phangnga

Ban Sam Phan
Khao Luang
1786 △

Tha Sala
LAEM TALUMPHUK

Thai Muang
Khok Kloi

Ko Luk Khao Phanom Bencha

Chawang

Nakhon Si Thammarat

Thalang

KO PHUKET

Krabi

1197 △

Khao Sam △ 663
Thung Song

Ban Ron Phibun

Pak Phanang

Ban Pak Phraek

Hua Sai

Phuket

Thom

Khlong

Ban Khuan Mao

KO LANTA YAI

Huai Yot

Phatthalung

Ranot

MALAY

KO TAO YAI

Sikao

Trang

Thale Luang

Pak Phayun

KO TALIBONS

Kantang

Thale Sap Songkhla

PENINSULA

Thung Wa

Rattaphum

Songkhla

Ban Khlong Kua Chana

Hat Yai

Pattani Yaring

Na Thawi

Khok Pho Sai Buri

Sadao

Satun

Thepha

Yala

Narathiwat

1145

Betong

THAILAND
MALAYSIA

Sungai Kolok

Bukit Bubus
Sungai Kolok

6°

© Rand McNally & Co.
A-563800-257   -1   -1   -1

THAILAND   Size of symbol indicates relative size of town

Elevations in metres

0   50   100   150   200 km

0   50   100   150 mi

scape, its vegetation and animal life, and its human uses.

Physiographic regions and drainage. The mountains, a continuation of the Himalayan system from India, Burma, and China, extend far southward in Thailand along the western border and the peninsula and into Malaysia. Long granitic ridges were formed when great masses of molten rock forced their way upward through the older sedimentary strata. Between the ridges lie relatively flat basins drained by the four principal tributaries of the Chao Phraya, Thailand's major river. Important provincial centres, or *changwats*, such as Chiang Mai, Lampang, Phrae, and Nan, grew up along these four streams. The alluvial soils of these intermontane basins provide fertile soil for the cultivation of rice, vegetables, tobacco, and fruit trees. Peaks average about 5,200 feet above sea level. Doi Inthanon, at 8,514 feet (2,595 metres) the highest in the kingdom, is southwest of the ancient city of Chiang Mai (Chiengmai), which is overshadowed by the peak of Doi Suthep, a tourist attraction and site of the royal resort palace, Phu Phing Ratchanivet. Many of the rugged limestone hills contain caves from which remains of prehistoric man have been excavated.

The mountains, the Khorat Plateau, and the southeast

The lower reaches of the mountains are rich in teak and other commercial timber, while the upper slopes are dotted with tea plantations. The rivers emptying through narrow valleys into the central plain are glutted by the monsoons, sweeping along in their steep descent great quantities of sediments that have produced vast, fan-shaped heaps of alluvial deposits along the flood plains at the foot of the mountainous regions.

The Khorat region, enfolded on three sides by Laos and Cambodia, consists of a two-sided geological fault that has been tilted rather than a uniform uplift of the underlying sedimentary rocks. At the western edge, the tilting produced north–south ranges whose escarpments look westward over the central plain. To the south, the tilting produced east–west ranges along the Cambodian border; these form steep escarpments that overlook the Cambodian plain. Surface elevations in the Khorat region are about 650 feet; the terrain is rolling, and the hilltops generally slope in conformity with the tilt of the land. Monsoon rains over the thin forest cover produce rapid runoff; flooding occurs almost yearly at Ubon Ratchathani at the junction of the Mun and Chi. These two major rivers have built up scattered alluvial lands that are used for rice growing.

Close to the Mekong River, which meanders across the north and east of the Khorat region and runs along most of the Laotian border, swampy land and lakes are common, in contrast to the aridity of much of the region. A high underground water table that can be tapped produces mostly unpalatable water, but the Thai government has done much to improve the freshwater situation in this part of the kingdom. The Mekong itself, from about 2,300 to 4,300 feet wide, is either studded with islands or broken up by impassable rapids. The governments of both Thailand and Laos, however, are planning for its use in agriculture and industry.

The generally rolling countryside of the southeast has high hills in the centre and along the eastern boundary with Cambodia. Notable peaks are Khao Khieo (2,614 feet [797 metres]), visible from the top of Phu Khao Thong (the Golden Mount) in Bangkok, and Khao Soi Dao ("Reaching for the stars"), which attains a height of 5,471 feet (1,668 metres). The mountains, reaching nearly to the sea, create a markedly indented coastline fringed with many islands, some of which are popular tourist resorts. The short, seaward-running streams have built up small alluvial basins and deltas along the coast, while the mouths of larger rivers consist of tidal flats and mangrove swamps. Long stretches of sandy beach make Chon Buri, Rayong, and some of the islands year-round resorts. On higher grounds plantations produce rubber, sugarcane, pineapples, and cassava.

The central plains and the peninsula

The central plains, which form the Thai heartland, consist of two regions—the heavily dissected rolling plains in the north and the Chao Phraya River Delta. A rolling plain in the north also is heavily dissected, principally by the three rivers—the combined Ping and Wang, the Yom, and the Nan—that merge to form the Chao Phraya and its delta. Like most deltas, that of the Chao Phraya, which stretches southward to the Gulf of Thailand, is braided into many small channels; it is joined by other rivers as it crosses the plains. The usual flooding of the flat delta in the wet season is an asset to the rice-growing activity, although higher ground on the extreme eastern and western edges of the delta requires irrigation. The entire delta was at one time covered by the Gulf of Thailand, but the water-borne sediments from the uplands to the north filled it in over many centuries. Such silting is a continuing obstruction to navigation channels of the Chao Phraya, but it also provides several feet of new land each year at the river's mouth—so much so that a temple once on an island now lies on the river's west bank.

The topography of the peninsula is rolling to mountainous, with little flat land. A gently sloping sandy coastline, the site of the famous beach Hua Hin, borders the Gulf of Thailand on the east. The Phet is one of several large rivers dammed for irrigation. Massive mountains on the west, reaching about 4,900 feet, contain difficult passes between Thailand and Burma. Toward Malaysia mountains look to the Andaman Sea to the west and to the South China Sea to the east. Off the rugged and much-indented west coast lie numerous major islands, including tin-rich Phuket and others rich in bird and fish life.

Climate. The major influences on Thailand's climate are its location on the Indochinese Peninsula within the sphere of the tropical monsoons and certain topographic features that modify the effects of the rains. Beginning in May, warm, humid air masses flow northeastward over the region from the Indian Ocean, depositing great quantities of rain that reach a maximum in September. Between October and February, the wind currents are reversed, and cold, dry air masses are driven in from the northeast. Stagnant air in March and April is associated with the hot, dry season.

Effects of the monsoons

Topographic effects are most noticeable on the peninsula, where Ranong on the west receives 188 inches (4,772 millimetres) of rain annually, and Hua Hin on the east receives only 40 inches (1,007 millimetres). Songkhla has its rainy season during the winter months, the result of moisture picked up from the Gulf of Thailand by the cold northeast air masses. In this area a true tropical rain-forest climate prevails.

Nationwide, temperatures are relatively steady throughout the year, averaging between 75° and 86° F (24° and

30° C). The greatest fluctuations are in the north, where frost may occur in December on higher elevations; maritime influences moderate the climate in the south. The cold, dry winter air produces frequent morning fogs that generally dissipate by midday.

Vegetation and animal life. About one-half of Thailand is forested, one-fifth covered by grass, shrub, and swamp, and the remainder under settlement or cultivation. Forests consist largely of such hardwoods as teak and members of the dipterocarp family of timber- and resin-producing trees. As elsewhere in Southeast Asia, bamboo, palms, rattan, and many kinds of fern are common. The southeastern forest is dense with undergrowth and aerial roots, while orchids climb the trunks of many trees. Grasses and shrubs have sprung up across many cutover areas, and lotuses and water lilies dot most ponds and swamps throughout the country.

Elephants, buffalo, cattle, horses, and mules are among the important domesticated animals for agriculture and transportation. Some elephants are still found wild in the west and the northeast. Although forestry is now done by machines, elephants remain helpful in difficult terrain. Agricultural machines are rapidly replacing draft animals, and horses and mules increasingly are used only as pack animals along the mountain trails of the north. Wild animals are decreasing in quantity and in number of species due to game hunting. The rhinoceros and tapir are almost extinct. Deer and antelope can still be found, but the big cats are becoming fewer in number. The Siamese cat is popular among foreigners.

Lizards live around houses and prey on insects. Frogs and toads (some of them edible) are numerous, and crocodiles are also found; a crocodile farm in Bangkok raises them for commercial and scientific purposes. Snakes abound, including the king cobra, numerous vipers, and dangerous water snakes. A snake farm in Bangkok raises many kinds for extracting venom. The green turtle of the sandy coast lays hundreds of eggs at a time, which are highly regarded as culinary delicacies.

Both freshwater and marine fish are abundant, as are edible crustaceans, such as shrimp, prawn, and sea crabs. The most useful insect is the silkworm. Many species are wild, but some are raised for the prosperous silk industry. Mosquitoes still carry malaria, although incidence of the malady is decreasing. White ants and moths are a scourge to clothing and books.

Human uses of the land. *Traditional regions.* In the traditional or popular sense, the regions of Thailand are the Lanna Thai, or northern Thailand; the Isan, or northeastern Thailand; the central plain; the southeast; the Pak Tai, or south Thailand; and west and southwest Thailand.

The people of the mountainous Lanna Thai speak a dialect similar to that of neighbouring Burma. The women wear simple blouses and knee-length sarong; the men wear loose trousers and cotton jackets called *mohom*. Most of the people live on glutinous rather than common rice. The people have a complexion that is fairer than that of other Thai. The fertile valley plains grow rice and such other crops as peanuts, beans, garlic, onions, corn, and tobacco on the irrigated lands. Tea, widely cultivated as a permanent crop, is consumed in the north as both a pickled and a drinking tea. Besides rice, the outstanding export of the region consists of teak and other commercial timbers. The mountains of the north are also the home of the mountain Thai, who migrate from Burma, Laos, and sometimes from southern China.

The Isan is situated on the undulating terrain bordered on the west and south by rather hilly topography. The people dress much like the northern Thai, except close to the Cambodian border, where the *pha chong kraben*—a side-rolled skirt for women, a broadly bloused and belted pantaloon-like garment for men—similar to the Hindu dress of India, is worn instead of trousers. The dialect is like that of Laos, although very similar to that of the central Thai. With some attention, however, the northerners and the northeasterners can understand one another. Agglutinous rice is consumed in most of the northeast, except near the Cambodian border. Besides rice, various kinds of timbers, jute, and cattle constitute important exports. In general, the people depend on agriculture, but the scanty rainfall and sandy soil make the living in the region difficult. As a result, migration from the northeast to other parts of the country is common. The highway to the northeast and thence to Laos makes the region a growing crossroads. It is probably the only part of the country to which the government is devoting both attention and money in an effort to raise the standard of living to that of the other regions.

The central plain, lying mostly on the undulating to flat delta region, is the major rice-producing area of the country, much of whose surplus is exported. Because of its central position, population and manpower are heavily concentrated, especially in Bangkok, and industrial and commercial enterprises have grown faster there than elsewhere. The eastern, western, and northern peripheries of the central plain, however, remain to be developed. The soil of the northern half of the plain is inferior. People from the northeast and other places have migrated to the central area in hope of a better living.

The southeast, lying close to the sea on an undulating to hilly region, is well watered. Close to the sea fishing predominates; plantations and gem mines are found on the inner hill and mountain slopes. Thai of Chinese descent live here in great numbers. Tapioca and sugarcane are the chief crops, and fish supply the Bangkok and the upper-country markets and are also exported. Chanthaburi and Trat are famous for their sapphires. The beaches are popular and attract foreign tourists.

The people of the Pak Tai region of the peninsula speak a dialect that has a different intonation from that of the central Thai. The extreme south consists of Thai who speak the Malay language, the majority of whom are Muslim. The southern economy depends on exports of tin and rubber. Fishing provides income for the people living close to the seas on both sides of the peninsula. Phuket and Songkhla are well-known for their fine beaches, which are lined with beautiful coconut groves.

The west and southwest, consisting mostly of hilly to mountainous terrain adjoining the Burmese border, is sparsely populated. The forest covers are chiefly mixed deciduous and bamboo. The soils are rich with minerals, such as tin, tungsten (wolfram), and fluorite. The Karen from Burma often migrate and live within the Thai border. They clear the land and cultivate the hill slopes in the same manner as the mountain Thai in northern Thailand. The region is also the chief supplier of the bamboo used in the curing of rubber.

Patterns of settlement. Hill settlements depend much on shifting cultivation of upland crops. Such mountain Thai as the Karen, Meo, Yao, Lahu, Lisu, and the lowland Thai who have migrated usually settle on the ridges and the slopes in groups ranging from two to three to 100 or more houses, depending on the resources of the area. The Meo are opium cultivators, preferring to live on high slopes where opium grows well in the cool climate. The Karen live along the stream valleys and grow rice on well-tended, terraced fields. The Thai who have migrated earn a living from their tea and coffee plantations.

No true plains villages exist in Thailand, although in the northeast the villages are scattered on the higher grounds to escape the floods; the lower grounds are used for rice farming. In the north, where the villages are found on the alluvial basins of major rivers, increased population and transportation have tended to disperse the villages away from the river toward the main railroads and highways, reducing the amount of rice-growing land.

The delta is densely settled, but only on the high ground that is free from flooding. The irrigation canals modify the pattern of settlement; with increasing facility in transportation offered by small motorboats, the villages tend to become dispersed away from the rivers in an east–west direction. New highways also tend to modify the pattern of settlement, especially at the crossings of canals and rivers by highways, where new towns grow up rapidly.

The southern and southeastern plantations, especially the fruit and rubber plantations, are scattered along the fertile slopes, alternating with the low and narrow rice fields, and the villages are therefore arranged according-

Interactions of the natural and human ecologies

Rural and urban Thailand

ly. Most of them are joined by good roads and highways. Alluvial deposits containing tin, no matter how isolated, are accessible to all kinds of land and sea communications. Settlement is almost continuous along both sides of the peninsula. Most of the people live by fishing, except in areas in which bird's-nest collecting (the jelly-like adhesive of which is the basis of a popular soup or sweet dessert) brings a good income. The coastal villages are connected both by land and sea highways.

Urban settlement in Thailand is found mostly on the plains and in the coastal areas rather than on the hills. Bangkok, for example, grew from a small settlement on the east bank of the Chao Phraya. In other large towns, such as Chiang Mai, the old, square city walls are still apparent, with numerous Buddhist temples scattered inside and outside the walls. Thus, urbanization in Thailand can be said to centre around the original sites of the palaces and the temples. Other interesting patterns of settlement can be observed in certain urbanized areas. Phitsanulok, for example, has a number of floating houses along both banks of the rivers. Chon Buri, a seaside town, has a trellis pattern of houses on islands that are accessible by footbridges. Such patterns of settlement reflect the strong demand for living space in the urban areas.

THE PEOPLE OF THAILAND

The diversity of ethnic, linguistic, and religious groups in Thailand is characteristic of most nations of Southeast Asia, where shifting political boundaries have done little to impede the centuries-long migrations of people from one area to another.

Composition of the population. *Ethnic groups.* Thai people are found not only in Thailand but also in Laos, Burma, India, both Vietnams, and in southern China. These Thai speak the Thai language, but with different accents and a few different words. Little difference exists between the Thai in Laos, Burma, and even in China and those of northern Thailand, but there is a noticeable difference between them and the Thai living in the central plain and close to Cambodia. The peninsular Thai also are much influenced by the Malay.

Geographical dispersion of Thai peoples

Wars between Thailand and Burma in the past brought many refugees and prisoners of war into Thailand. The Mon, a Burmese people, settled in many parts of the north, the centre, and the west; their distinctiveness is evident in their festivals and religious rites. Even the original Thai are not completely free from ethnic intermixture, and the ethnic origin of the modern Thai is even more complex when the Chinese and the Indian descendants are considered. Bangkok is the chief melting pot of the Thai race. Tracing true Thai blood in Bangkok should not be attempted, as a famous Thai scholar (himself of Chinese descent) has said, for what makes the Thai is the institution.

Except the Karen, who mixed rather easily with the northern Thai, the hill tribes, or the mountain Thai, prefer to keep themselves isolated. They occasionally come down to the markets to trade with the lowlanders. They are probably of purer stock than the modern Thai. Two small hill tribes of special interest, the Lawa and the Semang. The Lawa are believed by some historians to be the original dwellers of the delta plain, driven into the hills of the northwest by the Thai who conquered the area. The Semang of the southern mountains live by hunting with blowpipes and spears. Another ethnic group that often escapes attention is that of the Chao Nam, or sea dwellers. Rarely settling permanently, they live by fishing along the western coast and the adjacent islands of the peninsula.

Linguistic groups. The Thai, who live in almost all areas, comprise the majority linguistic group. The greatest concentration is in the Chao Phraya Delta. Burmese, Laotian, and Cambodian influences already have been noted. The people of Tak and Kanchanaburi, near the southwestern Burmese border, speak Karen and Mon. From Chumphon to the south, the Thai speak a southern dialect with much musical inflection. Most of the Thai have been in contact with one another, especially administrative officials and teachers, and the Thai living in

The mix of tongues and faiths

Thailand, Area and Population				
	area		population	
	sq mi	sq km	1960 census	1970 census*
Regions (*phaks*)				
Central				
Provinces (*changwats*)				
Ang Thong	379	981	198,000	217,000
Chachoengsao	2,093	5,422	323,000	338,000
Chainat	1,018	2,636	245,000	256,000
Chanthaburi	2,337	6,052	158,000	211,000
Chon Buri	1,732	4,485	392,000	542,000
Kanchanaburi	7,524	19,486	233,000	321,000
Lop Buri	2,544	6,588	336,000	433,000
Nakhon Nayok	932	2,414	154,000	161,000
Nakhon Pathom	841	2,178	370,000	411,000
Nonthaburi	241	623	196,000	254,000
Pathum Thani	578	1,497	190,000	233,000
Phet Buri	2,454	6,357	238,000	278,000
Phra Nakhon-Thonburi	598	1,549	2,136,000	2,633,000
Phra Nakhon Si Ayutthaya	958	2,480	479,000	501,000
Prachin Buri	4,554	11,795	335,000	421,000
Prachuap Khiri Khan	2,461	6,373	152,000	249,000
Rat Buri	1,977	5,120	411,000	464,000
Rayong	1,277	3,307	148,000	250,000
Samut Sakhon	324	840	166,000	158,000
Samut Songkhram	154	399	162,000	159,000
Samut Prakan	361	934	235,000	325,000
Sara Buri	1,144	2,963	304,000	342,000
Sing Buri	325	842	154,000	162,000
Suphan Buri	2,061	5,339	491,000	561,000
Trat	1,127	2,919	66,000	94,000
North				
Provinces				
Chiang Mai	8,878	22,993	798,000	1,024,000
Chiang Rai	7,260	18,803	812,000	1,086,000
Kamphaeng Phet	3,457	8,954	173,000	333,000
Lampang	4,833	12,518	472,000	616,000
Lamphun	1,702	4,407	250,000	318,000
Mae Hong Son	5,105	13,222	81,000	104,000
Nakhon Sawan	3,736	9,677	648,000	758,000
Nan	4,515	11,694	240,000	310,000
Phetchabun	4,311	11,166	320,000	513,000
Phichit	1,749	4,530	389,000	440,000
Phitsanulok	3,729	9,659	352,000	492,000
Phrae	2,258	5,847	299,000	365,000
Sukhothai	2,641	6,841	316,000	394,000
Tak	6,027	15,609	168,000	217,000
Uthai Thani	2,499	6,472	146,000	177,000
Uttaradit	2,940	7,614	260,000	321,000
Northeast				
Provinces				
Buriram	4,159	10,771	584,000	797,000
Chaiyaphum	4,165	10,788	486,000	626,000
Kalasin	2,954	7,650	427,000	573,000
Khon Kaen	5,175	13,404	844,000	1,025,000
Loei	4,222	10,936	211,000	326,000
Maha Sarakham	2,224	5,760	499,000	613,000
Nakhon Phanom	3,764	9,749	436,000	561,000
Nakhon Ratchasima	7,564	19,590	1,095,000	1,547,000
Nong Khai	2,789	7,223	257,000	442,000
Roi Et	3,033	7,856	668,000	780,000
Sakon Nakhon	3,683	9,539	427,000	598,000
Sisaket	3,403	8,813	601,000	790,000
Surin	3,392	8,784	582,000	747,000
Ubon Ratchathani	8,787	22,758	1,131,000	1,480,000
Udon Thani	6,411	16,605	744,000	1,118,000
South				
Provinces				
Chumphon	2,219	5,746	175,000	235,000
Krabi	1,785	4,624	94,000	148,000
Nakhon Si Thammarat	3,926	10,169	730,000	927,000
Narathiwat	1,632	4,228	266,000	326,000
Pattani	777	2,013	282,000	330,000
Phangnga	1,583	4,100	93,000	135,000
Phatthalung	1,262	3,269	234,000	298,000
Phuket	309	801	76,000	100,000
Ranong	1,323	3,426	38,000	59,000
Satun	1,031	2,669	70,000	131,000
Songkhla	2,576	6,673	500,000	621,000
Surat Thani	4,946	12,811	325,000	434,000
Trang	1,909	4,944	240,000	326,000
Yala	1,821	4,716	149,000	199,000
Total Thailand	198,455†	514,000	26,258,000‡§	34,152,000§

*Preliminary.   †Converted area figures do not add to total given because of rounding.   ‡Excludes an estimated 250,000 hill people who have never been enumerated.   §Figures do not add to total given because of rounding.
Source: Official government figures.

remote areas can understand the central Thai.
Chinese is the second major language. In the commer-

cial centres of Bangkok and other cities, Chinese or their descendants operate both large and small commercial enterprises. Those of Chinese descent also make a living as middlemen and storekeepers. Most of them speak Chinese, as do some of the northern hill tribes, such as the Meo and Ho.

Although no reliable statistics exist, English-speaking Thai probably make up the third major linguistic group. English is required in secondary schools and the university, and frequent contact with American military personnel also encourages the speaking of English. The prevalence of Indian dialects reflects the large number of Indian merchants and their descendants in the commercial centres. Other linguistic groups are found among the mountain Thai. Some of them can speak Chinese, although most of them understand the northern Thai dialect (see further TAI LANGUAGES).

Religious groups. The religious groups in Thailand, in order of size, are the Buddhists, the Muslims, the Confucians, the Christians, and the Sikhs. Buddhism, professed by more than 90% of the population, is considered the national religion, and Buddhists are scattered throughout the nation. Muslims live mostly in the south, whereas about one-half of the Christians live in the central region. Hindus and the Sikhs are concentrated in the central region, chiefly around Bangkok. Although several of the hill tribes have converted to Buddhism or Christianity, most remain animists. An interesting religious group in Thailand, although totalling only about 4,000 families, exerts much influence on the Thai religious life. These are the Brahmins. The royal and the official ceremonies are almost always directed or performed by the Brahmins, whose rites are blended harmoniously with those of the Buddhists. Brahmins are famous for their astrological experiences. The plowing ceremony, carried out in the presence of the king and queen by Brahmins and other officials, is believed to bring a good rice harvest. The Brahmins and the royal astrologers are also responsible for the preparation of the national calendar.

Contemporary demography. *Birthrates and mortality rates.* By the early 1970s, Thailand's population had more than doubled since World War II. Trends suggest that comparable growth will continue, since the government's attempts at family planning run counter to much social and religious tradition. The very high birthrate of about 33 per year per 1,000 people is about twice that of many Western nations, but, since Thailand is an agricultural country, the population pressure on the land is not as serious as it would be in an industrial country. The World Health Organization has helped to suppress such endemic diseases as malaria and tuberculosis. The death rate has been reduced from about 16 persons per 1,000 to about 7.0 per 1,000 since World War II.

Distribution of population. Productivity and location make the delta plain of the Chao Phraya the most densely populated area. The municipality of Bangkok-Thonburi alone had a population of about 3,200,000 persons in 1970. Population centres in the north and northeast generally follow the rivers. The southern population is concentrated along the eastern coast, where there are some wide strips of agricultural lands. Tin mining and smelting and shipping on the west coast make Phuket Island the most densely populated province of the south. The southeast coast is also another heavily populated area. Areas of forest, rugged topography, dry and infertile soils, or swampy vegetation are thinly populated.

Migratory patterns. Immigration, especially from China, is more significant than emigration. The government has felt that overpopulation by the Chinese in Bangkok and other commercial centres must be controlled. Although the quota has been brought down to 200 a year, the number of Chinese nationals in Thailand at present is about 400,000, not including Chinese who are Thai citizens. Of the Europeans, Americans, and Indians who take up residence for commercial purposes, only some of the Indians make Thailand their permanent home.

The northern hill tribes, of course, have immigrated from neighbouring countries. This influx continues, and in the early 1970s they numbered between 300,000 and

Brahmin religious influence

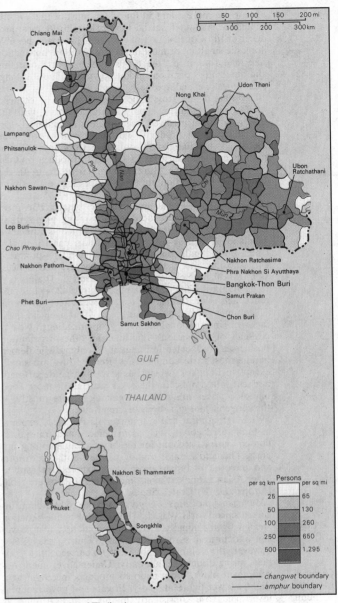

Population density of Thailand.
By courtesy of the Royal Thai Survey Department

500,000 persons. Their immigration can be traced to their need for more land to grow opium and other crops, to the demand for labour in the forest industry, and to political unrest in their original homeland.

Emigration of Thai doctors and nurses to other countries, especially to the United States, has resulted in serious shortages of medical personnel in Thailand.

THE NATIONAL ECONOMY

Thailand's economy is still based on the production of basic agricultural, mineral, forest, and other raw materials. Its gold and other foreign-exchange reserves increased by about 15% annually after 1957, and the Thai unit of currency, the baht, is among the world's most stable currencies.

The economic milieu. *Areas of economic activity.* Growing demands have encouraged a stronger and more diversified Thai agriculture. Rice is likely to remain as the major crop, unless radical dietary changes occur in Asia. Sweet corn, cassava, and plants yielding fibres are other major crops. Fine breeds of cattle and pigs have been introduced from the West. Hardwoods, such as teak and yang (a source of gurjun balsam), are major forest products; rubber trees—introduced into the country during the 19th century—are important. Fishery includes both marine species and freshwater fish caught in the rivers or in cultivation ponds.

Primary and fabricated products

There are more than 650 tin mines, most of them in the peninsula, making Thailand the world's third-largest producer of tin. Construction of a smelter has made possible domestic smelting of most of the ore. Iron-ore production rose manyfold during the 1960s. Other important mining and quarrying operations produce gypsum, fluorite, tungsten, limestone, and marble.

The share of the gross national product (GNP) contributed by manufacturing is only about 15 percent, with the major part of it involved in processing agricultural, forest, and mineral products. The main centres for large industry is the Bangkok-Thonburi metropolis, while numerous cottage industries in the north produce textiles, teak carvings, lacquer ware, and similar products. In the southeast, in addition to food processing, oil refining and gem cutting are carried on.

Thailand has several hydroelectric plants, but most electrical power is produced by generating plants using gas and solid fuels, such as lignite, which is mined in Thailand. A nuclear-power plant is under construction at Chon Buri. Small amounts of petroleum are produced domestically, and the government has granted concessions for offshore explorations in the Gulf of Thailand.

The Bank of Thailand, established in 1942, issues currency, acts as central banker to the government and to the 16 commercial banks, and serves as fiscal agent in dealing with international monetary organizations. Nearly one-half of the nation's retailing and other distribution businesses are located in Bangkok-Thonburi. Middlemen handle most farm commodities. Retail stores are small, except in Bangkok, which has several large department and cut-rate stores. In these, as well as in most food markets, prices are fixed; bargaining occurs mostly in the souvenir and gift shops of larger cities.

With agricultural and raw materials the basic exports, manufactured goods, such as machinery and transportation equipment, account for the highest value among imports. Thailand's major trading partner, both for exports and imports, is Japan; most other exports are sent to other Asian nations, whereas most other imports are from Europe and the United States.

Management of the economy. A huge public debt, incurred since World War II, is componded by the situation created by the rapidly increasing population that leaves less agricultural surplus for export. During the 1960s, however, the volume output of the Thai economy doubled, rising about 8% annually. Under government development plans, gross national products increased at a slightly lower figure annually. Private and governmental investment rose consistently in this period. Aiming at diversification, the government has supported a greater number of small industries since 1964. To encourage exports, duties are low, except on rice, to which a premium is attached to prevent domestic shortages.

Unions are prohibited, but the Labour Disputes Act of 1966 guarantees good working conditions and fair wages. Strikes are not allowed, unless management representatives fail to agree with employees and Labour Department mediators.

Transportation and communications. Bangkok is the centre of Thailand's water, land, and air transport. The rivers of the delta have been used for transport since antiquity, and modern irrigation canals have added to the inland-waterway mileage. Because of the rains, it is difficult to keep some highways open all year, especially in the peninsula. Mountain trails are often the only means of travel in remote areas. Where roads are inadequate, airplane and helicopter services often compensate. Rail lines radiate from Bangkok in several directions, one linking up with the Cambodian rail system.

The port of Bangkok, at Khlong Toei, is the largest and busiest of the 22 in the kingdom, handling 95% of imports and 85% of exports. It is congested, however, and expansion is planned. Don Muang Airport, north of Bangkok, is served by 28 international airlines, including Thai Airways International, a state-owned line. Over 20 smaller airports are located throughout the country.

There are some 8,000 post offices, performing both regular and ancillary services. Domestic and foreign telegraphic facilities are also available. The Telephone Organization of Thailand services well over 150,000 (a figure constantly rising) telephones and links 25 provinces with telephone and radio-relay cable.

ADMINISTRATION AND SOCIAL CONDITIONS

Structure of government. Following the revolution of 1932, a provisional constitution was promulgated, stating that supreme power lay in the hands of the people. The monarch, the National Assembly, the Commissariat of the People (later, the State Council), and the law courts were to exercise power on their behalf. Since then, several constitutions have been created because of changes of government, but the provisions are similar.

Under the present constitution, the king is head of state and of the armed forces. He is held to be sacred and inviolable, and in the name of the people he exercises legislative power, with the advice and consent of the Assembly. He also appoints the prime minister. Executive powers are vested in a Council of Ministers, judicial powers in the courts; both operate in the name of the king. The royal family is very much at the core of modern Thai society, being regarded as the symbol of national unity and the protector of national welfare and traditions.

In form, the Thai government resembles those of Western nations; various ministries are responsible for such matters as finances, agriculture, education, public health, communications, and justice.

The province, or *changwat*, of which there are 70, is the major unit of local government. Beneath these are districts, subdistricts, and communes and villages. The 120 municipalities in the kingdom are classified as cities, towns, or communes, according to their populations; they are run by an elected mayor and councillors.

Thai law has been influenced heavily by the Hindu code of Manu, which probably was transmitted through the ancient Mon kingdom located in central Thailand. Reform in the late 19th century introduced concepts of Western jurisprudence. All judges sitting in the 110 courts across the country are professionals, appointed without political consideration; they are bolstered by a system of judge trainees.

Under the king as commander in chief, the army, navy, and air forces are assisted by the Military Assistance Program, and by the Southeast Asia Treaty Organization (SEATO), of which Thailand is a member. Thai soldiers have fought in Korea and Vietnam, but in the early 1970s they were fully occupied in containing Communist infiltration from neighbouring countries.

The political process. Thailand has had only nine elections since 1932, and in those years 13 attempts have been made to overthrow the 16 cabinets, of which six were successful. The military has been involved in most of these attempts to influence the course of government. Dissatisfaction with the pace of Thailand's progress toward achieving standards of living comparable with those in most Western nations has been at the bottom of many of these coups, some originating from within the parliament. The successful coup of November 1971 was directed also at slowing the Communist insurgency within the country and at a rapidly rising crime rate.

The social milieu. The average per capita income in Thailand is about 3,400 baht (21 baht = $1 U.S.; 50.4 baht = £1 sterling, on December 1, 1970), with regional averages ranging from 4,800 in the central region to only 1,300 in the northeast. In the early 1970s almost half of the population was under 15 years of age, creating an enormous dependency rate. The cost-of-living index was also rising dramatically.

Thailand's health and welfare services remain far from adequate. The emigration of potential medical practitioners to more lucrative practices in the West has tended to undermine governmental attempts to upgrade services within the country. Mobile medical centres and helicopters attempt to alleviate the lack of widespread facilities. The doctor-patient ratio in the early 1970s was 15 per 100,000, and medical practice on the midwife level was common. Infant mortality and diseases of childbirth are leading causes of death, whereas malaria has been widely

Margin notes:

Constitutional framework and legal system

Government and economic planning

Health, welfare, housing, and education

reduced through the use of DDT, which has hastened the devastation of forest areas as a side effect.

Only Bangkok-Thonburi, and a few other large municipalities have housing shortages. The construction of government-financed housing cannot keep pace with demand, and slum areas have proliferated in some parts of the city.

A National Scheme of Education was introduced in 1960, requiring children under 15 to complete seven years of elementary education. Secondary education generally lasts five years, but when it is vocational it lasts six. Only a small minority of students go on to secondary training, however. The entrance without examination of some 60,000 students into newly opened Ramkhamhaeng University in 1971 nearly trebled the nation's university and teacher-training population. Eight other institutions, not including military academies, offer degrees in undergraduate and postgraduate fields.

CULTURAL LIFE AND INSTITUTIONS

According to many historians, the Thai's original home was in China, perhaps as far north as Mongolia. The Thai brought with them many cultural institutions of the Chinese. They began settlement in the Indochinese Peninsula about 800 years ago, at which time some Indian colonies already were established. Indian culture has been continuously absorbed into Thai life. Modifications were affected by the cultures of the Mon people, the Javanese, and the Khmer and Burmese people.

Traditional arts and customs

Thai arts are reflected in religion, architecture, porcelain and pottery, painting, music, drama, and literature. In religion artistic expression can be found in the sculpture of Buddha images. Thai architectural style is to be seen in the temples. Wood is usually the basic construction material. The ornamental parts are generally gilded and enriched with glass mosaic, gold leaf, porcelain, stucco, lacquer, and inlaid mother-of-pearl. The multiple-structured temple ground is a paradise for architects. Porcelain and pottery, although at first put to utilitarian uses, were later regarded as objects of art. Thai painting probably derived from India and Ceylon and is mostly religious; the artists are anonymous monks or dedicated laymen. The paintings are usually drawn on the temple walls, which are constructed with bricks and plaster.

Thai music is based on a unique system. It is not derived from the Chinese or Javanese systems, although the instruments used for playing may look the same.

The royal palace plays an important role in leading and preserving Thai culture through frequent royal functions and state ceremonies. Among these is the Kathin ceremony, a colourful pageant marking the end of the Buddhist Lent. It takes place with a procession of royal barges on the Chao Phraya, reconstructing a tradition dating from the earliest days of Buddhism. Thai temples hold ceremonies to mark the special events of Buddha's life. These are often accompanied by fun fairs to attract large crowds to the temples.

The University of Fine Arts teaches all Thai fine arts, including drama and music. It also designs architectural structures for the government as well as the religious institutions in a style that will preserve Thai forms. The Royal Institute of Thailand and the Siam Society are responsible for research and publication concerning the Thai way of life. The National Museum acts as an educational and information centre for the evolution of culture in the country.

The first type for printing Thai letters was devised by a British captain in 1828, and the first printing press was brought to Thailand by an American missionary in 1836. The Thai government made use of the printing press for the first time in 1839, when a royal proclamation banning opium smoking and trade was printed.

The communications media

The number of newspapers in the early 1970s—more than 15 in Bangkok printed in Thai, Chinese, and English, and some 50 in the provinces—was growing rapidly. Similarly, the number of radio and television sets was soaring: farmers often carried radios in the fields, and the roofline of many small towns sprouted a forest of antennas. About 30 radio transmitters, which cover most of Thailand, are operated by the government's Public Relations Department. In 1955 Thailand became the first nation of mainland Asia to have regular television programming, and in the early 1970s Bangkok had eight channels; three provincial stations reach over 30 provinces. Two Earth satellite stations were built at Si Racha in 1970 to facilitate overseas television links.

BIBLIOGRAPHY. The annual *Thailand Official Year Book* is the best source for current information. An excellent, well-illustrated pamphlet of the TRIBAL RESEARCH CENTER OF THAILAND, "Tribesmen and Peasants in North Thailand, 1967" (1969), briefly describes all the tribesmen in Thailand. The ROYAL THAI SURVEY DEPARTMENT, *Thailand National Resources Atlas* (1969), is the only atlas that can be used authoritatively as a reference. MASASHICHI NISHIO, "Public Health in Thailand," *Southeast Asian Studies*, vol. 11, no. 1 (1964; Eng. trans. JPRS 32217, 1965), based on scholarly research, gives a true picture of health conditions in Thailand. On physical geography, see ROBERT L. PENDLETON, *Report to Accompany the Provisional Map of the Soils and Surface Rocks of the Kingdom of Siam* (1953); and the SIAM, MINISTRY OF COMMERCE AND COMMUNICATIONS, *Nature and Industry* (1930).

(P.P.A.)

Thames River

The Thames, the principal river of England and the stream on the banks of which London was built, winds through six of the country's southern counties for 210 miles (338 kilometres), of which 92 miles are tidal, to the North Sea. Rising in the southwest in the Cotswolds of Gloucestershire at Thameshead, three miles from Cirencester, it broadens to 125 feet at Oxford and 250 feet at Teddington, the tidal head. At London Bridge it has widened to 750 feet, and 16 miles downstream, at Gravesend, it is 2,100 feet wide; and nearer the sea, between Sheerness and Shoeburyness, the estuary expands rapidly to 5½ miles. The average gradient from source to tidal water is 30 inches per mile (for related information see LONDON).

The first of its tributaries enters the stream 154 miles above London Bridge; this is the Churn, whose source at Seven Springs, four miles south of Cheltenham, has some claim to be the source of the Thames. Descending a broad vale, it accepts the waters of the Coln, the Windrush, the Evenlode, the Cherwell, the Ock, and the Thame before its valley becomes steep-sided as it divides the Chiltern Hills from the Berkshire Downs. At Pangbourne the river turns abruptly eastward and flows beneath beautifully wooded slopes, taking in the Kennet and the Loddon. Below Maidenhead the landscape flattens, save for Windsor's lone knoll, after which it is joined by the Colne, the Wey, and the Mole. Below Teddington Lock, 19 miles upstream from London Bridge, the river is tidal. Through Greater London it is embanked and spanned by 18 roads and six railway bridges. After the Tower Bridge and the Pool of London down the ten miles to Greenwich, the banks are given over to quays and docks, and tunnels replace bridges: Rotherhithe, Blackwall, Greenwich, and Woolwich, the latter two for pedestrians only. Along the next stretch to Tilbury and Gravesend, estuarine marshes alternate with factories and chalk bluffs; the Purfleet–Dartford Tunnel, connecting Essex and Kent, permits bypassing of London. Below Tilbury, the main outport, the wide estuary is coastal in nature.

Drainage pattern of the river basin

The Thames Basin divides distinctly in two, above and below the Goring Gap. The upper portion, on Jurassic strata of which older Lias and oolitic (round-grained limestone) series form the higher rim, is itself divided by a line of hills breached by the river at Oxford, where drainage converges. The lower basin consists of chalk downfolded into a syncline or depression, with a west–east axis and a covering of Eocene sands and clays.

The thick series of Mesozoic clays and limestones, of varying resistances to erosion, were subject at a later period to folding that created a downwarp along the line of the present Kennet-Thames. Individual streams flowing east toward the proto-Kennet-Thames were later captured by its more effective westward flow. The upper Thames itself developed as a west–east subsequent stream and captured southward-flowing Cotswold streams (see RIVERS AND RIVER SYSTEMS).

Eventually, the whole of this intricate pattern was profoundly influenced by the Ice Age with its climatic changes. Ice invaded the north and northeast of the basin, and in periods of melt and of heavy rain great floods poured down the valleys, which were successively deepened and finally left encumbered with gravel and alluvium upon which the present relatively small rivers meander. In addition, the lower Thames was pushed southward from the vale of St. Albans to a position near the southern chalk rim. Throughout the Thames system, tiers of river terraces were formed, often of sand and gravel of economic value. In the Middle Gravels of the Boyn Hill terrace at Swanscombe, a fragmentary skull was found, dating from the interglacial period and closely related to *Homo sapiens*.

A permeable basin and year-round rainfall ensure a regular flow. The monthly averages of the daily mean natural discharge at Teddington from a drainage basin of 3,812 square miles (9,873 square kilometres) vary from 4,900 cusecs (cubic feet per second) in January to 1,074 cusecs in August, with an annual mean of 2,703 cusecs (1 cusec = 0.0283 cubic metre per second). When the river runs full to its banks (with a flow of 9,114 cusecs), it temporarily floods the nontidal lowlands; during heavy floods the flow may exceed 19,000 cusecs. Floods occasionally threaten the embanked stretches in the centre of London when high-river spates pour toward the estuary at the same time that strong spring tides are running from the sea. Fears that the city may be inundated by rare "surge tides" thrust up the estuary by North Sea gales have led the London authorities to consider the erection of downstream barriers. Because the Thames is the chief water supply for London and its western suburbs (and also for districts around Oxford and Faringdon), drought, when the flow can drop below 300 cusecs, is also a matter for serious concern. The freshwater Thames has been controlled by the Thames Conservancy Board since 1857 and the tidal Thames below Teddington by the Port of London Authority since 1908.

Called the Tamesis by Julius Caesar and, by early English chroniclers, variously the Tamis, Tamisa, or Tamensim, the river has been sweetly sung of by bards throughout history. But in London after the mid-19th century it became more of an open sewer than a poetic stream. Starting in 1963 the freshwater and tidal authorities, aided by new regulations, began a battle against pollution that is visibly restoring the purity of the Thames.

The river became navigable by barges to Oxford and beyond by 1624 but with difficulty until locks were constructed above Staines in 1771. Locks between Staines and Teddington were added in 1810–15 by the London Corporation. Later improvements allowed boats drawing three feet to reach Lechlade. Some barge traffic uses the river above Teddington, especially to Kingston. Passenger steamers ply daily in summer between Oxford and Kingston, also from Westminster in London County upstream to Kew, Richmond, and Hampton Court, and downstream from Tower Pier to Tilbury, Southend-on-Sea, and Margate. Water-buses run between Greenwich and Putney. Ferries cross the Thames at Woolwich–North Woolwich and Gravesend–Tilbury. Pleasure boating is popular, especially on the freshwater Thames.

Some of the derelict canals that connect with the freshwater Thames were restored for pleasure boating in the 1960s; those off the tidal stretches are used commercially, including the Grand Union Canal to the Midlands. The Thames below Tower Bridge is one of the world's most important commercial waterways, its traffic supervised by the Thames Navigational Service.

BIBLIOGRAPHY. *The Thames Book* (1971), is a useful general guide, supplemented by K. FIDLER, *The Thames in Story* (1971) and ROY CURTIS, *Thames Passport* (1970). See also *The Thames Book* (annual), and the ASSOCIATION OF THAMES YACHT CLUBS, *Thames Handbook* (1956–60). *The River Thames: The Highway of the Port of London* (1970) covers the river's economic importance; while *The Oarsman's and Angler's Map of the River Thames . . . with Notes on Punting* (1927) deals with a recreational side.

(B.E.)

Thar Desert

The Thar Desert, or Great Indian Desert, consists of a tract of rolling sand hills lying partly in the Indian state of Rājasthān and partly in Pakistan. Covering 77,000 square miles (200,000 square kilometres) of territory, it is bordered by the irrigated Indus Plain to the west, the Arāvalli Range to the southeast, the Rann of Kutch to the south, and the Punjab Plain to the north and northeast. The desert results from the dryness of the prevailing monsoon winds, which do not bring sufficient rain to keep the region moist. The name Thar is derived from *t'hul*, the general term for the region's sand ridges. The Thar is inhabited by about 7,000,000 people, most of whom eke out a modest existence through subsistence agriculture.

Since the India-Pakistan waters agreement in 1960, both countries have undertaken major irrigation schemes in the region. Mineral deposits remain largely unexploited, however, and the economic emphasis remains on agriculture (for a related physical feature, see INDUS RIVER; see also DESERTS).

The landscape. *Geology.* The desert sands cover early Precambrian gneiss (granite-like metamorphic rocks formed in the oldest geological era, which began 4,600,000,000 years ago), sedimentary rocks from 570,000,000 to 2,500,000 years old, and more recent material deposited by rivers (alluvium). The surface sand is aeolian (wind-deposited) sand of the Quaternary Period (the most recent geological period, which began 7,000,000 years ago).

Relief. The desert presents an undulating surface, with high and low sand dunes separated by sandy plains and low, barren hills, or *bhakar*s, which rise abruptly from the surrounding plains. The dunes are in continual motion and take on varying shapes and sizes. Older dunes, however, are in a semistabilized or stabilized condition, and many rise to a height of almost 500 feet. Several playas (saline lakes), locally known as *dhand*s, are scattered throughout the region.

Drainage and soils. The drainage is mainly interior, except for the Indus River in the west and the Lūni River, which drains the southeast. Short, seasonal streams (wadis) are formed in the uplands only during the rains, but they soon die out in the sand.

The soils consist of seven main groups—desert soils; red desertic soils; sierozems (brownish-gray soils); the red and yellow soils of the foothills; the saline soils of the depressions; and the lithosols (shallow, weathered soils); and regosols (soft, loose soils) found in the hills. All these soils are predominantly coarse-textured, well-drained, and calcareous (calcium-bearing). A thick accumulation of lime often occurs at varying depths. The soils are generally infertile and, because of severe wind erosion, are overblown with sand.

Climate. The amount of annual rainfall in the desert tract is generally low, ranging from about 4 inches or less in the west to about 20 inches in the east. Precipitation is highly erratic, and there are wide fluctuations in the amount from year to year. About 90% of the total annual rain occurs during the season of the southwest monsoon, from July to September. At other seasons the wind blows from the northeast. May and June are the hottest months of the year, with temperatures rising to 122° F (50° C). During January, the coldest month, the mean minimum temperature ranges between 41° and 50° F (5° and 10° C), and frost is frequent. Dust storms and dust-raising winds, often blowing with velocities of 140 to 150 kilometres per hour (87 to 93 miles per hour), are common in May and June.

Vegetation and animal life. The desert vegetation is mostly herbaceous, or of stunted scrub; trees occasionally dot the landscape. On the hills, gum arabic acacia and euphorbia may be found. The *khajri* (*Prosopis cineraria*) tree grows throughout the plains; several other trees and shrubs, including the jujube, also occur. The stable sand dunes support a scanty vegetation of grasses, shrubs, and trees; a wild gourd, the *Citrullus colocynthis* (colocynth), is widespread.

Poetry and pollution of the Thames

The seven groups of soils

Game
animals

The thinly populated grasslands support the black buck, the chikara, and some feathered game, notably the francolin and quail. Among the migratory birds, sand grouse, ducks, and geese are common. The desert is also the home of the vanishing great bustard.

There are five major breeds of cattle in the Thar tract. Among these, the Tharparkar breed is the highest milk yielder, while the Kankre breed is good both as a beast of burden and as a milk producer. Sheep are bred for both medium-fine and rough wool. The camel is commonly used for transport, as well as for ploughing the land and other agricultural purposes.

The inhabitants. About 80% of the population of 7,000,000 are rural, and they are distributed in densities that vary from ten persons per square mile in Jaisalmer District in the south to 104 persons per square mile in Churu district in the east. Customs, rituals, and modes of dress are manifold. Both Islām and Hinduism are practiced, and the population is divided into complex economic and social groups. Many nomads are engaged in animal husbandry, crafts, or trade. They do not belong to a specific ethnic group, nor are they associated with a separate area; in general they are symbiotically related to the sedentary population and its economy.

Natural resources and their exploitation. *Grasses.* The grasses form the main natural resources of the desert. They provide nutritive and palatable pasturage, as well as medicines used locally by the inhabitants. Alkaloids, used for making medicine, and oils for making soap are also extracted.

Water. Water is very scarce. Whatever seasonal rain falls is collected in tanks and reservoirs and is used for drinking and domestic purposes throughout the year. Most groundwater cannot be utilized because it lies deep underground and is often saline. Recently, however, good aquifers (geological formations containing water) have been detected in the central part of the desert.

Minerals. Lignite (brown coal) is mined at Palana near Bīkaner, and natural gas has been located at Kamli Tal, northwest of the town of Jaisalmer. Deposits of gypsum now being exploited—located in Nāgaur, Jaisalmer, Bīkaner, and Barmer districts—are estimated at about 100,000,000 tons. Other minerals found in the region are limestone, bentonite (a clay formed from the decomposition of volcanic ash), glass sands, and minerals suitable for making ceramics. Salt is harvested from the saline lakes.

Irrigation. Apart from wells and tanks, canals are the main sources of water throughout the desert. When water is available, crops such as wheat, cotton, sugarcane, millet, sesame, castor beans, and chili peppers are grown. The Sukkur (Lloyd) Barrage on the Indus River, completed in 1932, irrigates the southern Thar region in Pakistan by means of canals, while the Gang Canal brings water from the Sutlej River to part of the northern region. The Rājasthān Canal, when completed in 1980, will irrigate 2,470,000 acres, mainly in the Bīkaner and Jaisalmer districts of India. The canal begins at the Harike Barrage—at the confluence of the Sutlej and Bēas rivers in the Indian Punjab—and continues in a southwesterly direction for 292 miles. It is hoped that it will provide agricultural land in the project area that will support about 2,000,000 people in place of the present (1970) 100,000 and will turn a substantial part of the dreary desert into a rich granary.

Power. Thermal power-generating plants, fuelled by coal and oil, are located only in the large towns and supply power only locally. Hydroelectric power is supplied by the Nangal power plant located on the Sutlej River in Punjab. When the Rājasthān Canal is completed it will generate about 22,000 kilowatts of hydroelectric power generated at big falls situated along its length.

Transport. Roads and railways are few. One railway line serves the southern part of the region from Lūni Junction, India, to Hyderābād, Pakistan. In the Indian part of the desert, a second line goes from Merta Road to Sūratgarh via Bīkaner, while another connects the towns of Jodhpur and Jaisalmer. In the Pakistani part of the desert, another railway line runs between Bahāwalpur and Hyderābād. There are few paved roads in the region.

The India-Pakistan waters agreement. The partition of India and Pakistan in 1947 left most of the irrigation canals fed by the rivers of the Indus System in Pakistani territory, while a large desert region remained unirrigated on the Indian side of the border. The Indus Water Treaty of 1960 fixed and delimited the rights and obligations of both countries concerning the use of waters of the Indus River system. Under the agreement, waters of the Rāvi, Bēas, and Sutlej rivers are to be made available to the Rājasthān Canal to irrigate mainly the desertic tract covering the Bīkaner and Jaisalmer districts in India.

Future prospects. Future economic development in the desert depends to some extent upon the harnessing of the sun's rays and the wind. Such possibilities as developing high-temperature solar furnaces for the production of electricity, and constructing windmills for lifting deep groundwater and powering flour mills, were investigated in the late 1960s with promising results. It has also been indicated that solar electricity can be generated from saline water contained in "solar ponds." Such developmental projects when completed would do much to enhance the living standards of the inhabitants of the region. (B.B.R./S.Pa.)

Theales

Theales constitutes one of the larger orders of the flowering plants, consisting of 21 families, with approximately 155 genera and 2,550 species. Theales plants vary in form, structure, and range of habitats and are related to many other plant orders. Some authorities suggest that at least a few of the related orders evolved from an ancestor that, if still extant, would be included within the Theales. From this viewpoint, therefore, the order is of considerable interest.

Another feature of interest is the distribution of the species within the families. Four families contain 400 or more species; one has about 120 species; and the other 16 are of somewhat equivocal status. None contains more than 40 species. Many authorities merge the 16 small families with one or another of the larger families or place them in other orders.

GENERAL FEATURES

Distribution and abundance. The order Theales is predominantly tropical in distribution, occurring in rain forests or in upland evergreen broad-leaved forests; few species occur in temperate regions. Members of the order are found almost worldwide; however, the centre of distribution is in Southeast Asia.

Importance. Members of one family, Dipterocarpaceae, are characteristic of the Malaysian rain forest, where species form the upper canopy at heights up to 250 feet (about 80 metres). Many species of this family are of economic importance for their timber; others produce valuable resins. *Camellia* (*Thea*) *sinensis*, the tea plant, is the most important economic species in the order. It has been cultivated for a long period of time in eastern India (Assam), Tibet, and China, the area to which it is probably native. Tea is also grown in several other areas (*e.g.*, Ceylon, Turkey, and the U.S.S.R.).

The tea plant

Other species of *Camellia* (*e.g.*, *C. japonica*) are widely cultivated as ornamentals in gardens in the temperate zone. *Gordonia, Stuartia* (both of the family Theaceae), *Hypericum* (Hypericaceae), *Ochna* (Ochnaceae), and many other genera are used as horticultural ornamentals.

Edible fruits include the souari nut (*Caryocar nuciferum*, family Caryocaraceae), the mammee apple (*Mammea americana*, Clusiaceae), and the mangosteen (*Garcinia mangostana*, Clusiaceae).

NATURAL HISTORY

Pollination. Not much is known about the pollination mechanisms in the order, but a number of notable structural developments seem to be related to pollination.

The most simple is the uniting of the stamens (male parts) either in a ring, as in the cultivated camellias, or in bundles, as in the common Saint-John's-wort (*Hypericum*) and in many tropical members of the order. In some members of the family Clusiaceae the stamens are united into very condensed groups known as phalanxes. A further adaptation, presumably effective in pollination, is the extreme elongation of the stamens of the family Caryocaraceae; these project considerably beyond the petals and are also united at the base.

The most remarkable pollination adaptations are found in members of the Marcgraviaceae, in which the floral bracts, small leaflike structures located just below the flowers, are transformed into nectar-secreting organs of various shapes, but always hollow and somewhat pitcher-like. In the simplest case (found in three genera), a bract subtends each flower. In the genus *Marcgravia*, however, the flower cluster is pendulous and umbellate —the flowers are on stalks that radiate from a common point, umbrella fashion. The central flowers of the umbel are sterile, and their bracts are enlarged to form erect, pitcher-like structures, superficially very like the insectivorous pitchers of *Nepenthes*, which hang below the outer ring of fertile flowers. These nectar-filled pitchers attract hummingbirds, which were once thought to pollinate the fertile flowers as they hovered, drinking the nectar. In at least two Guyanese species, the hummingbirds approach the pitchers from above the fertile flowers and do not come into contact with the stamens or the stigmata (female parts). In these two species, the stamens open in the late bud stage, and the flowers are actually self-fertilized.

Humming-
bird
flowers

Seed dispersal. Various dispersal mechanisms occur in the order, but only two are noteworthy. In most families, the aging sepals persist around the ripening fruit, and in various groups, notably the families Dipterocarpaceae and Lophiraceae, two or more of them enlarge above the fruit, producing a two-winged structure that is distributed by the wind.

The most remarkable development connected with the seeds occurs in the family Dioncophyllaceae. In this group the fruits open before ripening, and the developing seeds are pushed out from the fruit by the lengthened and hardened funiculi—the stalks on which the ovules grow within the ovary. The seeds continue to develop in this exposed position until ripe, when they fall, leaving the remains of the fruit and the funiculi. The function of this strange process, which is unique among flowering plants, is unknown.

Ecology. The order is extremely diverse in its habitat requirements. There are trees of the tropical rain forests (the family Dipterocarpaceae and others), climbers in the same forests (Marcgraviaceae), mangrove growth forms in coastal tidewaters (Pellicieraceae), trees and shrubs of the mountain evergreen broad-leaved forests (Theaceae and others), herbs and shrubs of various temperate habitats (Theaceae, Hypericaceae), and aquatics of tropical and temperate freshwaters (Elatinaceae). The morphological variability of the order is thus reflected in its ecology.

FORM AND FUNCTION

Vegetative characters. The order Theales is not well distinguished from other plant orders, and there are no conclusive diagnostic characters that will consistently serve to distinguish it. The following features occur frequently in the order, however, and, in combination, serve to characterize it in a general way.

The plants are usually woody, often with evergreen foliage. The leaves are usually simple, and resins are often present in the tissues. The bisexual flowers are mostly hypogynous; *i.e.*, the sepals, petals, and male parts (stamens) arise at the base of the ovary, a condition in which the ovary is described as "superior." The calyx consists of free sepals and the corolla of free petals, and the flower is radially symmetrical. The stamens are usually numerous, with a tendency to be united, either in a ring or in a number of separate bundles. The ovary is composed of two to many usually united segments called carpels, or simple ovaries, that each bear ovules—developing seeds—that attach along the central axis.

Resins are found in many members of the order, and some are of economic importance. In the family Hypericaceae, the resins occur in distinct, often globular glands, which may be yellow, orange, red, or black; similar glands occur in some of the smaller families (*e.g.*, Diegodendraceae and Tetrameristaceae). In the family Dipterocarpaceae, the resins are more generally distributed throughout the tissues.

Although most species of the order are evergreen trees or shrubs, the family Marcgraviaceae, found in the forests of tropical South America, is composed of climbers. These have a number of structural modifications, particularly in the genus *Marcgravia*, which shows shoot dimorphism, a condition that consists of two distinct types of vegetative growth patterns. The climbing shoots bear small leaves without stalks that are arranged in two rows (distichous) on the branches. Short adventitious (aerial) roots develop along these shoots and enable them to climb. The upper shoots, which bear pendulous flower clusters at their ends, have much larger, stalked, spirally arranged leaves, and lack the adventitious roots of the climbing stems. The transition between one shoot type and the other is often quite abrupt. The cause is unknown, but it is thought that the increase in the amount of light received by the shoots as they climb higher may be involved.

Variable
plant
organs

The family Dioncophyllaceae also shows remarkable vegetative modifications. In two of its genera, the leaves have two forms, one being "normal," the other terminating in two leathery hooks that presumably enable the plant to scramble over other vegetation. In the third genus, the leaves are of three forms, two as just described plus a third type with an elongation of the midrib, projecting beyond the blade and bearing glandular hairs. The function of the elongated part, which is called a rhabdode, is unknown, but the glandular hairs borne on it are very similar in structure to the "tentacles" of the insectivorous genus *Drosophyllum* of the order Nepenthales. The leaves of the Dioncophyllaceae have been compared both to the leaves of the Droseraceae and to the pitcher-bearing leaves of the family Nepenthaceae, but botanists agree that they are not insectivorous.

Floral characters. The flowers are exceptionally variable, and a wide range of structures occurs. There are usually distinct sepals and petals, though in some cases (family Dipterocarpaceae) the petals may be rather leathery and not brightly coloured. The sepals are usually four or five in number, free, and overlapping. In some groups, however, there is no sharp distinction between the sepals and the floral bracts and bracteoles—small green appendages just below the flowers—and the calyx appears to consist of a compressed spiral of several segments. This condition of the flower buds is called perulate. The flower petals vary from two to many, though four or five occur most commonly. They are normally free but may be fused to the ring formed by the united bases of the stamens.

The stamens are usually numerous (more rarely five to ten) and are centrifugally arranged (*i.e.*, they ripen from the centre of the flower toward the circumference). They are usually united, either into a ring, to which the petals are sometimes joined, or into distinct bundles. The anthers (pollen sacs) usually open by slits, but terminal pores occur in some groups (*e.g.*, Ochnaceae). The connective between the anthers is sometimes prolonged into an appendage (as in Dipterocarpaceae and Oncothecaceae).

The ovary consists of two or more (frequently five) carpels that are united, or, if apparently free, have a united style—the narrow upper portion. The ovules have two integuments, or coverings, and endosperm, a starchy nutrient tissue for the developing embryo, may be present or absent in the seed.

EVOLUTION

Fossil record. As with most flowering plant groups, the fossil record of the Theales order is both scanty and of little value in deducing the evolutionary history of the group. Noteworthy features include the occurrence of

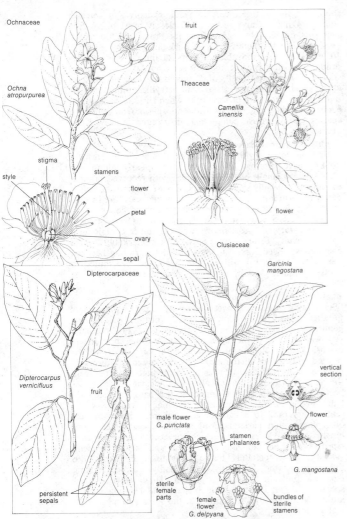

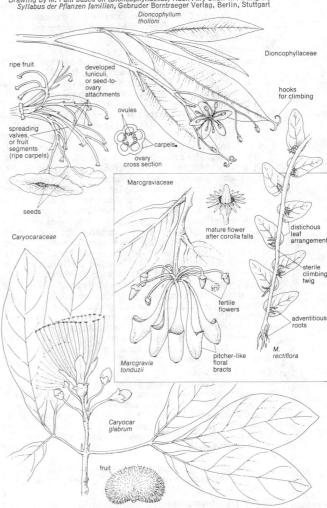

Figure 1: Vegetative, floral, and fruiting structures of four of the larger families of the order Theales.
Drawing by M. Pahl; *G. punctata* and *G. delpyana* based on A. Engler, *Syllabus der Pflanzen familien;* floral details of *G. mangostana* based on L.H. Bailey, *Manual of Cultivated Plants* (1949); the Macmillan Company

phiraceae. Similarly, the families Theaceae and Clusiaceae are linked by the Bonnetiaceae. Many of the smaller families included in the order are sufficiently similar to various of the larger families for them to be merged by various workers. Thus, the family Lophiraceae is usually included in the Ochnaceae; Bonnetiaceae, Asteropeiaceae, Tetrameristaceae, and Pellicieraceae in the Theaceae; and Hypericaceae in the Clusiaceae (the resulting large family, in the last instance, is often called Guttiferae). The remaining smaller families—Strasburgeriaceae, Ancistrocladaceae, Dioncophyllaceae, Diegodendraceae, Marcgraviaceae, Pentaphylacaceae, Caryocaraceae, Quiinaceae, Medusagynaceae, and Oncothecaceae—form a mixed group. Some of them are clearly allied to the large families within the order, whereas others are of more controversial status.

Drawing by M. Pahl based on (Dioncophyllaceae) Nach Airy Shaw in A. Engler, *Syllabus der Pflanzen familien,* Gebruder Borntraeger Verlag, Berlin, Stuttgart

Figure 2: Vegetative, floral, and fruiting structures of three of the smaller families in the order Theales.

fossils from families that are at present entirely tropical (Dipterocarpaceae and Clusiaceae) in deposits of Tertiary age (beginning about 65,000,000 years ago) in Europe and in the Mediterranean area.

Phylogeny. The difficulty of deducing evolutionary relationships of such a variable group is revealed by extreme affinities that have been suggested for it. It has been suggested by some authorities, for example, that the order is derived from early members of the family Dilleniaceae (order Dilleniales). Others stress this relationship by merging the Theales and Dilleniales, either completely or in part. Again, the similarity between the orders Theales and the Ericales leads to the view that the order Ericales was derived from the Theales. Some authorities, in fact, place the order Theales in a crucial position in their systems, suggesting that the origins of several other plant groups are to be found in a "thealaceous" ancestor. These groups are the orders Capparales, Primulales, Diapensiales, Salicales, Violales, Sarraceniales, and Malvales, and the family Lecythidaceae of the order Myrtales, as well as the Ericales already mentioned.

The problem of the precise meaning of phylogenetic origins occurs with this group. It cannot be denied that similarities exist among the orders mentioned, but many botanists are skeptical that all or even most of them arose from the Theales.

Within the order the problems of phylogeny are similar. A few indications as to the evolutionary relationships of the families emerge, however, even though they do not give a clear picture of evolution within the order.

The family Ochnaceae, for instance, appears to be linked to the Dipterocarpaceae through the family Lo-

Central evolutionary position of the Theales

CLASSIFICATION

Distinguishing taxonomic features. Some of the characteristics used in distinguishing the families have been mentioned. The curious bracts of the Marcgraviaceae and the enlarged and persistant calyx of Lophiraceae and Dipterocarpaceae, for instance, serve to diagnose these families. Because the group is so variable, many other characters are used in its classification; these include variations in habitat, leaf position and form, presence or absence of stipules, and floral characters.

Annotated classification. The following classification treats as separate families groups that have traditionally been considered as subfamilies or tribes of the larger families. Also included here are a few small families (Medusagynaceae, Oncothecaceae, and Elatinaceae) whose relationship to the rest of the order is somewhat doubtful. The affinities of these families have not yet been settled, and their inclusion here is based, to some extent, on taxonomic intuition.

ORDER THEALES

Trees, shrubs, or woody climbers, rarely herbs. Leaves alternate or opposite, usually simple and evergreen, with or without stipules. Flowers solitary or in inflorescences (clusters) of varying degrees of complexity and usually radially symmetrical and bisexual. Sepals sometimes 4 but usually 5 to many, usually free and overlapping, sometimes not distinguishable from the bracts and bracteoles. Petals usually 5, free or rarely united at the base (sometimes to the tube formed by the stamens) or the apex. Stamens usually numerous, maturing from the centre of the flower outward, often united in bundles or in a ring. Carpels usually 5, more rarely fewer or more numerous, usually united; when free they are still joined by means of the united styles. Placentation (ovule attachment) usually axile—to the central axis of the ovary. Seeds with or without endosperm. Twenty-one families with approximately 155 genera and 2,550 species. Distribution throughout the tropics, with extensions into subtropical and temperate regions of both hemispheres.

Family Ochnaceae

Trees, shrubs, or very rarely herbs. Leaves alternate, usually simple, with many pinnately arranged (*i.e.*, branching from a midrib), parallel, lateral secondary veins. Stipules are present but inclined to fall early and are sometimes deeply cut into narrow lobes. Flowers in racemes or panicles (simple- and complex-branched flower clusters, respectively), bisexual, usually radially symmetrical (rarely bilaterally symmetrical, at least with regard to the stamens). Sepals 4 or 5, or sometimes up to 10, free, usually overlapping. Petals sometimes 4, usually 5, but occasionally up to 10, free, contorted, or overlapping, falling early. Stamens usually numerous, in 3 to 5 whorls, free; in some genera sterile stamens (staminodia) are present. Filaments short, anthers (pollen sacs) usually opening by terminal pores, more rarely by longitudinal slits. Ovary variable, of 1 to 15 carpels. Two main types of ovary structure occur: (1) carpels united into a compound ovary with terminal style; (2) carpels free, borne on the fleshy receptacle (the expanded tip of the flower stalk bearing the flower parts), united by means of the single style. Ovules 1 to several in each carpel, placentation along the central axis of the ovary or on the inner walls. Fruit a capsule, usually splitting between the carpel segments in ovaries of type (1) or, in ovaries of type (2), a group of fleshy drupes (stone-seeded fruits) borne on a fleshy receptacle that enlarges with age. Seeds 1 to many, with or without endosperm, usually with a straight embryo. Twenty-seven genera and about 400 species widely distributed in the tropics of the world, with a few species in subtropical areas, notably in southern Africa. The largest genera are *Ouratea* (about 210 species) and *Ochna* (95 species).

Family Lophiraceae

Trees, with alternate, simple leaves with venation like that of the Ochnaceae. Flowers large, showy, in panicles. Sepals 5; petals 5; stamens numerous, anthers opening by short slits near the apex only. Ovary of 2 carpels, incompletely 2-chambered; styles 2, terminal, ovules 10 to 12 per chamber, placentation basal. Fruit a woody capsule, surrounded by the persistent calyx, of which the outermost segment is much enlarged and the next somewhat enlarged, producing an unequally 2-winged reproductive structure reminiscent of that of the family Dipterocarpaceae. One genus with 2 species, distributed in tropical Africa.

Family Dipterocarpaceae

Trees with resin. Leaves alternate, simple, with a covering of stellate (branched in star shapes) hairs or peltate (shieldlike) scales. Stipules present, falling early. Flowers bisexual, radially symmetric, often fragrant, arranged in panicles. Calyx of 5 overlapping or valvate (touching along the edges) sepals, free or united; may be joined to the ovary at the base. Petals 5, twisted, often leathery. Stamens numerous, anthers opening by slits, the connective (the apex of the filament between the anther sacs) prolonged, usually to a point. Ovary of 3 carpels, with 3 chambers; ovules 2 in each chamber, placentation axile. Style entire or 3-lobed. Fruit indehiscent (*i.e.*, it does not split open along definite seams), usually 1-seeded, surrounded by the persistent calyx, of which 2 or more lobes are much enlarged, forming a winged reproductive structure. Seeds without endosperm. Twenty-two genera and about 400 species distributed mainly in the Asian tropics but also with 2 genera (about 24 species) in tropical Africa.

Family Strasburgeriaceae

Trees with large, alternate, simple, remotely toothed leaves. Stipules present, each pair fused into a simple or 2-parted scale borne in the axil (upper angle between leaf stalk and shoot) of the leaf. Flowers bisexual, radially symmetrical, solitary, axillary. Calyx of up to 10 closely overlapping, free segments, not sharply distinct from the bracts and bracteoles, persistent in fruit. Petals 5, free, overlapping, fleshy. Stamens 10, with versatile (movable) anthers. A thick, lobed, nectar-producing disk is present, its 10 lobes alternating with the 10 stamens. Ovary 10-ribbed, of 5 united carpels; ovules 2 in each carpel, placentation axile. Fruit berrylike, pulpy throughout, indehiscent, more or less corky when ripe. Seeds 2 or 1 in each ovary chamber, winged, with endosperm. One genus and species (*Strasburgeria calliantha*), distributed in New Caledonia.

Family Ancistrocladaceae

Climbing shrubs with the ends of the branches forming hooks. Leaves alternate, simple, with small, early-falling stipules. Flowers small, borne in panicles with recurved branches, bisexual, radially symmetrical. Calyx of 5 segments, united below to form a tube, which at maturity becomes fused to the ovary. Sepals persistent and unequally enlarged and winglike in fruit. Petals 5, contorted, slightly fused at the base. Stamens 5 or 10. Ovary of 3 carpels, with one chamber containing a solitary ovule. Fruit a nut. Seed with remarkably folded cotyledons ("seed leaves"), the seed coat intruding between the folds. One genus with about 16 species, distributed in southern India, Ceylon, Southeast Asia, and tropical West Africa.

Family Dioncophyllaceae

Scrambling shrubs. Leaves alternate, simple, with many parallel lateral veins, dimorphic (2 forms), or, in one genus trimorphic; *i.e.*, the leaf forms are (1) "normal," (2) with hooks at the apex, or (3) bearing an elongate extension of the midrib covered with capitate (swollen-headed) glands (a rhabdode). Stipules absent. Flowers in cymose inflorescences (flower clusters that mature from the top downward), bisexual, radially symmetrical. Sepals 5, free or somewhat united at the base, persistent in fruit. Petals 5, free. Stamens 10 or many, free. Disk absent. Ovary of 2 to 5 carpels, 1-chambered, ovules numerous, placentation parietal. Fruit at first closed, later opening by 2 to 5 valves, from which the seeds project as they ripen, borne on elongate, thickened and woody funiculi (stalks). Seeds peltately borne (shieldlike, the stalk into the centre of the disk), disklike, broadly winged, hanging from the funiculi. Endosperm present. Three genera with 1 species each or 1 genus with 3 species, depending on the authority consulted. Distribution in the forests of west tropical Africa.

Family Diegodendraceae

Trees or shrubs (2 growth forms of the single species found in this family) with alternate, simple, entire, pinnately veined, leaves dotted with transparent depressions. Stipules present, very long, wrapped around the bud and falling early, leaving an annular (ring-shaped) scar. Flowers bisexual, radially symmetrical, in a cymose-paniculate terminal inflorescence (many-branched flower clusters maturing from the top downward). Sepals 5 or 6, unequal, overlapping, free, persistent. Petals 5, free, equal, deciduous (falling). Stamens many, free. Carpels 2 or 3, free, on a small receptacle, covered with peltate scales, united by the style, which divides above into 2 or 3 separate stigmata (pollen-receiving surfaces). Ovules 2 in each carpel, basal. Fruit unknown. This family, which was first described in the early 1960s, contains a single genus and species (*Diegodendron humbertii*), distributed in Madagascar.

Family Theaceae (Ternstroemiaceae)

Trees or shrubs with alternate, simple, mostly evergreen leaves without stipules. Flowers usually showy, solitary, or more rarely in racemes or panicles, radially symmetrical, mostly bisexual. Calyx of 5 or more sepals (when more than 5 these not distinguishable from bracts and bracteoles), overlapping, usually free. Stamens usually numerous, free, or shortly united in a ring, sometimes fused to the petal bases. Anthers usually opening by slits, rarely by terminal pores. Ovary 3- to 5-carpellate. Ovules 2 or more in each chamber, placentation axile; styles free or united. Fruit dehiscent or indehiscent. Seeds with folded or twisted embryo and scanty endosperm. Twenty-eight genera and about 575 species, distributed in tropical and temperate regions of the world.

Family Marcgraviaceae

Climbing or epiphytic (*i.e.*, not rooted in soil but living upon aerial surfaces) shrubs. Leaves alternate, simple, without stipules, sometimes dimorphic. Flowers bisexual, radially or bilaterally symmetrical, borne in racemes or pseudo-umbels, the bracts variously modified into nectar-producing, pitcher-like bodies that are sometimes winged. Sepals 5, overlapping. Petals 5, free or completely fused into a cap or head, which is shed as a whole when the flower opens. Stamens 5 to many, free or slightly united. Ovary of 2 or more united carpels, 2- to many-chambered, ovules numerous, in several rows in each chamber, placentation at first parietal, later appearing axile. Stigmata sessile ("perched"—no stalk or style) on top of the ovary. Fruit fleshy, more or less indehiscent. Seeds numerous, with or without endosperm. Five genera with about 120 species, distributed in the tropics of South America.

Family Pentaphylacaceae

Shrubs or trees. Leaves simple, alternate, entire, evergreen, without stipules. Flowers bisexual, radially symmetrical, borne in racemes or spikelike inflorescences. Sepals 5, free, overlapping, persistent. Petals 5, free, overlapping. Stamens 5, free, flexed inward in the bud, anthers opening by valves. Ovary 5-chambered, with 2 ovules in each chamber attached near the apex of the ovary along the central axis. Style 1, stigmas 5, small. Fruit a capsule that opens by means of a dorsal suture. Seeds winged, with scanty endosperm. One genus, with four species distributed in Malaysia and western China.

Family Tetrameristaceae

Trees with alternate, simple, leathery leaves without stipules and which are dotted beneath with black glands. Flowers bisexual, radially symmetrical, in axillary, umbel-like racemes. Sepals 4, overlapping in 2 series, persistent, the outer pair larger. Petals 4, overlapping, persistent. Stamens 4. Ovary 4-chambered, each chamber containing 1 ovule, placentation basal. Style single, with 4 stigmatic teeth. Fruit a berry, surrounded by the persistent perianth (sepals and petals). One genus with three species, distributed in Malaysia, Borneo, and Sumatra.

Family Caryocaraceae

Trees or shrubs. Leaves evergreen, opposite or alternate, with 3 fingerlike lobes. Flowers bisexual, radially symmetrical, in terminal racemes. Sepals 5 or 6, united below, the lobes overlapping. Petals 5 or 6, free, overlapping. Stamens many, in 5 or 6 series, sometimes shortly united at the base, much exceeding the perianth. The inner stamens are sometimes sterile (staminodia). Ovary 4- to 20-chambered, each chamber with 1 ovule, placentation axile. Fruit fleshy or splitting into woody sections. Seeds with scanty endosperm. Two genera with 25 species, distributed in tropical South America.

Family Asteropeiaceae

Similar to Theaceae, differing in having 10 to 15 stamens united at the base and an indehiscent fruit surrounded by the accrescent (enlarging with age), winglike calyx. One genus with 5 species, confined to Madagascar.

Family Pellicieraceae

Completely glabrous (smooth, no plant hairs or scales) trees. Leaves alternate, toothed, leathery, without stipules. Flowers axillary, solitary, sessile, included for a time in the 2 long bracteoles. Sepals 5, free, overlapping. Petals 5, free, overlapping. Stamens 5, the filaments free, the anthers elongate and adherent to the style. Ovary 10-grooved, 2- or 5- chambered, with 1 ovule in each chamber, placentation axile. Fruit 10-grooved, indehiscent, leathery. Seed 1 (by abortion of the other ovules), with no endosperm, and a long plumule (growing point of the embryo). One genus and species distributed in Panama and Colombia.

Family Quiinaceae

Trees, shrubs, or climbers. Leaves opposite or whorled, pinnately lobed or simple, with numerous lateral nerves and pinnately arranged tertiary nerves. Stipules present. Flowers bisexual or unisexual, in racemes or panicles, radially symmetrical or sometimes very slightly bilaterally symmetrical. Sepals 4 or 5, overlapping, free, unequal. Petals 4 to 8, free, overlapping. Stamens 15 to 150. Ovary of 2, 3, or 7 to 13 carpels; chambers as many as carpels, each with 2 almost basal ovules. Styles free, as many as carpels. Fruit berrylike, fleshy, but dehiscent at maturity. Seeds covered with silky hairs, without endosperm. Three genera and 37 species, distributed in the forests of tropical South America.

Family Medusagynaceae

Shrubs. Leaves opposite, simple, leathery, without stipules. Flowers in terminal panicles, bisexual, radially symmetrical. Sepals 5, overlapping, deciduous. Petals 5, overlapping, free. Stamens very many, anthers opening by slits. Ovary of 20 to 25 almost free carpels, each bearing a style on the upper, outer angle of the carpel, the styles of the whole ovary thus forming a ring. Ovules 2 in each carpel, 1 ascending, 1 descending, placentation axile. Fruit a capsule opening between the segments, the valves diverging from the base upward, and remaining attached to the top of the central column, the whole umbrella-like. Seeds winged. One genus and species (*Medusagyne oppositifolia*), occurring in the Seychelles.

Family Oncothecaceae

Small, glabrous trees. Leaves alternate, entire, evergreen. Flowers bisexual, radially symmetrical, in terminal paniculate inflorescences. Sepals 5, overlapping. Petals 5, fused at the base, with a rotate (circular in outline) limb of 5 overlapping lobes. Stamens 5, borne on the corolla (collection of petals) tube, anthers opening by slits, the connective prolonged into a hooked appendage. Ovary of 5 carpels, each carpel containing 2 ovules, placentation axile. Styles 5, recurved. Fruits not well-known but drupelike, with 5 to 10 seeds. One genus and species (*Oncotheca balansae*), distributed in New Caledonia.

Family Bonnetiaceae

Trees or shrubs. Leaves alternate, entire, without stipules. Flowers in terminal panicles or racemes, bisexual, radially symmetrical. Sepals 5, unequal, overlapping. Petals 5, contorted. Stamens numerous, free or united at the base or united into 5 bundles. Ovary of 3 to 5 united carpels, ovules numerous in each chamber, placentation axile. Style usually entire. Seeds with or without endosperm, sometimes winged. Five genera with about 20 species, distributed in South America and Southeast Asia.

Family Clusiaceae

Trees or shrubs. Leaves opposite, simple, without stipules. Inflorescence various, flowers radially symmetrical, unisexual or polygamous (unisexual and bisexual flowers on the same plant), rarely bisexual. Sepals occasionally 2, usually 4 or 5 or sometimes 6, overlapping, free. Petals as many as sepals, contorted or overlapping, free. Stamens numerous, mostly fused, at least in the lower part, into bundles (phalanxes) in the same number as and opposite to the petals. Staminodia frequently present in the female flowers. Ovary 1- to many-chambered, ovules 1 to many, placentation axile or parietal. Fruit various, dehiscent or indehiscent. Seeds without endosperm, often with arils (fleshy appendages). A large family of 41 genera and 460 species, with worldwide tropical distribution.

Family Hypericaceae

Trees, shrubs, subshrubs, or herbs, rarely climbers. Leaves opposite or in whorls, usually gland-dotted, without stipules. Plant hairs (when present) often stellate. Flowers bisexual, radially symmetrical, and mostly solitary or in panicles. Sepals usually 5, imbricate. Petals usually 5, overlapping, or contorted. Stamens many, often united into 3 or 5 bundles. Sepals, petals, and stamens often with black or amber glands. Ovary of 3 to 5 carpels, with 1 chamber or 3 to 5 chambers. Ovules numerous, placentation axile or parietal. Styles usually more or less free. Fruit a capsule or berry. Seeds numerous, without endosperm. Eight genera and about 440 species centred in the tropics, but with 1 genus (*Hypericum*) widely distributed in temperate regions.

Family Elatinaceae

Herbs or rarely low shrubs. Leaves opposite or in whorls, simple; stipules present. Flowers small, axillary, solitary or in cymes. Sepals 3 to 5, free, overlapping. Petals 3 to 5, free, overlapping, persistent. Stamens 3 to 5 or 6 to 10, free. Ovary 3- to 5-chambered; ovules numerous, with axile placentation. Fruit a capsule opening between the segments. Seeds horseshoe-shaped, without endosperm. Two genera with 45 species, mostly confined to aquatic or at least wet habitats throughout the world.

Critical appraisal. The order Theales is a variable group with a large number of unusual modifications. Thus, it is not surprising that taxonomic treatments of the 21 families included here vary.

Comparisons reveal a wide diversity of opinion as to which families the order Theales should contain, which groups should be regarded as families, and which orders are related to the Theales. The main conclusion arising from this lack of agreement is that the order Theales, as presented here, is variable and shows multiple relationships in many directions; for example, more than 60 plant families have been placed in the order Theales or have belonged to other orders that include genera at some time placed in the Theales as defined here. This represents about 13 percent of all flowering plant-families, an impressive number to be related to the 21 families. This large group is understandably difficult to divide so that all assumed relationships take their proper place.

Certain groups, however, show more or less clear affini-

The problem of determining relationships

ties with the Theales; these are the orders Dilleniales, Ericales, and Violales, with which the Theales are closely associated in all of the most authoritative classification systems.

When the content of the group is considered, it is clear that it may be viewed as one order, as is done here, or divided into a number of separate orders. Because there are no objective standards for satisfactorily defining orders, no final decision can be made. It seems, however, that within the large and variable Theales as presented here, some eventual subdividing is likely and would be useful.

Some of the authors of the various taxonomic systems dealing with the Theales recognize a large number of relatively small families, while others recognize a smaller number of relatively larger families. In view of the extreme variability of the group and its multiple relationships, the former treatment—the one followed here—seems to be a more accurate reflection of the natural situation, and it seems likely to gain wider acceptance.

Further study of the group, however, from many points of view, is likely to result in modifications. Many of the families comprising the Theales are small, tropical, and not well-known. Detailed studies of them may reveal unsuspected similarities or differences that will result in altered viewpoints. The habitats of many species in the group are in danger of extinction as a result of man's activities, and it is extremely important that they be preserved for study.

BIBLIOGRAPHY. H.K. AIRY SHAW, "On the Dioncophyllaceae, a Remarkable New Family of Flowering Plants," *Kew Bull.*, pp. 327–347 (1951), a detailed, well-illustrated study of this remarkable family, followed by anatomical notes by C.R. METCALFE (on pages 351–368); P.S. ASHTON, *A Manual of the Dipterocarp Trees of Brunei State* (1964), a comprehensive manual for identification; F.W. FOXWORTHY, "*Dipterocarpaceae* of the Malay Peninsula," *Malay. Forest Rec.*, no. 10 (1932), a manual for identification; H. GOTTWALD and N. PARARESWARAN, "Beiträge zur Anatomie und Systematik der Quiinaceae," *Bot. Jb.*, 87:361–381 (1967), a detailed study of the family; C.E. KOBUSKI, many papers, under the general title "Studies in the Theaceae," mostly in the *J. Arnold Arbor.*, but also in *Ann. Mo. Bot. Gdn.; Bot. Mag., Tokyo; Brittonia;* and *Kew Bull.* (1935–61), very full taxonomic treatments of many genera of Theaceae and allied groups; N.K.B. ROBSON, "The Genus Hypericum in Africa South of the Sahara, Madagascar and the Mascarenes," *Kew Bull.*, pp. 433–446 (1957), a taxonomic study by the foremost authority on the group; R. SCHMID, "Die systematische Stellung der Dioncophyllaceene," *Bot. Jb.*, 83:1–56 (1964), supplements, in detail, Airy Shaw's work on the same family; J.R. SEALY, *A Revision of the Genus Camellia* (1958), a well-illustrated taxonomic revision of this horticulturally important genus; B.G.L. SWAMY, "A Contribution to the Embryology of the Marcgraviaceae," *Am. J. Bot.*, 35:628–633 (1948), an embryological work, with notes on pollination; C.F. SYMINGTON, "Forester's Manual of Dipterocarps," *Malay. Forest Rec.*, no. 16 (1941), a manual of identification from the forester's viewpoint.

(J.Cul.)

Theatre, Art of

Although a wide range of entertainment is presented in arenas called theatres, the art of theatre is concerned almost exclusively with live performances in which the action is precisely planned to create a coherent and significant sense of drama. Though the word theatre is derived from the Greek *theaomai*, "to see," the performance itself may be directed either to the ear or to the eye, as is suggested by the interchangeability of the terms spectator (which derives from words meaning "to view") and audience (which derives from words meaning "to hear"). Sometimes the appeal is strongly intellectual, as in Shakespeare's *Hamlet*, but the intellectual element in itself is no assurance of good theatre. A good performance of *Hamlet*, for example, is extremely difficult to achieve, and a poor one is much less rewarding than a brilliant presentation of a farce. Moreover, a good *Hamlet* makes demands on the spectator that may be greater than he is prepared to put forward, while the farce may be enjoyed in a condition of comparative relaxation. The full participation of the spectator is a vital element in theatre.

There is a widespread misconception that the art of theatre can be discussed solely in terms of the intellectual content of the script. Theatre is not essentially a literary art, though it has been so taught in some universities and schools. The literary side of a theatrical production should be subordinate to the histrionic. The strongest impact on the audience is made by acting, singing, and dancing, followed by spectacle—the background against which those activities take place. Later, on reflection, the spectator may find that the meaning of the text has made the more enduring impression, but more often the literary merit of the script, or its "message," is a comparatively minor element. This is even more apparent in opera than in drama; the composer, the singers, and the conductor nearly always contribute more to the success of the event than the librettist.

Yet it is often assumed that the theatrical experience can be assimilated by reading the text of a play. In part, this is a result of the influence of theatrical critics, who, as writers, tend to have a literary orientation. Their influence is magnified by the fact that serious theatre cannot be made widely available—for each person who sees an important production, thousands of others will know it only through the notices of critics. Those who write the most widely read notices usually are most interested in textual and thematic values, and they underestimate or even ignore elements that are nearer to the heart of theatre. If great paintings were not available in reproduction, and if it were thus necessary to rely on descriptions of them by critics, the literary bias of those critics would have a profound effect on the art, as indeed it had through the writings of John Ruskin, for example, in 19th-century England. Theatre critics have had just this sort of influence on the taste of audiences.

The literary element of theatre

This is not to say that the contribution of the author to the theatrical experience is unimportant. The script of a play is the basic element of theatrical performance. In the case of many masterpieces it is the most important element. But even these dramatic masterpieces demand the creative cooperation of artists other than the author. The dramatic script, like an operatic score or the scenario of a ballet, is no more than the raw material from which the performance is created. The actors, rather than merely reflecting a creation that has already been fully expressed in the script, give body, voice, and imagination to what was only a shadowy indication in the text. The text of a play is as vague and incomplete in relation to a fully realized performance as is a musical score to a concert. The Hamlets of two great actors probably differ more than two virtuoso renditions of Bach's *Goldberg Variations* possibly can.

This article contains a treatment of the art of theatre in the most general terms, an attempt to illuminate what it is and why it has been regarded as a fundamental human activity throughout man's history. It makes no attempt to provide a systematic treatment of either the history of theatre or its constituent elements. The theatrical traditions of the various cultures of the world are considered at length in articles such as THEATRE, WESTERN; and DANCE AND THEATRE, EAST ASIAN; and in the theatre sections of articles such as SOUTH ASIAN PEOPLES, ARTS OF; and AFRICAN PEOPLES, ARTS OF. Much more extensive treatment of the elements of theatre will be found in articles such as STAGING AND STAGE DESIGN; THEATRES AND STAGES; ACTING; and DIRECTING. Genres of dramatic literature are discussed in TRAGEDY; COMEDY; and SATIRE, as well as in DRAMATIC LITERATURE.

ORIGINS

Exactly how the theatre came into being is not known. The earliest known theatrical works of major significance are the tragedies that were performed in Athens in the 6th century BC. They were presented as part of a festival in honour of the god Dionysus, a deity concerned with intoxication, with sex, with art. The Dionysiac festival was a spring festival, devoted to the thoughts and emotions evoked by the ending of winter and the return of fertility to the earth.

The festival had religious origins, although by the time

The Dionysiac festival

of the three great tragedians of ancient Athens, Aeschylus, Sophocles and Euripides, of the 5th century BC, it had become considerably secularized. The earlier religious character of the festival may have made it analogous to the rites of very primitive people, still to be observed in some parts of the world. Such primitive rites are at least in part dramatic: war dances, for instance, which are intended to frighten the enemy and to put courage into the hearts of the participants, imitate the battle itself, or at least the way in which the participants hope to see the battle develop. Other rites also have a practical purpose and a mimetic form; in rain dances, for example, the dancers imitate rain.

In the Orient, too, the theatre is closely tied to religion in its origins. Ritual dance-drama is traceable to about AD 100 in India, where the transition to theatre coincided with the advent of Buddhism in India in the 2nd century AD. A similar transition from dance-drama to theatre is discernible in China with the advent of Buddhism by the 6th century and in Japan by the 14th.

The art of theatre achieved its first full flowering in Athens in the 5th century BC. It is assumed that the classical drama of this period was a sophisticated elaboration of more primitive rites. At one time the performers were priests; from the form of the plays it is reasonable to assume that the principal feature of the stage was an altar and that the principal feature of the occasion was a sacrifice.

The ultimate sacrifice is the human being, and the original form of the drama may have been the ritual slaying of an important victim—a king's son, for example, or a young virgin. As the Athenian community became more civilized, however, the idea of human sacrifice, along with the idea of the savage kind of deity who would demand it, became unacceptable. Gradually, doubtless after many generations, even the sacrifice of an animal became abhorrent. In its place a symbolic sacrifice was offered—a story of sacrifice, in which the protagonist suffered on behalf of the community and died for the people. This idea is at the heart of the Greek tragedy, such as Sophocles' *Oedipus Rex*, in which King Oedipus must extirpate his own wrongs to redeem his people from the catastrophes that plague them.

Comedy, as well as tragedy, has roots in Athens of the 5th century BC. Along with deeply serious attempts of tragedians to discern a moral order at work in the universe, comic dramatists such as Aristophanes ridiculed the notion of any enduring significance in the acts of either gods or men. In addition to the genres of tragedy and comedy, classical Greece left to posterity a measure of specialization among the performers—between the actors, each of whom impersonated several characters of the play, and the chorus, who stood back from the action, commented upon it, and interpreted its significance for the audience.

Drama as an expression of its cultural milieu

Beyond these formal elements, however, classical drama offers a pattern of development that is re-enacted continually in other cultures throughout history. The rapid rise and decline of drama in ancient Athens parallels the rise and decline of the Athenian civilization itself. Great periods of achievement in theatre have tended to coincide with periods of national achievement, when man's breadth of vision expands to encompass the cosmos, as in Elizabethan England. Conversely, periods of excessive materialism, such as those of the decay of ancient Greece or ancient Rome, tend to produce theatre in which ostentation, spectacle, and vulgarity predominate.

When a great culture declines, its theatrical tradition need not die with it. Ancient Athenian tragedy experienced a rebirth in 17th-century France in the works of Racine and Corneille and, in the 20th century, in the plays of Jean Anouilh and Jean Cocteau. Similarly, there was a vogue for Shakespeare in 19th-century Germany. This cross-fertilization of theatrical tradition is a salient aspect of theatrical history. Probably more than in other arts, each theatrical style represents an amalgamation of diverse heritages.

The course of drama in the centuries since the Athenian drama reached its peak in the 5th century BC has added little that is fundamental to the art of theatre. That the heights achieved by ancient Greek drama have never been equalled stands as a powerful argument against an easy belief in the constant progress of mankind.

THEATRE AS EXPRESSION

Mimesis in theatre. The art of the theatre is essentially one of make-believe, or mimesis. In this respect it differs from music, which seldom attempts to imitate "real" sounds, except in so-called program music, such as Tchaikovsky's *1812 Overture*, which suggests the sounds of a battle. In this respect, the art of narrative in literature is much closer to that of the theatre. In a story, considerable attention must be paid to plausibility. Even if the story is not intended to be believed as having actually happened (*e.g., Don Quixote* or *Pilgrim's Progress*), plausibility is essential if the story is to hold the auditor's attention. The principal factor in plausibility is not precise correspondence with known facts but inner consistency in the story itself.

Drama also requires plausibility, but in drama it must be conveyed not by a narrator but by the actors' ability to make the audience "believe in" their speech, movement, thoughts, and feelings. This plausibility is based on the connection between the impression made by the actors and the preconceptions of the auditors. If the character Hamlet is to be plausible, the actor must make his audience believe that Hamlet could conceivably be as he is presented. This does not mean that the actor must make his audience believe that he literally is Hamlet; merely that he is plausibly and consistently making-believe to be Hamlet. The aim of a performance is not to persuade spectators that a palpable fiction is fact, that they are "really" there, out on those bitterly cold battlements of Hamlet's castle at Elsinore. Indeed, they are far more free to appreciate the play and to think about it if they are not "really" present. Knowing all the time that it is a figment, they are willing to enter into the make-believe, to be transported, if it is sufficiently convincing. Yet they know that, however thrilling or pleasurable the rapture, it may be shattered at any moment by some ineptitude or mistake on the stage or by a coughing neighbour in the audience.

Factors in dramatic plausibility

The rapture is sustained by an inner consistency in the performance, as long as the rules of the game are kept. The actor must not behave, even for a second, in such a way as to betray the audience's belief; for it is this sympathetic concentration by the audience that makes his performance possible.

That is the basic rule, or convention, of the make-believe of the theatre. The actor breaks the basic rule of the game if he forgets his words, or laughs at private jokes, or is simply incompetent, or is unsuited to his part. No audience can accept a vulgar, lumpish, elderly Hamlet, because Hamlet is a young prince whose lines are consistently thoughtful and witty. Yet it is not necessary that the actor playing Hamlet should "really" be all these things; he need only give the impression of being princely, witty, elegant, and young enough to sustain the credulity of the people sharing the make-believe.

Thus, in every performance there must be realism in some degree. At certain epochs and in certain kinds of play the aim has been to be as realistic as possible. In the early years of the 20th century, productions of the Moscow Art Theatre and of the Abbey Theatre in Dublin exemplified this aim to a high degree. But even the most realistic production, *e.g.*, Anton Chekhov's play *The Cherry Orchard* in Konstantin Stanislavsky's production at Moscow, made immense concessions to theatrical artifice. Conversation in real life often leads nowhere; it is full of vaguely inconclusive, meaningless, boring passages. It does not necessarily attempt, as every word in Chekhov's play must, to fit into a story, to be part of the expression of a theme, or to introduce and reveal a group of characters.

Degrees of realism in performance

Extreme realism continued to be a goal in theatre until the advent of motion pictures. Just as realistic painting declined when photographs achieved similar effects mechanically, so did staging that attempted to reproduce the actual world in every detail decline when such effects became commonplace in films.

Though most commercial, light comedies continue to be written and acted as realistically as possible, realistic theatre fell out of fashion in the first half of the 20th century as much as realistic painting. The most extravagantly unrealistic productions, however, inevitably retained certain quite realistic features; the actors still must be recognizably human, no matter how fantastic the script and settings may be.

Theatre as social expression. In different contexts, different aspects of humanity have seemed important and have therefore been stressed in theatrical representation. Renaissance drama, for instance, emphasized the individuality of each character, while in 17th-century theatre, which was much more restricted in its philosophy and in its setting, man was presented not as a creature proclaiming his unique importance in the universe but rather as one adapted to the quite limited environment of 17th-century society. The greatness of the Elizabethan theatre was the universality of its outlook and the breadth of its appeal; these have never been regained. Since the latter part of the 17th century the art of the theatre has been concerned with smaller themes and has aimed at a smaller section of society.

Upper-class characters of 17th–19th-century drama

From the 17th to the 19th centuries, the theatre's principal leading characters were persons of breeding and position; the "lower classes" only appeared as servants and dependents, mostly presented in terms of low comedy. Rustics were almost automatically ridiculous, although sometimes their simplicity might be shown as endearing or pathetic. The 17th-century plays of Molière are a good deal more egalitarian than English plays of similar date, or even of a century later; but even Molière never allowed the audience to forget that his plays were about, and for, persons of high station. A very clear line is drawn between employers and employed, and the latter, though often more intelligent, never seem to belong to quite the same species.

By the early 19th century the theatre had become more democratic, or at all events, more middle class. As far back as Oliver Goldsmith's *The Good-Natured Man* (first performed 1768) and *She Stoops to Conquer* (1773), the principal characters were persons of upper middle class rather than aristocrats. By the middle of the 19th century the whole European theatre had become at least as much a middle class as an aristocratic entertainment. Nevertheless, it was still thought important, especially in London, that the actors should suggest gentility. George Bernard Shaw in *Our Theatres in the Nineties* remarked that to be employed in a good production it was far less important that a young actor be talented than that he speak "well" and be beautifully dressed. The plays that succeeded throughout Europe were plays about men and women of good social position and the plots were concerned with some infringement, usually sexual, of the genteel code of behaviour: *The Second Mrs. Tanqueray* (1893) by Arthur Wing Pinero is an example.

After the Russian Revolution of 1917 the Soviet theatre made a clean break with gentility. The heroes and heroines of Soviet theatre were the splendid, muscular, idealistic workers; elegance, wit, and good tailoring were considered symptoms of decadence. In western Europe, however, gentility continued between the two world wars, the 1920s and the 1930s, to be the dominant aim of the fashionable theatre. In New York it received a setback at the time of the economic Depression of the 1930s. At a famous series of productions at the New York Group Theatre, a director, Harold Clurman, was in conscious revolt against the oppressive bourgeois gentility of the day. The theatre was not spectacularly successful, however, and stayed in existence for no more than a few years.

In Europe it was not until after World War II ended in 1945 that deep changes in social structure became apparent. By the 1950s the theatre everywhere was making efforts to reflect and to interest a wider section of society. By that time, however, audiences at all levels had lost the habit of theatregoing and were fast losing the habit of moviegoing, as television was becoming the popular medium of drama—indeed, of all entertainment. Theatre began to be directed not to any one class in society or to any one income group, but rather toward anyone who was prepared for the energetic collaboration in the creative act that the art demands.

ELEMENTS OF THEATRE

The theatrical hierarchy. Theatrical art demands the collaboration of the actors with one another, with a director, with the various technical workers upon whom they depend for costumes, scenery and lighting, and with the business people who finance, organize, advertise, and sell the product.

Collaboration among so many types of personnel presupposes a hierarchy. In the commercial theatre the most powerful person is usually the producer (American parlance), or manager (British parlance). He is responsible for acquiring the investment that finances the production. The rehearsal of the play is conducted by the director (American parlance), or producer (British parlance), who is responsible for interpreting the script, for casting, and for scenery and costumes. Under his general direction a stage manager, possibly with several assistants, looks after the organization of rehearsal and the technical side of the performance—light and curtain cues, properties, sound effects, and so on.

Producers, managers, and directors

Naturally, the hierarchy varies somewhat in different circumstances. In the National Theatre of Great Britain, for example, the apex of the pyramid is an artistic director, who is more concerned with guiding the policy of the theatre than with details of administration or the preparation of any single production—though he may, of course, also assume responsibility for the preparation of a number of productions.

An art that involves the close cooperation of so many people can scarcely express the views of all participants. A novel or a painting may bear the unmistakable hallmark of its authorship, but no work of theatrical art can be other than a compromise.

The dominant expression so far as the audience can tell is nearly always that of the actor with the most important part. It may, therefore, be wondered why theatres are no longer dominated by actor-managers, as they were in 19th-century London, where Sir Henry Irving managed the Lyceum for 21 years (1878–99) as its artistic director, administrator, producer-director, and leading actor. Since Irving's day theatrical business has become infinitely more costly and complicated. Budgets in Irving's time were only one-tenth as large; and he had no aggressive trade unions to deal with; and taxes were very much lower and less complex than in the 1970s.

Also, although the leading actor seems completely to dominate the performance, he is often only a mouthpiece; the words he speaks so splendidly were written by somebody else; the tailor and wigmaker must take some credit for his appearance; that he should play the part at all was usually not his own idea but that of a producer or director.

Even before the actors assemble for the first rehearsal, the producer, director, and designer, and—if he is available—the author, have conferred on many important decisions, such as the casting and the design of scenery and clothes. The capacity of the theatre that is selected determines the budget and therefore the scale of the production. Certainly the most lively part of the work still lies in the period of rehearsal, but much of it has been predetermined before it begins.

Although it might be supposed that the author would be the best person to direct a play, he usually is not, for several reasons. First, authors are apt to love their brainchildren not wisely but too well; and, like most parents, are not usually the most impartial judges of their character and quality. Also, authors rarely combine a knowledge of their own craft with a good working knowledge of the quite different craft of direction. Finally, the authors of many plays are dead or unavailable.

Role of the playwright

The role of the audience. It is partly because it is a collaborative art, involving so much compromise, that the theatre seems often to lag behind other arts, expressing dated views in a dated manner. There is another reason too: the theatre depends more than most arts upon audience response. If the house is not full, not only does the performance lose money, it loses force. It is unusual for new ideas, even for new ways of expressing old ideas, to be popular. With few exceptions, people apparently do not go to the theatre to receive new ideas; they want the thrilling, amusing, or moving expression of old ones.

If a performance is going well, the members of its audience tend to subordinate their separate identities to that of the crowd. This phenomenon can be observed not only at the theatre, but at concerts, bullfights, and prizefights. The crowd personality is never as intelligent as the sum of its members' intelligence, and it is much more emotional. Intelligent members of an audience lose, to an extraordinary degree, their powers of independent, rational thought; instead, unexpected reserves of passion come into play. Laughter becomes infectious; grave and solid citizens, as members of an audience, can be rendered helpless with mirth by jests that would leave them unmoved if they were alone.

This being the case, theatre audiences are virtually incapable of an intellectual consideration of the ideas presented to them unless those ideas are already familiar. Familiar ideas can be received effortlessly while the emotional or thrilling or amusing aspects of the presentation are enjoyed. This is why the effectiveness of a theatrical performance never depends solely upon the excellence of a text. It is also why the excellence of theatre is so difficult to convey in cold prose after the event. Irving's most thrilling performance was not in any of the many great plays in which he appeared but in *The Bells*, a script of negligible literary quality. Similarly, Laurence Olivier's performance as Shakespeare's *Richard III* was more exciting than his performances in many superior works of Shakespeare. Theatrical art succeeds to the degree that excitement is engendered in the audience, a factor that is unrelated to the intellectual merits of the text.

The effect of theatre structure. From the 17th century to the 20th century, few dreamed of building a theatre in other than the now traditional, proscenium style. This style consists of a horseshoe auditorium in several tiers facing the stage, from which it is divided by an arch—the proscenium—which supports the curtain. Behind the closed curtain, the backstage machinery facilitates quick changes of illusionistic scenery. This type of theatre was developed for Italian opera in the 17th century. It is ironic that opera, the least naturalistic of theatrical forms, should have given birth to the proscenium theatre, the stronghold of theatrical illusion. From its introduction, productions of plays of all themes have tended to exploit the audience's pleasure in its dollhouse realism.

The proscenium theatre separates the audience from the performers, not only by the proscenium arch but also by the footlights and by the pit holding the orchestra. In the theatres of Elizabethan England, the actors performed in the very midst of their audience. Their theatre had evolved from the courtyards of inns, in which a raised platform was erected for a stage. Some members of the audience stood around it while others watched from windows and galleries surrounding the inn yard.

In the early years of the 20th century, the English actor-manager William Poel suggested that Shakespeare should be staged so as to relate the performers and the audience as they had been on the Elizabethan stage. His ideas slowly gained in influence and, in 1953, the Shakespearean Festival Theatre at Stratford, Ontario, was built with just such an "open" stage, with no curtain, and with the audience sitting on three sides of it. A considerable success, it had a strong influence on subsequent theatre design.

It could no longer be taken for granted that the opera house with a proscenium was the right way to build a theatre. The open stage proved suitable not only for Elizabethan plays but for a wide repertoire. Probably it will never completely replace the proscenium, which remains more suitable for the countless plays that were written with such a stage in mind, such as the comedies of

The dominance of the proscenium

Advantages of the "open" stage

Molière or the highly artificial comedies of Richard Brinsley Sheridan and Oscar Wilde. On the other hand, the more realistic plays of Ibsen, Shaw, and Chekhov, all written for the proscenium theatre, lend themselves very well to the open stage.

There are three solid reasons for preferring the open stage. First, more people can be accommodated in a given cubic space if arranged around the stage instead of just in front of it. This is important not merely for the economic advantage of a larger capacity but also for artistic reasons —the closely packed audience generates more concentration and excitement.

A second reason for preferring the open stage is that the actors are nearer to more of their audience and can therefore be better heard and seen. This point is contested by adherents of the proscenium stage, who claim that the actor at any given moment must have his back turned to a large part of the house and, as a result, must be more difficult to see and hear. If the open stage is used efficiently, however, the actor's back will never be turned to anyone for more than a few seconds at a time.

The third reason is that members of an audience seated all around the stage are far more aware of the presence of the others than is the case in an opera house. The performance thereby is appreciated more as an event jointly shared and created by the audience and the actors.

The proscenium has come to be associated so closely with creating "illusion" that it has led to a misconception about the function of drama, and a misdirection of the energies of dramatists, players, and audiences. The single-minded attempt by the actors to create, or by the audience to undergo, illusion, reduces drama to a form of deception.

The art of the theatre is concerned with something more significant than creating the illusion that a series of quite obviously contrived events are "really" happening. *King Lear* is far more complex and interesting than that. Art is concerned not with deception but with enlightenment. The painter's art helps its audience to see and the musician's art helps it to hear in a more enlightened way: Rembrandt and Bach are trying not to deceive their audiences but to express and to share their deepest thoughts and feelings. Similarly, the art of the theatre is concerned with expressing the most profound thoughts and feelings of the performers about the story they are enacting, so that the audience may partake in this ritual event.

The influence of writing and scholarship. Like the other arts, the theatre has been the subject of a great deal of theoretical and philosophical writing, as well as criticism, both of a journalistic and of a less ephemeral character. Members of the theatrical profession have probably been influenced by the work of scholars and theorists more than they realize. Scholarship has made Shakespeare's work, for example, far more intelligible and coherent. On the other hand, many of the scholarly debates over small points seem irrelevant in the theatre.

A commendable example of scholarship is the emendation of Mrs. Quickly's description of Falstaff's death in Shakespeare's *Henry V* (Act II, Scene 3), from "a table of green fields," which, in the context, seems unintelligible, to "a [*i.e.*, he] babbled of green fields," which is not only comprehensible but touching. But it scarcely alters the way in which an actress will speak this phrase. It is one descriptive phrase among five or six others relating his fumbling with the sheets, playing with flowers, and smiling at his fingers' ends. It may be the greatest description of the moment of death in all literature; in the course of performance, however, an audience does not follow even so great a passage as this word by word.

A compelling actor playing Hamlet can ask whether 'tis nobler in the mind to suffer the "eggs and bacon" of outrageous fortune and few will be aware that he has not said "slings and arrows." And if Mrs. Quickly says "a table of green fields" with good accent and discretion, the musical flow and emotional effect of this marvellous speech will hardly be diminished.

Similarly, the highly respected English scholar Dover Wilson speculates whether Hamlet's too, too "solid" flesh ought rather to be read "sullied." The arguments have

Interaction
between
scholars
and
actors

little force in theatre because audiences can scarcely distinguish whether the actor has, in fact, said "solid" or "sullied."

The scholars and the theatre professionals live almost completely segregated from each other. Dover Wilson went to his first professional rehearsal when he was well over 70 and professed himself surprised at the illumination the actors seemed intuitively to bring to points that were obscure when regarded as solely literary conundrums. Conversely, the actors found he could give extremely useful advice and information about the meaning of certain passages and other matters relevant to their work.

Much journalistic criticism is marred by the difficulties imposed upon a writer who wants to be just without being dull. Justice demands reason and moderation, but such qualities are often less interesting to read than high-coloured opinion.

George Bernard Shaw was perhaps the greatest theatrical and musical critic in the English language, but he is again and again betrayed, in the pursuit of readership, into exaggeration, prejudiced partisanship, and facile jokes at the expense of actors' deficiencies, as in his *Our Theatres in the Nineties* (1931).

THE PLACE OF THEATRE IN CONTEMPORARY LIFE

Work, leisure, and theatre. There have been widely different opinions as to what the aim of the theatre should be. Some have insisted that it have a serious purpose; others regard it merely as a medium of entertainment; and still others see no reason why it should not be simultaneously entertaining and serious.

In general, mankind has regarded as serious the activities that help him to survive and to propagate his species —feeding and sheltering himself and his family. At all levels of sophistication, however, mankind's serious pursuits offer opportunities for entertainment. All of man's tools—whether made of bone, stone, iron, or bronze in the early stages of his development, or the ox, horse, steam engine, and atomic power in later stages—not only make his work easier or more efficient but also afford a means of self-expression. The ablest members of the human species have never made a clear-cut distinction between work and play. The best workers enjoy their work, be it surgery, carpentry, housework, or fieldwork. They engage themselves in work that permits, even demands, an expression of their invention and ingenuity. Indeed, the most valuable workers are not the most strenuous but the most ingenious and resourceful; and as their tasks increase in complexity and responsibility, the need for intelligence and imagination increases. These qualities will also be expressed in the play of such people.

In the times and places in which theatre has become frivolous or vulgar or merely dull, intelligent and imaginative people have stayed away from it. This was the case in London during the first half of the 19th century. There was very little significant writing for the theatre; Charles Dickens and William Makepeace Thackeray, whose talents were to a considerable degree histrionic, chose to write novels rather than plays. A similar movement away from the theatre by the intelligentsia occurred in New York City in the middle of the 20th century, as fewer and fewer serious productions were undertaken.

Of the many theories and philosophies propounded about the purposes of theatrical art, from the *Poetics* of Aristotle onward, most presuppose that the theatre is directed towards an elite consisting of the wealthier, more leisured, and better educated members of a community. In these theories, popular theatre is assumed to be noisily cheerful and egregiously sentimental, with very easy tunes, obvious jokes, and plenty of knockabout "business." In the 20th century, however, the distinctions between social classes have become progressively more blurred.

Egalitarian manners became fashionable, indeed obligatory; and the theories that gave serious art a role exclusively for the upper classes lost much of their force.

Thus, the theatre has come to face a dilemma: it has become necessary for it to re-examine the purposes of its existence. Paradoxically, while more people are enjoying more leisure than ever before, there has not been a proportional increase in theatrical attendance. Those engaged in the professions or employed in a managerial capacity, unlike the aristocrats of earlier times, generally allow themselves little leisure time. Of those engaged in industry, whose leisure time has increased, the enormous majority are engaged in dull and repetitive tasks that leave them tired and apathetic at the end of the day. Comparatively few make imaginative, intelligent, and decisive use of their leisure.

The
dilemma
of the
contem-
porary
theatre

The theatre's efforts to appeal to the whole community generally have been futile. There exists an ever-widening gulf: on one side, a small, enthusiastic, and highly vocal minority clamours for art galleries, symphony concerts, and drama; on the other, the vast majority is apathetic to such serious art.

The necessity for subsidies. A serious theatre, with or without massive public attendance, must be sustained by other financial support. Public funds have been used for this purpose throughout Europe and in much of Asia. The assumption behind such a subsidy is the realistic one that a serious theatre is now too costly to pay its way.

In Great Britain in 1940, under the threat of imminent invasion in World War II, the government took the first steps toward subsidizing theatre by guaranteeing a tour of the Old Vic Theatre against loss. Subsequently, its support of theatre increased continually, to the sum of millions of pounds annually.

In governmental support of the arts, the United States lagged considerably behind most of the civilized world. Until the middle of the 20th century, private patronage was still the sole support of legitimate theatre. With few exceptions, however, professional theatrical management in the United States has been strictly a commercial business. Its record has been blotted by numerous instances of greed and irresponsibility and an absence of a longer view than immediate personal advantage. Unions have sometimes pressed demands that have made professional theatrical production economically difficult.

Academic theatre. A significant new factor on the contemporary scene is the theatrical activity conducted by the universities with departments of drama. Their theatres, often handsomer and better equipped than professional houses, present plays of all sorts. Millions of people attend performances in university theatres each year, and the academic theatre is beginning to compete with the professional theatre for audiences. In serious planning and choice of programs its standards are far superior to professional theatre, since the aim is educational. The standard of performance is more debatable. Unfortunately, many leading parts, whether in classics or in potboilers, call for assured and authoritative actors, between 35 and 50 years of age. Academic theatre, therefore, is handicapped at the outset by the immaturity of most of its student-actors, though professional actors are sometimes hired for special productions or to become actors-in-residence.

Problems
of
academic
theatre

A more serious drawback is that the direction of drama departments and of university theatres is often entrusted not to theatre men but to academics, chosen in most instances for scholarly rather than theatrical distinction. Furthermore, most college theatres operate on extremely low budgets, and, while money without taste and intelligence cannot create good theatre, taste and intelligence without money can seldom do so either. The highest standards can, in certain instances, be achieved by sheer ingenuity, but, in general, shoestring budgets result in that desperate air of "making do"—almost a trademark of academic theatre.

It is a common error in universities to suppose that the mere production of a masterpiece must amount to an educational experience for players and audience alike. It is not so. Incompetent acting and direction can reduce the greatest masterpiece to suffocating, excruciating tedium. Moreover, in many schools, the theatre must be economically self-supporting, and each season one of the successful Broadway musicals of yesteryear is put on to redeem the losses incurred by Shakespeare, Molière, and O'Neill.

In Britain, the universities still, with few exceptions, take the view that theatrical art has no place in a university curriculum. If university students want to act, they must join a club and act in their spare time. The universities that do have theatre departments, such as Manchester and Bristol, aim to teach not professional skills but theatrical history, criticism, and theory.

The diminishing audience. In Great Britain, government subsidy has been made available to the National Theatre of Great Britain and the Royal Shakespeare Company, two institutions offering a predominantly classical program; to the Royal Court Theatre in London, producing new and experimental work; and to resident companies in most of the principal cities outside London. These companies present serious programs and play to excellent houses. In the short time since their establishment (mostly in the 1960s) they have created a revolution in the quality both of theatregoing and of theatrical organization. Still, there is a gulf between theatre audiences and the masses, and, more and more, theatre becomes a "mandarin" activity, designed for the edification of a select few.

In the communist world there is far less contrast between mandarin and popular art. In the Soviet Union the statistics of popular interest in art and literature are very impressive, but the level of creative work is kept low by censorship. Artistic creation is compelled to conform to party policy; and the political machinery often manipulates popular opinion. In the theatre, success can sometimes be assured to productions that are politically acceptable, denied to those that are not.

In both the East and the West tremendous efforts are being made towards more fruitful use of the leisure time that technology has made available. By the second half of the 20th century, theatre had become a regular leisure-time activity only to a small minority. Although the civilized world generally regarded a serious theatre as an essential activity, deserving of public support, the mere existence of an intelligent and imaginative theatre does not ensure such support. This can probably be achieved only by profound changes of belief concerning the purpose not merely of theatre but of human existence.

Prospects. It is not unreasonable to suppose that, by the end of the 20th century, the live theatre could cease to exist, in which case movies and television or possibly television alone would hold the dramatic field. In television, it is possible to anticipate not only many technical improvements—larger, less wobbly and distorted pictures, more subtle and credible colour—but, more important, an improvement in the method of distribution and the material that is distributed, including the widespread use of video cassettes. There may even be a demand for something more intellectually ambitious and spiritually nourishing than currently popular programs.

Another negative factor is the declining number of people with professional theatrical experience. Most of those who have furthered the art of theatre—actors, directors, managers, technicians—grew up in the theatre; even many of those who now devote most of their time and earn most of their money in movies and television spent their most impressionable years on the stage. Among the generations arising since World War II, however, there has been very much less theatrical experience and little interest in whether the theatre survives or not. As the years pass, fewer and fewer people, not just among the professionals but lay people as well, will have seen a play acted by live actors at a level higher than school or college theatricals.

Two factors, however, contribute to the perpetuation of theatre. First, there are the theatrical classics themselves, the classic dramas of different epochs and different cultures such as Racine's *Phèdre* (1677), Molière's *Le Tartuffe* (1664), Congreve's *Love for Love* (1695), Ibsen's *Peer Gynt* (published 1867), Shaw's *Saint Joan* (1923) —the instances could be multiplied countless times without exhausting the great works of the human spirit. Such works were written for the stage and can only be given full expression by stage representation.

Adaptations for the screen or television of material that was conceived in terms of the stage remain merely adaptations. If the original is a work of genius, the adaptation must seem presumptuously inadequate. It is possible that the adaptation of some stage pieces may excel the original: Puccini's opera *Madama Butterfly* is a more important work than the play by David Belasco from which it was adapted. But it can hardly be argued that Laurence Olivier's film adaptations of Shakespeare's *Henry V, Hamlet, Richard III,* or *Othello* were equal to the original stage productions. These films were justified in that thousands of people, who would not otherwise have had the opportunity, saw the adapted plays magnificently performed. The texts were necessarily garbled and hashed, however, and the acting and direction were adapted to suit a medium for which the originals were not conceived. Some part of the public will always believe that it is as important to see fine performances of theatrical masterworks as to see the originals of great achievements in painting, sculpture, and architecture, rather than mere photographic reproductions. As long as this is the case, there is a good reason for the continued existence of a live theatre.

The second reason for believing in the survival of theatre is that the live theatre can achieve a sense of occasion impossible for canned events. This sense of occasion is a heightening of everyday people and occurrences into a new vividness and significance: not just the heightening of characters and events of the drama but also a heightening of the people who take part, spectators as much as performers.

This can occur more effectively if the occasion is a great one, if the house is large and full, if the audience appears to be distinguished, and if celebrated performers are taking part. But the sense of occasion can be achieved more simply, more subtly, and less expensively. What matters is that, when the performance begins, the audience should be excited, receptive, and ready.

A live theatrical performance has a built-in sense of occasion. A first night at the Comèdie Française, the Bolshoi, the National Theatre in London, the Metropolitan Opera in New York, draws some hundreds of national figures, pacesetters in different fields. This is one of the things that the motion pictures aimed at but failed to achieve in any lasting way with their gala premieres. Yet the heart of the occasion lies not in the auditorium, however bedizened with celebrity, but on the stage. There, a troupe is about to create either a new work or a new interpretation of a classic. The sense of occasion is at its strongest when the cast is distinguished; but even unknown players in obscure performances can create it.

Activity is required of the theatre audience if the performance is to succeed; the audience is required to share with the performer, to assist him in the act of creation.

In films and in television, mistakes can be eliminated, unsuccessful scenes can be reshot, even rewritten, the whole work can be manipulated, edited, titivated, and set before the public with every detail in its proper place. The product has been prefabricated without the cooperation of its ultimate audience, which is therefore reduced to the status of a mere consumer.

In the theatre, on the other hand, every audience helps to create or to destroy the performance. To some extent, audiences get the performance they deserve.

Moreover, in every live performance is the imminence of disaster. An actor must be skilful and an audience must be imaginative if Macbeth, seeing a phantom dagger in the air, or Othello, falling down in an epileptic fit, is to be moving and impressive instead of merely ludicrous. Yet it is precisely this hairbreadth division between the sublime and the ridiculous that creates the sense of occasion.

Some dozens of immortally great expressions of the human spirit have been written for performance by live actors for live audiences and cannot be adequately experienced in any other medium. This is why, in spite of economic difficulties, in spite of far smaller technical resources and far greater distributive problems, the live theatre must survive. (T.G.)

BIBLIOGRAPHY. Few works have dealt extensively with the aesthetics of theatre as a body of knowledge or theory

Adaptations for the screen or television

The participating audience

unrelated to particular productions, schools of playwriting, or historical periods. Most philosophical writings or manifestoes—those of Aristotle, Castelvetro, and Victor Hugo, for example—deal almost entirely with the form and content of dramatic literature, though they have had great impact on all aspects of theatre over long periods of time. Notable modern exceptions are ANTONIN ARTAUD, *Le Théâtre et son double* (1938; Eng. trans., *The Theatre and Its Double*, 1958), which considers theatre in its broadest implications and has had enormous influence on avant-garde theatre since World War II; and JERZY GROTOWSKI, *Towards a Poor Theatre* (1968), an elucidation of personal artistic values by a director-teacher whose Polish Laboratory Theatre has been among the most controversial and innovative theatrical phenomena of the century. The ideas of one of this century's most important playwrights and directors emerge in *Brecht on Theatre: The Development of an Aesthetic*, ed. and trans. by JOHN WILLETT (1964). Perceptive analyses of aesthetic points of view represented in theatrical production include: MORDECAI GORELIK, *New Theatres for Old* (1940, reprinted 1962), a classic work on staging and design that covers the late 19th century and first four decades of the 20th; G.B. SHAW, *Our Theatre in the Nineties*, 3 vol. (1932), an incisive contemporary view of drama in the 1890s; and the writings of such major 20th-century critics as Harley Granville-Barker, Stark Young, and George Jean Nathan. Personal histories by leading theoreticians and practitioners, including KONSTANTIN STANISLAVSKY, *My Life in Art*, trans. from the Russian (1924, reprinted 1956); and HAROLD CLURMAN, *The Fervent Years* (1957), carry implicit commentaries on the art of theatre. Stanislavsky's *An Actor Prepares*, trans. from the Russian (1936, reprinted 1956); and T. COLE (comp.), *Acting: A Handbook of the Stanislavski Method*, rev. ed. (1957), though specialized, develop aesthetic points of view that have underlain much of the theatrical production in the West during the 20th century. A classic study of theatre in terms of its aesthetic intentions is contained in FRANCIS FERGUSSON, *The Idea of a Theatre* (1949), while PETER BROOK, *The Empty Space* (1968), is a brilliant analysis of theatrical values as they are manifested in such diverse areas as commercialized drama, the popular or "rough" theatre, and the dedicated avant-garde or "holy" theatre. An overview—outdated but still singular—of the many different forms and aesthetic conditions of Oriental theatre is contained in FAUBION BOWERS, *Theatre in the East* (1956). Discussions of the conditions under which theatrical forms have emerged appear in many anthropological works, including SIR JAMES FRAZER, *The Golden Bough*, 3rd ed., 12 vol. (1907–15), and those of Margaret Mead and others. Finally, such periodicals as *The Drama Review* (formerly, *Tulane Drama Review)* and the defunct *Theatre Arts* contain important reportorial, critical, and philosophical writing on theatre both as an artistic and a social expression. The entertainment sections of *The New York Times* and other journals often contain important analytical commentary or deliberately arranged clashes of aesthetic points of view toward theatre.

Theatre, Western

This article is divided into the following sections:

I. The origins of Western theatre

PRECLASSICAL ANTIQUITY

Religious ritual. *Imitation.* Drama as an art form emerged at a comparatively late stage in man's cultural evolution, but it is generally believed to have had its roots in primitive religious ritual, and there are patterns in the behaviour of primitive societies that can justifiably be called pre-theatrical. These patterns indicate something of the psychology of peoples standing face to face with what was mysterious and unknown in their environment, and they reveal an attempt to establish some sort of contact with those sources of power in nature that seemed most hurtful and destructive—violent phenomena such as excessive heat, cold, drought, fire, and flood. Backed up by ceremonies of propitiation, involving first human and later animal sacrifices, the rituals such peoples undertook were an appeal, made to deities supposed to control the various elements, for assistance or protection. Ritual activity was at first confined to simple imitation, either of the phenomena themselves or of objects observed to be associated with them: the consuming power of fire, for example, was sought through the ashes and the secret of fertility through evergreens. The rhythms of nature, as seen in the movement of the wind or of the sea, were simulated in the dance.

Transfiguration. Of special interest is the early use of masks and other ritual disguises to aid imitation, to fortify pretense. The imagination that could give rise to such a notion was already active by the Lower Paleolithic Period, because ancient cave paintings that date from this time (such as those that are to be seen at Lascaux in southern France) depict dancers who are half human, half beast. Persons involved directly in the celebration of the rite wore the forms of nature or emblems associated with the god to whom appeal was being made. A state of heightened emotional awareness was achieved by the frenzy of the dance, and in many of the primary rites it was supposed that the god took possession of the dancer at the height of his ecstasy. This was transfiguration rather than simple imitation. Among many tribes and peoples the priest, magician, or medicine man would employ special effects—smokes, smells, incantations, and the like—to achieve the desired trancelike state. Meanwhile, others would participate in the rite by forming processions, by executing certain steps and rhythms, or by clapping and perhaps by chanting. They thus assisted in the transformation, though they themselves were not transformed.

The role of the dance

Solemn and grotesque rites. Two basically different types of rite were celebrated: the solemn and the grotesque. Both had the effect of evoking terror, prompting the fear that arises when facing the inconceivable or utterly unknown. The solemn rites were part of a rigid tradition that had been evolved and handed down from generation to generation, and young members of the people or tribe were initiated into the rites step by step. A cultural system thus found coherence and protection by institutionalizing itself: not to observe the tradition was thought to bring about misfortune. The solemn rites were mainly an embodiment of death—the fear that is commonest among all individuals—and were attempts to ward off its evil. They chiefly concerned those elements of nature in which rebirth noticeably follows upon death—that is, on the solstices and seasons—and this fact accounts for the most persistent of all early theatrical imitations, the ritual slaying of the god of fertility (winter) and his subsequent resurrection (spring). Solemn rites were further concerned with propitiation for past misdemeanours or for assistance in future struggles.

The grotesque rites, on the other hand, were in the main evolved to give thanks for assistance received. Their celebration called for spontaneous reactions, and they were to a great extent impromptu. They were not marked by a coherent narrative pattern but were expressions of joy, and their most remarkable characteristic was, simply, excess. Whereas the solemn rites can be said to be the forerunner of Western tragedy, which has always tended to preserve some links with its religious origins, the grotesque rites led to secularized farces and, eventually, to the other two major dramatic genres in Western theatre, comedy and satire play.

ANCIENT NEAR EASTERN AND EGYPTIAN CIVILIZATIONS

The transition (which is still taking place in parts of the world in the 20th century) from tribal communities toward a society organized by the division of labour has imposed enormous strains, both physical and psychological, on man. It has, however, challenged all of the arts to serve not merely as a means of man's self-expression but also to become an integral part of his cultures as they evolve.

In ancient cultures, the gods were still thought of as more or less concrete, real authorities—a conception of their deity reflected in the various social and political structures that were set up, at first by a system in which the king was regarded as "chosen" by the god, and afterward by a system in which he was regarded (in Egypt) as the god himself. Only much later was there a "twilight of the gods" to rob them of their legislative power. Even then, other authorities had to be evoked, since something approaching a godlike supremacy was thought necessary to uphold a civilization. Extreme alternatives were dictatorship and anarchy, but there was also the possibility of the individual's being encouraged to participate in the evolution of society and being given the political means to do so. At all times theatre, as a community celebration and activity, has played an important part in this evolution, sometimes directly, sometimes simply by reflecting political change and development.

Mesopotamia. There is evidence of a Sumerian civilization dating from at least 3000 BC. The Sumerians, who were originally from the Caucasus, occupied Mesopotamia (the land lying between the rivers Tigris and Euphrates) and established city states there, with palaces and temples. Each city had its own god, whose priests were of great importance and influence in the community. The Sumerians' chief religious festival was that of the New Year, celebrated in the autumn and the spring with rituals symbolizing the peoples' hope that winter (when the god of fertility was dead) would not last forever and that the coming year would be prosperous. During the 1st Ur dynasty (c. 2650–2500 BC) a new custom was introduced at the spring festival, and it might well be a reflection of a constitutional change: a popular king ruled the city for a day, a lord of misrule—the custom later reappeared in Christian times, when the usual power structures were turned upside down for one day on the Feast

Sumerians' New Year festival

of the Holy Innocents—and on this occasion the high priest would also ritually slap the real king's face.

The Babylonian civilization borrowed wholesale the culture of the Sumerians and elaborated upon it, so that by the time of Nebuchadrezzar I (1124–1103 BC) the New Year was being celebrated in Babylon by most splendid processions, by a recitation of the myth of creation, and by pantomimic performances. Here, clearly, are signs of a germinating theatrical activity.

Egypt. There is much similarity between Egyptian and Mesopotamian mythologies and between the ways their civilizations developed. Because of the necessity of controlling the waters of the Nile, the two regions eventually became one kingdom, and Egyptian myths retained many characteristics that had belonged to the earlier Mesopotamian civilizations. To the early peoples inhabiting the region, a "god" was the spirit of the tribe, and for each there was a different god, taking an animal form—for one the falcon, for another the pig, and so on. This primitive belief later found expression in the animal-headed gods of Egypt: Horus the falcon headed, Thoth the ibis headed. The Egyptian pharaohs were not regarded as chosen by the god, they were thought to be the god himself. While alive, the pharaoh was the god Horus; after his death he was transformed into the god Osiris. Thus the myths relating to Osiris and Horus came to be especially important.

Since the end of the 18th century Egyptologists have sought to interpret the significance of what are known as the Pyramid Texts. These were found written on the inside walls of the pyramids, and the earliest dates from the 5th dynasty (c. 2494–c. 2345 BC). In 1882 it was suggested for the first time that these texts should be called dramas. Some scholars further suggested that priests, wearing animal masks, had given performances of the texts in the tombs and buildings attached to the pyramids. These views were much disputed, but there is more general agreement that one of them, known as the Abydos passion play, really was performed, though many prefer to regard it as expanded ritual rather than as drama. Its subject is the death and dismemberment of the god Osiris and the reassembling of his scattered limbs by his wife, the goddess Isis, and their son, Horus. No text survives, but there is an account left by a court official that describes a presentation of the play for which he was responsible between 1887 and 1849 BC.

The Pyramid Texts

GREECE

Greek drama originated in the festivals of the nature god Dionysus (who was particularly associated with the vine, the bull, and the goat), whose cult originally had gone to Greece from Egypt by such paths as trade routes. The great Dionysia festival at Athens, where the important theatrical events took place, was very much a religious festival. It is generally accepted that drama emerged from the ritual celebrations of religious festivals, but the steps by which it did so are not fully understood.

Dramatic genres. The classical Greek theatre divided drama into tragedy, comedy, and satyr play; there were dramatic masterpieces in each of the genres. The size and shape of theatre buildings were also a new concept largely influenced by Greek developments, while actors in character roles were separated from actors who commented, as a chorus, on the unfolding story, the latter being intermediaries, as it were, between audience and protagonist. Another feature was the use of strongly characterized masks worn by the actors. Early tragedy (originating at Athens in 534–531 BC and named after a connection with Greek *tragos*, "goat": that is, tragedy either originated as a song with a goat as prize or as a song connected with a goat's sacrifice) had a single actor–chorus–audience pattern like religious ritual's priest–initiates–congregation one. The parallel is reinforced by themes and structures of the earliest surviving plays, for tragedy dealt with the universe's moral regulation in a serious, formal way. The tragic poet was required to submit three tragedies on the same myth, along with a satyr play (a burlesque of the myth) to the festival competition. The only complete satyr play to sur-

Chorus in Greek drama

vive is Euripides' *Cyclops*. Comedy (from Greek *kōmos*: revel) developed later, its origins in spontaneous thanks to Dionysus for the fertility that aided agriculture.

Drama as a whole developed a tendency to occupy itself with more human, immediate concerns as time went on, and it has been argued that tragedy was formed, ennobled itself, and then lost its vigour while Athens was doing the same thing in its political life. Comedy began as broad political satire (old comedy), developed into social satire (middle comedy), and then developed into a comedy of manners with stereotyped characters in plots dependent on intrigue and situation. The only extant Greek tragedies are the collective 35 plays of Aeschylus, Sophocles, and Euripides. Aeschylus, the oldest of the three great tragedians, introduced a second actor to drama (both actors doubled in more than one part, however), marking a move away from convention patterned on religious ritual as new scope was opened up. Sophocles introduced a third actor, and in his and Euripides' hands the number of characters to a play further increased. Euripides went further, and the chorus was whittled away, in prominence as much as in numbers. Aeschylus started with a 50-strong chorus who, in addition to a purely dramatic task, sung a hymn to Dionysus at his festival; by Euripides' day the chorus was half the size and merely filled breaks in the action with lyrical odes.

In comedy, Aristophanes, the greatest old comedy playwright, used his chorus as formally as Sophocles, but Menander, the new comedy's chief exponent, had choruses introduce songs for their own sake. The realistic direction the theatre took changed both stage language and setting correspondingly, for early works consisted of choral odes interrupted by "episodes" of speech for individual actors but, with Sophocles' dialogue and chorus, achieved parity. The metrical rhythms were significant.

The theatre. The original setting for performances was a large dancing floor (or *orchēstra* in Greek), to which a dressing room (or *skēnē* in Greek, whence scene) was later added, then extended, permitting the use of revolving panels (*periaktoi*) bearing pictures announcing the place of action. The late-5th-century-BC theatre was an open-air one, with the now-customary three actors taking perhaps some ten parts among them, while a chorus of 15 (24 in comedy) was in attendance. Theatrical devices were sparse, and the actors' sumptuous dresses were a change from simple, everyday Greek clothes. Everybody on stage wore a mask, and a crane (or *mēchanē* in Greek, whence mechanical) was used to introduce flying gods. A movable platform (*ekkylēma*) suggested an indoor setting, but on the stage actors chiefly talked and did not use properties to any great degree. Action, sometimes gruesomely violent, was recounted by messengers, rather than staged.

Songs and dancing provided by the chorus divided the plays, short by modern standards, into "scenes," of which there might be four to a play. The actor would often remain while the chorus provided the interlude, so that though a greater amount of time could be thought to have elapsed dramatically than in actual fact, there was nothing like the modern curtain's power of speeding the action on by years. At suitable dramatic peaks, songs might replace spoken dialogue; Euripides, for instance, wrote long solos.

The Greek theatre was symbolic, with men impersonating women and with place identified by some token. In any case, the auditorium held 10,000 to 20,000 people, ranged steeply so as to appreciate the geometric configurations of the chorus dances by looking down on them, while the landscape beyond the *skēnē* compensated for any austerity of the orchestra.

Equipment and techniques of Greek theatre

ROME

Of the plays written and performed in Roman times, only a few have survived. But the Romans make little claim to originality in their drama, and on the whole their literary production was heavily dependent upon Greek models. Indeed, the Roman period is of interest in the history of Western theatre not so much for the way it flourished as for the way it declined—resulting in 400 years of seeming

death for organized theatre. Many factors must be taken into account in explaining why this happened, but perhaps the dominant reason lay in the political cynicism with which the Roman authorities used public games, at which theatrical performances took place, to divert the populace from economic and political dissatisfaction. The number of official festivals proliferated. They had little or no basis in religious tradition, and theatre lost its close ties with religious ritual, degenerating into theatricality and spectacle for its own sake.

Native theatrical tradition. There was at least the germ of a native theatrical tradition in Italy from early times, in what were known as the Fescennine verses, crude exchanges of ribaldry sung in a rough and improvised rhythm at harvest celebrations and other times of country merriment. Livy, the historian, says that in 364 BC Etruscan players were summoned to Rome at a time of pestilence to avert the wrath of the gods by their dancing and music. This tradition of early Etruscan influence is given some substance by the similarity of the Etruscan word for player, which was *ister*, to the Latin *histrio*. From the combination of Fescennine verse and Etruscan dance to the music of pipes, there apparently grew what Livy calls a "medley" (*satura*). This seems to have been a plotless entertainment, consisting of jests, horseplay, and songs. The Oscan inhabitants of Campania, in the Neapolitan region of Italy, also had a long established tradition of burlesque which was afterward carried to Rome and known under the title of *fabula Atellana* ("Atellan play," Atella being the name of a Campanian town). It has been suggested that the playwright Plautus (2nd century BC) was associated with this tradition before moving to Rome and presenting his plays at the state festivals there.

Imitation of Greek models. It was, however, the introduction of Greek plays that characterized the literary development of Roman theatre. In 240 BC Livius Andronicus, a Greek from Tarentum, who made his living at Rome as a teacher, first translated a Greek play for performance at the Roman games. Though the literary merit of his translations was slight, he himself is of some importance as a pioneer. The first signs of native genius shone in the comedies (and to a much lesser extent in the tragedies) of Gnaeus Naevius, whose first play was produced in 235 BC. The fragments of his work that survive reveal that they were Italian in spirit and dealt with low life, but that they retained a Greek setting. The kind of play so set was to be called *fabula palliata* ("play in Greek dress"). Naevius also showed striking evidence of his originiality by inventing the Roman historical play, dealing with legendary Roman heroes and events, afterward to be known as *fabula praetexta*. Naevius incorporated with his work sharp and outspoken attacks on the Roman nobility. As a result, it appears that he was punished with imprisonment or exile. Perhaps in view of this fate, the great poet Quintus Ennius, who followed him as a dramatist, adapted his talent to the social conditions of the time and tried, by his translations of Greek tragedies (his version of Euripides' *Medea* became especially famous), to satisfy the Hellenistic tastes of the contemporary nobility. Plautus and Terence, Rome's outstanding playwrights of the 2nd century BC, modelled their comedies upon the work of such Greek playwrights as Menander. More obviously Roman in theme and allusion, they nevertheless retained the Greek setting and dress. Native Latin comedy, dealing with Roman themes and set in Italy, seems to have come into being toward the end of the 2nd century BC, and the genre was distinguished as *fabula togata* ("play in Roman dress").

Seeds of decay. Plays were given as part of the free entertainment offered at public festivals. From the start, however, Roman theatre was dependent upon popular taste in a way that had never been known in Greece. If a play failed to please, the manager of the festival was obliged to return part of the subsidy from public funds. Thus, even in Republican times, there was some anxiety to give the public what it wanted—and this proved to be the sensational, the spectacular, and the crude. During imperial times, Roman emperors made even more cynical use of this knowledge, providing

The works of Gnaeus Naevius

"bread and circuses" (the withering phrase of the 1st-century-AD satirist Juvenal) to divert the people from their miserable and, therefore, politically dangerous lot. Buildings such as the Colosseum in Rome and amphitheatres erected throughout the empire were evidence of the power and grandeur of Rome but not of its artistic life and energy; there is little reason to believe that they were intended for anything but trivial and degrading display. At least in Republican days there had been a written text and a genuine attempt to expose vice and ridicule folly in as amusing a way as possible. But as the people's taste for spectacle came more and more to indicate what was put on in the arenas—gladiatorial combats to the death, water spectaculars with mock sea battles, wild beasts exhibited and encouraged to tear one another to pieces, Christians covered with pitch and used as human torches—it is not surprising that serious people avoided the theatre as demeaning and undignified and that writers were alienated from it. During the imperial age there was a fashion for tragedies to be written as closet drama or for recitation rather than for stage performance. Plays of this kind included the tragedies of Seneca, a Stoic philosopher and leading statesman under the emperor Nero, and they were to exercise enormous influence during the Renaissance, especially in England.

Mimic tradition. The most popular form of acted entertainment came to be the mime and pantomime, which relied upon the actors' improvisations and physical agility and offered ample opportunity for the audacious presentation of immorality and open obscenity. These entertainments had replaced Plautine comedy and Atellan farce in public favour even by Cicero's day, in the dying years of the Republic. By the time of the Christian persecutions under the emperors Nero and Domitian, mimes and pantomimes were used to ridicule the Christian faith on stage. In *Centunculus*, for example, a clown is baptized and martyred, being grotesquely crucified in a way calculated to burlesque his faith. It is not entirely surprising that, after the triumph of Christianity, theatrical performances were stopped in the 5th century, and the theatre was abominated by the Church Fathers as an art so debased through commercial exploitation as to have lost any relevance to the general good of society.

Christian Byzantium. The theatre of the ancient world thus survived only in fragments, like some river that has temporarily split itself into several channels. There were a few texts; a variety of theatre buildings, useful as quarries; some theoretical treatises; and groups of itinerant mimics, singers, and dancers who exercised their talents illicitly wherever a patron or passer-by could be found to look or listen.

The old Roman Empire was Christianized and split into two sectors, one based at Rome and the other at Constantinople (Istanbul). The Byzantine Church, centred at Constantinople, took on something of the stylistic refinement attached to court ceremonials of the Byzantine Empire. Public worship was marked by magnificent processions, some of them directed by the emperor's master of ceremonies. Homilies (sermons of edification) were often characterized by dialogue, revealing the influence of Oriental poetry. In 968, Bishop Liudprand of Cremona, who had been sent to Constantinople on a diplomatic mission from the German emperor, Otto I, left a description of theatrical performances at the Hagia Sophia. But almost all the detailed evidence of organized religious and secular drama that certainly developed within the Christian Church of Byzantium—long preceding the emergence of dramatic forms from the liturgy of the Western Church—has been lost and the subject is still a matter of some controversy.

II. The Middle Ages and the Renaissance

THEATRICAL REVIVAL IN THE MIDDLE AGES

Secular theatrical activity. Although the principal kinds of drama that flourished in the West during the Middle Ages were religious, inspired by the Christian's liturgy, there were other kinds of theatrical activity that existed side by side with the church, though not connected with it. Eventually they merged to create a theatre, religious in inception but recreational in its later development, that by the 16th century was healthy, full of initiative, and equipped to reanimate the newly discovered classical heritage of Greece and Rome.

Long before any organized theatre began to emerge in the 10th century, there were survivors of the Roman mimic tradition—singers, acrobats, dancers, jugglers—who seem to have formed themselves into a wandering fraternity. They would appear at festivals and other occasions when their presence was desirable, afterward to vanish again into the obscurity that has always characterized the wandering player's life. Their performances were not encouraged by the church, but neither do they seem effectively to have been banned. During the late Middle Ages these burlesque entertainers were to find a more secure place at princely courts and in the households of lords both spiritual and temporal, where they performed as actors or minstrels and musicians at their masters' festivities. The written texts that they evolved for performance were, especially in France, literate and often sharply satirical.

Old traditions and customs, too, flourished locally throughout the countries of Europe. While zealous monks and missionaries Christianized the West, often making use of former places of pagan worship to build their churches and adapting pagan rites to Christian use, it seems they did not Christianize existing theatrical traditions. It is difficult, today, to say just how far the people who took part in sword dances, masked carnival processions, May dances, spring festivals, wedding rites of sexual initiation, and the like were aware that these stemmed from pagan rites practiced by their forefathers. The subject is of primary interest to folklorists. In the clowning, jugglery, singing, dancing, mimicry, and burlesque that took place there would, however, sometimes come together the three basic components of drama: impersonation, dialogue, and action. The results were farces—called *soties* in France, *Fastnachtsspiele* in Germany, *kluchtspelen* in the Netherlands—usually dealing with such themes as foolish or cunning peasants, disgruntlement about work, the relationship between master and servant, husband and wife. Eventually these farcical scenes were included as interludes in the religious-inspired drama (which had by this time moved out of the churches into the villages and was no longer performed exclusively by the clergy), making the latter infinitely more vigorous, more effective as entertainment, and providing scope for dramatic irony and counterpoint.

Liturgical drama. During the 9th century there was a new impulse to increase the musical effect of the church's plainsong. Musical embellishments were added, for example, to the final syllable of the Alleluia, and whole texts eventually were elaborated as sequences to be sung during the mass. Antiphonal singing, in which the choir divides into two parts, is a form of choral drama and proved to be most important in the rebirth of organized drama. A text contained in a 10th-century manuscript from the monastery of St. Gall in Switzerland dramatizes antiphonally the visit of the three Marys to the tomb where Christ's body had been buried. They find the sepulchre empty and an angel (here angels) guarding it. The angels ask them, *"Quem quaeritis?"* ("Whom do ye seek?"), and a short dialogue follows. The part of the angel was sung by one division of the choir, the part of the women by another. This simple vocal dramatization of one event mentioned in the Easter liturgy led to much of the rest being presented in a more elaborate dramatic form, involving movement and "soloists." The aim seems always to have been to convey, in as vivid a way as possible and for the benefit of an uneducated laity, the deep significance of events ritually celebrated in liturgical worship. Gradually rules were drawn up in various dioceses through Europe governing gesture, vestments to be worn, and ways of suggesting locale. By the end of the 13th century not only the Easter liturgy but also that of the Passion and the Nativity (and also the messianic prophecies that form the liturgy of Advent, leading up to Christmas) had been so dramatized. The little religious plays that resulted were performed at different places

Closet drama in the imperial age

Survival of the Roman mimic tradition

Pedagogical aim of liturgical drama

within the church, then in the church grounds, finally in village and town itself. The vernacular was used alongside the Latin, again with the intention of making events as clear as possible, spoken scenes replaced chanted antiphons, and by the early 14th century the religious drama had in most places passed from the hands of the clergy into the hands of the laity.

Miracle plays. It is thought that trade guilds, which were also religious guilds, were the main avenue of transition. The plays became entirely vernacular, were much expanded from the original liturgical elaborations, and became known in Italy as *sacre rappresentazioni*, in Spain as *autos sacramentales*, in France as *mystères* (borrowed in England after 1800 as mysteries, this word derives from the Latin *ministerium*, meaning "service"), and in England as miracle plays. Performances were directed sometimes by one of the clergy, by a teacher, by the master of a craftsmen's guild. Each guild, indeed, would assume responsibility for one play of the "cycle" into which, by their final development in the 16th century, the individual plays had grown. Cycles covered the entire story of the redemption, from the fall of man up to the Last Judgment, but centring on the Passion and designed to stress the humanity as much as the divinity of Christ. Church vestments were replaced or supplemented by contemporary costumes suitable to the character being portrayed, scenery became more elaborate and ingenious (especially in Spain, Italy, and France; it remained fairly sparse in the northern countries of Europe). Most important of all, however, that use of the vernacular and the consequent relaxation of the strictly ritualized presentation which had characterized liturgical drama allowed comic interludes to be incorporated with the central religious theme. These interludes were the farces that had evolved from folklore customs; in the religious drama they were particularly (though not exclusively) associated with scenes in which devils or peasant characters appeared.

The theatre thus became as secular as that of classical antiquity, though it was consistently Christian in ethos. The kinds of play that evolved throughout Europe were distinct, national, and independent. Yet all reflected a common spirit of Christian man. Performances were closely linked to the feasts of the Christian calendar, themselves adapted from the earlier folk festivals of the agricultural year: Christmas (winter solstice); Shrovetide, Easter, and May Day (advent of spring); Ascension Day, Whitsunday, and Corpus Christi (summer solstice); St. Michael's Day and All Saints' Day (harvest thanksgiving and autumn). Modern observers may be surprised at the endurance of audiences willing to sit or stand all day for several days to watch simple but surprisingly dignified and profound plays. They had a rarity value, however, augmented by long months of preparation in which the entire community had been involved, and they were heightened by a sense of occasion.

Involvement of entire communities in miracle plays

Morality plays. The miracle plays reveal a faith and hope for salvation that does not appear in a later kind of medieval drama known as the morality play. Morality plays, which were commonly produced during the 15th century, reflect something of the sociological turmoil of an age in which the existing social framework was turned upside down. They are dramatized allegories, and their characters are abstractions such as mankind, good, evil, death, chastity, and lust. Vivid sermons focussing on the seductive power of evil to which Christian man is exposed, they show how he may nonetheless arrive at the day of judgment with an army of virtues rather than vices to settle his fate. In the plays scholarly theological learning, Christian allegory, and Old Testament themes predominate. Meant to provide moral education, they were performed by and for the new middle classes of the fast expanding towns.

This theatrical development is interesting in relation to other changes that took place in the age of the merchants' revolution, including a switch from payment in kind to the use of money (which alone had a tremendous effect on people, involving them in risks and investments with the great banking concerns that had begun to emerge).

There had also been a rise in trading, which paved the way for speculation and stemmed from the new financial profit system and the newly opened sea routes. The conflict between virtue and luxury became the principal theme of literature: man was urged to lead his life in accordance with Christian faith (plays about Lazarus); to endure suffering with patience (plays about Job); to be honest in his dealings with fellowmen (*Cenodoxus*); not to become the slave of luxury (*Everyman*); above all, to avoid committing the seven deadly sins. The morality plays present the dilemma of man faced with the reorganization of educational and economic systems and the breakdown of old political structures who was at the same time striving to hold fast to his soul.

CLASSICAL REVIVAL OF THE RENAISSANCE

Full of disgust and disdain for the decadence of life and society in 15th-century Italy, men began to desire a new kind of life in the manner of classical Roman times. The old ideals of Roman morality and humanity were sought for their elegance, wit, and knowledge of the world. Learning had traditionally been sought in the seclusion of the monasteries, but the "new learning" of the Renaissance was more dynamic. Scholars wished not only to understand the ideals of antiquity but to re-create them. They regarded this world not as something to be overcome in order to have life in the next but as something created to be enjoyed by man. They began to hunt for classical manuscripts and to study the other remains of antiquity. Even the papacy promoted these new humanistic aims. The Vatican Library amassed works embodying classical culture from all over the Christian world. The worldly popes of this period encouraged both artists and scientists of the highest renown to gather at their courts, even though their liberal ideas often clashed with Christian doctrines.

Italian Neoclassicism. During the 10th and 11th centuries, especially in Germany, Roman culture had enjoyed a mild renaissance, in the course of which a nun, Hrosvitha, had studied the comedies of Terence in her convent at Gandersheim (now Bad Gandersheim) in Germany, copied his style (which might have caused many a nun to blush with embarrassment), and produced her own Christian comedies. She substituted chaste Christian women, honest men, and constant Christian martyrs for Terence's bawds, slaves, and foolish old men. Although interesting in her own right, Hrosvitha did not have any practical influence on theatrical developments. During the true Renaissance, however, classical literature and drama—first that of Rome, especially the works of Plautus, Terence, and Seneca, later that of Greece—were discovered and not only became an object of research and reading but a starting point from which to recreate theatrical traditions of the past. In Rome itself, classical works of Roman antiquity were performed by Pomponius Laetus and his company; in 1486 Sulpitius Verulamus edited Vitruvius' *De architectura libri decem* (Marcus Vitruvius Pollio had dedicated this remarkable treatise on the architectural arts of the classical world, which included a description of ancient Greek and Roman theatres, to the Roman emperor Augustus). The whole educational system was meanwhile revolutionized by the invention of printing. Up to this time scholars had passed on their theological and scientific knowledge to succeeding generations either orally or via handwritten manuscripts. New works of learning could be made accessible to a rapidly growing number of educated men. The printed Latin texts of Vitruvius, Terence, Plautus, and Seneca were widely read and exerted a striking influence on further developments in the theatre. Throughout Europe, theatrical performances were given in learned and aristocratic society, in academies, private institutions, and religious societies. For many of these revivals, careful reconstructions of classical stages were erected. The printings of Vitruvius' work, by now published all over Europe and often appearing in translation, were provided with woodcuts showing ground plans and front elevations of classical stages. Not many "classical" theatres were actually built, however, but of these few the Teatro Olimpico at

The chaste Christian comedies of Hrosvitha

Vicenza (1585), designed and started by the Venetian architect Andrea Palladio and completed by Vincenzo Scamozzi, is one of the most beautiful. Early revivals of comedies by Plautus and Terence relied on the rather modest descriptions of the classical stage supplied by the scholar Aelius Donatus in his annotated edition of Terence.

It was not a great step from reviving Latin comedy to imitating it in the vernacular. The early Humanists, led by Ludovico Ariosto, were the first to do so, treating contemporary themes in a critical, sarcastic, yet humorous manner.

In this period, dramatists (and Humanist poets in general) had a political role to play, feared and at the same time courted. Sovereigns preferred to win their affection rather than take issue with them; in their comedies they could either belittle a man or praise him to the skies, merely by their words. Consequently, the most important personalities were invited to live at the courts, which thus became centres of the arts of the theatre and of poetry.

The Renaissance stage

The stages used in the Renaissance for performance of these works of the Italian classical period were based on the principles found in Vitruvius' work on classical architecture. In the matter of painted backdrop scenery, however, a new element was now introduced because Renaissance painters had mastered the rules of perspective. A facsimile of "nature" was the aim, but "nature" was to be more perfect on stage than in reality, for it could be freed from all the accidentals and impurities of real life. For the staging of pastoral plays (artificial evocations of the shepherd's sensitive life set in a pristine and wholly delightful landscape) a setting that depicted fields and woods was provided. The Renaissance tragedy setting was characterized by temples and palaces. For comedies, perspective settings depicted the houses of the "little" man of the middle and lower classes.

Opera. The birth of opera in the late 16th century stemmed from new information about the important part played by music in the classical theatre. It was realized that in their theatrical performances the Greeks had adopted a special declamatory vocal style (*recitativo*), different from the more solemn monologue (*aria*) and choruses. A group of Florentine patricians known as the Camerata (*c.* 1580) undertook a revival of Greek theatre as they imagined it to have been, and it is from their endeavours that the European opera arose. It is not entirely surprising that the first operatic compositions should have dealt with Greek myths (such as the stories of Orpheus and Eurydice, Daphnis and Chloë). Great scenic artists were engaged to create suitable settings, which took full advantage of the 16th-century mastery of perspective. Voices were to ravish the audience's ears, the beauty of the setting to please their eyes: the opera was a field in which artists—composers, singers, poets, technicians, and painters alike—surpassed nature and proved their creative abilities. Opera was given on sumptuous occasions, intended to make manifest the patron's power and wealth, and thus it was politically important. Indeed, while enjoying the artistic and aesthetic experience of a theatrical performance, patrons were at all times keenly aware of the political implications of such activities. Ambassadors' reports from the time show that an overall political climate was reflected in theatrical performance, even though the works might not deal specifically with a political subject (see OPERA).

Commedia dell'arte. Another kind of dramatic skill was also becoming appreciated at court: this was the delightful commedia dell'arte, a tradition of playing highly developed at this time and thought to be in direct descent from the Atellan plays of Roman antiquity—a link which cannot, however, be established by research. Commedia dell'arte ("comedy of art") is also known as *commedia all'improviso* ("improvised comedy"), so called to distinguish it from the *commedia erudita* ("comedy of learning") of the earlier Italian Renaissance period. It flourished during the 16th century and later. At first it was performed chiefly at the courts and only in the 18th century was it primarily associated with country fairs (*théâtre de la foire*) and suburban theatres in Italy

and Austria. The artistic demands made of actors in commedia dell'arte were considerable. As well as physical dexterity they had to be of a high educational standard, command several languages, be quick witted, and be able to react fast in improvised situations. On top of this, players were expected to have at their disposal a number of *lazzi* (short sketches, brought to a pitch of perfection, which could be inserted anywhere in the performance). Originally the main characters were supposed satirically to portray "types" of Italian citizen: there was Pantalone, an old lustful Venetian merchant; the Dottor, a learned doctor (*dottore*) of Bologna; a servant, Arlecchino, of Bergamo; the boastful Neapolitan Capitano, of Spanish origin (Naples having been conquered by the Spaniards). These "type" characters were masked, as in the pantomime of Roman times; the actors playing the lovers, however, were not (see COMMEDIA DELL'ARTE).

High demands made on actors of commedia dell'arte

Professional troupes. Only professional players were able to reach the high playing standards of commedia dell'arte, and so permanent troupes were formed, playing perfectly in ensemble. These troupes were paid to perform in Italian courts and in those abroad. The tradition flourished for nearly two centuries throughout Europe, inspiring such dramatists as Molière in France during the 17th century and Carlo Goldoni in Italy during the 18th century. Even the 20th-century theatre was stimulated by the example of commedia dell'arte in its efforts to revive a "theatrical theatre."

By the mid-16th century professional players had made organized theatre their own province, were in commercial competition with one another, and had thus made the theatre part of the general competitive profit system. This fact meant that the audience was able to exert great influence on further theatrical developments through its likes and dislikes. At this time, too, the first measures to achieve publicity were taken in order to win the public's attention and favour: heralds announced details of performances, playbills carried them. Licenses to play were dependent on magistrates' findings with regard to the moral standards of their repertoire—were they offensive to public morality, religion, or the state?—and thus the early workings of a public magisterial censorship were established.

Angelo Beolco of Padua, called Ruzzante, organized one of the earliest professional troupes in Italy. Already, since 1520, they had travelled throughout northern Italy, performing at the courts and in the markets. Keeping their Paduan dialect, they played rustic comedy, themes based on the social tensions between urban and rural life, and love farces or tragicomedies, usually with a pastoral background. After experimenting with Plautine comedy, Ruzzante's main achievement was to develop certain character "types" which may be considered the forerunners of the commedia dell'arte characters. He also introduced a more natural style of acting, drawn from life and observation of people—an approach that in this period was adopted in the other arts as well (François Rabelais in literature, Orlando di Lasso in music, Pieter Bruegel the Elder in painting).

Ruzzante's troupe

Courtly entertainments. During the 15th and 16th centuries the courts did not at first employ theatre specialists. Courtiers, noblemen holding a court appointment, court painters, musicians, and masters of ceremonies—all were involved in the organization and performance of courtly entertainment. Leonardo da Vinci (who ranks among the most famous theatre technicians, having designed by 1490 the first revolving stage, incorporating a movable planetary system) arranged the setting, masks, and costumes of *Festa del Paradiso*, an entertainment given during the wedding celebrations for Lodovico Sforza, duke of Milan. Raphael also painted much admired stage settings. The court poets were naturally expected to devise the texts, the master of ceremonies to organize the production. Equestrian ballets (to specially composed music by the court musician) and triumphal processions were a spectacular feature, needing careful preparation, and became the highlight of these displays of power and glory. Princes, dukes, and monarchs were invited to these festivals. They came with their suites, riding on horseback or else in ornate carriages, and even their arrival processions were sometimes choreographed, especially in France, where the *entrées solennelles*, entrance processions of great pomposity, were developed to a peak of elaboration and ceremonial. In England the masque, a short allegorical drama, became the favourite court diversion, reaching its climax under the reign of the Stuarts, when the designer Inigo Jones and the poet Ben Jonson joined forces.

Members of the court all had a thorough training in dancing, fencing, singing, instrumental music, and courtly ceremonial. They were therefore well equipped to perform in these masques and ballets, even to take the solo parts as well as appear in the choruses.

Jesuit drama. The continuous development of religious theatre was interrupted by the Reformation and Counter-Reformation which separated the Protestant north of Europe from the Catholic countries of the south. In the south it was the Society of Jesus (the Jesuits) that took particular interest in the theatre, being fully aware of the persuasive power inherent in performed action. It was also a means of teaching their pupils how to behave and express themselves in accordance with the requirements of the upper classes of society. Finally, theatre was considered an effective way of fulfilling the Jesuit order's professed missionary task. Thus it was that the Jesuits encouraged colourful theatrical activities in such Latin American countries as Brazil (*Auto de Santiago*, 1564), Venezuela (1566), Peru (1569; building upon traditions of Spanish religious and secular drama, established there since 1548), Bolivia (1578), Paraguay (1596; following up Corpus Christi plays and *autos sacramentales*, which had been introduced there *c.* 1544), and in Argentina, Ecuador, and Chile (1646).

The
Jesuit
theatre

During the 17th and 18th centuries—when the order was suppressed in many countries—the Jesuit theatre flourished, standing fast to its didactic intentions. Many of the most important theorists of Baroque theatre, moreover, were Jesuits or their pupils, especially in the field of scenic design. The Jesuit theatre made full use of the elaborate operatic stage, of its towering architecture and luxurious settings, and of its flying machinery and stage trapdoors. The Jesuits had their own composers and librettists of high rank, and Jesuit schools gave special training in grammar and rhetoric. Princes often took part in close of term performances at Jesuit colleges, and the Catholic emperors attended them.

Spain's Golden Age. During the second half of the 16th century professional troupes had been established in Spain and England. These troupes did not perform for one particular social class; members of high society attended professional performances in the Spanish *corrales* (courtyards), and in the English public playhouses the upper classes attended as well as the groundlings. Professional troupes were specially hired to act at court on certain occasions.

Since the process of Reformation had not affected Spain, the *autos sacramentales* continued to preserve the long tradition of religious drama. The prudent Spanish clergy had successfully purged religious drama of those elements that had laid it open to ridicule in other European countries. *Autos* were written by the most famous poets of the Spanish Golden Age. Early professional troups, such as that of Lope de Rueda, were of strolling players, and they introduced Italian culture and Humanist-inspired comedy to Spain. They were so poor that they were said to keep all their belongings "in a single sack." The traditional theatre of the strolling players also proved to be the father of Cervantes' *drama a noticia* (tragedies based on his own experiences in Algerian prison) and of his *entreméses* (comic interludes), which were performed by the professional troupes. The establishment of *corrales* meant a more secure livelihood for the actors and a better chance of control over theatrical entertainment on the part of church and town authorities. Naïve religious faith plus national pride, relish for an elegant way of life, and incomparable creativeness and versatility—these all distinguished the work of Lope de Vega, who wrote both secular comedies for the *corrales*

and *autos sacramentales* for Corpus Christi celebrations. The *gracioso*, a comic servant character, appeared in many of his dramatic works, originating from the Spanish tradition of strolling players and virtuoso actors. He is contrasted with the hero, and the relationship has much in common with that between Sancho Panza and Don Quixote in Cervantes' novel.

Not until the late Baroque period was Italian perspective setting introduced to the Spanish theatre. Thereafter, however, it played an equally important part in theatrical production as it had done in other European countries. During this Golden period, the Spanish theatre was distinguished by the work of poets of highest rank, including Calderón de la Barca, and that is one of the reasons why dramatic literature reached a height of perfection and refinement, able to integrate man with the "great theatre of the world," a hierarchical concept in which every man played his part before God, who held each class of society as equally important: the poor, the rich, the servant, his master, the sick, the healthy man, the ugly, and the good-looking; to each God gave life and each must prove himself worthy of it.

This world picture had already been accepted by progressive Spanish Jesuits and was even expressed in their motto *vox populi, vox dei* ("the voice of the people is the voice of God"). It meant that the Spanish (and also the Austrian) Baroque theatre differed widely from contemporary theatrical activities in other absolutist states. This divergence of attitude is also revealed in the fact that in Spain (and again, also Austria) comic characters, presented as an analogy to the hero, continued to play an important part on the stage: the servant is confronted with an experience equivalent to that of the master but reduced to an apt intellectual horizon and is, thus, a reflection of the hero's image. This conception of a corporate state, in which each class bears its appropriate responsibilities, was most clearly expressed in Calderón's *El gran teatro del mundo* (*The Great Theatre of the World*) and *La vida es sueño* (*Life Is a Dream*).

Continuing
importance
of comic
characters
as
reflec-
tions of
their
masters

The Elizabethan playhouse. In England during the Reformation, the theatre was active in disseminating Protestant propaganda, and several interludes mocking the traditions of the former religious stage made their appearance. Adapted from traditional miracle and morality plays, their performance frequently led to riots and disorders. Tudor governments, both Protestant and Catholic, were at various times forced to take legislative action against the theatre. Actors were placed under strict supervision and control; an increasingly vigorous censorship was imposed on play texts, in manuscript and in print; places of performance were made subject to license.

The influence of the Neoclassical drama of Italy was a long time reaching Protestant England, partly because of its association with Rome and the Latin language, partly because its plots of intrigue were less interesting to English audiences than topical debate, partly because a people tends to rely more on native resources at times when it is faced with the threat of foreign invasion. There was, however, a relaxation of this tension in 1587 after the execution of the Catholic Mary, Queen of Scots, and the defeat of the Spanish Armada the following year opened the door for new ideas in the arts and education. But by that time a distinctly English style had already grown out of the ashes of the old religious theatre. It was distinguished by a reliance on the symbolism derived from liturgical plays and from heraldry; it owed its narrative scheme and structure (of plot–subplot) to the miracle cycles and saint's plays; its emphasis on debate and parable to the moralities; and its professional character to the players of interludes who had been employed to perform at court since the end of the 15th century. Professionally organized and relying on the support of commercial speculators and the protection of sovereign and court officials, the theatre of Christopher Marlowe, Shakespeare, Jonson, and John Webster retained its links with the popular theatre and with its medieval heritage and was self-confident enough to draw what it wanted and no more from Neoclassical precepts.

During the reign of Elizabeth I (1558–1603) the first

regular playhouses were built in London, including the Globe, Swan, Fortune, Hope, and Red Bull. All of these were open to the air. The licenses to run them were usually granted to an entrepreneur belonging to the players' company, whose management aimed at making a profit. The spectators came from all walks of life. During the winter the company of actors would perhaps stay at the castle of one or more noblemen and perform for him. They were also engaged for court performances. Private theatres were opened in some of the old monasteries, suppressed under Henry VIII and now abandoned, including the Blackfriars (from 1576) and Whitefriars (after 1605). Later on, under the first Stuart kings, James I and Charles I, roofed theatres were built along Italian lines. But in 1642, the theatres were closed by the Puritans at the outbreak of the Civil War and remained closed during the Commonwealth period until 1660, when England took up once again her theatrical traditions at the Restoration of the monarchy. The theatre flourished but along lines quite different from those established in the age of Shakespeare.

Shakespeare and most of his famous colleagues were truly professionals of the theatre, usually being attached to a particular professional company. Their characters were written for particular actors, whose abilities and personalities were well-known to them. Their plays were efficiently designed to appeal to their audiences but did not merely present a tragic or comic "mirror of the world." They argued highly explosive political topics. In Shakespeare's histories, for instance, the subject of kingship is thoroughly examined in all its implications: both the rightful but incompetent sovereign and the usurping but strong monarch are scrutinized—a most daring undertaking in the days of Elizabeth.

Rough theatre in Germany. Monopolies, suppression, and withdrawal of playing licenses were some of the reasons why many troupes of actors left Tudor England and went to the European mainland. Unlike the commedia dell'arte troupes, who were mainly engaged by the courts, these English strolling players usually travelled from one fair to another, playing to an audience of rural folk. (Only very rarely did they perform at court, although there is a record of Christopher Marlowe's *Doctor Faustus* being given in 1608 at Graz, in Austria.) At first they adopted a rough style of acting, having to express themselves chiefly through mime because of language problems. They played in innyards, on primitive wooden platforms constructed on the spot, in market squares, or before the church. The German-speaking countries benefitted most from the importation of Elizabethan plays and stage conventions. By and by these troupes were reshaped and their repertoires extended to include plays given in the vernacular, though with an intermingling of many English words and phrases. Shakespearean drama included *Der bestrafte Brudermord* ("Fratricide Punished," based on *Hamlet*) and *Hieronimo, Marschalk in Spanien* (based on Thomas Kyd's *Spanish Tragedie*). There was also Italian pastoral comedy, French tragedies, and Spanish cloak-and-dagger drama. Favourite themes included tested virtue, human nobility, the courageous suffering of ill fortune or pain; the sudden change of man's fortune, the power of fate; pride, jealousy, lust for power, and malice of every kind. The style was bloody, bold, and melodramatic. From the mid-17th century, Dutch strolling players also visited Germany: though their playing was of a very high standard, they could not earn their living in their native country, and so they roamed throughout northern Germany and Scandinavia, performing *vertoonige* ("living tableaux") and contemporary comedies and tragedies, Spanish drama being much favoured. Italian travelling players in the main presented their marionette and puppet theatre in Austria and southern Germany. These "Pulcinella" players influenced Austrian popular theatre a good deal, much more so than the commedia dell'arte (called *wällische*) troupes who played in Austria from the end of the 17th century. Commedia dell'arte, however, had an enormous success at the Austrian courts, and their style of acting was much imitated (as, for example, in productions of

the *Edelknabenkomödien*, or "Comedies of the Pages," that were given at the court of Holy Roman emperor Leopold I, an ardent admirer and connoisseur of the theatre).

There were, of course, many who derided the strolling troupes and who contemptuously dismissed their repertoire as "debased cultural property." They considered the play *Der bestrafte Brudermord* as only a crude travesty of *Hamlet*. Such critics, however, did not appreciate the valuable results of the troupes' activities. Links were established between one country and another, and audiences were confronted with new outlooks on life and experience, on man and the world. And thus—in an age when compulsory education was still unknown, when few could read and write, when scientific knowledge and experience of the world were limited to a very few privileged people—the strolling players opened doors to the future and the past, to other peoples, and to other cultures. They conveyed new knowledge that enlarged the range of experience. This was the real achievement of the strolling players.

French Neoclassicism. In France sacred drama was forbidden by decree in 1548 to prevent its being used by the Protestants to bring Roman Catholicism into contempt. Continuity of theatrical tradition was thus lost, and French dramatists, deprived of their great heritage of religious plays and popular farces, began to ape Italian "academic" drama. The sterility of the results is one of the reasons why a taste for dancing and spectacle developed among court amateurs in France. New "rules" for the new drama were invented, the most notorious being that of the "unities" (of action, time, and place) that were to be observed in both tragedy and comedy. According to this rule, the play should consist of one central action, occurring at one time (not to exceed the time it takes to perform the play), and in one place. Plays that followed the rule were performed mainly in colleges and universities; at court, the queen Catherine de Médicis much preferred Italian poets and actors. But a permanent home for these was not established until 1598 at the Hôtel de Bourgogne.

In the 17th century under Cardinal Richelieu, French statesman and minister to Louis XIII, a special board was set up to bring new life to the theatre, and one of its tasks was to make the "regular" tragedy and comedy flourish. Another professional theatre was opened in the Marais district of Paris, keen competition ensued between it and the Bourgogne, by 1650 Italian stage machinery had been imported, and the playwrights Pierre Corneille, Molière, and Jean Racine had brought the French theatre to an eminence that many students believe eclipsed that of England and Spain. These masters brought to the theatre a degree of observation of both human foibles and human passion and suffering that sufficed to give a genuine vitality to the revived classical forms not attained before or since. Their influence was felt throughout Europe and was synthesized in the French poet and literary critic Nicolas Boileau-Despréaux's *L'Art poétique* (1674). The theatre once again assumed an educative role: people were to behave in a "courtly" manner, to master passion by means of reason, or to transform violent feelings into "noble passions."

Rise of the national theatres. French national pride being invoked, poets and theatrical artists were called upon to develop French styles of artistic expression. After a period of training in Italian art, the stage-struck kings now demanded French styles in opera, drama, and ballet. The Académie Royale de Musique (opera) was founded in 1669; the Comédie-Française, which may be considered the first national theatre, was established in 1680 with a mandate to pursue the cultural aims of France that has continued to the present day.

In the course of the succeeding centuries, national theatres were also established in many other European countries but not necessarily for the same reasons. German national theatres fought to shake off the infiltration of French culture and to develop a native theatre. It was the aim of Emperor Joseph II to institute national theatres for all the peoples of his empire so as to open up the possibility of becoming acquainted with the works of world literature in their own tongue. After establishing a German national theatre for the German-speaking population of Austria, Joseph II then supported the Czechoslovakians' efforts toward their own national theatre; later, a national theatre was founded in Budapest for the Hungarians. Gustav III created the Swedish national theatre. Catherine II the Great of Russia, like Joseph II, wished to educate her people by confronting them with the dramatic works of world literature performed in their own language. During the 19th and 20th centuries, however, as individual countries strove for autonomy, endeavours toward establishing national theatres became a political target. England managed to found a subsidized national theatre only in the second half of the 20th century—and then without a permanent home—a fact explained largely by the profit-system upon which the English theatre has traditionally operated.

The ballet. The triumphant progress of opera and the ballet during the 17th century is a major chapter in the history of theatrical development during the age of Baroque. At the beginning of the 17th century, ballets were often given as an interlude and curtain piece during the performance of an opera. Eventually they were integrated with the plots of the operas, though they were usually placed at the end of the acts. The "star" opera was inaugurated in Venice, giving pre-eminence to aria or a solo vocal part (as opposed to the Florentine tradition of chorus-dominated works). Composers made new demands on singers, who had to study for many years in order to meet them successfully. After the mid-17th century, singers exerted considerable influence on the structure of new works because they demanded showpiece arias at certain places in the text. The dramatic technique of Baroque opera adopted followed set rules: arias were to be sung front stage facing the audiences; the chorus was directed as a static body; the ornate setting was an elaborate decoration to please the eye rather than a functional definition of the acting area (see BALLET).

Decline of classicism. The influence of Molière and Racine, together with that of Corneille, was felt everywhere in Europe. Nowhere else, however, was their genius matched. Only in England was anything written that has survived the test of time in terms of frequent adaptation and revival and then only in comedy. English tragedy attempted to provide an equivalent of the French classical play in a genre known as rhymed heroic drama. Nevertheless, the English heroic play as written by John Dryden, Sir Robert Howard, and Nathaniel Lee was unclassical in its bombast and general lack of restraint, concentrating upon expressing the marvellous as well as exaggerating the passions in a quite unnatural manner. There were one or two exceptions—Joseph Addison's *Cato*, the early success of which was partly due to its relevance to current political crises, is thoroughly classical and held the stage for over a century. Comedy, on the other hand, classified as "comedy of manners," thrived for some decades in the hands of William Wycherley, William Congreve, and George Farquhar and at its best was elegant, witty, cynical, and sharply critical of contemporary society. In the rest of Europe, including France itself, nothing of much note was produced apart from lifeless imitations of French classical tragedy and comedy. This decay of the Neoclassic drama continued throughout the 18th century, flickered to life with the tragedies of Voltaire in France and Vittorio Alfieri in Italy, and finally gave way to a new spirit in both comedy and tragedy.

Restoration drama

III. The rise of a middle class theatre

THE 18TH CENTURY

The history of Western theatre in the 18th century is dominated by personalities. Everywhere it was actors and designers whose names counted with audiences rather than writers. The costume designs of Lodovico Burnacini, the perspective settings of the Bibiena family, whose members between 1680 and 1780 were unchallenged for originality and activity, define the Baroque spirit and its Rococo sequel that spread outward from dramatic representations to enhance the whole of aristocratic life. Theatre worthy of the name became a courtly or at least a metropolitan toy designed to kill time in a manner as costly as befitted its aristocratic patrons. Popular theatre dwindled into fairground improvisations and the meagre, eviscerated repertoires of strolling players.

Middle class drama. Reaction came neither from right nor left but from the centre—from the middle classes who had been denied a theatre for so long: by Puritan sentiment in England, by aristocratic privilege in France, by war and social unrest in the Low Countries and middle Europe, by stagnation in Spain, and by feudalism in Russia and Scandinavia. The new drama took the problems of middle class life as seriously as the old drama had treated the aristocracy.

In England, the cynical comedy of manners was displaced by the sentimental comedy of such dramatists as Colley Cibber and Richard Steele, in which middle class social and domestic problems were treated in moralizing scenes of pathos leading to a happy ending. Sincerely moral, if artistically inept, the sentimental comedy in England is related to the *comédie larmoyante* ("tearful comedy") in France, whose best representative is the playwright Pierre-Claude Nivelle de La Chaussée. George Lillo in England extended the accepted range of tragedy by making persons of the middle class the protagonists of his *The London Merchant, or the History of George Barnwell* (1731), something that had only been done previously by Thomas Heywood in *A Woman kilde with Kindnesse* (1603). Lillo's play inspired G-E Lessing in Germany to write *Miss Sara Sampson* (1755), in a deliberate attempt to free German drama from the dead hand of French Neoclassicism, and to create *bürgerliches Trauerspiel* ("middle class tragedy"). In France, the same extension of the tragic genre led to the *drame bourgeois* of Denis Diderot. All of the middle class plays were seriously written to enunciate moral truths, to preach against the crimes of civilization and conventional society, to advocate the strength and purity of the natural virtues, to express pity for the oppressed, and admiration for the solid, serious, virtuous middle class merchant.

Sentimental comedy

There was some opposition to the sentimental spirit in the drama, notably in England and Italy. Oliver Goldsmith tried to provide an alternative in the shape of what he called laughing comedy, with plays like *The Good-Natur'd Man* (1786) and *She Stoops to Conquer* (1773). The work of Richard Brinsley Sheridan was also fundamentally opposed to the lachrymose comedy, which is mocked (in the character of Lydia Languish) in his most famous play, *The Rivals* (1775).

In Italy, Carlo Goldoni and Carlo Gozzi both made use of the old commedia dell'arte traditions in their plays. Commedia dell'arte still survived in the fairs and suburban theatres of Italy and Austria but only as a shadow of its former vigorous self.

Nevertheless, despite this literate opposition, it was exploitation of the sentimental drama and of the new audiences' penchant for it that brought the tear-drenched successes of David Garrick, England's foremost actor, and first in the long line of actor-managers who were to dominate the establishment theatre in the 19th century. The feeling for spectacle and display which it engendered also fostered in that century the extravagant historico-realistic productions of Edmund Kean and John Philip and Charles Kemble (*i.e.*, the Kemble brothers) and supported the later development of pantomime, music hall, and extravaganza which flourished throughout the Victorian age.

Romantic movement. The Romantic reaction against Neoclassical insistence on cool reason was, in Germany, ushered in by the *Sturm und Drang* ("Storm and Stress") movement—headed by Johann Wolfgang von Goethe's *Götz von Berlichingen* (1773), a celebration of natural man, and closed by Friedrich Schiller's *Kabale und Liebe* (1784). Both these dramatists were involved in the court theatre established at Weimar, one of the many principalities of which Germany was made up at that period, where Goethe established a recognizable, if rather stiff, company style that was copied in other parts of Germany and was of great influence on young actors during the first part of the 19th century.

Beginnings of an American theatre. The spirit and form of the English theatre in the Restoration and Georgian periods dominated the start of professional theatre in North America. Actors, scenery, and repertory were imported to the American colonies around 1750, and early performances were given in existing halls or else in hastily erected quarters. For a long time, however, Puritan prejudice against the theatre proved difficult to overcome—one touring company announced their presentation of Shakespeare's *Othello* as "a moral dialogue in 5 acts."

THE 19TH CENTURY

Nineteenth-century interest in specialty entertainment

This was a century, above all, of progress in the theatre. There were especially significant advances in the field of stage lighting. More and more theatres were built. A quickening interest in specialty entertainment saw the rise of music hall and vaudeville; the actor-manager enjoyed his heyday. Toward the end of the century Western theatre was revolutionized by a number of "free" theatres that were seeking escape from the established systems of theatre management, production, and acting styles and were looking to promote a new kind of play.

A sharp increase in the number of theatre buildings matched a rapid growth in urban development. During the London winter season of 1807, for example, only ten theatres were operating; by 1870 there were 30. Most of the new theatres were smaller than hitherto. None rivalled the new Drury Lane in London, opened in 1794 to seat 3,600 people, about whose size the actress Mrs. Siddons had bitterly complained when her London debut there failed badly. England (1843) and France (1864) removed state censorship over who might and might not present plays, acts that encouraged the opening of new theatres.

In 1803 gas replaced candles as the source of illumination at London's Lyceum Theatre, and other theatres quickly followed suit. The advantages included control and brightness, to a degree never before known, while the obvious disadvantages were an appalling smell and an increased danger of fire from the naked jets of flame (between the introduction of gas illumination and the introduction of electric lighting systems toward the end of the century, some 400 theatres in Europe and North America were burned down). Experiments with electricity at first permitted certain "special" effects (lightning, sunrise, rainbows) and finally resulted in fully electric lighting systems. The first such was installed at the Paris Opéra in 1880–81.

Plays and players. Much of the drama performed during the 19th century derived from the movement initiated by the *Sturm und Drang* dramatists of the late 18th century in Germany. The works of Schiller and Goethe, for instance, gave rise to a spate of "fate dramas" between 1800 and 1825; in 1830 the performance of Victor Hugo's *Hernani* caused riots when it was presented in Paris at the conservative Comédie-Française playhouse, but it at last saw the rout of Neoclassical drama 50 years after the German dramatist Lessing had called for a return to the inward dramatic truthfulness of Shakespeare. Elsewhere in France, some good Romantic plays were written by dramatists such as Alfred de Musset. In England, almost nothing that repays serious attention was written for the theatre between the time of Sheridan and that of Oscar Wilde and George Bernard Shaw; in 1879, the poet and critic Matthew Arnold was able to observe with some justification that "In England we have no modern drama at all." It is not a far step from the Romantic imagination and its attitudes to romantic agony and attitudinizing—to crude, barnstorming melodrama, which reached its nadir in 19th-century England and the United States, where the popular section of audiences derived great pleasure from spectacular effects within plays that mixed sentimentality, villainy, and violence. Parodies of the classical theatre were also popular (*extravaganza*; *burletta*).

Melo-drama

Some individuals began to capitalize on their special talents as singers, dancers, mimics, jugglers, and to give solo performances in ale houses and taverns. These entertainments became so popular and so financially successful that, from the "music room" annex of the public saloon, a great chain of provincial and metropolitan theatres sprang up during the 19th century to be known in England as music hall and in the United States and elsewhere in Europe as vaudeville.

The actor-manager. Personalities also triumphed in the more orthodox dramatic genres, just as they had a century earlier. The 19th century, however, was the heyday of the actor-manager—star, licensee of the theatre (or theatres), and arranger of the performance. He dominated the forestage while his fellow actors were relegated to the background as a sort of mobile set dressing, but after the invention of gas lighting he was forced into retreat behind the proscenium arch to become part of the stage picture as a whole. Because of the technical difficulty in manipulating complicated special effects—storms, forest fires, earthquakes—the star was eventually obliged to hand over artistic control of the production to a neutral observer; thus the stage manager, who had not been of any special importance hitherto, was elevated to the status of *régisseur*, or director, and eventually became a theatre giant in his own right. Finally, the actor-manager's control over the business side of his productions was gradually replaced by that of financial speculators whose interest was in theatre real estate rather than in artistic triumphs.

Movement toward realism. After the actor retired from his forestage and the picture-frame stage had won the day, realism of an almost photographic kind became a main object of production. The Romantic movement had stimulated an interest in historical plays, and strenuous efforts to ensure total accuracy of costume and setting had been made since the early years of the century culminating in the extravagant and costly productions of Sir Henry Irving (died 1905) and Sir Herbert Beerbohm Tree in England. This development, however, meant that the gulf between realistic appearance and rhetorically overblown texts and their delivery was ludicrously apparent. Sacrifices that had to be made included the language of poetry in drama by the playwrights and extravagance of diction and determined bravura performances by the actor.

A move toward ensemble acting and away from virtuoso displays of talent was perhaps the logical continuation of efforts to establish realistic stage presentation in settings and costume. In England, Madame Vestris, an actress and stage singer whose real name was Lucia Elizabeth Mathews, had opened the intimate Olympic Theatre in 1831 and demanded natural movements and gestures from her players. Charles Kean was well-known for his handling of crowd scenes (the extras were split into groups and led by a competent actor). The leading company of German-speaking Europe, the Burgtheater in Vienna, was famous for its company spirit and style. But it was George II, the ruler of the tiny duchy of Saxe-Meiningen, who was the most significant individual in the modern development of ensemble acting. He assumed direct control of his state theatre company in 1866 and achieved a harmony and discipline of playing never before known. The company's extensive European tours between 1874 and 1890 influenced not only the actor-managers of the established theatre but also André Antoine (in Paris) and Konstantin Stanislavsky (in Moscow), both of whom were to be champions of the school of realism in acting and direction later in the century.

The new playwrights. In the established theatre, revivals of the classics were the order of the day, along with the undemanding "well-made plays" of such banal French playwrights as Eugène Scribe, Eugène Labiche, and Victorien Sardou. The new dramatists of the movement known as realism include Henrik Ibsen, Bjørnstjerne Bjørnson, and August Strindberg in Scandinavia; Anton Chekhov and Maksim Gorky in Russia; Gerhart Hauptmann and Frank Wedekind in Germany; Henry Becque in France. Their plays dealt with themes belong-

The "well-made play"

ing to a real, contemporary society, treated in action and dialogue that looked and sounded like everyday behaviour and speech. In one form or another they influenced the mainstream of Western drama up to the present day. In 1867 the French novelist Émile Zola called for a rejection of all artifice in the theatre arts as in the novel, demanding that plays be faithful records of behaviour, scientific analyses of life. This "slice of life" technique, an extreme form of realism, characterizes some of Strindberg's plays (such as *Miss Julie*) as well as those of Becque. The new generation of writers found their audience, small but sympathetic, in a number of "free" theatres that now began to appear throughout Europe.

The work of André Antoine

Théâtre Libre. In 1887, André Antoine, an enthusiastic amateur actor, who worked as a clerk for a Paris gas company, formed a small company that he called Théâtre-Libre (Free Theatre). His intention was to provide a showcase theatre for the young playwrights, both from France and abroad, who could find no other opportunity of bringing their work before the public. Antoine's first bill was a group of one-act plays, and it attracted the attention of leading avant-garde theatre intellectuals including Zola and Becque. In 1888 Leo Tolstoy's *The Power of Darkness* was presented, and Théâtre-Libre took on an international significance. Apart from the work of French writers such as Becque, Eugène Brieux, François de Curel, and Georges de Porto-Riche, the Théâtre-Libre also presented the plays of Ibsen, Strindberg, Bjørnson, and Hauptmann. Théâtre-Libre was an artistic triumph but a financial disaster, piling up debts until in 1894 Antoine gave up its direction. Although best known for his efforts to promote realistic drama and realistic production—he was famous for hanging real carcasses of meat in the stage setting of a butcher's shop—and although his production methods best suited the realistic plays of Ibsen and Strindberg, Antoine also presented many poetic dramas that were Romantic or semi-Romantic in approach. But to these, by presenting them without bombast, he gave a new humanity and dignity. All this was his primary achievement, but he also influenced theatre production elsewhere. In Paris, the Théâtre de l'Oeuvre was opened in 1893 by one of his former actors, Lugné-Poe, who had broadly the same aims as Antoine but who combined artistic sensibility with good business sense, so that his theatre prospered. The Vieux-Colombier, founded by Jacques Copeau in 1913, whose history belongs to 20th-century theatre, can also be considered in direct line of descent from Théâtre-Libre. But it was in Germany that Antoine's influence was most immediately evident.

Freie Bühne. Berlin had emerged as a leading centre of dramatic activity during the 1880s, with the foundation of two important theatres, the Deutsches Theatre and the Lessing Theatre. Neither at first presented the new drama of the realistic school. Antoine's work in Paris, however, was noted and admired and in 1889 a group of men headed by the theatre critic Otto Brahm formed a stage company, called Freie Bühne (Free Theatre) after its Paris counterpart. First productions were of Ibsen's *Ghosts* and Hauptmann's *Before Dawn*. Plays by other avant-garde dramatists followed, but the Freie Bühne effectively ceased to function in 1894—largely because of its own success, for the new drama was quickly accepted by theatres throughout Germany: in Berlin itself there were the Deutsche Bühne and the Freie Volksbühne (Free People's Theatre); others were established in Munich, Leipzig, Breslau (now Wrocław, Poland), Hamburg, and Vienna. Brahm's productions were marked by outstanding ensemble work, and his direction of realistic drama was widely acclaimed. But his range was not so wide as that of Antoine, and his revivals of the German classics were not successful when presented in the modern style. Freie Bühne avoided possible conflict with state and police censorship by presenting private, or club, performances to members only, again following Antoine's earlier example in Paris.

The independent theatre. Dissatisfaction with established systems of theatre, including the all-powerful actor-manager, also existed in England. Critics since Mat-

thew Arnold had further deplored the lack of worthwhile modern English drama. Experimental theatre in Paris and Berlin was watched with approval and interest. William Archer and George Moore were two of many writers who called for an English equivalent of the Théâtre-Libre. A Dutchman living in England, Jacob Grein, organized a group known as the Independent Theatre and in the spring of 1891 produced Archer's translation of Ibsen's *Ghosts*, provoking a storm of moral fury. One champion of the new group and its policies was the theatre critic George Bernard Shaw, whose play *Widowers' Houses* (on the subject of slum landlordism) was produced by the Independent Theatre in 1892. The theatre was supported by a small group of subscribers, many of them distinguished writers, and it ceased activity in 1897. But it prepared the way for the Stage Society, founded in 1899, which played chiefly at the Court Theatre in London, whose work is an important episode in the history of 20th-century British theatre.

Moscow Art Theatre. Probably more has been written about the Moscow Art Theatre than about any other stage company, while its director, Konstantin Stanislavsky, has perhaps had more widespread influence on 20th-century acting than any other theorist. Russian theatre during the early 19th century was one of the most backward in Europe, content to play a repertoire of stock theatrical pieces, mainly French comedies and farces or Russian imitations of them. Little time was spent in rehearsal; the plays were so similar that the same performances (and sets) could be used time and again. During a lengthy conversation in a Moscow restaurant, Stanislavsky, deeply interested in theatre from boyhood and with considerable amateur experience of the stage, and Vladimir Nemirovich-Danchenko, a playwright, teacher, and dramatic critic, talked over their vision of an ideal theatre group, its artistic policy, and its production methods. On the basis of their discussion they formed a theatre group, which they called the Moscow Art Theatre Company, going into rehearsal of a play by Tolstoy in summer of 1898. No great stir was made until, on December 17, 1898, they revived Anton Chekhov's play *The Seagull* (which had failed badly in an earlier production). It established the reputation of the theatre, as well as that of Chekhov and Stanislavsky. The intimacy and naturalness of the acting were something entirely new, and Stanislavsky developed his method of infinitely detailed production until he achieved a perfect surface naturalism. He then became dissatisfied with the narrow confines thus imposed and aimed instead for what he called the inner truth, or "realism of the spirit." This aim, whose achievement was to be sought in a variety of ways, is perhaps the only acceptable description of all 20th-century theatrical endeavour.

The influence of Stanislavsky

The American theatre. The first American plays, as has been said, were modelled on English drama. A native type, the shrewd, rural Yankee, first appeared in Royall Tyler's *The Contrast* (1787) which introduced also a favourite theme of an early American drama: the triumph of native honesty and worth over foreign sham and affectation. In 1798, William Dunlap, America's first professional playwright, dramatized recent American history in a blank-verse tragedy, *André*, in which George Washington is a principal character. The heroic Indian was added in John Augustus Stone's *Metamora* (1829), the tough city lad in Benjamin Baker's *Glance at New York in 1848* (1848), and the stout-hearted frontiersman in Frank Murdoch's *Davy Crockett* (1872). Native-born actors early performed in minor roles, and the native star, able to hold his own with the best on the London stage, appeared with Edwin Forrest in the 1820s and with Charlotte Cushman in the 1830s. Forrest's "American" style was characterized by muscular strength and vocal power. Theatre, first confined to the Eastern Seaboard, in 1815 expanded into the Ohio Valley and then to the Mississippi Valley.

To begin with, settings including all except a few pieces of furniture actually used by the actors were painted on wings shutters. The use of real instead of painted rugs and draperies and a full complement of furniture appeared in the production of Dion Boucicault's *London Assurance* (1841). Detailed historical accuracy in setting and costume first attracted attention in Charles Kean's production of *King John* (1846). In Edwin Booth's theatre in 1869 the box setting began to be used. In the next 30 years the detailed realistic setting was perfected by such producer-directors as Augustin Daly, Steele MacKaye, and David Belasco. Realistic production was stimulated by the introduction of gas lighting about 1825 and of electricity about 1885.

Realism in acting appeared in some of the characterizations of Yankee specialists such as George H. Hill in the 1830s and 1840s; in Francis S. Chanfrau's tough city boy in the '40s; in Matilda Heron's unconventional *Camille* in the '50s; in Edwin Booth's quieter acting of Shakespeare and Joseph Jefferson's "natural" Rip Van Winkle in the '60s; and was fully developed by William Gillette and Mr. and Mrs. James A. Herne in the '80s. James A. Herne's *Margaret Fleming* (1890) was the first realistic problem play in the manner of Ibsen. Herne could not, however, secure production of this "new" drama in a regular theatre.

Growth of civic companies

At the beginning of the 19th century each major city had a resident repertory company. As population grew and spread westward, so did the number of resident companies, and a leading actor found it profitable to set himself up as a star, playing brief guest engagements with one resident company after another. The proliferation of such stars and the rise of the long run, which was necessitated by increasingly expensive staging, eventually destroyed the resident company, which was replaced in the 1860s and 1870s, except in a few of the largest cities, by the travelling "combination." Originating usually in New York City, which since 1825 had been the leading theatre centre, hundreds of these combination companies, presenting either a smaller repertory or a single play, were providing entertainment the length and breadth of the land. Booking agencies were formed as liaison between companies and theatres. Several theatre owners, producers, and agents, of whom Charles Frohman was the best known, formed the Theatrical Syndicate in 1896, which by controlling booking in key cities gained a virtual monopoly of theatre throughout the country. The syndicate was not interested in plays with limited audience appeal. The theatre on all levels, from serious drama to burlesque, was the country's chief medium of entertainment. It was a big and prosperous business, and it was beginning to be attacked for "commercialism." The change from repertory to the single play and the rise of realistic production also shifted artistic control from the actor to the manager, who became the producer-director, or *régisseur*. In the last decades of the 19th century Augustin Daly, Steele MacKaye, and David Belasco not only selected and cast their plays and directed the rehearsals but also personally supervised all other aspects of production.

IV. 20th-century theatre

The late-19th-century movement toward realism had involved dramatists, designers, directors, and actors. But the term "realism" only approximately describes the work produced by the playwrights. Ibsen, for example, who had begun his career with poetic, visionary work such as *Brand* (published 1866; Eng. trans. 1891), turned to "realistic" plays such as *The Pillars of Society* (1877) and *Ghosts* (1881), which occupied him for some 15 years. Even these, however, were not dispassionate "slices of life" but artfully constructed, psychologically probing, and profound dramas. His later work from *The Master Builder* (1892) to *When We Dead Awaken* (1899) is invested more and more with symbolism. Strindberg did not allow himself to be restricted by naturalistic limitations: his later work, especially *A Dream Play* (1929), presents life strangely distorted in a way that is akin to the Expressionism of the German playwrights Georg Kaiser and Ernest Toller in the second decade of the 20th century, which strives to penetrate beyond the appearances of reality to approach emotional truth. The plays of Frank Wedekind defy classification. *Spring's Awaken-ing* (1891) used the scientific analysis of behaviour (the slice-of-life technique) in a "real" study of adolescence, yet its ending moves toward expressionism: one of two boy heroes returns to urge the other to commit suicide, while a man in a mask, representing life, urges him to live.

The quest for a new theatre toward the end of the 19th century, in fact, only seemed to go hand in hand with realism. For almost immediately, designers, playwrights, and directors were seeking ways of escape. There was a common desire that contemporary truth should be a keystone of contemporary theatre and that the world should be brought onto the stage. But there was little agreement over the means of achieving these aims. Western theatre in the early 20th century was eclectic, using a variety of means to escape from realism, though not reality.

ESCAPES FROM REALISM

The new stagecraft. Technological advances made in the late 19th century, which brought a variety of new stage machinery and opened up new possibilities in the art of stage lighting by electricity, gave rise to new theories of stagecraft. Leading theoreticians included two designers. In Switzerland, Adolphe Appia turned from opera to drama to expound his theory of design, which demanded a fully three-dimensional setting, with various stage levels, and the use of "living" light. All were to strengthen the dramatic action of the play and were to change and evolve as a counterpoint to it.

An Englishman, Edward Gordon Craig, the illegitimate son of the actress Ellen Terry, thought of the theatre as a place where "the inner beauty and the meaning of life" is revealed. Recognizing that the experience of theatre is a combination of many arts—acting, directing, music, movement, mime, design, makeup, lighting—his aim was "total theatre," with one man being responsible for harmonizing every aspect of the play produced so that it might achieve its fullest effect. He felt that a suggestion of reality could create in the imagination of the audience a physical reality: the one Gothic pillar, for instance, designed to stand alone and carefully lit, can suggest a church more effectively than can a cardboard and canvas replica faithful to the last detail.

The work of Max Reinhardt

The young Max Reinhardt was an actor in Otto Brahm's Freie Bühne company and had been allowed to direct there a number of experimental productions (of Strindberg, Oscar Wilde, Wedekind, Gorky, and others). In 1903 he left the company and opened his own at the Neues Theater, winning acclaim for his staging of *A Midsummer Night's Dream* (1905). Reinhardt brought his love of colour and gaiety, richness and display to his productions and was attacked by both the old school of directors and the realists. All disliked the "theatricality" of his work, a quality scrupulously avoided in their own low-key work. It was his great service to the European theatre, however, that he restored its vital theatricality without reinstating its old staginess. In so doing, he also revolutionized theories of acting: rejecting the idea of "one style," he demanded for modern plays a style realistic in feeling but avoiding the drab exactness of realism. In productions of the classics he demanded lively, supple speaking in place of the slow, ponderous delivery of the traditionalists. He made his actors think afresh about their characters instead of assuming ready-made characterizations.

In 1902 he opened his Kleines Theater in Berlin and initiated a movement that aimed to break down the separation of stage and auditorium and to restore intimacy between actor and audience. In his endeavours to rescue the players from their isolation behind the proscenium arch, he often took them out of the theatre to play in places that seemed eccentric settings for a theatrical entertainment—a square in Venice, a palace ballroom in Vienna, the Boboli Gardens in Florence, and the Domplatz (cathedral square), where every year he directed *Jedermann* (*Everyman*), by his contemporary Hugo von Hofmannsthal, at the Salzburg Festival. He produced *Oedipus Rex* (1910, Vienna) in a circus arena, using one end for gigantic architectural settings unframed by any proscenium. For his production of the mimed religious play, *The Miracle* (1911), he transformed the huge Olympia exhibition building in London into a cathedral so that the audience became part of the congregation. But although he was a master of spectacle, his versatility was such that he directed subtle and intimate plays in small theatres with equal skill. Until World War I his personality dominated the German stage; nearly all the young directors and actors had either worked in one of his companies or been trained in one of his schools.

Revolt in Russia. In Russia, the general European reaction against over-attention to the externals of realism in theatre production came at more or less the same time that Stanislavsky himself was beginning to feel he must seek new paths. In 1905 he founded a small studio theatre for experiment and research, appointing Vsevolod Meyerhold director. A member of the Moscow Art Theatre Company, Meyerhold had left in 1902 when he became a convert to the Symbolist movement. After months of preparation, Meyerhold staged two productions, but Stanislavsky disliked them so intensely that he closed the studio. He thought the actors had been used as puppets to illustrate Meyerhold's theories. Yet these productions had an important effect on him as a demonstration of the slavish obedience to which the dictatorial producer could reduce his actors. He determined that the actor should in future be his collaborator not his subordinate, and he began to develop a method of "inner realism" that became known as the Stanislavsky method (and remains the basic training of Russian actors).

After the Revolution in 1917 Stanislavsky refused to allow his theatre to become a platform for spreading propaganda. He believed that its mission was to maintain a standard of acting that other theatres might emulate when the first excesses of the Revolution had abated.

Effect of governmental influence on Stanislavsky

The official edict decreed that characterization, ideas, and emotions should be reduced to the simplest possible terms for the new audiences, many of them illiterate. This amounted to a command to actors to overact, abandoning all subtleties and returning to a crude, melodramatic style. Some of Stanislavsky's company were much taken by the enthusiasm with which the new audiences acclaimed their overacting, so he decided to take his company abroad and in 1922 left on a tour of Europe and the U.S. On returning (1924), deciding that the Moscow Art Theatre must adapt itself to the new audiences, he began to produce in bold, sweeping strokes, stressing the dramatic elements and enlivening comic scenes with tricks borrowed from vaudeville. Although far from subtle, this new style did not stoop to the crude exaggerations of the contemporary Soviet propaganda theatre.

Meyerhold had meanwhile become one of the most powerful influences in the Russian theatre. He declared that the principles of propagandist theatre conformed with those of Marxism because they attempted to underline "the elements which make prominent what is common to all men, the unindividual." Detailed portrayal of emotion was described as "worthless soul junk," and the actor was ordered to "forget his little rickety ego" and become "an instrument for social manifestos." Many other producers, educated to despise an individualistic society, exercised ingenuity to deprive actors of individuality. Aleksandr Tairov, founder of the Kamerny Theatre (1914), made his actors wear fantastically exaggerated makeup so that they would not resemble anyone in real life and thus become individuals to the audience. Tairov invented the "constructivist" setting, a gaunt scaffolding supporting bare platforms on different levels, with every strut and bolt exposed to view. The aggressive functionalism of this kind of setting was regarded as having considerable propaganda value when the Russians were being taught to revere the machine as part of their training to become a great industrial nation.

A more moderate director was Yevgeny Vakhtangov, a pupil of Stanislavsky. In 1914 he was in charge of one of the studios attached to the Art Theatre and in 1920 was appointed director of this subsidiary, renamed the Third Studio (or Workshop). But Vakhtangov was not altogether in accord with the quiet naturalness of the Art

Theatre. His natural exuberance impelled him toward a style of production that, while avoiding the extreme stylization and unrealism of Meyerhold and Tairov, nevertheless enlarged, heightened, and sharpened character, emotion, and gesture. He wanted to work in vivid colours instead of halftones. In place of Stanislavsky's inner realism he wanted what he called "outer-technique." He found the ideal actors for his purpose when Stanislavsky put him in charge of a group of Jewish players who in 1917 had formed a company for production of plays in Hebrew, calling themselves the Habima Players. In 1918 they became affiliated with the Art Theatre. Vakhtangov's masterpiece was his production of Rappoport Ansky's *The Dybbuk* (1922).

Revolt in Germany. The German theatre had been revitalized by the work of Max Reinhardt, and soon after World War I two former members of his company, Leopold Jessner and Erwin Piscator, became the leading directors. Their productions employed actors on a bare, darkened stage picked out by shafts of light against a black background; scenery was limited to one or two small pieces, symbolic rather than realistic. Stylized staging inevitably led to stylized acting, which in turn demanded stylized writing. Thus was created the German school of Expressionist drama, which was regarded not as a movement in art but as a reform of life. Its leading dramatists were Georg Kaiser and Ernst Toller. Characters became symbols instead of people, their lines stripped of all but key words and phrases. In the age of technology technical devices were used openly on stage. The actor was reduced to a puppet, into which he poured his life, to become a ritualized, priestly figure, celebrating not the unindividual but the super-individual. Marxist economic theory eventually replaced this theology, and the people who secularized the German theatre were all involved in politics. Later in the 1920s, when steel, timber, and other materials became more plentiful, Piscator directed a series of productions using elaborate and expensive machinery. The front of his stage was constructed on the conveyor-belt principle; in the centre a cantilever bridge moved up and down; lantern slides and motion-picture films were projected onto the back wall; above the proscenium slogans blazed in lights; the gigantic shadows of pulsating machines were thrown onto gauzes. Jessner, too, made free with building materials once postwar restrictions on their use had been lifted. His favourite setting was a vast flight of steps extending the entire width of the stage, rising steeply to a high platform at the back. He was greatly influenced by the new stagecraft of Craig and by the work of the Soviet directors of the immediate post-revolutionary period, whom he copied in oversimplifying characters and their motives, abandoning subtlety for elementary Symbolism. The political theatre to which Expressionist drama gave way was described by one of its leading personalities, Bertolt Brecht, as Epic Theatre. Brecht's theorizing was to be of enormous influence during the middle decades of the 20th-century Western theatre.

Contributions of Jessner and Piscator

Revolt in France. The reaction against realism was slower to reach France. The founding of the Théâtre du Vieux-Colombier by Jacques Copeau in 1913 initiated the reaction. Copeau was a literary critic who set up his own company. Like Reinhardt, he sought to break down the barrier between actor and audience. His stage was unframed; there were no wings and no line of demarcation between stage and auditorium. Decor was used sparingly; the atmosphere for each play was created almost entirely by lighting.

The work of Jacques Copeau

Before opening the Vieux-Colombier, Copeau took his company to Le Limon, where they improvised scenes and practiced exercises. They learned much from Charles Dullin, a singer in the Montmartre cafes and an exponent of traditional *comédie improvisée*, still popular in Parisian cabarets and provincial fairs. The acting at the Vieux-Colombier in a modern play was at first sight realistic, although the detail was minimized; but closer watching showed that gesture was being used selectively to give each gesture unusual significance. Copeau's productions of Molière and Shakespeare were notable for their lightness, grace, and gaiety. In 1924 he took a group of young actors to Burgundy, where, besides studying acting, they worked in the fields and in a carpenter's shop and took part in the local wine festival. The peasants called them "Les Copiaux," under which name they first appeared at Basel, Switzerland, in 1926. Their characteristic production was *La Danse de la ville et des champs*, written and produced by Michel Saint-Denis, who in 1930 took over the company, renamed the Compagnie des Quinze. It was disbanded in 1936 but had become internationally famous. The company had its own playwright, André Obey, who wrote to suit its methods and talents.

Revolt in Italy. The new technology of the 20th century is clearly reflected in theatrical activity in Italy during the early decades, especially in the Futurism of Filippo Tommaso Marinetti. Inspired by Bergson's philosophy of an élan vital, by Nietzche's philosophy of a superman, and by the new ecstacy of speed—with automobiles and airplanes as the symbols of speed and progress—his work was a celebration of man the machine and involved the use of inanimate objects as vital actors in his productions.

Anton Giulio Bragaglia initiated an experimental theatre in 1921, which borrowed from the Futurists but subordinated mechanics and technology to the play. He aimed to restore theatricality to the drama, using light, multidimensional space, intricate masks, and costume to surrealistic effect. He also wished his actors to master the acrobatic art of the commedia dell'arte as an antidote to cerebral acting. The dramatist Luigi Pirandello also challenged realism, with its stress on social environment shaping the individual, for he believed that the individual was capable of shaping his environment. His own Theatre of Art, opened in Rome in 1925 at the Odeschalchi Theatre, was an attempt to make the theatre something more than a place where an ironic tolerance of the human condition was developed, but one where people became aware of man himself.

The Irish national theatre

Ireland. The establishment of an Irish national theatre during the early years of the 20th century was not a reaction against existing forms in theatre but the result of a nationalist political movement and a desire to displace the cheaply sentimental plays in which the Irish had previously been presented to the world. The first step was taken in 1899, when the poet William Butler Yeats and the playwright Lady Augusta Gregory founded the Irish Literary Theatre, a society encouraging poetic drama. During the early years of the 20th century they and their associates achieved a recognizable company style in play and production. After a London appearance in 1903, Miss A.E.F. Horniman (pioneer of the British repertory movement) provided a permanent home for them in Dublin at the rebuilt Abbey Theatre. Their brilliant work there became world famous, with fine native actors and outstanding dramatists, including J.M. Synge and Sean O'Casey.

Britain. British theatre paid very little attention to the anti-realistic movements that characterized experimental theatre in the rest of Europe. Outstanding during the first decade was the work of Harley Granville-Baker and J.E. Vedrenne at the Court Theatre in Chelsea, who encouraged new writers uninterested in writing for an artificial theatre (they included George Bernard Shaw and John Galsworthy). An acting style evolved whereby characters "seem to live and move by the laws of their own being." Later, Granville-Barker's Shakespearean productions at the Savoy Theatre revolutionized the approach to directing and acting Shakespeare's plays, which he presented with simplicity, continuity, and speed. His method of production work was developed after his retirement by directors such as Basil Bean and Gerald du Maurier.

Equally significant for the British theatre was the pioneer work done by Miss Horniman when she founded the first provincial repertory theatre at the Gaiety, Manchester, in 1908. It introduced to England the work of a number of important continental dramatists and gave opportunities to promising British playwrights. The Playhouse, Liverpool, was founded in 1911 and developed a great number of talented actors. The most adventurous and distinguished repertory theatre, however, was founded at Birmingham by Sir Barry Jackson in 1913, where notable first performances were given of plays by Shaw, the Scottish dramatist James Bridie, J.B. Priestley, John Drinkwater, and others, as well as revivals of classic plays. The repertory movement continued with distinction but after World War II was regarded largely as a ground where actors gained experience before making an assault on the capital—an attitude that was not rectified until the late 1950s and 1960s.

United States. In the first decade of the 20th century realism dominated the American theatre; in the plays of Clyde Fitch, William Vaughn Moody, and Edward Sheldon; in the acting of Mrs. Fiske, Richard Mansfield, and Ethel Barrymore; and in the productions of David Belasco and Harrison Grey Fiske. At the same time, however, the pretty operettas of Victor Herbert and the brash musical comedies of George M. Cohan were popular. The first *Ziegfeld Follies* appeared in 1907. The New Theatre in New York City, with a resident company dedicated to art rather than business, was established in 1909 but collapsed after two seasons.

Visits of the Abbey Theatre in 1911, Reinhardt's *Sumurūn* in 1912, Granville-Barker's company in 1915, and Copeau's group from the Vieux-Colombier in Paris in 1917 provided exciting glimpses of the work of Europe's art theatres and of the "new stagecraft," thus adding to a growing dissatisfaction with the United States theatre.

The modern period on Broadway may be said to have begun in 1918 with the establishment of the Theatre Guild, the first commercially successful U.S. art theatre, and in the next decade there occurred a flowering that placed U.S. theatre for the first time on a par with the best theatre of Europe. Eugene O'Neill emerged from the Provincetown Players in 1920 with *Beyond the Horizon* to win worldwide fame. He was quickly followed by other playwrights including Robert Sherwood, Maxwell Anderson, Elmer Rice. Their plays provided an expression of American life that was unprecedented in its richness and variety. Besides the Theatre Guild, independent producers also staged the new American drama, as well as interesting new plays from abroad and some classics in the new style. Designers such as Lee Simonson, Norman Bel Geddes, and Jo Mielziner provided distinguished settings that were realistic, symbolistic, or expressionistic as required by the new drama. The Moscow Art Theatre company visited New York in 1923, and, impressed with the quality of ensemble acting they found there (which only a permanent organization could achieve), some of its members remained in New York to teach the Stanislavsky system. In 1926 Eva Le Galliene established a permanent repertory company that presented classics old and new. *Show Boat* appeared in 1927 and became a classic of the musical stage. Outside New York City, competition from motion pictures reduced the number of theatres open to travelling companies from 1,500 in the early 1900s to 500, but on Broadway the number of productions grew from 150 in 1920-21 to 280 in 1927-28.

Distinguished U.S. designers

MID-20TH-CENTURY THEATRE

The most exciting place in Europe during the 1920s was, arguably, Berlin. Countless stories and anecdotes celebrate the city in this decade. The stage had earlier been flooded by the despair and disillusion of postwar Europe, but during the 1920s an overtly political theatre emerged.

Bertolt Brecht. One of the dramatist-directors working at this time was Bertolt Brecht, whose theories of stage presentation perhaps exerted more influence upon the course of mid-century drama in the West than did those of any other individual. His theory of Epic Theatre was evolved in an attempt to appeal to his audience's mind instead of to its emotions—the theatre of argument instead of the theatre of empathy—and he derived inspiration from the popular theatre with its blatant theatricality rather than from the "realistic" theatre of illusion. His own early plays have something in common with the German Expressionist drama; he then embarked upon a number of jazz ballad-operas in collaboration with the composer Kurt Weill. His greatest original work was written during the late 1930s and early 1940s, while in exile from the Nazi regime, first in Norway, then in the United States. Like the Russian director Meyerhold, Brecht was vehemently opposed to illusive stage presentation. He did not wish his audience to appreciate his plays like gourmets enjoying a meal; he wanted to stir their critical faculties in such a way that they would be forced to think about their own lives. In illusive stage productions, such as those of Stanislavsky, there is a danger that the audience will identify emotionally with the play's characters as characters—that they will witness not their own real life but somebody else's real life. In an effort to free the audience from "the spell cast upon them by the witchcraft of realistic producers who make a dream world of reality," Brecht evolved what he called the "alienation effect" (*Verfremdungs-effekt*). This does not mean that he wished to alienate the audience; it refers to his constant use of anti-illusive techniques in order to remind the audience they were in a theatre and to emphasize his dictum that "the actual world exists and is our

Devices of Brechtian stagecraft

subject; but this play and this stage are not it." He flooded his stage with hard white light during the play, regardless of when the action might take place; he projected captions, slogans, and comments onto a gauze screen between scenes; important points raised during the action were driven home by songs that were otherwise unrelated to the play; Stanislavsky's doctrine that the actor must identify himself subjectively with the character he is playing was reversed, and Brecht demanded instead an objective style of acting in which the actor remains always aware of himself.

The influence of Brecht's frontal attack on the illusive theatre has since been evident, directly or indirectly, in the theatre of every Western country. But traditions and conditions vary so much from one country to another that, though it is possible to trace here this influence and there another, playwrights, designers, and directors have become sufficiently aware of one another's work to borrow whatever they want for a given purpose. The theatre in the Western world is vigorous, but it is a cross-fertilization of many styles that makes it so. Brecht's attack on illusive theatre by no means universally triumphed. Many fine new plays of today belong to the school of realism. By the 1950s, moreover, at least three other approaches to the staged presentation of life were commonly to be found.

The "Cruel" approach. In France during the early 1930s, Antonin Artaud elaborated a theory of a Theatre of Cruelty. A surreal theatre based on ritual and fantasy, it launches an attack on the audience's subconscious in an attempt to release deep-rooted fears and anxieties that are normally suppressed, forcing people to view themselves and their natures without the shield of civilization. In order to shock the audience and thus win the necessary response, the extremes of human nature (often madness, or perversion) are graphically portrayed on stage. The style of physical playing is here more important than the texts performed. Artaud's influence is apparent in the work of such French directors as Jean-Louis Barrault, Jean Vilar, and Roger Blin. It was obvious also in Peter Brook's direction for London's Royal Shakespeare Company of the *Marat/Sade* by a German dramatist, Peter Weiss. The one major playwright associated with the Theatre of Cruelty is Jean Genet. Many others, however, make use of "Cruel" elements in their plays, including the British playwrights Edward Bond and David Rudkin.

The "Absurd" approach. The plays of a number of dramatists, especially in France during the 1950s, offered a vision of humanity struggling vainly and therefore absurdly to control its fate in a world that seemed in any case bent on destruction. Although no two playwrights were much alike in style, certain recurring themes, especially of futility and hopelessness, caused them to be labelled the "Absurd" school. Theatre of the Absurd has been traced directly from the work of the French dramatist Alfred Jarry, whose play *Ubu roi* caused a sensation

Jarry's *Ubu roi*

when it was produced in Paris in 1896. Texts are of much more importance than they are in Theatre of Cruelty, even though many of them seek to convey the total inade-

quacy of words as a means of communication. Distinguished writers whose names have been linked with the Absurd school include Samuel Beckett, Eugène Ionesco (both writing in Paris), Harold Pinter (in Britain), and Fernando Arrabal (a Spanish refugee writing in the French language). Each of these, however, has developed his own distinctive approach to the theatre and defies a common classification. Inverted logic and verbal humour (puns, non sequiturs) were a feature of "Absurd" plays and have been absorbed—much diluted —into mainstream light entertainment.

The "Factual" approach. Another method of presenting contemporary truth on the stage has been called Theatre of Fact, or Documentary Theatre. During the social protest movement that arose during the years of depression in the 1930s, groups such as the Federal Theatre in the United States adopted what are called Living Newspaper techniques, borrowing inspiration from the cinema (especially in the use of short, succinct scenes fast cutting one to the next), to present a highlighted version of contemporary problems. The technique has had a long, if intermittent, life. Surprisingly effective in the theatre, real events are reconstructed and interpreted, either through fictional revisions so arranged that they carry the unemotional weight of genuine official documents or else through the use of authentic documentary material (transcripts of trials, official reports, lists of statistics). Well-known works of this sort include the plays of Rolf Hochhuth (*The Representative, Soldiers*), of Reinar Kipphardt (*In the Matter of J. Robert Oppenheimer*), of Michael Hastings (*The Silence of Lee Harvey Oswald*), and the Royal Shakespeare Company's *US*.

It is clear that the Brecht approach to stage presentation has something in common with the Theatre of Fact, and that the Theatre of the Absurd has elements in common with the Theatre of Cruelty. But "schools" of drama are more usually constructed by critics than by playwrights, and many individual theatrical presentations borrow techniques from more than one approach.

Germany. The exciting German theatre of the 1920s was swept away when the Nazis came to power in 1933. After World War II, a few people were able to return. Bertolt Brecht formed the Berliner Ensemble company in East Berlin, creating a brilliant company style for the presentation of his plays. After his death in 1956 his widow, the actress Helene Weigel, continued to train actors and to present her husband's work. The influence of this company on theatre throughout the West can hardly be overemphasized, but even before Brecht's death it had begun to lose its dynamic power and seemed more concerned to preserve its established, albeit brilliant, style than to tread new paths. In West Germany Fritz Kortner, who had worked as a young actor with Reinhardt and was a leading player with Jessner, returned to Germany in 1947 to direct a series of brilliant productions. His interpretations of classical plays and of modern drama can be regarded as the culmination of the German tradition begun by Otto Brahm in the 1890s.

Otherwise, in spite of the number of theatres and the money lavished upon them in government and municipal grants, there were few signs in the 1950s of any strongly progressive theatrical movement. Much of the best creative work was done in the opera houses. But, after a revival of German drama, mainly by Swiss-German playwrights (including Max Frisch and Friedrich Dürrenmatt) and Peter Weiss, the theatre throughout Germany began to revive. Later, the work of such dramatists as Günter Grass, Siegfried Lenz, Reinar Kipphardt, and Rolf Hochhuth provided more opportunity for original direction and staging.

Swiss-German dramatists

U.S.S.R. The youngest post-revolutionary director of importance was Nikolay Okhlopkov. His earliest productions were entertainments given during World War I on an improvised platform in the square of his home town to entertain the troops, who encircled the stage. As a result of this experience of the open stage, he found the proscenium theatre cramping and in Moscow experimented with ways of breaking down the barrier between actor and audience.

In 1932 he became director of the Realistic Theatre, where for his production of Aleksandr Serafimovich's *The Iron Flood* he converted the auditorium into a mountainous terrain, seating the audience among the rocks so that actors, playing in every part of the auditorium, mingled with audience. He made other experiments in staging, but in 1938 the Realistic Theatre was closed on the grounds that his work appealed too exclusively to intellectuals. In 1934 Meyerhold, censured for his "obsession with the vague abstractions of decadent art," and for being "the father of formalism," was deprived of his position. Tairov, rebuked for being out of touch with his audiences, had been relieved of the direction of the Kamerny Theatre and forced to work under a committee. It is true that their work was too cold and abstract to please audiences who wanted warmth, humanity, and reality. But under Stalinism the theatre virtually ceased to progress, since any originality was condemned as decadent. Scenery became more and more laboriously realistic, as a setting in any way impressionistic was condemned as belonging to "abstract art." Only the magnificent standard of acting remained unchanged.

After Stalin's death in 1953 the theatre was relieved of many shackles and there was a cautious return to experiment, particularly at the Satire Theatre. Okhlopkov, only survivor of the experimentalist producers of the 1920s, remained the most original and stimulating director, though at times under Stalinism his originality had displeased the authorities, and he had been criticized for too unruly an imagination.

Soviet theatre in the 1960s

In the 1960s the Soviet theatre was perhaps at its best in productions of the classic Russian authors, directed with meticulous care. Its unique feature was its gigantic scale —the vast number of theatres, the fact that there were companies playing in more than 50 languages, the size of the companies (100 actors was not unusual), the size of the repertoire of each theatre, the huge and superbly equipped stages showing a succession of elaborate scenes, the size of the theatregoing audience, and the vast state subsidies to theatres, so that they need not even attempt to pay their way and thereby could keep their prices low.

The professional theatre could not satisfy the demand for dramatic entertainment, and every encouragement was given to the amateur. Most theatres accepted responsibility for at least one amateur group, the members of the company giving much time to training and advising it. Amateur companies of outstanding merit were given the title "people's theatre." Most of these companies toured neighbouring towns, as well as playing in factories and collective farms. The close relations between professional and amateur were mutually beneficial, for professionals found that contact with the personnel of the amateur groups infused freshness and reality into their own performances. By the late 1960s there was an even greater loosening up; satire, even political, became increasingly dominant and methods and techniques increasingly experimental and symbolic.

France.   The influence of Jacques Copeau was extended through the productions of Louis Jouvet and Dullin, who left his company in 1922 to start their own theatres. Jouvet's productions of Molière were his most important contribution. He freed the plays from the weight of tradition that was stifling them. His *L'École des femmes* (1936) was hailed as a return to the spirit of Molière. While Jouvet was careful to subjugate himself to his author, Dullin's productions were strongly coloured by his own personality and tastes. He loved bright colours, music, movements, and his productions were in sharp contrast to the asceticism of Georges Pitoëff, who believed that the director's primary aim should be to focus attention on a play's central idea, and eliminate all details of decor and acting that might obscure it. His great contribution to the French theatre was the number of foreign dramatists whom he introduced to the Parisian public.

Jouvet, Dullin, and Pitoëff, with Gaston Baty, were known as Les Quatre ("The Four"). Baty had served his apprenticeship under Reinhardt. His pictorial sense was superb, and his groupings and movement were beautifully composed, but they existed for themselves rather than

for the play. He was often accused of over-elaborating the classics to display his own inventiveness.

Dullin's use of mime was elaborated in the productions of his pupil Jean-Louis Barrault, who left the Comédie-Française in 1946 to form, with his wife, the actress Madeleine Renaud, the Compagnie Renaud–Barrault, which played in the provinces and abroad and, in Paris, at the Théâtre Marigny. In 1959 he became director of the Théâtre de France, to which in 1966 the annual Théâtre des Nations was transferred. Much of his work is symbolistic—a combination of pantomime, rhythmic movement, and shadowgraph.

He became the chief exponent of "total theatre," a theory evolved by Gordon Craig. Another pupil of Dullin, Jean Vilar, in 1951 founded the Théâtre Nationale Populaire (TNP). His style was governed by the size of the Palais de Chaillot, a theatre seating nearly 3,000 with a stage 70 feet (about 20 metres) deep and a proscenium opening 80 feet (about 25 metres) wide. Vilar made no attempt to fill the stage with scenery. He did no more than suggest the background of the play and filled his stage with big, swirling movement. He trained his actors to use bold, simplified gestures and delineate character in powerful outline.

Until the 1950s theatrical activity was almost entirely concentrated in Paris but with government help theatrical centres were established at Strasbourg, Aix-en-Provence, Saint-Étienne, Toulouse, and Reims.

Great Britain.   A director who refreshed English acting and direction in the 1930s was Theodore (Fyodor) Komisarjevsky, who in 1919 went to England from Russia, where he had been director of the Imperial and State theatres. His direction of plays by Chekhov and other Russian authors set a new standard in the English theatre. His Shakespearean productions at Stratford-on-Avon often infuriated audiences accustomed to conventional presentation. They were full of invention, sometimes brilliant, amusing, and illuminating, sometimes merely wayward. In the same tradition was Tyrone Guthrie; a director with a superb theatrical imagination, who began in the 1930s at the Old Vic, London. Sometimes his inventiveness was used merely to surprise and shock the audience or to satisfy his own sense of humour. Other fine Shakespearean producers include Peter Brook, whose productions in the 1950s and early 1960s gave early evidence of rare talent, and Peter Hall. In the late 1950s the most influential British director was Joan Littlewood. In 1945 she had founded the Theatre Workshop company at Manchester for working class audiences. In 1953 it moved to the Theatre Royal, Stratford, in the East End of London. She encouraged audience participation; allowed actors to improvise—all her later productions were "collective" in that the actors shared in planning the presentation and often took liberties with the text—and borrowed techniques from music hall, such as impromptu asides to the audience and the introduction of topical songs and jokes. Her productions also owed much to Bertolt Brecht. George Devine set up the English Stage Company at the Royal Court Theatre in 1956 to allow novelists to try their hand as playwrights and to introduce new writers and modern foreign drama. Its club, the English Stage Society, gave Sunday performances without decor, so allowing experimental plays to be tried out. Most of the new English playwrights of the 1950s and 1960s had their works first produced by the English Stage Company, which has also given many directors, designers, and actors later outstanding in the West End their first chance.

The work of Joan Little-wood

There was no permanent dramatic company in London until 1960. To remedy this lack Peter Hall engaged a company (called from 1961 the Royal Shakespeare Company), on long-term contract to play at Stratford-on-Avon and at the Aldwych Theatre, London, presenting modern plays as well as Shakespeare and other classics, both often produced in experimental styles. Michel Saint-Denis became a co-director (with Brook and Hall) in 1962. The Aldwych is the summer home of a World Theatre Season, established in 1964 by Peter Daubeny.

Provincial and repertory theatre.   In the provinces the theatre divides into touring, repertory, and amateur. The touring theatres are visited by London companies either before or after they play in London and by companies engaged to tour a London success. At Christmas nearly all these theatres stage an elaborate pantomime, so popular that the run often extends for three or four months. In the early 1920s there were more than 250 touring theatres in England and Scotland. By 1966 the number had dwindled to little more than 20. Many had failed to survive the competition of motion pictures; others were destroyed during World War II; and after the war television proved a deadly rival. "Repertory" theatres in the provinces withstood competition more successfully. These repertory theatres had at first no right to the title, because they did not keep a repertoire of plays ready for production as do continental "repertoire" theatres, which give performances of several plays from their repertoire each week. But by the mid-1960s, the nature of provincial repertory had changed considerably, as a result of increased government grants and bigger audiences. Most theatres had replaced the giving of a play for a short run (after which the production was scrapped) by a limited form of continental repertoire. By the early 1970s it was evident that the efforts to promote the repertories as basic to the life of their local community had often brilliantly succeeded.

The "little theatre"

The third branch of the provincial theatre, the amateur "little theatre," also makes a valuable contribution to theatrical experiment in Great Britain. Actors, designers, and stagehands are amateur and often anonymous. One of the leading provincial little theatres is the Maddermarket, Norwich, built in 1921 as the only theatre in England with an Elizabethan stage. Several other amateur dramatic societies flourish throughout Britain, many of them associated with the British Drama League. In the 1930s, a number of experimental "club theatres" were opened. The first was the Gate (1925). Its policy of producing unlicensed or uncommercial plays and witty reviews made it one of the most important of the prewar club theatres. Also influential were the Mercury, Notting Hill Gate (1933), famous for producing poetic plays by T.S. Eliot, Christopher Fry, Ronald Duncan, and others; the Hampstead Theatre Club; the Arts and New Arts Theatre Clubs; the Unity, St. Pancras, which in 1936 declared its intention of replacing the "escapism and false ideology of the conventional theatre" with a left-wing "agitational theatre," carried out with first English productions of plays by Clifford Odets, Sean O'Casey, and Soviet dramatists.

The national theatre. In 1949 Parliament passed the National Theatre Act, empowering the Treasury to make a grant of £1,000,000 to build a national theatre. Successive governments put off building the theatre until, in 1963, the government decided to finance a National Theatre, which opened under the directorship of Sir Laurence Olivier, with the Old Vic as its temporary home. In 1966 the government agreed to contribute half the cost of a building containing two auditoriums, the Greater London Council contributing the rest.

Other European countries. In northern Europe in the 1960s the largest audience was in Finland, where more than a quarter of the population were regular theatregoers. The number of plays by native authors was unusually high. Few have been performed abroad because of lack of good translations. In Denmark, production of a Danish play was comparatively rare, but a variety of foreign plays was produced. In Sweden, where the number of native playwrights was increasing, good theatre spread over the country. Göteborg rivalled Stockholm, and both were challenged by Malmö, Uppsala, Norrköping, and Hälsingborg. The Norwegian theatre has spent most of its life in financial crisis, partly because audiences have been scanty. It had to rely on private enterprise—even the National Theatre was founded in 1899 without state or municipal aid—until in 1961 the government took over financial responsibility for the whole theatre. To take the theatre to the people it founded the State Traveling Theatre, which played even in small villages beyond the Arctic Circle.

In eastern Europe the most advanced theatres were in Poland and Yugoslavia. Both were molded by great producers whose work has been continued by their pupils. In Yugoslavia, Branko Gavella was for nearly 50 years a free-lance producer, striving to improve standards and encourage originality. In Poland the work of Leon Schiller, a disciple of Gordon Craig, was continued by his most brilliant pupil, Erwin Axer. In Bulgaria, Romania, and Czechoslovakia development was hampered by subservience to socialist realism, but by the 1960s playwrights were beginning to write with more freedom and sophistication, and Josef Svoboda, chief designer at the National Theatre, Prague, after 1950, was widely regarded as the world's leading scenic designer. After World War II the number of Romanian theatre companies increased from 18 to 32, and Czechoslovakian theatres more than trebled. The Hungarian theatre, perhaps because of its situation, was the most cosmopolitan in its choice of plays. Never respectful of the dictates of socialist realism, it was a gay and sardonic theatre, excelling in satirical topical revues.

United States. The stock-market crash of 1929 heralded the end of the unparalleled prosperity in the theatre and in the nation. The nation recovered from the ensuing economic depression, but the theatre, under increasing competition from motion pictures, radio, and television, did not. In the next 30 years travelling companies all but disappeared, and productions on Broadway shrank to 60 in 1949–50 and thereafter averaged between 60 and 70 a year. No new theatres were constructed. Nevertheless, live theatre continued to attract talented writers: from the social protest movement of the 1930s came Clifford Odets, Sidney Kingsley, Lillian Hellman, Thornton Wilder, and William Saroyan; Tennessee Williams, Arthur Miller, and William Inge emerged in the 1940s, Edward Albee in the 1960s.

Effects of the Great Depression on U.S. theatre

Rising costs and shrinking audiences necessitated longer runs of plays. Enterprises outside the standard pattern, however, enjoyed some success. The Group Theatre for ten years maintained a permanent company, developed new playwrights, and evolved a new acting style based on the Stanislavsky system. From 1935 to 1939 the Federal Theatre Project presented hundreds of productions of all sorts and showed that a large untapped audience existed for live theatre at low prices. From 1937 to 1939 Orson Welles and John Houseman maintained a permanent company and gave limited runs of plays at the Mercury Theatre. From 1947 the Actors Studio cultivated the "method," derived from Stanislavsky's system and practiced by many outstanding U.S. actors. In 1955 the first U.S. Shakespeare festival was held at Stratford, Connecticut, and it became more popular each summer. The American National Theatre and Academy (ANTA), chartered by Congress in 1935 and activated in 1946, encouraged theatre, professional and nonprofessional, throughout the country. As bulk theatre activity decreased, the producer declined in importance and the stage director rose. Among the important directors in the 1940–60 period were Elia Kazan, Robert Lewis, Harold Clurman, Joshua Logan, and José Quintero.

The musical show after 1930 gained in polish and sophistication. In 1935 George and Ira Gershwin turned the play *Porgy*, by DuBose and Dorothy Heyward, into America's first successful folk opera, *Porgy and Bess.* Later examples were: *Pal Joey* (1940), *Lady in the Dark* (1941), *Oklahoma!* (1943), *South Pacific* (1949), *My Fair Lady* (1956), and the star-vehicle productions *Hello, Dolly!* (Carol Channing), *Funny Girl* (Barbra Streisand), and *Fiddler on the Roof* (Zero Mostel), all in 1964.

Rise of the musical

Off-Broadway theatre. Plays have always been produced in small theatres outside as well as in the main theatrical district in New York. In 1915–18 the Washington Square Players, in the 1920s the Provincetown Players, and in the 1930s the New Playwrights drew audiences and critics off-Broadway. A new era began in 1952 with the successful revival of Tennessee Williams' *Summer and Smoke* at the Circle in the Square and gained momentum with productions at the Phoenix, the Theatre de Lys, and the Fourth Street Theatre. In 1961–62, *The New York Times* counted 100 off-Broadway productions, 34 more than on Broadway. From 1962–63 the number of off-Broadway productions declined. Revivals of classics and of recent plays that had failed on Broadway predominated at first, but the proportion of new plays increased. Since production often took place in improvised quarters under makeshift conditions, it showed styles and forms seldom seen on Broadway. Many productions were stages without a proscenium arch and with the audience on two or three sides of the playing area. Actors, directors, designers, and producers who achieved success off-Broadway were soon active on Broadway. And Broadway successes began to appear off-Broadway, attracted by the greater artistic freedom.

Summer theatre. Declining production on Broadway was accompanied by a growth of theatre in resort areas during the vacation season. In 1940, 80 summer theatres were open for a ten-week season, performing a different play or musical each week in tents, barns, and sometimes in regular theatre buildings. By the 1960s more than 200 "straw-hat" theatres were in operation. Resident companies, frequently augmented by visiting stars, usually performed recent Broadway successes. Occasionally, these summer theatres were used to test new plays for possible Broadway production.

The Negro in the U.S. theatre. In native plays, the Negro appeared first as a plantation hand, a minor comic character. Later he was frequently seen as a comic domestic servant. The slavery plays like *Uncle Tom's Cabin* (1852) and the Civil War plays like *The Reverend Griffith Davenport* (1899) were the first to treat the Negro seriously. Edward Sheldon's *The Nigger* (1909) was the first play to deal with Negro problems in modern society. After the Civil War, Negroes became popular in minstrel shows and in all-Negro musicals.

From 1910 on, individuals like Bert Williams were featured in musicals like the *Ziegfeld Follies;* the integrated musical appeared in the 1940s. Negroes gained recognition in serious drama somewhat later; Charles Gilpin in *The Emperor Jones* (1920), Richard Harrison in *The Green Pastures* (1930), Canada Lee in *Native Son* (1941), and Paul Robeson in *Othello* (1943). Playwrights who contributed to the drama of Negro life include Ridgely Torrence, DuBose and Dorothy Heyward, and Paul Green. Negro playwrights had little success on Broadway until Lorraine Hansberry's *Raisin in the Sun* became a hit in 1959. The racial ferment of the 1960s created an audience for accusatory melodramas such as *Dutchman* (1964), by the poet LeRoi Jones (Imamu Amiri Baraka) and *Blues for Mister Charlie* (1964) and *The Amen Corner* (1965), by the novelist James Baldwin. *In White America* (1964), a documentary of 300 years of Negro grievances, by Martin Duberman, became a propaganda piece of the civil rights movement.

Community theatre. Community theatre grew out of the little theatre movement and its art theatres that sprang up (*c.* 1900–25), inspired by the "free" theatres of Europe, in protest against the commercial theatre. The little theatres presented noncommercial plays, European and American, with the "new stagecraft," in small theatres for small audiences.

Changing function of community theatre

As road companies disappeared, most of these organizations became substitutes for professional theatre, presenting popular plays in larger theatres to larger audiences with more paid personnel. By the late 1960s three types of community theatre existed: (1) a growing number with paid actors and staff, like the Arena Stage, Washington, D.C., and the Minnesota Theater Company in Minneapolis, of which Tyrone Guthrie was artistic director; (2) a few more paid staff and a few paid actors, like the Cleveland Play House; and (3) the great majority with some paid staff only. A new form of subsidy in the 1960s was exemplified by Ford Foundation grants in the Alley Theater in Houston and the Actor's Workshop in San Francisco.

University theatre. Dramatic performances by students go back to the colonial period, but instruction in theatre subjects did not enter the curriculum until about 1900, largely in colleges of liberal arts and as part of the reaction against commercial theatre. After World War I there was a tremendous expansion of courses, departments, and degrees in theatre studies. The National Theatre Conference of leading university and community theatres was founded in 1932. The American Educational Theatre Association (AETA) was established in 1936 and after 1949 published the *Educational Theatre Journal.* By 1964–65 nearly 600 college theatres were producing annually about 3,000 plays for an audience of more than 7,000,000. Much of this growth was because of the disappearance of professional theatre outside New York City. Although the aims of university theatre have been primarily cultural, it has affected the professional theatre, especially off-Broadway. Its unique contributions have been the development of theatre for children and the popularization of arena and other forms of open staging.

BIBLIOGRAPHY

Reference works: B.M. BAKER, *Theatre and Allied Arts* (1952, reprinted 1967), a bibliography containing more than 6,000 items published between 1885 and 1945, with cross-references and indexes; D.F. CHESHIRE, *Theatre: History, Criticism, and Reference* (1967), a comprehensive bibliographical guide to the main branches of theatrical endeavour, excluding opera and ballet; F.M. LITTO, *American Dissertations on the Drama and the Theatre* (1969), a bibliography that covers the period from 1865–1965; *Theatre Documentation* (semiannual), an annotated bibliography of current publications; *Enciclopedia dello spettacolo*, 9 vol., 3 vol. appendixes (1954–68), the only work of reference that treats all fields of the theatre and the film (opera and ballet included) exhaustively; PHYLLIS HARTNOLL (ed.), *The Oxford Companion to the Theatre*, 3rd ed. (1967), a single-volume standard work with bibliography and illustrations; SIEGFRIED MELCHINGER, *The Concise Encyclopedia of Modern Drama* (1966), four main sections, chronology of first performances, illustrations, and bibliography; J. GASSNER and E. QUINN (eds.), *The Reader's Encyclopedia of World Drama* (1969), covers the drama of five continents from the origins to the present; ANATOLE CHUJOY and P.W. MANCHESTER (eds.), *The Dance Encyclopedia*, rev. ed. (1967), a comprehensive, single-volume reference; A. LOEWENBERG, *Annals of Opera, 1597–1940*, 2nd rev. ed., 2 vol. (1955).

Theatre history—general: KENNETH MACGOWAN and WILLIAM MELNITZ, *The Living State: A History of the World Theater* (1955), an exemplary, concise introduction to theatre history providing time-charts, many excellent illustrations, bibliography, and an index; GEORGE FREEDLEY and J.A. REEVES, *A History of the Theatre*, 3rd rev. ed. (1968), a new edition especially important for its additional sections on the theatre in South America, Canada, and Germany under Hitler; RICHARD SOUTHERN, *The Seven Ages of the Theatre*, 2nd ed. (1964), an imaginative but none the less cogent and precise introductory book accompanied by an excellent booklist; MORDECAI GORELIK, *New Theatres for Old* (1940), an original and stimulating introductory work that contains a valuable glossary of stage terms, bibliography, and a wealth of excellent photographs; GEORGE ALTMAN et al., *Theater Pictorial: A History of World Theater As Recorded in Drawings, Paintings, Engravings, and Photographs* (1953); S. D'AMICO, *Storia del teatro drammatico*, 4th rev. ed., 4 vol. (1958), contains a wealth of illustrations, both monochrome and colour; H. KINDERMANN, *Theatergeschichte Europas* (1957–), vol. 3 and 4 provide a comparative survey of the Baroque theatre in Europe—the chapters on the court theatres and festivals in Austria and Germany are of particular interest (extensive bibliography, indexes, and chronology of opera and ballet included).

Theatre history—national and special studies: ALLARDYCE NICOLL, *Masks, Mimes and Miracles: Studies in the Popular Theatre* (1931, reprinted 1963), a well-documented account of the unliterary drama from classical mime to the commedia dell'arte with illustrations, footnotes, and appendix; MARGARETE BIEBER, *The History of the Greek and Roman Theater*, 2nd ed. rev. (1961), a detailed, indispensable account of the rise and development of all streams of theatrical endeavour in the ancient world with many illustrations, chronology, and an extensive bibliography; GLYNNE WICKHAM, *Early English Stages, 1300–1660*, 3 vol. (1959–72), the standard work on the English theatre from 1300 to 1660; ALLARDYCE NICOLL, *Stuart Masques and the Renaissance Stage* (1937); and A.M. NAGLER, *The Theatre Festivals of the Medici, 1539–1637* (1964), two detailed studies of the theatre festivals of the Renaissance in England and Italy, respectively, providing copious illustrations; E.K. CHAMBERS, *The Elizabethan Stage*, 4 vol. (1923, reprinted 1951), still a standard work on the history of the British theatre from the beginning of Elizabeth's reign to the death of Shakespeare, with appendixes of documents, statistics, and lists of plays; G.E. BENTLEY, *The Jacobean and Caroline Stage*, 7 vol. (1941–68), a sequel to Chambers though even more detailed covering the period from 1616 to 1642; *The London Stage, 1660–1800* (1960–), a reference book with critical introductions to each volume recording all known performances of plays (with dates and cast lists); N.D. SHERGOLD, *A History of the Spanish Stage* (1967), a detailed account of the Golden Age in Spanish drama and its medieval heritage; JOSEPH S. KENNARD, *The Italian Theatre*, 2 vol. (1932, reprinted 1964), a history of the Italian theatre from its beginnings to 1930; D.C. MULLIN, *The Development of the Playhouse* (1970), a survey of theatre architecture from the Renaissance to the present; FREDERICK W. HAWKINS, *Annals of the French Stage from Its Origins to the Death of Racine*, 2 vol. (1884, reprinted 1968); and *The French Stage in the Eighteenth Century*, 2 vol. (1888, reprinted 1968), still the best history of the French theatre in chronological sequence available in English (vol. 2 provides a chronology of the French stage, 1699–1799); JOHN LOUGH, *Paris Theatre Audiences in the Seventeenth and Eighteenth Centuries* (1957), a succinct survey of the other side of the theatre and a complementary work to Hawkins; W.H. BRUFORD, *Theatre, Drama, and Audience in Goethe's Germany* (1950), a thorough account of the interaction between life and drama, dramatic performance, and its reception; M.H. WINTER, *Le Théâtre du merveilleux* (1962; Eng. trans., *The Theatre of Marvels*, 1964), a lavishly illustrated book mainly concerned with French melodrama and romantic ballets; GEORGE ROWELL, *The Victorian Theatre* (1956), a thorough study of the English theatre from 1792 to 1914; MARK SLONIM, *Russian Theater, from the Empire to the Soviets* (1961), the fullest and most objective history of the Russian theatre yet produced; BARNARD W. HEWITT, *Theatre U.S.A., 1668–1957* (1959), contemporary documents in chronological order linked by lucid commentary; *History of the Theatre from 1800 to the Present* (1970).

Theatres and Stages

The English word theatre derives from the Greek *theatron*, literally, "a place for seeing," and, in its most common usage, it has come to signify a building or place so arranged that people can see and hear a performance given by others. The part of such a building in which these others perform is usually called the stage. This article deals with the art of the theatre from the viewpoint of the structures in which it has traditionally been presented. Although stage design is often a factor in determining the structure of the theatre, that subject is treated more fully in the article STAGING AND STAGE DESIGN. Aspects of theatre design are also discussed in THEATRE, ART OF and are treated in articles such as THEATRE, WESTERN; DANCE; and THEATRE, EAST ASIAN.

In this article there are three major sections. In the first, the development of theatre as place and its implications through the centuries is described; the second section is given over to a description of theatre in Asia; the final section contains an outline of the historical development of Western theatre.

Theatre as place

The civilizations of the Mediterranean basin in general, of the Far East, of northern Europe, and of the Western Hemisphere before the voyages of Christopher Columbus in the second half of the 15th century have all left evidence of constructions whose association with religious ritual activity relates them to the theatre. Studies in anthropology suggest that their forerunners were the campfire circles about which members of a primitive people's community would gather to participate in tribal rites. Karnak in ancient Egypt, Persepolis in Persia, Knossos in Crete, Stonehenge in Britain all offer examples of architectural structures, purposely ceremonial in design, so arranged and of a size to accommodate large audiences. They were used as places of assembly at which a priestly caste would invoke communication with supernatural forces. The transition from primitive ritual, in which there was mass participation, to something approaching drama, in which a clear distinction is made between ac-

*Fore-
runners
of formal
theatre*

tive participants and passive onlookers, did not take place in societies that failed to mature. Where the distinction was made, however, the priestly caste and, eventually, the performer were in time physically set apart from the spectators. Thus, theatre as place emerged.

A development such as this not only was a vital element in the process of formalizing ritual, it also brought with it the possibility of intense and empathetic response to the performance on the part of a now statically positioned audience. An interplay of the communicative senses, particularly sight and sound, therefore assumed the major roles they have continued to play. (From time to time, the sense of smell has also been involved, as in the burning of incense.) Consideration of audience requirements, such as sight and sound, have, in fact, determined the essential physical requirements of theatre as place and have also influenced the aesthetic of theatre design. Spectators are able to see a static performer's facial expression clearly without artificial aid if they are within a distance of about 100 feet (30 metres) of him and if they are set within a viewing angle of 150°–180°. Unaided, the performer's natural speaking voice can be heard over a distance of approximately 80 feet (25 metres). Consciously projected, it is audible for up to approximately 120 feet (37 metres). The chanted or singing voice can be heard over distances of up to 240 feet (73 metres). But in every case the sound effectively travels in one direction, sustained only within a cone of 150°–160° in front of the vocalizing source.

VARIED USE OF THEATRE BUILDINGS

Even a cursory survey of world civilizations would reveal that Western theatre, beginning in Greece c. 600 BC, is rich and varied in terms of theatre building. The art of theatre in the West also became socially sophisticated and varied. The first fact stems from the second. Broadly speaking, changes in theatre building have kept a sometimes laggardly pace with the theatre's evolution from something religious in inspiration to something of wider social significance. The Greek dramatists of the Classical period (5th century BC), especially the tragedians, whose plays were performed at time-hallowed religious festivals, celebrated gods and heroes in work that was also an eloquent statement of Greek theology. The comic playwrights, on the other hand, began to explore the drama's potentiality for expressing biting social comment and political satire, thereby changing the significance and the direction of the ancient festivals. Aristophanes, for instance, made use of the existing form of Greek theatre building that had been devised for the presentation of tragedy, but there is reason to believe that his comedies demanded effects more overtly theatrical than had the older tragedies. The change in emphasis from a drama that was dominated by the chorus (as in the early tragedies) to one in which the speaking actor played an increasingly important part (as in the comedies) was one reason why, during the Hellenistic Age, the performers were physically set apart: the chorus remained in the circular arena (orchestra), while the actors were elevated to a high, narrow platform immediately in front of the stage (*skēnē*), which, at that time, was a high wall backing the orchestra and giving access to it by three doors. Drama itself became increasingly secular as it was exposed to "corrupting" social influences, and changes in the physical theatre reflected this. In particular, the Roman comedy of the playwrights Plautus and Terence, which appealed to an experience far more sensual than spiritual, demanded an intimate contact between performers and audience that the older theatre form of Greece could not provide. As a result, the height of the stage was lowered and the full circle of the orchestra reduced to a semicircle. A pattern thus established during Classical times has been continued throughout the history of Western theatre: the playhouse adapts, however unwillingly, whenever a new kind of work becomes sufficiently established to demand it.

Once theatre buildings became established in major cities of Greece and Rome, they began to be used not only for dramatic performances but also as the principal place

*Change in
dramatic
emphasis
during the
Hellenistic
Age*

of public assembly. Orators and politicians quickly appreciated the fact that theatre facilities enabled them to be properly seen and heard; the Acts of the Apostles records that St. Paul addressed the Ephesians in their theatre; there is every reason to believe that theatres became the accepted place of confrontation between ruler and ruled.

Extra significance of theatres. Theatre buildings in Greece were always sited with regard to religious significance, but, from Roman times onward, convenience was the only factor in choosing the location for a new theatre. Theatres have long been regarded as symbols of glory, at first of the gods. In Greece, many theatres were associated with precincts sacred to the gods Apollo and Dionysus. One of the most popular theatres of the ancient Mediterranean world stood at Delphi, the great oracle of Apollo, located on the flank of Mt. Parnassus, birthplace of the muses; and it remained in use from the time of Pericles almost until the fall of Rome. The great theatre of Dionysus in Athens, though much remodelled by both Greeks and Romans (and revered above all others in the Classical world as the birthplace of public drama), was located along with a small cult temple in the precinct sacred to Dionysus. During the Roman Empire, theatres were often dedicated to the emperors as physical symbols glorifying the reigning deity. The first Roman remodelling of the theatre of Dionysus in Athens, for example, was dedicated to the emperor Nero, who is believed to have appeared there as actor and musician in the 1st century AD. During the following century, the emperor Hadrian was especially renowned for building and restoring theatres in all parts of his empire. In the grounds of his private villa at Tivoli, a few miles east of Rome, he caused three theatres to be built: one for Greek tragedy, one for comedy, and a small roofed odeum for intimate poetry readings and concerts. Even the austere emperor Augustus, who had established the empire in 27 BC, had both a small open-air theatre and a covered odeum at his private villa at Posillipus (modern Posilipo) on the Bay of Naples. Private philanthropy was as important in the ancient world, where theatre building is concerned, as it is in modern times. Herodes Atticus, for example, a famous Greek orator who was the tutor of the Roman emperor Marcus Aurelius in the 2nd century, built a theatre in Athens dedicated to his wife, and others in Corinth and Patras; there were countless royal patrons of the performing arts from the Renaissance onward; the Rockefeller family today is associated with foundations such as the Lincoln Center arts complex in New York City.

Importance of private philanthropy

Audience comfort. The Greek theatre, essentially a religious festival building, was principally concerned with what was to be presented on the stage. There is no record or archaeological evidence of a lobby, courtyard, or other enclosure being provided as an amenity for the audience—in which, for example, people might pass the interval between the separate plays of a long trilogy. The Romans, however, once the social side of theatre was stressed rather than the religious, were always careful to make provision for the audience, and most of their theatres were built close by a public courtyard; if this was not done, then a new one was built specifically for the theatre, usually immediately behind the stagehouse and giving easy access to the seating. Baroque theatres of the 18th century and the Neoclassical buildings of the 19th century paid particularly lavish attention to the design of lobby amenities for the audience, in general, and for important royal visitors, in particular.

"Theatrical" theatres. The very location of a theatre can itself be "theatrical." One of the great vistas of the Classical world is at Pergamum, where King Attalus, during the Hellenistic period of the 2nd century BC, before the ascendancy of Rome in that part of the world, built a magnificent Greco-Hellenistic theatre on a hillside facing a great ceremonial way that led to the temple of Dionysus. The stage was built of wood, so that all or part of it was portable and could be moved out of the way for ceremonial state processions, which could then be viewed by the entire free population of the town who seated themselves in the auditorium of the theatre. There is

evidence that those Roman theatres lying along the marching route of victorious generals and emperors, returning in triumph with their armies from foreign wars, were used in a somewhat similar way. The spectacular pageantry attendant on "royal entries" during the Renaissance and Baroque periods, for which the main square became an outdoor theatre with triumphal arches and portable seating along the line of march, was akin to the processional ceremonial of Classical Rome.

The Renaissance and Baroque periods in western Europe in many ways surpassed even the Roman in the ostentatious theatricality of their buildings. From the Medici court of 16th-century Italy until the fall of the Romanov royal family in Russia during World War I, the public and private theatres of one court vied with those of another in efforts to outshine their rivals. More recently, this sort of grandiose scheme has been on the decline, though in Germany and Italy dictators Adolf Hitler and Benito Mussolini found theatres and similar constructions an excuse for autocratic indulgence in ceremonial architecture. The performing arts themselves tended to get crushed in the embrace of the heavy stone masonry.

Rejection of formal buildings. Recent tendencies in theatre building—and also in the form and content of the drama itself—indicate a movement, especially on the part of the younger generation, to break away from the traditional relationships that have developed over the centuries between performer and audience. The abolition of formal playwriting is advocated, along with the conception of formal theatre as a high art. Instead, impromptu happenings are favoured, in which rigorous artistic training and discipline give way to orgiastic, spur-of-the-moment improvisation involving the active participation of all those in attendance. For such proceedings there is little need of a theatre building in any formal sense. Indeed, a structure of any kind is not an essential requirement. This approach to theatre has been adopted by many young revolutionaries, who show a zeal that is almost medieval in its fervour. It has manifested itself in recent years as a street theatre and is sometimes called guerrilla theatre. Often its devotees, intensely political, are seeking to overthrow established government as well as theatre. But, in fact, their methods are not of themselves new and do not necessarily result in a new definition of the actor–audience relationship. In all probability, such methods will, if they develop true vigour, create their own form of theatre building, as has happened in the past. Essentially, the only difference between modern guerrilla theatre and commedia dell'arte, the popular, rough theatre of the late Renaissance and early Baroque periods, is that the modern version does not seek primarily to entertain. Both are of the streets, but the modern version can, by means of electronic sound amplification or the klaxon "bull horn," force its message into the consciousness of the most unwilling and disinterested urban passerby.

Radical break with tradition in modern buildings

OUTDOOR AND INDOOR THEATRES

Theatres logically divide between those designed for outdoor performance and those for indoor use. In ancient times an outdoor theatre, for reasons of visibility and structure, was the only practical kind. The ancient Chinese, Japanese, Indian, Greek, and Roman theatres were all outdoor, except for the small roofed odeums of the Greco-Roman period, and these had to be small because the architectural problem of spanning a very large enclosed space had not then been solved. The problem of lighting in odeums was variously overcome by windows in the sidewalls or even by omission of an entire wall, usually in the southern exposure, which was instead provided either with piers or columns to support the roof structure.

Outdoor acoustics. The problem of acoustics is always more difficult to overcome out of doors, because there are no surrounding surfaces to reflect and redirect the acoustical energy field toward the audience. Audibility also depends on quiet surroundings because many distractions can easily top the vocal power of the performers. Out-

Problems of large outdoor facilities

door theatres are also prey to adverse weather—too hot, too cold, or too wet—and this limits the time of year when any given facility may comfortably be used.

Outdoor theatre activity today is even more vulnerable, for modern society is noisy. To compensate, there is electro-acoustical amplification, but inferior equipment results in an artificial and unlifelike reproduction of speech and music. Outdoor theatre today very often aims at great size, as it has in all ages and all civilizations. As modern examples there are the Hollywood Bowl in California, the Red Rocks Park in Colorado, and the many outdoor music- and drama-festival theatres associated with national parks and rural developments, such as Tanglewood in Massachusetts and Blossom Center in Ohio. Here, symphony orchestras, opera, ballet companies, and, sometimes, drama companies can perform before large audiences, but it is generally recognized that such places are no substitute for good theatre buildings in an urban setting. Historically, the outdoor theatre has not been long-lived—even that of Shakespeare in England and that of Lope de Vega in Spain soon found their way into permanent buildings.

Indoor lighting and acoustics. It was not until the theatre moved indoors during the late Renaissance that the stage began to resemble that with which most audiences today are familiar, with provision for elaborate scenery, backstage machinery, lighting, and other trappings familiar in the modern theatre. Efficient lighting, however, did not arrive until the late 19th century, when electricity at last provided a safe as well as an artistically expressive means of illumination. Prior to that, there had been an ever-present danger of fire from the use of open-flame illuminants in close proximity to highly combustible scenery and, indeed, to the wooden constructions used in the buildings themselves. Between the early 17th and late 19th centuries, thousands of theatres were destroyed by fire.

The move indoors also helped to isolate theatres from distracting outside noises. It created a host of new acoustical problems, however, such as excessive volume, room shaping that caused unexpected reverberations and echoes, and other dislocations of sound that were not fully understood until the 20th century. Instrumentation and scientific method were then employed to measure, sort out, and identify these phenomena, so that steps could be taken to ensure there would be no repetition of previous errors in theatre design. For, whereas architects from the Renaissance onward had contributed many aesthetic innovations to theatre design—the horseshoe-shaped auditorium, for example—most of these did not contribute to the understanding and improvement of the relationship between audience and performer. Instead of concentrating on problems related to sight and sound, they had been preoccupied with surface detailing—Classic, Baroque, Neoclassical, Neo-Baroque, and a host of other inessentials. It was not until the late 1880s that theatres began to be designed in consultation with engineers and scientists, who devised the means by which interior spaces for performance could be built with some degree of assurance as to their efficiency in terms of sight lines and acoustics. The first theatre building to be so planned was at Bayreuth in Germany, built to house the composer Richard Wagner's music dramas. The project's technical consultant was Carl Brandt.

VERSATILITY OF THEATRE AS PLACE

There is nothing new in today's rejection of traditional relationships between spectator and performer. The history of Western theatre is one of constant improvisation with whatever methods and materials were to hand. Indeed, such improvising often resulted in a golden age of theatre—the Elizabethan theatre in England, for instance, which was the culmination of improvised performances in innyard and animal-baiting pit; or commedia dell'arte of the late Renaissance in Italy, which was spontaneous and skillfully improvised; or the miracle play cycles of the Middle Ages, which evolved from the simple enactment of events in the church's liturgical worship. The satyr plays of Greece and the improvised farces that

were performed in the Naples district of Italy from early Roman times were acted in marketplaces and in the streets for the delight of a popular audience; today, a radical element in society is exploiting the potentialities of street theatre as a kind of impromptu happening with political overtones. Experimental theatres are a striking feature of college and university theatres, the members of which work from, as it were, an architecturally uncommitted or empty space; this they arrange in whatever way the playwright, director, or designer requires.

In the past, however, what began as an improvisation from necessity usually resulted in an "established" form of theatre: the open stage eventually developed into the "confrontational" relationship between stage and auditorium; the pageant wagon stage of the Middle Ages developed into the fixed thrust stage, eventually surrounded on three sides by spectators. In the 20th century the confrontational proscenium stage has shown signs of giving way to the open and thrust stage. In all this flux, it has always been the basic requirement of an audience to see and to hear that has established some more or less static form of theatre and that has determined whether or not such a form works efficiently. **Fixed forms arising from improvisation**

Another reason for the theatre's tendency to mobility has been the limited availability of talented performers and the lack of widespread, adequate performance facilities. These factors depend on geography, the state of a given culture, and its relative wealth. A primitive country cannot support expensive theatre centres, and so performers have to become adaptable, ready to perform anywhere—on the flat part of a truck, a wagon, an easily erected and dismantled portable platform—with an audience gathered round in a more or less informal manner (a feature still characteristic of the theatre of Southeast Asia, where the steps of a temple or other public building become a stage for the performers). Ingenuity such as this can inspire the quality of performance, which inevitably becomes the focal point. Elaborate architectural buildings, on the other hand, have sometimes swamped what goes on in them, emphasizing instead the theatrical effect of vulgar ornament and ostentation of every kind. Manifestations of this phenomenon include the monumental architecture of Nazi Germany, the 19th century opera houses, the architectural display of ancient Rome, and the fantastic movie palaces of the 1920s and 1930s.

Theatre building today is in the midst of a dilemma. In the wealthy nations, large sums of money are spent on such cultural bodies as symphony orchestras, opera, dance, and theatre companies, and facilities for their use must likewise be provided. Thus, a long tradition of philanthropy and support for the arts is being continued—imperial, bourgeois, or state in origin. But a subculture is developing that wants no part of the tradition maintained by this vast amount of money, preferring to go back to the "primitive" approach in order to rediscover the roots of Eastern as well as Western cultural genius. And so the cycle renews itself. The means are available, with the hand trumpet and megaphone giving way to the electric guitar and the klaxon bull horn, and the performers are ready; but, in addition, an audience must be attracted, for without an audience no dramatic message has any meaning. No one, however, can say whether a genuinely new definition of encounter between performer and audience is possible—or even desirable.

Theatre of Asia
The ancient, rich, and varied cultures of Asia produced three distinct types of theatre: (1) the religious dance drama of the south, of which Vietnam, Cambodia, Java, Bali, and India are representative; (2) the music drama or opera of China; and (3) the classical and popular drama of Japan. Collectively and generally, they contrast with Western drama in form, substance, and style of presentation. None, however, exhibits the range, variety, and continuity of development that characterizes Western theatre. This is not to belittle either the cultural or the ethnic values of Eastern theatre as an art. It simply reflects the fact that, in many instances, public art in Asia took to other forms of expression. Of the three types of **Lack of range and variety in Eastern theatre**

Theatre of Japan

theatre mentioned, that of Japan is the most varied and shows the most sustained development.

The theatre of Japan is of two kinds: Nō, the classical or court theatre of the aristocracy, and Kabuki, the public theatre of the people. Nō drama originated in about 1350 and Kabuki around 1600. The literal meaning of Nō is Talent. Kabuki takes its name from a slang word of the day roughly meaning gaudy. Each has roots in a much older puppet theatre, in which most of the dramatic literature dealt with ancient legends. The acting styles of Nō and Kabuki theatre are in sharp contrast: whereas the principal characteristic of Nō is an uncompromising restraint, bordering on the austere, Kabuki employs deliberately exaggerated emotional posturing, broad playing, and bombastic declamation. Scenically, they are also a contrast. Nō, in the restrained manner of the Japanese print and wall screen, uses a few simple, formal, stylized elements; it is restrained and much given to understatement to achieve its effect. Kabuki delights in spectacle and trick effects, sometimes startling and bizarre. Nō invariably employs a static background, simply painted to suggest land, sky, and pine. Kabuki, however, strives for mobility, plasticity, and variety, employing trick effects achieved by mechanical lifts, trapdoors, and revolving stages (a Japanese invention). Both, as in the theatre of Shakespeare in the West, are essentially actors' theatres, achieving great intimacy and rapport with the audience despite their quite different artistic frameworks. Both, again as in the Shakespearean theatre, began in the open air but moved indoors with time. The smaller in size and the more formal is the open stage of Nō, with an attached left stage bridge extension. Kabuki favours an actor–audience confrontational approach, such as the Western proscenium stage permits, but also employs long runway extensions right and left of the stage at the point where it joins and bisects the main-floor audience seating area. The Nō auditorium is small and intimate, designed for a connoisseur audience of between 200–300; contemporary Kabuki auditoriums, however, often seat more than 2,000. Almost up to the end of the 19th century, Kabuki auditoriums provided only for the traditional cross-legged Japanese seating posture, on a flat floor covered with mats and split up into square boxes. There were no aisles, as such, providing access to and from the seating system. But, as the form developed, side and rear balconies were added to the auditorium; and the Western type of seating, ranged on a gently sloping floor, was

eventually provided in most parts of the theatre. Newly built Kabuki theatres, notably the national theatre in Tokyo (which was built after World War II), have all the most up-to-date stage machinery and lighting, and theatre design takes into account maximum acoustical efficiency.

Nō theatre, on the other hand, remains virtually untouched by 20th-century mechanical innovations, still depending, to a great extent, on exquisite detailing of costumes and hand props for theatrical effect. Kabuki actors wear heavily stylized makeup, whereas the Nō actors use finely detailed and traditional masks of intricate design. In this respect, it is somewhat similar to the Classical theatre of Greece, but no formal connection between the two has ever been established nor is likely to be (see DANCE AND THEATRE, EAST ASIAN; KABUKI THEATRE; and NO THEATRE).

Historical development of Western theatres

In the Western world, theatre building, like theatre art, separates into two main divisions. The first, beginning with the theatrical activity of primitive peoples *c.* 1st millennium BC, lasted until the fall of Rome in the Christian Era. There followed a long hiatus during the Byzantine period and the Dark Ages, when no theatres were built at all. Although drama revived in the Middle Ages, no theatres in a formal architectural sense were built. The second period of theatre building began with the Renaissance, when there was a widespread interest in the Classical heritage of Greece and Rome, and it was at first sponsored by the academies and ducal courts of northern Italy. Theatre building has continued unabated since that time.

Revival of drama in the Middle Ages

It is, however, notable and significant that periods of particularly intense theatre building in the West have, at all times, followed periods in which dramatic activity had already reached new heights. This clearly indicates that theatres are built to satisfy an existing demand; excellence creates theatres, not the other way about. The vigour of the Elizabethan theatre, for example, was developed in improvised performing facilities—animal-baiting pits, innyards. The familiar thrust stage of the permanent playhouses built in later Elizabethan and Jacobean times was the outcome of that existing vigour. Theatre building has also tended to flourish during periods of economic surplus, which has encouraged both private and public philanthropy: such philanthropy has not, however,

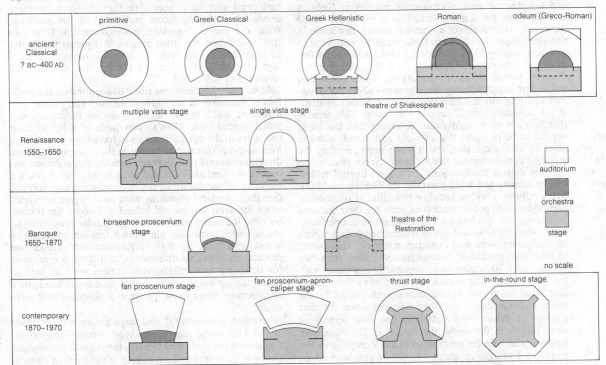

Figure 1: Form outline plans of Western theatres.

Figure 2: *Hellenistic theatre at Epidaurus, Greece.*
(Left) Reconstruction. (Right) Ruins of the theatre.
From (left) H. and R. Leacroft, *The Theatre* (1958);
Associated Book Publishers, and (right) Ewing Galloway

always been altruistic, the chief incentive often being profit, prestige, or political advantage.

The form of theatre building, particularly of the auditorium in relation to the stage, has undergone change and mutation, thus reflecting the progress of the drama itself. The changes have occasionally been due to some other factor, such as etiquette: during the Baroque period, for example, a system of stratified seating in the auditorium was dictated by the prevailing rigid class structure of society. Less often, change has been due to some startling innovation, notably, the introduction of electric light, that has changed the course of development more abruptly. Indeed, the development of buildings in which the Western world has housed its drama presents a sometimes contradictory, baffling, and occasionally obscure reflection of the cultural mainstream itself (Figure 1).

THEATRES OF ANCIENT GREECE AND ROME

Greek theatre. The temples of the ancient Egyptians may indeed have provided the setting for their dramas, and the theatral area adjoining the palaces at Knossos and Phaestus (in Crete) served as a place for ritual dances and ceremonies of a dramatic nature. But it was in ancient Greece that Western theatre can be said to have begun, emerging from rites sacred to the nature and fertility god Dionysus and reaching its first flowering in the Classical period of the 5th century BC. Those not taking active part in performance were grouped about the designated participants in such a way as to retain an empathetic yet vicarious sensual contact with them. This separation between actors and audience meant that the latter needed to be in direct line of sight and sound with the place of dramatic action, and it was almost certainly the repeated conjunction of these circumstances that led to the first theatre constructions. In a land blessed with a benign climate and a hilly terrain, the Greeks could utilize a hillside, a hollow between two hills, or some other natural bowl-shaped formation as a site for their theatres, positioning the spectators around and above the performers. During the Classical age in Athens, temporary wooden scaffoldings were used as audience seating. These seem to have been rectilinear in arrangement, rather than curvilinear—the latter plan being commonly associated with the later, Hellenistic period. Scholars have determined that these temporary constructions were placed in the agora (marketplace), and they thus constitute the first attempt at urban theatre design. The first permanent stone theatre in the world, the theatre of Dionysus, was built in Athens on the south slope of the Acropolis by the politician Lycurgus in about 330 BC. It consisted of an irregular, circular bank of seating, built of local stone

Primary importance of sight and sound in Greek theatre

placed on impacted earth, about a circular orchestra, and, from the start, it could probably accommodate from 6,000 to 12,000 spectators.

The stage. Most authorities agree that during the Classical period, in the 5th century BC, when the great tragedians Aeschylus, Sophocles, and Euripides flourished, all action performed by chorus and actors took place within the orchestra circle, with a beaten-earth surface like the threshing floors then to be found in countries of the Aegean. The stage (*skēnē*) was at that time not a raised platform but a low wooden barrier closing the back of the orchestra, behind which the actors and chorus removed for changes of mask and costume. Although archaeological evidence gives a clear picture of the auditoriums of Greek theatres after that built by Lycurgus, knowledge of the stage itself and of its subsequent development is less certain. The evidence suggests that all dramatic action continued to take place in the orchestra until the Hellenistic period, when a platform was raised in front of the permanent *skēnē*—by this time, a high wall that gave access to the orchestra by three doors. The speaking actors performed on the platform, while the chorus remained in the orchestra. It was in this period that the great theatre in Epidaurus (Figure 2) was built, with what is believed to have been a high, two-level stagehouse replacing the simpler wall structure of the *skēnē*.

Acoustics. Much recent study has centred on the problem of acoustics in the ancient theatre. The difficulty in achieving audibility to an audience of thousands, disposed around three-fifths to two-thirds of a full circular orchestra in the open air, seems to have been insoluble so long as the performer remained in the orchestra. A more direct, horizontal path between speaker and audience was therefore essential if unaided voice power was to reach a majority of spectators in the auditorium. Some contend that the acoustical problems were to a degree alleviated when the actor was moved behind and above the orchestra onto the raised platform, with a greater proportion of the audience being thus placed in direct line of sight and sound with him. By this time, the actors' masks had reached considerable dimensions, and there are grounds for believing that their mouth orifices were of help in concentrating vocal power—much as cupped hands or a rudimentary megaphone produce a simple sound-wave guide.

Increased architectural and engineering sophistication in the Hellenistic Age encouraged further innovations. The theatres of mainland Greece, the Aegean islands, and southern Italy (generally speaking, all older than those in Asia Minor) had been constructed on hillsides wherever

Sophistication of the Hellenistic Age

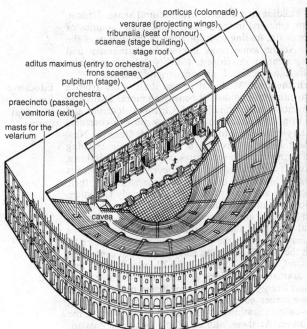

porticus (colonnade)
versurae (projecting wings)
tribunalia (seat of honour)
scaenae (stage building)
stage roof
aditus maximus (entry to orchestra)
frons scaenae
pulpitum (stage)
orchestra
praecincto (passage)
vomitoria (exit)
masts for the velarium
cavea

Figure 3: *Roman theatre.*
(Left) Reconstruction of a typical Roman theatre. (Right) Remains of the theatre at Ṣabrāth, Libya, 2nd century AD.
(Left) From H. and R. Leacroft, *The Theatre*, (right) UPI Compix

possible, so that excavation and filling were kept to a minimum; or, lacking a suitable slope, earth was dug out and piled up to form an embankment upon which stone seats were placed. By contrast, the cities of Asia Minor, which flourished during the Hellenistic Age, did not rely on a convenient hillside or other slope on which to locate their theatres. The principles of arch construction were understood, and theatres were built using vaulting as the structural support for banked seating. Archaeological remains and recent restoration of theatres at Perga, Side, Miletus, and other sites in modern Turkey exhibit this type of construction. By a third method of construction, auditoriums were hewn out of living rock. Of some six such Greek theatres extant, two excellent examples (both extensively remodelled in Roman times) are the great theatre at Syracuse in Sicily and that at Argos in the Peloponnese on the Greek mainland. The best preserved of all Greek theatres, also in the Peloponnese and now partially restored, is the magnificent theatre at Epidaurus, sacred city of Asclepius, the god of healing. It provided seats for some 12,000 people, and its circular orchestra is backed by a stagehouse and surrounded on three sides by a stone, hillside-supported bank of seats. Both chorus and actors performed in the orchestra, but only the actors used the two levels of the stagehouse. Theatre building flourished during the Hellenistic Age as never before in Classical times, and no city of any size or reputation was without its theatre.

Roman theatre. *Stage and auditorium.* The Romans inherited Greek tradition and technique in building generally and were the first to make theatres into true buildings. Their knowledge of engineering, moreover, and their supreme confidence in execution gave them an unlimited choice of sites when locating their theatres. Beginning by remodelling Greek and Hellenistic theatres, they eventually succeeded in giving architectural unity to auditorium and a single-level, raised stage. This they did by limiting the orchestra to a half circle and joining it to the auditorium, thereby improving acoustics over the Greek and Hellenistic theatres. They also brought to perfection the principles of barrel and cross vaulting, penetrating the seat bank at regular intervals with *vomitoria* (exit corridors) to provide a more convenient system of ingress and egress for the audience as well as to give sound structural support for the seating. The raised stage was at a single, much lower level than in the Hellenistic theatre. It was roofed, and entrances to it were increased to five: three, as before, in the wall at the rear of the stage and one at each side (Figure 3). The Romans' love of ostentatious

architecture led them to adorn the permanent background with profuse sculptures, a development that characterized all Roman stages built in imperial times. In some theatres a drop curtain, fixed in a trough across the front of the stage, was used to signal the beginning and end of performance. In some cases, a canvas roof was hoisted onto rope rigging in order that the audience be shaded from the sun. The best preserved Roman theatre, dating from about AD 170, is at Aspendus on the Mediterranean coast of modern Turkey.

In Roman theatres the stage alone was used by the actors. The orchestra became part of the auditorium in Rome, reserved by statute for those of privileged rank, who seated themselves there on a variety of portable chairs and litters. The orchestra was no longer needed as part of the performance area because the chorus had long since ceased to be an integral part of drama. The tragedies of Seneca, in the 1st century, of course included a chorus since they followed the example of their Greek models. But they never achieved the popularity of earlier comedies, especially those of Plautus and Terence. These had at first been performed on temporary wooden stages set up on a convenient slope and sometimes surrounded by temporary wooden seating.

Until the first triumvirate ("rule of three men," 60 BC), a puritanical Senate had banned all permanent theatre building within the city of Rome itself as decadent, not befitting a virile Roman society. Thus, theatre constructions there were temporary affairs, set up in the Campus Martius and taken down at the conclusion of the games at which they had been used. In 52 BC, however, the triumvir Pompey the Great built Rome's first permanent stone theatre. Another public theatre was built in Rome in 13 BC and named after Marcellus, son-in-law of the emperor Augustus. Like that of Pompey, it was a stone-vaulted structure. Both were used for the *scaenae ludi* ("scenic games"), which were part of religious festivities or celebrations of victory in war and which were paid for by triumphant generals and emperors. Archaeological remains of these two theatres are meagre. Only foundations remain of the theatre of Pompey, while the theatre of Marcellus was converted into a multiple dwelling during the late Middle Ages and survives in that form. During the empire, however, civic pride demanded that all important cities have theatres, amphitheatres, and, in many instances, a small, permanently roofed theatre (*theatrum tectum*, an odeum, or music hall). In fact, it is from outlying cities of the empire such as Arausio (Orange), Thamagadi (Timgad),

Incorporation of the orchestra into the auditorium

Leptis Magna, Ṣabrāth, and Aspendus that archaeological evidence provides most firsthand knowledge of Roman theatre building.

Vitruvius' treatise on architecture. Literary documentation complements and enhances archaeological knowledge of theatre building by the ancients. *De architectura libri decem* ("Ten Books on Architecture"), by the Roman architect Vitruvius (1st century BC), devotes three books to Greek and Roman theatre design and construction. The author gives general rules for siting an open-air theatre and for designing the stage, orchestra, and auditorium. These rules are based on principles of Euclidian geometry in matters of layout and proportion. His dictums on the provision of good sight lines from auditorium to stage are generally sound. Apart from that, however, his treatise is not very helpful. He mentions changeable scenery but is vague about what was involved. On this and on other subjects, notably acoustics, there has been much conjecture, but no archaeological remains provide sufficiently convincing proof of any interpretation. Vitruvius' notion of acoustics, which he claims is based on theory as well as practice, is vaguely associated with Greek ideas of musical theory but has since been proved to have no scientific or mathematical basis. Indeed, his views on this important matter were to cause problems for almost 2,000 years.

Vitruvius' principles of acoustics

The odeum. Vitruvius has nothing to say about the odeum, which, according to some authorities, represents the final refinement of theatre building in the ancient world. Modern studies in Classical archaeology have suggested that the roofed odeum was the high point of design and perfection of structure in ancient theatre building. Theatre history has, unfortunately, largely overlooked these buildings. Excavation work has revealed more than 30 of them, in a wide range of building materials. One of the most imposing, which also boasts the greatest span for a wooden trussed roof in the ancient world, was the Odeon of Agrippa, named after the emperor Augustus' civil administrator. A Roman building located in the Athenian agora, dating from about 15 BC, it is a beautifully detailed building, with an open southern exposure to light a stage surrounded by a truncated curvilinear bank of seating. It achieves an atmosphere of great dignity and repose, despite the vast size of the room. Odeums were apparently first built in Athens under Pericles (5th century BC). They continued to be built throughout the Hellenistic Age and also in the Roman Empire right up to the time of Emperor Severus Alexander (3rd century AD). They range in size from a minimum seating capacity of 300–400 to a maximum of 1,200–1,400. Experts who have studied these buildings in any detail disagree as to their specific purpose and use but claim they exhibited a refinement of detail and architectural sophistication found in no other Greco-Roman buildings devoted to the performing arts. They are usually found in Greek cities dating from Hellenistic times, on the grounds of private villas built by Roman emperors from Augustus to Hadrian, and in major cities of the empire usually dedicated to the emperors. In the dying years of the Roman Empire they were, it is claimed, the last remaining home of the performing arts, since by this time open-air theatres had long been given over to satisfying debased and perverted popular taste with sensational, crude, and, at times, bloody entertainments.

Greek and Roman theatre building is the basis of all later theatre design in the Western world. The theatres of the golden age of Spanish drama and of the English Elizabethan theatre in the 16th century—and the 20th century's avant-garde experiments with primitive theatre-in-the-round techniques—are, however, the exceptions.

THEATRE IN THE MIDDLE AGES

After the fall of Rome and the triumph of Christianity, organized theatre was suppressed during the 5th century as an art so debased as to serve no useful social or moral purpose. There were survivors of the Roman mimic tradition who formed a wandering fraternity of players. But, naturally enough, under such conditions there was no theatre building in a formal, architectural sense. Drama, at length, emerged in the Middle Ages from centuries of seeming death, finding its inspiration in the liturgy of the church. At the same time, interest in tournament and secular pageantry developed. (Such forms of entertainment, though theatrical, are not strictly dramatic.)

Church theatre. Medieval drama itself arose from a desire to educate. The task of conveying moral truths and a rudimentary understanding of Christian doctrine and dogma to a laity unable to read and write was considerable. The clergy began to dramatize events from the New Testament because this was a more dynamic teaching method than the static sculptures, stained-glass windows, and mosaics that for centuries had been the chief means of bringing home the meaning of these stories to their congregations and with which Byzantine, early Christian, and Gothic church buildings abound. It is doubtful whether there is any connection between the drama of Classical times and the new, rudimentary dramatizations that slowly grew into the miracle and mystery cycles of plays in the Middle Ages. As early as the 10th century in Switzerland, France, England, and Germany, short and simple dramatic renderings of parts of the Easter and Christmas liturgy of the mass were being performed. As the short scenes so dramatized grew in number, small stages—called mansions—were placed at the sides of the church nave. At these, stories of the Nativity, Passion, and Resurrection, depending upon the particular season of the Christian calendar, were acted out. The mansions were at first simply marked-off areas of the floor, but eventually small raised platforms, backed by curtains and simple scenery, came into use. At the conclusion of each scene, the congregation turned its attention to the next mansion, so following a succession of scenes set out at intervals around the nave, in much the same way as the 14 Stations of the Cross are placed for devotional purposes in the side aisles of churches today. Gradually, the performance of liturgical drama passed out of the hands of the clergy and into those of the laity, probably via the trade guilds of craftsmen, which were also religious fraternities. More and more secular interludes crept into the dramas—to such an extent that the dramas moved out of the church and onto the steps in front of it. Eventually, the plays moved away into the public square, which was thus turned into a theatre, and the individual plays performed became linked in cycles, often beginning with the story of the creation and ending with that of the Last Judgment. Each play within the cycle was performed by a different trade guild. Many of these cycles have survived and are valuable in their own right as dramatic literature. Another theme receiving dramatic attention in the Middle Ages was martyrdom of saints. Realistically acted scenes were performed in the public square on the appropriate saint's day as part of the feast-day celebrations.

Theatre in the marketplace. *Mansion stages.* The simplest way of presenting the plays was a straightforward development of the mansion system that had been used in the churches, as can be seen from a mid-15th-century engraving of the "Martyrdom of St. Apollonia" and from a 16th-century illustration of the Valenciennes mystery play (Figure 4). It appears that several mansions were erected about a raised platform, which was evidently the main acting arena, while the audience stood below the mansions (and possibly in the spaces between them). Some temporary seating was erected for the occasion, and no doubt nearby balconies and windows were also put to good use. Each episode in a play began in front of an appropriate mansion that depicted the setting for that scene; in the course of playing the scene, the actors spilled out in front of and around the mansion into the main acting arena. The principle is not unlike the modern theatre's "simultaneous setting," in which, for example, two or more locations are visible throughout, though only one may be lit or in use. The medieval settings were not usually realistic; place was suggested by a naïve artistic symbolism.

Pageant wagons. This was not necessarily the case, however, in another method of presentation, especially

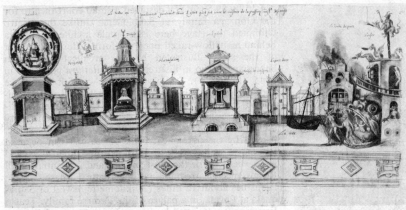

Figure 4: The setting for the Valenciennes mystery play, miniature by Hubert Cailleau, 1547.
In the Bibliothèque Nationale, Paris.
By courtesy of the Bibliothèque Nationale, Paris

popular in England and the Netherlands. There, the mansions were portable, in England called pageant wagons and in the Netherlands *wagonseel*. Beneath the raised platform was a curtained space with room for the actors. Although the number of settings available was the same as for the mansion presentation, in this case only one wagon was visible at a time; the audience remained where it was, and the pageant was wheeled to it. Sometimes the pageant wagons were far from simple structures; many incorporated practical effects to enliven the proceedings. A realistic replica of the ark, complete with animals and possibly floated on water, might be constructed for the story of Noah and the Flood; or an ingenious model of a whale, able to contain an actor within its belly, might be used for the story of Jonah; fire-breathing mechanics were employed for a representation of "Hell's Mouth" in Last Judgment plays.

Ingenious scenic effects of pageants

Courtly diversions. The religious drama performed on mansion or pageant wagon constituted the principal public theatre of the Middle Ages, and it flourished until the late 15th and early 16th centuries. At the same time, another kind of theatre was associated with the courts, where more or less impromptu and unrehearsed entertainments, deriving from the medieval love of tournament, were much in vogue. Essentially planned as diversions, they were most sumptuously costumed and caparisoned, with the emphasis on spectacle. In some cases, wooden seating arrangements were specially provided for spectators, many of them distinguished guests of the royal or ducal household. This type of theatrical entertainment grew in popularity throughout Europe, culminating during the 16th century with such buildings as the Boboli Gardens theatre in Florence, associated with the court of the Medici family. Another manifestation of this essentially courtly theatrical display took place on the triumphant return to a city in his own realm of some royal person and entourage after victory in war or on the occasion of a neighbouring ruler's visit. Public participation was then often invited and, sometimes, enforced, to help swell the sense of occasion. It was followed by private festivities held at court—disguisings and masquerades, with jugglers and troubadours. On occasion, a group of strolling players would also be invited to perform, improvised facilities being set up in the great hall or courtyard of the palace.

Like all primitive theatre, that of the Middle Ages was one of participation, and throughout its development it never lost the close proximity of actors and audience. It was a theatre of symbolism rather than of illusion, and, like the Classical theatre, it essentially took place in the open air, with none of the magic associated with enclosed space, where a half-darkened stage can bestow mystery and illusion upon scenic display.

THEATRES OF THE RENAISSANCE

The revival of theatre building, first sponsored by 16th-century ducal courts and academies in northern Italy, was part of the general Renaissance interest in the newly discovered Classical heritage of Greece and Rome. The ruins of Classical theatres were studied as models, along with Vitruvius' treatise on Classical architecture. There were, however, new conditions that fundamentally affected design as compared with the procedures of Classical architects. First of all, the theatre's move indoors gave rise to problems of lighting and room acoustics. The laws of geometric perspective were discovered and, when applied by artists to stage and scenic design, brought about a profound change in the effect of a stage on an audience. The first Renaissance theatres, like those of early antiquity, were temporary wooden constructions in gardens, ballrooms, and assembly halls. Sometimes, they were hastily erected affairs, put up to celebrate the birth and weddings of ducal offspring or to commemorate victories in war. The theatrical performances given were mostly of allegorical pageantry, but the scenic spectacle was calculated to dazzle the eye and often succeeded. One court vied with another for the services of clever innovators, painters, sculptors, and architects who could, on order, devise stages, audience-seating constructions, scenery, costumes, pageant wagons, fireworks displays, and the assorted trappings of theatrical extravaganza. Famous names from the world of art contributed their talents to the theatrical entertainments at the courts of popes, cardinals, dukes, and lesser nobility. Leonardo da Vinci, Michelangelo, Vasari, Bramante, Raphael, and a host of other Italian painters, sculptors, and architects, as well as poets, such as Tasso, and musicians, such as Monteverdi, strove to please and exalt the reputations, real or imaginary, of their princely patrons.

The Renaissance attempt to dazzle the spectators

First large-scale indoor theatres. A more sober attempt to revive the Classical theatre was made by the academies, organized by upper class gentlemen who assembled to read and, on occasion, to participate in and to support financially productions of Classical drama. The plays were generally of three kinds: contemporary poetic dramas based on ancient texts; Latinized versions of Greek dramas; and the works of Seneca, Terence, and Plautus in the original. The Olympic Academy in the little town of Vicenza, near Venice, commissioned a famous late Renaissance architect, Andrea Palladio, to design a theatre for them. This, the Teatro Olimpico, was the first permanent, modern, indoor theatre, and it has survived intact (Figure 5). Palladio thoroughly researched his subject (the outdoor Classical theatre of Rome) and without knowing it designed for his clients something very close to a Roman odeum. It is a scaled-down version of an outdoor Roman theatre, with shallow open stage and a heavily sculptured, pedimented, permanent background. A colonnade of heroic proportions, surmounted by sculptured figures, surrounds a steeply stepped bank of seating. Overhead is a painted sky. To promote an intimate stage–auditorium relationship, he used a flattened ellipse in planning the seating, rather than the classic half circle. The interior was to be lit by tallow candles mounted in wall sconces. Palladio died before the building was finished, and his follower Vin-

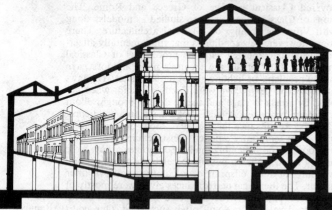

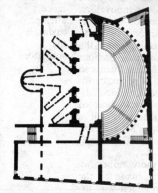

Figure 5: *The first permanent indoor theatre.*
Teatro Olimpico, Vicenza, Italy, designed by Andrea Palladio and completed by Vicenzo Scamozzi, 1585. (Top) View of stage and auditorium. (Centre) Section. (Bottom) Plan.
By courtesy of (centre, bottom) George C. Izenour; photograph, (top) Foto Tapparo e Trentin, Vicenza

cenzo Scamozzi completed the work (1585). Behind the five stage entrances (attributed to Scamozzi) are static, three-dimensional-perspective vistas of streets disappearing to their separate vanishing points; it is not certain whether this was the intent of the original design. In performance, the theatre is efficient if the auditorium is full, and speech carries quite well because of the small volume, flat ceiling, modulated sidewalls, excellent vertical sight lines, and direct hearing lines from all seats to the stage. The exterior is an ungainly, masonry-walled structure with wood-trussed, tiled roof. Inside this primary structure, the theatre is constructed of wood and plaster and bears scarcely any relation to the primary structure. This brings up a point fundamental even to modern theatre buildings. Because of its interior function, a theatre makes for ungainly, difficult, and, at best, anonymous exterior architecture. The problem central to successful theatre design concerns its interior functions, involving solution of sight lines, acoustics, provision of adequate stage facilities, audience comfort, and the like. This usually results in an exterior architecture that is oppressively monumental, formalistic, and characteristic of a "one-building-inside-the-other" construction.

In 1588–89 Scamozzi designed a small court theatre for the Gonzaga family at Sabbioneta. Unlike the Teatro Olimpico the stage here is a single architectural vista behind a shallow-raked open platform, after the manner of the stage illustrated by the architect-theoretician Sebastiano Serlio in his treatise *Architettura* published in 1545 (Figure 6). Serlio's influence was felt in France and England, notably in the work of Inigo Jones, architect to the court of King James I. At Sabbioneta, a divided horseshoe-shaped bank of seating leaves an empty arena, at floor level, in front of the stage. This space, backed by the permanent bank of seating, can be used for more seating, but it also permits other uses and paves the way for the most famous and influential of all Renaissance theatre buildings, the Teatro Farnese.

This lies about 12 miles (20 kilometres) west of Sabbioneta at Parma, in a palace of the Farnese family. Teatro Farnese was designed by the architect Giovanni Battista Aleotti and is the first proscenium theatre in the world to be designed for movable scenery (Figure 7). Designed and built in 1618 (but not used until 1628, to celebrate the marriage of a Medici daughter to a Farnese son), it is the earliest large-scale indoor facility for theatrical activities to have survived. It was severely damaged by fire bombing in World War II but has since been restored to its former glory. There has also survived an extensive catalog giving details of events held there, including some contemporary comment on performances. It describes the variety of use to which the theatre was put. Drama, opera, and ballet were performed on stage; equestrian acts and sumptuous balls were held in the spacious arena between stage and seating, which could also be flooded to a depth of 2 feet (0.6 metre) and used for mock naval battles. Other court functions requiring ceremony, such as reviews, ambassadorial receptions, proclamations of state, and a variety of princely extravaganzas, round out the theatre's multiple uses. Lighting was still a problem and remained so for all interior theatres until the 19th century. Teatro Farnese has windows (as did the Teatro Olimpico and the Teatro all'Antica at Sabbioneta before it) behind and above the banked seating. This helped to illuminate the space when used in daytime, but at night tallow candles or animal-fat lamps, in wall and overhead fixtures, were the source of illumination for all theatres until the introduction of gas lighting in the 19th century. Teatro Farnese set the style for stage and auditorium design over the next 250 years, except for the courtyard-patio (*corrales*) theatre in Spain and the Elizabethan and Jacobean theatre of England.

Scamozzi's theatre at Sabbioneta

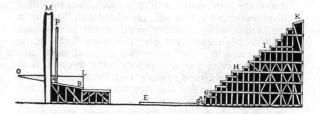

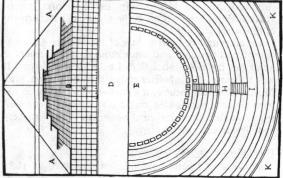

Figure 6: Sebastiano Serlio's design for a theatre, illustration from his *Architettura*.

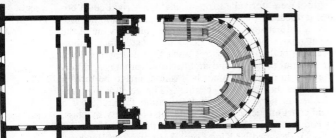

Figure 7: *The first proscenium theatre designed for movable scenery.*
Teatro Farnese, Parma, Italy, designed by Giovanni Battista Aleotti, 1918. (Top) View looking toward the stage. (Bottom) Plan.
By courtesy of (top) the Soprintendenza di Parma, (bottom) George C. Izenour; photograph, (top) Comm. Luigi Vagni, Parma

Shakespeare's theatre. Curiously, more is known about the theatres and stages of Greece and Rome than about those of Elizabethan England. Scholars have put forward a variety of theories about the origin of the theatre of Shakespeare. One theory suggests that it stemmed from the pits used for animal baiting, a popular Elizabethan sport; another has it as an elaboration of the 16th-century English innyard; yet another seeks to establish some connection with Vitruvian theory of theatre design. All are inconclusive, however, because of the lack of direct archaeological evidence. Literary documentation is limited, and graphic evidence consists of one poorly drawn sketch (the so-called DeWitt sketch) copied from a firsthand description by an artist who did not see the building it purports to show. Unlike the Italian court and academy theatres, it was a public theatre; the first, built by James Burbage in 1576, was called the Theatre. The Elizabethan stage is established beyond all doubt as being thrust forward, surrounded on three sides by the audience, backed by a stagehouse, or inner stage, which was, according to some authorities, on two levels (though on this point there has been much controversy). Behind the inner stage were dressing rooms, property rooms, and storage space for the limited scenic elements used in connection with plays in the repertoire. The thrust-platform stage was partially covered by a canopy, referred to as the heavens, supported by the primary structure upstage and two narrow columns about halfway downstage. A downstage trapdoor, or trapdoors, permitted appearances from below and could be used, for example, in graveyard scenes. Like the public theatre of Greece and Rome, it was open to the sky, subject to vagaries of weather. Britain's climate dictated time and length of the theatrical season. In all probability, an Elizabethan theatre like the Globe in London was essentially a wooden-framed, thatched-roofed building, seating and standing fewer than 1,800 persons in three tiered balconies and a ground floor referred to as the pit or yard (Figure 8).

"Golden Age" of Spanish theatre. The great flowering of Spanish theatre parallels that of Shakespeare in time, but its origins are still more obscure, with even less documentation upon which to base theories of its existence and appearance. Like its famous English counterpart, it was an open-air, public theatre. It was not, however, confined to one city, as theatre in England had been confined to London: all large urban centres in Spain had

By courtesy of (left) the Victoria and Albert Museum, London; (right) from H. and R. Leacroft, *The Theatre*

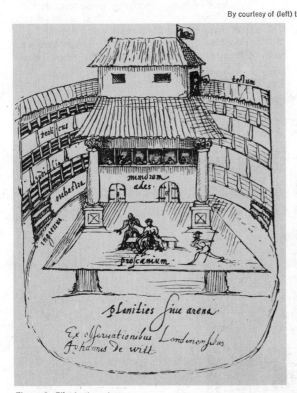

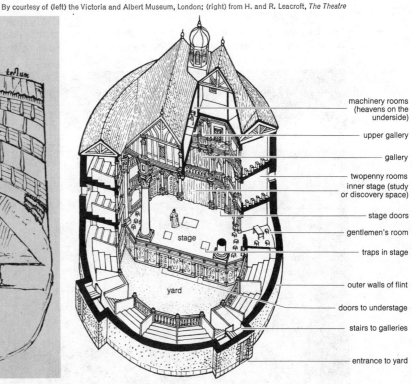

machinery rooms (heavens on the underside)
upper gallery
gallery
twopenny rooms
inner stage (study or discovery space)
stage doors
gentlemen's room
traps in stage
outer walls of flint
doors to understage
stairs to galleries
entrance to yard

Figure 8: *Elizabethan theatres.*
(Left) The Swan Theatre, London, drawing by Johann DeWitt, *c.* 1596. In the Victoria and Albert Museum, London. (Right) Conjectural reconstruction of the second Globe Theatre, London, 1614.

permanent theatres. The stage was an open platform set at one end of a rectangular patio or courtyard, and it was surrounded by shallow balconies on two levels. The ground-level area next to the stage was perhaps supplied with rough benches; if not, the audience in that part stood —as in the pit of a Shakespearean theatre. The background to the stage was, for the most part, architectural, probably somewhat simple and austere, containing entrances at two levels to an inner stage. Occasionally, a curtain might have been used to augment the scenic effect, being drawn aside to permit upstage action. As with Shakespeare, however, locale was suggested by poetic discourse rather than by visual symbolism. The stage was most probably in direct descent from the medieval wagon platform that had been used in the public square. Backstage were the actors' dressing rooms and stage property rooms. A shallow roof, supported by the primary backstage structure, extended some way over the platform, though probably not far enough to require any additional support. After a period of time, awnings were rigged over the seating, and, eventually, the addition of a permanent roof made it an indoor theatre. Seville at one time boasted seven permanent theatres; the most important in Madrid was the Corral de la Cruz, opened in 1579. This style of theatre finally succumbed to the importation of Italian Baroque, which became the rage for both public and private court theatres, as opera and ballet became the principal entertainments.

Commedia dell'arte.   The most popular public theatre of the late Renaissance was commedia dell'arte, literally, the "comedy of art," as opposed to the "comedy of learning" performed in the academies; it is referred to by some theatre historians as "the rough theatre of the Renaissance." It was not served by theatre building in any formal sense. Bands of strolling players, musicians, jugglers, and acrobats performed in public squares and in the courts, especially at carnival time in Venice, Rome, Florence, and other large cities where they were in great demand. Depending on what was at hand, they would perform on a flat wagon, a bare platform set up on trestles in the public squares, or simply on no stage at all. The technique of the commedia left its mark on acting styles, but it exerted no influence on stage or theatre architecture.

The "rough theatre of the Renaissance"

THEATRE OF THE BAROQUE

The Baroque style, beginning in Italy and spreading across Europe, dominated theatre building between about 1650 and 1790. Its chief characteristics are basically refinements in detail of the proscenium stage and of the Renaissance horseshoe-shaped auditorium and seating plan. As many as five shallow balconies were stacked vertically in the auditorium, but these were more closely coupled with the stage than had been the case in, for example, the Teatro Farnese. For the first time, an orchestra pit in front of the stage, sunk below ground level, made an appearance. At first, these new features were seen in private court theatres; later, they appeared in the large, new public theatres that were built in many capital cities of western Europe. Such buildings parallel the rise of grand opera and ballet, and they reveal a preoccupation with theatrical show and spectacle. Inventors and designers were called upon to provide elaborate, portable, perspective scenery and complicated stage machinery, both above and below stage, to effect scene changes (nearly always carried out in full sight of the audience). Famous names of this period include the Italians Giacomo Torelli and the Bibiena family, whose ingenious settings were unrivalled for originality. A rigid court etiquette dictated that the lines of perspective should provide a perfect stage picture from the point of view of the royal box, which directly faced the stage. Since, moreover, the building of theatres was controlled by the ducal or imperial purse, a rigid architectural formalism, differing only in detail, became the fashion, not to be broken until late in the 19th century. The auditorium was planned in tiers, a vertical stratification that reflected a rigid court etiquette and the ordering of society by class. A good example is the French court theatre at Versailles (1769), designed by King Louis XV's architect, Jacques-Ange Gabriel (Figure 9). For a court theatre, its stage is exceptionally well equipped, mechanized in the manner of the Bibiena family, with an overhead pulley system for flying drops and borders, while the flat wings and shutters making up the elaborate scene were mounted on frames attached to carriages that ran on rails beneath the stage and so could easily be changed. Engravings of the time indicate that the court theatres were used for balls, concerts, and the like, as well as for stage performance. Though of limited seating capacity, these costly little court theatres witnessed the first productions of many operas by composers such as Haydn and Mozart, and they also played an important part in sponsoring the development of classical ballet.

Public theatres.   *The opera house.*   There were two kinds of theatre in the 18th century. One was a logical

Figure 9: The court theatre in the palace of Versailles, France, designed by Jacques-Ange Gabriel in 1769 and restored in 1957.

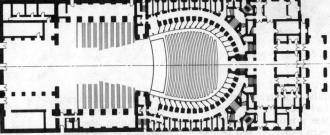

Figure 10: *The opera house.*
Teatro alla Scala, Milan, designed by Giuseppe Piermarini, 1776–78. (Top) View of the auditorium from the stage. (Bottom) Plan.
By courtesy of (bottom) George C. Izenour; photograph, (top) Erio Piccagliani

18th-century theatres

development of the earlier private court theatres and was the outcome of a sophisticated, urban, upper class demand for theatre as entertainment. The Teatro alla Scala of Milan in Italy is a good example of the style adopted (Figure 10). Built in 1776–78, it was one of many similar structures erected by 18th-century nobility in the major capitals of western Europe. Public theatres such as La Scala differ from private court theatres only in the size of auditorium and stage. Opera, generally including a ballet, was by this time the most popular form of entertainment, especially in Italy, demanding and receiving the ostentatious kind of production that styled it "grand." Whereas Versailles had seated fewer than 700 in the auditorium, La Scala seats more than 2,000.

The Restoration playhouse. The other kind of public theatre, peculiar to England, was the Restoration playhouse. The Baroque horseshoe-shaped auditorium, with its deep stage and orchestra pit, was generally in favour all over western Europe, fixing the design and style of opera houses, in particular. In it, the actor played in front of elaborately painted scenery and behind the proscenium arch. The Restoration playhouse, however, while borrowing the fully rigged stage of the Baroque theatre, provided, in addition, a deep apron stage thrusting out from the proscenium, upon which most of the action took place. Thus, the actor played, as it were, in the auditorium and away from the scenic backing; the English, with their Shakespearean tradition, were loath to abandon the intimate contact between actor and audience that the Elizabethan theatre had allowed. At either side of the forestage were doors by which actors entered; above these doors were additional boxes, for spectators, stacked one above the other in the Baroque manner.

Influence of lighting and technical achievements. Theatre lighting in this period was provided by wick-fed illuminants concealed behind the wings and proscenium arch and at the edge of the stage apron. In the auditorium either a large, single, central fixture, as at La Scala, or a number of smaller ceiling fixtures, as at Versailles, was the custom. All were kept burning during performance,

and the habit of lighting the auditorium persisted until late in the 19th century.

From the 18th century there survives some commentary on the subject of theatre design and construction, notably by the Italian count Francesco Algarotti, the Frenchman Pierre Patte, and the Englishman George Saunders. Algarotti, a diplomat by profession, comments as an interested amateur; Patte and Saunders are dilettante architects, neither of whom actually built a theatre. These treatises, which largely parrot one another, clearly demonstrate their authors' inability to go beyond Vitruvius' naïve technology. Pronouncements on sight lines and acoustics were limited to superficial geometrical details of the prevailing techniques for constructing horseshoe-shaped banked seating. There is no evidence that men of genuine science were at all involved or even interested in theatre problems. It is notable that, despite the intense theatre-building activity, the 18th and 19th centuries produced no innovation in auditorium design and made no significant addition to the basic knowledge of acoustics as derived from Greece and Rome. Another century was to pass before the shape of the auditorium and its relation to the stage was altered and before any real contribution was made toward an understanding of the acoustics of enclosed spaces.

THEATRE IN THE 19TH CENTURY

Theatre design in the 19th century continued the 18th-century horseshoe plan in auditorium design, and until late in the century there were few other changes apart from steady improvements in stage machinery, notably the overhead flying system for handling scenery.

Rejection of the Baroque theatre. There were two major departures from the norm, however. Richard Wagner's Festspielhaus, built at Bayreuth, in Germany, in 1876, and Adler and Sullivan's Auditorium theatre, in Chicago, built in 1889. Wagner's Festspielhaus, designed specifically for the composer's music dramas, is, for its time, an inexpensive brick and timber building in a rural setting. The Auditorium theatre is a massive, masonry-structured, wrought-iron, truss-spanned, multipurpose building for concerts, opera, drama, and other occasions requiring large assembly. It is the first example of an urban theatre as the principal component in a complex modern structure that also accommodates commercial office space and a hotel. Both the Festspielhaus and the Auditorium theatre rejected the Baroque stratified auditorium, returning instead to democratic, classical principles of auditorium design. The seating plan is in the shape of a fan, a belated recognition of the fact that good lateral sight lines are essential for comfortably watching performances on a proscenium stage. Bayreuth is the more radical departure, with a steeply stepped, fan-shaped auditorium in which all seats face the stage. Side boxes, another feature of the horseshoe plan, are also eliminated. At the rear of the auditorium, however, two shallow seating levels remain, the lower of which is divided into nine large boxes. Another striking feature is the absence of any radial or parallel aisle. Access to seating is via side aisles and two vomitory exits only, thereby further concentrating and compressing the main body of seats in front of the proscenium. The stage has a double proscenium, one behind the other, while the orchestra pit is deep and partially covered (Wagner called it "the mystic gulf"), so that the musicians are hidden from view of the audience. This design thus broke away completely from the prevailing seating plan and from the open orchestra pit favoured since the 17th century. It has exerted a powerful influence on proscenium theatre design ever since. Wagner's theatre was at first lighted by gas, both on the stage and in the auditorium. At Wagner's insistence, it was the first theatre to darken its auditorium during performance.

These new ideas were elaborated by a succession of German architects, principal among them Max Littman, who designed the Prinzregententheater in Munich, the Schiller Theatre in West Berlin, the Hoftheater in Weimar, and, at the turn of the century in collaboration with George Fuchs, the Künstler Theatre in Munich.

The Festspielhaus at Bayreuth

Figure 11: The Penthouse theatre at the University of Washington, Seattle, designed by John Ashby Conway; architect Carl F. Gould, 1940.
By courtesy of the School of Drama, University of Washington, Seattle

Further effects of technical achievement. Late in the 19th century, electric lighting was introduced, and, for the first time, stages could be brightly illuminated without the constant danger of fire that had existed while candles, oil lamps, and gas jets were in use.

Studies in acoustics. The problem of acoustics was not studied until the turn of the century, so the architect's chief concern until then was with interior detail and ornament, while his exterior vied for attention in the urban scene with other public buildings, such as churches, city halls, and railroad stations. The overthrow of principles of acoustics stemming from ancient Greece or based on architectural fancy and their replacement by a theoretical explanation of the acoustical field and the resulting mathematical analysis of the acoustics of enclosed spaces was achieved by Professor Wallace Sabine of Harvard University. In 1896 he discovered the reverberation equation, which is the foundation of all subsequent studies in acoustical engineering. Eighteenth- and 19th-century designers and theoreticians had repeated Vitruvius' theories on the subject, adding their own "commonsense" obser-

Sabine's reverberation equation

vations, thereby confusing the subject further. These men had been, for the most part, amateurs, whereas Sabine was a professional physicist. His contribution has since been expanded and refined by researchers in the United States, Great Britain, Germany, France, and Denmark. Now, detailed acoustical studies are usually undertaken concurrently with architectural planning before concert halls, opera houses, theatres, and other such buildings are designed.

The Festspielhaus at Bayreuth and the Auditorium theatre in Chicago also have excellent acoustics, which were achieved before Sabine's work. This is attributed to the great care which was taken to provide good sight lines to the stage from all seats and to eliminate all large, concave-shaped architectural elements in the flat-domed, horseshoe-shaped auditorium. Simple, flat, modulated surfaces were favoured instead. Modern acoustical theory since Sabine states that good sight lines are basic to good hearing lines. Scrutiny of these earlier designers' papers reveals no goal other than a desire that spectators should be able to have a clear view of the stage and that

By courtesy of Morris Gest

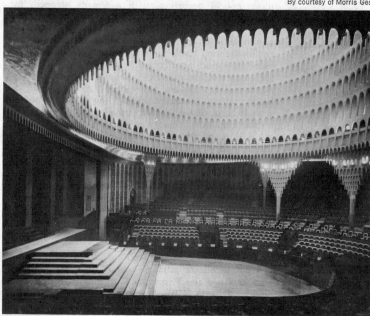

Figure 12: The Grosses Schauspielhaus, Berlin, designed by Hans Poelzig, 1919.

the auditorium design should distract from the performance as little as possible.

Auditorium reform. Theatre history indicates that, by the end of the 19th century, the time was ripe for change. Auditorium reform had already been proposed by German architects, beginning with Karl Friedrich Schinkel early in the 19th century and later by others. Chief among them was Gottfried Semper, who exerted great influence on Wagner and to whom the design of Bayreuth is sometimes erroneously attributed; in fact, a Dresden architect, Otto Brückwald, working with Wagner, is responsible for it. The United States, Great Britain, and France were slow to take up the idea of arranging seating in unbroken continuous rows, now called "continental seating," partly because of rigid interpretation of building codes. The Goodman Theatre at the Art Institute of Chicago (1925) represents the first use of "continental seating" in the United States, but it did not become really popular in the Western Hemisphere until after World War II.

20TH-CENTURY THEATRE: TRENDS IN MODERN DESIGN

Twentieth-century theatre design has followed two principal developments. First of all comes electromechanization of the proscenium stage, mainly for lighting and scenic control but sometimes introducing a flexible, mechanized apron and caliper stages in front of and to the right and left of the main proscenium stage. In these respects, Germany has led the way. Next, there has been an avant-garde movement away from proscenium theatre design altogether. The first manifestations were in France (*c.* 1920), then in the United States (*c.* 1930); they harked back to the open stage of the Renaissance, to the Shakespearean theatre, and, indeed, to the roots of theatre itself. Jacques Copeau was the first to design a nonrepresentational theatre, with Théâtre du Vieux-Colombier (Paris, 1913). Its intimate, architectural, open stage owed much to Palladio's Teatro Olimpico and to the stage of Shakespeare. In the 1920s Gilmor Brown, director of the Pasadena (California) Playhouse, designed a small, unconventional, private theatre (the "play-box theatre") and in so doing provided the United States with its first departure from the proscenium-style theatre. He was followed there by Glenn Hughes, who initiated theatre-in-the-round at the University of Washington at the Penthouse theatre designed in 1940 by J.A. Conway; C.F. Gould, architect (Figure 11). Their lead has been followed by others since World War II, particularly in the educational and regional repertory theatre.

Perfection of stage equipment. From a technical point of view, the perfection of electric light, its instrumentation and control, has exerted a more profound effect on contemporary theatre design than any other single invention. Stage lighting, as opposed to stage illumination, has now been raised to the status of an art form and has revolutionized stage decoration, stage design, and stage form, in that order. For the first time since theatre moved indoors at the Renaissance, adequate and safe illumination became possible. But, beyond mere function and safety, there is inherent in the medium a flexibility and subtlety that has allowed it to become an integral part of scenic effect and to heighten visual expression for artistic purpose. Early in the 20th century, pioneer work was done by Adolphe Appia in Switzerland and by Edward Gordon Craig in England. Though largely theoretical, it had a profound effect on design of and for the stage. Machinery was invented and instrumentation devised that made practical many of the theoreticians' ideas, and these were adapted by scenic designers, directors, and theatre engineers on both sides of the Atlantic. There was also a movement toward more plastic setting, and an effort was made to free the actor from the restrictions of the proscenium stage. As early as 1890 in Germany, first at Worms and later at the Hoftheater at Weimar, theatres began to incorporate mechanized orchestra-pit apron lifts, which provided a means for altering the point of contact between stage and auditorium (actor and spectator). At the same time, elevators, revolving stages, slip stages, and an expanded and more versatile overhead

flying system for handling scenice elements, both flat and plastic, were introduced. All this meant larger backstage facilities, higher fly towers, greater depth and width of stages, and increased understage volume. By World War I Germany led the Western world in mechanized stages and lighting systems, while in the auditorium even better sight lines were achieved and the continental seating system perfected.

By courtesy of (top) The Humanities Research Center, The University of Texas at Austin, Texas, and (bottom) Edith Lutyens Bel Geddes (Mrs. Norman Bel Geddes) for the Norman Bel Geddes Estate

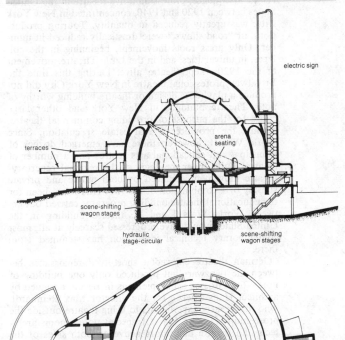

Figure 13: The project Theatre #14 designed by Norman Bel Geddes in 1922 for a theatre proposed for the Century of Progress Exposition, Chicago (1933-34). (Top) Model. (Centre) Section. (Bottom) Plan.

Setbacks to theatre building. Between the two world wars the live theatre faced increasing competition for public attention from the cinema, especially in the United States, where a gigantic industry, centred on Hollywood, produced motion pictures for worldwide distribution. The invention of sound on film created a demand for

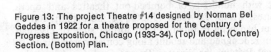

(Left margin notes)

Departure from proscenium-style stages

Competition from the cinema

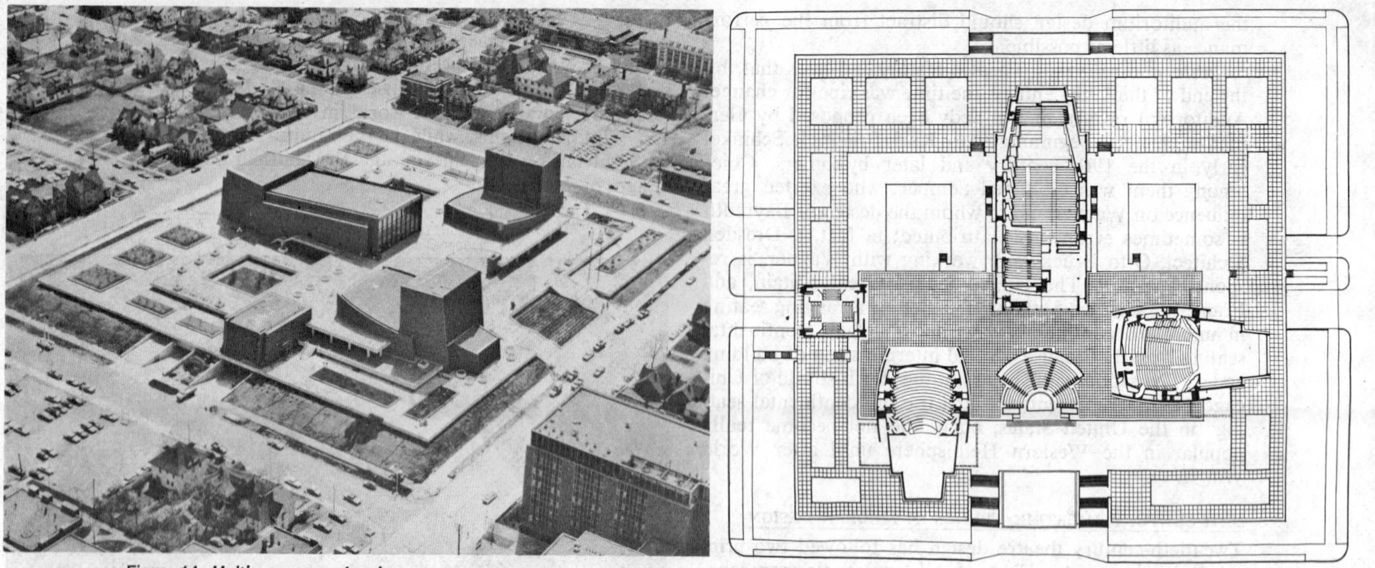

Figure 14: *Multipurpose performing arts centre.*
The Krannert Center for the Performing Arts at the University of Illinois, Urbana, designed by Max Abramovitz, 1969. (Left) Aerial view. (Right) Plan: (top left) studio theatre-in-the-round; (bottom left) drama theatre; (top centre) great hall; (bottom centre) amphitheatre; and (right) music theatre.
By courtesy of (left) the University of Illinois, Urbana–Champaign, (right) George C. Izenour

more cinema theatres with ever larger seating capacities, suited only for showing commercially canned products. As a consequence, professional live theatre in the United States between 1920 and 1940, concentrated in New York City, was greatly reduced in quantity. Touring productions, or "road shows," were drastically reduced in number. Only grass roots movement, beginning in the colleges, in universities, and in the Little Theatre movement of the 1920s, kept theatre alive. During this time the Broadway professional theatre in New York City did not produce a playhouse design or theatre building worthy of note. Theatre building, in New York and other large cities, for the purpose of providing commercial theatre, became the province of real estate speculation. Since World War II, however, there have emerged dozens of municipal and educational arts centres and a number of theatres built under the aegis of the regional repertory-theatre movement, financed by both public and private subsidy or a combination of the two. Had it not been for the educational theatre-building programs carried out between World Wars I and II, theatre building in the United States would have progressed scarcely at all; most contemporary technical innovation has stemmed from there.

German theatre enjoyed a short-lived renaissance between the two wars but produced only one building of note—the Grosses Schauspielhaus in Berlin, designed by architect Hans Poelzig for the director Max Reinhardt, who made early experiments to bring theatre outside the proscenium (Figure 12). Of special note among architects and theatre innovators active on both sides of the Atlantic were Walter Gropius (Germany) and Norman Bel Geddes (United States; Figure 13), both of whom produced theatre-design projects, though neither of them was to realize a building. The economic depression of the 1930s stifled further innovation, and the onset of World War II brought to an end all theatre-building activity on both sides of the Atlantic.

Postwar activity.   After World War II, Germany was left with hundreds of bombed-out theatres and opera houses; within 20 years (1950–70) more than 100 of them had been restored to their former state or else had been redesigned and rebuilt along contemporary lines. In Great Britain, the director Tyrone Guthrie advocated a return to the open-stage techniques in his productions of Shakespeare at the Edinburgh (Scotland) International Festival of Music and Dance. Moving to Stratford, Ontario (Canada), and assisted by stage designer Tanya Moiseyevich, Guthrie designed and built the Shakespeare Festival Theatre. This attempted a fusion of the classical

auditorium with the stage of Shakespeare. The experiment, with modifications, was repeated in 1963 at Minneapolis, where the Guthrie Theater was especially designed for him to work in. The Guthrie Theater, as indicated in the plan and section, while it is reminiscent of his earlier theatre at Stratford, exhibits a studied asymmetry in plan and section in place of the older theatre's ordered symmetry.

German theatre design after the war took up where Littman and others had left off: apron flexibility was further extended. The chief innovator in backstage design and mechanization was Walther Unruh, whose work is exemplified by the Deutsch Oper, West Berlin. Here, the stage is cruciform in plan, employing lifts under the main stage, a trapped revolving slip stage upstage, and slip stages right and left of the main stage: thus, it completes the process toward mechanization begun at the turn of the century by providing means for shifting complete and wholly plastic settings with great speed. The combination of 20th-century engineering, contemporary knowledge of auditorium design principles of sight and sound, and continental seating system makes this building the best modern opera house in the world.

North American initiative.   Beginning in the late 1950s, the United States and Canada constructed theatres, concert halls, and a variety of multipurpose facilities by the hundreds, in the greatest theatre building boom ever known in the Western Hemisphere. The two fundamentally opposing conceptions of theatre design—proscenium style and open stage—predominate. The Alley Theatre, Houston, Texas, is a fine example of the more radical school, favouring outright rejection of the proscenium along with its stagehouse and backstage machinery. The building, opened in 1968, houses two theatres: one is a modified thrust stage surrounded by a banked seating limited to a viewing angle of 90°; the other is an arena with in-the-round envelopment of stage by audience.

The opposing school, basing its main design principles on the proscenium form but making provision for an extended apron in front of a proscenium opening, is exemplified by the music and drama theatres of the Krannert Center for the Performing Arts, opened in 1969 at the University of Illinois in Champaign–Urbana (Figure 14). Between these extremes are many buildings that permit the flexible use of space, which can be arranged to mount productions in-the-round, on the thrust stage principle, or with the proscenium-apron relationship to an auditorium. Other buildings, especially those of the educational and regional repertory-theatre move-

Experimental Guthrie Theater in Minneapolis

ment, attempt a compromise between strict proscenium design and fixed theatre-in-the-round.

Public acceptance of radical departures from the traditional proscenium form was widespread during the 1960s, as private and public philanthropy together backed many successful theatre-building projects. Performing-arts centres began to appear throughout North America, usually sponsored in one of two ways: (1) as part of capital expansion in educational institutions (colleges and universities) and (2) as part of urban renewal by municipalities attempting to revitalize the decaying core of cities. There are either separate buildings for each of the performing arts (theatre, concert, recital, ballet, and so on) or else a single multipurpose building that, by electromechanical means and engineering design, can provide adequate facilities for all types of performance. In the United States, Canada, and elsewhere, gigantic arts complexes to house the performing arts are being sponsored by government and private philanthropy. Examples include the Canadian National Arts Centre at Ottawa, the Kennedy Center for the Performing Arts in Washington, D.C., and London's South Bank arts centre. Practically speaking, an argument can be advanced for concentrating on the building of sufficiently adjustable facilities that can be shared by all the performing arts in turn, and this has been the most outstanding development in theatre design, especially in the United States, since World War II. (An excellent example is the Jesse H. Jones Hall, in Houston, Texas.) Modern knowledge of building techniques, mechanization and control, understanding of room acoustics, and related problems of sight and sound has for the first time in theatre history made this kind of building a striking innovative reality.

BIBLIOGRAPHY

General works: GEORGE FREEDLEY and JOHN A. REEVES, *A History of the Theatre*, 3rd rev. ed. (1968), good, concise, factual information (moderately well illustrated) that places theatre building in proper perspective with theatre in a more general sense; PHYLLIS HARTNOLL (ed.), *The Oxford Companion to the Theatre*, 3rd ed. (1967), standard work on theatre history; ALLARDYCE NICOLL, *The Development of the Theatre*, 5th ed. rev. (1966), the best work in English on the physical theatre by the outstanding scholar of modern times (well illustrated); ROBERTO ALOI, *Architetture per lo spettacolo* (1958), a well-illustrated work on theatre building of all periods, including the cinema (written in Italian but captioned in English); DONALD C. MULLIN, *The Development of the Playhouse* (1970), an excellent student reference work; MARTIN HURLIMANN (ed.), *Das Atlantisbuch des Theaters* (1966), a collection of essays in German by recognized authorities in all branches of theatre including architecture, stage mechanics, and stage design among others (well illustrated); A.M. NAGLER, *Sources of Theatrical History* (1952), the recognized work in English for original source material in all branches of theatre.

Ancient theatres: MARGARETE BIEBER, *The History of the Greek and Roman Theater*, 2nd ed. rev. (1961), a profusely illustrated work by the recognized scholar in the field—translated and expanded from her earlier work in German (excellent for students because of its direct style of writing).

Medieval theatre: E.K. CHAMBERS, *The Mediaeval Stage*, 2 vol. (1903), an out-of-date but most exhaustive treatment of the subject, with a good bibliography.

Renaissance theatre: ALLARDYCE NICOLL, *Stuart Masques and the Renaissance Stage* (1937), excellent and exhaustive for advanced students interested in the fine points of scholarship of a difficult period in theatre history; GEORGE R. KERNODLE, *From Art to Theatre* (1944), interesting light on the subject of royal entries—also on pagentry, showing its derivation in the fine arts; A.M. NAGLER, *Theatre Festivals of the Medici, 1539–1637* (1964), profusely illustrated, footnoted, and cross-referenced from original documents of the period (not for beginners); CYRIL HODGES, *The Globe Restored* (1953), the best conjectural restorations of all the theatres of Elizabethan England, including excellent drawings and exhaustive graphic treatment of the subject.

Baroque theatre: JOHN L. HOTSON, *The Commonwealth and Restoration Stage* (1928), the best treatment of the period (illustrated); MARGARETE BAUR-HEINHOLD, *Theater des Barock* (1966; Eng. trans., 1967), the best work in English on this period, beautifully illustrated, much of it in colour, with excellent chronology and bibliography; PER BJURSTROM,

Giacomo Torelli and Baroque Stage Design (1961), complete documentation, literary and graphic, of one of the most prolific of the Baroque theatre designers; GIULIANA RICCI, *Teatri d'Italia* (1970), a beautifully illustrated work on Italian opera houses and their origin; A.M. NAGLER, *Shakespeare's Stage* (1958), a compilation of all the facts concerning Shakespeare's theatre.

19th- and 20th-century theatre: EDWIN O. SACHS and ERNEST A.E. WOODROW, *Modern Opera Houses and Theatres*, 3 vol. (1896–98, reprinted 1968), an exhaustive treatment of the subject, including drawings in plan and section—the definitive work on theatre-building activity of the century; MAXWELL SILVERMAN, *Contemporary Theatre Architecture*, with a checklist of theatre architectural publications (1946–64) by NED BOWMAN (1965), an excellent (but not critical) record of contemporary theatre building for general use—mostly photographs and drawings; J. MIELZINER, *The Shapes of Our Theatre* (1970), a good work by a famous designer of scenery; G. CALLWEY, *Theaterbau Aufgabe und Planung* (1968), an excellent short work that gives a good conception of German theatre building since World War II; WALTHER UNRUH, *Theater technik* (1969), a German text by the acknowledged master of the German stage and its engineering (good illustrations); HAROLD BURRIS-MEYER and EDWARD C. COLE, *Theatres and Auditoriums*, 2nd ed. (1964), the best work in English on theatre building in North America—designed as a handbook for architects and students; TYRONE GUTHRIE, *A New Theatre* (1964), a personal account of the building of the Guthrie Theater by its founder and artistic director; WALTER R. FUERST and SAMUEL J. HUME, *Twentieth-Century Stage Decoration*, 2 vol. (1927, reprinted 1967), the best general work detailing continental stagecraft and buildings of the period after World War I and before the 1930s.

(G.C.I.)

Theatrical Production

Any work presented to an audience at a particular time and place by living performers using themselves as the medium of presentation can be described as a theatrical production. The term theatrical production in general refers to the process of planning, rehearsing, and presenting such a work.

A theatrical production can be either dramatic or nondramatic. Whether it is the one or the other is determined by the kind of activity presented. It is often assumed that the distinguishing feature of drama is a written text; in fact, it is the fictional mimetic (from Greek *mimēsis*, "imitation, representation") nature of the performer's behaviour that makes a work dramatic. Thus, a person who walks a tightrope is performing an acrobatic act. A person who pretends to be an acrobat walking a tightrope is performing a dramatic act. Both performers are engaged in theatrical presentation. The difference between them is the difference between actual and illusory activity. Though a dramatic performance may include dancing, singing, juggling, and other nondramatic acts, it is mainly concerned with representing actual or imagined life.

In nondramatic theatrical presentation, on the other hand, there is no imitation of "another existence" but simply the pleasure or excitation of one human being by another. Whether acrobatic or musical, gestural or vocal, nondramatic activity is theatrical because it is presented by a living performer to an audience. But it remains nondramatic so long as it has a purely presentational quality rather than a representational one.

In any single theatrical production, one or another type of activity may so prevail that there is little difficulty in determining the aesthetic nature of the final work. A play by the 19th-century Norwegian dramatist Henrik Ibsen, with its depiction of middle-class behaviour, minimizes nondramatic activity; the recital of a song by the 19th-century Romantic composer Franz Schubert, by contrast, with its emphasis upon musical values, may ignore dramatic elements and, to a great extent, even the act of presentation itself. Between these extremes, however, there are many types of theatrical production where the aesthetic is not so simple to determine. Opera brings into relief the tenuous line between dramatic and nondramatic presentation, for in opera it is sometimes the dramatic values that are stressed and at other times the musical.

A further complication is the mixed nature of many theatrical productions. Within any one presentation, for

Dramatic and nondramatic theatrical production

instance, dramatic and nondramatic material may alternate. Vaudeville, or music hall, employs a succession of fictional sketches, musical and dance numbers, feats of dexterity, and other acts some of which are representational, others not. This variety is also characteristic of the Oriental stage, where dramatic moments are elaborated into dance-like exhibitions. Given this perspective, the definition of what constitutes "theatrical production" must remain elastic. The present article first examines the chief elements of theatrical production and then some of the ways in which these elements have at various times been combined to create distinctive kinds of theatrical production.

This article is divided into the following sections:

I. Elements of theatrical production

The central feature of a theatrical production is the living performer. There are, of course, many theatrical-like presentations, such as architectural and lighting displays, in which the performer is virtually eliminated, but these are occasional and special kinds of entertainment. In the main, theatrical production—whether it involves one person speaking directly to an audience in a nightclub or an ensemble of actors half-enveloped by scenery and viewed by spectators in a playhouse—has certain common elements: the living performer or performers, his or their acting in space (a stage of some sort) and time (a performance of some limited duration), and a producing process and organization.

The common elements

THE PERFORMER

In nondramatic theatre, the performer's nature is entirely his own. He presents his work in his own person and to an audience that exists in the same time and space as he does. This is true of the acrobat, the magician, the rock 'n' roll singer, the orator, and many other performers. By comparison, the dramatic actor exists in two worlds. He presents himself as a performer who is aware of an audience and sharing time and space with it. But the dramatic performer also presents himself as an actor of fictitious events and responses, as though living in another place and time. All dramatic theatre necessitates the double presentation of actor as performer and of actor as character.

Relation to the audience. Whether dramatic or nondramatic, the performer attempts to astonish the audience in some way, for an audience will observe him only so long as he offers an unusual spectacle. This is especially evident in the circus. When a freak of nature is exposed in a sideshow, the wonder, of course, resides in the performer himself. But more often the circus performer presents acts that are uncommon, acts that the average person in the audience cannot emulate. These may be acts of dexterity, such as tumbling, or of daring, such as lion taming.

Allied to the presentation of these uncommon feats is the enactment of a more ancient type of wonder: sympathetic magic. For some historians the roots of theatre are to be traced to such enactment. Ritual in form and secret in manner, the performance of traditional tribal acts had the double purpose of binding the collective and invoking hidden powers. Whether dance or mime or song, the actual behaviour was a means of releasing or manifesting forces that had to be approached with awe and caution.

Something of this magical property attaches to every theatrical performance.

On a third level, there is a type of wonder induced not by the unusualness or secretiveness of the performance but by its degree of perfection. In performance an actor or singer stirs admiration not so much by the rarity of the act (although that may be a factor) as by the quality of his rendition. This is somewhat different from the tumbler who, though graceful in movement, stirs response by the feats he can accomplish. The more naturalistic performance of actors, being inherently less wondrous, must compensate by being aesthetically more pleasing. The performer who presents more or less ordinary behaviour is likely to lose his audience's interest, a danger that is often circumvented by the content of the material he performs. Drama presents bizarre or extreme acts: the murder of husbands, the debates of gods, or the mistaken wooing of lovers. In the 19th century, when drama began to discard the more bizarre, melodramatic situations that had formerly been much presented, it substituted material that was calculated to shock or attack the audience, either because it was subject matter generally regarded as unsuitable for public presentation or because the material embodied social attitudes uncongenial to most of the playgoers. However the actor manages it, then, through the strangeness of his acts—the mystery they involve, the beauty they express, or the challenge they convey—the performer must work to provoke a response of wonder from his audience.

Impulse to create astonishment

Along with the impulse to create astonishment, the performer has an opposite impulse to display familiar acts. This is less true of the nondramatic performer than it is of the dramatic. Whereas the acrobat or the conjuror may deliberately, in a showman-like manner, seem to falter and thus remind his audience that they share a common frailty, this side of his act is of minimal importance. In drama, on the other hand, it is a very necessary part of the presentation that some features of recognizable behaviour be displayed so that even the most grotesque happenings find some echo in the audience and engage its sympathetic recognition and understanding. This may be done through familar events, emotions, allusions, or characters. A chorus provided the link between the familiar and wondrous in Greek tragedy. Secular interludes and miraculous events were combined in the medieval mystery play. Whatever the mixture, however, aspects of the strange and the familiar are present in every drama.

Skills and attributes. Occasionally, the performer himself can initiate a new style of presentation, but more frequently the demands of his times dictate the skills and attributes he must have. Skills include the specific physical and vocal behaviour that the performer can control and produce at will, such as a dance step or a facial reaction. Attributes refer to aspects of the performer's presence, which he projects to the audience but which he may or may not be able fully to control, such as degree of intensity. Certain performers are required to develop what may be a strictly limited skill (flying the trapeze or juggling balls) to a high pitch of proficiency. They systematically cultivate the necessary physical and temperamental qualities for performing such a traditional act, and, if able and talented, they may transcend its conventional features to create variations or elaborations. Success in this kind of nondramatic presentation, however, is not dependent upon skill alone. Showmanship —a broad term that describes any one or more attributes of personality, such as audaciousness, humour, charm— is equally necessary.

The high degree of physical skill associated with nondramatic performance can sometimes be found also in drama, particularly in the drama of East Asia. Chinese opera and Japanese drama alike require the actor to play one type of role for his entire professional life. He must play this role in a manner strictly determined by tradition, reproducing specific patterns of movement and speech that he can only master by first gaining control of complex and arduous physical skills. Later, if he is especially gifted, he may bring to his role certain refinements

The role of the actor in the Orient

of the tradition, and these refinements he hands down to a succeeding generation.

Western drama, however, does not usually provide the actor with quite so defined a repertory of movements and utterances. It is true that actors in the Italian commedia dell'arte specialized in one role and transmitted to their successors a body of situations, speeches, and *lazzi* (stage sketches, or routines). But, nevertheless, they seem to have had more leeway than their Oriental counterparts in exercising invention and expressing personal attributes. Great rhetorical skill has been demanded of the Western actor, however, for the metrical rhythms of Greek, Latin, French, English, and Spanish drama are intricate and were part of the glory of their respective theatres.

Naturalistic theatre, which flowered in the late 19th century, made rhetoric obsolete, and it expected the actor to hide his virtuoso performing skills by creating the illusion of everyday behaviour. This meant that more weight was given to the actor's attributes. Instead of exercising his personal magnetism through patterned behaviour, he had to do it through intense personal revelation. Among his attributes the actor counts a marked ability to focus his energies, to concentrate intently either upon the audience directly or upon a fellow actor and, thereby, indirectly upon the audience. All good actors, whatever their other limitations, can in one way or another project a concentrated force. This power of concentration became increasingly important to the actor in performance as set patterns of playing disappeared.

Actor-as performer. In nondramatic theatrical production the performer invariably acknowledges the presence of the audience. He plays directly to it. In dramatic theatre, on the other hand, the actor may or may not recognize the audience as audience. In Greek Old Comedy, an actor speaking for the author would at one point of the play cajole, advise, or challenge the spectators. By contrast, the naturalistic actor plays as though a fourth wall separates him from the audience. Between these two extremes fall a variety of relationships. At times, although direct contact is made, the audience is itself assumed to be playing a role, as in trial plays where the audience is treated as a jury or as spectators in the court of justice. At other times, the actor may address the audience one moment and play as though there were a fourth wall the next.

The nature of the actor's place and role

The quality of the contact between performer and audience is subtly modified by the nature of the performer's place and role in society. In the broadest terms, the performer may be seen as a celebrant, servant, or critic of society. As a celebrant, the actor performs a priestly function. In fact, at some points in history, he was a priest. He thus mediated between the audience and its faith. In Greek tragedy, Japanese Nō, and medieval mystery plays, the performer enacted quasi-religious actions. But the actor as celebrant need not be a "priestly" figure. Equally, the celebrants were the magnificent star performers of the 19th century, such as Sarah Bernhardt, who proved to be the apotheosis of Bohemian romanticism.

More often, the actor has been a servant, allied to the court jester and household retainer. In classical Rome he was a slave or lowly freedman. In Elizabethan England he was nominally a great man's underling or, if he lacked the protection of the nobility, was classified as a rogue and vagabond. Consequently, direct contact with the audience was invariably couched in supplicatory terms.

It was not until the 19th century that the actor as a rebel began to appear. Performing in plays critical of society, he himself addressed the audience indirectly and so avoided committing himself to the plays' views. But with the 20th century, direct assault on the audience occurs. Troupes such as the Living Theatre from the United States and writers such as the Austrian dramatist Peter Handke (one of whose plays is known in English as *Offending the Audience*) castigate the audience deliberately in order to force its members to choose sides in a sociopolitical struggle.

Actor as character. The second aspect of the dramatic performer's work has to do with mimesis, or representa-

tion. He is actor as character. In this sense, "character" includes both the enactment of representational behaviour and the portrayal of human types. In enacting representational behaviour, the performer adopts a fictional framework and acts according to his text's demands. When playing Macbeth, for instance, he behaves "as if" he sees the phantom dagger referred to in the text. Working carefully in rehearsal, he correlates selected gesture and vocal delivery with his sense of the character's internal processes in order to produce an image of Macbeth vainly endeavouring to grasp the dagger. In portraying character, the actor must often work within established categories of stock or generic types. Roman comedy, for instance, utilized a limited number of stock characters (including the cunning slave, the passionate young lover, the suspicious old father). The generic type is less specific in behaviour and sentiment than is the stock character. The king, the wise counsellor, the raging tyrant are examples coming from historical and biblical sources; the leading man, the juvenile, the ingenue, and the villain are examples from theatrical tradition itself.

Characters in "slice-of-life" drama

Some characters, however, do not stem from tradition but are native to a particular playwright. This is especially true in naturalistic "slice-of-life" drama, which modelled its roles on field observation or personal experience. Stock and generic types stressed those features of personality common to human beings. Naturalistic drama, however, sought to particularize each role in order to stress what separates one individual from another. At the same time, comprehensive theories of acting were evolved, notably those of Konstantin Stanislavsky, who was director of the Moscow Art Theatre. While the actor might start with a given "type" of the most general sort (a country doctor, for example), his efforts during rehearsal were bent on differentiating this doctor from any other. Directors encouraged external observation and internal probing as techniques to enable the actor to create a character whose behaviour is idiosyncratic and drawn from experience. This style of acting demanded extensive preparation, with the result that lengthy rehearsal periods of from six months to a year became the ideal.

Naturalistic acting raises questions about the relation between the actor's self and the role he performs. Does the actor merely simulate behaviour or does he experience the passions and thoughts of the character? Central to the actor's art though this question is, it has never been satisfactorily answered. Some theorists say that the actor must blend his own personality with features called for by the role, using techniques of emotional recall and psychological probing. Others say that the actor ought to rely upon his physical technique in order to create an illusion of life.

SPACE AND TIME

The distinction between actor as performer and actor as character is matched by a distinction between the presentational and representational nature of space and time in theatrical production.

The playhouse area. As a matter of geographical fact, performer and audience exist together in a common area. Within this common area there is a clearly delineated performing space (ring, stage platform, pit) and an audience space, the two structurally related. Some of the more common patterns of relationship are (1) an amphitheatre, with a bank of spectators half surrounding a playing area; (2) a circle of spectators standing or sitting about a ring in which the performance takes place; and (3) rows of seated spectators facing a raised platform. Theatre space is often associated with a special building, but this has not always been the case, nor is it always the case in modern times. Often theatre space has embraced a town square or even an entire town so that performers and audience are able to mingle. Modern attempts to create a space within which the distinction between performer and audience is blurred (called environmental theatre) echo earlier examples from the popular theatre.

Division of audience and performers

Isolation of performer. Yet, despite the innumerable variations in the form and use of geographical space in the theatre, it is possible to discern two conditions that all productions endeavour to meet. First, every production seeks to impart a special quality to the theatrical area. If a theatrical building is used, that in itself may provide a heightened sense of locale. Otherwise, special decoration of familiar locales (town, market square) or procession through them might transform them into ceremonial or festive spaces. Again, the urge to create wonder is at work. Next, every production tries to make the performer visible and audible to the audience. This is largely a practical matter. On flat ground, the circle or ring has often proved to be most efficacious. In hilly country, the amphitheatre is the readiest solution. When a playing area is to be permanent, some means of raising the performer above the level of the crowd is often introduced, such as boards laid over trestles. The degree to which the performer is to be isolated depends partly on how complete and detailed a view of the presentation the audience expects.

The isolation of the performer has, however, another property. Marking out a playing area was often a religious act: in classical Greece, for instance, the dancing circle surrounded the altar of the god Dionysus. Thus, the performing space had a symbolic character. Even when the direct religious tie was broken, stepping into the ring or onto the stage was still regarded as a passage from one world into another, a world of magical or spectacular properties. This is equally true of the sawdust ring of the circus and of the bare boards of the trestle stage. Existing traditional theatres, especially those of the Orient, still regard the act of preparing to go on stage (putting on makeup, for instance) as sacred. Because of this, the isolation of the actor is more than utilitarian; it is transformational. He becomes greater than life.

Illusion of place. In dramatic production, this geographical space takes on another dimension, a behavioral character: the magical property already belonging to it as a performing area is further augmented by the fictional action that now takes place. The stage becomes another locale by an act of imagination in which both actors and audience participate. It may be done simply, by speech: at the opening of a scene in *Twelfth Night*, one of the characters asks "what country, friends, is this?" and is told "this is Illyria, lady." Thus, the subsequent action is set firmly in the context of Illyria. It may be done visually, by the designer's ingenuity (the audience sees a room or a garden). The actor as character inhabits not the theatre but Illyria, the room, the garden. Although the audience may not be deluded into believing that it inhabits another place, it does gain a double vision. Its focal attention is fixed on the hypothetical locale, while its peripheral attention is fixed on the performing space. Apparently, though how it is not clear, human beings can sustain such paradoxical perception.

There are varying degrees to which the geographical or behavioral property of space dominates in any one theatrical production. In some productions, especially those that are inspired by the anti-naturalistic theories of the Russian director Vsevolod Meyerhold, the audience is constantly reminded that it is in a theatre. Naturalistic productions, in contrast, following the principles of Stanislavsky, put greater stress on behavioral space and encourage a clear distinction between performing area and viewing area. On the other hand, the theatre has often reconciled the paradoxical features of dramatic space. The Greek theatre combined the actor's platform with a more public dancing circle that gave ready access to an amphitheatre of seats. The 18th-century English stage moved out from a recessed picture of a representational locale to a projecting apron that merged with the auditorium. In both examples, the theatre found a physical convention for fusing geographical and behavioral space and for mediating between the actor and the audience.

Real and illusory time. Time likewise has a dual character in drama. The performer and audience exist together in chronological time. But the actor as character exists in a behavioral time that is generally different from the chronological time. Neoclassical drama of the 17th century, especially in France, endeavoured to make the dura-

tion of play going (chronological time) coincide with the duration of a play's action (behavioral time). But, as a rule, drama has achieved its effects by accentuating the discrepancy between "real" and "illusory" time.

On one hand, the performer projects a sequence of activity upon which the audience concentrates intensely. Because it is difficult to maintain full attention over very long periods, it must be modulated; that is, stimulated, relaxed, and stimulated again. Contrast and suspense give spice and direction to the audience's awareness of passing moments, thereby making the "real" time spent at a performance absorbing and deeply felt. These performing experiences are further heightened by the illusion that another time scheme is also operating, that of the fictional event. Some drama gains its effects by suggesting that chronological and behavioral time differ between scenes but not within scenes; that is, months may pass between Act I and II of *Three Sisters* by the Russian playwright Anton Chekhov, but within any act the time scale in which the actor as character exists is exactly the same as that in which the actor as performer operates. Shakespeare, however, presents a scene in *Othello* (Act II, scene 2) that takes about 25 minutes to play, yet during this scene an entire night has supposedly passed. One of the most extensive temporal schemes in drama is to be found in the medieval cycles of miracle plays, which unfolded over a period of two to four days and which covered the history of the universe from a time before Genesis to the Day of Judgment yet to come.

In contrast to this awesome inclusion of all time is the handling of time in Japanese Nō drama, in which "real" time, with its inevitable passage, is retarded to create a sensation of timelessness. The deliberate pace of the performer, the reiteration of the drum, and the unchanging facade of the stage all contribute to this impression. Here, again, the audience's awareness of real time passing accentuates the meaning of illusory time.

ARRANGEMENT OF PERFORMER, SPACE, AND TIME: THE PRINCIPLE OF CONTRAST

The fundamental elements of theatrical production, then, are performers and their activities, the space they fill, and the time they define. The aesthetician Suzanne Langer, in her book *Feeling and Form* (1953), describes how they are arranged to produce an effect of the imminent future, and, indeed, one of the liveliest feelings that drama can excite is that of expectation. In its more obvious manifestation such expectation is experienced as suspense. But imminence as a sensation exists in the spectator; the organizing principle that stimulates that sensation is contrast.

Being a temporal and spatial art, theatre employs both temporal and spatial contrast. A scene that builds from expectation of a crisis, through the crisis, and into the denouement exhibits temporal contrast. This contrast is experienced as degrees of intensity. A scene that reveals a prince dressed in black amidst a festive court, as in *Hamlet*, illustrates spatial contrast. In the composition of any presentation, theatrical production employs a mosaic of contrasts—dozens of temporal and spatial fragments are deliberately organized to create a total impression. The trapeze artist employs a spatial contrast (balance and imbalance) and a temporal one (a preliminary easy feat and a difficult finale). A play offers contrasts between one character and another, between actor as performer and actor as character, between actor and scenic space, and between a topical allusion and the audience's social awareness (all spatial). It also offers contrasts between the intensity of one moment and that of another, between the actor's appearance from one scene to another, between what a character thinks will happen and what an audience has been told will happen (all temporal).

Contrast, of course, is a principle of all art. Theatrical production, however, stresses its own peculiar contrasts, those between the fixed and the dynamic (static space and moving actor), the visible and the invisible (the actor's words and gestures and the character's thoughts and feelings), the actual and the fictional (what the actor does and what his acts represent), and finally the possible and

Transformation of locale through the actor's speech [margin note]

Deliberate slowing of time in Japanese Nō drama [margin note]

the impossible (an actor as character presenting the dead Romeo and the actor as performer being alive and well). It is by the artful manipulation of these contrasts that theatre produces its effects.

The principle of contrast in the cinema

The cinema, which is often mistakenly thought of as another theatrical form, shows quite a different handling of contrast. The fusion of the possible and impossible in the same act no longer obtains. Film is hypnotic; what is shown can be—in fact, exists, even if only as an image. Initiative shifts from the performer to the viewer; that is, to the camera's eye. In theatre the performer has to assert himself in a defined space. His energy, directed at the spatial frame, fellow performers, and the audience, shapes the performance. In the cinema this energy belongs to the lens. Its gaze, its shift of attention, its opening and fading play upon the surface of nature and of man as part of nature. Instead of emphasizing the essential contradiction of man's condition, which is so much a part of theatre, cinema harmonizes place and person within its visual frame. On film, only the expert technical eye can usually distinguish location from studio shots. Wherever the lens turns seems to be part of a unified sequence of viewing. On stage, no matter how skillful the scenic artist may be, the audience is aware of the tension between reality and appearance, a tension that does not exist in film, where all elements of the frame express a single visual reality.

Because the cinema's popularity has helped to reduce the amount of theatrical production, it is often asserted that the cinema is superior to the theatre as a performing art. But this superiority only applies to certain aspects of storytelling—those involving man's adventures, for instance. Storytelling is common to several literary and performing arts. The novel nurtures an interior sensitivity to unfolding events that is not quite shared by either theatre or film, while theatre fosters narrative dependent upon a character's assertiveness. Ultimately, it is not the superiority of one medium's stories to another that is pertinent but the distinctiveness of one mode of storytelling from another.

II. Methods of theatrical production

Aesthetically, the theatrical production of drama appears to involve autonomous persons enacting a fiction. The preparation and execution of a production, however, require the coordination of many individual contributions. These contributions may be discussed according to the people involved (actors, dramatists, designers, and so on) or according to the functions performed (devising a piece to be performed, playing the action, providing a theatrical setting, and so on). Theatrical personnel and their division of responsibilities have varied widely in the course of theatrical history. Function, however, tends to remain fairly constant.

THE PIECE AND ITS PERFORMANCE

Scenario or script. Traditionally, the dramatic piece has always been planned in advance and rehearsed, although there are degrees of advance planning and rehearsal. The theatre of the commedia dell'arte was basically impromptu. Nonetheless, it involved considerable preparation of constituent elements, such as character type, set speeches, and highly polished routines, even though the exact sequence and interplay of these elements would vary from performance to performance. Contemporary "happenings" reduce advance planning to a minimum but do not eliminate it completely. Normally, however, advance planning is so extensive that it appears in the form of a written script, perhaps devised by the actors, perhaps created by a single dramatist. Depending on the writer's involvement with the actors and the theatre as a whole, the script may be either a tentative prospectus for a piece to be created in rehearsal (a scenario) or a fairly finished blueprint of the final presentation (a play).

Whether scenario or play, a piece consists of segments of activity arranged in a meaningful sequence. More often than not it is a narrative sequence, and thus each segment of activity presents a step in the unfolding of a story. But the sequence may also be based on a common motif or recurrent characters. The segments of activity, usually termed episodes or scenes, can include many kinds of behaviour—such as persuasion of one person by another, delivery of a speech, singing of a song, engaging in hand-to-hand combat. According to the conventions of a theatre and the genius of its creative artists, dramatists and actors alike, these activities assume distinct form.

Determining the scope of the material

To a significant extent, theatrical tradition and social practice determine the scope of the material to be presented. In the theatre of ancient Greece, for example, legendary stories provided a fictional framework for its tragedy, while episodes of debate, lamentation, prophecy, and choral comment constituted the main activities. In other theatres, storytelling, singing, acrobatics, as well as a wide variety of passionate speeches make up the presentation. In short, the ingredients of a particular theatrical production already exist in the playing tradition. Whoever performs the function of maker of the piece (dramatist, manager, actor) operates within that context of performing routines and production conditions. With these he perhaps fuses material drawn from other arts (poetry, dance, architecture) and from other more personal experiences. While in the process of devising the piece, he may work closely with his fellow artists or he may compose the piece privately and leave its execution to others.

Relation of production to occasion. The nature of a theatrical production and the way in which it evolves are governed by the nature of the occasion for which it is presented. The occasion may exist prior to the theatrical production and give rise to it, or the production may be prepared in the expectation of finding an occasion for its presentation. Annual festivals, such as the Dionysia of ancient Greece or Corpus Christi in medieval Europe, are examples of established occasions that predate any specific theatrical production. Other such ready-made occasions may be civic or aesthetic in purpose rather than religious. Yet all normally possess social agencies that subsidize and, in part, manage production. There are also special events, such as royal entries or marriages, that provide unique occasions for some sort of production. When the occasion already exists, the type and subject matter of a production are frequently selected to glorify an accepted social and aesthetic ideal.

Commencing with the Renaissance, there developed a professional theatre of the marketplace. Productions were offered in large population centres or were taken to villages and towns where a potential audience already existed. With a shift from theatre devised for an independently existing occasion to speculative theatre, seeking to create its own occasion, there is a shift from a communal to a cosmopolitan audience. Instead of presenting plays at times that inherently held sacred or civic meaning and, therefore, drew together the entire populace, actors presented plays with some regularity and frequency in order to attract a public large enough to support them. Instead of fulfilling a recognized social purpose, the theatre had to justify itself and persuade people to attend by providing novelty and excitement.

Performing the piece. Occasion naturally determines the exact role of the actor with regard to his audience. Not only does it affect the manner in which the actor addresses the audience or represents a character, but it also influences the physical appearance of the actor. As a religious official or as descendant of a priest, a status belonging to performers in Japanese Nō drama and in the tragedy of classical Greece, the actor is often transformed by costume into an extrahuman or superhuman figure. Raised headdresses, painted or masked faces, enveloping robes, all contribute to the creation of a daemonic figure. As a servant, however—the status actors held in Elizabethan England—he often apes the master, playing the role not of hero or demigod but the epitome of contemporary society. Whatever the adornment, however, the actor's appearance is intimately connected with his social role, the image portrayed fulfilling audience expectation.

Earlier it was noted that the actor is the central figure in theatrical production, and indeed it is true that, while performing, he is the focus of attention. During the preparatory and rehearsal phases of production, however, he may be a subordinate. In the Renaissance, for instance, the actors themselves were in control of all phases of production, but with the coming of capitalism they yielded the reins to theatrical managers and, much later, to stage directors. Ultimately, they discovered that, if nonperformers control the production process, the performer's spontaneous interaction with the audience becomes subordinate to a prescribed scheme.

The importance of stage scenery in theatrical production is determined by the degree to which either the auditorium or playing area needs to be transformed for or during a performance. Four possibilities exist: little or no change is introduced into either area (as in the Elizabethan public theatre); the playing area remains unaltered while the audience area is changed (as in erecting banks of seating in a town square); the playing area is changed while the audience area remains fixed (as in proscenium theatre); both areas are transformed (as in Renaissance court theatre and contemporary environment theatre).

The fixed playing space often has greater or lesser emblematic significance. In Japan, the Nō stage had three pine trees symbolizing heaven, Earth, and man; the kabuki stage employed the convention that the right-hand side is more eminent than the left; the Elizabethan playhouse used trap doors for heaven and hell. The practice of changing the visual and physical arrangement of the playing area became widespread during the Renaissance. At first, designers generalized the correspondence between play and setting by devising scenery appropriate to tragic, comic, and pastoral dramas. Later they created a setting unique to one play alone. With the emergence of designed space and changeable scenery, there arose an entire profession of scenic architects and mechanics whose work at times overshadowed that of the actors in importance. By the 20th century the designer's task became so complex that it was often divided among scenic, costume, and lighting personnel and involved technicians, electricians, stagehands, prop masters, wardrobe mistresses, and many others working together.

COLLABORATION OF PARTICIPANTS:
PREPARING AND REHEARSING THE PIECE

Because it is a public art, theatre is buffeted by many forces external to the artistic process. Moreover, that process is itself subject to internal strain as various contributors to a performance strive to achieve their individual goals. Clashes of temperament are not unusual, and, given the intensity and intimacy of theatrical work, this is not surprising. Yet there are striking instances of close, harmonious, and enduring collaboration among theatre people.

No single pattern for production exists. There are too many social and personal variables at work during planning and rehearsals. What may be the procedure in one case or at one time may not be of use in another. Certain broad observations may be made, however.

First, any individual production is normally, though not invariably, part of a more continuous enterprise. The continuity may be provided by the civic or religious life of the community, the stable association of an acting troupe, the permanence of a producer's office, some other element, or a combination of these. Whatever it may be, it influences and even determines the mode of planning a production, conducting rehearsals, and giving performances.

Next, the production process tends to be either cooperative or hierarchical. True cooperation is rare, and there are few instances in theatrical history when it existed. The company for which Shakespeare wrote and to which he belonged seems to have been one of those rare collectives. A partnership of actors, it remained for more than 25 years a well-knit community of professional associates and friends. More usual is the hierarchical organization. Whether by force of talent, right of possession, or exercise of authority, a single individual takes the initiative

and controls a production. In most instances, the professional speciality of that leader is dictated by conditions of the particular theatre in which he works. In 17th-century France, for instance, the leader virtually had to be an actor (Molière was an actor turned actor-manager-dramatist); in 20th-century America he virtually has to be a producer or director.

Finally, the mode of planning and rehearsing a production may be influenced by the artistic concept of an individual or a group. As long as theatre was part of a continuing tradition, its mode of production varied little. The mode was partly conditioned by the social role of theatre and partly by the type of material the actor performed. Thus, the actor who played one type of role for his entire professional life concentrated on perfecting recurrent stage routines, while the actor who handled many different roles within a brief season had to work rapidly and with facility.

New theories of production evolved during the 19th century that affected both styles of performance and methods of rehearsal. Gradually, the idea of ensemble arose, an ensemble that stressed harmony of ideal and craft among the actors and between the actors and the stage environment in order to achieve a unity of effect. These ideas necessitated the careful orchestration of all elements of production. In the 18th and earlier 19th centuries, the charismatic figure was the star actor; it then became the star ensemble (the Moscow Art Theatre, for instance) and, through the ensemble, the director.

III. Kinds of theatrical production

The development of telecommunication and the complications of international relations have extended horizons in every field of art and science, including theatre. Not only do theatrical troupes travel readily from one part of the world to another, thereby giving audiences firsthand contact with an extensive repertoire, but these troupes, stimulating one another, are experimenting with a wide variety of theatrical forms. As a consequence, the concept of what constitutes theatrical production has broadened considerably.

To describe all the variations of theatrical production is hardly feasible, but it is possible to indicate some of the major historical and contemporary kinds of production. One kind may be differentiated according to what is produced (the nature of the production). Another kind may be classed according to whom and why a work is addressed (occasion and purpose); still another in terms of how a work is produced (the system of production); a fourth in terms of who dominates production (the guiding artist); and, lastly, in terms of distinguishing marks of the production (the style).

KINDS ACCORDING TO THEIR NATURE

Nondramatic.   Nondramatic productions include diverse oral and musical presentations, circus and vaudeville acts, and various types of pageantry.

As a form of presentation, circus is diverse, containing within its compass quite different orders of performance. These might be divided as to whether they are feats of daring, illusion, or drama. Acrobatics such as wire walking, flying the trapeze, or riding bareback excite wonder because of their difficulty and the dexterity they require. Presentation is rooted in a death-defying impulse. Lion taming, too, is a feat of daring and dexterity —though here the audience is mainly conscious of the audacity exhibited rather than the skill displayed. Feats of illusion involve conjuring of one sort or another. Whether the performer causes a woman to disappear or a body to levitate, skill in devising the act and carrying it off creates the illusion that the audience is seeing something happen that it knows is impossible. Dramatic feats usually involve only the clowns. In one sense this type of presentation properly belongs to the dramatic theatre. For convenience it is included here as a form of mime. It is allied to feats of illusion, as when a dozen clowns stream out of a tiny automobile. Generally, however, the clown engages in a highly refined and circumscribed dramatic activity (perhaps mimicking other nondramatic performers) of a ludicrous, often grotesque, and quite improbable nature (see CIRCUS).

Pageantry is an entirely different kind of production. It can be either nondramatic or dramatic. In either case it is communal in purpose and organization. Nondramatic pageantry includes civic processions (such as the Festival of Roses parade in Pasadena, California), as well as static displays (the gymnastic demonstrations common in eastern Europe and China). The appeal of nondramatic pageantry lies in visual spectacle, particularly spectacle that overwhelms the individual. The performer presents himself as a member of the collective, and, even where one person might be in focus, such as the Queen of the Roses, he or she is passive and wins attention merely as the apex of a broad pyramid of performers. In certain religious pageants the focal figure is not a living person at all but the icon or statue of a god or saint. By extension, one form of pageantry eliminates the living participants altogether. A *son et lumière* display, which emphasizes the visual grandeur of an architectural marvel or a natural wonder, is a form of pageantry halfway between visual art and theatre.

Dramatic pageantry has much in common with the nondramatic kind: there is communal involvement, stress on visual display, processional or static masses, and so on. It has, further, a fictional character. Either individual segments of the pageant illustrate a historical or hypothetical incident, or the pageant as a whole has a motif that may be historical or—more commonly in the past— mythic or allegorical. Performers in the U.S. re-enacting the dumping of tea into Boston Harbor exemplify historical pageantry; in England the assault on the Castle of Beauty by Knights of the Mount of Love, a pageant celebrating the marriage of Prince Arthur to Catherine of Aragon in 1501, exemplifies the allegorical type common at Renaissance courts. Pageantry of both the dramatic and nondramatic sort played and continues to play a significant role in the legitimization of political actions and the assertion of social prestige (see PAGEANT AND PARADE).

Dramatic. Central to dramatic production, of course, is the acted play involving, as described above, the performer-character in a fictional event. Dramatic production of this kind is divisible according to genre (including comedy, tragedy, farce), style (romantic, classical), or structure (architectonic unity of action, harmonic multiplicity of actions). There are, in addition, special examples of dramatic production distinguished by their alliance either to music or to dance.

Opera and musical comedy combine drama and music in varying degrees of dominance. Opera in particular straddles the border between these two arts, and much aesthetic discussion of this mode has concentrated on the relative importance of the enactment of the fiction or the elaboration of the music. The musical development of opera predominated in the 17th and 18th centuries, whereas emphasis since Richard Wager in the late 19th century has been increasingly on dramatic features. Operetta and musical comedy, the latter a peculiarly North American genre, are more closely allied to the theatre than to opera (see OPERA; POPULAR THEATRE).

Dramatic production stressing bodily or kinetic communication falls under the headings of dance and mime. Dance is the more clearly distinct art, though it shares so many features with the theatre that it is hard to say where one art ends and the other begins. Dance was a significant and essential element in the growth of Western drama; it was also a source and remains a feature of the Oriental. Traditional Chinese theatre, in fact, is a dance–song presentation of a fictional act, and the work of the U.S. choreographer and performer Martha Graham is properly dance-drama. When the fictional basis is slight or nonexistent and the movement of figures through space takes place within a relatively abstract framework, dance separates most evidently from drama. Thus, in ballet, the pas de deux often uses the drama as a point of departure for the kinetic exploration of space. Mime, on the other hand, remains closely connected to drama, being merely a highly specialized form of enactment. Relying on movement without words,

it enjoyed an immense vogue in imperial Rome, contributed to the style of commedia dell'arte, and has undergone a modest revival at the hands of such French performers as Jean-Louis Barrault and Marcel Marceau (see BALLET; MODERN DANCE).

Folk productions. Mention should be made of productions that combine dramatic and nondramatic characteristics and also of those verging on what might be termed folk production. The prime example of the combined form is the vaudeville or variety show. It may be offered in a regular theatre, a nightclub, or even a circus. It brings together pieces that contrast with one another in style and tone. In a single performance, the audience might witness feats of daring and illusion, dramatic sketches, musical offerings, and dancing. Its theatrical appeal lies not only in the individual acts but also in the way they are climactically arranged.

Folk production describes those communal events that, while social in character, include an element of presentation. Essentially, members of a community will offer a traditional piece as part of a larger festivity. Masked or costumed merrymakers may gather at or join a party, mix with the crowd or guests, give their piece, celebrate, and move on. The Feast of Fools, the *Purim-shpil*, and maypole dances exemplify this type of minimally produced theatrical play.

KINDS ACCORDING TO OCCASION AND PURPOSE

The principal types of theatrical occasion may conveniently be divided, as previously noted, between those that exist independently of any theatrical celebration and that are thus dependent upon communal production and those speculative presentations that create their own occasions and upon which commercial production thrives. Communal production is the responsibility of the social organism. It usually has civic, religious, educational, or cultural purposes or a combination of these. Commercial production principally has a recreational purpose, although it may also include any of the purposes of communal production. In the main, communal production is engaged in presenting a single performance to coincide with some extratheatrical event: a religious observance, a political ceremony, a military celebration. Commercial production requires continuing performance, frequency of presentation determined not by the nature of the occasion but by the size of the potential audience. The idea of a theatre season, an extended period of playing and producing, is a product of the commercial theatre.

Religious and civic. Among communal productions are those that are offered at a religious occasion. Though there are diverse theories about the origin of drama, most historians recognize that drama emerged from religious ritual, probably in order to heighten or celebrate significant stages of life, such as the maturation of the male or the change of a season. At what precise point the ritual act of religion gave way to the theatrical act of drama is uncertain, but formal drama is first met in ancient Greece.

Certainly, religious festivals gave rise to dramatic expression by re-enacting the passion and trials of the god or man-god on whom the religion centred. In Christian Europe, biblical plays became attached to particular festivities, the most notable being that of Corpus Christi. In the same way, the story of the assassination of Ḥusayn ibn ʿAlī, the Islāmic leader of the Shīʿite faction, was enacted at the Persian festival of Taʿziya. As in ancient Greece, these festivals would extend over many days during which all other communal activity ceased so that everyone could either participate in the play or join the audience.

Civic occasions are not usually so all-embracing. Under the term "civic occasions" fall those periodic celebrations connected with the life of a community, such as the Lord Mayor's pageant in London, or special celebrations determined by events, such as a military triumph in ancient Rome or a royal entry in 16th-century Brussels. Behind these productions lay the need and desire for social and political prestige. The occasion for seeing a production was also an occasion for seeing the general or the prince in all his splendour. In fact, the presentation

Non-dramatic pageantry

Opera and musical comedy

The vaudeville or variety show

was conceived as a frame for the ruler and the virtues he ostensibly exemplified.

Student productions

Educational. Initially, educational aims were subsumed under religious aims. But with the growth of educational institutions came theatrical performances given by students. A play might be enacted to enhance appreciation of its literary qualities, to celebrate a graduation, or to commemorate a national holiday. At first these productions were communal in character and occasional in presentation. Then, for brief periods in Elizabethan and Jacobean England, school and choral masters endeavoured to turn this communal activity into a commercial operation by utilizing boys as professional actors. During the 20th century, however, educationally based drama has concentrated upon younger students. While often having a recreational result in practice, in intent theatre for children has had an openly avowed educational purpose. The purpose might be to communicate a body of literature to the youngster, to inculcate a moral attitude, or to stimulate aesthetic and cultural appreciation. Sometimes this type of theatre has involved children as performers, sometimes adults. Although promoters of children's productions may be commercial managers, in general, sustained educational theatre has required communal support. Some countries, such as the Soviet Union, subsidize highly respected theatres for children and youth. The artists accept it as their principal responsibility to develop and prepare presentations for children of different age levels. The U.S. uses indirect means, such as educational grants from government sources, which partially subsidize productions for children.

Decline of communal productions

Theatre for specific and limited occasions is no longer widespread, however, as it once was. The performance of the Passion Play still occurs every ten years at Oberammergau in Germany, and the honouring of the Virgin Mary takes place annually at Elche in Spain, but such examples of communal production are rare. In their place continuous presentation, first pioneered by commercial operation, has now been adapted to renewed communal purposes. Where festivals appear, as they do with increasing frequency in the 20th century, they appear as cultural activities organized to make a body of dramatic literature, such as Shakespeare's works, available to the public. By enabling the audience to see a number of plays in a few days, they often succeed in immersing an audience in an atmosphere that counteracts the distractions of modern urban living.

KINDS ACCORDING TO SYSTEM OF PRODUCTION

Theatrical production may be further differentiated according to the system of planning, rehearsing, and performing a play. Any system varies with the social and artistic conditions, but on the whole three kinds of operation seem to recur in the history of production. There is the single-performance system related to a community or institution. There is the repertory system of a more or less permanent professional company offering a variety of plays. And, finally, there is the commercial system of single productions kept in a continuous run of performances over as long a period as is profitable. These systems, while overlapping in methods and objectives, are distinct enough to warrant individual examination.

Single performance. Single or limited performance of a presentation, as part of institutional or communal life, is fairly common on a number of levels. The Greek city-state (polis), the medieval town, the Japanese temple, the school, and the club are but a few of the groups that give or have given such dramatic performances. Often the mode of production merely imitates the prevailing theatre of the time. There have, however, been times when the single-performance mode was itself the prevailing system. Both the Greek city-state and the medieval town organized their productions in a strikingly similar way, with the municipality exercising control. For the Athenians, municipal officials supervised the selection of the plays to be produced at the festivals, appointed a *choregus* who financed each play, arranged for the dithyrambic choruses of citizens, and organized the procession and presentations during the festival.

Similarly, medieval town officers—really the assembled chief artisans of the local craftsmen's guilds—undertook to assign to each guild the play it was to perform and designated the stations or sites for the performances. Whether the town as a whole or merely the individual guild was responsible for securing the text of a play is uncertain, but there was overall agreement on what portions of the biblical story would be enacted by the guilds.

There was, however, one difference between the Greek and medieval production systems. Until at least the 4th century BC, the Athenians presented new plays every year, whereas the medieval townspeople would re-enact the same plays or variations of them. Yet in both systems, many aspects of production (the theatre space used, the pool of actors, the store of costumes, for instance) were the same from year to year so that, single performance notwithstanding, each individual offering relied upon an established tradition.

The court masque

This was less true of the court masque (an allegorical dramatic performance featuring music and especially dancing) in Renaissance times, which was also presented only once. Although each production belonged to a tradition of courtly entertainment, masques of the 16th and 17th centuries became increasingly lavish and novel. A court official was responsible for the overall piece and so has something in common with the later theatre manager or entrepreneur. It was he who recommended a dramatic poet to provide the text, hired the actors, made arrangements for stage scenery to be provided and painted, and approved the results before offering them to the sovereign. The most fundamental distinction between this kind of production and earlier institutional types is that the masque was devised for the delectation of the monarch, and therefore his taste and will dictated what was done and how much was expended.

Permanent companies. The development of a production system depending on a permanent company introduced a new element into theatre, that of professional virtuosity. The emergence of professional theatre companies was a feature of the Renaissance and the growth of townships. Various courts had maintained performers throughout the medieval period, but these were usually musicians or single performers. With the emergence of the town, the theatre company began to appear throughout Italy, France, Germany, England, and Spain, usually consisting of between five and 12 actors who devoted their lives to the perfection of their craft.

The repertory troupe. Initially, the company was obliged to tour, since neither court nor city could employ full-time professionals. As a result, the actors became accustomed to performing in all kinds of physical spaces: in halls, on outdoor platforms, in chapels, on village greens. To compensate for rudimentary scenic spectacle, the actors used a rich array of costumes—some traditional garments for recurrent characters or situations, some deliberately opulent for their own sake. At all times the actors kept a number of plays fresh in mind so that, if they played an extended engagement in one place, they could offer their plays in repertory—that is, a new play at each performance, repeating plays on request or as business warranted. When a troupe finally settled in one city, it continued this mode of presentation, and thus a true repertory system was born.

Within this very broad system two stylistic differences may be observed. Some permanent troupes performed pieces in which the actors portrayed stock figures. Each actor had his or her speciality. Italian commedia dell'arte and Japanese kabuki both utilized such types. Molière, though far less rigid in portraying stock types, led a company each of whose members specialized in one kind of characterization. English and Spanish troupes, however, used actors who were much more flexible and who enacted generic types in the many stories that were dramatized. Otherwise, the companies had a great deal in common. Actors bought plays from writers, hired any supporting personnel they needed, and took the profits. Usually, they worked on a share system, dividing the proceeds among themselves. Sometimes one person might be the acknowledged head of the troupe; sometimes a true partnership existed. In either case the operation was fundamentally the same.

Commercial management. The repertory troupe continued but eventually came to be managed by an individual. Initially, the manager was also an actor, and the actor-manager was in his heyday from the late 18th up to the beginning of the 20th century. With his appearance the production system changed. Instead of one's partner or fellow townsman at the head of the troupe, there was an employer. His concern was less with the continued living to be earned by the actor and more with the profit he could extract from the public. Gradually, out of this change emerged the stock company and the single-show association. The stock company was an acting troupe usually managed and organized for a limited period—called a season—to give a number of plays. Sometimes the manager would take the leading roles and engage others to support him. If he were not an actor himself, he would hire all the performers. The major shift in mode of production came when the stock companies stopped presenting plays in repertory—that is, a variety of plays given in alternation—and extended the run of a single play. This happened when city populations grew large enough to keep one play running for an indefinite time. At the end of the 17th century, a London play that had run eight performances was deemed a success. A generation later, however, the production of John Gay's *Beggar's Opera* in 1728 made theatrical history by running for 62 performances. By the mid-20th century, successful productions might run for five, six, and even seven years. One play, *The Mousetrap* by Agatha Christie, opened in 1952 and was still running in the early 1970s.

With the extended run there was little need to maintain a company of actors, even for a season. Instead, single-show contracts were negotiated. A manager or an actor would select a play that he thought might achieve an extended run, raise the necessary financial backing, hire actors, stage managers, scenic artists, a host of associates, and a theatre. Since a play was to be repeated indefinitely, it was feasible to invest a judicious amount of money in the accoutrements. Out of this system developed the need for someone who could coordinate the efforts of all the people involved and plan the final, overall effect. At first, the manager or actor-manager undertook this task. Later, individuals specializing in this work appeared.

With the stock company and especially with the single-show association grew the need for all the ancillary facilities of business and advertisement. Advertising, either by way of personal appearance, such as a parade through town before a performance, or by means of printed notices in newspapers and flyers, became extremely important in generating a sufficient audience for a show. Increasingly, in the late 19th and early 20th centuries, star actors became specially known for a single role or a small repertoire: Sarah Bernhardt for Marguérite Gautier in *Le Dame aux camélias*, Joseph Jefferson for Rip Van Winkle, Tommaso Salvini for Othello, James O'Neill (father of Eugene O'Neill) for the Count of Monte Cristo.

Modern repertory companies. During the rise of the stock company and single-show system, there continued to exist highly refined examples of the repertory ensemble. The Comédie Française, originally an amalgamation of two Parisian troupes, has endured from 1680 to the present. In opera the repertory system remains fundamentally unchanged. Toward the end of the 19th century, however, an idealization of the acting ensemble and the repertory system it supported became widespread throughout Europe. New theatres, devoted to naturalistic staging, were successfully established, and these, in time, became national theatres supported by the state. Most famous of these repertory theatres is the Moscow Art Theatre; others include the Abbey Theatre of Dublin, the Royal Shakespeare Company of Great Britain, and the Théâtre National Populaire of France. Meanwhile, traditional theatres such as the kabuki and Nō theatres of Japan have been declared national treasures. All of these theatres, because of government subsidy, maintain large staffs of actors, directors, designers, and other artists and craftsmen. Production is continuous. New plays or, more often, revivals of old plays enter the repertoire while former productions are dropped. The works of major national authors receive constant performance, thus establishing the main lines of tradition for the company. Often these repertory troupes conduct schools for training young people who might then enter the company. One of the chief aesthetic problems facing such companies is how to strike a balance between old and new. Theatre is, after all, a living art. By continuous repetition a production can atrophy. Yet it is the responsibility of these national theatres to offer their dramatic heritage to the people. Most theatres resolve this dilemma by bringing old productions up-to-date and by sponsoring studios and experimental activities where novel approaches may be tested. Where a dominant historical style has survived, as in the case of many Oriental dance and drama companies, maintenance of tradition rather than its adaptation to changing circumstances becomes the main objective.

Fringe productions. These regular, established modes of production are supplemented by a host of fringe productions. They are variously called experimental, underground, and off-Broadway plays. In general, they involve a mixture of professional, would-be professional, and amateur actors. Often their objectives are programmatic: they espouse a style, an author, a political viewpoint, or an aesthetic ideal. Depending on civic or labour regulations, they usually endeavour to assemble productions cheaply. Presentations are offered in lofts, chapels, and other kinds of makeshift spaces, as well as in small theatres. Their production mode can be either single show or repertory.

In addition, there is another kind of theatre that represents a distinct break with the past. Certain groups, such as the Living Theatre or the Polish Laboratory Theatre in Wrocław led by Jerzy Grotowski, adopt a communal way of life. They regard mere professional association as an inadequate basis either for personal existence or artistic creation. Instead, the actors live cooperatively, share a common point of view about life, and seek to reflect that view in their theatrical productions. This shared life is superficially reminiscent of the touring troupe, but the endeavour to achieve a company ethos is closer to the religious motive of an earlier day.

KINDS ACCORDING TO THE CONTROLLING ARTIST

The fourth kind of production can be distinguished according to the dominance of the constituent artist. As a collective art, theatre strives to achieve the ideal of a well-balanced presentation in which all the participating workers have their just place. In practice, however, one or another of the contributing artists or producers has dominated the production system.

Actor domination. Perhaps the supreme example of the actor-dominated production can be found in the commedia dell'arte tradition. Not only did the actor have financial and administrative control over production, but the very quality of performance was woven almost wholly out of the actor's art. At first, in the 16th century, the commedia troupe consisted of travelling actors; by the 17th century many of them had found permanent residence at the courts of Italy and elsewhere in Europe. Each actor had his special role (Arlecchino, Pantalone, Brighella, the *innamorato* or lover among others) with its attendant set speeches and traditional business. The young would learn the tradition appropriate to a role and, if talented, embroider upon that tradition. Thus prepared, the actors would improvise a presentation on the thread of a story selected by the troupe leader. Scenarios of commedia dell'arte plays did exist, but they were only pale shadows of the production itself, which only came to life in performance.

Other actor-dominated theatres include the Elizabethan theatre, Chinese opera, and kabuki. In these instances, however, the complete blending of administrative control and artistic pre-eminence characteristic of the commedia did not go so far. The Elizabethan professional company, for example, had a production system based upon actor control of the repertory, but the artistic character of the

Stock companies and single-show systems

Theatres with state subsidies

Experimental, underground, and off-Broadway productions

work was determined by the plays presented. However fine the actor's art, it was the dramatist's contribution that lent distinction to that theatre.

Dramatist and director domination. Rarely has the dramatist dominated a production system, unless, as occurred with Molière, he was also an actor. During certain periods the work of the dramatist, whatever his own responsibility, did determine the creative process in production. In ancient Greece the selection of a play was the first step in production. In the 19th and 20th centuries the acquisition of a script was also the preliminary step in establishing the single-show association. Only occasionally, as in the court theatre at Weimar, of which Johann Wolfgang von Goethe took charge during the late 18th century, did the dramatist as a dramatist take responsibility for establishing and conducting a theatrical enterprise.

In imperial Rome, the *dominus gregis* (manager of the festivals at which theatrical performances were given) controlled the lives and probably the art of the Roman comedians. During the 18th century the theatrical actor-manager came into prominence. But it was in the 19th century, with the rise of the stage director, that artistic, and in large measure, administrative control passed into the hands of a nonperformer. With the ideal of an artistically unified production there emerged one man to realize that unity—the director.

The stage director was responsible for modulating the acting, correlating the animate and inanimate aspects of production, and creating a single effect that inevitably became the expression of his own genius. At the turn of the 19th century, Edward Gordon Craig, illegitimate son of the British actress Ellen Terry, carried the ideal of unity even farther by recommending the merger of director and scenic designer and advocating the reduction of actors to automata completely responsive to the director-designer's vision. In this he was building upon the ideas of Adolphe Appia, a late-19th-century Swiss stage designer who saw in Richard Wagner's aspirations for music-drama the highest realization of the theatre's possibilities.

The designer's rise to special importance had begun during the Renaissance. In the first half of the 17th century, Inigo Jones was the driving force in creating the elaborate productions of the English court masque, while the machines of Nicola Sabbatini and the designs of Giacomo Torelli played significant roles in Italy and France.

The puppet show

A special form of theatrical technique, in which the manager, designer, and director are one, is the puppet show. The puppet is a general term that encompasses any inanimate figure manipulated by a human being. The figure may be a hand-operated puppet, either reduced or approaching life size, three-dimensional in form; a two-dimensional shadow puppet; or a string operated puppet called a marionette. They all share the common aesthetic whereby their movement in a highly restricted space creates the illusion of lifelikeness. In some cultures, such as the Javanese and the Turkish, the puppet show has been a major theatrical form. In Japan the *bunraku* doll theatre has competed successfully with the living actor of the kabuki theatre. In fact, many plays of the prominent writer Chikamatsu Monzaemon were originally for the puppet theatre (see PUPPETRY).

KINDS ACCORDING TO STYLE

A final method of categorizing production is according to style. This term is fraught with danger, for in theatre it has too often suggested actors' and directors' mannerisms rather than deeply ingrained characteristics of their work. Nevertheless, it is necessary to refer to style in order to distinguish the salient form of a particular theatre. Style, then, is the distinctive way in which the materials of a production (actor, script, space, time) are fused to project an impression upon the audience.

While the very word style suggests uniqueness, it is possible to speak about categories of style. For one thing a style of production may be composed of mixed modes of presentation or a single mode. Among styles of mixed modes are those that combine various media. Opera com-

bines drama and music; the court masque combines drama, music, dance, and changing scenery. Greek tragedy combines spoken words, choral chant, and dance. Other types of presentation mix tonalities (comedy and tragedy), agents (living stagehands and performing dolls in *bunraku*), or masked and unmasked performers (commedia dell'arte). All of these mixed modes contribute to a distinctive style of performance, just as the single modes of Neoclassical tragedy, 19th-century Realism, and the dancers of Bali in Indonesia achieve their recognizable styles.

At one time it was customary to describe historical productions in terms of a supposed mode of performing behaviour. Thus, ancient Greek tragedy was considered austere, English Restoration performance mannered, Romantic acting bombastic. More thorough study of the various periods, however, has rendered such easy generalizations suspect. Scholars now realize that all productions share certain common objectives. They all convey in some measure a sense of reality for the particular audience addressed, although the sense of reality for one age may not be the same for another. They all combine elements of that reality (the familiar) with elements of the wondrous (the *mirabilia*). They all arouse interest in some features of the presentation as presentation (the sensuousness of the poetry, the cleverness of the business, the pleasure of the song), and—at the same time—in the revelation of the representation, that is, the fictional life that is being enacted on the stage. Style is thus determined not by the presence of one or another of these features but by the way the acting and script create a unique configuration out of these elements. Greek tragic style, for instance, is a result of the alternation of song and scene within an amphitheatre that has the effect of both distancing and yet involving the spectator. It is further delimited by the peculiar feature of the scenes in which highly impassioned moments of suffering, argumentation, and challenge are contained within an extremely strict rhetorical form, thereby producing the impact of an explosion. This dialectic of strict form and fierce passion is further heightened by the stately appearance of the masked actor, as well as by the alternation of "cool" ode and "hot" episode. But these elements are only the preconditions for Greek tragic style; the style itself can only be experienced in the theatre as a series of striking contrasts. The same holds true for all other theatrical styles.

Greek tragic style

IV. Theatrical production as a coherent art

Theatrical production can now be seen not as an amalgam of separate arts but as a coherent art manifesting itself in divergent ways. Central to all production is the performer–audience relationship, cemented together by the activity the player projects and to which the spectator adjusts. Out of a distinctive treatment of that activity and the social context in which it is presented comes each of the expressions of the theatre: drama, opera, acrobatics, and so on. Drama thus is not the sum of acting plus script plus scenery but the exploitation of one aspect of performing—the mimetic, or representational—in terms of performing space and time. But, since the other aspects of performance, such as dexterity, daring, and illusion, are all inherent in the performing act and coexist with each other and with the mimetic, they are also part of drama. Hence, any single aesthetic form, such as drama or opera, that may appear to be an autonomous art is but the cultivation of one facet of a multifaceted art. That is why one form may grow out of another, as opera did out of drama, or may crystallize in one manner for a time, only to disintegrate and reunite with other expressions of theatre, as drama seems to be doing with acrobatics and music in the 20th century. Seen in this context, theatrical production is pre-eminently the art in which human beings test their imaginative and physical capabilities by presenting themselves to each other in dazzling, yet recognizable, shapes.

BIBLIOGRAPHY. DAVID CHESHIRE, *Theatre: History, Criticism, and Reference* (1967), an introductory reader's guide to theatre books in English with some emphasis on the British stage; OSCAR G. BROCKETT, *History of the Theatre* (1968), a reliable, modern general history; TOBY COLE and HELEN CHINOY (eds.), *Actors on Acting*, rev. ed. (1970), and *Directors on Directing* (1963), two collections of essays by actors and directors respectively—the latter has a good introductory essay on the emergence of the director; BARRETT H. CLARK (ed.), *European Theories of the Drama*, rev. ed. (1965), the standard compilation of extracts on dramatic theory from Aristotle to the present; ALLARDYCE NICOLL, *The Development of the Theatre*, 5th rev. ed. (1966), the standard history of theatre architecture and design; JOHN GASSNER, *Producing the Play* (1941), essays on major aspects of theatrical production by various specialists—reliable for a description of standard practice until the middle of the 20th century.

(B.Be.)

Thebes (Egypt)

Thebes, one of the famed cities of antiquity, the capital of the ancient Egyptian empire at its heyday, lay on either side of the Nile at approximately latitude 26° N; the modern town of Luxor, which occupies part of the site, is 419 miles south of Cairo. Ancient Thebes was about six miles square; the main part of the city was on the east bank; on the west bank was "the city of the dead"—the kings' mortuary temples, and the houses of those priests, soldiers, craftsmen, and labourers who were devoted to their service.

HISTORY

The ancient name of Thebes, Wase or Wo'se, was derived from the sacred *was* sceptre. The nome or province of Wase, the fourth of Upper Egypt, is known to have existed from the 4th dynasty onward. The earliest monuments that have survived at Thebes itself date from the 11th dynasty (2133–1991 BC), when the local nomarchs (governors) united Egypt under their rule. From this time Thebes became the royal capital and was called Nowe or Nuwe, "the city [of Amon]," after its chief god. The Greek name Thebes (Thebai) was derived from Ta-ope, the ancient Egyptian name for Luxor.

Age of prosperity

During the 12th dynasty (1991–1786 BC), the royal residence was moved to al-Fayyūm, but the kings of Egypt honoured Amon, their family god, and built temples at Thebes. The Hyksos invaders had little or no control over the area, and it was the kings of Thebes who finally drove them out of Egypt (*c.* 1560). Then began the era of greatest prosperity for Thebes. The 18th-dynasty pharaohs rebuilt it and made it their capital, embellishing its temples with the spoils of Asia and the tribute of Nubia. During the 15th century BC great palaces rose on either bank of the river, brightly painted and surrounded with gardens: noblemen had their estates round about, and in the crowded streets foreign traders and mercenaries mingled with the citizens. The pharaohs of the New Kingdom vied with each other in building great temples on the east bank and even larger mortuary temples on the west. The height of Theban prosperity was reached about 1400 BC in the reign of Amenhotep III, much of whose vast wealth from foreign tribute was poured into the temples of Amon. For a brief period in the reign of his son Akhenaton, Thebes fell on evil times; the city was abandoned by the court and the worship of Amon proscribed. With its restoration by Tutankhamen, however, Thebes soon regained its revenues and prestige and retained both through the reigns of Seti I and Ramses II, who still resided for part of every year in Thebes. The city continued to be richly endowed; according to ancient sources, Ramses III donated 86,486 slaves and vast estates to Amon's temples.

Decline

Under the later Ramessids Thebes began to decline; the government fell, it seems, into grave economic difficulties. In the reign of Ramses IX, about 1121 BC, a series of investigations into the plundering of royal tombs in the necropolis of western Thebes uncovered proof of corruption in high places, following an accusation made by the mayor of the east bank against his colleague on the west. The plundered royal mummies were moved from place to place and at last deposited by the priests of Amon in the tomb of Amenhotep II and in a tomb-shaft in Dayr al-Baḥrī. (The finding of these two hiding places was one of the great events of modern archaeological dis-

covery.) Such maladministration in Thebes led to unrest and there were strikes among the necropolis workers. Control of local affairs tended to come more and more into the hands of the high priests of Amon, leading to a situation in which, after the death of the last Ramses, the government of Egypt was shared between the pharaoh in Tanis and the high pontiff at Thebes. Intermarriage and adoption strengthened the ties between them, daughters of the Tanite kings being installed as "God's Wife of Amon" at Thebes, where they wielded greater power.

The Napatan (Nubian) pharaohs made Thebes their capital. Its fame among the early Greeks was such that Homer speaks of the wealth of "hundred-gated Thebes." In 661 BC, however, it was sacked by Ashurbanipal's Assyrians, and although rebuilt by the Saites it never fully recovered. In Strabo's time (*c.* 63 BC–*c.* AD 21) the city had dwindled to a mere village visited by tourists who came to see the ancient temples.

Adapted from *Westermann Grosser Atlas zur Weltgeschichte*; Georg Westermann Verlag, Braunschweig

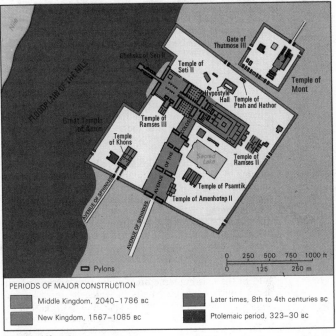

PERIODS OF MAJOR CONSTRUCTION

Middle Kingdom, 2040–1786 BC

New Kingdom, 1567–1085 BC

Later times, 8th to 4th centuries BC

Ptolemaic period, 323–30 BC

Temple of Karnak.

ARCHAEOLOGY

Luxor and Karnak. *The temples of Karnak.* Karnak, on the east bank of the Nile, is a village that has given its name to the most northerly part of Thebes, the quarter in which the great temples of Amon, Mut, and Khons were situated. Its ancient name was Ipet-isut, or Eptesowe, "Chosen of Places." The ruins of Karnak cover a considerable area and are still impressive, though nothing remains of the houses, palaces, and gardens that must have surrounded the temple precinct in ancient times. The temples are enclosed within three walls. The most northerly is that of the temple of Mont, the war god, of which little now remains but the foundations. The southern temple, which has a horseshoe-shaped sacred lake, was devoted to the goddess Mut, wife of Amon; this also is much ruined. It was built largely by Amenhotep III, whose architect was commemorated by statues in the temple.

Between these two precincts lay the largest of all Egyptian temples, and one of the largest in the world, the great metropolitan temple of the state god, Amon-Re. It is in fact not one temple but a complex of temples, added to and altered at many periods, and lacking, in consequence, a coherent plan. It has been called a great historical document in stone. In it are reflected the fluctuating fortunes of the Egyptian Empire. There are no fewer than ten pylons, separated by courts and halls, and nowadays numbered for convenience from west to east, Number 1 being the latest. The seventh and eighth pylons were erected by Thutmose III and Queen Hatshepsut; the ninth and tenth,

Temple of Amon-Re

(Left) The Colossi of Memnon, now about 65 ft high, are virtually the only remains of Amenhotep III's great mortuary temple in western Thebes. (Centre) Capitals and lintels of the massive hypostyle hall, temple of Amon-Re, Karnak. (Right) The mortuary temple of Queen Hatshepsut at Dayr al-Baḥri, western Thebes.

(Left) J. Allan Cash, (centre) EB Inc., (right) A.F. Kersting

of Horemheb's reign, formed a series of processional gateways at right angles to the main axis, linking the temple with that of Mut to the south, and further, by way of the avenue of sphinxes, with the temple of Luxor two miles away.

The history of the temple must be briefly sketched. The original Middle Kingdom temple has left no trace save a small jubilee shrine of Sesostris (Senusret) I, now reconstructed from fragments found inside the third pylon. At the beginning of the 18th dynasty, Thutmose I enclosed the 12th-dynasty temple and fronted it with two pylons, the fifth and fourth, with a pillared hall of gilded cedarwood between. Hatshepsut pierced the roof with two tall obelisks, one of which still stands. In the reign of Thutmose III the temple was greatly enlarged; not only did he add to the existing structures, and add a pylon and pillared courts containing halls in which he inscribed the annals of his campaigns, but he also built to the east of the Middle Kingdom area a transverse temple in the form of a jubilee pavilion. On the walls of one of the rear rooms of this temple is carved a kind of pictorial catalogue of the strange animals and plants he had brought home from Asia in the 25th year of his reign. He was probably also the builder of the wall that runs round the temple from the fourth pylon eastward, and of the sacred lake to the south of it, on which the bark of Amon floated. Small additions were made by his successors, and Amenhotep III added a pylon (Number 3) to the west and greatly embellished the temple.

Hypostyle hall

The most striking feature of the temple of Karnak is the hypostyle (pillared) hall that occupies the space between the third pylon and the second, built by Ramses I. The area of this vast hall, one of the wonders of antiquity, is 5,800 square yards. It was decorated by Seti I and Ramses II, to whom much of the construction must be due, though it may have been planned and begun earlier. Fourteen enormous columns, 78 feet high, raised the roofing slabs of the central nave above the level of the rest so that light and air could enter through a clerestory. Seven lateral aisles on either side brought the number of pillars to 140. Historical reliefs on the outer walls show the victories of Seti in Palestine and Ramses II defeating the Hittites at the Battle of Kadesh.

Ramses III built a small temple to Amon outside the Ramesside pylon and at right angles to it, confronting a triple shrine erected by Seti II. The Bubastite kings of the 22nd dynasty, in adding a vast court to the front of the temple, incorporated both these small temples. The Bubastite Gate at the southeast corner of this court commemorates the victories won by Sheshonk I, the biblical Shishak, in Palestine in the reign of Rehoboam. The Na-

patan pharaoh Taharqa planned a tall colonnade, of which one pillar still stands, and perhaps began the giant first pylon, 370 feet wide and 143 feet high, which was continued by King Nectanebos (Nekhtnebef) in the 4th century BC but never completed. Beyond it, an avenue of sphinxes dating from Ramses II's reign leads to the quayside.

Within the enclosure of the great temple of Amon-Re are included a number of other small shrines and temples. A temple to Ptah and Hathor, in the north side of the enclosure, was built by Hatshepsut and Thutmose III and added to by the Ptolemies, who also embellished the great temple by the addition of granite shrines and gateways. To the south, Ramses III dedicated a temple to Khons, the moon god, which merits attention. A small late temple to Opet, the hippopotamus goddess, adjoins it.

Karnak presents a continual problem to the architects who seek to preserve it, for the foundations are inadequate and moisture from the Nile's annual flood has disintegrated the sandstone at the base of walls and columns. The work of repairing and strengthening goes on continuously, and in carrying out this work new discoveries are constantly being made. In one of the pylons, thousands of fragments were found from a temple built at Thebes by Akhenaton to his god Aton; this temple was destroyed when the cult of Amon was restored.

The temple of Luxor. The southern part of Thebes grew up around the other great temple of Amon, Ope or Ipet, "the Harim [of Amon]." The modern name, in Arabic al-Uqṣur, means "the palaces" or perhaps, after the Roman *castra* (remains of which have been found in the neighbourhood), "the forts." Here, close to the Nile and parallel with the bank of the river, King Amenhotep III built his beautiful temple dedicated to Amon-Re, king of the gods, his consort Mut, and their son Khons.

A small pavilion is all that is left of earlier work, though there was probably a temple here earlier in the 18th dynasty if not before. It was completed by Tutankhamen and Horemheb and added to by Ramses II; smaller additions were made in Ptolemaic times. The hypostyle hall was at one time converted into a Christian church, and the remains of another Coptic church can be seen to the west of it.

The original part of the temple consisted of a large peristyle court and a complex of halls and chambers beyond; on the east side of the central hall was the birth room, a chapel whose walls were decorated with scenes of the mystical marriage of Queen Mutemuia, Amenhotep's mother, with the god of Amon and of the birth of the royal child with the assistance of goddesses. One of the halls contains a granite shrine of Alexander the Great.

The great court is surrounded on three sides by a double row of graceful papyrus-cluster columns, their capitals imitating the umbels of the papyrus plant in bud. An entrance flanked by the towers of a pylon was planned for the north end, but this design was altered, and, instead, the most striking feature of the temple, a majestic colonnade of 14 pillars, 52 feet high, was added. This colonnade, which also has papyrus-umbel capitals, may have been intended for the central nave of a hypostyle hall similar to that at Karnak, but the side aisles were not built; instead, enclosing walls were built down either side. Ramses II added an outer court, decorated with colossal statues of himself between the pillars of a double colonnade, and a lofty pylon on which he depicted festival scenes and episodes from his wars in Syria. In front of the pylon were colossal images of the pharaoh and a pair of obelisks, one of which still stands; the other was removed in 1831 and re-erected in the Place de la Concorde in Paris.

In the forecourt of the temple is the mosque of Shaykh Yūsuf al-Ḥaggāg, the local Muslim saint. His feast is celebrated with a boat procession resembling an ancient rite, the "Beautiful Festival of Ope," during which, on the 19th day of the second month, Amon was said to come from Karnak on his state barge to visit his other temple at Luxor, escorted by the people of Thebes in holiday attire. Reliefs on the walls of the great colonnade depict preparations for the procession of sacred barks during the festival.

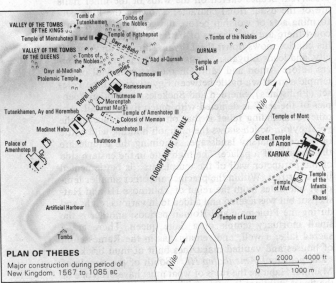

PLAN OF THEBES
Major construction during period of New Kingdom, 1567 to 1085 BC

Ancient Thebes, east and west banks.

Western Thebes. Across the Nile from Luxor and Karnak, on the western bank, was another Thebes, the abode of the dead. The Egyptians called the whole region the Western City, or Kheftet-her-nebes, "She who is opposite to her lord." In Greco-Roman and Coptic times it was called Djeme. The presiding deity was a goddess, Mert-Seger, "the Lover of Silence," who was thought to live on the peak that dominates the range of cliffs in which the tombs are hollowed. After death, both pharaohs and commoners were ferried across the river to be buried in the necropolis of the west. The earliest cemeteries are in the most northerly part of the area; nomarchs of the early 11th-dynasty built pyramid-tombs on the desert edge north of the present village of Qurnah, where the cliffs approach most nearly to the river. Their successors, the Mentuhoteps who ruled the whole country, had larger tombs farther to the south. The largest, that of Mentuhotep II, was built at the head of the Valley of Asasif, at a spot known as Dayr al-Baḥrī, "the northern monastery." Here, dwarfed by a semicircle of towering cliffs, a combined pyramid tomb and funerary temple were erected on three ascending terraces.

The kings of the New Kingdom, fearing for the safety of their rich burials, adopted a new plan, that of building only their mortuary temples in the low desert within view of the valley, and concealing their tombs in a lonely valley (Bībān al-Mulūk, "the Valley of the Tombs of the Kings") in the western hills behind Dayr al-Baḥrī. Here, in tombs sunk deep into the heart of the mountain, the pharaohs of the 18th, 19th, and 20th dynasties from Thutmose I onward were interred, and also one or two queens and officials of high rank. The plan of the tombs varies considerably but consists essentially of a series of descending corridors interrupted by deep shafts to baffle robbers and by pillared chambers or vestibules; at the farther end is the burial chamber with a stone sarcophagus in which the royal mummy was laid, and store chambers around which furniture and equipment were stacked for the king's use in the next world. The walls were in many cases covered with sculptured and painted scenes depicting the dead king in the presence of deities, especially the gods of the underworld, and with illustrated magical texts similar to those found in funerary papyri, designed to help him on his journey through the nether regions. There were a number of these texts; they represent differing but not necessarily conflicting views of the afterlife in which the king had to undergo trials and surmount perils. In the *Book of That Which Is in the Underworld*, for instance, he travels in the boat of the sun god through 12 caverns that represent the 12 hours of the night. In the *Book of Gates* giant serpents guard the portals through which the sun has to pass, and strange jinns and demons help or hinder the boat on its way. Astronomical figures often decorated the ceilings of the burial chambers, and the sky-goddess Nut herself is sometimes painted across the firmament of stars.

There are some 60 tombs in the valley, almost all of which were robbed in antiquity, many of them during the lifetime of the successors or of near descendants of the owners. In the time of Strabo, Greek travellers were able to visit 40. Only the little tomb of Tutankhamen on the floor of the valley, protected by a pile of rock chippings thrown down from a later Ramesside tomb, escaped pillage. The wonderful treasures exhumed from Tutankhamen's tomb, now in the Tutankhamen galleries of the Cairo museum, vividly indicate how rich the burial of a great pharaoh of the empire's heyday must have been. The longest tomb is Number 20, that of Queen Hatshepsut, whose burial chamber is nearly 700 feet from the entrance and descends 320 feet into the rock.

In the 19th and 20th dynasties, queens and a few favoured royal princes were buried in another valley today known as Bībān al-Ḥarīm, "the Valley of the Tombs of the Queens." It is situated at the southern end of the Theban necropolis, about 1½ miles west of the temple of Madīnat Habu. Here over 70 tombs have been found, very few of them inscribed and decorated. The earliest may be that of Sitre, wife of Ramses I. The most notable are those of Nefertari (Number 66), the favourite queen of Ramses II; of Prince Khaemwese (Number 44) and Prince Amonhirkhopshef (Number 55); and of a Ramesside queen called Titi (Number 52).

The limestone foothills that lie parallel to the river and about three miles away from it are honeycombed for a distance of over two miles with the tombs and tomb-chapels of high officials, mainly of the 18th, 19th, and 20th dynasties. The usual plan of these tombs included a forecourt, a transverse chamber, a long, corridor-like room, and, at the end, a chapel containing statues of the deceased and his family, in the floor of which a shaft or passage ran down to the burial chamber. After the funeral the shaft was filled in but the chapel and anterooms were kept open and visited by the family of the tomb owner. Near the villages of Dira 'Abū al-Nega' al-Asasif, al-Khūkhah Shaykh 'Abd al-Qurnah, Dayr al-Madīnah, and Qurnat Mura'i, several hundred tomb-chapels are still open to view. The walls are decorated with mural paintings, many of them wonderfully fresh and full of vivid interest, depicting the daily occupations of the ancient Egyptians. The dead are shown, in the outer rooms of these tombs, inspecting the workmen on their estates or in their hours of leisure hunting birds in the marshes or game in the desert, listening to music, or playing checkers

Valley of the tombs of kings

Tombs of officials

with their wives. In the infinite variety of these homely scenes, the whole cycle of the farmer's year, from plowing to harvest, is depicted—sculptors, metalworkers, weavers, and brickmakers ply their trades; and butchers, brewers, and cooks prepare food for the dead man's table. The treasurer goes on his rounds of inspection and the vizier receives foreign envoys to pharaoh's court. The gay patterns on the roofs derive from those in houses of the period. In the inner chapels fewer secular scenes are found. The funeral ritual is usually depicted: the cortège crossing the Nile, the ceremony of "Opening the Mouth" by the tomb door, the funerary feast; while in the innermost chamber there are representations of the deceased man and his wife in the company of Osiris and other gods undergoing the ordeal of judgment known as the "weighing of the heart" or being given nourishment by the goddess in the sacred sycamore. In the tombs of the late New Kingdom, purely religious scenes predominate.

The royal mortuary temples. In the New Kingdom, when the pharaohs hid their tombs in the secret valley, ostentation had to be concentrated in their mortuary temples, which rivalled each other in size and magnificence. Although they were designed for the performance of rites connected with the mortuary cult of the builder, they were all dedicated to Amon, the supreme god of Thebes, and had the character and essential form of a New Kingdom temple. They were built in western Thebes on the edge of the valley, in a sequence generally corresponding to a topographical arrangment from north to south. Only traces of most of the earlier ones remain. The most important will be mentioned here.

Temple of Hatshepsut 1. The temple of Hatshepsut at Dayr al-Baḥrī, which is the earliest large 18th-dynasty structure to survive and one of the most impressive. Here in the bay of cliffs, next to the pyramid-temple of Mentuhotep II mentioned above, the queen's architect Senenmut in about 1490 BC designed a series of colonnades and courts on three levels. The approach from the valley led through an avenue of sphinxes, and in the forecourt was a garden planted with trees and vines. On either side of the sloping ramp leading to the next level, against the terrace face, was a gallery whose roof was supported on a double row of columns; a similar gallery ran along the westward side of the court on the next level, with side chapels dedicated to Anubis and Hathor. The top terrace contained what may have been a hall of columns, with further chapels on either side and a sanctuary dug into the cliff behind. Many of the reliefs in the colonnades and chapels are of great beauty and considerable interest: one depicts the transport of two obelisks by barge from Aswān to Karnak, another the divine marriage of Queen Ahmes with the god Amon and the resultant miraculous birth of Hatshepsut herself, and a third the maritime trading expedition sent by the queen to Punt, the land of incense beyond the Red Sea.

Temple of Amenhotep III 2. The mortuary temple of Amenhotep III, which must have been the largest and most splendid of all the Theban temples. It was, however, almost completely demolished by later pharaohs and all that is left today are a few foundations, a huge *stela* 30 feet high, and the two great statues known as the Colossi of Memnon, which once flanked the gateway in front of the temple pylon but now sit like lonely sentinels in the middle of cultivated fields. The statues represent Amenhotep III; with their crowns they were nearly 70 feet high and each was hewn from a single block of stone. The northern one was the "singing Memnon" celebrated in classical times because on certain days, shortly after sunrise, it emitted a curious high note; numerous Roman tourists including the emperor Hadrian and his wife Sabina came to Thebes in order to hear this marvel, but in the reign of Septimius Severus the statue was patched with masonry and never "sang" again.

Temple of Seti I 3. The temple of Seti I at Qurnah, which survives only in part, the forecourt and pylon having disappeared. It was dedicated in part to the funerary cult of Ramses I, the father of Seti, and was completed by Seti's son, Ramses the Great, who figures largely in the reliefs. The walls are decorated with scenes of purely religious content in which the pharaohs make offerings to various gods or are favoured by them.

Temple of Ramses II 4. The Ramesseum, or mortuary temple of Ramses II (Ramses the Great), which, though much ruined, retains some of its ancient grandeur. The wide outer pylon is decorated with vigorous scenes of the king's wars against the Hittites in Syria, and the inner pylon with episodes from the Battle of Kadesh and scenes from the festival of the harvest god, Min. Tall figures of the king in the guise of Osiris decorate the pillars of the inner court. In the first court stood a seated colossus of Ramses II; only fragments of it are left, but enough to show that it was of enormous size. It must have been over 60 feet high and weighed about 1,000 tons. The hypostyle hall beyond the second court resembles that of the temple of Karnak; beyond were further pillared halls and a sanctuary that has now disappeared. Around the temple, within the high brick enclosure wall, are very extensive remains of vaulted buildings that must have been magazines, stables, workshops, and houses belonging to the temple staff. Diodorus Siculus describes the Ramesseum under the name of "the Tomb of Ozymandias" (i, 47–49).

Temple of Ramses III 5. The temple of Ramses III at Madīnat Habu. This is the latest and most southerly of the great New Kingdom mortuary temples. The general plan was modelled on that of the Ramesseum: a wide front pylon, an outer and an inner peristyle court separated by a second pylon, a large pillared hall and two smaller vestibules, and the sanctuary surrounded by smaller rooms. The hypostyle hall is partly ruined, the pillars having been dismantled to the level of the first or second drums, but the temple is otherwise well preserved. Scenes carved on the walls of the inner halls are of the usual ritual character, showing the king performing acts of worship before the gods, but in the first court there are also scenes of battle in which the king in his chariot mows down the Libyans, attacks an Amorite city, and leads Libyans, Asians, and sea raiders as prisoners before Amon and Mut. On the external wall of the temple a great sea battle between Egyptians and the Peleset (Philistines), Sherden and Shekelesh and other "peoples of the sea," is depicted with much lively detail. Another outstanding relief is that on the outer face of the great pylon, which shows the pharaoh hunting wild cattle in a reedy, marshy landscape. Adjoining the temple are the remains of a palace. The high gate in the eastern side of the perimeter wall of the temple area is battlemented like a fortress. Within the precinct are other smaller temples: one dates from the reign of Thutmose III and Hatshepsut but was altered and added to in various reigns and during the Ptolemaic and Roman periods; another is the small mortuary temple of a Saite queen. There are a sacred lake, a well, and remains, as in the Ramesseum, of houses and vaulted magazines built of mud brick.

The palace of Amenhotep III. South of the temple of Madīnat Habu lie the ruins of what must have been one of the finest buildings in western Thebes: the palace of King Amenhotep III and Queen Tiy at Malkata. It is in fact four palaces, one of which was occupied by the "great royal wife," for whom her husband constructed a huge lake on which she could sail in her barge. This lake has been identified with a great excavated basin, still traceable by a line of mounds to the southeast of Malkata; recent evidence, however, has thrown doubt on this: it may rather have been a harbour for shipping connected with the Nile.

In ancient Egypt there were other great cities, but none which has left so great a legacy to posterity. The great temples of Thebes with their historical scenes and inscriptions, the tombs with their wealth of illustration of daily life and religious belief, and the countless antiquities which now fill the museums and private collections of the world, are all aspects of that legacy. Few other sites have contributed more to our knowledge of early man than that of ancient Thebes.

BIBLIOGRAPHY. There are many good general descriptions of the antiquities of Thebes, among them G. LEGRAIN, *Les Temples de Karnak* (1929); and J. CAPART, *Thèbes, la gloire d'un grand passé* (1925; Eng. trans., *Thebes: The Glory of a Great Past*, 1926); the most recent, embodying research carried out since World War II, is C.F. NIMS' lavishly illustrated *Thebes of the Pharaohs* (1965). K. BAEDEKER,

Ägypten (1902; Eng. trans., *Egypt,* 8th ed., 1929), gives convenient plans and description of the monuments. Among the many archaeological publications special mention should be made of W.M.F. PETRIE, *Six Temples at Thebes* (1897); H.E. WINLOCK, *Excavations at Deir el Bahri, 1911–1931* (1942); E.H. NAVILLE, *The Temple of Deir el Bahari,* 7 vol. (1894–1908) and *The XIth Dynasty Temple at Deir el-Bahari,* 3 vol. (1907–13); and H.H. NELSON et al., *Medinet Habu,* 12 vol. (1930-57). Extensive references may be found in the detailed and invaluable volumes of B. PORTER and R.B.L. MOSS, *A Topographical Bibliography of Ancient Egyptian Hieroglyphic Texts, Reliefs, and Paintings,* vol. 1, pt. 1, *Private Tombs,* rev. ed. (1960); pt. 2, *Royal Tombs and Smaller Cemeteries,* rev. ed. (1964); vol. 2, *Theban Temples* (1929). For the cult of Amun at Thebes, G. LEFEBVRE, *Histoire des grands prêtres d'Amon de Karnak jusqu'à la XXIᵉ dynastie* (1929); and the more recent work of E. OTTO, *Egyptian Art and the Cults of Osiris and Amon* (1968), should be consulted (further bibliography in the latter work). For the history of Thebes, see the revised first volumes of the *Cambridge Ancient History,* 3rd ed. (1970–71), esp. the chapters by WILLIAM C. HAYES (vol. 1, ch. 20, and vol. 2, ch. 9).

(M.S.D.)

Theism

Theism is the view that all limited or finite things are dependent in some way on one supreme or ultimate reality of which one may also speak in personal terms.

Theism's view of God can be clarified by contrasting it with that of deism, of pantheism, and of mysticism. Deism closely resembles theism; but for the deist, God is not involved in the world in the same personal way. He has made it, so to speak, or set the laws of it—and to that extent he sustains it in being. But subject to this final and somewhat remote control, God, as the deist sees him, allows the world to continue in its own way. This view simplifies some problems, especially those that arise from the scientific account of the world: one does not have to allow for any factor that cannot be handled and understood in the ordinary way. God is in the shadows or beyond; and, though men may still in some way centre their lives upon him, this calls for no radical adjustment at the human or finite level. The deist proceeds, for most purposes at least, as if there were no God—or only an absent one; and this approach is especially true of man's understanding of the world. This is why deism appealed so much to thinkers in the time of the first triumphs of modern science. They could indeed allow for God, but they had "no need of that hypothesis" in science or in their normal account of things. Religion, being wholly superadded, was significant only in a manner that involved little else in the world or in the way man lives. The theist, on the other hand, questions this view and seeks in various ways (as noted below) to bring man's relation to God into closer involvement with the way he understands himself and the world around him.

Theism, pantheism, and mysticism

Theism also sharply contrasts with pantheism, which identifies God with all that there is; and with various forms of monism, which regards all finite things as parts, modes, limitations, or appearances of some one ultimate Being, which is all that there is. Some types of absolute Idealism, a philosophy of all-pervading Mind, while regarding every finite thing as comprising some limitation of the one whole of Being, seek also to retain the theistic element in their view of the world; and they do this normally—as in the works of A.E. Taylor, Andrew Pringle-Pattison, or G.F. Stout—by stressing the role of unifying finite centres, such as self-conscious human beings, in the way the universe as a whole functions. But there is no recognition here of the finality of what is technically known as "the distinctness of persons." The theist, by contrast, considers the world to be quite distinct from its Author or Creator, human life being thus in no sense strictly the life of God, while also making room for a peculiarly intimate involvement of God in the world and in human life.

Mysticism in practice comes close to theism; but mystical thought, and much of its practice, has often involved a repudiation of the proper reality of finite things and sometimes (as in a recent work by W.T. Stace, *Mysticism and Philosophy*) tends to dismiss all of the finite manifold or multiplicity of things as some wholly unreal phantasm that has no place in the one undiversified Being, which alone is real. Theism is very far removed from ideas of this kind.

THEISM IN WESTERN THOUGHT

God encountered as person. The idea that the world, as man understands it in a finite way, is dependent on some reality altogether beyond his comprehension, perfect and self-sustained but also peculiarly involved in the world and its events, is presented with exceptional sharpness and discernment in the Old Testament, whence it became a formative influence in Hebrew history and subsequently in Christianity and Islām. Behind the creation stories; behind the patriarchal narratives, like that of Jacob at Bethel (Gen. 28) or wrestling with his strange visitor at Penuel (Gen. 32); and behind the high moments of prophecy, like Isaiah's famous vision in the Temple (Isa. 6), and of moving religious experience in the Psalms, in the Book of Job, and (with remarkable explicitness) in some well-known passages, like the story of Moses at the burning bush (Ex. 3)—behind all of these there lies a sense of some mysterious, all-encompassing reality by which man is also in some way addressed and which he may also venture to address in turn. Moses wished to see God, to have some explicit sign that could convince the people and establish his own authority; but he was shown, instead, that this is just what he could not have: all that he could be assured of was that God is real and is bound to be—"I am who I am," he was told. On the other hand, in the throes of this humbling and staggering experience, Moses began to learn also what was expected of him and how his people should live and be led. The God who was so strange and elusive was somehow found to be a God who "talked" to him and with whom people could "walk." The same seemingly bewildering claim of remoteness, almost to the point of unreality, linked with a compelling explicitness and closeness, is also found in other cultures, as illustrated below. This claim presents the reflective thinker with the twofold problem of theism, viz., how, in the first place, a reality as remote and mysterious as the God of theism—the "wholly other," in the famous words of the German theologian Rudolf Otto—can be known at all; and, second, how, if it can be known, it can be spoken of in precise and intimate ways and encountered as a person.

Old Testament theophanies

The existence of God. There have been many attempts to establish the existence of one supreme and ultimate Being—whom in religion one speaks of as God—and some of these have been given very precise forms in the course of time.

The influence of Plato and Aristotle. The pattern for many of these was laid down in ancient Greece by Plato. He taught about God mostly in mythical terms, stressing the goodness of God (as in *The Republic* and *Timaeus*) and his care for man (as in the *Phaedo*); but in the *Phaedrus,* and much more explicitly in the *Laws,* he presented a more rigorous argument, based on the fact that things change and are in motion. Not all change comes from outside; some of it is spontaneous and must be due to "soul" and ultimately to a supreme or perfect soul. Whether God so conceived quite gives the traditional theist all that he wants, however, is not certain. For God, in Plato, fashions the world on the pattern of immutable Forms and, above all, on "the Good," which is "beyond being and knowledge"; *i.e.,* it is transcendent and beyond the grasp of thought. But Plato's combination of the notion of the transcendent, which is also supremely good, and the argument from change provided the model for much of the course that subsequent philosophical arguments were to take. Aristotle made the argument from motion more precise, but he coupled it with a doubtful astronomical view and a less theistic notion of God, who, as the unmoved mover, is the ultimate source of all other movement, not by expressly communicating it but by being a supreme object of aspiration, all appetite and activity being in fact directed to some good. Aristotle thus set the pattern for the more deistic view of God, whereas the theist, taken in the strict sense, turns more for his start and inspiration to Plato.

The causal argument. The argument for the existence of God inferred from motion was given a more familiar form in the first of the five ways of St. Thomas Aquinas, five major proofs of God that also owed much to the emphasis on the complete transcendence of God in the teaching of Plotinus, the leading Neoplatonist of the 3rd century AD, and his followers. (The word that Plotinus used for the ultimate but mysterious dependence of all things on God is emanation; but this characterization was not understood by him, as it has been by some later thinkers, as questioning the genuine independent existence of finite things.) In the first way, Aquinas put forward the view that all movement implies, in the last analysis, an unmoved mover; and though this argument, as he understood it, presupposes certain views about movement and physical change that may not be accepted today, it does make the main point that finite processes call for some ground or condition other than themselves.

This becomes more explicit in the second way, which proceeds from the principle that everything must have an "efficient cause"—*i.e.*, a cause that actively produces and accounts for it—to the notion of a first cause required to avoid an infinite regress, or tracing of causes endlessly backward. As normally found, the idea of efficient causality, in respect to change and process, has many difficulties; and some would prefer to speak instead of regular or necessary sequence. But a more serious objection stresses the apparent inconsistency of thinkers who invoke a general principle of causality and then exempt the alleged first cause. As the child is apt to put it, "Who then made God?" To this a defender of St. Thomas, or at least of the present approach to the idea of God, would reply that the first cause is not supposed to be itself a member of any ordinary causal sequence but altogether beyond it, an infinite reality not itself a part of the natural or temporal order at all. This point, in fact, is what the third way, starting from the contingency of the world, brings out more explicitly. Nothing explains itself, and all other explanations fall short of showing in any exhaustive way why anything is as it is, or why there is anything at all. But it is also hard to suppose that things just happen to be. Nothing could come out of just nothing, and so the course of events as men find and explain them points to some reality that is not itself to be understood or explained in the normal way at all: it is Explanation with a capital *E*, as it were, that is seen to be necessitated by all that there is—of whose nature, however, nothing may be directly discerned beyond the inevitability of its being as the ultimate or unconditioned ground of all else and in this way transcendent or utterly mysterious in itself.

This way of thinking of the being and necessity of God has been impressively presented in the mid-20th century by notable thinkers like Austin Farrer, E.L. Mascall, and H.P. Owen and also by the present writer (see below *Bibliography*). Generally known as the cosmological approach to the idea of God, it has much in common with the insistence on the transcendence of God in recent theology.

The ontological argument. Scholars have often converged upon the same theme in what appears to be a very different line of argument, namely the ontological one, with which are associated especially the names of St. Anselm, first of the Scholastic philosophers (in the 11th century), and René Descartes, first major modern philosopher (in the mid-17th century). Proponents of this argument try to show that the very idea of God implies his existence. God is the greatest or most perfect being. If the attribute of existence, however, is not included in man's concept of God, he can then think of something more perfect, viz., that which has existence as well. Critics, such as Gaunilo—a monk of Marmoutier—in Anselm's day and Immanuel Kant—one of the major architects of modern philosophy—many centuries later, have fastened on the weakness that existence is not a predicate or attribute in the same way, at least, as colour or shape; but there have been highly ingenious attempts by influential

religious thinkers of today to restate the argument in an acceptable form. (See especially the writings of Charles Hartshorne and Norman Malcolm.) Others find in the argument an oblique and needlessly elaborate way of eliciting the feeling that there must be some reality that exists by the very necessity of its own nature and to which everything else directs man's thought.

The reference to value and design. Attempts to arrive at the idea of God in somewhat more comprehensible terms are reflected in the references to value and design in the fourth and fifth ways of St. Thomas; this approach, however, has been given a more explicit presentation and critical discussion in the works of David Hume, a mid-18th-century Scottish Skeptic, and in Kant. The main idea of the teleological argument, as it is called, is that of the worth and purpose, or apparent design, to be found in the world. This purposiveness is taken to imply a supreme Designer. It has been questioned, however (by Kant, for example), whether this argument can really get started without presupposing some feature of the causal argument. The presence of seemingly purposeless features of the world and of much that is positively bad, like wickedness and suffering, while always embarrassing for a theistic view, presents peculiar difficulties here. For the arguer is now throwing hostages to fortune in the shape of a special assessment of the way things actually happen, which goes far beyond the mere requirement of some ultimate ground, whatever the world appears to be like. The arguments from worth and design have, however, one considerable advantage, viz., that they provide a fairly straightforward way of learning about the nature of God and of ascribing a certain aim and character to him from one's understanding of the phenomena that he is required to explain. The supreme Designer or Architect is known from his works, especially perhaps as reflected in the lives of men; and this approach opens up one way of speaking of God, not just as mysterious power behind the world but as some reality whom man may come to know in a personal way from the way the world goes and from his understanding of what it means.

Many thinkers in the late 19th and early 20th centuries sought to establish man's knowledge of God in the way suggested through his understanding of himself and the world, and of these the most notable and valuable still today are the British theists James Ward, a psychologist, and F.R. Tennant, a philosophical theologian. But the work of thinkers like Pierre Teilhard de Chardin, a Jesuit paleoanthropologist, and the spate of discussion that he has provoked are also relevant here; and such work, in turn, owes much—directly or otherwise—to the work of evolutionary thinkers like Samuel Alexander and Henri Bergson and of modern scientists like Julian Huxley.

The problem of particular knowledge of God. If the central theme of traditional theism, viz., that the finite world depends in some way on one transcendent and infinite Being, can be sustained, then a crucial problem presents itself at once: the question of how a being whose essence can never be known to man—who, as infinite, is bound to be beyond the grasp of reason and to remain wholly mysterious—how such a being can be said to be known at all, much less known and experienced in the close and intimate personal ways that the theist makes equally central to his claim. Part of the answer is that the theist does not claim to fathom the ultimate mystery of God or to know him as he is in himself. All that is claimed on this score is that man sees the inevitability of there being God in the contingent and limited character of everything else; and though this line of thought could not be adopted for any finite existence—since one could not normally affirm in any sensible way the existence of anything without specifying in some measure, however slight, what it is like—one can, nonetheless, regard the case of God as unique and not subject to the conditions of finite intelligibility. In these ways, an insight or intuition into the being of God may be claimed without a commitment to anything about his nature beyond the sort of completeness or perfection required to account for there being limited finite things. This insight is much in line with the "deliverances of religious

The five ways of Aquinas

The arguments of Anselm and Descartes

The views of Ward, Tennant, and Teilhard

consciousness" in which it is claimed that God is "hidden," is "past finding out," that his ways are not man's ways, that he is eternal, uncreated, and so on. But the theist still has a major problem on his hands, for he also makes a central issue of the claim that God can be known—"met" and "encountered" in some way—indeed, that some very bold affirmations about God and his dealings with men may be made.

Theism and natural theology. Theists have tried to deal with this problem in various ways. One of these ways is their use of the doctrine of analogy, which owes a great deal to the teaching of St. Thomas Aquinas. Various types of analogy are distinguished in the traditional doctrine; but the central claim is that certain predicates, such as "love," "faithfulness," or "justice," may be affirmed of God in whatever way may reflect his involvement as the author of the limited realities, such as man, of which such predicates may be affirmed in the normal, straightforward way. The difficulty with this procedure is that, whatever it yields, the content of faith is still very thin and remote, far from the warm fellowship of personal relations. Most of the traditional sponsors of the doctrine admit this and contend, therefore, that the findings of their "natural theology," as it is called, must be supplemented by that of revelation or of divine disclosure. Theism, in fact, is hardly conceivable without some doctrine of revelation. But even if the theologian says that God takes the initiative in communicating himself to man, the epistemological problem remains of how men's essentially finite minds can apprehend anything pertaining to infinite or eternal Being.

Revelation and authority

Theism and religious experience. At this point, recourse is sometimes had to authority, the authority of a sacred book, an institution, or a system of doctrines, or one of divinely implanted images. But there must at least be some initial justification of an authority, to say nothing of an evaluation of rival claims. A more attractive solution, then, especially for those who stress the personal involvement of God in men's lives, is one posed in terms of religious experience. Such experience is usually given prominence in theistic contexts. It is sometimes understood in terms of paranormal phenomena, like hearing voices or seeing visions, which have no natural origin, or like being in some peculiar psychical state. Some of the faithful believe that God literally speaks to them (or spoke in times past to prophets) in this way. A more subtle view holds that men have reason to regard certain experiences as their clue to what they should say of God in his relation to them. The question then arises of how these experiences should be recognized; and various answers are given, such as that which stresses the formative influence (within such experiences) of the initial insight into the being of God and the patterning of the experiences, in themselves and in wider ramifications, as a result. Much use is made in this context of the analogy with men's knowledge of one another. Men do not know one another's minds, it is alleged, as they know their own but only as mediated through bodily states and behaviour. So a man may come to know God, who in his essence is impenetrable to him, from the impact that he makes within experiences and events that one would otherwise understand and handle just as one does other finite occurrences. In the molding and perpetuating of such experiences, prominence is given to imagination and to the place of figurative terms and symbolism. These forms have therefore a place of special importance in theistic types of religion, the personal encounter being extended and deepened through art and literature, song, dance, myth, and ritual. This fact, in turn, presents problems for thought and practice, since the art forms and ritual must not be allowed to take wing on their own and thereby be loosed from the discipline and direction of the proper dynamic of religious life.

Theism and religious language. Preoccupation with the forms in which religious life expresses itself has led some theistic writers to lean heavily on the contribution made to religious understanding today by studies of religious language. In some cases this concern has carried with it, as generally in much linguistic philosophy of today, a skeptical or agnostic view of the transcendent factor in religion. It is hard to see, however, how attenuations of this kind could be strictly regarded as forms of theism; though clearly, within their more restricted scope, they can retain many of the other characteristics of theism, such as the stress on personal involvement and response. This tendency is very marked in some recent studies of religion, in which the inspiration and form of theism are retained without the substance—though how long and how properly are moot points. There are others who, while retaining the transcendent reference of theism, look for the solution of the central problem less in the substance of religious awareness and in varieties of experience than in the modes of articulation and religious language. Controversy centres, to a great degree, on which of these approaches is the most fruitful.

The question of transcendence in theism

In the work of some theists today, the preoccupation with language is also combined with the existentialist stress on personal involvement and commitment. A good example of this approach is found in the work of I.T. Ramsey, the bishop of Durham, who, in spite of his insistence on disclosure situations, in which something peculiarly significant becomes alive to man, seems to concede more than a theist should to the skeptical strain in recent studies of religious language.

The nature of God in modern thought. Modern thought has thrown new light on issues, both old and new, regarding the nature of God.

Theism and incarnation. The core of human personality has often been thought to be man's moral existence, and, accordingly, theists have often taken this fact to be the main clue to the way they are to think of divine perfection and to the recognition of a peculiar divine involvement in the world. Prominence is thus accorded to the high ethical teaching and character of saints and prophets, who have a special role to play in transmitting the divine message. In some religions this tendency culminates in doctrines of incarnation, of God manifesting himself expressly in refined or perfected human form. This trend is peculiarly marked in the Christian religion, in which the claim is usually made that a unique and "once for all" incarnation of God has occurred in Christ. Incarnational claims seem certainly to take their place easily in some main forms of theism. The vindication of such claims, however—especially today—relies much on consideration of the personal factor in religion generally.

For these and related reasons, the theist today may find himself calling to his aid certain other disciplines that centre upon men as persons, such as psychology and anthropology. Not all of the forms and findings of these studies favour the theist, and he should take special note of their challenge when they seem hostile, for they may touch him at his tenderest spot. He may, on the other hand, find in such studies, and certain general literature that borders on kindred themes, substantial help in reconstructing his case in the full context of contemporary thought and culture.

Humanism and transcendence. It is indeed from certain modern studies of man and his environment that some of the most disturbing challenges to the theist have come. For it has been argued that the very idea of God, as well as the more specific forms that it takes, emanate from man's emotional needs for succour and comfort. It is in fact man himself, it is said, who has created God in his own image, and the attempt is made to substantiate this view from accounts of the proclivity of men, especially in early times, to personify natural objects—rivers, trees, mountains, and so forth—and, in due course, to confer peculiar properties upon them, leading in time to the notion of some superbeing in whom these powers and properties are concentrated. The classical statement of this position appeared before the development of anthropology and the modern systematic study of religions, viz., in David Hume's essay "The Natural History of Religion" (1757). This short but splendidly lucid and challenging work set the pattern for the more scientific and empirical studies of religion that began to take shape in the 19th century in pioneer work by E.B. Tylor, a British ethnologist and anthropologist, in his *Primitive*

Role of the sciences of religion

Culture (1871), and by Sir James Frazer, an ethnographer and historian of religion, in his *Golden Bough* (1890–1915). But a corrective to this approach was soon provided by other scholars equally renowned, who started from the historical and empirical evidence available to them at the time. Andrew Lang, a Scottish litterateur, drew attention to the phenomenon among very early peoples, of the High God, a Supreme Being who created himself and the earth and dwelt at one time on earth. John H. King, in *The Supernatural: Its Origin, Nature and Evolution* (1892), stressed the importance of the element of mystery in all religions, and another pioneer of religious anthropology, R.R. Marett, showed how extensively the savage ascribes the mysteries of life and power to a supernatural source. Lucien Lévy-Bruhl, a French sociologist, noted the pervasiveness of prelogical factors in primitive mentality, and Rudolf Otto, the most famous name in this context, found evidence in early forms of religion of a response to "the wholly other," the *mysterium tremendum et fascinans*.

The idea of a finite God. Concern with the problem of evil—*i.e.*, with reconciling the existence of evil with that of a good God—becomes acute for thinkers who rest their case mainly on what they find in the world around them; and this has led many to retreat to the notion of a finite God, according to which the world may be under the direction of a superior being who is nonetheless limited in power, though not in goodness. This is a serious alternative to the idea of a supreme and unlimited source of all reality as found in the usual forms of theism. Indeed, it is a moot point whether the idea of a finite God should be classified as a form of theism. It does come close to traditional theism, however, in its insistence on the unity and absolute benevolence of God. There are clearly advantages in the notion of God as a limited being, especially where evil is concerned; for though one could still insist that God intends nothing that is not wholly good, he can now account for extensive suffering and other ills on the basis of the limits to God's power. He is doing his utmost, the finitist holds, but there are things—refractory materials or explicitly evil powers—that he has not yet subdued, though hopefully he will eventually do so. There is also induced in this way a sense of urgency in man's own obligation to cooperate with God—to be a "fellow worker." God will clearly need his help though he himself is in the vanguard of the battle against evil. Thus, those who incline to the idea of a finite God usually have been activist in thought and practice.

There are also grave difficulties to be met. For if a thinker has recourse to the idea of God simply to account for what is otherwise bewildering in the finite course of things, he may find no warrant for the inference involved and indeed may find himself desperately clinging to what is sometimes called "the God of the gaps" (*i.e.*, of the gaps in man's explanations). If, on the other hand, he starts from the inherently incomplete character of finite explanation as such, or from the contingency of finite things, nothing short of an infinite or absolute God will meet the case. In addition, the usual attitude of religious people, or of what is sometimes known as "the religious consciousness," is that of a profound assurance and serenity that presupposes that God is "all in all" and beyond any possibility of being thwarted. It is also questionable whether the attitude of worship is appropriate for a limited being, however superior he may be to man.

The views of James, Perry, and the process philosophers

Among the outstanding advocates of the idea of a finite God were, at the turn of the 20th century, the U.S. Pragmatist William James and some of his disciples, notably Ralph Barton Perry. Thus, it is not surprising that a closely similar notion arising in the mid-20th century finds its main inspiration and support in the United States, viz., in the work of process philosophers, such as Charles Hartshorne and Schubert Ogden, who have developed some of the leading ideas of A.N. Whitehead, an eminent metaphysician. In their view, God is himself in process of fulfillment in some kind of identification with the world, which at the same time leaves him distinct in some sense from the universe, which he permeates and unifies. There are grave and admitted para-

doxes in this view; and, in spite of the remarkable ingenuity of its advocates and their logical nimbleness, it is not clear that the paradoxes can be sustained nor that the difficulties that are shared with the simpler notion of a finite God can be overcome. Much in recent religious thought centres on this issue.

Theism in Islām. The Muslim faith owes much to the Semitic outlook from which the Old Testament and Christianity arose. It centres on a transcendent personal deity; but, in its regard for the holiness and majesty of God, it rejects incarnational doctrines as a form of blasphemy. There is, however, a paradoxical side to one form of Islām: while insisting that God is all in all, it sometimes tends to represent all of man's own actions as the action of God within him and thus has some tendency to identify man with God. This tendency, most marked in the mysticism of the Şūfīs, seems, as respects its monism, to veer away from theism but seems, as respects the sense of devotion and personal excitation that it inspires, to be in line with the more explicit forms of theism. In its main form, Islām, with its quite exceptional sense of the transcendence of God, is one of the most distinctively theistic religions, though at odds with the incarnational factor in Christian theism.

THEISM IN EASTERN THOUGHT

The trend toward the testing of theistic thought in the crucible of the special disciplines was continued not only in further anthropological studies (see *The Worship of the Sky-God,* by E.O. James) but also in extensive scholarly studies and translations of the sacred books of the great religions of the East.

Hindu theism. It was noted, for example, that the Vedic hymns that appear in the earliest Hindu scriptures contain significant intimations of a sense of "the wonder of existence," "the outpourings," as Savepalli Radhakrishnan, the former philosopher-president of India, has expressed it, "of poetic minds who were struck by the immensity of the universe and the inexhaustible mystery of life." Note was taken also of early manifestations of henotheism, a view that exalts several deities to the first place. The theme of some one supreme reality, the first principle, or the supreme self becomes more explicit in the *Upaniṣads,* ancient Hindu scriptures, while retaining a sense of its ineffableness. One hears of "the way of silence" and of the ultimate absorption of all into the one supreme reality, the "one who breathes breathless." This one is variously conceived in its relation to finite things; and although the transcendent reference is rarely absent, there is not the same recognition of the distinctness of finite beings that there is in Western theism or of the eternal self being involved in the world in a personal way. The *Upaniṣads* have, in fact, a variety of themes and emphases, tending generally toward a monistic and mystical philosophy; but on occasion the theistic element is very marked, as in the *Kaṭha* and the *Śvetāśvatara* books of the *Upaniṣads.* The absolutist and the theistic views are not always felt to be exclusive. This climate of thought has set the course for much of subsequent Hinduism, in which, along with the persistence of the monistic strain, the theistic note is sounded much more distinctly, especially in the doctrine and practice of *bhakti*—devotion to a personal God who bestows grace. In the famous *Bhagavadgītā* (probably 3rd or 4th century BC), a classic of religious literature, and in the teaching of the Brahmin Rāmānuja (11th century), considered the founder of the Viśiṣṭādvaita (qualified nondualism) school, the flowering of the more theistic side of Hinduism is found. In the Śaiva-siddhānta theology of South Indian Śaivism (a major cult of Hinduism), there is a firm insistence that the soul, in being united with God, is not annihilated or negated but only fused into the likeness of God, who, in turn, is always in loving pursuit of the soul. This doctrine makes the system "perhaps the highest form of theism that India was ever to develop" (R.C. Zaehner). In the closing words of the *Bhagavadgītā* is an insistence on a love of God for man and of man for God that represents a decisive turning point in the history of Hinduism:

Think on me, worship me, sacrifice to me, pay me homage,

Theism in the *Upaniṣads*

so shalt thou come to me, I promise thee truly, for I love thee well. Give up all things of *dharma*, turn to me only as thy refuge. I will deliver thee from all evil. Have no care.

This theology has been well reflected in the 20th century in the devotionalism of Gandhi and in the writings of Sri Aurobindo, a philosopher and Yoga devotee, which reflect an indwelling of the divine within the world and a summons to high moral endeavour on the part of man that comes close to theism without explicitly accepting it.

Buddhism and theism. The same diversity of strains is found in Buddhism. Though Buddhism was at one time regarded as an atheistic religion leading to total elimination of self in a state of Nirvāṇa, a close examination of the evidence—in the Pāli *Tipiṭaka*, for example, the canon of the Theravāda school of Buddhism—leads to a revision in favour of the view that the seeming negativism of early Buddhist scriptures and the rejection of metaphysics reflect chiefly the caution arising from a profound recognition of the characterless elusiveness of the transcendent. And although the Buddhist doctrine of compassion and its rigorous intellectual and moral discipline may lack something of the warmth of a close personal commitment, the Buddhist adoration of the Buddha and of the *bodhisattvas* (those on their way to Enlightenment) afforded much scope to the religious responses that find their full expression in overt theism. This trend became more marked in the more popular forms of Buddhism and in the mythologies that centre upon the idea of the *bodhisattva*s.

Theism in other religions. In the same way, the seeming agnosticism of Confucian religion is qualified by its teaching about a power from beyond the world working for justice within it, a "Heaven-ordained relationship" that provides the basis of ethics and induces a deep consciousness of individuality. This trend became intensified in the conflations that resulted from the extension of Buddhism into China.

Theism in Confucianism, Sikhism, and Jainism

In the doctrines of Sikhism, a religion of the eastern Punjab that combines certain Muslim and Hindu elements, stress is laid upon personal awareness of God as a central and unifying factor in religion. In doctrine though not always in practice, however, the Sikhs reject every notion of an avatar, or incarnation. The religion of the Jains is nontheistic in theory, but the great figures of its tradition come to function as gods in popular religion. For a period in ancient Persia, there was established in the teaching of Zoroaster (Zarathushtra) a form of ethical monotheism in which the god Ahura Mazdā is the creator of the physical and moral world—though limited, for a time at least, by an opposing principle of evil (Ahriman).

The clue to the theistic element in the religions of primitive peoples may well be found in an observation by H.H. Farmer, a British philosophical theologian:

We may surmise that at moments of living prayer and worship there is in primitive man a turning to *a* god as if he were in fact the one and only God, though without any expressly formulated denial of the existence of others; for the time being, the god worshipped fills the whole sphere of the divine.

BIBLIOGRAPHY. The classic recent statement of God's transcendence is A.M. FARRER, *Finite and Infinite*, 2nd ed. (1959), a difficult but essential book; C.A. CAMPBELL, *On Selfhood and Godhood* (1957), is an exceptionally lucid presentation that allows for the distinctness of finite beings; see also further statements in WILLIAM TEMPLE, *Nature, Man and God* (1934); H.H. FARMER, *God and Men* (1947); and H.D. LEWIS, *Philosophy of Religion* (1965). A. SETH PRINGLE-PATTISON presents the more traditional Idealist view in *The Idea of God in the Light of Recent Philosophy* (1920). An Idealism stressing the immediate awareness of other minds and of God is found in W.E. HOCKING, *The Meaning of God in Human Experience* (1912); a presentation similarly starting from Empiricism and science that culminates in a "Cosmic Teleology" is that of F.R. TENNANT, *Philosophical Theology*, 2 vol. (1928–30). E.S. BRIGHTMAN, *The Problem of God* (1930), treats God as a limited being (finitism).

Mysticism and theism: An excellent account of many types of mysticism is provided in DAVID KNOWLES, *The English Mystical Tradition* (1961). A comprehensive account (including Eastern mysticism), with profound reflections on mysticism's relation to theistic claims, is in R.C. ZAEHNER, *Mysticism, Sacred and Profane* (1957).

Theism and Idealism: Typical statements are A.E. TAYLOR, *The Faith of a Moralist*, 2 vol. (1930, reprinted 1968); G.F. STOUT, *God and Nature* (1952); A.C. EWING, *Idealism* (1934, reprinted 1950); JOSIAH ROYCE, *The World and the Individual*, 2 vol. (1900, reprinted 1959); and BRAND BLANSHARD, *Reason and Goodness* (1960). For difficulties Idealism poses for theism, see H.D. LEWIS, *The Elusive Mind*, ch. 14 (1969).

Arguments for God's existence: An excellent account appears in F.C. COPLESTON, *History of Philosophy*, vol. 2, ch. 34 (1950). For what lies behind the arguments (and their importance for God's transcendence), E.L. MASCALL, *He Who Is*, ch. 4–6 (1945), is unrivalled. See also the readings in ALVIN PLANTINGA, *The Ontological Argument* (1965); and *God and Other Minds* (1967); and in JOHN HICK, *The Many-Faced Argument* (1967). For its current revival, see CHARLES HARTSHORNE, *The Logic of Perfection* (1962); and NORMAN MALCOM, "Anselm's Ontological Arguments," *The Philosophical Review*, 69:41–62 (1960). For substantial articles on the traditional arguments, see *Religious Studies*, vol. 4, no. 2 (1969). The best recent account of the cosmological argument and transcendence is given by I.M. CROMBIE, "The Possibility of Theological Statements," in BASIL MITCHELL (ed.), *Faith and Logic* (1957). For the arguments from design and value, see H.P. OWEN, *The Moral Argument for Christian Theism* (1965); his exhaustive defense in *The Christian Knowledge of God* (1969); and ILLTYD TRETHOWAN, *Absolute Value* (1969).

Idea of a finite God: WILLIAM JAMES, *Pragmatism and the Will of God*, ch. 8 (1917), is the classical statement. See also R.B. PERRY, *Realms of Values* (1954, reprinted 1968); and the celebrated advocate of this view, E.S. BRIGHTMAN, *The Problem of God* (1930). For criticism, see C.A. CAMPBELL, *Scepticism and Construction*, ch. 8 (1931).

Process theology: Process theology stems from A.N. WHITEHEAD, *Process and Reality* (1929, reprinted 1969). Its most notable exponents are CHARLES HARTSHORNE in *The Logic of Perfection* (1962); and SCHUBERT OGDEN in *The Reality of God* (1966).

Religious experience: The pioneer work is WILLIAM JAMES, *The Varieties of Religious Experience* (1902, reprinted 1961). H.H. FARMER, *Revelation and Religion* (1954), maps out various religious attitudes and considers them in relation to a typical theistic view. Questions about the vindication of religious experience are discussed in *Our Experience of God* by H.D. LEWIS (1959 and 1969).

Religious language: The theistic position in linguistic religious philosophy is best represented in I.T. RAMSEY, *Religious Language* (1957). See also the masterly work by W.K. MUNDLE in *A Critique of Linguistic Philosophy* (1970).

World religions: See R.C. ZAEHNER, *At Sundry Times* (1958) and *Hinduism*, 2nd ed. (1966); R.L. SLATER, *World Religions and World Community* (1963); HANS JOACHIM SHOEPS, *Wesen und Geschichte* (1961; Eng. trans., *The Religions of Mankind*, 1968); and E.G. PARRINDER, *Worship in the World's Religions* (1961) and *Avatar and Incarnation* (1970).

(H.D.L.)

Themistocles

Themistocles, the creator of Athenian sea power and chief saviour of Greece from subjection to the Persian Empire in the invasion of 480 BC, is often unfavourably viewed by early writers. Admittedly a master strategist, he is often depicted as a slick politician, bent on enriching himself even in the crisis of the great war. The reason for this bias is perhaps that he was a strong democrat, hated by the Athenian upper classes; and their views, passed on to their friend the historian Herodotus and to Plato, himself an aristocrat, colour the whole tradition. Herodotus introduces him only at the onset of the crisis as "newly come to the front" (which is wrong) and drops him from his story at the end of 480. Only the historian Thucydides does him justice and calls the darkest charges against him "alleged."

Themistocles was born, at latest, about 524 BC. His father Neocles came of the aristocratic Lycomid family and was not poor; but his mother was a concubine, non-Athenian, possibly non-Greek. He thus owed his citizenship to the legislation of Cleisthenes, which, in 508, had made citizens of all free men of Athens. This no doubt contributed to his democratic sympathies. In 493 he was elected archon, the chief judicial and civilian executive

Themistocles, Roman copy of a Greek herm, possibly c. 465–460 BC. In the Scavi di Ostia Museum.
By courtesy of the Gabinetto Fotografico Nazionale del Ministero Della Publica Instruzione, Rome

officer in Athens; this is the first recorded event of his life. As archon, he sponsored the first public works destined to make the defensible rocky bays of Piraeus, five miles from Athens, into harbours, replacing the nearer but unprotected beaches of Phaleron. He must also have been concerned in the trial of Miltiades, the great colonial Athenian prince, who arrived in flight from the Chersonese (Gallipoli) and was prosecuted by aristocratic rivals for having ruled as a monarch. Themistocles himself took a cool view of Miltiades' autocratic character; but his judgment was not at fault if he helped to save the strategist and tactician who, in 490, beat off the first Persian attack on Athens at Marathon.

After Marathon, most Athenians thought that the danger was past, but not so Themistocles. He also saw that Marathon—a victory for Athens' spearmen, middle class men who could afford the costly bronze panoply —could not be repeated if the enemy, strong in archers and cavalry, came again in much greater force. The only hope was to exploit the invader's supply difficulties, which would be great if Persia's naval allies, including the formidable Phoenicians, could be beaten at sea. But for this strategy Greece needed far more warships—the newly developed, specialized triremes—than it then had. Themistocles urged that the Athenian fleet, then 70 strong, be doubled or trebled; but he was opposed. The opposition was not without political overtones; for triremes would have to be paid for by those who had money, whereas armour, once one had it, cost nothing to maintain; and also, a strong navy would give political weight to the men who rowed the galleys, the poorer voters, as compared with the armoured-infantry middle class.

The 480s were a period of intense political struggle. Miltiades died in disgrace (489), and from 487 to 483 other leaders were successively ostracized. Though never himself defeated, Themistocles must have been attacked repeatedly; he was the man accused by his enemies of being a danger to the established order. Nonetheless, in 483 he won his greatest triumph. The state-owned silver mines near Sunium were the site of a rich strike; and he persuaded the assembly, instead of "declaring a dividend," to devote the whole surplus to increasing the navy. Thus when Xerxes I, the Persian king, marched in 480, Athens had 200 triremes, though many of the rowers were still untrained.

Themistocles further succeeded in selling his naval strategy to the Peloponnesians, headed by Sparta, who could

Advocacy of a large navy

raise another 150 triremes. The combined fleet was to fight not on their own doorstep, as Greeks preferred to do, but as far forward as possible, exploiting the geographical situation. Serving under a Spartan admiral (since Corinth and Aegina would not serve under an Athenian), Themistocles conducted the main fleet to the straits north of Euboea. Here their presence forced the enemy to approach en masse down a coast with few beaches; and a typical north Aegean storm there inflicted losses that probably, in the end, proved decisive. But the Greeks were still outnumbered. In the Battle of Artemisium, fighting in a defensive half-moon formation, they suffered as well as inflicted heavy losses, and they knew that they must retire even before they heard that their small holding force on land had been destroyed at Thermopylae.

One hope remained. Themistocles had persuaded the Athenians to evacuate women and children to the Peloponnese and, in the last resort, to retire to Salamis. If the Persians attacked that island citadel, a battle in the narrow sound might yet give a chance to the Greeks, with their armoured marines and heavier ships, against the better sailing ships commanded by the Persians. Persuading the Peloponnesians to join the Athenian fleet, Themistocles then lured Xerxes by a false message, suggesting that he himself was ready to change sides, into ordering an all-out attack. The Greeks enveloped the head of the Phoenician column as it emerged from the narrowest part of the strait and destroyed it; and though most of the other Asian contingents in the rear escaped, Xerxes had lost for good the command of the sea.

Sparta honoured Themistocles with a great ovation; but Athens, led during the crisis by the Areopagus, or council of nobles, gave the chief commands in 479 to the recalled exiles, Aristides and Xanthippus; and Themistocles' postwar history was a sad one. He outwitted the Spartans when they attempted to prevent Athens from rebuilding its defensive walls, but he failed to induce the people either to transfer their capital to Piraeus or, at that time, to reduce the powers of the Areopagus. The people, after their tremendous war effort, were in a mood of reaction. Though praised (not by name) in Aeschylus' *Persians* (472), Themistocles was at last ostracized. He lived at Argos for some years, during which democracy made headway in some parts of the Peloponnese. Then Sparta accused him of complicity in alleged intrigues with Persia. He escaped, and, until his death in about 460, served as governor of some Asian Greek cities still subject to the son of Xerxes.

Battle of Salamis

BIBLIOGRAPHY. The histories by HERODOTUS and THUCYDIDES are primary. The *Life* by PLUTARCH is based on sources of various quality and must be used critically. Full discussions and a bibliography may be found in PETER GREEN, *The Year of Salamis, 480–479 B.C.* (1970), who uses and often disagrees with A.R. BURN, *Persia and the Greeks* (1962).

(A.R.Bu.)

Theodoric the Great

As the Ostrogothic king of Italy from 493 to 526, Theodoric the Great was one of the most remarkable rulers of early medieval Europe. He conquered Italy, in which the control by the Roman Empire had disintegrated late in the 5th century, and ruled it peacefully for 33 years. His wish to impose racial harmony in his kingdom was the dominating feature of his rule and makes him uniquely great among the Germanic rulers who supplanted Roman administration in the West.

Theodoric was born about 454/455, the son of the Ostrogothic chieftain, Theodemir, and as a boy lived as a hostage in Constantinople, then the capital of the Eastern Roman Empire. Although he thus had some of the advantages of a Roman upbringing, he was said to have remained illiterate. This is undoubtedly an exaggeration: what is meant is that he never attained the skill in calligraphy that was expected of a ruler in the 5th and 6th centuries. At the time of his birth the Ostrogoths had recently escaped from the empire of the Huns, who had fiercely oppressed them, uprooting them from their homes in the Ukraine, transferring them to Pannonia, and taking away

Early life

Theodoric, detail of a fresco, 14th century. In the Church of Santa Maria in Porto Fuori, Ravenna.
Alinari

their grain. For more than 30 years after Theodoric's birth, the chief aim of the Ostrogoths was to find new land upon which they could settle and live in peace. In northern Pannonia they fought endlessly against other Germanic peoples, acted for and against the emperors at Constantinople, and sometimes received and sometimes were refused financial subsidies from the imperial government. On the death of his father in 471, Theodoric became his successor and soon led his people to new homes in Lower Moesia (in what is now Bulgaria), where they entered into relations, usually hostile, with another group of Ostrogoths led by Theodoric Strabo. Conditions in the Balkan provinces at this time were chaotic. Theodoric guided his people through the confusion with considerable skill but was unable to settle them safely and permanently on the land. The emperor Zeno gave him the title of patrician and the office of master of the soldiers and even appointed him as consul in 484; but in vain efforts to achieve his aims Theodoric frequently ravaged the imperial provinces and actually threatened Constantinople itself. In 488 Zeno ordered him to make his way to Italy, overthrow its barbarian ruler Odoacer, and govern the peninsula in the Emperor's name. With his people, who may have numbered 100,000 persons, Theodoric arrived in Italy in late August 489. In the following year he defeated Odoacer in three pitched battles and won control of nearly all Italy, but he could not take Ravenna, where Odoacer held out for more than three years. This war caused untold damage to city and country alike in northern Italy.

The circumstances of Odoacer's death illustrate the crueller side of Theodoric's character, a side he normally concealed. When the Ostrogoths had failed to take Ravenna, the two leaders agreed to govern Italy jointly, and Odoacer admitted Theodoric into the impregnable city on March 5, 493. In the palace of Lauretum ten days later, two Goths, pretending to be suppliants, suddenly seized Odoacer by the hands, and Theodoric cut him down with a sword. Theodoric went on to murder the dead man's wife and son and to massacre his followers remorselessly throughout northern Italy.

Whether Theodoric governed Italy as an independent king or as an official of the Roman emperor at Constantinople has been much debated. The truth appears to be that in theory he recognized the overlordship of the Eastern emperor; in practice, however, he was king both of the Romans and of the barbarians in Italy. In his official documents, he is simply "king" without qualification; he never defined of whom or of what he was the king. But there were some limits to his powers. He could not appoint legitimate consuls without confirmation by the emperor; he could issue edicts but not laws, though in practice there was little difference between the two; he could not confer Roman citizenship upon a Goth or appoint a Goth to a Roman civilian office or to the Senate; and his

Theodoric's strengths and limitations

people could not legally intermarry with Romans. Early in his reign Theodoric put aside the skins or furs that Germanic rulers usually wore and surrounded his throne with something of Byzantine pomp. Unlike Odoacer, he dressed himself in the purple of the emperors.

Theodoric maintained peace in Italy throughout his 33-year reign. The Goths were settled in northern and central Italy, while Sicily and southern Italy as far north as Naples were free of them; but some of them lived in such overseas Ostrogothic dominions as Dalmatia and Pannonia. The Goths were divided from the Romans by language, for Gothic in the middle of the 6th century was both a spoken and a written language, used both for secular and for ecclesiastical matters. And they were further divided from the Romans by religion because they were Arian Christians, not Catholics, and they accepted the doctrines of the 4th-century heretical Gothic bishop Ulfilas.

Early in the 6th century Theodoric published his *Edict,* a collection of 154 rules and regulations. With one or two exceptions, these were not new laws but brief restatements in simple language of Roman laws that were already in existence. The *Edict* was a handbook issued for the convenience of judges, and it covered the cases that in the King's opinion were likely to come most frequently before the courts. The rules of the *Edict* applied to Goths as well as to Romans: in other words, the Goths were to be subject to Roman law, though not to Roman judges, and no provision was made for the recognition of their own national customs and usages. This was a discrepancy in Theodoric's policy of keeping Goths and Romans separate and of preventing fusion of the two nationalities.

Goths alone served in the army, and Romans were forbidden to carry arms. The Goths lived on the income of the estates on which they had been planted and also received an annual donative from the King. The warriors apparently went each year to Ravenna or wherever the King happened to be to receive the money from his own hand. On these occasions Theodoric would review the deeds of his troops, praising the brave and reprimanding the cowardly. Gothic soldiers on active service also received rations, either in kind or in the equivalent cash. Thus, the Ostrogoths of Theodoric's reign lived a very different life from that of their forebears, who had starved under the rule of the Huns; entering the Roman Empire and taking over one of its provinces had been profitable for them. The Romans of the kingdom continued to be governed by the old Roman civil service, which continued to exist more or less unchanged.

The great aim of Theodoric's administration was to preserve harmony between Goths and Romans. He was never guilty of religious persecution. In his letters of appointment and elsewhere, he stressed above all else that the Goths must not oppress the Roman population, must not plunder their goods or ravage their fields, and must try to live amicably with them. He made endless high-minded appeals to the warriors to behave decently. He even stooped to point out that "it is in your interests that the Romans should be undisturbed, for while they enrich our Treasury they multiply your donatives." In fact, the animosity of the Gothic rank and file against the Romans was made clear over and over again, and no plea that might have held it in check was left unused by the King. He never missed an opportunity to propagate the idea of *civilitas* ("civilized life" or "civilization"), a concept that includes the maintenance of peace and order, racial harmony, and the outlawing of oppression and violence. "We do not love anything that is uncivilized," says one of his documents, "we hate wicked pride and its authors. Our Piety execrates men of violence. In a law suit let justice prevail, not the strong arm."

The end of Theodoric's reign was disgraced by the murder of the Roman scholar Boethius, which the King later regretted. Theodoric died on August 30, 526, and was buried in a remarkable tomb that still exists in Ravenna. He was succeeded by Athalaric, the son of his daughter Amalasuntha.

Preservation of racial harmony

BIBLIOGRAPHY. No good biography of Theodoric has been published in English in recent years, and we must still rely on THOMAS HODGKIN, *Italy and Her Invaders*, vol. 3–4 (1885), which, however, is excellent. See also WILHELM ENSSLIN, *Theoderich der Grosse* (1947), a sound, reliable work.

(E.A.T.)

Theodosius I the Great

The Roman emperor Theodosius I (called the Great in Christian tradition) successfully maintained the unity of the disintegrating empire during his lifetime and greatly strengthened Christianity as the official religion of the state.

Giraudon

Theodosius I, detail from an embossed and engraved silver disk, late 4th century. In the Real Academia de la Historia, Madrid.

Background and youth. Theodosius was born January 11, 347 (possibly 346), near Cauca in the province of Gallaecia in northwestern Spain. His father was to become the general Flavius Theodosius; his mother's name is unknown. His grandparents, like his parents, were probably already Christians. Theodosius, who grew up in Spain, did not receive an extensive education but was intellectually open-minded and acquired a special interest in the study of history.

While on his father's staff, he participated in his campaigns against the Picts and Scots in Britain in 368–369, against the Alemanni in Gaul in 370, and against the Sarmatians in the Balkans in 372–373. As a military commander in Moesia, a Roman province on the lower Danube, he defeated the Sarmatians in 374. When his father was sentenced to death and executed as a result of political intrigues by enemies at court, Theodosius withdrew to his Spanish estates. At the end of 376, he married Aelia Flacilla, also a Spaniard. His first son, the future emperor Arcadius, was born in 377, and his daughter Pulcheria in 378. Immediately after the catastrophic defeat of the emperor Valens, who perished at the hands of the Visigoths and other barbarians on August 9, 378, near Adrianople, the emperor Gratian unexpectedly summoned Theodosius to his court. When Theodosius had once again proved his military ability by a victory over the Sarmatians, Gratian proclaimed him coemperor on January 19, 379. His dominion was to be the eastern part of the empire, including the provinces of Dacia (present-day Romania) and Macedonia, which had been especially infiltrated by barbarians in the preceding few years.

First years as emperor. In 379 and 380 Theodosius resided chiefly in Thessalonica. He sought first to rebuild the army, the discipline of which was considerably impaired, and to consolidate Rome's position on the Balkan peninsula. Military unpreparedness could not be overcome by conscription alone, which applied only to certain classes. Theodosius therefore directed that large numbers of Teutons, who had been barred from military service, be accepted by the army. By 379, however, when foreigners had already intermingled extensively with the rest of the army, both among the troops and in all ranks of the officer corps, Theodosius did no more than many of his predecessors to encourage this process. In contrast to the West, in Theodosius' provinces both Romans and Teutons were among the leading generals.

Recognizing that the barbarians, who had invaded the provinces as early as 375, could no longer be expelled by force and that he could count on Gratian for only limited assistance, Theodosius sought new possibilities for coexistence. This resulted in the friendly reception of the Visigoth Athanaric in 381 and the conclusion of a treaty of alliance, or *foedus*, with the main body of the Visigoths in the fall of 382. The Goths, who pledged themselves to lending military assistance, were assigned territory for settlement between the lower Danube and the Balkan mountains. Under this novel arrangement, an entire people was settled on imperial soil while retaining its autonomy. Theodosius may have hoped that the Goths would become integrated, as had a group of Goths who in *c.* 350 had settled near Nicopolis in Moesia; their leader, Bishop Ulfilas, undertook missionary work among the parties to the *foedus* of 382.

Treaty of alliance with the Visigoths

Some historians have regarded Theodosius as biassed in favour of the Goths. He has even been accused of having contributed decisively, through the treaty of 382, to the downfall of Rome. Yet, it should be noted that the policy of that treaty, which was undertaken in the justified expectation of raising Roman military strength and recultivating tracts of wasteland, by no means became customary. Instead, the Emperor took strict measures against further invasions by Teutonic bands and did not permit any doubts to arise as to Roman claims of superiority over the barbarians.

Theodosius' situation was complicated by the sharp antagonism that arose around 379 between disciples of the Nicene Creed (according to which Jesus Christ is of the same substance as God the Father) and several other Christian groups in his part of the empire. Theodosius himself, the first emperor who did not assume the title of *pontifex maximus* (supreme guardian of the old Roman cults), believed in the Nicene Creed, despite his Baptism only after a serious illness in the fall of 380. Out of political as well as religious motives, he energetically undertook to bring about unity of faith within the empire. His position was improved by the fact that during 379 the followers of the Nicene Creed gained ground, whereupon Theodosius on February 28, 380, without consulting the ecclesiastical authorities, issued an edict prescribing a creed that was to be binding on all subjects. Only persons who believed in the consubstantiality of God the Father, Son, and Holy Spirit were henceforth to be considered Catholic Christians, a designation that here appears for the first time in a document.

First designation of Catholic Christians

There is no doubt that the principle of religious intolerance was proclaimed in this edict. When assessing the edict, however—which should not be viewed simply as an isolated measure—it must be remembered that to the Christians Theodosius was emperor by the grace of God. While thus committed to defend the true faith, he by no means carried out his stated intention by force. The creed, prescribed in 380, was again defined at the beginning of 381 and ecclesiastically sanctioned, as it were, by a church council summoned to Constantinople by Theodosius in the summer of 381. That gathering is considered the second ecumenical council. The Symbolum Nicaeno-Constantinopolitanum (*i.e.*, the Niceno-Constantinopolitan Creed [or Symbol]), which is still used by most Christians, along with the ranking by the council fathers of the bishop of Constantinople directly after the bishop of Rome, can thus be traced back to Theodosius. Henceforth, the emperor's authority in matters of faith was to be recognized by the bishops of the East. There is no ground, however, for speaking of a rigidly organized imperial church controlled by the emperor.

The period when Theodosius stayed mainly in Constantinople, dating from the end of 380 to 387, is that to which most of his measures to improve the capital may be attributed. The plan for the Forum Tauri, the largest public square known in antiquity, designed after the model of Trajan's Forum in Rome, is outstanding. It is unclear, however, to what extent the Emperor encouraged the flowering of art and literature in his time.

The middle years. In 383, Maximus, a Spaniard who had been proclaimed emperor by the troops in Britain, asserted himself as ruler in the Western provinces (*praefectura Galliarum*). Suspicions that Theodosius was in collusion with the usurper and thus implicated in the death of Emperor Gratian in August 383 are unfounded. Theodosius, who had to acknowledge the sovereignty of Gratian's stepbrother Valentinian II, born in 371 and the nominal ruler in Italy since the end of 375, could not interfere with Maximus, for he lacked both sufficient military strength and secure borders. Yet, when Maximus invaded Italy in 387 and Valentinian was forced to flee to Thessalonica, Theodosius soon decided upon countermeasures. His decision was perhaps hastened through the influence of Valentinian's mother, whose daughter Galla he had married at the end of 387, having been a widower since 386. Theodosius' position by that time had become stronger. Long-standing negotiations with the Persians over the division of power in Armenia had resulted in a treaty that was to become the basis for a long period of peace on the eastern border. Having ordered one army division from Egypt to Africa and sent Valentinian with a fleet to Italy, Theodosius set out in the spring of 388 with the main body of troops to move against Maximus' army, which had invaded Pannonia in the Balkans. By July the enemy was defeated. When Maximus surrendered at the end of August he was branded as a usurper, but his followers were generally treated with leniency.

In the same year, Theodosius again relinquished the West to his coemperor Valentinian but secured his own influence by placing the Frankish general Arbogast, a man he trusted, at Valentinian's side as principal adviser. By remaining in Italy until the spring of 391, where he resided mostly in Milan, Theodosius emphasized his claim to supreme authority throughout the empire. In 389 he visited Rome, where, accompanied by his four-year-old son Honorius, he made a triumphant entry. In Milan, Theodosius found in Bishop Ambrose an ecclesiastic who was intent upon cooperating effectively with the Emperor and even upon forming a friendship with him, although Ambrose pointed out to Theodosius the limits of the power of temporal rulers more clearly than had others. A conflict had already arisen between them in 388 over Theodosius' punishment of orthodox fanatics who had set fire to a synagogue and to the shrine of a sect. As a devout Christian, Theodosius finally acceded to the Bishop's wishes in the matter but took pains to make him understand that he was not willing to grant the Bishop greater influence in affairs of government.

A new conflict arose in 390 when, following the murder of one of his generals in Thessalonica, Theodosius issued an order for brutal retaliation. It was rescinded too late, so that a horrible massacre resulted among the population there. Ambrose had the Emperor's action condemned in a church council and bade him do public penance. After a prolonged hesitation, Theodosius complied with the order and was readmitted to communion at Christmas 390. His penance should not be construed as a victory of the church over the Emperor but only as a demonstration of the power of atonement over the penitent sinner. The claims that arose in future centuries that the church had been placed above the temporal power derived not from Theodosius' act of penance but only from the myth generated by it. Although Theodosius had gained an important ally in Ambrose, he continued intent on preserving the emperor's authority in the face of Ambrose and other bishops. While maintaining an entirely friendly attitude toward the church, Theodosius still took care in his legislation to see that the material interests of the state were sacrificed only to a very limited extent to church or clergy. In addition, Theodosius decided to enforce more strongly against the pagans the religious policy he had pursued since 379. In February 391 he prohibited sacrifices and the visiting of temples. Up to that time, he had basically tolerated the pagans and had entrusted adherents of the old cults with the highest offices.

Quarrels between his second wife Galla and his son Arcadius, as well as his own view of the eastern capital as the centre of the empire, prompted Theodosius to move his residence back to Constantinople, where he arrived in November 391.

Victory over pagan usurpers. A new crisis arose for Theodosius three months after Valentinian's death on May 15, 392. Arbogast treacherously proclaimed as emperor of the West a former rhetoric teacher, Eugenius, who had close connections with the pagan aristocracy of the Senate. Theodosius, who did not yet dare to risk a civil war, delayed reception of a legation requesting recognition of Arbogast's puppet. On November 8, 392, he made his edicts of 391 more stringent by completely prohibiting the worship of the pagan gods. He left no further doubts as to his position when he elevated his son Honorius to Augustus in January 393 and thereby demonstrated that he would no longer tolerate any emperor other than himself and his sons. Because he still refrained from military action, his enemies occupied Italy in the spring of 393. Led by Nicomachus Flavianus, the forces striving to preserve the pagan cults gathered around Eugenius.

The now inevitable struggle for power was thus at the same time a struggle that would decide whether pagan religions would once again be tolerated within the empire alongside Christianity. Theodosius did not set out from Constantinople until May 394. As in 388, he made his way toward the Danube and then the Sava with his powerful army. His force consisted largely of barbarians and their allies, one of whose heads was Stilicho, a man of Vandal origin who had been married since 384 to the Emperor's niece Serena. Theodosius' sons Arcadius and Honorius stayed behind in the capital. Arcadius, who had been given the right to promulgate laws independently, was supposed to direct the government in the East.

Theodosius first met the enemy at the Frigidus River on the eastern border of Italy. Although Theodosius' advance guard, composed almost entirely of Visigoths, suffered heavy losses during an attempted breakthrough on September 5, 394, the Emperor ventured to attack the following day and was victorious. Later Christian tradition, emphasizing Theodosius' piety and trust in God, essentially interpreted the victory as a divine judgment: the god of the Christians had triumphed over the old Roman gods. After the deaths of Eugenius, Arbogast, and Nicomachus Flavianus, Theodosius showed himself lenient and strove to achieve the settlement between opposing forces necessary to strengthen imperial unity.

Probably as a result of the exertion of the campaign, Theodosius fell ill. He went to Milan, where he summoned Honorius in order to present him formally as Augustus of the West. Because Theodosius had appeared to recover, his death on January 17, 395, was generally unexpected. On his deathbed he had entrusted Stilicho, promoted to generalissimo after the victory at the Frigidus, with the care of his two sons. From Ambrose's funeral oration, filled with praise of the Christian ruler, it is evident that contemporaries had no doubt as to the continuing unity of the empire, for the question of succession seemed to have been settled in the best possible way. Yet, all too soon it was to become apparent that Theodosius had not chosen his advisers with sufficient care and that the men who were guiding the sickly Arcadius were unwilling to cooperate with Stilicho, who remained loyal to the dynasty. After his death, Theodosius' body was borne in state to Constantinople and interred in the mausoleum erected by Constantius II.

BIBLIOGRAPHY. A brief modern biography is A. LIPPOLD, *Theodosius der Grosse und seine Zeit* (1968). Still useful is A. GUELDENPENNING and J. IFLAND, *Der Kaiser Theodosius der Grosse* (1878). W. ENSSLIN, *Die Religionspolitik des Kaisers Theodosius d. Gr.* (1953), is fundamental for Theodosius' religious policy; it can be supplemented by N.Q. KING, *The Emperor Theodosius and the Establishment of Christianity* (1961). The Emperor's Gothic policy, especially in the light of contemporary sources, is discussed by M. PAVAN in *La politica Gotica di Teodosio nella pubblicistica del suo tempo* (1964). Useful information may also be found in J.B. BURY, *History of the Later Roman Empire*, new ed., vol. 1 (1923); and A.H.M. JONES, *The Later Roman Empire, 284–602*, 2 vol. (1964).

(A.Lip.)

War against Maximus

War against Eugenius

Significance of Theodosius' penance

Theology

Theology, meaning literally the study of God, is a discipline of religious thought that is restricted in its narrower sense, because of origination and format, to Christianity, but in its broader sense, because of its themes, to other religions. The themes of theology are God, man, the world, salvation, and eschatology (or the study of last times).

Nature of theology. The concept of theology that is applicable as a science in all religions and that is therefore neutral is difficult to distill and determine. The problem lies in the fact that theology as a concept had its origins in the tradition of the Greeks but that it obtained its content and method only within Christianity. Thus, theology, because of its peculiarly Christian profile, is not readily transferable in its narrow sense to any other religion. In its broader thematic concerns, theology as a subject matter is germane to other religions.

The Greek philosopher Plato (c. 428–348/347 BC), with whom the concept emerges for the first time, associated with the term theology a polemical intention—as did his pupil Aristotle. For Plato theology described the mythical, which he allowed may have a temporary pedagogical significance that is beneficial to the state but is to be cleansed from all offensive and abstruse elements with the help of political legislation. This identification of theology and mythology also remained customary in the later Greek thought. In distinction to philosophers, "theologians" (as, for example, the poets of myth—e.g., the 8th-century-BC Greeks Hesiod and Homer—or the cultic servants of the oracle at Delphi [Greece] and the rhetors of the Roman cult of emperor worship) testified to and proclaimed that which they viewed as divine. Theology thus became significant as the means of proclaiming the gods, of confessing to them, and of teaching and "preaching" this confession. In this practice of "theology" by the Greeks lies the prefiguration of what later would be known as theology in the history of Christianity. In spite of all the contradictions and nuances that were to emerge in the understanding of this concept in various Christian confessions and schools of thought, a formal criterion remains constant: theology is the attempt of adherents of a faith to represent their statements of belief consistently, to explicate them out of the basis (or fundamentals) of their faith, and to assign to such statements their specific place within the context of all other worldly relations (e.g., nature and history) and spiritual processes (e.g., reason and logic).

Here, then, the above indicated difficulty becomes apparent. In the first place, theology is a spiritual or religious attempt of "believers" to explicate their faith. In this sense it is not neutral and is not attempted from the perspective of removed observation—in distinction to a general history of religions. The implication derived from the religious approach is that it does not provide a formal and indifferent scheme devoid of presuppositions within which all religions could be subsumed. In the second place, theology is influenced by its origins in the Greek and Christian traditions, with the implication that the transmutation of this concept to other religions is endangered by the very circumstances of origination. If one attempts, nevertheless, such a transmutation—and if one then speaks of a theology of primitive religions and of a theology of Buddhism—one must be aware of the fact that the concept "theology," which is uncustomary and also inadequate in those spheres, is applicable only to a very limited extent and in a very modified form. This is because some Eastern religions have atheistic qualities and provide no access to the *theos* ("god") of theology. If one nonetheless speaks of theology in religions other than Christianity or Greek religion, he implies—in formal analogy to what has been observed above—the way in which representatives of other religions understand themselves.

Relationship of theology to the history of religions and philosophy. *Relationship to the history of religions.* If theology explicates the way in which the believer understands his faith—or, if faith is not a dominating quality, the way in which a religion's practitioners understand their religion—this implies that it claims to be normative, even if the claim does not, as in Hinduism and Buddhism, culminate in the pretention to be absolutely authoritative. The normative element in these religions arises simply out of the authority of a divine teacher, or a revelation (e.g., a vision or auditory revelation), or of any other kind of spiritual encounter over against which one feels committed. The newly evolving discipline of the history of religions, which encompasses also religious psychology, religious sociology, and religious phenomenology as well as philosophy of religion, has emancipated itself from the normative aspect in favour of a purely empirical analysis. This empirical aspect, which corresponds to the modern conception of science, can be applied only if it functions on the basis of objectifiable (empirically verifiable) entities. Revelation of the kind of event that would have to be characterized as transcendent, however, can never be understood as such an objectifiable entity. Only those forms of religious life that are positive and arise out of experience can be objectified. Wherever such forms are given, the religious man is taken as the source of the religious phenomena that is to be interpreted. Understood in this manner, the history of religions represents a necessary step in the process of secularization. Nevertheless, it cannot be said that theology and the history of religions only contradict one another. The "theologies"—for want of a better term—of the various religions are concerned with religious phenomena, and the adherents of the religions of the more advanced cultures are themselves constrained—especially at a time of increasing cultural interdependency—to take cognizance of and to interpret theologically the fact that besides their own religion there are many others. In this regard, then, there are not only analytical but also theological statements concerning religious phenomena, particularly in regard to the manner in which such statements are encountered in specific primitive or high religions. Thus, the objects of the history of religions and those of theology cannot be clearly separated. They are merely approached with different categories and criteria. If the history of religions does not surrender its neutrality, since such a surrender would thereby reduce the discipline to anthropology in an ideological sense (e.g., religion understood as mere projection of the psyche or of societal conditions), theology will recognize the history of religions as a science providing valuable material and as one of the sciences in the universe of sciences.

Relationship to philosophy. The relationship of theology to philosophy is much more difficult to determine, because it is much more complicated. The problems can here only be mentioned. If one does not adhere to the narrow concept of philosophy that reduces it positivistically to logic or epistemology (theory of knowledge) but rather understands philosophy as the discipline that attempts to explicate the totality of being, the difference between this latter interpretation of philosophy in relation to theology becomes apparent. If theology is responsible to an authority that initiates its thinking, speaking, and witnessing—e.g., a document containing revealed truth, as well as the spiritual testimony related to it—philosophy bases its arguments on the ground of timeless evidence, an evidence with which autonomous reason understands itself to be confronted. Since, on the other hand, theology also uses reason and systematically develops its tenets—however much its critical reflections are based on religious convictions—there are many common areas that have partly complementary significance but that partly also lead to polemical tensions.

The significance of theology. *The religious significance of theology.* Just as in the case of religions themselves, so also their theological reflections are not limited to a special religious sphere, separated from common life. Whoever speaks of God and the gods speaks at the same time of man and of the meaning of existence. He makes therewith statements about the world, its conditions of being created, its estrangement from the purpose of creation (e.g., sin), and its determined goal (eschatology or view of the last times). Out of these state-

(marginal notes)

The terminological problem

Limitations

Contributions of the history of religions to theology

The scope of theological reflections

ments result normative directives for life in the world, not only for the purpose of gaining access to salvation but also for concrete ethical behaviour in the context of the I-Thou (or person to person) relationship, of the clan, of the nation, and of society. In ancient times, all aspects of life (*e.g.*, relationship between the sexes, hygiene, work, and other aspects) were determined religiously and permeated by cultic forms and practices. In this regard, every religion contains the totality of being that its "theology" intends to express—if one also includes certain rudiments of reflection in primitive religion in the concept "theology."

In primitive religions the tribe represents the pivot around which all world relations turn. The primeval (or mythical) time to which the tribe traces its own origins is also the time of salvation and fulfillment. Therefore, primitive religions primarily concern themselves with the ancestral cult. Involved in tribal concerns in the realm of religious thought are conceptions of *mana* (spiritual power, or force); *i.e.*, the teaching that tribal heads, medical men, and sorcerers are subjects of special charisma (spiritual power or influence) and more potent powers of life. In Eastern religions, as in Western religions, this understanding is infinitely refined, developed, and theologically reflected. In regard to the relationship of man to the world, many Eastern religions (especially Hinduism) have a definite skeptically tinged negative view of all reality, which is especially pronounced in contrast to the Christian doctrine of creation. Though this doctrine points to a "happy event" in Christianity, the call to life and reality is understood in Eastern thought in the opposite manner:

> To be man implies being cut off from all true reality. Creation should have never happened, and its faults should be eliminated as soon as possible . . . The illusion that I am is a calamity. Not death is to be explained, but rather birth. (Stephen Neill).

The cultural importance of theology. Since theology does not remain restricted to transcendent statements and to an esoteric and sacred realm, and since it rather encompasses all worldly dimensions (cosmology, anthropology, historiology, and other areas), it has always had important significance for cultural evolution and general intellectual life. Western historians hardly need to be reminded of the fact that the Old Testament prophetic theology of history (*e.g.*, the 8th-century-BC Hebrew prophets Amos and Isaiah) has decisively influenced the origins of the concept "history" and, indeeed, has made this concept possible in the first place. On Old Testament theology of history is based the understanding of history as a linear process, as directed to a goal (*i.e.*, the Kingdom of God) and qualified by the characteristic of singularity. This view of history contrasts with a cyclical understanding of successive events; *i.e.*, the view that history repeats itself. The fact that university and school were originally initiated by the church (as is still very often the case in mission fields) is based on the fact that theology has thematized in its various subjects the various dimensions of life (nature, history, ethics, and other disciplinary areas). Also, much of modern philosophy has emerged out of theological themes and categories—in such modern thinkers as the existential philosophers Martin Heidegger and Jean-Paul Sartre and even in the Communist thinker Karl Marx remnants of this fact are still observable. Modern philosophy has, by and large, only gradually emancipated itself from this theological origin, but this emancipation also took place in a manner that retained the dialectical relationship of theology and philosophy. That theological questions in the modern age of secularism are less openly posed than in the time of the Middle Ages does not reduce their lasting significance. They always re-emerge, often in disguised form, such as in the quest for the meaning of life and existence or in the nihilistic resignation over against that quest; furthermore, they re-emerge in the quest for the dignity of human existence, for the inviolability of life, the determination of human rights, and many other such questions. A theologian such as the German-American thinker Paul Tillich (1886–1965) has investigated specifically the secular

(margin left:) Man and the world

(margin left:) The emergence of theological questions in a secular age

realm in view of the relevance of these latent theological questions that are posed by modern man in his relationship to a constantly changing world.

Theological themes. The themes discussed by theology are of universal dimensions. They encompass the doctrine of God, of man, and of the world. Even when no "doctrine of God" exists in the strict sense of the term, as in the case of what are sometimes called "atheistic" religions (*e.g.*, certain areas of Hinduism and Buddhism), man and the world are understood in the context of finality and therefore have religious aspects. The inclusion of the world in theological discussion also implies that behaviour in the world—that is, ethics—is included in theology; in some areas (*e.g.*, Confucianism) it gains a dominating position. Ethical conceptions—derived from theological concepts in the broad meaning of theology—are developed in contradictory forms: they can lead to ascetic world denial but also to a definite world affirmation. The first form is realized in Buddhism and Hinduism, the second in Confucianism. In Christianity both forms are represented. The theological theme of the relation of man and the world has been described by the 17th-century French scientist and thinker Blaise Pascal as the doctrine of the "dignity and poverty of man"—*i.e.*, the doctrine of creation and fall—and, related to this, the proclamation of salvation and the presentation of a path to salvation. This path leads, in the various religions, into greatly diverging directions. It can be placed under the exclusive direction of divine grace (as in Amida Buddhism and in Protestant Christianity); it can be left to the activity and initiative of man (as in Confucianism), or it can be characterized by a combination of both (as in Zen Buddhism and in the Roman Catholic combination of grace and merit). Finally, theology also includes among its various themes statements concerning the process and goal of history (eschatology), especially concerning the relation of secular history and history of salvation.

Functions of theology. The vastness of theological interests and aspects implies that theology can master the material with which it is confronted only within a broad spectrum of partial disciplines. Since theology is based on authority (revelation), and since this authority is documented in the Holy Scriptures (especially in Christianity), it is constrained to engage in philological and historical studies of these sources and, related to these studies, also with hermeneutical (critical interpretive) questions. This historical task broadens into a concern with the history and tradition of the religion that a particular theology represents. In this concern many difficult and controversial questions arise: whether and to what extent the canon (scriptural standard) of the sources of revelation is glossed over and modified by tradition and what normative value the modifying tradition has or should have. These problems play an important part in the relationship between Protestantism and Catholicism, even though the problems are also treated independently by each confession.

(margin right:) Controversial questions in theology

The question of truth posed by theology requires the constitution of a discipline that specifically concerns itself with fundamental questions (systematic theology). Its task can be determined in the following manner: (1) It has to develop the totality of religious teachings (dogmatics, or the doctrine of faith). (2) It has to interpret man's existence in the world and, related to this, to determine the norms (ethics derived from faith) for action in the world—*e.g.*, for the disposition toward one's fellow man and toward societal and political structures and institutions. (3) It further has to represent its claim to truth in the context of confrontation with other claims to truth and with other criteria of verification (apologetics, polemics). As part of this concern, theology's task is to explain reasonably, in view of historical relativism, the absolute claim of the truth that it represents. Related to this is the modern-day task of coordinating its doctrine of creation or its doctrine of the revelation of the transcendent (*e.g.*, the Christ event in Christianity) with the world view of modern natural science and its thesis of the immanency of being—*i.e.*, of being that is self-contained. Another aspect of this task is the confrontation with other religions' claim to truth, which can lead to vastly different results: either—this is noted only as an example—it can lead to the thesis of the complementary positions of individual religions and therefore to tolerance (as for example in Hinduism as well as in some schools in the West) or to one's own religion's claim to be absolute (as in Christianity, at least among the most important of its representatives). But also, in the last mentioned situation, such a claim is widely modified. It can manifest itself by a total rejection of other religions as "devil's work," but it can also understand other religions as first steps to and as seeds of a religious development, the completion of which it knows itself to be.

The vast dimension of theological themes implies that theology is, with its many disciplines, a microcosmic image of the university. Even though it is a science in which the believer or the adherents of a religion explicate and critically analyze the truth that is represented by them, it nevertheless has to remain free within the framework of this commitment, and it has to fulfil the responsibility of its scientific task on the basis of its own autonomy. The opposite of this freedom would arise when an institution (*e.g.*, the church) restricts this freedom with normative claims, forcing it therewith to assume ideological functions. The struggle concerning the freedom and limitations of theology—*i.e.*, concerning responsible criticism and authority—is a struggle that has accompanied the history of theology from the very beginnings to the present.

BIBLIOGRAPHY. FRIEDRICH SCHLEIERMACHER, *Schleiermachers kurze Darstellung des theologischen Studiums*, 2nd ed. (1830; Eng. trans., *Brief Outline on the Study of Theology*, 1850 and later), is still the best picture of theology as a whole and all its parts. KARL RAHNER and HERBERT VORGRIMLER, *Kleines theologisches Wörterbuch* (1961; Eng. trans., *Theological Dictionary*, 1965); and JOHN MACQUARRIE, *Twentieth-Century Religious Thought* (1963), together cover a vast range of topics and themes of theology, past and present. GERHARD VON RAD, *Theologie des Alten Testaments*, 2 vol. (1957–60; Eng. trans., *Old Testament Theology*, 2 vol., 1962–65); and RUDOLF BULTMANN, *Theologie des Neuen Testaments*, 2 vol. (1948–53; Eng. trans., *Theology of the New Testament*, 2 vol., 1952–55; 1-volume edition, 1965), are the most important texts dealing with Holy Scripture in modern times. MIRCEA ELIADE, *Le Mythe de l'éternel retour* (1949; Eng. trans., *Cosmos and History*, 1959); and OSCAR CULLMANN, *Christus und die Zeit*, 3rd rev. ed. (1962; Eng. trans., *Christ and Time*, 3rd rev. ed., 1962), deal with Christianity as a historical religion in contrast to non-historical interpretations of religion. ADOLF VON HARNACK, *Lehrbuch der Dogmengeschichte*, 3rd ed., 3 vol., 1893; Eng. trans., *History of Dogma*, 7 vol., 1900, reprinted 1961), is the classic study of the history of Christian theology in relation to Greek thought. The new disciplines of religious study, namely, the history and the phenomenology of religions, are introduced and illustrated by RUDOLF OTTO, *Das Heilige*, 9th ed. (1922; Eng. trans., *The Idea of the Holy*, 2nd ed., 1957); and *The History of Religions: Essays in Methodology*, ed. by MIRCEA ELIADE and JOSEPH KITAGAWA (1959). Modern theology, from the 18th century to the present, is treated in contrasting new ways by KARL BARTH, *Protestant Thought from Rousseau to Ritschl* (Eng. trans. 1959) and *Church Dogmatics*, 4 vol. (Eng. trans. 1936–61); and PAUL TILLICH, *Perspectives on 19th and 20th Century Protestant Theology* (1967) and *Systematic Theology*, 3 vol. (1951–63), are exhaustive treatments of the most fully developed theologies in Catholic and Protestant churches.

(H.Th.)

Theosophy

Theosophy is a religious philosophy with definite mystical concerns that can be traced to the ancient world but is of catalytic significance in religious thought in the 19th and 20th centuries. The term theosophy is derived from the Greek *theos*, "god," and *sophia*, "wisdom" and is usually translated as "divine wisdom." The literal translation of the term, however, indicates its meaning only in a general sense. Confusion may be avoided by a recognition of two usages of the word. In modern times it has been widely identified with the doctrines promoted by the Russian-born religious mystic Mme Helena Petrovna Blavatsky (1831–91) through the Theosophical Society,

founded by her and others in 1875. The term may also be employed in a more general sense to refer to a certain strain of mystical thought to be found in such thinkers as the Greek philosophers Pythagoras (6th century BC) and Plato (5th–4th century BC); the Gnostic teachers (adherents of a dualistic religious-philosophical movement) Simon Magus (1st century AD) and Valentinus (2nd century AD); the Neoplatonist philosophers Plotinus (3rd century AD) and Proclus (5th century AD); the medieval north European mystics Meister Eckehart (*c.* 1260–*c.* 1328) and Nicholas of Cusa (1401–64); the Renaissance speculative mystics Paracelsus (*c.* 1490–1541) and Giordano Bruno (1548–1600); the German philosophical mystic Jakob Böhme (1575–1624); and the German Romantic philosopher Friedrich Schelling (1775–1854). The wide variety of viewpoints represented suggests the looseness of such a usage. Modern theosophists follow Mme Blavatsky in claiming to have revived this ancient mystical tradition in the modern era.

Nature and significance. Despite its diversity, theosophical speculation reveals certain common characteristics. The first of these is an emphasis on mystical experience. Whether ancient or modern, theosophical writers have agreed that a deeper spiritual reality exists and that man may establish direct contact with that reality through intuition, meditation, revelation, or some other state transcending man's normal consciousness. A second emphasis is that of esoteric doctrine. A distinction between an inner, or esoteric, teaching and an outer, or exoteric, teaching is commonly accepted, and much attention is devoted to deciphering the hidden meaning concealed in sacred texts. Modern theosophists claim that all the historic world religions, including Christianity, contain such an inner teaching. A third interest is that in occult phenomena. Most theosophical speculation reveals a fascination with supernatural or other extraordinary occurrences and with the achievement of higher psychic and spiritual powers. It is held that knowledge of the divine wisdom gives access to the mysteries of nature and man's deeper being. A fourth characteristic is that of a preference for monism—the view that reality is constituted of one principle, such as mind or spirit. Despite a recognition of basic distinctions between the exoteric and esoteric, between the phenomenal world and a higher spiritual reality, and between man and the divine, which suggests dualism, most theosophically inclined writers have affirmed an underlying, all-encompassing unity that subsumes all differentiation. Finally, theosophical speculation shows an affinity for religious and philosophical conceptions identified with Asian thought. The striking similarities between certain theosophical and Oriental doctrines have led to vigorous scholarly debate, particularly with regard to ancient and medieval thinkers. Though some scholars have attributed these similarities to the diffusion of Eastern conceptions westward, most now argue for a parallel but independent development. There is, however, no question about the validity of the claim of direct Asian influence upon modern theosophical thought, since Mme Blavatsky lived in India for a number of years and often expressed admiration for Oriental doctrines.

History, beliefs, and practices. *Theosophical speculation before 1875.* The beginnings of theosophical speculation may be traced back at least to Pythagoras in the 6th century BC. He founded a religious brotherhood at Croton in southern Italy, where he taught such doctrines as the transmigration of souls, the unity of all forms of life, and the importance of ascetic purification. Elements of theosophical speculation have also been traced in Plato's thought and in such early religious movements as the pre-Christian Greek philosophical-mystical movement known as Orphism and the heretical 2nd-century Christian dualistic and esoteric form of Gnosticism. The connection of theosophical speculation and Gnosticism would seem especially important since the latter had much influence on the early Christian Fathers. The Gnostics regarded the material world as intrinsically evil and believed that deliverance would come only through spiritual enlightenment.

General characteristics of theosophical speculation

Classical
theosoph-
ical
speculation

Classical theosophical speculation may be said to have climaxed in the works of Plotinus in the 3rd century AD. Inspired by Plato and the teachings of the 2nd-century philosopher Ammonius Saccas (who, like many great reformers, left no writings), he developed the Neoplatonic philosophy; after the death of Plotinus, his student Porphyry gathered and published his teachings in the *Enneads* (Concerning the One). Plotinus conceived of reality as an ideal world consisting of three principles, or hypostases: the One (*to hen*), the Intellect (*nous*), and the Soul (*psychē*). The three principles formed a descending hierarchy. The One, or the Good, embodied the supreme sphere of being, beyond human comprehension, transcendent to all differentiations and forms, and yet the source of all. Man was viewed as potentially divine through his participation in the One; he might achieve mystical union with the One through contemplation and self-purification.

With the increasing ascendancy of an antimystical orthodox Christian viewpoint in Europe during the Middle Ages, theosophical speculation tended to decline for a time. It surfaced again in the 13th century, however, in the sermons and writings of the great German mystic Meister Eckehart. Trained in the Dominican order and always an avowed Christian, his views nevertheless reveal certain theosophic overtones. One of his major doctrines was the distinction between God conceived in personal terms and God as the ultimate reality, which he called the Godhead. Believing that all words must fail in describing God, he was driven to the use of a negative terminology, sometimes referring to the deity as "Nothing." A number of Western students have noted the remarkable parallels between this "negative theology" and the Advaita Vedānta (nondualistic) system of the 9th-century Indian philosopher Śaṅkara. Describing Brahman, the ultimate reality, the follower of Vedānta declares in almost identical words, "*neti-neti,*" "not this, not that"—*i.e.*, that it cannot be conceived or expressed in terms of finite, existing things.

The revival of classical learning during the Renaissance in Europe led to the rediscovery of the writings of Plato and Plotinus, which in turn apparently encouraged a new burst of theosophical speculation. Most notable were Nicholas of Cusa, Paracelsus, and Giordano Bruno, whose writings reflect the curious Renaissance fusion of mysticism and materialism. The result was a flowering of investigations in alchemy, magic, and occultism. In addition to Platonism (dealing with the nature of reality) and Neoplatonism (dealing with levels of reality), there was also an intense interest in the Kabbala (a widespread Jewish mystical movement) and Hermeticism (a Hellenistic mystical, occultic, astrological, and alchemical movement). Bruno went so far as to affirm that Christ had been a magus (magician) and that the Hermetic religion of the ancient Egyptians was superior to Christianity.

In the period since the Renaissance, the two most significant names are those of the shoemaker and mystic Jakob Böhme, who died in the early 17th century, and the 19th-century German Romantic philosopher Friedrich Schelling. Drawing upon intense personal mystical experiences, Böhme developed a conception of God as the *Ungrund*, the primal ground of being, and a dialectical conception of reality as the interplay of opposites. "In yes and no all things subsist," he declared. Though his voluminous writings seem to suggest acquaintance with Plotinus and Meister Eckehart, he apparently came to these views largely on his own. Significantly, he entitled one of his works, *Six Theosophic Points*; the term theosophic is applied to his views more often than to those of any other Western mystic. A more systematic thinker than Böhme, Schelling recast much of the theosophic viewpoint within an idealistic and Romantic framework. At the same time he reaffirmed the mystical premise of all theosophical speculation—*i.e.*, that God must be experienced, must be known directly to be known at all.

The
relation-
ship of
opposites

It should be noted that theosophical speculation has not been confined to Western thought. Indeed, the richest and most profound source of such views has been Indian thought, where it may be traced from the earliest Vedas

(Hindu scriptures involving nature mysticism) through the *Upaniṣad* (philosophical-speculative scriptures) and the *Bhagavadgītā* ("The Lord's Song") to modern times. Where the theosophic current has been but one among many currents in the West, it has been the mainstream of Indian thought. Elements of theosophy may also be found in the other Asian religions, especially in Islāmic Ṣūfism, Buddhism, and Taoism.

The Theosophical Society. Since 1875, theosophy has been largely identified with the Theosophical Society founded in that year in New York City by Helena Petrovna Blavatsky and Henry Steel Olcott. A woman of noble Russian descent, Mme Blavatsky had immigrated to the United States in 1873 after many years of travel and occultist investigations throughout Europe and the Middle East. Olcott (1832–1907), an American lawyer, newspaperman, and student of spiritualism, soon fell under her sway. The two moved to India in 1878, eventually establishing their base of operations at Adyar, near Madras, which still serves as the international headquarters for the Theosophical Society today. During the later 19th century, branch societies were established throughout much of India and in the major cities of Europe. Mme Blavatsky, meanwhile, authored a series of often obscure works that have since been accepted as classic expositions of theosophical doctrine; best known are her two-volume *Isis Unveiled*, published in 1877, and *The Secret Doctrine*, also in two volumes, published in 1888.

The Theosophical Society affirms the following objectives: (1) to form a nucleus of the universal brotherhood of humanity, without distinction of race, creed, sex, caste, or colour; (2) to encourage the study of comparative religion, philosophy, and science; and (3) to investigate unexplained laws of nature and the powers latent in man. The society insists that it is not offering a new system of thought but merely underscoring certain universal concepts of God, nature, and man that have been known to wise men in all ages and that may be found in the teachings of all the great religions. One of the society's most controversial claims concerns the existence of a brotherhood of Great Masters or Adepts, who, it is asserted, have perfected themselves and are directing the spiritual evolution of humanity.

According to Mme Blavatsky, a theosophist accepts three fundamental principles:

1. An Omnipresent, Eternal, Boundless, and Immutable Principle on which all speculation is impossible, since it transcends the power of human conception and could only be dwarfed by any human expression or similitude. It is beyond the range and reach of thought—in the words of *Māṇḍūkya* (an *Upaniṣad*), "unthinkable and unspeakable."

2. The Eternity of the Universe *in toto* as a boundless plane; periodically "the playground of numberless Universes incessantly manifesting and disappearing," called "the manifesting stars," and the "sparks of Eternity."

3. The fundamental identity of all Souls with the Universal Over-Soul, the latter being itself an aspect of the Unknown Root; and the obligatory pilgrimage for every soul—a spark of the former—through the Cycle of Incarnation (or "Necessity") in accordance with cyclic and karmic (causal) law, during the whole term (from *The Secret Doctrine*).

The
fundamen-
tal
principles
of the
Theosoph-
ical Society

In addition to these principles, most modern theosophists subscribe to a rather elaborate cosmogony (theory of the origin of the universe). There are, it is believed, seven worlds or planes through which the universe evolves. In ascending order these are the physical plane; the emotional, or astral, plane; the mental plane; the intuitional, or Buddhic, plane; the spiritual, or Atmic, plane; the monadic, or Anupadaka, plane; and the divine, or Adi, plane. As a phase of this evolutionary process, it is held that man undergoes the same septenary (sevenfold) progression, eventually reaching perfection. Reincarnation and karma (the law of cause and effect) govern the evolution. Man must expect to undergo a series of rebirths or reincarnations in the course of his spiritual ascent since the law of evolution is determined by karma. Each action, desire, or thought produces a result. This is not, it is insisted, a fatalistic viewpoint; each man is free to choose his own course. One's future life, however, will be determined by the actions in the present life. The result is that "As a man soweth, so shall he also reap."

Despite its beginnings in America, the Theosophical Society almost expired in the United States in the years following Mme Blavatsky's and Olcott's removal to India. During the 1880s and 1890s it was revived by William Q. Judge (1851–96), an Irish-born American mystic, who succeeded in making the American section the most active unit in the international movement. The American wing, however, was to be repeatedly disrupted by schisms in later years. Following Mme Blavatsky's death in 1891, tensions rapidly escalated between Judge and Olcott, culminating in the secession of the American movement from Indian control in 1895. After Judge's death in 1896, Katherine Tingley (1847–1929) succeeded to the headship of the American section; at her instigation the American headquarters was transferred to Point Loma in California and the focus of the movement's work recast along more practical lines. In 1950–51 the headquarters was moved to Pasadena, California. A new schism developed, with still a third group claiming to represent theosophy in America. Such sectarianism has declined in recent years.

Though Judge came to dominate the American work after 1891, Olcott maintained an uneasy control over the international movement. Upon his death in 1907, he was succeeded as president in India by the magnetic Englishwoman Annie Besant (1847–1933), whose leadership gave Indians a sense of pride in that they were exporting ideas of importance to the West. A forceful writer, her many books still provide one of the best expositions of theosophical belief. In 1911 she proclaimed Jiddu Krishnamurti, an obscure Indian youth, as the vehicle of a coming World Teacher, an act that led to much controversy. Krishnamurti subsequently renounced any claims to being a World Teacher and entered upon a career of writing and teaching. Since the 1920s he has spent much time in the United States and Europe, where his books have enjoyed considerable popularity. Though theosophical societies continue to exist, they have lost much of the vitality of their early years; the total membership of all divisions today is relatively small—e.g., the Theosophical Society in America, with headquarters in Wheaton, Illinois, numbers about 5,000.

Influence of the Theosophical Society

Conclusion. The influence of the Theosophical Society has been rather significant, however, despite its small following. The movement has been a catalytic force in the 20th-century Asian revival of Buddhism and Hinduism and a pioneering agency in the promotion of greater Western acquaintance with Eastern thought. In the United States it has influenced a whole series of religious movements, including the Mighty I Am movement, Rosicrucianism, the Liberal Catholic Church, Psychiana, Unity, and sections of the New Thought movement. In the estimation of some scholars, no other single organization has done more to popularize Asian religious and philosophical ideas in the West than the Theosophical Society (see also NEW THOUGHT).

BIBLIOGRAPHY. Two classic works on Western mysticism that include much material relevant to an understanding of theosophical speculation are: EVELYN UNDERHILL, *Mysticism* (1911), and WILLIAM RALPH INGE, *Christian Mysticism* (1899). More recent studies include: RUDOLF OTTO, *Mysticism, East and West* (1932); SARVEPALLI RADHAKRISHNAN, *Eastern Religions and Western Thought* (1939); and R.C. ZAEHNER, *Mysticism, Sacred and Profane* (1957). For the Theosophical Society, see the old but still valuable account in J.N. FARQUHAR, *Modern Religious Movements in India*, pp. 209–291 (1915); for a recent full-scale history, see *The Theosophical Movement, 1875–1950* (1951). GERTRUDE WILLIAMS, *Priestess of the Occult: Madame Blavatsky* (1946), provides a modern critical biography of the central figure in the movement. For an exposition of the doctrines of the Theosophical Society, see MADAME BLAVATSKY, *The Secret Doctrine* (1888), and *The Key to Theosophy* (1889); ANNIE BESANT, *The Ancient Wisdom* (1897); and C.W. LEADBEATER, *An Outline of Theosophy* (1902). C.W. BRADEN, *These Also Believe* (1949), gives an excellent brief summary of the teachings. ALDOUS HUXLEY, *The Perennial Philosophy* (1946), provides evidence that theosophical thought remains very much alive in the 20th century.

(C.T.J.)

Therapeutics

Therapeutics, as the treatment and care of a patient for the purpose of combatting disease or injury, is concerned with the total management of the patient, including the supervision of diet and fluid intake; the employment of symptomatic and supportive measures to relieve pain and ease discomfort; the administration of drugs, vaccines, and antitoxins; the surgical repair or removal of diseased parts; the supply of artificial or natural tissues and organs; the use of drugs or irradiation; the application of physical agents such as heat and remedial exercises; nursing care; psychiatric treatment; the provision of activity for the development of muscle strength and motor skills; and the application of human sympathy and understanding, as well as the deployment of social services to cope with the social consequences and hardships with which disease is so frequently associated.

Classification by body systems and structures. Textbooks of therapeutics are segregated into those dealing with medical and those with surgical treatment. They deal with the various aspects of treatment primarily according to the body systems and structures. Thus, in books of medical treatment, besides chapters dealing with principles of treatment, antimicrobial therapy, corticosteroid therapy, and infectious diseases and immunization, there are chapters on diseases of the blood, diseases of the reticuloendothelial system, and leukemia; bleeding disorders and thrombosis; diseases of the heart and circulation; diseases of the alimentary tract; renal (kidney) diseases and disturbance of acid–base balance; metabolic and nutritional diseases; diseases of the nervous system; psychiatric diseases; diseases of the endocrine (ductless) glands; disorders of connective tissue, muscles, and joints; respiratory diseases; diseases of the skin; diseases of the eye; tropical diseases and infestations; venereal diseases; diseases of children; and domestic and industrial poisoning. Textbooks of medical therapeutics include advice on the prevention and management of diseases induced by drugs. Surgical treatment is generally considered in separate textbooks, and radiation therapy is generally included as a part of surgical treatment in textbooks.

Types of therapeutics

Classification by techniques. Therapeutics can also be considered under the various techniques and materials used, such as drugs, irradiation, surgery, physical therapy, occupational therapy, psychiatric treatment, and social therapy. This is the pattern that will be followed for the most part in this review. The most important and potent part of medical treatment is drug therapy, or clinical pharmacology.

Pharmacology embraces the physical and chemical properties, biochemical and physiological effects, mode of action, absorption, distribution, and excretion of drugs, and their therapeutic uses. The physician is interested not only in drugs that are useful in the prevention, diagnosis, and treatment of human disease—that is, in pharmacotherapeutics—but he is naturally also concerned with the biochemical and physiological effects of drugs and their mechanism of action and interaction—that is, pharmacodynamics.

The science of therapeutics. Medicine began with the Greeks, and the Greek physician Hippocrates (400 BC) is generally considered to have been the "father of medicine." Until as late as the latter part of the 19th century, therapeutics was entirely empirical and largely directed toward the relief of symptoms. At this time advances in experimental pathology and pharmacology began to establish therapeutics on a rational basis. Nevertheless, authority, tradition, and prejudice prevented the correct assessment of the value of many specific forms of therapy until the advent of the controlled clinical trial near the midpoint of the 20th century. In setting up such trials, researchers face the fact that two factors tend to prejudice the correct assessment of any form of treatment. The

Controlled clinical trial

first is the psychological effect on a patient of taking drugs, and the second is the observer error of the physician. The simple act of taking medicine may seem to be sufficient to improve the health of many persons, and the beneficial effects of treatment are likely to be more marked in persons with favourable attitudes toward doctors and medicine in general than in those who are skeptical. This is why in any clinical trial it is important that so-called dummy tablets with no pharmacological effect be introduced. Such a trial is called a blind trial. Doctors, too, are capable of suggesting to themselves that pharmacological effects have arisen from a dummy tablet, and if a doctor is involved in a therapeutic trial of a drug about which he is enthusiastic he is likely to make errors in assessing symptomatic improvement in patients known to have taken the drug. It is a natural wish of every doctor that his treatment should be successful, and this may even be projected into the conversation with the patient when he attempts to convince the patient that he has improved. Ideally, therefore, the assessing doctor should be unaware of which person in the trial is receiving an active drug and which is receiving the dummy tablet. Such a trial is called a double blind trial. Such complicated therapeutic trials were not necessary to establish the value of insulin in diabetes mellitus, streptomycin in tuberculosis, or penicillin in pneumonia. The value of these drugs was immediately apparent. Therapeutic problems are usually more complex, however, and a common problem is to assess the advantages of various types of drugs over their predecessors. If methods of treatment can be assessed in comparable groups of patients in a double blind fashion, the efficacy of a drug can be scientifically established. This is now common practice in the assessment of new forms of therapy that can be compared either with the previously established form of therapy or, if there is doubt about the efficacy of the previous form of treatment, with a dummy form of treatment.

Sources of drugs
In the early part of the 20th century most drugs were either (1) vegetable drugs obtained from leaves, roots, seeds, or barks—*e.g.*, belladonna (the active principle of which is the alkaloid atropine) and foxglove (the active principle of which is the glycoside digoxin); (2) mineral salts such as ferrous sulfate, potassium bromide, sodium chloride, or calcium gluconate; (3) animal products such as insulin, thyroid extracts, and animal extracts of some pituitary hormones, such as adrenocorticotrophic hormone.

More recently it has become possible to synthesize drugs, and most drugs used today do not occur in nature but are the product of the synthetic chemist.

Mechanisms of drug action. Most drugs produce their effects by combining with enzymes, cell membranes, or other specialized functional components of cells called receptors. Interaction between drug and body cell alters the function of some cell component and causes biochemical or physiological effects. Subsequent events are called the effects of the drug. Drugs frequently have multiple effects. Digitalis, for example, affects three fundamental processes in the heart: there is an action on the contractile protein of the heart muscle fibre, an effect on the passage of electrolytes (substances that in solutions separate into positive and negative ions) through the muscle fibre membrane, and an effect on the utilization of energy by the muscle cell. Thus many drugs alter the course of disease by stimulating or depressing biochemical processes or physiological functions. Such drugs are called pharmacodynamic agents. Other drugs have effects on bacteria, viruses, or parasites without any significant effect on man: these drugs are called antimicrobial or chemotherapeutic agents.

Types of action

Routes of administration of drugs. Drugs may be given (1) by mouth, (2) by injection into muscle tissue or subcutaneously (under the skin), or (3) by injection into a vein.

Drugs are usually given by mouth, and a few are absorbed in the mouth, but most are swallowed and absorbed through the stomach or small intestine. Occasionally a drug may be given as a suppository and absorbed through the rectum.

When a drug is given by injection into muscle tissue, its absorption is more rapid and more predictable, which is an advantage when patients are unconscious or uncooperative. Strict precautions are necessary to avoid introducing infection. Drugs can be injected subcutaneously (beneath the skin) if they are not irritants, which has the advantage that the patient can give himself the injection, as many diabetics do with their insulin. Intramuscular injections are given deep into muscle tissue, and it is almost impossible to use this method on oneself.

Intravenous injections are given directly into a vein, and only aqueous solutions of drugs are given in this way, which offers the advantage of a quick effect, particularly desirable when inducing anesthesia. On the other hand, the rapid access into the circulation makes the method dangerous enough that it is reserved for emergency situations or when a rapid effect is essential.

Decisions involved in the formulation of therapeutic regimen

THE ACTIVITY STATUS TO BE ASSIGNED

Before the advent of specific forms of therapy and before techniques were available for the study of the body's responses to disease, it was generally accepted that rest was beneficial in almost all disease states. During the past third of a century this view has been questioned, and it is now believed that rest, like all other facets of therapy, should be prescribed only when its advantages can be demonstrated. The benefits of rest can be summarized as follows:

1. Rest reduces the tissue demands for nutrients including oxygen, and it reduces the formation of metabolic waste products by these tissues.
2. Rest may permit healing to occur more rapidly (as in the healing of fractured bones).
3. Rest may permit compensatory mechanisms to come into effect (as in the development of collateral circulation after obstruction of an artery or vein).
4. Rest reduces the pain that results from movement of damaged or diseased tissues.

At the same time it has been realized that there are disadvantages of immobilizing tissues or of resting the whole body. Bed rest results in defective drainage of the lungs and bladder and in reduced spontaneous bowel actions. Minerals, including calcium, are lost from bones when they are rested.

Harmful effects of bed rest
The peripheral circulation of blood in veins stagnates, and as a result clotting may occur. If a person is immobile, pressure due to the weight of the body may result in damage to the skin and, ultimately, in bed sores. Local rest of limbs may result in wasting of muscles, loss of bone minerals, loss of dexterity of movement, and stiffening of joints and may ultimately lead to permanent contractures. Pressure ulceration of dependent parts may occur, and in many cases fluid collects in dependent parts if these are not regularly moved.

The value of rest in the treatment of many internal diseases has also been examined; it has been found, for example, that recovery from some conditions of the kidney and liver is not accelerated by resting in bed. Hence prolonged bed rest is no longer considered to be an essential part of the treatment of acute inflammation of the liver or the kidney. In general the person who is unwell will require rest in bed, and in certain circumstances rest may be beneficial for those who do not feel unwell. On most occasions, however, more is apparently lost by unnecessary rest than by continued activity.

THE DIET AND FLUID INTAKE

Opinions have also altered on the value of specific dietary regimens in therapy. There are certain essentials for an adequate diet in health and disease, and these may be particularly important during illness, when deviations are more likely to occur and when their consequences may be especially severe as a result of the body's abnormal requirements for nutrients. An adequate intake of calories is necessary to provide energy requirements. The contribution of protein, fat, and carbohydrate to the total calorie content is probably of secondary importance but may lead to malnutrition if grossly abnormal. An

Diseases
benefitted
by specific
diets

adequate intake of certain essential dietary constituents must be maintained, although deficiencies can usually be tolerated for a short period. These essential substances include minerals (such as calcium and iron), salt, and the vitamins.

There are relatively few diseases in which specific diets are of proven benefit. A high content of certain dietary constituents may be required to replace abnormal losses as experienced in the protein-depletion types of intestinal and kidney disease and the salt-losing types of kidney and adrenal gland disease. On the other hand, it may be necessary to curtail certain dietary components. Thus a low intake of salt may be of great benefit in the treatment of heart failure and in some disorders of the liver and kidneys. Even normal quantities of protein may be harmful in other types of liver and kidney disease. Finally, there are a few rather unusual conditions in which an attempt must be made to eliminate a substance completely from the diet. Such substances include foods causing allergic reactions. A well-known example is shellfish, but there are less common sources of allergic reaction such as milk or gluten, the protein present in wheat and grain products. Rare and often familial inborn deficiencies of certain enzymes that are essential for the utilization of food constituents lead to accumulation of harmful substances when these foodstuffs are eaten. These conditions must be detected early in life before permanent harm is done, and treatment is usually by complete elimination of certain foods from the diet. Examples of such "inborn errors of metabolism" include phenylketonuria, in which the lack of a certain essential body enzyme leads to accumulation of injurious substances if the amino acid phenylalanine is ingested; this leads to brain damage and to permanent mental impairment. Another example is known as galactosemia, in which damage to the brain and eyes can occur if the sugar galactose is taken in the diet.

Although the proportion of the diet contributed by individual types of food is not particularly important in health, there are some conditions in which certain types of food must be restricted. The prime example is diabetes mellitus, a disease in which the body's handling of carbohydrates, and particularly of sugar, is impaired by an absolute or relative deficiency of insulin. Maintenance of a normal level of glucose in the blood is assisted by limiting the quantity of sugar and other carbohydrates taken in the diet.

Ineffective
thirst
mech-
anism

The quantity and type of fluid in the diet are usually ignored in health, since they are adequately controlled by variations in thirst. The thirst mechanism is effective in controlling the intake of fluid, and the kidneys are able to retain or excrete fluid to maintain a delicate balance between intake and body requirements. In disease, however, either the thirst mechanism or the kidney function may be abnormal. The ill person may ignore his sensation of thirst and the unconscious person may be unaware of it; very sick persons may be unable to respond to their thirst by drinking fluids. Maintenance of a sufficient intake of fluids is then an essential part of therapy. Diseased kidneys may fail to conserve fluid, and dehydration can occur in spite of a normal intake of fluid. Alternatively, the kidneys may fail to excrete fluids, in which case the intake of fluid must be restricted. Very ill persons frequently receive fluid other than by mouth, by means of transfusion or by way of a tube passed through the mouth into the stomach. In these circumstances, the intake of fluid is not controlled by the thirst mechanism, and a careful record of fluid administration and of fluid excretion is necessary to avoid underhydration or overhydration.

SYMPTOMATIC AND SUPPORTIVE MEASURES

Symptomatic and supportive measures are employed in therapy to relieve unpleasant symptoms and to maintain a person's general condition and morale during an illness. They may at times be the only therapeutic measures needed, for a great many illnesses require no specific treatment, and a majority of patients are cured without the intervention of the doctor. Relief of symptoms may result from specific therapy of the disease (such as the use of an

antibacterial drug to treat a bacterial sore throat) or may require separate measures. These may in themselves be healing (such as immobilizing a broken bone in a plaster cast), but in other cases they may be potentially detrimental to the patient. Thus powerful pain-killing drugs may be required after severe injury, although they may carry the risk of causing unwanted effects such as reducing the level of consciousness or depressing the movements of the lungs. Certain symptoms may have to be relieved even if they are not primarily a part of the disease process. Important examples are anxiety and pain. Anxiety is almost unavoidable in the case of illness. It is often relieved by explanation, encouragement, and reassurance. Drugs that act upon the nervous system to suppress anxiety are being increasingly used for this purpose, and unwanted side effects from these drugs are becoming common. When anxiety is accepted as a normal response to illness, treatment with drugs may not be required. Pain is often relieved by measures such as rest for an inflamed or injured part but may, if severe, require drug treatment. Simple pain-killing drugs (analgesics) such as aspirin are widely used to treat minor pains. More severe pain is treated with a number of powerful drugs (such as pethidine or morphine), most of which have the additional property of causing drowsiness. If pain is confined to one region of the body, it is sometimes possible to interrupt the pain-carrying fibres that travel in peripheral nerves by injecting anesthetic drugs into the nerve itself or into the relevant area of the spinal cord. The many other symptoms that may arise during the course of an illness and may require treatment cannot be listed in full, but most are amenable to therapy with simple measures. There are occasions, however, when a physician will decide that a distressing symptom may have to remain untreated because the risk entailed in treatment may be greater than is justified by the severity of the underlying condition.

Relief of
pain

Fever, a result of many diseased states, rarely requires treatment in itself, though on rare occasions, and particularly in children, the body temperature rises to a very high level and in these circumstances may cause damage, particularly to the brain. The body temperature can be reduced artificially by exposure of the body to cool air and by sponging with cold water. The normal response of the body to high fever is perspiration, however, and this in itself causes a reduction of body temperature by the heat lost when perspiration evaporates from the skin. Certain drugs, such as aspirin, have an antipyretic (antifever) effect and are often useful in viral infections for which no specific therapy is available.

Reduction of body temperature to subnormal levels (hypothermia) is a valuable aid to therapy in certain conditions. This treatment is based upon the observation that the requirements of the tissues for oxygen, and the rate at which they produce waste products, fall as the temperature is reduced. Thus tissues that are receiving a barely adequate oxygen supply or that are deficient in oxygen may survive longer at lower temperatures. The technique of induced hypothermia, for example, permits complete interruption of the blood flow to the brain during heart surgery or brain surgery for a period that would cause irreversible damage at normal temperature. The same technique has been employed to increase the time available for natural recovery after injury or loss of blood supply to the brain and to other tissues.

EMPLOYMENT OF SPECIFIC MEASURES

Although it is generally agreed that prevention is better than cure, preventive medicine is often neglected. Epidemiology is the study of disease patterns with the object of establishing the cause of disease. Once the cause of a disease is known, it may be possible to apply methods to ensure its prevention, often at relatively small cost. It is as a result of preventive methods that smallpox, cholera, poliomyelitis, diphtheria, and many other infectious diseases have largely been eliminated from Western communities. More recently, therefore, attention has focussed on preventive aspects of the noninfective diseases. Examination of cervical smears (specimens from the opening into the uterus) can detect cancer of the womb at an early and therefore potentially curable stage. Population surveys and routine examinations of population groups that are relatively accessible, such as school children, pregnant mothers, old people in homes, and industrial groups, can detect diabetes mellitus, anemia, high blood pressure (hypertension), and breast cancer at an early stage.

Programs for preventive regimens depend on the local health situation in the country concerned. In African and Indian countries the main need is to combat the infectious diseases by better sanitation, the eradication of disease carriers (such as malaria-carrying mosquitoes), better education of the people, and immunization and vaccination programs. Infections conveyed by water or food are preventable by public health measures. Effective systems of sewage disposal and the provision of pure water have eradicated cholera and typhoid in many countries. Among the diseases controllable by active immunization are smallpox, diphtheria, whooping cough, poliomyelitis, tuberculosis, tetanus, typhoid, paratyphoid, cholera, yellow fever, and rabies, and to some extent even influenza.

Correction of environmental deficiencies

Preventive measures may be primarily concerned with the environment; these include better housing, clean water supply, adequate nutrition, and fluoridation of water. Such measures may alternatively be concerned primarily with the individual and involve immunization against infectious disease or testing for presymptomatic disease, such as routine X-rays for the detection of early tuberculosis or urine testing for diabetes mellitus.

Other measures considered in specific methods for the alleviation of disease include what is known as social medicine. Much disease has a social origin and is therefore caused in part by social factors: poverty, overcrowding, and chronic fatigue are especially relevant. Furthermore, disease has social consequences, and social services are an important part of the therapeutic program. These may include the provision of meals and nursing care for those ill at home without the necessary facilities available, the care of the young children of the sick mother, and even the provision of domestic help.

MODIFICATION OF REGIMENS TO FIT THEM TO THE SICK

The principles upon which treatment of most common illnesses is based are fairly well defined. Such treatment can be described as if it were applicable to all patients with this disease, but this is rarely the case. The skills of therapeutics consist not only of administering the recognized forms of treatment but also of modifying the treatment according to the individual patient. The following factors are among those that usually influence the exact form of therapy.

1. The severity of the illness and its impact upon the individual affect decisions, for example, as to the risks that should be taken in therapy, for many forms of effective modern treatment occasionally cause complications and must inevitably carry a degree of risk. Such considerations also affect the necessity for utilizing a kind of therapy that will lead to rapid cure, possibly with greater risk, as opposed to more leisurely treatment with less risk.

2. The age of the patient influences many decisions, such as the advantages of rest or of immobilization. Bed rest is particularly likely to lead to complications in the elderly and is difficult to enforce in children unless they are extremely ill. The response to certain drugs and the risk of side effects are also related to age, not only because of variations of dosage but also because of differences in susceptibility to certain complications. The response to irradiation of tissue depends to some extent upon age, and the risks of inducing cancerous changes as the result of X-rays are usually taken more seriously in children than in the elderly. At the extremes of life, anesthesia, necessary for surgery, carries an increased risk. The reaction to hospitalization varies greatly with age. Young children have been shown to suffer considerably from the deprivation of parental care while in the hospital, and old people frequently become confused and disorientated when they leave their normal environment. Age also raises ethical problems, such as the difficult decision as to whether or not intensive treatment should be

given an elderly person who is suffering from a degenerative or ultimately fatal condition.

3. The effect of ethnic group, social class, and family background upon the outcome of the illness is usually considered. Many ethnic groups tolerate certain illnesses poorly or more poorly than others. Tuberculosis, for example, may be particularly dangerous in certain races. The social effects of absence from work during or after treatment and the effects of loss of earnings and of residual disability are also taken into account, as is the effect of the illness on the family of the patient.

4. The doctor has to consider the best place in which to carry out treatment. The majority of illnesses are satisfactorily treated while the ill person continues his day-to-day life or remains in his home with his family. When special medical or nursing care is required, a decision must be made as to whether he should be treated in a hospital or in a nursing home. This decision is made after consideration of family and personal preferences, financial implications, and the availability of adequate treatment elsewhere. The age of the patient is again important, old people and young children responding poorly to removal from their environment and their families, especially at times of illness. The decision as to the place of treatment will influence the treatment thereafter, for many forms of therapy, such as those involving transfusion or special procedures or observations, may be impractical at home.

Home and hospital care

5. The religious beliefs of patients may influence the choice of therapy, particularly in regard to such things as the attitudes of certain religions about therapeutic abortion or about blood transfusion.

6. The patient's attitude to his disease will also affect the type and place of therapy on many occasions. The apprehensive patient may feel more secure when in a hospital or may, on the other hand, have his anxieties increased by the need to enter a hospital. An excessive fear of surgical treatment may justify alternative nonsurgical forms of therapy.

7. The response to previous therapy may provide valuable guidance to the likely result of further treatment for the same or related conditions. This is of particular importance when complications or adverse effects have followed previous treatment, and unexpected or unusual response to therapy may recur if the treatment is repeated. In the case of allergies to drugs, for example, the reactions may be extremely severe if the drug is used again. Some forms of therapy carry an increased risk when carried out for a second or subsequent time. Examples are the cumulative toxicity of repeated administration of the antibiotic chloramphenicol, and risks resulting from the technical difficulties of operating for a second time on organs such as the thyroid. Such decisions are influenced to a great extent by the age of the patient.

8. Concurrent therapy is frequently a factor to be taken into account. There is an increasing awareness of the importance of interactions between different drugs in the body. Such interactions may increase, diminish, or otherwise alter the response to drugs given at the same time. Patients frequently take medicines for conditions other than that currently being investigated and treated. Important examples are the potentially dangerous interactions between some antidepressant drugs and many commonly used remedies, and the effect of barbiturate sleeping tablets upon the effectiveness of anticoagulant drugs. Previously established drug therapy must be taken into account in the choice of drugs in many illnesses.

9. Other diseases may be present. Many persons suffer from conditions other than the one under treatment, and these conditions may modify their response to subsequent forms of treatment. Examples are the preference for nonsurgical forms of treatment for patients with severe heart or lung disease, because of the risk of anesthesia and of complications in the postoperative period. Forms of treatment that require long periods of bed rest for old patients or for those with joint disease are avoided. Preexisting disease may also modify the response to drugs. Persons with diseases of the kidneys or liver commonly excrete or inactivate drugs more slowly than normal,

therefore require smaller doses for equivalent effect, and risk toxic effects if the drug is given in normal doses. Persons with chronic lung disease may develop sometimes fatal depression of their breathing when given doses of certain analgesics that have no such effect upon people with healthy lungs.

Major therapeutic techniques

SURGICAL TREATMENT

The great scope of modern surgery can only be suggested in this section. In general, surgical procedures can be categorized as follows:

Outline of surgical procedures

1. Repair of abnormalities resulting from:
  a. Congenital defects (*e.g.*, birthmarks, heart deformities)
  b. Trauma (*e.g.*, laceration of tissues, fracture of bones)
  c. Disease processes (*e.g.*, peptic ulcers, rheumatic scarring of heart valves)
  d. Degenerations (*e.g.*, hernias, prolapses)
2. Excision of abnormal tissues
  a. After trauma (*e.g.*, amputation of a severely damaged limb)
  b. After damage by disease (*e.g.*, removal of a kidney irreparably damaged by infection)
  c. Tumours, benign or malignant
3. Aspirations of collections of fluid
    Drainage of the contents of abscesses and cysts or of collections of fluid in body cavities.
4. Removal or bypass of obstructions to hollow organs
  a. Removal of an inhaled object from the lung or throat
  b. Relief of mechanical obstruction of the gut (due to tumour, torsion, or paralysis of movement of the gut)
  c. Relief of obstruction of blood vessels (by blood clot), kidneys and ureters (by stones), bladder (by enlargement of the prostate or stricture of the urethra)
  d. Relief of obstruction to the flow of cerebrospinal fluid (the various forms of hydrocephalus)
5. The supply of natural or artificial tissues and organs
  a. Natural tissues (skin grafts from other sites of the body; transplantation of kidneys or cornea or of segments of blood vessels from live or dead human donors)
  b. Artificial tissues (replacement of damaged or diseased tissues by artificial ones, such as artificial heart valves made of metal or plastic, metal or plastic artificial hip joints, synthetic grafts for blood vessels)

BIOLOGICAL THERAPY

Materials from human, animal, or plant sources have been used since the earliest days of therapeutics. During the last half-century an increasing number of therapeutic substances have been synthesized chemically, but a number of important materials are still obtainable only from biological sources.

Blood products. Human blood is used widely in therapy, either as whole blood or as one of the constituents of blood. Red blood cells, white blood cells, and platelets can be separated to some extent from whole blood and can be used for certain purposes. Plasma, which is all of the blood except its cells, is of great value in some situations because it can be stored for long periods. Some of the protein constituents of plasma have been separated from blood and used for special purposes, such as the treatment of bleeding disorders (*e.g.*, hemophilia) that result from deficiencies of these substances. Separation of blood components has the advantage that deficiencies can be remedied without the unnecessary administration of blood products that are not required by the patient. This also leads to more efficient usage of existing supplies of blood. Blood is most commonly used, however, as for transfusion to replace loss due to bleeding, and in these circumstances whole blood is usually preferred.

The products of blood serum (the blood minus its cells and coagulation factors) are used in medicine as a source of immune antibodies. Antibodies are produced by humans and animals as a response to infections. They circulate in the blood, and serum from the blood can be used to provide antibodies to prevent or counter these infec-

tions in man. Antibodies are known to reside in certain proteins of the blood (immunoglobulins), and concentrates of these proteins may be used to provide a high concentration of antibody in a small volume. Normal human serum has few applications in medicine, but serum collected from healthy people after their recovery from an infective illness may be of value in preventing or treating that illness in other people. More commonly, however, immunoglobulins concentrated from such serum are used. Immunoglobulin administered by injection is used on occasion for the prevention of certain virus diseases, including hepatitis (liver inflammation), measles, and chickenpox. Human immunoglobulin is also used in certain deficiency states in which normal immunoglobulins are reduced or absent from the blood. Persons with lower levels of immunoglobulins are unduly susceptible to infections, and this susceptibility can be overcome by administering concentrates of immunoglobulin from healthy people. Immune serum prepared in animals is used only in the treatment of tetanus and diphtheria, and its use is avoided if possible because of the risk of producing severe reactions to the foreign protein.

Immunoglobulins

Vaccines. Vaccines, produced in various ways from micro-organisms such as bacteria or viruses, are widely used in the prevention of infectious diseases. In general, vaccines consist either of (1) killed or inactivated micro-organisms (such as diphtheria, whooping cough, or influenza vaccines) or (2) living organisms that have been modified so that they can induce antibody production without producing disease (smallpox vaccination, oral poliomyelitis vaccines). In either case, the objective is to simulate a natural infection with these micro-organisms and thereby induce the formation of antibodies against them. The antibodies circulate in the blood and prevent further infection with that micro-organism or neutralize the effects of infection if this should occur.

PHARMACODYNAMIC THERAPY

Most of the drugs used in modern therapeutics can be looked upon as acting by stimulating or depressing physiological or biochemical processes within the body. The actions of drugs are often complex, and in many cases the exact mode of action is unknown. Any drug may have actions other than those desired in the context of its use.

A necessarily incomplete summary of some of the types of drug action utilized in therapeutics for diseases of different body systems follows.

The nervous system. *The brain.* Drugs that stimulate the central nervous system have relatively few uses in therapeutics. Drugs such as strychnine now have no applications in medicine but are of considerable historic interest. Stimulants are occasionally used to counter depression of the nervous system resulting from overdose of drugs. Drugs such as caffeine or amphetamine have a stimulant action upon the brain, and caffeine, for example, produces a more rapid and clearer flow of thought and allays drowsiness and fatigue. The amphetamine group of drugs has been used for this purpose in the past, but the danger of addiction limits their use.

Depression of brain activity is widely used in therapeutics. Sedatives reduce brain activity, hypnotics produce sleep, and anesthetics produce loss of consciousness. All act by inhibiting electrical activity within the brain, though the methods by which they work may vary widely. Probably the best known drugs of this type are the barbiturate drugs, which are used, in various dosage and preparations, as sedatives, hypnotics, or anesthetics.

Sedatives, hypnotics, and anesthetics

Selective or preponderant actions on certain parts of the brain or on certain types of brain activity are exerted by certain drugs.

Anticonvulsant drugs are used for the treatment or, more often, the prevention of epileptic attacks. The most widely used drugs of this type for this purpose include phenobarbital and hydantoinate drugs such as diphenylhydantoin.

Drugs are used to inhibit involuntary movements (*e.g.*, the drugs used in the treatment of Parkinson's disease). These include synthetic compounds related to atropine.

Many pain-killing drugs, analgesics, are known. These

drugs work by selectively or preponderantly inhibiting pain-receiving centres in the brain. Aspirin is an effective analgesic for minor pain, but more severe pain may require drugs with more powerful action, such as meperidine hydrochloride. The more powerful analgesic drugs, particularly those of the morphine group, produce addiction and are reserved for the treatment of severe pain. In addition to their analgesic action, they inhibit brain activity and produce drowsiness and sleep, or even coma.

In recent years many drugs have been introduced that have a specific antidepressant effect. In some cases the mode of action is known—for example, inhibition of brain enzymes by the monoamine oxidase inhibitor drugs—but in other cases the biochemical basis of antidepressant therapy remains uncertain.

A number of compounds are known to have a beneficial effect in psychotic states such as schizophrenia. The first of these compounds to be introduced, and one still widely used, is chlorpromazine, but many other compounds have been introduced since the discovery of this drug.

Peripheral nervous system. Local anesthetic drugs inhibit the conduction of impulses through peripheral nerves. They are usually used to inhibit pain sensations. The best known examples include procaine and lignocaine. These drugs are usually injected into the skin or tissues or in the vicinity of nerves that are conducting painful stimuli. Some local anesthetic drugs, such as cocaine, are effective when used locally in the eye, on mucous membranes, or on the skin.

The autonomic nervous system (visceral or vegetative nervous system) is widely distributed throughout the body and provides the innervation of the heart, blood vessels, endocrine glands, abdominal viscera, and smooth (nonvoluntary) muscles. The autonomic nervous system is composed of two divisions, the sympathetic and parasympathetic nervous systems. The sympathetic nervous system was originally so called because it coordinates bodily functions and teleologically is concerned with the responses to emergency situations in the external environment, such as the preparation for fight or flight. The mobilization of carbohydrate reserves and the increase in blood pressure and heart rate are preparatory measures. The parasympathetic nervous system, on the other hand, is concerned with bodily welfare at less stressful times and has its major influence on digestive glands.

Effector substances

Pharmacological stimulation of the autonomic nervous system is rarely used in therapeutics. The effector substances released where autonomic nerve fibres terminate on end organs have been isolated, however, and derivatives of these effector substances are widely used in medicine. These simulate the actions of the sympathetic or the parasympathetic nerves. The former type, the so-called sympathomimetic drugs, includes epinephrine and ephedrine, and parasympathomimetic drugs include acetylcholine and carbachol. Inhibition of the sympathetic nervous system is possible with a number of compounds acting in different ways. Inhibition of sympathetic activity acting on peripheral arteries forms the basis for most types of treatment for hypertension (elevated blood pressure) at the present time. Drugs have recently become available that selectively inhibit sympathetic activity on the heart, and these are of value in angina. Inhibition of parasympathetic activity is carried out with drugs of the atropine type. These drugs, among other effects, reduce the activity of the intestinal tract.

Relaxation of voluntary muscles. There are no clinically useful drugs that increase the power of muscles (except when weakness is due to the rare disease myasthenia gravis). Drugs that paralyze muscles are used to produce muscular relaxation during surgical operations. Curare is the best known drug of this type.

The cardiovascular system. *The heart*. Certain drugs influence the function of the heart in a number of different ways. Drugs that increase the power of contraction of the failing heart include drugs of the digitalis group. These are among the oldest drugs in medicine. As squill, they were used as medicines by the ancient Egyptians and by the Romans. Digitalis, derived from the foxglove plant, is mentioned in writings as early as 1250 and was intro-

duced into medical treatment in 1785. Digitalis has a number of effects on the heart; one of its most valuable actions is to increase the power of muscular contraction of the failing heart. Many preparations are available, but digoxin is the one most commonly used.

Drugs can increase the rate of heartbeat. Drugs that mimic the activity of the sympathetic nervous system or inhibit parasympathetic nervous activity will, as a result, increase the heart rate. These drugs are of value in the occasional case in which the heartbeat is unduly slow.

Drugs can slow the heart rate. Drugs of the digitalis group slow the heart rate when the speed is unduly fast as a result of certain abnormalities of heart rhythm or as a result of failure of the heart. In the absence of heart failure or an abnormal rhythm, an excessively rapid heartbeat can be slowed by inhibiting sympathetic nervous activity or by stimulating parasympathetic activity, although the latter method is rarely used in practice.

Electrical conductivity of heart

Drugs are available that reduce the rate of electrical conduction within the heart. Electrical activity spreads through the heart from the upper part (the atria) to the lower part (the ventricles). In certain conditions, abnormally rapid contraction of the atria results in an excessive pulse rate. This abnormality can be controlled either by reducing the atrial activity or by reducing the rate of conduction of impulses within the conducting system of the heart. Digitalis drugs are of particular value in the latter respect.

Drugs are available that reduce electrical excitability of the heart. Electrical impulses that lead to the contraction of the heart muscle normally arise from a focus in the atria. If the cardiac muscle is unduly excitable, abnormal focusses of electrical activity may arise elsewhere and result in an abnormal heart rhythm. This may reduce the efficiency of the heart, produce heart failure, and even cause death. Electrical excitability of the heart may be reduced by a number of drugs.

Drugs can relieve cardiac pain. Cardiac (heart) pain results from insufficient arterial blood supply to the heart muscle. It can be relieved by using powerful analgesic drugs (such as morphine), but other preparations that are not analgesic as such are available that act by increasing the blood supply to the myocardium and reducing its oxygen needs.

The arteries. The calibre of medium and small arteries throughout the body can be varied as a result of activity of the sympathetic nervous system that causes constriction of small arteries. Arteries can be further constricted by the administration of sympathomimetic drugs, and these compounds are sometimes used to counter a fall in blood pressure. Arteries can be dilated by the use of drugs that oppose sympathetic activity. These drugs find their prime use in the treatment of hypertension. The earlier drugs of this type acted to inhibit both sympathetic and parasympathetic activity, but more recently drugs such as guanethidine and methyldopa have been developed that selectively inhibit sympathetic activity. These compounds effectively lower the blood pressure.

The respiratory system. Drugs acting upon the respiratory system include drugs that affect breathing, drugs that act upon coughs, and drugs that relieve obstruction of the air passages. Drugs that increase the breathing rate have few clinical applications. Nikethamide is occasionally used as a respiratory stimulant when respiration has been depressed as a result of overdose of other drugs or as a result of disease. Morphine and its derivatives are powerful depressants of respiration, but there are very few clinical situations in which depression of respiration is required.

Coughing results from irritation of the air passages and is a valuable protective reflex. It needs to be suppressed only when it is tiring and is serving no useful function. Few drugs are known with a specific cough-suppressant activity, and most of the effective cough suppressants are derived from the analgesics. Expectorants are drugs that act to liquefy sputum and hence ease its expectoration. Dehydration, one of the commonest causes of thick sputum, can be countered without the use of drugs.

Narrowing of the air passages is a feature of many

Opening obstructed air passages

illnesses (such as asthma and bronchitis). In the case of asthma this narrowing is potentially reversible, but many persons with bronchitis—inflammation of the bronchi—have irreversible obstruction of their air passages. Obstruction is frequently the result of infection that can be countered by the use of appropriate antibiotics. Spasm of the muscle of the bronchial wall may cause obstruction, however, and this may be reversed by treatment with sympathomimetic drugs (such as adrenaline). Asthmatic persons frequently develop constriction of bronchi as a result of allergic mechanisms. This constriction can be inhibited by anti-allergic drugs, but before these drugs are used it is necessary to attempt to remove the cause of the allergy from the patient's environment.

The digestive tract. Drugs that act upon the digestive tract include drugs that affect gastric acidity, drugs that stimulate or decrease activity of the lower bowel, and drugs that reduce or prevent vomiting. Since the pancreas is partially involved in the digestive process, it, too, is included in this section.

When ulcers in the stomach and duodenum arise from excessive production of acid by the stomach, they are cured and symptoms relieved by reduction of the gastric acidity. Most antacids (e.g., sodium bicarbonate) act by chemically neutralizing gastric acid.

Cathartics, drugs used to stimulate contraction of the lower bowel and thereby produce a bowel action, are the most abused drugs in medical practice. Constipation, unless extremely severe, is rarely harmful, and the habit of taking drugs to produce a daily bowel action is usually condemned. Cathartics may act either by stimulating the lower bowel, by retaining fluids within the bowel, by increasing the bulk of the bowel contents, or by a lubricant action (as by mineral oils). The use of mineral oils (such as liquid paraffin) is potentially dangerous and has resulted in many complications.

Drugs that decrease the activity of the lower bowel are used in the treatment of diarrhea. Most of the effective drugs act by inhibiting the parasympathetic nervous system and are derived from atropine. Kaolin is an inert powder that increases the solidity of the stools in patients with diarrhea. In some cases, in which diarrhea has a specific cause (such as infection), specific treatment with antibiotic or other drugs is also required.

Vomiting is frequently a symptom of underlying disease and is not treated by nonspecific anti-emetics unless such disease has been excluded. Certain drugs have anti-emetic activity, among which are a number of antihistamine drugs and chlorpromazine and its derivatives.

Drugs that cause vomiting are rarely required in therapy but are occasionally used in an attempt to remove ingested poisons from the stomach. A strong solution of common salt is one of the most effective emetics and usually causes vomiting.

The pancreas. The pancreas has two main functions. It synthesizes and excretes enzymes for digestive processes. There are no drugs in clinical use that predictably increase or suppress this activity. The pancreas also produces insulin, essential for the metabolism of carbohydrates and lacking in many cases of diabetes mellitus. Insulin itself is used in therapy (see below *Substitution therapy*), and a number of drugs that increase the output of insulin by the pancreas are of value in treating diabetic persons who still have the potential to produce insulin from the pancreas.

Stimulation of the pancreas

The urinary tract. Drugs may affect or modify the function of the kidneys in a number of ways. Drugs that increase the flow of urine are known as diuretics and are used in treating conditions in which fluid is abnormally retained in the body. This may occur as a result of disease of the heart, the liver, or the kidneys themselves. Many available diuretics act at different sites within the kidney and can be used in combination to treat patients who have severe fluid retention. Drugs that reduce the flow of urine are of no clinical application, unless urine flow is abnormally high as a result of deficiency of pituitary antidiuretic hormone.

A number of drugs are known to alter the excretion of substances by the kidney. Among those that are of thera-

peutic value are probenecid, which not only increases the excretion of uric acid and can be used in the treatment of gout but also reduces the excretion of penicillin and is therefore used to aid penicillin therapy.

Physicians seldom prescribe drugs to cause contraction of the bladder, but when this is required parasympathomimetic drugs are used.

The blood-forming organs and the blood. No drugs are available that act by a pharmacological means to stimulate production of all formed elements of the blood. Abnormalities of the blood, and particularly of the red cells, may result from deficiency of iron, vitamin B_{12}, and folic acid, and in these circumstances replacement therapy with these compounds may correct the anemia.

Drugs that inhibit production of formed elements of the blood are used in the treatment of leukemia (excess of white cells) or polycythemia (excess of red cells).

Anticoagulants are widely used to inhibit clotting of blood in arteries and veins. The most widely used compounds act by interrupting the synthesis of substances that are essential for the clotting process.

The endocrine glands. Endocrine glands produce and secrete hormones that circulate in the bloodstream and have actions at many and distant sites in the body. Many endocrine glands, such as the thyroid, adrenal, and sex glands, are controlled by hormones released from the pituitary. Pituitary hormones available for clinical use can be used to stimulate the respective target glands. When overactivity of an endocrine gland is the result of pituitary overactivity, the pituitary gland itself is sometimes suppressed or destroyed by surgery or by radiation. Alternatively, it may involve less risk to the patient to control the activity of the target gland by direct surgical attack or by drugs. Many hormones have been isolated and in some cases synthesized; these are used in therapy to replace deficiencies.

The thyroid gland. Persons having an underactive thyroid gland are treated by administration of thyroid hormone. Overactivity of the thyroid gland may be treated with a number of antithyroid drugs that act by interfering with the chemical synthesis of thyroid hormone.

Adrenal (suprarenal) glands. The adrenal glands may be stimulated by giving the pituitary hormone (adrenocorticotropic hormone) or its synthetic equivalent. The adrenal glands produce a number of hormones, of which cortisol, the most important, is essential for life. Another hormone, aldosterone, is required to maintain a normal blood pressure. The production of cortisol can be inhibited only by suppressing the pituitary gland, but the effects of aldosterone can be counteracted by the use of the drug spironolactone. Corticosteroid drugs, which are synthetic derivatives of cortisol, have many actions in therapeutics dependent upon their anti-inflammatory effects and are also used to replace deficiencies of adrenal function.

The testes. The testicular hormone testosterone has been synthesized, for clinical use in the treatment of testicular deficiencies resulting either from damage or disease of the testes or from pituitary dysfunction.

The ovaries. Therapy with gonadotropins, hormones from the pituitary, has been effectively applied to the treatment of female infertility, since these hormones stimulate ovarian activity. It is possible to inhibit ovarian function by the use of ovarian hormones themselves, and various combinations of them are used as oral contraceptives. They act by inhibiting ovulation.

The pituitary. Several pituitary hormones are now available for therapeutic purposes. Adrenocorticotropic hormone (ACTH) stimulates the adrenal glands to produce cortisone. Growth hormone may be used to stimulate growth in children who are deficient in the natural pituitary hormone. Gonadotropins are used to treat infertility due to deficient ovulation. Vasopressin, the hormone of the posterior pituitary, is used to replace a deficiency of this hormone in the condition known as diabetes insipidus.

ACTH and growth hormone

Drugs that alter metabolic processes. Many drugs affect metabolic processes in the body. The use of insulin in the treatment of diabetes has been mentioned. Gout, which is associated with excess production of uric acid, is sometimes treated with allopurinol, a drug that interrupts the synthesis of uric acid. High levels of cholesterol in the bloodstream, which may be associated with premature arterial degeneration, are often lowered by the use of the drug clofibrate. Vitamin D, like the other vitamins, has its main application in the treatment of specific vitamin deficiencies but may be used to correct abnormally low concentrations of calcium in the blood, even though they are not caused by a deficiency of this vitamin.

Drugs that act on inflammation. Certain drugs modify or suppress the inflammatory responses of the tissues to infection or other injury, and this action is widely used in therapy. Aspirin, though primarily an analgesic, has anti-inflammatory properties that are particularly valuable in the treatment of inflammation of the joints, as in rheumatic fever and rheumatoid arthritis. Other synthetic drugs have anti-inflammatory and analgesic properties and are of value in the treatment of joint disease.

Cortisol, the hormone produced naturally by the adrenal glands, has a powerful anti-inflammatory action and in addition modifies many types of allergic response. Many synthetic preparations, known as corticosteroids, also possess these properties. The most widely used at present are prednisone, prednisolone, cortisone, and hydrocortisone. These powerful drugs are effective in a wide range of disorders. They act either by suppressing inflammation or by interfering in some way with allergic or immune processes. Corticosteroids may be taken by mouth or by injection, and they are effective when applied to the skin, eyes, or mucous membranes. Complications of prolonged corticosteroid therapy are common, and prolonged therapy is usually avoided if a safer method of treatment is available or unless corticosteroid treatment is essential for survival or maintenance of health.

CHEMOTHERAPY

Definition of chemotherapy

The term chemotherapy is applied to the use of drugs that destroy micro-organisms or parasites in or on the body of the patient or inhibit their multiplication. Antimicrobial chemotherapeutic drugs usually act by selective inhibition of biochemical processes essential to the micro-organisms. Some of the toxic effects of these drugs on man are due to inhibition of similar processes in human cells. Chemotherapy is available against many bacteria, some viruses, some fungi, and many parasites.

Antibacterial drugs. Drugs effective against bacteria have been known since the development of penicillin in the 1940s. They differ in potency, range of activity, toxicity, and cost. In general, antibiotics can be divided into those that have activity against comparatively few bacteria (narrow spectrum) and those that are active against a larger number of bacteria (broad spectrum). The broad-spectrum antibiotics may be less effective against a particular type of micro-organism than a narrow-spectrum antibiotic to which it is sensitive.

The choice of antibacterial agent involves the physician in the consideration of several factors. Recovery from many bacterial infections occurs without antibacterial therapy; recovery may not always be hastened by such therapy. In some situations antibacterial drugs have been shown to delay cure, particularly in certain infections of the intestinal tract, such as cholera, and in carriers of typhoid bacilli. The choice of an antibiotic drug depends upon the known or suspected bacterium causing the infection, its known or anticipated range of antibiotic sensitivities, the severity of the infection, and the likely outcome of the illness without chemotherapy, as well as the known side effects of the available antibacterial drugs and the frequency with which they occur.

The efficacy of many antibacterial drugs has been reduced by the emergence of bacteria resistant to the action of antibiotics to which they were once sensitive. This is believed to be the result of excessive and incorrect use of antibacterial drugs, often for conditions that required no such therapy. The development of bacterial resistance can usually be avoided if adequate doses of drugs are given for a sufficient time and by the occasional combined use of two or more drugs. Bacterial resistance,

which at one time threatened to remove the valuable weapon of antibiotic therapy from therapeutics, has now been checked by more judicious use of drugs and by the synthesis of many new antibacterial compounds. Nearly all bacterial infections may be effectively treated by one or more antibiotics; as a result primary bacterial infections now cause relatively few deaths in developed countries where these drugs are available. The length of time needed for antibiotic treatment depends upon a number of factors including the potency of the antibiotic and the ease with which it can gain access to the site of infection. Most acute infections are adequately treated by one or two weeks' antibiotic therapy; other infections, such as tuberculosis, may require prolonged treatment.

Antiviral drugs. Few antiviral drugs are available for therapeutic purposes, but it is likely that effective drugs will be developed within the next few years. It is likely that these drugs will be more effective when given before the development of symptoms and will therefore have a greater prophylactic than therapeutic value. Methisazone, recently introduced, has been shown to be highly effective in protecting persons who have come in contact with smallpox. Idoxuridine is a drug active against herpes virus (the cause of "cold sore" and other inflammations) and has been used to treat herpetic infections of the cornea of the eye. Of the large number of drugs known to be active against many viruses, most act by interfering with essential metabolic processes of viruses or of the cells that they infect. The great majority of the antiviral drugs tested have proved too toxic for clinical use, but increasing knowledge of the biochemistry of viruses and of their infections is expected to lead to the discovery of less toxic and more active agents.

Treating smallpox and herpes

Drugs active against fungus infections. Many fungi cause infections in man. Some troublesome infections of the skin are treated with the drug griseofulvin, and dangerous systemic fungus infections with amphotericin B. The fact that the importance of fungus infections in man has only recently been recognized probably accounts for the scarcity of drugs active against pathogenic fungi.

Antiparasitic agents. A large number of parasitic agents infect man, and specific therapy is available against many of these. This therapy is used in conjunction with such measures as the eradication of mosquitoes for the control of malaria and the control of animal carriers of other diseases. Drugs have therefore been used partly to kill carriers such as insects and also as prophylaxis and therapy of infection. Antimalarial drugs are used as prophylaxis when regular administration is required throughout the period of exposure or for the treatment of established malaria. Drugs are also available for the treatment of amebiasis, trypanosomiasis, and many other parasitic diseases.

SUBSTITUTION THERAPY

The replacement of substances in which the body is deficient forms an important part of therapy.

Restoration of substances lost from the body. Loss of blood occurs from bleeding, and loss of fluids from severe diarrhea or vomiting. Minerals and proteins may be lost because of kidney or bowel disease. The method of replacement usually depends on the nature of the loss. Blood, for example, cannot be given by mouth.

Deficiencies of dietary constituents. These deficiencies may occur as a result of inadequate intake in the diet, impaired absorption of substances from the intestinal tract, or excessive bodily requirements for certain dietary constituents. Inadequate intake of essential substances can sometimes be corrected by improving the diet, but often it is necessary to administer pure preparations of the deficient substance or substances. Examples are vitamin deficiencies or deficiency of iron, both of which may, on occasion, result from inadequate intake. Poor absorption of substances present in normal concentrations in the diet may result from disease of the intestinal tract or from removal of parts of the intestines by surgery. It is rarely possible to correct this type of deficiency by increasing the intake of foods rich in the deficient substances, and treatment consists of administering these

Iron deficiencies

substances in pure form. If absorption is severely disturbed, it may be necessary to give such replacements by injection. Deficiencies in calcium, potassium, iron, vitamin B_{12}, and folic acid may all occur as a result of impaired absorption from the gut. Increased requirements for certain dietary constituents may occur during pregnancy or during periods of rapid growth, and this may lead to deficiencies. Supplements of pure preparations of the deficient substance are usually used in treatment. An example is the treatment of the increased demand for iron, folic acid, and calcium during pregnancy.

Deficiencies of hormones can, in most cases, be corrected by the administration of a synthetic or semisynthetic preparation of the hormone that is lacking. Preparations are available of thyroid, adrenal, testicular and ovarian hormones, and of some of the pituitary hormones. Insulin is administered by injection for the treatment of diabetes mellitus, a condition in which the production of insulin by the pancreas is insufficient to maintain a normal level of glucose in the blood.

RADIATION THERAPY

Forms of radiation

Radiation therapy is the treatment of disease by ionizing radiation (radiation that forms positively and negatively charged particles in the substance that it encounters). X-rays, gamma rays, and corpuscular radiation such as alpha or beta rays all have the ability to produce ionization in living matter. There is no fundamental difference in these forms of radiation, whether they are produced in modern generators such as linear accelerators or whether they are emitted by radioactive elements. It is the energy of the radiation that is important, because penetration into the tissues depends on the energy. The effects of irradiation are destructive. Some cells are killed directly and in others the ability to reproduce is destroyed. Cells that are rapidly growing and reproducing are more vulnerable to irradiation than those that are less actively dividing. Hence, the most important practical applications for radiation therapy are in the treatment of cancer. The object of radiation therapy is to provide adequate and uniform irradiation of a tumour while sparing healthy tissue. This requires accurate localization of the tumour and precise distribution of the irradiation. As cancer is second only to heart disease as the most common cause of death, the uses of radiation therapy are numerous. Nevertheless, surgery remains the first line of attack in most localized cancers, and radiation therapy is generally reserved for those cases not amenable to direct surgery. Radiation therapy is also used in certain nonmalignant disorders, which include certain skin conditions, and in some rheumatic disorders; radiation from radioactive isotopes (forms that emit radiation while changing to a different element) is used for the treatment of certain cases of overactivity of the thyroid gland and in some patients with polycythemia, in which the bone marrow produces too many blood cells.

Local irradiation to an organ or tissue can be achieved by the oral or intravenous administration of certain radioactive isotopes that are concentrated in that particular organ. Iodine, for example, is almost selectively concentrated in the thyroid gland. When the radioactive form of iodine is administered (iodine-131 is commonly used), it is concentrated in the gland and emits beta particles. The particles are completely absorbed within the thyroid, causing ionization in its tissues. This destroys a proportion of the thyroid cells and, when an appropriate dose is given, can restore a hyperactive gland to normal. Radioactive iodine can also be used for certain types of thyroid cancer, though surgery and external irradiation are more appropriate in most cases. Phosphorus is concentrated in bone, for bone is the major phosphate pool in the body. When radioactive phosphorus (phosphorus-32) is given intravenously, it is concentrated in bone; the beta particles emitted irradiate the bone marrow. When an appropriate dose is given, this will control certain states of bone marrow overactivity, in which the bone marrow production of red cells is excessive. Several radioactive isotopes can be made up into needles for implantation so that the emission of radiation can be uti-

lized locally. Radium in this form has long been used for the treatment of cancer of the neck of the womb. Radioactive tantalum, because it can be bent into any shape or form, is particularly useful for implantation as wire into curved surfaces such as the bladder, for the treatment of local cancer.

PHYSICAL THERAPY

Physical agents such as heat, cold, muscular exercises, and faradic current (an unsymmetrical alternating current) to stimulate wasted muscles are of greatest use in patients with the rheumatic diseases and with certain neurological disorders, in which muscle wasting occurs after damage to its nerve supply.

Heat, which relieves pain by its action as a counterirritant, can be applied in a variety of ways—the heat lamp, electric pad, and warm baths. Generalized heat is particularly advantageous for the patient with rheumatoid arthritis with extensive joint involvement and also has the advantage of stimulating the circulation. Infrared waves, short waves, and ultrasonic waves are electromagnetic waves that penetrate the skin and warm the deeper tissues and require more sophisticated equipment and greater skill. Short waves are high-frequency alternating currents that produce heat by causing rapid oscillation of ions in the patient's tissues. Ultrasonic waves are sound waves with a very high frequency that are undetectable by the human ear. Faradism is an electric current that will stimulate motor nerves and cause tetanic contraction of muscle. It thus will stimulate wasted muscles to recover.

Uses of heat

Remedial exercises may be active or passive. Passive exercises are used to promote the mobilization of stiff or inflamed joints and to prevent deformities. Even acutely inflamed and painful joints should be put through as full a range of movements as pain permits. As soon as possible, patients with arthritis should progress to active exercises so that muscle tone is maintained. Hydrotherapy in the form of supervised exercises in a warm pool plays an important part in the modern treatment of arthritis. The warmth relaxes the muscles, and the buoyant effect of the water makes movement easier.

OCCUPATIONAL THERAPY

Occupational therapy is the treatment of physical or mental disorders by the use of occupation or recreation, with the object of promoting recovery or creating new habits and of preventing deterioration. That work helps to maintain health is generally recognized; it is also of value in disease, especially in the more chronic disorders and in psychiatric illnesses; it is particularly important in children. Doctors recognize that it is important to relieve the boredom and to stimulate the interest of the chronically ill person and to promote self-confidence in the depressed schizophrenic patient. Occupational therapy in the form of craft work and recreational activities plays a large part in the recovery of such patients.

Occupational therapy may also help to mobilize stiff joints and to increase muscle power by graduated exercises and work under supervision. Remedial occupational therapy aims to minimize the disability that may follow illness or injury and help the patient prepare himself for other useful employment if he is unable to return to his previous industry. Such treatment is particularly useful to the person who has suffered injury in an accident and also to the person with arthritis. Many of the physical measures already considered form part of this treatment, and the remainder may be summarized as rehabilitation. Unstable joints may require splinting or other support. Deformities are prevented and remedial exercises practiced to make full use of the undamaged muscle. Basketry, carpentry, pottery, and others of the less physically demanding crafts may be taught and practiced.

BIBLIOGRAPHY. C.W.H. HAVARD (ed.), *Fundamentals of Current Medical Treatment*, 3rd ed. (1970), covers the whole field of medical treatment; a selected bibliography is provided at the end of each chapter. D.R. LAURENCE, *Clinical Pharmacology*, 3rd ed. (1966), is intended for medical students, with references given at the end of each chapter. *Cecil-Loeb Textbook of Medicine*, 12th ed. by P.B. BEESON and W. MCDER-

MOTT (1967), is a medical classic not confined to therapeutics; covers the etiology, diagnosis, and treatment of disease.
(C.W.H.H./J.E.St.)

Thermionic Devices

Thermionic devices convert heat directly into electricity by means of thermionic emission—the ejection of electrons from a heated surface—rather than by changing it first to some other form of energy. Heat for the device is supplied by chemical, solar, or nuclear sources. It differs somewhat from the vacuum diode, primarily in the source of heat for the cathode.

Thermionic emission is the liberation of electrons from a hot cathode, or emitter. The emitted electrons travel through a vacuum or gas-filled space to a cool anode, or collector. Useful electrical power can be extracted by a load—a resistor or other impedance device—connected between the cathode and anode. The phenomenon was first observed in the middle of the 18th century by Charles DuFay, a French experimenter, who noted that gas near a heated solid conducts electricity. In 1853 Edmund Becquerel, a French physicist, reported that a measurable electric current could be produced by a potential of a few volts in air if the air was heated between hot platinum electrodes. Toward the end of the 19th century in Germany, Julius Elster and Hans Geitel, experimenting on a sealed device that contained two electrodes, noted that charges flowed from the heated electrode to the cooled electrode.

Thermionic emission was identified by Thomas A. Edison in 1883 when he observed that a current passed from a heated filament of an incandescent electric lamp to a conductor in the same glass bulb. Later, W.H. Preece and J.A. Fleming, two English scientists, showed that this effect was produced by electrons flowing through the vacuum from the heated cathode to the anode. J.J. Thomson, an English physicist, in 1897 recognized that electrons exist in solids and described thermionic emission as the "boiling off" of free electrons from solids into a vacuum cavity (see also ELECTRON TUBE).

Thermionic work function — Another English physicist, O.W. Richardson, in 1916 identified the thermionic work function (a measure of the energy required for an electron to free itself from the surface of the metal) and determined emission current density with the aid of kinetic theory. His theory was subsequently corrected by S. Dushman, a U.S. scientist (1930), following the discovery by Enrico Fermi of electron properties in metals (1927). The basic expression for emission current is thus called the Richardson-Dushman equation.

The development of thermionic converters was delayed until the 1950s when the impetus of space exploration promoted renewed interest. A vacuum thermionic converter and the cesium-filled thermionic converter were developed shortly after 1955.

EFFICIENCIES

A thermionic converter is a device with a heated electron emitter (cathode) electrically insulated from a cooled collector (anode), with the gap between them either a vacuum or filled with a metallic vapour. The elements are placed in a gas-tight envelope, with provisions for connecting a heat source to the cathode, a coolant to the anode, and electrical leads to a load.

Typically, the emitter operates at a temperature near 2,000° K (1,727° C), and the collector at 1,000° K (727° C).

The operation of a thermionic converter is influenced by a number of physical characteristics:

Fermi energy. The Fermi energy, or Fermi level, of a solid is the maximum energy that electrons in a solid may reach, even at absolute zero, because of the crowding of electrons.

Work function. The work function is the energy that must be imparted to an electron near the Fermi level of a solid to get the electron out of the solid into a cavity. The work function of tungsten, a typical material for emitters, is 4.52 electron volts (eV), but a collector work function of 0.6 eV has been obtained.

Ionization potential. The ionization potential is the energy that must be imparted to an atom to remove an atomic electron and move it an infinite distance away, making it a free electron. The atom is then said to be ionized.

Thermionic current density. The thermionic current density J_e of a solid is given by the Richardson-Dushman equation in the form:

$$J_e = AT^2 \exp\left(-1.6 \times 10^{-19}\, \Psi/kT\right) \text{ amperes/cm}^2$$

based on the projected area of the electrode, in which $A = 120.4$ amperes per square centimetre °K^2 for an ideal metal, for T in degrees Kelvin; Ψ is the work function in electron volts; k is the Boltzmann constant, with the numerical value 1.38×10^{-23} joule/°K. (If the temperature T is measured in degrees Kelvin, the quantity kT has the dimensions of an energy and is usually called the thermal energy.) At 300° K (room temperature), $kT/1.6 \times 10^{-19} = 0.0259$ electron volt. Among real materials, A varies: 60.2 for tungsten, molybdenum, and tantalum; 330 for zirconium; 17,000 for platinum; 1.4 for alumina; 1.1×10^{-5} for magnesia.

THE VACUUM CONVERTER

In a thermionic converter with a vacuum gap between the electrodes, the electron gas is boiled out of the heated cathode at a high temperature and passed through the vacuum to a colder anode. The electron gas is then condensed at the anode, which is cooled to maintain a lower temperature than the cathode. The electron gas then passes through the external circuit and back to the cathode side to deliver electric power.

Electrons pass through a retarding electrostatic field. The base line corresponds to the potential of the electron in the cathode or the emitter. Heat lifts some of these electrons over the work function barrier at the surface of the emitter, Ψ_E. As soon as an electron escapes the surface of the emitter, it enters into the vacuum gap with other emitted electrons, encountering a retarding potential or space charge potential because of repulsion by other electrons in the gap. Only those electrons with initially sufficient energy to pass over the peak of the potential can reach the anode side. The anode also emits at its temperature, but the net electron flow is from the cathode to the anode (or collector), whose work function is Ψ_c. The net output voltage is V, given by the difference in electric potentials produced by these work functions and after deducting the space charge potential.

To limit the space charge effect, the vacuum gap or interelectrode spacing has to be 0.001 inch (0.025 millimetre) or less. With both electrode surfaces of tungsten impregnated with oxides of barium, aluminum, and calcium, a maximum current density of three amperes per square centimetre can be obtained with a cathode temperature of 2,308° F and an anode temperature of 1,000° F. These conditions yield a maximum output of one watt per square centimetre at 0.7 volts, giving an efficiency of 12 to 13 percent. An output of 10 to 30 watts per square centimetre at 15 percent efficiency is obtainable.

Reduction of space charge effect — Because of the limitations of the vacuum converter and the difficulty in maintaining a small gap (down to 0.0004 inch [0.01 millimetre]), various methods of reducing space charge have been studied. Space charge can be reduced by suitably applied magnetic fields and auxiliary electric fields; by introducing another grid, as in the triode; and by neutralizing the space charge with metallic vapour. The last has proven to be by far the most successful.

GAS-NEUTRALIZED CONVERTERS

The most efficient thermionic converters are filled with a cesium vapour, chosen because of its low ionization potential (3.87 eV). Other metals, such as rubidium and potassium, produce similar results. Metals with a high ionization potential permit a high collector temperature and still have less back emission of electrons compared to cesium. Emitter materials of tungsten, molybdenum, tantalum, and rhenium have been tested. A collector of molybdenum is common. Heat lifts some of the thermionic electrons over the work function barrier at the surface of the emitter. As soon as an electron escapes, it is accelerated by the potential created by cesium ions just outside of the emitter (emitter sheath drop). A small portion of these electrons helps produce cesium ions, Cs^+, but the majority flows through the nearly neutral plasma (equal number of Cs^+ ions and electrons) to the collector, a slight energy loss resulting from the collision with ions and atoms of cesium. The loss is reduced by keeping the gap between the electrodes small.

Cesium vapour contributes to satisfactory performance because (1) cesium ions neutralize the space charge effect of electrons; (2) adsorbed cesium produces a low work function of the collector Ψ_c, thus providing greater output voltage; (3) adsorbed cesium in the emitter adjusts its work function to permit an optimum number of electrons to escape.

The cesium pressure is controlled by a liquid cesium reservoir in the converter system. Depending on the cesium pressure used, there may be two different designs:

1. High-pressure devices. When cesium pressure is several millimetres of mercury, the cathode is covered by cesium. A small interelectrode spacing of one mil is required to limit the loss from back scattering of electrons. A suitable cathode temperature is in the 1,500° to 1,800° C range.

2. Low-pressure devices. A low cesium pressure of 10^{-2} millimetres of mercury or lower, in conjunction with high emitter temperature of above 1,800° C, results in a cesium-free cathode. A larger interelectrode spacing (from two to ten mils) is permissible because of negligible electron scattering. In a low-pressure device with the emitter temperature lowered to 1,200° C, arcing occurs and ions are generated by impact ionization of cesium. Part of the electric energy output is dissipated in the arc (called "ball of fire").

The thermionic converter is a low-voltage, high-current device. A typical cesium vapour-filled device, with cylindrical electrodes one inch (25.4 millimetres) long and one-half inch (12.7 millimetres) in diameter, produces 0.7 volt at 70 amperes; a flat converter 1¼ inch (31.8 millimetres) in diameter, heated by focussed solar energy, produces 1.3 volts at 64 amperes. In laboratory units, 15 to 17 percent efficiency has been achieved; units with 20 percent efficiency are easily built.

DEVICES AND APPLICATIONS

The fact that a thermionic converter is a high-temperature heat engine suggests various applications: an electrical power source for space vehicles; a device for utilizing high temperatures, such as the initial high-temperature steam, utilizing a maximum temperature higher than the permissible steam temperature, in a nuclear power plant; a compact power plant for mobile or stationary applications; and a compact portable electrical generating system.

The heat for a thermionic device may come from any convenient source, and may be nuclear, chemical, or solar in origin. Nuclear fuel is attractive because of the large energy yield per pound of fuel and because the high temperature at which the heat energy can be delivered matches the desirable temperatures in thermionic converters. Because of critical mass, minimum economical unit capacity is limited when heat is supplied by nuclear fission. In the form uranium dioxide, UO_2, uranium-233 is preferred to uranium-235, the minimum for both being around a 50-kilowatt level. Control is similar to that of fission nuclear reactors (*q.v.*). When a fuel element is needed for emitters, a combination of carbides such as UC-ZrC (uranium carbide-zirconium carbide) or uranium carbide alone is used. For low unit capacity below one kilowatt and up to the multikilowatt range, radioactive isotopes may be employed for heating. If low cost, penetrating radiation, and long life are important, cobalt-60, strontium-90, and cesium-137 in the form of cobalt metal, strontium oxide, strontium difluoride, and strontium titanate may be employed. For short-lived application, cerium-144 and rubidium-106 in the form of the cerium oxide may be used; for long-lived weak radiation, plutonium-238 in the form of the oxide or promethium-147 may be

used; and for short-lived, weak radiation, gaseous krypton-85, polonium-210, or curium-242 may be used.

Designs may take the form of in-reactor or out-of-reactor systems. The latter simplifies problems of constructing the enclosure to avoid permanent change in dimensions (creep) and rupture due to the extremes of temperature and radiation environment inside the reactor. The in-reactor system, however, is more compact. The successful use of nuclear thermionic devices depends upon the containing and maintaining of the dimensional stability of the isotope and fission heat source. Reactor lifetime is limited by the reactivity of fuel or fuel element swelling.

Solar-powered thermionic systems are designed mainly for space applications. Combustion heated systems are designed for ground and power plant applications.

In spacecraft. Thermionic devices can be applied in space as uncomplicated and lightweight power sources in the following manner:

1. For electrostatic or electromagnetic propulsion. This may require units from 1,000 to 10,000 kilowatt of electric power (kWe). The most likely design would be a thermionic converter in a reactor, with liquid-metal heat transfer to the radiator.

2. Space auxiliary power for manned spacecraft. The power demand would range from 10 to 50 kWe and could be met with a thermionic converter on the surface of a reactor.

3. Instrumentation and control. Requiring up to 10 kWe, the choice could be a solar-heated thermionic converter or an isotope-heated system.

When selecting a nuclear source for a space mission, both fuel and launch costs must be considered. Around 100 kW, cobalt-60 shows promise as a leading heat source for multikilowatt power in space. A cobalt-60 kernel with shielding will prevent loss of the radioactive material by diffusion or chemical attack. Its weight is comparable to a plutonium-238 heat source and costs are substantially lower.

A typical thermionic reactor element for space applications is the so-called fast spectrum (of neutrons) flashlight reactor, having a wet cell thermionic fuel element with the sheath insulator in a cesium environment (cesium is isolated from the sheath insulator in the dry cell). Subassemblies of cells, containing emitters of one diode and collectors of the next, are enclosed in a long bilayer type of insulator and sheath. A three-cell series-connected diode has approximately 20 square centimetres of emitter area for 300 watts (140 amperes at 2.1 volts) normally. A full length element consists of 10 to 12 diodes in series for 1 kW at 8 volts. The fuel elements are assembled to form a cylindrical core. For 100 kWe the overall size is 24 in. (61 cm) diameter × 26 in. (66 cm) high, and 2,400 lb weight (7,200 lb total, including radiation shield and auxiliaries). A single coolant loop flows through the reactor at a liquid metal temperature of 600° to 700° C. Other concepts are moderated "flashlight" reactor with a fuelled moderator element such as uranium zirconium hydride, providing a reduced minimum critical size; externally fuelled coolants in tubes, a unit cell "pancake" (flat) concept; out-of-core, using a heat pipe (see HEAT EXCHANGERS) with a reactor of uranium nitride or tungsten and gas as a heat transfer fluid; and a direct-radiating reactor with the anode arranged outside of the reactor for radiation into space.

A 108-watt thermionic generator of 7.6 percent efficiency for space applications has been tested for 3,000 hours.

Solar-powered thermionic generator modules, with five converters in each module (4.33 cm² emitter area yielding 8 watts/cm² at 2,000° K), have been constructed. The emitter is tantalum and the collector is molybdenum, with two-mil spacing using low-pressure cesium. Each module is heated by a solar concentrator measuring five feet in diameter. The specific power is 440 lb/kW for a 1.5 kW total. Although technically demonstrated and proven for a two-year lifetime, this solar-heated device was not employed.

For a space propulsion system of 1,000 kWe of power, both a nuclear steam-turbine power plant and a nuclear

High- and low-pressure devices

The fast spectrum reactor

thermionic power plant have been proposed. Since the only cooling available is by radiation into space, the condenser, or cooler surface area, can be made smaller as the condenser temperature is increased. A realistic condenser temperature could be 400° K because the strength of the turbine blades limit inlet temperature to 1,000° K. The top or cathode temperature of a thermionic system could be 2,000° K, and the anode or cooler temperature 1,200° K.

Aside from other considerations, the radiator area of such a thermionic power plant would be only 1/81 as large as that in a steam power plant.

Comparison with other energy conversion devices

Unlike conventional heat power devices—such as Rankine cycle, Brayton cycle, and Stirling cycle power plants—thermionic devices, like other direct energy conversion devices, have no rotating or reciprocating parts, thus eliminating the need for attended operation. Other advantages include the ability to tolerate large acceleration higher than 30 times the force of gravity, low system weight, and the fact that efficiency of operation is largely independent of unit capacity.

When compared to other direct energy conversion devices (fuel cells, thermoelectric devices, solar cells, MHD [magnetohydrodynamic] generators), thermionic devices have the lowest specific weight: 1 lb per kWe is practical, compared to 1,000 for solar cells, 250 for thermoelectric devices, and 100 for chemical fuel cells. Thermionic devices are best suited for high temperatures (1,500° K, compared to the 800° C maximum temperature for a thermoelectric system). In a nuclear isotope space power system of 4 kWe, a thermionic system has highest efficiency (10–12 percent), smallest radiator area (20–25 ft²), and lowest system weight. A thermionic system with the converters in the core of a reactor has a specific weight of 7 lb/kWe for the 100- to 1,000-kWe range, including shielding.

When utilizing solar heat, a thermionic system with a solar concentrator is again less than one-half the weight of a solar-cell system of similar capacity.

process of lowering the temperature to that required for the steam turbine (maximum 700° C). This is called "topping," and the technique can increase power output by 20 percent or more.

Flame-heated thermionic converters have been developed for 5 to 200 watts. The combustion chamber is a silicon carbide-coated molybdenum cup, the outside acting as an emitter. With an emitter area of 6 cm², 5 watts/cm² were produced at 1,300° C. A 70-watt unit using a silicon carbide envelope, impermeable to combustion products, has functioned for 1,200 hours. Portable units, a 300- to 600-watt backpack and 1- to 3-kW base-site power system, have also been produced.

For power generation, a nuclear thermionic system does not differ markedly from that of a fossil fuel system. The treatment and removal of fission products are similar in all nuclear reactors.

A large quantity of fission products is generated in a nuclear fuel element in a year of operation. Disposal methods depend on the type of fuel and emitter materials, operating temperature, and design. Gaseous and volatile fission products may be removed directly from the emitter and the interelectrode space through an exhaust system, by diffusion through the emitter or by venting from the emitter. Some build up of fission product concentration in the cesium is tolerable because of the small electron scattering cross section of xenon, the most abundant fission product.

For ground applications the fission products are treated as in any nuclear reactor system.

Inaccessible regions other than space. Nuclear-fuelled thermoelectric systems have been selected for use in remote radio stations, but for the power range, thermionic systems could serve as well. A small nuclear thermionic electric power source is particularly useful in remote locations.

Among developments of special interest is the ISOMITE unit. This isotope battery (see the Figure) is a relatively low-temperature thermionic converter powered by a radioisotope. It operates at a very low cesium pressure, about 10^{-3} to 10^{-2} torr (millimetres of mercury). Power ranges are 100 μW, 10 mW, and up to 1 W, fuelled by promethium-147 oxide Pm_2O_3. Typical data are as given in the Table.

Isotope-powered converter

anode (connected to collector and to housing)

tantalum collector

electrode gap

niobium support

alumina insulator

nickel housing

zirconia insulation

alumina insulator

formed nickel closure

alumina insulator

secondary container (tantalum emitter)

promethia fuel

primary container

cesium reservoir

insulation

shroud

cathode (connected to nickel closure)

By courtesy of McDonnell Douglas Astronautics Company

A 10-milliwatt thermionic converter fuelled by promethium-147. Arrows indicate direction of electron flow.

Typical Characteristics of an Isotope-Powered Thermionic Converter		
output	1 μW	10 mW
Total heat output (W)	0.27	3.6
Curies of activity	750	10^4
Fuel capsule diameter (cm)	0.71	1.76
Emitter area (cm²)	3.0	14.6
Interelectrode spacing (cm)	0.013	0.0063
Total volume (cm³)	0.28	4.28
Total weight (gm)	11	87
Emitter temperature (° K)	780	870
Collector temperature (° K)	700	703
Collector work function (eV)	1.42	1.48
Maximum power (mW)	0.780 at 0.1 V	19 at 0.145 V
Efficiency (percent)	0.29	0.55

Battery life is normally five years; with plutonium-238 (Pu-238) fuel, 10 years of life can be expected.

A small power unit such as this has many applications, such as a satellite power source for deep space probes, in underwater power supplies, and in remote terrestrial applications.

LIMITATIONS

Thermionic converters lack moving parts, but there are sources of deterioration in the devices. Vapour pressure of the emitter material, for example, produces evaporation or sputtering. Also, the electrode materials are subject to creep (permanent change in mechanical dimensions) and to rupture under thermal cycling and from stress corrosion.

Some form of power conditioning is usually needed in a thermionic converter to change direct-current (dc) to alternating-current (ac) electricity. Dc can be changed to ac

Ground power stations. Thermionic devices can be employed effectively in ground power stations. Energy in the form of electricity can be extracted from high-temperature steam by a thermionic converter during the

by applying a small modulating signal or by switching, using an electromagnetic field or plasma injection.

FUTURE POSSIBILITIES

In large power applications for space (above 1,000 kWe), the nuclear thermionic system appears to have advantages over a vapour cycle turbine system, partly because of its inherent compactness.

In terrestrial nuclear power systems thermionic conversion is superior to either the magnetohydrodynamic (MHD) generator or the thermoelectric system for power plant topping. With fossil power, however, the MHD system may be a more attractive topping technique.

Extensive undersea applications, both small power and large power, still await development. For this use the thermionic converter is substantially more efficient than the thermoelectric system.

BIBLIOGRAPHY. S.L. SOO, *Direct Energy Conversion* (1968), a modern text dealing with all aspects of direct energy conversion, devices, comparison, and long-range prospects, including an extensive bibliography; S.N. LEVINE (ed.) *Selected Papers on New Techniques for Energy Conversion* (1961), an overall survey and collection of important papers on progress made to 1960; E. BLUE and J.H. INGOLD, "Thermionic Energy Conversion," in G.W. SUTTON (ed.), *Direct Energy Conversion*, pp. 239–335 (1969), a discussion of recent surveys, emphasizing basic theories of plasma physics and solid-state physics; and G.C. SZEGO and J.E. TAYLOR (eds.), *Space Power System Engineering* (1966), a general survey including comparison of various devices, selection and range of application, and costs for space emissions.

For information on recent developments, see the *Proceedings of the Intersociety Energy Conversion Engineering Conference* (annual).

(S.L.S.)

Thermodynamics, Principles of

Thermodynamics is that part of physical science that is concerned with the conditions that material systems may assume and the changes in conditions that may occur either spontaneously or as a result of interactions between systems, including interactions such as heat, which cannot be described in terms of mechanics. It is basic to the distinction between mechanics and thermodynamics that according to mechanics all the energy of a system in any state is convertible to work, whereas according to thermodynamics only a fraction of the energy of a system in most states is convertible to work without other effects. The scope of thermodynamics has been steadily broadening since early in the 19th century as a result of a better understanding that has grown up of its underlying principles.

The word thermodynamics was derived from the Greek words *thermē* ("heat") and *dynamis* ("force"). The beginnings of the study of thermodynamics are found in the early 19th century in the study of the motive power of heat; that is, the capability of hot bodies to produce mechanical work. These early studies revealed several underlying principles, the most important of which are the first and second laws of thermodynamics. The discovery and clear enunciation in 1850 of the two laws by Rudolf Julius Clausius, a German mathematician and physicist, broadened greatly the scope of the subject. Throughout the rest of the 19th century it developed into a science, now known as classical thermodynamics, concerned primarily with physical systems in or passing through stable equilibrium states (the terms system and state are defined below). More recently thermodynamics has been extended to include physical systems in nonequilibrium states.

Although the development of thermodynamics, in contrast to other aspects of the study of physics, has progressed without regard to the details of the microscopic structures of physical systems, many scientists, beginning with Ludwig Eduard Boltzmann, Austrian physicist, have felt that the laws of thermodynamics might be justified and explained by means of detailed microscopic descriptions of matter and the laws of mechanics (classical or quantum) and statistics. Work in this direction has resulted in the development of the branch of

thermodynamics known as statistical thermodynamics, which, though it plays an important role in the evaluation of properties of systems, has not achieved one of its original goals, namely, the derivation of the laws of thermodynamics from the laws of mechanics. In particular, it now appears that the second law of thermodynamics is an independent law of nature. This particular point will be clarified below.

This article is divided into two parts. In the first part, the general principles of thermodynamics that apply to any physical system in any state—and the corollaries of these principles—are presented without reference to the detailed microscopic structure of matter. The presentation, therefore, encompasses both classical and nonequilibrium thermodynamics. In the second part, the detailed microscopic structures of physical systems are considered, and the states of such systems are discussed in the light of the laws of both quantum mechanics and thermodynamics. Quantum mechanics and thermodynamics are shown to be complementary parts of physical science, and they are neither separable nor are they derivable one from the other.

This article is divided into the following sections:

I. Brief history of classical thermodynamics

Temperature is probably the earliest thermodynamic concept to attain operational status. Early in the 17th century Galileo, an Italian astronomer and physicist, devised a thermoscope that was a rudimentary thermometer. Soon thereafter a liquid-expansion thermometer with bulb and stem, open at the top, was devised in France by Jean Ray. In 1640 the grand duke Ferdinand II of Tuscany, one of the founders of the Florentine Academy of Experiment, invented the sealed-stem alcohol thermometer. Such devices were put to clinical (determining degrees of fever), agricultural (incubation), and meteorological uses.

The purpose of these instruments was to measure a quantity, that had as yet been undefined, that was more objective in nature than the physiological sensations of hotness and coldness. An equilibrium concept was probably involved; namely, that all bodies exposed to the same atmosphere would ultimately attain the same degree of hotness or coldness, despite any contrary evidence of the senses. An associated concept of the equilibrium concept was that temperature is a driving potential that causes some influence to pass from one body to another of unequal hotness or coldness. Thus, when a body is taken from a warm room to the cold outdoors, its length begins immediately to decrease.

What was it that passed from one body to another at different temperatures? Was it temperature itself that was

Early
attempts
to
measure
temperature

transmitted? The English philosopher and scientist Francis Bacon as early as 1620, and the Florentine Academy a few years later, began to make this distinction between this influence and temperature; but it was more than a century before Joseph Black, a chemist at the University of Glasgow, in 1770 made the distinction sharply. He showed by mixing equal masses of pairs of liquids of different temperatures that the temperatures of the two substances often changed by radically different amounts. Indeed, a large change in temperature of a solid body produced no change at all in the temperature of a mixture of ice and water or of water and steam. Temperature was not necessarily conserved or even transmitted in the process.

Black established the science of calorimetry, which led to the establishment of the caloric theory, based upon the following postulates: (1) Caloric is an all-pervading elastic fluid, the particles of which repel one another strongly. (2) Particles of caloric are attracted by particles of matter. (3) Caloric is conserved. (4) Caloric is either sensible (*i.e.*, change in caloric is associated with change in temperature) or latent. (5) Caloric has weight. These postulates were intended to account for expansion and contraction upon heating and cooling, variations in heat capacity, calorimetry, latent heat, and gain in weight of certain metals when heated in air (calcined). Frictional heating was subsequently accounted for by postulating that friction reduced the attraction between caloric and matter.

Toward the end of the 18th century, Count Rumford (Benjamin Thompson), an expatriate American colonial engineer and physicist, attacked the validity of the caloric theory on the basis of experiments intended to show that caloric could be created and, therefore, was not conserved. More refined measurements on the generation of heat by frictional work were made nearly a half century later by an English physicist, James Prescott Joule.

In 1824 Sadi Carnot, a French military engineer, introduced the concept of the heat-engine cycle, a concept that permitted a sharp distinction to be made between interactions of systems and changes in their states. Carnot then proved from conservation of caloric and the impossibility of the production of work without compensating changes in the environment that (1) a reversible cyclic engine is the most efficient possible means of producing work from heat, and (2) all reversible cyclic engines operating between the same pair of heat reservoirs must have the same efficiency. Although the proof, as it turned out, was invalid, Clausius asserted in 1850 that Carnot's principle is itself a basic postulate and is, in effect, what came to be known as the second law of thermodynamics.

Carnot's heat engine

In the decade of the 1840s Joule laid the foundations of the first law of thermodynamics by showing that the amount of work required to bring about a given change of state is independent of the kind of work (whether mechanical, electric, or magnetic), the rate of doing work, or the method of delivering it. Joule concluded that work can be converted into heat, with a fixed ratio of one to the other, and that heat can be converted into work. In 1844 Julius Robert von Mayer, a German physicist, postulated that in a work-producing cycle the heat introduced must exceed the heat rejected by an amount proportional to the work. He deduced the value of the proportionality constant from calculation of cycles in a gaseous system.

In 1849 Lord Kelvin (William Thomson), an engineer of Glasgow, pointed out the conflict between the caloric basis of Carnot's arguments and the conclusions reached by Joule. In 1850 Clausius resolved the difficulty by stating explicitly the first and second laws of thermodynamics. Within a few years Clausius defined and named the property entropy that is conserved in all reversible processes, and derived from the second law the principle of increase of entropy.

The first law was stated by Clausius as follows: In all cases in which work is produced by the agency of heat, a quantity of heat is consumed that is proportional to the work done; and, conversely, by the expenditure of an equal quantity of work, an equal quantity of heat is produced. He applied this statement to a cyclic process in a system (a concept with which he credits Carnot) in order to obtain a statement of the first law in terms of work and heat without reference to alteration in the state of the system. This led naturally to a definition of the property energy—called mechanical energy by Kelvin and contracted to energy by J. Willard Gibbs, an American mathematician and physicist. Clausius stated the second law in the following terms: A passage of heat from a colder to a hotter body cannot take place without compensation.

Clausius' paper of 1850 marked the birth of the science of thermodynamics. Immediately thereafter, Kelvin, who had previously displayed an interest in the theory of temperature, proposed and discussed various definitions for thermodynamic temperature scales, including the one that now bears his name. James Clerk Maxwell, a physicist of Edinburgh and Cambridge, averred that two bodies each equal in temperature to a third body are equal in temperature to each other. This statement, which is sometimes called the zeroth law of thermodynamics, is an incomplete version of a condition for equilibrium, subsequently derived by Gibbs and others, that is a corollary of the second law. Maxwell also devised a number of mathematical relations that now bear his name. Kelvin and Max Planck, a German physicist, later restated the second law, so as to avoid the undefined term compensation used by Clausius, in terms of the impossibility of a perpetual-motion machine of the second kind (see below).

In the years 1873–78 Gibbs published three papers that proved to be definitive as regards the conditions for equilibrium. These papers provided a mathematical method so orderly and systematic that they have served as the foundations of physical chemistry and many subsequent applications of classical thermodynamics.

At the turn of the century, the French mathematician Henri Poincaré addressed the problem of definition of temperature and heat and the statement of the first and second laws. In 1909 Constantin Carathéodory, a Greek mathematician teaching in Germany, presented an alternative logical structure in which he shunned use of the term heat. It is closest in method and spirit to that used here. He states the two laws as follows: First, an extensive property exists the increment in which is the work received by the system while surrounded by an adiabatic wall (an adiabatic wall being one that permits only work interactions between the system and its surroundings). Second, in the neighbourhood of any prescribed initial state are states that cannot be reached by an adiabatic process.

In 1918 Walther Nernst, a Nobel-Prize winning chemist of Germany, stated the Nernst heat theorem, treated below, which is essentially the third law of thermodynamics, which rounds out the exposition of classical thermodynamics by providing a common base for values of entropy for all atoms or molecules that can be formed from simpler species.

II. Basic concepts and laws of thermodynamics

SYSTEMS, STATES, AND PROPERTIES

The description of physical phenomena is based on the concept of state of a system and the changes of state that occur either spontaneously or because of interactions with other systems. Knowledge of the states of a system is equivalent to knowledge of the outcomes of all possible observations on the system; namely, observations of all its properties.

The term system means any identifiable collection of matter that can be separated from everything else by a well-defined surface so that changes in everything else need not affect the condition of the collection. Examples of systems are a number of water molecules confined within a watertight container, a thermonuclear plasma (a special collection of charged particles) confined by a suitably designed magnetic field, and the vapour of a solid within a cavity in the solid.

The particles of a system may have a finite rest mass, as do molecules, atoms, or electrons, or zero rest mass, as do photons. The number of particles of a system can be large, as in a cubic centimetre of tungsten, or small, as in a hydrogen atom.

At any instant of time a system is in a condition called a state, which encompasses all that can be said about the results of any measurements or observations that can be performed on the system at that time. The state at a given instant of time determines the properties of the system. A property is any quantity the value of which depends upon the state but not the history of the system. For a given state the value of a property can be determined by some type of measurement (some physical operation or test). When the values of all properties of two states are identical, the two states are identical; otherwise they are different.

Because of unavoidable quantum mechanical considerations, a simple measurement, no matter how nearly perfect, will not yield the precise value for a property. In general, a very large number of measurements of the same kind is required to yield the precise value, each measurement performed on a duplicate of the system in the given state and each yielding a different result. The value of a property is defined, therefore, as the sum of all the results of the measurements of the property divided by the number of measurements (in other words, the arithmetic average or expectation value of all the results of the measurements of the property). It will be shown below that a state can be described by a set of weighting factors, or probabilities, that enter into the evaluation of all properties.

Although an indefinite number of properties can be associated with a state, the values of these properties are not all independent of each other. The number of independent properties is finite and is either small or large, depending on the type of state in question; that is, on whether or not it is a stable equilibrium state. The meaning of the terms that define the various types of states will be given below.

WORK AND NONWORK

An interaction between two systems such that whatever happens in each of the interacting systems could have been brought about while the sole effect external to each system was the change in level of a mass in a gravity field will be defined as work; that is, work is an interaction that must satisfy a test: each of the interacting systems is separately required to experience the same changes as in the actual interaction, but, through alteration of circumstances external to that system, the effect outside of it is solely the rise or fall of a mass. If this test can be satisfied in the case of both systems, then the original interaction is work.

It can be shown from experimental evidence that the following interactions conform to the definition just cited and are, therefore, work interactions: (1) the displacement of a point on the boundary of a system at which point a force is exerted in the direction of the displacement by another system (this is essentially the definition of work in mechanics, which is less general than the one given here, which covers interactions other than those considered in mechanics; the present definition implies that the force applied on a body by a stationary force field, such as gravity or an electrostatic field, results in no work, even though the body is in motion—for example, freely falling); (2) the electromagnetic interactions between primary and secondary coils of a transformer; and (3) the exchange of radiation emitted by lasers. Such radiation consists of wave particles, which are in order relative to each other as contrasted with those, for example, from an incandescent lamp, which are randomly arranged. On the other hand, it can be shown by virtue of the second law that the exchange of radiation between a hot system and a cold system (such as blackbody radiation) does not conform to the requirement stated in the definition of work and is not, therefore, a work interaction.

Work is one of several distinguishable types of interaction that can occur between two systems. Any interaction that is not work will be hereinafter called nonwork. A special type of nonwork interaction that will be treated below in detail is a heat interaction. In general, an interaction is fully specified if the exact sequence of states, called the path, of each of the interacting systems is specified. In turn, the path of one of the systems and the interactions that occur specify the process experienced by the system. In an interaction that satisfies the definition of work, each system is said to be experiencing an adiabatic process.

The state and, therefore, the values of the properties of a system can change either spontaneously or as a result of interactions with other systems. During changes of state the values of certain properties are subject to limitations imposed by the laws of physics. The limitations imposed by thermodynamics are consequences of the first and second laws, which will be stated here in an unusually general way.

FIRST LAW

The first law is a statement of existence of a property called energy. It is based on the concept of work and can be stated as follows: For any process involving no effects external to the system except displacement of a mass between specified levels in a gravity field, the magnitude of that mass is fixed by the end states of the system and is independent of the details of the process. This law has many implications or corollaries, some of which are as follows.

1. *Uniqueness of work values.* By virtue of the first law a unique number can be assigned to a work interaction between two systems. This number is n when n arbitrarily selected units of mass are displaced between two arbitrarily specified levels in a gravity field. The sign of work is selected positive when work is done by a system—that is, when the sole external effect would be the rise of a weight.

2. *Definition of energy.* By virtue of the first law, the work in an adiabatic process depends on the initial and final, or end, states only. It follows that a property of a system can be defined, called energy, such that its change of value between states A_1 and A_2 is equal to the work W_{12}^a involved in an adiabatic process that has A_1 and A_2 as end states. In terms of symbols, if E_1 and E_2 denote the energies of states A_1 and A_2, respectively, and W_{12}^a the work done in any adiabatic process connecting A_1 and A_2, the difference $E_2 - E_1$ is equal to the negative of W_{12}^a; i.e.,

$$E_2 - E_1 = -W_{12}^a. \qquad (1)$$

Energy is only partially defined by equation (1) because the difference between E_1 and E_2 does not specify the values of E_1 and E_2. An arbitrary value such as zero, however, can be assigned to E_0 of some reference state A_0, so that the energies of all other states are fixed by equation (1).

It will be shown below that by virtue of the second law of thermodynamics certain interactions that cause change of energy cannot be described as work. The corresponding process is, by definition, a nonadiabatic process. Because energy is a property, the energy change associated with any nonadiabatic process will equal numerically the work in any adiabatic process between the same end states.

Because work values are additive, energy is an additive or extensive property; that is, the energy of a whole is equal to the sum of the energies of its parts.

3. *Conservation of energy.* The magnitude of the work in an adiabatic process can be positive, negative, or zero, depending on the end states of the process, but zero adiabatic work does not necessarily imply identical end states. An adiabatic zero-work change of state may occur spontaneously in a system, as, for example, when an electrical capacitor discharges through an internal resistor. During such a process, equation (1) requires that the energy of the system remain invariant. This is the so-called law of conservation of energy, which is a consequence of the first law of thermodynamics. The

Measurements and values compared

Consequences of the first law

first law, on the other hand, cannot be deduced from the law of conservation of energy.

A system that experiences an adiabatic, zero-work process is said to be isolated from all other systems in the environment.

4. *Impossibility of perpetual-motion machine of the first kind.* A perpetual-motion machine of the first kind (PMM1) is any system that undergoes a cycle and has no external effect except the rise of a weight. The term cycle (or cyclic process) is defined as a process in which the initial and final states of the system are identical.

By virtue of the first law, the work of an adiabatic cycle must be equal to zero and, therefore, a PMM1 is impossible.

5. *The first law and relativity.* According to the general theory of relativity, the energy E of a system is equal to the product of its mass m and the square of the speed of light c in a vacuum, namely,

$$E = mc^2. \qquad (2)$$

By virtue of the first law, the energy E of an isolated system is conserved. Therefore, equation (2) requires that the mass m of the system is also conserved, regardless of the processes occurring within the system (such as chemical reactions, nuclear reactions, and creation and annihilation of particles). Moreover, if the energy of a system is altered by virtue of an adiabatic or nonadiabatic interaction, the mass of the system must also be altered in accordance with equation (2). In most applications the energy transferred to or from a system is so much smaller than the total energy mc^2 of the system that the change in mass is negligible.

Conservation of mass

SECOND LAW

The second law is a statement of existence of stable equilibrium states and of special processes that connect these states to others. More than the first law, the second law distinguishes thermodynamics from other parts of physics. Because it has far-reaching implications concerning the properties and behaviour of matter, it is frequently invoked in discussions of philosophy as well as in discussions of physics.

Of the many statements of the second law, those of Clausius, Planck, and Carathéodory are the most notable. All of these statements imply the existence of a stable equilibrium state for given values of energy, the number of particles, and the constraints (see below)—an implication that is here taken to be the essential element of the second law.

The term equilibrium state means a state that does not change with time while the system is isolated from all other systems in the environment. Equilibrium state is sometimes confused with steady state: a steady state does not change with time even though the system, rather than being isolated, is interacting with other systems.

If a system is in an equilibrium state, a finite change of state may be caused by interactions with the environment, including those that leave no finite net effects in the environment. Several types of equilibrium states can be distinguished. Among these is the stable equilibrium state for which a finite change of state cannot occur, regardless of interactions that leave no net effects in the environment.

Consistent with its nature, a system might assume any one of a set of possible states, but some of the possible states may be prohibited by restrictions imposed by the environment. These restrictions are called constraints. For example, a given amount of gas may assume any of a large number of states. The same amount of gas, however, confined in a gas-tight container of fixed volume is restricted to states with volumes smaller than or equal to the volume inside the container. The possible states of the system that are consistent with the constraints will be called allowed states.

Constraints on systems

The second law can now be stated as follows: Among all the allowed states of a system with given values of energy, numbers of particles, and constraints, one and only one is a stable equilibrium state. Such a state can be reached from any other allowed state of the same energy,

numbers of particles, and constraints and leave no effects on the state of the environment.

The second law cannot be derived from the laws of mechanics (either classical or quantum). The second law asserts that a stable equilibrium state exists for each value of the energy, whereas in mechanics the only stable state is that of minimum energy, what is known as the ground state.

Some corollaries of the second law are as follows.

1. *State principle.* By virtue of the second law, stable equilibrium states exist, and a unique stable equilibrium state corresponds to each set of values of energy, numbers of particles, and constraints. The uniqueness implies the following corollary: the value of any property of a system in a stable equilibrium state may be expressed as a function of the values of the energy, numbers of particles, and constraints only. This corollary is known as the state principle.

2. *Reversible and irreversible processes.* A process is reversible if the system and its environment can be restored to their initial states, except for differences of smaller order of magnitude than the maximum changes that occur during the process.

According to the second law, a system may start from any allowed state and reach the corresponding stable equilibrium state with no net effect on the environment. Such a process could not be reversible. For if it were, the system, starting from the stable equilibrium state, could undergo a process that ends at another state with no net effect on the environment. This conclusion, however, violates the definition of a stable equilibrium state. It follows that irreversible processes exist.

3. *Impossibility of perpetual-motion machine of the second kind.* It can be shown from the definition of a stable equilibrium state that a system in such a state can receive but cannot produce work. The plausibility of this corollary will be evident from the observation that work can always be used to change from any state to a nonequilibrium state by creating relative velocity of parts or compression to a smaller volume. If a system in a stable equilibrium state were to produce work, that work could be used to cause the system itself to end in a nonequilibrium state with no net effects on the environment—contrary to the definition of its initial state.

This corollary applies strictly only to systems of which the energy can be increased indefinitely, such as any system with particles free to move from one place to another or any system with translational degrees of freedom. Most practical systems satisfy this requirement. The generalization to systems that do not satisfy the requirement, such as a nuclear-spin system, is discussed below under *Negative temperature.*

A perpetual-motion machine of the second kind (PMM2) is any device that would deliver net work; *i.e.*, raise an external weight, while undergoing a cycle and interacting with a single system in a stable equilibrium state. A perpetual-motion machine of the second kind is a device that permits a system to violate the corollary stated above and is, therefore, impossible.

Prior to the discussion of the fourth corollary, it is necessary to define the terms mutual stable equilibrium and reservoir. Two systems A and B are said to be in mutual stable equilibrium if the combined system AB is in a stable equilibrium state. It can be readily verified that if two systems are in mutual stable equilibrium, each system must be in a stable equilibrium state. Moreover, if the two systems are brought into communication so that interactions are not prohibited, no interactions will occur unless the allowed states of at least one of the systems are altered.

A reservoir R is a special kind of a system that provides useful reference states for applications of the second law and satisfies the following conditions: (1) it is closed to the transfer of rest mass—*i.e.*, its boundaries cannot be crossed by material particles; (2) its constraints are invariant with time—for example, its volume has the same value at all times; (3) it passes through stable equilibrium states only; and (4) in the course of finite interactions it remains in mutual stable equilibrium with a dupli-

Reservoirs as systems

cate of itself that experiences no such interactions. An example of a reservoir is a mixture of solid, liquid, and vapour water in mutual stable equilibrium while enclosed in a container.

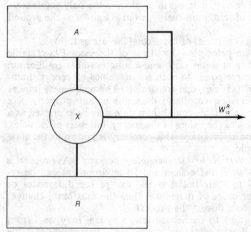

Figure 1: Production of work by a system A interacting with a reservoir R through an intermediate device X (see text).

4. *Work done reversibly by a system in combination with a reservoir.* A system A in combination with a reservoir R can experience a work interaction with other systems either directly or through an intermediate device X, or both, while X is undergoing a cyclic process (Figure 1). During this work interaction no rest mass is exchanged between A and R while the state of A changes from A_1 to A_2. The work done is denoted by W_{12}^R for processes in general and by $(W_{12}^R)_{rev}$ for processes that are reversible.

By virtue of the second law it can be shown that for a given change of state from A_1 to A_2, the work $(W_{12}^R)_{rev}$ is the same for all reversible processes and for all reservoirs in mutual stable equilibrium with each other; that is, $(W_{12}^R)_{rev}$ is fixed by the end states A_1 and A_2. Moreover, W_{12}^R cannot exceed $(W_{12}^R)_{rev}$ when both correspond to the same change of state from A_1 to A_2.

ENTROPY

The two laws of thermodynamics imply the existence of a property called entropy that is conserved in all reversible processes. Its definition is based on another property called available work.

Available work. Because for a given system and reservoir $(W_{12}^R)_{rev}$ depends on the end states of the system only, a property can be defined called available work (symbolized Ω, omega), such that its change of value between states A_1 and A_2 is equal to the work $(W_{12}^R)_{rev}$; that is (using the symbol $\equiv$ to imply definition),

$$(\Omega_2 - \Omega_1) \equiv -(W_{12}^R)_{rev}. \qquad (3)$$

It can be easily verified that available work is an additive or extensive property.

Definition of entropy. Because both energy and available work are extensive properties, the difference between them is also an extensive property. Entropy will be defined as the extensive property S the change of which, DS, in a change of state is equal to a positive constant c_R times the difference between the corresponding changes of energy DE and available work $D\Omega$ evaluated with respect to a standard reservoir. This definition can be written in the form of an equation; *i.e.*,

$$DS \equiv c_R (DE - D\Omega). \qquad (4)$$

The symbol D denotes a change, finite or infinitesimal, in magnitude of the property the symbol of which it precedes.

The standard reservoir may be chosen to be a mixture of solid, liquid, and vapour water in mutual stable equilibrium, and an arbitrary value, as explained below, may be assigned to the constant c_R. Subject to subsequent considerations, an arbitrary value may be assigned to the entro-

py of an arbitrarily selected reference state of the system. Thereafter, by means of equation (4), a value may be found for any state, equilibrium or nonequilibrium, once values for E and Ω have been determined by appropriate measurements.

Entropy changes in adiabatic processes. If the process from state A_1 to state A_2 in system A is adiabatic—that is, system A experiences only work interactions—then the work done by A must, by equation (1), equal the decrease in the energy of A. For a reversible adiabatic process the work done must, by equation (3), also equal the decrease in available work, so that the difference between the decrease in energy and the decrease in available work must be equal to zero. It follows from equation (4) that for a reversible adiabatic process the entropy change of the system is equal to zero; that is, the entropy is invariant. Moreover, because the fourth corollary states that the work for any adiabatic process cannot exceed that for the reversible adiabatic process, it follows that for an adiabatic process in general the entropy change must be greater than or at least equal to zero. In terms of symbols these conclusions can be written as

$$(DS)_{rev}^a = 0, \text{ for reversible adiabatic processes,} \qquad (5)$$

and

$$(DS)^a \geq 0, \text{ for adiabatic processes} \qquad (6)$$

(the symbol $>$ means "greater than," and $\geq$ means "greater than or equal to").

Principle of increase of entropy. When equation (6) is applied to any process in an isolated system—*i.e.*, to an adiabatic process for which the work is zero—it becomes

$$DS \text{ (isolated)} \geq 0. \qquad (7)$$

Thus, the entropy of an isolated system may remain constant or may increase, but a decrease of entropy in an isolated system is impossible. Because any process in any system may be conceptually changed to a process in an isolated system by including in the isolated system all systems with which the original system interacts, the conclusion represented by equation (7) is of great generality. Equation (7) is known as the principle of increase of entropy, although it may be more strictly said to be the principle of the impossibility of a decrease of entropy. According to this principle, whenever any process occurs in nature, the total entropy of all systems involved in the process must either increase or, if the process is reversible, remain constant.

STABLE EQUILIBRIUM

Criterion for stable equilibrium. Changes of state in an isolated system can occur only until the system reaches the unique stable equilibrium state consistent with the given values of energy, numbers of particles, and constraints. It follows from equation (7) that the entropy of the stable equilibrium state must be larger than that of any equilibrium or nonequilibrium state with the same values of energy, numbers of different particles, and constraints. By the same token, a criterion for stable equilibrium is that the entropy should be at its maximum value for fixed values of energy, numbers of particles, and constraints.

Equations relating properties for stable equilibrium states. By virtue of the state principle, the simplest illustrations of the laws of thermodynamics are provided by applications to systems in or passing through stable equilibrium states. For the properties and the relations between properties of systems in such states can be expressed by means of relatively simple mathematical forms.

The term numbers of particles, as used in the state principle, implies certain species of particles. The set of species selected must be a minimum set in terms of which the composition of all allowed states may be described. Such a minimum set of species, which will be unique in the number of members for a given system regardless of the choice of species to make up the set, is called a set of components.

For a system A with given fixed values E of energy,

$n_1, n_2, \ldots, n_k$ of the numbers of particles of components 1, 2, ..., k of the set of k components, and $\beta_1, \beta_2, \ldots, \beta_s$ of constraints 1, 2, ..., s of the set of s constraints, the uniqueness of the corresponding stable equilibrium state implies that the value of any property of A in that state must be fully and uniquely determined by the given fixed values. Moreover, for all stable equilibrium states, the values of a property F may be expressed as a mathematical function having a single value for each single set of values $E, n_1, n_2, \ldots, n_k, \beta_1, \beta_2, \ldots, \beta_s$.

$$F = F(E, n_1, n_2, \ldots, n_k, \beta_1, \beta_2, \ldots, \beta_s). \quad (8)$$

Several relations like equation (8) for several properties may be manipulated mathematically to express the values of any property as a function of the values of any set of independent properties of stable equilibrium states. A set of independent properties is such that the value of each property in the set can be varied without affecting the values of the remaining properties in the set.

Expressions for entropy and energy

Two functions of interest to subsequent considerations are those that relate the values of entropy S to the values of $E, n_1, n_2, \ldots, n_k, \beta_1, \beta_2, \ldots, \beta_s$, and the values of energy E to the values of $S, n_1, n_2, \ldots, n_k, \beta_1, \beta_2, \ldots, \beta_s$. These functions are denoted as

$$S = S(E, n_1, n_2, \ldots, n_k, \beta_1, \beta_2, \ldots, \beta_s) \quad (9)$$

and

$$E = E(S, n_1, n_2, \ldots, n_k, \beta_1, \beta_2, \ldots, \beta_s). \quad (10)$$

In general, the change of entropy per unit change of energy, or of any of the numbers of particles, or of any of the constraints can be evaluated with the help of equation (9). The same remark applies to energy and equation (10). Such changes are called partial derivatives and are used to define a number of useful properties that have meaning for stable equilibrium states only.

Mutual stable equilibrium of closed systems. If two systems A and B that are closed to the transfer of rest mass taken together constitute a system in a stable equilibrium state, then the entropy of that system must be at a maximum for the value of its energy. One of the consequences of this requirement will be seen from a possible variation—a conceptual alteration of state consistent with the description of the system and the constraints imposed on it and its parts A and B by the environment —in which the energy of A is increased by a small amount denoted by dE_A, and that of B is decreased by the same amount, while both A and B pass through stable equilibrium states without changes of values of their constraints. The entropy of part A is correspondingly altered by the amount dS_A. This amount can be expressed as

$$dS_A = \left(\frac{\partial S_A}{\partial E_A}\right)_{n,\beta} dE_A,$$

in which $(\partial S_A/\partial E_A)_{n,\beta}$ denotes the rate of change of S_A per unit change of E_A as A passes through stable equilibrium states while its numbers of particles (n) and its constraints (β) are held constant, namely, the partial derivative of S_A with respect to E_A. A similar expression can be written for the entropy change dS_B of B, so that the alteration dS of combined system AB is given by the expression

$$dS = \left(\frac{\partial S_A}{\partial E_A}\right)_{n,\beta} dE_A + \left(\frac{\partial S_B}{\partial E_B}\right)_{n,\beta} dE_B. \quad (11)$$

It can be shown that if the entropy S is to be at a maximum for the given fixed value of energy $E_A + E_B$ of the combined system AB and for both positive and negative variations dE_A, then it is necessary that the two partial derivatives $(\partial S_A/\partial E_A)_{n,\beta}$ and $(\partial S_B/\partial E_B)_{n,\beta}$ be equal to each other, namely,

$$\left(\frac{\partial S_A}{\partial E_A}\right)_{n,\beta} = \left(\frac{\partial S_B}{\partial E_B}\right)_{n,\beta}. \quad (12)$$

The quantity $(\partial S/\partial E)_{n,\beta}$ of a system may be thought of as a potential that governs the tendency of energy to pass from one system to another. It can be shown that

it is a "capturing tendency" in that if

$$\left(\frac{\partial S_A}{\partial E_A}\right)_{n,\beta} > \left(\frac{\partial S_B}{\partial E_B}\right)_{n,\beta},$$

then dE_A may be greater than zero (energy may pass from system B to system A) in an actual process but not less than zero (because less than zero would be contrary to the principle of increase of entropy). Conversely, the reciprocal quantity $(\partial E/\partial S)_{n,\beta}$ may be thought of as an "escaping tendency."

"Capturing" and "escaping" tendencies

Temperature. The potential that governs the flow of energy is called temperature. A scale of temperature may be defined in terms of any function of $(\partial S/\partial E)_{n,\beta}$ or $(\partial E/\partial S)_{n,\beta}$ that continuously increases or decreases with either. The scale commonly used in thermodynamics is the Kelvin scale of temperature. It is denoted by T and defined as

$$T \equiv \left(\frac{\partial E}{\partial S}\right)_{n,\beta}, \quad (13)$$

so that T becomes a measure of the escaping tendency of energy. The necessary condition, equation (12), for mutual stable equilibrium between two systems A and B is equivalent to an equality between the temperatures T_A and T_B of A and B, namely,

$$T_A = T_B. \quad (14)$$

From the observations that the work produced by the combination of systems A, X, and R used in the definition of entropy change is the decrease in energy of the combination AR and that for a reversible process the entropy of that combination is conserved, it is readily shown that the constant c_R in equation (4) is equal to the partial rate or derivative $(\partial S_R/\partial E_R)_{n,\beta}$ of the entropy of the reservoir R or the inverse of the temperature T_R of the reservoir. Because the magnitude of constant c_R is arbitrary, a selection of a value for it for a simple reservoir fixes not only the scale of entropy but also that of the Kelvin temperature. By international agreement the value of T for solid, liquid, and vapour water in mutual stable equilibrium is 273.16° K. Among the reasons for the selection of this five-digit figure is that it causes the temperature interval between the freezing and boiling points of water under a pressure of one atmosphere to be almost exactly 100 degrees. If any other reservoir R' is used with X and A, the change in entropy found from equation (4) for a change in state of system A from A_1 to A_2 will be the same as that found using R if constant $c_{R'}$ is taken equal to the inverse temperature of the reservoir R'.

Entropy constant

When the number 273.15 is subtracted from the value of any given Kelvin temperature T, the result will be the Celsius temperature t, or t (degrees Celsius) $\equiv T - 273.15$.

Heat. An argument will now be outlined to prove that certain nonwork interactions are entirely distinguishable from work in that no fraction of any one such interaction will satisfy the definition of work.

If two systems A and B are in stable equilibrium states and each is under constant constraints, but they are not in mutual stable equilibrium, then an interaction could occur between them. By virtue of the third corollary of the second law, any such interaction must be a nonwork interaction; that is, its effects on at least one system, say A, could not have been produced with the sole external effect was the rise of a weight. In general, however, the effects on A could be produced while weights external to A are raised and, in addition, a change of state of B takes place. It can be shown that maximum work will be delivered to the weights if the process is carried out reversibly and each system passes through stable equilibrium states. A reversible cyclic device X (Figure 2) interposed between systems A and B will permit these conditions to be fulfilled. The device X may produce work, but the reversible interactions experienced by A with X and X with B cannot be work by virtue of corollary 3 of the second law.

For the reversible process just described it can be shown from the functions that relate energy to entropy and other independent properties that the work δW that will be delivered to the weights is equal to the negative of the energy change dE_A of system A times the ratio $(T_A - T_B)/T_A$. This conclusion can be written as an equation; i.e.,

$$\delta W = -\frac{T_A - T_B}{T_A} dE_A. \tag{15}$$

In equation (15), the symbol d denotes an infinitesimal change of the value of a property, whereas δ denotes an

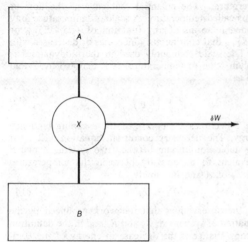

Figure 2: Production of work by a reversible cyclic device X that undergoes reversible nonwork interactions with systems A and B (see text).

infinitesimal amount of a quantity that is not a property or state function. Work is not a property of any system, and therefore δW is the appropriate way to indicate an infinitesimal amount of W.

Because dE_A is a measure of the magnitude of the interaction experienced by A with X, equation (15) expresses the work produced as a fraction of the magnitude of that interaction. As systems A and B approach mutual stable equilibrium, temperatures T_A and T_B approach equality, a necessary condition, and the fraction that represents the ratio of δW over dE_A approaches zero; that is, the work that can be obtained from the interaction between A and B through X becomes a vanishingly small fraction of the magnitude of the interaction. Moreover, it can be shown that then the interactions between A and X and between X and B are exactly equal, and each may be expressed as a product of temperature and entropy change $T_A\,dS_A$ and $T_B\,dS_B$.

In the limit, therefore, as T_A approaches T_B, the cyclic device X is no longer required, and the nature of the interaction approaches something completely distinguishable from work. It is this special kind of interaction that is called heat and denoted by the symbol Q. Moreover, for any process for which a system passes only through stable equilibrium states of fixed constraints and for a change of state corresponding to changes dS in entropy and dE in energy, the infinitesimal amount of heat $(\delta Q)_{rev}$ received by the system is given by the relations

$$(\delta Q)_{rev} = T\,dS = dE. \tag{16}$$

If the interacting systems pass only through stable equilibrium states, then the process will be reversible.

Heat is not a property of a system. Accordingly, the symbol δQ is used to denote an infinitesimal amount of heat but not the change in value of a property. Nor is heat contained within a system. Being an interaction, its magnitude depends upon the arbitrary selection of boundaries between systems.

Meaning of heat   The term heat is used here in a special sense that is quite foreign to the popular conception of its meaning. A different term might have been used were it not for the historical association of the word heat with thermodynamics. It will be observed from the context that the word heat is reserved here for a very special kind of interaction between systems, which only by virtue of the second law

is entirely distinguishable from all other kinds of interactions, including the special kind called work. If a less restrictive definition had been used, then some of the relations between heat and entropy given here would not always hold.

Heat and flow of entropy.   When a heat interaction occurs between two systems A and B that pass through stable equilibrium states, the process is reversible. For the combined system AB the process may be considered an adiabatic process for which the work is zero, so that, in accordance with equations (5) and (7) expressed in terms of subsystems A and B, $DS_A + DS_B = 0$. Because, from equation (16), DS_A is equal to $(\delta Q_A/T)_{rev}$ and different from zero, the heat interaction is associated with a flow of entropy from A to B if heat flows from A to B and conversely. By way of contrast, work in a reversible process leaves the entropies of the interacting systems unaltered.

To system B may be added a part that is not in a stable equilibrium state and that may experience an irreversible process without affecting the state of the other part or the interaction between A and B. Although the process as a whole is no longer reversible, the interaction is the same as before and could appropriately be called heat. A flow of entropy from A to B is still associated with the flow of heat from A to B, but the increase of entropy in B exceeds the amount that has flowed from A; that is, the statement $dS > \delta Q/T$ may be written for the irreversible process, and

$$dS \geq \frac{\delta Q}{T} \tag{17}$$

for processes in general.

For an adiabatic process equation (17) reduces to equation (6). For other processes equation (17) will apply provided that the only nonwork interactions are heat; that is, at least locally where the interaction occurs, the behaviour on each side of the boundary is the same as if both systems were passing through stable equilibrium states, with identifiable temperatures, and the process was reversible. It can readily be shown that certain nonwork interactions when used in place of δQ will not satisfy equation (17).

Inequality of Clausius.   An inequality that was first stated by Clausius bears his name. It is as follows: For an irreversible cycle the sum of ratios, each of which is a heat δQ received by the system divided by the temperature T at which the heat is received, is always less than zero. When each amount of heat δQ is very small, the sum of the ratios $\delta Q/T$ can be represented by a cyclic integral, and the inequality of Clausius is given by the relation

$$\left(\oint \frac{\delta Q}{T}\right)_{irrev} < 0. \tag{18}$$

(The symbol $\oint$ means to integrate over a closed path, the complete cycle.) The inequality of Clausius follows directly when the inequality of equation (17) is applied to each step of an irreversible cycle and summed up for all the steps, because dS, being the change in a property, sums up to zero. Application of the inequality of Clausius is restricted, of course, to processes for which all nonwork interactions are heat.

Work, heat, and change of energy.   If work and heat interactions occur successively, then the total energy change dE will be the sum of the work effect $(-\delta W)$ and the heat effect δQ; or, by equations (1) and (16),

$$dE = \delta Q - \delta W, \tag{19}$$

the minus sign resulting from the conventions regarding the signs for heat and work.

In practice it is not always necessary that work and heat should be successive in time. For example, if simply by shifting a boundary between systems a process can be made either adiabatic or heat only, then simultaneous heat and work are identifiable and may be used together in equation (19).

Expression (19) for change of energy is applicable, of course, only to those processes for which the interactions are identifiable as heat and work. Because heat and work are limiting cases of actual processes, equation (19) is strictly applicable only where all interactions have been carried to these limits.

Reversible cyclic engine. By reference to the definition of heat, it will be observed that the reversible interactions between A and X and between X and B in Figure 2 are heat interactions in which one part of X is in equilibrium with A and another part with B, whether or not A and B are close to mutual stable equilibrium. Because the process for the combined system AXB is adiabatic, it can be shown that the heat δQ_B received by B is equal to the heat δQ_A received by A times the negative of the ratio T_B/T_A; namely,

$$\delta Q_B = -\frac{T_B}{T_A}\delta Q_A. \tag{20}$$

The work produced by cyclic device X is, by equation (19), equal to the negative of the sum $\delta Q_A + \delta Q_B$, and, because of equation (20),

$$\delta W = -\delta Q_A - \delta Q_B = \frac{T_A - T_B}{T_A}(-\delta Q_A). \tag{21}$$

It is seen from equation (21) that X will produce positive work if $T_A > T_B$ and $\delta Q_A < 0$; that is, if heat flows from the hotter system to X and from X to the cooler system. The efficiency η with which X converts to work the heat it receives from the hotter system is thus

$$\eta = \frac{T_A - T_B}{T_A}. \tag{22}$$

Reversible cyclic engines

This quantity is called the Carnot efficiency after Carnot, who, before the discovery of the first and second laws of thermodynamics, made the following statements concerning the efficiency of engines working between reservoirs at specified levels of temperature: The efficiency of a reversible engine has a fixed value that is the same for all reversible engines and is greater than that of any irreversible engine.

An example of a reversible cycle in which a system receives all heat at one temperature and rejects all heat at another with reversible adiabatic changes between the two temperatures is the Carnot cycle, devised by Carnot. Its efficiency is given by equation (22).

Work-producing systems and devices. A problem of economic and social importance in heat engineering is the production of work to be used for practical purposes such as lifting weights, driving electric generators, propelling vehicles, or operating cutting tools. Work can be obtained from any system that is not in a stable equilibrium state as it changes toward a stable equilibrium state without changes in constraints. For example, work may be obtained by lowering a weight inside a closed system while causing—through appropriate levers, belts, and pulleys—a weight to rise outside. The production of work need not end until the internal weight has reached the lowest position in the gravity field that the configuration of the system permits. Similarly, an electric storage battery may produce work until it is completely discharged. The maximum work that can be produced by the system adiabatically will be obtained if the process is executed reversibly—that is, at constant entropy. By virtue of the second law the maximum work is only a fraction of the energy of the system. This fraction is larger the farther the system is initially from stable equilibrium; *i.e.*, the larger the difference between the maximum entropy corresponding to the initial energy and the entropy of the initial nonstable state. The fraction is equal to zero when the difference in entropy just described is equal to zero—namely, when the system is initially in a stable equilibrium state.

On the other hand, a system in any state, including a stable equilibrium state, can produce work when combined with a system in the environment that passes through stable equilibrium states but is not in mutual stable equilibrium with the first. The maximum work that can be obtained is the maximum possible decrease in the available work when the system in the environment acts as a reservoir, or it is the maximum possible decrease of one of the other availability functions discussed below when other conditions are imposed by the environment. In order to obtain this maximum, the work-producing process must be completely reversible. For example, if the system with the elevated weight described in the preceding paragraph is at a higher or lower temperature than the atmosphere, then further work may be obtained by interposing a Carnot heat engine between the system and the atmosphere, so that the system is gradually cooled or heated to the temperature of the atmosphere as heat flows to the engine and produces work. If the whole process is executed reversibly, then the maximum possible work will be produced.

The greatest sources of work are fuels found in nature that are either not themselves in stable equilibrium states—for example, uranium in a reactor—or are not in mutual stable equilibrium with the atmosphere from which they have been isolated in the course of geologic history—for example, the fossil fuels coal and petroleum. In either case, the maximum work can be obtained only by a reversible approach to stable equilibrium or mutual stable equilibrium.

In the case of uranium, a reversible nuclear reaction is required; for the fossil fuels, a reversible chemical reaction. A close approximation to a reversible chemical reaction is found in lead storage batteries used in automobiles for starting and for lighting. No close approximation to a reversible nuclear reaction has yet been realized in practice, although in principle such a reaction is possible.

Because the cost of work includes not only fuel costs but also capital costs that usually increase as irreversibility in the process is reduced, the economical means of producing work may in some respects depart radically from the reversible means. For example, in fossil-fueled central power stations, fuel and oxygen in the air enter into an irreversible chemical reaction that raises the temperature of the resulting products by about 2,000 degrees on the Kelvin scale and reduces the work available by about one quarter. Energy from these hot products is then transferred irreversibly across a large temperature difference to appear as heat added to liquid and vapour water that is the working fluid of a heat engine. The loss in work available is again about one quarter of that of the original fuel and air. Irreversibility in the heat-engine cycle accounts for another 10 percent, so that about 40 percent is actually realized as work delivered to the electrical distribution system.

Economical production of work

A Carnot cycle is an obvious but usually impractical means to produce work from heat interactions with hot products of chemical or nuclear reactions. Most commonly used is the Rankine cycle, in which heat is used to generate vapour from a liquid; the vapour is expanded through a work-producing engine, condensed to liquid as it rejects heat to the environment, and pumped back into the vapour generator. The Stirling cycle, which has had only limited application, passes through gaseous states only.

III. Simple systems

STABLE EQUILIBRIUM STATES

A closed simple system is one in which the numbers of particles of the various components are fixed and the only constraint provided by the environment is an upper value for the volume of the system. By virtue of the state principle, volume (regardless of shape) and energy become sufficient to determine a stable equilibrium state, and the number of independent properties is two. A system that is not influenced by capillarity and external force fields is a simple system. These conditions may be satisfied despite capillarity and gravity fields if homogeneous parts of the system are large, so as to have small surface-to-volume ratio, yet shallow in the vertical direction of the gravity field and free of electric and magnetic fields created by external bodies.

Definition of a simple system

For stable equilibrium states of a closed simple system, entropy S or any other property can be regarded as fixed by the two independent properties volume V and energy

U; therefore, S can be expressed as a function of V and U of the form

$$S = S(V,U). \qquad (23)$$

For a number of reasons the energy E of a simple system is denoted by a different symbol U and is called the internal energy. Alternatively, equation (23) may be solved for U in terms of S and V to give

$$U = U(S,V). \qquad (24)$$

The energy change dU between two neighbouring stable equilibrium states can be expressed in terms of the corresponding entropy and volume changes, dS and dV, respectively, by means of the relation

$$dU = \left(\frac{\partial U}{\partial S}\right)_V dS + \left(\frac{\partial U}{\partial V}\right)_S dV. \qquad (25)$$

The first partial differential coefficient has already been identified (by equation 13) as the Kelvin temperature. The second is the rate of energy change (the rate of receiving work) with change in volume in reversible adiabatic compression or expansion. It can be shown to be the negative of the pressure p that the system exerts on constraining walls. Substitution of the temperature T and the pressure p in equation (25) results in the equation

$$dU = TdS - pdV, \qquad (26)$$

in which the first term in the right-hand member represents the heat and the second the work of a reversible process. It may be observed, however, that equation (26) holds for any change between neighbouring stable equilibrium states regardless of the nature of the process, because it is a relation between properties and changes in values of properties. But for the general process, the terms (TdS) and $(-pdV)$ are not in general equal to the respective heat and work that may be involved in the process.

By means of the criterion of stable equilibrium and equation (26), it can be shown that not only the temperature but also the pressure must be uniform throughout a simple system in a stable equilibrium state.

Representation of states on diagrams. Because a stable equilibrium state in a simple system is determined by two independent properties, all such states may be represented by points on a surface in a space in which two of the three coordinates represent independent properties and the third the dependent property. Alternatively, the traces

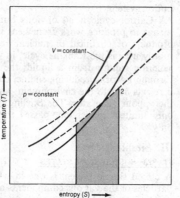

Figure 3: *Relationships between thermodynamic properties of systems.*
(Left) Relationships of pressure and volume of systems maintained at fixed temperature *(T)* or at fixed entropy *(S)*. (Right) Relationships between temperature and entropy of systems maintained at fixed pressure *(p)* or at fixed volume *(V)*.

of planes of constant value of one property may be shown on a two-dimensional chart in which the coordinates represent the other two properties. Two common choices of the latter class are pressure–volume (p–V) and temperature–entropy (T–S) charts. An example of the former is shown in Figure 3 (left), with traces of planes of constant temperature from the pressure–volume–temperature space and of planes of constant en-

tropy from the pressure–volume–entropy space. On the p–V chart the area under a curve of states represents the work done on a slowly moving piston that confines the fluid in a cylinder. On the T–S chart (Figure 3 [right]) the area under the curve represents the heat received by the system in a reversible process passing through the states represented by the curve. Because the change of energy of a system undergoing a cycle is equal to zero, it is seen from equation (19) that the cyclic integral $\oint \delta Q$ must be equal to the cyclic integral $\oint \delta W$. For a reversible cycle, TdS may be substituted for δQ and pdV for δW so that

$$\oint TdS = \oint pdV. \qquad (27)$$

For any cycle, therefore, the area enclosed by the representation on the T–S chart is equal to that on the p–V chart; for example, the areas enclosed by the representations of the Carnot cycle in the p–V and T–S charts (Figure 4 [left] and 4 [right]) are equal.

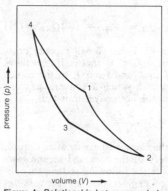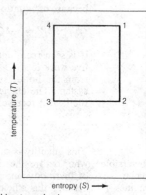

Figure 4: *Relationship between work done and heat received by a fluid undergoing a Carnot cycle.*
The lines from state 1 to state 2 represent reversible and adiabatic expansion of the fluid; from 2 to 3, reversible compression at fixed temperature accompanied by heat rejection; from 3 to 4, reversible and adiabatic compression; from 4 to 1, reversible expansion at fixed temperature accompanied by heat reception. The enclosed area (left) represents the net work done by the fluid during the complete cycle; it is exactly equal to the enclosed area (right) that represents the net heat flow to the fluid.

Reversible constant-pressure process. The reversible process at constant pressure, because of its practical importance, warrants special consideration. Because for constant pressure the change in the product pV is also p times the change in V, pdV, it can be shown that the expression for the heat $(\delta Q)_p$ received by the system is equal to the change of an extensive property called enthalpy, which is defined by the relation $H \equiv U + pV$; that is,   Enthalpy

$$(\delta Q)_p = dH. \qquad (28)$$

Thus, in any heating of a simple system in such a way (for example, under a piston loaded by a weight) that its boundary expands slowly as it maintains constant pressure, the enthalpy of the system increases by the amount of heat added.

MAXWELL RELATIONS

For a closed simple system that assumes only stable equilibrium states, it can be shown that the partial derivative $(\partial T/\partial V)_S$ is equal to the negative of the partial derivative $(\partial p/\partial S)_V$, thus,

$$\left(\frac{\partial T}{\partial V}\right)_S = -\left(\frac{\partial p}{\partial S}\right)_V.$$

This relation is one of the Maxwell relations, named for the man who first stated them.

Enthalpy, Helmholtz free energy, and Gibbs free energy are, respectively, defined as follows:

$$H \equiv U + pV, \qquad (29)$$
$$\Psi \equiv U - TS, \qquad (30)$$
$$Z \equiv H - TS. \qquad (31)$$

These properties can be manipulated mathematically to obtain the following equations:

$$\left(\frac{\partial T}{\partial V}\right)_S = -\left(\frac{\partial p}{\partial S}\right)_V, \tag{32}$$

$$\left(\frac{\partial T}{\partial p}\right)_S = \left(\frac{\partial V}{\partial S}\right)_p, \tag{33}$$

$$\left(\frac{\partial S}{\partial V}\right)_T = \left(\frac{\partial p}{\partial T}\right)_V, \tag{34}$$

$$\left(\frac{\partial S}{\partial p}\right)_T = -\left(\frac{\partial V}{\partial T}\right)_p. \tag{35}$$

These equations are Maxwell relations. They relate the entropy to the relatively easily measured properties pressure, volume, and temperature.

PHASE RULE

An intensive property of system A is defined as a property of which the value at a spatial point in a part of A approaches a limit independent of the size of the part as the size is reduced until it can no longer be identified as a system. As a system is subdivided into smaller and smaller parts, at some point a part becomes so small as compared with the extent of force fields between the parts that it is no longer isolatable and may not, therefore, be considered a system.

For certain stable equilibrium states of a simple system, parts of the system may assume different values of intensive properties; for example, liquid and vapour water may coexist in mutual stable equilibrium for which liquid and vapour parts have the same pressure and temperature but radically different densities. Each such part is called a phase. More generally, a phase of a system is the collection of all homogeneous parts open to the transfer of rest mass and having identical values of their intensive properties.

In the absence of chemical reactions and membranes that are permeable to one substance and not to another, the number of components of a phase of a multiphase system will be identical with the number of molecular species present in the whole system. As soon, however, as a chemical reaction is permitted in which some of these species may be formed from others, then the number of components is reduced by one.

A closed simple system has two independent properties; a simple system open to the transfer of rest mass will have these same two plus the number n of components for the system, because the quantity of each component may be independently varied. On the other hand, the number of independent properties of the same simple open system is also equal to the sum $F + r$, in which F denotes the number of independent intensive phase properties and r the number of phases, because the F intensive properties fix the intensive states of the phases, and the r masses of the r phases fix the size of the system. From these remarks it follows that F is given by the relation

$$F = n + 2 - r. \tag{36}$$

The Gibbs phase rule

This is the phase rule of Gibbs. It reveals, for example, that for a single-component open system, such as water, the number of independent intensive properties may be 2, 1, or 0 if the number of phases present is 1, 2, or 3, respectively. Thus, for water vapour, temperature and pressure are independent properties; *i.e.*, after the value of one is arbitrarily selected, the value of the other may be arbitrarily selected. For coexisting liquid and vapour, either pressure or temperature may be considered the independent property; for coexisting solid, liquid, and vapour (the triple point), the values of all intensive phase properties are fixed by the nature of the substance, and the value of none may be arbitrarily selected.

SIMPLE ONE-COMPONENT SYSTEMS

Phases. All systems that consist of a single pure molecular species, such as argon, oxygen, or water, exhibit largely common patterns of coexisting phases. A closed system of this kind, being a simple system, has two independent properties and the relationships between proper-

ties for stable equilibrium states may therefore be shown as a surface in three-dimensional space. The projection of one such surface onto the pressure–temperature plane is shown in Figure 5 (top) and onto a pressure–volume plane in Figure 5 (bottom). It will be evident from these

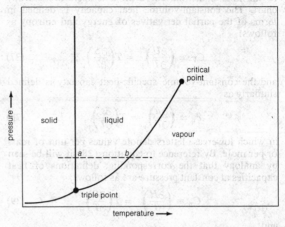

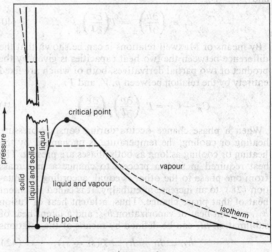

Figure 5: *Relationships between phases of a pure substance.* (Top) The horizontal broken line through a and b represents the effects of absorption of heat by a substance at a constant pressure. (Bottom) The broken line from lower right to upper left represents the effects of compressing a substance, initially entirely vaporous, while keeping the temperature fixed (an isothermal process).

figures that the solid may be heated under constant pressure until some liquid appears. Further heating increases the proportion of liquid present at constant temperature until the solid vanishes, leaving only liquid. Further heating increases the temperature of the liquid until vaporization begins, provided that the pressure is less than the critical pressure. Continued heating increases the proportion of vapour present at constant temperature until the liquid vanishes, leaving only vapour. The vapour may then be raised in temperature indefinitely or until chemical dissociation destroys the assumed purity of the molecular species.

At the critical pressure the coexisting liquid and vapour states are identical, and the vaporization process contracts to an infinitesimal process. At higher pressures no vaporization occurs. It becomes clear, then, that liquid and vapour states differ in degree rather than in kind, because any liquid state can be transformed to any vapour state by a process for which the system remains in a single-phase condition throughout. The same cannot be said of the transition from solid states to either liquid or vapour states.

Processes at constant volume and at constant pressure. When a simple system is heated at constant volume, no work occurs at the boundaries, so that the heat, according to equation (23), is equal to the increase in energy as

Heat capacities

well as to the product of temperature and increase in entropy:

$$(\delta Q)_v = dU = TdS.$$

The heat of a constant-volume process is therefore equal to the area under the curve on a temperature–entropy chart. The constant-volume heat capacity is defined in terms of the partial derivatives of energy and entropy as follows:

$$C_V \equiv \left(\frac{\partial U}{\partial T}\right)_V = T\left(\frac{\partial S}{\partial T}\right)_V; \qquad (37)$$

and the constant-volume specific-heat capacity is defined similarly as

$$c_v \equiv \left(\frac{\partial u}{\partial T}\right)_v = T\left(\frac{\partial s}{\partial T}\right)_v, \qquad (38)$$

in which lowercase letters denote values per unit of mass or per mole. By reference to equation (28) it will be seen by analogy that the corresponding definitions of heat capacities at constant pressure are as follows:

$$C_p \equiv \left(\frac{\partial H}{\partial T}\right)_p = T\left(\frac{\partial S}{\partial T}\right)_p \qquad (39)$$

and

$$c_p \equiv \left(\frac{\partial h}{\partial T}\right)_p = T\left(\frac{\partial s}{\partial T}\right)_p. \qquad (40)$$

By means of Maxwell relations it can be shown that the difference between the two heat capacities is given by the product of two partial derivatives, both of which are fixed entirely by the relation between p, V, and T:

$$C_p - C_V = T\left(\frac{\partial p}{\partial T}\right)_V\left(\frac{\partial V}{\partial T}\right)_p. \qquad (41)$$

When a phase change occurs during constant-pressure heating or cooling, the temperature is unchanged by the heating or cooling as long as both phases are present. The heat required in such a process to change a unit mass from one phase to the other is equal, according to equation (28), to an increase in enthalpy. It is called the latent heat of that phase change. Thus, a latent heat of fusion h_{jl}, a latent heat of vaporization h_{fg}, and a latent heat of sublimation h_{ik} can be defined by means of the relations

$$h_{jl} = h_l - h_j = T(s_l - s_j), \qquad (42)$$
$$h_{fg} = h_g - h_f = T(s_g - s_f), \qquad (43)$$
$$h_{ik} = h_k - h_i = T(s_k - s_i), \qquad (44)$$

in which subscripts j, l, f, g, i, and k refer, respectively, to solid in equilibrium with liquid, liquid in equilibrium with solid, liquid in equilibrium with vapour, vapour in equilibrium with liquid, solid in equilibrium with vapour, and vapour in equilibrium with solid.

In a two-phase region the change in any extensive property is directly proportional to the corresponding change in any other for a fixed value of temperature, and the pressure is a function of temperature only. From these observations and Maxwell relations (33) or (34), it follows that the rate of change of pressure with temperature change for a two-phase mixture is equal to the ratio of the entropy change to the volume change when a fixed quantity of the substance is changed from one phase to the other—e.g., from liquid state to vapour state. Alternatively, the ratio of enthalpy change to volume change gives the rate of change of pressure with change in the natural logarithm (ln) of temperature:

The Clapeyron relation

$$\frac{dp}{dT} = \frac{s_2 - s_1}{v_2 - v_1} \qquad (45)$$

$$\frac{dp}{d(\ln T)} = T\frac{dp}{dT} = \frac{h_2 - h_1}{v_2 - v_1}. \qquad (46)$$

These equations are used to express the Clapeyron relation.

Equation of state. The mathematical relation between the pressure, volume, and temperature for stable equilibrium states of a closed simple system is called its equation of state. Although it will be subsequently shown to be a relation that does not completely specify the nature of the system, the mathematical relation is an important

one because the three properties it relates are relatively easily measured.

Experimentally it is found that the relation between the pressure, volume, and temperature of a system is extremely complicated. No explicit mathematical expression has ever been devised that represents all the stable equilibrium states of any one simple system. Instead, equations have been proposed, each of which represents some limited range of states of a particular system. The complexity of equations of state ranges from that for a perfect gas with a single constant to those for liquid and vapour states, of which that for water is an example, which often have between 10 and 100 constants, the values of which must be determined so as to fit experimental data.

For the range of liquid and vapour states of a pure molecular species, the general pattern of the p-v-T relation is best shown by drawing a graph of the quantity pv/RT versus the ratio of pressure to critical pressure. If v is taken to be the specific volume (the volume per unit mass) and R is chosen so that pv/RT becomes unity at zero pressure and infinite specific volume for any temperature, then a coincidence occurs: pv/RT is unity for every temperature for that substance, provided only that the specific volume is infinitely large. The constant R is called the gas constant of the molecular species.

The molecular weight of oxygen is 32 and the molecular weight M for any species is inversely proportional to the gas constant R of the molecular species. Thus, the molecular weight M of any species can be defined as 32 times the ratio of the gas constant of oxygen and the gas constant of the species:

$$M \equiv 32\frac{R \text{ (for } O_2)}{R}. \qquad (47)$$

It follows that the volume occupied by a molecular weight of a gas at very low pressure is the same for all gases for any selected pair of values of p and T. Moreover it is directly proportional to T and inversely proportional to p.

The product of molecular weight M and gas constant R is the same for all gases and is called the universal gas constant (denoted by $\mathbf{R}$). The result is an equation, called the perfect-gas equation of state, that appears frequently in the literature of thermodynamics; that is,

The universal gas constant

$$pv/RT = 1, \qquad (48)$$

in which v is the volume occupied by one molecular weight, or one mole, of gas.

The equation of state (48) applies, therefore, to any pure molecular species in states for which the specific volume is extremely large and the pressure, at finite temperature, is therefore extremely small. It holds within 2 percent for water vapour at a pressure of one atmosphere and with correspondingly better precision as the pressure is lowered. A gas that conforms to equation (48) is called a semiperfect gas.

By means of Maxwell relations and equation (23) it can be shown in the case of a semiperfect gas that internal energy, enthalpy, and both heat capacities are functions of temperature only and are independent of the effects of volume or pressure. Moreover, the difference $c_p - c_v$ between the specific-heat capacities is equal to the gas constant R when all three quantities are defined in terms of unit mass or, alternatively, in terms of molecular weight.

When quantum effects are not important, an approximate expression for the specific-heat capacity may be obtained from statistical thermodynamics. It is

$$c_v = \frac{f}{2}R, \qquad (49)$$

in which f denotes the number of active degrees of freedom of the molecule (the number of independent ways in which the space configuration of the molecule may change). For a mass concentrated in a point, f would be three (corresponding to the three directions of translation), and c_v would be $3R/2$. With spatial distribution of the mass, additional degrees of freedom appear by virtue of rotation and vibration of the molecule. The number of such degrees of freedom active in a molecule depends, in accordance with quantum theory, on the temperature. In Table 1 are shown the molal heat capac-

Table 1: Molal Specific Heat Capacities of Gases at Room Temperature

	c_v	c_p	$c_v/(\frac{1}{2}R)$	$c_p/(\frac{1}{2}R)$	$k = c_p/c_v$
He*	2.979	4.965	3.000	5.000	1.667
H_2	4.88	6.87	4.92	6.91	1.406
O_2	5.02	7.00	5.05	7.04	1.406
N_2	4.97	6.96	5.01	7.00	1.400
CO	4.97	6.96	5.01	7.00	1.400
H_2O	6.02	8.01	6.07	8.06	1.330
CO_2	6.81	8.80	6.86	8.85	1.292

*And all other monatomic gases.

ities of several gases at room temperature along with the corresponding number of degrees of freedom $c_v/(\frac{1}{2}R)$. For a monatomic gas this number of degrees of freedom proves to be three almost exactly; for diatomic gases it is nearly five (corresponding to two degrees of rotational freedom); and for more complex molecules, a number in excess of five, which implies vibrational degrees of freedom. For all except the monatomic molecule, the value of c_v increases with temperature as new degrees of freedom become active.

The expressions for energy, enthalpy, and entropy of a semiperfect gas are as follows:

$$u = \int_{T_0}^{T} c_v dT + u(T_0), \tag{50}$$

$$h = \int_{T_0}^{T} c_p dT + u(T_0) + RT_0, \tag{51}$$

$$s = \int_{T_0}^{T} c_v \frac{dT}{T} + R \ln \frac{v}{v_0} + s(T_0, v_0)$$

$$= \int_{T_0}^{T} c_p \frac{dT}{T} - R \ln \frac{p}{p_0} + s(T_0, p_0); \tag{52}$$

in these equations the subscript 0 refers to an arbitrarily selected state.

Perfect gas

The perfect gas is a special case of the semiperfect gas —namely, that for which the heat capacities are independent of temperature. The integrals of the previous expressions can now be resolved to give the following:

$$u = c_v(T - T_0), \tag{53}$$

$$h = c_p T - c_v T_0, \tag{54}$$

$$s = c_v \ln \frac{T}{T_0} + R \ln \frac{v}{v_0} + s_0$$

$$= c_p \ln \frac{T}{T_0} - R \ln \frac{p}{p_0} + s_0, \tag{55}$$

in which s_0 denotes the arbitrary value of s at T_0 (for which u is zero) and at p_0.

For a reversible adiabatic process in a perfect gas, the following relations hold: $pv^k =$ constant, $Tv^{k-1} =$ constant, and $pT^{-k/(k-1)} =$ constant, and k is the ratio c_p/c_v.

In 1873 the Dutch physicist Johannes van der Waals proposed the following equation, which in a qualitative way describes the liquid and vapour states of a pure species:

Van der Waals' equation

$$p = \frac{RT}{v - b} - \frac{a}{v^2}, \tag{56}$$

in which a and b are constants for any one species. Not only does this equation approach that of the semiperfect gas as v goes to infinity, but the equation also provides for a region of coexisting states that is capped by a critical state, as in actual substances. Below the temperature T_c (equal to $8a/27Rb$), three values of v correspond to each value of p. Pairs of high-volume and low-volume states, such as P and R (Figure 6), may be found at each pressure–temperature combination. The one pair for which the areas $PQbP$ and $QaRQ$ are equal can be shown

to be the pair that can coexist in mutual stable equilibrium.

An approximate justification of the van der Waals equation can be made based in part on the Newtonian equation of motion for a collection of particles having the following characteristics: (1) the particles are uniform rigid spheres; (2) their diameters are appreciable fractions of the mean distances between them, except at infinite specific volume; and (3) they exert finite attractive forces, which vary with the distance between them, as well as infinite repulsive forces upon contact.

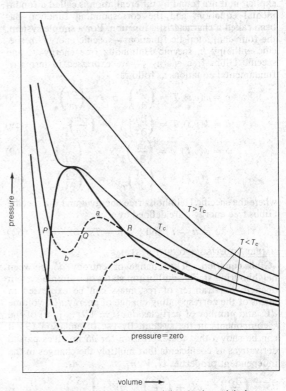

Figure 6: Relations between pressure (p) and volume (v) of liquid and vapour states of a pure molecular species at different temperatures according to the van der Waals equation (see text).

Equations of state, by proper assignment of values of constants, can be made to represent quantitatively (as contrasted with qualitatively for the van der Waals equation) the properties of many molecular species with fair precision. An equation has been developed that represents the properties of water within the precision of virtually all experimental measurements on liquid and vapour water.

A general type of equation of state, which can be made to fit almost any range of gaseous states at the expense of indefinite increase in the number of constants, is the virial form. It may be written as

Virial equations of state

$$\frac{pv}{RT} = 1 + B\rho + C\rho^2 + D\rho^3 + \ldots, \tag{57}$$

in which ρ denotes the density, and the coefficients B, C, D, . . . , called the second, third, fourth, . . . virial coefficients, are functions of temperature only. Substantial progress has been made in determining the forms of the functions B and C for the simpler molecular structures by means of models of the structure and force fields between them.

Critical point. In recent decades the relationships between the various properties of a pure molecular species at and near the critical point have been the subject of many studies. It appears from these that certain mathematical singularities occur at the critical point, including an infinite value for the heat capacity at constant volume, which indicate that no continuous equation (such as the van der Waals equation) relating pressure, volume, and temperature can represent the actual variation in these properties for states closer than a few degrees in temperature to the critical point. A so-called scaling law has been devised to cope with the mathematics of this region.

Fundamental equations. As was implied above by the development of the equation of state for a semiperfect gas, such an equation alone is not adequate to yield the values of energy u, enthalpy h, and entropy s. It must be supplemented by a knowledge of the variation of heat capacity with temperature.

A type of equation for which any of the properties p,T,u,v,s (or any algebraic combination of these) not explicit in it are found by differentiation is called a fundamental equation, and the corresponding function has been called a characteristic function. For a simple system, the four characteristic functions—specific energy u, specific enthalpy h, specific Helmholtz free energy ψ, and specific Gibbs free energy ζ—are expressed in terms of fundamental equations as follows:

$$u = u(v,s),\ T = \left(\frac{\partial u}{\partial s}\right)_v,\ p = -\left(\frac{\partial u}{\partial v}\right)_s, \tag{58}$$

$$h = h(p,s),\ T = \left(\frac{\partial h}{\partial s}\right)_p,\ v = \left(\frac{\partial h}{\partial p}\right)_s, \tag{59}$$

$$\psi = \psi(v,T),\ p = \left(\frac{\partial \psi}{\partial v}\right)_T,\ s = -\left(\frac{\partial \psi}{\partial T}\right)_v, \tag{60}$$

$$\zeta = \zeta(p,T),\ v = \left(\frac{\partial \zeta}{\partial p}\right)_T,\ s = -\left(\frac{\partial \zeta}{\partial T}\right)_p, \tag{61}$$

where the specific Helmholtz free energy ψ and the specific Gibbs free energy ζ are defined by

$$\psi \equiv u - Ts \text{ and } \zeta \equiv h - Ts. \tag{62}$$

SIMPLE MULTICOMPONENT SYSTEMS

Gibbs equation. The change of entropy dS between neighbouring stable equilibrium states of a simple system open to the transfer of rest mass can be expressed in terms of the corresponding change of energy dU, volume dV, and number of particles dn_i ($i = 1,2,\ldots,k$) of the k components in the system. By use of equation (9) it can be shown that the expression for dS involves partial derivatives as coefficients that multiply the changes in the independent properties $U, V, n_1, n_2, \ldots, n_k$:

$$dS = \left(\frac{\partial S}{\partial U}\right)_{V,n} dU + \left(\frac{\partial S}{\partial V}\right)_{U,n} dV + \left(\frac{\partial S}{\partial n_1}\right)_{U,V,n} dn_1 + \ldots + \left(\frac{\partial S}{\partial n_k}\right)_{U,V,n} dn_k, \tag{63}$$

in which subscript n denotes all of $n_1, n_2, \ldots, n_k$ that can be held constant. Upon identifying, as in equation (23), the first two partial derivatives in terms of pressure p and temperature T and introducing a new quality μ_i to be defined shortly, equation (63) becomes what is called the Gibbs equation:

$$dS = \frac{1}{T}dU + \frac{p}{T}dV - \frac{\mu_1}{T}dn_1 - \ldots - \frac{\mu_k}{T}dn_k. \tag{64}$$

Chemical potential

The quantity μ_i, which is called the chemical potential of component i in the system, is defined as follows:

$$\mu_i \equiv -T\left(\frac{\partial S}{\partial n_i}\right)_{U,V,n} \quad \text{for } i = 1,2,\ldots k. \tag{65}$$

Mutual stable equilibrium. Upon seeking the conditions that must be satisfied in order that two or more phases should be in mutual stable equilibrium while open to transfer of rest mass between them, it is unnecessary to consider any states for which any one phase would be in a nonequilibrium state if it were suddenly isolated. It is unnecessary because any change of state that could occur spontaneously while the phase was isolated would be one of many allowed changes of state when it was not isolated and would, therefore, serve as an indication that at least one spontaneous change is possible and that equilibrium does not exist.

It is sufficient, therefore, to consider only those states for which the individual phases are in stable equilibrium states when isolated. The Gibbs equation provides a general statement of the change of entropy of a simple phase that may exchange component substances with neighbouring phases as it passes through stable equilibrium states. If the formation of any new part unlike the existing parts is prohibited by the definition of the phase, then a set of stable equilibrium states is prescribed for which the Gibbs equation expresses changes in entropy between states in the set.

A heterogeneous system may be considered to be made up of several homogeneous phases, within each of which the formation of a new part is prohibited as proposed above. The states that these phases may assume consistent with mutual stable equilibrium may now be found by seeking out the state of maximum entropy of the whole system for a given volume and energy. This kind of procedure was used above to show that the phases of such a system must have equal temperatures. By similar reasoning it can now be shown that the phases must have equal pressures and equal values of the chemical potential μ_i of each component i present in all the phases. That is, among the necessary conditions for stable equilibrium of a multiphase simple system (*i.e.*, in the absence of force fields and capillarity) is uniformity throughout the multiphase system of temperature, pressure, and chemical potential of each component present in all the phases.

Of these conditions the one most open to exception is equality of pressure. In order for it to apply, an encroachment of the volume of each phase upon every other, for constant energy and composition of each phase, must be an allowed variation in state of the system. Wherever phases are separated by a rigid boundary, which may be permeable to one or more components, then equality of pressure between such phases is not necessary to mutual stable equilibrium.

If two phases are separated by a wall that is permeable to some components but not permeable to others, then equality of chemical potential of those other components across the wall is not necessary. An exception can be made as regards the potentials T, p, and μ_i in cases in which a transfer of energy, volume, and component i can occur at stable equilibrium in one direction but not in the other direction. Then a condition for mutual stable equilibrium becomes, because entropy is to be maximized, that the temperature in the phase that can receive energy but cannot supply it may be greater than or equal to the temperature in phases that can both receive and supply energy. Similar statements can be made in regard to pressure and the transfer of volume and in regard to chemical potential of component i and the transfer of that component.

These statements imply that potentials T, p, and μ_i are escaping tendencies for energy, volume, and component i, respectively. For equilibrium each escaping tendency must be balanced as between phases, unless the escape of one flux has reached its upper limit for a phase so that no further escape is possible. For such a phase it is necessary for equilibrium that the escaping tendency be not less than in other phases, but it may be more. This consideration is relevant for certain quantum effects at low temperature, for two phases separated by a movable solid boundary that has come up against a stop and behind which the pressure may be greater than in front (but not less), and for exhaustion of a phase as regards one component.

From the definitions of enthalpy H (29), Helmholtz free energy Ψ (30), and Gibbs free energy Z (31), it is readily shown that the chemical potential can be expressed in alternative forms; that is,

$$\mu_i = \left(\frac{\partial U}{\partial n_i}\right)_{V,S,n} = \left(\frac{\partial H}{\partial n_i}\right)_{p,S,n} = \left(\frac{\partial \Psi}{\partial n_i}\right)_{V,T,n} = \left(\frac{\partial Z}{\partial n_i}\right)_{p,T,n} \tag{66}$$

The last of these is known as the partial Gibbs free energy ζ_i of component i in the phase. In view of the definition of Z, μ_i may also be expressed in terms of the partial enthalpy h_i and the partial entropy s_i; thus,

$$\mu_i = \left(\frac{\partial Z}{\partial n_i}\right)_{p,T,n} = \left(\frac{\partial H}{\partial n_i}\right)_{p,T,n} - T\left(\frac{\partial S}{\partial n_i}\right)_{p,T,n} = \zeta_i = h_i - Ts_i. \tag{67}$$

In general, lowercase symbols with subscript i denote the partial property. For a phase of pure component i, any partial property is identical with the corresponding specific property—that is, the value of the property per unit mass, which is here taken to be the mole. The chemical potential of a component i in a mixture containing i is equal to the specific Gibbs free energy of i in a phase of pure i in equilibrium with the mixture through a membrane permeable to i alone.

A semipermeable membrane such as the one just proposed is one across which the pressure need not be balanced for equilibrium. By definition of the membrane, encroachment of the mixture phase into the volume of the pure phase cannot occur, but the reverse encroachment can occur. The membrane must, of course, have sufficient structural strength to support the pressure difference.

The expression for the chemical potential of a semiperfect gas in terms of temperature and pressure is found from equations (67), (51), and (52). It proves to be the sum of a simple function of pressure p and temperature T plus a relatively complicated function $f_i(T)$ of temperature as follows:

$$\mu_i = RT \ln p + f_i(T), \qquad (68)$$

in which the function $f_i(T)$ is different for different semiperfect gases i. For a given temperature, however, equation 68 indicates that the chemical potential increases with increase in pressure. That is, temperature being fixed, the escaping tendency increases as the pressure increases.

Three equations will be recorded here but not derived.

1. The Gibbs equation as an expression for the change in Gibbs free energy of a phase between neighbouring stable equilibrium states:

$$d\mathbf{z} = V dp - S dT + \sum_i \mu_i\, dn_i. \qquad (69)$$

In the equation the short notation $\sum_i \mu_i\, dn_i$ has been used

to denote $\mu_1 dn_1 + \mu_2 dn_2 + \cdots + \mu_k dn_k$, in which subscript $i = 1, 2, \ldots, k$ denotes a component substance.

2. The Gibbs free energy as a summation of products of chemical potentials and numbers of moles of component substances i of a phase:

$$\mathbf{z} = \sum_i \mu_i\, n_i. \qquad (70)$$

Gibbs–Duhem equation 3. The Gibbs–Duhem equation, which relates for a phase the changes between stable equilibrium states in temperature, pressure, and numbers of moles of components:

$$S dT - V dp + \sum_i n_i\, d\mu_i = 0. \qquad (71)$$

Mixtures of gases. *Gibbs–Dalton rule for mixtures.* Gibbs revised the earlier rule of the 18th- and 19th-century English physicist John Dalton for determining the properties of a mixture of gases from the properties of the pure components. Two equivalent statements of the Gibbs–Dalton rule for mixtures are as follows: (1) The pressure in a mixture of different gases is equal to the sum of the pressures of the different gases as existing each by itself at the temperature of the mixture and with the same value of the chemical potential as it has in the mixture. (2) The pressure of a mixture of different gases is equal to the sum of the pressures of the pure components each existing as a phase in equilibrium with the mixture through a membrane permeable to the component.

Using single subscripts to refer to components in the mixture and double subscripts to refer to pure component phases, the Gibbs–Dalton rule takes the form

$$p = p_{11} + p_{22} + p_{33} + \cdots \qquad (72)$$

for

$$T = T_{11} = T_{22} = \ldots, \qquad (73)$$

and

$$\mu_1 = \mu_{11}, \ \mu_2 = \mu_{22}, \ldots. \qquad (74)$$

In this notation p_1 would have no "operational" meaning because no instrument has been devised that can measure the pressure of component 1 when it is part of a mixture.

It can now be shown from the Gibbs–Dalton rule and the Gibbs–Duhem equation that the number c_i of mass units of component i in unit volume of the mixture (the concentration c_i of i in the mixture) is equal to the density ρ_{ii} or the inverse of the specific volume v_{ii} of i in the pure phase in mutual stable equilibrium with the mixture. The concentration c_i denotes the ratio of mass n_i of i in the mixture to the volume v of the mixture. It follows immediately that the density ρ (or $1/v$) of the mixture is the sum of the densities ρ_{ii} (or $1/v_{ii}$) of the pure phases.

Further application of the Gibbs–Duhem equation yields the following expressions for extensive properties:

$$U = nu = \sum_i n_i\, u_{ii},$$

$$H = nh = \sum_i n_i\, h_{ii},$$

$$S = ns = \sum_i n_i\, s_{ii},$$

$$\Psi = n\psi = \sum_i n_i\, \psi_{ii}, \text{ and}$$

$$\mathbf{z} = n\zeta = \sum_i n_i\, \zeta_{ii} = \sum_i n_i\, \mu_{ii} = \sum_i n_i\, \mu_i. \qquad (75)$$

In these equations the mass n_i of component i in the mixture will be identical with n_{ii} the mass of i in the pure phase if the volume of the pure phase ii that is in mutual stable equilibrium with the mixture is made equal to the volume of the mixture. The result is in accord with Dalton's concept that each component behaves as if it were present alone.

A further conclusion that can be reached is that a Gibbs–Dalton mixture of semiperfect gases is itself a semiperfect gas. That is, for the mixture the ratio pv/RT is equal to unity if v is the volume per mole of all components and R the universal gas constant. If a specific gas constant is used and v is the volume per unit mass, then the mixture behaves as a semiperfect gas with a molecular weight M that is the mass m of the mixture divided by the total number n of moles of all components. It is also the average of the molecular weights M_i of the components, each weighted proportionately to the mole fraction y_i of that component in the mixture:

$$M = \frac{m}{n} = \sum_i y_i\, M_i.$$

Mixing gases. Some further results of the Gibbs–Dalton rule will be given here without proof. If a number of pure species are confined by thin partitions in separate parts of an insulated volume V in such quantities that their pressures are equal when their temperatures are equal, then when the partitions are removed (or destroyed), the gases will mix irreversibly without change in temperature, pressure, energy, or enthalpy. The change of entropy ΔS is greater than zero, as is appropriate for an adiabatic irreversible process. It is given by the negative of the product of the number n of moles of all components multiplied by the gas constant R and a mean logarithmic mole fraction:

$$\Delta S = -nR \sum_i y_i \ln y_i, \qquad (76)$$

in which y_i denotes the mole fraction of the species i in the final mixture. Both the Helmholtz free energy and the Gibbs free energy decrease in the mixing process.

The Gibbs–Dalton rule holds in regions of state in which the pressure is low relative to the critical pressure of every component. Outside these regions an equation of state for a mixture may be devised from the equations of state of its components, with varying degrees of precision, by means of certain combining rules. One of these rules, proposed by the 19th- and 20th-century French physicist Émile-Hilaire Amagat, states that the volume of a mixture is the sum of the volumes of the pure components—each at the pressure and temperature of the mixture. A 20th-century U.S. chemist, James Alexander Beattie, later proposed a rule of more general application that prescribes how the coefficients in the Beattie–Bridgman equations for the pure components may be combined in order to obtain the corresponding coefficients for the mixture.

Vapour pressures of pure liquids. The vapour of a pure species may be in mutual stable equilibrium with its liquid at a flat interface at the normal or saturation vapour pressure corresponding to its temperature. The vapour may also, however, be in mutual stable equilibrium at a nonwetting porous wall that is permeable to vapour but not to liquid or at a curved interface, either of which can support a pressure difference between liquid and vapour. The effect of change in pressure of the liquid on the corresponding vapour pressure is called the Poynting effect. It is found by equating chemical potentials of liquid and vapour. For an incompressible liquid and a semiperfect vapour, the Poynting effect proves to be approximately proportional to the change in pressure on the liquid. For water at 40° C (104° F) the equilibrium pressure of the vapour increases by 1 percent when the pressure on the liquid is increased by a factor of 200.

The Poynting effect

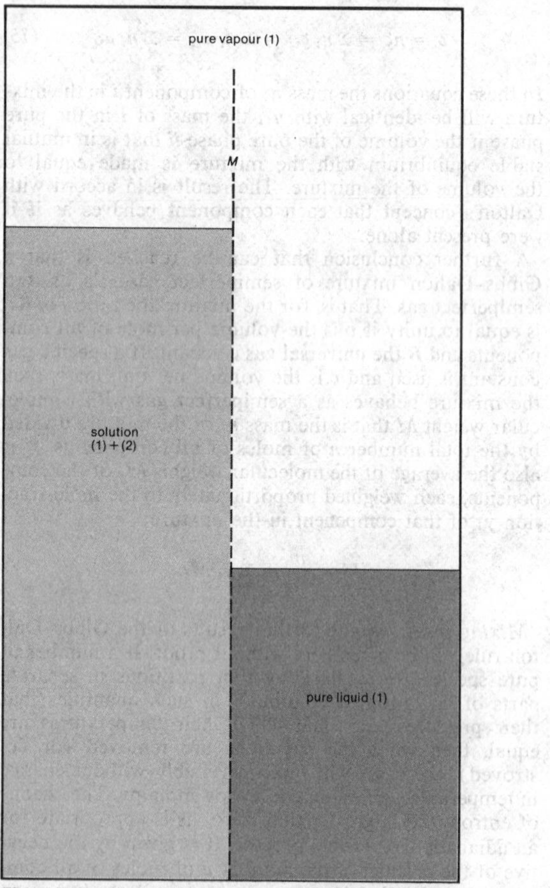

```
┌─────────────────────────────────────┐
│           pure vapour (1)            │
│                    ╎                 │
│                    ╎                 │
│                   M╎                 │
│                    ╎                 │
│                    ╎                 │
│     solution       ╎                 │
│     (1) + (2)      ╎                 │
│                    ╎─────────────────│
│                    ╎                 │
│                    ╎  pure liquid (1)│
│                    ╎                 │
└─────────────────────────────────────┘
```

Figure 7: Equilibrium between a pure volatile liquid (1), a solution of nonvolatile substance (2) in liquid (1), and the vapour of substance (1). Substance (1) can pass through the membrane (*M*), but substance (2) cannot. The difference in the vapour pressures of solvent and solution causes the liquid levels to be unequal. The difference in pressure between pure liquid and solution is called the osmotic pressure (see text).

Ideal solutions. When a solute is added to a volatile solvent, the volatility of the solvent is reduced. The effect is to reduce the pressure of solvent vapour that is in equilibrium with the liquid in proportion to the reduction in the mole fraction of solvent in the solution. Thus the effect on the volatility is the same for equal numbers of moles of different solutes in solution, the mole being measured as described by equation (47). This observation, which holds only for dilute or ideal solutions, is

expressed in Raoult's rule. The rule states that at given pressure p and temperature T the pressure p_1^v of pure solvent vapour in equilibrium with the solution is equal to the product of the mole fraction x_1 of solvent in the solution and the vapour pressure p_1^o of pure liquid solvent at the pressure and temperature of the solution. By ignoring the small Poynting effect on the vapour pressure of the solvent, the rule of boiling-point raising may be derived from Raoult's rule by mathematical deduction. It is that the rate of change of boiling temperature T with mole fraction x_2 of solute 2, as solute is added to a dilute solution, is equal to the rate of change of boiling temperature of pure solvent 1 with the logarithm of the pressure p_1^o on the pure solvent. The mathematical statement of the rule of boiling-point raising is given by the relation

Raoult's rule

$$\left(\frac{\partial T}{\partial x_2}\right)_{x_2 \to 0} = \left[\frac{dT}{d(\ln p_1^o)}\right]_{x_2 = 0}. \tag{77}$$

For water at 25° C (77° F) the value of $(\partial T/\partial x_2)$ is about 17° C (31° F) or, more practically, 0.17° C for each mole percent of solute regardless of the nature of the solute.

Figure 7 depicts a container in which volatile solvent liquid 1 is separated from a solution containing nonvolatile solute 2 by a wall M permeable to 1 only. The wall extends only part way to the top, leaving a vapour space with free access of vapour 1 from one liquid surface to the other. Because the pressure of vapour in mutual stable equilibrium with the solution is less, by Raoult's rule, than that in equilibrium with the pure solvent, the height of the solution surface must be greater than that of the pure liquid by enough to provide the appropriate hydrostatic head of vapour between them. The corresponding hydrostatic head of liquid, of course, is much greater and accounts, except for the head of vapour, for a substantial difference between the pressure of the solution and the pressure of the solvent with which it is in equilibrium through the semipermeable wall. This difference in pressure, which is required to prevent migration of solvent into the solution, is called osmotic pressure. With the usual approximations for a dilute solution and a perfect vapour, it can be shown by equating chemical potentials of solvent across the wall that the osmotic pressure P is approximately equal to the product of gas constant R, temperature T, and number of moles c_2 of solute per unit volume of solution.

Osmotic pressure

By means of the Gibbs–Duhem equation (71) and the assumption of perfect vapours for the two components of a binary solution, it can be shown that Raoult's rule requires that the pressure p_2^v of solute vapour in equilibrium with a solution is proportional to the mole fraction x_2 of solute in the solution; that is, p_2^v is equal to

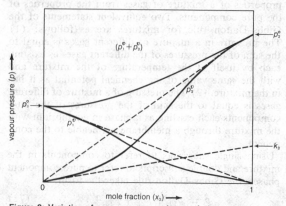

Figure 8: Variation of vapour pressure above solutions of two completely miscible volatile substances, 1 and 2, from pure 1 ($x_2 = 0$, $P_1^v = p_1^o$) to pure substance 2 ($x_2 = 1$, $P_2^v = p_2^o$). The Henry's rule constant, k_2, is shown as the tangent to the graph of p_2^v at $x_2 = 0$.

$k_2 x_2$, k_2 being a constant of proportionality. This relation is known as Henry's rule. Unlike Raoult's rule, in which the coefficient of x_1 is the vapour pressure of the pure solvent, the proportionality constant k_2 bears no simple relation to the properties of the components. Of course, if Raoult's and Henry's rules were to hold over the whole range of x_2 from 0 to 1, then k_2 would be the vapour pressure of pure solute. In general, however, the laws hold only for dilute solutions; that is, for x_2 nearly zero. An example of the variation of vapour pressures of a binary mixture of two completely miscible volatile species is shown in Figure 8, in which the distinction between

Henry's rule constant k_2 and the vapour pressure p_2° of pure solute is made evident.

Equation (68) for the chemical potential of a semiperfect gas can be used in combination with Raoult's and Henry's rules to show that any change in chemical potential of solvent in a solution between two states at the same temperature is proportional to the change in $RT \ln x_1$. Similarly, the change in chemical potential of solute is proportional to change in $RT \ln x_2$. Expressions for the chemical potentials, therefore, are

$$\mu_1 = RT \ln x_1 + \mu_1^{\circ} \qquad (78)$$

$$\mu_2 = RT \ln x_2 + \mu_2^{\circ}, \qquad (79)$$

in which μ_1° is the chemical potential of pure solvent $(x_1 = 1)$ at the pressure and temperature of the solution. The quantity μ_2° is the chemical potential of pure solute in a hypothetical ideal-solution state for which x_2 is unity. Equations (78) and (79) indicate that the logarithm of the mole fraction of a component is the measure of the escaping tendency of that component.

When to an ideal solution at a given pressure and temperature is added some pure solvent starting from the same pressure and temperature, it can be shown that the total volume occupied by solution and solvent remains unchanged by the process of dissolving. Similar statements may be made concerning the total energy and total enthalpy. One consequence is that no heat flows to or from the fluids during this process of solution; thus, the heat of solution is zero, and the process is adiabatic. The total entropy, on the other hand, increases during the process of solution, as would be expected from equation (6) for an irreversible adiabatic process. In general, a similar addition of pure solute to an ideal solution will result in change in total volume, energy, and enthalpy, and the heat of solution will not be zero. The change in volume, energy, and enthalpy per unit of solute added will be independent of the composition of the solution over the range of ideality.

BULK FLOW

A kind of transfer of matter in which each elementary piece of the flowing fluid can be considered to be a closed and separable system bounded by a prescribed surface is called bulk flow. Contrasting with this definition is transfer of material by molecular diffusion, in which the flowing molecules cannot be considered to be closed and separable systems.

Figure 9 shows a system A enclosed within a fixed boundary σ and an infinitesimal adjacent mass dm separated from A by a part of σ that is penetrable by A. The mass dm may be pushed across σ to join the larger mass inside. The work done by the surroundings on the combined system comprising A and dm will be equal to the product $pv\,dm$—namely, the pressure p multiplied by the specific volume v and the mass dm. This statement must be qualified by limiting it to slow motion of the boundary of dm and to zero shear effects in the fluid.

It can now be shown from equation (19) that the change in energy found within the boundary σ is the initial value of $E + pV$ for the mass dm, or $(e + pv)\,dm$, e denoting energy per unit mass. To this must be added any heat δQ that crosses the boundary of the combined system, and from it must be subtracted any work δW_x, called shaft work, that crosses boundary σ by virtue of

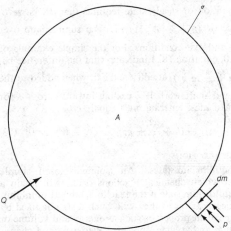

Figure 9: Schematic calculation of the change in energy of system resulting from the introduction of additional mass (see text).

torque in a rotating shaft or the equivalent. The corresponding statement for the energy change dE within σ when an infinitesimal mass of fluid dm crosses σ is

$$dE = (e + pv)\,dm + \delta Q - \delta W_x. \qquad (80)$$

Equation (80) is sufficiently general to apply to otherwise simple systems that may change level in a gravity field and that depart from equilibrium to the extent that elementary parts acquire the uniform velocity ϕ. Then it may be shown by consideration of work in adiabatic processes that the energy e of unit mass is the sum of the internal energy u, the kinetic energy $\phi^2/2$, and the gravity potential energy gz for height z above a datum level $z = 0$, g denoting the gravity constant, which has the dimensions of acceleration:

$$e = u + \frac{\phi^2}{2} + gz. \qquad (81)$$

Equation (80) may now be repeated after substituting the enthalpy symbol h for $u + pv$:

$$dE = \left(h + \frac{\phi^2}{2} + gz\right) dm + \delta Q - \delta W_x. \qquad (82)$$

A special case of the problem of bulk flow is one for which inward flow and outward flow occur, each in one or more channels, and the state of the fluid within the control volume is the same at all times. The state of the control volume for which this assumption holds is called a steady state, and the flow condition is called steady flow. A simple example with single entry and single exit is shown in Figure 10. It would apply to a boiler, for which W_x is zero, and to a steam turbine, for which Q is nearly zero, as well as to many other engineering devices.

Steady flow

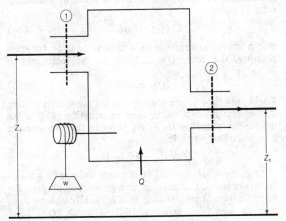

Figure 10: A system in a steady state in which the state of the fluid between boundaries 1 and 2 is the same at all times. The net mass flux across the entire boundary of the system must be zero. The heights of boundaries 1 and 2 above a datum are denoted Z_1 and Z_2 (see text).

The condition of steady state requires that dE be zero. The value of $(h + \frac{\phi^2}{2} + gz)dm$ is then summed up over all entry and exit conditions. For the simple example of Figure 10, equation (82) indicates that the difference between $(h + \frac{\phi^2}{2} + gz)$ at entry and exit when added to the heat Q' and shaft work W_x' passing inward across σ for each unit of mass entering must equal zero:

$$(h + \frac{\phi^2}{2} + gz)_1 - (h + \frac{\phi^2}{2} + gz)_2 + Q' - W_x' = 0. \quad (83)$$

CHEMICAL REACTIONS

Stable equilibrium states. An isolated closed simple system in which chemical reactions occur will attain a stable equilibrium state if the reactions are left uninhibited to proceed as far as they will. Such a state is fixed by two independent properties such as energy and volume or temperature and volume, and it is called a state of chemical equilibrium. Among the properties of the chemical equilibrium state fixed by the two independent properties are the proportions of the molecular species present.

When a chemical reaction proceeds at such a rate that chemical equilibrium is not achieved, each state passed through may be considered, for the purposes of analysis, to be a stable equilibrium state for which an anticatalyst has prevented chemical reaction. Between these states the system may experience chemical reaction in such degree as to produce a certain chemical aggregation in a second state different from that in the first. These states may be considered to have been achieved by successively removing and replacing an agent, such as an anticatalyst, that prohibits a chemical reaction. In the presence of such an agent each stable equilibrium state would correspond to a different set of proportions of species that would constitute a system with its own set of allowed states. To identify the state, therefore, it is necessary to add to the two independent properties required by the state principle an additional property that identifies the system. For example, for a mixture of molecules of nitrogen (N_2), hydrogen (H_2), and ammonia (NH_3) and the chemical reaction of formation of ammonia from the elements N_2 and H_2,

$$\frac{1}{2}N_2 + \frac{3}{2}H_2 \rightleftarrows NH_3,$$

the energy, volume, and some measure of the degree to which this reaction has proceeded in one direction or the other would be required to identify the system and its stable equilibrium state.

Heat in chemical reactions. For any chemical reaction in a simple system, for which heat Q and work W are the only interactions, the energy change ΔE is given, according to equation (19), by the difference between heat and work: $\Delta E = Q - W$. For a chemical reaction in a system held at constant volume, the heat $(Q)_V$, in the absence of other interactions, is given by the increment in energy:

$$(Q)_V = \Delta E. \quad (84)$$

For a chemical reaction in a system held at constant pressure, the heat $(Q)_p$ is given by the increment in enthalpy:

$$(Q)_p = \Delta H. \quad (85)$$

For steady flow between entry section 1 and exit section 2, the heat interaction, in view of equation (83), is the increase in enthalpy $H_2 - H_1$ between the two sections plus any shaft work W_x:

$$Q = H_2 - H_1 + W_x.$$

For a chemical reaction at constant volume in an isolated system, no change in energy occurs despite the large change in temperature that is usually observed, as may be seen from equation (84) in which $(Q)_V$ (and therefore ΔE) is equal to zero for an isolated system.

When values are sought in the literature for the properties E and H for use in the preceding equations or for S and Z for use in other equations, it is found that for

different molecular species they are not available on a common base—that is, an arbitrarily selected zero state is used for each separate species independently of that for any other. It is necessary, therefore, to supplement data for the molecular species with data on change in values of properties when each species is formed from the chemical elements without change in pressure or temperature.

Equilibrium between chemically reacting species. Included in the description of a system is the set of possible states that the system may assume. The choice of this set is often arbitrary and may be made to suit convenience in approximating a real system and its behaviour. For example, a system consisting of a mixture of hydrogen and oxygen gases may or may not have included among its possible states those in which water has been formed by chemical reaction.

The description of a multicomponent system may or may not permit a certain chemical reaction in which some species are formed from others. Whenever a reaction is permitted that was not permitted before, the number of components, each of which must be independently variable, decreases by one. Moreover, one new kind of change of state is introduced—namely, a variation in which certain species leave phases in which they are actual components to form other species in phases in which these others are actual components.

From O.A. Hougen, K.M. Watson, and R.A. Ragatz, *Chemical Process Principles*, 2nd ed. (1957), used with permission of John Wiley and Sons, Inc.

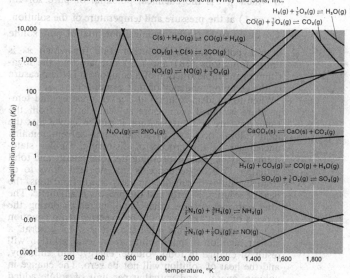

Figure 11: Variation in equilibrium constant, K_p, with variation in temperature for several chemical reactions (see text).

For a reaction such that a moles of A combine with b moles of B, etc., to form k moles of K plus l moles of L, etc., the stoichiometric (chemical-reaction) statement is

$$aA + bB + \ldots \rightleftarrows kK + lL + \ldots. \quad (86)$$

This statement implies that the change Δn_A in number of moles of species A resulting from the reaction, when divided by the coefficient a, is numerically identical with similar quotients for the other species; i.e.,

$$\frac{\Delta n_A}{a} = \frac{\Delta n_B}{b} = \ldots = -\frac{\Delta n_K}{k} = -\frac{\Delta n_L}{l} = \ldots = -\Delta\xi. \quad (87)$$

The common value of the ratios, sometimes called the degree of reaction, is denoted by $\Delta\xi$. The stable equilibrium state in a system for which reaction (86) is allowed must be the state for which the entropy is at a maximum for all the states having given values of energy and volume of each phase. By reference to the Gibbs equation (64), it can be shown that this maximum is attained when the chemical potentials μ_A, μ_B, $\ldots$, μ_K, μ_L, $\ldots$ of species A, B, $\ldots K$, L, $\ldots$ are related as in the following equation, which is called the equation of chemical equilibrium:

$$a\mu_A + b\mu_B + \ldots - k\mu_K - l\mu_L - \ldots = 0. \quad (88)$$

Because for each component of a Gibbs–Dalton mixture

of semiperfect gases the chemical potential may be simply expressed, as in equation (68), in terms of the logarithm of the partial pressure of the species in the mixture, the condition for stable equilibrium becomes such that a product of powers of the partial pressures p_A, p_B, ..., p_K, p_L, ... is the same for a given temperature regardless of the proportions of the components that make up the mixture. This product is called the equilibrium constant in terms of pressure. For reaction (86) it is given by

$$\frac{p_K^k \, p_L^l \cdots}{p_A^a \, p_B^b \cdots} = K_p(T). \tag{89}$$

The variation of K_p with variation in temperature for a number of familiar reactions is shown in Figure 11.

For a chemical reaction among the components of an ideal solution, a similar equilibrium constant is found for which the mole fraction x_I of component I is substituted in equation (89) for the partial pressure of component I:

$$\frac{x_K^k \, x_L^l \cdots}{x_A^a \, x_B^b \cdots} = K_x(T). \tag{90}$$

When a gas mixture is not a Gibbs–Dalton mixture or a solution is not ideal, then a property called the fugacity takes the place of pressure in equation (89), and one called activity takes the place of mole fraction in (90). (For the definitions of these properties, see SOLUTIONS AND SOLUBILITY.)

Because each of these so-called equilibrium constants changes with change in temperature, some knowledge of the rate of change of the value of K with temperature is of great value. This rate is expressed most simply as the rate of change of ln K with temperature, and it proves to be equal to the quotient of the change in enthalpy when the reaction occurs at constant pressure and temperature and the product RT^2. In non-ideal mixtures (or solutions) the change in enthalpy must be measured between a reactants state for which the fugacity (or activity) of each reactant species is unity and a product state for which the fugacity (or activity) of each product is unity:

$$[d(\ln K_\alpha)/dT]_p = \frac{\Delta H^\circ}{RT^2}. \tag{91}$$

AVAILABILITY FUNCTIONS

The economic and engineering importance of a system in a given state is often determined by its available work Ω_R with reference to ambient systems as a reservoir. The function Ω_R, which was used above to introduce and define entropy, proves to be one of a number of availability functions (all of which were stated or implied by Gibbs in his papers of 1873 and 1877–78).

The decrease in Ω_R between two states of a system is the maximum work that can be obtained from the system and a reservoir at T_0, no net changes of state occurring in any other systems aside from, for example, the rise of an external weight. The maximum work is also the value of the work produced by system and reservoir in a reversible process and is a value common to all reversible processes joining the two prescribed states of the system. In view of equation (4) and the definition of the entropy constant c_R, the decrease in available work Ω_R may now be identified as the decrease in the quantity $(E - T_0 S)$, in which the subscript 0 is introduced to refer to the reservoir. The value of Ω_R itself may be taken to be the maximum possible decrease in $(E - T_0 S)$, which is also the decrease when the system changes to a state of mutual stable equilibrium with the reservoir.

If the system is surrounded by an atmosphere at temperature T_0 that applies a constant pressure p_0 at all interfaces with other systems, then some of the work discussed in the previous paragraph is associated with change in volume of the atmosphere. The net maximum useful work, $(W_u)_{max}$, that can be delivered by system and atmosphere to other things for a change from state 1 of the system to state 2, no net changes in state occurring in any other things aside from the rise of a weight, is given by the decrease in an availability function Φ defined as $E + P_0 V - T_0 S$:

$$(W_u)_{max} = \Phi_1 - \Phi_2.$$

The function Φ is useful in evaluating the performance of a work-producing device that changes volume as it uses up its capacity for doing work.

A less well known availability function is that for a system exposed as before to a large reservoir at fixed pressure p_0 and temperature T_0 with which the system can exchange (through permeable or semipermeable membranes) component species; that is, transfer of these species can occur until the chemical potential of each in the system equals that in the reservoir. This availability function, denoted by Ξ, has a minimum value of zero. It is given by the relation

$$\Xi \equiv E + p_0 V - T_0 S - \sum_i \mu_{i0} n_i, \tag{92}$$

μ_{i0} denoting the chemical potential of component i in the reservoir.

NEGATIVE TEMPERATURE

In the interest of simplicity, the third corollary of the second law was stated above as follows: A system in a stable equilibrium state can receive but cannot produce work. Although this statement is satisfactory for all ordinary systems, which are also called normal systems, recent developments in the theory of nuclear spins—the spinning of neutrons and protons of the atomic nucleus that contributes to both the angular momentum and the magnetic moment of the atom—have shown that some systems, which will be called special systems, in stable equilibrium states can produce work but cannot receive work.

A special system requires the following characteristics: (1) the energy of its allowed states has a finite upper limit; and (2) it must be coextensive in space with another system that shields it from work interactions that would change its volume or the velocity of its parts. For example, a lithium fluoride crystal may be considered to contain two distinct systems occupying the same space. The first, a special system, consists of the nuclear spins of the atoms of the crystal and has the energy of these spins. The second, a normal system, consists of the same atoms in the crystal, but its energy does not include that of the nuclear spins of the atoms. The stable equilibrium states of the two systems can be identified and distinguished because each comes to equilibrium in itself much more rapidly than they together approach mutual stable equilibrium.

It can be shown by reference to the second law of thermodynamics that for a closed special system the entropy–energy diagram is as shown in Figure 12. The

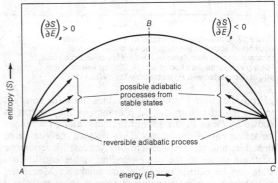

Figure 12: Entropy-energy diagram for a closed special system, for which negative absolute temperatures exist (see text).

curve ABC represents stable equilibrium states as well as the upper boundary for the region of all allowed states for given values of constraints β. Normal stable equilibrium states, which a special system may assume, are those on the AB part of the curve. Special stable equilibrium states are those on the BC part of the curve, and for these special equilibrium states the energy decreases with increase of entropy. In view of the definition of tempera-

Equilibrium constants

Characteristics of special systems

ture (equation [13]), the temperature is therefore represented by a negative number.

The significance of negative temperatures on the scale of hotness and coldness can best be described in terms of the reciprocal Kelvin scale τ, in which $\tau \equiv 1/T$. The possible range of values of τ is from minus infinity to plus infinity, with the hottest temperature possible at minus infinity and the coldest temperature possible at plus infinity. Thus, negative temperatures correspond to hotter levels (the direction of heat flow being from hot to cold) than plus infinity on the Kelvin scale. The so-called absolute zero on the Kelvin scale becomes plus infinity on the τ scale of temperature.

THIRD LAW

Valid calorimetric experiments at temperatures near zero on the Kelvin scale invariably are in accord with the following postulate, which is the third law of classical thermodynamics: The entropy of any finite system approaches a noninfinite value as the temperature on the Kelvin scale approaches zero.

The third law applies only to stable equilibrium states and implies that the heat capacity at constant constraints must go to zero at zero temperature. It follows that a substance cannot be treated as a perfect gas at temperatures near zero, because for a perfect gas the specific heat capacity at constant volume is constant, and the entropy, as given by equation (55), approaches minus infinity. For crystalline substances near zero temperature, the variation of heat capacity is often found to be proportional to T^n, n being greater than unity.

From the third law in combination with the second law, it can be shown that for any finite system all paths of stable equilibrium states for fixed values of constraints β_i must converge on a single value of entropy as they approach zero temperature, as shown in Figure 13.

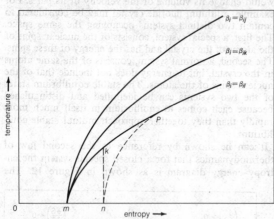

Figure 13: Convergence of values of entropy of stable equilibrium states of a system upon a single value at very low temperatures, as postulated by the third law of thermodynamics. For a given value β_{II} of constraint β_i, Pm represents stable equilibrium states and Pn metastable states (see text).

From the curve of stable equilibrium states for constant values β_{II} of constraints β_i, a branching may occur, as shown by Pn of Figure 13, but the states along Pn cannot be stable equilibrium states. They may be metastable or unstable, and the constant-entropy process nk from one of these states to the corresponding stable equilibrium state can be neither reversible nor adiabatic. Moreover, the change at zero temperature from n to m may be a spontaneous irreversible change to a stable equilibrium state. It follows that, as the temperature approaches zero, the magnitude of the entropy change in any isothermal reversible process approaches zero. This is the Nernst heat theorem, named for the Nobel-Prize winning German chemist, which is a corollary of the third law as stated above. An equivalent statement is that, as the temperature approaches zero, the magnitude of the entropy change between any pair of stable equilibrium states at the same temperature approaches zero.

Because the change between stable equilibrium states

may involve a change in value of a constraint, such as the volume, all states that can coexist in stable equilibrium at zero temperature must have the same minimum value of the entropy for the same mass. Moreover, if a system consisting of chemically reacting species can be brought into a stable equilibrium state by imposing appropriate electrostatic forces in an electrolytic cell, then the system must have the same minimum value of entropy whether in the reactants state or the products state.

It is appropriate now to assign the value zero to the minimum value of the entropy for a given system. The energy at any finite temperature for given values of constraints β may be found from the experimentally determined relation between the heat capacity C_β and temperature by integrating the product $C_\beta dT$ from temperature zero to temperature T:

$$[E - E_{(T=0)}]_\beta = \int_{T=0}^{T=T} C_\beta dT.$$

Similarly, the entropy at any finite temperature may be found by integrating the product $(C_\beta/T)dT$:

$$S_\beta = \int_{T=0}^{T=T} \frac{C_\beta}{T} dT.$$

It is possible, therefore, to determine the values of Gibbs free energy $(E + pV - TS)$ for chemically reacting species at some standard pressure and temperature and, from these values, the conditions for chemical equilibrium, including the equilibrium constants—all without experimental values for the chemical reaction as such between the species.

IV. Force fields

NONRELATIVISTIC EFFECTS

When to the conditions for a simple system, gravitational, electrical, and magnetic constraints in the form of applied force fields are added, an additional term appears in the Gibbs equation for each additional constraint. Each added term is a product similar to the product pdV in that it represents the work done in a reversible process in which the value of a constraint is varied.

When a gravity field is applied to a system of mass small enough so that the field is affected by it only negligibly, a gravity potential γ may be defined as the increase in energy per unit mass of an elementary system as it is moved from a reference level ($\gamma = 0$) to the given level while entropy, number of particles, and volume constraint are held constant. The Gibbs equation (64) for a system of mass m then becomes

$$dS = \frac{1}{T}[dE + pdV - \sum_i \mu_i dn_i - md\gamma]. \quad (93)$$

A simple and familiar condition for stable equilibrium that can be deduced from the Gibbs equation in form (93) is that for an otherwise simple fluid system in a gravity field, the rate of change of pressure with vertical distance is proportional to the density of the fluid. The proportionality factor proves to be g, the so-called acceleration of gravity.

A modification of the Gibbs equation similar to but more complicated than that given above for a gravity field has been devised to apply to a dielectric material, a material of which the electrically charged component species cannot move from one position in the material to another as it changes between neighbouring stable equilibrium states in an electric field between the plates of a capacitor. Another has been devised for a magnetic material in a magnetic field. (They will not be given here.)

RELATIVISTIC EFFECTS IN A GRAVITY FIELD

In an extremely intense gravity field, relativistic effects cannot be ignored. By combining the Einstein relation between energy and mass ($E = mc^2$) with the first and second laws, the following two conclusions are reached: (1) For stable equilibrium in a vertical column, it is necessary, as in nonrelativistic systems, that the temperature, $(\partial E/\partial S)_{n\beta}$, be uniform. (2) If a system is held at

(Left margin notes:)

States to which the third law is applied

Nernst heat theorem

constant volume and lifted reversibly and adiabatically —that is, at constant entropy S—the pressure and temperature of the system both increase. More specifically, the increase in the natural logarithm of the pressure when the system is lifted from the level at which the gravity potential γ is arbitrarily assigned the value zero to a level at which it has the value γ is equal to the quotient of γ and the square of the speed of light c. A similar statement holds for temperature. Since the square of the speed of light c is a very large number, the effect on pressure and temperature will be small except in very intense gravitational fields.

The relation between temperature and gravity potential may be derived by consideration of a cycle in which a pure molecular species in a triple-point state (for example, solid, liquid, and vapour in mutual stable equilibrium) is lifted reversibly, adiabatically, and at constant volume from the reference level $\gamma = 0$ to the level γ, heated reversibly at constant temperature, lowered reversibly and adiabatically to $\gamma = 0$, and cooled to the original state. Because of the increase in mass in the heating process, the work of descent will exceed the work of ascent. The efficiency of this cycle may then be equated to that of a Carnot cycle in terms of temperature, as in equation (22), to obtain the desired relation.

V. Steady rate processes

Many applications of thermodynamics involve interactions between systems some or all of which are passing through nonequilibrium states. For example, chemical and nuclear reactions and flow of energy and matter are processes occurring in systems passing through nonequilibrium states.

Problems of analysis of nonequilibrium states

The analysis of nonequilibrium states is more difficult, both conceptually and numerically, than that of stable equilibrium states. For example, because the number of properties required for the description of nonequilibrium states is larger than that for stable equilibrium states, the mathematical relations between properties are correspondingly more complicated.

In the interest of simplicity, the following applications are restricted to systems in steady states having fixed time rates of change of extensive properties. These applications will be called steady rate processes.

APPROACH TO MUTUAL STABLE EQUILIBRIUM

If two systems I and II are each in a stable equilibrium state but not in mutual stable equilibrium, a process in which they change toward mutual stable equilibrium will occur if they are connected by an intermediate system M. Depending upon the nature of the three systems and their states, the process that occurs may be caused by the transfer through M of energy alone or of matter with energy. The rate at which such transfer occurs will depend upon the initial departure from mutual stable equilibrium of systems I and II. By means of the first and second laws of thermodynamics and one additional postulate to them, a number of useful relationships between rates and potential differences or gradients may be determined for a substantial variety of rate processes, most of which are irreversible.

Generally it is possible to conceive of the process in M as being caused by two systems I and II, each of which would immediately assume a stable equilibrium state if the communication with M were suddenly stopped. To meet this requirement, the conductivity of matter or energy in I and II must be very great, so that whatever the influence on I of interaction through M with II, that influence will be felt uniformly through I and similarly with II. If the region is fluid, this result could be attained by minimal stirring of the fluid.

Under these circumstances, values of properties may be assigned to I and II. Region M, on the other hand, is in a nonequilibrium state. Nevertheless, values of intensive properties such as temperature and chemical potential of component i can be assigned to a point A in the region M by the method of local isolation. This method consists of isolating a region comprising point A and measuring the intensive property for this region when it reaches a stable equilibrium state. The value of the property in the limit as the size of the region is reduced to the smallest consistent with isolation may be taken to be the value at point A.

Region M will be assumed to be in a steady state; that is, the rate of change of any intensive property of I, II, or M is negligible. Extensive properties of I and II, on the other hand, may change at a finite rate, and any such rate is called a flux. Thus, an energy flux J_u is defined as the negative of the change of energy of I per unit time and, because of steady state in M, the change of energy of II per unit time:

$$J_u \equiv -\frac{dU_I}{dt} = \frac{dU_{II}}{dt}. \tag{94}$$

Similarly a flux of component i is denoted by J_i and is given by

$$J_i \equiv -\frac{dn_{iI}}{dt} = \frac{dn_{iII}}{dt}. \tag{95}$$

Under the steady-state conditions assumed and with I and II each held at constant volume, any one flux must depend upon those differences in intensive properties between I and II that measure the departure from stable equilibrium. Among these may be differences in temperature, pressure, mole fraction of component i, potential of component i, etc. The choice of differences that is made is governed by the postulate to be employed. It is made by expressing the rate of entropy generation in the process in terms of the Gibbs equation and using the resulting expression to define conjugate pairs of fluxes and forces. Each flux is then expressed in terms of all the forces so defined.

The region M between I and II may be subdivided into vertical laminas dM, over any face of which, for interaction in one direction only, the values of all intensive properties are uniform. For any one lamina, therefore, constant-volume stable equilibrium regions I and II may be substituted for material adjoining M without altering the process in the lamina (Figure 14).

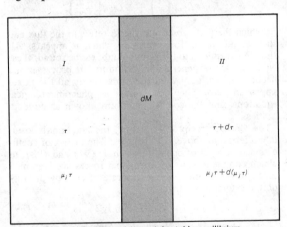

Figure 14: Two systems, I and II, each in stable equilibrium but not in mutual stable equilibrium, interacting through a thin intermediate system dM, which is in a nonequilibrium state. The symbol τ represents the quantity $1/T$, the reciprocal of the absolute temperature (see text).

For steady state in dM the rate of entropy generation in the process will be wholly accounted for by changes of entropy in I and II. Because the Gibbs equation (64) states the entropy change of a phase such as I or II in terms of the temperature, chemical potentials of components, change in energy, and change in masses of components, it will yield an expression for the rate of entropy change in terms of temperature, chemical potentials, and rates of change of energy and masses. These rates of change are the fluxes, J_u and J_i, of energy and of component, as indicated above. Because of the steady-state condition these fluxes may prove to be identical for regions I and II, but they will differ at most only infinitesimally for an infinitesimal thickness of the lamina dM.

The rate of entropy generation in the whole process is

found by summing for regions I and II the rates of entropy change, one of which will be negative and the other positive, to get an infinitesimal difference between two finite rates. This rate of entropy generation will then be the sum of products of fluxes and differences between I and II of potentials. These products are $J_u d(1/T)$ and $J_i d(-\mu_i/T)$, symbol d denoting the difference between the value in II and the value in I of the potential in parentheses. Thus the expression for the rate of entropy generation $d\dot{S}$ is

$$dS = J_u\, d\left(\frac{1}{T}\right) + \sum_i J_i\, d\left(-\frac{\mu_i}{T}\right), \qquad (96)$$

in which $\sum_i$ denotes summation over all component substances $i = 1, 2, \ldots k$.

This last expression serves the purpose of identifying conjugate fluxes and forces; that is, for energy flux J_u the difference $d(1/T)$ is the conjugate force, etc.

Each flux J_u, J_i of equation (96) is a function of the state of one of the stable equilibrium regions I or II and of the forces $d(1/T)$, $d(-\mu_i/T)$, with the further condition that, whatever the state, the flux will be zero when all forces are zero—that is, for mutual stable equilibrium. Purely mathematical considerations indicate that the functional relation between a flux such as J_u and the forces $d(1/T)$, $d(-\mu_i/T)$ is a very simple one, provided that the fluxes are small; *i.e.*, provided that the departure from mutual stable equilibrium is small. This functional relation is that the flux is equal to the sum of terms each consisting of a force multiplied by a coefficient L. From thermodynamic considerations it can be shown that the magnitudes of the coefficients L are fixed once the nature and states of regions I and M are fixed. They are independent of the magnitudes of the forces $d(1/T)$ and $d(-\mu_i/T)$. The functional relation is thus given by

$$J_u = L_{uu}\, d\left(\frac{1}{T}\right) + \sum_i L_{ui}\, d\left(-\frac{\mu_i}{T}\right) \qquad (97)$$

$$J_i = L_{iu}\, d\left(\frac{1}{T}\right) + \sum_i L_{ii}\, d\left(-\frac{\mu_i}{T}\right), \qquad (98)$$

in which the first subscript on an L refers to the flux and the second to the force term in which it appears. Although exceptions to them may doubtless be found, these equations are of general application to rate processes and become increasingly valid the more nearly all the fluxes approach zero. They are known as phenomenological equations, and the coefficients L are known as conductivities.

The Onsager reciprocal relation, the additional postulate referred to above, is as follows: The matrix of coefficients L of a set of equations such as (97) and (98), in which conjugate pairs of fluxes and forces are identified through expression (96) for the rate of entropy production, is symmetrical; that is,

$$L_{ij} = L_{ji} \text{ for } i, j = u, 1, 2 \ldots. \qquad (99)$$

Lars Onsager, a Norwegian–American theoretical chemist, stated this new law in 1931 in an argument based on a principle of statistical mechanics called the principle of microscopic reversibility and a postulate that is closely related to the second law of thermodynamics. The new law was subsequently shown to be of general application in irreversible processes and was extended to a wide variety of phenomena.

The phenomenological equations reduce to special forms for various special systems and force conditions and are known under different names. For example, Fourier's law of heat conduction (for the 19th-century French mathematician and physicist Jean-Baptiste Fourier), Ohm's law of electric current flow (for the 19th-century German physicist Georg Simon Ohm), Fick's law of neutral particle diffusion (for the 19th-century German physiologist Adolf Eugen Fick), and the law of ambipolar diffusion of positive and negative charges are all special cases of the linear phenomenological equations. The constants appearing in the laws just cited, such as

The Onsager reciprocal relation

Phenomenological equations

electric resistance in Ohm's law, may be expressed easily in terms of the conductivities L of the phenomenological equations.

FLOW OF A SUBSTANCE THROUGH A BARRIER

A relatively simple application of the thermodynamics of rate processes is to the flow of a single-component substance through a barrier M under conditions such that the phenomenological equations (97) and (98) are valid. An example would be the flow of helium through a rubber membrane between two stable equilibrium regions I and II. The Onsager reciprocal relation is simply that $L_{u1} = L_{1u}$, subscript 1 referring to helium.

The two forces are the differences across the membrane $d(1/T)$ and $d(\mu_1/T)$. When the flux of helium is zero, then the difference $d(1/T)$ causes its conjugate energy to flow downgrade in temperature and upgrade in $1/T$. When the temperature difference and $d(1/T)$ are zero, then its conjugate helium will flow downgrade in chemical potential and in μ_1/T. Each of these forces, however, tends to cause its nonconjugate flux, as well as its conjugate flux, in one or the other direction. This behaviour is called coupling. In the absence of coupling, the coefficients L_{u1} and L_{1u} would both be zero.

By virtue of coupling, the two forces may be set in relation to each other so as to stop the flow of helium because of a balance between the opposing influences of the two forces. Such a steady state will be attained spontaneously if a temperature difference is maintained between I and II for a long enough period of time while the volumes of I and II are held constant. The flow of helium will eventually cease—or at least approach zero as a limit as time proceeds. A flow of energy will persist, however, in the steady-state condition by virtue of the temperature difference.

It can be seen from the second phenomenological equation (98) that the ratio L_{1u}/L_{11} is equal to the ratio of forces $d(\mu_1/T)/d(1/T)$ when J_1 is zero. From the two equations (97) and (98) taken together it can be seen that the ratio L_{u1}/L_{11} is equal to the ratio of fluxes J_u/J_1 when $d(1/T)$ is zero. Because the Onsager reciprocal relation requires that L_{1u} be equal to L_{u1}, it follows that the ratio of forces when J_1 is zero must equal the ratio of fluxes when the temperatures of I and II are equal.

By means of a simple thermodynamic analysis, the ratio of forces $d(\mu_1/T)/d(1/T)$ may be expressed in terms of the ratio of pressure difference to temperature difference dp/dT, which then proves to be proportional to the excess of J_u/J_1 for dT equal to zero over the enthalpy h_1 of helium in region I. The actual relation is

$$\left(\frac{dp}{dT}\right)_{J_1=0} = -\frac{1}{v_1 T}\left[\left(\frac{J_u}{J_1}\right)_{dT=0} - h_1\right]. \qquad (100)$$

This relation gives the ratio of the pressure gradient to the temperature gradient for which the particle flow is stopped. Because it can be shown that for simple bulk flow J_u/J_1 is h_1 for fluid crossing any section in which the temperature is uniform in the direction of flow, it follows from equation (100) that bulk flow may be stopped even in a temperature gradient by zero pressure gradient. Whenever the energy flux per unit particle flux differs from h_1 in constant-temperature flow, then a pressure gradient is necessary to stop flow in a temperature gradient.

Application of equation (100) to the flow of a perfect gas may be made for a porous plug with pore sizes very small compared with the mean distance travelled by gas molecules between collisions or compared to flow between emitting and receiving surfaces separated by a distance that is very small compared with the mean distance between collisions. For both of these the result is the same and can be shown to be

$$\left(\frac{dp}{dT}\right)_{J_1=0} = \frac{1}{2}\frac{p}{T} \qquad (101)$$

or, for a finite length,

$$\left[\frac{p^I}{p^{II}} = \sqrt{\frac{T^I}{T^{II}}}\,\right]_{J_1=0}. \qquad (102)$$

The Knudsen effect

These relations describe what is known as the Knudsen effect.

The excess over the enthalpy flux of the energy flux across the barrier per unit of matter flowing when dT is zero is called the heat of transport and is denoted by q_1^*:

$$q_1^* \equiv \left(\frac{J_u}{J_1}\right)_{dT=0} - h_1. \qquad (103)$$

It is the direct heat interaction that must be provided between regions II and I (Figure 14) when one unit of mass flows from I to II through M if the temperatures of I and II are to be maintained equal. Its magnitude can be found, in accordance with (100), by a measurement of the ratio dp/dT that corresponds to a flux J_1 of zero. The value found in this way for the heat of transport through a rubber membrane for nitrogen is −260 calories per gram mole and for hydrogen +100.

VI. Statistical thermodynamics

The mechanical theory of heat was developed concurrently with thermodynamics. It relates heat to changes in the motion of the atoms and molecules of matter. The history of the theory can be traced back to the Greek philosophers Democritus (*c.* 400 BC) and Epicurus (*c.* 300 BC). The French philosopher Pierre Gassendi developed in the 17th century a theory in which all material phenomena are attributable to the indestructible motion of atoms. Although the English philosopher Robert Hooke, the German philosopher and mathematician Gottfried Wilhelm Leibniz, and the Swiss mathematician and physicist Daniel Bernoulli improved upon it in the 17th and 18th centuries the theory was not firmly established until Joule demonstrated experimentally in the 19th century, that a quantitative relation exists between heat and work when they produce identical effects.

After Joule's demonstration the theory developed rapidly into a science of major importance that became known as statistical mechanics or statistical thermodynamics. Its subject is the relation between the laws of thermodynamics and the details of the structure of matter. Its development, which can be traced through Hermann Ludwig Ferdinand von Helmholtz, a German physicist and anatomist; Clausius; Maxwell; and Boltzmann, culminated in the work of Gibbs, who in 1901 presented an exposition of statistical thermodynamics that excels in completeness, rigour, and generality. Although the exposition of Gibbs is stated in terms of classical mechanics, it is better adapted to quantum mechanics, which in some ways it anticipates.

Perhaps because Gibbs's contribution was not fully understood, a less general and less rigorous molecular statistics prevailed in the literature, with few exceptions, until after World War II.

GIBBSIAN STATISTICS

According to classical mechanics, the state of a system having N degrees of freedom (independent ways in which the space configuration of the system may change) is fully specified by the values of N position coordinates $q_1, q_2, \ldots, q_N$, and N momentum coordinates $p_1, p_2, \ldots, p_N$. For example, the state of a system consisting of n point particles (particles without internal structure and therefore without internal degrees of freedom) is specified if the position coordinates along three Cartesian axes x, y, and z and the corresponding momentum coordinates along these same axes for each of the particles are specified. For such a system the number N of the degrees of freedom is equal to three times the number n of the particles of the system.

The position of a particle in space may be represented geometrically by a point in three-dimensional space having coordinates x, y, and z. The state of the particle involves not only the values of the coordinates x, y, and z but also the values of momentum component (which fixes the velocity component) p_x in the x direction, p_y in the y direction, and p_z in the z direction. These considerations suggest a mental extension of the concept of space to six dimensions, having coordinates x, y, z, p_x, p_y, and p_z. The state of the particle could then be completely described by a point in the six-dimensional space for which the values of x, y, z, p_x, p_y, and p_z are appropriately fixed.

The particle just discussed is said to have three degrees of freedom, and its state can be represented by a point in a six-dimensional space. A collection of two such particles might have six degrees of freedom, and the representation of its state would call for a 12-dimensional space. The number of degrees of freedom of a more complex system is the number of independent kinds of displacement to which it is subject. The state of such a system having N degrees of freedom may be represented geometrically in classical mechanics by a point in $2N$-dimensional space having as coordinates $q_1, q_2, \ldots, q_N$, $p_1, p_2, \ldots, p_N$. This $2N$-dimensional space was called by Gibbs phase space.

According to Gibbs, the term thermodynamic state of a system with N degrees of freedom does not necessarily correspond to a unique point in phase space, but to a set of probabilities of the system being in any one of the allowed points consistent with the constraints imposed on the system. Because any set of allowed states in classical mechanics forms a continuum, Gibbs introduced a probability density or distribution P, which he called the coefficient of probability, such that the product $Pdq_1dq_2 \ldots dq_N dp_1 dp_2 \ldots dp_N$ is equal to the probability of the system being in states having values of coordinates between q_1 and $q_1 + dq_1$, q_2 and $q_2 + dq_2, \ldots, q_N$ and $q_N + dq_N$ and values of momenta between p_1 and $p_1 + dp_1$, p_2 and $p_2 + dp_2, \ldots$, and p_N and $p_N + dp_N$. For a given thermodynamic state, the distribution P will be a corresponding function of q's and p's. Furthermore, because a system must be at some one of the allowed states, the sum of all the probabilities must always be equal to unity or, by the same token, the integral of the distribution P over all q's and p's must be always equal to unity.

Various types of thermodynamic states correspond to particular mathematical forms of the distribution P. For example, Gibbs assumed without proof that, for the stable equilibrium states of a system with N degrees of freedom, the coefficient of probability P corresponding to the state $q_1, q_2, \ldots, q_N, p_1, p_2, \ldots, p_N$ of energy ε is equal to the number 2.718282 (the base of natural logarithms) raised to the $(\Psi - \varepsilon)/\Theta$ power, in which Ψ and Θ are constants; in other words, P is given by the exponential relation

$$P = \exp\left(\frac{\Psi - \varepsilon}{\Theta}\right). \qquad (104)$$

He called this distribution of probabilities a canonical distribution. Further discussion of Gibbsian statistics will be omitted because the quantum statistical thermodynamics discussed below, though based on Gibbsian ideas, is more complete.

QUANTUM STATISTICAL THERMODYNAMICS

Definition of state. In contrast to classical mechanics, a fundamental premise of quantum mechanics is that at a given time the most that can be said about results of measurements on a system is the probability of finding particular values of properties, such as coordinates and momenta, rather than the particular values that will be observed. This premise reflects the principle of indeterminacy first introduced by the German physicist Werner Heisenberg. It requires a description of the state of a system in terms of probabilities.

The principles of quantum mechanics may be stated by means of a number of mathematical formulations. Among these, the best known are the wave formulation by the German physicist Erwin Schrödinger, the vector formulation by the English physicist P.A.M. Dirac, and the matrix formulation by Heisenberg. The matrix formulation is especially suited to the exposition of quantum statistical thermodynamics and is adopted below (for a discussion of matrices in general, see the article ALGEBRA, LINEAR AND MULTILINEAR).

Any property of a system that in classical mechanics

Early mechanical theories of heat

Phase space

Matrices
and
eigen-
values

may be expressed as a function of position and momentum coordinates is expressed in quantum mechanics by a matrix. For example, the Hamiltonian function of classical mechanics, which is the energy of the system, is represented by the Hamiltonian matrix. Matrix representations are used also for properties (such as spin) that have no classical analogue. The method of calculation of elements of matrices is specified by the principles of quantum mechanics.

Each matrix possesses eigenvalues; that is, a set of numbers that can be found by solving the characteristic equation of the matrix. The eigenvalues of the matrix of a property are real, as distinguished from complex, in the mathematical sense. Each one corresponds to a possible outcome of a measurement of the property performed on the system. For example, a measurement of the energy of a system in a given condition will yield any one of the real eigenvalues of the Hamiltonian matrix of the system. The number of eigenvalues of a property may be either finite, as with spin, or infinite, as with energy for most systems.

According to quantum mechanics, it is impossible to predict from knowledge of the condition of a system which eigenvalue a measurement will yield. Instead, the most that can be said at any instant of time is the probability that a measurement will yield a given eigenvalue.

The state of a system is defined as the set of all probabilities for the outcomes of all measurements that may be performed at a given instant of time. That is, the state of a system is represented by Table 2, in which $\overline{F}$, $\overline{G}$,

Table 2: State of a System

property	$\overline{F}$	$\overline{G}$	$\overline{H}$	
Probabilities	$W(F_1)$	$W(G_1)$	$W(H_1)$	...
	$W(F_2)$	$W(G_2)$	$W(H_2)$	...
	•	•	•	
	•	•	•	
	•	•	•	

$\overline{H}$, ... denote observable properties and in which $W(F_1)$ denotes the probability that any one measurement of property $\overline{F}$ will yield the eigenvalue F_1, ..., $W(G_1)$ denotes the probability that any one measurement of property $\overline{G}$ will yield the eigenvalue G_1, ... and so forth. It can be shown that these probabilities can be combined to form a matrix $[\rho]$, called the density matrix or statistical matrix. Conversely, a systematic procedure exists for determining from a given density matrix $[\rho]$ the probability $W(E_n)$ that a measurement of energy corresponding to the Hamiltonian matrix $[E]$ will yield the energy eigenvalue E_n of $[E]$. Again, the procedure yields the probability $W(F_m)$ that a measurement of property $\overline{F}$ corresponding to matrix $[F]$ will yield the eigenvalue F_m of $[F]$.

Expectation values of properties. Because measurements of a property $\overline{F}$ of a system in a given state yield different eigenvalues F_m, each with a probability $W(F_m)$ specified by the density matrix $[\rho]$ that represents the state, an expectation value or simply a value of the property corresponding to the given state is defined as the weighted average of the various possible eigenvalues, each eigenvalue being weighted by the probability that it will be observed. Symbolically, the value F of a property $\overline{F}$ may be represented as a sum over many terms, each of which is the product of a probability $W(F_m)$ and the eigenvalue F_m; that is,

$$F = \sum_m W(F_m)F_m, \quad (105)$$

in which the symbol $\sum_m$ denotes summation over all eigenvalues, and each eigenvalue is represented by a different symbol (different value of the subscript m) even when two or more eigenvalues have the same value. (For some matrices several distinct eigenvalues may have identical numerical values. The eigenvalues are then called degenerate.)

Reversible equation of motion. Quantum mechanics provides an equation, called the equation of motion, from which can be found the rate of change of the density matrix $[\rho]$ with time for each of the numerous processes that are reversible and adiabatic. The equation will not be given here.

Conditions for equilibrium are found from the equation of motion. If the eigenvalues of the density matrix $[\rho]$ for an equilibrium state are denoted by $x_1, x_2, \ldots, x_m, \ldots$ and the eigenvalues of the Hamiltonian matrix $[E]$ by $E_1, E_2, \ldots, E_m, \ldots$, it can be shown that, in the absence of irreversibilities, a necessary and sufficient condition for equilibrium is that the first eigenvalue x_1 be equal to the probability $W(E_1)$, that a measurement of the energy will yield the first eigenvalue E_1, the second eigenvalue x_2 be equal to $W(E_2)$, etc. Moreover, for equilibrium states the expectation value of the energy E can be expressed as a sum of terms each of which is the product of x_m and E_m; that is,

$$E = \sum_m x_m E_m. \quad (106)$$

General expression for entropy. According to the first and second laws of thermodynamics, entropy is a property or state function of a system. Moreover, it must be invariant in any reversible adiabatic process. From these two conditions and the requirement that it is an extensive property, the expectation value S of entropy can be shown to be proportional to a mean of the natural logarithms of the eigenvalues of the density matrix. When $y_1, y_2, \ldots, y_m, \ldots$ denote the eigenvalues of the density matrix $[\rho]$ (corresponding to an arbitrary state, which is not necessarily equilibrium or stable equilibrium), the mean is calculated by weighting each $\ln y_m$ with the value y_m. In mathematical form this statement is expressed

$$S = -k \sum_m y_m \ln y_m, \quad (107)$$

in which k is a universal constant that proves to be the Boltzmann constant.

Pure states. A pure state is defined as one for which the eigenvalues of the density matrix $[\rho]$ are all equal to zero, except for one that is equal to unity. It follows from equation (107) that the entropy of a pure state is equal to zero.

It can be shown that any pure state may be described also by means of a wave function of quantum mechanics; and, conversely, states that can be described by wave functions correspond to zero entropy. In general, however, the entropy of a system is not equal to zero, and the state of the system cannot in general, therefore, be described by a wave function.

Stable equilibrium states. In the language of quantum statistical thermodynamics, the criterion for stable equilibrium (see above *Stable equilibrium*) implies that the density matrix for a stable equilibrium state be such that the entropy (equation [107]) is at its maximum for given expectation values of energy and numbers of particles. When this criterion is applied to a system of which the numbers of particles are known without uncertainty (the probability of the value for the number of particles of a given kind that is found by a measurement is unity), it yields the eigenvalues $x_1^\circ, x_2^\circ, \ldots, x_m^\circ, \ldots$ for the stable equilibrium states as functions of the energy eigenvalues $E_1, E_2, \ldots, E_m, \ldots$ of the Hamiltonian matrix of the system and the temperature of the stable equilibrium state in question. The various mathematical functions are as follows:

$$x_1^\circ = \frac{\exp(-E_1/kT)}{\sum_m \exp(-E_m/kT)}; x_2^\circ = \frac{\exp(-E_2/kT)}{\sum_m \exp(-E_m/kT)}; \ldots \quad (108)$$

$$T \equiv \left(\frac{\partial E}{\partial S}\right)_\beta, \quad (109)$$

$$E = \sum_m x_m^\circ E_m = \frac{\sum_m E_m \exp(-E_m/kT)}{\sum_m \exp(-E_m/kT)}, \quad (110)$$

and

$$S = -k \sum_m x_m^\circ \ln x_m^\circ$$
$$= k \ln \left[\sum_m \exp(-E_m/kT) \right] + \frac{E}{T}. \quad (111)$$

Because the eigenvalues $x_1, x_2, \ldots, x_m, \ldots$ of the density matrix for any equilibrium state and, therefore, the eigenvalues $x_1^\circ, x_2^\circ \ldots, x_m^\circ, \ldots$ of the density matrix for any stable equilibrium state represent probabilities that measurements of energy will yield eigenvalues $E_1, E_2, \ldots, E_m, \ldots$, respectively, equation (108) can be thought of as analogous to the canonical distribution postulated by Gibbs, provided that the two constants Θ and Ψ in equation (104) are expressed in terms of the temperature T and the energy eigenvalues $E_1, E_2, \ldots, E_m, \ldots$. It can be shown that Θ and Ψ are given by the relations

$$\Theta = kT \quad (112)$$

and

$$\Psi = kT \ln \left[\sum_m \exp(-E_m/kT) \right]. \quad (113)$$

It can be readily verified from equations (111) and (113) that the function Ψ is equal to the Helmholtz free energy of the system; i.e., equal to $E - TS$. Moreover, because the energy eigenvalues $E_1, E_2, \ldots, E_m, \ldots$ are in general functions of the values of the constraints, the Helmholtz free energy Ψ is a function of temperature and the constraints and, therefore, a characteristic function. This means that in quantum statistical thermodynamics the problem of evaluating the properties of any system with numbers of particles that are known without uncertainty and in a stable equilibrium state reduces to the problem of evaluating the energy eigenvalues as functions of the constraints. The evaluation of the energy eigenvalues is a difficult mathematical task that has been carried out for only a very few systems. The difficulty, however, is in the calculation rather than in the conception of the evaluation.

The **canonical partition function**

The quantity Q_c, called the canonical partition function, is defined as the sum of $\exp(-E_1/kT)$, $\exp(-E_2/kT)$, $\exp(-E_3/kT)$, etc. It appears in the expressions for many properties of systems in stable equilibrium states. For example, because

$$Q_c \equiv \sum_m \exp(-E_m/kT), \quad (114)$$

it follows that the probability x_m° of observing an energy eigenvalue E_m is the quotient of $\exp(-E_m/kT)$ and Q_c, that the Helmholtz free energy per mole is the product of (kT) and the logarithm of Q_c, and that the entropy is the sum of the product $k \ln Q_c$ of k and logarithm of Q_c and the quotient E/T of the expectation value of the energy and the temperature:

$$x_m^\circ = \frac{\exp(-E_m/kT)}{Q_c}; \ \Psi = kT \ln Q_c; \text{ and } S = k \ln Q_c + \frac{E}{T}.$$

STATISTICS OF GRAND SYSTEMS

Stable equilibrium states. In many systems the numbers of particles may be uncertain either because the system is open to the transfer of rest mass or because particles can be created and annihilated within the system. The terminology of Gibbs suggests that such systems be called grand systems.

By definition, uncertainty in the numbers of particles means that measurements of these numbers for a grand system in a given state yield different particle-number eigenvalues. This uncertainty is analogous to that associated in general with the energy. It follows that an expectation value rather than a dispersion-free value (that is, rather than a unique value that is observed as a result of every measurement) is assigned to the number of particles of each component of a state of a grand system. Without discussion of the matrix formalism for grand systems, some results applicable to stable equilibrium states will be given.

A stable equilibrium state of a grand system is fully described by the set of eigenvalues $x_1^\circ, x_2^\circ, \ldots, x_m^\circ, \ldots$

of the density matrix that maximizes the entropy of the system at given expectation values of energy, numbers of particles of the components, and constraints. The mth eigenvalue x_m° is equal to the probability that a suitable measurement will yield the mth energy eigenvalue E_m and the mth number-of-particle eigenvalues $n_{1m}, n_{2m}, \ldots, n_{km}$ for the set of k components of the system. It can be expressed as a function of the energy eigenvalues $E_1, E_2, \ldots, E_m, \ldots$ of the Hamiltonian matrix of the system, the eigenvalues $n_{11}, n_{12}, \ldots, n_{1m}, \ldots$ of the number of particles of component number one, the eigenvalues $n_{21}, n_{22}, \ldots, n_{2m}, \ldots$ of the number of particles of component number two, $\ldots$, the total potential $\mu_1, \mu_2, \ldots, \mu_k$ of the k components $1, 2, \ldots k$, and the temperature T of the stable equilibrium state in question. It is given by the relation

$$x_m^\circ = \frac{\exp[(n_{1m}\mu_1 + n_{2m}\mu_2 + \ldots + n_{km}\mu_k - E_m)/kT]}{\sum_m \exp[(n_{1m}\mu_1 + n_{2m}\mu_2 + \ldots + n_{km}\mu_k - E_m)/kT]}. \quad (115)$$

The sum in the denominator of (115) is called the grand partition function Q_g; i.e.,

$$Q_g \equiv \sum_m \exp[(n_{1m}\mu_1 + n_{2m}\mu_2 + \ldots + n_{km}\mu_k - E_m)/kT]. \quad (116)$$

It appears in many relations between properties for grand systems in stable equilibrium states. For example, for a grand system with volume V as the only independent constraint, the equation of state is given by the relation

$$pV/kT = \ln Q_g. \quad (117)$$

Equation (117) applies to grand systems in gaseous, liquid, or solid states.

The one-particle approximation for one-component systems. Because of mathematical difficulties, the energy eigenvalues of most systems can be computed only approximately. A class of approximations that consists in expressing each energy eigenvalue of the system as a sum of energy eigenvalues of suitably defined subsystems, each having one particle only, is called the one-particle approximation. It is valid for some crystals and for dilute gases at such low densities that short-range interparticle forces (forces between two particles that act only when the two particles are very near each other) can be neglected, and long-range forces on each particle are independent of the positions of other particles. Some results of the analysis applicable to dilute gases will be given below.

In the context of the one-particle approximation, each of the energy eigenvalues $E_1, E_2, \ldots, E_m, \ldots$ of a dilute gas having one component only (namely, consisting of a number of particles of a single type) is expressed as a sum of terms such that each term is a positive integer multiplied by an energy eigenvalue of a system that has one particle only and for which the eigenvalues can be evaluated. For example, if $\nu_{m1}, \nu_{m2}, \ldots, \nu_{mj}, \ldots$ denote the positive integers that appear in the sum for the mth eigenvalue E_m and $\varepsilon_1, \varepsilon_2, \ldots, \varepsilon_j, \ldots$, the energy eigenvalues of the system with the one particle, then E_m is given by the relation

$$E_m = \nu_{m1}\varepsilon_1 + \nu_{m2}\varepsilon_2 + \ldots + \nu_{mj}\varepsilon_j + \ldots$$
$$= \sum_j \nu_{mj}\varepsilon_j \text{ for all values of } m. \quad (118)$$

Equation (118) is interpreted as meaning that of the n_m particles associated with the energy eigenvalue E_m, ν_{m1} have energy ε_1, ν_{m2} have energy ε_2, $\ldots$, ν_{mj} have energy $\varepsilon_j, \ldots$. From this interpretation it follows that the sum of all the positive integers $\nu_{m1}, \nu_{m2}, \ldots, \nu_{mj}, \ldots$ must be equal to n_m; i.e.,

$$\nu_{m1} + \nu_{m2} + \ldots + \nu_{mj} + \ldots = \sum_j \nu_{mj} = n_m. \quad (119)$$

Fermions and bosons

The values that each integer ν_{mj} can assume are restricted by the nature of the particles in question. For certain particles, called fermions, each ν_{mj} may be either zero or unity for all values of the subscripts m and j; i.e., for any energy eigenvalue E_m of the overall system and any energy eigenvalue ε_j of the auxiliary one-particle system. For example, because electrons are fermions a grand system consisting of electrons has, for a state with an energy eigenvalue E_m, at most one electron of one-particle energy eigenvalue ε_j. (This restriction is equivalent to Pauli's exclusion principle of atomic physics.) On the other hand, for certain particles called bosons, each of the integers ν_{mj} may have any positive integral value as well as the value zero. In a grand system consisting of photons—which are bosons—in a state with energy eigenvalue E_m, any number of photons from zero to n_m may have a particular energy ε_j.

When the allowed numerical values of the integers ν_{mj} are considered, the properties of a dilute gas in a stable equilibrium state can be expressed as functions of the one-particle energy eigenvalues $\varepsilon_1, \varepsilon_2, \ldots, \varepsilon_j, \ldots$ rather than the eigenvalues $E_1, E_2, \ldots, E_m, \ldots$ of the overall system.

For example, the expectation or average value ν_j of the number of particles that can be thought of as having one-particle energy ε_j—namely, the expectation value ν_j of the integers $\nu_{1j}, \nu_{2j}, \ldots, \nu_{mj}, \ldots$—is defined as the sum of terms each being an integer ν_{mj} multiplied by the probability x_m° that a suitable measurement will yield the energy eigenvalue E_m.

It can be shown that, if μ denotes the total potential of the single component of the grand system, then ν_j is given by the relations

$$\nu_j = \sum_m x_m^\circ \nu_{jm} = \frac{1}{\exp[(\varepsilon_j - \mu)/kT] + 1} \text{ for fermions} \quad (120)$$

and

$$\nu_j = \sum_m x_m^\circ \nu_{jm} = \frac{1}{\exp[(\varepsilon_j - \mu)/kT] - 1} \text{ for bosons.} \quad (121)$$

Relation (120) is called the Fermi–Dirac distribution, and the corresponding dilute gas is said to obey Fermi–Dirac statistics. Relation (121) is called the Bose–Einstein distribution, and the corresponding dilute gas is said to obey Bose–Einstein statistics.

Again, for a system with volume V as the only constraint, it can be shown that the equation of state, (117), and the expectation value n of the number of particles are given by the relations

$$\frac{pV}{kT} = \sum_j \ln \{1 \pm \exp[(\mu - \varepsilon_j)/kT]\}^{\pm 1} \quad (122)$$

and

$$n = \sum_j \{[\exp(\varepsilon_j - \mu)/kT] \pm 1\}^{-1}, \quad (123)$$

in which the plus sign in $\pm$ applies to fermions and the minus sign to bosons.

Fundamental equation for one-component simple systems. For a system for which both sets of eigenvalues $E_1, E_2, \ldots, E_m, \ldots$ and $\varepsilon_1, \varepsilon_2, \ldots, \varepsilon_j, \ldots$ are functions of volume V only, equations (122) and (123) indicate that p and n are functions of volume V, temperature T, and potential μ only. In principle, the p and n functions can be combined so as to eliminate volume V and obtain a fundamental equation that gives the total potential as a function of n, p, and T. But because equations (122) and (123) are transcendental, the derivation of such a fundamental equation is a difficult mathematical task. Under certain conditions it can be done with the aid of some approximations that are additional to the one-particle approximation.

For example, for a dilute gas in which the molecules have three translational degrees of freedom and of which the temperature is sufficiently high and pressure sufficiently low, it can be shown that the potential μ can be approximated by the expression

$$\mu = kT\ln p - \frac{5}{2}kT\ln T - kT\ln q_s - kT\ln \frac{k(2\pi mk)^{3/2}}{\hbar^3}, \quad (124)$$

in which m denotes the mass of each particle of the system; $\hbar$, an alternate form of Planck's constant; and q_s, the partition function associated with the energy eigenvalues $\bar\varepsilon_i$ for the internal structure of each molecule:

$$q_s = \sum_i \exp(-\bar\varepsilon_i/kT).$$

Such a gas is called a semiperfect gas. Consistent with the relations found for a semiperfect gas above without reference to the detailed structure of the molecules of the system, its fundamental equation is independent of n. This result reflects conformity with the definition of a simple system, which excludes capillarity. In contrast with equation (68), equation (124) gives the chemical potential per particle instead of per mole. It includes, therefore, the Boltzmann constant k, which is related to a single molecule and which is equal to the universal gas constant R divided by the number of molecules contained in a mole.

As indicated earlier, the heat capacities of a semiperfect gas are functions of temperature. From equation (124) may be found the following expressions for specific heat capacities per molecule:

$$c_p = \frac{5}{2}k + 2kT\frac{\partial \ln q_s}{\partial T} + kT^2\frac{\partial^2 \ln q_s}{\partial T^2}$$

and

$$c_v = \frac{3}{2}k + 2kT\frac{\partial \ln q_s}{\partial T} + kT^2\frac{\partial^2 \ln q_s}{\partial T^2},$$

in which $\partial^2 \ln q_s/\partial T^2$ denotes the partial derivative of $\partial \ln q_s/\partial T$ with respect to T. Because q_s is a function of T, both specific heat capacities are functions of T.

A particular semiperfect gas is one for which c_p and c_v are independent of temperature. As stated above, such a gas is called a perfect gas. A gas behaves as a perfect gas either when the molecules have no internal structure, so that q_s is unity, or when q_s can be approximated by the product $g \exp(-\bar\varepsilon_0/kT)$, in which g and $\bar\varepsilon_0$ are constants.

Electronegativity of atoms and molecules. An atom or a molecule may be regarded as a grand system with electrons as its only component particles because it can exchange energy and electrons while reacting chemically with other atoms and molecules.

An atom A of atomic number z contains z units of positive electric charge in addition to its electrons. It has all the energy eigenvalues of the neutral atom and of each of the multiply (positively) charged ionized atoms. Consideration will be limited to atoms having energy eigenvalues corresponding to a singly charged negative ion; i.e., an ion with $z + 1$ electrons.

The eigenvalues n_i of the number of electrons in atom A are such that

$$n_i = i = 0, 1, 2, \ldots, z, z + 1;$$

that is, the atom can be fully ionized ($i = 0$), partially ionized ($i < z$), neutral ($i = z$), or singly negatively charged ($i = z + 1$).

For each n_i a number g_{i_0} of energy eigenvalues will have the minimum numerical value E_{i_0}, in which g_{i_0} may be one or greater than one. Each of the g_{i_0} identical eigenvalues E_{i_0} represents the energy of the so-called ground state of A with exactly n_i electrons. Moreover, an infinite number of energy eigenvalues E_{ij} ($j = 1, 2, \ldots$), each with a multiplicity or degeneracy g_{ij}, correspond to the excited states for each n_i.

For a stable equilibrium state at temperature T, the expectation value n of the number of electrons of the atom is given in terms of the above notation by the relation

$$n = \frac{\sum_{i,j} n_i g_{ij} \exp[(n_i\mu - E_{ij})/kT]}{\sum_{i,j} g_{ij} \exp[(n_i\mu - E_{ij})/kT]}, \quad (125)$$

in which the symbol $\sum_{i,j}$ denotes a double summation, one over all values of i from zero to $z + 1$ and the other over all values of j from zero to infinity. The number n may assume any value between 0 and $z + 1$, although n_i can assume only integral values.

For given n and T values equation (125) can be solved for the value of the potential μ. Although the solution is numerically tedious, some general results are readily established: (1) For a fully ionized state (that is, for the minimum value $n = 0$) μ is minus infinity, and for a singly charged negative-ion state (that is, for the maximum value $n = z + 1$) μ is plus infinity, both for all

Boltzmann constant

values of T. Such extreme values of μ are always obtained when the value of the number of particles of the grand system is either minimum or maximum. They are consistent with the interpretation of the potential μ as an escaping tendency. (2) For values of n in the range between z and $z + 1$, the potential μ is positive. For all other values the potential μ is negative. (3) For a neutral atom state (that is, for $n = z$), in the limit as T approaches zero, μ is equal to one-half the difference between the energy eigenvalues of the ground states of the singly charged negative ion and the singly charged positive ion. It can also be written in the form

$$\mu = -\frac{I_1 + A_1}{2}, \qquad (126)$$

in which I_1 and A_1 are, respectively, the first ionization energy and the electron affinity of the atom. For example, for the hydrogen atom the first (and only) ionization energy is equal to 13.6, the electron affinity is 0.7, and, therefore, the potential μ is -7.15, all in electron-volt units.

Since μ is a measure of the escaping tendency, $-\mu$ is a measure of a capturing tendency or power to attract. The power of an atom to attract electrons is called the electronegativity of the atom. The preceding analysis indicates that electronegativity can be identified with the potential $-\mu$ of electrons in an atom, and its value can be computed by means of statistical thermodynamics. Similar results can be obtained for molecules and for solid surfaces.

VII. Concluding remarks

The concepts of a system and states of a system adopted throughout this article are more general than are usually adopted in the science of thermodynamics. In the first part of the article, in which the microscopic structure of the particles that constitute the system is ignored, the many relations for systems in stable equilibrium states that are well-known to classical thermodynamics are derived. The method, however, lends itself well to the treatment of states other than stable equilibrium inasmuch as the values of entropy may be found for such states.

In the second part, the microscopic structure is brought into consideration but without loss of the concept of an unambiguous stable equilibrium state. This result is achieved through the quantum-mechanical interpretation of measurement as an operation that yields definite eigenvalues with certain probabilities. The results are, first, many relations familiar to statistical mechanics that permit evaluation of properties of a system from the known structure of the particles and, secondly, a means of applying the laws of thermodynamics to systems that are large or small, simple or complex. The limitation of thermodynamics, frequently applied in the past, to macroscopic systems no longer applies. To illustrate this generality, thermodynamic ideas are applied above to a single atom in order to discover the meaning of the previously recognized quantity electronegativity.

BIBLIOGRAPHY. E. MENDOZA (ed.), *Reflections on the Motive Power of Fire by Sadi Carnot; and Other Papers on the Second Law of Thermodynamics, by É. Clapeyron and R. Clausius* (1960), on the original theoretical development of the first and second laws; J.R. MAYER, "Bemerkungen über die Kräfte der unbelebten Natur," *Annln. Chemie Pharmacie*, 42:233–240 (1842), perhaps the first attempt to demonstrate the conversion of heat into work; *The Scientific Papers of J.P. Joule*, vol. 1 (1884), on the experimental foundations of the first law; W.D. NIVEN (ed.), *The Scientific Papers of J.C. Maxwell* (1890), includes the development of the Maxwell relations; *The Collected Works of J. Willard Gibbs*, 2 vol. (1928), the definitive treatment of equilibrium statistical mechanics in terms of classical mechanics; MAX PLANCK, *Vorlesungen über Thermodynamik*, 7th ed. (1921; Eng. trans., *Treatise on Thermodynamics*, 3rd ed., 1927), on the connection between the second law and the concept of reversibility and statement of impossibility of perpetual motion of the second kind; HENRI POINCARE, *Thermodynamique* (1892), definitions of temperature and heat and statements of the first and second law; C. CARATHEODORY, "Untersuchungen über die Grundlagen der Thermodynamik," *Math.*

Annln., 67:355–386 (1909), a rigorous mathematical exposition marked by avoidance of undefined terms such as heat and temperature; G.N. LEWIS and MERLE RANDALL, *Thermodynamics*, rev. ed. by K.S. PITZER and LEO BREWER, 2nd ed. (1961), extensive application of the Gibbsian conditions of equilibrium to heterogeneous systems; W.M. LATIMER, *The Oxidation States of the Elements and Their Potentials in Aqueous Solutions*, 2nd ed. (1952), experimental data on chemical reactions; N.F. RAMSEY, "Thermodynamics and Statistical Mechanics at Negative Absolute Temperatures," *Phys. Rev.*, 103:20–28 (1956), on special systems that can assume negative temperatures on the Kelvin scale; A.B. PIPPARD, *The Elements of Classical Thermodynamics for Advanced Students of Physics* (1957), a concise and consistent application of principles to systems in equilibrium; G.N. HATSOPOULOS and J.H. KEENAN, *Principles of General Thermodynamics* (1965), a broad, rigorous, and logically complete exposition of classical thermodynamics, including the application of entropy to nonequilibrium systems, the combination of the postulates of thermodynamics, and of statistical mechanics through the use of information theory; S.R. DEGROOT, *Thermodynamics of Irreversible Processes* (1951), general and extensive application of the Onsager reciprocal relations and the theory of rate processes; R.C. TOLMAN, *The Principles of Statistical Mechanics* (1938), a scholarly exposition of classical and quantum statistical mechanics, including the density matrix; R.H. FOWLER, *Statistical Mechanics*, 2nd ed. (1936, reprinted 1955), written from the viewpoint of molecular statistics, and with E.A. GUGGENHEIM, *Statistical Thermodynamics* (1939, reprinted 1956), extensive applications to terrestrial physics and chemistry.

(J.H.K./G.N.Ha./E.P.G.)

Thermoelectric Devices

Thermoelectric devices are devices that either convert heat directly into electricity—in the case of thermoelectric generators—or provide cooling by passing an electric current through appropriate materials—in the case of thermoelectric refrigerators. Both devices are based on thermoelectric effects involving interactions between the flow of heat and of electricity through solid bodies. Although the effects themselves were discovered in the first half of the 19th century, it is only in recent years that the devices based on them have begun to compete with conventional generators and refrigerators. The growing knowledge of solid-state physics in general, and semiconducting materials in particular, has made possible such applications as a refrigerator the size of a thimble and a nuclear-powered generator on the Moon to provide electrical power for equipment that sends moonquake information back to the Earth.

The two most important thermoelectric effects are the Seebeck effect and the Peltier effect. In the Seebeck effect, an electrical current or voltage is produced in a circuit made of two different conducting materials if the two junctions (points of contact) are held at different temperatures. The flow of heat from the hot to the cold junction gives rise to an electrical current; this effect is the basis for thermoelectric generation of electricity from heat. In the Peltier effect, when a direct electric current flows through a circuit made of two different conductors, one junction between the two materials is cooled while the other is heated, depending on the direction of current flow. This effect, which may be considered the inverse of the Seebeck effect, is the basis for thermoelectric refrigeration.

The Seebeck and Peltier effects

A major advantage of thermoelectric devices is that they involve only the motion of heat and electricity, rather than the motion of mechanical parts as in rotating machinery such as turbines, dynamos, motors, or compressors used in more familiar generators and refrigerators. The major disadvantages of thermoelectric devices are that they are often less efficient to operate and more expensive to produce than conventional machines and so are usually used in specialized applications rather than as replacements for large-scale power generating plants or air-conditioning equipment.

HISTORY

Thomas Johann Seebeck, a German physicist, discovered the effect which bears his name in 1821. He found that a magnetic compass needle held close to a circuit made of two different conductors was deflected (indicating a flow of current) when the two junctions in the circuit were held at different temperatures.

The second major thermoelectric effect was discovered in 1834 by Jean-Charles-Athanase Peltier, a French watchmaker turned scientist, who, when he passed a current through the junction between two conductors, observed that heat was either absorbed or was emitted at the junction, depending on the direction of the current flow.

The thermodynamic relationship between these two thermoelectric effects was established by the English physicist Lord Kelvin (William Thomson) in 1857. He also discovered a third effect, related to the other two but more difficult to detect. The Thomson effect is the absorption or evolution of heat when an electrical current flows in a uniform conductor along which there is a temperature gradient.

The Seebeck effect is the basis for the thermocouple, a device that is widely used to measure temperatures. This was the only application of thermoelectricity for more than a century after the discoveries of Seebeck and Peltier. The theory of thermoelectric power generation was developed by a German scientist, E. Altenkirch, in 1909. In the following year he calculated the performance that could be achieved with thermoelectric refrigeration and heating, though useful devices based on his calculations were not feasible with the materials available at that time. In the multiplication of research efforts on semiconductor materials that followed the invention of the transistor in 1947, it was realized that these materials are best suited for thermoelectric applications. In the Soviet Union, Abram F. Ioffe and a group in Leningrad made important contributions to the field and, in the early 1950s, produced some of the first useful generators and refrigerators using semiconductors such as bismuth telluride (a compound of the elements bismuth and tellurium represented by the chemical formula Bi_2Te_3). In England, H.J. Goldsmid and his coworkers independently discovered that bismuth telluride could produce useful cooling. They achieved a temperature drop of 40° C (72° F) below room temperature in 1955 and 65° C (117° C) in 1958. In another independent effort, a group in the United States discovered that lead telluride (PbTe) and related semiconductors could be used effectively for thermoelectric generators.

Basic materials

These materials—bismuth telluride and lead telluride —remain the basis of thermoelectric materials most widely used for refrigeration and electric-power generation today. As a result of extensive materials research in many laboratories around the world in the 1950s and 1960s, only two other important materials were developed. Alloys of silicon and germanium, investigated in 1962, were found to be useful at higher temperatures, and bismuth–antimony alloys, investigated in 1962–63, were found best for use at low temperatures.

BASIC PRINCIPLES

Thermoelectric effects. The thermoelectric effects are concerned with the interactions between the flow of heat and of electricity in conducting solids. A very familiar effect is the production of heat in a wire when an electrical current flows through it, as in an electric heater or toaster. This phenomenon is called Joule heating; the amount of heat is proportional to the square of the current and is independent of the direction of the current flow. Although Joule heating is not itself a thermoelectric effect, it does, however, play an important role in thermoelectric devices.

In Figure 1, the flow of heat and the flow of electrical current through a conductor (A) are associated with two driving forces, the temperature difference along the conductor and the voltage applied to the ends of the conductor. The current is proportional to the applied voltage and inversely proportional to the resistivity of the material—i.e., its opposition to flow of electricity. Resistivity is denoted by the Greek letter rho (ρ). Similarly, the heat flow from the hotter to the colder regions of a material is pro-

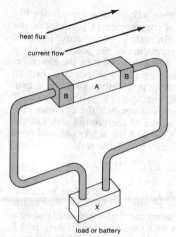

Figure 1: Basic thermoelectric circuit (see text).

portional to the temperature gradient and to the thermal conductivity of the material—that is, its ability to conduct heat. This quantity is represented by the Greek letter kappa (κ).

In the first thermoelectric effect, a voltage is produced by the temperature gradient, the magnitude of the voltage depending on a characteristic of the material known as the Seebeck coefficient (S), expressed in volts per degree Celsius. This coefficient is often called the thermoelectric power, and it is usually measured in microvolts (10^{-6} volt) per degree Celsius. This voltage can be of either polarity, depending on the material.

According to the second thermoelectric effect, there is a flow of heat proportional to the electrical current and depending on a characteristic of the material known as the Peltier coefficient (Greek pi, π). This heat flow, unlike Joule heating, can be in either direction, depending on the material (π, like S, can be positive or negative), and the heat flow reverses when the current is reversed. The thermoelectric coefficients S and π have been defined here as properties of a particular material, but the observation of these effects depends on the presence of junctions between two different materials, A and B. If the two junctions between A and B in Figure 1 are at different temperatures, then there is a voltage developed across A and a voltage developed across B. If X is a voltmeter in the circuit, it will read the difference between these voltages.

If X in Figure 1 is a battery that drives a current around the circuit, then a quantity of heat flows across each unit of cross-sectional area of A, and a different quantity flows in B. At the junctions, there is a difference of heat flow that is absorbed at one junction (cooling) and evolved at the other (heating) depending on the direction of current flow. In effect, heat is removed from one junction and delivered to the other. The circuit acts as a heat pump— that is, it pumps heat from one junction to the other if the two materials are different.

In the Peltier experiment, if the two junctions are at different temperatures and the Peltier coefficient of material A varies with temperature, then the heat absorbed at one junction will not be the same as that evolved at the other. The difference must appear within the material A. This is the Thomson effect, the third thermoelectric effect, which is the absorption or emission of heat in a single material at a rate proportional to the current flow and the temperature gradient.

Thomson effect

The Thomson coefficient is proportional to the change of the Peltier coefficient with temperature. The first two thermoelectric effects are also related to each other. The laws of thermodynamics lead to the "Kelvin relation," which states that, for any material, the Peltier coefficient is equal to the product of the Seebeck coefficient and the absolute temperature: $\pi = ST$.

Electronic origin. The origin of the thermoelectric effects can be understood in terms of the motion of the electrons or holes (a hole is equivalent to a positive charge, as it results from the absence of an electron) that carry the electrical current in a conductor. For a detailed discussion of these effects, see the articles ELECTRICITY; and THERMODYNAMICS, PRINCIPLES OF.

The Seebeck coefficient is small in most metals, typically a few microvolts (10^{-6} volt) per degree Celsius. Semiconductors (materials which are neither good electrical conductors nor good insulators) have much larger values of the coefficient, in the range of hundreds or thousands of microvolts per degree Celsius. A semiconductor material is made *n*-type (*i.e.*, given an excess of negative charges) by the addition of a small amount of impurity that introduces an excess of electrons in the crystalline structure of the semiconductor. The addition of an impurity that produces a deficiency of electrons, or holes, yields *p*-type (*i.e.*, with an excess of positive charges) material. A junction between *n*-type and *p*-type material is called a *p-n* (or *n-p*) junction.

The number of excess electrons or holes determines the electrical resistivity of a metal or semiconductor. In general, the larger the concentration of carriers, the lower the resistivity. The resistivity of a semiconductor is much higher than that of most metals, since it contains fewer charge carriers.

Thermal conduction Thermal conduction also depends on these carriers, increasing with increasing concentrations of electrons or holes. In metals, most of the heat is carried by the electrons or holes. In any solid, heat is also carried from hot to cold regions by the vibrations of the atoms about their normal positions in the crystal structure or lattice. This so-called lattice thermal conductivity is the most important mechanism operating in semiconductors with small numbers of electrons or holes—less than one per 10,000 atoms.

Basic thermoelectric devices. Semiconductors have relatively large thermoelectric powers and are thus preferable to metals as the active materials for most thermoelectric applications. In a basic device, two bars of semiconductor, called thermoelements, one *n*-type and one *p*-type, are joined with metal connections into a circuit, as shown in Figure 2. In an elementary refrigerator, X is a battery that drives an electron current around the circuit, as shown. Cooling occurs at both junctions J_2

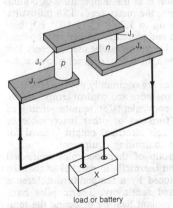

Figure 2: An elementary thermoelectric device (see text).

and J_3, so that the *n*-type and *p*-type effects are added. Heat is evolved at junctions J_1 and J_4. If these are kept near room temperature by attaching air-cooled fins or a water-cooled heat sink (a device for disposing of heat), then the cooled junctions will be well below room temperature. With the best available semiconductors, arranged in this simple circuit, if the hot junctions are maintained at 20° C (68° F), the cold junctions can reach −50° C (−58° F), a difference of 70° C (126° F). Much lower temperatures can be achieved by "cascading" a thermoelectric refrigerator, an effect that is achieved by building several stages, each of which acts as the heat sink for the next.

In an elementary thermoelectric generator, X in Figure 2 is an electrical load such as a motor or an electronic circuit. If the top junctions, J_2 and J_3, are heated while

the lower junctions, J_1 and J_4, are kept near room temperature, a current will flow through the load. Again the effects of the two types of semiconductor are added, and increased conversion efficiency is obtained. With the best available materials, heat can be converted into electrical energy with an efficiency near 10 percent, or somewhat higher if several stages are cascaded.

Figure of merit. In both types of device, the performance depends on the properties of the two semiconducting materials. In a refrigerator, the Peltier effect (and therefore, by the Kelvin relation, the thermoelectric power S) must be large to maximize the cooling effect; the resistivity (ρ) must be small to minimize Joule heating; and the thermal conductivity (κ) must be small so that a large temperature difference can be maintained. Similarly, in a generator, a large thermoelectric power (S) is required to maximize the voltage produced by the temperature gradient; a small ρ results in minimum waste of electrical power by Joule heating; and low κ prevents the heat from flowing wastefully through the thermoelements.

In either device, when the efficiency or performance is calculated, the material parameters always occur in a certain combination: $Z = S^2/\kappa\rho$, where Z is known as the figure of merit since the device efficiency improves with increasing Z. This equation states that the figure of merit of a semiconductor material is given by the square of its Seebeck coefficient divided by the product of its resistivity and its thermal conductivity.

If both materials have properties that are identical except for the sign of S, this figure of merit (Z) applies to each material separately and also to the couple as a whole. If the properties are different, Z for the couple must be calculated.

The figure of merit enters, along with the absolute temperatures of operation of the device, into various calculations of device performance. Important characteristics are as follows:

1. Efficiency of a generator, symbolized by the Greek letter eta (η), is the ratio of the maximum electrical power delivered to a load to the rate of heat flow through the thermoelements. For infinitely large Z, this becomes the maximum efficiency attainable in thermodynamic theory—the so-called Carnot efficiency—and is always less than 100 percent.

2. The maximum temperature difference (symbolized ΔT_{max}) that can be achieved with a single-stage refrigerator which is one-half the product of the figure of merit and the square of the cold junction temperature: $\Delta T_{max} = \frac{1}{2}ZT_c^2$.

3. The coefficient of performance of a refrigerator is the ratio of the heat removed from a load to the electrical power used in the device. For infinitely large Z this becomes the thermodynamic limiting efficiency, which can be larger than 100 percent because electricity is being used to pump heat from one place to another, not to generate heat.

The improved performance that can be achieved in multiple-stage devices can also be expressed in terms of Z and the various temperatures involved.

THERMOELECTRIC MATERIALS

In order to maximize the figure of merit, it is necessary first to choose the best semiconducting materials and then to control their properties by proper additions of impurities. The first obvious advantage of semiconductors is their large available thermoelectric powers, both *n*-type and *p*-type. Since the smaller the density of electrons or holes is, the larger the Seebeck coefficient will be; the addition of impurities is minimized to increase the figures of merit. If, however, the density of the charge carriers (electrons or holes) becomes too low, the electrical resistivity will rise so high that the figure of merit is reduced. The figure of merit therefore reaches a maximum at some intermediate density of electrons or holes, which is about one per 10,000 atoms, or 10^{19} per cubic centimetre. The Seebeck coefficient is then near 200 microvolts per degree Celsius.

Some thermal conductivity at this level is due to the charge carriers, but in most semiconductors even more

Figure of Merit of Various Semiconductor Materials

material	conductivity type	figure of merit $Z\ (1{,}000°\ K)^{-1}$	at temperature $T(°K)$
Bi_2Te_3	n	2.8	300
Bi_2Te_3	p	2.2	300
90% Bi_2Te_3 + 5% Sb_2Te_3 + 5% Sb_2Se_3	n	3.2	300
25% Bi_2Te_3 + 72% Sb_2Te_3 + 3% Sb_2Se_3	p	3.4	300
PbTe	n	1.9	500
PbTe	p	1.8	600
75% PbTe + 25% SnTe	n	1.7	900
70% Si + 30% Ge	n	0.9	1,100
70% Si + 30% Ge	p	0.7	1,000
88% Bi + 12% Sb	n	6.0	80
88% Bi + 12% Sb + magnetic field	n	8.6	100

heat is carried by the vibrating atoms, in the phenomenon called lattice thermal conductivity. Lattice thermal conductivity can vary by a factor of 1,000 between different semiconductors (semiconducting diamonds have the highest room temperature thermal conductivity known; silver antimony telluride, $AgSbTe_2$, conducts heat almost as poorly as glass or plastics). Lattice thermal conductivity is, therefore, the most important variable in selecting the optimum thermoelectric material.

Materials made up of heavy atoms generally have low lattice thermal conductivities. For this reason, compound semiconductors such as bismuth telluride and lead telluride are useful thermoelectric materials (lead and bismuth are the heaviest of the common nonradioactive elements).

Effect of atomic disarrangement on thermal conductivity

Another factor that influences thermal conductivity is the orderliness of the atomic arrangement in the crystals that make up the material. Disordered solids, such as glasses, have lower thermal conductivities than do perfectly ordered crystals. Disorder may be introduced into crystals by mixing two similar materials. If the atoms involved are different in their masses but chemically similar (i.e., if they come from the same column of the periodic table), then the resultant alloyed material will have electronic properties similar to those of the pure materials, but the lattice thermal conductivity may be as much as ten times lower. In bismuth telluride, replacing some of the bismuth atoms with antimony or of tellurium with selenium gives rise to useful improvements in the figure of merit, as shown in the Table. Similar results are obtained by alloying lead telluride with lead selenide or germanium telluride. In these materials, the excess electrons for negative-type behaviour are obtained by adding a very small amount of an element, such as iodine, that takes the place of tellurium in the crystal but has one more electron per atom. Small additions of elements with fewer electrons, such as cadmium, result in positive-type conductivity.

The bismuth telluride–antimony telluride–bismuth selenide system provides the best available materials for use in refrigerators, and these are also used in generators that operate over a fairly small range above room temperature, up to about 200° C (400° F). For generators that have their hot junctions up to 500° C (900° F), lead telluride-based materials are best. At higher temperatures, the figure of merit of these materials drops to very low values because the thermoelectric power decreases. For high-temperature use, different semiconductor alloys are used. Alloys of silicon and germanium, the semiconductors most commonly used for transistors, are the best available materials for use up to 1,000° C (1,800° F).

At temperatures far below room temperature, another group of materials, bismuth–antimony alloys (e.g., 88 percent bismuth, 12 percent antimony), are best. In the range from −200° to −100°C (−330° to −150° F) they have larger figure-of-merit values than any other known materials, and, in single crystals of these alloys, a properly oriented magnetic field can raise the figure of merit even higher.

Greatest efficiency in a thermoelectric generator is obtained by operating with the largest possible temperature difference between junctions. It would be useful to fabricate the hottest sections of the device using silicon–germanium alloys, the intermediate sections with lead

telluride, and the sections near room temperature with bismuth–telluride alloys. For practical reasons, commercial generators are usually made as single-stage devices using a single material, the choice depending on the range of temperatures to be used.

APPLICATIONS

Temperature measurement. The oldest and most familiar thermoelectric device is the thermocouple that is used to measure temperature. In the circuit of Figure 1, if one junction between the two different conductors is held at a known temperature, then the voltage developed by the Seebeck effect and measured by the meter at X will depend on the temperature of the other junction. If this dependence is calibrated using known temperatures, such as the melting points of pure substances, this simple circuit provides a convenient and accurate means of temperature measurement.

Principles of the thermocouple

Efficiency of energy conversion is not important in this application, and the materials A and B are most useful in the form of long fine wires; the materials used, therefore, are usually metals rather than brittle semiconductors. Material B, for example, may be copper and material A an alloy known as constantan, composed of 60 percent copper and 40 percent nickel. With these metals, the measured voltage for temperatures near room temperature is about 40 microvolts per degree Celsius. With the reference junction held at 0° C (32° F) in an ice-water bath, if the measuring junction is at the temperature of boiling water (100° C, 212° F), the meter reads 4.28 millivolts. For high temperatures up to 1,700° C (3,100° F) thermocouples of platinum and platinum–13 percent rhodium are commonly used. Other alloys can be used for very low temperatures—i.e., down to a few degrees above absolute zero.

Metallic thermocouples are commonly used in laboratories and in industry to measure and control temperatures. They are particularly convenient for remote sensing of high temperatures in furnaces or other inaccessible or hazardous locations. Their electrical output is ideal for electronic temperature-controlling equipment.

A thermopile is a group of thermocouples connected electrically in series and thermally in parallel so that the Seebeck voltages produced by a temperature difference are added for increased sensitivity. Thermopiles have been used to measure radiant heat by detecting the temperature rise of a blackened cap which is heated by the radiation.

Thermopiles

Metallic thermopiles can also be used in thermoelectric generators for applications in which economy and simplicity are more important than efficiency. Thus, in an experimental telephone repeater for use in remote regions where no electricity was available, heat from burning propane gas was converted into electrical power using a thermoelectric generator made with many metallic wires. A few watts of power were obtained in this experiment with 0.5 percent efficiency in 1954. Ten years later, in a similar application, 200 watts were generated at about 5 percent efficiency, using semiconductor thermoelements. This generator provided power for a microwave repeater on a mountain peak, where the propane tanks were replenished only twice a year.

Thermoelectric generators. Thermoelectric generators have several advantages over more conventional machines for converting heat into electricity. First, they have no moving parts to suffer wear and require maintenance. Second, they are silent and vibration free. Third, they can be scaled down to very small size with no loss of efficiency. Large steam generating plants have efficiencies as high as 40 percent, but the efficiency drops drastically as they are reduced in size. For power requirements up to a few kilowatts, the 5 to 10 percent efficiencies obtained with thermoelectric generators are at least as high as those of steam generators or internal combustion engines.

There are a number of applications in which these advantages can be used today, in spite of the relatively high initial costs. These include remote terrestrial equipment with moderate power requirements, such as the telephone repeaters mentioned above, unattended lighthouses and navigation buoys, and Arctic weather stations. Heat for these applications may be provided by burning any kind of available fuel or by nuclear energy. Power for space applications can also be provided by thermoelectric generators with nuclear or solar energy as the heat source. Some typical applications are described below.

Kerosene lamp generator. In some remote areas of the Soviet Union, no electricity is available and kerosene lamps are used for home lighting. These lamps also provide a useful quantity of heat which can be converted into electrical power for radio receivers or even transmitters. A cylindrical arrangement of thermoelements is mounted over the glass chimney of such a lamp. The hot combustion gases heat the inner junctions while the outer junctions are cooled by a set of cooling fins with large surface area. The temperature difference of about 300° C (540° F) results in a few watts of electrical power for the radio. Similar generators developed in the United States are used in remote areas of many of the world's underdeveloped countries.

In Leningrad, where the first kerosene lamp generator was developed, larger generators have also been built for use in the far north. These use all types of fuel, from gasoline to firewood. One such generator provides 200 watts of electrical power for communications use and consumes about two kilograms (4.4 pounds) of firewood per hour.

Liquid- or gas-fuelled (portable) generators. A number of companies have developed thermoelectric generators in the 10- to 100-watt range. The fuel for these is typically propane, kerosene, or gasoline, burned either with a conventional flame or in a flameless "catalytic burner." The thermoelements are made with bismuth telluride, lead telluride, or silicon–germanium alloys, and the operating temperature range is matched to the choice of materials. Natural air convection is usually used to cool the cold junctions. The measured efficiency of such a generator may be only 4 percent, although the materials are capable of 10 percent conversion efficiency. The extra loss occurs in the burners, which may deliver only 40 percent of the heat theoretically obtainable from the burning fuel. In spite of the need for engineering improvements, such generators are already competitive in efficiency and in weight with portable gasoline internal combustion generators.

Generators of this type are used in many countries for communications applications. Another important use is in corrosion protection of oil and gas pipelines. Corrosion is an electrochemical process and is greatly reduced if the vulnerable metal is kept at an appropriate electrical potential with respect to its surroundings. Using a negligible amount of fuel from the pipeline, a thermoelectric generator provides this electrical potential.

Nuclear-powered generators. Heat produced by the decay of radioisotopes (see RADIOISOTOPES, APPLICATIONS OF) or by a small nuclear reactor (*q.v.*) has been converted into electricity for various space and terrestrial applications. In the U.S. SNAP program (Systems for Nuclear Auxiliary Power), the various generators are designed SNAP-3, SNAP-10A, etc.

In the radioisotope power sources, a radioactive material with a reasonably long half-life (the length of time it takes the radioactivity to decrease to half its initial value)

is carefully sealed inside a metal container so that none of the decay particles can escape. As it absorbs the energy produced by the radioactive decay, the container is heated to a high temperature. The thermoelements surround this hot container and they, in turn, are surrounded by cooling fins which dissipate heat either by air or water convection or by radiation into space. Some useful radioisotopes are strontium-90, polonium-210, plutonium-238, and curium-242.

One American generator is a 60-watt strontium-90-fuelled device that uses lead telluride thermoelements to provide power for a floating weather station contained in a large buoy. Similar generators have been installed in automatic weather stations near the North and South poles, where the entire units, buried in snow, are designed to operate unattended for two years and to transmit weather data automatically every six hours.

In England, similar generators using plutonium-238 and silicon–germanium thermoelements, provide a few watts of power for bright pulsed marine lights in inaccessible unmanned lighthouses.

Since 1961, when a grapefruit-sized radioisotope-fuelled generator was the first thermoelectric device to orbit the Earth, there have been several similar generators used

Figure 3: (Foreground) Radioisotope thermoelectric generator installed on the moon in 1971. Astronaut's shadow is on the lower right. Some of the equipment powered by this generator is visible in the background.

in a variety of space applications. One used plutonium-238 and lead telluride thermoelements to provide 2.5 watts of power. A much more ambitious device has produced over 500 watts using a nuclear reactor heat source and a silicon–germanium thermoelectric generator.

In one successful space application a radioisotope-fuelled generator was placed on the surface of the Moon on November 19, 1969, and in 1971 it was still performing perfectly in powering a number of lunar experiments and radio transmission equipment. In the generator, plutonium-238 provides 1,500 watts of heat at 600° C (1,100° F) at the hot junctions of the lead telluride thermoelements, and a large finned beryllium radiator cools the cold junctions to about 275° C (530° F; there is no air for convection cooling). The electrical output is about 75 watts, corresponding to 5 percent efficiency. This generator is expected to provide about 65 watts of power after ten years of operation, the drop being due only to the decay of the radioisotope and not to the deterioration

SNAP series of thermo-electric generators

Generator on the Moon

of the thermoelectric device. Similar generators have been placed on the Moon in several Moon landings since 1963 (see Figure 3).

Solar generators. Experimental thermoelectric generators have been used as alternatives to solar batteries to convert sunlight into electricity. These generators, for use in space applications, are of two types. In the first, large panels, rolled or folded during launching, are extended in space to capture sunlight on one surface and radiate heat from the other. In the second type, a large mirror is deployed in space to concentrate sunlight onto a compact generator. This type sometimes includes some form of heat storage such as a meltable solid that gives up its stored heat during dark periods to provide continuous power without storage batteries. Besides this continuous power capability, the advantages of solar thermoelectric generators are their light weight and resistance to radiation damage.

Special applications. There are a number of special applications besides communications and navigation in which thermoelectric generators have been used.

A very widespread but seldom appreciated use for tiny thermoelectric generators is in the automatic control system of home gas furnaces in which heat from a pilot flame is used to generate an electrical current by means of lead telluride thermoelements. This current is used to hold the main gas valve open against a closing force. If the pilot flame should go out, the current is no longer generated and the valve automatically closes, providing a "fail safe" operation.

In electronics, a small bismuth telluride generator has been used to convert alternating current electricity via heat into smooth, ripple-free direct current for special components. It has also been demonstrated that such a generator can be used to convert direct current at one voltage to direct current at a different voltage.

In a medical application, a tiny radioisotope thermoelectric generator has been implanted in the human body to provide power for an implanted electronic "pacemaker," which triggers the heart beat of patients suffering from tachycardia. This eliminates the need for repeated operations to replace the batteries normally used. It is expected that they will have a life of up to 10 years.

Thermoelectric refrigerators. The advantages and disadvantages of thermoelectric refrigerators are similar to those mentioned above for generators. The absence of moving parts leads to greater reliability and silent operation. The available efficiency, or coefficient of performance, is lower than that of large mechanical refrigerators or air conditioners, but it is the best available for small, special-purpose coolers.

Bismuth telluride alloys are used in all of the thermoelectric cooling devices developed in England, Japan, the United States, the Soviet Union, and several other countries. Single-stage coolers can achieve a temperature drop of about 70° C (126° F) below room temperature. With a small second stage on a larger first stage (for example, a single couple with its hot junctions cooled by eight similar couples), a temperature drop greater than 100° C (180° F) can be achieved. Using eight stages, the coldest three of which make use of the magnetically enhanced Peltier effect in bismuth–antimony alloys mentioned above, a temperature drop of 171° C (308° F) below room temperature has been achieved in an experimental device. This is more than halfway down toward absolute zero.

Small-scale cooling and temperature control. The most important applications of thermoelectric cooling devices are in the area of small-scale special instruments for laboratory and industrial use. In electronics, spot coolers have been used to improve the performance of many solid-state devices, including transistors, lasers, light-emitting diodes, and microwave parametric amplifiers. The eight-stage device mentioned above was designed to cool a tiny, ultrasensitive infrared detector.

Small ovens are often used to control the temperature of such devices as quartz crystal oscillators to within one-thousandth of a degree at a fixed temperature well above the maximum ambient temperature. Thermoelectrically cooled chambers are used instead of these ovens to achieve the same control at room temperature or below to improve the long-term performance of these oscillators. In such temperature-control devices, active heating as well as cooling can be achieved by reversing the current through the thermoelements.

When metallic thermocouples are used for precise temperature measurement, as described above, the reference junction is usually maintained at exactly 0° C (32° F) in an ice water bath. This inconvenient bath has been replaced by a thermoelectrically cooled water cell, which automatically keeps a constant mixture of ice and water and needs no maintenance. When some of the water freezes in this cell, it increases in volume, and the expansion is used to operate a switch on the cooling device so that a fixed ratio of ice to water is maintained.

In oil-pumped vacuum systems, the vacuum can be improved by using a "cold trap" in the form of a thermoelectrically cooled baffle between the pump and the vacuum chamber to condense the residual oil vapours.

An early application that makes use of a single semiconductor couple is an automatic dew-point hygrometer, in which a tiny polished silver mirror reflects a beam of light away from a detector; when the mirror is cooled to the dew point by the thermoelements, droplets of water form on the mirror and reflect light into the detector. The temperature of the mirror is recorded, and the current in the thermoelements is automatically reversed; the dew evaporates and the procedure is repeated.

In biological research, thermoelectric coolers have been used for maintaining specimens such as blood plasma, antibiotics, and sperm cells at low temperatures during storage and transport. Other applications include freezing-point determinations of biological fluids, refrigeration of microtome platforms to freeze tissues that are to be sliced into very thin microscopic specimens, and cold probes to stimulate individual nerve cells within a living cat's brain.

Large-scale refrigeration. Because of their high cost, thermoelectric refrigerators have not made any large impact on the consumer market. Many demonstration units have been developed, however, and, in a few cases, these have been produced for actual use because of their special advantages. Among the demonstrations have been full-sized household refrigerator-freezers and smaller refrigerators for use in boats and trailers, water coolers, and room air conditioners. In large-scale uses, at least one building in the United States, the Johnson Wax Building in Wisconsin, was completely air conditioned with thermoelectric cooling panels because standard units could not be conveniently installed. In one hotel, every room has been equipped with its own thermoelectric ice maker, more for the novelty of the device than for its economic advantages. The largest thermoelectric devices made have been nine-ton submarine air conditioners built for the United States Navy. In this application, noiseless operation was the most important advantage.

Thermoelectric heating. Any thermoelectric cooling device can act as a heater if the current through the thermoelements is reversed. In the temperature-control devices mentioned above, this heating mode is often used, as well as the cooling mode. Consumer applications that use both heating and cooling have also been demonstrated. A thermoelectric baby-bottle cooler, for instance, has been designed with a built-in clock. At a preset time, the current in the cooler can be reversed so that the bottle is warmed to the ideal drinking temperature by the time the alarm wakes the baby's mother. In a thermoelectric "hostess cart" or "buffet bar," heating and cooling are used simultaneously in two adjacent compartments of a rolling cart, to keep food hot or cold, ready to serve.

The same air conditioner that cools a house in the summer can be used to heat it during the winter. A large thermoelectric heat pump can move heat either into the house or out of it, depending on the direction of current flow through the device. In either direction, the efficiency can be greater than 100 percent if the temperature difference to be achieved is not too large. In mild climates, this type of home heating could, therefore, be more eco-

Single-stage and multistage coolers

Biological applications

nomical to operate than normal electrical heating. Again, as in most large-scale applications, the initial cost of the device is relatively high.

Future prospects. Thermoelectric devices in ever-increasing numbers will continue to be used in various small-scale specialized applications for which they are ideally suited. Many large-scale applications have been suggested, from home heating and air conditioning to central power plants and automotive generators to replace internal combustion engines. These schemes will become practical only if further research in solid-state physics leads to new, inexpensive materials with much larger values for the thermoelectric figure of merit than those presently available.

BIBLIOGRAPHY. H.J. GOLDSMID, *Applications of Thermoelectricity* (1960), a brief readable monograph covering the field of thermoelectric effects, materials, devices, and applications, and *Thermoelectric Refrigeration* (1964), a more detailed account of thermoelectric refrigeration devices, with emphasis on materials for use below room temperature; R.R. HEIKES and R.W. URE, JR., *et al.*, *Thermoelectricity: Science and Engineering* (1961), a multi-authored review of all aspects of thermoelectric devices from basic thermodynamics and crystal growth methods to refrigerator and generator design technology; A.F. IOFFE, *Semiconductor Thermoelements, and Thermoelectric Cooling* (1957), a classic work translated from the Russian, emphasizing the important contributions made at the Institute for Semiconductors in Leningrad; C.R. RUSSELL, *Elements of Energy Conversion* (1967), a work covering various types of heat-to-electricity converters, including thermoelectric generators, with particular emphasis on the SNAP nuclear powered devices; R. WOLFE, "Magneto-thermoelectricity," *Scient. Am.* 210:70–82 (1964), a simple account of the improvements achieved in low temperature thermoelectric devices by the application of magnetic fields to semimetallic thermoelements.

(Ja.H.W./Ra.W.)

Thermometry

Thermometry is the science of measuring temperature. Any instrument used for this purpose is a thermometer. Pyrometry, a special case of thermometry, is, loosely, the science of measuring high temperatures. The term pyrometry has undergone a gradual change in meaning since its introduction in 1731 until it now usually refers to radiation thermometry (measurement of heat radiated from a body), even though recent infrared-radiation pyrometers are not restricted to high-temperature measurements.

There are many definitions of temperature (see HEAT; THERMODYNAMICS, PRINCIPLES OF). In lay terms, temperature is a measure of the hotness or coldness of a system, or a measure of the ability of a system to transfer heat to another system. More scientifically, it may be defined as the property of a system that determines whether it is in thermal equilibrium with other systems. If two isolated systems at different temperatures are placed in intimate contact (*e.g.*, a piece of hot metal in a pail of cold water), the hotter system will transfer heat to the colder until both are at the same temperature, intermediate between their original temperatures; that is, until thermal equilibrium is reached. Temperature is not a measure of the total quantity of heat in a system.

Temperature is one of the seven basic physical quantities in terms of which all other physical quantities are defined. It differs from the others (such as length and mass) by being "intensive," whereas the others are all "extensive." Length, for example, is additive: two separate one-metre lengths placed end to end establish a two-metre length. Temperature, being intensive, is not additive, however: one litre of water at 20° C (68° F) added to another litre of water at 20° C gives two litres of water still at 20° C. This phenomenon has fundamental implications for the establishment of a practical scale of temperatures. The scale or its unit cannot be established at a single temperature and extrapolated to others; it must be carefully defined over the whole range of temperatures.

Temperature measurement and control play an integral role in a wide variety of industrial, scientific, and domestic activities. Those industries where the need is especially obvious include agriculture, aircraft and automobile indus-

Impor-
tance of
thermom-
etry

tries, heating and air conditioning, refrigeration, electronics industries, mining and metallurgy, manufacturing. A familiar and important application of precise thermometry in science is in medicine. Domestically, nearly every household has at least one thermometer, be it on the furnace or the kitchen range.

HISTORY OF THERMOMETRY

Early history. Although the ancient Greeks conceived of degrees of hot and cold and performed various simple experiments which could, in retrospect, have formed the basis of a thermometer, not until the late 16th century did the first thermoscope appear; most authorities attribute its invention to the Italian scientist Galileo (Galilei), probably in 1592. Probably not provided with a scale, the thermoscope measured only changes in temperature and these only qualitatively (see illustration, top left). Gali-

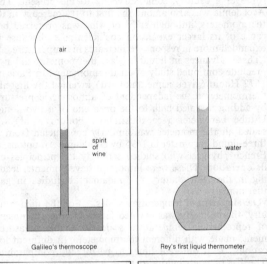

Galileo's thermoscope   Rey's first liquid thermometer

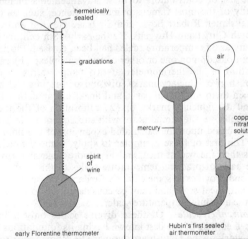

early Florentine thermometer   Hubin's first sealed air thermometer

Early thermometers.

leo's thermoscope consisted simply of a large glass bulb with a long, narrow, openmouthed neck inverted over a vessel of coloured water or spirit of wine (alcohol). After some air had been driven out of the bulb, the liquid rose a short distance into the neck; subsequent changes in the temperature of the bulb produced expansion or contraction of the air in it, which in turn produced changes in the level of the liquid in the neck. The idea of providing such a thermoscope with a scale, thus producing a thermometer, probably originated with Sanctorius Sanctorius, a colleague of Galileo, in 1611. He noted the level at which the liquid stood when the bulb was surrounded by melting snow and again when it was heated by a candle and divided the intervening distance into 110 equal parts.

By 1632 Jean Rey, a French physician, apparently unaware of the earlier Italian work, had invented the first thermometer with a liquid instead of air as the indicating

The
first
mercury
thermom-
eter

fluid (see illustration, top right). He simply filled a flask having a long, slender neck with water until the liquid level lay in the neck. Changes in the temperature of the bulb produced corresponding changes in the liquid level.

In succeeding years the sensitivity of these thermometers to barometric pressure was observed. This difficulty was first overcome in about 1644 by the grand duke Ferdinand II of Tuscany, who conceived the idea of hermetically sealing the end of a liquid-filled thermometer of the Rey type (see illustration, bottom left). Ferdinand contributed further to the advance of thermometry by promoting the establishment in 1657 of the Accademia del Cimento in Florence. During the ten years of its existence this society conducted extensive thermometric experiments while its workmen became highly skilled in the manufacture of thermometers of reproducible dimensions. These Florentine thermometers were widely used for over a century, some surviving to the present. The Accademia was also among the first to try mercury in its thermometers, although spirit of wine was preferred because of its larger expansion coefficient; i.e., because it expanded more in response to increases in temperature.

These advances in liquid-in-glass thermometry did not preclude continued study of air thermometers. In Paris in 1672 Hubin (given name unknown) invented the first air thermometer to be independent of atmospheric pressure by adding a sealed bulb to the open end of a two-liquid U-tube barometer (see illustration, bottom right). A sealed air thermometer was similarly constructed from a three-liquid barometer in 1695 by Guillaume Amontons, a French physicist who studied seriously the principles of its operation. These were important developments, leading in the 19th century to fundamental studies in gas thermometry.

Development of temperature scales. For the next century, thermometry was devoted largely to the attainment of reproducible temperature scales to enable measurements made with different thermometers, in different locations, or at different times to be directly comparable. The list of contributors to these advancements includes many of the most famous names of science, such as the Englishmen Robert Boyle and Sir Isaac Newton and the Dutch Christiaan Huygens. By the early 18th century as many as 35 temperature scales had been devised, most of them based upon one or other of two principles: (1) calibration of the thermometer at two temperatures to establish two fiduciary marks, division of the interval between them into equal parts, and linear extrapolation beyond the fiduciary marks, or (2) calibration of the thermometer at one temperature with subsequent scale divisions based upon the calculated expansion of the fluid in it. The first of these is simpler to apply, is more precise, was then the widest used, and in a more general form is the basis of practical temperature scales to this day. The second provides to some extent a fundamental rather than an empirical scale and may be considered the forerunner of the absolute temperature scale.

Fahrenheit scale. Of these diverse scales only a few survived, one of the best known having its foundations in the work of the Danish astronomer Ole Rømer. For several years before his death in 1710, Rømer turned his attention to thermometry. He calibrated his standard thermometers according to principle (1) above, assigning the value 60 (degrees) to the boiling point of water and 7½ (later 8) to the melting point of ice, these serving as his two fixed points. For his meteorological observations he seldom used the upper part of his scale, and therefore he changed his upper reference temperature to that of blood heat, labelling it 22½. Rømer's scale is important only insofar as it influenced Daniel Gabriel Fahrenheit, a Dutch instrument maker of German descent. Fahrenheit became justly famous in the period 1700–30 for the quality of his mercury thermometers and for the agreement among them when they were calibrated on his scale. Preferring finer scale divisions than Rømer used, he chose 32 for the melting point of ice and 96 for blood heat. On this scale he determined the boiling point of water to be 212 degrees, although he did not use it as one of his fixed points. The Fahrenheit scale commonly used in the En-

The
two
principles
of
thermom-
eter
scales

glish-speaking world today derives from the original one but uses 32 and 212 rather than 32 and 96 for its two fixed points. Thus, the unit of temperature (Fahrenheit degree, ° F) on this scale is 1/180 of the difference between the boiling and freezing points of water. It is a tribute to the skill of Fahrenheit that the presently accepted value for the body temperature of a healthy person (98.6° F) is so consistent with his original scale.

Réaumur scale. At about the same time (1730), a scale based on principle (2) above was developed by the French scientist René-Antoine Ferchault de Réaumur. Though it is not absolutely clear how he proceeded, it seems he chose for his thermometric fluid spirit of wine diluted with some particular amount of water, assigned 0° Re to its level at the freezing point of water, and graduated the thermometer so 1° was 1/1000 of the total volume occupied by the fluid at 0° Re. The alcohol was so diluted as to boil at about 80° Re, but because of confused reporting it was believed that this was the boiling point of water. Thus, what has been handed down as the Réaumur scale uses 0° Re as the freezing and 80° Re as the boiling point of water. But for this historical accident Réaumur might have been credited with establishing the first centigrade scale (i.e., one with the fundamental interval divided into 100 parts), because, on his original scale, the boiling point of water would have been near 100° Re. The Réaumur scale found widest acceptance in Germany.

Celsius scale. The first truly centigrade scale is generally attributed to the Swedish astronomer Anders Celsius in 1742. Earlier workers, including Fahrenheit, had already been aware that the temperature of boiling water is dependent upon atmospheric pressure, but Celsius was the first to allow for this explicitly in his calibrations. For his scale he assigned 0° to the level at which the mercury stood when the thermometer bulb was immersed in water boiling at a particular barometric reading and 100° to the level when the bulb was immersed in melting snow. Shortly thereafter the inverted form of Celsius' scale (i.e., 0° for the freezing point and 100° for the boiling point of water) made its appearance in Sweden and in France. It later spread throughout most of the world and was known for two centuries as the centigrade scale until, in 1948, the name of Celsius was officially attached to it.

Absolute temperature scale. All of the temperature scales described above are essentially empirical. The basis for a fundamental scale, however, had already been laid by experiments on the properties of gases. In 1661 Robert Boyle observed that the product of the pressure (P) and volume (V) of a given quantity of air at constant temperature was constant over a moderately wide range of pressures. What is now known as Boyle's law may therefore be written

Boyle's
law

$$PV = \text{constant.}$$

Further experiments many years later showed that Boyle's law is only approximately true except in the limit of very low pressures, in which case it is exactly true for all gases.

In about 1800, Jacques-Alexandre-César Charles and Joseph-Louis Gay-Lussac concluded from independent experiments that the volume occupied by any gas increases linearly with increase in temperature when the gas is maintained at constant pressure. Known as Charles's law, this result may be expressed in the form

$$V = V_0 (1 + \alpha t),$$

where V is the volume at temperature $t°$ C, V_0 is the volume at 0° C (32° F), and the constant symbolized by the Greek letter alpha, α, is the coefficient of thermal expansion. According to Charles and Gay-Lussac, α has the same value for every gas; just as before, the law is only approximate but becomes exact in the limit of low pressures, in which case α has the value 0.003661 = 1/273.15. If this value is inserted in the above equation, it follows that, when $t = -273.15°$ C, the gas has no volume at all. For this reason the temperature $-273.15°$ C is called the absolute zero; no lower temperature is possible. This statement of zero volume should not be interpreted literally; what it approximately means is that at

−273.15° C the molecules comprising the gas are so tightly packed that no space is left between them. In practice, all substances at this temperature are in the liquid or solid state, for which the law no longer applies anyway.

If now a new temperature scale is defined so that temperatures T on it are given by $T = t + 273.15$, Charles's law may be rewritten in the form

$$\frac{V}{T} = \text{constant.}$$

This, when combined with Boyle's law, results in the general gas law (see GASEOUS STATE)

$$\frac{PV}{T} = \text{constant.}$$

It is evident from this equation that, if either the pressure or the volume of a given quantity of gas is held constant, measurement of the other may be used to determine temperature. This condition is the basis of the gas thermometer. A gas for which the general gas law holds is called *ideal*, or *perfect*; the scale on which the temperature T was defined is called the absolute temperature scale, or the ideal-gas temperature scale.

Kelvin scale. Because no real gas behaves exactly as an ideal gas, most of the early experiments utilizing these principles produced slightly different scales, not only for different gases but also for the constant pressure and constant volume modes of operation. The need remained for a truly fundamental temperature scale independent of the properties of any particular substance. This need was met by the British physicist William Thomson (later Lord Kelvin), who proposed in 1848 to define a thermodynamic temperature scale in terms of the efficiency of an ideal heat engine described by the French physicist Sadi Carnot in 1824 (see THERMODYNAMICS, PRINCIPLES OF). A heat engine may be described as a machine that converts heat into mechanical work, such as a steam or an internal-combustion engine. To produce continuous work, the machine performs a given cycle of operations over and over again. Any heat engine operates on the principle that during one part of its cycle the working substance absorbs heat from a reservoir at a high temperature, and during another part, after using some of this heat to do the work, it rejects a lesser quantity of heat to a reservoir at a lower temperature. In the case of the steam engine, for example, the working substance is water vapour, the high-temperature reservoir is the boiler, and the low-temperature reservoir is the condenser. No heat engine can be perfectly efficient; *i.e.*, can convert all of the heat extracted from the high-temperature reservoir into useful work. Carnot's contribution was to show that his ideal engine worked at the maximum possible efficiency and, further, that this efficiency was independent of the nature of the working substance and dependent only upon the temperatures of the two reservoirs.

Thomson (Lord Kelvin) showed that for the Carnot engine, if Q_1 units (joules) of heat are extracted from the hot reservoir and Q_2 joules of heat are returned to the cold reservoir, a temperature scale could be defined such that

$$\frac{T_1}{T_2} = \frac{Q_1}{Q_2},$$

where T_1 and T_2 are the temperatures assigned to the hot and cold reservoirs, respectively, on his thermodynamic temperature scale. This is often also called the Kelvin scale, in his honour. Thomson went on to establish that the temperatures so defined are identical with those defined by the ideal-gas laws; *i.e.*, the absolute and thermodynamic temperature scales are the same.

To establish the size of the unit on the Kelvin scale, Thomson pointed out that in principle one temperature could be defined arbitrarily, and, by the above equation, all others would be measured in terms of it. This was impractical in his day. As an alternative and to keep the scale compatible with those already in use, he accepted the Celsius principle of setting the difference between the freezing and boiling points of water equal to 100 kelvins

(the name now used for the unit on the Kelvin scale). Thus, the kelvin (symbol K without the degree sign °) has the same magnitude as the degree Celsius, and the two scales are related by

$$T\,(\text{K}) = t(°\text{C}) + 273.15.$$

(The degree sign is still occasionally used with the symbol K when referring to temperatures or temperature differences on the kelvin scale.)

This definition of the kelvin suffers the disadvantage that the position of the two fundamental reference points relative to the absolute zero (*i.e.*, the number 273.15) must be determined by experiment. Suppose this value can be found to within 0.01° K; then the freezing point of water on the Kelvin scale (273.15° K) is uncertain by about one part in 27,000. A very low temperature, such as the boiling point of liquid helium (4.2° K), however, is uncertain by about one part in 400. For scientific work such a large uncertainty in converting from one scale to the other is undesirable. For this reason Kelvin's first proposal for defining the kelvin is preferred.

Rankine scale. It is of course possible to set up an absolute temperature scale with a degree the same size as the Fahrenheit degree. If this is done, the absolute zero is found to occur at −459.67° F. The absolute Fahrenheit scale is defined by setting $T(°\text{R}) = t(°\text{F}) + 459.67$; it bears the same relation to the Kelvin scale as the Fahrenheit does to the Celsius. This scale is commonly called the Rankine scale, in honour of W.J.M. Rankine, a famous 19th-century Scottish engineer and one of the founders of the science of thermodynamics.

Advances in thermometer technology. Coincident with these fundamental developments, advances in thermometer technology continued. Any property of a substance that changes with temperature may in principle form the basis of a thermometer; properties other than the expansion of liquids and gases are capable of higher sensitivity and wider range. The English scientist Sir Humphry Davy reported in 1821 that the electrical resistance of a metal is dependent upon temperature. The German scientist Sir William Siemens proposed in 1871 to exploit this phenomenon to build an electric resistance thermometer. His choice of platinum for the material of the sensor was superb; as perfected by the British physicist Hugh Longbourne Callendar and others, the platinum resistance thermometer is the most stable and accurate thermometer available. It is described in detail later; at this point it is important for the role it plays in the present International Practical Temperature Scale, below.

Another electric thermometer, called a thermocouple, is based upon the discovery by Thomas Johann Seebeck in Germany in 1822 that an electric current is generated in a simple closed circuit consisting of two dissimilar metals (*e.g.*, copper and iron) when the two junctions are held at different temperatures. Thermocouples (also described below) composed of platinum and an alloy of 10 percent rhodium in platinum have been developed into precise instruments, especially for reading high temperatures; they, too, form a part of the International Practical Temperature Scale.

That the temperature of a hot object might be measured by suitably sampling the heat it radiates was recognized by the 19th century. Various theoretical attempts to establish a relation between the emitted radiation and the temperature of the object culminated in 1900 in the famous law of the German physicist Max Planck. For the very special case of a blackbody (*i.e.*, a body that totally absorbs all of the radiation incident upon it), Planck developed the equation

$$L_\lambda(T) = c_1\lambda^{-5}/(e^{c_2/\lambda T} - 1),$$

where $L_\lambda(T)$ is the spectral radiance of the source (*i.e.*, the energy radiated per unit time per unit of projected area per unit solid angle at a fixed wavelength symbolized by the Greek letter lambda, λ), T is the thermodynamic temperature, and c_1 and c_2 are the first and second radiation constants, respectively. Not only has this law been found to describe the spectral distribution of the energy emitted by a blackbody accurately, but it

Ideal gas

Establishment of the Kelvin unit

Planck's law

also marked the beginning of the quantum theory of radiation. For his discovery Planck received the Nobel Prize for Physics in 1918. It is important that the same temperature appears in Planck's equation as in Kelvin's thermodynamic scale, so that radiation thermometry, in addition to gas thermometry, provides a practical means of measuring thermodynamic temperatures. Planck's law as applied to a particular radiation thermometer, the optical pyrometer, is also an integral part of the International Practical Temperature Scale.

International temperature scales. Although the thermodynamic scale as propounded by Kelvin was recognized as fundamental, there were practical difficulties in using it. Gas thermometers were cumbersome and unsuited to many applications. Furthermore, in many cases, knowledge of the thermodynamic temperature was not as important as the precise reproduction of temperature or temperature intervals on some practical scale. A multiplicity of such scales was obviously undesirable. Thus, in 1927 all countries adhering to the International Committee on Weights and Measures adopted the International Temperature Scale. This scale was defined basically by extending the principle (1) listed earlier. Because of improvements in measurements and techniques, the International Temperature Scale was replaced in 1948 by the International Practical Temperature Scale of 1948 (IPTS-48), in 1960 by a revised version, and in 1968 by the currently used International Practical Temperature Scale of 1968 (IPTS-68).

The IPTS-68 recognizes the thermodynamic temperature as the basic temperature and defines its unit (the kelvin) to be 1/273.16 of the triple point (equilibrium among the solid, liquid, and vapour phases) of water (see the Table). The IPTS-68 itself is so constructed as to

Defining Fixed Points of the International Practical Temperature Scale of 1968*

fixed point	T_{68} (°K)	t_{68} (°C)
Equilibrium among the solid, liquid, and vapour phases of equilibrium hydrogen (triple point of equilibrium hydrogen)	13.81	−259.34
Equilibrium between the liquid and vapour phases of equilibrium hydrogen at a pressure of 33,330.6 newtons per square metre (25/76 standard atmosphere)	17.042	−256.108
Equilibrium between the liquid and vapour phases of equilibrium hydrogen (boiling point of equilibrium hydrogen)	20.28	−252.87
Equilibrium between the liquid and vapour phases of neon (boiling point of neon)	27.102	−246.048
Equilibrium among the solid, liquid, and vapour phases of oxygen (triple point of oxygen)	54.361	−218.789
Equilibrium between the liquid and vapour phases of oxygen (boiling point of oxygen)	90.188	−182.962
Equilibrium among the solid, liquid, and vapour phases of water (triple point of water)	273.16	0.01
Equilibrium between the liquid and vapour phases of water (boiling point of water)	373.15	100.00
Equilibrium between the solid and liquid phases of zinc (freezing point of zinc)	692.73	419.58
Equilibrium between the solid and liquid phases of silver (freezing point of silver)	1,235.08	961.93
Equilibrium between the solid and liquid phases of gold (freezing point of gold)	1,337.58	1,064.43

*All of the assigned boiling and freezing point temperatures are for a pressure of one standard atmosphere (101,325 newtons per square metre). The freezing point of tin (t_{68} = 231.9681° C) may be used as an alternative to the boiling point of water.

closely approximate thermodynamic temperatures; its unit is also called the kelvin, or the degree Celsius, which has the same size. Temperature (T_{68}) on the IPTS-68 is defined by assigning numerical values to 11 reproducible fixed points and interpolating between them in prescribed ways. The IPTS-68 is not defined below −259.34°

C. The 11 fixed points of the IPTS-68 and their assigned temperatures are listed in the Table.

An important but subtle point regarding these scales is worth noting. By definition, the unit for thermodynamic temperatures is the same in all temperature regions; this is not necessarily so for the IPTS-68. Even if the temperatures assigned to the fixed points are their true thermodynamic values, it has not yet been established that the assigned interpolating formulas will exactly reproduce thermodynamic temperatures except above the gold point. Thus, the unit on the practical scale may not be constant; a degree in one temperature region may be of different size from that in another. Hence, the accurate determination of thermodynamic temperatures in all temperature regions is the major task of modern thermometry.

METHODS OF TEMPERATURE MEASUREMENT

Temperature measurements are required over such a wide range and in such a wide variety of situations that a very large number of types of thermometers have been developed. The principles of the more important of these are outlined below. Many considerations influence the choice of thermometer for a particular task, among them cost, durability, size, speed of response, accuracy, sensitivity, and temperature range.

Gas. Gases are used in several ways as thermometric fluids. In the gas thermometer they provide the best means of measuring thermodynamic temperatures over the wide range from about −263° to 1,000° C (−441° to 1,800° F). Only for very low temperatures, however, is the gas thermometer a practical measuring device.

The three forms of the gas thermometer. The gas thermometer may be constructed in one of three forms: constant-volume, in which the pressure of a given quantity of gas confined to a constant volume is measured as a function of temperature; constant-pressure, in which the volume of a given quantity of gas maintained at constant pressure is measured as a function of temperature; and constant-temperature, in which both the pressure and volume of a given quantity of gas at temperature T are measured and then measured again when a known fraction of this gas has been transferred to a reference volume. In all three cases one of the temperatures is a known reference (frequently the triple point of water), and the others are determined relative to it. Most gas thermometers in use are of the first type. In a typical installation a quartz or metal bulb containing the gas is held at a constant temperature and connected to a pressure-measuring device through a complex network of capillary tubing. An appropriate standard IPTS-68 thermometer placed so as to be at the same temperature as the bulb allows a direct comparison of the practical with the thermodynamic scale. The gas is usually helium, especially at low temperatures, but hydrogen, nitrogen, argon, and others have been used at high temperatures.

A number of small but important effects must be considered if accurate temperatures are to be obtained. The volume of the bulb itself, for example, and hence of the gas in it changes with temperature; the amount of change can be calculated if the thermal-expansion coefficient (fractional increase in volume for a 1° C rise in temperature) of the material of the bulb is known; metals are preferred over glasses in this regard. Again, a small portion of gas is not in the bulb but in the connecting capillary, which usually is exposed to a temperature gradient. This volume and its temperature distribution must be measured. Many possibilities for errors arise. Perhaps the most important are adsorption of gas on and desorption of gas from the walls of the bulb. These result in the nature and quantity of the gas not being constant. The uncertainties in temperatures measured with very good gas thermometers vary from a few thousandths of a degree below 100° C to a few tenths of a degree at 1,000° C.

Vapour-pressure thermometry. Gases are also used in vapour-pressure thermometry. From thermodynamic principles the equilibrium pressure of the vapour over a liquid surface may be related to thermodynamic temperature by an equation involving the latent heat of

Factors leading to error

ty (χ)—*i.e.*, a parameter that indicates the extent to which a material is susceptible to magnetization—of paramagnetic salts, which is expressed by

$$\chi = \frac{C}{T - \theta,}$$

where C and θ (theta) are constants. Cerium magnesium nitrate obeys this relation down to about 0.006° K. Below that point the equation defines a magnetic temperature, which must be related to thermodynamic temperature by some kind of auxiliary measurements. The susceptibility is usually determined by placing a spherical single crystal or a small cylindrical powdered specimen of the salt inside a coil, the mutual inductance of which is measured with an alternating-current bridge. The constants C and θ are determined above 1° K by comparison with another type of thermometer and the equation extrapolated below.

Magnetic thermometers with other salts (*e.g.*, gadolinium sulfate) make convenient interpolating instruments from 1° to 30° K. They are calibrated at two or three temperatures over the range, and intervening temperatures are interpolated using the above or some other simple relation between χ and T. It is interesting that the extension of this principle to nuclear magnetism (as distinct from atomic paramagnetism) will measure the lowest temperatures yet attained, below 10^{-5}° K.

Thermal noise. In any electrical conductor the electrons move about randomly, the extent of their motion increasing with temperature. Because they are charged particles, their motion produces a small fluctuating voltage; it commonly manifests itself, for example, as noise or static in electronic circuits. From thermodynamic principles it has been shown that this thermal-noise voltage is systematically related to temperature. A thermal-noise thermometer takes advantage of this relationship to measure thermodynamic temperatures. Generally, two platinum resistors connected to an electronic amplifier are used, the first at a known reference temperature and the second at an unknown temperature. The noise generated in the two resistors is compared, and one is attenuated until they are equal. Or, alternatively, one resistance may be varied until the noise voltages are equal. In either case an inherent difficulty is to separate the noise generated in the amplifier itself from that generated in the resistors. Variations of these techniques have been proposed; *e.g.*, rather than attenuate the noise from the resistor at the higher temperature, one may inject noise into the one at the lower temperature, with the advantage of reducing the dependence upon amplifier noise. Noise thermometers may be operated at temperatures from a few degrees Kelvin to above 1,000° C.

Pyroelectric. Crystals of certain solids, such as tourmaline and triglycine sulfate, exhibit spontaneous polarization when their temperature is changed (*i.e.*, they become electrically charged with opposite faces having charges of opposite polarity). The magnitude and polarity of the induced voltage is dependent upon the magnitude and direction of the temperature change. This phenomenon, called pyroelectricity, has been suggested as the basis of a differential thermometer but had not yet been fully exploited in the early 1970s. Extreme sensitivity is clearly possible, for in some materials a 1° C temperature change generates several hundred volts. Temperature changes smaller than 10^{-5}° C have been measured in this way, and 10^{-7}° C appears possible. Pyroelectric thermometers will not measure temperature itself, because the voltage gradually disappears when the crystal is maintained at constant temperature.

Gas viscosity. A gas-viscosity thermometer depends upon the resistance offered by a capillary tube to the flow of gas through it. In one such device the flow of argon through a variable-length capillary at a reference temperature is matched to the flow through a ceramic capillary at a high temperature as sensed by a differential manometer (pressure-measuring instrument). At balance, the pressure drop along both capillaries is the same, and under these conditions a simple equation relates the resistance of the reference capillary to the temperature of

the ceramic capillary. The temperature is then obtained from an independent calibration of the instrument.

Temperature indicators. Certain materials give one single indication of a temperature. Crayons or paints that melt or change colour within a very small temperature range may be applied to any surface and will indicate when the surface reaches a specified temperature. Pellets that melt and tapes that turn black are similarly applied. More than 100 such temperatures between 40° and 1,800° C may be measured in this way by suitable choice of indicator. The accuracy is typically within 1 percent. Pyrometric cones, small clay cones, their axes inclined slightly from the vertical, soften and bend at particular temperatures and are much used in the ceramic industries. Cholesteric liquid crystals, which indicate temperature by changing their colour, differ from the other indicators in that the colour change is reversible, and the crystals may traverse a range of colours to indicate more than one temperature. Sensitivity is high; a 0.1° C temperature change is detectable.

Thermography. Thermography, or mapping of external temperature distributions over extended areas, can be accomplished with the indicators described above or by photography, especially with infrared-sensitive emulsions. Scanning and recording with infrared pyrometers is common in meteorological applications. Another method employs phosphors that emit visible light when irradiated with ultraviolet. The intensity of the emitted radiation is temperature-dependent. The phosphor may be painted on a surface, irradiated, and the temperature distribution observed visually or photographed.

Shadowgraph, Schlieren, and interferometer techniques when applied to transparent mediums, such as high-temperature gases, can be employed to map internal temperature distributions. These techniques exploit the temperature dependence of the index of refraction, that property determining the direction and velocity with which a light ray traverses a medium. In the shadowgraph and Schlieren techniques an extended uniform beam of light is shone through the medium; temperature gradients within cause small displacements of individual rays within the beam. These effects are reproduced as variations in the intensity of the emergent beam and may be displayed by suitable projection on a screen or photographic plate, where they appear as shadows. In the interferometer an initial monochromatic beam is split so that only one portion traverses the medium, is subsequently reunited, and is then projected on a screen. Interference fringes, indicating contours of constant temperature, result from the velocity changes undergone by the individual rays in one beam relative to those in the other. This method is capable of quantitative evaluation.

BIBLIOGRAPHY. The most complete references for thermometry, covering all phases of the subject and giving extensive bibliographies, is the series, *Temperature: Its Measurement and Control in Science and Industry,* 4 vol. (1941–72). Among textbooks dealing in whole or in part with some part of thermometry, two that give the most complete coverage are H.D. BAKER, E.A. RYDER, and N.H. BAKER, *Temperature Measurement in Engineering,* 2 vol. (1953–61); and M. TERNY, *La Mesure des températures au laboratoire et dans l'industrie* (1962). A review emphasizing measurements of reasonably high precision is R.E. BEDFORD, T.M. DAUPHINEE, and H. PRESTON-THOMAS, "Temperature Measurement," in *Tools and Techniques in Physical Metallurgy,*" ed. by F. WEINBERG vol. 1, ch. 1 (1970). Cryogenic thermometry is ably reviewed in C.A. SWENSON, "Low Temperature Thermometry, 1 to 30 K," *Critical Reviews in Solid State Sciences,* 1:99–136 (1970). Two excellent accounts of the history of thermometry are H.C. BOLTON, *Evolution of the Thermometer: 1592–1743* (1900); and W.E.K. MIDDLETON, *A History of the Thermometer and its Uses in Meteorology* (1966). Two extensive bibliographies of research papers dealing with all phases of thermometry published from 1953 through 1962 are C. HALPERN and R.J. MOFFAT, "Bibliography of Temperature Measurement: January 1953 to June 1960," *National Bureau of Standards Monograph 27* (1961); and C. HALPERN, "Bibliography of Temperature Measurement: July 1960 to December 1962," *ibid.,* suppl. 1 (1963). The complete text of the IPTS-68 appears in "The International Practical Temperature Scale of 1968," *Metrologia,* 5:35–44 (1969).

(R.E.Be.)

Mapping internal temperature distributions

The phenomenon of pyroelectricity

Thermoreception

Thermoreception is a process in which different levels of heat energy (temperatures) are detected by living things.

GENERAL FEATURES

Adaptive function. Temperature has a profound influence upon living organisms. Active life among animals is feasible only within a narrow range of body temperatures, the extremes being about 0° C and 45° C. On the Fahrenheit scale the same range is 32° F and 113° F. Limitations depend on the freezing of tissues at the lower temperature and on the chemical alteration of body proteins at the higher end of the range. Within these limits the metabolic rate of the animal tends to increase and decrease in parallel with its body temperature.

Body temperature and metabolism among more highly evolved animals (*e.g.*, birds and mammals) are relatively independent of direct thermal influences from the environment. Such animals can maintain considerable inner physiological stability under changing environmental conditions (see HOMEOSTASIS) and are adaptable to substantial geographic and seasonal temperature fluctuations. A polar bear, for example, can function both in a zoo during summer heat and on an ice floe in frigid Arctic waters. This kind of flexibility is supported by the function of specific sensory structures called thermoreceptors (or thermosensors), which enable the animal to detect thermal changes and to adjust accordingly.

Temperature of the body directly reflects that of the environment among cold-blooded (poikilothermic) animals, such as insects, snakes, and lizards. These creatures maintain safe body temperatures mainly by moving into locations of favourable temperature (*e.g.*, in the shade of a desert rock). Warm-blooded (homoiothermic) organisms, such as the polar bear, normally keep practically constant body temperature, independent of environment. Homoiothermic animals, including man, are able to control their body temperature not only by moving into favourable environments but also through the internal regulatory (autonomic) effects of the nervous system on heat production and loss. Such autonomic adjustments depend on lower brain centres; the behavioral (movement) responses require the function of the brain's outer layers (the cerebral cortex).

A variety of behavioral responses is elicited through stimulation of thermoreceptors, including changes in body posture that help regulate heat loss and the huddling together of a group of animals in cold weather. In some species, thermoreceptors are also involved in food location and sexual activities. Bloodsucking insects, such as mosquitoes, are attracted by thermal (infrared) radiations of warm-blooded hosts; such snakes as pit vipers can locate warm prey at considerable distance by means of extremely sensitive infrared receptors. Man has achieved the widest range of adaptability to extremes in temperature, since his technology allows him to protect himself under a considerable variety of thermal conditions on earth and even in outer space.

Perceptual aspects of thermoreception are found in evidence that man and other animals have conscious temperature sensations and emotional experiences of thermal comfort and discomfort (see FATIGUE; SENSORY RECEPTION, HUMAN). The effects of temperature on productive efficiency and behaviour (*e.g.*, on one's ability to think) have led to the installation of heat-regulating equipment in homes, public buildings, factories, and similar shelters for people, livestock, and other animals.

Thermoreception can be studied in different ways: (1) on the basis of reports of temperature sensations and thermal comfort by human subjects; (2) through observations of behavioral responses to variations in temperature by all kinds of animals; (3) by the measurement of compensatory autonomic responses (*e.g.*, sweating or panting) to thermal disturbances in the environment; and (4) by recording electrical impulses generated in the nerve fibres of thermoreceptors in laboratory animals and human subjects.

General properties of thermoreceptors. The concept of thermoreceptors derives from studies of human sensory physiology, in particular from the discovery reported in 1882 that thermal sensations are associated with stimulation of localized sensory spots in the skin. Detailed investigations reveal a distinction between hot spots and cold spots; that is, specific places in the human skin that are selectively sensitive to warm stimuli or to cold. To this extent the different thermoreceptors exhibit sensory specificity. Modern neurophysiological methods show thermoreceptors also to be biophysically specific, in that they include nerve endings that are excited only by or primarily by thermal stimuli.

Extending far beyond the context of conscious temperature sensation as reported by humans, the biophysical definition holds for any thermoreceptive structure. Clearly, electrical responses from thermoreceptors are observable whether conscious sensations are reported by the animal (as in the case of a person) or whether they are not (as in the case of a laboratory rat). Although they are closely related, the concepts of sensory and biophysical specificity are not identical, the criterion being the quality of inner experience (sensation) in the first case and the quality of the neurally effective stimulus in the second. To make the distinction clear, a receptor that is neurally excited by cooling as well as by the application of a chemical (*e.g.*, menthol) might be classified only as a specific (cold) thermoreceptor in terms of human sensation; biophysically, however, it manifestly is a chemoreceptor as well (see CHEMORECEPTION).

Most of the modern understanding of thermoreceptors is based on biophysical (electrophysiological) investigations. This approach, introduced in 1936 for recording the electrical signals from single thermosensitive nerve fibres in the tongue of the cat, had been applied by 1960 to similar recordings from single thermoreceptors in the skin of human subjects. Such investigations are made by dissecting single nerve fibres under the microscope and placing them on electrodes or by inserting very fine wires (*e.g.*, tungsten microelectrodes) directly into the intact nerve or receptor. As in the case of other sensory nerve fibres, the electrical signals generated by the activity of thermoreceptors are brief impulses of about one millisecond duration and roughly constant amplitude. They follow in a more or less regular sequence, modulations (changes) in the frequency of which reflect differences in the intensity of the stimulus. (Frequency modulation is widely applied in such devices as radios for information processing.) Sensory structures are called specific thermoreceptors if they respond biophysically to temperature stimuli yet are practically insensitive to such other kinds of stimulation as mechanical pressure.

The general properties of thermoreceptors in the external parts of the body are found to be similar for any species of animals investigated. Thermoreceptors can be divided into well-defined classes as cold and as warm receptors. At constant temperatures (within an appropriate range), cold receptors are continuously active electrically, the frequency of the steady discharge (static response) depending on temperature. In most cases the static activity reaches a maximum at temperatures between 20° and 30° C (68° and 86° F). On sudden cooling to a lower temperature level, the cold receptors respond with a transient increase in frequency (dynamic response); if the lower temperature is maintained, the frequency drops to a level of static discharge in adaptation. When the receptor is warmed up again, a transient decrease in electrical activity is seen, after which the frequency rises again and finally adapts to the initial static value. Warm receptors are also continuously active at constant temperatures, with a maximum at 41° to 46° C (about 106° to 115° F). On sudden temperature changes, warm receptors respond in the opposite direction from that of cold receptors, temporarily overshooting adaptation frequency on warming and showing transient inhibition on cooling. Thermoreceptors are thus selectively sensitive to specific ranges of temperature as well as to rate of temperature change.

Some receptor cells in the skin of fishes and amphibians respond both to mechanical and to thermal stimulation. In the skin of cat, monkey, and man, receptors have been

Early
investigations of
thermoreception

Cold
receptors
and warm
receptors

Cold-
blooded
and
warm-
blooded
animals

found that are excited both by mechanical stimuli and by cooling. It seems, however, that these nerve endings are primarily mechanoreceptors (see MECHANORECEPTION), their sensitivity to cooling being much lower than that of specific cold receptors.

THERMORECEPTION IN INVERTEBRATES

Insects placed on a surface that provides a temperature gradient (warmer at one end and cooler at the other) often congregate in a narrow band of temperature, providing behavioral evidence of sensitive thermoreception. Honeybees (*Apis mellifera*) normally choose a temperature range of 35° ± 1.5° C (95° ± 2.7° F); when repeatedly replaced at the warm end of the gradient, individual bees follow their average chosen temperature within ±0.25° C (±0.45° F). Bees also accurately regulate temperature in the hive between 35° and 36° C (95° and 97° F) by behavioral patterns (*e.g.*, beating wings to circulate air) in the brood season.

Among invertebrates other than arthropods, the leech (*Hirudo medicinalis*) can make temperature discriminations with an accuracy of 1° C (about 2° F). The slug (*Agriolimax reticulatus*) reacts at temperatures below 21° C (70° F) by increased locomotor activity in response to 0.3° C (0.5° F) cooling over a period of five minutes.

The temperature sensitivity of bloodsucking arthropods (*e.g.*, lice) is considerably greater than that of nearly all other arthropods; the warmth of the victim's body is the primary influence in stimulating and guiding such blood feeders. The so-called castorbean tick (*Ixodes ricinus*), which sucks blood from sheep, responds when its front legs, which are the primary site of thermal sensitivity, are warmed up by 0.5° C (0.9° F). The bloodsucking assassin bug (*Rhodnius prolixus*) responds with direct movement toward any warm stimuli; *e.g.*, when a glass tube warmed 15° C (27°F) above air temperature is kept within about four centimetres (1.5 inches) of its antennae. Similarly, mosquitoes (*Aedes aegypti*) fly readily to a warm, odourless, inanimate surface as if it were that of a warm-blooded creature. The mosquito's antennae are probably the site of the thermosensors, and the animals manifest sensitivity to changes in air temperature of about 0.5° C. In most insects the thermoreceptors appear to be located in the antennae, since they show impairment of thermoreceptive behaviour when part or all of the antennae are removed. Behavioral studies represent a rather gross method of localizing thermosensitive structures, however. A more direct approach to thermoreceptor function in insects has been achieved by electrophysiological methods. Microelectrodes with tips of very small diameter are inserted near the presumed thermosensitive cells. Any electrical nerve impulses elicited by temperature stimuli are amplified and recorded. This method permits, for example, the study and identification in various insects of receptors that are sensitive to cooling. Cockroaches (*Periplaneta americana*) have two whiplike antennae consisting of 120 to 180 ring-shaped segments that grow thinner and longer with increasing distance from the animal's head. There are about 20 cold receptors per antenna; these are located on the thicker segments (Figure 1), with rarely more than one per segment. Each cold receptor consists of a delicate hairlike structure (sensillum) emerging from a ring-shaped wall. The cold sensilla are mechanically protected by large bristles covering the segments of the antenna. At constant

Studies with micro-electrodes

temperatures the cold receptor is continuously active, the average maximum frequency of its discharge being about 16 impulses per second at a temperature near 28° C (82° F). At higher and lower temperatures, the steady frequency becomes lower. When the receptor is rapidly cooled, its discharge frequency rises steeply up to 300 impulses per second and then declines gradually to a much lower constant level. On rapid warming, the opposite response is seen; *i.e.*, there is a transient inhibition of the receptor discharge, followed by a gradual restoration of the steady activity. The cold receptor is thus sensitive to constant temperatures as well as to the rate of temperature changes.

Caterpillars of various moths (*Lasiocampidae, Saturniidae, Sphingidae*) have cold-receptor cells in their antennae and mouthparts (maxillary palps). Electrophysiological investigations with microelectrodes suggest that just three receptor cells located in the third antennal segment and probably not more than one receptor cell in the maxillary palp are sensitive to cooling. At constant room temperatures, static neural activity from such cells is observed; this activity increases in frequency when the temperature is lowered. During rapid cooling, the frequency rises steeply to a transient maximum of up to 300 impulses per second, while rapid warming produces a temporary inhibition of the discharge. Since only a few cells out of the 20 or 30 that comprise the thermoreceptor structure exhibit the typical electrical response to cooling, specific thermoreceptive function among caterpillars is strongly indicated.

Electrophysiological evidence for the presence of thermosensitive structures also is available for the antennae of honeybees and of migratory locusts (*Locusta migratoria migratorioides*). Temperature-induced changes in the spontaneous electrical activity within the central nervous system of honeybees also have been recorded. Other sensory structures in these animals also can be influenced by temperature, but their primary functions appear to be chemoreceptive or mechanoreceptive.

THERMORECEPTION IN VERTEBRATES

Fish. Many species of modern bony fish (teleosts) are sensitive to very small changes of temperature of the water in which they live. Various marine teleosts, such as the cod (*Gadus gadus*), have been trained to swim half out of water up a long sloping trough in response to changes of as little as 0.03° to 0.07° C (0.05° to 0.13° F) in the temperature of the water flowing over them.

More detailed conditioning experiments with freshwater fish show that they can distinguish warm from cold, discrimination being made on the basis of thermal change rather than on absolute temperature. Temperature sensitivity persists in these animals when the nerve supplying the lateral line (see MECHANORECEPTION) is cut but is abolished after transection of the spinal cord. When freshwater fish are trained to seek food in response to a change in water temperature, they are found to discriminate differences of less than 0.1° C (0.2° F). Goldfish (*Carassius*) have been trained to discriminate between warm and cold metal rods placed in their tanks. Consistent responses are obtained only when the rod is at least 2° C (3.5° F) colder or warmer than the water. Practically the whole surface of the fish, including the fins, is found to be thermosensitive. This mode of temperature discrimination need not be ascribed to the function of specific thermoreceptors; it could depend on skin receptors that are sensitive to combined mechanical and thermal stimulation. Indeed, electrophysiological recordings from nerve fibres originating in the skin of fish support the latter view. Changes in the electrical activity of these fibres are elicited only when the skin is touched by some solid object; yet the frequency of this mechanically elicited neural discharge is heavily influenced by the temperature of the object used in touching the fish.

Temperature discrimination in goldfish

Elasmobranchs, such as rays and sharks, have distinctive sense organs, called ampullae of Lorenzini, that are highly sensitive to cooling. These organs consist of small capsules within the animal's head that have canals ending at the skin surface. The capsules and their canals are filled

From *Zeitschrift für Vergleichender Physiologie* (1968)

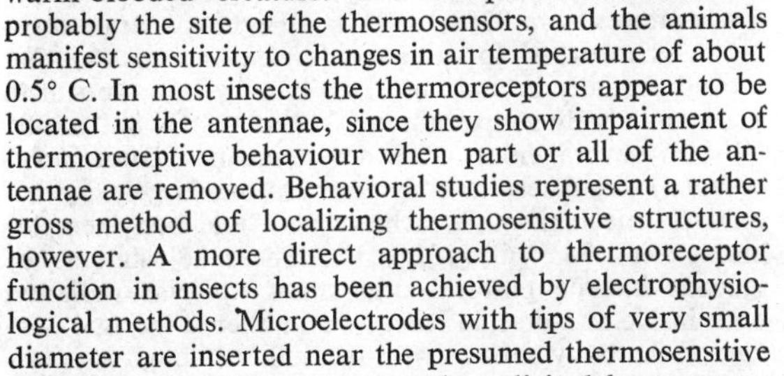

Figure 1: (Left) Portion of cockroach antenna showing location of cold receptor. (Right) Magnification of a single cold receptor of a cockroach.

with a jellylike substance, sensory-receptor cells being situated within each capsule. Recordings of impulses from single nerve fibres supplying the ampullae of Lorenzini in rays (*Raja*) and dogfish (*Scyliorhinus*) reveal steady activity of the receptors at constant temperatures between 0° and 30° C (32° and 86° F), the average frequency maximum appearing near 19° C (66° F). Rapid cooling causes transient overshooting of the stabilized discharge frequency, while rapid warming produces transient inhibition of the impulses. In some single fibres, cooling by 3° C (5.5° F) leads the frequency to overshoot by about 100 impulses per second. It remains an open question, however, whether the ampullae of Lorenzini are to be called specific thermoreceptors, since they also respond to mechanical stimuli and to weak electrical currents.

Amphibians and reptiles. Rattlesnakes (*Crotalus*) and related species of pit vipers (Viperidae) have a pair of facial pits (Figure 2), sense organs on the head below and in front of the eyes, which are most sensitive thermo-

From *Journal of Physiology* (1956)

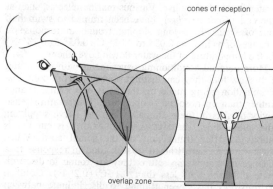

Figure 2: (Top) Partially dissected head of rattlesnake showing heat-sensitive membrane inside pit organ. (Bottom) Cones of reception, directions from which heat energy can be detected (see text).

receptors indeed. The pit organs act as directional distance receptors and make it possible for the reptile to strike at warm prey even when the snake's eyes and nose are covered and its tongue has been cut off. Each pit is a cavity about five millimetres deep, equally as wide at the bottom, and narrowing toward the opening at the surface of the head. Inside and separated from the bottom by a narrow air space is a densely innervated membrane of about ten microns thickness stretching between the walls of the pit. A direct connection between the air space beneath the membrane and the open air maintains equal pressure on both sides of the membrane. Warm-sensitive receptors distributed over the membrane consist of treelike structures of uninsulated (unmyelinated) nerve fibres. Infrared radiation (heat energy) reaches the membrane from an external source through the narrow open-

ing of the pit, permitting the snake not only to detect heat but also to localize coarsely the position of the stimulus. The fields of direction (cones of reception) from which each pit can receive infrared radiation from the environment extend to the front and sides of the head, with a narrow zone of overlap in the middle, as shown in Figure 2.

Under resting conditions, there is an irregular, steady discharge of nerve impulses from the pit organ. Rapid warming by as little as 0.002° C (0.004° F) at the nerve endings elicits a significant increase in impulse frequency; cooling produces an inhibition of the resting discharge. In contrast to the warmth receptors in mammals, the reptile's pit receptors are practically insensitive to steady temperatures, despite their high sensitivity to rate of thermal change. The distinctive consequence in the snake's adaptive behaviour is that gradual variations in air temperature tend to occur without detection, only the more rapid changes in infrared radiation being discriminated. Sensitivity to rapid temperature changes is enhanced by the very limited heat capacity of the receptive membrane (since it is so thin). When an animal that is 10° C (18° F) warmer than the environmental background appears for half a second at a distance of 40 centimetres (about 16 inches) in front of the snake, the heat energy radiated is enough to elevate significantly the frequency of receptor discharge in the pit organ. Indeed, behavioral experiments show that under these conditions the snake is able to discover warm prey through the victim's infrared radiations.

As poikilotherms, reptiles have practically no internal neural or metabolic mechanisms for maintaining their body temperature within physiologically safe limits. Nevertheless, such reptiles as snakes and lizards are able to keep their body temperature near these safe levels through behavioral regulation (*i.e.*, by moving to cooler or warmer places as necessary). The body temperatures of two samples of lizards (*Sceloporus magister* and *Cnemidophorus tesselatus*), for example, were found to be 34.9° ± 0.6° C (94.8° ± 1.1° F) and 41.3° ± 0.2° C (106.3° ± 0.4° F), respectively, although the average air temperatures were 33° C (91° F). Highly accurate regulation is recorded for a snake (*Crotalus cerastes*) that moved partially in and out of its burrow into the sun to maintain a body temperature of 31° to 32° C (88° to 90° F) over several hours. The desert iguana (*Dipsosaurus dorsalis*) regulates its body temperature largely by behavioral mechanisms to achieve and hold body temperatures near 38.5° C (101.3° F). These adjustments by iguanas include postural orientation to solar radiation both inside and outside burrows and altered thermal contact of the body surface with the soil. Although supporting direct evidence remains to be more fully developed, it appears that reptiles have thermosensitive nerve structures in the brain as well as in the skin.

There is some electrophysiological evidence of thermal sensitivity among amphibians, but only to relatively large temperature changes. The lateral-line organs in frogs (*Xenopus laevis*), which, as in fish, are sensitive to minute water turbulence, also respond to static temperatures and to temperature changes. Whether these responses have any adaptive, behavioral significance for temperature detection remains to be demonstrated. It has been reported, however, that a frog placed in a pan of cool water will not jump out as the pan is heated, if the temperature changes are gradual enough. Indeed, frogs are recorded to remain in the water this way until they are boiled to death.

Birds. Birds are homoiothermic, normally maintaining their body temperature within a range of less than 1° C (2° F). Investigations of temperature regulation in birds suggest the existence of thermosensors both in the lower part of the brain (hypothalamus) and in the skin. Direct electrophysiological evidence of thermoreceptors has been obtained in the tongues of chickens and in the skin of pigeons by recording from individual fibres of nerves serving the receptors. At a constant temperature of 20° C (68° F), a high level of static activity was observed for cold receptors in the chicken's tongue. When

Detection of warmth of their prey by snakes

the temperature of the tongue was maintained at 44° C (111° F), individual cold fibres showed a low, steady-state frequency of two to four impulses per second. A temperature drop of 9° C (16° F) was found to elicit an initial response of 30 impulses per second, which gradually declined to a new static frequency of eight impulses per second. Rewarming of the tongue resulted in a cessation of detectable electrical activity for several seconds; no specific warm receptors were found. There is some electrophysiological evidence of cold and warm receptors in the skin of pigeons.

Megapodes, large-footed birds such as the Australian mallee fowl (*Leipoa*), or brush turkey, bury their eggs. They depend on the thermal sensitivity of their face or mouthparts to guide their efforts in controlling the temperature of the eggs during hatching. The eggs are incubated in mounds where heat is generated through the fermentation of rotting vegetation and by irradiation from the sun. For extended periods of time the male bird is busy covering and uncovering the eggs, normally keeping the temperature almost constant at 34 ± 1° C (93 ± 2° F) over the unusually long incubation period (as much as 63 days) that characterizes this family of birds.

Mammals. Detailed information is available from electrophysiological investigations of single thermosensitive nerve fibres in the skin of mammals, particularly cats and monkeys. The nose of a cat contains numerous cold and warm receptors that are highly specific in responding to thermal stimuli; they are not excited by mechanical deformation of the skin. As a rule, each thermoreceptor is connected with a single nerve fibre. By using very finely tipped thermal stimulators, investigators can locate precisely the sites of warm and cold receptors in the skin; the details of the underlying cellular structure at these spots have been studied by electron microscopy. At the site of a cold-sensitive spot in the cat's nose, a thin, myelinated (insulated) nerve fibre penetrates the dermis and divides

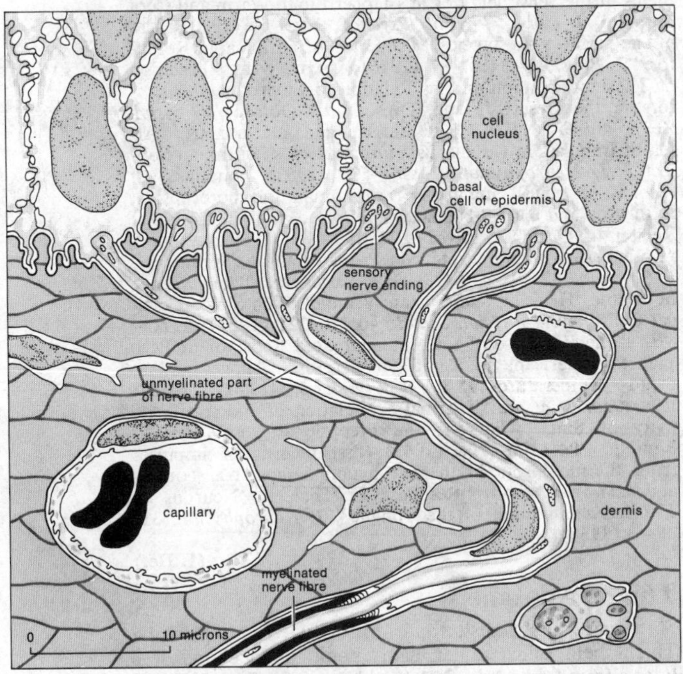

Figure 3: Cold receptor in the skin of a cat as seen with electron microscope.

into several unmyelinated branches about 70 microns beneath the skin surface (Figure 3). The tips of these branches have been shown to be the cold-sensitive nerve endings proper; they come into close contact with the basal cells of the epidermis. In most cases the nerve endings are embedded in small concavities on the lower surface of the basal cells. Warm receptors remain to be identified; they appear to be situated in a deeper layer of the skin. In monkeys and, presumably, in man, warm receptors are innervated by unmyelinated nerve fibres

(diameter one micron, impulse conduction velocity of 0.5 to 1.5 metres [1.5 to five feet] per second); cold fibres are served either by unmyelinated fibres or by thin myelinated fibres (diameter two to four microns, conduction velocity three to 20 metres [ten to 66 feet] per second).

At constant skin temperatures in the normal range, cold fibres in mammals are found to be continuously active. The average maximum frequency of the static discharge is observed at 27° C (81° F), the extreme limits of the normal range of static activity being 5° and 42° C (41° and 108° F). At skin temperatures above 45° C (113° F), cold receptors again can be activated. This so-called paradoxical discharge corresponds to the similar paradoxical sensation of cold in man when a hot object is touched or the hand is put into hot water. On sudden cooling, temporary overshooting can be 30 times higher than the static frequency of eight impulses per second. Warm receptors in the cat's nose start to show their activity at skin temperatures of 30° C (86° F) and reach an average maximum of 35 impulses per second at 46° C (115° F). Above this temperature the discharge suddenly falls off.

Similar populations of cold and warm receptors have been found in monkey skin, which has an additional group of warm fibres distinguished by an average static maximum at 41° C (106° F). The transient overshooting of warm-receptor activity can be several times higher than the static maximum frequency. When cold stimuli of the same magnitude (*e.g.*, 3° C [37° F]) are rapidly applied to the warmer skin, the degree of overshooting reaches a maximum at a skin temperature of 27° C (81° F). This temperature corresponds to that which elicits maximum static discharge from the cold fibres. Overshooting on rapid warming of warm receptors follows the same general rule: the temporary maximum occurs at temperatures for which the static discharge frequency also appears at a maximum.

Distinctive properties of cold receptors are found in hibernators. European hamsters (*Cricetus cricetus*) tend to maintain body temperatures of about 5° C during hibernation. Further cooling, however, elicits arousal reactions from the animal that indicate thermoreceptive function is intact. Electrophysiological investigations have shown that myelinated cold fibres serving the hamster's nose are continuously active at very low temperatures, having a static maximum near 4° C (39° F). In contrast to these findings, myelinated cold fibres in mammals that do not hibernate are blocked at temperatures below 10° C (50° F).

Relatively little is known about the processing of information from skin thermoreceptors in the central nervous system (brain and spinal cord). Responses to cooling the tongue have been recorded from single nerve cells (neurons) of the brain's thalamus in monkeys. In addition to a few brain neurons that are excited both by mechanical stimulation and cooling of the tongue, there are also numerous nerve cells in the thalamus that respond only to cooling. The latter neurons exhibit a static discharge in the temperature range (at the tongue) between 15° and 44° C (59° and 111° F), the maximum frequency being at 21° to 31° C (70° to 88° F). Rapid cooling of the tongue causes considerable transient overshooting in frequency from thalamic nerve cells over the entire range of preadapting temperatures used; by contrast, warming of the tongue results in a transient inhibition but not an increase in the rate of a discharge of any nerve elements in the brain. Thus, the activity of thalamic nerve cells activated by cooling the tongue closely reflects the behaviour of the peripheral (*e.g.*, tongue or skin) cold receptors. Even in the outer layers of the brain (cerebral cortex), nerve cells that respond specifically to cooling of the skin have been found. Other individual cortical neurons in the cat, however, receive signals not only from peripheral thermoreceptors but from mechanoreceptors and taste receptors as well.

Cats can be trained to respond behaviorally to thermal stimulation (*e.g.*, they will press a bar or lever). These experiments reveal cats to be relatively insensitive in discriminating warm and cold stimuli applied to the furred skin of the trunk or the legs, requiring temperature differ-

Mound building to regulate nest temperatures

Thermal information processing in the monkey brain

ences amounting to several degrees Celsius. This does not necessarily mean that cats have no finer thermal sensitivity than their grossly observable behaviour suggests. Indeed, autonomic regulatory responses, such as increased blood flow to the ear, can be elicited by mild warming of the paws, even though such warming is inadequate as a signal for training behavioral responses. In contrast to the low thermal sensitivity of their skin elsewhere in the body, cats have been found to manifest behavioral responses when the nose and upper lip are warmed or cooled by only 0.1° to 0.2° C (0.2° to 0.4° F). This corresponds to levels of thermal sensitivity of the face in human subjects and also is in accordance with electrophysiological evidence of high thermal sensitivity of the cat's nasal region.

Mammalian thermoreceptor structures, each containing elements sensitive to warm and cold, are to be found in the skin, in the deep tissues of the body, and in the hypothalamus and spinal cord. While much of the evidence of thermosensors in the central nervous system derives from experiments in neural temperature regulation within the body, in 1963 microelectrodes were used to record directly the activity of thermosensitive neurons in the frontal part of the cat hypothalamus. Many investigations made with this method show that most neural elements in the cat and rabbit hypothalamus are practically insensitive to directly applied temperature stimuli. There are, however, two smaller populations of thermosensitive neurons, one of which responds to local warming and the other to local cooling of the brain tissue.

Warm-sensitive brain neurons in cats and rabbits increase the frequency of their static impulse discharge in direct proportion to the degree that hypothalamic temperature is raised above normal. Similarly, the cold receptors there respond with an increase in impulse frequency when the temperature of the hypothalamus falls below the normal value for the animal's body. Since temperature in the deeper tissues of the body (e.g., the brain) varies quite slowly, the activity of hypothalamic thermosensors seems to be almost entirely a function of the level of temperature alone and not of the rate of temperature change. By contrast, the thermoreceptors in mammalian skin are highly sensitive to rapid changes in temperature. Intervening elements in the nervous system have been identified that integrate temperature signals from the hypothalamus and from the skin. Thermosensors are also found to be localized in the midbrain of rabbits and in various parts of the spinal cord in guinea pigs and dogs. These findings are in good agreement with observations that thermoregulatory responses such as shivering or panting can be influenced by local temperature changes in the spinal region of the animal.

Signals from hypothalamic thermosensors, from deep-body thermosensors, and from those in the skin are integrated in thermoregulatory centres located mainly in the mammal and bird hypothalamus. The integrated signals provide information about the inner (core) temperature of the body and about thermal changes at the periphery (body surface). Such information serves to activate internal mechanisms that maintain body temperature within the normal range of values. When signals from warm receptors (especially from those in the hypothalamus) prevail over signals from cold sensors, such heat-loss mechanisms as sweating, panting, and widening of blood vessels (vasodilatation) in the skin act to reduce body temperature. When signals predominate from cold receptors (particularly from those in the skin), heat-conservation mechanisms are initiated. Heat production rises as muscles expend energy in shivering and through other metabolic reactions (nonshivering thermogenesis); heat loss is reduced by mechanisms that narrow the blood vessels (vasoconstriction) in the skin and that fluff out hairs or feathers to enhance thermal insulation. All these involuntary, or autonomic, regulatory changes continue even without the function of the cerebral cortex; thus, they do not require consciousness, persisting during light anesthesia or during sleep.

In human beings, the function of thermosensors is closely involved in the highly emotional experiences of thermal comfort and discomfort. Whereas temperature sensations are mainly related to the activity of warm and cold receptors in the human skin, thermal comfort and discomfort reflect the general state of the thermoregulatory system, involving signals not only from thermoreceptors in the skin but from thermoreceptors in deep-body regions and in the hypothalamus as well. Thus, the same temperature at the skin can be experienced as comfortable or uncomfortable, depending on the thermal condition of the person's whole body. When one is overheated, an ice bag applied to the head may be perceived as pleasant; but, if someone is generally chilled just to the point of shivering, the same cold stimulus can be most unpleasant.

BIBLIOGRAPHY. J. BLIGH and H. HENSEL, "Modern Theories on Location and Function of the Thermoregulatory Centers in Mammals Including Man," in *Advances in Biometerology*, vol. 1 (1973), covers thermosensors in the central nervous system; H. HENSEL, "Physiologie der Thermoreception," *Ergebn. Physiol.*, 47:166–368 (1952), a comprehensive review with references, *Allgemeine Sinnesphysiologie: Hautsinne, Geschmack, Geruch* (1966), discusses skin receptors, with comprehensive references, and "Cutaneous Thermoreceptors," in *Handbook of Sensory Physiology*, vol. 2 (1973), describes thermoreceptors in the skin; R.W. MURRAY, "Temperature Receptors," *Advances Com. Physiol. Biochem.*, 1: 117–175 (1962), covers the comparative physiology of thermoreceptors; H. PRECHT, J. CHRISTOPHERSEN, and H. HENSEL, *Temperatur und Leben* (1955), a comprehensive review on temperature and life, covering micro-organisms, plants, man, and other animals; Y. ZOTTERMAN, "Thermal Sensations," in J. FIELD (gen. ed.), *Handbook of Physiology*, sect. 1, *Neurophysiology*, 1:431–458 (1959), and "Specific Action Potentials in the Lingual Nerve of Cat," *Skand. Arch. Physiol.*, 75:105–120 (1936), a classic showing first electrical records from specific thermosensitive nerve fibres; M. BLIX, "Experimentela bidrag till lösning av fragan om hudnervernas specifika energi," *Uppsala LäkFör. Förh.*, 18:87–102 (1882–83), reports on the discovery of cutaneous hot and cold spots; E.A. BREARLEY and D.R. KENSHALO, "Electrophysiological Measurements of the Sensitivity of Cat's Upper Lip to Warm and Cool Stimuli," *J. Comp. Physiol. Psychol.*, 70:5–14 (1970); T.H. BULLOCK and F.P.J. DIECKE, "Properties of an Infrared Receptor," *J. Physiol.*, 134:47–87 (1956); C.B. DE WITT, "Precision of Thermoregulation and Its Relation to Environmental Factors in the Desert Iguana, Dipsosaurus Dorsalis," *Physiol. Zoöl.*, 40:49–66 (1967); H. HENSEL and K.K. BOMAN, "Afferent Impulses in Cutaneous Sensory Nerves in Human Subjects," *J. Neurophysiol.*, 23:564–578 (1960), contains first records of neural impulses from human thermoreceptors; H. HENSEL and D.R. KENSHALO, "Warm Receptors in the Nasal Region of Cats," *J. Physiol.*, 204:99–112 (1969); A. IGGO, "Cutaneous Thermoreceptors in Primates and Subprimates," *J. Physiol.*, 200:403–430 (1969); S. LANDGREN, "Convergence of Tactile, Thermal, and Gustatory Impulses on Single Cortical Cells," *Acta Physiol. Scand.*, 40:210–221 (1957); R. LOFTUS, "The Response of the Antennal Cold Receptor of Periplaneta Americana to Rapid Temperature Changes and to Steady Temperature," *Z. Vergl. Physiol.*, 59:413–455 (1968); T. NAKAYAMA et al., "Thermal Stimulation of Electrical Activity of Single Units of the Preoptic Region," *Am. J. Physiol.*, 204:1122–1126 (1963), first records of impulses from thermosensors in the cat hypothalamus; D.A. POULOS and R.M. BENJAMIN, "Response of Thalamic Neurons to Thermal Stimulation of the Tongue," *J. Neurophysiol.*, 31: 28–43 (1968).

(H.He.)

Thiers, Adolphe

Statesman, journalist, and historian, Louis-Adolphe Thiers held office under King Louis-Philippe and was later a founder and the first president of the French Third Republic. A clever, essentially conservative, and sometimes unscrupulous politician, he was equally noted for his financial acumen. In conjunction with his stockbroker father-in-law, Alexis Dosne, he made many profitable speculations based on information he acquired through his close relations with those in power.

Thiers was born in Marseille on April 18, 1797, officially the son of a sea captain who married his mother on May 13 and deserted her four months later. Educated at first at the Marseille school that now bears his name, he studied law at Aix-en-Provence, where he met his lifelong friend, the historian François Mignet. In 1821 he went to

Sweating, panting, and shivering

Early life and career

Thiers, portrait by Léon Bonnat, 1876. In the Louvre, Paris.
Archives Photographiques

Paris and became a contributor to the influential newspaper the *Constitutionnel*. In January 1830 he helped found a new opposition newspaper, the *National*, which almost openly advocated a change of dynasty should the reactionary king Charles X attempt to circumscribe public liberties. During the revolution of July 27–29, 1830, which overthrew King Charles, he took refuge in a Paris suburb and returned on the 29th to win support for Louis-Philippe, duke of Orléans. He was rewarded by being made a member of the Council of State and was elected to the Chamber as a deputy for Aix-en-Provence.

Under the Orleanist monarchy, Thiers was undersecretary of state for the treasury (1830), minister of the interior (1832, and 1834–36), and minister of trade and public works (1833–34). During those years, he was the most notable representative of the Party of Resistance (conservative moderates). He mercilessly crushed all insurrections, in particular those of the legitimists under the Duchesse de Berry in 1832 and of the Republicans in 1834. Premier and minister of foreign affairs (1836 and 1840), in his second term of office his support of the Egyptian pasha Muḥammad 'Alī almost led to war with England because of a conflicting Near Eastern policy. Forced to resign by King Louis-Philippe's determination to avert war, Thiers nevertheless remained a leader of the resistance party.

After the Revolution of February 1848, Thiers returned to the Assembly as a representative for Seine Inférieure. Though he helped elect Prince Louis-Napoleon to the presidency of the Second Republic (1849), the two later became estranged. Exiled from 1851 to 1853, Thiers again became a deputy under the Second Empire, and was originally one of those who favoured war with Prussia in 1870. During the war crisis, however, Thiers changed his views and became an opponent of the aggressive policy that he had previously advocated. This swing stood him in good stead after the French defeat in September 1870; he thus became the wise man who had foreseen the folly of pursuing such a policy without adequate military power. He was clever enough to remain out of the national defense government set up after the fall of the Empire (September) and thus had no responsibility for the final French surrender in January 1871. In February he was elected simultaneously for 26 *départements* and on February 17 became "chief of the executive power of the French Republic." In August 1871 he became president of the republic. Thiers believed that France could be united under a conservative republic and tried to win the monarchist opposition over to this view. His first major task was to restore political order. In concert with the Germans, he ruthlessly used troops to defeat the Paris insurrection known as the

Commune (March–May 1871), thus destroying for many years the strength of French Socialists and workers' movements. But even this did not win him the support of the monarchists, and in 1873 he resigned. Meanwhile, his financial skill had enabled France to pay off ahead of time the indemnity due the Germans. But his military law of 1872 failed to establish an adequate professional army and the five years' conscription period he introduced seriously depleted the labour force.

Thiers joined the republican opposition in what was now a mainly royalist Assembly. He died suddenly on September 3, 1877, at Saint-Germain-en-Laye, just outside Paris, while preparing an election manifesto.

Thiers probably achieved greater power and wealth than any French politician of his time, but his ability was not greatly appreciated by those whom he served. His *Histoire de la révolution française*, which appeared in ten volumes between 1823 and 1827, and his *Histoire du consulat et de l'empire*, published in 20 volumes between 1845 and 1862, made a notable contribution to the growth of nationalism in France. In addition, his effecting the return of Napoleon's body to France from St. Helena in 1840 fostered the Napoleonic legend. Of himself, Thiers fairly successfully promoted the image of an old, shrewd, and wise patriot, although, by those of left-wing sympathies, he was never regarded as anything but an inveterate enemy of social reform.

Assessment

BIBLIOGRAPHY. HENRI MALO, *Thiers 1797–1877* (1932); and CHARLES H. POMARET, *Monsieur Thiers et son temps* (1948), are two biographies that give an overly favourable interpretation of Thiers's work. A recent and more balanced biography is ROBERT CHRISTOPHE, *Le Siècle de Monsieur Thiers* (1966). R.L. DREYFUS, *La République de M. Thiers, 1871–1873* (1930), also very favourable, provides an account of Thiers's policies during the first years of the Third Republic. The four books of HENRI GUILLEMIN on the origin of the Commune explain the policies of Thiers during the Franco-German War and the internal crisis that followed: *Cette curieuse guerre de 70* (1956); *L'Héroïque défense de Paris (1870–1871)* (1959); *La Capitulation (1871)* (1960); and *L'Avènement de M. Thiers et réflexions sur la Commune* (1971). The best studies on Thiers in English are the recent contributions of CHARLES POUTHAS and J. NERE in the *New Cambridge Modern History*, vol. 10–11 (1960–62). JOHN MAUDGRIDGE SNOWDEN ALLISON, *Thiers and the French Monarchy* (1926, reprinted 1968), remains an interesting study.

(J.Vi.)

Thirty Years' War

The Thirty Years' War is a conventional and largely misleading name for that part (1618–48) of the 50 years' struggle for the European balance of power (*c.* 1610–60) in which the Austrian Habsburgs and the German princes and cities were involved.

The usual picture of the Thirty Years' War, as painted by German historians and accepted uncritically by most English and American scholars, can be summarized as follows: (1) the war was one continuous struggle, fought almost exclusively on German soil, beginning with the Bohemian Revolt in 1618 and ending with the Peace of Westphalia in 1648; (2) it was the last and greatest of the Wars of Religion kindled by the German and Swiss Reformation of the 1520s, which the non-German powers, namely Denmark, Sweden, and France, together with the half-Spanish Habsburgs, exploited for political ends of their own; (3) it completely destroyed the German economy, leaving behind an impoverished near-desert that had lost one-third, one-half, or even two-thirds of its population; and (4) it dealt a mortal blow to the intellectual, moral, and artistic life of Germany.

Interpretations

Every one of these assertions can be challenged. First, there was not one uninterrupted war, but about a dozen wars, fought at different times, in different parts of Europe, by different belligerents, for different aims, interrupted by years of truce or peace affecting different regions.

Second, the religious differences between the German Protestants and Catholics were indissolubly bound up with constitutional and political questions. While it is impossible to assess the ratio of religious, political, constitu-

Sites associated with the Thirty Years' War.

From *Grosser Historischer Weltatlas*, vol. 3, Neuzeit, 2nd ed. (1962); Bayrischer Schulbuch—Verlag, Munich

tional, and economic considerations that determined any particular move, religious questions, more often than not, merely provided ideological and propagandist grounds for very secular war aims and peace proposals. The involvement of non-German powers was due to the geographical position of Germany in the heart of Europe and to a number of factors that would have remained even if there had been no religious conflict. The head of the Austrian Habsburgs, for instance, king of Bohemia and of Hungary and ruler of his house's ancient patrimony on the Danube, in the Alps, and on the Upper Rhine was also Holy Roman emperor, nominal sovereign over the whole *Reich*, or empire (that is, over all the other German princes); and the German princes were anxious to resist any expansion of his authority. At the same time, the emperor's Spanish Habsburg cousins, to whom he was closely bound by family ties, were nominally members of the empire insofar as they held Franche-Comté and the Netherlands (though the northern Netherlands had been in open revolt against Spain since 1572); and Spain was furthermore in dispute with France over certain Italian principalities of which the emperor was nominally overlord. The king of Denmark likewise was a member of the empire in his capacity as duke of Holstein and, eventually, as director of the Lower Saxon Circle of the empire. The Hohenzollerns of Brandenburg, electors of the empire, were vassals not only of Bohemia for certain fiefs in Silesia but also of Poland for their Duchy of Prussia. Finally, Sweden's Baltic policy led to encroachment on the Pomeranian part of the empire. These and other dynastic or territorial questions provided reasons or pretexts for German princes to call in foreign powers as well as for

foreign powers to take sides in German or so-called German affairs.

Finally, the social, economic, and cultural effects have been misinterpreted. Seen in their true perspective, they will be found on a par with the results of every war.

The present article is divided into sections as follows:

Survey of political aspects
    Western Europe
    Northern Europe
    Eastern Europe
    Germany
    Great Britain
Survey of religious aspects
Events
    War of the Jülich Succession (1609–14)
    Bohemian and Palatine War (1618–23)
    Struggle for Graubünden (1620–39)
    Swedish-Polish War (1621–29)
    Danish War (1625–29) and the Edict of Restitution
    War of the Mantuan Succession (1628–31)
    Swedish War (1630–35) and the Peace of Prague
    War of Smolensk (1632–34)
    French and Swedish War (1635–48)
    Swedish-Danish War (1643–45)
    Peace of Westphalia (1648)
    Franco-Spanish War (1648–59)
    First Northern War (1655–60)
German civilization
    The population
    Economic life
    Literature and the arts
Conclusion

The first two sections allude to matters elucidated in the third section. Throughout the article the new style is used for dating, even where English, Swedish, or Russian historians use the old.

SURVEY OF POLITICAL ASPECTS

Western Europe. The uniting aspect of this period in the history of western Europe is the struggle of the French monarchy and of the Dutch republic, or United Provinces of the Netherlands, against the two branches of the House of Habsburg: Spain and Austria.

Habsburg encirclement of France

The later wars of aggression, waged by Louis XIV of France and by Napoleon I, tend to obscure the fact that from the middle of the 16th to the middle of the 17th century France was the victim of a deliberate policy of encirclement by the Habsburg powers. In the south, possession of Roussillon gave Spain a firm foothold north of the Pyrenees. In the southeast, the Republic of Genoa was a Spanish satellite and the Duchy of Milan was Spanish territory. Genoa and Milan guaranteed a short and safe line of communication from Spain to Austria proper as well as to the Spanish possessions along the eastern borders of France, namely, Franche-Comté (contiguous with Austrian Alsace) and the Low Countries (Luxembourg, Hainaut, and Artois on the French frontier, with Flanders, Brabant, and the rest of the Netherlands in their immediate hinterland). After the successes of the Dutch rebellion, from 1572, the overland route from Genoa to Brussels was the more important because the final link of the chain around France had snapped after the death of Mary I of England (1558): the fate of the Armada in 1588 had demonstrated the insecurity of the northern sea route from Spain to the Netherlands.

The breaking of this Habsburg stranglehold was the foremost task of French statesmanship. It was first undertaken when Henry IV of France resisted the attempt by the Habsburgs, in 1609, to acquire Jülich-Cleves-Mark-Berg, as this attempt threatened to deal the deathblow to the independence of the United Provinces of the Netherlands and to lay open France's northern frontier. Henry's policy, interrupted by his assassination (1610) and by the pro-Spanish appeasement of the French regency under Marie de Médicis, was resumed by Cardinal de Richelieu, in power from 1624 until his death in 1642, and was continued by his successor, Cardinal Mazarin. France, at first too weak to wage open war against the Habsburgs, began by making treaties with powers hostile to them (or to their satellites in Germany or in eastern Europe), namely, with the United Provinces (1624), with Sweden (1631), and with Russia (1632); but the defeat of the United Provinces' ally Denmark (Peace of Lübeck, 1629) the withdrawal of Russia (Peace of Polyanov, 1634), the defeat of the Swedes (Battle of Nördlingen, 1634), and the defection of Sweden's German allies (Peace of Prague, 1635) forced Richelieu to declare open war on Spain (1635), after which Catalonia and Portugal (1640) and later Great Britain (1657) also joined the French camp. The modest French military successes were surpassed at the conference table: the Peace of Westphalia (1648) established the preponderance of France and France's allies throughout central and northern Europe; the formation of the League of the Rhine (1658) gave France a decisive voice in the affairs of the empire; and the Peace of the Pyrenees (1659) enlarged and secured France's frontiers and marked the end of Spain as a great power.

Twelve years' Truce of Antwerp

For the Dutch, the period of the Thirty Years' War forms part of their Eighty Years' War against Spain (1568–1648). The 12 years' Truce of Antwerp (April 9, 1609) can now be seen as the de facto recognition of the independence of the United Provinces; but contemporary Dutch statesmen foresaw that the Spanish crown would not easily abandon the hope of reducing the rebellious heretics and recovering its richest European province. In fact, Philip IV of Spain, whose accession in 1621 coincided with the expiry of the truce, immediately renewed the war. But whereas at the outbreak of the rebellion Spain had been the leading maritime, commercial, and colonial power, superiority in all these spheres had passed to the Netherlands. The only weakness of the maritime republic was its lack of land forces; but the States-General had no difficulty in enlisting foreign mercenaries or paying subsidies to foreign princes. Whereas the interest of Spain demanded the localization of every conflict so that resources might be concentrated against the Dutch, the interest of the Dutch was served best by extending the war so as to engage Spain's power away from their borders. Religious and constitutional affinities gave the Calvinist Dutch republicans additional zest in their support (1) of the Calvinist elector John Sigismund of Brandenburg in his struggle for Jülich; (2) of the semirepublican nobles of Bohemia in their fight against Austrian absolutism; and (3) of the generals who, from 1621, continued the Bohemian War, nominally on behalf of the Calvinist elector Frederick V of the Palatinate. But practical political considerations made the United Provinces the focal point of every anti-Habsburg coalition: the Franco-Dutch Treaty of Compiègne (June 20, 1624) was the prelude of the Treaty of The Hague (1625), which effectively brought Denmark into the war against the emperor Ferdinand II; and, after Denmark's defeat, Dutch diplomacy and subsidies aided Richelieu in enlisting Gustavus II Adolphus of Sweden as the military champion of the anti-Habsburg cause (1630–32).

From the middle of the 1630s, the French superseded the Dutch as leaders of the anti-Habsburg struggle. The conquest of Alsace and of Breisach by France's protégé Bernhard of Saxe-Weimar in 1638 and the secession of Portugal in 1640 shook Spain into preferring to come to an arrangement with the Dutch; and the latter, having smashed the Spanish Navy in the English Channel (1639) and off Pernambuco (1640), thereby putting an end to Spanish overseas expansion, now considered France and the Portuguese colonial empire greater rivals to their mercantile interests than Spain. Disregarding the alliance with France, which they had made in 1635, the Dutch on Jan. 30, 1648, signed a separate peace with Spain.

Struggle for Baltic supremacy

Northern Europe. Viewed from northern Europe, the first half of the 17th century comprises the attempts of the two Scandinavian kingdoms, Denmark and Sweden, to obtain what the diplomatic language of the time called the *dominium maris Baltici* ("lordship of the Baltic Sea"); *i.e.,* the possession of the leading Baltic ports through whose customs sheds the raw materials of the North German, Polish, and Russian hinterlands found their way into the West.

Denmark's repeated attempts to overpower Sweden failed, and the Danish outposts in the eastern Baltic were lost. King Christian IV's attempt to make himself supreme in Lower Saxony by acquiring the German bishoprics of Bremen, Verden, Minden, and Hildesheim led to the Danish War (1625–29), in which the superior generalship of his adversaries outweighed the subsidies granted to him by the Dutch and the British. The Peace of Lübeck (1629) finished Denmark as a European power of consequence.

Denmark's decline was emphasized by the simultaneous rise of Sweden. The Peace of Knäred (1613) made only transitory concessions to Christian IV of Denmark, who had attacked Sweden in 1611. Thenceforward, King Gustavus II Adolphus systematically began to close the ring of Swedish possessions around the Baltic. After preliminary gains at the expense of Muscovite Russia, whose access to the Baltic he closed (1617), he successfully attacked the Baltic provinces of Poland and of Poland's vassal, Prussia (1621–29). Besides pursuing this Baltic ambition, he may also have been aspiring to supplant his Catholic cousin, Sigismund III Vasa, on the Polish throne. Any such design, however, had to be abandoned: on the one hand the Swedish nobility objected to it; on the other, the king's Baltic policy was challenged by the advance of imperial armies along the southern shore from the west, which drew him into intervening in German affairs. The Swedish-Polish Truce of Altmark (1629) was followed by alliance with France (Treaty of Bärwalde, Jan. 23, 1631).

The alliance with France survived the death of Gustavus Adolphus and remained the sheet anchor of his successors' position until Sweden's collapse as a great power (1721). Sweden reaped the fruits of this policy; first in the Peace of Brömsebro at the end of the Swedish-Danish War of 1643–45; then in the Peace of Westphalia (1648);

and finally in the Peace of Roskilde (1658), with Denmark in the course of the First Northern War. By the end of this period Sweden had achieved dominance in the Baltic area.

Eastern Europe. The first half of the 17th century also embraces the first attempt by Poland to force Orthodox Muscovy (Russia) into the orbit of Latin Christianity as well as the first attempt on the part of the House of Romanov to enter the comity of western Europe. Poland, tied to the Habsburgs by religion and tradition, hostile to Sweden by religion and dynastic rivalry, and implacably hostile to Muscovy by history and religion, exploited the "troubles" that convulsed Russia after the death of Boris Godunov (1605). The experiment of ruling Russia through a Polish puppet, the first False Dmitry, failed in 1606 when the usurper succumbed in an outbreak of Russian nationalism and Orthodox fanaticism. But Poland came nearest to making Russia a satellite when in 1610 Sigismund III had his son, the future Wladyslaw IV of Poland, elected as tsar: the Polish dictatorship in Moscow lasted two years.

In 1609, the first Russo-Swedish alliance had been concluded by the tsar Vasily III Shuysky; and, despite Sweden's later aggressions, the new Romanov dynasty (from 1613) continued to regard Sweden as Russia's natural ally against Poland. England and the United Provinces acted as intermediaries at the Russo-Swedish Peace of Stolbova (1617), and 13 years later French envoys brought about Muscovy's indirect support of Gustavus Adolphus' war in Germany. Russia, however, did not want to be involved directly in Germany, and the Russo-Polish War of Smolensk (1632–34) remained a sideshow. After Gustavus Adolphus died, Swedish-Russian relations cooled, as the Swedish chancellor Axel Oxenstierna correctly assessed Russia as potentially more dangerous than Poland.

The Russo-Polish Peace of Polyanov (1634), which included Wladyslaw IV's final resignation of his claim to the Russian throne, freed Poland to resume hostilities against Sweden and, by thus tying down Swedish troops, contributed to the Swedish disaster at Nördlingen.

Germany. All these European conflicts affected Germany more often and more deeply than any of the other contestants. Germany was the only country where the Reformation had resulted in a permanent split into three religious factions—Catholic, Lutheran, and Calvinist. As these religious divisions largely marched with political frontiers, they were sustained and aggravated by dynastic rivalries, such as that between the Catholic Wittelsbachs in Munich (Bavaria) and the Calvinist Wittelsbachs in Heidelberg (the Palatinate) or that between the Calvinist Kassel branch and the Lutheran Darmstadt branch of the House of Hesse. In turn, these political and religious dissensions were partly exacerbated and partly overlaid by constitutional problems: the Holy Roman emperor, a Habsburg and a Catholic, wanted to establish monarchical absolutism in the empire; the electors, Catholics and Protestants alike, wanted to maintain what they called the "electoral preeminence" in the empire's affairs; and lastly, the other princes wanted to overthrow the ascendancy of both the emperor and the electors, so as to obtain complete freedom of action for themselves.

Each of the rivals found it easy and profitable to call in some foreign power. On the whole, the emperor relied on his Spanish cousins; the Protestant towns and smaller princes relied on Sweden, on France, and on the Dutch; Catholic Bavaria, with its satellites Cologne, Liège, Münster, Paderborn, and Hildesheim, usually blackmailed the emperor, while inclining to France and opposed to Spain; Lutheran Saxony disliked all foreign entanglements, but regarded the Calvinists as worse than the Catholics and generally found it most profitable to side with the emperor (since repeated endeavours to rally a neutralist "third force" never succeeded); and Protestant Brandenburg was weak and irresolute until 1640, when Frederick William, "the Great Elector," began to play off emperor, Swedes, Dutch, Poles, and French with such skill that by 1660 he had raised Brandenburg-Prussia to the rank of a great German and minor European power.

Great Britain. From the death of Queen Elizabeth I (1603) to the passing of the first Navigation Act by Cromwell's Parliament (1651), Great Britain's influence upon European affairs was negligible. The European policy of the government was vacillating between Spain, France, and the United Provinces, while Parliament and public opinion were enthusiastically anti-Spanish but unwilling to transform brave words into hard cash.

James I originally wanted to continue Elizabeth's pro-French and pro-Dutch policy, but assented to peace with Spain (1604). In 1613 he gave his daughter Elizabeth in marriage to Frederick V of the Palatinate, leader of the Protestant anti-Habsburg faction in Germany; but twice, in 1617 and in 1623, he tried to obtain a Catholic Spanish Habsburg princess for his son Charles before betrothing him, in 1624, to a Catholic French Bourbon.

James had at least not dissuaded his son-in-law from accepting the Bohemian crown (1619), but his dislike of the Czech nobility's republican sympathies and religious radicalism, combined with his desire to appease the Spaniards, prevented him from giving tangible support to Frederick during the war in Bohemia. It was only when Frederick had lost the Palatinate and when the Spanish marriage project had collapsed that a cautious parliamentary grant for the preparation of war against Spain gave expression to the English public's lively sympathy for the Protestant cause. An expedition to the Palatinate was hopelessly bungled.

Charles I, on succeeding his father, undertook the war against Spain and also associated himself with the Dutch in the Treaty of The Hague (Dec. 9, 1625) for the support of Christian of Denmark against the emperor and the Catholic League in Germany. But the naval expedition against Cádiz (1625) was a failure; and Charles failed to pay Denmark the promised £360,000 per annum, after the first installment of £46,000. Soon afterward, he squandered ships, troops, and money on the disastrous expedition of 1627 to help the Huguenot rebels of La Rochelle against his brother-in-law, Louis XIII of France. Thereafter Charles's devious foreign policy was hampered by lack of funds, which forced him to conclude peace both with France (1629) and with Spain (1630), and by lack of interest in foreign affairs on the part of his most capable adviser, Strafford. In 1636 and again in 1641, Charles offered to the Habsburgs an alliance against the Dutch in return for the restoration of the Palatinate to his nephew Charles Louis; but the Habsburgs declined this offer because Bavaria objected to it. Richelieu likewise in the same years preferred for France an understanding with Bavaria to a possible rapprochement with England.

SURVEY OF RELIGIOUS ASPECTS

Religious issues were insolubly interwoven with political and constitutional problems. For Germany the whole question stemmed from the Peace of Augsburg of 1555, a compromise between the Catholic and Lutheran Estates (members) of the empire. Neither party was satisfied, neither meant to abide by it. It fixed the religious frontiers as they had existed in 1552; *i.e.*, at the lowest ebb of Protestant fortunes. It gave the sovereign lay princes the right to change with their own religion that of their subjects; but it prohibited any Catholic bishopric or free city from adhering in future to the Lutheran creed. It expressly excluded Calvinists from the toleration granted to Lutherans. Above all, it failed to lay down any criteria by which the many doubtful points might be interpreted or to create any machinery to enforce its observance.

One of the many points left in suspense by the Peace of Augsburg concerned the right of the Protestant gentry in town and country under Catholic sovereigns to keep Protestant pastors and hold Protestant services. This issue played a part in the revolts of the Austrian and Bohemian nobility against their Habsburg overlords, which began in 1609 and ended with the Bohemian War in 1620. The ecclesiastical reservation that forbade the "reform" of Catholic bishoprics prevented Cologne from turning Protestant together with its archbishop, Gebhard, in 1583. Gebhard's deposition was the basis of the greatness of the House of Wittelsbach: Bavarian princes held the archbishopric of Cologne continuously from 1583 to 1761, the bishoprics of Hildesheim and of Liège almost uninterrupt-

Russia's "Time of Troubles"

Dynastic rivalry

Peace of Augsburg

edly throughout the same period, and the bishoprics of Paderborn and of Münster with but few more interruptions. Thus the undisputed leadership of Catholic Germany by the Wittelsbach Maximilian I of Bavaria was grounded on the pre-eminence of his house not only in the south but also in the northwest of Germany, where Jülich and Berg in the hands of his brother-in-law fortified his house.

The distribution of the religious parties in the empire during the first half of the 17th century, according, be it understood, to the sovereign's choice of religion, was approximately as follows: the whole of northern, northeastern, and central Germany, with the exception of the bishopric of Hildesheim and the abbey of Fulda, was Protestant; northwestern, western, and southeastern Germany, with the exception of the Rhenish Palatinate in the west, was Catholic, as were all the Habsburg dominions (Austria and Tirol, Bohemia-Moravia and Silesia, a portion of Swabia). Württemberg in Swabia, Ansbach and Bayreuth in Franconia, and nearly all the free cities, even those in otherwise Catholic districts, adhered to the Protestant faith. The nobility and townspeople in Bavaria and the Habsburg countries, nearly all of whom had been Protestants, had been recatholicized or expelled by about 1625.

The historian must not doubt the strength and sincerity with which the champions of the contesting factions and their humblest followers believed in the exclusive truth of their church: the emperor Ferdinand II, Maximilian of Bavaria, Tilly, and Richelieu were devout Catholics; Gustavus Adolphus, Bernhard of Weimar, the electors of Brandenburg, Saxony, and the Palatinate were unswerving Protestants; Wallenstein is perhaps the only personality of note who seems to have been entirely indifferent to religious distinctions, astrology having largely supplanted Christianity as his creed. Motives other than religious zeal, however, were the factors determining political allegiance.

The subordination of religion to politics

Pope Urban VIII and the cardinals Richelieu and Mazarin were unbending in their opposition to Catholic Spain and to the Catholic emperor. The Lutheran elector of Saxony and the Lutheran landgrave of Hesse-Darmstadt were firm adherents of the emperor so long as circumstances permitted. Lutheran Saxony and Catholic Bavaria were consistently anti-Spanish and anti-Swedish. Calvinist Hesse-Kassel was Lutheran Sweden's most reliable ally and, together with Bavaria, mostly pro-French. The struggle for the Baltic brought the Lutheran Gustavus Adolphus into conflict with Orthodox Russia, with Catholic Poland, and with Lutheran Denmark; but his fight in Germany made him the ally of Catholic France and of Orthodox Russia. Maximilian of Bavaria extended his power at the expense alike of the Lutheran cities in Swabia and in Franconia, of the Calvinist elector Palatine, and of the Habsburg emperor and did so mostly in conjunction with Lutheran Saxony and Catholic France. The bishops of Würzburg and of Bamberg were the first to abandon the Catholic interest at the peace congress of Münster. Protestant as well as Catholic princes, prelates, and cities were susceptible to French subsidies. Of none of the belligerents can it be said that religious motives were responsible for any major decision. The secret debates (1629–30) in the Swedish council about entry into the war are revealing: the security and defense of Sweden and the conquest of Germany were declared the war aims; the king was expressly warned against speaking of a war of religion since France might take umbrage.

Success of monarchy

The suppression of Protestantism by Ferdinand II in Austria and in Bohemia and by Richelieu in France was undertaken mainly on political considerations. The Protestants not only infringed the spiritual unit of the country (a tenet still held by every government) but also were the chief opponents of royal absolutism and, not without cause, were suspected of republican tendencies on Dutch and Swiss models. Their defeat therefore paved the way for that spiritual and administrative uniformity that became the hallmark of 17th- and 18th-century monarchy.

Similarly, the contest of the emperor against the Protestant princes and cities was to a large extent a contest to decide whether the empire was to be a monarchy, with the emperor at its head and the princes as his vassals, or a federation of more or less independent princes, with the emperor as its titular president. So long as Ferdinand II was willing to concede to the six electoral princes their traditional prerogatives in the government of the empire, these electors (including Lutheran Saxony and Calvinist Brandenburg) sided with him against the lesser princes. When Ferdinand in 1629 unmasked his real intentions by the Edict of Restitution, the electors, led by Catholic Bavaria, turned against him. The Peace of Westphalia brought about the triumph of the lesser princes, with whom the electors now identified themselves against any recurrence of imperial centralism.

In fact, the Peace of Westphalia proved the interdependence of the problems, religious and constitutional, political and economic, that again and again were used as interchangeable counters. The recognition of the adherents of the Reformed (Calvinist) religion as being of equal right with those of the Lutheran faith was largely a by-product of the dispute over Pomerania between Brandenburg and Sweden. The emperor sacrificed the north German bishoprics to the Protestant claimants (Sweden, Brandenburg, Saxony, Mecklenburg, and Brunswick) and Alsace and the bishoprics of Metz, Toul, and Verdun to France; and in return Sweden and France renounced their claims to Austrian territory in Silesia and in Swabia respectively and assented to the exclusion of the Austrian Protestants from the treaty's clauses on restitution and toleration. The attitude of the Catholic princes to Pope Innocent X's protest against any formal agreement with the Protestants is characteristic of the trend toward excluding denominational considerations from political decisions: the first secret intimation that the nuncio gave to the emperor and to the Catholic princes in November 1647 was answered with evasive excuses; and the formal protocol handed over on Christmas Eve did not even receive an answer from any prince, temporal or ecclesiastical. A special "anti-protest clause" in the peace treaty was signed by all parties: it declared Innocent's condemnation of the peace invalid and ineffective and thus demonstrated the complete emancipation of secular politics from ecclesiastical tutelage. The religious questions left unanswered by the Peace of Augsburg in 1555 were solved in 1648 in the modern spirit of the "reason of state."

EVENTS

War of the Jülich Succession (1609–14). The settlement that the Peace of Augsburg had formulated for Germany was shaken in 1607–08 when Maximilian I of Bavaria annexed and recatholicized the Lutheran city of Donauwörth. Some of the German Protestant states concluded a military alliance, the Union, on May 14, 1608. The death of Duke John William of Jülich on March 25, 1609, opened a crucial question of succession over which war broke out. On July 10, 1609, a Catholic military alliance, the League, was formed.

Catholic League and Protestant Union

The wealth of John William's lands—Cleves, Jülich, Mark, and Berg—and their strategic position attracted not only the powerless legitimate heirs, namely, John Sigismund of Brandenburg and Wolfgang Wilhelm of Palatinate-Neuburg but also every powerful neighbour. The Habsburgs wished to install an Austrian prince who would have placed the lands at the disposal of the Spaniards in their struggle with the Dutch and would incidentally have counteracted the predominance of Bavaria in northwestern Germany. France, the United Provinces, and England naturally objected to any strengthening of the Spaniards in that region. The assassination of Henry IV of France (May 14, 1610) prevented the war from becoming a European contest, though Spanish, Austrian, and Dutch troops repeatedly invaded the duchy in pretended support of one or the other of the heirs. The Protestant Union, which John Sigismund had joined by turning Calvinist, and the Catholic League, of which Wolfgang Wilhelm had become a member by entering the Roman Church and marrying a sister of Maximilian, brought about a compromise that excluded all foreign claims (Oct. 24, 1610) and led to the partition of the inheritance between Brandenburg and Neuburg (Treaty of Xanten, 1614).

Bohemian and Palatine War (1618–23). This war began with the insurrection, in 1618, of the Bohemian and Austrian Estates against the future emperor Ferdinand II, whose intention was to impose absolutist rule and to enforce the Catholic Counter-Reformation. The Bohemian nobles toyed with the idea of setting up a republic in order to secure the support of the Dutch but eventually, in August 1619, elected as their king the elector Frederick V of the Palatinate in the hope of obtaining the aid of the Protestant Union and Great Britain. Their expectations proved fallacious. Frederick failed to discipline the haughty Bohemian nobles or to rally the Bohemian townsmen and peasants (whom he did nothing to relieve from harsh oppression by their feudal lords) and was abandoned by his German allies as well as by his father-in-law, James I of Great Britain. Ferdinand, although in a very weak position, succeeded in buying the support of Maximilian of Bavaria and the Catholic League at a heavy price in money and land. In a campaign of a few months, the League's troops under Johann Tserclaes von Tilly crushed the Austrian Estates and broke the rule of Frederick in the Battle of the White Mountain, near Prague (Nov. 8, 1620). The conquest of Glatz (Klodzko) on Oct. 25, 1622, completed the subjugation of the lands of the Bohemian crown.

Battle of the White Mountain

In the meantime, the Spaniards from their bastions in Luxembourg and in Franche-Comté had since 1620 been overrunning the Rhenish Palatinate, where Tilly joined them in 1662, after he and Maximilian had in 1621 subdued the Upper Palatinate (north of Bavaria and west of Bohemia). Tilly also overcame the badly coordinated actions of several German princelings and generals who, in the pay of the United Provinces, Denmark, and England, still upheld Frederick's cause, notably, Ernst von Mansfeld and Christian of Brunswick. Whereas the Protestant Union had dissolved itself (May 1621), Lutheran Saxony, which had never adhered to the Union, was won over to the emperor by the offer of Lusatia. The defeat of Christian of Brunswick by Tilly at Stadtlohn (Aug. 6, 1623) left the situation as follows: the emperor was in undisputed control of his Austrian and Bohemian territories; Maximilian of Bavaria, who was created elector, had become the leading power in southern and northwestern Germany; the Spaniards were in possession of the Rhenish Palatinate; and Frederick was a landless exile, living on the bounty of the Dutch.

Struggle for Graubünden (1620–39). The Valtellina, leading from the northern frontier of the Duchy of Milan through the Alps toward Tirol, opened the shortest and safest land route between Spanish Italy and the Austrian territories in Germany, whence the Spaniards could reinforce their troops in the Netherlands and in the Palatinate. It belonged to Graubünden, or the Grisons, a union of leagues in loose relations with the Swiss. Spain and Austria obviously wanted to bring the Union's lands under their own control; France and Venice naturally opposed the forging of this link, which would have completed encirclement of both of them by the Habsburg powers. The political and military issues were here poisoned by religious, personal, local, and clannish rivalries, of which Georg Jenatsch was the stormy centre. A Spanish occupation of the Valtellina (1620), reinforced by an Austrian incursion into the other territories of Graubünden (1621), provoked French and Venetian protests, which led to the nominal "deposit" of the Valtellina in the hands of the papacy (1623)—in fact a veiled means of prolonging Spanish control there. Then Richelieu ventured on the first French occupation of Graubünden (1624–26); but the internal weakness of France, where Richelieu's regime was challenged on the one hand by the pro-Spanish faction of Catholic zealots (the Parti Dévot) and on the other by the Huguenots, made it impossible to maintain this indirect attack on Spain. The Treaty of Monzón (1626) made Graubünden into a sort of Franco-Spanish protectorate, with papal troops in occupation. During the War of the Mantuan Succession, the Habsburgs again overran the country (1629–31). A final French occupation (from 1635) was ended in 1639 by a reaction of Graubünden against the French. Eventually the Peace of

The Valtellina

Milan (Sept. 3, 1639), between Spain and Graubünden, brought the country into virtually complete dependence on Spain.

Swedish-Polish War (1621–29). From 1611, Gustavus Adolphus had taken advantage of the "Time of Troubles" and its aftermath in Muscovite Russia; and by the Peace of Stolbova (1617) he had acquired Karelia and Ingria, which together constituted the land bridge between Swedish Finland and Swedish Estonia, so that the Gulf of Finland was converted into a Swedish lake. He then turned against Poland (1621). His conquest of Livonia gave him Riga, the chief Baltic port (though the Swedish nobles possessed themselves of the largest land properties in the country, to the detriment of the Swedish crown); and from the Duchy of Prussia, Poland's vassal, he took the ports of Memel and Pillau, the latter commanding the approach to Königsberg. Sweden's position in the Baltic, however, was eventually endangered by the course of the Danish War, as the imperial general Wallenstein conquered Mecklenburg (with the ports of Wismar and Rostock) and threatened moreover to conquer Pomerania; and in summer 1628 Swedish forces were sent to help the port of Stralsund, which Wallenstein was besieging. Finally, the Truce of Altmark (Sept. 25, 1629) was concluded between Sweden and Poland, largely thanks to French mediation. Livonia and the Prussian ports were left in Sweden's possession.

Danish War (1625–29) and the Edict of Restitution. Christian IV of Denmark had observed strict neutrality during the Bohemian War despite repeated Dutch attempts to enlist his help on behalf of Frederick of the Palatinate. In 1624, however, he began to contemplate offensive action. His motives were rivalry of Sweden in the Baltic regions and the wish for Danish supremacy in the estuaries of the Elbe and Weser. The king's election, in spring 1625, as director of the Lower Saxon Circle of the empire furnished him with the legal pretext for interference in Germany. The Treaty of The Hague (Dec. 9, 1625), in the negotiation of which the British statesman George Villiers, 1st duke of Buckingham, played a major part, promised British and Dutch subsidies for a military effort by Denmark on Frederick's behalf, in cooperation with the German generals who had already tried to uphold the latter's cause; and this Protestant coalition could expect the sympathy of the Habsburgs' other enemies—prince Gábor Bethlen of Transylvania, the Ottoman Turks, and also Catholic France.

Protestant coalition

The coalition's plan seems to have envisaged a fourfold advance: Christian of Brunswick was to overpower the Wittelsbach bishoprics and duchies in Westphalia and in the lower Rhineland; Christian IV of Denmark was to make himself master of Lower Saxony; Ernst von Mansfeld, generalissimo of the coalition, was to press forward into Bohemia, Silesia, and Moravia; and Bethlen was to sally forth from Hungary and join forces with Mansfeld.

On the opposite side were ranged the veteran troops of the Catholic League under Tilly, who was to deal with Christian of Brunswick and with Christian IV of Denmark, and the imperial army of Wallenstein, who was to repel Mansfeld and Bethlen.

On both sides the generals were on bad terms with one another and never effectively coordinated their efforts. But Tilly and Wallenstein had the advantage of fighting on interior lines and could therefore tackle their adversaries in turn. The coalition, on the other hand, was weakened by the faithless policy of Charles I of Great Britain, who failed to honour his financial obligations and let Buckingham embark on a foolish expedition against France in aid of the Huguenots of La Rochelle (June–November 1627). Wallenstein forced Mansfeld out of northern Germany (Battle of Dessau, April 25, 1626); and Mansfeld, though he held a strong position in Silesia, neither made full use of anti-Habsburg movements (apart from discontent in the Bohemian lands, a peasants' revolt broke out in Austria in May) nor effected a junction with Bethlen and the latter's Turkish auxiliaries. Wallenstein outmanoeuvred Bethlen, and Mansfeld died on his way to Venice (Nov. 29, 1626), whence he hoped to receive fresh subsidies. Isolated Danish troops maintained themselves in Silesia until the autumn of 1627, when Wallenstein overwhelmed them.

Meanwhile, Tilly was favoured by the untimely death of Christian of Brunswick (June 16, 1626) and by the military incompetence of Christian IV of Denmark. The Danish Army suffered a crushing defeat in the Battle of Lutter (Aug. 27, 1626). In 1627 Tilly pursued the beaten Danes into Holstein; and Wallenstein, who joined him, continued the pursuit into Jutland. Mecklenburg, whose dukes had sided with Christian, was given by the emperor to Wallenstein, who immediately set about obtaining bases on the Baltic for an imperial navy. His attempt to add the Pomeranian port of Stralsund to his Mecklenburg ports of Wismar and Rostock led to the intervention of Gustavus Adolphus.

Wallenstein's contact with maritime affairs changed his whole outlook. His first sight of large river barges on the Oder had made him believe that they were oceangoing capital ships; but he now realized the importance of sea power and overseas trade and reassessed the political position that the emperor might take up with regard to the Hanse towns, Denmark, the Netherlands, England, and Spain. Denmark, which he wished to draw into the emperor's interest, profited by his mediation: at the Peace of Lübeck (May 22, 1629) Christian IV had only to renounce further participation in the affairs of the empire.

The defeat of the anti-Habsburg coalition raised the position of the emperor to its greatest height since Charles V's victory over the League of Schmalkalden in 1547. **Edict of Restitution** Ferdinand II's Edict of Restitution (March 6, 1629), prescribing the recovery by the Catholics of all ecclesiastical lands in which Protestantism had been established since 1552, was more than an act of reparation of the damage suffered by the Catholic Church since Luther's time: it was an unambiguous assertion of the imperial prerogative in all matters pertaining to the constitutional structure of the empire. At the Electoral Diet of Regensburg (1630) the opposition, led by Lutheran Saxony (anxious to retain its threatened acquisitions) and by Catholic Bavaria (determined to counteract the emperor's aggrandizement) forced Ferdinand to dismiss Wallenstein and so to make himself defenseless at the very moment when Gustavus Adolphus had landed on German soil.

War of the Mantuan Succession (1628–31). The death of Vincenzo II Gonzaga, duke of Mantua and Montferrat, on Dec. 26, 1627, led to the first direct clash between the Habsburgs and France, albeit on a secondary theatre of war. The claims of the legitimate Gonzaga heir, Charles, duc de Nevers, whom France supported, were overridden by Ferdinand II, supreme lord of the imperial fiefs in Italy; and Spain lent military aid to Ferdinand so as to keep a French vassal away from the approaches to Milan. Richelieu, however, was soon stronger. The Huguenot rebels of La Rochelle capitulated to Louis XIII (autumn 1628); Savoyard forces, which attempted to block the French king's way into Piedmont, were defeated at Susa (March 6, 1629); and the Peace of Susa with England (April 14), followed by the submission of the Huguenot rebels in Languedoc to the Peace of Alais (June 28), secured the French rear. The Habsburg forces withdrew from Casale in October 1630; and Richelieu, who in November triumphed over the pro-Spanish faction in France (the so-called Day of Dupes), achieved full success. By the Treaty of Cherasco (1631), the French candidate was installed in Mantua. Meanwhile, Savoy had ceded the fortress of Pinerolo to France; and Pope Urban VIII, determined opponent of the Habsburgs, annexed Urbino, another vacant imperial fief. The Austro-Spanish monopoly in Italy was broken.

Swedish War (1630–35) and the Peace of Prague. The suspension of hostilities between Sweden and Poland freed Gustavus Adolphus to intervene in Germany. After landing at Usedom (July 6, 1630), he quickly occupied the whole duchy of Pomerania and restored Wallenstein's duchy of Mecklenburg to its hereditary dukes. He concluded the Treaty of Bärwalde (Jan. 23, 1631) with France, whereby he was to receive annual subsidies of 1,000,000 livres to enable him to campaign for the restoration of the "liberty" of the German princes "oppressed"

by the emperor. In these circumstances an immediate objective for Gustavus was to stop the enforcement of the Edict of Restitution on Magdeburg, which commanded a strategic crossing point on the Elbe; but his advance into central Germany was impeded by the hardly veiled hostility of the electors George William of Brandenburg and John George I of Saxony. Saxony tried at the Convent, or Conference, of Leipzig (February 1631) to establish a neutral party between the emperor and Sweden, which proved unacceptable to either. Though Gustavus stormed the Brandenburg fortress of Frankfurt an der Oder (April 13), thereby both securing his left flank against the Poles and intimidating the two electors, the delay led to the fall of Magdeburg to Tilly (May 20). Brandenburg and Saxony now yielded to the Swedish threats, especially as Tilly imprudently invaded Saxony and treated it as enemy country. Alliances with Brandenburg (June 20) and with Saxony (September 11) protected Gustavus' rear and virtually rendered the electorates Swedish satellites. The defeat of Tilly at Breitenfeld (September 17) and the conquest of Prague (November 15) by the Saxons under Hans Georg von Arnim opened southern Germany to the Swedes. **Battle of Breitenfeld**

The smaller German Protestant princes, such as Bernhard of Saxe-Weimar, flocked to Gustavus' standards; by April 1632 Gustavus had advanced as far as Munich, and his armies had reached Lake Constance to the south and Mainz to the west. The archbishopric of Mainz and the Rhenish Palatinate were placed under Swedish administration; the bishoprics of Würzburg and Bamberg were given to Bernhard as a Swedish fief under the name of Duchy of Franconia. The king's war aims gradually widened: his agreements with the German princes became more onerous, and the stipulations that the Treaty of Bärwalde had made for the protection of France's friends and of the Catholic religion were treated lightly. Gustavus did not aim at the imperial crown, but his secret negotiations with Wallenstein show that he thought of placing the Habsburg dominions under the rule of Swedish puppets.

The recall of Wallenstein to the leadership of the imperial army completely changed the situation: Gustavus was manoeuvred out of southern Germany and shortly afterward was killed in the Battle of Lützen (Nov. 16, 1632). While the conduct of Swedish military operations then fell to Johan Banér and subsequently Lennart Torstenson, the direction of policy was undertaken by the chancellor, Axel Oxenstierna, who, by the Treaty of Heilbronn (April 23, 1633), consolidated the Swedish alliance with the German princes, albeit without Brandenburg and Saxony. Wallenstein's victory at Steinau in Silesia (October 11) and Bernhard's capture of Regensburg (November 14) cancelled each other out, and Wallenstein's machinations to make himself the arbiter of affairs caused the emperor to have him murdered (Feb. 25, 1634); but the Swedish defeat at Nördlingen (Sept. 5–6, 1634) led to the dissolution of the League of Heilbronn and to the open defection of most German princes, led by Saxony, from the Swedish cause.

The Peace of Prague (May 30, 1635) reconciled the emperor and nearly all the German opponents of the Edict of Restitution, which it modified by making the year 1627 the criterion of rightful possession of ecclesiastical lands (instead of 1552). Thenceforth, Sweden played only a subordinate part in the war. The leading role fell to France.

War of Smolensk (1632–34). From c. 1628, Gustavus Adolphus and Richelieu had been trying to bring about alliances with Russia, Turkey, Transylvania, the Crimean Tatars, and the Ukrainian Cossacks, who were to engage the emperor and Poland on their eastern frontiers. Concerted action, however, proved difficult to achieve. But Moscow gave Gustavus considerable indirect aid by selling to Sweden, on a cash-and-carry basis at an artificially low price, cereals that the Swedes resold in Amsterdam at considerable profit: between 1628 and 1633 the Swedes bought Russian grain at a cost of 100,000 talers per annum and sold it at 400,000 talers per annum (the latter sum being equal in amount to the direct subsidy received annually from France). Russo-Swedish military coopera- **Swedish-Russian cooperation**

tion was eventually achieved, largely through the efforts of Sweden's envoy Alexander Leslie (later earl of Leven in the peerage of Scotland): the Russians invaded Poland in autumn 1632 and besieged Smolensk, while Gustavus Adolphus moved eastward and ordered his general Carl Gustav von Wrangel to prepare an offensive from his bases in Prussia.

The great scheme came to nought. The deaths of Gustavus Adolphus and of the Moscow patriarch Philaret (October 1633), who had been the two chief architects of Swedish-Russian cooperation, removed the mutual goodwill as the basis for a real alliance. Turkey, moreover, was committed in a war with Persia; the Tatars of the Crimea turned against Muscovy instead of Poland; and the revolt of the Ukrainian Cossacks against their Polish overlords was delayed. Finally, an insurrection of the peasants in central Russia forced Tsar Michael's government to conclude the Peace of Polyanov with Poland (June 14, 1634).

French and Swedish War (1635–48). The near-collapse of the Swedish system in Germany in 1634–35 forced Richelieu to abandon his cautious policy of nonintervention. He concluded offensive and defensive alliances with the United Provinces (Feb. 8, 1635) and with Sweden (Treaty of Compiègne, April 28), sent a French army to the Valtellina (March–April), and declared war on Spain (May 19). He then secured an alliance with Savoy and Parma (League of Rivoli, July 11); mediated the 20-year Truce of Stuhmsdorf between Sweden and Poland (September 12); and took the best of the German generals still serving Sweden, Bernhard of Saxe-Weimar, into French pay (October 27).

In 1636 the invasion of northern France from the Spanish Netherlands by Ottavio Piccolomini, whose capture of Corbie (August 15) threatened to expose Paris, was outweighed by a series of Swedish victories over Saxon and imperial forces, culminating in Banér's defeat of Melchior von Hatzfeldt at Wittstock (October 4), which reestablished Swedish supremacy in northern and central Germany. A careless northward movement of the imperial commander in chief, Matthias Gallas, in 1637, laid southern Germany open to the French; and Bernhard of Saxe-Weimar, having overrun Alsace, in 1638 conducted a brilliant campaign in the course of which he took the key fortresses of Rheinfelden (March 23), Freiburg (April 6), and Breisach (December 17). Before Bernhard's death, the incompetence of the French led to Piccolomini's great victory of Thionville (June 7, 1639), which, however, was to be the last success of the Austro-Spanish armies. The outbreak, in 1640, of revolution both in Catalonia and in Portugal compelled the Spaniards to limit their commitments outside the Iberian Peninsula. The capitulation of the great stronghold of Arras to the French (Aug. 9, 1640) endangered the Spanish position in the Netherlands, and a Spanish counteroffensive into Champagne ended with the French victory at Rocroi (May 19, 1643), won by the young duc d'Enghien (Prince de Condé).

In Germany the various commanders—French, Swedish, Bavarian, and imperial—waged war almost on each one's own responsibility: no coherent pattern can be found in those campaigns, which were nearly always small-scale raids with limited objectives. The Swedish victory over Saxon and imperial forces at Breitenfeld (Nov. 2, 1642) and the capture of the Little Town quarter of Prague by the Swedes (July 26, 1648) are—besides the Swedish campaign against Denmark—the most notable military events of these years. They were overshadowed by the diplomatic activity that began in 1640 and ended in 1648 with the Peace of Westphalia.

During the French and Swedish War, death had removed three great figures from the international scene: the emperor Ferdinand II on Feb. 15, 1637, leaving the succession to his son Ferdinand III; Richelieu on Dec. 4, 1642; and Louis XIII of France on May 14, 1643. Richelieu's place was taken by Cardinal Mazarin during the regency for Louis XIV.

Swedish-Danish War (1643–45). The precarious situation of the imperial cause after Breitenfeld and the Danish jealousy and fear of Sweden brought about an understanding between Ferdinand III and Christian IV; and Sweden's decision to wage a preventive war against Denmark gave the emperor a respite, since the Swedish army under Torstenson had to abandon its march on Vienna (September 1643) and to turn northward instead. In a lightning campaign (December 1643–January 1644) Torstenson conquered Schleswig-Holstein and Jutland. When an imperial army under Gallas came to the succour of the Danes, Torstenson at once marched against him, destroyed his army at Jüterbog (Nov. 23, 1644), and invaded Bohemia, where another imperial army was wiped out at Jankov (March 6, 1645). By the Peace of Brömsebro, signed on Aug. 23, 1645, Denmark ceded Jämtland and Härjedalen on the Norwegian frontier, Halland on the Kattegat, and the Baltic islands of Gotland and Ösel to Sweden.

Peace of Westphalia (1648). Treaties signed in the Westphalian towns of Münster and Osnabrück terminated both the Eighty Years' War between Spain and the United Provinces of the Netherlands (Jan. 30, 1648) and the war between France, Sweden, and the German Protestants on the one side and the emperor and the German princes on the other (October 24). The Peace of Prague (1635) between the emperor Ferdinand II and the majority of the German princes had proved abortive: it expressed too much the temporary ascendancy of the emperor, took little account of Sweden, and completely disregarded France, which at that very moment openly took up arms against Spain and the emperor. No general peace was possible without the participation of Sweden, France, and Spain; and in 1640 the parties began in earnest to prepare the summoning of a peace congress. The emperor Ferdinand III entered into secret negotiations with Sweden in Hamburg; the Imperial Diet demanded a universal congress instead of bilateral transactions. The renewal of the Franco-Swedish alliance on June 30, 1641, included the stipulation that two congresses be held simultaneously in neighbouring Westphalian towns: the Catholic envoys were to meet in Münster, the Protestant envoys, in Osnabrück.

In 1643–44 Sweden and France sent out the first invitations, and the congress began to take shape. The slow and tortuous negotiations about procedure and substance, protocol and ceremonial, the admission or rejection of envoys and mediators—all these fumblings, which went on right to the actual signing of the treaties—were mostly due not to obstruction but to inexperience. By trial and error the congress had to explore and define the methods of modern international diplomacy. The 150 representatives (about 110 Germans and 40 foreigners) lacked any precedent for their tasks, starting, as it were, from scratch every time a fresh topic turned up. They gradually developed a kind of esprit de corps, which cut across political and religious frontiers and contributed not a little to the realistic settlement, which was satisfactory to all but a few diehards.

Though the plenipotentiaries were bound fairly narrowly by instructions from their governments, a few figures stand out to whom the successful outcome was largely due. The imperial ambassador, Maximilian Graf von Trauttmansdorff, outshone the rest; he had been the architect of the Peace of Prague and became the main author of the Peace of Westphalia. He and his chief secretary, Isaac Volmar, were converts to the Roman faith and therefore understood the opposing positions and did their best to check the firebrands in the Catholic camp. France was brillantly represented by the duc de Longueville (Henry d'Orléans) and his duchesse (Anne Geneviève de Bourbon-Condé), but as members of the princely faction they were suspect to Mazarin. Mazarin also mistrusted France's principal actual negotiator, Claude de Mesmes, comte d'Avaux, whereas the latter's equally skillful but more ruthless colleague, Abel Servien, enjoyed the cardinal's confidence; their mutual antagonism, however, in no way impaired their efficiency as representatives of the French crown. Similar dissensions rent the Swedish mission: Johan Oxenstierna, the chancellor's son, stood for the policy of conquest sponsored by the Swedish nobility, whereas Johan Adler Salvius, a gifted and experienced

The negotiators

diplomat of humble birth, sided with the young queen Christina in wishing for peace at almost any price. The Spanish ambassadors, the conde de Peñaranda (Gaspar de Bracamonte) and Antonius Brun, succeeded in terminating the war with the Dutch (Jan. 30, 1648) with great sacrifice to Spanish power but without loss to Spanish honour.

The Brunswick counsellor, Jacob Lampadius, stands out as the expert in all legal problems and the Lübeck envoy, David Gloxin, as the champion of the mercantile interest. Johann Rudolf Wettstein, of Basel, was accredited only as a representative of the Swiss Protestant cantons but acted on behalf of the whole Swiss Confederation. Lastly, the two unofficial mediators must be mentioned—the papal nuncio Fabio Chigi (later Pope Alexander VII) and, especially, the Venetian diplomat Alvise Contarini: they employed their good offices for smoothing out factional divisions and keeping alive the mutual interests of the European comity of nations.

Territorial settlement. The territorial clauses of the peace treaty all favoured France, Sweden, and their allies.

Sweden obtained the largest share: Hither Pomerania (Vorpommern), with Stettin and sole control over the Oder estuary; the Mecklenburg port of Wismar; and the archbishopric (but not the city) of Bremen and the bishopric of Verden, with control over the Elbe and Weser estuaries. In addition, there was the "satisfaction" of the Swedish Army, amounting to 5,000,000 talers guaranteed collectively by the members of the empire.

French gains

France incorporated the cities and bishoprics of Metz, Toul, and Verdun in Lorraine (French protectorates since 1552) and added to them the suzerainty over the secular vassals of the three bishops. France also obtained the ill-defined feudal rights exercised by the emperor over various towns, villages, and districts in Alsace (excluding Strassburg but including the bridgehead of Breisach), and the permanent right to garrison Philippsburg, on the right bank of the Rhine south of Speyer. These gains appeared modest. The possession of Breisach and Philippsburg, however, laid all southern Germany open to French arms; and the deliberate vagueness of the clauses relating to the cessions in Lorraine and Alsace later provided the legal or casuistical pretexts for the wars of aggression waged by Louis XIV.

The only major setback that France suffered was the conclusion of the separate peace between Spain and the United Provinces. This deprived France of an ally in the rear of the Spanish Netherlands and prolonged the Franco-Spanish War by a decade.

The gains and losses of the German princes were determined by the convenience of the principal powers: France, Sweden, and Austria. These used the claims of their lesser partners as pawns mainly for adjusting differences among themselves at somebody else's expense.

Brandenburg obtained Farther Pomerania (Hinterpommern); the bishoprics of Kammin, Halberstadt, and Minden; the county of Hohnstein; and the reversion of the archbishopric of Magdeburg on the death of the existing administrator, Augustus of Saxony (which occurred in 1680). Bavaria was to keep the Upper Palatinate and the electoral dignity, but the Rhenish Palatinate was restored to Frederick V's heir, Charles Louis, for whom a new electorate was created. Saxony retained what had been secured at the Peace of Prague, namely, Lusatia and Magdeburg, but the latter only for the lifetime of the present administrator. Hesse-Kassel ousted Hesse-Darmstadt from the district of Marburg and incorporated the abbey of Hersfeld and the county of Schaumburg. The Welfs of Brunswick obtained the right to have one of their princes elected as Protestant administrator of Osnabrück in alternation with a Catholic bishop. Mecklenburg was compensated for the loss of Wismar by the bishoprics of Schwerin and Ratzeburg.

Finally, the United Provinces of the Netherlands and the Swiss Confederation were released from their legal obligations toward the empire and so recognized as independent republics.

Political and religious settlement for Germany. For Germany, the Peace of Westphalia brought to a conclusion the century-old struggle between the monarchical tendencies of the emperor and the federalistic aspirations of the princes. Ferdinand II had made considerable progress in revitalizing the imperial power: without consulting the electors or princes, he had arrogated to himself the outlawry of Frederick V of the Palatinate and the transfer of the latter's electoral dignity to Maximilian of Bavaria (1623) and the deposition of the dukes of Mecklenburg (1628); on his own authority, he had interpreted, that is, in fact, rescinded, the Peace of Augsburg by the Edict of Restitution (1629), thereby superseding the legislative authority of the Imperial Diet; and by the Peace of Prague (1635), he had transformed all princely troops into contingents of an army under his supreme command and abolished the princes' traditional right to conclude alliances among themselves or with foreign powers.

The Peace of Westphalia completely reversed this trend. It confirmed the full sovereignty of the members of the empire, including their right to form alliances, restricted only by the meaningless proviso "except against the emperor and *Reich.*" It bound the emperor to the decisions of the Imperial Diet in all matters concerning war and peace. The Diet, which during the past 40 years had met only three times (1608, 1613, 1640–41), increased its sphere of competence at the expense of the emperor as well as the electors; the Protestant administrators of the secularized bishoprics were admitted with full voting rights. From 1663 the Diet remained in permanent session at Regensburg.

The peace established equality of rights between Catholics, Lutherans, and Calvinists: the supreme court of the empire was to be staffed by 26 Catholics and 24 Protestants, and Protestants were admitted to the Aulic Council in Vienna. The Edict of Restitution was repealed, and 1624 was declared the "standard year" according to which territories should be deemed to be in Catholic or Protestant possession. Except in the Habsburg dominions, where toleration was not granted to non-Catholics, dissidents were allowed private worship, liberty of conscience, and the right of emigration. Religious disputes were not to be decided by majority vote of the Imperial Diet but to be solved amicably between the Corpus Evangelicorum (the Protestant states collectively) and the Corpus Catholicorum, organized under the directorate of Saxony and of Mainz respectively.

Franco-Spanish War (1648–59). The conclusion of a separate peace with the United Provinces helped Spain to continue the struggle against France; and Condé's victory over the Spaniards at Lens (Aug. 20, 1648) was offset by the outbreak of the Fronde. During these civil wars in France (1649–53), the rebel leaders, including Condé, even made treaties of their own with Spain. Success came to the French from 1655, especially after the outbreak of hostilities between Spain and England and the conclusion of Anglo-French treaties of friendship (Sept. 5, 1656) and of alliance (March 23 and May 9, 1657). Robert Blake's exploits in the Mediterranean and in the Caribbean (1655–57), followed on land with the Battle of the Dunes (June 14, 1658) and the capture of Dunkerque (June 25) and Gravelines (Aug. 24, 1658), broke Spain's resistance. In the Franco-Spanish Treaty of the Pyrenees (Nov. 7, 1659), France obtained Roussillon and northern Cerdagne (thus establishing the frontier along the line of the Pyrenees), Artois, and a number of frontier fortresses in the Netherlands and Luxembourg. Spain had ceded to France the first place among the great powers of Europe.

Treaty of the Pyrenees

First Northern War (1655–60). The last decade of the 50-year period here surveyed witnessed another conflict in northern Europe. It arose, however, from the start of the Thirteen Years' War between Russia and Poland (1654–67), which is best considered as belonging to a later historical period, characterized by the decline of Poland and by the rise of Russia and of Brandenburg-Prussia. In so far as it reaffirmed certain tendencies of the earlier period, it may be briefly summarized here.

The question of the Ukraine led to war between Russia and Poland in 1654. Charles X of Sweden took advantage of this war to attack Poland in July 1655. The elector Frederick William of Brandenburg took the Swedish side from 1656 to 1657 but changed to the Polish in 1658. Russia began war against the Swedes in June 1656 but concluded the Truce of Valiesari in December 1658. In 1657 the emperor Ferdinand III's heir, Leopold I, allied Austria with Poland. Frederick III of Denmark attacked Sweden in June 1657.

Baltic settlement

By the Peace of Roskilde (Feb. 26, 1658), Denmark was forced to cede to Sweden not only Trondheim on the North Sea coast of Norway but also Bohuslän on the Swedish coast at the end of the Skagerrak, Skåne on the eastern side of the Sound, with adjacent Blekinge, and the island of Bornholm, thus forfeiting all hope of the "lordship of the Baltic." Denmark, however, subsequently refused to close the Baltic to Western shipping and was attacked by Sweden again in summer 1658. The Dutch, in their own commercial interests, came to Denmark's support, and the Treaty of Copenhagen (June 6, 1660) restored Bornholm and also Trondheim to Denmark, but otherwise confirmed the settlement of Roskilde.

The Peace of Oliva (May 3, 1660), between Sweden on the one hand and Poland, Austria, and Brandenburg on the other, assigned Livonia to Sweden and recognized Brandenburg's full sovereignty over ducal Prussia, both these stipulations being made at Poland's expense. The Russo-Swedish Peace of Kardis (July 1, 1661) re-established the terms of the Peace of Stolbova (1617).

France had played an active role in mediating the Baltic settlement. Habsburg Austria had gained nothing from the conflict and was meanwhile confronted by the League of the Rhine (Aug. 14, 1658), organized by Mazarin, whereby France, Sweden, the electoral archbishoprics (Mainz, Cologne, and Trier), Münster, Brunswick-Lüneburg, Palatinate-Neuburg, and Hesse-Kassel guaranteed the Peace of Westphalia against Habsburg revisionism.

GERMAN CIVILIZATION

The population. Any estimate of the movement of population of Germany between 1600 and 1650 is hampered by the absence of any census before the 18th century and the vagueness of the territory to which any statistics could be applied. All assertions of a decline of the population during the war by one-third or even more are therefore baseless guesswork. The computation of the population of "Germany" as a whole at the beginning or the end of the war would differ by about one-quarter or more according to the inclusion or exclusion (either of which can be defended on historical grounds) of certain territories, such as the Netherlands, Switzerland, Schleswig-Holstein, Brandenburg's Polish fief of Prussia, Spain's French-speaking possessions in Luxembourg and in Franche-Comté, French-speaking Lorraine, the Slav-speaking parts of Austria's possessions (Bohemia, Moravia, Carniola, Styria), and the Italian-speaking Trentino.

Such statistical surveys as were occasionally made for a small district were nearly always prompted by the wish to support some special pleading: to obtain a grant-in-aid, to reduce a tax assessment, to avoid military service or statute labour. The main sources on which historians have drawn are the reports of chroniclers and, rarely, parish registers of death—to the virtual exclusion of registers of marriage and baptisms. In view of the huge birthrate this neglect amounts to 30 to 50 percent; *i.e.*, to that one-third or one-half by which the population is said to have been reduced.

Death on the battlefield can be left out of count because the armies of the time, and consequently their losses, were very small. The Catholic League had an effective strength of about 15,000 men; Gustavus Adolphus landed in Germany with 15,000 men; Bernhard of Saxe-Weimar received French pay for 18,000 men; the strongest French army employed in Germany (in 1645) numbered 12,000; the first imperial army raised by Wallenstein in 1625 consisted of 15,000 foot and 6,000 horse.

The most serious losses were caused by epidemics, especially typhoid, the plague, and venereal diseases, spread by soldiers and refugees and intensified by lack of hygiene and the incompetence of doctors. A few chance survivals of accurate lists of victims make it certain, however, that during the worst outbreaks of the "pest" (the generic name applied to every epidemic) the mortality reached only 12 percent, and that in thickly populated towns. The average annual mortality rate seems to have been around 6 to 8 percent.

Internal migration

The most plausible explanation of the depletion of certain parts of Germany is to be found in an extensive internal migration, chiefly from the agrarian village to the industrial town and from the economically declining to the economically prosperous town (as for instance from Cologne to Frankfurt). But there was also a considerable fluctuation of refugees and evacuees from open country to the safety of the walled town: Kiel and Lübeck served as refuges for the gentry of Holstein. A typical example of this temporary dislocation of the population can be seen in five Thuringian rural districts for which accurate statistics have been computed: numbers declined during the years 1631–49 between 66 and 87 percent, and increased in the decade 1649–59 by between 78 and 125 percent. The net result of this redistribution of population was an all-around though small increase of the total population such as is characteristic of every predominantly agricultural society. Bearing in mind the elasticity of the term Germany, one can assume a population of 15,000,000–17,000,000 in 1600 and one of 16,000,000–18,000,000 in 1650, as may be inferred from the figure (fairly well attested) of 10,000,-000–17,000,000 for the Empire in 1700.

Economic life. The years around 1620 saw German economic life at its lowest point. For centuries its strength, like that of Italy, had lain in the flourishing towns, where industry, banking, and trade (import and export) were concentrated. From the middle of the 16th century, the heyday of their prosperity was over. Politically, the free cities succumbed to the growing power of the territorial princes; only a few—Lübeck, Hamburg, Bremen, Danzig, Nürnberg, Augsburg, Frankfurt—maintained more than an outward semblance of independence.

Economically the Hanse towns of northern Germany were severely hit by the Muscovites' destruction of Novgorod (1570), by the Spaniards' sack of Antwerp (1585), and by Queen Elizabeth I's closing of the London Steelyard (1598); and the separation of the United Provinces from Spain gave to the Hanse's Dutch rivals a free hand to break its monopoly in the Baltic. The southern German cities, whose bankers were deeply involved in the financial transactions of both Austrian and Spanish Habsburgs, were largely ruined by the repeated bankruptcies of the Spanish crown (1557, 1575, 1596, 1607); the insolvency of the Augsburg firm of Welser in 1614 was only the most spectacular debacle of many.

Inflation

The collapse of the old order was made evident in the big inflation of the years 1619–23, which brought utter ruin to the classes dependent on savings, annuities, or fixed incomes but provided colossal gains to versatile financiers and industrialists as well as to unscrupulous speculators and profiteers. The emperor Ferdinand II, who lent his active support to a combine of ruthless racketeers, and the dukes of Brunswick-Wolfenbüttel were conspicuous among the "legal" counterfeiters. When the currency was stabilized again in 1624, a thoroughgoing transfer of capital had occurred: none of the old-established and sometimes decadent firms survived, and their place was taken by pushing upstarts. This changeover of family and business fortunes continued: the proscription of Wallenstein and his adherents in 1634 permitted the Viennese courtiers and generals to acquire for a song the richest Bohemian and Silesian estates.

In fact, the inflation of 1619–23 was the turning point. The outward sign of economic recovery was the establishment of the big clearing banks of Hamburg (1619) and Nürnberg (1621); the Hamburg Mark Banko was for two centuries the most stable international currency unit until the pound sterling superseded it.

In German agriculture, too, a regrouping of ownership and profits rather than a general decline is to be noted. The steady rise of corn prices from the mid-16th century made large-scale farming and bulk selling more profitable; and from the end of the 16th century the feudal owners of big estates practiced wholesale evictions of peasants and forced acquisition of peasant lands, thereby depopulating the countryside and obliterating hundreds of villages. As far as can be ascertained, those villages that were wholly or partly burned down by the soldiery in the course of the war were all rebuilt and even enlarged before the end of it; and the same is true of Magdeburg, the only town of any size to be severely damaged by enemy action. The wars themselves proved a source of gain to the big landowners, who supplied victuals, grain, and livestock to the contending armies, whereas the small farmers could not compete with the lord of the manor and, moreover, endured greater hardship from marauding troops than did the townsman. Especially in those areas that suffered least from the military invasions—Prussia, Pomerania, Brandenburg, and Mecklenburg—the formerly-free farmers were reduced to virtual or legal serfdom.

Apart from the destructive effect of every war, it must be borne in mind that all the campaigns of the first half of the 17th century were of short duration and almost invariably centred around the same focal points that, by their geographical position, have been fought over again and again from time immemorial: the Alpine passes, the Rhine crossings, the bridgeheads of Regensburg on the Danube and Magdeburg on the Elbe, the plains of Leipzig and Brabant. The resilience of the people of these districts, however, has always been equal to their plight—as can be seen, for instance, at Leipzig. That city went bankrupt in 1625, was bombarded and stormed in 1631, 1632, 1633, 1637, and 1642, witnessed the major battles of Breitenfeld (1631 and 1642) and Lützen (1632) before its very gates, and was under Swedish occupation from 1642 to 1650; but in these years the annual Leipzig Fair established itself as the centre of European trade, and in 1640 the town council reported regular trade relations with Italy, Poland, England, Brabant, Scandinavia, the Ukraine, and the intermediate countries. Parts of Germany were affected by hostilities for a few weeks, others not at all. Most towns never saw an enemy within their walls.

Atrocity
stories

Of all the wild exaggerations concerning the moral degeneration of the German people caused by the Thirty Years' War, that of cannibalism due to famine and starvation has a morbid appeal, which few writers have been able to withstand. The refutation of these stories is the more difficult as the original accusations were vague, the source material is buried in the files of rural magistrates' courts, and critical investigations are scattered in obscure journals. It seems that one case of cannibalism can be taken as established: it occurred among the starving garrison of Breisach during the long seige in 1638. A second case proved in court is that of a Silesian bandit tried in 1654: having killed a pregnant woman, he ate her unborn child's heart in order, as he confessed, to make himself "stronger and fiercer"—a clear example of a form of superstitious magic known to anthropologists. Every other story of cannibalism that has been investigated can be shown to be the adaptation of some classical or medieval fable, if not simply a journalistic stunt. Thus, a contributor to a popular serial in 1639 startled his readers with the rhetorical question: "Has Germany become America? Cannibals now openly walk about. . . ." The vicar of a Palatine village, asking his co-religionists abroad for donations, asserted that "food is so scarce that the dead are no longer safe in their graves." This unsubstantiated hint proved so effective that thenceforth no appeal to charity dispensed with references to body snatching and cannibalism.

The
Baroque

Literature and the arts. The great impetus of the Renaissance and the intellectual fervour of the Reformation had exhausted themselves by 1570, just when Italy, France, England, Spain, and the Netherlands entered upon a fresh period of cultural grandeur. From the general European point of view, Germany was overshadowed and virtually ceased to count as an independent contributor in the cultural field. The picture of the years 1600–50, however, is different when studied from the narrower German angle. From the start of the 17th century onward, German scholars, scientists, musicians, writers, and poets were coming again to the fore and producing works that were to have lasting influence upon German culture.

The legend of the cultural exhaustion and desolation of Germany during and after the Thirty Years' War is solely due to the aesthetic standards of 19th-century historians, who despised the Baroque style and so could not appreciate the work of Baroque artists and writers. Moreover, the huge spate of German translations, chiefly of Italian, Spanish, and French scholars and scientists, prose writers, and poets, tends to be overlooked.

Italian influence was especially prominent in the German theatre of the time, in which decor, stage effects, and music were combined to produce operatic showpieces: the plays (in Latin) of the Jesuit Jakob Bidermann (1578–1639) and the Passion play of Oberammergau first performed in 1634 are spectacular examples. The composer Heinrich Schütz (1585–1672) helped to establish the fashion for Italian music in Germany with his madrigals, symphonies, and oratorios as well as the first German opera (*Dafne*, 1627) and the first German ballet (*Orpheus und Eurydice*, 1638).

German language and literature had enthusiastic though somewhat pedantic nurseries in the literary societies modelled on the Florentine Accademia della Crusca, of which the Weimar Fruchtbringende Gesellschaft (1617) was the oldest and most influential, followed by the Hamburg Teutschgesinnte Genossenschaft (1643), the Nürnberg Pegnitzorden (1644), and others. Aiming at a purification of the German language, the encouragement of writers, and an improvement of manners and morals, they listed among their members numerous leaders of society and every literary figure of note. Martin Opitz with his *Buch von der deutschen Poeterey* (1624) and Justus Georg Schottel (1612–76) with his *Teutsche Sprachkunst* (1641) standardized the theory of New High German poetics and grammar for 150 years. Opitz's own poetry is unoriginal and largely modelled on the French poets of the Pléiade; but as he tried his hand in every type of fashionable literature and was a prolific translator, his influence was considerable throughout 17th-century Germany. The mystical poems of Friedrich Spee (1591–1635), the epigrams of Friedrich von Logau (1604–55), the Latin odes of Jakob Balde (1604–68), the satirical novels of J.M. Moscherosch (1601–69), the hymns of Simon Dach (1605–59) and of Paul Gerhardt (1607–76), the occasional and patriotic poems of Georg Rudolf Weckherlin (1584–1653), the plays of Andreas Gryphius (1616–64), and the novel, *Die Adriatische Rosemund*, of Philipp von Zesen (1619–89)—these highlights of the German literature of the war years are still read. Their testimony to a flourishing literary life is further supported by the expansion of the two leading German printers and publishers, Endter in Nürnberg and Stern in Lüneburg, whose books, pamphlets, hymnals, calendars, etc., were bought by the middle and lower classes in, at least, every Protestant region of the empire.

The outstanding figure in German science is the astronomer Johannes Kepler, who discovered the laws of the planets while serving successively the emperor Rudolf II, the Estates of Upper Austria, and Wallenstein. Otto von Guericke, who as councillor and burgomaster of Magdeburg supervised the reconstruction of the city after 1631, was the inventor of the air pump and manometer. The Naturwissenschaftliche Gesellschaft, founded in Rostock in 1622, was the first learned society to devote itself primarily to the advancement of science. The English physician William Harvey chose a Frankfurt publisher to bring out his discovery of the circulation of the blood (1628).

In art and architecture, the influence of Palladio and Bernini was strong enough to Italianize all building in the south of Germany, whereas the northwest fell under Dutch influence. Maximilian of Bavaria patronized the Dutchman Peter Candid, a pupil of Giorgio Vasari, as painter and builder for his palaces in Munich and Schleissheim. All the palaces, cathedrals, and churches built in the 17th century by the Habsburg rulers and their courtiers in Vienna, Salzburg, Graz, Innsbruck, and Prague were the work of Italian designers, as were Wallenstein's palaces in Prague, Jicin, and Sagan. On the whole, however, there was little incentive for new building, since the great buildings of the prosperous first three-quarters of the 16th century still served the need of the majority of their owners. Most private houses of the less well-to-do are artistically insignificant and have therefore failed to gain entry in the histories of architecture. A lively interest in architecture, however, is attested by the success of several textbooks for the instruction of builders and their clients, such as that by Rüdiger Kossmann of Cologne (1630, re-edited in 1644 and 1653) and three by Josef Furttenbach of Ulm (1628, 1640, and 1641).

CONCLUSION

The European struggle against the predominance of Spain is the main topic of all the hot and cold wars, diplomatic moves and alignments, religious and constitutional tensions that fill the history of the first half of the 17th century. The Thirty Years' War, so called, is merely a segment of this general upheaval. The result, in the peace treaties of Westphalia and of the Pyrenees, can be summed up as follows.

In the field of international as well as of German politics, the sovereignty and independence of the individual state was established as the principle on which, thenceforth, the European comity of nations and, in the narrower German context, the framework of the Holy Roman Empire were to be based. For Germany this structure survived, with modifications (notably in the Napoleonic period), until the foundation of the German Empire under Prussian hegemony in 1871; and for western Europe the principle was maintained into the second half of the 20th century. The medieval conception of the theoretical unity of the *respublica Christiana* with the Roman emperor and the Roman pope as its temporal and spiritual heads was formally abandoned in favour of a community of sovereign, independent states, of equal status, regardless of form of government or confession of faith, though united by a common adherence to certain fundamental principles of law and order. This was a first, tentative step toward a European community in which, however, Great Britain and Russia were not included.

BIBLIOGRAPHY. Major works on the Thirty Years' War are S.H. STEINBERG, *The Thirty Years War and the Conflict for European Hegemony, 1600–1660* (1966); HENRI HAUSER, *La Prépondérance espagnole, 1559–1660* (1933), useful for background material; C.V. WEDGWOOD, *The Thirty Years War* (1938, reprinted 1961 and 1969); GEORGES PAGES, *La Guerre de Trente Ans, 1618–1648* (1939); R.R. ERGANG, *The Myth of the All-Destructive Fury of the Thirty Years' War* (1956); and GUNTHER FRANZ, *Der Dreissigjährige Krieg und das deutsche Volk*, 3rd rev. ed. (1961). For a Marxist interpretation, see JOSEF V. POLISENSKY, *Třicetiletá válka a česky národ* (1960; Eng. trans., *The Thirty Years War*, 1972). Studies of the Peace of Westphalia include ERNST HOVEL (ed.), *Pax optima rerum* (1948); MAX BRAUBACH, *Der Westfälische Friede* (1948), an excellent brief account; and FRITZ DICKMANN, *Der Westfälische Frieden*, 2nd ed. (1965), a standard work for the period 1630–48.

(S.H.ST.)

Thomas, Dylan

It would seem probable that more myths have been spun about Dylan Thomas and therefore more rubbish written than about any other English-language poet since Lord Byron, a century and a half earlier. For this he was, himself, in some measure responsible. "Bewilder 'em," he said, and his earlier verse did, though it is hard now to see why. He wrote, as he put it, about birth, copulation, and death—the common concerns of man—and, although his imagery is sometimes dense, it is ultimately comprehensible. He also claimed to be "the drunkest man in the world," which he certainly was not, for he had a weak head and really preferred to drink beer. Finally, his wit was fantastic and fraught with puns and other wordplay, so that what he said was often slightly askew. A small, rather sickly man all his life, he assumed in public a Casanova-like role, which was directly contradictory to his long marriage (1936 until his death, early in his 40th year) to his Irish wife, Caitlin Macnamara, who bore him two sons and a daughter. Nevertheless, the myth of the insatiable amorist was added to the others. When he told the journalists in New York that he had come to

The myth of Dylan Thomas

Thomas, 1952.
Rollie McKenna

America as part of his endless quest for naked women in wet mackintoshes, they were, of course, delighted. In fact, his American trips, on the last of which he died in a New York hospital, were made solely to earn money. Throughout his poetic career he was haunted by the thought of death, and perhaps his chief contribution to English poetry was his vision that life and death form part of a great process shared with all nature by the poet's body.

Dylan Marlais Thomas was born on October 27, 1914, in Swansea, in southwest Wales, and it was there that he spent his childhood. His father was the English teacher at Swansea grammar school, which in due course the boy attended. Dylan's mother was a small farmer's daughter, so that he had a country home he could go to when on holiday. His poem "Fern Hill" (1946) describes its joys. His mother took him as a child to chapel, which became a source of some of his imagery, although he was not a religious poet in any conventional sense. He always and correctly referred to himself as a Welsh poet, though he had no knowledge of the Welsh language. He also and incorrectly at times maintained that he was of working class origin. His family was well-educated middle class. From his earliest days the father read Shakespeare rather than children's books aloud to the boy at bedtime. Later he arranged that Dylan have elocution lessons to improve, which in this context meant to anglicize, his diction. He himself was to refer to his "cut glass" voice, and anybody who has heard him knows how perfectly he spoke English. Indeed, as a very young amateur actor, he considered taking up the stage as a profession. Those who saw him "performing" later in his life would probably agree that acting was in fact always his second profession—second to that of the poet, of course.

Education and youth

He did badly at school. Indeed, he was always intellectually lazy with regard to any subject that did not directly concern him, but when it did he was exactly the reverse. His knowledge of English poetry, for instance, was enormous, not in the theory but in the practice. He once said that he was not interested in poetry, only in poems. He had begun writing them at a very early age, and scholars have shown that the bulk of his poetic output was completed, at least in embryonic form, by the time he moved to London at the age of 21. This fact is not surprising if it is recalled that he was in youth essentially a lyric poet, and most lyrics are written by very young men.

Dylan Thomas, in Swansea with his and his father's books, was perhaps the last of the Romantic poets, heir to a tradition that stretched back through Rupert Brooke and Siegfried Sassoon, English poets of World War I, to John Keats and Percy Bysshe Shelley, in the 19th century, and beyond that to Thomas Chatterton, in the 18th. As did all of the poets of that tradition, he had to experiment with words. He was perhaps the last major poet to do so, hence the bewilderment when his early poems were first published in the mid-1930s. Much later he was to write more "epic" work, but never in what anybody could call the classical tradition. He knew most of John Milton by heart, and at the end of his life he was preoccupied with similar themes (*e.g.*, the nature of good and evil in war, the innocent death of a child or an old man murdered by a casual bomb). Among these was an opera libretto based on the epic concept of the atomic destruction of the world, followed by the re-creation of the first man and woman and their discovery of language. This major work, however, is one of the might-have-beens of literature.

First
publica-
tions His first book, *18 Poems*, appeared in 1934, followed by *Twenty-five Poems*, two years later. London was his home for some ten years from about 1936. (He made tentative approaches to life in the capital before that, and it also took him some time to move out.) He was famous in literary circles, sociable, and very poor, with a wife and growing family to support. His attempts to make money—with the British Broadcasting Corporation and as a film scriptwriter—were not sufficiently remunerative. He managed, as far as anyone could, to avoid the war (he was excused from military service because of a lung condition), for he regarded himself in those days as a pacifist and occasionally burbled about being a Communist, though his ignorance of politics was as total as was his knowledge of English language poetry. He had, however, an instinctive aversion to the rich and smug and a sympathy for the poor and oppressed. More disastrous than his political ignorance was his total lack of any sort of business acumen. He became badly behind with his income tax returns, and what money he managed to make was snatched from him, at source, by the British Exchequer. He took to drinking more heavily and to borrowing from richer friends. Nevertheless, he continued to work, though with increased knowledge the composition of his poems became an ever slower and more painstaking business—he was nearing the end of the treasure chest compiled in his early youth—while the London or London-based atmosphere became increasingly dangerous and uncongenial both to him and to his wife. As early as 1946 he was talking of emigrating to the United States, but, without any money, how? In the following year he had

Nervous
breakdown what would seem to be a nervous breakdown but refused psychiatric or other medical assistance. He moved to Oxford, where he was given a cottage by A.J.P. Taylor, a distinguished historian. His trips to London, however, principally in connection with his BBC work, were gruelling, exhausting, and increasingly alcoholic.

In 1949 Mrs. Taylor financed the purchase of a cottage, the Boat House, Laugharne, and he returned to Wales. In the following year his first American tour was arranged, and for a while it seemed as if a happy compromise had been arranged between American money and Welsh tranquillity. It was then that he wrote his "play for voices," *Under Milk Wood,* an idea with which he had been playing at least since 1945. It was presented at the Poetry Center in New York in 1953, and its final version was broadcast by the BBC in 1954. He also published his *Collected Poems* (1952), an immediate success on both sides of the Atlantic. But, because of the insistence of the Inland Revenue, he still had no money. Indeed, he had come to hate money, and what he could earn or borrow he squandered. Furthermore, he found his American tours exhausting: in Wales it was beer, in the United States and Canada it was whiskey. There were far too many people who seem to have derived pleasure from making the famous poet drunk. Despair mounted, his marriage was in peril, and at last, far from his Welsh home, he took such an overdose of hard liquor that he died, on November 9, 1953. He was on his way to California, to stay with Igor Stravinsky, to write the epic opera he had in mind.

MAJOR WORKS

POETRY: *18 Poems* (1934), including "The Force That Through the Green Fuse Drives the Flower," "Light Breaks Where No Sun Shines," "I See the Boys of Summer," and "Especially When the October Wind"; *Twenty-five Poems* (1936), including "To-day, This Insect," "Hold Hard, These Ancient Minutes in the Cuckoo's Mouth," and "Altarwise

by Owl-Light"; *The Map of Love* (1939), including "We Lying by Seasand," "After the Funeral," and "Twenty-four Years"; *Deaths and Entrances* (1946), including "A Refusal To Mourn the Death, by Fire, of a Child in London," "Do Not Go Gentle into That Good Night," "Poem in October," "Ceremony After a Fire Raid," and "Ballad of the Long-legged Bait"; *In Country Sleep* (1952), including the title poem and "Over Sir John's Hill," "Lament," and "In the White Giant's Thigh"; *Collected Poems 1934–52* (1952).
SEMI-AUTOBIOGRAPHICAL PROSE: *Portrait of the Artist As a Young Dog* (1940); *Adventures in the Skin Trade* (1955).
SHORT STORIES: *A Prospect of the Sea* (1955).
DRAMA: *Under Milk Wood* (1954), a radio play for voices.
BROADCASTS: *Quite Early One Morning* (1954).
MOTION PICTURE SCRIPT: *The Doctor and the Devils* (1953), adapted from the story by Donald Taylor.

BIBLIOGRAPHY. J. ALEXANDER ROLPH, *Dylan Thomas: A Bibliography*, with a foreword by DAME EDITH SITWELL (1956), is a most scholarly work. It should be used, however, in conjunction with RALPH MAUD, *Dylan Thomas in Print: A Bibliographical History* (1970). CONSTANTINE FITZGIBBON, *The Life of Dylan Thomas* (1965), is the official biography of the poet, commissioned by his trustees and approved by his widow. This is also true of the *Selected Letters of Dylan Thomas,* ed. by FITZGIBBON (1966). Omitted from *Selected Letters* are most of the *Letters to Vernon Watkins,* ed. with an introduction by VERNON WATKINS (1957), which cast a great deal of light on Thomas' mental activities as a poet, particularly in his earlier years. *Dylan Thomas in America* (1955) is a biographical study by JOHN MALCOLM BRINNIN, who was Thomas' friend and American agent. See also Thomas' *Early Prose Writings*, ed. by WALFORD DAVIES (1971).

(C.Fi.)

Thomas Aquinas, Saint

St. Thomas Aquinas was a Christian philosopher who developed his own conclusions from Aristotelian premises, notably in the metaphysics of personality, creation, and Providence; a theologian responsible in his two masterpieces, the *Summa theologiae* and the *Summa contra gentiles,* for the classical systematization of Latin theology; and a poet who wrote some of the most gravely beautiful eucharistic hymns in the church's liturgy. Although many modern Roman Catholic theologians do not find him altogether congenial, he is recognized by the Catholic Church as its foremost Western philosopher and theologian.

Alinari—Art Reference Bureau

"Apotheosis of St. Thomas Aquinas," altarpiece by Francesco Traini, 1363. In the Sta. Caterina, Pisa.

Early years.   Thomas was born in 1224/1225, at Roccasecca, near Aquino, on the road from Rome to Naples, where his parents were in possession of a modest feudal domain on a boundary constantly disputed by the emperor and the pope. His father was of Lombard origin; his mother was of the later invading Norman strain. His people were distinguished in the service of Emperor Frederick II during the civil strife in southern Italy between the papal and imperial forces. Thomas was placed in the monastery of Monte Cassino near his home as an oblate (*i.e.*, offered as a prospective monk) when he was still a young boy; his family doubtless hoped that he would someday become abbot to their advantage. In 1239, after nine years in this sanctuary of spiritual and cultural life, young Thomas was forced to return to his family when the Emperor expelled the monks because they were too obedient to the Pope. He was then sent to the University of Naples, recently founded by the Emperor; the university provided an environment that was wide open to the scientific and philosophical works that were being translated from the Greek and the Arabic. In this setting Thomas decided to join the Friars Preachers, or Dominicans, a new religious order founded 30 years earlier, which departed from the traditional paternalistic form of government for monks to the more democratic form of the mendicant friars (*i.e.*, religious orders whose corporate as well as personal poverty made it necessary for them to beg alms) and from the monastic life of prayer and manual labour to a more active life of preaching and teaching. By this move he took a liberating step beyond the feudal world into which he was born and the monastic spirituality in which he was reared. A dramatic episode marked the full significance of his decision. His parents had him abducted on the road to Paris, where his shrewd superiors had immediately assigned him so that he would be out of the reach of his family but also so that he could pursue his studies in the most prestigious and turbulent university of the time.

Entry into the Dominican order

Studies in Paris. Thomas held out stubbornly against his family despite a year of captivity. He was finally liberated and in the autumn of 1245 went to Paris to the convent of Saint-Jacques, the great university centre of the Dominicans; there he studied under Albertus Magnus, a tremendous scholar with a wide range of intellectual interests.

Escape from the feudal world, rapid commitment to the University of Paris, and religious vocation to one of the new mendicant orders all meant a great deal in a world in which faith in the traditional institutional and conceptual structure was being attacked. The encounter between the gospel and the culture of his time formed the nerve centre of Thomas' position and directed its development. Normally, his work is presented as the integration into Christian thought of the recently discovered Aristotelian philosophy, in competition with the integration of Platonic thought effected by the Fathers of the Church during the first 12 centuries of the Christian Era. This view is essentially correct; more radically, however, it should also be asserted that Thomas' work accomplished an evangelical awakening to the need for a cultural and spiritual renewal not only in the lives of individual men but also throughout the church. Thomas must be understood in his context as a mendicant religious, influenced both by the evangelism of St. Francis of Assisi, founder of the Franciscan order, and by the devotion to scholarship of St. Dominic, founder of the Dominican order.

Study of Aristotle's works

When Thomas arrived at the University of Paris, the influx of Arabian–Aristotelian science was arousing a sharp reaction among believers; and several times (in the years 1210, 1215, 1231, and 1245) the church authorities tried to block the naturalism and rationalism that were emanating from this philosophy and, according to many ecclesiastics, seducing the younger generations. Thomas did not fear these new ideas, but, like his master Albertus Magnus (and Roger Bacon, also lecturing at Paris), he studied the works of Aristotle and eventually lectured publicly on them.

For the first time in history, Christian believers and theologians were confronted with the rigorous demands of scientific rationalism. At the same time, technical progress was requiring men to move from the rudimentary economy of an agrarian society to an urban society with production organized in trade guilds, with a market economy, and with a profound feeling of community. New generations of men and women, including clerics, were reacting against the traditional notion of contempt for the world and were striving for mastery over the forces of nature through the use of their reason. The structure of Aristotle's philosophy emphasized the primacy of the intelligence. Technology itself became a means of access to truth; mechanical arts were powers for humanizing the cosmos. Thus, the dispute over the reality of universals —*i.e.*, the question about the relation between general words such as "red" and particulars such as "this red object"—which had dominated early Scholastic philosophy, was left behind; and a coherent metaphysics of knowledge and of the world was being developed.

During the summer of 1248, Thomas left Paris with Albertus, who was to assume direction of the new faculty established by the Dominicans at the convent in Cologne. He remained there until 1252, when he returned to Paris to prepare for the degree of master of theology. After taking his bachelor's degree, he received the *licentia docendi* ("license to teach") at the beginning of 1256 and shortly afterward finished the training necessary for the title and privileges of master. Thus, in the year 1256 he began teaching theology in one of the two Dominican schools incorporated in the University of Paris.

Years at the papal Curia and return to Paris. In 1259 Thomas was appointed theological adviser and lecturer to the papal Curia, then the centre of Western humanism. He returned to Italy, where he spent two years at Anagni at the end of the reign of Alexander IV and four years at Orvieto with Urban IV. From 1265 to 1267 he taught at the convent of Santa Sabina in Rome and then, at the request of Clement IV, went to the papal Curia in Viterbo. Suddenly, in November 1268, he was sent to Paris, where he became involved in a sharp doctrinal polemic that had just been triggered off.

The works of Averroës, the outstanding representative of Arabic philosophy in Spain, who was known as the great commentator and interpreter of Aristotle, were just becoming known to the Parisian masters. There seems to be no doubt about the Islāmic faith of the Cordovan philosopher; nevertheless, he asserted that the structure of religious knowledge was entirely heterogeneous to rational knowledge: two truths—one of faith, the other of reason—can, in the final analysis, be contradictory. This dualism was denied by Muslim orthodoxy and was still less acceptable to Christians. With the appearance of Siger of Brabant, however, and from 1266 on, the quality of Averroës' exegesis and the wholly rational bent of his thought began to attract disciples in the faculty of arts at the University of Paris. Thomas Aquinas rose in protest against his colleagues; nevertheless, the parties retained a mutual esteem. As soon as he returned from Italy, Thomas began to dispute with Siger, who, he claimed, was compromising not only orthodoxy but also the Christian interpretation of Aristotle. Thomas found himself wedged in between the Augustinian tradition of thought, now more emphatic than ever in its criticism of Aristotle, and the Averroists. Radical Averroism was condemned in 1270, but at the same time Thomas, who sanctioned the autonomy of reason under faith, was discredited.

Opposition to the Averroists

In the course of this dispute, the very method of theology was called into question. According to Aquinas, reason is able to operate within faith and yet according to its own laws. The mystery of God is expressed and incarnate in human language; it is thus able to become the object of an active, conscious, and organized elaboration in which the rules and structures of rational activity are integrated in the light of faith. In the Aristotelian sense of the word, then (although not in the modern sense), theology is a "science"; it is knowledge that is rationally derived from propositions that are accepted as certain because they are revealed by God. The theologian accepts authority and faith as his starting point and then proceeds to conclusions using reason; the philosopher, on the other hand, relies solely on the natural light of reason. Thomas was the first to view theology expressly in this way or at least to present it systematically, and in doing so he raised a storm of opposition in various quarters. Even today this opposition endures, especially among religious enthusiasts for whom reason remains an intruder in the realm of mystical communion, contemplation, and the sudden ecstasy of evangelical fervour.

The literary form of Thomas' works must be appreciated in the context of his methodology. He organized his teaching in the form of "questions," in which critical research is presented by pro and con arguments, according to the pedagogical system then in use in the universities. Forms varied from simple commentaries on official texts to written accounts of the public disputations, which were significant events in medieval university life. Thomas' works are divided into three categories: 1) commentaries on such works as the Old and New Testaments, the *Sentences* of Peter Lombard (the official manual of theology in the universities), and the writings of Aristotle; 2) disputed questions, accounts of his teaching as a master in the disputations; 3) two *summae* or personal syntheses, the *Summa contra gentiles* and the *Summa theologiae*, which were presented as integral introductions for the use of beginners. Numerous *opuscula* ("little works"), which have great interest because of the particular circumstances that provoked them, must also be noted.

The logic of Thomas' position regarding faith and reason required that the fundamental consistency of the realities of nature be recognized. A *physis* ("nature") has necessary laws; recognition of this fact permits the construction of a science according to a *logos* ("rational structure"). Thomas thus avoided the temptation to sacralize the forces of nature through a naïve recourse to the miraculous or the Providence of God. For him, a whole "supernatural" world that cast its shadow over things and men, in Romanesque art as in social customs, had blurred men's imaginations. Nature, discovered in its profane reality, should assume its proper religious value and lead to God by more rational ways, yet not simply as a shadow of the supernatural. This understanding is exemplified in the way that Francis of Assisi admired the birds, the plants, and the Sun.

The inclusion of Aristotle's *Physics* in university programs was not, therefore, just a matter of academic curiosity. Naturalism, however, as opposed to a sacral vision of the world, was penetrating all realms: spirituality, social customs, and political conduct. About 1270, Jean de Meun, a French poet of the new cities and Thomas' neighbour in the Rue Saint-Jacques in Paris, gave expression in his *Roman de la Rose* to the coarsest realism, not only in examining the physical universe but also in describing and judging the laws of procreation. Innumerable manuscripts of the Roman poet Ovid's *Ars amatoria* ("The Art of Loving") were in circulation; André le Chapelain, in his *De Deo amoris* ("On the God of Love") adapted a more refined version for the public. Courtly love in its more seductive forms became a more prevalent element in the culture of the 13th century.

At the same time, Roman law was undergoing a revival at the University of Bologna; this involved a rigorous analysis of the natural law and provided the jurists of Frederick II with a weapon against ecclesiastical theocracy. The traditional presentations of the role and duties of princes, in which biblical symbolism was used to outline beautiful pious images, were replaced by treatises that described experimental and rational attempts at government. Thomas had composed such a treatise—*De regimine principum* ("On the Government of Princes")—for the King of Cyprus in 1266. In the administration of justice, juridical investigations and procedures replaced fanatical recourse to ordeals and to judgments of God.

In the face of this movement, there was a fear on the part of many that the authentic values of nature would not be properly distinguished from the disorderly inclinations of mind and heart. Theologians of a traditional bent firmly resisted any form of a determinist philosophy which, they believed, would atrophy liberty, dissolve personal responsibility, destroy faith in Providence, and deny the notion of a gratuitous act of creation. Imbued with Augustine's doctrines, they asserted the necessity and power of grace for a nature torn asunder by sin. The optimism of the new theology concerning the religious value of nature scandalized them.

Although he was an Aristotelian, Thomas was certain that he could defend himself against a heterodox interpretation of "the Philosopher," as Aristotle was known. Thomas held that human liberty could be defended as a rational thesis while admitting that determinations are found in nature. In his theology of Providence, he taught a continuous creation, in which the dependence of the created on the creative wisdom guarantees the reality of the order of nature. God moves sovereignly all that he creates; but the supreme government that he exercises over the universe is conformed to the laws of a creative Providence that wills each being to act according to its proper nature. This autonomy finds its highest realization in the rational creature: man is literally self-moving in his intellectual, volitional, and physical existence. Man's freedom, far from being destroyed by his relationship to God, finds its foundation in this very relationship. "To take something away from the perfection of the creature is to abstract from the perfection of the creative power itself." This metaphysical axiom, which is also a mystical principle, is the key to St. Thomas' spirituality.

Last years at Naples. At Easter time in 1272, Thomas returned to Italy to establish a Dominican house of studies at the University of Naples. This move was undoubtedly made in answer to a request made by King Charles of Anjou, who was anxious to revive the university. After participating in a general chapter, or meeting, of the Dominicans held in Florence during Pentecost week and, having settled some family affairs, Thomas resumed his university teaching at Naples in October and continued it until the end of the following year.

Although Thomas' argument with the Averroists had for years been matched by a controversy with the Christian masters who followed the traditional Augustinian conception of man as fallen, this latter dispute now became more pronounced. In a series of university conferences in 1273, Bonaventure, a Franciscan friar and a friendly colleague of Thomas at Paris, renewed his criticism of the Aristotelian current of thought, including the teachings of Thomas. He criticized the thesis that philosophy is distinct from theology, as well as the notion of a physical nature that has determined laws; he was especially critical of the theory that the soul is bound up with the body as the two necessary principles that make up the nature of man and also reacted strongly to the Aristotelians' denial of the Platonic–Augustinian theory of knowledge based upon exemplary Ideas or Forms.

The disagreement was profound. Certainly, all Christian philosophers taught the distinction between matter and spirit. This distinction, however, could be intelligently held only if the internal relationship between matter and spirit in individual human beings was sought. It was in the process of this explanation that differences of opinion arose—not only intellectual differences between idealist and realist philosophers but also emotional differences. Some viewed the material world merely as a physical and biological reality, a stage on which the history of spiritual persons is acted out, their culture developed, and their salvation or damnation determined. This stage itself remains detached from the spiritual event, and the history of nature is only by chance the setting for the spiritual history. The history of nature follows its own path imperturbably; in this history, man is a foreigner, playing a brief role only to escape as quickly as possible from the world into the realm of pure spirit, the realm of God.

Thomas, on the contrary, noted the inclusion of the history of nature in the history of the spirit and at the same time noted the importance of the history of spirit for the history of nature. Man is situated ontologically (*i.e.*, by his very existence) at the juncture of two universes, "like a horizon of the corporeal and of the spiritual." In man there is not only a distinction between spirit and nature but there is also an intrinsic homogeneity of the two. Aristotle furnished Thomas with the categories necessary for the expression of this concept: the soul is the "form" of the body. For Aristotle, form is that which makes a thing to be what it is; form and matter—that out of which a thing is made—are the two intrinsic causes that constitute every material thing. For Thomas, then, the body is the matter and the soul is the form of man.

The objection was raised that he was not sufficiently safeguarding the transcendence of the spirit, the doctrine that the soul survives after the death of the body.

In January 1274 Thomas was personally summoned by Gregory X to the second Council of Lyons, which was an attempt to repair the schism between the Latin and Greek churches. On his way he was stricken by illness; he stopped at the Cistercian abbey of Fossanova, where he died on March 7, 1274. In 1277 the masters of Paris, the highest theological jurisdiction in the church, condemned a series of 219 propositions; 12 of these propositions were theses of Thomas. This was the most serious condemnation possible in the Middle Ages; its repercussions were felt in the development of ideas. It produced for several centuries a certain unhealthy spiritualism that resisted the cosmic and anthropological realism of Thomas Aquinas.

Assessment. The biography of Thomas is one of extreme simplicity; it chronicles little but some modest travel during a career devoted entirely to university life: at Paris, the Roman Curia, Paris again, and Naples. It *Importance* would be a mistake, however, to judge that his life was *of the* merely the quiet life of a professional teacher untouched *university* by the social and political affairs of his day. The drama *environ-* that went on in his mind and in his religious life found *ment* its causes and produced its effects in the university. In the young universities all the ingredients of a rapidly developing civilization were massed together, and to these universities the Christian Church had deliberately and authoritatively committed its doctrine and its spirit. In this environment, Thomas found the technical conditions for elaborating his work—not only the polemic occasions for turning it out but also the enveloping and penetrating spiritual milieu needed for it. It is within the homogeneous contexts supplied by this environment that it is possible today to discover the historical intelligibility of his work, just as they supplied the climate for its fruitfulness at the time of its birth.

Thomas was canonized a saint in 1323, officially named doctor of the church in 1567, and proclaimed the protagonist of orthodoxy during the modernist crisis at the end of the 19th century. This continuous commendation, however, cannot obliterate the historical difficulties in which he was embroiled in the 13th century during a radical theological renewal—a renewal that was contested at the time and yet was brought about by the social, cultural, and religious evolution of the West. Thomas was at the heart of the doctrinal crisis that confronted Christendom when the discovery of Greek science, culture, and thought seemed about to crush it. William of Tocco, Thomas' first biographer, who had known him and was able to give evidence of the impression produced by his master's teaching, says:

Brother Thomas raised new problems in his teaching, invented a new method, used new systems of proof. To hear him teach a new doctrine, with new arguments, one could not doubt that God, by the irradiation of this new light and by the novelty of this inspiration, gave him the power to teach, by the spoken and written word, new opinions and new knowledge.

MAJOR WORKS

THEOLOGICAL TREATISES: *Scriptum super IV libros Sententiarum* (1254–56); *De veritate* (1256–59); *Summa contra gentiles* (c. 1258–64; *On the Truth of the Catholic Faith*, 1955); *Summa theologiae* (1265 or 1266–73; incomplete); *De potentia Dei* (1259–68; *On the Power of God*, 1932–34); *De malo* (undated; *On Free Choice*); *De spiritualibus creaturis* (undated; *On Spiritual Creatures*, 1949); *De anima* (undated; *The Soul*, 1949); *De unione Verbi incarnati* (undated); *De virtutibus* (1269–72; *On the Virtues in General*, 1951).
BIBLICAL COMMENTARIES: *Expositio in Evangelium S. Matthaei* (1269–72); *Expositio in Job ad litteram* (1261–64); *Expositio in Evangelium Joannis* (1269–72); *Exposition in S. Pauli Apostoli epistolas* (undated; incomplete); *In psalmos Davidis expositio* (1272–73).
COMMENTARIES ON ARISTOTLE: *In octo libros Physicorum expositio* (1268–71; *Commentary on Aristotle's Physics*, 1963); *In tres libros De anima* (undated; *The Commentary of St. Thomas Aquinas on Aristotle's Treatise on the Soul*, 1946); *In librum De sensu et sensato expositio* (1270–71); *In decem libros Ethicorum expositio* (1271–72; *Commentary on the Nicomachean Ethics*, 1964); *In duodecim libros Meta-*

physicorum expositio (c. 1272; *Commentary on the Metaphysics of Aristotle*, 1961); *In libros De caelo et mundo expositio* (1272–73); *In libros Posteriorum analyticorum expositio* (undated; probably late).
OTHER WORKS: (PHILOSOPHICAL TREATISES): *De ente et essentia* (before 1256; *On Being and Essence*, 1949); *Contra impugnantes Dei cultum et religionem* (1256; *An Apology for the Religious Orders*, 1902); *De regno* (*De regimine principum*) *ad regem Cypri* (1266; *On Kingship*, 1949); *De perfectione vitae spiritualis* (1269–70); *De unitate intellectus contra Averroistas* (1270; *The Unicity of the Intellect*, 1946); *De aeternitate mundi contra murmurantes* (1270–72); *De substantiis separatis, seu de angelorum natura* (undated; *Treatise on Separate Substances*, 1959). (HYMNS AND LITURGICAL COMPOSITIONS): "Pange, lingua, gloriosi" (1264); "Verbum supernum prodiens" (1264; "The Word of God Proceeding Forth"); office for the Feast of Corpus Christi (c. 1264), including the sequence "Lauda Sion Salvatorem" ("Praise, O Zion, thy Salvation").

BIBLIOGRAPHY. Thomas' first biography was that of his disciple, WILLIAM OF TOCCO, published in *Acta Sanctorum*, vol. 1, pp. 656–686 (March 1865); new ed., with other biographies, *Fontes vitae S. Thomas Aquinatis*, 6 fasc. (1912–37); and A.M. WALZ, *San Tommaso d'Aquino. Studi biografici* (1945; Eng. trans., *Saint Thomas Aquinas: A Biographical Study*, 1951).
Latin editions of the Opera omnia: Rome (17 vol., 1570), called *Piana* because they were published under Pius V; new and rev. ed., 25 vol., Parma (1852–73, reprinted 1948–50); then in Paris, Vivès ed. (34 vol., 1871–80); in progress, a critical edition, called *Leonina* because it was requested by Leo XIII (1882–   ). Of all his works, the *Summa theologiae* has been the most frequently re-edited. A recent, excellent edition was published by the Institute of Medieval Studies in Montreal, 5 vol. (1941–45).
English translations: The two *Summae*, by the English Dominicans (22 vol., 1911–34); selections, by THOMAS GILBY, *Philosophical Texts* (1951), and *Theological Texts* (1955); and A.C. PEGIS, *Basic Writings of St. Thomas Aquinas* (2 vol., 1945).
A bibliography was published by PIERRE MANDONNET and JEAN DESTREZ, *Bibliographie thomiste*, 2nd ed. (1960); it has been continued by the *Bulletin thomiste* since 1924. Also, V.J. BOURKE, *Thomistic Bibliography, 1920–1940*, as a supplement to vol. 21 of *The Modern Schoolman* (1945, complemented in 1948 and 1950).
Studies: ETIENNE GILSON, *Le Thomisme* (1922; Eng. trans. of the 1st ed., *The Philosophy of St. Thomas Aquinas*, 1924; rev. Eng. trans., *The Christian Philosophy of St. Thomas Aquinas*, 1956); M.D. CHENU, *Introduction à l'étude de Saint Thomas Aquin* (1950; Eng. trans., with revisions, *Toward Understanding St. Thomas*, 1964); M.C. D'ARCY, *St. Thomas Aquinas* (1953). On historical and doctrinal contexts: PIERRE MANDONNET, *Siger de Brabant et l'averroïsme latin au XIII*e *siècle*, 2nd ed. (1911); ETIENNE GILSON, *L'Esprit de la Philosophie médiévale*, 2 pt. (1932; Eng. trans., *The Spirit of Medieval Philosophy*, 1936, reprinted 1965); *History of Christian Philosophy in the Middle Ages* (1955); M.D. CHENU, *La Théologie au XII*e *siècle* (1957; Eng. trans., *Nature, Man and Society in the Twelfth Century*, 1968); FERNAND VAN STEENBERGHEN, *La Philosophie au XIII*e *siècle* (1966).

(M.-D.Ch.)

Thomson, Sir Joseph John

Sir Joseph John Thomson, the British physicist, helped revolutionize the knowledge of atomic structure by discovering the electron, which is a fundamental unit of all matter. This discovery, at the close of the 19th century, had far-reaching consequences for 20th-century science. Moreover, under his leadership the Cavendish Laboratory at Cambridge University achieved distinction as a centre of scientific training and research.

Thomson was born on December 18, 1856, the son of a bookseller in a suburb of Manchester. When he was only 14, he entered Owens College, now the Victoria University of Manchester. He was fortunate in that, in contrast with most colleges at the time, Owens provided some courses in experimental physics. In 1876 he obtained a scholarship at Trinity College, Cambridge, where he remained for the rest of his life. After taking his B.A. degree in mathematics in 1880, the opportunity of doing experimental research drew him to the Cavendish Laboratory. He began also to develop the theory of electromagnetism. As set forth by James Clerk Maxwell, electricity

Thomson, pencil drawing by Walter
Monnington, 1932. In the National Portrait
Gallery, London.
By courtesy of the National Portrait Gallery, London

and magnetism were interrelated; quantitative changes in one produced corresponding changes in the other.

Prompt recognition of Thomson's achievement by the scientific community came in 1884, with his election as a fellow of the Royal Society of London and appointment to the chair of physics at the Cavendish Laboratory. Thomson entered physics at a critical point in its history. Following the great discoveries of the 19th century in electricity, magnetism, and thermodynamics, many physicists in the 1880s were saying that their science was coming to an end like an exhausted mine. By 1900, however, only elderly conservatives held this view, and by 1914 a new physics was in existence, which raised, indeed, more questions than it could answer. The new physics was wildly exciting to those who, lucky enough to be engaged in it, saw its boundless possibilities. Probably not more than a half dozen great physicists were associated with this change. Although not everyone would have listed the same names, the majority of those qualified to judge would have included Thomson.

Discovery of the electron

Thomson's most important line of work, interrupted only for lectures at Princeton University in 1896, was that which led him, in 1897, to the conclusion that all matter, whatever its source, contains particles of the same kind that are much less massive than the atoms of which they form a part. They are now called electrons, although he originally called them corpuscles. His discovery was the result of an attempt to solve a long-standing controversy regarding the nature of cathode rays, which occur when an electric current is driven through a vessel from which most of the air or other gas has been pumped out. Nearly all German physicists of the time held that these visible rays were produced by occurrence in the ether—a weightless substance then thought to pervade all space—but that they were neither ordinary light nor the recently discovered X-rays. British and French physicists, on the other hand, believed that these rays were electrified particles. By applying an improved vacuum technique, Thomson was able to put forward a convincing argument that these rays were composed of particles. Furthermore, these rays seemed to be composed of the same particles, or corpuscles, regardless of what kind of gas carried the electric discharge or what kinds of metals were used as conductors. Thomson's conclusion that the corpuscles were present in all kinds of matter was strengthened during the next three years, when he found that corpuscles with the same properties could be produced in other ways; *e.g.*, from hot metals. Thomson may be described as "the man who split the atom" for the first time, although "chipped" might be a better word, in view of the size and number of electrons. Although some atoms contain many electrons their total mass is never so much as 1/1000 that of the atom.

By the turn of the century most of the scientific world

had fully accepted Thomson's far-reaching discovery. In 1903 he had the opportunity to amplify his views on the behaviour of subatomic particles in natural phenomena when, in his Silliman Lectures at Yale, he suggested a discontinuous theory of light; his hypothesis foreshadowed Einstein's later theory of photons. In 1906 he received the Nobel Prize for Physics for his researches into the electrical conductivity of gases; in 1908 he was knighted; in 1909 he was president of the British Association for the Advancement of Science; and in 1912 he received the Order of Merit.

Work at Cavendish Laboratory

Thomson was, however, by no means a scientific recluse. During his most fruitful years as a scientist, he was administrative head of the highly successful Cavendish Laboratory. (It was there that he met Rose Elizabeth Paget, whom he married in 1890.) He not only administered the research projects but also financed two additions to the laboratory buildings primarily from students' fees, with little support from the university and colleges. Except for its share of a small government grant to the Royal Society to aid all British universities and all branches of science, the Cavendish Laboratory received no other government subsidy, nor were there contributions from charitable corporations or industry. A gift from a devoted staff member made possible the purchase of a small liquid-air machine essential for Thomson's research on positive rays, which greatly increased knowledge of the recently discovered atomic nuclei.

Thomson was, moreover, an outstanding teacher; his importance in physics depended almost as much on the work he inspired in others as on that which he did himself. The group of men he gathered around him between 1895 and 1914 came from all over the world, and after working under him, many accepted professorships abroad. Seven Nobel Prizes were awarded to those who worked under him. Thomson took his teaching duties very seriously: he lectured regularly to elementary classes in the morning and to postgraduates in the afternoon. He considered teaching to be helpful for a researcher, since it required him to reconsider basic ideas that otherwise might have been taken for granted. He never advised a man entering a new research field to begin by reading the work already done. Rather, Thomson thought it wise that he first clarify his own ideas. Then he could safely read the reports of others without having his own views influenced by assumptions that he might find difficult to throw off.

Thomson demonstrated his wide range of interests outside science by his interest in politics, current fiction, drama, university sports, and the nontechnical aspects of science. Although he was not athletic, he was an enthusiastic fan of the Cambridge cricket and rugby teams. But his greatest interest outside physics was in plants. He enjoyed long walks in the countryside, especially in hilly regions near Cambridge, where he searched for rare botanical specimens for his elaborate garden. In 1918 Thomson was made master of Trinity College. This position, in which he remained until his death, gave him the opportunity of meeting young men, most of whom were not interested in science. He enjoyed these meetings and made many new friends.

To a large extent, it was Thomson who made atomic physics a modern science. The studies of nuclear organization that continue even to this day and the further identification of elementary particles all followed his most outstanding accomplishment, his discovery of the electron in 1897. Although this new physics has continued to raise more theoretical questions than can be answered at present, from the start it rapidly gave rise to practical applications in technology and industry. Thomson's interest in science continued unabated until his death in Cambridge on August 30, 1940.

BIBLIOGRAPHY

Works: J.J. THOMSON and G.P. THOMSON, *Conduction of Electricity Through Gases,* 3rd ed., 2 vol. (1928–33); J.J. THOMSON, *Recollections and Reflections* (1936).

Biographies: R.J.S. RAYLEIGH, *Life of Sir J.J. Thomson, O.M.* (1942); G.P. THOMSON, *J.J. Thomson and the Cavendish Laboratory in His Day* (1964).

(G.P.T.)

Thoreau, Henry David

Thoreau's greatness lies in the power of his principal ideas. He had only a few—that a man must follow his conscience regardless of cost, that life was too dear to be wasted in making a living, that the world of woods and streams was good, while the world of streets or crowds was bad. None could be called original. Yet his lucid, provocative writing invited everyone to read and be convinced. To many, the more man's culture has homogenized, the more cogent Thoreau's views have seemed. Their influence has been augmented by his two famous symbolic actions, both movingly described in his prose: his passing a night in jail for civil disobedience and his living for two years in a cabin at Walden Pond, not only to show that a man could be his own master but that doing so could be richly rewarding.

Thoreau, portrait by Samuel Worcester Rowse, 1854. In the Concord Free Public Library, Massachusetts.
By courtesy of the Corporation of the Free Public Library, Concord, Massachusetts

To all appearances, he himself lived a life of bleak failure. His neighbours viewed him with familiarity verging on contempt. He had to pay to have his first book, *A Week on the Concord and Merrimack Rivers*, printed; when it sold a mere 220 copies, the publishers dumped the remaining 700 on his doorstep. His second book (he published only two during his life) was *Walden; or, Life in the Woods*; it fared less badly but still took five years to sell 2,000 copies. When after his death it was proposed that his journals be printed, the local squire, Samuel Hoar, snorted in amazement. For most of his life Thoreau responded to his neighbours with prickly independence; in fact, he called *Walden* his cockcrow to the world. Yet by the time he died he was ready to yield to the world's verdict, saying sadly, for instance, of the *Week*, "Do not suppose that I rate it too high."

Early life.   Thoreau was born on July 12, 1817, in Concord, Massachusetts. Though his family moved the next year, they returned in 1823, not to move again. Even when he grew ambivalent about the village after reaching manhood, it remained his world. For he never grew ambivalent about its lovely setting of woodlands, marshes, streams, and meadows. "I think I could write a poem to be called 'Concord,' " he declared. Little distinguished his family. He was the third child of a feckless small businessman named John Thoreau and his bustling, talky wife, Cynthia Dunbar Thoreau. Such evidence as exists suggests that the family showed an interest in natural history and in books. His parents sent him to infant school, to grammar school, and then in 1828 to Concord Academy. There his playmates thought him standoffish—nicknaming him "the Judge"—but he impressed his teachers and so was permitted to prepare for college.

The curriculum was devised to ready local boys for Harvard. When he graduated from the academy, his favourite subjects were the Greek and Roman classics, natural history, and mathematics; and his favourites they

stayed. At Harvard he made a good record but not an outstanding one. He found at least a few friends, attended a few clubs, and joined in a few rowdy demonstrations. Looking back later, he remarked dryly that he got little benefit from the faculty or from his fellow students, but that the library meant a good deal to him. Graduating in 1837, he searched for a teaching job and secured one in Concord at his old grammar school. No disciplinarian, he lasted two shaky weeks. Though he applied elsewhere, writing to schools as far away as Virginia and upstate New York, he came up with nothing. While applying, he worked for his father in the family pencil-making business. In June 1838 he started a small school with the help of his brother John. Despite its progressive nature, it lasted for three years, until John fell ill.

Years at Harvard

During the summer vacation of 1839, he and John took a canoe trip along the Concord and Merrimack rivers. The experience was beautiful, indeed inspiring. It confirmed him in the opinion that he ought to be not a schoolmaster but a poet of nature. That meant living in nature as well as writing about it; that also meant, as the ancient Greeks had taught him, living a life of integrity. As the 1840s opened, he took up the profession of poet. He struggled to stay in it and succeeded throughout the decade, only to falter in the 1850s.

Friendship with Emerson and the beginning of his literary career.   Sheer chance made his entrance to writing easier, for he came under the benign influence of the essayist and poet Ralph Waldo Emerson, who had settled in Concord during Thoreau's sophomore year at Harvard. By the autumn of 1837, they were becoming friends. Fourteen years older than Thoreau and at the onset of his magnificent prime, Emerson sensed in him a true disciple—that is, one with so much Emersonian self-reliance that he would still be his own man. Thoreau saw in Emerson a guide, a father, and a friend. Early on, he abandoned the guide as needless and began contradicting the father. But he always esteemed the friend.

With his magnetism Emerson attracted others to his home and village. Out of their heady speculations and affirmatives came New England Transcendentalism. In retrospect it was one of the most significant literary movements of 19th-century America, with at least two authors of world stature, Thoreau and Emerson, to its credit. Essentially it combined romanticism with reform. It celebrated the individual rather than the masses, emotion rather than reason, nature rather than man. It conceded that there were two ways of knowing, through the senses and through intuition, but asserted that intuition transcended tuition. Similarly, it conceded that matter and spirit both existed. It asserted, however, that the reality of spirit transcended the reality of matter. It strove for reform yet insisted that reform begin with the individual, not the group or organization. Emerson refused to send a penny to charitable societies, convinced that they were going about reform in exactly the wrong way. Thoreau, before the anti-slavery crusade engulfed his sympathies, coolly advised the Abolitionists to free themselves before they tried to free the Negro slave.

Onset of New England Transcendentalism

In Emerson's company Thoreau's hope of becoming a poet and managing to live as one often looked not only proper but feasible. Late in 1837 he began a journal that covered thousands of pages before he scrawled the final entry two months before his death. He soon polished some of his old college essays and composed new and better ones as well. He penned some poems—a good many in fact—for several years. Captained by Emerson, the Transcendentalists started a magazine, *The Dial*; and the inaugural issue, dated July 1840, carried Thoreau's poem "Sympathy" and his scrap of essay on the Roman poet Aulus Persius Flaccus.

The Dial published more of Thoreau's poems and then, in July 1842, the first of his outdoor essays, "Natural History of Massachusetts." Though disguised as a book review, it showed that a nature writer of distinction was in the making. Then followed more lyrics, and fine ones, such as "To the Maiden in the East." There were also some translations from the Greek poets Aeschylus and Anacreon, some excerpts from Oriental scriptures (fore-

Thoreau's one romance

casting his interest in Oriental philosophy), and another nature essay, remarkably felicitous, "A Winter Walk." *The Dial* died with the issue of April 1844. Before it expired, however, it let Thoreau publish a richer variety of writing than any other magazine ever would.

By then, he had channelled his emotional life into his writing. His one romance had come in 1840, when he wanted to marry an attractive visitor to Concord named Ellen Sewall. She said yes, but her father uttered a grating no. Some of Thoreau's best poems and some highly charged prose resulted from the romance. "To the Maiden in the East," for example, is surely about Ellen. For two periods, 1841–43 and 1847–48, he stayed mostly at the Emerson house, where he found in Emerson's wife, Lidian, a sympathetic older woman he could dream of loving. Otherwise he was married to his writing.

In spite of Emerson's heady encouragement to live as a poet, Thoreau sometimes had to live as a workman. He made several reluctant attempts to find a job in the early 1840s. No one could have been more generous than Emerson in inviting Thoreau to live at his home with a minimum of duties and a maximum of freedom, and the invitation seemed to solve the problem. Yet Thoreau grew restless. His restlessness was accentuated by grief over the death in January 1842 of his brother John, who died of lockjaw after cutting his finger. Henry, too, soon suffered from lockjaw symptoms, failing to recover until the end of April. By the following May, he was staying on Staten Island as tutor in the household of Emerson's brother, William. The idea was that he could teach and write and, in the intervals, cultivate the New York literary market. The teaching and writing went indifferently, however, and the effort to conquer New York failed. "My bait will not tempt the rats," he wrote sourly. By the end of 1843 he was home again.

Move to Walden Pond. Back he went to making pencils and grinding graphite. By early 1845 he felt more restless than ever, until he decided to take up an idea of Stearns Wheeler's. Wheeler, a Harvard classmate, had once built a waterside hut, where he could loaf or read, and Thoreau had spent a short time there. In the spring he picked a spot by Walden Pond, two miles from Concord, on land Emerson owned. With Emerson's permission he chopped down some of its pines, hewed the timbers, and with the help of friends fashioned a small cabin. On July 4, his personal Independence Day, he moved in.

From the outset the move gave him profound satisfaction. It provided him with enough time to ponder what the world was really like. With his "Realometer," he said, he could now ascertain whether the world was basically good or bad, noble or mean. The move provided him with time to meet his simple wants. He could easily grow his own beans, never mind if he dined out often. And, most valuable, it provided him with time to write.

He stayed for two years. Before the first one ended, he finished the full draft of *A Week on the Concord and Merrimack Rivers* (published 1849). Before the second was over, he finished the initial draft of *Walden; or, Life in the Woods* (published 1854), which announced that the world was good. In between, he composed some lively essays, including a long one on the British writer Thomas Carlyle, and hundreds of pages of journals. His stay at Walden proved to be his most productive period.

Still, he was by no means the literary hermit that tradition has pictured him. He entertained many a guest—in fact he titled a chapter of *Walden* "Visitors"—and many a day he walked to Concord. In the summer of 1847 Emerson invited him to stay with Lidian and the children again, while Emerson himself went to Europe. Thoreau accepted. On September 6, 1847, hopeful that he had more lives to live, he left his cabin forever.

Midway in his Walden sojourn he spent his night in jail. On an evening in July 1846, he was accosted by Sam Staples, the constable and tax gatherer. Sam asked him amiably to pay his poll tax, which he had omitted paying for several years. He declined and Sam locked him up. The next morning a still unidentified lady, perhaps his aunt, Maria, paid the tax. Thoreau reluctantly

emerged, did an errand, and then went huckleberrying. A single night, he decided, was enough to make his point.

Civil disobedience

His point was that he could not support a government that endorsed slavery and waged an imperialist war against Mexico. He was becoming involved; he was shifting from his first position that reform was mainly a matter for the individual. His imprisonment set Concord tongues wagging, and so he concluded that justifying his action would make an instructive lecture for the Concord Lyceum. He gave it twice, ultimately titling it "Civil Disobedience," and then his bluestocking friend Elizabeth Peabody printed it, in May 1849, in a volume she edited called *Aesthetic Papers*. Understandably, it was ignored. But by the end of the 19th century it had begun to make itself felt, and, by the middle of the 20th, it had an eager audience. To many, its message still sounds timely: there is a higher law than the civil one, and the higher law must be followed even if a penalty ensues. So does its consequence: "Under a government which imprisons any unjustly, the true place for a just man is also a prison."

Late life and works. When Thoreau left Walden, he passed the peak of his career, and his life lost much of its illumination for today. In spite of his hopefulness on leaving, he would complain by July 1852, "My life is almost altogether outward, all shell and no tender kernel." Slowly his Transcendentalism drained away. He turned naturalist and surveyor. He collected botanical specimens for himself and reptilian ones for Harvard, jotting down their descriptions in his journal. He established himself in his neighbourhood as a sound man with rod and transit. He spent more time in the family business; after his father's death he took it over entirely. He made excursions to the Maine woods, to Cape Cod, and to Canada, using the trips as raw material for three series of magazine articles: "Ktaadn [sic] and the Maine Woods," in *The Union Magazine* in 1848; "Excursion to Canada," in *Putnam's Monthly* in 1853; and "Cape Cod," in *Putnam's* in 1855.

When he became less of a Transcendentalist he became more of an activist. As the 1850s jolted along he became, above all, a dedicated Abolitionist. As much as anyone in Concord, he helped to speed fleeing slaves north on the so-called Underground Railroad. He lectured and wrote against slavery, with "Slavery in Massachusetts," a lecture delivered in 1854, as his hardest indictment. In the Abolitionist John Brown he found a father figure beside whom Emerson paled; the fiery old fanatic became his ideal. By now Thoreau was in poor health; and when Brown's raid on Harpers Ferry failed and he was hanged, Thoreau suffered a psychic shock that probably hastened his own death. He died, apparently of tuberculosis, on May 6, 1862. Yet it should be added that, according to Sam Staples' testimony, he died in peace.

MAJOR WORKS

PHILOSOPHICAL AND POLITICAL: *A Week on the Concord and Merrimack Rivers* (1849); "Resistance to Civil Government" (first published 1849, then as "Civil Disobedience" in *A Yankee in Canada* (1866); *Walden; or, Life in the Woods* (1854); "Life Without Principle," published posthumously in *The Atlantic Monthly* (1863).

TRAVEL AND NATURAL HISTORY: "Walking" (1862); *Excursions* (1863); *The Maine Woods* (1864); *Cape Cod* (1865); *A Yankee in Canada with Anti-Slavery and Reform Papers* (1866); *Early Spring in Massachusetts* (1881); *Summer* (1884); *Winter* (1888); *Autumn* (1892); *Poems of Nature* (1895).

OTHER WORKS: *Letters to Various Persons*, ed. by Ralph Waldo Emerson (1865); *Familiar Letters of Henry David Thoreau*, ed. by Frank B. Sanborn (1865, enlarged 1894); *Journal* (1906).

BIBLIOGRAPHY. FRANCIS H. ALLEN (comp.), *A Bibliography of Henry David Thoreau* (1908), the prime source up to 1908, continued by WILLIAM WHITE (comp.), *A Henry David Thoreau Bibliography, 1908–1937* (1939); and PHILIP E. BURNHAM and CARVEL COLLINS (comps.), "Contribution to a Bibliography of Thoreau, 1938–1945," *Bulletin of Bibliography*, 19:16–18, 37–39 (1946). Current bibliography appears in each issue of the quarterly *Thoreau Society Bulletin*, cumulated in *A Bibliography of the Thoreau Society Bulletin Bibliographies, 1941–1969*, ed. by WALTER HARDING (1971). The chief storehouses of Thoreau manuscripts and other materials are the Berg Collection in the New York Public Library; the Concord, Massachusetts Public Library; the Harvard University Library; the Henry E. Huntington Library in San Marino, California; and the J. Pierpont Morgan Library in New York.

Editions and correspondence: The Writings of Henry Thoreau, 20 vol. (1906), is the standard "Walden" collection of his finished work and journal, to be replaced by the new edition being prepared by a group of Thoreau specialists. The *Collected Poems of Henry Thoreau*, ed. by CARL BODE (1943; rev. ed., 1964), is the standard collection of the poems. *The Correspondence of Henry David Thoreau*, ed. by WALTER HARDING and CARL BODE (1958), is the standard collection, containing all available letters to Thoreau as well as from him. *Consciousness in Concord*, with notes and commentary by PERRY MILLER (1958), is a small but previously missing part of the journal, edited exhaustively by Miller.

Biography and criticism: The definitive life is WALTER HARD-ING, *The Days of Henry Thoreau* (1965). Its still useful predecessor is HENRY S. CANBY, *Thoreau* (1939). The best general critical study is SHERMAN PAUL, *The Shores of America: Thoreau's Inward Exploration* (1958). The prime study of *Walden* alone is CHARLES R. ANDERSON, *The Magic Circle of Walden* (1968).

(Ca.B.)

Thought Processes, Theories of

In everyday language the word thinking covers several distinct psychological activities. It is sometimes a synonym for "tending to believe," especially with less than full confidence. ("I think that it will rain, but I am not sure.") At other times it denotes attentiveness ("I did it without thinking"); or it denotes whatever is in consciousness, especially if it refers to something outside the immediate environment. ("It made me think of my old grandmother.") In the sense on which psychologists have concentrated, thinking is intellectual exertion aimed at finding an answer to a question or a means of achieving a desirable practical goal.

The psychology of thought processes concerns itself with activities similar to those usually attributed to the inventor, the mathematician, or the chess player; but psychologists have not reached agreement on any definition or characterization of thinking. For some it is a matter of modifying "cognitive structures" (*i.e.*, perceptual representations of the world or parts of the world). Others view thinking as internal problem-solving behaviour, as a means of arriving at adaptive behaviour (*i.e.*, behaviour with rewarding or biologically valuable consequences) through manipulation of symbols.

Perhaps the most satisfactory provisional conception of thinking is one that applies the term to any sequence of covert symbolic responses (*i.e.*, occurrences within the human organism that can serve to represent absent events). If such a sequence is aimed at the solution of a specific problem and fulfills the criteria for reasoning, it is called directed thinking. Reasoning, of which rudimentary forms can be inferred to occur in infrahuman mammals, is a process of piecing together the results of two or more distinct previous learning experiences to produce a new pattern of behaviour. Directed thinking contrasts with other symbolic sequences that have different functions; *e.g.*, the autistic (or free-associative) thinking of the daydream or the psychoanalytic session and the simple recall (mnemonic thinking) of a chain of past events.

In the past, psychologists and laymen often identified thinking with conscious experiences. But as the scientific study of behaviour came to be recognized generally as the task of psychology, the limitations of introspection as a source of data have become widely apparent. It thus has become more usual to treat thought processes as intervening variables or constructs with properties that must be inferred from relations between two sets of observable events. These empirically available events are inputs (stimuli, present and past) and outputs (responses, including bodily movements and speech). For many psychologists such intervening variables are of interest as aids in dealing with and in making sense of the immensely complicated network of associations between stimulus conditions and responses, the analysis of which otherwise would be prohibitively cumbersome. Others are con-

cerned, rather, with identifying cognitive (or mental) structures that are held to underlie a human being's observable behaviour without his necessarily being aware of them.

ELEMENTS OF THOUGHT

The prominent use of words in thinking ("silent speech") has encouraged the belief, especially among behaviourist and neobehaviourist psychologists, that to think is to string together linguistic elements subvocally. Early experiments (largely in the 1930s) by E. Jacobson and L.W. Max revealed that evidence of thinking commonly is accompanied by electrical activity in the muscles of the thinker's organs of articulation. This work later was extended with the help of more sophisticated electromyographic equipment, notably by A.N. Sokolov. It became apparent, however, that the muscular phenomena are not the actual vehicles of thinking but represent rather a means of facilitating the appropriate activities in the brain when an intellectual task is particularly exacting. The identification of thinking with speech was assailed by L.S. Vygotski and by J. Piaget, both of whom saw the origins of human reasoning in the ability of children to assemble nonverbal acts into effective and flexible combinations. These theorists insisted that thinking and speaking arise independently, although they acknowledged the profound interdependence of these functions, once they have reached fruition.

Following different approaches, a 19th-century Russian physiologist (I.M. Sechenov), the U.S. founder of the behaviourist school of psychology (J.B. Watson), and a 20th-century Swiss developmental psychologist (Piaget) all arrived at the conclusion that the activities that serve as elements of thinking are internalized or fractional versions of motor responses; that is, the elements are considered to be attenuated or curtailed variants of neuromuscular processes that, if they were not subjected to partial inhibition, would give rise to visible bodily movements.

Sensitive instruments can indeed detect faint activity in various parts of the body other than the organs of speech; *e.g.*, in a person's limbs when the movement is thought of or imagined without actually taking place. Such findings have prompted statements to the effect that we think with the whole body and not only with the brain, or that "thought is simply *behaviour*—verbal or nonverbal, covert or overt" (B.F. Skinner). The logical outcome of these and similar statements was the peripheralist view (Watson, C.L. Hull) that thinking depends on events in the musculature, feeding proprioceptive impulses back to influence subsequent events in the central nervous system, ultimately to interact with external stimuli in determining the selection of a course of overt action. There is, however, evidence that thinking is not precluded by administering drugs that suppress all muscular activity. Furthermore, it has been pointed out (*e.g.*, by K.S. Lashley) that thinking, like other more-or-less skilled activities, often proceeds so quickly that there is simply not enough time for impulses to be transmitted from the central nervous system to a peripheral organ and back again between consecutive steps. So the centralist view that thinking consists of events confined to the brain (though often accompanied by widespread activity in the rest of the body) was gaining ground in the third quarter of the 20th century. Nevertheless, each of these neural events can be regarded both as a response (to an external stimulus or to an earlier neurally mediated thought or combination of thoughts) and as a stimulus (evoking a subsequent thought or a motor response).

The elements of thinking are classifiable as "symbols" in accordance with the conception of the sign process ("semiotic") that has grown out of the work of some philosophers (*e.g.*, C.S. Peirce, C.K. Ogden, I.A. Richards, and C.R. Morris) and of psychologists specializing in learning (*e.g.*, C.L. Hull, N.E. Miller, O.H. Mowrer, and C.E. Osgood). The gist of this conception is that a stimulus event x can be regarded as a sign representing (or "standing for") another event y if x evokes some part, but not all, of the behaviour (external and internal) that would have been evoked by y if it had been present. When a

Directed, autistic, and mnemonic thinking

Thinking as a brain function

stimulus that qualifies as a sign results from the behaviour of an organism for which it acts as a sign, it is called a "symbol." The "stimulus-producing responses" that are said to make up thought processes (as when one thinks of something to eat) are prime examples.

This treatment, favoured by psychologists of the stimulus-response (S-R) or neo-associationist current, contrasts with that of the various cognitivist or neorationalist theories. Rather than regarding the components of thinking as derivatives of verbal or nonverbal motor acts (and thus subject to laws of learning and performance that apply to learned behaviour in general), adherents of such theories see them as unique central processes, governed by principles that are peculiar to them. These theorists attach overriding importance to the so-called structures in which "cognitive" elements are organized. Unlike the S-R theorists who feel compunction about invoking unobservable intermediaries between stimulus and response (except where there is clearly no other alternative), the cognitivists tend to see inferences, applications of rules, representations of external reality, and other ingredients of thinking at work in even the simplest forms of learned behaviour.

The Gestalt school of psychologists held the constituents of thinking to be of essentially the same nature as the perceptual patterns that the nervous system constructs out of sensory excitations. After mid-20th century, analogies with computer operations acquired great currency; in consequence, thinking frequently is described in terms of storage, retrieval, and transmission of items of information. The information in question is held to be freely translatable from one "coding" to another without impairing its functions. The physical clothing it assumes is regarded as being of minor importance. What matters in this approach is how events are combined and what other combinations might have occurred instead.

THE THOUGHT PROCESS

Laws of association: contiguity, similarity

According to the classical empiricist-associationist view, the succession of ideas or images in a train of thought is determined by the laws of association. Although additional associative laws were proposed from time to time, two invariably were recognized. The law of association by contiguity states that the sensation or idea of a particular object tends to evoke the idea of something that has often been encountered together with it. The law of association by similarity states that the sensation or idea of a particular object tends to evoke the idea of something that is similar to it. The early behaviourists, beginning with Watson, espoused essentially the same formulation but with some important modifications. The elements of the process were conceived not as conscious ideas but as fractional or incipient motor responses, each producing its proprioceptive stimulus. Association by contiguity and similarity were identified by these behaviourists with the Pavlovian principles of conditioning and generalization.

The Würzburg school, under the leadership of Külpe, saw the prototype of directed thinking in the "constrained-association" experiment, in which the subject has to supply a word bearing a specified relation to a stimulus word that is presented to him (e.g., an opposite to an adjective, or the capital of a country). Their introspective researches led them to conclude that the emergence of the required element depends jointly on the immediately preceding element and on some kind of "determining tendency" such as Aufgabe ("awareness of task") or "representation of the goal." These latter factors were held to impart a direction to the thought process and to restrict its content to relevant material. Their role was analogous to that of motivational factors—"drive stimuli," "fractional anticipatory goal responses"—in the later neobehaviouristic accounts of reasoning (and of behaviour in general) produced by C.L. Hull and his followers.

Külpe, Hull, and Selz

Hull's theory resembled G.E. Müller's earlier "constellation theory" of constrained association. Hull held that one particular response will occur and overcome its competitors because it is associated both with the cue stimulus (which may be the immediately preceding thought process or an external event) and with the motivational condition (task, drive stimulus) and is thus evoked with more

strength than are elements associated only with the one or the other. O. Selz pointed out that in many situations this kind of theory would imply the occurrence of errors as often as correct answers to questions. It thus was untenable. Selz contended that response selection depends rather on a process of "complex completion" that is set in motion by an "anticipatory schema," which includes a representation of both the cue stimulus and the relation that the element to be supplied must bear to the cue stimulus. The correct answer is associated with the schema as a whole and not with its components separately. Selz's complex completion resembles the "eduction of correlates" that C.E. Spearman saw as a primary constituent of intellectual functioning, its complement being "eduction of relations," that is, recognition of a relation when two elements are presented.

The determination of each thought element by the whole configuration of factors in the situation and by the network of relations linking them was stressed still more strongly in the 1920s and 1930s by the Gestalt psychologists on the basis of W. Köhler's experiments on "insightful" problem solving by chimpanzees, and on the basis of later experiments by M. Wertheimer and of K. Duncker on human thinking. They pointed out that the solution to a problem commonly requires an unprecedented response or pattern of responses that hardly could be attributed to simple associative reproduction of past behaviour or experiences. For them, the essence of thinking lay in sudden perceptual restructuring or reorganization, akin to the abrupt changes in appearance of an ambiguous visual figure.

Thinking as perceptual reorganization

The Gestalt theory has had a deep and far-reaching impact, especially in drawing attention to the ability of the thinker to discover creative, innovative ways of coping with situations that differ from any that have been encountered before. This theory, however, has been criticized for underestimating the contribution of prior learning and for not going beyond rudimentary attempts to classify and analyze the structures that it deems so important. Later discussions of the systems in which items of information and intellectual operations are organized have made fuller use of the resources of logic and mathematics. Merely to name them, they include the "psychologic" of Piaget, the simulation of human thinking with the help of computer programs using list-processing languages and tree structures (H.A. Simon and A. Newell), and extensions of Hull's notion of the "habit-family hierarchy" (I. Maltzman).

A further development of consequence is a growing recognition that the essential components of the thought process, the events that keep it moving in fruitful directions, are not words, images, or other symbols representing stimulus situations; rather, they are the operations that cause each of these representations to be succeeded by the next, in conformity with restrictions imposed by the problem or aim of the moment. In other words, directed thinking can reach a solution only by going through a properly ordered succession of "legitimate steps." These steps might be representations of realizable physicochemical changes, modifications of logical or mathematical formulas that are permitted by rules of inference, or legal moves in a game of chess. This conception of the train of thinking as a sequence of rigorously controlled transformations is buttressed by the theoretical arguments of Sechenov and of Piaget, the results of the Würzburg experiments, and the lessons of computer simulation.

Implicit trial and error

Early in the 20th century both E. Claparède and John Dewey suggested that directed thinking proceeds by "implicit trial-and-error." That is to say, it resembles the process whereby laboratory animals confronted with a novel problem situation try out one response after another until they sooner or later hit upon a response that leads to success. In thinking, however, the trials were said to take the form of internal responses (imagined or conceptualized courses of action, directions of symbolic search); once attained, a train of thinking that constitutes a solution often can be recognized as such without the necessity of implementation through action, followed by sampling of external consequences. This kind of theory, popular among behaviourists and neobehaviourists, was stoutly opposed by the Gestalt school whose insight theory stressed discovery of a solution as a whole and in a flash.

The divergence between these theories appears, however, to represent a false dichotomy. The protocols of Köhler's chimpanzee experiments and of the rather similar experiments performed later under Pavlov's auspices show that insight typically is preceded by a period of groping and of misguided attempts at solution that soon are abandoned. On the other hand, even the trial-and-error behaviour of an animal in a simple selective-learning situation does not consist of a completely blind and random sampling of the behaviour of which the learner is capable. Rather, it consists of responses that very well might have succeeded if the circumstances had been slightly different.

Heuristic (probabilistic) thinking; computer simulation

A. Newell, J.C. Shaw, and H.A. Simon pointed out the indispensability in creative human thinking, as in its computer simulations, of what they call "heuristics." A large number of possibilities may have to be examined, but the search is organized heuristically in such a way that the directions most likely to lead to success are explored first. Means of ensuring that a solution will occur within a reasonable time, certainly much faster than by random hunting, include adoption of successive subgoals and working backward from the final goal (the formula to be proved, the state of affairs to be brought about).

MOTIVATIONAL ASPECTS OF THINKING

The problem to be taken up and the point at which the search for a solution will begin are customarily prescribed by the investigator for a subject participating in an experiment on thinking (or by the programmer for a computer). Thus, prevailing techniques of inquiry in the psychology of thinking have invited neglect of the motivational aspects of thinking. The conditions that determine when the person will begin to think in preference to some other activity, what he will think about, what direction his thinking will take, and when he will regard his search for a solution as successfully terminated (or abandon it as not worth pursuing further) barely are beginning to attract investigation. Although much thinking is aimed at practical ends, special motivational problems are raised by "disinterested" thinking, in which the discovery of an answer to a question is a source of satisfaction in itself.

In the views of the Gestalt school and of F.C. Bartlett, the initiation and direction of thinking are governed by recognition of a "disequilibrium" or "gap" in an intellectual structure. Similarly, Piaget's notion of "equilibration" as a process impelling advance from less equilibrated structures, fraught with uncertainty and inconsistency, toward better equilibrated structures that overcome these imperfections, was introduced to explain the child's progressive intellectual development in general. Piaget's approach may also be applicable to specific episodes of thinking. For computer specialists, the detection of a mismatch between the formula that the program so far has produced and some formula or set of requirements that define a solution is what impels continuation of the search and determines the direction it will follow.

Neobehaviourists (like psychoanalysts) have made much of secondary reward value and stimulus generalization; i.e., the tendency of a stimulus pattern to become a source of satisfaction if it resembles or has frequently accompanied some form of biological gratification. The insufficiency of this kind of explanation becomes apparent, however, when the importance of novelty, surprise, complexity, incongruity, ambiguity, and uncertainty is considered. Inconsistency between beliefs, between items of incoming sensory information, or between one's belief and an item of sensory information evidently can be a source of discomfort impelling a search for resolution through reorganization of belief systems or through selective acquisition of new information.

The motivational effects of such factors have been receiving more attention since the middle of the 20th century, mainly because of the pervasive role they have been found to play in exploratory behaviour, play, and aesthetics. But their role in all forms of thinking also began to be appreciated and studied in relation to curiosity, conflict,

and uncertainty. As evidence accumulates about the brain processes that underlie fluctuations in motivational state, and as psychophysiological equipment with which such fluctuations can be monitored comes in for increasing use, future advances in the theory of thinking are likely to correct the present imbalance and give due prominence to motivational questions.

BIBLIOGRAPHY.   R. THOMSON, *The Psychology of Thinking* (1959), a readable summary account of experimental approaches to thinking; P.C. WASON and P.N. JOHNSON-LAIRD (eds.), *Thinking and Reasoning* (1968), a more recent collection of reprinted readings by many of the leading contributors to the field; G. HUMPHREY, *Thinking: An Introduction to its Experimental Psychology* (1951), a scholarly and thorough critical review of all but the most current theoretical treatments. The most influential directions in 20th-century theorizing may be found in M. WERTHEIMER, *Productive Thinking*, ed. by S.E. ASCH *et al.* (1945), on Gestalt theory; O.H. MOWRER, *Learning Theory and the Symbolic Processes* (1960), on S-R or neo-associationist behaviour theory; A. NEWELL and H.A. SIMON, "Computer Simulation of Human Thinking," *Science*, 134:2011–2017 (December 22, 1961); JEAN PIAGET, *La psychologie de l'intelligence* (1947, Eng. trans. 1950), a compressed account of the first 20 years of this author's work; F.C. BARTLETT, *Thinking* (1958), the treatment of thinking as a form of skill, sometimes known as the "information-processing" approach; and L.S. VYGOTSKI, *Thought and Language* (1962; orig. pub. in Russian, 1934), the fountainhead of most Soviet research on the topic. D.E. BERLYNE, *Structure and Direction in Thinking* (1965), reviews experimental findings, discusses crucial problems, and attempts a synthesis that draws on S-R behaviour theory, Piaget's ideas, and modern Soviet research, among other developments.

(D.E.B.)

Thought Processes, Types of

Thought processes are inner (private or covert) activities of people that may be elicited by stimuli arising intrinsically (from within the body) or extrinsically (from the surrounding environment). While intrinsic stimulation (*e.g.*, feeling sad) may exert a major influence at a particular time, the course of thinking in general depends on stimuli from all sources. The practice of considering behaviour by specifying the instigating origin (stimulus) and the observable act (response) has led some psychologists to identify thinking as a mediating (or intervening) activity, or, in other words, as an unobservable activity that links (or mediates) observable stimuli and responses. The public, scientific study of thinking thus is concerned with investigating the properties and effects of mediation (see THOUGHT PROCESSES, THEORIES OF).

There is no sharp distinction between thinking and other aspects of covert (private, unobservable) behaviour, such as remembering or perceiving, the differences seeming to be largely those of degree. Thinking is characterized to some degree as an organizing function that produces "new" information derived from the original data of experience. In remembering, the information carried by experience is stored for later retrieval. To perceive is to interpret or give meaning to an immediate sensory stimulus. Since covert representations of experience (mediating and symbolic activities) seem to enter into all aspects of observable behaviour, psychologists search for principles that govern cognitive processes (the activities of knowing) in general.

Expressive and disciplined thinking

The spectrum or range of thinking reflects the relative intensity of intrinsic and extrinsic influences. When intrinsic processes operate strongly and are relatively free of environmental constraints, a person thinks expressively: he imagines, fantasizes, dreams, hallucinates, or has delusions. As his thinking becomes dominated by external stimuli, he tends to become more logical, directed, disciplined; the process then is identified by such terms as judging, conceptualizing, and problem solving.

Sigmund Freud recognized this distinction between expressive and disciplined function in contrasting what he called primary and secondary process thinking. Freud held that one's impulses and wishes arise from unconscious sources and determine primary process thinking, while the pursuit of exterior objects and goals determines secondary process thinking, which he associated with planning, rational control, and continuous organization. These two aspects of thinking also can be called, respectively, autistic (determined by subjective emotional–motivational activities) and realistic (oriented toward the external environment). The terms are not mutually exclusive but rather correspond to relative degrees of influence of different conditions that enter into thinking.

In a broad sense, then, activities called thinking are internally adaptive responses to intrinsic and extrinsic stimuli; not only do they express inner impulses but they also serve to generate environmentally effective, goal-seeking behaviour.

REALISTIC THINKING

Convergent thought processes. It has been proposed that certain forms of thinking call on one's abilities to assemble and organize information. The result of such thinking satisfies a defined goal in the achievement of an effective solution to a problem. These forms are called convergent thinking and become apparent when situations arise in which one's ability to cope with a task demands resources beyond the explicit stimuli presented; *i.e.*, converges the components of one's past and present experience in organizing or directing one's response.

Experimental approaches. In studying thinking experimentally, investigators often use standardized tasks that have measurable outcomes; for example, a human subject (say, a young child) may be shown three levers—one black, the other two white. Initially, the standard task may be for the child to discover that for pulling the black lever he will receive some reward (perhaps something good to eat) but that for pulling either white lever he will get no reward at all. Orderly procedures are established under which experimental changes can be introduced to observe their effects on the thinker's performance. The results are compared with those obtained under a standard control condition without the changes.

Among the variables that can be manipulated are the amount of information available to the individual (*e.g.*, the black lever may also be illuminated); the kind or degree of incentives under which he works (*e.g.*, a larger or better tasting reward); the order or arrangement of objects (*e.g.*, black lever in the middle or on the right); the instructions provided; the subject's familiarity or degree of prior experience with the task; and the stress under which he functions, such as punishment for mistakes or the threat of failure. The thinker's personality characteristics provide another set of variables for study; for example, subjects who typically exhibit high levels of anxiety can be compared in their task performance with those who ordinarily show little anxiety; or the performance of a person who shows a compelling need to achieve success can be compared with that of a person who exhibits strong fears of failure.

Conditions that affect realistic thinking

Research results indicate that any condition that increases the complexity of a task requiring convergent thinking tends to make the solution more difficult and time-consuming. The more multiple choices (*e.g.*, ten levers instead of three) a thinker is offered, the more difficult the solution of the task is likely to be. Irrelevant items of information, such as the illumination of all levers, may complicate a problem; and as irrelevant data become more numerous or as relevant information becomes less accessible to or discoverable by the thinker, the solution becomes more difficult.

Finding a solution is helped by providing the thinker with cues, guidelines, rules, or other appropriate ways of orienting himself toward the problem (*e.g.*, he may be pointed toward the right lever). Performance is uncertain to the degree that the individual must discover these directions by his own efforts. When separate cues must be combined (*e.g.*, the colour of the lever and the presence or absence of illumination), the more suitable they are for the required relationship, the more efficient the process of solution tends to be.

Individual traits and factors. Conditions that increase the thinker's motivation, such as incentives and special instructions, tend to improve performance. A person's response to these conditions, however, depends on his personality characteristics; very anxious people typically show particularly impaired performance when the task is difficult or stressful. An important consideration is the set (or expectation) of the person; a person's tendency toward rigidity—inability to adapt readily to changing conditions of the task—is likely to have adverse effects on his performance. Instruction or special training that aids one in overcoming his prior sets fosters his ability to achieve correct solution.

Realistic thinking may be aided or hindered by the individual's strategies and cognitive or perceptual style. Such characteristics include the way a person attends to and uses sensory information; he may, for example, focus on inessentials, may fail to observe details accurately, or may be disturbed by complexities in the task stimuli. Also important to convergent thinking are the individual's abilities to analyze and to synthesize sensory information.

Realistic thinking tends to be elicited when the individual perceives no obvious or immediate path to a desired goal. It is likely to begin with his recognition of a problem—otherwise, his behaviour would simply indicate the operation of habits or the automatic production of responses. Realistic thinking continues with one's consideration of alternatives, each marked by some uncertainty or risk. He next begins processing information (including pertinent past experience) by analyzing, combining, and organizing available and potential resources for reaching his goal. In the final phase of the process he produces a response; it may be a wrong solution, a partial solution, or a correct solution. Recycling of these phases (recognition, considering alternatives, processing data, and responding) may continue in a complex way until the goal finally is reached or until the process ends in failure.

Phases of realistic thinking

The explicitness of these phases varies with the complexity of the task, as well as with the problem-solving skills of the individual. In this connection, the individual may show evidence of "learning how to learn"; that is, he may exhibit a progressive increase in skill as he encounters a series of similar problems.

Judgment. A simple form of realistic thinking that lends itself well to controlled experimentation is inferred from one's ability to discriminate discrete objects or items of information (*e.g.*, distinguishing a lion from a tiger). The outcome is a judgment, and the process may be called decision making. The availability of information, the rate at which it is presented, the set (expectancy) of the judge, and the number of alternatives available to him influence the efficiency of his judgment. Redundancy (or surplus) of information facilitates judgment; for example, the lion may be discriminated on the basis of a number of different sensory cues: he is tan or brown, he lacks stripes, he has a mane, and so on.

Within what is called the general theory of adaptation level, the decision-making response is considered to be a weighted average of various stimuli: focal (the specific sensory properties of the lion and tiger), contextual (the background in which they are observed), and residual (such intrinsic or experiential factors as memory for other brown or striped objects). Variations in one or more of these three types of stimuli shift the judge's decision in one direction or another in relation to his immediately preceding judgment.

Concept attainment. A more complex form of realistic thinking is inferred when an individual is asked to identify or use a *class* of items, as in selecting several different kinds of triangle from an array of other geometric figures. The individual may proceed to link together in his thinking a newly experienced group of objects according to one or more of their common properties. He thus may be able to give them a general name, as in first learning the meaning of the term triangle, or he may determine whether a newly given object fits a category he already knows. Physical objects are multidimensional; that is, they may vary in shape, size, colour, their location in relation to other objects, their emotional significance, or their connotative meaning. How a person identifies such dimensions, develops hypotheses (or tentative conclusions) about which of the specific dimensions define a class, arrives at the rules of class membership, and how

Linking by common properties

he tests various hypotheses all reflect his ability to grasp concepts. Successful performance in all these processes leads to his formulation of pertinent rules based on his ability to classify specific items (see CONCEPT FORMATION).

Problem solving. Still more complex forms of realistic thinking seem to occur when tasks are presented in which the goal is impossible (or very difficult) to achieve directly. In such situations, people commonly appear to pass through intermediate stages of exploring and organizing their resources; indeed, one may first need to exert himself in understanding the problem itself before he can begin to seek possible directions toward a solution. Familiar examples of problem-solving tasks include anagrams (*e.g.*, rearrange "lpepa" to spell "apple"); mathematical problems; mechanical puzzles; verbal "brain teasers" (*e.g.*, Is it legal for a man to marry his widow's sister?); and, in a more practical sense, design and construction problems. Also of interest are issues of human relations, games, and questions pertinent to economics and politics.

Trial and error. Problem-solving activity falls broadly into two categories: one emphasizes simple trial and error; the other requires some degree of insight. In trial and error, the individual proceeds mainly by exploring and manipulating elements of the problem situation in an effort to sort out possibilities and to run across steps that might carry him closer to the goal. This behaviour is most likely to be observed when the problem solver lacks advance knowledge about the character of the solution, or when no single rule seems to underlie the solution. Trial-and-error activity is not necessarily overt (as in one's observable attempts to fit together the pieces of a mechanical puzzle); it may be implicit or vicarious as well, the individual reflecting on the task and symbolically testing possibilities by thinking about them.

Solutions through insight. In striving toward insight, a person tends to exhibit a strong orientation toward understanding *principles* that might bear on the solution sought. The person actively considers what is required by the problem, noting how its elements seem to be interrelated, and seeks some rule that might lead directly to the goal. The insightful thinker is likely to centre on the problem to understand what is needed, to take the time to organize his resources, and to recentre on the problem (reinterpret the situation) in applying any principle that seems to hold promise.

Understanding, organizing, and applying principle

Direction and flexibility characterize insightful problem solving. The thinker directs or guides his steps toward solution according to some plan; he exhibits flexibility in his ability to modify or to adapt procedures as required by his plan and in altering the plan itself. Both characteristics are influenced by the thinker's attitudes and by environmental conditions. If, for example, the task is to empty a length of glass tubing of water (without breaking it) by removing wax plugs about a half-inch up the tube from each end, and the only potential tools are a few objects ordinarily found on a desk top, the usual appearance and functions of such common objects may make it difficult for the problem solver to see how they can be adapted to fit task requirements. If a paper clip is perceived as holding a sheaf of papers in the usual way, such perception would tend to interfere with the individual's ability to employ the principle that the clip's shape could be changed: straightened out for use in poking a hole in the wax.

Formal, logical processes. A special form of problem solving employs formal, systematic, logical thinking. The thinker develops a series of propositions, often as postulates; *e.g.*, the shortest distance between two points is a straight line. He builds a structure of arguments in which statements are consistent with each other in reaching some goal, such as defining the area of a triangle. This kind of logical, mathematical reasoning applies formal rules in supporting the validity of successive propositions.

Inductive and deductive thinking

Both inductive and deductive processes may be used by a problem solver. In inductive thinking one considers a number of particular or specific items of information to develop more inclusive (or general) conceptions. After aspirin was synthesized, for example, some people who swallowed the substance reported that it relieved their *particular* headaches. Through induction, the reports of these *specific* individuals were the basis for developing a more inclusive notion: aspirin may be helpful in relieving headaches in general.

Deduction is reasoning from general propositions—or hypotheses—to more specific instances or statements. Thus, after the general hypothesis about the effectiveness of aspirin had been put forward, physicians began to apply it to specific, newly encountered headache cases. The deduction was that, if aspirin is *generally* useful in managing pains in the head, it might also be helpful in easing pains elsewhere in the body. Although a person may deliberately choose to use induction or deduction, people typically shift from one to the other, depending on the exigencies of the reasoning process.

Students of problem solving almost invariably have endorsed some variety of mediation theory in their efforts to understand realistic thinking. The assumptions in that kind of theory are that implicit (internal) representations of experience are stored in and elicited from memory and are linked together during the period between the presentation of a stimulus and the implementation of a response. Those theorists who prefer to avoid the use of unobservable "entities" (*e.g.*, "mind") increasingly have been invoking the nervous system (particularly the brain) as the structure that mediates such functions.

Creative thinking. Divergent (or creative) thinking has been defined as an activity that leads to new information, or previously undiscovered solutions, rather than to a predetermined, correct solution (as in convergent thinking). Some tasks call for flexibility, originality, fluency, and inventiveness, especially for problems in which the individual must supply his own, unique solution. The "problem" might be a personal, emotional difficulty that needs resolution or expression.

Four progressive stages. A number of processes or phases have been identified as typical of creative thinking. In what logically would be the first phase (*i.e.*, preparation), the thinker assembles and explores his resources and perhaps makes preliminary decisions about their value in solving the problem at hand. Incubation represents the next period, in which he mulls over possibilities and shifts about from one to another relatively free of any rigid rational or logical preconceptions and constraints. Incubation seems to be at least partly unconscious, proceeding without the individual's full awareness. Illumination occurs when resources fall into place, and a definite decision is reached about the result or solution. Verification (refinement or polishing), the process of making relatively minor modifications in committing ideas to final form, follows. Often enough, objective standards for judging creative activity (*e.g.*, musical composition) are lacking; an important criterion is the emotional satisfaction of the creator. Although the four phases have been ordered in a logical sequence, they often vary widely and proceed in different orders from one person to the next. Many creative people attain their goals by special strategies that are not neatly describable.

Preparation, incubation, illumination, verification

The phases of preparation, incubation, illumination, and verification are characteristic of creative thinkers generally but do not guarantee that a worthwhile product will ensue. Results also depend on whether an individual has the necessary personality characteristics and abilities; in addition, the quality of creative thinking stems from the training of the creator. The artist who produces oil paintings needs to learn the brushing techniques basic to the task; the scientist who creates a new theory does so against a background of previous learning. Further, creativity intimately blends realistic (objective) and autistic (subjective) processes; the successful creator learns how to release and to express his feelings and insights.

Creative thinking is a matter of using intrinsic resources to produce tangible results. This process is markedly influenced by early experience and training. School situations, for example, that encourage individual expression and that tolerate idiosyncratic or unorthodox thinking seem to foster the development of creativity.

Artistic versus scientific creativity. While the processes of creative thinking in artistic and scientific pursuits have much in common, there are also distinctive differences. The artist places more importance on feeling and individual expression, often going to extremes to divorce himself from environmental constraints. The scientist relies more on disciplined, logical thinking to lead him in new directions. Artistic endeavour is dominantly expressive (although clearly oriented toward a goal), while scientific inventiveness is dominantly disciplined (although flexibly receptive to feelings and to imaginative experiences).

Thinking in groups. It might be supposed that greater efficiency should be achieved if several people collaborate to solve a problem than if only one individual works on it. Such results are by no means invariable.

Although groups often may increase the motivation of their members to deal with problems, there is a counterbalancing need to contend with conflicts arising among members of a group and with efforts to give it coherent direction. Problem solving is facilitated by the presence of an effective leader who not only provides direction but permits the orderly, constructive expression of a variety of opinions; much of the leader's effort may be devoted to resolving differences. Success in problem solving also depends on the distribution of ability within a group. Solutions simply may reflect the presence of an outstanding individual who might perform even better by himself.

Although groups may reach a greater number of correct solutions, or may require less time to discover an answer, their net man-hour efficiency is typically lower than that achieved by skilled individuals working alone.

A process called brainstorming has been offered as a method of facilitating the production of new solutions to problems. In brainstorming, a problem is presented to a group of people who then proceed to offer whatever they can think of, regardless of quality and with as few inhibitions as can be managed. Theoretically these unrestricted suggestions increase the probability that at least some superior solutions will emerge. Nevertheless, studies show that when individuals work alone under similar conditions, performance tends to proceed more efficiently than it does in groups.

Under special circumstances, however, a group may solve problems more effectively than does a reasonably competent individual. Group members may contribute different (and essential) resources to a solution that no individual can readily achieve alone; such pooling of information and skills can make group achievements superior in dealing with selected problems. Sometimes social demands may require group agreement on a single alternative, as in formulating national economic or military policies under democratic governments. When only one among several alternative solutions is correct, even if a group requires more time, it has a higher probability of identifying the right one than does an individual alone.

One difference between problem solving by a group and by an individual is the relative importance of covert or vicarious processes. The group depends heavily on verbal communication, while the individual, in considerable degree, attacks the problem through implicit, subjective, silent activity.

AUTISTIC THINKING

When the intensity of extrinsic (or environmental) influence is greatly reduced and intrinsic (or internal) influences dominate, thought processes tend to become autistic; these include so-called free association, fantasy (and reverie), dreaming, and pathological thinking. In such processes, thinking is especially responsive to emotional and motivational impulses. Often seeming to arise from wishes or needs, autistic thinking may represent an activity through which the individual symbolically gains gratification that the environment does not provide. For instance, one's wishes may be fulfilled only in dreaming. According to Freud, autistic thinking is especially influenced by unconscious tendencies that otherwise might find no expression.

Free association. A person freely associates by responding verbally when the usual constraints of logic,

goal orientation, or controlled sequence of thinking are removed or reduced. His responses are likely to reflect aroused emotional activity or impulses; for example, during free association, ordinarily forgotten and repressed past experiences seem to be more readily remembered. What is actually produced in free association (as in other forms of autistic thinking) may not always seem to be particularly coherent or meaningful. Some theorists suggest that such responses are likely to symbolize rather than to state an impulse directly. Thus a psychoanalytic theorist might imagine that a young woman's verbal associations about being run over by a beer truck symbolically disguise a socially unacceptable wish to be seduced in some illicit romantic encounter.

One technique that is claimed to be helpful in uncovering an individual's latent or repressed tendencies is the word-association test, devised by Carl Jung, a Swiss psychiatrist. The test taker is presented with a list of words, to each of which he is supposed to respond by saying whatever he thinks of first. It is theorized that especially significant responses may be identified by such clues as the person's delay in responding, by his use of words that indicate strong emotion, or by unusual or bizarre responses. The word chair for example, prompts many people to say table; the analyst is likely to be alerted if the response is *criminal* or *blood*.

Fantasy. Fantasizing is definable as comparatively well organized sequences of thinking in which sensory imagery prevails. When a person who is otherwise awake tends to lose contact with the environment and his thinking proceeds with little or no concern for logical considerations, conditions become favourable for fantasizing. The activity may also take on a problem-solving character, especially when the thinker periodically monitors the process to evaluate the degree to which he may have progressed toward a solution. Fantasy tends to be highly egocentric, dramatic, pleasurable, and free flowing; it may range from vaguely conscious reverie to vivid, almost hallucinatory visual, auditory, or tactual daydreams.

Psychologists have tried to infer the details of such covert processes by asking people to respond to ambiguous stimuli in whatever way they wish, and by so doing to project their inner experiences. Well-known projective methods include the Rorschach Test, in which inkblots in black and white and colour are used as stimuli; and the so-called Thematic Apperception Test (TAT), in which pictures (of people, for example) are shown, about which the subject is asked to make up stories. The Rorschach Test is believed by some to provide evidence of a person's originality, of the balance he maintains between emotional and logical thinking, and of typical ways in which he perceives the environment; some psychologists assert that the TAT may yield clues to a person's motivational characteristics, his inner conflicts, and his attitudes toward other people. Others hold that those projective methods are most untrustworthy and that their use can lead to dangerously misleading conclusions (as in mistakenly committing people to psychiatric hospitals).

Certain marginal states of consciousness seem especially favourable for autistic thinking. An example is the drowsy (hypnagogic) period experienced just before falling asleep; at such times, images and apparently random thinking may well up and "float" freely. Similar (hypnopompic) experiences that emerge on awakening also have been reported. Roughly equivalent activities may occur even when one seems fully awake, but when autistic processes hover between full fantasy and conscious orientation to the environment.

Drugs may induce a variety of alterations in thinking; there may be heightened sensitivity to sensory stimuli and responsiveness to inner states through enhanced imagery and unusual ideational activity. Dosed with some drugs, people seem completely to withdraw from the environment and may show evidence of hallucinatory and delusional experiences (see HALLUCINOGEN).

Dreaming. Autistic thinking during sleep is called dreaming. Reduction in external stimulation while one is asleep permits intrinsic activities to exert a strong influence on thought processes. Some psychoanalytic theo-

Margin notes:

Brainstorming for new solutions

Rorschach and other projective tests

Freud's theories of dreams

rists interpret dreaming as a mechanism for maintaining sleep and fulfilling wishes. Freud held that impulses may be expressed in disguised form when one dreams, particularly if their frank expression would be in conflict with the dreamer's moral and social standards. Freud wrote that the original wish that prompts dreaming corresponds to the dream's latent content. Such latent content is to be inferred from the dream as it is directly experienced (the manifest content). The meaning of any dream, according to Freud, lies in its latent content; to the extent that the latent wish is unacceptable to or threatens the dreamer, he is said to employ mechanisms of symbolic imagery, condensation, displacement, and secondary elaboration to disguise it. Condensation refers to the combining of elements; by itself, a knife may suggest a hostile weapon, but dreamed of in combination with other eating utensils it appears innocuous. In displacement the dreamer shifts an impulse from one object to another; he may dream of slicing a melon (manifest) rather than an enemy (latent). Secondary elaboration is the process of imposing structure to increase the coherence and logic of the dream.

Other theorists suggest that in many instances dreams do not hold the latent or hidden significance that Freud assigned them. These critics indicate that dreams may simply be the result of random remembering or of imagery that wells up during sleep. In such dreaming, the sequence of dream elements would represent little more than transient associations (see DREAMS).

Physio-logical studies of dreaming

In their efforts to study dreaming in terms of more objective evidence, some investigators record electrical activity generated by the brains of sleeping people. People are most likely to say they have been dreaming if they are awakened during a period of so-called rapid eye movement, at which times distinctive changes in brain activity are observable. When people are chronically wakened whenever such signs of dreaming appear, they tend to develop symptoms of psychological disturbance (e.g., hallucinatory activity) during daylight hours. When later permitted to sleep without interruption, they give evidence of dreaming intensively, as if to compensate for previous deprivation. It would appear that dreaming may meet some fundamental physiological need.

Although dreaming largely seems to express intrinsic activity, it can be influenced by external stimuli and is likely to include experiences that symbolize such stimuli. A light tap on the foot of a sleeper, for example, might prompt him to dream of buying a new pair of shoes (see also SLEEP).

Pathological thinking. One popular system for classifying disturbances in personality is based on general patterns or categories of activity called behaviour disorder, neurosis, and psychosis.

Behaviour disorders. Individuals who are judged to show difficulty in self-control, in ability to withstand stress, or who hold unorthodox moral and social standards are likely to be labelled as exhibiting behaviour disorders. The thinking of such people appears to be essentially "normal" in that they show efficient awareness of the environment. Behaviour disorder is displayed mainly in antisocial acts, stemming from what many observers consider to be the individual's deviant evaluation of what is "right" or "wrong," or of what is socially acceptable.

Neurosis. According to some theories, persons classified as neurotic are thought to suffer deep-lying conflicts, controlled in varying degrees by repression. Their tensions are held to produce feelings of anxiety and guilt and to lead to emotion-laden thinking (or worrying). Such theories also posit the operation of so-called ego-defense mechanisms, or activities believed to allow the individual to keep his distressing, repressed impulses from his own awareness. Thus his reasoning may be altered, as in dreaming. Defense mechanisms include rationalization, which justifies actions on a false basis, as when a soldier who enjoys killing feels he does so through patriotism; projection, which attributes to others one's own impulses, as when a hater feels hated; denial, or refusal to admit unacceptable or embarrassing aspects of experience; reaction formation, in which one acts contrary to his repressed impulses, as when he drowns his lecherous ten-

dencies in excessive piety; and rigidity, or excessively careful, fixed thinking (see also PSYCHONEUROSES).

Psychosis. When one's thinking seems grossly disturbed over an appreciable period, he is usually classified by psychiatrists as psychotic. Severe personality disorders of this sort may result from environmental stress, bodily disease, chemical or toxic factors, or any number of experiential influences (e.g., combat experiences, loss of loved ones). The relation between thinking and environmental constraints seems grossly distorted in some forms of psychosis; the effect may be disorientation in time, in space, or in personal identity. In significant degree, the psychotic's emotional and cognitive processes appear to the observer to be independent of what is happening in the surrounding environment.

Bizarre symptoms of psychosis

Some ideational symptoms observed among psychotics are bizarre hallucinatory activities such as those reflected in vivid visual or auditory experiences (e.g., hearing "voices") perceived by the individual as coming from the environment; delusions, ostensibly false beliefs that dominate thinking, such as notions of being persecuted or of having a special identity or a mission (as of being appointed to destroy the world); stereotyped, repetitive ideation or actions, such as the incessant recurrence of silly, emotionless "laughter" or detailed rituals resembling peculiar kinds of calisthenics.

Psychotic persons also may show signs of amnesia, inability to understand what others are saying, failures of attention, disorganization of thinking as expressed in meaningless or incoherent speaking or writing. Among psychotics who are likely to be identified as schizophrenics, speech tends to become odd, fragmented, and difficult to follow rationally; their idiosyncratic use of words is common, along with apparently meaningless phrases and sometimes disregard for sentence structure. Instances of what some claim to be "second sight," divine inspiration, possession by spirits, or extreme detachment from ordinary concerns all are likely, in psychiatric settings, to be interpreted as temporary psychotic episodes.

Thought processes cover a remarkably wide range of types; many are poorly understood or may not even be known to professional psychologists. It seems clear, however, that any kind of thinking mediates between intrinsic (bodily) activities and extrinsic (external) sources of stimulation, each type of thought process representing a resultant of autistic and environmental influences.

BIBLIOGRAPHY. General background for the psychoanalytic view of thinking is provided by SIGMUND FREUD, *A General Introduction to Psychoanalysis,* ed. by J. RIVIERE (1938); D. RAPAPORT, "Toward a Theory of Thinking," in *Organization and Pathology of Thought,* pp. 689–730 (1951); and C.S. HALL and G. LINDZEY, "Freud's Psychoanalytic Theory," in *Theories of Personality,* pp. 29–75 (1957). Several general textbooks cover a variety of thought processes. W.E. VINACKE, *The Psychology of Thinking* (1952), discusses such topics as logic, concept formation, problem solving, imagination, creative thinking, and attitudes; a 2nd edition (in press), pays special attention to mediation theory, information theory, and motivational influences on thinking. D.M. JOHNSON, *The Psychology of Thought and Judgment* (1955), deals with problem solving and the experimental study of decisions and judgment. F.C. BARTLETT, *Thinking* (1958), gives interesting examples of thought as a "gap-filled" and steplike process, with attention to "adventurous" thinking. A systematic treatment, based on modern behaviourist ("neo-associationist") conceptions is D.E. BERLYNE, *Structure and Direction in Thinking* (1965). Historically important formulations of insightful processes are K. DUNCKER, *Zur Psychologie des Produktiven Denkens* (1935; Eng. trans., *On Problem-Solving,* 1945); and MAX WERTHEIMER, *Productive Thinking,* ed. by *Michael Wertheimer* (1959). A wide variety of authors discuss special topics in E. HARMS (ed.), *Fundamentals of Psychology: The Psychology of Thinking* (1961). A thorough review of problem solving by groups is H.H. KELLEY and J.W. THIBAUT, "Group Problem Solving," in G. LINDZEY and E. ARONSON (eds.), *The Handbook of Social Psychology,* 2nd ed., vol. 4 (1969). E.J. MURRAY, *Sleep, Dreams, and Arousal* (1965), is a good source for experimental work; and C.T. TART (ed.), *Altered States of Consciousness* (1969), presents chapters on imagery, the effects of drugs, meditation, and other unusual forms of thinking.

(W.E.V.)

Thucydides

Thucydides, the greatest of Greek historians, was perhaps the first person to apply a highly refined intellect to a large-scale examination of the nature of political power and the way in which state policies are made. His *History of the Peloponnesian War*, though incomplete, is a military, political, but most important, a psychological account of the war between Athens and Sparta that lasted from 431 to 404 BC, and of the inevitable moral attrition brought about by the war. His influence on all subsequent historians has been incalculable. All that is certainly known (perhaps all that ancient scholars knew) of his life is what he reveals about himself in the course of his narrative. He was an Athenian, old enough when the war began to estimate its importance and judge that it was likely to be a long one and to write an account of it, observing and making notes from its beginning. He was probably born, therefore, not later than 460—perhaps a few years earlier since his detailed narrative begins, just before 431, with the events which provoked the war. He was certainly over 30 when he was elected *stratēgos*, a military magistrate of great importance, in 424. Hence, he belongs to the generation younger than that of the Greek historian Herodotus. His father's name was Olorus, which is not known as an Athenian name; Olorus was probably of Thracian descent on his mother's side. Thucydides was related in some way to the great Athenian statesman and general Miltiades, who had married the daughter of a Thracian prince of this name. He himself had property in Thrace, including mining rights in the gold mines opposite the island of Thasos, and was, he tells us, a man of influence there.

Thucydides, detail of a Roman bust after a Greek original. In Holkham Hall, Norfolk, England.

He was in Athens when the great pestilence of 430–429 raged; he caught the disease himself and saw others suffer. Later, in 424, he was elected one of the ten *stratēgoi* of the year, and, because of his connections, was given command of the fleet in the Thraceward region, based at Thasos. He failed to prevent the capture of the important city of Amphipolis by the Spartan general Brasidas, who launched a sudden attack in the middle of winter. Because of this blunder, Thucydides was recalled, tried, and sentenced to exile. This, he says later, gave him greater opportunity for undistracted study for his *History* and for travel and wider contacts, especially on the Peloponnesian side—Sparta and its allies. He lived through the war, and his exile of 20 years ended only with the fall of Athens and the peace of 404. The time and manner of his death are uncertain, but that he died shortly after 404 is probable, and that he died by violence in the troubled times following the peace may well be true, for the *History* stops abruptly long before its appointed end. His tomb and a monument to his memory were still to be seen in Athens in the 2nd century AD.

Scope and plan of the "History." The *History*, which is divided into eight books, probably not by Thucydides' design, stops in the middle of the events of the autumn of 411 BC, more than six and a half years before the end of the war. This much at least is known: that three historians, Cratippus, a younger contemporary; Xenophon, who lived a generation later; and Theopompus, who lived in the last third of the 4th century, all began their histories of Greece where Thucydides left off. Xenophon, one might say, began the next paragraph nearly as abruptly as Thucydides ended his. So it is certain that Thucydides' work was well-known soon after publication and that no more was ever published other than the eight books that have survived; it may reasonably be inferred from the silence of the available sources that no separate section of the work was published in his lifetime. It may also be inferred that parts of the *History*, and the last book in particular, are defective, in the sense that he would have written at greater length had he known more and that he was trying still to learn more—*e.g.*, of internal Athenian politics in the years of "uneasy truce." His existing narrative is in parts barely understandable without some imaginative guesswork.

It may be assumed, then, that there are three fairly definable stages in his work: first, the "notes" he made of events as they occurred; secondly, the arrangement and rewriting of these notes into a consecutive narrative, as a "chronicle," but by no means in the final form that Thucydides intended; thirdly, the final, elaborated narrative—of the preliminaries of the war (Book i), of the "Ten Years' War," and of the Athenian expedition to conquer Sicily. Thucydides supplemented his "note" stage throughout the project; even the most elaborated parts of the *History* may have been added right up to the time of his death—certainly many additions were made after the war was over.

All this is significant because Thucydides was writing what few others have attempted—a strictly contemporary history of events that he lived through and that succeeded each other almost throughout his adult life. He endeavoured to do more than merely record events, in some of which he took an active part, and in all of which he was a direct or indirect spectator; he attempted to write the final history for later generations and, as far as a man can and as no other man has, he succeeded. It is obvious that he did not rush his work; the last of the complete narrative (stage three, above) took him to the autumn of 413, eight and a half years before the end of the war, the last of stage two, to six and a half years before. During these last years he was observing, inquiring, writing his notes, adding to or modifying what he had already written; at no time before the end, during all the 27 years of the war, did he know what that end would be nor, therefore, what would be the length and the final shape of his own *History*. It is evident that he did not long survive the war since he did not leave any connected account, even at stage two, of the last six years. But in what he lived to complete, he wrote a definitive history.

Character studies. Besides the political causes of the war, Thucydides was interested in and emphasized the conflict between two types of character: the ever-active, innovating, revolutionary, disturbing Athenians and the slower-moving, more cautious Peloponnesians, especially the Spartans, "not excited by success nor despairing in misfortune," but quietly self-confident. Thucydides was not really concerned with individuals but rather with the actions, sufferings, and the characters of states ("the Athenians," "the Syracusans," etc.); but he did understand the significance of personalities. Besides depicting by their words and deeds the characters of some who influenced events, such as Cleon, the harsh demagogue of Athens; Hermocrates, the would-be moderate leader in Syracuse; the brave Nicostratus; and the incompetent Alcidas, he goes out of his way to give a clear picture of the characters and influence of four men: Themistocles (in a digression, the Athenian hero of the Second Persian War), Pericles, Brasidas, and Alcibiades. All four of them were of the active, revolutionary type. Pericles of Athens was indeed unique for Thucydides in that he combined caution and moderation in action and great stability of character with a daring imagination and intellect; he was a leader of the new age. During the war each of them

—Pericles and Alcibiades in Athens, Brasidas in Sparta —was in conflict with a conservative, quietist opposition within his own country. The conflict between the revolutionary and the conservative also extended between the generally daring Athenian state and the generally cautious Peloponnesians. It is a great loss that Thucydides did not live to write the story of the last years of the war, when Lysander, the other great revolutionary Spartan, played a larger part than any other single man in the defeat of Athens. This defeat was, in one aspect, the defeat of intellectual brilliance and daring by "stolidity" and stability of character (this last the quality most lacking in Alcibiades, the most brilliant Athenian of the second half of the war); but it was largely brought about by Brasidas and Lysander, the two Spartans who rivalled the Athenians in daring and intellect.

Study of the war's technical aspects. Thucydides was also interested in the technical aspect of the war. The most important problems in the war, besides protecting food supplies during land fighting, centred around the difficulties and possibilities of war between an all-powerful land force (Sparta and its allies) and an all-powerful naval force (Athens). Thucydides also studied the details of siege warfare; the difficulties of the heavily armed combat in mountain country and of fighting against the fierce but unruly barbarians of the north; an army trying to force a landing from ships against troops on shore; the one great night battle, at Syracuse; the skill and the daring manoeuvres of the Athenian sailors and the way these manoeuvres were overcome by the Syracusans; the unexpected recovery of the Athenian fleet after the Sicilian disaster—in all these aspects of the war he took a keen professional interest.

In Thucydides' introductory pages on the early history of Greece he lays much stress on the development of sea trading and naval power and on the accumulation of capital resources: they help to explain the great war between a land power and a sea power.

Style and historical aims. Thucydides was himself an intellectual of the Athenian kind; markedly individualist, his style shows a man brought up in the company of Sophocles and Euripides, the playwrights, and the philosophers Anaxagoras, Socrates, and the contemporary Sophists. His writing is condensed and direct, almost austere in places, and is meant to be read rather than delivered orally. He explains in a scientific and impartial manner the intricacies and complexities of the events he observed. Only in his speeches does he sometimes fall short of the lucidity of the narrative prose; his fondness for abstract expressions and the obscurity of his rhetorical antithesis often make the passages difficult to understand.

In a prefatory note near the beginning of the *History*, Thucydides speaks a little of the nature of his task and of his aims. It was difficult, he says, to arrive at the truth of the speeches made—whether he heard them himself or received a report from others—and of the actions of the war. For the latter, even if he himself observed a particular battle, he made as thorough an enquiry as he could— for he realized that eyewitnesses, either from faulty memory or from bias, were not always reliable.

Use of speeches

He wrote the speeches out of his own words, appropriate to the occasion, keeping as closely as possible to the general sense of what had actually been said. He could never have omitted them, for it is through the speeches that he explains the motives and ambitions of the leading men and states; and this, the study of the human mind in time of war, is one of his principal aims. (The omission of speeches from the last book is a great loss and is caused, no doubt, by the difficulty he had in getting information about Athens at this period.) They are reported as though directly quoted but are Thucydides' own words and are written in his own unique style, partly because he could not pretend that they were exact reports and partly because long passages in indirect speech would be scarcely tolerable and no more "authentic." He avoided, he says, all "storytelling" (this is a criticism of Herodotus), and his work might be the less attractive in consequence;

but I have written not for immediate applause but for posterity, and I shall be content if the future student of these events, or of other similar events which are likely in human nature to occur in after ages, finds my narrative of them useful.

This is all that he expressly tells of his aim and methods. Moreover, in the course of his narrative (except for the pestilence of 430 and his command in 424) he never gives his authority for a statement. He does not say which of the speeches he actually heard, which of the other campaigns he took part in, what places he visited, or what persons he consulted. Thucydides insisted in doing all the work himself; and he provides, for the parts he completed, only the finished structure, not the plans or the consultations.

His authority is hardly equalled by that of any other historian. He kept to a strict chronological scheme, and where it can be accurately tested by the eclipses that he mentions, it fits closely. There are also a fair number of contemporary documents recorded on stone, most of which confirm his account both in general and in detail. There is the silent testimony of the three historians who began where he left off, not attempting, in spite of much independence of opinion, to revise what he had already done, not even the last book, which he clearly did not complete. Another historian, Philistus, a Syracusan who was a boy during the Athenian siege of his city, had little to alter or to add to Thucydides' account in his own *History of Sicily*. Above all, there are the contemporary political comedies of Aristophanes—a man about 15 years younger than Thucydides with as different a temper and writing purpose as could be—which remarkably reinforce the reliability of the historian's dark picture of Athens at war. The modern historian of this war is in much the same position as the ancient: he cannot do much more than translate, abridge, or enlarge upon Thucydides.

Authority of his work

For Thucydides kept rigidly to his theme: the history of a war—that is, a story of battles and sieges, of alliances hastily made and soon broken, and, most important, of the behaviour of peoples as the war dragged on and on, of the inevitable "corrosion of the human spirit." He vividly narrates exciting episodes and carefully describes tactics on land and sea. He gives a picture, direct in speeches, indirect in the narrative, of the ambitious imperialism of Athens—controlled ambition in Pericles, reckless in Alcibiades, debased in Cleon—ever confident that nothing was impossible for them, resilient after the worst disaster. He shows also the opposing picture of the slow steadiness of Sparta, sometimes so successful, at other times so accommodating to the enemy. His record of Pericles' speech on those killed in the first year of the war is the most glowing account of Athens and Athenian democracy that any leading citizen could hope to hear. It is followed (in, of course, due chronological order) by a minutely accurate account of the symptoms of the pestilence ("so that it may be recognized by medical men if it recurs") and a moving description of the demoralizing despair that overtook men after so much suffering and such heavy losses—probably more than a quarter of the population, most of it crowded within the walls of the city, died.

Equally moving is the account of the last battles in the great harbour of Syracuse and of the Athenian retreat. In one of his best-known passages he analyzes by a most careful choice of words, almost creating the language as he writes, the moral and political effects of civil strife within a state in time of war. By a different method, in speeches, he portrays the hard fate of the town of Plataea due to the long-embittered envy and cruelty of Thebes and the faithlessness of Sparta, and the harsh brutality of Cleon when he proposed to execute all the men of the Aegean island city of Mytilene. Occasionally, he is forced into personal comment, as on the pathetic fate of the virtuous and much-liked Athenian Nicias.

He had strong feelings, both as a man and as a citizen of Athens. He was filled with a passion for the truth as he saw it, which not only kept him free from vulgar partiality against the enemy but served him as a historian in the accurate narrative of events—accurate in their detail and order and also in their relative importance. He does not, for example, exaggerate the significance of the campaign he himself commanded, nor does he offer a self-defense for his failure. Characteristically, he mentions his exile not as an event of the war but in his "second preface"— after the peace of 421—to explain his opportunities of wider contacts.

Subsequent fame. The story of his later fame is a curious one. It has been mentioned above that in the two generations after his death three historians began their work where he had left off; but apart from this silent tribute and late stories of his great influence on the orator Demosthenes, Thucydides is nowhere referred to in surviving 4th-century literature, not even in Aristotle, who, in his *Constitution of Athens*, describes the revolution in Athens in 411 and diverges in many ways from Thucydides' account. It was not until the end of the 4th century that the philosopher Theophrastus coupled Thucydides with Herodotus as a founder of the writing of history. Little is known of what the scholars of Alexandria and Pergamum did for his book; but copies of it were being made in considerable numbers in Egypt, and so, doubtless, elsewhere, from the 1st to the 5th centuries AD. By the 1st century BC, as is clear from the writings of Cicero and Dionysius (who vainly disputed his pre-eminence), Thucydides was established as the great historian, and since that time his fame has been secure wherever he has been known.

BIBLIOGRAPHY

Texts: "Oxford Classical Series," by H. STUART JONES and J.E. POWELL, 2 vol. (1953–55); "Teubner Series," by C. HUDE, editio major (1901), new ed. by O. LUSCHNAT (1954–   ); in "Budé Series," by JACQUELINE DE ROMILLY, with French trans. (1953–   ).

Commentaries: That of T. ARNOLD, 4th ed., 3 vol. (1857), is still worth consulting; important for the interpretation of language are J.M. STAHL's edition (in Latin, 1882–88); and that of J. CLASSEN, rev. by J. STEUP (1900–22); for books i-ii only, A. CROISET (1886). See also A.W. GOMME, *Historical Commentary*, 3 vol. (1945–56).

English translation: That of THOMAS HOBBES (1629), is well worth reading. Modern translations include an accurate and vigorous translation by R. CRAWLEY (1874; in Everyman's Library, 1910, and reprinted in "Great Books of the Western World," vol. 6, 1952); and a lively one by REX WARNER (1954).

Studies and special aspects: J.B. BURY, *The Ancient Greek Historians*, ch. 3–4 (1909, reprinted 1958), old, but still valuable and useful; SIR F.E. ADCOCK, *Thucydides and His History* (1963), quite brief but with some novel theories; J.H. FINLEY, *Thucydides*, 2nd ed. (1942, reprinted 1963), a suave, bland account by probably the most eminent American student of Thucydides; JACQUELINE DE ROMILLY, *Thucydide et l'impérialisme athénien* (1947; Eng. trans., *Thucydides and Athenian Imperialism*, 1963), a profound and searching analysis, not narrowly concerned with imperialism; C.N. COCHRANE, *Thucydides and the Science of History* (1929, reprinted 1965), detects a profound influence on Thucydides by the Hippocratic school of scientific medicine of his time —particularly in regard to such things as "cause" and "symptom."

(A.W.Ge.)

Thunderstorms

A thunderstorm is a short-lived storm produced by clouds of great vertical extent and always accompanied by lightning and thunder. A thunderstorm often produces strong, gusty winds, heavy rain, and sometimes hail. Almost invariably, thunderstorms are associated with cumulonimbus clouds, dense rain clouds with exceptional vertical development that look like mountains or huge towers. In an advanced stage, their summits have a smooth, fibrous appearance and sometimes resemble a huge anvil (Figure 1). The base of a cumulonimbus cloud is usually dark because it has great depth. Sometimes, particularly in the mountainous areas of the western United States, water drops from a thunderstorm are small, and they evaporate before reaching the ground as precipitation (*q.v.*).

Within a cumulonimbus cloud there are strong updrafts that carry cloud particles and raindrops to the cold upper parts of the clouds. The interaction of water and ice particles causes the separation of electrical charge. In general, positive charge is concentrated in the upper regions of the cloud and negative charges near the central regions. When the accumulated electric charge becomes sufficiently large, a lightning (*q.v.*) discharge occurs. The massive surge of current in the lightning channel causes tremendous heating and sudden expansion of the air, and the resultant shock wave becomes the sound wave known as thunder.

Thunderstorms generally occur in warm, moist air. Although all of them have certain common features, in some ways they differ greatly. Some storms may be less than three kilometres (1.9 miles) in diameter, last less than half an hour, deposit no rainfall at the ground, and exhibit only one lightning flash. In other cases, lines of thunderstorms hundreds of miles long can sweep across the country causing torrential rain and hail, extremely strong winds, and tornadoes. When this happens, the storms pose great hazards to man, animals, crops, and property.

The damage to property and crops by hail in the United States is estimated to average about $200,000,000 a year. In northern Italy, southwestern U.S.S.R., Argentina, and many other countries, hail does tremendous damage to fruit orchards, vineyards, and grain fields. Lightning kills, maims, and burns every year. According to figures published by the U.S. Forest Service, lightning-caused forest fires destroy more than 500,000 acres per year in the United States.

The tornado, spawned by thunderstorms, is the most violent of atmospheric phenomena. On the average, tornadoes, whirlwinds, and waterspouts (*q.v.*) kill about 250 people each year and do tens of millions of dollars in damage.

Clearly, severe thunderstorms sometimes cause great destruction and misery, but they also do a great deal of good. In most regions of the world, rainfall during the growing season is supplied by thunderstorms. If heavy showers did not occur over the corn and wheat fields of the United States, Canada, and the Ukraine, there would be catastrophic shortages of food.

Society would benefit greatly if thunderstorms could be more accurately predicted, more precisely observed and tracked, and if they could be artificially controlled. If rainfall intensities and winds could be reduced, if lightning and hail could be suppressed, and if tornadoes could be eliminated, man would reap the benefits without suffering the disasters. Atmospheric scientists in the second half of the 20th century were actively working toward these difficult but not impossible goals.

CAUSES OF THUNDERSTORMS

Thunderstorms occur when the atmosphere has a property termed instability. In essence, when a weather system is unstable, a small displacement leads to a larger one. When the atmosphere is unstable, a volume of air having an upward displacement for any reason will continue moving upward at an accelerating rate. If a sufficiently large mass of air begins rising, the result will be the formation of an updraft. If the air is moist as well as unstable, a cloud will form; and further growth can lead to precipitation and lightning.

The earth's atmosphere becomes unstable when the temperature decreases rapidly with height, this change coming about most often as a result of solar heating of the earth's surface and of the air in the lowest layers of the atmosphere. Some of the heat is transported upward by means of molecular motion and small-scale turbulent eddies of air. If the incoming energy exceeds that being transported upward, the temperatures in the lowest layers rise, causing the temperature lapse rate, the rate of temperature decrease with height, to continue increasing. When the lapse rate exceeds certain specific values depending on the humidity properties of the air, the atmosphere becomes unstable. If upward air motion is initiated by a mountain ridge, for example, a rising convection current is set in motion. The ascending stream of air will be warmer and more buoyant than the surrounding air. Heat and moisture are carried upward. Countercurrents transport cooler

Instability and convection

Figure 1: Cumulonimbus cloud with anvil, a classic
thunderstorm
Louis J. Battan

and drier air downward. For the reasons just cited, the
puffy clouds that start as cumulus and may become cumulonimbus are called convective clouds.

Such clouds may be initiated in a variety of ways. Some
early studies often indicated that convective clouds and
thunderstorms were started as a result of excessive warming of certain surface areas. The temperature differences
were attributed to differences in the colour and hence the
absorption properties of various soils and rocks. Sometimes thermals may be traced to such hot spots, but evidence indicates that most thunderstorms are set off as a
result of organized lifting of the air.

As noted previously, mountain ridges are important in
generating thunderstorms. Not only do they serve as a
barrier that forces the air to rise, but also they become
what are sometimes called high-level heat sources. Solar
heating of the high terrain causes the air close to them to
be warmer than the air at the same altitudes over the
adjacent valleys. Because the warm air is less dense, it
rises through the surrounding cooler and heavier air. The
importance of this effect is shown by the fact that, even in
mountainous areas, most thunderstorms occur during the

afternoon and early evening hours when it is warmest.

Thunderstorms are often initiated when a cold front
advances toward moist, unstable air (see WINDS AND
STORMS), which is forced to rise over the frontal surface.
Sometimes lines of thunderstorms occur above and nearly
parallel to a cold frontal surface. More often, particularly
over the central United States, long lines or zones of
thunderstorms develop in the warm air many tens of
miles, sometimes several hundred miles, ahead of the cold
front. The tendency of these so-called prefrontal squall
lines to be more or less parallel to the front has suggested
that they have been initiated by a dynamic mechanism
related to the front.

In the tropics, weather fronts of the kinds so commonly
noted at higher latitudes are almost never observed. Air
masses of contrasting temperature do not come into contact, as is the case at the polar front, when air from the
polar regions encounters air from the tropics. Nevertheless, the regions of maximum thunderstorm frequency
occur in equatorial and tropical regions (Figure 2). These
storms are triggered by air rising as a result of converging
wind systems. When the northeast trade winds meet the
southeast trades, the air at the zone of confrontation must
rise. Because it is both moist and unstable, showers and
thunderstorms are produced in abundance.

A variety of disturbances in the low-altitude wind field
may lead to convergence and ascending air. Such disturbances occur often in equatorial areas and at higher latitudes as well and lead to cumulonimbus clouds and thunderstorms.

TYPES OF THUNDERSTORMS

At one time it was common to classify thunderstorms
according to where they occurred; for example, as air-
mass, frontal, or orographic (mountain-related) thunderstorms. During the 1960s, it was found more meaningful
to classify them according to the chief characteristics of
the storms themselves; the characteristics depend largely
on the properties of the environment in which a given
thunderstorm develops.

Isolated thunderstorms, especially those that occur under
atmospheric conditions such that the wind velocity does
not change markedly with height, are sometimes called

Weather
fronts

By courtesy of the World Meteorological Organization

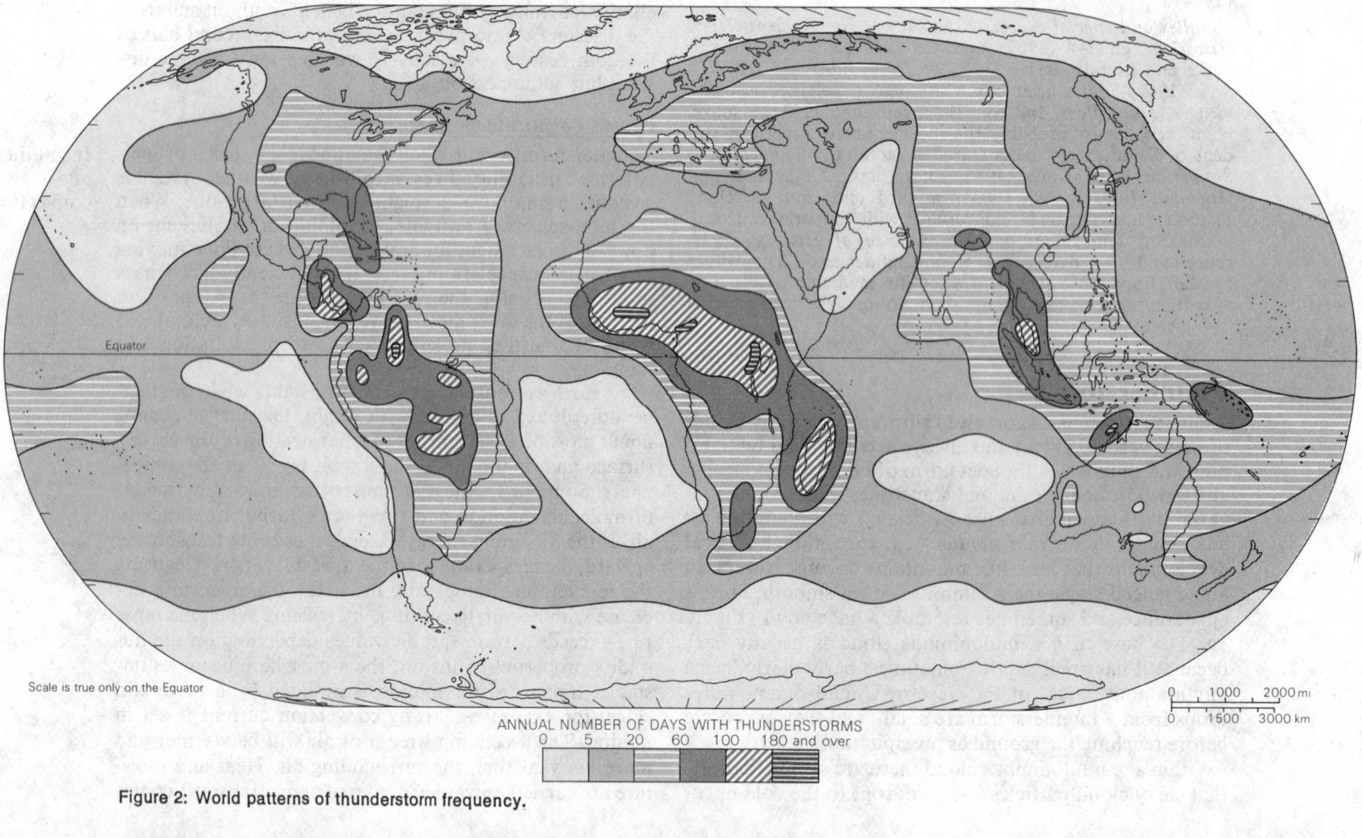

Scale is true only on the Equator

ANNUAL NUMBER OF DAYS WITH THUNDERSTORMS
0   5   20   60   100   180 and over

0   1000   2000 mi
0   1500   3000 km

Figure 2: World patterns of thunderstorm frequency.

air-mass, or local, thunderstorms. They are mostly vertical in structure, relatively short-lived, and usually do not produce violent weather at the ground level. Extensive flight measurements indicate that such thunderstorms are composed of one or more individual cells, each of which passes through a definable life cycle. Early in the growth of the cloud, air motions are mostly upward not as a steady, uniform stream but as one that is composed of a series of rising eddies. The precipitation particles grow as the cloud grows; when the accumulated water and ice becomes excessive, a downdraft is started. At maturity a local storm may be composed of intense updrafts and downdrafts side by side (Figure 3). In its later stages the

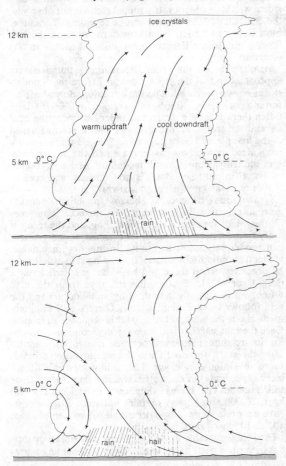

Figure 3: *Thunderstorm models.*
(Top) Mature stage of an isolated thunderstorm cell.
(Bottom) Cross section through a hail-producing organized thunderstorm.

updraft spreads throughout the cell and diminishes in intensity as the precipitation falls out.

Organized storms

Violent weather at the ground level usually results from a type of thunderstorm that is sometimes called an organized storm. Over the central United States, it commonly occurs when the winds in the middle layer of the atmosphere are from the southwesterly quadrant and are strong. Although there is still considerable debate about the structure of such storms, many authorities are convinced that in such thunderstorms the updraft is tilted from the vertical. Such storms may have a duration of many hours, remaining in a constant state of regeneration because moist, unstable air is drawn into the lower part of the cloud. Long swaths of hail can be produced by these storms; strong, gusty winds are common; and tornadoes sometimes are generated.

ENERGY OF THUNDERSTORMS

The energy to drive thunderstorms is supplied by a variety of sources, but most of it comes from the heat released when water vapour condenses to form cloud droplets. For every gram of water condensed, about 600 calories of heat are made available. When the water freezes in the upper

parts of the cloud, another 80 calories of heat per gram of water are released. This energy goes to increase the temperature of the updraft and, in part, is converted to kinetic energy of upward and downward air movement. If the quantity of water that is condensed in and then precipitated from a cloud is known, then the total energy of a thunderstorm can be calculated. In an average thunderstorm, the energy emitted amounts to about 10^7 kilowatt-hours, which is equivalent to a 20-kiloton atomic bomb. A large, severe thunderstorm might be 10 to 100 times more energetic.

PHYSICAL CHARACTERISTICS OF THUNDERSTORMS

An individual thunderstorm cell may be perhaps 3 km (less than 2 mi) in diameter, may extend to an altitude of 8 to 10 km (26,000–33,000 ft), and may last less than 30 minutes. A larger local thunderstorm would be composed of many cells in varying stages in their life history. Such a storm can be tens of kilometers in diameter, its summit may extend to altitudes exceeding 18 km (59,000 ft), and its duration may be many hours.

When referring to the diameter of a thunderstorm, it is necessary to specify what is being measured. The quantities cited above refer to the diameter of the cloud at middle altitudes, the distance observed by an airplane flying through the cloud at an altitude of perhaps 5 km (16,000 ft). In such a penetration, the aircraft might encounter several updrafts and downdrafts. The most extensive measurements of thunderstorm properties by means of airplanes were made by the Thunderstorm Project conducted in 1946 and 1947 by the U.S. Weather Bureau in collaboration with the U.S. Navy and Army Air Forces.

Updrafts and downdrafts.   Although updrafts and downdrafts encountered in Ohio and Florida thunderstorms sometimes had diameters exceeding 4 km (13,000 ft), most often they were between about 500 and 2,500 m at the altitudes between 3 km and 8 km (10,000–26,000 ft). At flight levels near 1,500 m (5,000 ft) the drafts tended to have a greater diameter and be weaker than at greater heights in the clouds.

Updraft speeds measured by the Thunderstorm Project ranged to a maximum of 26 metres per second (m/sec) (85 ft/sec) but usually were less than half that much. They increased with height and averaged 5.0, 7.3, and 8.4 m/sec (16.4, 24.0, and 27.6 ft/sec) at altitudes of 1.5 (5,000 ft), 4.5 (15,000 ft), and 7.6 km (25,000 ft), respectively. At the same altitudes, downdraft speeds were 4.6, 6.1, and 7.3 m/sec (15.1, 20.0, and 24.0 ft/sec), respectively. At greater altitudes, higher updraft speeds have been measured by aircraft and radar and have been inferred on theoretical grounds. Updrafts exceeding 20 m/sec (65 ft/sec) are not considered unusual in the upper parts of large thunderstorms. Airplanes flying through them at altitudes about 10 km (33,000 ft) have measured updrafts exceeding 30 m/sec (100 ft/sec). The strongest updrafts have been observed in severe organized thunderstorms, which often are many tens of kilometres in diameter. Lines or zones of such storms sometimes extend for many hundreds of miles.

Vertical extent of thunderstorms.   The heights of thunderstorms have been measured by radar and by aircraft flying over their tops. They commonly extend to altitudes over 11 km (36,000 ft) and sometimes to over 20 km (66,000 ft). On very unstable days when the atmosphere is moist, the upper limit of the thunderstorm cloud is determined by the depth of the troposphere, that part of the atmosphere lying below the stratosphere. On such occasions the rising updraft air would be warmer than its environment until it penetrates through the base of the stratosphere. Since this layer is characterized by air temperatures that are nearly constant or may increase with height, it has great stability. The momentum of an updraft would carry it into the stratosphere, but after a short penetration the rising air would be cooler and heavier than the surrounding air. The resulting downward force would stop further upward motion.

The base of the stratosphere varies with latitude and season of the year. In general, it ranges from about 10 to 20 km (33,000 to 66,000 ft) with the higher found in the summer at lower latitudes. When the rising cloud air encounters the stable stratosphere, it spreads outward and forms the anvil cloud so characteristic of thunderstorms. If winds are light, the anvil may extend in all directions around the cloud. Most of the winds at the anvil altitudes carry cloud material downwind.

Thunderstorm tops do not usually reach the stratosphere. More often their vertical extent is determined by a stable layer in the troposphere. For a number of reasons, layers may be formed where the temperature is constant or increases with height. Sometimes the air temperature decreases only slowly with height. Regions where the temperature decreases slowly or increases with height are stable layers, and a rising volume of air encountering them often cannot penetrate them. As a result the stable layer determines the maximum vertical extent of the cloud and the altitude where the cloud spreads out to form the anvil.

Turbulence. An airplane flying through a thunderstorm is commonly carried upward and downward by the drafts in the storm. In addition, it often is buffeted from side to side and up and down. This motion is called turbulence, which is caused by large changes in air motions over distances comparable to the dimensions of the airplane. Turbulence not only contributes to crew and passenger discomfort but also subjects the aircraft to undesirable stresses. In severe turbulence, structural damage may result, most likely when the turbulence stresses are augmented by forces caused by airplane manoeuvres. For example, if the pilot tries to maintain altitude for an airplane in a very strong downdraft that contains so-called sharp-edge gusts that produce turbulence, he will impose additional forces on the wings, adding to those imposed by the gusty air. In the limiting case, a wing may collapse.

Turbulence may be expressed in various units. Commonly, the g unit, equal to the acceleration of gravity of the earth, is used. A gust of 1 g will cause severe aircraft turbulence. In the upper part of violent thunderstorms, vertical accelerations of about 3 g have been reported.

Movement of thunderstorms. The motion of a thunderstorm is determined largely by the average wind velocity in the layer of the atmosphere in which the storm develops. The average speed of 120 thunderstorms observed in Florida and Ohio was 20 kilometres per hour (12.4 miles per hour), but some storms moved much faster. In extreme circumstances thunderstorms may move at 65 to 80 km/hr (40 to 50 mph).

When considering the movement of a thunderstorm, the dynamic character of it must be taken into account. Most storms are in a constant state of change, with new cells developing while old ones dissipate. When wind speeds are light, an individual cell may move very little, less than 2 km (1.2 mi), during its lifetime; but new cells forming downwind may give the illusion of rapid cloud motion. This type of behaviour is often observed in mountainous areas. The first storms of the day generally form over the ridges. As the day progresses, new clouds develop near the existing ones but closer to the valleys. An observer who sees the nearest edge of the clouds getting closer may readily assume that the original clouds are moving over the valley.

Although new cloud developments generally occur downwind of an existing storm, this is not necessarily the case. Sometimes they grow on the flanks and, as a result, visual observations may lead to the notion that there is little relation between the winds and thunderstorm motion. As would be expected, this view is most likely to arise when wind speeds are low.

WEATHER UNDER THUNDERSTORMS

Wind
velocities
and
temper-
ature

The air in a thunderstorm downdraft descends from altitudes where the temperature is lower than at the ground. Moreover, the downdraft is maintained at a cooler temperature than its environment by the evaporation of water and ice particles. The sinking air is not only heavier than the surrounding air, but its so-called horizontal momentum also differs from that of the surrounding air. If the descending air originated at an altitude of 10 km (6.2 mi), for example, it would reach the ground with a horizontal

velocity that somewhat resembles the wind velocity at its level of origin. When the air strikes the ground, it usually moves outward ahead of the storm at a higher speed than the speed of the storm itself.

In extreme circumstances, the outrushing, cool air may reach velocities of 100 kilometres per hour (62 miles per hour) or more and do extensive damage to property and vegetation. This severe wind most often occurs when organized lines of severe thunderstorms form in an environment where the middle level winds are very strong. When serious wind damage is produced by such a storm, the victims may suspect that it was caused by a tornado. Of course, if a funnel cloud is observed, then the nature of a storm would be obvious. If a funnel cloud is not observed, the character of the damage can be revealing. Tornadoes blow debris in a tight circular pattern, whereas the outflowing air from a thunderstorm pushes it mostly in one direction.

An observer on the ground watching a thunderstorm approach can feel the gusty, cool air before the thunderstorm passes overhead. The outspreading, downdraft air forms a pool some 500 to 2,000 m (1,600 to 6,600 ft) deep. Often there is a very distinct boundary between the cool air and the warm, humid air in which the storm formed in the first place. The passage of such a boundary is easily recognized as wind speeds increase and the air temperature suddenly drops. Over a five-minute period, a cooling of 10° F (more than 5° C) is not unusual, and cooling that is twice as great is not unknown.

By the time the cool air begins spreading over the ground, rain usually is reaching the surface. Sometimes all the raindrops evaporate while falling, and the result is a dry thunderstorm. At the other extreme, thunderstorms can produce the most torrential downpours imaginable. Under a cumulonimbus cloud, impending rain usually can be predicted when the cloud base darkens, indicating a deep layer of cloud obscuring the rays from the sun. Often, but not usually, a flash of lightning occurs and the rain follows several minutes later. There is still disagreement about the interpretation of this sequence of events. Once the rain starts, it builds up rapidly, commonly reaching its maximum intensity between five to ten minutes after the start. In small Ohio thunderstorms, the maximum five-minute rate was 122 millimetres (about 4.8 inches) per hour but most often was less than one-tenth of this amount. The average thunderstorm yielded 2×10^8 kg (220,000 short tons) of rain, but some large storms gave ten times more. Large organized storms can produce 10^{10} to 10^{12} kg of rain.

The following table lists certain extreme rainfall quantities in various parts of the world. They represent measurements at a single point.

Precipita-
tion from
storms

Some Extreme Rainfall Rates*					
date	place	duration	amount		average rate (mm/hr)
			(inches)	(cm)	
April 5, 1926	Opids Camp, Calif.	1 min	0.65	1.65	990
Sept. 30, 1925	Haughton Grove, Jamaica	3 min	1.6	4.07	814
Nov. 29, 1911	Porto Bello, Panama	5 min	2.5	6.37	765
May 12, 1916	Plumb Point, Jamaica	15 min	8.0	20.3	812
June 22, 1947	Holt, Mo.	42 min	12.0	30.5	436
July 14–15, 1947	Baguio, P.I.	24 hr	46.0	117.0	487
*Probably from thunderstorms, but not documented.					

As the duration of the rainfall increased, the average rates decreased but were extreme in every case shown. Such rapid accumulations of water invariably cause flooding; greater damage is, of course, associated with longer durations and greater quantities.

OCCURRENCE OF THUNDERSTORMS

Thunderstorms are most likely to occur in a moist, unstable atmosphere. Air masses having these properties are commonly formed over equatorial and tropical areas. When a body of air moves over low-latitude oceans, it is humidified by evaporation from the underlying water surface. Heat is transferred from the warm ocean water to the air. In addition, the nearly direct rays from the sun warm the moist, lowest layers of the atmosphere. As a consequence of these processes, moist, tropical air masses develop suitable properties for thunderstorm formation.

Disturbances in the wind field caused by pressure perturbations or changes in topography leading to an upward displacement of the air initiate the development of thunderstorms. All the conditions necessary for their occurrence are most often met over the land areas in the equatorial zone between ten degrees north and south latitudes where the average number of days with thunderstorms exceeds 100 per year. In certain places in equatorial Africa and South America, there are more than 180 thunderstorm days in an average year (Figure 2).

Frequency of storms

At higher latitudes, the frequency of thunderstorms depends on the character of the topography and the frequency of invasions of moist, tropical air. Since this happens most often in the spring and summer, the Northern Hemisphere experiences most of its thunderstorms between May and September, whereas thunderstorm maximums are found some six months later in the Southern Hemisphere.

Over the large continental area of North America, thunderstorms occasionally occur, even in the winter, in the states along the coast of the Gulf of Mexico. As summer approaches, moist, tropical air gradually extends to higher latitudes and thunderstorms do likewise. By July and August they occur on the average on more than six days per month over the flatlands of central Canada.

During midsummer, areas of high thunderstorm frequency are centred over the Florida peninsula and northern New Mexico where 18 to 20 thunderstorm days per month are experienced. The frequent thunderstorms in the New Mexico-Colorado area are initiated as warm, humid air is forced to rise on the east slope of the Rocky Mountains. On a yearly basis there are about 90 thunderstorm days in central Florida.

Thunderstorms constitute a common feature of the summer monsoons (*q.v.*) in many parts of the world, particularly over southern Asia. As the continent is warmed by solar radiation, an ocean-to-land air current is established. Moist, unstable air from the Indian Ocean is carried inland and is forced to rise up the steep slopes of the Himalayas. As a result, showers and thunderstorms are produced in great abundance. Record high rainfalls occur. The annual average precipitation at Cherrapunji, India, is about 11.6 m (457 in.) per year with about 10 m falling during the period from May to September.

In cold regions, poleward of about 60° latitude, thunderstorms are scarce or nonexistent because of the cold air near the ground and the stable atmospheric conditions. There also are few thunderstorms over those parts of the earth dominated by semipermanent high-pressure centres. See CYCLONES AND ANTICYCLONES. In these regions, which correspond to the great deserts of the world, the air generally descends. This causes a drying of the air and a stabilization of the atmosphere; as a result, thunderstorm development is inhibited.

OBSERVATIONS OF THUNDERSTORMS

Most of the existing data on thunderstorms have been accumulated by weather observers. Unfortunately, by visual observations, it is difficult and often impossible to obtain quantitative information about the characteristics of the clouds that produce the thunder. When widespread thunderstorms occur, the sky commonly is overcast with many intermingled layers of clouds of various types. Cloud summits are frequently obscured.

Advances in aviation, and in particular the development of airplanes of high structural integrity, have made it possible to fly through thunderstorms to measure their internal properties. High-flying airplanes have yielded accurate data on the vertical extent of thunderstorms.

Radar observation of storms

The development of radar during World War II contributed a great deal to the store of knowledge about thunderstorms. Most of the available statistics on thunderstorm dimensions and movements have been obtained by means of

radar. Conventional radar sets measure the location and reflectivity of water and ice particle concentrations. By noting changes in the intensity, size, or position of radar echoes, it has been possible to infer the nature of the motions in the thunderstorms.

By courtesy of the National Severe Storms Laboratory, ESSA

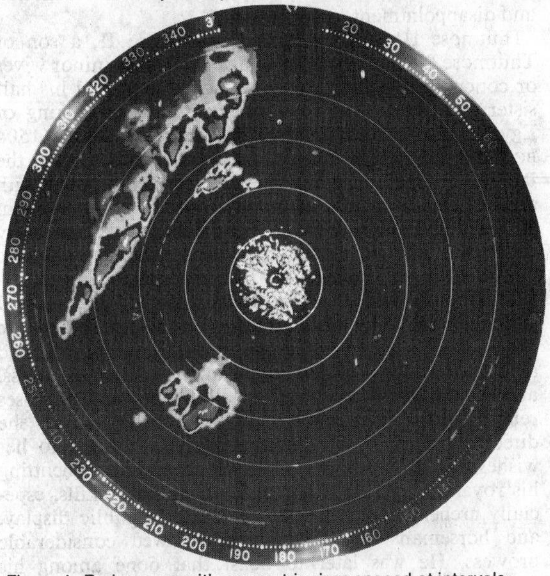

Figure 4: Radarscope with concentric rings spaced at intervals of 20 nautical miles. A line of thunderstorms is oriented northeast–southwest. Another large isolated storm is located southwest of the centre. The varying shades of gray show the varying intensity of the radar echo.

Networks of radar sets are employed by the civil and military weather services in several countries to detect and track thunderstorms. All commercial airliners are now equipped with radar to allow the pilots to observe thunderstorms and take evasive action and thereby reduce flight hazards and increase passenger comfort.

Since about 1960, atmospheric scientists have begun to use pulsed-Doppler radar sets. Such equipment not only can make the same observations as were made by earlier radars but can measure the instantaneous fields of motion of the precipitation particles. In certain circumstances, this information can be used to measure the speeds of updrafts and downdrafts. Furthermore, it is sometimes possible to infer the size of the precipitation particles.

Weather satellites photograph cloud patterns and telemeter the pictures back to earth (see WEATHER FORECASTING). Radiometers on board the satellites supply information on the temperatures of the clouds (*q.v.*) that are observed. On the basis of appearance and temperature, it is possible to infer when a cloud is a cumulonimbus and, hence, probably a thunderstorm source. At the present time, satellite data are revealing patterns of convective cloud and thunderstorm development on a scale never seen before. The information has been particularly valuable over the vast, low-latitude oceanic areas that were never adequately observed in the past. It is anticipated that, in time, satellite data coupled with radar and aircraft data will lead to more realistic models of thunderstorms than exist today.

BIBLIOGRAPHY. D. ATLAS *et al., Severe Local Storms,* Met. Monogr., vol. 5, no. 27 (1963), a series of authoritative articles at an advanced level; H.R. BYERS and R.R. BRAHAM, *The Thunderstorm* (1949), the final report of the most comprehensive investigation of thunderstorms ever attempted; W.J. HUMPHREYS, *Physics of the Air* (1940, reprinted 1964), a classic in atmospheric physics; G.T. TREWARTHA, *An Introduction to Climate,* 4th ed. (1968), an intermediate-level book discussing thunderstorm formation and distribution; L.J. BATTAN, *The Nature of Violent Storms* (1961), a nontechnical discussion of thunderstorms, tornadoes, and hurricanes; M.A. UMAN, *Lightning* (1969), an advanced, up-to-date treatment; P.E. VIEMEISTER, *The Lightning Book* (1961), a nontechnical discussion of all aspects of lighting.

(L.J.B.)

Thutmose III

Perhaps the greatest of the pharaohs of ancient Egypt, Thutmose III is generally regarded as the architect of the Egyptian empire. His reign marked the beginning of the greatest epoch in the country's history. But the first 21 years of his reign must have been filled with frustration and disappointment.

Thutmose III was the son of Thutmose II, a son of Thutmose I; his mother was one of the King's minor wives or concubines, named Isis. Thutmose II married his half sister Hatshepsut and was crowned the fourth king of Egypt's 18th dynasty. Before his untimely death (1504 BC) Thutmose II made some show of arms against the Palestinian Bedouin and crushed a rebellion in Nubia with severity. Since there was no prince with a better claim to the throne, the boy was crowned king on the early death of his father; he was about ten at the time and was *Thutmose's* betrothed to the heiress, his half sister Neferure. Nefe-*minority* rure's mother, Hatshepsut, the daughter of Thutmose I and wife and sister of Thutmose II, acted as regent. In the second year of his reign this strong-minded and ambitious woman herself assumed the attributes, dress, and insignia of a king and to all intents and purposes reigned in his stead. As one of her courtiers says, "she directed the affairs of the whole land according to her wishes." Still, Thutmose was given an education befitting his royal station. He was taught all military skills, especially archery, which he demonstrated in public display, and horsemanship, in which he showed considerable prowess. He was later to boast that none among his followers could equal him in physical strength and in marksmanship.

Hirmer Fotoarchiv, Munchen

Thutmose III smiting the Asiatics, limestone relief from the Temple of Amon at Karnak, 1490-36 BC.

As he grew up, Thutmose may even have been entrusted with command of the army on campaign in Nubia; whether he also fought in Palestine is doubtful. His grandfather Thutmose I had penetrated into northern Syria; Thutmose II, though far from a weakling, had not followed this success, and Hatshepsut, as a woman, may have been unwilling to send an army into the field. Thus, through inaction, Egyptian influence in Syria and Palestine had declined. The sons and grandsons of the Syrian princes who had surrendered to Thutmose I no longer sent tribute, and the king of Mitanni, a powerful Mesopo-

tamian kingdom with its capital beyond the Euphrates, was able to extend his control westward to the Mediterranean.

In the 22nd year of Thutmose's reign, a formidable coalition was formed against Egypt, led by the king of Kadesh in northern Syria, and no doubt supported by the Mitanni. At this moment of crisis Hatshepsut died. Her death was opportune; whether her nephew was responsible is a matter of surmise only, but later in his reign, he decreed that her name be obliterated on all her monuments, her statues smashed, and her figure erased from reliefs.

After a few months' preparation the King was ready to *First* march at the head of his army. The first campaign is *Syrian* recorded in some detail on the walls of the temple he built *campaign* at Karnak in Thebes that depict the march to Gaza and thence to Yahmai south of the Carmel Range, the Council of War, and the King's bold decision to surprise the enemy encamped at Megiddo, northeast of Carmel and about 18 miles southeast of the modern city of Haifa. Thutmose's approach was by the route least expected, a narrow defile over the mountain. It was successful. The enemy was defeated and Megiddo was taken after a siege of eight months. In subsequent campaigns, which are less fully described in the annals, ports on the Phoenician coast were converted into Egyptian supply bases, and Kadesh and other cities in al-Biqāʿ (Beka) Valley were taken.

In the 33rd year of Thutmose's reign, the time was at last ripe for his most audacious move, an attack on the kingdom of Mitanni itself, which had grown stronger since the day when Thutmose I had taken its army by surprise. Thutmose planned the campaign well; pontoon boats were transported across Syria on oxcarts for the crossing of the Euphrates River. The ensuing encounter, which must have taken place on the eastern bank, is not described by the annalist; it resulted in the precipitate flight of the Mitannian king and the capture of thirty members of his harem and some hundreds of his soldiers. Triumphantly, Thutmose set up his commemorative inscription by the river's edge, next to that of his grandfather Thutmose I. It was his farthest point of advance. On the homeward journey he also hunted elephant in the land of Niy, in the Orontes Valley, and on his return he celebrated a great triumph at Thebes and dedicated prisoners and booty to the temple of the state god Amon.

In later campaigns (there were 17 in all), Thutmose III was content to consolidate what he had won and to lay the foundations of an imperial organization of his Asian possessions. Native rulers, members of local ruling dynasties, were henceforward set to govern their own territories as vassals of Egypt and were bound by solemn oath to keep the peace, render annual tribute, and obey the Egyptian representative in the region, the "overseer of foreign lands." Their sons were sent as hostages to Egypt and educated at court, so that in due course they might return to rule their inheritance, Egyptianized in outlook and sympathies. Fortresses were built, and Egyptian garrisons were stationed at key points along the coast and in the highlands.

To the south, Thutmose extended the limits of Egyptian domination over Nubia as far as Napata, near the Gebel Barkal, where he built a temple to Amon. He thoroughly subdued the turbulent Nubian tribes and employed many of them in the gold mines, which from his reign on became the basis of Egyptian wealth in foreign exchange with the princess of western Asia. For the last 12 years of his reign, he was content to enjoy the fruits of his victories. The tribute of Syria and Palestine and of the Sudan poured into his treasury; the annals list huge quantities of timber and metal ores, cattle, and grain delivered by the conquered. Minoan Crete and Cyprus, Babylonia, Assyria, and the Hittites sent gifts. The tombs of high officials of the reign are decorated with scenes depicting the reception of foreign envoys coming from places as far away as the Aegean and the Greek mainland to lay their rich and exotic gifts at the feet of the pharaoh. The prestige of Egypt had never been so high.

The new prosperity is reflected in the remarkable program of building undertaken by the King's architects. The Temple of Amon at Karnak in particular was enlarged and enriched by many new buildings and a number of obelisks. Two of the splendid granite obelisks that he erected there are now in Istanbul and Rome; of the two, now known as Cleopatra's Needles, with which he adorned the temple of the sun-god at Heliopolis, one is in New York's Central Park, and the other on the Thames embankment in London. During his reign art and craftsmanship received new impetus from his patronage. The exotic birds, beasts, and plants that he brought back from his campaigns in Asia are depicted on the walls of his Festival Hall at Karnak; among the gifts sent him from abroad were a live bear, an elephant, a giraffe, and "birds that give birth every day"—probably domestic hens, which were rare in the Near East at that time.

During the last year of his life, feeling his strength failing, Thutmose appointed his son Amenhotep II, the son of his second wife, Hatshepsut's daughter Meryetre, as co-regent. When he died, in 1450 BC, he was laid to rest in a remote corner of the Valley of the Tombs of the Kings in western Thebes. Along with many other royal burials, this tomb was later looted by robbers and the mummy of the pharaoh was one of those discovered in 1889, in a hiding place where the priest-kings of the 21st dynasty had hidden them for safety. Of the rich furniture that must originally have been placed in the tomb, only a few fragments were found. His mortuary temple, which was built on a terrace at Dayr al-Baḥrī beside that of Hatshepsut, was discovered in 1962.

Nearby, the burial place of three members of his harem was found; judging by their names, they were Syrian princesses, and though of minor rank their jewelry and equipment were extremely lavish.

Of all the kings of ancient Egypt, Thutmose III is perhaps the one who, for the modern historian, most nearly comes to life. His records, though couched in the boastful and extravagant terms thought befitting a pharaoh's exploits, leave little doubt not only of his ability as a soldier and a statesman, but also of his abilities as an athlete and a hunter of lion, wild cattle, and elephant. From his mummy it is known that he was a small man, not above five feet three inches in height. His statues show a resolute face with a large, high-bridged nose and pleasantly smiling mouth.

His fame lived after him. His name, inscribed on countless amulets, was thought to bring power and protection to the wearers. A popular hymn celebrating his triumphs became a model for later paeans of victory; in it the god Amon-Re says:

I set thy glory and the fear of thee in all lands, and the terror of thee as far as the four supports of the sky. . . . the rulers of all foreign countries are gathered together within thy grasp. I stretch out my hands to bind them for thee.

BIBLIOGRAPHY. There is no separate life of Thutmose III. His career and achievements are described in some detail in general histories such as J.H. BREASTED, *A History of Egypt from the Earliest Times to the Persian Conquest* (1905, reprinted many times); and, more recently, A.H. GARDINER, *Egypt of the Pharaohs* (1961). The newly revised edition of *The Cambridge Ancient History*, vol. 2, pt. 1 (1971), contains chapters by WILLIAM C. HAYES on the early part of the 18th dynasty; and by MARGARET S. DROWER on the Egyptian Challenge and Egypt in Asia. The bibliographies to these chapters are very full. The text of Thutmose's annals and other inscriptions may be found in J.H. BREASTED (ed.), *Ancient Records of Egypt*, vol. 2 (1906). For a better translation of the more important texts, see J.B. PRITCHARD, *Ancient Near Eastern Texts Illustrating the Old Testament*, 3rd ed. (1966); the fullest commentary on the Asian campaigns is that of H.W. HELCK in *Die Beziehungen Ägyptens zu Vorderasien im 3. und 2. Jahrtausend v. Chr.* (1962). Statues of the king, some of which may be portraits, are illustrated by C. ALDRED in *New Kingdom Art in Ancient Egypt During the Eighteenth Dynasty, 1590 to 1315 B.C.* (1951), no. 25, 35–37, 39.

(M.S.D.)

Thysanoptera

Members of the order Thysanoptera, among the smallest of the winged insects, are abundant in the tropical and temperate regions of the world. The approximately 5,000 species that have been described so far are also known as thrips. Thrips have an economic importance, for some species transmit plant viruses, and by their feeding reduce seed production, disfigure flowers and fruits, and damage plant leaves. In warm areas a number of them cause plant galls and leaf rolls. On the other hand, a few species prey on destructive mites and scale insects, and a number may aid in the pollination of flowers and, indirectly, in the formation of leaf mold.

Most thrips are 1.5 to 3 millimetres in size, with the smallest being about 0.6 millimetres and the largest about 15 millimetres. Because of their minute size they can enter the smallest flowers or tiniest cracks in stems and bark. Their wings, when present, are narrow and fringed, hence the name Thysanoptera (Latin, "fringed wings"). Despite their Lilliputian size, thrips are often elaborately ornamented with hexagonal designs, spines, or body flanges. The bristles (setae) of some are expanded at the tips or elongated, or the body wall may be expanded into prongs or forks. The larvae of thrips tend toward bright colours (red, orange, or yellow); the adults range from whitish to browns or black. Adults have extensible bladders on the tarsi of the legs, as suggested by the common name bladder feet.

General features

Natural history. *Life cycle.* The development of thrips takes place in the egg, in two larval stages, during which all the immature feeding occurs, and in one, two, or three pupal stages in which no feeding has ever been observed.

Although the changes that occur in pupae of Thysanoptera resemble those that occur in insects to undergo complete metamorphosis, thrips are said to undergo only simple metamorphosis.

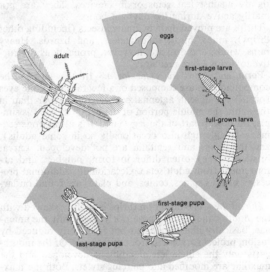

Figure 1: Life cycle of pear thrips.

The primary method of reproduction among thrips is by bisexual union. The males frequently are shorter lived than females, and mating often takes place early in the life span, when the adults first appear. Reproduction by unfertilized eggs (parthenogenesis) has been known to occur occasionally.

Thrips in the suborder Terebrantia always lay eggs, as do most thrips in the more advanced suborder Tubulifera. Hatching of eggs within the female (ovoviparity), occurs in some highly evolved members of the Tubulifera. Eggs are elongated, oval to kidney shaped, faintly to distinctly sculptured, and, as is the case in other minute insects, are proportionately large, often occupying two or three abdominal segments of the female before laying. Ordinarily, eggs of the Terebrantia are inserted into living plant tissue in a slit prepared by the sawlike ovipositor of the female. By contrast, eggs of the Tubulifera, whose females have no ovipositor, are pushed under bark, in or between flowers and leaf sheaths, or are glued onto leaf or bark surfaces. Eggs take from three to 16 days to hatch according to the species and conditions.

Egg laying

Although similar in overall form to the adult, the larvae of thrips are weaker and simpler in structure. The long anal bristles characteristic of larvae may hold droplets of excreted liquid that are deposited on leaf surfaces. The presence of dark coloured spots of excreta adjacent to light coloured feeding zones are some typical signs of thrips damage.

The first stage is short (a few days); the second may last up to many months when estivation or hibernation occurs. In the Terebrantia the second stage larva transforms into a prepupa, whereas in the Tubulifera an abbreviated form, the primipupa, is part of the sequence of development and is followed by the prepupal form. The prepupal stage is of short duration (a few hours to several days) and gives rise to the final pupal stage, of short or long duration, that eventually produces the adult. Pupation takes place in the ground in earthen cells (in the case of many advanced Terebrantia), in cocoons (in many primitive Terebrantia), or on a host plant (in many advanced Terebrantia and the Tubulifera). Some thrips, for example, the pear thrips, have only one generation per year; others such as the onion thrips may have several generations each growing season.

Ecology. In regions having winter cold, thrips hibernate as adults or immature forms in detritus, hollow stems, or in the ground. Those that perish with the cold are replaced each year by spring migrants from warmer areas. In the tropics many thrips exhibit seasonal fluctuations, being more active in the wet than in the dry seasons. Some thrips are sensitive to relative humidity. Larvae are generally found in shady locations, on the underside of leaves or branches. Adults occasionally occur on the upper side of leaves in bright light. Most thrips rest tightly against leaf veins or in crevices. They are primarily active during the daylight hours.

Thrips are preyed upon by many insects (including other thrips), mites, birds, salamanders, and lizards. Heavy rains, winds, and dust are, however, probably as destructive to thrips as are predators.

Form and function. *The larva.* In the larvae, the compound eyes are composed of a few facets, simple eyes (ocelli) are absent, antennal segments are fewer than in the adult, the middle portion of the body (thorax) is simple, the lower part of the leg (tarsus) is always one segmented (although also occasionally so in some adults), and the wings and genitalia are not developed. Larval bristles (setae) often differ in form, number, and arrangement from adult setae. Occasionally additional processes such as spines, combs, and plates are found on larvae.

The adult. The head of a thrips is slightly skewed with the mouth cone directed posteriorly. Generally the antennae, basically nine-segmented but frequently reduced by fusion, project forward in front of the eyes. Of the mouthparts only the single left mandible is developed and the maxillae are modified into piercing stylets. Both the maxillae and the labium bear segmented sensory projections (palps).

The middle portion of the body (thorax) bears the legs. The first part of the thorax (prothorax) of thrips bears the fore legs, the inner parts (coxae) of which may exhibit ridges that when rubbed with spurs from the lower parts (femurs) supposedly emit sound. The remainder of the thorax (pterothorax) bears the wings as well as the mid and hind legs. The wings are usually fairly simple and straplike. At rest they are laid over the abdomen but never folded. Typically the wings have long posterior fringes with shorter fringes occurring on the leading edge of the wings.

The abdomen is elongated and generally flattened dorso-ventrally, especially in the Tubulifera. There are ten distinctive segments with a rudiment of the 11th. The first and eighth abdominal segments bear breathing holes (spiracles). Often in the Tubulifera, several setae on the back are S-shaped and hook into the wing fringes to hold the wings at rest. In the Terebrantia the terminal segment is rounded in the males and split ventrally up to the eighth segment in the females. In the Tubulifera the terminal segment is tubelike.

The male genital organs are composed of paired appendages and an unpaired copulatory organ (aedeagus), all of which retract into the abdomen. The paired testes and accessory glands with their ducts occur in the posterior half of the abdomen. The female of the Terebrantia usually has an ovipositor composed of two pairs of sawlike blades. These are absent in the Tubulifera. There are eight egg sacs (ovarioles) and spherical, often pigmented, seminal receptacle for storage of sperm acquired during mating.

Evolution, paleontology, and classification. The Thysanoptera are part of the Psocoptera or Corrodentia-Hemiptera phyletic line of insects. Their origin may have been correlated with the development of the left mandible as an efficient chisel for piercing pollen granules. Possibly during the period when ancestral types were pollen feeders early thrips proliferated into a distinct order, which has since become diverse. Because of their small size, the development of fringe wings seemingly was favoured to overcome disproportionate drag on the uplift of the wings.

The earliest fossil, *Permothrips longipennis*, seems closest to the family Aeolothripidae, the most generalized and perhaps ancestral type. All extant families are known from fossils embedded in amber. The most advanced groups are the families Thripidae and Phlaeothripidae. The terebrantian families mostly retain their habit of feeding on vascular plants and pollen. Many members of the single extant tubiferan family Phlaeothripidae have adjusted to feeding in moldy debris.

Distinguishing taxonomic features. Although no particular structure is absolutely indicative of a taxonomic level, many features are useful in separating the major groups of Thysanoptera. The form of the antennae and its appendages, the shape and structure of the forewing, abdominal characters including form of the ovipositor in females, and glandular and setal location are important characters for determining the familial relationships. At the generic and species level antennal details, mouthparts, and body sculpturing are useful taxonomic characters, along with colour and bristle arrangement.

Annotated classification. The classification presented here is based on that of H. Priesner (1957, 1960).

ORDER THYSANOPTERA

Insects averaging about 2 mm; unique in that the right mandible is atrophied, resulting in an asymmetrical mouthcone; wings, when present, bear long fringes. Extensible bladders on the tarsi of the adults.

Suborder Terebrantia

The 10th and last abdominal segment, rarely tubelike, always split ventrally, major anal setae arising from subapical region, never from separate platelets; with sawlike ovipositor in female; wings usually with fine hairs (micotrichia) and at least 1 longitudinal vein; larvae with intermediate antennal segments bearing rings and microsetae; pupae with antennal sheaths either extended forward of head or lying over head; eggs without polar thickenings. 2 fossil families, Permothripidae and an undetermined family are, respectively, from Permian and Jurassic periods. Present families include the following.

Family Aeolothripidae

Oligocene (Baltic amber) to present. Worldwide. Antennae 9-segmented; ovipositor may be upturned or straight; forewings broad and rounded at tips, surface with microtrichia and several longitudinal and cross veins; antennal sensors on intermediate segments in form of linear or circular disks.

Family Merothripidae

Oligocene (Baltic amber) to present. Worldwide. Antennae 8- or 9-segmented; ovipositor downturned, often weakly developed; forewings narrow, surface smooth; antennal sensors on intermediate segments disclike.

Family Heterothripidae

Cretaceous (Cedar Lake amber) to present. Western Hemisphere and India. Antennae nine-segmented; ovipositor downturned; forewings narrow, surface with microtrichia; antennal sensors on intermediate segments as flat discs or protruding peglike cones.

Family Thripidae

Oligocene (Baltic amber) to present. Worldwide. Antennae 6- to 9-segmented; ovipositor downturned, rarely weakly developed; forewings narrow, with microtrichia; antennal sensors on intermediate segments as simple or forked sense cones.

Suborder Tubulifera

The 10th abdominal segment tubelike, never split, major anal setae arising from separate plates adjacent to the tube; females without ovipositor; wings without longitudinal veins or fringe; larvae with antennal segments smooth not ringed; pupae with antennal sheaths hornlike or curved around (not over) head; eggs often with a tubercule on anterior pole.

Family Phlaeothripidae

This is the only family currently assigned to the suborder. Representatives occur throughout the world are known from Oligocene (Baltic amber) to the present.

Critical appraisal. The subordinal disposition of the thrips is well established, but the ranking of family groups as given above is disputed by some who would raise the families to superfamily rank. The order was earlier (1838) designated the Physapoda by H. Burmeister, given in allusion to the swollen tarsi, the so-called bladder feet.

BIBLIOGRAPHY. The literature on Thysanoptera is widely scattered throughout numerous entomological journals with occasional summaries given in monographs or lists. The monographs are predominantly faunal studies, though they often include regional revisions of some of the taxa. Only a few complete generic revisions have been published. Some of the latest, though not necessarily recent, faunal monographs are: S.F. BAILEY, "The Thrips of California, Part 1: Suborder Terebrantia," *Bull. Calif. Insect Surv.*, vol. 4, no. 5, pp. 143–220 (1957); H.E. COTT, *Systematics of the Suborder Tubulifera (Thysanoptera) in California* (1956); L.J. STANNARD, "The Thrips, or Thysanoptera, of Illinois," *Bull. Ill. Nat. Hist. Surv.*, vol. 29, no. 4, pp. 215–552 (1968); G.D. MORISON, "Thysanoptera of the London Area," *Lond. Nat.*, reprint no. 59 (1947–49). Two comprehensive catalogues and annotated synopses are C.F. JACOT-GUILLARMOD, "Catalogue of the Thysanoptera of the World (Part 1)," *Ann. Cape Provincial Museums* (*Nat. Hist.*) (1970); and L.J. STANNARD, *The Phylogeny and Classification of the North American Genera of the Suborder Tubulifera (Thysanoptera)* (1957). Proposals for the classification of the thrips that have received general acceptance are those by H. PRIESNER, "Zur Vergleichender Morphologie des Endothorax der Thysanoptera," *Zool. Anz.*, vol. 159, no. 7–8, pp. 159–167 (1957), and "Das System der Tubulifera (Thysanoptera)," *Anz. öst. Akad. Wiss.*, 13:283–296 (1960). Morphological treatments of the Thysanoptera are found in R.G. DAVIES, "Observations on the Morphology of the Head and Mouthparts in the Thysanoptera," *Proc. R. Ent. Soc. Lond.* (A), vol. 33, no. 7–9, pp. 97–106 (1958); and P. PESSON, "Ordre des Thysanoptera," in P. GRASSE, *Traité de zoologie*, vol. 10, no. 2, pp. 1805–1869 (1951). A source of ecological information on thrips is that by L. CEDERHOLM, *Ecological Studies on Thysanoptera* (1963).

(L.J.S.)

Tiberius

Tiberius, Rome's second emperor, whose reign was initially marked by wise and beneficent measure, ended his life as a tyrannical recluse. Yet he left behind him institutions that helped to ensure the survival of the empire. Tiberius Claudius Nero Caesar Augustus was a man of puzzlingly conflicting qualities. He had the training and talent to be a great administrator and a victorious general. Rome—the state, not the city—flourished under Tiberius. The rebellious borders were subdued, the treasury grew fat, and the provinces were prosperous and well governed. The city itself was less fortunate. By the time Tiberius became emperor he was 56 years old. He had lost every person he ever loved, and he had himself experienced insults, threats, and exile. Tiberius, or those who spoke in his name and employed his power, brought to the city of Rome an accelerating reign of insecurity and terror that threatened almost every major figure and destroyed many of them.

Background and youth. Tiberius was born on November 16, 42 BC. His father, also named Tiberius Claudius Nero, a high priest and a magistrate, was a former fleet captain for Julius Caesar. His mother, the beautiful Livia Drusilla, was her husband's cousin and may have been only 13 years old when Tiberius was born. (Many dates during that era of civil strife cannot be accurately determined.) In the civil wars following the assassination of

Tiberius, sculpture by an unknown artist. In the Vatican Museum.
Alinari

Julius Caesar, the elder Tiberius gave his allegiance to Mark Antony, Caesar's protégé. When Augustus, Caesar's grandnephew and heir, fell out with Antony and defeated him in the ensuing power struggle, the elder Tiberius and his family became fugitives. They fled first to Sicily and then to Greece, but by the time Tiberius was three years old an amnesty was granted and the family was able to return to Rome.

In 39 BC Augustus had the power, if not yet the title, of emperor. Attracted by the beauty of Livia, who was at that time pregnant with a second son, Augustus divorced his own wife, who was also pregnant, and, forcing the elder Tiberius to give up Livia, married her. The infant Tiberius remained with his father, and, when the younger brother, Drusus, was born a few months later, he was sent to join them.

At the death of his father, Tiberius was nine years old and, with Drusus, he went to live with Livia and the Emperor. The two boys and the Emperor's daughter, Julia, between them in age, studied together, played together, and took part in the obligatory ceremonials of temple dedication and celebration of victories. They were joined by their cousin Marcellus, the son of Augustus' sister, Octavia.

In the absence of a clear law designating Augustus' successor as emperor, all three boys were trained accordingly. They were instructed in rhetoric, literature, diplomacy, and military skills, and soon they also began taking a ceremonial role in the affairs of state. As oldest, Tiberius was the first to do so.

In the triumph following Augustus' victory over Cleopatra and Antony at Actium, the 13-year-old Tiberius rode the right-hand horse of Augustus' chariot in the procession. Though not a striking figure, he conducted himself well.

Serious by nature, he had become a shy youth, though he was sometimes called sullen. His rhetoric teacher, Theodorus the Gadarene called him "mud, kneaded with blood." His great talent was application. With the best teachers in the empire at his disposal and, above all, as a participant in the life of the palace, the centre of the civilized Western world, he learned rapidly. By the age of 14, Tiberius was used to dining with client kings of the empire, to conducting religious services over the heads of powerful men five times his age, and even to seeing his own face and form in marble statues.

Years in the shadow of Augustus. He was not handsome. As a teen-ager he was tall and broad-shouldered, but his complexion was bad. His nose had a pronounced hook, but that was typically Roman: his beautiful moth-

(margin) Life with Augustus

er, Livia, had the same nose. His manner was disconcerting. He had a slow, methodical way of speaking that seemed intended to conceal his meaning rather than make it plain. But he was diligent. He may not have known he would be emperor, but he cannot have doubted that he would be at least a general at a rather early age and thereafter he would be a high official in the government of Rome. In 27 BC, when Tiberius was 15 years old, Augustus took him and Marcellus to Gaul to inspect outposts. They experienced no fighting, but they learned a great deal about how to rule the marches, keep fortifications intact, and keep garrisons alert. When they returned, Augustus gave Marcellus his daughter Julia as wife.

Marriage to Vipsania   Then Tiberius himself married. Love matches were infrequent in imperial Rome, but Tiberius' marriage to Vipsania Agrippina was one. She was the daughter of Marcus Agrippa, Augustus' son-in-law and lieutenant. During Tiberius' long life, there are hardly a dozen years when he could have been said to be happy: the years of his marriage to Vipsania. Besides his love for his wife and for his brother Drusus, now growing into manhood, he was occupied with important work. His first military command at the age of 22, resulting in the recovery of standards of some Roman legions that had been lost decades before in Parthia, brought him great acclaim. As a reward he asked for another active command and was given the assignment of pacifying the turbulent province of Pannonia on the eastern shore of the Adriatic Sea.

Tiberius not only conquered the enemy but so distinguished himself by his care for his men that he found himself popular and even loved. His fellow officers gave him the affectionate nickname of "Biberius Caldius Mero," which was a Latin play on his own name signifying "drinker of wine with no water added." When he returned to Rome, he was awarded a triumph.

But Tiberius' happy years were coming to an end. His beloved brother, Drusus, broke his leg in falling from a horse while campaigning in Germany. Tiberius was at Ticinum, on the Po River, south of what is now Milan, 400 miles away. Riding day and night to be with his brother, he arrived just in time to see Drusus die. Tiberius escorted the body back to Rome, walking in front of it on foot all the way.

Shortly after the death of Drusus, he had to give up his wife, Vipsania, the other person he loved. Augustus' daughter Julia had become a widow for the second time. Her first husband, Marcellus, had died, and the emperor had married her to Agrippa (who, as Vipsania's father, was Tiberius' father-in-law). When Agrippa died in 12 BC, Augustus wanted her suitably married at once and chose Tiberius as her third husband. Tiberius had no more choice than his father had had when Augustus decided to marry Livia. Tiberius was as obedient as his father. He divorced Vipsania and married Julia.

Marriage to Julia   Tiberius' new wife has come down in history with a reputation for adultery and licentiousness. It is not certain how much of the reputation she deserved. Roman historians often dealt in gossip and had axes to grind, inventing scandal when there was none; but in Julia's case they had good reason for their opinion.

When Julia married Tiberius, he was 30. She was 27, twice a widow, the mother of five children (not all surviving). She was pretty, light-minded, and liked the society of men. She did not get along with her mother-in-law (who was also her stepmother), Livia, and after the first few months she did not get along with Tiberius. It is certain that she committed adultery, and this presented Tiberius with an immense problem, not only personal but political. A law of Augustus himself required a husband to denounce a wife who committed adultery. But Julia was the Emperor's beloved child, and, as Augustus knew nothing of her vices, to denounce her would be to wound him greatly, and that was dangerous.

With no good course of action to follow, Tiberius fled the dilemma. He asked for and received fighting commands away from Rome. When once in Rome between battles, he chanced to see Vipsania at the home of a friend. She had, at Augustus' orders, been remarried to a senator. Tiberius was so overcome with sorrow that he followed her through the streets, weeping. Augustus heard of it and ordered Tiberius never to see her again.

Although Augustus heaped honours on Tiberius, they did not compensate for Julia's behaviour. In 6 BC Tiberius was granted the powers of a tribune (one of the highest Roman offices) and shortly thereafter went into a self-imposed exile on the island of Rhodes, leaving Julia to frolic in Rome.

Tiberius was now 36 years old and at the pinnacle of his power. He was capable of ruling an empire, conducting a great war, or governing a province of barbarians. In Rhodes he had nothing to do. From this point on, all of his ability and strength appear to begin to turn inward, into strange and unpleasant behaviour. From this point begins the story of Tiberius the monster. It is impossible to know whether the picture of an evil, sadistic, ultimately all-powerful old man that began to take shape then is justified. The histories of Tiberius' reign—written either by flatterers, like his old war comrade Velleius Paterculus, or by enemies—are not wholly trustworthy. **Exile in Rhodes**

Yet there can be no question that a change took place in Tiberius at this time. The loving husband and brother, the keen student, and the victorious general all began to disappear. What emerged was a man who seemed interested only in his own satisfactions and the increasingly perverse ways to find them. On Rhodes Tiberius became a recluse —unassuming and amiable at first, resentful and angry later on.

Though Tiberius had left Rome for Rhodes of his own free will, daring the Emperor's wrath, he could not return without Augustus' permission. Augustus withheld that permission for the better part of a decade. Tiberius has no history during those years, for he had nothing to do. He walked and talked with his astrologer, Thrasyllus, and with other guests, servants, and clients of his estate. He read Greek poetry, Egyptian pornography, histories of warfare, and treatises on science. He bathed, and dined, and grew older.

In Rome Julia caroused with many lovers; Seneca says she practiced "every shamelessness in the arms of the first passerby." At last Livia secured proofs of Julia's many adulteries and took them to Augustus, who was shocked and then furious. Under his own law she should have been executed, but he did not have the heart for that; instead, he exiled her for life to the tiny island of Pandateria. But even then Tiberius was not recalled. There were three young men whom the Emperor appeared to favour as heirs, all sons of Julia. One of them, Postumus, reportedly no more than a boor, fell into disfavour with Augustus and was sent into exile with his mother. The other two, Lucius and Gaius, were clearly candidates to succeed. But in 2 BC Lucius died, in Massilia (Marseilles), and the Emperor relented. He called Tiberius back to Rome.

By AD 4 he was in possession of all his honours again, and in that year Gaius was killed in a war in Lycia. Tiberius had become the second man in Rome. Augustus did not like him, but he adopted him as his son. "Poor Rome, doomed to be chewed by those slow-moving jaws," Augustus complained; but he had no choice. He was growing old. Tiberius was the least objectionable successor left.

Tiberius became proud and powerful. His statues had been torn down and defaced while he was in Rhodes. Now they were rebuilt. He was given command of an army to quell Arminius, who had destroyed three Roman legions in Germany in AD 9; he succeeded wholly. He was succeeding at everything now, and in AD 14, on August 19, Augustus died.

Tiberius, now supreme, played politics with the Senate and did not allow it to name him emperor for almost a month, but on September 17 he succeeded to the principate. He was 56 years old.

Reign as emperor. The opening years of Tiberius' reign seem almost a model of wise and temperate rule. They were not without displays of force and violence, of a kind calculated to secure his power. The one remaining possible contender for the throne, Postumus, was murdered, probably at Tiberius' orders. The only real threat to his power, the Roman Senate, was intimidated by the concentration of the Praetorian Guard, normally dispersed all over Italy, within marching distance of Rome.

Apart from acts such as these, Tiberius' laws and policies were both patient and far-seeing. He did not attempt great new conquests. He did not move armies about or change governors of provinces without reason. He stopped the waste of the imperial treasury, so that when he died he left behind 20 times the wealth he had inherited, and the power of Rome was never more secure. He strengthened the Roman navy. He abandoned the practice of providing gladiatorial games. He forbade some of the more outlandish forms of respect to his office, such as naming a month of the calendar after him, as had been done for Julius Caesar and Augustus. He ruled so well that the German historian Theodor Mommsen, for instance, calls him "the ablest of all the sovereigns the empire ever had."

There were, to be sure, occasional wars and acts of savage repression. Tiberius' legions put down a provincial rebellion with considerable bloodshed. In Rome itself, on the pretext that four Jews had conspired to steal a woman's treasure, Tiberius exiled the entire Jewish community of the city. Four thousand of the strongest men were impressed into the army and sent to Sardinia to die of malaria and neglect; the remaining 6,000 persons were banished.

The most ominous and least defensible aspect of Tiberius' first years as emperor was the growth of the practice called "delation." Most crimes committed by well-to-do citizens were, under Roman law, punished in part by heavy fines and confiscations. These fines contributed in large part to the growth of the imperial treasury, but the money did not all go to the fiscus. Because there were no paid prosecutors, any citizen could act as a volunteer prosecutor and, if the person he accused was convicted, collect a share of the confiscated property. These volunteers, called *delatores*, made a profitable career of seeking out or inventing crime. Many of the prosecutions were based on rumour or falsified evidence, and there were few Romans who were so honoured or so powerful that they did not need to fear the attack of the *delatores* on any suspicion, or on none at all.

Death of Drusus

In AD 23 Tiberius' son died. Young Drusus, named after the favourite brother who had died in Germany, had not been loved by his father and seems not to have earned much love. Devoted to blood sports of all kinds, he loved watching executions and gladiatorial displays, and spent his leisure time in hunting wild game. He does not appear to have possessed a great deal of intelligence. Nevertheless, his death saddened Tiberius. From then on he spared less and less thought to the work of empire. More and more he delegated his authority in the actual running of affairs over to the man he had entrusted with the important command of the Praetorian Guard, Sejanus. Before long it was Sejanus who ruled Rome, and Tiberius was emperor only in name.

Ironically, the death of Drusus, the event that brought Sejanus to power, may have been Sejanus' own doing. Apparently Sejanus seduced the wife of the younger Drusus, Livilla, and induced her to become his accomplice in murdering her husband. The evidence is not absolute and has been questioned by many historians, but, when it eventually appeared, it was not questioned by Tiberius. In AD 27, at the age of 67, Tiberius left Rome to visit some of the southern parts of Italy. En route he paused to go to the island of Capri. His intention appears to have been only to stay for a time, but he never returned to Rome.

It is the remaining decade or so of Tiberius' life that has given rise to the legend of Tiberius the monster. It seems probable, to begin with, that Tiberius, never handsome, had become repulsively ugly at about the time of his removal to Capri. First his skin broke out in blotches, and then his complexion became covered with pus-filled eruptions, exuding a bad smell and causing a good deal of pain. He built himself a dozen great villas ringing Capri, with prisons, underground dungeons, torture chambers, and places of execution. He filled his villas with treasure

Life on Capri

and art objects of every kind and with the enormous retinue appropriate to a Caesar: servants, guards, entertainers, philosophers, astrologers, musicians, and seekers after favour. If the near-contemporary historians are to be believed, his favorite entertainments were cruel and obscene; but the historians' venom ascribes to him every imaginable vice. Even under the most favourable interpretation, he killed ferociously and almost at random. It is probable that by then his mind was disordered.

He had not, however, lost touch with the real world. He came to realize just how strong he had made Sejanus and how weak he had left himself. In AD 31 he had allowed himself to be elected consul of Rome for a fifth time and had chosen as his co-consul Sejanus. He gave Sejanus permission to marry Livilla, the widow of Tiberius' son, Drusus. Now Sejanus not only had the substance of power but its forms as well. Golden statues were erected to him. His birthday was declared a holiday. Animals were sacrificed in his honour.

But Tiberius had come to fear and mistrust him. With the aid of Macro, Sejanus' successor as commander of the Praetorians, Tiberius smuggled a letter to the Senate denouncing Sejanus and calling for his execution. The Senate was shocked and taken aback by the swift change, but it complied instantly. Perhaps moved by the justice of Tiberius' charges or by the strength of the Praetorian Guard, it condemned Sejanus to death. Sejanus woke that morning the most powerful man in the Western world, but by nightfall he was dead and his body lay, covered with spittle, by the Tiber.

Execution of Sejanus

Apparently Tiberius now reached a peak of denunciation and torture and execution that lasted for the remaining six years of his life. In the course of this reign of terror his *delatores* and torturers found evidence for him of the murder of his son, Drusus, by Livilla and Sejanus. Many great Roman names were implicated, falsely or not, and while that inquisition lasted no one on Capri was safe. A casual guest arriving to see Tiberius was mistaken for a suspect and went to the torturers.

Tiberius' chief remaining concern for the empire was who would rule it when he was gone. There were few living successors with any real claim, and Tiberius settled, as Augustus had done before him, on the least offensive of an undesirable lot. His choice was Gaius Caesar, still a young boy and known by the nickname the Roman legions had given him when he was a camp mascot, Caligula, or Little Boots. Caligula, a great-grandson of Augustus through Julia and her daughter, had a claim to the throne as good as any. If his morals and habits were less attractive, Tiberius did not seem to mind. "I am nursing a viper in Rome's bosom," Tiberius observed, and named Caligula his adopted son and successor.

On March 15, AD 37, Tiberius took part in a ceremonial game that required him to throw a javelin. He wrenched his shoulder, took to his bed, became very ill, and lapsed into a coma.

His physicians, who had not been allowed to examine him for nearly half a century, now studied his emaciated body and declared that he would die within the day. The successor, Caligula, was sent for. The Praetorian Guard declared their support for the new emperor. The news of the succession was proclaimed to the world. Then Tiberius recovered consciousness, sat up, and asked for something to eat. Caligula fled in terror. The notables of Rome, hasty to declare their fidelity to the new Caesar, were thrown into confusion. Only the Praetorian commander, Macro, kept his head. The next day, March 16, he hurried to Tiberius' bed, caught up a heap of blankets, and smothered Tiberius with them.

As an infant Tiberius had been a fugitive and then a pawn in large affairs. As a grown man he had been a popular and victorious general and then an exile. He came to supreme power already growing old. When he died he left the Roman Empire prosperous and stable, and the institution of the principate was so strong that for long it was able to survive the madness and excesses of his successors. Without him the later history of Rome might have been less colourful, lacking a Caligula or a Nero, but probably it would also have been far shorter.

BIBLIOGRAPHY. GREGORIO MARANON, *Tiberio: historia de un resentimiento,* 2nd ed. (1942; Eng. trans., *Tiberius: A Study in Resentment,* 1956), on the personality of Tiberius as seen by a psychologist and medical doctor; G.P. BAKER, *Tiberius Caesar* (1928), popularized, more dogmatic than the evidence always warrants, but illuminating; TACITUS, *The Annals and The Histories,* trans. from the Latin by ALFRED JOHN CHURCH and WILLIAM JACKSON BRODRIBB (1952), a classic source in a workmanlike and reliable translation; SUETONIUS, *The Twelve Caesars,* trans. from the Latin by ROBERT GRAVES (1957), a basic source, elegantly translated by a great novelist; ROBERT SAMUEL ROGERS, *Studies in the Reign of Tiberius* (1943), a basic source for dates and chronologies.

(F.Po.)

Tiber River

One of the great historic rivers of Europe and the second-longest Italian river after the Po, the Tiber (Italian Tevere) flows through a countryside rich in traces of ancient Etruscan civilization and in associations with classical Roman times. It is on the banks of the Tiber that the city of Rome stands. The river is 252 miles (405 kilometres) long, and its waters rise at a height of 4,590 feet (1,400 metres) above sea level on the slope of Monte Fumaiolo, a major summit of the Appennino Tosco-Emiliano. Twisting in a generally southerly direction through a series of scenic defiles and broad valleys, the Tiber enters the Tyrrhenian Sea of the Mediterranean near Ostia Antica. Some ancient writers allege that it was known originally as Albula—a reference to the whiteness of its waters—but it was renamed Tiberis after Tiberinus, a king of Alba Longa (an area centred on Lago Albano, south of Rome) who was drowned in it (for related information, see ROME).

The naming of the river

The course of the river. From its source, the Tiber plunges precipitously to the south, widening as it swings southeast into the broad alluvial basin of the Val Tiberina. Bearing south-southwest at Ponte San Giovanni, it is joined from the left by the Chiascio and its tributary the Topino and also, from the right, by the Nestore. At Todi it bends west toward Orvieto, south of where it is joined by another right-bank tributary, the Paglia. It then flows in a south-southeasterly direction to its junction (near Orte) with the Nera, its most important tributary, which runs in from the left. Below the confluence, it skirts the picturesque foothills of the Monti Sabini, then turns south-southwest at Passo Corese, to be joined, again from the left, by the Aniene near the sprawling city of Rome. Below Rome, the Tiber branches out into a delta, the main channel being the Fiumara, with the Fiumicino functioning as a distributary branch on the north side.

Climate and hydrology. The hydrological regime of the Upper Tiber is influenced by the Mediterranean type of climate, which produces an irregular flow, dependent largely on snow and rainfall, with a spring maximum. Conversely, the lower course of the Tiber is so augmented by the waters of the Nera and the Aniene, whose combined catchment and springwater may amount to over 650,000,000 cubic yards (500,000,000 cubic metres), that the river remains navigable at Rome even during prolonged summer droughts. Though little rainfall derives from the brief storms that, in November and December, break over the mountains of the lower basin, floods occasioned by the river's absorption of underground water may last for several days. Descending from valley to valley at a comparatively gentle rate—between five and six feet per mile in the stretch of its course lying between the confluence of the Chiascio and the Nera, one or two feet per mile between the Nera and the Fara in Sabina, and one and a half feet per mile between the Fara in Sabina and Rome—the Tiber meanders in great loops and curves over its floodplain.

Historical associations. Although the Romans made some effort to control its lower course, their ignorance of hydraulic principles prevented the development of adequate protection against floods. It is only in modern times that the Tiber has flowed through Rome between high stone embankments. Though the river varies in depth between seven and 20 feet, there is some evidence that navigation upstream to the Val Tiberina was significant for the grain trade as long ago as the 5th century BC. Later, the shipment of building stone and also of timber became important. In its zenith, classical Rome was supplied with vegetables grown in the gardens of riverside villas.

The importance of the Lower Tiber was first recognized in the 3rd century BC, when Ostia was made a naval base during the Punic Wars. It later became a commercial centre for the import of Mediterranean wheat, oil, and wine. Successive attempts to maintain Ostia, on the Fiumara, and the port of the emperors Claudius and Trajan, on the Fiumicino, were defeated by the processes of silting and by the deposition of sandbars at the river mouths. In later centuries, several popes tried to improve navigation on the Lower Tiber, and ports were built at Rome in 1692, 1703, and 1744. Navigation and trade upon the Lower Tiber flourished again between the late 18th and mid-19th centuries, when further dredging took place on the lower course.

Silting problems

Silting has, nevertheless, continued with such persistence that, by the 1970s, the Tiber was only navigable at Rome itself. The Tiber Delta, meanwhile, has advanced about two miles seaward since Roman times. Whatever the problems occasioned by the seemingly inexorable processes of nature, the contemporary Tiber continues to contribute much to the beauty of the landscapes through which it passes.

BIBLIOGRAPHY. ROBERTO ALMAGIA, *L'Italia,* vol. 1, pp. 481–488 (1959), a standard general textbook in Italian on the geography of Italy, with good historical references; J.M. HOUSTON, *The Western Mediterranean World,* pp. 408–410, 547–555 (1964), a geographical description of the landscapes of the western Mediterranean, with a broad survey of the Tiber Valley; JOEL LE GALL, *Le Tibre, fleuve de Rome dans l'antiquité* (1953), an authoritative French study of the Tiber, its role in prehistory and classical terms, its hydrology, modifications made by man, and its commercial significance.

(J.Ho.)

Tibet

Tibet, an autonomous region (*tzu-chih-ch'ü*) of China since 1965, is often referred to as "the roof of the world." It occupies about 471,700 square miles (1,221,700 square kilometres) of the plateaus and mountains of Central Asia, including the world's highest known peak, Mt. Everest. It is bordered by the Chinese provinces of Szechwan to the east, Yunnan to the southeast, Tsinghai to the northeast, the Chinese autonomous region of Sinkiang to the northwest, the state of Jammu and Kashmir to the West, and India, Nepal, Sikkim, Bhutan, and Burma to the south. The population was estimated at 1,500,000 before annexation by China in 1951; the 1971 estimate was 1,300,000. Lhasa is the capital city.

The Tibetan name for the region is Bod. The name Tibet is derived from the Mongolian Thubet, the Chinese Tufan, the Tai Thibet, and the Arabic Tubbat.

Before the 1950s Tibet was a unique entity that sought isolation from the rest of the world. It comprised a cultural and religious whole, marked by the Tibetan language and Tibetan Buddhism. Little effort was made to facilitate communication with other countries, and economic development in Western terms was minimal. Under Chinese administration, Tibet remains veiled from the outside world. Tibetans in exile speak of destruction of the Tibetan way of life, while the Chinese have announced some industrial development of the area. Because of the lack of information since the mid-1950s, much of the material in this article deals with Tibet before the Chinese occupation. For history see TIBET, HISTORY OF. For religion see BUDDHISM; and BUDDHISM, HISTORY OF. For the capital city, see LHASA. For related physical features, see BRAHMAPUTRA RIVER; EVEREST, MOUNT; GANGES RIVER; HIMALAYAN MOUNTAIN RANGES; HUANG HO (RIVER); INDUS RIVER; KUNLUN MOUNTAINS; MEKONG RIVER; and YANGTZE RIVER.

(T.W.D.S.)

THE LANDSCAPE

The natural landscape. *Relief features.* Tibet is on a high plateau surrounded by mountain masses. The rela-

TIBET

tively level northern part of the plateau is called the Byang-thang (Ch'iang-t'ang), or Northern Plain, which extends more than 800 miles from west to east at an average elevation of 15,000 feet. The Byang-thang is dotted with brackish lakes, remnants of the Tethys Sea, which covered Asia Minor during the Eocene Epoch from 54,000,000 to 38,000,000 years ago. There are, however, no river systems there. Approximately at longitude 92° E, the Byang-thang begins to descend in elevation. The mountain ranges in eastern Tibet transverse from north to south creating meridional barriers to travel and communication. In central and western Tibet, the ranges run from northwest to southeast with deep or shallow valleys forming innumerable furrows.

The Byang-thang Plateau is bordered on the north by the Kunlun Mountains extending from longitude 77° to 93° E, with the highest peak, Ulugh Muz Tagh (Ulugh Muz Mountain), reaching 25,338 feet (7,723 metres). North of the Kunlun range lies the Tsaidam Basin, averaging 9,000 feet and bordered in turn by the Astin Tagh and Nan Shan (mountains). The western and southern border of the Plateau of Tibet is formed by the Himalayan mass that stretches from Nanga Parbat (26,660 feet [8,126 metres]) in the northwest to Namcha Barwa (25,446 feet [7,756 metres]) in the southeast. The highest peak is Mt. Everest, which rises to 29,028 feet (8,848 metres) on the Tibet–Nepal border.

North of Lake Manasarowar and stretching eastwardly is the Trans-Himalaya, or Kailas Range, with clusters of peaks, several exceeding 20,000 feet. The Trans-Himalayas are separated from the Himalayas by the Brahmaputra River, which flows across southern Tibet from longitude 82° to about 95° E then cuts south through the mountains to India. (T.V.W.)

Drainage and soils. Tibet is a prime source of water supply for Central Asia. The Indus River, known in Tibet as the Seng-ge Kha-'bab ("out of the lion's mouth"), has its source in western Tibet near Mt. Kailas, a mountain sacred to Buddhists and Hindus; it then flows eastward across Kashmir to Pakistan. Three other rivers also begin in the west. The Glang-chen Kha-'bab ("out of the elephant's mouth") flows south to become

the Sutlej in western India; the Rma-bya Kha-'bab ("out of the peacock's mouth") becomes the sacred Ganges; and the Rta-mchog Kha-'bab ("out of the horse's mouth") flows east and, after joining the Skid Chu (Happy River) south of Lhasa, forms the Brahmaputra.

The Salween River has its source in central Tibet as the Dngul Chu River, which flows through eastern Tibet and then enters Burma. The Mekong River begins in northern Tibet as two rivers—the Ngom Chu and the Rdza Chu—which flow through eastern Tibet, merge at Chamudo (Ch'ang-tu), and enter Laos and Thailand. The 'Bri Chu River rises in the northeast and is the source of the Yangtze River, and the Huang Ho, or Yellow River, of China first obtains its waters from the Rma Chu, which also rises in northeastern Tibet.

Among the country's lakes, the largest are Manasarowar, in the west, which is sacred to both Buddhists and Hindus, and the Zi-ling mtsho and Gnam-mtsho phyug-mo (Na-mu Hu), the Yar-'brog gyu-mtsho, or Yar-'brog, and the Mtsho Skya-rengs and Sngo-rengs in central Tibet.

Soils are alluvial and are often composed of sand that is blown by the wind to form a layer above gravels and shingles. Colour varies from light brown to gray, according to the humus content, which is generally poor.

Climate. Although Tibetans refer to their country as Gangs-ljongs or Kha-ba-can (Land of Snows), the climate is generally dry, and most of Tibet receives only 18 inches of rain and snow annually. The Himalayas act as a barrier to the monsoon (rain-bearing) winds from the south, and precipitation decreases from south to north. The perpetual snow line lies at about 16,000 feet in the Himalayas but rises to about 20,000 feet in the northern mountains. Humidity is low, and fog is practically nonexistent.

Temperatures in the higher altitudes are cold, but the lower valleys and the southeast are mild and pleasant. Seasonal variation is minimal, and the greatest temperature differences occur during a 24-hour period. Lhasa, which lies at an elevation of 11,830 feet (3,606 metres), has a maximum daily temperature of 45° F (7° C) and a minimum of 18° F (−18° C). The bitterly cold tem-

The rugged terrain

Temperature ranges

peratures of the early morning and night are aggravated by the gale winds that blow throughout most of the year. Because of the cool dry air, grain can be safely stored for 50 to 60 years, dried raw meat and butter can be preserved for over one year, and epidemics are rare.

Vegetation and animal life. The windswept Byang-thang is devoid of trees and larger forms of vegetation. Its arid climate supports little except grasses. The varied plant life of Tibet is found in the river valleys and in the lower, wetter regions of the south and southeast. Plant life includes weeping and Alpine willows; white and black poplars; junipers; spreading yews; pines, firs, spruces, teak, rhododendrons, oaks, birches, elms; bamboo, sugar-cane; babul trees; thorn trees; azaleas; tea bushes; *gro-ba* (a small white tree that grows mainly in hilly regions); *'om-bu* (a bushlike tree with red flowers that grows near water); *khres-pa* (a strong durable forest tree used to make bowls and food containers); *glang-ma* (a large willow tree used for basketry); and *rtsi-shing* (the seeds of which are used for making varnish). Fruit-bearing trees include the peach, walnut, apple, pear, apricot, banana, crabapple, and wild rose. Nettles, rhubarb, mushrooms, sweet potatoes, and certain roots are used for food, as are the leaves of the *lca-wa, khumag,* and *sre-ral,* all of which grow in the low, wet regions.

Both wild and domestic flowers flourish in Tibet. Among the wild flowers are the blue poppy, lotus, wild pansy, oleander, orchid, *tsi-tog* (a light pink flower that grows at high altitudes), *shang-dril* (a bell-shaped flower, either white, yellow, or maroon, that also grows at high altitudes), and *ogchu* (a red flower that grows in sandy regions). Domestic flowers include the rose, hollyhock, marigold, petunia, sweet pea, hydrangea, pansy, nasturtium, iris, tiger lily, dahlia, poppy, chrysanthemum, sunflower, carnation, gladiolus, and magnolia.

Forest animals

Animal life in the forest regions includes tiger, leopard, bear, wild boar, wild goat, stone marten (a kind of cat), langur (a slender, long-tailed monkey), lynx, porcupine, jackal, wild buffalo, weasel, *pha-ra* (a small member of the jackal family), and *gsa'* (a spotted cat that is smaller than a leopard).

In the high grasslands and dry bush areas, there are brown bears, deer, wild and big-horned sheep, mountain antelope, musk deer, wild asses, wild yaks, foxes, wolves, marmots, rabbits, rats, snakes, scorpions, lizards, and *dre-tse* (members of the wolf family). Water life includes various types of fish such as trout and catfish, frog, crab, otter, and turtle.

Undisturbed by aircraft or hunters, the bird reigns supreme in the Tibetan sky. Among the many kinds to be seen are the vulture, eagle, jungle fowl, ptarmigan, pheasant, cuckoo, dove, owl, spotted tinamou, mynah, robin, hawk, raven, crow, hoopoe, sparrow, lark, and nightingale. Other kinds include the gull, crane, sheldrake, cinnamon teal, *sing-bya* (a tiny, owllike bird), *khra* (a crow-sized, hawklike bird), *bya-long* (a blind bird about the size of a duck), and *skya-ka* (a black and white, crow-sized bird). The *rmos-'debs*—a small, gray bird that inhabits agricultural regions—gives a call that signals the opening of the planting season.

Traditional regions. Tibet is traditionally divided into three regions, or *Chol-kha-gsum* (*Chol-kha* means "region"; *gsum* means "three"). The Dbus-Gtsang region stretches from Mng'a-ris skor-gsum at the border of Jammu and Kashmir to Sog-la skya-bo near the town of Sog. The Khams, or Mdo-stod, region consists of the territory between Sog-la skya-bo and the upper bend of the Huang Ho (Yellow River; Tibetan Rma-chu), now located in Tsinghai Province. The A-mdo, or Mdo-smad, region reaches from the Huang Ho to Mchod-rten dkarpo in Kansu Province, China. Tibetans say that the best religion comes from Dbus-Gtsang, the best men from Khams, and the best horses from A-mdo.

The landscape under human settlement. Within the three *Chol-kha-gsum,* approximately 30 percent of the area is uninhabitable, 18 percent is roamed by nomads, 25 percent is occupied by semi-nomads, 22 percent is held by agriculturalists, and 5 percent is claimed by trappers in the forest belt.

Nomads, from November to March, occupy semipermanent base camps. Located between 14,000 and 17,000 feet above sea level, these camps are no more than about half a mile apart and are composed of large yak-hair tents. Between April and October, when the men take their animals in search of pasturage, they carry smaller, portable tents. The semi-nomads live between 12,000 and 14,000 feet above sea level in villages of about 150 families. The single- or two-story houses are built of stone and brick. Water mills, trees, and thornbushes are typical features of the villages, which are surrounded by small fields. The semi-nomads become nomadic between April and October. The villages of the agriculturalists are similar to those of the semi-nomads. They are located, however, at elevations of 8,000 to 12,000 feet in river valleys. The southern forest dwellers occupy wooden houses, with stone foundations and slate roofs, that are grouped into villages. Hunting and forestry are supplemented by agriculture; cultivation is carried out on narrow terraces.

Rural settlement patterns

The largest urban settlement was Lhasa, with an estimated population of 70,000 in the 1950s. Other cities include Jih-k'a-tse (Zhikatse) (population 20,000) and Chiang-tzu (Gyangtse) (10,000).

PEOPLE AND POPULATION

Language. The Tibetan and Burmese languages are related, although they are mutually unintelligible in their modern forms. Spoken Tibetan has developed a pattern of regional dialects and subdialects, which can be mutually understood. The dialect of Lhasa is used as a lingua franca. There are two social levels of speech—*zhe-sa* (honorific) and *phal-skad* (ordinary); their use depends upon the relative social status between the speaker and the listener. Chinese has been imposed on the Tibetans since the 1960s.

Tibetan is written in a script derived from that of Indian Gupta in about AD 600. It has a syllabary of 30 consonants and five vowels; six additional symbols are used in writing Sanskrit words. The script itself has four variations—*dbu-can* (primarily for Buddhist textbooks), *dbu-med* and *'Khyug-yig* (for general use), and *'bru-tsha* (for decorative writing).

Religion. Bon is considered to be the first known religion in Tibet, although there is some argument as to the time of its establishment. It is a form of shamanism, encompassing a belief in gods, demons, and ancestral spirits who are responsive to priests, or shamans. With the rise of Buddhism, Bon adopted certain Buddhist rituals and concepts; the Buddhists also adopted certain features of Bon, so that the two religions have many points of resemblance.

Although Chinese Buddhism was introduced in ancient times, the mainstream of Buddhist teachings came to Tibet from India. The first Buddhist scripture may have arrived in the 3rd century AD, but active promulgation did not begin until the 8th century. In later centuries, numerous Buddhist sects were formed, including the Dge-lugs-pa sect, which emphasizes monastic discipline; in the 17th century this sect, known also as the "Yellow Hats," gained political supremacy.

Tibetan Buddhism

In recent times the overwhelming majority of Tibetans have traditionally been Buddhists. Before the Chinese occupation, prayer flags flew from every home and adorned the mountain slopes. Monasteries were established throughout the country, and the Dalai Lama (the spiritual head of Tibetan Buddhism) was the supreme political head of the nation. A small minority, however, were adherents of either Islām, Hinduism, Bon, or Christianity. The Chinese have attempted to eliminate the influence of religion in Tibetan life. The Dalai Lama was forced into exile in 1959, temples were closed, religious artifacts and scriptures were destroyed, and prayer flags were taken down.

Population groups. The majority of Tibetans have the same ethnic origin, have traditionally practiced the same religion, and speak the same language. The population is, however, divided into social and economic strata.

The basic economic groups have been the nomads (*'brog-pa*), semi-nomads (*sa-ma-'brog*), agriculturalists (*zhing-pa*), and forest dwellers (*rong-pa*). There are also traders (*tshong-pa*), craftsmen (*lag-shes-pa*), government officials (*gzhung-zhabs*), monks (*grwa-pa*), and nuns (*a-ne*). In Lhasa there was a special group of outcastes (*ro-rgyab-pa*) who earned their living by begging and by disposing of corpses. These groupings did not, however, constitute rigid castes; monks, for example, could be government officials, and nomads or agriculturalists could be traders.

The Tibetan nobility

Social divisions existed between the nobility and the peasantry. Membership in the nobility is based on heredity. Of the more than 175 noble families in Tibet, six were descended from the families of the Dalai Lamas, and a few were descended from early kings and rulers. The remainder were families descended from those who had been ennobled for service to the government of the Dalai Lama. The overwhelming majority of the population were members of the peasantry.

THE ECONOMY

Although Tibet is rich in mineral resources, its economy has remained underdeveloped. Because of the difficult terrain and severe climate, agricultural development remained on a subsistence level. Trade was minimal, minerals were unexploited, and forestry was hampered by lack of transportation. Since the Chinese occupation, roads have been constructed, apparently more for military than for economic purposes.   (T.W.D.S.)

The extent and distribution of resources.   *Mineral resources.* A scientific investigation of western Tibet was conducted by Swami Pranavananda, an Indian who made surveys in the 1930s and 1940s in the Mt. Kailas and Lake Manasarowar districts. He discovered extensive goldfields in the district of Sankora; radium, iron, titanium, and emery on the eastern shores of Manasarowar and at nearby Rakas Tal; lead near Gebuk on the Ma-chüan Ho; arsenic and serpentine (a green mineral composed of a hydrous magnesium silicate) near Kungri-bingri Pass; and large deposits of borax on the shore of Tseti Tsho (Lake Tseti).

Following the occupation of Tibet, the geological section of the Chinese Academy of Science dispatched investigation teams who reported the existence of oil shale, asphalt, iron, manganese, magnesium, copper, lead, zinc, molybdenum (a metallic element that resembles chromium and tungsten), antimony, salt, soda, borax, Glauber's salt (the crystalline decahydrate of sodium sulfate, used in dyeing and as a laxative), sulfur, alum, mica, barite (barium sulfate, a white, yellow, or colourless mineral), graphite, talc, gypsum, jade, and china clay. A belt of iron deposits was located on the western bank of the Mekong River stretching for almost 25 miles south of Chamudo. Graphite was obtained from Ningtsin, and coal was reported plentiful around Chamudo. Iron deposits containing ore in concentrated seams of high quality and extractable depth were also found in the T'angku-la Shan-mo on the border of Tibet and the province of Tsinghai. Three rich crystal deposits were found in the glaciers of the Sane Range. Oil-bearing formations, a reserve of oil shales, and coal were unearthed, as well as lead, zinc, and manganese.

Biological resources. The most valuable woodland is the Khams district, though extensive forest-clad mountains are also found in the Sutlej River Valley in the west and in the Chumbi Valley in the south. The Spo-smad area in Khams is estimated to contain 17,300 square miles (44,800 square kilometres) of virgin forests. In the late 1950s, 30 kinds of trees including those of comparatively high economic value, such as varnish trees, spruce, and fir were discovered. Conifers averaging 90 feet high and some as high as 200 feet with a girth of five feet were reported, and the estimated total of forest timber resources in that part of Tibet alone was placed at more than 3,510,000,000 cubic feet.

Power resources. The swift-flowing rivers and mountain streams have enormous hydroelectric power potential. Especially promising are the Brahmaputra, Skyid, and Nyang rivers. The coal deposits and forests represent possible sources of thermal-power production.   (T.V.W.)

Sources of income.   *Agriculture and forestry.* The staple crops are barley, wheat, and pulses; other important crops include millet, buckwheat, *rgya-bra* (a grain similar to buckwheat), beans, hemp, and mustard. Butter from the yak (large, long-haired ox) or the *mdzo-mo* (a crossbreed of the yak and the cow) is the main dairy product. The diet is supplemented by a variety of garden vegetables including radishes, turnips, carrots, potatoes, peas, parsley, lettuce, tomatoes, and cabbage. Garlic, onions, mint, celery, cauliflower, pumpkins, squash, and eggplant are also grown. Some rice is raised in the southeast. The only imported foods are tea, sugar, and rice.

Agriculture is on a subsistence level and is limited by climate and elevation. During periods of bad harvest, the food kept in storehouses is adequate to meet the country's needs. Most cultivation is carried out in the river valleys and in the southeast. Most farmers keep domestic animals such as yaks, horses, mules, donkeys, and goats, and meat is obtained from cows, sheep, pigs, and chickens.

Agricultural problems

Because of the inaccessibility of Tibet's forests, forestry is largely undeveloped. The forest dwellers, however, derive their main source of income from the production of such wood products as planks, beams, wooden printing blocks, and kitchen utensils. Tibetans do not usually fish.

Mining. Traditional beliefs that mining would diminish the natural strength of the land and that the deities, being disturbed, would bring harm to men and animals discouraged the general exploitation of mineral resources. Some gold was mined in the west by placer techniques. It was reported that iron and coal mines were in production in the Nag-chu-kha region in the late 1950s.

Industry. Before the 1950s, Tibet had no modern industries. There were, however, small handicraft centres that were owned either individually or collectively and that produced scroll paintings, metal images, wooden block prints, and religious images. For these crafts, the *lag-shes-pa*, or craftsmen, had to be well versed in literature and mathematics. There were also carpet weavers, tanners, potters, goldsmiths and silversmiths, carpenters, tailors, and incense-stick makers—all of whom learned their trade through apprenticeship. Because the government rewarded outstanding artists and craftsmen with official titles, estates, and money, the arts and crafts of Tibet were well preserved.

Handicraft industries

In 1952 an ironwork and woodwork factory was opened in Lhasa; this was followed by the establishment of an automobile repair shop in 1957 and of a tannery in 1958.

Energy. Under the Chinese government, the small hydroelectric power station at Lhasa was repaired and reinforced with three generators. A new thermal station was installed in Jih-k'a-tse. Hydrographic stations in Lhasa and various parts of the country were established to determine the hydroelectric potential of the Brahmaputra, Skyid, and Nyang rivers.

Financial services. There were no banks before 1951. Small loans to be paid with interest could be obtained from local merchants, and the Tibetan government loaned public funds at interest as a means of collecting revenue. The Chinese have established branches of The People's Bank of China in Lhasa, Jih-k'a-tse, Chiang-tzu, Chamudo, and Gartok (Ka-erh). They have also extended agricultural and commercial credit and introduced Chinese currency.

Foreign trade. Tibet's major exports included wool, yak tail, musk, bear bile, deer horn, salt, borax, mica, sheep, medicinal herbs, and the skins of yak, fox, sheep, marmot, and lynx. Woollen cloth, felt, blankets, rugs, incense, dried fish, mules, and ponies were some of the minor export items.

Tibet imported tea, porcelain, brocades, and silks from China. India was the source of textiles, sugar, rice, tobacco, medicines, fuels, and dried nuts. Rice and dried fruit were imported from Nepal and Bhutan.

Management of the economy. Under the Tibetan government, the economy operated under a free enterprise system dependent upon supply and demand. Currency was allowed to float on the market for foreign exchange purposes.

The major government expenditure, 29 percent of the

Government expenditures

budget, was spent on religion and education. Monasteries were given land, grain, and butter for consumption by the monks and nuns, for use in exchange for labour, and for prayer gatherings. About 27 percent of the budget was allocated to defense, 22 percent to development, 10 percent for health services, 4 percent for maintenance of the government, and 8 percent for emergency and miscellaneous requirements.

Government tax revenues were mainly paid in the form of goods. Agriculturalists and nomads paid with services or in kind, and businessmen paid with the goods they handled. Taxes were collected by district administrators and by travelling tax collectors.   (T.W.D.S.)

Transport and communications. *Roads.* Before 1951, travelling in Tibet was done either on foot or on the backs of animals. Coracles (small boats made of wicker and hides) were used to cross the larger rivers. The Tibetan government obstructed the development of modern transportation to make access to the country difficult for outsiders. For trading, the Tibetans relied on the centuries-old caravan routes leading to Lhasa, of which the most important were from Tsinghai (via Nag-chu-kha) and Szechwan (via Chamudo), India (via Kalimpong and Sna-gdong [Ya-tung]); Nepal (via Skyid-grong and Nya-lam rdzong); and Kashmir (via Leh and Gartok).

Under the Communist Chinese, a network of motor roads was constructed, notably the Tsinghai and Szechwan highways. Many secondary roads were under construction.

Air transport. The first air communication between Tibet and Peking, China was inaugurated in 1956. The airport is located north of Lhasa. There is unscheduled service with Cheng-chou, China, via Yü-shu, Tsinghai Province. Military airfields have been constructed at Chamudo, Jih-k'a-tse, Dingri (Ting-jih), and Gartok.

Railways. There were no railways in Tibet before the Chinese occupation. After making an aerial survey, the Chinese carried out a land survey for a railroad from Tsinghai to Tibet. The proposed railway was to be 807 miles long, with Hsi-ning, Tsinghai Province, and Jih-k'a-tse, Tibet, as terminals. It would pass through complicated geological and topographical regions, and its average altitude would be more than 12,000 feet.

Postal and telegraph service. The first telegraph line was strung between Kalimpong and Gyangtse by the British in 1904. In the 1920s another line connecting Gyangtse with Lhasa was erected, this being the only telegraph system in use until the Chinese took over in 1951. Some 50 postal and telecommunication stations in Tibet, including mobile units, serve remote border areas and geological, hydrological, and construction teams.
                                                            (T.V.W.)

ADMINISTRATION AND SOCIAL CONDITIONS

The theocratic system of government

Government structure. *The Tibetan government.* Tibet had a theocratic government of which the Dalai Lama was the supreme religious and temporal head. He was chosen for life, in accordance with religious traditions and ceremonies, as a reincarnation of his predecessor. When he was unable to assume his position because of his youth, a regent was chosen from among the highest ranking monks by the National Assembly. The regent had full ruling powers, which he exercised until the Dalai Lama attained his majority between the ages of 16 and 18.

Next in line to the regent or the Dalai Lama were two prime ministers, one a monk and one a layman. Beneath them was the four-member Bka'-shag (Council of Ministers). In the late 1950s the collective function of the Bka'-shag was altered by the assignment of separate portfolios to each member. There were four ministries of home affairs, foreign affairs, defense, and economic affairs.

Parallel to the secular Bka'-shag was the Department of Religious Affairs (Yig-tsang), which was headed by a lord chamberlain (*spyi-skyabs mkhan-po*). The department was composed of four monks who held the title of secretary general; the entire departmental staff was also composed of monks. They dealt with the internal affairs

of the monasteries and cases involving monks. The lord chamberlain was also the head of the Department of Forestry and of the Dalai Lama's personal affairs.

Four laymen, known as *rtsis-dpon*, headed the Finance Department and the Revenue Department. They were also in charge of all lay governmental personnel. A council of the four secretaries general and the four finance secretaries (the *drung-rtse*) met with the Bka'-shag on important political issues. The members of this council were also permanent spokesmen of the National Assembly.

There were two assemblies. The National Assembly was composed of about 350 members, all government officials: the abbots and former abbots of the Se-ra, 'Bras-spungs, and Dga'-ldan monasteries; representatives of previous regencies; and representatives of the people. A smaller assembly known as the Rag-sdus rgyas-pa was composed of approximately 60 key members of the National Assembly, who represented governmental departments. The agendas of the assemblies were drafted by the Bka'-shag and the *drung-rtse*. When decisions were made, they were forwarded to the Dalai Lama, who could either accept or reject them.

The 105 districts (*rdzong*) and approximately 70 subdistricts (*gzhis-sdod*) were headed separately by eight governors (*spyi-skyabs*). In certain border regions and vassal territories, administrative offices were hereditary; governors and district officials were otherwise appointed.

All lay officials were appointed by the Bka'-shag and the Dalai Lama. Monk officials were selected by the Department of Religious Affairs and the Dalai Lama.

Contact between villages and the central government was maintained by a liaison official, or *rgan-po*, appointed by each village. Groups of villages appointed a liaison official known as a *gtso-drag*. Nomads had little contact with the government and were ruled by hereditary leaders.

The Chinese government. Since 1965, Tibet has been administered as an autonomous region (*tzu-chih-ch'ü*) of China. It is ruled by a revolutionary committee, which is headed by the local party chief and the military commander of Tibet. The region is divided into the municipality (*shih*) of Lhasa and five special districts (*chuan-ch'ü*), which are subdivided into 70 counties (*hsien*).

The judicial system has remained largely the same in structure. The army consists of more than 300,000 regular Chinese troops under a Chinese military commander, who is stationed at Lhasa. There are military cantonments in major towns along the borders with India, Nepal, and Bhutan. Tibetans have been forcibly recruited into regular, security, and militia regiments.
                                                            (T.W.D.S.)

The social sector. *Education.* There were a few secular schools in Tibet before the Chinese occupation. The monasteries were the main seats of learning, and some of the larger ones were similar in operation to theological universities. The doors of the monasteries were open to all, and no age limit or educational qualifications were set for admittance. The monks pursued a prescribed curriculum in Buddhist literature and, upon completion, became fully ordained. The intelligent ones could pursue an additional course of study in advanced philosophical works, usually requiring six to seven years to finish. If the candidate successfully passed the final examinations, he was given the coveted title of *dge-bshes*. A *dge-bshes* was respected for his education and was qualified to serve as a monk official in the government or on the administrative board of the monasteries.

Monastic education

Not all of the enrolled monks intended to acquire a serious education, and some came for vocational training as calligraphers, printers, painters, and craftsmen. A large number specialized in performing rituals for the sick. It was considered an honour to send at least one son to become a monk, and this was often done when the boy was only seven or eight years old.   (T.V.W.)

Health and welfare services. Under the health program of the Tibetan government, medical advice and medicine were provided free to expectant mothers. In addition to free vaccinations, sacred pendants known as

Massive walls of stone bricks and mud built in Chiang-tzu (Gyantse), Tibet, to defend the city from Mongol attacks.
Fosco Maraini—Monkmeyer

rims-srungs were distributed annually to prevent epidemics. The construction and maintenance of proper drainage systems, wells, and canals—and security facilities to guard against pollution of water sources—were undertaken through the health program. Care of the kinless aged and handicapped persons was also undertaken. The Chinese have built modern hospitals, improved the drainage system, and placed mobile health units at key locations. (T.W.D.S.)

Housing. The finest dwellings were those of the nobility. These were built of stone around a rectangular courtyard, on three sides of which were stables and storehouses. On the fourth side, opposite the gate, was the mansion itself, usually three stories high. The family quarters and chapel were located on the third floor, where the rooms, unlike the dark and ill-ventilated rooms below, may have had glass windows and doors. The walls and ceiling were painted with iconographic pictures and auspicious designs.

The peasants lived in one- or two-story buildings. The roof was flat and made of clay like the earthen floor. Windows were plentiful, but glass was rare and the windows were covered by waxed paper or other translucent material, which was protected by strong wooden shutters. The houses of the village peasants were, as a rule, solid and substantial, with walls of stone or sun-dried bricks, though occasionally of clods of earth. Flat roofs of beaten earth were common throughout the Tibetan highland, but, in the Chumbi Valley and other rainy districts, the roofs were gently sloped. Where pine trees grew, the roofs were constructed of pine shingles, kept in position by heavy stones. The nomadic pastoralists dwelled in tents of yak hair, rectangular in shape and ranging from 12 to 50 feet in length. An aperture of about two feet in width along the middle of the roof lets out smoke. (T.V.W.)

Social conditions. Under the Tibetan government there were no wages in the sense of monetary remuneration. Government officials and those who gave service to the government were paid in land. Monk officials received payments of barley, tea, butter, and cloth. District officials received a minimal payment. Labourers received food or clothing in payment for their services.

The social importance of land

The ownership of land was an indication of social status. Large estates were held by government officials and the hereditary nobility, while only a few peasants owned small plots of land. Most Tibetans were either tenant farmers or hired agricultural labourers.

CULTURAL LIFE

The arts. Tibet is most renowned for its religious scroll paintings (*thang-ka*), metal images, and wooden block prints. There are three categories of images—representing the peaceful, moderate, and angry deities—and three schools of painting—the *Sman-thang, Gong-dkar Mkhan-bris,* and *Kar-ma sgar-bris*—which are differentiated by colour tones and depicted facial expressions.

The rich and ancient culture is based on religion. The *Gar* and the *'cham* are stylistic dances performed by monks; they re-enact the behaviour, attitudes, and gestures of the deities. Ancient legendary tales, historic events, classical solo songs, and musical debates are elaborately staged in the open air in the form of operas, operettas, and dramas. The folk songs and dances of local regions abound with colour, joy, and simplicity: the *bro* of the Khams region, the *sgor-gzhas* of the *dbus-gtsang* peasants, and the Kadra of the A-mdo area are spectacles that are performed in groups; on festive occasions they continue for several days. These cheerful performances tell of the people's loves and celebrate their faith in their religion, the beauty of their country, and the brave deeds of their ancestors.

Customs. Traditional marriage ceremonies involve consultations with both a lama and an astrologer in order to predict the compatibility of a couple. The signing of a marriage contract is followed by an official ceremony at the home of the bridegroom. Appearance in a temple or before a civil authority is not required. After a couple is officially wedded, prayer flags are hoisted from the bride's side of the family upon the rooftop of the bridegroom's house to symbolize the equality of the bride in her new home. Although polygamy and polyandry were practiced on a limited scale, monogamy was the predominant form of marriage.

Tibetan marriage practices

When a death occurs, the family members make charitable contributions in the hope of ensuring a better reincarnation for the deceased. In the case of the death of an important religious figure, his corpse is preserved in a tomb. Otherwise, tradition calls for the corpse to be fed to the vultures, as a symbol of charity. The customs of burial and cremation exist but are seldom practiced.

A white scarf (*kha-btags*) is offered during greetings, visits to shrines, marriage and death ceremonies, and other occasions. This beautiful and unique tradition was derived from the ancient custom of offering clothes to adorn the statues of deities. Gradually, it became extended into a form of greeting, and the white scarf offering, symbolizing purity, became customary. Another unique tradition is the hoisting of prayer flags on rooftops, tents, hilltops, and almost anywhere a Tibetan can be found. These flags signify fortune and good luck.

Food and drink. The staple Tibetan food is barley flour (*rtsam-pa*), which is consumed daily. Other major foods include wheat flour, yak meat, mutton, and pork. Dairy products such as butter, milk, and cheese are also popular. The people in the higher altitudes generally consume more meat than those of the lower regions, where a variety of vegetables are available. Rice is generally restricted in consumption to the well-to-do families, southern border farmers, and monks.

Two beverages—tea and barley beer (*chang*)—are particularly noteworthy. Brick tea from China and local

Tibetan tea leaves are boiled in soda water. The tea is then strained and poured into a churn, and salt and butter are added before the mixture is churned. The resulting tea is light reddish white and has a thick buttery surface. *Chang*, which is mildly intoxicating, is thick and white and has a sweet and pungent taste.

Festivals. Festivals are both national and local in character. The many local celebrations are varied; national festivals, though fewer, are marked with a spirit of unity and lavishness.

The first day of the first month of the Tibetan calendar (February or March of the Gregorian calendar) is marked by New Year celebrations all over Tibet. Monasteries, temples, *stūpas* (outdoor shrines), and home chapels are visited at dawn, and offerings are made before statues and relics of deities and saints. A special fried cookie known as *kha-zas* is prepared in every home. Either a real or an artificial head of a horned sheep adorns the offerings. A colourful container filled with barley flour and wheat grain and another container of *chang* are presented to all visitors, who take a pinch of the contents and make an offering to the deities by throwing it in the air.

The New Year celebrations are almost immediately followed by the Smom-lam ("prayer") festival, which begins three days after the New Year and is celebrated for 15 days. The festival marks the victory of Buddha over his six religious opponents through debates and the performance of miracles. During this festival, special prayers are offered daily. Prayers, fasting, and charitable donations mark *sa-ga zla-ba*, the celebration of the anniversary of Buddha's birth, enlightenment, and death—three events that all occurred on the 15th day of the fourth month of the Tibetan calendar.

The death of Tsong-kha-pa Blo-bzang grags-pa, founder of the Dge-lugs-pa sect, is celebrated on the 25th day of the tenth month by the burning of butter lamps on the roofs and windowsills of every house. This festival is known as *lnga-mchod*. The *dgu-gtor* festival, or festival of the banishment of evil spirits, takes place on the 29th day of the last month of the Tibetan year. At night a bowl of flour soup and a bunch of burning straws are taken into every room of every house, and the evil spirits are called out. Outside, on a distant path, the bowl of soup and the burning straws are thrown and left to burn.

Superstitions. Superstition is prominent in Tibet. A traveller who encounters either a funeral procession, the source of running water, or a passerby carrying a pitcher of water is considered to have good fortune awaiting him. If a vulture or an owl perches on a rooftop, it is believed that death or misfortune will soon befall the household. If snow falls during a marriage procession, it is believed that the newlyweds will face many misfortunes or difficulties. A snowfall during a funeral, however, symbolizes an impediment to death in the family for a long period of time. (T.W.D.S.)

BIBLIOGRAPHY. The most knowledgeable Western sources on the political and social affairs of Tibet are SIR CHARLES BELL, *Tibet: Past and Present* (1924); and HUGH E. RICHARDSON, *A Short History of Tibet* (1962). CHANDRA DAS, *Journey to Lhasa and Central Tibet* (1902); and TSEPON W.D. SHAKABPA, *The Sacred Relics in Tibet* (1951), focus on the religious influence in Tibet. Books that give firsthand experience of turmoil in Tibet since the Chinese invasion are DALAI LAMA (the fourteenth), *My Land and My People* (1962); NGAWANG THUTOB, *Tibet Today* (1966); and KUNSANG PALJOR, *Tibet, the Undying Flame* (1970). The OFFICE OF H.H. THE DALAI LAMA, *Tibetans in Exile* (1969), is an official report of the work done, from 1959 to 1969, for the rehabilitation of Tibetan refugees in India. TURRELL V. WYLIE, *The Geography of Tibet According to the 'dZam-gling-rGyas-bShad* (1962), is an authoritative geography of Tibet.

(T.W.D.S./T.V.W.)

Tibet, History of

According to legend the Tibetan people originated from the union of a monkey and a female demon. The Chinese T'ang annals (10th century) place the Tibetans' origin among the nomadic, pastoral Ch'iang tribes recorded about 200 BC as inhabiting the great steppe northwest of China. That region, where diverse racial elements met and mingled for centuries, may be accepted as the original homeland of the Tibetans; but, until at least the 7th century AD, they continued to mix, by conquest or alliance, with other peoples. From that heritage two strains in particular stand out—the brachycephalic, or roundheaded, peoples and the dolichocephalic, or longheaded, peoples. The former, which predominate in the cultivated valleys, may have derived from the Yellow River basin and be akin to the early Chinese and Burmese; the latter, found mainly among the nomads of the north and in the noble families of Lhasa, seem to have affinities with the Turkic peoples, whose primitive wandering grounds were farther to the north. In addition, there are Dardic and Indian strains in the west, and, along the eastern Himalayan border, there are connections with a complex of tribal peoples known to the Tibetans as Mon. A common language and a single faith diffused a common culture that blended the several elements into a population consciously and recognizably Tibetan.

From the 7th to the 9th century, the Tibetan kingdom was a power to be reckoned with in Central Asia. When that kingdom disintegrated, Tibetans figured there from the 10th to the 13th century only casually as traders and raiders. The patronage of Tibetan Buddhism by the Mongol Yüan dynasty of China made it a potential spiritual focus for the disunited tribes of Mongolia. This religious significance became of practical importance only in the 18th century, when the Dzungars, who professed Tibetan Buddhism, threatened the authority of the Ch'ing dynasty throughout Mongolia. In the 19th century, Tibet was a buffer between Russian imperial expansion and India's frontier defense policy. Today, with Sinkiang, Tibet forms part of China's bastion—or salient—between its Indian and Soviet neighbours.

Historiographic sources. Contemporary sources for the early period (600–900 AD) consist of fragmentary annals, chronicles, and administrative documents, mostly from the cave library at Tun-huang. Some edicts inscribed on stone pillars also survive, and the Chinese T'ang annals provide invaluable evidence. Thereafter, there is little until the flowering of Buddhism in the 13th century, when monk-scholars began to compose religious histories (*chos-'byung*) and royal genealogies (*rgyal-rabs*). Whatever was known of earlier history tended to be overlaid with hagiography. Buddhist literature (there is virtually no other) also produced biographies of holy men that often contain historical matter. There are also local histories, lists of monasteries, guidebooks to sacred places, and a few secular family histories. Only a fraction of this material was ever accessible to foreign scholars; and the Tibetans, until their exodus to India in 1959, knew nothing of Western critical methods. Today, though the rich monastery libraries of Tibet have been lost, new material is sometimes found in the possession of refugees or in little-known monasteries in Nepal, Bhutan, and Ladākh, and from Mongolia.

EARLY HISTORY TO THE 9TH CENTURY

The Tibetan kingdom. A 9th-century chronicle traces the rulers of Tibet through some 36 generations from a semidivine figure Nyag-khri btsan-po, or 'O-lde spu-rgyal, beyond whom extends a shadowy lineage of deities. Later, Buddhist chroniclers piously sought the first ancestor in India, either among the legendary Pāṇḍavas or in the family of the Buddha. Though both periods are incredibly remote, it is not impossible that some adventurous warrior later crossed the Himalayas and won acceptance as leader of a Tibetan clan. The T'ang annals offer another, plausibly dated, theory that in AD 414 a fugitive prince of the Turkic, Southern Liang dynasty in north Szechwan made himself ruler of some Tibetan tribes.

Credible history begins late in the 6th century, when three discontented vassals of one of the princes among whom Tibet was then divided conspired to support the neighbouring lord of Yar-lung, whose title was Spu-rgyal btsan-po. *Btsan-po* ("mighty") became the designation of all kings of Tibet; *rgyal* means "king"; and *spu*, the meaning of which is uncertain, may refer to a sacral quality of

Religious celebrations

Impact of Tibet on Asian history

the princes of Yar-lung as divine manifestations (*lha-'phrul*) that might have inspired the conspirators' choice of a figurehead. Their dynamic championship led not only to the defeat of their old master but also to the rapid transformation of the new one, Gnam-ri slon-btsan, from a princeling in a small valley into the ruler of a vigorously expanding military empire.

Gnam-ri slon-btsan (*c.* 570–*c.* AD 619) imposed his authority over several Ch'iang tribes on the Chinese border and became known to the Sui dynasty (581–618) as the commander of 100,000 warriors. But it was his son, Slon-brtsan-sgam-po (*c.* 608–650), who brought Tibet forcibly to the notice of T'ai Tsung (reigned 626–649), founder of the T'ang dynasty. Slon-brtsan-sgam-po is traditionally believed to have been 82 years old when he died, but the earliest evidence suggests that he was quite young in AD 632, when he shook off ministerial tutelage and led an army against China. To pacify him, T'ang T'ai Tsung granted him a princess as his bride. She and a Nepalese princess whom Slon-brtsan had previously married, as well as a Tibetan lady, are credited with introducing Buddhism into Tibet, though later writers believe Buddhism was implanted several generations earlier. Slon-brtsan-sgam-po is famed as the first *chos-rgyal* ("religious king") and for his all-important influence on Tibetan culture, the introduction of writing for which he borrowed a script from India, enabling the texts of the new religion to be translated. He extended his empire over Nepal, western Tibet, the T'u-yü-hun, and other tribes on China's border; and he invaded north India.

For 50 years after Slon-brtsan-sgam-po's death a regency was imposed by his great minister, Mgar Stong-brtsan yul-bzung (died 667), and his able and aggressive sons. Peace with China was broken in 670, and for two centuries Tibetan armies in Ch'ing-hai and Sikang kept the frontier in a state of war. In alliance with the western Turks, the Tibetans challenged Chinese control of the trade routes through Central Asia.

In 698 the Mgar regency was broken by King 'Dus-srong (676–704), but the militaristic spirit went unchanged. There were calm periods, as in 710, when another marriage alliance was concluded between a Chinese princess and 'Dus-slon's young successor, Khri-lde-gtsug-brtsan (704–754). But the next reign, that of Khri-slon-lde-brtsan (755–797), marked the peak of Tibetan military success, including the exaction of tribute from China and capture of its capital, Ch'ang-an, in 763. Tibetans were also in contact with the Arab conquerors of Iran and penetrated into northern India.

But it was as the second religious king and champion of Buddhism that Khri-slon-lde-brtsan was immortalized by posterity. Buddhism, hitherto confined mostly to the royal household, had suffered proscription during the King's minority; but in 763 when he was 21, he invited Buddhist teachers from India and China to Tibet, and *c.* 779 he established the great temple of Bsam-yas, where Tibetans were trained as monks.

Buddhism did not at once become the national religion. Bitter differences between masters of Chinese and Indian doctrines were publicly debated and resolved, perhaps for political reasons, in favour of the Indian school. Internally, Buddhism foreshadowed the end of "Spu-rgyal's Tibet." The kings did not fully appreciate that its spiritual authority endangered their own supernatural prestige or that its philosophy was irreconcilable with belief in personal survival. They tried to combine old and new, patronizing Buddhist foundations but retaining their claims as divine manifestations and the rite of tumulus burial.

When a Buddhist monk could be appointed chief minister with precedence over all laymen, ecclesiastical influence was certain to become a factor in the rivalry between noble families. Increasing dissension caused a setback to Buddhism even before the death of Khri-slon-lde-brtsan. It recovered *c.* 805 with the accession of Khri-lde-slon-brtsan (died 815) and reached its climax under his successor, Ral-pa-can, whose blind devotion left the administration to a monk-minister. Military activity did not slacken, and a treaty with China in AD 821

acknowledged frontiers favourable to Tibet. But *c.* 836, hostile nobles, after removing the monk-minister, assassinated the King and enthroned his brother Glang-dar-ma. Reputed to have persecuted Buddhism almost to extinction, he was killed in 842 by an avenging monk.

Buddhist tradition records a contested succession involving a posthumous son by one queen, who is regarded as continuing the royal line, and the adopted son of another queen. But there are many inconsistencies, and contemporary Chinese histories indicate that Glang-dar-ma left no son and that Tibetan unity and strength were destroyed by rivalry between generals commanding the frontier armies. Early in the 9th century a scion of the old royal family migrated to western Tibet and founded successor kingdoms there, and by 889 Tibet was a mere congeries of separate lordships.

Culture of early Tibet. The rugged, warlike society—in which, however, women held an honoured place—centred around clan loyalty to chiefs who were bound by oath to the king. While preserving nomadic habits, Tibetans by the 6th century were also cultivating barley around stone-built, flat-roofed dwellings.

Buddhism competed for a foothold with earlier magical and animist rites (generally known as Bon), many of which—excluding blood sacrifices—were incorporated in later religious practice.

As attested in the Chinese annals, the Tibetans soon applied the new writing to translating not only Sanskrit religious texts but also to native chronicles, aphoristic poetry, and other works and to administrative purposes. Edicts were inscribed on impressive stone pillars, and surviving manuscripts show that the empire was based on sound organization.

In the arts Tibetans excelled at goldwork and silverwork and in fine armour. Their massive, boldly proportioned architecture, evident in the remains of early castles, was adapted to Buddhist temples in a characteristically Tibetan style; but the decorative arts probably owed much to Nepalese influence and to Chinese painting; as, for example, in the cave temples of Tun-huang. Contact with China brought paper, silk, jade, porcelain, and tea.

DISUNITY, 9TH TO 14TH CENTURY

With the disintegration of the kingdom, Tibetan generals and chieftains on the eastern border established themselves in separate territories. Some supported religious communities; others invited as leader a member of the old royal family. The acknowledged successors of the religious kings prospered in their migration to the west and maintained contact with Indian Buddhist universities through Tibetan scholars, notably the famous translator Rin-chen bzang-po (died 1055). In central Tibet, nobles and royal collaterals held on in their rival estates; but there, whether through persecution or apathy, Buddhism, which had probably not penetrated deeply into society, suffered an eclipse. As calm and prosperity returned, Buddhism trickled back, first from the east *c.* 978 and later, with greater force, from the west. A missionary journey by the renowned Indian pandit Atīśa in 1042 rekindled the faith through central Tibet, and from then onward Buddhism increasingly spread its influence over every aspect of Tibetan life.

Inspired by Atīśa and by other pandits whom they visited in India, Tibetan religious men formed small communities and expounded different aspects of doctrine. Atīśa's own teaching became the basis of the austere Bka'-gdams-pa sect. The Tibetan scholar Dkon-mchog rgyal-po established the monastery of Sa-skya (1073), and a series of lamas (Tibetan priests) founded several monasteries of what is generally called the Bka'-brgyud-pa sect.

Hermits such as Mi-la ras-pa (1040–1123) shunned material things; but the systematized sects became prosperous through the support of local lords, often kinsmen of the founding lama, and, except for the Bka'-gdams-pa, each developed its own system of keeping the hierarchical succession within a noble family. In some sects, particularly the Karma-pa and 'Bri-gung-pa, the principle of succession through reincarnation was evolved. Al-

Slon-brtsan's reign

Establishment of Buddhism in Tibet

The arts of early Tibet

though lamas of different schools studied amicably together, their supporters inevitably indulged in worldly competition. This tendency was intensified by the intervention of a new Asian power, the Mongols.

Relations with the Mongols

Timely submission by the Tibetans in 1207 averted invasion by the world-conquering Genghis Khan; but their failure to pay tribute to the Mongols after Genghis Khan's death resulted in punitive raids, and in 1247 a religious leader, the Sa-skya lama, was summoned to Mongolia, where he did homage and was appointed the Mongols' viceroy for Tibet. His nephew 'Phags-pa, who succeeded him, won great influence with Kublai Khan, the Mongol conqueror of China and founder in 1279 of the Yüan dynasty, with whom the relationship of Tibet to China was stated as a personal bond between the lama as priest and the emperor as patron (*yon-mchod*).

A series of Sa-skya lamas, living at the Chinese court, thus became rulers of Tibet on behalf of the Mongols. Administration was left to selected Tibetan officers, but the Mongols prescribed a reorganization of the many small estates into 13 myriarchies (administrative districts each comprising, theoretically, 10,000 families), nominally under their viceroy. The ideal was a single authority; but other monasteries, especially 'Bri-gung and Phag-mo-gru of the Bka'-brgyud-pa sect, whose supporters controlled several myriarchies, actively contested Sa-skya's supremacy, which was further weakened by domestic dissension.

The collapse of the Yüan dynasty in 1368 also brought down Sa-skya after 80 years of power. Indeed, already in 1358 a dynamic rival, Byang-chub rgyal-mtshan of Phag-mo-gru, who was dedicated to the elimination of Mongol influence and the restoration of the Tibetan ethos, had displaced the Sa-skya hierarch as effective master of Tibet. Consequently, when the native Chinese Ming dynasty evicted the Mongols, Tibet had regained its actual independence; for over 100 years the Phag-mo-gru-pa line continued to govern in its own right.

Some of the Ming emperors courted Tibetan lamas, but external support was no longer a factor in Tibetan politics; the changes of regime that occurred in 1481 and 1565 were purely internal matters. Indeed, the Chinese often seemed unaware of where real power in Tibet actually lay.

A proliferation of scholars, preachers, mystics, hermits, and eccentrics, as well as monastic administrators and warriors, accompanied the revival of Buddhism. Literary activity was intense. Sanskrit works were translated with the help of visiting Indian pandits; the earliest codifiers, classifiers, biographers, and historians appeared. In an outburst of monastic building, the characteristic Tibetan style acquired greater extent, mass, and dignity. Chinese workmen were imported for decorative work, such as tiled roofs and gilded ornaments. Temple walls were covered with fine frescoes; huge carved and painted wooden pillars were hung with silk and with painted banners (*thang-ka*). Chapels abounded in images, great and small, of gold, gilded copper, or painted and gilded clay; some were decorated with stucco scenes in high relief; in others the remains of deceased lamas were enshrined in silver or gilded stupas. Under Nepalese influence, images were cast and ritual vessels and musical instruments made in a style blending exuberant power and sophisticated craftsmanship; wood-carvers produced beautiful shrines and book covers, and from India came palm-leaf books, ancient images, and bell-metal stupas of all sizes.

Foreign influence on the arts

Many monks visited China, and the emperors lavished offerings of jewels, gold seals, jade, porcelain, and brocades on high lamas and their monasteries. Chinese inspiration, as well as Indian and Nepalese, shows in the style of painting and in decorative motifs, but specifically Mongolian influences, apart from administrative organization, seem confined to details of dress and ornament.

Although the earlier Bon continued in places, Buddhism, with its impressive externals and patronage, now became the popular religion. Some of the new prosperity may have filtered down to the common people; at least there is no hint of popular discontent.

TIBET, 14TH–19TH CENTURY

The Dge-lugs-pa (Yellow Hat) order. For 70 peaceful years Byang-chub rgyal-mtshan (died 1364) and his two successors ruled a domain wider than that of the Sa-skya-pa. Thereafter, although the Phag-mo-gru Gong-ma (as the ruler was called) remained nominally supreme, violent dissension erupted again; and in 1481 power was seized by the lay princes of Rin-spungs, ministers of the Gong-ma and patrons of the increasingly influential Karma-pa sect. Already a new political factor had appeared in the Dge-lugs-pa sect. Its founder was a saintly scholar, Blo-bzang grags-pa (died 1419), known, from his birthplace near Koko Nor, as Tsong-kha-pa. After studying with leading teachers of the day, he formulated his own doctrine, emphasizing the moral and philosophical ideas of Atīśa rather than the magic and mysticism of Sa-skya—though he did not discard the latter entirely. In 1409 he founded his own monastery at Dga'-ldan, devoted to the restoration of strict monastic discipline.

Although many monks lived truly religious lives, prosperity and political involvement inevitably undermined monastic behaviour, and Tsong-kha-pa's disciplinary reform appealed to people weary of rivalry and strife between wealthy monasteries. Tsong-kha-pa probably did not imagine that his disciples would form a new sect and join in that rivalry, but, after his death, devoted and ambitious followers built around his teaching and prestige what became the Dge-lugs-pa, or Yellow Hat, order, which was gradually drawn into the political arena.

The Dge-lugs-pa, who early adopted the practice of hierarchical succession through reincarnation, gradually built a number of monasteries. Although they won influence by mediating between more powerful sects, they met irreconcilable dislike from the Karma-pa, the allies of the Rin-spungs princes and their successors, the Gtsang kings, who displaced them in 1565.

In 1578 the Dge-lugs-pa, repressed in their homeland, took a step destined to bring foreign interference once more into Tibetan affairs. The older orders had failed to pursue their missionary opportunities in Mongolia after the fall of the Yüan dynasty. Now, the third Dge-lugs-pa hierarch, Bsod-nams-rgya-mtsho, was invited to visit the powerful Tümed Mongol leader Altan Khan, with whom he revived the patron–priest relationship that had existed between Kublai Khan and 'Phags-pa. From this time dates the title of Dalai ("Oceanwide") Lama, conferred by Altan and applied retrospectively to the two previous hierarchs. The holder is regarded as the embodiment of a spiritual emanation of the *bodhisattva* Spyan-ras-gzigs (pr Chenrezi)—Avalokiteśvara. The succession is maintained by the discovery of a child, born soon after the death of a Dalai Lama, into whom the spirit of the deceased is believed to have entered. Until 1642 the Dalai Lamas were principal abbots of the Dge-lugs-pa, and in that year acquired temporal and spiritual rule of Tibet. With Altan's help virtually all the Mongols became Dge-lugs-pa adherents, and on Bsod-nams-rgya-mtsho's death they acquired a proprietary interest in the order and some claims on Tibet itself when the fourth Dalai Lama was conveniently discovered in the Tümed royal family.

To support their protégé the Mongols sent armed bands into Tibet, bringing a new dimension into sectarian enmity. Their opponents were the Red Hat Lama, head of a Karma-pa subsect, and his patron the Gtsang king. The lama's personal title has misled some Western writers into thinking that the Yellow Hats were opposed by all the older sects, inaccurately lumped together as Red Hats.

That phase of rivalry ended inconclusively with the early death of the fourth Dalai Lama and the decline of Tümed Mongol authority in Mongolia. The next came when Gushi Khan, leader of the Khoshotd tribe, which had displaced the Tümed, appeared as champion of the Dge-lugs-pa. In 1640 he answered an appeal from Bsod-nams chos-'phel, the energetic minister of the fifth Dalai Lama, Ngag-dbang-rgya-mtsho and invaded Tibet, where after fierce fighting he defeated the Gtsang king and his Karma-pa supporters.

The unification of Tibet. Once more the priest found a patron. In 1642, with exemplary devotion, Gushi enthroned the Dalai Lama as ruler of Tibet, appointing Bsod-nams chos-'phel as minister for administrative affairs and himself taking the title of king and the role of military protector. These three forceful personalities methodically and efficiently consolidated the religious and temporal authority of the Dge-lugs-pa. Lhasa, long the spiritual heart of Tibet, now became the political capital as well. Gushi's troops enforced the Dalai Lama's rule from K'ang-ting in the east to the Ladākh border. Dge-lugs-pa supremacy was imposed on all other orders, with special severity, but without savagery, toward the Karma-pa. A reorganized district administration, largely under nominees of the Dalai Lama, reduced the power of the lay nobility.

The grandeur and prestige of the regime were enhanced by reviving ceremonies attributed to the religious kings, by enlarging the nearby monasteries of 'Bras-spungs, Se-ra, and Dga'-ldan, and by building the superb Potala palace, completed by another great figure, Sangs-rgyas rgya-mtsho (1679–1705), who succeeded as minister regent just before the death of his patron the Dalai Lama. By then a soundly based and unified government had been established over a wider extent than any for eight centuries.

Relations with the Manchus

The installation of the fifth Dalai Lama at Lhasa (1642) and the Manchu Ch'ing dynasty in China (1644) were almost synchronous. The two had previously been in communication, and Gushi had had earlier relations with the Manchus. In 1653 the Dalai Lama, having been invited by the emperor, visited the Chinese court as an independent ruler.

Good relations with Tibet were important to the Manchus because of the Dalai Lama's prestige among the Mongols, from whom a new threat was taking shape in the ambitions of the powerful Dzungars of western Mongolia. During the fifth Dalai Lama's lifetime, Tibetan influence was generally favourable to Chinese interests.

Elsewhere, Lhasa's expanding authority brought disagreements with Bhutan, which held its own against Tibetan incursions in 1646 and 1657, and with Ladākh, where a campaign ended in 1684 in Tibetan withdrawal to an accepted frontier when the Ladākhī king appealed for help to the Muslim governor of Kashmir.

In 1707, Capuchin fathers from Nepal reached Lhasa. Jesuit missionaries had found their way briefly to western Tibet (1624–41) and Shigatse (1628–30), and two Jesuits from China passed through Lhasa itself in 1661. The Capuchin mission continued with a few interruptions until 1745, and from 1716 to 1721 a famous Jesuit scholar, Ippolito Desideri, was also at Lhasa.

Tibet under Chinese overlordship. The Dalai Lama's death in 1682 and the discovery of his five-year-old reincarnation in 1688 were concealed by Sangs-rgyas rgya-mtsho, who was intent on continuing the administration without disturbance. He informed the Chinese only in 1696. Emperor K'ang-hsi (reigned 1662–1722), already suspicious because of Tibetan collusion with the hostile Dzungar leader, Dga'-ldan, was incensed at the deception. In 1703 he discovered an ally in Tibet and an antagonist to Sangs-rgyas rgya-mtsho when Lha-bzang Khan, fourth successor of Gushi, sought to assert rights as king that had atrophied under his immediate predecessors. The behaviour of the sixth Dalai Lama, Tshangs-dbyangs-rgya-mtsho, who preferred poetry and libertine amusements to religion, gave Lha-bzang his opportunity. In 1705, with the Emperor's approval, he attacked and killed Sangs-rgyas rgya-mtsho, deposed Tshangs-dbyangs-rgya-mtsho as a spurious reincarnation, and dispatched him toward China, on which journey he died. Lha-bzang then installed, as rightful incarnation, a mature lama. The Tibetans angrily rejected him and soon recognized in east Tibet the infant reincarnation of Tshangs-dbyangs-rgya-mtsho.

In 1717 the Dzungars, nominally Dge-lugs-pa supporters, took advantage of Tibetan discontents to intervene in a sudden raid, ostensibly to avenge the Dalai Lama and Sangs-rgyas rgya-mtsho. They defeated and killed Lha-bzang and, seizing power at Lhasa, behaved with outrageous rapacity.

Fear of hostile Mongol domination of Tibet compelled the Emperor to send troops against the Dzungars. After an initial reverse, his armies drove them out in 1720 and were welcomed at Lhasa as deliverers, all the more because they brought with them the new Dalai Lama, Bskal-bzang-rgya-mtsho, of whom the Emperor had skillfully secured possession. Then and for the next 200 years there was no fighting between Tibetans and Chinese; but after evicting the Dzungars the Emperor decided to safeguard Chinese interests by appointing representatives—generally known as Ambans—at Lhasa, with a small garrison in support.

The Tibetans, interpreting this as another patron and priest relationship, accepted the situation, which, for the most part, left them to manage their own affairs. It was only in recurring crises that Chinese participation became, briefly, energetic. The first occasion was a civil war in Tibet from 1727 to 1728, when, by a change of Imperial policy, Chinese troops had been withdrawn. Fear of renewed Dzungar interference necessitated another expedition to restore order. The Chinese wisely supported an able lay nobleman, Pho-lha Bsod-nams sttobs-rgyas, who, for 30 years until his death in 1747, governed Tibet peacefully, in virtual independence but with due respect for Chinese suzerainty.

Pho-lha's son and successor rashly conspired with the Dzungars, and in 1750 he was assassinated as a preventive measure by the Ambans. They, too, were immediately killed by infuriated Tibetans; but order was quickly restored by the Dalai Lama, and a small Chinese expedition found nothing to do.

The Gurkha invasion

The third crisis was the invasion of Tibet in 1792 by the militant Gurkhas, who had ruled Nepal since 1768. They were driven out and pursued into Nepal itself by the Manchu general, Fu-k'ang-an.

That led to nominally stricter Chinese control over Tibet; but, as Manchu energy declined, the Tibetans became increasingly independent, though still recognizing the formal suzerainty of the Emperor, behind which it sometimes suited them to shelter. At no time did the Ambans have administrative power, and after 1792, when Tibet was involved in wars with Ladākh (1842) and Nepal (1858), the Chinese were unable to help or protect them.

Administration and culture under the Manchus. No Dalai Lama until the 13th approached the personal authority of the "Great Fifth." The seventh incarnation was overshadowed by Pho-lha; the eighth was diffident and retiring. But after the Pho-lha family's regime, Dge-lugs-pa churchmen resumed power and held on to it through a series of monk regents for about 145 years. Some check on them existed in the Panchen Lamas of Bkra-shis lhun-po, the second-ranking line of incarnations, whom the Chinese since 1727 had built up to counterbalance the authority of Lhasa.

The original austerity of Tsong-kha-pa's order was diluted by power, wealth, and numbers. There were, of course, disciplinarians and saints and many scholars also. The older sects, free from political responsibilities, were often renowned for piety and discipline and produced scholars and mystics with wide-ranging religious views.

Chinese contacts affected Tibetan culture less than might be expected. They helped to shape the administrative machinery, army, and mail service, which were based on existing institutions and run by Tibetans. Chinese customs influenced dress, food, and manners; china and chopsticks were widely used by the upper classes.

The arts of painting, wood carving, and casting figures continued on traditional lines, with much technical skill but few signs of innovation. An important effect of Manchu supremacy was the exclusion of foreigners after 1792. That ended the hopes of Christian missionaries and the diplomatic visits from British India, which had been started in 1774. Tibet was now closed, and mutual ignorance enshrouded future exchanges with its British neighbours in India.

TIBET IN THE 20TH CENTURY

In the mid-19th century the Tibetans repeatedly rebuffed overtures from the British, who at first saw Tibet as a trade route to China and later as countenancing Russian advances that might endanger India. Eventually, in 1903, after failure to get China to control its unruly vassal, a political mission led by Col. Francis Younghusband with strong military support was dispatched from India to secure understandings on frontier and trade relations. Tibetan resistance was overcome by force, the Dalai Lama fled to China, and the rough wooing ended in a treaty at Lhasa in 1904 between Britain and Tibet without Chinese adherence.

In 1906 the Chinese by skillful diplomacy achieved a treaty with Britain, without Tibetan participation, which recognized their suzerainty over Tibet, although that suzerainty was clearly ineffective and had not been acknowledged in the Lhasa treaty. Success emboldened the Chinese to seek direct control of Tibet by using force against the Tibetans for the first time in ten centuries. In 1910 the Dalai Lama again was forced to flee, this time to India.

Declaration of Tibetan independence. That dying burst by the Manchu dynasty converted Tibetan indifference into enmity; and, after the Chinese Revolution in 1911, they expelled all Chinese from Tibet, declared their independence of the new republic, and looked to Britain for support. The British government, doubting Tibet's ability to maintain complete independence, persuaded the Chinese to join in a tripartite conference aimed at a settlement that might guarantee Tibetan autonomy under nominal Chinese suzerainty. Though a convention was initialled by the three representatives, the Chinese, ostensibly dissatisfied on the frontier issue, withdrew before final signature. Thereupon the British and Tibetans jointly declared the convention between themselves binding, denying the Chinese all advantages under it unless they also signed.

The effects of this agreement were differently interpreted by the several parties. The Chinese denied its validity; but Tibet functioned in practice as an independent government until 1951 and defended its frontier against China in occasional fighting as late as 1931. A British representative at Gyantse conducted friendly, if distant, communications with Lhasa. But the Chinese, though continuing to claim Tibet as their territory, were allowed no presence there in any capacity from 1913 until 1935.

In 1935 the Tibetans, weakened by the death of the resolute 13th Dalai Lama, admitted a Chinese "condolence mission." Once at Lhasa, it established a small office and sought to arrange the return, under Chinese protection, of the sixth Panchen Lama, who had left Tibet in 1923 after disagreements with the Dalai Lama. The British government sent Sir Basil Gould, political officer in Sikkim, to observe that development, which contravened their agreements with Tibet. After his departure in 1937, a small, temporary British mission remained at Lhasa. In 1947 it was taken over by the new government of India, together with its predecessor's rights and responsibilities toward Tibet.

The independent regime of the Tibetan government continued unchanged. The sixth Panchen Lama died in China. The 14th Dalai Lama was discovered in 1939. In World War II Tibet preserved its neutrality in spite of pressure from China and its allies to use the country as a supply route. In 1947 an attempted coup by a former regent, suspected of Chinese sympathies, was frustrated. In 1949, in view of Communist successes in China, the Tibetans evicted the Chinese mission from Lhasa.

The Chinese conquest. But the Communists were not to be diverted. In 1949 the "liberation" of Tibet was heralded, and in October 1950 they launched an invasion of east Tibet. The poorly equipped Tibetan troops were overwhelmed. An appeal by the Dalai Lama to the United Nations was denied, and expected support from India and Britain was not forthcoming. A Tibetan delegation summoned to China in 1951 had to sign a treaty dictated by the conquerors. It professed to guarantee Tibetan autonomy and religion but also allowed the establishment at Lhasa of Chinese civil and military headquarters. Unremitting pressure was exerted to bring Tibetan society

Expulsion of the Chinese

Chinese occupation

and government into line with those of Communist China. The unique authority of the Dalai Lama was undermined by dividing Tibet into three regions.

To soften the loss of independence, the Tibetans were offered some modern benefits, such as hospitals, new agricultural methods, schools (under Chinese supervision), and rudimentary local industries. But the greater progress was in making roads and bridges, an innovation for the Tibetans, who had no wheeled vehicles, and a necessity for the extension of Chinese control.

Smoldering resentment at the strain on the country's resources from the influx of Chinese soldiery and civilians was inflamed in 1956 by reports of savage fighting and oppression in districts east of the upper Yangtze, outside the administration of Lhasa but bound to it by race, language, and religion. Refugees from the fighting in the east carried guerrilla warfare against the Chinese into central Tibet, creating tensions that exploded in a popular rising at Lhasa in March 1959. The Dalai Lama, most of his ministers, and many followers escaped across the Himalayas; and after days of fighting and bloodshed the rising was fiercely suppressed.

The Tibetan government was replaced by a military dictatorship intent on imposing the pattern of China. It immediately demolished the framework of Tibetan society and the influence of church and nobility by confiscating all private property. The country was reorganized into peasant associations in preparation for collectivization and communes. To give an appearance of Tibetanness, the new Panchen Lama, a creature of the Chinese, was appointed chairman of an interim administration, and a few of the countless Buddhist temples were maintained as showplaces. The rest were abandoned, and the monks fled, were imprisoned, or reverted to lay life. Strict regimentation, monopoly of agricultural production, prevention of travel by Tibetans, severe punishments, and forced labour for suspected opponents were aggravated in 1961 and 1962 by near famine resulting from the upheaval. More refugees fled to India, guerrilla activities continued, and the Panchen Lama, rapidly disillusioned, was dismissed and disgraced in 1964.

The events of 1959 intensified disagreements with India, which had given asylum to the Dalai Lama, and, in 1962, Chinese forces proved the efficiency of the new communications by invading northeast Assam.

In 1966 and 1967 the Chinese position was shaken by Red Guard excesses and internecine fighting when the Cultural Revolution reached Lhasa. Military control was restored by 1969; and in 1971, although resistance was officially admitted and former collaborators of any status had disappeared, a new local government committee, containing 14 Chinese and three Tibetan nonentities, was announced. Between 1963 and 1971 no foreign visitor was allowed to enter Tibet, and only a few Nepalese traders remain. There has since been a trickle of information to indicate that the Chinese have destroyed all overt traces of Tibetan religion and submerged the old culture and religion, now openly preserved only by some 70,000 Tibetan refugees in India, Nepal, Bhutan, and Sikkim.

Relations with India

BIBLIOGRAPHY. W.D. SHAKABPA, *Tibet: A Political History* (1967), the first history of its kind by a Tibetan; TIEH-TSENG LI, *The Historical Status of Tibet* (1956), a Chinese view; HUGH E. RICHARDSON, *Tibet and Its History* (1962), a British view; DAVID L. SNELLGROVE and HUGH E. RICHARDSON, *A Cultural History of Tibet* (1968); JACQUES BACOT, FREDERICK W. THOMAS, and CHARLES TOUSSAINT, *Documents de Touen-houang relatifs à l'histoire de Tibet* (1940), translation of the earliest Tibetan records; PAUL PELLIOT, *Histoire ancienne du Tibet* (1961), translation of contemporary Chinese accounts of 7th to 9th-century Tibet; LUCIANO PETECH, *China and Tibet in the Early 18th Century: History of the Establishment of Chinese Protectorate in Tibet* (1950), brilliant documentation of a turning point in Tibetan history; ALASTAIR LAMB, *Britain and Chinese Central Asia* (1960), fully documented examination of the years 1767–1905; H.H. THE DALAI LAMA, *My Land My People* (1962), a personal account of recent events; GEORGE GINSBURGS and MICHAEL MATHOS, *Communist China and Tibet* (1964), draws on all available sources regarding Chinese actions in Tibet from 1951 to 1962.

(H.E.R.)

Tides

Sea-level oscillations of approximately daily, or diurnal, and twice daily, or semidiurnal, period are a worldwide phenomenon observed at continental coasts and islands. According to Newton, this motion is caused by the difference of the gravitational attraction between celestial bodies and the centrifugal acceleration of their rotation. These differences of accelerations are called tide-generating accelerations, and the motion itself is called tides.

Because these tide-generating accelerations act on the particles in the atmosphere and in the Earth as well as on the water masses of the ocean, there are atmospheric tides, Earth tides, and ocean tides. Tidal oscillations are periodic because they are related to the motion of the Earth, the Sun, and the Moon. The tides on the Earth are not influenced by other celestial bodies. It is customary in the English language to refer sometimes to certain phenomena that do not arise from tide-generating forces as tides, for instance meteorological tides and tsunamis (*i.e.*, great sea waves produced by submarine earthquakes or volcanic eruptions).

For centuries efforts have been directed toward understanding the physics and hydrodynamics of the tides in the sea. Amplitudes of tidal oscillations are largest there; atmospheric and Earth tides are less significant. At most coastal or island locations the interval between successive high waters is about 12 hours and 25 minutes, which is half the time of the Moon's apparent revolution around the Earth. In some areas, such as the China Sea, the interval is approximately 24 hours. The first are called semidiurnal tides, the second diurnal tides. If there is a prevailing semidiurnal tide, the difference between the high-water time and the time the Moon crosses the meridian of the location is approximately constant, and this difference is known as the high-water interval for the particular location.

In addition to semidiurnal and diurnal tides, there are also long-period tides. Periods of 14 days to 19 years exist as a result of the motion of the Sun, Moon, and Earth. A fourth group of tides, not of direct astronomic origin, consists of the shallow-water tides that result from the interaction of the semidiurnal and diurnal and other tides.

The difference in sea level between successive high water and low water, called the range of tide, may vary from day to day in a certain place; within a fortnight it reaches a maximum value, known as spring tide, and a minimum value, known as neap tide. In the open sea distances of high- and low-water level from undisturbed sea level are more or less equal to one another. The vertical tidal motion of the sea level is combined with components of horizontal motion. The water particles moved by harmonic tidal currents oscillate on an ellipse within one tidal period. The times between maximum and minimum currents are about six hours and 12 minutes. In shallow waters, especially in tidal rivers, the incoming tidal current, called the flood current, passes upstream with increasing maximum current and decreasing duration. The maximum velocity of the seaward-directed current or ebb current becomes progressively less going up the river and flows for an increasingly larger time. If the tide is entering a very shallow river the wave as a whole does not proceed as fast as the water particles do, according to the tidal currents. The result is a wall-like wave, called a bore, or a mascaret, which travels up the river.

In some areas—*e.g.*, the Mediterranean and the Baltic—the tidal range for both diurnal and semidiurnal tides is quite small. In other areas the range increases, and in the Bay of Fundy it reaches more than 15 metres (50 feet). Most of tidal sea-level records originate from the coasts of the continents and from islands. Available measurements taken in the open sea are insufficient to permit understanding of the tidal processes in that region, which constitutes the greater part of the surface of the world's oceans. For this reason, theoretical tidal studies are of great importance; they lead to a physical understanding of tidal processes in the sea. This article treats the causes of tides and tidal currents, and their prediction by means

of hydrodynamic–numerical (HN) models: For other motions of the sea, see WATER WAVES and OCEAN CURRENTS; and for the general interaction of these motions and their world character, see OCEANS AND SEAS. See also ESTUARIES and LAKES AND LAKE SYSTEMS for further information on these water bodies, which are also affected by the tides.

THE CAUSES OF TIDES

The gravitational attraction of two bodies such as the Earth and the Moon is proportional to the product of their masses and inversely proportional to the square of the distance between their centres. Their gravitational attraction tends to force them to approach one another, but this is inhibited by the centrifugal force of rotation around their joint centre of gravity. If it is assumed that the mass of each body is concentrated in its centre, then the two forces balance each other. There is an important difference between these two forces, gravitational attraction and the centrifugal force of rotation. The first depends on distance and consequently varies for different particles on the Earth; the second is constant for all points of the Earth. If a single water particle of the ocean is considered, there is no balance; the gravitational attraction of the Moon may be different from the centrifugal force of rotation.

These differences are the tide-generating forces. In the same way, tide-generating forces are caused by the gravitational attraction of the Sun; they are determined by the motions of the Sun, the Earth and the Moon, the distance, the mass, and the volume. The tide-generating forces are vectors (*i.e.*, they are physical quantities that have magnitude and direction). One component is directed to the centre of the Earth and coincides in direction with the gravitational force of the Earth itself, altering this only in a very small amount (the ratio is 1:9,000,000). The other components are situated on a tangential plane at the sea surface and drive the water masses in the direction of the Moon and Sun, respectively.

Tide-
generating
forces

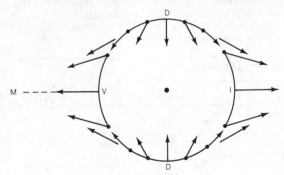

Figure 1: Tide-generating forces (see text).

Figure 1 shows the distribution of the tide-generating forces on the Earth. The lengths of the arrows are proportional to the magnitudes of the forces. M is the direction of the Moon; the water masses tend to build a deviation toward the Moon (Point V), as well as in the opposite direction (Point I). At point D there is a lowering of the sea level. A deformation of the sea level is similarly caused by the tide-generating forces of the Sun. The tide potential V of the Moon at the sea surface based on the relationship of the distance between and positions of the Earth and Moon is expressed as follows:

$$V = 26{,}206 \left[\left(\frac{c}{r}\right)^3 \left(\cos 2\,\delta + \frac{1}{3}\right) \right.$$
$$\left. + 0.002598 \left(\frac{c}{r}\right)^4 (5 \cos 3\,\delta + 3 \cos \delta) \right] \frac{cm^2}{sec^2},$$

in which c is the average distance of the Moon and r the distance between the centre of the Moon and the centre of the Earth, δ is the angle between the line joining the centres of the Moon and the Earth and the line from the centre of the Earth to the point on the Earth's surface that is being considered. A similar equation is valid for the tide potential of the Sun.

From M.N. Hill (ed.), *The Sea*, vol. 1 (1962); John Wiley & Sons, Inc.

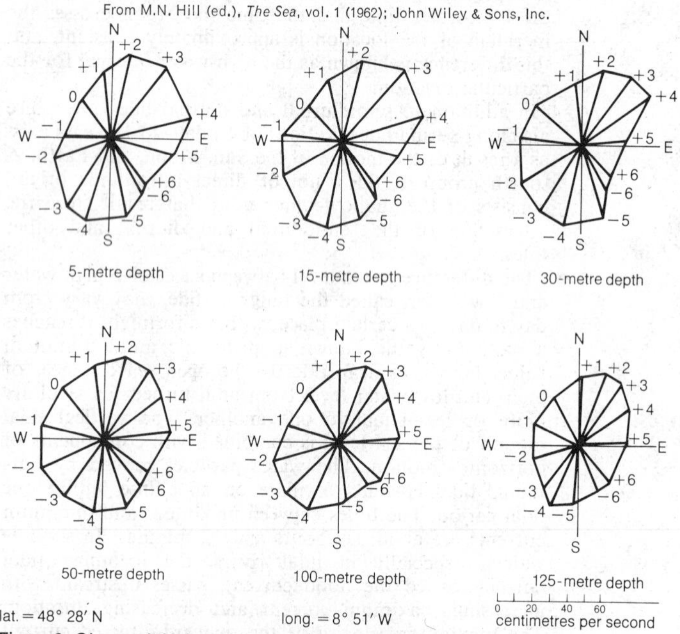

The
equilib-
rium tide

The differential quotients of the tide potential yield the tide-generating acceleration. The dimension of the potential V is centimetres squared per second squared. If V is divided by the acceleration of gravity (which has the dimension centimetres per second squared) a term remains, $\bar{\xi}$, which has the dimension centimetres. The surfaces of equal acceleration of gravity are disturbed by this value $\bar{\xi}$. Figure 1 indicates a maximum elevation at points V and I and a maximum depression at point D. This shape of the sea surface would occur in an ocean covering the whole Earth, if the Earth were completely rigid and the tide potential remained constant. This type of tide, called equilibrium tide, is fictitious but accurately represents tide-generating forces at the surface of and within the Earth. In such a case the slope of the surface of the sea would be balanced by the tide-generating acceleration, and there would be no tidal currents.

In investigating the dynamics of the tides, the tide-generating acceleration may be replaced by the acceleration caused by the slope of the equilibrium tide.

The maximum elevation of the equilibrium tide of the Moon is 35.6 centimetres (14.0 inches), and the greatest depression would be 17.8 centimetres (7.0 inches). The natural tidal range in the sea is quite different from these values of the equilibrium tide, and accordingly the conclusion that there are no tidal currents in the sea is completely unrealistic.

TIDAL ANALYSIS

Tidal harmonics. The tide potential of the Moon and the Sun are functions of the following variables: the Earth's speed of rotation, γ; the mean motion of the Moon, σ; the mean motion of the Sun, η; the speed of revolution of the Moon's nodes, N; the mean motion of the Moon at its closest approach—the lunar perigee, ω; and the time. These speeds are incommensurable (*i.e.*, they are not divisible, in whole numbers, by each other), and they may serve as independent variables in representing the tide potential by means of a Fourier series (a mathematical series of terms consisting of the trigonometric functions, sine and cosine), each term in which is called a tide or a tidal constituent; the most important are given in Table 1.

Table 1: Tidal Constituents

name	symbol	speed (° per hour)	coefficient	speed
Diurnal species				
Lunisolar	K_1	15.041	0.265	γ
Larger lunar	O_1	13.943	0.189	$\gamma - 2\sigma$
Larger solar	P_1	14.959	0.088	$\gamma - 2\eta$
Semidiurnal species				
Principal lunar	M_2	28.984	0.454	$2\gamma - \sigma$
Principal solar	S_2	30.000	0.211	2γ
Larger lunar elliptic	N_2	28.440	0.088	$2\gamma - 3\sigma + \omega$
Lunisolar	K_2	30.082	0.058	2γ

The coefficient is proportional to the equilibrium amplitude within the given species and indicates the magnitude of a constituent.

Besides the diurnal and semidiurnal constituents there are long- and short-period constituents. Tidal oscillations of high frequency may be important in shallow-water areas.

Tidal constituents. As long as tidal motions are linear (*i.e.*, no interaction occurs between different constituents), the constituents of the Fourier series may be investigated separately. Table 1 shows that the principal lunar (M_2) tide is the predominant one. The nature of the tide potential gives rise to a similar development of the observed sea level into harmonic series (a series of terms whose reciprocals form an arithmetic progression, $1, \frac{1}{2}, \frac{1}{3}, \ldots 1/n$). The frequencies are taken from the tide potential, and, for a given place, measurements of the sea level within a time interval are used to determine amplitudes and phases by various mathematical methods. After amplitudes and phases are known, the measurements may be reproduced. Furthermore, it becomes

possible to synthesize the tide for any time, past, present, or future. This harmonic method may be used to predict tides and the components of tidal currents, but only for places for which sufficient long-term records of sea-level elevations are available. Harmonic-tide predictions are fairly good for deepwater ports; in shallow-water areas, especially in tidal estuaries, special corrections are needed in order to get precise results, or non-harmonic methods must be applied.

Special machines have been developed to synthesize tidal constituents and especially to determine high- and low-water height and time. The first to design such a tide-predicting machine was a Scottish physicist, Lord Kelvin, in 1872. In 1930, H. Rauschelbach constructed a machine containing 62 tidal constituents. Such analogue machines have been replaced by digital computers, which are much faster. Predicted high- and low-water time and water heights for important ports all over the world are published in tide tables prepared by hydrographic offices in the different countries.

Tide-
predicting
machines

In a similar way it is possible to predict tidal currents, but normally no such predictions are available.

Tidal measurements. Along the coastlines of continents and islands a large number of tide gauges are in permanent operation. The harmonic analyses of these sea-level records are collected and published by the International Hydrographic Bureau (IHB) in Monaco. Measurements of tidal currents are available for only a few places. The same is true of sea-level observations in the open sea. Recently developed instruments provide the first measurements of the vertical tidal components in the deep sea.

5-metre depth   15-metre depth   30-metre depth

50-metre depth   100-metre depth   125-metre depth

lat. = 48° 28′ N   long. = 8° 51′ W

0 20 40 60 centimetres per second

Figure 2: Observed tidal currents at the entrance to the English Channel, and their variation with water depth. Positive and negative values shown indicate the number of hours after and prior to the Moon's transit of Greenwich.

The tidal harmonics for Immingham, in the North Sea, and Do Son, in the South China Sea, are given in Table 2.

In the North Sea the tides are semidiurnal; in the South China Sea they are diurnal. Considering tidal currents, the amplitude and phase may vary from the surface to the bottom. Figure 2 represents tidal currents as a function of time for different depths, as revealed by records made west of the entrance to the English Channel.

The elements of tidal current ellipses, including the amounts, direction, and time of maximum velocity, may be shown on maps. The large axes of the tidal current ellipses in Figure 3 are proportional to the maximum speed of the tidal current, and their orientation coincides with the direction of the maximum tidal current in the North Sea. Small axes refer to the minimum speed of the tidal currents. Full lines indicate the time of max-

Table 2: Harmonic Tidal Constituents for Immingham and Do Son

symbol	speed (° per hour)	coefficient	Immingham phase	Immingham amplitude (cm)	Do Son phase	Do Son amplitude (cm)
M₂	28.984	0.454	161°	223	113°	4
S₂	30.000	0.211	210°	73	140°	3
N₂	28.440	0.088	141°	45	100°	1
K₂	30.082	0.058	212°	18	140°	1
K₁	15.041	0.265	279°	15	91°	72
O₁	13.943	0.189	120°	16	35°	70
P₁	14.959	0.088	257°	6	91°	24

imum speed of tidal currents referred to Moon's transit in Greenwich. Maps of this type provide an idea of the geographical distribution of the tidal currents in the sea. The time of the occurrence of high water and the

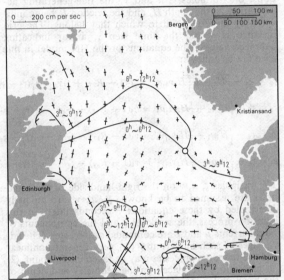

Figure 3: Major and minor axes of tidal current ellipses in the North Sea (see text).

tidal range and their geographical distribution are also of interest. But because tidal sea-level records originate primarily from harbours and other coastal locations and because no measurements from the open sea are available, it is difficult to draw maps containing cotidal and corange lines (along a cotidal line the time of high water is constant, and along a corange line the tidal range is constant). In several cases such lines in the open sea have been constructed by means of an interpolation of coastal values. If no measurements are available, then the distribution of cotidal lines in the open sea remains uncertain. Corange lines have not been drawn. In order to overcome these difficulties, theoretical methods have been used. One powerful available tool developed by Walter Hansen since 1939 is the hydrodynamic–numerical method, which will be considered later.

TIDAL DYNAMICS AND PREDICTION

Tides and tidal currents are best explained by the mathematical–physical laws that govern the tidal motion in the sea. These laws are expressed as hydrodynamical differential equations, a system that consists of the equations of motion and the continuity equation. The equations of motion express the several forces that produce tidal accelerations. The continuity equation expresses the fact that the volume of any body of water must remain constant despite its motion. The density of the seawater is assumed to be constant.

Conditions required for tidal prediction Under certain conditions the hydrodynamic equations make it possible to determine the tides and tidal currents in an estuary, in a sea, or even in the world ocean. These conditions are: (1) the tide-generating accelerations are given quantitatively as functions of time and space; (2) the distribution of the depth and the shape of the coast-

line of the sea are considered to be known; (3) boundary conditions must be defined, especially those which relate to the coastline: no flow normal (perpendicular) to the coast.

Condition (1) is fulfilled because the tide potential is known very precisely. Condition (2) is normally met by existing pilot charts. With respect to condition (3), there are two types of boundaries. The first is represented by a coastline, and the condition is: no water transport into or out of the land; consequently, the normal component of the tidal current must be zero. The world ocean is an example of a sea totally surrounded by land. The advantage of this coastal boundary condition is that the tides are uniquely determined without using any tidal measurements. The second type is the open boundary. If the sea level is prescribed along a line around the open sea, then the tides within the area bounded by this line are uniquely determined. In natural seas both of these boundary conditions normally occur. The second condition can be applied in cases of neighbouring seas.

Tidal prediction using analytical methods. In the past, mathematicians and physicists developed analytical solutions of the hydrodynamic equations, partly in Cartesian, partly in spherical coordinates. For this purpose it was necessary to simplify the equations, especially with regard to the depth and the shape of the water body considered. In recent years tides in oceans bounded by meridians have been investigated by two English oceanographers, Joseph Proudman and Arthur Doodson, but it has not been possible to reproduce the natural tide quantitatively by means of these analytical solutions.

A very simple solution is obtained by assuming the tidal currents to be zero. In this case the tide-generating accelerations are balanced by the shape of the sea surface, and the equilibrium tide is reproduced. There is no real possibility of reproducing natural tides in such a simple way.

There exists a large number of solutions concerned with tides in areas of very simple geometry. Amplitudes and phases depend on the ratio of the frequency of the tide-generating acceleration to the eigenfrequency (characteristic frequency) of the basin. The amplitudes increase if this ratio approaches one. Friction inhibits the unlimited increase of the amplitude if frequencies are equal to each other. The eigenfrequencies depend on the geometry of the basin.

A tide-generating constituent in a narrow canal that is closed on both ends causes simple harmonic oscillations to occur. These tides are called independent tides. In a canal closed on one side and open on the other, tidal oscillations may be caused by co-oscillation with the water masses beyond the open end of the canal. These tides are called co-oscillating tides. In many adjacent and marginal seas the co-oscillating tide is much more important than the independent tide.

The distinction between completely and partly closed seas is important in the view of tide reproduction. In the case of completely closed basin, tides and tidal currents can be determined quantitatively without using any measurements. In a sea with partly open boundaries, such as the North Sea or the Gulf of St. Lawrence, it is necessary to prescribe the sea level as a function of time on or along the open boundary. Completely closed seas, then, are well suited to checking the results derived from hydrodynamic equations against measurements from the sea under consideration.

Although the world ocean fits these conditions, it is too complicated to use in such an analytical investigation. There are no other completely closed seas on Earth, and the tides of lakes, such as Lake Baikal, are small. Other seas that are almost completely closed have, like lakes, only very small tides: the Black Sea, Baltic Sea, and even the Mediterranean Sea are examples.

Therefore, in order to check hydrodynamic theories, it is necessary to restrict the investigations to seas with boundaries that are not too open. The tides within such an area should be appreciable. Although a full check of the quality of hydrodynamic theories is not possible in such cases, because the solution of these equations is influenced by the prescribed sea level, the computed tides

Finite
difference
method

in the interior of the area may be compared with the measurements in corresponding locations, and in this way the quality of the solution may be tested.

Tidal prediction using hydrodynamic–numerical methods. *Tides in natural seas of small width.* Solutions of the hydrodynamic equations, taking into account arbitrary depth and coastline distribution, are developed as follows: time is eliminated by assuming that the sea level is a pure harmonic function of time. The derivatives in space direction are then replaced by finite differences. Finally, a system of linear equations remains to be solved. The tides in canal-like seas have been investigated using this difference method in one dimension. As a boundary condition, the tidal currents are assumed to be zero at the closed end, and the amplitude and phase are prescribed at the open end. The numerical computation is a simple one, and no mathematical difficulties appear. The Austrian oceanographer Albert Defant and others have applied these or similar methods to several canal-like adjacent areas, among them the Adriatic Sea, the Red Sea, and the Persian Gulf. Figure 4 represents Defant's results for the Red Sea. The qua-

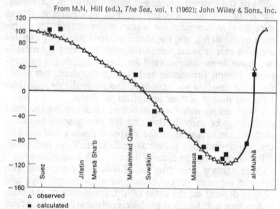

Figure 4: Range of observed and calculated values of the M_2 tidal constituent in the Red Sea.

lity of the reproduction of the tidal measurements is remarkable; furthermore, these investigations yield an understanding of tidal processes in elongated canals. The way in which the resulting amplitudes and phases are related to the geometry of canal-like seas is clear.

Defant also considered the North Sea, and even the Atlantic, as an elongated canal in order to apply the one-dimensional method, but it was not possible to reproduce the measurements quantitatively. Numerical methods for solving tidal problems in two dimensions were developed. First, the boundary value method was performed, the time dependency again assumed to be harmonic. After eliminating the components of tidal currents, for the sea-level variation there remains a partial differential equation of the second order and of elliptic type. This differential equation is replaced by a system of linear equations that relate sea level to the points of a grid placed upon the sea under investigation. The tide is determined if the sea level is defined by the grid points on the boundary. It is also possible to transfer the hydrodynamical equation, after introducing a time factor, into a system of linear equations without eliminating the components of the tidal currents.

Boundary
value
method

In water that is not too shallow this boundary value method yields a sufficient reproduction of measured tides. There are, however, a number of disadvantages. Different tidal constituents must be computed separately. The resulting sea level is a pure harmonic function of time. Because the equations are linear, no nonlinear interaction can be taken into account. Especially in shallow-water areas, such as tidal estuaries, tides and tidal currents may differ strongly from a harmonic function of time. Furthermore, it is impossible to investigate the interaction between different tidal constituents and among tides, surges, and gradient currents.

General prediction of tides. Attempts to design more general numerical methods, as a continuation of the

boundary value method but avoiding its disadvantages, have been made since 1945. These efforts resulted in the hydrodynamic–numerical methods (abbreviated HN methods), which also may be called initial boundary value methods.

The method is fairly general and is applicable to all kinds of processes of motion in the deep ocean and in shallow waters. Nonlinearity and nonharmonic time dependency can be taken into account, and the method yields not only tidal motion but any motion in the sea turbulence.

The hydrodynamic–numerical (HN) model in a simple quadratic area is derived as follows. The sea under consideration is first covered by a grid. The sea level ζ is indicated by $+$ points, the west–east component u by $\bullet$ points, and the south–north component v of the tidal currents are determined at x points. The hydrodynamic differential equations are replaced by difference equations, the variables ζ, u and v, the tide-generating acceleration X, the depth H, and the friction R being indicated by the grid point to which they belong. The grid distance is 1 and the time step τ, a bar indicating averaged values. The equations of the HN model in this case are as follows:

$$\zeta_2' = \zeta_1 - \frac{\tau}{1}H_2 u_2 + \frac{\tau}{1}H_4 v_{41} u_2' = u_2(1 - R_2\tau) + f\tau\bar{v}_2 - q\frac{\tau}{1}(\zeta_3 - \zeta_1) - \tau X_{21}$$

$$\zeta_3 = \zeta_3 + \frac{\tau}{1}H_2 u_2 + \frac{\tau}{1}H_5 v_{51} u_4' = u_4(1 - R_7\tau) + f\tau\bar{v}_7 - q\frac{\tau}{1}(\zeta_8 - \zeta_6) - \tau X_{71}$$

$$\zeta_6 = \zeta_6 - \frac{\tau}{1}H_7 u_7 - \frac{\tau}{1}H_4 v_{41} v_4' = v_4(1 - R_4\tau) - f\tau\bar{u}_4 - q\frac{\tau}{1}(\zeta_1 - \zeta_6) - \tau X_{41}$$

$$\zeta_8 = \zeta_8 + \frac{\tau}{1}H_7 u_7 - \frac{\tau}{1}H_5 v_{51} v_5' = v_5(1 - R_5\tau) - f\tau\bar{u}_5 - q\frac{\tau}{1}(\zeta_3 - \zeta_8) - \tau X_5.$$

The variables ζ, u, v on the right-hand side of the equations are assumed to be known, ζ', u', v' are uniquely determined by these equations τ seconds later. In this iteration process, the sea level ζ and the components of tidal currents u and v are computed step by step. The advantages of such models are: (1) very general nonlinear and even random processes may be taken into account, (2) no restrictions are placed on the geometry and depth of the basin under consideration, and (3) the large amount of numerical work is performed by electronic computers.

Prediction of tides in the North Sea, Atlantic, and the world ocean. Computers are not initially available for computation work with hydrodynamic–numerical models, and it was not possible to start investigations with the world ocean. Tidal estuaries, adjacent, and marginal seas were therefore treated first.

As an example, the tide in the North Sea has been computed by means of a hydrodynamic–numerical model. In this area tides along the coast and tidal currents in the open sea are fairly well known, and a comparison between computed and measured values is possible.

Tides
in the
North
Sea

Figure 5 shows the corange and cotidal lines of the principal lunar (M_2) tide of the North Sea, obtained by hydrodynamic–numerical-model computation. The correlation of observed and computed sea levels is excellent.

The influence of the depth distribution and the rotation of the Earth is indicated in the results of two HN models that accounted for these assumptions. Figure 6 shows the cotidal and corange lines of the tide in the North Sea with a constant depth of 80 metres (260 feet); Figure 7, the cotidal and corange lines with the depth constant (80 metres = mean depth of the North Sea), but the Coriolis acceleration (that due to rotation of the Earth) assumed to be zero, hence the effect of the rotation of the Earth is neglected. The results show that the high tidal range along the British coast is not caused by the rotation of the Earth as had been assumed in earlier investigations. HN models make it clear that the depth of the North Sea is predominantly responsible for observed distribution of the range.

Corange and cotidal lines that are drawn for the tides in a rectangular basin of constant depth, which, as a very rough first approximation, represents the North Sea reveal amplitudes and phases of the principal lunar (M_2) tide that are quite different from the tides discussed immediately above. This demonstrates in a distinctive way

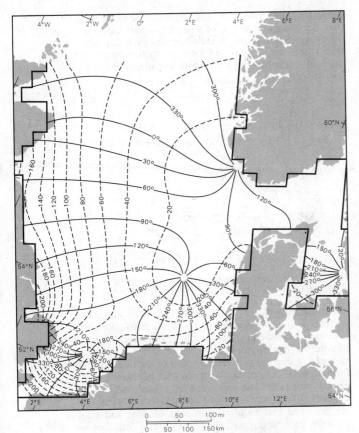

Figure 5: Cotidal and corange lines in North Sea according to HN computation. Measured range and time of high water in coastal locations. Zero time equal to Moon's transit in Greenwich. Amplitudes in centimetres.

the important influence of the coastal configuration, and that it is not possible to reproduce the tides in natural seas by investigating basins of simple geometry.

Before considering the world ocean, it is useful to examine tidal prediction in a body of water of intermediate size like the Atlantic Ocean. Figure 8 shows the computed sea level at the time of the Moon's transit in Greenwich and three hours six minutes later, compared with the measured sea level along the coasts of the Atlantic Ocean. Again, the hydrodynamic–numerical method can be considered successful.

Tides in the world ocean

Figure 9 represents the world ocean including amphidromic points of the principal lunar (M_2) tide delivered by a 6° model. Amphidromic points, characterized by zero tidal range, are points at which the sea level remains unchanged by the tides. Dashed lines are referred to zero sea level at the time of the Moon's transit in Greenwich, and full lines correspond to zero sea level at three hours six minutes after the time of the Moon's transit in Greenwich. Because the hydrodynamic–numerical model does not require any tidal measurement, the results are independent of sea-level records. On the other hand the grid size of 6° in this model is relatively large, and, consequently, not all the fine structure of the ocean's depth and coast is sufficiently accounted for. For example, the shelf configuration may drop through the grid system because of the wide spacing. The response of the shallow-water areas on tides is important for the distribution of tidal amplitudes and phases. The grid distance should be about 50 kilometres (30 miles); it is more than 600 kilometres (400 miles) in this model.

Accuracy of hydrodynamic–numerical methods. Using hydrodynamic–numerical models it is possible to perform tidal predictions of sea level and tidal currents for an entire sea with only one computation. At the open boundary, the tidal constituents given in Table 1 (at least M_2, S_2, N_2, K_2, K_1, O_1, P_1) are prescribed by their amplitudes and phases. By means of these constituents the tides on the boundary are predicted. The model deter-

mines tides and tidal currents as a function of time at all grid points in the interior of the basin. This prediction method has been tried for several areas and Figure 10 shows the model computation compared with tidal prediction for selected points around the North Sea; similar results have been obtained for the Gulf of St. Lawrence and for Kuwait in the Persian Gulf. Tidal currents are predicted by the same computation. Because only measurements on the boundary are needed, hydrodynamic–numerical model tidal prediction provides a maximum of information with a minimum of measurements.

Effect of shallow water. In shallow-water areas the nonlinear terms in the hydrodynamical equations become increasingly important. Different tidal constituents, such as M_2 and S_2, cannot be treated separately, and the sea level is no longer a simple harmonic function of time. For tidal currents in the harmonic case, a water particle returns to its original location within a tidal period, thus describing a tidal ellipse. But in the nonlinear case the water masses do not return to their origin within one tidal period. Consequently, a periodic process on the open boundary of the sea results in a nonperiodic motion like a permanent transport in the interior of the sea under consideration. Figure 11 shows such a residual transport in the North Sea caused by the principal lunar (M_2) tide prescribed on the open boundaries as a simple harmonic function of time. Tides and surges also must be investigated within one process; separate treatment delivers only a first approximation. Little is known about the interaction of tides and the strong permanent currents in the world ocean, such as Gulf Stream, Kuroshio, and the equatorial countercurrent and undercurrent.

Residual currents

Tidal currents. Tidal current measurements show the variation of velocity as a function of depth (see Figure 2). Attempts have been made to determine the tidal current as a function of depth. In estuaries and in narrow straits with alternating tidal currents, it was found that the true velocity is approximated by the formula:

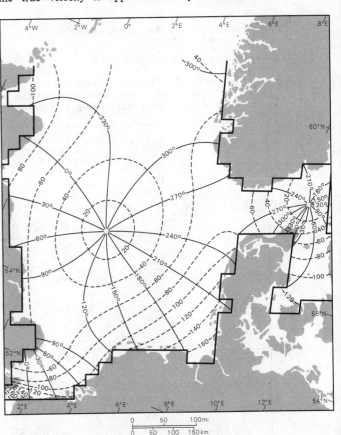

Figure 6: Tides in a North Sea basin of constant depth (80 metres), with the Earth's rotation taken into account. Solid lines are cotidal lines referred to Moon's transit in Greenwich. Dashed lines are amplitudes in centimetres.

$U = U_{ob}\left(\dfrac{Z}{H}\right)^{\alpha}$, in which U_{ob} is the surface velocity, Z is depth, H the total depth, and α is a coefficient that varies from $\tfrac{1}{5}$ to $\tfrac{1}{7}$.

If the water in the sea is stratified, there are layers each

motion is called internal waves; the oscillations are irregular, but there are periods of a day or of half a day. Hydrodynamic–numerical models are designed for stratified water masses, but not enough measurements are available for comparing computations and measurements.

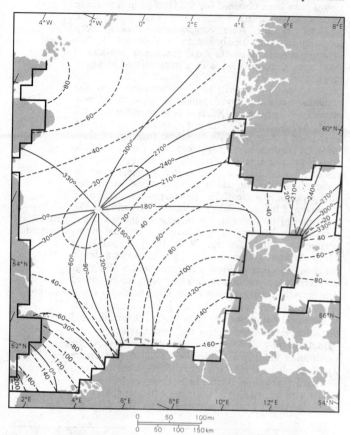

Figure 7: Tides in a North Sea basin of constant depth (80 metres) without taking into account the Earth's rotation. Solid lines, cotidal lines, refer to Moon's transit in Greenwich. Dashed lines are amplitudes in centimetres.

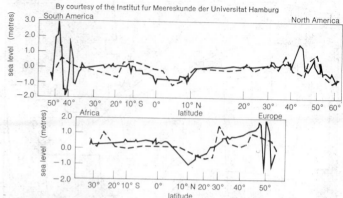

By courtesy of the Institut fur Meereskunde der Universitat Hamburg

Figure 8: M₂ constituents along the Atlantic coast, showing computed (broken lines) and measured (solid lines) sea level.

Practical aspects. The knowledge of tides and tidal currents may serve important purposes. Navigators approaching a coast and steaming into a river need information on the depth in these areas; moreover, it is advantageous for a ship to sail in the direction of the tidal current flow. Coastal-engineering work is also intensively concerned with tides. The regulation of a tidal estuary, the damming of a tidal river, or the construction of a harbour are problems that require knowledge of tides and tidal currents; such work may change the natural condition to such a degree that unwanted effects arise. As an example, the damming of a tidal river may cause flood current of very short duration and high velocity and, consequently, an ebb current of long duration and low velocity. A river in a sand-bed channel allows transport of such bottom material landward during each tidal period, but if the ebb current is extremely small, this material will not return to the sea within the same tidal period. The result is that the depth of such a tidal river decreases within a short time, and ultimately the river cannot be used as a waterway for ships. Information on the behaviour of the tides in a river that will result from artificial construction is therefore of great practical value, and hydrodynamic–numerical

with its own density, which may oscillate at their interfaces. Amplitudes may become remarkable and can be expected to be on the order of tens of metres. This type of

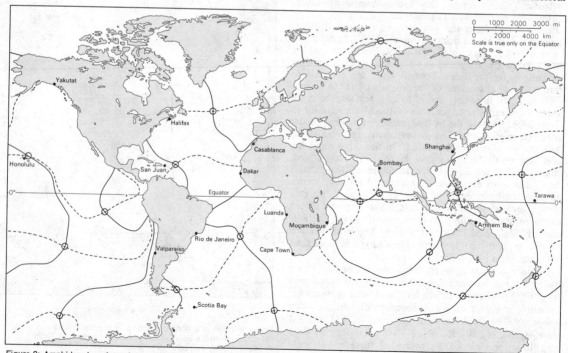

Figure 9: Amphidromic points of the M₂-tide in the world ocean (see text).

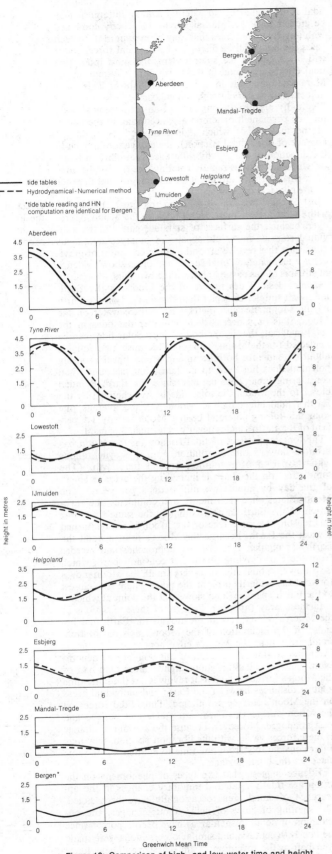

tide tables
Hydrodynamical - Numerical method

*tide table reading and HN
computation are identical for Bergen

Aberdeen

Tyne River

Lowestoft

IJmuiden

height in metres

Helgoland

Esbjerg

Mandal-Tregde

Bergen*

Greenwich Mean Time

Figure 10: Comparison of high- and low-water time and height
in the North Sea based on computation by the HN method
and on tide tables.
By courtesy of the Institut fur Meereskunde der Universitat Hamburg

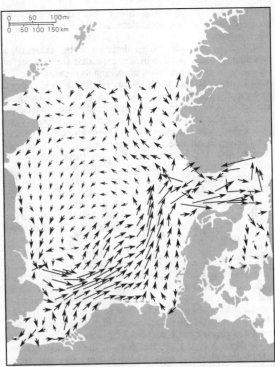

Figure 11: Residual current caused by the M$_2$ tide on the
boundaries of the North Sea.

in the open sea. It has been pointed out that tides in
shallow water cause a permanent transport, and polluted
water masses may be transported by tides without any
support by other currents. Similarly, tidal motion may be
important for fishery, especially in cases of stratified water masses.

Complicating factors. Ocean currents and sea-level
variations not caused by tide-generating accelerations are
observed in the ocean. Among these are storm tides, tsunamis, surface waves, gradient currents, and others; each
of these phenomena may be periodic or nonperiodic.

Meteorological effects are caused by several forces.
The wind stress on the sea surface and the air-pressure
gradients act on water masses from the surface to the
bottom. Radiation and backradiation, evaporation, and
precipitation influence temperature and salinity of the
seawater; the density of the water is a function of the last
two conditions. Horizontal-density gradients are responsible for gradient currents. In the ocean, the meteorological effects are in near correlation with the large ocean
currents, such as the Gulf Stream, Kuroshio Current, and
others. The current systems as a first approximation are
considered to be constant. In adjacent and marginal seas,
storms may from time to time cause storm tides involving
sea-level elevations of up to several metres. Under normal conditions the wind velocity decreases after several
hours. Such an elevation of sea level is neither a permanent nor a periodic one, but it may be a complicated
function of time, especially in areas where the storm
surge interacts with the tides. In shallow-water areas this
interaction is expected to be nonlinear. Tides and storm
surges in several areas have been successfully reproduced
by means of hydrodynamic–numerical models. Hitherto
it has been assumed that the mass of the ocean water is
constant. A considerable amount of frozen water is stored
in polar areas, however, and given proper variation of the
climate of the Earth, this amount of ice and the elevation
of sea level will change. Another potential cause of sea-
level change is the vertical motion of the land.

The amplitudes of the tides depend to some extent on
water depth; climatic changes may therefore cause
changes in tidal amplitudes. It was previously pointed out
that the tidal potential can be represented by a Fourier
series. The assumption is that the motion of the Sun, the
Earth, and the Moon as a celestial system is unchanged.
According to some theories of the Moon's development,

Changes
in climate
and
length
of day

models may be useful in such cases. Other practical aspects of tide information are related to efforts to convert
the energy of tides into electric energy, and the problems
that arise from the pollution of water in coastal areas and

the distance between the Moon and the Earth has changed. Under such conditions the tidal potential also has changed.

The ocean tides have been determined by assuming a completely rigid Earth, which means that the surface of the Earth is unchanged. But according to measurements it may be assumed that the elasticity of the Earth is comparable to the elasticity of steel, which is the reason there are bodily, or Earth, tides as well as water tides. Measurements indicate that the ratio of ocean tides to Earth tides plus ocean tides is about 0.7. There are other factors influencing Earth tides and ocean tides. It has been discovered that the length of a day has increased by one to two seconds within the last 120,000 years. This decrease in the Earth's rotation is partly explained by the friction of tidal currents. The friction term in the hydrodynamical equation is inverse to the depth. Therefore, much tidal energy is dissipated in shallow-water areas such as the Siberian Shelf, Bering Sea, Irish Sea, and the Patagonian Shelf.

TIDES IN THE ATMOSPHERE AND SOLID EARTH

Atmospheric tides. Like the water, the atmosphere is under the influence of the tide-generating acceleration, and air tides are to be expected. In the layers of air near the surface, pressure oscillations of the principal lunar (M_2) as well as principal solar (S_2) frequencies have been determined for a number of places. Because of the lesser density of the air, the tides in the atmosphere are much smaller than those in the ocean. Analysis yields larger amplitudes for S_2 than for M_2 atmospheric tides, which is explained by the fact that daily heating and cooling is responsible for these oscillations. Because the frequency is precisely the same as the frequency of the tidal-generating oscillation, it is not possible to separate the effects. The M_2 amplitude of atmospheric tides is of the order of magnitude of 0.06 millimetre (0.002 inch) mercury.

In the ionosphere there are different layers that oscillate with lunar or solar frequencies; the amplitudes may be of the order of several hundred metres.

Earth tides. The tidal potential also acts on the solid body of the Earth, the lithosphere. Whereas it is possible in the case of ocean tides to assume that the depth of the ocean is small compared with its horizontal dimensions, the density variation and other properties of the lithosphere make the determination of bodily tides more difficult than determination of ocean tides.

Knowledge of the precise nature of the solid body of the Earth as a whole is limited, but it is known to be influenced by the tide-generating acceleration in two different ways. First, these accelerations act on the particles of the solid body of the Earth, which behaves as an elastic body, so that tides are developed within it. In addition, the tides of the ocean, especially the water masses transported by tidal currents, cause a periodic loading and unloading, a process that results in indirect tides. If the solid body of the Earth were completely rigid, no bodily tides would occur, and, at least in principle, the tide-generating forces could be measured; in this case they would be in agreement with the equilibrium tide. Measurements indicate that the theoretical values are not reached and that the elasticity is comparable to the elasticity of a steel sphere the same size as the Earth.

Tide-generating accelerations are a space-wide phenomenon acting on the particles of celestial bodies. If there are oceans on other planets, it is possible, in principle, to determine the tides in such oceans, and, if all the astronomical parameters are known, the bodily tides of the planets also can be calculated. (W.Hn.)

ASTRONOMICAL TIDES

Tidal effects on the planets and other bodies in the solar system, like those on the Earth, are caused by differences in the pull of gravity exerted by one body on various parts of another. The gravity difference can cause an elongation through stress if the subject body is deformable; if it is not, the stress set up may cause some adjustment of the distribution of material. In extreme cases,

tidal force caused by an external gravity difference may be greater than the internal gravity of a body combined with any cohesive forces that may be present in it. In such cases the body will be disrupted by the tidal force, and it will break up. In the solar system, the most interesting tidal effects are found in the Earth–Moon system, in the Mars satellites, and in the rings of Saturn. Tides also influence stars, star clusters, and galaxies.

A tidally produced elongation of an astronomical body may be permanent or temporary, according to the nature of the material of which it is composed. Also, in the absence of drag (tidal friction), the elongation may be in the direction of the gravity difference (equilibrium tide), or, when the body is rapidly rotating, the tidal bulge may be carried forward around it by an amount that depends on the physical conditions.

Just as the Moon raises tides on the Earth, the Earth, with its far greater mass, raises tides on the Moon. Moreover, because the surfaces of stars are gaseous, the individual stars of many close pairs in binary star systems (two stars that revolve around a common centre of gravity) are elongated by tidal forces and often show evidence of streams of gas passing between the two stars.

Effect of the Earth on the Moon

Lunar tides. Tides raised on the Moon by the Earth are much simpler to depict than those raised on the Earth by the Moon. Because there is no surface water on the Moon, it is only necessary to consider the tides in the solid material; that is, the bodily tides. Solar tides can be neglected for the Moon. The solar tide-raising potential is about the same for both Earth and Moon, but tide-raising potential does not need to be taken into account when considering lunar tides because since the Earth is much closer to the Moon, the solar tide is overwhelmed by the Earth's tidal effect on the Moon. On the average, the solar tide-raising potential on the Moon is only 1.5 percent of the Earth's and is never greater than 3 percent.

The long-term effect of tidal friction on the Moon has been to slow its rate of rotation until it is synchronous with its period of revolution around the Earth. (The same effect on the Earth is increasing the average length of the day by about two milliseconds per year.) The Moon rotates once each month and completes one revolution of the Earth in approximately the same time. For this reason, the same face of the Moon is always turned toward the Earth. Because the Moon's orbit around the Earth is irregular, it alternately approaches and recedes from the Earth. While rotating at constant speed, which is so slow that tidal friction is very small, the Moon moves forward fastest in its orbit at the point where it is closest to the Earth (perigee) and slowest at the point at which it is farthest away (apogee). Because of these variations in the Moon's rate of revolution around the Earth and because of the inclination of the Moon's axis of rotation, small areas near the Moon's edge appear and disappear from time to time. As a result of this oscillatory phenomenon, which is called libration, slightly more than half of the Moon's surface is seen as it revolves. At the same time relative distances between the Earth and individual areas on the Moon's surface are altered. Thus, tidal forces on the Moon due to the Earth are greatest at perigee and least at apogee. Moreover, because the amount of change in these forces varies with the libration position, they may differ considerably from one time to another at the same place on the lunar surface.

Evidence suggests that two types of phenomena on the Moon are tidally related. Temporary changes in the appearance of small areas occasionally have been noted. The sighting of glows of light, colour changes, and obscuration of detail in such areas have been reported since the late 18th century, and similar observations were made even before the invention of the telescope. These lunar transient events seem to occur unpredictably, but statistically they are observed more frequently at perigee, when the overall tidal effect of the Earth on the Moon is greatest.

In 1970 the discovery of seismic signals, which measure interior disturbances in the Moon, heightened interest in lunar tides. One type of signal, called type A, occurred at each perigee and was found to originate at very nearly the same place each time. Because it was extremely unlikely that meteorites would fall precisely at each perigee in the same place, it was concluded that the disturbances that caused the A-type signals were moonquakes, triggered by extreme tidal conditions. A second group, type B, were believed to be tidally related because they were found to occur sometimes at perigee and also at apogee.

The relative frequencies of the two types are so similar that it now appears certain that the lunar events are related to moonquakes of a kind similar to those with which the seismic signals were associated; the glows and obscurations may represent the appearance of small quantities of gas and dust, tidally released through cracks in the Moon's surface. This idea is supported also by the small amounts of gases that have been detected on the Moon.

The Roche limit. Although a tidal force on a planet or satellite in the solar system is essentially disruptive, it amounts to only a small fraction of that body's own gravitational forces. If, however, such forces are sufficiently large, they may overcome the combined effect of internal gravity and the cohesive forces that hold a body together. The body will then begin to break up.

If a natural satellite (a moon) moves closer to its planet through time, the effect of the planet's tide-generating force increases rapidly, and the spherical shape of the satellite becomes distorted. If the satellite is sufficiently deformable, it will become more and more elongated. Finally, if it comes close enough to the planet, the satellite will break up completely.

A French scientist, Édouard Roche, calculated the shape that a small satellite would assume if it were free to adapt itself to tidal stresses under conditions similar to those just described. Roche also determined how close such a satellite could approach its planet without breaking up. In order to change its shape freely the satellite would have to be a fluid, composed either of a gas or a liquid. Although this situation is quite artificial, it can be used as a first approach to find the absolute limits in some real examples.

He found that the limiting figure, or shape, of such a liquid or gaseous satellite is a prolate spheroid—a nearly egg-shaped body in which the longest axis is slightly more than twice the length of either of the shorter ones. The satellite is least likely to break up when it moves with its long axis pointing directly toward the centre of the planet. Roche also proved that when the satellite and the planet have the same density, the satellite will break up, in the absence of any internal cohesive forces, at a distance of 2.44 times the planet's radius, or 1.44 times the radius above the planet's surface. In other words, for a planet and satellite of the same density, the satellite cannot exist permanently inside a sphere drawn around the planet at 2.44 times its radius, or 1.44 times the radius above its surface. The limiting distances, or Roche limit, in any such situation depends on the relative densities of the planet and satellite as well as the planet's radius; it would be nearer to the planet for higher planetary density and farther away for a satellite that is denser than its planet.

Although the Moon is well outside the Roche limit of the Earth, many small artificial satellites have been put into orbits much closer, and some of them have lasted for several years. Eventually, though, the satellites lose energy through atmospheric drag and spiral toward the Earth. If, however, the parts of the satellite were not rigid and rigidly held together by rivets, screws, and the like, the satellite's internal gravity would not be sufficient to prevent the parts from gradually separating. The case of a nose cone and a space vehicle, or of two space vehicles travelling together, perhaps illustrates the point. Unless the units are physically joined by a clamping device, continual small adjustments in speed must be made to keep them together, or else they will slowly drift apart.

The rings of Saturn   Saturn possesses ten satellites, all of which orbit outside the Roche limit. In addition, the planet also has around it a remarkable series of broad flat rings, the nature of which remained a puzzle for some 200 years following their discovery in the 17th century. The rings are inclined to Saturn's orbital plane and also to the orbital plane of the Earth (the ecliptic). Most of the time the rings appear as concentric ovals that change in shape; occasionally, they disappear from view. Because this happens whenever the Sun or the Earth passes through the plane of the rings, it indicates that the material of the rings is confined very closely to a plane.

Because the whole system of rings is inside the equal-density Roche limit, the existence of the rings can be directly attributed to tidal forces. This was recognized by Roche in 1848 and was explained in mathematical terms in 1859 by the Scottish physicist James Clerk Maxwell. Saturn has such an extremely low density that a piece of it would float in water. If, on the other hand, the ring material is solid, it must be heavier than the material of which Saturn is composed, and the actual Roche limit must be beyond the rings. It appears that the rings are indeed composed of small, separate, rocklike particles revolving in free orbits and held together by internal cohesion only. The particles probably collide occasionally and thus erode very slowly into smaller and smaller particles. Even if such a flat system as Saturn's rings could exist temporarily as a single continuous sheet, it would be unstable, and the tidal force of the planet would break it up.

The Mars satellites   Mars has two satellites, Deimos and Phobos. Deimos is relatively far removed from the planet, but the orbit of Phobos is close to Mars, at a mean distance of 2.75 Martian radii. The density of Mars is known to be 3.97; if the densities of Phobos and Mars are in about the same proportion as those of the Moon and the Earth, the Roche limit will be about 2.86 times the planet's radius. Thus, Phobos revolves at just about the limit of stability.

In 1970 the image of the little satellite was recorded by chance by a spacecraft circling Mars. The spacecraft, which was engaged in photographing the planet itself, was more distant than Phobos from the planet. Silhouetted against the body of the planet, Phobos was seen to be elliptical. It measures 14 miles (23 kilometres) in diameter along the orbital and 11 miles (18 kilometres) in the perpendicular direction. Eventually, it may be broken up by the tidal action of Mars.

Tides in stars and galaxies. Tidal disturbances are present in many binary star systems. Observations show that stars in such systems are usually ellipsoidal rather than spherical in shape. The amount of distortion can be measured in terms of the ellipticity of the star; in general, the shorter the period of rotation of one star about the other, the greater the ellipticity. Because the period, in turn, depends on the size of the orbit and because the square of the period is proportional to the cube of the mean distance between the stars, the ellipticity depends strongly on the distance. This effect is at least partly tidal, though in some binary star systems—particularly those containing very hot (young) stars—another factor, rapid rotation, may also be active. In such cases, the two possible causes of ellipticity would reinforce each other.

In many binary systems, spectral measurements show that streams of gas pass from one star to the other. The best known systems with gas streams of this kind are Beta Lyrae (the second brightest star in the constellation Lyra, the Lyre) and W Ursa Majoris (the variable, W, in the constellation of Ursa Major, the Great Bear). In Beta Lyrae, only one star can be seen; the other is too faint. Nevertheless, the gas streams that have been detected (as bright mission lines in the spectrum) are flowing from the bright, early type star to the fainter, which is believed, therefore, to be the more massive. In addition to showing tidal distortion, the bright star also rotates rapidly, and this increases the instability of the system.

Disintegration of star clusters   The stars in a cluster are in continuous motion and interact gravitationally with one another. Close chance encounter between the stars in a cluster, however, may change any star's motion sufficiently for it to escape from the group. The differential rotation of a galaxy and its tidal action on the cluster both act to separate the innermost and outermost parts of the cluster; in time, the less massive stars are lost, and the cluster progressively disintegrates. For the Pleiades, the time needed for disintegration is about 10^9 years; for a looser group, or stellar association, the so-called O-B class (hot and bright) of stars, very much less time is needed.

Some external galaxies occur in pairs or groups. When the pairs are quite close in the sky, it is sometimes found that jets and streams of bright material extend from one to the other. The inference in these cases is that the pairs are actually close in space and are interacting tidally. In spiral galaxies with companions, radio observations of neutral hydrogen have shown some asymmetries that are also believed to be due to tidal distortions. One such example is known as M101 (NGC 5457). Similar but rather smaller asymmetries have been found by radio measurement of the hydrogen gas in the galaxy called the Andromeda Nebula and its nearby companions; others are believed to exist in the Milky Way, which has as close companions the Magellanic Clouds. On the other hand, bright galaxies without close companions are apparently undistorted at radio wavelengths. A recent optical study of bright galaxies revealed that about 20 percent have close companions and exhibit distorted optical features.

(B.M.M.)

BIBLIOGRAPHY. W. HANSEN, "Tides," in M.N. HILL (ed.), *The Sea: Ideas and Observations on Progress in the Study of the Sea*, vol. 1 (1962), is a summary of modern research on tides. The same author's "Hydrodynamical Methods Applied to Oceanographic Problems," the proceedings of a symposium on mathematical–hydrodynamical methods of physical oceanography at the Institut für Meereskunde, Universität Hamburg (1962), gives a general introduction to the Hydrodynamical–numerical (HN) Method. Standard textbooks on the subjects indicated by their titles are: A. DEFANT, *Physical Oceanography*, vol. 2 (1961); H. LAMB, *Hydrodynamics*, 6th ed. (1959); J. PROUDMAN, *Dynamical Oceanography* (1953); and H.U. SVERDRUP, M.W. JOHNSON, and R.H. FLEMING, *Oceans: Their Physics, Chemistry, and General Biology* (1942). P. SCHUREMANN, *A Manual of the Harmonic Analysis and Prediction of Tides* (1924), is a United States Coast and Geodetic Survey handbook on the technique of harmonic analysis; on the principles of harmonic analysis of tides, see W. HORN, "Gezeiten des Meeres," in *Landolt-Börnstein*, vol. 3 (1952). J. BARTELS and W. HORN, "Gezeitenkrafte," *ibid.*, contains a deduction of the tide-generating potential of the Moon and Sun. Astronomical tides are discussed in G.H. DARWIN, *The Tides and Kindred Phenomena in the Solar System* (1962), based on lectures given in 1897; O. STRUVE, *Stellar Evolution* (1950); B.M. MIDDLEHURST, "An Analysis of Lunar Events," *Rev. Geophys.*, 5:173–189 (1967); R. MEISSNER, G. SUTTON, and F. DUENNEBIER, "Mondbeben," *Umschau*, 71:111–115 (1971); and in the NASA reports for Apollo 12 (1970).

(W.Hn./B.M.M.)

Tien Shan (Mountains)

The Tien Shan, a Chinese name meaning "Celestial Mountains," forms one of the great mountain systems of Central Asia. Situated in the U.S.S.R. and China, it stretches for about 1,800 miles (3,000 kilometres) from west-southwest to east-northeast. It is about 300 miles wide in places at its eastern and western extremities but narrows to about 220 miles in width at the centre.

The Tien Shan are bounded to the north by the Dzhungarian and southern Kazakhstan plains and to the southeast by the Tarim Basin; to the southwest, the Gissar-Alai Mountains form part of the Tien Shan, making the Alai (Alayskaya), Surkhandarya (Surkhobskaya), and Gissar (Gissarskaya) valleys the boundaries of the system with the Pamir mountain ranges. The Tien Shan Range also includes the Chu-Ili Mountains (Chu-Iliyskiye Gory) and the Karatau Range (Khrebet), which extend far to the northwest into the Kazakhstan lowlands. Within these limits the total area of the Tien Shan is about 386,000 square miles (1,000,000 square kilometres).

The highest peaks The highest peaks are a central cluster of mountains forming a knot, from which ridges extend along the boundary between China and the Soviet Union; these peaks are the Pobeda Peak (Pik Pobedy, or Victory Peak), which is 24,406 feet (7,439 metres) high, and the Khan-Tengri Peak, which is 22,949 feet (6,995 metres) high. (For an associated physical feature, see ISSYK-KUL, LAKE.)

The natural environment. *Physiography.* The relief is characterized by a combination of mountain ranges and intervening valleys and basins, trending generally from east to west. The deepest depression in the eastern Tien Shan is the Turfan Depression, within which is the lowest point in Central Asia—505 feet (154 metres) below sea level. Thus, the differences in elevation in the Tien Shan are extreme, exceeding four and a half miles. The eastern extension of the Turfan Depression is the Ha-mi Basin; both basins are bounded on the north by the Po-ko-to Shan, with elevations of up to 17,864 feet (5,445 metres), and by the eastern extremity of the Tien Shan, the K'o-erh-lei-k'o Shan, which reaches heights up to 16,158 feet (4,925 metres).

The ranges are of the Alpine type, with steep slopes; glaciers occur along their crests. The basins are bounded on the south by the low rising Chiao-lo Shan. West of the Turfan Depression is one of the greatest mountain knots of the eastern Tien Shan: the O-ha-pu-t'e Shan, which reaches elevations of up to 18,208 feet (5,550 metres). The ridge has considerable glacial development, as well as numerous forms of relief indicating ancient glaciation.

West of 84° east, the eastern Tien Shan ridges fork, trending in southwestern and northwestern directions, and enclose the vast Ili Depression (Iliyskaya Vpadina), which gradually widens and loses height as it proceeds westward. It is bounded on the north by the Po-lo-ho-lo Shan, which has glaciers in the eastern part and is characterized by steeply sloping ridges. This range also gradually descends westward, where, at a height of 6,801 feet (2,073 metres), lies the great undrained lake of Sai-li-mu Hu. The Ili Depression is bounded on the south by the highest mountains in the eastern Tien Shan—the K'a-erh-li-k'o Shan, reaching heights up to 22,346 feet (6,811 metres), and the isolated Ketmen Range (Khrebet Ketmen), which rises to an elevation of 11,936 feet (3,638 metres) in the central part of the depression.

The Ili Depression

The northern extremity of the Soviet part of the Tien Shan forms the Dzhungarian Alatau Range (14,645 feet [4,464 metres]), which is subject to considerable glacial action. To the south, the Trans-Ili Alatau Range rises abruptly above the Ili Depression to a height of 16,315 feet (4,973 metres). The successive transition of climatic zones, determined by altitude, from arid and dry steppe at lower levels to glacial at the summit is evident on the northern slopes of this range. The Kirgiz (Kirgizsky) and Talas (Talassky) Alatau ranges, rising above 13,000 feet and located farther west, also belong to the outer chain of the northern Tien Shan. There is a great difference in elevation between these outer mountain ridges and the plains at their base. Streams, therefore, usually plunge down the mountainsides through deep gorges and, as they flow out onto the plains, form vast fan-shaped deposits of silt and mud. On the fertile land thus formed are located many oases and population centres, including the cities of Alma-Ata and Frunze in the Kazakh and the Kirgiz Soviet Socialist republics (q.q.v.). The Kungey-Alatau and Terskey-Alatau ranges also belong to the northern Tien Shan. They rise to a height of 17,100 feet and border the vast Issyk-Kul Basin, the centre of which is filled by Lake Issyk-Kul.

The Aksay River (T'o-shih-kan Ho in Chinese) Basin and most of the Naryn River Basin are situated within the inner Tien Shan. This region is characterized by the alternation of comparatively short mountain ranges and valleys, both extending east and west. The predominant elevations of the mountains vary from about 10,000 to 15,000 feet, while the elevations of the depressions that separate them vary from between about 6,000 to 10,500 feet. The most important ranges are Borkoldoy (16,565 feet [5,049 metres]), Dzhetym (16,178 feet [4,931 metres]), Atbashi (15,702 feet [4,786 metres]), and the Kok Shaal-Tau Range, in which Dankov Peak reaches a height of 19,626 feet (5,982 metres).

The elevation of the mountains increases in the Sarydzhaz River (called K'un-a-li-k'o Ho in Chinese) Basin area in the central Tien Shan, lying to the east of the Akshiyrak Range. The ranges gradually converge, forming the high-altitude mountain knot already mentioned,

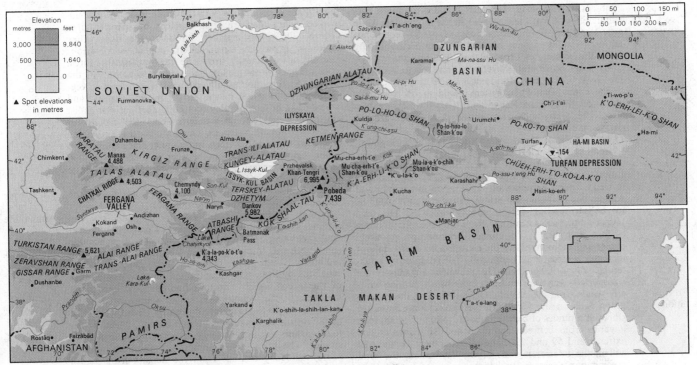

The Tien Shan.

<table>
<tr><td>The Fergana Range</td></tr>
</table>

which includes the Khan-Tengri crests and Pobeda (Victory) Peak.

In contrast to most of the Tien Shan ranges, which run approximately east–west, the Fergana Range (Fergansky Khrebet), separating the inner region from the western and southern Tien Shan, extends from southeast to northwest. Its maximum elevation is 15,354 feet (4,680 metres). The southwestern slopes display a variety of climatic zones in the course of their gradual descent.

The western Tien Shan ranges lie north of the Fergana Valley (Ferganskaya Dolina). Several short but high and steep ranges running southwest–northeast here meet the southern sides of ranges running westward and northwestward. The highest peak is the Chatkal Ridge (14,773 feet, or 4,503 metres), and the predominant elevations vary from about 7,500 to 10,500 feet.

The southern Tien Shan ranges (including Turkistan, Zeravshan, and Alai, among others) border the Fergana Valley on the south and extend chiefly east and west. The maximum elevation is 18,441 feet (5,621 metres), with several peaks above 15,000 feet. To the south, the Tien Shan meets the Pamirs. Foothills approach the northern slopes of the ranges; there are oases on the plains below the mountains.

Glaciers. The total area of the Tien Shan glaciers exceeds 3,800 square miles, of which more than four-fifths is in the Soviet Union. Largest among the several glacier areas are the Khan-Tengri-Pobeda region and the O-ha-pu-t'e Shan. There are also many glaciers in the Kok Shaal-Tau Range, the Akshiyrak Range, the Trans-Ili Alatau Range, and the southern Tien Shan. The largest glacier in the Tien Shan is Inylchek Glacier (Lednik), which is approximately 37 miles long; it descends from the western slopes of the Khan-Tengri massif and branches into numerous tributaries. Other large glaciers in this area include North (Severny) Inylchek (24 miles) and Mu-cha-erh-t'e Shan-k'ou (21 miles). The length of the largest Tien Shan glaciers elsewhere is usually between six and 12 miles; the most usual size is that of the relatively small valley glaciers, from about one and a half to three miles long.

The glaciers are usually fed by snowfall upon the glaciers themselves or by snow avalanches from the surrounding slopes. Glacial action in the Tien Shan is apparently decreasing; most glaciers are either receding or standing still. During recent decades, however, large glaciers in the inner Tien Shan region have made short-term

<table>
<tr><td>Largest glacial areas</td></tr>
</table>

advances. The glaciers of Tien Shan feed many large rivers, including the Naryn, Sarydzhaz, Ili, and Zeravshan.

Rivers and lakes. The rivers of the Tien Shan flow into major inland depressions, such as the Azalskaya and Tarim. The largest rivers are the Ili and Chu in the northern Tien Shan, Narym in inner Tien Shan, Sarydzhaz in central Tien Shan, and Zeravshan in southern Tien Shan. Their maximum flows occur at the end of spring and in summer. Freshets sometimes cause catastrophic flows of mud and stone. Much water is diverted for irrigation. Hydroelectric power plants are being constructed on the Narym, the largest river of the Tien Shan.

The largest lake is the undrained Issyk-Kul, situated at 5,279 feet (1,609 metres). The lake, which has an area of 2,425 square miles, is saline and does not freeze in the winter; it is used for navigation and is a popular resort and tourist attraction. Po-ssu-t'eng Hu (533 square miles in area) is situated in the eastern Tien Shan.

Geology. The mountains of Tien Shan are composed in the main of crystalline and sedimentary rocks of the Paleozoic Era (from 570,000,000 to 225,000,000 years ago). The intermontane basins are filled with sediments from the Mesozoic (225,000,000 to 65,000,000 years ago) and Cenozoic (65,000,000 years ago to the present) eras. These sediments were chiefly formed by erosive river action. Granite-like rocks crop out over much of the area in the north and east of the Tien Shan.

The north and east portions of the region underwent folding during the mountain-building period that occurred during the Early Paleozoic Era; it has been uplifted dry land since, and its original sedimentary cover has been almost completely obliterated by erosion. The southern and western parts of the Tien Shan, however, consist principally of sedimentary metamorphosed (structurally changed by heat and pressure) rock and, to a lesser degree, of intrusive and volcanic rock. These regions experienced folding during the Late Paleozoic Era.

A new stage of development began in the middle of the Tertiary Period (about 26,000,000 years ago) and has continued to the present time. It has been characterized by sudden movements of the Earth's crust. Loose fragments of rock have slid into the valleys and formed accumulations; those in the Fergana Valley are almost five miles thick. Shallow lakes were formed in many valleys and later evaporated, leaving behind salty deposits.

Subsequently, glaciers deposited boulder moraines (accumulations of earth and stones) in the mountains, while gravel and loess (wind-borne deposits) strata accumulated in the valleys. Zones of deep faulting occur, usually along the boundaries between the ridges and the valleys. Large-scale horizontal movements have occurred along the great Talas Fergana fault, which traverses nearly the entire Tien Shan system along the northeastern slopes of the Fergana Range and its northwestern extension. The deep faults are associated with catastrophic earthquakes that occurred at Verny (1887), at Kashgar (1902), in the northern Tien Shan chains (1911), and at Chatkal (1946), and Khait (1948).

Climate. The position of Tien Shan in the centre of Eurasia governs its sharply continental climate, characterized by great extremes of temperature in summer and winter. The characteristic aridity of the region is manifest in the surrounding deserts and dry regions. The area absorbs much solar heat, and there are about 2,500 hours of sun each year. The climate becomes progressively cooler and more humid as the elevation of the mountains increases. Permafrost (perennially frozen subsoil) is extensive above 9,000 feet. The prevalent air masses are transported over the Tien Shan by moisture-bearing westerly winds from the Atlantic Ocean. Most of the precipitation falls on the windward western and northwestern slopes at altitudes of between about 7,500 and 9,000 feet; it varies from between about 28 and 31 inches at one extreme and 59 and 79 inches at the other. To the east and in the interior regions of the Tien Shan, the total precipitation decreases to between eight and 12 inches, and it amounts to less than four inches in places. Maximum precipitation falls on the southern Tien Shan in March and April, and the summer is dry. In western and northern Tien Shan most of the rain falls during the warm period of the year, with a maximum in April or May. Most of the rain in the inner and eastern Tien Shan regions falls during the summer months. Many mountain valleys here are used as winter pastures because of the small amount of snow that falls in wintertime.

Temperatures vary in the Tien Shan, mostly depending on height. Summer is hot in the foothills: the mean temperature in July in Fergana Valley may reach 81° F (27° C); in the Ili Depression it may reach 73° F (23° C); and up to 93° F (34° C) to the east, in the Turfan Depression, where the climate is even more continental. The temperature in July at a height of about 10,500 feet in inner Tien Shan drops to 41° F (5° C), and frost is possible throughout summer. The mean temperature in January in Fergana Valley is 25° F (−4° C); in the Ili Depression it is 14° F (−10° C); and it drops to −9° F (−23° C) in the Alpine regions of inner Tien Shan, while in places (in particular, Aksay Valley) temperatures of −58° F (−50° C) have been recorded.

Plant and animal life. The characteristics of the living world of the Tien Shan are largely determined by the region's distinct zones of elevation, which provide a diverse distribution of soils and vegetation. In the foothills and plains at the base of the mountains semidesert and desert areas have usually developed; these zones continue to heights of between 5,250 and 5,800 feet. In the Tien Shan they are characterized by ephemeral vegetation growths that die out at the beginning of summer; xerophyte (adapted to a scant supply of water) grasses, wormwood, and the desert shrub ephedra are generally distributed. The most common landscape in the Tien Shan is steppe, which occurs at elevations of between about 3,500 and 11,000 feet.

The forests of the Tien Shan alternate with steppes and meadows. They are principally on the northern slopes and extend to an elevation of 9,000 to 9,800 feet. On the lower slopes of the outer ranges the forests are principally deciduous, consisting of maple and aspen, with extensive admixtures of wild fruit trees (apples and apricots). Vast areas of the southwestern slopes of the Fergana Range are occupied by very ancient nut-bearing forests. Stands of pistachio, walnut, and juniper are found up to 7,500 feet on the shaded slopes of several western and southern Tien Shan ranges. North and east of the Fergana Valley, coniferous forests predominate. At the upper boundary they are often replaced by sparse juniper forests. The water meadow forests in the river valley bottoms, in which aspen, birch, poplar, and various brushwoods ordinarily grow, lie far outside the forest zone. The forest glades and areas adjacent to the upper tree line are usually covered with meadow vegetation. Sub-Alpine meadows of mixed grasses and cereals extend up to almost 10,000 feet on the moist northern slopes but on southern slopes are usually replaced by mountain steppes. There are short-grass Alpine meadows up to 11,500 feet. In the inner and eastern Tien Shan regions, at elevations between 11,500 and 12,000 feet and sometimes higher, the level areas and gentle slopes are "cold deserts," with sparse and short vegetation. Mosses and lichens are found in the areas of the glacial zone that are free of snow and ice.

Animals in the Tien Shan include the wolf, fox, and ermine. There are also many typical Central Asian species, inhabiting chiefly the high mountains; these include snow leopard, mountain goat, Manchurian roe, and mountain sheep. The forest–meadow–steppe zone is inhabited by bear, wild boar, badger, field vole, members of the jerboa family (nocturnal jumping rodents), and members of the Ochotonidae family (short-eared mammals related to the rabbits). The many birds include the mountain partridge, pigeon, Alpine chough, crow, mountain wagtail, redstart, Himalayan snow cock, and other species. The lower zones—desert and semi-arid regions—are visited by animals from the neighbouring plains, such as antelope, gazelles, Tolai hares, and gray hamsters. Lizards and snakes are also found. (Y.Y.R.)

The human imprint. *The inhabitants.* Several million people live in the Tien Shan. The Fergana Valley is the most densely populated, with more than 500 persons per square mile in places. Most of the Tien Shan is occupied by the Kirgiz and Uighur ethnic groups. Tadzhiks, Uzbeks, Kazakhs, and Mongolians reside along the periphery of the region. Substantial Russian and Ukrainian populations have been established in the Soviet part of the Tien Shan in recent decades; Chinese populations live in the eastern Tien Shan. Irrigated agriculture has developed in the valleys and on the mountain slopes, and livestock herding is practiced in the mountains.

After the Russian Revolution of 1917, the nomadic Kirgiz and Kazakhs adopted a settled way of life. Their principal occupation is the herding of livestock; in the summer herds of horses, sheep, and cattle are driven to the mountain pastures. Where conditions permit, agriculture is developed. The Uighurs live principally by irrigated agriculture, supplemented by handicraft production. Except for the Mongolians, the other peoples of the Tien Shan also engage in agriculture. (S.I.B.)

Exploration. The Russian Geographical Society played a major role in the scientific exploration of the Tien Shan. From 1856 to 1857 the Russian geographer P.P. Semyonov-Tyan-Shansky gave the first scientific description of many regions of northern and inner Tien Shan, while the expeditions of another Russian geographer, G.Y. Grum-Grzhimaylo, in the 1880s, contributed greatly to the exploration of the eastern Tien Shan. The peak of Khan-Tengri was ascended for the first time in 1931 by a Soviet expedition led by M.T. Pogrebetsky. Pobeda Peak, the highest point, was conquered in 1956 by another Soviet expedition led by V.M. Abalakov.

Prospects for the future. Industry has been developing rapidly in the Soviet part of the Tien Shan; this development has been accompanied by a corresponding increase in the urban population in the valleys, which increased from 20 percent of the total population in 1942 to 40 percent in 1970. Further economic growth depends on the expansion of the area of irrigated lands; on hydroelectrical development, on the extraction of mineral deposits (which include copper-molybdenum and lead zinc ores in the western Tien Shan and antimony-mercury in the southern Tien Shan), and on the development of the exceptional recreational and touristic potential of parts of the region, especially for mountain climbing. (Y.Y.R.)

Tientsin

Tientsin (Wade–Giles romanization T'ien-ching, Pinyin romanization Tian-jing or Tian-jin), the third largest city of the People's Republic of China after Peking and Shanghai, is located in eastern Hopeh Province at the northeastern extremity of the North China Plain. It lies about 60 miles southeast of Peking and about 35 miles inland from the Gulf of Chihli (Po Hai) of the Yellow Sea. The Tientsin Municipality covers an area of about 1,500 square miles (4,000 square kilometres), and the municipality contains a total population of about 4,300,000. Tientsin (meaning literally Heavenly Ford) has been an important transport and trading centre since the Yüan dynasty (1279–1368). It is China's second largest manufacturing centre after Shanghai, and the leading port in North China.

Tientsin was famous as a cosmopolitan centre long before the arrival of the European trading community in the 19th century. Its maritime orientation and its role as the commercial gateway to Peking fostered the growth of an ethnically diverse population that was commercially innovative and culturally distinctive. The city is noted for its woven handicraft products, terra-cotta figurines, and extensive seafood cuisine.

History. The marshy, poorly drained area surrounding contemporary Tientsin was sparsely populated until the Sung dynasty (960–1126), when the settlement of Chiu-san-han-k'ou was built on the west bank of the Hai Ho (Hai River). The original settlement was later joined by the larger town of Chih-ku, built on high ground at the confluence of the Tzu-ya and Hai rivers. Chih-ku grew rapidly as a port and commercial centre, and it became the chief storage, transfer, and distribution point for grain and other foodstuffs from central and South China.

In recognition of the importance of Chih-ku (then called Hai-chin) as a shipping centre, the Yüan (Mongol) government (1279–1368) established offices for the regulation of navigation and customs and expanded the town's warehouse and harbour facilities. The city also became a major salt producer when salterns were constructed along the Hai Ho.

The development of modern Tientsin began during the Ming dynasty (1368–1644), when the national capital was shifted from Nanking to Peking. In 1368 the settlement became a garrison town and was named T'ien-chin-wei (Defense of the Heavenly Ford). A large military base was built and a rectangular wall constructed in 1425. The town prospered as it became the main gateway to Peking, and its population was swelled by immigrants from Shantung, Kiangsu, and Fukien provinces.

By the beginning of the Ch'ing (Manchu) dynasty (1644–1911), Tientsin had become the leading economic centre of North China because of its location at the northern terminus of the Grand Canal (Yün Ho). As better inland waterway connections were established,

Origins of the city

there was a steady increase in the city's volume of trade. Members of the first Dutch diplomatic mission to China in the mid-17th century commented favourably on the well-constructed 25-foot-high wall surrounding the city and noted the many temples and the large commercial and marketing area.

Economic prosperity declined temporarily during the mid-19th century when the European nations trading with China unremittingly pressed their demands for commercial and diplomatic privileges. The Treaty of Tientsin, which ended the second Anglo-French War (1856–58) against China, was signed by the British, French, and Chinese in 1858. Among its provisions, it authorized the establishment of British and French concessions in Tientsin. Between 1895 and 1902 concessions were given to Japan, Germany, Russia, Austria-Hungary, Italy, and Belgium. Hostilities were resumed in Tientsin in 1860, and the city was shelled by the British and French; the Convention of Peking then declared Tientsin an open trading port. Ten years later, a violent expression of Chinese anti-foreign feeling erupted in the city when the French Catholic orphanage and cathedral were attacked. In 1900 renewed anti-foreign demonstrations led to the shelling and occupation of the city by Allied (Western) forces and the destruction of the old city wall.

By the end of the 19th century, Tientsin had grown to more than 200,000 people, with about half the population residing within the old Chinese city. Living conditions for the Chinese were in sharp contrast to those in the spacious, well-tended European quarters that were distributed to the southeast and along the riverbanks.

Tientsin became an important ocean shipping centre by 1900. The Huang Ho (Yellow River) shifted its course, and the Grand Canal became silted up in the early 1850s, thereby restricting inland waterway traffic through the city, and shipping operations were shifted eastward along the banks of the Hai Ho. Facilities were also built at Ta-ku and T'ang-ku at the mouth of the Hai Ho.

Under the Republic of China (1911–49), Tientsin became a special municipality (*shih*) under the direct administration of the National government. In 1935 the Japanese attempted to extend their control over North China by establishing an autonomous area in eastern Hopeh Province, which was to be administered by Japanese military authorities in Tientsin. One year later, the Japanese presented demands to the Chinese authorities that were designed to weaken Chinese control over the area. With the opening of the Sino-Japanese War (1937–45), Tientsin was occupied by the Japanese, and in 1939 the Japanese blockaded the British and French concessions in response to anti-Japanese demonstrations.

During the Communist Revolution (1945–49), Tientsin remained under Nationalist control until mid-January 1949, when the city was captured by the Communists. Since then, Tientsin's growth as a trading and manu-

The period of foreign control

The Chinese Republic period

From *Chine, Pays de Charme et de Beaute*, Shanghai

Central Tientsin, with the Hai Ho in the foreground.

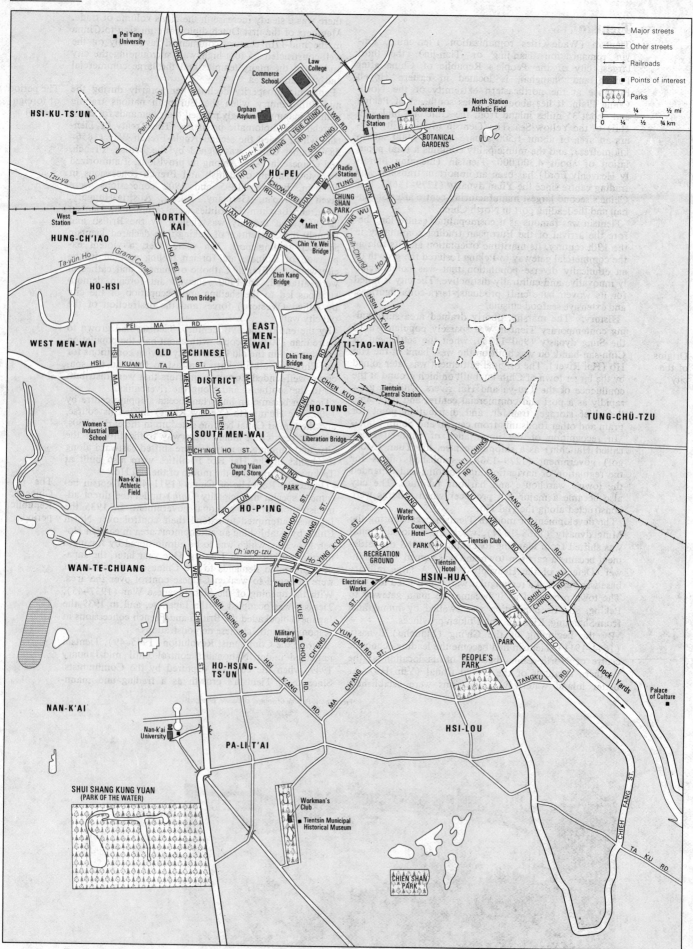

The city of Tientsin.

facturing centre has been responsive to internal development needs. Despite its proximity to Peking, the city retains a distinctive character, attributable to its functional and utilitarian origins.

The contemporary city. *The city site.* Central Tientsin is located at the point where the Yung-ting, Ta-ch'ing, Tzu-ya, Nan-yün, and Pei-yün rivers converge before merging into the Hai Ho, which then flows eastward into the Gulf of Chihli. The city stands at an elevation of less than 15 feet above sea level on a level alluvial plain. Some low-lying areas east of the city are only about six feet above sea level, and about 80 percent of the built-up area is below 12 feet.

The area of the Tientsin Municipality encompasses approximately 1,500 square miles (4,000 square kilometres), while the city and immediate suburbs cover approximately 675 square miles (1,750 square kilometres). The municipality borders on the Tientsin Special District (T'ien-ching Chuan-ch'ü) on the north and west, the Ts'ang-chou Special District (Ts'ang-chou Chuan-ch'ü) on the south, and the Gulf of Chihli on the east. Between 1955 and 1967 Tientsin was a subprovince-level city, which served as the capital of Hopeh Province. Its jurisdiction extended over the built-up urban core and eastward along the Hai Ho to include the port at T'ang-ku. At that time, Tientsin city was administratively separate from the Tientsin Special District, which had its seat at Yang-liu-ch'ing, southwest of central Tientsin.

In 1967 Tientsin Municipality was made a first-order, province-level administrative unit, and the area under its immediate control was expanded to include counties (*hsien*) formerly under the special district. The city simultaneously became the special district seat but lost its position as provincial capital. It was estimated in the early 1970s that 13 wards (*ch'u*) were included within greater Tientsin, which was administratively responsible to the central government in Peking. It was not clear, however, how many rural or suburban counties (*hsien*) were administratively tied to the municipality.

The environment. Despite Tientsin's proximity to the sea, it has a distinctly continental climate with sharp daily and seasonal temperature fluctuations. It is subject to the full effects of the cool, dry Siberian high-pressure system during the winter (October to April), while in the summer (May to September), the high pressure system over the North Pacific Ocean brings hot and rainy weather. Winter precipitation is minimal, and the air is dry, with relative humidity averaging 50 percent. In summer, moist, rain-bearing southerly winds prevail, and the average relative humidity exceeds 70 percent. The average annual temperature is 56° F (13° C), with a January average of 39° F (4° C) and a July average of 84° F (29° C). Severe winter storms are common, but typhoons seldom occur. Both the Hai Ho and the port of T'ang-ku freeze over for approximately 80 days during the winter. Ice appears at the beginning of December and usually thaws by the end of February.

Flood-control measures

The Hai Ho was long subject to frequent flooding. As the main outlet for the rivers of the North China Plain, it frequently became heavily silted during the spring and summer months; during the winter season its water level was often too low for navigation. Extensive water conservation began in 1897. The river was straightened to facilitate tidal action and to shorten the distance to the sea. Locks were constructed to regulate the flow of water from the river into its many canals, the river and the sand bars at its mouth were dredged, and silt-laden water was diverted into settling basins.

Since 1949 multipurpose flood-control, irrigation, and navigation improvements have been in progress over an area of some 15,200 square miles. Construction of the Kuang-ting Reservoir on the Yung-ting Ho near Peking has helped alleviate flood damage within metropolitan Tientsin. New diversion channels have also been built to control the floodwaters of the Ta-ch'ing and Tzu-ya rivers to the southwest.

The marshy lakes and floodplains around Tientsin abound with numerous varieties of reeds, bulrushes, and shrubs, such as tamarisk. Closer to the seashore, Russian thistle, glasswort, and artemisia (herbs and shrubs with strong-smelling foliage) can be found. Freshwater fish (including silver and golden carp) are raised in the ponds and marshy depressions.

The city plan. The urban core of Tientsin extends for about seven miles from east to west and about nine miles from north to south. Ho-p'ing, the central district, is located on the west bank of the Hai Ho, just below the large bend of the Hai Ho. It is the main commercial and financial centre, and its two main streets of Ho P'ing Lu (Ho P'ing Road) and Chieh Fang Lu have several large department stores, restaurants, and hotels.

The central district

The old Chinese district is situated immediately to the northwest of Ho P'ing Lu. It is bounded by the four wide boulevards of Tung, Hsi, Pei and Nan Ma Lu that follow the course of the old rectangular wall. The street pattern in the old town is winding and irregular, in contrast to the more regular gridded pattern in the foreign-developed zones to the south and west. The district is subdivided into four smaller sections, each of which in traditional times had special marketing and commercial functions.

North and west of the old Chinese town and continuing across the Nan-yün Ho is the mixed residential and industrial Hung-ch'iao district. It extends to the confluence of the Tzu-ya Ho, Pei-yün Ho, and Hai Ho. The northern outskirts contain workers' housing developments, and the area is famous for its domestic handicrafts.

The newer western and southern districts of Hsin-hua, Ho-hsi, and Nan-k'ai were built on what (until it was drained) was marshy, low-lying land. Hsin-hua, at the bend of the Hai Ho well south of the central district, is the main trading, shipping, and administrative area. It has extensive shipping facilities and is the site of the customs office, the central post office, the harbour bureau, and the central police headquarters. Residential sections have been built in the southern part of this district. Ho-hsi and Nan-k'ai districts in the west and southwest are given primarily to residential and recreational use, and Nan-k'ai is also a major university centre.

The eastern districts of Ho-pei and Ho-tung, east of the Hai Ho, centre on industry and transport. Ho-pei has a few technical and vocational educational institutions in addition to its residential quarters, while Ho-tung is mainly industrial.

Transportation. Tientsin is North China's leading transport centre. The Ching-p'u railway runs south from Tientsin to Shanghai via Chi-nan, Shantung Province, and Süchow, Kiangsu Province. The Ching-shan railway runs north from Peking through Tientsin and Shan-hai-kuan on the Hopeh–Liaoning border to Mukden (Shen-yang), Liaoning Province. The lines are served in Tientsin by three railway stations, classification yards, and extensive maintenance and repair facilities.

Railway services

Heavily traversed inland waterways radiate to the south and southwest along the Grand Canal and Tzu-ya and Ta-ch'ing rivers; they connect the city with Pao-ting, Ts'ang-chou, and Heng-shui in southern Hopeh Province. The Ching-t'ang highway from Peking through Tientsin to T'ang-ku is the main all-weather freight road to the sea. Other main roads extend southward along the Ching-p'u railway into Shantung Province, westward to Shansi Province, and northward to Ch'in-huang-tao, northeastern Hopeh, and the Northeast (formerly Manchuria).

Intra-urban transport has expanded since 1949. About 120 miles of trolley, electric-trolleybus, and motorbus routes connect the city's railway stations and extend to the suburbs of Pei-ts'ang in the north, Hui-tui in the east, and Li-ch'u-chuang in the south.

Tientsin is the main collection point and transshipment centre in North China for goods manufactured for export and is the chief port of entry for heavy machinery and other capital-intensive imports. About one-fourth of China's total foreign trade by value is handled through Tientsin's outport and fishing port of T'ang-ku, which was enlarged and modernized in the early 1950s.

The population. The total population of the Tientsin Municipality was estimated in 1970 at about 4,300,000. The majority lives in the central city, where densities are probably in the range of 15,000 to 75,000 persons per square mile. Statistical information is not available on the suburban population or the population in rural areas that extend to the municipal borders.

Before 1949 most people were engaged in commercial or service occupations. Since then the occupational structure of the city has changed, and about half the population is employed by industry and only about 17 percent in commerce. An additional 7 percent are involved in construction, 8 percent in transport and communications, 7 percent in administration, and 10 percent in education, public health, and social welfare.

Ethnic minorities compose about 3 percent of the population, the largest groups being Tungans, Koreans, Manchus, and Uighurs. Most of them live in the central city in areas that have special historical associations. The largest single community of Tungans is in the northern suburb of T'ien-mu-ts'un.

Housing and architecture. The provision of housing for Tientsin's work force has been a major concern of the municipal authorities. The emphasis since 1949 has been on suburban development, although residential areas in the central city have also been rehabilitated. Before World War II many of the suburban residential areas were built on marshy, poorly drained land subject to flooding, and sanitary conditions were especially bad. Most of the new complexes have been constructed near industrial zones on the outskirts of the city.

Many of the large commercial and administrative buildings in the central city were built by foreign concessionaires. They are typical of European and Japanese colonial architecture of the 1920s and 1930s, with buildings of contrasting architectural styles juxtaposed helter-skelter, without any plan. Some of the public buildings dating from the 1950s were built in imitation of the Soviet monolithic style, and housing complexes are usually standard two- or three-story rectangular blocks. The best known is a commercial structure, the Ch'un-yeh-ch'ang building in the heart of the central business district.

Economic life. Since 1949 heavy industry has been developed and the existing industrial base consolidated for greater productivity. Major activities are the production of heavy machinery, chemicals, and iron and steel and shipbuilding and repair. The Tientsin Heavy Machine-building plant employs about 5,000 workers and is one of China's largest manufacturers of mining equipment. Other products include machinery for textile mills and agriculture, machine tools, electrical equipment, bicycles, tractors, elevators, precision instruments, trucks, and watches.

The chemical complex at Ta-ku, T'ang-ku, and also at Han-ku (north of T'ang-ku on the rail line to T'ang-shan) produces agricultural fertilizers and pesticides, pharmaceuticals, chemicals and petrochemical products, plastics, artificial fibres, dyestuffs, and paints. The Yung-li alkali products plant at T'ang-ku accounts for 40 percent of China's total output of purified soda, some of which is exported to Japan.

Tientsin's light industries

Textiles are the chief light industry. Other such products include processed foods, hides, rubber goods, and paper. Tientsin's industry is largely under the jurisdiction of the municipality, with about 40 percent of production subject to local price setting, planning, and raw-material allocation.

Financial services include branches of the People's Bank of China, the Joint State-Private Bank, the Agricultural Bank of China, and The People's Insurance Company of China. Retail and wholesale trade is managed by commerce bureaus that are responsible to municipal and provincial authorities. Pricing and personnel matters are managed locally, while the distribution of commodities, long-range planning, and high-level financial management are handled by provincial-level bureaus.

Political and government institutions. The Tientsin Municipal Revolutionary Committee is the city's chief administrative body. It was established in 1967 during the political disruption of the Great Proletarian Cultural Revolution (1966–69). Prior to 1967 responsibility for the management of the city's affairs was shared by a

The Municipal Revolutionary Committee

number of bureaus under both party and governmental control. Since then, it is difficult to gauge the level of administrative autonomy that the committee—composed of representatives of the army and the mass revolutionary organizations (representing peasants, workers, and students) and of former Communist Party officials—can exercise relative to the Hopeh provincial government and the central government in Peking.

Until 1967, and perhaps currently, the Tientsin Municipal Planning Commission played a key role in managing industry and commerce. It controlled the supply and distribution of industrial raw materials, set production levels, allocated funds for capital investments, determined manpower needs, supervised product research and development, and coordinated transportation and public utility use.

Public utilities. Major public works projects since 1949 have helped alleviate chronic flood damage and have improved the city's water supply and sewage disposal systems. Marshy, low-lying lands have been drained and converted to agricultural and recreational use, new roads have been constructed, and streetlights have been installed.

The city's water supply

The supply of fresh water has always been a problem because of the city's location near the sea at low elevation. Several freshwater reservoirs have been built in the southwestern and northeastern suburbs. Swampy lowlands to the southwest have been drained; one of the most extensive was converted into the large recreational area of the Shui-shang Kung-yüan (Park on the Water).

Thermal electric power plants (fuelled with coal) are capable of generating more than 100,000 kilowatts of electricity, and the city is connected by a power grid with Peking and T'ang-shan, Hopeh.

Health and safety. Tientsin has more than 40 Western-style and Chinese hospitals, with separate facilities for children, workers, and members of ethnic minorities. Factories and recreational and convalescent centres also provide health care services through their associated clinics.

Tientsin was one of the first cities to establish women's committees to assist working women in household maintenance and child care and to disseminate public health information. Since the program began in 1962 as an outgrowth of the urban commune movement, more than 1,500 committees with some 28,000 housewives have been operating.

Education. By 1960 about one-sixth of Tientsin's population was enrolled in educational institutions. This figure was undoubtedly smaller in the 1970s as a result of the drastic educational reforms of the 1960s. Emphasis is now on practice as well as theory, and students are expected to participate in productive activities while undergoing formal courses of study. The general universities of Nan-k'ai, Hopeh, and Tientsin are located in a new university quarter in Nan-k'ai, on the southwestern periphery of the city. Other higher educational institutions include the Polytechnic Institute, the Central Conservatory of art and music, a medical school, and a teacher training school. Work–study schools attached to factories supplement formal educational programs.

Cultural life. The city has several museums and a major library. The Museum of Fine Arts is noted for its collection of Yüan, Ming, and Ch'ing dynasty paintings, while the Tientsin Municipal Historical Museum and the Tientsin People's Science Hall have more contemporary displays. The Tientsin Municipal Library, with 840,000 volumes, is the city's largest library.

Special exhibits are held at the Palace of Exhibitions and the National Minorities Cultural Palace, and the People's Festival Hall is used for operas, plays, and concerts. The largest movie house is the Peace Cinema. There is also an astronomical observatory.

As in other large Chinese cities, billboards, the cinema, telephone directories, newspapers, and magazines are the main advertising media. The chief newspaper is the *T'ien-ching jih-pao* ("Tientsin Daily"). There is also a television station. Radio and television broadcasts are in Mandarin.

There are more than 30 parks and recreation centres. Victory Park and the Children's Park are in the centre of the city, and the Hsi-ku, Nan-k'ai, People's, Chien-shan, and Shui-shang parks are in the suburbs. Recreational clubs have also been built for industrial workers, and there are four stadiums.

BIBLIOGRAPHY. Although there are no recent works dealing specifically with Tientsin, AUDREY G. DONNITHORNE, *China's Economic System* (1967); BARRY M. RICHMAN, *Industrial Society in Communist China* (1969); and JOHN WILSON LEWIS (ed.), *The City in Communist China* (1971), refer to the organization and management of the city's industry, trade, and financial institutions. *Nagel's Encyclopedia-Guide to China* (1968) gives a brief description of the city.

(B.Bo.)

Tiepolo, Giovanni Battista

After a long period in the 19th century in which his reputation was in eclipse, Giovanni Battista Tiepolo has come to be recognized as the greatest painter of 18th-century Italy. His huge decorative works formed a perfect complement to the Rococo churches and palaces of his time. Described by one of his contemporaries as being "all spirit and fire," he worked with astonishing verve, and his output of ceilings, murals, easel compositions and portraits, sketches, and etchings is so huge as to invite the suspicion of superficiality. Yet there is an underlying melancholy in all his best works that give them a profundity rarely found in other art of his time. Critics now rank him with the great painters of all ages.

Alinari

"Story of Anthony and Cleopatra," fresco by G.B. Tiepolo. In the Palazzo Labia, Venice.

Giovanni Battista, or Giambattista, Tiepolo was born in Venice on March 5, 1696; his father, who had been engaged in the shipping business, died the following year, leaving his wife and five children in comfortable circumstances. His mother entrusted Giambattista to Gregorio Lazzarini, a painter of decorative, academic taste, who taught his young pupil the basic techniques of his profession. Tiepolo was drawn to a melancholic style with strong contrasts of light and shade, or chiaroscuro. Such strong shadings of light and dark, coupled with a genuine dramatic feeling, may be seen in his first public work, "The Sacrifice of Isaac" (1716), for the church of Sta. Maria dei Derelitti, or Ospedaletto. Tiepolo's name first appears on the lists of the Venetian painters' guild as an

independent painter in 1717. The fact that his studio was thriving at this time is attested by his marriage to Cecilia Guardi, the sister of the painters Giovanni Antonio and Francesco.

During this period, Tiepolo was influenced by the robust plastic modelling of his Venetian contemporary Giovanni Battista Piazzetta, as in such works as the monumental "Madonna of Carmelo and the Souls of Purgatory" (*c.* 1720). His artistic education, however, was complex and varied: he examined the works of both Venetian and foreign contemporaries and studied older painters as well, as demonstrated by his large production of etchings after 16th-century subjects. Through his intense artistic activity, Tiepolo mastered a wide variety of forms and moods, ranging from the drama of such works as "The Crucifixion" (1723–24), in the Oratory of Sta. Barbara Burano, to the narrative humour of the four mythological scenes now in the galleries of the Accademia in Venice. It seems unlikely that the young Tiepolo left Venice, and therefore he did not see the great decorative cycles that other Venetian painters were executing throughout Europe. Nevertheless, he understood their methods. His maturity of technique and originality of formal invention were already evident in his first frescoes, the "Glory of St. Theresa" in the Church of the Scalzi and "The Force of Eloquence" on the ceiling of the Palazzo Sandi-Porto (now Cipollato). It was not, however, until the frescoes of the Palazzo Arcivescovile of Udine, executed sometime after 1726, that Tiepolo, then about 30, reached full maturity of expression. In these frescoes, he gave up the chiaroscuro of his early works and greatly brightened his colour, while preserving his form intact. The decoration was commissioned by Dionisio Dolfin, the patriarch of the town of Aquileia, and Tiepolo probably began work with the ceiling above the main staircase, depicting the "Fall of the Rebelling Angels" in vigorous, dramatic forms; in the gallery, within the Baroque perspective framings of Mengozzi Colonna, his faithful collaborator, he narrated biblical episodes of varying complexity, in bright colour and with bold brush play.

At this same time, or shortly thereafter, in a melodramatic and agitated style, Tiepolo executed for the Dolfin family's Venetian palace ten scenes of Roman history. The enrichment of his colour during this period became particularly tasteful in his smaller paintings, such as the two versions of "Apelles Painting the Portrait of Campaspe" (Montreal Museum of Fine Arts and the National Gallery, London), both of which are subtle, almost ironic re-enactments of the classical episode.

By the 1730s, Tiepolo's fame had gone beyond Venice. He was called to Milan in 1731, and there he decorated the Palazzo Archinto (destroyed by bombing in World War II) with mythical scenes, of which marvellous small models remain, and the Palazzo Dugnani, for which he painted graceful episodes from history within Baroque settings. In autumn of that same year, he began the decoration of the Cappella Colleoni at Bergamo, depicting stories of John the Baptist (1732), into which he introduced airy landscape backgrounds that marked an innovation in his style. In the fall of 1734, working "day and night without rest," as he himself put it, Tiepolo decorated the Villa Loschi, now known as Zileri dal Verme, at Biron, near Vicenza, for which he prepared a famous and very beautiful series of drawings. Indeed, Tiepolo was a tireless and prodigious sketcher, capable of suggesting with pen and skillful watercolouring the rapid conception of structures and images that he would later carry out in frescoes and paintings.

In 1736, Count Tessin, who had to select a painter to decorate the royal palace in Stockholm, described Tiepolo this way: "full of spirit . . . of infinite fire, dazzling colour, and astonishing speed." This is a fitting portrait of both the painter and the man. But Tiepolo would not leave the city of Venice, where the nobility and the clergy were by now contending for his work and where he was being praised as "the most famous of the virtuosi." Rather, he preferred to send his works abroad, as in the case of "The Adoration of the Trinity by Pope Clement" (*c.* 1735), which was sent to Nymphenburg and is now in the

Alte Pinakothek in Munich, or "The Martyrdom of St. Sebastian" (1739), which was sent to the church in Diessen. Sometime toward the end of the 1730s, Tiepolo painted the "Institution of the Rosary" on the large ceiling of the Church of the Gesuati (or Sta. Maria del Rosario), at Zattere, covering an enormous amount of space and reviving the triumphal taste of Roman Baroque decoration.

In the decade from 1740 to 1750, Tiepolo created works based on secular themes in which he experimented with forms and appearances of the great luminosity that was rediscovered in Venetian painting from 1730 by Piazzetta, Canaletto, and Guardi. During this time he became a close friend of Count Algarotti, an important personality in the international cultural life of the time. Tiepolo's general education had been unpretentious and provincial, but his meeting with Algarotti drew him closer to the classical taste of the time. Nevertheless, the world he depicted in his works of the period on the theme of the tales of Cleopatra ("The Banquet of Cleopatra" [1744; National Gallery of Victoria, Melbourne], two canvases [1747], in Arkhangelskoye, near Moscow, and the fresco complex at the Palazzo Labia in Venice [shortly before 1750]) is a fanciful image of antiquity; formally, this image is derived from the Venetian Renaissance master Veronese and parallels the melodramas on classical themes that were popular in the 18th century.

An invitation to decorate some of the rooms of the Residenz in Würzburg came to Tiepolo at one of the happiest moments of his career, in the full maturity of his artistic genius, and he went there in 1750 with his two sons, 23-year-old Giovanni Domenico and 14-year-old Lorenzo. They painted a cycle of frescoes in marvellous accord with the style of Balthasar Neumann, the architect. The ceiling of the Kaisersaal, with its "Wedding Allegory," is the most boldly luminous work of Tiepolo's career. The wall frescoes narrate events of the Middle Ages with a supreme naturalness and a total indifference to history. The "Olympus," an assemblage of mythological and allegorical representations on the enormous ceiling of the main staircase, has been said to symbolize and exalt the humanistic aspirations of the 18th century. The rhythmic grandeur of these decorative sequences is also reflected in the solemn "Adoration of the Magi" (1753; Alte Pinakothek, Munich). (The influence of Rubens has been seen in these works, and it is possible that Tiepolo's stay in Germany did, indeed, give him the opportunity to become acquainted with artists such as Rubens and Rembrandt, neither of whom was well represented in Venetian collections.) Almost in direct contrast to the grandeur of this official production, the artist pursued an almost romantic, poetic theme, portraying episodes taken from the Italian Renaissance poet Tasso in four magnificent canvases depicting the story of Rinaldo and Armida, now in the Art Institute of Chicago. In their new treatment of landscape and their inclination toward lyric warmth, these canvases are direct precursors of his decoration for Villa Valmarana, near Vicenza (1757), in which the personality of his son Giovanni Domenico asserted itself in exotic rural scenes of carnival season. For the first time since his earliest attempts in 1748–49, Giovanni Domenico achieved something more than his previous depersonalized collaborations with his father and was able to express his own peculiar anecdotal and realistic–grotesque vein. The elder Tiepolo, on the other hand, drew on the poetry of Homer, Virgil, Ariosto, and Tasso to execute a nucleus of feelings ranging between the dramatic and the passionate, on an idyllic but sensually moving plane. This stay on dry land after his close contact with Venice gave him the magnificent new graphic observations documented in the lyrically intense landscape of the great altarpiece he executed for the Cathedral of Este in Italy, "St. Tecla Freeing Este from the Plague" (1759).

Tiepolo was now on the eve of his departure for Spain, from which he would never return. Before leaving Italy for the last time, he accepted the task of celebrating the last dream of power of a noble Venetian family, the Pisani family, who had built their own belated but splendid Versailles. In Tiepolo's magnificent "Apotheosis

of the Pisani Family," the most attractive section is an array of children's portraits and a frieze of male and female satyrs, which give a stamp of sensual existentialism to the decorative ensemble. Interspersed among his many decorations, Tiepolo painted many portraits. A unique example is the superb portrait of the "Procurator Giovanni Querini (?)," owned by the Galleria Querini-Stampalia of Venice; it represents not only a man but also an undermined aristocracy destined to fall.

Venice's political equilibrium was shattered in 1756 by the Seven Years' War, but Spain remained outside the conflict, and Carlos III invited Tiepolo to Madrid to enhance the glory of the Spanish monarchy at the Palacio Nacional. Tiepolo arrived in 1762 with his active collaborators, Giovanni Domenico and Lorenzo. In 1764, this team finished the decoration, in which the elder Tiepolo continued to define, and in part carry out, the complex thematic conception of the three ceilings. Unfortunately, the concepts did not fit in with the architectural environment, and the chromatic vividness of the beautiful sketches was not completely realized in the finished work. Nevertheless, in "The Power of the Spanish Monarchy," "The Apotheosis of the Spanish Monarchy," and "Aeneas Led to the Temple of Venus," Tiepolo dared to create bold perspective inventions, sustained by rich chromatic orchestration. In contrast to the solemnity that pervaded the Spanish court, Tiepolo presented a poetic art of light and colour, based on an inner feeling of almost romantic melancholy, as may be seen in the religious canvases executed for Aranjuez and in the various sequences of the "Flight into Egypt" executed for private patrons. The ceilings were Tiepolo's last major undertaking; he died in Madrid on March 27, 1770.

The hostile attitude of the official Spanish milieu seems to have resounded in the 19th century, when connoisseurs and critics rejected Tiepolo, along with the Baroque and Rococo styles, in general. He was considered an unhealthy and bizarre genius. But the change in taste brought about by Impressionism late in the century prepared the way for the rediscovery of the great Venetian. Generations of critics in Italy and elsewhere have worked to reconstruct his enormous pictorial output and to reassemble his prodigious mass of quick sketches and brilliant etchings. Modern taste accepts him without reservation and without need for either historical perspective or cultural justification.

MAJOR WORKS

PAINTINGS: "The Sacrifice of Isaac" ("The Sacrifice of Abraham"; 1715–16; Sta. Maria dei Derelitti or Ospedaletto, Venice); "Repudiation of Hagar" (1717–19; Rasini Collection, Milan); "The Madonna of Carmelo and the Souls of Purgatory" (c. 1720; Brera, Milan); "Glory of St. Theresa" (c. 1720; Church of the Scalzi, Venice); "The Force of Eloquence" (c. 1724–25; Palazzo Cipollato, Venice); frescoes (c. 1726; Palazzo Arcivescovile, Udine, Italy); ceiling frescoes (1731, now destroyed; Palazzo Archinto, Milan); "The Adoration of the Christ Child" (1732; St. Mark's, Venice); frescoes (1732; Cappella Colleoni, Bergamo); frescoes, Chapel of S. Vittore (1737; S. Ambrogio, Milan); vault frescoes (c. 1739; Church of the Gesuati, Venice); frescoes (1740; Palazzo Clerici, Milan); vault frescoes (1743–44, now destroyed; Church of the Scalzi, Venice); frescoes (1743; Villa Cordellina, Montecchio Maggiore, Vicenza); "Time Revealing Truth" (frescoes, 1744–45; Palazzo Barbarigo, Venice); "Allegory of Fortitude and Wisdom" (frescoes, 1744–45; Ca' Rezzonico, Venice); "Story of Anthony and Cleopatra" (frescoes, before 1750s; Palazzo Labia, Venice); "The Glorification of Francesco Barbaro" (fresco, c. 1750; Metropolitan Museum of Art, New York); "Gifts Offered to Cleopatra" (fresco, c. 1750; Necchi Collection, Pavia); "Timocleia and the Thracian Commander" (fresco, c. 1750; National Gallery of Art, Washington, D.C.); frescoes, Kaisersaal (1750–52; Residenz, Würzburg); "Olympus" (1753; Residenz, Würzburg); vault frescoes (1754–55; Church of the Pietà, Venice); frescoes for Villa Contarini, Mira (c. 1756; Musée Jacquemart-André, Paris); frescoes (1757; Villa Valmarana, Vicenza); "Apotheosis of the Pisani Family" (frescoes, 1762; Villa Pisani, Stra, Italy); "Apotheosis of the Spanish Monarchy" throne room (1764; Palacio Nacional, Madrid).

OIL SKETCHES: These exist in many museums, including the Isabella Stewart Gardner Museum, Boston; National Gallery, London; Frick Collection, New York; Museum of Fine Arts,

Movement toward the classical

Last years in Spain

Boston; and the Cleveland Museum of Art. Tiepolo also produced a great number of drawings and etchings.

BIBLIOGRAPHY. Contemporary sources and those of the late 18th century recognized the greatness of Tiepolo: VINCENZO DA CANAL, *Vita di Gregorio Lazzarini* (1732; ed. by G.A. MOSCHINI, 1809); A. LONGHI, *Compendio delle vite dei pittori veneziani storici più rinomati* (1762); FRANCESCO ALGAROTTI, *Opere*, 8 vol. (1764–65); A.M. ZANETTI, *Della pittura veneziana* (1771); LUIGI A. LANZI, *Stória pittorica della Italia*, 3 vol. (1795–96). Neoclassicism brought a disregard for the artist, who was often cited in negative criticisms and was admired only in evaluations of certain writers and painters of the second half of the 19th century, such as Gautier and Degas. It is necessary to come to the beginning of our century to discover a re-evaluation and a reconstruction of the work of Tiepolo in numerous monographs: POMPEO G. MOLMENTI, *G.B. Tiepolo: La sua vita e le sue opere* (1909); EDUARD SACK, *Giambattista und Domenico Tiepolo* (1910); ANTONIO MORASSI, *Tiepolo*, 2nd ed. (1950; Eng. trans., *G.B. Tiepolo: His Life and Work*, 1955); *A Complete Catalogue of the Paintings of G.B. Tiepolo* (1962); GUIDO PIOVENE and ANNA PALLUCCHINI (eds.), *L'opera completa di Giambattista Tiepolo* (1968). There are many studies on the painting cycles of the artist: ANTONIO MORASSI, *Tiepolo e la villa Valmarana* (1945); RODOLFO PALLUCCHINI, *Gli affreschi di Giambattista e Giandomenico Tiepolo alla Villa Valmarana di Vicenza* (1945); M.H. VON FREEDEN and CARL LAMB, *Das Meisterwerk des Giovani Battista Tiepolo: Die Fresken der Würzburger Residenz* (1956); PAOLO D'ANCONA, *Gli affreschi di Palazzo Clerici: Tiepolo a Milano* (1956); CARLA GUGLIELMI FALDI, *Tiepolo alla Scuola dei Carmini di Venezia* (1960). Catalogs from expositions have contributed to the diffusion of knowledge about the artist: GIULIO LORENZETTI, *Mostra del Tiepolo* (1951); ALDO RIZZI, *Catalogo della mostra del Tiepolo a Udine*, 2 vol. (1971). Important studies on his drawings are: DETLEV VON HADELN (ed.), *Handzeichnungen von G.B. Tiepolo*, 2 vol. (1927; Eng. trans., *The Drawings of G.B. Tiepolo*, 2 vol., 1928, reprinted 1970); GIORGIO VIGNI, *Disegni del Tiepolo* (1942); GEORGE KNOX, *Catalogue of the Tiepolo Drawings in the Victoria and Albert Museum* (1960); TERISIO PIGNATTI, *Le acqueforti dei Tiepolo* (1965); ALDO RIZZI, *Catalogo della mostra dei desegni del Tiepolo* (1965); *Tiepolo: A Bicentenary Exhibition, 1770–1970*, catalog by GEORGE KNOX (1970); ALDO RIZZI (ed.), *L'opera grafica dei Tiepolo. Le acqueforti* (1971; Eng. trans., *The Etchings of the Tiepolos*, 1972); ANNA PALLUCCHINI, *Giambattista Tiepolo* (1971), in Italian; H.D. RUSSELL, *Rare Etchings by Giovanni Battista and Giovanni Domenico Tiepolo* (1972).

(R.Pal.)

Tiglath-pileser III

Tiglath-pileser III was the brilliant king mainly responsible for the creation of the last Assyrian Empire. During his reign (745–727 BC), he reformed the civil administration, bringing about the internal stability and peace that enabled the army he had reorganized to extend control over Syria and Palestine for the first time. He thus held sway from the Egyptian border to the Persian Gulf and over Cilicia, southern Anatolia, and western Iran.

His biography can be reconstructed from his annals, correspondence, and building inscriptions. He was the first to have annals (as opposed to formal inscriptions)

Tiglath-pileser III, relief from Nimrūd, 8th century BC. In the British Museum.

written on the sculptured slabs adorning his palace walls at Calah (Nimrūd).

Since the days of Tiglath-pileser's father, Adad-nirari III, Assyria had been politically and militarily weak, for its northern neighbour, Urartu, dominated the states controlling its main trade routes to the Mediterranean and to the Iranian plateau. Some portions of the empire had ceased to pay the tribute required by treaties. In the spring of 745 BC a rebellion against the weak Ashur-nirari V, a son of Adad-nirari III, brought another son, who was then governor of Calah, to power. This new ruler assumed the throne name of Tiglath-pileser (the Hebrew form of the Assyrian Tukulti-apil-esharra, "My trust is in the son of [the temple] Esharra"). This may have been a deliberate reference to an illustrious forebear, Tiglath-pileser I, *c.* 1100 BC, who had also had to rescue his country from the incursions of Aramaean and Caucasian tribesmen. The new ruler, an intelligent and vigorous man, acted swiftly. *Usurpation of the throne*

He rearranged territorial governorships by subdividing the larger provinces that had tended to strive for independence from the central power. Outside the immediate home territory he appointed Assyrian officials to be directly responsible to him as well as to support their local ruler. By 738 there were 80 such provinces. The Assyrians had to report directly to the King, who thus was able to check continuously on the loyalty and efficiency of all of his civil servants. They were responsible for local taxation, the storage of military supplies, and the calling up of local forces to support the new Assyrian Army, now a skilled professional force compared with its predecessor, which had relied on somewhat haphazard conscription. A new intelligence system, using reports transmitted by staging posts, was also created.

Tiglath-pileser was thus prepared to break the stranglehold of the surrounding tribes. He first moved eastward against Zamua (modern Sulaymānīyah), then north against the Medes. Both were brought back under control of the adjacent provincial governors. The tribal lands of Puqudu, northeast of Baghdad, were joined to the Arraphka (Kirkūk) province, thereby holding the Aramean tribes in check. This and contiguous operations strengthened the hands of Nabu-nasir (Nabonassar), the native king of Babylon, who maintained peace until his death in 734. All this was facilitated by Tiglath-pileser's policy of mass resettlement. Groups whose loyalty was assured, since they were now dependent on the King for protection in a foreign environment, were settled in troublesome border regions. In 742–741 alone tens of thousands were thus resettled. *Military campaigns*

Tiglath-pileser next attacked the Urartian ruler Sardur III and his neo-Hittite and Aramaean allies, whom he defeated in 743 BC. Advance westward was, however, barred by the capital of Arpad, which had to be besieged for three years—a technique now feasible to a standing army. The victory in 741 was far-reaching, as noted in the Bible (Isa. 37:13), and was to stem the barbarian pressures from the north that, after Tiglath-pileser, were to threaten the whole civilized world. Tribute was brought to him at Arpad from Damascus, Tyre, Cilicia, and other cities and regions. Before Menahem, ruler of Israel, died, he sent 1,000 talents of silver, collecting it from male Israelites on a per capita equivalent of the current price of a slave at Nineveh (II Kings 15:19–22).

The Assyrian king's skill is best seen in his handling of affairs in Syria and Palestine. From an independent military headquarters he bypassed the rebels' ringleader at Damascus, won over most coastal cities, cut off supplies of Lebanon timber from Egypt, and sent a force to Ashke-lon and Gaza. In 734 the border with Egypt was sealed. The tribes of Ammon, Edom, and Moab, who, with Israel, had attacked Ahaz of Judah—a vassal of Assyria—now had to pay tribute. Over the next two years Tiglath-pileser systematically broke the power of Damascus. Israel was made subject through the assassination of Pekah (Pakaha) and his replacement by a pro-Assyrian vassal Hoshea (Ausi; *cf.* II Kings 15:29–30). Galilee was taken from Israel and made part of an adjacent province.

The Assyrian sensed that these rebels were encouraged by Ukin-zer, the Chaldean chief who, in 734, had seized the throne of Babylon. Using consummate diplomacy, Tiglath-pileser sowed discord among other Aramean tribes, one of whose chiefs he won over. His strategy now paid off. He could move the Assyrian Army through areas held by loyal governors or vassals east of the Tigris. One force seized Babylon and another the rebel stronghold of Sapia. It proved a fitting culmination that in 729–728 Tiglath-pileser himself took over the throne of Babylon using his personal (or perhaps Babylonian) name of Pulu (II Kings 15:19; I Chron. 5:26). He died soon afterward, having set Assyria on the road it was to follow to its end.

BIBLIOGRAPHY. No definitive life of Tiglath-pileser has been written. The *Cambridge Ancient History*, vol. 3 (1925), was based on PAUL ROST, *Die Keilschrifttexte Tiglat-Pilesers III* (1893), which is to be replaced by H. TADMOR, *The Inscriptions of Tiglath-pileser III of Assyria* (in prep.), a critical edition with introduction and commentary. New texts are given by H.W.F. SAGGS, "The Nimrud Letters, 1952," *Iraq*, 17:21–50, 126–154 (1955); and D.J. WISEMAN, "A Fragmentary Inscription of Tiglath-pileser III from Nimrud," *Iraq*, 18:117–129 (1956). RICHARD D. BARNETT and MARGARETE FALKNER, *The Sculptures of . . . Tiglath-pileser III* (1962), gives illustrations of the King and his campaigns.

(D.J.W.)

Tigris–Euphrates River System

The two greatest rivers of western Asia have widely separated sources in the mountains of eastern Turkey and travel in a southeasterly direction through north Syria and Iraq to the head of the Persian Gulf. The total length of the Euphrates (Akkadian Purattu; Turkish Firat; Arabic Furāt; Biblical Perath) is approximately 1,700 miles (2,700 kilometres)—that of the Tigris (Akkadian Idiklat; Biblical Hiddekel; Turkish Dicle; Arabic Dijla) about 1,180 miles (1,900 kilometres). Both rivers traverse two-thirds of their courses before reaching the fringes of the Mesopotamian Plain—the silt-filled depression that must be regarded as their combined delta. To the north of this an upper and a middle course is usually distinguished for each river; each upper course is restricted to the valleys and gorges of east Anatolia, at altitudes diminishing from those of their sources at 6,000–10,000 feet above sea level; each middle course proceeding more tranquilly through the uplands of north Syria and Iraq at elevations varying from 1,200 feet at the foot of the so-called Kurdish Escarpment to 170 feet where the alluvium begins at the head of the delta.

The Tigris and Euphrates derive the bulk of their water from the winter rains and snow of the Güneydoğu Toroslar and Zagros mountains. Both, in their middle courses, are joined by substantial left-bank tributaries. Tributary streams of the Tigris, the Great and Little Zab, which are fed in the spring with snow-melt waters from the high ranges of Iraqi and Iranian Kurdistan, are both more powerful and more unpredictable than the Balīkh and the (western) al-Khābūr, which flow into the Euphrates from springs beneath the Escarpment. The Tigris, therefore, is a more copious and swifter stream than the Euphrates, its character being reflected in the Arabic name Dijla, meaning arrow. Geologically, the most striking feature of both streams is the heavy content of silt which they carry in flood-time. At this season their mean discharge in Iraq is reckoned at about 175,000 cubic feet per second, and their water carries as much as 3,000,000 tons of eroded material from the highlands in a single day. The fact that little of this sediment reaches the sea explains the vast tract of alluvial soil of which the Mesopotamian Plain is composed.

The Tigris–Euphrates basin. After reaching the Syrian frontier 250 miles apart, the rivers in their middle courses gradually converge until they are separated only by a triangle of barren limestone desert, known as al-Jazīrah (the Island). On either side of this they have cut deep and permanent beds in the Tertiary rock, so that their courses have remained virtually unchanged since prehistoric times and are punctuated at frequent intervals by the ruins of ancient cities. The Tigris here

traverses the homeland of the Assyrians, whose three great capitals—Nineveh, Calah (modern Nimrūd), and Ashur—still overlook the river. By contrast, when the alluvial plain is reached, the rivers are found to have so frequently bifurcated or altered their beds that their earlier courses, and the canals dependent upon them, can sometimes be traced only by the lines of *talls* ("mounds") representing ancient settlements. The *talls* increase in number as the territory of Babylonia is reached, and the mounds marking the sites of the great Sumerian cities in the extreme south suggest a pattern of occupation almost unrelated to the present system of waterways.

The two rivers, in their lower courses, tend to build up their beds to a level considerably above the plain across which they flow. They are, furthermore, confined between artificial bunds (embankments) to prevent the inundation of the adjacent agricultural lands in the high-water season. Consequently, when, in the past, these bunds have proved ineffectual or have been damaged intentionally, not only have vast areas of surrounding country been flooded but on occasion the rivers have changed their main courses. The high level of the rivers has nevertheless made possible the system of irrigation to which the country owes its prodigious agricultural potential.

The Euphrates has no major right-bank tributaries in its delta, but is joined on its left bank by the Gharrāf Channel, which branches off from the Tigris at al-Kūt. The Tigris has two major left-bank tributaries. It is joined near Baghdad first by al-'Uzaym and then by the even larger Diyālā. This produces a volume of water in excess of the river's capacity, which dissipates itself in extensive marshes on either side of its lower course. To the west the marshes merge into the waters of a great shallow lake, the Hawr al-Hammār. The Euphrates flows through this lake before uniting with the Tigris in a single channel, the Shatt al-'Arab, which reaches the sea over 100 miles further south.

Physiography. *The Euphrates.* The headwaters of the Euphrates comprise two confluent streams known as the Murat and Kara Su. From their sources near Erzurum, Turkey, they traverse the high lava plain to the northwest of Lake Van and meet eventually at Keban, near Elâzığ, where, spanning a deep gorge, the rockfill Keban Dam is due to be completed in 1974. The stream, after breaking through the range of Güneydoğu Toroslar, drops down through the foothills of the ancient district of Commagene. Approaching to within 100 miles of the Mediterranean, it flows by Birecik in Turkey, where it is spanned by road, and Jarābulus on the Syrian side of the frontier, where it is crossed by the Iraqi Railway. From here its southeasterly course across Syria is through barren and thinly populated country, where its cultivable valley is no more than a few miles wide. After the western al-Khābūr joins the Euphrates, it flows through a broader agricultural province until it reaches Abū Kamāl, near the Iraqi frontier, after which the valley narrows again to a strip of alluvium between limestone escarpments. At intervals in the reach between the frontier and Hīt, small towns such as 'Ānah and Rāwah occupy islands in mid-stream, subsisting upon a riparian system of cultivation that uses ingenious waterwheels for irrigation. Below Hīt, the rivercliffs recede and from this point onward irrigation begins on a large scale. Just south of the river below ar-Ramādī lies Lake Habbānīyah, a large depression, enclosed on three sides by low hills, that has been converted into a controlled escape, to minimize the danger of floods and to be used for storage during the low-water period. Between ar-Ramādī and al-Hindīyah, over a distance of about 140 miles, the mouths of all the main controlled irrigation canals as well as most of the pumping installations are to be found. At al-Hindīyah itself, until early in the present century, the river split into two branches, al-Hillah and al-Hindīyah, each of which, over the centuries, had alternately assumed importance. In 1908 a barrage was built to canalize and control al-Hilah branch, thus making al-Hindīyah the main river channel. Below al-Kifl the river enters an unstable area where effective control is difficult. It bifurcates twice before reappearing above as-Samāwah as a single stream, which still maintains its

Use of embankments

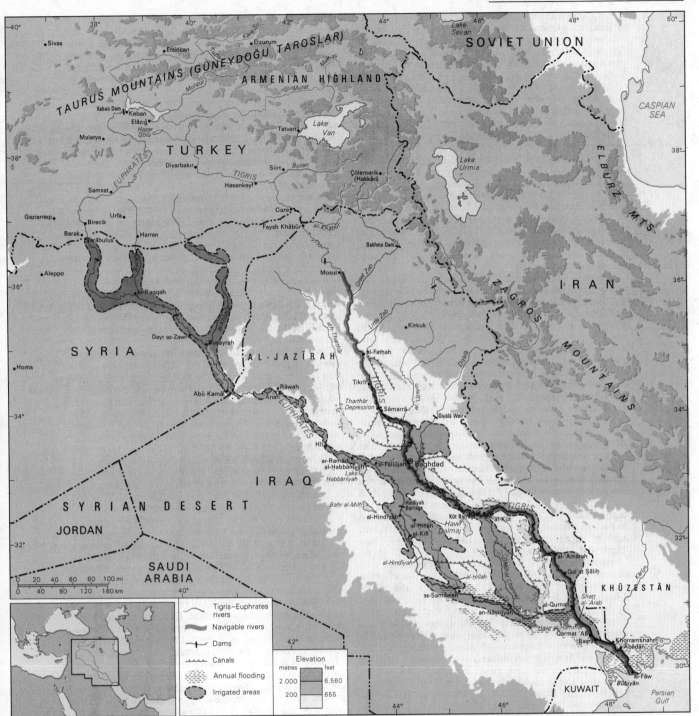

Tigris–Euphrates river system.

elevation above the surrounding marshes. Below an-Nāṣ-rīyah, numerous channels dispose of the waters, which make their way into the Hawr al-Ḥammār, from which, in turn, the outflow finds its way to the Shaṭṭ-al-'Arab.

The Tigris. The Tigris rises in a small mountain lake, Hazar Gölü, southeast of Elâzığ, Turkey. Minor tributaries, flowing into it, drain a wide area extending eastward into Hakkârı il (province). Passing beneath the great basalt walls of Diyarbakir, and by a troglodyte settlement at Hasankeyf, it reaches the Syrian frontier at its junction with the eastern al-Khābūr near Cizre (Jazīrat ibn 'Umar), entering Iraq a few miles beyond at Faysh Khābūr. After passing Mosul, with the ruins of Nineveh on its left bank, the Tigris is joined by its two main tributaries, the Great and the Little Zab, which drain the mountain area of Iraqi Kurdistan. During the season of melting snows, the Zabs, laden with silt, double the volume of the main stream. The river next passes through

the al-Fatḥah gorge, where rapids impede navigation, after which a further reach of 60 miles brings the Tigris to the head of the alluvial plain near Sāmarrā'. Here there is a barrage and a regulated escape that diverts surplus water into the Tharthār Depression to the west. From Baghdad onward, after receiving the waters of al-'Uẓaym and the Diyālā, the Tigris is increasingly confined between artificial embankments, from which the southward overspill keeps the great Hawr Dalmaj (Dalmaj Marsh) almost perennially supplied with water. At al-Kūt, 200 miles downstream from Baghdad, there is a barrage and the Shaṭṭ al-Gharrāf (Shaṭṭ al-Hai) Channel branches off southward. The Shaṭṭ al-Hai is a very ancient bed of the river, irrigating a wide interfluvial area before merging its surplus water with that of the Euphrates where it enters the Hawr al-Ḥammār. The main stream, meanwhile, both above and below al-'Amārah, again splits into a number of channels that disperse their water over rice-growing

From Baghdad to Basra

areas and extensive marshes on either bank. At al-Qurnah it joins an old bed of the Euphrates, now fed by the outflow of these same marshlands to become Shaṭṭ al-ʿArab. At Zarmat ʿAlī, a little above Basra, the main stream is joined by more waters from the Euphrates that have filtered through the Hawr al-Ḥammār.

Shaṭṭ al-ʿArab. On either side of the Shaṭṭ al-ʿArab, both above and below Basra, close settlement is limited to a belt of cultivation between one and three miles wide. These lands are irrigated by a network of creeks that fill with water from al-ʿArab when the sluices are opened at high tide and are famous for their groves of date palms, from which the fruit is exported all over the world. At Khorramshahr, al-ʿArab is joined by the Kārūn River, which flows southward from Khuzistan in Iran. From here to the sea an uneasy political agreement gives equal rights of navigation to Iraq and Iran. Basra on the right bank is, of course, the principal seaport of Iraq, while Khorramshahr, on the left bank, is Iranian. Two further ports on the lower course of al-ʿArab, Abadan (Iran) and al-Fāw (Iraq) are no more than specialized discharge points for exporting oil.

Climate. The countries traversed by the Tigris and Euphrates have a continental sub-tropical climate, with extremes of heat and cold in summer and winter, respectively, and a scanty rainfall. In the alpine regions, where the rivers have their upper courses, winter winds are weak and variable, and much of the light precipitation falls in the form of snow, which lies for four or more months in the higher valleys. At this season the mean temperature is much below freezing, so that agriculture is at a standstill and communications are restricted. After the snowfields melt in the spring the rivers are in spate. The mounting volume of their waters is augmented in their middle courses by seasonal rainfall, which reaches its maximum between March and May. Although in the rivers' lower courses intermittent rains continue during the winter months, the total rainfall rarely exceeds eight inches annually, and from May onward rain ceases altogether. In the alluvial plain, the most conspicuous climatic feature is the extreme heat of the summer months, with day temperatures rising as high as 120° F (49° C), and with the relative humidity as low as 15 percent. The fertility of the delta is therefore entirely dependent upon the seasonal flooding of the Tigris and Euphrates.

Vegetation and animal life. Dense communities of common reed and the narrowleaf cattail are found in the wide areas of marshland through which the rivers flow in south Iraq. The young shoots of both are used by Marsh Arabs for fodder. Along the rivers themselves in their lower courses the Euphrates poplar and a species of willow grow in small belts. The poplar is used for practical purposes such as boat building. Undergrowth in these riverain thickets is composed chiefly of five-stamen tamarisk and mesquite, which also extends northward to the middle course of the Tigris and to its tributaries, up to an altitude of 3,000 feet. It is often accompanied by licorice, from whose roots an exportable product is obtained.

Wild pigs are widespread in the marshes adjoining the rivers throughout their courses. In southern Iraq, jackals and occasional hyenas are to be seen among the riverside gardens, and a very large form of Indian jungle cat inhabits the more remote tamarisk thickets. The smaller Eastern wild cat is less common. Among smaller animals are several species of gerbils and the agile jerboa, which may be seen as far north as central Anatolia. Buxton's mole-rat, which covers the entrance to its burrow with a mound of earth, is also found in the riverbanks. Many birds migrating between Europe and Asia fly along the rivers' course.

Locally resident birds include babblers, bulbuls, scrub warblers, and sandgrouse. Among the larger species that frequent the marshes and occasionally breed there are pelicans, flamingoes, herons (including the huge giant heron), storks, spoonbills, and two kinds of bustard. Winter visitors are geese, white-fronted or graylag, and innumerable ducks, including all the common European kinds as well as the red-crested pochard and marbled duck. Gray cranes breed on the upper reaches of the Euphrates. Brilliant European bee-eaters visit the riverbanks on passage, and Persian bee-eaters remain to breed. Both the European and the Indian rollers nest in the vicinity of the rivers, particularly in the vertical banks of water channels.

Among the freshwater fish characteristic of the Tigris-Euphrates system, the carp family is the most conspicuous. The rivers harbour a variety of genera in this family, including small-scale forms recalling the Indian mahseer. A barbel genus is recorded as attaining a weight of 300 pounds. Besides carp, there are a few varieties of catfish as well as the spiny eel with its curious tubular nostrils.

Human ecology. With the exception of city dwellers, the Arab population on the rivers' banks live either by stock breeding or by agriculture. Their way of life varies from the nomadism of the desert bedouin to the settled condition of the peasantry (fellahin) in the agricultural districts. Both bedouin and fellahin, together with semi-settled Arabs, may be included within the organization of a single tribe. Over the past half century, however, tribal associations have begun to disintegrate. Among the fellahin an improved system of land settlement and legal reforms are breaking the authority of feudal landlords and encouraging the syndication of small holdings.

The uniform simplicity of village life among the fellahin extends to the limits of the delta. Almost the only variation is to be found among the Maʿdan, or Marsh Arabs, who occupy the vast triangle of swampland between an-Nāṣirīyah, al-ʿAmārah, and Basra. A distinctive culture emerges from their seminomadic life. They raise water buffalo and hunt wildfowl or pigs from their mashuf canoes. The giant mardi reeds found in these swamps reach a height of up to 25 feet, providing them with building material for their characteristic architecture.

The Marsh Arabs

North of al-Fatḥah gorge, the Tigris and its tributaries pass through country in which pure Arabs are increasingly in a minority. In the 17th century this region provided winter pasture for the Kurdish tribes but was then settled with Turkmen by Sultan Murad IV, in order to secure his lines of communication with Baghdad. To the north the Turkmen merge with the Iraqi Kurds, whose orchards and vegetable gardens are found along the Tigris tributaries and their smaller affluents. In their upper courses, both the Tigris and the Euphrates pass through mountain country whose inhabitants were once predominantly Kurdish. Today, however, the Kurds have become assimilated into the Anatolian population. Until recently the highland provinces, where both rivers have their sources, were underpopulated as a result of the departure of the Armenians early in the 20th century.

History of the rivers. History has little to record regarding physiological changes in the upper and middle courses of the two rivers. In the delta, by contrast, the pattern created by complex hydrological developments over a period of several millennia is available for study, even if it is as yet only partially understood. Different explanations, for example, have been given for the way in which the plains were formed and the present coastline created. Until recently it was thought that the head of the Persian Gulf once extended as far as the apex of the delta but must have receded southward until, in early historic times, it corresponded roughly to a line drawn through al-ʿAmārah and an-Nāṣirīyah. Nearer to the present coastline, meanwhile, the westward outflow from the Kārūn River had built up a barrier of silt, behind which a great lake formed. The lake had then gradually filled with alluvium, until only the Hawr al-Ḥammār and the marshes around it remained. In 1952, this long-accepted interpretation was refuted by geologists who detected a gradual subsidence in the basal rocks beneath the Euphrates estuary at a rate that was enough to maintain the alluvial deposit at a constant level. They accordingly concluded that the coastline had remained almost unchanged since historic times—a contention that still requires to be reconciled with conflicting archaeological evidence.

The tangle of waterways and ancient irrigation channels with which the Mesopotamian Plain appears to be covered, especially when seen from the air, gives an exaggerated impression of ancient prosperity, modified only if one remembers that at no time in the past were all these channels in simultaneous use. Of the major canal systems on which the country depended in early medieval times, for instance, some are today re-used and extended, while others are obsolete and forgotten. The five great Euphrates canals (Isa, Sarsar, Malik, Kutha, and Nil), on which the fertility of central Iraq depended in 'Abbāsid times, have modern counterparts, but their overflow can no longer drain into the Tigris because of a change in level. East of the Tigris, now long neglected and dry, is the great Nahrawān Canal, which irrigated an area extending almost to the Persian frontier. Leaving the Tigris just north of Sāmarrā' and utilizing an ancient bed of the main river, this canal collected the waters of al-'Uẓaym and the Diyālā, carrying them southeastward almost to al-Kūt. It was abandoned after the Mongol invasions, and only a small part of its former dependent territory is now supplied with water by the Diyālā Weir. The old Ishaqi-Dujaylah Canal that irrigated the farmlands west of the Tigris in the same era also now lies derelict.

Hydrology. The rivers have two well-marked flood periods; the first, an irregular rise mainly due to the rain, that lasts from November to the end of March; the second, that of the main flood in April and May. During the second period, the rivers' combined discharge may reach 175,000 cubic feet per second, but the volume drops rapidly in June and rarely exceeds one-tenth of that amount in later summer and autumn. From the point of view of agriculture, the rivers are high at the wrong time of year for most crops (except rice), so that cultivation by direct inundation cannot be generally practiced.

Furthermore, the sheer volume of flood water endangers the bunds within which the rivers are confined in their lower courses. The primary requirement of river control is therefore to maintain an effective system of diversion and storage, both as a precaution against the kind of inundation that threatened the existence of Baghdad as recently as 1954 and as a means of retaining the flood waters for distribution in the hot season. To this end, in the early decades of the present century, barrages were built at al-Hindīyah and al-Kūt, and an important weir constructed on the Diyālā east of Baghdad. The diversionary escapes at ar-Ramādī on the Euphrates and at Sāmarrā' on the Tigris were both completed in 1956. An even larger storage basin has been created by the construction of a dam at Dukān on the Little Zab in 1958, and yet another is being built at Bakhma on the Great Zab.

Irrigation. The districts of northern Iraq and Syria, together with the piedmont area of southeastern Anatolia, through which the two rivers flow in their middle courses, have a milder climate than the plains in the south and sufficient rainfall to raise a crop of winter grain without irrigation. North of 'Ānah on the Euphrates and of Tikrīt on the Tigris date palms disappear and are replaced by vines, olives, tobacco, and temperate fruits. There are no major canal systems in this area, and such irrigation as is required is supplied by mechanical lifts. By contrast, in the south the principal crops are wheat, barley, millet, and rice, as well as dates, all of which are dependent upon irrigation. Irrigation takes three forms. Water is distributed from rivers and canals by direct flow onto the land through small channels; by lifting water mechanically into such channels; and by direct inundation. The second of these methods is limited to land relatively close to rivers and canals; the third is useful only for rice cultivation. The relative importance of each method may be judged by the figures for 1942, an average and comparatively recent year; out of a total area cropped by irrigation, 1,700,000 acres were dependent on lifts, 1,500,000 on canals, and 250,000 on inundation. Canals are of two kinds; controlled canals, which receive water from regulators on the main river at all seasons, and uncontrolled canals, which are fed only when the river level reaches the canal head—an eventuality that unfortunately occurs mainly at the season when water is least in demand.

While the Tigris, at the northern extremity of the delta, flows at a slightly higher level than the Euphrates, before reaching Baghdad the relationship is reversed, and the Euphrates becomes the higher of the two by about 30 feet. There is a second reversal before the Tigris reaches al-Kūt. In antiquity, advantage was taken of these characteristics, which permitted irrigation from one river and drainage into the other, and the situation is still partially reflected in the operation of the controlled canal zones of the present irrigation system.

Five areas are dependent upon irrigation from large canals, controlled by barrages and sluice gates. The canal systems are the following: (1) the five left-bank Euphrates canals, running generally eastward between ar-Ramādī and al-Musayyib. Irrigation is perennial and is by free flow. (2) The Euphrates canals, depending directly on the Hindīyah Barrage. (3) The Diyālā canals, whose flow is maintained in summer by the Diyālā Weir. (4) The canal system on the Kūt Barrage, including the Gharrāf Canal, and the Dujaylah (an old bed of the Tigris). (5) Canals and spillways from al-'Amārah to Qal'at Ṣāliḥ, on the left bank of the Tigris. Uncontrolled canal irrigation and inundation are predominantly practiced in rice-growing areas, such as in ash-Shāmīyah district (through which run the two branches of al-Hindīyah channel of the Euphrates) along the lower Euphrates around as-Samāwah, from an-Nāṣirīyah to the Hawr al-Ḥammār, and along the Lower Tigris below al-Kūt. Water-lifting machinery, consisting either of oil pumps or more primitive types of apparatus, is in use throughout the middle and lower courses of both rivers. Among the traditional devices in use, particularly on the middle Euphrates, are tall waterwheels, driven by the force of the current, which raise the water in earthenware jars attached to their rims. On the Tigris the height of lifts vary from six feet in the lowest reaches to 40 feet at Baghdad.

In the great irrigated areas of lower Mesopotamia, where the system of extensive cultivation has traditionally been practiced, a primary threat is the gradual salinization of the soil. The irrigation water from the rivers is slightly saline and the heavy residue left by evaporation in hot weather is augmented by salt forced to the surface by groundwater. The resultant deterioration of the soil has been promoted by the pattern of irrigation canals, whose dikes, created by dredging, have divided the low-lying ground into small units, making it difficult to drain off water before evaporation occurs. Philologists have found evidence in cuneiform texts to suggest that the deterioration of land through salinization was already well understood as early as the third millennium BC, when the centres of agricultural prosperity began to shift northward from the original homeland of the Sumerians.

Navigation and river crossings. In 1836 a British expedition, led by Col. Francis Chesney, navigated the Euphrates by steamship from an-Nāṣirīyah to al-Qurnah, north of the Hawr al-Ḥammār. Today the Euphrates is not navigable except by local craft. From Basra to Baghdad, however, the Tigris is navigable by steamers with draughts of 4 ft 6 in. in the high water season and 4 ft at low water. Above Baghdad small steamers of three foot draught can, with some difficulty, reach Mosul. Much of the downstream traffic on rivers consists of *kalaks*—rafts of timber and brushwood supported on inflated skins. *Kalaks* carry loads of up to 35 tons and take three or four days to cover the 275 miles from Mosul to Baghdad. Upon arrival, the timber is sold and the skins returned by road to their starting-point. Sailing craft include *muhaylahs* and *safīnahs* 30–80 feet long, with a capacity of up to 50 tons. Carrying smaller loads are *balams*—long, narrow double-ended, flat-bottomed craft with a shallow draft. Until recently *guffahs*—huge circular coracles of basketwork, coated with bitumen and capable of carrying up to 20 men—were in regular use in the vicinity of Baghdad.

The ancient trade route from the Persian Gulf to the

Dams and Reservoirs					height		length		installed power capacity (MW)	reservoir capacity	
name	location	type*	completion date	purpose	feet	metres	feet	metres		000 ac ft	000,000 cu m
Euphrates											
Keban Dam	Elâziğ, Turkey	RG	1974†	power, irrigation	679	207	3,598	1,097	1,240	25,100	31,000
Tabqah Dam	ar-Raqqah, Syria	RG	1983†	power, irrigation	165	50	7,500	2,300	1,070	6,000	7,400
Hindīyah Barrage	al-Hindīyah, Iraq	B	1913‡	irrigation, flood control	25	8	779	238	...	...	...
Ḥabbānīyah Lake Escape	ar-Ramādī, Iraq	N	1956	storage, flood control	—	—	—	—	—	2,000	2,500
Tigris and tributaries											
Sāmarrā' Barrage and Tharthār Outlet	Wādī ath-Tharthār, Iraq	N	1956	power, irrigation flood control	39	12	827	252	...	69	85
Dukān Dam	Little Zab River, Iraq	CA	1958	power, irrigation flood control	381	117	1,181	360	...	5.5	6.8
Darband-e Khan Dam	Diyālā River, Iraq	R	1962	power, irrigation	459	140	1,411	430	...	2	3
Diyālā Weir	Diyālā River, Iraq	C	1940	irrigation	36	11	1,342	409	—	...	...
Kūt Barrage	al-Kūt, Iraq	C	1939	irrigation	34	10.5	1,663	507	—	...	...
Bakhma Dam	Great Zab River, Iraq	...	†	storage	...	...	...	...	—	...	...

... Not available. — None, or not applicable. *R-rockfill, G-gravity, B-brick, C-concrete, N-natural depression. †Under construction. ‡Enlarged 1922.

Mediterranean followed the right bank of the Euphrates almost to Aleppo. The modern road and railway, after crossing the river at as-Samāwah, are diverted at al-Ḥillah toward Baghdad, but the road returns from Baghdad to the important Euphrates crossing at al-Fallūjah, after which it runs across the desert to Damascus. From Baghdad, with its four modern bridges over the mainstream, the railway follows the right bank of the Tigris to Mosul, then turns northwestward across the corner of Syria known as the "Bec-de-Canard" to follow the Turco-Syrian frontier to the Euphrates crossing at Jarābulus. On its way, it passes near the ruins of Haran (modern Harran), the "crossroads city" of the ancient world, and intersects a road that runs due north from ar-Raqqah to cross the headwaters of Euphrates once more at Samsat.

Among the mountains of east Anatolia, railways follow, in part, the upper course of the Tigris and both confluents of the Euphrates, bridging the Euphrates near Malatya.

Future prospects. In spite of recent engineering accomplishments, the full exploitation of the Tigris–Euphrates water supplies and the coordination of efforts between the three countries through which the rivers pass, have yet to be achieved.

In Iraq, where it has been estimated that 60 percent of the irrigated land suffers from some degree of salinity and a proportion of the cultivated land has had to be abandoned from this cause, it has been necessary to move away from piecemeal schemes of irrigation and toward the adoption of a single coordinated scheme for water use. An irrigation plan for the entire Tigris–Euphrates region, adopted by intergovernmental agreement, would allow further progress. At the moment, apart from an arrangement established in 1946 by which Turkey transmits flood warnings to Iraq, no intergovernmental water control agreements have been reached.

BIBLIOGRAPHY. R.M. ADAMS, *Land Behind Baghdad* (1965), a detailed study of the Nahrawān Canal and its history; ADMIRALTY, NAVAL INTELLIGENCE DIVISION, *Turkey*, 2 vols. (1942-43), *Iraq and Persian Gulf* (1944), excellent maps; M.A. BEEK, *Atlas of Mesopotamia* (1962), a text dealing with salinization and delta formation, including primarily historical or archaeological maps; W.C. BRICE, *A Systematic Regional Geography*, vol. 8 of the "South West Asia Series" (1966), a reliable contemporary work; F.R. CHESNEY, *Expedition for the Survey of the Rivers Euphrates and Tigris*, 2 vol. (1850); J. HANSMAN, "Charax and the Karkheh," *Iranica Antiqua*, 7:21–58 (1967), an article on the changing coastline north of the Shaṭṭ al-'Arab, and on the discharge of the Tigris and Euphrates; M.G. IONIDES, *The Régime of the Rivers Euphrates and Tigris* (1937), once a standard work but now outdated; G.M. LEES and N.L. FALCON, "The Geographical History of the Mesopotamian Plains," *Geogr. J.*, 118:24–39 (1952), an article presenting new information on the question of the formation of the coastline of Iraq; B. LEWIS, *The Emergence of Modern Turkey* (1962), relevant hydro-

logical material; A. MUSIL, *The Middle Euphrates* (1927), an erudite study of historical geography in this region; A. SOUSA, *Irrigation in Iraq* (1945); W. THESIGER, *The Marsh Arabs* (1964), photographs of reed architecture.

(S.H.F.L.)

Tilak, Bal Gangadhar

Scholar, mathematician, and philosopher, Bal Gangadhar Tilak is remembered best as a man of action, who laid the foundation of India's independence by building his own defiance of British rule into a national movement. The popular leader of a militant school of nationalism, he was also the movement's chief theoretician, articulating its ideals and devising its programs. Passive resistance, the boycott of British goods, the organization of mass opinion, and other forms of effective political action that Gandhi later adopted were first introduced by Tilak.

Camera Press—Publix

Tilak.

Tilak was born on July 23, 1856, into a cultured, middle-class, Brahmin family at Ratnāgiri, on the west coast of India. His father was an educator and noted grammarian. After taking his university degree, Bal studied law but then decided to teach mathematics in a private school in Poona, which was to become the centre of his political career. He developed the school into a university college after founding the Deccan Education Society (1884), which aimed at educating the masses, especially in the English language, which Tilak and his associates considered a powerful force for the dissemination of liberal and democratic ideals. The life members of the society were supposed to follow an ideal of selfless service, but when some members began to keep their outside earnings for themselves, Tilak resigned. He then turned to the task of awakening the political consciousness of the people through two weekly newspapers: *Kesari* ("The Lion"), published in Marathi, and *The Mahratta,* published in English, of which he had become owner and editor.

Organization of religious festivals

In an attempt to rekindle the people's pride in their own history, religion, and culture, he organized two important festivals, Ganesh, in 1893, and Shivaji, in 1895. Gaṇeśa (Ganesh) is the elephant-headed god worshipped by all Hindus; Śivajī (Shivaji), the first Hindu hero to fight against Muslim power in India, was the founder of the Marāthā state, which in the course of time overthrew Muslim power in India. It was characteristic of Tilak that he sought inspiration in India's history, while Gandhi found his in Tolstoy and the Bible, and Nehru in the Socialist ideology of the English Fabian Society.

His activities aroused the nation and soon brought him into conflict with the British government, which prosecuted him for sedition and sent him to jail in 1897. The trial and sentence made him the idol of the country and earned him the title Lokamanya (Beloved Leader of the People). Fifty more years were to elapse before India achieved liberty, but the psychological change brought about by the trial laid the foundation for its independence.

Support of boycott and passive resistance

When Lord Curzon, viceroy of India, partitioned Bengal in 1905, Tilak strongly supported the Bengali demand for the annulment of the partition and advocated a boycott of British goods that soon became a movement sweeping the nation. The following year he set forth a program of passive resistance, known as the Tenets of the New Party, that he hoped would lead to the establishment of a parallel government and destroy the hypnotic influence of British rule and prepare the people for sacrifice in order to gain independence.

This was strong meat for the moderate party in the National Indian Congress, which believed in making "loyal" representations to the government for small reforms. Tilak aimed at Swarajya (independence), not piecemeal reforms, and attempted to persuade the Congress to adopt his militant program. On this issue, he clashed with the moderates at the Surat session of the Congress in 1907. Taking advantage of the split in the nationalist forces, the government again prosecuted Tilak on a charge of sedition and inciting terrorism and deported him to Mandalay, Burma, to serve a sentence of six years' imprisonment.

His major work, the *Bhaga-wadgita-Rahasya*

In Mandalay jail, Tilak, primarily a scholar and a politician only by necessity, settled down to write his magnum opus, the *Bhagawadgita-Rahasya* ("Secret of the *Bhagavadgītā*"), a daringly original exposition of the most sacred book of the Hindus. Tilak discarded the orthodox interpretation that the *Bhagavadgītā* taught the ideal of renunciation; in his view it taught selfless service to mankind. Earlier, in 1893, he had published an essay on the antiquity of the Vedas entitled *Orion,* which showed by astronomical calculations that certain hymns in the *Ṛgveda,* the oldest Hindu scripture, could not have been composed later than 4000 BC. In the sequel to *Orion,* published ten years later and called *The Arctic Home in the Vedas,* he attempted to prove that the North Polar region was the original home of the Aryans, the prehistoric ancestors of the Hindus and other Indo-Germanic peoples. He held therefore that "Aryan civilisation must be supposed to date back several thousands of years before the oldest Veda period."

On his release in 1914, on the eve of World War I, he once more plunged into politics and launched the Home Rule League with the rousing slogan: "Swarajya (independence) is my birthright and I will have it." In 1916 he rejoined the Congress and signed the historic Lucknow Pact, a Hindu–Muslim accord, with Mohammed Ali Jinnah, the future founder of Pakistan. In historical perspective, the partition of India might have been averted if, after Tilak's death in 1920, the Indian leadership had

not departed from the ideal embodied into the pact of uniting Hindus and Muslims under a common Indian nationalism.

Tilak visited England in 1918 as president of the Indian Home Rule League. He realized, as no other Indian leader had before him, that the Labour Party was a growing force in British politics, and he established firm relationships with its leaders; his foresight was justified: it was a Labour government that granted independence to India in 1947.

When Tilak returned home in 1919, he attended the meeting of the Congress at Amritsar and advised the delegates to follow his policy of "responsive co-operation," in carrying out the Montagu–Chelmsford reforms which introduced a certain degree of Indian participation in regional government. But before he could give the new reforms a decisive direction, he died in Bombay on August 1, 1920. In their tributes, Mahatma Gandhi called him "the Maker of Modern India" and Jawaharlal Nehru, "the Father of the Indian Revolution."

BIBLIOGRAPHY. The first authoritative biography in English published outside India is D.V. THAMANKAR, *Lokamanya Tilak* (1956); S.L. KARANDIKAR, *Lokamanya Bal Gangadhar Tilak: The Hercules and Prometheus of Modern India* (1957), is a chronological treatment.

(D.V.T.)

Tillich, Paul

An eminent 20th-century theologian and philosopher who illuminated and bound together the realms of religion and culture, Paul Tillich was a central figure in the intellectual life of his time both in his native Germany and later in his adopted homeland, the United States. It is generally held that the 20th century has been marked by a widespread breakdown of traditional Christian convictions about God, morality, and the meaning of human existence in general. In assessing Tillich's role in relation to this development, some critics have regarded him as the last major spokesman for a vanishing Christian culture, a systematic thinker who sought to demonstrate the reasonableness of the Christian faith to modern skeptics. Others have viewed him as a forerunner of the contemporary cultural revolution, whose discussions of the meaning of God and faith served themselves to undermine traditional beliefs.

Henri Dauman—LIFE Magazine, © Time Inc.

Tillich, 1965.

Tillich himself believed he was a "boundary man," standing between the old and the new, between a heritage imbued with a sense of the sacred and the secular orientation of the new age. He asserted that his vocation was to mediate between the concerns voiced by faith and the imperatives of a questioning reason, thus helping to heal the ruptures threatening to destroy Western civilization. He believed that from the beginning life had prepared him for such a role, and his long career as a theologian, educator, and writer—in Germany and the U.S.—was devoted to this task with single-minded energy.

Early life

Born in Starzeddel, a village in the Prussian province of Brandenburg, on August 20, 1886, Paul Tillich spent his boyhood years in Schönfliess, a small community east of the Elbe, where his father served as minister and diocesan superintendent in the Prussian Territorial Church. Life in Schönfliess—a walled town founded in the Middle Ages and surrounded by fertile fields and dark forests—left indelible marks on the impressionable boy: a strong sense of historical continuity, a feeling of intimacy with nature and its processes, and a deep attachment to the church as the bearer of sacred meaning in the centre of community life.

This life style, epitomized for Tillich in the person of his authoritarian and theologically conservative father, was challenged when Tillich first attended the humanistic secondary school in Königsberg-Neumark, where he was introduced to the classical ideal of free thought, untrammelled by anything except the rules of reason. He accepted that ideal enthusiastically. When his father was transferred to Berlin in 1900, he responded with the same enthusiasm to the kind of freedom that life in a thriving metropolis made possible.

Tillich's love of freedom, however, did not make him forget his boyhood commitment to a rich and satisfying religious tradition; and how to enjoy the freedom to explore life without sacrificing the essentials of a meaningful tradition became his early and lifelong preoccupation. It appears as a major theme in his theological work: the relation of heteronomy to autonomy and their possible synthesis in theonomy. Heteronomy (alien rule) is the cultural and spiritual condition when traditional norms and values become rigid, external demands threatening to destroy individual freedom. Autonomy (self-rule) is the inevitable and justified revolt against such oppression, which nevertheless entails the temptation to reject all norms and values. Theonomy (divine rule) envisions a situation in which norms and values express the convictions and commitments of free individuals in a free society. These three conditions Tillich saw as the basic dynamisms of both personal and social life.

His early attempts to solve the problem took the form of working out an independent position in relation to his conservative father; in this context he learned to examine personal experiences in terms of philosophical categories, for the elder Tillich loved a good philosophical argument. But the decisive, seminal encounter with the problem came during his theological studies at the University of Halle (1905–12), where he was forced to match the doctrinal position of the Lutheran Church, based on the established confessional documents, against the theological liberalism and scientific empiricism that dominated the academic scene in Germany at the beginning of the new century.

In his search for a solution Tillich found help in the writings of the German philosopher F.W.J. von Schelling (1775–1854) and the lectures of his theology teacher Prof. Martin Kähler. Schelling's philosophy of nature, which appealed to Tillich's own feeling for nature, offered a conceptual framework interpreting nature as the dynamic manifestation of God's creative spirit, the aim of which is the realization of a freedom that transcends the dichotomy between individual life and universal necessity. Kähler directed his attention to the doctrine of justification through faith, laid down by Saint Paul and reiterated by Martin Luther.

The "Protestant principle"

Tillich now concluded that this doctrine, which he called the "Protestant principle," could be given a far wider scope than previously had been thought. Not limited to the classical religious question of how sinful man can be acceptable to a holy God, it could be understood to encompass man's intellectual life as well, and thus all of man's experiences. As the sinner is declared just in the sight of God, so the doubter is possessed of the truth even as he despairs of finding it, and so cultural life in general is subject both to critical negation and courageous affirmation. The rigid formulas of the Lutheran Church could thus be rejected while their essential content was affirmed.

Tillich's first attempts to work out the details of this insight were in the form of Schelling studies, dissertations for a doctorate in philosophy (1911) and a licentiat in theology (1912). In the latter work especially, *Mystik und Schuldbewusstsein in Schellings philosophischer Entwicklung* ("Mysticism and Consciousness of Guilt in Schelling's Philosophical Development"), one can discern a probing of the implications of the Protestant principle for the very nature and structure of reality, especially in his explication of Schelling's view of sin and redemption as a cosmic event embracing all existence.

Ordained a Lutheran clergyman on the conclusion of his university studies, Tillich served as a military chaplain during World War I. The war was a shattering experience to him, not only for its carnage and physical destruction but as evidence of the bankruptcy of 19th-century humanism and the questionableness of the adequacy of autonomy as sole guide. The chaotic situation in Germany after the armistice made him certain that Western civilization was indeed nearing the end of an era.

The concept of *kairos*

His practical response to this crisis was to join the Religious-Socialist movement, whose members believed that the impending cultural breakdown was a momentous opportunity for creative social reconstruction, a time that Tillich characterized by the New Testament term *kairos*, signifying a historical moment into which eternity erupts, transforming the world into a new state of being. But ideas, rather than political activity, were his main interest. At teaching posts in the universities of Berlin, Marburg, Dresden, Leipzig, and Frankfurt he participated eagerly in discussion groups searching for a new understanding of the human situation. He also wrote extensively, publishing over 100 essays, articles, and reviews in the period 1919–33.

In most of these writings Tillich was using the insight he had gained at Halle as a norm in analyses of religion and culture, the meaning of history, and contemporary social problems. The remarkable work, *Das System der Wissenschaften nach Gegenständen und Methoden* ("The System of the Sciences according to their Subjects and Methods," 1923), was his first attempt to render a systematic account of man's spiritual endeavors from this point of view. As early as 1925, in Marburg, he was also at work on what was to become his major opus, *Systematic Theology* (3 vol., 1951–63).

Tillich's passionate concern for freedom made him an early critic of Hitler and the Nazi movement, and in retaliation he was barred from German universities in 1933—the first non-Jewish academician "to be so honoured," as he wryly put it. He then accepted an invitation to join the faculty at Union Theological Seminary in New York, and despite initial difficulties with a new language and adapting his thought pattern to pragmatic American mental habits, he emerged as an "apostle to the skeptics" in his new homeland during the years following World War II. At Union Seminary (1933–55), Harvard University (1955–62), and the University of Chicago (1962–65), he engaged graduate and undergraduate students in searching dialogue concerning the meaning of human existence. His public lectures and books reached large audiences who did not usually show an interest in religious questions. In his most widely read books, *The Courage to Be* (1952) and *Dynamics of Faith* (1957), he argued that man's deepest concern drives him into confrontation with a reality that transcends his own finite existence. Tillich's discussion of the human situation in these books shows a profound grasp of the problems brought to light by modern psychoanalysis and existentialist philosophy.

Systematic Theology

The publication of his *Systematic Theology* made available the results of a lifetime of thought. The most novel feature of this work is its "method of correlation," which makes theology a dialogue relating questions asked by man's probing reason to answers given in revelatory experience and received in faith—theonomy's answers to autonomy's questions. The dialogue of *Systematic The-*

ology is in five parts, each an intrinsic element in the system as a whole: questions about the powers and limits of man's reason prepare him for answers given in revelation; questions about the nature of being lead to answers revealing God as the ground of being; questions about the meaning of existence are answered by the New Being made manifest in Jesus Christ; questions about the ambiguities of human experience point to answers revealing the presence of the Holy Spirit in the life process; and questions about human destiny and the meaning of history find their answers in the vision of the Kingdom of God. Readers of this and other works by Tillich have been impressed by the broad reach of his thought but also baffled by the philosophical terminology that he used in discussing God and faith. Those who see him as an advocate of agnosticism or atheism, however, may have misunderstood his intent. He rejected the anthropomorphic "personal God" of popular Christianity, but he did not deny the reality of God, as the conventional atheist has done. Modern "Christian atheists" who cite Tillich in support of their "God is dead" claim overlook the fact that for Tillich the disappearance of an inadequate concept of God was the beginning of a grander vision of God. Like Spinoza, he was a "God-intoxicated man" who wanted to help his fellow human beings recapture a relevant and dynamic religious faith.

In his last years Tillich expressed some doubts about the viability of any systematic account of man's spiritual quest. But he never abandoned the insight that came to him at the University of Halle—that all of man's cultural and spiritual life could be illuminated by the "Protestant principle" of justification by faith; he was still working out its implications at his death on October 22, 1965.

BIBLIOGRAPHY. Autobiographical essays may be found in Tillich's writings: *The Protestant Era*, trans. by J.L. ADAMS (1948); *My Search for Absolutes* (1967); *On the Boundary* (1966); and *My Travel Diary: 1936*, ed. by J.C. BRAUER (1970). A good biographical study is ARNE UNHJEM, *Dynamics of Doubt: A Preface to Tillich* (1966).

The *Gesammelte Werke*, 11 vol. (1959-69), a collection of Tillich's writings, makes available his early and mostly untranslated works, including in vol. 1, *Frühe Hauptwerke*. *Systematic Theology*, 3 vol. (1951-63), is Tillich's major statement of the meaning of Christian faith, together with *The Courage to Be* (1952), and *The Dynamics of Faith* (1957).

Two important critical studies are CHRISTOPH RHEIN, *Paul Tillich: Philosoph und Theologe* (1957), with emphasis on Tillich's early development; and J.L. ADAMS, *Paul Tillich's Philosophy of Culture, Science, and Religion* (1965), the best overall view of Tillich's thought published in English. Other studies include: C.W. KEGLEY and R.W. BRETALL (eds.), *The Theology of Paul Tillich* (1952); D.H. KELSEY, *The Fabric of Paul Tillich's Theology* (1967); W.L. ROWE, *Religious Symbols and God: A Philosophical Study of Tillich's Theology* (1968); and R.P. SCHARLEMANN, *Reflection and Doubt in the Thought of Paul Tillich* (1969).

(A.U.)

Timbuktu

Timbuktu, or Tombouctou, is a West African city, important as the terminus of a trans-Saharan caravan route and as a centre of Islāmic culture in the period *c.* 1400–1600. It is located in the Republic of Mali, on the southern edge of the Sahara about eight miles north of the main bed of the Niger River.

History. In the almost total absence of archaeological data, knowledge of the city prior to the 19th century is based on local Arabic chronicles and on some references in the works of North African historians and travellers. Timbuktu was probably founded about AD 1100 as a seasonal camp by Tuareg nomads who came down from their winter grazing grounds at Arawan to pasture on the banks of the Niger during the summer. Gradually the encampment attracted traders and other travellers, who erected semipermanent straw huts around the Tuareg tents. Later, mud houses and a mosque were built, and a thorn stockade was replaced by a low wall.

At an uncertain date, but probably in the late 13th century, Timbuktu was incorporated within the expanding Mali Empire. In 1325 it was visited by the Mali sultan, Mansa

Mūsā, as he returned from a lavish pilgrimage to Mecca. He built a tower for the Great Mosque (Djingereyber) and a royal residence, the Madugu (the former has since been rebuilt many times, and of the latter no trace now remains). Shortly after this the city was annexed by the Mossi kingdom of Yatenga, but when the North African traveller Ibn Baṭṭūṭah visited in 1353, he found it again governed by Mali.

Harrison Forman

Sankorey Mosque in Timbuktu, the focus of Islāmic scholarship from the 15th century.

Timbuktu only began to assume real commercial importance in the mid-14th century. Although scarcely remarked on by Ibn Baṭṭūṭah, by 1375 it was indicated on a Catalan map. The growth of Timbuktu is to be associated with two factors. First, during the late 14th century, Dyula merchants from Mali began to open up routes from Jenne, south of Timbuktu, to the gold fields of the Begho area (modern Ghana–Ivory Coast border). Second, the route from central Mali to North Africa through Walata began to decline; in its place grew up the Jenne-Timbuktu route along the Niger, and the two cities became focal points in the gold-salt barter trade.

In the wake of increased trade and the influx of North African merchants, came the settlement of Muslim scholars and saints, who were to earn Timbuktu its wide renown in the 15th–16th centuries. It made little difference that the Tuareg regained control of the city in 1433; they ruled from the desert and, though they plundered periodically, trade and learning suffered little.

In 1468 Timbuktu was conquered by Sonni 'Alī, the Songhai ruler, during a movement of westerly expansion. He was generally ill-disposed to the city's Muslim scholars, but his successor—the first ruler of the new Askia dynasty, Mohammed I Askia of Songhai (reigned 1493–1528)—reversed the policy and used the scholarly elite as legal and moral counsellors. The Askia period as a whole (1493–1591) saw Timbuktu at the height of its commercial and intellectual development. Merchants from Wadan, Tuwat, Ghudāmis (Ghadames), Augila, and the cities of Morocco gathered there to buy gold and slaves in exchange for the Saharan salt of Taghaza and for North African cloth and horses. The city's scholars, many of whom had studied in Mecca or Egypt, attracted students from a wide area to their courses in Arabic grammar, Qur'ānic exegesis, theology, law, and other Islāmic sciences delivered in and around the Sankorey mosque. Although the city had a resident governor and tax collector appointed by the Askia, its judge (*qāḍī*) enjoyed considerable freedom of action, and his word carried weight with the Songhay rulers.

The year 1591 saw an abrupt change of fortune when a small but well-equipped force sent by Sultan Aḥmad al-Manṣūr of Morocco entered the city. The Moroccans already had defeated the Askia's army near Gao, and they now made Timbuktu the centre of their new administration. Two years later the city's scholars were arrested on suspicion of disaffection; some were killed during a struggle, others—mostly of the Aqit family, whose mem-

Commercial importance

The Moroccan conquest

bers had filled the office of *qāḍī* for a century—were exiled to Morocco.

The Moroccan conquest heralded an era of instability and stagnation that led to the commercial and intellectual decline of Timbuktu. The small Moroccan garrisons could not effectively protect the Niger Bend, which became prey to attacks from the Bambara, Fulani, and Tuareg. Intergroup rivalry among the Moroccans led to frequent changes of pasha (governor), especially after 1618, from which date the Moroccans in Timbuktu appointed from among their own number without reference to Marrakech.

In 1670 Timbuktu fell to the rising power of the Bambara kingdom of Segu. A century later (1787) the city was overrun by the Tuareg. Throughout the 17th and 18th centuries there were few decades untouched by either famine or epidemic, so that the population of Timbuktu had fallen from 25,000–40,000 in the 16th century to below 10,000 by *c.* 1800.

The 19th century saw other invasions. In 1826 the Fulani of Macina brought Timbuktu within their expanding theocratic state. On the death of their leader Shehu Ahmadu Lobbo (1844), an agreement was reached whereby the city regained a large measure of autonomy under the Moorish Kunta chief al-Bakkā'ī. It was again at the mercy of the Tuareg in 1893, when the French captured it.

French rule

The French presence was firmly established in 1894 by Maj. (later Field Marshal) Joseph Joffre, who constructed Fort Bonnier (now Fort el-Bekkay)—named after a French colonel killed by the Tuareg earlier that year. Timbuktu then began a new career as headquarters of a *cercle* (province) of French West Africa.

Timbuktu's history under French occupation is undistinguished. The French partly restored the city from the desolate condition in which they found it, but despite romantic illusions, no railway or tarmac road ever reached it. In 1960 it became part of the newly independent Republic of Mali.

It was in the 19th century that Europe obtained its first eyewitness accounts of Timbuktu since the publication of Leo Africanus' *Description of Africa* in 1550. The first European visitor to return alive (1828) was the Frenchman René Caillié, who stayed there in disguise (his British precursor, Maj. Alexander Gordon Laing, had been murdered by the Tuareg in 1826). The fullest description of Timbuktu is that of Heinrich Barth, a German scholar sent by the British government, who spent seven months in Timbuktu under the protection of al-Bakkā'ī in 1853–54.

Timbuktu today. Timbuktu is an administrative centre of the Republic of Mali. Small salt caravans from Taoudenni still arrive in winter, but there is no gold to offer in exchange, and trans-Saharan commerce is, in effect, dead. Apart from a recently introduced air service, the city still remains most easily accessible by camel and boat. Islāmic learning survives among a handful of aging scholars, and a Lycée Franco-Arabe teaches Arabic to the younger generation.

BIBLIOGRAPHY. Three locally written Arabic chronicles form the basis of our knowledge of Timbuktu prior to 1800. They are: AL-SAʿDI, *Ta'rīkh as-Sūdān*; KATI, *Ta'rīkh al-Fattāsh*; and the anonymous *Tadhkirat an-Nisyān*. All have been published with French translations (1900, 1913, and 1890 respectively). No book has been specifically devoted to the history of Timbuktu, but parts of H. BARTH, *Travels and Discoveries in North and Central Africa*, 5 vol. (1858; reprinted 4 vol., 1965); J.P. ROUCH, *Contribution à l'histoire des Songhay* (1953); and E.W. BOVILL, *Golden Trade of the Moors*, 2nd ed. rev. by R. HALLET (1968), contain useful material. A very readable if somewhat flamboyant account of Timbuktu and its history was written by a French journalist, FELIX DUBOIS, *Timbuctoo the Mysterious* (Eng. trans. 1897), often drawing on the local chronicles. More scholarly and up-to-date information may be found in J.F.A. AJAYI and M. CROWDER (eds.), *A History of West Africa*, vol. 1, ch. 3, 7, and 13 (1971).

(J.O.H.)

Time

One facet of human consciousness is the awareness of time. Men feel the passage of time in their personal ex-

perience, both psychic and physical, and observe it in their environment, both human (social) and nonhuman (animate and inanimate). Time, as experienced, is a one-way flow at a pace that is slow enough to be perceptible. (Actually, only material fluids flow; but, like psychic experiences in general, that of time can be described only in the language of material phenomena.) Men feel and think in the time flow. They also act in it, either seizing opportunities or missing them.   (A.J.T.)

The flow of time and man's experience of duration

I. Time and its role in the history of thought and action

NATURE AND DEFINITION OF TIME

Time appears to be more puzzling than space because it seems to flow or pass or else men seem to advance through it. But the passage or advance seems to be unintelligible. The question of how many seconds per second time flows (or one advances through it) is obviously an absurd one, for it suggests that the flow or advance comprises a rate of change with respect to something else—to a sort of hypertime. But if this hypertime itself flows, then a hyper-hypertime is required, and so on, ad infinitum. Again, if the world is thought of as spread out in space–time, it might be asked whether man's consciousness advances up a timelike direction of this world and, if so, how fast; whether future events pop into existence as the "now" reaches them or are there all along; and how such changes in space–time can be represented, since time is already within the picture. (Ordinary change can, of course, be represented in a space–time picture: for example, a particle at rest is represented by a straight line and an oscillating particle by a wavy line.)

In the face of these difficulties, philosophers tend to divide into two sorts: the "process philosophers" and the "philosophers of the manifold," respectively. Process philosophers—such as Alfred North Whitehead, an Anglo-American metaphysician who died in 1947—hold that the flow of time (or man's advance through it) is an important metaphysical fact. Like the French intuitionist Henri Bergson, they may hold that this flow can be grasped only by nonrational intuition. Bergson even held that the scientific concept of time as a dimension actually misrepresents reality.

Process philosophers versus philosophers of the manifold

Philosophers of the manifold hold that the flow of time or man's advance through time is an illusion. They argue, for example, that words such as past, future, and now, as well as the tenses of verbs, are indexical expressions that refer to the act of their own utterance. Hence, the alleged change of an event from being future to being past is an illusion. To say that the event is future is to assert that it is later than this utterance; then later yet, when one says that it is in the past, he asserts that it is earlier than that other utterance. "Past" and "future" are not real predicates of events, in this view; and change in respect of them is not a genuine change.

Again, although process philosophers think of the future as somehow open or indeterminate, whereas the past is unchangeable, fixed, determinate, philosophers of the manifold hold that it is as much nonsense to talk of changing the future as it is to talk of changing the past. If a person decides to point left rather than to point right, then pointing left *is* what the future was! Moreover, this thesis of the determinateness of the future, they argue, must not be confused with determinism, the theory that there are laws whereby later states of the universe may be deduced from earlier states (or vice versa). The philosophy of the manifold is neutral about this issue. Future events may well exist and yet not be connected in a sufficiently lawlike way with earlier ones.

One of the features of time that puzzled the Platonist Augustine, in the 5th century AD, was the difficulty of defining it. In contemporary philosophy of language, however (influenced by Ludwig Wittgenstein, a Cambridge philosopher), no mystery is seen in this task. Learning to handle the word "time" involves a multiplicity of verbal skills, including the ability to handle such connected words as "earlier," "later," "now," "second," and "hour." These verbal skills have to be picked up in very complex ways (partly by ostension), and it is not surprising that the meaning of the word "time" cannot be distilled into a neat verbal definition. (It is not, for example, an abbreviating word like "bachelor.")

The philosophy of time bears powerfully on men's emotions. Not only do they regret the past, they also fear the future, not least because the alleged flow of time seems to be sweeping them toward their deaths, as swimmers are swept toward a waterfall. (J.J.C.S.)

PRESCIENTIFIC CONCEPTIONS OF TIME AND THEIR INFLUENCE

Temporal existence, death, and survival

The individual's experience and observation of time. The irreversibility and inexorability of the passage of time is borne in on a human being by the fact of death. Unlike other living creatures, he knows that his life may be cut short at any moment and that, even if he attains the full expectation of a human life, his growth is bound to be followed by eventual decay and, in due time, death.

Although there is no generally accepted evidence that death is not the conclusive end of life, it is a tenet of some religions (*e.g.*, of Zoroastrianism, Judaism, Christianity, and Islām) that death is followed by everlasting life elsewhere—in *sheol*, hell, or heaven—and that eventually there will be a universal physical resurrection. Others (*e.g.*, Buddhists, Orphics, Pythagoreans, and Plato) have held that people are reborn in the time flow of life on Earth and that the notion that a man has only one life on Earth is the illusion of a lost memory. It is said that the Buddha recollected all of his previous lives. The Greek philosophers Pythagoras and Empedocles, of the 6th and early 5th centuries BC, whose lives probably overlapped that of the Buddha, are likewise said to have recollected some of their previous lives. Such rebirths, they held, would continue to recur any number of times unless a person should succeed in breaking the vicious circle (releasing himself from the "sorrowful wheel") by strenuous ascetic performances.

The belief that a man's life in time on Earth is repetitive may have been an inference from the observed repetitiveness of phenomena in his environment. The day-and-night cycle and the annual cycle of the seasons dominated the conduct of human life until the recent harnessing of inanimate physical forces in the Industrial Revolution made it possible for work to be carried on for 24 hours a day throughout the year—under cover, by artificial light, and at an artificial temperature. There is also the generation cycle, which the Industrial Revolution has not suppressed: the generations still replace each other, in spite of the lengthening of life expectancies. In some societies it has been customary to give a man's son a different name but to give his grandson the same name. To name father and son differently is an admission that generations change; but to name grandfather and grandson the same is perhaps an intimation that the grandson is the grandfather reincarnate.

Thus, though every human being has the experience of irreversible change in his own life, he also observes cyclic change in his environment; hence the adherents of some religions and philosophies have inferred that, despite appearances, time flows cyclically for the individual human being, too.

Interpretations of time in different ages and lands

The human experience and observation of time has been variously interpreted. Parmenides, an Italiote Greek (Eleatic) philosopher (6th–5th century BC) and Zeno, his fellow townsman and disciple, found that change is logically inconceivable and that logic is a surer indicator of reality than experience; thus, despite appearances, reality is unitary and motionless. In this view, time is an illusion. The illusoriness of the world that "flows" in time is also to be found in some Indian philosophy. The Buddha and, among the Greeks, Plato and Plotinus, all held that life in the time flow, though not wholly illusory, is at best a low-grade condition by comparison, respectively, with the Buddhist Nirvāṇa (in which desires are extinguished) and with the Platonic world of Ideas; *i.e.*, of incorporeal timeless exemplars, of which phenomena in the time flow are imperfect and ephemeral copies.

It has been held, however—*e.g.*, by disciples of the Greek philosopher Heraclitus—that the time flow is of the essence of reality. Others have held that life in the time flow, though it may be wretched, is nevertheless momentous; for it is here that a man decides his destiny. In the Buddhist view, a person's conduct in any one of his successive lives on Earth will increase or diminish his prospects of eventually breaking out of the cycle of recurrent births. For those who believe in only one earthly life, however, the momentousness of life in the time flow is still greater because this life will be followed by an everlasting life at a destination decided by conduct in this brief and painful testing time. The view that life in time on Earth is a probation for weal or woe in an everlasting future has often been associated—as it was by the Iranian prophet Zoroaster (*c.* 600 BC)—with a belief in a general judgment of all who have ever lived to be held on a common judgment day, which will be the end of time. The belief in an immediate individual judgment was also held in pharaonic Egypt. Both of these beliefs have been adopted by Jews, Christians, and Muslims.

Cyclic view of time in the philosophy of history. The foregoing diverse interpretations of the nature and significance of the individual human being's experience and observation of time differ sharply from each other, and they have led to equally sharp differences in views of human history and of ultimate reality and in prescriptions for the conduct, both collective and individual, of human life. Thinkers have been divided between holders of the cyclic view and holders of the one-way view of time and between believers in the different prescriptions for the conduct of life that these differing views have suggested. Variations in the two basic views of time and in the corresponding codes of conduct have been among the salient characteristics distinguishing the principal civilizations and philosophies and higher religions that have appeared in history to date.

Environmental recurrences and religion. The cyclic theory of time has been held in regard to the three fields of religion, of history (both human and cosmic), and of personal life. That this view arose from the observation of recurrences in man's environment is most conspicuously seen in the field of religion. The observation of the generation cycle has been reflected in the cult of ancestors, important in Chinese religion and also in older civilizations and in precivilizational societies. The observation of the annual cycle of the seasons and its crucial effect on agriculture is reflected in a ceremony in which the emperor of China used to plow the first furrow of the current year; in the ceremonial opening of a breach in the dike of the Nile to let the annual floodwaters irrigate the land; and in the annual "sacred marriage," performed by a priest and priestess representing a god and goddess, which was deemed to ensure the continuing fertility of Babylonia. A cycle longer than that of the seasons is represented by the recurrent *avatāra*s (epiphanies, incarnate, on Earth) of the Hindu god Viṣṇu (Vishnu) and in the corresponding series of buddhas and *bodhisattva*s (potential buddhas). Although the only historical Buddha was Siddhārtha Gautama (6th–5th century BC), in the mythology of the northern school of Buddhism (the Mahāyāna), the identity of the historical Buddha has been almost effaced by a long vista of putative buddhas extending through previous and future times.

In contrast to northern Buddhism and to Vaiṣṇava Hinduism, Christianity holds that the incarnation of God in Jesus was a unique event; yet the rite of the Eucharist, in which Christ's self-sacrifice is held by Catholic and Eastern Orthodox Christians to be reperformed, is celebrated every day by thousands of priests and the nature of this rite has suggested to some scholars that it originated in an annual festival at the culmination of the agricultural year. In this interpretation, the bread that is Christ's body and the wine that is his blood associate him with the annually dying gods Adonis, Osiris, and Attis—the divinities, inherent in the vital and vitalizing power of man's crops, who die in order that men may eat and drink and live. "Unless a grain of wheat falls into the earth and dies, it remains alone; but, if it dies, it bears much fruit" (John 12:24).

Seasons, generations, eons

The cyclic view in various cultures.   The cyclic view of history, both cosmic and human, has been prevalent among the Hindus and the pre-Christian Greeks, the Chinese, and the pre-Columbian peoples of Central America; and it has reappeared in the modern West, although this civilization was originally Christian—that is, was nurtured on a religion that sees time as a one-way flow and not as a cyclic one.

Yin–Yang,
Love–
Strife,
kalpas

The Chinese, Hindus, and Greeks saw cosmic time as moving in an alternating rhythm, classically expressed in the Chinese concept of the alternation between Yin, the passive female principle, and Yang, the dynamic male principle. When either Yin or Yang goes to extremes, it lops over into the other principle, which is its correlative and complement in consequence of being its opposite. In the philosophy of Empedocles, an early Greek pluralist, the equivalents of Yin and Yang were Love and Strife. Empedocles revolted against the denial of the reality of motion and plurality that was made by his Eleatic predecessors on the strength of mere logic. He broke up the Eleatics' motionless, and therefore timeless, unitary reality into a movement of four elements that alternately were harmonized by Love and set at variance by Strife. Empedocles' Love and Strife, like Yin and Yang, each lopped over into the other when they had gone to extremes.

Plato translated Empedocles' concept from psychological into theistic terms. At the outset, in his view, the gods guide the cosmos, and they then leave it to its own devices. But when the cosmos, thus left to itself, has brought itself to the brink of disaster, the gods resume control at the eleventh hour—and these two phases of its condition alternate with each other endlessly. The recurrence of alternating phases in which, at the darkest hour, catastrophe is averted by divine intervention is similarly an article of Vaiṣṇava Hindu faith. In guessing the lengths of the recurrent eons (kalpas), the Hindus arrived, intuitively, at figures of the magnitude of those reached by modern astronomers through meticulous observations and calculations. Similarly, the pre-Columbian Mayas rivalled the modern Westerners and the Hindus in the scale on which they envisaged the flow of time, and they kept an astonishingly accurate time count by inventing a set of interlocking cycles of different wavelengths.

Plato and Aristotle took it for granted that human society, as well as the cosmos, has been, and will continue to be, wrecked and rehabilitated any number of times. This rhythm can be discerned, as a matter of historical fact, in the histories of the pharaonic Egyptian and of the Chinese civilizations during the three millennia that elapsed, in each of them, between its first political unification and its final disintegration. The prosperity that had been conferred on a peasant society by political unity and peace turned into adversity when the cost of large-scale administration and defense became too heavy for an unmechanized economy to bear. In each instance, the unified state then broke up—only to be reunited for the starting of another similar cycle. The Muslim historian Ibn Khaldūn, writing in the 14th century AD, observed the same cyclic rhythm in the histories of the successive conquests of sedentary populations by pastoral nomads.

Cultural
mor-
phology
in Vico
and
Spengler

In the modern West, an Italian philosopher of history, Giambattista Vico, observed that the phases through which Western civilization had passed had counterparts in the history of the antecedent Greco-Roman civilization. Thanks to a subsequent increase in the number of civilizations known to Western students of cultural morphology, Oswald Spengler, a German philosopher of history, was able, in the early 20th century, to make a comparative study of civilizations over a much broader spectrum than that of Vico. The comparison of different civilizations or of successive periods of order and disorder in Chinese or in pharaonic Egyptian history implied, of course, that, in human affairs, recurrence is a reality.

The application of the cyclic view to the life of a human being in the hypothesis of rebirth was mentioned earlier. This hypothesis relaxes man's anxiety about being annihilated through death by replacing it with a no less agonizing anxiety about being condemned to a potentially endless series of rebirths. The strength of the reincarnation-ist's anxiety can be gauged by the severity of the self-mortification to which he resorts to liberate himself from the "sorrowful wheel." Among the peoples who have not believed in rebirth, the pharaonic Egyptians have taken the offensive against death and decay with the greatest determination: they embalmed corpses; they built colossal tombs; and, in the Book of the Dead, they provided instructions and spells for ensuring for that portion of the soul that did not hover around the sarcophagus an acquittal in the post mortem judgment and an entry into a blissful life in another world. No other human society has succeeded in achieving this degree of indestructibility despite the ravages of time.

One-way view of time in the philosophy of history. When the flow of time is held to be not recurrent but one-way, it can be conceived of as having a beginning and perhaps an end. Some thinkers have felt that such limits can be imagined only if there is some timeless power that has set time going and intends or is set to stop it. A god who creates and then annihilates time, if he is held to be omnipotent, is often credited with having done this with a benevolent purpose that he is carrying out according to plan. The omnipotent god's plan, in this view, governs the time flow and is made manifest to man in progressive revelations through the prophets—from Abraham, by way of Moses, Isaiah, and Jesus, to the prophet Muḥammad (as Muslims believe).

Salvation
history
and the
"axis age"

This belief in *Heilsgeschichte* (salvational history) has been derived by Islām and Christianity from Judaism and Zoroastrianism. Late in the 12th century, the Christian seer Joachim of Fiore saw this divinely ordained spiritual progress in the time flow as unfolding in a series of three ages—those of the Father, the Son, and the Spirit. Karl Jaspers, a 20th-century Western philosopher, has discerned an "axis age"—*i.e.*, a turning point in human history—in the 6th century BC, when Confucius, the Buddha, Zoroaster, Deutero-Isaiah, and Pythagoras were alive contemporaneously. If the "axis age" is extended backward in time to the original Isaiah's generation and forward to Muḥammad's, it may perhaps be recognized as the age in which men first sought to make direct contact with the ultimate spiritual reality behind phenomena instead of making such communication only indirectly through their nonhuman and social environments.

The belief in an omnipotent creator god, however, has been challenged. The creation of time, or of anything else, out of nothing is difficult to imagine; and, if God is not a creator but is merely a shaper, his power is limited by the intractability of the independent material with which he has had to work. Plato, in the *Timaeus*, conceived of God as being a nonomnipotent shaper and thus accounted for the manifest element of evil in phenomena. Marcion, a 2nd-century Christian heretic, inferred from the evil in phenomena that the creator was bad and held that a "stranger god" had come to redeem the bad creator's work at the benevolent stranger's cost. Zoroaster saw the phenomenal world as a battlefield between a bad god and a good one and saw time as the duration of this battle. Though he held that the good god was destined to be the victor, a god who needs to fight and win is not omnipotent. In an attenuated form, this evil adversary appears in the three Judaic religions as Satan.

Evolu-
tionary and
dialectical
views

Observation of historical phenomena suggests that, in spite of the manifestness of evil, there has in truth been progress in the history of life on this planet, culminating in the emergence of man, who knows himself to be a sinner yet feels himself to be something better than inanimate matter. Charles Darwin, in his theory of the selection of mutations by the environment, sought to vindicate apparent progress in the organic realm without recourse to an extraneous god. In the history of Greek thought, the counterpart of such mutations was the swerving of atoms. After Empedocles had broken up the indivisible, motionless, and timeless reality of Parmenides and Zeno into four elements played upon alternately by Love and Strife, it was a short step for the Atomists of the 5th century BC Leucippus and Democritus to break up reality still further into an innumerable host of minute atoms moving in time through a vacuum. Granting that one single atom had once made a single slight swerve, the build-up of observed phenomena could be accounted for on Darwinian lines. Democritus' account of evolution survives in the fifth book of *De rerum natura*, written by a 1st-century-BC Roman poet, Lucretius. The credibility of both Democritus' and Darwin's accounts of evolution depends on the assumption that time is real and that its flow has been extraordinarily long.

Heraclitus had seen in phenomena a harmony of opposites in tension with each other and had concluded that War (*i.e.*, Empedocles' Strife and the Chinese Yang) "is father of all and king of all." This vision of Strife as being the dominant and creative force is grimmer than that of Strife alternating on equal terms with Love and Yang with Yin. In the 19th-century West, Heraclitus' vision has been revived in the view of G.W.F. Hegel, a German Idealist, that progress occurs through a synthesis resulting from an encounter between a thesis and an antithesis. In political terms, Heraclitus' vision has reappeared in Karl Marx's concept of an encounter between the bourgeoisie and the proletariat and the emergence of a classless society without a government.

Apocalyptic views In the Zoroastrian and Jewish–Christian–Islāmic vision of the time flow, time is destined to be consummated—as depicted luridly in the Revelation to John—in a terrifying climax. Present-day man has recently become aware that history has been accelerating—and this at an accelerating rate. The present generation has been conscious of this increase of acceleration in its own lifetime; and the advance in man's knowledge of his past has revealed, in retrospect, that the acceleration began about 30,000 years ago, with the transition from the Lower to the Upper Paleolithic Period, and that it has taken successive "great leaps forward" with the invention of agriculture, with the dawn of civilization, and with the progressive harnessing —within the last two centuries—of the titanic physical forces of inanimate nature. The approach of the climax foreseen intuitively by the prophets is being felt, and feared, as a coming event. Its imminence is, today, not an article of faith; it is a datum of observation and experience.   (A.J.T.)

EARLY MODERN AND 19TH-CENTURY
SCIENTIFIC PHILOSOPHIES OF TIME

Isaac Newton distinguished absolute time from "relative, apparent, and common time" as measured by the apparent motions of the fixed stars, as well as by terrestrial clocks. His absolute time was an ideal scale of time that made the laws of mechanics simpler, and its discrepancy with apparent time was attributed to such things as irregularities in the motion of the Earth. Insofar as these motions were explained by Newton's mechanics (or at least could not be shown to be inexplicable), the procedure was vindicated. Similarly, in his notion of absolute space, Newton was really getting at the concept of an inertial system. Nevertheless, the notion of space and time as absolute metaphysical entities was encouraged by Newton's views and formed an important part of the philosophy of Immanuel Kant (died 1804), a German critical philosopher, for whom space and time were "phenomenally real" (part of the world as described by science) but "noumenally unreal" (not a part of the unknowable world of things in themselves). Kant argued for the noumenal unreality of space and time on the basis of certain antinomies that he claimed to find in these notions—that the universe had a beginning, for example, and yet (by another argument) could not have had a beginning. In a letter dated 1798, he wrote that the antinomies had been instrumental in arousing him from his "dogmatic slumber" (pre-critical philosophy). Modern advances in logic and mathematics, however, have convinced most philosophers that the antinomies contain fallacies.

Static versus dynamic systems Newtonian mechanics, as studied in the 18th century, was mostly concerned with periodic systems that, on a large scale, remain constant throughout time. Particularly notable was the proof of the stability of the solar system that was formulated by Pierre-Simon, marquis de Laplace, a mathematical astronomer. Interest in systems that develop through time came about in the 19th century

as a result of the theories of the British geologist Sir Charles Lyell, and others, and the Darwinian theory of evolution. These theories led to a number of biologically inspired metaphysical systems, which were often—as in the French evolutionary philosopher Henri Bergson and the Anglo-American process philosopher Alfred North Whitehead—rather romantic and contrary to the essentially mechanistic spirit of Darwin himself (and also of present-day molecular biology).   (J.J.C.S.)

II. Time as systematized in modern scientific society

TIME MEASUREMENT: GENERAL CONCEPTS

Time measurement involves two quantities: (1) epoch, which specifies the moment when an instantaneous event occurs in the sense of time of day, and (2) time interval, or duration of a continued event. The progress of any phenomenon that undergoes regular changes may be used to measure time. Such phenomena occur in astronomy, physics, chemistry, geology, and biology. To measure time some quantitative process is necessary. Two such processes have been adopted, and these define two, independent, fundamental measures of time.

Dynamical and atomic time distinguished The concept of dynamical time is based on the laws of motion and gravitation published by Isaac Newton in 1687; this kind of time could be obtained in theory from the motions of any bodies subject only to the force of gravitation. It is obtained in practice from the orbital motions of planets and satellites for which nongravitational forces are negligible or small and is called Ephemeris Time (ET). (An ephemeris is a table that lists positions of such bodies as planets and satellites as functions of time.)

Electromagnetic time, the other measure of time, is based on the laws of electricity announced by James Clerk Maxwell in 1864. As measured through the operation of an atomic clock by counting cycles of electromagnetic radiation, it is called atomic time (AT). A fundamental distinction between the two types of time is that dynamical time involves the motions of material bodies whereas electromagnetic time does not.

Rotational time. Rotational time, in forms such as sidereal (measured by the stars) and mean solar time, is based on the rotation of the Earth about its axis. It is not dynamical time in the sense defined above; variations in rotational speed with a range of one part in 10,000,000 have occurred since 1820, for example, with respect to Ephemeris Time and atomic time. The speed of rotation is affected by winds, tides, turbulent motions within the Earth's core, and other geophysical phenomena, the effects of which cannot be computed as accurately as can those of gravitation. Rotational time, even if it is variable with respect to Ephemeris and atomic times, remains in common usage because it is of necessity required for civil purposes, navigation, geodetic surveying, and space-vehicle tracking.

Under the present system of time measurement, epoch is stated in terms of mean solar time and time interval in terms of atomic time. Ephemeris Time is used in celestial mechanics but not for common purposes.

Newtonian time and relativity. Time in the Newtonian sense was mentioned above as if there were a single absolute time. According to this concept, all events that occur anywhere in the universe could be arranged in a single, ordered sequence. Thus, of two events, *A* and *B*, either *A* would occur before *B*, *B* before *A*, or the two would be simultaneous. This intuitive concept of time was altered drastically by Albert Einstein in 1905. According to the theory of special relativity, separate coordinate systems in uniform relative motion each have a different time system, and none is preferred. Absolute simultaneity disappears in relativity, and it is possible that event *A* occurs before *B* as measured by the clocks of one coordinate system but that the reverse occurs according to the clocks of another system.

A multiplicity of times exists in relativity, and the role of time in the physical universe is more complex under relativity than under Newtonian mechanics. Fortunately, however, all time measurements of which man has knowledge have been made on or near the surface of the

Earth and for the most part do not involve relativity. This section of the article, therefore, begins with an investigation of time as if it were single valued. Relativistic effects are discussed later.

Astronomical time divisions. Measures of astronomical time are based upon (1) the rotation of the Earth about its axis, (2) the orbital motion of the Earth about the Sun, and (3) the orbital motion of the Moon about the Earth. The Earth's axis undergoes motions similar to the progressive and oscillating motions of a top. In consequence of these motions and their combinations, numerous kinds of days, months, and years are defined, including those listed in the accompanying Table. Those of

Astronomical Time Divisions

day	month	year
mean solar	synodic	tropical
apparent solar	sidereal	sidereal
mean sidereal	anomalistic	Besselian
true sidereal	draconic	eclipse
ephemeris	tropical	Julian

chief interest are: the mean solar day; the synodic month, the interval from New Moon to New Moon; and the tropical year, the interval from equinox to the corresponding equinox. (Equinoxes, two of which occur each year, are the moments when the Sun crosses the celestial Equator.) Seasons are repeated, on the average, at intervals of a tropical year.

The week is not specifically related to any astronomical cycle. The period may have originated as an interval for market days; weeks of five, six, and 10 days have been observed. The seven-day week was in use in ancient times in Chaldea and was established as a measure of time in biblical times under the Mosaic Law. It may be related to the fact that the successive phases of the Moon (*e.g.*, new, first quarter, full, and last quarter) are nearly seven days apart; the average is 7.38. It is desired that the average number of calendar days in a year (Y_c) shall nearly equal the number of mean solar days in a tropical year (Y_t). This is achieved by designating some years as leap years. Values of Y_c are 365.25 in the Julian calendar and 365.2425 in the Gregorian calendar. The quantity Y_t varies slowly; its value in 1970 was about 365.24219 mean solar days. Because of variations in speed of rotation, Y_t cannot be predicted accurately for many centuries in advance beyond the fourth decimal. Hence, attempts to improve the calendar by modifying the leap-year rule are of doubtful value (see CALENDAR).

> The calendar days in a tropical year

ROTATIONAL TIME

The Earth's rotation causes the stars and the Sun to appear to rise each day in the east and set in the west. The apparent solar day is measured by the interval of time between two successive passages of the Sun across the observer's meridian, a great circle in the sky passing through the zenith and through the celestial poles. One sidereal day (very nearly) is measured by the interval of time between two similar passages of a star. Fuller treatments of astronomical reference points and planes are given in the articles ASTRONOMICAL MAPS; and MECHANICS, CELESTIAL.

The plane in which the Earth revolves about the Sun is called the ecliptic. As seen from the Earth, the Sun moves eastward on the ecliptic 360° per year, almost one degree per day. As a result, an apparent solar day is nearly four minutes longer, on the average, than a sidereal day. The difference varies, however, from 3 minutes 35 seconds to 4 minutes 26 seconds during the year because of the Earth's elliptical orbit, in which at different times of the year it moves at slightly different rates, and because of a 23½° inclination of the ecliptic to the Equator. In consequence, apparent solar time is nonuniform with respect to dynamical time. A sundial indicates apparent solar time but becomes slightly fast or slow by civil, or mean solar (clock), time according to the time of year.

The 17th-century introduction of clocks and watches that marked a uniform rate of the passage of time

made apparent solar time unsuitable for civil use. Therefore, mean solar time was introduced; it is defined as a measure of the rotation of the Earth. The difference between apparent solar time and mean solar time, called the equation of time, varies from zero to about 16 minutes.

The measures of sidereal, apparent solar, and mean solar time are defined by the hour angles of certain points, real or fictitious, in the sky. Hour angle is the angle, taken to be positive to the west, measured along the celestial equator between an observer's meridian and the hour circle (a great circle passing through the poles) on which some celestial point or object lies. Hour angles are measured from zero through 24 hours.

Sidereal time is the hour angle of the vernal equinox, a reference point that is one of the two intersections of the celestial equator and the ecliptic. Because of a small periodic oscillation, or wobble, of the Earth's axis, called nutation, there is a distinction between the true and mean equinoxes. The difference between true and mean sidereal times, defined by the two equinoxes, varies from zero to about one second.

Apparent solar time is the hour angle of the centre of the true Sun plus 12 hours.

Mean solar time is 12 hours plus the hour angle of the centre of the fictitious mean Sun. This is a point that moves along the celestial equator with constant speed and that coincides with the true Sun on the average. In practice, mean solar time is not obtained from observations of the Sun. Instead, sidereal time is determined from observations of the transit across the meridian of stars, and the result is transformed by means of a quadratic formula to obtain mean solar time.

> Mean solar time

Time units. The mean solar day is divided as follows: one mean solar day equals 24 mean solar hours; one mean solar hour equals 60 mean solar minutes; one mean solar minute equals 60 mean solar seconds; thus one mean solar day equals 86,400 mean solar seconds. Analogous divisions are used for other kinds of time—for example, for sidereal, Ephemeris, and atomic time.

Reckoning of days and hours. The day begins at midnight and runs through 24 hours. In the 24-hour system of reckoning, used in Europe and by military agencies of the United States, the hours and minutes are given as a four digit number. Thus 0028 means 28 minutes past midnight, and 1240 means 40 minutes past noon. Also, 2400 of May 15 is the same as 0000 of May 16. This system allows no uncertainty as to the epoch designated.

In the 12-hour system there are two sets of 12 hours; those from midnight to noon are designated AM (ante meridiem, "before noon"), and those from noon to midnight are designated PM (post meridiem, "after noon"). The use of AM and PM to designate either noon or midnight can cause ambiguity. To designate noon, either the word noon or 1200 should be used. To designate midnight without causing ambiguity, the two dates between which it falls should be given unless the 24-hour notation is used. Thus, midnight may be written: May 15-16 or 0000 May 16.

Mean solar time of the Greenwich (England) meridian is denoted Universal Time (UT). Equivalent designations are Greenwich Mean Time (GMT), used in air and sea navigation, and Z, used in communications. The term UT is used in astronomy and other scientific work.

Zone time. Local mean solar time depends upon longitude; it is advanced by one hour for every 15° to the east. To avoid the inconvenience of numerous differences in local times, an international system of 24 time zones was adopted in 1884. Standard time is the same everywhere within a zone, the boundaries of which may zigzag. The time in any standard zone differs from UT by an integral number of hours: minutes and seconds are the same.

The International Date Line is a zigzag line in the mid-Pacific Ocean near 180° longitude. When travelling across it westward a calendar day is added; one day is dropped in passing eastward.

During World War I, daylight-saving time was adopted in various countries; clocks were advanced one hour to save fuel by reducing the need for artificial light in evening hours. During World War II, all clocks in the United

States were kept one hour ahead of standard time for the interval February 9, 1942–September 30, 1945, with no changes made in summer. Since then, the time in a large part of Europe has been kept one hour ahead of standard zone time without any change during summer. Beginning in 1967, by act of Congress, the United States observes daylight-saving time in summer, though state legislatures retain the power to pass exempting laws, and a few have done so.

Practical determination of rotational time. The determination of time is a specialized branch of astronomy that is usually conducted by a government observatory. The basic definitions concerning time determination are standardized by the International Astronomical Union. The Bureau International de l'Heure (International Time Bureau) at Paris provides data needed for the uniform reduction of observations, and it coordinates results.

The determination of Universal Time (UT) requires (1) a telescope for observing or automatically recording the crossing of a star of known position over a celestial reference line, usually a meridian; and (2) a clock on which the time of crossing is recorded. The observations give the difference between UT and the clock. One may then obtain UT thereafter by applying the difference to the clock time.

Coordinated time. The initial values of Universal Time obtained at various observatories, denoted UT0, differ slightly because of polar motion. A correction is added for each observatory to convert UT0 into UT1. An empirical correction to take account of annual changes in the speed of rotation is then added to convert UT1 to UT2.

Coordinated Universal Time, denoted UTC, is obtained from an atomic clock that is adjusted in epoch so as to remain close to UT2; the frequency of a clock on UTC is constant, that of atomic time.

The leap second

Beginning January 1, 1972, the practice was adopted of keeping UTC within about 0.5 second of UT2 by resetting a clock on UTC by exactly one second when necessary. Clocks on UTC had been retarded about once per year. Normally, the last second of each day is 23 hours 59 minutes 59 seconds, and the next second is 0 hour 00 minute 00 second of the next day. When clocks are to be retarded, however, that next second is designated 23 hours 59 minutes 60 seconds of the same day, and the second immediately following is designated 0 hour 00 minute 00 second of the next day. The day on which the leap second is inserted is selected by the International Time Bureau.

Precise clocks are maintained to indicate UTC, and time signals are broadcast on this system. In consequence, Universal Coordinated Time is the reference for time in common use.

EPHEMERIS TIME

Ephemeris Time (ET) may be obtained from the orbital motion of any planet or satellite. The orbital motion of the Earth about the Sun, as developed mathematically in the American astronomer Simon Newcomb's *Tables of the Sun* (1895), has been adopted to define the basic measure of ET. (The Earth and Sun are 180° apart; that is, opposite each other in the plane of the ecliptic, so that an observation of the Sun with respect to the stars gives the orbital position of the Earth.) Newcomb's *Tables* are used to form a solar ephemeris, or a table that gives the Sun's coordinates for successive values of Ephemeris Time.

An observed position of the Sun is obtained with a meridian circle, an instrument that works on the same principles as a surveyor's transit but is somewhat larger. The time at which such a position should be reached is found from the solar ephemeris, and this is the Ephemeris Time at which the Sun had the observed position.

Values of Ephemeris Time are also obtained from observations of the Moon by using the lunar ephemeris for the observed position. The lunar ephemeris, however, contains an empirical, nongravitational term, which arises from tides raised in the Earth by the Moon. The value of Ephemeris Time obtained from the Moon is, there-

fore, not strictly dynamical time, and the lunar ephemeris must be brought into accord with the solar ephemeris from time to time. In practice, the Moon is generally used to determine Ephemeris Time because of its rapid orbital motion. Very accurate positions of the Moon are obtained visually by observations of occultations of stars (an occultation is the passage of the Moon across the line of sight to the star, so that the star vanishes for a short time). Its position can also be measured with a meridian circle or photographically.

PRINCIPLES OF TIME MEASUREMENT

Chronometers. Time-measuring instruments can be astronomical, mechanical, or atomic depending upon the physical level to which reference is made.

Astronomical time-measuring instruments. The type of telescope formerly used to obtain accurate star positions from which to calculate precise times consisted of a small, visual transit instrument that could be moved only in the plane of the meridian. As much the same principles are still used, a brief description of them is of value here. An observer generated a signal at the instant that the image of the star was seen to cross a spider thread (the thinnest-possible cross hair obtainable up to the 1930s) in the meridian plane. This instrument has been largely replaced by two other, more accurate instruments that determine latitude as well as time.

Zenith tube and astrolabe

The first is the photographic zenith tube (usually called the PZT). It was adapted to determine time in 1934 at the United States Naval Observatory. The PZT is fixed with the telescope tube vertical; it photographs only stars that transit near the zenith. A motor drives the photographic plate so as to track the stars. Four exposures are made with the lens and plate reversed 180° between exposures. Signals initiated by the moving plate are recorded by a clock. Reflection from the surface of a mercury basin determines the vertical direction automatically and very accurately.

The second instrument, called an astrolabe, was designed about 1956 and utilizes a 60° prism and a basin of mercury to form the direct and reflected images of a star. These images coincide when the altitude of the star is exactly 60°. An observer manipulates a motor so as to keep the two images parallel to a spider thread (see above: a real spider thread was used in the 19th century as the best and thinnest cross hair; the term is now used for any such hair, no matter what the material used). The instant when the altitude is 60° is recorded automatically.

Mechanical clocks. A clock is a device that indicates intervals or the passage of time. It consists of two parts: (1) a part that vibrates or one in which some other repetitive event occurs at equal intervals of time; and (2) a counting part, which indicates the total count for an interval usually with hands and a dial or in digital form. An important achievement in timekeeping history was the discovery, about 1583, by Galileo that the oscillation period of a pendulum is virtually independent of the amplitude of its swing. The Dutch mathematician-astronomer Christiaan Huygens derived the theory of the pendulum and had the first pendulum clock constructed in 1656. Numerous improvements were subsequently made, and pendulum clocks reached a fairly high stage of precision by about 1925. The rates of the best pendulum clocks are constant to about 0.001 second per day. Pendulum clocks, not long ago the most exact timepieces known in the world, no longer are used in precise timekeeping, which for modern purposes in the 1970s must reach even higher precision. For detailed information concerning the phenomena on which atomic time is based, see ATOMIC STRUCTURE; ELECTROMAGNETIC RADIATION; ELECTRICITY; SPECTROSCOPY, PRINCIPLES OF. In the following sections, only a general summary can be made.

Quartz-crystal clocks. Quartz-crystal clocks work by exerting an extremely accurate control of the frequency of vibrations that measure time. A quartz crystal, if deformed, acquires a difference in electric potential across certain of its faces. Conversely, a difference in electric potential applied across these faces will deform the crystal. This property, known as the piezoelectric effect, enables a quartz crystal to control the frequency of an electrical circuit; the frequency is that of the mechanical vibration of the crystal. Frequency f and period p of a cyclic occurrence are related, the frequency being the inverse of the period. In symbols, $f = 1/p$. Frequency is measured in cycles per second (cps); this unit is alternatively called the hertz (Hz). Frequently used multiple units are: kilohertz (kHz, 10^3 cps); megahertz (MHz, 10^6 cps); gigahertz (GHz, 10^9 cps); and terahertz (THz, 10^{12} cps).

Quartz-crystal clocks were introduced into timekeeping about 1930. Early performance was relatively poor; clocks were subject to large accelerations in rate and to frequent stoppages, often accompanied by sudden changes in rate. Performance improved, and, by 1960, highly reliable, precise quartz-crystal clocks were available. The best of them had very low accelerations, about one part in 10^{11} per day, which, however, could not be predicted accurately.

Atomic clocks. A new era in timekeeping was introduced with the development of the atomic clock. An atomic clock uses quantum transitions (energy changes) within atoms to produce extremely regular waves of electromagnetic radiation; like the recurrent events in other kinds of clocks, these waves are then counted. To be useful, the waves from individual atoms or molecules must be in phase with one another. Such radiation is called coherent (see LASER AND MASER).

Use of
microwave
spectral
linesThe frequency, ν, of the radiation produced by a particular quantum transition depends upon the initial energy E_1 and the final energy E_2, and, if h is the number known as Planck's constant, the frequency is the difference between E_1 and E_2 divided by Planck's constant. In symbols this can be written: $\nu = (E_1 - E_2)/h$. Each transition produces a spectral line. The frequency of visible radiation (light waves) is about 5×10^{14} Hz, too high to permit counting of individual cycles. The development of methods of generating frequencies on the order of 10^{10} Hz opened the possibility of using spectral lines in the one-centimetre microwave region of the spectrum for frequency control. In 1946 principles of the use of spectral lines in the construction of an oscillator were described, and in 1947 an oscillator controlled by a quantum transition of the ammonia (NH_3) molecule was constructed. An ammonia-controlled clock was built in 1949 at the National Bureau of Standards, Washington, D.C. In 1954, an oscillator of higher precision, called a maser, which also utilized ammonia, was developed.

Cesium clocks. About 1939 a technique of projecting a beam of atoms and molecules was developed to facilitate their study. This led to several attempts to construct a cesium-beam atomic clock. In June 1955 a cesium-beam atomic standard of high precision was first placed in operation at the National Physical Laboratory, Teddington, England. From 1955 to 1958 a joint experiment was carried out by the National Physical Laboratory and the United States Naval Observatory to determine the relationship between the frequency of cesium and the second of Ephemeris Time as determined from observations of the Moon with a dual-rate moon camera. The value obtained for the ephemeris second was 9,192,631,770 cycles. Cesium-beam oscillators were subsequently constructed at a number of laboratories. Small commercial models weighing about 65 pounds (30 kilograms) and accurate to about two parts in 10^{12} have been made.

Hydrogen clocks. Hydrogen masers of very high stability have been developed at Harvard University. These have stabilities of about one part in 10^{14}. The absolute frequency, however, is uncertain by a larger amount. The frequency of hydrogen is 1,420,405,751.8 Hz.

Rubidium clocks. Gas cells of high stability using rubidium have been developed. The frequency depends on construction and adjustments, so that they do not have the absolute precision of cesium-beam clocks.

Precision in dealing with time. Assiduous efforts have been made in recent decades to define, correlate, and disseminate astronomical and atomic time with the utmost precision.

Precision of the concept of the second. The fundamental unit of time interval in the metric system was, by usage but not by formal adoption, the second of mean solar time: 1/86,400 of the mean solar day. Because of variations in speed of rotation of the Earth and, consequently, in the length of the mean solar day, this unit became unsatisfactory. In 1955 the International Astronomical Union defined the second of Ephemeris Time (ET) as 1/31,566,925.9747 of the tropical year for 1900 January 0 (same as December 31, 1899) at 12 hours ET. The length of the tropical year (see above *Astronomical time divisions*) changes according to the epoch because of gravitational perturbations, so that it must be defined for a particular period in time. This definition was adopted by the International Committee of Weights and Measures in 1956 and ratified by the General Conference of Weights and Measures in 1960. In 1964 the conference also defined an atomic second as 9,192,631,770 periods of radiation of a particular cesium-133 transition. In 1967 this became the sole definition of the second in the International System of Units (SI), the modern form of the metric system. The second of ET remains as the unit of time interval in the system of constants adopted by the International Astronomical Union in 1964.

In 1970 the atomic second was shorter than the mean solar second by about three parts in 10^8, and an atomic clock gained about one second per year on a clock showing mean solar time. The length of the mean solar day, which is always 86,400 mean solar seconds, was then 86,400.0026 seconds of atomic time.

Atomic-time scales. Using the preceding definition of the atomic second, any atomic clock can be used to generate an atomic-time scale after an initial epoch has been specified. The time scale obtained will depend, to some extent, on the clocks used. That determined by the International Time Bureau, denoted TAI, is based on about 50 highly accurate atomic clocks about the world.

Variations in the Earth's rotation. Variations in the Earth's rotation are classified as (1) secular, (2) irregular, and (3) periodic.

Variations in the difference between Universal Time (UT) and Ephemeris Time (ET) in modern terminology were found by astronomers from studies of ancient observations—in particular, of solar and lunar eclipses. By 1875 the American astronomer Simon Newcomb suspected that the discrepancies were caused by variations in speed of rotation rather than by irregularities in the Moon's motion. This idea was established as correct in 1939. About this time attempts to detect annual and semiannual periodic variations were initiated. Quartz-crystal clocks were good enough by about 1955 to give sufficiently reliable values of time intervals for the very small periodic changes to be detected.Difference
between
Universal
Time and
Ephemeris
Time

It was thought formerly that the irregular variation consisted of abrupt changes in speed, as large as three parts in 10^8 (three milliseconds per day). The comparison of UT with atomic time since 1955, however, shows that sudden changes in speed do not occur. Instead, sudden changes in acceleration and deceleration occur about every five years. The cause is not certain.

Tidal friction causes a progressive deceleration. Other geophysical effects are present, however, which can cause either a long-period acceleration or retardation—*e.g.*, changes in sea level from melting ice. These effects were under study in the early 1970s.

Tidal friction retards the speed of rotation but does not affect the orbital motion of the Earth. Hence, the number of mean solar days in one year must have been larger in the past than at present. An accurate extrapolation cannot be made, however, because the strength of tidal friction in the remote past is not known. A study of coral fossil growth rings, however, tends to indicate that several hundred million years ago there were about 400 days in a year. The age of the coral can be determined by radioactive dating, but there is difficulty in recognizing yearly growth patterns, superimposed on the daily pattern.

Time and frequency dissemination. Precise time and frequency are broadcast by radio in many countries.

Transmissions of time signals began as an aid to navigation in 1904; they are now widely used for many scientific and technical purposes. The seconds pulses are emitted on Coordinated Universal Time (see above), and the frequency of the carrier wave is maintained on some multiple of atomic frequency. Radio stations that provide such transmissions include those whose call signs are NBA (Panama Canal Zone); WWV (Fort Collins, Colorado); and GBR and MSF (Rugby, Warwickshire). The radio navigational systems Loran-C and Omega also provide precise time and frequency.

The accuracy obtainable from the signals varies from about one millisecond on high frequency to one microsecond for Loran-C. Frequency may be calibrated to about one part in 10^{11} in one day with transmissions of very low frequency and about one part in 10^{12} with Loran-C. The United States Naval Observatory also provides a service for synchronizing clocks around the world to about one microsecond through use of portable atomic clocks. Artificial satellites of the Earth also have been used in experiments to synchronize widely separated clocks to about 0.1 microsecond.

Radioactivity and time measurement. Atoms of a radioactive element (for details, see RADIOACTIVITY) decay at a rate that is independent of temperature, pressure, and other environmental factors. A clock could be constructed that would be based on radioactive decay, but it would not measure time interval with high precision. The process is useful, however, for measuring long intervals of time up to many millions of years.

Carbon-14 dating makes possible the age determination of objects containing carbon over the range of 100 to 50,000 years. Carbon-14, produced in the atmosphere by cosmic rays, enters living matter in a fairly constant ratio to carbon-12, which does not decay. The ratio of carbon-14 to carbon-12 in an object determines its age.

RELATIVISTIC AND COSMOLOGICAL EFFECTS

Relative motion. Let A and B be a pair of clocks fixed relative to each other and whose readings have been related by the exchange of electromagnetic (light) signals. Let the pair be in uniform motion relative to a clock C, which coincides successively with A and B. Then, as a consequence of Einstein's postulates of special relativity, the time interval of transit as measured by the single clock C will be less than that given by the difference in readings of the pair (see RELATIVITY). This holds irrespective of whether C is considered to be moving or at rest. The statement often made that, in effect, a moving clock runs slowly compared to the clock of a stationary observer, is misleading; three clocks should be included in the comparison. Several effects outside the scope of special relativity (which deals with nonaccelerated, linear motions) have been predicted; some have been confirmed.

Gravitational potential. A clock in a weaker potential (gravitational) field runs faster than one in a stronger field. Near the surface of the Earth the frequency increases about one part in 10^{16} per metre, and a clock 100 metres (330 feet) higher than a second clock will have a frequency higher by one part in 10^{14}.

Clocks on the Earth are affected by orbital motion about the Sun and by the gravitational potential of the Sun. The net effect is an average lowering in frequency of 1.5×10^{-8} plus an annual term with coefficient 3.3×10^{-10}, compared to a clock at rest at infinity. These effects are the same for all clocks on the Earth. They might be detected, possibly, by a comparison of atomic time with that derived from observations of certain pulsars that emit rapidly and uniformly varying radio-frequency radiation, because pulsars are external to the solar system.

Around-the-world experiment. A clock carried eastward around the world in an airplane should differ, at the end of the trip, from one fixed on the Earth because (1) the two clocks are in rotation at different speeds about nonrotating axes at the centre of the Earth and (2) there is a difference in gravitational potential. Moreover, effect (1) will be different for clocks carried eastward and westward at the same speed relative to the

Earth, because the Earth rotates eastward. In experiments carried out in 1971 with atomic clocks of the U.S. Naval Observatory, the eastward-flying clock lost 0.06 microsecond and the westward one gained 0.27 microsecond, which confirmed the predicted relativistic effects.

Basis of Ephemeris Time. Newcomb's 1895 mathematical development of the orbital motion of the Earth (mentioned above) is based on celestial mechanics, which in turn is based on the laws of motion and gravitation of Newton; this development includes the disturbing gravitational effects (called perturbations) of the planets. The observations used to obtain the constants in the solution were obtained from observations of angles only. Modern studies of the Earth's orbital motion allow for effects predicted by general relativity and take into account extremely precise astronomical measurements of planetary distances by radar reflection. As a result, more precise measures of Ephemeris Time can be expected.

Cosmological theories have been proposed in which the gravitational constant, G, diminishes slowly, about one part in 10^{10} or 10^{11} per year, with respect to electrical constants. If such hypotheses are correct, then the frequency of an atomic clock with respect to Ephemeris Time would increase secularly. No secular change has been found thus far, however; G is constant within the errors of observation, four parts in 10^{10} per year.

(W.Ma.)

III. Contemporary philosophies of time
TIME IN 20TH-CENTURY PHILOSOPHY OF PHYSICS

Time in the special theory of relativity. Since the classic interpretation of Einstein's special theory of relativity by Hermann Minkowski, a Lithuanian–German mathematician, it has been clear that physics has to do not with two entities, space and time, taken separately, but with a unitary entity space–time, in which, however, timelike and spacelike directions can be distinguished. The Lorentz transformations, which in special relativity define shifts in velocity perspectives, were shown by Minkowski to be simply rotations of space–time axes. The Lorentz contraction of moving rods and the time dilatation of moving clocks turns out to be rather analogous to the fact that different-sized slices of a sausage are obtained by altering the direction of the slice: just as there is still the objective (absolute) sausage, so also Minkowski restores the absolute to relativity in the form of the invariant four-dimensional object, and the invariance (under all mathematical transformations) of the space–time interval and of certain fundamental physical quantities such as action (which has the dimensions of energy times time, even though neither energy nor time is separately invariant).

Process philosophers charge the Minkowski universe with being a static one. The philosopher of the manifold denies this charge, saying that a static universe would be one in which all temporal cross sections were exactly similar to one another and in which all particles (considered as four-dimensional objects) lay along parallel lines. The actual universe is not like this, and that it is not static is shown in the Minkowski picture by the dissimilarity of temporal cross sections and the nonparallelism of the world lines of particles. The process philosopher may say that change, as thus portrayed in the Minkowski picture (*e.g.*, with the world lines of particles at varying distances from one another), is not true Bergsonian change, so that something has been left out. But if time advances up the manifold, this would seem to be an advance with respect to a hypertime, perhaps a new time direction orthogonal to the old one. Perhaps it could be a fifth dimension, as has been used in describing the de Sitter universe as a four-dimensional hypersurface in a five-dimensional space. The question may be asked, however, what advantage such a hypertime could have for the process philosopher and whether there is process through hypertime. If there is, one would seem to need a hyper-hypertime, and so on to infinity. (The infinity of hypertimes was indeed postulated by John William Dunne, a British inventor and philosopher; but the remedy seems to be a desperate one.) And if

Time dilatation in special and general relativity

Minkowski space–time and Lorentz transformations

Possible fifth-dimensional hypertime

no such regress into hypertimes is postulated, it may be asked whether the process philosopher would not find the five-dimensional universe as static as the four-dimensional one. The process philosopher may therefore adopt the expedient of the French intuitionist Henri Bergson, saying that temporal process (the extra something that makes the difference between a static and a dynamic universe) just cannot be pictured spatially (whether one supposes four, five, or more dimensions). According to Bergson, it is something that just has to be intuited and cannot be grasped by discursive reason. The philosopher of the manifold will find this unintelligible and will in any case deny that anything dynamic *has* been left out of his world picture. This sort of impasse between process philosophers and philosophers of the manifold seems to be characteristic of the present-day state of philosophy.

The theory of relativity implies that simultaneity is relative to a frame of axes. If one frame of axes is moving relative to another, then events that are simultaneous relative to the first are not simultaneous relative to the second, and vice versa. This paradox leads to another difficulty for process philosophy over and above those noted earlier. Those who think that there is a continual coming into existence of events (as the present rushes onward into the future) can be asked "Which present?" It therefore seems difficult to make a distinction between a real present (and perhaps past) as against an as-yet-unreal future. Philosophers of the manifold also urge that to talk of events becoming (coming into existence) is not easily intelligible. Enduring things and processes, in this view, can come into existence; but this simply means that as four-dimensional solids they have an earliest temporal cross section or time slice.

When talking in the fashion of Minkowski, it is advisable, according to philosophers of the manifold, to use tenseless verbs (such as the "equals" in "2 + 2 equals 4"). One can say that all parts of the four-dimensional world exist (in this tenseless sense). This is not, therefore, to say that they all exist *now*, nor does it mean that Minkowski events are "timeless." The tenseless verb merely refrains from dating events in relation to its own utterance.

The clock paradox

The power of the Minkowski representation is illustrated by its manner in dealing with the so-called clock paradox, which deals with two twins, Peter and Paul. Peter remains on Earth (regarded as at rest in an inertial system) while Paul is shot off in a rocket at half the velocity of light, rapidly decelerated at Alpha Centauri (about four light-years away), and shot back to Earth again at the same speed. Assuming that the period of turnabout is negligible compared with those of uniform velocity, Paul, as a four-dimensional object, lies along the sides AC and CB of a space–time triangle, in which A and B are the points of his departure and return and C that of his turn-around. Peter, as a four-dimensional object, lies along AB. Now, special relativity implies that on his return Paul will be rather more than two years younger than Peter. This is a matter of two sides of a triangle not being equal to the third side: AC + CB < AB. The "less than" —symbolized < —arises from the semi-Euclidean character of Minkowski space–time, which calls for minus signs in its metric (or expression for the interval between two events), which is:

$$ds = \sqrt{c^2 dt^2 - dx^2 - dy^2 - dz^2}.$$

The paradox has been held to result from the fact that, from Paul's point of view, it is Peter who has gone off and returned; and so the situation is symmetrical, and Peter and Paul should each be younger than the other—which is impossible. This is to forget, however, the asymmetry reflected in the fact that Peter has been in only one inertial system throughout, and Paul has not; Paul lies along a bent line, Peter along a straight one.

Time in general relativity and cosmology. In general relativity, which, though less firmly established than the special theory, is intended to explain gravitational phenomena, a more complicated metric of variable curvature is employed, which approximates to the Minkowski metric in empty space far from material bodies. Cos-

mologists who have based their theories on general relativity have sometimes postulated a finite but unbounded space–time (analogous, in four dimensions, to the surface of a sphere) as far as spacelike directions are concerned, but practically all cosmologists have assumed that space–time is infinite in its timelike directions. Kurt Gödel, a contemporary mathematical logician, however, proposed solutions to the equations of general relativity whereby timelike world lines can bend back on themselves. Unless one accepts a process philosophy and thinks of the flow of time as going around and around such closed timelike world lines, it is not necessary to think that Gödel's idea implies eternal recurrence. Events can be arranged in a circle and still occur only once.

The general theory of relativity predicts a time dilatation in a gravitational field, so that, relative to someone outside of the field, clocks (or atomic processes) go slow. This retardation is a consequence of the curvature of space–time with which the theory identifies the gravitational field. As a very rough analogy, a road may be considered that, after crossing a plain, goes over a mountain. Clearly, one mile as measured on the humpbacked surface of the mountain is less than one mile as measured horizontally. Similarly—if "less" is replaced by "more" because of the negative signs in the expression for the metric of space-time—one second as measured in the curved region of space–time is more than one second as measured in a flat region. Strange things can happen if the gravitational field is very intense. It has been deduced that so-called black holes in space may occur in places where extraordinarily massive or dense aggregates of matter exist, as in the gravitational collapse of a star. Nothing, not even radiation, can emerge from such a black hole. A critical point is the so-called Schwarzschild radius measured outward from the centre of the collapsed star—a distance, perhaps, of the order of 10 kilometres. Something falling into the hole would take an infinite time to reach this critical radius, according to the space–time frame of reference of a distant observer, but only a finite time in the frame of reference of the falling body itself. From the outside standpoint the fall has become frozen. But from the point of view of the frame of the falling object, the fall continues to zero radius in a very short time indeed—of the order of only ten or a hundred microseconds. Within the black hole spacelike and timelike directions change over, so that to escape again from the black hole is impossible for reasons analogous to those that, in ordinary space–time, make it impossible to travel faster than light. (To travel faster than light a body would have to lie—as a four-dimensional object—in a spacelike direction instead of a timelike one.)

Dilatation of time in gravitational fields and black holes

As a rough analogy two country roads may be considered, both of which go at first in a northerly direction. But road A bends round asymptotically toward the east; *i.e.*, it approaches ever closer to a line of latitude. Soon road B crosses this latitude and is thus to the north of all parts of road A. Disregarding the Earth's curvature, it takes infinite space for road A to get as far north as that latitude on road B; *i.e.*, near that latitude an infinite number of "road A northerly units" (say, miles) correspond to a finite number of road B units. Soon road B gets "beyond infinity" in road A units, though it need be only a finite road.

Time beyond infinite time

Rather similarly, if a body should fall into a black hole, it would fall for only a finite time, even though it were "beyond infinite" time by external standards. This analogy does not do justice, however, to the real situation in the black hole—the fact that the curvature becomes infinite as the star collapses toward a point. It should, however, help to alleviate the mystery of how a finite time in one reference frame can go "beyond infinity" in another frame.

Most cosmological theories imply that the universe is expanding, with the galaxies receding from one another (as is made plausible by observations of the red shifts of their spectra), and that the universe as man knows it originated in a primeval explosion at a date of the order of 10×10^9 years ago. Though this date is often loosely

Expanding universe; creation; τ time

called "the creation of the universe," there is no reason to deny that the universe (in the philosophical sense of "everything that there is") existed at an earlier time, even though it may be impossible to know anything of what happened then. (There have been cosmologies, however, that suggest an oscillating universe, with explosion, expansion, contraction, explosion, etc., ad infinitum.) And *a fortiori*, there is no need to say—as Augustine did in his *Confessions* as early as the 5th century AD—that time itself was created along with the creation of the universe, though it should not too hastily be assumed that this would lead to absurdity, because common sense could well be misleading at this point.

A British cosmologist, E.A. Milne, however, proposed a theory according to which time in a sense could not extend backward beyond the creation time. According to him there are two scales of time, "τ time" and "t time." The former is a time scale within which the laws of mechanics and gravitation are invariant, and the latter is a scale within which those of electromagnetic and atomic phenomena are invariant. According to Milne τ is proportional to the logarithm of t (taking the zero of t to be the creation time); thus, by τ time the creation is infinitely far in the past. The logarithmic relationship implies that the constant of gravitation G would increase throughout cosmic history. (This increase might have been expected to show up in certain geological data, but apparently the evidence is against it.)

Time in microphysics. Special problems arise in considering time in quantum mechanics and in particle interactions.

Quantum-mechanical aspects of time. In quantum mechanics it is usual to represent measurable quantities by operators in an abstract many-dimensional (often infinite-dimensional) so-called Hilbert space. Nevertheless, this space is an abstract mathematical tool for calculating the evolution in time of the energy levels of systems—and this evolution occurs in ordinary space–time. For example, in the formula $AH - HA = i\hbar(dA/dt)$, in which i is $\sqrt{-1}$ and $\hbar$ is $\frac{1}{2}\pi$ times Planck's constant, h, the A and H are operators, but the t is a perfectly ordinary time variable. There may be something unusual, however, about the concept of the time at which quantum-mechanical events occur, because according to the Copenhagen interpretation of quantum mechanics the state of a microsystem is relative to an experimental arrangement. Thus energy and time are conjugate: no experimental arrangement can determine both simultaneously, for the energy is relative to one experimental arrangement, and the time is relative to another. (Thus, a more relational sense of "time" is suggested.) The states of the experimental arrangement cannot be merely relative to other experimental arrangements, on pain of infinite regress; and so these have to be described by classical physics. (This parasitism on classical physics is a possible weakness in quantum mechanics over which there is much controversy.)

The relation between time uncertainty and energy uncertainty, in which their product is equal to or greater than $h/4\pi$, $\Delta E \Delta t \geq h/4\pi$, has led to estimates of the theoretical minimum measurable span of time, which comes to something of the order of 10^{-24} second and hence to speculations that time may be made up of discrete intervals (chronons). These suggestions have not been vigorously followed up, however, and are open to a very serious objection, viz., that the mathematics of quantum mechanics makes use of continuous space and time (for example, it contains differential equations). It is not easy to see how it could possibly be recast so as to postulate only a discrete space–time (or even a merely dense one). For a set of instants to be dense, there must be an instant between any two instants. For it to be a continuum, however, something more is required, viz., that every set of instants earlier (later) than any given one should have an upper (lower) bound. It is continuity that enables modern mathematics to surmount the paradox of extension framed by the Pre-Socratic Eleatic Zeno—a paradox comprising the question of how a finite interval can be made up of dimensionless points or instants.

Time in particle interactions. Until recently it was thought that the fundamental laws of nature are time symmetrical. It is true that the second law of thermodynamics, according to which randomness always increases, is time asymmetrical; but this law is not strictly true (for example, the phenomenon of Brownian motion contravenes it), and it is now regarded as a statistical derivative of the fundamental laws together with certain boundary conditions. The fundamental laws of physics were long thought also to be charge symmetrical (for example, an antiproton together with a positron behave like a proton and electron) and to be symmetrical with respect to parity (reflection in space, as in a mirror). The experimental evidence now suggests that all three symmetries are not quite exact but that the laws of nature are symmetrical if all three reflections are combined: charge, parity, and time reflections forming what can be called (after the initials of the three parameters) a CPT mirror. The time asymmetry was shown in certain abstruse experiments concerning the decay of K mesons that have a short time decay into two pions and a long time decay into three pions.

Time in molar physics. The above-mentioned violations of temporal symmetry in the fundamental laws of nature are such out-of-the-way ones, however, that it seems unlikely that they are responsible for the gross violations of temporal symmetry that are apparent in the visible world. An obvious asymmetry is that there are traces of the past (footprints, fossils, tape recordings, memories) and not of the future. There are mixing processes but no comparable unmixing process: milk and tea easily combine to give a whitish brown liquid, but it requires ingenuity and energy and complicated apparatus to separate the two liquids. A cold saucepan of water on a hot brick will soon become a tepid saucepan on a tepid brick; but the heat energy of the tepid saucepan never goes into the tepid brick to produce a cold saucepan and a hot brick. Even though the laws of nature are assumed to be time symmetrical, it is possible to explain these asymmetries by means of suitable assumptions about boundary conditions. Much discussion of this problem has stemmed from the work of Ludwig Boltzmann (died 1906), an Austrian physicist, who showed that the concept of the thermodynamic quantity "entropy" could be reduced to that of randomness or disorder. Among philosophers in this tradition may be mentioned Hans Reichenbach, a German–U.S. Positivist, Adolf Grünbaum, a contemporary U.S. philosopher, and Olivier Costa de Beauregard, a contemporary French philosopher-physicist. There have also been many relevant papers of high mathematical sophistication scattered through the literature of mathematical physics. Reichenbach (and Grünbaum, who improved on Reichenbach in some respects) explained a trace as being a branch system; *i.e.*, a relatively isolated system, the entropy of which is less than would be expected if one compared it with that of the surrounding region. For example, a footprint on the beach has sand particles compressed together below a volume containing air only, instead of being quite evenly (randomly) spread over the volume occupied by the compressed and empty parts.

Another striking temporal asymmetry on the macro level, viz., that spherical waves are often observed being emitted from a source but never contracting to a sink, has been stressed by Sir Karl Popper, a contemporary Austrian and British philosopher of science. By considering radiation as having a particle aspect (*i.e.*, as consisting of photons), Costa de Beauregard has argued that this "principle of retarded waves" can be reduced to the statistical Boltzmann principle of increasing entropy and so is not really different from the previously discussed asymmetry. These considerations also provide some justification for the common-sense idea that the cause–effect relation is a temporally unidirectional one, even though the laws of nature themselves allow for retrodiction no less than for prediction.

A third striking asymmetry on the macro level is that of the apparent mutual recession of the galaxies, which can plausibly be deduced from the red shifts observed in their spectra. It is still not clear whether or how far this asymmetry can be reduced to the two asymmetries already discussed, though interesting suggestions have been made.

The statistical considerations that explain temporal asymmetry apply only to large assemblages of particles. Hence, any device that records time intervals will have to be macroscopic and to make use somewhere of statistically irreversible processes. Even if one were to count the swings of a frictionless pendulum, this counting would require memory traces in the brain, which would function as a temporally irreversible recording device.

TIME IN 20TH-CENTURY PHILOSOPHY OF BIOLOGY AND PHILOSOPHY OF MIND

Organisms often have some sort of internal clock that regulates their behaviour. There is a tendency, for example, for leaves of leguminous plants to alter their position so that they lie in one position by day and in another position by night. This tendency persists if the plant is in artificial light that is kept constant, though it can be modified to other periodicities (e.g., to a six-hour instead of a 24-hour rhythm) by suitably regulating the periods of artificial light and darkness. In animals, similar daily rhythms are usually acquired, but in experimental conditions animals nevertheless tend to adapt better to a 24-hour rhythm than to any other. Sea anemones expand and contract to the rhythm of the tides, and this periodic behaviour will persist for some time even though the sea anemone is placed in a tank. Bees can be trained to come for food at fixed periods (e.g., every 21 hours), and this demonstrates that they possess some sort of internal clock. Similarly, man himself has some power to estimate time in the absence of clocks and other sensory cues. This fact refutes the contention of the 17th-century English philosopher John Locke (and of other philosophers in the Empiricist tradition) that time is perceived only as a relation between successive sensations. The U.S. mathematician Norbert Wiener has speculated on the possibility that the human time sense depends on the α-rhythm of electrical oscillation in the brain.

Temporal rhythms both in plants and animals (including man) are dependent on temperature, and experiments on human subjects have shown that, if their temperature is raised, they underestimate the time between events.

Despite these facts, the Lockean notion that the estimation of time depends on the succession of sensations is still to some degree true. People who take hashish and mescalin, for example, may feel their sensations following one another much more rapidly. Because there are so many more sensations than normal in a given interval of time, time seems to drag, so that a minute may feel like an hour. Similar illusions about the spans of time occur in dreams.

It is unclear whether most discussions of so-called biological and psychological time have much significance for metaphysics. As far as the distorted experiences of time that arise through drugs (and in schizophrenia) are concerned, it can be argued that there is nothing surprising in the fact that pathological states can make people misestimate periods of time, and so it can be claimed that facts of this sort do not shed any more light on the philosophy of time than facts about mountains looking near after rainstorms and looking far after dust-storms shed on the philosophy of space.

The idea that psychological studies of temporal experience are philosophically important is probably connected with the sort of Empiricism that was characteristic of Locke and still more of the Empiricists George Berkeley and David Hume and their successors. The idea of time had somehow to be constructed out of men's primitive experience of ideas succeeding one another. Nowadays, concept formation is thought of as more of a social phenomenon involved in the "picking up" of a language; thus, contemporary philosophers have tended to see the problem differently: men do not have to construct their concepts from their own immediate sensations. Even so, the learning of temporal concepts surely does at least involve an immediate apprehension of the rela-

tion of "earlier" and "later." A mere succession of sensations, however, will go no way toward yielding the idea of time: if one sensation has vanished entirely before the other is in consciousness, one cannot be immediately aware of the succession of sensations. What Empiricism needs, therefore, as a basis for constructing the idea of time is an experience of succession as opposed to a succession of experiences. Hence, two or more ideas that are related by "earlier than" must be experienced in one single act of awareness. William James, a U.S. Pragmatist philosopher and also a pioneer psychologist, popularized the term "specious present" for the span of time covered by a single act of awareness. His idea was that at a given moment of time a person is aware of events a short time before that time. (Sometimes he spoke of the specious present as a saddleback looking slightly into the future as well as slightly into the past, but this was inconsistent with his idea that the specious present depended on lingering short-term memory processes in the brain.) He referred to experiments by the German psychologist Wilhelm Wundt that showed that the longest group of arbitrary sounds that a person could identify without error lasted about six seconds. Other criteria perhaps involving other sense modalities might lead to slightly different spans of time, but the interesting point is that, if there is such a specious present, it cannot be explained solely by ordinary memory traces: if one hears a "ticktock" of a clock, the "tick" is not remembered in the way in which a "ticktock" 10 minutes ago is remembered. The specious present is perhaps not really specious: the idea that it was specious depended on an idea that the real (nonspecious) present had to be instantaneous. If perception is considered as a certain reliable way of being caused to have true beliefs about the environment by sensory stimulation, there is no need to suppose that these true beliefs have to be about an instantaneous state of the world. It can therefore be questioned whether the term "specious" is a happy one.

Two matters discussed earlier in connection with the philosophy of physics have implications for the philosophy of mind: (1) the integration of space and time in the theory of relativity makes it harder to conceive of immaterial minds that exist in time but are not even localizable in space. (2) The statistical explanation of temporal asymmetry explains why the brain has memory traces of the past and not of the future, and hence helps to explain the unidirectional nature of temporal consciousness. It also gives reasons for skepticism about the claims of parapsychologists to have experimental evidence for precognition; or it shows, at least, that if these phenomena do exist they are not able to be fitted into a cosmology based on physics as it exists today.

(J.J.C.S.)

BIBLIOGRAPHY

Time in the history of thought and action: (*Eastern*): CHARLES ELIOT, *Hinduism and Buddhism*, 3 vol. (1921, reprinted 1962); FUNG YU-LAN, *A History of Chinese Philosophy*, 2nd ed., 2 vol. (Eng. trans. 1952–53); R.C. ZAEHNER, *The Dawn and Twilight of Zoroastrianism* (1961). (*Pre-Socratic*): HENRI FRANKFORT et al., *The Intellectual Adventure of Ancient Man* (1946); JOHN BURNET, *Greek Philosophy, Thales to Plato* (1914, reprinted 1964). (*Classical Greek*): W.K.C. GUTHRIE, *A History of Greek Philosophy*, 3 vol. to date (1962–69), to 5th century BC inclusive; JACQUELINE DE ROMILLY, *Time in Greek Tragedy* (1968); NORMAN W. DE WITT, *Epicurus and His Philosophy* (1954). (*Christian and Muslim*): JAMES BARR, *Biblical Words for Time* (1962); OSCAR CULLMANN, *Christus und die Zeit*, 3rd rev. ed. (1962; Eng. trans., *Christ and Time*, rev. ed., 1962); SAINT AUGUSTINE, *Confessions* (many English translations), the most important work of Greco-Roman thought on the problems of experienced time and the difficulty of grappling with them; IBN KHALDUN, *al-Muqaddimah* (written in the early 14th century; Eng. trans., *The Muqaddimah: An Introduction to History*, 3 vol., 1958), undoubtedly the greatest work of its kind. (*18th and 19th centuries*): GIOVANNI BATTISTA VICO, *Principi di una scienza nuova*, 3rd ed. (1744; Eng. trans., *The New Science*, trans. by THOMAS G. BERGIN and MAX H. FISCH, 1948), a seminal work on the ontal significance of history; G.W.F. HEGEL, *The Logic of World and Idea*, trans. by H.S. MACRAW (1929), and *Science of Logic*, trans. by W.H. JOHNSTON and L.G. STRUTHERS (1929); KARL MARX, *Selected Works of Marx and Engels*, by C.P. DUTT, 2 vol. (1942); CHARLES DARWIN, *On the Origin of Species by Means of Natural Selection* (1859, many later editions). (*20th-century studies*): OSWALD SPENGLER, *Der Untergang des Abendlandes*, 2 vol. (1919–22; Eng. trans., *The Decline of the West*, 2nd ed., 2 vol., 1934); the symposium volume, *History and the Concept of Time* (*History and Theory: Beiheft* 6, 1966); S.G.F. BRANDON, *History, Time, and Deity* (1965); STEPHEN TOULMIN and JUNE GOODFIELD, *The Discovery of Time* (1965), history of the changing attitude toward time that arose from the geology and biology of the 19th century; MIRCEA ELIADE, *Le Mythe de l'éternel retour* (1949; Eng. trans., *Cosmos and History: The Myth of the Eternal Return*, 1959); FRANCIS C. HABER, *The Age of the World: Moses to Darwin* (1959).

Time as systematized in modern scientific society: Astronomical times are treated in the *Explanatory Supplement to the Astronomical Ephemeris and the American Ephemeris and Nautical Almanac*, by the Nautical Almanac Offices of the United Kingdom and United States (1961); and *Spherical Astronomy*, by EDGAR W. WOOLARD and GERALD M. CLEMENCE (1966); the former also discusses calendars. ROBERT R. NEWTON, *Ancient Astronomical Observations and the Accelerations of the Earth and Moon* (1970), discusses eclipses; G.P. KUIPER and BARBARA M. MIDDLEHURST (eds.), *Telescopes* (1960), describes astronomical instruments; IVAN I. MUELLER, *Spherical and Practical Astronomy* (1969), concerns practical usages.

Contemporary pure studies of time: The two major reference works in the study of time are G.J. WHITROW, *The Natural Philosophy of Time* (1961); and J.T. FRASER (ed.), *The Voices of Time* (1966). Both contain extensive references and the latter extensive bibliographies. See also numerous issues of the journal *Studium Generale* (monthly since 1955); and G.J. WHITROW, *The Nature of Time* (1972). (*Multidisciplinary symposia*): J.T. FRASER *et al.* (eds.), *The Study of Time: Proceedings of the First Conference of the International Society for the Study of Time* (1972); ROLAND FISCHER (ed.), *Interdisciplinary Perspectives of Time* (1967); RUDOLF W. MEYER (ed.), *Das Zeitproblem in 20. Jahrhundert* (1964); JOSEPH CAMPBELL (ed.), *Man and Time* (1957). (*Emphasis on philosophy*): Two books of readings with extensive bibliographies are RICHARD M. GALE (ed.), *The Philosophy of Time* (1967); and J.J.C. SMART (ed.), *Problems of Space and Time* (1964). See also the UNIVERSITY OF CALIFORNIA, BERKELEY PHILOSOPHICAL UNION, *The Problem of Time* (1935), and individual philosophers mentioned in the text. (*Literature and the arts*): GEORGE KUBLER, *The Shape of Time* (1962); ERWIN PANOFSKY, *Studies in Iconology* (1962); GEORGES POULET, *Études sur le temps humain* (1950; Eng. trans., *Studies in Human Time*, 1956); HANS MEYERHOFF, *Time in Literature* (1960). (*Psychology*): JEAN PIAGET, *Le Développement de la notion de temps chez l'enfant* (1946; Eng. trans., *The Child's Conception of Time*, 1969); JOHN E. ORME, *Time, Experience and Behaviour* (1969); PAUL FRAISSE, *Psychologie du temps* (1957; Eng. trans., *The Psychology of Time*, 1963); NORMAN O. BROWN, *Life Against Death: The Psychoanalytical Meaning of History* (1959); JOHN COHEN, *Psychological Time in Health and Disease* (1967). (*Biology and medicine*): NATIONAL INSTITUTE OF MENTAL HEALTH, *Biological Rhythms in Psychiatry and Medicine* (1970); CURT P. RICHTER, *Biological Clocks in Medicine and Psychiatry* (1965); ERWIN BUNNING, *The Physiological Clock* (1964); GEORG SCHALTENBRAND (ed.), *Zeit in Nervenärztlicher Sicht* (1963); J.L. CLOUDSLEY–THOMPSON, *Rhythmic Activity in Animal Physiology and Behaviour* (1961); *Biological Clocks*, the Cold Spring Harbor Symposia on Quantitative Biology, vol. 25 (1960). (*Physics*): ADOLF GRUENBAUM, *Philosophical Problems of Space and Time* (1963), discusses many important issues including that of temporal asymmetry; his *Modern Science and Zeno's Paradoxes* (1967) provides an up-to-date discussion of problems concerned with the continuity of time. See also OLIVIER COSTA DE BEAUREGARD, *Le Second Principe de la science du temps* (1963); RICHARD SCHLEGEL, *Time and the Physical World* (1961); and THOMAS GOLD (ed.), *The Nature of Time* (1967). For process philosophy, see MILIC CAPEK, *The Philosophical Impact of Contemporary Physics* (1961).

(A.J.T./W.Ma./J.J.C.S.)

Time Perception

Man experiences continual change; nights succeed days, winters follow summers; some die, others are born; nothing halts the flow of the river. Let man seek to free himself of these exterior changes and he will meet them again within himself in the tensions and satisfactions of his own bodily needs. Even were he to take refuge in thinking or in reverie, he again would find ceaseless introspective change.

Man subsumes the continuing quality of experience by saying that he lives in time (the dimension of his becoming) even as he lives in space (the dimension of his movements).

The human experience of change is complex. One primary element clearly is that of a succession of events; but distinguishable events are separated by more or less lengthy intervals that are called durations. Sequence and duration are fundamental aspects of what is perceived in change.

Manifestly, duration is relative to the events people isolate in the sequences through which they live: the duration of a kiss, of a meal, of a trip. A given interval always can be subdivided into a sequential chain delimiting briefer durations, as with the regular units that provide empirical measures of time: the second, the day, the year.

Indeed, human experience is not simply that of one single series of events, but of a plurality of overlapping changes. The duration of a radio program, for example, can combine with that of a breakfast, both being inserted within the longer period of an ocean voyage.

Man seems to be unable to live without some concept of time. Ancient philosophies sought to relate the concept of time to some objective reality to which it would correspond. René Descartes (1596–1650) inaugurated a critical era of philosophy by stressing the ancient problem of the origin of ideas, including the idea of time. Immanuel Kant (1724–1804), providing a radical answer to the epistemological problem of time, wrote that we do not appreciate time objectively as a physical thing; that it is simply a pure form of sensible intuition. Other philosophers of the 18th and 19th centuries sought to explain the notion of time as arising from association and memory of successive perceptions.

Early philosophical views of time

A move to empirical psychology emerged with the growth of research on the introspective data of experience. From about mid-19th century, under the influence of the psychophysical notions of Gustav Theodor Fechner, psychologists conducted experiments to study the relationship between time as perceived and time as measured in physics. Their work with adults gradually spread to the study of children and of animals. The psychologists then broadened their investigations of time to cover all forms of adaptation to sequence and duration.

SEQUENTIAL ACTIVITIES

Adaptation to successive events. One may respond to stimulation in an immediate way (as in unconditioned reflex action) without taking the element of time into account. Stimulation, however, can also signal an event to follow; then it has meaning only as part of the sequence of which it is the first term: bell announcing dinner, a road sign, or an approaching danger. People react to such stimuli with anticipatory behaviour that is adapted to a stimulus or action that has not yet occurred. The principles that govern such time-binding adaptation are none other than those of conditioning. One event becomes conditioned as the signal for another stimulus that is to be sought or avoided.

Time-binding adaptation as conditioning

The bottle-fed infant who initially reacts to the nipple on his lips with a simple sucking reflex is gradually conditioned to stop crying when he sees the bottle (the signal for feeding). Later he may learn to react to even more secondary signals that announce the arrival of the bottle; *e.g.*, being lifted from the crib or hearing the sounds of his mother warming the milk in the kitchen. His behaviour has come to incorporate the temporal dimension of the events.

According to the principles of instrumental conditioning, one stimulus becomes the signal for an ensuing event only if the second stimulus elicits an adaptive reaction (consummatory or aversive) and only if the order of the sequence is repeated. Conditioning tends to be established most rapidly when the interval between the signal (conditioned stimulus) and the unconditioned stimulus is quite brief. Ivan P. Pavlov estimated that the optimum interval for such a sequence was 0.5 second, which corresponds approximately to the intervals characteristic of sequences that are most accurately discriminable perceptually (see below).

Aside from adapting the individual to the order of a sequence, conditioning also adapts to the duration between signal and immediately effective stimulus. Response to signal tends to occur after about the same interval that separated the two stimuli during conditioning. Thus, an animal may be trained to delay a response for some time after the signal (delayed conditioning).

This form of adaptation is most pervasive in human behaviour, permitting people to anticipate sequences of events in their environment so that they can prepare to cope appropriately with what is yet to happen.

Adaptation to periodic change. In 1912 one of Pavlov's students (I.P. Feokritova) demonstrated that a dog accustomed to being fed every 30 minutes would begin to drool toward the end of each half-hour period. It was clear evidence of conditioning to time; the between-feedings interval itself served as a conditioned stimulus.

That discovery underscores the ever-present periodicity of daily living, especially on the biological level: rhythms of activity and sleep, rhythms of eating and lovemaking. As conditioning intervenes, anticipatory experiences of hunger, fatigue, or arousal serve our adaptation to ecological demands.

Allowance should also be made for the daily, or circadian, rhythms in metabolic activity (*e.g.*, daily cycles of temperature change). There is evidence that these fundamental biological functions can synchronize with the rhythmic phases of environmental (exogenous) change. Thus within a few days after a factory worker has been assigned to the night shift, highs and lows of his daily fluctuations of temperature will be inversed. The rhythmic changes in body temperature persists, nevertheless, suggesting an innate (endogenous) basis for circadian phenomena. Such a hypothesis would mean that the gradual establishment of human circadian rhythms of sleep or temperature results from maturation of the nervous system rather than from conditioning in the strict sense. Experiments in 1962, in which men lived in caves or other enclosures for months deprived of temporal cues from the environment, also demonstrated the enduring nature of rhythms in body temperature and in sleep–wakefulness. The rhythmic periods, however, sometimes expanded, the subject beginning to live on an approximately two-day cycle without being aware of it.

Through conditioning to time and by way of circadian rhythms, human physiology provides a kind of biological clock that offers points of reference for temporal orientation (see also PERIODICITY, BIOLOGICAL).

PERCEPTION OF SEQUENCE AND DURATION

The psychological present. To perceive is to become aware of stimulation. Awareness of sequence or duration may, at first glance, seem inconsistent with the definition of perceiving. In a mathematical sense, certainly, the present is only a point along the continuum of becoming, an instant when future is transformed into past. Nevertheless, there is indeed a more prolonged psychological present, a brief period during which successive events seem to form a perceptual unity and can be apprehended without calling on memory. There is a perceptual field for time just as there is a visual field. The rate or speed of a sequence determines the limits of the time field.

When a metronome ticks two or three times a second, one perceives an integral sequence, becoming aware of a rhythmic auditory series characterized by a perceptually distinct frequency. When the ticks come less often, however—at intervals of three seconds, say—the frequency or sequence no longer is perceived. Each physically discrete sound impulse remains an isolated perceptual event; each tick is no longer perceived as belonging to the same temporal field as the one that follows. Similar effects can be achieved by playing a recording of music or speech at a very slow rate. Music or spoken sentences are recognizable only when their elements (melody, rhythmic patterns, phrase) are presented at an optimal speed that

permits significant perceptual unity; that is, only when they belong to the relative simultaneity of the psychological present.

The perceived field of time also depends on the number of stimulus elements presented. When a clock strikes three or four times, one knows without counting that it is three or four o'clock. At noon one must count; the first chimes no longer belong to the psychological present that includes the last. Most people also can repeat a series of letters or numbers they hear, so long as there are no more than seven or eight elements. This ability varies with the degree of perceptual (*e.g.*, semantic) organization among the elements. While most adults can apprehend only about eight letters, they can grasp and repeat without fault sentences of 20 to 25 syllables (see also ATTENTION).

Perception of sequence. A series of physically discrete stimuli that impinge too rapidly on a sensory structure (*e.g.*, flashes of light on the retina) may produce perceptual fusion; the flashes will be indiscriminable and will appear to be uninterrupted light. The experience of fusion yields to one of discontinuity over distinctive critical ranges of frequency for some of the senses: visual flicker appears under prescribed experimental conditions at about 60 flashes per second, auditory flutter at about 1,000 interruptions per second, and tactual vibration at about 4,000 pulses per second. These values depend on differences in the persistence of the receptor systems (*e.g.*, how long an image is seen after removal of the stimulus).

The question of perceiving sequence hardly has meaning for the senses of taste and smell. Hearing appears to be particularly adapted to temporal perception, since the pattern of auditory excitement shows little inertial lag, closely following the physical duration of successive stimuli. Tactual function can give comparable results, but hearing has the practical superiority in everyday experience of reception at a distance.

When two heterogeneous stimuli (*e.g.*, a flash and a click) are successively presented, the critical threshold for passing from perceived simultaneity to an awareness of succession is found for intervals that vary between 0.02 to 0.1 second, depending on the training of the subjects. The maximum interval for perceiving sequence is more difficult to measure. The minimum time intervals are largely determined by the immediate physiological conditions of direct perceiving, while the maximum intervals are obscured by the effects of other cognitive activities. Determining when direct perception ends and when memory takes over is difficult.

At any rate, awareness of unitary sequence ceases for pairs of auditory or visual stimuli when the interval between them increases to approximately two seconds. For perceptually organized stimuli (as in a rhythm, a melody, or a phrase) the interval may reach five seconds, as indicated by one's ability to reproduce the pattern.

Between the upper and lower limits there are optimal values that seem most likely to produce perception of sequence. In the simple case of two homogeneous stimuli the optimum interval seems to be about 0.6 to 0.8 second. This is inferred from a series of clues: the same interval defines the tempo most frequently adopted in spontaneous motor activity (*e.g.*, tapping, walking) and corresponds to the heart rate. It is the interval that is most precisely reproduced by subjects in experiments; shorter intervals tend to be overestimated and longer ones underestimated. Stimuli repeated at that rate are subjectively judged to proceed most comfortably, without appearing to rush each other as in faster tempos and with no tendency to be separately perceived as at slower frequencies.

Perceived duration. Duration, the interval between two successive events, may be distinguished as full or empty (filled or unfilled) in terms of the sensory stimulation that intervenes. An empty interval is bounded by two perceptually discrete stimuli (*e.g.*, two clicks in succession); a duration is full when there is continous stimulation, being delimited by an onset and cessation (*e.g.*, a light stays on throughout the interval). To experience an empty duration is to perceive sequence, while full duration corresponds to the temporal length of a stimulus.

Circadian rhythms in metabolic activity

Relation of perceived time to number of elements presented

Full and empty duration

Human subjects need a minimum of about 0.1 second of visual experience or about .01 to .02 second of auditory experience to perceive duration; any shorter experiences are called instantaneous. Direct, unitary perception of duration occurs up to a maximum period of approximately 1.5 to 2 seconds from the beginning to the end of a continuous sensory stimulus.

This roughly two-second maximum for directly perceived duration seems to have a biological basis and can be considered the upper temporal limit of some sort of integrated neural mechanism. The immediate physiological process triggered by a stimulus endures beyond the period of stimulation, and may be measured as the duration of electrical impulses (e.g., in the optic nerve) evoked by simple stimulation. This initial activity appears to be integrated subjectively into a cognitive unit that embraces the rapidly ensuing perceptual processes as well. The optimum range of 0.6 to 0.8 second noted earlier seems to represent the typical duration of this integrating mechanism, as inferred from studies of sensory physiology and from reaction-time experiments.

At any rate, only within these limits can the quality and precision of direct human perception (as opposed to estimation and recall) of duration be studied. Such perception can be absolute or relative. Absolute perception corresponds to estimates expressed in subjectively qualitative terms as long or short. In making such estimates, people can discriminate four to five different durations between 0.1 and 1.0 second and six to seven between 0.5 and 5.0 seconds. In studies of relative perception, subjects attempt to reproduce intervals that are presented, or are told either to produce durations of specified length or to compare two successively presented durations. These tasks, especially comparison, give rise to constant time-order errors; that is, errors in estimation that depend on which interval is presented first.

Experimentally, the perception of empty duration is found to vary with the sense that marks the limits. With duration constant, interval estimates tend to be greater (1) when the limits are visual rather than auditory or tactual, (2) when they are of low intensity, or (3) when auditory limits are higher pitched. If the unfilled limits are defined by successive stimuli from different places, duration appears longer when the distance between the two sources is greater; this is called the S effect or kappa effect. The reverse is the tau effect, in which the distance is perceived as being wider when the interval between successive stimuli is longer.

Kappa and tau effects

The perception of filled duration also varies with the stimulus. Holding the interval constant, interrupted stimulation (e.g., several successive clicks) appears to last longer than does a continuous stimulus; and auditory stimuli appear to last longer than visual. Filled durations seem longer as stimulus intensity (e.g., loudness) or auditory pitch rises.

One interval can be perceived as longer or shorter than the next when the difference is about 7 to 10 percent (both full and empty durations). This relative difference threshold is lowered by practice. Such studies also reveal that apparent duration remains proportional to the objectively measured length of the interval.

ESTIMATING DURATION

When an interval lasts more than a few seconds, it no longer is directly perceivable as a whole, but its length can be estimated on the basis of memory function. Since common experience shows how imprecise these estimates are, people generally calculate time from such indicators as the position of the sun or with clocks and watches. Duration then is inferred rather than perceived.

Estimates, however, often are made, including those of absolute duration in which an activity is appreciated as brief or prolonged. Lacking a watch, one may make crude estimates based on such quantitative aspects of activity as distance travelled, number of dishes washed, or number of pages read. Or one may estimate directly as in subjectively counting seconds.

Factors that affect time estimation. *Type of activity.* The more often a task is broken up or interrupted, the longer it seems to take. As a corollary, a period of doing nothing appears longer than when one is doing something. Similarly, relatively passive activities appear longer than do those requiring active participation; e.g., time passes faster for the student who is taking notes than for one who passively listens.

Level of motivation. The more one is motivated by a given task, the shorter it appears to last. Clearly, motivation and the type of activity pursued are interdependent factors. Lack of motivation tends to interrupt attention to a task; a task in which perceptual focus frequently shifts rarely corresponds to one for which there is strong motivation. The more one notices change during an interval, the longer it is judged to be. More generally, it may be said that time has subjective duration only when one notices it; e.g., in awaiting the arrival of a friend (as opposed to the actual meeting) or in hoping to finish a task (in contrast to working at it).

Change as a factor in judging time

Personality traits. Although inadequacies in quantifying personality traits and difficulties in studying estimates of time spans exceeding a few seconds have hampered scientific study, simple observation reveals marked individual differences in the ability to estimate time. Sex differences have not been reliably established, but the influence of age is well known. Experimental data indicate that children use the same criteria as do adults, but give more variable estimates of duration. One reason for this seems to be that they are less able to compensate for differences in the nature of a task or in personal motivation; also they are inexperienced in making inferences based on the volume of work they have accomplished. Elderly people tend to find time shorter, probably since they are likely to notice long-accustomed changes less frequently.

Children are as accurate as adults in reproducing various series of metronome clicks that last about two seconds or less. But estimates of longer intervals require processes for organizing experience that develop only with age, and very young children seem to depend only on limited criteria: "It lasts because it's longer; because there's more of it; because it goes faster." According to Jean Piaget, estimates based on more or less explicit comparison with standard units of duration imply concrete cognitive operations that are developed only after about the age of seven or eight. Adolescents typically construct more sophisticated notions of time abstracted from such concrete experimental data.

Physiological effects: drugs. The precision with which time is perceived has not been found to be related to heart rate or to electroencephalographic data. It has been shown, however, that perception of time as in clapping or counting accelerates or decelerates with the rise and fall of body temperature. The precise metabolic basis for such temperature effects awaits further study.

The influence of body temperature

Ethical considerations sharply limit the dosage level of drugs employed for experiments on human beings. Understanding of the interactions between drug effects and personality traits in studies of time estimation is, therefore, quite incomplete. Within the dosage ranges investigated, however, stimulating drugs (e.g., thyroxine, caffeine, amphetamines) produce overestimates of duration, while depressants and anesthetics (e.g., barbiturates, nitrous oxide) promote underestimates. Under the influence of hallucinogens (e.g., marijuana, mescaline, LSD), subjects tend to estimate absolute duration as very long. In addition, a marijuana user may underestimate the speed of a motor vehicle, increasing the chances of accident.

Sensory deprivation and hypnosis. Relatively complete sensory deprivation (e.g., prolonged stays in experimental isolation chambers) compresses the experience of time to the point that short or long intervals (from about a minute to a day) seem to pass about twice as fast as usual. Time spent under these unpleasant conditions paradoxically seems shorter than normal time. Thus, the 58 objective days of a subject's first stay in a cave were underestimated as 33 days.

Under hypnosis, durations ordinarily are estimated at least as precisely as ever. Time distortion, however, can be readily induced among hypnotized subjects by simple suggestion. Such a subject, for example, may be exposed to two clicks that delimit an objective, 10-second interval but be told that it lasts 10 minutes. On being asked to count objects for 10 minutes, he may report having counted several hundreds without difficulty over what the experimenter's stopwatch shows to have been 10 seconds.

BIBLIOGRAPHY. P. FRAISSE, *Psychologie du temps* (1957; Eng. trans., *The Psychology of Time*, 1963), provides the most complete synthesis of the psychological works on time. A comparison with M. STURT, *The Psychology of Time* (1925), shows how this problem has developed and evolved. The collective works edited by J.T. FRASER, *The Voices of Time* (1966); and R. FISHER, "Interdisciplinary Perspectives of Time," *Ann. N.Y. Acad. Sci.*, vol. 138, article 2 (1967), present the most varied aspects of the problem of time, ranging from religious conceptions to scientific data from physics and biology. E. BUNNING, *The Physiological Clock* (1964), provides a very sound study of the problems of the temporal regulation of organisms. M. SIFFRE, *Hors du temps* (1963; Eng. trans., *Beyond Time*, 1964), reports the psychological disorientation of a subject who stays for a long period in an environment deprived of temporal references. L.F. COOPER and M.H. ERICKSON, *Time Distortion in Hypnosis* (1954); and M. FRANKENHAEUSER, *Estimation of Time* (1959), present original researches. The point of view of genetic epistemology is developed by JEAN PIAGET, *Le développement de la notion de temps chez l'enfant* (1946; Eng. trans., *The Child's Conception of Time*, 1969).

(P.F.)

Timur

A Turkic conqueror, of Islāmic faith, whose nomad hordes ranged from China to the Mediterranean, Timur (or Tamerlane) is remembered chiefly for the barbarity of his conquests and the cultural achievements of his dynasty.

By courtesy of the Topkapı Sarayı Museum, Istanbul

Timur, miniature, 16th century. In the Topkapı Sarayı Museum, Istanbul.

Timur was born in 1336 in an oasis valley between Samarkand (Samarqand) and the Hindu Kush (mountains) in Central Asia, a member of the Turkic Barlas clan, not of imperial Mongol origin. He first led a small nomad band and by guile and force of arms established dominion over the lands between the Oxus and Jaxartes rivers (Transoxiana) by the 1360s. He then, for three decades, led his mounted archers to subdue each state from Mongolia to the Mediterranean. He was the last of the mighty conquerors of Central Asia to achieve such military successes as leader of the nomad warrior lords, ruling both agricultural and pastoral peoples on an impe-

Military campaigns

rial scale. The poverty and desolation caused by campaigns gave rise to many legends, which in turn inspired such works as Marlowe's *Tamburlaine the Great*.

By defeating the Ottoman sultan Bayezid at Angora (modern Ankara) in 1402 and thus preventing him from extending his domain into Europe, the fall of Constantinople and the death agony of Byzantium were delayed half a century by this Muslim nomad.

Timur's impact on the grand duchy of Moscow was also great, for he routed the Golden Horde, the descendants of the Mongol conqueror Genghis Khan, whose dominion stretched from Siberia to the Caucasus.

The name Timur Lenk signified Timur the Lame, a title of contempt used by his Persian enemies, which became Tamburlaine, or Tamerlane, in Europe. He was heir to a political, economic, and cultural heritage rooted in Central Asia. His nomad stock cultivated the military arts and discipline of Genghis Khan and, as mounted warriors, scorned the settled peasants. Irrespective of his ability, his victories were not fortuitous. He started his campaigns when remnants of the great Khan's empire were weakened by factional strife. Moreover, a long-term shift in the weather patterns of Central Asia brought rain to hitherto desert areas that provided fresh pasture for livestock, oases for the caravan trade, and bases for flourishing nomad societies.

Timur never took up a permanent abode. Continually in the saddle, he personally led his almost constantly campaigning forces, enduring extremes of desert heat and lacerating cold. When not campaigning he moved with his army according to season and grazing facilities. His court travelled with him, including his household of one or more of his nine wives and concubines. He strove to make his capital, Samarkand, the most splendid city in Asia, but when he visited it he stayed only a few days and then moved back to the pavilions of his encampment in the plains beyond the city.

In 1404 he returned to Transoxiana to celebrate his victories and to prepare his grandest campaign—that waged against the Ming dynasty in China. He assembled the entire forces of the steppes and all his booty. Here were the caravans of elephants and treasure from the plains of the Punjab and the sultanate of Delhi; the loot of the Volga region and the steppes; the tribute from Egypt of gold, ostriches, and a giraffe; florins from Byzantium; tapestries from Castile; master craftsmen from Damascus; scholars from Baghdad; captive Turks from Anatolia; merchants from the bazaars of the Mediterranean and from China. From Hormuz, on the Indian seaboard, to Chistopol, on the Volga, lay the ruins of intransigent towns and regions, with towers built by Timur's warriors from the skulls of their victims. Later in the year he set out to conquer China with an enormous expedition, still suffering from the excesses of his celebrations. He died in February 1405, near Chimkent, probably from a fever provoked by excessive drinking.

He was unlettered but not ignorant; his physical vigour was matched by his mental vitality. He delighted in the company of scholars and in playing chess. He could discuss with the leading scholars of Islām questions of history, religious dogma, and practical science. He was above all master of the military techniques developed by Genghis Khan, using every weapon in the military and diplomatic armory of the day. He never missed an opportunity to exploit the weakness (political, economic, or military) of the adversary or to use intrigue, treachery, and alliance to serve his purposes. The seeds of victory were sown among the ranks of the enemy by his agents before an engagement. He conducted sophisticated negotiations with both neighbouring and distant powers. which are recorded in diplomatic archives from England to China. In battle, mobility and surprise were his major weapons of attack, but this chess-playing nomad knew when to hold back and wait. His disposition was such that he could change course or target whenever circumstances provided superior alternatives. The French Orientalist René Grousset criticized Timur's campaigns on the grounds that they lacked geographical coherence, but this was irrelevant to flexible nomadic tactics. The demands

Personality and assessment

of Islām to wage war against the infidel, the needs of his kingdom in Central Asia, and the predatory appetites of the nomad lords provided Timur with the necessary elements for successful aggressive campaigns.

Few records of him have survived five centuries of strife, but those that have are richly varied. Court records of the campaigns were composed in Persian prose and Turkic verse. The great Arab historian Ibn Khaldūn left an account of meetings with Timur at the time of the Syrian campaign. The Spanish ambassador describes his experiences at Timur's court in Samarkand, as does the Pope's envoy. Some of his diplomatic correspondence is preserved in the archives of Oriental and Western capitals, and there are collections of coins struck by Timur, showing his triangular device, in many museums. His living memorials are the Timurid monuments of Samarkand, covered in azure, turquoise, gold, and alabaster mosaics; these are dominated by the great cathedral mosque, ruined by an earthquake but still soaring to an immense fragment of dome. His mausoleum, the Gūr-e Amīr, is one of the gems of Islāmic art. Within the sepulchre he lies under a huge but broken slab of jade. Beside him are his chief divine and some of his descendants. The tomb was opened in 1941, having remained intact for half a millennium. The Soviet Archaeological Commission found the skeleton of a man who, though lame in both right limbs, must have been of powerful physique, tall for a Tatar, and of haughty bearing. With these remains there were bristles of a chestnut moustache. From this evidence a bust was reconstructed that probably gives a more realistic impression of his appearance than do the finely drawn features in the Persian miniatures.

Sons and grandsons fought over the succession when the Chinese expedition disbanded, but Timur's dynasty survived in Central Asia for a century in spite of fratricidal strife. Samarkand became a centre of scholarship and science. It was here that Ulūgh Beg, his grandson, set up an observatory and drew up the astronomical tables that were later used by the English royal astronomer in the 17th century. During the Timurid renaissance of the 15th century, Herāt, southeast of Samarkand, became the home of the brilliant school of Persian miniaturists. At the beginning of the 16th century, when the dynasty ended in Central Asia, his descendant Bābur established himself in Kābul and then conquered Delhi, to found the Muslim line of Indian emperors known as the Great Mughals.

Timur's successors

BIBLIOGRAPHY. The most scholarly study of the evidence relating to Timur's life is in the English translation of v.v. BARTHOLD, *Four Studies on the History of Central Asia*, vol. 1, *A Short History of Turkestan: History of Semirechyé* (1956), and vol. 2, *Ulugh-beg* (1958). Based substantially on this work is the account of his life given in HILDA HOOKHAM, *Tamburlaine, the Conqueror* (1962), which also contains the fullest available bibliography of works in English. Another account of Timur is given in HAROLD LAMB, *Tamerlane, the Earth Shaker* (1929).

(H.H.H.)

Tinamiformes

The Tinamiformes, or tinamous, are a group of ground-dwelling, chicken-like birds of Central and South America. They have a superficial resemblance to partridges and quail (gallinaceous birds) but are placed in a distinct order related to the much larger rheas. Tinamous long have interested scientists because of many peculiar features of their skeleton and biology that link them to the large flightless birds or ratites: the ostriches, emus, cassowaries, and rheas.

Tinamous, considered by hunters to be among the finest game birds in sport and in palatability, are heavily hunted in many parts of South America. Market hunting has been curtailed by law but is still practiced in some countries. Frozen tinamous from Argentina were formerly sold in the United States under the name South American quail. Although no species of tinamou was listed as endangered in the 1971 list of the International Union for the Conservation of Nature, habitat destruction and heavy hunting have reduced many populations.

General features. The 46 species of tinamous range in size from that of a small quail, about 15 centimetres (6 inches) long and about 150 grams (5 ounces) in weight, to that of a large grouse, 45 centimetres long and about 2 kilograms (4 pounds) in weight. Tinamous are rather uniform in body proportions and stance, resembling guinea fowl (Numididae). The head is small and the bill medium sized, relatively thin, and slightly downcurved. The long, slender neck is clothed in short feathers. The body is heavy, with a high rump outline from the enormous development of rump feathers, which generally hide the extremely short or even rudimentary tail. The short, rounded wings are inconspicuous on the standing bird; the primary flight feathers are hidden by the full plumage of the flanks. The bare legs are rather thick and of medium length. There are three short front toes, with the hindtoe elevated or absent.

The sexes are alike, except that the female is generally slightly heavier and has brighter coloration. The plumage coloration is highly concealing, in spotted or barred patterns of brown, gray, rufous, or tan, depending on the environment. The crested tinamous of the genus *Eudromia* have a long, slender crest that the bird directs forward when it is excited. The colour of the legs or of the bill is vivid and diagnostic in several species, such as the yellow-legged tinamous (*Crypturellus noctivagus*).

Protective coloration in spotted or barred patterns

Natural history. *Locomotion.* Highly adapted for ground dwelling, tinamous normally walk rapidly (especially the savanna species) and can run with amazing swiftness. If forced into extended running, however, as when chased by men or dogs, they tire quickly and are likely to stumble and fall. They are best able to escape notice by standing motionless with the neck extended or by quietly slipping away, making use of all available cover. Some species may crouch or feign death, rising in flight only when almost stepped upon. Small tinamous that live in open terrain sometimes hide in animal holes, such as the burrows of armadillos.

The flight of tinamous is clumsy but swift and accompanied by an easily audible rumbling or whistling noise produced by the stiff, curved primaries. The elegant crested tinamou (*Eudromia elegans*) of the open tableland of Argentina alternates periods of flapping with short glides. When flushed, forest species sometimes collide with branches and tree trunks and may injure themselves. If forced to make several flights in short succession, tinamous soon become exhausted, apparently because of a low circulation rate, related in turn to the surprisingly small size of the heart and lungs. The flight muscles are well developed, but the circulatory system seems to be insufficient for sustained activity.

Unlike the gallinaceous birds, tinamous sleep on the ground at night. Exceptions are members of the genus *Tinamus*, which roost in trees, choosing thick, horizontal branches of tangled lianas high above ground.

Vocalizations. The voices of tinamous are among the strongest and most pleasant of any in the neotropics. They consist of loud, stereotyped, but melodious whistles, varying from the long and astonishingly songlike sequence of the brown tinamou (*Crypturellus obsoletus*) —astonishing because most relatives of the tinamous do not produce elaborate vocalizations—to the monosyllabic call of the cinereous tinamou (*C. cinereus*). The calls of the male and female are similar but discernibly different to the human ear. The female solitary tinamou (*Tinamus solitarius*) has a special call given during the time before egg laying, and another call is uttered by both sexes of this species after perching at dusk.

Habitat selection and food habits. Collectively, tinamous are adapted to many types of habitat, including dense woodland, thickets, open woodland, savanna, and even to the brunchgrass-covered plateaus of the high Andes, where they occupy the ecological niche held by the grouse in other parts of the world. In some forest regions as many as five species of tinamou coexist, inhabiting slightly different types of plant communities. The grassland tinamou do not occur north of the Amazon River; there the tinamou niche is occupied by the crested bobwhite (*Colinus cristatus*), a quail.

The food taken by tinamous varies with the season and habitat. In summer the red-winged tinamou (*Rhynchotus rufescens*), for example, eats mainly animal material —largely insects, but its mouth is large enough to swallow mice. In the stomach of one bird 707 termites were counted. In winter this species shifts over to vegetable food. It occasionally becomes a pest in agricultural areas, using its strong bill to dig up the roots of manioc, or cassava (*Manihot esculenta*). The small tinamous of the genus *Nothura* take mostly seeds, but the spotted tinamou (*Nothura maculosa*) occasionally eats ticks in pastures. The forest-inhabiting solitary tinamou prefers small fruits and berries, collected on the ground, but is not above taking a frog when it finds one. Members of the genus *Nothoprocta* are considered beneficial to agriculture because of their large consumption of insects. Young tinamous of all species are more dependent upon insects than are adults. Unlike the gallinaceous birds, tinamous do not scratch for food, as is evident by their weak toes and short nails; instead, they turn over leaves and other debris with the bill or dig with it.

Reproduction. Courtship behaviour has been described for only a few species of tinamous. Certain species have well-defined breeding periods, and others breed throughout the year. Courting birds are reported to raise the thickly feathered rump and display the brightly coloured undertail coverts. A similar display can be seen in a frightened *Crypturellus:* it presses the breast to the ground, raises the rump, spreads the terminal feathers like a fan, and exhibits the sharply marked undercoverts. Courting birds have been observed to chase each other around on the ground.

Multiple mating is the rule among tinamous, although a few species such as the ornate tinamou (*Nothoprocta ornata*) maintain stable pairs. All forms of polygamy exist, the conditions varying between and even within species. Many species have uneven sex ratios; preponderance of males seems to be more frequent, the ratio reaching four to one in the variegated tinamou (*Crypturellus variegatus*). The ratio in the ornate tinamou is

about one to one. For the solitary tinamou, on the other hand, there appears to be a preponderance of females.

The nest, a shallow depression in the ground, is constructed and defended by the male. The eggs are among the most beautiful of all bird eggs, always monochromatic and highly glazed. The colours include light chocolate brown, near black, purple, dark bluish green, light yellowish green, and gray when laid, but the shell pigments fade when exposed to light. One hen, or more, places her eggs in the nest of a male; when several females provide the eggs, the clutch may become quite large, eight to 16 eggs. Incubation, which lasts 19 to 20 days, is done entirely by the male, who broods and guides the chicks for several weeks after hatching. The chicks, blotched and streaked like the young of the rheas, are able to run as soon as they are hatched. When frightened, they squat and freeze, becoming almost invisible.

Paleontology and classification. There is no doubt that the tinamous represent one of the oldest stocks of birds on the South American continent. Three genera of fossil tinamous, of one species each, have been described from a single deposit from the upper Pliocene of Argentina (about 4,000,000 years ago). Most other fossil tinamous, mostly representing species still extant, have been found at scattered sites from the upper Pleistocene (less than 1,000,000 years ago) of South America.

Many authors have noted anatomical and biological resemblances between the tinamous and rheas, or nandus (Rheidae). The structure of the bony palate, an important feature in the taxonomy of ratite birds, quite clearly links the two groups, but most authorities prefer to maintain them as separate orders, Rheiformes and Tinamiformes, each with a single family, respectively, Rheidae and Tinamidae.

BIBLIOGRAPHY. P. BRODKORB, "Catalogue of Fossil Birds," *Bull. Fla. St. Mus. Biol. Sci.,* 7:179–293 (1963), a checklist of fossil birds, stating that ratites and carinates could have arisen from a tinamou-like stock; D.A. LANCASTER, "Biology of the Brushland Tinamou, *Nothoprocta cinerascens*," *Bull.* *Am. Mus. Nat. Hist.,* 127:271–314 (1964), one of the few comprehensive life histories of tinamous—the species inhabits the lowlands east of the Andes in northern Argentine, living in thorn woods; W. BEEBE, "The Variegated Tinamou, *Crypturus variegatus variegatus* (Gmeln)," *Zoologica,* 6:195–227 (1925); K.C. PARKES and G.A. CLARK, JR., "An Additional Character Linking Ratites and Tinamous, and an Interpretation of Their Monophyly," *Condor,* 68:459–471 (1966), ratites and tinamous share a conformation of the rhamphoteca not found in other birds; A.K. and O.P. PEARSON, "Natural History and Breeding Behaviour of the Tinamou *Nothoprocta Ornata*," *Auk,* 72:113–127 (1955), life history of a tinamou that lives in grass-covered hills of southern Peru at considerable heights in the Andes; H. SICK, "Tinamou," in A.L. THOMSON (ed.), *A New Dictionary of Birds* (1964), a survey of the principal characteristics of the whole group.

(H.S.)

Tin Products and Production

Tin (chemical symbol Sn, from the Latin *stannum*) is a soft, bluish-silver-white element that is highly malleable and ductile but has little mechanical strength. The main uses of tin are as thin coatings on steel sheet to be used as containers; in alloys such as bronze, solder, bearing metals, pewter, and type metal; and as chemical compounds. The most common alloying elements are copper, antimony, lead, and bismuth.

Relatively rare despite its worldwide use, tin is found in the ore cassiterite, or tinstone, the oxide of tin, either in lodes or alluvial deposits. The chief producing countries are Malaysia, Bolivia, U.S.S.R., Thailand, China (mainland), and Indonesia. Tin exists in two crystalline forms; common or white tin (beta tin), which is stable at temperatures above 13.2° C (55° F), and gray tin (alpha tin), the transformation product. When white tin disintegrates into a gray tin in powder, the condition is known as tin pest or tin disease. Although the transformation temperature is moderate (13.2° C), the change from white to gray tin does not occur unless the metal is of great purity and has been exposed to temperatures well below 0° C (32° F). Small amounts of bismuth, antimony, and lead, the impurities normally present in commercial grades of tin, retard such transformation. Thus, the spontaneous appearance of gray tin at low temperatures is a rare occurrence.

Tin has a highly crystalline structure, demonstrated when a sheet of tin is bent: the squeaking sound (tin cry) is produced by the twisting of the crystals. White tin—its industrial form—crystallizes in a tetragonal structure, and gray tin in a diamond-type cubic structure. The atomic number of tin is 50; its atomic weight is 118.69; the specific gravity of white tin is 7.28 and of gray tin is 5.75; melting point is 231.9° C (449.4° F) and boiling point is 2,270° C (4,118° F). It appears in group IVa of the periodic table. Further information on the physical and chemical properties of tin can be found in the article CARBON GROUP ELEMENTS AND THEIR COMPOUNDS.

History. Tin, in the form of its alloy bronze, was widely used in ancient times. Bronze implements with tin contents of 10 to 18 percent dating from about 3500 BC have been found in Ur (Iraq). Tin mining was reported in Caucasia as early as 1500 BC, and later in Persia (now Iran), Great Britain, France, and Spain. The Phoenicians are believed to have played an important part in spreading the early bronze culture by their trade in tin, which their ships brought to the eastern Mediterranean from Great Britain and Spain at least as early as 1100 BC. The Cornish tin mines were famous by the time the Romans conquered Great Britain in the 1st century AD. Tin-producing areas gradually opened up in other parts of the world, in Malaya (now West Malaysia) and China in the 9th century and in Indonesia and Thailand in the 18th century. Bolivia, Republic of Zaire, and Nigeria became important sources by the early 20th century.

Pliny the Elder in AD 79 described two alloys of tin and lead, now commonly called solder. The Romans are known to have used solder and tinned-copper vessels. Tinned-iron vessels appeared in Bohemia in the 14th century. Tinned-steel sheet (tinplate) was manufactured in England and Saxony by the middle of the 17th century.

Table 1: World Mine Production of Tin*

	1960	1961	1962	1963	1964	1965	1966	1967	1968	1969	1970	1971†
Malaysia	52,811	56,924	59,541	60,906	60,964	64,689	69,988	73,275	76,270	73,325	73,795	75,445
U.S.S.R.	16,256‡	17,272‡	17,272‡	21,336‡	22,352‡	23,368‡	24,384‡	25,400‡	26,416‡	27,433‡	27,433‡	28,449‡
Bolivia	19,718	20,735	21,836	22,564	24,708	23,405	26,036	27,320	29,408	30,047	29,380	27,881
Thailand	12,273	13,482	14,914	15,834	15,847	19,352	22,926	22,850	24,057	21,092	21,779	21,689
China (mainland)	28,448‡	30,480‡	28,448‡	28,448‡	25,400‡	25,400‡	22,352‡	20,320‡	20,320‡	20,321‡	20,321‡	20,321‡
Indonesia	22,958	18,871	17,587	13,134	16,607	14,934	12,726	13,815	16,828	17,413	19,062	19,722
Australia	2,237	2,789	2,758	2,906	3,700	3,911	4,915	5,675	6,756	8,722	9,512	9,515
Nigeria	7,798	7,903	8,341	8,863	8,861	9,700	9,504	9,489	9,798	8,741	7,959	7,117
Zaire	8,774	6,415	6,985	6,993	5,190	6,425	5,117	4,739	7,005	6,647	6,458	6,503
Brazil	1,581	591	743	1,168	803	1,839	1,885	1,761	1,861	2,650	3,315	2,601
Others	10,433	11,582	11,161	11,955	12,332	11,614	12,081	13,017	12,856	12,956	14,105	13,973
Total	183,287	187,044	189,586	194,107	196,764	204,637	211,914	217,661	231,575	229,347	233,119	233,216

*Expressed in terms of metal obtainable from ore in metric tons (1 metric ton = 1.1023 short tons). †Preliminary. ‡U.S. Bureau of Mines estimate.
Source: U.S. Dept. of Interior, Bureau of Mines, *Minerals Yearbook, 1964, 1967, 1969, 1971 Preprint.*

The development of modern high-speed machinery and rail transportation was facilitated by the invention in 1839 of Babbitt metal, an alloy containing 89 parts of tin, 9 of antimony, and 2 of copper; the antimony combined with the tin to form hard particles in the otherwise soft matrix. The metal was developed to provide bearings for steam engines.

The 20th century has witnessed a proliferation of applications of tin in both pure and alloy form. Its principal uses, in addition to tinplate, include piping, wire, tubes, sheet, foil, and anodes for electroplating. By 1971 the world production was about 233,000 metric tons (257,000 tons), of which more than one-third was used for tinplate.

Economic importance. Ninety percent of the world's production of tin comes from nine countries, with the leading producer Malaysia. Table 1 shows the principal producers. Small tonnages are also produced in Canada, Japan, Portugal, and Spain. Tin is especially important to the economy of Bolivia and the producing countries in Southeast Asia.

The principal user of tin is the U.S., which imports about one-third of all the primary tin produced and augments this supply with secondary tin recovered from scrap. Industrial requirements for tin in the U.S.S.R. have been rising; in the early 1970s imports amounted to about 5,000 metric tons (5,510 tons) a year. Consumption of tin by countries is given in Table 2.

Table 2: Primary Tin Consumption for 1968
(metric tons)

	tinplate	solder	bronze	Babbitt metal	tinning	sub-total	total
U.S.*	31,888	16,103	4,269	2,223	2,240	56,723	64,307
(percent)	50	25	7	3	3	88	
Japan	11,557	7,729	2,006	1,405	547	23,244	24,663
(percent)	47	31	8	6	2	94	
U.K.†	9,559	1,485	2,417	3,316‡	1,405	18,182	21,174
(percent)	50	8	13	18	7	96	
West Germany	3,817	1,557	270	351	1,304	7,299	12,277
(percent)	31	13	2	3	11	60	
France	4,960	2,583	807	713	553	9,616	10,518
(percent)	47	25	8	7	5	92	
U.S.S.R.	—	—	—	—	—	—	30,968§

*U.S. Bureau of Mines Tin Report. †Figures include secondary tin consumption; 1968 tin consumption—primary, 17,145 tons, secondary, 2,000 tons. ‡White metal. §Estimated total consumption for U.S.S.R.

MINING, REFINING, AND RECOVERY

Cassiterite the major tin ore The mineral cassiterite, or tin dioxide, is the major tin ore of the world. In lode deposits, as found in Bolivia, tin sulfide minerals such as stannite, teallite, cylindrite, and canfieldite are found with the cassiterite in granite and quartz.

Because cassiterite is both heavy and chemically resistant, it forms large placers, or residual concentrations, from which lighter, less stable materials have been removed by various natural forces. Alluvial placers, by far the largest in number and most productive, are deposited in streams where the water flow is slack. Almost 60 percent of the tin production in Southeast Asia comes from alluvial deposits, which yield about 0.4 pound of tin metal per cubic yard.

Residual placers form on top of a bedrock source of cassiterite as chemical decay removes other minerals. In Zaire, residual placers grade downward into weathered lodes and are mined either as placers or open-pit lodes.

Eluvial placers occur at the bottom of slopes after the gravity separation of cassiterite from the decayed tin-bearing rock debris that has been washed or wind blown down the slope. Marine placers lie beneath seawater. Seagoing dredges work such placers off the coasts of Thailand and Indonesia.

Mining techniques. Alluvial deposits lend themselves to mining by water-washing methods and gravity separation of the cassiterite. Lode deposits require the more complex operations, including rock blasting and crushing prior to gravity separation.

Placer tin is mined either by marine methods, using bucketline dredges and gravel pumps, or through land-mining techniques, especially open-pit methods. Bucketline dredges are quite similar to the floating dredges that are used to mine other types of placer deposits (see MINING AND QUARRYING). The tin-bearing mud is excavated at depths down to 140 feet (43 metres) below the water level. In either method, final concentration and removal of associated minerals is carried out on shore using a variety of techniques. Final concentrates, ready for direct smelting, contain almost pure cassiterite (between 70 and 77 percent tin).

In gravel-pump and hydraulic mining methods, water jets break up the tin-bearing material, and the material is then conveyed by various methods to the washing apparatus, or launders. In gravel-pump mining, a pump elevates the watery mud up to a wooden trough, or palong. In hydraulicking, a natural head of water flushes the ore down the gently sloping palong, trapping the heavy tin oxide particles behind wooden slats, or riffles. The preliminary rough concentrates are collected periodically and transferred to dressing sheds for final concentration. In open-pit operations the material is excavated dry by power shovels and transported via conveyor belt to a washing plant and dressing shed.

Underground lode deposits can be found at high altitudes (12,000 to 15,000 feet [3,700 to 4,600 metres] above sea level in Bolivia) or low ones (down to 1,300 feet [400 metres] below sea level, as in Cornwall, England). The lodes are reached by lateral passages driven into the side of a mountain or by vertical shafts. The ore is broken up by blasting and drilling and then taken above ground for further crushing and grinding. The finely divided ore is then concentrated by the same types of separations used for alluvial deposits.

Ore beneficiation. Concentrates from alluvial deposits are smelted without further beneficiation, or further concentration through refinement. Lode deposits of only 40 to 60 percent tin, on the other hand, must be roasted and acid-leached (see below) to remove sulfur and other metallic impurities.

Roasting. Typically, the crushed concentrates are loaded into the top of a six-hearth so-called Herreshoff furnace and are moved down to succeeding lower hearths by rotating rakes (rabble arms) and the force of gravity. Temperatures inside the gas-heated furnace range from 315° C (600° F) in the lowest discharge hearth to 760° C (1,400° F) in the middle hearths. Most of the roasting is done in two-hour stages between 650° C (1,200° F) and 760° C (1,400° F). This step of the process removes most of the sulfur and some of the arsenic; the sulfides of iron, copper, bismuth, and zinc are converted to oxide; and lead sulfide is oxidized to sulfate. Adding 1 to 5 percent salt removes some of the volatile chlorides of lead, bismuth, arsenic, antimony, and silver in the fume; the chlorides remaining are water soluble.

Some Bolivian ores contain up to 9 percent tungsten, which is recovered by mixing sodium carbonate with the roasted concentrate and heating it to 600° C (1,100° F) to form sodium tungstate, a water-soluble compound from which the tungsten can be recovered by evaporation.

Acid leaching. The roasted concentrates are leached with hydrochloric acid to remove most of the iron, zinc, lead, silver, bismuth, and copper impurities. After washing and drying, the purified concentrate is ready for smelting.

Problems of tin metallurgy

Smelting. The metallurgy of tin is comparatively simple, though it does present a few problems: (1) the temperature required to reduce tin dioxide with carbon also reduces the oxides of other metals in the ore (reduced iron, for example, forms hard compounds with tin); (2) since tin at smelting temperatures is extremely fluid, it finds the most minute openings for escape and soaks into porous refractories; (3) tin reacts with furnace linings, thus producing slags that must be retreated.

Because of those problems and the resulting high tin content of the slag, smelting is accomplished in two stages: (1) primary smelting in either reverberatory or blast furnaces and (2) retreatment of slags (unwanted hard compounds of tin and iron) and refinery dross. Most large tin-smelting plants use reverberatory furnaces for both primary smelting and retreatment processes. Operations are more easily controlled, and cleaner slags are produced than in the older blast furnaces (see METALLURGY). Loss of tin dust is much smaller when the reverberatory furnace is used to smelt finely divided ores and concentrates.

The reverberatory tin-smelting furnace is a relatively new and special type of blast furnace, in which heat is reflected from the roof of the furnace onto the material. Thus, the material does not come into contact with the fuel. The hearth slopes toward a taphole that is near the centre and to one side and low enough to drain the furnace completely. The size of the hearth varies, the largest being 30 to 40 feet (9 to 12 metres) long and 12 to 15 feet (3.7 to 4.6 metres) wide. The larger reverberatory furnaces will take an 8- to 15-ton load that contains tin concentrates, 15 to 20 percent anthracite, and smaller amounts of limestone, slag, sand, and by-products from the refining steps.

Batch operations. Tin smelting is a batch operation in which one load is smelted and tapped before the next is added. The furnaces are operated at 1,200° to 1,300° C (2,200° to 2,400° F); the time for each load is 10 to 12 hours. The batch is stirred at intervals. It is customary to limit the amount of reducing agent in the primary furnace and to permit a considerable amount of tin to flow out as slag. This practice produces metallic tin low in iron.

The completed batch is tapped into a settler, from which the slag usually overflows into cast-iron pots. The molten tin is cast from the bottom of the settler into slabs of about 75 pounds (34 kilograms) and is ready for further refining.

The slag, containing 10 to 25 percent tin, is resmelted in the same kind of furnace used for smelting the ore. But a higher temperature, up to 1,480° C (2,700° F), is required because the reduction of the tin silicate in the slag is more difficult than the reduction of the tin oxide in the ore. Fine anthracite coal serves as the reducing agent; limestone flux and metallic iron may be added to aid in the reduction. The aim is to produce a discardable slag

containing no more than 2 percent tin. During the resmelting considerable iron–tin compound is formed and returned to the system.

Electric smelting. Electric furnace smelting was first used in 1934 at Geomines in Shaba (formerly Katanga), now in Zaire. The modern three-phase Héroult electric-arc furnaces, rated at 1,000 kilovolt-amperes, are cylindrical shells lined first with insulating brick and then with firebrick. The graphite electrodes are 1.3 feet (40 centimetres) in diameter (see METALLURGY).

Refining. The crude tin produced by smelting must be refined by further heat or by an electrolytic process. Heat treatment includes two steps: liquation and boiling.

Liquation and boiling

In liquation, crude tin placed on the sloping hearth of a small reverberatory furnace is heated to just above its melting point. The fluid tin runs into a boiling kettle, while metals whose melting points are sufficiently higher than that of tin remain on the hearth as dross. Iron is largely removed, and arsenic, antimony, and copper are partly removed; but lead and bismuth, also with low melting points, flow with the tin into the kettle, where the final refining (boiling) is carried out.

The molten tin in the boiling kettle is agitated with steam, compressed air, or poles of green wood, which produce steam. The remaining impurities form a light scum, which is removed and recirculated through the smelting cycle. The pure tin is cast in iron molds, usually in the form of 100-pound (45-kilogram) ingots. The purity of grade A tin is guaranteed to exceed 99.8 percent tin.

Electrolytic refining. Electrolytic refining produces a purer grade of tin than that obtained by fuel-fired heat refining; but costs are higher and the demand for pure grades (99.99+ percent) is low. One modern electrorefining facility has developed an economical method by processing low-grade concentrates. First it upgrades them by roasting, leaching, and fire refining, to give a crude tin of approximately 93 percent tin, 3 percent antimony, 2 percent lead, 1 percent arsenic, and 0.5 percent copper. The final electrolytic process produces a metal in the range of 99.97 percent tin.

Recovery from scrap. Several thousand tons of tin are recovered each year from metal scrap, mostly in the form of tin-bearing alloys and clean tinplate clippings. In the U.S. secondary tin metal recovered from scrap may average 3,050 metric tons annually, while 18,300 metric tons of tin are recovered in the form of tin alloys and tin compounds. Other major consuming countries have similar salvage programs.

Detinning tinplate scrap

In salvage operations, often called detinning, clean tinplate scrap is placed in perforated steel-plate drums that revolve in a vat of hot caustic soda solution, containing an oxidant such as sodium nitrate or nitrite. Steam coils maintain a temperature of 96° to 99° C (205° to 210° F). The tin dissolves, forming sodium stannate in solution, which can be treated in three ways: (1) evaporation of the solution to crystallize the sodium stannate; (2) electrolysis to recover tin metal; or (3) acidification by carbon dioxide, sulfuric acid, or acidic gases to precipitate tin hydrate that can be further processed to tin oxide, smelted to tin metal, or converted to tin chemicals. About 711,000 metric tons (784,000 tons) of tinplate scrap are treated in this way annually in the United States.

Tin-bearing alloy scrap is handled by secondary smelters as part of the production of primary metals and alloys. Lead refineries recover metals from solder and tin dross, Babbitt metal, and type metal. Copper refineries rework scrap tin, bronze, and tin-containing brass.

METALLIC TIN PRODUCTS

Smelters control purity of tin between 99.8 and 99.98 percent; about 90 percent of all tin produced is Grade A, which has a minimum purity of 99.8 percent. Ingots of 28, 56, and 100 pounds are purchased from metal brokers by steel mills, copper and lead refiners, solder and bearing manufacturers, and metal and alloy dealers. Smaller consumers may purchase individual ingots of pure or alloyed tin from metal dealers; or they may purchase fabricated products such as sheet, tube, or powder. The primary industrial use of tin is for tinplate and tin coatings on iron, copper, and other metals; other uses are as alloys, chemical compounds, and pure tin products.

Pure metal. As a first step in the production of tin products, ingots often must be remelted. Tin, because of its low melting point, can be remelted in cast-iron or steel pots, which resist corrosion by molten tin. The tin may be poured, ladled, or pumped into open molds or hinged molds of cast iron, sand, plaster, rubber, or other materials. Shrinkage on solidification is about 3 percent. Cast bars or slabs are readily rolled into sheet and foil, extruded into tubes and pipe, or drawn into wire. Tin is pliable during cold-working and does not harden when worked.

Tin pipe. Molten tin is cast into a cylindrical tubing mold that forms the chamber of an extrusion machine. After the metal solidifies, a ram descends into the chamber and extrudes the metal through a die. The most common diameter sizes for tubes are from about 0.25 inch (6.3 millimetres) up to about 0.75 inch (19 millimetres).

Tin piping is used for conveying distilled water and for draft-beer tubing from barrels to counter taps. Ancillary equipment for these operations requires tin-lined brass valves and fittings. In lining valves, the tin metal is cast into the fluxed, cleaned body, and the openings are machined out. Brass pipe can be tin-lined by inserting tin tubing into the pipe and drawing a steel ball through the tube to expand the tin against the wall in a tight bond.

Tin wire. Cylindrical billets with a diameter of 2 to 3 inches (51 to 76 millimetres) are extruded as wire from a press at a diameter of about 3/16 inch (4.8 millimetres). This wire can be reduced on normal wiredrawing machines to as fine as 0.2 millimetre. Tin wire is used for electrical fuses and other special purposes.

Collapsible tubes. Collapsible tubes of tin, in which shaving cream, toothpaste, and other pastelike materials are packaged, are formed by impact extrusion. Cone-shaped slugs or disks of tin containing about 0.2 percent copper as a hardener are oiled and fed into the die of the press, which is capable of exerting hundreds of tons of pressure per square inch. The ram of the press descends on the slug, squeezing tin out through the narrow annulus, or ringlike opening, of the die and forming a tube enveloping the ram. The tin-clad ram then returns upward out of the die, swings forward, and is simultaneously cleared of the tin by a blast of compressed air. The tubes are hand-stacked vertically over close-fitting pegs on a conveyor belt. The nozzles may be formed with their screw threads in this same operation. The tubes are printed and dried while still on the pegs.

Collapsible tubes are light; a body of 4½ inches (114 millimetres) in length and 1 inch (25 millimetres) in diameter weighs only 1/40 pound (12 grams). Wall thickness ranges from 0.005 to 0.01 inch (0.13 to 0.25 millimetre).

Tin-coated lead tubes, cheaper than all-tin, can also be impact extruded from slugs. A slab of lead is placed between two sheets of tinfoil of a thickness proportional to that desired on the wall of the tubes. Two roll passes weld the tin to the lead. The extrusion process is the same as for all-tin tubes.

Tin sheet and foil. In producing sheet and foil, tin is cast into slabs in either open or book molds. The slabs are rolled soon after casting because the grain size can enlarge on standing. The first pass through the rollers reduces thickness to one-half. The next pass, which sometimes is made across the direction of the first rolling, reduces the thickness by one-half again. Successive reductions to sheet or foil are about nine-tenths on each pass. On the way to the reelers, the foil passes over high-speed polishing rollers. A smear of pure olive oil serves as a lubricant in the early stages.

Tin anodes. Tin anodes for electroplating processes can be cast, extruded, or rolled from billets to any shape or size. Connector hooks are attached by drilling and tapping. Large, 9,000-pound anodes for tinplate production are cast in iron molds.

Tin powder. Tin powder is produced by spraying molten tin from nozzles under slight pressure in a vertical tower in which an inert atmosphere is maintained. The

tower is sufficiently high to allow the atomized powder to solidify and cool in its downward path. The fine powder is graded and classified by screening.

Tin in glass manufacture. Clear, flat glass is produced by allowing molten glass to solidify while it floats on a pool of molten tin, avoiding the costly polishing and grinding required in making plate glass (see GLASS PRODUCTS AND PRODUCTION).

Tinplate. Tinplate is a low-carbon steel sheet (see STEEL PRODUCTION) thinly coated with pure tin. The strength and formability of steel are combined with the corrosion resistance, solderability, and appearance of tin. Tinplate is ductile and can be drawn and folded into complicated shapes. The tin surface can be enamelled, lacquered, or painted. Tinplate is used for food cans because tin is nontoxic and resists corrosive attack by air and by food acids. Oxygen or dry air combines with tin to form an invisible and protective oxide film on the surface that thickens as the temperature is raised. In vacuum packing (in the absence of oxygen), tin resists a wide range of acids by retaining a film of hydrogen.

World production of tinplate in 1968 was more than 11,000,000 metric tons (12,000,000 tons) containing about 75,000 tons of pure tin. About 93 percent of world tinplate production is by electrolytic tinning and 7 percent by hot-dip tinning.

Electrolytic tinning. A coating of tin can be deposited on most metals in high-speed electroplating processes. Tin alloy coatings can be achieved by including salts of other metals such as copper, lead, zinc, cadmium, and nickel in the electrolyte. The world's first commercial electrolytic tinplate line was installed at the United States Steel Corp. plant in Gary, Indiana, in 1937.

In the halogen tin-plating process, using the halogen compounds stannous chloride and alkali fluorides with addition agents as the electrolyte, the sheet travels at 1,500 to 2,000 feet per minute horizontally instead of following vertical paths in individual plating vats or cells. One side of the sheet is plated on one level; the direction is then reversed, and the other side is plated on an upper level. An alkaline process is based on an alkaline solution of sodium stannate and sodium hydroxide that functions as the electrolyte. The plating speed (500 feet per minute) is lower than that in the other processes. The Ferrostan process uses a stannous sulfate bath containing phenol sulfonic acid and addition agents.

The cold-reduced steel is handled as a continuous band through all operations, including electrolytic cleaning, treatment with dilute acid (light pickling), electrodeposition of the tin coating, rinsing and drying, brightening of the dull matte coating by induction heating, chromate treatment, rinsing and drying, oiling with a thin film of dioctyl sebacate, and coiling. Shipped coils weigh up to 20,000 pounds (9,000 kilograms). Coils may be diverted to shears that cut the finished tinplate into sheets 20 × 14 inches (51 × 36 centimetres).

Electrolytic tinplate is produced in five grades, with tin-coating thickness ranging from 0.000015 inch (0.00038 millimetre) on both sides of 0.25-pound (0.11-kilogram) tinplate to 0.00006-inch (0.0015 millimetre) on both sides of one-pound (0.45-kilogram) tinplate. Differential tinplate with a heavier coating on the surface that is to form the inner side of a container in which corrosive foods are to be packed is also produced.

Double-reduced tinplate, introduced in the 1960s, involves a base sheet that has been cold-rolled a second time to reduce its thickness to about 0.006 inch (0.15 millimetre) and bring out the inherent strength of the steel.

Hot-dip tinning. Molten tin wets and adheres to most metals and is highly fluid, draining rapidly from an article before solidification and leaving a thin, even coating that is bright, lustrous, and nontoxic. The coating protects the underlying metal from oxidation and chemical attack from weak acids, alkalies, and electrolytes; the coating also has lubricating properties and aids in forming and drawing operations; and the tin coating makes possible the joining of metals that are difficult to solder. The hot-dip process, though it is used to make less than 1 percent of the total tinplate produced in the U.S., is important in other countries.

A modern hot-tinning unit comprises a thermostatically controlled vessel of molten tin held at about 316° C (600° F). A submerged mechanism of rollers and guides conducts clean, cold-reduced steel sheets downward through a layer of zinc chloride flux into the tin and then upward and out of the tin through a thick covering layer of palm oil. The sheets are subjected to the squeegeeing action of immersed tinned-steel rollers that regulate coating thickness. The tinned sheets are cooled by an air blast and then cleaned and polished, usually by a combination of washing with alkaline detergent and dry cleaning.

Hot-dip tinplate is used primarily for packaging corrosive foods such as acid fruits. It has a minimum tin-coating thickness of 1.25 pound per 31,360 square inches. Special grades with coating thickness up to three pounds of tin per 31,360 square inches are produced for noncontainer uses such as gas meters, light engineering parts, kitchen utensils, and electrical equipment.

Other tin-coated articles. Fabricated articles made of cast iron, steel, copper, and copper alloys are given a smooth, bright tin coating by immersion in liquid tin. Coatings also may be electroplated, using either acid or alkaline electrolytes. The dull-plated tin can be brightened in hot oil, but proprietary bright-tinning processes are in commercial use. The coating thickness on fabricated articles is usually in the range of 0.0001 to 0.002 inch, depending on requirements and corrosion protection desired.

For tin-coated copper vessels and cast-iron bearing shells, liquid tin is poured onto the surface and wiped smooth with a cloth pad. Copper tubing and aluminum pistons can be protected from corrosion with a thin tin coating applied by immersion in a solution of tin salts.

Alloys and alloy-coated products. Tin is easily alloyed. Copper, antimony, bismuth, cadmium, and silver when alloyed to tin increase its hardness, mechanical strength, corrosion resistance, and workability. High-tin alloys are noted for their conformability, low coefficient of friction, retention of oil films on the surface, and good casting properties. When tin is a minor constituent in alloys, it can provide specific or unusual effects. (For bronze, bell metal, and gunmetal see COPPER PRODUCTS AND PRODUCTION. The principal constituent of those alloys is copper.)

Solder. After tinplate, the largest use of tin is in solders for joining metals at temperatures below 427° C (800° F); tin also is used in filler metals (materials for filling in holes and dents in automobile bodies) that melt well below that temperature. Tin–lead alloy solders constitute the largest portion of all solders in use. Alloys ranging from 2 to 70 percent tin, with the balance lead, and melting between 183° and 312° C (361° and 594° F) are used for joining copper, brass, nickel–silver, iron, tinplate, and other coated metals. For special purposes, tin–antimony, tin–antimony–lead, tin–silver, tin–zinc, and lead–tin–silver alloys are used. Special low-melting alloys (fusible alloys) melting below 150° C (300° F) contain bismuth, cadmium, tin, lead, and indium. The composition, melting characteristics, and applications of commonly used solders are given in the article WELDING, BRAZING, AND SOLDERING. The melting characteristics are given in terms of the temperature below which the alloy is completely solid (its solidus) and above which it is completely molten (its liquidus). With the melting points of both tin and lead low and fairly close together, they can be alloyed in iron pots or crucibles.

Because of the large differences in the specific gravities of tin and lead (7.28 and 11.34, respectively), mechanical stirring is necessary throughout melting and casting to keep the lead from sinking to the bottom. Molten solder may be poured into separate molds to solidify into ingots or may be cast continuously by feeding the molten metal into a water-cooled graphite die at such a rate that billets are produced without interruption. A travelling saw divides the issuing billet into convenient lengths. Billets may be remelted to form solder strip that can be rolled to solder foil and then cut to any shape. Short billets may be

extruded through a die, coiled, and drawn to form wire solder in sizes ranging in diameter from 0.128 inch (10 standard wire gauge) to 0.028 inch (22 standard wire gauge).

Hollow wire or tubes of various shapes, diameters, and configurations are manufactured containing a flux core that is introduced as a warm liquid during drawing and solidifies when cold. The flux can be noncorrosive or corrosive.

Solder also is made in powder form as paste solder, an alloy suspended in a mixture of emulsifying material and flux. It is particularly useful in mechanized soldering, in which premeasured quantities of solder and flux are applied automatically.

Fusible alloys. Alloys that melt at temperatures below the melting point of tin are formed mainly with metals of similarly low melting points, such as bismuth, cadmium, lead, and indium. They are termed fusible alloys because they melt rapidly when the melting temperature is reached. Two groups of alloys stand out. The first, containing 15.5 percent tin, 52.5 percent bismuth, and 32 percent lead, melts at 96° C (205° F); the second, containing 13.1 percent tin, 49.5 percent bismuth, 27.3 percent lead, and 10.1 percent cadmium, melts at 70° C (158° F).

Contraction of alloys during solidification results in castings of dimensions smaller than those of the mold. But alloys containing bismuth and antimony may expand as well as contract during solidification, depending on the proportion of the metals present. Fusible alloys that are dimensionally stable with the mold are suitable for making foundry patterns and dies. Fusible alloys play a key role in safety devices that operate when the surrounding temperature reaches their melting points—*e.g.*, fire alarms, water-sprinkler devices, and fire-door closers. Other uses include: low-temperature soldering, to avoid damaging heat-sensitive materials; and tube bending, in which the alloy is poured into the tube, which is then bent and the alloy melted out.

Babbitt metal. Babbitt metal (tin and lead-base bearing metals or white-metal bearing alloys) serves as the lining for bearing shells of cast iron, steel, bronze, or gunmetal. Babbitt metal, which is white in colour and has very low friction, may be made of: (1) high-tin alloys that are substantially lead-free; (2) intermediate alloys in which some tin is replaced by lead; and (3) high-lead alloys. All are low-melting materials consisting of hard compounds in a soft matrix. The compounds found in each group are similar; it is in the composition and properties of the matrix that they differ. Typical compositions are given in Table 3. In compounding bearing metal, the tin is melted first; the copper and antimony strips are then dipped in tinning flux and lowered into the molten tin, where they dissolve below 400° C (752° F) without oxidation. Sometimes master alloys, 50 percent antimony and 10 percent copper, instead are immersed in the tin. When lead is added, the molten metals must be well stirred. Users of Babbitt metal usually buy ingots of the required composition and melt them in iron kettles from which they can ladle or pump the molten alloy.

The bearing shell or backing is precoated with tin for tin-base bearings or with lead–tin for lead-base bearings. While the coating is still molten, the white metal is cast onto the backing and allowed to solidify from the bond inward to prevent contraction cavities at the bond and to restrict the growth of intermetallic compound (alloy layer) at the interface between the bearing shell and the white metal alloy. Pouring temperatures are usually 50° C (122° F) above the point at which the metal is completely molten. The lining is machined to a mirror-bright finish and specified thickness.

High-tin alloy bearings are used for high unit loads and high operating temperatures. They hold oil films and readily adapt their shapes to conform to the shaft. Foreign matter not carried away by the lubricant is embedded below the surface and rendered harmless. Lead-base alloy bearings are prone to separate into elemental lead and tin and have a lower thermal conductivity than tin-base bearings.

Varieties of tin coatings [margin note]

Lining bearing shells [margin note]

Table 3: Composition and Uses of Tin Alloys

trade name or type	composition (percent)											uses
	Cu	Sn	Pb	Sb	Ni	Al	Si Ti	Zr	Cr	Fe		
Tin base and lead base												
Babbitt metal (grade 1)	4.5	91		4.5								turbines, centrifugal pumps
Babbitt metal (grade 2)	3.5	89		7.5								automotive bearings
Babbitt metal (grade 3)	8	84		8								
Babbitt metal (grade 4)	3	75	10	12								
Babbitt metal (grade 5)	2	65	18	15								bearings
Jeweler's white metal		92		8								costume jewelry
Pewter (casting)	0.5	92		7.5								plates, domestic utensils
Pewter (spinning)	2	91		7								tea and coffee service, trays, tankards
Pewter (soft)	2	95		3								
Britannia metal	1–3	90–95		4–8								castings, ornamental objects
Linotype		3–5	balance	11–12								type metal
Stereotype		6–8	balance	13–15								type metal
Monotype		7–8	balance	15–17								type metal
Foundry type		10–13	balance	20–25								type metal
Aluminum base												
Alcoa 80S	1	6.5			0.5	balance	1.5					solid bearings subject to high loads
Aluminum–Tin	1	20				balance						automotive bearings-connecting rod, main camshaft
Miscellaneous												
Alpha titanium		2.5				5	balance					structural material for aircraft and spacecraft
Zircaloy-2		1.5					0.05	balance	0.10	0.12		nuclear power reactor fuel cladding
Superconducting Nb₃Sn		33.4										solenoid magnets
Dental amalgam*		12										fillings

*Plus mercury, silver balance.

Aluminum–tin bearing alloys. Aluminum–tin bearing alloys are of two types. The 6.5 percent tin alloy, usually the material in sand or gravity die castings, is rarely bonded to a stronger backing. Its high fatigue strength enables it to carry higher fluctuating loads than either the tin-base or softer copper–lead alloys, but its ability to embed foreign matter is low. The finished bearings, usually electroplated with tin, serve as connecting rod and main bearings for tractors and heavy-duty gasoline and diesel engines.

The other type of aluminum–tin alloy (20 percent tin) is used for connecting rod, main, and camshaft bearings for passenger cars, especially in Europe. This type of bearing withstands high loads and fatigue at elevated temperatures. The aluminum–tin alloy in sheet form can be bonded directly to a soft steel backing. Both surfaces are scratchbrushed and rolled together in a single pass so that the total reduction is at least 45 percent. By annealing for one hour at 350° C (662° F), the tin is distributed throughout the aluminum matrix in discrete particles and provides a constant bearing surface.

Pewter. Pewter is an alloy of tin hardened with antimony and copper. Modern pewter compositions are given in Table 3. The best grades contain no lead.

Pewter played an important part in the development of civilization as a medium of artistic expression and as a material from which domestic utensils were fashioned (see METALWORK). Pewter exceeds most other metals in ductility and ease of working. It may be stretched, compressed, and bent into almost any desired shape; and it does not harden sufficiently on cold working with tools to make annealing necessary. Pewter is melted and cast like other tin-base alloys. Slabs for rolling can be cast in open or hinged molds, which may be of cast iron, plaster of paris, wood, papier-mâché, or rubber. Articles also can be cast in sections and assembled by soldering.

Pewter ingots are rolled to sheet, which is a starting material for articles made by simple forming, spinning (forming while rapidly rotating), stretching, or hammering. Modern pewter can be given a mirror-bright finish or a soft satin sheen by polishing, and it retains its brightness indefinitely. It is used for tankards, domestic utensils, plates, trays, and tea and coffee services. Reproductions of objects from the 17th and 18th centuries are often made, some cast from the original molds.

Type metal. Type metal compositions are shown in Table 3. Different kinds of typecasting and printing processes each require special alloy properties that are obtained by altering, within fairly narrow limits, the proportions of tin, antimony, and lead (see PRINTING).

Alloyed cast iron. Alloyed cast iron, with a 0.1 percent tin content, is used in automotive engine blocks, transmissions, and heat-resistant applications. The tin acts as a stabilizer. The iron has a higher and more uniform hardness, better machinability, and better wear resistance with tin. The pure tin is added to the ladle in the form of shot or pieces of wire just before casting.

Miscellaneous alloys. Alpha-type titanium alloys are particularly suitable for structural materials in aircraft and spacecraft because of their light weight, strength, weldability, and resistance to creep.

Zircaloy-2, an alloy of tin and zirconium, is technically feasible for use in all nuclear power reactors using pressurized water as a coolant and moderator. The low neutron absorption of zirconium makes it an attractive structural material and fuel cladding for nuclear power reactors, but it has low strength and highly variable corrosion behaviour. The addition of 1.5 percent tin overcomes these disadvantages.

Niobium–tin is important in the construction of high-field superconducting solenoid magnets. The alloys are excellent superconducting materials at low temperatures.

Tin-alloy-coated articles. Coatings of tin–lead alloys containing 63 percent or more tin can be applied to articles by hot dipping and by electrodeposition from a special electrolyte. The solderability of the coating is useful, particularly in the electronics industry, for parts made of copper, brass, or steel. Tin-alloy coatings on fabricated articles are generally harder, brighter, and more resistant to corrosion than pure tin coatings.

Tin–copper-coated articles (12 percent tin) have the appearance of 24-karat gold. Tin–zinc coated articles (75 percent tin) are readily solderable and have excellent corrosion resistance. Tin–nickel plated articles (66 percent tin) have decorative and functional uses. The coating is used to resist etching of certain areas in the manufacture of printed circuits.

Terneplate is low-carbon steel sheet or strip coated with terne metal, a lead–tin alloy. Lead alone does not alloy with iron, but, when from 7 to 20 percent tin is added, the

Tin as a stabilizer of cast iron

Terne metal

tin readily wets the steel and forms a solid solution with the lead. A composition of 80 to 85 percent lead and 20 to 15 percent tin is usually preferred. The clean, cold-reduced, mild-steel strip is coated by hot dipping, as in the tin-plating process, except at a higher temperature (370° C [700° F]). Its main uses are for roofing materials, automotive parts, casket linings, and packaging for paints and greases.

CHEMICAL COMPOUNDS

Tin compounds have been known since 1605 when Andreas Libavius, the 16th-century German author of the first textbook on chemistry, described a method of preparing tin tetrachloride. This compound was widely used for weighting silk fabrics until the 1930s, when synthetic fibres supplanted silk. Large amounts of white tin oxide were produced to give opacity to pure white ceramic glazes on bathroom fixtures until cheaper substitutes, such as zirconium oxide, appeared.

In the early 1940s, production of inorganic tin chemicals surged with the invention of the continuous electrolytic tin-plating processes for can stock. In the same period, the organotin stabilizer was invented. Organotin compounds, in which a tin atom carries one, two, three, or four alkyl or aryl groups, are prepared from tin tetraalkyl or tetraaryl compounds. When about 2 percent of an organotin compound is added during the heat processing of clear polyvinyl chloride polymers, decomposition and darkening are prevented, and the polyvinyl chloride is stabilized against degradation by sunlight. In the early 1970s, about 10 percent of the total production of vinyl chloride polymers was stabilized with tin compounds.

In the 1950s a Dutch chemist, G.J.M. Van der Kerk, discovered that trialkyltin and triaryltin compounds had biocidal and fungicidal properties; he concluded that toxicity results when the tin atom combines directly with three carbon atoms and reaches a maximum when the total number of carbon atoms in the molecule is about 12. Hundreds of tons of tin compounds have come into use as industrial fungicides in wood preservation, papermaking, and textile manufacture; as disinfectants in hospitals; as antifoulants for paint; and as agricultural sprays for root crops, fruit, and nut trees.

About 60 percent of tin chemicals are by-products of the process of detinning tinplate scrap. The United States, Great Britain, West Germany, The Netherlands, and Japan are the principal producers of tin chemicals.

Inorganic compounds. About 15 inorganic tin compounds of industrial importance are produced from either pure tin or basic tin compounds—sodium stannate and hydrated tin oxide—obtained from detinning tinplate scrap. Sodium stannate and hydrated tin oxide react with hydrochloric acid to form stannous chloride, an important intermediate in making other tin compounds.

Stannous chloride. Stannous chloride is made by dissolving granular tin in hydrochloric acid. When the solution is evaporated, crystals of hydrated stannous chloride are formed. The hydrate melts and decomposes at 38° C (100° F).

Uses of
stannous
chloride

Stannous chloride is a constituent of tin-plating electrolytes, the tin–nickel-alloy-plating electrolytes, and immersion-tinning processes. It is used as an activator for plating plastics and for silvering mirrors, an additive to drilling muds, an antisludge agent for oils, a stabilizer of perfume in soaps, and a catalyst in organic reactions. Careful neutralization of a solution of stannous chloride precipitates stannous oxide, a starting material for other tin compounds.

Stannous fluoborate. When stannous oxide is dissolved in fluoboric acid, stannous fluoborate is produced. This product, a salt, is sold commercially as a 47-percent solution for use in preparing the tin fluoborate electrolyte used in tin-plating.

Stannous fluoride. Stannous fluoride is obtained by dissolving stannous oxide in hydrofluoric acid. The chief use of this salt is in toothpaste formulations for preventing demineralization of teeth.

Stannous oxide. Stannous oxide is prepared by precipitating the hydrate from a solution of stannous chloride

with alkali carbonate. Its principal use is as an intermediate in preparing other stannous chemicals, such as stannous fluoride. It also is essential to the manufacture of gold–tin and copper–tin ruby glass.

Stannous pyrophosphate. Stannous chloride and sodium pyrophosphate combine to form the salt stannous pyrophosphate, which acts as a polishing agent in fluoride toothpastes and plays a part in electroplating with copper–tin alloy (bronze).

Stannous sulfate. There are two methods of producing stannous sulfate: (1) from stannous oxide and sulfuric acid, or (2) by reacting granulated tin with an excess of sulfuric acid at 100° C (212° F) and evaporating in a vacuum. Stannous sulfate is the principal ingredient in the Ferrostan electroplating solution (see above *Electrolytic tinning*). It has found a large use in "liquor finishing," in which a copper–tin coating is applied to steel wire by immersion in a solution of stannous sulfate and copper sulfate. The coating acts as a lubricant in drawing the wire to thinner gauges and protects the wire from oxidation in storage.

Stannic bromide. The reaction of tin with bromine produces stannic bromide, which is thermally stable and can be purified by distillation at a boiling point of 202° C (396° F). Because of its low melting point (31° C [88° F]) and the high specific gravity (3.34 at 35° C [95° F]) of the compound it is used in heavy-media separation of minerals in metallurgical processes.

Stannic chloride. The commercial preparation of stannic chloride is by direct chlorination of tin under pressure. The chlorine must be dry and the temperature in the vessel not over 38° C (100° F). The liquid is purified by distillation and can be shipped in steel drums of special design to keep out moisture.

Stannic chloride (with pyrophosphates) acts as a replacement for the gum extracted during the processing of silk (weighting silk). It acts as a colour fixative in the dyeing of silk. Its largest application in the early 1970s was in the preparation of other inorganic tin compounds and organotin compounds. When sprayed on glass and fired, it forms a conductive coating and strengthens the glass. Minor uses are in stabilizing the perfume in soaps, as an additive to diesel oils and transformer oils, and in making blueprint paper.

Uses of
stannic
chloride

Stannic oxide. In the industrial production of stannic oxide, tin metal is atomized and the finely divided metal burned. It is also prepared by calcining (heating to a high temperature) the hydrated oxide obtained by the hydrolysis (by boiling or by treatment with weak acid) of sodium stannate.

The soft white colour of fired porcelain enamel coatings opacified with stannic oxide is considered most desirable for the highest quality finish on bathtubs and other vitreous products. Stannic oxide is also used in making coloured ceramic glazes such as chrome–tin pink and vanadium–tin yellow. Substantial quantities of stannic oxide are consumed as a putty powder for polishing marble and granite.

Potassium stannate. Potassium stannate is prepared by dissolving tin in potassium hydroxide or by decomposing tin hydrate in potassium hydroxide. Potassium stannate is an ingredient in high-speed, high-conductivity tin-plating and tin-alloy-plating baths. It is the basis of a process for tin-plating aluminum pistons by immersion.

Sodium stannate. The commercial preparation of sodium stannate is accomplished by detinning scrap tinplate in a hot caustic soda solution containing oxidizers. The stannate is recovered by purifying the solution by evaporation and crystallization. Sodium stannate formed the basis of the first successful alkaline-tin electroplating bath. The plating speed and current-carrying capacity are less than those of the potassium stannate bath, but the process is cheaper and popular in job-plating shops.

Metal stannates. Ceramic dielectric bodies are made from alkaline earth and heavy metal stannates, particularly stannates of barium, cadmium, copper, lead, and nickel. A soluble salt of the metal is reacted with sodium or potassium stannate, and the insoluble compounds are recovered.

Organotin compounds. Stabilizers, biocides and fungicides of varying toxicity, and catalysts all are industrially important organic tin (organotin) compounds.

Reaction processes. The commercial production of stabilizers and biocidal compounds depends on either the Grignard or the modified Wurtz processes. In the Grignard process, a tin tetrahalide reacts with an excess of alkylmagnesium halide to produce tetraalkyltins, the starting materials for many organotin compounds. Under the modified Wurtz method, dibutyltin dichloride, butyl chloride, and sodium react to yield tetrabutyltin. Tetrabutyltin can be converted to dibutyltin dichloride by treatment with stannic chloride and part of the product recycled.

Organotin compounds can also be prepared by reacting aluminum alkyls with stannic chloride or by direct synthesis in which tin metal reacts with alkyl halides in the presence of suitable catalysts at elevated temperatures to produce dialkyltin halides.

Stabilizers. A number of different organotin compounds are useful as chemical stabilizers, to prevent various types of deterioration. One of these is dibutyltin dilaurate, prepared from the dichloride, which is hydrolyzed with caustic soda to form dibutyltin oxide. The oxide is then treated with lauric acid to yield dibutyltin dilaurate. This was one of the first compounds used as a stabilizer for polyvinyl chloride plastics. It also is added to poultry feed to control worms in chickens.

Biocidal and fungicidal compounds. The toxic properties of many tin compounds make them useful as insecticides and fungicides. Some of the more important of these compounds are as follows:

1. Bis-tributyltin oxide manufactured by the caustic hydrolysis of tributyltin chloride and industrially available in a number of formulations for use in antifouling paints, sanitary formulations, and for the control of micro-organisms in industrial-process water. Various proprietary formulations serve other purposes: tributyltin sulfide for ship-bottom paints; tributyltin benzoate and salicylate for treating textiles and leather against mildew, fungi, and gram-positive bacteria; and linoleate compounds for the similar treating of plastics.

2. Tributyltin chloride, as a rodent repellent, especially in coatings for exposed electrical cables.

3. Triphenyltin hydroxide, for controlling potato blight, leaf spot on sugar beets and celery, and pecan blight; it is used also on cotton and other crops. The acetate derivative, obtained by reacting the hydroxide with acetic acid, also is effective.

4. The hydroxide of tricyclohexyltin chloride, as a control of plant-feeding mites; its low order of mammalian toxicity allows its use on apple, pear, and citrus trees, as well as on vegetables and some field crops.

Catalysts. Stannous octoate, a stannous soap, acts as a catalyst in curing silicone oil emulsions. When mixed with certain amines, it catalyzes production of polyurethane foam rubber. Proprietary formulations for stannous soaps derived from the reaction of stannous oxide and oleic and stearic acid also are used as catalysts in foam rubber production. Stannous oxalate is one type of catalyst utilized in the hydrogenation of coal.

BIBLIOGRAPHY. C.J. FAULKNER, *The Properties of Tin* (1954), a comprehensive tabulation of established constants for the mechanical, thermal, electrical, magnetic, physical, and nuclear properties of tin; E.S. HEDGES (ed.) *Tin and Its Alloys* (1960), individual chapters written by specialists, covering the physical metallurgy, chemical behaviour, practical metallurgy in the alloy field, tin and tin alloy coating practices, and applications for tin products; W.E. HOARE, E.S. HEDGES, and B.T.K. BARRY, *The Technology of Tinplate* (1965), a profusely illustrated guide for manufacturers and users of tinplate; J.G.A. LUIJTEN and G.J.M. VAN DER KERK, *Investigations in the Field of Organotin Chemistry* (1955), a review of the theory of organotin chemistry, synthesis, and preparation of compounds, with numerous references; C.L. MANTELL, *Tin: Its Mining, Production, Technology and Applications*, 2nd ed. (1949, reprinted 1970), a comprehensive coverage of tin involving the history, the geology and sources of tin deposits, mining and metallurgy, properties of tin and tin alloys, analysis, and applications; P.A. WRIGHT, *Extractive Metallurgy of Tin* (1966), an up-to-date treatise on the physical chemistry of tin-smelting processes linked by a discussion of the economics involved; NATIONAL PRODUCTION AUTHORITY, U.S. DEPT. OF COMMERCE, *Materials Survey: Tin* (1953), a detailed textual and statistical study of the tin industry; D. HANSON and W.T. PELL-WALPOLE, *Chill Cast Tin Bronzes* (1951), a text dealing with the history, constitution, melting and casting, and heat treatment of tin bronzes; B.N. OSBURN and G.O. WILBER, *Pewter: Spun, Wrought and Cast* (1947), an explanatory text covering metal composition, designing, casting, and working with pewter; T.S. MACKEY, "The Electrolytic Tin Refining Plant at Texas City, Texas," *J. Metals*, 2:32–43 (1969), a description of a modern refinery for tin metal recovery from low-grade concentrates including by-product recovery; R.K. INGHAM, S.D. ROSENBERG, and H. GILMAN, "Organotin Compounds," *Chem. Rev.*, 60:459–539 (1960), a review and tabulation of the methods of preparation, physical and chemical properties, and industrial applications of organotin compounds, with an extensive list of references; manuals of the TIN RESEARCH INSTITUTE, Columbus, Ohio, on the subject of tin coating and alloying processes, electroplating, analysis, corrosion behaviour, research and development, uses and applications for tin products.

(R.McK.MacI.)

Tintoretto

Tintoretto (Jacopo Robusti), one of the greatest artists of the late Renaissance, was a painter with a wholly personal, constantly evolving technique and vision. Although it is almost certain that his family was originally from Lucca, Tintoretto (a nickname meaning "little dyes" [after his father's profession of silk dyer, or *tintore*]) is considered a Venetian painter, not only by birth but because he always lived in Venice and because with his innumerable works he contributed to creating the face of that city. He was not only an exponent of the witness to the life of the city, of the sacred and profane complex pictorial developments of Venetian art but a myths of a society that formed a part of the dramatic history of 16th-century Italy.

Giraudon

Tintoretto, self-portrait, oil painting. In the Louvre, Paris.

Background and early life. The exact date of Tintoretto's birth is not known. A death certificate, dated in May 1594, gives his age as 75. In a portrait of the year 1588, his age is given as 70. Taking into account the known dates of his career, the hypothesis that he was born in 1518 seems warranted. In a will of 1539 he called himself an independent professional man—not a surprising description in view of his imposing and forceful personality. No documents have survived regarding Jacopo's artistic education. His biographers, among them Carlo Ridolfi, whose book was published in 1648, speak of an apprenticeship of Tintoretto with Titian that was broken off because of the master's resentment of the pupil's proud nature and exceptional accomplishment. On the other hand, a contemporary pointed out that Tintoretto's style was formed by studying formal elements of the Tuscan school, especially those of Michelangelo, and of pictorial elements derived from Titian. This explains a story of a sign that Tintoretto reportedly placed in his

Grignard and Wurtz processes

studio: "Il disegno di Michelangelo e'l colorito de Tiziano." The story, however, in no way does justice to the development of a style of painting that was in fact much more complex.

Apprenticeship and early influences

Most probably, Jacopo's precocious talent prompted his father to place him in the workshop of some undistinguished painter, but one with a solid artisan tradition so that Tintoretto might learn the foundations of his craft. Traces of an absolute style in his youthful works tend to corroborate this hypothesis. But he soon became aware of the variety of approaches tried by painters working between 1530 and 1540 in Venice and already reacting against the style of Giorgione, who was the first to merge forms and to subordinate local colour in a picture to its pervading tone. It was above all the emigration of Roman artists to Venice in 1527 after the sack of Rome by imperial troops, as well as subsequent contacts with painters from Tuscany and Bologna, that induced the painters of the Venetian school to return to greater plasticism, without altering the fundamental chromatic nature of the Venetian tradition. The influence of Michelangelo, the visit of the art historian Giorgio Vasari to Venice in 1541, and the journeys of Venetian artists to central Italy renewed Venetian painting in depth, giving it means of expression adapted to different types of pictures. In the renewed idiom, form and colour were blended in a synthesis in which light dominated so as to express a richly fantastic and visionary spirit. Thus the early works of Tintoretto were affected by all of these Venetian influences. Critics have identified a group of youthful works of Tintoretto, above all *Sacre Conversazioni*, the most important of which is in the Wildenstein Collection, New York. Painted in 1540, it represents the Virgin with the Child on her knees, facing away from her, and six saints. While the style echoes various elements of the Venetian art of Tintoretto's time, it also shows a definite Michelangelesque influence.

Career. A group of 14 octagonal ceiling paintings with mythological themes in Modena, at the Galleria e Museo Estense (originally painted for a Venetian palace), with their singular refinement in perspective and narrative clarity, also belong to Tintoretto's first phase. Among other influences, they recall the fashion of partitioned ceiling paintings imported to Venice by Vasari. At this time Tintoretto probably had greatly enlarged his circle of clients and had formed friendships with literary men and artists.

This was also the period of Tintoretto's closest collaboration with Andrea Meldolla (called Lo Schiavone); together they decorated the Palazzo Zen with frescoes. The fresco technique had an important part in the formation of Tintoretto's idiom, for it suggested to him the quickness of execution that was to become fundamental to his manner of painting. Unfortunately only some 18th-century prints of his frescoes and a few fragments of the numerous frescoed facades that adorned Venice survive.

Tintoretto's drawing exercises were made from nature, from statues, and from small wax models posed in various ways and artificially illuminated, as in tiny stage sets. These methods were suited to the painter's concern with resolving problems of form and light. Not much of his abundant graphic work has survived: individual figures, some groups, many sketches of details. Only one complete graphic composition still exists (now in the Kupferstichkabinett, Berlin), which Tintoretto drew for the painting "Vulcan Surprising Venus and Mars" (in the Alte Pinakothek in Munich). The indefatigable draftsman acquired a narrative fluency that allowed him to trace with a brisk brushstroke and fanciful inspiration the series of biblical stories (now in Vienna), the mythological episodes for the poet Pietro Aretino's house in Venice (1545), and sacred compositions such as "Christ and the Adulteress," in which figures set in vast spaces in fanciful perspectives are illuminated in a distinctly Mannerist style. Tintoretto returned to an earlier form of composition in his masterpiece of 1547, the "Last Supper" of S. Marcuola, in which the choice of rough and popular types succeeds in endorsing the scene with a portrayal of ordinary everyday reality struck with wonder by the revelation of the miracle.

A few months later Tintoretto became the centre of attention of artists and literary men with his "S. Marco Freeing the Slave." A letter from Aretino, full of praise, yet also intended to temper Tintoretto's youthful exuberance, confirmed the fame of the 30-year-old painter. Relations between Tintoretto and Aretino did not come to an end at this point, even though one of Aretino's letters contains hints of dissension, for which apparently Titian was responsible. Although Aretino was no longer to write laudatory letters to Tintoretto, he commissioned him to execute family portraits. And after his death, his likeness was to appear in Tintoretto's huge "Crucifixion" of the Scuola Grande di S. Rocco (1565). The painting "S. Marco Freeing the Slave" is so rich in structural elements of post-Michelangelesque Roman art that it is reasonable to assume that Tintoretto had visited Rome.

Early fame

Tintoretto mastered a precise and varied complex Manneristic style that enabled him to conceive the fanciful scene of the "S. Rocco Among the Plague-Stricken" for the church of S. Rocco (1549), a work that had earned Vasari's praise. That style is also evident in the altarpiece "St. Augustine Healing the Plague-Stricken," in which a realistic study from life dissolves into fanciful arabesques of contorted and deformed bodies.

But Tintoretto did not interrupt his artistic experiments. Stories from Genesis, painted for the Scuola della Trinità (1550–53), show a new attention to Titian's manner of painting as well as a palpable awareness of nature. The masterpiece of this phase is undoubtedly "Susanna Bathing"; the light creates Susanna's form in crystalline clarity against a background evoked with a fresh poetic sense.

In 1555 Tintoretto, now a famous and sought-after painter, married Faustina Episcopi. The young wife, affectionate and devoted, bore him eight children. At least three of them, Marietta, Domenico, and Marco, learned their father's trade and became his associates. Although Marietta is known to have been an able painter and musician, no record of her work is extant. On the other hand, innumerable works by Domenico are known; they exhibit a certain independence of style from his father, above all in portraiture.

Marriage and family

An artist of indefatigable activity, of a veritable fury of creativity, Tintoretto spent most of his life in the bosom of his family and in his workshop. But the love of solitude to which his biographer alludes did not prevent the painter from forming friendships with several artistic personalities, including the composer Gioseffo Zarlino, who created new polyphonic and choral structures. These men undoubtedly shared Tintoretto's highly innovative and anticonformist outlook.

This particular period in Tintoretto's career, marked by greater vivacity of colour, by a predilection for a variegated perspective, and by a highly decorative quality, coincided with his growing admiration for the art of Paolo Veronese, who had been working in the Doges' Palace. The assimilation and transformation of the Veronesian elements in Tintoretto's work are discernible in his very beautiful ceiling paintings of Bible stories, now in the Prado. In these fabulous tales, such as "Joseph and Potiphar's Wife" and "The Finding of Moses" (*c.* 1555), Tintoretto created the most significant documents of Venetian Mannerism, painting the figures in subtly luminous colours and achieving harmony by the use of elegant linear arabesques.

Influence of Veronese

The use of a colour that absorbs light yielded new possibilities for suggesting spaces no longer structured by the pure play of perspective. And in those spaces the painter introduced crowds in harmonized order with the rest of the picture, a feature that had until then been missing in Venetian art. It was at that time that Tintoretto began to participate in the decoration of the church of the Madonna dell'Orto and the private chapel of the Contarini family contained within it, which in 1563 became the final resting place of the great Cardinal Gasparo, who played an important role in the city's religious life. Tintoretto's works for the Madonna dell'Orto, which occupied him for approximately a decade, also give an idea of the evolution of the idiomatic elements of his art: the "Presentation of the Virgin in the Temple" (1552) was according to Vasari "a highly finished work, and the best executed and most successful painting that there is in the place"; in "St. Peter's Vision of the Cross" and in "The Decapitation of St. Paul" (c. 1556), the figures stand out dramatically on a space suffused with a vaporous, unreal light. In the two enormous canvases depicting the Jews worshiping the golden calf while Moses on Mt. Sinai receives the tables of the law and a Last Judgment, Tintoretto painted two works of the highest rank with a great richness of narrative means, with an awareness of the thematic link between the two scenes that attests to a knowledge of scripture and of contemporary spiritual movements. The high figurative quality of the two paintings implies that Tintoretto made a number of experiments in this decade. Proof of this is, above all, the dramatic style in which the scenes are executed, a style that firmly impresses their romantic pathos on the beholder. Tintoretto's spatial conception has a dynamic character. As a modern critic has noted, Tintoretto conveys a feeling of an almost precipitate falling forward or of an equally swift rise. The contrasted movements give the figures a similar instability. To achieve such effects Tintoretto used formulas that were invariably different: in "The Pool of Bethesda" in the church of S. Rocco (1559), the evangelical episode is realized in a compressed space through which the foreshortened ceiling seems to weigh upon the milling crowd; in the "St. George and the Dragon," Tintoretto sets the fable in a landscape of considerable depth, intersected by the white walls of the city. A series of canvases that the philosopher and physician Tommaso Rangone, grand guardian of the Scuola di S. Marco, commissioned from Tintoretto in 1562 contains similar elements. Of these pictures the most beautiful is probably the "Finding of the Body of St. Mark," now in the Brera in Milan.

In May 1564 the councillors of the Scuola Grande di S. Rocco decided to have the Sala dell'Albergo decorated with paintings, in place of the movable decorations used during feast days. S. Rocco (St. Roch) is the protector against plagues; the numerous epidemics of that period had given new impetus to the cult of the saint and caused great riches to flow to the Scuola, which built a splendid centre to assist the poor and the infirm. When Tintoretto presented the Scuola with his oval painting the "Glorification of S. Rocco," the directors decided to entrust him with the decoration of the Sala. Vasari relates that designs were invited from various prominent artists, including Paolo Veronese, but Tintoretto, who presented his work already installed in the Sala, won hands down over his competitors. Similar episodes are counted by contemporary sources as proof that when it came to his work the painter knew no scruples. He was indeed a man devoured by the passion for painting and not for pecuniary gain, for he committed himself to grandiose undertakings for exceedingly modest remuneration.

The question of who assisted Tintoretto in his dizzying activity is still open: at that time Marietta was only about nine and Domenico four. But it is known that in 1560 his studio began to be visited by young painters, especially from the Netherlands and Germany. In 1565 his immense "Crucifixion" was displayed in the Sala dell'Albergo of the Scuola Grande di S. Rocco. Around Christ, in the centre, many figures revolve in a livid light that, muting the picture's colours, invests it with dramatic power. The decoration of the chamber was completed in 1567; it included other scenes of Christ's Passion, remarkable for their thematic innovations. Although working on the *teleri* for the walls of the Scuola, Tintoretto also executed between 1566 and 1567 a "Last Judgment" for the Sala del Scrutinio of the Doges' Palace (which was destroyed by the fire of 1577); painted the "S. Rocco in Prison" for the church of S. Rocco; and for the church of S. Cassiano, finished the "Crucifixion" and the "Descent of Christ into Limbo," paintings in which the powerful realism of the portraits of the donors contrasts with fanciful inventions.

Vasari, who visited Venice in 1566 to bring his *Lives of the Most Eminent Italian Architects, Painters and Sculp-*

tors up to date, thus had an opportunity to follow Tintoretto's work in progress. Undoubtedly he had the painter's most recent works in mind when he wrote that Tintoretto was "the most extraordinary brain that the art of painting has produced." For all his fundamental reservations about Tintoretto's style, Vasari sensed his greatness.

In 1576, with renewed zeal, Tintoretto resumed the decoration of the Scuola Grande di S. Rocco. He had finished the huge central panel of the upper hall with "The Erection of the Brazen Serpent" in time for the feast of the saint on August 16 and promised to paint a certain number of canvases, "wishing to demonstrate the great love that I bear for the saint and our venerable school, because of my devotion to the glorious Messer San Rocho." In 1581 all the ceiling paintings were completed (ten ovals and eight rhomboid chiaroscuro panels; the latter restored in the 18th century) and ten *teleri* on the walls. Certainly the fundamental idea goes back to the conception elaborated in the rough illustrations of the *Biblia Pauperum*—i.e., the concordance of the Old and New Testaments. It is not known who assisted Tintoretto in choosing the themes of this work, but it can be assumed that the painter himself devised, with the aid of religious texts, the complex iconographic structure by means of which he succeeded in composing his biblical poem with the greatest freedom, completely disregarding the commands of the Counter-Reformation censuring "the abuses of painters."

In his work Tintoretto exalted the charitable purpose of the Scuola and the theme of salvation from the physical and moral miseries of the human condition. The three huge paintings on the ceiling—"The Erection of the Brazen Serpent," "The Gathering of Manna," "Moses Striking the Rock"—allude to miraculous liberation from illness, hunger, thirst, while the canvases on the walls, depicting the life of Christ, celebrate the victory over spiritual evils through the institution of "baptism" (water), of "communion" (bread), as well as the certainty of victory over temptation ("The Temptation of Christ") and over death ("Resurrection"). In comparison to the works in the Sala dell'Albergo, in which the spatial relationship of the composition was precisely defined and the colour was still rich, in the great Sala the use of colour is reduced to much more emphatic chiaroscural contrasts.

In the ten *teleri* of the walls the painter's inexhaustible powers of invention created several of the masterpieces of his career. In "The Nativity," dividing the picture into two superimposed planes, he achieved a multiplicity of vision. In "The Baptism of Christ" the threadlike throng is evoked in a landscape in depth; "The Last Supper," rich in realistic detail, unfolds in an ample space created by the foreshortened table, while "The Ascension" remains one of the most spontaneous and visionary compositions, foreshadowing the fantasies of El Greco, Tintoretto's real spiritual heir. The order of execution of these paintings, which were finished in 1581, has not been established.

It seems almost impossible that in the same year the painter should have executed the four mythological allegories for the Doges' Palace, of which the most famous is that of "Ariadne, Bacchus, and Venus." All are works of great elegance, with an almost academic finishing touch. But the real Tintoretto is certainly to be found in S. Rocco, where he bears witness to his great faith and, like the medieval mosaicists, offers an illustrated Bible to the crowds of the poor who frequented the beneficent institution. His deep but independent faith in the religious myths, unrestricted by any rules of the Counter-Reformation, is apparent as much in the striking sketch of "The Council of Trent" (Turin, private collection), executed for the Doge Da Ponte, as in the altarpiece of S. Trovaso, executed in 1577 for Milledonne, a participant and historian of the Council, with the semi-nude women who tempt St. Anthony.

By 1577 Marietta, born around 1556, and Domenico, born in 1560, already officers of the painters' guild, could help their father, together with other future artists of the close of the 16th and the beginning of the 17th century. Certainly the presence of collaborators is obvious in two

Continuing experiments in dramatic style

Work for the Scuola Grande di S. Rocco

Vasari's judgment of Tintoretto

Workshop productions

cycles: the eight scenes of the "Gonzaga Cycle" (Alte Pinakothek, Munich), with vivid scenes of battles, painted between 1579 and 1580, and the many paintings for the halls of the Scrutinio and of the Maggior Consiglio in the Doges' Palace, which the Republic wanted to adorn with new canvases after the fire of 1577. It was certainly more his wish to finish his immense work in the decoration of S. Rocco than it was his advanced age that induced the painter to leave the canvases of the Doges' Palace largely to his workshop.

In the canvases executed between 1583 and 1587 for the lower hall of the Scuola Grande di S. Rocco, depicting episodes of the life of Mary and Christ, Tintoretto follows a new direction: light in its most lyrical meaning dominates the paintings, dissolving the colour in a flash of diaphanous brushstrokes. Space is multiplied in unlimited successions of perspectives; the scenery at times prevails over the human figure, as in the two great works in the ground floor hall, with the "St. Mary of Egypt" and the "St. Mary Magdalene" immersed in an incandescent hazy atmosphere in which things are animated with a life of their own: an invitation to the contemplative life of the 70-year-old painter, more than ever leaning toward the view of man and his destiny offered by the Christian faith. A marvelous model (in the Louvre) of the "Paradise" for the Doges' Palace (executed later with different aims and with the help of many assistants) and "The Last Supper" of S. Giorgio Maggiore, with the incorporeal apparitions of angelic creatures, finished a few months before his death, are proof of Tintoretto's deep spiritual bent. He died on May 31, 1594, and was buried in the church of Madonna dell'Orto next to his favourite child, Marietta.

Assessment. His work as a portrait painter has often been underestimated in comparison to the work of Titian. Tintoretto's portraits, often incorporated in his compositions, can be dated from 1545 up to almost the end of his activity. If the early ones are marked by a Mannerist elegance, reminiscent of painters of the Tuscan school—e.g., his "Portrait of a Young Man" at Hampton Court —the artist very soon places the stamp of his almost brutal introspective force on that extraordinary group of the Soranzo family. At times he seems to approach the chromatic softness of Titian, as in the "Portrait of a Woman in Black." And he knows how to clothe authoritative personages with solemnity and majesty, such as "Doge Alvise Mocenigo and Family Before the Madonna and Child" or the victor of Lepanto, "Sebastiano Venier" (private collection, Turin). But, above all, his portraits of old men are unforgettable, with that inner spiritual force that conquers physical decay—from the "Bearded Man with Fur" (Kunsthistorisches Museum, Vienna) to the spectral image of the "Old Man" (formerly in the Cook Collection, Richmond, Surrey). His self-portraits together with the witty verbal portrait that was left by one of his contemporaries in a letter give an idea of what Tintoretto looked like.

Tintoretto's art was much discussed and highly appreciated in 17th-century Venice, above all in the acute evaluations of Marco Boschini, the great 17th-century critic of Venetian painting. Roger de Piles, following in the latter's footsteps, exalted Tintoretto's luministic idiom. But to the 18th century, the closer it drew to 19th-century Neoclassical rationality, Tintoretto appears excessive and too remote from its own sensibility. Ruskin's romantic enthusiasm inaugurated a new attitude toward the art of Tintoretto. And modern art historiography will come to recognize in him the greatest representative of that wide-ranging European movement that was Mannerism, interpreted in accordance with the great Venetian tradition.

MAJOR WORKS

RELIGIOUS, MYTHOLOGICAL, AND HISTORICAL SUBJECTS: "Madonna and Child with Six Saints" (1540; Wildenstein Collection, New York); 14 ceiling paintings (c. 1540; Galleria e Museo Estense, Modena); "Supper at Emmaus" (c. 1540; Museum of Fine Arts, Budapest); "Apollo and Marsyas" (1544–45; Wadsworth Atheneum, Hartford, Connecticut); "St. Demetrius Altarpiece" (c. 1545; S. Felice, Venice); "Christ and the Adulteress" (c. 1547; Gemäldegalerie, Dresden); "Last Supper" (1547; S. Marcuola, Venice); "Christ Washing the Feet of the Apostles" (1547; Prado, Madrid); "S. Marco Freeing the Slave" (1548; Accademia, Venice); "Esther Before Ahasuerus" (1548; Hampton Court Palace, Middlesex); "St. Martial with SS. Peter and Paul" (1549; S. Marziale, Venice); "S. Rocco Among the Plague-Stricken" (1549; S. Rocco, Venice); "St. Augustine Healing the Plague-Stricken" (c. 1549; Museo Civico d'Arte e Storia, Vicenza, Italy); "Susanna Bathing" (c. 1550; Kunsthistorisches Museum, Vienna); "St. George and the Dragon" (c. 1550; National Gallery, London); "Presentation of the Virgin in the Temple" (1552; Madonna dell'Orto, Venice); "Miracle of the Loaves and Fishes" (late 1550s; Contini Bonacossi Collection, Florence, replica in the Metropolitan Museum of Art, New York); "The Finding of Moses" (1555; Prado); "Joseph and Potiphar's Wife" (c. 1555; Prado); "The Pool of Bethesda" (1559; S. Rocco, Venice); "Finding of the Body of St. Mark" (c. 1562; Brera, Milan); "The Law and the Golden Calf" (c. 1562; Madonna dell'Orto, Venice); "The Last Judgment" (c. 1562; Madonna dell'Orto, Venice); "Crucifixion" (1565; Scuola Grande di S. Rocco, Venice); "S. Rocco in Prison" (1567; S. Rocco, Venice); "Descent of Christ into Limbo" (1568; S. Cassiano, Venice); "Crucifixion" (1568; S. Cassiano, Venice); "Doge Alvise Mocenigo and Family Before the Madonna and Child" (c. 1573; National Gallery of Art, Washington, D.C.); ceiling paintings, upper hall and walls (1564–81; Scuola Grande di S. Rocco, Venice); "The Virgin and Child Adored by SS. Mark and Luke" (c. 1570–80; Staatliche Museen Preussischer Kulturbesitz, Berlin); "Ariadne, Bacchus, and Venus" (1581; Doges' Palace, Venice); "Glorification of S. Rocco" (finished 1588; Scuola Grande di S. Rocco, Venice); "Paradise" (1588–90; Doges' Palace, Sala del Maggior Consiglio, Venice); "A Battle Between Turks and Christians" (1580s; Prado); "The Last Supper" (1594; S. Giorgio Maggiore, Venice).

PORTRAITS: "Portrait of a Young Man" (1545; Hampton Court Palace, Middlesex); "Self-Portrait" (c. 1546; Victoria and Albert Museum, London); "Portrait of a Man" (1547; Rijksmuseum Kröller-Müller, Otterlo); "Knight of Malta" (c. 1551; Hampton Court Palace); "Portrait of a Young Lady" (c. 1551; Kunsthistorisches Museum, Vienna); "Portrait of a Woman in Black" (c. 1553; Gemäldegalerie, Dresden); "Portrait of a Venetian Gentleman" (1555; National Gallery of Ireland, Dublin); "Portrait of a Gentleman with a Gold Chain" (c. 1556–60; Prado); "Portrait of Jacopo Sansovino" (c. 1556; Uffizi, Florence).

BIBLIOGRAPHY. For documentation of the works and an examination of the artist, see the following Venetian sources: CARLO RIDOLFI, *La Vita di Giacopo Robusti detto il Tintoretto* (1642) and *Le maraviglie dell'Arte*, 2 vol. (1648; rev. by DETLEY VON HADELN, 1914–24); MARCO BOSCHINI, *La Carta del Navegar pitoresco* (1660; ed. by ANNA PALLUCCHINI, 1966); and ANTONIO M. ZANETTI, *Della pittura veneziana . . .* (1771). At some distance from the historiography of the 17th century is JOHN RUSKIN, *The Stones of Venice*, 3 vol. (1851–53; abridged ed. by J.G. LINKS, 1960), which approaches Tintoretto with a new interpretation, inaugurating the tradition of Anglo-Saxon studies. The following works have all contributed to an understanding of Tintoretto: BERNHARD BERENSON, *The Venetian Painters of the Renaissance*, 3rd ed. (1897); JOHN B. STOUGHTON HOLBORN, *Jacopo Robusti, Called Tintoretto* (1907); EVELYN M. PHILLIPPS, *Tintoretto* (1911); FRANCIS P.B. OSMASTON, *The Art and Genius of Tintoretto*, 2 vol. (1915); and ERIC NEWTON, *Tintoretto* (1952).

German critical work, primarily philological, has made an important contribution. It was initiated with the fundamental volume of HENRY THODE, *Tintoretto* (1901). M. DVORAK, *Geschichte der Italienischen Kunst im Zeitalter der Renaissance*, vol. 2 (1929), identified the inclination toward a Mannerist element in Tintoretto's work, comparing it to Michelangelo. ERICH VON DER BERCKEN, *Die Gemälde des Jacopo Tintoretto* (1942), uses this presupposition to make a catalog of his works. MARY PITTALUGA, *Il Tintoretto* (1925), adds to the historical position adopted by Thode. LUIGI COLETTI, *Tintoretto*, 3rd ed. (1951), enlarges the critical examination of Tintoretto's work, making it the major representation of the Mannerist tendency in Venice. RODOLFO PALLUCCHINI, *La giovinezza del Tintoretto* (1950), is also attracted by this concept as a means of describing the formation of the artist. LUIGI RUDRAUF, "Vertiges, chutes et ascension dans l'espace pictural du Tintoretto," in *Venezia e l'Europa* (1955), examines the new concept of Tintoretto's space. HANS TIETZE and ERICA TIETZE-CONRAT, *The Drawings of the Venetian Painters in the 15th and 16th Centuries* (1944), is essential for an understanding of Tintoretto's drawing activities. A well-written monograph is HANS TIETZE, *Tintoretto: The Paintings and Drawings* (1948).

For the school of San Rocco, see RODOLFO PALLUCCHINI, *Tintoretto a San Rocco* (1937); and EDOUARD HUTTINGER, *Die*

Bilderzyklen Tintorettos in der Scuola di San Rocco zu Venedig (1962). Particularly noteworthy contributions are F. ARCANGELI, "La 'Disputa' del Tintoretto a Milano," *Paragone*, 6:21–35 (1955); and ANNA PALLUCCHINI, "Considerazioni sui grandi 'teleri' del Tintoretto alla Madonna dell' Orto," *Arte Veneta*, 23:54–68 (1969). A complete edition of the work of Tintoretto is offered in CARLO BERNARI and PIERLUIGI DE VECCHI, *L'opera completa del Tintoretto* (1970).

(R.Pal.)

Tirpitz, Alfred von

Alfred von Tirpitz, as an admiral, created the German high-seas fleet in the 17 years before World War I and, in his political role, exerted a dominant influence on German foreign policy of the period.

Tirpitz, 1915.
By courtesy of the Archiv fur Kunst und Geschichte

Tirpitz was born at Küstrin in Brandenburg, Prussia, on March 19, 1849, the son of a Prussian civil servant. He enlisted in the Prussian Navy as a midshipman in 1865, attended the Kiel Naval School, and was commissioned in 1869. After serving as commander of a torpedo-boat flotilla and as inspector general of the torpedo fleet, he demonstrated his technical ability and devised the tactical principles that developed systematically when he became chief of staff of the Navy High Command. Promoted to rear admiral in 1895, Tirpitz was sent to command the German cruiser squadron in East Asia from 1896 to 1897 and selected Tsingtao as a future German naval base in China. In June 1897 Tirpitz became secretary of state of the Imperial Navy Department, an appointment that marked the beginning of his two-decade buildup of the German fleet in close collaboration with Emperor William II.

In 1898 Tirpitz introduced the First Fleet Act, for the reorganization of Germany's sea power. The nucleus of the navy was intended only for coastal defense and consisted of armoured vessels for tactical operations, light reconnaissance ships, and torpedo-boat flotillas for escort duty. Only seven battleships, two heavy cruisers, and seven light cruisers were newly ordered, but they enabled Germany to have one squadron of eight ships in both the Baltic and the North seas and to have one squadron in reserve. In addition, a few overseas stations were manned. While the 1898 act was designed to meet the need for a high-seas battle fleet, Tirpitz's Second Fleet Act of 1900 laid down an ambitious program—to build a larger and more modern oceangoing fleet—that the navy was never able to fulfill. Tirpitz knew how to stimulate public interest in a bigger navy and, a secretary of state from 1897, he displayed great skill as a parliamentarian. Tirpitz was ennobled in 1900 and awarded the Order of the Black Eagle; and in 1911 he rose to the rank of grand admiral.

In the meantime not even the 1900 navy law had evoked any significant political response in Britain. The reactions were late in coming: not until the British formed their

Early career and rise to power

alliances of 1904 (with France) and 1907 (with Russia) and launched the "Dreadnought" (1906) in an an effort to score an important technical advantage by constructing oversized capital ships. Their building program turned out to be a miscalculation, however, because not only all the other great powers but even many countries with small navies such as Chile and Turkey immediately followed suit. Nevertheless, because Britain had had a head start since 1905, when it had an edge of seven capital ships over its principal rival, Germany, and because of rapidly increasing British and declining German construction, there were 49 British battleships either in service or being built in 1914 as against 29 German vessels of the same type.

The decisive question in considering Tirpitz's objectives is whether it was good policy to augment the navy laws to the point where they could not be implemented and must inevitably result in political difficulties. From 1900 onward, when the so-called *Risikoflotte* ("risk fleet"—*i.e.*, a deterrent for potential attackers) was established under the second navy law, it became obvious that the navy was intended not only for actual defense, but also as an alliance asset in time of peace. The Emperor and Tirpitz hoped to be able, through mounting financial and military pressure, to force Britain to loosen its alliances. But when the British war minister Lord Haldane finally arrived in Berlin in 1912 for talks, political concessions were no longer obtainable from Britain. By that time Germany had discontinued its four-per-year naval vessel production rate and had abandoned the naval armament race with Britain. Thus, Tirpitz's naval policy was no longer an actual threat, but it may have continued to play such a role in the minds of the British public.

Tragically, the incipient *détente* between Germany and England had advanced no further by July 1914, when war was declared. However eagerly Tirpitz may have wanted the high-seas fleet to go into action in World War I, he was forced to realize that, given the vastly superior naval strength of the Allies, his policy of naval deterrence had failed and that the conditions for a decision at sea were unfavourable to Germany. Even unlimited submarine warfare, which he favoured but for which the necessary vessels had still to be built, could no longer have had any more than a temporary impact. Faced with mounting opposition, Tirpitz drew the correct conclusion from the failure of his plans by resigning in March 1916. With anxiety he saw the loss of morale on the home front; he thus became cofounder of the patriotic rallying movement known as the Fatherland Party, which, however, made only a small impact on an increasingly war-weary nation. Once again Tirpitz sat in the Reichstag, from 1924 to 1928 as a deputy of the German National People's Party. But, as circumstances had changed completely, he had lost the power to persuade. He retired to Upper Bavaria, where he died, at Ebenhausen near Munich, on March 6, 1930.

Tirpitz was, by the standards of his time, a modern naval officer. He possessed a sound knowledge of the world, a dedicated mind, and an active interest in technology, and he was a brilliant organizer. He was obsessed by his work; he therefore tended to be biassed and, once he had enunciated his principles, raised them to the status of a doctrine. The continuous and steady implementation of the naval laws took priority over other technical, tactical, and political considerations. Naval construction and its impact were to determine how the navy was to be used and hence its political value and not vice versa. With the largest German navy, which under him became the world's second largest, Tirpitz forged an efficient military weapon that did not see the action for which it was intended in the war and finally collapsed from within.

Critique of Tirpitz's policy

Assessment

BIBLIOGRAPHY. ALFRED VON TIRPITZ, *Erinnerungen* (1919; Eng. trans., *My Memoirs*, 2 vol., 1919), and *Politische Dokumente*, 2 vol. (1924–26), were composed and published by Tirpitz to justify himself. ULRICH VON HASSELL, *Tirpitz, sein Leben und Wirken* (1920), is the first Tirpitz biography based on family papers. ADOLF VON TROTHA, *Grossadmiral von Tirpitz: Flottenbau und Reichsgedanke* (1932), explains the naval policy from the viewpoint of the collaborator. More recent studies of Imperial German naval policy include WALTHER HUBATSCH, *Die Aera Tirpitz* (1955) and *Der Admiralstab* (1958); WILHELM SCHUESSLER (ed.), *Weltmachtstreben und Flottenbau* (1956); and JONATHAN STEINBERG, *Yesterday's Deterrent: Tirpitz and the Birth of the German Battle Fleet* (1965).

(W.C.H.)

Tissue Culture

Tissue culture, which is a method of research, involves removing from animals or plants small fragments of tissue, called explants, and placing them in an environment in which they can survive outside the parent organism. A tissue in culture may consist of a population of cells (a cell culture) or a part of an organ in which different cell types retain their natural relationships to each other (an organ culture). The life of plants and animals, which (except for the simplest forms) contain many kinds of highly specialized cells, requires the coordination and interdependence of the functions of all cell types. Cells in culture may grow in the sense that they increase in size and number; they may differentiate from simple cells into cells with specialized functions; or they may perform specialized functions. Cultures of muscle cells, for example, may contract; those of specialized cells in the pancreas may produce the hormone insulin; and cultures of cells from the deadly nightshade plant produce the alkaloid compound atropine.

Cultures of cells and organs or organ fragments are useful in studying functions, behaviour, and interactions of specific cells. In addition, the large-scale development of animal-cell culture techniques has been of value in the production of viral vaccines that provide immunity to several viral diseases when given to man. Cell and organ cultures have been extensively used to study cancerous cells from animals and plants; experiments concerned with basic analyses of differences between normal and cancerous cells, the process by which normal cells transform into malignant ones, and tumour-inhibiting drugs have all been especially valuable.

General background. *Important terms.* The cell, the ultimate unit of autonomous life, contains at least one nucleus, in which is found the genetic material, deoxyribonucleic acid (DNA), in units called chromosomes. The nucleus is surrounded by a highly structured and dynamic environment called cytoplasm, in which many of the metabolic and specialized functions of the cell are carried out. The process by which somatic cells (*i.e.*, body cells as distinguished from reproductive cells) increase in number is called mitosis. During mitosis, the structures of the parent cell replicate and are divided between two or more daughter cells, which thus carry the genetic information and capabilities of the parent cell. Cells in tissue cultures sometimes produce daughter cells with abnormal numbers of chromosomes; such cells, for example, may have double the normal number of chromosomes or a number different from, but not an exact multiple of, the normal number.

A tissue is a structural and functional aggregation of cells and intercellular material; *e.g.*, muscle and connective tissue are tissues found in animals; cambium and xylem are tissues found in plants. An organ is a more complex structural unit, usually well-defined, and composed of several tissues; *e.g.*, lung, liver, and brain are organs of animals, root and stamen are organs of plants. A clone is a population of cells derived from a single cell. Clones derived from somatic cells and grown as cells in culture generally remain similar to the parent cell, unless a change in the genetic material by mutation or unequal cell division results in a modification of the daughter cells.

Types of media

The medium, or milieu, of cells in culture substitutes for the nutritional environment normally provided by blood and interstitial fluids in animals or by sap in plants. Media are either of biological origin (*i.e.*, composed of natural fluids derived from animals or plants) or of chemical origin (*i.e.*, synthetic mixtures of nutrient substances). A synthetic medium may be supplemented with natural fluids; the mixture is called a semidefined medium.

History. In 1839 a German zoologist, Theodor Schwann, suggested that individual cells could probably be grown outside an organism; actual demonstration of the growth of cells in this way, however, was dependent on the development of suitable techniques. An early observation of living cells undergoing mitosis outside an organism occurred about 1887, when white blood cells, or leukocytes, were collected from a frog and transferred to glass dishes for microscopic study. The first attempt to grow cells from higher plants in nutrient media was made about 1902. By 1907, the successful demonstration (by an American zoologist, Ross G. Harrison) of the growth of processes from frog nerve cells in a medium of clotted lymph had made it clear that the technique of tissue culture was not only feasible but that it could be useful in biological research. A student of Harrison developed the cell culture technique and applied it to cells of birds and mammals, using a medium containing clotted blood plasma. He collaborated with the Nobel Prize-winning surgeon and experimentalist Alexis Carrel in developing many refinements in cell culture methodology, particularly the use of embryonic tissue extracts combined with blood plasma.

The media first used for tissue cultures were composed of biological fluids; *e.g.*, lymph, blood serum, plasma, and tissue extracts for animal cells and coconut milk for plant cells. About 1911, the first attempts to culture animal cells in a synthetic medium consisting of salts, carbohydrates, and other nutrients were followed by studies of the effects on the cells of variations in certain components of the medium. It was recognized that the study of cell behaviour would best be carried out in a controlled environment; *i.e.*, a completely defined medium. These initial studies resulted in the development and use of numerous chemically defined nutrient media containing salts, amino acids, vitamins, and other components necessary for the growth of specific cells; *e.g.*, hormones, fatty acids, and trace metals.

Chemically defined media for plants, whose requirements are less complex than those of animal cells, were introduced in the U.S. about 1934 by Philip R. White, a leader in the development of tissue culture, and in France about 1939 by Roger Gautheret. Various semidefined media for animal cells, containing small amounts of proteins and tissue extracts, began to appear in the 1930s, and the first completely defined animal-cell culture media became available about 1949.

The technique of growing cells in a blood plasma-embryonic tissue extract medium made possible the successful culture of organs, both whole embryonic organs, such as bone, and fragments of larger organs, such as pituitary or mammary glands.

Organ culture

An English school of organ culture developed at the Strangeways Research Laboratory in Cambridge from about 1929; other European pioneers of organ culture work in The Netherlands, France, and Yugoslavia. Many laboratories in the U.S. and Japan now use organ culture techniques. Plant cultures are usually organ, rather than cell cultures, unless specific methods are used to separate cells from each other. A clonal culture of tomato root was maintained for more than 30 years, during which weekly transfers of small pieces of root were made into fresh chemically defined medium.

Advantages and disadvantages of cell culture techniques. *Advantages.* Early cell culture work was based on the premise that cells should be placed in an environment imitating as closely as possible the local environment in the organism from which the cells were removed (*i.e.*, in vivo condition); hence the early use of such biological media as blood plasma and tissue extracts. The use of biological media whose composition is complex and variable allows a greater degree of experimental control than that attainable with organs or tissues under conditions of limited survival, but a lesser degree of experimental control than that attainable with organs or tissues grown in chemically defined media.

Cells in culture, especially those grown in single layers on a glass or plastic surface, can be examined directly by light microscopy and photographed using the techniques of photomicrography and cinephotomicrography, which includes time-lapse moving pictures that emphasize cell

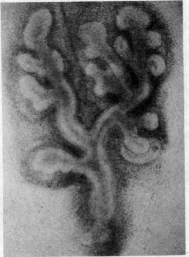

Organ cultures.
Chick embryo lung (left) 24 hours in culture, (centre) 48 hours in culture. (Right) Hairs from mouse embryo skin in culture for 13 days.
By courtesy of (left, centre) Norman K. Wessells, (right) Margaret H. Hardy

movements and behaviour; specialized optical systems make possible the detailed study of individual living cells. Cells in culture can also be fixed (*i.e.*, killed so that the structural parts of the cells remain as similar as possible to those in the living cells) and then either selectively stained so that specific structures can be studied, or sliced into very thin sections so that detailed ultrastructural features can be examined.

Cells in culture may be treated experimentally in numerous ways; cancer-producing chemicals or viruses, for example, may be added, as well as vitamins, hormones, drugs, and disease-causing micro-organisms; cells may be irradiated. The ability of particular cells to act as hosts for viruses may be studied with cells in culture, and the effects of viral infections upon the metabolism of host cells may be investigated. Cells from cell cultures also can be injected into animals or used for biochemical investigations. Tissue culture makes possible the study of the interactions of one cell type with another. One application of cell-to-cell interaction is cell hybridization; *i.e.*, the combination of nuclei from two cells into one nucleus within one cytoplasm. Using cell culture techniques, the genetic material (chromosomes) of two different cells, which may be from two such different species as man and mouse, can be placed within the cytoplasm of one cell. Specific human chromosomes are lost in human-mouse hybrid cells, but specific genetic properties of the remaining human chromosomes, difficult to investigate by other methods, can be studied.

Cells from different species or genetically different members of the same species are normally rejected when transplanted from a host to a recipient. This tissue discrimination is minimal, however, in vertebrate cells grown in cultures; hybrid organs (for example, a mouse-duck testicle) have been grown in organ culture.

Special properties of particular cell types can be identified in cell cultures. Skin cultured in the absence of vitamin A, for example, hardens; that is, it becomes keratinized. Keratinization stops in the presence of vitamin A, and active secretion of mucous substances takes place; the process can be studied using tissue culture techniques. Cultures of endocrine glands are useful in studying hormone production and the means by which the secretory functions of these specialized organs can be enhanced or diminished. The reactions of particular cell types to viruses, their responses to drugs, and comparisons between normal and cancerous cells of similar origin are other special properties that can be studied with cell cultures.

Techniques have been developed by which cells may be stored in a condition of suspended life for long periods of time at very low temperatures in liquid nitrogen; such cells can be grown again in cell cultures after months or years in cold storage.

Disadvantages. The principal disadvantages of cell and organ culture are the reverse of the advantages; *e.g.*, examined microscopically, living cells in culture look unfamiliar to the pathologist accustomed to observing sections of fixed and stained, dead cells. Although cells in culture are no longer subjected to the regulatory controls normally exercised upon them in the organism and therefore behave differently in culture, this sometimes is regarded as the justification for the cell culture technique.

Cell culture techniques. *Apparatus.* Cultures are usually grown either as single layers of cells (monolayers) on a solid surface such as glass or plastic or as a suspension in a fluid medium. Cellulose sponges have been used to grow cells in order that some of the normal three-dimensional characteristics of tissue growth can be maintained; foam prepared from a protein called fibrin, which is responsible for normal blood clotting, also has been used for this purpose. Monolayer cultures may also be grown on semisolid supporting materials; *e.g.*, gels, blood clots, or surfaces coated with the protein collagen. Cells in suspension culture are kept from settling to the bottom of the growth vessel by various devices that stir, shake, or rotate the cells in their fluid medium.

Because the kinds of media that support cell growth are also good nutrients for contaminant organisms (*e.g.*, bacteria, pleuropneumonia-like organisms, and fungi), sterile media, glassware, and plasticware must be used in cell culture work; in addition, cultures must be prepared and handled in a very clean environment, which is created by filtering the air and disinfecting all working surfaces. The addition of antibiotics to tissue culture media has somewhat reduced the need for stringent sterility conditions, at least for cultures that are grown for only a short time, and has made obsolete some previously used extreme precautions, modified from hospital procedures used during surgery. Apparatus for growing cells and organs may be very simple or very complex. A culture that will be used only a short time, for example, may be prepared simply as a hanging drop; *i.e.*, in a drop of fluid or semisolid medium on a small square piece of glass inverted over a piece of glass with a depressed area in the centre, a depression slide. Monolayer cultures, growing in media contained in flasks, bottles, tubes, or dishes, can be maintained for longer periods. After the cells have exhausted the nutrients in a medium, it may be replaced by fresh medium, and culture growth continued. Cultures may be maintained in this way for long periods of time, often months or years. As the number of cells in a cell culture increases, it also may be subdivided into daughter cultures, thus allowing the propagation of numerous cultures of specific types of useful cells. Organs in organ cultures can be grown in simple devices; *e.g.*, watch glasses, depression slides. It is often desirable to grow organ

Cell hybridization

Types of apparatus

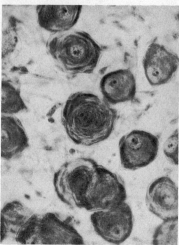
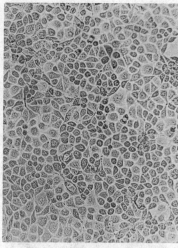
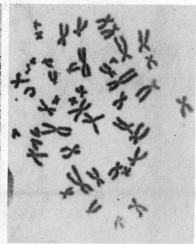

Animal tissue cultures.
(Left) Neurons of chick dorsal root ganglion in culture. (Centre) Monolayer culture of mouse fibroblasts grown in a completely defined medium. (Right) A human cell showing chromosomes during cell division.
By courtesy of (left) Edith R. Peterson, (centre) Charity Waymouth, (right) Keen A. Rafferty, Jr.

cultures on, rather than in or under, the nutrient medium; in this case, the tissue fragments may be floated on paper or rayon or supported on expanded metal grids. Special equipment that permits continuous microscopic observation of cells, as well as time-lapse filming of their activities, may be designed to allow the addition of fresh medium to the growth vessel or the injection of drugs into the organ without disturbing the position of the culture. Complex equipment developed for maintaining cells in continuous culture on a large scale permits periodical harvesting of the cells and continuously supplies fresh nutrients and gases. Monitoring devices attached to some equipment automate the continuous operation.

Nutrient media. Although media for cell and organ culture may be of many different kinds, minimal conditions for the culture of particular cell types, rather than the best conditions, often are achieved. For example, some survival, growth, differentiation, and function of many cell types can be accomplished in cell cultures maintained in biological media; *i.e.*, blood serum, blood plasma, and tissue extracts. Many chemically defined nutrient media have been designed for particular cell types or cells whose growth requirements are not very strict. Since all of the minor requirements of cells with exacting needs are not yet known, a defined medium is commonly supplemented with small amounts of blood serum, and the medium is considered a semidefined one. Every nutrient medium must contain (1) such major inorganic ions (charged particles) as sodium, potassium, calcium, magnesium, chloride, and phosphate, which are necessary to maintain normal fluid balance and to act with certain enzymes (biological catalysts); (2) energy sources, usually glucose or another simple sugar for animal cells, sucrose for plant cells; sugars also provide a major source of carbon atoms for the formation of certain cell constituents (*e.g.*, lipids, polysaccharides); (3) nitrogen-containing compounds, mainly the amino acids, which are the basic building blocks for proteins and nucleic acids of the cell; (4) essential enzymes, which require water-soluble vitamins and traces of certain metal ions (*e.g.*, iron, copper, zinc); (5) certain hormones, which may be required to influence specific functions of particular cell types; (6) special substances, other than hormones, required for specific functions (*e.g.*, certain proteins, fat-soluble vitamins, fatty acids); (7) respiratory gases necessary to sustain life, oxygen for animal cells and carbon dioxide for those of green plants; and (8) water. Biological media may not supply these requirements in the best proportions to sustain particular cell types. Many of the numerous chemically defined media are available commercially throughout the world.

Not only must media for cell culture have an appropriate chemical composition, with proper proportions of the various components, but they also must be appropriately acid or alkaline—*i.e.*, most animal cells require slightly alkaline conditions, while plant cells require acid conditions. The pressure exerted by media used for cultures of vertebrate animal cells should not cause the cells to shrink or swell. For invertebrate animals such as insects, the optimum pressure of the media varies with the species over a wide range.

Because plant cells are capable of synthesizing complex nitrogen-containing compounds from simple sources, the large number of amino acids required by animal cells in culture is not needed in media for plant culture. The simplest amino acid (glycine) and an inorganic nitrogen compound may provide sufficient nitrogen for growth, although the addition of other amino acids may be beneficial, and other organic nitrogen sources (*e.g.*, arginine, urea, asparagine) may be substituted for glycine.

Initiation and growth of cultures. Cultures may be initiated from fragments of a tissue or from a tumour taken from the parent organism. Sometimes, the tissue is broken down into a cell suspension by various mechanical, chemical, or enzymatic means that separate the cells from each other. Blood leukocytes, normally found in the blood of animals, may be used to initiate cultures, especially if abnormalities of the hereditary material (chromosomes) are of interest. Leukocytes usually are forced to undergo cell division (mitosis) by treatment with products called phytomitogens, which are found in the red kidney bean, in *Phytolacca americana* (pokeweed), and in several other plants; at a stage in mitosis when the chromosomes become visible microscopically, the process is stopped by adding a compound originally isolated from the autumn crocus (*Colchicum autumnale*), colchicine.

After cells or organs have been placed in or on a nutrient medium, they are incubated at a temperature either close to that of the organism from which they were removed, for animals or plants without a temperature-regulating mechanism, or close to that of the normal environment of the organism, for animals with a constant body temperature; *e.g.*, 39° C for chick; 37° C for man, rabbit, or mouse; 28° C for mosquito; 20° C for oyster; 22° C for plant cells. Media for animal cells usually contain the compound sodium bicarbonate and carbon dioxide gas to maintain the correct degree of alkalinity; the vessels in which the cultures are grown, therefore, must be either closed with an airtight seal or placed in a special incubator containing air fortified with carbon dioxide to prevent the escape of carbon dioxide gas. Efforts to develop animal-cell culture media employing nonvolatile compounds in place of carbon dioxide show promise. Plant tissues, which grow in much more acid media than do those of animals, use atmospheric carbon dioxide.

As stated previously (see above *Apparatus*), cultures can be grown in a variety of vessels—from small hanging

Composition of nutrient media

Use of leukocytes

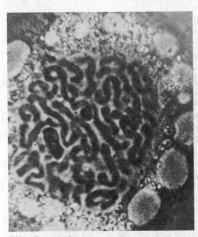  

Plant tissue cultures.
(Left) Prophase nucleus of a blood-lily endosperm. (Centre) Section through bacteria-free crown-gall tumour of a sunflower. (Right) Developing ovary of a columbine.
By courtesy of (left) Andrew Bajer, (centre) Philip R. White, (right) Sanford S. Tepfer

drop or test-tube cultures to flasks or bottles capable of yielding large quantities of cells weighing several grams. An early method of measuring growth, which involved measuring the area of outgrowth of cells from explants in blood-plasma clots, is unreliable as a measure of increase in cell mass or number because most of the increase is the result of migration of pre-existing cells from the explant; the number of mitoses in the areas of outgrowth, however, provides a rough measurement of culture growth. More commonly used methods for growth measurement involve growing cells as monolayers or in suspension, harvesting, and counting them in measured samples of cell suspension, either directly (under the microscope or with an electronic cell counter) or indirectly; *e.g.*, by measuring packed cell volume in a small tube within which the cells can be spun in a centrifuge; or by chemical assay of protein or DNA content. Large cultures, especially plant cultures, may be weighed. Certain types of animal organ cultures are suitable for direct growth measurements; *e.g.*, increases in length and thickness of bone explants.

In some tissue cultures, growth rate, or any measurement involving increase in number or size of cells, may not be an important criterion; in cell or organ cultures from endocrine glands, for example, the production of a specific hormone may be the measurement of choice. In other cases, morphological and developmental changes and the progress of differentiation of cells or organs are the important criteria. Sometimes functional capacity may be the criterion of choice; *e.g.*, the ability of muscle cells to contract, the production of antibodies by specific cells. The ability of cells to generate tumours may be the important criterion; it is tested by implanting the cells into appropriate animal or plant hosts.

Experimentation. The changes that can occur in cells when they are grown in culture can be studied in a population of cells derived from a single cell (clone). Clones

Use of clones

may be produced either by enclosing a cell in a restricted environment in which it can divide and give rise to a large population or by placing small numbers of cells on a semisolid medium and allowing each cell to give rise to a small colony of cells that can be isolated and used to grow a clonal population. Clones of human cells with a normal chromosome complement, however, usually undergo only a limited number of successive cell divisions in culture, after which the cells either die or undergo chromosomal changes that make them abnormal. Human cells containing the normal chromosome number are widely used to prepare vaccines against such diseases as poliomyelitis, measles, and influenza. Caution is necessary in such procedures, however, because human cells may carry infective viruses other than those against which a vaccine is developed.

With time-lapse moving pictures, the direct effects of light, heat, ionizing radiations, drugs, and chemicals, including oxygen and other gases, may be readily seen. In addition, moving pictures are used to record the interac-

tions between two or more cell types; *i.e.*, cell fusions, one cell entering another and moving around in its cytoplasm, and the effects of micro-organisms on different cells. Although the process of phagocytosis, or cell eating, has long been recognized as a means by which certain scavenger cells remove debris and bacteria from tissues, the related process of pinocytosis, or water uptake by cells, was discovered only after studies of time-lapse moving pictures of cells in culture.

The process of mitosis is significant in understanding the ways by which the components of the cell are able to replicate. An important experimental procedure, therefore, is to treat cells in culture so that their mitoses are synchronized; *e.g.*, cycles of cooling and warming or treatment with certain chemical substances, which block specific processes in the mitotic cycle so that mitosis occurs at the same time in many cells. Such bursts of mitoses permit the detailed study of biochemical events associated with mitosis; in addition, synchronized cells behave more uniformly than a population of cells in which all stages of cell division are occurring at any given time.

The use of radioactive chemicals, which may be incorporated into proteins, nucleic acids, and other important cellular constituents, has made possible the detailed mapping of chemical changes that occur during a complete cycle of growth and division of cells in culture (see CELL AND CELL DIVISION).

Importance. *Biological research.* Cell and organ culture techniques have made possible detailed investigations, under controlled conditions, of the nutrition and metabolism of many kinds of cells. Many cell types from vertebrate animals are grown in cell cultures; *e,.g.*, muscle, kidney, spleen, lung, liver, skin, bone, bone marrow, intestine, brain, nerve, testis, ovary, uterus, retina, tongue, salivary glands, pancreas, adrenal, pituitary, thymus, blood leukocytes. Although embryonic cells of vertebrates usually are easier to grow in culture than are those of adult tissues, many cells from adults also are grown. Cultures of cells of various invertebrate animals, including insects and their larvae, mollusks (such as oysters and mussels), and such annelid worms as the earthworm, are useful in studying agents that may have economic importance in agriculture and marine ecology. Plant tissues (*e.g.*, from root and stem tips, flower and fruit parts, callus tissue derived from cambium, phloem, or xylem of woody plants) also are grown in culture and studied to increase knowledge of plant growth and metabolism, viral specificity, and transformation of normal cells to cancerous ones. Tumours removed from plants and animals and grown in cultures provide opportunities to compare normal and cancerous growth. Features common to cancer in plant and animal cells have been studied extensively, in the hope that knowledge of the mechanisms that cause abnormal growths of one type of organism will help to clarify the nature of cancerous changes in another.

It is possible to select and grow cells with particular

Types of cells studied

biochemical properties; *e.g.*, nutritional variants may or may not require certain specific nutrients (amino acids such as asparagine or arginine, vitamins such as biotin or inositol), antigenic variants may or may not react to the presence of certain substances. Cells also may differentiate in culture; *i.e.*, primitive cells with many potential functions may give rise to cells capable of performing only specific functions. In addition, biochemical mechanisms important to mitosis may be studied with synchronized cell cultures, as can hereditary properties, which can be manipulated in cell cultures in ways that are not possible with whole organisms. At one time, it was generally thought that cells were potentially immortal and could divide indefinitely, that death could be regarded as a breakdown at the organizational, rather than at the cellular, level. Evidence gathered from cells in culture, however, indicates that normal cells (as contrasted with cancerous cells) can age; in addition, a general correlation is found between the degree of differentiated function of a cell and its potential for growth; *i.e.*, highly differentiated cells such as those of the brain lose the capacity to divide, and other cells such as those found in connective tissue retain the capacity to regenerate in the organism (as in wound healing) or to produce many generations of daughter cells in culture.

Growth and development can be studied in cultures; the earliest stages of hair development in the mouse, for example, which occur before the mouse is born, have been elucidated in organ culture. The early phases of feather formation, which occur before birds hatch, have been studied in cultures of chick embryo skin. Whole plants have been produced from single cells of such plants as carrot and phlox.

Culture techniques allow the development of fertilized mammalian eggs to many-celled stages. Animals with four parents have been created through the fusion, in culture, of fertilized eggs from two animals whose hereditary material may not be the same. Fused eggs may be implanted in foster mothers and undergo normal development and birth; the animals may have unusual and interesting genetic patterns, which are unattainable by normal methods of reproduction.

Applied research. The demonstration, in 1949, that the causative agent of a viral disease, poliomyelitis, would grow in cultures of human cells resulted in the preparation of vaccines that provide immunity against several viral diseases, including poliomyelitis, influenza, measles, and mumps. Cells in culture are also used to demonstrate and diagnose the damaging effects of viruses on cells. A naturally occurring viral inhibitor, called interferon, formed in response to the stimulus of a viral infection, as well as several other viral inhibitor agents, have been produced in cell cultures. The effects of these inhibitors upon cells containing viruses also has been examined in cell cultures.

Many of a large group of inherited disorders in man, so-called inborn errors of metabolism, are known to be caused by the lack of a specific enzyme (biological catalyst), which, in turn, prevents a biochemical reaction. Cells from persons with, or suspected of carrying, such disorders have been isolated so that the biochemical nature of specific defects can be studied. In some cases, the disorder can be corrected by medical treatment; even if treatment is not feasible, however, the identification of persons carrying, but not necessarily exhibiting, detrimental hereditary traits is useful to couples whose children might inherit a disorder.

Culture techniques for treating growing cells (*e.g.*, from blood, from a small piece of skin, or from the uterine fluids of a pregnant woman) so that the chromosomes of dividing cells can easily be counted and examined were developed about 1952; in 1956, the normal chromosome number in man was found to be 46, not 48 as had been previously believed. Defects associated with mental deficiency (*e.g.*, mongolism) may be identified by examination of cells cultured from a pregnant woman.

Other diagnostic applications of cell cultures include classification of brain tumours and identification of a chromosome of unusual conformation, called the Philadelphia chromosome, which is associated with a cancerous condition of white blood cells (chronic granulocytic leukemia). Cells from a type of virus-related cancer first found in African children (Burkitt's lymphoma) also carry a characteristic chromosome, called a marker chromosome, which is similar to the marker chromosome in the cells of patients with infectious mononucleosis, a noncancerous viral disease.

Tissue culture has made many contributions to the understanding of the transformation of normal cells into malignant ones, which may occur both in cultures of cells and in animals as a result of the influence of certain viruses and chemical carcinogens, or without the intervention of a known agent. Air pollutants from smog have been added to cell media in tests for the presence of carcinogenic chemicals in them; although the smog material alone is relatively ineffective, a combination of smog with viruses is more effective in effecting a malignant transformation of cells than are the viruses alone.

Tissue culture techniques are of increasing value in the production of hormones from cultures of cells or organs. Attempts once were made to grow organ cultures of parathyroid glands removed from unborn humans and to transplant them into patients with underactive glands or none at all. Limited success was achieved by this method because such transplants, like others, suffered from the probability of tissue rejection. Tissue culture methods, which are used to determine compatibility between a potential donor and a recipient in tissue transplants, involve the examination of mixed cultures of one type of white blood cells (lymphocytes) from the two persons. The previously mentioned techniques for fertilizing eggs with sperm and following early development of the embryo now are used to test the efficiency of antifertility agents.

BIBLIOGRAPHY. E.N. WILLMER, *Tissue Culture*, 3rd rev. ed. (1958), an easily understood, introductory text; R.C. PARKER, *Methods of Tissue Culture*, 3rd ed. (1961); P.R. WHITE, *The Cultivation of Animal and Plant Cells*, 2nd ed. (1963); and J. PAUL, *Cell and Tissue Culture*, 4th ed. (1970), more advanced textbooks; D.J. MERCHANT, R.H. KAHN, and W.H. MURPHY, *Handbook of Cell and Organ Culture* (1964), a laboratory handbook; M.R. MURRAY and G. KOPECH, *A Bibliography of the Research in Tissue Culture, 1884–1950*, 2 vol. (1953), a comprehensive reference source for early literature on tissue culture; C.V. RAMAKRISHNAN (ed.), *Tissue Culture* (1965); C. WAYMOUTH (ed.), *Advances in Tissue Culture* (1970); and D.A.T. NEW, *The Culture of Vertebrate Embryos* (1966), reviews on specialized topics; M. HARRIS, *Cell Culture and Somatic Variation* (1964); E.N. WILLMER (ed.), *Cells and Tissues in Culture*, 3 vol. (1965–67), *Cytology and Evolution*, 2nd ed. (1970); and V.J. CRISTOFALO and G.H. ROTHBLAT (eds.), *Nutrition and Metabolism of Cultured Cells* (1971), advanced books concerned with the entire field of tissue culture and its theories and implications.

(C.Wh.)

Tissues and Fluids, Animal

As the smallest structural and functional component of an organism, the cell is the basic unit of life. Although some animals and plants, such as protozoans and certain algae, consist of only one cell, they can, nevertheless, exist independently and may even have highly specialized parts that are analogous to tissues of more complex organisms. By definition, however, a tissue is a collection of cells having similar structures and performing special, as well as similar, functions. Those tissues, such as muscle, that consist almost entirely of cells devoted to a single purpose are known as simple tissues. Other tissues, such as those lining the alimentary canal (digestive tract) of higher animals, may serve a variety of functions; therefore, they are called composite tissues.

Very early in the evolution of animals, different tissues tended to become aggregated into organs, and the organs themselves divided into specialized parts. The simple pouchlike outgrowth of glandular cells from the side of the alimentary canal of amphioxus, a primitive chordate animal, for example, is now represented in complex vertebrates by a separate liver, pancreas, and gallbladder. Thus, an animal can be considered as a collection of tissues that are often, but not always, united into organs

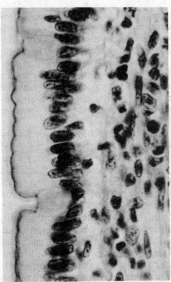
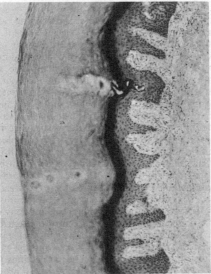
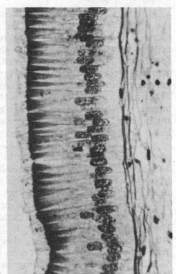

Figure 1: *Photomicrographs of epithelial cells.*
(Left) Simple columnar epithelium of small intestine showing striated (grooved) border. (Centre)
Stratified squamous epithelium of the skin of the fingertip. (Right) Ciliated epithelium from
the alimentary tract of a mussel.
Don W. Fawcett, M.D.

and organ systems. The fluids that are produced by tissues and in which they are bathed usually are considered as tissues only when, as in the case of blood, they have a definite and continuing cell content.

CLASSIFICATION OF TISSUES

Anatomical classification. The classification of tissues has always been determined by the methods available for their study. Hence, because early investigators were accustomed to dividing an animal body into its organ systems, tissues were first classified anatomically according to the organ system from which they came—*i.e.*, nervous tissues, digestive tissues, reproductive tissues, and so on. This system proved inadequate, however, when it became obvious that there were more tissues than could be accounted for by the few types that were peculiar to a specific organ system. This realization led to an attempt to classify tissues according to the cell types of which they are composed: tissues composed of epithelial cells covered the outside of organs; those composed of endothelial cells lined the inside of organs; and those consisting of stroma cells were thought to serve as a functionless matrix in which other functional cells were embedded. Tissues that did not have an obvious function were collectively called connective tissue because it was thought that their sole purpose was to connect one type of cell to another. This category included the elastic tissue of tendons, the cartilage of joints, the main skeletal elements, and even blood, although there appears to be no logical connection in structure or function between blood and bone. Despite such seeming inconsistencies, however, this method of classification was useful in drawing attention to the similarities that occur throughout the animal body. A particular type of epithelial cell, for example, may be found in many different locations and in many kinds of organs.

Embryological classification. The great surge in structural embryology (the study of the formation and development of the embryo in plants and animals) that occurred when tissues were being classified according to cell types led to a system of tissue classification based on embryological origin. In the course of embryological development in most animals, it is fairly easy to recognize those cells that originate on the outside of the embryo (ectodermal cells), those that originate on the inside of the embryo (endodermal cells), and those that lie between the inside and outside of the embryo (mesodermal cells). This classification, although valuable for the information it reveals concerning evolution, is of far less value when applied to specific tissues. The epidermal and mesodermal elements of skin, for example, are confused; how

far back the mouth ectoderm goes by infolding before true endoderm starts has been the subject of endless semantic arguments.

Functional classification. The most useful of all systems is to classify tissues according to the functions that they perform. On this basis tissues can be divided into three distinctive classes and a miscellaneous class. One of the distinctive classes contains those tissues that are used for assimilation, storage, transport, and excretion of food or waste products—*i.e.*, those tissues that serve an animal's needs for growth, repair, and energy. Involved in assimilation are the alimentary tissues, which not only break down food products to derive energy but also transform energy into utilizable sources that can be stored and released as required (see DIGESTION AND DIGESTIVE SYSTEMS). In any but the smallest animals the products secured by the alimentary tissues or liberated from the storage tissues are transported to other areas of the body, a function that is performed by blood and lymph. The role of tissues such as those in the lung and kidney is to excrete waste products from the body.

Another group of tissues classified according to function contains those used for coordination. This group includes those tissues that coordinate the organism in relation to its external environment as well as those that coordinate the parts of the organism internally. External coordination is performed by the central nervous system (brain and spinal cord) and its associated sense organs; internal coordination, though aided by the sense organs, is largely the responsibility of the chemical secretions (hormones) of specialized endocrine glands.

The third distinctive group of tissues according to the functional classification contains those required for support and movement, the skeletal and muscular tissues. The fourth group includes tissues used for reproduction; the hemopoietic tissues, which are concerned with the production of blood cells; and tissue fluids.

TISSUES FOR ASSIMILATION, STORAGE, TRANSPORT, AND EXCRETION

Alimentary tissues. The principal tissues involved in assimilation lie along the alimentary canal, the anterior end of which is the mouth. Lining the mouth is a simple form of covering tissue, or epithelium, known as squamous (scaly) epithelium because it consists of flattened, overlapping cells. It is also called stratified epithelium because there are several layers of cells. In such an arrangement, which is necessary in an area of rough usage like the mouth, cells that are detached from the surface can be replaced quickly by those underneath. Because they are in direct contact with the

Inadequacies of classification systems

air, these tissues must be kept moist. Interspersed among the epithelial cells, therefore, are numerous cells that secrete a slimy fluid called mucus. In many animals these cells are aggregated into small glands. Surface tissues (epithelia) containing mucous cells are called mucous membranes; irrespective of the type of epithelium involved, such membranes line the entire alimentary canal.

Tongue and salivary glands

The mouth of terrestrial animals also contains the tongue, which is the main food-gathering organ of many amphibians, some reptiles, and even a few mammals. Regardless of the organism, the interior of the tongue invariably consists of a mass of well-vascularized (blood-filled), interlacing muscle fibres; the tissues covering the surface of the tongue, on the other hand, differ from one group of animals to another. The squamous epithelium on the upper surface of most, if not all, animals is cornified epithelium; it is capable of producing keratin, the tough material that comprises horns, hooves, and nails. The surface of the mammalian tongue contains pits that extend down to the underlying mucus-producing tissues, from which arise pillars of various shapes. With this arrangement, sensory nerve endings in the pits can be kept constantly moist; yet, the organ itself is so tough on the surface that it can be used for scraping or rasping.

Mammals require such large quantities of mucus to moisten food and to protect oral membranes that they have developed specialized glands, the salivary glands, with ducts leading into the mouth. Anatomically, these glands are botryoidal; physiologically, they are merocrine; and biochemically, they are mixed. These terms also apply to many other glands. A botryoidal gland is one with many branching ducts, each of which finally terminates in a hollow spherical gland, thus giving the appearance of a bunch of grapes. A merocrine gland is one in which no part of the cytoplasm (the part of a cell exclusive of the nucleus) of the secreting cell is lost; all the granules of the secreted product pass through the cell membrane and into the lumen (cavity) of a duct, in which they are dissolved and distributed. A mixed gland is one that produces a number of products; thus, the salivary glands yield a serous fluid called mucus, which is a dispersion of a protein in water, and small quantities of the digestive enzymes ptyalin and maltase. (Enzymes are proteins that control chemical reactions in living matter.) The total of all these secretions is saliva, the importance of which is indicated by the fact that its daily output in man exceeds that of urine.

Esophagus and stomach

After leaving the mouth, food passes down the esophagus, a muscular tube that histologically—i.e., in terms of its tissue structure—is little more than an extension of the mouth. Internally, the esophagus is lined with a thick coat of the same type of stratified squamous epithelium as is found in the mouth. There is a longitudinal layer of striated muscle (muscle in which the bands, or striations, represent areas of different composition), the contractions of which control swallowing, and a thin circular layer of nonstriated muscle that is separated from the epithelium-lined lumen by a cushion of connective tissues. The esophagus enters the stomach, an organ of variable tissue construction in different animals; it is primarily a sack, or a series of sacks, that holds, churns, and partially digests the contents. In the human stomach the entire inner surface is covered with a simple columnar-shaped epithelium from which thousands of pits, or gastric glands, descend into the underlying layer of connective tissue. In the stomachs of some animals the glands are confined to small areas, and much of the inner stomach wall is composed of stratified squamous, and even occasionally keratinized, epithelium. The outer stomach wall consists of three layers of nonstriated muscle fibres that run longitudinally, circularly, and diagonally.

Interesting tissues in the stomach are the gastric glands, which are simple in structure but complex in cellular makeup and function. In most organisms the glands are S-shaped tubular structures, but sometimes they are branched. The cells forming the glands are of four types. In the gastric pit, the part of the gland that opens into the stomach, the cells resemble the general epithelial lining and are active secretors of mucus. Just below the pit

is the isthmus, a section of the gland containing a few mucus-producing cells and many hydrochloric-acid-secreting ones; the acid is necessary in the digestive process. Between the isthmus and the base of the gland is the neck, which contains additional mucus cells and a few that produce hydrochloric acid. The base of the gland consists mostly of cells that secrete an enzyme that catalyzes the breakdown of proteins in the stomach; the base also includes several of another type of cell, the exact function of which is still in doubt.

Small intestine

After partial digestion in the stomach, from which only a very few simple substances are absorbed, the food passes to the small intestine. In higher vertebrates all the tissues and structures of the small intestine are modified for the sole purpose of absorption, which is a direct function of surface area. The inner wall of the small intestine consists of a series of connecting ridges. Arising from the ridges are millions of finger-like projections called villi, the centre of each of which contains blood vessels that remove absorbed materials. The tightly packed epithelial cells covering the villi are themselves covered with even smaller projections (microvilli). This combination of villi and microvilli results in a total absorptive surface of the small intestine that is approximately 10,000 times greater than that of a smooth tube. The tissues of the remaining length of the alimentary canal are primarily devoted to the recycling of water. They do not have villi and are usually covered with a simple epithelium containing numerous mucus-secreting cells.

In lower vertebrates the glands that produce the enzymes necessary to convert food substances into absorbable molecules are found along the entire length of the small intestine. In all higher forms, however, the larger surface area creates a greater demand for enzymes. As a result, the glands are located in a completely separate organ, the pancreas, which, in tissue structure and secretory function, closely resembles a salivary gland.

Fatty tissue

Digested food materials of all types, as well as undigested droplets of fat, are picked up by the blood from the small intestine and transported to other parts of the body either for storage or for immediate use. Fat is stored in fat cells, which develop from undifferentiated cells in connective tissue. At an early stage of their development, the undifferentiated cells become filled with small fat droplets; later, these coalesce into a large single fat droplet. In some lower vertebrates, particularly amphibians, fat cells are localized, forming fat bodies that are distinct from the surrounding tissue. In most higher forms, however, fatty (adipose) tissue is dispersed throughout the body, although fat cells do tend to aggregate into fat masses in certain areas, particularly in the layers beneath the surface of the skin.

Liver tissues. The bulk of nutrient-bearing blood goes to the liver, which is probably the most important single tissue in the maintenance of the mammalian body. The evolutionary mechanism by which the liver reached this important function is not entirely clear. Many invertebrates and such lower vertebrates as amphioxus have outgrowths from the anterior region of the alimentary canal, apparently for the purpose of increasing the secretory area. In the cyclostomes (e.g., lamprey, hagfish) the lumen of a much-branched outgrowth remains open; hence, the liver in these animals is a series of intercoiled tubes. In higher forms, however, there is no lumen; instead, the liver consists essentially of many-sided (polygonal) cells so closely pressed together that all trace of a tubular origin is lost. The cells cluster about much-branched blood vessels, from which phagocytes (cells that ingest and destroy foreign materials) migrate and become interspersed among the liver cells. There is also a network of branching ducts, originating as intercellular spaces, that collect bile (a fluid secreted by the liver that aids in digestion) and form the bile duct, which leads to the gallbladder. Despite the fact that they perform a multiplicity of functions, all liver cells appear to be of the same type.

When blood reaches the liver from the small intestine, its carbohydrate content is adjusted either by the removal of excess sugars and their conversion to glycogen particles that are stored in the liver or by the addition of sugar through the breakdown of previously stored glycogen. Poisonous substances carried by the blood are either detoxified, if possible, or removed from the blood and stored. Partially broken down erythrocytes (red blood cells), arriving from the spleen at the rate of about 3,000,000 per second, are picked up by the phagocytes and broken down further; the breakdown products are either recycled or, as in the case of excess pigments, excreted through the bile. Liver cells also control the synthesis and distribution of fat in the form of large molecules composed of both lipid and protein (lipoprotein); the synthesis of all proteins in blood plasma; and the synthesis of urea, a nitrogenous waste that is subsequently excreted by the kidney.

Blood and lymph. To refer to blood as a tissue is a semantic, not a scholarly, definition, because in some invertebrates (*e.g.*, annelids) the blood is almost acellular (lacking in cells), and in the great majority of invertebrates it contains at the most only a few leukocytes (white blood cells). Only at the vertebrate level do the oxygen-carrying pigments of the blood become localized in specific blood cells, and only at the mammalian level do they lose their nuclei. The acellular portion of blood is called plasma when it is in a blood vessel and lymph when it passes out through the walls of capillaries (tiny blood vessels) to bathe the cells in surrounding tissues (see BLOOD AND LYMPH).

Respiratory pigments

The most important function of blood is to carry oxygen, which is transported by a respiratory pigment; the best known pigments are the hemoglobins. These compounds, which contain iron, are found in all vertebrates and also in many annelids, insects, and a few mollusks. Other respiratory pigments include the hemocyanins, which contain copper, and the hemovanadins, which contain vanadium. All of these pigments function in much the same manner: they pick up oxygen from the air and transport it to the cells, where it is released. The blood of most animals also contains leukocytes of various forms and functions.

Blood plasma contains approximately 7 percent dissolved proteins, including the globulin fraction, which is of great immunological importance; other constituents include nutrients and hormones. The most important function of plasma is to maintain a proper fluid balance among the various tissues of the body. The lymph that passes through the walls of capillaries and bathes the tissues collects in lymph vessels and is recycled back into the bloodstream.

Kidney tissues. The original function of the vertebrate kidney was to remove water from the body cavity (coelom) of aquatic animals. The primitive kidney consisted of little more than a longitudinal duct opening at its posterior end into the cloaca (a passage into which waste products are discharged) and contained at its anterior end a series of funnels with cilia (lashing hairlike projections) to remove the excess fluid. This type of kidney is found in the larvae (*e.g.*, tadpoles) of many vertebrate animals. Early in the evolutionary history of aquatic vertebrates a tissue was developed that permitted excess blood fluids to be removed by a similar mechanism: a small, tangled mass of capillaries (the glomerulus) entered a pouch in the side of the longitudinal coelomic duct. With the adaptation of early vertebrates to terrestrial life, however, it was necessary that water be conserved; the coelomic funnel disappeared, and the glomerulus with its pouch (Bowman's capsule) no longer led directly into the excretory duct but into a highly complex series of tubules designed to concentrate and recycle water while permitting the removal of some water-soluble wastes.

Adult vertebrates known as the anamniota (fishes and amphibians) have a kidney structure very much like that of the embryo; the adult kidney of amniotes (reptiles, birds, and mammals), however, is derived from the posterior end of the embryonic kidney (see EXCRETION AND EXCRETORY SYSTEMS). In the anamniotic kidney, venous blood goes directly into a large sinus (a cavity or hollow space within a structure of the body). Located in this sinus are branched, tangled tubules, each of which terminates in a Bowman's capsule containing arterial blood that comes directly from the heart through a series of branches of the main artery in the body. After its passage through the glomerulus, the arterial blood empties into the sinus, which, at its anterior end, drains into a large vein.

Embryonic amniotes have a very similar structure, but a pouched outgrowth from the posterior end of the collecting tubule develops completely new units around it. This outgrowth becomes the ureter (the duct that carries urine from the kidney to the urinary bladder), and the pouch becomes the renal pelvis (a saclike cavity at which the ureter is attached to the kidney). The excretory units (nephrons), each of which consists of a Bowman's capsule, glomerulus, and tubule, then develop in the surrounding tissue and become attached through one or more branches to the renal pelvis. Arterial blood enters the kidney through the renal artery directly from the dorsal aorta (the main posterior artery from the heart). It then passes through arterioles (tiny arteries) to the glomerulus in the Bowman's capsule; a great deal of water and all but the largest molecules in the blood are forced through the walls of the glomerulus by the high pressure of the blood. (The human kidney excretes about two gallons [7.5 litres] of water an hour through the glomeruli; of course, most of this is subsequently reabsorbed.) Blood leaves the glomerulus through another set of arterioles that form a network of capillaries around the coils of the kidney tubules; it then returns to the heart through the venous system.

Nephrons

Histologically, the kidney tubule is divided into three parts: a thick proximal section that is adjacent to the Bowman's capsule and consists of columnar or cubical epithelial cells with large numbers of microvilli on their surface; a distal portion of very similar structure that leads to the collecting duct; and, between the two, a long, but variable, length of thin-walled tubule. The proximal portion of the tubule has the dual function of reabsorbing materials to be recycled—*e.g.*, water, glucose, amino acids, ascorbic acid, sodium, chlorides, and bicarbonates—and of removing from the blood in the arterioles surrounding the tubule those substances that do not pass through the walls of the glomerulus. The thin-walled portion of the tubule further concentrates the urine, and in the final convoluted section the water, sodium, and phosphate contents of the urine are adjusted to the requirements of the body.

Apart from the capillaries and tubule cells described, there are a few specialized tissues in the kidney. Located around the neck of each arteriole, where it enters the glomerulus, is a cuff of juxtaglomerular cells; these are thought both to control the flow of blood into the glomerulus and to secrete an enzyme. Another interesting cellular adaptation is the presence of podocytes in the walls of the Bowman's capsule. As the name podocytes indicates, these are "footed" cells that protrude from the wall of the capsule and press against the glomerulus, thereby improving fluid flow by maintaining a clear space between the blood vessels of the glomerulus and the wall of the capsule.

Lung tissues. Animal tissues to secure oxygen and excrete carbon dioxide are extremely variable (see RESPIRATION AND RESPIRATORY SYSTEMS). In many small invertebrates, gas exchange takes place directly through the body wall or through external gills, which are thin, often tufted extensions of the body wall through which the blood circulates. The protected gill first appears in the pelecypod mollusks (*e.g.*, clam, oyster, scallop); it is a folded sheet of parallel anastomosing (connecting) blood vessels that are covered first by the mantle (the tissue covering the soft body organs of a mollusk) and then the shell. Adaptation for life on land, however, required the development of the lung, an internal sac with a heavily vascularized wall into which air could be drawn and from which waste gases could be expelled by the expansion and contraction of adjacent structures. The first such organ appears in the gastropod mollusks (*e.g.*, snail, slug, whelk); an analogous structure, in the form of an outgrowth from the anterior end of the alimentary canal,

Respiratory structures in animals

was developed by the lungfish and persists in most adult amphibians, in which the walls of the sac begin to show folding. The increased demand for oxygen occasioned by rapid movement on land resulted in the evolution of multilobed, heavily vascularized lungs in reptiles, birds, and mammals. Gases were inhaled and exhaled first by the simple contraction of the thoracic (chest) walls and later with the assistance of the diaphragm (a muscular partition that separates the thoracic cavity from the abdominal cavity).

Two other mechanisms for gas exchange were developed by the arthropods (*e.g.*, insects, spiders, crustaceans). In scorpions the interior surface of a series of four pairs of ventral pouches is folded into a number of lamellae (thin plates). Because of the pagelike appearance of this arrangement, it is called a book lung. In insects and a few other groups (*e.g.*, onycophorans and centipedes), thin-walled ducts, supported by rings of chitin (a horny substance), conduct atmospheric gases to small pouches that are in direct contact with tissues. That this system is extremely efficient in small animals is indicated by its ability to meet the extraordinary oxygen demands of, for example, the flight muscles of many insects. But because it cannot be adapted to large organisms, terrestrial arthropods that use this system have never reached the sizes attained by those animals that have lungs.

TISSUES FOR COORDINATION

None of the tissues so far described would be able to function satisfactorily were they not coordinated in relation to both the external and the internal environment of the animal. Coordinating tissues are broadly classified into those that are physical (nervous and sensory tissues) and those that are chemical (endocrine tissues).

Physical coordinators. It may be stated as a broad generalization that both physical and chemical coordination in invertebrates are performed by the same tissues, because the nervous tissues of many invertebrates also serve as hormone sources. Hormones, chemical substances secreted into the bloodstream by endocrine glands, have specific effects on other organs). In vertebrates most endocrine functions are isolated in specialized glands, several of which, such as the pineal and hypophysis in the brain, are derived from nervous tissue. The basic unit of all nervous tissue is the neuron, which, with few exceptions, consists of a cell body from which protrude numerous branching cytoplasmic processes (dendrites) and one long fibre (the axon). The dendritic fibres act as interconnections between neurons; the axon either transmits impulses to an organ (efferent axon) or collects impulses from sensory organs (afferent axon; see NERVE IMPULSE; NERVES AND NERVOUS SYSTEMS). Internally, the cell body of the neuron contains considerable quantities of what were once called Nissl bodies, which consist of stacks of rough-surfaced endoplasmic reticulum (a convoluted membranous network in cells) with large numbers of ribosomes (granular structures consisting of protein and ribonucleic acid—RNA) sandwiched between them. The presence and structure of the Nissl bodies indicate that RNA plays a major role in the functioning of the nerve cell and is probably responsible for the storage of information (memory). Aggregations of neurons are known as ganglia.

In addition to neurons, and also associated with the central nervous system, ganglia, and the axon itself is a tissue that may be either in the form of glia cells or Schwann cells. The former, which are also known as neuroglia cells, constitute a special type of connective tissue that is interspersed among nerve cells and fibres. The Schwann cells are large, flattened cells that are wrapped in such a tight spiral around the axon that most of their cytoplasm has been squeezed out through their membrane. In effect, the axon is wrapped in many layers of membrane with only a little cytoplasm on the inner and outer surfaces. Membranes have a central lipid (fatty) layer; the nerve, therefore, is covered by an insulating layer of lipids that is commonly known as the myelin sheath.

There are three principal types of neuroglia cells: astro-

cytes, which, as the name indicates, are star-shaped cells with numerous branches at their ends; oligoglia (also called oligodendroglia or oligodendrocytes), which have fewer but thicker branches than astrocytes and are generally smaller; and microglia, which are the smallest of the three. It was once thought that these cells serve merely as connective tissue to support neurons. Evidence is accumulating, however, that they may play a more active role not only in transmitting nutrients and forming enzymes but also in the conduction of neural impulses. Because the short ends of some oligoglia are wrapped tightly around the capillaries in the brain, they could form a direct conducting path for hormones. The astrocytes become active principally when there is neural damage, at which time they assume a phagocytic function.

A slice across the brain or spinal cord shows it to be divided into two regions, descriptively called gray matter and white matter. The former, which is on the outside of the brain and on the inside of the spinal cord, contains the neurons; the white matter owes its appearance to the lipid content of the myelin sheaths around the nerves of which it is largely composed. A typical neuron has about 100 dendritic branches; these may form junctions (synapses) either with dendritic branches from other cells (axodendritic synapses) or with the surface of another neuron (axosomatic synapses). Impulses originating in one neuron may or may not be transmitted through the synapses to other neurons; the mechanism of such selective transmission, on which depend thought, reason, and memory, is not at present fully understood.

A neuron not only receives and transmits impulses to other dendrites but it may also receive an impulse from a sense organ in an outlying part of the body or transmit an impulse to an outlying muscle. The bundles of axons through which these impulses are carried are called nerves. At the terminal end of a transmitting axon in, for example, a muscle, there is a short spray of branches known as axonal telodendria, each of which terminates in a structure called a bouton. When an impulse reaches the boutons, they secrete the chemical acetylcholine, which, because the boutons are in molecular contact with the membrane of the muscle, causes the muscle to contract. Although the nerves leading to the abdominal muscles of the viscera are structurally similar, they operate by a different method. Because visceral muscles are not anchored to joints or bones, they are in a constant state of partial contraction, and movement is produced either by increasing (exciting) or decreasing (depressing) this state. The excitatory nerves mediate their action through the release of acetylcholine; the depressant nerves, through the release of adrenaline or noradrenaline.

There are a few specialized types of neurons in the central nervous system. In many invertebrates and vertebrate larvae, giant neurons carry impulses directly across areas at which they would otherwise be interrupted. Another highly specialized type of giant neuron, the Purkinje cell, lies at the junction of the cerebral cortex and the medulla of the cerebellum, an area in the brain that coordinates locomotor functions and is most highly developed in birds and mammals. Each Purkinje cell has many dendritic branches that ramify through the whole of the outer (molecular) layer of the cerebral cortex. The only afferent nerves leaving the cerebral cortex are those that are made up of the axons of Purkinje cells. In the inner (granule) layer of the cerebellar cortex are large numbers of small granular cells, the dendritic branches of which receive impulses from the axons of incoming (afferent) nerves. Each granular cell has a single axon that rises vertically through the molecular layer and then divides into two branches that run in opposite directions and synapse with the dendrites of some of the Purkinje cells. The union of all the Purkinje cells with the granular cells, which has been likened to a telephone distribution system, is the mechanism for the transmission of the extremely complex nervous impulses required for the locomotor responses of mammals and birds.

Afferent nerves (those that conduct impulses toward the brain and spinal cord) reaching other areas of the central nervous system come from sense organs (receptors) that

The neuron

Types of neuroglia cells

Chemo-
receptors

receive either internal or external stimuli. For higher animals the most important of these are the photoreceptors, the light-sensitive nerve endings located in the rods and cones of the retina of the eye (see PHOTORECEPTION). Chemoreceptors, or taste buds, usually consist of two types of cell pressed together into a small, pear-shaped Y. The receptor cells, which are elongated into an apical process that is in contact with the medium to be tasted, are heavily innervated by terminal buds of the afferent nerves; they are separated from each other by the sustentacular (supporting) cells that lie beneath the surface and are not innervated. There is considerable argument as to whether the human perception of sweet, sour, salty, metallic, and bitter are sensed by the same nerve endings or by different ones; there is still more argument as to which of these senses are present in lower vertebrates. Catfish have "taste buds" in slender projections on their lips, called barbels, and insects have very similar structures both in their antennae and, in the case of butterflies, in their feet (see CHEMORECEPTION).

The vibroreceptors (those sensitive to mechanical vibrations) apparently are present in relatively few animals. Except for the ear, the most developed of such organs are located in the fish, in which they extend in lines along the length of the body (see MECHANORECEPTION and SOUND RECEPTION). Although the function of sensory structures in animals other than man is difficult to determine, it appears that most organisms possess heat and cold receptors, which are different organs; each apparently consists of a single cell permeated by a terminal treelike branching of a nerve. Pressure sensors, on the other hand, usually consist of a fluid-filled cavity and several cells bunched around the end of a nerve. In man these receptors, called pacinian corpuscles, are very large (up to four millimetres, or 0.2 inch); they are found in the deeper layers of the skin and throughout the body, at points at which pressure sensation is necessary—e.g., joints, tendons, ligaments.

Chemical coordinators. In many invertebrates chemical stimulators are secreted by the neurons themselves and then move to their place of action along the axon. Such is the case with the hormone in crustaceans that controls the lightening or darkening of the body in response to the environment. The hormonal activities of neurons, however, are nowhere better shown than in the insects, the principal endocrine glands of which are the corpora allata (wing-shaped bodies) and the corpora cardiaca (heart-shaped bodies) that lie alongside the brain. Neurons in the brain secrete large colloidal (jellylike) granules that pass beyond the axon to the heart-shaped bodies and then to the wing-shaped bodies. Some evidence indicates that these colloid granules are also liberated directly into the hemolymph (the fluid in invertebrate tissues and body cavities).

Endocrine
glands

The principal endocrine tissues of the higher vertebrates are the thyroid gland, parathyroid glands, endocrine constituents of the pancreas, interrenal chromaffin tissues of the adrenal gland, and the pituitary gland (see ENDOCRINE SYSTEMS). Of these the thyroid gland presents the clearest evolutionary and histological picture. In mammals this gland secretes not only the hormone thyroxine (tetraiodothyronine) but also smaller quantities of another hormone, triiodothyronine; both have a powerful effect on both rate of maturation and general metabolism. A similar product (monoiodotyrosine) is synthesized by many algae, and both monoiodotyrosine and diiodotyrosine are found in all invertebrates, in many of which the synthesis is apparently centred in the pharyngeal region (the portion of the digestive tract lying between the mouth and the esophagus and forming the respiratory organs of aquatic vertebrates). In the most primitive vertebrates (the cyclostomes) there appears, as an outgrowth of the pharyngeal region, an exocrine gland (one that secretes through a duct, as for example, the digestive glands) that is not unlike a salivary gland in structure. In all higher forms, embryological development of the thyroid gland begins with a duct connected to the pharynx, just as in the lower vertebrates. Ultimately, however, it becomes a ductless (endocrine) gland that is divided into

lobes and lobules, which are small, spherical collecting pouches surrounded by cells that secrete the hormone into the lumen of the pouch. Blood vessels in the organ pick up the thyroxine and transport it around the body. The thyroid is chemically linked to the pituitary gland by a system of negative feedback; that is, as the secretory activity of one increases, that of the other decreases.

The parathyroids are also pharyngeal derivatives that are represented in most teleost (bony) fishes by structures called ultimobranchial bodies and in higher forms by four small endocrine glands imbedded in the back part of the thyroid, two on each side. These glands, which have completely lost their lobular structure, consist of a tangled mass of cellular cords, the secretory products of which pass directly to capillaries. The secretions appear to have their principal effect on the calcium–phosphorus ratio in blood.

The endocrine portions of the pancreas (a large gland located behind the stomach that secretes digestive enzymes as well as hormones) are called the islets of Langerhans. In some lower vertebrates, however, the islets are individual glands, completely separated from the pancreas. Like the parathyroids, the islets also consist of tangled cords; they contain four kinds of cells that are designated by the first four letters of the Greek alphabet —alpha, beta, gamma, and delta. The alpha cells are filled with dense masses of granules that yield the hormone glucagon, which, because it it antagonistic to the hormone insulin, prevents the synthesis of glycogen, protein, and fat. The beta cells, which are the most numerous cells in the islets, also consist of large masses of granules that produce insulin, a hormone that controls the sugar (glucose) content of the blood. The function of the gamma and delta cells is not yet known.

Although in mammals interrenal and chromaffin cells are combined into the adrenal gland, the former being the cortex (outside) and the latter the medulla (inside), both tissues are quite distinct. (There are two adrenal glands in mammals, one associated with each kidney.) The interrenal tissues, which exist as separate glands in all vertebrates except birds and mammals, secrete hormones, of which cortisone is a typical example. The cells of these tissues are usually distinguished by the presence in their cytoplasm of large vesicular mitochondria (granular or rodlike bodies, which, in this case, contain fluid-filled cavities). Chromaffin cells, which occur in most animals as scattered clumps, secrete the hormones adrenaline and noradrenaline. The cells are large and ovoid, resembling neurons in all but their lack of axons and dendrites.

The pituitary, which has a dual origin and a dual function, is the most important endocrine gland of the body. It originates from two separate locations: one part, the adenohypophysis, develops as an upgrowth from the roof of the mouth; the other part, the neurohypophysis, develops as a downgrowth from the floor of the brain. The adenohypophysis is divided into three regions, the anterior lobe, the intermediate lobe, and a third lobe that connects to the neurohypophysis. Like most endocrine glands, the anterior lobe consists of tangled masses of cords with numerous types of secreting cells. The hormones secreted by this region mostly interact with the secretions from other endocrine glands to control the internal environment of the body. The neurohypophysis not only has direct axonic connections with the brain but also contains numerous neurosecretory cells (neurons that produce one or more hormones). The products of these cells pass directly to the anterior lobe, the activities of which they control. Thus, through the neurohypophysis the brain can control the secretions of the anterior lobe and thereby adjust the internal environment to the external environment, conditions of which are communicated to the brain by the sense organs. A typical example of such control is found in birds. When the brain becomes aware of increasing day length through impulses from the eye, it stimulates the neurohypophysis to secrete neurohormones. These, in turn, stimulate the anterior lobe to release hormones that cause the rapid development of the gonads, thus assuring that the bird will be in condition to breed in the spring.

Neuro-
hormones

TISSUES FOR SUPPORT AND MOVEMENT

Connective tissues.   Connective tissues hold the body together. Most such tissue is of the white fibrous type, which is divided into two kinds, loose and dense, although the two actually grade imperceptibly into each other. White fibrous connective tissue has several roles—it envelops and often penetrates organs to hold them together, encloses muscles, and forms a considerable proportion of the spongy layers of the skin. It is composed of a loose meshwork of a relatively inelastic fibrous protein (collagen), the fibres of which are interspersed in a gelatinous matrix that contains numerous leukocytes derived from the blood. When glandular organs contain considerable quantities of connective tissue—as do, for example, the spleen and thymus—the leukocytes increase in number and become star-shaped cells, the terminal processes of which anastomose to form a loose three-dimensional network. This is best seen in such invertebrates as flatworms, in which a stellate reticulum (a network of star-shaped cells) fills all the space not occupied by discrete internal organs. Mucoid connective tissue, which contains much more gelatinous substance than connective tissue, is found in all embryos as the initial stage in the development of connective tissue; and though rare in adult animals, it does form in the main bulk of such outgrowths as cockscombs and turkey wattles.

Connective tissue of great structural strength consists of almost pure collagen fibres arranged in parallel layers, as in tendons. In ligaments, fibres of elastin, a fibrous protein that is brownish in colour, are mixed with collagen fibres, in which case the tissue is often called yellow elastic connective tissue.

Cartilage.   Although usually classified as connective tissues, cartilage and bone are better regarded as supportive in function. Cartilage is the product of cells known as chondrocytes, which secrete around themselves a clear, jellylike mass of a sugar-like substance containing sulfur, (chondroitin sulfate). Cartilage of this type, which is found in the adult skeletons of cyclostomes as well as in small sharks and rays, is called hyaline cartilage. In larger sharks the deposition of calcium salts modifies the hyaline cartilage into calcified cartilage, which, because it resembles bone in composition but not in structure, must be clearly differentiated from bone. Another modified form of cartilage is fibrous cartilage, which grades almost imperceptibly into fibrous connective tissue at, for example, the junction of tendons with bone or cartilaginous joints. Elastic cartilage (Figure 2) contains yellow elastic fibres; one of the places at which this type of cartilage appears as a supporting structure is in the outer ears of mammals.

Cartilage is also found in some invertebrates, such as in the cranial capsule (head covering) of cephalod mollusks (*e.g.,* squid, octopus), but the principal skeletal substance of invertebrates is chitin—a hard, waterproof, inelastic nitrogenous polysaccharide. Among the animals in which it is found are cnidarians (*e.g.,* hydroids, corals, sea anemones), mollusks, bryozoans ("moss animals"), nematodes (roundworms), and acanthocephalians (spiny-headed worms) as well as the better known arthropods (see SKELETAL SYSTEMS).

Bone.   Bone is derived from cells called osteoblasts, which lay down crystals of calcium phosphate known as apatite, in bone. When calcium phosphate is deposited in connective tissue, the resulting structure is called direct bone; when it is deposited as a replacement for cartilage, the resulting structure is called indirect bone. Because the osteoblasts move into a thick, fibrous sheet of white connective tissue during direct bone formation, the somewhat misleading term of membrane bone is often used. At the beginning of direct bone formation, the osteoblasts produce columnar structures (trabeculae) arranged so as to provide the maximum support for the bone that forms on both sides. The space between the trabeculae is filled with red bone marrow. As the osteoblasts become encased in bone, they turn into stellate cells known as osteocytes, which maintain contact with each other through long, branching surface projections. Because the osteocytes cluster around blood vessels, a cross section through a bone appears as a

Chitin

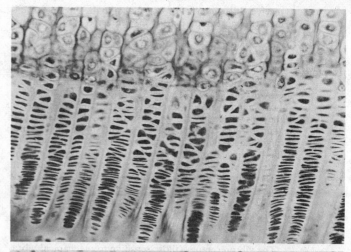

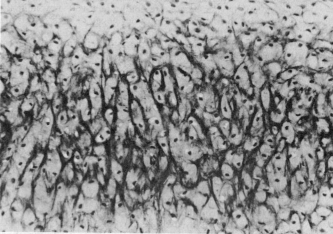

Figure 2: *Photomicrographs of cartilage.*
(Top) Hyaline cartilage of the epiphyseal plate (rabbit tibia).
(Bottom) Elastic cartilage.
Don W. Fawcett, M.D.

series of concentric rings with a small opening in the centre, called the haversian canal; this opening is actually the space occupied by the blood vessel. Membrane bones, such as those of the growing skull, frequently change their shape with the aid of cells known as osteoclasts. Osteoclasts break down the existing bone into material that can be redistributed to new positions by osteoblasts.

Indirect bone formation, in which bone replaces cartilage (Figure 2), occurs in the shaft bones (those of the arms and legs) of all animals and in the jawbones of most of them. A cell known as chondroclast dissolves the chondroitin sulfate, leaving a soft mucus-like material into which the osteoblasts move. As in the case of direct bone formation, the osteoblasts first build internal trabeculae and then encase them with solid bone. On the shank of bones (the long portion between the ends) there is always a lamellar layer of bony plates wrapped around the outside.

Muscle.   Muscle, a relatively simple tissue of complex function, has primarily two kinds of cells. One cell type, found in smooth muscle, contains one nucleus; it is controlled by the autonomic nervous system (the nerves outside the central nervous system that control involuntary body functions, such as breathing and digestion) and is concerned with the maintenance of the body's interior environment. The other cell type makes up striated (striped) muscle, which is also known as skeletal muscle; it is a multinucleate cell (cell with many nuclei) innervated by the central nervous system. Because the latter is under voluntary control, it can coordinate the organism with its external environment. Although cardiac (heart) muscle consists of striated cells (fibres) that are branched and interlocking, this type of muscle is under autonomic nervous control and has a unique system for the conduction of nerve impulses (see MUSCLE SYSTEMS; MUSCLE CONTRACTION).

Smooth muscle tissue generally occurs in simple sheets that are wrapped around, or run along, internal organs. At points at which the cell membranes are fused, the individual cells are interconnected by projections (called nexuses) that run from one cell into the other. Only a relatively few cells contain nerve endings, the impulses being transmitted from cell to cell through the nexuses. This arrangement can readily result in such rhythmic movements as the peristalsis (wavelike muscle contractions) of the intestine.

The striated cells that make up skeletal muscles are very different from those of smooth muscle cells. Each cell consists of numerous long, minute, threadlike structures (myofibrils) that are of two kinds: large fibrils composed of the protein myosin give rise to dark-banded striations; thin fibrils composed of the protein actin give rise to light-banded striations. The myosin bands are designated as the A bands and the actin bands as the I bands after the manner in which they refract (bend) light. When a muscle cell contracts, the thin actin fibres slip in between or coil around the thick myosin fibres; even when fully stretched, the actin fibres still slightly overlap the myosin fibres. This system permits a large degree of extension and contraction without breaking cytoplasmic continuity.

Because striated muscle cells have several nuclei, it is customary to refer to them as muscle fibres rather than cells. These fibres are grouped together into strands, each surrounded by a thin layer of connective tissue. The strands, in turn, are gathered into bundles that are connected by a thicker layer of connective tissue, and the bundles are held together as a muscle. At each end of a muscle the tissue is infiltrated by white fibrous connective tissue, which itself becomes a ligament for attachment. Unlike smooth muscle, in which only a few cells contain nerve endings, each fibre of a striated muscle is in contact with the terminal of an afferent nerve.

The muscles of the heart were, until very recently, regarded as a single large syncytium (a multinucleate mass of cytoplasm resulting from a fusion of cells). It now appears, however, that fine divisions do exist between the fibres. The muscle fibres in this organ branch and are interlaced; they continue to contract rhythmically long after all connections to the nervous system have been severed.

OTHER TISSUES

Reproductive tissues. The most important of the reproductive tissues, the gonads (ovaries and testes) produce the gametes (eggs and sperm, respectively). These organs are simplest in the teleost fishes, in which each gonad consists of a simple closed sac, the anterior wall of which carries the spermatogonia (the precursors of mature sperm) in the male and the oogonia (the precursors of mature eggs) in the female. These gamete-producing cells are inactive except during the breeding season, when they proliferate so rapidly that the distended sac often occupies 60 percent of the total body space.

In all other vertebrates the testes develop as an independent body of tubules surrounding a lumen. The distal end of the tubules contains spermatogonia, and the resulting sperm accumulate in many different forms in a central area in the testes. The network of tubules leads to a duct that may, in some forms, have both a spermatheca (a small bulbous sac) for the accumulation of sperm and an ejaculatory pouch for the expulsion of seminal fluid (the sperm and the liquid secretions in which they are carried). In addition to the seminiferous tubules (those in which the sperm are formed), the testes of vertebrates contain interstitial cells (undifferentiated connective tissue cells lying between the testicular tubules) that secrete male hormones (Figure 3). In vertebrates the sperm duct (vas deferens) joins with the kidney duct (ureter) just before leaving the body. In some invertebrates, notably flatworms, the testes are diffuse structures, actually clumps of spermatogonia scattered throughout the body with ducts leading to a short vas deferens. Although many annelids (*e.g.*, earthworms) contain two or more

Myofibrils (margin note)

Male reproductive tissues (margin note)

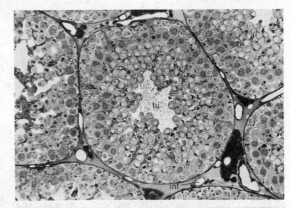

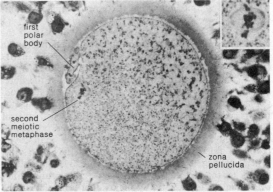

Figure 3: *Photomicrographs of reproductive tissues.*
(Top) Testicular tissue showing the seminiferous tubules (tu) and interstitial cells (int). (Bottom) A recently ovulated human egg with its first polar body.
(Top) Don W. Fawcett, M.D., (bottom) L. Zamboni

pairs of segmentally arranged tests, the sperm still leaves the organism by a single duct.

The principal features of the male reproductive system —testes and sperm duct—are common throughout the animal kingdom, but in all groups there are many accessory sexual glands, some of unknown function. In mammals the main accessory glands are the prostate and Cowper's gland. In the former, which is a mass of branched tubules embedded in a matrix of fibrous connective tissue, the secreting tubules open by numerous ducts into the urethra (the duct that conducts urine from the urinary bladder to the exterior); it is the excretion of the prostate that forms the main mass of seminal fluid. Cowper's glands also lead into the urethra; they consist of branched tubules that secrete a thick, viscous substance for which no useful function has yet been found in most mammals. In rodents, however, the substance forms a vaginal plug that apparently helps to keep the sperm in the vagina of the female.

In many animals in which fertilization occurs outside the body, the female reproductive system consists of an egg-producing gland (the ovary) and a tube (the oviduct) to convey the eggs to the exterior. In all vertebrates except bony fishes, no direct connection exists between the ovary and the oviduct; the latter terminates internally as an open funnel that is pressed against the ovary only at the time of ovulation (release of the egg from the ovary). In both oviparous and viviparous forms, the tissues of the oviducts are divided into specific areas for specific functions. In oviparous vertebrates (those that lay eggs) the upper portion of the duct is lined with a mucous epithelium containing simple tubular glands that secrete a dense albuminous fluid, a protein that constitutes egg white. As the egg twists in its passage through this region, each of the ends of the thick albumin is twisted into a chalaza, one of the two spiral cords for holding the egg in the centre of the shell. The next region of the oviduct contains two types of tubular glands that are sometimes branched. One set of these glands secretes additional albumin; the other set of glands secretes a substance that constitutes the liquid portion of the egg white. The next oviduct region

Female reproductive tissues (margin note)

lays down a coat of keratin as the base over which the next section deposits the calcareous shell.

In viviparous mammals (those who bear live young) the term oviduct is usually applied only to the region that lies between the internal funnel and the uterus (the organ in which the embryo and fetus develop). The tissues of this oviduct are quite simple, consisting of ciliated epithelium, with a few mucus-secreting cells, thrown into longitudinal folds that fill most of the lumen. At the time of ovulation the blood vessels in the oviduct become engorged with blood, and a circular band of smooth muscle contracts rhythmically so that the lip of the open funnel strokes the ovary and thus secures the egg. The epithelium of the uterus is also deeply folded and contains numerous blood vessels and mucus-secreting glands. The vagina is a simple tubular structure that, in virgins, is coated with ciliated epithelium; ultimately, this is replaced at its distal end with stratified epithelium that becomes cornified in some mammals.

The ovarian tissue is one of the most complex in the body. It consists essentially of a surface epithelium in which the oogonia are developed and a central matrix composed largely of collagen fibres and fibroblasts (cells in the connective tissue that form and maintain the fibres in such tissue). Oocytes (cells derived from mature oogonia that eventually become eggs) are budded into the matrix, in which each is surrounded by a flattened layer of what are called nurse cells. As the egg matures, it becomes surrounded by a membrane and lies into a small cavity (follicle) filled with a fluid secreted by the nurse cells. When the egg is fully mature (Figure 3), the follicle moves to the surface of the ovary and ruptures, after which the egg is taken up by the oviduct. The cleft in the follicle then closes, and because it becomes filled with yellow pigmented cells, it is known as the corpus luteum, or yellow body. The luteal cells secrete a hormone that both inhibits further egg production and assists in preparing the uterus for implantation of the egg. In such animals as the frog, in which large quantities of eggs are produced at the same time, no corpora lutea are formed; instead, the remnants of the ovary survive as a shrivelled body that does not commence egg production again until the next breeding season. In forms having heavily yolked eggs, such as birds, a dense mesh of blood vessels surrounds the follicle; yolk is transferred to the egg through the nurse cells, which remain in contact with the outer surface of the egg.

Hemopoietic tissues. Hemopoietic tissues, which produce the cellular components of blood, have an interesting evolutionary history. In the cyclostomes they appear in scattered masses throughout the intestinal wall, but by the time the level of lungfish is reached, the tissues have become aggregated into a rather well-defined mass in the wall of the stomach. In amphibians and reptiles the hemopoietic tissues are segregated as a distinct organ, the spleen; it is filled with a red pulp consisting primarily of large cells (hemocytoblasts) from which are differentiated all the various types of blood cells. The spleen in these organisms is permeated by arteries that divide into extremely thin-walled arterioles through which the white cells enter the blood; there is still some argument, however, concerning the manner in which the red cells get into the blood.

In mammals the spleen has lost entirely its hemopoietic function; its sole concern is to sort out and destroy erythrocytes that are no longer useful. The production of the cellular constituents of blood has been transferred to the red bone marrow, which fills the spaces in trabecular, or spongy, bone. Here are produced large cells called myeloblasts, which, as the need develops, differentiate into three types of leukocytes; into erythroblasts, from which the erythrocytes are formed; or into multinucleate megakaryocytes, which ultimately produce the blood platelets (minute granular bodies that function in blood clotting). In a normal human, erythrocytes are produced at the rate of about 3,000,000 per second, a figure that may double following serious injury and blood loss. Simultaneous with production, 3,000,000 erythrocytes per second are broken up in the spleen and the pieces passed to the

Production and destruction of blood cells

liver, where they are broken down further. Excess pigments are excreted as bile pigments; the remainder are recycled.

Tissue fluids. The most important tissue fluid is lymph, which, as mentioned previously, is a colourless substance derived from blood that filters through the walls of capillaries to bathe the cells in all the tissues of the body. Lymph is returned to the bloodstream by lymph vessels, some of which, particularly those in the vicinity of the principal veins into which they lead, form lymph hearts. These are little more than slightly muscularized tubes with a valve at each end to secure a one-way flow of the returning lymph. Lymph is also conducted by the vessels to lymph nodes, which consist essentially of sinusoids (enlarged areas in channels of the circulatory system) that are lined with cubical epithelium and in which the composition of the lymph is adjusted in a manner that is not yet well understood.

Another blood fluid of great importance but of little-known function is cerebrospinal fluid. This colourless watery substance, which fills the cavities of the brain and spinal cord, is, to all intents and purposes, identical with the aqueous fluid that fills the eye. Cerebrospinal fluid is a specialized form of lymph; as such, it contains a few lymphocytes, a type of white blood cell that is formed in lymphoid tissues found in such organs as the spleen, tonsils, and lymph nodes. The fluid reaches the cavities of the central nervous system through a complex of tangled capillaries known as the choroid plexus, which is located in the roof of one of the brain cavities. It is through the walls of the finer blood vessels in the choroid plexus that the lymphocytes get into the cerebrospinal fluid.

A third body fluid of immense importance is that secreted by the milk-producing glands located in the breasts of female mammals. These are actually greatly enlarged sebaceous glands (saclike structures, usually opening into hair follicles, which secrete an oily fluid that lubricates the skin and hair); it is the large fat drops secreted by these glands into the fluid of the breasts that produces the familiar white emulsion known as milk. In most mammals the glands are activated by a hormone contained in the placenta (the vascular organ that connects the fetus with the maternal uterus), which is eaten by the mother shortly after the birth of its young. Hormones from the corpus luteum of the ovary also enter into the mechanism for initiating milk production. In primitive mammals, such as the duck-billed platypus, milk is not elaborated; instead, the secretion of slightly enlarged sebaceous glands is licked from the surface of the skin by the newborn, which, unlike other mammals, are hatched from eggs. Some birds also produce "milk," so called because of its opaque white appearance; female pigeons, for example, grind grain in the gizzard (a muscular enlargement of the alimentary canal), predigest it to a milky substance, and then regurgitate it for the young.

Milk

BIBLIOGRAPHY. WILLIAM BLOOM and DON W. FAWCETT, *A Textbook of Histology*, 9th ed. (1968); and WILFRED M. COPENHAVER, *Bailey's Textbook of Histology*, 15th ed. (1964), standard textbooks that emphasize human tissues; DONALD I. and GAIL R. PATT, *Comparative Vertebrate Histology* (1969), one of the few works covering other vertebrates in addition to man; ANNA-MARY CARPENTER, *Human Histology* (1968), a very fine colour atlas; W. PENFIELD (ed.), *Cytology and Cellular Pathology of the Nervous System* (1932), still the standard work in this field; but ALF BRODAL, *Nevro-anatomi i relasjon til klinisk nevrologi* (1943; Eng. trans., *Neurological Anatomy in Relation to Clinical Medicine*, 2nd ed., 1969), deals with the topic more broadly; JACK H. PRINCE et al., *Anatomy and Histology of the Eye and Orbit in Domestic Animals* (1960), a comprehensive reference work, but the same author's *Comparative Anatomy of the Eye* (1956) is easier for the general reader to understand; HANS S. HELLER, *Neurohypophysis* (1957), for those with a special interest in the pituitary gland; G. FORTEZA BOVER and R.B. CANDELA, *Atlas de citología sanguínea* (1963; Eng. trans., *Atlas of Blood Cytology: Cytomorphology, Cytochemistry, and Cytogenetics*, 1964), the most comprehensive work on blood; GARTH CHAPMAN, *Body Fluids and Their Functions* (1967), a good treatment of body fluids; JEAN OLIVER, *Nephrons and Kidneys* (1968), for comparative kidney structure.

(Pe.G.)

Tissues and Fluids, Plant

The plant body is constructed of various types of cells usually organized to form tissues. Tissues have been classified on the basis of their position in the plant, the types of cells they contain, and the function of these cells. No single criterion, however, adequately expresses the complex interaction of cells and their association in the form of specific tissues.

Tissues with cells that continuously divide to produce new cells are termed meristematic tissues. They give rise to the mature tissue systems of the plant of which three can be distinguished: (1) the dermal tissue system, which makes up the outer layers or protective tissue of the plant; (2) the vascular tissue system, which includes the water- and food-conducting tissues, xylem and phloem, respectively; and (3) the fundamental or ground tissue system, which includes all other tissues exclusive of dermal and vascular. Although mature tissues may consist of one cell type (simple tissues), they more often are made up of a variety of cell types (complex tissues).

MERISTEMATIC TISSUES

All tissues of the plant are derived from cell-producing tissues called primary tissue meristems, which begin to form early in embryonic development. The primary tissue meristems are designated protoderm, procambium, and ground meristem. Protoderm functions to produce the dermal or "skin" tissue system of the plant; procambium gives rise to the vascular or conducting tissue system; and ground meristem is the precursor of the fundamental or ground tissue system.

As the young embryo develops, protoderm tissue, which forms from the peripheral cells, is clearly delimited from the other tissues as the embryo elongates and becomes bilaterally symmetrical—that is, with mirror-image halves. At this stage procambium is also evident. The ground meristem originates from the embryonic tissue situated between protoderm and procambium.

The cotyledons or first leaves (seed leaves) are the first organs formed. Soon after they begin to develop, the shoot apical meristem forms between them. At the end of the embryo opposite the cotyledons, the root apical meristem forms. The root and shoot apical meristems continuously contribute cells to the primary tissue meristems, which, following differentiation and maturation, give rise to the primary tissues and the primary plant body. The primary tissues include primary xylem, primary phloem, cortex, pith, and epidermis. In young stems the arrangement of tissues as seen in cross section is as follows: outermost tissue, the epidermis; cortex; primary phloem; and primary xylem. The pith occupies the centre of the stem (see Figure 1).

In many plants vegetative development is essentially complete when the primary tissues have matured. This is true in many lower vascular plants such as club mosses, horsetails, and some ferns; in monocotyledons (flowering plants with parallel-veined leaves, such as grasses, orchids, and palms); and in some nonwoody dicotyledons (flowering plants with net-veined leaves, such as violets and poppies). In other herbaceous dicotyledons, however, and in woody plants, formation of new tissues continues after primary growth is complete. The production of these tissues and the continuation of growth in such plants are attributable to the lateral meristems, regions of cell division that contribute to growth in stem thickness. These meristems, called the vascular cambium and the cork cambium, are responsible for producing the secondary tissues—secondary xylem, secondary phloem, and periderm—that form the secondary plant body (see Figure 2). The vascular cambium is chiefly responsible for increasing the diameter of the plant.

Apical meristems.   The cells of the shoot and root apical meristem are organized in precise patterns that are characteristic of various plant groups. Knowledge of the arrangement and organization of cells at the apex is useful for descriptive purposes and for making structural comparisons between plants. Apical organization, however, is known to vary during normal development and is often influenced by seasonal changes.

Root and shoot systems *(margin note)*

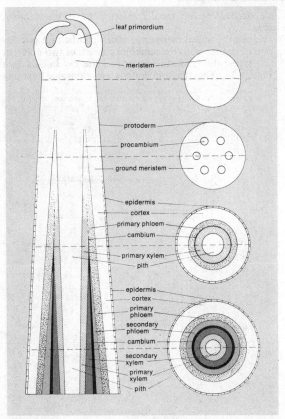

Figure 1: *Tissue organization in a stem tip.*
(Left) Longitudinal section. (Right) Cross sections at different levels.

Reprinted with permission of The Macmillan Company from *Botany* by W. Muller. Copyright © 1968 by Walter H. Muller

Various regions of the apex can be distinguished from each other by examination of such features as cell and nucleus size, frequency and planes of cell division, and wall thickness. At the summit of the shoot apex a group of meristematic cells constitutes a so-called initiation zone, which gives rise to cells of the surface layer and a region below, the zone of central mother cells, which divide infrequently. Surrounding the latter zone is the peripheral zone, within which most of the apical activity takes place—cell divisions are frequent and leaf primordia and procambium cells are initiated. Below the central mother cell zone lies a zone termed the rib meristem, whose cells are arranged in radial, regular, longitudinal rows and divide transversely; much of the fundamental tissue system is derived from the rib meristem. Various kinds of mature tissues are produced in the plant body because the cells of the shoot apex divide at different rates and in different planes. Although in some plants, apical meristems lack distinguishable zones, the cells of the shoot apex retain the ability to divide at different rates and in different planes.

Despite the structural differences in apical meristems of various groups of plants, they function in similar ways. All apical meristems (1) produce cells that differentiate into primary-tissue meristems, which in turn produce the primary tissues of the plant; (2) initiate organs, primarily leaves and branches, in a coordinated manner and in a genetically determined pattern; and (3) contribute to the increase in length of the plant.

Lateral meristems.   The vascular cambium, which produces xylem and phloem cells, originates from procambium that has not completely differentiated during the formation of primary xylem and primary phloem. The cambium is thought to be a single row of cells that produces new cells: externally, the secondary phloem, and internally, the secondary xylem. Because it is not possible to distinguish the cambium from its immediate cellular derivatives, which also divide and contribute to the formation of secondary tissues, the cambium and its immedi-

Function of apical meristems *(margin note)*

ate derivatives are usually referred to as the cambial zone.

Unlike the apical meristems, which consist of a population of similar cells, the cambium consists of two different cell types; the fusiform initials and the ray initials (see Figure 2). The fusiform initials are elongated tapering

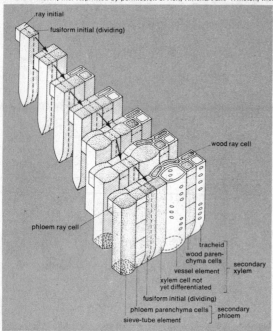

Figure 2: Production of secondary xylem and phloem cells by cambial initials.

cells that give rise to all cells of the vertical system of the secondary phloem and xylem. The ray initials are isodiametric cells—about equal in all dimensions—and they produce the vascular rays, which constitute the horizontal system of secondary tissues. The fusiform and ray initials of the cambium divide in a tangential plane (*i.e.*, parallel to the stem surface) generating xylem mother cells toward the inside and phloem mother cells toward the outside. These cells in turn continue to divide tangentially, producing new cells that add to the xylem and to the phloem. Divisions of the cambium cells and xylem and phloem mother cells do not result in the production of equal amounts of secondary xylem and secondary phloem; because the cambium produces more cells internally than externally, more secondary xylem is produced than secondary phloem. Because divisions in the fusiform and ray initials are primarily tangential, new cells are regularly arranged in well-defined radial rows, a characteristic pattern for secondary vascular tissues.

Divisions in the cambium not only produce secondary vascular tissues but also increase the circumference of the cambium. As new cells are continuously added to the inside of the cambium, the cambium increases laterally (in circumference) to keep pace with the growth of the stem. In some plants this is accomplished simply by radial division of the fusiform and ray initials. In other plants, the mechanism for increasing cambial diameter or increasing the number of cambial cells is more complex. If cambial activity is extensive, the primary tissues lying outside the cambium, such as primary phloem, cortex, and epidermis, may be crushed by the pressure of new secondary tissue growth or become torn and obliterated because they cannot accommodate to the rapidly increasing diameter of the plant.

As growth proceeds the cork cambium forms in living cells of the epidermis, cortex, or, in some plants, phloem and produces a secondary protective tissue, the periderm. The cork cambium is, like the vascular cambium, a lateral meristem that produces cells internally and externally by tangential divisions. Unlike the cambium, the cork cambium consists of one cell type.

Intercalary meristems. Another type of meristem active in certain plants, especially horsetails and grasses, is the intercalary meristem. These cells possess the ability to divide and produce new cells, as do apical and lateral meristems. They differ, however, in being situated between regions of mature tissue, such as at the base of grass leaves, which are themselves located on mature stem tissue. In many instances intercalary meristems function for only a short time and eventually completely differentiate into mature tissues. Intercalary meristems are usually located at positions on the stem where leaves have emerged (nodes) and are largely responsible for elongation in grass shoots and leaves.

MATURE TISSUES

Dermal (protective) tissues. *Epidermis.* The epidermis, or surface cell layer, which covers all organs of the plant including stem and root, leaf, flower, fruit, and seed, functions in a variety of ways. It limits transpiration —evaporation of water from the surface of the plant, especially the leaf. Specialized cells facilitate gaseous exchange between the outside air and internal tissues. The epidermis also serves as a protective barrier, restricting insect and bacterial invasion of the underlying cells. In view of the many functions of this tissue, it is not surprising that it is also structurally variable. The epidermis may consist of either one cell layer or several. Function of epidermis

The epidermis forms from protoderm, one of the primary tissue meristems. In addition to cellulose, the main carbohydrate component of wood, epidermal cells produce a fatty substance, cutin, which permeates the cell wall, eventually forming an outer layer, the cuticle. Although a cuticle covers the epidermis of all higher plants, the extent to which it develops depends on the plant species and the environment in which it grows. The cuticle is responsible for the protective functions of the epidermis. In some plants wax is also deposited on the cuticle and within the matrix of the cell wall. Waxy deposits may occur as thin layers or as thick layers such as those seen on leaves of the Brazilian wax palm, *Copernicia cerifera*, from which the commercially important carnauba wax is collected. The wax covering further serves to control water loss. Other substances, such as lignin, crystals, and mucilage, occur in epidermal cell walls of certain plants.

The epidermis is not continuous over the surface of the plant but is interrupted by pores that serve as channels to the interior tissues. The pores are bordered by specialized, often kidney-shaped epidermal cells, called guard cells. The combination of pore and guard cells is referred to as the stoma. Two to several epidermal cells, called accessory cells, may be adjacent to the guard cells and participate in stomatal opening and closing. The accessory cells and the stoma constitute the stomatal apparatus. There is considerable variation in the development, structure, and distribution of the stomatal apparatus in plant species. The size, shape, and wall thickenings of the guard cells are important in stomatal function and gaseous exchange.

Another important group of structurally modified epidermal cells includes hairs (trichomes) which occur as outgrowths of epidermal cells and, when present, are usually characteristic of the particular plant. Trichomes may be either glandular, consisting of a stalk terminating in a globular head, or nonglandular, consisting simply of elongated, often tapering structures. Both types may be single celled or multicellular. The glandular trichomes usually produce and secrete volatile and nonvolatile substances, such as volatile oils, mucilages, and resins. In addition, trichomes on many carnivorous plants produce digestive enzymes (biological catalysts). Nonglandular trichomes, which may function in reducing transpiration and excessive water loss, are variable in structure and occasionally provide commercially important products, such as cotton and kapok.

Hairs are found on the surfaces of roots. Root hair cells are initiated behind the meristematic zone of the root apex and continue to elongate as the distance of the epidermal cells from the meristem increases. Root hairs usu- Root hairs ally live and function only for a few days; the sequential nature of the production near the root apex, however, insures a continuous supply. Root hairs increase the water absorbing ability of the plant.

Periderm. In plants in which substantial secondary growth—increase in stem thickness—occurs, a protective tissue, the periderm, forms. It arises from the activity of a cork cambium and is a complex tissue consisting largely of cork cells. Periderm serves the secondary plant body in much the same way as the epidermis serves the primary plant body, restricting water loss from the tissues within, protecting against attack by organisms—particularly after tissue damage—and preventing mechanical injury to the underlying tissues. The protective nature of periderm results largely from the properties of cork cells, many layers of which form on the outer side of the cork cambium. Cork cells produce a fatty substance known as suberin, which is deposited over the primary cellulose walls; in addition, some wax may also be deposited. The combination of wax and suberin makes the cork relatively impermeable to the passage of water and gases. In certain plants some cork cells remain thin walled and alternate with thick-walled cells. Neither cell type is alive when mature. At maturity all cork cells become filled with air or, in some instances, with resins or tannins that produce the dark pigmentation characteristic of certain types of cork and may have a protective function.

As secondary growth continues, the outer periderm layers crack and peel, and new layers of periderm form in tissues underlying the older periderm. In certain parts of the periderm, loosely arranged groups of cells often project above the other cells, forming prominent markings on the outer surface of the plant. These groups of cells, called lenticels, are similar to stomata in that they provide for passage of air to the interior tissues. The term bark is a nontechnical one usually referring to all tissues outside the vascular cambium. It may include parts of the phloem, cortex, and epidermis as well as periderm.

Vascular (conducting) tissues. All vascular plants, such as ferns, gymnosperms, and angiosperms, possess a well-developed vascular system that conducts water and food materials through the plant axis to the various organs; it usually also functions in support. The vascular system consists basically of two complex tissues, the xylem and phloem (see Figure 3). The two tissues are

Reprinted with permission of The Macmillan Company from *Botany* by W. Muller. Copyright © 1968 by Walter H. Muller

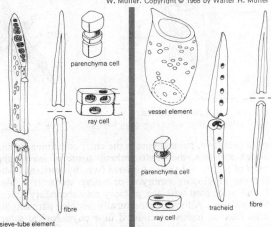

parenchyma cell

ray cell

vessel element

parenchyma cell

fibre

sieve-tube element and companion cell

ray cell

tracheid

fibre

Figure 3: Cells of the (left) phloem and (right) xylem.

distinctive, each being made up of several different cell types and each functioning in its own way. Movement of water and dissolved salts from the root system to other parts of the plant takes place through the xylem. Transfer of food materials produced in photosynthetic tissue or accumulated in storage organs occurs through the phloem (see also PLANT INTERNAL TRANSPORT).

Vascular tissue is usually classified into primary xylem and primary phloem, which are produced by the procambium, and secondary xylem and secondary phloem, which are produced by the cambium. The first cells of

Function of xylem and phloem tissues

primary xylem and primary phloem to differentiate, called protoxylem and protophloem, are followed by additional vascular elements called metaxylem and metaphloem. Because protoxylem and protophloem ordinarily mature while the axis is elongating, they are often partially or completely destroyed during growth. Since metaxylem and metaphloem mature after elongation is complete, the cells composing them are not destroyed. In grasses and some other monocotyledons, the vascular tissues are formed until all the procambium has differentiated; the vascular bundle is then said to be closed to further development. In other vascular plants, however, residual procambium is present, and the bundle is said to be open to additional growth. The cambium formed from this procambium continues to produce new xylem and new phloem. Differentiation of vascular tissues in roots is similar to that in stems.

Xylem. The xylem (wood) of most angiosperms is made up of cells called tracheids, vessel elements, and wood fibres collectively known as tracheary elements. It also contains parenchyma cells, which are often relatively simple thin-walled cells (see Figure 3). During development the walls of primary xylem cells thicken in a characteristic way. The thick walls of the first formed cells of protoxylem are deposited in discrete rings. These annular or sometimes helical thickenings become stretched and extended by the elongation of the tissue, occurring at this time. The deposition of thick walls of later formed cells of metaxylem is much more complete. The thickened bands join to form scalariform and reticulate thickenings. The newest cells of metaxylem have their entire inner surface covered by thick walls except for regions containing thin places, the pit areas. These pitted elements are characteristic of the latest formed primary xylem and of the secondary xylem.

Tracheids and vessel elements are elongated cells, which, at maturity, have thickened lignified walls, usually bearing numerous pits. They contain no living material (protoplast), and water flows unimpeded through the cell lumen (interior). Vessel elements differ from tracheids in being perforated at their ends; tracheids are imperforate cells that communicate only through the pits between overlapping walls of adjacent cells. The perforations usually occur on the end walls but may also form on the side walls. In either case this area of the cell wall is known as a perforation plate. Vessel elements, usually arranged in longitudinal rows, one above the other, form a connected series of elements known as a vessel. Vessels provide the major pathway for longitudinal conduction of water in most angiosperms. The length of a vessel varies, and the end members are imperforate. If vessel length is limited, a continuous network of overlapping vessels that transports water to terminal parts of the plant is maintained. Water moves longitudinally through the vessels and also through the pits on the lateral walls of the vessels into adjacent vessels. This combination of lateral and longitudinal flow is necessary for effective water transport. In certain primitive angiosperms and in gymnosperms (conifers) and some lower vascular plants that lack vessels (*e.g.*, certain ferns and club mosses), the movement of water occurs entirely through pits on lateral walls of tracheids to adjacent elements.

Water movement

The bulk of tissue in most trees is secondary xylem or wood. Perhaps the most conspicuous feature of secondary xylem and one that commonly distinguishes it from primary xylem is the presence of vascular rays. These form a transverse (extending from the stem centre to the surface) system of living tissue intimately associated with the tracheary elements. The extent of secondary xylem development is dependent on the activity of the cambium. Its activity, like that of most other meristems, is usually periodic, and the tracheary elements produced during the beginning of the growth period are distinct from those produced toward the end of the growth period. The periodic activity of the cambium is thus apparent in the structure of the xylem. The amount of xylem produced during one growth period is called a growth ring; when growth rings concide with annual growth activity, the term annual ring is often employed.

Phloem. Because of its importance in long distance translocation of food, the phloem has been extensively studied. Despite the information that has accumulated, the characteristics of the functioning phloem cells are not yet known. The major difficulty is that when phloem tissue is injured or killed, as it must be for most studies, changes occur in the conducting cells. Because intact phloem cells are under a positive pressure, any injury results in a rearrangement of the cell contents. The position and physical state of the cellular components in an injured cell may differ considerably from those of the intact, functioning cell. Although it has not yet been possible to describe fully a functioning conducting cell, the components that are present can be described, and the features that have been consistently observed can be indicated.

In angiosperms, phloem is composed of sieve-tube elements and companion cells together with other cells such as phloem fibres (see Figure 3). Sieve-tube elements are arranged end-to-end in a connected series, forming a sieve tube. In gymnosperms the equivalent of sieve-tube elements and companion cells are the sieve cells and albuminous cells. Sieve cells differ from sieve-tube elements primarily in the nature of their sieve areas, which are thin places in the cell wall with pores through which conducting strands link adjacent cells. In sieve cells the sieve areas are unspecialized; that is, clusters of pores similar in size and number are distributed on the lateral and tapering end walls. In sieve-tube elements, on the other hand, a few sieve areas on the end walls usually have larger pores and are termed sieve plates. In the sieve tube the individual sieve-tube elements join at their sieve plates. In tissue containing sieve cells, the cells overlap one another, and the sieve areas of adjacent cells are associated, forming a continuous link from cell to cell.

The pores in sieve areas contain callose, a carbohydrate. The amount of callose in the pores increases as the cell ages or after the cell has been chemically or mechanically treated. Deposits of callose are believed to plug the sieve areas and to interfere with food conduction. Whether or not callose deposition in sieve areas occurs in functioning conducting elements remains controversial. Evidence suggests that callose, ordinarily present in small quantities, increases in amount after tissue manipulation. Its presence in fixed material (*i.e.*, tissues prepared for microscopic examination) is a diagnostic feature of phloem.

The nature of the conducting strands is not yet clearly understood. Presumably they are composed of cytoplasm and are similar in some ways to plasmodesmata—cytoplasmic connections from cell to cell. The conducting strands may be larger than plasmodesmata and often are packed with protein in fixed material. In mature sieve cells and sieve-tube elements, the vacuolar membrane (*i.e.*, the membrane surrounding the internal watery sac in the centre of the cell) breaks down, resulting in a mixing of cytoplasm and vacuolar contents. Protein initially present in the cytoplasm may move through sieve areas and be continuous from cell to cell. It has been difficult to determine whether or not the protein plays a role in the transfer of food. Phloem protein (P-protein), once called slime, is often observed in conducting cells of the phloem where it forms slime plugs that lie against the sieve areas. It is essential that the relationship between protein and the conducting strands be clarified before the mechanism of transport through phloem can be fully explained. Although sieve-tube elements and sieve cells commonly lose their nuclei as they mature, they do retain functional cytoplasm. The companion cells and albuminous cells of the phloem are also thought to be essential for translocation of food.

Phloem cell contents

Fundamental (ground) tissues. The axis of most plants is composed of relatively large amounts of fundamental, or ground, tissues. The most common are parenchyma, collenchyma, and sclerenchyma (see Figure 4). These are simple tissues, but parenchyma and sclerenchyma are often found as components of complex tissues.

Parenchyma. Parenchyma is made up of thin-walled, commonly polyhedral (many-sided) living cells. The most common tissue in vascular plants and perhaps the

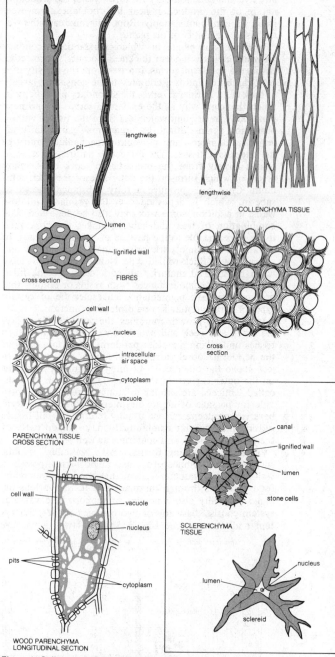

Figure 4: Cell types and tissues.
From T. Weier, C. Stocking, and M. Barbour, *Botany* (1970); John Wiley & Sons

most primitive, parenchyma is the chief constituent of the cortex and pith, the photosynthetic tissue of leaves, the pulp of fruits, and the endosperm (starchy nutrient tissue for the developing embryo) of many seeds. It is also found associated with the primary and secondary xylem and phloem. Although structurally simple, parenchyma cells may be highly specialized in a physiological sense. Some cells, especially those of the leaf and cortex, contain chloroplasts, which are small membrane-enclosed pigment bodies active in photosynthesis. Parenchyma containing chloroplasts is known as chlorenchyma. Other parenchyma cells may function in the production and storage of food substances necessary for maintenance of the plant. Parenchyma cells containing starch, lipid (fats), or protein are common in fruits, seeds, and especially in storage organs, such as rhizomes (creeping horizontal stem structures), bulbs, and tubers (underground storage stems, such as potatoes). Some parenchyma cells synthesize and accumulate other products such as crystals of calcium oxalate, tannins, mucilages, and resins. In addition, water, pigments, and soluble salts are found within parenchyma cells. Parenchyma tissue is therefore of primary importance to the plant.

Collenchyma. Collenchyma is basically a supporting tissue that provides structural rigidity for many plant organs. It is found chiefly in the cortex of stems and in leaves. For many herbaceous plants it is the chief supporting tissue, especially during early stages of development. In plants in which secondary growth occurs, the collenchyma tissue is only temporarily functional and becomes crushed as woody tissue develops. Collenchyma is located along the periphery of stems beneath the epidermal tissue. It may form a complete cylinder or occur as discrete strands that constitute the ridges and angles of stems and other supporting structures of the plant.

Collenchyma cells, polygonal in cross section, are much longer than parenchyma cells. The strength of the tissue results from the unevenly thickened cell walls and the longitudinal overlapping and interlocking of the cells. The cells have protoplasts, often containing chloroplasts, and they produce a thick cellulose wall. The wall is not uniformly thick in all cells, and thickening may occur predominately in longitudinal strips at the corners of the cell, on the tangential (*i.e.*, outer, toward the stem exterior) surface of the cell, or around the spaces between adjacent cells. Pits are present and provide a mechanism for intercellular communication. An important feature of collenchyma is that it is extremely plastic—the cells can extend and thus adjust to increase in growth of the organ.

Sclerenchyma. The major function of sclerenchyma is support. Unlike collenchyma, mature cells of this tissue are generally nonliving and have heavily thickened walls containing lignin. The size, shape, and structure of sclerenchyma cells are not uniform. Two distinct types of cells occur: those that are greatly elongated are termed sclerenchyma fibres; those that are essentially uniform in diameter are called sclereids (see Figure 4). The division is arbitrary, and intermediate and overlapping types of sclerenchyma cells commonly occur, even within one plant organ.

Fibres may occur singly or in groups of few to many cells with their long, tapering ends interlocked, thus providing maximum support. They may be found almost anywhere in the plant body and are classified according to position. Cortical fibres and phloem fibres are characteristic of the stems and roots of many plants. Fibres also partially or completely surround vascular bundles in leaves and in the plant axis. Most fibres have extremely thick cell walls containing pits, and the cell lumen is very narrow or completely obscured.

Sclereids occur singly or in groups and are present in various tissues of the plant such as periderm, cortex, pith, xylem, and phloem. They also occur in leaves and fruits and constitute the hard shell of nuts and the outer hard coat of many seeds. Sclereid walls are commonly pitted, and the pits may be extensively branched. Sclereids are extremely variable in form and are classified according to shape. Brachysclereids or stone cells are isodiametric; macrosclereids are rod shaped; osteosclereids are bone shaped; that is, elongated with enlarged ends; and asterosclereids are star shaped or otherwise branched. The utility of this classification is limited by the occurrence of sclereids that do not fit into any of the categories.

Endodermis. The endodermis, another kind of ground tissue, usually consists of a layer of cells surrounding the vascular system and separating it from the cortex. The endodermis is a prominent feature of the roots in most vascular plants and of shoots of many lower vascular plants. The endodermal cells have distinctive wall markings caused by the deposition of suberin in a strip along the transverse and radial walls (*i.e.*, on all walls except the inner and outer ones that are parallel to the root surface) of the cells; it is known as the Casparian strip. The Casparian strip is often impregnated with lignin. The combination of suberin and lignin in the cellulose matrix of the wall restricts the passage of water and solutes. In some plants, as a result of the continued deposition of encrusting materials, these endodermal cells appear to be thick walled. Cells adjacent to the xylem that fail to thicken are identified as passage cells. The functional

Location of collenchyma wall thickenings

Casparian strips

significance of the endodermis tissue remains obscure despite the attention given it by many investigators.

BIBLIOGRAPHY. College-level textbooks on this subject include: A.J. EAMES and L.H. MACDANIELS, *An Introduction to Plant Anatomy*, 2nd ed. (1947); K. ESAU, *Plant Anatomy*, 2nd ed. (1965); A. FAHN, *Plant Anatomy* (1967; orig. pub. in Hebrew, 1962); and W.H. MULLER, *Botany*, 2nd ed. (1969). A comprehensive review for the specialist is K. ESAU, "The Phloem," in the *Encyclopedia of Plant Anatomy* (1969); P.M. RAY, *The Living Plant* (1963), is an introductory treatment in paperback.

(A.E.D./C.L.W.)

Titanium Products and Production

Titanium, a metallic element of light weight—0.163 pounds per cubic inch (4.51 grams per cubic centimetre)—and of high strength particularly in alloy form, is used extensively in many aerospace applications; and because of its excellent corrosion resistance, it has many applications in the chemical-process industries. Although the element titanium had been known since its initial discovery in 1791 by William Gregor in England, and its identification in rutile in 1795 and in ilmenite in 1797, it was not until William Justin Kroll, a German refugee in the U.S., invented a magnesium-reduction process in 1936 that the production of metallic titanium became feasible. The process, which Kroll gave to the U.S. Bureau of Mines for development, remains in its original form or modifications thereof, the principal method used today for winning titanium metal from its ores.

Mining. Titanium ores are plentiful, and numerous deposits of highly concentrated titanium minerals are readily accessible and easily mined. Rutile in the beach sands of Florida and Australia is merely scooped up and shipped to a mill for processing. Ilmenite, such as occurs in many near-surface deposits in North America, is similarly mined with large, mechanical shovels and transported to the processing plant.

Rutile and ilmenite are the two important ores of titanium. Rutile is almost pure (98–99 percent) titanium dioxide (TiO_2), containing small amounts of iron, silicon, and other elements as impurities. Ilmenite is a combined iron(II)-titanium dioxide usually expressed as iron(II) titanate ($FeO \cdot TiO_2$) containing about 32 percent titanium and 37 percent iron. Rutile is the preferred ore for the production of titanium because of its high titanium content and the ease with which titanium tetrachloride, the starting material for the production of metallic titanium, can be produced from it (see Table 1).

Most of the world's rutile supply comes from the beach sands of New South Wales and Queensland along the east coast of Australia. Other sources include Florida, India, Brazil, and South Africa. Ilmenite is much more abundant than rutile, and large deposits are known to exist in the United States, Canada, South America, Africa, and Europe, including the U.S.S.R. (See Table 1.) In addition to rutile and ilmenite, many other minerals contain titanium but not in sufficient concentration to be of commercial importance.

Refining and recovery. The production of titanium metal from its ores is accomplished in several steps, each involving chemical reactions and each designed to eliminate the gaseous elements oxygen and nitrogen from the chemical reactions. Titanium dioxide is produced from rutile or ilmenite by dissolving the ore in a sulfuric acid solution and precipitating the iron compounds. The solution is then hydrolyzed, producing a hydrous titanium oxide, which is washed and calcined. Titanium has a great affinity for oxygen and nitrogen, and unlike other metals, it actually dissolves oxygen and nitrogen in both the liquid and the solid states in addition to reacting to form oxides and nitrides. To eliminate oxygen and nitrogen from the titanium production processes, the oxide prepared from the ore is first converted to titanium tetrachloride ($TiCl_4$) by reacting the titanium dioxide with chlorine gas in the presence of a reducing agent, usually carbon.

The resultant titanium tetrachloride—a liquid when at room temperature—contains many impurities, principally other metal chlorides, and it must be purified before being

Titanium ores

Table 1: World Production of Titanium Concentrates (Ilmenite and Rutile) (short tons)

key: NA—not available; W—withheld to avoid disclosing individual company confidential data.

country*	1965	1966	1967	1968	1969†
Ilmenite					
Australia (shipments)‡	494,385§	575,420§	604,438	622,861	785,065
Brazil‖	10,796	14,920	16,498	19,710	19,842
Canada (titanium slag)¶	545,916	524,773	602,455	672,867	749,281
Ceylon	54,222	45,415♀	58,573	82,238	91,328
Egypt	—	2,507§	1,171	NA	NA
Finland	117,947	129,588	139,883	154,323	152,339
India	33,132	33,253	45,840	64,733	56,708
Japan (titanium slag)	3,190	3,867	6,293	4,624	5,617
Malagasy Republic	6,957	6,821	2,047	—	—
Malaysia♀	136,154	130,364	100,097	138,698	143,300
Norway	311,017	407,553§	464,039	471,083	540,903δ
Portugal	83	530§	590	610	220δ
Senegal	—	—	—	NA	NA
Spain	22,167§	46,548	41,728	43,583	44,092δ
United States□	969,459	965,378	935,091	978,509	931,247
Total ilmenite	2,705,425§	2,886,937§	3,018,743§	3,261,684	3,530,745
Rutile					
Australia	243,410	273,122§	306,236	323,608	396,080
Brazil‖	397	37	313	126	110
Ceylon	—	—	—	1,270	1,213
Egypt	—	37	7	NA	NA
India	1,452	2,002	2,798	2,961	2,751
Senegal	—	—	—	NA	NA
Sierra Leone	—	—	27,713	10,582	14,275
United States	W	W	W	W	W
Total rutile°	245,259	275,198§	337,067§	338,547	414,429

*Titanium concentrates are produced in U.S.S.R., but no reliable figures are available. †Preliminary. ‡Includes small quantities of leucoxene concentrates. §Revised. ‖Production—Comissao Nacional de Energia Nuclear only. ¶Containing approximately 70–72 percent TiO₂. ♀Exports. δEstimate. □Includes a mixed product containing ilmenite, leucoxene, and rutile. °Total is of listed figures only.

Source: U.S. Department of the Interior, Bureau of Mines, *Minerals Yearbook · 1969*.

reduced to titanium metal. A sequence of distillations at temperatures above or below the boiling point is used to remove these undesired compounds. The high-purity titanium tetrachloride produced is reduced to metallic titanium by reaction with magnesium or sodium. The Kroll process, which uses magnesium, and modifications that use sodium, as the reducing agents, are batch processes conducted in large reactors. An argon or helium atmosphere is used within the reactor because all air and moisture must be excluded from the reaction to prevent oxygen, nitrogen, or hydrogen contamination of the final product. Both processes produce titanium in the form of a highly porous material, termed titanium sponge, with magnesium chloride or sodium chloride entrapped in the pores. This sponge is crushed to a suitable size for handling and then leached with water and acid or heated in a vacuum to remove the entrapped chlorides. Titanium sponge is the raw material from which ingots of titanium and titanium alloys are melted. The sponge's purity is dependent on the purity of the titanium tetrachloride from which it was made, the purity of the magnesium or sodium reducing agent, and the purity of the atmosphere during the reduction process. Common impurities in sponge titanium are oxygen, nitrogen, carbon, hydrogen, and iron.

The Kroll process (margin note)

The metal and its alloys. Titanium in pure form is a soft, ductile metal. It has a density of 4.51 grams per cubic centimetre (0.163 pounds per cubic inch), which is about midway between aluminum (2.70 grams per cubic centimetre) and iron (7.86 grams per cubic centimetre). It has a silvery gray colour and can be polished to a high lustre. It is not, however, as lustrous as chromium or stainless steel. Titanium melts at 1,675° C (3,045° F). The common impurities, carbon, oxygen, and nitrogen, raise the melting point; most metallic impurities, such as iron, manganese, chromium, and copper, lower the melting point. There are two crystal structures of titanium. At tempera-

tures below 882° C (1,620° F), titanium has a hexagonal close-packed structure; this form is known as the alpha phase. At temperatures between 882° C and its melting point, titanium has a body-centred cubic structure, known as the beta phase (see below). Titanium is paramagnetic and has very low electrical and thermal conductivity. It occurs in three valence forms, 2, 3 and 4, the most stable of which is 4. The most common oxide is titanium dioxide, TiO_2.

Like stainless steel and aluminum, titanium, because of the formation of an oxide surface film that is relatively inert chemically, has excellent corrosion resistance, in many environments. Titanium will resist corrosive attack by oxidizing acids such as nitric acid and aqua regia, organic acids, moist chlorine gas, chloride solutions, dilute solutions of sulfuric acid and hydrochloric acid, and dilute solutions of alkalies. Although at room temperatures titanium is resistant to oxidizing atmospheres, at elevated temperatures it reacts with the oxygen in the air. At temperatures as low as 260° C (620° F), the surface of titanium becomes tarnished, forming an oxide film that ranges in colour from blue to gold. At higher temperatures, a thicker, yellow-brown oxide film, or scale, is formed. The rate of oxidation increases as the temperature is increased, but it is not until temperatures are above about 1,200° F (648° C) that oxidation becomes a problem if long-time exposures are involved. At temperatures between 1,200° and 2,200° F (1,215° C), short-time heating can be carried out in air. Forging and fabrication of titanium alloys are done at these temperatures with no detrimental effects as long as the oxide scales are removed after fabrication. In the liquid state, however, titanium is very reactive and reduces all known refractories.

Corrosion resistance (margin note)

Titanium will ignite and burn in dry chlorine gas and is attacked by hydrofluoric and phosphoric acids and moderate concentrations of the alkalies. Titanium is severely attacked by fuming red nitric acid. The corrosion resistance of titanium is outstanding in marine atmospheres and seawater. No noticeable corrosion of titanium has been found after exposure to seawater for over three years.

Perhaps the most important property of titanium is its ability to be alloyed with most of the other metals and many of the nonmetals. Alloying additions increase the strength of titanium both at room temperatures and at elevated temperatures. Pure titanium has a tensile strength of about 40,000 pounds per square inch (psi). By alloying it, tensile strengths as high as 200,000 psi can be obtained, thus making it useful as a structural metal.

The major alloying elements that are added to titanium are aluminum, vanadium, molybdenum, manganese, iron, and chromium. All of the titanium-base alloys contain one or more of these elements. The gaseous elements—oxygen, nitrogen, and hydrogen—and carbon are present in small quantities in almost all titanium alloys.

Titanium alloys can be classed in three basic types: alpha, alpha-beta, and beta alloys. Alpha alloys contain elements that dissolve in the hexagonal close-packed alpha phase. Alpha-beta alloys contain limited quantities of elements that dissolve in the body-centred cubic beta phase resulting in a two-phase alpha-beta alloy. Beta alloys contain large quantities of elements that dissolve in the beta phase resulting in an all-beta structure. Alpha alloys have medium strengths (120,000 to 150,000 psi) and good elevated-temperature strengths, can be welded, and are used mostly as forgings. Alpha-beta alloys are the most versatile. In the annealed condition, they have medium strengths but can be heat treated to very high strengths. These alloys have good forming characteristics and can be used in both sheet and bar-stock form. Generally, they are not weldable. Beta alloys have medium strengths and excellent forming characteristics but contain large quantities of high-density alloying additions. They also can be heat treated to high strength levels. Compositions and properties of typical alloys are listed in Table 2.

Titanium has long been used as a deoxidizer in steel, to which it is added as a ferrotitanium or a ferrocarbontitanium alloy. More recently, it has been used as an alloy-

Table 2: Typical Alloys

type of alloy	composition (balance titanium)	tensile strength (psi)	elongation (percent)
Alpha	5% Al–2.5% Sn	130,000	15
Alpha-beta	6% Al–4% V	140,000	15
Alpha-beta (heat treated)	6% Al–4% V	180,000	7
Beta	13% V–11% Cr–3% Al	150,000	15
Beta (heat treated)	13% V–11% Cr–3% Al	200,000	6

Table 3: U.S. Statistics on Titanium Sponge, Ingot, and Mill Products
(000 lb)

year	titanium sponge			titanium ingot (includes alloys)	
	domestic production	imports	domestic consumption	domestic production	mill product (net shipments)
1960	10,622	4,462	10,974	16,594	10,142
1961	13,454	4,980	13,982	19,262	11,242
1962	13,460	1,850	14,272	20,800	13,042
1963	15,758	2,936	17,730	22,276	12,224
1964	18,600	4,078	22,262	27,928	15,417
1965	19,000*	6,268	24,210	30,588	18,716
1966	27,000*	10,450	39,354	48,506	27,992
1967	30,000*	14,288	40,124	51,920	27,268
1968	30,000*	6,886	28,474	38,468	23,800

*Estimate.
Source: U.S. Department of the Interior, Bureau of Mines, *Minerals Yearbook 1968*.

ing addition to many steels to reduce grain size and control carbon content in stainless steel. In aluminum it is used to refine the grain size, while in copper it produces a precipitation-hardening alloy. In high-temperature nickel–cobalt–chromium alloys, titanium is added to produce a precipitation-hardening reaction providing high strengths at temperatures up to 1,500° F (815° C). Titanium is used in permanent magnet alloys of the iron–cobalt–nickel–titanium type.

Chemical compounds: preparation and uses. Titanium dioxide (TiO_2) is the most important compound of titanium. It is used extensively in the pigment industry because of its excellent hiding power or opacity. A pure white compound having high reflectivity, it is ideal for use in white paints, enamels, and lacquers and can be used in conjunction with other compounds in coloured paints.

Use in the pigment industry

It is also used in pigments for rubber, paper, oilcloth, leather, textiles, inks, and cosmetics. The two main sources for titanium dioxide are rutile and ilmenite. Since less pure titanium dioxide can be used in pigments than can be used in producing titanium metal, most of the titanium dioxide produced from ilmenite is used by the pigment industry. The preparation of titanium dioxide for the pigment industry follows the same procedures as those already described.

Titanium tetrachloride, the raw material for producing titanium metal, is the next most important compound. It is produced by chlorinating titanium dioxide, or titanium ores, in the presence of carbon. The minor amounts of iron, silicon, oxygen, and other impurities remaining after chlorination are removed by fractional distillation. Titanium tetrachloride is used, along with titanium dioxide, as a catalyst in many chemical reactions and as a smoke-producing compound for skywriting or smoke screens. Titanium carbide, a compound produced by reacting carbon with a titanium compound, is used in conjunction with a tungsten carbide in cutting tools and dies. Thin coatings of pure titanium carbide (3,800 on the Vickers diamond hardness scale as compared to about 1,300 for tungsten carbide) are applied by vapour deposition on tools, dies, punches, and other components. Many other compounds of titanium exist, but their uses are limited.

Economic importance. Titanium became an important structural metal with the advent of the space age. Its primary uses are as components in the compressor sections of jet engines, and as structural and nonstructural components of airframes and space-vehicle systems. These applications exploit the high strength-to-weight ratios of titanium alloys and their retention of strength in moderately high temperatures. In addition, titanium and its alloys are used in chemical-process equipment in which the excellent corrosion resistance can be used to advantage.

In the early days of titanium-sponge production (the 1950s), titanium sponge sold for about $5 per pound. As the quantity of titanium-sponge production increased, the price of sponge gradually fell until it sold at about $1.30 per pound with mill products selling for $3 to $20 per pound, depending on the complexity of the production process.

Titanium sponge is produced in the United States, Japan, U.S.S.R., and Great Britain. United States consumption (see Table 3) of sponge increased annually from 1960 to 1967, the year that government stockpiling was stopped; production in that year peaked at about 30,000,000 pounds. U.S. production accounted for about two-thirds of consumption, the remainder being imports principally from Japan. The prognosis for the titanium industry remained favourable, with predictions of increased consumption through the 1970s.

BIBLIOGRAPHY. A.D. and M.K. MCQUILLAN, *Titanium* (1956), a classic text describing the metallurgy of titanium and its alloys, relating properties to metallurgical phenomena; J. BARKSDALE, *Titanium: Its Occurrence, Chemistry and Technology* (1949), on the geology, extraction, and chemistry of titanium minerals, metal, and compounds; S.C. WILLIAMS, *Report on Titanium, The Ninth Major Industrial Metal* (1965), a modern review of the titanium industry with emphasis on technical-economic factors involved in the production and uses of titanium; S. ABKOWITZ, J.J. BURKE, and R.H. HILTZ, JR., *Titanium in Industry* (1955), a general review of the properties and applications for titanium and its alloys in the aerospace and other industries; H. CONRAD (ed.), *Applications Related Phenomena in Titanium Alloys* (1968), a compilation of papers describing metallurgical phenomena that influence the performance characteristics of titanium alloys in practical applications.

(H.R.O.)

Titian

Titian was recognized early in his own lifetime as a supremely great painter, and his reputation has never suffered a decline in the intervening centuries. The art theorist Giovanni Lomazzo in 1590 declared him "the sun amidst small stars not only among the Italians but all the painters of the world." The universality of Titian's genius is not questioned today, for he was surpassingly great in all aspects of the painter's art. In his portraits he searched and penetrated human character and recorded it in canvases of pictorial brilliance. His religious compositions cover the full range of emotion from the charm of his youthful Madonnas to the tragic depths of the late "Crucifixion" and the "Entombment." In his mythological pictures he captured the gaiety and abandon of the pagan world of antiquity, and in his paintings of the nude Venus ("Venus and Adonis") and the Danae ("Danae with Nursemaid") he set a standard for physical beauty and often sumptuous eroticism that has never been surpassed. Other great masters—Rubens and Nicolas Poussin, for example—paid him the compliment of imitation.

EARLY LIFE AND WORKS

The traditional date of Titian's birth was long given as 1477, but today most critics favour a later date of birth —1488/1490. Titian (in Italian Tiziano Vecellio), son of a modest official, Gregorio di Conte dei Vecelli, and his wife, Lucia, was born in the small village of Pieve di Cadore, located high amid mountain peaks of the Alps, straight north of Venice and not far from the Austrian Tyrol. At the age of nine he set out for Venice with his brother, Francesco, to live there with an uncle and to become an apprentice to Sebastiano Zuccato, a master of mosaics. The boy soon passed to the workshop of the Bellini, where his true teacher became Giovanni Bellini, the greatest Venetian painter of the day. Titian's early works are richly evident of his schooling and also of his association as a young man with another follower of the elderly Giovanni Bellini, namely, Giorgione of Castelfranco (1477–1510). Their collaboration in 1508 on the frescoes of the Fondaco dei Tedeschi (the German Exchange) is the point of departure for Titian's career, and it explains

Influence of Giorgione

Titian, self-portrait, oil painting. In the
Staatliche Museen Preussischer Kulturbesitz,
Berlin.
By courtesy of the Staatliche Museen Preussischer
Kulturbesitz Gemaldegalerie Berlin (West)

why it is difficult to distinguish between the two artists in
the early years of the 16th century. Only ruined outlines
of the frescoes survive, the "Allegory of Justice" being
the chief scene assigned to Titian. The etchings (1760) of
the frescoes by Antonio Maria Zanetti, already in a much
faded condition, give a better notion of the idealism and
the sense of physical beauty that characterize both artists'
work. The problem of distinguishing between the paintings of Giorgione and the young Titian is virtually insuperable, for there is little solid evidence and even less
agreement among critics about the attribution of several
works. The present tendency among Italian writers is to
assign far too much to Titian in his youth.

It is certain that Titian's first independent commission
was for the frescoes of three miracles of St. Anthony of
Padua. The finest in composition is the "Miracle of the
Speaking Infant"; another, the "Miracle of the Irascible
Son," has a very beautiful landscape background that
demonstrates how similar in topography and mood were
Titian's and Giorgione's works at this time. In fact, after
Giorgione's death in 1510, Titian assumed the task of
adding the landscape background to Giorgione's unfinished "Sleeping Venus" (Gemäldegalerie, Dresden), a
fact recorded by a contemporary writer, Marcantonio
Michiel. Still Giorgionesque is the somewhat more lush
setting of Titian's "Baptism of Christ" (c. 1515, Capitoline Museum, Rome), in which the donor, Giovanni
Ram, appears at the lower right.

The authorship of individual portraits is the most difficult of all to establish, but the "Gentleman in Blue" (so-
called "Ariosto") is certainly Titian's because it is signed
with the initials T.V. (Tiziano Vecellio). The volume and
the interest in texture in the quilted sleeve seem to identify Titian's own style. On the other hand, "The Concert"
has been one of the most debated portraits, because since
the 17th century it was thought to be most typical of
Giorgione. The pronounced psychological content as well
as the notable clarity of modelling in the central figure
has led 20th-century critics to favour Titian. Technique
and the clear intelligence of the young Venetian aristocrat in the "Young Man with Cap and Gloves" has led
modern critics to attribute this and similar portraits to
Titian.

The earliest compositions on mythological or allegorical themes show the young artist still under the spell of
Giorgione in his creation of a poetic Arcadian world
where nothing commonplace or sordid exists. The inspiration lies in the idyllic world of the love lyrics of the
16th-century Italian poets Jacopo Sannazzaro and Pietro
Bembo. "The Three Ages of Man," where the erotic relationship of the young couple is discreetly muted and a
mood of tenderness and sadness prevails, is one of the
most exquisite of these. The contemporary "Sacred and
Profane Love" is likewise set in a landscape of extraordinary beauty, but here the allegory is less easily understood. The most generally accepted interpretation holds
that the two women are the twin Venuses, according to
Neoplatonic theory and symbolism. The terrestrial Venus, on the left, stands for the generative forces of nature,
both physical and intellectual, while the nude Venus, on
the right, represents eternal and divine love. Essentially
an ideally beautiful young woman rather than a cruel
biblical antiheroine is the lovely "Salome."

MATURE LIFE AND WORKS

Sometime in the early 1520s Titian brought to his house
in Venice a young woman from Cadore whose name was
Cecilia. Two sons were born in 1524 and 1525, first Pom-   *Marriage*
ponio, who became a priest, and second Orazio, later a
painter and Titian's chief assistant. During Cecilia's grave
illness in 1525, Titian married her. She recovered and
later gave birth to two daughters, Lavinia (born
1529/30) and another who died in infancy. On Cecilia's
death in 1530, the artist was disconsolate and he never
remarried.

Mythological paintings. Titian's fame had spread
abroad, and Alfonso I d'Este sought him as one of the
chief masters in a cycle of mythological compositions for
his newly rebuilt rooms called the Alabaster Chambers in
the castle at Ferrara. Two of the canvases are now in the
Prado at Madrid: the "Worship of Venus" and "The
Andrians"; one of the most spectacular, the "Bacchus
and Ariadne," is in the London National Gallery. The
gaiety of mood, the spirit of pagan abandon, and the
exquisite sense of humour in this interpretation of an
idyllic world of antiquity make it one of the miracles of
Renaissance art. Warmth and richness of colour help to
balance the intentionally asymmetrical grouping of the
figures, placed in richly verdant landscape that is also an
integral part of the design. At this time Titian partially
repainted the background of Giovanni Bellini's "Feast of
the Gods" (National Gallery of Art, Washington, D.C.),
so that the picture would better fit the series in the same
room at Ferrara.

The standard for the reclining nude female obliquely
placed in the picture space was established by Giorgione
in the "Sleeping Venus." In Titian's "Venus of Urbino"
the ideal rendering of the body and the position remain
virtually unchanged, except that the goddess is awake and
reclines upon a couch within the spacious room of a
palace. For sheer beauty of form these two works were
never surpassed. Despite the inherent eroticism of the
subject, Titian managed it with restraint and good taste.
Variations on the theme recur throughout his career.

Religious paintings. Among the religious paintings Ti-   *The*
tian produced between 1516 and 1538 is one of his most   *"Assump-*
revolutionary masterpieces, the "Assumption" (1516–   *tion"*
18). This large and at the same time monumental composition occupies the high altar of Sta. Maria dei Frari in
Venice, a position that fully justifies the spectacular
nature of the Virgin's triumph as she ascends heaven-
ward, accompanied by a large semicircular array of
angels, while the startled Apostles gesticulate in astonishment at the miracle. When the painting was unveiled it
was quickly recognized as the work of a very great
genius.

The posture of the Madonna in the "Assumption" and
the composition of Titian's "Madonna and Child with SS.
Francis and Alvise and Alvise Gozzi as Donor" reveal the
influence of Titian's contemporary Raphael; and the pose
of St. Sebastian in the "Resurrection Altarpiece," the influence of Michelangelo. These influences, however, are
of secondary importance since the landscapes, the physical types, and colour are totally Titian's own.

In the "Pesaro Madonna" (1519–26) Titian created a
new type of composition, in which the Madonna and
Saints with the male members of the Pesaro family are
placed within a monumental columnar portico of a
church. The picture is flooded with sunlight and shadows.
This work established a formula that was widely followed by later Venetian Renaissance painters and served
as an inspiration for some Baroque masters, including
Rubens and Van Dyck.

Such a quantity of masterpieces by Titian followed that only a few can be mentioned. The poetic charm of the artist's pictures with landscape continues in the "Madonna and Child with St. Catherine and a Rabbit" and the "Madonna and Child with SS. John the Baptist and Catherine of Alexandria" (c. 1530). The "Entombment" is his first tragic masterpiece, where in a twilight setting the irrevocable finality of death and the despair of Christ's followers are memorably evoked. The stately "Presentation of the Virgin in the Temple," a very large canvas, reflects the splendour of Venetian Renaissance society in the great architectural setting, partly in the latest style of the contemporary architects Serlio and Jacopo Sansovino. The pageantry of the scene also belongs to well-established tradition in Venetian art, but the organization, with its emphasis on verticals and horizontals, constitutes Titian's interpretation of the High Renaissance style.

Portraits. One of Titian's great triumphs came when he answered the call to Bologna in 1530 at the time of Charles V's coronation as Holy Roman emperor. In 1531, in keeping with his social state, he moved to a Venetian palace known as the Casa Grande, which survives as a 20th-century slum. Titian returned to Bologna to portray Charles V again on the occasion of the second meeting of Charles V and Pope Clement VII in the winter of 1532–33. The portrait of "Charles V in Armour" (1530) and another painted in January 1533 are lost, while only a less important work, "Charles V with Hound" (1532–33, Prado, Madrid), a copy of a portrait by Jakob Seisenegger, survives. Charles was so pleased with Titian's work that in May 1533 he bestowed upon the artist the most extraordinary honour of knighthood. Thereafter, the Austrian-Spanish Habsburgs remained Titian's most important patrons. Charles attempted to induce Titian to go to Spain in 1534 to prepare a portrait of the Empress, but the artist wisely refrained from undertaking the arduous journey.

Titian's other portraits in the 1520s and 1530s provide a gallery of the leading aristocrats of Italy. A splendid example is "Alfonso d'Avalos, Marques del Vasto" (1533), brilliantly rendered in gleaming armour ornamented with gold. He is accompanied by a small page whose head reaches his waist. The introduction of a secondary figure to give scale is a device frequently adopted by Titian. Another refulgent portrait in armour, but without the secondary figure, is that of "Francesco Maria della Rovere, Duke of Urbino" (1536–38). Emphasis here is given to the Duke's military career, not only by the armour but also by baton in hand and the three others in the background. These works are essentially idealized state portraits, although the heads are very convincingly rendered. "Doge Andrea Gritti" is to a greater extent a symbol of the office—that is, that of ruler of Venice. The gigantic body in a canvas of large size is sweeping in design and commanding in presence. In later works, too, Titian very effectively managed the scaling of a figure to appear massive by filling the space of the canvas—in his portraits of Pietro Aretino, for example, where he gives his subject a leonine bulkiness. Allowing more space around the figure in "The Englishman," he projected a personality of cultivated elegance and human warmth.

LATE LIFE AND WORKS

Travels and commissions. *Portraits.* The large number of masterpieces in portraiture that Titian continued to create throughout the rest of his life is astounding. Pope Paul III and his grandson, Cardinal Alessandro Farnese, began to compete with Emperor Charles V for Titian's services. At the request of the Pope, the painter travelled to Bologna in May 1543 and there prepared the celebrated official portrait of "Pope Paul III Without Cap." Although a state symbol of the Pontiff, the characterization of the crafty statesman, bent with age, comes through.

Titian's next major association with the Farnese came in 1545–46, when he made his only visit to Rome, lodged in the Belvedere Palace of the Vatican. For the first time

Titian was able to see the archaeological remains of ancient Rome and also the Renaissance masterpieces of Michelangelo, Raphael, Sebastiano del Piombo, and others. The effect upon the master's own style was relatively slight, understandably enough, since he was already a mature and world famous artist.

Of portraits of the Farnese family carried out at this time, few remain. The most celebrated of all is "Paul III and His Grandsons Ottavio and Cardinal Alessandro Farnese" (1546; Museo e Gallerie Nazionali di Capodimonte, Naples). A painting of a family group, it is most searching in psychological revelation. The feeble Pope, then aged 78, appears to turn suddenly in his chair toward Ottavio Farnese, his 22-year-old grandson. Ottavio's overobsequious bow and his shrewd Machiavellian profile demonstrate Titian's sheer genius in understanding and recording character. As a foil, the great churchman Cardinal Alessandro Farnese stands quietly by. It is no wonder that the portrait is not completely finished, for Paul III must have found it too revealing of the feud within the Farnese family.

If one were forced to name Titian's two greatest portraits, the choice might fall upon the Farnese group and upon another, "The Vendramin Family." Here the situation is quite different, for the two heads of the clan kneel in adoration of a reliquary of the Holy Cross, accompanied by seven sons ranging from about eight to 20. This monumental portrait group is a tour de force in technical brilliance, richly beautiful in colour, running the emotional gamut from gravity to the innocence of childhood.

On his departure from Rome, in June 1546, Titian's association with the Farnese ended. He received no payment for his pictures, and his hopes for recompense in the form of a benefice for his son Pomponio were never realized. Titian decided to throw in his lot with the Habsburgs. Consenting to undertake the arduous journey to Augsburg, he set out in the depths of winter in January 1548 to cross the Alps to reach the Emperor's court. There he carried out one of his most memorable works, the equestrian "Emperor Charles V at Mühlberg," designed to commemorate the Emperor's victory over the Protestants the year before. It is the great state portrait par excellence, intended to show the Emperor as a Christian knight, as he wished posterity to remember him. Titian minimized the disfiguring lantern jaw and gave great dignity of bearing to his subject. In sheer mastery of the painter's art, the picture is unsurpassed. The handsome armour, with its gleaming highlights and reflected colour, the rose sash across the chest (a symbol of the Catholic party and the Holy Roman Empire), and the superb sunset landscape all contribute to make it one of the masterpieces of all time.

In December 1548 Charles instructed Titian to proceed to Milan to prepare likenesses of Prince Philip on his first trip outside of Spain. Once again, in the fall of 1550, Charles obliged Titian to travel to Augsburg to remain until May 1551, when he executed one of his greatest state portraits, the "Philip II" in full length. In this portrait of Philip, when still a prince aged 23, Titian achieved another tour de force in sheer beauty of painting, and he treated gently the surly face of the arrogant young man.

Religious paintings. Like some of Titian's earlier religious paintings, "Christ Before Pilate" is a work in which Titian managed a large crowd in a processional manner leading to the focal point, the figure of Christ at the left. Here the people are in a state of turmoil as they demand Christ's crucifixion. The composition, however, marks a new phase in Titian's development, far removed from the Renaissance serenity of the "Presentation," which is not explainable by the subject alone. The compact massing of figures, the oblique position of the steps and the wall at the left, and the general effect of excitement are indicative of the mid-16th-century style known as Mannerism. Titian assimilated and recreated, however, to produce a masterpiece far surpassing anything of which the Mannerist artists were capable.

Titian's religious compositions after his visit to Rome in 1545—46 reveal to some degree his contact with ancient

(margin notes: Titian and Charles V; "Paul III and His Grandsons"; "Christ Before Pilate")

art and the works of Michelangelo. In "Christ Crowned with Thorns" the burly muscular figures are thus explained, as perhaps is the violence of the whole interpretation.

Last years in Venice. On his return to Venice in 1551, Titian remained there for the rest of his life except for summer visits to his native city of Pieve di Cadore. In his last 25 years his productivity was undiminished in quantity and in creative ideas.

Portraits. Among his portraits is the full-length, dashingly rendered figure of the Duke of Atri, who is dressed in red velvet. One of the latest and most dramatic was "Jacopo Strada," in which this brilliant antiquarian, writer, and art collector is shown presenting to the spectator a small statue, a Roman copy of an Aphrodite of Praxiteles. Here again, the scope and variety of Titian's invention is astonishing in this new composition, so notable for lively action, psychological preception, and pictorial beauty. One must not forget Titian's "Self Portrait," in which he presents himself with great dignity, wearing the golden chain of knighthood. The intelligent, tired face is fully rendered, while the costume is sketched in lightly with a free brush. One of the most remarkable late works is the "Triple Portrait Mask" or "Allegory of Prudence," in which Titian, gray-bearded and wearing a rose-coloured cap, represents old age, his son Orazio, maturity, and presumably Marco Vecellio stands for youth.

Religious paintings. The "Trinity" (or "La Gloria"), painted for Charles V's personal devotion, reflects central Italian art to a lesser degree than the earlier "Christ Crowned with Thorns." The glowing richness of colour predominates in this adoration of the Trinity in which Charles V and his family appear among the elect. The "Martyrdom of St. Lawrence" marks a further step in new compositional directions that culminate in Baroque form in the following century. St. Lawrence upon his gridiron is placed obliquely in space, and the steps reverse the direction to the right. Although dramatic power invests the main action in the foreground, the night scene with the tall flares and mysterious light suggests the supernatural. In his late religious pictures Titian veils the human forms in shadowy light and so increases the dominant mood of spirituality. One sees this effect in the late "Entombment," in which muted colour prevails, and in the awesome tragedy of the "Crucifixion." The "Christ Crowned with Thorns," employing essentially the same composition as in the earlier version, is now seen through a veil of darkness, and the colour is broken into tiny spots and areas. All is miraculous in the "Annunciation," in which Gabriel rushes in and an assembly of angels in glory hovers about the Virgin. Titian's final word and last testament is the "Pietà," intended for his own burial chapel but left unfinished and completed by Palma il Giovane. The master and his son, Orazio, appear as tiny donors on the small plaque to the right. The monumentality of the composition is established by the great architectural niche flanked by Moses and the Hellespontic sibyl, while the figures are grouped in a long diagonal. The subdued colour befits the all-prevailing sorrow and the immutability of death in this, one of the artist's most profound achievements.

Mythological paintings. The "Venus and Cupid with an Organist" and the "Venus and the Lute Player" are variations on the theme of the earlier "Venus of Urbino." Aside from the emphasis on the idealized beauty of the nude goddess, it is generally believed that symbolism is involved in these pictures, although the precise meanings have been variously interpreted. Beauty of sound (music) and beauty of vision are common to both. In the first example, a Renaissance garden with fountain and trees in perspective, completes the background, which is separated from the figures by a dark red velvet curtain. More symbolism of an erotic nature is present in the embracing couple, a stag, and the satyr on the fountain. In the second picture, the background consists of a broad river valley and the distant Alpine peaks so dear to Titian's heart. This late landscape, painted in the artist's free illusionistic style, is extraordinarily beautiful.

The "Venus with a Mirror" (National Gallery of Art,

Washington, D.C.), the one original among several versions, is a natural theme for the goddess of love and beauty. Yet Titian is the first artist to show her with a mirror held by Cupid. Her form is somewhat more heroic than hitherto, and her head to a limited degree is inspired by ancient sculpture. The superb quality of the flesh tones is enhanced by the cloak of dark red velvet, trimmed with fur.

A group of several important pictures of mythological themes was created by the master in 1554—62 for Charles's successor, Philip II of Spain, who never bothered to remunerate Titian for any of them. From the letters of the artist to the King, it is clear that he planned the paintings in pairs, but otherwise they do not constitute a comprehensive iconographic program. The first pair (still in Madrid) consists of the "Danae with Nursemaid" and the "Venus and Adonis." The magnificent nude Danae lies upon her couch, knees raised, as Jupiter descends to her in the form of golden rain, and her nursemaid rather amusingly attempts to catch the coins in her apron. This work (of which there exist numerous replicas and copies) is undoubtedly the most voluptuous in Titian's entire repertory. In colour and technique, as well, the "Danae" is one of Titian's greatest achievements; one is tempted to say that no other artist ever equalled him in imagination and in the depiction of sheer beauty of this work. In the "Venus and Adonis," the goddess, depicted from the back, attempts to restrain her muscular young lover as he is about to depart for the hunt, his dogs straining at the leash. The rose of his costume and the red velvet cushion beneath Venus are foils in the colour composition to the flesh tones and the sunlit landscape.

The "Perseus and Andromeda" was intended to be a companion to "Medea and Jason," according to Titian's letter, but for some reason the second picture was never carried out. Andromeda, bound to the rock at the left, awaits deliverance as Perseus descends from the sky to slay the monster. Her powerful physique reflects Titian's familiarity with the work of Michelangelo, yet Andromeda's body is more feminine and graceful than any of the Florentine's masculine-looking women. Titian's sensitivity to female beauty is unfailing.

"The Rape of Europa" is surely one of the gayest of Titian's "poesies," as he called them. Taken by surprise, Europa is carried off, arms and legs flying, on the back of Jupiter in the form of a garlanded white bull. A putto (chubby, naked little boy) on the back of a dolphin appears to be mimicking her, and cupids in the sky follow the merry scene. Titian's fondness for oblique compositions is most successfully applied here, for it contributes to the sense of movement, and it allows for the extensive seascape and the mountainous shore. The sheer wizardry of Titian's technique is nowhere more fully demonstrated than in the misty distances shot through with blues and sunset rose and in the expanse of sea with its iridescent lights.

In "The Rape of Europa" Titian reached the climax of his powers, and by good fortune the picture has survived in almost perfect condition. On the contrary, two other great "poesies" done for Philip II are sadly abused by time and restorers, paticularly the "Diana and Callisto," and less so the "Diana and Actaeon." The assembly of female nudes in a variety of poses, befitting the action, illustrates two episodes of the Diana legend as told by Ovid in his *Metamorphoses*, books II and III. "Diana and Actaeon" depicts Actaeon, the youthful hunter of heroic body, just as he is unwittingly happens upon Diana and her nymphs as they are bathing (and before Diana punishes him by transforming him into a stag). Behind him is a great rose-coloured curtain. A landscape of extraordinary beauty and a vaulted passage form the setting within which the maidens are gathered. The organization of the rather complex design once more presages Baroque compositional methods. In the companion picture, the goddess discovers that Callisto, one of her maidens who had taken the vow of chastity, is pregnant. Though she was deceived by Jupiter's trickery, she is, nevertheless, banished and later, according to the legend, transformed into a bear. A standing and rather fulsome nude rips the drap-

Margin notes: "Self Portrait" "Pietà" "The Rape of Europa"

ery from the reclining Callisto. The golden canopy in the trees above Diana is the cloth of honour referring to her divinity. The glorious deep blue sky with golden clouds and the green branches of the tree supply the backdrop for the nude bodies. Diana, tall and imperious, is magnificent, despite the surface damage that has destroyed much of the paint. Subtleties abound in every movement and every gesture.

The latest of these compositions carried out for Philip II was the "Tarquin and Lucretia," a dramatic work of great vigour that proves that the aged master had lost none of his creative powers. Rather than Lucretia's suicide because of her rape by Tarquin, which is the more common subject, Titian chose to represent Tarquin's violent attack upon her. Again the rich colour is equally as important as the action. Against the green curtain and white sheets the rose velvet breeches of Tarquin and his green and gold doublet stand out in rich brilliancy.

The end came on August 27, 1576, when the great master died of old age, while a plague was raging in Venice. He was interred in the church of Sta. Maria dei Frari, where two of his most famous works may still be seen.

Through his long life Titian was highly successful in all branches of the painter's art. In his interpretation of Christian iconography he was infused in his youth with the poetic styles of the elderly Giovanni Bellini and his contemporary Giorgione. Titian created new compositions such as the "Assumption" and the "Pesaro Madonna" and later in his life the "Martyrdom of St. Lawrence," and he carried out a never-ending succession of new conceptions as his career matured. He gained international fame as a portraitist, beginning as a Giorgionesque painter and developing into a major creator of the state portrait for the glorification of rulers. The revival of the culture of the ancient world lies at the root of Renaissance culture in the arts and in literature; inspired by the ancient poets such as Ovid, Catullus, and Theocritus, Titian recreated pictorially the legends of Greece and Rome in a series of incomparable masterpieces.

MAJOR WORKS

RELIGIOUS PAINTINGS: frescoes of three miracles of St. Anthony of Padua (1510-11; Scuola del Santo, Padua); "Gipsy Madonna" (c. 1510; Kunsthistorisches Museum, Vienna); "Salome" (c. 1515; Galleria Doria-Pamphili, Rome); "Assumption" (1516–18; Sta. Maria dei Frari, Venice); "Madonna and Child with SS. Francis and Alvise and Alvise Gozzi As Donor" (signed 1520; Pinacoteca, Ancona); "Resurrection Altarpiece" (signed 1522; SS. Nazaro e Celso, Brescia); "Pesaro Madonna" (1519–26; Sta. Maria dei Frari, Venice); "Entombment" (1526–32; Louvre, Paris); "Madonna and Child with St. Catherine and a Rabbit" (c. 1530; Louvre, Paris); "Madonna and Child with SS. John the Baptist and Catherine of Alexandria" (c. 1530; National Gallery, London); "The Presentation of the Virgin in the Temple" (1534–38; Accademia, Venice); "Christ Before Pilate" (signed 1543; Kunsthistorisches Museum, Vienna); three Old Testament subjects (1543–44; Sta. Maria della Salute, ceiling of the sacristy, Venice); "Christ Crowned with Thorns" (1546-50; Louvre, Paris); "Martyrdom of St. Lawrence" (1548–57; Gesuiti, Venice); "Trinity" ("La Gloria") (1554; Prado, Madrid); "Crucifixion" (1558; S. Domenico, Ancona); "Entombment" (1559; Prado, Madrid); "Magdalen" (c. 1560; Hermitage, Leningrad); "Annunciation" (1560–65; S. Salvatore, Venice); "Madonna and Child in Evening Landscape," (1562–65; Alte Pinakothek, Munich); "Christ Crowned with Thorns" (1570–76; Alte Pinakothek, Munich); "St. Jerome" (1575; Nuevos Museos, Escorial); "Pietà" (1576; Accademia, Venice).

MYTHOLOGICAL PAINTINGS: "Sacred and Profane Love" (1512–15; Borghese Gallery, Rome); "Flora" (c. 1515; Uffizi, Florence); "The Three Ages of Man" (c. 1515; National Gallery of Scotland, Edinburgh, lent by the Duke of Sutherland); "Bacchus and Ariadne" ("Ferrara Bacchanals," 1520–23, National Gallery, London); "Worship of Venus" (1518–19) and "The Andrians" (1523–24; both in Prado, Madrid); "Venus Anadyomene" (c. 1525; National Gallery of Scotland, Edinburgh, lent by the Duke of Sutherland; "Venus of Urbino" (1538–39; Uffizi, Florence); "Jupiter and Antiope," so-called "Venus of El Pardo" (c. 1540, perhaps finished c. 1560; Louvre, Paris); "Venus and Cupid with an Organist" (signed c. 1550; Prado, Madrid); "Venus with a Mirror" (1550–55; National Gallery of Art, Washington, D.C.); "Danae with Nursemaid" (1553–54; Prado, Madrid); "Venus and Adonis" (1553–54; Prado, Madrid);

"Perseus and Andromeda" (1554–56; Wallace Collection, London); "Diana and Actaeon" and "Diana and Callisto" (1559; National Gallery of Scotland, Edinburgh, lent by the Duke of Sutherland); "The Rape of Europa" (c. 1559–62; Isabella Stewart Gardner Museum, Fenway Court, Boston); "Venus and the Lute Player" (c. 1560; Metropolitan Museum of Art, New York); "Nymph and Shepherd" (c. 1570; Kunsthistorisches Museum, Vienna); "Tarquin and Lucretia" (1571; Fitzwilliam Museum, Cambridge); "The Flaying of Marsyas" (c. 1570–76; Uměleckohistorické Muzeum, Kroměříž, Czech.).

PORTRAITS: "The Concert" (1510–12; Pitti Palace, Florence); "Gentleman in Blue," so-called "Ariosto" (signed c. 1512; National Gallery, London); "Young Man with Cap and Gloves" (1512–15; Earl of Halifax Collection, Garrowby Hall, London); "Man with a Glove" (1520–22; Louvre, Paris); "Federico II Gonzaga, Duke of Mantua" (c. 1523; Prado, Madrid); "Alfonso d'Avalos, Marques del Vasto" (1533; Marquis de Ganay Collection, Paris); "Francesco Maria della Rovere, Duke of Urbino" (1536–38; Uffizi, Florence); "Doge Andrea Gritti" (1535–38; National Gallery of Art, Washington, D.C.); "The Englishman," so-called (1540–45; Pitti Palace, Florence); "Pietro Aretino" (c. 1545; Pitti Palace, Florence); "Clarice Strozzi" (1542; Staatliche Museen Preussischer Kulturbesitz, Berlin); "Pope Paul III Without Cap" (1543; Museo e Gallerie Nazionali di Capodimonte, Naples); "The Vendramin Family" (1543–47; National Gallery, London); "Paul III and His Grandsons Ottavio and Cardinal Alessandro Farnese" (1546; Museo e Gallerie Nazionali di Capodimonte, Naples); "The Emperor Charles V at Mühlberg" (1548; Prado, Madrid); "Giovanni Battista Castaldo" (1548; Becker Collection, Dortmund); "Self Portrait" (c. 1550; Staatliche Museen Preussischer Kulturbesitz, Berlin); "Philip II" (1550–51; Prado, Madrid); "Giovanni Francesco Acquaviva, Duke of Atri" (1552; Staatliche Kunstsammlungen Kassel); "Lavinia with Fan," so-called (1555–60; Gemäldegalerie, Dresden); "Jacopo Strada" (1567–68; Kunsthistorisches Museum, Vienna); "Triple Portrait Mask," "Allegory of Prudence" (c. 1570; National Gallery, London).

BIBLIOGRAPHY. SIR JOSEPH A. CROWE and GIOVANNI B. CAVALCASELLE, Titian: His Life and Times (1877), the first major monograph on the artist; ADOLFO VENTURI, Storia dell' arte italiana, vol. 9, pt. 3, pp. 93–386 (1928), with summary of documents; HANS TIETZE, Tizian: Leben und Werk, 2 vol. (1936; shorter editions in English in 1 vol., 1937 and 1950); THEODOR HETZER, "Tiziano Vecellio," Allgemeines Lexikon der bildenden Künstler . . . , vol. 34, pp. 158–172 (1940), bibliography and documentation, but excessively restrictive in attribution; BERNARD BERENSON, Italian Pictures of the Renaissance, Venetian School, pp. 183–192 (1957), a list of authentic works, and illustrations; ANTONIO MORASSI, "Titian," Encyclopedia of World Art, vol. 14, col. 133–157 (1967), many doubtful attributions and dates; RODOLFO PALLUCCHINI, Tiziano, 2 vol. (1969), fully illustrated; ERWIN PANOFSKY, Problems in Titian, Mainly Iconographic (1969); HAROLD E. WETHEY, The Paintings of Titian, vol. 1, The Religious Paintings (1969), vol. 2, The Portraits (1971), vol. 3, Mythological and Historical Paintings (in prep.), a complete corpus with catalogue raisonné.

(H.E.W.)

Titicaca, Lake

Lake Titicaca (Lago Titicaca), the world's highest lake navigable to large vessels, lies at 12,500 feet (3,810 metres) above sea level in the Andes mountains of South America, astride the border between Peru to the west and Bolivia to the east. Second largest lake of South America (after Maracaibo), Titicaca covers 3,205 square miles (8,301 square kilometres) and runs in a northwest to southeast direction for a distance of 120 miles. It is 50 miles across at its widest point. A narrow strait, Tiquina, separates the lake into two bodies of water. The smaller, in the southeast, is called Lago Uiñaimarca; the larger, in the northwest, Lago Chucuito.

Titicaca (its meaning is uncertain, but it has been variously translated as Rock of the Puma or Crag of Lead) lies between Andean ranges in a vast basin (about 22,400 square miles in area) that comprises most of the Altiplano (High Plateau) of the nothern Andes. From the snow-covered Cordillera Real Range on the northeast (Bolivian) shore of the lake, some of the highest peaks in the Andes rise to heights of more than 21,000 feet.

The lake averages 328 feet in depth, but the bottom tilts sharply toward the Bolivian shore, reaching its greatest recorded depth of 913 feet (281 metres) off Isla Soto in the northeast corner of the lake. In contrast, the small arm of the lake beyond Tiquina averages less than 33 feet.

More than 25 rivers empty their waters into Titicaca; the largest, the Ramis, draining about two-fifths of the entire Titicaca Basin, enters the northwest corner of the lake. One small river, the Desaguadero, drains the lake at its southern end. This single outlet empties only 5 percent of the lake's excess water; the rest is lost by evaporation under the fierce sun and strong winds of the dry Altiplano.

Titicaca's level fluctuates both seasonally and over a cycle of years. During the rainy season (summer, from December to March) the level of the lake rises, normally to recede during the dry winter months. The extreme difference between high and low levels may be as much as 16 feet. It was formerly believed that Titicaca was slowly drying up, but in the early 1970s studies seemed to refute this, indicating a more or less regular cycle of rise and fall.

Titicaca's waters are limpid and only slightly brackish, with salinity ranging from 52 to 55 parts in 1,000. Surface temperatures average 56° F (14° C); from a thermocline (a layer of water separating an upper, warmer, oxygen-rich zone from a lower, colder, oxygen-deficient zone) at 66 feet temperatures drop to 52° F (11° C) at the bottom. Analyses show measurable quantities of sodium chloride, sodium sulfate, calcium sulfate, and magnesium sulfate in the water.

As in other Alpine lakes, fish life is restricted, consisting principally of two species of killifish (*Orestias*)—a kind of small fish, usually striped or barred with black—and a catfish (*Trichomycterus*). In 1939, and subsequently, trout were introduced into Titicaca. Rainbow trout predominated and, finding no competition, gorged on the native fishes. Within a few years trout of 25 to 35 pounds were common. In 1961 a fish cannery started operations, netting fish from the lake and at the mouth of spawning streams. Other canneries followed, and the catch fell off rapidly. Today a trout of eight pounds is considered large. The Peruvian and Bolivian governments now prohibit the taking of trout by any method, but poaching is frequent. A large frog (*Telmatobius*), which may reach a length of nearly a foot, inhabits the shallower regions of the lake.

Forty-one islands, some of them densely populated, rise from Titicaca's waters. The largest, Isla de Titicaca (or Isla del Sol), lies just off the tip of the Copacabana Peninsula.

Ruins on shore and on the islands attest to the previous existence of one of the oldest civilizations known in the Americas. The chief site is at Tiahuanaco, Bolivia, at the southern end of the lake. No one knows with certainty who erected the temples, stelae, and stone figures, which antedate the Christian era. On the Isla de Titicaca ruins of a temple mark the spot where, according to the tradition of the Incas (a Quechuan people of Peru who established an empire about 1100), the legendary founders of the Inca dynasty, Manco Capac and Mama Ocllo, were sent down to earth by the Sun, the Inca god.

Aymara Indians have dwelt on the shores of Titicaca since before recorded history. Pockets of Quechua-speaking Indians scattered around the lake probably descend from peoples transferred to the high plateau by the Inca conquerors.

The Altiplano Indians, short, dark, and barrel-chested, have been the subjects of medical research because of their extraordinary adaptation to high-altitude living. Studies show their hearts, lungs, and spleens are larger than those of men who live at sea level, while their bone marrow manufactures more red corpuscles to capture oxygen molecules from the rarefied air.

The Aymara still practice their ancient methods of agriculture on stepped terraces that predate Inca times. They grow barley, quinoa (a kind of pigweed that produces a small grain), and the potato, a New World tuber that was unknown in Europe before the discovery of America and that originated on the Altiplano. The highest cultivated plot in the world was found near Titicaca—a field of

barley growing at a height of 15,420 feet above sea level. At this height the grain never ripens, and the stalks furnish forage for llamas and alpacas, the American relatives of the camel that serve the Indians as beasts of burden and as a source of meat.

Remnants of an ancient people, the Uru, still live on floating mats of dried totora (a reedlike papyrus that grows in dense brakes in the marshy shallows). From the totora, the Uru and other lake dwellers make their famed balsas—boats fashioned of bundles of dried reeds lashed together that resemble the crescent-shaped papyrus craft pictured on ancient Egyptian monuments.

In 1862 the first steamer to ply the lake was prefabricated in England and carried in pieces on muleback up to the lake. Today a ship of 2,000 tons is the flagship of three vessels making regular crossings from Puno, on the Peruvian shore, to the small Bolivian port of Guaqui. A narrow-gauge railway connects Guaqui with La Paz, capital of Bolivia. The world's second highest railway runs from Puno down to Arequipa and the Pacific, completing land-bound Bolivia's principal link with the sea.

Because of its great height and the vast amount of water held by Titicaca, various schemes have been proposed for the production of hydroelectric power. Some would channel the lake waters into the Amazon Basin to the east; others would take advantage of the rapid fall to the comparatively close Pacific to the west. In either case, the water would have to traverse canals and tunnels to cross the height of the land. Estimates of the potential output of energy vary from 2,300 to 4,500,000,000 kilowatts.

BIBLIOGRAPHY. Literature concerning Lake Titicaca is scattered and sparse. See FELIX MONHEIM, *Beiträge zur Klimatologie und Hydrologie des Titicacabeckens* (1956), a well-documented, detailed treatment of the hydrological and climatological aspects of the lake and its basin; PERU, MINISTERIO DE MARINA, *Informe sobre Estudio Realizado en el Lago Titicaca durante Diciembre de 1969* (1970), a summary of the latest investigations on the chemical properties of Titicaca's waters, the vertical and lateral temperature distribution, and a detailed profile of depths; WASHINGTON CANO, *El Lago Titicaca* (1952), a general, popular monograph including legends and traditions surrounding the lake.

(Lu.M.)

Tito

Josip Broz Tito was the leader of the Yugoslav Partisans who fought against Hitler in World War II and for a Socialist regime in Yugoslavia. In 1945, he became the first president of the new Yugoslav state and directed the modernization of his country with a firm hand. He challenged all the great world powers and became the first successful heretic in the Communist world when he defied the Soviet Union in 1948. He preached the doctrine of equality of large and small states and proclaimed the right of every Socialist country to pursue its own way to Socialism.

Josip Broz ("Tito" was added in 1934) was born on May 7, 1892, in the village of Kumrovec on the border of Croatia and Slovenia, the seventh of 15 children of a poor peasant family. His father was a Croat, his mother a Slovene. (Tito's official birthday is celebrated on May 25: the exact birth dates of children are often overlooked under the poor conditions of large peasant families.)

At the age of 13 Tito went to the town of Sisak as an apprentice locksmith, and as a youth he was employed as a metalworker in Trieste, Bohemia, and Germany. On his journeys he joined the metalworkers' trade unions and the Social Democratic Party of Croatia. The outbreak of World War I found him in the 25th Regiment in Zagreb, which was sent against Serbia in August 1914. Accused of spreading anti-war propaganda, Tito was arrested and kept in the Petrovaradin jail; but in January 1915 the charges were dropped, and he was sent with his regiment to the Carpathian front, where he was later decorated for bravery. But when his regiment was transferred to the Bukovina front, he was seriously wounded—stabbed by a Cossack's lance—and captured by the Russian Army.

It was not until 1920 that Tito returned from Russia to Croatia with his Russian wife (divorced 1935) to work in a mill near Bjelovar as a mechanic. Having joined the Communist Party (CPY), he was arrested in 1923 but was acquitted. He lived in poverty and lost two children. Working in the shipyards at Kraljevica, he was arrested again in 1925 and sentenced to seven months' probation. In April 1927 he was given membership in the Zagreb Committee of the CPY, which supported the Comintern's Open Letter against factions in the CPY. In 1928 he was appointed deputy of the Politburo of the Central Committee of the CPY and secretary general of the Croatian and Slavonian committees. On August 4, 1928, he was again arrested. At his trial he denied the right of tribunal to judge him; he was sentenced to five years.

Upon his release from prison in 1934, he became a member of the Central Committee of the Communist Party of Yugoslavia (CPY) and then of the Politburo of the Central Committee. Subsequently he travelled from Yugoslavia to Moscow, Paris, Prague, and Vienna. For conspiratorial reasons, he adopted several pseudonyms, among which "Tito" was most frequently used. He worked in Moscow in 1935 in the Balkan section of the Comintern and participated in its Seventh Congress. In August 1936 Tito was named organizational secretary of the CPY Politburo. In 1937 Premier Joseph Stalin initiated a purge of Yugoslav Communists living in the Soviet Union, and about 800 were liquidated. The CPY was saved from dissolution by the high ranking Comintern official Georgi Dimitrov, and late in 1937 Tito was appointed secretary general by the Executive Council of the Comintern. Tito returned to Yugoslavia and reorganized the party, taking into its leadership young revolutionaries, such as Edvard Kardelj, Milovan Djilas, Aleksander Ranković, and Ivo Ribar. In October 1940 the Fifth Party Conference was held clandestinely in Zagreb, attended by 105 members. Tito was formally chosen secretary general of the CPY Central Committee. The party then numbered 6,000 members plus 30,000 members of the Young Communist League. In 1937 Tito helped send some 1,300 Yugoslav volunteers to fight for the Republicans in the Spanish Civil War. These volunteers later formed the nucleus of the national liberation forces in Yugoslavia.

Germany attacked Yugoslavia on April 6, 1941. Early that June Serbian peasants in Hercegovina rose spontaneously against the Croatian Ustashe—members of a separatist terrorist organization that aided the Germans. Tito's resistance began after June 22, when Germany invaded the Soviet Union.

Tito issued a proclamation for a general uprising. Calling for brotherhood and unity among the Yugoslav peoples, he promised them equality after independence was won. The uprising grew so swiftly that by the end of the summer almost half of Yugoslavia was liberated; the liberated area in Serbia and Montenegro was held primarily by the Yugoslav Army of the Fatherland (often referred to as the Chetniks) and not by Tito's Partisans. Tito established his general headquarters at Užice in western Serbia. Against the wishes of Moscow, a new revolutionary administration was created in liberated areas; this and other issues deepened the conflict between Tito and the exiled royal government and its representative in the country, Dragoljub Mihajlovíc, called Draža. Using troops from the Russian front and Greece, the Germans launched an offensive against the Užice region at the end of November, driving out the Partisans. There were heavy casualties, and Tito, the last to leave resistance headquarters, was nearly captured fighting his way through the advancing German lines. This was the first of seven major German offensives against Tito's forces.

The Partisan movement spread throughout Yugoslavia, however, and in December Tito organized special proletarian brigades comprised of extremely mobile guerrilla shock units. Alarmed by the growth of the Partisans, Hitler launched two major offensives in early 1943—the Neretva and Sutjeska—against the main body of the Partisans and their headquarters. More than ten German divisions participated, aided by six Italian and quisling units. The Partisans, though having to transport more than 4,000 wounded through the mountains in winter,

broke through all the German encirclements. These were the decisive battles of the Yugoslav revolution. At the Sutjeska battle, the Partisans lost more than 6,000 men, and many were wounded, including Tito.

After the capitulation of Italy in September 1943, the Partisans numbered over 250,000. Tito, without informing any of the great powers (including Moscow), decided to convene a Partisans Parliament (the Anti-Fascist Council of the National Liberation Committee of Yugoslavia), which set up the provisional revolutionary government and declared Yugoslavia a federal community of equal peoples. Tito was given the title of marshal of Yugoslavia. At the Teheran Conference, the Allied leaders granted the Partisans the status of allies and decided to send military missions and aid. On May 25, 1944, Hitler ordered a surprise parachute and tank attack on the Partisan headquarters at Drvar in Bosnia, and Tito once again narrowly escaped. Stalin and Winston Churchill, seeking to unify the Yugoslav émigré government with Tito's revolutionary government, agreed that each should have equal influence in Yugoslavia (the so-called 50–50 agreement). Tito showed remarkable diplomatic skill in preventing the realization of these schemes, both in his meetings with Churchill in Naples during August 1944 and with Stalin in Moscow during September of that year. Although German military power had capitulated on all fronts by May 9, 1945, German units in Yugoslavia received orders to continue fighting. They and pro-German Yugoslavs offered resistance until May 15, when they were finally annihilated.

The war had devastated the country. War dead amounted to more than 11 percent of the population, and war damages were extensive and costly. Toward the end of the war Tito found himself at loggerheads with the West because of his attempts to seize Trieste, his support of the Communists in the Greek Civil War, his shooting down of two United States planes over Slovenia, and his establishment of an undisguished Communist regime in Yugoslavia. Nevertheless, on June 28, 1948, when Tito's relations with the West could not have been worse, Stalin broke with Tito by ejecting the CPY from the Cominform.

This conflict with Stalin arose out of Tito's determination to preserve Yugoslav independence. Stalin hoped to take advantage of Yugoslavia's isolation by trying to bring Tito down through economic blockade, sedition, border incidents, and threats of military invasion. These threats united the Yugoslav people behind Tito even more than in the days of World War II.

With Stalin's death in 1953, the new Soviet leaders changed their approach, and a Soviet official state and party delegation, led by Soviet premier Nikita Khrushchev, visited Belgrade on June 2, 1955, where it formally rejected Stalin's policy and acknowledged Tito's concept of the right of equality of states and their rights to choose their own road to Socialism.

Tito's conception of Yugoslav Socialism was embodied in his constitutional reforms. The first Yugoslav constitution (1946) was modelled on the Soviet constitution. Many rights obtained by each republic of Yugoslavia during the Partisan struggle were yielded to the central government, which also established administrative control over the economy. But after the break with Stalin, new reforms decentralized administration and established workers' councils in the factories. The republic was granted a greater freedom and a Council of Nationalities was created. On January 13, 1953, Tito was elected as the first president of Yugoslavia. A new constitution was enacted on April 7 for the Socialist Federative Republic of Yugoslavia. The relationship between the federation (a joint and equal community of all nationalities in Yugoslavia) and the republic (the five major Yugoslav nationalities, each constituting a sovereign Socialist republic) was to be "between two essentially equal and mutually dependent and interlinked social and political communities."

Abroad Tito conducted a policy of nonalignment with either the Soviet Union or the United States. His neutralist policy led Tito to closer ties with the conference of 25

Communist Party activities in the 1920s

Organization of the resistance movement

Marshal of Yugoslavia

The conflict with Stalin

The
policy of
nonalign-
ment

nonaligned states convened by Tito, Jawaharlal Nehru of India, and Gamal Abdel Nasser of Egypt. The conference adopted a 27-point declaration denouncing colonialism; demanding an end to the armed action against dependent peoples, endorsing the struggle of the Algerians, and condemning the apartheid system in South Africa.

In the pursuit of this policy Tito travelled extensively in Africa, Asia, and Latin America between 1962 and 1970. In August 1968 Tito denounced the invasion of Czechoslovakia by the Soviet Union, stressing that this act "violated the sovereignty of a socialist country and dealt a grave blow to socialist and progressive forces all around the world." He followed this up by proposing the creation of Partisan units and territorial defenses in all parts of the country, in order to strengthen the regular army. A new law made males eligible for military service up to the age of 65, while women between the ages of 19 and 40 could be assigned to military and civil defense units. In September 1970, at the age of 78, Tito announced a plan forming a collective leadership to succeed him.

The qualities that made Tito a successful resistance leader—decisiveness, adaptability, moral and physical stamina, and a ready sense of humour—enabled him to provide Yugoslavia with nearly three decades of stable leadership. Tito travelled frequently, in Yugoslavia as well as abroad. His third wife, Jovanka Budisavljević, a former Partisan fighter, usually accompanied him on state visits both in and out of the country. In the early 1970s, he had achieved the status of an elder statesman and lived, with his wife, either in Belgrade or the island resort of Brioni. Tito's hobbies included photography, hunting, and fishing. He was considered one of the best dressed statesmen in Europe and a fine pianist.

BIBLIOGRAPHY. PHYLLIS AUTY, *Tito* (1970), is an up-to-date scholarly biography with notes, index, photographs, and four maps, by an acknowledged specialist. FITZROY MacLEAN, *Disputed Barricade: The Life and Times of Josip Broz-Tito* (1957), is a well-written straightforward biography bringing forward the subject against his political background, with map, photographs, and an index; the same author's *Eastern Approaches* (1949), an eye-witness account of the writer as observer or participant in events in the U.S.S.R., Asia, and Yugoslavia, devotes its third and last section to a brilliant account of the British mission, headed by himself, to Tito and his Partisans in Yugoslavia in 1943–45. See also VLADIMIR DEDIJER, *Josip Broz Tito—Prilozi za Biografiju* (1953), a biography with photographs and an index; and the same author's *Tito Speaks* (1952), a closeup account of Tito by one who knew him that makes use also of first-hand recollections of others and of Tito's own words to construct a vivid portrait. H.F. ARMSTRONG, *Tito and Goliath* (1951), concentrates on the significance in theory and in practical politics of Tito's career, as does F.W. NEAL, *Titoism in Action: The Reforms in Yugoslavia After 1948* (1958), an account of Tito's political and economic direction of Yugoslavia since World War II.

Tobacco Production

Tobacco is the common name of the plant *Nicotiana tabacum*, and, to a limited extent *N. rustica*, and the cured leaf that is used, usually after aging and processing in various ways, for smoking, chewing, snuffing, and extracting of nicotine. The common name was derived from an American Indian word applied both to a tube for inhaling the smoke and to a cylinder of leaf prepared for smoking. This article deals with the history of tobacco, its culture, curing, grading, and marketing, the manufacture of tobacco products, controls, world production and consumption, economic statistics, and health hazards.

Tobacco is produced commercially as a field crop in certain areas of the world where soils and climate combine to yield a product possessing certain recognized characteristics. The tobacco industry obtains various kinds of leaf from these areas for use in manufacturing products acceptable to consumers. Nicotine and the related alkaloids contained in tobacco are generally recognized as habit forming and narcotic, characteristics that help account for the worldwide popularity of tobacco products.

Though tobacco is tropical in origin, it is cultivated throughout the world. The crop is grown in the U.S.S.R.

around 50° N latitude, and in Australia and New Zealand at about 40° S latitude. *N. tabacum* requires a frost-free period of 100 to 130 days from date of transplanting to maturity in the field. *N. rustica*, which is grown to some extent in the U.S.S.R. and India, matures in advance of *N. tabacum*.

HISTORY

When Christopher Columbus discovered America, he found the natives using tobacco in much the same manner as it is used today. The American Indians believed it to possess medicinal properties, which was the main reason for its introduction in Europe. Tobacco was important in Indian ceremonials, such as the smoking of the pipe of peace. Evidently the natives of North and South America had developed crude methods of tobacco culture. Its extension to practically all parts of the world began with its introduction to Europe: France, 1556; Portugal, 1558; Spain, 1559; and England, 1565. Jean Nicot, the French ambassador to Lisbon, Portugal, in whose honour the genus *Nicotiana* was named, is said to have sent the seed of *N. tabacum* to Catherine de Médicis, the queen of France. Portuguese and Spanish sailors took tobacco from Europe to all parts of the world.

There are no available records as to early culture outside Europe, but the beginnings of culture by European settlers in colonial America took place in the following areas on the dates indicated: Santo Domingo, 1531; Cuba, 1580; Brazil, 1600; Jamestown, Virginia, 1612; Maryland, 1631. Tobacco soon became the chief commodity exchanged by the colonists for European manufactured articles.

Overproduction was an economic problem from the beginning. After the American Revolution tobacco culture expanded from the colonial areas in Virginia and Maryland into Kentucky, Tennessee, North Carolina, Ohio, and Missouri. Originally the tobacco was air cured—left to dry in a barn or shed for several weeks. Later smoke from a wood fire was used (fire curing). This enabled the leaf to withstand long ocean voyages by sailing ship. About 1825 the fire-curing method was modified in parts of Virginia and North Carolina by use of charcoal, which eliminated the effect of smoke on the taste and aroma of the leaf. The method was further modified after the American Civil War by the introduction of a furnace with metal flues.

A light, air-cured leaf known as White Burley appeared about 1864, when a farmer in Brown County, Ohio, found individual tobacco plants that were deficient in green colouring. These plants, when cured, manifested a light yellowish-red colour that was porous, extremely absorptive, and highly suitable for use in manufacturing mixtures for chewing and smoking. It has also been suitable for use in manufacturing the popular American blended cigarette.

White
Burley

THE MODERN INDUSTRY

Cultivation. The prime requisite for successful tobacco culture is a supply of well-developed, healthy seedlings at the proper time for transplanting. Orinoco strains of seed are sown to grow leaf for flue curing. The Pryor group are grown to produce the dark air-cured and fire-cured types. Burley and Maryland strains are seeded for the production of light, air-cured tobaccos. Broad-leaf and seed-leaf strains, Havana seed, Cuban, and Sumatra varieties are for the production of cigars. The variety grown for production of Perique resembles the Cuban-like variety used in Puerto Rico. Aromatic varieties are grown for production of this type of leaf and in some degree resemble the Cuban varieties.

Soil for a plant bed should be fertile, of good tilth and drainage, protected from chilling winds, and exposed to the sun. The soil is usually partially sterilized by burning, steaming, or using chemicals such as methyl bromide to control diseases, weeds, insects, and nematodes (a class of worms). In warm regions the small germinating seedlings are produced outdoors in cold frames covered with thin cotton cloth or a thin mulch, such as chopped grass in Rhodesia, straw, or pine needles. Glass or plastic is used in colder regions, and close attention is given to watering and ventilation. The usual rate of seeding—*i.e.*, 28 grams of cleaned seed of high germination to 200 square yards (167 square metres) of seed-bed area can be expected, under favourable conditions, to produce 15,000 to 25,000 plants for transplanting. High analysis mixtures of commercial fertilizers are usually applied before seeding at the rate of one-half to two pounds per square yard of seed-bed area. The soil must be finely pulverized and level so the seed can be lightly covered with soil by rolling or trampling. Uniform distribution of seeds is important. In eight to ten weeks the seedlings are four to seven inches in length and ready for transplanting in the field.

Seed-bed diseases, such as blue mold, anthracnose, bacterial leaf spots, damping off, and virus are controlled by sanitation and application of sprays. Insecticides may be applied simultaneously to control insects such as flea beetles.

Transplanting machines are used extensively (see Figure 1), but most of the world's tobacco is planted by hand. When the soil is dry, adding water helps a high percentage of transplants to survive. Fumigation of soil prior to transplanting is a common practice in many areas where nematodes are common, to reduce their damage.

Figure 2: Tobacco cultivated under artificial shading cloth to produce leaves suitable for cigar wrappers, Cuba.
Eastfoto

By courtesy of the U.S. Department of Agriculture

Figure 1: Two-row transplanter used to plant tobacco seedlings, Pennsylvania.

Soil and fertilizer requirements vary widely with the type of tobacco grown. Well-drained soil with a structure that assures good aeration is desirable. Flue-cured, Maryland, cigar binder, and wrapper types of tobacco are produced on sandy and sandy-loam soil, with a sandy and sandy-clay subsoil where local conditions permit. Burley, dark air-cured, fire-cured, cigar-filler, and cigar-binder types are grown on silt-loam and clay-loam soils, with clay subsoils. The type of tobacco, soil, and climate determine fertilizer requirements. If any of the chemical elements essential for growth are lacking, the tobacco plant develops nutritional deficiency symptoms. Though nitrogen, phosphoric acid, and potash may be applied in the shade cigar-wrapper area of Florida–Georgia, very little fertilizer is used on eastern European fields of aromatic tobacco, where rich soils can make the leaf grow too large and rank to be desirable commercially.

Soil must be prepared and cultivated to control weeds and promote the early and continuous growth of tobacco. For production of cigar-wrapper leaf, a unique method of culture is practiced in Cuba and the U.S., under artificial cheesecloth shade (see Figure 2). A high moisture content is maintained in soil and air to produce a thin, elastic leaf. In Sumatra and Java under the prevailing conditions of soil and climate, tobacco for cigar wrapper is produced for one or two years following the clearing of jungle growth. Climatic and soil conditions characterized by a moist atmosphere appear to be associated with the production of acceptable cigar-wrapper tobacco. Cuban leaf for cigar filler is produced on certain soils from special varieties in the prevailing climatic conditions.

Cigar-wrapper leaf

Aromatic tobacco culture in Turkey, Greece, Bulgaria, Yugoslavia, and other areas differs from that of most of the large-leafed tobaccos in that the plants are rarely topped and preferably are grown on soils of low productivity. The most acceptable aromatic leaf is produced in the Mediterranean climate, maturing during dry periods on upland soils.

Spacing of plants in the field varies widely according to the type of tobacco. Flue-cured tobacco rows are 4 feet (1.2 m) apart with plants 20 to 24 inches (50 to 60 cm) apart in the row. Burley and cigar tobaccos are 3 to 3½ feet by 15 to 27 inches. Dark air-cured and fire-cured tobaccos may be planted on the square with hills 3½ feet apart. Maryland may be planted 36 to 32 inches or closer. Aromatic tobaccos are spaced in rows 15 to 24 inches apart with 3 to 8 inches between plants in the row. Perique is spaced the widest with rows 5 feet apart and 36 to 42 inches between plants.

Large-leaf tobaccos grown in the United States and in several other countries are topped—that is, the terminal growth is removed—when the plant has reached the desired size, usually at or shortly after flowering. The number of leaves remaining varies widely. Dark air-cured and fire-cured tobaccos may have 10 to 16 leaves; Burley, flue-cured, Maryland, and cigar types may have 16 to 20 leaves. After topping, the suckers, or lateral shoots are removed to increase leaf development, providing increased yields. The work may be done by hand, in which case it must be repeated regularly, or by application of sucker-suppressing chemicals.

Diseases and pests. Common diseases are black-root rot, fusarium wilt, tobacco-mosaic, bacterial-leaf spot, downy mildew or blue mold, black shank, broomrape, and witch weed. These may be controlled by sanitation, crop rotation, the use of sprays and fumigants, and breeding of disease-resistant strains. Resistance to bacterial-leaf spot, fusarium wilt, mosaic, black shank, and black-root rot have been accomplished by breeding. Some resistant varieties of tobacco in general use have been produced by blending desired characteristics from *N. longiflora, N. debneyi, N. glutinosa,* and others with some strain of *N. tabacum.*

Common insect pests are the green June beetle larvae, cutworms, and flea beetles in the plant bed; hornworms, grasshoppers, flea beetles, cutworms, budworms, and aphids in the field. The cigarette, or tobacco, beetle damages the stored leaf and sometimes the manufactured product. Insect pests are controlled on the growing crop by using sprays and dusts, on the stored product by fumigating and trapping. Biological control often is effective. Fumigation controls nematodes in the field.

Harvest. Tobacco is harvested 70 to 130 days after transplanting by one of two methods: (1) the entire plant is cut and the stalk split or speared and hung on a tobacco stick or lath, or (2) the leaves are removed at intervals as they mature. The leaves of cigar-wrapper and aromatic tobaccos are strung using a needle, and leaves to be flue-cured are looped, using a string tied to a lath or stick that is hung in the curing barn. To prevent breakage and bruising during the handling necessary in curing, it is desirable for the leaf to wilt without sunburning. Tobacco may be left in the field from a few hours to two days to wilt.

Curing.   The three common methods of curing are by air, fire, and flue. A fourth method, sun curing, is practiced with aromatic types and to a limited extent with air-cured types. Curing entails four essential steps: wilting, yellowing, colouring, and drying. These involve physical and chemical changes in the leaf and are regulated to develop the desired properties. Air curing (see Figure 3)

By courtesy of the U.S. Department of Agriculture

Figure 3: Hanging Maryland tobacco, cured on the stalk, in a curing barn.

is accomplished mainly by mechanical ventilation inside buildings. Coke, charcoal, or liquid petroleum gas may be burned to provide heat when conditions warrant. Air curing, which requires from one to two months' time, is used for many tobaccos, including dark air-cured types, cigar, Maryland, and Burley.

The fire-curing process resembles air-curing except that open wood fires are kindled on the dirt floor of the curing barn after the tobacco has been hanging for two to six days. The smoke imparts a characteristic creosote aroma. The firing process may be continuous or intermittent, extending from three weeks to as long as ten weeks until curing is complete and the leaf has the desired finish.

The barns for flue curing are small and tightly constructed with ventilators and metal pipes, or flues, extending from furnaces around or under the floor of the barn. Fuels used are wood, coal, oil, and liquid petroleum gas. If oil or gas heaters are used, flues are not needed. Heat is applied carefully with attention to the chemical and physical changes in the leaf. Flue-curing requires from four to eight days' time and is used for Virginia, or bright, tobacco. In bulk curing, the leaves are loaded evenly in racks in a curing chamber.

Grading and marketing.   After curing, the leaf may be piled in bulk to condition for a time before it is prepared for sale. The preparation consists usually of grading the

Air curing, fire curing, and flue curing

leaf and putting it in a bale or package of convenient size and weight for inspection and removal by the buyer. Except during humid periods, the leaf must be conditioned in moistening cellars or humidified rooms before it can be handled without breakage. Type of leaf and local custom determine the fineness of grading. At its most elaborate, grading may be by position of the leaf on the plant, colour, size, maturity, soundness, and other recognizable qualities; flue-cured tobacco in the United States and Rhodesia is graded this way, and each grade bulked or baled separately. Much simpler grading is usual in developing countries, where the buyer is as much concerned with the proportions of each grade as he is with the quality of the entire lot; aromatic tobaccos are an example of this. Most tobaccos entering world trade, except the aromatic, are assembled before sale into bundles or hands of 15 to 30 leaves and tied with one leaf wrapped securely around the butts.

Most United States, Canadian, Central African, and Australian tobacco is sold by farmers at auction warehouses. Buyers visiting farms or local villages purchase other tobaccos by private treaty. The purchase of entire crops under preplanting contracts is less common than bale or package buying. Much of the world's tobacco is sold noncompetitively by farmers in countries where a state monopoly is the sole purchaser. Indonesian and Cameroon cigar leaf is bought from farmers by private treaty, by middlemen who resell overseas, in Bremen and Paris, to the ultimate manufacturers.

Most tobaccos, except aromatic and cigar, are regraded if necessary and usually redried after purchase; then the exact amount of moisture needed for aging is added and the tobacco is securely packed in cases or hogsheads. Exported tobacco is shipped in this form. The trend is for the packing factories to stem the leaf—that is, remove most of the stem leaving the lamina—usually by threshing machines but sometimes by hand, before redrying it. The aging process, particularly with cigar tobaccos, is sometimes hastened by forced fermentation procedures. After purchase, aromatic tobaccos are manipulated; that is, they are factory-graded, baled, and subjected to an elaborate, in-the-bale, fermentation process before going to the ultimate manufacturer.

Manufacture of products.   If leaf tobacco is not bought in ready-stemmed form, the first step in turning it into a product that the consumer can smoke, chew, or take as snuff is to remove midribs (central veins). For most products, manufacturers blend leaf of various types, origins, grades, and crop years to obtain the qualities they require and assure uniformity over the years. Cigarette manufacturers usually add sweetening preparations and flavourings, and process the tobacco in a variety of secret ways before it is fed, as finely shredded rag, into the cigarette-making machines. Preparation of tobaccos for pipe smoking and chewing is as varied as the assortment of these products. Their manufacture may involve the incorporation of additives and the application of pressure and heat. Snuff is usually made by fermenting fire-cured leaf and stem, and grinding it; salts and flavourings may be added. Cigars are made by wrapping a binder leaf around a bunch of cut filler leaf and overwrapping with a fine wrapper leaf; on all but the finest cigars the work is largely mechanized.

In the United States and increasingly elsewhere, stems and scrap are used for nicotine extractions or are ground down and made into reconstituted sheet in a process akin to papermaking. The sheet may be used as a substitute cigar binder or, more rarely, as wrapper, or it may be finely cut and used to supplement natural tobacco in cigarettes.

Production control.   In an effort to correct overproduction problems, controls of various kinds have been instituted in several countries, notably the U.S., Turkey, Rhodesia, Canada, and Japan.

WORLD PRODUCTION AND CONSUMPTION

About 80 countries produce tobacco. The total production fluctuates from year to year partly because of weather and growing conditions, partly because of world demand, between about 9,000,000,000 and 10,000,000,000 pounds. The yearly production of the United States for 1960–

64 averaged 2,178,400,000 pounds; in 1967 it was 1,967,-911,000 pounds; in 1968, 1,715,573,000 pounds; and in 1970, an estimated 1,906,000,000 pounds.

The preferential duty extended by the British Government to tobacco produced in Commonwealth countries greatly stimulated production in Canada, Rhodesia, and other countries under British influence. Rhodesia shows a decline in production, possibly due to Commonwealth sanctions.

Most tobacco is consumed in the countries where it is produced. During the years 1960–64, the principal countries that exported 1,685,340,000 pounds also imported 1,536,742,000 pounds. Cigarette tobaccos, such as the flue-cured and aromatic types, are increasingly in demand in world-trade channels, as are cigar tobaccos.

A high and rising proportion of all the world's tobacco is consumed in cigarette form. Cigarettes comprise almost all tobacco consumed in Mexico and Brazil; seven-eighths in Great Britain and Italy; three-quarters or more in the U.S., France, Canada, and Argentina. Even such traditionally cigar-smoking countries as Denmark and The Netherlands take half their tobacco as cigarettes and only about a quarter as cigars.

Tobacco consumption has risen faster in the developing countries than in the advanced ones. In the advanced countries consumption fell off with the publication of reports connecting smoking with cancer but quickly recovered. The ultimate effect is not yet clear. India and parts of Africa consume only about two pounds (0.9 kilograms) per adult per year, or in terms of cigarettes, about 910. The comparable figure in Great Britain is 6½ lbs (3 kg). In the U.S. 10½ lbs (4.8 kg) were consumed per adult in 1968, which was down from 12 lbs in 1962. In Switzerland 12 lbs (5.4 kg) of tobacco were consumed per adult.

ECONOMIC AND SOCIAL ASPECTS

Revenue. Tobacco has long been a source of revenue in many countries of the world. This revenue is derived from taxes on the stored leaf and on the manufactured products as in the U.S., from duties on imports as in the U.K., or from profits from the operation of government monopolies that have been in effect in many European countries, Japan, and elsewhere. In many countries the income of the governments in tax revenue collected on manufactured tobacco products, particularly cigarettes, exceeds the sale value received by farmers for the crop. In the U.S., in addition to the revenue collected by the federal and state governments, a number of cities exact a tax on tobacco products.

Tobacco and health hazards. The contention that smoking is a health hazard is almost as old as the use of tobacco. In 1604 King James I of England issued the first official condemnation of tobacco, "A Counterblaste to Tobacco." One of the first published reports on the subject, issued in 1859, showed that of 68 patients in a hospital at Montpellier, France, who had cancer of the lips, tongue, tonsils, or other parts of the mouth, all used tobacco and 66 of them smoked short-stemmed clay pipes. This type of pipe fell from favour following the release of the report.

Interest in the relationship between tobacco and health waned until cigarette smoking became widespread following World Wars I and II, when health authorities reported that in countries in which cigarette smoking was popular, deaths from lung cancer and certain other diseases were climbing at an alarming rate.

In 1954 the American Cancer Society and the British Medical Research Council reported independently, following separate three-year statistical studies, that death rates were higher for cigarette smokers than for nonsmokers. In 1962 the Royal College of Physicians of London summarized the evidence on the disease-tobacco relationship and called cigarette smoking a serious hazard to health. The British government then inaugurated a program of public education aimed at reducing the use of tobacco. In 1963 a second American Cancer Society report cited evidence showing that the death rate for cigarette smokers increases as the amount of smoking in-

creases. Despite the unfavourable medical reports and adverse publicity given to smoking, the per capita consumption of cigarettes in the U.S. in 1970 was 4,000, only slightly down from 4,258 in 1965. In January 1964 a special advisory committee appointed by the United States Surgeon General ended a two-year study by reporting that cigarette smoking was associated with the 70% increase in the lung cancer death rate for American males in 1950–60. The committee described cigarette smoking as a health hazard and urged controls. The report found that cigarette smoking was associated with lung cancer, coronary artery disease, chronic bronchitis, and emphysema. Pipe smoking, the report added, is linked with lip cancer. In 1965 Federal legislation was passed requiring that all cigarette packages sold after January 1, 1966, carry health hazard warning labels. Cigarette advertising on television was banned beginning January 1, 1971, while the American Cancer Society and Heart Association used television to mount an intensive campaign against smoking.

To gather additional information on the association between health and smoking, the U.S. Department of Health, Education and Welfare in 1964 began awarding funds for research. In the same year, six tobacco companies gave the American Medical Association $10,000,000 for research. These studies are continuing on an expanded basis. Meantime the tobacco industry has been manufacturing filter and extra-length cigarettes in an attempt to lessen the health hazard of cigarette smoking.

BIBLIOGRAPHY

History: J.E. BROOKS, *The Mighty Leaf: Tobacco Through the Centuries* (1952); J.C. ROBERT, *The Story of Tobacco in America* (1949); B.C. AKEHURST, *Tobacco* (1968); R.K. HEIMANN, *Tobacco and Americans* (1960); H.I. HITIER and L. SABOURIN, *Le Tabac*, 3rd rev. ed. (1965); W.A. PENN, *The Soverane Herbe: A History of Tobacco* (1901); N.M. TILLEY, *The Bright-Tobacco Industry, 1860–1929* (1948). An early denunciation of the use of tobacco was presented by JAMES I, KING OF ENGLAND, in *A Counterblaste to Tobacco* (1604); a contemporary evaluation is given in *Smoking and Health,* Report of the Advisory Committee to the Surgeon General of Public Health Service (1964).

Culture, production, and marketing: C.E. GAGE, "American Tobacco Types, Uses and Markets," *Circ. U.S. Dep. Agric. 249* (1942); W.W. GARNER, *The Production of Tobacco,* rev. ed. (1951); P. GISQUET and H.I. HITIER, *La production du tabac: principes et méthodes* (1961); J.B. HUTSON, "Consumption and Production of Tobacco in Europe," *Tech. Bull. U.S. Dep. Agric. 587* (1937); J.E. MCMURTREY, JR., "Tobacco Production," *Agric. Inform. Bull. 245* (1961); C.A. WERNER, *A Textbook on Tobacco: An Exhaustive Technical Treatise on the Culture, the Manufacture and the Merchandising of Tobacco and Tobacco Products,* 4th ed. (1914); A. PROVOST, *Technique du Tabac* (1959); J.B. KILLIBREW and H. MYRICK, *Tobacco Leaf: Its Culture, Cure, Marketing, and Manufacture* (1897).

Diseases: G.B. LUCAS, *Diseases of Tobacco,* 2nd ed. (1965); E.E. CLAYTON and J.E. MCMURTREY, JR., "Tobacco Diseases and Their Control," *Fmrs. Bull. U.S. Dep. Agric. 2023* (1950); J.E. MCMURTREY, JR., "Nutrient Deficiencies in Tobacco," in H.B. SPRAGUE (ed.), *Hunger Signs in Crops,* pp. 99–141 (1964); F.A. WOLF, *Tobacco Diseases and Decays,* 2nd ed. rev. (1957).

Statistics: U.S. DEPARTMENT OF AGRICULTURE, *Agricultural Statistics* (annual), *The Tobacco Situation* (1954), and *Estimated World Production of Leaf Tobacco* (1954).

(J.E.McM.)

Tocharian Language

Tocharian (Tokharian), also called Tocharish, is an Indo-European language that was spoken in northern Chinese Turkistan (Tarim Basin) during the latter half of the 1st millennium AD. Documents from about AD 500–700 attest to two dialects: Tocharian A, from the area of Turfan in the east; and Tocharian B, chiefly from the region of Kucha in the west but also from the Turfan area.

Discovery and decipherment. The first Tocharian manuscripts were discovered in the 1890s. The bulk of the Tocharian materials were carried to Berlin by the Prussian expeditions of 1903–04 and 1906–07, which explored

Government warnings

the Turfan area, and to Paris by a French expedition of 1906–09, which investigated chiefly in the area of Kucha. Smaller collections are in London, Leningrad, and Japan.

Tocharian is written with a north Indian syllabary (a set of characters representing syllables) known as Brāhmī, which was also used in writing Sanskrit manuscripts from

Translation and analysis

the same area. The first successful attempt at grammatical analysis and translation was made by the German scholars Emil Sieg and Wilhelm Siegling in 1908 in an article that also established the presence of the two dialects, provisionally called A and B. The Berlin collection consisted of both dialects, whereas all other manuscripts discovered were in B.

The German name Tocharisch was proposed, and the language was demonstrated to be Indo-European.

Characteristics. Tocharian forms an independent branch of the Indo-European language family not closely related to other neighbouring Indo-European languages (Indo-Aryan and Iranian). Rather, Tocharian shows a closer affinity with the western (*centum*) languages: compare, for example, Tocharian A *känt*, B *kante, känte* "100," and Latin *centum* with Sanskrit *śatám*; A *klyos-*, B *klyaus-* "hear," and Latin *clueo* with Sanskrit *śru-*; A *kus*, B *kuse* "who," and Latin *qui, quod* with Sanskrit *kas*. In phonology, Tocharian differs greatly from the other Indo-European languages in that all of the Indo-European stops of each series fall together, resulting in a system of three (voiceless) stops, *p, t,* and *k*.

The Tocharian verb reflects the Indo-European verbal system both in stem formations and in personal endings. Especially noteworthy is the wide development of the mediopassive form in *r* (as in Italic and Celtic); *e.g.,* Tocharian A *klyoṣtär* "is heard." The 3rd person preterit plural ends in *-r*, similar to Latin and Sanskrit perfect forms and the Hittite preterit. The noun, however, shows little trace of the original Indo-European inflection. Instead, it is built up by the addition of postpositions to the oblique (accusative) form. This type of inflection (agglutination) has been attributed to the influence of non-Indo-European languages (Turkish, Finno-Ugric).

The vocabulary shows a remarkable influx of loanwords —from Turkish, Iranian, and, later, Sanskrit. Chinese has had little influence. Many of the most archaic elements of the Indo-European vocabulary are retained—*e.g.,* A *por*, B *puwar* "fire" (Greek *pyr*, Hittite *paḫḫur*); A and B *ku* "dog" (Greek *kyōn*); A *tkaṃ*, B *keṃ* "earth" (Greek *chthōn*, Hittite *tekan*), and especially, nouns of relationship: A *pācar, mācar, pracar, ckācar,* B *pācer, mācer, procer, tkācer,* "father," "mother," "brother," and "daughter," respectively.

Literature. Tocharian literature is Buddhistic in content, consisting largely of translations or free adaptations of Jātakas, of Avadānas, and of philosophical, didactic, and canonical works. In dialect B there are also commercial documents, such as monastery records, caravan passes, medical and magical texts, and the like. These are important source materials for the social, economic, and political life of central Asia.

The "Tocharian problem." Since the appearance of Sieg and Siegling's article, the appropriateness of the name Tocharian for the language has been disputed. According to Greek and Latin historical sources, the Tochari (Greek Tócharoi, Latin Tochari) inhabited the basin of the upper Oxus River (modern Amu Darya) in the 2nd century BC and were probably Iranians. Sieg and Siegling's identification of this language as belonging to these people was probably in error.

Identification of the Tocharian-speaking people

There have, of course, been numerous attempts to identify the speakers of Tocharian with this or that people or tribe mentioned in Chinese annals or in other documents dealing with the area in and around the Tarim Basin during the last half of the 1st millennium AD. One such identification that gained some adherents was with the Wu-sun. Neither this nor any other identification, however, would appear to be more than mere speculation.

Furthermore, the name *ārśi* (*ārśiype* "Arśi-country," *ārśikäntu* "Arśi-language"), once accepted as the native name in dialect A, is probably a loanword through Irani-

an from Sanskrit *ārya*. The question of the name is, however, of little linguistic importance. Tocharian, even if generally accepted as a misnomer, will probably remain. For dialect A and dialect B, the substitution of Turfanian and Kuchean, or of East Tocharian and West Tocharian, has been suggested.

Of greater importance, at least from the linguistic point of view, is the relationship of the Tocharian language to the other Indo-European languages and the interrelationship of the two dialects themselves. In the former regard, in spite of superficial resemblances to Italic and Celtic (see above), the more fundamental shared features —*e.g.,* common vocabulary, certain verbal categories (*s*-aorists, preservation of the perfect active participle), and possible relics of common phonological developments— would appear to align Tocharian with the more southeastern branches of Indo-European; that is, with Thracian and Phrygian or even with Greek and Armenian. Those features shared with the Baltic and Slavic languages (certain present and preterit formations in particular) might be the result of later contacts.

With regard to the interrelationship of the two dialects, it is possible that dialect A was, at the time of documentation, a dead liturgical language preserved in the Buddhist monasteries in the east, whereas dialect B was a living language in the west (note that commercial or at least nonliturgical documents are found in that dialect). The presence of manuscripts in B mixed with those in A in the monasteries of the east can be accounted for by ascribing the B manuscripts to a new missionary invasion of those monasteries by Buddhist monks from the west.

BIBLIOGRAPHY. E. SIEG and W. SIEGLING (eds.), *Tocharische Sprachreste* (1921), gives the transcription of all the manuscripts in dialect A. A small companion volume, *Tafeln*, reproduces a number of the best preserved leaves in facsimile. E. SIEG, W. SIEGLING, and W. SCHULZE, *Tocharische Grammatik* (1931), is an exhaustive grammar of dialect A, with a verbal index identifying and listing all verb forms in that dialect. H. PEDERSEN, *Tocharisch vom Gesichtspunkt der indoeuropäischen Sprachvergleichung* (1941), is still the best overall comparative study from the Indo-European point of view, even though extensive published materials in dialect B were not available. E. SIEG and W. SIEGLING, *Tocharische Sprachreste, Sprache B*, 2 pt. (1949–53), contain all the Berlin manuscripts in dialect B plus a few from other collections (especially the Hoernle collection in London). Part 1 is an edition of the Udānālaṅkāra fragments with translation and glossary. W. KRAUSE, *Westtocharische Grammatik*, vol. 1, *Das Verbum* (1952), is indispensable for the verb in dialect B (a second volume was never published). W. KRAUSE and W. THOMAS, *Tocharisches Elementarbuch*, vol. 1, *Grammatik* (1960), vol. 2, *Texte und Glossar* (1964), including both dialects, now replace all earlier introductions to the study of Tocharian. Two articles by G.S. LANE, "On the Interrelationship of the Tocharian Dialects," in H. BIRNBAUM and J. PUHVEL (eds.), *Ancient Indo-European Dialects* (1966); and "Tocharian: Indo-European and Non-Indo-European Relationships," in G. CARDONA, H.M. HOENIGSWALD, and A. SENN (eds.), *Indo-European and Indo-Europeans* (1970), attempt to solve some of the problems concerning the varied uses of the two dialects and the general problem of the position of Tocharian within the Indo-European family of languages.

(G.S.L.)

Tocqueville, Alexis de

The French political scientist, historian, and politician Alexis de Tocqueville remains today best known as the author of the classic *De la démocratie en Amérique* (*Democracy in America*), an acute description and often prophetic analysis of the American political system in the early part of the 19th century.

Alexis-Charles-Henri Clérel de Tocqueville was born in Paris on July 29, 1805, of an old Norman family. He was a great-grandson of the statesman Chrétien de Malesherbes, a liberal aristocratic victim of the French Revolution and a political model for the young Tocqueville. Almost diminutive in stature, acutely sensitive, and plagued by severe bouts of anxiety since childhood, he remained close to his parents throughout his life. Outwardly proud and cold among strangers, Tocqueville was yet able to form deep and lasting friend-

Tocqueville, oil painting by T. Chassériau
(1819–56). In the Musée de Versailles.
H. Roger-Viollet

application en France (1833; Eng. trans., On the Penitentiary System in the United States and Its Application in France, 1833); Beaumont's Marie, ou l'esclavage aux États-Unis (1835; Eng. trans., Marie, or Slavery in the United States, 1958), on America's race problems; and the first part of Tocqueville's De la démocratie 1835–40; Eng. trans., Democracy in America, 1835–40). On the basis of observations, readings, and discussions with a host of eminent Americans, Tocqueville attempted to penetrate directly to the essentials of American society and to highlight that aspect—equality of conditions—that was most relevant to his own philosophy. Tocqueville's study analyzed the vitality, the excesses, and the potential future of American democracy. Above all, the work was infused with his message that a society, properly organized, could hope to retain liberty in a democratic social order.

The first part of De la démocratie won an immediate reputation for its author as a political scientist. This period probably was the happiest and most optimistic of his life. Hailed as the Montesquieu (the famous 18th-century philosopher) of the century, within the next few years Tocqueville was named to the Legion of Honor, the Academy of Moral and Political Sciences (1838), and finally the French Academy (1841). With the prizes and royalties from the book, he was even able to rebuild his ancestral chateau in Normandy. Within a few years his book had been published in England, Belgium, Germany, Spain, Hungary, Denmark, and Sweden. In America, while it was sometimes viewed as having been derived from politically biased sources, it was newly accorded the status of a classic. But the greatest immediate honour came from across the English Channel. In England, which he had visited as an unknown in 1833, he was welcomed, after his book was published, in the highest political and intellectual circles when he returned in 1835. He established lifelong friendships there and found the political atmosphere so congenial that England became intellectually his second home. The tie was to be reinforced by his marriage in 1836 to Mary Mottely, an Englishwoman. The English journey also awakened his interest in the problems of industrialization, and his first essay on the old regime in France was written as a result of his conversations with the philosopher and radical reformer John Stuart Mill.

Returning to France, Tocqueville spent four more years on the final portion of De la démocratie, which was published in 1840. Its composition took far longer, moved farther afield, and ended far more soberly than Tocqueville had originally intended. American society slid into the background, while Tocqueville now attempted to complete a picture of the influence of equality itself on all aspects of modern society. France increasingly became his principal example, and what he saw there altered the tone of his work. He observed the curtailment of liberties by the Liberals who had come to power in 1830 as well as the growth of state intervention in economic development. Most depressing to him was the increased political apathy and acquiescence of his fellow citizens in this rising paternalism. His chapters on democratic individualism and centralization in De la démocratie contained a new warning based on these observations. A mild, stagnant despotism now seemed to him democracy's greatest danger.

This was also the period in which Tocqueville fulfilled his lifelong ambition to enter politics. He lost his first bid for the Chamber of Deputies in 1837, due largely to his fear of compromising his independence by accepting government support or by running an undignified campaign to woo his rural bourgeois electors. He soon broke down suspicion caused by his aloofness and aristocratic background and won the following election in 1839. Eventually, Tocqueville built up an enormous personal influence in his constituency. He won every election after the first by more than 70 percent of the vote and became president of his departmental council (a local representative body). Characteristically, at the level of local politics his quest for pre-eminence was completely fulfilled. But his need for uncompromised dignity and independence deprived him of influence in the Chamber for a much longer time.

Politics

ships. He was most comfortable in small, informal groups, where he was listened to with respect. This ability to influence those closest to him led him to project his own experience on to the social framework and to envision local government and small-scale association as the best form of political organization.

Given the choice of a variety of careers, it is not surprising that Tocqueville chose the one most congenial to him: that of politician. Despite a frail voice in a fragile body, distaste for the daily demands of parliamentary existence, and long periods of illness and nervous exhaustion, he adhered to his original choice until he was driven from office. His decision in favour of a public career was made with some assurance of success. His father was a loyal royalist prefect and in 1827 was made a peer of France by Charles X, who had earlier called him to Versailles. At that time, young Tocqueville moved easily into government service as an apprentice magistrate. There he prepared himself for political life while observing the impending constitutional confrontation between the Conservatives and the Liberals with growing sympathy for the latter. He was strongly influenced by the lectures of the historian and statesman François Guizot, who asserted that the decline of aristocratic privilege was historically inevitable. And finally, after the manner of Liberals under the autocratic regime of the restored Bourbon kings, Tocqueville began to study English history as a model of political development.

Government service

He entered public life in the company of a close friend who was to become his alter ego—Gustave de Beaumont. Their life histories are virtual mirror images. Of similar backgrounds and positions, they were companions in their travels in America, England, and Algeria; coordinated their writings; and ultimately entered the legislature together.

The July Revolution of 1830 that put the "citizen king" Louis-Philippe of Orléans on the throne was a turning point for Tocqueville. It deepened his conviction that France was moving rapidly toward complete social equality. Breaking with the older liberal generation, he no longer compared France with the English constitutional monarchy but with democratic America. Of more personal concern, despite his oath of loyalty to the new monarch, his position had become precarious because of his family ties with the ousted Bourbon king. He and Beaumont, seeking to escape from their uncomfortable political situation, asked for and received official permission to study the uncontroversial problem of prison reforms in America. They also hoped to return with knowledge of a society that would mark them as especially fit to help mold France's political future.

America and democracy

The two men spent nine months in the United States during 1831 and 1832, out of which came first their joint book, Du système pénitentiaire aux États-Unis et de son

A good committee reporter on large nonpartisan issues—prison reform, slavery, colonial policy—he could not adapt himself to the give and take of perpetual bargaining and coalitions with those whom he regarded as mediocre or untrustworthy politicians. He was neither able to follow the leadership of others nor did his oratorical style win him quick recognition as a leader himself. As a result, he had no major legislative accomplishment to his credit during the reign of Louis Philippe. His speech prophesying revolution only a few weeks before it took place in February 1848 fell on deaf ears. The biting sketches of friend, foe, and even himself in his *Souvenirs* (1893; "Recollections"), reflect his feeling of the general mediocrity of political leadership before and after 1848.

February Revolution of 1848

The February Revolution brought about a new political situation for France and for Tocqueville. Having for years decried apathy as the chief danger for France, Tocqueville recognized even before the Revolution that France was faced with a politically awakened working class that might well propel French politics into socialist and revolutionary channels. Tocqueville considered economic independence as necessary to the preservation of his own intellectual independence. He thus viewed pressures of the dependent poor for state welfare, and of the unemployed for state employment, as the initial steps to a universal and degrading dependence on the state by all social classes. Unsympathetic to revolutionaries and contemptuous of socialists before the Revolution, Tocqueville opposed the demands of the Parisian workers during the June days of 1848, when their uprising was bloodily suppressed by the military dictator General Louis Cavaignac, as well as in the debates over the constitution of 1848. The only intellectual change produced in Tocqueville by the events of 1848 was a recognition of the strength of socialist ideas and of the problematic nature of the proprietary society. But while he had sought to reconcile the aristocracy to liberal democracy in *De la démocratie*, he rejected social democracy as it emerged in 1848 as incompatible with liberal democracy.

Politically, Tocqueville's own position was dramatically improved by the February Revolution. His electorate expanded from 700 to 160,000 under universal manhood suffrage. He was elected as a conservative Republican to the Constituent Assembly by 79 percent of the voters and again in 1849 by more than 87 percent. Along with Beaumont, he was nominated to the committee that wrote the constitution of the Second Republic, and the following year he became vice president of the Assembly. He served as minister of foreign affairs between June and October of 1849. During his short tenure he worked cautiously to preserve the balance of power in Europe and to prevent France from extending its foreign involvements. His speeches were more successful and his self-confidence soared, but the results gave him little more durable satisfaction than those he had attained during the July Monarchy under Louis Philippe.

In June 1849 a government crisis produced by French armed intervention to restore papal authority in Rome was the occasion for Tocqueville's brief appointment to the Ministry of Foreign Affairs. Shortly after his dismissal from the ministry by President Louis-Napoleon in October 1849 he suffered a physical collapse. After a slow recovery he performed a final service for the Second French Republic. As reporter for the constitutional revision committee he attempted to avert the final confrontation between the President and the legislature, which ended with an executive seizure of dictatorial power. Briefly imprisoned

Coup of 1851

for opposing Louis Napoleon's coup d'etat on Dec. 2, 1851, Tocqueville was deprived of all political offices for refusing his oath to the new regime. He was thrown back on a small circle of political allies and friends and felt a deeper sense of isolation and political pessimism than ever before.

Seeking to re-enter politics, he reverted to the strategy of his youthful success—the publication of a book on the fundamental themes of liberty and equality. This time he chose as his subject the French Revolution. *L'Ancien Régime et la Révolution* (*The Old Regime and the Revolution*) appeared in 1856, after years of research and intermittent illness, as the first part of his project study. In this work, Tocqueville sought to demonstrate the continuity of political behaviour and attitudes that made postrevolutionary French society as prepared to accept despotism as that of the old regime. In this final study the traumatic events of the years 1848–51 were clearly the source of his emphasis on the durability of centralization and class hostility in French history. France seemed less the democratic society of the future he had glimpsed in America than the prisoner of its own past. Against the pessimism of his analysis of French political tendencies, *L'Ancien Régime* reaffirmed the libertarian example of the Anglo-American world. The acclaim that greeted this study briefly dispelled the gloom of his last years. Once again his book made him a public figure. His visit to England in 1857, culminating in an audience with the prince-consort, was the last public triumph of his life. He returned to his work; but before he could finish his study of the Revolution, he collapsed and died at Cannes on April 16, 1859.

Tocqueville's reputation in the 19th century reached its high point during the decade following his death, as the great European powers accommodated themselves to universal suffrage. He died just at the onset of a revival of liberalism in France. The nine-volume publication of his works, edited by Beaumont (1860–1866), was received as the legacy of a martyr of liberty. In England his name was invoked during the franchise reform debates of the 1860s, and in Germany it was linked to controversies over liberalization and federalization in the years preceding the empire devised by Bismarck. After 1870 his influence began to decline, a process not substantially reversed either by the posthumous publication of his *Souvenirs* in 1893 or that of his correspondence with his friend, the diplomatist and philosopher Arthur de Gobineau. By the turn of the century he was almost forgotten, and his works were generally regarded as outdated classics. They seemed too abstract and speculative for a generation that believed only in ascertained knowledge. Moreover, Tocqueville's prediction of democracy as a vast and uniformly levelling power seemed to have miscarried by not foreseeing both the extent of the new inequalities and conflicts produced by industrialization and those produced by European nationalisms and imperialism. The classless society had failed to appear in Europe and even America seemed to have become European by becoming nationalist and imperialist rather than vice versa. In France, Tocqueville's name was too closely identified with a narrowly defined Liberal tradition, which rapidly lost influence during the Third Republic. While his work as an innovative historian was acknowledged, it is significant that the revival of his ideas and reputation as a political sociologist owes so much to American, English, and German scholarship.

Reputation

The 20th-century totalitarian challenge to the survival of liberal institutions produced by two world wars and by the Great Depression of the 1930s fostered a "Tocqueville renaissance." The outdated facts of his books seemed less significant than the political philosophy implicit in his search to preserve liberty in public life and his strategies for analyzing latent social tendencies. His work was found to display a wealth of fruitful philosophical and sociological hypotheses. At a popular level, the renewed upsurge of social democracy of Europe after 1945 also combined with the polarization of the Cold War to the view of Tocqueville in the West as an alternative to Marx as a prophet of social change. Again, as in the late 1850s and 1860s, Tocqueville rose to heights of great popularity. Whether changes in social and intellectual climate will cause another levelling off only time will tell. It seems certain, however, that henceforth Tocqueville will continue to be invoked as an authority and inspiration by those sharing his contempt of static authoritarian societies as well as his belief in the final disappearance of class divisions and in liberty as the ultimate political value.

BIBLIOGRAPHY. Tocqueville's major works have all been published in the new *Oeuvres complètes*, ed. by J.P. MAYER (1951–   ): vol. 1, *De la démocratie en Amérique*; vol. 2,

L'Ancien Régime et la révolution; and vol. 12, the *Souvenirs*. Recent English translations of these works are: *Democracy in America*, 2 vol., ed. by P. BRADLEY (1945), another one volume edition of the same work, ed. by J.P. MAYER and M. LERNER (1966); *The Old Regime and the French Revolution*, trans. by S. GILBERT (1955); and *The Recollections of Alexis de Tocqueville*, ed. by J.P. MAYER and A.P. KERR (1970). A new English edition of *Du système pénitentiaire aux États-Unis, et de son application en France* (1833; *On the Penitentiary System in the United States and Its Application in France*), was published in 1964.

There are three 20th century biographies of Tocqueville: R.P. MARCEL, *Essai politique sur Alexis de Tocqueville* (1910); A. REDIER, *Comme disait M. de Tocqueville . . .* (1925); and J.P. MAYER, *Alexis de Tocqueville: A Biographical Essay in Political Science*, rev. ed. (1960). G.W. PIERSON, *Tocqueville and Beaumont in America* (1938), marked the beginning of a generation of intense Tocqueville scholarship. There is nothing approaching a definitive biography, nor is one likely to appear until work on the new publication of his *Oeuvres* reaches the volumes on Tocqueville's private and political correspondence. For the author's correspondence with Gobineau, see *The European Revolution and Correspondence with Gobineau*, ed. and trans. by J. LUKACS (1959). With the exception of his early years, however, and the more intricate details of his personal and political life, the important episodes of his life and the periods of his creative writings have been carefully analyzed. The best study of his private life remains that of Redier, despite its avowed antiliberal and antidemocratic bias. E.T. GARGAN, *De Tocqueville* (1965), also contains an analysis of his formative studies before 1830. Tocqueville's special relationship with Beaumont is studied in Pierson, in great detail for the earlier period; and in S. DRESCHER (ed.), *Tocqueville and Beaumont on Social Reform* (1968). See also their correspondence, ed. by A. JARDIN in vol. 8 of the new edition of Tocqueville's *Oeuvres* (1968). Pierson thoroughly covers Tocqueville's journey through the United States leading to the publication of *De la démocratie*. The influence of his English visits is dealt with in S. DRESCHER, *Tocqueville and England* (1964). Tocqueville's own travel notes are ed. by J.P. MAYER and A. JARDIN as vol. 6 of Tocqueville's *Oeuvres*. They are translated as *Journey to America* (1960), and *Journeys to England and Ireland* (1958). On Tocqueville's early political career see Marcel (cited above); M. LAWLOR, *Alexis de Tocqueville in the Chamber of Deputies* (1959); and various essays in *Alexis de Tocqueville: livre du centenaire, 1859–1959* (1960). E.T. GARGAN, *Alexis de Tocqueville: The Critical Years, 1848–1851* (1955), analyzes the period of the Second Republic; R. HERR, *Tocqueville and the Old Regime* (1962), covers the period of Tocqueville's study of the French Revolution.

Interpretations of Tocqueville's thought include: J. LIVELY, *The Social and Political Thought of Alexis de Tocqueville* (1962); R. ARON, *Essai sur les libertés* (1965); M. ZETTERBAUM, *Tocqueville and the Problem of Democracy* (1967); J. FELDHOFF, *Die Politik der egalitären Gesellschaft: Zur soziologischen Demokratie-Analyse bei Alexis de Tocqueville* (1968); S. DRESCHER, *Dilemmas of Democracy: Tocqueville and Modernization* (1968); and I. ZEITLIN, *Liberty, Equality, and Revolution in Alexis de Tocqueville* (1971).

(S.Dr.)

Togo

Togo, a sovereign West African republic, consists of that part of the former German colony of Togoland that was made French mandated territory after World War I. Situated on the Gulf of Guinea, it has a total area of about 22,000 square miles (57,000 square kilometres), and a population of about 2,000,000. From its 32-mile coastline, Togo extends northward for about 320 miles between Ghana to the west and Dahomey to the east to its boundary with Upper Volta in the north. Unlike some other French-speaking African countries, Togo has refrained from extending preferential trade treatment to France. Lomé, the capital, has a population of about 150,000 and is the largest city and port in the country. (For historical aspects see WEST AFRICA, HISTORY OF.)

The landscape. *Relief, drainage, and soils.* Togo consists of six geographical regions. The coastal region is narrow and consists of a low-lying, sandy beach region with a series of inland lagoons, the largest of which is Lac Togo. Beyond the coast lies the Ouatchi Plateau, which stretches about 20 miles inland at an altitude of about 200 to 300 feet. This is the region of the so-called *terre de barre*, a lateritic (reddish, leached, iron-bearing) soil.

Togo's six geographical regions

To the northeast of the plateau region is a higher tableland, with the highest altitudes reaching 1,300 to 1,500 feet. This region is drained by the Mono River and its tributaries, as well as by other smaller rivers, including the Haho and Sio. From the tableland region the terrain gradually rises toward the Chaîne du Togo, which runs across the country from the southwest to the northeast. Part of a mountain chain that begins in the Chaîne del' Atacora of Dahomey, the range ends in the Akwapim Hills of Ghana. Pic Baumann, which rises to about 3,235 feet (986 metres), is the highest mountain of Togo. Beyond it, to the north lies the Oti River Sandstone Plateau. This is a savanna (grassy parkland) region and is drained by the Oti River, one of the main tributaries of the Volta River. To the far northwest is a higher region that is mainly composed of granite and gneiss (a granite-like metamorphic rock); here are located the Dapango Cliffs, a distinctive feature.

Climate. Togo has a tropical climate in which rainy and dry seasons alternate. The rainy seasons occur from mid-April to mid-July and—in the south—from October to November. The coastal zone is the driest region, which receives about 24 to 36 inches of rain annually. The region of Palimé, about 65 miles inland, receives the highest amount of rain—about 70 inches annually. The north has only one rainy season with an average rainfall of about 45 inches from April to July; during the rest of the year the warm, dry harmattan (a dust-laden wind) predominates. The mean national temperature is 78° F (26° C). Minimum temperatures of about 68° F (20° C) are recorded in the mountains in August. Maxima of about 92° F (33° C) occur in the north during March and April at the end of the long dry season.

Vegetation and animal life. Savanna-type vegetation is the dominant feature of Togo. On the southern plateaus large trees, including the baobab, are common, while they are rare in the north. The southwestern regions, in which rainfall is heaviest, are covered with tropical forests, also found along the river valleys. Because of the lagoons, the coastal zone is dotted with several mangrove and reed swamps.

Wild animals are not found in great numbers, especially in the southern and central regions. A few lions, leopards, and elephants can be seen in the north. Monkeys, snakes, and lizards are numerous in many areas, and crocodiles and hippopotamuses abound in the rivers. In the game reserve of Tchanaga, near Sansanné-Mango in the north, there are wild herds of buffalo, asses, warthogs, antelopes, and deer. All kinds of reptiles, particularly snakes and lizards, and several varieties of birds and insects can be found in many areas. Fish caught off the coast include mackerel, bass, seabream, red snapper, triggerfish, dorado, ray, and sole, while crustaceans include shrimp and lobster.

The landscape under human settlement. Only 13 percent of Togo's population live in urban centres. The majority live in small villages scattered throughout the rural areas.

Rural settlement. In the coastal zone, the most familiar landscape is that of rectangular houses built either of clay and timber or of coconut or palm branches and topped by double-eaved thatched roofs. Scattered throughout the coconut plantations, they are not far from the sandy beaches, on which lie the fishermen's dugout canoes. Inland in the south, thatched rectangular huts made of adobe are clustered around big trees and surrounded by either earthen walls or fences made of palm branches. These clusters are linked by narrow lanes that converge toward the main roads and highways.

Regional architecture

In the north, the traditional adobe or stone huts are circular and are topped by conical roofs or thatched turrets. They are usually gathered in units corresponding to family groups; often enclosed by earthen walls, they are sometimes interlinked. One of the distinctive features of the northern Kara region is the high density of villages that stretch along the highway or climb up the slopes of the many hills.

Urban settlement. Lomé, the largest urban centre, is widely spread along the coast. At its centre, there is a

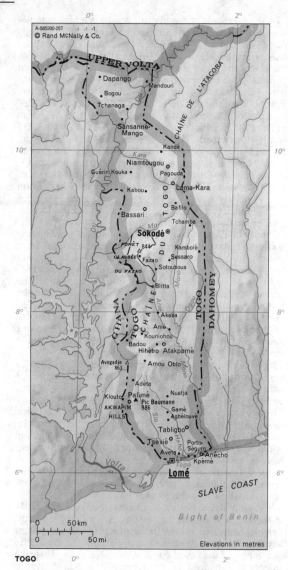

16th centuries, form the major ethnic group. There are also some scattered Yoruba, mainly Ana. Groups who emigrated from present-day Ghana and Ivory Coast since the 17th century include the Ane (or Mina), who are members of the Ge group, and who have adopted a variant of the Ewe language; the Ga-Adangme, who speak a dialect similar to the Ga language of Ghana; the Kepelle (Kpesi) and the Anyana; the Chakossi; and the Dagomba. The northern groups of the Tem (Kotokoli and Temba), Gurma, and Mossi came from the north, mainly from areas in Upper Volta. *The Ewe immigrants*

Most of the nation's 4,000 aliens live in Lomé. Mainly French, they include a few mulattoes of Brazilian, German, and French ancestry. Brazilians, or Portuguese of Brazilian birth, constituted the original trading settlement in Togo, and today Brazilian mulattoes are closely associated with economic and political development.

Religious affiliations. Although Christianity has profoundly marked the country, about three-quarters of the

mixture of old and new commercial and administrative buildings. To the west, the residential area along the shore contains most of the white population. Eastward and northward are residential areas with modern houses and bungalows. The traditional housing unit is the big, walled compound composed of a group of isolated rooms, each opening onto a courtyard.

Anécho, another coastal town, was once the country's European trade centre but is now declining. Other main towns include Palimé, Tsévié, and Atakpamé in the plateau region; Sokodé and Bassari in the central region; and Sansanné-Mango and Dapango in the north.

People and population. *Ethnic and linguistic groups.* The population of Togo is composed of about 30 ethnic groups, many of whom are immigrants from other parts of West Africa. The groups indigenous to Togo live in the north and southwest. The northern groups include the following Gur-speaking Voltaic peoples: the Gurma; the Natimba, Dye, Bu-Bankam, Bu-Kombong, and Konkomba; the Tamberma; the Basari; the Moba; the Naudeba (Loso), who speak Moré, the language of the Mossi of neighboring Upper Volta; the Kabre and the Logba; and the Namba (Lamba), whose language, Tem-Kabre, is similar to that of the Kabre; a small number of West Atlantic-speaking Fulani; and the Kebu (Akebu) who are a Kwa-speaking people of central Togo. In the southwest the indigenous Kwa peoples also belonging to the central Togo group are the Akposo, the Adele, and the Ahlo.

The immigrants came from east, west, and north. The Ewe, who emigrated from Nigeria between the 14th and

Togo, Area and Population

	area		population	
	sq mi	sq km	1970 census	1971 estimate
Regions				
Centrale				
Circonscriptions				
Bafilo	362	938	29,000	...
Bassari	2,444	6,330	95,000	...
Sokodé	2,198	5,692	106,000	...
Sotouboua	2,892	7,490	68,000	...
De La Kara				
Circonscriptions				
Kandé	653	1,692	42,000	...
Lama-Kara	419	1,085	96,000	...
Niamtougou	432	1,120	52,000	...
Pagouda	180	465	45,000	...
Des Plateaux				
Circonscriptions				
Akposso	1,692	4,382	132,000	...
Atakpamé	2,373	6,145	106,000	...
Nuatja	1,412	3,658	157,000	...
Palimé (Klouto)	1,077	2,790	77,000	...
Des Savanes				
Circonscriptions				
Dapango	1,869	4,840	181,000	...
Mango	1,453	3,762	58,000	...
Maritime				
Circonscriptions				
Anécho	275	712	121,000	...
Lomé	133	345	231,000	...
Tabligbo	483	1,250	72,000	...
Tsévié	1,289	3,338	156,000	...
Vogan	290	750	132,000	...
Total Togo	21,926	56,785	1,956,000	1,994,000

Source: Official government figures.

population still adhere to traditional animistic beliefs. There are about 400,000 Christians and 150,000 Muslims. The main Protestant (Calvinistic) church has been governed for a long time by Togolese moderators. Since independence, the Roman Catholic Church in Togo has been headed by a Togolese archbishop.

Demography. The population numbers about 2,000,000, the majority of which are women. The coast is the most populated region, and numbers generally decrease northward. The average annual growth rate is 2.5 percent. The rate of population growth ranges from 1.7 percent in the central region to 3.4 percent in the plateau region. Density of population averages 89 persons per square mile but is only about 65 per square mile in the savanna region of the extreme north, compared with 500 or more in some coastal areas. Togo's population is comparatively young; 54 percent of the total are under 20 years of age.

The national economy. Togo is essentially an agricultural country. Agriculture, including animal husbandry, fishing, and forestry, accounted for 58 percent in 1963 and 47 percent in 1966 of the country's gross domestic product and employs about 85 percent of the economically active population. Exports of agricultural products account for almost 66 percent of the country's total exports. The contribution of agriculture, however, has declined steadily since the 1960s because of the growing importance of mining, manufacturing, public utilities, and commerce.

Agriculture. A great variety of soils and climates enables Togo to grow a whole range of intertropical African products. Export crops include cocoa, palm kernels, peanuts (groundnuts), and cotton, while staple crops are corn, cassava, rice, yams, sorghum, and millet. Only one-fifth of the land area is cultivated, while one-fifth is left fallow. Greater production could be obtained by extension of the cultivated area, coupled with the widespread adoption of improved methods of cultivation.

Cattle, sheep, and pigs are raised in the plateau region and the north. Fishing is carried out on the coast and in the well-stocked inland rivers and ponds. Most of the catch is consumed locally. Forests, which cover about 10 percent of Togo's total area, are a source of tropical hardwoods and other products.

A government agency, the Office of Agricultural Products (Office des Produits Agricoles du Togo; OPAT) has a monopoly on the foreign sale of Togolese products. Export sales are made by local firms in Paris and London, acting as agents of the Office.

Mineral resources and exploitation. Phosphate is the major mineral resource and the country's second leading export item after cocoa. The deposits, which are estimated at 50,000,000 tons, are mined by the Compagnie Togolaise des Mines du Bénin, in which a United States firm holds 47 percent of the shares. Marble, with deposits of considerable size, is being quarried by SOTOMA (Société Togolaise de Marbres et de Materiaux), a mixed economy company with shares held by the Togolese government and an Italian firm.

The phosphate industry

Potential mineral resources include oil, iron ore, bauxite, uranium, chromite (an oxide of iron and chromium), gold, diamonds, rutile (titanium dioxide), manganese oxide, and kaolin (China clay). While the iron ore reserves are large, the metal content is only slightly more than 50 percent. The bauxite has a low mineral content.

Manufacturing. Manufacturing increased during the 1960s when a textile plant and a brewery were added to such existing enterprises as a tapioca and starch mill and a palm oil mill.

Foreign trade. The value of exports more than doubled during the 1960s, partly because of the rapid increase in phosphate exports. Coffee and cocoa, the leading agricultural export crops, represented 59 percent of the value of recorded exports in 1970. Togo's main customers are France, The Netherlands, West Germany, Belgium, and Luxembourg. There are also unrecorded exports, represented, for example, by the cocoa that is smuggled over the frontier for sale in Ghana.

Main imports include foodstuffs, beverages, tobacco, capital goods, raw materials and intermediate products, manufactured consumer goods, and fuel. The major sources of imports are France, the United Kingdom, and Japan.

Foreign financial aid. During the 1960s foreign financial assistance took the form of grants for investment, technical assistance, agricultural development and diversification, social investment, and education. The major donors were France, West Germany, other European Economic Community countries, the United States, and the United Nations.

Management of the economy. Economic development planning has been carried out by the National Commission for Planning, a governmental agency.

Under the first five-year plan (1966 to 1970), public investment was used to develop roads and other facilities and to improve education, as well as to promote rural development; a substantial part of private investment was devoted to housing, town planning, trade, and industry. The second five-year plan (1971–75) aims at continuing progress toward economic independence, while maintaining the present growth rate of the gross domestic product at 7 percent per annum.

In order to encourage foreign and domestic private investment, the Investment Code of 1965 guarantees foreign investors the right of freely transferring abroad all investment capital and income. The code also provides for tax benefits for priority enterprises.

Taxation. Indirect taxes, almost entirely on imports and exports, account for most of the government's ordinary budget revenues. Direct taxes consist of an income tax, a progressive tax on all profits, a tax on wages paid by employers, a tax on rental values, a land tax, and a head tax.

Economic prospects. Judging from the improvements made during the first five-year plan, further economic progress is anticipated. Unlike other former French territories, Togo has not extended preferential trade treatment to France and subsequently to the European Economic Community. This open-door, nondiscriminatory trade policy—together with the expanded production of phosphate and tropical produce—will, it is hoped, contribute toward development.

The open-door trade policy

Transport and communications. *Roads.* The road network covers more than 4,450 miles. The three main road systems are the coastal road between Ghana and Dahomey, which carries international traffic between Ghana and Nigeria; the road from Lomé north to Upper Volta; and roads serving the cocoa and coffee producing area of Palimé, Badou, and Atakpamé. This network includes about 1,000 miles of national highways and 3,300 miles of regional roads; about 3 percent of the roads are paved.

Rail system. The government-owned national railway consists of three main lines. These are the line carrying cocoa from Palimé to Lomé, the copra line from Anécho to Lomé, and the cotton line from Blitta to Lomé. The network is about 300 miles long and is of metre gauge. There is a project to build a 12-mile railroad to link Avéta, the site of a planned cement factory, with the Lomé–Blitta line. There is also a 16-mile private system, which links the phosphate mine in Kpémé with Lomé.

Port facilities. Lomé is Togo's principal port. Its artificial harbour, inaugurated in 1968, has an annual capacity of 500,000 tons. A second port at Kpémé, about 22 miles northeast of Lomé, is used exclusively to handle phosphate shipments.

Air transport. An airport at Lomé is open to jet traffic. It is used by domestic and foreign airlines. There are local airports in Atakpamé, Sokodé, Sansanné-Mango, and Dapango.

Communications. A department of posts and telecommunications is a governmental agency that manages the main post office in Lomé, in addition to 24 post offices throughout the country and several part-time post offices and rural delivery circuits.

The central telephone system in Lomé is connected with all other cities. A telecommunications link is to be established between Lomé and Accra in Ghana. International connections can be made by telephone or telegraph.

Administration and social conditions. *National government.* Since the coup d'etat of 1967 the constitution has been abolished and the National Assembly dissolved. The Togolese People's Rally (Rassemblement du Peuple Togolais), the only political party, was established in 1969. The chief executive and head of state appoints the members of his government and can dismiss them as well. He presides over a Council of Ministers with which he occasionally associates the central committee of the party.

Local government. The country is divided into four regions—Maritime, des Plateaux, Centrale, and des Savanes—which are supervised by inspectors who are appointed by the president. (For purposes of economic planning, however, the country is divided into five regions; the fifth region of de La Kara is created from Centrale and des Savanes.) The four regions are subdivided into 19 *circonscriptions*, each of which is headed by a district chief assisted by a district council. Seven communes have been established—for the cities of Anécho, Atakpamé, Bassari, Lomé, Palimé, Sokodé, and Tsévié, respectively.

Traditional authorities and justice. The administrative apparatus still has to reckon with traditional authorities, which include tribal kings or chiefs, village chiefs, and heads of family groups. These traditional authorities play a role in the judicial system, dealing with certain questions of customary law. The judicial system, headed by a Supreme Court, consists of a number of law courts in which civil, commercial, administrative, and criminal cases are heard.

Education. Education is modelled after the French system. Togolese teachers, who are replacing French personnel in increasing numbers, are expected to adapt the system to the Togolese context. Primary and secondary education is provided by public or parochial schools. The rate of school attendance, which in the early 1970s amounted to about 45 percent of the school-age population, has increased steadily since the mid-1960s.

Technical courses are given mainly by government-operated technical colleges at Lomé and at Sokodé. There are also private professional schools. Training is also organized by government agencies, and a number of Togolese technicians are trained abroad. A Regional Training Centre for Heavy Equipment is located at Lomé. Because of its bilingual (French and English) teaching, the centre receives students from about 20 African countries.

While continuing to send university students abroad on scholarships, mainly to France, Togo opened its own university in 1970. Some courses in the liberal arts and sciences are given in Lomé to some 400 students. In the early 1970s there were 16 hospitals, and some 60 doctors of whom 45 were Togolese.

Cultural life. *Radio and press.* The government operates three centres from which radio programs are transmitted throughout the country; they may also be heard in the whole of West Africa and Central Africa. Most programs are broadcast in French, the official language; a few are in English and in the main Togolese languages—Ewe, Kotokoli, Kabre, Basari, and Moba. Most weekend radio programs are devoted to cultural themes. There is no television.

Togo's only daily newspaper, *Togo-Presse,* is published by a governmental agency in French and Ewe. It is widely distributed throughout the country. Other publications include the government's *Journal Officiel; Espoir de la Nation,* an illustrated monthly magazine; *Présence Chrétienne,* a bimonthly published by the Catholic Church; and *Realités Togolaises,* a monthly printed in Dahomey.

The arts. Like other African peoples, the Togolese have a strong oral tradition. Little has been done, however, to promote vernacular literature. Before independence there were a few Togolese writers using French. Since independence, regional literature emerged with the works of several novelists and playwrights. Founded in 1967, the *Ballets Africains du Togo* has aimed at popularizing the finest traditional dances of the various ethnic groups.

The military government (margin note)

Traditional culture (margin note)

Prospects. Since the military coup d'etat of 1963—the first to occur in an African state south of the Sahara—Togo has not known the kind of political stability that promotes economic progress. Some progress toward economic development—such as the opening of the harbour at Lomé—has, however, been achieved. The government entertains hopes that the formation of the Togolese People's Rally may foster national reconciliation and unity, thus encouraging further economic progress.

BIBLIOGRAPHY. ROBERT CORNEVIN, *Histoire du Togo,* 3rd ed. (1969), an exhaustive work on the history of Togo, including some geographic data; *The World and Its Peoples: Africa South and West,* 2 vol. (1967), includes a detailed article on Togo.

(M.K.P.)

Tokugawa Ieyasu

Tokugawa Ieyasu, who founded a dynasty that was to give Japan more than two centuries of uninterrupted peace, was born in 1543 into the family of a local warrior situated several miles east of modern Nagoya, one of many such families struggling to survive in a brutal age of endemic civil strife. At his death 73 years later he was the ruler of a tranquil and prospering Japan. In the course of his rise to power he fashioned a political system that his successors inherited, modified, and managed with sufficient skill to preserve the Tokugawa hegemony and the peace of Japan until 1867.

By courtesy of the International Society for Educational Information, Tokyo, Inc.

Tokugawa Ieyasu, colour on paper by an unknown artist. In the collection of the Daiyo-ji (Daiyo Temple), Tokyo.

Early life and fortunes. Ieyasu's childhood was scarcely auspicious. His father was involved in a network of shifting alliances that repeatedly drew him into battle. When Ieyasu was two his mother was permanently separated from his father's family because of one such change in alliances, and when he was seven military adversity compelled his father to send him away as hostage to the Imagawa family, powerful neighbours headquartered at Sumpu (modern Shizuoka) to the east.

Conditions at Sumpu were more settled, and Ieyasu was trained in the military and governmental arts and developed a great love for falconry. In the late 1550s he took a wife, fathered the first of several sons, and began to acquire military experience by leading forces on behalf of Imagawa. Despite his personal comfort, however, Ieyasu's years at Sumpu had been worrisome ones. He had learned that his father had been murdered by a close vassal in 1549 and had observed helplessly from afar the subsequent disintegration of his family fortunes.

In 1560 Imagawa was slain during a battle with Oda Nobunaga, a powerful neighbour to the west, and young

Ieyasu
head of the
Tokugawa

Ieyasu seized the opportunity to return to his family's small castle and assume control of his surviving relatives and vassals. Within months he took steps to ally himself with Nobunaga, at the same time pacifying the new and inept leader of the Imagawa house long enough to recall his wife and son from Sumpu. Freed for a few years from warring with neighbours, he directed his military efforts to crushing rebellious Buddhist sectarian groups within his domain. Concurrently, he devoted much energy to improving his small army's command structure, appointing civil administrators, and formulating and enforcing procedures of taxation, law enforcement, and litigation.

During the later 1560s the Imagawa domain disintegrated, and Ieyasu expanded to the east as opportunity permitted. In 1570 this expansion led him to move his headquarters eastward to Hamamatsu, a small coastal town that he developed into the commercial and strategic centre of a thriving domain. Relying heavily on his alliance with the mighty Nobunaga, Ieyasu survived the vicissitudes of endemic war and slowly extended his territory until, by the early 1580s, he had become an important daimyo (feudal baron), in control of the fertile and populous area stretching from Okazaki eastward to the mountain barrier at Hakone.

Rise to pre-eminence. In 1582 Nobunaga was murdered by a rebellious subordinate, and Toyotomi Hideyoshi, his most brilliant general, quickly avenged the murder and moved to assume Nobunaga's pre-eminent political position. Ieyasu, then in the prime of life, emerged as his principal rival. After a few bloody but indecisive skirmishes, however, the cautious Ieyasu offered a vow of fealty, and Hideyoshi was content to leave Ieyasu's domain intact. During the rest of the 1580s, while Hideyoshi busily extended his control over the daimyo of southwestern Japan, Ieyasu strengthened himself as best he could. He continued to enlarge his vassal force, increase his domain's productivity, and improve the reliability of his administration. And in 1586, for greater security, he moved his headquarters even farther to the east, away from Hideyoshi, to Sumpu, the town he had known years before as a hostage.

Conquest
of the Hōjō

In 1589 Hideyoshi determined to obtain vows of subordination from the Hōjō daimyo, who held a large district east of the Hakone mountain barrier. When Hōjō refused to submit, Hideyoshi and Ieyasu mobilized a great army and navy that blockaded the Hōjō forces in their seaside castle at Odawara. After a long and patient siege the Hōjō were starved into capitulation. At Hideyoshi's suggestion Ieyasu then surrendered his coastal provinces west of Hakone in return for the Hōjō domain to the east. As rapidly as possible he moved thousands of vassals, their military equipment, and their households to the little fort and farmlands near the fishing village of Edo (modern Tokyo), nearly a month's march from Hideyoshi's headquarters near Kyōto.

During the 1590s Ieyasu, unlike several great daimyo from western Japan, avoided involvement in Hideyoshi's two disastrous military expeditions to Korea. Instead he grasped the opportunity afforded by his transfer to his new lands to deploy his forces rationally and to make his domain as secure as possible. He stationed his most powerful vassals on the perimeter of his territory and along main access routes, keeping the least powerful—and least dangerous to himself—nearer Edo. He then placed large tracts of land close by the town under direct administration by appointed officials, thereby assuring his castle inhabitants easy access to the largest possible supply of foodstuffs, and made detailed land and property surveys in order to regularize taxation. He also confiscated the weapons of all villagers, thereby reducing the likelihood of peasant rebellion, and moved vigorously to attract skilled artisans and businessmen to his new castle town. He undertook engineering projects to enlarge his castle, facilitate urban growth, and assure a water supply for the town populace. When Hideyoshi died in 1598, Ieyasu had the largest, most reliable army and the most productive and best organized domain in all Japan.

Hideyoshi's death precipitated another daimyo power struggle, and Ieyasu, as the most powerful and most respected of Hideyoshi's former vassal advisers, became the head of one faction in that struggle. The armies assembled in the autumn of 1600 at Sekigahara, some 50 miles (80 kilometres) northeast of Kyōto, and in the ensuing battle Ieyasu's eastern army triumphed.

This triumph left Ieyasu the undisputed master of Japan, and he moved swiftly to make his mastery permanent. Just as, in earlier years, he had consistently secured every military gain by adjusting administrative arrangements to fit his new needs, so, after the battle of Sekigahara, he initiated an extensive project of shifting daimyo about. In the process he stripped many erstwhile enemies of their lands, placed a number of his allies in strategic locations near surviving enemies, and secured for himself and his most faithful vassals direct control of much of central Japan. Then, having secured the strategic heartland, he proceeded over the next several years to make his control more sure by issuing regulations and establishing supervisory organs to constrain daimyo, imperial court nobles, and clerics, as well as his own vassals.

Ieyasu
master
of Japan

In 1603 the powerless but prestigious imperial court, which over the years had dutifully assigned Ieyasu titles that reflected his growing power, appointed him shogun (generalissimo), thereby acknowledging that this most powerful daimyo in Japan was the man officially authorized to keep the peace in the emperor's name. Two years later Ieyasu formally retired, left Edo for the more pleasant surroundings of his old home at Sumpu, and had the shogunal title assigned to his son Hidetada, intending thereby to assure that the title was recognized as a hereditary Tokugawa prerogative.

Consolidation of the dynasty. As shogun, and then as retired shogun, Ieyasu assumed responsibility for foreign affairs, a responsibility he seems to have welcomed. Because the Ming dynasty in China was faltering and was without much influence abroad, the conduct of Japanese foreign affairs, which would normally have been mainly with China, involved responding to Portuguese, Dutch, and English requests for trade and to Portuguese and Spanish requests for the right to proselytize in Japan. Ieyasu welcomed the trade, seeing in it a means of acquiring firearms, commercial profits, and general information. By 1612, however, certain diplomatic incidents had convinced the old soldier that the missionaries were, potentially at least, part of a secular threat to the political order that he had so labouriously constructed, and in the next two years he took steps to stop missionary activity and discourage the practice of their religion. Ieyasu started a trend that his successors were to pursue for three decades, until Christianity was nearly eradicated in Japan and only a token foreign trade survived at Nagasaki.

Ieyasu's daimyo transfers and political reforms of the years after the battle at Sekigahara had greatly strengthened his position, but he remained wary of the daimyo, and from 1604 until 1614 he had his son Hidetada keep them at work building and enlarging the castle at Edo. Thousands of ships and tens of thousands of men were employed for years on end hauling huge stones and great logs from distant points to Edo. By the time of his death Ieyasu had built the largest castle in the world, a sprawling network of broad moats, towering stone walls, long wooden parapets, huge gatehouses, and great fireproof warehouses full of rice and coin. Around it lay mansions in which the daimyo lived as hostages. Edo became a bustling town and port, full of artisans, traders, clerks, and labourers.

This great construction effort left Ieyasu stronger, and the cost involved left the daimyo much poorer. Yet Ieyasu still did not feel that his family fortunes were secure, for he knew full well that the undoubted military might of the Tokugawa family must evolve into undoubted political right. Although Hidetada was shogun, that did not necessarily settle the question of rightful authority, because Hideyoshi had been survived by a child son, Hideyori; and even as he was growing up in his great castle at Ōsaka, the boy gradually acquired more warrior followers and began to appear as a real threat to Tokugawa legitimacy. By 1614, however, many of the powerful former followers of Hideyoshi had died, and Ieyasu appar-

Elimination of
remaining
rivals

ently felt that he could safely undertake to destroy this last potential rival. After sufficient tension had developed, he mobilized his armies, and in two desultory and unimpressive campaigns, the old warrior finally reduced the great castle and destroyed its inmates. He then made more territorial adjustments favourable to the Tokugawa forces and returned again to his home at Sumpu. A year later, in 1616, he sickened and died, having accomplished what a century of warriors had attempted and failed: he brought enduring pre-eminence to his own family and a lasting peace to Japan.

BIBLIOGRAPHY. A.L. SADLER, *The Maker of Modern Japan: The Life of Tokugawa Ieyasu* (1937), is the only extended work in English; contains mostly battle stories and anecdotes. C.D. TOTMAN, *Politics in the Tokugawa Bakufu, 1600–1843*, ch. 1 (1967), summarizes the administrative aspects of Ieyasu's rise to power. KOYA NAKAMURA, *Ieyasu den* (1965), is a sympathetic scholarly biography by the pre-eminent scholar of Ieyasu (in Japanese).

(C.D.T.)

Tokyo–Yokohama Metropolitan Area

The Tokyo–Yokohama metropolitan area is an urban agglomeration on the Pacific coast of central Japan, including the capital city of Tokyo, the port city of Yokohama, and the manufacturing centre of Kawasaki. Tokyo means eastern capital, the name given the city when the capital of Japan was moved eastward in 1868 from Kyōto, meaning capital. The name Yokohama derives from the fact that the original fishing village was situated on a lateral (*yoko*) beach (*hama*) of Tōkyō-wan (Tokyo Bay).

The inmost part of the Tokyo–Yokohama metropolitan area is the central city of Tokyo (with a 1970 population of 9,000,000), a part of the urban prefecture (*fu*) of Tokyo, with a population of more than 11,000,000—comprising Tokyo, neighbouring industrial and residential cities, and rural districts, including the Bonin Islands (Ogasawaraguntō) in the Pacific. Tokyo-fu is not entirely contained in the Tokyo–Yokohama metropolitan area, which is a conurbation comprised of Tokyo proper, Yokohama, Kawasaki, and their contiguous urbanized municipalities; the metropolitan area's population in 1970 was over 22,000,000.

HISTORY OF THE TOKYO AREA

The eastern part of the present central city of Tokyo was originally called Edo ("estuary"), because it stood at the point where the Sumida-gawa (Sumida River) enters Tōkyō-wan. A castle was built overlooking the marshy lowland of the river in 1457. The river separated the ancient provinces of Musashi in the west and Shimohusa in the east, and the castle occupied an important strategic position.

The area had been inhabited in prehistoric times by peoples of the Jōmon (2500–250 BC) and the Yayoi (250 BC–250) cultures. The Yayoi lived on uplands and cultivated rice on marshy deltas and in valley bottoms. With the consolidation of a Japanese empire in the 6th century, the area became part of Musashi Province. Musashi and its surrounding regions were peripheral because the central government was located farther west. They rose in importance when the Tokugawa shoguns (supreme military commanders) established their military government in Edo in 1603. The old castle was rebuilt and enlarged. The town was laid out in the 17th century and became the residence of the whole Tokugawa hierarchy. By the mid-19th century Edo had become a metropolis with a population of 1,200,000. After the fall of the Tokugawa shoguns and the re-establishment of the authority of the emperor, the capital of Japan was moved from Kyōto to Edo in 1868; the city was then renamed Tokyo.

Growth of Tokyo area The municipal area of Tokyo city at the end of the 19th century consisted of 15 wards (*ku*). Together with the surrounding counties, it formed Tokyo Urban Prefecture. It had become not only the political but the commercial and financial centre of the country. Its growth was checked by the great earthquake and fire of

September 1, 1923, which severely damaged the downtown areas of Tokyo and Yokohama. During Tokyo's reconstruction the streets were widened, and many steel-and-concrete buildings were put up. At the same time, there was a growth of suburbs. At the beginning of the 1930s Tokyo city had 2,000,000 people and the suburban municipalities 3,000,000. In 1932, 20 new wards were added. During World War II, metropolitan Tokyo (Tōkyō-to), was established by amalgamating the city and its surrounding suburbs and counties. Large parts of Tokyo and Yokohama were destroyed by U.S. air raids in 1944 and 1945. After the war, starting in the 1950s, the Tokyo area grew enormously with the expansion of the Japanese economy.

The port of Kanagawa (later Yokohama), which was opened in 1859, expanded along with Japan's export trade. The city was completely new and Western in its characteristics. In 1872 it was connected to Tokyo by railroad. Along with Tokyo it was largely destroyed in the great earthquake and fire of 1923 and severely damaged by U.S. air raids in 1945. By 1970 Yokohama was the third largest city in Japan, after Tokyo and Ōsaka.

Kawasaki, situated between Tokyo and Yokohama, was formerly a post town on the Tōkaidō Highway. The Tokyo–Yokohama railway had a station there, and it became a centre of industrial development. The city expanded rapidly during the 1930s, was almost completely destroyed in World War II, and was subsequently rebuilt. The coastal area is the centre of heavy industry, including iron and steel, petroleum refining, chemicals, and thermoelectric power. Electrical machinery, food, and other light industries are in the centre of the city. In the 1970s Kawasaki was the leading industrial city of Japan. Its inland area was becoming a residential suburb of Tokyo.

THE CONTEMPORARY CITY

The Tokyo–Yokohama metropolitan area extends inland from the western coast of Tōkyō-wan. The city of Tokyo lies at the mouth of the Sumida-gawa. To its east, around the northern end of Tōkyō-wan, are suburbs comprising the prefecture of Chiba, which is separated from Tokyo by the Edo-gawa (Edo River). To the north of Tokyo city are the suburbs of Saitama Prefecture (Saitama-ken). South of Tokyo, separated from it by the Tama-gawa, is the great industrial centre of Kawasaki. The port of Yokohama (Yokohama-kō) lies southwest of Kawasaki. Still farther south, on Miura-hantō (Miura Peninsula) and around Sagami-wan (Sagami Bay), are other municipalities that are part of the Tokyo–Yokohama metropolitan area. The metropolitan boundary in the southwest is roughly delimited by the Sagami-gawa.

Terrain The original terrain consisted mostly of marshy river deltas and a few areas of sand dune. The present coastline is lined with warehouses, docks, and industrial sites. To the southeast of Yokohama is the rocky coast of Miura-hantō, with the naval harbour of Yokosuka (Yokosuka-kō). Farther south, on Sagami-wan, are the historic town of Kamakura and other resort places. The southern coast of Sagami-wan is crowded with vacationers in summer.

Soil and environment. The east side of the Sumida-gawa consists of thick alluvial soil, which has settled as much as 13 feet in some places as the groundwater has been drawn off for industrial purposes. In the early 1970s efforts were being made to contain this process by regulating the use of groundwater. Higher land in the metropolitan area consists of layers of volcanic origin on top of sand and gravel, sloping gently upward toward the mountains in the west.

To the south of Tokyo lies a hilly section varying in height from 164 to 656 feet. In the 1960s it was developed as a residential area expected to accommodate a population of 500,000. Farther south and west, these plains and hills end in the steep Okutama and Chichibu mountains, consisting of old geologic formations cut by the Tama-gawa and its tributary valleys. The steeper slopes are wooded, and the foothills are terraced with cultivated fields; the river supplies water to Tokyo. The mountains form part of the Chichibu-Tama National Park.

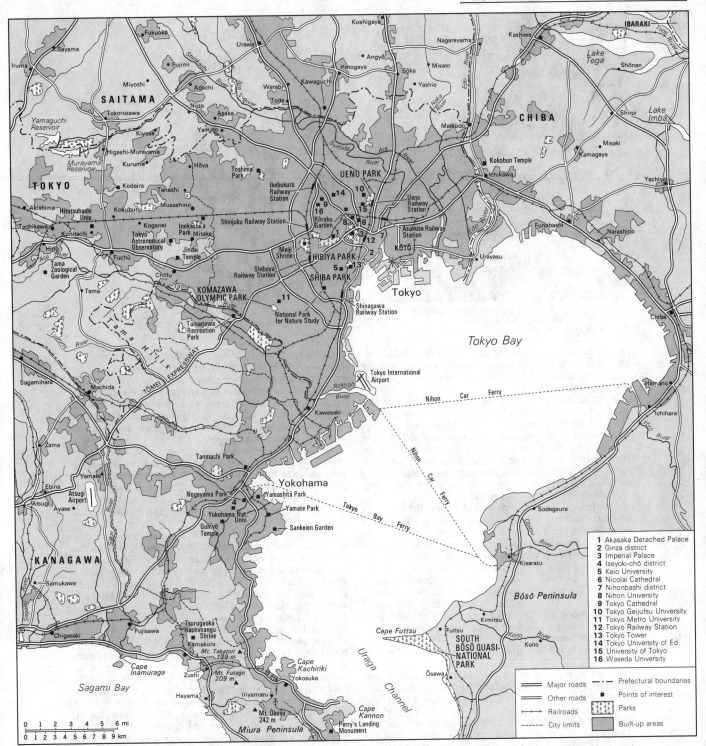

The Tokyo–Yokohama metropolitan area.

1 Akasaka Detached Palace
2 Ginza district
3 Imperial Palace
4 Iseyoki-chō district
5 Keio University
6 Nicolai Cathedral
7 Nihonbashi district
8 Nihon University
9 Tokyo Cathedral
10 Tokyo Geijufsu University
11 Tokyo Metro University
12 Tokyo Railway Station
13 Tokyo Tower
14 Tokyo University of Ed.
15 University of Tokyo
16 Waseda University

Major roads	-·-·-	Prefectural boundaries
Other roads	■	Points of interest
Railroads		Parks
City limits		Built-up areas

The climate of Tokyo is generally mild, although the summers are hot and humid. The annual mean temperature is 58.5° F (14.7° C). The January mean is 38.7° F (3.7° C), and the August mean is 79.5° F (26.4° C). Japan's climate is controlled by the summer and winter monsoons: in summer, masses of warm, humid air from the Pacific; in winter, a flow of cold, dry air from Siberia. There are rainy seasons in early summer and mid-autumn. Tokyo usually experiences two or three typhoons a year during the rainy seasons. The average annual rainfall is about 62 inches (1,563 millimetres), compared to 25–32 inches in London and about 40 inches in New York.

In mid-winter, temperatures may fall below freezing in the mornings. From January to March there are several snowfalls. The plum and camelia bloom in January on the southern coast of the metropolitan area, and Tokyo's spring reaches its climax in March and April with cherry blossoms and many varieties of flowers. The iris and azalea blossom in May, followed by the gloomy monsoon month of June. In the summer months the blue and purple hydrangea appear. After the autumnal rains, the trees begin to turn—the maples red, the ginkgo yellow. This is the season when chrysanthemum shows are held.

Wild animals are rare in the metropolitan area, except in the mountains where wild boars, foxes, and monkeys are found. Trout live in the mountain streams; in the lowlands the streams are too polluted for fish. Birds are relatively abundant in the residential areas, particularly doves, sparrows, crows, gulls, and swallows that winter in southern countries. The Imperial Palace moats are visited by several kinds of duck from northern regions. The

The Imperial Palace with the Niju-bashi (Double Bridge), used only on formal state occasions and on national holidays, in the foreground.
Shinichiro Morimoto—Orion Press

Japanese bush warbler, great tit, dusky thrush, bull-headed shrike, grey starling, and others are seasonal visitors, and in the suburbs one can see the white egret and hear the song of the skylark.

Industrialization, motorization, and population growth have brought water and air pollution. Fujiyama (Mt. Fuji), about 55 miles away, used to be visible on a clear day in winter from the centre of Tokyo, but today it can be seen only when the factories are shut down for the January holidays or when a strong wind blows away the smog. The prefectural and municipal governments have established Public Damage or Environment Conservation offices in an effort to combat pollution.

City plan. The inner part of Tokyo was the old town of Edo. The town was dominated by the castle of Edo, now the Imperial Palace where the emperor lives. The castle and the adjacent area where the high feudal lords had their dwellings was encircled by two moats, the *uchibori* ("inner moat") and *soto-bori* ("outer moat"). Unlike European medieval cities, Japanese castle towns had no walls. The warriors and lords lived between and outside the moats, forming the *yashiki-machi* ("residential town"). Along the roads and in the town area were merchants' shops and the houses of nonwarriors, comprising the *machiya* ("town house") section. Shintō shrines and Buddhist temples formed *tera-machi* ("temple town") on the urban fringes. These religious buildings were not only places of worship, amusement, and shopping on festival days but were also used for defense.

The castle and the residences of the feudal lords had beautiful gardens, some of which have been preserved and are now open to the public. The town area was divided into rectangular blocks named after various occupational groups: *gofuku-chō* ("silk-goods town"), *sakana-machi* ("fish town"), *kaji-chō* ("blacksmith town"). The residential areas of the lower samurai class also had their functional names: *okachi-machi* ("infantry town"), *takasho-machi* ("hunters with hawk"). There were also landscape names: *ta-machi* ("paddy town"), *hayashi-chō* ("wood town"), *komagome* ("horse grazing"), and *fujimi-chō* ("town from which Fujiyama can be seen"). Some of these names are preserved today, but most have disappeared with urban reorganization.

The centre of trade was Nihonbashi ("Japan Bridge"), from which five main highways began and which is still the zero-mile mark of the national-highway system. Nihonbashi and its vicinity was a busy wholesale marketplace and also a retail and financial area. The banks of the rivers and canals were crowded with boats coming from Ōsaka and other coastal regions of Japan. On the highways there were post towns every few miles. The first

post towns from Edo were Shinagawa, Shinjuku, Itabashi, and Senju, all now part of Tokyo city.

The marshy downtown area had to be drained with canals, and the Tone and Ara rivers had to be prevented from flooding. As Edo grew, water for its 1,000,000 inhabitants was brought in by aqueduct and distributed through wooden pipes; this system became the basis of modern Tokyo's water supply.

The early houses were made of wood, and Edo was so repeatedly in flames that fires were called the flowers of Edo. A great fire in 1657 damaged large parts of Edo, destroyed the main tower of the castle, and killed 100,000 inhabitants. After the earthquake and fire of 1923, the downtown area was largely rebuilt, and it was rebuilt again after World War II.

The main shopping street is Ginza Street, running northeast to southwest and lighted brightly at night. A stroll on the Ginza is popularly known as Ginbura. The northern extension of Ginza is Nihonbashi Street, a busy central shopping area that includes the best department stores. It passes through Tokyo's financial district. From Ginza a street leads westward to Hibiya Park and the Imperial Palace. Nearby are the government-office district and the Yūrakuchō amusement centre.

To the east of the Imperial Palace, separated from it by broad gardens and a moat, lies the Marunouchi business district, the heart of Japanese business activity, with offices and banks, the Chamber of Commerce, the railroad station, the Central Post Office, and the International Telephone and Telegraph Corporation building.

Tokyo's Metropolitan Government Office is situated at the southern end of Marunouchi district. To the north, across the outer moat, is the Kanda area, with many universities, bookstores, publishers, and hospitals. Other important areas are Taitō, in the north, and Shiba, in the south—commercial and residential areas of high population density. To the east of the Sumida-gawa is Kōtō, a low-lying marshy area drained by canals that create a checkerboard effect, which is an industrial and working class district.

In the western part of Tokyo is the uplands residential area, a quiet, tree-shaded section where most foreign embassies are located. The University of Tokyo, Waseda University, Keio University, and other universities and research institutes are in this area. Farther west, and southwest, of the Yamanote electric railroad, are middle class residential neighbourhoods the growth of which began after the earthquake of 1923 when city dwellers moved outward into the upland fields. In these areas the houses are generally frame, with some multistoried apartment houses. With the improvement of commuting

Plan of the old city

The Marunouchi district

Yokohama harbour.
Takanori Ishii—Bon

Yokohama

facilities, Tokyo's eastern and northeastern suburbs have also been growing as middle class residential areas.

The growth pattern of Yokohama and Kawasaki has been similar to that of Tokyo. The whole area within 20 to 30 miles of Tokyo's central station has become a commuting area. Older towns have become suburbs of Tokyo. Yokohama's business district is concentrated around its port. At the northern end of the business district, near Sakuragi Street Station, is the central shopping street of Isezaki. South of the business district is the hilly Yamate residential area, separated by Moto-machi Street where there are many exotic shops. The northern coast of Yokohama is an industrial area. Just south of the port, new industrial and port facilities have been established along the coast at Honmoku and Negishi.

Tokyo and Yokohama are divided into wards (*ku*), composed of towns (*machi*) having several thousand inhabitants each; some towns are further divided into smaller towns or districts known as *chō*. Originally these towns and districts were neighbourhood units, but they now function only as postal addresses and for purposes of registration. The older towns each have a tutelary deity (*uji-gami*) with a shrine. Residents of a town visit the shrine on festival days to pray for safety and prosperity. These festivals are full of colour: stalls are set up, and there is music and dancing. Among the more famous shrines are the Asakusa, Sano, Kanda Myojin, Nezu, and Fukagawa, dating from the Edo period. The Meiji Shrine in Tokyo, dedicated to the Emperor Meiji and his consort, is a kind of national monument and centre of pilgrimage for the whole country.

Transportation.   Tokyo is the national traffic centre; it is also an important international nodal point of the western Pacific and the Far East. The metropolitan area is spanned with a dense network of electric railways, bus lines, and motor highways. Tokyo Station is not only the central railroad station of the metropolis but also central for all Japan. Trains to Ōsaka and beyond start from Tokyo Station. Another important Tokyo terminal is Ueno Station, from which lines run to various parts of northern Japan. Shinjuku Station is the terminus of trains from central Honshu and some trains from the east. Interurban service in the Tokyo area is by the Japan National Railways and various privately owned electric lines.

Tokyo and Yokohama formerly had trains that have now been replaced by buses and subway lines. The Tokyo subway system had 80 miles of line in the early 1970s. A subway was under construction in Yokohama.

Tokyo's system of automobile expressways consists of a loop around the central business district and seven radial lines connecting with the national expressways. There were 2,025,000 registered automobiles of all kinds in greater Tokyo in the late 1960s, and in the Yokohama area there were 724,000. The ratio of persons to automobiles in Tokyo was about 10.1 to one.

The Tokyo International Airport is at Haneda, about eight miles southwest of the city. It is the terminus of overseas airlines from Asia, North and South America, Australia, and Europe, as well as of domestic lines from Ōsaka, Fukuoka, Okinawa, Chitose on Hokkaido, and many other cities. Atsugi Airport, west of Yokohama, is used by some domestic lines. A new international airport under construction near Narita, 30 miles east of Tokyo, was opened in 1972.

The city's airports

Tōkyō-wan has four major ports. Yokohama is the largest, handling 163,000 tons of cargo annually in the late 1960s. Kawasaki and Chiba are industrial ports, with tonnages of 61,000 and 51,000 respectively. The port of Tokyo handled 40,000 tons of cargo. Ferryboats carrying cars have several lines across Tōkyō-wan.

Building styles.   In Tokyo Urban Prefecture there were 3,100,000 dwellings in the late 1960s. The city of Yokohama had 500,000 and Kawasaki 250,000. These dwellings vary from the tiny wooden house of two or three stories sandwiched between high office buildings to the large suburban homes of the well-to-do. Some people live over their shops or behind them. The best residential area is in the Yamanote Loop, once the site of feudal residences in the Edo period but now given over to middle class frame houses with gardens. As part of social and economic reforms instituted after World War II, the large estates in this area were subdivided into small lots or adapted to such other uses as clubs or restaurants; some of them became public gardens. The uplands are now being invaded by office buildings and apartment houses. Throughout the metropolitan area there are many housing developments, ranging in size from several hundred homes to more than 10,000. Building is carried on by the Japan Housing Corporation, municipalities, prefectures, and private companies.

About three-fourths of the dwellings in Tokyo Urban Prefecture are made of wood, although the number of fireproof concrete-and-steel houses is increasing. Building styles are a mixture of Eastern and Western. While few purely Japanese buildings remain, even a modern apartment will have one or two rooms with a tatami (reedmat) floor and sliding doors. In Kawagoe, an old castle town about 23 miles from Tokyo, are traditional merchant houses with heavy tile roofs and plaster walls.

The central business districts of Tokyo, Yokohama, and other cities consist mainly of steel-and-concrete buildings. Their maximum height was formerly limited to about 100 feet to prevent earthquake damage, but taller buildings were permitted in the late 1960s. In 1971 Tokyo had three 40-story office buildings. Outside of the central business district, buildings tend to be small in area because of the high price of land.

Central Tokyo. In the governmental district of Kasumigaseki, southwest of the Imperial Palace, one can study building styles by eras. The Sakurada Gate, formerly one of the entrances to the castle of the shoguns, leads across the moat to the outer garden of the palace. The entrance passage is crooked for reasons of defense. To the left, in Hibiya Park, is the Supreme Court building of reddish brick, put up in the 19th century; to the right of it are the dun-coloured Metropolitan Police Board and the ministry of local government, built in the 1920s. Next to the latter is the ministry of foreign affairs, a postwar building with wide glass windows and central heating and air conditioning. The National Diet Building beyond is made of granite from the islands of the Inland Sea (Seto-naikai). Overlooking these governmental buildings is the Kasumigaseki Building, rising 482 feet (147 metres).

Government buildings (margin note)

Toichi Sakakibara

The Kasumigaseki Building, overlooking the Shinkansen express train, which runs through downtown Tokyo.

The Marunouchi district to the east of the Imperial Palace was developed as a business centre on vacant land formerly owned by the government. Marunouchi means inside castle; in this district is the outer-moat zone of the Edo castle, where the feudal lords had their mansions. A commercial centre was built there around the turn of the

20th century, consisting of red-brick buildings of three or four stories. These gave way in the 1920s and 1930s and after World War II to steel-and-concrete office buildings that are resistant to fire and earthquake. The Mitsubishi Bank and the Dai-Ichi Life Insurance Building are in Renaissance style. The postwar buildings are of lighter and taller construction, an example being the Tokyo Metropolitan Government Office. The former Imperial Hotel, designed by Frank Lloyd Wright in 1916, withstood the earthquake of 1923 and was torn down in 1967 and replaced by a plainer, taller structure in 1970.

The uptown area to the south has changed much less; many older buildings are still preserved. The old lecture hall of Keio University, of wooden construction with black-and-white-checkerboard walls, belongs to the early Meiji period. The Akasaka Detached Palace was completed in 1909.

To the north, near the Kanda-gawa (Kanda River), one finds a contrast of building styles and civilizations in the Seidō (a Confucian shrine rebuilt in 1935), the Kanda Myojin Shrine (a Shintō shrine rebuilt in 1934), and the Nicolai Cathedral (Greek Orthodox, dating from 1884).

New building. Recent buildings include the Palace-side Building adjacent to the northern moat, occupied by the Mainichi Press; Tokyo Cathedral with a sky-piercing tower, and the National Theatre. One of the highest structures in the world is a 1,092-foot (333-metre) TV tower, erected in 1958 and modelled on the Eiffel Tower in Paris; it dominates the Tokyo skyline. The Shinjuku Railway Station on the western Yamanote line was being developed in the early 1970s as a civic centre. The complex includes the station, two department stores, and other buildings with offices and shops. Nearby will be a second Marunouchi commercial district. Towering above it is the 46-story Keio Plaza Hotel. Similar complexes were being developed elsewhere in the metropolitan area —for example, at the Shimbashi Station in the central business district and at Yokohama Station. Department stores have decentralized by locating at railway stations throughout Tokyo—Shinjuku, Shibuya, Ikebukuro, Veno, and Asakusa—where they compete with the stores of the central business district of Ginza–Nihonbashi.

The Shinjuku development (margin note)

Demography. The total population of the Tokyo–Yokohama metropolitan area in 1970 was about 22,-000,000. The city of Tokyo proper had slightly less than 9,000,000; Yokohama had about 2,200,000, and Kawasaki had nearly 1,000,000. Each day another 1,000,000 entered the area to work. The average population density of Tokyo proper was 40,207 persons per square mile. The density for Yokohama was 13,761 and for Kawasaki 19,399.

The population of the metropolitan area is growing, partly through migration from other parts of Japan and partly from natural increase. While the central city's population declined slightly from 1965 to 1970, that of other parts increased; growth rates were highest in the outer suburbs, some of which increased by more than half in the period 1965–70. Generally speaking, the western part of Tokyo and the uplands are middle and upper class residential areas. Blue-collar workers live east of the Sumida-gawa and in the industrial areas of Kawasaki and Yokohama. Tokyo is a melting pot for all Japan, and in the downtown area one can hear the Kwansai (Ōsaka–Kyoto) accent and the Tōhoku (northeastern region) dialect. Most of the many foreigners in the metropolis do not live in national enclaves. Exceptions are the Chinese in Yokohama and Koreans in several areas.

Economic life. The Tokyo metropolitan area is the largest commercial centre of Japan, and its port of Yokohama is the country's largest. Most important businesses and banks have their head offices in the central business district, as do foreign companies and banks. Before World War II, Tokyo was Japan's second industrial city after Ōsaka, but since the war Ōsaka has declined in comparison to Tokyo. In the late 1960s Tokyo Urban Prefecture accounted for 12.1 percent of the country's annual manufactures and Kanagawa Prefecture (including Yokohama, Kawasaki, and neighbouring cities) for another 10.4 percent.

Manufacturing. The Tokyo–Kawasaki–Yokohama manufacturing zone, also known as Keihin, is one of the four major industrial agglomerations in Japan. In the late 19th century, manufacturing developed within the cities of Tokyo, Kawasaki, and Yokohama. It later expanded into the suburbs: along the Tōkaidō Line (a railroad) to the southwest; westward to Sagamiōno, Tachikawa, Hino, and Hachiōji; along the Ara-kawa to the northwest; along the Takasaki and Tōhoku rail lines to the north; along the Jōban line to the northeast; and around the northeastern coast of Tōkyō-wan into Chiba Prefecture. If one includes in this industrial area the four prefectures of Tokyo, Kanagawa (Yokohama), Saitama (to the west of Tokyo), and Chiba (to the northeast), there were in the early 1970s a total of about 130,000 manufacturing enterprises with more than 2,800,000 workers.

Tokyo itself has much light manufacturing, including textiles, toiletries, and printing and publishing. It is a centre of cultural activity and information. It also produces goods requiring an abundant labour force, such as electrical products, cameras, and automobiles. A large proportion of the establishments are family-size or relatively small shops with fewer than 30 workers, most of them subcontracting to larger concerns. The Yokohama–Kawasaki district is an area of heavy industry specializing in chemicals, machinery, metallurgy, petroleum refining, ships, motor cars, and fabricated metal products. A new centre for iron and steel, petroleum refining, petrochemicals, electric power, and other heavy industries is the Chiba–Ichihara coast at the northeast end of Tōkyō-wan. Another heavy-industrial centre has sprung up at Kashima about 60 miles northeast of Tokyo on the Pacific coast. The machinery and light industries have been decentralizing inland from Tokyo in the area 30 to 60 miles from the city, where a number of industrial parks have been established.

Commercial and service industries. Tokyo is a centre of wholesaling, drawing goods from all over the country and abroad and distributing them into the surrounding area. It is also Japan's financial centre. The banks, insurance companies, stockbrokers, and similar establishments are concentrated in the central business district.

Harumi Street in Tokyo's Ginza district, a principal shopping area located in the eastern part of the city.

Utilities. The water used in Tokyo, Yokohama, Kawasaki, and other parts of the metropolitan area is supplied by aqueduct systems. Local waterworks and private industrial and residential systems supplement the supply. Tokyo draws its water from the Tama and Edo rivers; there are reservoir dams at Murayama and Yamaguchi and at Ogōchi on the upper Tama. To meet increasing demand, new dams have been built on the upper Ara and Tone rivers, which are connected by a canal with the Murayama–Yamaguchi reservoirs. Yokohama, Kawasaki, Yokosuka, and neighbouring towns get their water from the Sagami-gawa, which is dammed at two points. Most of the metropolitan area is supplied with gas by the Tokyo Gas Company. Gas plants are located mainly on the coast, where domestic and imported coal, petroleum, liquid gas, and natural gas are brought in by ship. Petroleum and bottled propane gas are also widely used for heating and cooking.

The Tokyo Electric Company serves the whole Kantō region, as well as Yamanashi Prefecture and the eastern half of Shizuoka Prefecture. About 35 percent of the power comes from hydroelectric stations on the Tone and Kinu rivers in Kanto, the rivers Katsura, Shinano, and Azusa in central Honshu, and Inawashiro-ko (Lake Inawashiro) in the Tohoku region of northern Honshu. Another 65 percent of the Tokyo area's power comes from thermal stations located on Tōkyō-wan and at Kashima to the northwest. To meet future needs of the metropolitan area, one 960,000-kilowatt hydroelectric station and three thermoelectric stations with a combined output of 2,700,000 kilowatts were under construction in the early 1970s. Tokyo also drew from two atomic power stations, one at Tokai, 65 miles northeast, and another on the Fukushima coast, 120 miles northeast, of Tokyo.

The city's electric supply

Public institutions and services. Tokyo is not only the national capital but also the centre of the Kanto region, which comprises the prefectures of Ibaraki, Tochigi, Gumma, Saitama, Chiba, and Kanagawa. It houses all the institutions of the national and regional governments, as well as the offices of the local government and of government corporations, such as the telephone and telegraph corporation. Most of these are located near the Imperial Palace. Foreign embassies and international institutions have their offices in the central business district and in the western part of the city.

Because Tokyo is the place of political decision, nearly all of Japan's prefectures have offices there. Major cities and towns have their Tokyo offices. Federations of local government, such as the Mayors' Association, are located in Tokyo, as are the headquarters of political parties and many other semigovernmental institutions.

Efforts to break up and decentralize this massive agglomeration of power have never succeeded. The migration of governmental offices out of Tokyo will apparently be limited to research sections. In the early 1970s a new university-and-research town was under construction in Tsukuba, about 40 miles northeast of Tokyo.

Public health. The Tokyo–Yokohama metropolitan area shares the problems of other large urban areas with respect to pollution, noise, and lack of air and sunlight. Its inhabitants nevertheless live better than people in small cities and towns because they enjoy superior medical care and social services.

Because the population is relatively young, the birth rate in Tokyo, Kawasaki, and Yokohama is higher than the national average; in 1969 the birth rate in Tokyo Urban Prefecture was 20.3 per thousand, and in Kanagawa Prefecture it was 22.7, as compared with the 1969 national average of 18.5. The death rate was likewise lower, being 4.9 per thousand in both prefectures as compared with the national average of 6.8. The infant mortality rates were 12.0 and 11.9 per 1,000 live births, a little lower than the national average of 14.2. In 1970 there were about 758 persons for every physician in the prefecture of Tokyo and 1,174 in the prefecture of Kanagawa. In Tokyo city there were 105 persons per hospital bed. These ratios are very low for an Asian country and compare favourably with those of western Europe. The medical school of the

Komazawa Olympic Park, Tokyo.
Shinichiro Morimoto—Orion Press

University of Tokyo, founded in the latter part of the 19th century, is known for its Institute of Medical Science. The medical school of Keio University is another research hospital. A number of university hospitals in Tokyo are open to the public, but most hospitals are run by the national, prefectural, and municipal governments or public organizations such as the Red Cross. There are special hospitals for children, the aged, and patients suffering from cancer, tuberculosis, or heart disease.

Tokyo has always been a city of fires, stemming from crowded conditions and flammable building materials. In Tokyo Urban Prefecture there were 8,844 fires in 1969. The fire departments of all Japanese municipalities fight fires and other hazards such as traffic accidents, floods, and earthquakes. Tokyo has a metropolitan police agency to maintain order in the capital city. There are also mobile police that can be called in case of large-scale violence. Kanagawa Prefecture has its own police force, as do Yokohama and other large municipalities.

Education. In Tokyo as in other large cities more than 90 percent of the ninth-year graduates go on to high school. In the late 1960s there were more than 1,600 primary schools with 1,265,000 pupils in Tokyo and Kanagawa prefectures together; more than 1,000 junior high schools with 554,000 pupils; and more than 550 high schools with 598,000 students. There are also public and private kindergartens.

Colleges and universities
In the early 1970s the Tokyo metropolitan area had 116 universities and 110 junior colleges, with enrollments in the late 1960s of 608,000 and 75,000 students respectively. Almost half of all Japan's university and college students are to be found in the prefectures of Tokyo and Kanagawa. The century-old University of Tokyo has ten faculties and many research institutes. Other leading universities are Tokyo Kogyo University (engineering), Hitotsubashi University (trade and commerce), Tokyo University of Education, and Tokyo Geijutsu University (music and arts). There are also national universities for industry and agriculture, languages, medicine, dentistry, the merchant marine, and other fields. The prefectural and municipal universities are Tokyo Metropolitan and Yokohama Municipal. Among private universities, Waseda and Keio are the oldest and most highly regarded, especially in the fields of literature, politics, and business. The largest university is Nihon, with 72,000 students.

Culture and recreation. Tokyo is at the centre of national cultural activity. It is also the home of various institutions for national and international cultural communication. Modern Japan has been strongly influenced by the West, to which Tokyo and Yokohama have been gateways; Western technology and life styles first took root in those cities.

If Tokyo has been less a centre of Japanese traditions than have Kyōto, Ōsaka, and Nara, it has many valuable cultural properties from the past. The Imperial Household Agency Library and the Tôyô Bunko hold collections of classical books. There are the National Archives and the National Diet Library. The National Museum in Ueno Park concentrates on the art and history of Japan and Asia. The Kokuritsu Kagaku Hakubutsukan (National Science Museum), the Zoological Garden, and the National Museum of Western Art are also located in Ueno Park, as is the Metropolitan Gallery of Fine Art. Elsewhere in Tokyo there are numerous smaller collections and galleries. Near the Imperial Palace are the National Museum of Modern Art and the Technical and Engineering Museum. Tokyo and Yokohama also have their own local historical records and exhibits, such as the museum of folkways, in the city of Musashino, and the museum of old houses, in Kawasaki.

Museums

A whole range of theatre is available, from the traditional Kabuki to modern drama. Symphonic works, operas, and various other kinds of Western music and dance are performed.

The media. Tokyo is the information centre of Japan. Nationwide radio and TV programs originate there. The three largest nationwide newspapers, *Asahi, Mainichi,* and *Yomiuri shimbun,* are issued in Tokyo. A daily economic newspaper, several English-language papers, and papers in Korean are all published there. Hundreds of other daily and weekly papers are printed and distributed, as well as more than 40 weekly magazines.

In the early 1970s Tokyo had seven television channels, including two UHF channels. There were 65 radio stations, including two FM and one shortwave. Colour TV was rapidly becoming popular.

Parks

Recreation. Tokyo's parks are not as large as those of European and American cities, but they are numerous. Among the better known are the outer garden of the Imperial Palace, Hibiya Park, Ueno Park (with its zoo), and the Meiji Shrine's Outer Garden (with its baseball stadium and other playing fields). The latter along with Komazawa Olympic Park and Yoyogi Sports Centre, was one of the main centres of the Olympic Games in 1964. In the western part of Tokyo are the smaller natural parks of Inokashira, Zenpukuji, and Shakujii, with lakes. Some of the larger private gardens of the Edo period are now open to visitors. The most impressive of these is the Inner Garden of the Meiji Shrine with its irises and water lilies, a favourite spot of the emperor Meiji. There are also several botanical gardens.

In Yokohama, the best parks are Nogeyama and Yamate, on hills overlooking the harbour, and Yamashita Park on the coast. Sankei-en (Sankei Garden), formerly a private estate, contains a collection of historic buildings brought from other parts of the country.

Suburban recreation areas include the Tama Zoological Garden, where visitors can ride by bus through the lion section, and near it the *kodomo-no kuni* ("children's country"). Places of excursion from Tokyo and Yokohama include the Okutama and Sagami valleys, the Chichibu and Tanzawa mountains, the Fuji-Hakone-Izu National Park, the Izu-hantō (Izu Peninsula) with its many hot springs, the islands of Oshima and Miyake, the Miura-hantō, and many others. There are also amusement parks with roller coasters and similar rides, such as Kōrakuen, Tamagawa, Toshimaen, and Yomiuri.

The most popular sport in Japan is baseball. Tokyo has four professional teams and Kawasaki one. There are also university teams, and the Waseda–Keio games are followed intently. There are a number of golf courses in the suburbs.

BIBLIOGRAPHY. A comprehensive source, in English, is the INTERNATIONAL GEOGRAPHICAL UNION, REGIONAL CONFERENCE, *Geography of Tokyo and Its Planning* (1957), although now somewhat dated. The ASSOCIATION OF JAPANESE GEOGRAPHERS, *Japanese Cities* (1970), contains many useful studies of Tokyo. A German-language discussion is S. KIUCHI, "Tokio als Weltstadt," in J.H. SCHULTZE (ed.), *Zum Problem der Weltstadt* (1959). The TOKYO METROPOLITAN GOVERNMENT has published an atlas, *Regional and City Planning for Tokyo* (1964). H. AONO and S. BIRUKAWA, *Tokyo-to* (1967), is an academically written study of the Tokyo region (in Japanese). S. KIUCHI, *Tokyo* (1968) and *Kanagawa, Saitama, Chiba* (1969), contain colour photographs and maps. K. KODAMA and H. SUGIYAMA, *Tōkyō-to ne rekishi* (1969), is a history (in Japanese). Statistical data may be found in the *Statistical Yearbook of Japan*, published by the national government, and the *Yearbook of the City of Tokyo*, published by the Tokyo Metropolitan Government.

(S.K.)

Tolstoy, Leo

The enduring fame of Leo Tolstoy, Russian author, reformer, and moral thinker, rests mainly on two novels, *War and Peace* and *Anna Karenina*. A deeply contradictory man, Tolstoy was an individualistic aristocrat who in his later years tried unsuccessfully to lead the life of a poor peasant, a sensualist who ended up as an intransigent puritan, a man of singular vitality who feared death at almost every step. This extraordinary duality of character led him in middle life to abandon his career of a mere writer of fiction to become a radical Christian who propagated his belief in a life of love and faith and his rejection of property and such man-made institutions as governments and churches by a stream of essays and pamphlets and largely didactic short stories and plays.

Early years and marriage. Lev Nikolayevich, Count Tolstoy, was born on September 9 (August 28, old style), 1828, on his family's estate at Yasnaya Polyana, about 100 miles (160 kilometres) south of Moscow, in Tula Province. Tolstoy's parents died when he was a child, and he was raised by relatives. Private tutors had charge of his early education. At 16 he entered the Kazan University (now Kazan [V.I. Lenin] State University), but, disappointed with the formal instruction there, he returned to

Tolstoy
The Bettmann Archive

Yasnaya Polyana in 1847 to manage his estate and conduct his own education. In neither did he achieve much success, preferring the social whirl of Moscow and St. Petersburg to life in the country. In his diary, which he kept during most of his life, he recorded his moral transgressions. In his youthful entries there is already evidence of an unusual analytical talent in his realistic probing into the suppressed motives of his own behaviour.

Disgusted with this shiftless existence, Tolstoy in 1851 joined his soldier brother Nikolay in the Caucasus. In the following year he also entered the army and acted with bravery in several engagements against the hill tribes. Much of his leisure he spent in writing, completing his first published work, *Detstvo* (*Childhood*), which appeared in the magazine *Sovremennik* ("The Contemporary"). The material of *Childhood* is treated with conventional realism, except for digressive lyrical passages in the manner of the English novelist Laurence Sterne, whose *Sentimental Journey* Tolstoy partially translated at this time. He is autobiographical in this and in later works, for he often draws upon his own life, or the lives of those he knew well, for the content of his fiction; but what captivates readers of *Childhood* is its fresh and precise choice of significant detail and the amazing reliving of forgotten common experiences of childhood that, once recalled, exert a nostalgic charm. Sequels to *Childhood—Otrochestvo* (*Boyhood*) and *Yunost* (*Youth*)—lack this special charm, perhaps because an analysis of the moral failings of youngsters tends to dominate these two works. Tolstoy's experiences in the Caucasus are reflected in "Nabeg" ("The Raid") and "Rubka lesa" ("The Woodfelling"), his first short stories dealing with war. The theme is treated in a youthful spirit, but the exacting realistic analysis of military activity is tinged with that critical awareness of false heroics that became a central feature of his *Sevastopolskiye rasskazy* (1855–56; *Sevastopol*).

Sketches of military life

Transferred to the Danube front in 1854, Tolstoy participated in the siege of Sevastopol during the Crimean War. He described these experiences in his *Sevastopol* sketches, in which he contrasted the simple heroism of the common soldier with the false heroics of military leaders. At the end of the fighting in 1856, he left the army and went to St. Petersburg, where he became the idol of competing literary groups that sought his support of their social and aesthetic views. A pronounced individualist, he rebuffed the coteries and left for Yasnaya Polyana.

He went abroad in 1857, to France, Switzerland, and Germany. The criticism of stories based on his travels (*e.g.*, "Lyutsern" ["Lucern"]) caused him to lose interest in literature. Yet he continued to write. Between 1855 and 1863 he wrote a series of short stories—including

Early short stories

"Zapiski markera" ("The Memoirs of a Billiard-Marker"), "Dva gusara" ("Two Hussars"), "Albert," "Tri smerti" ("Three Deaths"), "Semeynoye schastye" ("Family Happiness"), "Polikushka," and "Kholstomer" (not published until 1886)—in which he concentrated mainly on moral problems. These stories anticipate his later concern with the harm a materialistic society inflicts on the natural, unspoiled man but represented no artistic advance on his earlier writing. In fact, the subjective moralistic emphasis is a defect, although many passages are persuasively argued. Only in the "Two Hussars" did Tolstoy avoid this pervasive subjectivism. There, the evil influences of society on one of the characters are artistically suggested rather than didactically argued. "Kholstomer," a satire on human beings from the point of view of a horse, is also something of an exception, for by his art Tolstoy somehow convinces the reader that the noble horse's natural life is superior to man's absurd, unnatural existence. The contrast between the natural man and the spoiled product of sophisticated society deeply interested Tolstoy, and he treated the theme with brilliant artistry in *Kazaki* (*The Cossacks*). The highly civilized protagonist suffers in comparison with the freedom-loving uninhibited Cossacks of the village in which he lives. Several of them are among Tolstoy's most memorable characterizations.

In the late 1850s Tolstoy became concerned with the poor state of education among the peasantry, and, on returning from his travels, he started a school for peasant children at Yasnaya Polyana. The success of his original teaching methods, which anticipated modern progressive education, drew him deeper into pedagogical studies. He journeyed to Europe again in 1860–61, visiting Germany, France, Italy, England, and Belgium and investigating educational theory and practice. Absorbed by this interest, he published an educational magazine, in which he developed his pedagogical theories, and compiled textbooks that won wide acceptance because of their simplicity and attractive approach.

In 1862 Tolstoy married Sonya (Sofya) Andreyevna Bers, a girl from a middle class family with wide intellectual interests. He dropped his educational activities and for the next 15 years devoted himself with all his ardent nature to married life. For the most part it was an intense but happy existence, and 13 children were born. He now managed his estate with much success and resumed writing, creating his two greatest masterpieces, *Voyna i mir* (*War and Peace*) and *Anna Karenina*.

The great novels. It took Tolstoy almost seven years to write his vast epic *War and Peace,* generally regarded as one of the two or three greatest novels in world literature. In this supreme effort he went far beyond his previous writings both in scope and treatment. In it, all the stuff of life is woven in enormous tapestry, and the rich material and numerous characters are handled with unsurpassed objectivity. Perhaps in no other novel does the mastery of realistic detail and the amazing subtlety and variety of psychological analysis so successfully create the total impression of life being lived completely and naturally.

The scheme of *War and Peace*

War and Peace, covering the period 1805–14, is primarily concerned with the histories of five aristocratic families, the members of which are portrayed against a vivid background of Russian social life and the titanic struggle of clashing armies during Napoleon's invasion of Russia. In this huge panorama appear the aristocracy and the peasantry, officers and privates of the army, the Russian and French emperors, diplomats and courtiers, town life and country life, and realistic pictures of war. The theme of war, however, is subordinated to the story of family existence, which at that time involved Tolstoy's optimistic belief in the life-asserting pattern of the natural stages of man—birth, childhood, maturity, love, marriage, birth again, and death. As models for two of the families, Tolstoy drew upon members of his own family, and the unforgettable heroine Natasha is modelled on his sister-in-law Tanya Bers. One has only to read her published diary, however, to realize how the witchery of his art has transformed her into the vital, poetic, "natural" woman

of the novel. The moral conflict between two of the main protagonists (bumbling, questing Pierre and polished, intellectually proud Andrey) is also Tolstoy's—Andrey's conviction that one should live for the sake of doing good for oneself being opposed to Pierre's ultimate belief that one should live for the sake of serving others. Tolstoy varied his realistic method of individualizing characters in accordance with the human types portrayed: it may be brilliant externalization, as in the case of a shallow society beauty; or psychological analysis in depth, as in that of an emotionally complex woman supposedly patterned after Tolstoy's mother; or acute symbolism, as in the creation of the peasant Platon Karatayev, who exists as a personification of the simplicity and truth living in the gray masses of Russia.

The sections of the novel that critics have frequently objected to are those in which Tolstoy set forth his philosophy of history and theorized about war and its architects. He anticipated these objections, and in 1868 he published an article explaining his views on these matters. There are two kinds of actions, he declared: those that do, and those that do not, depend upon individual will. In the historical process, he wrote, there is a minimum of freedom; the actions of so-called makers of history and leaders of war depend on the actions of countless other people and to this extent are predetermined. What troubled him was the historians' practice of fixing responsibility for what occurs in life upon individuals whom they call "great men" and endow with heroic virtues and vices. On the contrary, Tolstoy argued, natural law—the principles of right or justice regarded by many thinkers as common to all mankind and thus independent of formal law—determines the lives of human beings no less than the processes of nature itself. There is no free choice; all is ruled by an inexorable historical determinism. But it can hardly be denied that his labouring of such subjects interferes with the unity of *War and Peace* and represents an artistic lapse.

Though it is similar to *War and Peace* at least in narrative method and style, *Anna Karenina* has more artistic unity. Tolstoy's philosophy of life was in the process of changing between the writing of the two books. *War and Peace* is a life-loving, optimistic novel, and its main characters are morally robust and masters of their inner conflicts; *Anna Karenina*, which deals with Russian society in the 1860s, is pessimistic, and the inner conflicts of its characters, often unresolved, sometimes bring about human disaster. There is an inevitability about the tragic fate that hangs over the adulterous love of Anna and Vronsky. "Vengeance is mine, I will repay" is the epigraph of the novel and the leitmotiv of the whole story. Anna pays not so much because she transgresses the moral code but because she refuses to observe the proprieties customarily exacted in such liaisons by the hypocritical high society to which she belongs. Her love for Vronsky is a deep and lasting passion, and, unable to play the hypocrite, she unhesitatingly confronts high society with the sincerity of her love. Society's smug condemnation assures the tragic consequences of the affair. The sinful romance of Anna and Vronsky is effectively contrasted with the happy love and marriage of Kitty and Levin, which appears to have been inspired by Tolstoy's own experiences in marriage. Further, Levin's anguished doubts about the meaning of life, his haunting thoughts of suicide, and his desire to sympathize with the peasants are clear echoes of Tolstoy's own struggle at this time.

The moral basis of *Anna Karenina*

Last years as Christian reformer. Though happily married, famous as a novelist, and enjoying a large income, Tolstoy had become dissatisfied with himself by the time he finished *Anna Karenina*. An incessant probing into the purpose of life, which had troubled him since his youth, drove him to a state of spiritual crisis. In *Ispoved* (*A Confession*) he poignantly relates the moral and spiritual suffering he endured in his search for an answer to the meaning of life. The crisis came to a head in 1879. At one point he contemplated suicide. He found little help in the writings of philosophers, theologians, and scientists that he systematically examined, but the peasants, for whom he felt a deep sympathy, gave him a clue. One must serve God, they told him, and not live for oneself.

Ultimately Tolstoy became convinced that the teachings of Christ, as revealed in the New Testament, contained the answer to his question about the meaning of life. There is a power in each of us, he declared, that enables us to discern what is good, and we are in touch with that power. Our reason and conscience flow from it, and the purpose of our conscious life is to do its will; that is, to do good. From what he believed to be Christ's real utterances, corrected as he felt they should be if they were to retain their original substance, he formulated five commandments to guide him: do not be angry; do not lust; do not bind yourself by oaths; resist not him that is evil; be good to the just and the unjust. These commandments, with some modifications, became the basis for his future activities and teachings.

Conversion to Christian anarchism

Tolstoy's new convictions took a form of Christian anarchism that led him to disavow immortality and reject the authority of the church, which in turn was to excommunicate him in 1901. Further, he opposed organized government because it maintained itself through coercion, and he condemned private property because he believed that ownership was secured by force. He would have preferred to divest himself of his own property, but, bowing to the wishes of members of his family, he legally transferred his estate to them.

Following his spiritual crisis, Tolstoy devoted much time after 1880 to writing books, pamphlets, and articles on various aspects of his religious, social, moral, and artistic views. Though they lack the absorbing interest of the personal experience he related in *A Confession*, they are written in the same clear prose and often reveal his remarkable gift for logical and persuasive argumentation. The most important of these many discursive writings are *Kritika dogmaticheskogo bogoslaviya* (*An Examination of Dogmatic Theology*), a powerful attack on the Russian Orthodox Church; *V chyom moya vera* (*What I Believe*), an attempt to systematize his views on religion; *Tak chto zhe nam delat?* (*What Then Must We Do?*), a vivid account of his experiences in the slums of Moscow and an analysis of the causes of poverty; and *Tsarstvo bozhiye vnutri vas* (*The Kingdom of God is Within You*), the fullest statement of his Christian anarchism, in which he developed his belief in nonresistance to evil and reached the conclusion that governments exist largely for the sake of the rich and powerful and by their use of force persecute the masses of mankind and murder them in the violence of war. Some essays attack specific social and governmental practices, such as the use of intoxicants and tobacco in "Dlya chego lyudi odurmanivayutsya?" ("Why Do Men Stupefy Themselves?") and the execution of revolutionists in "Ne mogu molchat!" ("I Cannot Be Silent!"). Others call for reforms, advocating, for instance, the land tax proposed by the American economist Henry George (*Pisma o genre dzhorzhe* [*Letters on Henry George*]).

Religious and social essays

In 1897 Tolstoy completed *Chto takoye iskusstvo?* (*What is Art?*), an attempt to develop an aesthetic system in terms of his religious, moral, and social views. He maintained that a work is art only when it "infects" the reader, hearer, or viewer with the condition of the artist's soul. If there is no union between the artist and his audience through "infection"—that is, if a communication of sympathetic feelings is not conveyed—then the work has failed as art. Among the several degrees of art that Tolstoy recognized, the highest is "religious art"— that which infects people with feelings "flowing from the love of God and man." On this basis, he rejected as art some of the works of, for example, Shakespeare and Wagner. With that maddening consistency that is as much the hallmark of pride as of humility, he relegated his own great works of fiction up to this point to the category of "bad art," because they did not conform to the moral purpose of his new theory.

After his spiritual crisis Tolstoy, apart from his voluminous nonfiction, wrote several tales with a moral purpose, in a bare style devoid of the abundant details of his previous fiction. "Chem lyudi zhivy" ("What Men Live By"), "Dva starika" ("Two Old Men"), "Vrazhye lepko, a bozhye krepko" ("Evil Allures, but Good Endures"), "Mnogo li cheloveku zemli nuzhno?" ("How Much Land Does a Man Need?"), and "Tri voprosa" ("Three Questions") are cast in this new manner. These little masterpieces of construction, which focus on peasant life, belong to his category of "good universal art." Though a moral is present, it is never allowed to obtrude on the artistic unity of the story. Another series of tales, different in manner because they are intended to appeal to educated readers, are closer to the style of his earlier fiction. The finest are the unfinished "Zapiski sumasshedshego" ("Notes of a Madman"), a mystical treatment of man's despair in the face of life's defeats, and "Smert Ivana Ilicha" ("The Death of Ivan Ilich"), in which the hero, a symbolic Everyman, discovers the inner light of faith and love only when confronted by death. The problem of sex, which deeply concerned Tolstoy in his new belief that man's moral health depended on his ability to approach closer to the ideal of chastity, becomes the central theme of "Kreytserova Sonata" ("The Kreutzer Sonata"), a convincing artistic study of jealousy and ill-tempered polemic against society's sexual education of young men and women. Sex is also the main concern of "Dyavol" ("The Devil"), a story inspired by an episode in Tolstoy's life: a man, deeply in love with his young wife, cannot overcome his lust for a pretty peasant girl. The husband's despairing struggle with carnal desire is told with all Tolstoy's psychological mastery.

Sexual themes

A full-length novel, *Voskreseniye* (*Resurrection*), written when he was 71, was Tolstoy's major artistic effort after his "conversion." It is the story of a nobleman who seduces a young girl. She becomes a prostitute and is convicted of a crime that she did not commit, and the conscience-stricken hero, determined to marry her, follows her to Siberia. Though his love redeems her, in the end she refuses to marry him. There are many fine things, especially in the first part, where the account is cast in a bewitching poetic atmosphere. And the trial scene is a brilliant piece of realistic narrative. But *Resurrection* represents a marked falling off, artistically, from *War and Peace* and *Anna Karenina*. It bears evidence of haste, and the moral preaching and sharp attacks on the judicial and penal systems—however deserved—and on the religious services of the church are in the spirit of Tolstoy the polemicist rather than the literary artist.

After his "conversion" Tolstoy strove, by no means with complete success, to bring his daily existence into conformity with his altered views. He abandoned smoking and drinking, became a vegetarian, and often dressed in simple peasant clothes. Since he now believed that no one should depend upon the labour of others, he became as self-sufficient as possible, cleaning his own room, working in the fields, and making his own boots. In the hope of approaching closer to his ideal of chastity, he tried to conquer fleshly desires in his relations with his wife. He also engaged in philanthropic activities, such as the organization of famine relief. The eloquence of Tolstoy's moral and religious writings, his fame, and his vital personality attracted many adherents. Disciples organized colonies in which they endeavoured to live together according to his precepts. Tolstoy distrusted such organized efforts. The truth that brings happiness cannot be preached, he declared; it can be achieved only by individuals who honestly look within themselves. As his own reputation increased and knowledge of his views spread throughout Russia and abroad, hundreds of people from all over the world made their way to Yasnaya Polyana to see and talk with him.

But the older sons, and his wife especially, had little sympathy for Tolstoy's views and his altered way of life. Endless visits of "converts"—the "dark people," his wife called them—and the interference of one of them, V.G. Chertkov, in family affairs caused frequent quarrels between husband and wife. Contrary to his hopes, she refused to surrender her possessions and join him in a life of comparative asceticism. In fact, to secure the family's comfortable existence, she obtained, much against his will, the copyrights of his works printed before 1880, and these writings provided considerable income from editions that she herself published.

During the last part of his life Tolstoy withheld from publication various works, either because he was dissatisfied with them or because he wished to avoid quarrelling with his wife over copyright ownership. In 1911, a year after his death, several of them appeared; they are among his best creations. One is a short novel, *Khadzhi-Murat*, the story of a brave Caucasian warrior who deserts to the Russians and is killed attempting to see his son in secret. The vivid narrative method and psychological revelation of mutual misunderstandings entitle it to a place among the most superb examples of his art. Equally effective, though shorter, are "Otets Sergy" ("Father Sergius"), the story of an aristocrat who conquers his lust and spiritual pride and becomes a hermit-monk; "Falshivy kupon" ("The False Coupon"), a study in fictional form of how the example of goodness, in contrast with the evil-begetting power of evil, inspires good deeds; and "Alyosha Gorshok," a perfect short story of a peasant youth who finds contentment with his lot through submission to all adversities.

Post-
humous
stories
and plays

Several plays were included in the first posthumous collection of his works. Tolstoy believed that drama was "probably the most influential province of art," and at various periods he devoted much effort to writing plays. But he lacked certain of the qualifications necessary to the dramatist, and, though in some instances he succeeded, his plays are inferior, artistically, to his fiction.

Vlast tmy (*The Power of Darkness*), Tolstoy's highest achievement in drama, was first performed in 1888. It is a realistic tragedy of peasant life conceived as an illustration of one of his favourite later themes, suggested by the subtitle, "If a Claw is Caught, the Whole Bird is Lost." The initial evil action of the protagonist—his seducion of another man's wife—leads him to commit further sins, including the final sin of murder. A striking contrast is *Plody prosveshcheniya* (*The Fruits of Enlightenment*), a comedy that genially satirizes the foibles of aristocratic society. Tolstoy never finished *I svet vo tme svetit* (*The Light Shines in Darkness*), though it had a special autobiographical importance, for it concerns the hero's failure to convince his family of the wisdom of his beliefs. *Zhivoy trup* (written 1902; *The Living Corpse*) deals with the tragedy of a drunkard. Conscience stricken over the harm he has caused his wife, he pretends to have died so that she may marry the man she loves. When the police reveal that he is actually alive, he kills himself. The moralizing that appears in Tolstoy's writing in his old age is absent from his play, which is filled with kindness and sympathetic understanding of the erring ways of mankind.

The aging Tolstoy felt keenly the painful contradiction between the life of ease that the family lived and the life he wanted to live—the simple existence of a religious hermit, free of worldly goods and dedicated to service to others. He realized that his position made a mockery of his professed faith. Finally, the worsening domestic situation forced him to leave home stealthily one night, accompanied by his doctor and youngest daughter, Aleksandra, in search of, he hoped, a refuge where he could live quietly and closer to God. A few days later, on November 20 (November 7, O.S.), 1910, he died of pneumonia at the remote railway junction of Astapovo, in Ryazan Province.

Assessment. Tolstoy's eminence as a literary artist has never been seriously questioned by critics; he is universally accepted as one of the greatest writers of fiction in the world. Although never dependent on preceding Russian authors, he may have been influenced by foreign writers, such as Jean-Jacques Rousseau, Sterne, Stendahl, and later, William Thackeray. But there has never been unanimity about his reputation as a thinker. The dualism of Tolstoy's moral and intellectual development, however, has come to be more thoroughly understood by modern students of his thought. In his tireless search for truth he sought for absolutes in a world of incomplete knowledge and imperfect men. As a consequence, his unwillingness to compromise, his compulsive need to achieve the ulti-

mate rational explanation, often led him to push theory to the limits of absurdity, which many believe he came very close to doing in his views on history, nonviolence, education, and art. But any systematic study of his thought reveals its relation to the concepts of 19th-century liberalism. He believed that the whole history of the last 2,000 years had been shaped essentially by the moral development of individuals and the demoralization of governments. Tolstoy placed his faith in the moral development of the people as a final answer to what he regarded as the universal oppression of the many by the few. For him, the progressive movement toward a classless and stateless condition of mankind depended, contrary to the economic determinism and violent class struggle of Marxism, upon the growing moral perfection of each individual through observance of the supreme law of love and the consequent repudiation of every form of violence. Despite the extreme to which he carried his rationalism, Tolstoy is today generally considered to be among the foremost thinkers of the 19th century.

MAJOR WORKS

NOVELS: *Voyna i mir* (1865–69; *War and Peace*, trans. by Louise and Aylmer Maude in "Great Books of the Western World," vol. 51, 1952; trans. by Constance Garnett, 1961); *Anna Karenina* (1875–77; trans. by R.S. Townsend, 2 vol., 1958); *Voskreseniye* (1899; *Resurrection*, trans. by Louise Maude, 1957).

STORIES: *Detstvo* (1852; *Childhood* in *Childhood, Boyhood, Youth*, trans. by R. Edmonds, 1964); "Nabeg" (1853; "The Raid," trans. by Constance Garnett in *Tolstoy Tales*, 1947); *Otrochestvo* (1854; *Boyhood*); "Rubka lesa" (1855; "The Woodfelling" in complete works: *Tolstoy Centenary Edition*, trans. by Louise and Aylmer Maude, 1928–37); "Dva gusara" (1856; "Two Hussars" in complete works); *Yunost* (1857; *Youth*); "Kholstomer" (written 1863, first published 1886; in complete works); *Kazaki* (1863; *The Cossacks; The Death of Ivan Ilyich; Happy Ever After*, trans., by R. Edmonds, 1960); "Chem lyudi zhivy" (1881; "What Men Live By" in *Tolstoy Tales*, trans. by Louise and Aylmer Maude, 1947); "Dva starika" (1885; "Two Old Men"); "Mnogo li cheloveku zemli nuzhno?" (1886; "How Much Land Does a Man Need?"); and "Tri voprosa" (1903; "Three Questions") —all in translation in complete works; "Zapiski Sumasshedshego" (1884; "Notes of a Madman" in *Notes of a Madman and Other Stories*, trans. by S.S. Kotelianisky, 1943); "Smert Ivana Ilicha" (1886; "The Death of Ivan Ilich" in complete works); "Kreytserova sonata" (1891; "The Kreutzer Sonata" in *The Kreutzer Sonata, The Devil, and Other Tales*, trans. by Aylmer Maude, 1940) "Dyavol" (1889; "The Devil" in *The Kreutzer Sonata*); "Otets Sergy" (written 1898, first published 1911; "Father Sergius" in complete works); *Khadzi-Murat* (written 1904, first published 1911; trans. in complete works); "Falshivy kupon" (written 1904, first published 1911; "The False Coupon" in complete works); "Alyosha Gorshok" (written 1905, first published 1911; "Alyosha the Pot").

PHILOSOPHICAL AND SOCIAL WRITINGS: *Ispoved* (written 1878–79, first published 1882; *How I Came to Believe*—"*My Confession*," trans. 1921); *Kritika dogmaticheskoga bogoslaviya* (written 1880, first published 1891; *An Examination of Dogmatic Theology*); *V chyom moya vera* (written 1883, banned 1884; *What I Believe*, trans. by Aylmer Maude, 1940); *Tak chto zhe nam delat?* (finished 1886, first published 1902; *What Then Must We Do?*); *Tsarstvo bozhiye vnutri vas* (1894; *The Kingdom of God Is Within You*); "Dlya chego lyudi odurmanivayutsya" (1890; "Why Do Men Stupefy Themselves?"); "Ne mogu molchat!" (1908; "I Cannot Be Silent!"); *Pisma o genre dzorzhe* (1897; *Letters on Henry George*); and *Chto takoye iskusstvo?* (1898; *What Is Art?*) —all translations in complete works.

BIBLIOGRAPHY

Editions, selections, letters, and diaries: В.Г. ЧЕРТКОВ (ed.), *Л.Н. Толстой: полное собрание произведений*, 90 vol. (1928–58), is the most complete Russian edition of Tolstoy's works, the so-called Jubilee Edition, including his letters, notebooks, and diaries. Of editions in English translations none is complete; the most useful are *The Complete Works of Count Tolstoy*, trans. by LEO WIENER, 24 vol. (1904–05); and *Tolstoy Centenary Edition*, trans. by LOUISE and AYLMER MAUDE, 21 vol. (1928–37). Translations of single fictional works are also available in the Everyman's Library and in Penguin Classics. See also *The Journal of Leo Tolstoi, 1895–1899*, trans. by ROSE STRUNSKY (1917); *The Diaries of Leo Tolstoy: Youth, 1847–1852*, trans. by C.J. HOGARTH and A. SIRNIS (1917); *Leo Tolstoy: Last Diaries*, ed.

by LEON STILMAN (1960); PAUL BIRYUKOV (ed.), *Tolstoi's Love Letters*, trans. by S.S. KOTELIANSKY and VIRGINIA WOOLF (1923); *The Private Diary of Leo Tolstoy, 1853–1857*, trans. by LOUISE and AYLMER MAUDE (1927); *The Letters of Tolstoy and His Cousin Countess Alexandra Tolstoy, 1857–1903*, trans. by LEO ISLAVIN (1929).

Recollections of Tolstoy: S.A. BERS, *Recollections of Count Leo Tolstoy*, trans. by C.E. TURNER (1893); *Reminiscences of Tolstoy, by His Son Count Ilya Tolstoy*, trans. by GEORGE CALDERON (1914); MAXSIM GORKY, *Reminiscenes of Leo Nicolayevitch Tolstoi*, trans. by S.S. KOTELIANSKY and LEONARD WOOLF (1920); *The Autobiography of Countess Sophie Tolstoi*, trans. by S.S. KOTELIANSKY and LEONARD WOOLF (1922); A.B. GOLDENVEIZER, *Talks with Tolstoi*, trans. by S.S. KOTELIANSKY and VIRGINIA WOOLF (1923, reprinted 1969); COUNT LEON L. TOLSTOI, *The Truth About My Father* (1924); AYLMER MAUDE (ed.), *Family Views of Tolstoy* (1926); *The Diary of Tolstoy's Wife, 1860–1891*, trans. by ALEXANDER WERTH (1928); *The Final Struggle: Being Countess Tolstoy's Diary for 1910*, trans. by AYLMER MAUDE (1936); T.A. KUZMINSKAYA, *Tolstoy As I Knew Him*, trans. by NORA SIGERIST et al. (1948); *The Tolstoy Home: Diaries of Tatiana Sukhotin-Tolstoy*, trans. by ALEC BROWN (1951); SERGEI TOLSTOY, *Tolstoy Remembered by His Son*, trans. by MOURA BUDBERG (1961); VALENTIN BULGAKOV, *The Last Year of Leo Tolstoy*, trans. by ANN DUNNIGAN (1971). See also TATIANA SUKHOTIN-TOLSTOY *Sur mon père* (1960).

Biographies: P.A. SERGEENKO, *How Count L.N. Tolstoy Lives and Works* (1899; orig. pub. in Russian, 1898); AYLMER MAUDE, *The Life of Tolstoy*, 2 vol. (1908–10; rev. ed., 1930), one of the best accounts of Tolstoy's post-confessional years; P.I. BIRYUKOV, *Leo Tolstoy: His Life and Work* (1911); V.G. CHERTKOV, *The Last Days of Tolstoy*, trans. by N.A. DUDDINGTON (1922), a valuable account of the family struggle of the last years; A.I. NAZAROV, *Tolstoy: The Inconstant Genius* (1929); E.J. DILLON, *Count Leo Tolstoy: A New Portrait* (1934); DERRICK LEON, *Tolstoy: His Life and Work* (1944); ERNEST J. SIMMONS, *Leo Tolstoy* (1946); ALEXANDRA TOLSTOY, *Tolstoy: A Life of My Father*, trans. by E.R. HAPGOOD (1953); HENRI TROYAT, *Tolstoï* (1965; new ed., 1967; Eng. trans., 1967), the best work on Tolstoy's life. See also CYNTHIA ASQUITH, *Married to Tolstoy* (1960).

Criticism and interpretation: C.E. TURNER, *Count Tolstoi As Novelist and Thinker* (1888); AYLMER MAUDE, *Tolstoy and His Problems*, 2nd ed. (1902); D.S. MEREZHKOVSKI, *Tolstoi As Man and Artist* (1902, reprinted 1970), a classic interpretation that has exercised great influence; A.H.G. CRAUFURD, *The Religion and Ethics of Tolstoy* (1912); G.R. NOYES, *Tolstoy* (1918, reprinted 1968); JANKO LAVRIN, *Tolstoy: A Psycho-Critical Study* (1924; rev. as *Tolstoy: An Approach*, 1944); HELEN E. DAVIS, *Tolstoy and Nietzsche* (1929); G. WILSON KNIGHT, *Shakespeare and Tolstoy* (1934); H.W. GARROD, *Tolstoi's Theory of Art* (1935); DERK BODDE, *Tolstoy and China* (1950); ISAIAH BERLIN, *The Hedgehog and the Fox: An Essay on Tolstoy's View of History* (1953), one of the best books on Tolstoy's world view; GEORGE STEINER, *Tolstoy or Dostoevsky: An Essay in the Old Criticism* (1959), a vivid account of the man and his work; THEODORE REDPATH, *Tolstoy*, 2nd ed. (1969), including a note on recent Russian work on Tolstoy; R.F. CHRISTIAN, *Tolstoy's "War and Peace"* (1962), a valuable source study, and *Tolstoy: A Critical Introduction* (1969); see also THOMAS MANN, *Goethe und Tolstoi* (1932); К. ЛОМУНОВ, *Драмтургия Л.Н. Толстого* (1956); Н.К. ГУДЗИ, *Лев Толстой*, 3rd rev. ed. (1960); А.А. САБУРОВ, *Война и мир* (1959), a representative Soviet study; NADESHDA LUDWIG (ed.), *L.N. Tolstoi: Aufsätze und Essays zum 50. Todestag* (1960); and NICOLAS WEISBEIN, *L'Évolution religieuse de Tolstoï* (1960) and *Europe, novembre-décembre* (1960).

(E.J.Si.)

Tool and Die Making

Tool and die making is the industrial art of manufacturing stamping dies, plastics molds, and jigs and fixtures to be used in producing parts on a mass-production basis. The words "tool" and "die" are generic, and strictly speaking, redundant, because dies are also tools.

History. The development of modern tools and dies can be traced to the American inventor and manufacturer Eli Whitney, who was the first man to implement the concept of the planned manufacturing of interchangeable parts. Each part was manfactured to prescribed dimensions with the aid of tooling, so that the highly skilled craftsmen previously required for manufacturing were no longer needed since no additional fitting or selective assembly of the parts was necessary.

Whitney's tooling consisted of templates (tool-guiding patterns) and rudimentary fixtures—the antecedents of today's tools and dies—and he successfully demonstrated the feasibility of manufacturing interchangeable parts by mass-producing firearms for the War of 1812.

The successful introduction of interchangeable manufacturing and the development of machine tools, both in the 19th century, brought the modern machine shop into being. Then, as still in the early 1970s, the independent machine shop was called a job shop, which meant that it had no product of its own but served large industrial facilities by fabricating tooling, machines, and machine-part replacements. Eventually, some machine shops began to specialize in tooling to the exclusion of other work.

The development of the power press gave rise to a demand for another form of tooling, the press die, the function of which is to cut and form sheet metal into predetermined shapes and configurations. The work of fabricating press dies is similar to, but not identical with, that of producing jigs, fixtures, and other tooling, which led to many of the specialized machine shops labelling themselves tool and die shops.

The 20th-century developments of die casting and injection molding have brought about the demand for still other forms of tooling—the dies used in die casting and plastic molding. The making of these tools has also been taken over by the tool and die shops.

In the second half of the 20th century, however, the traditional tool and die shop was gradually replaced by specialized job shops that produce only one form of tooling. This trend can be attributed to the growing sophistication of tooling, for shops with the skills and equipment necessary to fabricate one form of tooling are seldom equipped for another. Even the single form of toolmaking called diemaking is becoming specialized; some shops now limit themselves to dies for special applications, such as automotive body dies. There is also a trend, although not a strong one, toward specialization according to die material. Some shops make tungsten carbide dies only; others exclude tungsten carbide entirely and work only with tool steel.

Despite the trend toward specialization, the fabrication of the tools of mass production is still referred to as tool and die making and its practitioners as tool and die makers.

Pressworking dies. The fabrication of pressworking dies constitutes the major part of the work done in tool and die shops. Most pressworking dies are utilized in the fabrication of sheet-metal parts that range in size from the finger stop on a dial telephone to the panels of an automobile body. Each pressworking die consists of two sections, called punch and die, or male and female. Both sections are mounted firmly in an electrically or hydraulically driven press. In a working cycle the press ram, on which the male section is mounted, descends into the fixed female section. Any metal interposed between the sections is cut or shaped to a prescribed form.

Like the dies, the presses range in size from extremely small to gigantic. A bench press is often small enough to be picked up manually; but the press that stamps out the roof of a car is generally about three stories high and capable of exerting tons of force.

Blanking dies. The most basic and fundamental of the pressworking dies, the blanking die, is designed to cut a shaped part out of a flat piece of sheet metal. The punch, driven downward by the press ram, pierces a flat part out of an incoming strip of sheet metal. The stamping thus produced is usually subjected to subsequent operations in more complex dies.

Forming dies. A sectional view of a forming die is shown in Figure 1, a simple example, presented here to show the elements and principles involved. As with blanking dies, the press tool consists of a male punch and a female die section. In this case, however, the descending punch forms a precut blank into a desired configuration. Correct positioning of the blank prior to forming is effected by gauges mounted on the lower die section.

Draw dies. Drawing, one of the most difficult but most frequently encountered press operations, requires a die

Contribution of Eli Whitney

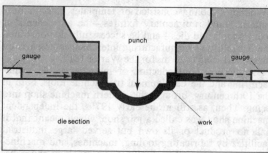

Figure 1: Forming die.

capable of inducing plastic flow in a sheet-metal part. The need for plastic flow stems from the fact that some parts cannot be formed by bending. A metal cup, a cartridge case, and the rear quarter panel of an automobile are examples. The reason that these parts cannot be formed without plastic flow is that flat sheet metal forced onto a curvilinear die surface cannot resist wrinkling. This problem can be visualized by attempting to force a sheet of paper into a drinking tumbler so that it adheres evenly and with uniform thickness to the surfaces of the sides and bottom.

A solution to the problem is found in a device called a holding ring, or binder (Figure 2). Before the punch contacts the metal to force it into the die cavity, the holding ring—which is pressurized—grips the edges of the metal sheet. Since the metal is restrained, the descending punch sets up a plastic flow process that enables the metal to be drawn into the die. While the physics involved in this process is rather complex, it may be said that sheet metal can be made to flow into a difficult configuration if sufficient binding pressure is exerted upon it. Without this capability, fabrication of complex sheet-metal shapes such as the modern automobile body would be difficult if not impossible. The square-cut look of vintage automobiles is not due to the early designer's preferences but to the fact that the draw process was not perfected in the early days of the automobile.

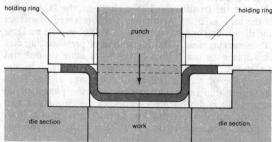

Figure 2: Draw die.

Coining dies. These dies impart embossed configurations to sheet metal parts. Obvious examples are the dies used in making coins. A strip of metal is fed through a die mounted in a small press. With each cycle of the press, an inscription is made on the sheet. Subsequently, the inscribed area is cut from the sheet by blanking to produce a coin.

Progressive dies. Such basic operations as blanking, forming, and drawing are normally performed individually. Depending on their complexity, some parts must go through a sequence of as many as 20 different operations, requiring as many as 20 different dies.

During World War I it was discovered that many different operations can be combined in a single die. The result was the progressive die, so named because the part is made by advancing through a progressive sequence of operations.

The design rationale of the progressive die is that a part outline can be defined in an incoming strip of metal by blanking or cutting away certain portions of the strip. The strip serves to carry the part through the sequence of operations, the last of which is a cutoff operation that severs the completed part. The implications of this form

of tooling can be appreciated by considering that in a ten-station progressive die the press cycles ten times before the first part emerges from the die. But starting with the tenth "hit," a finished part is produced with every cycle.

Press brake dies. This form of tooling is designed for bending and forming relatively long, slender parts, such as the frames and casements of steel and aluminum windows. The dies used to form these elements may have a length-to-width ratio of 100:1, hence a specialized press is required. Called a press brake, this machine has a very narrow, bladelike ram. A variety of extremely complex forming operations can be performed in press brake operations.

Hydroforming. This recently developed process replaces the upper die half with a fluid pressure-forming chamber as shown in Figure 3. As the ram of the Hydro-

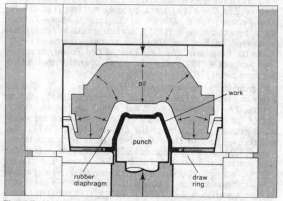

Figure 3: Hydroform die.

form machine descends, the diaphragm of the pressure chamber contacts the workpiece and forces it over a punch located in the lower half of the press. The operation performed is essentially that of drawing, but the capabilities of Hydroforming vastly exceed those of conventional drawing.

Plastic molds. The fabrication of plastic molds is another of the many forms of tool and die making. They are not properly referred to as dies, however, even though in many cases there is a visual resemblance.

The major plastic molding processes are injection molding, compression molding, transfer molding, and casting. The principal distinction between the molding processes and casting is that molding requires force while casting does not. Otherwise, the tooling involved is often quite similar.

Injection molding. As in sheet metal pressworking, two units are required—one mounted on a stationary platen, the other on a movable platen. The latter resembles the ram in a metalworking press, although the configuration of the machine is horizontal rather than vertical.

Design of the two mold halves is such that—when brought together—they make up a system of closed cavities linked by passages called runners. The runners, in turn, are linked to a central orifice called a sprue. Upon closure of the two mold units, a device called a reciprocating screw forces liquid plastic into the sprue. Continuing pressure from the screw forces the plastic into the runners, then into the cavities. The plastic then solidifies, the molds open, and the finished parts—along with their connecting runners—are ejected.

Parts formed by injection molding can be either thermoplastic or thermosetting. The distinction is that a thermoplastic can be resoftened by the application of heat whereas a thermosetting material cannot. This makes relatively little difference in mold design, but it does make a substantial difference in the design of the injection-molding machine.

Compression molding. Seldom used for thermoplastics, compression molding is one of the more commonly used methods of processing thermosetting materials. In this technology a plastic material in powdered form is placed in a mold. The mold halves then close, subjecting the powder to high compressive forces. At the same time, heat emanating from the dies liquefies the plastic, causing it to fill all recesses of the mold. Subsequent cooling by water circulating through the mold causes the plastic to harden. The mold then opens and the finished part is removed.

Fabrication of these molds is relatively simple. They must be highly polished, however, since any imperfection in the mold cavity is duplicated in the finished product. Polishing is generally accomplished by buffing the surfaces with diamond dust.

Other plastics molds. Casting, blow molding, extrusion molding, and high-pressure laminating are other plastics-working processes that require tooling fabricated in tool and die shops. It is worth noting, however, that the increasing specialization previously referred to has resulted in the emergence of the mold shop. These shops generally limit the work they accept to jobs associated with the plastic-fabricating industries.

Die-casting dies. Die-casting dies are of basically the same design as the injection mold. Two die halves are used; the two units establish a system of runners and cavities when closed. Liquid metal, usually zinc, is forced into the system by a plunger. Once in the cavities, the molten metal solidifies into a number of parts connected by solidified metal from the runners. The die-casting machine, a variation of the press, then opens and the parts are freed.

Jigs and fixtures. These two forms of tooling now constitute a small portion of the work done in tool and die shops. They are still important, but their range of applications is diminishing.

Drill jigs. Drill jigs are used when holes must be drilled in a specified relationship to various part features. Generally—although not always—a jig is a receptacle in which the workpiece can be placed and securely clamped. Precision guidance of the drill is accomplished with drill bushings. These are hardened steel devices just large enough for the drill to enter.

The ultimate form taken by any drill jig depends upon part shape and size, which means that the number of possibilities is infinite. The advent of numerically controlled machining in the early 1950s, however, largely obviated the need for jigs. In many cases hole patterns are now programmed into punched tape. Acting upon tape instructions, the machine table automatically moves the workpiece for precise positioning relative to a machine spindle, which is then activated—also by taped instructions—to machine the hole.

Fixtures. No really consistent semantic distinction separates a jig from a fixture. The drill jig previously discussed is often referred to as a "drill fixture." A fixture designed exclusively for drilling operation is a jig, which means that the phrase "jigs and fixtures" is as implausible as "apples and fruit." Nonetheless, this is the terminology of the industry.

When a workpiece is of such a shape that it cannot be held in a standard work-holding device such as a vise or a chuck, a special fixture is necessary. Fixtures are used to locate and position parts for virtually all machining operations, as well as for assembly and welding operations.

Tool-and-die-making facilities. *Contract shops.* Tools and dies are generally fabricated by job shops that work on a contract basis. The shops, which in many countries are family-owned, may have as few as ten men and as many as 100. For the most part they obtain their contracts to fabricate tooling through a process of competitive bidding.

To be competitive a tool and die shop must be equipped with all of the standard types of machine tools for the machining of metal parts to precise dimensions. It must also have adequate inspection devices. Finally, if a shop is in the business of building stamping dies, it must be equipped with one or more tryout presses. Thus even a small shop represents a sizable capital investment.

When a contract for a job is obtained, the superintendent orders the necessary steel and stock parts (screws, dowel pins, die shoes, etc.), and assigns the job to a leader, who in turn assigns it to a bench hand who subdivides it among his crew. The various parts—now referred to as details—are then laid out according to the customer's blueprint and routed to the machine leaders. After machining, the details are returned to the leader. Subsequently, they are sent to a heat-treating facility for hardening. After hardening, they are finish-ground to specified size and assembled into the finished tool.

If the job is a stamping die, it must be proved acceptable by successful operation in a tryout press. This phase of the operation is often the most difficult because it is virtually impossible to predict die performance.

Manufacturing plants. Every manufacturing plant that uses tools and dies must maintain a small tool and die facility. The work performed in these facilities is generally limited to tool maintenance. The only exceptions to this are certain very large manufacturers who can maintain a continuous flow of work in their shops and may wish for security with respect to new designs, since design plans are revealed with blueprints are released for bidding.

BIBLIOGRAPHY. H.W. BREDIN (ed.), *Tooling Methods and Ideas* (1967), a compilation of noteworthy examples of jigs and fixtures, previously published in *Machinery* magazine; D.B. DALLAS, "Automated Pressworking: An Installation in Action," *Manufacturing Engineering and Management*, pp. 27–30 (Aug. 1970), a description of an unusual three-dimensional transfer die; C.W. HINMAN, *Die Engineering Layouts and Formulas* (1943), an authoritative treatise on die engineering and die making; F.W. WILSON (ed.), *Die Design Handbook*, 2nd ed. (1965), articles by many industrial experts treating all phases of die engineering and die-making practice, *Handbook of Fixture Design* (1962), articles by many industrial experts covering the fundamentals of jig and fixture design, and including numerous examples of conventional and outstanding designs.

(D.B.D.)

Topological Groups and Differential Topology

The interaction of classical and modern mathematical methods have been most productive in that area of analysis (see ANALYSIS, REAL; ANALYSIS, COMPLEX; ANALYSIS, FOURIER; ANALYSIS, FUNCTIONAL) in which topological methods (see TOPOLOGY, GENERAL) play a role. In turn, the result has stimulated much work in topology and other branches of mathematics and has important applications in theoretical physics.

It is advantageous to consider topological methods in analysis under three headings and in rather different manners. The first section, the theorems of Tikhonov (also spelled Tychonoff) and Ascoli, considers two basic theorems that can be proved in a quite general setting and the importance of which cannot be overstressed. The second section, continuous groups, after some preliminary remarks, starts from the definition of a topological group and develops a theory that is gradually seen to encompass a whole range of general results. The third section, analysis on manifolds, is largely concerned with working from some important problems in classical analysis, discusses the methods topologists have employed in tackling them, and shows how the body of theory so developed has built itself into a coherent whole. Then in the discussion of differential topology, basic concepts, methods, and classification of manifolds are treated in detail. In this way a broad view of the areas of topological groups and differential topology is presented.

Before proceeding, however, some elementary and general remarks on the role of topology in analysis will be helpful. A distinctive feature of topological arguments in analysis is that they are qualitative and non-numerical. A simple instance of topological reasoning is the following. A ball is thrown vertically upward and a few moments later it falls back to its starting point: one deduces that at some point on the way it must have been stationary. This observation depends, of course, on certain preconceptions about gravity and the continuity properties of space and time. When suitably formulated, they form the foundation of analysis and topology. Now in such a simple example as a falling ball an elementary ap-

Use of punched tape for hole patterns

Shop routine

The use of topology in analysis

plication of the Newtonian calculus will give full information about the whole motion, while the topological argument merely asserts the obvious. If, however, a single ball is now replaced by a large number of balls, moving in more complicated ways, then direct analytical computation may become too lengthy or difficult. In such a situation one may settle for some qualitative aspects of the various motions, which may be derived by topological arguments but which may be far from self-evident because of the complexity of the situation. In fact, if the various balls are replaced by planets and one proceeds to study the Newtonian motion of several bodies under their mutual gravitational attraction, extremely difficult and unsolved mathematical problems are met. It was precisely the analytical difficulties of the many-body problem that motivated the French mathematician Henri Poincaré in his pioneering work on topology around the beginning of the 20th century.

This article is divided into the following sections:

Topological methods in analysis
  The theorems of Tikhonov and Ascoli
  Continuous groups
  Analysis on manifolds
Differential topology
  Basic concepts: the differentiable category
  Problems and methods of differential topology
  Results on the classification of manifolds

Topological methods in analysis

THE THEOREMS OF TIKHONOV AND ASCOLI

These theorems of the 20th-century Soviet mathematician Andrey Nikolayevich Tikhonov and of the 19th-century Italian mathematician Giulio Ascoli, which have far-reaching consequences throughout analysis, both make statements about the compactness of a topological space following hypotheses of compactness of spaces from which the space is constructed. A topological space is compact if every covering by open sets has a finite subcovering, and, in the case of a metric space (a space in which one can define a distance between any two points; see further TOPOLOGY, GENERAL), this is equivalent to every sequence having a convergent subsequence. If $\{X_\lambda : \lambda \in \Lambda\}$ is an arbitrary family of topological spaces, then the product topology on the product set (consisting of all functions x on Λ such that $x(\lambda) \in X_\lambda$ for each λ in Λ; see Box, equation 1) is that family containing all sets that are unions of sets of the form $\pi\{T_\lambda : \lambda \in \Lambda\}$, in which all of the sets T_λ are open in X_λ and all but a finite number of the sets T_λ are such that $T_\lambda = X_\lambda$. When the family consists of only two spaces X_1 and X_2, the product topology on $X_1 \times X_2$ consists of sets that are unions of sets of the form $T_1 \times T_2$ in which T_1 is open in X_1 and T_2 is open in X_2. Tikhonov's theorem states that the topological space consisting of the product set X with the product topology is compact whenever each X_λ is compact.

Because of the importance of compact spaces, it is often useful to be able to imbed a topological space as a subspace of a compact space, thus obtaining a compactification of the original space. The construction of the compactification due to the 20th-century Czech mathematician Eduard Čech and the 20th-century U.S. mathematician M.H. Stone, which is the one most frequently employed in analysis, leans heavily on Tikhonov's theorem. It imbeds an arbitrary completely regular Hausdorff space [that is, a Hausdorff space X such that, for each element x in X and each open set U in X containing x, there exists a continuous real-valued function f such that $f(x) = 0$ and $f(X - U) = 1$] in a topological space that is a product of compact intervals of the real line. Another application of Tikhonov's theorem is in proving that the set of linear functionals of norm less than or equal to unity (one) is compact in the Banach space Y of all bounded linear functionals on a Banach space Z when Y is given the weak-star topology.

Suppose now that F is a family of continuous functions f from a topological space X to a uniform space Y. The compact-open topology on F is that topology generated by sets of the form of the set of all f such that f

Compact spaces

$$
\begin{array}{ll}
(1) & X = \Pi\{X_\lambda : \lambda \in \Lambda\} \\[1em]
(2) & \{f : f \in F \quad \text{and} \quad f(C) \subset U\} \\[1em]
(3) & f(T) \subset \{y : y \in Y \quad \text{and} \quad (f(x), y) \in V\}
\end{array}
$$

belongs to F and the map of f of C is contained in U (see 2) in which C is a compact subset of X and U is an open subset in the uniform topology on Y. F is said to be an equicontinuous family if, for each x in X and for each entourage V of the uniformity on Y, there exists an open set T in X containing x such that $f(T)$ is contained in the collection of all y such that y belongs to Y and the pair $f(x)$ and y belongs to V (see 3) for each $f \in F$. A general form of Ascoli's theorem asserts that when the family G of all continuous functions from X to Y is made into a topological space by being given the compact-open topology, and when F is an equicontinuous subfamily closed in this topology and such that $\{f(x) : f \in F\}$ is a compact subset of Y for each x in X, then F is a compact subset of G. One important application of Ascoli's theorem is in proving the existence of eigenvalues of Fredholm operators (see ANALYSIS, FUNCTIONAL) in the theory of integral equations. (An integral equation is one in which a function to be determined appears in the integrand of some integral.)

The English mathematician Peter John Collins has shown that both Tikhonov's theorem and Ascoli's theorem are corollaries of a single very general compactness theorem.
                                     (Ed.)

CONTINUOUS GROUPS

The name continuous groups has been employed since the 19th century for a variety of mathematical structures, some of which are not even groups. Roughly speaking, the study arose from situations in which there is an infinite number of symmetries present. The set of symmetries is called "the group of transformations admitted by" the situation. In the early days of the theory, which was fathered largely by the Norwegian mathematician Sophus Lie, much of the research was devoted to applications to the theory of differential equations. (A differential equation is an equation involving one or more derivatives of some function to be determined; see DIFFERENTIAL EQUATIONS.) As one might expect, the presence of symmetries serves to reduce many difficulties by drastically limiting possibilities. Toward the end of the 19th century, the work of a French mathematician, Élie-Joseph Cartan, shifted the course of investigation toward a deeper analysis, both algebraic and topological, of the continuous group itself. So fruitful were some of Cartan's ideas that they molded some of the basic notions of algebra and topology. The threefold structure of continuous groups—algebraic, topological, and analytic—has attracted a variety of methods of attack, some of them marked by brilliant developments. The work of Lie and of Cartan had revealed many of the fundamental properties of continuous groups before the end of the 19th century. Rather than retrace their steps, this section begins by introducing some 20th-century terms; the early developments in the relations between groups and differential equations are presented later.

The work of Élie-Joseph Cartan

Topological groups.   A topological group G is a group G the elements of which are the points of a topological space for which the group operations are continuous. In greater detail, the multiplication and inverse defined in G satisfy the postulates:

G1. The associative law: $(xy)z = x(yz)$ for all x, y, z, of G.
G2. Existence of an identity: There is an identity element 1, such that $1x = x1 = x$ for every x of G.
G3. Existence of an inverse: for every x of G there is an element x^{-1} such that $x^{-1}x = xx^{-1} = 1$, in which 1 is the identity element.
G4. The mapping $x \rightarrow x^{-1}$ from G to G is continuous.
G5. The mapping $(x, y) \rightarrow xy$ from $G \times G$ to G is continuous.

The conditions (G1)–(G3) say that G is a group. The condition that G is a topological space for which the group operations are continuous means that there is a notion of "nearness" among the various elements of G so that if x' is near x then x'^{-1} is near x^{-1} (G4) and if y' is near y then $x'y'$ is near xy (G5).

The following are familiar examples of topological groups:

Example 1. G is the set of all real numbers with addition as the group product.

Example 2. G is the set of all complex numbers z with $|z| = 1$ and with multiplication as the group product.

Example 3. G is the set of all rigid motions in Euclidean space (the space of ordinary geometry; see TOPOLOGY, GENERAL) that keep some point O fixed. Here the group product is taken as composition of motions; that is, if T_2 and T_1 are in G, $T_2 \cdot T_1$ is the motion that takes any point p into $T_2(T_1(p))$.

Example 4. G is the group of all $n \times n$ matrices with complex coefficients and nonzero determinant, the group product being the usual matrix multiplication.

The groups in examples 1 and 2 above are Abelian; that is, $xy = yx$ for any two elements x and y. The groups in examples 2 and 3 above are compact; that is, any infinite sequence of elements $x_1, x_2, \cdots, x_n, \cdots$ contains a subsequence converging to an element of the group. The group in example 4 above is neither Abelian nor compact, but it is locally compact; that is, each element has a compact neighbourhood. Each of the groups in the examples is locally Euclidean; that is, each point has a neighbourhood resembling topologically a solid ball in Euclidean space of dimensions 1, 1, 3 and n^2, respectively.

The theory of topological groups has developed in three principal directions: the theory of the algebraic structure, of the topological structure, and of representations by transformation groups.

The algebraic structure of a topological group is especially accessible to investigation in case the group operations are analytic. In greater detail, in a topological space, a continuous function can be defined as any real-valued function f with the property that $f(x')$ is close to $f(x)$ if x' is close to x. One cannot speak, however, of differentiable or analytic functions on a locally Euclidean topological space in a self-consistent fashion unless one is given a rule by which to pick out from the totality of continuous functions the differentiable and analytic functions. A locally Euclidean space with such a rule is called a differentiable or analytic manifold, as the case may be. For simplicity, this article deals with analytic manifolds.

An analytic coordinate system around a point p in an analytic manifold is a finite sequence of functions $(x_1, \cdots, x_k)$ defined near p with the property: a function f is analytic around p if, and only if, it is expressible as a convergent power series in $x_1 \cdots, x_k$ in some neighbourhood of the point p. In an analytic manifold M there is of course an analytic coordinate system around each point, but in general the coordinate system is not defined throughout the manifold.

If $(x_1, \cdots, x_k)$ is an analytic coordinate system, the map $\Phi: p \to (x_1(p), \cdots, x_k(p))$ is a map of a neighbourhood of p onto a neighbourhood in Euclidean k-space E^k and the map Φ is a topological equivalence or homeomorphism of some neighbourhood of p onto a solid ball in E^k.

A map φ (taking possibly many points into a single point) of a manifold M into a manifold N is called an analytic map if for any analytic function f defined in a region of N, the composite function $f \circ \varphi$ is analytic in M [note that $f \circ \varphi(m) = f(\varphi(m))$].

A Lie group G is a topological group of a special kind: the underlying space is an analytic manifold for which the group operations are analytic. That is, the map $(x, y) \to xy$ of the analytic manifold of ordered pairs $G \times G$ into G is an analytic map, and the map $x \to x^{-1}$ of G into G also is analytic.

Infinitesimal transformations. One of the basic notions in the theory of Lie groups is that of infinitesimal transformation. If M is an analytic manifold and m is a point of M, then it is possible to speak of a tangent vector to M at m. In case M is a surface in Euclidean space, a tangent vector to a surface is regarded as a vector in the containing Euclidean space.

It is possible, however, to make a mathematically satisfactory intrinsic definition of a tangent vector to a manifold (*i.e.*, without reference to a containing Euclidean space) by means of the following consideration: a tangent vector X is completely determined once it is known how functions vary along it; that is, the directional derivative of functions along X. Hence for all purposes the notion of tangent vector X can be equated with the operation of taking the directional derivative along X. In this pragmatic spirit the following definition is adopted: a tangent vector X to a manifold M at a point m is an operator that assigns to each real-valued function f analytic around m a real number Xf, called the directional derivative of f along X, such that the effect of X upon the sum of two functions, the product of two functions, and a constant times a function are specified by certain formulas (see 4).

$$(4) \quad \begin{cases} X(f+g) = Xf + Xg \\ X(fg) = (Xf)g(m) + f(m)X(g) \\ X(af) = aXf, \text{ for analytic functions } f, g \text{ and constant } a \end{cases}$$

$$(5) \quad \partial/\partial x_i = (\partial y_1/\partial x_i)(\partial/\partial y_1) + (\partial y_2/\partial x_i)(\partial/\partial y_2) + \cdots + (\partial y_k/\partial x_i)(\partial/\partial y_k)$$

$$(6) \quad \begin{cases} X(f+g) = Xf + Xg \\ X(fg) = Xf \cdot g + f \cdot Xg \\ X(af) = aXf \end{cases}$$

It is easily proved that the set of all tangent vectors at a point m of a k-dimensional manifold constitutes a linear or vector space the dimension of which is k (over the field of real numbers). This linear space is called the tangent space to M at m, and it is denoted by $\dot{M}_m$. A vector field on a manifold M is a rule that assigns to each point m of M an element of $\dot{M}_m$. To illustrate, let $(x_1, \cdots, x_k)$ be an analytic coordinate system on a neighbourhood V of manifold M; $(\partial/\partial x_i)(m)$ denotes the operator that assigns to the analytic function $f(x_1, \cdots, x_k)$ the value of $\partial f/\partial x_i$ at the point m. Then $(\partial/\partial x_i)(m)$ is a tangent vector to M at m, and $(\partial/\partial x_1)(m), \cdots, (\partial/\partial x_k)(m)$ form a base for the vector space $\dot{M}_m$. $\partial/\partial x_i$ denotes the vector field $p \to (\partial/\partial x_i)(p)$ on the neighbourhood V. The most general vector field on V has the form $\Sigma_i A_i \partial/\partial x_i$, in which $A_1, \cdots, A_k$ are functions on V. An infinitesimal transformation on an (analytic) manifold is a vector field X such that for any analytic function f on M, the function $Xf: p \to X(p)f$ is analytic. An infinitesimal transformation on the neighbourhood V above is any vector field $X = \Sigma A_i \partial/\partial x_i$ such that the functions $A_1 \cdots, A_k$ are analytic. If $(y_1, \cdots, y_k)$ is a second coordinate system, then $\partial f/\partial x_i = \Sigma_j (\partial f/\partial y_j)(\partial y_j/\partial x_i)$, so that the form of the differential transformation is determined (see 5). An infinitesimal transformation X can also be equated with the operation $f \to Xf$ taking any analytic function f into the analytic function Xf. Indeed, any operation X assigning to any analytic function f an analytic function Xf such that the algebraic properties already specified for the directional derivative hold (see 6) for any analytic functions f and g, a being any constant, determines a unique infinitesimal transformation.

A map φ of an analytic manifold M into an analytic manifold N induces a map of the tangent space $\dot{M}_m$ into the tangent space $\dot{N}_{\varphi(m)}$ called the differential of φ at M and denoted by $d\varphi_m$, as follows: $d\varphi_m(X)f = X(f\varphi)$ for any function f analytic in M around the point m.

For example, if φ is an analytic curve in N—*i.e.*, an analytic map of the manifold of real numbers (t) into

N—then $d\varphi_t((d/dt)(t))$ is the tangent vector at the point $\varphi(t)$ that assigns to any function f on N the value $df(\varphi(t))/dt$; $d\varphi_t((d/dt)(t))$ is called the tangent to the curve φ at the point $\varphi(t)$. In case φ is a map of an analytic manifold into the real numbers—i.e., φ is a real-valued function on M—then for any tangent vector X in $\dot{M}_m$, $d\varphi(X)$ is a numerical factor of the tangent vector $(d/dt)(\varphi(m))$; the numerical factor is also denoted by $d\varphi(X)$. By this convention, $d\varphi$ becomes a real-valued function of tangent vectors in case φ is an analytic (or differentiable) real-valued function on M; this $d\varphi$ coincides with the classical definition of differential.

If X is an infinitesimal transformation on an analytic manifold M, then, by the fundamental existence and uniqueness theorem of ordinary differential equations, there passes through each point p of M a unique trajectory to X with initial point p; that is, an analytic curve $\varphi(p, t)$ in M with $\varphi(p, o) = p$ and the tangent to the curve at any point q coinciding with the tangent vector $X(q)$; more explicitly, $df(\varphi(p, t))/dt = Xf(\varphi(p, t))$ for any t and for any function f analytic in M. The notation exp tX is used to denote the map $p \rightarrow \varphi$ (p, t); for any point p, exp tX is defined for suitably small values of t (but not necessarily all). Thus an infinitesimal transformation can be thought of as the velocity field of a steady flow on a manifold, and exp tX is the displacement of points after t units of time.

In the special case that M is the set of real numbers and $X = \partial/\partial x = d/dx$, $(d/dt)x(\exp tX(p)) = dx/dx = 1$ and exp $tX(p) = p + t$. If $X = x^2 d/dx$, then exp $tX(p)$ is the trajectory to $dx/dt = x^2$, and exp $tX(p) = p/(1 - pt)$, which is not defined for $t = 1/p$. The term infinitesimal transformation owes its origin to the fact that for small values of the parameter t, the transformation exp tX consists of the displacement (see 7) up to infinitesimals of order t^2 if $X = \Sigma_i A_i \partial/\partial x_i$. If X is an infinitesimal transformation on a manifold, then $f(\exp tX(p)) = \Sigma(1/n!)t^n X^n f(p)$, the sum taken from $n = 0$ to ∞, whenever both sides are defined. This identity can be stated in a more familiar form when the following notational convention is adopted: if φ is a map of a space M into a space N, $\varphi(f)$ denotes the composite function $f \circ \varphi$ where f is a function on N. Thus by definition, $f(\varphi(m)) = (\varphi(f))(m)$. By this convention φ is regarded not only as a map of points of M into points of N but also as the equivalent indicated map of functions on N into functions on M. Adhering to this convention, the identity above states the formal expansion of the exponential (see 8) as operators on analytic functions on M, whenever both sides can be applied.

It is clear from (8) that a point m is fixed under the transformation exp tX for all t if, and only if, the point m is a zero of X; i.e., $X(m) = 0$ or $Xf(m) = 0$ for any analytic function f.

Local (pseudo-) groups of transformations. If G is a topological group and M a topological space and $P(M)$ denotes the set of all permutations of M (i.e., all transformations of M onto M which have inverses), then an operation of G on M is a rule T that assigns to each g in G an element $T(g)$ in $P(M)$ in such a way that multiplication in G corresponds to composition in $P(M)$ (see 9). Moreover, the element $T(g)(m)$ should depend continuously on g and m. If G is a Lie group and M is an analytic manifold, an operation is called analytic if the point $T(g)(m)$ depends analytically on g and m. An important variation on this idea is that of a local pseudo-group (sometimes called simply local group) operating on a manifold. Briefly, a local Lie group is a structure that resembles a neighbourhood N of the identity in a Lie group; products are not always defined but, when they are, the group postulates are fulfilled. The celebrated first and second fundamental theorems of Lie describe the relation between local Lie groups on a manifold and infinitesimal transformations.

An analytic family N of transformations of M is a one-to-one map T of N into $P(M)$ such that $T(n)(m)$ depends analytically on n and m. It is assumed that for some n_0 in N, $T(n_0)$ is the identity transformation of M. The map T_n is considered, which assigns to each tangent vector

$$(7) \qquad (x_1, \cdots, x_k) \rightarrow (x_1 + tA_1, \cdots, x_k + tA_k)$$

$$(8) \qquad \exp(iX) = \sum_0^\infty (n!)^{-1} i^n X^n$$

$$(9) \qquad T(g_1 g_2) = T(g_1) \circ T(g_2)$$

$$(10) \qquad T_n(X)(m) = d\phi_n(X)$$

$$(11) \qquad \begin{cases} X = \Sigma_i A_i \dfrac{\partial}{\partial x_i}, \qquad Y = \Sigma_i B_i \dfrac{\partial}{\partial x_i} \quad \text{and} \\[2mm] [X, Y] = \Sigma_{ij}\left(A_j \dfrac{\partial B_i}{\partial x_j} - B_j \dfrac{\partial A_i}{\partial x_i}\right)\dfrac{\partial}{\partial x_i} \end{cases}$$

$$(12) \qquad \begin{cases} [X, Y] = -[Y, X] \quad \text{and} \\[1mm] [[X, Y], Z] + [[Y, Z], X] + [[Z, X], Y] = 0 \end{cases}$$

$$(13) \qquad \exp(t_1 X_1) \cdot \exp(t_2 X_2) \cdot \ldots \cdot \exp(t_r X_r)$$

$$(14) \qquad \{\exp X; X \in \mathfrak{F}\}$$

$X \in \dot{N}_n$ an infinitesimal transformation $T_n(X)$ by the rule that involves the differential of φ (see 10) in which $\varphi: p \rightarrow (T(p) \cdot T(n)^{-1})(m)$ maps N into M and n into m. Roughly speaking, the infinitesimal transformation $T_n(X)$ describes how $T(p)$ differs from $T(n)$ as the point p moves away from the point n along a path the tangent vector of which at n is X.

Lie's first fundamental theorem states that $T_n(\dot{N}_n)$ is independent of the point n if, and only if, N is a local Lie group and T is an analytic operation of N on M. If this is the case, the family of infinitesimal transformations $T_n(\dot{N}_n)$ is called the infinitesimal generator of the local Lie group of transformations $T(N)$.

[Lie's first fundamental theorem]

It is readily verified that if X and Y are infinitesimal transformations on M, the operator $XY - YX$ is an infinitesimal transformation. $XY - YX$ is denoted by $[X, Y]$ and is called the Poisson bracket of X and Y. If $(x_1, \cdots, x_k)$ is an analytic coordinate system on a neighbourhood in M, then the specific forms for the infinitesimal transformations X and Y lead to an explicit structure in the Poisson bracket (see 11).

Directly from definitions, it may be seen that two identities follow (see 12); the latter one is known as the Jacobi identity.

If $\mathfrak{F}$ is a set of infinitesimal transformations it is called a Lie algebra of infinitesimal transformations if (1) $\mathfrak{F}$ is a linear family—that is, $\mathfrak{F}$ contains any linear combination of its elements with constant coefficients; and (2) $\mathfrak{F}$ contains the Poisson brackets of any of its elements.

Lie's second fundamental theorem states that a family of infinitesimal transformations $\mathfrak{F}$ is the infinitesimal generator of a finite-dimensional local Lie group of transformations if, and only if, $\mathfrak{F}$ is a finite-dimensional (over the field of constants) Lie algebra of infinitesimal transformations. The corresponding local Lie group of transformations is the set of all transformations of the form of a product of exponentials (see 13) in which $X_1, \cdots, X_r$ is a base for $\mathfrak{F}$ and $t_1, \cdots, t_r$ is any set of real numbers that are suitably small. The elements of the corresponding local group can also be described as the set of all transformations of exponential type with X belonging to the family of infinitesimal transformations (see 14). It may happen that the corresponding local group G is indeed a genuine group. In that case neither the elements of the form (6) nor (7) necessarily exhaust G; they merely cover a neighbourhood of the identity in G in general.

[Lie's second theorem]

In case the family $\mathfrak{F}$ of Lie's second fundamental theorem is infinite-dimensional, there arises a so-called infinite Lie pseudo-group. These pseudo-groups were studied extensively by Cartan, but basic questions about the nature of such structures were left unanswered. In the

1950s several independent investigations into some of these questions were initiated. In this article, however, the term Lie group is reserved for the finite-dimensional case alone.

With the help of his second fundamental theorem, Lie was able to determine all the local groups of transformations depending on a finite number of parameters (constants that distinguish special cases) that operate on the line, plane, and, in certain cases, on higher dimensional spaces. For example, it is relatively easy to show that the only finite-dimensional Lie algebras of infinitesimal transformations on the line that have no common zeros have in suitable coordinates one of three bases (see 15). These are the generators of three basic groups (see 16). These three are thus up to equivalence the only finite-dimensional local Lie groups operating transitively on the line.

The last example shows clearly that a local group of transformations of the line need not be a piece of a global group of transformations of the line. It is true, however, that any local Lie group has a neighbourhood of its identity that is *in abstracto* isomorphic (in a one-to-one correspondence) to a neighbourhood of the identity in some genuine (global) Lie group.

The Lie algebra of a Lie group. Consider now a Lie group G. For each g in G, $T(g)$ denotes the left translation map $x \to gx$ of G onto G. Then T is an analytic operation of G on G. By Lie's first fundamental theorem, the group $T(G)$ has an infinitesimal generator, and by Lie's second fundamental theorem, the infinitesimal generator is a Lie algebra of infinitesimal transformations; this infinitesimal generator is denoted by $\dot{G}$ and is called the Lie algebra of G. It is readily proved that $\dot{G}$ consists of precisely those infinitesimal transformations on G that are left unchanged by the right translations $x \to xg$ of G into G. It follows at once that each infinitesimal translation in G is uniquely determined by its value at the origin. Thus as a linear space, $\dot{G}$ is equivalent to $\dot{G}_e$, the tangent space of G at the identity element e. If X is an element of $\dot{G}_e$, and $\bar{X}$ is the element of G determined by X, then one defines $\exp \bar{X}(e)$. Also, $[X, Y]$ is defined to be the value at e of $[\bar{X}, \bar{Y}]$, in which $\bar{X}$ and $\bar{Y}$ are the elements of G with $\bar{X}(e) = X$ and $\bar{Y}(e) = Y$.

In the special case that G is the group $GL(n)$ of all inversible linear transformations of an n-dimensional linear space V_n over the real numbers, the tangent space to G at the identity element can be identified with the set of all linear transformations of V_n. Then for any $X \in \dot{G}_e$, $\exp X$ coincides with the classical exponential of the transformation X; that is, $\exp X = \Sigma_i \ X^i/i!$. For any X and Y in $\dot{G}_e$, $[X, Y] = XY - YX$, in which the multiplication on the right is the usual multiplication of linear transformations.

If the algebraic structure alone is abstracted from $\dot{G}$, it is seen to be an algebra with Poisson brackets as multiplication. This multiplication is nonassociative, but the structure of such algebras is capable of a virtually exhaustive description. On the other hand, there is a very close connection between the algebraic structure of a Lie group and the algebraic structure of its Lie algebra. Indeed, there is a one-to-one correspondence between the subalgebras of the Lie algebra $\dot{G}$ and the connected Lie subgroups of G, the correspondence being: a connected Lie subgroup H corresponds to the subalgebra of $\dot{G}$ that is determined by the tangent subspace H_e to H at the identity. A connected Lie subgroup H is normal in G if, and only if, the corresponding subalgebra $\dot{H}$ is an ideal in $\dot{G}$; that is, $[\dot{G}, \dot{H}]$ is contained in $\dot{H}$. To the commutator subgroup of G generated by the elements of the form $xyz^{-1}y^{-1}$, there corresponds the derived subalgebra that is generated by the elements $[X, Y]$ with X and Y in $\dot{G}$. In particular, a connected Lie group G is Abelian if, and only if, $[X, Y] = 0$ for all X and Y in $\dot{G}$.

The most elementary type of Lie algebra is one wherein the multiplication is trival; *i.e.*, $[G, G] = 0$. Such

a Lie algebra is called Abelian. Next in complexity is a Lie algebra wherein the product of some finite number of any elements is zero; *i.e.*, if setting $G^{(1)} = G$, $G^{(n+1)} = [G^{(n)}, G]$, then $G^{(n)} = 0$ for some n. Such a G is called nilpotent. One step more complex are Lie algebras G that have a decreasing sequence of ideals, $G \supset G_1 \supset \cdots \supset G_n \cdots$ with the quotient algebra G_i/G_{i+1} Abelian and $G_n = 0$ for some n; such a Lie algebra is called solvable. The maximum solvable ideal of a Lie algebra is called its radical. If G is a Lie algebra and R denotes its radical, then G/R has no nonzero radical; such a Lie algebra is called semisimple. If a Lie algebra has no nonzero properly smaller ideal, it is called simple. The basic theorems describing the structure of Lie algebras over any field of characteristic zero areas may be stated as follows:

Any Lie algebra is a semidirect sum of its radical and a semisimple subalgebra.

Any semisimple Lie algebra is a direct sum of simple Lie algebras.

Any simple Lie algebra over the field of complex numbers is one of the following type:

A_n: the Lie algebra of the group of all $n + 1$ by $n + 1$ complex-valued matrices of determinant 1.

B_n: the Lie subalgebra of A_{2n} that annihilates the quadratic form composed of a sum of squares of $\{x_k\}$ (see 17).

C_n: the Lie subalgebra of A_{2n-1} that annihilates the alternating bilinear form (see 18).

D_n: the Lie subalgebra of A_{2n-1} that annihilates the quadratic form composed to a sum of squares of $\{x_k\}$ (see 19).

The five exceptional simple Lie algebras G_2, F_4, E_6, E_7, E_8 discovered by the mathematician W. Killing are of dimensions 14, 52, 78, 133, 248, respectively. This remarkable classification is achieved by a study of the so-called root diagram of the Lie algebra.

Although each Lie group has a unique Lie algebra, a Lie algebra in the abstract (*i.e.*, divorced from its presentation as the infinitesimal generator of a Lie group) may arise from inequivalent or nonisomorphic groups. For example, the one-dimension Abelian Lie algebra over the field of real numbers is the Lie algebra of both example G1 and example G2 above. The problem of determining the relation between the various connected Lie groups having abstractly isomorphic Lie algebras was solved by the mathematician Otto Schreier.

The situation may be described in this way: to each abstract Lie algebra g (over the field of real numbers) there corresponds a unique (up to isomorphism) simply connected Lie group G—that is, a connected Lie group in which every closed curve can be deformed continuously to a point; any other Lie group G_1 the Lie algebra of which is isomorphic to g is obtained from G by a homomorphism with a discrete kernel. Thus G_1 is evenly covered by G, and all connected Lie groups the Lie algebras

Theorems describing the structure of Lie algebras

(15) (a) $\dfrac{d}{dx}$; (b) $\dfrac{d}{dx}, x\dfrac{d}{dx}$; or (c) $\dfrac{d}{dx}, x\dfrac{d}{dx}, x^2\dfrac{d}{dx}$

(16) $\begin{cases} (a)\text{ one-parameter translation group: } x \to x + t \\ (b)\text{ two-parameter affine group: } x \to ax + b \\ (c)\text{ three-parameter projective group: } x \to \dfrac{ax+b}{cx+d} \\ \quad \det\begin{vmatrix} a & b \\ c & d \end{vmatrix} \neq 0 \end{cases}$

(17) $x_1^2 + x_2^2 + \cdots + x_{2n+1}^2$

(18) $x_1 y_{n+1} - y_1 x_{n+1} + x_2 y_{n+2} - y_2 x_{n+2} + \cdots + x_n y_{2n} - y_n x_{2n}$

(19) $x_1^2 + \cdots + x_{2n}^2$

of which are isomorphic to G have the same simply connected covering group. The spin representation of physics provides another example of this phenomenon.

It should be emphasized, however, that in a neighbourhood of the identity, any two Lie groups having isomorphic Lie algebras are isomorphic. This can be seen from the Baker–Campbell–Hausdorff formula (see 20) that identifies the product of exponentials with the exponential of an algebraic form involving an infinite sum of terms built from X and Y with Poisson brackets. By a process known as complexification it can be proved that the classification of complex simple Lie algebras also applies to compact Lie groups.

The topological structure of Lie groups. It has been shown that to a given abstract Lie algebra there may correspond Lie groups that are not topologically equivalent. Therefore, it cannot be expected that the abstract Lie algebra $\dot{G}$ of a Lie group G determines the topological structure of G completely. One of the greatest contributions of Cartan to mathematics, however, was his demonstration that the Lie algebra $\dot{G}$ determines the important topological invariants called Betti numbers of the group G in the very important case that the Lie group G is compact and connected.

Cartan's researches on this problem led him to invent his theory of exterior differential forms and to conjecture the celebrated de Rham theorems, which were proved by his student Georges de Rham.

Exterior differential calculus. If V is a vector space, then the exterior algebra over V is understood to be an associative algebra $E(V)$ generated by the elements of V together with a unit element 1 such that the product of p elements $x_1 \cdot x_2 \cdots x_p$ is not zero in $E(V)$ if, and only if, $x_1, \cdots, x_p$ are linearly independent in V. Because $x^2 = 0$ for any x in V, it follows that $x \cdot y = -y \cdot x$ for any x and y in V. If V^* denotes the dual space of linear functions on V, then $E(V^*)$ can be identified in a natural way with the set of skew-symmetric multilinear functions on V, the product of two forms φ_p and Ψ_q, respectively p-linear and q-linear, being given by a formula (see 21). The algebra $E(V^*)$ is called the Grassmann algebra of V—after the 19th-century German mathematician Hermann Günther Grassmann. An exterior differential p-form on an analytic manifold M is a rule that assigns to each point m of M an element of degree p of the Grassmann algebra $E(\dot{M}_m{}^*)$, $\dot{M}_m$ being the tangent space to M at m. In the language of tensors, an exterior differential p-form is a covariant skew-symmetric tensor field of degree p. The novel operation introduced by Cartan is exterior differentiation of exterior differential forms. This operation assigns to any exterior differential p-form w a $(p + 1)$-form dw such that:

D1. d is linear.

D2. d applied to a function or zero form is the usual differential.

D3. $d(w_1 \cdot w_2) = dw_1 \cdot w_2 + (-1)^p w_1 \cdot dw_2$, in which p is the degree of w_1.

D4. $ddw = 0$ for any form w.

For example, if w is given as a differential of degree one or two, its differential is easily computed (see 22). The geometric significance of exterior differentiations is seen in the generalized Green-Stokes theorem (named after the 19th-century British mathematicians George Green and George Gabriel Stokes): If S is a p-dimensional hypersurface bounding the $(p + 1)$-dimensional solid region R, then the surface integral of w and the volume integral of dw are equal (see 23).

Exterior differentiation has the fundamental property that it commutes with maps. That is, suppose that φ is a map of a manifold M into a manifold N, and that ω is an exterior differential p-form on N. Extending the notational convention that was adopted above, one denotes by $\varphi(\omega)$ the p-form on M that is the "pullback" of the exterior differential p-form ω (see 24). It follows from the properties D1 through D4 that for any analytic map φ, this maps the differential into the differential of the "pullback" (see 25). In addition, because φ preserves the addition and multiplication of exterior forms, it is possible to say that φ yields a differential algebra homomorphism.

An exterior differential form ω is called closed if $dw = 0$; it is called exact if $w = du$. Because $d^2 = 0$, every exact form is closed. Conversely, if w is exact, then in any suitably small neighbourhood V there is a form u such that $du = w$ in V. Nevertheless, a closed form does not necessarily have to be exact. The set of closed forms constitutes a vector space and the set of exact forms is a subspace. *(Closed forms)*

De Rham's theorem states that the quotient space of closed exterior p-forms by the exact p-forms is the p-dimensional Betti group, so that the dimension of this space is the pth Betti number of M, which is denoted $\beta_p(M)$. Because, locally, every closed form is exact, the number $\beta_p(M)$ must clearly depend on the global structure of M. Cartan showed that for a compact connected Lie group G, $\beta_p(G)$ is determined by the Lie algebra $\dot{G}$. This success of Cartan encouraged a closer study of the topological structure of Lie groups in an attempt to determine for them the various finer topological invariants that were being introduced in topology.

The central position occupied by compact groups in topological questions concerning Lie groups was clearly established when it was discovered that any Lie group with a finite number of connected components is topologically a product of any of its maximal compact subgroups and a Euclidean space. Thereby the question of topological structure of Lie groups was reduced to the case of compact Lie groups, which are more amenable to topological treatment.

The principal results on topological structure of compact groups are that the structure called a cohomology ring with real coefficients of a compact Lie group is isomorphic to the cohomology ring of a direct product of spheres; but a compact Lie group is not, in general (even in the simply connected case), topologically equivalent to a direct product of spheres. This last result follows from a computation of the Steenrod reduced power operations in compact Lie groups that was carried out in 1954 by the mathematicians Armand Borel (Swiss) and Jean-Pierre Serre (French).

The torsion groups of nearly all compact Lie groups have also been determined. The compact Lie groups $So(n)$ and $Sp(n)$ (the special unitary group and symplectic group, respectively) have no torsion; Spin (n), the two-sheeted covering group of the orthogonal group, has no torsion for $n \leq 6$. $So(n)$ $(n \geq 3)$ and Spin (n) $(n \geq 7)$ have 2-torsion and all their torsion coefficients are equal to 2.

Representations as transformation groups. It is natural to compare general topological groups with special ones, and in particular much attention has been devoted to the study of homomorphisms of topological groups into groups of linear transformations or matrix groups. This study has achieved far-reaching results that throw fresh light on the classical Fourier transform (see ANALYSIS, FOURIER) and the theory of special functions (see DIFFERENTIAL EQUATIONS). Only two results will be mentioned here.

A. The theorem of the 20th-century mathematicians Fritz Peter (German) and Hermann Weyl (German-born U.S.) states that any compact Lie group is isomorphic to a subgroup of the unitary group.

B. The theorem of the Russian mathematician I. Ado states that any real Lie algebra is isomorphic to a Lie algebra of matrices. Thus any Lie group has a neighbourhood of its identity in which multiplication is isomorphic to multiplication in some matrix group.

Turning now to more general types of representations, there have been several investigations of the global relations between topological groups and the types of spaces in which they can operate as groups of continuous transformations, as well as special properties of the operations themselves. In order to indicate the scope of such investigations, several of the results may be mentioned; these are as follows:

A. The only two-dimensional surfaces on which a Lie group can operate transitively (*i.e.*, carrying any point into any other point) are the plane, sphere, torus (a doughnut-shaped object), projective plane, cylinder, Möbius band (a one-sided surface; see TOPOLOGY, GENERAL), and Klein bottle (a one-sided surface in the shape of a bottle).

B. A compact connected Lie group operating transitively and effectively (*i.e.*, so that each element other than the identity moves some point) on an even-dimensional sphere is simple; more generally, if M is a manifold the Euler-Poincaré characteristic of which $(\Sigma(-1)^p\beta_p(M))$ is a prime number, then any compact connected Lie group operating on M is simple.

C. If a Lie group G operates transitively on a compact simply connected space M, then some compact subgroup of G operates transitively on M.

D. If a Lie group operates transitively on a space M having no "holes," then M is topologically Euclidean space.

E. If a compact Lie group G operates on a manifold M, then the operation is topologically equivalent to the operation of a group of rotations of some (higher dimensional) Euclidean space on a subspace that is topologically equivalent to M.

F. If a compact connected Abelian Lie group operates on Euclidean space, then it must leave some point fixed, and the set of fixed points resemble a plane topologically in three or more dimensions.

Hilbert's fifth problem. Among the celebrated 23 problems for research that were proposed by the German mathematician David Hilbert in his address to the International Mathematical Congress of 1900 was the conjecture that any locally Euclidean topological group can be given the structure of an analytic manifold so as to become a Lie group. In 1929, the Hungarian-born United States mathematician John von Neumann was able to exploit the theory of integral equations on a Lie group that had been developed in 1927 by Peter and Weyl because he was able to introduce integration on general compact groups; thereby von Neumann succeeded in solving the Hilbert problem for compact groups.

The next great inroad on this problem came with the discovery by the Hungarian mathematician Alfréd Haar in 1932 that in any locally compact topological group one can introduce a measure and an integral invariant under all group translations $x \to yx$; that is, for any function f defined on a locally compact group G, the integral over G, $\int f(x)\,dx$, satisfies, in addition to the usual rule of linearity, also the condition that it equals the integral over G of the same function with yx substituted for x (see 26).

In 1934 the Soviet mathematician Lev Semyonovich Pontryagin was able to prove Hilbert's conjecture for Abelian groups as a by-product of his theory of characters on locally compact Abelian groups.

The final complete solution of Hilbert's fifth problem came in 1952 as a result of the work of the U.S. mathematicians Andrew Mattei Gleason, Deane Montgomery, and Leo Zippin. Indeed, it was found that any locally compact topological group is a limit of Lie groups. This profound result affirmed the central position of Lie groups in the theory of continuous groups.

Algebraic linear groups. An algebraic linear group is a subgroup of the group of all nonsingular $n \times n$ matrices $L(n)$ defined by the vanishing of polynomials (see ALGEBRA, ELEMENTARY AND MULTIVARIATE) in the matrix coefficients (see ALGEBRA, LINEAR AND MULTILINEAR), which is a subgroup of $L(n)$ that is the intersection of $L(n)$ with an algebraic variety. If the underlying field is the field of real or complex numbers, then any algebraic linear group is a Lie group, but not conversely. On the other hand, most of the questions involving linear groups that arise in mathematics reduce to problems concerning groups that are algebraic. It is natural, therefore, to seek the special properties that characterize algebraic linear groups and their Lie algebras. This study was initiated by the mathematician L. Maurer in the 19th century and resumed in mid-20th century by the mathematician Claude Chevalley, and others.

The theory of algebraic linear groups has thrown fresh light on the relation between an arbitrary Lie group and the set of all its finite-dimensional linear representations;

$$(20) \quad (\exp X)(\exp Y) = \exp(X + Y - \tfrac{1}{2}[X, Y] + \cdots)$$

$$(21) \quad \begin{cases} \phi_p \cdot \psi_q(X_1, \cdots, X_{p+q}) \\ \quad = (p+q)!^{-1} \sum_\sigma (-1)^{\epsilon(\sigma)} \phi_p(X_{\sigma(1)}, \cdots, X_{\sigma(p)}) \cdot \\ \qquad \cdot \psi_q(X_{\sigma(p+1)}, \cdots, X_{\sigma(p+q)}) \\ \text{where } \sigma \text{ ranges over all permutations of } 1, \cdots, p+q \\ \text{and } \epsilon(\sigma) = \pm 1 \text{ is the sign of } \sigma \end{cases}$$

$$(22) \quad \begin{cases} w = P\,dx + Q\,dy + R\,dz, \qquad dw = \left(\dfrac{\partial Q}{\partial x} - \dfrac{\partial P}{\partial y}\right) dx\,dy + \\ \quad + \left(\dfrac{\partial P}{\partial y} - \dfrac{\partial Q}{\partial z}\right) dy\,dz + \left(\dfrac{\partial P}{\partial z} - \dfrac{\partial R}{\partial x}\right) dz\,dx; \\ \text{if} \quad w = R\,dxdy + Q\,dydx + P\,dzdx, \quad \text{then} \\ dw = \left(\dfrac{\partial P}{\partial x} + \dfrac{\partial Q}{\partial y} + \dfrac{\partial R}{\partial z}\right) dx\,dy\,dz. \end{cases}$$

$$(23) \quad \int_S w = \int_R dw$$

$$(24) \quad \phi(\omega)(X_1, \cdots, X_p) = \omega(d\phi(X_1), \cdots, d\phi(X_p))$$

$$(25) \quad \phi(d\omega) = d(\phi(\omega))$$

$$(26) \quad \int_G f(yx)\,dx = \int_G f(x)\,dx$$

$$(27) \quad w_1 = \cdots = w_n = 0$$

this development was initiated by the mathematician T. Tannaka in an effort to generalize Pontryagin's duality theory of characters, and it was carried further by the mathematicians Gerhard Paul Hochschild and George Daniel Mostow.

Chevalley's theory of algebraic groups was carried out for arbitrary ground field, even fields of prime characteristic p. This theory in characteristic p rested on very different considerations from the classical theory in characteristic zero but arrived at identical conclusions about the classification of simple groups. Moreover, Chevalley's work established a significant connection between finite simple groups and simple Lie groups.

Invariants of an exterior differential system. The principal application of continuous groups to the solution of differential equations consists in forming first integrals of a system of differential equations from the infinitesimal generators of a group admitted by the system. The number of unknowns involved in the system is thereby reduced.

For simplicity of illustration, only systems of the type characterized by all $\{w_k\}$ vanishing (see 27) will be considered, in which $w_1, \cdots, w_n$ are independent differential 1-forms (*i.e.*, linear differential forms) on an $(n+1)$-dimensional manifold. The solutions of (27) are called integral curves, functions that are constant on solutions are called first integrals, and differential forms expressible in terms of first integrals and their differentials are called invariant forms. A first integral is thus an invariant 0-form. The system (27) is said to admit a transformation φ if φ carries solutions of (27) into solutions and to admit the infinitesimal transformation X if it admits the transformation $\exp tX$ for all small t.

The passage from groups of transformations admitted by (27) to first integrals of (27) is via invariant forms of (27). There are three simple principles for the formation of invariant forms out of given ones:

(A) If w is an invariant form, then dw is also invariant.

(B) If the system (27) admits the infinitesimal transformation X, and if w is an invariant form, then Xw is an invariant form.

(C) Under the hypotheses of (B), the form $\partial_X w$ is an invariant form, in which, for any p-form w, $\partial_x w$ is the $(p-1)$-form defined by "contraction" of the p-form w with x (see 28).

Suppose the system (27) admits an n-dimensional Lie group of transformations G whose Lie algebra G has a base $X_1, \cdots, X_n$ such that the determinant $w_i(X_j)$ is not zero.

The forms $w_1, \cdots, w_n$ are replaced by linear combinations $w_1', \cdots, w_n'$ such that $w_i'(X_j) = \delta_{ij}$—for i, $j = 1, \cdots, n$. The linear forms $w_1', \cdots, w_n'$ are invariant forms of (27) and are called the forms dual to $X_1, \cdots, X_n$. If $[X_i, X_j] = \Sigma_s c_{ijs} X_s$, then $dw_s' = -\Sigma_{ij} c_{ijs} w_i' w_j'$. It follows that if G is solvable, then the equation (27) can be solved by n successive quadratures. This is an analogue of the 19th-century French mathematician Évariste Galois's celebrated theorem on the solution of algebraic equations by radicals. Consider, for example, the specific equation (29) that is invariant under the group G generated by translations along the x-axis and by uniform stretching; this second-order differential equation is put in form (27) by introducing the new variable y' and (29) then becomes two equations in differentials (see 30).

The group G operates in (x, y, y')-space, and its infinitesimal generators are the differential operator with respect to x and a generator that is formed with differential operators with respect to x and y (see 31). The dual forms are expressed in terms of F (see 32). Because $[X_1, X_2] = X_1$, it follows that the differentials (see 33) are such that w_2' is exact and gives by integration the first integral u_2 with $du_2 = w_2'$. On the surface $u_2 = C_1$, $w_1' = 0$, and thus $w_1' = 0$ can be integrated. The results of the two successive integrations are expressed in terms of exponentials with integrals involving the function F (see 34).

The Poincaré invariant integral and Cartan's associated form. The French mathematician Henri Poincaré has shown that for any Hamiltonian system (see 35) the form $w = \Sigma_i dp_i dq_i$ has the property that $\int_D w$ over any two-dimensional manifold D in $(p_1, \cdots, p_n, q_1, \cdots, q_n)$-space is independent of t. A differential form with such a property is called a Poincaré integral invariant. If $F(x_1, \cdots, x_k, t, dx_1, \cdots dx_k)$ is a Poincaré integral invariant of a system in which derivatives are identified with functions of the variables and t (see 36), then $F(x_1, \cdots, x_k, t, dx - A_1 dt, \cdots, dx - A_k dt)$ is an invariant form of the system expressible in terms of differentials and the functions A_k (see 37) and it is called the associated Cartan form.

The associated Cartan form of $\Sigma_i dp_i dq_i$ is therefore expressible in terms of the differentials of H (see 38). This Cartan form is not only an invariant of the system in associated differential form (see 39), but it also actually determines the system, which is the first Pfaffian (or associated characteristic) system of w'. Any infinitesimal transformation admitted by the equations of motion leads to an invariant 1-form by way of the principle in (C) applied to w'. Quite frequently, such 1-forms are exact, and by integration first integrals are obtained. In this way the known first integrals of the n-body problem can be derived.

Poisson parentheses and contact transformations. A nondegenerate bilinear form B on a finite-dimensional vector space V determines a one-to-one linear map B_1 of V onto its dual space of linear functions V^* by the rule that $B_1(v)(w) = B(v, w)$. This map produces, out of functions on V, functions on V^*. In particular, it is the case that the function B produces the bilinear function B^* in V^* (see 40).

Now if M is a manifold (necessarily of even dimension) on which there is defined an exterior differential closed 2-form β that is nondegenerate at all points and if f and g are functions on M, it is possible to form the function (f, g) in terms of differentials (see 41); the function (f, g) is called the Poisson parentheses of f and g with respect to β. In the neighbourhood of any point, coordinates $(p_1, \cdots, p_n, q_1, \cdots, q_n)$ can be found such that $\beta = \Sigma_i dp_i dq_i$. A simple computation gives the Poisson parentheses (see 42). The function (f, g) is character-

$$(28) \qquad \partial_x w(X_1, \cdots, X_{p-1}) = w(X, X_1, \cdots, X_p)$$

$$(29) \qquad y\frac{d^2y}{dx^2} = F\left(\frac{dy}{dx}\right)$$

$$(30) \qquad \begin{cases} dy - y' dx = 0 \\ y \, dy' - F(y) dx = 0 \end{cases}$$

$$(31) \qquad X_1 = \frac{\partial}{\partial x}, \qquad X_2 = x\frac{\partial}{\partial x} + y\frac{\partial}{\partial y}$$

$$(32) \qquad \begin{cases} w_1' = dx - \dfrac{x}{y}\,dy - \dfrac{y - xy'}{F(y')}\,dy' \\ w_2 = \dfrac{dy}{y} - \dfrac{y'}{F(y')}\,dy \end{cases}$$

$$(33) \qquad \begin{cases} dw_2' = 0 \\ dw_1' = w_1' \, w_2' \end{cases}$$

$$(34) \qquad \begin{cases} y = C_1 \exp \displaystyle\int \frac{y' \, dy'}{F(y')} \\ x = C_1 \exp\left(\displaystyle\int \frac{1}{F(y')}\left(\exp\int \frac{y' \, dy'}{F(y')}\right)dy'\right) + C_2 \end{cases}$$

$$(35) \qquad \begin{cases} \dfrac{dp_i}{dt} = -\dfrac{\partial H}{\partial q_i} \\ \dfrac{dq_i}{dt} = \dfrac{\partial H}{\partial p_i}, \qquad i = 1, \cdots, n \end{cases}$$

$$(36) \qquad \frac{dx_i}{dt} = A_i(x_1, \cdots, x_k, t), \qquad i = 1, \cdots, k$$

$$(37) \qquad \frac{dx_1}{A_1} = \frac{dx_2}{A_2} = \cdots = \frac{dx_k}{A_k}$$

$$(38) \qquad \begin{cases} w' = \displaystyle\sum_i \left(dp_i + \frac{\partial H}{\partial q_i}\,dt\right)\left(dq_i - \frac{\partial H}{\partial p_i}\,dt\right) \\ = \Sigma_i \, dp_i dq_i - dH \, dt \end{cases}$$

$$(39) \qquad \frac{dp_1}{-\dfrac{\partial H}{\partial q_i}} = \cdots = \frac{dq_n}{\dfrac{\partial H}{\partial p_n}}$$

$$(40) \qquad B^*(x, y) = B(B_1^{-1}(x), B_1^{-1}(y)), \qquad x, y \in V^*$$

$$(41) \qquad (f, g) = \beta^*(df, dg)$$

$$(42) \qquad (f, g) = \sum_i \frac{\partial f}{\partial p_i}\frac{\partial g}{\partial q_i} - \frac{\partial f}{\partial q_i}\frac{\partial g}{\partial p_i}$$

$$(43) \qquad df \cdot dg \cdot \beta^{n-1} = (f, g)\beta^n$$

ized by an identity (see 43) in which the dot is exterior multiplication and $2n = \dim M$. Poisson parentheses may be defined alternatively in terms of Poisson brackets (see 44). Transformations of a manifold of dimension $2n$ or $2n + 1$ preserving an exterior 2-form β of maximum possible rank were called by Lie restricted nonhomogeneous contact transformations with respect to β. Lie studied more general nonhomogeneous contact transformations that preserve the equation $w = 0$ in which w is a differential 1-form on a $(2n + 1)$-dimensional manifold such that $w(dw)^n \neq 0$; also, homogeneous contact transformations of a $2n$-dimensional manifold preserving a 1-form w such that $(dw)^n \neq 0$. The best example of a one-parameter group of restricted nonhomogeneous contact transformations is given by the movement of a wave front according to the principle of Christiaan Huygens, a 17th-century Dutch mathematician and physicist.

Another example is the motion of a conservative dynamical system in Hamiltonian form—the mathematical foreshadowing of quantum mechanics (see MECHANICS, QUANTUM). If H is the Hamiltonian of a conservative dynamical system, then the infinitesimal transformation defined by equations (35) is the operator X_H, in which X_g denotes the infinitesimal transformation defined by the operator $f \to (g, f)$, parentheses being with respect to the Poincaré integral invariant $\beta = \Sigma_i dp_i dq_i$. The most general (analytic) infinitesimal transformation of $(p_1, \cdots, p_n, q_1, \cdots, q_n)$-space that preserves β is of the form X_g with g an arbitrary analytic function. The Hamiltonian form (39) of the equations of motion is preserved by any contact transformation with respect to β, and the equations (39) admit the infinitesimal contact transformation X_g only if g is a first integral or if X_g preserves the associated Cartan form of β. Thus if g_1 and g_2 are first integrals of (39), then their Poisson parentheses are a first integral by principle (B).   (G.D.M.)

ANALYSIS ON MANIFOLDS

Traditional analysis, the integral and differential calculus, is of a local character; that is to say, it deals primarily with small variations of the numbers or parameters involved. This section concentrates on global analysis, in which topological considerations play a significant role. For example, the study of geometry on a small piece of the Earth's surface involves only local analysis, whereas the study of great circles right around the Earth involves global analysis. The most important areas in which topological ideas have been applied in problems of global analysis are now considered.

Morse theory. One of the most basic questions in the differential calculus has always been the investigation of maxima and minima of functions. For a function $f(x)$ of a real variable this means investigating the points for which the first derivative df/dx vanishes. For a function $f(x_1, x_2)$ of two variables, both partial derivatives $\partial f/\partial x_1$ and $\partial f/\partial x_2$ must vanish, but in this case the conditions also occur at saddle-points. For example, if f gives the height above sea level, then maxima are mountain peaks, minima are in the valleys, and saddle-points are mountain passes.

On an idealized Earth in which f is smooth and nondegenerate (see below) there is a global formula (see 45) and an inequality (see 46) in which m_0, m_1, m_2 are, respectively, the numbers of minima, saddle-points, and maxima. This is a simple example of the global theory of critical points initiated by the U.S. mathematician Marston Morse around 1930. In general this theory deals with a smooth real-valued function f defined on a closed n-dimensional manifold M (the higher-dimensional analogue of a surface) and relates the number of critical points of f with the topology of the manifold. Near any point p of M, local coordinates $(x_1, x_2, \cdots, x_n)$ can be chosen; and p is called critical if all partial derivatives $\partial f/\partial x_i$ vanish there: it is called nondegenerate if the matrix $H(f)$ of second derivatives $\partial^2 f/\partial x_i \partial x_j$ at p has a nonzero determinant. In this case the local coordinates can always be chosen so that, near p, f is given by the formula expressed as a combination of squares of the coordinates (see 47) in which r is some integer between 0 and n called the index of the critical point. A maximum has index n while a minimum has index 0. In dimension 2 a saddle-point has index 1. Formula (45) for the 2-dimensional sphere generalizes to give an expression for the alternating sum of the numbers m_r of critical points of index r (see 48), in which the alternating sum $E(M)$ is an integer depending only on M and not on the particular function f.

Moreover, $E(M)$ is the famous Euler-Poincaré characteristic that is defined as the alternating sum of the Betti numbers $b_r(M)$ (see 49). The Betti number $b_r(M)$ is the number of independent r-dimensional cycles with respect to homology. Thus, for the 2-di-

Betti numbers

mensional sphere, $b_0(M) = b_2(M) = 1$, and $b_1(M) = 0$ so that $E(M) = 2$; and for the 2-dimensional torus (surface shaped like a bicycle tire), similar values can be computed (see 50). Formula (48) for these two cases can be applied, for instance, to the height function when the sphere or bicycle tire is resting on the ground. Exterior points are maxima and minima; interior ones are saddle-points. Thus for the sphere and for the bicycle tire the values of the m_k can be computed (see 51 and 52). In this simple example $m_r = b_r(M)$, but in a more complicated situation this does not hold, as illustrated by a kidney-shaped surface in which there are two maxima, one minimum, and one saddle-point so that $m_2 > b_2(M)$; but still the alternating sum of the m_r equals the alternating sum of the $b_r(M)$ as indicated by formulas (48) and (49). In general, it is always the case that $m_r > b_r(M)$ and, on the lines of formula (47), there are further inequalities (see 53).

$$(44) \quad \begin{cases} X_f = B_1^{-1}(df), \quad X_g = B_1^{-1}(dg) \\ [X_f, X_g] = X_{(f,g)} \end{cases}$$

$$(45) \quad m_0 - m_1 + m_2 = 2$$

$$(46) \quad m_1 - m_0 \geqslant -1$$

$$(47) \quad f(x_1, \cdots, x_n) = -x_1^2 - x_2^2 - \cdots - x_r^2 + x_{r+1}^2 + \cdots + x_n^2$$

$$(48) \quad m_0 - m_1 + m_2 - m_3 + \cdots + (-1)^n m_n = E(M)$$

$$(49) \quad b_0(M) - b_1(M) + b_2(M) - \cdots = E(M)$$

$$(50) \quad b_0(M) = b_2(M) = 1, \qquad b_1(M) = 2, \qquad E(M) = 0$$

$$(51) \quad \text{sphere: } m_0 = m_2 = 1, \qquad m_1 = 0$$

$$(52) \quad \text{bicycle tire: } m_0 = m_2 = 1, \qquad m_1 = 2$$

$$(53) \quad \begin{cases} m_0 \geqslant b_0(M) \\ m_1 - m_0 \geqslant b_1(M) - b_0(M) \\ m_2 - m_1 + m_0 \geqslant b_2(M) - b_1(M) + b_0(M) \\ \cdots \end{cases}$$

What has been described so far is the basic elementary part of Morse theory. It connects critical points of a function with the homology of a manifold (the Betti numbers). A manifold, however, has much more structure than just homology and more invariants than Betti numbers. It has a homotopy structure and finally a differential structure, each giving rise to more refined invariants. One of the remarkable features of Morse theory has been the success that it has achieved in connecting these deeper aspects of a manifold with the behaviour of nondegenerate functions. More than just the critical points are involved at this stage. Essentially, consideration is given to the way in which the level surfaces $f =$ constant alter as the constant is varied, paying particular attention to the levels containing critical points. It is interesting to observe that the whole viewpoint is now reversed; whereas traditionally Morse theory considered a general function f on a given manifold M, the Betti numbers of which were assumed known, and derived restrictions on the behaviour of f, the modern development by the U.S. mathematician Stephen Smale and others has been to construct a nice function f on any M and deduce properties of M from those of f. This program has now led to very substantial progress in the general problem of classifying manifolds.

In another direction, also initiated by Morse, the theory was applied to the study of the loop space ΩM of M; that is, the space the points of which represent closed paths on M beginning and ending at a fixed point. If M is endowed with a metric (for example, if it sits inside a high-dimensional Euclidean space) the length of a path can be defined, and in this way a function f obtained on the loop space ΩM. The critical points of f correspond to geodesics on M (paths that locally minimize length); the study of these is an old and basic question of differential geometry. One would like to apply Morse theory on ΩM so as to relate questions about geodesics on M to the homology of ΩM. Unfortunately, ΩM is infinite-dimensional and so Morse was led to approximate ΩM by finite-dimensional manifolds based on the approximation of any path by a piecewise geodesic path, analogous to the way one approximates a plane curve by a polygon. This method proved successful and was later applied by the Hungarian mathematician Raoul Bott to derive homotopical properties of the loop space. More recently, with the development of more confidence in the treatment of infinite-dimensional manifolds, it has been shown that the original Morse program can be carried out directly on ΩM without resorting to approximations.

Hodge–de Rham theory. One of the most important branches of analysis on manifolds concerns the periods of integrals. As a basic example consider first a function of one variable $f(x)$. This has an indefinite integral, namely, the function $g(x)$ (see 54) and satisfying therefore the relation that is basic to calculus (see 55). If the interest is in periodic functions, $f(x)$ has to satisfy the equation that identifies its values for argument displaced by 2π (see 56). Then the function $g(x)$ will also be periodic provided the mean value of f is zero (see 57). If x is interpreted as the angular coordinate on a circle, then the periodicity condition on $f(x)$ simply asserts that it is a well-defined single-valued function on the circle. The expression $f(x)dx$ is called a differential form on the circle, and the integral of $f(x)$ from 0 to 2π (see 57) is called its period. The equation setting $f(x)$ equal to the derivative of $g(x)$ (see 55) is written equivalently as $dg(x) = f(x)dx$, and $dg(x)$ is called the differential of $g(x)$. It is possible to say, briefly, that a differential form ω on the circle is the differential of a function if, and only if, its period vanishes.

The systematic extension of these notions to higher dimensions was carried out by de Rham in the early 1930s. The circle is replaced by an arbitrary manifold of n dimensions, and p-fold multiple integrals are considered for any integer p between 0 and n. The theory allows one to say that the homology properties of a manifold are completely mirrored in the calculus of differential forms, the connection being made via the periods. For a discussion of de Rham's theorem, see above *Exterior differential calculus*.

An important refinement of the de Rham theory was introduced by the British mathematician Sir William Vallance Douglas Hodge and has led to extremely fruitful developments. In the Hodge theory the manifold is assumed closed and endowed with a Riemannian metric. Using the metric, one then defines a second-order differential operator Δ acting on differential forms. For Euclidean n-space with its usual flat metric this coincides with the Laplace operator (see 58) applied to each component of the form. In analogy with the theory of harmonic functions, a differential form φ is said to be harmonic if it satisfies the equation $\Delta\varphi = 0$. The main theorem of Hodge then asserts that there is a unique harmonic form with prescribed periods; *e.g.*, on the 2-dimensional torus parameterized by angular coordinates (x, y) modulo 2π and with the natural flat metric, dx and dy are the unique harmonic 1-forms with periods $(2\pi, 0)$ and $(0, 2\pi)$ on the basic circles, and $dxdy$ is the unique harmonic 2-form with total integral $4\pi^2$. The theory of harmonic forms has particularly interesting applications in the case of complex manifolds, considered below.

Curvature and characteristic classes. A large class of analytical problems with global topological implications arises in Riemannian geometry. Among these are those related to the notion of curvature. For an oriented surface M in three-dimensional Euclidean space, the Gauss curvature K is a function on M defined geometrically as

follows. For each point p of M a unit vector $n(p)$ is drawn through the origin in a direction perpendicular to the tangent plane to M at p. As p moves over a very small portion A of M around a fixed point, p_0, $n(p)$ moves over a corresponding portion $n(A)$ of the unit sphere. The curvature $K(p_0)$ is defined as the ratio of the area of $n(A)$ to A. Thus for a sphere of radius a the curvature is a constant function equal to a^{-2}.

The Gauss-Bonnet theorem for a closed surface asserts that the total integral of the Gauss curvature is independent of the metric and is always equal to $2\pi E$, in which E is the Euler-Poincaré characteristic. For a sphere, $E = 2$ and so $\int K = 4\pi$.

In higher dimensions the curvature is described not simply by a function but by a suitable tensor. Taking certain polynomial functions of this tensor produces closed differential forms of various degrees. The generalized Gauss-Bonnet theorem asserts that the periods of these differential forms over any given cycle are independent of the metric and so define invariants of the manifold that generalize the Euler-Poincaré characteristic. These invariants are called characteristic classes and are viewed formally as elements in the cohomology groups of the manifold, the duals of the homology groups. Characteristic classes can also be defined purely topologically by investigating the global motion of the tangent space as the manifold is traversed. They measure to some extent the failure of the manifold to possess a globally defined notion of parallelism: for example, a global parallelism exists on the torus in which $E = 0$, but not on the 2-dimensional sphere in which $E = 2$.

A large class of interesting Riemannian manifolds in which much explicit work has been done are the homogeneous manifolds, those that admit rigid motions taking any point into any other point. All the rigid motions form a group (in fact, a Lie group), and the curvature and characteristic classes can be expressed in terms of the group theory. Many of the familiar manifolds such as spheres and projective spaces fall within this class.

Complex manifolds. Just as a differentiable manifold is a space with a collection of real local coordinates, so a complex manifold has complex local coordinates. The important characteristic is that the change from one coordinate system to another is effected by holomorphic transformations; that is, by convergent power series. Thus complex manifolds are the natural domain in which to develop a global theory of analytic functions of several complex variables. They arise naturally in algebraic geometry. Thus an algebraic curve, given by a polynomial equation (see 59), defines a one-dimensional complex manifold provided it has no singularities; that is, provided the equations requiring that the function value vanish along with its first two partial derivatives (see 60) have no common solution. If equation (59) is regarded as defining z_2 as a function of z_1 (an algebraic function), then this complex manifold appears as a multi-sheeted covering of the complex z_1 plane, and this is the original point of view concerning Riemann surfaces. If "points at infinity" are added in the equation for an algebraic curve (see 59), the passing to the projective plane has the effect of making the Riemann surface closed (or compact), and algebraic geometry is mainly connected with the theory of compact complex manifolds.

All the topics discussed so far, differential forms, harmonic forms, curvature and characteristic classes, acquire further refinement in the presence of a complex structure. Thus differential forms can now be expressed in terms of dz and $d\bar{z}$ if $z = x + iy$, instead of dx and dy; and a differential r-form is said to be of type (p, q), in which $p + q = r$, if it involves products of p of the dz_i and q of the $d\bar{z}_i$. Thus on a Riemann surface 1-forms can be of type $(1, 0)$ or $(0, 1)$. Hodge showed that this decomposition into types extended to the harmonic forms provided a metric is used that is appropriately related to the complex structure. In this way he was led to introduce the space $H^{p,q}(M)$ of harmonic forms of type (p, q) and its dimension $h^{p,q}(M)$ as new invariants of a complex manifold. They are related to the Betti numbers

$b_r(M)$ by a formula (see 61). In addition, they satisfy the symmetry condition $h^{p,q} = h^{q,p}$. The case $q = 0$ is particularly interesting because the space $H^{p,q}(M)$ turns out to be just the space of holomorphic differential p-forms; that is, forms involving only the dz^i and the coefficients of which are holomorphic functions.

The tangent space of a complex manifold is naturally a complex vector space, and so the obstruction to finding a global complex parallelism can be studied. This leads to a more refined set of characteristic classes than in the real case. More precisely, there is one class c_i (the ith Chern class) in each even dimension. Every monomial in the c_i of total dimension equal to the real dimension of M gives rise to an integer invariant of M (by integration of the corresponding differential form over the whole of M). An important problem, unsolved for many years, was to find relations between the numbers given by Chern classes and the numbers $h^{p,q}(M)$. This will be explained shortly.

Sheaf theory. In complex analysis the basic questions concern the existence of holomorphic or meromorphic functions with given properties. For example, a classical problem on a compact Riemann surface M is to find how many independent meromorphic functions exist with a given set of poles. Locally all such functions are known (given by power series in a local complex coordinate), but the problem is how to piece together local solutions to obtain a global solution. More precisely, if M is covered by a finite collection of coordinate patches U_i and if local solutions φ_i are taken in each U_i, then the differences $f_{ij} = \varphi_i - \varphi_j$ measure the obstruction to getting a global solution. If holomorphic functions g_i in U_i can be found so that the differences equal the measure of the obstruction (see 62), then $\varphi_i - g_i = \varphi_j - g_j$ in the intersection $U_i \cap U_j$, and so the functions $\varphi_i - g_i$ give a global solution. In any case, the functions f_{ij} clearly satisfy the equation that requires the sum of the functions to equal zero in a certain region (see 63). Now equations (62) and (63) are formally similar to those used in defining homology, or rather cohomology, the only difference being that the g_i and f_{ij} are now holomorphic functions rather than constants. Proceeding with this analogy, a new kind of cohomology group can be defined by taking collections of functions f_{ij} satisfying (63) modulo the subgroup (see ALGEBRAIC STRUCTURES) of those for which (62) has a solution. These new cohomology groups provide a convenient formal framework in which global analytic obstructions can be treated. The general setting here is that of the cohomology theory of sheaves. Interestingly enough, although this theory was first developed by the French mathematician Jean Leray in a purely topological context, its most significant application has been in the domain of complex analysis in which it has become an indispensable tool following the pioneering work of Cartan and Serre in the 1950s.

A sheaf S on a space X is, roughly speaking, some class of functions characterized by local properties. Cohomology groups $H^q(X, S)$ are then defined for each integer $q \geq 0$, $H^0(X, S)$ being just the global functions of the class. If S is the sheaf of constant functions, the usual cohomology groups (dual of homology) is obtained; but if S is the sheaf of holomorphic functions on a complex manifold M, the groups indicated above are obtained. More generally, the sheaf Ω^p of holomorphic p-forms on M can be taken. The resulting groups $H^q(M, \Omega^p)$ are finite-dimensional if M is compact and turn out to be isomorphic to the Hodge groups $H^{p,q}(M)$ when M is algebraic. Sheaf theory thus provides an alternative or supplement to harmonic form theory.

The meromorphic functions with given poles also form a sheaf S. The main interest is in the global functions $H^0(M, S)$, but the higher cohomology groups intervene automatically in many places. For example, it is difficult in general to compute the dimension of $H^0(M, S)$, but the alternating sum of the dimensions for higher cohomology groups (see 64) is much easier to deal with. The famous Riemann-Roch theorem, as generalized and proved by the German mathematician Friedrich Ernst

$$(54) \qquad g(x) = \int_0^x f(t)\, dt$$

$$(55) \qquad \frac{dg(x)}{dx} = f(x)$$

$$(56) \qquad f(x + 2\pi) = f(x)$$

$$(57) \qquad \int_0^{2\pi} f(x)\, dx = 0$$

$$(58) \qquad \Delta = \sum_{i=1}^n \frac{\partial^2}{\partial x_i^2}$$

$$(59) \qquad f(z_1, z_2) = 0$$

$$(60) \qquad f(z_1, z_2) = 0, \qquad \frac{\partial f(z_1, z_2)}{\partial z_1} = 0, \qquad \frac{\partial f(z_1, z_2)}{\partial z_2} = 0$$

$$(61) \qquad b_r(M) = \sum_{p+q=r} h^{p,q}(M)$$

$$(62) \qquad f_{ij} = g_i - g_j$$

$$(63) \qquad f_{ij} + f_{jk} + f_{ki} = 0 \quad \text{in} \quad U_i \cap U_j \cap U_k$$

$$(64) \qquad \chi(M, S) = \sum_q (-1)^q \dim H^q(M, S)$$

$$(65) \qquad \dim H^0(M, S) - \dim H^1(M, S) = 1 - g + d$$

$$(66) \qquad \sum_q (-1)^q h^{0,q}(M) = T_n(c_1, \cdots, c_n)$$

$$(67) \qquad T_1 = \frac{c_1}{2}, \qquad T_2 = \frac{c_1^2 + c_2}{12}, \qquad T_3 = \frac{c_1 c_2}{24}$$

Peter Hirzebruch in 1954, gives an explicit topological formula for $\chi(M, S)$ in terms of the Chern classes of M and the homotopy class of the set of poles. For a Riemann surface this formula reduces to a difference of dimension for two cohomology groups expressed in terms of g and d (see 65) in which g is the genus of M and d is the number of poles. The term involving H^1 is called the index of specialty (of the set of poles) and is known to vanish when $d > 2g - 2$. For a general algebraic manifold M the Hirzebruch formula applied just to the sheaf of holomorphic functions (no poles) gives a formula in terms of c_i and I_n (see 66) in which the c_i are the Chern classes of M and T_n ($n = 1, 2, \cdots$) is a certain sequence of polynomials now known as the Todd polynomials (after the English mathematician John Arthur Todd, who introduced them in the 1930s). Examples of T_n with n equal to one, two, and three are easily displayed (see 67). It is a remarkable fact that these Todd polynomials, originating in algebraic geometry, and certain other closely related polynomials have played a very important role in the study and classification of manifolds. Their arithmetical properties, which involve the Bernoulli numbers, reflect in a deep and mysterious manner the differential properties of manifolds. For instance, the 28 different differentiable structures that have been shown to exist on the seven-dimensional sphere by the U.S. mathematician John Milnor and others are distinguished by numerical invariants based essentially on the Todd polynomials.

Sheaf theory in complex analysis has a very wide range of application far beyond algebraic manifolds. In particular, it can be applied on non-compact manifolds and also to complex analytic spaces, in which singularities are allowed. Because such spaces do not have good systems of local coordinates, the Hodge theory of harmonic

Other applications of sheaf theory

forms does not exist in this context. On the other hand, the methods of partial differential equations, of which the Hodge theory is a noteworthy case, are not restricted to complex manifolds and have therefore considerably greater flexibility, as will be explained below.

Elliptic operators. The Laplace operator (see 58) and its generalization by Hodge to the Riemannian case are examples of elliptic partial differential operators. They are characterized by a non-degeneracy condition on their highest order terms, which for the Laplace operator is just the fact that the equation identifying a sum of squares of the ξ_i with zero (see 68) has no real solutions except for $\xi_i = 0$ (all i). All elliptic operators share certain basic features, notably the finite-dimensionality of their spaces of solutions on a compact manifold. Moreover, the adjoint D^* of an elliptic operator D is also elliptic, and the index of D, defined as the difference between the number of independent solutions of the equations $Du = 0$ and $D^*u = 0$, has the property of being stable under small perturbations of D. On a Riemann surface M if D is taken to be the Cauchy-Riemann operator (see 69) the solutions of $Du = 0$, $D^*u = 0$ can be identified with the sheaf cohomology groups $H^0(M, S)$, $H^1(M, S)$, in which S is the sheaf of holomorphic functions. Thus the Riemann-Roch theorem gives in this case a formula for the index in topological terms, namely, index $D = 1 - g$. Quite generally the Hirzebruch-Riemann-Roch theorem can be viewed as giving a formula for the index of a certain elliptic operator (generalizing the Cauchy-Riemann operator) in terms of characteristic classes.

(M.F.A.)

Differential topology

The aim of differential topology primarily is the study of differentiable manifolds and of differentiable maps between them. It also is concerned with geometric objects (such as vector fields, foliations, group actions), which one can associate with manifolds. Differential topology is thus in a position midway between differential geometry on the one hand and classical differential calculus on the other. The chief divergence from the spirit of differential geometry is that the latter only considers manifolds equipped with more precise structures (*e.g.*, Riemannian metrics, connections) and has thus a basically quantitative aspect, whereas differential topology is purely qualitative in its aims. It borders on analysis in the study of differentiable maps and their singularities: this is the subject that one could call differential analysis and is the study of maps that are required to be only differentiable, rather than analytic. Differential analysis was not yet recognized as an independent subject in the 1970s.

Differential topology has been studied as such only since the mid-1930s. Mathematicians have from the start made use of low-dimensional manifolds (such as points, curves, surfaces), but the idea of developing a general theory of objects defined by conditions that are merely differentiable, as opposed to analytic or algebraic, was slow to appear. The French mathematician Joseph-Louis Lagrange in his *Mécanique Analytique* (1788; "Analytic Mechanics") considers such manifolds as the phase spaces of a dynamical system, and the canonical transformations met with in dynamics contain the idea of structure-preserving coordinate transformations. It is only in the work of the 19th-century German mathematician Bernhard Riemann, however, that the general notion of an *n*-dimensional manifold is first formulated. He called it an "*m-fach ausgedehnte Mannigfaltigkeit*" (*m*-fold extended manifold). The impetus of Italian algebraic geometry, the theory of algebraic surfaces and of analytic ones led the German-born U.S. mathematician Hermann Weyl, in *Die Idee der Riemannischer Fläche* (1913; Eng. trans. *The Concept of a Riemann Surface,* 1964), to the first precise definition, within the particular context of an algebraic curve, of a manifold defined by coordinate charts and transformations, and thus to the idea of analytic structure. Only a little later, the theory of general relativity, with its insistence on the concept of curved space-time, gave a tremendous impulse to tensorial differential geometry. At the same time, the topological

Early definitions [margin note]

theory of Lie groups, due to Cartan, also drew attention to the notion of manifolds. The first modern definition of a manifold, by local coordinate systems and transformations, is due to the mathematicians Oswald Veblen (U.S.) and Henry Whitehead (British). It is with the fundamental work of Hassler Whitney in 1935 that differential topology as such was born.

From that time on differential topology took its inspiration from two opposite sources: on the one hand, differential analysis brought very powerful tools to bear, from 1935–40 onward: the theorem on the zero measure of the set of critical values of a differentiable map (since referred to as Sard's theorem, although Anthony Paul Morse had previously proved it in special cases); the extension theorem and spectral theorem of Whitney; then later the generalization of the implicit function theorem known as the transversality lemma (a lemma is a theorem, usually proved to use in the proof of another theorem); and, finally, a C^∞ (a C^∞ mapping is a mapping that is continuously differentiable an infinite number of times) generalization of the Weierstrass preparation theorem for analytic maps. On the other hand, algebraic topology was itself developing at the same time: the foundations of singular homology and cohomology theories; the theory of fibre spaces and of their characteristic classes; spectral sequences; and homotopy theory. So, about 1950, the techniques necessary for a detailed investigation of differentiable manifolds were available.

By 1935 Marston Morse had shown by means of his theory of critical points of functions and the inequalities that bear his name what sort of purely topological information about a manifold M could be deduced just from an inspection of the singularities of a real-valued function $f : M \to \Re$. A more detailed study of his methods, making use of gradient trajectories, has succeeded in an extremely direct fashion in associating to a generic function $f : M \to \Re$ a partition of M into cells, each cell of dimension k having its centre in a critical point of f, of index k; and in fact this cellular decomposition satisfies the homotopy-theoretical properties of a C–W complex. This representation of any manifold as a union of balls was to play a basic role in the appearance of surgery techniques (see below *Surgery techniques*), which study the possibility of transforming a given manifold M into another M' of the same dimension, generalizing the process by which one passes from a sphere to a torus by adding a handle.

An outline of the principal stages in the development of differential topology is given in the *Bibliography*. In the 1970s, the status of the subject is a little ambiguous. Many important problems, connected with the classification of manifolds up to diffeomorphism, remain unsolved; these problems, however, are hard, and in general they are not decidable; it seems more likely that differential topologists will turn more toward the topological study of groups of diffeomorphisms, introducing a new point of view into functional analysis. The works of the French mathematician Jean Cerf provide an excellent example of this trend, which seems very promising.

BASIC CONCEPTS: THE DIFFERENTIABLE CATEGORY

If $\Re^n$ and $\Re^p$ are Euclidean spaces, with coordinates $(x_1, \cdots, x_n)$ and $(y_1, \cdots, y_p)$, respectively, a system of functions expressed in terms of f_j (see 70) defines a mapping F from $\Re^n$ to $\Re^p$. If all the f_j are r-times continuously differentiable, then the mapping is said to be of class C^r. It is to be noted that if F and G (see 71) are two such mappings, then the composite mapping $G \circ F$ (see 72) is also of class C^r.

A mapping $F : \Re^n \to \Re^n$ is known to be locally invertible at 0 if the Jacobian determinant (see 73) is non-zero at 0 (inverse function theorem). F is then said to be a local diffeomorphism.

The notion of a jet. Two germs of mappings $\Re^n \overset{F}{\underset{G}{\rightrightarrows}} \Re^p$ [F defined by (f_i) and G by (g_i)] are said to be equivalent to rth order if $D_\omega f_i(0) = Dg_i(0)$ for every multi-index $\omega = (i_1, \cdots, i_d)$, of total degree $d(\omega) = d \leq r$. This defines an equivalence relation on germs of mappings. The set of equivalence classes, which is parameterized by the values c_ω^i $(d(\omega) \le r)$ of the partial derivatives, makes up the space $J^r(n, p)$ of local jets of $\mathfrak{R}^n$ into $\mathfrak{R}^p$ of order r. In particular, a germ of a curve is a germ of a mapping $(\mathfrak{R}', 0) \to (\mathfrak{R}^n, 0)$; the space of all first-order jets $J'(1, n)$ consists of the usual tangent vectors to $\mathfrak{R}^n$ at 0.

If F is a differentiable mapping of $\mathfrak{R}^n$ into $\mathfrak{R}^p$, it can be extended in a canonical manner into a mapping from the set of tangent vectors $T(\mathfrak{R}^n)$ into the set of tangent vectors $T(\mathfrak{R}^p)$: if the tangent vector z is represented by the curve $f : \mathfrak{R}' \to \mathfrak{R}^n$, $F(z)$ is the equivalence class of the composite curve $F \circ f$.

In a general way, if X, Y are open subsets of $\mathfrak{R}^n$, $\mathfrak{R}^p$, respectively, the space of jets of rth order of $\mathfrak{R}^n$ into $\mathfrak{R}^p$ is defined as being the set of local jets of C^r mappings that take a point x of X into a point y of Y; it is thus just the product $X \times Y \times J^r(n, p)$; the projection map $r : z \to (x, y)$ is the mapping that takes a jet z into its source x and its target y.

For a given mapping $F : X \to Y$, of class C^r, to every point $x \in X$ can be associated in $J^r(n, p)$ the jet $J^r(F_x)$ of the germ of F at x; one also has defined a section of the (trivial) vector bundle r over the graph of F; this section is the rth derivative of F.

Imbedded manifolds and intrinsic manifolds. An n-dimensional Euclidean space $\mathfrak{R}^n$ is considered, with coordinates $(x_1, \cdots, x_n)$, together with a system of $p \le n$ differentiable functions $(f_1, \cdots, f_p)$, and the equations that result by setting the functions equal to zero (see 74): If V denotes the subset $V \subset \mathfrak{R}^n$ defined by the vanishing of these equations and at a point $x \in V$ at least one of the minors of order p of the Jacobian matrix $J = D(f_1, \cdots, f_p)/D(x_1, \cdots, x_n)$ is nonzero, say the one relative to the first p coordinates $(x_1, \cdots, x_p)$, then, according to the implicit function theorem, there is a neighbourhood of x in $\mathfrak{R}^n$ such that the system (E) may be resolved in terms of the variables $(x_{p+1}, \cdots, x_n)$, thus transforming into an equivalent linear system (see 75).

In other words, a neighbourhood W of x in V is $(n - p)$-dimensional, parameterized by the values of the $(n - p)$ variables $(x_{p+1}, \cdots, x_n)$. In this case one says that, locally at x, V is an imbedded manifold of dimension $(n - p)$ and codimension p. If at all points x of V it is possible to choose such a nonzero Jacobian minor so that every point has such an $(n - p)$-dimensional neighbourhood, then V is said to be an imbedded manifold, of dimension $n - p$. V is said to be closed if V, imbedded in $\mathfrak{R}^n$, is compact (i.e., bounded). A set of functions such as $x_{p+1}, \cdots, x_n$ is a system of local coordinates; it defines a diffeomorphism of a neighbourhood W of x onto an open subset $U \subset \mathfrak{R}_{n-p}$. Any such diffeomorphism is called a coordinate chart about x. For an imbedded manifold, there exist a great many local coordinates (in fact, any set of functions $y_1, \cdots, y_d$ with $dy_1 \wedge \cdots \wedge dy_d \ne 0$ at x defines a coordinate chart about x).

Now two coordinate charts U, U' at x satisfy the following property: that on the open subset $U_1 \subset U$ in which the composite $f' \circ f^{-1}$ is defined, it is a diffeomorphism onto an open subset $U' \subset U'$, hence the following intrinsic definition of a manifold.

A differentiable n-dimensional manifold of class C^r is a (Hausdorff paracompact) topological space X such that every $x \in X$ has a neighbourhood V, together with a homeomorphism $h : V \to U$ onto an open neighbourhood U of 0 in $\mathfrak{R}^n$ (coordinate chart). Whenever two local charts V_1 and V_2 have a non-empty intersection, then the mapping $h_2 \circ h^{-1}$, taking $h_1(V_1 \cap V_2) \subset U_1$, onto $h_2(V_1 \cap V_2) \subset U_2$, which is anyway a homeomorphism, is required to be a diffeomorphism, of class C^r. It is to be noted that if three charts V_1, V_2, and V_3 have a non-empty intersection, then the transition functions $h_{ij} = h_i \circ h_j^{-1}$ satisfy $h_{31} = h_{32} \circ h_{21}$ where they are all defined. In the case in which the diffeomorphisms h_{ij} are in fact analytic, then the manifold is said to be an analytic manifold. A C^0 manifold is a topological manifold.

Manifolds with boundaries. A manifold with boundary M^{n+1}, of class C^r, is a topological space that has an n-dimensional manifold ∂M of class C^r as a subspace, in such a way that:

(A) the complement $(M - \partial M)$ is an $(n + 1)$ manifold, of class C^r;

(B) every point $x \in \partial M$ has a neighbourhood W in M, together with a homeomorphism h of W into Euclidean upper half space (see 76) mapping W onto an open neighbourhood U of the origin, mapping $W \cap \partial M$ diffeomorphically onto a set of specific structure (see 77), and $M \cap W$ diffeomorphically onto another set of specific structure (see 78).

Isomorphisms of differentiable structures. A differentiable structure (class C^r) on a manifold M is completely determined by the knowledge of the set $(\mathfrak{H})$ of differentiable functions on M. Two structures (ζ) and (ζ') are said to be equivalent if there exists a homeomorphism h taking the set $(\mathfrak{H})$ into the set $(\mathfrak{H}')$.

The fundamental theorems of Whitney. In his basic articles of 1935–36, Hassler Whitney establishes that every differential manifold (n-dimensional, paracompact—i.e., the union of countably many compact sets) can be imbedded in a Euclidean space $\mathfrak{R}^n$, of sufficiently high dimension.

The proof is in fact fairly simple: one first establishes that for the manifold M equipped with a locally finite covering $\mathfrak{R}$ by coordinate neighbourhoods U_i, one can always construct a subordinate partition of unity $\{\mathfrak{R}_i\}$. This allows the extension of every coordinate function x_i, originally only defined on the coordinate neighbourhood U_i, into a function globally defined on M. This gives an imbedding i of M into a large-dimensional Euclidean space $\mathfrak{R}^N$ (one may map two of the x_i's onto the same coordinate of $\mathfrak{R}^N$ if their supports are disjoint); it now remains to cut down $\mathfrak{R}$ as far as possible. A general position argument concerns linear projections

$$(68) \quad \sum_{i=1}^{n} \xi_i^2 = 0$$

$$(69) \quad \frac{\partial}{\partial x} + i \frac{\partial}{\partial y}$$

$$(70) \quad y_i = f_i(x_1, x_2, \cdots, x_n)$$

$$(71) \quad \mathfrak{R}^n \xrightarrow[f_i]{F} \mathfrak{R}^p \xrightarrow[g_j]{G} \mathfrak{R}^q$$

$$(72) \quad z_k = g_k(f_j(x_i))$$

$$(73) \quad D(f_i)/D(x_j) = \det |\partial f_i/\partial x_j|$$

$$(74) \quad \begin{cases} f_1(x_1, \cdots, x_n) = 0 \\ f_2(x_1, \cdots, x_n) = 0 \\ \quad \cdot \\ \quad \cdot \\ \quad \cdot \\ f_p(x_1, \cdots, x_n) = 0 \end{cases}$$

$$(75) \quad \begin{cases} x_1 = g_1(x_{p+1}, \cdots, x_n) \\ \quad \cdot \\ \quad \cdot \\ \quad \cdot \\ x_p = g_p(x_{p+1}, \cdots, x_n) \end{cases}$$

$$(76) \quad H^{n+1} = \{x \in \mathfrak{R}^{n+1} | x_{n+1} \ge 0\}$$

$$(77) \quad U \cap \{x | x_{n+1} = 0\}$$

$$(78) \quad U \cap \{x \in \mathfrak{R}^{n+1} | x_{n+1} \ge 0\}$$

(see 79). The composite $L \circ i$ is an imbedding for properly chosen L. In fact, the dimension can even be pushed down as far as $2n$, by a surgery type of argument, which can eliminate any possible points of self-intersection.

Whitney's work also contains smoothing theorems. Every C^1 manifold M is also a C^r manifold, the C^r structure inducing a C^1 structure equivalent with the original one; one can even provide M with an analytic structure. The idea here is the following: one imbeds the manifold M into a Euclidean space $\mathfrak{R}^N$ and constructs a tubular neighbourhood of M in $\mathfrak{R}^N$ using a field of transverse $(N - n)$-planes F_x of class C^{r-1}. This defines a locally surjective map (see 80). One then smooths this field of $(N - n)$-planes F into a nearby field F', keeping it transverse to $i(M)$. On taking another tube $\mathfrak{I}'(M)$, possibly smaller, one can pass to the quotient by the planes defined by F', thus providing M with a C^r-structure.

PROBLEMS AND METHODS OF DIFFERENTIAL TOPOLOGY

The differentiable category has as objects differentiable manifolds, and as morphisms differentiable maps. The problems concerning the objects are those of topology; those concerning the morphisms belong more to the realm of analysis.

Problems about differentiable manifolds. The essential problem is that of equivalence: given two manifolds M and M' (say imbedded ones for definiteness), to be able to recognize whether M and M' are isomorphic; and in a general way, to organize algebraically (if possible) the set of equivalence classes.

For M and M' to be isomorphic, they must at least be homeomorphic as topological spaces, so that they must have the same topological invariants: dimension; fundamental group π_1; homology groups; homology type. It is known that in its most general form, this problem is not decidable; it is therefore quite reasonable to make simplifying hypotheses (in particular on the group π_1) to make the problem more accessible. Among the weaker equivalence relations between manifolds, that which has turned out to be the most accessible is that known as cobordism (see below *Cobordant manifolds*).

A second type of problem is that of invariance. To what extent are the invariants of a manifold, constructed using the differentiable structure, in fact invariant under topological equivalence? Historically, this problem has arisen especially in the context of characteristic classes of the tangent bundle.

A third type of problem is that of the existence and classification of further structures that can be put on a given manifold. The most interesting problems here concern complex or almost complex structures, foliations, and imbeddings or immersions between two given manifolds.

Problems concerning the morphisms. The problem of the topological equivalence of two maps between manifolds is a difficult problem and is possibly not sufficiently motivated. It has not been systematically tackled up to now. An extensive literature, however, does exist concerning the local problem of to what extent the topological type of a germ of a mapping is determined by its jet. As far as differential equivalence (modulo diffeomorphism of the domain and the range) is concerned, a complete theory has now been developed by the mathematician J. Mather, which answers the question, at least in principle. The fundamental problem here is that of the density of topologically stable maps; some results on this subject have been announced.

In a general way, the theory of differentiable mappings requires an elucidation of the structure (in a nontechnical sense) of the set of singular points and values. This study was started by Whitney, who described the generic singularities of certain mappings (see 81). A particular case, the theory of functions, is included in Morse theory. An essential tool of this subject is the notion of stratified set in Euclidean space; here again, Whitney's work on the stratification of analytic sets played a decisive role. The notion of stratified set allows a considerable extension of the transversality techniques, which will now be taken up.

The methods. From analysis, differential topology has borrowed the technique of transversality; from algebraic topology, that of the universal object. It is not an exaggeration to say that the combination of these two techniques has provided differential topology with its most powerful tools.

The idea of the universal object had its origin in homotopy theory; its use in the classification of vector bundles on a given space is a typical example, although it is known how to prove the existence of universal objects in much greater generality.

The technique of transversality is in principle nothing more than an intrinsic reformulation of the implicit function theorem: given a submanifold $Q \subset \mathfrak{R}^n$, of codimension q, at each pt $y \in Q$, Q is defined by a local morphism $\pi : U \to \mathfrak{R}^q$, which is a submersion (see 82). A differentiable mapping $f : M \to \mathfrak{R}^q$ is said to be transverse to Q if for all points $x \in f^{-1}(Q)$, the composite map (see 83) has maximal rank $[= \max (m, q)]$. If f is a transversal mapping, then $f^{-1}(Q)$ is a submanifold of M, of codimension q, and with normal bundle induced by f from the normal bundle of Q in $\mathfrak{R}^n$. In the space of differentiable mappings $C^r(M, \mathfrak{R}^n)$ $(r \geq m)$, the set of mappings transverse to Q is a dense open set; in other words, transversality is a generic property.

Transversality techniques admit two types of generalizations:

(A) One may replace the smooth manifold Q by a set with singularities, such as analytic or algebraic sets. This is the starting point of the theory of stratified sets.

(B) Considering, instead of the map f itself, its derivative $J^r(f)$ in the space of jets, if $\mathfrak{J}$ is a submanifold of the space of jets $J^r(m, n)$, then generically the derivative $J^r(f)$ is transversal to $\mathfrak{J}$.

The notion of transversality is nothing but a formulation of the old notion of general position, well-known in algebraic geometry and combinatorial topology. Note that if f and g are both transversal to Q and if they can be imbedded in a homotopy itself transversal to Q, when considered as a mapping (see 84), then the inverse images $f^{-1}(Q)$ and $g^{-1}(Q)$ are isotopic in M. (The same theorem can even be extended to the case of Q a set with singularities.) Mather has introduced for differentiable mappings the notion of infinitesimal stability: if $f : X \to Y$ is a differentiable map, denoting θ_f the vector bundle induced on X by the f from $T(Y)$ certain maps result (see 85). A section σ of $\pi : \theta_f \to X$ is an infinitesimal deformation of f, because it associates to every point $x \in X$ a tangent vector to Y at $y = f(x)$; f is said to be infinitesimally stable if all infinitesimal deformation σ can be written in the form $\sigma = f(\xi) + f^{*-1}(\eta)$, in which ξ and η are sections of π_X and π_Y, respectively.

The fundamental results of Mather's theory are the following:

(A) Every infinitesimally stable mapping belonging to an open $W \subset (X, Y)$ is stable (*i.e.*, two nearby maps g, f are connected by diffeomorphisms of X and Y).

(B) The infinitesimal stability of a mapping f is equivalent with the transversality of its derivative $J^r(f)$ to the orbits in $J^r(n, p)$ defined by the action of the groups of local diffeomorphisms of the domain and the range.

An important special case of these results is the fibration theorem of C. Ehresmann: if $f : X \to Y^n$ is a proper morphism, f everywhere of maximal rank n, then f is a fibration.

Surgery techniques. Of a more elementary nature (in principle), but nevertheless extremely powerful, surgery of manifolds is based on a generalization of the construction of a surface of genus p from one of genus $p - 1$, by the addition of a handle. Here, the basic model comes from Morse theory: one considers a function $f : M^n \to \mathfrak{R}$, taking a point O into 0, and having there a critical point of a rank k that is expressible in terms of local coordinates about zero (see 86). Letting M^+ and M^- be the level manifolds $f^{-1}(\pm \varepsilon)$, respectively, and considering the trajectories of the gradient field of f, the trajectories ending at O from $f(\leq \varepsilon)$ form a ball of dimension k the boundary of which in M^- is a $(k - 1)$ sphere σ^{k-1}. Similarly, the gradient trajectories starting from O form an $(n - k)$

ball the boundary of which in M^+ is an $(n - k - 1)$ sphere σ^{n-k-1}. A tubular neighbourhood of σ^{k-1} in M^-, of boundary $S^{n-k-1} \times \sigma^{-1}$, is mapped (by following the gradient trajectories [not going through O]) onto a tubular neighbourhood of σ^{k-n-1} in M^+. One has therefore passed from M^- to M^+ by the following operation: one chooses a sphere σ^{k-1} with trivial normal bundle, the boundary of the tubular neighbourhood of which is therefore $\sigma^{k-1} \times S^{n-k}$. One then replaces this tubular neighbourhood $\sigma^{k-1} \times D^{n-k}$ by the product $D^k \times \sigma^{n-k-1}$. In this process the cycle σ^{k-1} has been killed because it can now be contracted to zero across the new D^k; of course, one has introduced a new cycle σ^{n-k-1}.

Example of surgery. If M is an oriented manifold of dimension $n \geq 4$, one can, by a succession of surgeries of index 1, kill the whole fundamental group π_1 of M. Indeed, if any generator g of π_1 is considered, realized as an imbedded circle S^1, with trivial normal bundle, this cycle can be killed by an elementary surgery. This introduces a new cycle of dimension $n - 1 - 1 \geq 2$, and so this operation does not introduce anything more into π_1. If M' is the new manifold, obtained by this surgery from M, then $\pi_1(M')$ is the quotient of $\pi_1(M)$ by the normal subgroup generated by g.

A refinement of the technique is provided by Smale's theory of handlebodies, in which one associates the manifold $f \leq -\varepsilon$ to the effect of surgery on $f = -\varepsilon$.

Cobordant manifolds. Two open manifolds M^n and M'^n are said to be cobordant if there exists a manifold with boundary W^{n+1} such that an acceptable restrictive relationship holds (see 87). This defines an equivalence relation between manifolds, and the set of equivalence classes is provided (by topological sum) with the structure of an Abelian group denoted Ω^n.

Morse theory applied to a function g on W with $g(M) = 0$, $g(M') = 1$ shows that every cobordism can be realized as a finite sequence of surgeries; conversely, a sequence of surgeries gives a cobordism. If f and g are two homotopic mappings of X into Y, transverse on a submanifold Q of Y, then the submanifolds $f^{-1}(Q)$ and $g^{-1}(Q)$ are cobordant (as can be seen if one considers a homotopy from f to g, transverse to Q). Consequently, the cobordism class of such an inverse image is homotopy invariant of the mapping f. (In the case where dim $X = $ dim Y, Q reduced to a point, dim $f^{-1}(Q) = 0$ and Browder's notion of the degree of the mapping f is recovered.)

The concept of cobordism between manifolds is a weakening of the notion of homotopy equivalence. The transition between the two is the notion of h-cobordism: two manifolds M^n and M'^n are said to be h-cobordant if there exists a manifold with boundary W^{n+1} (see 87) such that each of the manifolds M and M' is a deformation retract of W^{n+1}.

RESULTS ON THE CLASSIFICATION OF MANIFOLDS

Cobordism. The essential tool of cobordism theory is the Pontryagin-Thom construction; given a manifold M^n imbedded in a sphere S^{n+k} of possibly high dimension, one considers the normal bundle $T_\nu(M^n)$, the class of which does not depend on the chosen imbedding for k large enough; y is the mapping of M into the Grassmannian $G(k)$ of k-planes in $\mathfrak{R}^{n+k}$, which induces the normal bundle $T_\nu(M)$ from the universal vector from the universal vector bundle U. Denote by $MSO(k)$ the so-called Thom space, constructed by compactifying the space U by one point at infinity. The map y can then be extended into a mapping $\bar{y}$ from a tubular neighbourhood of M into U; $\bar{y}$ can then be extended into a mapping $\bar{\bar{y}} : S^{n+k} \to MSO(k)$. From the general theorem it now can be seen that two manifolds M and M^1 are cobordant if, and only if, the corresponding maps $\bar{\bar{y}}$ and $\bar{\bar{y}}_1 : S^{n+k} \to MSO(k)$ are homotopic. Consequently an equality involving Ω_n holds (see 88) for k large.

Topological product makes the Abelian group $\Omega = \Sigma \Omega_n$ into a graded ring. The structure of the algebra Ω has been studied at length. The ring $\mathfrak{R}$ of cobordism classes of manifolds without orientation $\mathfrak{R}_m = \pi_{m+k}((MO)(k))$ can also be considered, as before. The structure of $\mathfrak{R}_n$ can be completely determined because the homotopy groups

(79) $\qquad L : \mathfrak{R}^N \to \mathfrak{R}^{2n+1}$

(80) $\qquad \mathfrak{I}(M)|_W \to \mathfrak{R}^N$

(81) $\qquad \mathfrak{R}^n \to \mathfrak{R}^{2n}, \qquad \mathfrak{R}^{2n} \to \mathfrak{R}^{2n-1}, \qquad \mathfrak{R}^2 \to \mathfrak{R}^2$

(82) $\qquad U \cap Q = \pi^{-1}(0)$

(83) $\qquad \pi_y \circ f : M_x \to \mathfrak{R}^q$

(84) $\qquad M \times I \to \mathfrak{R}^n \times I$

(85)
$$\begin{array}{ccc} & T(X) \xrightarrow{f} \theta_f \xrightarrow{f^*} T(Y) & \\ \pi_X & \searrow \quad \downarrow \quad \downarrow \pi_Y & \\ & X \to Y & \end{array}$$

(86) $\qquad f = -X_1^2 - X_2^2 - \cdots - X_k^2 + X_{k+1}^2 + \cdots + X_n^2$

(87) $\qquad \partial W^{n+1} = M^n - M'^n$

(88) $\qquad \Omega_n = \pi_{n+k}(MSO(k))$

(89) $\qquad \Omega \to \Omega \to W \to \Omega \to \Omega \to W \cdots$

(90) $\qquad z \in H_i(M; Z_2), \qquad i < \dfrac{n}{2}$

(91) $\qquad \varphi^* H_n(X) \to H_{n+N}(T(\nu))$

$\pi_{n+k}((MO)(k))$ can be calculated. It is a polynomial algebra over Z_2 having one generator in every dimension not of the form $2^m - 1$. The algebra $\Omega \otimes_Z Q$, with real coefficient is a polynomial algebra with one generator u in every dimension of the form $4k$.

There is an exact sequence involving W (see 89) in which W is the subring of $\mathfrak{M}$ consisting of those classes that admit a representative for which the W_1-Stiefel-Whitney class can be represented as an integral class. The ring Ω has been determined by the English mathematician Charles Terence Clegg Wall; the nonprojective generators of $\mathfrak{R}$ have been constructed by the German mathematician Albrecht Dold.

Cobordism theory has had many extensions; in particular, the complex cobordism groups, $\pi_{n+k}(MU(k))$, as well as the spin-cobordism ring have been calculated.

The complexes $MSO(k)$ are useful for resolving the problem of realizing homology classes as submanifolds. The following are the principal results: it is possible to specify classes z that (see 90) can be realized as a submanifold (not necessarily oriented). In real cohomology, the classes of dimension less than 7 are realizable, but there do exist homology classes of dimension 7 that are not realizable. Finally, the cobordism class of a manifold is determined by a knowledge of its characteristic numbers: a manifold, all of the characteristic numbers of which vanish, necessarily bounds. (A characteristic number is the value taken by a characteristic class on the fundamental cycle of the manifold.)

Classification up to homotopy. Remarkable results of the mathematicians P.S. Novikov and W. Browder have allowed a characterization of the homotopy types of manifolds.

Given a Poincaré complex X (*i.e.*, a complex satisfying Generalised Poincaré Duality), with fundamental class $z \in H_n(X)$, one can associate to it (Spivak's theorem) a topological vector bundle ν playing the role of a normal bundle; now suppose that this normal bundle admits an orthogonal structure. One can construct the Thom complex $T(\nu)$ of the vector bundle ν, and thus obtain a mapping $f : S^{n+N} \to T(\nu)$ such that the image $f^*(s)$ of the fundamental class s is the image $\varphi(Z)$ of Z by a bundle isomorphism (see 91). If one then takes a mapping

$f_1 : S^{n+k} \to T_X(\nu)$ transverse to X, and homotopic to f, one constructs a manifold $M_1 = f_1^{-1}(X)$ that is mapped onto X by a map f_1 of degree one. The problem is then to simplify M, as far as possible by surgery, to make it have the same homotopy type as X. If M is simply connected, this can be done except possibly for the middle dimension, in which one meets an obstruction. If this obstruction vanishes, then the homotopy type of X as a manifold can be realized. These results have been extended to piece-wise linear and topological manifolds.

Classification up to diffeomorphism. An essential result is the so-called h-cobordism theorem, which generalizes results of Smale. If M and M' are two simply connected manifolds of dim ≥ 5, and there exists an h-cobordism W between them, then W is a product $M \times I$, and M and M' are diffeomorphic. A particular case is the Poincaré conjecture in dimension ≥ 5; every manifold M^n, $n \geq 5$, homotopy equivalent to a sphere S^n, is in fact homeomorphic to one. The proof of the h-cobordism theorem is by a surgery argument, which eliminates critical points in pairs of index i, $i - 1$. In the case $\pi_1(M) \neq 0$, the theorem no longer holds. One can then define an obstruction to the elimination of the critical points of a Morse function, defined by Whitehead torsion of the h-cobordism (s-cobordism theorem).

The problem of classification of manifolds, at least of those that are simply connected, is thus reduced to the problem of recognizing whether two given manifolds are h-cobordant; this problem reduces to the problem of simplifying a given cobordism into an h-cobordism. Here again, obstructions are met in the middle dimension. This is in fact the origin of Milnor's examples of exotic spheres, a discovery that has been at the source of all subsequent progress, in particular Michel Kervaire's construction of a manifold of dimension 10, which can be triangulated, but which does not admit a differentiable structure. The general problem of the classification of manifolds, stuck in dimensions three or four (because the Poincaré conjecture is still open in these dimensions), has been attempted in dimensions five and six by C.T.C. Wall. The considerable algebraic difficulties, however, have not allowed a great deal of progress.

Finally, it is as well to add that all these techniques have been generalized to the piecewise linear and topological categories, which has permitted the solution of major problems, such as the Hauptvermutung. (R.F.T.)

BIBLIOGRAPHY. The reader interested in topological groups may wish to consult some of the following works: LEV PONTRYAGIN, *Topological Groups*, 2nd ed. (1966); DEANE MONTGOMERY and LEO ZIPPIN, *Topological Transformation Groups* (1955); CLAUDE CHEVALLEY, *Theory of Lie Groups*, vol. 1 (1946), and *Théorie des groupes de Lie*, vol. 2–3 (1951–55); ECOLE NORMALE SUPERIEURE, *Séminaire "Sophus Lie": le année 1954/1955* (1955); HERMANN WEYL, *Classical Groups*, rev. ed. (1946), and *Gruppentheorie und Quantenmechanik*, 2nd rev. ed. (1931; Eng. trans., *Theory of Groups and Quantum Mechanics*, 1931); LYNN H. LOOMIS, *An Introduction to Abstract Harmonic Analysis* (1953); ANDRE WEIL, *L'Intégration dans les groupes topologiques et ses applications* (1940); EUGEN WIGNER, *Gruppentheorie und ihre Anwendung auf die Quantenmechanik der Atomspektren* (1931); LUTHER P. EISENHART, *Continuous Groups of Transformations* (1933); EDMUND T. WHITTAKER,. *Treatise on the Analytical Dynamics of Particles and Rigid Bodies*, 4th ed. (1937); ELIE CARTAN, *Oeuvres complètes*, 3 vol. (1952–55), *Leçons sur les invariants intégraux* (1922), and *Les Systèmes différentiels extérieurs et leur applications géométriques* (1945); SOPHUS LIE and FRIEDRICH ENGEL, *Theorie der Transformationsgruppen*, 3 vol. (1888–93, reprinted 1930); LOUIS AUSLANDER and CALVIN C. MOORE, *Unitary Representations of Solvable Lie Groups* (1966).

The following works are references dealing with analysis on manifolds: F. HIRZEBRUCH, *Neue topologische Methoden in der algebraischen Geometrie*, 2nd ed. (1962; Eng. trans., *Topological Methods in Algebraic Geometry*, 3rd ed., 1966), a good survey of modern topological techniques as applied to algebraic geometry; JOHN MILNOR, *Morse Theory* (1963), a simple and good introduction to the theory of critical points; W.V.D. HODGE, *The Theory and Applications of Harmonic Integrals*, 2nd ed. (1952), a classic work; GEORGES de RHAM, *Variétés différentielles* (1955), a good treatment of the Hodge-de Rham theory; ROBERT C. GUNNING and HUGO ROSSI, *Analytic Functions of Several Complex Variables* (1965), for sheaf theory applied to complex analysis; SIGUROUR HELGASON, *Differential Geometry and Symmetric Spaces* (1962), a treatment of curvature and related topics, in particular spaces connected with Lie groups.

Some references on differential topology are: SERGE LANG, *Introduction to Differentiable Manifolds* (1962); SHLOMO STERNBERG, *Lectures on Differential Geometry* (1961), two books on differential geometry that treat differentiable manifolds—some of the original articles remain highly recommended reading; HASSLER WHITNEY, "Differentiable Manifolds," *Ann. Math*, 37:645–680 (1936); R. THOM, "Quelques propriétés globales des variétés différentiables," *Comment. math. helvet.*, 28:17–86 (1954), on cobordism; JOHN MILNOR, "On Manifolds Homeomorphic to the 7-Sphere," *Ann. Math.*, 64:399–405 (1956), on exotic differentiable structures; and STEPHEN SMALE, "Generalized Poincaré's Conjecture in Dimensions Greater Than Four," *Ann. Math.*, 74:391–406 (1961). As for differential analysis and singularity theory, the results are far too recent to allow for a complete exhaustive presentation. RALPH ABRAHAM and JOEL ROBBIN, *Transversal Mappings and Flows* (1967); and FREDERIC PHAM, *Introduction à l'étude topologique des singularités de Landau* (1967), are introductions to the subject. BERNARD MALGRANGE, *Ideals of Differentiable Functions* (1966), covers the foundations of differential analysis. JOHN N. MATHER, "Stability of C^∞ Mappings, IV," *Publs. math. Inst. ht. Étud. scient.*, 37:223–248 (1969), is a basic article on the differentiable equivalence theory of singularities. Additional references are JOHN L. KELLEY, *General Topology* (1955); EDUARD CECH, "On Bicompact Spaces," *Ann. Math.*, 38:823–844 (1937); and M.H. STONE, "Applications of the Theory of Boolean Rings to General Topology," *Trans. Am. Math. Soc.*, 41:321–364 (1937).

(G.D.M./M.F.A./R.F.T.)

Topology, Algebraic

Topology is a branch of mathematics that deals with selected properties of collections of related physical or abstract elements. It had its beginnings in the study of those properties that endure when the collection undergoes distortion but remains intact.

Topology is so fundamental that its influence is apparent in almost every other branch of mathematics. It has even been found useful in disciplines that are not considered parts of mathematics proper. An intimate relation exists between aspects of topology and symbolic logic. Applications of so-called fixed-point theorems (see below) are made in mechanics. Topology contributes to the design of geographical maps; of networks for the distribution of electrical power, water, and natural gas; and of systems for industrial automation, guided missiles, and automobile traffic control.

To assign a topological character to a collection, it is sufficient to identify the subcollections that are to be open sets; that is, the subcollections that are similar in certain features (excluding the precise shape) to the interiors of circles in the familiar Euclidean plane. A collection so assigned a topological character is called a topological space. Topological spaces, on the other hand, are not limited to a Euclidean framework, because any collection at all may be made a topological space by assigning the open sets. These assignments are usually made with a definite object in view, such as an application to some particular problem in mathematics, physics, or technology. Consequently, in practice the characterization of a particular topological space is usually accomplished with the help of axiomatic methods.

Algebraic topology applies algebraic methods to study certain questions about topological spaces. The questions studied are usually of a qualitative nature, and the phenomena studied are usually "global"; that is, they belong to the space as a whole but are not inherent in any small part of it.

Certain intuitive notions can be analyzed, clarified, and classified topologically. A plane closed curve that does not cross itself has an inside and an outside; this intuitive idea can be made precise and can even be proved. The properties of knottedness and unknottedness of closed curves in three-dimensional space can be defined and analyzed, and this analysis is far from trivial.

Topology deals not only with spaces but also with maps;

The
fixed-
point
theorem

that is, continuous functions from one space to another. The notation $f: X \to Y$ means that f is a map taking points of X to points of Y. Consider, for example, the Brouwer fixed-point theorem, asserted by the 20th-century Dutch mathematician L.E.J. Brouwer: if D^n is the unit disc in coordinate n-space R^n, it can be defined by an inequality (see Box, inequality 1). The theorem states that any map from the disc to itself has a fixed point (see 2). This asserts that a given equation has a solution, a useful conclusion.

More can be proved. With any map $f: X \to X$ (intuitively a function that redistributes the points of X) satisfying suitable assumptions such as continuity, the Lefschetz number $L(f)$ can be introduced. On the one hand, this is the total number of fixed points of f, counted with appropriate multiplicities; in particular, if $L(f)$ is nonzero, then f has a fixed point. On the other hand, $L(f)$ can be calculated without detailed knowledge of f; for example, if $X = D^n$, then $L(f) = 1$ for all f.

The Lefschetz number is a first example of an algebraic invariant to be discussed immediately below.

Invariants. A quantity depending on a space X or a map is an invariant if it is not changed when X or f is changed in some specified way. Invariants play a central role in the classification of spaces or maps. To prove the existence of a space or map satisfying specified requirements, it is usually possible to construct it; to prove the nonexistence of some hypothetical space or map, it may be possible to show that if it did exist, some invariant would be involved in a contradiction.

A suitable example of an invariant is the degree (to be defined) of a map $f: S^1 \to S^1$ from the unit circle S^1 to itself. If the argument point x moves once around the circle, then the image point $f(x)$ will move around the circle some whole number of times, say $d(f)$. This integer $d(f)$ is called the degree of f. On this foundation can be based almost the whole of plane topology. The "winding number," for example, of a closed plane curve Γ around a point x can be defined. If Γ is simple, its outside is the set of points x around which the winding number is zero.

The unit sphere S^{n-1} in n-space R^n is defined by an equation (see 3); it is the boundary of the unit disc D^n. The degree of a map from the sphere to itself can be

defined; for $n - 1$ greater than 1 this is usually done using homology theory (see below *Homology and cohomology*). The Lefschetz number of a map is easily stated (see 4). The degree of a map from the unit sphere to itself is unchanged by small perturbations of f. This leads to the notion of homotopy.

Homotopy theory. If X and Y are two spaces, and f_0 and f_1 two maps from X to Y, then it is said that f_0 and f_1 are homotopic, and $f_0 \sim f_1$ is written, if f_0 can be perturbed or deformed continuously into f_1. More precisely, homotopy requires that there should be intermediate maps (see 5). Such a family of maps f_t is called a homotopy.

The relation $f_0 \sim f_1$ is an equivalence relation; thus it is possible to classify the maps from X to Y into homotopy classes. It is usual to write $[X, Y]$ for the set of such homotopy classes. Take, for example, both X and Y to be the circle S^1, or more generally the sphere S^n, and assign to each map its degree. This assignment gives a one-to-one correspondence between the set $[S^n, S^n]$ of homotopy classes and the set Z of integers.

In homotopy theory those questions are studied in which it makes no difference if all the maps in sight are replaced by homotopic ones. Two spaces X and Y, for example, are definable as homotopy-equivalent (see 6). A map between two homotopy-equivalent spaces is called a homotopy-equivalence; it is analogous to a homeomorphism, except that equality of maps has been replaced by homotopy. A space X is called contractible if it is homotopy-equivalent to a point.

For various reasons, the domain of homotopy theory is larger than might be expected. First, invariants of a map f usually take values in some algebraic object, such as the group of integers; typically it is discrete. If an invariant $d(f)$ of f is continuous in any sense, then $d(f_t)$ must be constant as t varies, so that $d(f_0) = d(f_1)$, and homotopic maps must have the same invariant. This is the case for the Lefschetz number and for all the most usual invariants; thus they belong to homotopy theory.

Second, the so-called extension problem starts with a space X, a subspace A of X, and a map $g: A \to Y$ from the subspace A to Y. (A space X together with a subspace A is often called a pair X, A.) It can be asked whether there is a map from the whole space X to the same image space Y that extends the given map g of A in a specific way (see 7). (It is usual to write $g = f|A$.) As a special case, it is possible to take X as the unit n-dimensional ball, Y as its boundary, A as identical to Y, and g as the identity mapping of S^{n-1} onto itself (see 8). The problem then asks whether there is a so-called retraction of the ball on its boundary. If the Brouwer fixed-point theorem is assumed to be false, it is easy to show that such a retraction would exist. It can be proved (using the degree) that there is no such retraction; and this immediately implies the Brouwer fixed-point theorem. Many other appealing geometric problems can be reduced to extension problems.

Extension
problems

Extension problems belong to homotopy theory, at least for suitable pairs X, A. This classification follows from Borsuk's so-called homotopy extension theorem (see 9), which implies that given two homotopic maps of A, either they both extend, or neither does.

Third, numerous geometrical problems that do not appear to lie in homotopy theory have been successfully reduced to homotopy theory. This is done, for example, for the classification of fibre bundles by a classification theorem (see below *Fibrings*); it is also done for the computation of groups called cobordism groups by another theorem. Reduction to homotopy theory whenever possible is now a standard method in differential and geometric topology.

To obtain concrete results in homotopy theory, it is normal to require invariants that are computable. This requirement leads to homology.

Homology and cohomology. The basic idea of homology theory, which goes back to the French mathematician Henri Poincaré, is to divide a space up into points, line segments, triangles, and other geometric components and then to measure the number and the interrela-

---

(1) $\quad x_1^2 + \cdots + x_n^2 \leqslant 1$

(2) $\quad \begin{cases} \text{Fixed point theorem for the disk } D^n: \\ \text{Given } f: D^n \to D^n, \text{ there exists } x \text{ in } D^n \text{ such that} \\ f(x) = x. \end{cases}$

(3) $\quad S^{n-1}: x_1^2 + \cdots + x_n^2 = 1$

(4) $\quad \text{If } f: S^{n-1} \to S^{n-1} \text{ then } L(f) = 1 - (-1)^n d(f).$

(5) $\quad \begin{cases} \text{Requirement of homotopy: There should be } f_t: X \to Y \\ \text{for } 0 < t < 1 \text{ such that } f_t(x) \text{ is a continuous function of} \\ \text{the two variables } t \text{ and } x \text{ for } 0 \leqslant t \leqslant 1, x \text{ in } X. \end{cases}$

(6) $\quad \begin{cases} X \text{ is homotopy-equivalent to } Y \text{ if and only if there are} \\ \text{maps } f: X \to Y \text{ and } g: Y \to X \text{ such that } fg \sim 1: Y \to Y \\ \text{and } gf \sim 1: X \to X. \end{cases}$

(7) $\quad \begin{cases} \text{For subspace } A \text{ of } X, \text{ the map } f: X \to Y \text{ extends} \\ g: A \to Y, \text{ if } f(a) = g(a) \text{ for } a \text{ in } A. \end{cases}$

(8) $\quad \begin{cases} X = E^n \\ A = Y = S^{n-1} \\ g: S^{n-1} \to S^{n-1} \end{cases}$

(9) $\quad \begin{cases} \text{Borsuk's homotopy extension theorem: Given a map} \\ f_0: X \to Y, \text{ and a homotopy } g_t: A \to Y \text{ starting from the} \\ \text{restriction of } f_0 \text{ to } A, g_0 = f_0|A, \text{ the theorem extends the} \\ \text{homotopy from } A \text{ to } X \text{ so as to give a homotopy } f_t \text{ of } f_0. \end{cases}$

The
Euler
characteristic

tionships of these parts in a suitable algebraic way. If, for example, a surface M^2 is divided into vertices (V in number), edges (E in number), and triangular faces (F in number), then the Euler characteristic of M^2, which is also the Lefschetz number of the identity map $1: M^2 \rightarrow M^2$, may be defined as $V - E + F$.

The simplest figure obtained by connecting two points is a simplex in one dimension, a line segment. Adjoining one point in a second dimension results in a two-dimensional simplex (triangle). To this, the adjunction of a point in a third dimension yields a three-dimensional simplex (tetrahedron). To this, the adjunction of a point in a fourth dimension yields a four-dimensional simplex, and so on. More generally, the standard n-simplex σ^n can be precisely defined (see 10). The ith face of σ^n is the subspace $x_i = 0$. A finite simplicial complex is a space that can be assembled from a finite number of simplexes in the obvious way. Homology theory was first set up for finite simplicial complexes; but starting in the 1930s it was extended to maps from compact spaces to finite simplicial complexes and later to maps from simplexes to all spaces.

The modern approach to homology theory is axiomatic. The business of homology theory is to assign to each space some invariants that are (Abelian) groups and to assign to each map some invariants that are homomorphisms of groups (see 11). In the construction of these groups and homomorphisms, it can be proved that they satisfy seven axioms of the U.S. mathematicians Samuel Eilenberg and Norman E. Steenrod. Everything else follows from these axioms.

From the axioms, theorems can be deduced that allow the calculation of homology groups of all the spaces arising in practice. The study of position in manifolds, for example, is based on theorems that relate the (co)homology of a subspace to the homology of its complement, a result due to a number of mathematicians. Homology provides the first weapon in geometrical problems of homotopy theory (see above *Homotopy theory* and below *Further homotopy theory*). Singular homology can be constructed (see 12).

The
difference
between
cohomology
and
homology

Cohomology differs from homology formally, in that a map induces a homomorphism in the opposite direction from that in homology (see 13). At the same time, cohomology can be introduced with coefficients in an Abelian group G (see 14).

Cohomology operations give extra structure to cohomology groups and can be used to resolve geometric problems. A good example is the Steenrod square, which is a homomorphism Sq^i mapping one cohomology group to another (see 15).

Homotopy groups. If it is desired to study maps from a simplicial complex W to a space X, it is natural to divide the problem into two parts: first, to study the possible ways of mapping simplexes into X; and, second, to assemble the information about maps of simplexes so as to obtain information about maps of the whole complex W. Homotopy groups serve to formalize the first part of the problem; obstruction theory serves to formalize the second part.

In what follows, it is convenient to agree that spaces have base points and that maps and homotopies preserve the base points. If X, A is a pair, it is possible to consider maps (see 16) from the cell E^n to X that carry the boundary sphere S^{n-1} into the subspace A. It is usual to take the set of homotopy classes of such maps; by geometrical constructions with the cell E^n, this set is turned into a group $\pi_n(X, A)$ (see 17). For $n \geq 3$ it is Abelian. If A is taken to the base point, the absolute homotopy group, written $\pi_n(X)$, is obtained. It coincides with $[S^n, X]$, the homotopy classes of maps from the sphere S^n to the space X. It is Abelian for $n \geq 2$. For $n = 1$ it coincides with what is called the fundamental group of X, introduced by Poincaré. For example, $\pi_n(S^n)$ is the group of integers Z.

A map $f: X, A \rightarrow Y, B$ induces a homomorphism of relative homotopy groups. Each pair X, A gives rise to an exact sequence, which is called the exact homotopy sequence of the pair (see 18).

(10) $\begin{cases} \text{The standard } n\text{-simplex } \sigma^n \text{ is the subspace of } R^{n+1} \\ \text{given by: } x_1 + \cdots + x_{n+1} = 1, \quad x_1 \geq 0, \cdots, x_{n+1} \geq 0. \end{cases}$

(11) $\begin{cases} \text{Relative homology groups can be assigned to pairs} \\ X, A. \text{ The homology group said to be in dimension } n \text{ is} \\ \text{written } H_n(X, A). \text{ The subspace } A \text{ may be the empty set} \\ \phi, \text{ in which case } H_n(X) \text{ can be written for } H_n(X, \phi). \\ \text{For example, } H_n(S^n) \text{ turns out to be the group of} \\ \text{integers } Z \text{ (if } n > 0). \text{ If } X, A \text{ and } Y, B \text{ are two pairs,} \\ \text{it is usual to write } f: X, A \rightarrow Y, B \text{ to mean that } f \text{ is a} \\ \text{map from } X \text{ to } Y \text{ which carries the subspace } A \text{ into } B. \\ \text{Homology-theory is then used to define the induced} \\ \text{homomorphism } f_*: H_n(X, A) \rightarrow H_n(Y, B). \text{ If } f \text{ maps for} \\ \text{example } S^n \text{ to } S^n, \text{ then the induced homomorphism } f_* \text{ is} \\ \text{an endomorphism of } H_n(S^n) \cong Z; \text{ it must be} \\ \text{multiplication by some integer } d; \text{ this integer } d \text{ is the} \\ \text{degree of } f. \end{cases}$

(12) $\begin{cases} \text{To construct singular homology, it is usual first to take} \\ \text{the set of all maps } f: \sigma^n \rightarrow X. \text{ The free Abelian group} \\ \text{generated by these maps is the chain group } C_n(X). \text{ By} \\ \text{using the faces of } \sigma^n \text{ it is possible to define a} \\ \text{boundary homomorphism } d_n: C_n(X) \rightarrow C_{n-1}(X). \text{ The} \\ \text{homology group } H_n(X) \text{ is then defined as } \ker d_n/\operatorname{im} d_{n+1}. \end{cases}$

(13) $\begin{cases} \text{In cohomology a map } f: X, A \rightarrow Y, B \text{ induces a} \\ \text{homomorphism } f^*: H^n(Y, B) \rightarrow H^n(X, A). \end{cases}$

(14) $\begin{cases} \text{In the construction of cohomology } H^n(X, A; G) \text{ with} \\ \text{coefficients in an Abelian group } G, \text{ the chain groups} \\ C_n(X) \text{ are replaced by the cochain groups} \\ C^n(X; G) = \hom(C_n(X), G). \end{cases}$

(15) $Sq^i: H^n(X, A; Z_2) \rightarrow H^{n+i}(X, A; Z_2)$

(16) $f: E^n, S^{n-1} \rightarrow X, A$

(17) $\begin{cases} \text{The set of homotopy classes of maps } f, \text{ defined in (16),} \\ \text{is turned by geometrical construction into a group} \\ \text{called the } n\text{th relative homotopy group of } X \text{ mod } A, \text{ and} \\ \text{written } \pi_n(X, A). \end{cases}$

(18) $\cdots \rightarrow \pi_n(A) \xrightarrow{i^*} \pi_n(X) \xrightarrow{j^*} \pi_n(X, A) \xrightarrow{d} \pi_{n-1}(A) \rightarrow \cdots$

(19) $\begin{cases} \text{A space } X \text{ or pair } X, A \text{ is said to be } n\text{-connected if the} \\ \text{homotopy groups } \pi_r(X) \text{ or } \pi_r(X, A) \text{ are zero for } r \leq n. \\ \text{The Hurewicz isomorphism theorem states that if } X \text{ is} \\ (n-1)\text{-connected, where } n \geq 2, \text{ then an isomorphism} \\ \pi_n(X) \cong H_n(X) \text{ is obtained.} \end{cases}$

(20) $\begin{cases} \text{Examples: } \pi_3(S^2) = Z; \quad \pi_6(S^3) = Z_{12}, \\ \text{The group of integers modulo 12.} \end{cases}$

(21) $\begin{cases} \text{Freudenthal suspension theorem states that the} \\ \text{homotopy group } \pi_{n+r}(S^n) \text{ is independent of } n \text{ for} \\ n > r+1; \text{ more precisely, there is an isomorphism} \\ \pi_{n+r}(S^n) \cong \pi_{n+r+1}(S^{n+1}). \end{cases}$

The isomorphism theorem due to the U.S. mathematician Witold Hurewicz states that for a certain space X, such as the sphere, an isomorphism is obtained between the first nonvanishing homotopy and homology groups (see 19). There is a corresponding theorem for relative groups.

If the spheres are treated as some of the most basic spaces in homotopy theory, it is natural to seek the structure of the homotopy groups of spheres. Some examples are known (see 20). Although much effort has been devoted to this problem, no pattern or general formula has been produced.

Stability and suspension. A phenomenon in algebraic topology is said to be stable if it happens in the same way in any dimension or in any sufficiently large dimension. The suspension theorem due to the Dutch mathematician

The
Hurewicz
isomorphism
theorem

Hans Freudenthal provides an example expressed in terms of an isomorphism (see 21). This isomorphism is given by the geometrical construction of suspension. The suspension SX of X is the union of two cones with common base X, for which simple examples exist (see 22). Further reasoning is technical (see 23). It is useful to give sets of homotopy classes an algebraic structure whenever it is possible (see 24).

The homology and cohomology groups of a suspension can be given (see 25), and homology and cohomology are considered stable. The Steenrod square (see 15) is a homomorphism between cohomology groups that is defined in every dimension and commutes with the suspension isomorphism; it is therefore considered stable.

Fibrings. If $p:E \rightarrow B$ is a map, then the counter-images $p^{-1}b$ of the points in B are called the fibres of p; they are regarded as a continuous family of subspaces in E, indexed or parameterized by the points of B. It may be required that each fibre be homeomorphic to a fixed space F; even so, it may not be possible to choose the homeomorphisms to vary continuously as the parameter b is varied. Further structure or further axioms may be required.

The Möbius band

The Möbius band, for example, may be regarded as a family of intervals, parameterized by the points of a circle. Another example is given by the family of tangent spaces to a manifold. In this example every fibre is a vector space; such examples are called vector bundles; they are important in differential topology. Whitney sums can be defined (see 26). A vector bundle with fibres of (real) dimension n is a fibre bundle with structural group $GL(n, R)$, in the sense of Steenrod.

In the applications, it is important to be able to classify the bundles over X with group G. This is a problem in homotopy theory; such bundles are in one-to-one correspondence with homotopy classes of maps $f:X \rightarrow BG$. Here BG is a space called the classifying space of G; its characteristic property is that there is a fibring $EG \rightarrow BG$, called the universal bundle, in which EG is contractible and G acts freely on EG, with quotient BG.

The most practical invariants of a bundle, ξ, over X with group G are characteristic classes (see 27). These classes have convenient properties, and many results in the topology of manifolds are expressed in terms of them. Characteristic classes defined for G-bundles and satisfying an obvious naturality axiom are in one-to-one correspondence with elements of $H^*(BG)$; and $H^*(BG)$ has been calculated for the most useful groups G (see below *Spectral sequences*).

In a lifting problem, it is usual to give a map $f:X \rightarrow B$ and ask whether there is a map $g:X \rightarrow E$ such that $pg = f$. The problem, for example, of finding a continuous field of nonzero tangent vectors on a manifold is a problem of this type. Lifting problems belong to homotopy theory; this classification is guaranteed by what is called the homotopy lifting theorem, the statement of which is analogous to that of the homotopy extension theorem (see 9). It follows from the homotopy lifting theorem that a fibring gives rise to an exact homotopy sequence (see 28). It is possible therefore to obtain information on homotopy groups from fibrings that arise in nature, so to speak, such as the Hopf fibrings.

The French mathematician Jean-Pierre Serre proposed that the word fibring should be used for any map that has the homotopy lifting property. He thus greatly increased the range of useful fibrings by admitting fibrings involving function spaces, particularly loop spaces (see 29). There is a natural relationship involving loop spaces such that suspension theory may be reduced to the study of loop spaces (see 30).

Fibring involving function spaces

Serre used essentially similar constructions to show that any map $f:X \rightarrow Y$ may be factored in the form $X \xrightarrow{e} E \xrightarrow{p} Y$, in which e is a homotopy-equivalence and p is a fibring. This factoring provides enough fibrings for all the purposes of homotopy theory.

Sheaf cohomology. A sheaf over a space X may be viewed in two lights. The first is the viewpoint of the case of functions on a Riemann surface X. To each open set U in X can be associated the ring of complex functions analytic on U; but as U gets bigger the ring gets smaller, and vice versa. In general, it is possible to associate to each open set U in X a ring or group $\Gamma(U)$ satisfying suitable axioms. Second, it is possible to view a sheaf as a parameterized family of coefficient groups indexed by the points of X. To a point x of a Riemann surface, for example, can be associated the group of those functions that are analytic around x.

The sheaves over X may be considered as the objects of a category; homological algebra can then be done in this category. The entity called a function that associates to each sheaf Γ the group $\Gamma(X)$ of functions on the whole space is not exact, but it has derived functors. These provide the cohomology groups $H^n(X; \Gamma)$ of X with coefficients in the sheaf Γ. From the point of view of algebraic topology, this situation is the appropriate version of cohomology when the coefficient group is replaced by a sheaf.

Cohomology with local coefficients

Sheaf cohomology is useful in algebraic geometry. A simple special case is that in which the sheaf is a fibring, so that the coefficient groups corresponding to the different points of x are all isomorphic to a fixed group. This gives cohomology with local, or twisted, coefficients, useful, for example, in studying nonorientable manifolds.

Spectral sequences. Since the pioneering work of the French mathematician Jean Leray and the celebrated work of Serre, algebraic topology has made much use of spectral sequences. A spectral sequence is an algebraic construct comparable with an exact sequence, but more complicated. Although the existence of a spectral sequence may not provide an algorithm or rule for computing the groups concerned, the experts succeed with it more often than not.

(22) Example: $SS^n = S^{n+1}$

(23) A map $f:X \rightarrow Y$ induces a map $SF:SX \rightarrow SY$. This yields a function $S:[X, Y] \rightarrow [SX, SY]$. The space Y may be $(n-1)$-connected; when this is the case it can be shown that this function is a bijection if X is at most $(2n-2)$-dimensional, a surjection if X is $(2n-1)$-dimensional.

(24) If SX is a suspension, then the set of homotopy classes $[SX, Y]$ may be made into a group. The common value of the groups $[S^{m+r}X, S^mY]$ for sufficiently large values of m is the group $\{X, Y\}_r$ of "stable homotopy classes of maps from X to Y."

(25) The homology and cohomology groups of a suspension: $\tilde{H}_{n+1}(SX) \cong \tilde{H}_n(X)$; $\tilde{H}^{n+1}(SX) \cong \tilde{H}^n(X)$. (Here the "reduced" homology of X is defined by $\tilde{H}_n(X) = H_n(X, pt)$.)

(26) If $p:E \rightarrow B$ and $q:E' \rightarrow B$ are vector bundles; their Whitney sum is a vector-bundle, in which the fibre over b is the direct sum $(p^{-1}b) \oplus (q^{-1}b)$.

(27) If G is a unitary group $U(n)$ the Chern classes $c_i(\xi) \in H^{2i}(X; Z)$ are obtained; if G is an orthogonal group $O(n)$ the Stiefel-Whitney classes $w_i(\xi) \in H^i(X; Z_2)$ and the Pontrjagin classes are obtained.

(28) $\cdots \rightarrow \pi_n(F) \rightarrow \pi_n(E) \rightarrow \pi_n(P) \rightarrow \pi_{n-1}(F) \rightarrow \cdots$

(29) If X is a space with base-point x_0, then the path-space LX is the space of maps $\omega:I \rightarrow X$ from the unit interval I to X such that $\omega(0) = x_0$ (paths starting at the base-point). A map $p:LX \rightarrow X$ is defined by $p(\omega) = \omega(1)$; it is a fibering with LX contractible; it is analogous to the fibering $EG \rightarrow BG$. The loop-space ΩX is the fibre $p^{-1}(x_0)$; that is, the space of paths starting and finishing at the base-point.

(30) $[SX, Y] \cong [X, \Omega Y]$

A spectral sequence consists of groups together with boundary homomorphisms between these groups (see 31). The spectral sequence is said to converge toward a limit, if certain conditions are satisfied (see 32).

Suppose, for example, there is a fibring with fibre F, total space E, and base B. The result is the Serre spectral sequence (see 33), which converges toward the homology of the total space, and its initial term is the homology of the base with coefficients in the homology of the fibre. There is a similar spectral sequence in cohomology.

Since the introduction of the Serre spectral sequence, mathematicians have been able to work effectively with the homology of fibrings. One application, originally due to Borel, led to the calculation of the cohomology of the classifying space BG for each of the classical Lie groups G. This calculation led to a complete understanding of the theory of characteristic classes. If, for example, G is the unitary group $U(n)$, then the cohomology ring $H^*(BU(n))$ is a polynomial algebra generated by the Chern classes $c_1, \cdots, c_n$ of the universal bundle.

Other spectral sequences are also useful. A celebrated calculation of the cohomology of Eilenberg–MacLane spaces by Henri Cartan of France (see below *Further homotopy theory*) led eventually to the Rothenberg-Steenrod spectral sequence (see 34). In this case the cohomology of a classifying space BG (with coefficients in a ring R) can be computed using a spectral sequence, in which the initial term is obtained from the homology of G by homological algebra.

The Eilenberg–Moore spectral sequence To proceed in the opposite direction, there is obtained the Eilenberg–Moore spectral sequence (see 35), in which the homology of a loop space ΩX can be computed from that of X using homological algebra and a spectral sequence. In fact, Eilenberg and Moore also give their result at what is called the chain level and give their spectral sequence in greater generality, to compute the homology of induced fibrings.

Further homotopy theory. A considerable advance in homotopy theory became possible by using spectral sequences to prove results on the homology of fibrings (following Serre). An example (see 36) in suspension theory leads to an easy proof of the result mentioned above in *Stability and suspension*. More advanced results in suspension theory have been obtained in England from the study of loop spaces by the United States mathematician George W. Whitehead and English and Japanese, respectively, mathematicians Ioan Mackenzie James and Hiroshi Toda.

A process similar to the calculation of the cohomology of classifying spaces but involving many steps instead of one led, in the hands of Serre and Cartan, to the calculation of the homology of Eilenberg–MacLane spaces. A space Y is an Eilenberg–MacLane space of type (π, n) if its homotopy groups are all zero except for the nth, which is π. The circle S^1, for example, is an Eilenberg–MacLane space of type $(Z, 1)$. If Y is of type (π, n), then its loop space is of type $(\pi, n-1)$. If Y is of type (π, n), then $[X, Y] = H^n(X; \pi)$; the group of homotopy classes of maps from X to Y is isomorphic to the nth cohomology group of X with coefficients in π. It follows that the cohomology of the Eilenberg–MacLane space Y gives an enumeration of those cohomology operations that can be defined on $H^n(X; \pi)$ for all X. In particular, for any prime p, the mod p Steenrod algebra A is defined to be the set of all stable cohomology operations defined on cohomology with coefficients Z_p: its structure is determined by the results on Eilenberg–MacLane spaces.

Use of Eilenberg–MacLane spaces Any space X can be approximated by an iterated fibring in which the building blocks are Eilenberg–MacLane spaces of type $(\pi_n(X), n)$, which is the Postnikov decomposition of X. In principle, then, if the homotopy groups of X were known, the homology of these Eilenberg–MacLane spaces would be known, and thus the homology groups of X could be calculated. In practice, the method is usually applied in the reverse direction, by knowing the homology of X, and by calculating its first few homotopy groups. This is the so-called method of killing homotopy groups of Cartan and Serre.

The method of killing homotopy groups may be applied

to gain general information without computing specific groups. This method leads to Serre's C-theory, by which it can be shown on a priori grounds that the homotopy groups of a given space are finite, or finitely-generated. The theorems also show that different primes play independent roles in homotopy theory; the 3-primary component of a given group can be calculated without considering its 2-primary component.

In stable homotopy theory, it is possible to formalize the method of killing homotopy groups. The Adams spectral sequence can be obtained (see 37). As a result, the groups of stable homotopy classes of maps can be computed, starting from homological data, using homological algebra and a spectral sequence. This spectral sequence has been used to compute stable homotopy groups of spheres and (following the method of the mathematician John W. Milnor of the United States) to compute cobordism groups.

Generalized homology. A generalized homology or cohomology theory is a functor that assigns to any space X groups $K_n(X)$ or $K^n(X)$ and that satisfies the first six axioms of Eilenberg and Steenrod already referred to (see above *Homology and cohomology*) but that does not necessarily satisfy the seventh axiom, which would restrict the resulting groups when X is a point. One example of such a functor that has become important in algebraic topology is the K-theory of Alexander Grothendieck of France, Michael F. Atiyah of the United States, and others. The groups $K^n(X)$ are constructed in terms of vector bundles. The isomorphism classes of complex vector bundles over X, for example, form a monoid or semigroup under Whitney sum. Consider all homomorphisms that map this semigroup to an Abelian group; among them is one that is universal: the group into which it maps is the 0th K-cohomology group $K^0(X)$.

Further examples are provided by bordism and cobordism. It is possible to construct the singular homology group $H_n(X)$ by using maps from the n-simplex to X; it is also possible to construct the bordism group $MSO_n(X)$ by a comparable use of maps from oriented n-manifolds to X. These functors are often relevant in questions on the topology of bundles and manifolds, and they have been used to prove geometrical results of a nontrivial nature. Bordism and cobordism

Calculation of generalized homology groups is often based on the spectral sequence of G.W. Whitehead–Atiyah–Hirzebruch (see 38). This sequence starts from the ordinary homology groups of X with coefficients in the generalized homology of a point and converges to the generalized homology of X (similarly for cohomology). To apply this sequence, it is necessary to know the generalized homology of a point; that is, the groups $K_q(pt)$. In the case of K-theory, these groups are determined by the Bott periodicity theorem.

There is an analogy between the group $K^n(X)$ and the set $[X, Y]$ of homotopy classes of maps from X to a fixed space Y. If $f: A \rightarrow X$ is a map, it is possible to construct $X \cup {}_fCA$ by taking X and the cone CA with base A and identifying each point a in A with $f(a)$ in X. The sequence $A \xrightarrow{f} X \longrightarrow X \cup_f CA$ is called a cofibring. If either the group $K^n(X)$ or the set $[X, Y]$ is taken and X is varied along a cofibring, an exact sequence is obtained.

The representability theorem of E.H. Brown, a mathematician of the United States, gives necessary and sufficient conditions on a functor K from spaces to sets in order that it have the form $K(X) = [X, Y]$. These conditions are always satisfied by the groups $K^n(X)$ of a generalized cohomology theory. For complex K-theory, for example, it follows that $K^0(X) = [X, BU]$, in which BU is the "limit" as $n \rightarrow \infty$ of the classifying spaces $BU(n)$.

Conversely, ideas from generalized cohomology are useful in stable and, to a less extent, in unstable homotopy theory. The set of homotopy classes $[X, Y]$, or the group of stable homotopy classes $\{X, Y\}_r$, is considered as a generalized cohomology functor of X; the spectral sequence of G.W. Whitehead–Atiyah–Hirzebruch then serves as a modern substitute for obstruction-theory.

(31) $\left\{\begin{array}{l}\text{A spectral sequence consists of groups } E^r_{p,q} \\ \text{(depending on three indices } p, q, r\text{), together with} \\ \text{boundary homomorphisms } d^r: E^r_{p,q} \to E^r_{p-r,q+r-1} \\ \text{between these groups.}\end{array}\right.$

(32) $\left\{\begin{array}{l}\text{It is usual to start with the groups } E^2_{p,q} \text{ for } r=2. \text{ The} \\ \text{higher terms } E^r_{**} = \sum_{p,q} E^r_{p,q} \text{ are determined by} \\ E^{r+1}_{**} = \ker d_r / \operatorname{im} d_r \text{ as } r \text{ tends to infinity the group } E^r_{p,q} \\ \text{tends to } E^\infty_{p,q}. \text{ The spectral sequence is said to converge} \\ \text{toward } L_* = \sum_n L_n \text{ if the groups } E^\infty_{p,q} \text{ with } p+q=n \text{ are} \\ \text{the subquotients arising from a suitable filtration of } L_n. \\ \text{The notation } E^2_{p,q} \Rightarrow L_n \text{ indicates such a spectral} \\ \text{sequence.}\end{array}\right.$

(33) $\left\{\begin{array}{l}\text{The Serre spectral sequence:} \\ H_p(B; H_q(F)) \Rightarrow H_n(E).\end{array}\right.$

(34) $\left\{\begin{array}{l}\text{The Rothenberg-Steenrod spectral sequence:} \\ \operatorname{ext}_{H_*(G;R)}(R,R) \Rightarrow H^*(BG;R).\end{array}\right.$

(35) $\left\{\begin{array}{l}\text{The Eilenberg-Moore spectral sequence:} \\ \operatorname{cotor}^{H_*(X,R)}(R,R) \Rightarrow H_*(\Omega X, R).\end{array}\right.$

(36) $\left\{\begin{array}{l}\text{In suspension-theory there is a bijection} \\ [SY, Z] \cong [Y, \Omega Z]. \text{ In particular (taking } Z = SY\text{) the} \\ \text{identity map } 1: SY \to SY \text{ corresponds to an embedding} \\ \text{of } Y \text{ in } \Omega SY. \text{ It can be shown that if } Y \text{ is } (n-1)\text{-} \\ \text{connected, then the pair } (\Omega SY, Y) \text{ is } (2n-1)\text{-connected;} \\ \text{that is, } Y \text{ and } \Omega SY \text{ are the same in a certain sense} \\ \text{throughout a large range of dimensions.}\end{array}\right.$

(37) $\left\{\begin{array}{l}\text{If } X \text{ and } Y \text{ are spaces, and } p \text{ is a prime, it is possible to} \\ \text{obtain the Adams spectral sequence:} \\ \operatorname{ext}^{**}_A(\tilde{H}^*(Y;Z_p), \tilde{H}^*(X;Z_p)) \Rightarrow {}_p\{X,Y\}_*. \\ \text{Here } {}_pG \text{ means the } p\text{-component of the group } G; \text{ the} \\ \text{algebra } A \text{ is the mod } p \text{ Steenrod algebra; and the} \\ \text{reduced cohomology groups } \tilde{H}^*(Y;Z_p), \tilde{H}^*(X;Z_p) \text{ are} \\ \text{considered as modules over } A.\end{array}\right.$

(38) $\left\{\begin{array}{l}\text{The spectral sequence of G.W. Whitehead-Atiyah-} \\ \text{Hirzebruch:} \\ H_p(X; K_q(pt)) \Rightarrow K_n(X).\end{array}\right.$

Present outlook. In the 1970s, progress in the central and older parts of algebraic topology has been less rapid than in the past. Although, for example, detailed calculations of the homotopy groups of spheres $\pi_r(S^n)$ have been carried out for a reasonable range of dimensions, no pattern has emerged that might lead to new insights and theorems not yet suspected. The most flourishing and hopeful areas are in general the borderlines with other subjects, in which a cross-fertilization of ideas often leads to new advances.

On the frontier with algebra, ideas developed in algebraic topology have evidently had an important influence in the development of category theory, homological algebra, and algebraic K-theory. Conversely, ideas from all these subjects have proved stimulating and useful in algebraic topology; for example, the work on finiteness obstructions and surgery obstructions relies essentially on algebraic K-theory.

Similarly, on the frontier with algebraic geometry, ideas from algebraic topology have evidently had an important influence on the modern school of algebraic geometry associated with Grothendieck. Equally, ideas from modern algebraic geometry have led to significant work in algebraic topology.

The advances in the topology of manifolds made possible by a celebrated breakthrough of Kirby and Siebenmann consist of work that is geometrical in interest and method but has a large interrelation with algebraic topology.

The celebrated work of Atiyah and Singer lies on the borderline of algebraic topology and analysis. The study of systems of partial differential equations on a manifold is generalized to the study of an elliptic operator. The theorem of Atiyah and Singer, in its first form, related the behaviour of this operator to the topology of the underlying manifold. The proof used the principle that a discrete invariant does not change when the operator is continuously perturbed. A later form of the theorem embodies a far-reaching generalization of the Lefschetz number. Perhaps, while the best contemporary work often draws together several subjects, it sometimes reveals new potentialities in the most basic ideas of algebraic topology.

BIBLIOGRAPHY. EDWIN H. SPANIER, *Algebraic Topology* (1966); and DALE HUSEMOLLER, *Fibre Bundles* (1966), are two of the most generally useful standard texts. The scope of Spanier is wider; that of Husemoller is more limited. It is not easy for a student to read Spanier as a first text, but mathematically it is excellent. JOHN F. ADAMS, *Algebraic Topology: A Student's Guide* (1972), has a much longer bibliography, with a survey article and a guide to the literature.

Topology, General

An offshoot of geometry, topology was originated during the 19th century. A simple (but not entirely accurate) definition has often been used: Topology is the study of those properties that an object retains under deformation, specifically, bending, stretching and squeezing, but not breaking or tearing. Thus a triangle is topologically equivalent to a circle but not to a straight line segment. Similarly, a solid cube made of modelling clay could be deformed into a ball by kneading. It could not, however, be molded into a solid torus (ring) unless a hole were bored through it or two surfaces were joined together. A solid cube is therefore not topologically equivalent to a finger ring.

More precisely, if there are given two geometric objects or sets of points, and if some two-way transformation (or operation or mapping) takes each point p of either set into one and only one point p' of the other, and if the transformation is continuous in the sense (which can be made precise) that points close to p become points close to p', then the transformation is called a homeomorphism and the two sets are said to be topologically equivalent. Topology is, then, the study of properties that remain invariant under homeomorphisms.

This definition is intended to make it clear that the deformation concept has certain limitations. If two figures are given in Euclidean two-dimensional space, called $\Re^2$—that is, the space of ordinary plane geometry—and if one of them consists of a circle tangent internally to a larger circle, and the other consists of two externally tangent circles, then a homeomorphism exists that transforms one figure into the other, and therefore the two figures are topologically equivalent. One figure cannot, however, be changed to the other by distortion in $\Re^2$. It is possible to turn one of the circles through 180° around the common tangent line as axis, thus carrying it into three-dimensional space $\Re^3$, and effect the deformation. The extra dimension may or may not be available, depending on the conditions of the problem. An internally tangent sphere in $\Re^3$ could be continuously deformed to bring it to a position of external tangency by a rotation in hypothetical four-dimensional space $\Re^4$, which might present no difficulty mathematically but would be impossible to achieve or even visualize in a physical application. The mathematical context may also prevent the use of an additional dimension: In any case, the deformation concept is not used or needed in defining topology.

Examples of problems, methods, and applications of topology. *Euler's theorem.* An example of a topological invariant is provided by Euler's classic theorem on polyhedra. A three-dimensional polyhedron without holes or handles may be considered (it is topologically a ball). If the numbers of faces, edges, and vertices on its surface are F, E, and V, respectively, then $F - E + V = 2$. Thus a cube, with six faces, 12 edges, and eight vertices, satisfies the property; and so do all polyhedral balls, however complicated and irregular. Furthermore, if a point is removed from a face of the surface of the polyhedral ball and the remainder is suitably mapped onto a planar figure, the property still holds, being topologically invariant; and in fact the theorem is most readily proved with the aid of such a mapping.

Though topology deals with some very generalized sets in abstract spaces that do not resemble point sets of the "real world," there are applications of topology to physics and the other sciences.

The fixed-point theorem. The fact that every direction is south to a person standing at the North Pole is a defect of the system of latitude and longitude. Because the polar regions have become more important places than they once were, it might be convenient to adopt a coordinate grid on which there would be no such singular point anywhere on Earth. On the other hand, such a grid is impossible. It is also true that at any instant there is always at least one place on the Earth's surface where the wind is not blowing. These two facts, seemingly very different from each other, are both direct consequences of the fixed-point theorem, which states that every homeomorphism of a round spherical surface onto itself either leaves at least one point fixed or sends some point into its diametrically opposite. A three-dimensional ball also has the fixed-point property: If one continuously stirs a pot of glue, no matter how long and thoroughly, and even induces slippage along the sides of the pot, so that each particle is moved about, and then stops, there will always be some particle of the glue that has returned to its starting point.

The Möbius band. A driving belt may wear because of friction over the wheels. If such a belt is given a 180° twist before the ends are sewn together, it may last longer because it wears equally on both sides. In fact, it has only one side and one edge. Such a belt is a model of a Möbius band (see MATHEMATICS AS A CALCULATORY SCIENCE). Cutting a Möbius band down the middle gives it a second edge and returns it to a single two-sided surface (with twists).

Jordan's theorem. A simple closed curve in the plane does not cross itself. (A figure-8 curve is not simple.) Jordan's theorem states, in effect, that every simple closed curve divides the plane into two compartments, one inside the curve and one outside it; and that it is impossible to pass continuously from one to the other without crossing the curve. This seemingly trivial and self-evident state of affairs has many important consequences.

The classical "utility problem" or "cranky neighbour problem" asks whether it is possible for three houses (A, B, and C) each to be connected to three utility plants, 1, 2, and 3, without having any of the lines cross. The negative answer is derived from topological considerations. It must be recognized at the outset that it makes no essential difference how the houses and plants are oriented. The lines from houses A and B to utilities 1 and 2 form a simple closed curve.

If the third house C is now placed inside the curve, it can be satisfactorily connected to 1 and 2; but then the inside will be compartmented, and no matter where 3 is placed, it will be cut off in terms of Jordan's theorem from one of A, B, or C. The same argument holds if C is placed outside.

This method of solution finds serious application in the theory of stamped electrical circuits. The lines of such stamped circuits cannot be permitted to cross. The question of what noncrossing circuits are possible is an extension of the problem of the three utilities.

The role of topology in mathematics. The applications of topology to mathematics itself are much deeper and more far-reaching than the above examples would indicate. Most of those who work in topology are not searching for immediate applications. They study it because of the challenge it offers and because they wish to learn more about the properties of real or abstract spaces. They wish to know whether one set of properties implies another set of properties. They wish to know what is true and what is possible. Topological notions and methods underlie much of modern mathematics, and the topological approach has illuminated and clarified very basic structural concepts in diverse branches of the subject.

In the same way that the Euclidean plane satisfies certain axioms or postulates, it can be shown that certain abstract spaces have definite properties without examining these spaces individually. By approaching topology from this abstract point of view, it is possible to use its methods to study things other than collections of points. Collections of entities that are of concern in analysis or algebra or collections of geometric objects can be treated as spaces and the elements in them as points.

Much use is made of the notion of open sets (subsets of a space that satisfy certain axioms) in studying topological spaces. A point p is said to be a limit point of a set Y in a topological space X, for example, if each open set in X that contains p contains a point of Y other than p. In determining whether or not p is a limit point of Y, it is of no concern whether p belongs to Y (which is stated symbolically as $p \in Y$). In physical terms, this means that p is infinitely close, in a certain sense that can be made precise, to other points of Y. The set of points that are either points or limit points of Y is called the closure of Y and is designated by $\bar{Y}$. A set is called closed if it contains each of its limit points. *The closure of a set*

Examples are useful in topology; they help a mathematician to discover theorems that are likely to be true and aid him in labelling others as false. Giving a counter-example is a convincing way of showing that a "proof" is wrong or that a conjecture is false. Examples of some useful topological spaces are described below, some of them being quite different from those studied in geometry.

Building topological spaces. Certain topological spaces are of historical interest because they have been widely used in the past. Others are studied because they illustrate an interesting property. On many occasions the mathematician "manufactures" a topological space to meet his immediate needs.

A topological space X is built up of a collection of sets $\{U\alpha\}$ called a basis. This collection of sets together with all their possible unions is called the open sets of the topology. In the plane, for example, each open set is the union of interiors of circles. The set of interiors of circles, therefore, is a basis for the plane. The set of interiors of rectangles is another basis. In determining whether a point p is a limit point of a set X, it makes no difference whether each interior of a circle that contains p or each interior of a rectangle that contains p contains a point on X other than p. For the line, one basis is the collection of open intervals. For Euclidean three-dimensional space, one basis is the collection of interiors of balls, and another is the collection of interiors of rectangular solids. If a distance is defined for a topological space, the basis is usually taken as the interiors of balls in which the interior of the ball with centre at p and radius r is the set of all points that have distance from p less than r.

A look at several well-known topological spaces may indicate how topological spaces are constructed and suggest which topological spaces have been considered important. *Well-known topological spaces*

Euclidean n-dimensional space. Points of this space are n-tuples of numbers $(x_1, x_2, \cdots, x_n)$. Basis elements are the interiors of balls in which the distance between $p = (x_1, x_2, \cdots, x_n)$ and $q = (y_1, y_2, \cdots, y_n)$ is the square root of $(y_1 - x_1)^2 + (y_2 - x_2)^2 + \cdots (y_n - x_n)^2$.

Hilbert space. Points of real Hilbert space are sequences of numbers $x_1, x_2, \cdots$ such that the infinite sum Σx_i^2 is finite. Elements of the basis are the interiors of balls in which the distance between $p = (x_1, x_2, \cdots)$ and $q = (y_1, y_2, \cdots)$ is the square root of $\Sigma (y_i - x_i)^2$.

Discrete spaces. For a collection of objects that is to be regarded as a topological space with its elements as points, it is sufficient to describe the subsets of the collection that are to be called open sets. One possibility is to define all subsets as open, even the one-point sets. The resulting topology is called the discrete topology. It is not very useful from the topological point of view because a discrete space has no limit points.

Linear spaces. If the elements of a collection are ordered, which means that for any two elements one precedes the other, this ordering can be used to give the collection a linear topology. Basis elements are of three sorts: the set of points between some two points, the set of points before some point, and the set of points after some point. The line and interval are two conspicuous examples of linear spaces. Another example is given below.

A lexicographically ordered square. If I^2 is a square in the plane with its sides parallel to the axes, then each point p of I^2 may be designated by coordinates (x, y), and it is possible to write $p = (x, y)$. The points of I^2 are so ordered that if $p_1 = (x_1, y_1)$ and $p_2 = (x_2, y_2)$, then p_1 precedes p_2 if either $x_1 < x_2$ or $x_1 = x_2$, and $y_1 < y_2$. In this ordering the lower left-hand corner is the first point and the upper right corner is the last. Such points of I^2 are said to be the points of the lexicographically ordered square because the order is analogous to that found in a dictionary. The topology is linear. While the lexicographical square shares some properties with an interval, it differs in that it contains an uncountable collection of disjoint open sets.

Function spaces. If A and B are topological spaces, a function f that maps A into B, which is stated symbolically as $f:A \to B$, is a rule that assigns an element of B to each element of A. The point b of B associated with the point a of A is designated by $f(a)$; b is called the image of a. If $\{f_\alpha\}$ is a collection of such functions, it is sometimes convenient to regard this collection as a topological space the points of which are the functions. A collection of subsets of the collection must be selected to serve as open sets. There are many ways of doing this; the description of two of them follows.

Topologies for function space
In the first topology given for $\{f_\alpha\}$, the open sets are made to be large by restricting the basis elements with respect to only a finite number of points of A. A basis element is determined by a particular function belonging to the space—that is, an $f\alpha_0 \in \{f_\alpha\}$—a finite number of points $a_1, a_2, \cdots, a_n$ of A; and a finite collection of open sets $U_1, U_2, \cdots, U_n$ in B, such that $f\alpha_0(a_i) \in U_i$ for $i = 1, 2, \cdots, n$. The basis element determined by $f\alpha_0$, these a_i's and these U_i's, is the set of all f's in $\{f_\alpha\}$ such that $f(a_i) \in U_i = 1, 2, \cdots, n$. Other basis elements are determined by other elements of $\{f_\alpha\}$, other finite subsets of A, and other finite collections of open sets in B.

In the second topology given for $\{f_\alpha\}$ it is supposed that B is the interval $[0, 1]$ of the real line $\Re^1$. The distance between each pair of elements f_β, f_γ of $\{f_\alpha\}$ is defined to be the least upper bound of $|f_\beta(x) - f_\gamma(x)|$, x varying over A. Basis elements are open balls.

Something can be learned from the fact that different topologies can be chosen for $\{f_\alpha\}$. A topology can be chosen to suit certain needs, and the choice of topology is usually made with a definite object in mind. In dealing with differentiable functions, for example, it may be advantageous to define distance so that for two functions to be close, their derivatives must also be close.

For the function spaces just described, no use was made of the topology of A; it might just as well have been discrete. The function spaces are related to Cartesian-product spaces, which are covered below.

Cartesian-product spaces. Starting with a pair of topological spaces X_1, X_2, the Cartesian product of X_1 and X_2 (written $X_1 \times X_2$) may be constructed as follows: The points of $X_1 \times X_2$ are ordered pairs (a, b) in which $a \in X_1$ and $b \in X_2$. Basis elements of $X_1 \times X_2$ are sets of the form $U_1 \times U_2$ in which U_1 is a basis element of X_1; U_2 is a basis element of X_2; and $U_1 \times U_2$ denotes the set of all points (x_1, x_2) of $X_1 \times X_2$ in which $x_1 \in U_1$, $x_2 \in U_2$. In a certain sense, the plane $\Re^2$ is the Cartesian product of two lines. Also $\Re^{m+n}$ is the Cartesian product of $\Re^m$ and $\Re^n$.

Cartesian products of topological spaces
Instead of the Cartesian product of just two spaces, the Cartesian product of a collection $\{X_\alpha\}$ of topological spaces can be studied. In this case a point in the Cartesian-product space is a collection $\{p_\alpha\}$ such that $p_\alpha \in X_\alpha$. The collections $\{p_\alpha\}$ and $\{X_\alpha\}$ have like subscripts. To get a basis element, a collection $\{U_\alpha\}$ is considered in which U_α is an open set in X_α and all but a finite number of the U_α's are the whole of the corresponding X_α. The basis element corresponding to U_α is the set of all points $\{q_\alpha\}$ of the Cartesian-product space such that $q_\alpha \in U_\alpha$.

Topological spaces. The collection of open sets of a topological space is axiomatically required to have the following properties:

1. Each point in the space is an element of (belongs to) some open set.
2. The union of any collection of open sets is an open set.
3. If two open sets share a common point, their intersection is open.

It may be shown that $\Re^n$, Hilbert space, discrete spaces, linear spaces, function spaces, and Cartesian-product spaces are all topological spaces. The basis elements were chosen to make this true. Had they been indiscriminately chosen, a topological space might not have resulted. The line would not be a topological space, for example, if its basis elements were defined as closed intervals. The third requirement would not be satisfied.

An unusual topology of the line. The points of an unusual topology called "E^1-bad" are the points of a horizontal line. Basis elements are half-open intervals open on the right—that is, sets of the form $[p, q)$ in which p, q are points of the horizontal line with p to the left of q, and $[p, q)$ is the set consisting of p and all points strictly between p and q. While the space E^1-bad has the same points as a line, its topology is different. It does not have the linear topology. No point of E^1-bad is a limit point of the set of points to the left of it. It will be shown below that E^1-bad differs from $\Re^1$ in other respects.

Topological properties. Although in what follows mention is made of such topological properties as connectedness, separability, being homeomorphic with another space, regularity, normality, and compactness, these are only a sampling of many such topological properties, many others of which can be found in textbooks on topology. Homeomorphisms preserve all topological properties, but it may be shown that mappings preserve some of them; for example, connectedness, separability, and compactness.

Mappings. Suppose A, B are topological spaces and $f:A \to B$ is a function that maps A into B. If $p \in A$, f is continuous at p if for each open set U in B containing $f(p)$ there is an open set V in A containing p such that f sends each point of V into U. This property of f is expressed imprecisely by saying that points close to p are sent close to $f(p)$. The function f is continuous if it is continuous at each point of A. Continuous functions are called mappings. Topologists are concerned with what properties are preserved by mappings. They are interested in whether or not mappings can be extended. They classify certain mappings as being differentiable, piecewise linear, or homeomorphic.

Homeomorphisms. Two topological spaces are called topologically equivalent, or homeomorphic, if there is a one-to-one correspondence between them that is continuous both ways. The vertical projection shown in Figure 1 sets up such a one-to-one correspondence between the straight interval X and the curved interval Y. If A and B

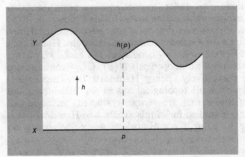

Figure 1: Vertical projection showing a one-to-one correspondence between the straight interval X and the curved interval Y (see text).

512 Topology, General

Topological equivalence

are topologically equivalent, there is a function $h: A \to B$ such that h is continuous, h is onto (each point of B is the image of a point of A), h is one to one, and the inverse function, h^{-1}, is continuous. Thus h is called a homeomorphism.

Topological properties are properties such that if one topological space has the property and a second space is topologically equivalent to the first, then the second has the property also. Properties having to do with size or straightness are not topological properties. Various topological properties will be examined in what follows.

Suppose Y is a point set in a topological space X. Regard Y as a subspace of X the open sets of which are the intersection of Y with open sets in X. The set Y has a topological property if it has the property when regarded as a subspace. A function on Y is called continuous if it is continuous when Y is regarded as a subspace.

Connectedness. A topological space X is connected if each map of it into the two-point space $\{0, 1\}$ takes all of X into one of 0 or 1. This is a complicated positive way of saying what is usually stated in a simple negative way. A space is connected if it is not the sum of two (non-null) sets neither of which contains either a point or a limit point of the other. Intuitively, this means that the space is all in one piece. It may be shown that $\Re^n$, Hilbert space, and the lexicographically ordered square are connected but that E^1-bad is not.

The Suslin problem. It is important to know what set of properties characterizes a line. It is known that a line is a connected linear space with no first or last point. The lexicographically ordered square with its end points removed, however, also has these properties.

Separability

A topological space is called separable if it contains a countable set of points such that each open set in the space contains some point of the countable set. It is possible to prove that any separable, connected linear space with no first or last point is topologically equivalent to a line. The Suslin problem asks whether the conditions of separability can be replaced by the condition that the space does not contain an uncountable collection of disjoint open sets. It has been shown that within the framework of the ordinary axioms of set theory, a proof cannot be constructed to show that this replacement is possible. This limitation results partially because these axioms permit the assumption that a set does not exist unless an algorithm is available for describing it and permits the labelling of some subsets of a countable model as uncountable merely because the function is missing from the model being used to match the set one to one with the integers.

Spaces like Hilbert space. Is Hilbert space homeomorphic with $\Re^1 \times \Re^1 \times \cdots$, the Cartesian product of countably many real lines? This question has been of interest, but the answer was hard to obtain. If there were a homeomorphism, it would not be direct by associating the point $(a_1, a_2, \cdots)$ in $\Re^1 \times \Re^1 \times \cdots$ with the point $(a_1, a_2, \cdots)$ in Hilbert space. The point all coordinates of which are 1 lies in $\Re^1 \times \Re^1 \times \cdots$ but not in Hilbert space. The set of points with precisely one coordinate 1 and all others 0 has a limit point in $\Re^1 \times \Re^1 \times \cdots$ but no limit point in Hilbert space. It was shown in 1966 by the U.S. mathematician R.D. Anderson, however, that, contrary to earlier claims, there is indeed a homeomorphism between Hilbert space and $\Re^1 \times \Re^1 \times \cdots$. Investigations are under way to determine what other spaces are homeomorphic with Hilbert space.

Hausdorff spaces. A topological space is called Hausdorff (after the German mathematician Felix Hausdorff) if it satisfies the following condition: For each two points, p, q there are disjoint open sets $U(p)$, $U(q)$ containing p and q, respectively. Being Hausdorff is a topological property. Not all topological spaces are Hausdorff, but most of those that are seriously studied, including all those mentioned so far in this article, are Hausdorff. It is possible to build a non-Hausdorff space by adding an ideal point to an interval as follows.

A non-Hausdorff interval with two right ends. Let pq be a closed interval with the ordinary linear topology. Basis elements are either open intervals or half-open in-

tervals that contain either p or q. An interval is constructed with two right ends by adding another right end q' to pq. A point of this enlarged space is either q' or a point of pq. A basis element is either a basis element of the original interval pq or the union of the one-point set $\{q'\}$ and an open interval of pq with q as an end. The enlarged space is not Hausdorff because there are no disjoint open sets containing q, q'.

Other separation properties. The Hausdorff property is one of the separation properties. Two sets A, B can be separated if these two sets lie in disjoint open sets. A space is Hausdorff, therefore, if each two points can be separated. A space is regular if each point can be separated from a closed set not containing it. A space is normal if each pair of disjoint closed sets can be separated.

Sometimes a topological space has to be constructed that has one topological property but not another. To build a space that is Hausdorff but not regular, the topology of a line can be changed. Rather than using ordinary open intervals as the basis elements, they can be the set of points consisting of the centre and irrational points of open intervals. While no basis element then has more than one rational point, any closed set containing it has many rational points.

The plane is normal: If A, B are disjoint closed sets, the set of points closer to A than to B is an open set (as is the set of points closer to B than to A). The upper half-plane space described below, however, is regular but not normal.

The upper half-plane space. The points of this space are the points of the plane on or above the x-axis. The basis elements are of two sorts: the interiors of circles above the x-axis, and the union of interiors of circles tangent to the x-axis from above together with the point of tangency (see Figure 2). Physically this space may be regarded as points of an upward flow in which the rate of flow is one unit per second at the x-axis and less above. If p is a point and $r > 0$, the open set generated by p and r

Figure 2: *Two sorts of basis elements for the upper plane space.*
(A) The interiors of circles tangent to the x-axis from above the point of tangency and (B) the interiors of circles above the x-axis (see text).

can be regarded as the set of points to which a person could swim from p in less time than from r if he swims at the rate of one unit per second. The current would prevent him from swimming between any two points of the x-axis. No basis element contains two points of the x-axis in the upper half-plane space.

To see that the upper half-plane space is not normal, one could assign coordinates to the x-axis and let A be the set of points with rational coordinates and B the set of those with irrational coordinates. A rather involved argument shows that it is impossible to separate A from B.

Cartesian products of normal spaces. It can be seen that the Cartesian product of regular spaces is regular. Until the 1970s, one of the unsolved questions in topology asked whether the Cartesian product of a normal space and a straight-line interval is normal. In 1970 the mathematician Mary Ellen Rudin of the United States constructed an example (using box products) of a normal Hausdorff space whose Cartesian product with an interval is not normal.

The first axiom of countability. This axiom is modelled after the fact that if p is any point in the plane and U is an open set containing p, then there is an integer n such that the open ball with centre at p and radius $1/n$ lies in U. A topological space X satisfies the first axiom of countability provided the following condition holds: For each point p in X there is a sequence of open sets $U_1, U_2, \cdots$ each containing p, such that if U is any open

Non-Hausdorff spaces

A space regarded as points of a flow

set whatsoever containing p, then there is an integer n such that U_n is contained in U, symbolically, $U_n \subset U$. Each of $\mathfrak{R}^n$, Hilbert space, discrete spaces, the lexicographically ordered square, E^1-bad, and the upper half-plane space satisfy the axiom. Some Cartesian-product spaces do not satisfy the axiom at any point whatsoever. To get another Hausdorff space not satisfying this first axiom of countability the topology of the line $\mathfrak{R}^1$ can be changed as follows. The basis elements are defined to be of two sorts: any one point set other than the origin, or the complement of a finite set of points. Then the first axiom of countability is not satisfied at the origin.

The second axiom of countability. A topological space satisfies the second axiom of countability if it has a countable basis. The plane has a countable basis (interiors of circles with radii and centres represented by rational numbers). Neither the lexicographically ordered square, E^1-bad, nor the upper half-plane space does. One very useful theorem in topology is that any space that is regular and that satisfies the second axiom of countability is normal.

Compactness. A topological space is called compact in the limit-point sense (called countably compact by some or merely compact by others) if each infinite set of points has a limit point.

A collection $\{U_\alpha\}$ of open sets is called a covering of a topological space X if each point of X lies in some U_α. A space is called compact in the covering sense (sometimes called bicompact or even merely compact) if each open covering contains a finite number of elements that cover. It may be shown that any space that is compact in the covering sense is compact in the limit-point sense; but the converse is not necessarily true. For a space to be compact in the covering sense, it is necessary and sufficient that each infinite subset Y have a limit point p such that for each open set U containing p, $U \cap Y$ has as many points as Y. For some important spaces (such as metrizable spaces; see below *Moore spaces*), the two kinds of compactness are equivalent so that there is no confusion in omitting qualifications.

There are examples of two topological spaces such that each is compact in the limit-point sense but their Cartesian product is not. (These spaces could not satisfy the first axiom of countability.) The Tikhonov theorem, however, states that if $\{X_\alpha\}$ is any collection (perhaps even an uncountable collection) of topological spaces, the Cartesian product of the X_α's is compact in the covering sense if and only if each X_α is.

Cardinality of compact spaces. The Tikhonov theorem shows that the number of points in a compact topological space can be arbitrarily large. If one forms spaces by taking big Cartesian products, however, the first axiom of countability is not satisfied. Until the late 1960s, one of the unsolved questions in topology asked how many points there could be in a first-axiom topological space that was compact in the covering sense. In 1969 the Russian mathematician A.V. Arkhangelsky showed that no such space could have more points than there are real numbers.

Some kinds of spaces have been more widely studied than others. Metrizable spaces, decomposition spaces, Moore spaces, and uniform spaces, all to be covered below, are Hausdorff spaces with a particularly rich history.

Metrizable spaces. A topological space X is metrizable if one can assign a suitable distance $D(x, y)$ to each pair of its points x, y. This distance function is required to satisfy the following properties:

1. $D(x, y) \geq 0$, the equality holding if and only if $x = y$;
2. $D(x, y) = D(y, x)$ (symmetry condition);
3. $D(x, y) + D(y, z) \geq D(x, z)$ (triangle condition); and
4. D preserves the topology of X.

The fourth condition means that the open balls under the distance function form a basis for X.

One of the standard theorems in topology states: A necessary and sufficient condition that a separable, regular Hausdorff space be metrizable is that it have a countable basis. This theorem permits the supposition that any

Marginal note (left): First and second axioms of countability

Marginal note (left): The Tikhonov theorem

regular Hausdorff space satisfying the second axiom of countability is metrizable and shows, for example, that certain decomposition spaces are metrizable (even though it would be hard to assign them a metric) and that all theorems that hold in metrizable spaces are true in these spaces.

Not all metrizable spaces are separable. In the late 1940s, working independently in the Soviet Union, Japan, and the United States, three topologists—Y.M. Smirnov, J. Nagata, and R.H. Bing, respectively—came up with closely related sets of necessary and sufficient conditions that a Hausdorff space be metrizable. This work was probably triggered by that of another topologist, A.H. Stone, working in England.

A topological space to which a distance function has already been assigned is called a metric space. Two spaces may be topologically equivalent even though they have been assigned quite different metrics. (The whole plane and the interior of a circle in the plane are examples of topologically equivalent spaces the ordinary metrics of which are quite different.) Any metric, however, is a handy tool to use in studying a space (though some may be better than others), so that it is of interest to determine which topological spaces are metrizable.

Decomposition spaces. Suppose a topological space X is decomposed into a disjoint collection G of closed sets, each compact in the limit-point sense such that if $g \in G$, and U is an open set in X containing g, then there is an open set U' in U containing g such that U' is the union of elements of G. Such a decomposition is called an upper semi-continuous decomposition. Breaking a square into vertical intervals gives an example of such a decomposition. One can build a topological space by regarding the elements of G as points and choosing certain subcollections of G as open sets. The usual selection defines a set of (generalized) points to be open in the decomposition space if and only if the union of the closed sets identified with these points is open in X. In the case of the decomposition of the square mentioned above, the decomposition space would be homeomorphic to an interval. In general, if X is regular, the decomposition space is regular, and if X satisfies the second axiom of countability, then the decomposition space does also. Hence it can be assigned a metric even though this metric might not be readily determined.

The study of collections of closed sets as points of a decomposition space is yet another illustration of how topology can be used to study collections other than ordinary point sets.

One of the interesting properties of decomposition space is that if an upper semi-continuous decomposition of the plane is such that the elements of the decomposition are connected and do not separate the plane, then the decomposition space is topologically equivalent to the plane. Efforts to extend this result to higher dimensions have resulted in some interesting research and some unsolved problems.

Moore spaces. Robert Lee Moore introduced a kind of space that has been widely studied. Moore spaces are more restrictive than first-axiom regular Hausdorff spaces and more general than metrizable spaces. They share many of the properties of metrizable spaces, and many theorems that hold in metrizable spaces can be shown to hold in Moore spaces.

If X is a topological space, $x \in X$, and G is an open covering of X, Star (x, G) denotes the union of the elements of G containing x. A Moore space may be defined as a regular Hausdorff space X with a sequence of open coverings, G_1, G_2, $\cdots$ such that if $p \in X$ and U is an open set containing p, then there is an integer n (a function of p and U) such that Star $(p, G_n) \subset U$. It may be noted that a metric space is a Moore space because G_i can be taken to be the set of open sets with diameters less than $1/i$. The upper half-plane space, however, is a Moore space, but it is not normal and hence not metrizable.

For many years topologists tried to decide whether all normal Moore spaces are necessarily metrizable. It is now known that some of the same considerations that

Marginal note (right): Conditions that a Hausdorff space be metrizable

Marginal note (right): Collections other than point sets

prevent one from obtaining an affirmative answer to the Suslin problem by using the ordinary axioms of set theory make it impossible to show by using these axioms that even all separable normal Moore spaces are metrizable.

Uniform spaces. With each covering of a space X there may be associated a subset U of $X \times X$, in which U is the set of all points $(x, y) \in X \times X$, such that x and y lie in the same element of G. The set U is called a neighbourhood of the diagonal because it contains all points of $X \times X$ the two coordinates of which are equal. A collection of neighbourhoods of the diagonal is called a uniformity if it satisfies a certain set of requirements. These requirements, not listed here, were fashioned so as to be useful in studying functions defined on X. Any space for which a uniformity has been selected is called a uniform space.

Some mathematicians are more interested in studying the continuous functions that can be defined on a space than they are in studying the space itself. Uniform spaces are particularly interesting to them because by using the uniformity they can consider functions on the uniform spaces that share many of the properties of uniformly continuous functions on metric spaces.

Problems of current interest. Many of the problems of research interest in topology are concerned with manifolds and involve an interplay between the methods of general topology and those of algebraic topology (see TOPOLOGY, ALGEBRAIC). An n-manifold $\mathfrak{M}^n$ is a separable metric space such that each point of $\mathfrak{M}^n$ lies in an open set homeomorphic with $\mathfrak{R}^n$. Some interesting results obtained after 1950 and some open questions are given below without defining all terms.

Planar fixed-point problem. The following has been called the most interesting unsolved problem in plane topology: Does each compact continuum that is the intersection of a decreasing sequence of disks have the fixed-point property?

Polyhedral Schoenflies problem. It was shown in 1960 by Morton Brown of the United States that an $(n-1)$-sphere in $\mathfrak{R}^n$ is tame under certain conditions. A set in $\mathfrak{R}^n$ is tame if there is a homeomorphism of $\mathfrak{R}^n$ onto itself that takes the set onto a polyhedron. The polyhedral Schoenflies question asks whether each polyhedral $(n-1)$-sphere in $\mathfrak{R}^n$ bounds a piecewise linear n-ball. The answer is known to be affirmative if $n = 1, 2, 3$, but the problem is unsolved in higher dimensions.

Triangulation problem. It was shown in 1952 by E.E. Moise of the United States that all three-dimensional manifolds can be triangulated, or divided into dimensional triangles (or tetrahedra). It was announced in 1969, however, that not all n-manifolds ($n \geq 6$) have a combinatorial triangulation. Which (if any) higher dimensional manifolds can be triangulated?

Free-surface problem. Is a two-dimensional sphere S^2 in $\mathfrak{R}^3$ tame if for each $\varepsilon > 0$, there are ε-maps f_1, f_2 of S^2 into opposite components of $\mathfrak{R}^3 - S^2$? It was shown in 1961 by the U.S. mathematician R.H. Bing that the answer is in the affirmative if f_1 and f_2 are homeomorphisms. It was shown that S^2 is tame if each component of $\mathfrak{R}^3 - S^2$ is locally 1-connected.

Approximating surfaces. It was shown in 1959 by R.H. Bing that if $\mathbb{C}^2$ is a two-dimensional complex and h is a homeomorphism of $\mathbb{C}^2$ into a combinatorial three-dimensional manifold $\mathfrak{M}^3$, then for each $\varepsilon > 0$ there is a piecewise linear homeomorphism h' of $\mathbb{C}^2$ into $\mathfrak{M}^3$ such that h' is within ε of h. If $\mathbb{C}^2$ is a connected two-dimensional manifold and $\mathfrak{M}^3$ is connected, it was shown that h' can be a side approximation in that if $h(\mathbb{C}^2)$ separates $\mathfrak{M}^3$, and U is a component of $\mathfrak{M}^3 - h(\mathbb{C}^2)$, h' could be selected so that each component of $h'(\mathbb{C}^2) - U$ is of diameter less than ε. To what extent do these results extend to higher dimensions?

Poincaré conjecture. The axioms of plane geometry give a geometric characterization of the plane. It is known that a connected compact two-dimensional manifold is topologically a two-dimensional sphere if each topological circle in it separates it. It is natural to seek a nice characterization of a three-dimensional sphere. A con-

jecture rich in history is that a compact connected three-dimensional manifold $\mathfrak{M}^3$ is topologically a three-dimensional sphere if each map of the boundary of a disk into $\mathfrak{M}^3$ can be extended to send the whole disk into $\mathfrak{M}^3$. A variation of this conjecture that turned out to be false was proposed by the French mathematician Henri Poincaré in 1900. Numerous unsuccessful attempts have been made to answer the question. It is known that $\mathfrak{M}^3$ is a three-dimensional sphere if each simple closed curve in $\mathfrak{M}^3$ lies in a topological three-dimensional ball in $\mathfrak{M}^3$. Solutions by C.D. Papakyriakopoulos of the United States to Dehn's lemma and the loop theorem have facilitated the study of three-dimensional manifolds. Although the Poincaré problem still remains unsolved, it is of interest that in 1960 two U.S. mathematicians Stephen Smale and John Stallings gave independent solutions of a higher dimensional version of the Poincaré conjecture in $\mathfrak{M}^n$, $n \geq 5$.

BIBLIOGRAPHY. Among elementary treatments of topology with material understandable to those at the advanced high-school level are: B.H. ARNOLD, *Intuitive Concepts in Elementary Topology* (1962); R.H. BING, *Elementary Point Set Topology* (1960); RICHARD COURANT and HERBERT ROBBINS, *What Is Mathematics?* (1941); and L.A. STEEN and J.A. SEEBACH, JR., *Counterexamples in Topology* (1970). Although Arnold's approach is intuitive, some theorems are proved. Bing gives some topological examples and discusses the axiomatic approach to topology. Courant and Robbins' book discusses aspects of several branches of mathematics, and chapter 5 is devoted to interesting theorems and problems in topology. The book of Steen and Seebach contains examples prepared by teams of students working under the authors' direction. Intermediate-level books suitable for those with the background of a course in calculus include: J.D. BAUM, *Elements of Point Set Topology* (1964); M.C. GEMIGNANI, *Elementary Topology* (1967); ROBERT H. KASRIEL, *Undergraduate Topology* (1971); KAZIMIERZ KURATOWSKI, *Wstęp do teorii mnogści i topologii* (Eng. trans., *Introduction to Set Theory and Topology*, 1962); and M.H. NEWMAN, *Elements of the Topology of Plane Sets of Points*, 2nd ed. (1951). The first three of these are especially suitable as texts for an undergraduate course in topology. Newman's book gives an elementary treatment of many of the topological properties of the Euclidean plane. WACLAW SIERPINSKI, *Topologia ogólna* (1928; Eng. trans., *General Topology*, 2nd ed., 1956), was the text that introduced many graduate students to the study of topology. JOHN L. KELLEY, *General Topology* (1955), followed as a widely used graduate text. It treated general topology in a way particularly useful to those working in analysis. Although DICK WICK HALL and GUILFORD L. SPENCER, *Elementary Topology* (1955), is labelled elementary, it has a careful treatment of some of the difficult properties of the plane not easy to understand. J.G. HOCKING and G.S.YOUNG, *Topology* (1961), has been widely used as a graduate text and not only treats general topology but also introduces many geometric ideas useful in the study of manifolds. More recent texts include JAMES DUGUNDJI, *Topology* (1965); RYSZARD ENGELKING, *Zarys topologii ogólnej* (1965; Eng. trans., *Outline of General Topology*, 1966); S.T. HU, *Introduction to General Topology* (1966); KAZIMIERZ KURATOWSKI, *Topologie*, 4th ed., vol. 1 (1958; Eng. trans., *Topology*, new ed., vol. 1, 1966); and STEPHEN WILLARD, *General Topology* (1970).

(R.H.Bi.)

Tornadoes, Whirlwinds, and Waterspouts

Tornadoes, whirlwinds, and waterspouts are atmospheric vortices, or rotating funnel-cloud air masses of small diameter. They are differentiated from each other by the intensity of their rotation and by the surfaces that they traverse. Though tornadoes and whirlwinds both travel over landmasses, whirlwinds are atmospheric systems smaller than tornadoes. Waterspouts are tornadoes that form or pass over a water surface.

Tornadoes. The name tornado comes from the Spanish *tronada* ("thunderstorm"), which supposedly was derived from the Latin *tornare* ("to make round by turning"). The most violent of atmospheric storms, a tornado is a powerful vortex or "twister" whose rotational speeds are estimated to be near 300 miles (480 kilometres) per hour but may occasionally exceed 500 miles (800 kilometres) per hour. The direction of rotation in the North-

Figure 1: *Tornadoes of the midwestern United States.*
(Left) A typical killer tornado photographed in Tracy, Minnesota, on June 13, 1968; it travelled
13 miles along the ground. (Right) Twin funnels, in one of the worst recorded tornado
outbreaks, crossing a highway south of Elkhart, northern Indiana, on April 11, 1965; debris can
be seen falling out of the left funnel.
(Left) Eric Lantz, (right) Paul Huffman

ern Hemisphere is usually, though not exclusively, counterclockwise.

The first visible indication of tornado development is usually a funnel cloud (Figure 1) or "tuba," which extends downward from the cumulonimbus cloud of a severe thunderstorm. As this funnel dips earthward, it becomes darker because of the debris that is forced into its intensifying vortex. Some tornadoes give no visible warning until their destruction strikes the unsuspecting victims.

Tornadoes often occur in groups or series, and several twisters sometimes descend from the same cloud base (Figure 1). An outbreak in the United States in the late afternoon and evening of April 11, 1965, is an example of such a series. This outbreak was the most destructive tornado disaster in the United States in 40 years. A system of at least 37 deadly whirls caused destruction in the states of Iowa, Wisconsin, Illinois, Indiana, Michigan, and Ohio; 271 persons were killed, and more than 3,000 were injured. Property damage was estimated at $300,-000,000. The death total was surpassed only by that of a tornado on March 18, 1925, which killed 689 persons in Missouri, Illinois, and Indiana.

The forward speed of an individual tornado is normally 30 to 40 miles (48 to 64 kilometres) per hour but may range from nearly zero to 70 miles (zero to 112 kilometres) per hour. The direction of motion is usually from the southwest to the northeast, although tornadoes associated with hurricanes may move from the east. The paths of twisters average only several hundred yards in width and 16 miles (26 kilometres) in length, but large deviations from these averages may be expected; *e.g.*, the disastrous 1925 tornado was at times 1 mile (1.6 kilometres) wide, and its path length was 219 miles (352 kilometres).

In the short time that it takes to pass, a tornado causes fantastic destruction. There have been cases reported in which blades of straw were embedded in fence posts; a schoolhouse with 85 pupils inside was demolished and the pupils carried 150 yards (137 metres) with none killed; and five railway coaches, each weighing 70 tons, were lifted from their track and one coach was moved 80 feet (24 metres).

Although much remains to be learned about tornado formation and movement, remarkable advances have been made in the effectiveness of tornado detection and warning systems. These systems involve analyses of surface and upper-air weather, detection and tracking of atmosphere changes by radar, and spotting severe local storms.

Waterspouts. When a tornado forms or passes over a water surface it is called a waterspout. Like tornadoes, waterspouts may assume a variety of shapes and often occur in series or families. Measurements of their forward speeds are scarce, but estimates vary from a few

miles an hour to speeds as high as 40 to 50 miles per hour. Contrary to popular opinion, a waterspout does not "suck up" water to great heights, though it may lift the water level a few feet. The main visible cloud consists mostly of freshwater clouds produced by condensation of water vapour; however, a sheath of spray often rotates around the lower portion of the vortex tube (Figure 2).

B.J. Oram

Figure 2: Waterspout in Tampa Bay, Florida, showing cloud and disturbed water surface. It was one of a series of spouts that occurred on June 25, 1964.

One of the largest and most famous waterspouts, observed near Massachusetts on August 19, 1896, was witnessed by thousands of vacationers and several scientists. Its height was estimated to be 3,600 feet (1,095 metres) and its width 840 feet (256 metres) at the crest, 140 feet (43 metres) at centre, and 240 feet (73 metres) at the base. The spray surrounding the vortex tube near the water surface was about 700 feet (200 metres) wide and 400 feet (120 metres) high. The spout lasted 35 minutes, disappearing and reappearing three times. Most waterspouts are smaller, with much shorter lives. This outstanding spout is an example of one that apparently was spawned by thunderstorm-squall conditions, similar to those that produce tornadoes over land.

There are few authentic cases of large ships ever being destroyed by a spout, although spouts are a dangerous hazard to small vessels; and a few intense waterspouts have caused deaths when they moved inland over populated areas. The belief that firing a cannonball or other projectile into a spout can "break it up" has no scientific foundation.

Whirlwinds. A whirlwind, in the general sense, is any rotating mass of air or atmospheric vortex. The term is, however, commonly restricted to atmospheric systems smaller than a tornado but larger than the eddies of microscale turbulence. The whirlwind is usually named after the visible phenomenon associated with it; thus there are dust whirls, or dust devils; sand whirls, or sand pillars; and fire, smoke, and even snow whirls, or spouts.

In contrast to the pendant form of the tornado funnel, a dust or sand devil develops from the ground upward, usually under hot, clear-sky conditions. The whirl shape is normally that of a cylindrical column or an inverted cone. The axis of rotation is usually vertical, but it may be inclined. The direction of rotation may be either clockwise or counterclockwise. Vortices with a horizontal axis of rotation are sometimes called rolls or rotors. Dust and sand whirls are not nearly as violent as tornadoes, although jackrabbits have been lifted by the more intense vortices. The whirls measure in diameter from a few inches to several hundred feet, and visible heights from a few feet to at least 5,000 feet (1,500 metres). This is probably not the upper limit, for sailplane pilots have used their spirally ascending currents to soar to above 15,000 feet. Like tornadoes and waterspouts, dust and sand devils often appear in groups or series. Eleven of them were simultaneously sighted in Ethiopia; and in the Mojave Desert a series of smaller whirls followed in the wake of a larger primary vortex. Such secondaries are sometimes referred to in India as "dancing devils."

Fire whirlwinds are a problem to the forest rangers who must cope with them. A historical example of a great fire vortex, produced by war, is that which formed over Hamburg, Germany, following a massive aerial bombing during the night of July 27–28, 1943. The fire fueled a counterclockwise rotation storm one to two miles in diameter and three miles high, with winds estimated to be more than 100 miles per hour in some sections.

Treated in this article are the occurrence, physical characteristics, and theories of formation of tornadoes and allied phenomena. For further information on atmospheric motions associated with severe storms, see WINDS AND STORMS; and CYCLONES AND ANTICYCLONES. See also, THUNDERSTORMS; and HURRICANES AND TYPHOONS.

OCCURRENCE AND DISTRIBUTION

Tornadoes. Tornadoes strike in many areas of the world, but nowhere are they as frequent or as fierce as in the U.S., where an average of 628 per year was reported during the period 1953–65. Direct comparisons of relative tornado frequencies in various countries are biased, because observational data are often lacking in sparsely settled regions. It appears, however, that Australia, where several hundred per year have been reported, has the dubious honour of second place. Other countries reporting tornadoes include, but are not limited to, Great Britain, Canada, China, France, Germany, The Netherlands, Hungary, India, Italy, Japan, the Soviet Union, and even Bermuda and the Fiji Islands.

Distribution and frequency of U.S. tornadoes A total of 898 tornadoes were counted in the United States during the year 1965 alone. This peak may not be the all-time high, because in earlier years when the population density was less, the observational network was more crude. For the same period, 1953–65, the annual average number of days on which one or more tornadoes occurred (tornado days) was 158. A vast "tornado belt" embracing the Great Plains and the southeastern portion of the country is threatened by tornadoes every year (Figure 3). Every state in the nation, including Alaska and Hawaii, has experienced twisters. The average frequency varies from 109 in Texas to less than three in the far western and most of the northeastern states.

A more important criterion for gauging tornado severity is the average number of tornadoes in a unit area, such as a square mile or a two-degree square on a map. Computations of this tornado density for a 45-year period show that the greatest concentration of tornadoes per unit

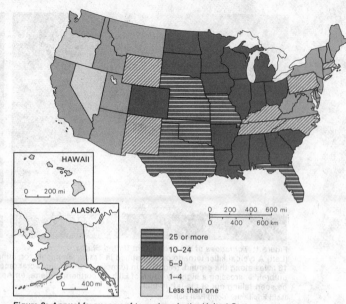

Figure 3: Annual frequency of tornadoes in the United States. (Based on 1953–65 data.)

area is found in the states of Oklahoma and Kansas. The area with the greatest potential for casualties is that which combines a high tornado incidence rate with a thick population concentration. Southwestern Oklahoma, for example, has the highest tornado incidence per unit area but because it is thinly populated, compared with the Chicago area, which has less than one-half its tornado incidence, casualty potential for Chicago is much greater. Over a 45-year period the potential casualties for Chicago are nine people per square mile, compared with one person per square mile in southwestern Oklahoma. Although the probability that a specific locality will be struck by a tornado in any one year is very small, this low probability does not mean that such an event will not happen. An extreme example of an apparent defiance of probability statistics took place in Codell, western Kansas, a small town hit by tornadoes on the same date, May 20, in three successive years, 1916, 1917, and 1918.

Seasonal and diurnal variation Tornadoes may occur during any month of the year. Normally, for the United States as a whole, the month with the most tornadoes is May; and more than half the year's total occurs during the three months of April, May, and June (Figure 4). The lowest frequency is in December and January. No season of the year is free from tornadoes, but in spring and summer they are five times as numerous as in winter and fall.

Tornadoes are generated from severe thunderstorms,

By courtesy of U.S. Department of Commerce

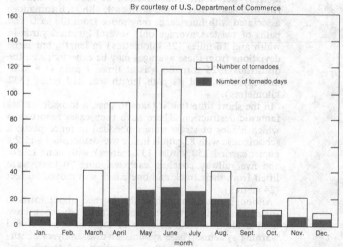

Figure 4: Frequency chart showing the number of tornadoes and the number of tornado days per month for the United States. (Based on 1953–65 figures.)

which form readily between warm, moist air from the south or southwest and contrasting cool, dry air from the west or northwest. A squall line of severe local storms often develops along this boundary, and sometimes a family of tornadoes is spawned. In February, warm, moist air from the Gulf of Mexico begins to penetrate the Gulf states. As it continues its northern and eastern penetration, tornado frequencies reach their peaks during April over the southern Atlantic states, during May over the southern Plains states, and during June over the area extending from the northern plains to western New York state. In the summer and fall the decreasing contrast between the air masses results in a reduction of tornado incidence in most sections, although they may develop from the severe thunderstorms associated with unstable air masses, especially in Florida, where tornadoes are often associated with hurricanes. During December and January, cold air dominates the country, and the moisture–temperature relationships required for tornado genesis are not usually present.

Although tornadoes may strike at any hour of the day or night, they generally form during the middle or late afternoon, between 3 to 7 PM, the period most favourable for the development of severe thunderstorms (q.v.), from which they are bred.

Waterspouts. The worldwide distribution of waterspouts is difficult to determine because ·most of them occur over oceans and their detection depends upon observations from coasts or from ships or airplanes. They are most frequent over tropical and subtropical waters; many of them have been observed over the Gulf of Mexico, off the coast of Florida and the Bahamas, and over the Gulf Stream. The spouts are common off the west coast of Africa near the Equator and off the coasts of China and Japan; but they may appear in unexpected places, such as the Grand Banks of Newfoundland and even near Seattle, Washington. As mentioned earlier, one of the largest observed waterspouts occurred off the coast of Massachusetts. A broad spout estimated to be 100 feet high and 700 feet thick appeared off the California coast in 1914, and one offshore from New South Wales, Australia, had a measured height of over 5,000 feet.

The most common season for waterspouts in the Northern Hemisphere is between May and October, but they may appear at any time of the year or of the day or night.

Whirlwinds. Every summer hundreds of thousands of dust and sand devils travel across the arid and semi-arid regions of the world. Only an extremely small fraction of such whirls are observed by man, however, because desert areas are sparsely settled. Observers report that whirlwinds are sighted almost daily during the hot season over the Sahara and the arid regions of Australia and southwestern United States. They are also common over sections of India and the Middle East. An extensive scientific census of dust devils near Tucson, Arizona, was taken from June 23 to July 28, 1962. A total of 1,663 whirls were spotted, and the daily average was near 80.

Dust devils may, at times, develop in more temperate weather and have even been observed as far north as the subarctic. The planet Mars, too, might have them, a theory having been proposed that the dust clouds in the Martian atmosphere may be produced by the action of dust devils.

Diurnal frequency and duration Dust and sand devils are usually most active over desert areas in the early afternoon, 12:30 to 2:00 PM, local standard time. These times precede by several hours those at which the maximum air temperature is recorded in a standard, shaded instrument shelter five feet above the ground. One reason for this apparent anachronism is that the much hotter sand surface attains its peak temperature earlier than the air at the five-foot (1.5-metre) level.

The life of a dust or sand devil may be longer than visual observations indicate, because the vortex itself does not depend upon the visible material forced into it. Durations vary from several seconds to about seven hours, but most dust devils probably last less than five minutes, and few persist for more than an hour. The larger, more vigorous whirls have a longer lifetime than the smaller vortices. One large dust devil, with a height of

about 2,500 feet (750 metres), lasted for seven hours as it travelled 40 miles (64 kilometres) on salt flats in western Utah. And in northwestern Mexico a large whirl formed at the end of an embankment and remained there for four hours.

PHYSICAL CHARACTERISTICS OF THE VORTICES

Although the visible characteristics of tornadoes, waterspouts, and other atmospheric vortices are well known, details regarding the distribution of velocity, pressure, energy, and particulate matter within them are lacking.

Tornadoes and waterspouts. Tornadoes destroy all standard measuring instruments; hence, most values given for velocity, pressure, and energy distribution have depended upon theory and engineering damage estimates. Since the 1940s, however, radar, instrumented aircraft, and photogrammetric techniques have provided some quantitative data for analysis of the vortex structure.

Velocity distribution

The first quantitative observation of the distribution of tangential and vertical speeds within a tornado was made from scaled movies of the debris and cloud fragments in a tornado in Dallas on April 2, 1957. The tornado was fairly stable and relatively small, with a spotty damage path. The variation of the tangential (rotational) velocity with radius at the 1,000-foot (300-metre) level is shown in Figure 5, in which the tangential velocity is seen to rise

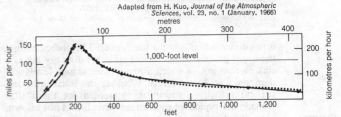

Adapted from H. Kuo, *Journal of the Atmospheric Sciences*, vol. 23, no. 1 (January, 1966)

Figure 5: Variation of the tangential velocity with radius at the 1,000-ft. level in the Dallas tornado on April 2, 1957. Dashed and dotted line represents the theoretical values; solid line represents observed values.

steeply from zero at the centre of the vortex to 150 miles (240 kilometres) per hour at about 200 feet (60 metres) from the centre and then fall off more gradually. This type of velocity distribution closely resembles the Rankine (theoretical) combined vortex (dashed and dotted lines in the figure), in which the inner core is assumed to rotate with a constant angular speed, designated by the Greek omega (Ω), and corresponding to the rotation of a solid body. The tangential velocity is the product of the constant angular speed times the radius of the vortex. This is expressed in the equation $v_1 = \Omega r_1$, in which v_1 indicates tangential velocity and r_1 the radius distance. Hence, for this particular tornado, the tangential velocity in the inner core at the 1,000-foot level was almost directly proportional to the radius until the maximum speed (indicated by vm) was reached at the corresponding radius (rm). At this point, $vm = \Omega rm$.

The tangential velocity distribution in the outer portion of this two-celled vortex follows closely the relation $v_2 r_2 = C = $ constant. Hence, $v_2 = C/r_2$, or the velocity is inversely proportional to the radius. The velocity profiles for the 300- and 100-foot levels showed somewhat greater deviation from the Rankine (theoretical) vortex, possibly because of frictional effects near the ground. The peak tangential speed for this tornado was 170 miles (274 kilometres) per hour, at a radius of 130 feet (40 metres) and elevation of 225 feet (69 metres).

Vertical speeds are measured by tracking debris in the air and correcting for free-fall velocities (which are not related to the tornado-derived speeds). Isotachs (lines of equal value of wind velocity) of these vertical speeds are depicted in Figure 6, in which distances are in metres and speeds in metres per second (one metre per second equals 2.24 miles per hour). A jet of strong vertical flow extends upward from a high-speed centre at 135 feet (41 metres), but the jet disappears near the 1,000-foot (300-metre) level. Above this altitude the line of zero velocity values at any one time appears to coincide with a zone of mois-

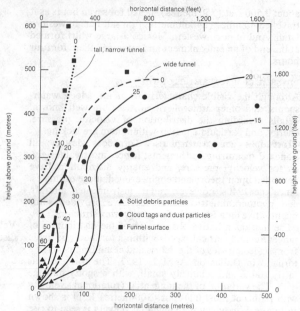

Figure 6: Distribution of the vertical wind velocities (in metres per second) in the Dallas tornado on April 2, 1957.
Adapted from H. Kuo, *Journal of the Atmospheric Sciences*, vol. 23, no. 1 (January, 1966)

Pressure, heat flux, and energy

ture condensation around the funnel. This indicates that the upper portion of the funnel probably does not act as a sink mechanism, in which air condenses at high levels and then sinks to lower levels. Whether the horizontal and vertical velocity distributions presented for the Dallas tornado are typical of most other tornadoes is not known.

No direct measurements have been made of pressures within a tornado, although barographs outside the zone of destructive winds have recorded the sudden drops of pressure associated with the tornado passage. By the use of theoretical relationships between wind and pressure and evaluation of damage patterns, however, some estimate of the distribution of pressure may be obtained.

Although standard barographs are not designed to register the rapid changes of pressure produced by a tornado, there have been cases in which barographs or aneroid barometers on the fringes of the zones of maximum winds have done so. Pressure drops of 100 millibars, about 10 percent of normal atmospheric pressure, are not uncommon, and a fall of 200 millibars has been reported. Because these changes may occur within an interval of less than 30 seconds, the normal pressure inside a building does not have time to adjust to the fast reduction of pressure outside, causing explosive or "suction" effects. Roofs are lifted and walls are blown outward.

The heat flux and energy distribution within a tornado have never been measured directly. Calculated values for the kinetic energy of a typical tornado vary from 10^{10} to 10^{13} joules (10^4 to 10^7 kilowatt-hours). The energy input required to generate this organized motion is probably 10 to 100 times as great. For comparison, the total energy (including radiation) of the 20-kiloton nuclear bomb dropped upon Hiroshima was about 10^{13} joules (10^7 kilowatt-hours). Any theory of tornado development must explain how the potential energy of the environment is converted into the organized kinetic energy of the tornado vortex.

The lower portion of a tornado funnel often appears as a mass of dust and debris picked up by the vortex. The rim of the funnel is usually rendered visible by clouds produced by the condensation of water vapour. The inner core is almost cloudless. Heavy rains and hail are often associated with the severe thunderstorms from which tornadoes develop. Waterspouts sometimes draw fish and frogs into the vortex and then drop them onto land.

Velocity distribution

Dust devils and "fair-weather" waterspouts. Until quite recently few detailed measurements of horizontal and vertical velocities in dust devils had been made. Quantitative data on "fair-weather" waterspouts are still more

sparse, but it is probable that the velocity distributions are similar to those of dust devils in many respects.

Recent measurements in dust devils indicate that the variation of the tangential velocity with radius corresponds closely to that of the Rankine vortex, as described earlier. Tangential speeds of 25 miles (40 kilometres) per hour have been measured and are probably common in moderately strong vortices. Velocities of over 50 miles (80 kilometres) per hour probably occur in some of the larger, more vigorous dust devils. Sailplane pilots have measured vertical speeds of 10 miles (16 kilometres) per hour in moderate whirls and 20–30 miles (32–48 kilometres) per hour in stronger vortices.

A recent study indicates that the mature dust devil may be divided into three vertical regions. Region 1 is a shallow frictional layer near the ground. It is here that the air and dust are entrained into the core of the whirl. Above this shallow boundary layer is Region 2, a stable vortex in which the pressure force and centrifugal force are in balance. Region 3 begins where the top of the vortex becomes unstabilized and the turbulent air diffuses radially with height.

Pressure drops of a few millibars are typical in dust devils. Details regarding the pressure distribution are not known, but there is good evidence that pressure in the well-defined vortex (Region 2) follows a radial distribution similar to that of the Rankine vortex.

The main energy source for a dust or sand devil is the heat flux from the hot surface, although, under certain circumstances, dust or sand devils can be formed in a moderate surface temperature environment, provided that other necessary meteorological conditions are fulfilled. A heat transport (flux) of 0.7 calories per square centimetre per minute was measured over a desert dry lake in California. For a circular area with a 10-metre (30-foot) diameter, this flux would correspond to a net upward heat transport of about 50,000 watts. A dust devil moving over a heated surface utilizes this energy to maintain itself. When dissipative forces, such as surface friction and eddy interaction with the environment, exceed the available energy, the whirlwind is destroyed.

THEORIES OF VORTEX FORMATION: THE GENERATION OF TORNADOES, WATERSPOUTS, AND WHIRLWINDS

At present, meteorologists have not generally agreed on any particular quantitative theory for complete explanation of the formation and maintenance of tornadoes, waterspouts, and other vortices. The literature on vortex theory is extensive; therefore this review will be concerned mainly with some of the more recent theories that seem to fit atmospheric observations and laboratory simulation experiments. Any theory of vortex formation must explain, quantitatively, how the potential energy of the environment is converted into the organized rotational motion of the vortex.

Downward development theory. One kind of tornado formation theory assumes that the tornado vortex develops downward from the parent thunderstorm cloud. It is known that the bases of cumulonimbus clouds associated with severe thunderstorms have stronger rotation than those of ordinary thunderstorms. Further, the visible funnel appears to work downward toward the ground. This visible aspect does not necessarily mean, however, that the tornado vortex itself must originate at upper levels since spirally rising air currents could produce a cloud sheath resulting from condensation of water vapour in the rising air.

Vortex-contraction theory. During the last 25 years radar has been extensively employed in the detailed analysis of severe storms. The use of radar in this area is based on the fact that clouds and precipitation "backscatter" the emitted radiation, producing an "echo" that is photographed on a radarscope. Areas of relatively clear air ("echo-free") are delineated by contrast. Radar meteorologists have contributed significantly to both theories of tornado development and methods of warning.

A photograph of a historically significant echo associated with an Illinois tornado is reproduced in Figure 7. A projection from the mother thunderstorm lengthened and

The "hook" echo

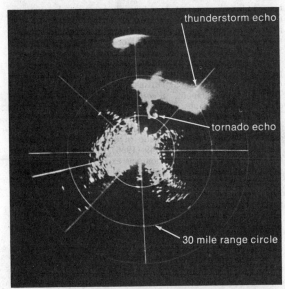

thunderstorm echo

tornado echo

30 mile range circle

Figure 7: Hook echo of a tornado in Champaign, Illinois, photographed on a radar scope on April 9, 1953. This was the first occasion on which the hook echo, an important clue in the tornado warning system, was recognized and photographed.
By courtesy of the Illinois State Water Survey, Urbana, Illinois; photograph, Donald W. Staggs

curved in a counterclockwise manner to form an echo resembling a "figure 6" or "hook." The hook itself is not the tornado, but tornadoes are often associated with echoes of this shape. An analysis of echo alignments and motions and of surface pressure and wind distribution revealed that this distribution corresponded to that of a "tornado cyclone" detected in 1948. This kind of cyclone is a small low-pressure area of about 5 to 25 miles in cross section; the 1948 tornado funnel was one to two miles south of the cyclone centre, and it has been suggested that the contraction of this cyclone would result in an increase in angular momentum and a large upward motion, producing condensation within the tornado cyclone.

Severe local-storm theory. A model for severe local storms that may produce tornadoes is shown in Figure 8.

Adapted from K.A. Browning, *Journal of the Atmospheric Sciences,* vol. 21, no. 6 (November, 1964)

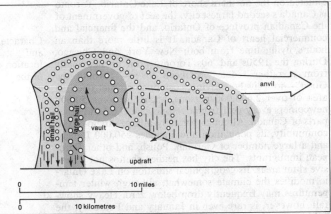

anvil

large hail

vault

updraft

0   10 miles

0   10 kilometres

Figure 8: Vertical section illustrating precipitation trajectories in different parts of a severe storm travelling to the right of the prevailing winds in the middle troposphere.

This model includes a strong shearing of wind (scissor-like action) veering (turning, in clockwise sense) with height. It is based partly upon radar range-height scope photographs of a severe hailstorm in southeast England in July 1959 and of tornadoes in Oklahoma on May 4, 1961. Numerous surface observations were also utilized. The essential features of the model are the following:

1. An updraft of warm, moist air, in which most of the streamlines (lines following flow paths) turn counterclockwise (cyclonically) through about 270 degrees.

2. A downdraft within the precipitation areas ahead of the updraft.

3. An extensive overhanging radar echo ahead of the storm.

4. A region of low reflectivity or "vault" in which there is a persistent strong updraft. The largest hail usually falls in the area of intense echo surrounding the vault.

5. A hook-shaped echo that has a definite counterclockwise circulation. When a tornado forms, it is usually near the forward edges of the hook. It is believed that the hook-shaped echo results from rotation within the strong updraft. Large hail, frequently associated with tornado-breeding storms, requires a vigorous updraft for its formation. The development of a core of rotation within the updraft appears to be required for the genesis of severe storms moving to the right of the environmental winds in the troposphere. It has been suggested that the necessary core of rotation within the updraft could develop only when the updraft was strong enough to generate the growth of giant hail.

Electricity theory. It is known that lightning (*q.v.*), when it accompanies a tornado, has peculiar characteristics. The high-voltage discharges have been described as brighter and bluer than those from other storms. A farmer who had looked up into the core of a tornado later described the walls as constantly illuminated by lightning flashes that "zigzagged" from side to side. So it is not strange that lightning has been hypothesized as the source of energy for the genesis or maintenance of tornadoes. Electrical theories for tornado formation are not new, but have been revived in modern studies.

The lightning hypothesis

Electrical energy is assumed to be transferred to the vortex or the incipient vortex by mechanisms such as the electromagnetic acceleration of ions or heat released from lightning strokes. These electrical transfer mechanisms have been analyzed on the basis of theory and the use of simulated tornado vortex experiments. It has been concluded that the electrodynamic acceleration of ions is unimportant for either the genesis or maintenance of a tornado. Although the heat released from lightning could initiate updrafts, this lightning energy would have to persist for several minutes in order to generate a tornado. Laboratory experiments indicate that electrical discharges in the centre of an intense vortex inhibit, rather than strengthen, its circulation.

These negative results do not mean that electrical phenomena might not produce important indirect effects: the rate of release of latent heat from condensation and precipitation could be influenced by the electrodynamic acceleration of charged particles in the vortex.

General vortex theory. Because of the complex interrelationships of the meteorological factors that must operate together to develop a tornado, a quantitative dynamic theory for generation and maintenance of these twisters is very difficult to formulate.

A theory, nevertheless, has been formulated for the dynamics of atmospheric vortices, which applies not only to tornadoes but also to milder twisters, such as dust devils and other whirlwinds. This model is based on the preexistence of two atmospheric conditions considered to be essential for the genesis and maintenance of the vortices: (1) a thick layer of unstable stratification, either with or without the influence of the latent heat of condensation; and (2) existence of vorticity. The first factor produces sinking because vertical instability aids strong updrafts and the rising air mass is replaced by horizontally converging air. The second factor provides a source of momentum for the development of a stronger tangential velocity as the air converges into a smaller radius. Thus tornadoes and waterspouts, because they are basically convective in nature, are similar to dust devils and fire whirlwinds. For all of these vortices the ratio between horizontal extent and vertical extent (ranging from $\frac{1}{5}$ to $\frac{1}{50}$) is small in comparison to that for hurricanes and extratropical cyclones (from about 10 to 200). Because only the general mechanisms that govern the vortices were of concern, differences depending upon atmospheric structural details were disregarded and it was assumed that all of these small-scale vortices are governed by the same simple model.

From a set of equations for atmospheric vortex motions,

the effective radius of the innermost cell, assumed to be developing into a vortex, was found to be inversely proportional to the one-third power of the initial vorticity, and directly proportional to the one-third power of the product of the eddy viscosity coefficient and the effective depth of the unstable layer. When this layer is shallow, only relatively small and weak whirlwinds, such as dust devils, can be produced.

For a steady state (equilibrium) circular vortex, two solutions were derived. The first was a two-cell type, with descending motion in the centre and ascending motion in the outer part; the second was a one-cell type. The theoretical descending motion in the centre is compatible with the observed sparseness of particulate matter in the cores of tornadoes and dust whirls.

The two-cell solution also indicates that the pressure distribution in the outer portion of the vortex is the same as the flow in the outer part of the Rankine combined vortex described earlier.

Other solutions for a steady state vortex are possible, but it appears that all of them have the following common characteristics:

1. The maximum vertical speed is proportional to a stability factor and increases linearly with height in the unstable layer.

2. The maximum tangential speed is proportional to the angular momentum and the square root of the stability factor; it is inversely proportional to the square root of the coefficient of eddy viscosity, but it is almost independent of the height.

3. The radius of the maximum tangential wind is proportional to the square root of the eddy viscosity coefficient divided by the stability factor.

4. The tangential flow outside the radius of the maximum tangential wind closely approximates the relation in which the product of velocity and radius is a constant $(vr = C)$.

The theoretical results of the dynamic–model theory agree quite well with observations of tornadoes and dust devils.

BIBLIOGRAPHY

Books and monographs: T.F. MALONE (ed.), *Compendium of Meteorology* (1951), an excellent historical reference work, with valuable bibliog., see particularly pp. 673–680, "Tornadoes and Related Phenomena" by E.M. BROOKS; H.P. GERRISH, *Mesoscale Studies of Instability Patterns and Winds in the Tropics* (1967), a discussion of a revised climatology of tornadoes and waterspouts in the Florida area; H.P. GREENSPAN, *The Theory of Rotating Fluids* (1968), a monograph that unifies the theory of rotating fluids, special attention given to laboratory experiments, contains an extensive bibliog.; C.W. NEWTON, "Severe Convective Storms," in *Advances in Geophysics* ed. by H.E. LANDSBERG, vol. 12 (1967), short but excellent summary of theoretical advances in this field, long bibliog.; E.H. PALMEN and C.W. NEWTON, *Atmospheric Circulation Systems: Their Structure and Physical Interpretation* (1969), a general treatment; R.W. FAIRBRIDGE (ed.), *The Encyclopedia of Atmospheric Sciences and Astrogeology*, in the "Encyclopedia of Earth Sciences Series," vol. 2 (1967), articles on tornadoes, waterspouts, whirlwinds, and related cross references.

Popular books and booklets: L.J. BATTAN, *The Nature of Violent Storms* (1961), a popular, but scientifically accurate book that includes descriptive material and non-mathematical theories for extratropical and tropical cyclones, thunderstorms, tornadoes, and related whirlwinds; S.D. FLORA, *Tornadoes of the United States*, 2nd ed. (1954), a standard work on tornadoes and related whirlwinds, detailed descriptive matter; *Tornado Preparedness Planning* (March 1968), a booklet of the U.S. Weather Bureau with practical suggestions for minimizing tornado and severe thunderstorm losses, contains valuable descriptive and statistical information.

Articles: A. BARCILON, "Theoretical and Experimental Model for Dust Devil," *J. Atmos. Sci.*, vol. 24, no. 5, pp. 453–466 (1967), theory presented and experimental flows described, using air and a rotating cylinder; E.M. BROOKS, "The Tornado Cyclone," *Weatherwise*, vol. 2, pp. 32–33 (April 1949), emphasizes the importance of detecting and tracking the mesocyclone connected with tornado development; K.A. BROWNING, "Airflow and Precipitation Trajectories Within Severe Local Storms Which Travel to the Right of the Winds," *J. Atmos. Sci.*, vol. 21, no. 6 (1964), an illustrated model for

tornado-breeding storms, based mainly on radar observations, reviews other studies of severe local storms that travel to the right of the winds in the lower and middle troposphere; C.H.V. EBERT, "The Meteorological Factor in the Hamburg Fire Storm," *Weatherwise*, vol. 16, no. 2, pp. 70–78 (1963), describes the meteorological conditions preceding and accompanying the great fire vortex produced by aerial bombing during World War II; C.E. FETHERSTON, "A Weather Fan—the Tampa Bay Waterspout," *Weatherwise*, vol. 17, no. 4 (1964), excellent photographs; W.D. FLOWER, "Sand Devils," *Prof. Notes Met. Off., Lond.*, no. 71 (1936), a classical article on theory and observations of dust and sand whirlwinds; J.G. GALWAY, "The Topeka Tornado of 8 June 1966," *Weatherwise*, vol. 19, no. 4, pp. 144–149 (1966), analyzes meteorological and safety factors and contains excellent photographs of tornado and aerial photographs of damage; J.H. GOLDEN, "Waterspouts at Lower Matecumbe Key, Florida, 2 September 1967," *Weather*, vol. 23, pp. 103–115 (March 1968), coloured aerial photographs; W.H. HOECKER, JR., "Wind Speed and Air Flow Patterns in the Dallas Tornado of April 2, 1957," *Mon. Weath. Rev. U.S. Dep. Agric.*, vol. 88, no. 5, pp. 167–180 (1960), distribution of rotational and upward air speeds in a tornado observed for the first time by use of high-quality movies; S. THORARINSSON and B. VONNEGUT, "Whirlwinds Produced by the Eruption of Surtsey Volcano," *Bull. Am. Met. Soc.*, vol. 45, no. 8, pp. 440–443 (1964), unique photographs show the wide variety of forms that volcanic whirlwinds assume; U.S. WEATHER BUREAU, "The Palm Sunday Tornadoes of 1965," *Weatherwise*, vol. 18, no. 3, pp. 122–127 (1965), an illustrated account of the disastrous series of tornadoes that struck the Midwest on April 11, 1965; B. VONNEGUT and J.R. MEYER, "Luminous Phenomena Accompanying Tornadoes," *Weatherwise*, vol. 19, no. 2, pp. 66–68 (1966), presents possibly the first photograph of luminous phenomena accompanying tornadoes, contains a short history of electromagnetic theories for tornado formation or maintenance and a short list of references dating back to Francis Bacon; E.M. WILKINS, "Role of Electrical Phenomena Associated with Tornadoes," *J. Geophys. Res.*, vol. 69, no. 12, pp. 2435–2447 (1964), presents results of theoretical analyses and laboratory experiments to determine whether the unusual electrical phenomena associated with tornadoes might be important in the life cycle of the tornado; N.R. WILLIAMS, "Development of Dust Whirls and Similar Small-Scale Vortices," *Bull. Am. Met. Soc.*, vol. 29, no. 3, pp. 106–117 (1948), summarizes observations over Mojave Desert, California, presents theory for vorticity generation.

(N.R.W.)

Toronto

Situated on the northern shore of Lake Ontario, Toronto is Canada's second largest city, the seat of government of the Canadian province of Ontario, and the financial and commercial heart of Canada. It is little more than an hour's flying time from both New York and Chicago. During the 1950s and '60s Toronto grew phenomenally from a rather sedate provincial town—"Toronto the Good"—to a lively, thriving, cosmopolitan metropolitan area of over 2,600,000 persons, attracting some 50,000 newcomers every year from overseas, the U.S., and other parts of Canada. Although basically a large Anglo-Saxon community, its population now includes 250,000 Italians and a large number of German, Polish, and other European immigrants. The city has neither ghettos nor extensive slum areas. Its geographical situation on Lake Ontario modifies the climate somewhat, although winter temperatures may frequently drop below zero. Heavy snowfall, however, is rare even in January and February, the coldest months. July and August are humid, with temperatures in the 90s (°F; 30° C).

History.   The first known settlement in the Toronto area, Teiaiagon, inhabited first by the Seneca and later by the Mississauge Indians, was on the east bank of the Humber River. In the 17th century it became a trading post, strategically situated at the crossing of ancient Indian trails going west to the Mississippi and north to Lake Simcoe and beyond into vast wilderness areas. These land and water routes were followed by explorers, fur traders, missionaries, and others intent upon opening up and exploiting the resources of the Great Lakes region.

By the mid-18th century the name Toronto had come to be commonly used for one of three tiny forts built (1720–50) in the area by the French to defend their trade with

Character and location of the city

the Indians against English and other European competitors. The French were defeated in 1759 and the forts were subsequently destroyed, but the settlement survived as a trading post.

At the end of the Seven Years' War with France (1763), Canada came under British sovereignty and during the next decade was a haven for those American colonists who, after the U.S. War of Independence, preferred British rule to that of the new Republic. Some 40,000 "Empire Loyalists" are said to have settled in the Great Lakes and St. Lawrence areas at this time, and during the 19th century large numbers of immigrants came from Britain.

In 1787 Lord Dorchester, governor in chief of Canada, opened negotiations with three Indian chiefs for the purchase of a site for the future capital of Ontario; about 250,000 acres fronting the lake were acquired in exchange for £1,700, bales of cloth, axes, and other trading goods.

Ontario's first parliament met in 1792 at Niagara, but in 1793 Col. John Simcoe, lieutenant governor of Upper Canada, selected the present site of Toronto for his capital because of its fine harbour, strategic location for defense and trade, and the rich potential of its wilderness hinterland. He changed its name from Toronto to York; two years later (1795) Ontario's capital consisted of only 12 cottages and a small military establishment on the edge of the wilderness.

Occupation by U.S. forces in 1813

While the British were engaged with France in Europe, the United States declared war on Britain; and York, with a population of 700 and practically defenseless, was taken (1813), pillaged and occupied by U.S. forces for 11 days before being retaken. The Speaker's Mace was carried off but was returned in 1934; the Royal Standard is still in the U.S. Naval Academy, Annapolis, Maryland.

Economic depression in Britain following the Napoleonic Wars drove many overseas, and York's population increased from 720 (1816) to about 9,000 in 1834, when the city was incorporated and the old name of Toronto restored. In 1849 there was a disastrous fire that destroyed some 15 acres of the downtown area, including St. James' Cathedral, St. Lawrence Market, and many offices, stores, and warehouses, but the city soon recovered.

Rapid development followed the coming of the Grand Trunk and Great Western railways in the 1850s, and for a decade prosperity was enhanced by a treaty with the United States (1854) that gave certain of Canada's products free entry to markets south of the border. The timber resources of the province were exploited, and large areas of land were converted to farming. Thus, Toronto grew rapidly as an industrial, trading, and distributing centre; its population was 45,000 in 1861, 208,000 in 1901, and 522,000 in 1921.

Prosperity and security were reflected in civic improvement, great building activity, and cultural progress. Between the city's incorporation (1834) and Canada's national confederation under the British North America Act of 1867, many of Toronto's buildings of historical and architectural importance were constructed, including the new St. James' Cathedral, St. Lawrence Hall, and University College, all of which are still extant. A Grand Opera House (since demolished) was opened in 1874, a stolid successor to the numerous small theatres of mid-century that were mostly converted barns. King's College (founded 1827), later to become the University of Toronto, was constructed in 1843 on the site of the present Ontario Parliament Buildings (1886).

During the 50 years from 1834 to 1883, the city maintained its boundaries virtually unchanged. Some reclamation near the lake improved lakeshore properties and docking facilities. Largely by the annexation of adjacent villages and towns, the area of the city was doubled by 1900 and doubled again by 1920. In 1930 the metropolitan area included the central city, four towns (Leaside, Mimico, New Toronto, and Weston), three villages (Forest Hill, Longbranch, and Swansea), and five townships (Etobicoke, East York, North York, Scarborough, and York).

The depression years of the 1930s caused severe financial problems for suburban Toronto. Capital debt payments could not be met, and expenditure on public services—sewage and piped water supply in places remote from the lake, for example—had to be postponed. A rapid increase in population after World War II added to the municipal burden, and many solutions were investigated. In 1953 the Ontario Municipal Board recommended for the 13 municipalities the establishment of a federated form of government unique in North America. The Municipality of Metropolitan Toronto Act was passed, and a twenty-five-man Council of Metropolitan Toronto met for the first time on January 1, 1954. One of the first tasks of the council was to find ways and means of dealing with common major problems by united action, meanwhile permitting local matters to be handled independently. Since the joint credit of the combined municipalities was much greater than the sum of their credits as individual authorities, financing was greatly simplified. A common level of assessment and tax rate on property—the main source of revenue—was agreed upon by each municipality. A most significant feature of the system was that members of the Metropolitan Council were appointed by virtue of their election to office either as mayors, aldermen, or controllers of a particular municipality, thus ensuring a high degree of coordination and good communication between the central body and the local municipalities.

Uniting of the metropolitan area

The Metropolitan Council worked well: it resolved many of the difficult sewage and water problems; it greatly improved transportation by constructing expressways and roads, a new airport terminal building (1962), and an excellent subway; new schools were built and old ones improved; a regional parks system was introduced in an attempt to control future development.

In 1967 the Metropolitan Toronto Corporation was reorganized. The 13 municipalities were reduced to six, and the council increased to 33 members—12 representing the city of Toronto, 20 for the five suburban boroughs, plus the chairman. The council considerably extended its responsibilities in education and the social services, adding, for example, urban renewal, waste disposal, and ambulance and library services.

Administrative reorganization of 1967

The contemporary city. *Layout.* The site of the city is almost uniformly flat, although three to four miles inland there is a fairly sharp rise of some 40 feet—the shoreline elevation of the former glacial Lake Iroquois. Streets are laid out in a grid, although the pattern is modified to some extent by diagonal roads roughly following the shoreline. The central business areas are located around Bloor and Yonge streets and Yonge and Queen streets. The central financial district, with its numerous insurance and banking offices and the Toronto Stock Exchange, is on Bay Street south of the old City Hall (1899).

The skyline of the downtown area is dominated by the Toronto-Dominion Centre and Commerce Court, two major office and banking complexes rising over 50 stories. Other buildings of note are the new City Hall (1958) designed by the Finnish architect Viljo Revell; the Science Centre; Ontario Place; Scarborough College, Massey College, and several other university buildings; and many commercial and industrial buildings of high quality.

Toronto is a major Great Lakes port and, through the St. Lawrence Seaway, an ocean port as well. It handles over 6,000,000 tons of freight annually. The lakefront is separated from the downtown area by railway tracks and an expressway, but planned lakefront developments should radically change this situation. Ferry service connects the dock area and the Toronto Islands, about one-half mile from the shore, which contain yacht clubs, parks, and other recreational facilities.

To the north of the central business district is a fashionable shopping area. Immediately south of Bloor Street is a vestigial, park-like area, the site of the Ontario Parliament Buildings and the University of Toronto. Large expanses of grass and tall shade trees make this a pleasant central area, complementing the ravines that form so important an element in the metropolitan parks system. One of the most attractive residential areas is

Downtown Toronto, with the City Hall in the centre.
Dick Huffman—Pix

Rosedale, an older neighbourhood of dignified houses and winding, tree-lined streets quite close to the downtown area, which itself contains many residential streets of modest, well-designed houses.

Population. During part of the 1950s and 1960s Toronto became one of the fastest growing urban areas in North America, the metropolitan population expanding from 1,174,000 in 1953 to 2,628,000 in 1971. The influx of European immigrants transformed the character of the city: traditionally Protestant and largely of British origin, by 1961 less than half the inhabitants of the central city were of British extraction. The largest groups of immigrants came from Germany and Italy, but there were also substantial numbers from Greece, Portugal, and other countries.

Transportation. Policy for all means of public transportation—buses, tramcars, and subways—is coordinated by the Metropolitan Toronto Planning Board. Sophisticated computer models have been worked out to facilitate the flow of passenger and goods traffic in the metropolitan area, and the plan envisages a rapid transit network of commuter rail lines, extended subway and bus services, expressways, and arterial and collector roads. From 1953 to 1969 Metro Toronto expended some $377,000,000, and its road system alone totals 375 miles. Traffic signals at some 900 intersections are computer coordinated, and a 25 percent improvement in efficiency is claimed.

The modern, efficient subway consists of two lines running north–south and east–west. Seventeen miles west of the centre of the city is Toronto International Airport, Canada's busiest air terminal.

Economic life. Toronto enjoys the economic benefits of its position on the Great Lakes system, which makes it readily accessible to trade with major industrial centres in the United States and, via the St. Lawrence Seaway, to oceangoing shipping. As the capital of Canada's richest and most populous province, the city has a widely diversified economy. Ontario produces over 50 percent of Canada's manufactured goods and about 80 percent of its

manufactured exports; it has immense resources of raw materials—minerals, timber, water, agricultural products, and hydroelectric power. In North America, the Toronto Stock Exchange stands fifth in value of trading.

In 1964 the city's labour force of 711,748 was distributed thus: manufacturing, 228,401; construction, 35,989; transportation, 54,901; wholesale trade, 45,412; retail trade, 104,917; financial services, 76,669; personal and recreational, 50,353; government and community, 108,357.

Culture and recreation. The city is an important cultural centre. The Toronto Symphony Orchestra and other musical groups have an international reputation. There are three major theatres, together with many small experimental theatres. The Art Gallery of Ontario and the Royal Ontario Museum have excellent collections, and there are numerous privately owned galleries. Two important recent additions are the Ontario Science Centre (1970), with its imaginative working exhibits, and Ontario Place (1971), a series of connected exhibition buildings on man-made islands in the lake that are an extension to the permanent Canadian National Exhibition. The city has two major universities—the University of Toronto with its colleges, Erindale and Scarborough, and York University with Glendon College. Ryerson Polytechnic Institute will shortly achieve university status, and the Ontario College of Art offers a wide diversity of excellent programs. Discotheques, coffeehouses, boutiques, movie theatres, night clubs, and the Toronto Maple Leafs ice hockey team all add to the colour and vitality of this vigorous community.

There is an active winter season of cultural activities, with a rich fare of concerts, theatre, opera, ballet, and films. Lectures, seminars, evening classes, and meetings of all kinds cover a multitude of subjects, and the religious life of the community is sustained by a variety of churches, synagogues, mosques, temples, and other meeting places. Many ethnic groups organize traditional festivals, balls, entertainments, and social activities, often in their own language.

In 1967 the Metropolitan Toronto Corporation assumed responsibility for the Canadian National Exhibition, claimed to be the world's largest annual exhibition, which was first launched in 1879 as the Toronto Industrial Exhibition. An international air show, agricultural, animal, and flower displays, theatrical and musical events, and a fairground attract over 3,000,000 visitors in the late summer each year. The permanent buildings are used for trade shows and other special events between seasons.

The Metropolitan Toronto Parks Department administers approximately 7,000 acres of parkland, and ambitious plans have been made for the development of Toronto's waterfront. The Metropolitan Toronto and Region Conservation Authority is an important joint provincial–municipal agency concerned with the development of recreational areas, flood control, and the conservation of existing woodlands and waterways. Established in 1957, it has jurisdiction over some 1,000 square miles and is responsible for the implementation of a large part of Toronto's waterfront-development plan. The authority also offers assistance and technical advice to rural land owners.

Toronto is the main regional tourist centre serving Muskoka, the Haliburton Highlands, and Georgian Bay, all magnificent lakeland and forest areas with fine hunting, fishing, and camping facilities. Recently there has been a remarkable increase in winter sports, and although Ontario's highest point is only 2,183 feet, good ski facilities are available within easy reach of the city. Algonquin Provincial Park is some 163 miles to the north, Niagara Falls is 80 miles south, and the city is surrounded by beautiful rolling farmland, with well-marked sites of historical and architectural interests. Camping, cottaging, boating, and fishing in summer and skiing, ice hockey, and curling in winter are the most popular forms of outdoor recreation.

BIBLIOGRAPHY. The most useful recent works are DONALD KERR and JACOB SPELT, *The Changing Face of Toronto* (1965), a succinct account of the growing city; and ROBERT

Margin notes:

Distribution of the labour force

Local recreational areas

A. MURDIE, "Factorial Ecology of Metropolitan Toronto 1951–1961," *University of Chicago, Dept. of Geography, Research Paper,* no. 116 (1969). The Metropolitan Planning Board annually publishes an excellent brochure on the activities of its constituent departments, *Metropolitan Toronto* and a statistical report, *Metropolitan Toronto Key Facts.* See also HAROLD KAPLAN's essay on social geography, *Urban Political Systems: A Functional Analysis of Metro Toronto* (1967); and FRANK SMALLWOOD's short critical appraisal, *Metro Toronto: A Decade Later* (1963). A beautifully illustrated architectural history for the general reader is ERIC ARTHUR, *Toronto, No Mean City* (1964).

Other useful books are: D.C. MASTERS, *The Rise of Toronto, 1850–1890* (1947); JESSE E. MIDDLETON, *The Municipality of Toronto: A History,* 3 vol. (1923); HENRY J. SCADDING, *Toronto of Old* (1873; abr. ed., 1966); CHARLES P. MULVANY, *Toronto: Past and Present* (1884); EDWIN C. GUILLET, *Toronto from Trading Post to Great City* (1934); LARRY S. BOURNE, *Private Redevelopment of the Central City: Spatial Processes of Structural Change in the City of Toronto* (1967); and EDITH G. FIRTH, *The Town of York, 1793–1815: A Collection of Documents of Early Toronto* (1962).

(Th.Ho.)

Torts, Law of

Tort is a legal term used in both common- and civil-law systems to describe various wrongs that may give rise to civil proceedings, mainly in the form of an action for damages. The law of torts is concerned with the prevention of or compensation for harm sustained by a person through the unlawful or dangerous activity of others. The word tort has its origin in the Latin *tortus,* which means "twisted or crooked." It thus describes vividly the irregularity of the harmful conduct for which the law of torts provides a remedy.

The law of torts regulates a wide variety of unlawful behaviour, ranging from direct physical attack and dangerously negligent conduct to the most subtle forms of violation of values, such as social reputation or affection for next of kin. In modern times it has become one of the most important branches of the legal order, since scientific and technical progress, in, for example, the field of industrial processes or transport, has exacted an ever growing toll of life, limb, and property.

Civil- and common-law approaches to tort law

The common features of such a wide range of wrongs can be described only in general terms, which accounts for the vagueness of the statutory provisions dealing with tortious liability in many codified legal systems on the European continent and in Latin America. In contrast, the common-law countries have adhered to a system of special types of particular torts: "a set of pigeon-holes, each bearing a name, into which the act or omission of the defendant must be fitted before the law will take cognizance of it and afford a remedy," as one commentator has aptly described it.

THE NATURE OF TORT

Tort and crime. A tort is a species of civil wrong and must be distinguished from a criminal wrong giving rise to criminal proceedings, which have for their object the punishment of the wrongdoer. The function of criminal law is to protect the interests of the entire public by punishing an offender. The purpose of the law of torts is to protect the interests of individuals by granting compensation for damages they have suffered. Criminal proceedings are commenced and maintained by the state in the form of a criminal prosecution. Civil proceedings arising from a tort, on the other hand, are brought by the injured persons as private plaintiffs. The distinction between tort and crime thus lies in the interests at stake and the remedies afforded by the law. The same wrong, however, often constitutes a crime against the state and a tort against an individual. Thus, the thief who steals a piece of jewelry commits both the crime of larceny and the tort of conversion. Not infrequently, tort and crime even bear the same name, such as "trespass," "assault," "battery," or "libel"; and the same act can frequently be made the subject of proceedings of both kinds.

The distinction between crime and tort and punishment and compensation is in practice somewhat blurred by the fact that in many legal systems the idea of punishment is of some importance in the field of torts. This becomes particularly clear in the award of "punitive" or "exemplary" damages in addition to compensation under English or American law, in cases in which the wrongdoer has acted intentionally and deliberately. The same idea can be found in other legal systems—the German, Swiss, and Turkish, for example—with regard to serious violations of "personality rights," such as defamation (see below).

Concepts of the function of tort in Socialist legal systems

Closely linked to this punitive function of tort law is the ideological proposition of legal systems in Socialist countries that tortious liability must aim to deter and to educate the wrongdoer. The emphasis placed on the deterrent function of damages reflects the view that any violation of the rules of Socialist society can be explained as a relic of bourgeois-capitalist ideology that must be exterminated. In order to ensure the deterring effect of damages, Soviet law has gone as far as to prohibit liability insurance. This "educational" function of tortious liability might suggest that the amount of compensation, like the degree of punishment, should be proportionate to the wrongdoer's fault. Socialist legal systems, however, adhere expressly to the principle of full compensation irrespective of the degree of fault. The requirement of fault is completely abandoned with respect to certain particularly hazardous activities, such as the operation of automobiles. Socialist legal systems, like their Western counterparts, have thus retained the concept of liability without fault, although this would seem to be incompatible with the deterrent function of tort law.

Tort and breach of contract. A tort must be distinguished from a breach of contract. Whereas a contractual duty springs from an agreement of the parties, a tortious duty is imposed upon the parties by the law itself without regard to their consent. Every man, in principle, is free to enter into contractual relations with another. But he has no choice as to the obligations that the law imposes on him if he drives an automobile on a public highway. The purpose of contractual liability is to protect a specific interest in the performance of the promises of the contracting parties. The purpose of the law of torts on the other hand, is to protect very diverse legally recognized interests by providing compensation for losses suffered in respect of violation—by anyone—of such interests. The same facts, however, frequently may give rise to an action in tort and one for breach of contract. This situation may occur whenever a person voluntarily binds himself by a contract to perform some duty that is already imposed upon him by operation of law independently of any agreement. A surgeon, for example, who negligently treats his patient may be held liable for breach of an implied term in his contract to take reasonable care as well as for a tort of negligence committed by invasion of the interest in freedom from physical harm. Concurrent liability in tort and contract is not, however, universally recognized. Some legal systems—the French system for example—in principle restrict the injured person to an action for breach of contract when the wrongdoer was violating a contractual obligation.

Immunity from tortious liability. Under certain circumstances a civil wrong does not give rise to tortious liability because the wrongdoer is granted immunity. Such immunity from liability for conduct that would otherwise be tortious has in most legal systems traditionally been conferred upon the state. The general immunity of the state from liability for illegal conduct of its organs has been upheld with particular tenacity in the common-law countries. The judicial reluctance to impose vicarious liability upon governmental entities for the wrongs of their officers and employees can be explained as a result of the fear that tortious liability might unduly hamper or interfere with public administration and impose intolerable financial burdens upon the treasury. Modern developments, however, have proved that such fears were largely exaggerated. The threat of tortious liability, wherever it has been introduced, has not affected the smooth functioning of public entities. To a certain extent it may even be perceived as a stimulus to a more efficient and careful public administration. The ever growing use of motor vehicles by government officials and the corresponding necessity of compensating accident victims has led to a further erosion of the immunity doctrine.

Tortious liability of public entities is thus now the rule, although certain exceptions are admitted. These are largely in the area of adverse effects on individuals of government policies, of judicial acts, of acts of state relating to other sovereign states, of certain military activities, and of malfunctions of postal services.

The erosion of the traditional-immunity doctrine is not restricted to Western countries: the same trend can be noted in Socialist legal systems. The civil code of a constituent republic of the Soviet Union (Russian Soviet Federated Socialist Republic [R.S.F.S.R.]) of 1922, for example, exempted state institutions from tortious liability unless contrary provision was established by law. The new civil code of the R.S.F.S.R. of 1964, however, has adopted the opposite position: article 446 expressly declares state institutions liable for injury caused to citizens by improper official acts in the sphere of administrative management unless otherwise provided by special statute.

Inasmuch as tortious liability is based on the requirement of fault, immunity is also conferred upon certain wrongdoers on account of their age or state of mind. Infants and insane persons under certain circumstances thus enjoy exemption from tortious liability. The extent to which such immunity is granted varies. Common law, on the whole, seems to be less reluctant than civil-law systems and the Socialist legal orders to recognize tortious liability of infants or lunatics.

THE HISTORICAL AND SOCIAL CONTEXT OF TORT-LAW DEVELOPMENT

Historical background. Problems of tortious liability have arisen ever since life in a common society led to the development of law. The law of torts in the earlier stage of its evolution usually consisted of a miscellaneous and more or less unconnected group of specific rules protecting a few particular interests against harmful interferences of a particular kind. Roman law, for example, knew three principal torts: *iniuria* (intentional interference with the person), *furtum* (intentional interference with property), and the rule of the *lex Aquilia* covering losses caused by negligence.

Tort law is more deeply imbedded in the past than any other branch of the common law. It abounds in historical curiosities, seemingly arbitrary distinctions, and strange inconsistencies. The reason for most of these anomalies lies in the ancient system of legal procedure with its "forms of action." Until comparatively recent times a plaintiff under common law could sue in tort only if he could fit his claim into one of the recognized forms of action for which some particular writ of summons was available (see PROCEDURAL LAW).

The earliest tortious actions in common law

The first writs that were available for tortious causes of action were those of trespass and of "trespass upon the case." The action of trespass, recognized about the year 1250, was restricted to direct and immediate injuries to land, goods, or persons, such as those occasioned by throwing a log that hits another man or his property. Indirect or consequential injuries, such as those suffered by someone who stumbles over the log, became remediable 100 years later by "actions of trespass upon the case." A considerable variety of injuries eventually became recoverable by applying for such a writ on the case, and it lay within the discretion of the judges whether they would consider the wrong concerned a good cause of action.

In striking contrast to the development in the common law, tort law in legal systems based on the civil law seems to have advanced much further from its historical roots. The great jurists of the law of nature in the 17th and 18th centuries enunciated the general principle that everybody shall be held liable for the damage caused by his fault, and this principle has been embodied in various forms in many civil codes. An example is presented by article 1382 of the French Code Napoléon or Code Civil of 1804.

Many other civil codes based on the French model have subsequently adopted similar provisions. Other legal systems in the civil-law sphere have chosen somewhat more restrictive solutions. The German Civil Code, for example, grants protection to various specifically mentioned interests.

Apart from general provisions dealing with liability for losses occasioned by one's fault, the civil codes usually contain specific rules imposing liability for the harmful acts of one's servants and for pursuing certain hazardous activities, such as keeping an animal or operating an automobile.

The difference between tort law in the common-law countries and in the civil-law sphere is not in practice as important as it may appear at first sight. Theoretically, the range of application of the abstract provisions in a civil code is much larger than the pigeonhole system of Anglo-American case law. It must be borne in mind, however, that behind the screen of the general terms of a civil code the courts develop a bulk of so-called case law that in many ways resembles its counterpart in the common law. Although the means by which a certain solution to a legal problem is reached may be strikingly different, the results tend to be very much the same under common- and civil-law influence.

Approaches to the problem of liability. The purpose of the law of torts is the adjustment of certain losses that are the inevitable result of living together in a common society. Such losses might, in principle, be borne by the individuals who suffer them. The law of torts, however, attributes liability for certain losses to persons other than the injured individuals. It enables the victims of harm resulting from the socially unreasonable conduct of others to demand compensation from the wrongdoers.

A major problem that has to be solved by the law of torts arises whenever a particular wrongdoer cannot be ascertained or when his fault cannot be proved. In such circumstances the victim of an accident might remain without compensation. The same situation might occur whenever the financial means of someone committing a tort are insufficient to compensate his victim. Two areas in which such problems of determining liability have been particularly acute are industrial and traffic accidents.

Industrial accidents. Traditional solutions to the social problems raised by contemporary accident rates lie within the scope of tort law that has been described above. Some countries, however, in regard to certain categories of risk, have increasingly adopted a scheme of compensation that is totally independent of any tortious liability of a particular wrongdoer. Modern systems of social insurance, for example, provide extensive protection against the harmful consequences of personal injuries. The pressing need for granting help to the victims of accidents irrespective of tortious claims was first felt with regard to industrial accidents. Under common law as well as under most other legal systems, by far the greater proportion of such accidents remained uncompensated. Among other factors, the difficulty of proving the employer's fault and the delay and expenses of litigation turned industrial accidents into personal disasters for the injured persons and their dependents. In order to provide a remedy for such blows of fate, the German legislature in 1884 introduced a system of social insurance for industrial accidents—an example that has been followed all over the world. In the Soviet Union as well as in other Socialist countries, the enactment of social-insurance laws was one of the first measures of the newly established governments. Despite considerable resistance, workmen's compensation acts have also been adopted by all United States jurisdictions. These acts usually charge the employer with the injuries attributed to the risks of the employment without regard to questions of the negligence of employer or employee. This form of strict liability is supplemented by a system of compulsory liability insurance, which distributes the losses over the entire industry. Although workmen's compensation acts rely on the employer's tortious liability in order to protect the employees, the system in its practical consequences results in a distribution of risks, which is the characteristic feature of insurance.

Extension of tortious liability by workmen's compensation acts

Contemporary trends all over the world show a tendency to widen the scope of social insurance beyond the field of industrial accidents. Many countries, especially in western Europe and in the Socialist sphere of influence, have adopted collective systems of health and general accident insurance. Under such systems the victims of personal injuries may obtain at least partial compensation for the losses they have suffered. Claims for compensation are directed against the social-insurance agency: the problem of tortious liability is thus irrelevant in this context. Some legal systems, however, provide that the social-insurance agency may take over the rights of the victim against the tort perpetrator in order to recover its payments.

Traffic accidents. Despite the progress of social-insurance systems, the regulation of traffic accidents in most countries has remained primarily the task of tort law. Due to the ever-increasing rate of traffic injuries, this function has turned into one of the heaviest burdens born by the legal system. The existing rules of tortious liability in some respects do not correspond to the needs of the times.

Common-law countries have generally adhered to the principle that liability for traffic injuries presupposes a wrongdoer's fault. This means in practice that victims of traffic accidents must prove that their injuries were the result of another's negligence. This and other obstacles have resulted in only a comparatively small proportion of traffic victims eventually obtaining compensation. By way of contrast, civil-law countries, including France, Germany, Italy, Switzerland, Scandinavia, Turkey, Spain, and Japan, as well as the Socialist countries, have adopted a rule of strict liability with regard to the operation of motor vehicles—that is, the driver of a motor vehicle is liable for compensation regardless of fault. Even this system leaves something to be desired from the point of view of the victim, since compensation is excluded when the accident is caused by an "act of God." It is at least reduced in cases of contributory negligence.

Tortious liability for traffic injuries—no matter whether founded on negligence or strict liability—also presents the problem that compensation can sometimes not be obtained because the person being sued (the tort-feasor) does not have sufficient financial means. With the strange exception of Soviet Russia and several states in the U.S., most countries have tried to minimize such risks by introducing compulsory liability insurance. Following the French example, many legal systems have gone so far as to grant to traffic victims a direct claim for compensation against the automobile operator's insurance company. Even compulsory third-party insurance, however, does not necessarily ensure full compensation to injured persons, for frequently the amount of damages recovered from the wrongdoer is limited by the extent of the offending party's insurance cover.

"No-fault" insurance as a substitute for tortious claims

The various deficiencies of the traditional principles of tortious liability with regard to the adjustment of traffic accidents have led to numerous reform projects in several countries. Strong criticism of the "forensic lottery" of tort liability as a system of personal-injury compensation in automobile accidents was first raised in the United States and has resulted in various plans aimed at the replacement of tort law by a system of compulsory automobile accident insurance. Such schemes provide for recovery of personal injuries for all victims of automobile accidents without regard to fault.

Redistribution of the burdens of tortious liability. The interplay of tort law and modern insurance practices has resulted in a socialization of the risks and losses that are inevitable in modern society. The ancient starting point of tort law—"the loss lies where it falls"—has largely been replaced by its modern counterpart—"the loss lies with the community." Judges and, above all, juries cannot be expected to remain indifferent to the question of which party to a lawsuit might best be able to bear the loss concerned: mere knowledge of the fact that one party is insured can influence their decisions considerably. In automobile-accident cases especially, this factor has led to a natural tendency to favour the plaintiff at the expense

of the defendant, who is usually protected by liability insurance. In view of this, the jury in most parts of the United States may not be informed whether the defendant is insured or not.

The inclination of courts to consider the relative capacity of the respective parties to bear the loss has brought about a certain erosion of the traditional principles of tortious liability. The requirement of fault in automobile-accident cases under common law, for example, has largely been abolished in practice by overstraining the standards of care applied to the defendant's conduct. The result is that negligence is almost always found. The extension of the manufacturer's liability (see below) to the ultimate consumer of his product can equally be explained by the tendency to favour the poor against the rich.

Another important change in tort law resulting from the social policy of shifting losses to defendants who might reasonably be expected to bear the burden without being ruined is the growth of "strict liability." During the course of the 19th century the principle "no liability without fault" had won worldwide recognition. One of the first exceptions to this doctrine related to the keeping of animals, and many legal systems, including the common law, contain a rule of strict liability for harm done by certain animals. Another exception was recognized by some civil-law countries with regard to the owner of a building that has collapsed.

Development of doctrines of strict liability

One of the most important events in the development of the common law regarding strict liability was the English decision in the case of *Rylands* v. *Fletcher* (1868). According to the rule of this case, which has been recognized by most jurisdictions in the United States, a defendant, without regard to his fault, is strictly liable for the damage caused by abnormal and unduly dangerous things and activities, such as the storage of a large quantity of explosives or inflammable liquids. The doctrine of strict liability that developed from this case is confined to extraordinary risks and does not apply to such things as water in a cistern or gas or electricity in household pipes or wires. The principle of strict liability has further been extended by statute or modification of the common law to industrial accidents, to the manufacture or sale of food, and to aviation. Most civil-law countries have adopted the principle of strict liability for the operation of railways, motor vehicles, and nuclear plants.

A SURVEY OF MODERN TORT LAW

A basic distinction adopted by the common law in the course of the 19th century was based on the wrongdoer's will. Modern tort law distinguishes between intentional injuries and those that are merely negligent; that is, caused without the intent of the tort-feasor. Civil-law systems, on the other hand, usually treat intention and negligence alike, as two different kinds of fault for which tortious responsibility must be assumed. In practice, however, the rules relating to intentional, as opposed to negligent, wrongdoing reveal significant differences in civil law systems. Most of the wrongs falling under the various torts classified in their common-law form and described below give rise in civil-law countries to tortious liability according to the relevant provisions of particular civil codes.

Personal injury. Tort liability based on the wrongdoer's intent can arise from the interference with the person or the property of another. Intentional personal injuries under common law fall under several specific torts.

Battery. A defendant's conduct constitutes the tort of battery if he intentionally causes some physical contact with the person of the plaintiff without the latter's consent. The law relating to battery thus protects the interest in freedom from physical contact with another. The contact need not be directly with the plaintiff's body; contact with things attached to the person of another (throwing over a chair on which he is sitting, for example) will be sufficient. The contact need not entail actual physical harm: knocking off another's hat or spitting in his face amounts to battery, as does kissing a woman without her consent. The last example illustrates one of the most important and intricate problems of the action for battery. In order to be liable for battery, the defendant must have acted without the plaintiff's consent. Consent may either be expressly declared, as when one agrees to a surgical operation, or it may be inferred from the circumstances of the case, as when one participates in a game of football. The plaintiff's consent is assumed for ordinary contacts that are common in social life, such as a friendly blow on the shoulder or a gentle touch to attract the attention of a stranger.

The problem of consent in surgical operations

The problem of the validity and the extent of a plaintiff's consent frequently arises in connection with surgical operations on patients who are unconscious or of unsound mind. If the plaintiff is incapable of giving valid consent because of a mental disturbance, for example, he will be able to bring an action for damages. If he has given valid consent to a particular operation, and the surgeon in the course of his treatment discovers the desirability of extending the operation to another area, the mere medical indication will not justify the surgeon in going ahead. Unless the consent given prior to the operation was sufficiently general in its terms, or unless an unforeseen emergency has arisen during the operation that allows the assumption that the patient would consent if he could be asked, the surgeon by extending the operation exceeds the express or implied consent of the patient and may be held liable for battery.

Assault. Closely related to the tort of battery is the tort commonly called assault. In contrast to battery, which protects the interest in freedom from physical contact with another, the action for assault is designed to protect the interest in freedom from a particular form of mental anxiety; that is, freedom from apprehension of harmful or offensive contact with another. The difference between assault and battery is, thus, that between threat and its realization. The apprehension of physical contact need not result in fear on the part of the plaintiff. Only the apprehension of an immediate contact, however, amounts to assault. There must thus usually be some threatening action, such as the shaking of a fist or wielding of a gun. Mere words—threats of future violence, for example—do not usually constitute an assault under common law.

Battery and assault in civil-law systems are not considered as special types of civil wrongs. Along with various other injuries, they fall within the range of application of the general provisions of civil codes on tortious liability. The different theoretical approach, however, does not in practice seem to entail substantially different results.

False imprisonment. The interest in freedom from confinement is protected by the tort of false imprisonment. There are many different ways in which this tort can be committed. An action for false imprisonment may arise from the plaintiff's confinement to a vehicle, to a house, a prison, or to an entire city. The barriers used for the confinement need not be physical. Restraint on movement in a street by a mere threat of force can constitute false imprisonment. There must, however, be a total restraint. If the plaintiff's movement is blocked in one direction only—by the closing of a bridge, for example—he has no remedy arising from a tort of false imprisonment. The tort can be committted by mere omission, such as failure to let a prisoner out of jail when he has served his sentence.

False imprisonment is, of course, excluded in cases of lawful arrest by police officers or, under certain circumstances, by private citizens who have witnessed the commission of a crime. Even if the confinement is authorized by the law, the prisoner may resort to an action for malicious prosecution; that is, for the groundless instigation of criminal proceedings. In order to obtain compensation the plaintiff must prove that the defendant maliciously and without probable cause had occasioned criminal proceedings that were terminated in favour of the plaintiff.

Mental suffering. As pointed out above, mere words do not constitute a cause of action for assault. And defamation (see below) does not provide protection from

insults directed at the injured party that are not also communicated to a third person. It is quite possible, however, that a person might suffer a harm by being subjected to abuse that does not threaten physical violence and that is not heard by a third party. This gap in the common law has in more recent years been filled step by step by the recognition of a separate cause of action for the intentional infliction of mental or emotional disturbance. Tortious liability of this kind was first imposed on common carriers who had insulted their passengers and was subsequently extended to innkeepers and other persons offering their services to the general public. The new tort has further been applied to outrageous jokes, such as telling a woman facetiously that her husband has been killed. In other instances mishandling of dead bodies has been recognized as a valid cause of action for the survivors whose personal feelings were hurt. Under certain circumstances harms inflicted on a third person can amount to a tort of causing mental disturbance in those who have indirectly suffered fright or shock—at the sight of the mutilated corpse of a murdered sister, for example. Liability is restricted to mental suffering of a very serious kind and cannot be extended to trifling injuries.

Violations of property rights. Tort liability can arise from an intentional interference with another's property. There are various wrongs that fall under this category of the law of torts.

Trespass to land. A defendant is liable for trespass to land when he intentionally enters or remains on land in the possession of another without his permission. The same liability accrues from the intentionally caused intrusion of any physical matter into the plaintiff's land. It is not the function of tort law to protect ownership as such. The action for trespass to land purports to protect the interest in exclusive possession of land in its intact, physical condition. Thus, the tenant—not the landlord—sues if a third person enters land he occupies. Trespass to land can be committed by such acts as walking on the plaintiff's soil, flooding it with water, throwing rocks or rubbish on it, or by attracting a crowd of spectators eager to watch the landing of a balloon. Trespass to land can further be committed by invasion of that portion of the air space above the plaintiff's land that is requisite for its full use. The exact limits of this zone have been the subject of much discussion due to the rapid expansion of aviation. There can be no doubt, however, that the flight of an aircraft at a reasonable height above the ground does not constitute trespass to land. Similar problems as to the upward extent of the possessor's rights arise with regard to intrusions below the surface by mining or construction activities.

Nuisance. The enjoyment of land and the premises thereon is also protected by the tort of nuisance. Activities that produce excessive dust, noise, stenches, insects, fumes, seepage, gases, smoke, vibrations, or severe emotional disturbances—invasions more subtle and more persistent than those required for trespass—may give rise to an action for nuisance. The court may award damages, order the nuisance to be stopped by means of an injunction, or both.

Trespass to chattels. The counterpart to the tort of trespass to land, as far as movable property is concerned, is the tort of trespass to chattels. This action arises from any intentional, physical interference with a chattel in the possession of another—by damaging or removing it, for example. The plaintiff is entitled to compensation for the loss he has suffered. When he has been permanently deprived of his goods, he may recover their value by way of damages. The plaintiff will be entitled to something less than the full value of his property if, for example, his horse is beaten or his automobile is used without his consent.

Conversion. By far the most important action for intentional interference with the chattels of another arises from the tort of conversion. Conversion may be defined as an intentional dealing with a chattel in a manner that is seriously inconsistent with the right of the person entitled to it.

Conversion can be committed by acquiring possession

of goods without legal justification and with the intention of exercising dominion over them. Stealing a chattel is conversion, as is its purchase from the thief or its seizure under legal process without justification. Merely to remove goods from one place to another may amount to trespass to chattels but is not necessarily conversion. Destroying or altering a chattel will constitute a conversion if done intentionally, as, for example, by shooting the annoying dog of a neighbour or by making wine from another's grapes. Even a mere erroneous delivery of a good to the wrong person can be conversion. Conversion can further be committed by a refusal to surrender a chattel upon lawful and reasonable demand, as in the case of a finder who refuses to hand over the property to the rightful owner. Furthermore, the mere use of a chattel without causing the least damage to it can amount to conversion if it is done in obvious defiance of the owners' rights.

The classification of torts relating to intentional interference with property under common law has no equivalent in civil-law systems. It should be noted that the range of application of the common-law action for conversion covers situations that in civil-law systems are regarded as partly nontortious.

Actions based on negligence. By far the greatest number of civil actions for tort and, possibly, the majority of civil actions as a whole are brought by injured persons to recover compensation for damage suffered through the negligent conduct of the defendant.

Negligence as a separate tort under common law was not recognized before the 19th century. Its development from the ancient action of trespass on the case coincided with the increasing use of dangerous machinery during the course of the Industrial Revolution. The growing rate of industrial and traffic accidents gave rise to social problems that the existing rules of tortious liability were unable to solve. The principle "no liability without fault," designed to further the interests of risk-taking entrepreneurs in the early capitalist economy, obstructed the evolution of strict liability as a means of providing compensation for the victims of such accidents. In order to meet the demands of social justice, lawyers directed their attention to the task of expanding the notion of fault from its traditional meaning. This led to a distinction between intentional and unintentional injuries and to an awareness of negligence as a separate basis of tort liability.

Legal systems based on civil law have reacted to the same problems by recognizing strict liability for various ultrahazardous activities. Insofar as rules of liability without fault were not developed, stress was laid instead upon negligence as a ground for imposing tortious liability. The relevant general provisions of civil codes, expressly or implicitly, have admitted that negligence may give rise to tortious liability under the same conditions as intentional wrongdoing. Civil law, in contrast to common law, thus treats negligence as simply another kind of fault for which a defendant may be held liable. Many of the principles that have been developed under common law as specific rules relating to negligence as a separate tort, such as the rules of proximate cause or contributory negligence, are under civil law treated as general topics of tort law that bear on any kind of tort liability, no matter whether the wrongdoer's conduct was intentional or unintentional.

Definitions of negligence. Negligence may be described as a failure to comply with that standard of care that would correspond to the conduct expected of a reasonable man of ordinary prudence under similar circumstances. Any conduct that falls below that standard of behaviour is considered to be negligent. In order to find out whether the particular conduct of a particular person can be called negligent, his conduct must be compared with the supposed behaviour of a purely fictitious person who meets the requirements of an ideal citizen. This mythical person, who is always a model of prudence and care, can be found in most legal systems. He is extremely versatile: if the conduct of the driver of an automobile is to be considered, the reasonable man will be the motorist of ordinary sense using ordinary care and skill; if the

fatal outcome of a surgical operation gave rise to the issue, he will be the prudent surgeon of the skill and knowledge commonly possessed by members of the surgical profession in good standing; and if the person who has caused injury to another lacks one of the physical attributes of ordinary people his behaviour will be compared with that of an ideal man who is equally physically disabled.

The mere failure to comply with the standard of care that has just been described is not sufficient to constitute the tort of negligence. As an English judge has put it: "In strict legal analysis, negligence means more than heedless or careless conduct, whether in omission or commission; it properly connotes the complex concept of duty, breach, and damage thereby suffered by the person to whom the duty was owing." (*Lochgelly Iron & Coal Co.* v. *M'Mullan* [1934].)

According to this definition, negligence requires a legal duty of care that is imposed on the wrongdoer and that is owed to the group of persons to which the plaintiff belongs. Liability for negligence, under common law, in other words, presupposes that the defendant was under an obligation to take reasonable care for the benefit of the plaintiff. "A man is entitled to be as negligent as he pleases towards the whole world if he owes no duty to them." (Lord Esher in *Le Lievre* v. *Gould,* [1893]). The requirement of a duty of care may be illustrated by a famous American case, *Palsgraf* v. *Long Island Railroad Co.* (1928): a railway passenger was trying to get into a train that had already begun to move. One of the defendant's employees assisted him, and a package containing fireworks fell from the passenger's arms upon the rails. The shock caused by the ensuing explosion upset some scales at the other end of the platform. The scales fell upon the plaintiff and injured her. The majority of the court held that there was no liability in negligence because, although the conduct of the defendant's servant was careless, no duty was owed to the plaintiff against this remote hazard. The decision in the Palsgraf case clearly reflects the view that common law does not recognize remote duties and that, therefore, no duty of care can be owed to the unforeseeable plaintiff. It must be noted, however, that the scope of duties recognized under common law is fairly wide. Any motorist, for example, is considered to be under an obligation to take reasonable care for the benefit of all other persons on the road.

In order to support an action for damages based on negligence, the plaintiff further has also to show that the defendant failed to comply with his duty of care. A breach of duty can be assumed when the defendant failed to do what a reasonable man of ordinary prudence would do under the same or similar circumstances. A defendant cannot be held responsible for his passive inaction unless this was contrary to a specific duty to act. Common law seems on the whole reluctant to impose such duties. A motorist is thus not required to walk to a nearby telephone booth to summon medical aid for the victim of a road accident whom he sees lying on the ground in urgent need of help.

The third element necessary to an action based on negligence is causal connection between the defendant's carelessness and the damage suffered by the plaintiff. Legal problems relating to causation are among the most difficult and most controversial issues of the law of torts. There is no doubt that a person committing a tort can be held liable for the immediate consequences of his wrongdoing, such as fracture of the leg of a pedestrian who has been hit by his automobile. Great difficulties arise, however, when the injured person in the ensuing course of events suffers further damage—when the pedestrian catches an infectious disease during a stay in the hospital, for example. Although the fact of causation may be clearly established, the wrongdoer's liability must somehow be limited. This limitation of responsibility, under common law, is performed by the doctrine of "proximate cause." It excludes liability for those consequences of the defendant's conduct that are "too remote" to be attributed to him. A precise definition of this rule cannot be offered. Which consequences are deemed too remote to be within the limits of a particular tort-feasor's liability must in practice be decided by means of a sense of justice rather than by means of logical reasoning.

Contributory negligence. Liability of a defendant arising from negligence can be excluded if the plaintiff was equally at fault—if he was reading a newspaper while he was crossing a street and was hit by an inattentive motorist, for example. Under common law, a plaintiff who fails to conform to the standard of care to which he is required to conform for his own protection is in principle denied recovery. This doctrine of "contributory negligence" can lead to highly unsatisfactory results when the negligence of both parties has been of equal importance in causing the harm or, even worse, where the defendant's negligence has been gross whereas the plaintiff's negligence has been relatively slight. Civil-law systems avoid such hardship by providing for an apportionment of damages according to the relative fault of the parties. A similar rule has been adopted in Great Britain by the Law Reform (Contributory Negligence) Act, 1945. Various statutes of similar effect operate in the United States. Where such "comparative negligence" statutes have not been enacted, the ancient common-law rule of contributory negligence has been modified considerably by the so-called doctrine of "last clear chance." This rule was developed by an English court in 1842 in the case of *Davies* v. *Mann* (1842). The plaintiff had negligently left his ass, fettered by its forefeet, in a highway. The defendant drove his wagon into it and killed it. It was held that, despite of his own negligence, the plaintiff could recover damages because the defendant could have avoided the harmful consequences of that negligence.

The defense of assumption of risk

Closely related to the doctrine of contributory negligence is the defense of assumption of risk. Liability for negligence, according to this rule, is excluded when the injured person expressly or implicitly agreed to assume the risk of the defendant's negligence. A spectator watching an ice-hockey match thus implicitly consents to the risk of being hurt by the puck, which may be hit out of the rink in the course of the game.

Effect of intervention of third parties. An intervening act of a *third party* in the production of damage does not necessarily relieve the defendant from liability. Inasmuch as such intervention could reasonably have been foreseen, it cannot be considered a superseding cause that will free the defendant from his responsibility. This is of considerable practical importance with regard to negligent medical treatment of an injured victim: the defendant is liable for all ordinary forms of professional negligence on the part of the doctor who treats the person he injured. He will be relieved from liability only if the intervening third person's conduct was so unusual that the defendant could not reasonably have foreseen it.

Negligence and industrial accidents. The working of the common-law rules on negligence caused considerable hardship with regard to industrial accidents. By far the greater proportion of injuries suffered in the course of employment remained uncompensated because the injured employees were unable to prove their employer's negligence. Even when negligence could be proved, the employer in many instances successfully raised the defenses of contributory negligence or assumption of risk on the part of the employee. The employer's liability was further restricted by the effect of the "fellow servant" rule, which relieved the employer from responsibility for injuries that had been caused by the negligence of a fellow servant. As described above, the social problems arising from these rules have largely been solved by the adoption of workmen's compensation acts.

The development of the rules of the manufacturer's liability to the consumer bears analogy to the evolution of tortious liability for the benefit of injured workmen. At first, the interests of consumers who had been injured by defective products did not find protection in the law of torts. In order to invoke the producer's liability based on negligence, the plaintiff would have to show that he had suffered harm by a breach of a duty owed to him by the defendant. But until the beginning of the 20th century, common-law courts failed to recognize the existence of a duty of care imposed on the manufacturer for the benefit of the consumer. This position has gradually been abandoned. Since the leading cases of *MacPherson* v. *Buick Motor Co.* (1916) in the United States and *Donoghue* v. *Stevenson* (1932) in Great Britain, the consumer, under certain circumstances, has had a direct claim based on negligence for compensation from the producer for injuries suffered as a result of defective goods. There is a growing tendency in American legal literature to hold the manufacturer more strictly liable for the harm caused by his products. If this trend prevails the plaintiff will be relieved from proving the defendant's negligence.

The development of manufacturer's liability in common law has exercised considerable influence on legal thinking and judicial practice in civil-law countries. The traditional position of many civil-law systems had failed to recognize special rules of tortious liability enabling the consumers who had been injured by defective products to obtain compensation from the producer. Following the example presented by the evolution of the common law, legal writing and judicial reasoning in civil-law countries have been building a system of manufacturer's liability that in its practical results in many respects resembles the solutions reached under common law.

Protection of intangible personal interests. *Defamation.* The interest in reputation and good name is covered by the law of defamation, which is made up of the torts of libel and slander. The distinction between libel and slander is based on the medium that is used to communicate a defamation. Libel, in general, is written, and slander, in general, is oral. Defamation by radio or television in common-law countries is increasingly regarded as libel. In contrast to slander, libel is always actionable per se; that is, without proof that damage has actually occurred. This difference may lead to strange results. Defamatory words in a letter regarding a third person but that have merely been read by the addressee make the sender liable for libel without proof of any actual damage to the plaintiff. A defamatory speech before an audience of 1,000 people, on the contrary, merely gives rise to an action based on slander, which, subject to certain exceptions, requires proof of actual damage. The distinction between both types of defamation is the result of a historical development peculiar to the common law. It has no equivalent in civil-law systems.

Distinction between libel and slander

Rights of privacy. Personal rights other than reputation have gained judicial protection in the United States by recognition of a so-called right of privacy.

The concept of a legal right to privacy had its origin in a review article by the American jurists Samuel D. Warren and Louis Brandeis, published in 1890. The authors postulated a "right to privacy"; that is, a legal principle

which may be invoked to protect the privacy of the individual from invasion either by the too enterprising press, the photographer, or the possessor of any other modern device for recording or reproducing scenes or sounds.

This farsighted view today has gained support in most jurisdictions of the United States. English courts, however, up to the early 1970s have not followed the American example.

In practice, however, the different legal situation does not seem to have created any striking discrepancies between the extent of protection afforded to human personality on either side of the Atlantic. As far as civil-law systems are concerned, the French seem to have had the least difficulties in coping with modern menaces to intangible personal interests. Civil-law systems that are based on a more restrictive enunciation of tortious liability, such as the German system, on the other hand, have had some trouble in adjusting themselves to modern needs relating to protection of the integrity of personality. There has, however, been a recognition of a "general personality right" that may be regarded as a step toward safeguarding the individual from the intrusions of the mass media.

Tort law, to some extent at least, also provides protection for the interest of freedom from interference with family relations. A husband whose wife has been injured in an accident may thus claim compensation for the resulting loss of her household services and company. Similarly, he may sue an adulterer who interfered with the marital relation.

BIBLIOGRAPHY. WILLIAM L. PROSSER, *Handbook of the Law of Torts*, 3rd ed. (1964); and FOWLER V. HARPER and FLEMING JAMES, JR., *The Law of Torts*, 3 vol. (1956), are among the best modern treatises on tort law. A concise survey of the present English law of torts is offered by HARRY STREET in *The Law of Torts*, 4th ed. (1968). *Clerk and Lindsell on Torts*, 13th ed. (1969); *Pollock's Law of Torts*, 15th ed. (1951); *Salmond on the Law of Torts*, 14th ed. (1965); and *Winfield on Tort*, 8th ed. (1967), are classic works that have appeared in numerous editions under the supervision of various successors to the original authors. The subject has been treated on a comparative basis by KONRAD ZWEIGERT and HEIN KOETZ in *Einführung in die Rechtsvergleichung auf dem Gebiete des Privatrechts*, vol. 2 (1969); and, with regard to tort law in the European Economic Community, by ANDREAS HELDRICH in *Die allgemeinen Rechtsgrundsätze der ausservertraglichen Schadenshaftung im Bereich der Europäischen Wirtschaftsgemeinschaft* (1961). As regards tort law in Socialist countries, see JOHN N. HAZARD, ISAAC SHAPIRO, and PETER B. MAGGS, *The Soviet Legal System*, rev. ed. (1969); GUYLA EORSI, "The Adaptation of Civil Liability to Modern Needs," *Review of Contemporary Law*, 10:11–24 (1963); and BERNHARD RUDDEN, "Soviet Tort Law," *New York University Law Review*, 42:583–630 (1967). Modern trends relating to the protection of traffic victims are reflected in ALFRED F. CONARD *et al.*, *Automobile Accidents Costs and Payments* (1964); LEON GREEN, *Traffic Victims: Tort Law and Insurance* (1958); and TERENCE G. ISON, *The Forensic Lottery: A Critique on Tort Liability As a System of Personal Injury Compensation* (1967).

(A.F.A.H.)

Totemism

Totemism is a system of belief in which man is believed to have kinship with a totem or a mystical relationship is said to exist between a group or an individual and a totem. A totem is an object, such as an animal or plant that serves as the emblem or symbol of a kinship group or a person. The term totemism has been used to characterize a cluster of traits in the religion and in the social organization of many primitive peoples.

Totemism is manifested in various forms and types in different contexts, especially among populations with a mixed economy (farming and hunting) and among hunting communities (especially in Australia); it is also found among tribes who breed cattle. Totemism can in no way be viewed as a general stage in man's cultural development; but totemism has certainly had an effect on the psychological behaviour of ethnic groups, on the manner of their socialization, and on the formation of the human personality.

Origin of the term totem

The term totem is derived from *ototeman* from the language of the Algonkian tribe of the Ojibwa (in the area of the Great Lakes in eastern North America); it originally meant "his brother–sister kin." The grammatical root, *ote*, signifies a blood relationship between brothers and sisters who have the same mother and who may not marry each other. In English, the word totem was introduced in 1791 by a British merchant and translator who gave it a false meaning in the belief that it designated the guardian spirit of an individual, who appeared in the form of an animal—an idea which the Ojibwa clans do indeed portray by their wearing of animal skins. It was reported at the end of the 18th century that the Ojibwa name their clans after those animals that live in the area in which they live and appear to be either friendly or fearful. The first accurate report about totemism in North America was written by a Methodist missionary, Peter Jones, himself an Ojibwa chief, who died in 1856 and whose report was published posthumously. According to Jones, the Great Spirit had given *toodaims* ("totems") to their clans; and because of this act, it should never be forgotten that members of the group are related to one another and on this account may not marry among themselves.

Generally speaking, totemistic forms are based on the psychomental habits of the so-called primitives, on a distinctive "thought style" which is characterized, above all, by an "anthropopsychic" apprehension of nature and natural beings, for instance, ascribing to them a soul like man's. Beasts and the things of nature are again and again thought of as "persons," but mostly as persons with superhuman qualities.

THE NATURE OF TOTEMISM

It is advisable to define totemism as broadly as possible but concretely enough so that some justice can be done to its many forms. Totemism is, then, a complex of varied ideas and ways of behaviour based on a world view drawn from nature. There are ideological, mystical, emotional, reverential, and genealogical relationships of social groups or specific persons with animals or natural objects, the so-called totems. It is necessary to differentiate between group and individual totemism. These forms exhibit common basic characteristics, which occur with different emphases and not always in a complete form. The general characteristics are essentially the following: (1) viewing the totem as a companion, relative, protector, progenitor, or helper—superhuman powers and abilities are ascribed to totems and totems are not only offered respect or occasional veneration but also can become objects of awe and fear; (2) use of special names and emblems to refer to the totem; (3) partial identification with the totem or symbolic assimilation to it; (4) prohibition against killing, eating, or touching the totem, even as a rule to shun it; and (5) totemistic rituals.

General characteristics

Though it is generally agreed that totemism is not a religion, in certain cases it can contain religious elements in varying degrees, just as totemism can appear conjoined with magic. Totemism is frequently mixed with different kinds of other beliefs—the cult of ancestors, ideas of the soul, beliefs in powers and the spirits. Such mixtures make the understanding of particular totemistic forms difficult. The cultic veneration of definite animals and natural things and powers by all those who belong to an ethnic unit do not belong to totemism itself.

Group totemism. Group (social or collective) totemism is the most widely disseminated form of totemism. Though the following characteristics can belong to it, they must not be taken to be part of a whole system: (1) mystic association of animal and plant species, natural phenomena, or created objects with unilineally related groups (lineages, clans, tribes, moieties, phratries) or with local groups and families; (2) hereditary transmission of the totems (patrilineal or matrilineal); (3) names of groups that can be based either directly or indirectly on the totem (the same holds true for personal names used within groups); (4) totemistic emblems, symbols, and taboo formulas are, as a rule, a concern of the entire group, but they can also belong to subdivisions of that group. Taboos and prohibitions can apply to the species itself or they can be limited to parts of animals and plants (partial taboos instead of partial totems). (5) Totems for groups are sometimes connected with a large number of animals and natural objects (multiplex totems) whereby a distinction can be made between principal totems and subsidiary ones (linked totems). Totems are associated or coordinated on the basis of analogies or on the basis of myth or ritual. (Just why particular animals or natural things—which sometimes possess absolutely no recognizable worth for the communities concerned—were selected as totems is often hard to fathom and may be based on eventful and decisive moments in a people's past which are no longer known.) (6) Accounts of the nature of totems and the origin of the societies in question are informative, even if they are sometimes valuable only as supplementary rationalizations; they are especially informative with regard to their presuppositions. If, for example, one group supposes that it is derived directly or indirectly from the totem, this may be recounted (as a rationalization) that an animal progenitor was changed into a human being who then became the founder of the group or that the ancestral lord of the group was descended from a conjugal union between a man and a representative of the animal species. Groups of men and species of animals and plants can also have progenitors in common. In other cases, there are traditions that the human progenitor of a kin group had certain favourable or unfavourable experiences with an

Characteristics of group totemism

animal or natural object and then ordered that his descendants had to respect the whole species of that animal.

Group totemism is now found especially among peoples in Africa, India, Oceania (especially in Melanesia), North America, and parts of South America who farm rather than simply gather food from nature. Peoples with hunting and partly harvesting economies who exhibit this form of totemism include, among others, the Australian Aborigines (hunters who occupy a special position due to the many forms of totemism among them), the African Pygmies, and various tribes of North America—such as those on the northwest coast (predominantly fishermen), in parts of California, and in northeast North America. Moreover, group totemism is represented in a distinctive form among the Ugrians and west Siberians (hunters and fishermen who also breed reindeer) as well as among tribes of herdsmen in north and Central Asia.

Individual totemism. Individual totemism is expressed in an intimate relationship of friendship and protection between a person and a particular animal or a natural object (sometimes between a person and a species of animals); the natural object can grant special power to its owner. Frequently connected with individual totemism are definite ideas about the human soul (or souls) and conceptions derived from them, such as the idea of an al-

Nagualism

ter ego and nagualism—from the Spanish form of the Aztec word *naualli*, "something hidden or veiled"—which means that a kind of simultaneous existence is assumed between an animal or a natural object and a person; *i.e.*, a mutual, close bond of life and fate exist in such a way that in case of the injury, sickness, or death of one partner, the same fate would befall the other member of the relationship. Consequently, such totems became most strongly tabooed; above all, they were connected with family or group leaders, chiefs, medicine men, shamans, and other socially significant persons. In shamanism, an earlier trait of individual totemism is often ascertained: the animalistic protective spirits can sometimes be derived from individual totems. To some extent, there also exists a tendency to pass on an individual totem as hereditary or to make taboo the entire species of animal to which the individual totem belongs. In this can perhaps be seen the beginning of the development of totems that belong to a group. Many tales about the origins of the group totem could, perhaps, point in this direction.

Individual totemism is widely disseminated. It is found not only among the tribes of hunters and harvesters but also among farmers and herdsmen. Individual totemism is especially emphasized among the Australian Aborigines.

SOME EXAMPLES OF TOTEMISM

Wiradjuri. (New South Wales, Australia) Totem clans are divided among two subgroups and corresponding matrilineal moieties. The group totem, named "flesh," is transmitted from the mother. In contrast to this,

Individual totems

individual totems belong only to the medicine men and are passed on patrilineally. Such an individual totem is named *bala*, "spirit companion," or *jarawaijewa*, "the meat (totem) that is within him." There is a strict prohibition against eating the totem. Breach of the taboo carries with it sickness or death. It is said: "To eat your *jarawaijewa* is the same as if you were to eat your very own flesh or that of your father." The medicine man identifies himself with his personal totem. Every offense or injury against the totem has its automatic effect upon the man who commits it. It is a duty of the totem to guard the ritualist and the medicine man while he is asleep. In the case of danger or the arrival of strangers, the animal goes back into the body of the medicine man and informs him. After the death of the medicine man, the animal stands watch as a bright flickering light near the grave. The individual totem is also a helper of the medicine man. The medicine man emits the totem in his sleep or in a trance so that it can collect information for him. Finally, black magic (sorcery) is also practiced by the medicine man; by singing, for instance, the medicine man sends out his totem. To kill an enemy, the totem enters the chest of the enemy and devours his viscera. The transmission of the individual totem to novices is done through the father or the grandfather who, of course, himself is also a medicine man. While the candidate lies on his back, the totem is "sung into" him. The blood relative who is transmitting the totem takes a small animal and places it on the chest of the youngster. During the singing, the animal supposedly sinks slowly into his body and finally disappears into it. The candidate is then instructed on how he has to treat the animal that is his comrade, and he is further instructed in song and the ritual concentration that is necessary to dispatch the totem from his body.

By courtesy of the Australian News and Information Bureau, New York

Australian Aborigines dancing a corroboree. In dancing a corroboree the Australian natives imitate birds, animals, fish, and men, and also the movements of storms and floods.

Nor-Papua. (Murik Lakes, west of the mouth of the Sepik River, north New Guinea) Patrilineal, exogamous groups (consanguineous sibs) are spread over several villages and are associated with animals, especially fish. They believe that they are born from totems and they make them taboo. Children are able to decide during their initiation whether they will respect the paternal or maternal totem. Each group of relatives has a holy place to which the totem animal brings the souls of the dead and from which the souls of children also come. Totem animals are represented as spirit creatures in sacred flutes, in disguises, and in figures preserved in each man's house. At the end of initiation ceremonies, the totems are mimicked by the members of the group.

Iban. (Sungai Dayak, Sarawak, Malaysia) Among these peoples, individual totemism is clearly discernible. Particular persons dream of a spirit of an ancestor or a dead relative; this spirit appears in a human form, presents himself as a helper and protector, and names an animal (sometimes one of the natural objects) in which he is manifested. The Iban then observe the mannerisms of animals and recognize in the behaviour of the animals the embodiment of their protector spirit (*ngarong*). Sometimes, members of the tribe also carry with them a part of such an animal. Not only the particular animal, but the whole species of the animal is given due respect. Meals and blood offerings are also presented to the spirit animal. Young men, who wish to obtain such a protector spirit for themselves, sleep on the graves of prominent persons or seek out solitude and fast so that they may dream of a helper spirit. Actually, only a few persons can name such animals as their very own. Individuals with protector spirits have also attempted to require from their descendants the respect and the taboo given the animal representing the spirit. As a rule, such descendants do not expect special help from the protector spirit, but they observe the totemistic regulations anyway. Thus it can be concluded that particular families or groups of relatives of the Iban represent totem communities.

Birhor. (Munda-speaking hunter and harvester tribe that resides in the jungle of Chotanāgpur Plateau, northeast Deccan, India) The Birhor are organized into patrilineal, exogamous totem groups. According to one imperfect list of 37 clans, 12 are based on animals, ten on plants, eight on Hindu castes and localities, and the rest on objects. The totems are passed on within the group, but no account of their origin is available. From tales about the tribe's origins, it appears that the totem had a fortuitous connection with the birth of the ancestor of the clan. The Birhor think that there is a temperamental or physical similarity between the members of the clan and their totems. Prohibitions with regard to taboo are sometimes cultivated to an extreme degree. In regard to eating, killing, or destroying them, the clan totems are regarded as if they were human members of the group. Moreover, it is believed that an offense against the totems through a breach of taboo will produce a corresponding decrease in the size of the clan. If a person comes upon a dead totem animal, he must smear his forehead with oil or a red dye, but he must not actually mourn over it; he also does not bury it. The close and vital relationship between the totem and the clan is shown in a definite ceremony: the yearly offering to the chief spirit of the ancestral hill. Each Birhor has a tradition of an old settlement—thought to be located on a hill in the area. Once a year, the men of each clan come together at an open place. The elder of the clan functions as the priest who gives the offering. A diagram with four sections is drawn on the ground with rice flour. In one of these, the elder sits while gazing in the direction of the ancestral hill. The emblem of the particular totem is placed in one of the other places of the diagram; depending on the circumstances, this emblem could be a flower, a piece of horn or skin, a wing, or a twig. This emblem represents the clan as a whole. If an animal is needed for such a ceremony, it is provided by the members of another clan who do not hold it as a totem. The Birhor show great fear of the spirits of the ancestral hill and avoid these places as far as possible.

Kpelle. (Liberia, West Africa) In this society, there is not only group totemism but individual totemism as well. Both categories have the same designations, namely, "thing of possession," "thing of birth," "thing of the back of men." These phrases express the idea that the totem always accompanies man, belongs to him, and stands behind him as a guide and warner of dangers. The totem also punishes the breach of any taboo. The totems are animals, plants, and natural phenomena. The kin groups that live in several villages were matrilineal at an earlier time, but they are beginning to exhibit patrilineal tendencies. The group totems, especially the animal totems, are considered as the residence of the ancestors; they are respected and are given offerings. Moreover, a great role is played by individual totems that, in addition to being taboo, are also given offerings. Animal personal totems can be transmitted from father to son or from mother to daughter; on the other hand, individual plant totems are assigned at birth (plants of a tree of life for the child) or later. The totem also communicates magical powers. It is even believed possible to alter one's own totem animal; further, it is considered an alter ego. Persons with the same individual totem prefer to be united in communities. The well-known leopard confederation, a secret association, seems to have grown out of such desires. Entirely different groups produce patrilineal taboo communities which are supposedly related by blood; they comprise persons of several tribes. The animals, plants, and actions made taboo by these groups are not considered as totems. In a certain respect, the individual totems in this community seem to be the basis of group totemism.

A SHORT HISTORY OF TOTEMISTIC THEORY

From McLennan to Levi-Strauss. There are a number of theories or hypotheses concerning totemism. Many of them are marked by methodological deficiencies, preconceived ideas, and a prejudiced selection of source documents; nevertheless, some of these theories contain points of view that deserve consideration.

The first theory was proposed by the Scottish ethnologist John Ferguson McLennan. Following the vogue of 19th-century research, he wanted to comprehend totemism in a broad perspective, and in his study "The Worship of Animals and Plants" (1869, 1870) he did not seek to explain the specific origin of the totemistic phenomenon but sought to indicate that all of the human race had in ancient times gone through a totemistic stage.

In 1899 McLennan's theories were criticized by E.B. Tylor, an English anthropologist who rejected the confusion of totemism with mere worship of animals and plants. Tylor claimed to find in totemism the tendency of the human spirit to classify the world and its things. He thus viewed totemism as a relationship between one type of animal and a clan. But he was opposed to the idea of seeing totems as the basis of religion.

Views of
E.B. Tylor,
Andrew
Lang, and
James G.
Frazer

Another Scottish scholar, Andrew Lang, early in the 20th century advocated a nominalistic meaning for totemism, namely that local groups, clans, or phratries, in selecting totem names from the realm of nature, were reacting to a need to be differentiated. If the origin of the names was forgotten, there followed a mystical relationship between the objects—from which the names were once derived—and the groups that bore these names. Lang wanted to explain the relationship through nature myths according to which animals and natural objects were considered as the relatives, patrons, or ancestors of the respective social units. Thoughts by the tribes on these matters led eventually to taboos. Group exogamy first originated in the formation of totemistic associations.

The first comprehensive work on totemism was *Totemism and Exogamy*, published in 1910 in four volumes by the British anthropologist Sir James George Frazer. It presented a meritorious compilation of the then known worldwide data on the subject.

Basing his view on research done among primitives in Australia and Melanesia, Frazer saw the origin of totemism as one possibility in the primitive interpretation of the conception and birth of children ("conceptionalism"). According to this primitive idea, women become impregnated when a spirit of an animal or a spiritual fruit enters into their wombs. Since the children therefore participate in the nature of the animal or plant, these plants or animals take on significance. These ideas were hereditary and resulted in the beginning of totem clans derived from a particular natural creature.

A Russian–American ethnologist, Alexander Goldenweiser, subjected totemistic phenomena to sharp criticism. This critical work had lasting importance, especially in the United States, where it engendered a skeptical attitude concerning totemism. Goldenweiser saw in totemism three phenomena that could exist singly and actually coincided only in the rarest of cases. These phenomena were: (1) clan organization; (2) clans taking animal or plant names or having "emblems" obtained from nature; and (3) belief in a relationship between groups and their totems. Goldenweiser did not perceive these phenomena as a unity, since any of them could exist apart from the others.

In another treatise published in 1910, a German ethnologist, Richard Thurnwald, claimed to recognize in totemism the expression of a specific way of thinking among the primitives. Primitives judge the natural environment according to its external appearance without analyzing it any closer and assume that there are sympathetic connections and combinations of natural things; from these ideas come lasting rules of behaviour (like taboos, respect, and social relationships). For the psychology of totemism, Thurnwald later (1917–18) put forth a detailed, systematic presentation; by means of concrete examples, he also raised questions about the connections of totemism with ancestor worship, notions of souls, belief in power, magic, offerings, and oracles.

The founder of a French school of sociology, Émile Durkheim, in a general work concerning the elementary forms of religion (1912), also examined totemism from a sociological and theological point of view. Durkheim hoped to discover a pure religion in very ancient forms and generally claimed to see the origin of religion in totemism. For Durkheim, the sphere of the sacred is a reflection of the emotions that underlie social activities, and the totem was, in this view, a reflection of the group (or clan) consciousness, based on the conception of an impersonal power. The totemistic principle was then the clan itself, and it was permeated with sanctity. Such a religion reflects the collective consciousness that is manifested through the identification of the individuals of the group with an animal or plant species; it is expressed outwardly in taboos, symbols, and rituals that are based on this identification.

In further contributions, Goldenweiser in 1915–16 and 1918 criticized Lang, Frazer, and Durkheim and insisted that totemism had nothing to do with religion; that man in no way viewed his totem as superior to himself or as a deified being but viewed it as his friend and equal. Goldenweiser also rejected Frazer's thesis of "conceptionalism" as an explanation of totemism. On the other hand, Goldenweiser was of the opinion that all totemistic manifestations do have at least something of a kind of religion, but he was not inclined to include the guardian spirit conception within totemism.

In 1916, an American ethnologist, Franz Boas, posited a theory of totemism as an "artificial" unity, existing only in the thinking of ethnologists. For Boas, totemism exhibited no single psychological or historical origin; since totemistic features can be connected with individuals and all possible social organizations, and they appear in different cultural contexts, it would be impossible to fit totemistic phenomena into a single category. Boas was against systematizing and thought it senseless to ask questions about the origins of totemism.

The first theoretician of the Vienna school of Ethnology, Fritz Graebner, attempted to explain the forms of both individual totemism and group totemism and designated them as a moderately creedal or semireligious complex of ideas according to which individual members or subgroups of a society are thought to be in an especially close (but not cultic) relationship to natural objects. According to Graebner, with the help of the cultural–historical method, one can establish (1) the extent to which totemistic forms belong to one definite cultural complex, (2) which forms are "older" or "younger," and (3) the extent to which forms belong together genetically. Graebner tried to work out a "totemistic" complex (a "culture circle") for the South Seas. This complex entailed a patrilineal group totemism as well as the material, economic, and religious elements that, in his opinion, appear to be combined with the totemism in that area.

Another member of the same school, Bernhard Ankermann, in 1915–16 championed the view that all totemisms, regardless of where they are found, contained a common kernel around which new characteristics are built. As seen from the standpoint of what was found in Africa, this kernel appeared to him to be the belief in a specific relationship between social groups and natural things—in a feeling of unity between both—a relationship he believed to be spread throughout the world, even if only in a modified or diminished form. Magical and animalistic ideas and rites are merged with totemism in a strong inseparable unity. The genesis of this type of relationship presupposes a state of mind that makes no distinction between man and beast. Although magic can be closely connected with totemism, the feeling of unity between man and beast has nothing to do with magic, which was connected with it only later. According to Ankermann, the totems are not something perilous, something to be shunned, but, on the contrary, totems are something friendly; and since this is directly due to kinship, a totem is thought to be like a brother and is to be treated as such. The totemistic taboo is believed to be due to the fact that the totem is a relative. Ankermann was inclined to see the formation of totemism in a "lower" form of hunting, in an emotional animal–man relationship, in animalistic behaviour. Men of early times, he thought, might have imitated those animals that attracted their attention most of all. According to Ankermann, pretension and reality, however, for the "primitives" are blurred into one thing. Primitive man identifies himself with the animal while he is imitating it; the habit of so doing could lead to a continuing identification. Early man imitated all animals that interested him, but he imitated those that shared his place of habitation above all.

In 1915–16 Wilhelm Schmidt, then the leader of the Vienna school of Ethnology, viewed totemism strictly according to the then-existing schemes of culture circles (today long abandoned); because totemism was disseminated throughout the world, he thought of it as a closed cultural complex in spite of local differences. He maintained that the differences in totemism shown by earlier theories are exaggerated and could, moreover, be due to the lack of particular elements of totemism, to the loss of certain forms of totemism, to incursions from the outside, or to different stages of the development of totemism, none of which would exclude a unified origin for all of totemism. Schmidt believed that the cultural–historical school of ethnology had produced proof that the older, genuine totemism occurred as an integral part of a culture located in a definite area and that it was "organically" connected with definite forms of technology, economy, art, and world view. From a "pure" totemism, Schmidt wanted to separate similar forms, such as sex and individual totemism. Moreover, though he did not designate totemism as a religion, he saw that it did have some sort of religious meaning. Schmidt (in opposition to Ankermann) wanted to regard the higher form of hunting as the economic basis for the totemistic "culture circle."

The leading representative of British social anthropology, A.R. Radcliffe-Brown, took a totally different view on the totemistic problem. Like Boas, he was skeptical of the reality of totemism. In this he opposed the other pioneer of social anthropology in England, Bronisław Malinowski, who wanted to admit the reality of totemism in some way and looked at it more from a biological and psychological point of view than from an ethnological one. According to Malinowski, totemism was not a cultural phenomenon but was the result of trying to satisfy basic human needs within the natural world. As far as Radcliffe-Brown was concerned, totemism was composed of elements that were taken from different areas and institutions, and what they have in common is a general tendency to characterize segments of the community through a connection with a portion of nature. In opposition to Durkheim's theory of sacralization, Radcliffe-Brown took the point of view that nature is introduced into the social order rather than secondary to it. At first, he shared with Malinowski the opinion that an animal becomes totemistic when it is "good to eat." He later came to oppose the usefulness of this viewpoint since many totems—such as crocodiles and flies—are dangerous and unpleasant.

In 1952, when Radcliffe-Brown rethought the problem, he found that the similarities and differences between species of animals are to a certain degree translated into ideas of friendship and conflict, or close relationships and opposition among people. The natural world is represented in the form of social relationships to the extent that these social relationships become valid in primitive societies. The structural principle which Radcliffe-Brown believed he had discovered at the end of his comparative study is based on the fusion of the two contrary ideas of friendship and animosity. Thus totemism speaks in its own way of interrelationships and antitheses, ideas that are also found in moieties. So totemism is formulated as a general problem in which the contrasts in nature serve to create an integral whole. Thinking in terms of opposing things is, according to Radcliffe-Brown, an essential structural principle for evaluating totemism.

The most incisive critique of totemistic phenomena, one that denied the reality of totemism, was supplied by the French ethnologist Claude Lévi-Strauss in *Le Totémisme aujourd'hui* (English translation, *Totemism*, 1963). As a chief representative of modern structuralism, Lévi-Strauss was especially stimulated by Radcliffe-Brown, whose views he further attempted to expand. Lévi-Strauss believed that he was to approach the apparent, acknowledged difficulties in the study of totemism from the viewpoint of a study of structure. In order to study the structure of totemism, Lévi-Strauss devised a scheme to illustrate the abstract polarities that he saw in totemism as a phenomenon in human culture. This scheme was implemented in a table of oppositions or polarities, or mutual relationships. The basic opposition, or relationship, was between nature and culture. On the one hand, there were in nature certain natural realities such as species of animals or plants and specific animals or plants. On the other hand, there were in culture various groups and individuals who identified themselves with particular species or with specific animals or plants. Lévi-Strauss distinguished four kinds of opposition, or relationship, between nature and culture within totemism: (1) a species of animal or plant identified with a particular group, (2) a species of animal or plant identified with an individual, (3) a particular animal or plant identified with an individual, and (4) a particular animal or plant identified with a group.

According to Lévi-Strauss, each of these four combinations corresponds to the phenomena that are to be observed in one people or another. The first antithesis holds good, for example, for the Australians, for whom natural things are associated with cultural groups (moieties, sections, subsections, phratries, clans, or the association of persons from the same sex). As an example of the second combination, there is the individual totemism of North American Indians, in which a person is correlated with a species of nature. For the third type of combination, Mota in the Banks Islands of Melanesia is cited: the individual child is thought of as the incarnation of a particular animal, plant, or natural creature that was found and consumed by the mother at the time that she was conscious of her pregnancy. For the fourth type of correlation, Lévi-Strauss cited examples from Polynesia and Africa where definite individual animals formed the object of group patronage and veneration.

Lévi-Strauss also critiqued the findings of A.P. Elkin, a specialist on Australia, where totemism had already played a special role in the formation of theories and where it exhibits an abundance of forms for expressing totemism. Elkin had differentiated the following forms: (1) individual totemism; (2) social totemism—i.e., totemism that is in a family, moiety, section, subsection, patrilineal clan, or matrilineal clan; (3) cultic totemism with a religious content that is patrilineal and "conceptional" in form; (4) dream totemism—totemistic content in dreams—found in social or individual totemism. Elkin denied the unity of totemism, but (according to Lévi-Strauss) wanted to preserve its reality on the condition that he might trace it back to a multiplicity of types. For Elkin, there is no longer "one" totemism but many totemisms, each in itself a single irreducible whole.

In connection with the Australian material, Lévi-Strauss argued that matrilineal clan totemism—that passed on the "flesh" or "blood"—and the patrilineal clan totemism—based on dreaming—were in no way heterogeneous but were to be thought of as being mutually complementary. They were different means of connecting the material and spiritual world; they were two different, but correlative, types that express the relationship between nature and society.

Lévi-Strauss concluded that not the similarities but the dissimilarities correspond to the so-called totemism. Such a pattern was clearly expressed in the basic model of the contrasts of the natural with the cultural (that were outlined above). Depending on the ideas of Radcliffe-Brown, Lévi-Strauss claimed to perceive antithetical thinking as a crucial structural principle in totemism and believed that the similarity among totemistic ideas in various cultures lay in similarities between both systems of differences—those documented in the natural sphere and those in the culturally defined social groups. Lévi-Strauss concluded that the distinction between the classes of man and animal serves as the conceptual basis for social differences. For Lévi-Strauss, totemism is therefore an "illusion" reduced to a form of thinking, and this so-called totemism is connected with understanding the demands that it answers as well as the way in which it seeks to satisfy those demands. Since it is a "logic that classifies," totemism in this sense has nothing of the ar-

chaic itself. Its picture is projected onto the material (the natural phenomena), not taken from it. It does not take its substance from without.

Present situation and emerging trends. From the publications of Lévi-Strauss and the contributions of his predecessors, it is obvious that difficulties stand in the way of an adequate interpretation of the intricate profusion of totemistic phenomena. But it seems fair to many authorities to ask whether it is possible to dispose of totemism simply as an illusion, whether the very abstract structural interpretation of the facts is actually legitimate. To those who question the position, it seems clear that even though all totemistic forms of expression can hardly be seen under one common denominator, reality cannot be totally denied to totemism. A specific relationship between man and nature, one that serves as a basic scheme of classification, seems to be at the basis of all the various forms of totemism. Indeed, this can be regarded as the prevailing characteristic of totemism in the form in which it manifests itself. A special problem, however, must be taken into consideration: since totemism can be connected with different ideas and practices, of religious, magical, or ideological natures, it is difficult to decide what is "totemistic" and what is "nontotemistic."

BIBLIOGRAPHY. FRANZ BOAS, "The Origin of Totemism," *Am. Anthrop.*, 18:319–326 (1916), contains a variety of ideas and objects defined as totemism, and thus maintains little unity; A.P. ELKIN, "Studies in Australian Totemism: The Nature of Australian Totemism," *Oceania*, 4:113–131 (1933–34); E.E. EVANS-PRITCHARD, "Nuer Totemism," *Annali Lateran.*, 13:225–248 (1949), describes the manifestations of totemism combined with the conception of the spirit in the "Nilot" tribe; J.V. FERREIRA, *Totemism in India* (1965), a critical evaluation of hitherto existing works on totemism in general and that of India in particular; R. FIRTH, "Totemism in Polynesia," *Oceania*, 1:291–321, 377–398 vol. 1 (1930–31), a useful survey article; J.L. FISCHER, "Totemism on Truk and Ponape," *Am. Anthrop.*, 59:250–265 (1957), describes and interprets the highly contrasting forms of totemism found in Micronesia, using not only the unusual sociological–ideological organization but also containing psychological aspects; G. FOSTER, "Nagualism in Mexico and Guatemala," *Acta Am.*, 2:85–103 (1944), deals with important borderline cases of totemism with particular regard to the problem of personal totemism; J.G. FRAZER, *Totemism and Exogamy*, 4 vol. (1910) and *Totemica: A Supplement to "Totemism and Exogamy"* (1937), comprehensive and informative reference works although the hypotheses are now out of date; A.A. GOLDENWEISER, "Totemism: An Analytic Study," *J. Am. Folklore*, 23:179–293 (1910); "Totemism," *Encyclopaedia of the Social Sciences*, vol. 14 (1934); J. HAEKEL, "Der heutige Stand des Totemismusproblems," *Mitt. Anthrop. Ges. Wien*, 82:33–49 (1952), attempts to give a critical examination with concrete examples of the question, complex in its various forms; CLAUDE LEVI-STRAUSS, *Le Totémisme aujourd'hui* (1962; Eng. trans., *Totemism*, 1963), contains a detailed critical evaluation of existing hypotheses of Anglo-American and French authors; R. PIDDINGTON, *An Introduction to Social Anthropology* 1:200–206 (1950), offers a short but sufficient characterization of the totemic phenomena, the difficulty in defining it, its great variability, and some concrete examples.

(Jo.H.)

Toulouse-Lautrec, Henri de

Henri de Toulouse-Lautrec exerted a great influence on French art of the late 19th and early 20th centuries by his use of new kinds of subjects, his ability to capture the essence of an individual with economical means, and his stylistic innovations. Although his legs were severely deformed following two accidents in his youth, and his body was later weakened by alcoholism and mental collapse, Toulouse-Lautrec nonetheless helped set the course of avant-garde art well beyond his early and tragic death at the age of 36.

Childhood and education. Henri-Marie-Raymond de Toulouse-Lautrec-Monfa was born November 24, 1864, at Albi. His family was wealthy and had a lineage that extended without interruption back to the time of Charlemagne. Toulouse-Lautrec grew up amid his family's typically aristocratic love of sport and art. Most of the boy's time was spent at the Château du Bosc, one of the family estates located near Albi. Henri's grandfather, fa-

"At the Moulin Rouge" (centre self-portrait and portrait of Dr. Tapié de Céleyran in the background), oil on canvas by Henri de Toulouse-Lautrec, 1892. In the Art Institute of Chicago. 1.21 × 1.41 m.
By courtesy of the Art Institute of Chicago

Crippling accident

ther, and uncle were all talented draftsmen, and thus it was hardly surprising that Henri began sketching at the age of ten. His interest in art grew as a result of his being incapacitated in 1878 by an accident in which he broke his left thighbone. His right thighbone was fractured a little over a year later in a second mishap. These accidents, requiring extensive periods of convalescence and often painful treatments, left his legs atrophied and made walking most difficult. As a result, Toulouse-Lautrec devoted ever greater periods to art in order to pass away the frequently lonely hours.

Toulouse-Lautrec's first visit to Paris occurred in 1872, when he enrolled in the Lycée Fontanes (now Lycée Condorcet). He gradually moved on to private tutors, and it was only after he had passed the baccalaureate examinations, in 1881, that he resolved to become an artist.

His first professional teacher in painting was René Princeteau, a friend of the Lautrec family. Princeteau's fame, such as it was, arose from his depiction of military and equestrian subjects, done in a 19th-century academic style. Though Toulouse-Lautrec got on well with Princeteau, he moved on to the atelier of Léon Bonnat at the end of 1882. In Bonnat, Toulouse-Lautrec encountered an artist who fought vehemently against deviation from academic rules, condemned the slapdash approach of the Impressionists, and judged Toulouse-Lautrec's drawing "atrocious." His work received a more positive reaction in 1883, when he joined the studio of Fernand Cormon.

Work in Cormon's studio

In the early 1880s, Cormon enjoyed a moment of celebrity, and his studio attracted such artists as Vincent van Gogh and the Symbolist painter Émile Bernard. Cormon gave Toulouse-Lautrec much freedom in developing a personal syle. That Cormon approved of his pupil's work is proved by his choosing Toulouse-Lautrec to assist him in illustrating the definitive edition of the works of Victor Hugo. In the end, however, Toulouse-Lautrec's drawings for this project were not used.

Despite this approval, Toulouse-Lautrec found the atmosphere at Cormon's studio increasingly restrictive. "Cormon's corrections are much kinder than Bonnat's were," he wrote his uncle Charles on February 18, 1883. "He looks at everything you show him and encourages one steadily. It might surprise you, but I don't like that so

much. You see, the lashing of my former master pepped me up, and I didn't spare myself." The academic regimen of copying became insufferable. He made "a great effort to copy the model exactly," one of his friends later recalled, "but in spite of himself he exaggerated certain details, sometimes the general character, so that he distorted without trying or even wanting to." Soon Toulouse-Lautrec's attendance at the studio became infrequent at best. He then rented his own studio in the Montmartre district of Paris and concerned himself, for the most part, with doing portraits of his friends.

The documentor of Montmartre. Thus it was that in the mid-1880s Toulouse-Lautrec began his lifelong association with the bohemian life of Montmartre. The cafés, cabarets, entertainers, and artists of this area of Paris fascinated him and led to his first taste of public recognition. He focussed his attention on depicting popular entertainers such as Aristide Bruant, Jane Avril, Loie Fuller, May Belfort, May Milton, Valentin le Désossé, Louise Weber (known as La Goulue, or the Glutton), and clowns such as Cha-U-Kao and Chocolat.

In 1884 Toulouse-Lautrec made the acquaintance of Bruant, a singer and composer who owned a cabaret called the Mirliton. Impressed by his work, Bruant asked him to prepare illustrations for his songs and offered the Mirliton as a place where Toulouse-Lautrec could exhibit his works. By this means and through reproductions of his drawings in Bruant's magazine *Mirliton*, he became known in Montmartre and started to receive commissions.

Toulouse-Lautrec sought to capture the effect of the movement of the figure through wholly original means. For example, his contemporary Edgar Degas (whose works, along with Japanese prints, were a principal influence on him) expressed movement by carefully rendering the anatomical structure of several closely grouped figures, attempting in this way to depict but one figure, caught at successive moments in time. Toulouse-Lautrec, on the other hand, employed freely handled line and colour that in themselves conveyed the idea of movement. Lines were no longer bound to what was anatomically correct; colours were intense and in their juxtapositions generated a pulsating rhythm; laws of perspective were violated in order to place figures in an active,

Artistic originality

unstable relationship with their surroundings. A common device of Toulouse-Lautrec was to compose the figures so that their legs were not visible. Though this characteristic has been interpreted as the artist's reaction to his own stunted, almost worthless legs, in fact the treatment eliminated specific movement, which could then be replaced by the essence of movement. The result was an art throbbing with life and energy, that in its formal abstraction and overall two-dimensionality presaged the turn to schools of Fauvism and Cubism in the first decade of the 20th century.

The originality of Toulouse-Lautrec also emerged in his posters. Rejecting the notion of high art, done in the traditional medium of oil on canvas, Toulouse-Lautrec in 1891 did his first poster, "Moulin Rouge—La Goulue." This poster won Toulouse-Lautrec increasing fame. "My poster is pasted today on the walls of Paris," the artist proudly declared. It was one of more than 30 he would create in the 10 years before his death. Posters afforded Toulouse-Lautrec the possibility of a widespread impact for his art, no longer restricted by the limitations of easel painting; and they enhanced the success he had enjoyed in the preceding year when his works were shown in Brussels at the Exposition des XX (the Twenty), an avant-garde association, and in Paris at the Salon des Indépendants.

Toulouse-Lautrec is most important for his success in going beyond a representation of superficial reality to a profound insight into the psychological makeup of his subjects. He turned to the lithograph after 1892 as a medium well suited to this goal. Among more than 300 lithographs produced in the final decade of his life were an album of 11 prints entitled "Le Café Concert" (1893); 16 lithographs of the entertainer Yvette Guilbert (1894); and a series of 22 illustrations for Jules Renard's *Les Histoires naturelles* (1899). But none of these works is more significant than "Elles," a series done in 1896, presenting a sensitive portrayal of brothel life. Toulouse-Lautrec spent lengthy periods observing the actions and behaviour of prostitutes and their clients. The resulting 11 works revealed these individuals as human beings, with some of the same strengths and many of the weaknesses of other members of society. A masterpiece of this genre is "Au Salon de la rue des Moulins" ("At the Salon"). This painting evokes sympathy from the spectator as he observes the women's isolation and loneliness, qualities which the young Toulouse-Lautrec had so often experienced himself. "At the Salon" is a brilliant demonstration, therefore, of his stated desire to "depict the true and not the ideal," in which truth is based not on a careful representation of detail but rather on capturing, in a few brief brushstrokes, the essential nature of a subject.

Physical and mental decline

The appearance of "Elles" coincided with a growing deterioration in his physical and mental condition. Toulouse-Lautrec's figure, even among the great human diversity found in Montmartre, remained unmistakable. His fully developed torso rested on dwarfish legs. Not quite five feet one inch tall, his size seemed further diminished because of his practice of associating with unusually tall men, such as his fellow students Maxime Dethomas and Louis Anquetin and his cousin and close friend Gabriel Tapié de Céleyran. His frequently ironic tone failed to mask a fundamental dislike of his physical appearance, and his letters contain many derogatory remarks about his body and references to an increasing number of ailments, including syphilis. Drinking heavily in the late 1890s, when he reputedly helped popularize the cocktail, he suffered a mental collapse at the beginning of 1899. The immediate cause was the sudden, unexplained departure of his mother from Paris on January 3. He was always close to his family, particularly to his mother, who had always supported his ambitions; and he interpreted her leaving as a betrayal. The effect on his weakened system was severe, and he was committed shortly thereafter to a sanatorium in Neuilly-sur-Seine. This decision was made by the artist's mother, against the advice of relatives and friends of the artist, in the hope of avoiding a scandal.

Toulouse-Lautrec remained formally committed until March 31, 1899, though he chose to stay on at the sanatorium until mid-May. While there he was able to demonstrate his lucidity and power of memory by preparing a number of works on the theme of the circus. These works, however, lack the force and intensity of his earlier compositions. In the spring of 1900 he started drinking heavily again. On September 9, 1901, less than three months before his 37th birthday, he died at Château de Malromé.

Assessment. Toulouse-Lautrec was not a profound intellectual. Tapié de Céleyran wrote that he read little and when he did it was usually at night, because of insomnia. But he was a great satirist of pretense and convention. In typical fashion, he passed off his initial, unsuccessful attempt at the baccalaureate by having name cards printed "Henri de Toulouse-Lautrec, flunker of the arts." This iconoclasm surfaced also when he parodied Puvis de Chavannes' serious Symbolist work "The Sacred Grove" by turning it into a boisterous scene filled with rowdy friends (1884; Henry Pearlman Collection, New York City). Yet he also could push himself in pursuits like swimming and boating, and toward the end of his life he installed a rowing machine in his studio. In his enthusiasm for sports he once accompanied a French bicycling team on a trip through England. Toulouse-Lautrec was, as two observers have concluded, a "sensitive, deeply affectionate man, conscious of his infirmity but wearing a mask of joviality and irony."

Although recognized today as a major figure in late-19th-century art, Toulouse-Lautrec's status in his lifetime was disputed. Indeed, the artist's father, who took slight interest in his son after his disabling injuries, regarded his son's work as only "rough sketches" and could never accept the idea of a member of the aristocracy betraying his class by turning from a "gentleman" artist to a professional one. Stung by such criticism and hampered by his infirmities, Toulouse-Lautrec persevered to emerge as a prolific artist whose work would help shape the art of decades to come.

MAJOR WORKS

PAINTINGS: "Mme la Comtesse A. de Toulouse-Lautrec" (c. 1881–82; Musée Toulouse-Lautrec, Albi); "Au Salon de la Rue des Moulins" ("At the Salon," 1894; Musée Toulouse-Lautrec); "Portrait of Mrs. Suzanne V." (1885; Ny Carlsberg Glyptotek, Copenhagen); "Mme la Comtesse A. de Toulouse-Lautrec, mère de l'artiste" (1887; Musée Toulouse-Lautrec); "Girl in the Artist's Studio" (1888; Kunsthalle Bremen); "In Batignolles" (1888; Tate Gallery, London); "In the Circus Fernando: The Ringmaster" (1888; Art Institute of Chicago); "Monsieur Samary, de la Comédie-Française" (1889; private collection, Paris); "At the Nouveau Cirque: Five Stuffed Shirts" (1891; Philadelphia Museum of Art); "À la mie" (1891; Museum of Fine Arts, Boston); "At the Moulin de la Galette" (1891; Stedelijk Museum, Amsterdam); "La Goulue at the Moulin Rouge" (1891–92; Museum of Modern Art, New York); "At the Moulin Rouge" (1892; Art Institute of Chicago); "The Moulin Rouge" (1892; Národní Galerie, Prague); "Quadrille at the Moulin Rouge" (1892; National Gallery of Art, Washington, D.C.); "Jane Avril dansant" (1892; Louvre, Paris); "Jane Avril Leaving the Moulin Rouge" (1892; Wadsworth Atheneum, Hartford, Connecticut); "Portrait of L. Delaporte" (1893; Ny Carlsberg Glyptotek, Copenhagen); "Le Docteur Tapié de Céleyran dans un couloir de théâtre" (1894; Musée Toulouse-Lautrec); "Femme tirant son bas, ou femme de maison" (c. 1894; Louvre); "La Danse de la Goulue, ou les Almées" (1895; Louvre); "Women in a Brothel" (1895; Szépművészeti Múzeum, Budapest); "La Clownesse Cha-U-Kao" (1895; Louvre); "May Belfort" (1895; Cleveland Museum of Art); "Chilpéric" (1895–96; John Hay Whitney Collection, New York); "La Toilette" (1896; Louvre); "At the Bar" (1898; Kunsthaus, Zürich); "The Tête-à-Tête Supper" (1899; Courtauld Institute Galleries, London); "Aux courses" (1899; Musée Toulouse-Lautrec).

POSTERS: "Moulin Rouge—La Goulue" (1891); "Reine de joie" (1892); "Le Divan japonais" (1892); "Aristide Bruant dans son cabaret" (1893); "Confetti" (1894); "May Belfort" (1895).

BIBLIOGRAPHY. The definitive biographical study of Toulouse-Lautrec remains the French work by the artist's lifelong friend, MAURICE JOYANT, *Henri de Toulouse-Lautrec*, 2 vol. (1926–27, reprinted 1968). Other biographies of the artist, though often with romantic, exaggerated texts, are HANS TIETZE, *Toulouse-Lautrec* (1953); JACQUES LASSAIGNE, *Toulouse-Lautrec* (1939; Eng. trans., 1953); PHILIPPE HUISMAN and M.G. DORTU, *Lautrec par Lautrec* (Eng. trans. 1964); GERSTLE MACK, *Toulouse-Lautrec* (1938); LAWRENCE and ELIZABETH HANSON, *The Tragic Life of Toulouse-Lautrec* (1956); and EDOUARD JULIEN, *Lautrec* (Eng. trans. 1959). There is no catalogue raisonné. For valuable discussions of the artist's work, see the introduction by JEAN ADHEMAR and THEODORE REFF to LUCIEN GOLDSCHMIDT and HERBERT SCHIMMEL, *Unpublished Correspondence of Henri de Toulouse-Lautrec* (1969); DOUGLAS COOPER, *Henri de Toulouse-Lautrec* (1955); HANSPETER LANDOLT, *Henri de Toulouse-Lautrec: Drawings and Sketches in Colour* (1955); and L.F. JOHNSON, "Time and Motion in Toulouse-Lautrec," *College Art Journal*, 16:13–22 (1956).

(A.C.Bi.)

Toussaint-Louverture

An outstanding individual in black history, usually regarded as the greatest figure in the history of Haiti, François Dominique Toussaint began life as a slave. He became virtual dictator of the island of Hispaniola (now Haiti and the Dominican Republic) and displayed statesmanship, military and diplomatic genius, and an understanding of economics. His supreme goal was the termination of Negro slavery. He also stood for the reconciliation of whites, mulattoes, and blacks, for republican principles, for the adaptation of blacks to French culture, and for Haitian independence.

Toussaint was born on Bréda plantation near Cap Français (now Cap-Haïtien), capital of the French colony of Saint-Domingue (Haiti), probably in 1743. The son of an educated slave, he acquired through Jesuit contacts some knowledge of French, though he wrote and spoke it poorly, usually employing the Creole patois and African tribal language. Winning the favour of the plantation manager, he became a livestock handler, healer, coachman, and finally steward. Legally freed in 1777, he married a humble woman who bore him two sons. Toussaint was homely, short, and small framed. He was a fervent Catholic, opposed to voodoo. He dressed simply and was abstemious and a vegetarian. Although he slept little, his energy and capacity for work were astonishing. As a leader he inspired awe and adulation.

Participation in a slave revolt

A sudden slave revolt in the north province (August 1791) found him uncommitted. After hesitating a few weeks, he helped his former master escape and then joined the black forces who were burning plantations and killing many whites and mulattoes. He soon discerned the ineptitude of the rebel leaders and scorned their willingness to compromise with white radicals. Collecting an army of his own, Toussaint trained his followers in the tactics of guerrilla warfare. In 1793 he added the name of Louverture.

When France and Spain went to war in 1793, the black commanders joined the Spaniards of Santo Domingo, the eastern two-thirds of Hispaniola. Knighted and recognized as a general, Toussaint demonstrated extraordinary military ability and attracted such renowned warriors as his nephew Moïse and two future monarchs of Haiti, Jean-Jacques Dessalines and Henry Christophe. Toussaint's victories in the north, together with mulatto successes in the south and British occupation of the coasts, brought the French close to disaster. Yet, in May 1794, Toussaint went over to the French, giving as his reasons that the French National Convention had recently freed all slaves, while Spain and Britain refused, and that he had become a republican. He has been criticized for the duplicity of his dealings with his onetime allies and for a slaughter of Spaniards at a mass. His switch was decisive; the governor of Saint-Domingue, Etienne Laveaux, made Toussaint lieutenant governor, the British suffered severe reverses, and the Spaniards were expelled.

By 1795 Toussaint-Louverture was world famous. Adored by the blacks and appreciated by most whites and mulattoes, he did much to restore the economy. Defying French Revolutionary laws, he allowed many émigré planters to return, and he used military discipline to force the former slaves to work. Convinced that people were naturally corrupt, he felt that compulsion was needed to prevent idleness. Yet the labourers were no longer whipped: they were legally free and equal, and they shared the profits of the restored plantations. Racial tensions were eased because Toussaint preached reconciliation and believed that blacks, a majority of whom were African born, must learn from whites and Europeanized mulattoes.

Elimination of rivals

Though he worked well with Laveaux, Toussaint eased him out in 1796. Léger-Félicité Sonthonax, a terrorist French commissioner, also allowed Toussaint to rule and made him governor general. But the ascetic black general was repelled by the proposals of this white radical to exterminate the Europeans, and he was offended by Sonthonax's atheism, coarseness, and immorality. After some devious manoeuvres, Toussaint forced Sonthonax out in 1797.

Next to go were the British, whose losses caused them to negotiate secretly with Toussaint, notwithstanding the war with France. Treaties in 1798 and 1799 secured their complete withdrawal. Lucrative trade was begun with Britain and also with the United States. In return for arms and goods, Toussaint sold sugar and promised not to invade Jamaica and the American South. The British offered to recognize him as king of an independent Haiti; but, scornful of pompous titles, and distrustful of the British because they maintained slavery, he refused.

Toussaint soon rid himself of another nominal French superior, Gabriel Hédouville, who arrived in 1798 as representative of the Directory. Knowing that France had no chance of restoring colonialism as long as the war with England continued, Hédouville attempted to pit against Toussaint the mulatto leader André Rigaud, who ruled a semi-independent state in the south. Toussaint divined his purpose and forced Hédouville to flee. Succeeding Hédouville was Philippe Roume, who deferred to the black governor. Then a bloody campaign in 1799 eliminated another potential rival to Toussaint by driving Rigaud out and destroying his mulatto state. A purge that was carried out by Jean-Jacques Dessalines in the south was so brutal that reconciliation with the mulattoes was impossible.

Controlling all Saint-Domingue, Toussaint turned to Spanish Santo Domingo, where slavery persisted. Ignoring commands to the contrary by Roume and by Napoleon Bonaparte, who had become first consul of France, Toussaint overran it in January 1801, freed the slaves, and amazed the nonblacks with his magnanimity.

Command of Hispaniola

In command of the entire island, Toussaint dictated a constitution that made him governor general for life with near absolute powers. Catholicism was the state religion, and many revolutionary principles received ostensible sanction. There was no provision for a French official, however, because Toussaint professed himself a Frenchman and strove to convince Bonaparte of his loyalty. He also described his success in restoring order and prosperity in epistles that, like all his writings, were ungrammatical yet testify to the grasp, incisiveness, and depth of a formidable intellect.

Bonaparte had confirmed Toussaint-Louverture's position but saw him as an obstacle to the restoration of Saint-Domingue as a profitable colony. Toussaint knew Bonaparte despised Negroes and planned to reinstitute slavery; aware that Bonaparte would seek to intimidate the island upon making peace with England, he drilled a huge army and stored supplies. Yet Toussaint behaved ambiguously: venerating France, fearing Bonaparte, aging and growing weary, he trusted no one and failed to clarify his purposes. He desired above all to prevent a restoration of slavery while preserving the society he had built. Whites and mulattoes looked hopefully to France to repress the huge black majority; on the other side, many black leaders, like Moïse, wanted to expel all whites and divide the plantations. Some blacks were alienated by Toussaint's perfidies and equivocations, his mysteriousness, and the occasional atrocities he thought necessary amid such dangers.

A French invasion under Gen. Charles Leclerc began in January 1802 in far greater force than expected. Most whites and mulattoes defected to him; after a few weeks of furious fighting, so did the chief black leaders, even Christophe and Dessalines. In May Toussaint formally agreed to lay down his arms, in exchange for Leclerc's promise not to restore slavery. Perhaps he foresaw that yellow fever would destroy the French, as it did in the following year.

Leclerc gave Toussaint a spectacular welcome. The black leader retired in honour to a plantation. A few weeks later he attended a parley to discuss his personal situation. Suspected of plotting an uprising, he was seized and sent to Ft. de Joux in the French Alps, where he was confined and interrogated repeatedly, and where he died on April 7, 1803.

BIBLIOGRAPHY. Biographical accounts favourable to Louverture include: C.L.R. JAMES, *The Black Jacobins: Toussaint L'Ouverture and the San Domingo Revolution*, 2nd ed. rev. (1963), sound but with a Marxist bias; RALPH KORNGOLD, *Citizen Toussaint* (1944), a detailed study; and T. LOTHROP STODDARD, *The French Revolution in San Domingo* (1914), a classic work favourable despite its anti-Negro bias. A critical study is STEPHEN ALEXIS, *Toussaint Louverture, libérateur d'Haiti* (abridged Eng. trans., *Black Liberator: The Life of Toussaint Louverture*, 1949), a work that is credulous in places.

(J.E.F.)

Toyotomi Hideyoshi

Toyotomi Hideyoshi, a feudal lord of peasant origin, completed the unification of Japan begun by Oda Nobunaga; he did so by defeating the remaining powerful feudal barons (daimyo). He was born on February 6, 1537, in Nakamura, Owari Province (present-day Aichi Prefecture), the son of a peasant.

Early career

When he was still a boy, he left home for Tōtōmi Province (present-day Shizuoka Prefecture) and became page to a retainer of the Daimyo of Tōtōmi. After a short period, he returned home to become a foot soldier for the great Japanese leader Oda Nobunaga. His cheerful nature, tactful manner, and intelligence helped him to be promoted to samurai (a military retainer of a daimyo). When Nobunaga began his campaign to subjugate central Japan in 1568, Hideyoshi fought in many of the important battles.

By courtesy of the International Society for Educational Information, Tokyo, Inc.

Toyotomi Hideyoshi, detail of a portrait by an unknown artist, 1599. In a private collection.

In September 1573, by overthrowing two powerful daimyo, Hideyoshi became a lord of Nagahama, Ōmi Province, and subsequently took the name of Hashiba-chikuzen-no-kami.

From 1577, by order of Nobunaga, Hideyoshi embarked on the suppression of San-in and San-yo (Chugoku district), in the course of which he invaded Bitchū Province. Operating from a base at Himeji Castle in Harima Province, he besieged the daimyo Mōri Terumoto at Takamatsu. In 1582, Oda Nobunaga died after an attack by his retainer Akechi Mitsuhide; Hideyoshi immediately made peace with Mōri, and then moved

east to avenge Nobunaga by killing Mitsuhide, which he accomplished at the Battle of Yamazaki.

At a conference of the Oda family's chief retainers, Hideyoshi insisted that Nobunaga's grandson succeed as head of the Oda family in opposition to two powerful vassals of their late leader who supported Nobunaga's third son. In 1583, Hideyoshi defeated one of these vassals in a battle and allowed him to commit suicide. After subduing a number of important strongholds, Hideyoshi in the same year built a castle in Ōsaka and embarked on his attempt to conquer the whole of Japan in an effort to complete Nobunaga's work of unifying the country after more than two centuries of feudal warfare. In the following year he fought a battle with Tokugawa Ieyasu, a powerful daimyo and a supporter of Nobunaga's second son. After an inconclusive fight, the two leaders concluded an alliance.

In 1585 Hideyoshi was appointed *kampaku* (chief adviser to the emperor) and later became *dajō-daijin* (chief minister). He was awarded the family name of Toyotomi by the Emperor, and he thus came to bear the name Toyotomi Hideyoshi. Shortly thereafter, he made peace with Mōri Terumoto, who had again become his antagonist, and then conquered the large islands of Shikoku and Kyushu, which constituted most of western Japan. He achieved some of his victories with Tokugawa Ieyasu's assistance. After subduing, with Ieyasu's aid, the Kantō and Ōu districts in the east in 1590, he became head of an alliance of daimyo that constituted a government of national unification.

Administrative innovations

At first he imposed such measures as *katana-kari* ("sword hunting") in order to enforce the prohibition of the use of arms by farmers, merchants, and monks and *shiro-wari* (destruction of castles or reducing the number of castles), to destroy unnecessary strongholds throughout Japan. He also introduced *shi-nō-kō-shō,* freezing class distinctions by rigidly separating warriors, farmers, artisans, and tradesmen, and by allowing each class to live in different areas of a town or village to promote the orderly establishment of a feudal society. In addition, he conducted *kenchi* (land surveys) and abolished road checkpoints in order to promote transportation. Development of mineral resources was encouraged so that the resulting coinage would help to further trade.

Upon conquering the whole of Japan, Hideyoshi entrusted the position of *kampaku* to his nephew, Toyotomi Hidetsugu, henceforth assuming the title of *taikō*, the designation of a retired *kampaku*. He then prepared to invade Korea. His ultimate purpose was reportedly the conquest of China, the Philippines, and India, but even control of the Korean peninsula, which he first invaded in 1592, was not possible because of Japan's entirely inadequate forces for an undertaking of such magnitude. After a temporary peace with China, which eventually broke down, Hideyoshi in 1597 staged a second invasion of Korea. He died at the age of 62 on August 18, 1598, deeply perturbed by the unfavourable results of the Korean war.

There were no children born to Hideyoshi by his formal wife, but he had a son by a concubine. At Hideyoshi's death, however, the son was only six years old, and Tokugawa Ieyasu took the reins of government, to become five years later the founder of the Tokugawa shogunate, or military government.

Assessment

Because of Hideyoshi's lowly beginnings, he was said to be illiterate and uncultured. He did, however, secretly attempt to educate himself, showing a facility for composing poetry. He performed well in Nō plays and avidly studied tea ceremony with a prominent master, frequently holding such ceremonies to demonstrate his skill. After his death his policies of national unification were followed by Tokugawa Ieyasu, and they became the basis of the peaceful Tokugawa era, which lasted until 1868.

(T.Ku.)

Track-and-Field Sports

Track-and-field sports consist of competitions in running, walking, jumping, and throwing events. Although these contests are called track and field (or simply track) in the United States, they are generally designated as athletics in British Commonwealth countries and the equivalent of this term in non-English-speaking nations.

This article covers the history of track and field, the organization and administration of the sport at various levels, the conduct of competitions, and the rules and techniques of the individual events that comprise a track-and-field meet. The article also contains descriptions of the controversies surrounding the sport, and the recreational and fitness activities that are offshoots of the competitive sport.

For related articles, see ATHLETIC GAMES AND CONTESTS, including tables of Olympic events and champions in the section *Olympic record;* for world records, see also SPORTING RECORD in the *Ready Reference and Index*.

Track-and-field athletics are the oldest forms of organized sport, having developed out of man's most basic activities—running, walking, jumping, and throwing. Track and field has become the most truly international of sports, with nearly every country in the world engaging in some form of competition. Most nations now send representative teams both of men and women to the quadrennial Olympic Games, which have become the official world championships of track and field. There also are several continental and intercontinental championship meets held, including the European, British Commonwealth, African, Pan-American, and Asian.

Within the broad title of track and field come as many as two dozen distinct events, which have been standardized by national and international governing bodies of the sport. These events, generally held outdoors with running and walking events on a quarter-mile (440-yard) or 400-metre oval track, and field events (jumping and throwing) either inside the track's perimeter or in surrounding areas, make up a "meet," or "meeting" in British usage.

In many parts of the world, notably the U.S., Canada, and Europe, track and field moves indoors during the winter; because of limited space, some events are modified, and several are eliminated altogether.

Also within the general scope of track-and-field athletics come separate but related competitions that are not contested on the track. Cross-country running competition is carried out on various types of countryside and park land. Marathons (races of 26 miles 385 yards) and races of other long distances are run on roads, and many of the long-distance race walks are contested on measured road courses.

With rare exceptions, only amateur athletes (*i.e.,* those who compete for no financial gain) are allowed to enter track-and-field meets. The rules of amateurism and of competition are established and enforced by the International Amateur Athletic Federation (IAAF) and its member body from each nation. These bodies also maintain both the world and the national records in the standard events.

General considerations

HISTORY

Track-and-field sports can be traced back as far as man's evolution into an upright animal. The activities that make up the modern track-and-field events are as basic and simple, yet as essential to him as his instincts to move and to survive. Running, walking, jumping, and throwing are intimately tied in with his urge to ensure self-preservation. And long before any formal contests were staged, it is more than likely that young men matched their skills in these natural activities against each other—and employed them in play—as boys and girls will do without any urging or formal instruction.

Early history, decline. There is little in the way of definitive records of track and field's early days as an organized and formalized sport. Egyptians and several Asian civilizations, however, were known to have engaged in track and field contests many centuries before the Christian Era. As early as 1829 BC, Ireland was the scene of the Lugnasad or Tailteann Games involving various forms of track-and-field activity.

The sport's first big push came from the Greeks. Athlet-

ic contests were common features of their religious festivals. The Olympic Games traditionally date from 776 BC and continued through 11 centuries—finally ending in *c.* AD 393 on orders from the Roman emperor Theodosius. The earliest reported Olympic event was the "stade"—a run of a little over 200 yards. A long jumper named Chionis holds an important position in track-and-field history because he has the oldest known measured mark, having leaped 23 feet 1½ inches in the long jump at the Olympic Games of 656 BC.

The ancient Olympics

These ancient Olympics were strictly men-only affairs. Greek women were reputed to have formed their own Games, the Heraea Games, which—like the Olympics—were held every four years. The events included foot races of about 165 yards. Numerous other athletic festivals included the Pythian, Isthmian, and Nemean games (see further ATHLETIC GAMES AND CONTESTS).

The imperial edict that ended the Olympics in the 4th century AD apparently left the world without organized track-and-field activity for hundreds of years. If there were any organized contests during the early Middle Ages, no reports of them have survived.

Revival in England. Track and field as it is practiced today was born and grew to maturity in England and, later, its colonies and former colonies. The first historical mention of the sport comes from England in 1154, when practice fields were established in London. Later, however, during the 1300s, King Edward III banned athletic events, claiming they interfered with the practice of archery. Not until the following century, when Henry VIII was the reigning monarch, was track and field given official approval. This king reputedly was an accomplished hammer thrower.

During the 17th century, English men of means entertained themselves by matching their footmen in distance races and wagering on the outcome. Outstanding distance running times arose from these competitions, known as "pedestrianism," as early as the 1600s and 1700s. In 1653 a man known only as "a butcher from Croydon" was said to have run 20 miles in 1½ hours. Considering the fact that this time exceeds the current world record by several minutes, there is considerable doubt as to the accuracy of the course measurement and timing. Another early mark of note was a 4½-minute mile reported by Horace Walpole in 1787.

Development of organized sport. This, however, was the prehistory of track-and-field athletics. The development of the modern sport has come only since the early 19th century. In 1825 amateur races were held at Uxbridge and also at Lord's Cricket Ground in London. The English public schools and universities played a big part in the organization of the sport. Eton College established a 100-yard hurdle race in 1837 and added sprints and a steeplechase six years later. These were interclass meetings limited to students at the school.

Emergence of "gentleman amateurs"

The Royal Military Academy at Woolwich in 1849 promoted the first regularly organized track-and-field competition of modern times. Activity developed on many fronts in the decade to come, but it was the 1860s when track and field enjoyed its biggest surge to that date.

In 1862 the West London Rowing Club organized the first track-and-field meet that was open to all amateurs. Two years later, Oxford and Cambridge universities inaugurated their annual match. Then, in 1866, the Amateur Athletic Club was founded and conducted the first English championships. The emphasis in all these competitions was to provide a meeting place for "gentleman amateurs"—well-to-do athletes who received no financial compensation for their efforts. The rules of these meetings served as a basis of current regulations governing amateurism.

In 1880 the Amateur Athletic Club yielded governing power to the Amateur Athletic Association (AAA), which took charge of overseeing men's track-and-field athletics in England and Wales and conducting the annual national championships.

Track and field in North America. The development of track and field in North America came at about the same time but proceeded at a slower rate. The first meeting on that continent took place near Toronto in 1839. The San Francisco Olympic Club became the first organized team when it was founded in 1860. It was, however, the New York Athletic Club (NYAC), formed in 1868, that gave the sport its major thrust in the Western Hemisphere. The NYAC put together the world's first indoor track-and-field meet, on Nov. 11, 1868, at the Empire City Skating Rink in New York City. Actually, it could barely qualify as an indoor affair. The floor had not yet been laid, and runners competed on an eight-laps-to-the-mile track that had been staked out on the firm ground. The building lacked a roof, and canvas provided temporary cover. By 1876 the NYAC was promoting what could be considered the first national track-and-field competitions, though participation was limited. The club started a movement that led to the formation in 1879 of the National Association of Amateur Athletes (NAAA), consisting of 14 clubs, mostly in the New York–New Jersey area but also including one from Boston and the San Francisco Olympic Club, to conduct national championships. Beginning in 1879, the NAAA meets, all in New York City, continued for ten years. As a result of accusations of laxity in enforcing amateur rules, the Amateur Athletic Union (AAU) took over as the national governing body and conducted its first championships, in Detroit, in 1888. The AAU has continued its outdoor meets annually, adding the yearly indoor championships in 1906.

Meanwhile, intercollegiate competition was thriving in the United States. College championships began in 1876 under the auspices of the Intercollegiate Association of Amateur Athletes of America (IC4A). Ten colleges and universities from the northeastern U.S. made up the charter membership. Collegiate track and field reached national stature in 1921 with the staging of the first National Collegiate Athletic Association (NCAA) championships.

Development of international sport. The first international meeting of consequence came a year before the revival of the Olympic Games when, in 1895, the NYAC faced the London AC. But not until the Olympic Games in Athens, Greece, in 1896 did track-and-field athletics have the focal point necessary to become an international sport. Although the Olympic rebirth was rather insignificant by today's standards, it provided the inspiration and standardizing influence that were to make track and field the most international of sports. The Games grew steadily and by the 1908 Olympics in London had a representative field of 22 nations.

In 1913 athletic spokesmen from 16 countries met in Berlin to draw up the charter for the International Amateur Athletic Federation (IAAF). The main outcome of this meeting was the adoption of a set of standard rules for amateurism and conduct of competition and to approve the first set of world records. Membership in the international governing body now has grown to over 130 countries.

Women's track and field. The emphasis in track and field's early days was almost exclusively on men's athletics. Women have a considerably shorter modern athletic history, stretching back just over a half century. The first women's national governing body came into existence in 1917 with the formation of the French Women's Sports Federation. Two years later, organized women's competition began in England.

An international women's governing body called the Fédération Sportive Féminine Internationale (FSFI) got its start in 1921 with Britain, Czechoslovakia, France, Italy, Spain, and the U.S. as cofounders. The FSFI sponsored women's world championships at Paris in 1922; Göteborg, Sweden, in 1926; Prague, Czechoslovakia, in 1930; and London in 1934, following the inter-Olympic plan of the women's Games in ancient Greece. Meanwhile, the International Olympic Committee refused to consider adding women's events for the 1924 Olympic Games, but under an agreement providing for dual control by the FSFI and the IAAF five events for women were included in the Games in 1928. In 1936 the IAAF became the governing body of women's track and field and the FSFI was dissolved.

Growing interest and participation. International games other than the Olympics came into being before World War II, notably the British Empire Games (started in 1930 at Hamilton, Ontario), and the European Championships (first held at Turin, Italy, in 1934). Not until after the war, though, did track and field enjoy its greatest period of growth. Easier international travel and communications, increased emphasis on the sport, and improved equipment, facilities, and techniques have coupled with other factors to push both the scope and quality of the sport to unprecedented levels.

Performances have improved radically, with no modern world record surviving from before 1959. The 110-metre high hurdle time (13.2 seconds) set by Martin Lauer of West Germany that year (a mark that has since been tied several times) is the oldest one on the books.

Participation has increased on all levels. This is particularly evident among the newly emerging nations of the world. Whereas Europe, the United States, Australia, and New Zealand formerly monopolized world track-and-field power, Asians, Africans, and Latin Americans began producing world class athletes after World War II. African runners from newly independent nations, for instance, won five races in the 1968 Olympic Games. No black athlete representing an African nation ever had won an Olympic title before 1960.

In an age of jet travel and instant communications, interest in track-and-field competition has spread around the world. The effects on the sport have been profound.

ORGANIZATION AND ADMINISTRATION

The international governing body for track-and-field sports is the International Amateur Athletic Federation (IAAF). The IAAF defines an amateur athlete as "one who competes for the love of the sport and as a means of recreation, without any motive of securing any material gain from such competition." This definition is subject to various interpretations among member nations, and it has been the source of many controversies and conflicts. But in its broadest sense it means that athletes are to receive no direct monetary payment for their athletic efforts. Most of the individuals involved in the administration of the sport also are not paid for their work. The organization comprises "duly elected national governing associations or federations of countries, in control of amateur track and field athletics, cross-country running and walking, which agree to abide by the rules and regulations of the IAAF. Only one member from each country can be affiliated."

National track-and-field groups such as the United States' Amateur Athletic Union (AAU) and the British Amateur Athletic Association (AAA), along with the governing bodies of about 130 other countries, are represented in the IAAF.

The primary functions of the international body are to adopt and enforce a set of rules that are uniform throughout the world, to promote international competition, and to maintain world records in the various events.

The IAAF has established regulations for the conduct of the Olympic Games, continental and group championships such as the Pan-American Games, British Commonwealth Games, and European Championships and matches involving two or more member nations. Other competitions are conducted under the auspices of the ruling body of the nation where the meet is held. The rules governing these competitions are in substance nearly identical to those set up by the IAAF. In other words, the international group sets the policies that its members (each being the sole ruler of the sport in its country) follow.

Each IAAF member nation has its own national set of rules and maintains its own set of records in line with international guidelines. The amateur athletic federations of individual countries conduct their own national championships—usually annually—in men's and women's track and field, cross-country, race walking, and events such as the marathon run. These national ruling bodies also have the obligation of selecting representatives for international meets.

Rebirth of Olympics and formation of IAAF

Amateur defined

The national groups delegate the power to conduct individual meets within their boundaries, assuring, however, that these competitions meet their rules and regulations.

In the United States, for example, the AAU alone has the power to select international teams (except for the Olympic team, which is under the jurisdiction of the United States Olympic Committee), to establish rules, and to accept or reject records. It also conducts the national championships and other competitions. The nonchampionship meets generally involve either nonschool athletes or a mixture of students and nonstudents.

Meets in which participation is restricted to college or university athletes usually are governed by the rules of the National Collegiate Athletic Association (NCAA), National Association of Intercollegiate Athletics (NAIA), or one of two junior (two-year) college groups. Most secondary or high schools of the United States come under the aegis of the National Federation of State High School Athletic Associations and its subordinate units in each state.

Unlike most other countries, where competition among athletic clubs predominates, the bulk of U.S. track-and-field meets involve high school, college, and university individuals and teams. The schools typically are the spawning ground of the vast majority of athletes. It is normally only after they leave school that they join club and military teams or participate in AAU competition as "unattached" individuals.

Questions of payments to amateurs

Under IAAF rules, athletes can receive no direct payment for competing. Most member nations, however, do provide considerable support to amateur athletes who are potential international competitors. This support may consist of special training facilities for top-flight athletes, expense-paid travel and lodging, military duty with special privileges and duty exemptions, favourable occupational arrangements in eastern European countries, and, in the United States, the so-called athletic scholarships for athletes attending colleges and universities.

As amateur athletes, all that winners may accept as material rewards are prizes that are "of lasting value, are intended for the athlete himself and shall not exceed the value of U.S. $100 (or its equivalent in other currencies)." Usually these awards consist of trophies, medallions, jewelry, or merchandise.

Truly professional track-and-field athletes, who were prominent when match footraces for stakes were popular, have become rare in the 20th century. A relatively few exist in Australia, where handicap running events involving wagering are held and runners are paid for their efforts. England also supports a few such races. In the late 1960s, several American and European businessmen attempted to form professional track-and-field leagues, or circuits, featuring high-level performers. But their efforts were not successful.

The best of the world's track-and-field athletes remain in the amateur ranks, as evidenced by the fact that only one professional record exceeds that of amateurs. That is the relatively unnoticed and rarely held 100-mile track run, in which the professional athlete George Perdon of Australia set the record of 12 hours 25 minutes and 9 seconds in 1970.

Conduct of competition

The details of conducting track-and-field competitions vary, depending on location and the level and type of meet. But the basic format of the sport has been standardized to a great degree by the rules of the IAAF and subordinate bodies, and by tradition. The purpose of this section is to discuss the general organization and conduct of track and field meets.

Facilities. Outdoor track-and-field meets take place on or around oval-shaped running tracks that to meet official specifications must be either 440 yards (one-quarter of a mile) or 400 metres in circumference. With the exceptions of marathon runs and road walks held in conjunction with track meets, all running and walking events occur on the track.

Track compositions vary greatly. Whereas they were formerly almost exclusively made up of natural materials dirt, clay, cinders, and crushed brick being the most common) many new surfaces have been developed since 1960. Many tracks now feature toppings of asphalt-rubber mixtures and of synthetic compounds. These new track materials provide a consistent, resilient surface that stays "fast" in all weather conditions and needs little maintenance.

All-weather tracks and runways

These tracks, generally with "all-weather" toppings, have helped athletes on all levels achieve faster times. One of these surfaces, having a plastic-resin base, got its first international test in the 1967 Pan-American Games at Winnipeg, Manitoba, and was later used at the Olympic Games in Mexico City. That was the first Olympics to be conducted on an artificial surface. Nearly a dozen world records fell during the men's and women's competition there.

Field event athletes also are getting the benefit of improved footing. In an earlier era, jumpers and throwers launched themselves and their implements from dirt, cinders, or similar soft surfaces. Now the jumpers and javelin throwers generally use all-weather surfaced runways for their approaches. Shot-putters and hammer and discus throwers lob their implements from a circle of concrete or similar solid, smooth materials. With the improvement in takeoff areas there has been a corresponding improvement in putting and throwing records.

The field events normally are held on the area inside or adjacent to the track. With jumping, throwing, and running events all taking place at the same time, the stadium often takes on the appearance of a multiring circus with all rings operating at once.

Indoor track-and-field meets adapt themselves to meet the specifications of the arena where the meet is held. Because of the space limitations, several events must be dropped, including the javelin, discus, and hammer throws. Indoor tracks have a wide variety of sizes, shapes, and surfaces. But generally none is as big as the outdoor 400-metre/440-yard type. For the big meets in the United States and Europe—where the indoor sport centres and flourishes—tracks are usually wooden, with raised (banked) turns that facilitate running the cramped curves. Track sizes generally range from 140 to 220 yards in circumference, or eight to 12 laps to the mile. The straightaway for the short races usually is in the middle of the arena, inside the boundaries of the track, and the jumping and throwing also is done inside this perimeter.

Cross-country running utilizes any terrain that is available in the area where it is being run. This ranges from parklands, to golf courses, to forests, to farming country. Runners follow a course laid out for them—generally covering from 2 to 10 miles—and take natural obstacles as they come to them.

Running across country and on roads

Road running, such as the marathon race, road races, and the long-distance walking events occur on city streets and country roads that have been measured and marked according to official specifications. Often these races start and finish on the track. This is particularly true when they accompany track-and-field meets; *e.g.*, in the Olympic Games.

Equipment. Every event has items of equipment that are essential to the conduct of the event. All athletes, for example, require shoes that give traction, protection, and minimum weight. The quality of shoes has improved steadily, becoming at the same time lighter, more colourful, and more specialized in purpose. Both the spiked shoes worn by runners and jumpers and the flat-soled shoes of throwers have contributed to record breaking.

Other items of equipment—which have been modified and improved as well—include the starting blocks used by sprinters and hurdlers, hurdles, vaulting poles, and the implements employed in the various throwing events.

Timing and measurements. Exacting timing and measurement of performances are a vital part of track and field, not only to determine winners at the meet in question but also to provide marks that can be compared for record purposes. Official timekeepers record the times in the running and walking races, using either hand-held stopwatches or more precise electrical timing devices. In races of one mile and less times are taken in tenth-second increments. Distances above one mile are recorded in fifth-seconds (although they are published as .2, .4, etc., rather than ⅕, ⅖).

For a time to be accepted as a record, it must be clocked by three officials, or by an automatic timer, and must meet other specifications in regard to wind assistance, competitive conditions, and proper certification. In running events through 200 metres, as well as the long and triple jumps, the assisting wind may not exceed two metres per second (about 4.473 miles per hour) in the direction of the runners.

Accepted measurement standards

Metric measurements are the official standard in international competition. Field event performances are recorded to the centimetre in all events except the discus, javelin, and hammer throws; these are measured in even-numbered centimetres.

The United States is one of the last remaining countries to retain the "English" system of measurement, as Great Britain and most of the rest of the British Commonwealth nations in the early 1970s joined the world's majority on the metric system. But while the U.S. clings to the traditional feet, inches, yards, and miles for domestic track and field, it shifts to metres in the international arena. In the running and walking events, this means switching from events such as 100 yards to 100 metres, from three miles to its equivalent 5,000 metres, and so on. In the field events, the performer sees his marks measured in metres and centimetres rather than feet and inches.

The IAAF recognizes world records in the "English" running and walking events, but all field event records must be measured in metric terms.

Official world records are maintained only in men's and women's outdoor track-and-field events. Because competitive areas vary so much, there are no recognized marks for cross-country and road races or for indoor events. In the United States, however, the AAU keeps official American indoor records.

Basic rules. Track-and-field meets generally occur during one- or two-day periods, although major championships such as the Olympic Games may stretch out over a week or more.

In running events up to and often including 5,000 metres, preliminary competitions, called heats, often are necessary to eliminate all but the best individuals. Key championship meets, for instance, may include as many as three qualifying rounds to advance runners to the final race. Athletes are placed in these qualifying heats according to their best performances, and only the heat leaders advance to the next race. The number reaching the final race varies according to the size of the track and the distance of the race, but generally it ranges from 8 runners in the 100-metre sprint to 12 or 15 in the 5,000-metre run. Races above 5,000 metres seldom if ever require preliminaries.

Qualifying heats and trials

An official fires a gun to start all races. In those runs of up to one lap of the track athletes are required to stay within marked lanes throughout the race. In multilap races, after leaving the starting line, the runners and walkers string out in single file or run along side by side on the inside edge of the track. The runner or walker whose torso reaches the finish line first is the winner. Two or more athletes may have identical times and still be separated in the placings.

Field event participants have two types of qualifying competitions. In most meets, all but the high jumpers and pole-vaulters (who are eliminated as they progress from one height to the next) are allowed three preliminary jumps or throws if there are more than eight competitors. Then the leaders at that point are allowed three more attempts to improve themselves. High jumpers and pole-vaulters are eliminated after three successive failures at a given height.

In major championship meets, however, the number of entrants is often so large that qualifying throws and jumps are required to cut the field to a manageable size. These usually consist of each man or woman trying to meet a minimum requirement. The leaders advance to the finals, where they follow normal field event procedures just as if there hadn't been an earlier round.

All field events have rules for breaking ties. In the high jump and pole vault, the jumper requiring the fewest attempts wins. In all other field events, the victory goes to the athlete with the superior second effort.

The men's decathlon consisting of a combination of ten running, hurdling, jumping, vaulting, and throwing events and the women's pentathlon consisting of a combination of five running, hurdling, jumping, and throwing events are spread over two days each. Athletics in these events get only three attempts in each of the throws and in the long jump and are arbitrarily divided into heats for the running portions. They receive points for each performance—the better the mark, the higher the point total—and the winners are those scoring the highest total. The IAAF has charge of establishing standard scoring tables.

Team scoring. Although track and field is basically an individual sport, with each event being something of a separate entity, an offshoot of this is the team scoring aspect.

Much public attention is given to the national scores in the Olympic Games, but these totals are strictly unofficial. Team scoring comes into play primarily in matches between nations, clubs, and school teams. U.S. universities, colleges, and high schools give particular emphasis to these combined scores.

The points allotted to individual events and places vary from meet to meet. A national competition may give ten points for a first-place finish, eight for second, six for third, and so on down to one for sixth. Scoring in an international dual match is five points for first, three for second, two for third, and one for fourth. The points scored in all events are totalled, and the team with the highest total wins.

Point scoring

Cross-country, road running, and walking meets utilize an entirely different scoring method. In these races, the first-place finisher receives one point, second place gets two, etc. The team's leaders, three to five athletes depending on the meet, have their finish positions totalled, and the team with the lowest score wins.

Seasons. The outdoor track season in the Northern Hemisphere normally begins on a major scale in March and continues through September, making it a spring and summer sport. The bulk of activity in the United States concludes with the closing of high schools and colleges in June, while the European season starts and finishes later. In the Southern Hemisphere—notably Australia, New Zealand, and South Africa—the track-and-field season falls in the November to April period because of the reversal of seasons.

Indoor track and field is concentrated in the winter months, mainly January through March. This phase of the sport developed as a cold-weather alternative to outdoor track and field. As it has gained in popularity, however, it has spread to areas that could conduct outdoor meets at this time of year. California, scene of several of the world's major indoor meets, is a prime example of a warm climate with indoor meets.

Cross-country running occupies the fall and winter months. In the United States, the sport centres on the September to November period. European runners carry on their activity almost from the end of one track season, October or November, to the start of the next, in March or April of the following year. Southern Hemisphere athletes run cross-country during their fall and winter. Road runs and walks are year-round sports. Events are held in every month of the year, from the heat of summer to the cold and snow of winter.

CONFLICTS AND CONTROVERSIES

Track and field, a sport that occupies centre stage at all international games, generates its share of conflicts, some of which revolve around the struggle for national prestige among the countries involved. Some nations as well as individuals stake much on the outcome of these events, and emotions run high on such occasions. The temptation to break, or at least bend, rules exists.

Conflicts often centre on definitions of amateurism. Ostensibly, all track-and-field athletes are amateurs. They compete "for enjoyment" and are not allowed to profit financially from the sport, according to the IAAF definition of an amateur.

Although athletes are not openly paid for their participation, many top-quality performers are supported in a variety of ways, some legal and some questionable. Eastern European nations have given rise since World War II to a class of competitor often referred to as the state amateur. World class athletes receive preferential treatment from their respective governments in return for their athletic performances. Such direct government subsidies are not given in other nations of the world, but nearly every country hoping to field Olympic contenders has a system that supports athletes. In the United States, the colleges and universities assume this role by granting so-called athletic scholarships to relieve the athlete of the financial burden of going to school, thereby allowing the track-and-field performer ample time for training and competing. To some extent, the branches of the military service also provide this support by providing athletes with choice duty assignments. In Japan, industries see to the needs of outstanding athletes. In Scandinavian countries, special training camps are offered.

Complaints about payment of athletes

The IAAF has placed limits on the amount of expense money an athlete may receive while competing in meets around the world, as well as defining the type and value of awards allowed. Several athletes have been penalized for overextending these limits. Celebrated cases have involved famed distance runners. The world record holders Paavo Nurmi (Finland) and Gunder Hägg (Sweden) were forced into early retirement for allegedly violating amateur rules, as was the miler Wes Santee (U.S.).

Rumours of others accepting "under-the-table" payments are heard regularly in track circles. One well-publicized case involved shoe companies offering large sums of money to Olympic athletes at the 1968 Games. In return, the athletes were expected to display conspicuously the company's products during competition.

Political bickering among nations also is part of international sport; so much so that an early four-minute miler and Olympian, Chris Chataway of Great Britain, wrote a book about it entitled *War Without Weapons*. That title aptly describes the situation that sometimes seems to exist on the worldwide track-and-field scene.

At its first Olympics in 1952, the Soviet Union insisted that its athletes be housed apart from other athletes and threatened to pull out of the Games if its demands were not met. In an extension of "Cold War" politics, the Soviets also cancelled a meet with the United States in 1966, blaming U.S. involvement in the Vietnamese war.

Arguments extend as well to which nations should be allowed to enter international competition and which should not. This has been a particular problem among countries split apart by wars and revolutions. Following World War II, East and West Germany competed as one combined unit until 1964, then each fielded a separate team in 1968, but only after an agreement that neither's national anthem would be played nor flag flown. South Korea competed in the Olympics, but not North Korea; South Vietnam, but not the North; Nationalist China (Taiwan), but not mainland China.

An explosive issue during the 1960s was the status of the Republic of South Africa. The nation was excluded from the 1964 Olympics because of apartheid racial practices existing in that country. The International Olympic Committee tentatively agreed to readmit the South Africans to the 1968 Olympics. But when a majority of black African nations threatened to boycott en masse, South Africa again was barred from competing.

Individual athletes also have participated in boycott activities. Many American Negroes claimed before the 1968 Games that they would refuse to compete in protest over racial discrimination they said existed in their home country. The boycott, however, failed to materialize. A boycott by the West Germans the next year went ahead. When a countryman was barred from competing in the 1969 European Championships, the West German contingent voted not to compete.

Several countries, particularly the U.S., have had lasting disputes over control of the sport by various governing bodies. In the United States, the conflict between the AAU and NCAA has attracted the attention of the federal government.

Drug use

Another area of considerable controversy has been the use of drugs. IAAF rules prohibit the use of any chemical substance that might aid an athlete in the performance of his event—be it a strength-building, relaxing, or "pep" drug. But despite the rules, and despite tests developed to detect certain types of drug use, all available evidence indicates that intake of such substances is increasing.

One of the most popular drugs is the anabolic steroid variety. "Steroids" reportedly materially increase an athlete's strength and weight within a rather short period of time, when combined with a wholesome diet and heavy training. This makes this type of drug, taken in pill or injection form, particularly in demand among athletes in the throwing events, where size and power are prime requisites. Use of the drug is almost impossible to detect through standard tests. Other types of drugs, however, leave obvious traces, and at the Olympics and other major meets athletes are tested for drug usage.

Another type of athletic testing has caused considerable comment among athletes and the sports public alike. This is the testing of women to determine if they indeed meet the requirements of their sex. Several cases of men posing as women have been uncovered, one involving a German high jump champion during the 1930s.

Determination of sex even on the basis of the highly sensitive and accurate chromosome test is not as clearcut as it might appear, and disputes have arisen over the verdicts of doctors assigned to the testing at international events. One side effect of the tests has been the ruination of the careers and reputations of several athletes involved in the testing. After failing a chromosome test, a Polish sprinter of the 1960s retired. Many other athletes who for one reason or another avoided taking the tests have become the subject of normally unfounded rumours and insinuations.

RECREATION AND FITNESS

Since the actions involved in track-and-field athletics are the basic ingredients in nearly all sports, it is to be expected that a number of related recreational and physical fitness activities should grow up around the sport. In themselves, running, walking, jumping, and throwing lead to excellent physical conditioning as well as providing enjoyable recreation.

The jogger

Running—or jogging as slow running often is called—and walking enjoyed a considerable return to popularity during the 1960s both for their recreational and their fitness aspects. Numerous experts in the fields of exercise physiology and preventive and rehabilitative medicine proved there is a distinct correlation between the lack of endurance exercise (such as running, walking, and other continuous activities) and disease, particularly heart disease. They recommended jogging, walking, bicycling, and the like, both to prevent disabling illnesses and attacks and to recover from them.

Perhaps the best known exponent of this type of exercise is Kenneth Cooper, a United States Air Force medical officer who tested his theories on nearly 1,000,000 airmen and other volunteers. In his best-selling book, *Aerobics*, he heartily endorsed moderate forms of distance running and walking for persons of all ages and both sexes.

One result of jogging's popularity has been a tremendous growth in low-level distance running competition. Evidence of this can be seen in the Boston Marathon race, which in the early 1960s had fields in the range of 200 runners and by the end of the decade was drawing nearly 1,200 persons.

Many of the runners at Boston and elsewhere are runners who started in the sport rather late in life, or persons who have remained active over a long period of time. In both the United States and Europe, competitions began to accommodate men beyond the age of 40. Plans were underway to organize an unofficial "Veterans' Olympics" for these athletes.

Accompanying the growth of running in the older age

Figure 1: (Left) Start of the women's 100-m. final, 1968 Olympics, Mexico City. (Top to bottom) Chi Cheng (Taiwan), Raelene Boyle (Australia), Wyomia Tyus (U.S.), winner, Margaret Bailes (U.S.), Barbara Ferrell (U.S.), Miguelina Cobian (Cuba), Irene Kirszenstein Szewinska (Poland), Dianne Burge (Australia). (Centre) Willie Davenport (U.S.), first over the hurdle on his way to win the 110-m. race of the Dr. Martin Luther King Jr. International Freedom Games, 1969. (Right) Jim Hines (279), anchor man on U.S. 400-m. relay team, runs for a new world record of 38.2. East German anchor man Harold Eggers takes baton while speeding toward the finish during the 1968 Olympics.
(Left) UPI Compix, (centre) Albert Session—Track and Field News, (right) Wide World Photos

groups is competition for the young athletes. This is particularly evident in the United States, where boys and girls as young as five years old compete regularly against athletes in their own age groups.

Another offshoot of competitive track is competition in extralong endurance runs. Athletic history is rich with reports of such feats of endurance. During the 1920s, a number of athletes twice attempted trans-United States runs known as Bunion Derbies. Interest in this sort of running revived in 1964 when the South African Don Shepherd ran unaccompanied across the U.S. in 173 days. Bruce Tulloh (Great Britain) broke that "record" in 1969 when he made the almost 3,000 miles in less than 65 days, accompanied by a small caravan of aides.

The Scandinavians devised a sport that employs elements of cross-country running, hiking, and land navigation. This increasingly popular sport called orienteering involves travelling an unmarked course through natural terrain. The runner–hiker checks in at various control points along the route, which he finds by using a map and compass. Thus, navigational skill takes on equal importance with running ability.

Track-and-field events

Recognized track-and-field events

As many as 25 events may make up a men's track and field meet, and a women's competition may contain as many as 15 separate contests. A men's meet may include any of the following recognized events, with championship meets including most of them: 100-, 200-, 400-, 800-, 1,500-, 5,000-, and 10,000-metre runs (in the United States, 100-, 220-, 440-, 880-yard, and one-, three-, and six-mile runs); 110- and 400-metre (120- and 440-yard) hurdles; the 3,000-metre steeplechase; the 400- and 1,600-metre (440-yard and one-mile) relays with four members per team; the high jump, long jump (or broad jump), triple jump, and pole vault; the shot put, discus, hammer, and javelin throws; a race walk of from one mile to 50 kilometres; and a decathlon in which an individual competes in ten events. Women's competition may include the 60-metre (60-yard) run and 100- through 1,500-metre (100-yard through one-mile) runs; 80-, 100-, and 200-metre hurdles; 400- and 800-metre (400- and 880-yard) four-member team relays, and 2,400-metre three-member team relays; high jump and long jump; shot put, discus, and javelin throws; and the five-event pentathlon.

This section will examine the basic technical facets and historical highlights of these running, race walking, jumping, and throwing events.

RUNNING

Running events range in distance from the 50-yard dash to continuous superendurance runs as long as 24 hours in duration. Some are on the track, others on roads and over the open countryside, and some require hurdling barriers.

Sprinting. The sprint, or dash, distances are those involving an all-out or nearly all-out burst of speed that is sustained throughout the event. Sprinting generally encompasses events from 50 to 440 yards and their metric equivalents. Races below 100 yards are limited mainly to indoor meets, and often to competitions involving younger athletes. Outdoors, both men and women sprint 100 yards or 100 metres, 220 yards or 200 metres, and 440 yards or 400 metres as their most common events. These distances are run in championship meets.

Until 1884, all sprinters started from a standing or leaning position. That year Bobby Macdonald, a Maori residing in Scotland, began a trend that was to become universal in sprinting by starting from a crouched position. This method, now used by nearly all sprinters, involves taking a preliminary position (on the starter's command, "On your marks") with one knee on the ground, one foot several inches in front of the other and both hands resting behind the starting line. On the command "Set," the runner raises his knee from the ground and leans forward. As the gun sounds, he drives powerfully from his mark and accelerates to full speed.

An athlete's start, and the quickness of his reaction time, can very well determine his result in races as short and exacting as these. The German sprinter Armin Hary, the 1960 Olympic 100-metre champion and first man to run 10.0 seconds for that distance, reputedly was one of the all-time best starters. He got off the line so quickly that he was widely accused of "beating the gun." Sprinters, all runners in fact, are allowed one false start. When one runner jumps the gun, a second shot sounds and all of the runners return to the starting line. Once an athlete is charged with his second false start, he is disqualified.

Another significant development in sprinting was the invention of starting blocks in 1927. The U.S. track coach George Bresnahan patented the blocks (adjustable metal or wood devices to support the feet at the starting line) that year and, using them, George Simpson ran the 100 yards in a world record time of 9.4 seconds in 1929. The record wasn't accepted, however, because the implement was not legal at that time. Most sprinters continued to start from holes dug in the track until starting blocks were legalized in the 1930s. Jesse Owens, the great sprinter and hurdler from the United States, set his many world records in that decade starting out of holes. Use of starting blocks

Little distance separates sprinters at the end of high-quality races. To obtain the advantage at this crucial point they develop special techniques of finishing. In the 1920s, American world record-holding sprinter Charles Paddock was known to fling his arms wide and leave the ground in a flying leap at the end of races. Present-day sprinters rely on well-timed leaning finishes—which often leave them sprawled face down on the track later—to get their torsos to the line first.

Because of the shortness of these races in terms of time,

improvement is difficult to see and to measure. But improvement does come. For example, John Owen (U.S.) sprinted the first less than 10-second time for 100 yards in 1890, doing 9⅘ seconds (at that time, records were kept in fifth-seconds instead of current tenths). Not until 1929 did Simpson break through the 9½-second barrier with his unrecognized 9.4, which Frank Wykoff (U.S.) matched in 1930. It was another 33 years until Robert Hayes (U.S.) moved the record down another three-tenths-second to 9.1. At 100 metres, the case is similar. Luther Cary (U.S.) first broke 11 seconds in 1891, and the record didn't go below 10-flat until James Hines (U.S.) ran 9.9 in 1968. The slow, yet regular, improvement is more obvious as the distance increases.

Success at 100 and 200 metres (or 100 and 220 yards) often goes hand in hand, while 400-metre men and women are usually specialists at that distance.

Top short sprint men include Percy Williams (Canada), Eddie Tolan (U.S.), Jesse Owens (U.S.), and Bobby Morrow (U.S.): all won Olympic championships at both 100 and 200 metres. In the women's realm, Marjorie Jackson (Australia), Fanny Blankers-Koen (The Netherlands), Betty Cuthbert (Australia), Wilma Rudolph (U.S.), and Renate Stecher (East Germany) have accomplished a similar feat. Cuthbert also won at 400 metres in a later Olympiad.

The 400-metre dash, like the 200, is run around the track's turn(s) and in lanes all the way. This requires a start that is "staggered," all athletes starting progressively farther up the track with each line away from the inside, to equalize the total distances covered.

Staggered starts

All-time standouts in the one-lap (400-metre or 440-yard) sprint have been Ben Eastman (U.S.), who in 1932 improved the world record by a full second to 46.4; Otis Davis (U.S.) and Carl Kaufmann (Germany), the first men to break 45 seconds for 400 metres when they did 44.9 simultaneously at the 1960 Olympics; and Lee Evans (U.S.), 1968 Olympic champion who in Mexico City with 43.8 first broke 44-flat in the 400-metre run.

The women first ran 400 metres at the Olympics in 1964. Perhaps the greatest woman 400 runner ever, however, never ran in the Games. Sin Kim Dan (North Korea) tied or improved the world record five times during her career, to a low of 51.2 seconds in 1964, but her country was ineligible for the Olympics.

Middle-distance running. As distances exceed 400 metres, fatigue becomes an increasingly greater factor, and it becomes essential for the runner to regulate his pace. The aim is to take maximum advantage of his speed while harbouring strength for the final burst.

The middle-distance races—those in the range of 800 to 2,000 metres—are still run quite rapidly, but the factor that distinguishes them from the sprints is the controlled pace. The most common middle distances are 800 metres or 880 yards, and 1,500 metres or one mile, for both men and women. Olympic events are conducted at 800 and 1,500 metres for both men and women—women running the longer distance for the first time in 1972.

Undisputed focal point of middle-distance running has been the mile. Although this has long been the classic American and British Commonwealth distance, interest in the event has spread to countries that normally use only metric distances. The quest for the magic four-minute mile involved not only Americans, Englishmen, and Australians but also Swedes, Frenchmen, and others.

Even before World War II, speculation was beginning to grow about the possibilities of a runner breaking through the four-minute barrier. Glenn Cunningham (U.S.), who played a big role in the prewar flurry of interest, raced to a 4:04.4 effort indoors in 1938. Then came a series of war-years matches between the Swedes Gunder Hägg and Arne Andersson. They traded records several times, with Hägg finally bringing it down to 4:01.4 in 1945. The mark remained there for nine years.

The four-minute mile

May 6, 1954, was one of track-and-field's historic days. On a cool and blustery day at Oxford, England, medical student Roger Bannister (Great Britain) cracked the four-minute mark for the first time with 3:59.4. About six weeks later, Australia's John Landy knocked the rec-

ord down further to 3:58.0, then lost to Bannister in a monumental match between the two at the British Empire Games later that summer.

Bannister and Landy opened the gates for a flood of sub-four-minute clockings. By the end of the 1960s, such runners as Derek Ibbotson (Great Britain), Herb Elliott (Australia), Michel Jazy (France), Peter Snell (New Zealand), and Jim Ryun (U.S.) had led a parade of almost 200 men who had broken the once seemingly impregnable barrier. The record has come down to Ryun's 3:51.1, yet four minutes remains an important landmark for all milers, and one indicating world class potential.

Perhaps because of this interest in the mile race, the equivalent 1,500 metres (or metric "mile") normally claims top billing in any Olympics or other international meet. Olympic 1,500-metre champions are numbered among the all-time greats of track and field; they include Paavo Nurmi (Finland), Jack Lovelock (New Zealand), Herb Elliott (Australia), Peter Snell (New Zealand), and Kipchoge Keino (Kenya).

Milers/1,500-metre runners show a tendency either to be fast in the shorter distances or to be strong in the longer ones. Among the first group are several athletes who have won Olympic titles at both 800 and 1,500 metres. They include Edwin Flack (Australia), James Lightbody (U.S.), Mel Sheppard (U.S.), and Albert Hill (Great Britain), all of whom accomplished it in 1920 or earlier, and Snell in the 1964 Games. Ryun also falls into the sprinter category, having held world records at 880 yards as well as 1,500 metres and the mile. Paavo Nurmi is the only athlete to have won the Olympic 1,500 and a longer distance. Other prominent examples of the endurance-type miler are Jazy and Keino, both of whom have held world records at distances up to 5,000 metres.

As indicated, some 800-metre men double in the 1,500 or mile. Others fall into the sprinter category, being quite proficient in the one-lap event as well as the two-lap. No athlete ever has won both the Olympic 400- and 800-metre titles, but 800 champions James Meredith, Mel Sheppard, Mal Whitfield, and Tom Courtney (all U.S.) have contributed to winning 4 × 400-metre relay teams.

World records in all middle-distance events have improved drastically in the 20th century, and particularly since World War II. The higher level of competition, better pacing, and improved tracks and running shoes can share in the credit for this. But the key reason is training techniques, which are of higher quality and quantity than ever before. In the 1930s and earlier, middle-distance runners seldom totalled more than 10 or 20 miles of training per week. Today's runners seldom do less than 50, and many go well beyond 100 miles a week.

Training techniques and improved records

Several athletes and coaches have made their unique contributions to training techniques. The Swedes Hägg and Andersson popularized the *fartlek* (or "speed play") method involving a mixture of slow and fast cross-country running. The Germans and eastern Europeans brought "interval" training into vogue during the late 1940s and 1950s. This method consists of a series of short (200- to 800-metre), timed runs on the track, broken up by periods of jogging or slow running and walking. Elliott brought "resistance" training, with running in soft sand and heavy weight lifting, into prominence. Finally, Snell used long and rather slow road running—100 miles a week—to get the basis for his record breaking. Athletes now use one or the other of these various methods, or a combination of them.

Pacing, as mentioned earlier, is crucial in middle-distance racing. An athlete must keep himself in a position where he can win, yet he must not squander his limited resources too soon. He also must avoid becoming trapped by other runners, since they all run as closely as possible to the inside lane and often in tight bunches.

Many runners prefer to get out in front at the start and dictate a pace. The majority, however, seem to prefer following the leader, conserving their strength, and relying on a fast finishing burst to win. Pacing styles have changed over the years, and this is particularly evident in mile running. The early style was to start fast, relax somewhat during the middle two laps, then finish as rap-

Pace and strategy

idly as possible. Walter George (Great Britain) ran this way during his record mile in 1886. Nurmi believed in evenly paced laps and ran this way during his 1923 record race of 4:10.4. Hägg, Bannister, and Landy all ran fastest on their first laps. But by the time Ryun got his record, the style had become even, conservative pacing over the first three-quarters, then a powerful finishing sprint. Ryun ran his last 440 yards in 53.5 seconds.

Comparative Records of Great Mile Runners

quarter	George (U.K.) 1886	Hägg (Sweden) 1945	Bannister (U.K.) May 1954	Landy (Australia) June 1954	Ryun (U.S.) 1967
1st 440	58.5	56.6	57.5	58.5	59.2
2nd 440	63.25	61.9	60.7	60.2	59.8
3rd 440	66.0	61.2	62.3	58.5	58.6
4th 440	65.0	61.7	58.9	60.7	53.5
Mile	4:12.75	4:01.4	3:59.4	3:58.0	3:51.1

The entry of women into international middle-distance running has come only recently on any kind of major scale. Women ran 800 metres at the 1928 Olympics, but the event wasn't revived until 1960. The 1,500-metre event for women was included for the first time at the 1972 Games. With the record for 800 metres standing at just under 2:00 (1:58.3, set in 1971; although Sin Kim Dan had run 1:58.0 in 1964, her marks were never accepted as records) and the 1,500 at about 4:05, two minutes and four minutes became significant barriers for women.

Long-distance running. The long distances are those from 3,000 metres to 30,000 metres (the longest event in which records are recognized by the IAAF) and the marathon. Runs at longer distances have been held and sometimes runs are held for distance covered in a specified time interval, ranging from 1 to 24 hours, but this discussion is concerned with the standard competitive events. Included here are flat-track races, the steeplechase, cross-country, and road runs. The most common of these events—which are almost exclusively the province of male athletes—are the 3,000-metre (or two-mile), 5,000-metre (or three-mile), 10,000-metre (or six-mile) runs, the 3,000-metre steeplechase, and the marathon road run of more than 26 miles. Olympic distances are the 5,000- and 10,000-metre runs, the steeplechase event, and the 26-mile 385-yard marathon.

Pure, basic speed, although important to all running events, becomes progressively less a dominant factor as distance increases, while endurance training and tactics take on greater importance. The training techniques mentioned in the middle-distance section become all the more vital for athletes who run long distances. Training quantities increase accordingly; for instance, long-distance runners rarely average less than 100 training miles a week, and many go 200 or higher. Before the 1968 Olympic Games, Australian marathoner Derek Clayton reportedly averaged 210 miles a week. American Ted Corbitt indicated he was regularly logging 300 per week in preparation for a 100-mile race in 1969.

Pacing tends to level out in long distance races, with each mile or kilometre being covered in about the same time as all others. Track races of 3,000 to 10,000 metres still feature a fast burst on the later laps, but this begins to disappear with more distance until it becomes all but nonexistent in the marathon.

Accordingly, with improved training and techniques, times have improved startlingly. Using the 50 years from 1920 to 1970 as end points, the two-mile world record had dropped from above nine minutes to below 8:20; records at 5,000 metres and three miles were each more than a minute faster than they were in 1920, and the 10,000-metre and six-mile marks had come down more than three minutes.

The history of long-distance running is rich with stories of athletes who have held multiple world records. This is understandable for two reasons: (1) all track distance runs are closely related in terms of the abilities, techniques, and training required, and (2) long distance run-

(margin: Endurance and tactics)

ners normally have careers of ten or more years, offering them many opportunities for fast times. Track runners who stand out most prominently in this respect are Walter George (Great Britain), Alfred Shrubb (Great Britain), Hannes Kolehmainen (Finland), Nurmi, Ville Ritola (Finland), Hägg, Emil Zátopek (Czechoslovakia), Vladimir Kuts (U.S.S.R.), Sandor Iharos (Hungary), and Ron Clarke (Australia). Although he never won an Olympic championship, Ron Clarke broke world records more than two dozen times during his long international career, he held marks at two, three, and six miles, and 5,000 and 10,000 metres when he retired in 1970.

One of the sport's unique events is the one-hour track run, the only official event whose object is running for distance within a set time rather than seeing how fast a man can go for a standard distance. Gaston Roelants (Belgium) averaged better than 4 minutes 42 seconds per mile when he covered 12 miles 1,478 yards—a world record—in the allotted time.

The steeplechase combines long-distance running with hurdling and negotiating a water hazard. Scattered over the 3,000 metres (slightly less than two miles) are 28 barriers and seven water jumps, or four barriers and one water clearance per lap. All barriers are three feet in height and are solidly constructed, allowing athletes either to hurdle the barrier or step on top. On the water obstacle, the barrier stands in front of a 12-foot-long pool that is 2½ feet deep immediately in front of the barrier and slopes up to ground level. Runners place one foot on top of the barrier, push off, then land—either beyond the pit or, usually, with one foot in the shallow end of it. Steeplechasing requires outstanding distance running ability as well as hurdling skill. Many of the top runners, notably Ritola and Roelants, have held world records for flat races as well as for the steeplechase.

(margin: Steeplechase and marathon)

The marathon race commemorates the feat of a Greek soldier who in 490 BC supposedly ran from Marathon to Athens to bring news of his countrymen's victory over the Persians. The race between the same two Greek cities became part of the Olympic Games in 1896 and covered about 40 kilometres, or just under 25 miles. In 1908, the distance was standardized at its present 26 miles 385 yards. Traditionally, this long road race ends the track and field portion of the Olympics and is generally a highlight of the Games. Many athletes who have had success on the track attempt to make the big step upward from six to 26 miles, but only two have done it totally successfully. Kolehmainen won the 5,000- and 10,000-metre runs in the 1912 Games and won the marathon in the 1920 Games, eight years later. In 1952, Zátopek completed one of the greatest feats in long-distance-running history by winning all three events, the 5,000- and 10,000-metre runs and the marathon, in the same Games. Only one athlete has managed to win the Olympic marathon twice—Abebe Bikila of Ethiopia, in 1960 and 1964. And each time he ran the fastest time ever recorded for the distances.

Since marathon courses vary greatly in composition and terrain, no official record for the distance is maintained. For comparative purposes, however, statisticians have kept lists of the best performances. As with other track and field records, marathon times are continually being lowered. Jim Peters (Great Britain) in 1953 accounted for the first marathon under 2 hours and 20 minutes when he was timed at 2 hr 18 min 40.2 sec. Fourteen years later, Derek Clayton (Australia) brought the best time down below 2:10 with a clocking of 2:09:36.4. This represents 26.2 miles at less than five minutes each.

Many international marathons—as well as shorter and longer road races—are held annually throughout the world. The most famous are the Boston Athletic Association race, held each April since 1897, the Japanese Open at Fukuoka, and the Polytechnic, which covers a course from Windsor to Chiswick, England.

Cross-country running varies according to locality of the race. In Great Britain, where races of this type are extremely popular and often bring together as many as 1,000 runners, runs are up to nine miles in length. Races cover whatever terrain is available, often involving cross-

(margin: Cross-country running)

ing creeks, running through plowed fields, and jumping fences. Europeans favour cross-country runs that resemble steeplechases. Races of several laps often are run over horse-racing courses, complete with barriers, and at shorter distances than those employed in England. Cross-country running in the United States typically is on golf courses and parklands, at distances up to 10,000 metres.

The sport of cross-country has its own championships, the International, held annually in March or April. Standard men's distance for this race is 12,000 metres or about 7½ miles. Women run 2½ miles or roughly 4,000 metres.

Except for cross-country, women compete in long-distance running only sporadically and never on a championship level. Women nevertheless have accomplished commendable long-distance feats. A 16-year-old American girl, Caroline Walker, in 1970 ran what is believed to be the fastest marathon ever recorded by a woman—3 hours 2 minutes and 53 seconds. Several women have completed the 54-mile Comrades Marathon in South Africa.

Hurdling. These events combine sprinting with negotiating a series of obstacles called hurdles. Men run the 110-metre (or 120-yard) high hurdles, over 10 barriers 106.7 centimetres (42 inches) high and 9.14 metres (10 yards) apart, and the 400-metre (or 440-yard) intermediate hurdles, also over 10 barriers but 91.4 centimetres (36 inches) in height, and 35 metres (38.25 yards) apart. The 110- and 400-metre distances are the standard international events. Low hurdling, over 30-inch (76.2-centimetre) barriers at distances of 220 yards and 200 metres, has all but disappeared as a standard event.

Women, through 1968, had only one hurdle race—80 metres over eight barriers about 76 centimetres (30 inches) high. Beginning in 1969, the hurdles were raised to about 84 centimetres (33 inches), the distance was lengthened to 100 metres, and an additional 200-metre race was added to the women's program. The 100- and 200-metre races both contain ten obstacles, the long race using 76-centimetre hurdles.

The object in hurdling is to spend the least possible time in the air, and to make the hurdling action smooth and rhythmic so as not to disrupt forward progress. Hurdling, therefore, is more a quick stepping action than a floating jump. A.C.M. Croome of Oxford University is credited with developing in about 1885 the economical hurdle clearance involving a straight front leg, forward lunge of the trunk, and snapping action of the trailing leg. This "step-over" action is the basis of modern hurdling technique.

Hurdle design

The modern L-head hurdle (which in the 1930s replaced the heavy, inverted T style) is designed so that a force of eight pounds (3.6 kilograms) on the top edge of the crossbar is required to overturn them. A hurdler may knock down an unlimited number of barriers without penalty. If, however, he trails a leg or foot alongside any hurdle instead of clearing it properly, or if he intentionally knocks down a hurdle with his hand, he is disqualified.

Leading hurdlers combine a sprinter's speed with suppleness and hurdling technique, since they must take the strides between barriers and then to clear the hurdles while travelling at an all-out pace. Starting and finishing techniques are as important here as in the flat sprints.

To support the claim that top hurdlers also must be top sprinters is the case of Harrison Dillard (U.S.). He was favoured to win the 1948 Olympic hurdle championship but he failed to qualify for the United States' team as a hurdler. Rather than be left out completely, he attempted the 100 metres and made the team. Dillard won the flat race at the London Olympic Games. Four years later, he returned to capture the Olympic high hurdles gold medal.

Strangely, in an era where records at all distances fall regularly, the high-hurdle mark recently has been the most stable in track and field. Martin Lauer (Germany) established the current record of 13.2 seconds in 1959, and Lee Calhoun (U.S.), the only man ever to win two Olympic titles in the event, tied it a year later. Though equalled several times since, Lauer still claims a share of the record.

The one-lap hurdle race places a premium on endurance and striding patterns as well as on speed and hurdling technique. Four-hundred-metre or 440-yard hurdlers require the speed of a quarter miler and the strength of a longer distance man. Specialists in this event tend to be high-quality long sprinters rather than top high hurdlers. The two-time Olympic champion Glenn Davis (U.S.) typifies this sort of athlete, having held the world record in the 440-yard flat race as well as in the hurdles.

Striding patterns

In the 400-metre hurdles, athletes normally take 15 strides between hurdles, but fatigue and varying track conditions often complicate this pattern and force improvisation. Running on the springy track in the high altitude of Mexico City, Dave Hemery (Great Britain) took only 13 steps between hurdles for most of the distance and ended up breaking the then existing world record by a full second with 48.1 seconds.

The roll of women's 80-metre hurdle Olympic champions and record holders includes many of the sport's outstanding athletes: Mildred Didrikson (U.S.), Blankers-Koen, Shirley Strickland De La Hunty (Australia), and Irina Press (U.S.S.R.).

Relay running. Standard relays usually involve four-man teams, each running equal and specified distances before passing a baton to a teammate. Most common of the relay events for men are the 440-yard, 880-yard, one-mile, two-mile, and four-mile as well as their metric equivalents. These are often referred to as the 4 × 110, 4 × 220, etc. In the Olympic Games and other international competitions, men and women run the 400- and 1,600-metre relays, women running the longer distance for the first time in the Olympics in 1972.

Except for the baton-passing and baton-carrying aspect, the running techniques in relays are identical to those of the comparable individual events. The baton is a hollow wooden, metal, or plastic implement about one foot in length. It must be handed from man to man within a specified take-over zone that extends 20 metres. In events of 880 yards and less, athletes may begin their run an additional 10 metres before the take-over zone but may not accept the baton until they reach the legal 20-metre area.

Baton passing

Baton passing is an exacting operation that decides the outcome of most races of 400 metres. Ideally, the incoming man hands off to the outgoing one while both are travelling at optimum speed and are a maximum distance apart. This requires constant practice and split-second timing so as to avoid losing momentum, running out of the exchange zone (which results in disqualification), or dropping the baton. Runners employ two basic passing methods—the blind pass (in which the outgoing runner does not look back) in the shorter events, and the safer visual pass (outgoing runner watches incoming one until pass is completed) at longer distances, where fatigue may lead to a costly drop.

Relays are primarily an outgrowth of the United States school system, which puts heavy emphasis on this sort of team competition. College and university teams on both coasts were running relay events before 1900. In 1895 a number of eastern schools competed in the first annual Pennsylvania Relay Carnival. That meet has expanded through the years to take in high school, club, and other athletes and now includes more than 3,000 athletes competing annually. Similar relay carnivals take place in other areas of the U.S., and the normal schedule has the 400- and 880-yard relays, the mile, two-mile, four-mile, and the sprint (legs of 440-, 220-, and 880-yards) and distance (440-yard, 880-yard, three-fourths mile, and one-mile) medleys. These all follow the rules and procedures described earlier. Another event, the 480-yard high-hurdle relay, is unique. This is run in "shuttle" fashion, with one runner travelling the normal direction on the track and his teammate returning the opposite way. No baton is carried; the outgoing runner simply starts when the incoming one crosses his finish line.

Because of its abundance of sprinting talent and emphasis on relay racing, the United States has dominated this phase of the men's sport in Olympic and other international competition.

Figure 2: (Left) Dick Fosbury (U.S.), high jumping in style known as the "Fosbury flop," wins the event at the NCAA Indoor Track and Field Championships, 1968. (Centre) Barbara Inkpen (England) takes a spectacular leap in the senior long jump during the Women's Amateur Athletic Association Championship, Crystal Palace, 1969. (Right) Bob Seagren (U.S.), champion pole vaulter, on his way up to clear the bar at the Los Angeles Invitational Track Meet, 1967.
(Left) Wide World Photos, (centre) Central Press—Pictorial Parade, (right) Ernest E. Schworck—UPI Compix

Race walking. This facet of track and field bears little resemblance to the actions and speed of hiking or casual strolling. Top race walkers travel at a maximum rate of just over six minutes per mile, or ten miles per hour; *i.e.*, more than twice the speed of a hiker.

Walkers develop a special technique to carry them along at this rapid rate. Elements of the distinctive style are a rapid pulling motion with the legs, pronounced and rhythmic motion of the hips, and exaggerated arm and shoulder movement.

Race walking rules stipulate that (1) the walker must maintain unbroken contact with the ground (one foot always touching), and (2) the leg must be straightened (*i.e.*, the knees locked rather than bent) for an instant while it is in contact with the ground. When walkers are travelling at a high rate of speed, the temptation is strong to break contact with the ground or to make bent-legged contact. Both infractions are difficult to detect, since the steps occur within fractions of seconds, and make the judging of walking races both an important and exacting task. Walkers may receive one warning of impending violation and are disqualified for violation of the rules.

The IAAF and its member bodies recognize only marks made at selected distances: international race walking primarily follows the Olympic lead and uses the 20- and 50-kilometre distances as standard events in major competitions. Twenty kilometres equals roughly 12½ miles, and 50 kilometres is just over 31 miles. Both are relatively recent additions to the Olympic program, the "50" beginning in 1932, and the "20" in 1956.

Walking is primarily the domain of the Europeans, and only one athlete from outside that continent and Great Britain—Norman Read of New Zealand in the 1956 "50"—has managed to win an Olympic championship. Other 50-kilometre standouts have been the Olympic titlists Don Thompson (Great Britain), Abdon Pamich (Italy), and Christoph Hohne (East Germany). Among 20-kilometre walkers, Vladimir Golubnichy of the Soviet Union is outstanding, with a record of winning two Olympic races (in 1960 and 1968) contested at this distance.

Besides the Olympics, walkers compete in the Lugano Cup competition, which is the equivalent of the world walking championships. The team event contains walks of 20 and 50 kilometres. The cup goes to the nation with the best cumulative performance.

JUMPING

Men compete in four jumping events, the high jump, long jump, triple jump, and pole vault, while women compete only in the high jump and long jump.

High jumping. There is but one stipulation placed on the method an athlete chooses to get himself over the crossbar, which is perched atop two standards. He must leave the ground from one foot, not two.

The crossbar is raised progressively higher as athletes jump over it. High jumpers are allowed three attempts at clearing each height. On the third miss, they are out of the competition. They may enter the competition at any point. In fact, if they begin when the bar is at a higher level, this may work in their favour because of the "countback" rule for breaking ties. The rule works this way: (1) first officials check the athlete's number of attempts at the height where the tie occurred; (2) if two or more men are still tied, the total number of *failures* throughout the competition is computed; (3) if they remain tied, a count is made of the total number of *jumps* in the competition. In each of the three cases, the athlete with the lowest total is the winner. This puts a premium on taking as few jumps as possible.

Inflated or foam-rubber-cushion landing pads have replaced sawdust pits. These cushions are two or more feet thick and have both reduced the threat of injuries and made possible refinements of technique. Another boon to the high jumper has been the development of durable, all-weather takeoff areas that provide a consistent surface for the run-up and all-important foot placement preceding the jump.

Jumping styles have evolved in the 20th century as records have progressed. One of the earliest and most basic techniques was the scissors, in which the jumper approached the bar from the right side and jumped off the left foot, with his torso upright when he crossed the bar. But neither this style nor its variants are employed to any appreciable extent in modern competition, and no athlete has topped seven feet using them. Another now rather rare jumping method is the western roll, sometimes called the belly roll, in which the jumper approaches the bar from the left and jumps off the left foot, "rolling" his torso over the bar. Its leading exponent, Gene Johnson (U.S.) has cleared 7 feet 1 inch (2.16 m).

The most common method employed is the straddle. With this style, the athlete approaches the bar at an angle, extends his lead leg upward toward the crossbar, drapes himself facedown and parallel to the bar at the height of his jump, then lands on his side or back in the pit. Charles Dumas (U.S.) used this technique in 1956 when he became the first man to break another of track and field's "magical barriers"—seven feet.

The straddle style's leading exponents include Valery Brumel (U.S.S.R.) and Ni Chihchin (China). Brumel, whose brilliant career was cut short in 1965 by a motorcycle accident that shattered his leg, accounted for six world record improvements and the 1964 Olympic championship. Ni never competed in the Games and his records are not officially recognized because his nation is not an IAAF member.

Brumel and Ni are examples of men who have taken maximum advantage of their size and leg power. Brumel is 1.85 m (6 feet ⅞ inch) tall, yet he has jumped 2.28 m (7 feet 5¾ inches). Ni is 1.84 m (6 feet ½ inch) in

Rules of heel and toe racing

Jumping styles

height and has a high jump best of 2.29 m (7 feet 6¼ inches). Few jumpers have been able to exceed their own height by as much as Brumel's and Ni's 43 to 45 cm (17-inch-plus) differential. Pat Matzdorf (U.S.), 1.70 m (6 feet 3 inches) jumped 2.29 m (7 feet 6¼ inches) for a recognized world record in 1971.

Though straddle stylists claim the best marks, a more recent development in jumping technique has created more excitement. Dick Fosbury (U.S.) is credited with developing a style that involves approaching the standards from almost straight ahead, then twisting on takeoff and going over head first with the back to the bar, finally landing on the shoulders. The style, referred to as the "Fosbury flop," gained wide exposure and increasing acceptance when Fosbury used it to win the 1968 Olympic championship. Though many jumpers had successfully converted to this style by 1970, none had yet bettered Fosbury's best height of 2.24 m (7 feet 4¼ inches).

The "Fosbury flop"

Easily the leading female high jumper of all time is Iolanda Balas (Romania). Miss Balas, 1.71 metres (5 feet 7¼ inches) tall, used the complicated eastern cutoff style of jumping, characterized by bringing the trailing leg under the lead leg and down to the pit first. The shoulders and head are brought to the left (when the jumper leads with his right leg) and down, thus lifting the hips and buttocks up to clear the bar. Beginning in 1957, she tied or improved the world record 14 times, taking it from 1.75 m (5 feet 9 inches) to 1.91 (6 feet 3¼ inches). Her career included two Olympic championships. The "Fosbury flop" even came to the women's sport in the late 1960s. Debbie Brill (Canada), winner of the 1970 British Commonwealth Games, was the first to reach 1.83 m (6 feet)—still a rare feat for women—using her version of this technique.

The standing high jump went out with the 1912 Olympics, but mention should be made of Ray C. Ewry (U.S.). After being confined to a wheelchair as a youth, he developed the leg strength and spring to win eight Olympic championships in the standing jumps—three in the high jump, three in the long jump, and two in the triple jump.

Pole vaulting. The origins of this event can be traced back to the days when men used poles to assist them in clearing obstacles such as ditches, creeks, and fences. Present pole-vaulting competition is organized along the lines of the high jump—*i.e.*, vaulters attempt to get over a crossbar placed on uprights, they get three tries at each height, the "countback" rule is employed to break ties, and they land in a pit that now generally is of rubber composition or inflated.

IAAF rules state that pole-vaulting poles "may be of any material or combination of materials, and of any length or diameter." In the 1960s, fibre glass came into general use for vaulting poles because of the flexibility and catapulting action of that substance. The use of this pole revolutionized the event, as will be discussed later. Previously, more rigid bamboo and metal poles had been used.

Early in the history of pole vaulting, poles were equipped with spikes at one end. They dug into the ground as the vaulter planted his pole. Early in the 20th century, a slotlike box for pole placement became part of standard vaulting equipment. This box, which is sunk below ground level at the base of the uprights, is about eight inches deep and six inches wide at the point where the pole stops.

Pole-vaulting technique

Pole-vaulting technique involves the following. The vaulter takes an approach run of 30–45 metres (100–150 feet), carrying the pole with his hands about 0.75 m (2½ feet) apart and the pole roughly parallel to the ground. After planting the pole, he leaves the ground and pulls himself upward until he is almost doing a handstand on the pole. He twists as he approaches the bar and arches over feet first and facedown. The pole is released just before the flyover and is given a push backward to prevent its knocking off the bar; the athlete then lands on his back in the pit.

The fibre-glass vaulting pole brought revolutionary changes in the event, both in styles and performances. The new pole put more emphasis on gymnastic agility than the rigid types, where sheer speed and power were at a premium. Fibre-glass vaulters hang upside down early in their vaults, waiting for the right instant when the bowed pole recoils to give them their vital lift.

Before the advent of the fibre-glass pole it took 13 years (1927 to 1940) for the world record to progress from 14 to 15 feet (4.26 to 4.57 metres). John Uelses (U.S.), using fibre glass, accomplished the first outdoor 16-foot (4.88 metre) vault in March 1962. Just 18 months later, John Pennel (U.S.) surpassed 17 feet (5.18 metres). And in 1970, Christos Papanicolaou (Greece) pushed the world record over 18 feet (5.49 metres).

Cornelius Warmerdam (U.S.) was perhaps the leading pole vaulter of the pre-fibre-glass era, but he never competed in the Olympics because World War II intervened during his peak years. In 1940, Warmerdam achieved the world's first 15-foot vault. He improved that mark five more times in the next two years, reaching a height of 4.77 m (15 feet 7¾ inches) that no one bettered for 15 years. Warmerdam also went 15 feet 8½ inches indoors, but indoor marks are not counted as world records.

The next great vaulter, Bob Richards (U.S.), never bettered Warmerdam's marks. But Richards was the only man ever to win two Olympic pole-vault titles, his victories coming in 1952 and 1956. Others who excelled before the fibre-glass revolution of the early 1960s were Bob Gutowski (U.S.), who broke Warmerdam's world record, and Don Bragg (U.S.), the 1960 Olympic champion.

Bragg won his Olympic title at 4.70 m (15 feet 5 inches). By 1964, fibre glass had taken over, and that year's champion Fred Hansen (U.S.) vaulted 5.10 m (16 feet 8¾ inches). Another Olympiad passed, and the 1968 Mexico City Olympic winner, Bob Seagren (U.S.), did almost a foot better than that.

Throughout the event's history, United States athletes have dominated—never losing an Olympic title and rarely being without a world record. The exceptions, since the 1920s, have been Charles Hoff (Norway), Pentti Nikula (Finland), Wolfgang Nordwig (East Germany), and Christos Papanicolaou (Greece), the first to top the 18-foot barrier with 18 feet ¼ inch (5.49 m) in 1970.

Long jumping. Formerly known in many areas as the broad jump and, for many years, as the running broad or long jump, this is competitive jumping for distance. An Englishman named J. Howard reportedly leaped 29 feet 7 inches (9.02 metres) in 1854—which is better than the existing record. But he employed aids that have since become illegal. Howard carried five-pound weights in each hand, and hurled them backward on takeoff to gain extra momentum, and he jumped from a slightly elevated block.

Long-jumping rules now state that an athlete can carry nothing in his hands and that the takeoff board must be level with the landing pit. The board marks the point where he breaks contact with the ground. He may step on the board, but he is charged with a foul if any part of his foot goes past the forward edge. The jumper lands in a sand-filled pit, and his distance is measured from the front of the takeoff board to the closest point of body contact in the pit.

A crucial part of long jumping, as with all jumping events, is the approach run. Not only is high speed required to achieve maximum momentum but the athlete also must arrive precisely at the takeoff point without breaking stride and on the proper foot. In the long and triple jumps, there is the additional problem of hitting the takeoff board. If the jumper starts too far back, he loses valuable distance; if he runs too far, he oversteps the board and has a foul charged against him. Athletes in these events normally measure their approaches carefully and place pegs alongside the runway as check points.

The approach run in long jumping

Long jumpers employ two basic styles. One is the "hang" (or "tuck") technique, where the knees simply are tucked under the body in midflight. The other is the more complicated "hitch-kick" style, which involves taking a long step in midair. The latter, which resembles walking on air, is the most popular among modern athletes.

Two distinct landmarks stand out in the history of long jumping. The first centres on the spectacular day Jesse

Owens (U.S.) ran and jumped through on May 25, 1935. Owens raised the world long-jump record to 26 feet 8¼ inches (8.13 m), and he also tied the world record for the 100-yard dash and set new world records for the 220-yard, and 200-metre runs on the flat, and for the 220-yard and 200-metre low hurdles. Not unil 25 years later did Owens—winner of four events at the 1936 Olympics—lose his long jump record.

During most of the 1960s, Ralph Boston (U.S.) led long jumpers. It was Boston who finally broke Owens' long-standing record and pushed the world record past 27 feet (8.23 metres). On Oct. 18, 1968, in the rarified atmosphere of Mexico City, Bob Beamon (U.S.) touched down at 8.90 metres (29 feet 2½ inches). No one had done better than 8.35 metres (27 feet 5 inches) previously. In 33 years, the world record had gone up less than nine inches (22.86 centimetres). Then, in one day, Beamon improved it by almost two feet (60.96 centimetres). Many track and field experts called this jump at the 1968 Olympics the greatest single performance in track and field history.

The event joined the women's Olympic program relatively recently, in 1948. Before that, the event's leader had been Blankers-Koen of The Netherlands, who had jumped 6.25 metres (20 feet 6 inches) in 1943.

Two ladies starred during the 1960s. Mary Rand (Great Britain), like Blankers-Koen a woman of many track-and-field talents, became the world's first female 22-foot jumper when she landed 6.76 metres (22 feet 2¼ inches) from the board to win the 1964 Olympics. Tatyana Shchelkanova (U.S.S.R.) never won the Olympic title but set numerous world records, with a best jump of 21 feet 11¾ inches (6.70 m) in 1964.

Triple jumping. In some quarters, this event has been known as the hop, step, and jump, which describes the combination of actions involved. A triple jumper takes an approach run similar to that in the long jump, although slightly slower because he must maintain control in order to execute the three phases of the leap. The first segment is a hop, in which the jumper must take off and land on the same foot. Then he goes into an elongated step, landing on the opposite foot. Both of these have been completed while still on the runway. The final phase is the jump into the pit, which resembles a long jump and ends with a two-footed landing. As an example of how far the triple jumper travels during each of the leaps, the longtime world record holder Józef Schmidt (Poland) had these marks during his 17.03-metre (55-foot 10½-inch) effort in 1960: hop—19 feet 8¼ inches; step—16 feet 5¾ inches; jump—19 feet 8½ inches (6.00, 5.02, and 6.01 metres).

Rules governing the triple jump are identical to those in the long jump in regard to the takeoff board, measurements, and number of efforts allowed. Early triple jumpers performed with two hops and a jump. James Connolly (U.S.) jumped in this manner when he won the 1896 Olympic championship, but rules prescribing the present method were adopted before the next Games.

Two athletes have stood out in the post-World War II period—Adhemar Ferreira da Silva (Brazil) and Schmidt. Da Silva was one of South America's rare world class track-and-field athletes (another has been Nelson Prudencio, also a triple jumper and also from Brazil). Da Silva's career included two Olympic titles, 1952 and 1956, and five world record performances. Between 1950 and 1955, he boosted the record from 52 feet 6 inches to 54 feet 3¾ inches (16.00 to 16.55 metres).

Schmidt won two Olympic—1960 and 1964—and two European championships. He placed only seventh in the 1968 Olympic Games, with a leg injury hampering him. Even at that, he nearly equalled his world record, which had stood for eight years.

The Games at Mexico City featured the greatest triple jumping in history, as five men—Victor Saneyev (U.S.S.R.), Prudencio, Giuseppe Gentile (Italy), Art Walker (U.S.) and Nikolay Dudkin (U.S.S.R.)—all went beyond Schmidt's former mark of 55 feet 10½ inches (17.03 metres). Olympic competitive pressure, the fast and springy artificial runway, and the lowered air resistance of Mexico City's 7,500-foot (2,300-metre) elevation all contributed to the onslaught. Within 24 hours, Gentile accounted for the first-ever 56-foot (17.07-metre) jump, and Saneyev—the winner—bounded over 57 feet with five-eighths inch to spare (17.39 metres).

THROWING

The four standard throwing events—shot put, discus, hammer, and javelin—all involve the use of implements of various weights and shapes hurled for distance. Women compete in only the shot, discus, and javelin.

Shot putting. This event, which evolved from stone putting, is not a "throwing" event strictly speaking. The action involved here is better described as shoving the weight, since the rules state that the arm may not extend behind the shoulders during the putting action.

The shot is spherical and has a smooth outer surface of metal (iron, brass, or a substance not softer than brass). In indoor competition, athletes may use a soft rubber-, plastic-, or leather-coated shot filled with metal pellets. The men's implement weighs 16 pounds (7.256 kg) and measures about five inches (12.7 cm) in diameter. Women put a 4-kilogram (8-lb 13-oz) shot, about 10 cm (4 in.) in diameter.

Shot-putters launch the ball from a ring 7 ft (2.134 m) across. The ring is equipped with a toeboard on the front. During competition, an athlete may not step on top of or over any portion of the circle (though he may touch the sides), or leave the ring before the shot hits ground. If he does so, or leaves from the front half of the circle at any time, he is charged with a foul. In present-day competition, the ring usually is mounted on concrete or a similar hard surface that provides solid, dependable footing. Athletes put into a sector with right and left boundaries that are approximately 65 degrees apart. Measurements are from the front of the ring to the point where the shot first touches ground.

Shot-putters are among the largest athletes in track and field, usually well over 200 pounds (90 kg). And they have grown even bigger in recent years through the use of heavyweight lifting training, which adds both bulk and explosive strength. This form of training came into general usage during the 1950s, and combined with a new putting technique to revolutionize the event.

Before the early 1950s conventional shot-putting style involved making a 90-degree turn while crossing the ring. Parry O'Brien (U.S.) is credited with developing a style that included a full 180-degree turn. O'Brien began his put at the back of the ring, with his back to the toeboard. He crouched low, with the implement tucked near his chin, as he moved across the circle. Gathering momentum as he turned, he took full advantage of his speed and strength as legs and putting arm straightened explosively at the release. O'Brien officially improved the world record ten times between 1953 and 1959, won two Olympic championships, and was the first man to better 59, 60, 61, 62, and 63 feet (17.98, 18.29, 18.59, 18.90, and 19.20 m). His form, with minor variations, was adopted almost universally.

Before the O'Brien era, the key men in the event had been Ralph Rose (U.S.) and Jack Torrance (U.S.). Rose, an Olympic champion in 1904 and 1908, put the shot past 50 feet (15.24 m) for the first time a year after winning his second Olympics. It took 19 years for Rose's mark of 51 feet 0 inch to fall. Progress came slowly until the emergence of Torrance in the mid-1930s. Torrance, who weighed nearly 300 pounds (136 kg), improved the world record to 57 feet 1 inch (17.40 m), a mark that lasted 14 years.

Following O'Brien's exploits of the 1950s, Bill Nieder (U.S.) and Dallas Long (U.S.) each assumed the spotlight briefly. Nieder was the first man to better 65 feet (19.81 m) and won the 1960 Olympic crown, while Long, the 1964 Olympic king, first bettered 66 and 67 feet (20.12 and 20.42 m). They preceded another of the sport's supermen, Randy Matson (U.S.). Matson, nearly 6 feet 7 inches tall and weighing 270 pounds (122.5 kg), broke through the 70-foot (21.34-m) barrier in 1965, and two years later was able to surpass 71 feet (21.64 m).

Hop, step, and jump

Physical requirements of shot-putters

Figure 3: (Left) Jay Silvester (U.S.), preparing to release the discus at the 1969 National AAU meet. (Centre) Hal Connolly (U.S.), hurling the hammer during the 1970 National AAU meet. (Right) Yanis Lusis (U.S.S.R.) throws the javelin at dual competitions with the U.S., 1969.
(Left and centre) Don Chadez, (right) Tass—Sovfoto

Through the end of 1970, no other athlete had been able to exceed 69 feet.

Shot putting was not a part of the women's phase of the Olympic Games until 1948. A pioneer on a par with O'Brien in the women's shot was Tamara Press (U.S.S.R.). Press, 220 pounds (100 kg), thoroughly dominated the event while at her prime, winning the 1960 and 1964 Olympic titles and becoming the first woman to better both 55 and 60 feet (16.76 and 18.29 m). Even her records proved to be vulnerable, however. By 1968, Margitta Gummel (East Germany) had pushed the record out to 64 feet 4 inches (19.61 m) while winning the Olympic championship.

Discus throwing. This event, the throwing of a plate-like implement, is the classic event of track and field. In his writings, many centuries before the birth of Christ, the Greek poet Homer made numerous references to discus throwing, and a form of it was popular in the ancient Grecian Olympics.

The Greek technique, as it was deduced from study of famous statues, consisted of throwing a four- to five-pound (1.8 to 2.3 kg) discus from a standing position on a pedestal and using a highly stylized form; a separate event using this style was part of the 1908 Olympics. But the style proved to be so artificial that it gave way completely to the modern technique. This involves starting by facing the back of the throwing circle and taking 1½ quick turns before releasing the discus. The circle is 8 feet 2½ inches (2½ metres) in diameter. Present rules stipulate that the sides and back of the ring must be surrounded by a cage for the protection of other athletes, officials, and spectators. The boundaries of the sector into which the discus is thrown are 60 degrees apart.

The discus for men is 4 pounds 6½ ounces (2 kg) in weight, about 8¾ inches (22.23 cm) in diameter, 1¾ inches (4.45 cm) thick in the centre tapering to one-half inch (1.27 cm) on the outer edges; the women's discus is 2 pounds 3¼ ounces (1 kg) in weight, about 7¼ inches (18.42 cm) in diameter, 1½ inches (3.81 cm) thick in the centre tapering to one-half inch (1.27 cm). The implement is constructed of wood "or other suitable materials" and has a metal rim around the outer edge. Rules of the competition, training techniques, and the physical dimensions of the athletes involved are similar to those in the shot put. In fact, many athletes double successfully in the two events. The discus places slightly more emphasis on speed and agility, however, and discus throwers tend to be a bit taller and leaner than shot-putters, though still normally weighing well above 200 pounds (90 kg).

The first great discus thrower of the 20th century was Martin Sheridan (U.S.), who won the Olympic championships in 1904 and 1908 (the former in a throwoff after tying with the shot-put champion Ralph Rose) and had

improved the world record from 129 feet (39.30 m) to 144 feet (43.88 m) by 1909.

During and just after World War II, the record-setting task fell into the hands of a durable veteran, Adolfo Consolini (Italy). Consolini set his final world mark, 181 feet 6½ inches (55.32 m), in 1948, the same year he won the Olympic title and set a European record of 186 feet 11 inches (56.98 m) in 1955 when he was nearly 39.

The quest for 200 feet (60.96 m) began in earnest in the 1950s, by the Americans Fortune Gordien and Sim Inness. Gordien ended up with the highest mark of the two —194 feet 6 inches (59.28 m), but Inness won the 1952 Olympic title.

This was the background of one of the most spectacular stories in Olympic and track and field history—the career of Al Oerter (U.S.). Oerter's international competition began at the 1956 Olympics in Melbourne. He upset Gordien for the championship there. Four years later, he added a second Olympic title. He achieved a third gold medal at Tokyo, and finally a fourth at Mexico City. He is the only athlete ever to have won four consecutive titles in a single event. Also, in 1962, Oerter recorded the first 200-foot (60.96-m) performance.

Although Oerter beat him in Olympic competition, Ludvik Daněk (Czechoslovakia) exceeded Oerter's world record and became the first 210-foot (64.00-m) thrower. Daněk in turn surrendered the record to Jay Silvester (U.S.), first man to throw more than 220 feet (67.06 m).

Eastern Europeans—primarily athletes from the Soviet Union—have maintained almost complete dominance in women's discus throwing. From 1939 to 1952, the Soviet thrower Nina Dumbadze increased the world record from 158 feet 6 inches (48.30 m) to 187 feet 1¾ inches (57.04 m). Her countrywoman Nina Ponamanyeva twice won Olympic titles, in 1952 and 1960.

Tamara Press (U.S.S.R.), better known as a shot-putter, broke Nina Dumbadze's world record in 1960 and later extended the women's mark to 195 feet 10½ inches (59.70 m). The West German Liesel Westermann had the honour of making the first toss over 200 feet.

Hammer throwing. The so-called hammer actually is a ball similar to the shot, attached by a length of steel wires slightly under four feet (1.22 m) long to a handle that can be gripped with both hands. The hammer thrower takes several spins before letting the implement fly, and since it weighs 16 pounds (7.26 kg) its centrifugal force carries it a considerable distance.

The event's predecessors are among the oldest events in track and field. Legends trace it back to the Tailteann Games, about 2000 BC. In those games, Celtic heroes were said to have gripped a chariot wheel held by its axle, whirled it around their heads and thrown it. Wheel hurling was replaced later by throwing a boulder attached to a wooden handle. During the 16th century,

The Greek technique of discus throwing

Early precursors of the hammer throw

King Henry VIII of England became proficient in an athletic event that involved throwing a blacksmith's hammer. The name remained, even though the nature of the implement changed.

Hammer throwing has been an Olympic Games event since 1900. Throwers compete from a circle that is the same size as the one used for shot putting—seven feet in diameter. They throw into a sector identical to that of the discus—60°. As with the discus throw, a wire-fence cage surrounds three sides of the hammer ring to protect observers. Hammer-throwing technique requires great strength combined with sure balance. Within the small ring, athletes make three turns. While spinning, the hammer is at arms' length and is creating a strong centrifugal pull that the athlete must counteract. Upon releasing the implement, he must guard against losing his balance and stepping out of the circle, which results in a foul.

Irish-bor athletes made this event their stronghold from the 1880s until almost 1950. Two enjoyed particular prominence. John Flanagan, a United States citizen, raised the world record 14 times from 1895 to 1909, and took it from 145 feet (44.20 m) to over 184 feet (56.08 m) during that period. He also won three consecutive Olympic championships—1900, 1904, 1908. Patrick O'Callaghan (Ireland) accounted for Olympic gold medals in 1928 and 1932 and was the first man over 190 feet (195 feet 4¾ inches [59.56 m] in 1937).

During the 1950s and 1960s, eastern Europeans displayed conspicuous strength in the event. But their dominance was not total. A Norwegian, Sverre Strandli, first broke 200 feet (60.96 m). Mikhail Krivonosov (U.S.S.R.) did much of the record breaking during the mid-1950s, improving the mark six times. In the 1956 Olympics, however, he lost to Harold Connolly (U.S.). Connolly, whose left arm was considerably smaller and weaker than his right arm because of a childhood injury, improved the world record seven times to a peak of 233 feet 9½ inches (71.26 m).

More recent hammer competition has featured the duels of Romuald Klim (U.S.S.R.) and Gyula Zsivótzky (Hungary). After finishing second in the 1960 Olympics, Zsivótzky repeated that placing 1964 as Klim won. The Hungarian, however, twice improved the world record before the 1968 Games and got his long-sought gold medal after a dramatic confrontation with Klim. Ironically, Zsivótzky lost the world record a short time later —to Klim.

Cramped indoor facilities do not allow for hammer throwing. But in the United States a similar weight event is substituted. In this event the athlete uses a 35-pound implement with a triangular handle attached directly to the weight. Leading throwers toss it in the range of 70 ft (21.34 m). A limited amount of outdoor competition also is conducted with a 56-pound weight, which is of similar construction; this competition was discontinued as an AAU event in 1959.

Javelin throwing. The art of spear throwing was introduced to the ancient Olympics in 708 BC as part of the pentathlon. Modern javelin throwing involves the use of a spearlike implement that is hurled with an over-the-shoulder motion at the end of an approach run. Javelins consist of three parts—the metal tip, which is weighted and pointed so that it will stick into the ground; the metal or wooden shaft; and the grip, which is the binding in the centre of the implement that the athlete holds while carrying out the throw. Men's javelins are about 8½ ft (260 cm) long and weigh roughly 1 lb 12 oz (800 g). The women's implement measures about 7½ ft (220 cm) and weighs 1 lb 5 oz (600 g).

This event is the only one of the throws that uses a runway (about 100 ft or 30 m long) rather than a ring for the approach. On his approach the thrower runs down the runway carrying the javelin at about shoulder height. Just before reaching the foul line, he alters his step pattern and turns so that the nonthrowing side is in front of the one with the implement. He makes a half-turn back toward the throwing area and follows through as the throw is executed. The javelin is not required to stick in the ground as it comes back to earth, but the point must

come down first. It must land within a 30-degree sector.

Throwers from Scandinavian countries have played a major role in this event as far back as the 19th century. Erik Lemming of Sweden established his first world record in 1899 and his final one—just under 200 ft (60.96 m) in 1912. Within this period, he captured two Olympic championships. The next two Olympic titles went to Jonni Myyrä (Finland), who did most of the record breaking through 1920. Myyrä's countryman, Matti Järvinen, 1932 Olympic titlist, improved the world record 10 times during his career to a peak of 253 ft 4½ in. (77.22 m) in 1936.

In the 1950s, Richard Held (U.S.) developed a javelin with improved glider-like aerodynamic qualities, with which his brother Franklin set world records of 263 ft 10 in. (80.40 m) in 1953 and 268 ft 2 in. (81.75 m) in 1955. The design principle came into general usage at the 1956 Olympics where Egil Danielsen (Norway) first surpassed 280 ft (85.34 m) with 85.71 m (281 ft 2½ in.). The design was formalized, with some changes, under specifications adopted by the IAAF in 1960 and, following minor improvements in performance by several athletes, Norwegian Terje Pedersen made a dramatic breakthrough by going from 285 ft 10 in. to 300 ft 11 in. (87.12 m to 91.72 m) within two months of 1964. Pedersen, however, never was a serious contender for Olympic honours. The 1964 title went to Pauli Nevala (Finland), and in 1968 the winner was Yanis Lusis (U.S.S.R.), one of the greatest competitors in the event's history. Nevala, Lusis, Jorma Kinnunen (Finland), and Mark Murro (U.S.) all joined Pedersen in the select 300-foot (91.44-m) category.

In the women's event, the all-around athlete Mildred ("Babe") Didrikson won the first Olympic championship in 1932. A later winner of the Olympic crown was Dana Zátopek, wife of four-time distance running champion Emil Zátopek of Czechoslovakia. Among women javelin throwers, 200 feet is on a par with 300 feet for men. Elvira Ozolina (U.S.S.R.) first bettered that barrier in 1964. Two months later, however, she lost the Olympic title to a 17-year-old Romanian, Mihaela Penes, who fell just shy of 200 feet.

DECATHLON AND PENTATHLON

Men and women both participate in multi-event competitions in which each of their performances earn points. The allotment of points is established by the IAAF and depends on the quality of the marks (i.e., the better the mark the higher the point total). The men's ten-event decathlon and the women's five-event pentathlon are all-around tests involving running, hurdling, jumping, and throwing, and are part of the Olympic Games program.

Decathlon. Competition in the decathlon extends over two days and includes four running and six field events. Each day begins and ends with runs, and the field events come between them. The order is, on the first day: 100 metres, long jump, shot put, high jump, and 400 metres; on the second day: 110-metre high hurdles, discus throw, pole vault, javelin, and 1,500 metres.

Decathlon rules vary slightly from those in individual events. For instance, each athlete gets only three attempts in each of the throwing events and the long jump; he may make a false start twice rather than once before being disqualified from a run; aiding wind does not affect a mark for record purposes. The IAAF has revised its scoring tables three times since the event's inception, most recently in 1962. Top decathlon performers average at least 800 points per event.

Emphasis is on overall consistency and high point production in every event rather than concentration on individual event victories. In a very real sense, the athlete is competing against himself and the scoring tables as much as with the man beside him. It is possible for him to go through the ten events without having the best mark in any one, yet still to come out ahead in the combined scoring. In practice, the best decathlon athletes normally have an individual event or two in which they might be close to world class, plus no glaring weaknesses in the remainder. As an example, Bill Toomey, the world record

The
modern
javelin

Decathlon champions

holder at the end of the 1960s, displayed the ability to win open 100-metre and 400-metre races and long jumping competitions, and he had more than adequate talent in the other seven events. An Olympic decathlon champion, because of his versatility, often is referred to as the world's greatest athlete. This title may have originated at the 1912 Olympics, where the King of Sweden reportedly said to decathlon winner Jim Thorpe (U.S.), "You, sir, are the world's greatest athlete."

Even though he later was relieved of his Olympic titles (pentathlon as well as decathlon) because he had played professional baseball, Thorpe earned recognition as the first great ten-event specialist. Others have been Harold Osborn (U.S.), Paavo Yrjölä (Finland), Glenn Morris (U.S.), Bob Mathias (U.S.), Rafer Johnson (U.S.), Toomey, and Nikolai Avilov (U.S.S.R.), all of whom achieved world records as well as won Olympic championships. Mathias is the only man to have won the Olympics twice, the first time in 1948, when he was 17 years old.

Pentathlon. The women's five-event contest, like the decathlon, is a two-day affair. The first day's competition includes the 100-metre hurdles (which replaced the 80-metre event following the 1968 Olympics), shot put, and high jump. The long jump and 200 metre come on the second day. On the IAAF scoring table for women, the leading performers score more than 5,000 points.

Pentathlon competition became part of the women's Olympic program in 1964, as the first championship went to Irina Press (U.S.S.R.). Press, also a world record hurdler, is part of the most famous family in women's track and field. Her sister, Tamara, held world records in the shot put and discus throw, and between them they won five Olympic titles.

Men's pentathlon and all-around

A five-event pentathlon for men was dropped from the Olympic Games program after 1924, but such competitions (not to be confused with the multisport Modern Pentathlon, which includes fencing, swimming, horseback riding, shooting, and running) still are held occasionally. All five events—the long jump, javelin throw, 200-metre, discus throw, and 1,500-metre—are held on the same day. Male pentathletes use the same table as in the decathlon; best performances are well over 4,000 points.

Another non-Olympic multi-event competition is the all-around, which is peculiar to the United States and conducted by the AAU. It is a one-day competition with ten events—100-yard dash, shot put, high jump, 880-yard walk, hammer throw, pole vault, 120-yard high hurdles, 56-pound weight throw, long jump, and mile run.

BIBLIOGRAPHY

History and general: M.F. WATMAN (comp.), *The Encyclopaedia of Athletics*, 2nd ed. (1967), information on the background of track and field, rules and records, and biographical data on athletes; J. HOPKINS, *The Marathon* (1968), historical background on the event; R.L. QUERCETANI, *World History of Track and Field Athletics, 1864–1964* (1964), the development of the sport to its present state.

Rules: INTERNATIONAL AMATEUR ATHLETIC FEDERATION (IAAF), *Official Handbook* (annual), rules governing international track-and-field competition, and world and Olympic Games records, *Scoring Tables (Men)* and *Scoring Tables (Women)*, point tables for the conduct of the decathlon and pentathlon.

Technique: J.W. ASPLAND and H. HATHAWAY, *Starting and Timekeeping* (1969), rules and techniques for officiating running events; K.H. COOPER, *Aerobics* (1968), suggestions for carrying out a jogging program; J.K. DOHERTY, *Modern Training for Running* (1964), various methods of training for long and middle distance events, *Modern Track and Field*, 2nd ed. (1963), training and competitive techniques for all events; T. ECKER and F. WILT (eds.), *International Track and Field Coaching Encyclopedia* (1970), training and competitive techniques for all events; R. GANSLEN, *Mechanics of the Pole Vault*, 7th ed. (1970), a complete book on the event; G.P. MEADE, *Athletic Records: The Whys and Wherefores* (1966), reasons why records are regularly improving; R. PICKERING, *Strength Training for Track and Field Athletics* (1969), use of weight training and other strength-building exercises as they relate to track and field events; W. ROSS, *The Hurdler's Bible* (1966) a complete book on the event; F. WILT, *Run, Run, Run* (1965), technical explanations of various running theories and practices.

Records and statistics: ASSOCIATION OF TRACK AND FIELD STATISTICIANS, *International Athletics Annual* (annual), and WOMEN'S TRACK AND FIELD WORLD, *Handbook* (annual), lists of records and all-time leading performers; D.H. POTTS and R.L. QUERCETANI, *1968 Olympic Track and Field Handbook* (1968), containing results of all Olympic Games events from 1896.

Biographical information: R. BANNISTER, *First Four Minutes* (1955), events leading up to Bannister's significant breakthrough; J. HENDERSON, *Road Racers and Their Training* (1970), information on long distance and marathon runners; C. NELSON, *Track and Field: The Great Ones* (1970), data on record performers; F. WILT, *How they Train* (1959), a collection of short descriptions about the personal and running statistics of hundreds of leading middle- and long-distance runners.

(B.Ne.)

Trade, International

International trade transactions are extremely diverse and include the purchase and sale of consumer goods; consumer services, such as travel; industrial raw materials and services; producer and capital goods, such as plant and machinery; securities in such forms as promissory notes and stock-ownership certificates; and gold. The only distinguishing characteristic of an international trade transaction is that it reaches across a national boundary. In the typical exchange, an individual or business firm in one nation receives a foreign good, service, or security, in exchange for which some small part of that nation's domestic currency is allowed to pass into foreign hands. The other nation exports part of its production or assets, receiving in exchange what is to it a foreign currency. The transfer of money into foreign hands poses special problems, as does the export of goods or the import of goods. This article reviews the origin and function of such international transactions in the light of international trade theory, and it examines the principal issues and problems that are posed by international trade.

THE THEORY OF INTERNATIONAL TRADE

History. Accounts of barter of goods or of services among different peoples can be traced back almost as far as the record of human history. International trade, however, is specifically an exchange between members of different nations, and accounts and explanations of such trade begin (despite fragmentary earlier discussion) only with the rise of the modern nation-state at the close of the European Middle Ages. As political thinkers and philosophers began to examine the nature and function of the nation, trade with other nations became a particular subtopic of their inquiry. It is, accordingly, no surprise to find one of the earliest attempts to describe the function of international trade within that highly nationalistic body of thought now known as "mercantilism." Mercantilist analysis, which reached the peak of its influence upon European thought in the 16th and 17th centuries, focussed directly upon the welfare of the nation. It insisted that the acquisition of wealth, particularly wealth in the form of gold, was of paramount importance for national policy. Mercantilists took the virtues of gold almost as an article of faith; consequently, they never undertook to explain adequately why gold deserved such a high priority in their economic plans.

Mercantilism

The trade policy dictated by mercantilist philosophy was accordingly simple: encourage exports, discourage imports, and take the proceeds of the resulting export surplus in gold. Because of their nationalistic bent, mercantilist writers either brushed aside or else did not realize that, from an international viewpoint, this policy would necessarily prove self-defeating. The nation that successfully gains an export surplus must ordinarily do so at the expense of one or more other nations that record a matching import surplus. Mercantilists' ideas often were intellectually shallow, and indeed their trade policy may have been little more than a rationalization of the interests of a rising merchant class that wanted wider markets—hence the emphasis on expanding exports—coupled with protection against competition in the form of imported goods. Yet mercantilist policies, as will be noted later, are by no means completely dead today.

Comparative advantage analysis. The British school of "classical economics" began in no small measure as a reaction against the inconsistencies of mercantilist thought. Adam Smith (1723–90) was the founder of this school; his famous work, *The Wealth of Nations*, is in part an antimercantilist tract. In *The Wealth of Nations*, Smith emphasized the importance of specialization as a source of increased output, and he treated international trade as a particular instance of specialization: in a world where productive resources are scarce and human wants cannot be completely satisfied, each nation should specialize in the production of goods it is particularly well equipped to produce; it should export part of this production, taking in exchange other goods that it cannot so readily turn out. Smith did not expand these ideas at much length; but David Ricardo (1772–1823), the second great classical economist, developed them into the "principle of comparative advantage," a principle still to be found, much as Ricardo spelled it out, in every international trade text.

Simplified theory of comparative advantage. For clarity of exposition, the theory of comparative advantage is usually first outlined as though only two countries and only two commodities were involved, although it is by no means limited to such cases. Again for clarity, the cost of production is usually measured only in terms of labour time and effort; the cost of a unit of cloth, for example, might be given as two man-days. The two countries will here be A and B, and the two commodities wine and cloth. The labour time required to produce a unit of either commodity in either country is as follows:

Cost of Production (labour time)

	country A	country B
wine (1 unit)	1 man-day	2 man-days
cloth (1 unit)	2 man-days	6 man-days

As compared with country A, country B is productively inefficient. Its manpower needs more time to turn out a unit of wine or a unit of cloth. This relative inefficiency may result from differences in climate, in worker training or skill, or in the amount of available tools and equipment, or from numerous other possible reasons. Ricardo took it for granted that such differences do exist, and he was not concerned, for purposes of his comparative-advantage analysis, with their origins.

One's first inclination is to conclude that in such circumstances country B could not possibly compete with country A, and indeed that if trade were to be opened up between them, country B would be competitively overwhelmed. Ricardo insisted that this conclusion is false. The critical factor is that country B's disadvantage is less pronounced in wine production, in which its workers require only twice as much time for a single unit as do the workers in A, than it is in cloth production, in which the required time is three times as great. This means, Ricardo pointed out, that country B will have a *comparative* advantage in wine production. Both countries will profit, in terms of the real income they enjoy, if country B specializes in wine production, exporting part of its output to country A, and if country A specializes in cloth production, exporting part of its output to country B. Paradoxical though it may seem, it is preferable for country A to leave wine production to country B, despite the fact that A's workers can produce wine of equal quality in half the time that B's workers can do so.

To illustrate this conclusion, one might consider that country A's total labour force consists of 300 men. Disregarding the possibility of trade with B, A then has a choice of various daily outputs of cloth and of wine, depending on the number of men engaged in each of the two occupations. This range of choices is illustrated by the line DEF in the Figure. If all 300 men work on cloth production, total daily cloth output will be 150 units (point D in the diagram), since each such unit requires two days' labour. At the other extreme, if all labour works on wine production, daily wine output will be 300 units (point F). Any

intermediate point on the line DEF is possible. Point E, for example, indicates 80 units of cloth produced daily (160 men so employed) and 140 units of wine (employing the other 140 men). DEF is country A's daily "production possibility" line. If it does not trade with country B and so can consume only what it produces itself, DEF will also be country A's "consumption possibility" line; it must choose some point thereon, depending on the preferences of its citizens for wine and cloth. DEF represents the limit of production and consumption possibilities; points above and to the right of DEF are unattainable.

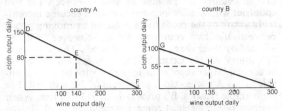

Production possibilities for cloth and wine (see text).

In the right-hand diagram, the line GHJ has exactly the same production and consumption significance for country B—assuming its total force to be 600 men (so as to make it roughly equal to A in total output capacity). The position of the line GHJ reflects the fact that manpower in country B requires two days to produce a unit of wine, and six days for a unit of cloth.

One may consider that A and B are initially isolated from one another. Country A has chosen point E (80 cloth, 140 wine) as its production–consumption point. Country B has chosen point H (55 cloth, 135 wine). The opportunity of free trade between the two countries is now opened up. If both countries wish to attain the higher levels of production and consumption available to them through specializing on and trading of the product for which they have a comparative advantage, Country A will shift its entire labour force to cloth production, and Country B will shift its entire labour force to wine production. A possible barter rate (setting aside the detail of how this would be worked out) would be one cloth for two and one half wine. Country A might then choose to export 60 units of its total daily cloth output of 150, keeping the other 90 for domestic consumption. In exchange for this 60 cloth (at the 1-for-2½ exchange rate) it would receive 150 wine. A's real income position is thus improved in comparison with pretrade point E: cloth for domestic consumption has risen from 80 to 90, and wine consumption has risen from 140 to 150. Country B enjoys a similar gain. In comparison with pretrade point H, its daily cloth consumption has risen from 55 to 60, and wine consumption has risen from 135 to 150.

The incentive to export and to import can be explained in price terms. In country A (before international trade), the price of cloth ought to be twice that of wine, since a unit of cloth requires twice as much labour effort. If this price ratio is not satisfied, one of the two commodities will be overpriced and the other underpriced. Labour will then move out of the underpriced occupation and into the other, until the resulting shortage of the underpriced commodity drives up its price. In country B (again, before trade), a cloth unit should cost three times as much as a wine unit, since a unit of cloth requires three times as much labour effort. Hence, a typical before-trade price relationship, matching the underlying real cost ratio in each country, might be as follows:

	country A	country B
Price of wine per unit	$5	£1
Price of cloth per unit	$10	£3

The absolute levels of price do not matter at all. All that is necessary is that in each country the ratio of the two prices should match the labour-cost ratio.

As soon as the opportunity of exchange between the two countries is opened up, the difference between the wine–cloth price ratio in country A (namely, 5:10, or 1:2) and that in country B (which is 1:3) provides the opportunity

Price incentives to trade

of a trading profit. Cloth will begin to move from A to B, and wine from B to A. A trader in A, starting with a capital of \$10 for example, would buy a unit of cloth, sell it in B for £3, buy 3 units of B's wine with the proceeds, and sell this in A for \$15. (This example assumes, for simplicity, that costs of transporting goods are negligible or zero. The introduction of transport costs complicates the analysis somewhat, but it does not change the conclusions, unless these costs are so high as to make trade impossible.)

So long as the ratio of prices in country A differs from that in country B, the flow of goods between the two countries will steadily increase as traders become increasingly aware of the profit to be obtained by moving goods between the two countries. Prices, however, will be affected by these changing flows of goods. The wine price in country A, for example, can be expected to fall as larger and larger supplies of imported wine become available. Thus A's wine–cloth price ratio of 1:2 will fall. For comparable reasons, B's price ratio of 1:3 will rise. When the two ratios meet, at some intermediate level (in the example earlier, at 1:2½), the flow of goods will stabilize.

At a later stage in the history of comparative-advantage theory, the English philosopher and political economist John Stuart Mill showed that the determination of the exact after-trade price ratio was a supply-and-demand problem. At each possible intermediate ratio (within the range of 1:2 and 1:3), country A would want to import a particular quantity of wine and export a particular quantity of cloth. At that same possible ratio, country B would wish to import and export particular amounts of cloth and of wine. For any intermediate ratio taken at random, however, A's export–import quantities probably will not match those of B. Ordinarily, there will be just *one* intermediate ratio at which the quantities *do* correspond; that is the final trading ratio at which quantities exchanged will stabilize. (Once they have stabilized, there is no longer any profit in exchanging goods. Even with such profits eliminated, however, there is no reason why A producers should want to stop selling part of their cloth in B, since the return there is as good as that obtained from domestic sales. Any falloff in the amounts exported and imported would reintroduce profit opportunities.)

In the elementary labour-cost example used above, there will be *complete* specialization: country A's entire labour force will move to cloth production and country B's to wine production. More elaborate comparative-advantage models recognize "real" production costs other than labour (that is, the costs of land and of capital). In such models, part of country A's wine industry may survive and compete effectively against imports, as may also part of B's cloth industry. The models can be expanded in other ways: to take account of more than two countries, or more than two commodities, and of transport costs. The essential conclusions, however, remain those obtained from the elementary model used above, so that this model, despite its simplicity, still provides a workable outline of the theory. (It should be noted that even the most elaborate comparative-advantage models continue to rely on certain simplifying assumptions without which the basic conclusions do not necessarily hold. These assumptions are discussed below.)

As noted earlier, the effect of this analysis is to correct any false first impression that low-productivity countries are at a hopeless disadvantage in trading with high-productivity ones. The impression is false, that is, if one assumes, as comparative advantage theory does, that international trade is an *exchange* of goods between countries. It is pointless for country A to sell goods to country B, whatever its labour-cost advantages, if there is nothing that it can profitably take back in exchange for its sales. With one exception, there will always be at least one commodity that a low-productivity country such as B can successfully export. Country B must of course pay a price for its low productivity, as compared with A; but that price is a lower per capita domestic income and not a disadvantage in international trading. For trading purposes, absolute productivity levels are unimportant; country B will always find one or more commodities in which it

enjoys a *comparative* advantage; that is, a commodity in the production of which its absolute disadvantage is *least*. The one exception is that case in which productivity ratios, and consequently pretrade price ratios, happen to match one another in two countries. Such would have been the case had country B required four man-days (instead of six) to produce a unit of cloth. In this particular circumstance, there would be no incentive for either country to engage in trade, and no gain from trading. In a two-commodity example such as that employed, it might not be unusual to find matching productivity and price ratios. But as soon as one moves on to cases of three and more commodities, the statistical probability of encountering precisely equal ratios becomes very small indeed.

The major argument derived from comparative-advantage analysis is that each country should specialize in those occupations in which it is relatively efficient; it should export part of that production and take in exchange those goods in whose production it is, for whatever reason, at a comparative disadvantage. The theory of comparative advantage thus provides a strong argument for free trade—and indeed for a laissez-faire attitude with respect to trade. The supporting argument is simple: specialization and free exchange among nations yield higher real income for the participants.

The fact that a country will enjoy higher real income as a consequence of the opening up of trade does not mean, of course, that every family or individual within the country must share in that benefit. Producer groups affected by import competition obviously will suffer, to at least some degree. Comparative-advantage theorists concede that free trade would affect the relative income position of such groups, and perhaps even their absolute income level. But they insist that the special interest of these groups clashes with the total national interest, and the most that they are usually willing to concede is the possible need for temporary protection against import competition, in order that the persons affected may have sufficient time to move to another occupation.

In actual fact, of course, nations often maintain permanent tariff and similar protectionist measures. The reasons for this clash between comparative-advantage reasoning and particular national policies are discussed below.

As already noted, the British classical economists made no attempt to explain *which* commodities a country would export or import. They simply accepted the fact that productivity differences do exist between countries, and they explored the consequences of that fact. Thus far, the only systematic attempt to explain the background of relative productivity conditions has been that of the Swedish economists Eli Heckscher and Bertil Ohlin. Ohlin's book, *Interregional and International Trade*, built on the foundations of Heckscher's work, was first published in 1933.

According to the Heckscher–Ohlin theory, comparative-advantage positions derive primarily from differences in each nation's endowment of productive inputs—that is, land, labour, and capital. The United States, for example, possesses a relatively large quantity of capital goods—relative to its own stock of land and of labour and relative also to the proportions of land, labour, and capital possessed by other nations. Any given commodity, so it is asserted in Heckscher–Ohlin analysis, typically requires for efficient production a given "mix" of inputs. A country will have a comparative advantage in the production and sale of a commodity if and when its endowment of factors exists in the proportions needed for its production. Some commodities, for example, are considered to be "capital intensive"—that is, their manufacture demands the use of relatively large amounts of capital equipment. A country like the United States, possessing proportionately large quantities of capital (again, relative to other countries), can be expected to have a comparative advantage in such capital-intensive commodities. Other products will be labour intensive; still others, land intensive. Thus, comparative-advantage positions are parcelled out according to relative factor endowments. Ohlin suggested one or two other sources of trading advantages, but these he treated as being of minor importance.

Sources
of comparative
advantage

Evaluation of international trade theory.

International trade analysis, like the greater part of economic theory, is strongly deductive in its construction. Attempts to test the conclusions of this theory empirically are still in their infancy. Some attempts have been made to test Heckscher–Ohlin theory by examining the composition of actual exports and imports. The results (although far from conclusive) suggest that United States exports are more labour intensive than United States imports. This is in flat contradiction of the Heckscher–Ohlin theory, which says that the United States must export capital-intensive commodities and import labour-intensive ones, since it possesses a relatively large amount of capital and a relatively small amount of labour (as compared with the situation in most other countries). It has been suggested that differences in labour productivity might explain this contradiction. The productivity of U.S. labour is so much higher than elsewhere that its relative scarcity is more than compensated for.

If labour productivities vary markedly among countries, then the *size* of the labour force is not necessarily an important factor in evaluating its productive competence; that is, size is not really as important a factor in the distribution of comparative-advantage positions as the Heckscher–Ohlin theory suggests. There is, moreover, probably no room in Heckscher–Ohlin theory for any concept of "corrected size," size of the labour force adjusted up or down to allow for markedly high or low productivity. *Any* trade pattern, no matter how violently in opposition to Heckscher–Ohlin reasoning, could always be made to conform to that reasoning by making a suitable after-the-event "productivity correction." If *any* trade pattern is so explainable, then Heckscher–Ohlin analysis is reduced from a theory to a tautology, losing all predictive power.

Most international trade economists still cautiously recognize the Heckscher–Ohlin doctrine—possibly because of the lack of any coherent alternative—but it must be considered as a speculative and unverified hypothesis.

The earlier comparative-advantage principle rests on a more secure analytic base. It cannot, however, be viewed as a comprehensive theory of international trade; it is instead an outline of some basic truths and a refutation of some elementary fallacies. To bring out these truths, the analysis makes some considerable simplifying assumptions. The more important of these assumptions are the following: (1) Full employment is assumed to prevail in both or all countries at all times; there are no problems of unemployment or recession. (2) Within each country, resources are assumed to be "occupationally mobile"; that is, in terms of the example earlier employed, the labour, capital, and land employed in wine production can move to cloth production or vice versa, if required to do so by competitive pressures. (3) The exchange of goods is treated as a *balanced* exchange—indeed, almost to the point that it might be a barter exchange. No consideration is given to the special problems arising out of balance-of-payments surpluses or deficits or out of the maintenance of a particular exchange rate. (4) Each country is assumed to have a *given* resource stock and a *given* technology.

The use of such assumptions is necessary but unfortunate. It is necessary because without them it would be impossible to bring out the fundamental truth of comparative-advantage positions. It is unfortunate because it conveys the impression that comparative-advantage theorists wish to brush aside as inconsequential many of the issues with which a nation must sometimes deal in its policies toward international trade. Nations have been known, for instance, to try to cope with unemployment by erecting barriers to international trade; or they have maintained such barriers because the occupational mobility of resources (their transfer to a different employment) is sometimes a slow and difficult process.

A more fundamental objection to comparative-advantage theory is its neglect of the fact that the composition and development of a nation's stock of productive resources may be changed by international trade. Comparative-advantage theory treats the resource stock as *given*. In point of fact, as a country becomes deeply involved in international trade, its resource stock (the size and nature of its capital stock, the training of its labour force) grows and changes in order to meet the particular demands of that trade. Comparative-advantage theory says that a nation's international trade situation—the pattern of its exports and imports—is what it is because of the nature of its resource supply, but sometimes one may say with equal truth that the nation's resource supply is what it is because of its involvement in international trade.

Insofar as the purpose of the analysis is to explain the gains in real income that accrue from the opening up of free international trade, the assumption of a given resource supply is convenient and defensible. If the intent, however, is the more ambitious one of furnishing a statement of the nature and consequences of international trade, the assumption is less satisfactory. Comparative-advantage theory is probably best viewed as simply an outline of some fundamental principles of international exchange. A more sophisticated theory of such exchanges remains to be built on this foundation.

STATE INTERFERENCE IN INTERNATIONAL TRADE

Methods of interference. Regardless of what comparative-advantage theory may say about the virtues of unrestricted trade, all nations interfere with international exchanges to at least some degree. Tariffs may be imposed on imports—in some instances making them so costly as to bar completely the entry of the good involved. Quotas may limit the permissible volume of imports. State subsidies may be offered to encourage exports. Money-capital exports may be restricted or prohibited. Investment by foreigners in domestic plant and equipment may be similarly restrained.

These interferences may be simply the result of special-interest pleading, for as already noted, particular groups suffer as a consequence of import competition. Or a government may impose restrictions because it feels impelled to take account of factors that comparative advantage sets aside. It is of interest to note that insofar as goods and services are concerned, the general pattern of interference follows the old mercantilist dictum of discouraging imports and encouraging exports.

Reasons for interference. The more important considerations that prompt governmental regulation are summarized below.

Revenue. Underdeveloped nations in particular often lack the institutional machinery needed for effective imposition of income or corporation taxes. The governments of such nations may then finance their activity by resort to tariffs on imported goods, since such levies are relatively easy to administer. The amount of tax revenue obtainable through tariffs, however, is always limited. If the government tries to increase its tariff income by imposing higher duty rates, this may choke off the flow of imports and so reduce tariff revenue instead of increasing it.

Protection of domestic industry. Probably the commonest argument for tariff imposition is that particular domestic industries need tariff protection for survival. Comparative-advantage theorists will of course argue that the industry in need of such protection ought not to survive and that the resources so employed ought to be transferred to occupations having greater comparative efficiency. The welfare gain of citizens taken as a whole would more than offset the welfare loss of those groups affected by import competition; that is, total real national income would increase. An opposing argument would be, however, that this welfare gain would be widely diffused, so that the individual beneficiaries might not be conscious of any great improvement. The welfare loss, in contrast, would be narrowly and acutely felt. Although resources *can* be transferred to other occupations, just as comparative-advantage theory says, the transfer process is sometimes slow and painful for those being transferred. For such reasons, comparative-advantage theorists rarely advocate the immediate removal of all existing tariffs. They argue instead against further tariff increases—since increases, if effective, attract still more resources into the wrong occupation—and they press for gradual reduction of import barriers.

Simplifying assumptions of comparative-advantage analysis

Unemployment. A variant of the industry-protection argument is that tariffs or quotas are needed to maintain domestic employment—particularly in times of recession. Today, there is near-unanimity among economists that proposals to remedy unemployment by means of tariff increases are misguided. Insofar as a higher tariff is effective for this purpose, it simply "exports unemployment": the rise in domestic employment is matched by a drop in production in some foreign country. That other country, moreover, is likely to impose a retaliatory tariff increase. Finally, the tariff remedy for unemployment is a poor one because it is usually ineffective and because more suitable remedies are now available. Today it is recognized that unemployment is far more efficiently dealt with by the implementation of proper fiscal and monetary policies.

Economic development. The comparative-advantage principle supports, as indicated earlier, free-trade and laissez-faire policies. Ordinarily, a mature and developed country, with widely diversified and self-confident industries, has no great difficulty in accepting the validity of this principle, with the exception of those producers who are afflicted by import competition.

Considerations are quite different for an underdeveloped country—that is, a country with a low per capita income, with limited industry, and typically relying on the export of one or two agricultural or mineral primary products. Today, all such underdeveloped countries are forced to direct their policies toward growth and higher real living standards. Progress is commonly viewed in terms of industry growth and diversification. These countries, however, are unlikely to think in laissez-faire terms. The less privileged nations may vary in the extent of their belief that growth and development can and should be fostered by governmental action, but that some such action is needed is almost universally accepted. The leaders of such countries are thus inclined to regard laissez-faire comparative-advantage theory as an apology for the status quo devised by the more affluent countries. Many underdeveloped nations are thus in a painful position: they depend on their exchanges with richer countries for survival, and yet they suspect that this foreign trade is a form of exploitation, whether so intended or not, that keeps them in a subservient position as "hewers of wood and drawers of water" and that prevents the development of their domestic industries.

Weakness of comparative-advantage theory

Unfortunately, comparative-advantage theory is deficient on precisely this matter of the growth and expansion of resources. As noted earlier, the concern of this theory is with the best possible use of a *given* stock of industrial and other resources. It is thus difficult to resolve the issues involved. In general, the poorer nations have had limited success in the attempt to foster the development of their domestic industries by means of restrictions on foreign trade, and most economists are disdainful of the "infant industry" argument that tariffs and similar protection are effective means of generating industrial growth. A comprehensive evaluation of such attempts at development must await a more complete theory of the sources and effects of international trade.

National defense. A common appeal made by an industry seeking tariff or quota protection is that its survival is essential in the national interest: its product would be needed in wartime, when the supply of imports might well be cut off. The verdict of economists on this argument is fairly clear: the national-defense argument is frequently a red herring, an attempt to "wrap oneself in the flag," and insofar as an industry *is* essential, the tariff is a dubious means of ensuring its survival. Essential industries ought instead to be given a direct subsidy to enable them to meet foreign competition, with explicit recognition of the fact that the subsidy is a price paid by the nation in order to maintain the industry for defense purposes.

Autarky, or self-sufficiency. Many demands for protection, whatever their surface argument may be, are really appeals to the autarkic feelings that prompted mercantilist reasoning. (Autarky is defined as the state of being self-sufficient at the level of the nation.) A proposal for the restriction of free international trade can be described as "autarkic" if it appeals to those half-submerged feelings that "we" (citizens of the nation involved) form a community sharing a common welfare and common interests, whereas "they" (foreigners) have no regard for such welfare and interests and might even be actively opposed thereto. And it is quite true that a country that has become heavily involved in international trade has given hostages to fortune: a part of its industry has become dependent upon export markets for income and for employment. Any cutoff of these foreign markets (brought about by recession abroad, by the imposition of new tariffs by some foreign country, or by numerous other possible changes) would be acutely serious; and yet it would be a situation largely beyond the power of the domestic government involved to alter. Similarly, another part of domestic industry may rely on an inflow of imported raw materials, such as oil for fuel and power. Any restriction of this import inflow could have the most serious consequences. The vague threat implicit in such possibilities often results in a yearning for autarky, for national self-sufficiency, for a life free of dependence on the hazards of the outside world.

In point of fact, no nation in today's world, no matter how rich and varied its endowment of resources, could really practice self-sufficiency, and attempts in that direction could produce sharp drops in real income. Nevertheless, protectionist arguments—particularly those made "in the interests of national defense"—often draw heavily on the strength of such autarkic sentiments.

Balance-of-payments difficulties. Governments may interfere with the processes of foreign trade for a reason quite different from those thus far discussed: shortage of foreign exchange. Today, most governments try to maintain fixed exchange rates between their own currencies and those of other countries. Even if not absolutely fixed, the exchange rate is ordinarily allowed to fluctuate only within a narrow range of values. Fixed exchange rates are held to facilitate trade because they eliminate the uncertainty arising out of a fluctuating rate. If the rate fluctuates, either the exporter is uncertain as to the revenue he will earn from his sale or else the importer is uncertain as to what his purchase will cost him in terms of domestic currency.

The maintenance of a fixed exchange rate requires each government to keep a foreign exchange reserve, typically maintained in gold or in a major currency such as the United States dollar or the British pound sterling. This reserve is drawn upon whenever the country's total imports outrun its total exports in value. An import surplus means that the demand for foreign currencies (to pay for imports) outruns the supply of foreign currencies (earned through exports).

If balance-of-payments difficulties arise and persist, the government's foreign-exchange reserve will run low. In a crisis, this situation may force the government to devalue the nation's currency; that is, to give it a new and lower value in the foreign exchange markets. But typically, before being driven to this extremity, it will try to redress the balance by restricting imports or encouraging exports, in much the old mercantilist fashion.

The threat of trade restriction prompted by reserve shortages has grown more acute in recent years. The total volume of international transactions has risen steadily, but there has not been a corresponding increase in the supply of international reserves. International debate still goes on as to whether the needed reserve increase should be furnished by increasing the price of gold, which would increase the reserve power of any given physical quantity of gold; by the creation of "paper gold" through the International Monetary Fund or a similar agency; or by greater resort to the use of a national currency such as the pound sterling or the dollar. Meanwhile, nations are inclined to hoard their reserves: they regard any depletion with alarm while welcoming any increase. Thus they are drawn toward the old mercantilist policy of reserve accumulation, even though they know that it is not in the interest of expanded international trade that they do so. (For a more detailed discussion of this topic, see EXCHANGE AND PAYMENTS, INTERNATIONAL.)

"Paper gold" and other suggested remedies

A company that finds itself barred from an attractive foreign market by tariffs or quotas may be able to leapfrog the barrier simply by establishing a manufacturing plant within that foreign country. This policy of foreign plant investment has expanded enormously since the close of World War II. United States companies have taken the lead, investing particularly in western Europe, Canada, and South America. Industry in other developed countries has followed a similar pattern—some foreign companies establishing plants within the United States as well as in other areas of the world.

Foreign ownership of domestic industry

The governments of countries subject to this new investment find themselves in an ambivalent position. The establishment of new foreign-owned plants may mean more than simply the creation of new employment opportunities and new productive capacity; it may also mean the introduction of new technologies and superior business-control methods. But the government that welcomes such benefits must also expect complaints of "foreign control," an argument that will inevitably be pressed by domestic owners of older plants who fear a new competition that cannot be blocked by tariffs. Many governments are still wrestling with this problem, particularly insofar as investment by U.S. firms is involved. Countries such as Great Britain and Canada have been liberal in their admissions policy; others, notably Japan, impose tight restriction on foreign-owned plants.

PATTERNS OF TRADE

Degrees of national participation. Nations vary considerably in the extent of their foreign trade. As a very rough generalization, it may be said that the larger a country is in physical size and population, the less its involvement in foreign trade, mainly because of the greater diversity of raw materials available within its borders and the greater size of its internal market. Thus the participation of the United States is relatively low, its export and import totals each being just over 4 percent of its gross national product, and that of the U.S.S.R. even lower. The U.S. gross national product, however, is so immense by world standards that the United States still ranks as one of the world's most important trading countries. Some of the smaller countries of western Europe (such as The Netherlands) have export and import totals that approach 40 percent of their gross national products.

Trade among developed countries. The greatest volume of trade occurs among the developed, capital-rich countries of the world, especially among the industrial leaders known as the "Group of 10" (Belgium, Canada, France, Germany, Italy, Japan, The Netherlands, Sweden, the United Kingdom, and the U.S.). Generally, as a country matures economically its participation in foreign trade grows more rapidly than its gross national product.

Trade within the EEC

The European Economic Community (EEC, or Common Market) affords an impressive instance of the gains to be derived from freer trade. In economic terms, the EEC is simply a plan for unrestricted movement of goods, labour, and capital across the boundaries of its member countries (Belgium, France, Italy, Luxembourg, The Netherlands, and West Germany). A major part of the increases in real income in EEC countries is almost certainly attributable to the removal of trade barriers. The EEC's formation cannot, however, be interpreted as reflecting an unqualified dedication to the free-trade principle. EEC rules require member countries to maintain a common and often substantial tariff against goods from outside the Community.

Trade among developed and underdeveloped countries. Difficult problems frequently arise out of trade between developed and underdeveloped countries. Many less-developed countries are tropical, frequently relying heavily for income upon the proceeds from export of one or two crops, such as coffee, cocoa, sugar. Markets for such goods are highly competitive (in the sense in which economists use the term *competitive*)—that is, prices are extremely sensitive to every change in demand or in supply. Prices of manufactured goods, the typical exports of developed countries, are commonly much more stable. Hence, as the price of its export commodity fluctuates, the tropical country experiences large fluctuations in its "terms of trade," the ratio of export prices to import prices, often with painful effects on the domestic economy. With respect to almost all important primary commodities, efforts have been made at price stabilization and output control. These efforts have met with varied success.

Comparable problems arise when the underdeveloped country exports a mineral such as petroleum or copper. The initiative in developing such a resource is often taken by a foreign company from a developed country that owns (in part if not in full) the extracting capital facilities. Particularly since the mineral resource is exhaustible, charges of exploitation are common. The matter is a continuing source of political strife and may on occasion lead to expropriation of the mineral properties.

Several underdeveloped countries have joined in creating organizations for the promotion of trade between themselves. Notable examples include the Central American Common Market (1961), the Latin American Free Trade Association (1961), and the Common Afro-Malagasy-Mauritanian Organization.

Soviet foreign trade. The Soviet Union's involvement in foreign trade, measured as before by comparing exports or imports against gross national product, is even lower than that of the United States. The U.S.S.R. is not in general an important trader in world markets, but it has made occasional large-scale entries, such as its grain purchases during years of domestic crop shortage in the 1960s and early 1970s.

Since the 1917 Revolution, Soviet policy has clearly been influenced by autarkic feelings, further reinforced by its suspicions of the capitalist world and by its strong desire for centrally directed planning. Today, the U.S.S.R. appears to be showing a greater interest in expanded trade connections, doubtless because of growing industrial maturity.

The attitude of the U.S.S.R. toward foreign trade was forced to undergo some change when that country acquired influence over the eastern European countries after World War II. It established the Council for Mutual Economic Assistance (Comecon) to direct trade with and among its satellite neighbours. Comecon, however, appears to be primarily a device for implementing and integrating central development plans among member countries—unlike the European Common Market, which was planned to facilitate the unrestricted movement of goods and productive inputs. Exchanges among Comecon countries do not appear to be directed by the same considerations of price and quality that govern trade in the Western world; at any rate, the patterns of Comecon trade are often difficult for an outsider to interpret. Some satellite countries, it appears, would willingly trade more freely with the West, but they are restrained by demands that they first of all fulfill their obligations to the Comecon organization.

Comecon

BIBLIOGRAPHY. The classic works in the field of international trade theory are: ADAM SMITH, *An Inquiry into the Nature and Causes of the Wealth of Nations*, 2 vol. (1776); DAVID RICARDO, *On the Principles of Political Economy and Taxation* (1817); JOHN STUART MILL, *Principles of Political Economy*, 2 vol. (1848); and BERTIL G. OHLIN, *Interregional and International Trade* (1933, rev. ed. 1967). Particularly useful international trade textbooks include: C.P. KINDLEBERGER, *International Economics*, 4th ed. (1968); D.A. SNIDER, *Introduction to International Economics*, 4th ed. (1967); and P.B. KENEN, *International Economics*, 2nd ed. (1967).

(R.R.)

Trademark Law

A trademark is a mark or a sign that distinguishes the goods of one manufacturer or trader from those of another. The sign must be one that can identify a product as originating from one source and, thus, distinguish it from those coming from another source. It may be a word or a device or combination of both. It may be an invented word like Kodak for cameras, a coined word like Coca-Cola for a soft drink, a fanciful word like Arpège ("arpeggio" in music) for a perfume, or a common word like Volkswagen ("people's car") for an automobile. And it may also be a word that is originally a descriptive word but by continued and exclusive use by a manufacturer or trader becomes distinctive of his goods—for instance, Dry Ice.

What the law everywhere does require is that the mark must be "distinctive"; *i.e.*, that it allows the owner to communicate symbolically with the public in identifying his product and in assuring them that they are getting his product when the mark appears thereon. The concept of distinctiveness is not interpreted uniformly in the various parts of the world. Moreover, it has been expanded as a result of the evolution of the conditions of trade and new needs of protection. Particularly, there is now recognition and protection of so-called service marks, which identify and distinguish not products but services offered or performed by persons. The most familiar of these are marks used to identify transportation services, communication services, cleaning services, hotel services, and the like.

There are also collective or association marks, which are trade or service marks used by an association of producers or traders or by a cooperative or any other collective group. These serve to distinguish the products or services of the members of the group or to indicate membership in a union, association, or other organization.

In addition, there are the so-called certification marks used in connection with goods of persons other than the owner of the mark to certify regional or other origin, material, mode of manufacture, or other characteristics. The principles that apply to trademarks used on goods apply generally to the other kinds of marks as well.

An international definition

There has always been a felt need for an international definition that could be agreed upon by the various countries. One such was adopted in 1963 by the International Association for the Protection of Industrial Property, which describes the mark generally as "capable of distinguishing the products or services of a person or of a group of persons. The distinctive character of a mark, in respect of the goods or services designated by it, arises from the nature of the sign or of the use which has been made of it." What follows is an enumeration of a number of things that, if distinctive, can serve as trademarks: words or groups of words, letters, numerals, devices, names, the shape or other presentation of products or their packages, colour combinations with signs, combinations of colours, and combinations of any of the enumerated signs. The International Bureau for the Protection of Industrial Property established in Geneva has prepared a model trademark law for developing countries that defines a trademark in general terms as "any visible sign intended to distinguish the goods or services of one enterprise from those of another."

GENERAL CONSIDERATIONS

The purposes served by trademarks. The observation made by an American judge asserts that "it is not settled whether a trademark is to be primarily regarded as protecting the trademark owner's business from a species of unfair competition or as protecting the public from imitations." The truth, of course, is that a trademark purports to protect both, though often the law or the tribunals in interpreting and applying the law may appear to give primary weight to one or the other. Trademark law in fact looks upon four classes of interests and claims: the interest of the manufacturer or merchant who adopts and uses a trademark to identify or distinguish the goods he puts on the market to prevent the diversion of prospective customers; the interest of competitors who wish to prevent undue monopolization of effective symbols or signs or expressions giving information about the goods; the interest of the consumer not to be deceived or confused about the goods he wishes to buy; and the general public interest, which would be seriously affected if producers of goods could not ensure the benefit of their labour and investment and if consumer deception were tolerated.

The competing interests

Main characteristics of trademark. The primary function of a trademark is to identify the origin of the article to which it is affixed. This is the basic difference between a patent and a trademark. The purpose of the patent is not to indicate origin of the product but to protect a new product or a new process by which the

product is made irrespective of the origin. A trademark is not necessarily an invention. It may sometimes be forced upon the producer by the public. A certain fortuitous sign may be liked by the public and eventually become a trademark, although it was not so intended at first. The trademark need not be novel. It may be in use in one industry and subsequently be adopted in another. A mark that has been a trademark in the past and abandoned may be readopted and used again as a trademark.

Guarantee of quality

Besides the primary function of indicating origin, the trademark has certain additional functions. One of these is to guarantee the quality of the products bearing the mark. The public may not know or care about the identity of the producer of a commodity but the mark identifies for them goods associated with certain experiences or assumed characteristics in composition, ingredients, quality, and the like. It gives assurance that goods bearing the same trademark at the next purchase will have the same characteristics. This is called the guarantee function of the trademark. It means also that the owner need not actually participate in the production of the goods. It is sufficient if he exercises control over the quality of the goods.

The source of products bearing a trademark is sometimes uncertain, varied, or fluid. Traders' trademarks may be affixed on products from divergent sources, and manufacturers' trademarks may be affixed on products made for the manufacturers in whole or in part by various suppliers or subcontractors.

The guarantee function of trademarks is particularly relevant when they are used in different territories since the owner of a trademark, to satisfy local requirements of the public's tastes or preferences, may not sell the identical goods in each area. Importation of the differing products of one country into the territory of another may interfere with the trademark's guarantee of quality and may injure the goodwill of the owner as well as deceive the expectations of the public. The same guarantee function is involved in cases of licensing trademarks where the law requires control and supervision by the owner of the trademark with respect to the methods of manufacture and the finished goods.

The mark also performs an advertising function. Once it has acquired goodwill and consumer response because it symbolizes real or assumed value of the product concerned, it constitutes a kind of advertisement. By constant repetition the mark is impressed on the consumer's mind to the point where its mere display suffices to remind the public of the standards or other properties of the product with which the owner has permeated the market.

Relationship of trademark to unfair competition. Trademarks have their origin in the rule that no man has the right to put up his goods for sale as the goods of another person, either by direct or indirect representation. By using the trademark of a rival person, even without making a direct false representation to the purchaser, the seller, in effect, tells him a lie and commits the tort of passing off, or unfair competition. A trademark is only one of the badges or indicia by which the trade of a person and the goods he deals in are identified with him and distinguished from the trade and goods of another. There are numerous other indicia, such as, the name under which one trades, the manner and packaging in which the goods appear on the market, the showing of prizes or medals that have been bestowed for the particular goods, and marketing or advertising devices.

How far the use of particular indicia, other than a trademark, does or does not amount to representing one's goods as those of someone else must always be a question of evidence before the courts. The growth and development of the concept of unfair competition rests upon notions of civil responsibility, principles of honest customs in trade, and disapproval of questionable practices. All such attitudes, of course, depend on the degree of community pressure for the suppression of unfair conduct in business.

Trademark law, while a part of the law of unfair competition deriving from the fundamental rule against passing off, has gradually crystallized in the recognition of trademarks as property. Since this law grants the trader, who uses a mark to identify his goods and distinguish them from others, an exclusive right in the use of such mark, this right exists quite apart from a legal inquiry as to passing off. Legislation everywhere that defines and protects this property has given the trademark the characteristic of a special monopoly right in the sense that it prevents its use for another's similar goods in exactly the same way as it protects any other kind of private property. Thus the trademark law, within more or less fixed technical boundaries, prohibits acts that might not be calculated to deceive. Using the identical trademark of a registered proprietor of a trademark for identical or similar goods is prohibited regardless of whether such use is likely to deceive purchasers.

On the other hand, the security given by the law for the recognition and protection of trademark rights, is given in exchange for compliance with certain technical formalities, and failure to comply with such requirements deprives the claimant of the special protection of the trademark law. In such cases, the trademark owner may still be protected by the unfair competition law if the use of his trademark by another is likely to result in passing off by confusing the purchaser. The unfair competition law is an all-inclusive basic concept of which the law of trademarks is a particular branch. This is another way in which trademarks differ from patents. An inventor of a new product or a new process who has not obtained a patent cannot stop another person from making or using the same product or process, nor can he claim unfair competition against the second party. But the owner of a trademark who failed to register his mark may still be protected against its use by another under the conditions of a passing-off action.

This concept of the trademark law as a part of the law of unfair competition, while true of the United States, British-law countries, and a number of civil-law countries, is not universal. In many other countries, for example those of Latin America, there is either no unfair competition law at all or such law as there is exists apart from trademark law and is limited in application to specified acts of deception or fraud through other means. In such countries the one way to protect a trademark against unauthorized use by another is by registration as provided for by law.

THE SUBSTANTIVE LAW OF TRADEMARKS

Acquisition of trademarks. The value as well as the ownership of a trademark springs from its adoption and use with respect to the products it serves to distinguish and individualize. The law does not protect the material sign or mark itself as a creation or invention of the user but the value and the use of that sign or mark in connection with the business in the goods concerned. Because of this, the *right* in a trademark was, until recently, generally acquired by prior adoption and use, registration being only declaratory of *property* in a trademark. It followed that the registered proprietor of a trademark was only the prima-facie owner and anyone could show a prior use of such trademark and cause the cancellation of the registration. Generally speaking, this is no longer true. There remain comparatively few countries where registration of a trademark is merely declaratory of property therein.

In the United States the situation is a special one. Congress has no power to legislate generally on the subject of trademarks, and protection rests fundamentally on the common law. A trademark right is created by use of a trademark, and the common law protection attaches to such right, irrespective of registration. Federal registration gives the registrant only certain procedural advantages such as a presumption of ownership, a right to sue in the federal courts, a right to claim treble damages in case of willful infringement, and the right to claim protection in foreign countries in certain situations. The only other country where the law is the same is the Philippines, which derives its trademark law from the United States. In Canada, which has a legal position derived partly from British law and partly from American law, actual use of a mark is a condition of registration. In a few civil-law countries right in a trademark may be acquired by user apart from registration, but even in those countries this

rule has been mitigated. In Belgium, Luxembourg, and The Netherlands, where, until recently, use alone was the source of ownership, the position is now changed under the unitary Benelux law, which establishes registration as the source of ownership. In Great Britain and the nearly 40 other jurisdictions that derive their trademark law from British law, the common law has been modified and registration gives substantive rights.

Use alone as a basis of ownership in trademarks thus has been abandoned today in the vast majority of countries. This is explained by modern commercial conditions under which the market for any given industry or commercial enterprise is no longer confined within definite boundaries. An industry or trade may start with a mark extending over a small part of a country's territory, then extend to the whole territory of that country, and later reach any number of foreign countries. Under these circumstances the need has arisen for an enterprise adopting and using a new mark to give notice of its claim in a form that will protect its market beyond the boundaries in which notice is given by mere use of the mark. This not only provides protection for the person adopting a new mark but gives security to other manufacturers or traders who may consult the register to avoid adopting a trademark already in use. With prior use and adoption for the whole territory predicated on the registration of the trademark, registration may well be considered as the basis of ownership. The law may require the person who first adopts and uses the trademark in connection with his business to register it; unless he does so, he cannot complain of anyone else registering or using the same trademark since he failed to give notice to the public of his claim. Unless the later user of the mark acts fraudulently, he acquires a property right by registering the trademark himself. This is the law in a large number of countries today.

A position that entirely disregards rights created by use and grants ownership to the person who first applies for registration could result in injustice and in deception of the public. This has encouraged the development of a third system for acquisition of property in trademarks, which is particularly appropriate with respect to their international protection. In practice, the requirement of prompt registration in every country is nearly impossible in many cases. There must necessarily be a waiting period for a commercial or industrial enterprise to consider whether it will be able to do sufficient business with a certain trademark in a particular foreign country to require registration. The enterprise may have to consider what the prospects are of its exporting goods to a foreign country. It may have to test the market by trial shipments, engage in publicity, seek agents and distributors, etc. This is equally true in a single country, where the enterprise may adopt and use different trademarks in connection with several products. It may be preferable to test the market for a particular product before applying to register the mark. Or the trademark may not be registrable at first until it acquires distinctiveness by use. For these reasons a system has been developed under which registration gives ownership in a trademark only when uncontested for a stated period of time, during which the prior user may have his claim of ownership enforced.

A prior user has two remedies. He may file opposition against an application for registration of a mark by showing that he had a prior user right in the same or a similar mark. But in such cases he must generally show not only use, but that he has acquired a reputation as a user that would make the use of the applicant's mark deceptive or confusing and therefore disentitled to protection in a court of justice. Or else he must show that the mark applied for is his mark and that the applicant is therefore acting in defraud of his rights or that the applicant is not entitled to claim proprietorship of the mark. If the prior user fails to oppose registration in the name of another, he may still move to cancel the registration as an aggrieved person, but if he fails to do so within seven years from the date of registration, such registration becomes conclusive against him. This is the legal position today in all British-law countries, and, with some qualifications, represents the general principle elsewhere. In most other countries

Use versus registration

the term within which a registration becomes incontestable as against a prior user is even shorter, between three and five years.

Even in the United States, the Lanham Trademark Act of 1946 introduced the principle of incontestability of registration after five years, although in practice there are many conditions and limitations. In France as well, where formerly ownership of a trademark was acquired by the user and an adverse registration could be cancelled at any time by a prior user, the law has changed in recent years. Ownership is now acquired by registration uncontested within five years, and it may be contested only by a person who has used his mark in France to such an extent that it has become well known to the public.

Distinctiveness of the mark

Registrability. A corollary to the importance of registration is that the mark must be such that it is entitled to valid registration. The primary requirement, of course, is that the mark must be distinctive, but in some countries certain subject matter cannot be registered as a trademark regardless of distinctiveness. In most important commercial countries, however, it is now provided that a mark that may not have been distinctive at the time of its adoption and first use may become distinctive if used exclusively for a sufficiently long time to have come to identify and distinguish the goods of the proprietor. This is particularly the case with respect to descriptive terms or subject matter that is not primarily distinctive, such as letters, numerals, colours, devices, and the general appearance of products or containers. The procedure for proving distinctiveness of such matters differs in the various countries, but the basic consideration is whether the mark has acquired what is called secondary meaning. This means that while the primary meaning of a certain trademark is, for instance, descriptive, the mark has developed a new secondary meaning designating and identifying certain goods as originating from a certain source.

In a number of countries the question of whether a trademark is distinctive or has acquired distinctiveness is not examined at the time application is filed for registration. The mark is registered and then it is up to the court to decide in a given case that may be brought before it whether the mark was validly registered. In many other countries the patent office examines the question of registrability both with regard to objective compliance with the legal requirements of registration, and with regard to prior registered marks of other persons. In most of these countries the decision of the patent office to allow the application for registration is published, allowing any interested person to oppose the application and ask that it be refused. This is the system that operates in the United States and in British-law countries.

Infringement. Ownership of a trademark confers both the positive right to use it and the negative right of precluding third parties from interfering with the proprietor's exclusive right. Interference with this exclusive right constitutes what is technically called infringement, which is one of the most important problems in the protection of trademarks. The issue as to whether or not there is infringement arises under various circumstances: (1) at the time of application by a newcomer to register a trademark and the registrar or the previous owner objects that such mark is infringing, (2) when an action is brought for cancellation of a registration, or rectification of the register to expunge a junior mark on the ground that it infringes a senior one, (3) in an infringement action when the plaintiff claims that the defendant is wrongfully using his mark.

In all of these instances the question is whether the resemblance to the plaintiff's mark is likely to deceive or confuse purchasers of the particular goods. Notwithstanding differences of law in the various countries, criteria for making such a judgment are generally alike. The general impression of the ordinary purchaser should serve as a guide. The mark should be looked at as a whole, since the ordinary purchaser will not stop to dissect it; the similarities rather than the differences should be considered. The two marks should not be viewed side by side, since the ordinary purchaser relies only upon his memory of the plaintiff's mark. Also the nature of the goods plays a role in the judgment; if the value of the goods concerned

is high, the purchaser may be discriminating and cautious in looking at a mark, while in the case of common and inexpensive goods, no great thought is given. If purchasers are children or illiterate persons or foreign to the language of the mark, any doubt as to similarity should be resolved in favour of the owner of the old mark as against a newcomer. If a trademark is one combining a verbal and a figurative element, the verbal element is deemed more important because it is this that the public ordinarily recognizes and calls for. But there are exceptions to this rule when the figurative element dominates a trademark by its use, colour, etc.

The protection of famous marks

Infringement involves not only confusing similarity of trademarks but also similarity of the goods for which the two marks are used. There is considerable variety in the various countries as to the scope of protection of a trademark with respect to the type of goods. The general principle is that the goods of the two parties are deemed similar or conflicting if the public could attribute them to the same origin. The physical or essential characteristics of the goods as to form, composition, or quality is not necessarily the primary test. The fact that the goods are intended to satisfy the same need, are sold through the same channels, and are offered to the same class of customers is granted more importance. There has also been a recognition, both in theory and case law, that this general rule of similarity of goods is inadequate for the protection of certain marks enjoying a great reputation and that such marks should be protected against use by others even for quite dissimilar products. This view is based on several considerations.

In the first place, a mark that enjoys wide publicity in identifying certain products of outstanding quality becomes associated in the mind of the public with a certain origin. Use of the same trademark by another person even on dissimilar goods is likely to create an erroneous belief that the products of the newcomer come from the same origin, or that there is some relationship or connection between the two parties. Second, use by another person of such a mark for dissimilar products destroys the uniqueness and originality or distinctive power of the trademark, which is thus diluted and weakened, to the injury of the owner. Third, a newcomer who appropriates and uses a mark of great reputation is being permitted to obtain an unfair advantage or unjust enrichment from the efforts, expenses, and investment of the original owner.

In many countries the courts are granting protection to famous trademarks on any or all of the above mentioned grounds. But they are also conscious of the danger that they may be called upon to give this extended protection to marks that merely become widely known through unusually heavy advertising and publicity financed by owners with great resources. The courts are therefore leaning more and more on the extent to which the mark is known outside the relevant field of competition. The more memorable the mark is to members of the trade and the consuming public, the more likely its use may cause confusion as to origin or sponsorship, impair its economic value to the owner, and produce an unearned profit for the newcomer.

Transfer of rights in trademarks. A trademark is an asset of the proprietor, which may be disposed of as any other asset. If the proprietor is a human person, on his death the mark passes to his heirs. If a company, its trademark is transferred to the purchaser or liquidator with the rest of the assets of the business. For a long time it was thought that since a trademark is attached and owes its value to the goodwill and reputation of a business in which it is used, it cannot be transferred apart from the goodwill of the business; otherwise purchasers of the goods would be deceived. In fact, this theory is not true in many cases. Under modern conditions of trade a business is frequently built around a trademark, with the goodwill of the business inseparable from the trademark itself. In this situation the assignment of the trademark without the business in which it is used need not result in deception of the public. At any rate, in most of the world today, a trademark may be assigned without the goodwill of the business, provided that the use of the mark by the assignee does not deceive the public. In most countries an assignment of a trademark must be recorded in the patent office in order to give legal notice to the public that there has been a change in the proprietorship of the mark.

Licensing arrangements

Even more important than the transfer of trademarks, particularly in the international field, is the licensing of trademarks. The proprietor generally finds it advantageous not to part with his trademark but rather to grant to another person the right or authorization to use the trademark in whole or in part on an exclusive or non-exclusive basis. In international trade, particularly, there are enterprises in various countries that seek licenses to use a mark enjoying an international reputation that would benefit the sale of their goods. This is a short cut to commercial success that saves investment and expense in promoting a new trademark. Manufacturers also find it advantageous to license their trademarks to foreign enterprises. This overcomes import restrictions, customs barriers, and foreign exchange difficulties, enables them to obtain royalties for the use of their mark from the licensee, and at the same time creates valuable goodwill for their trademarks through use by the licensee. In international arrangements this licensing frequently involves the sharing of secret know-how or special technological information and assistance that promotes economic development.

Here again, there once were objections to the licensing as unlawful, or at least improper, since the trademark was no longer associated with the proprietor's business, and its use by the licensee might result in deception of the public with regard to the origin of the goods. These objections have long since been overruled by practice and subsequently by law. As a result, in most countries today a trademark may be licensed, provided that the trademark proprietor controls and supervises the standards and specifications of the goods for which the mark is used so that they are equivalent to those under which the proprietor has used it. In many countries the law requires that the license be recorded in the patent office to provide notice to the public.

LOSS OF TRADEMARK RIGHTS

Just as a trademark right is acquired under conditions prescribed by law, it may also be lost under certain conditions. A registered trademark may be lost as a result of legal action annulling the registration either on objective grounds attacking the registrability of the mark or on grounds relating to prior rights of others. It may also be lost by renunciation or abandonment, affirmative or tacit, such as failure to renew the registration. More serious causes of loss of trademark rights come from failure to use a registered trademark and from the transformation of a trademark into a generic term.

In countries in which a trademark is acquired by use and the proprietor has not sought to obtain registration, the right continues so long as the mark has not been abandoned. Abandonment involves two elements: discontinuance of use of the mark and intention to abandon the mark. When the mark is registered, the obligation of the owner to use it is clear. The law has established a registration system and protects a registered trademark on the assumption that the proprietor has a bona-fide intention to use such a mark and that he does actually use it. Difficulties arise in the application of this principle, but generally the law does prescribe that the registration of a trademark may be forfeited if the mark is not used for a prescribed period of years. Usually this is between three to five years, with some countries requiring use even within a shorter time. In a number of countries, however, there is no requirement of use, and a few still retain old systems permitting registration of so-called defense and reserve marks, but these are gradually amending their law to require use.

The trademark lost by success

Loss of the right in a trademark also occurs when it is transformed, or degenerates, into a generic word. In this field there is considerable diversity in the law of various countries.

In the United States there have been spectacular cases of

loss of trademark rights regarding such famous trademarks as Aspirin, Cellophane, Shredded Wheat, Thermos, and others. The position of U.S. courts, broadly speaking, is that a designation that is initially a trademark ceases to be such when it comes to be generally understood as a generic or descriptive designation of the type of goods in connection with which it is used. It makes no difference whether this transformation is made as a result of the action or negligence of the trademark owner or whether he has done everything possible to avoid this result. The courts consider only whether the public still recognizes the word as a trademark or whether it understands it as a description of the article. In difficult cases there may be a minority of the public or a substantial portion of the trade who still recognize the designation as a trademark indicating specific origin. In such cases the courts seek to balance the equities of the claimant for the mark, of his competitors, and of the public.

The law of British countries looks more to what the view of the mark is to the trade rather than to the general public. Once it has been established that there is a trade use of the mark in a generic or descriptive meaning, the mark may be declared lost.

In a contrary direction is the law of civil-law countries that generally considers the right in a trademark as equivalent to the right in movable property. It will not allow a mark to be expropriated for public and general use so long as the owner has not renounced his right, and any use of the mark by the trade or by the public without authorization of the owner is considered abusive. So long as the owner retains the registration of the mark and keeps it alive by renewal the mark cannot be lost.

A middle position is held by the Scandinavian countries, where, if the owner tolerates the use of his trademark in such a manner that it becomes a commonly used indication for goods of a certain kind, he loses his right in the mark.

Mention may also be made of the possible loss of trademark rights by confiscation—with or without the business to which they are attached—as a result of state action. The law of the state that has taken such action governs the legal position of the trademark within that country, but insofar as the confiscation purports to extend to trademarks registered in foreign countries, it generally meets the resistance of interested persons who claim that their business has been expropriated without proper indemnification. Many cases of such expropriation occurred after World War II in the Socialist states of eastern Europe. In many cases the owners of the business involved have emigrated to the West, where they have generally succeeded before the courts in preventing the state enterprise of such countries from claiming ownership of the trademarks registered in the countries of western Europe.

INTERNATIONAL INSTITUTIONS FOR THE PROTECTION OF TRADEMARK RIGHTS: THEIR PROVISIONS AND EFFECT

International Convention for the Protection of Industrial Property. During the 19th century, the increase of importance of trademarks in international trade led many countries to enter into bipartite conventions providing for the reciprocal protection of trademarks of their nationals. Such provisions also were included in various treaties of commerce, treaties of friendship, etc. The position under such treaties continued, however, to be insecure, varied, and fluid, especially since the protection of trademarks was bound up with the uncertain duration of such treaties. The great demand for stability and security in international trade finally led to the conclusion in Paris in 1883 of the International Convention for the Protection of Industrial Property, generally called the Paris Convention. This has been revised successively through the years, most recently at Lisbon in 1958. Many countries have acceded to this convention through the years with the result that at the present time nearly 80 countries are party to it, which makes it, in effect, an international charter for the protection of industrial property rights, and specifically of trademarks, in a large part of the world.

Basic principles of the convention

The convention establishes two basic principles. The first is the "national treatment" principle, which means that the persons entitled to the benefits of the convention are treated in each country as that country treats its own nationals. They therefore have all the rights, advantages, and protection enjoyed by nationals, subject only to compliance with the conditions and formalities applicable to nationals. No discrimination is allowed between foreigners and nationals, and no reciprocity is required, which means that country A is bound to protect the trademarks of nationals of country B without being permitted to inquire whether country B does the same for the rights of the nationals of country A. This replaced the old system of reciprocity that created great uncertainty and variety in the international protection of trademarks.

The second principle of the convention is called the "unionist treatment." It provides that certain rights and benefits stipulated by the convention must be made available to persons entitled to its benefits, irrespective of whether or not these are provided for under the law of the country involved. Among the specific benefits and rights granted is the right of priority, under which an applicant for a trademark in one of the member countries may claim the priority of the filing date of his first application in his own country, provided he files for the same trademark in the other countries within six months from the first application. As a result of this important priority right, the claimant has time to protect his trademark in the other countries and prevails over an intervening applicant or any intervening user.

Another right is the so-called validation of trademarks, which means that a trademark registered in the country of origin must be accepted for registration and protected in the other countries, subject only to certain stated exceptions relating to prior rights or to marks that are devoid of any distinctive character or are generic or descriptive. The third important right provides that a member country must refuse or cancel the registration and prohibit the use of a trademark that infringes a foreign mark considered to be well known in the country where protection is sought. The complaining party is allowed up to three years to seek cancellation of an infringing mark.

Several other rights are provided, including a period of grace for the renewal of registration, the right to assign a foreign trademark without assignment of the trademark or the business in the home country, the right to contest the registration of a trademark by a foreign agent or representative of the owner, and the right to demand seizure on importation or prohibition of importation or seizure within the country of goods illegally bearing the trademark of another. Provisions for the protection of trade names and for protection against acts of unfair competition are also subjects of the convention.

The Paris Convention has a central organ for the administration and development of the international system of industrial property. This is the International Bureau, located in Geneva, which has been actively functioning for nearly a century in the interest of the Union for the Protection of Industrial Property established by the convention.

Pan-American trademark conventions. There have also been a series of Pan-American conventions for the protection of industrial property rights and particularly of trademarks, the most important of these being the General Inter-American Convention for Trademark and Commercial Protection concluded in Washington in 1929. This convention has been ratified and is now in effect among 10 of the 21 American republics. Some of these republics are still bound by the earlier Convention of Buenos Aires of 1910, to which five additional countries are a party. The convention of 1910 was a rather poor substitute for the Paris International Convention, whereas the Washington Convention of 1929 is an extensive document that contains the same two general principles as the Paris Convention; *i.e.*, the national treatment principle and the "unionist" principle. It does not provide for a right of priority but it does provide that a prior user of a trademark in any contracting country may contest the registration of the same or a confusingly similar mark in any other country if the newcomer had knowledge or ought to have had knowledge of the existence or use of the prior mark in its country of origin, if there has been prior use in the country where protection is sought, or if the newcomer failed to use the mark for a specified period after registration. The convention also provides for registration and protection of a mark already registered in the country of origin, subject to certain exceptions; and it contains full provisions for the protection of commercial names, for the suppression of acts of unfair competition, and for matters relating to false indications of origin.

Madrid arrangements. The other principal institution for the protection of trademark rights is the Madrid Arrangement for the International Registration of Trademarks. Originally concluded in Madrid in 1891, this arrangement has been revised through the years, and the present treaty is one adopted at Nice in 1957.

The main features of the arrangement revolve around a central filing system under which the owner of a trademark registration obtained in his country of origin may request his patent office to transmit an application for international registration to the International Bureau at Geneva. On receipt of this application the bureau registers the mark in the International Trademark Register and informs the countries that are party to the arrangement. These countries have a term of one year within which to declare whether they refuse protection to such a mark. If no such refusal is made, the mark is deemed registered in the particular countries as if the application were filed and the mark registered directly in each of them. If a country refuses protection to such a mark, the applicant may attempt to overcome the refusal by taking direct action in the particular country under the law of that country.

The membership of this arrangement includes 21 countries. Most of them are European, but also included are Morocco, Tunisia, Egypt, and South Vietnam. About two-thirds of all international marks registered are of French, German, and Swiss nationals.

The United States, British-law countries, Scandinavian countries, Latin-American countries, and the majority of non-European countries are not party to this arrangement.

While the advantages of a central filing for marks with a minimum of formalities and expense are obvious, there are a number of serious disadvantages. The basic objection to the whole system is the automatic extension of an international registration to twenty countries regardless of whether or not the applicant has a bona-fide intent, or indeed an interest, to have his mark protected in all of them. As a result of the multiplication of businesses and products in the present stage of international trade, there is a severe shortage of symbols, words, and devices available for adoption and registration as trademarks. Because of this, it is important that the trademark registers of the world be unencumbered by registrations for marks that are not really used or intended to be used. The contracting countries conscious of this disadvantage inherent in the automatic extension of international registrations, added a provision in 1957 that a supplemental fee be paid for each country, if the contracting countries should so provide. This fee, however, is so small that it has not had the result of reducing the encumbrance of the registers. Another disadvantage is that an applicant for an international registration is not limited to registering a mark for the goods for which he uses or intends to use the mark; he may cover any or even all classes of goods, which again narrows the field for subsequent bona-fide users of marks.

Finally, the requirement that the mark must have been first registered in the country of origin works to the disadvantage of nationals of countries where marks are submitted to very careful examination. In those countries the applicant may not obtain his registration for months or years before he can apply for an international registration, whereas in countries where there is no prior examination, a class including most of the members of the Madrid Arrangement, applicants may apply for an international registration promptly upon filing their marks at their national patent office.

Proposals are now underway for a new trademark arrangement that will avoid the disadvantages and pitfalls of the Madrid Arrangement.

Disadvantages of universal filing

There is a second Madrid Arrangement for the repression of false indications of origin. This particularly concerns the so-called appellations or origin—geographical names entitled to be used only by products whose quality and characteristics are due exclusively or essentially to natural or human factors of the particular geographical area. These include the well-known names of wine products, cheeses, beer, and other foodstuffs. An additional arrangement was concluded in Lisbon in 1958 to permit international registration or appellations of origin at the International Bureau under procedures analogous to those for the international registration of trademarks.

The European Economic Community and trademarks. The Rome treaty of 1958 establishing the European Economic Community, or what is generally called the Common Market, has no specific provisions on trademarks or trademark law. It does, however, touch upon the subject of trademarks indirectly in two ways. In the chapter dealing with the elimination of restrictions as between member states to ensure freedom of movement of goods between them, there is an exception in article 36 to the effect that prohibitions or restrictions of importation, exportation, and transit may be justified on certain grounds, including the protection of industrial and commercial property. Thus, if a certain trademark is owned in one of the member countries by one person and in another country by a different person, the goods bearing it cannot lawfully be imported from the one country to the other. This is reinforced by the general provision of Article 222 that the treaty shall in no way prejudice the system existing in member states in respect of property—and this, of course, includes property in trademarks.

The diversities of the trademark law in the member countries of the Common Market and the diverse ownership of trademarks in such countries do constitute legal barriers to the free movement of goods and to the economic integration that is the principal object of the Common Market. To prevent agreements and practices between enterprises that may have the effect of extending these legal barriers, the treaty has antitrust provisions in its chapter on Rules Governing Competition that affect agreements relating to trademarks.

Nevertheless, the treaty does aspire to eliminate the diversities of law and diverse rights in trademarks. Article 100 provides that the Council of Ministers of the Common Market "shall issue directives for the approximation of such legislative and administrative provisions of the member States as have a direct incidence on the establishment and functioning of the Common Market." And Article 235 provides that if action by the community appears necessary to achieve one of the aims of the community, the council shall enact the appropriate provisions. Thus the Council of Ministers of the Common Market may issue directives for the harmonization of trademark legislation and regulations of the Common Market countries, and eventually may enact a uniform law of trademark rights.

As a matter of practical fact, however, the council would not attempt to do this in such a technical field unless the member countries were really agreed that uniformity or unity of law is necessary and desirable. That is already being done with respect to patent law in the Common Market, by a special committee of experts from each of the six member countries, and will probably be followed by a similar effort for the adoption of a single trademark law.

Marginal note: Action on unification

BIBLIOGRAPHY. In the U.S., H.D. NIMS, *The Law of Unfair Competition and Trade-marks* (1917), was the basic work in the field until W.J. DERENBERG published his comprehensive book, *Trade-mark Protection and Unfair Trading* (1936). More recent information may be found in R. CALLMANN, *The Law of Unfair Competition, Trade-marks, and Monopolies*, 3rd ed. (1967). There is abundant analysis and critical exposition on many topics of trademark law in legal reviews, and particularly in the *Trademark Reporter* (monthly), published by the U.S. Trademark Association. In England, the standard reference is D.M. KERLY, *Law of Trade Marks and Trade Names*, 9th ed. (1966). In Germany, E. REIMER, *Wettbewerbs und Warenzeichenrecht*, 4th ed. (1966); and in France, E. POUILLET, *Traité des marques de fabrique et de commerce*, 6th ed. (1912), are standard reference books. P.ROUBIER, *Le Droit de la propriété industrielle*, 2 vol. (1952–54), has given a new dimension to juristic writing in France. A good book in Spanish is P.C. BREUER MORENO, *Tratado de marca de fábrica y comercio*, 2nd ed. (1953). S.P. LADAS, *The International Protection of Industrial Property* (1930), is a particularly useful work for a comparative view of the international protection of trademarks.

(S.P.L.)

Trade Unionism

To be understood in its international context, trade unionism must be examined as part of a wider concept—the labour movement as a whole. That movement consists of several more or less intimately related organizations such as labour parties, workers' mutual insurance organizations, producers' or consumers' cooperatives, and workers' education and sports associations. All have the common objective of improving the material, cultural, and social status of their members.

What distinguishes one organization from another is the particular aspect of that broad objective it is endeavouring to pursue, and the particular method it employs. The relationship among the various parts of the labour movement varies from country to country and from period to period. Not all countries have produced the entire gamut of organizations referred to above; in some countries the term "labour movement" is virtually synonymous with "trade unionism."

ORIGINS AND BACKGROUND OF THE TRADE UNION MOVEMENT

Early forms of labour organizations. Unions originated, mainly in Great Britain and the U.S. in the late 18th and early 19th centuries, as associations of workers using the same skill. There is no connection between trade unions and medieval craft guilds, for the latter were composed of master craftsmen who owned capital and often employed several workers. The early unions were formed partly as social clubs but soon became increasingly concerned with improving wages and working conditions, primarily by the device of collective bargaining. Progressing from trade to trade within the same city or area, the clubs formed local associations, which, because they carried on their main activities on a purely local level, were almost self-sufficient. With industrial development, however, local associations sooner or later followed the expansion of production beyond the local market and developed into national unions of the same trade. These in turn formed national union federations.

Factors favouring unionism. The unions of the early 19th century were almost exclusively based upon a particular craft. But as mass production industries—which required large numbers of rapidly trained, semiskilled workers—developed, a trend toward large-scale union organization grew, and toward the end of the 19th century Great Britain was including unskilled workers. Unions that recruited members from such groups—whose ranks were expanding rapidly as a result of new technologies—emerged either as industrial unions or as general unions. Industrial unions attempted to organize all workers employed in producing a given product or service, sometimes including even the general office or white-collar workers. General unions included skilled workers and labourers of all grades from different industries, even though they usually started from a base in one particular industry. But changing technologies, union mergers, and ideological factors led to the development of various kinds of unions that would not fit easily into any of the above categories.

Obstacles to union organization. In most Western countries, labour movements arose out of the protest of workers and intellectuals against a social and political system based upon discrimination according to ancestry, social status, income, and property. Such a system offered few avenues for individual or collective advancement. Discrimination in political franchise (restrictions on or outright denials of the vote) and a lack of educational opportunities, anti-union legislation, and the whole spirit

Marginal note: Labour unions as protest movements

of a society founded upon acknowledged class distinctions were the main sources of the social protest at the root of modern labour movements.

Anti-union laws such as the Combination Laws in Britain, the French Loi Le Chapelier (forbidding combination), similar laws in most Germanic countries, and court decisions under common law in the United States in the 19th century made it inevitable that reformers would first turn their energies to the removal of those legal impediments. The demand for equal voting rights became an early preoccupation of the labour movements, partly because of a desire for recognition of the working man as a full citizen, and partly to give the worker political power to remove anti-union laws and to obtain legislation for improving working conditions, especially for children and women. At a much later stage, when democratic equality was substantially achieved, unification of unions that had been divided according to political or religious sympathies became the next goal of the labour movements, with less attention paid to anticapitalist ideologies.

UNION DEVELOPMENT IN INDUSTRIALIZED NATIONS

General differences. Among the various labour movements, the roles assigned to collective bargaining and to labour legislation vary substantially; such differences even occur within a single movement. In Great Britain and the United States the role of collective bargaining is stressed. Legislation is regarded primarily as a device to bring about, facilitate, and supplement orderly collective bargaining. Most continental European countries, though with considerable variations among them, rely on substantive labour legislation to a far higher degree than Great Britain or the U.S.

Collective agreements in Britain and many other Western countries, either traditionally or under the impact of tight labour markets, frequently designate the minimum wages allowable; the actual wage rates may be considerably above those listed in the contract. Prolonged full employment and high prosperity may tend to weaken the allegiance of workers to their union, because wages then tend to rise more from an increasing demand for labour than from union pressure. Such a weakening of allegiance to the union is particularly noticeable among younger members who did not live through the "heroic era" of a union's early struggles for recognition and improvements in low wages and poor working conditions.

Changes in the character of unions

The "generation problem" within the unions is complicated by rapid and substantial changes in the structure of the labour force in the industrial countries. The decline in agricultural jobs, the emergence of the semiskilled workers in the mass production industries, and the rise in the numbers of white-collar workers and employed women have changed not only the economic and social milieu within which the unions operate but also their recruiting potential and their character. White-collar workers have formed or joined unions in increasing numbers, though in lesser proportions than their blue-collar colleagues. A number of "quasi-unions" also have emerged—professional associations that, while often refusing to be classified as unions, increasingly behave as unions do and are sometimes prepared to cooperate with or even join confederations of manual workers.

Great Britain. *Early history.* Britain was a pioneer in the development of modern industry, and its unions are among the oldest in the world. They go back to the late 18th century when artisans, threatened by the establishment of mechanized factories, formed local clubs for their common defense. Their efforts soon met with government hostility, based at first upon the common law concept that unions were in "restraint of trade." Later, under the impact of the French Revolution, the Combination Acts of 1799 and 1800 declared unions to be criminal conspiracies against the public. Even after those laws were repealed in 1824, legal and administrative measures against unions continued for a long time.

In 1834, for example, six Dorsetshire labourers from the village of Tolpuddle (the "Tolpuddle Martyrs") were sentenced to seven years transportation to a penal colony in Australia for organizing trade union activities. It was only in 1871 that legislation was passed that exempted unions from prosecution because of "restraint of trade." Local trade clubs had survived intermittent prosecution, and in 1834 the reformer and socialist Robert Owen attempted, without lasting results, to organize them in a national movement—the Grand National Consolidated Trades Union.

In 1851 the Amalgamated Society of Engineers established the pattern for the "new model" unions—national associations of skilled workers who had passed through a regular apprenticeship. Their main economic weapon was their ability to restrict the number of apprentices, thereby limiting the supply of skilled labour. They also functioned as "friendly societies"; that is, they provided mutual assistance in case of sickness or for emigration.

During the same period, some of the leaders of the craft unions formed the so-called "Junta," which engaged in political action and joined Marx's International Workingmen's Association (the First International), even though most of them failed to understand—much less approve—the principles of Marxian socialism. This was not the first attempt of labour leaders to engage in political action. In the 1830s some unionists had joined a small group of radical members of Parliament in drawing up a petition for universal male suffrage, which became part of the platform of the Chartist reform movement. The Chartists were concerned mainly with electoral reform, but trade unions played an important part in their activities. Chartism was the first specifically working-class national movement in Britain. But the emergence of the working class as a major political force had to await the entrance of the miners into the political arena, the extension of the right to vote to large numbers of workers, and the organization of less skilled workers.

The legalization of unionism. After passage of the Trade-Union Act of 1871, which effectively legalized trade unions, unions of agricultural workers, seamen, gas workers, general and municipal workers, and dock workers were organized. This period of union activity culminated in the successful dock workers' strike of 1889. The new unions emphasized nation-wide collective bargaining and demanded a legal minimum wage and an eight-hour day. Socialist ideas entered the movement, and political organizations of the working class—such as the Independent Labour Party—came to play an increasing role. Shortly after the turn of the century, the Labour Party was born.

"Contracting out" and "contracting in"

The legal status of unions became endangered by the Taff Vale court decision of 1901, which held that unions could be sued for losses incurred by employers as a result of union action. That decision was nullified by the Trade Disputes Act of 1906. Shortly before World War I financial support of the Labour Party by trade unions was legalized, provided that individual union members could "contract out." This meant that union members could choose not to pay the so-called political levy; that is, not make a contribution to the special fund that most unions established for support of the Labour Party. After the unsuccessful General Strike of 1926, that provision was changed into the "contracting in" system, which required union members to state expressly their wish to pay the political levy. As a result, a sizable proportion of union members failed to pay the levy, and in 1945 the newly elected Labour government once again established the "contracting out" principle.

The growth of union membership. Between 1910 and 1920 trade union membership more than trebled, from 2,565,000 to 8,334,000. But the postwar slump of 1921 and the return to the gold standard in 1925 led to a great crisis in the history of British trade unionism—the General Strike of 1926. The failure of the strike resulted in widespread disillusionment, which was intensified by the start of the Great Depression in 1930. By 1933 union membership had fallen to 4,392,000, half of what it had been in 1920. Afterward union membership gradually increased until by 1969 it stood at more than 10,000,000, about 9,500,000 of whom were affiliated with the Trades Union Congress (TUC), the national organization representing British trade unions. The diversity in size and organization of British unions is tremendous. They range from small local craft groups to giant general unions with memberships in excess of 1,400,000. A trend toward large-scale union mergers became apparent in the 1960s.

Dual system of bargaining. The basic institutional factor underlying problems of industrial relations in Britain is the existence of two bargaining systems: the industry-wide contract negotiated by the union and the employers' association, and the unofficial agreements arrived at in the various plants by managers, shop stewards, and individual workers. The terms reached under the unofficial system are consistently more favourable for the workers than those in the official contract. Such a dual system has its roots in the failure of most unions to control the shop stewards, and of the employers' associations to control the plant managers.

Union control over the shop stewards proved weak during World War I when the stewards assumed an authority that often brought them into conflict with the union leadership. World War II, and the long period of full employment that followed, reinforced that trend. The Industrial Relations Act of 1971 brought the first comprehensive legislation in this field in the country's history. It provided, among other things, for legally enforceable collective agreements between unions and employers.

Role of government. Caught between rising earnings, rising prices, and a great reluctance to permit a devaluation of the currency, the post-World War II governments embarked upon a series of experiments with methods of wage restraint. The first, undertaken in 1948–50, had ended in failure; and from 1951 to 1964 the Conservative governments made several attempts to limit wage and salary increases, but the unions refused to cooperate. When a Labour government was returned in 1964, some of the unions became more willing to accept an incomes policy. As a result, union (and business) representatives took their places on a Prices and Incomes Board empowered to investigate and suggest reforms, which were mainly related to enhancing productivity.

A searching investigation of the entire industrial relations system by the Donovan Commission (Royal Commission on Trade Unions and Employers' Associations) was also undertaken. Among other things, the commission recommended an obligatory 28-day conciliation period before any unofficial strike (any walkout not sanctioned by the official union leadership) could begin, and also a poll of the union's members if a major official strike was imminent and if the government doubted that the union leaders had rank-and-file support.

Various emergency measures were taken when the exchange rate of sterling was threatened in 1966 and again after sterling's devaluation in 1967. They included the suspension of all wage, price, and dividend increases for various periods. But in 1970 a government white paper admitted that "the use of a productivity, prices, and incomes policy for short-term purposes can only have a short-term effect. The long-term role of the policy is essentially an educational one."

The incomes policy put the responsibility for wage restraint on the unions. But, as mentioned above, effective earnings are determined not so much by the unions as by shop stewards, whose activities the union leaders do not entirely control. It was hardly surprising, therefore, that the incomes policy proved ineffective. Nor was it conceivable that the unions, created to improve their members' earnings, could for long be turned into devices for preventing their members from obtaining the wage increases that management was willing to concede. The creation of an Industrial Relations Commission and of a Commission for Industry and Manpower in 1969–70 indicated that new means were being sought to promote and preserve collective bargaining under conditions of full employment while at the same time keeping price increases at an acceptable rate.

United States. *The beginnings.* Unionism in the United States goes back to the early days of national independence when craftsman employees in various trades—carpenters, masons, shoemakers, and printers—formed local groups to obtain shorter hours and higher wages. The Mechanics' Union of Trade Associations formed in Philadelphia in 1827 represented an early attempt to combine unions of different crafts on a local level. The first steps toward extending the organization beyond the local area were made in the 1830s but were only temporarily successful. Much emphasis was placed on political action and the formation of labour parties. The main objectives included free education and the abolition of property restrictions on the right to vote, which had survived from Colonial times in some states down to the Jacksonian era (1828–36). Once those objectives were achieved in the Northern states, the labour parties disappeared. Most of the unions—including the National Trades Union formed in 1834—were dissolved in the depression of 1837.

In the 1850s a new departure occurred. With improvements in transport and the consequent expansion of markets beyond local areas, unions in the same trade began to expand their fields of operation and to establish regional or even national federations. The National Typographical Union was formed in 1852 and was followed by five others. Concentration on job-connected problems rather than on broad, ideological issues was characteristic of this period.

The Knights of Labor. The only large reform movement among the early labour organizations was backed by the Noble Order of the Knights of Labor, founded in 1869. Its objectives, many of them more political than industrial, were vague and moderate and included the eight-hour day and the abolition of child labour. Its rise was spectacular, especially after it won a strike against the Wabash Railroad, controlled by Jay Gould, a New York multimillionaire, in 1885. But after that victory, the organization soon declined—in part because of a growing anti-radical mood in the country. That mood was intensified by the Haymarket bomb episode in Chicago (1886), in which seven policemen were killed, and with which the Knights were quite unjustly associated. A more significant factor in their decline was the fact that the Knights combined skilled and unskilled workers in one organization. The mass immigration of unskilled workers weakened their economic power to the point that union victories could be won only with the assistance of skilled workers; and when they were no longer willing to give battle on behalf of the unskilled immigrants, the decline of the Knights became inevitable.

The American Federation of Labor. In the meantime, however, the American Federation of Labor began to supplant the Knights as a national federation of unions of skilled workers. Started with modest success as the Federation of Organized Trades and Labor Unions of the United States and Canada in 1881, it was transformed into the American Federation of Labor (AFL) five years later. Samuel Gompers, a cigar maker, was elected president, and his personality decisively shaped the AFL's evolution. It was to be a practical, non-ideological movement, accepting the existing social system but attempting to change it in favour of the organized skilled workers. The main instrument of change was to be collective bargaining. The affiliated organizations were to be autonomous within their "jurisdiction"; that is, the job territory over which their charter gave them full authority. Organization was limited to skilled workers, who alone were regarded as capable of forming effective unions.

Membership of the AFL grew only slowly until the turn of the century, partly because of a predominantly unfavourable economic situation and partly because of government hostility. Between 1900 and the outbreak of World War I, however, membership expanded from less than 600,000 to about 2,000,000. The war itself opened new opportunities for organized labour. Pres. Woodrow Wilson's administration gave Gompers semi-official status by making him a member of a small advisory commission to the Council of National Defense; and the President himself appeared at the 1917 AFL convention. By 1920 the membership of AFL-affiliated unions had doubled to 4,000,000.

The next decade was a period of crisis and stagnation

Rise of
anti-union
sentiment
in the
1920s

for unionism. Serious opposition to Gompers arose in 1921 in the person of John L. Lewis, newly elected head of the United Mine Workers. Gompers won, but his death in 1924 brought William Green, a member of the mine workers' union, to the presidency. The liquidation of the war industry, and a sharp anti-union offensive by many employers—who were supported by conservative U.S. presidents, hostile courts, and anti-labour sentiments of great sectors of the general public—combined to bring about a sharp decline in union membership. Under the slogan of the "open shop," by the use of so-called yellow dog contracts that required workers not to join unions, and by court injunctions against unions, employers staged a major offensive against organized labour. This not only kept the unions out of the steel industry but also reduced union membership to little more than its prewar level.

The "Wobblies." The 1920s also saw the decline of an important union movement that had attempted to organize unskilled workers into industrial unions—the Industrial Workers of the World (IWW). The "Wobblies," as they were popularly known, had been founded in 1905 in Chicago in response to the AFL's opposition to unionism for unskilled workers. Consisting largely of itinerant industrial labourers, the IWW had concentrated on militant strike action, especially against employers hostile to unionism.

The movement included a considerable ideological element and eventually came under the control of anarchists and syndicalists. That fact, together with the IWW's strong opposition to World War I, led to the suppression of its press and to prosecutions under the Espionage and Sedition Acts of 1917 and 1918. After World War I, many states adopted legislation outlawing the IWW, thus driving it underground. It was further weakened by disputes with the Communists, so that by the mid-1920s it had ceased to be a significant force within the labour movement.

The Depression and New Deal. The Great Depression, which began in 1929, almost destroyed some of the unions, but it also gave unionism a new start. The reasons for this new turning point were several. With the depression and the shifting political climate, there came a radical change in labour legislation—the Norris-LaGuardia Act of 1932, which removed the legal basis for the use of court injunctions in labour disputes. (In a partial reinterpretation of that 1932 act, the U.S. Supreme Court in 1970 ruled that unions could be enjoined from permitting walkouts in violation of no-strike pledges contained in their contracts.)

The New Deal legislation that followed the victory of Franklin D. Roosevelt in the presidential election of 1932 guaranteed the right of workers to join unions of their own choosing and required management to engage in collective bargaining if the majority of the workers so desired. A National Labor Relations Board was set up to enforce the law. Although the law was revised later by the Taft-Hartley Act and the Landrum-Griffin Act, its basic principle that collective bargaining is the most desirable way of determining wages and working conditions was not changed. Even when strikes threaten national security, only delaying action is legally provided for; in some situations, however, governmental pressure to avoid or settle strikes has, in fact, come close to coercion. Minimum wage legislation was passed on both the federal and state levels, and government encouragement of unionism was manifested not only during the New Deal but repeatedly throughout the presidencies of Harry S. Truman, John F. Kennedy, and Lyndon B. Johnson.

A basic
change in
unionism
itself

The change in the governmental attitude toward unionism was accompanied by a basic transformation of unionism itself. Adjusting itself to the new, enlarged role of the government in economic affairs, as well as to the catastrophic consequences of the Great Depression, the AFL abandoned its traditional distrust of government regulation of industrial relations. With some reluctance it accepted and finally supported a government-sponsored social security system providing for gradual expansion of old age pensions, unemployment benefits, and—much later—health insurance.

The Congress of Industrial Organizations. No less important was the belated adjustment of the structure of unions to accommodate the growing number of semi-skilled workers in the mass production industries, whose employees the traditional craft unions of the AFL had failed to organize. Under the leadership of the United Mine Workers' president John L. Lewis, eight unions within the AFL promoted organizing drives to establish industrial unions in such industries as steel, automobiles, rubber, and chemicals. When endorsement of his plan was defeated at the AFL convention in 1935, Lewis set up a Committee for Industrial Organization, which three years later was transformed into the Congress of Industrial Organizations (CIO). For having formed a rival organization the unions of the CIO were expelled by the AFL.

The decisive battles of the new organization were fought in the steel and automobile industries. A favourite weapon of the organizers—mainly mine workers' leaders assisted by intellectuals and a few Communists—was the sit-down strike, a strike during which workers do not walk out of the plant but remain idle at their work positions, thus paralyzing the plant and making it necessary for management to make an immediate response to their demands. Victories in the largest steel and automobile companies in 1937 were finally crowned by the capitulation of the Ford Motor Company in 1941.

World War II and after. The new competition induced the AFL in turn to engage in organizing drives. Total union membership grew from 2,900,000 in 1933 to 9,000,000 in 1939. By the end of World War II it had risen to 15,000,000, more than one-third of total nonagricultural employment. Just as had World War I, World War II induced union expansion, partly because of government assistance offered in return for a no-strike pledge.

The World War II era also witnessed a growth in anti-union sentiment, though not quite as sharp as that following the first World War. The passage of the Smith-Connally (War Labor Disputes) Act of 1943 over President Roosevelt's veto, and of the Taft-Hartley Act four years later over President Truman's veto, both of which introduced new government controls over unions, was evidence of a changed public opinion. In spite of the postwar economic expansion, union membership stagnated—partly because of the shift toward white-collar employment that the unions found difficult to cope with. Jurisdictional disputes between unions affiliated to the two competitive federations led to a waste of union resources.

On the other hand, the departure of the union leaders who had initiated and continued the AFL-CIO split removed some of the difficulties in the way of merging the two organizations. The expulsion of the Communist-dominated unions by the CIO in 1949 and the withdrawal of the United Mine Workers from the AFL also facilitated unification. In 1955 the AFL and CIO merged under the combined leadership of George Meany and Walter Reuther. The new organization (AFL-CIO) represented some 15,000,000 members at its birth. Not included in the new federation were the mine workers, some railroad unions, and various smaller organizations expelled for Communist domination; others were expelled later for corrupt practices—including the International Brotherhood of Teamsters with its more than 1,500,000 members.

Merger
of the
AFL and
CIO

The AFL and CIO had been instrumental, even before the merger, in setting up the International Confederation of Free Trade Unions (ICFTU) to combat the Communist-dominated World Federation of Trade Unions (WFTU). But issues of international policy soon caused sharp internal frictions between Meany and Reuther. While Meany criticized the ICFTU for failing to combat Communism with enough vigour, Reuther criticized Meany for complacency, for excessive concentration on a negative anti-Communist policy out of line with the thinking of most European unions, and for lack of imaginative leadership for social change. Personal rivalries intensified the conflict. In 1968 Reuther's United Automobile Workers left the AFL-CIO and combined with the Teamsters and two smaller unions and formed the Alliance for Labor Action (ALA) to engage in new organizing drives and to operate on a wider range of issues. The ALA had barely established itself when it lost its main driving force with the death of Walter Reuther in an airplane accident in 1970.

Unions of public employees. By means of an executive order issued in 1962 the Kennedy administration gave federal public employees the right to organize and bargain collectively, though not to strike. That action, together with some legislation at the state level, led to a rapid expansion of unionism among public employees. But the problem of how bargaining could be conducted effectively without the ultimate sanction of the strike remained to be solved.

A number of professional associations, though refusing to regard themselves as unions, began in the late 1960s to engage in collective bargaining and even, occasionally, to go out on strikes. The outstanding example was the influential National Education Association, several of whose affiliates carried out successful strikes. A whole class of quasi-unions was thus developing outside the traditional labour movement.

Western Europe. Unionism on the Continent shares some features with unionism in Britain: early persecution by government and courts, reliance upon government intervention and mediation in disputes; a tendency for unions to carry on collective bargaining with employers' associations rather than with individual companies, and a general acceptance of the terms of agreements as a floor upon which higher effective earnings are achieved by various devices. A distinguishing characteristic of European trade unionism has been, and to a large extent still

is, its tendency toward ideologically oriented unions, most of which were established by political parties or religious organizations in the 19th century. After World War II, a trend in the direction of unified trade unions, combining different ideological currents under one roof, manifested itself and has achieved considerable success.

Germany. Trade unionism began to gather momentum in Germany only after the fall of Otto von Bismarck in 1890. Under Socialist inspiration the bulk of the unions formed a national federation in that year. The Catholic Centre Party followed in 1894 with the establishment of a much smaller federation of Christian unions. Nationalist- and, for a brief period, Communist-led unions, as well as separate white-collar unions came into being at various times before World War I. There were some successes in collective bargaining, but unions remained fairly insignificant during this period.

After World War I, the Socialist-inspired unions organized in three main federations: the Allgemeiner Deutscher Gewerkschaftsbund, ADGB (General Confederation of German Trade Unions), for the manual workers, the AFA for white-collar employees, and the ADB for civil servants. Collective agreements for an industry or trade set minimum wages, which in turn were supplemented by the efforts of workers' councils in the plants. The council members were elected by all workers and white-collar employees, whether union members or not. Legally, and often in fact, councils were independent of the unions. Unionism flowered during the short period of prosperity in the 1920s but was destroyed by the Nazi takeover in 1933. The Labour Front, established and totally controlled by the National Socialist (Nazi) Party, was not a union by any definition of the term. Immediately after World War II, a powerful trade union movement came into being in West Germany. It was based on a merger of 16 Socialist and Christian industrial unions in a unified Deutscher Gewerkschaftsbund (DGB). Its membership, whose turnover is high, has levelled off at 6,500,000 workers in 1970 after a rapid rise. In addition, there are union federations for white-collar workers and civil servants. A small separate Catholic federation has had little success.

Under the slogan of "codetermination" the unions have

acquired direct representation in management. Legislation enacted in 1951 provides that in the coal and steel industries stockholders shall elect five members of an 11-man supervisory board of the company, and workers another five. Two of the workers' representatives come from the enterprise, a third is appointed by the union, and two more by the union federation, usually the DGB. The 11th member is jointly elected by the ten others. In addi-

tion, one of the three members of the *Vorstand* (management), which actually runs the enterprise, must be selected with the approval of the workers' representatives; that member is in charge of labour relations. In other large firms, outside the coal and steel industries, labour holds one-third of the seats on the supervisory boards. The DGB has been campaigning for an extension of the coal and steel system to all large firms. A committee of social scientists appointed by the government to study the question in a 1970 report supported the DGB demand, though with some significant modification.

France. Ever since the merger in 1895 between syndicalist and Marxist trade unions, the French labour movement has suffered persistently from internal cleavages and organizational divisions. The main union federation, the Confédération Générale du Travail (CGT), was set up in that year. It represented a coalition of anarchists and syndicalists, who put their trust in a revolutionary general strike to destroy capitalism and the state, together with a group of Marxists, who aimed at obtaining control of the state by a revolution. The syndicalists organized local union federations, mostly of an industrial nature.

Syndicalism broke down in the World War I wave of patriotism that engulfed French workers; after 1918 the Communists inherited a large part of the syndicalist following. For most of the time ever since, the French labour movement has been divided into three main (and several smaller) ideologically inspired organizations: the CGT under Communist control, the mostly Socialist FO (Force Ouvrière, Workers' Strength), and the formerly Christian CFDT (Confédération Française Démocratique du Travail, French Democratic Confederation of Labour), which has been trying to overcome its religious origins and the limits those origins set to its expansion among the main body of French workers.

Although most French workers are not organized, and those who are union members pay their dues only irregularly, the elections of workers' councils and shop stewards (*délégués du personnel*) roughly indicate worker allegiances. It would thus appear that a small majority supports the CGT and somewhat fewer the CFDT and FO. White-collar workers are organized in the CGC (Confédération Générale des Cadres). Other unions remain outside all confederations.

In view of the fragmentation in the French labour movement, it is not surprising that collective bargaining developed late—after 1936. It is still less significant than labour legislation and administrative action in determining wages and working conditions. Workers' councils, to provide worker participation in management, and the shop steward system, to handle grievances in the plant, were both established by law. But by the early 1970s, dwindling union strength had weakened both institutions to the point that they were not functioning in large numbers of enterprises. The great strike movement of the late 1960s, which was organized more for political reasons than as a collective bargaining tactic, developed outside the unions. Later on, however, the unions finally succeeded in controlling it.

Italy. In Italy, much the same as in France, the unions have remained weakened and divided by ideologies and religion. The late economic and political development of Italy directed labour's attention toward radical and political solutions. Soon after the resurgence of unions that followed the downfall of Mussolini's Fascist regime, the old tendency toward multiple and changing divisions within the movement reasserted itself.

Three major confederations emerged after World War II: the Confederazione Generale Italiana del Lavoro (CGIL), led by a coalition of Communists and left-wing II: the Confederazione Generale Italiana del Lavoratori (CISL), representing the Catholic labour movement, but with some Socialists as well; and the Unione Italiana del Lavoro (UIL) under Social Democratic leadership. The CGIL claims some 3,500,000 members, the CISL 2,500,000, and the UIL 500,000, but usually such figures are exaggerated. In plant committee elections the CGIL usually obtains a slim majority of the votes, with the CISL getting 30 percent and the UIL about 15 percent. In the wide-scale strikes of 1969–70, the unions persuaded far more than their members to join the so-called rolling strikes—short walkouts, one after the other, in different industries.

When labour agreements are reached, they usually are national in scope, and some cover benefits and conditions for all industries. In 1962 the unions obtained the additional right to conclude supplementary agreements at the plant level.

Scandinavia. The consolidation of local unions into national organizations paralleled the advance of industrialization in Norway, Sweden, and Denmark during the second half of the 19th century. That trend toward centralized unionism received support at the Scandinavian Labour Congress of 1897; and, by 1900, all three countries had small but firmly rooted federations of national trade unions. Employers' associations followed similar development from a local to national scale.

Agreement on basic principles

By the late 1930s the federations of workers and employers in the three countries had agreed on certain basic principles in the conduct of labour relations. Agreements between the labour and management federations, besides placing limitations on sympathetic lockouts and strikes, provide for orderly negotiations by upholding the right to organize for collective bargaining and by laying down procedures for discussion. The broad measure of understanding between labour and management and their common desire to keep government intervention at a minimum has facilitated responsible collective bargaining. Strikes and lockouts have not been entirely eliminated, but their occurrence has become less frequent, although a reversal of this trend manifested itself beginning in 1968. Full collective bargaining rights, including the right to strike, have been extended in Sweden to government employees of all kinds.

In Scandinavia collective bargaining is highly centralized in comparison with the United States or Great Britain. The influence of the federations of labour in conducting negotiations or determining national policy far surpasses that exerted by the AFL-CIO or the British TUC. The federations have the power to ensure that their basic decisions are implemented in the industry agreements. They have acquired an important role in political affairs through their close alliance with the Labour and Socialist parties. In Sweden, the federation has pursued a policy of establishing skill and industry differentials—the so-called solidarity policy—but effective wages have often departed from contract rates, thus counteracting the solidarity policy.

Norwegian and Swedish unions are organized chiefly on an industrial basis, whereas the Danish unions—comparable to the British in this respect—are both general and industrial. Although it is not compulsory, union membership is widespread, even among white-collar workers.

Yugoslavia. After its break with the Soviet Union in 1948, Yugoslavia commenced a program of economic reforms combining the profit motive, public ownership of most means of production, and a gradual decentralization of economic decision making.

The system of centrally directed state-managed enterprises has been progressively replaced by a workers' self-management system under which relatively free economic decisions are made. The concept of workers' self-management, recognizing the system's potential conflict of interest between management and workers, stresses the role of workers as coproducers in the enterprise. Management is exercised by a director, who is under the supervision of a workers' council elected by the employees of the enterprise.

Coproducer role for workers

To the extent that workers' councils actually represent the workers' interests, they have superseded the role of the trade union within the enterprise. Union functions have consequently been reduced to such activities as assisting individual workers in personal matters, obtaining better training and education for workers, and exercising a modest participatory role in various enterprise deliberations.

The unions appear to be attempting to offset the decline in their traditional functions within an enterprise by enhancing their influence at provincial and national levels. There, the trade unions endeavour to participate in decisions on social and economic issues within the framework set by the political system.

Soviet Union. The Russian labour movement owes its origin to the strikes of the 1890s, in which revolutionary students and workers cooperated against the tsarist regime and capitalist business owners. Hampered by a hostile government, the trade union movement slowly developed on the general pattern of the German labour organizations. With the Russian Revolution in 1917, however, the entire basis of the developing labour movement changed. Under Lenin's strategy, the unions became one of the links connecting the Communist Party—a small, close-knit elite of professional revolutionaries—with the large mass of industrial workers on whose behalf the party would operate.

The role of unions under Communism. A key question arose after the Bolshevik takeover. What role would unions perform in a Socialist system in which capitalism had ceased to operate? A long and involved debate followed. The unions themselves endeavoured to fill the traditional role of trade unions: to maintain or improve the living standards of their members. Leon Trotsky argued, however, that the unions should be transformed into "production agents" so that they would serve the workers' interests by fostering increased productivity of labour, promoting economic reconstruction, and providing increased quantities of consumer goods. Unions were thus to be instruments of economic administration, with only a subsidiary role in setting wages and working conditions. Another more radical role was proposed by the Workers' Opposition, which urged that the trade unions should dominate the state and manage the economy.

The answer to the question of what role unions were to play in the new Communist state was, in fact, dictated by an overall economic policy that called for the commitment of all possible resources to industrialization. The destruction of much of the productive equipment of the country in World War I, the civil war, and the ensuing foreign intervention made it impossible for the shattered economy to satisfy even the most elementary needs of the population. Moreover, the failure of Germany to abolish capitalism, as the Bolsheviks had hoped, required a complete revision of Bolshevik strategy. In the absence of victorious revolutions in the industrially advanced nations, the "dictatorship of the proletariat" in the Soviet Union was doomed unless that country could be rapidly industrialized. Thus, the growth of a working class to build an industrial base in the Soviet Union became the main task of both party and unions.

Such a program, however, required that real wages be kept to a minimum so that all possible resources could be devoted to capital formation. Consequently, unions could not be permitted to assist workers in raising their living standards. Instead, they became instruments of the state to increase output and speed industrialization. That production-oriented role gave rise to a trade union structure appropriate to the machinery of Soviet economic administration and adaptable to its changes.

Unions as instruments of the state

Pattern of unionism. Soviet trade unions are strictly industrial in nature. All persons employed in any one factory, state farm, or other undertaking belong to the same union; and that same union comprises all of the employees of similar factories, farms, or other enterprises everywhere else in the Soviet Union. Horizontal coordination occurs at the republic, regional, and local levels; but just as the economic administration has been closely centralized, so the national organs of the trade unions exercise effective authority over all lower levels of the union. More than 90 percent of industrial workers belong to unions, mainly because of the considerable advantages, such as social insurance benefits, available to members.

Other socio-economic functions. Soviet trade unions do not limit their activities to industry and plant matters alone. Their other functions include legislative initiative in labour matters; participation in national economic planning and wages policy; the administration of social insurance; the organization of cultural and recreational facilities; and cooperation in the education and vocational training of workers.

Moves in the 1960s toward decentralization in economic planning and administration, the use of incentives, and the assignment of greater authority to local managers have given rise to an increase in union influence at the lower levels. Among the unions' new roles are greater participation in the settling of grievances and in application of the wage system at the plant level. Some observers have discerned a tendency for the Soviet industrial relations system to evolve in the direction of those of other advanced industrial nations. Nevertheless, like all other organizations in the Soviet Union, the trade unions remain in all essentials under the complete control of the Communist Party.

Japan. Japanese labour unions are mainly the product of the post-World War II period. With the support of the U.S. occupation forces, the Japanese government adopted a drastic labour-protection policy immediately after the war. Its constitution was amended in 1946 so that workers' rights "to organize and to bargain and act collectively" were guaranteed. The phenomenal postwar economic growth of Japan has resulted in a great increase in employment. Trade union membership in 1970 was estimated at 11,500,000, approximately one-third of its potential.

Unions enterprise-oriented. Union structure in Japan differs sharply from the Western pattern. The enterprise —not a craft or industry—provides the base of union organization. One of the main features of enterprise unionism is "lifetime" employment. Employers do not, as a rule, lay off workers either permanently or temporarily; on the other hand, workers are not expected to move from one company to another. Typically, the enterprise recruits and trains young workers immediately after their graduation from school, and continues to employ them until they reach retirement age, usually 55. Educational background and length of service in a given company are the key factors in wage determination. Under such a system collective bargaining naturally focusses on particular enterprises or companies.

National confederations. Most of the enterprise unions are combined in national unions or in federations that are affiliated with national confederations. Major confederations are Sōhyō (General Council of Trade Unions of Japan), with 4,200,000 members; Dōmei (Japanese Confederation of Labour), with 1,900,000; and Chūritsurōren (Liaison Council of Neutral Trade Unions), with 1,400,000 members. The national confederations participate very little in bargaining with employers; their major function is the guidance and coordination of their affiliated enterprise unions. Each spring, the national confederations form a special committee for Shunto (the spring offensive). The committee plans the amount of the wage increase to be demanded, the period of negotiations, and the dates of industry-wide strikes.

National unions and confederations play an even more important role in politics by allying themselves with one of the parties—Nippon Shakaitō (Socialist), Minshato (Democratic Socialist), and Kyosanto (Communist).

The new mobility. Some changes in the system seem to be resulting from Japan's high economic growth rates. Because the labour market, especially for young workers, has become extremely tight, and because labour mobility has increased, the lifetime employment system has begun to be eroded. Rapid technological changes have made obsolete the traditional system of basing wages on length of service. Young workers with a modern school education are more suitable for many of the new jobs. Partly because of the high rate of economic growth and partly because of the Shunto bargaining targets, the unions have been successful in obtaining high wage increases. Thus the main emphasis of the Japanese labour movement has begun to shift from politics to economics.

Australia and New Zealand. Early settlers, who had brought the ideal of unionism along with them from England, established the first workingmen's organizations in Australia and New Zealand in the 1830s in the form of small trade societies. The foundations of modern unionism in Australia were not laid until two or three decades later, however, when urban craft unions for skilled workers began to emerge in the 1850s and 1860s. During that period and until 1890 "mass" or "industrial" unions were formed, first by the coal miners and subsequently by others, including gold miners, seamen, and wool shearers. Economic growth and a labour shortage favoured union expansion. With manhood suffrage already a reality, the union movement devoted its attention to such essentially economic issues as the eight-hour day.

Two distinctive features of present-day trade unionism, namely, political participation and compulsory arbitration, can be traced back to the serious strike setbacks and the economic depression of the 1890s. The Australian Labor Party, created and largely financed by the unions, has been a significant force on the Australian political scene since it first gained office in 1910. The Labour Party of New Zealand also derives much of its strength from trade union support.

Compulsory arbitration. Before 1890 unions had opposed the idea of compulsory arbitration. After losing a number of major strikes in which union recognition had been the main issue, the unions adopted a more favourable attitude toward arbitration, which would force employers to recognize them. Despite the retention of state arbitration systems in some form since passage of the first Commonwealth Conciliation and Arbitration Act of 1904, the focus of attention and activity has gradually shifted to the federal sphere. By the 1970s industrial relations were dominated by compulsory arbitration, yet collective bargaining continued, generally under close union control. Nor was strike action precluded by compulsory arbitration. Indeed, by international standards, the frequency of strikes in Australia has been relatively high, although with a short average duration.

In pre-Commonwealth days the need for close coordination for the successful pursuit of labour's objectives was expressed in successive Intercolonial Trade Union congresses, beginning in 1879. Their direct descendant is the Australian Council of Trade Unions (ACTU), founded in 1927.

Membership. In 1970 there were 305 unions in Australia with a total membership of 2,315,000, or 50 percent of the country's wage and salary earners. In 1969 119 unions with a total membership of 1,472,000 were affiliated with the ACTU, including all of the major unions. Two other central labour bodies, functioning on behalf of white-collar and professional unions, had an affiliated membership of 377,777. A much closer association has been developing between the ACTU and both of these bodies. A Council of Commonwealth Public Service Organizations claims a membership of about 100,000.

Later developments in New Zealand. Trade unions developed in Australia and New Zealand along broadly similar lines. In New Zealand, however, 1936 legislation provided for compulsory unionism. This took the form of providing that every employer bound by an award of the Court of Arbitration, or by any industrial agreement, could not employ a worker subject to the award or agreement unless that worker was a member of the union also bound by the award or agreement. This resulted in a considerable expansion and strengthening of the union movement. In 1961 the 1936 legislation was amended. Compulsory membership was made subject to agreement between employer and union or to a demand by more than 50 percent of the employees in an industry for compulsory unionism. Provision was made also to allow any worker conscientiously objecting to union membership to apply for a certificate of exemption. In the absence of a compulsory membership agreement, provision was made for the preferential hiring of unionists over non-unionists.

DEVELOPMENT OF TRADE UNIONS IN EMERGING NATIONS

The Indian subcontinent. *India.* According to a 1961 census, India's wage earners totalled 24,000,000, or 13 percent of its labour force, most of which was engaged in subsistence agriculture. Of the 24,000,000 wage earners,

Marginal notes: Miners among the first "mass" unions · Half of all employees in unions · "Lifetime" jobs for workers

about 4,000,000 (17 percent) were estimated to be organized in unions.

The weakness of Indian trade unionism is related to the country's slow industrialization. Historically, Indian unions were closely linked to the independence movement. The Indian National Congress Party took the initiative for the formation in 1920 of the first national body of trade unions, the All-India Trade Union Congress (AITUC), but this soon split into several factions.

The history of the trade union movement in India is one of conflicts and splits resulting mainly from ideological rivalries. Inter-union rivalry has hindered its development, and membership, which had increased rapidly after independence, stagnated during the 1960s and 1970s.

Collective bargaining is ineffective in India because the unions are not strong enough to force settlements; union rivalry makes the situation worse. As a result, unions tend to turn to the government for intervention. The Industrial Disputes Act of 1947 empowered the central or provincial governments to refer an industrial dispute for adjudication. In addition, wage boards have been set up for the determination of wages.

Pakistan. Though the nonagricultural sector of the Pakistan economy has expanded considerably since independence was achieved in 1947, some 20 years later (prior to separation from Bangladesh) approximately 68 percent of the total labour force of 40,000,000 was still engaged in agriculture. Of the approximately 14,000,000 wage earners, only 500,000 are organized; thus, the degree of unionization is only 3.5 percent, compared with India's 17 percent.

Low level of union membership

The All-Pakistan Confederation of Labour, established in 1950, has been recognized by the government as the sole representative of the workers in Pakistan. Many other trade union federations, however, have sprung up. Just as its Indian counterpart, the Pakistan labour movement is divided, and inter-union rivalry is a major handicap to its development. Collective bargaining is extremely difficult; when agreements are concluded they usually result from voluntary concessions made by progressive employers. Unilateral employer's decisions and government intervention play a dominant role in industrial relations.

Latin America. The highest rate of population increase of any area in the world not only has put a heavy strain on the educational systems of most Latin American countries but also has produced excess supplies of common labour. As a result, advances in wages and working conditions have been exceedingly difficult. Accordingly, one of the main objectives of Latin American trade unions has been to protect and insulate the employed labour force from the consequences of an excess supply of unemployed labour. Various job-protection devices have been developed, mainly based upon a system of severance pay proportionate to the length of an employee's service. Such a system makes dismissal expensive for the employer.

Ideological orientations. Labour movements in Latin America consistently have taken on an ideological colouring. In the early 1970s there were three main groupings of unions: those affiliated with the mildly progressive ORIT (Organización Regional Interamericana de Trabajadores), which in turn belongs to the International Confederation of Free Trade Unions (see below); the CLASC (Confederación Latinoamericana de Sindical Cristiana), a radical Christian movement strongly opposed to what is described as the American dominance of ORIT; and finally, the largely underground organizations, dominated by Communist parties or Communist sympathizers.

Mexico. Among the Latin American labour movements Mexico's is the most successful, partly as a result of the high growth rates of the Mexican economy during and after World War II. Although collective bargaining has been practiced for many years and is fairly well developed, the trade unions have succeeded in welding a close relationship to Mexico's governing party; the unions, in fact, constitute one of the three main divisions of the party organization. Thus, the success of the Mexican labour movement since about 1920 has depended mainly on relationship to the government party.

Elaborate labour legislation based on Article 123 of the Mexican Constitution gives labour courts powerful means to intervene in disputes. They may declare a strike lawful or unlawful, and by their decision the outcome of a strike is more or less settled. Unlawful strikes have few chances of success, but a lawful strike is almost certain to bring advances to the union.

Decisive role of labour courts

Africa. During most of the colonial period in sub-Saharan Africa, unionism, when it existed at all, was limited to white workers. Attempts of black workers to form unions—usually for the purpose of obtaining wages and working conditions similar to those of white workers—were frequently treated as rebellious political movements and suppressed. Black workers were thus compelled to engage in strikes and demonstrations without having a stable organization at their disposal. Violence often accompanied these short-lived movements.

In the late 1930s, and especially during and after World War II, colonial governments altered their policies and introduced trade unionism in their territories. Usually these unions were patterned after the model of the mother country, and in many cases they were simply branches of metropolitan unions. In some areas—as for instance Guinea and Kenya—close cooperation developed in due course between the unions and the national liberation movements. Political leaders were also often union leaders, or closely associated with them. In other parts of Africa—in Rhodesia, for example—the national liberation movements ignored the unions, the membership of which was rather small and which were therefore not in a position to offer financial or mass support to political movements.

After independence was achieved, unions consistently abandoned the patterns inherited from the former metropolitan territories. Western-style unionism was clearly inappropriate in sub-Saharan Africa with its low level of literacy, a labour force with a large migratory component, few educated working-class leaders, low living standards, and a poorly developed labour market. The unions, however, were rarely given an opportunity to develop new autonomous forms of organization and action. Almost everywhere the government party, by a combination of rewards and pressures, took over the unions under the slogan of "African socialism" and turned them into instruments to enhance production and restrict the wage demands of their members.

Only sporadically, mostly in North Africa, did autonomous unions survive. In most cases they formed the nucleus of the opposition to the government, as is the case in Morocco.

INTERNATIONAL ORGANIZATIONS

The large trade union movements of various countries for many years have maintained loose alliances by joining international organizations of labour; federations of unions, rather than individual unions, usually hold membership. In 1901, the International Federation of Trade Unions was established, chiefly under the guidance of German unions. It proved to be ineffective and disappeared during World War I. In 1919 it was revived at Amsterdam, but immediately came into collision with the Red International of Labour Unions, established by the new government of the Soviet Union. The Communist organization had a brief period of expansion but soon dwindled away and had disappeared before 1939.

Unity and division. At a 1945 conference in London a new organization came into being, the World Federation of Trade Unions (WFTU). Its principal organizers were the British Trades Union Congress, the U.S. Congress of Industrial Organizations, and the Soviet Russian Labour Federation. It made a vigorous but unsuccessful attempt to reconcile the differences between the Communist and non-Communist factions. The U.S. announcement of the Marshall Plan for economic aid to Europe, in which the Soviet Union and other Communist states declined to participate, provided the occasion for the withdrawal of the non-Communist faction.

Ideological cleavage of the international labour movement

In 1949, in London, the non-Communist groups created the International Confederation of Free Trade Unions

(ICFTU). At the first session, 70 labour organizations of 53 nations, claiming to represent 50,000,000 workers, became "founding members." The ICFTU was readily accepted by nearly all of the non-Communist-led labour organizations of the world; and after ten years it had grown to include 138 organizations located in 103 different countries, representing more than 57,000,000 workers.

The announced purposes of the ICFTU include: striving for world peace, the spreading of democratic institutions, increasing the standard of living for workers everywhere, a worldwide strengthening of free trade unions, and support to colonial people in their struggle for freedom. The ICFTU consistently opposed Fascist as well as Communist dictatorships, and implemented that policy by giving such aid as was possible to free labour in Spain and certain Latin American countries. It also furnished direct financial assistance to workers in Hungary and Tibet and campaigned against racialist policies in South Africa.

Failures and successes of the ICFTU. Lack of homogeneity among affiliates hindered the activity of the ICFTU in many fields, chiefly because of differences among its affiliates in the approach to unions in Communist-controlled countries. It found its work to be most effective in the area of international education. By 1960 it had created an International Solidarity Fund of $2,000,000 to aid workers who became victims of oppression and to promote democratic trade unionism in economically underdeveloped countries. Problems of union organization were discussed at ICFTU seminars in various parts of the world, with experienced labour leaders and labour spokesmen from the less industrialized countries participating.

To facilitate the functioning of its widespread activities, the ICFTU established headquarters in Brussels, Belgium, with regional or subregional offices in many other countries. From one or more of those centres it conducted numerous educational conferences, maintained a residential trade union training college in Calcutta, India, and assisted in founding an African Labour College in Kampala, Uganda. It provided assistance to inexperienced workers in areas in the first stages of industrialization and sent organizers to Lebanon, Okinawa, Cyprus, Cameroon, India, Indonesia, Nigeria, and elsewhere.

Worldwide program of training industrial workers

It has been the consistent policy of the ICFTU to cooperate with the United Nations Educational, Scientific, and Cultural Organization and with the International Labour Office in Geneva. It is wholly financed by contributions from its affiliates.

Communist and Catholic federations. The WFTU, meanwhile, has continued to be completely dominated by the Communists. It claimed to represent more than 90,-000,000 workers by 1960, more than one-half in the Soviet Union and a large part of the remainder in Soviet satellite nations. It also has substantial affiliates in France and Italy. The WFTU has adhered strictly to the Communist Party line and has not cooperated with other organizations, serving more as a political instrument than as an economically oriented federation of unions.

A much smaller international organization, the International Federation of Christian Trade Unions (IFCTU), now called the WCL (World Confederation of Labour), is made up largely of Catholic labour unions in France, Italy, and Latin America. The ICFTU, at its founding congress in 1949, invited the affiliates of the IFCTU to join, but the invitation was rejected. On the international scene, the WCL has been a comparatively ineffective organization, its influence limited to a few countries in Europe and Latin America.

BIBLIOGRAPHY. The classic works on this subject are: SIDNEY and BEATRICE WEBB, *History of Trade Unionism*, rev. ed. (1920), *Industrial Democracy* (1920); JOSEPH SCHUMPETER, *Capitalism, Socialism, and Democracy*, 3rd ed. (1950); C. KERR *et al.*, *Industrialism and Industrial Man* (1960); S. PERLMAN, *A Theory of the Labor Movement* (1949); and J.T. DUNLOP, *Industrial Relations Systems* (1959).

The international labour movement is well presented (up to 1950) in L.L. LORWIN, *The International Labor Movement: History, Policies, Outlook* (1953).

Surveys of the literature may be found in A.M. ROSS (ed.), "Literature on Industrial Relations and Economic Development," in *Industrial Relations and Economic Development* (1967); and A. STURMTHAL, "The Labor Movement Abroad," in N.W. CHAMBERLAIN *et al.* (eds.), *A Decade of Industrial Relations Research, 1946–1956* (1958).

Larger areas are treated on a comparative basis in H.A. CLEGG, *A New Approach to Industrial Democracy* (1960); W. GALENSON (ed.), *Comparative Labor Movements* (1952); E.M. KASSALOW, *Trade Unions and Industrial Relations* (1969); A. STURMTHAL (ed.), *Contemporary Collective Bargaining in 7 Countries* (1957), *The Tragedy of European Labor, 1918–1939* (1951), and *Unity and Diversity in European Labor* (1953).

The bulk of the literature is devoted to individual countries. Among the outstanding works are: S.B. LEVINE, *Industrial Relations in Postwar Japan* (1958); V.R. LORWIN, *The French Labor Movement* (1955); KENNETH F. WALKER, *Australian Industrial Relations Systems* (1970); J.P. WINDMULLER, *Labor Relations in the Netherlands* (1969); I. BERNSTEIN, *The Lean Years: A History of the American Worker, 1920–1933*, and *The Turbulent Years: A History of the American Worker, 1933–1941* (both 1960); E.C. BROWN, *Soviet Trade Unions and Labor Relations* (1966); A. FLANDERS, *Trade Unions*, 7th rev. ed. (1968); D.L. HOROWITZ, *The Italian Labor Movement* (1963); INTERNATIONAL LABOUR OFFICE, *The Trade Union Situation in Sweden* (1961), *The Trade Union Situation in the United Kingdom* (1961), *The Trade Union Situation in the U.S.S.R.* (1960), *The Trade Union Situation in the United States* (1960); and T.L. JOHNSTON, *Collective Bargaining in Sweden* (1962).

(A.F.St.)

Traffic Control

Traffic is the movement of people, goods, or vehicles between separated points, and traffic control involves the attempts to make these movements as fast, efficient, and safe as possible with minimum damage to the environment. Traffic control may thus involve planning automobile, truck, bus, and pedestrian movements through the congested streets of a large city; the design of navigation systems for aircraft takeoff, flight, and landing; and mechanized handling of freight for cargo ships. Inadequate control is characterized by congestion, pollution, and accidents.

The kinds of traffic present in a transportation system result from established patterns of activity. The principal land traffic systems, surface and underground, were over roads and railways, though other kinds are developing. Pipelines provide a unique continuous-flow means of moving an increasing variety of materials; though somewhat inflexible, often limited to single commodities, and directional in use, they have the important advantage of being practicable for almost any type of terrain. Cableway and conveyor systems are being developed for pedestrian use in high-density pedestrian traffic areas.

Sea and air transport are the other major types of transportation, but a number of hybrids are under development. Hovercraft (vehicles able to travel over land or water supported on a cushion of air), for example, have added a whole range of potential applications to vehicle technology since their development in 1955. Hovercraft control has aspects in common with both sea and land vehicles and, because of their high speeds, with air traffic (see AIR-CUSHION MACHINES).

The main recent changes in air transport relate to the possible development of supersonic transports and, as in the case of shipping, increasing vehicle size. An especially promising development is the potential reduction in size of airports. Now requiring thousands of acres, they may be reduced in size by vertical-takeoff and associated aircraft types. In shipping there is more specialization of carriers: in some, the cargo is divided up into individual shipping units, as in barges; others unload from a parent ship in small self-propelled units; and others carry cargoes in submarine plastic containers.

The more mixed the traffic to be controlled is, either by type or performance, the greater are the control problems in maximizing vehicle flow and assuring safety. Control is usually exercised by a particular supervising agency for specific types of traffic; problems of competition and regulation arise between these agencies.

ROAD TRAFFIC CONTROL

The following discussion is limited to questions affecting traffic control. For a complete treatment of road design, construction, and maintenance, see ROADS AND HIGHWAYS.

History. Traffic congestion, often bad enough to require drastic control measures, was a feature of city life at least as early as Roman times. A basic cause, then as now, was poor city planning, with roads laid out in such a way as to bring traffic from all quarters to a central crossing point. In the 1st century AD Julius Caesar banned wheeled traffic from Rome during the daytime, a measure gradually extended to cities in the provinces. Late in the 1st century AD the emperor Hadrian was forced to limit the total number of carts entering Rome.

The problem moderated with the decline of commerce in the early Middle Ages, but reappeared during the resurgence of city life in the high Middle Ages, when road maintenance and traveller safety were more paramount problems than traffic control. About 1500 Leonardo da Vinci, envisioning a revolutionary solution to urban traffic problems, then acute in the crowded and busy Italian cities, proposed separating wheeled and pedestrian traffic by creating routes at different levels. Except for the railways, however, very few segregated route systems were established before the 20th century.

Congestion was severe enough in European cities of the 17th century to require ordinances prohibiting parking on certain streets and establishing one-way traffic. The advent of the railroad brought temporary relief to the growing problem of road traffic control, though it created congestion at terminals inside cities. The automobile, with its increase, first in speed and then in numbers over horse-drawn transport, rapidly created a new situation that was to become one of the characteristic problems of urban industrialized society in the 20th century.

Traffic elements. Much motor traffic is still carried on roads that were conceived, if not used, for the horse-drawn vehicles of another age, though roads designed primarily and exclusively for motor traffic are not only easier, safer, and more efficient to drive on but facilitate the best form of traffic control. The essential features of major routes include separation of types of traffic and levels (grade separation), control of access, and design standards suited to the types of vehicle and drivers expected to use the routes. Most of these characteristics are included to permit "free-flowing" traffic on autobahns (Germany), autostradas (Italy), autoroutes (France), freeways and expressways (U.S.), and motorways (U.K.). Early examples of such motor roads were the Avus in Berlin opened in 1919, the Bronx River Parkway in New York opened between 1921 and 1924, Lake Shore Drive freeway in Chicago in 1933, Frankfurt-Darmstadt autobahn in 1935, and several privately financed motor routes built around Milan between 1922 and 1930. The U.S. interstate system, due for completion in the 1970s, is now the most comprehensive highway network in the world.

The elements of road traffic and their various functions are many and often conflicting. In all countries, the needs of pedestrians are quite different from those of vehicles. Vehicles themselves may wish to move at high speed, to manoeuvre and circulate through congested areas, to stop frequently for loading and unloading. Policy makers try to plan traffic-control systems to minimize such conflicts.

Problems. The principal problems associated with road traffic are those which relate to its impact on city dwellers and on commuters while in the city (see also TRANSPORTATION, URBAN). Individual mobility and the desire for travel in the developed countries are increasing at such a rate that demand for roads invariably outstrips supply. Congestion and a continuous worsening of public transport facilities is the result, and this in turn tends to affect urban land use. Cities spread out in patterns determined more by the motor car than by human social needs. New areas lack a cohesive structure. Administration of these huge urban-suburban areas is a continuing problem. Of more immediate significance is the worldwide toll in death and injury that results partly from the failure of road users or their vehicles and partly from

improper road design. Furthermore, the growing public awareness of the noise, atmospheric, and visual pollution caused by road vehicles makes it imperative to review vehicles, roads, and their relationship.

Government regulation. All nations regulate vehicles and drivers on their highways. Drivers are regulated by age, types of vehicle driven, and financial provisions; vehicles are controlled by specifications pertaining to registration, ownership, mechanical worthiness, required accessories, sizes, and weights. Further regulations determine the manner of operation of vehicles on the public highways. Uniform Traffic Acts and Model Municipal Ordinances have been developed to guide traffic legislation throughout the U.S. The nations of western Europe have cooperated effectively in highway and driver regulation. A notable success is the European system of road signs, which employs symbols instead of words to overcome the language barrier. In the underdeveloped countries, where roads and highways are now considered to be critical to economic progress, government takes an even larger role.

Conventional control techniques. Among the principal types of highway control are rules limiting the use of streets. The one-way street was one of the earliest measures and is still in widespread use. Traffic flow can be thought of as possessing properties analogous to frictional materials. The capacity of an undivided street is thus increased if traffic is allowed to move in only one direction. Furthermore, if side streets are used to handle complementary flows, the capacity of the traffic network is further increased. Other general benefits include a reduction in accidents and shorter journey times. Similar considerations apply to the banning of turns, particularly those which require crossing major traffic streams.

The traffic engineer attempts to ensure a homogeneous traffic flow in order to encourage a greater degree of consistency in traffic behaviour. Speeds can be limited with maximum allowable speeds established for specific locations. Another set of restrictions involves loading and unloading, and parking. Curbside parking seriously reduces the potential flow in a street and thus limits its capacity, and often increases the accident rate. Further, parked cars may block the way of public safety vehicles such as fire trucks. Loading, unloading, and parking are controlled by the designation of parking areas, no parking zones, loading zones, time limits on parking, etc. Increasingly important are control measures aimed at improving the flow and regularity of public transit vehicles, particularly in downtown areas.

Traffic-control devices are often used to inform the driver of various conditions affecting road use. These can be divided into categories. Regulatory devices may be either prohibitory (no entry, speed limit, no waiting) or mandatory (stop, keep left, yield). Warning devices are used to warn the road user of hazardous conditions, unusual traffic movements, or special local conditions (children playing, junctions, slippery road surfaces). A final group is that of guidance or informative devices giving route and other pertinent information (destinations, parking and service areas, information offices). The principal devices are road signs and carriageway markings. To ensure effectiveness, these must compel attention and quickly convey their meaning and adequate time must be allowed for driver response. Signs must furthermore command respect and be sited to minimize accidental collision. Ensuring maximum performance is related to uniformity of siting and layout, and the development of correct habitual responses is important. Uniform national standards have been adopted in most countries and an international system in western Europe as noted above. International standards have been drawn up in a United Nations Protocol on Road Signs.

Road traffic signals have improved in effectiveness since their introduction 100 years ago. Their purpose is to promote the orderly movement of traffic and reduce the frequency of accidents. In large cities it is necessary to synchronize street networks in order to maximize traffic flow. Traffic signal controllers are either pretimed or traffic-actuated. Pretimed controllers, widely used in Eu-

"Free-flowing" traffic

Traffic-control devices

rope and the U.S., allocate a specific time interval to each stream of traffic in an orderly repeating sequence. Extensively used in Britain for many years, traffic-actuated signals vary the time allocation and sequence in response to actual traffic demands as measured by traffic detectors. Individual signal units have an illuminated red, yellow (amber) and green lens mounted in a signal head, directionally sited on poles or wires. At least two signal heads are visible to a traffic stream. Pedestrian signals which indicate when to walk are often added. Today's designers, however, prefer to segregate pedestrians and vehicles by constructing overhead or underground walkways.

Cycle length, that is the time required for a complete sequence of signal indications, normally varies between 30 and 150 seconds. A short cycle length reduces the overall capacity of the intersection. The alternative, a long cycle, may provoke some impatience but a driver is not concerned merely with the time lost at a single junction as much as with the speed and smoothness of his whole journey. Considerable research in recent years has been aimed toward limiting delay in traffic control systems. Early coordinated movement patterns were developed with fixed-time signals to allow compact groups of vehicles to progress along a street together. This simultaneous system required that all colour indications be alike at the same time, and had the unfortunate effect of causing drivers to exceed speed limits without achieving high overall journey speeds. This disadvantage was overcome to some extent by an alternate system in which all signals changed indication simultaneously, but adjacent signals showed opposite colours. Problems arose because, since the greens and reds must be of approximately equal duration, the system is suited only to uniformly spaced blocks with cross flows approximately equal to those progressing down the street. A better compromise is the limited progression system which uses a master controller to offset the start of each green phase to enable a speed progression to be maintained by vehicles. A more advanced master controller can operate the flexible progressive system which permits a variation of progression plans by remote control, for example to cover peak hour operation, or to favour directional movements of traffic at particular times of day.

Area traffic control Digital computers have made possible more complete and more extensive forms of control. Computer control of large networks of roads is generally called area traffic control (Figure 1). Information is obtained by a variety

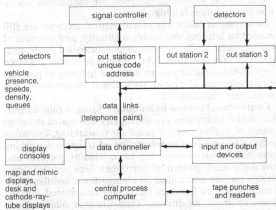

Figure 1: Relationship of elements in a road-traffic area-control system.

of traffic detectors installed in the street system, which measure the presence of vehicles, traffic flow rates, stopped time, speeds, and turning movements. The greater the number of detectors and measurements being made the more complex and expensive the system becomes as items of data are fed over special lines, or are coded and carried on standard telephone cables. Information is processed by the central computer which can then determine settings for all the traffic signals in the network based on some optimization of time, speed, or flow for all traffic or for a particular segment of the flow.

Ideally, such control is dynamically responsive to all changes in the state of traffic flow. Few, if any, systems operate at this level. The more usual arrangement is for a computer to scan the data inputs and compare what it deduces of the current situation with past experience and then select the nearest suitable set of control plans, built up by trial and error over a time period and stored. The selected plan may be modified by further computation to fit a current traffic situation more precisely. Thereafter the computer directly or indirectly operates the switching system that controls the signals.

In the control centres information is printed out on teleprinters; often display diagrams indicate the current state of all signal settings, flows, and journey speeds along routes. These displays may be further supplemented by tabular information on cathode-ray (television) tubes and by closed-circuit television surveillance. This latter facility enables the controllers to monitor the smooth operation of the system and simultaneously, to recognize situations such as accidents which the computer cannot understand.

Electronic control on important high capacity routes of a freeway or motorway is becoming a normal feature of such roads. Its essential purposes are to facilitate traffic merging from entrance ramps into the available gaps of the main stream and to redistribute traffic to adjacent streets if the capacity of the route is being impaired by too many vehicles entering. It is also necessary to warn drivers of hazards and of the consequences resulting from emergencies. Information about gaps in the traffic stream, breakdowns, or hazardous weather are collected by surveillance systems and relayed to a local or central processing point. Detectors coupled with auxiliary equipment are capable of deducing traffic flow and speed. Radio telephones and closed-circuit television may be used as supplementary aids, the latter sometimes being triggered and directed to locations in the system when other types of detectors indicate unusual outputs. New types of signals, capable of displaying various messages such as lane closures, accidents, fog warnings, and speed control, can be set automatically and remotely from integrated control centres which maintain emergency services and receive information continuously from surveillance equipment and both ground and air police patrols.

New concepts in control. Several experimental automatic road-vehicle systems have been built in the U.S. and Europe. While a standard of exceptional reliability is a basic requirement of a practical system, and while present costs are high, improvements in micro-electronics and in solid-state microwave sources indicate that costs might be more than offset, in the 1970s, by reduced accident rates and more efficient use of highways. The latter characteristic may be achieved by a high-speed electronic guidance system which could achieve a fivefold increase in present lane capacity, from 2,000 to 10,000 vehicles per hour, at speeds from 60 to 75 miles per hour (96–120 kilometres per hour). One concept, involving electronically coupled automobiles moving like the cars of a railroad train, could raise highway capacity to 40,000 vehicles per hour.

Steering systems Steering systems are operated by mounting two magnetic field detectors at the front end of the vehicle equidistant from the centre of its longitudinal axis. A guidance cable, installed in the road, sets up a surrounding circular magnetic field. Any movement of the vehicle, from the travel axis, is measured as a transverse error causing corrective operation of the electrohydraulic steering mechanism. For further control purposes a speed signal is emitted from a buried cable; deviations from correct speed cause either acceleration or braking of the car. Particular difficulties with these systems involve the design of transitions from manual control areas to fully automatic areas and the achievement of technical reliability. In addition, difficulties of unlocking traffic jams in which vehicle densities are five times those at present, may be extraordinary.

Several semi-automatic systems offer stepping stones to full automation. One of the principal problems, which both limits driver performances and increases road accidents, is the saturation of a driver's visual processes with a multiplicity of signs and signals. Improved methods of conveying the most important information have been developed in research programs. "Talking" signs for example, are activated by a signal from an approaching vehicle; their taped information is transmitted to the vehicle receiver for the driver's response. Receivers can be built so that they respond only to the roadside transmitters if the driver requires it but an override can be installed to permit the relay of important information such as traffic holdups ahead, accidents, changes in weather conditions, and information on parking.

Experiments have also been made with automatic routing systems. Traffic detectors linked to a computer measure flows and compute journey times on all parts of the road system. Control information is relayed to signs that display the most suitable routes to be used by approaching drivers to reach important destinations. One experimental project offers an individual route guidance system. The driver inserts a punched card, coded with destination and route requirements, into a transmitter which triggers a matching code transmitter at the approach to each intersection. A low-frequency response signal switch switches a visual display monitor on the vehicle's control panel indicating the turns required.

RAIL TRAFFIC CONTROL

History. The first slow and cumbersome horse-drawn rail traffic posed few control problems not resolved by follow-the-leader principles. It was only after the development of swifter steam-driven trains, in the early years of the nineteenth century, that more frequent trains and their proximity to each other created dangers of collisions. The smooth contact between tracks and iron wheels allowed higher speeds and greater loads to be hauled at the same time that the low friction necessitated long stopping distances. Engines were fitted with brakes and, later, manned brake vans, whose guard could apply the brakes when the engine driver signalled with a whistle.

Trackside control also developed slowly with the first signalman, or "railway policeman," located at passenger and goods depots, or stations, sited along the line. These men indicated, by means of hand signals, the state of the track ahead. Red taillights were mounted at the rear of trains at night to improve safety. Later, signal flags were often replaced by swivelling coloured boards, or disks, for daytime use and with coloured lights at night. Later, signals were located well ahead of stopping points, giving rise to the term "distant signal." As was the case with other modes of transport, the need for control increased with greater traffic movements and faster operating speeds; in the early period, elaborate signalling was unnecessary since the frequency of service was such as to still permit adequate train spacing. The first real method of control was the development of a time-interval system of train spacing. In the event of breakdown or accident, however, there were no means of delaying a following train from entering a section of track except by a physical check on entry and exit by sections; *e.g.*, a brakeman with a flag or lantern.

First introduced for railway use in England between Euston and Camden in 1837 the electric telegraph, permitted communication between fixed signal points. Each signalman was responsible for a portion of track known as a block section. Bell codes were used to describe the class and route of the train to be passed by the signalman to the next block section or to accept or reject a train from the preceding section. Generally, only one train was permitted in a section at one time; under poor visibility conditions a section was normally kept empty between every two trains. Many decisions of precedence were left to the individual signalman, and with only limited information at their disposal, signalmen often made incorrect decisions causing excessive delay. At the same time, standard codes and rules were established by most railway companies and safety was further improved by the introduction of Westinghouse air brakes about 1870.

Because concise and standardized information was needed by the engineer, mechanical semaphore arm sig-

nals, operated remotely by wires from a lever in a signal box, were developed in 1841 as a principal means of communication. The angle of the arm indicated stop, proceed with caution, or clear ahead. For night use coloured lenses, mounted near the pivot of the arm, are passed across a light source, thus displaying, for the different arm angles, either the familiar red for stop, yellow for caution (approach, reduce speed), and green for clear (proceed as authorized). Similarly the remote control and setting of points, in a block, was transferred from the trackside to the charge of the signalman. Interlocking devices were designed in the 1850s to prevent conflicting settings of points and signals. The time losses due to poor acceleration and deceleration characteristics of trains were obviated, to some extent, by the increasing use of presignals, informing the driver that the signal ahead might be at stop and requiring him to reduce speed or proceed slowly from a stop. Thus the more violent fluctuations were smoothed out; similar control arrangements have now been adopted for use in European cities to control road traffic.

Traffic elements. Railways in most countries are classified as either private or common carriers. Private carriers are in the minority, operating mostly in lumbering, industrial plants, and mining. Further operational classifications are made on the basis of the type of traffic carried. Principal subdivisions are intercity routes (linehaul), intracity route networks (commuter), switching services for warehousing and industrial plants, and general terminal operators.

Rail traffic is divided into passenger and freight, and, although both normally operate over the same system, there are special control problems particular to each. In recent years it has been clear that it is necessary to consider the total journey made by the rail passenger rather than simply the time he spends in the train. The integration of rail services with other forms of transport is essential, particularly in locating stopping points and in designing mainline terminals or commuter stations.

Freight is now a predominant factor in all rail operations. Although the heart of the freight control system is still the so-called marshalling yard, where individual wagons are collected for train makeup, recent years have seen the development of bulk trains, designed specifically for single train loads and running from a private siding to a similar destination siding. The rolling stock is often semipermanently coupled and the handling equipment at the terminals is usually designed for continuous operation of the system at a high capacity.

New systems management and control methods are still needed to improve the speed, regularity, and comfort of rail services while safeguarding established high standards of safe operation. The required resources are often beyond the capability of an outdated industry to provide; direct injection of capital, by national governments, is a worldwide phenomenon.

Conventional control techniques. Modern railway traffic-control techniques are principally automated developments of earlier systems based on timetabling, operating rules, and signals. The scheduling of trains in a working timetable predetermines the basic running patterns and the daily work pattern of personnel. Unscheduled operations require controllers to change the schedules. Minimum intervals between trains are determined, on the basis of track conditions. Time–distance diagrams are often used to compare running conditions with those in the timetable and to indicate when and what type of regulatory intervention is needed.

Colour light signals have now largely superseded semaphore types. Because they are operated electrically, colour light signals can be sited at distances remote from the signal box. Combinations of light colours can be used to indicate different requirements to the driver. High intensity lights, visible over great distances, are particularly advantageous in poor weather. Searchlights use a single lens and bulb with different colours displayed by means of panels on colour filters rotated in front of the lamp. Lights can be more appropriately sited in relation to the driver's cab position and permit a greater variety of infor-

Telegraph communications (margin)

Colour light signals (margin)

mation to be efficiently displayed. With the development of hydraulic, pneumatic, and electrical methods of switching, the problems of distance are overcome and the displacement of mechanical devices from the local signal box enables many more sets to be controlled from a central point.

The basic element in automatic control is an electric circuit built into the track which operates track signals. When a train enters a section of track it causes the current to detour through the locomotive's wheels and axles, instead of completing its normal circuit, altering signals ahead.

When a train has passed a section, the signal behind it is automatically switched by a track circuit immediately ahead to indicate danger. As the train advances to the next section, the first signal can automatically be changed to a lower state of warning and so on until a full clearance signal is set at a given number of sections behind the train. The number of intermediate sections left behind a train is determined by train speeds and section lengths, and influences the capacity of a track.

Today, manual signal boxes have generally been replaced by a few centralized boxes controlling large areas of track. All operations are performed with pushbuttons and the system is designed with full interlocking plant preventing any mis-setting of switches, points, and signals. Each movement can be made only in a predetermined and safe way, eliminating the setting of conflicting routes and signals. Operation of all devices is monitored and relayed from the trackside to an illuminated display on a track diagram. Newer systems also monitor all train movements with individual identity and location indicated by lights supplemented by cathode-ray tubes.

Additional automation has been carried to the cab. Relays, tuned to the transmission of a particular frequency, feed back an activating signal rearward. Similarly each track circuit is set to control the signals. Coded circuits operate other train-borne devices by the installation of suitable receiving coils mounted, above the track, at the front of the locomotive. In this way trackside signal displays are transferred to the cab, reducing the risk of a crew missing a signal. Greater safety margins are provided by the addition of audio signals. Various methods of providing coded impulses include systems in which drivers must respond to audio warnings with an acknowledgment signal. Automatic train stopping is provided by the same means, and in addition, the brakes may be automatically applied if a driver fails to respond to track restrictions. Another form of visual display makes use of a moving map continuously indicating a spot position.

Radio communications

The first recorded moving train two-way radio was used by the New York Central Railroad in 1928. Radio offers a number of advantages in improving communications between train crews and control dispatchers or maintenance gangs on the track. It also establishes a direct link between trains and obviates the need for crews to use wayside telephones. Equipment failures can be reported directly and because of this and other advantages, particularly in automated marshalling yards, delay is reduced. Most railways throughout the world are equipped to some extent with two-way train radios.

A further development is the automation of route-setting procedures. These enable a controller to notify the computer at the beginning and end of the required route; thereafter, all intervening signals and points are automatically established. Storage of a working timetable in program form can be used to initiate the route settings for each subsequent track movement and as each train clears appropriate sections of the track. At the same time identities of trains may be transmitted from one control to another in the form of unique labels, known as head codes. Thus, in addition to changing the signals behind it to red as it proceeds from section to section, a train can remotely generate complete new control sequences.

The development of computer-controlled freight transit is incomplete until a corresponding organizational and documentation process for the dispatch and receipt of goods has been integrated within the total system. A customer may, for example, transcribe orders to the transport system, specifying commodity type, consignment identity, consignor and consignee information, payment instructions, priorities, etc. Information can then be relayed to and from the computer and prices indicated for a particular consignment. In the next stage, trains are made up after each wagon has been loaded and, if required, part-load consignments can be allocated a space number in a specified wagon. Train makeup takes into account engine types, routing, overall weights and lengths, numbers and types of cars, and braking power for all trains leaving a siding. The information is then relayed to points down the line by telephone, telegraph, or teleprinter for the reverse process of train breakup. The grouping of consignments for common destinations into single cars reduces transshipment costs and time losses. Where placement lists of all loads are stored in a computer, optimization programs can be developed to minimize subsequent trucking distribution movements.

Sorting freight cars is a complex operation. Various control systems have been installed in marshalling yards enabling cars to be pushed over a raised track, known as a hump, so that the car travels freely down a grade and over switching points to its correct berth. Automatic humping includes sensors to detect car speed and weight, from which car rolling resistance is estimated. Once the uncoupled car has been allocated a train and siding, automatic switching sets the points along its predetermined path. Simultaneously the computer calculates the speed required for the car to reach the end of the train. Automatic braking devices or boosters reduce or increase the car's speed off the hump to that needed to reach its train coupling point in the siding.

Other, more refined, methods remotely control the pushing locomotive. The spacing of cars rolling off the hump, the automatic control of the pushing speed, and the control of retarders or speed boosters are all directly controlled by computer. Identification of car destinations is an essential part of the process. Manual checking in the yard with radio links to the yardmaster have been displaced by closed-circuit television checking off the train against the makeup list forwarded by teleprinter.

The final scheduling and control of the freight train is integrated into the comprehensive rail control system, and computers permit the computation of alternative strategies with an assessment of benefits. Controllers finally impose their selection of priorities. In the 1970s many of these systems were becoming universal.

New concepts in control. Modern signalling systems have improved the safety, efficiency, and operating economies of railways by providing better track capacity and more flexibility. In West Germany alone more than 10,000 hand signal boxes in 1945 had been reduced to fewer than 3,500 in 1971, and the process is continuing throughout the world. Future control systems are largely developments of existing concepts, but wider area traffic control will be available as the reliability of components is improved and methods of optimizing large networks with multicommodity flows develop.

Modern signalling systems

Difficulties occur when trains are run at different speeds under the same control system. The location of signals, for instance, is determined on the basis of the number of sections required for the fastest train to brake from full speed. This distance is excessive for slower moving trains and hence, because density cannot be maintained, line capacity is reduced. The greater the disparity, the more exaggerated the loss of efficiency will be. Because time is important to passengers, train speeds are rising; on the New Tōkaidō Line, a 500-kilometre section between Tokyo and Osaka carries 200 trains a day with more than 50 travelling at speeds up to 210 kilometres per hour.

A method of overcoming disadvantages of mixed traffic is the so-called moving block. In this system the fixed track block is replaced by a moving zone in the front and the rear of the train, the length of the zone determined by the speed of the train. If a train enters another train's zone, signals appear in the cab and at the same time automatically decelerate the train. The moving block system can be applied to express traffic while the conventional system is preserved for slower traffic.

Separating trains by an optimum minimum headway (distance between two trains moving in the same direction) requires the following train controller to have continuous information on the track ahead, including train positions and hazards. This information can be supplied by radar, overhead lines, and other methods.

These developments lead toward automation of the whole system, including driverless trains. A particularly interesting application of these principles is used in new urban rapid transit railways of which the Bay Area Rapid Transit railway in San Francisco is an example. A full system concept is being developed under complete surveillance, with computer processing and monitoring of all aspects ranging from automatic revenue collection to absolute traffic protection (insurance of no collisions) and automatic protection in case of computer failure. Operating speeds are up to 130 kilometres per hour at headways of 90 seconds.

Traffic control and communication is divided into three subsystems, line supervision, traffic protection, and automatic traffic operation. Unlike other control systems mentioned earlier, this system dispenses with central control and operates on the basis of car-carried traffic control, station and trackside control, central supervisory control, and the traffic telephone system.

Failure
rates

Failure rates have been assessed for each subsystem based on component failure rates and, in turn, their failure consequences determined for the overall degradation of the system. Fail-safe operation and the minimization of delay were essential considerations. Maintainability has been the key to design of diagnostic apparatus. Other considerations have included a study of customer-created problems through the misuse of automatic ticket machinery (see also RAILROADS AND LOCOMOTIVES).

AIR TRAFFIC CONTROL

History. In the early days of flying, man depended mainly on his own senses aided by primitive controls borrowed from the mariner. The penalties of failure were severe. The first step toward improvement was to end the basic hazard of the aircraft pilot's isolation by installing a communication system. After World War I commercial aircraft were regularly equipped with radios for communication between ground and air. Positioned information and estimated times of arrival were relayed to the ground. Ground stations, in turn, transmitted weather and instructions to the aircraft. With the development of regular routes, networks of ground stations were established so that positions could be determined with known direction-finding techniques: the beaming of an aircraft's radio signal was simultaneously plotted on maps at two or more ground stations, and the resulting positional intersect of the bearings was relayed to the aircraft's radio operator. This technique permitted course corrections to be made when the ground was obscured by clouds. In the late 1920s, the development of radio beams enabled a pilot to follow a track to his destination. (For a detailed discussion of this subject, see NAVIGATION.)

With all these methods, however, control still depended largely on the pilot and, in those early days of aircraft radio, interference, topography, and weather often obliterated the transmissions. Terminal control was limited to the use of light signals by the ground control officers. Later the radio link was added to the system.

While air travel expanded steadily, it was not until World War II that the need to handle large numbers of aircraft brought the development of much more sophisticated types of control. Night bombing led to the development of so-called en route control in which pilots were given time checkpoints along the flight path and at the target point. The problem of returning to a darkened home base many hours later and perhaps, in very different weather conditions, led to the use of the standard beam approach in which the pilot located himself once his aircraft entered a signal beam emitted by a ground transmitter. The wide, fan-shaped beam, tapering to a point at the end of the runway, was divided into two halves, one of which was dots, the other dashes. The plane followed the path where dots and dashes over-

lapped, forming a continuous note. As an aid to the pilot in determining his position and the point at which to begin a descent, additional transmitters, emitting a vertically directed signal of different intensity, were provided.

Improved ground control methods were also necessary in wartime because of the large number of aircraft returning to a base at the same time. Aircraft and bases exchanged radio identities and sequences of landing were established, including stacking, directing returning aircraft to circle at 1,000-foot (300-metre) altitude intervals. The lowest aircraft was designated the next in turn to land, with each higher aircraft descending through a one-thousand-foot step to its next altitude until the last had been accommodated by the controller on a specified runway. Ground controllers also established "talk-down" methods. One such system developed at the time was called controlled descent through cloud and has led to a modern version, ground-controlled approach.

Traffic elements. Aircraft are flown today for numerous purposes ranging from scheduled airliners to unscheduled airliners, military aircraft, bulk cargo carriers, and such independents as private business and sport planes, crop sprayers, weather craft, and traffic controllers. Operational control of aircraft depends primarily on their service use, on whether they fly near the ground or in adverse climates away from bases, and whether they operate from land, water, or ice. Aircraft have high operating costs and, with increasing sophistication, represent larger investment problems and fly from complex and costly ground bases. Helicopters and the newer generation of vertical-takeoff aircraft have somewhat different characteristics and, therefore, individual control problems.

Lengths and widths of runways are classified according to the type of traffic they handle. Principal types include private, secondary, feeder, continental, and intercontinental airports.

Problems. Collision avoidance remains a critical traffic control problem. Systems are developed and can act as a supplementary aid in terminal areas, as well as the principal sensor in airways lacking ground surveillance equipment. Considering the high closing (approaching) speeds of modern aircraft (20 miles, or 30 kilometres, per minute) the somewhat lower ascent or descent rates (two miles, or three kilometres, per minute and four miles, or six kilometres, per minute, respectively) and aircraft capability for rapid acceleration, it is necessary to be able to specify required avoidance manoeuvres quickly from among available options. Simple proximity warning indicators detect aircraft presence, within certain ranges, in the surrounding airspace and warn the pilot, but avoidance ultimately depends on visual sighting of the intruder. Newer types of instruments, operating on a common frequency, transmit regular interrogation pulses; other aircraft respond with an identity "label." This is in a digital code form, presenting such information as altitude and rate of change in altitude, together with range-finding signals. Extremely accurate atomic clocks are synchronized in order to measure the time elapsed between the sending and receiving of signals and to deduce the interval of time separating the two aircraft. Without directional location, avoidance options are limited to a vertical plane of escape, but both aircraft must make the correct decision relative to the other; generally one moves up and the other down.

Thunderstorms ahead of aircraft are readily detected by airborne radar, but ice particles and other turbulences in the upper altitudes are not. While airports are usually sited to avoid frequent fog situations, as many as one in fifty landings must be aborted because of visibility conditions. New electronic automatic landing systems, using radio altimeters in conjunction with a computer, have been perfected, and it is likely in the future that fog will be more of a hazard on the journey to and from the airport. Accidents and pollution problems, including smoke, turbulence, and noise, have grown increasingly important. (See also TRANSPORTATION, AIR.)

Regulation. Late in World War II a number of Allied and neutral nations convened in Chicago to determine the

Collision
avoidance

arrangements necessary for the safe and orderly development of international air transport. They established the International Civil Aviation Organization to study and report on customs facilities, traffic control, aircraft maintenance, and the important need for standardization. Air-transport terminals, unlike those of other transport modes, are likely to be used more frequently by the vehicles of another nation than those of the host country. Accordingly, standards have been laid down by member nations for all essential matters; factors of lesser import are subject to recommended practices. English has become the international language of control. The rules adopted are updated by regular conventions of the international organization.

Conventional control techniques. The purpose of air traffic control is to regulate flight movements, ensuring that collision courses are avoided and that safe distances are maintained between aircraft. The separation of aircraft is governed by International Civil Aviation Organization rules specifying lateral (angular distance), horizontal (distance or time interval), and vertical (different flight levels) intervals.

Airspace is divided by flight levels into upper, middle, lower, and controlled airspace. Controlled airspace includes that surrounding airports and airways, which define the corridors of movement between them with minimum and maximum altitudes. The degree of control varies with the importance of the airway and may, for private light aircraft, be represented only by ground markings. Airways are usually divided by 1,000-foot (300-metre) and 500-foot (150-metre) levels with aircraft assigned specific operating levels, according to direction and performance. Normally all such movements are controlled by air traffic control centres. In upper airspace, above about 25,000 feet (7,500 metres) pilots may be allowed free route choices provided that flight tracks and profiles have been agreed on in advance. In middle airspace all pilots entering or crossing controlled airspace are obliged to accept control and notification must therefore be given to control in advance. Radar advisory services are often available in middle airspace but not generally below 5,000 feet (1,500 metres) in lower airspace. Besides vertical spacings, in airways, horizontal separations are important, usually taking the form of a minimum time interval of ten minutes between aircraft on the same track and elevation with a lateral spacing, typically, of ten miles (16 kilometres).

The simplest form of flight control is called the visual flight rule. Aircraft in controlled airspace must remain at least one nautical mile (1,852 metres) horizontally and 1,000 feet (300 metres) vertically away from all clouds and visibility must not be less than five nautical miles (9,260 metres). Outside controlled airspace, the aircraft must be flown clear of clouds and within sight of land or water. In congested airspace all pilots must obey the instrument flight rule; that is, they must depend principally on instruments for their safety. In poor visibility and at night instrument flight rules invariably apply. At airports, in control zones, all movements are subject to permission and instruction from Air Traffic Control when visibility is typically less than five nautical miles or the cloud ceiling is below 1,500 feet (450 metres).

Procedural control starts with the aircraft's captain receiving meteorological forecasts together with a briefing officer's listings of radio-frequency changes along the flight path and notices to airmen. Flight plans are checked and possible exit corridors from the flight path, in case of emergency, are determined. Flight plans are relayed to control towers and approach control centres. As the aircraft taxis out, under instructions from the ground-movement controller, the pilot awaits his turn to be fitted into the overall pattern of incoming and outgoing movements. Controllers allocate an outgoing track which enables aircraft separation to be maintained; this is determined from a check of the more recently used standard departure clearances. As the aircraft climbs to its initial altitude, on an instructed heading, the departure controller identifies the image caused by the aircraft on the radar screen before allowing any new takeoffs or landings. Further instructions clear the aircraft for its final climb to the en route portion of the flight and the pilots' first reporting point marked by radio devices. This portion of the flight may also be under radar surveillance.

Progress reports on the en route portion of the flight are required, and the aircraft may be tracked on radar. Pairs of transmitters define each leg of the airway. At several points along his route the captain reports altitude, time and the estimated time of arrival at the next listed reporting point. Flight progress strips are made up on boards from the filed flight plans and include all traffic on an airway under that centre's control. Information includes call signs, flight details, and estimated times of arrival at reporting points. As each report is received actual times are entered and the estimated times of arrival are adjusted for subsequent reporting points; altitudes are also checked. Each aircraft has a separate strip for each reporting point. The progress of all aircraft is thus adjusted as the flights proceed, and updating estimates are made of the future state enabling the controller, in direct communication with the flight by radio, to maintain separations and to permit pilots a safe change of course or altitude if these are required.

Since the introduction of long-range tracking radar, the flight progress board has been used as a backup system immediately available in the event of instrument failures. Whereas tabulating reported information only represents a succession of reports on an aircraft's position, radar gives continuous coverage of flight movements allowing safe reductions to be made in separations and, thus, increasing capacity (see also RADAR).

At a reporting point en route the receiving control centre takes over the flight from the departure centre, and all further reports and instructions are made to the new control centre. Descent instructions are relayed to arrange the incoming aircraft at separations of perhaps five miles (eight kilometres), in effect, on a slanting line. As the aircraft closes in speed adjustments or lengthening of flight paths may be necessary to maintain separations of three nautical miles over the airport boundary. Controllers determine the landing sequences and stacking instructions and may adjust takeoffs to handle surges in the incoming flights. The final stage is initiated by transfer of control to an approach controller. Under radar surveillance the final directions are given for landing. In the landing sequence, control passes to the control tower where precision radar is used to monitor the landing, and ground movement controllers issue taxiing instructions (Figure 2).

Marginal notes: Airspace   Flight progress strips

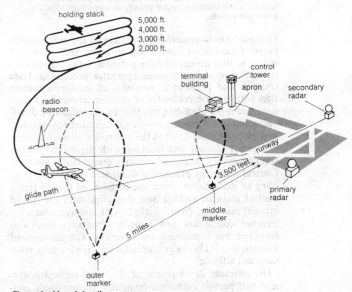

Figure 2: *Aircraft landing sequence.*
Control tower receives information on an airplane's approach via radar, allocates a runway, and issues final instructions so that the aircraft will intersect the glide-path beam of the instrument-landing system. Markers (dashed-line hoops) indicate to the pilot fixed distances from the runway.

The control tower handles the initial and terminal parts of the flight. Other tower functions include the operational control of high-intensity approach lights, emergency services, taxiing movements, and continuous broadcasts of airport information on runways in use and weather details. Besides a clear viewing position of the whole runway area, immediate and direct communication is an important requirement, particularly in coordinating activities with area and approach control centres. Smaller airport towers, with fewer traffic movements, may combine the functions of approach and final control.

New concepts in control. Air traffic control is still a manual operation controlled by humans. Semi-automatic systems are currently being installed, but if air travel is to continue its development, and effective airport and airway capacities with adequate safety are to be achieved, fully automatic systems will be required. Controllers are believed to be at, or near, the limit in the use of radar for aircraft surveillance and sequencing and voice communication for instructing aircrews and receiving information. Information is often limited and lacking in precision, both in terms of the ground controllers and the air crew and, furthermore, can be dangerously ambiguous. Because of this situation controllers and pilots may spend most of their time exchanging information. Decisions are thus in danger of being taken on the basis of incomplete data. The principal objective is to automate both the information and control systems, within a data-processing complex of specified reliability.

Flight data processing

The first essential component of an automated system is a means for processing flight data information. Flight plans, subsequent amendments, weather data, and notices to airmen may be entered directly into a central computer (Figure 3). Information from other centres is carried

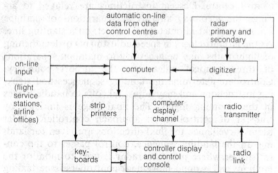

Figure 3: *Elements of an automated in-flight control system.*
The information from other control centres and from radar is entered in the computer, which already contains flight plan and weather data.

via data links to remote input devices of the central computer. Operational data, from primary and secondary radar, is first processed into a digital form for onward transmission and subsequent computer processing. Data transfer and printout is available at equipped remote sites within a control centre or at other terminals. Target data and flight plan data can thus be correlated by developing suitable computer programs. Comprehensive information can be displayed to the controller giving automatic aircraft identity and tracking with flight information simultaneously displayed on the controller's consoles. Central computer processing eliminates the manual handling of information from one member of the air traffic control team to another and thus eliminates the use of manual marking. Pictorial displays of airways, obstacles, weather conditions, and boundary markers may also complete the comprehensive coverage. Ground-derived information is always available for positive identity, position, and altitude.

The ultimate development of this semi-automatic system will permit automatic computer ground-to-air control with simultaneous information and display to both ground controller and aircraft pilot for monitoring purposes. Full control will have passed from man to machine (see also TRANSPORTATION, AIR).

WATER TRAFFIC CONTROL

History. Navigation is still the principal means of controlling the paths of ships; direction measurements are made by a navigator using, as of old, a knowledge of the movements of the sun and stars and, since the Middle Ages, the magnetic compass or the later development, the gyroscopic compass (see also NAVIGATION; COMPASS; and TRANSPORTATION, WATER). From early times the need to exchange information between ships and with land stations, led to the development of visual and audible signal systems. Markers were carried by ships and also laid in channels, and the transmission of messages was accomplished through flag, semaphore, horn, bell, whistle, and light signals leading to the establishment of first national and later international codes. The invention and use of radio, at the beginning of this century, brought a marked improvement in ship communication.

Considerable advances in mapping were made over the centuries; modern navigation charts show all coasts, submerged obstacles, sea depths, and navigational aids such as lighthouses, lightships, buoys, and radio beacons (see also HYDROGRAPHIC CHARTING).

New forms of steam propulsion and the design of iron ships in the 19th century led to increased ship size. The growth in world trade brought to the fore the problem of establishing consistent avoiding action when vessels approached each other. International rules of the road at sea were laid down in 1863 and have since been periodically updated.

Traffic elements. Ships can be broadly divided into tramps, specialized vessels, and liners. Tramps are mostly conveyors of bulk cargo, trading internationally, and operating without fixed sailing schedules, generally committed on the basis of time, or for a specific voyage. Specialized carriers include tankers and a rapidly growing group of carriers designed for the movement of iron ore, sugar, and other bulk commodities. Container ships, ferries, and belships, capable of lifting awkward loads of up to 250 tons with large derricks, are among other specialized vessels. Liners are vessels operated as common carriers on scheduled services between ports.

Problems. A fundamental difference of scale exists between the potential size of vessels designed for operation on land and sea. Severe load limitations exist for land vehicles whereas at sea the million-ton ship is by no means unrealistic in the 1970s. The principal traffic problems of harbours and approaches are related to the increasing size of cargo ships and the growing numbers of small craft used for recreation. Many of these difficulties can be overcome by separating one type of operation and craft from another and by more rigorous demarcation of areas of use. Often the siting and establishment of new marinas, away from crowded shipping lanes and established ports, reduces the problems and permits the special needs of the leisure user to be fulfilled.

Water pollution

But a vast and urgent control problem has been created by the increasing pollution of the earth's water. At sea, improved sewage disposal methods and a reduction in air pollution can be effected by waste processing before discharge as required on land for other industrial operations. Reducing oil pollution is a more serious difficulty, long recognized by governments in legislation prohibiting oil discharge within 50 miles (80 kilometres) of land and in the designation and control of ocean dumping grounds. Such control is effected internationally through a United Nations agency, the Inter-Governmental Maritime Consultative Organization, and methods of instituting court proceedings against offenders have resulted from international conventions. Victims of pollution damage are also enabled to claim compensation from ship owners and insurers.

The redesign and development of control systems to prevent oil spillage are important in tanker design. Difficulties have arisen with some new systems due to the explosive dangers of residual vapour in the tanks. Apart from the "creeping" pollution arising from oil discharge during normal operations, the main problem is the danger of collision or shipwreck, in which massive quantities of crude oil or other harmful materials may be released to pollute vast coastal areas. New methods of treatment are being investigated and disaster procedures laid down, enabling authorities to undertake swift clearing operations.

Regulations, international and national. International regulations control ship construction and use. All important routes are now governed by regional agreements. Shipowners have developed the liner conference system that regulates sailings and ports of call and establishes a common tariff for freight and passenger movements. Postal administrations also contract with shipping companies, through the shipping conferences, for mail handled as a commodity on a tonnage basis. Coastal shipping is usually subject to governmental control. Tramp shipping is based on market chartering of ships or space therein, for the carriage of all types of cargo to and from all ports. The largest of these markets is the Baltic Mercantile and Shipping Exchange in London.

Generally there are obligations for ship constructors and owners to comply with rules, established nationally and internationally, governing classification of ships. These affect ship design, particularly elements concerned with safety standards, including lifesaving equipment, waterproof and fireproof bulkheads, gangways, navigational aids, and construction standards. The maritime nations regularly hold international conventions to consider the problems of safety at sea, including all aspects of navigation. National regulations impose survey systems to check vessels for seaworthy conditions, and societies, such as Lloyd's Register of Shipping (U.K.), American Bureau of Shipping (U.S.), Registro Italiano (Italy), Germanischer Lloyd (West Germany), and Bureau Veritas (France), today classify and survey most of the world's mercantile fleet.

Conventional control techniques. Control of ships on the open sea still remains exclusively with the master of the vessel; when other ships are met established rules of steering are practiced. This ancient arrangement, primitive by comparison with the sophisticated and centralized air traffic-control system, has survived thanks to the expanse of sea and the relatively few ships sailing upon it. Communication between ships is, therefore, vital in their control, both at sea and with the confined channels of inland waterways. The principal methods of transmitting a signal are visual (that is, by flag, semaphore, or light) or audible (by means of horns or radio). The revised International Code of 1934 includes alphabetic, numeral, and answering flags. Urgent messages can be communicated by single flags while three-letter groups are used for compass points, bearings, and times. Semaphore signalling employs hand flags, while Morse can be transmitted visually by searchlights equipped with horizontal control slats, or by radio. Ships also use sirens for "in sight" conditions, to indicate impending course changes and, generally, for warning purposes in bad visibility.

The control of ships near coasts is facilitated, both for warning and navigational purposes, by the use of lightships and lighthouses. Channels on the approach to ports are clearly marked by floating buoys, usually fitted with lights and equipped with sound signals (horns, bells, and whistles) for use in bad weather or at night. The proper provision of buoys and beacons, anchored in their correct position and their subsequent maintenance, is essential for control and safety purposes.

Buoys are classified by their functional role into categories denoted by shape, markings, and colour. The approach to an estuary for example, is marked by a landfall buoy and main channels by red can-shaped or black cone-shaped buoys. Where channels fork, at junctions, spherical buoys are used to indicate direction either to port or starboard. Other special buoys denote wreck positions, danger areas, and middle ground, the region near the centre of the channel where ships can safely move.

Marine and harbour radar was first developed during World War II in the United Kingdom. Subsequent developments have permitted much shorter wavelengths to be used, employing narrow beam scanners, that give an immediate measurement of bearing and range with accuracies better than 30 seconds and 20 yards (18 metres).

Shipborne marine radar assists navigation and helps to reduce collisions at sea, providing map-type information both in darkness and fog of other objects, adjacent coastlines, icebergs, and some types of approaching storms. Harbour radar permits information to be radioed to ships to position themselves clear of channels in controlled anchorages and, entering or leaving port, allows determination of position relative to navigational markers. It also enables irregularities to be monitored by harbour masters and the movements of harbour vessels to be controlled by radio instructions to tug and other masters (see also RADAR).

Collisions occur at sea even in cases in which vessels have clearly sighted each other. This happens when, despite radio and radar equipment, erroneous deductions are made. Some collisions result from the slow response and poor manoeuvrability of ships; this is particularly true of the new supersized ships. Furthermore, because of their great size, new ships congest the few deep channels near coasts or leading to harbours. The mechanization of cargo handling and docks has concentrated the huge new ships into a few ports and their narrow approaches. Such natural shipping lanes as the English Channel, where nearly 1,000 ships a day pass through straits less than 25 miles (40 kilometres) wide, and other heavily used man-made systems such as the Kiel Canal in Germany, which passes some 90,000 ships a year, create the need for new control systems.

The first type of physical control system to be applied after the establishment of a basic set of rules for a given area is to segregate opposing directions of movement. A working party from the various navigational organizations of Europe has agreed on a sea-lane three miles (five kilometres) wide, separated by a safety zone two miles (three kilometres) wide, at several European locations. As in all international developments where the rights of nations, or even individuals, have become established over the centuries, the pace and manner of changes are usually exceedingly slow.

Whereas navigational control of a ship refers to its position relative to natural features, operational control refers to the governing of its movements in relation to that of other vehicles and along prescribed channels. A return echo, received from the emission of pulsed radio energy and transmitted by the rotating aerial of a marine radar, is displayed on a cathode-ray tube in a plan position indicator. Ships and channel markers are thus displayed at various selected ranges, from about 1 to 100 nautical miles (1 nautical mile = 1,852 metres), dependent on the power radiated by the installation and aerial characteristics. Newer equipment provides for an automatic plotting of the data aligned to standard charts.

New concepts in control. The development of a new navigation system was based on the principle that if two radio stations transmitted different signals, a receiver, equipped to pick them up simultaneously, could compare the differences and obtain an estimate of its range from the two stations. Such a system has been designed and manufactured using a master station, transmitting two or three slightly different signals at frequencies around 100,000 cycles per second (see NAVIGATION). Over 30 chains of stations are being erected throughout the world's most crowded shipping areas, covering approaches to western Europe, the U.S. and Canadian western seaboards, the Persian Gulf and Indian Ocean areas, and the waters around Japan and South Africa. Other systems, operating over much greater oceanic distances, are being developed from early versions of long-range navigators, but lack the precision of the closer, lower frequency chains.

While many of the problems of the control of inland waterways concern the maintenance of channels and locks, the increasing growth of traffic on major canals, inland seas, and lakes demands more advanced forms of traffic control than hitherto. Many of the most important waterways only offer single-lane operation for the larger ships, with carefully regulated speed control to inhibit erosion. An example of control is that maintained for the busy Kiel Canal, where a speed limit of 15 kilometres per

Rules of steering (margin)

Collisions at sea (margin)

Control of lakes (margin)

hour permits about 180 ships to be accommodated at one time in the canal, with control exercised by stations at either end. The stations monitor and log data on ships' movements, coordinating a flow of information from visual observations made at locks and sidings along the canal's length. By constructing time–distance diagrams, controllers attempt to optimize the traffic flow by using the sidings to organize priorities.

Currently research is being undertaken to test a digital computer system for making the control decisions. Favoured is a simulation technique in which each ship's movements would be forecast in advance; if a conflict threatened between two ships, signals would automatically be set to stop one or the other vessel, according to a minimum delay criterion, in the previous siding.

With the advent of nuclear-powered vessels the avoidance of collision at sea has become even more paramount in control development. For the present, while the automation of crew operations by the provision of monitoring and control systems is growing, it is likely that ships will remain primarily self-controlled at sea. But the improvement of satellite communications, for the tracking and control of air traffic over the oceans, will probably lead in future years to a joint-use system shared with ships at sea.

BIBLIOGRAPHY. W.W. HAY, *Transportation Engineering* (1961), deals comprehensively with basic engineering principles; J.R. MEYER, J.F. KAIN, and M. WOHL, *The Urban Transportation Problem* (1965), covers many of the social and economic aspects controlling urban transport; M. WOHL and B.V. MARTIN, *Traffic Systems Analysis* (1967), describes the transportation process in depth; P.M. DANFORTH, *Transport Control* (1970), is a modern general review of the technology of control relating transport systems to the environment of man. General texts on railroad-traffic control include W.W. HAY, *Railroad Engineering* (1953); J.R. DAY and B.K. COOPER, *Railway Signalling Systems*, 2nd ed. (1963); and H. SAMUEL, *Railway Operating Practice* (1962). Air-traffic control is more subject to international requirements than either roads or railways. The principal publications are issued by the INTERNATIONAL CIVIL AVIATION ORGANIZATION (*Aeronautical Telecommunications* and *Communication Procedures, etc.*): and by the INTERNATIONAL AIR TRANSPORT ASSOCIATION: *e.g., Aviation's Role in Future Transportation* (1968). For a general descriptive text of the process of air-traffic control, see D.E. CHARLWOOD, *Take-Off to Touchdown* (1967); and on the regulatory aspects, J.L. GRUMBRIDGE, *Marketing Management in Air Transport* (1966); and S. WHEATCROFT, *Air Transport Policy* (1964). International aspects of shipping are covered in publications of the UNITED NATIONS CONFERENCE ON TRADE AND DEVELOPMENT (UNCTAD); the INTERNATIONAL CHAMBER OF SHIPPING; and the INTERNATIONAL SHIPPING FEDERATION. The INSTITUTE OF SHIPPING RESEARCH (BERGEN) publishes a wide range of shipping texts. General shipping texts include A.E. BRANCH, *The Elements of Shipping* (1964); and E.F. STEVENS, *Shipping Practice*, 8th ed. (1967). More specialized aspects of control include L. OUDET, *Emploi du radar pour prévenir les abordages* (1959); Eng. trans., *Radar and Collision*, 1960); F.J. WYLIE (ed.), *Use of Radar at Sea*, 4th rev. ed. (1968).

(F.D.H.)

Tragedy

Although the word tragedy is often used loosely to describe any sort of disaster or misfortune, it more precisely refers to a work of art, usually a play or novel, that probes with high seriousness questions concerning the role of man in the universe. The Greeks of Attica, the ancient state whose chief city was Athens, first used the word in the 5th century BC to describe a specific kind of play, which was presented at festivals in Greece. Sponsored by the local governments, these plays were attended by the entire community, a small admission fee being provided by the state for those who could not afford it themselves. The atmosphere surrounding the performances was more like that of a religious ceremony than entertainment. There were altars to the gods, with priests in attendance, and the subjects of the tragedies were the misfortunes of the heroes of legend, religious myth, and history. Most of the material was derived from the works of Homer and was common knowledge in the Greek communities. So powerful were the achievements of the three greatest

Greek dramatists—Aeschylus (525–456 BC), Sophocles (c. 496–406 BC), and Euripides (c. 480–406 BC)—that the word they first used for their plays survived and came to describe a literary genre that, in spite of many transformations and lapses, has proved its viability through 25 centuries.

Historically, tragedy of a high order has been created in only four periods and locales: Attica, in Greece, in the 5th century BC; England in the reigns of Elizabeth I and James I, from 1558 to 1625; 17th-century France; and Europe and America during the second half of the 19th century and the first half of the 20th. Each period saw the development of a special orientation and emphasis, a characteristic style of theatre. In the modern period, roughly from the middle of the 19th century, the idea of tragedy found embodiment in the collateral form of the novel.

Four great periods of tragedy

This article focusses primarily on the development of tragedy as a literary genre. Further information on the relationship of tragedy to other types of drama will be found in the article DRAMATIC LITERATURE; its place in the development of literature in general is discussed in LITERATURE, WESTERN; and its role in the growth of theatre is discussed in THEATRE, WESTERN. Related material will also be found in the articles NOVEL and COMEDY.

THE DEVELOPMENT OF TRAGEDY

Origins in Greece. The questions of how and why tragedy came into being and of the bearing of its origins on its development in subsequent ages and cultures have been investigated by historians, philologists, archaeologists, and anthropologists with results that are suggestive but conjectural. Even the etymology of the word tragedy is far from established. The most generally accepted source is the Greek *tragōidia*, or "goat-song," from *tragos* ("goat") and *aeidein* ("to sing"). The word could have referred either to the prize, a goat, that was awarded to the dramatists whose plays won the earliest competitions or to the dress, goat skins of the performers, or to the goat that was sacrificed in the primitive rituals from which tragedy developed.

In these communal celebrations, a choric dance may have been the first formal element and perhaps for centuries was the principal element. A speaker was later introduced into the ritual, in all likelihood as an extension of the role of the priest, and dialogue was established between him and the dancers, who became the chorus in the Athenian drama. Aeschylus is usually regarded as the one who, realizing the dramatic possibilities of the dialogue, first added a second speaker and thus invented the form of tragedy. That so sophisticated a form could have been fully developed by a single artist, however, is scarcely credible. Hundreds of early tragedies have been lost, including some by Aeschylus himself. Of some 90 plays attributed to him, only seven have survived.

Four Dionysia, or feasts of the Greek God Dionysus, were held annually in Athens. Since Dionysus once held place as the god of vegetation and the vine, and the goat was believed sacred to him, it has been conjectured that tragedy originated in fertility feasts to commemorate the harvest and the vintage and the associated ideas of the death and renewal of life. The purpose of such rituals is to exercise some influence over these vital forces. Whatever the original religious connections of tragedy may have been, two elements have never entirely been lost: (1) its high seriousness, befitting matters in which survival is at issue and (2) its involvement of the entire community in matters of ultimate and common concern. When either of these elements diminishes, when the form is overmixed with satiric, comic, or sentimental elements, or when the theatre of concern succumbs to the theatre of entertainment, then tragedy falls from its high estate and is on its way to becoming something else.

Two vital elements

As the Greeks developed it, the tragic form, more than any other, raised questions about man's existence. Why must man suffer? Why must man be forever torn between the seeming irreconcilables of good and evil, freedom and necessity, truth and deceit? Are the causes of his suffering outside himself, in blind chance, in the evil designs of others, in the malice of the gods? Are its causes within him, and does he bring suffering upon himself through arrogance, infatuation, or the tendency to overreach himself? Why is justice so elusive?

Aeschylus: the first great tragedian. It is this last question that Aeschylus asks most insistently in his two most famous works, the *Oresteia* (a trilogy comprising *Agamemnon, Choephoroi,* and *Eumenides*) and *Prometheus Bound* (the first part of a trilogy of which the last two parts have been lost): is it right that Orestes, a young man in no way responsible for his situation, should be commanded by a god, in the name of justice, to avenge his father by murdering his mother? Is there no other way out of his dilemma than through the ancient code of blood revenge, which will only compound the dilemma? Again: was it right that in befriending mankind with the gifts of fire and the arts, Prometheus should offend the presiding god Zeus and himself be horribly punished? Aeschylus opened questions whose answers in the Homeric stories had been taken for granted. In Homer, Orestes' patricide is regarded as an act of filial piety, and Prometheus' punishment is merely the inevitable consequence of defying the reigning deity. All of the materials of tragedy, all of its cruelty, loss, and suffering, are present in Homer and the ancient myths but are dealt with as absolutes—self-sufficient and without the questioning spirit that was necessary to raise them to the level of tragedy. It remained for Aeschylus and his fellow tragedians first to treat these "absolutes" critically and creatively in sustained dramatic form. They were true explorers of the human spirit.

In addition to their remarkable probing into the nature of existence, their achievements included a degree of psychological insight for which they are not generally given credit. Though such praise is usually reserved for Shakespeare and the moderns, the Athenian dramatists conveyed a vivid sense of the living reality of their characters' experience: of what it felt like to be caught, like Orestes, in desperately conflicting loyalties or to be subjected, like Prometheus, to prolonged and unjust punishment. The mood of the audience as it witnessed the acting out of these climactic experiences has been described as one of impassioned contemplation. From their myths and epics and from their history in the 6th century, the people of Athens learned that they could extend an empire and lay the foundations of a great culture. From their tragedies of the 5th century, they learned who they were, something of the possibilities and limitations of the spirit, and of what it meant, not merely what it felt like, to be alive in a world both beautiful and terrible.

Aeschylus has been called the most theological of the Greek tragedians. His *Prometheus* has been compared to the Book of Job of the Bible both in its structure (*i.e.,* the immobilized heroic figure maintaining his cause in dialogues with visitors) and in its preoccupation with the problem of suffering at the hands of a seemingly unjust deity. Aeschylus tended to resolve the dramatic problem into some degree of harmony, as scattered evidence suggests he did in the last two parts of the *Promethiad* and as he certainly did in the conclusion of the *Oresteia.* This tendency would conceivably lead him out of the realm of tragedy and into religious assurance. But his harmonies are never complete. In his plays evil is inescapable, loss is irretrievable, suffering is inevitable. What the plays say positively is that man can learn through suffering. The chorus in *Agamemnon,* the first play of the *Oresteia,* says this twice. The capacity to learn through suffering is a distinguishing characteristic of the tragic hero, pre-eminently of the Greek tragic hero. He has not merely courage, tenacity, and endurance but also the ability to grow, by means of these qualities, into an understanding of himself, of his fellows, and of the conditions of existence. Suffering, says Aeschylus, need not be embittering but can be a source of knowledge. The moral force of his plays and those of his fellow tragedians can hardly be exaggerated. They were shaping agents in the Greek notion of education. It has been said that from Homer the Greeks learned how to be good Greeks; from the tragedies they learned an enlarged humanity. If it cannot be

Aeschylus' view of the problem of suffering

proved that Aeschylus "invented" tragedy, it is clear that he at least set its tone and established a model that is still operative. Even in the 20th century, the *Oresteia* has been acclaimed as the greatest spiritual work of man, and dramatists such as T.S. Eliot, in *The Family Reunion* (1939), and Jean-Paul Sartre, in *The Flies* (1943), found modern relevance in its archetypal characters, situations, and themes.

Sophocles: the purest artist. Sophocles' life spanned almost the whole of the 5th century. He is said to have written his last play, *Oedipus at Colonus,* at the age of 90. Only seven of his plays, of some 125 attributed to him, survive. He won the prize in the tragic competitions 20 times and never placed lower than second.

Sophocles has been called the great mediating figure between Aeschylus and Euripides. Of the three, it might be said that Aeschylus tended to resolve tragic tensions into higher truth, to look beyond, or above, tragedy; that Euripides' irony and bitterness led him the other way to fix on the disintegration of the individual; and that Sophocles, who is often called the "purest" artist of the three, was truest to the actual state of human experience. Unlike the others, Sophocles seems never to insinuate himself into his characters or situations, never to manipulate them into preconceived patterns. He sets them free on a course seemingly of their own choosing. He neither preaches nor rails. If life is hard and often destructive, the question Sophocles asks is not how did this come to be or why did such a misfortune have to happen but rather, given the circumstances, how must a man conduct himself, how should he act, what must he do?

His greatest play, *Oedipus the King,* may serve as a model of his total dramatic achievement. Embodied in it, and suggested with extraordinary dramatic tact, are all the basic questions of tragedy, which are presented in such a way as almost to define the form itself. It is not surprising that Aristotle, a century later, analyzed it for his definition of tragedy in the *Poetics.* It is the nuclear Greek tragedy, setting the norm in a way that cannot be claimed for any other work, not even the *Oresteia.*

In *Oedipus,* as in Sophocles' other plays, the chorus is much less prominent than in Aeschylus' works. The action is swifter and more highly articulated; the dialogue is sharper, more staccato, and bears more of the meaning of the play. Though much has been made of the influence of fate on the action of the play, later critics emphasize the freedom with which Oedipus acts throughout. Even before the action of the play begins, the oracle's prediction that Oedipus was doomed to kill his father and marry his mother had long since come true, though he did not realize it. Though he was fated, he was also free throughout the course of the play—free to make decision after decision, to carry out his freely purposed action to its completion. In him, Sophocles achieved one of the enduring definitions of the tragic hero—that of a man for whom the liberation of the self is a necessity. The action of the play, the purpose of which is to discover the murderer of Oedipus' father and thereby to free the city from its curse, leads inevitably to Oedipus' suffering—the loss of his wife, his kingdom, his sight. The messenger who reports Oedipus' self-blinding might well have summarized the play with "All ills that there are names for, all are here." And the chorus' final summation deepens the note of despair: "Count no man happy," they say in essence, "until he is dead."

But these were not Sophocles' ultimate verdicts. The action is so presented that the final impression is not of human helplessness at the hands of malign gods nor of man as the pawn of fate. Steering his own course, with great courage, Oedipus has ferreted out the truth of his identity and administered his own punishment, and, in his suffering, learned a new humanity. The final impression of the *Oedipus,* far from being one of unmixed evil and nihilism, is of massive integrity, powerful will, and magnanimous acceptance of a horribly altered existence.

Some 50 years later, Sophocles wrote a sequel to *Oedipus the King.* In *Oedipus at Colonus,* the old Oedipus, further schooled in suffering, is seen during his last day on earth. He is still the same Oedipus in many ways: hot-

Sophocles' emphasis on action

tempered, hating his enemies, contentious. Though he admits his "pollution" in the murder of his father and the marriage to his mother, he denies that he had sinned, since he had done both deeds unwittingly. Throughout the play, the theme of which has been described as the "heroization" of Oedipus, he grows steadily in nobility and awesomeness. Finally, sensing the approach of the end, he leaves the scene, to be elevated in death to a demigod, as the messenger describes the miraculous event. In such manner Sophocles leads his tragedy toward an ultimate assertion of values. His position has been described as "heroic humanism," as making a statement of belief in the human capacity to transcend evils, within and without, by means of the human condition itself.

Tragedy must maintain a balance between the higher optimisms of religion or philosophy, or any other beliefs that tend to explain away the enigmas and afflictions of existence, on the one hand, and the pessimism that would reject the whole human experiment as valueless and futile on the other. Thus the opposite of tragedy is not comedy but the literature of cynicism and despair, and the opposite of the tragic artist's stance, which is one of compassion and involvement, is that of the detached and cynical ironist.

Euripides: the dark tragedian. The tragedies of Euripides test the Sophoclean norm in this direction. His plays present in gruelling detail the wreck of human lives under the stresses that the gods often seem willfully to place upon them. Or, if the gods are not willfully involved through jealousy or spite, they sit idly by while man wrecks himself through passion or heedlessness. No Euripidean hero approaches Oedipus in stature. The margin of freedom is narrower, and the question of justice, so central and absolute an ideal for Aeschylus, becomes a subject for irony. In *Hippolytus*, the goddess Artemis never thinks of justice as she takes revenge on the young Hippolytus for neglecting her worship; she acts solely out of personal spite. In *Medea*, Medea's revenge on Jason through the slaughter of their children is so hideously unjust as to mock the very question. In the *Bacchae*, when the frenzied Agave tears her son, Pentheus, to pieces and marches into town with his head on a pike, the god Dionysus, who had engineered the situation, says merely that Pentheus should not have scorned him. The Euripidean gods, in short, cannot be appealed to in the name of justice. Euripides' tendency toward moral neutrality, his cool tacking between sides (*e.g.*, between Pentheus versus Dionysus and the bacchantes) leave the audience virtually unable to make a moral decision. In Aeschylus' *Eumenides* (the last play of the *Oresteia*) the morals of the gods improve. Athena is there, on the stage, helping to solve the problem of justice. In Sophocles, the gods are distant, but their moral governance is not questioned. *Oedipus* ends as if with a mighty "So be it." In Euripides the gods are destructive, wreaking their capricious wills on defenseless man. Aristotle called Euripides the most tragic of the three dramatists; surely his depiction of the arena of human life is the grimmest.

Many qualities, however, keep his tragedies from becoming literature of protest, of cynicism, or of despair. He reveals profound psychological insight, as in the delineation of such antipodal characters as Jason and Medea, or of the forces, often subconscious, at work in the group frenzy of the *Bacchae*. His Bacchic odes reveal remarkable lyric power. And he has a deep sense of human values, however external and self-conscious. Medea, even in the fury of her hatred for Jason and her lust for revenge, must steel herself to the murder of her children, realizing the evil of what she is about to do. In this realization, Euripides suggests a saving hope: here is a great nature gone wrong—but still a great nature.

Later Greek drama. After Euripides, Greek drama reveals little that is significant to the history of tragedy. Performances were given during the remainder of the pre-Christian era in theatres throughout the Mediterranean world, but with the decline of Athens as a city-state, the tradition of tragedy eroded. As external affairs deteriorated, the high idealism, the exalted sense of human capacities depicted in tragedy at its height yielded more

Euripides' view of justice

and more to the complaints of the skeptics. The Euripidean assault on the gods ended in the debasement of the original lofty conceptions. A 20th-century British classical scholar, Gilbert Murray, used the phrase "the failure of nerve" to describe the late Greek world. It may, indeed, provide a clue to what happened. On the other hand, according to the 19th-century German philosopher Friedrich Nietzsche, in *The Birth of Tragedy* (1872), a quite different influence may have spelled the end of Greek tragedy: the so-called Socratic optimism, the notion underlying the dialogues of Plato that man could "know himself" through the exercise of his reason in patient, careful dialectic—a notion that diverted questions of man's existence away from drama and into philosophy. In any case, the balance for tragedy was upset, and the theatre of Aeschylus, Sophocles, and Euripides gave way to what seems to have been a theatre of diatribe, spectacle, and entertainment.

The long hiatus. The Roman world did not succeed in reviving tragedy. Seneca (4 BC–AD 65) wrote nine tragedies, mostly adaptations of Greek materials, such as the stories of Oedipus, Hippolytus, Medea, and Agamemnon, but with little of the Greek tragic feeling for character and theme. The emphasis is on sensation and rhetoric, tending toward melodrama and bombast. The plays are of interest in this context mainly as the not entirely healthy inspiration for the precursors of Elizabethan tragedy in England.

The long hiatus in the history of tragedy between the Greeks and the Elizabethans has been variously explained. In the Golden Age of Roman literature, roughly from the birth of Virgil in 70 BC to the death of Ovid in AD 17, the Roman poets followed the example of Greek literature; although they produced great lyric and epic verse, their tragic drama lacked the probing freshness and directness fundamental to tragedy.

With the collapse of the Roman world and the invasions of the barbarians came the beginnings of the long, slow development of the Christian Church. Churchmen and philosophers gradually forged a system, based on the Christian revelation, of the nature and destiny of man. The mass, with its daily re-enactment of the sacrifice of Jesus Christ, its music, and its dramatic structure, may have provided something comparable to tragic drama in the lives of the people.

With the coming of the Renaissance, the visual arts more and more came to represent the afflictive aspects of life, and the word tragedy again came into currency. Chaucer (1340–1400) used the word in *Troilus and Criseyde*, and in *The Canterbury Tales* it is applied to a series of stories in the medieval style of *de casibus virorum illustrium*, meaning "the downfalls" (more or less inevitable) "of princes." Chaucer used the word to signify little more than the turn of the wheel of fortune, against whose force no meaningful effort of man is possible. It remained for the Elizabethans to develop a theatre and a dramatic literature that reinstated the term on a level comparable to that of the Greeks.

Elizabethan tragedy. The long beginning of the Elizabethan popular theatre, like that of the Greek theatre, lay in religious ceremonials, probably in the drama in the liturgy of the two greatest events in the Christian year, Christmas and Easter. In the Early Church, exchanges between two groups of choristers, or between the choir and a solo voice, led to the idea of dialogue, just as it had in the development of Greek tragedy. The parts became increasingly elaborate, and costumes were introduced to individualize the characters. Dramatic gestures and actions were a natural development. More and more of the biblical stories were dramatized, much as the material of Homer was used by the Greek tragedians, although piously in this instance, with none of the tragic skepticism of the Greeks. In the course of generations, the popularity of the performances grew to such an extent that, to accommodate the crowds, they were moved, from inside the church to the porch, or square, in front of the church. The next step was the secularization of the management of the productions, as the towns and cities took them over. Day-long festivals were instituted, involving, as in

Tragedy and the Christian mass

Cycles of
miracle
and
mystery
plays

the Greek theatre, the whole community. Cycles of plays were performed at York, Chester, and other English religious centres, depicting in sequences of short dramatic episodes the whole human story, from the Fall of Lucifer and the Creation to the Day of Doom. Each play was assigned to an appropriate trade guild (the story of Noah and the Ark, for example, went to the shipwrights), which took over complete responsibility for the production. Hundreds of actors and long preparation went into the festivals. These "miracle" and "mystery" plays, however crude they may now seem, dealt with the loftiest of subjects in simple but often powerful eloquence. Although the audience must have been a motley throng, it may well have been as involved and concerned as those of the Greek theatre.

Once the drama became a part of the secular life of the communities, popular tastes affected its religious orientation. Comic scenes, like those involving Noah's nagging wife, a purely secular creation who does not appear in the Bible, became broader. The "tragic" scenes—anything involving the Devil or Doomsday—became more and more melodramatic. With the Renaissance came the rediscovery of the Greek and Roman cultures and the consequent development of a world view that led away from moral and spiritual absolutes and toward an increasingly skeptical individualism. The high poetic spirits of the mid-16th century began to turn the old medieval forms of the miracles and mysteries to new uses and to look to the ancient plays, particularly the lurid tragedies of Seneca, for their models. A bloody play, *Gorboduc*, by Thomas Sackville and Thomas Norton, first acted in 1561, is now known as the first formal tragedy in English, though it is far from fulfilling the high offices of the form in tone, characterization, and theme. Thomas Kyd's *Spanish Tragedie* (c. 1589) continued the Senecan tradition of the "tragedy of blood" with somewhat more sophistication than *Gorboduc* but even more bloodletting. Elizabethan tragedy never freed itself completely from certain melodramatic aspects of the influence of Seneca.

Marlowe and the first Christian tragedy. The first tragedian worthy of the tradition of the Greeks was Christopher Marlowe (1564–93). Of Marlowe's tragedies, *Tamburlaine* (1587), *Doctor Faustus* (c. 1588), *The Jew of Malta* (1589), and *Edward II* (c. 1593), the first two are the most famous and most significant. In *Tamburlaine*, the material was highly melodramatic—Tamburlaine's popular image was that of the most ruthless and bloody of conquerors. In a verse prologue, when Marlowe invites the audience to "View but his [Tamburlaine's] picture in this tragic glass," he had in mind little more, perhaps, than the trappings and tone of tragedy: "the stately tent of war," which is to be his scene, and "the high astounding terms," which will be his rhetoric. But he brought such imaginative vigour and sensitivity to bear that melodrama is transcended, in terms reminiscent of high tragedy. Tamburlaine, a Scythian shepherd of the 14th century, becomes the spokesman, curiously enough, for the new world of the Renaissance—iconoclastic, independent, stridently ambitious. Just as the Greek tragedians challenged tradition, Tamburlaine shouts defiance at all the norms, religious and moral, that Marlowe's generation inherited. But Tamburlaine, although he is an iconoclast, is also a poet. No one before him on the English stage had talked with such magnificent lyric power as he does, whether it be on the glories of conquest or on the beauties of Zenocrate, his beloved. When, still unconquered by any enemy, he sickens and dies, he leaves the feeling that something great, however ruthless, has gone. Here once again is the ambiguity that was so much a part of the Greek tragic imagination—the combination of awe, pity, and fear that Aristotle defined.

Conflict
between
tradition
and
individual-
ism

In *Doctor Faustus* the sense of conflict between the tradition and the new Renaissance individualism is much greater. The claims of revealed Christianity are presented in the orthodox spirit of the morality and mystery plays, but Faustus' yearnings for power over space and time are also presented with a sympathy that cannot be denied. Here is modern man, tragic modern man, torn between the faith of tradition and faith in himself. Faustus takes

the risk in the end and is bundled off to hell in true mystery-play fashion. But the final scene does not convey that justice has been done, even though Faustus admits that his fate is just. Rather, the scene suggests that the transcendent human individual has been caught in the consequences of a dilemma that he might have avoided but that no imaginative man *could* have avoided. The sense of the interplay of fate and freedom is not unlike that of *Oedipus*. The sense of tragic ambiguity is more poignant in Faustus than in *Oedipus* or *Tamburlaine* because Faustus is far more introspective than either of the other heroes. The conflict is inner; the battle is for Faustus' soul, a kind of conflict that neither the Greeks nor Tamburlaine had to contend with. For this reason, and not because it advocates Christian doctrine, the play has been called the first Christian tragedy.

Shakespearean tragedy. Shakespeare was a long time coming to his tragic phase, the six or seven years that produced his five greatest tragedies, *Hamlet* (c. 1601), *Othello* (c. 1602), *King Lear* (c. 1605), *Macbeth* (c. 1605), and *Antony and Cleopatra* (c. 1606). These were not the only plays written during those years. *Troilus and Cressida* may have come about the same time as *Hamlet*; *All's Well That Ends Well*, shortly after *Othello*; and *Measure for Measure*, shortly before *King Lear*. But the concentration of tragedies is sufficient to distinguish this period from that of the comedies and history plays before and of the so-called romances afterward. Although the tragic period cannot entirely be accounted for in terms of biography, social history, or current stage fashions, all of which have been adduced as causes, certain questions should be answered, at least tentatively: What is Shakespeare's major tragic theme and method? How do they relate to classical, medieval, and Renaissance traditions? In attempting to answer these questions, this proviso must be kept in mind: the degree to which he was consciously working in these traditions, consciously shaping his plays on early models, adapting Greek and Roman themes to his own purpose, or following the precepts of Aristotle must always remain conjectural. On the one hand, there is the comment by Ben Jonson that Shakespeare had "small Latin and less Greek," and Milton in "L'Allegro" speaks of him as "fancy's child" warbling "his native wood-notes wild," as if he were unique, a sport of nature. On the other hand, Shakespeare knew Jonson, who knew a great deal of Latin and Greek, and is said to have acted in Jonson's *Sejanus* in 1603, a very classical play, published in 1605 with a learned essay on Aristotle as preface. It can be assumed that Shakespeare knew the tradition. Certainly the Elizabethan theatre could not have existed without the Greek and Roman prototype. For all of its mixed nature—with comic and melodramatic elements jostling the tragic—the Elizabethan theatre retained some of the high concern, the sense of involvement, and even the ceremonial atmosphere of the Greek theatre. When tragedies were performed, the stage was draped in black. Modern studies have shown that the Elizabethan theatre retained many ties with both the Middle Ages and the tradition of the Greeks.

Shakespeare's earliest and most lighthearted plays reveal a sense of the individual, his innerness, his reality, his difference from every other individual, and, at times, his *plight*. Certain stock characters, to be sure, appear in the early comedies. Even Falstaff, that triumphant individual, has a prototype in the braggadocio of Roman comedy, and even Falstaff has his tragic side. As Shakespeare's art developed, his concern for the plight or predicament or dilemma seems to have grown. His earliest history plays, for instance (*Henry VI*, Parts I, II, III), are little more than chronicles of the great pageant figures—kingship in all its colour and potency. *Richard III*, which follows them, focusses with an intensity traditionally reserved for the tragic hero on one man and on the sinister forces, within and without, that bring him to destruction. From kingship, that is, Shakespeare turned to the king, the symbolic individual, the focal man, to whom whole societies look for their values and meanings. Thus Richard III is almost wholly sinister, though there exists a fascination about him, an all but tragic ambiguity.

Tragic
elements
in
Shake-
speare's
comedies
and
histories

Although Shakespeare's developing sense of the tragic cannot be summed up adequately in any formula, one might hazard the following: he progressed from the *individual* of the early comedies; to the *burdened* individual, such as, in *Henry IV*, Prince Hal, the future Henry V, who manipulates, rather than suffers, the tragic ambiguities of the world; and, finally, in the great tragedies, to (in one critic's phrase) the *overburdened* individual, Lear being generally regarded as the greatest example. In these last plays, man is at the limits of his sovereignty as a human being, where everything that he has lived by, stood for, or loved is put to the test. Like Prometheus on the crag, or Oedipus as he learns who he is, or Medea deserted by Jason, the Shakespearean tragic heroes are at the extremities of their natures. Hamlet and Macbeth are thrust to the very edge of sanity; Lear and, momentarily, Othello are thrust beyond it. In every case, as in the Greek plays, the destructive forces seem to combine inner inadequacies or evils, such as Lear's temper or Macbeth's ambition, with external pressures, such as Lear's "tiger daughters," the witches in *Macbeth*, or Lady Macbeth's importunity. Once the destructive course is set going, these forces operate with the relentlessness the Greeks called Moira, or Fate.

At the height of his powers, Shakespeare's tragic vision comprehended the totality of possibilities for good and evil as nearly as the human imagination ever has. His heroes are the vehicles of psychological, societal, and cosmic forces that tend to ennoble and glorify humanity or infect it and destroy it. The logic of tragedy that possessed him demanded an insistence upon the latter. Initially, his heroes make free choices and are free time after time to turn back, but they move toward their doom as relentlessly as did Oedipus. The total tragic statement, however, is not limited to the fate of the hero. He is but the centre of an action that takes place in a context involving many other characters, each contributing a point of view, a set of values or antivalues to the complex dialectic of the play. In Macbeth's demon-ridden Scotland, where weird things happen to men and horses turn cannibal, there is the virtuous Malcolm, and society survives. Hamlet had the trustworthy friend Horatio, and, for all the bloodletting, what was "rotten" was purged. In the tragedies, most notably *Lear*, the Aeschylean notion of "knowledge through suffering" is powerfully dramatized; it is most obvious in the hero, but it is also shared by the society of which he is the focal figure. The flaw in the hero may be a *moral* failing or, sometimes, an excess of virtue; the flaw in society may be the rottenness of the Danish court in *Hamlet* or the corruption of the Roman world in *Antony and Cleopatra*; the flaw or fault or dislocation may be in the very universe itself, as dramatized by Lear's raving at the heavens or the ghosts that walk the plays or the witches that prophesy. All these faults, Shakespeare seems to be saying, are inevitabilities of the human condition. But they do not spell rejection, nihilism, or despair. The hero may die, but in the words of the novelist E.M. Forster to describe the redeeming power of tragedy, "he has given us life."

Such is the precarious balance a tragedian must maintain: the cold, clear vision that sees the evil but is not maddened by it, a sense of the good that is equally clear but refuses the blandishments of optimism or sentimentalism. Few have ever sustained the balance for long. Aeschylus tended to slide off to the right, Euripides to the left, and even Sophocles had his hero transfigured at Colonus. Marlowe's early death should perhaps spare him the criticism his first plays warrant. Shakespeare's last two tragedies, *Macbeth* and *Antony and Cleopatra*, are close to the edge of a valueless void. The atmosphere of *Macbeth* is murky with evil; the action moves with almost melodramatic speed from horror to horror. The forces for good rally at last, but Macbeth himself steadily deteriorates into the most nihilistic of all Shakespeare's tragic heroes, saved in nothing except the sense of a great nature, like Medea, gone wrong. *Antony*, in its ambiguities and irony, has been considered close to the Euripidean line of bitterness and detachment. Shakespeare himself soon modulated into another mood in his last plays,

Cymbeline (c. 1609), *The Winter's Tale* (c. 1610), and *The Tempest* (c. 1611). Each is based on a situation that could have been developed into major tragedy had Shakespeare followed out its logic as he had done with earlier plays. For whatever reason, however, he chose not to. The great tragic questions are not pressed. *The Tempest*, especially, for all Prospero's charm and magnanimity, gives a sense of brooding melancholy over the ineradicable evil in mankind, a patient but sad acquiescence. All of these plays end in varying degrees of harmony and reconciliation. Shakespeare willed it so.

Decline in 17th-century England. From Shakespeare's tragedies to the closing of the theatres in England by the Puritans in 1642, the quality of tragedy is steadily worse, if the best of the Greek and Shakespearean tragedies are taken as a standard. Among the leading dramatists of the period—John Webster, Thomas Middleton, Francis Beaumont, John Fletcher, Cyril Tourneur, and John Ford— there were some excellent craftsmen and brilliant poets. Though each of them has a rightful place in the history of English drama, tragedy suffered a transmutation in their hands.

The Jacobean dramatists—those who flourished in England during the reign of James I—failed to transcend the negative tendencies they inherited from Elizabethan tragedy: a sense of defeat, a mood of spiritual despair implicit in Marlowe's tragic thought; in the nihilistic broodings of some of Shakespeare's characters in their worst moods—Hamlet, Gloucester in *Lear*, Macbeth; in the metaphoric implication of the theme of insanity, of man pressed beyond the limit of endurance, that runs through many of these tragedies; most importantly, perhaps, in the moral confusion ("fair is foul and foul is fair") that threatens to unbalance even the staunchest of Shakespeare's tragic heroes. This sinister tendency came to a climax about 1605 and was in part a consequence of the anxiety surrounding the death of Queen Elizabeth I and the accession of James I. Despite their negative tendencies, the Elizabethans, in general, had affirmed life and celebrated it; Shakespeare's moral balance, throughout even his darkest plays, remained firm. The Jacobeans, on the other hand, were possessed by death. They became superb analysts of moral confusion and of the darkened vision of humanity at cross purposes, preying upon itself; of lust, hate, and intrigue engulfing what is left of beauty, love, and integrity. There is little that is redemptive or that suggests, as had Aeschylus, that evil might be resolved by the enlightenment gained from suffering. As in the tragedies of Euripides, the protagonist's margin of freedom grows ever smaller. "You are the deed's creature," cries a murderer to his unwitting lady accomplice in Middleton's *Changeling* (1622), and a prisoner of her deed she remains. Many of the plays maintained a pose of ironic, detached reportage, without the sense of sympathetic involvement that the greatest tragedians have conveyed from the beginning.

Some of the qualities of the highest tragedians have been claimed for John Webster. One critic points to his search for a moral order as a link to Shakespeare and sees in his moral vision a basis for renewal. Webster's *Duchess of Malfi* (c. 1613) has been interpreted as a final triumph of life over death. Overwhelmed by final unleashed terror, the Duchess affirms the essential dignity of man. Despite such vestiges of greatness, however, the trend of tragedy was downward. High moral sensitivity and steady conviction are required to resist the temptation to resolve the intolerable tensions of tragedy into either the comfort of optimism or the relaxed apathy of despair. Periods of the creation of high tragedy are therefore few and short-lived. The demands on artist and audience alike are very great. Forms wear out, and public taste seems destined to go through inevitable cycles of health and disease. What is to one generation powerful and persuasive rhetoric becomes bombast and bathos to the next. The inevitable materials of tragedy—violence, madness, hate, and lust—soon lose their symbolic role and become perverted to the uses of melodrama and sensationalism, mixed, for relief, with the broadest comedy or farce.

These corruptions had gone too far when John Milton,

Total vision of Shakespeare's tragedies

The Jacobean transmutation

29 years after the closing of the theatres, attempted to bring back the true spirit and tone of tragedy, which he called "the gravest, moralest, and most profitable of all other Poems." His *Samson Agonistes* (1671), however, is magnificent "closet tragedy"—drama more suitable for reading than for popular performance. Modelled on the *Prometheus*, it recalls Aeschylus' tragedy both in its form, in which the immobilized hero receives a sequence of visitors, and in its theme, in which there is a resurgence of the hero's spirit under stress. With Restoration comedy in full swing, however, and with the "heroic play" (an overly moralized version of tragedy) about to reach its crowning achievement in John Dryden's *All for Love* only seven years later (published 1678), *Samson Agonistes* was an anachronism.

Neoclassical tragedy. *Corneille and Racine.* Another attempt to bring back the ancient form had been going on for some time across the English Channel, in France. The French Classical tragedy, whose monuments are Pierre Corneille's *Cid* (1637) and Jean Racine's *Bérénice* (1670) and *Phèdre* (1677), made no attempt to be popular in the way of the Elizabethan theatre. The plays were written by and for intellectual aristocrats, who came together in an elite theatre, patronized by royalty and nobility. Gone were the bustle and pageantry of the Elizabethan tragedies, with their admixtures of whatever modes and moods the dramatists thought would work. The French playwrights submitted themselves to the severe discipline they derived from the Greek models and especially the "rules," as they interpreted them, laid down by Aristotle. The unities of place, time, and action were strictly observed. One theme, the conflict between Passion and Reason, was uppermost. The path of Reason was the path of Duty and Obligation (noblesse oblige), and that path had been clearly plotted by moralists and philosophers, both ancient and modern. In this sense there was nothing exploratory in the French tragedy; existing moral and spiritual norms were insisted upon. The norms are never criticized or tested as Aeschylus challenged the Olympians or as Marlowe presented, with startling sympathy, the Renaissance overreacher. Corneille's *Cid* shows Duty triumphant over Passion, and, as a reward, hero and heroine are happily united. By the time of *Phèdre*, Corneille's proud affirmation of the power of the will and the reason over passion had given way to what Racine called "stately sorrow," with which he asks the audience to contemplate Phèdre's heroic, but losing, moral struggle. Her passion for her stepson, Hippolyte, bears her down relentlessly. Her fine principles and heroic will are of no avail. Both she and Hippolyte are destroyed. The action is limited to one terrible day; there is no change of scene; there is neither comic digression nor relief—the focus on the process by which a great nature goes down is sharp and intense. Such is the power of Racine's poetry (it is untranslatable), his conception of character, and his penetrating analysis of it, that it suggests the presence of Sophoclean "heroic humanism." In this sense it could be said that Racine tested the norms, that he uncovered a cruel injustice in the nature of a code that could destroy such a person as Phèdre. Once again, here is a world of tragic ambiguity, in which no precept or prescription can answer complicated human questions.

The English "heroic play." This ambiguity was all but eliminated in the "heroic play" that vied with the comedy of the Restoration stage in England in the latter part of the 17th century. After the vicissitudes of the Civil War, the age was hungry for heroism. An English philosopher of the time, Thomas Hobbes, defined the purpose of the type: "The work of an heroic poem is to raise admiration, principally for three virtues, valor, beauty, and love." Moral concern, beginning with Aeschylus, has always been central in tragedy, but in the works of the great tragedians this concern was exploratory and inductive. The moral concern of the heroic play is the reverse. It is deductive and dogmatic. The first rule, writes Dryden (following the contemporary French critic, René Le Bossu) in his preface to his *Troilus and Cressida* (1679), is "to make the moral of the work; that is, to lay down to yourself what that precept of morality shall be, which

you would insinuate into the people. . . ." In *All for Love* the moral is all too clear: Antony must choose between the path of honour and his illicit passion for Cleopatra. He chooses Cleopatra, and they are both destroyed. Only Dryden's poetry, with its air of emotional argumentation, manages to convey human complexities in spite of his moral bias and saves the play from artificiality—makes it, in fact, the finest near-tragic production of its age.

The eclipse of tragedy. Although the annals of the drama from Dryden onward are filled with plays called tragedies by their authors, the form as it has been defined here went into an eclipse during the late 17th, the 18th, and the early 19th centuries. Reasons that have been suggested for the decline include the politics of the Restoration in England; the rise of science and, with it, the optimism of the Enlightenment throughout Europe; the developing middle class economy; the trend toward reassuring deism in theology; and, in literature, the rise of the novel and the vogue of satire. The genius of the age was discursive and rationalistic. In France and later in England, belief in Evil was reduced to the perception of evils, which were looked upon as institutional and therefore remediable. The nature of man was no longer the problem; rather, it was the better organization and management of men. The old haunting fear and mystery, the sense of ambiguity at the centre of man's nature and of dark forces working against him in the universe, were replaced by a new and confident dogma. Tragedy never lost its high prestige in the minds of the leading spirits. Theorizing upon it were men of letters as diverse as Dr. Samuel Johnson, David Hume, Samuel Taylor Coleridge, and Percy Bysshe Shelley and German philosophers from Gotthold Lessing in the 18th century to Friedrich Nietzsche in the 19th. Revivals of Shakespeare's tragedies were often bowdlerized or altered, as in the happy ending for *Lear* in a production of 1681. Those who felt themselves called upon to write tragedies produced little but weak imitations. Shelley tried it once, in *The Cenci* (1819), but, as his wife wrote, "the bent of his mind went the other way"—which way may be seen in his *Prometheus Unbound* (1820), in which Zeus is overthrown and man enters upon a golden age, ruled by the power of love. Goethe had the sense to stay away from tragedy: "The mere attempt to write tragedy," he said, "might be my undoing." He concluded his two-part *Faust* (1808, 1832) in the spirit of the 19th-century optimistic humanitarianism. It was not until the latter part of the 19th century, with the plays of a Norwegian, Henrik Ibsen, a Russian, Anton Chekhov, a Swede, August Strindberg, and, later, an American, Eugene O'Neill, that something of the original vision returned to inspire the tragic theatre.

A new vehicle: the novel. The theme and spirit of tragedy, meanwhile, found a new vehicle in the novel. This development is important, however far afield it may seem from the work of the formal dramatists. The English novelist Emily Brontë's *Wuthering Heights* (1847), in its grim Yorkshire setting, reflects the original concerns of tragedy: *i.e.*, the terrifying divisions in nature and human nature, love that creates and destroys, character at once fierce and pitiable, destructive actions that are willed yet seemingly destined, as if by a malicious fate, yet the whole controlled by an imagination that learns as it goes. Another English novelist, Thomas Hardy, in the preface to his *Woodlanders* (1887), speaks of the rural setting of this and other of his novels as being comparable to the stark and simple setting of the Greek theatre, giving his novels something of that drama's intensity and sharpness of focus. His grimly pessimistic view of man's nature and destiny and of the futility of human striving, as reflected in his novels *The Return of the Native* (1878), *Tess of the D'Urbervilles* (1891), and *Jude the Obscure* (1895), is barely redeemed for tragedy by his sense of the beauty of nature and of the beauty and dignity of human character and effort, however unavailing.

The work of the Polish-born English novelist Joseph Conrad (1857–1924) provides another kind of setting for novels used as vehicles of the tragic sense. *Lord Jim* (1900), originally conceived as a short story, grew to a full-length novel as Conrad found himself exploring in

The return to Greek models

Inductive and deductive morality

Thomas Hardy's pessimism

ever greater depth the perplexing, ambiguous problem of lost honour and guilt, expiation and heroism. Darkness and doubt brood over the tale, as they do over his long story *The Heart of Darkness* (1899), in which Conrad's narrator, Marlow, again leads his listeners into the shadowy recesses of the human heart, with its forever unresolved and unpredictable capacities for good and evil.

Dostoyevsky's tragic view. In Russia, the novels of Fyodor Dostoyevsky, particularly *Crime and Punishment* (1866) and *The Brothers Karamazov* (1880), revealed a world of paradox, alienation, and loss of identity, prophetic of the major tragic themes of the 20th century. More than any earlier novelist, Dostoyevsky appropriated to his fictions the realm of the subconscious and explored in depth its shocking antinomies and discontinuities. Sigmund Freud, the founder of psychoanalysis, frequently acknowledged his indebtedness to Dostoyevsky's psychological insights. Dostoyevsky's protagonists are reminiscent of Marlowe's Doctor Faustus, caught between the old world of orthodox belief and the new world of intense individualism, each with its insistent claims and justifications. The battleground is once more the soul of man, and the stakes are survival. Each of his major heroes —Raskolnikov in *Crime and Punishment* and the three Karamazovs—wins a victory, but it is in each case morally qualified, partial, or transient. The harmonious resolutions of the novels seem forced and are neither decisive of the action nor definitive of Dostoyevsky's total tragic view.

The American tragic novel. In America, Nathaniel Hawthorne's novel *The Scarlet Letter* (1850) and Herman Melville's *Moby Dick* (1851) are surprisingly complete embodiments of the tragic form, written as they were at a time of booming American optimism, materialistic expansion, and sentimentalism in fiction—and no tragic theatre whatever. In *The Scarlet Letter*, a story of adultery set in colonial New England, the heroine's sense of sin is incomplete; her spirited individualism insists (as she tells her lover) that "what we did had a consecration of its own." The resulting conflict in her heart and mind is never resolved, and, although it does not destroy her, she lives out her life in gray and tragic isolation. Melville said that he was encouraged by Hawthorne's exploration of "a certain tragic phase of humanity," by his deep broodings and by the "blackness of darkness" in him, to proceed with similar explorations of his own in *Moby Dick*, which he dedicated to Hawthorne. Its protagonist, Captain Ahab, represents a return to what Melville called (defending Ahab's status as tragic hero) a "mighty pageant creature, formed for noble tragedies," whose "ponderous heart," "globular brain," and "nervous lofty language" prove that even an old Nantucket sea captain can take his place with kings and princes of the ancient drama. Shakespearean echoes abound in the novel; some of its chapters are written in dramatic form. Its theme and central figure, reminiscent of Job and Lear in their search for justice and of Oedipus in his search for the truth, all show what Melville might have been—a great tragic dramatist had there been a tragic theatre in America.

Some American novelists of the 20th century carried on, however partially, the tragic tradition. Theodore Dreiser's *American Tragedy* (1925) is typical of the naturalistic novel, which is also represented by the work of Stephen Crane, James T. Farrell, John Steinbeck. Though showing great sensitivity to environmental or sociological evils, such works fail to embody the high conception of character (as Melville describes it above) and are concerned mainly with externals, or reportage. The protagonists are generally "good" (or weak) and beaten down by society. The novels of Henry James, which span the period from 1876 to 1904, are concerned with what has been called the tragedy of manners. The society James projects is sophisticated, subtle, and sinister. The innocent and the good are destroyed, like Milly Theale in *The Wings of the Dove* (1902), who in the end "turns her face to the wall" and dies but in her death brings new vision and new values to those whose betrayals had driven her to her death.

The trend in American fiction, as in the drama, contin-

ued in the 20th century, toward the pathos of the victim —the somehow inadequate, the sometimes insignificant figure destroyed by such vastly unequal forces that the struggle is scarcely significant. F. Scott Fitzgerald's Gatsby in his novel *The Great Gatsby* (1925) is betrayed by his own meretricious dream, nurtured by a meretricious society. The hero of Ernest Hemingway's novel *A Farewell to Arms* (1929), disillusioned by war, makes a separate peace, deserts, and joins his beloved in neutral Switzerland. When she dies in childbirth, he sees it as still another example of how "they"—society, the politicians who run the war, or the mysterious forces destroying Catherine—get you in the end. The tone is lyric and pathetic rather than tragic (though Hemingway called the novel his *Romeo and Juliet*). Grief turns the hero away from, rather than toward, a deeper examination of life.

Only the novels of William Faulkner, in their range and depth and in their powerful assault on the basic tragic themes, recall unmistakably the values of the tragic tradition. His "saga of the South," as recounted in a series of novels (notably *Sartoris*, 1929; *The Sound and the Fury*, 1929; *As I Lay Dying*, 1930; *Sanctuary*, 1931; *Light in August*, 1932; *Absalom, Absalom!* 1936; *Intruder in the Dust*, 1948; *Requiem for a Nun*, 1951), incorporates some 300 years of Southern history from Indian days to the present. At first regarded as a mere exploiter of decadence, he can now be seen as gradually working beyond reportage and toward meaning. His sociology became more and more the "sin" of the South—the rape of the land, slavery, the catastrophe of the Civil War and its legacy of a cynical and devitalized materialism. Increasingly he saw the conflict as internal. The subject of art, Faulkner said in his 1949 Nobel Prize speech, is "the human heart in conflict with itself." His insistence is on guilt as the evidence of man's fate, and on the possibility of expiation as the assertion of man's freedom. Compassion, endurance, and the capacity to learn are seen to be increasingly effective in his characters. In the veiled analogies to Christ as outcast and redeemer in *Light in August* and in the more explicit Christology of *A Fable* (1954), in the pastoral serenity following the anguish and horror in *Light in August*, and in the high comedy of the last scene of *Intruder in the Dust*, Faulkner puts into tragic fiction the belief he stated in his Nobel speech: "I decline to accept the end of man."

TRAGEDY AND MODERN DRAMA

Tragic themes in Ibsen, Strindberg, and Chekhov. The movement toward naturalism in fiction in the latter decades of the 19th century did much to purge both the novel and the drama of the sentimentality and evasiveness that had so long emasculated them. In Norway Henrik Ibsen incorporated in his plays the smug and narrow ambitiousness of his society. The hypocrisy of overbearing men and women replace, in their fashion, the higher powers of the old tragedy. His major tragic theme is the futility, leading to catastrophe, of the idealist's effort to create a new and better social order. The "problem play" —one devoted to a particular social issue—is saved in his hand from the flatness of a sociological treatise by a sense of doom, a pattern of retribution, reminiscent of the ancient Greeks. In *Pillars of Society* (1877), *The Wild Duck* (published 1884), *Rosmersholm* (published 1886), and *The Master Builder* (published 1892), for example, one sacrifice is expiated by another.

In Sweden, August Strindberg, influenced by Ibsen, was a powerful force in the movement. *The Father* (1887) and *Miss Julie* (published 1888) recall Ibsen's attacks on religious, moral, and political orthodoxies. Strindberg's main concern, however, is with the destructive effects of sexual maladjustment and psychic imbalance. Not since Euripides' *Medea* or Racine's *Phèdre* had the tragic aspects of sex come under such powerful analysis. In this respect, his plays look forward to O'Neill's.

Anton Chekhov, the most prominent Russian dramatist of the period, wrote plays about the humdrum life of inconspicuous, sensitive people (*Uncle Vanya*, 1899; *The Three Sisters*, 1901; and *The Cherry Orchard*, 1904, are

[margin notes] Paradox, alienation, loss of identity in Dostoyevsky

Guilt and expiation in Faulkner

typical), whose lives fall prey to the hollowness and tedium of a disintegrating social order. They are a brood of lesser Hamlets without his compensating vision of a potential greatness. As in the plays of the Scandinavian dramatists, Chekhov's vision of this social evil is penetrating and acute, but the powerful, resistant counterthrust that makes for tragedy is lacking. It is a world of victims.

American tragic dramatists. In little of the formal drama between the time of Ibsen, Strindberg, and Chekhov and the present are the full dimensions of tragedy presented. Some critics suggested that it was too late for tragedy, that modern man no longer valued himself highly enough, that too many sociological and ideological factors were working against the tragic temperament. The long and successful career of Eugene O'Neill may be a partial answer to this criticism. He has been called the first American to succeed in writing tragedy for the theatre, a fulfillment of his avowed purpose, for he had declared that in the tragic, alone, lay the meaning of life —and the hope. He sought in Freud's concept of the subconscious the equivalent of the Greek idea of fate and modelled his great trilogy, *Mourning Becomes Electra* (1931), on Aeschylus' *Oresteia*. Although the hovering sense of an ancient evil is powerful, the psychological conditioning controls the characters too nakedly. They themselves declare forces that determine their behaviour, so that they seem almost to connive in their own manipulation. *Desire Under the Elms* (1924) presents a harsh analysis of decadence in the sexual and avaricious intrigues of a New England farmer's family, unrelieved by manifestations of the transcendent human spirit. *The Great God Brown* (1926) and *Long Day's Journey into Night* (1939–41; first performance, 1956) come closer to true tragedy. In the latter, the capacity for self-knowledge is demonstrated by each member of the wrangling Tyrone family (actually, O'Neill's own; the play is frankly autobiographical). The insistent theme of the "death wish" (another example of Freud's influence), however, indicates too radical a pessimism for tragedy; even the character of Edmund Tyrone, O'Neill's own counterpart, confesses that he has always been a little in love with death, and in another late play, *The Iceman Cometh* (1939), the death wish is more strongly expressed. Although he never succeeded in establishing a tragic theatre comparable to the great theatres of the past, O'Neill made a significant contribution in his sustained concentration on subjects at least worthy of such a theatre. He made possible the significant, if slighter, contributions of Arthur Miller, whose *Death of a Salesman* (1949) and *A View from the Bridge* (1955) contain material of tragic potential that is not fully realized. Tennessee Williams' *Streetcar Named Desire* (1947) is a sensitive study of the breakdown of a character under social and psychological stress. As with Miller's plays, however, it remains in the area of pathos rather than tragedy.

Other serious drama. The 20th century has produced much serious and excellent drama, which, though not in the main line of the tragic tradition, deserves mention. In British theatre, George Bernard Shaw's *Saint Joan* (1923) and T.S. Eliot's *Murder in the Cathedral* (1935) dramatized with great power both doubt and affirmation, the ambiguity of human motives, and the possibility of fruitless suffering that are true of the human condition as reflected by tragedy. During the Irish literary revival, the work of J.M. Synge (*Riders to the Sea*, 1904) and Sean O'Casey (*Shadow of a Gunman*, 1923), like Faulkner's work, sought a tragic theme in the destiny of a whole people. The masterpiece of this movement, however, is not a tragedy but a comic inversion of the ancient tragedy of *Oedipus*—Synge's *Playboy of the Western World* (1907).

The drama of social protest—exemplified in such works as the Russian Maksim Gorky's *Lower Depths* (1902), the German Bertolt Brecht's *Threepenny Opera* (1928) and *Mother Courage* (1941), and the American Clifford Odets' *Waiting for Lefty* (1935)—shares the tragedians' concern for evils that frustrate or destroy human values. The evils, however, are largely external, identifiable, and, with certain recommended changes in the social order, remediable. The type shows how vulnerable tragedy is to dogma or programs of any sort. A British author, George Orwell, suggested in *Nineteen Eighty-four* that tragedy would cease to exist under pure Marxist statism. Brecht's fine sense of irony and moral paradox redeem him from absolute dogmatism but give his work a hard satiric thrust that is inimical to tragedy. Traditional values and moral imperatives are all but neutralized in the existentialist worlds of the dramas and novels of Jean-Paul Sartre and Albert Camus, two outstanding philosopher-dramatists of the post World War II era. In their works, the protagonist is called upon to forge his own values, if he can, in a world in which the disparity between the ideal (what man longs for) and the real (what he gets) is so great as to reduce the human condition to incoherence and absurdity. Plays that led to the coinage of the term the theatre of the absurd are exemplified by *Waiting for Godot* (1952) and *The Killer* (1959), respectively by the Irish writer Samuel Beckett and the Romanian Eugène Ionesco, both of whom pursued their careers in Paris. Here, the theme of victimization is at its extreme, the despair and defeat almost absolute.

A coherent and affirmative view of man, society, and the cosmos is vital to tragedy—however tentative the affirmation may be. Unresolved questions remain at the end of every tragedy. There is always an irrational factor, disturbing, foreboding, not to be resolved by the sometime consolations of philosophy and religion or by any science of the mind or body; there is irretrievable loss, usually though not necessarily symbolized by the death of the hero. In the course of the action, however, in the development of character, theme, and situation and in the conceptual suggestiveness of language, tragedy presents the positive terms in which these questions might be answered. The human qualities are manifest, however limited; man's freedom is real, however marginal. The forces that bear him down may be mysterious but actual—fate, the gods, chance, the power of his own or the race's past working through his soul. Though never mastered, they can be contended with, defied, and, at least in spirit, transcended. The process is cognitive; man can learn.

Absence of tragedy in Oriental drama. In no way can the importance of a conceptual basis for tragedy be better illustrated than by a look at other drama-producing cultures with radically different ideas of the individual, his nature, and his destiny. While the cultures of India, China, and Japan have produced significant and highly artistic drama, there is little here to compare in magnitude, intensity, and freedom of form to the tragedies of the West.

In Buddhist teaching, the aim of the individual is to suppress and regulate all those questioning, recalcitrant, rebellious impulses that first impel the Western hero toward his tragic course. The goal of Nirvāna is the extinction of those impulses, the quieting of the passions, a kind of *quietus* in which worldly existence ceases. Western tragedy celebrates life, and the tragic hero clings to it: to him, it is never "sweet to die" for his country or for anything else, and the fascination for Western audiences is to follow the hero—as it were, *from the inside*—as he struggles to assert himself and his values against whatever would deny them. In Oriental drama, there is no such intense focus on the individual. In the Japanese Nō plays, for instance, the hero may be seen in moments of weariness and despair, of anger or confusion, but the mood is lyric, and the structure of the plays is ritualistic, with a great deal of choral intoning, dancing, and stylized action. Although a number of Nō plays can be produced together to fill a day's performance, the individual plays are very short, hardly the length of a Western one-act play. Nō plays affirm orthodoxy, rather than probing and questioning it, as Western tragedies do.

The drama in India has a long history, but there too the individual is subordinated to the mood of the idyll or romance or epic adventure. Perhaps one reason why the drama of India never developed the tragic orientation of the West is its removal from the people; it has never known the communal involvement of the Greek and Eliz-

---

O'Neill: pessimism too radical for tragedy

Tragedy in works of social protest

abethan theatres. Produced mainly for court audiences, an upper class elite, it never reflected the sufferings of common (or uncommon) humanity. Only recently has the drama in China embraced the vigour and realism of the common people, but the drama is in the service not of the individual but of a political ideology, which replaces the traditional themes of ancestor worship and filial piety. In all this, the mighty pageant figure—Oedipus, Prometheus, Lear, or Ahab standing for the individual as he alone sees and feels the workings of an unjust universe—is absent.

Tragedy in Nō drama

An example from the Nō plays will illustrate these generalizations. In *The Hoka Priests*, by Zenchiku Ujinobu (1414–99), a son is confronted with Hamlet's problem—*i.e.*, that of avenging the death of his father. He is uncertain how to proceed, since his father's murderer has many bold fellows to stand by him, while he is all alone. He persuades his brother, a priest, to help him, and disguising themselves as priests, they concoct a little plot to engage the murderer in religious conversation. There are a few words of lament—"Oh why,/ Why back to the bitter World/ Are we borne by our intent?"—and the Chorus sings lyrically about the uncertainties of life. The theme of the conversation is the unreality of the World and the reality of Thought. At an appropriate moment, the brothers cry, "Enough! Why longer hide our plot?" The murderer places his hat on the floor and exits. The brothers mime the killing of the murderer in a stylized attack upon the hat, while the Chorus describes and comments on the action: "So when the hour was come/ Did these two brothers/ By sudden resolution/ Destroy their father's foe./ For valour and piety are their names remembered/ Even in this aftertime" (translated by Arthur Waley, *The Nō Plays of Japan*, 1921).

Thus the Nō avoids directly involving the audience in the emotions implicit in the events portrayed on the stage. It gives only a slight hint of the spiritual struggle in the heart of the protagonist—a struggle that is always speedily resolved in favour of traditional teaching. In play after play the action does not take place before our eyes but is re-enacted by the ghost of one of the participants. Thus, the events presented are tinged with memory or longing—hardly the primary emotions that surge through and invigorate Western tragedy at its best.

Loss of viability in the West. The absence, even in the West, of a great tragic theatre in the 20th century may be explained by the pantheon of panaceas to which modern man has subscribed. Politics, psychology, social sciences, physical sciences, nationalism, the occult—each offered a context in terms of which he might act out his destiny, were it not crowded out by the others. Modern man is not tested but harried and not by gods but, too often, by demons. In the dramas of Athens and England, tragedy was born of the impossibility of a clear-cut victory in man's struggle with powers greater than himself. In the modern drama, the struggle itself seems impossible.

The would-be hero is saved from a meaningful death by being condemned to a meaningless life. This, too, however, has its tragic dimension, in its illustration of the power of evil to survive from millennium to millennium in the presence or the absence of the gods.

Tragedy is a means of coming to terms with that evil. To assume that tragedy has lost viability is to forget that this viability was seriously questioned by the first Western philosopher to address himself to the problem. An account of the development of the theory of tragedy will reveal a resourcefulness in man's critical powers that can help to compensate, or occasionally even supersede, his lapsing creative powers.   (R.B.S.)

THEORY OF TRAGEDY

Classical theories of tragedy. As the great period of Athenian drama drew to an end at the beginning of the 4th century BC, Athenian philosophers began to analyze its content and formulate its structure. In the thought of Plato (*c.* 427–347 BC), the history of the criticism of tragedy began with speculation on the role of censorship. To Plato (in the dialogue on the *Laws*) the state was the noblest work of art, a representation (*mimēsis*) of the

fairest and best life. He feared the tragedians' command of the expressive resources of language, which might be used to the detriment of worthwhile institutions. He feared, too, the emotive effect of poetry, the Dionysian element that is at the very basis of tragedy. Therefore, he recommended that the tragedians submit their works to the rulers, for approval, without which they could not be performed. It is clear that tragedy, by nature exploratory, critical, independent, could not live under such a regimen.

Ethics and art—Plato and Aristotle

Plato is answered, in effect and perhaps intentionally, by Aristotle's *Poetics*. Aristotle (384–322 BC) defends the purgative power of tragedy and, in direct contradiction to Plato, makes moral ambiguity the essence of tragedy. The tragic hero must be neither a villain nor a virtuous man but a "character between these two extremes, . . . a man who is not eminently good and just, yet whose misfortune is brought about not by vice or depravity, but by some error or frailty [*hamartia*]." The effect on the audience will be similarly ambiguous. A perfect tragedy, he says, should imitate actions that excite "pity and fear." He uses Sophocles' *Oedipus the King* as a paradigm. Near the beginning of the play, Oedipus asks how his stricken city (the counterpart of Plato's state) may cleanse itself, and the word he uses for the purifying action is a form of the word catharsis. The concept of catharsis provides Aristotle with his reconciliation with Plato, a means by which to satisfy the claims of both ethics and art. "Tragedy," says Aristotle, "is an imitation [*mimēsis*] of an action that is serious, complete and of a certain magnitude . . . through pity and fear effecting the proper purgation [catharsis] of these emotions." Ambiguous means may be employed, Aristotle maintains in contrast to Plato, to a virtuous and purifying end.

To establish the basis for a reconciliation between ethical and artistic demands, Aristotle insists that the principal element in the structure of tragedy is not character but plot. Since the erring protagonist is always in at least partial opposition to the state, the importance of tragedy lies not in him but in the enlightening event. "Most important of all," Aristotle said, "is the structure of the incidents. For tragedy is an imitation not of men but of an action and of life, and life consists in action, and its end is a mode of action, not a quality. . . ." Aristotle considered the plot to be the soul of a tragedy, with character in second place. The goal of tragedy is not suffering but the knowledge that issues from it, as the denouement issues from a plot. The most powerful elements of emotional interest in tragedy, according to Aristotle, are reversal of intention or situation (*peripeteia*) and recognition scenes (*anagnōrisis*), and each is most effective when it is coincident with the other. In *Oedipus*, for example, the messenger who brings Oedipus news of his real parentage, intending to allay his fears, brings about a sudden reversal of his fortune, from happiness to misery, by compelling him to recognize that his wife is also his mother.

Later critics found justification for their own predilections in the authority of Greek drama and Aristotle. For example, the Roman poet Horace (65–8 BC), in his *Ars poetica* (*Art of Poetry*), elaborated the Greek tradition of extensively narrating offstage events into a dictum on decorum forbidding events such as Medea's butchering of her boys from being performed on stage. And where Aristotle had discussed tragedy as a separate genre, superior to epic poetry, Horace discussed it as a genre with a separate style, again with considerations of decorum foremost. A theme for comedy may not be set forth in verses of tragedy; each style must keep to the place alloted it.

On the basis of this kind of stylistic distinction, the *Aeneid*, the epic poem of Virgil, Horace's contemporary, is called a tragedy by the fictional Virgil in Dante's *Divine Comedy*, on the grounds that the *Aeneid* treats only of lofty things. Dante (1265–1321) calls his own poem a comedy partly because he includes "low" subjects in it. He makes this distinction in his *De vulgari eloquentia* (1304–06; "On the Vernacular Tongue"), in which he also declares the subjects fit for the high, tragic style to be salvation, love, and virtue. Despite the presence of these subjects in this poem, he calls it a comedy because his style of language is "careless and humble" and because it is in the vernacular tongue rather than Latin. Dante makes a further distinction:

> Comedy . . . differs from tragedy in its subject matter, in this way, that tragedy in its beginning is admirable and quiet, in its ending or catastrophe foul and horrible . . . From this it is evident why the present work is called a comedy.

Fate and will in comedy and tragedy

Dante's emphasis on the outcome of the struggle rather than on the nature of the struggle is repeated by Chaucer and for the same reason: their belief in the providential nature of human destiny. Like Dante, he was under the influence of *De consolatione philosophiae* (*Consolation of Philosophy*), the work of the 6th-century Roman philosopher Boethius (*c.* 480–524) that he translated into English. Chaucer considered Fortune to be beyond the influence of the human will. In his *Canterbury Tales*, he introduces "The Monk's Tale" by defining tragedy as "a certeyn storie . . ./of him that stood in greet prosperitee,/ And is y-fallen out of heigh degree/ Into miserie, and endeth wrecchedly." Again, he calls his *Troilus and Criseyde* a tragedy because, in the words of Troilus, "all that comth, comth by necessitee . . ./ That forsight of divine purveyaunce/ Hath seyn alwey me to forgon Criseyde."

Elizabethan approaches. The critical tradition of separating the tragic and comic styles is continued by the Elizabethan English poet Sir Philip Sidney, whose *Defence of Poesie* (also published as *An Apologie for Poetrie*) has the distinction of containing the most extended statement on tragedy in the English Renaissance and the misfortune of having been written in the early 1580s (published 1595), before the first plays of Shakespeare, or even of Marlowe. Nevertheless, Sidney wrote eloquently of "high and excellent tragedy, that . . . with stirring the affects of admiration and commiseration teacheth the uncertainty of this world and upon how weak foundations gilden roofs are builded."

Since the word admiration here means awe, Sidney's "admiration and commiseration" are similar to Aristotle's "pity and fear." He differs from Aristotle, however, in preferring epic to tragic poetry. The Renaissance was almost as concerned as Plato with the need to justify poetry on ethical grounds, and Sidney ranks epic higher than tragedy because it provides morally superior models of behaviour.

Sidney goes further than mere agreement with Aristotle, however, in championing the unities of time and place. Aristotle had asserted the need for a unity of time: "Tragedy endeavors, as far as possible, to confine itself to a single revolution of the sun, or but slightly to exceed this limit." Sidney, following the lead of a 16th-century Italian Neoclassicist, Ludovico Castelvetro, added the unity of place: "the stage should always represent but one place, and the uttermost time presupposed in it should be, both by Aristotle's precept and common reason, but one day . . . ." Sidney also seconds Horace's disapproval of the mingling of styles, which Sidney says produces a "mongrel tragicomedy."

Shakespeare's opinion of the relative merits of the genres is unknown, but his opinion of the problem itself may be surmised. In *Hamlet* he puts these words in the mouth of the foolish old pedant Polonius: "The best actors in the world, either for tragedy, comedy, history, pastoral, pastoral-comical, historical-pastoral, tragical-historical, tragical-comical-historical-pastoral; scene individable, or poem unlimited . . ." (Act II, scene 2). As to the classical unities, Shakespeare adheres to them only twice and neither time in a tragedy, in *The Comedy of Errors* and *The Tempest*. And through the mouths of his characters, Shakespeare, like Aristotle, puts himself on both sides of the central question of tragic destiny—that of freedom and necessity. Aristotle says that a tragic destiny is precipitated by the hero's tragic fault, his "error or frailty" (hamartia), but Aristotle also calls this turn of events a change of "fortune." Shakespeare's Cassius in *Julius Caesar* says, "The fault, dear Brutus, is not in our stars, / But in ourselves . . . ," and in King Lear, Edmund ridicules a belief in fortune as the "foppery of the world." But Hamlet, in a comment on the nature of hamartia, is a fatalist when he broods on the "mole of nature," the "one

defect" that some men are born with, "wherein they are not guilty," and that brings them to disaster (Act I, scene 4). Similarly, Sophocles' Oedipus, though he says, "It was Apollo who brought my woes to pass," immediately adds, "it was my hand that struck my eyes." These ambiguities are a powerful source of the tragic emotion of Athenian and Elizabethan drama, unequalled by traditions that are more sure of themselves, such as French Neoclassicism, or less sure of themselves, such as 20th-century drama.

Neoclassical theory. In the Neoclassical period Aristotle's reasonableness was replaced by rationality, and his moral ambiguity by the mechanics of "poetic justice." In the 17th century, under the guise of a strict adherence to Classical formulas, additional influences were brought to bear on the theory of tragedy. In France, the theological doctrine of Jansenism, which called for an extreme orthodoxy, exercised a strong influence. In England, the restoration of the monarchy in 1660, with the reopening of the theatres, introduced a period of witty and lusty literature. In both nations, the influence of natural law—the idea that laws binding upon humanity are inferable from nature—increased, along with the influence of the exact sciences. Critics in both nations declared that Aristotle's "rules" were made to reduce nature into a method.

In his 1679 preface to Shakespeare's *Troilus and Cressida*, Dryden says, "we lament not, but detest a wicked man, we are glad when we behold his crimes are punished, and that Poetical justice is done upon him." Similar sentiments, calling for the punishment of crimes and the reward of virtue, were expressed in France. Catharsis had become vindication. Thomas Rymer, one of the most influential English critics of the time, in *The Tragedies of The Last Age* (1678), wrote that

Vindication rather than catharsis

> besides the purging of the passions, something must stick by observing . . . that necessary relation and chain, whereby the causes and the effects, the vertues and rewards, the vices and their punishments are proportion'd and link'd together, how deep and dark soever are laid the Springs, and however intricate and involv'd are their operations.

The effect was to rob tragedy of a great deal of its darkness and depth. The temper of the age demanded that mystery be brought to the surface and to the light, a process that had effects not merely different from but in part antipathetic to tragedy. Nicolas Boileau, the chief spokesman of the French Neoclassical movement, in his discussion of pity and fear in *Art Poétique* (1674), qualified these terms with the adjectives "beguiling" and "pleasant" (*pitié charmante, douce terreur*), which radically changed their meaning. The purged spectator became a grateful patient.

In his preface to *Phèdre* (1677), Racine subscribed to the *quid pro quo* view of retribution.

> I have written no play in which virtue has been more celebrated than in this one. The smallest faults are here severely punished; the mere idea of a crime is looked upon with as much horror as the crime itself.

Of Phèdre herself, his greatest heroine, he says,

> I have taken the trouble to make her a little less hateful than she is in the ancient versions of this tragedy, in which she herself resolves to accuse Hippolytus. I judged that that calumny had about it something too base and black to be put into the mouth of a Princess . . . This depravity seemed to me more appropriate to the character of a nurse, whose inclinations might be supposed to be more servile. . . .

For Aristotle, pity and fear made a counterpoint typical of Classicism, each tempering the other to create a balance. For Racine, pity and fear each must be tempered in itself. In the marginalia to his fragmentary translation of Aristotle's *Poetics*, Racine wrote that in arousing the passions of pity and fear, tragedy

> removes from them whatever they have of the excessive and the vicious and brings them back to a moderated condition and conformable to reason.

Corneille contradicted Aristotle outright. Discussing *Le Cid* he said, in *A Discourse on Tragedy* (1660),

> Our pity ought to give us fear of falling into similar misfortune, and purge us of that excess of love which is the cause of their disaster . . . but I do not know that it gives

us that, or purges us, and I am afraid that the reasoning of Aristotle on this point is but a pretty idea . . . it is not requisite that these two passions always serve together . . . it suffices . . . that one of the two bring about the purgation. . . .

The accommodation of tragedy to Neoclassical ideas of order demanded a simplification of tragedy's complexities and ambiguities. The simplifying process was now inspired, however, by the fundamental tenet of all primitive scientific thought namely, that orderliness and naturalness are in a directly proportionate relationship. Racine declared the basis of the naturalistic effect in drama to be a strict adherence to the unities, which now seem the opposite of naturalistic. In his preface to *Bérénice* (1670), he asked what probability there could be when a multitude of things that would scarcely happen in several weeks are made to happen in a day. The illusion of probability, which is the Aristotelian criterion for the verisimilitude of a stage occurrence, is made to sound as if it were the result of a strict dramaturgical determinism, on the grounds that necessity is the truest path to freedom.

Racine and Corneille both contradicted Dante and Chaucer on the indispensability of a catastrophic final scene. "Blood and deaths," said Racine, are not necessary, for "it is enough that the action be grand, that the actors be heroic, that the passions be aroused" to produce "that stately sorrow that makes the whole pleasure of tragedy" (preface to *Bérénice*).

Milton was artistically much more conservative. He prefaced his *Samson Agonistes* (1671) with a warning against the

error of intermixing Comic stuff with Tragic sadness and gravity; or introducing trivial and vulgar persons: which by all judicious hath been counted absurd; and brought in without discretion, corruptly to gratify the people.

He bypassed Shakespeare for the ancients and ranked Aeschylus, Sophocles, and Euripides as tragic poets unequalled yet by any others. Part of the rule, for Milton, was that which affirmed the unities. In his concurrence with the Classical idea of the purgative effect of pity and fear, Milton combined reactionary aesthetics with the scientific spirit of the recently formed Royal Society.

Nor is Nature wanting in her own effects to make good his assertion [Aristotle on catharsis]: for so, in Physic things of melancholic hue and quality are used against melancholy, sour against sour, salt to remove salt humours.

Dryden spoke against a delimiting conception of either the genres or the unities. Speaking in the guise of Neander in *Of Dramatick Poesie, an Essay* (1668), he said that it was

to the honour of our nation, that we have invented, increased, and perfected a more pleasant way of writing for the stage, than was ever known to the ancients or moderns of any nation, which is tragi-comedy.

The French dramatists, he felt, through their observance of the unities of time and place, wrote plays characterized by a dearth of plot and narrowness of imagination. Racine's approach to the question of probability was turned completely around by Dryden, who asked:

How Many beautiful accidents might naturally happen in two or three days, which cannot arrive with any probability in the compass of twenty-four hours?

Johnson's definitive critique

The definitive critique of Neoclassical restrictions was not formulated, however, until the following century, when it was made by Samuel Johnson and was, significantly, part of his 1765 preface to Shakespeare, the first major step in the long process of establishing Shakespeare as the pre-eminent tragic poet of post-Classical drama. On genre he wrote:

Shakespeare's plays are not in the rigorous and critical sense either tragedies or comedies, but compositions of a distinct kind; . . . expressing the course of the world, in which the loss of one is the gain of another; in which, at the same time, the reveller is hasting to his wine, and the mourner burying his friend. . . . That this is a practice contrary to the rules of criticism will be readily allowed; but there is always an appeal open from criticism to nature.

And on the unities:

The necessity of observing the unities of time and place arises from the supposed necessity of making the drama credible. [But] the objection arising from the impossibility of passing the first hour at Alexandria, and the next at Rome, supposes, that when the play opens, the spectator really imagines himself at Alexandria . . . Surely he that imagines this may imagine more.

Johnson's appeal to nature was the essence of subsequent Romantic criticism.

Romantic theories of tragedy. Lessing was the first important Romantic critic. He stated one of Romanticism's chief innovations in his *Hamburg Dramaturgy* (1767–69):

The names of princes and heroes can lend pomp and majesty to a play, but they contribute nothing to our emotion. The misfortune of those whose circumstances most resemble our own, must naturally penetrate most deeply into our hearts, and if we pity kings, we pity them as human beings, not as kings.

Within a generation, revolutions in Europe and America offered social expression of this literary precept, and a dramatic tradition dominant for 22 centuries was upturned. From the time of Aristotle, who thought that the tragic hero should be highly renowned and prosperous, the tragic hero had been an aristocrat, if not a man of royal blood. With the exception of their minor or peripheral characters, the tragic dramas of Athens, England, and France told nothing of the destinies of the mass of mankind. All this was now changed.

But it is not certain that what was good for the revolution was good for tragedy. Coleridge in his critical writings of 1808–18 said that:

there are two forms of disease most preclusive of tragic worth. The first [is] a sense and love of the ludicrous, and a diseased sensibility of the assimilating power . . . that in the boldest bursts of passion will lie in wait, or at once kindle into jest. . . . The second cause is matter of exultation to the philanthropist and philosopher, and of regret to the poet, . . . namely, the security, comparative equability, and ever-increasing sameness of human life.

In accord with this distaste for an excess of the mundane, Coleridge attacked the new German tragedies in which "the dramatist becomes a novelist *in his directions to the actors,* and degrades tragedy to pantomime." To describe, or rather indicate, what tragedy should ideally be, Coleridge said "it is not *a copy* of nature; but it is an imitation."

Coleridge's operative words and phrases in his discussions of tragedy were "innate," "from within," "implicit," "the being within," "the inmost heart," "our inward nature," "internal emotions," and "retired recesses." The new philosophical dispensation in Coleridge, like the new social dispensation in Lessing, reversed the old priorities; and where there were once princes there were now burghers, and where there were once the ordinances of God and the state there were now the dictates of the heart. By means of this reversal, Coleridge effected a reconciliation of the "tragedy of fate" and the "tragedy of character" in his description of the force of fate as merely the embodiment of an interior compulsion different in scale but not in kind from the interior compulsions of character. In Classical tragedy, he said the human "will" was "exhibited as struggling with fate, a great and beautiful instance and illustration of which is the Prometheus of Aeschylus; and the deepest effect is produced, when the fate is represented as a higher and intelligent will. . . ."

According to Coleridge, Shakespeare used the imaginative "variety" that characterizes man's inward nature in place of the mechanical regularity of the Neoclassical unities to produce plays that were "neither tragedies nor comedies, nor both in one, but a different genus, diverse in kind, not merely different in degree,—romantic dramas or dramatic romances." In his preoccupation with the mixture of genres and his distinction between the "mechanical" (Neoclassicism) and the "organic" (Shakespeare), Coleridge was influenced by *Lectures on Dramatic Art and Literature* (delivered 1808–09, published 1809–11), by August Wilhelm von Schlegel, perhaps the most influential of German Romantic critics.

Coleridge's reconciliation of fate and character

Like Coleridge and most Romantic critics of tragedy, Schlegel found his champion in Shakespeare, and, also like them, he was preoccupied with the contrast between Classic and Romantic. Like Coleridge, Schlegel emphasized Shakespeare's inwardness, what Coleridge called his "implicit wisdom deeper even than our consciousness." It is in Shakespeare's most profound insights that Schlegel locates one of the principal distinctions between Classical and Shakespearean tragedy, in what he calls Shakespeare's "secret irony." The irony in *Oedipus the King* consists in the relation between the audience's knowledge of the protagonist's situation and his own ignorance of it. But Shakespeare's "readiness to remark the mind's fainter and involuntary utterances" is so great, says Schlegel, that "nobody ever painted so truthfully as he has done the facility of self-deception, the half self-conscious hypocrisy towards ourselves, with which even noble minds attempt to disguise the almost inevitable influence of selfish motives in human nature."

The irony Schlegel sees in Shakespeare's characterizations also extends to the whole of the action, as well as to the separate characters. In his discussion of it he suggests the reason for the difficulty of Shakespeare's plays and for the quarrelsome, irreconcilable "interpretations" among Shakespeare's commentators:

> Most poets who portray human events in a narrative or dramatic form take themselves apart, and exact from their readers a blind approbation or condemnation of whatever side they choose to support or oppose. . . . When, however, by a dexterous manoeuvre, the poet allows us an occasional glance at the less brilliant reverse of the medal, then he makes, as it were, a sort of secret understanding with the select circle of the more intelligent of his readers or spectators; he shows them that he had previously seen and admitted the validity of their tacit objections; that he himself is not tied down to the represented subject but soars freely above it. . . .

In Greek tragedy, the commentary by the chorus was an explicit and objective fact of the drama itself. In the presentation of Shakespeare's plays, such a commentary is carried on in the separate minds of the spectators, where it is diffused, silent, and not entirely sure of itself. When the spectators speak their minds after the curtain falls, it is not surprising that they often disagree.

In *Oedipus the King*, which Aristotle cited as the model of Classical tragedy, the irony of the protagonist's situation is evident to the spectator. In *Hamlet*, however, according to the American philosopher George Santayana, writing in 1908, it is the secret ironies, half-lights, and self-contradictions that make it the central creation of Romantic tragedy. As has been noted, Coleridge objected to the dramatist's giving directions to the actors, but part of the price of not having them is to deny to the audience as well an explicit indication of the playwright's meaning.

George Wilhelm Friedrich Hegel (1770–1831), the immensely influential German philosoper, in his *Aesthetik* (1820–29), proposed that the sufferings of the tragic hero are merely a means of reconciling opposing moral claims. The operation is a success because of, not in spite of, the fact that the patient dies. According to Hegel's account of Greek tragedy, the conflict is not between good and evil but between goods that are each making too exclusive a claim. The heroes of ancient tragedy, by adhering to the *one* ethical system by which they molded their own personality, must come into conflict with the ethical claims of another. It is the moral one-sidedness of the tragic actor, not any negatively tragic fault in his morality or in the forces opposed to him, that proves his undoing, for both sides of the contradiction, if taken by themselves, are justified.

The nuclear Greek tragedy for Hegel is, understandably, Sophocles' *Antigone*, with its conflict between the valid claims of conscience (Antigone's obligation to give her brother a suitable burial) and law (King Creon's edict that enemies of the state should not be allowed burial). The two claims represent what Hegel regards as essentially concordant ethical claims. Antigone and Creon are, in **Tragedy as** this view, rather like pawns in the Hegelian dialectic—his **Hegelian** theory that thought progresses from a thesis (*i.e.*, an **dialectic** idea), through an antithesis (an idea opposing the origi-

nal thesis), to a synthesis (a more comprehensive idea that embraces both the thesis and antithesis), which in turn becomes the thesis in a further progression. At the end of *Antigone*, something of the sense of mutually appeased, if not concordant, forces does obtain after Antigone's suicide and the destruction of Creon's family. Thus, in contrast to Aristotle's statement that the tragic actors should represent not an extreme of good or evil but something between, Hegel would have them too good to live; that is, too extreme an embodiment of a particular good to survive in the world. He also tends to dismiss other traditional categories of tragic theory. For instance, he prefers his own kind of catharsis to Aristotle's—the feeling of *reconciliation*.

Hegel's emphasis on the correction of moral imbalances in tragedy is reminiscent of the "poetic justice" of Neoclassical theory, with its similar dialectic of crime and punishment. He sounds remarkably like Racine when he claims that, in the tragic denouement, the necessity of all that has been experienced by particular individuals is seen to be in complete accord with reason and is harmonized on a true ethical basis. But where the Neoclassicists were preoccupied with the unities of time and place, Hegel's concerns, like those of other Romantics, are inward. For him, the final issue of tragedy is not the misfortune and suffering of the tragic antagonists but rather the satisfaction of spirit arising from "reconciliation." Thus, the workings of the spirit, in Hegel's view, are subject to the rationalistic universal laws.

Hegel's system is not applicable to Shakespearean or Romantic tragedy. Such Shakespearean heroes as Macbeth, Richard III, and Mark Antony cannot be regarded as embodiments of any transcendent good. They behave as they do, says Hegel, now speaking outside of his scheme of tragedy, simply because they are the kind of men they are. In a statement pointing up the essence of uninhibited romantic lust and willfulness Hegel said: "it is the inner experience of their heart and individual emotion, or the particular qualities of their personality, which insist on satisfaction."

The traditional categories of tragedy are nearly destroyed in the deepened subjectivities of Romanticism of the 19th-century German philosophers, Arthur Schopenhauer and his disciple Friedrich Nietzsche. In Schopenhauer's *Die Welt als Wille und Vorstellung* (1819; *The World as Will and Idea*, much more than the social or ethical order is upturned. In place of God, the good, reason, soul, or heart, Schopenhauer installs the will, as reality's true inner nature, the metaphysical to everything physical in the world. In Schopenhauer, there is no question of a Hegelian struggle to achieve a more comprehensive good. There is rather the strife of will with itself, manifested by fate in the form of chance and error and by the tragic personages themselves. Both fate and men represent one and the same will, which lives and appears in them all. Its individual manifestations, however, in the form of such phenomena as chances, errors, or men, fight against and destroy each other.

Schopenhauer accordingly rejects the idea of poetic justice: "the demand for so-called poetical justice rests on entire misconception of the nature of tragedy, and, indeed, of the nature of the world itself. . . . The true sense of tragedy is the deeper insight, that it is not his own individual sins that the hero atones for, but original sin, *i.e.*, the crime of existence itself. . . ." Schopenhauer distinguishes three types of tragic representation: (1) "by means of a character of extraordinary wickedness . . . **Schopen-** who becomes the author of the misfortune"; (2) "blind **hauer's** fate—*i.e.*, chance and error" (such as the title characters in **three types** Shakespeare's *Romeo and Juliet* and "most of the tragedies of the ancients"); and (3) when "characters of ordinary morality . . . are so situated with regard to each other that their position compels them, knowingly and with their eyes open, to do each other the greatest injury, without any one of them being entirely in the wrong" (such as, "to a certain extent," *Hamlet*).

This last kind of tragedy seems to Schopenhauer far to surpass the other two. His reason, almost too grim to record, is that it provides the widest possible play to the destructive manifestations of the will. It brings tragedy, so to speak, closest to home:

those powers which destroy happiness and life are such that their path to us also is open at every moment; we see the greatest sufferings brought about by entanglements that our fate might also partake of, and through actions that perhaps we also are capable of performing . . . ; then, shuddering, we feel ourselves already in the midst of hell.

Schopenhauer finds tragedy to be the summit of poetical art, because of the greatness of its effect and the difficulty of its achievement. According to Schopenhauer, the egoism of the protagonist is purified by suffering almost to the purity of nihilism. His personal motives become dispersed as his insight into them grows; "the complete knowledge of the nature of the world, which has a quieting effect on the will, produces resignation, the surrender not merely of life, but of the very will to live."

Schopenhauer's description has limited application to tragic denouements in general. In the case of his own archetypal hero, the hero's end seems merely the mirror image of his career, an oblivion of resignation or death that follows an oblivion of violence. Instead of a dialogue between higher and lower worlds of morality or feeling (which take place even in Shakespeare's darkest plays), Schopenhauer posits a succession of states as helpless in knowledge as in blindness. His "will" becomes a synonym for all that is possessed and necessity-ridden.

Nietzsche's *Geburt der Tragödie aus dem Geiste der Musik* (1872) was deeply influenced by Schopenhauer. The two elements of tragedy, says Nietzsche, are the Apollonian (related to the Greek god Apollo, here used as a symbol of measured restraint) and the Dionysian (from Dionysus, the Greek god of ecstasy). His conception of the Apollonian is the equivalent of what Schopenhauer called the individual phenomenon—the particular chance, error, or man, the individuality of which is merely a mask for the essential truth of reality which it conceals. The Dionysian element is a sense of universal reality, which, according to Schopenhauer, is experienced after the loss of individual egoism. The "Dionysian ecstasy," as defined by Nietzsche, is experienced "not as individuals but as the *one* living being, with whose creative joy we are united."

Nietzsche dismisses out of hand one of the most venerable features of the criticism of tragedy, the attempt to reconcile the claims of ethics and art. He says that the events of a tragedy are "supposed" to discharge pity and fear and are "supposed" to elevate and inspire by the triumph of noble principles at the sacrifice of the hero. But art, he says, must demand purity within its own sphere. To explain tragic myth, the first requirement is to seek the pleasure that is peculiar to it in the purely aesthetic sphere, without bringing in pity, fear, or the morally sublime.

The essence of this specifically aesthetic tragic effect is that it both reveals and conceals, causing both pain and joy. The drama's exhibition of the phenomena of suffering individuals (Apollonian elements) forces upon the audience "the struggle, the pain, the destruction of phenomena," which in turn communicates "the exuberant fertility of the universal." The spectators then "become, as it were, one with the infinite primordial joy in existence, and . . . we anticipate, in Dionysian ecstasy, the indestructibility and eternity of this joy." Thus, he says, there is a desire "to see tragedy and at the same time to get beyond all seeing . . . to hear and at the same time long to get beyond all hearing."

The inspired force of Nietzsche's vision is mingled with a sense of nihilism:

"only after the spirit of science has been pursued to its limits, . . . may we hope for a rebirth of tragedy . . . I understand by the spirit of science the faith that first came to light in the person of Socrates—the faith in the explicability of nature and in knowledge as a panacea."

Nietzsche would replace the spirit of science with a conception of existence and the world as an aesthetic phenomenon and justified only as such. Tragedy would enjoy a prominent propagandistic place. It is "precisely the tragic myth that has to convince us that even

the ugly and disharmonic are part of an artistic game that the will in the eternal amplitude of its pleasure plays with itself." And, consummately: "we have art in order that we may not perish through truth."

Tragedy in music. Musical dissonance was Nietzsche's model for the double effect of tragedy. The first edition of his book was titled *The Birth of Tragedy out of the Spirit of Music,* another influence from Schopenhauer, for whom music differed from all the other arts in that it is not a copy of a phenomenon but the direct copy of the will itself. He even called the world "embodied music, . . . embodied will." Nietzsche's theorizing on the relation of the tragic theme to art forms other than the drama was in fact confirmed in such operas as Mussorgsky's version of Pushkin's tragedy *Boris Godunov,* Verdi's of *Macbeth* and *Othello,* and Gounod's *Faust.* In contrast to these resettings of received forms, Wagner, Verdi, and Bizet achieved a new kind of tragic power for Romanticism in the theme of the operatic love-death in, respectively, *Tristan and Isolde, Aida,* and *Carmen.* Thus, the previous progression of the genre from tragedy to tragicomedy to romantic tragedy continued to a literary-musical embodiment of what Nietzsche called "tragic dithyrambs."

An earlier prophecy than Nietzsche's regarding tragedy and opera was made by the German poet Friedrich von Schiller in a letter of 1797 to Goethe:

I have always trusted that out of opera, as out of the choruses of the ancient festival of Bacchus, tragedy would liberate itself and develop in a nobler form. In opera, servile imitation of nature is dispensed with . . . here is . . . the avenue by which the ideal can steal its way back into the theatre.

Critical theory in the 20th century. In the 20th century, discussion of tragedy was sporadic until the aftermath of World War II. Then it enjoyed new vigour, perhaps to compensate for, or help explain, the dearth of genuine tragic literature, either in the novel or in the theatre. In the 1950s and 1960s countless full-length studies, articles, and monographs variously sought the essence, the vision, the view of life, or the spirit of tragedy out of a concern for the vital culture loss were the death of tragedy to become a reality. They also attempted to mediate the meaning of tragedy to a public that was denied its reality, save in revivals or an occasional approximation. Since the Romantic critics first ventured beyond the Aristotelean categories to consider tragedy, or the tragic, as a sense of life, there was an increasing tendency to regard tragedy not merely as drama but as a philosophical form. It is noteworthy that the Spanish philosopher Miguel de Unamuno's influential book, *The Tragic Sense of Life* (1921), barely mentions the formal drama.

From the time of Aristotle, tragedy has achieved importance primarily as a medium of self-discovery—the discovery of man's place in the universe and in society. That is the main concern of Aristotle in his statements about reversal, recognition, and catharsis, though it remained for the Romantic critics to point it out. The loss of this concern in the facile plays of the 19th and 20th centuries resulted in the reduction of tragic mystery to confused sentimentalism. Critics of the 20th century, being less certain even than Schopenhauer or Nietzsche of what man's place in the scheme of things may be, experimented with a variety of critical approaches, just as contemporary dramatists experimented with various "theatres." Although these critics lacked the philosophical certainties of earlier theorists, they had a richer variety of cultures and genres to instruct them. The hope of both critics and dramatists was that this multiplicity would produce not mere impressionism or haphazard eclecticism but new form and new meaning. (L.C.)

BIBLIOGRAPHY. A lengthier development of many of the points made in this article may be found in R.B. SEWALL, *The Vision of Tragedy* (1959). Among the works examining the origins of tragedy in ancient Greece are H.D.F. KITTO, *Greek Tragedy,* 3rd ed. (1961); and J. JONES, *On Aristotle and Greek Tragedy* (1962). Works concentrating on modern tragedy include: GEORGE STEINER, *The Death of Tragedy* (1961); WALTER KERR, *Tragedy and Comedy* (1968); and RAYMOND WILLIAMS, *Modern Tragedy* (1966). Special aspects of tragedy are treated in J.M.R. MARGESON, *The Origins of English Tragedy* (1967); EUGENE VINAVER, *Racine and Poetic*

Nietzsche's division of tragedy in two elements

Tragedy (1955); A.C. BRADLEY, Shakespearean Tragedy (1904); and GEORGE LUKACS, The Historical Novel, ch. 2 (1962), a Marxist view. A useful anthology of writings on tragedy is LIONEL ABEL (ed.), Moderns on Tragedy (1967). Other recent works on the subject include: RICHMOND HATHORN, Tragedy, Myth, and Mystery (1962); MURRAY KRIEGER, The Tragic Vision: Variations on a Theme in Literary Interpretation (1960); and DOROTHY KROOK, Elements of Tragedy (1969).

Trajan

Trajan, the first Roman emperor to have been born in the provinces, revived expansive imperialism, built magnificently, and, in reaction against the despotism of Domitian, one of his predecessors, took care to maintain correct relations with the Senate.

Trajan, wreathed portrait bust of gilt bronze, early 2nd century AD. In the Museum of Archeology, Ankara.
By courtesy of the Museum of Archeology, Ankara

Origins and early career. Marcus Ulpius Traianus was born, probably on September 15, AD 53, at Italica (modern Santiponce, near Seville) in the Roman province of Baetica, southern Spain. Although his ancestors, whether or not original settlers, were undoubtedly Roman, or at least Italian, they may well have intermarried with natives. While his family was probably well-to-do and prominent in Baetica, his father was the first to have a career in the imperial service. He became a provincial governor and in 67–68 commander of a legion in the war the future emperor Vespasian was conducting against the Jews. In 70, Vespasian, by then emperor, rewarded him with a consulship and a few years later enrolled him among the patricians, Rome's most aristocratic group within the senatorial class. Finally, he became governor, successively, of Syria and Asia.

Early military career

Although there is little documentation of Trajan's early life, presumably the future emperor grew up either in Rome or in various military headquarters with his father. He served ten years as a legionary staff tribune. In this capacity he was in Syria while his father was governor, probably in 75. He then held the traditional magistracies through the praetorship, which qualified him for command of a legion in Spain in 89. Ordered to take his troops to the Rhine to aid in quelling a revolt against the emperor Domitian by the governor of Upper Germany, Trajan probably arrived after the revolt had already been suppressed by the governor of Lower Germany. Trajan clearly enjoyed the favour of Domitian, who in 91 allowed him to hold one of the two consulships, which even under the empire remained most prestigious offices.

When Domitian had been assassinated by a palace conspiracy on September 18, 96, the conspirators had put forward as emperor, and the Senate had welcomed, the elderly and innocuous Nerva. His selection represented a reaction against Domitian's autocracy and a return to the cooperation between emperor and Senate that had characterized the reign of Vespasian. Nevertheless, the imperial guard (the praetorian cohorts) forced the new em-

peror to execute the assassins who had secured the throne for him. There was also discontent among the frontier commanders. Therefore, in October 97, Nerva adopted as his successor Trajan, whom he had made governor of upper Germany and who seemed acceptable both to the army commanders and to the Senate. On January 1, 98, Trajan entered upon his second consulship as Nerva's colleague. Soon thereafter, on January 27 or 28, Nerva died, and Trajan was accepted as emperor by both the armies and the Senate. Before his accession, Trajan had married Pompeia Plotina, to whom he remained devoted. As the marriage was childless, he took into his household his cousin Hadrian, who became a favourite of Plotina.

Domestic policies as emperor. Trajan deified Nerva and included his name in his imperial title, which took the form Imperator Caesar Divi Nervae Filius Nerva Traianus Augustus (Emperor Caesar, Deified Nerva's Son, Nerva Trajan Augustus). In 114, he placed before Augustus the adjective Optimus (Best). This was undoubtedly intended, by recalling the epithets Optimus Maximus, applied to Jupiter, to present Trajan as the god's representative on earth.

Trajan listed after his names the republican powers and offices borne by his predecessors. To this traditional sequence he added, but only in the provinces, proconsul, a title that indicated a military command. Although the emperor Augustus, whose power had rested on control of the armies, had avoided any suggestion of the military basis of his control, after a century of imperial rule, such a title probably caused no offense, particularly when avoided in Italy and Rome, which had traditionally been exempt from the presence of legions or of military commands. Thus Trajan's formula followed the pattern set by his predecessors, and his slight changes and additions need not be regarded as evidence for an autocratic view of his position.

Despite his outward "constitutionality," Trajan was in fact a much more positive ruler than Nerva had been during his short reign. Instead of returning to Rome at once to accept from the Senate the imperial powers, he remained for nearly a year on the Rhine and Danube, either to make preparations for a coming campaign into Dacia (modern Transylvania and Romania) or to ensure that discipline was restored and defenses strengthened. He sent orders to Rome for the execution of the praetorians who had forced Nerva to execute the conspirators who had brought him to the throne. He gave the soldiers only half the cash gifts customary on the accession of a new emperor, but in general, he dealt fairly, if strictly, with the armies.

Relations with Senate and people

When he returned to Rome in 99, he behaved with respect and affability toward the Senate. He was generous to the populace of Rome, to whom he distributed considerable cash gifts, and increased the number of poor citizens who received free grain from the state. For Italy and the provinces, he remitted the gold that cities had customarily sent to emperors on their accession. He also lessened taxes and was probably responsible for an innovation for which Nerva is given credit—the institution of public funds (alimenta) for the support of poor children in the Italian cities. Such endowments had previously been established in Italy by private individuals, notably by Trajan's close friend, the orator and statesman Pliny the Younger, for his native Comum (modern Como) in northern Italy.

For the administration of the provinces, Trajan tried to secure competent and honest officials. He sent out at least two special governors to provinces whose cities had suffered financial difficulties. One was Pliny the Younger, whom he dispatched to Bithynia-Pontus, a province on the northern coast of Asia Minor. The exchange of letters between Pliny and Trajan during the two years of Pliny's governorship are preserved as the tenth book of his correspondence. They constitute a most important source for Roman provincial administration. In one exchange, Pliny asked Trajan how he should handle the rapidly spreading sect of Christians, who, refusing to conform to normal religious practices, suffered from great unpopularity but were, as far as Pliny could see, harmless. In his reply, a model of judiciousness, Trajan advised Pliny not to ferret out Christians nor to accept unsupported charges and to punish only those whose behaviour was ostentatiously recalcitrant. Clearly in Trajan's time the Roman government did not yet have (and, indeed, was not to have for another century) any policy of persecution of the Christians; official action was based on the need to maintain good order, not on religious hostility. The corrrespondence also illustrates the wasteful expenditure of cities on lavish buildings and competition for municipal honours, an indication that the finances of the empire were already beginning to show inflationary trends.

Public works

Trajan undertook or encouraged extensive public works in the provinces, Italy, and Rome: roads, bridges, aqueducts, the reclamation of wastelands, the construction of harbours and buildings. Impressive examples survive in Spain, in North Africa, in the Balkans, and in Italy. Rome, in particular, was enriched by Trajan's projects. A new aqueduct brought water from the north. A splendid public bathing complex was erected on the Esquiline Hill, and a magnificent new forum was designed by the architect Apollodorus of Damascus. It comprised a porticoed square in the centre of which stood a colossal equestrian statue of the Emperor. On either side, the Capitoline and Quirinal hills were cut back for the construction of two hemicycles in brick, which, each rising to several stories, provided streets of shops and warehouses. Behind the square was a public hall, or basilica, and behind this a court flanked by libraries for Greek and Latin books and backed by a temple. In this court rose the still-standing Column of Trajan, an innovative work of art that commemorated his Dacian Wars. Its cubical base, decorated with reliefs of heaps of captured arms, later received Trajan's ashes. The column itself is encircled by a continuous spiral relief, portraying scenes from the two Dacian campaigns. These provide a commentary on the campaigns and also a repertory of Roman and Dacian arms, armour, military buildings, and scenes of fighting. The statue of Trajan on top of the column was removed during the Middle Ages and replaced in 1588 by the present one of St. Peter.

Military campaigns. Trajan's civil accomplishments were impressive but, except for the *alimenta*, not innovative. He is renowned chiefly for abandoning the policy, established by Augustus and generally adhered to by his successors, of not extending the Roman frontiers. Despite his title Germanicus, his first year on the Rhine–Danube frontier was not marked by any major conquest. In 101, however, he resumed the invasion of Dacia that Domitian had been forced to abandon by Decebalus, the country's redoubtable king. In two campaigns (101–102 and 105–106), Trajan captured the Dacian capital of Sarmizegethusa (modern Varhély), which lay to the north of the Iron Gate in western Romania; Decebalus evaded capture by suicide. Trajan created a new province of Dacia north of the Danube within the curve of the Carpathian Mountains. This provided land for Roman settlers, opened for exploitation rich mines of gold and salt, and established a defensive zone to absorb movements of nomads from the steppes of southern Russia.

Invasion of Dacia

Trajan's second major war was against the Parthians, Rome's traditional enemy in the east. The chronology of his campaigns is uncertain. In preparation for them, in 105/106, one of his generals annexed the Nabataean kingdom, the part of Arabia extending east and south of Judaea. Next, about 110, the Parthians deposed the pro-Roman King of Armenia, whereupon, in 113/114, Trajan campaigned to reinstate him. In the following year (115) he annexed upper Mesopotamia and, in the same or next year, moved down the Tigris to capture the Parthian capital of Ctesiphon. He reached the Persian Gulf, where he is said to have wept because he was too old to repeat Alexander's achievements in India. Late in 115, Trajan barely escaped death in an earthquake that devastated Antioch. In 116, revolts broke out both in the newly conquered territories and in Jewish communities in several of the eastern provinces. Trajan, discouraged and in ill health, left Antioch for Rome. He died in his 64th year on August 8 or 9, 117, at Selinus (modern Selindi) on the southern coast of Asia Minor. His ashes were returned to Rome

Death and succession

for a state funeral and burial in the base of his column. Just before his death was made public, it was announced that he had adopted Hadrian, who in 100 had married Trajan's favourite niece. Although Hadrian differed completely in temperament from Trajan and initially had not been advanced with any unusual speed, Trajan, a few years before his death, had made him governor of Syria, where he was responsible for the logistical support of the Parthian campaign. But Trajan did not then adopt him or give any indication of a choice of successor. Hence contemporary gossip stamped the announcement of Hadrian's last-minute adoption as a fiction put out by the empress Plotina, though it was probably a genuine deathbed decision.

Assessment. The lack of adequate historical sources for Trajan's reign makes it difficult to give an estimate of his personality and policies. Although he has been regarded by some as having brought to the rule a provincial point of view, his upbringing had been in upper class Roman circles and in the imperial administration. His portraits in busts and on coins show a very individual face, hair brushed forward, making him look "low browed," whose large, strong features suggest a man of decision and action, not one of culture and thought like his successor, Hadrian. By the opening of the 2nd century, the empire had become monarchical—whatever outward respect was paid by "good" emperors to the tradition of Augustus that the *princeps,* the "first man" in the state, was an agent of the Senate and Roman people. Trajan's coins, inscriptions, and monuments emphasize his mission to bring happiness, security, equity, justice, and well-being to the empire. Pliny the Younger's *Panegyric* of AD 100 portrays him as the ideal ruler, the best and wisest of men who, most like the gods in character and intelligence, governs with the cooperation of other good men and in the service of the state. Possibly Pliny was holding up to Trajan a "mirror of the prince" to persuade him to conform to this characterization. In any case, Trajan, though confident of his personal abilities and ambitious for military glory, appears sincerely to have tried to maintain and improve the commonwealth.

Later Romans, dazzled by Trajan's achievements and buildings, regarded his reign as the apogee of the early empire. Under Hadrian, the historian Florus felt that the empire, senescent during the 1st century, had been rejuvenated by Trajan. In the 4th century another historian, Eutrupius, stated that the highest compliment that the Senate could pay to an emperor was to hail him as *felicior Augusto, melior Traiano,* "more fortunate than Augustus, better than Trajan." A medieval legend mentioned by Dante told how Trajan's justice and pity toward a poor widow moved Pope Gregory the Great (*c.* 600) to pray successfully for Trajan's admission to paradise. The modern Romanians claim, rightly or wrongly, descent from the Romans whom Trajan settled in Dacia.

Modern historians differ in their judgments of Trajan both as a ruler and as a conqueror. Some think that he genuinely wished to govern in cooperation with the Senate; others, that behind a facade of constitutionality he was actually autocratic. Some hold that his Dacian campaigns redeemed the costly fiasco of Domitian's defeat, brought the empire new revenues, and strengthened the Danubian frontier. Others regard his success as having been prepared by Domitian and his Parthian war as having overstrained the resources of the empire because of his megalomanic desire for military glory. Certainly, despite the Dacian gold, the financial and general economic condition of the empire began during his reign to show signs of breakdown. Moreover, his operations on the northern and eastern frontiers brought no enduring peace. To the north, barbarian pressure increased throughout the following century. Although Hadrian abandoned the eastern annexations, later emperors resumed without marked success the effort to conquer Parthia. Thus his reign may be taken either as the brilliant high noon of internal peace and external success or as a splendid sunset presaging the stormy midnight of the 3rd century.

BIBLIOGRAPHY. B.W. HENDERSON, *Five Roman Emperors,* ch. 8 (1927); *Cambridge Ancient History,* vol. 9, ch. 5–6

(1936), with bibliography; R. SYME, *Tacitus*, 2 vol., ch. 2, 4–5, 19–20 (1958); R. PARIBENI, *Optimus Princeps*, 2 vol. (1926–27), in Italian; and W.H. GROSS in *Paulys Realencyclopädie der classischen Altertumswissenschaft*, suppl. 10, pp. 1035–1113 (1965), have not been superseded. For further bibliographical references, see "Trajan," and "Ulpius Traianus," in the *Oxford Classical Dictionary*, 2nd ed., pp. 1088–1089, 1103 (1970). P. VON ROHDEN and H. DESSAU, *Prosopographia imperii romani saec*, vol. 3, articles 574 and 575 (1898), on Ulpius Traianus and the Emperor, summarize in Latin the ancient evidence. See also: several essays in A. PIGANIOL and H. TERRASSE (eds.), *Les Empereurs romains d'Espagne* (1965); L. ROSSI, *Trajan's Column and the Dacian Wars* (1971); R. SYRNE, "The Fame of Trajan," in *Emperors and Biography* (1971).

(M.Ha.)

Tranquillizer

The tranquillizers, or tranquillizing drugs, are used to allay mental states characterized by anxiety, tension, and hyperactivity. The introduction of these agents in the mid-1950s effectively revolutionized the handling of mental patients. Drugs acting on the nervous system had long been known. These included depressants (such as anesthetics and sedative-hypnotic drugs) and stimulants, or convulsants. The tranquillizers proved to be uniquely useful because of their ability to moderate anxiety while producing a minimum of other effects on the nervous system. The use of the term tranquillizer has been somewhat controversial, and the action of these compounds has been variously referred to as psychotherapeutic ("mind-curing"), phrenotropic ("mind-affecting"), neuroleptic ("nerve-seizing"), ataractic ("tending to tranquillize"), psycholytic ("mind-easing"), and psychosolytic ("psychosis-easing"). Generally, the tranquillizers are placed in two main categories depending upon the chief clinical uses to which they are put. Antipsychotic tranquillizers, used to treat psychoses, are reserpine (and other alkaloids from *Rauwolfia serpentina*) and chlorpromazine (and related phenothiazines); antineurotics, used to treat various classes of neurosis, include meprobamate and chlordiazepoxide (and the related diazepam).

Sites and nature of action. Very little is known about the sites and modes of action of tranquillizers, but it is generally agreed that the antipsychotic tranquillizers act solely on the brain itself, whereas antianxiety agents act on the spinal cord as well. Studies of the site of action of the latter drugs have been carried out by severing the spinal cords of experimental animals at various points to determine where activity occurs. The antipsychotic drugs have been found to affect the levels of the so-called transmitter substances, chemical agents that assist in the transmission of nerve impulses across the gaps between nerve cells. Prominent among the transmitter substances are a number of complex organic nitrogen-containing compounds, particularly serotonin and the catecholamines, epinephrine and norepinephrine.

Biological disposition. *Chlorpromazine.* Absorption, metabolism, and excretion of chlorpromazine may be taken as typical of the phenothiazine tranquillizers. Chlorpromazine is well absorbed in man after either oral administration or injection. It would appear that all tissues take up the drug very rapidly after it has reached the bloodstream; because of this, blood concentrations are usually quite low. Scarcely any of the drug is detectable in the tissues 24 hours after administration.

The availability of radioactively labelled chlorpromazine has permitted extensive studies of its metabolism, or chemical conversion, in the tissues of the body, since the label remains with the compound as it is transformed. The chief metabolic transformation products, or metabolites, are those in which (1) the sulfur atom in the molecule has been oxidized to a sulfoxide, (2) methyl groups have been removed from the terminal nitrogen atom, or (3) a hydroxyl group has been introduced into one of the rings of the molecular structure, often with other groups, called conjugates, attached. The principal metabolite, quantitatively, is chlorpromazine sulfoxide, a compound much less biologically active than the parent drug. The compound from which nitrogen-methyl groups have been removed is only slightly less active than chlorpromazine,

Effect on transmitter substances

but the other metabolites are either much less active or completely inactive.

Chlorpromazine is presumed to cross the blood-brain barrier easily, and the highest concentration of labelled drug administered to rats was found in the cortex of the large hemispheres. After oral administration to rats only about 60 percent of the drug was absorbed, the rest being excreted unmetabolized in the feces within eight or nine days. After subcutaneous injection, metabolic products were found in the urine, and four days later, 97.4 percent of the administered dose had been excreted.

Reserpine. In contrast to chlorpromazine, reserpine is inefficiently absorbed after an oral dose, somewhat less than one percent of the dose being taken up per day. The principal metabolic products are the two main components of the drug molecule, methyl reserpate and trimethoxybenzoic acid. Despite the profound and prolonged tranquillizing action of reserpine and its depletion of serotonin and other transmitter substances in the brain, the level of reserpine detectable in the brain is both low and transient.

Meprobamate. Meprobamate is not attacked by the normal enzymes of digestion, so that—as shown by animal studies—about 10 percent of the orally administered drug is excreted unchanged in urine, along with certain metabolites (glucuronides). Similar results are seen in man. The drug is readily absorbed from the gastrointestinal tract of animals including man, and distribution in the body takes place rapidly after administration. About 60 percent of the ingested dose is excreted by experimental dogs as a metabolite bearing a hydroxyl group. In humans, there is a stimulation of meprobamate metabolism by the drug itself, suggesting that enzyme induction plays an important role in the development of tolerance.

Chlordiazepoxide. Blood levels of chlordiazepoxide are low, even after high oral doses. The unchanged drug is excreted in the urine to the extent of 1 percent to 2 percent of the administered dose each day; a further 3 to 6 percent is excreted in combined form. Excretion continues at a low rate for several days after administration is stopped. By measuring the fluorescence of chlordiazepoxide in human blood plasma at regular intervals after administration of oral doses of 15–30 milligrams, investigators found a half-life of about 24 hours for the drug; tracer studies give a similar result. The half-life of urinary excretion is 20 hours, and about 20 percent of the dose can be recovered in the feces. The major metabolite in the urine is the demethylaminated product, traces of which are also present in the plasma.

Tranquillizers in the management of psychoses. The two classes of tranquillizers used in the treatment of psychoses are different chemically and have different histories; yet they were introduced into modern Western medical practice at about the same time. Crude *Rauwolfia* root had been used in India for centuries as a sedative and hypotensive agent; the isolation of the active principle, reserpine, was accomplished in 1952. Its use (initially as the ground root) in Western medicine began in 1953. Chlorpromazine, a synthetic compound, was first used as a temperature lowering drug and then as an antivomiting agent. During an investigation of its sedative side effect, its utility in the treatment of psychoses was discovered, and it has been in use for this purpose since 1954. The introduction of reserpine and, shortly afterward, chlorpromazine into psychotherapeutic practice greatly altered the climate in mental institutions, generally changing them from custodial establishments into true therapeutic hospitals. Due largely to these new drugs, mentally disturbed patients were treated earlier and more effectively. In 1956 a long-term trend in rising mental hospital admissions was reversed; from 1956 to 1969 the resident mental patient population in the United States declined 19 percent while the total population of the country increased 20 percent. Similar results were obtained in Europe as well.

Reserpine. Although reserpine has been synthesized, the drug used for medical purposes is obtained from plant sources. Various crude, pure, or partially purified preparations are employed. High doses of reserpine can pro-

Introduction of tranquillizers

duce depression in patients; for this and other reasons, reserpine is not used extensively today in the treatment of psychoses. It is used, however, in the treatment of hypertension, in which much lower doses can be given. Side effects of the drug include gastric irritation, slowing of the heart, increased salivation, nasal congestion, and edema.

Chlorpromazine. Chlorpromazine is prepared synthetically (by the reaction of *m*-chlorodiphenylamine with sulfur, followed by alkylation with 3-dimethylaminopropylchloride). The product is crystallized in the form of one of its salts; and the drug is administered in this form.

Chlor-
promazine,
the
reference
compound

The utility of chlorpromazine in the treatment of psychoses is well established, although the mechanism of its action is still obscure. A variety of chemical and neurological changes have been cited to explain the antipsychotic effect, but no definite connection has been established. Chlorpromazine is generally considered the standard, or "reference," compound in the treatment of psychotic patients. It is used to control agitation, to modify delusions and hallucinations, and to restore or increase the patient's response to psychotherapy. In some cases, psychiatric patients treated with chlorpromazine in institutions must be maintained on lower doses of the drug after discharge to prevent relapse. In other cases, however, once the acute phase of the psychosis has been treated, it is possible gradually to reduce the use of the drug and eventually to eliminate it altogether.

Among the conditions treated with chlorpromazine are: chronic delirium, nausea and vomiting, mania, melancholia, conceptual disorders, hypermotor activity, diminished emotional response, lack of verbal communication, catatonia, and paranoia. Many so-called psychosomatic conditions that are complicated by stress, such as arthritis, severe tension headache, gastrointestinal disorders, dermatological conditions, and asthmatic states, have responded to chlorpromazine. The drug has also been found useful in treating chronic alcoholics and mental defectives and in facilitating withdrawal from narcotics or other drugs. Chlorpromazine and other phenothiazines are used to reduce the need for preanesthetic and postanesthetic medication in general surgery and to reduce the amounts of narcotics and other analgesics needed in childbirth, thereby lowering the risk of respiratory depression for the mother and infant.

Chlorpromazine and other phenothiazines produce hepatic obstruction in a small percentage of patients, but this disappears after discontinuance of the drug. A very few cases of agranulocytosis (destruction of certain blood cells) have been noted. With large doses of phenothiazines a few persons may exhibit neuromuscular reactions resembling parkinsonism. Other side effects observed are skin pigmentation, lactation, photosensitivity, weight gain, and absence of menstrual discharge.

Tranquillizers used in the management of anxiety. *Meprobamate.* Meprobamate is used primarily in the treatment of anxiety and tension states, with such associated symptoms as irritability, restlessness, insomnia, and muscle tension. It may be used to facilitate psychotherapy. Although meprobamate is used predominantly in the treatment of certain neurotic conditions, it has also been used successfully in the treatment of psychotics in combination with phenothiazines. It has, however, little value in the treatment of delusions or hallucinations. Other conditions in which meprobamate has been successfully employed are behavioral disorders in children, headaches associated with emotional disturbances, preoperative and postoperative anxiety, and premenstrual tension. It is also used during childbirth and as an adjunct in the treatment of dermatological conditions.

Mepro-
bamate
in
anxiety
treatment

Meprobamate has been employed in the treatment of allergic states and gastrointestinal disturbances of emotional origin. It relieves insomnia, but it is not a true hypnotic. In orthopedic disorders and rheumatic conditions, meprobamate is often used to relieve muscular spasms. It is also useful in reducing spasticity and improving motor performance in patients suffering from cerebral palsy or spinal cord injuries. Meprobamate is helpful in certain patients suffering from minor epileptic attacks, although it is ineffective in cases of severe epileptic seizures.

Physical dependence on meprobamate may be produced after high doses for prolonged periods. Otherwise, the drug has only minor side effects, such as skin rashes, drowsiness, and allergic reactions.

For commercial use meprobamate is prepared synthetically. (The appropriate propanediol is made by condensation of formaldehyde with 2-methylvaleraldehyde or by reduction of the corresponding malonic ester with lithium aluminum hydride. It is then converted to meprobamate by ester exchange with urethane.)

Benzodiazepines. Two benzodiazepines, chlordiazepoxide and diazepam, are used clinically in the treatment of anxiety. Chlordiazepoxide and diazepam are both employed in a variety of clinical conditions, including convulsive states and neuromuscular and cardiovascular disorders. They have been used to moderate alcohol-withdrawal symptoms to help rehabilitate the chronic alcholic. They have also been employed to aid in preoperative and postoperative sedation and to relieve anxiety in dental patients. The drugs do not affect delusions or hallucinations, but they render the patient more accessible to psychotherapy. They are used adjunctively in antidepressant and anticonvulsant therapy. The most common side effects are drowsiness and ataxia (lack of muscular coordination), but skin rashes, nausea, dizziness, constipation, fainting, and headaches have been observed. Physical dependence also can occur and is a cause for caution in prolonged use.

Used to
treat
alcoholism

The benzodiazepine tranquillizers were discovered as the result of an unexpected chemical rearrangment observed when a synthetic procedure that had been expected to yield a certain complex organic nitrogen compound—a quinazoline derivative—gave instead another product, which proved to be a benzodiazepine.

BIBLIOGRAPHY. D.H. EFRON (ed.), *Psychotomimetic Drugs* (1970); M. GORDON (ed.), *Psychopharmacological Agents*, 2 vol. (1964–67), and with G.E. ULLYOT, "Psychopharmacological Agents," in the *Kirk-Othmer Encyclopedia of Chemical Technology*, vol. 16, pp. 640–679 (1968); NATIONAL INSTITUTES OF HEALTH, *Summary of Research at the National Institute of Neurological Diseases and Blindness*, research profile no. 1, *Cerebrovascular Disorder (Strokes)*, research profile no. 2 (1967); I.J. PACHTER and A.A. RUBIN, "Anti-Psychotic and Anti-Anxiety Agents," in *Annual Reports in Medicinal Chemistry, 1968* (1969); E. USDIN and D.H. EFRON, *Psychotropic Drugs and Related Compounds*, Public Health Service Publication No. 1589 (1967).

(M.Go.)

Transfer of Training

Will one's knowledge of English help him learn German? Are skillful table-tennis (Ping-Pong) players generally good court-tennis players? Can a child learn to multiply if he does not know how to add? These questions represent the problems of transfer of training: the influence the learning of one skill has on the learning or performance of another.

KINDS OF TRANSFER

Basically three kinds of transfer can occur: positive, negative, and zero. The following examples from hypothetical experiments, purposely uncomplicated by distracting detail, illustrate each. Suppose a group of students learn a task, B, in ten practice sessions. Another group of equivalent students, who previously had learned another task, A, is found to reach the same level of performance on task B in only five practice sessions. Since the average number of practice sessions required to learn B was reduced from ten to five, transfer of training from task A to task B is said to be positive $(10 - 5 = +5)$. Many successful training aids, such as those that simulate the cockpit of an airplane and that are applied to teach people how to use instruments for flying blind without leaving the ground, produce positive transfer; when students who have preliminary training in such trainers are compared to those who do not, those with preliminary training almost invariably require less practice in achieving the desired level of skill.

Positive,
negative,
and zero
transfer

Sometimes the effect of transfer of training is to hamper effectiveness in subsequent activity. If after learning task A a group of people need 15 practice sessions to learn task

B whereas only 10 sessions are required for those without any previous training in task A, then task A is said to lead to negative transfer of training on task B (10 − 15 = −5). Having learned to drive on the right side of the road often is observed to produce negative transfer for the tourist from Japan or continental Europe or North America when he is travelling in Great Britain, where cars are to be driven on the left-hand side of the road.

The degree to which transfer of training occurs between two different tasks is often minimal and may be so small that it is called zero transfer. If learning task B with or without previous training in task A requires ten practice sessions, then the amount of transfer from one task to the other is said to be zero (10 − 10 = 0). Learning to knit Argyle socks is apt to produce zero transfer of training in learning to sing an operatic aria in French.

Although in contemporary psychology transfer of training is a distinct topic of investigation with its own experimental designs and procedures for measurement, its implications pervade practically all of psychology, from conditioning to personality development. The Russian physiologist Ivan P. Pavlov (1849–1936) discovered that when a dog is conditioned to salivate in response to a sound wave of 1,000 cycles per second, it will also salivate if it is next exposed to a tone of 900 cycles per second, although typically the volume of saliva will be slightly reduced. In this case, transfer of training occurs between two similar auditory stimuli; in general, phenomena of this sort are called stimulus generalization. At the very root of modern theories of personality development is the assumption that what a person learns during his childhood will show a pervasive degree of transfer to his adult behaviour. In some cases stimulus generalization mediates this transfer. Some cases of excessive fears may have their origins in unpleasant experiences during early life.

EDUCATION AND TRANSFER

The experimental study of transfer of training has historical roots in problems of educational practice. Educators in Western countries at the end of the 19th century widely endorsed the doctrine of formal discipline, contending that psychological abilities, called "mental faculties" by such philosophers as Saint Thomas Aquinas (1225–74), could be strengthened, like muscles, through exercise. By learning geometry, one was expected to improve his ability to reason; studying Latin was held to "strengthen" the so-called faculty of memory, and so on. Although what contemporary educators have demoted from the doctrine to the theory of formal discipline once seemed reasonable to many, experimental tests have refuted it. When the reasoning abilities of groups of mathematics students in secondary schools were compared with those of other equally talented students who had not had the same mathematical training, no differences in general logical effectiveness were observed between the groups.

An alternative theory of identical elements was proposed in which it was postulated that transfer between activities would take place only if they shared common elements or features. Thus it was predicted that one's training in addition would transfer to his ability to learn how to multiply. It was reasoned that both tasks share identical features, multiplication basically requiring a series of successive additions, and that both tasks demand the individual's concentration.

But the identical-elements formulation soon came under attack when experimental results suggested that one's understanding of general principles, rather than the presence of identical task elements, has substantial effects on transfer of training. In one notable experiment, two groups of boys practiced throwing darts at a target placed under about a foot of water. Only one group, however, was instructed about the principle that water bends (refracts) light. According to this principle, the apparent position of the target should vary with the depth of the water. When the target depth was reduced to four inches, the group that had been taught the general principle of refraction adjusted rapidly to the change and exhibited substantial positive transfer; the other boys showed comparative difficulty in learning to hit the target at the shallower level.

These formulations (formal discipline, identical elements, and general principles), when considered carefully, might be recognized as points of view rather than as rigorously specified theories that could lead to unequivocal predictions of the results of new experiments in transfer of training. For example, failure to demonstrate positive transfer between mathematical training and general reasoning ability could be attributed to ineffective teaching of mathematics; in such case, the results need not be interpreted as refuting the theory of formal discipline. If the then-traditional manner of teaching mathematics could be changed to emphasize logical thinking (rather than routinized application of formulas), it was argued that perhaps mathematical training could improve reasoning ability in general. Some theorists also suggested that the positive transfer observed to result when boys learned the principle of refraction was consistent with the hypothesis of identical elements; these theorists observed that a general principle may be considered an element common to many tasks. According to this line of reasoning, the group of boys who exhibited positive transfer with the shift to a new target depth shared the principle of refraction as an element in common with the previous task, along with those of aiming and throwing. By contrast, the youngsters who performed without the benefit of knowing about refraction were held to have gained positive transfer from throwing but to have suffered negative transfer as a result of aiming incorrectly.

EXPERIMENTAL ANALYSIS OF TRANSFER OF TRAINING

The indeterminate character of the broad theoretical formulations offered to account for transfer of training and the often unsuccessful ways in which they were applied to the practical problems of classroom teaching led some psychologists to retreat to the laboratory in the hope of identifying more clear-cut, fundamental processes in transfer of training. As a result, a number of different transfer-of-training phenomena were discovered, several of which may be reviewed as follows.

Stimulus and response similarity. The method of paired-associate learning, in which a person is asked to learn to associate one syllable or word with another (*e.g., complete–hot, safe–green, wild–soft*), encouraged the investigation of the influence of stimulus and response similarity on transfer of learning. Typically these pairs of verbal items are presented to the laboratory subject so that the first, or stimulus, member (*e.g., complete*) is exposed alone, followed after a short interval by the second, or response, member (*e.g., hot*). The subject's task is to respond to the stimulus term before the response term appears, as when an English-speaking student in learning French is supposed to respond to *le livre* with *the book*.

When two successive lists of paired associates are learned in which the stimulus elements are the same but the response terms are changed (*e.g., complete–hot* in the first list and *complete–new* in the second), negative transfer typically results. Apparently, in learning the second list the subject tends to respond to the stimulus term (*e.g., complete*) with the previously learned correct response term (*e.g., hot*), the result being interference with new learning to produce negative transfer. If he were learning the second list without having learned the first, the subject would not be so handicapped.

Another question concerns the sort of transfer that results when response terms are different and stimulus elements are similar but not identical; for example, *entire* is similar to *complete*. After one has learned *complete–hot*, the experimental evidence is that his ability to learn *entire–new* becomes definitely more difficult. Both *entire* and *complete* seem to have a tendency to evoke the response *hot* and to be incompatible with subsequently learning the association of *entire* with *new*. The principle that appears to operate in such situations is that the greater the similarity in stimulus elements, the greater the degree of negative transfer.

The influence of response (rather than stimulus) similarity on transfer of training is more complex; in paired-asso-

Theories
of transfer

ciate learning, the subject needs to learn the response term of each pair (response learning) and then to remember that it is linked with its appropriate stimulus partner (associative learning). When response terms are relatively difficult to learn (as in the case of unfamiliar or foreign words), the subject tends to profit considerably from learning the first list. But when response terms already have been learned (or are easy to learn), little if any positive transfer is likely to occur. The degree of transfer between lists that contain similar response terms depends both on how similar they are and on their level of difficulty; increasing the similarity between response terms is most likely to increase positive transfer when the response terms are relatively difficult to learn.

Although attempts have been made to formulate an all-embracing theory that would account for the effects of similarity among paired associates on transfer of training, a major obstacle that has prevented fully satisfying results is that the degree of positive or negative transfer is typically a product of many interacting influences beyond those of stimulus and response similarity. For example, the amount of training that the subject receives also has significant effects on transfer. When initial training is given on a simulated task (*e.g.*, learning to operate a set of dummy controls in preparation for a second task of acquiring a complicated skill, such as flying an airplane), negative transfer effects frequently appear during the initital stages of learning the second task and then give way with further training to generally positive transfer effects.

Another stumbling block in developing theoretical explanations has to do with the meaning of the central concept of similarity. In such experiments as those in which the salivary reflex is conditioned to different auditory stimuli, similarity is measured in terms of physical stimulus properties (*e.g.*, pitch or loudness); in other studies, as in paired-associate learning, similarity typically is expressed in terms of verbal meaning. In neither case has a universally adopted method yet been devised to measure similarity in a reliable and precise way; perhaps none can be, simply since there are so many different aspects of physical and linguistic or semantic similarity. Despite these difficulties, efforts to analyze transfer experimentally in terms of the properties of stimulus and response events have been productive in identifying conditions that can be varied to alter the direction and the degree of transfer of training.

Retroactive and proactive inhibition.   Closely related to stimulus and response similarity are phenomena called retroactive inhibition and proactive inhibition; these demonstrate how forgetting seems to result from interfering activities.

In a study of retroactive inhibition, both the experimental and control groups of people learn task A (for example, a list of adjectives) and are tested for their ability to recall A after a specified time interval. The groups differ in what they are asked to do during the interval; the experimental group learns a similar task B (say, another list of words), while the control group is assigned some unrelated activity (for example, naming a series of coloured chips) designed to prevent them from rehearsing task A. The results of numerous studies of retroactive inhibition show that the experimental subjects typically are poorest in recalling information from task A. The interpolated activity, particularly a comparable one such as memorizing a second list of adjectives, apparently interferes with one's ability to recall words from the first list. Habit competition, or what is sometimes called interference, between the items of the original and the interpolated word lists at the time of recall is considered to be one of the major sources of the negative transfer exhibited in retroactive inhibition.

Experimental designs for demonstrating proactive inhibition differ from those used for showing retroactive inhibition in that the experimental group learns task B before, instead of after, task A. Whereas B was a task that was interpolated between the learning and the recall of task A in the retroactive inhibition study, B is a task that precedes the learning of task A in the proactive inhibition

study. To evaluate the effects on the experimental subjects of their having learned B prior to A, the control people are instructed to relax during the time the experimental group is learning B. Typically an experimental subject's ability to recall from task A is inferior to that of a control person, the degree of inferiority depending in part on how similar the two tasks are; the greater the similarity, the poorer the recall tends to be. Although proactive inhibition, so called to indicate that it acts forward from the first-learned task to the second, produces appreciably less forgetting than does retroactive inhibition, they both support the theory that interference can produce forgetting (see MEMORY: RETENTION AND FORGETTING: *Theories of forgetting*).

Stimulus predifferentiation.   Educational films can be considered as everyday examples of stimulus predifferentiation, in which the individual gets preliminary information to be used in subsequent learning. The student who sees a film describing the various parts of a microscope is likely to be better prepared to learn the requisite skills when confronted with the instrument itself. In laboratory studies of stimulus predifferentiation, the subject is given experience with a particular stimulus situation ahead of time; later he is asked to learn new responses in the same situation. In one illustrative study, subjects first practiced labelling four different lights and then later were asked to learn to press selectively one of four switches, each connected to one light. The rate at which they learned the appropriate pressing reactions was related to how well they had learned to label the lights.

The results of a large number of experiments covering a variety of stimulus predifferentiation techniques suggest that when a learner has an opportunity to become generally acquainted with an environment, he retains some information about its different components that prepares him for learning to make new responses to them. Various explanations have been offered to account for this facilitation; some investigators suggest that the process of labelling enhances the distinctiveness of environmental stimuli for the labeller; others hold that perceptual acquaintance can more sharply differentiate an environment into its component parts for the perceiver or that it may encourage appropriate responses of observing or attending. Nevertheless, no single process has been identified as fundamental in stimulus predifferentiation. Perhaps a number of these processes operate in different combinations from one stimulus-predifferentiation transfer experiment to another, each process representing a different method by which a learner can become familiar with the details of his environment.

Transposition.   Another phenomenon that has received considerable attention in theories of transfer of training is called transposition. An initial report of transposition came from a study in which chickens were trained by rewards to respond to the darker of two gray squares. After this discrimination task was learned, the chickens were shown the originally rewarded gray square along with one that was still darker. They seemed to prefer the darkest gray to the square that had been previously rewarded. This finding was interpreted to support the hypothesis that the birds had initially learned to respond to a relationship (what a human being would call the concept "darker") and that this response to a relationship had been transposed or transferred to the new discrimination. This relational interpretation later was challenged by theorists who offered a formulation to show, on the basis of principles of stimulus generalization, how a response to a relational stimulus could be explained by assuming that organisms do indeed respond to the absolute properties of the stimuli. Both explanations were found to be too simple for the variety of findings obtained with transposition studies. As a result, the interest of many investigators shifted away from demonstrating the relative merits of absolute versus relational interpretations to identifying conditions that seem to influence transposition behaviour. Within this context, newer, more sophisticated formulations have been proposed that consider both the absolute and relational characteristics of the stimuli in transposition studies.

Obstacles to a unified theory of similarity in transfer

Interference theory

Transfer among animals

Learning to learn. When people are asked to learn successive lists of words, their performance tends to improve from one task to another so that much less time is commonly required to learn, say, the tenth list than was needed for mastering the first list. This improvement suggests that information beyond the specific content of lists of words is also learned. It would seem as if the subjects are learning how to learn; that is, they seem to be acquiring learning sets, or expectancies, that transfer from list to list to produce continually improving performance.

Some of the most intensive work on learning sets has been carried out with monkeys that were learning how to solve several hundred discrimination problems in succession. In each problem, the monkey learned which one of two objects (for example, a bottle cap and a cookie cutter) consistently contained a piece of food. Although the solution of each successive problem required the animals to discriminate between two previously unfamiliar objects, performance tended to improve on successive tasks; the monkeys made increasing numbers of correct choices on the second trial of each problem as the process continued. Manifestly there was no cue to indicate the correct choice on the first trial of any specific problem. If the animal responded correctly on the first trial, then on the second trial it would only have to choose the same object to be correct thereafter; if the monkey made an error on the first trial, then the other object would inexorably be the one that should be chosen next. During their efforts to solve the first few problems the monkeys were correct approximately half the time on the second attempt to solve each problem. This success increased to an average of 80 percent correct after each animal had solved 100 problems, to 88 percent after 200 correct solutions, and eventually to 95 percent after 300. Thus, after a long series of separate tasks, all of the same type, the monkey's first response to the next problem usually provided sufficient information for the animal to make the correct choice.

Since each of the successive discrimination problems was different, what actually was being transferred from problem to problem? In these discrimination problems, the monkeys seemed to have several items of information to learn in addition to which one of the two objects contained the rewarding bit of food. The animals apparently had to learn to pay attention to that part of their environment where the objects were placed. To make the correct choice, it would seem that a monkey would have to learn to abandon any preference it might exhibit for objects on either the left or the right; indeed, the animals usually did show such preferences. (The correct object was shifted from side to side in a random sequence to control for these preferences.) Ostensibly, the monkeys also had to learn that one object consistently contained food while the other was always empty. Although these learning sets by themselves would not serve to identify the correct object in each new discrimination problem, it seems likely that they could help the animal locate the reward very rapidly by eliminating initially unprofitable responses.

Reversal learning. In reversal learning, the individual first learns to make a discrimination, such as choosing a black object in a black–white discrimination problem, and then is supposed to learn to reverse his choice— i.e., to choose the white object. Such reversals tend to be difficult for most learners since there are negative transfer effects; e.g., the individual tends to persist in responding to the black object that was originally correct. Eventually, however, one's tendency to make the originally learned selection typically becomes weaker, and he makes the competing response (e.g., to white) more frequently until a point is reached where it is almost consistently evoked. Reversal learning can be accomplished very rapidly when a laboratory animal, such as a monkey, is presented with a series of reversal-learning problems in which the same sequence of shifts is repeated (as when black is initially correct, then white, then black, then white, and so on). After extended reversal training, some animals are able to make the next reversal in the sequence in one trial. They behave as if they have mastered the abstract concept of alternation or of regular sequence.

The speed with which representatives of a given species of animal, including human beings, can be taught to make a reversal of this kind seems to be related to the place biologists assign them in a hierarchy of evolutionary development. On first being exposed to a reversal-learning problem, normally competent adult humans who can use language are likely to achieve a solution with great rapidity. Monkeys can learn to perform equally well after a relatively longer series of reversal-learning tasks; but isopods such as pill bugs or sow bugs, small relatives of crabs and shrimp, have such primitive brains that they seem to be unable to improve their performance at all during a series of reversal-learning tasks.

Evolution and transfer

DEVELOPMENTAL PROCESSES AND TRANSFER

The manner in which a problem is learned seems to have an effect on what is transferred. This conclusion is supported by experiments in which comparisons are made of the relative ease with which children of different ages execute reversal and so-called extradimensional shifts (see CONCEPT FORMATION). In performing both kinds of shift, experimental subjects learn two successive discriminations between two pairs of objects that vary simultaneously in two aspects or dimensions—e.g., white triangle versus black square, and black triangle versus white square. In training subjects initially, discrimination of only one dimension (for example, black–white) is made relevant, with the child's selection of one of the cues (for example, white) being rewarded, while the other (black) is incorrect. After they have learned this, the children are shifted to the second discrimination. In the case of a reversal shift, the same stimulus dimension (black–white) remains relevant, but the child is now to learn to reverse his initial choice; black choices are now rewarded, and white selections become incorrect. For an extradimensional shift, the initially irrelevant dimension (square–triangle) is given relevance by rewarding selection of one of its alternatives and by failing to reward choices for the other.

The relative ease with which human beings learn to make extradimensional and reversal shifts is related to how old they are. Reversal shifts are relatively difficult for young children to learn and are relatively easy for adults to master. As people gain maturity, the relative ease with which they execute a reversal shift tends to increase in comparison with their ability to achieve an extradimensional shift.

Age and transfer

Explanations for these developmental changes seem to be found in the manner in which the individual solves a discrimination problem. Very young children and laboratory animals tend to learn simple habits when faced with a discrimination problem for the first time; for example, they are most likely to learn simply to approach black objects and to avoid white. Reversal shift is often extremely difficult for them, and negative transfer effects are substantial. Subjects who primarily learn simple habits are faced with the task of eliminating one habit (e.g., to choose black) that has been rewarded and then of developing another habit (e.g., to choose white) that previously has not been rewarded.

Human adults, on the other hand, generally find a reversal shift relatively easy; they do not behave as if they simply associate their choices to the relevant stimuli (e.g., white and black) but instead appear symbolically (or conceptually) to react to both of them in terms of their common characteristic (brightness). A similar kind of symbolic or logical response is appropriate in solving reversal-shift problems; since the relevant dimension remains the same, this kind of shift tends to be easier to make than is one involving extradimensional shift, which requires the individual to switch to a new symbolic response (e.g., from brightness to size). In short, when they respond concretely, learners favour their potentials for achieving extradimensional transfer; those who tend to respond symbolically enhance the probability for reversal transfer.

Whatever the validity to be found in theoretical explanations of this sort, review of how transfer phenomena may be influenced suggests that no single principle or simple theory thus far put forward accounts for all of the observed data. Instead, the evidence is that several interacting processes underlie transfer of training and that their relative influence depends both on the nature of the tasks between which transfer takes place as well as on the characteristics of the learning organism. If one seeks to control the degree of transfer, as one does in educational settings, it seems useful to analyze transfer behaviour in terms of a number of component processes—e.g., in the light of notions about stimulus and response similarity, stimulus predifferentiation and response learning, and the symbolic abilities of the learner.

THE PHYSIOLOGY OF TRANSFER OF TRAINING

Although available evidence for a physiological basis of transfer of training is limited, some impressive data already are recorded. Some central (brain and spinal-cord) mechanisms seem to control transfer of training. A long-established transfer phenomenon is cross education, in which there is positive transfer of a skill learned with one part of the body to another, untrained part. For example, a person who learns to throw a dart with his preferred hand exhibits positive transfer to his non-preferred hand.

Cross education

Since different muscles are involved in the equivalent action of opposite limbs, positive transfer resulting from cross education cannot be attributed simply to common muscular movements; instead it would seem that cross education depends on central processes that control the actions of both limbs.

Among highly evolved animals, transfer of training between limbs from opposite sides of the body evidently is mediated through a massive system of neural fibres, known as the corpus callosum, that connects the two hemispheres of the brain. One of the many ways in which the validity of this principle may be demonstrated is first to train blindfolded cats to discriminate with one paw between two different pedals (by feeling raised horizontal lines on one pedal and by detecting raised vertical lines on the other). Since each eye sends some of its nerve impulses to both hemispheres of the cat's brain while each paw only directs impulses to the hemisphere of the brain on the same side of the animal's body, this procedure feeds the sensory information to just one hemisphere. After learning to make the discrimination with one paw (e.g., reward being given only for the pedal with the horizontal pattern), a cat that is confronted with making the same discrimination with the other front paw, which has its connections with the ostensibly "untrained" brain hemisphere, will nevertheless exhibit positive transfer. Indeed, even when the corpus callosum is surgically severed immediately after learning (to "disconnect" the two hemispheres), positive transfer will take place from one front paw to the other; manifestly, transfer of training takes place between connected hemispheres while the animal is learning. If the cat's corpus callosum is severed before it initially learns to discriminate the two pedals, however, no transfer occurs between the animal's limbs; the untrained paw fails to exhibit any benefit from what has been learned with the other paw. In other words, by severing the cat's corpus callosum, the surgeon splits the brain into two independently functioning units. The same kinds of behaviour are observable among other split-brain animals, including chimpanzees and people.

The physiological foundations of transfer of training are not limited merely to the anatomical considerations of the central nervous system. To better understand how physiological processes mediate transfer of training means also to be able to specify more fully the anatomic, electrical, and chemical basis of learning in general, a goal that remains incompletely achieved. Many physiologists and psychologists hold that the search for the neurophysiological foundations of learning can be pursued most profitably by measuring physical and chemical changes that influence the transmission of nerve impulses. It has long been established that chemical changes are part of the process of neural transmission; and it is widely agreed that, in some way, biochemical activities also are responsible for all forms of learning, including transfer of training.

One popular theory in the 1960s was that learning and remembering depend on changes in the molecular structure of such chemicals as ribonucleic acid (RNA) and peptides that are incorporated in the cells of the body, including nerve cells. Some researchers have theorized that memory traces are physically coded within the molecules of cells.

Reports of experiments have been published offering evidence that skills have been transferred from one individual to another by injecting materials taken from the brains (or even other parts of the body) of trained animals into the bodies of untrained organisms (e.g., flatworms, rats, hamsters). These reports have encouraged many to hope that someday one might be able to learn a foreign language, for example, by simply taking a pill instead of through the usual time-consuming practice. Subsequent efforts to repeat such experiments sometimes have given positive results but more often have yielded no evidence of chemical transfer of training from one individual to the next. In view of such inconsistent findings, this question had become a matter of considerable controversy by the 1970s. Many investigators seemed inclined to dismiss the notion that organisms can learn by swallowing chemicals or through injection as another of those oversimplified interpretations that continue to be offered in efforts to account for complex psychophysiological phenomena.

BIBLIOGRAPHY. Introductory psychology texts that discuss transfer of training as an experimental phenomenon and its implications for a wide variety of behaviour are H.H. KENDLER, *Basic Psychology*, 2nd ed. (1968); and H.H. and T.S. KENDLER, *Basic Psychology: Brief Edition* (1971). H.C. ELLIS, *The Transfer of Learning* (1965), presents a general analysis of transfer and includes reprints of important journal articles on the topic. Undergraduate texts that review theories and experimental evidence concerning transfer of training are J. DEESE and S.H. HULSE, *The Psychology of Learning*, 3rd ed. (1967); and J.F. HALL, *The Psychology of Learning* (1966). H.W. REESE, *The Perception of Stimulus Relations: Discrimination Learning and Transposition* (1968); and D.A. RILEY, *Discrimination Learning* (1968), are accounts of how transfer of training influences discrimination learning.

(H.H.K.)

Transition Elements and Their Compounds

The so-called transition elements constitute a group of 56 (the majority of the 105 known elements); while the term transition has no particular chemical significance, it is a convenient name by which to distinguish the similarity of the atomic structures and resulting properties of the elements so designated. They occupy the middle portions of the long periods of the periodic table of elements (see Figure 1) between the groups on the left-hand side

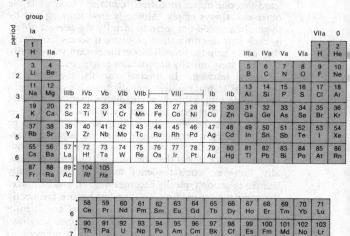

Figure 1: Transition elements in the periodic table.

and the groups on the right. Specifically, they form Groups IIIb, IVb, Vb, VIb, VIIb, and Ib. Of these 56 transition elements only 24 are treated in this article (see Table 1 for list of names), the others being treated elsewhere as explained below.

The article is divided into the following sections:

I. The transition elements as a group

The most striking similarities shared by the 24 elements treated here are that they are all metals and that most of them are hard, strong, and lustrous, have high melting and boiling points, and are good conductors of heat and electricity. The range in these properties is considerable, therefore the statements are comparative with the general properties of all the other elements.

Table 1: Abundance of the Transition Elements in the Earth's Solid Crust

(in grams per ton)

Titanium	5.7×10^2	Ruthenium	0.001
Vanadium	135	Rhodium	0.001
Chromium	102	Palladium	0.01
Manganese	950	Silver	0.07
Iron	5.63×10^3	Hafnium	3.0
Cobalt	25	Tantalum	2.0
Nickel	75	Tungsten	1.5
Copper	55	Rhenium	0.001
Zirconium	165	Osmium	0.001
Niobium	20	Iridium	0.001
Molybdenum	1.5	Platinum	0.005
Technetium	~ 0	Gold	0.004

GENERAL PROPERTIES

Many of the elements are technologically important: titanium, iron, nickel, and copper, for example, are used structurally and in electrical technology. Second, the transition elements form many useful alloys, with one another and with other metallic elements. Third, most of these elements dissolve in mineral acids although a few, such as platinum, silver, and gold, are called "noble"— that is, are unaffected by simple (nonoxidizing) acids.

Without exception, the elements of the main transition series (*i.e.*, excluding the lanthanides and actinides as specified below) exhibit variable valence and form stable compounds in two or more formal oxidation states (valence and oxidation states are explained in the following section). For most transition elements, the compounds formed in at least one oxidation state are coloured and are typically, though not uniformly, paramagnetic (capable of being weakly magnetized). In many of the simple solid compounds, such as some of the oxides, sulfides, and fluorides and in several of the pure metals themselves, complex magnetic behaviour, such as ferromagnetism (capability of being strongly magnetized) or antiferromagnetism, is observed at normal temperatures.

The transition elements may be subdivided into two main types according to the electronic structures of their atoms, which are simply indicated here but fully explained in the section immediately following.

The three main transition series are called the first, second, and third transition series. The first series consists of the nine elements from scandium (symbol Sc, atomic number 21) to copper (symbol Cu, atomic number 29). The second series includes the elements yttrium (symbol Y, atomic number 39) to silver (symbol Ag, atomic number 47). The third series extends from lanthanum (symbol La, atomic number 57) to gold (symbol Au, atomic number 79). Scandium, yttrium, and lanthanum might be excluded from the category of transition elements, because formation of their compounds is somewhat different, but, for convenience and tradition, they are here regarded as transition elements.

There are also two inner transition series. One of these comprises the elements from cerium (symbol Ce, atomic number 58) to lutetium (symbol Lu, atomic number 71); these elements are called the lanthanides because the chemistry of each closely resembles that of lanthanum. Lanthanum itself is often regarded as one of the lanthanides. The other inner transition series can be considered to begin with either actinium (symbol Ac, atomic number 89) or protactinium (symbol Pa, atomic number 91) and to end with lawrencium (symbol Lr, atomic number 103). The elements of this group are called the actinides. These inner transition series are covered by the articles RARE-EARTH ELEMENTS AND THEIR COMPOUNDS and ACTINIDE ELEMENTS AND THEIR COMPOUNDS. This article treats only the three main transition series, which are included in the set of 27 elements often called the *d*-block transition elements. Because scandium, yttrium, and lanthanum actually do not form compounds analogous to those of the other transition elements and because their chemistry is quite homologous to that of the lanthanides, they too are excluded from this article, which, then, specifically treats only the 24 elements in the three series titanium–copper, zirconium–silver, and hafnium–gold. The *d*-block transition elements and some of their characteristic properties are listed in Table 2.

d-block elements

Electronic structure and position in the periodic table. The relative locations of the transition elements in the periodic table and their chemical and physical properties can best be understood by considering their electronic structures and the way in which those structures vary as atomic numbers increase. The details of atomic structure necessary for comprehension of the properties are fully covered in the articles ATOMIC STRUCTURE; MOLECULAR STRUCTURES; CHEMICAL REACTIONS; and CHEMICAL BONDING. Only a brief summary of these subjects can be given here, with emphasis upon those aspects of atomic structure relevant to the transition elements.

Atomic structure. All of the elements exist as atoms, characteristic for each element, that combine, or form bonds, in various ways to form millions of compounds. An atom has a nucleus composed of protons (subatomic particles with a single positive electrical charge) and neutrons of about the same mass, but no charge. The number of protons or positive charges on the nucleus is the atomic number of that element. The number of neutrons varies, and atoms with the same atomic number but different numbers of neutrons are called isotopes of that element. The sum of neutrons and protons is the atomic mass number. Thus, an atom of iron has 26 protons and may have 28, 30, 31, or 32 neutrons, making the atomic number of iron 26 and the atomic masses of its isotopes 54, 56, 57, and 58. The iron isotope with mass 56 is represented as iron-56 or as ^{56}Fe.

Electrons and chemical bonding. The nucleus of an atom is surrounded by as many electrons, negatively charged particles with negligible mass, as there are protons, making the atom as a whole electrically neutral. If the elements are examined in order of increasing atomic number, it is found that the increasing number of electrons are arranged in an orderly and periodic fashion; that is, certain features of the arrangements recur. Some electronic structures of atoms are more stable than others

Table 2: Some Properties of the Transition Elements

	symbol	atomic number	atomic mass	density g cm⁻³, 20° C	melting point °C	boiling point °C	type of crystal packing*	electrical resistivity microohm-cm	heat of atomization, at 298°, kJmole⁻¹	1st ionization potential electron volts
1st main series										
Titanium	Ti	22	47.90	4.507	1,668	3,260	hcp, bcc	42(0°)	473	6.82
Vanadium	V	23	50.94	6.11	1,890	3,000	bcc	24.8(20°)	515	6.74
Chromium	Cr	24	52.01	7.19	1,875	2,199	bcc, hcp	12.9(20°)	397	6.763
Manganese	Mn	25	54.938	7.44	1,244(±3)	2,097	complex	185(20°)	281	7.432
Iron	Fe	26	55.847	7.873	1,536(±1)	3,000	ccp, bcc	9.71(20°)	416	7.90
Cobalt	Co	27	58.94	8.90	1,493	3,100	ccp, bcc	5.68(0°)	425	7.86
Nickel	Ni	28	58.71	8.908	1,453	2,730	ccp, hcp	6.84(20°)	430	7.633
Copper	Cu	29	63.54	8.94	1,083	2,582	ccp	1.68(20°)	339	7.724
2nd main series										
Zirconium	Zr	40	91.22	6.506	1,850	4,377	bcc, hcp	40.0(0°)	611	6.984
Niobium	Nb	41	92.91	8.58	2,468(±10)	4,927	bcc	15.22(0°)	774	6.88
Molybdenum	Mo	42	95.94	10.22	2,610	5,560	bcc, hcp	7.2(0°)	659	7.10
Technetium	Tc	43	†	11.49	2,170	5,030	hcp	—	649	7.28
Ruthenium	Ru	44	101.1	12.45	2,310(±20)	4,080(±100)	hcp, ccp	6.71(0°)	669	7.364
Rhodium	Rh	45	102.91	12.41	1,960	3,700	ccp	4.33(0°)	577	7.46
Palladium	Pd	46	106.4	12.02	1,552	2,020	ccp	9.93(0°)	381	8.33
Silver	Ag	47	107.870	10.5	960.8	2,210	ccp	0.616(0°)	286	7.574
3rd main series										
Hafnium	Hf	72	178.50	13.29	2,230	5,200	hcp, bcc	35.5(20°)	703	7.9‡
Tantalum	Ta	73	180.95	16.65	2,996	5,427	bcc	13.6(0°)	781	7.88
Tungsten	W	74	183.85	19.3	3,410	5,930	bcc, complex	5.5(20°)	837	7.98
Rhenium	Re	75	186.22	21.04	3,170	5,630	hcp	19.14(0°)	791	7.87
Osmium	Os	76	190.2	22.61	3,050(±30)	5,020(±100)	hcp, ccp	8.12(0°)	728	8.7
Iridium	Ir	77	192.2	22.65	2,443	4,500	ccp	4.71(0°)	690	9
Platinum	Pt	78	195.09	21.45	1,769.3	4,100	ccp	9.85(0°)	566	9.0
Gold	Au	79	196.967	19.32	1,063	2,808	ccp	2.06(0°)	368	9.22

*hcp—hexagonal close-packed; ccp—cubic close-packed; bcc—body-centred cubic.   †Does not occur in nature. The only isotope that has been obtained on a macroscopic scale has a mass number of 99.   ‡Estimated value; nearly all are estimated or extrapolated values.

Ions

and atoms tend to give up or add electrons to achieve electronic configurations of greater stability, thereby becoming ions—i.e., positively or negatively charged particles. An ion is represented by the symbol of the element with the electrical charge in superscript: Fe^{3+}. All metals tend to lose electrons to form positive ions, or cations, whereas nonmetals tend to gain electrons to form negatively charged ions, or anions. Oppositely charged ions attract one another and form compounds with electrovalent or ionic bonds between the ions; the solid structure of an ionic compound has no theoretical size limit because every ion holds around itself oppositely charged ions with equal bonding force. Atoms may also share electrons in covalent bonds to form polyatomic species that may be either neutral molecules (e.g., water) or electrically charged ions (e.g., ammonium, NH_4^+, or sulfate, SO_4^{2-}). In a third major type of bonding, called the metallic bond, electrons are freed from the parent bonding nuclei so that they can move about among the atoms unclaimed by any particular atom. Atoms of the transition elements interact with one another and with atoms of other elements in all three of these ways.

Chemical formulas. The composition of every chemical species is represented by a formula in which the symbol for an element stands for an atom of that element and the number of atoms of that element present is specified by a subscript. If a species consists of discrete, neutral molecules, the formula indicates their atomic composition; e.g., benzene exists as molecules composed of six atoms of carbon and six of hydrogen and its formula is C_6H_6. Diammonium hydrogen phosphate is a crystalline solid composed of many ammonium ions (NH_4^+) and hydrogen phosphate ions (HPO_4^{2-}); each ion is a discrete entity, but no ammonium ion is associated with a particular hydrogen phosphate ion, and there are no individual species having the composition represented by the formula $(NH_4)_2HPO_4$, which specifies only the composition of the individual ions and the ratio (two to one) in which they are present.

Valence and oxidation number. All changes in electron structures of atoms, whether in the single state or bonded into groups, are chemical reactions, and the electrons accepted, donated, or shared in these processes are called valence electrons. The electronic state of an atom, alone or in combination with others, is specified by the oxidation number, the number of electrons removed from the neutral atom in changing it to the ionic level at which it is present in the species in question.

Atomic orbitals. The electrons associated with an atomic nucleus are localized, or concentrated, in various specific regions of space called atomic orbitals, each of which is characterized by a set of symbols (quantum numbers) that specify the volume, the shape, and orientation in space relative to other orbitals. An orbital may accommodate no more than two electrons. The energy involved in the interaction of an electron with the nucleus is determined by the orbital that it occupies, and the electrons in an atom distribute themselves among the orbitals in such a way that the total energy is minimum. Thus, by electronic structure, or configuration, of an atom is meant the way in which the electrons surrounding the nucleus occupy the various atomic orbitals available to them. The simplest configuration is the set of one-electron orbitals of the hydrogen atom, summarized in Figure 2. The orbitals can be classified, first, by principal quantum number, and the orbitals have increasing energy as the principal quantum number increases from 1 to 2, 3, 4, etc. (The sets of orbitals defined by the principal quantum numbers 1, 2, 3, 4, etc., are often referred to as shells designated K, L, M, N, etc.) For principal quantum number 1 there is but a single type of orbital, called an s orbital. As the principal quantum number increases, there are an increasing number of different types of orbitals, or subshells, corresponding to each: s, p, d, f, g, etc. (see Figure 2). Moreover, the additional orbital types each come in larger sets. Thus, there is but one s orbital for each principal quantum number, but there are three orbitals in the set designated p, five in each set designated d, and so on, as indicated at the top of Figure 2. For the hydrogen atom, the energy is fully determined by which orbital the single electron occupies. It is especially notable that the energy of the hydrogen atom is determined solely by the principal quantum number of the orbital occupied by the electron (except for some small effects that are not of concern here); that is, in hydrogen, the electron configurations of the third shell, for example, are equi-energic (of the same energy, whichever one the electron occupies), which is not the case with any of the other atoms, all of which contain two or more electrons.

The Aufbau principle. To understand the electron configurations of other atoms, it is customary to employ the *Aufbau* (German: "building up") principle, the basis of which is that, to achieve a multi-electron configuration, the required number of electrons must be added to the orbitals one at a time, filling the most stable orbitals

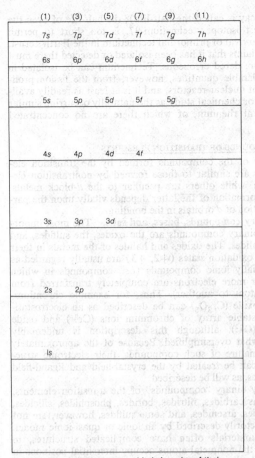

(1)	(3)	(5)	(7)	(9)	(11)
7s	7p	7d	7f	7g	7h
6s	6p	6d	6f	6g	6h
5s	5p	5d	5f	5g	
4s	4p	4d	4f		
3s	3p	3d			
2s	2p				
1s					

Figure 2: The hydrogen atom orbitals in order of their energies (see text).

first, until the total number has been added. There is one restriction upon this conceptualization, namely, the Pauli exclusion principle, which states that only two electrons may occupy each orbital. Thus there can be no more than two electrons in any s orbital, six electrons in any set of p orbitals, ten electrons in any set of d orbitals, etc. In carrying out this process, however, one cannot simply use the ordering of electron orbitals that is appropriate to the hydrogen atom as shown in Figure 2; as electrons are added they interact with each other as well as with the nucleus, and as a result the presence of electrons in some orbital causes the energy of an electron entering another orbital to be different from what it would be if this electron were present alone. The overall result of these inter-electronic interactions (sometimes referred to as shielding) is that the relative order of the various atomic orbitals is different in many-electron atoms from that in the hydrogen atom; in fact, it changes continuously as the number of electrons increases.

As multi-electronic atoms are built up, the various subshells s, p, d, f, g, etc. of a principal quantum number cease to be equi-energic; they all drop, although not by equal amounts, to lower energies. Overall lowering of energy occurs because the shielding from the nuclear charge that an electron in a particular orbital is given by all of the other electrons in the atom is not sufficient to prevent a steady increase in the effect that the charge in the nucleus has on that electron as the atomic number increases. In other words, each electron is imperfectly shielded from the nuclear charge by the other electrons. In addition the different types of orbitals in each principal shell, because of their different spatial distributions, are shielded to different degrees by the core of electrons beneath them; accordingly, although all of them decrease in energy, they decrease by different amounts, and thus their relative order in energy continuously changes. In order to specify the electron configuration of a particular atom, it is necessary to use the order of orbitals appropriate to the specific value of the atomic number of that atom. The

Shielding (margin note)

behaviour of the various d and f orbitals is to be especially noted in regard to where the transition elements occur in the periodic table.

The argon atom (atomic number 18) has an electron configuration $1s^2 2s^2 2p^6 3s^2 3p^6$ (i.e., it has two electrons in the s orbital of the first shell; two in the s and six in the p orbitals of the second shell; two in the s and six in the p orbitals of the third shell: this expression often is abbreviated [Ar] especially in specifying the configurations of elements between argon and krypton, because it represents a common part of the configurations of all these elements). The $3d$ orbitals are more shielded from the nuclear charge than is the $4s$ orbital, and, consequently, the latter orbital has lower energy. The next electrons to be added enter the $4s$ orbital in preference to the $3d$ or $4p$ orbitals. The two elements following argon in the periodic table are potassium, with a single $4s$ electron, and calcium, with two $4s$ electrons. Because of the presence of the $4s$ electrons, the $3d$ orbitals are less shielded than the $4p$ orbitals; therefore, the first regular transition series begins at this point with the element scandium, which has the electron configuration [Ar] $4s^23d^1$. Through the next nine elements, in increasing order of atomic number, electrons are added to the $3d$ orbitals until, at the element zinc, they are entirely filled and the electron configuration is [Ar] $3d^{10}4s^2$. The $4p$ orbitals are then the ones of lowest energy, and they become filled through the next six elements, the sixth of which is the next noble gas, krypton, with the electron configuration $1s^22s^22p^63s^23p^64s^23d^{10}4p^6$, or [Kr].

First transition series (margin note)

Throughout the next period the pattern of variation of the orbital energies is similar to that immediately preceding. When the configuration of the noble gas, krypton, has been achieved, the $5s$ orbital is more stable than the $4d$ orbitals. The next two electrons therefore enter the $5s$ orbital, but then the $4d$ orbitals fall to lower energy than the $5p$ orbitals, and the second regular transition series commences with the element yttrium. Electrons continue to be added to the $4d$ orbitals until those orbitals are entirely filled at the position of the element cadmium, which has an electron configuration [Kr] $4d^{10}5s^2$. The next six electrons enter the $5p$ orbitals until another noble gas configuration is attained at the element xenon. Analogously to the two preceding periods, the next two electrons are added to the next available orbital, namely, the $6s$ orbital, producing the next two elements, cesium and barium. At this point, however, the ordering of orbitals becomes more complex than it previously had been, because there are now unfilled $4f$ orbitals as well as the $5d$ orbitals, and the two sets have approximately the same energy. In the next element, lanthanum (atomic number 57), an electron is added to the $5d$ orbitals, but the immediately following element, cerium (atomic number 58), has two electrons in the $4f$ orbitals and none in the $5d$ orbitals. Through the next 12 elements the additional electrons enter the $4f$ orbitals, although the $5d$ orbitals are of only slightly higher energy. This set of elements from lanthanum, where the $4f$ orbitals were still vacant or about to be filled, through lutetium, in which the $4f$ orbitals are completely filled by 14 electrons, makes up the lanthanides, mentioned above.

Second transition series (margin note)

At this point the next available orbitals are the $5d$ orbitals, and the elements hafnium through gold, the third regular transition series, correspond to the successive filling of these $5d$ orbitals. Following this series there are again p orbitals ($6p$) to be filled, and when this is accomplished the noble gas radon is reached.

Third transition series (margin note)

Molecular orbitals. If two atoms are close together, some of their orbitals may overlap and participate in the formation of molecular orbitals. Electrons that occupy a molecular orbital interact with the nuclei of both atoms: if this interaction results in a total energy less than that of the separated atoms, as is the case if the orbital lies mainly in the region between the two nuclei, the orbital is said to be a bonding orbital and its occupancy by electrons constitutes a covalent bond that links the atoms together in compound formation and in which the electrons are said to be shared. If the occupation of an orbital by electrons raises the energy of the system, as is the case if the orbital lies mainly outside the region between the two nuclei, that orbital is said to be antibonding; the presence of electrons in such orbitals tends to offset the attractive force derived from the bonding electrons.

A bonding or an antibonding molecular orbital may be disposed along the line passing through the two nuclei (Figure 3A), in which case it is designated by the Greek letter σ (sigma); or it may occupy regions approximately parallel to that line (Figure 3B and 3C) and be designated π (pi).

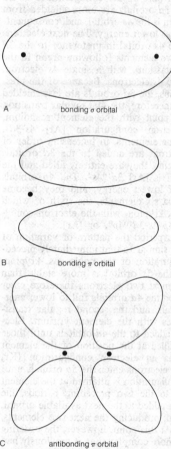

A   bonding σ orbital

B   bonding π orbital

C   antibonding π orbital

Figure 3: Electron distributions in molecular orbitals (see text).

Terrestrial abundances and discovery of the transition elements. The most abundant transition element in the Earth's solid crust is iron, which is fourth among all elements and second (to aluminum) among metals in crustal abundance. The elements titanium, manganese, zirconium, vanadium, and chromium also have abundances in excess of 100 grams (3.5 ounces) per ton. Some of the most important and useful transition elements have very low crustal abundances—*e.g.*, tungsten, platinum, gold, and silver. Table 1 lists the abundances of the transition elements.

Four of the regular transition elements were known to the ancients: iron (*ferrum*), copper (*cuprum*), silver (*argentum*), and gold (*aurum*). Their chemical symbols (Fe, Cu, Ag, Au), in fact, are derived from their alchemical (Latin) names rather than their contemporary names. The other regular transition elements were discovered (or recognized as elements) after the early 18th century. The transition element most recently discovered in nature is rhenium (atomic number 75), which in 1925 was detected in platinum ores and in the niobium mineral columbite.

Technetium (atomic number 43) is the only *d*-block element that has not been isolated from the Earth's crust. All isotopes (*i.e.*, all atoms with 43 protons and any number of neutrons) of technetium are radioactive (*i.e.*, they decay spontaneously by emitting certain particles and radiation; the time it takes one-half of a sample

to decay is called the half-life); the half-life of even the stablest isotope, technetium-97, is too short to permit the survival of primordial technetium in the Earth's crust, and claims that it has been isolated or detected there must be considered erroneous. Technetium can be isolated in considerable quantities, however, from the fission products of nuclear reactors, and it is at least as readily available for chemical study as the naturally occurring similar element rhenium, of which there are no concentrated ores.

COMPOUNDS OF TRANSITION ELEMENTS

Many of the compounds formed by the transition elements are similar to those formed by nontransition elements, while others are peculiar to the *d*-block metals. The formation of the latter depends vitally upon the participation of *d* orbitals in the bonding.

Binary compounds, bases, and salts. The most important binary compounds are the oxides, the sulfides, and the halides. The oxides and halides of the metals in their lower oxidation states ($+2$, $+3$) are usually regarded as essentially ionic compounds (*i.e.*, compounds in which one or more electrons are completely transferred from one atom to another). Thus, for example chromium-(III) oxide (Cr_2O_3) can be described as an electrostatically stable array of chromium ions (Cr^{3+}) and oxide ions (O^{2-}), although this description is undeniably somewhat oversimplified. Because of the approximately ionic nature of such compounds, their electronic structures can be treated by the crystal-field and ligand-field theories, as will be described.

Many binary "compounds" of the transition elements, such as carbides, nitrides, borides, phosphides, silicides, selenides, arsenides, and some sulfides, however, are not satisfactorily described by an ionic or quasi-ionic model. Such materials often have complicated structures, in which the nonmetal atoms occupy interstitial positions in metal lattices (*i.e.*, the regular geometrical arrangements of the metal atoms) or form elaborate two- and three-dimensional networks within an array of metal atoms. It is not uncommon for such substances to be markedly nonstoichiometric (*i.e.*, the component elements do not combine in characteristic proportions). For example, the cobalt (Co) telluride (Te) system forms a structural phase that is stable over the entire range of compositions from one in which the proportions of cobalt and tellurium are equal, CoTe, to one in which the proportions are 1:2, cobalt to tellurium, $CoTe_2$. Composition can vary continuously from the former to the latter by progressive loss of cobalt atoms from alternate planes in the structure until finally, at $CoTe_2$, every other plane of cobalt atoms present in CoTe is absent. Among borides on the other hand, it is a multiplicity of phases, rather than non-stoichiometry, that makes the structural situation complex. (A phase is a homogeneous, physically distinct portion of matter in a heterogeneous system.) With low boron-to-metal ratios, as those in substances with apparent formulas such as M_4B, M_5B, M_2B, M_5B_2, and M_7B_3 (in which M represents an atom of an unspecified metal and B an atom of boron), the structures contain isolated boron atoms. As the boron-to-metal ratio increases, bonding between boron atoms themselves become important. For example, there are pairs of boron atoms in trivanadium diboride, V_3B_2; and in tetranickel triboride, Ni_4B_3, two thirds of the boron atoms are linked into endless, zigzagging chains. In the many metal–boron compounds designated M_3B_4 there are double chains or bands, while in MB_2 compounds the structure consists of alternating layers of close-packed metal atoms and sheets of boron atoms.

All of the transition metals form bases (*i.e.*, chemical compounds that yield the hydroxide ion, OH^-, in solution) or hydroxides, although in some cases it is doubtful if the compound is other than an amorphous hydrous (*i.e.*, containing water) oxide. Whether such substances are true hydroxides or simply hydrous oxides, however, they are precipitated from aqueous solutions of the cations (*i.e.*, positive ions) in the usual oxidation states ($+2$ or $+3$) and redissolve in acid to regenerate the cations. Nearly all of the transition metals, in one or more oxi-

Non-stoichiometric substances

dation states, form salts of the common oxo anions (negative ions containing oxygen atoms), such as nitrate, sulfate, and perchlorate. These salts are usually obtained as crystalline hydrates (compounds, formed by combination of water with another substance, in which water retains its molecular state as H_2O) by evaporation of aqueous solutions.

Coordination compounds. One of the most characteristic features of the chemistry of the transition elements in their normal oxidation states (generally +1 to +4) is the formation of coordination compounds or complexes. These are species in which a metal ion is surrounded by and bonded to groups of anions or molecules called ligands. The essential feature of a ligand is that it contains a donor atom, such as nitrogen or oxygen, that has an unshared pair of electrons that can be used to form a bond to a metal ion. In the classic picture of a ligand-to-metal bond the donor atom of the ligand is so oriented as to localize the donated electron pair between the donor atom and the metal ion, and a donor, or dative, bond is thus formed. The localization of electrons between a specific pair of atomic nuclei is the same phenomenon that constitutes covalent bond formation involving a sigma molecular orbital, but the fact that both electrons are supplied by the donor atom results in the transfer of negative charge to the metal atom and development of positive charge upon the donor atom so that the dative bond has considerable electrovalent (ionic) character.

Depending on the number and charges of the ligands, which need not all be the same, a coordination complex may be charged either positively or negatively or it may be neutral. Some examples are the following three complexes formed by the element cobalt: hexamminecobalt(II), $[Co(NH_3)_6]^{2+}$; trichlorotriamminecobalt(III), $[Co(NH_3)_3Cl_3]$; tetrachlorocobaltate(II), $[CoCl_4]^{2-}$. Even in the absence of deliberately added ligand species, a cation in water or other solvent is in fact part of a complex in which solvent molecules are the ligands. In water these solvent complexes are the aquo ions, of which the one with chromium (Cr), hexaquochromium(III), is representative: $[Cr(H_2O)_6]^{3+}$. The set of donor atoms around the central cation is called the coordination sphere or coordination polyhedron of the cation. The number of atoms in a coordination sphere is called the coordination number. It varies from two to nine among the regular transition metal ions, but coordination numbers 4–6 are by far the most common. For most coordination numbers, several geometric arrangements are possible as shown in the structural formulas. For coordination number 4, the two most symmetrical arrangements are square (**1**) and tetrahedral (**2**); for coordination number 6 the only important arrangement is the octahedral one (**3**):

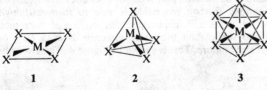

1 **2** **3**

The coordination number 5 is also common; it shows two important geometrical arrangements: the trigonal bipyramid (**4**) and the square pyramid (**5**), which are quite similar in energy.

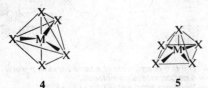

4 **5**

Each ligand atom need not belong to a separate ion or molecule. A ligand that has only one donor atom is called a monodentate or unidentate ligand. The halide ions (ions of the halogens: fluorine, chlorine, bromine, iodine, and astatine), the cyanide ion (CN⁻), water (H_2O), ammonia (NH_3), and hydroxide ion (OH⁻) are important monodentate ligands. There are also many types of polydentate or chelating ligands (a chelate is a coordination compound in which the central atom is joined to two or more atoms in the same ligand group). For example, ethylenediamine ($H_2NCH_2CH_2NH_2$) can form two nitrogen-to-metal (N–M) bonds, closing a five-membered chelate ring (**6**); thus ethylenediamine is a bidentate ligand. Some other bidentate ligands are the oxalate ion (see diagram **7**), the acetylacetonato ion (see diagram **8**), and the dimethylglyoximato ion, which is shown incorporated into the well-known bis(dimethylglyoximato)nickel complex (diagram **9**).

Chelation

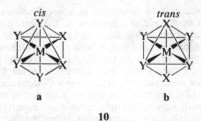

6 **7** **8**

9

Isomerism. In complexes containing two or more types of donor atoms the occurrence of isomers (molecules having the same number and kinds of atoms but differing in structure) becomes an important phenomenon. For octahedral complexes, the study of isomers has been carried out in great detail. Any octahedral complex in which there are two donors of one kind (X) and four of another (Y) can exist in two isomeric forms, *cis* and *trans* (see **a** and **b**, diagram **10**), called geometrical isomers.

cis *trans*

a **b**

10

The fact that there are only two geometrical isomers of MX_2Y_4 complexes is consistent with the octahedral shape of the coordination polyhedron but inconsistent with several other coordination polyhedra (*e.g.*, a plane hexagon or a trigonal prism), and observations of this kind contributed some of the earliest evidence for octahedral coordination geometry in complexes of chromium(III), cobalt(III), and platinum(IV). As the number of different donors increases, the number of isomers generally increases also. For an octahedral complex of the type expressed as $MX_2Y_2Z_2$, there are five geometrical isomers.

For square complexes, *cis* and *trans* isomers are also possible as in the case of the dichlorodiammineplatinum(II), $[PtCl_2(NH_3)_2]$, complexes (**11a** and **11b**).

cis *trans*

Cl NH₃ Cl NH₃
  Pt   Pt
Cl NH₃ H₃N Cl

a **b**

11

The occurrence of optical isomers—that is, complexes that are geometrically the same except that one is the mirror image of the other and the two mirror images are not superimposable—is of particular interest. A sample containing only one of the two isomers, or at least more

Optical isomerism

of one than of the other, has the power to rotate the plane of polarized light; hence the term optical isomers. The two optical isomers have equal rotatory powers but cause rotation to occur in opposite directions.

Optical isomers are most commonly found in complexes containing chelating ligands. Thus, a complex in which there are two ethylenediamine ligands and two unidentate ligands, with the latter in a *cis* relationship, exists in two non-superimposable mirror-image forms, as shown in diagram 12 for the case of dichlorobis(ethylenediamine)-cobalt(III), $[Co(H_2NCH_2CH_2NH_2)_2Cl_2]^+$.

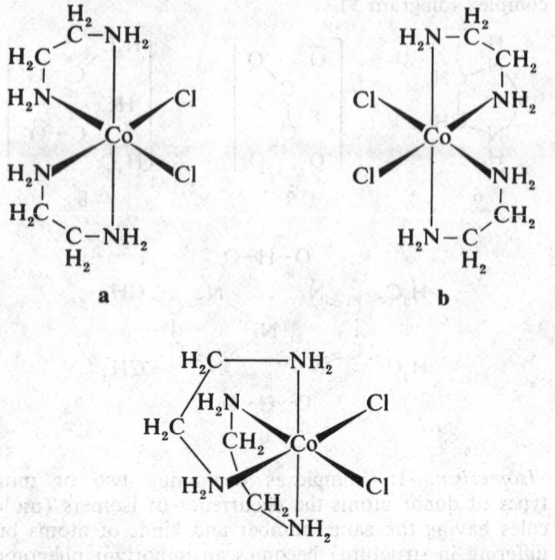

12

In diagram 12, **a** and **b** are mirror images; **b** and **c** are identical, and the comparison of **a** with **c** shows very clearly that the mirror-image structures are not superimposable.

The formation of complexes in aqueous solution upon addition of ligands to a solution of the aquo ion is an important phenomenon. Such complexes form in a step-wise fashion, so that the coordinated water molecules are successively replaced by the ligand. For example, when ammonia is slowly added to a solution of nickel(II) ions, a series of ammonia complexes forms. Comparison of the stability of the ammonia complexes with that of the complexes with ethylenediamine reveals an important phenomenon called the chelate effect. When the two ammonia (NH_3) ligands are tied together to form one bidentate ligand, ethylenediamine, the displacement of two water molecules is about 540 times more favourable than when the ammonia molecules are separate unidentate ligands. The formation of chelate rings increases the degree of complex formation, other factors being equal. This is the major reason that polydentate ligands such as ethylenediaminetetraacetate (EDTA) are so important and useful in transition-metal chemistry as powerful complexing agents that reduce the concentrations of metal ions in aqueous mediums.

Oxo anions. Many of the transition metals in their highest oxidation states form anions of the type MO_4^{n-}, in which M is the metal atom and n takes the values 2 for the Group VI elements and 1 for the Group VII elements. Some important examples are the ions of chromium: chromate(VI), CrO_4^{2-}; of molybdenum: molybdenum(VI), MoO_4^{2-}; and of tungsten: tungstate(VI), WO_4^{2-}; and of manganese: manganate(VII), MnO_4^-; of technetium: technetate(VII), TcO_4^-; and of rhenium: rhenate(VII), ReO_4^-. Osmium and ruthenium form the neutral compounds osmium(VIII) oxide, OsO_4, and ruthenium(VIII) oxide, RuO_4, which, even though they are uncharged, are closely related with respect to structure and bonding to the oxo anions. The stability of higher oxidation states increases, and the oxidizing power of oxo anions thus decreases, as each group in the periodic table is descended; thus the chromate(VI) ion and

the manganate(VII) ion of the first transition series are powerful oxidizing agents, whereas the tungstate(VI) ion and the rhenate(VII) ion of the third transition series have no significant oxidizing power.

The chromate(VI) and manganate(VII) ions are widely used in analytical chemistry for the volumetric determination of reducing agents. In acidic solution, the chromate(VI) ion dimerizes (*i.e.*, forms a larger ion by the union of two simple ones):

$$2CrO_4^{2-} \quad + \quad 2H^+ \quad \longrightarrow \quad Cr_2O_7^{2-} \quad + \quad H_2O.$$
chromate(VI) ion   hydrogen ion   dichromate(VI) ion   water

The Group V and Group VI elements, especially vanadium, molybdenum, and tungsten, form complex polynuclear oxo anions, called isopolyanions. In highly basic solutions the simple mononuclear species (*e.g.*, WO_4^{2-}) are stable, but as the solution is made more acidic the polynuclear species appear. These isopolyanions are formed by the joining of metal–oxygen octahedra (MO_6) through shared vertices and edges. The ultimate products of the aggregation process, in very strongly acidic solution, are the hydrous oxides such as tungsten(VI) oxide, $WO_3 \cdot 2H_2O$, molybdenum(VI) oxide, $MoO_3 \cdot 2H_2O$, and vanadium(V) oxide, V_2O_5. When the condensation reactions leading to polynuclear species are carried out in the presence of other elements, such as phosphate ions, silicate ions, or metal ions (*e.g.*, nickel(II), manganese(II), or cerium(IV)), the heteropolyacids, or their anions, are formed. In these, the metal–oxygen octahedra are fitted together around a central site that may be either a tetrahedron or an octahedron, occupied by the phosphorus, silicon, or metal atom, which is designated the hetero atom. A typical heteropolyanion is the 12-molybdophosphate ion, $[PMo_{12}O_{40}]^{3-}$, in which 12 molybdate octahedra are interconnected to surround a phosphorus atom that lies at the centre, joined to four tetrahedrally arranged oxygen atoms.

Metal carbonyls and nitrosyls. The metals of the main transition series form complexes in which the carbon monoxide molecule, CO, functions as a ligand. For the most part these complexes, which are called metal carbonyls, contain metal atoms in very low ($+1$, 0, -1) formal oxidation states. According to current theoretical views, the special ability of the *d*-block transition metals to bind carbon monoxide (and, in a similar manner, nitric oxide, NO) is attributable to the presence of electrons in *d* orbitals that have the shape and energy necessary to engage in formation of pi molecular bonds with the CO group. Only the *d*-block atoms in low oxidation states meet this requirement.

Carbon monoxide differs from most other ligands in that the simple donation of one of its unshared electron pairs to an electron pair acceptor does not result in strong bonding. Carbon monoxide is able to form carbonyls with transition metals because the bonding of those metals to the carbon monoxide molecule is of a dual or synergic nature. This is shown in Figure 4. The electrons

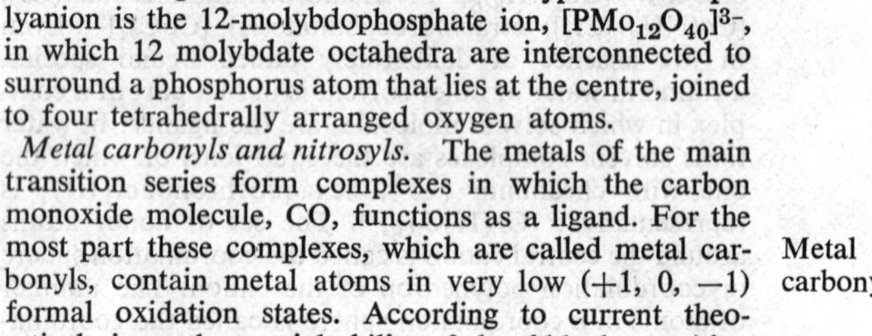

Figure 4: *The two components of a bond between a metal atom and a carbon monoxide molecule.*
(A) shows the sigma bond and (B) the pi bond.

in a sigma orbital on the carbon atom form a donor bond to the metal atom. This is not a very effective bond by itself, but it leads to a polarization, whereby the carbon monoxide group becomes positive and the metal atom, negative. The metal atom can then donate electron den-

Side notes in margins:
The chelate effect

Iso-polyanions

Metal carbonyls

sity from filled *d* orbitals to the empty pi antibonding orbitals of carbon monoxide. This process produces a polarity opposite to the first one. The two processes thus tend to be mutually reinforcing, or synergic, and as a result stable bonds are formed.

Some representative metal carbonyls are hexacarbonylchromium, $Cr(CO)_6$; decacarbonyldimanganese, $Mn_2(CO)_{10}$; nonacarbonyldiiron, $Fe_2(CO)_9$; and dodecacarbonyltetrairidium, $Ir_4(CO)_{12}$. In addition to binary metal carbonyls (*i.e.*, those containing only metal atoms and carbon monoxide groups), there are thousands of substances containing some CO ligands along with others.

The first metal carbonyl, tetracarbonylnickel, $Ni(CO)_4$, discovered in 1890, is the only one that can be formed readily by direct reaction of the metal with carbon monoxide, and it found almost immediate industrial application in the purification of nickel. The process is still in limited use today, affording metal of 99.90–99.99 percent purity. Impure metal reacts at 50° C (about 120° F) to form tetracarbonylnickel, which is decomposed at 200° C (about 400° F) to regenerate the metal. During the next 20 years carbonyls of iron, cobalt, and molybdenum were synthesized. Many metal carbonyl molecules of very complicated structures have been synthesized, including those formulated $M_3(CO)_{12}$ (M = iron, Fe, ruthenium, Ru, and osmium, Os), which contain triangles of metal atoms; $M_4(CO)_{12}$ (M = cobalt, Co, rhodium, Rh, and iridium, Ir), which contain tetrahedral groups of metal atoms; and $Rh_6(CO)_{16}$, which has an octahedron of metal atoms.

The simplest metal carbonyls are those in which a single metal atom is surrounded by an array of four, five, or six carbon monoxide groups. The latter are always bound to the metal through the carbon atom in the synergic manner explained above. In many, but not all, of the polynuclear (*i.e.*, containing two or more metal atoms per molecule) metal carbonyls there is another type of carbonyl group—*i.e.*, a bridging CO, in which the carbon atom forms normal covalent single bonds to two metal atoms. There are even a few cases in which a carbon monoxide group lies symmetrically over a triangle of metal atoms and is bonded to all three, thus forming a triple bridge.

Most metal carbonyls react fairly easily with phosphines, amines, and olefins, forming products in which one or more of the CO groups is replaced by these ligands. Nickel carbonyl, for example, reacts with phosphines, R_3P, in which R is an organic radical (a combining group derived by removal of a hydrogen atom from an organic compound) and P is phosphorus, to produce, for example, tricarbonyl(triphenylphosphine)nickel, $Ni(CO)_3[(C_6H_5)_3P]$, and dicarbonylbis(triphenylphosphine)nickel, $Ni(CO_2[(C_6H_5)_3P]_2$.

The formulas of the simpler metal carbonyls can all be understood by postulating that the total number of valence electrons around each metal atom, counting those in both sigma and pi orbitals, should be equal to 18. Each carbon monoxide group is considered to contribute two electrons. Thus, if a metal atom has initially *n* electrons of its own it will form bonds to $(18 - n)/2$ carbon monoxide groups. This is illustrated by pentacarbonyliron, $Fe(CO)_5$: the iron atom, with an electron configuration $[Ar]3d^64s^2$, possesses a total of eight valence electrons; thus ten more are needed and these are supplied by five CO groups, each of which adds two electrons. When the metal has an odd number of electrons it must also interact with some univalent group, such as a halogen atom or another metal atom, thereby acquiring a share in one more electron. Manganese, for example, has seven electrons. By forming a bond to one halogen—*e.g.*, chlorine (Cl)—and to five CO groups, or to one other manganese atom and to five CO groups, the molecules chloropentacarbonylmanganese, $ClMn(CO)_5$, or bis(pentacarbonylmanganese), $(OC)_5Mn—Mn(CO)_5$ are formed.

The nitric oxide molecule, NO, is very similar to the carbon monoxide molecule except for the presence of an additional electron, which can be donated to, or at least shared with, the metal atom in addition to the two electrons on the nitrogen atom that are analogous to the two

electrons on the carbon atom of carbon monoxide. The nitric oxide molecule also possesses the necessary pi antibonding orbitals with which to accept electrons from metal *d* orbitals. It can, therefore, exhibit ligand behaviour similar to that of carbon monoxide. Because nitric oxide can contribute three electrons whereas carbon monoxide donates only two, two NO groups can replace three CO groups; or an NO group can replace one CO group plus a metal-to-metal bond or one CO group plus a metal-to-ligand single bond. In this way, the composition of dicarbonyldinitrosyliron, $Fe(CO)_2(NO)_2$, can be related to that of pentacarbonyliron, $Fe(CO)_5$, and the compositions of both tetracarbonylnitrosylmanganese, $Mn(CO)_4(NO)$, and carbonyltrinitrosylmanganese, $Mn(CO)(NO)_3$, can be understood in relation to those of bis(pentacarbonylmanganese) and chloropentacarbonylmanganese. Metal nitrosyls

There are other ligands, particularly certain PR_3 groups, in which R may be any of several monovalent atoms or groups that resemble carbon monoxide in combining sigma donation with pi acceptance in their interaction with metal atoms. Phosphorus trifluoride, PF_3, is very similar to carbon monoxide in its bonding capabilities, and it forms an extensive series of complexes comparable in composition to the metal carbonyls—*e.g.*, tetrakis(phosphorus trifluoride)nickel, $Ni(PF_3)_4$.

The toxicity of carbon monoxide is due to its ability to form a complex with the iron atom of hemoglobin, thus blocking its function as an oxygen carrier. Phosphorus trifluoride is also highly toxic for the same reason.

Organometallic compounds. Scarcely any organometallic compounds of the transition elements were known (if the term organometallic is understood to imply the presence of direct metal-to-carbon bonds) prior to 1951. In that year the discovery of dicyclopentadienyliron, $(C_5H_5)_2Fe$, commonly known as ferrocene, was announced; the following year the correct molecular structure of the compound was determined. As shown in Figure 5A, it is a kind of "molecular sandwich," the two cyclopentadienyl rings lying parallel and the metal atom occupying the midpoint between them.

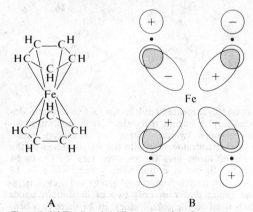

Figure 5: (A) The "sandwich" structure of the ferrocene molecule ($C_5H_5)_2Fe$; (B) sketch showing how the pi-type ring orbitals and an iron *d* orbital overlap to give a component of the metal-to-ring bonding. The view is of a section through the molecule, perpendicular to the ring planes.

The bonding of the cyclopentadienyl rings to the iron atom in ferrocene is due primarily to the overlap of pi orbitals of the organic group with *d* orbitals of the metal. The principal component of this bonding consists of the interaction of the incompletely filled pi type orbitals with the d_{xz} and d_{yz} orbitals, as shown in Figure 5B. Soon after the nature of the ferrocene molecule was clarified it was shown that the cyclopentadienyl group (the C_5H_5 ring) could form similar bonds to almost all of the other transition metals. More importantly, it was recognized that the basic type of interaction, which can be broadly described as donation of pi electrons from an organic molecule, radical, or anion to *d* orbitals of a transition metal, could occur with a great number of unsaturated organic species. Thus ligands derived from ring systems other than cyclopentadiene—*e.g.*, cyclopropene, cyclobutadiene, benzene, and cycloheptatriene—containing 3-, 4-, 6-, and 7-membered rings, respectively—have been shown to form very similar bonds to transition metal atoms. Moreover, non-aromatic olefin and polyolefin systems of many kinds can also form bonds to transition metals by using their pi electrons, much as conventional ligands use their electron pairs, to form donor bonds.

Many of the organometallic compounds in which olefins are attached to transition metal atoms through their pi electrons contain carbonyl groups. In such molecules, the metal atoms generally attain an 18-electron configuration, as they do in the metal carbonyls themselves. In counting electrons, each carbon–carbon double bond is treated as a donor of two electrons. Some representative molecules are shown in diagrams 13–17. In diagram 13

13

14

15

16

17

there is one cyclopentadienyl group (a five-electron donor), one allyl group (a three-electron donor), and two carbonyl groups (which donate two electrons each). These 12 electrons, together with the six possessed by the molybdenum atom, give the required total of 18. In **14** the organic ligand is a butadiene group, while in **15** there are both a cyclopentadienyl group and a cyclooctatetraene group that uses only two of its double bonds to attach itself to the cobalt atom. In **16** there is a benzene ring serving as a six-electron donor in place of three CO groups of a hexacarbonylchromium molecule, $Cr(CO)_6$.

The first organometallic compound of a transition metal (diagram **17**) was characterized as long ago as 1830. The nature of this and related compounds became clear, however, only in the 1950s. Simple metal–carbon sigma bonds also are formed by transition metals, but are stable only under special circumstances.

Transition-metal catalysts. One important use of transition metals and their compounds is as catalysts for a variety of industrial processes, mostly in the petroleum and polymer (plastics, fibres) industries, in which organic molecules are isomerized, built up from simple molecules, oxidized, hydrogenated, or caused to polymerize.

Only a few of the most important such processes and their catalysts can be mentioned here. Catalysts are of two physical types: homogeneous (*i.e.*, dissolved in the reaction mixture) and heterogeneous (*i.e.*, constituting a solid phase separate from and insoluble in the reaction

mixture). Both types are represented on the industrial scene, but the latter are much more common.

The introduction of catalysts that allow polymerization to be carried out at relatively low temperatures and pressures revolutionized the production of polyethylene and polypropylene. Previously polyethylene had to be made by a process requiring pressures of about 1,000 atmospheres, and polypropylene of useful properties was not commercially important. The catalysts devised and applied during the early 1950s are prepared from titanium tetrachloride and an aluminum alkyl such as triethylaluminum: the precipitated, titanium-containing solid, plus the excess aluminum alkyl in solution, constitutes the catalyst. A very different sort of catalyst, consisting of chromium(VI) oxide dispersed on silica-alumina, performs similarly in polymerizing ethylene but cannot produce a useful form of polypropylene.

Chromium in the form of chromium(III) oxide on alumina is the major industrial catalyst for transforming saturated hydrocarbons (*i.e.*, those in which all available valence bonds of the atoms are attached to other atoms) to useful olefins (unsaturated organic compounds), chiefly *n*-butane to butylene and butadiene.

Iron-containing catalysts are used in various processes of which the most notable is that for producing ammonia from nitrogen and hydrogen. This process, developed early in the 20th century, represents the first major industrial application of transition metal catalysis. The catalyst is magnetic triiron tetroxide (Fe_3O_4), "promoted" by the addition of small quantities of potassium oxide, aluminum oxide, calcium oxide, and silica.

Molybdenum in molybdenum(VI) oxide–aluminum oxide mixtures or in cobalt oxide–molybdenum oxide–aluminum oxide mixtures finds many applications, such as desulfurizing gases and liquids; removing lead, nickel, and vanadium from petroleum refinery feed stocks; and in modifying, or "reforming," crude petroleum fractions to increase their octane rating.

Olefins that are free of such impurities as carbon monoxide, sulfur, halogen, and compounds of arsenic or lead (catalyst poisons), can be hydrogenated (*i.e.*, combined with hydrogen) at atmospheric pressure and room temperature, using various types of active nickel preparations as catalysts.

Copper is a component of a variety of catalysts, of which the copper chromites, used for selective hydrogenation of carbonyl groups (compounds containing the divalent organic radical $>CO$), are perhaps the most important. Fats and oils can also be hydrogenated to alcohols using copper catalysts. Palladium chloride together with copper(I) salts forms a homogeneous catalyst for oxidizing ethylene to acetaldehyde (Wacker process), but commercial use of this process has been abandoned. Metallic platinum has a broad spectrum of catalytic activities. One of the most important in terms of tonnage production is in catalytic reforming of petroleum fractions to improve antiknock quality of gasoline. Silver oxide, on an inactive, refractory support, catalyzes oxidation of ethylene to ethylene oxide.

The oxo process (also called hydroformylation), in which certain olefins react with carbon monoxide and hydrogen to give aldehydes (a class of organic compounds that contain the group —CHO), requires a homogeneous catalyst containing a transition metal. The first practicable one was hydrogen tetracarbonylcobaltate(-I), $HCo(CO)_4$, which is formed in the reaction mixture by action of hydrogen on octacarbonyldicobalt, $Co_2(CO)_8$. More recently rhodium complexes have been found to have greater activity at lower temperatures and pressures and to be more easily recovered. The net reaction in the oxo process is represented by

$$RCH=CH_2 \quad + \quad CO \quad + \quad H_2 \longrightarrow RCH_2CH_2CHO.$$

a terminal olefin carbon monoxide hydrogen an aldehyde

Biological functions of transition metals. Several transition elements are important to the chemistry of living systems, the most familiar examples being iron, cobalt, copper, and molybdenum. Iron is by far the most widespread and important transition metal that has a function in living systems; proteins containing iron participate in two main processes, oxygen transport and electron transfer (*i.e.*, oxidation–reduction) reactions. There are also a number of substances that act to store and transport iron itself.

Heme proteins. The chief heme proteins are the hemoglobins, myoglobins, cytochromes, and certain enzymes (enzymes are catalysts for the chemical reactions of biological processes), such as catalase and peroxidase. In all of these the iron is present as a particular type of porphyrin complex called heme (see Figure 6). Hemoglobin

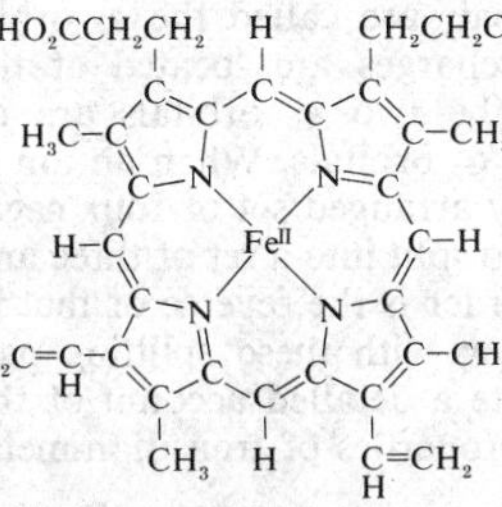

Figure 6: The structure of the heme group in hemoglobin.

Function of hemoglobin has two functions: it binds oxygen molecules to its iron atoms and transports them from the lungs to the muscles, where they are transferred to myoglobin molecules that store them until required for biological oxidations; and it binds carbon dioxide and carries it back to the lungs. It is believed that iron is not involved in the latter function.

The effectiveness of hemoglobin as an oxygen carrier depends on cooperative interactions between the subunits, whereby the binding of molecular oxygen to one heme group increases the binding ability of the next, and so on. The coordination stereochemistry of the iron is a significant factor in the mechanism of this enhancement. Deoxyhemoglobin—*i.e.*, hemoglobin not bound to oxygen—contains iron(II) in a state in which the bonding radius of the iron is so great that it cannot fit into the plane of the four nitrogen atoms of the porphyrin ring but instead lies about 0.75 Å (angstrom; an angstrom is a unit of length equal to 10^{-10} metre) out of that plane. When an oxygen molecule is bound, the bond radius of the iron atom decreases, and it slips back into the plane of the nitrogen atoms. Thus, attachment of a molecule of oxygen to the iron atom moves it about 0.75 Å; when it moves the motion is then transmitted to certain remote parts of the subunit to which this iron atom belongs. As a result of the changes that are thus induced in one subunit, structural changes are caused in other subunits, which increase the affinity for oxygen at the other heme units.

Cytochrome *c* is the most abundant of the cytochromes, a class of important organic compounds with the ability to combine with metals, particularly iron and magnesium. It is a type of heme protein that serves as an electron carrier. The cytochrome *c* molecules in a great range of organisms are very similar, indicating an early evolutionary development with little subsequent change.

Iron–sulfur electron-transfer proteins. The relatively small proteins (molecular weights of 6,000–12,000) known as iron–sulfur electron-transfer proteins contain iron bound by sulfur atoms present in structural units derived from the amino acid cysteine. Such proteins appear to occur in all green plants, including algae, in all photosynthetic bacteria, and in some anaerobic (*i.e.*, living or acting only in the absence of oxygen) bacteria and are evidently essential in the electron-transfer processes involved in photosynthesis, but explicit chemical specification of their activities is still lacking. The ferridoxins vary in chemical type; some contain as few as two iron atoms, others as many as eight. A substance called rubredoxin, which appears to work in conjunction with ferridoxins at least in some micro-organisms, contains only one iron atom in a molecule that has a molecular weight of approximately 6,000. Proteins called hemery-

thrins, involved in respiratory functions of several groups of invertebrate animals, contain iron that is not bound to heme structures. Little is yet known about the chemical basis of their activity.

In man and other higher mammals, iron is stored and transported by ferritin and haemosiderin, which are present in liver, spleen, and bone marrow. Ferritin is a water-soluble substance consisting of a roughly spherical protein sheath approximately 75 Å in inside diameter and 120 Å outside diameter, within which is a structural unit of colloidal, hydrous iron(III) phosphate: as much as 23 percent of the dry weight is iron. Haemosiderin contains even larger proportions of "iron hydroxide." Transferrin is a protein that binds trivalent iron very strongly and transports it between ferritin and red blood cells.

Other transition metals in biological systems. Though cobalt is understood to be an essential trace element in animal nutrition, the only detailed chemical knowledge of its biochemical action has to do with vitamin B_{12} and related co-enzymes. These molecules contain **Vitamin** one atom of cobalt bound in a macrocyclic ring (*i.e.*, **B_{12}** one consisting of many atoms) called corrin, which is similar to a porphyrin ring. Copper is found in both plants and animals, and numerous copper-containing proteins have been isolated. The blood of many lower animals, such as mollusks, cephalopods, gastropods, and decapods, contains respiratory proteins called hemocyanins, which contain copper atoms (but no heme) and appear to bind one oxygen molecule per two copper atoms. Human serum contains a glycoprotein called ceruloplasmin, the molecule of which contains eight copper atoms; its biological function is still uncertain. Other proteins, called cerebrocuprein, erythrocuprein, and hepatocuprein, that are found in the mammalian brain, erythrocytes, and liver, respectively, contain about 60 percent of the total copper in those tissues; their functions are still unknown. There are a number of copper-containing enzymes; examples are (1) ascorbic acid oxidase (an oxidase is an oxidizing enzyme), which contains eight atoms of copper per molecule; it is widely distributed in plants and microorganisms; (2) cytochrome oxidase, which contains heme and copper in a 1:1 ratio; (3) tyrosinases, which catalyze the formation of melanin (brownish-black pigments occurring in hair, skin, and retina of higher animals) and were the first enzymes in which copper was shown to be essential to function.

Vanadium occurs widely in petroleum, notably that from Venezuela, and can be isolated as porphyrin complexes, the origin of which is not known. Vanadium is present in high concentrations in blood cells (vanadocytes) of certain ascidians (sea squirts), apparently in a curious, complex, and poorly understood protein-containing substance called hemovanadin, thought to serve in oxygen transport. Molybdenum is believed to be a necessary trace element in animal diets, but its function and the minimum levels have not been established. Nitrogen-fixing bacteria utilize enzymes that contain both **Nitrogen** molybdenum and iron. One such enzyme, or at least a **fixation** part of it that has been isolated in the crystalline state, contains two atoms of molybdenum and 40 atoms of iron. This protein in association with another, which contains only iron, can catalyze the reduction of nitrogen gas to nitrogen compounds.

THEORIES OF TRANSITION-METAL COMPLEXES

As has been noted, partially filled *d* orbitals account for the characteristic chemical properties of the regular transition elements, both as a class and as individuals. The interpretation and understanding of the chemical and physical properties of these elements thus depends heavily upon the description of these d^n (*n* is one or more but fewer than ten) electron configurations. The five orbitals of each *d* shell, regardless of principal quantum number, have the shapes and designations shown in Figure 7. The radial extent or size changes with principal quantum number, but the shapes are characteristic for all sets.

For an atom or ion in free space and not subject to any electromagnetic field, the five orbitals of a set have equal energies; but in chemical compounds, the surrounding

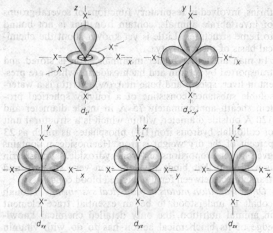

Figure 7: The shapes of the d orbitals and their conventional designations. The symbols X$^-$ represent some or all of a set of six octahedrally located anions.

d-orbital subsets

atoms cause the set to separate into subsets, differing in energy. This separation has a profound influence upon the spectroscopic properties (including colour) and magnetic properties of the substance, and the analysis of such effects has stimulated a great deal of theoretical and experimental effort. The most common situations to be considered are those in which a transition-metal ion occurs in an octahedron or a tetrahedron of surrounding anions or other ligands. Such cases illustrate the handling of the problem of the electronic structure of transition-metal ions in compounds.

Three different theoretical approaches have been used: (1) the valence-bond treatment, pioneered in the United States by Linus Pauling; (2) the crystal-field or ligand-field theory, first proposed by Hans Bethe and developed extensively by the U.S. physicist J.H. Van Vleck; and (3) the molecular orbital theory, the application of which to transition-metal complexes was first discussed by Van Vleck. The second and third methods are used almost exclusively, and only those two will be outlined here.

Crystal-field and ligand-field theories. The crystal-field theory (CFT) employs an extreme electrostatic model, in which the ligands are treated as point charges (i.e., as if the entire negative charge were concentrated at a single point in space) if they are anions or as point dipoles (i.e., pairs of particles having equal and opposite charges that are separated by a finite distance) if they are neutral molecules. These extreme approximations are useful because they preserve certain essential features of the actual physical condition and yet reduce the mathematical problem to one that can be solved. Since the CFT treatment makes no allowance for covalence in the metal–ligand bonds, it necessarily does not account for all aspects of the electronic structures of complexes, even the most ionic ones. It can be amended, however, by empirical adjustment of certain parameters, to allow for some of the effects of covalence, without sacrificing mathematical convenience. This version of the theory, which can correlate much of the data on complexes of metals in their normal oxidation states, is called ligand-field theory (LFT).

Orbital splitting patterns. Crystal-field theory treats the question of how the energies of a set of d electrons or orbitals are split when a set of ligands is placed around a central metal ion; it does so by treating the ligands as a set of negative charges. The simplest case to consider is that of an ion with a single d electron, surrounded by six negative charges at the vertices of an octahedron. This arrangement is defined, relative to a set of Cartesian axes, x, y, z, shown in Figure 8. By comparing the shapes of the d orbitals (see Figure 7) with this arrangement, it can be seen that the d_{xy}, d_{xz}, and d_{yz} orbitals have equivalent relationships to the set of charges. Thus, the electron will be repelled to the same extent by the negative charges regardless of which of the three orbitals it occupies. The three orbitals thus have equal energy and are called triply

Octa-hedral complexes

degenerate. It is not particularly obvious from a pictorial argument, but mathematical analysis shows that each of the other two orbitals, d_{z^2} and $d_{x^2-y^2}$, causes the electron to experience the same amount of electrostatic repulsion from the surrounding charges; they are described as doubly degenerate. Thus, the first important conclusion of the crystal-field theory is that the spatial relationships of the d orbitals to the surrounding charges cause the set of five d orbitals to be split into two subsets; the orbitals within each subset are equivalent to each other and are thus degenerate, but they are no longer degenerate with those in the other subset. Those in the subset consisting of the d_{xy}, d_{yz}, and d_{zx} orbitals are known as the t_{2g} orbitals; the d_{z^2} and $d_{x^2-y^2}$, pair are called the e_g orbitals. When the surrounding charges are located at the vertices of an octahedron, the two e_g orbitals are of higher energy than the three t_{2g} orbitals. When an ion is surrounded by a tetrahedrally arranged set of four negative charges, the d orbitals also split into a set of three and a set of two, but the energy order is the reverse of that in the octahedral case. Beginning with these splitting patterns it is possible to elaborate a detailed account of the magnetic and spectroscopic properties of transition-metal ions in their compounds.

Tetra-hedral complexes

Magnetic and spectroscopic properties. Discussion of magnetic properties must begin with the basic question of how many unpaired electrons will be present. This is decided by the competition between two factors: (1) the electrons tend to occupy separate orbitals since this minimizes repulsions between them; and (2) the electrons also tend to occupy orbitals of lower energy in preference to higher ones. For ions with one, two, and three d electrons in octahedral fields, the first factor dictates, without opposition from the second, that the electrons occupy separate t_{2g} orbitals; such ions therefore always have 1, 2, and 3 unpaired electrons. Similarly, for configurations of eight and nine d electrons, the only possibilities are six electrons in t_{2g} orbitals and two in e_g orbitals, and six electrons in t_{2g} orbitals and three in e_g orbitals ($t_{2g}^6 e_g^2$ and $t_{2g}^6 e_g^3$), and such ions must always have 2 and 1 unpaired electrons, respectively. For cases of d^4, d^5, d^6, and d^7 configurations, the number of unpaired electrons depends on which of the two factors dominates. If the splitting (the energy difference between e_g and t_{2g} orbitals) is relatively small, control by the first factor produces the high-spin configurations, $t_{2g}^3 e_g$, $t_{2g}^3 e_g^2$, $t_{2g}^4 e_g^2$, and $t_{2g}^5 e_g^2$, which have 4, 5, 4, and 3 unpaired electrons, respectively. When the difference is relatively large, control by the second factor produces the low-spin configurations t_{2g}^4, t_{2g}^5, t_{2g}^6, and $t_{2g}^6 e_g$, with 2, 1, 0, and 1 unpaired electrons, respectively. In tetrahedral complexes the splitting is always sufficiently small so that the first factor dominates and high-spin states are always obtained. Once the number of unpaired electrons is known, numerical values of the magnetic moments are calculated by taking account of the interaction of the orbital-angular momentum with the spin-angular momentum.

Factors influencing magnetic properties

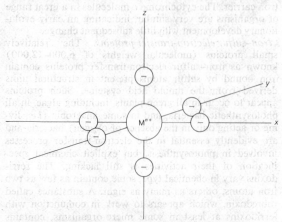

Figure 8: An octahedrally arranged set of negative charges in relation to a set of Cartesian coordinates with a positively charged metal ion (M^{n+} at the centre).

The spectra emitted by the electronic structures of transition-metal ions, which are responsible for their colours, can be understood in terms of the CFT splitting patterns. For a d^1 ion in an octahedral field, a single electronic transition, $t_{2g} \rightarrow e_g$, is expected; that is, the absorption of light raises the energy of an electron and causes it to pass from the low-energy t_{2g} orbital to the high-energy e_g orbital. The titanium(III), Ti^{3+}, ion, for example, has just a single absorption band in the visible region of the spectrum, at a wavelength of about 5,000 nanometres, corresponding to an energy of 20,000 cm^{-1}, which is assigned to this transition. This says that the orbital energy difference for Ti^{3+} in $[Ti(H_2O)_6]^{3+}$ is 20,000 per centimetre. For configurations with more than one d electron, electronic interactions require that an elaborate treatment, which cannot be explained here, be used.

The difference in the colours of hexaquonickel(II) ion, $[Ni(H_2O)_6]^{2+}$ (green), and tris(ethylenediamine)nickel(II) ion, $[Ni(H_2NCH_2CH_2NH_2)_3]^{2+}$ (purple), reflects the fact that the six nitrogen atoms cause a greater splitting than the six oxygen atoms.

In general, the relative magnitudes of d orbital splittings for a given ion with different ligand sets fall in a consistent order. This ordering of ligands according to their ability to split the d orbitals was discovered empirically in the 1930s and is called the spectrochemical series. A short list of ligands in order of their splitting power is fluoride (weakest), water, thiocyanate, pyridine or ammonia, ethylenediamine, nitrite, cyanide (strongest).

Jahn-Teller effect. According to the Jahn-Teller theorem, any molecule or complex ion in an electronically degenerate state will be unstable relative to a configuration of lower symmetry in which the degeneracy is absent. The chief applications of this theorem in transition-metal chemistry are in connection with octahedrally coordinated metal ions with high-spin d^4, low-spin d^7, and d^9 configurations; in each of these cases the t_{2g} orbitals are all equally occupied (either all half filled or all filled) and there is a single electron or a single vacancy in the e_g orbitals. Either an e_g or an e_g^3 configuration gives rise to a doubly degenerate (E) ground state, and thus a distortion of the octahedron is expected. In other words, high-spin d^4, low-spin d^7, and d^9 ions should be found in distorted, not regular, octahedral environments. It has been found by experiment that, with few possible exceptions, this is the case. The exceptions do not necessarily constitute violations of the Jahn-Teller theorem, because the slightness of the distortions may be within experimental error.

Distorted complexes By far the most common form of distortion in the three cases given above is an elongation of the octahedron along one of its fourfold axes. Thus, two opposite ligands are farther from the metal ion than the other, coplanar (*i.e.*, lying in one plane) set of four. Such effects have been observed in compounds and complexes of high-spin chromium(II) and manganese(III) ions, $(t_{2g}^3 e_g)$; low-spin cobalt(II) and nickel(III) ions, $(t_{2g}^6 e_g)$; and copper(II) and silver(I) ions $(t_{2g}^6 e_g^3)$. The greatest body of data available is for copper(II) compounds, and some representative sets of copper–ligand distances are copper(II) chloride, four chloride ions at 2.30 Å and two at 2.95 Å; copper(II) bromide, four bromide ions at 2.40 Å and two at 3.18 Å.

Molecular-orbital theory. The molecular-orbital (MO) treatment of the electronic structures of transition-metal complexes is, in principle, a more flexible approach than the CFT or LFT treatments. Because a great many complexes and compounds in the ordinary oxidation states (II, III) of the transition metals are substantially ionic, the CFT and LFT treatments are useful though not exact. In the MO method, the ligand-atom orbitals and all of the valence-shell orbitals of the metal atom are presumed to interact to form molecular orbitals.

The interaction of a metal ion from the first transition series and an octahedral set of ligands that interact only through orbitals directed toward the metal ion results in the separation of the d orbitals of the metal ion into two sets of molecular orbitals; a t_{2g} set and a higher energy e_g set. This is the same pattern as that obtained in the CFT

treatment, but the difference is that now the t_{2g} and e_g orbitals are regarded not as pure d orbitals but as molecular orbitals, having both metal d orbital and ligand orbital components. Thus, the modifications of CFT that lead to LFT—that is, inclusion of covalence effects—are in harmony with the basic ideas of the MO treatment.

II. The chemistry of the individual transition elements

Although the transition elements have many general chemical similarities, each one has a detailed chemistry of its own. The closest relationships are usually to be found among the three elements in each vertical group in the periodic table, although within each group the element of the first series usually differs more from the other two than they differ from each other. Most of the first series elements are more familiar and technically important than the heavier members of their vertical group. Thus, it is convenient to discuss first each of the metals of the first transition series and then to discuss the remaining ones in pairs.

THE ELEMENTS OF THE FIRST TRANSITION SERIES

Before considering in detail the chemistry of the individual elements, a few of the chemical trends to be found in the first transition series may be summarized.

General chemical trends of the first transition series

1. From titanium to manganese the highest valence exhibited, which usually is found only in oxo compounds, fluorides, or chlorides, corresponds to the total number of $3d$ and $4s$ electrons in the atom. The stability of this highest oxidation state decreases from titanium(IV) to manganese(VII). Following manganese—that is, for iron, cobalt, and nickel—oxidation states corresponding to the loss of all $3d$ and $4s$ electrons do not occur; higher oxidation states in general become progressively more difficult to attain because the increasing nuclear charge causes the $3d$ electrons to be more tightly bound. Very high oxidation states occur only for chromium(V, VI), manganese(V, VI, VII), and iron(V, VI) and apart from the fluorides, such as chromium(V) fluoride, CrF_5, and chromium(VI) fluoride, CrF_6, and oxofluorides such as manganese(VII) trioxide fluoride, MnO_3F, the main chemistry in these oxidation states is that of oxo anions such as manganate(VII), MnO_4^-; chromate(VI), CrO_4^{2-}; and ferrate(VI), FeO_4^{2-}. All of these compounds are powerful oxidizing agents.

2. The oxides of each element become more acidic with increasing oxidation number, and the halides become more covalent and susceptible to hydrolysis.

3. In the oxo anions characteristic of the higher valence states the metal atom is tetrahedrally surrounded by oxygen atoms, whereas in the oxides formed in the lower valence states the atoms are usually octahedrally coordinated.

4. In the oxidation states II and III, complexes in aqueous solution or in crystals are usually four-, five- or six-coordinated.

5. Oxidation states lower than II are not found in the ordinary chemistries of the transition elements, except for copper. The lower oxidation states are, however, attainable for all the elements using ligands of the carbon monoxide type.

It should be emphasized that the occurrence of a given oxidation state, as well as the stereochemistry of the compounds formed in that state, depend very critically on the experimental conditions and that species having no independent existence under ordinary conditions of temperature and pressure in air may well be the dominant species under other conditions. Thus a transition-metal ion may be obtained in a particular configuration that is difficult to produce by other means through incorporation of the ion into a crystalline host lattice, as well as by using ligands of rigid geometry. Therefore, the principal types of compounds and stereochemistries mentioned in the following descriptions are not the only ones possible for the elements, though they are the most common.

The oxidation state II is important for all of the elements in the first transition series, which form well-defined binary compounds such as oxides and halides that are essentially ionic in nature in that oxidation state. With the exception of titanium, they also form well-defined aquo ions formulated $[M(H_2O)_6]^{2+}$.

Oxidation states

All of the elements form some compounds in oxidation state III. That is the highest oxidation state known for copper and is not a stable one in its aqueous chemistry;

oxidation state III is important, however, in the normal chemical compounds of the elements. The fluorides and oxides of those elements in oxidation state III are generally ionic in nature, although the chlorides and bromides have more covalent character. The oxidation state IV is important only for the earlier elements, namely, titanium and vanadium: for chromium, manganese, iron, cobalt, and nickel, the state IV is found mainly in fluorides, fluoro complex anions, and some other unusual situations.

For the ions of the first transition series, the spectroscopic and magnetic properties can be accounted for quite well using crystal- or ligand-field theory; magnetic properties are due primarily to the unpaired spins with only secondary effects from orbital angular momentum superimposed. For the heavier transition elements, the interpretation of magnetic properties is much more difficult.

Titanium. The preparation of pure titanium is difficult because of its reactivity. Titanium cannot be obtained by the common method of reducing the oxide with carbon because a very stable carbide is readily produced, and, moreover, the metal is quite reactive toward oxygen and nitrogen at elevated temperatures. Therefore, special processes have been devised. One of the ores, such as ilmenite ($FeTiO_3$) or rutile (TiO_2), is treated at red heat with carbon and chlorine to yield titanium tetrachloride, $TiCl_4$, which is fractionally distilled to eliminate impurities such as ferric chloride, $FeCl_3$. The $TiCl_4$ is then reduced with molten magnesium at about 800° C (1,500° F) in an atmosphere of argon, and metallic titanium is produced as a spongy mass from which the excess of magnesium and magnesium chloride can be removed by volatilization at about 1,000° C (1,800° F). The sponge may then be fused in an atmosphere of argon or helium in an electric arc and be cast into ingots. On the laboratory scale, extremely pure titanium can be made by vaporizing the tetraiodide, TiI_4, in very pure form and decomposing it on a hot wire in vacuum.

The atoms are arranged in a hexagonal, close-packed lattice in titanium, which resembles other transition metals such as iron and nickel in being hard, refractory, and a good conductor of heat and electricity. It is quite light in comparison to other metals of similar mechanical and thermal properties, however, as well as unusually resistant to certain types of corrosion, and therefore it has come into demand for special applications in engineering.

Although titanium is rather unreactive at ordinary temperatures, it combines directly with many nonmetals, such as hydrogen, the halogens, oxygen, nitrogen, carbon, boron, silicon, and sulfur at elevated temperatures. The resulting nitride (TiN), carbide (TiC), and borides (TiB and TiB_2) are interstitial compounds that are very stable, hard, and refractory. Titanium is not attacked by mineral acids at room temperature or by hot aqueous alkali; it dissolves in hot hydrochloric acid, giving trivalent titanium species, and hot nitric acid converts it into a hydrous oxide that is rather insoluble in acid or base. The best solvents for the metal are hydrofluoric acid or other acids to which fluoride ions have been added; such mediums dissolve titanium and hold it in solution because of the formation of fluoro complexes.

Divalent titanium. The chemistry of divalent titanium is rather restricted. The well-defined compounds are titanium(II) chloride ($TiCl_2$), bromide ($TiBr_2$), iodide (TiI_2), and oxide (TiO). The halides are best obtained by reduction of the tetrahalides with titanium metal or by the decomposition of the trihalides at high temperature. The oxide, which can be made by heating TiO_2, titanium(IV) oxide, with titanium, has the same type of crystal structure as sodium chloride, but it is usually non-stoichiometric (*i.e.*, the component substances are not characteristically proportional).

Trivalent titanium. Many compounds are formed by trivalent titanium, both in the solid state and in solution. The more important solid compounds are the trichloride, which occurs in several crystalline forms, and the oxide, Ti_2O_3. One form of the trichloride, formed from the tetrachloride, is particularly important as a catalyst in the

stereospecific polymerization of propylene to make the useful polymer polypropylene.

Aqueous solutions of trivalent titanium containing the hexaquotitanium(III) ion, $[Ti(H_2O)_6]^{3+}$, can be readily obtained by reducing aqueous quadrivalent titanium either electrolytically or with zinc. The violet solutions are oxidized by atmospheric oxygen and must therefore be kept in an inert atmosphere; they often are used as fairly rapid, mild reducing agents in volumetric analysis. Titanium in the trivalent state also forms a number of octahedral complexes, such as hexafluorotitanate(III) ($TiF_6{}^{3-}$), hexachlorotitanate(III), ($TiCl_6{}^{3-}$), and a number of others containing neutral ligands.

Tetravalent titanium. Oxidation state IV is the most important one for titanium. The dioxide, TiO_2, occurs in three crystal modifications, rutile, anatase, and brookite, all found in nature, and in all the crystal forms the dioxide is colourless when pure and is often employed as a white pigment. A hydrated form of the dioxide is obtained by adding a base to solutions of quadrivalent titanium.

The four halides, TiF_4, $TiCl_4$, $TiBr_4$, and TiI_4, are known. The most important, the tetrachloride, is a colourless liquid—melting point −23° C (−9° F), boiling point 136° C (277° F)—with a pungent odour that fumes strongly in moist air and is vigorously, though not violently, hydrolyzed by water to give the dioxide and hydrochloric acid.

A characteristic reaction of aqueous solutions of tetravalent titanium is the development of an intense orange colour when hydrogen peroxide is added, and this reaction can be used for the colorimetric determination of either titanium or hydrogen peroxide.

Tetravalent titanium forms a number of complexes, including such species as hexafluorotitanate(IV), $TiF_6{}^{2-}$, and hexachlorotitanate(IV), $TiCl_6{}^{2-}$, and many molecular complexes that form upon the addition of two neutral ligands to $TiCl_4$. Examples of the latter are tetrachlorobis(diethyl ether)titanium(IV), $TiCl_4[O(C_2H_5)_2]$, and tetrachlorobis(triethylphosphine oxide)titanium(IV), $TiCl_4[OP(C_2H_5)_3]_2$.

Other compounds of tetravalent titanium include anhydrous titanium(IV) nitrate, $Ti(NO_3)_4$ (a volatile compound made by the action of dinitrogen pentoxide, N_2O_5, on the hydrated form of the compound), which is an extremely reactive oxidizing agent toward organic substances, and the sulfate, the structural nature of which is not known.

Vanadium. The preparation of very pure vanadium is difficult because the metal is quite reactive toward oxygen, nitrogen, and carbon at elevated temperatures. Because the major commercial use of vanadium is in steel and cast iron, to which it lends ductility and shock resistance, vanadium is produced commercially mainly in the form of an iron alloy called ferrovanadium. When the very pure metal is required, it may be obtained by processes described in the foregoing discussion of titanium. Very pure vanadium metal resembles titanium in being quite corrosion resistant, hard, and steel gray in colour. In the massive state it is not attacked by air, water, alkalies, or nonoxidizing acids other than hydrofluoric acid. It dissolves in nitric acid, concentrated sulfuric acid, or aqua regia and at high temperatures will combine with nearly all nonmetals. For vanadium the important oxidation states are II, III, IV, and V.

Divalent vanadium. The chemistry of the divalent state is rather limited. The black vanadium(II) oxide, VO, has a rocksalt type of structure but shows a marked tendency to be non-stoichiometric: it can be obtained with from 45 to 55 atom-percent oxygen. It has a metallic lustre and rather good electrical conductivity of a metallic nature and dissolves in mineral acids to give solutions containing the vanadium(II) ion, V^{2+}. Electrolytic or zinc reduction of acidic solutions of vanadium in its higher oxidation states produces violet, air-sensitive solutions that also contain the V^{2+} ion, which is present as an octahedral hexaquo species, $[V(H_2O)_6]^{2+}$. Such solutions are very strong reducing agents and attack even water, with evolution of hydrogen. The hexaquo ion is

Titanium production

Titanium tetra-chloride

Preparation and uses of vanadium

present in various salts as, for example, the type of double sulfate known as Tutton salts, $M_2[V(H_2O)_6](SO_4)_2$, in which M is an alkali-metal ion.

Trivalent vanadium. The chemistry of the trivalent state is more extensive. All four halides are known as well as the black, refractory vanadium(III) oxide, V_2O_3, which can be made by reduction of vanadium(V) oxide, V_2O_5, with hydrogen or carbon monoxide. The trioxide has a pronounced tendency to be non-stoichiometric, and it is entirely basic in nature, dissolving in acids to give solutions of the vanadium(III) ion, V^{3+}, or its complexes. A hydrous form of the oxide can be precipitated upon addition of hydroxides to such solutions. The hexaquovanadium(III) ion, $[V(H_2O)_6]^{3+}$, is blue in colour and subject to oxidation by air. There are a variety of complexes of the V^{3+} ion, especially with anions, such as tris-(oxalato)vanadate(III), $[V(C_2O_4)_3]^{3-}$; hexacyanovanadate(III), $[V(CN)_6]^{3-}$; and hexakis(isothiocyanato)vanadate(III), $[V(NCS)_6]^{3-}$.

Tetravalent vanadium. The oxidation state IV of vanadium is the most stable under ordinary conditions. The most important compounds of tetravalent vanadium are those containing the vanadyl(IV) (VO^{2+}) unit, which can persist through a variety of chemical reactions. It readily unites with either four or five ligands to form either five- or six-coordinated complexes. The aqueous pentaaquovanadyl(IV) ion, $[VO(H_2O)_5]^{2+}$, is blue and occurs in a number of salts. The vanadium–oxygen bond is essentially a double bond with a length in the range of 1.5–1.6 Å. Vanadium(IV) fluoride (VF_4), chloride (VCl_4), and bromide (VBr_4) are stable solid compounds, but there is only indirect evidence for the existence of the iodide, VI_4, in the vapour phase. The dark blue vanadium(IV) oxide, VO_2, can be prepared by mild reduction of vanadium(V) oxide, V_2O_5.

Pentavalent vanadium. In oxidation state V, vanadium has an extensive chemistry. Vanadium(V) oxide, V_2O_5, is obtained by burning the finely divided metal in an excess of oxygen but is generally contaminated with small amounts of the lower oxides. It is amphoteric in character; *i.e.*, it dissolves in either acids or bases. Solutions so obtained are moderately strong oxidizing agents as indicated, for example, by the fact that chlorine is evolved when the oxide V_2O_5 is dissolved in hydrochloric acid. In sodium hydroxide solution, V_2O_5 dissolves to give colourless solutions containing vanadate ions. On addition of acid to about pH 6.5 the solutions become bright orange and remain so until, at around pH 2, a brown precipitate of V_2O_5 is formed; the precipitate redissolves when more acid is added and the dioxovanadium ion, VO_2^+, is formed. Vanadate solutions are quite complex in nature and still not completely understood; available data indicate the presence of mono-, di-, and trinuclear species, formulated $[VO_3OH]^{2-}$, $[V_2O_6(OH)]^{3-}$, and $[V_3O_9]^{3-}$, in basic solution, and polyvanadate ions, such as $V_{10}O_{28}^{6-}$, in acid solution.

The only halide of pentavalent vanadium is white vanadium(V) fluoride, VF_5, which is very volatile—melting point 19.5° C (67.1° F), boiling point 48° C (118° F). The action of halogens on the oxide V_2O_5 results in the formation of the oxohalides, vanadyl(V) fluoride (VOF_3), chloride ($VOCl_3$), and bromide ($VOBr_3$), which all have structures that are polymeric in the solid because of bridging halogen atoms.

Chromium. The name of the element chromium (from Greek *chrōmos*, "colour") connotes the pronounced and varied colorations of chromium compounds. The red colour of ruby and the green colour of emerald, to mention only gems, are due to small amounts of chromium. The free metal is never found in nature; most ores consist of the mineral chromite, the ideal formula of which is $FeCr_2O_4$. Natural deposits are usually contaminated with magnesium, aluminum, and silica and their chromium content varies from 42 to 56 percent. One of the chief uses of chromium is in ferrous alloys, for which the pure metal is not required. Accordingly, chromite is often reduced with carbon in a furnace, producing the alloy ferrochromium, which contains iron and chromium in an atom ratio of approximately 1 to 2. To obtain pure chromium, chromite is first treated with molten alkali and oxygen, converting all of the chromium to the alkali chromate, and the latter is dissolved in water and eventually precipitated as sodium dichromate, $Na_2Cr_2O_7$. The dichromate is then reduced with carbon to chromium(III) oxide, Cr_2O_3, and that oxide in turn reduced with aluminum to give the chromium metal.

The metal is white, hard, lustrous, and brittle and is extremely resistant to ordinary corrosive reagents; this resistance accounts for its extensive use as an electroplated protective coating. Chromium metal dissolves rather readily in nonoxidizing mineral acids—for example, hydrochloric or sulfuric acids; it does not dissolve in cold aqua regia or in nitric acid because of a curious phenomenon known as passivation, in which the metal presumably becomes covered with a thin unreactive coating. At elevated temperatures chromium unites directly with the halogens or with sulfur, silicon, boron, nitrogen, carbon, or oxygen.

While chromium forms compounds in all formal oxidation states from -2 to $+6$, the oxidation states $+2$, $+3$, and $+6$ are of principal importance.

Binary compounds. The important binary compounds of chromium are the halides and the oxides. Divalent chromium forms all four halides, with chromium(II) chloride, $CrCl_2$, being the most common and important of these. It dissolves in water to give a blue solution containing the chromium(II) ion, Cr^{2+}. Trivalent chromium also forms all four halides, but again only the chloride is important. The anhydrous substance, chromium(III) chloride, $CrCl_3$, which can be prepared by the action of thionyl chloride, $SOCl_2$, on the hydrated chloride, sublimes in a stream of chlorine gas at about 600° C (about 1,100° F); but if heated to such a temperature in the absence of chlorine it decomposes to chromium(II) chloride ($CrCl_2$) and chlorine. The flaky appearance of $CrCl_3$ is a consequence of its crystal structure, which is of an unusual type. It consists of close-packed layers of chloride ions with metal ions present only between every other layer; because the layers between which there are no metal ions are only weakly held together, the crystal has pronounced cleavage parallel to the layers. The only stable halides formed in higher oxidation states are the tetrafluoride, pentafluoride, and hexafluorides (CrF_4, CrF_5, and CrF_6, respectively).

Three oxides of chromium are important, Cr_2O_3, CrO_2, and CrO_3. The green oxide, Cr_2O_3, which has the same structure as corundum (aluminum oxide), is formed on burning the metal in oxygen, on thermal decomposition of CrO_3 or of ammonium dichromate, or by roasting the hydrous oxide, $Cr_2O_3 \cdot nH_2O$. The latter, commonly called chromic hydroxide despite its variable water content and the lack of direct evidence that it contains hydroxide ions, is precipitated on addition of alkali hydroxide to solutions of chromic salts. If Cr_2O_3 is ignited strongly it becomes inert toward both acid and base, but otherwise it and its hydrous form are amphoteric (capable of acting either as an acid or as a base), dissolving readily in acid to give the hexaaquochromium(III) ion, $[Cr(H_2O)_6]^{3+}$, and in concentrated alkali to form anions the exact natures of which are not known. The oxide Cr_2O_3 can be fused with the oxides of several bivalent metals to give compounds of general formula $M^{2+}Cr_2O_4$ (M^{2+} representing a dipositive ion), which are mixed metal oxides having the spinel structure (spinel is a natural oxide of magnesium and aluminum, $MgAl_2O_4$); many of these mixed oxides are of interest because of their magnetic properties.

Chromium(IV) oxide, CrO_2, which is normally synthesized by hydrothermal reduction of CrO_3, is ferromagnetic and has metallic conductance.

Chromium(VI) oxide, CrO_3, is obtained as an orange-red precipitate upon adding sulfuric acid to solutions of sodium or potassium dichromate. The red solid is thermally unstable above its melting point, 197° C (387° F); after various intermediate stages, it loses oxygen and transforms to Cr_2O_3; and it is readily soluble in water, producing highly poisonous solutions that constitute the usual medium for the electrodeposition of chromium.

Vana-dium(V) oxide (margin)

Oxides of chromium (margin)

Solutions of CrO_3 react vigorously and sometimes explosively with organic matter; however, such solutions are often used for controlled oxidations in organic synthesis, for which purpose solutions in acetic acid are very convenient.

As noted in the foregoing, chromium oxides supported on other oxides, such as alumina, have important applications as industrial catalysts.

Aqueous chemistry. The aqueous chemistry of chromium centres around the Cr^{2+} ion, the Cr^{3+} ion, the complexes of these ions, and the chromates, CrO_4^{2-} and $Cr_2O_7^{2-}$. Aqueous solutions of the chromium(II) ion, Cr^{2+}, which is sky-blue in colour, are best prepared by dissolving chromium metal in dilute mineral acids in the absence of oxygen, but they may also be prepared by reducing solutions of trivalent chromium with zinc amalgam or electrolytically. Various hydrated salts can be crystallized from these solutions—*e.g.*, $CrSO_4 \cdot 5H_2O$, $CrCl_2 \cdot 4H_2O$, and $Cr(ClO_4)_2 \cdot 6H_2O$.

The chromium(II) ion is readily oxidized by air, and therefore solutions must be protected. Even so they decompose, at rates varying with the acidity and the anions present, reducing water with the liberation of hydrogen.

In nearly all chromium(II) compounds the coordination is octahedral. Because of the electronic structure of the chromium(II) ion, however, the octahedron is generally quite distorted because of the Jahn-Teller effect (see above). In nearly all compounds of chromium(II), that ion is in the high-spin electronic configuration, and occupation of one of the antibonding e_g orbitals by a single electron leads to a lengthening of two of the bonds in the octahedron.

The chemistry of trivalent chromium is very extensive. There are literally thousands of complexes that are, with almost no exceptions, of octahedral stereochemistry. The principal characteristic of these complexes in aqueous solution is their relative kinetic inertness. The hexaaquochromium(III) ion, $[Cr(H_2O)_6]^{3+}$, which has a regular octahedral structure, occurs in aqueous solution and in numerous salts, such as the violet hydrate, $[Cr(H_2O)_6]Cl_3$, and in an extensive series of chromium alums represented by the formula $MCr(SO_4)_2 \cdot 12H_2O$, in which M represents an alkali cation such as potassium, K^+. The aquo ion is readily hydrolyzed (*i.e.*, transformed by reaction with water) to the hydroxopentaaquochromium ion, $[Cr(H_2O)_5OH]^{2+}$, and as acidity is further decreased that substance condenses to give a dimeric hydroxo-bridged species and, ultimately, polymeric materials of high molecular weight that precipitate as dark green gels.

The chromium(III) ion has a particular affinity for ammonia and other ligands in which amine-type nitrogen atoms are coordinated. An enormous number of such complexes, called ammines, have been prepared and their chemistry investigated in considerable detail. In addition, many other complexes, including anionic ones such as hexafluorochromate(III), CrF_6^{3-}, and hexacyanochromate(III), $Cr(CN)_6^{3-}$, are formed. The slow reactivity of chromium(III) complexes in ligand replacement reactions accounts in part for the enormous variety of known complexes, because many that are not thermodynamically stable can nevertheless be isolated.

The electronic, spectral, and magnetic properties of the octahedrally coordinated chromium(III) ion are relatively uncomplicated but are of considerable importance. All compounds containing octahedrally coordinated chromium(III) ion are paramagnetic (weakly magnetizable) because of the presence of three unpaired electrons in the t_{2g} orbitals. The visible absorption bands that account for the colour of the chromium(III) ion in its various compounds are attributable to electronic transitions from the ground (*i.e.*, lowest energy) state. The presence of chromium(III) ions replacing some aluminum ions in α-Al_2O_3 accounts for the red colour of the mineral ruby. In addition, however, there is another important aspect to the electronic behaviour of the chromium(III) ion in this environment. Besides the transitions that cause the red colour, there are two transitions that give rise to extremely sharp, though weak, lines. In the

high-energy states that result from these sharp transitions, there is but a single unpaired electron. These states play a key role in the operation of the laser that uses ruby crystals.

The chromate(VI), CrO_4^{2-}, and dichromate(VI), $Cr_2O_7^{2-}$, ions have been mentioned previously as examples of oxo ions of the transition elements. They are the most important species formed by chromium in its six-valent state. The pH-dependent equilibrium between the chromate and dichromate ions is quite labile (*i.e.*, readily undergoes change), and upon the addition of cations (*e.g.*, barium ion, Ba^{2+}; lead ion, Pb^{2+}; and silver ion, Ag^+) that form insoluble chromates, the chromate, not the dichromate, ion is precipitated. Solutions of chromates and dichromates are powerful oxidizing agents and are often so used in preparative chemistry and in analytical chemistry. Unlike the analogous oxo species of molybdenum and tungsten, the chromates have little tendency to form more complex polynuclear oxo species, although trichromates, $Cr_3O_{10}^{2-}$, and tetrachromates, $Cr_4O_{13}^{2-}$, are known.

Manganese. As with titanium, vanadium, and chromium, the highest oxidation state ($+7$) of manganese corresponds to the total number of $3d$ and $4s$ electrons. That state occurs only in the oxo species manganate(VII) (MnO_4^-), manganese(VII) oxide (Mn_2O_7), and manganese(VII) trioxide fluoride (MnO_3F), which show some similarity to corresponding compounds of the halogens—for example, in the instability of the oxide. Manganese in oxidation state $+7$ is powerfully oxidizing, usually being reduced to divalent manganese. The intermediate oxidation states are known, but, except for some compounds in the $+3$ and $+4$ states, they are not particularly important.

Manganese, first recognized as an element by the Swedish chemist Carl Wilhelm Scheele in 1774, is second only to iron among the transition elements in its abundance in the Earth's crust and is roughly similar to iron in its physical and chemical properties but is harder and more brittle. Although it is widely distributed, manganese occurs in a number of substantial deposits, mainly the oxides, of which the mineral pyrolusite (manganese(IV) oxide, MnO_2) is the most important. Manganese is quite electropositive, dissolving very readily in dilute non-oxidizing acids. Although relatively unreactive toward nonmetals at room temperature, it reacts with many at elevated temperatures. Thus manganese burns in chlorine to give manganese(II) chloride, $MnCl_2$; reacts with fluorine to give manganese(II) and (III) fluorides, MnF_2 and MnF_3; and burns in nitrogen at about $1,200^\circ$ C ($2,200^\circ$ F) to give manganese(II) nitride, Mn_3N_2, and in oxygen to give trimanganese tetroxide Mn_3O_4. Manganese also combines directly with boron, carbon, sulfur, silicon, or phosphorus, but not with hydrogen. The most important oxidation states for manganese are $+2$, $+3$, $+7$.

Divalent manganese. The most important and generally the most stable oxidation state of manganese is $+2$, exhibited in neutral or acid aqueous solution in the very pale pink hexaquomanganese(II) ion $[Mn(H_2O)_6]^{2+}$, which is quite resistant to oxidation. In basic mediums, however, manganese(II) hydroxide, $Mn(OH)_2$, is formed, which is rather easily oxidized even by air. The important binary compounds include the oxide (MnO), the four halides (MnF_2, $MnCl_2$, $MnBr_2$, and MnI_2), the sulfide (MnS), the selenide ($MnSe$), and the telluride ($MnTe$). In addition to the anhydrous halides, hydrated species are readily formed. Although divalent manganese forms many complexes, it is not as strongly bound to ligands as are other divalent cations in the first transition series. The coordination geometry for complexes of Mn^{2+} is usually octahedral, although certain tetrahedral complexes are known. The manganese(II) ion in tetrahedral environments has a green fluorescence and is often used in making commercially important phosphors. For example, Mn^{2+} ions can be substituted for some of the zinc ions (Zn^{2+}) in zinc orthosilicate, Zn_2SiO_4.

Trivalent manganese. Oxidation state $+3$ occurs in the oxide Mn_3O_4, which as a mineral is called haussmannite (which also contains Mn^{2+}), in manganese(III) oxide hydroxide, MnO(OH), and in the mineral braunite (manganese(III) oxide, Mn_2O_3); it also occurs in a number of mixed metal oxide systems. The halides of trivalent manganese are limited to the fluoride, a red-purple solid instantaneously hydrolyzed by water, and the black trichloride, which is not stable above $-40°$ C ($-40°$ F). The manganese(III) ion, Mn^{3+}, can be obtained in aqueous solution by oxidation of Mn^{2+} solutions (by electrolysis or by treatment with the persulfate ion) or by reduction of the manganate(VII) (permanganate) ion, MnO_4^-, under appropriate conditions; but it cannot be obtained in high concentrations because it is capable of oxidizing water. Manganese(III) ion also has a strong tendency to disproportionate, giving Mn^{2+} and manganese(IV) oxide, but it can be stabilized by the formation of certain complexes.

Tetravalent manganese and higher oxidation states. There is a rather restricted chemistry for tetravalent manganese, but one such compound, manganese(IV) oxide (manganese dioxide, MnO_2), is the black mineral pyrolusite, an important ore. A tetrafluoride and the sulfate, $Mn(SO_4)_2$, as well as a few complexes are also known, but there is no aqueous chemistry of tetravalent manganese. In higher oxidation states, one of the best known manganese compounds is potassium manganate-(VII) (permanganate), $KMnO_4$. The manganate(VII) ion and its salts have an intense purple colour, and crystalline materials appear almost black. Potassium manganate(VII) is manufactured on a large scale by electrolytic oxidation of basic solutions of lower valent manganese compounds. Solutions of manganate(VII) are unstable and decompose slowly when acidic, but decomposition of neutral or slightly alkaline solutions is immeasurably slow. The decomposition is catalyzed by light so that standard manganate(VII) solutions must be stored in dark bottles. The manganate(VII) ion is a powerful oxidizing agent in both acid and basic solutions and is often used as an oxidant, both for preparative purposes and in analytical chemistry.

Iron. Hundreds of mineral species contain iron as a constituent, and igneous rocks average 5 percent iron content. The major iron ores are the minerals hematite [iron(III) oxide, Fe_2O_3], magnetite [triiron tetroxide, Fe_3O_4], limonite [iron(III) oxide hydroxide, FeO(OH)], and siderite [iron(II) carbonate, $FeCO_3$].

For the element iron the trends already noted in the relative stabilities of oxidation states among elements of the first transition series are continued, except that there is no compound or chemically important circumstance in which the oxidation state of iron is equal to the total number of its valence shell electrons, eight; the highest known oxidation state is $+6$, which is rare and unimportant. Even the trivalent state, which is important at the position of chromium in the periodic table, loses ground to the divalent state at the position of iron. This trend continues in the remaining elements with the sole exception of trivalent cobalt, which is stable in a host of complexes.

The Mössbauer effect. Iron compounds are amenable to study by taking advantage of a phenomenon known as the Mössbauer effect (the phenomenon of a gamma ray being absorbed and reradiated by a nucleus without recoil). Although the Mössbauer effect has been observed for about one-third of the elements, it is particularly for iron (and to a lesser extent tin) that the effect has been a major research tool for the chemist. In the case of iron the effect depends on the fact that the nucleus of iron-57 can be excited to a high energy state by the absorption of gamma radiation of very sharply defined frequency that is influenced by the oxidation state, electron configuration, and chemical environment of the iron atom and can thus be used as a probe of its chemical behaviour.

Pure iron is a white, lustrous metal that is not particularly hard and is quite reactive. As commonly available, however, iron almost always contains small amounts of carbon, which modify its properties greatly. In a very finely divided state metallic iron is pyrophoric (*i.e.*, it ignites spontaneously). It combines vigorously with chlorine on mild heating and also with a variety of other nonmetals, including all of the halogens, sulfur, phosphorus, boron, carbon, and silicon (the carbide and silicide phases play major roles in the technical metallurgy of iron). Metallic iron dissolves readily in dilute mineral acids. With nonoxidizing acids and in the absence of air divalent iron is obtained; with air present or when warm dilute nitric acid is used, some of the iron goes into solution as the iron(III) ion, Fe^{3+}. Very strongly oxidizing mediums, for example, concentrated nitric acid or acids containing dichromate, passivate iron (*i.e.*, cause it to lose its normal chemical activity), however, much as they do chromium (see above). Air-free water and dilute air-free hydroxides have little effect on the metal, but it is attacked by hot concentrated sodium hydroxide.

Under normal atmospheric conditions iron rusts to form hydrated oxides, a process that occurs in two steps: first, iron dissolves in the acid solution produced by the moisture and the carbon dioxide of the air, to form ferrous iron—*i.e.*, iron(II)—and liberate hydrogen; second, oxygen from the air oxidizes the ferrous iron to form hydrated iron(III) oxide.

The stable structure of iron up to $766°$ C ($1,411°$ F) is that of a crystal form called body-centred cubic, and it is ferromagnetic (*i.e.*, capable of being permanently magnetized). Above this temperature the structure is retained but the magnetic properties change to simple paramagnetic (*i.e.*, capable of being only weakly magnetized and only as long as the magnetizing field is present). At $906°$ C ($1,663°$ F) the structure changes to a crystal form called cubic close-packed; but there is another structural change at $1,401°$ C ($2,554°$ F), and iron reverts to the body-centred cubic structure.

Iron oxides. Despite differences in oxidation state, it is convenient to discuss the oxides of iron together because there are fundamental structural relationships between them. Three iron oxides are known, all of which have some tendency to occur in a non-stoichiometric condition, but the ideal compositions of the phases are FeO, Fe_2O_3, and Fe_3O_4. Iron(II) oxide, FeO, can be obtained, by thermal decomposition of iron(II) oxalate in a vacuum, as a pyrophoric black powder that becomes less reactive if heated to higher temperatures. The crystalline substance can be obtained only by establishing equilibrium conditions at high temperature and then rapidly quenching the system, because at lower temperatures iron(II) oxide is less stable than iron and triiron tetroxide, and slow cooling allows disproportionation (*i.e.*, separation into the more oxidized and the more reduced substances). FeO has the rock-salt structure. It is almost always encountered in an iron-deficient condition, typically having a composition of $Fe_{0.95}O$ (*i.e.*, in the proportion of 95 atoms of iron to 100 atoms of oxygen). Essentially stoichiometric FeO (*i.e.*, having the atomic ratio of one to one) has been prepared from $Fe_{0.95}O$ and iron metal at $777°$ C ($1,431°$ F) and 50 kilo-atmospheres pressure.

Hydrous iron(III) oxide, which can be precipitated from solutions of iron(III) (ferric) ion by ammonia and other bases, exists in several forms that depend on the method of preparation. Upon heating any of these forms above $200°$ C (about $400°$ F), the water is driven off and the final product is the red-brown compound designated α-Fe_2O_3, which is identical to the mineral hematite. It has the same structure as corundum (Al_2O_3), in which the oxide ions form a hexagonally close-packed array (in each layer of the array, every ion is tangent to six others) with the metal ions occupying octahedral interstices. By careful oxidation of triiron tetroxide, Fe_3O_4, or by heating a mineral called lepidocrocite (one of the modifications of FeO(OH)) another type of iron(III) oxide, designated γ-Fe_2O_3, is obtained. The structure of the latter phase can be regarded as a cubic close-packed array (every ion is tangent to four others) of oxide ions with iron(III) ions distributed randomly over both the octahedral and the tetrahedral interstices.

Finally, there is triiron tetroxide, Fe_3O_4, a mixed iron(II)–iron(III) oxide that occurs in nature in the form of black, octahedral crystals of the mineral magnetite; it can

(Marginal notes:)
Potassium manganate (VII)

Rusting of iron

be made by ignition of Fe_2O_3 above 1,400° C (2,550° F) and has a structure related to that of the mineral spinel ($MgAl_2O_4$), in which the iron(II) ions all occupy octahedral interstices while the iron(III) ions are half in tetrahedral and half in octahedral interstices of a cubic close-packed array of oxide ions. Magnetite has electrical conductivity 10^6 times that of Fe_2O_3, probably because of rapid oscillation between oxidation states of iron atoms occupying different sites in the structure.

Divalent iron. The four halides of divalent iron are all known in both anhydrous and hydrated forms. Iron(II) iodide and iron(II) bromide can be prepared by direct reaction of the elements; iron must be present in excess in the case of the bromide, $FeBr_2$. For the fluoride, FeF_2, and the chloride, $FeCl_2$, it is necessary to use hydrogen fluoride, HF, or hydrogen chloride, HCl, rather than fluorine or chlorine in order to avoid formation of the trihalides. Iron metal dissolves in the aqueous hydrohalic acids, and from these solutions the hydrated halides $FeF_2 \cdot 8H_2O$ (colourless), $FeCl_2 \cdot 6H_2O$ (pale green), and $FeBr_2 \cdot 4H_2O$ (pale green) may be crystallized.

Divalent iron forms salts with virtually every stable anion, and the salts are generally green, hydrated, crystalline substances, isolated by evaporation of aqueous solutions. Iron(II) (ferrous) iron exists in aqueous solution as the hexaquoferrate(II) ion $[Fe(H_2O)_6]^{2+}$, which also occurs in many of the crystalline salts, such as the sulfate and the perchlorate. An important double salt that contains this ion is Mohr's salt, $(NH_4)_2SO_4 \cdot FeSO_4 \cdot 6H_2O$, which is fairly stable toward both air oxidation and loss of water and is commonly used in volumetric analysis to prepare standard solutions of ferrous iron. Most other ferrous compounds are more or less susceptible to superficial oxidation by air or loss of water of crystallization, or both, behaviour that is well illustrated by $FeSO_4 \cdot 7H_2O$, which slowly effloresces and becomes yellow brown. The carbonate, hydroxide, and sulfide of divalent iron may be precipitated from aqueous solutions of ferrous salts. Both the carbonate and the hydroxide are white, but they quickly darken in the presence of air as a result of oxidation. The sulfide undergoes slow oxidation. Iron(II) hydroxide, $Fe(OH)_2$, is somewhat amphoteric, readily redissolving in acids and also in concentrated sodium hydroxide. If 50 percent sodium hydroxide is boiled with finely divided iron and then cooled, blue-green crystals of tetrasodium hexahydroxoferrate(II), $Na_4[Fe(OH)_6]$, are obtained.

Aqueous solutions of the iron(II) ion are pale blue green in colour and susceptible to oxidation by molecular oxygen. Iron(II) forms a number of complexes, most of them octahedral; one particularly important example is the hexacyanoferrate(II) (ferrocyanide) ion, $Fe(CN)_6^{4-}$, which is extremely stable. Nearly all iron(II) complexes are high-spin with four unpaired electrons, but $Fe(CN)_6^{4-}$ is low-spin with a t_{2g}^6 configuration.

Trivalent iron. Iron(III) occurs in salts with most anions except those with which it is incompatible because of their character as reducing agents. Thus, no triiodide exists; the only trihalide commonly encountered is the chloride, and that is usually the hexahydrate, which forms as a yellow mass on evaporation of aqueous solutions of iron(III) (ferric) chloride. Salts with oxo anions, such as the perchlorate, nitrate, and sulfate, are generally pale pink to nearly white hydrates obtained by evaporation of aqueous solutions.

Among the most conspicuous and important features of the chemistry of trivalent iron in aqueous solution are its tendency to hydrolyze and to form complexes. Ferric iron has a high-spin d^5 configuration ($t_{2g}^3 e_g^2$) like that of divalent manganese; however, unlike manganese, its solutions generally exhibit a pronounced yellow to orange colour unless they are very strongly acidic. The cause of this colour is partial hydrolysis to hydroxo complexes such as those formulated $[Fe(H_2O)_5(OH)]^{2+}$, $[Fe(H_2O)_4(OH)_2]^+$, and $[Fe(H_2O)_4(OH)_2Fe(H_2O)_4]^{4+}$. Even at the rather acidic pH of 2 the extent of hydrolysis is considerable, and in order to have solutions that contain at least 99 percent of the iron in the form of the pale purple hexaquoferrate(III) ion, $[Fe(H_2O)_6]^{3+}$, the

Iron(III) complexes [left margin note]

pH must be reduced to zero or less. As the pH is raised above 3, more highly condensed species begin to form, attainment of equilibrium becomes sluggish, and colloidal gels are formed. Ultimately, hydrous iron(III) oxide is precipitated as a red-brown gelatinous mass. There is no evidence of the existence of any definite iron(III) hydroxide, $Fe(OH)_3$.

Trivalent iron forms a large number of complexes, most of them octahedral, and the octahedron may be considered its characteristic coordination polyhedron. The affinity of trivalent iron for amine ligands is very low, and no simple complexes with such ligands exist in aqueous solution. Chelating amines, such as ethylenediaminetetracetic acid, form definite complexes, however, and iron may be sequestered (*i.e.*, rendered relatively unreactive) by the addition of such chelating agents to solutions containing small amounts of iron. In general, trivalent iron has its greatest affinity for ligands that coordinate through oxygen atoms—*e.g.*, phosphate ions, polyphosphate ions, and polyols such as glycerols and sugars —and forms fairly strongly complexes with the fluoride ion but not with the chloride ion. In extremely concentrated hydrochloric acid solutions the tetrahedral ion, tetrachloroferrate(III), $FeCl_4^-$, is formed and may be isolated as solid salts by using large cations. The complexes with thiocyanate have an intense red colour, a fact employed in sensitive qualitative and quantitative analytical tests for the iron(III) ion.

The cyanide ion forms the complex hexacyanoferrate(III), $[Fe(CN)_6]^{3-}$, which is exceedingly poisonous, in contrast to hexacyanoferrate(II) $[Fe(CN_6]^{4-}$. The reason for the difference lies in the kinetic lability of the iron(III) complex, $[Fe(CN)_6]^{3-}$, which dissociates rapidly, thereby supplying cyanide ions; whereas the iron(II) complex, $[Fe(CN)_6]^{4-}$, is kinetically inert.

It has long been known that treating a solution of trivalent iron with $[Fe(CN)_6]^{4-}$ yields a blue precipitate called Prussian blue and that treating a solution of divalent iron with $[Fe(CN)_6]^{3-}$ yields a blue precipitate called Turnbull's blue. These substances are actually identical, and their true formula is $MFe_2(CN)_6$, in which M is sodium (Na^+), potassium (K^+), rubidium (Rb^+), but not lithium (Li^+), which is too small, or cesium (Cs^+), which is too big. The structure is made up of a cubic array of iron ions with cyanide ions along cube edges. Every other cube contains an M ion at its centre.

Prussian blue [right margin note]

Cobalt. The trends toward decreased stability for very high oxidation states and increased stability of the +2 state relative to the +3 state, which have been evident through the series titanium, vanadium, chromium, manganese, iron, persist with cobalt. In fact there is a complete absence of oxidation states higher than +4 under chemically significant conditions, and even the latter may be represented by only a few incompletely characterized compounds. The +3 state is relatively unstable in simple compounds, but forms a host of low-spin complexes, most of them involving ammonia or amines as ligands. The oxidation state +1 is perhaps better known for cobalt than for any other element in the first transition series except copper.

The abundance of cobalt in the Earth's crust is relatively low, and the element is widely distributed; even the best cobalt ores contain only low concentrations of the element and require complex processing to concentrate and extract it. In general, little cobalt ore is mined for the cobalt content: the metal is recovered as a by-product from the ores of other metals, particularly copper and nickel.

Cobalt is a hard, bluish-white metal and, along with iron and nickel, is one of the three metals that are ferromagnetic at room temperature. It dissolves slowly in dilute mineral acids, does not combine directly with either hydrogen or nitrogen, but will combine, on heating, with carbon, phosphorus, or sulfur. Cobalt is also attacked by oxygen and by water vapour at elevated temperatures, with the result that cobalt(II) oxide, CoO, is produced.

Cobalt salts and oxides. In aqueous solutions that contain no complexing agents, the cobalt(III) (cobaltic) ion, Co^{3+}, is very unstable in comparison to the cobalt-

(II) (cobaltous) ion, Co^{2+}. Electrolytic or ozone oxidation of cold, acidic perchlorate solutions of Co^{2+}, however, yields the aqueous Co^{3+} ion, which appears to have a half-life of about a month at 0° C (32° F). At room temperature the cobalt(III) ion is rapidly reduced by water.

Oxides of cobalt
Cobalt forms only two well-defined oxides. Cobalt(II) oxide, an olive-green substance, is easily prepared by reaction of the metal with oxygen at high temperatures, by thermal decomposition of the carbonate or nitrate, and in other ways. It has the rock-salt structure and is antiferromagnetic at ordinary temperatures. When cobalt(II) oxide is heated at 400°–500° C (750°–900° F) in an atmosphere of oxygen, tricobalt tetroxide, Co_3O_4, is produced, a spinel-type compound containing Co^{2+} ions in tetrahedral interstices and diamagnetic Co^{3+} ions in octahedral interstices. There is no evidence for the existence of pure cobalt(III) oxide, Co_2O_3. Some oxide materials of uncertain composition, obtained by oxidation of cobalt(II) hydroxide, $Co(OH)_2$, with air or ozone, are known.

There are hydrated cobalt(II) salts with all common anions; they are easily obtained, for example, by reaction of cobalt(II) hydroxide, $Co(OH)_2$, with the appropriate acid. Virtually all such salts are red or pink and contain octahedrally coordinated cobalt(II) ions (Co^{2+}), in many cases the hexaquocobalt(II) ion, $[Co(H_2O)_6]^{2+}$. The hydroxide, $Co(OH)_2$, may be precipitated by strong bases as either a blue or pink solid, depending on conditions, but only the pink form is permanently stable. It is amphoteric, dissolving in acids to give cobalt(II) salts and in very concentrated alkali to give a deep blue solution containing the tetrahydroxocobaltate ion $[Co(OH)_4]^{2-}$. Cobalt(II) sulfide, CoS, can be precipitated from aqueous solutions as a black solid.

Few simple cobalt(III) salts are known. Anhydrous cobalt(III) fluoride, CoF_3, can be prepared by fluorination of the metal or of cobalt(II) chloride, $CoCl_2$, and the hydrate $CoF_3 \cdot 3.5H_2O$ is also known as a green powder that separates from electrolyzed solutions of Co^{2+} in 40 percent aqueous hydrofluoric acid. The blue cobalt(III) sulfate octadecahydrate, $Co_2(SO_4)_3 \cdot 18H_2O$, can be isolated by oxidation of solutions of cobalt(II) salts in sulfuric acid, and the hexaaquocobalt(III) ion, $[Co(H_2O)_6]^{3+}$, is also found in the alums such as dipotassium cobalt(II) sulfate dodecahydrate, $K_2Co(SO_4)_2 \cdot 12H_2O$.

Cobalt complexes. Divalent cobalt forms numerous complexes of several structural types. Octahedral and tetrahedral ones are most common, but there are a fair number of square ones as well as some that are five-coordinate. Divalent cobalt has a greater tendency to form tetrahedral complexes than any other transition metal, at least in part because, for an ion with seven d electrons, ligand-field stabilization energies are less unfavourable to the tetrahedral configuration relative to the octahedral than is the case for the ion of any other transition metal. The cobalt(II) ion is in fact the only commonly occurring ion with a configuration of seven d electrons. The hexaaquocobalt(II) ion $[Co(H_2O)_6]^{2+}$, is one of the most important octahedral complexes of divalent cobalt. Cobalt differs from all of the other first-row transition elements in that its aqueous solutions contain a small amount of the tetrahedral tetraaquo ion along with the octahedral hexaaquo ion.

Tetrahedral complexes of cobalt are formed by all of the halide ions—e.g., with chloride, the tetrachlorocobaltate(II) complex, $CoCl_4^{2-}$—as well as by the thiocyanate, (SCN^-), and azide, (N_3^-), ions, alone or in combination with two neutral ligands such as phosphines or amines, e.g., dichlorobis(triphenylphosphine)cobaltate(II), $Co[(C_6H_5)_3P]_2Cl_2$.

All tetrahedral complexes of divalent cobalt have three unpaired electrons, as do most of the octahedral ones. In a few cases, however, low-spin complexes are produced, but these are not expected to have regular octahedral structures because of distortion arising from the Jahn-Teller effect. In fact, those so far structurally characterized appear either to be five-coordinate rather than six-coordinate or to be dinuclear as in deca(methyl isocyanide)dicobalt(II) perchlorate, $[Co_2(CNCH_3)_{10}](ClO_4)_4$.

The complexes of trivalent cobalt are numerous. Because of the great variety of complexes that can be prepared and that undergo ligand exchange reactions at a rate slow enough to be conveniently measurable, they have been extensively studied and have provided much fundamental knowledge about isomerism, modes of reaction, and general properties of octahedral compounds as a class.

Cobalt-(III) complexes

Trivalent cobalt shows a particular affinity for ligands that donate through the nitrogen atom, and the majority of its complexes contain ammonia, amines, nitro groups, etc., either alone or in combination with halide ions, water molecules, and other ligands. These complexes are generally synthesized by oxidation of divalent cobalt in the presence of the desired ligands.

Except for a few cases, complexes of trivalent cobalt are octahedral, and with the exception of trifluorotriaquocobalt(III), $[Co(H_2O)_3F_3]$, and hexafluorocobaltate(III), $[CoF_6]^{3-}$, which are paramagnetic with four unpaired electrons, all octahedral complexes of trivalent cobalt are diamagnetic.

Nickel. Typical compounds of nickel in nature, in which it occurs primarily as minerals in combination with arsenic, antimony, and sulfur, are nickel(II) sulfide, NiS; nickel(III) arsenide, NiAs; nickel(III) antimonide, NiSb; nickel(III) diarsenide, $NiAs_2$; nickel(III) thioarsenide, NiAsS; and nickel(III) thioantimonide, NiSbS. Some commercially important deposits contain the mineral garnierite, a magnesium–nickel silicate of variable composition. Also certain varieties of the iron mineral pyrrhotite contain 3 to 5 percent nickel. Elemental nickel is found alloyed with iron in many meteors, and the central regions of the Earth are believed to contain considerable quantities. The free metal is never found in the Earth's crust. The metallurgy of nickel is complicated in its details, many of which vary widely, according to the particular ore being processed. In general the ore is transformed to nickel(III) sulfide, Ni_2S_3, which is roasted in air to give nickel(II) oxide, NiO, which is then reduced with carbon to obtain the metal. Some high-purity nickel is made by the carbonyl process mentioned earlier.

Nickel is a silver-white metal with high electrical and thermal conductivity and it can be fabricated readily by the use of standard hot and cold working methods. The metal is fairly resistant to attack by air or water at ordinary temperatures when compact and is therefore often electroplated as a protective coating. Nickel reacts only slowly with fluorine, eventually developing a protective coating of the fluoride, and therefore is used as the pure metal or in the form of alloys such as Monel metal (which contains some 60 to 70 percent nickel, 30 to 40 percent copper, and small amounts of other metals such as iron) in equipment for handling fluorine gas and corrosive fluorides. Nickel is ferromagnetic at ordinary temperatures, although not as strongly so as iron, and is less electropositive than iron but dissolves readily in dilute mineral acids.

Properties and reactions of nickel

The only important oxidation state in the ordinary chemistry of nickel is the $+2$ state; but the stereochemistry of divalent nickel compounds and complexes is quite complicated and elaborate.

Binary nickel compounds. Nickel(II) oxide, NiO, is a green solid with the rock-salt structure; it is formed upon heating the hydroxide, carbonate, oxalate, or nitrate and is insoluble in water but dissolves readily in acids. Addition of alkali metal hydroxides to aqueous solutions of divalent nickel salts precipitates nickel(II) hydroxide, $Ni(OH)_2$, as a voluminous green gel that becomes crystalline on prolonged storage. The hydroxide is readily soluble in acids and also dissolves in aqueous ammonia, because of the formation of complexes, but it is not amphoteric. Sulfide ions precipitate nickel(II) sulfide, NiS, from aqueous solutions of divalent nickel. The sulfide is initially soluble in acid, but on exposure to air it becomes insoluble due to oxidation to nickel(III) hydroxide sulfide, Ni(OH)S.

All four nickel halides are known in the anhydrous and hydrated states. Except for the fluoride, which is best made indirectly, the halides can be prepared by direct reaction of nickel with the halogens. All of the halides are soluble in water (although the fluoride is only moderately so) and can be crystallized from aqueous solutions.

Nickel(II) cyanide, $Ni(CN)_2$, is precipitated in the green hydrated form on addition of cyanide ions to aqueous solutions of divalent nickel, and it can be converted to the anhydrous yellow-brown compound on heating at 180° to 200° C (360° to 400° F). The green precipitate readily dissolves in an excess of cyanide to form the yellow tetracyanonickelate(II) ion, $[Ni(CN)_4]^{2-}$, and many hydrated salts of this ion—such as $Na_2[Ni(CN)_4]\cdot 3H_2O$—may be crystallized from such solutions.

Other binary nickel compounds, not all of which are stoichiometric, may be obtained by direct reaction of nickel with various nonmetals, such as phosphorus, arsenic, antimony, sulfur, selenium, tellurium, carbon, and boron. The existence of a hydride is doubtful although the finely divided metal absorbs considerable amounts of hydrogen.

Aqueous chemistry of nickel. In addition to its halides, nickel forms a large number of salts with oxo acids; most commonly the salts occur as hydrates—for example, the nitrate $Ni(NO_3)_2\cdot 6H_2O$ and the sulfate $NiSO_4\cdot 7H_2O$. Aqueous solutions of nickel salts that do not contain strong complexing agents contain the green hexaaquonickel(II) ion, $[Ni(H_2O)_6]^{2+}$, which also occurs in most of the hydrated salts of oxy acids such as the foregoing two examples.

Nickel complexes. Divalent nickel forms a large number of complexes, encompassing coordination numbers 4, 5, and 6 and all of the main structural types—i.e., octahedral, trigonal bipyramidal, square pyramidal, tetrahedral, and square. It is also characteristic of the complexes of divalent nickel that complicated equilibria, which generally depend upon the temperature and sometimes upon the concentration, often exist between the structural types.

The maximum coordination number of nickel is 6, and a large number of six-coordinate octahedral complexes are known. Ammonia and many organic amines displace water molecules from the coordination shell to give amine complexes. Such complexes characteristically have blue or purple colours in contrast to the bright green colour of the hexaaquo ion, because the stronger crystal fields provided by these ligands shift the absorption bands to higher energies, as already described under *Crystal-field and ligand-field theories.* Octahedral nickel(II) complexes have rather simple magnetic behaviour resulting from the presence of two unpaired electrons.

Nickel forms a considerable number of complexes in which its coordination number is 5. The structure may be trigonal bipyramidal, square pyramidal, or some intermediate arrangement. Depending on the strength of the ligand field, these complexes may be either high-spin (that is, with two unpaired electrons) or low-spin (that is, diamagnetic, with no unpaired electrons). The low-spin complexes tend to occur regardless of the arrangement of the molecules if the ligand set consists mainly of heavier atoms such as phosphorus, arsenic, sulfur, selenium, bromine, or iodine.

With coordination number 4, both tetrahedral and square arrangements occur depending on the type of ligand involved. Tetrahedral complexes can often be recognized by their spectroscopic and magnetic properties. They tend to be strongly coloured, either blue or green, and invariably have two unpaired electrons. The majority of four-coordinate nickel complexes, however, have square geometry. All square complexes are diamagnetic, and they are frequently red, yellow, or brown. An important square complex is the tetracyanonickelate(II) ion already mentioned; another is the bis(dimethyglyoximato) complex, which is bright red and highly insoluble in water and has long been used as both a qualitative and quantitative analytical test for nickel. The nickel complex with phthalocyanine has an intense, deep blue colour and has been used as a pigment.

The complicated changes among different atomic ar-

rangements of nickel complexes are generally caused by the tendency of many nominally four-coordinate and five-coordinate complexes to add additional ligands or to associate with sharing of ligand atoms so as to increase the coordination number of each nickel atom to 5 or 6. In some cases also there are equilibria between square and tetrahedral four-coordinate complexes. Since the two types have different magnetic and spectroscopic properties, such equilibria, which may vary with temperature and environment, can cause dramatic colour changes.

Higher oxidation states of nickel. There are a few known compounds in which nickel has oxidation states +3 and +4. Although there is no evidence for anhydrous oxides of nickel in those oxidation states, there are a number of hydrous oxides and mixed metal oxides, some of considerable complexity, that contain nickel in oxidation states +3 and +4. The best defined is perhaps the compound designated beta-nickel(III) oxide hydroxide, β-$NiO(OH)$, a black powder obtained by oxidation of divalent nickel nitrate solutions with bromine in aqueous potassium hydroxide. Electrochemical oxidation of nickel(II) hydroxide in alkaline solution gives a black oxide that does not appear to have a unique stoichiometry and that also retains some alkali metal.

It may be noted that the Edison, or nickel–iron alkaline, battery (voltage approximately 1.3 V), which uses potassium hydroxide as an electrolyte, is based on the reaction

$$Fe \quad + \quad 2NiO(OH) \quad + \quad 2H_2O$$

iron   nickel(III) oxide hydroxide   water

$$\xrightleftharpoons[\text{charge}]{\text{discharge}} Fe(OH)_2 \quad + \quad 2Ni(OH)_2.$$

iron(II) hydroxide   nickel(II) hydroxide

The detailed mechanism and the true nature of the oxidized nickel species are not fully understood.

Lower oxidation states of nickel. The most important compound of nickel in a lower oxidation state is tetracarbonylnickel, $Ni(CO)_4$. There are a number of other compounds of zero-valent nickel, such as bis(1,5-cyclooctadiene)nickel(0) and various derivatives of tetracarbonylnickel in which some of the carbon monoxide groups are replaced by phosphines or phosphites. These have been intensively studied as actual or potential catalysts for molecular transformations of olefins.

Copper. Copper is distributed widely in nature in the form of the free metal, sulfides, arsenides, chlorides, and carbonates. It is extracted by oxidative roasting and smelting, followed by electrodeposition from sulfate solutions, and it is technologically important, particularly in alloys, as an electroplated coating and as an exceptionally good conductor of heat and electricity. The pure metal is soft, tough, ductile, and characteristically reddish in colour and is second only to silver in thermal and electrical conductivity. Metallic copper is only superficially oxidized in air, sometimes acquiring a green coating that is a mixture of hydroxo-carbonate, hydroxosulfate, and small amounts of other compounds.

Copper is a moderately noble metal, being unaffected by nonoxidizing or noncomplexing dilute acids in the absence of air; it will, however, dissolve readily in nitric acid and in sulfuric acid in the presence of oxygen and is also soluble in aqueous ammonia or potassium cyanide in presence of oxygen, because of the formation of very stable cyano complexes upon dissolution. The metal will react at red heat with oxygen to give copper(II) oxide, CuO, and, at higher temperatures, copper(I) oxide, Cu_2O. It reacts on heating with sulfur to give copper(I) sulfide, Cu_2S.

Copper forms compounds in the oxidation states +1 and +2 in its normal chemistry, although under special circumstances some compounds of trivalent copper can be prepared. It has been shown that trivalent copper survives no more than a few seconds in aqueous solution.

Monovalent copper. Copper(I) (cuprous) compounds are all diamagnetic and, except in cases of colour resulting from the anion or from ultraviolet bands, they are colourless. The important binary compounds of copper(I) are the oxide, Cu_2O; the sulfide, Cu_2S; and the halides—cuprous chloride, CuCl; cuprous bromide, CuBr; and cuprous iodide, CuI. The chloride and bromide can be made by boiling an acidic solution of the copper(II) salt with excess of copper. Copper(I) iodide, CuI, forms upon addition of iodide ion to a solution of copper(II) ion. Copper(I) fluoride, CuF, is unknown. The three halides are highly insoluble in water, and it is to this fact that they owe their stability (see below). Two other fairly common compounds of univalent copper are the cyanide, CuCN, and the sulfate, Cu_2SO_4.

Only low concentrations of free cuprous ion can exist in aqueous solution because the equilibrium $Cu^{2+} + Cu \rightleftharpoons 2Cu^+$ lies far to the left. The equilibrium can be displaced in either direction by the addition of ligands or anions, which complex or precipitate insoluble salts of either univalent or divalent copper. The cuprous halides are stable because of their insolubility.

Stabilities of copper(I) and copper(II) The relative stabilities of copper(I) and copper(II) also vary with solvent, as is well illustrated by the vastly increased stability of the copper(I) ion in acetonitrile, CH_3CN. In this medium, the copper(I) halides have high solubilities, and the copper(I) ion is so much more stable than the copper(II) ion that the latter is, in fact, a fairly powerful oxidizing agent. The copper(I) ion forms many complexes; those with simple ligands, such as halide ions and amines, are almost invariably tetrahedral. Copper(I) forms a number of polynuclear complexes of which the earliest to be recognized were those of composition $Cu_4I_4L_4$, in which L is a trialkylphosphine or trialkylarsine ligand. In such complexes, the four copper atoms lie at the vertices of a tetrahedron, one iodine atom lies over each face of the tetrahedron, and one of the ligands is coordinated to each copper atom.

Copper(I), but not copper(II), forms a number of organometallic compounds. The simple alkyls, such as methyl- or ethylcopper, are generally unstable, whereas some of the aryls—*e.g.*, phenylcopper, C_6H_5Cu—are stable to well above room temperature. Organometallic compounds of the type $Li(CuR_2)$, in which R represents an alkyl group, are useful synthetic reagents that react with alkyl, vinyl, or aryl halides to form carbon-to-carbon, or C–C, bonds. The copper(I) ion also interacts with alkenes and alkynes to form pi complexes.

Divalent copper. The divalent state is the more important one, giving rise to a well-defined aqueous chemistry of the copper(II) ion, Cu^{2+}, and a large number of salts of various anions, many of which are water soluble. In addition there are a great number of complexes of copper(II).

The stereochemistry of copper(II) is very characteristic. The d^9 configuration makes the ion Cu^{2+} subject to Jahn-Teller distortion if placed in an environment of cubic (that is, regular octahedral or tetrahedral) symmetry. For this reason there are virtually no regular octahedral or tetrahedral complexes of the copper(II) ion; most commonly the structure found is one in which a set of six ligands forms an elongated octahedron, with two opposite copper-to-ligand bonds being very much longer than the other four. This effect is found also in simple salts and binary compounds, because its origin is inherent in the d^9 configuration of the dipositive copper ion. The four-coordinate complexes either are square or have distorted tetrahedral structures.

The important binary compounds of divalent copper are the black oxide, CuO, which is obtained by thermal decomposition of the nitrate or other oxo salts; above about $800°$ C $(1,500°$ F) it loses oxygen to form copper(I) oxide, Cu_2O. From solutions of the copper(II) ion the hydroxide is precipitated as bulky blue solid, which is amphoteric and redissolves in acids to give the Cu^{2+} ion and also in alkali hydroxide to give deep-blue solutions containing hydroxo anions. The three halides—copper(II) fluoride, CuF_2; copper(II) chloride, $CuCl_2$; and copper(II) bromide, $CuBr_2$—are known, but as noted above the iodide is unstable and cannot be isolated.

The most familiar cupric compound is the blue, hydrated sulfate, $CuSO_4 \cdot 5H_2O$, which may be completely dehydrated to the virtually white anhydrous sulfate upon heating. The hydrated nitrate is also known but cannot be entirely dehydrated without decomposition. The anhydrous nitrate can, however, be prepared by dissolving the metal in a solution of dinitrogen tetroxide, N_2O_4, in ethyl acetate, from which the salt formulated $Cu(NO_3)_2 \cdot N_2O_4$ crystallizes; when it is heated to $90°$ C $(190°$ F) the salt loses N_2O_4 to give $Cu(NO_3)_2$.

Most copper(II) salts dissolve readily in water and give the aquo ion, hexaaquocopper(II) $[Cu(H_2O)_6]^{2+}$, but it is notable that the octahedron of water molecules about the copper is almost certainly distorted so that two of them are farther from the metal atom than the other four. Addition of ligands to such aqueous solutions leads to the formation of complexes such as tetraamminecopper(II), $[Cu(NH_3)_4]^{2+}$.

Copper(II) forms a considerable number of compounds that are magnetically anomalous. For an ordinary mononuclear complex of the copper(II) ion, magnetic behaviour characteristic of the presence of one unpaired electron per ion is to be expected. In many cases, however, of which the acetate, $Cu(CH_3CO_2)_2 \cdot H_2O$, is typical, the magnetic moment found at room temperature is lower than expected and decreases rapidly as the temperature is lowered. The cause of this behaviour is an interaction between pairs of copper ions that are held in proximity by bridging acetate groups, with the result that the unpaired electrons on the two copper atoms do not behave independently. Instead they interact in such a way that the most stable state, which can be reached at very low temperatures, is that in which the two spins are oppositely directed, thereby leading to diamagnetism.

ELEMENTS OF THE SECOND AND THIRD TRANSITION SERIES

While the elements in the second and third transition series for a given group have chemical properties similar to those of the element in the first series, they nevertheless show definite differences from the lighter element of the group. The following examples illustrate this point: (1) Although cobalt (of the first series) forms a considerable number of tetrahedral and octahedral complexes in its divalent state, and that valence state is characteristic in ordinary aqueous chemistry, divalent states of rhodium (second series) and iridium (third series) are rare and relatively unimportant. (2) The manganese(II) ion (Mn^{2+}) is very stable and of principal importance in the chemistry of manganese, but for technetium and rhenium the oxidation state +2 is little more than a laboratory curiosity. (3) Trivalent chromium forms a great number of complexes, which make up one of the best known aspects of the chemistry of the element; whereas trivalent molybdenum and tungsten are not particularly stable states under any conditions and form only a few complexes. (4) The oxy anions of the first-row elements in their higher oxidation states—for example, chromate(VI) and manganate(VII)—are powerful oxidizing agents the chemistry of which is essentially restricted to that function; whereas their stoichiometric analogues, such as molybdate(VI), tungstate(VI), technetate(VII), and rhenate(VII), are quite stable and have an extensive and diverse chemistry. There are, however, some cases in which quite valid and useful analogies can be found between the chemistry of the lighter element and the two heavier elements of the group. For instance, the chemistry of trivalent rhodium complexes is, in general, quite similar to that of trivalent cobalt complexes. On the whole, however, there are differences more consistently than there are similarities between the first element and the heavier elements of each group.

Differences in properties of elements in the second and third series from those of the first

For the heavier transition elements, higher oxidation states are generally more stable than is the case for the elements in the first transition series; this is true not only, as has been mentioned, for the properties of the oxo anions but for the higher halides as well. Thus the heavier elements form compounds such as ruthenium(VIII) oxide, RuO_4; tungsten(VI) chloride, WCl_6; platinum(VI) fluoride, PtF_6, etc., which have no analogues among the first-row elements, whereas the chemistry of aquo ions of lower valence states, especially +2 and +3, which is such a dominant part of the chemistry of the lighter elements, is relatively unimportant for most of the heavier ones.

One of the reasons for the generally close similarity in chemistry between the second and third transition series elements of a given group is the so-called lanthanide contraction. As already described in this article, the series of elements known as the lanthanides comes between the second and third regular transition series and is formed by the filling of the 4f orbitals. The 5d and 6s orbitals, which are the valence shell orbitals for the third transition series elements, are imperfectly shielded by the 4f electrons from the increased nuclear charge. There is, consequently, a steady contraction in the size of these orbitals through the lanthanide series of elements, with the net result that the atomic and ionic radii of hafnium, which immediately follows the lanthanide series, are almost identical to the corresponding radii of the zirconium atom, which lies just above it in Group IV. Because the zirconium and hafnium atoms have almost identical sizes as well as analogous electron configurations in all of their oxidation states, their chemistry and the properties of their compounds are exceedingly similar; indeed, it is very difficult to separate the two elements because of the great similarity in properties of their compounds. In moving along the third transition series, there is a steady but slow divergence in the properties of the second and third elements in each group so that, at the end, considerable differences exist between those of palladium and platinum and of silver and gold. The differences are not as great, however, as might have been expected had the lanthanide contraction not intervened to preclude greater disparity in the orbital sizes. Although niobium and tantalum are not quite as similar as zirconium and hafnium, the differences between them are slight, and, similarly, molybdenum and tungsten, technetium and rhenium, ruthenium and osmium, and rhodium and iridium show marked similarities in their chemistries.

Zirconium and hafnium. Zirconium occurs widely in the Earth's crust, but not in concentrated deposits. The mineral zircon, $ZrSiO_4$ (zirconium orthosilicate), which is generally found in alluvial deposits in stream beds, ocean beaches, or old lake beds, is the only commercial source of zirconium. Baddeleyite, which is essentially pure zirconium(IV) oxide, ZrO_2, is the only other important zirconium mineral. These zirconium minerals generally have a hafnium content that varies from a few tenths of 1 percent to several percent. For some purposes separation of the two elements is not important: zirconium containing about 1 percent of hafnium is as acceptable as pure zirconium. In the case of the largest single use of zirconium, however, namely, as a structural and cladding material in atomic reactors, it is essential that the zirconium be essentially free of hafnium, because the usefulness of zirconium in reactors is based on its extremely low absorption cross section for neutrons. Hafnium, on the other hand, has an exceptionally high cross section, and accordingly even slight hafnium contamination nullifies the intrinsic advantage of the zirconium. Pure hafnium in fact is also used in some atomic reactors as a control element material because of its high neutron-capture cross section.

Separation of hafnium and zirconium is generally accomplished by a liquid–liquid countercurrent-extraction procedure. In the procedure, crude zirconium(IV) chloride is dissolved in an aqueous solution of ammonium thiocyanate and methyl isobutyl ketone is passed countercurrent to the aqueous mixture, with the result that the hafnium(IV) chloride is preferentially extracted.

Either of the metals, or a mixture of the two, is produced by the same process as that described in the section *Titanium* (see above). Both the metals have extremely high melting points: zirconium 1,850° C (3,362° F) and hafnium 2,230° C (4,046° F). Hafnium and zirconium are fairly resistant to acids and are best dissolved in hydrofluoric acid, in which procedure the formation of anionic fluoro complexes is important in stabilizing the solution. At normal temperatures neither metal is particularly reactive, but both become quite reactive with a variety of nonmetals at elevated temperatures.

Chemical properties. The atomic radii of zirconium and hafnium are 1.45 and 1.44 Å, respectively, while the radii of the ions are Zr^{4+}, 0.74 Å, and Hf^{4+}, 0.75 Å. The virtual identity of atomic and ionic sizes, resulting from the lanthanide contraction, has the effect of making the chemical behaviour of these two elements more similar than for any other pair of elements known. Although the chemistry of hafnium has been studied less than that of zirconium, the two are so similar that only very small quantitative differences—for example, in solubilities and volatilities of compounds—would be expected in cases that have not actually been investigated.

The most important respect in which these two elements differ from titanium is that lower oxidation states are of minor importance; there are relatively few compounds of hafnium or zirconium in other than their tetravalent states. The increased size of the atoms makes the oxides more basic and the aqueous chemistry somewhat more extensive, and permits the attainment of coordination numbers 7 and, quite frequently, 8 in a number of zirconium and hafnium compounds.

Oxides and halides. The four tetrahalides of each element are known, the most important being the tetrachlorides, because of their use in the separation and purification of the elements. The tetrachlorides may be prepared by chlorination of the heated metals, metal carbides, or mixtures of the metal oxides and charcoal. The tetrachlorides fume in moist air and are hydrolyzed vigorously by water. Hydrolysis proceeds only part way at room temperature, yielding the stable oxochlorides, $MOCl_2 \cdot 8H_2O$ (in which M is the metal atom). The bromides and iodides of zirconium and hafnium are similar to the chlorides but the fluorides are much less volatile and have different crystal structures.

The addition of a hydroxide to solutions of tetravalent zirconium and hafnium causes the precipitation of the white gelatinous hydrated dioxides, which are converted on strong heating to hard, white, insoluble anhydrous dioxides, ZrO_2 and HfO_2. Zirconium dioxide is exceptionally resistant to attack by both acids and alkalies and has good mechanical properties; thus it is used in crucibles and furnace cores. At least four structurally different forms of ZrO_2 have been observed, one of which is the mineral baddeleyite already mentioned.

A number of compounds called zirconates may be made by combining oxides, hydroxides, nitrates, etc., of other metals with similar zirconium compounds and firing the mixtures at 1,000° to 2,500° C (1,800° to 4,500° F). As is the case with their titanium analogues, the products are mixed metal oxides. No discrete zirconate ions are known.

By far the most important complexes of zirconium and hafnium are those with fluoride ions. Although salts of the hexachloro ions (MCl_6^{2-}) are known, they are unstable in solution, whereas fluoro complexes are stable in solution and are sources of a great range of solid crystalline substances. Those of zirconium have been extensively investigated, and octahedral hexafluorozirconate(IV) (ZrF_6^{2-}) ions, as well as heptafluorozirconate(IV) (ZrF_7^{3-}) ions, with either pentagonal bipyramidal or capped trigonal prismatic structures, have been observed. Octafluorozirconate (ZrF_8^{4-}) units of several types have also been found; dicopper(II) octafluorozirconate(IV) dodecahydrate, in $Cu_2ZrF_8 \cdot 12H_2O$, there are discrete square antiprisms; in other cases there are square antiprisms sharing edges.

Zirconium dioxide, ZrO_2, is more basic than titanium dioxide, TiO_2, and is virtually insoluble in excess base. There is an extensive aqueous chemistry of zirconium because of its lower tendency to hydrolysis; nevertheless, hydrolysis does occur, and it is doubtful that the zirconium(IV) (Zr^{4+}) aquo ion exists, even in the most strongly acid solutions. The hydrolyzed ion is often referred to as the zirconyl ion and written as ZrO^{2+}, but there is little if any evidence for the actual existence of such an oxo ion, either in solution or in crystalline salts; no such group has ever been observed by X-ray diffraction methods. Substances for which the formula might suggest the presence of a zirconyl ion are invariably found to have more complex structures. The best known of all zirconyl salts, for example, is formulated $ZrOCl_2 \cdot 8H_2O$; it actually contains a very complex tetranuclear cation, $[Zr_4(OH)_8(H_2O)_{16}]^{8+}$, in which the zirconium atoms lie in a distorted square linked by pairs of hydroxo (OH^-) bridges.

Zirconium and hafnium solutions with sulfate anions show considerable difference from those containing chloride, nitrate, or perchlorate ions. Even at low acidity there appear to be very stable neutral and anionic complexes, some of which may be polymeric. Crystalline materials with compositions $Zr(SO_4)_2 \cdot nH_2O$, in which n equals 4, 5, and 7, have been characterized; they have complex structures in which the zirconium atoms are coordinated by eight oxygen atoms from water and sulfate groups.

The chemistry of these elements in lower oxidation states is limited to the nonaqueous chemistry of lower halides and a few complexes thereof. The best known compounds in such states are the trichlorides (MCl_3), tribromides (MBr_3), and triiodides (MI_3), which can generally be prepared by reduction of the tetrahalides with hydrogen or excess metal. The hafnium triiodide phase has a marked tendency to be non-stoichiometric. There are halides in even lower oxidation states, but these have not been well characterized, and a substantially pure zirconium(II) chloride ($ZrCl_2$) phase appears to exist, but its structure is unknown. The valence 1 compounds ZrCl and HfCl are reported to be isotypic (*i.e.*, analogous in chemical formula and crystal structure) and to have very metallic properties, but little else is known about them.

Niobium and tantalum. Although not quite as similar to each other as are hafnium and zirconium, niobium and tantalum differ but little in their chemistry, and, thus, separation problems are significant. Due to their great chemical similarity and consequent close association in nature, in fact, the establishment of the individual identities of the two elements was very difficult. Niobium was probably first discovered in 1801, in an ore sample from Connecticut, by an English chemist, Charles Hatchett, who named the element columbium in honour of the country of its origin, Columbia being a synonym for the United States. In 1844 a German chemist, Heinrich Rose, discovered what he considered to be a new element occurring along with tantalum and named it niobium after Niobe, the mythological goddess who was the daughter of Tantalus. After considerable controversy it was decided that columbium and niobium were the same element, and eventually international agreement was reached to adopt the name niobium. The name columbium is often seen, however, even today, especially in the metallurgical literature.

Niobium is roughly ten times more abundant in the Earth's crust than tantalum. The main commercial sources of both elements are the columbite–tantalite series of minerals, in which columbite ($FeNb_2O_6$) and tantalite ($FeTa_2O_6$) occur in highly variable ratios. Niobium is also obtainable from pyrochlore, a calcium sodium niobate. The production procedures for the metals are complex, the major problem being separation of the two elements, which is solved mainly by use of a liquid–liquid extraction process. The metals themselves are obtained by either electrolysis of fused salts or reduction of fluoro complexes with a very reactive metal such as sodium. Both metals are bright, have high melting points (niobium, 2,468° C [4,474° F], tantalum, 2,996° C [5,425° F]), and are quite resistant to acids. They can best be dissolved in a mixture of nitric and hydrofluoric acids.

Compounds of niobium (V) and tantalum (V). For niobium and tantalum the most important oxidation state is +5. Niobium(V) oxide, Nb_2O_5, and tantalum(V) oxide, Ta_2O_5, are dense white powders that are relatively inert chemically and are scarcely, if at all, attacked by acids except concentrated hydrofluoric acid. The hydrous oxides, which vary in water content, are gelatinous white precipitates obtained upon neutralizing acid solutions of pentavalent niobium and tantalum halides; the anhydrous

oxides can be obtained by heating the hydrous oxides or by roasting certain other compounds in the presence of excess oxygen. When the oxides are fused with excess alkali hydroxide or carbonate, and the melts dissolved in water, isopolyniobates and isopolytantalates (analogous to the isopolyanions mentioned earlier) are obtained. The solutions are stable only when strongly alkaline and appear to consist mainly of the $M_6O_{19}^{8-}$ ions and protonated (*i.e.*, that have had one or more hydrogen ions, H^+, added) derivatives thereof. A large number of "niobates" and "tantalates" are known: they are almost entirely mixed metal oxides with the niobium and tantalum atoms occupying octahedral interstices in close-packed arrays of oxygen atoms. There are, however, a few compounds, such as scandium niobate, $ScNbO_4$, that contain discrete tetrahedral oxo anions, MO_4^{3-}.

Both niobium and tantalum form all four pentahalides, of which the fluorides and chlorides are the most important. The pentafluorides are readily made by direct fluorination of the metals, the pentoxides, or the pentachlorides and are volatile white solids that have, in the crystal and evidently also in the melt, polymeric structures in which fluoride ions are shared between metal atoms so as to give each metal atom a coordination number of 6. When dissolved in aqueous hydrofluoric acid the metals and the pentoxides form fluoro complexes, the composition of which varies markedly with conditions of temperature and concentration. A great variety of fluoro and oxofluoro complexes—*e.g.*, the anions NbF_6^-, TaF_6^-, TaF_7^{2-}, and TaF_8^{3-}—may be precipitated by the addition of various cations. In solutions of lower acidity, niobium readily forms the oxopentafluoroniobate ion, $NbOF_5^{2-}$. All the pentahalides can be sublimed (*i.e.*, converted directly from solid to gaseous state) without decomposition in an atmosphere of the appropriate halogen; in the vapour they are monomeric (*i.e.*, simple in structure and low in molecular weight) and presumably have trigonal bipyramidal structures.

There are also a number of oxohalides, such as those having the formulas $NbOCl_3$, $TaOCl_3$, $NbOBr_3$, $TaOBr_3$, $NbOI_3$ and NbO_2I. These oxohalides, which often arise in the preparation of the pentahalides when the systems are not scrupulously free of oxygen, are less volatile than the pure halides and are thus left behind upon fractional sublimation.

Compounds of lower oxidation states. The only certain lower oxides are those of niobium, NbO and NbO_2. Substances of tantalum–oxygen composition TaO_x, in which x represents the range 2 to 2.5, are in fact tantalum(V) oxide, Ta_2O_5, phases with interstitial tantalum atoms, not discrete phases or compounds. Niobium(IV) oxide, NbO_2, has the rutile-type (*i.e.*, that of natural titanium dioxide, TiO_2) structure with pairs of fairly close niobium atoms that are presumably bonded to each other. Niobium(II) oxide, NbO, has a metallic lustre and excellent electrical conductivity of the metallic type. There are also complex series of sulfides of lower oxidation states of both niobium and tantalum.

All of the eight possible tetrahalides are known with the exception of tantalum(IV) fluoride, TaF_4. Niobium(IV) fluoride, NbF_4, is a black, nonvolatile, paramagnetic substance that differs from the other six. The tetrachlorides and tetrabromides are all brown-black or black diamagnetic solids, with structures such that pairs of metal atoms form weak metal–metal bonds, thus eliminating all unpaired electrons. The tetrahalides form a number of complexes with ligands containing nitrogen, oxygen, and sulfur donor atoms.

In addition to the halides of tetravalent niobium and tantalum, there is a considerable number of halide compounds in which the formal oxidation numbers of the metals range from +2 to about +3.1. Direct metal-to-metal bonds, metal atom clusters, and non-stoichiometry are characteristic features among these compounds.

Many of the lower halides of niobium and tantalum are built up of $[M_6X_{12}]^{2+, 3+}$ units, in which M is the metal atom. The M_6X_{12} unit is a metal atom cluster consisting of an octahedron of metal atoms with a bridging halogen atom along each edge as shown in diagram **18**.

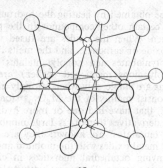

18

Such units are characteristic of, though not entirely restricted to, the chemistry of the lower oxidation states of niobium and tantalum.

Molybdenum and tungsten. Molybdenum (Mo) and tungsten (W) are very similar chemically, although there are some differences that are not easy to explain. They have similar abundances and occur in nature in the same sorts of compounds; neither occurs as a free metal. For molybdenum the chief ore is molybdenite—molybdenum(IV) sulfide, MoS_2—but molybdates such as lead molybdate, $PbMoO_4$ (wulfenite), and $MgMoO_4$ are also found. Although tungsten occurs as tungstenite—tungsten(IV) sulfide, WS_2—the important ores in this case are the tungstates such as scheelite (calcium tungstate, $CaWO_4$), stolzite (lead tungstate, $PbWO_4$), and wolframite—a solid solution or a mixture or both of the isomorphous substances iron(II) tungstate, $FeWO_4$, and maganese(II) tungstate, $MnWO_4$.

The small quantities of molybdenite in molybdenum ores are concentrated by foam flotation processes and roasted to give molybdenum(VI) oxide, MoO_3, which, after purification, can be reduced with hydrogen to the metal. For tungsten the ores are concentrated by magnetic and mechanical processes and the concentrate then fused with alkali. The crude melts are leached with water to give solutions of sodium tungstate, from which hydrous tungsten(VI) oxide is precipitated upon acidification, and the oxide is then dried and reduced to metal with hydrogen. The metals are quite refractory, the melting points being 2,610° C (4,730° F) for molybdenum and 3,410° C (6,170° F) for tungsten. Both metals are rather resistant to attack by acids, except for mixtures of concentrated nitric and hydrofluoric acids, and both can be attacked rapidly by alkaline oxidizing melts, such as fused mixtures of potassium nitrate and sodium hydroxide or sodium peroxide; aqueous alkalies, however, are without effect. The metals are inert to oxygen at normal temperature, but combine with it readily at red heat, to give the trioxides, and are attacked by fluorine at room temperature, to give the hexafluorides. Both elements form hard, refractory, and chemically inert interstitial compounds with boron, carbon, nitrogen, and silicon upon direct reaction with those elements at high temperatures. Tungsten carbide is extensively used for high-speed cutting tools; tungsten metal itself has wide application as a lamp filament, and molybdenum is used in a number of small-scale applications in which high resistance to erosion at high temperatures is required—*e.g.*, in jet engines, combustion liners, and afterburner parts.

Oxides of molybdenum and tungsten. Most of the chemistry of these elements is that of the higher oxidation states, although a few lower valent compounds are of interest because of the presence of metal atom clusters or metal–metal bonds of a high order (*i.e.*, involving several pairs of electrons).

A considerable number of molybdenum and tungsten oxide phases are known. The simpler and more important oxides are the trioxides, MoO_3, WO_3, the dioxides, MoO_2, WO_2, and an intermediate oxide of molybdenum, Mo_2O_5.

The ultimate products of heating the metals or other compounds, such as the sulfides, in oxygen are the trioxides, which are not attacked by acids but which dissolve in bases to form solutions of molybdate and tungstate ions. The dioxides are obtained by reducing the trioxides with hydrogen and ammonia at moderate temperatures; they are dark solids with metallic lustre and structures similar to that of rutile but are highly distorted as a result of the formation of relatively strong, direct metal–metal bonds.

The simple molybdate ion, $MoO_4{}^{2-}$, and tungstate ion, $WO_4{}^{2-}$, which are formed by dissolving the trioxides in strong alkali, condense and polymerize (*i.e.*, form giant molecules by the union of simpler molecules with one another) into the complex polymolybdate and polytungstate species that have been mentioned above.

The reduction of oxide compounds of hexavalent molybdenum and tungsten results in several classes of interesting compounds, which contain the element in average oxidation states between +5 and +6. One such class of substances is the tungsten bronzes. The reduction of sodium tungstate in hydrogen at red heat produces a chemically inert substance with a bronze-like appearance, and similar materials are obtained by vapour-phase reaction of alkali metals with tungsten(VI) oxide, WO_3. The tungsten bronzes are non-stoichiometric substances of general formula M_nWO_3, in which M is the alkali metal and n is between 0 and 1. The colours vary greatly with composition, from golden yellow to blue-violet. The tungsten bronzes have metallic lustre and excellent electrical conductivity in which the charge carriers are electrons; those with very low concentrations of alkali metal are only semiconductors. When acidified solutions of molybdates and tungstates are reduced by mild reducing agents, such as tin(II) (stannous) ion or sulfur dioxide, bright-blue materials called blue oxides are obtained (a detailed explanation for the blue colour has not been given). Similarly, when heteropolytungstates and molybdates are subjected to mild reduction, blue materials called heteropolyblues are obtained. In these cases the phenomena occur in solution, and it can be shown that the oxidation–reduction reactions involved are reversible.

Sulfides and halides. Molybdenum(IV) sulfide, MoS_2, and tungsten(IV) sulfide, WS_2, which occur in nature, have been noted. In addition tungsten forms tungsten(VI) sulfide, WS_3, and molybdenum forms a number of other sulfides. Molybdenum(IV) sulfide, MoS_2, has an unusual structure, built of close-packed layers of sulfur atoms stacked so as to create trigonal prismatic interstices that are occupied by molybdenum atoms. The stacking permits easy slippage of alternate layers, and thus MoS_2 has the property of lubricity similar to that of graphite and is employed as a lubricant in specialized applications.

Both elements form a variety of halides and oxohalides in various oxidation states. By direct reaction of the metals with halogens the hexahalides MoF_6, WF_6, WCl_6, and WBr_6 can be obtained. There is not as yet any confirmed report of molybdenum(VI) chloride, $MoCl_6$, but direct reactions of the elements produce molybdenum(V) chloride, $MoCl_5$, and molybdenum(V) bromide, $MoBr_5$. The hexahalides are colourless, volatile substances; the pentafluorides and pentachlorides are well-characterized compounds that have an interesting structural difference. The pentafluorides polymerize in the solid state to cyclic tetramers (*i.e.*, molecules formed, in this case in a ring, by the union of four identical molecules), whereby each pair of metal atoms is bridged linearly by one fluorine atom. The pentachlorides, on the other hand, form dimeric (*i.e.*, formed by the union of two identical simpler molecules) units in which there are two angular chloride bridges between each pair of metal atoms. The known tetrahalides and trihalides include nearly all of the possibilities, with the conspicuous exception of tungsten(III) fluoride, WF_3.

Of particular scientific interest are the dihalides, which actually have a complex structure that contains metal atom clusters similar to but different in detail from those formed by niobium and tantalum. The key structural unit has six metal and eight halogen atoms, written M_6X_8, and is illustrated in diagram **19**. As in the case with the analogous niobium and tantalum compounds, there is an octahedral cluster of metal atoms, but in this case there are only eight bridging halogen atoms and they

Tungsten bronzes

Dihalides of molybdenum and tungsten

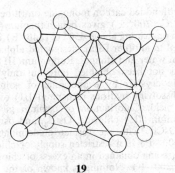

19

lie over faces of the octahedron. In the dihalides these units are linked together by the additional halide ions that serve as bridges. Tungsten compounds of this type are considerably less stable than those of molybdenum and tend to be readily oxidized.

Both elements form oxohalides in several oxidation states. In oxidation state +6, the stoichiometric types are MOX_4 and MO_2X_2, in which M is the metal atom, O the oxygen atom, and X the halogen atom. The oxohalides are readily obtained as by-products in the halogenation of the metals, unless the metal is first scrupulously reduced and the reaction system purged of oxygen. For oxidation state 5, the stoichiometric type is MOX_3, in which X may be Cl or Br.

Complexes. Molybdenum and tungsten form a variety of complexes. Molybdenum, but not tungsten, forms complexes of the type MX_6^{3-}, which are strong reducing agents. Both molybdenum and tungsten form the dinuclear complexes $M_2X_9^{3-}$, the structure of which can be considered as two octahedra sharing a face. In such systems there is some direct interaction between the metal atoms, which is quite strong in the case of tungsten. The elements also form hexahalo complexes in their higher oxidation states, particularly the hexafluoro complexes, MF_6^-.

For molybdenum, though not to any appreciable extent for tungsten, there are many important complexes containing metal–oxygen double bonds or metal–oxygen–metal bridge bonds. Molybdenum(VI) oxide dissolves in aqueous hydrochloric acid to give the dioxotetrachloromolybdate(VI) anion, $[MoO_2Cl_4]^{2-}$. Complexes of the dioxo type are particularly prevalent for molybdenum, additional examples being $[MoO_2F_4]^{2-}$ $[MoO_2(ligand)_2]$, in which the ligand may be an anion derived from any of various organic compounds.

Both molybdenum and tungsten in oxidation states +4 and +5 form a series of octacyano complexes, $M(CN)_8^{3-,\ 4-}$. The geometrical arrangement of the cyano groups around the metal atoms is variable, the geometry changing, depending on the surroundings, from dodecahedral to square antiprismatic. The cyano complexes are the most important, but not the only, octacoordinate complexes of these elements.

Finally, it is notable that molybdenum forms several complexes in the divalent state that are binuclear and contain very short molybdenum–molybdenum bonds, which are quadruple bonds, having four electron pairs shared between the metal atoms. Among the most important compounds containing such quadruple bonds are dimolybdenum tetraacetate, which can be obtained by boiling molybdenum carbonyl in acetic acid, and the salts of the octachlorodimolybdate ion, $Mo_2Cl_8^{4-}$, which is obtained from the acetate by treatment with hydrochloric acid. Thus far no tungsten analogue of these species has been definitely characterized. Both molybdenum and tungsten form the unusual molecules $[(CH_3)_3SiCH_2]_3M\equiv M[CH_2Si(CH_3)_3]_3$, in which there are metal-to-metal triple bonds (indicated as $M\equiv M$).

Technetium and rhenium. As has been noted, technetium does not occur in nature; nor does rhenium occur free in nature or as a compound in any distinct mineral; instead it is widely distributed in small amounts in other minerals. Rhenium is generally isolated from flue dusts and gases obtained on the roasting of molybdenites that contain rhenium. Such gases can be leached or scrubbed

with water to dissolve the oxide, Re_2O_7, which can be converted to ammonium rhenate(VII) (perrhenate), NH_4ReO_4, and then reduced to the metal with hydrogen. The melting point of rhenium, 3,170° C, is exceeded only by those of tungsten and carbon.

Technetium and rhenium are very similar chemically and differ greatly from manganese. Their most characteristic and important compounds are formed in the oxidation states +4 and +7, although compounds are known in all formal oxidation states from −1 to +7. Rhenium has only minor uses; for example, as an alloy with tungsten in flash bulb filaments; technetium, by the early 1970s, had essentially none.

Compounds of technetium and rhenium. Rhenium forms a variety of oxides, formulated $Re_2O_3\cdot xH_2O$, ReO_2, ReO_3, Re_2O_5, and Re_2O_7, while the only authenticated oxides of technetium are TcO_2 and Tc_2O_7. Of these, the heptoxides, which are obtained by burning the metals, are of greatest importance. They are quite volatile, and, if acid solutions containing the pertechnetate ion, TcO_4^-, are evaporated, technetium(VII) oxide is driven off, a fact that may be utilized to isolate and separate technetium. Rhenium(VII) oxide is not lost from acid solutions on evaporation at 100° C (212° F) but can be distilled from hot concentrated sulfuric acid. The heptoxides of rhenium and technetium readily dissolve in water to give acidic solutions. Both TcO_2 and ReO_2 have distorted rutile structures.

For rhenium particularly, the formation of oxo compounds is of major importance, especially in the higher oxidation states, +5 and +7. The pertechnetates, containing the ion TcO_4^-, and perrhenates, containing ReO_4^-, are among the most important compounds formed by these elements. The pure acids, which have not been isolated, are very strong acids in aqueous solutions. The oxo anions are quite stable in both acid and alkaline solution and are relatively weak oxidizing agents. There are oxohalides of both rhenium and technetium in the oxidation state +7—*e.g.*, ReO_3F, ReO_3Cl, and TcO_3Cl —that are readily hydrolyzed. Technetium trioxide chloride, TcO_3Cl, however, can be prepared under aqueous conditions by adding hydrochloric acid to potassium technetate(VII), $KTcO_4$, in sulfuric acid and extracting the product into chloroform. In oxidation state +6 oxohalides of the type MOX_4 are known; and in oxidation state +5, those of the type MOX_3.

Rhenium complexes. Of the many complexes containing oxorhenium species perhaps the most important are those of the type $ReOCl_3(PR_3)_2$, in which PR_3 represents a phosphine ligand. These compounds form a starting point for the preparation of a large number of complexes of rhenium in oxidation states between +3 and +6. In addition to forming double bonds to oxygen, rhenium also forms double and triple bonds to nitrogen. Typical compounds of these types are represented in diagrams **20** and **21**.

Both technetium and rhenium form the metal hydride ions formulated as MH_9^{2-}, which are the only pure hydrido complexes of transition metals, although many related species that contain other ligands along with the hydride ions are known. Rhenium also forms a series of complexes in which the nitrogen molecule is present as a ligand. These are among the best characterized complexes of this singularly unreactive molecule.

Finally, it should be mentioned that rhenium in oxidation state +3 has a pronounced tendency to form binuclear compounds containing rhenium–rhenium quadruple bonds as well as trinuclear clusters in which there are rhenium–rhenium double bonds. The compounds containing rhenium(III) and chlorine, bromine, or iodine all have Re_3X_9 as their true molecular formulas and contain

Oxides of rhenium and technetium

Hydride complexes

Molybdenum and tungsten multiple bonds

20 **21**

triangular arrays of doubly bonded metal atoms. On treatment of the halides with various ligands, complexes are formed in which these triangular clusters are preserved. The quadruple bonds mentioned occur in the ions $Re_2X_8^{2-}$, in which X represents Cl, Br, or SCN, and also in the carboxyl-bridge species $Re_2(O_2CR)_4X_2$, in which R is an alkyl or aryl group and X is a halogen. The first quadruple bond to be discovered was found in the octachlorodirhenate(III) ion, $Re_2Cl_8^{2-}$.

Ruthenium and osmium. Both ruthenium and osmium have low crustal abundances of about 0.001 part per million. They occur in nature along with the other platinum metals, and processes for isolating them are an integral part of the metallurgical art that applies to all of them and is discussed elsewhere.

Ruthenium and osmium are hard, bright metals having high melting points and resistance to chemical attack. They are the most noble of the platinum metals, and cold and hot acids, even including aqua regia, are without effect on them. They can be dissolved by fused alkalies, especially if an oxidizing agent such as sodium chlorate is present. Osmium will react at 200° C (about 400° F) with air or oxygen to form the volatile tetroxide, OsO_4. Although ruthenium tetroxide, RuO_4, has similar stability and volatility to osmium tetroxide, OsO_4, it differs in that it cannot be formed from the elements.

The chemistries of ruthenium and osmium are generally similar and differ markedly from that of iron. The higher oxidation states +6 and +8 are much more readily obtained than for iron, and there is an extensive chemistry of the tetroxides, oxohalides, and oxoanions. For both elements there is little, if any, evidence that simple aquo ions exist, and virtually all their aqueous solutions, whatever the anions present, may be considered to contain complexes. In addition to carbonyl and organometallic compounds in the low oxidation states −2, 0, and +1, both elements form compounds in every oxidation state from +2 to +8. The most important oxidation states, however, are +2, +3, +4, +6, and +8.

Oxides. Ruthenium(VIII) oxide and osmium(VIII) oxide (RuO_4 and OsO_4) both form crystalline solids. They are extremely poisonous with penetrating ozone-like odors. Osmium(VIII) oxide is a particular hazard, especially to the eyes, because of its ready reduction by organic matter to a black oxide in a lower oxidation state. Ruthenium(VIII) oxide is obtained when acid solutions containing ruthenium are heated with powerful oxidizing agents such as iodate(VII), manganate(VII), or cerium(IV) ion and can be distilled from the solutions or swept out by a gas stream. Osmium(VIII) oxide, as noted previously, can be obtained by burning the metal and also by oxidation of osmium solutions. Both tetroxides have a tetrahedral structure, are extremely soluble in carbon tetrachloride, and can be extracted from aqueous solutions with this solvent. Osmium(VIII) oxide finds limited use in organic chemistry.

Both metals form dioxides that have the rutile structure as well as some hydrous oxides, such as black $Ru_2O_3 \cdot nH_2O$, ruthenium(III) oxide, obtained from ruthenium(III) chloride solutions upon addition of bases. Aqueous solutions of the tetroxide can be reduced by hydrogen to give hydrous forms of the dioxide.

Halides. Ruthenium and osmium both form hexafluorides that are relatively volatile substances containing octahedral molecules. Both will dissociate into lower fluorides upon heating. The pentafluorides are dark-green solids that have cyclic tetrameric structures in which there are linear bridging fluoride ions giving each metal a coordination number of six. The pentafluorides are very reactive and readily hydrolyzed. Tetrafluorides and difluorides are also known; they are made by various reductive procedures. For example, osmium(VI) fluoride can be reduced with hexacarbonyltungsten to osmium(IV) fluoride, while ruthenium(V) fluoride can be reduced by iodine under mild conditions to give the ruthenium(IV) fluoride or at 250° C (480° F) to give ruthenium(III) fluoride.

The chemistry of the chlorides, bromides, and iodides of ruthenium and osmium is rather complex. The action of chlorine with added carbon monoxide on ruthenium metal at 370° C (700° F) gives beta-ruthenium(III) chloride, which on heating above 450° C (840° F) in chlorine is converted to another form, designated alpha, which is insoluble in water and ethanol. Ruthenium(III) bromide, $RuBr_3$, has not been obtained pure but only as green, hygroscopic crystals by evaporation of solutions prepared by dissolving hydrous ruthenium(III) oxide in hydrobromic acid. Chlorination of osmium gives a mixture of osmium(III) chloride, $OsCl_3$, and osmium(IV) chloride, $OsCl_4$, with the former predominating below 500° C (900° F) in a restricted supply of chlorine, and pure $OsCl_4$ being obtained in an excess of chlorine above 650° C (1,200° F). Nothing is known of the structures of either of these materials, and their chemistry has not been much investigated. Osmium also forms osmium(III) bromide, $OsBr_3$, osmium(IV) bromide, $OsBr_4$, and osmium(III) iodide, OsI_3, all of which apparently decompose on heating to substances having the composition of lower halides, but nothing is known about their true nature.

Divalent ruthenium and osmium. The chemistry of ruthenium and osmium in oxidation state +2 is exclusively that of complexes and is very complicated. These complexes are usually prepared by the reduction of solutions of the elements in higher oxidation states in the presence of the desired ligands. All complexes of divalent ruthenium and osmium are octahedral, diamagnetic, and usually kinetically inert. These characteristics are consistent with a t_{2g}^6 configuration. The reduction of almost any ruthenium compound in ammoniacal solution with zinc dust yields a solution from which orange crystals of hexammineruthenium(II) chloride, $[Ru(NH_3)_6]Cl_2$, separate. This substance is a powerful reducing agent. On the other hand, ruthenium forms the complex cation tris(dipyridyl)ruthenium(III), $[Ru(dipy)_3]^{2+}$ (in which dipy represents the bidentate organic ligand dipyridyl), which is extremely stable and forms a vast number of salts to all of which it lends an intense red colour. Osmium forms a similar dipyridyl complex. Other important complexes are the very stable hexacyano anions.

The first complex of molecular nitrogen discovered was pentamminenitrogenruthenium(II), $[Ru(NH_3)_5N_2]^{2+}$.

Trivalent and tetravalent states. Complexes of ruthenium and osmium in oxidation state +3 are virtually all octahedral with low-spin (t_{2g}^5) configurations. They are among the best characterized complexes of these elements and include the hexachloro, $[MCl_6]^{3-}$; hexammine, $[M(NH_3)_6]^{3+}$; tris(oxalato), $[M(C_2O_4)_3]^{3-}$; and tris(2,4-pentanediono), $[M(CH_3COCHCOCH_3)_3]$ species. The most notable complexes of ruthenium(IV) and osmium(IV) are the oxo bridged dinuclear anions having the structure $[Cl_5M-O-MCl_5]^{4-}$, prepared by reduction of the tetroxides by hydrochloric acid. These are diamagnetic because of coupling of electron spins through the M–O–M bridge system.

Nitric oxide complexes of ruthenium. Formation of nitric oxide complexes is a prominent feature of ruthenium chemistry. Ruthenium solutions or compounds that have ever been treated with nitric acid or any other source of the NO group must be suspected of containing RuNO groups, which can be detected by their absorption of infrared radiation of characteristic energy.

Rhodium and iridium. Rhodium and iridium occur in nature in association with the other platinum metals, and their separation and refinement form part of the overall metallurgical processing of the group, which is discussed elsewhere. These metals are somewhat more reactive than ruthenium and osmium. Rhodium will dissolve in hot concentrated sulfuric acid and both dissolve in concentrated hydrochloric acid containing sodium perchlorate at 125°−150° C (260°−300° F). Both will dissolve in aqua regia.

For both elements, the most important chemistry is that of the oxidation states +1 and +3, although iridium forms some complexes in oxidation state +4 and rhodium forms the dirhodium tetraacetate, $Rh_2(O_2CCH_3)_4$ and various derivatives containing two additional ligands —e.g., water, pyridine, or triphenylphosphine—in oxidation state $+2$. Complexes in oxidation state $+1$ chiefly contain carbon monoxide, olefins, and phosphines as ligands. Hexachloroiridate(IV), $IrCl_6{}^{2-}$, and hexabromoiridate(IV), $IrBr_6{}^{2-}$, are the only notable chemical species containing tetravalent iridium.

Binary compounds. Rhodium and iridium form several fluorides; rhodium(VI) fluoride, RhF_6, and iridium(VI) fluoride, IrF_6, are highly reactive molecular substances formed by direct reaction of the elements. The pentafluorides are cyclic tetramers having the formulas $[RhF_5]_4$ and $[IrF_5]_4$. Rhodium(IV) fluoride, rhodium(III) fluoride, and iridium(III) fluoride are also known.

Halides of rhodium and iridium

The only important halides, other than the fluorides, are the trihalides; rhodium(III) chloride, $RhCl_3$, and iridium(III) chloride, $IrCl_3$, can both be made by direct chlorination of the metals, while lower halides are obtainable only by removal of water from their hydrates, which octahedral and have $t_{2g}{}^6$ configurations.

Hydrous oxides having the formulas $Rh_2O_3 \cdot nH_2O$, $RhO_2 \cdot nH_2O$, $Ir_2O_3 \cdot nH_2O$, and $IrO_2 \cdot nH_2O$ can be precipitated from aqueous solutions; anhydrous compounds having the formulas M_2O_3 and MO_2 are also known. The latter have the rutile structure.

The monovalent state. Both four-coordinate (square) and five-coordinate complexes of rhodium(I) and iridium(I) are formed, and the criteria for stability of four- versus five-coordinate species are not well established. Bis[chlorodicarbonylrhodium(I)], $[RhCl(CO)_2]_2$, easily prepared by passing carbon monoxide saturated with ethanol over rhodium(III) chloride trihydrate, $RhCl_3 \cdot 3H_2O$, at $100°$ C, is an important reactant in the preparation of other univalent rhodium compounds. Thus it is cleaved by various donors L (*e.g.*, phosphines or chloride ion) to give mononuclear complexes of the type $RhCl(CO)_2L$. Action of triphenylphosphine on solutions of rhodium(III) chloride in ethanol produces the compound $RhCl(CO)[P(C_6H_5)_3]_2$, which can then be converted by action of sodium borohydride to the hydrido complex, $RhH(CO)[P(C_6H_5)_3]_3$, which is an extremely useful catalyst for homogeneous hydrogenation of olefins and for several other reactions.

Vaska's compound

The iridium complex having the formula *trans*-$IrCl(CO)[P(C_6H_5)_3]_2$, often called Vaska's compound, and related ones in which chloride is replaced by bromide or iodide, and triphenylphosphine is replaced by other phosphines, has a remarkable ability to bind small molecules such as oxygen, nitrogen, and sulfur dioxide and to add others such as iodomethane and chlorine. These reactions have been extensively studied because they are convenient models for a wide range of such reactions.

The trivalent state. A large number of complexes, cationic, neutral, and anionic, is known for both rhodium and iridium in oxidation state $+3$. The cationic and neutral complexes of trivalent rhodium are generally kinetically inert, while the anionic ones are usually labile; for iridium all three types are usually quite inert. In all cases, the complexes are diamagnetic because they are octahedral and have $t_{2g}{}^6$ configurations.

Rhodium forms the cation hexaaquorhodium(III), $[Rh(H_2O)_6]^{3+}$, when hydrous rhodium(III) oxide is dissolved in cold acids, and the deliquescent perchlorate having the formula $[Rh(H_2O)_6](ClO_4)_3$ can be isolated.

Both elements give amine complexes having the compositions $[M(NR_3)_6]^{3+}$, $[M(NR_3)_5X]^{2+}$, and $[M(NR_3)_4X_2]^+$, in which M represents rhodium or iridium, (NR_3), an amine or ammonia, and X, a halide; chloropentamminerhodium(II) chloride, $[Rh(NH_3)_5Cl]Cl_2$, is a typical example. These are similar to the corresponding cobalt complexes. The most important anionic complexes are hexachlororhodate(III), $RhCl_6{}^{3-}$, and hexachloroiridate(III), $IrCl_6{}^{3-}$, which have no cobalt analogues.

Rhodium(III) chloride is an important compound that is a starting material for the preparation of many others, in various oxidation states. In aqueous emulsions it can catalyze a number of useful organic reactions.

Palladium and platinum. Platinum and palladium are more abundant than any of the other platinum metals. Platinum is by far the best known and technologically the most important. Both palladium and platinum are more reactive than the other platinum metals. Palladium is readily attacked by concentrated nitric acid and in its sponge form will dissolve even in hydrochloric acid in presence of chlorine or oxygen. Platinum is not attacked by any single mineral acid, but it dissolves readily in aqua regia and slowly in hydrochloric acid in presence of air. Both metals are rapidly attacked by fused alkali oxides and peroxides and also by fluorine and chlorine at about $500°$ C ($900°$ F). They also combine with a number of nonmetallic elements on heating, such as phosphorus, arsenic, antimony, silicon, lead, sulfur, and selenium.

Both metals, but especially palladium, are capable of absorbing large volumes of hydrogen. At $80°$ C ($180°$ F) and one atmosphere, palladium will absorb up to 900 times its own volume. The absorption causes both the electrical conductivity and magnetic susceptibility to decrease. These and other observations have led some investigators to conclude that there is a definite palladium hydride phase, although its structure and ideal composition are not firmly established.

Binary compounds. The oxides of platinum and palladium are of little importance. Hydrous palladium(II) oxide is a yellow gelatinous precipitate that turns brown and then black on drying and cannot be completely dehydrated without decomposition. When a solution of hexachloroplatinate(IV), $PtCl_6{}^{2-}$, is boiled with sodium carbonate, hydrous platinum(IV), oxide, $PtO_2 \cdot nH_2O$, is formed. It can be dehydrated to PtO_2, anhydrous platinum(IV) oxide, which decomposes above about $200°$ C.

Platinum forms a hexafluoride as well as the tetrameric pentafluoride, $[PtF_5]_4$, and the monomeric tetrafluoride PtF_4, whereas palladium is the only one of the platinum metals that forms no hexafluoride. Palladium forms the tetrafluoride, PdF_4, and the difluoride, PdF_2. Platinum(IV) chloride, $PtCl_4$, bromide, $PtBr_4$, and iodide, PtI_4, are all known but have no palladium analogues. Platinum(IV) chloride is important as a starting material in preparing complexes of tetravalent platinum. The dihalides of both metals (chlorides, bromides, and iodides) are all known, and the chlorides are important compounds. Both dichlorides exist in two forms. The beta forms are isostructural and consist of M_6Cl_{12} units, like those in lower halides of niobium and tantalum except that the metal–metal distances are so great as to preclude significant metal-to-metal bonding. The compound Pt_6Cl_{12} dissolves in benzene. The alpha form of palladium(II) chloride consists of very long chains of $PdCl_2$ units in which pairs of bridging chlorine atoms give square coordination about each metal atom. The structure of the alpha form of platinum(II) chloride is uncertain but appears to be different from that of the alpha form of palladium dichloride.

Platinum(VI) fluoride, PtF_6, reacts with oxygen to give a compound having the formula $[O_2{}^+]\,[PtF_6{}^-]$. This reaction was first observed in 1962 by N. Bartlett, who reasoned that because xenon has an ionization potential almost identical to that of molecular oxygen, a similar reaction might occur between platinum(VI) fluoride and xenon. He confirmed this by obtaining a red solid, of variable composition $Xe[PtF_6]_x$, in which x ranges between 1 and 2. This discovery led others to examine the reaction of xenon with fluorine and thus the chemistry of the noble gases was discovered.

Reactions with the noble gases

The divalent state. The characteristic stereochemistry of platinum(II) and palladium(II) is square though a few five- and six-coordinate species are known. Palladium forms an ion, tetraquopalladium(II) $[Pd(H_2O)_4]^{2+}$, which is obtained when hydrous palladium(II) oxide dissolves in dilute nitric, perchloric, or sulfuric acids; platinum does not form the analogous ion. Palladium also dissolves in glacial acetic acid containing some nitric acid and, after boiling, brown crystals of the acetate, which has the formula $Pd_3(O_2CCH_3)_6$, can be obtained. The molecule of this compound contains a triangle of palladium atoms with two acetate groups bridging each edge. An anhydrous nitrate can also be obtained by action of nitrogen pentoxide, N_2O_5, on the hydrated nitrate.

The most common compounds of divalent platinum and palladium are salts of the red tetrachloropalladate(II),

$PdCl_4^{2-}$, and the tetrachloroplatinate(II), $PtCl_4^{2-}$, ions. From these, by substitution reactions, a great variety of other square complexes can be made. Some representative compounds have the formulas $K[Pd(NH_3)Cl_3]$, $Pt(NH_3)_2Cl_2$ (cis and trans isomers), $[Pt(NH_3)_4][PtCl_4]$, $[Pd(NH_3)_4][Pd(SCN)_4]$, $Pt[P(C_6H_5)_3]_2Cl_2$. Bridged binuclear species such as those shown in diagrams **22** and **23** are also well-known.

The compound $[Pt(NH_3)_4][PtCl_4]$, tetraammine platinum(II) tetrachloroplatinate(II), is known as Magnus' green salt. It has a structure in which the square cations and anions are stacked alternately in infinite columns and the colour is due to interactions between the metal atoms. A number of similar compounds are also known.

The tetravalent state. Oxidation state +4 is not a very stable one for palladium; only a few complexes are known and they are not common or important. Platinum, however, has an extensive chemistry in this oxidation state, and in all such compounds the platinum has octahedral coordination. The most extensive series of complexes of quadrivalent platinum are those in the series having the formulas $[Pt(NR_3)_6]X_4$, $[Pt(NR_3)_5X]X_3$, ... $M[Pt(NR_3)X_5]$, $M_2[PtX_6]$, in which (NR_3) represents an amine or ammonia, X is a halide, thiocyanate (SCN^-), or nitrite (NO_2^-) ion, and M is an alkali metal cation.

There are no compounds containing trivalent palladium or platinum, even though some substances have stoichiometry that might suggest this oxidation state. Thus, for example, the compound having the formula $Pt(NH_3)_2Br_3$ actually consists of molecules of compounds formulated $Pt(NH_3)_2Br_4$ and $Pt(NH_3)_2Br_2$ stacked in linear chains.

Other compounds of platinum. Platinum, and to a smaller extent palladium, forms a number of interesting compounds containing negatively charged organic groups or the hydride ion, H^-, as ligands; it also forms some phosphine complexes in which it is formally zero-valent. Many of the organic and hydride complexes are white substances formulated $Pt(PR'_3)_2XR$, in which X stands for Cl, Br, I, and R and R', for H or an alkyl or aryl group. Among the most stable of organometallic compounds are those formulated $[(CH_3)_3PtX]_4$, in which there are four $(CH_3)_3Pt^+$ groups at alternate vertices of a cube with the remaining vertices occupied by triply bridging chloride, bromide, iodide, or hydroxide ions (represented by X in the preceding formula). These compounds can be degraded with preservation of the $(CH_3)_3Pt$ moiety to give mononuclear complexes, such as cyclopentadienyltrimethylplatinum(IV), $C_5H_5Pt(CH_3)_3$.

Neither platinum nor palladium forms a simple carbonyl analogous to tetracarbonylnickel, but platinum forms $Pt(PF_3)_4$, tetrakis(phosphorus trifluoride)platinum, as well as a number of polynuclear mixed carbonylphosphine derivatives having formulas such as $Pt(CO)(PR_3)_3$, $Pt_3(CO)_3(PR_3)_4$, and $Pt_4(CO)_5(PR_3)_4$. Of particular interest are the triphenylphosphine complexes designated $Pt[P(C_6H_5)_3]_n$, $n = 2, 3, 4$, which are interconvertible in solution by varying the triphenylphosphine concentration. Bis(triphenylphosphine)platinum, $Pt[P(C_6H_5)_3]_2$ can bind a number of small molecules such as oxygen and sulfur dioxide and react with others such as chloromethane and bromine. The oxygen complex $Pt[P(C_6H_5)_3]_2O_2$ acts as an oxidant toward carbon monoxide, sulfur dioxide, triphenylphosphine, and other substances.

Silver and gold. Silver and gold are two of the noblest —that is, least chemically reactive—of the transition elements, and both are found in nature in the free state. For silver the more important deposits commercially are such compounds as the mineral argentite (silver sulfide, Ag_2S), which is usually associated with other sulfides such as those of lead and copper, as well as several other

sulfides, some of which contain antimony as well. Silver is found generally in lead ores, copper ores, and cobalt arsenide ores and is also frequently associated with gold in nature. Most silver is derived as a by-product from ores that are mined and processed to obtain these other metals. Gold is most commonly found free, the only compounds of gold in nature being various tellurides.

Silver is a white, lustrous metal and is among the most ductile and malleable ones known. Pure silver has the highest electrical and thermal conductivities of all metals. Gold is a soft, yellow metal that has the highest ductility and malleability of any element.

Silver is less reactive chemically than copper except toward sulfur and hydrogen sulfide, which rapidly blacken silver surfaces. The metal will dissolve in oxidizing acids and in solutions containing cyanide ions in the presence of oxygen or peroxides. Gold is much less reactive and is not attacked by oxygen or sulfur, although it will react readily with halogens or with solutions containing or generating chlorine, such as aqua regia. It also will dissolve in cyanide solutions in presence of air or hydrogen peroxide. Dissolution in cyanide solutions is attributable to the formation of the very stable dicyanoargentate(I), $Ag(CN)_2^-$, and dicyanoaurate(I), $Au(CN)_2^-$, ions.

As does copper, the elements silver and gold have a single s electron outside a completed d shell, but in spite of the similarity in electronic structures and ionization potentials there are few close resemblances between silver and gold on the one hand and copper on the other.

Both silver and gold find their chief applications in the form of the metals themselves, but silver is also of unique utility as silver chloride in photographic emulsions. Despite the relatively high cost of the material no satisfactory substitute has ever been found.

For silver the pre-eminently important oxidation state in all of its ordinary chemistry is the state +1, although the states +2 and +3 are known. With gold, on the other hand, the state +1 is generally quite unstable, and most of the chemistry of gold involves the state +3.

Silver compounds. The silver(I) (argentous) state is represented by a large number of compounds, most of which are insoluble in water. Silver nitrate, silver chlorate, silver perchlorate, and a few other salts with less common anions such as tetrafluoroborate, BF_4^-, hexafluorophosphate, PF_6^- and trifluoromethanesulfonate, $CF_3SO_3^-$, are readily soluble in water, and silver sulfate and acetate are sparingly so. Silver fluoride, AgF, is also water soluble and can be crystallized in the form of hydrates such as that formulated $AgF \cdot 4H_2O$, but it is an uncommon compound. The other halides are all insoluble in water, increasingly so in the sequence silver chloride, silver bromide, silver iodide. Silver chloride can be obtained as rather tough sheets that are transparent throughout much of the infrared region and have been used for optical purposes in infrared spectroscopy. The sensitivity to light of chloride and bromide as well as many other silver compounds accounts for their importance, particularly that of the chloride, in photography.

Other important silver compounds include the oxide, which is obtained as a dark brown precipitate upon addition of alkali hydroxides to solutions of the silver(I) ion, Ag^+. The addition of hydrogen sulfide or other soluble sulfides to solutions of the Ag^+ ion precipitates black silver sulfide, Ag_2S, which is the least soluble in water of all silver compounds. The black coating on tarnished silver articles is composed of this sulfide.

The silver(I) ion forms a great variety of complexes in both solution and the solid state. For the most part the coordination number of Ag^+ in its complexes is 2, and the complexes have the linear structure L–Ag–L. Because of this structure chelating ligands cannot readily form simple complexes and thus tend to give complicated polynuclear products. The coordination number of silver does in some cases exceed 2 and complexes of general stoichiometry AgL_3 and AgL_4 can exist. It is, of course, highly probable that in solution even the formally linear species, such as the ion $Ag(CN)_2^-$, contain water molecules bonded to the silver ion in the plane perpendicular to the axis. Silver forms its most stable complexes with ligands containing the donor atoms nitrogen, phosphorus, arsenic, sulfur, and selenium, and with cyanide. It has a low preference for oxygen ligands. Many silver salts, except for the most insoluble ones (the sulfide and the iodide), dissolve readily in aqueous ammonia as the result of formation of the diamminesilver ion, $Ag(NH_3)_2^+$. Another very important ligand for the silver(I) ion is the thiosulfate ion, $S_2O_3^{2-}$, which is employed in photography to fix the image by removing from the photographic plate the silver chloride grains that have not been photochemically reduced to metallic silver by light.

Silver(II) and silver(III) The oxidation state $+2$ is much less stable for silver than for copper, but there is a significant amount of chemistry for it. The ion Ag^{2+} can exist in strongly acid solutions, but it is a powerful oxidizing agent, and such solutions are gradually reduced by water. Many oxidations which are carried out by the peroxodisulfate ion, $S_2O_8^{2-}$, are catalyzed by added silver(I) ion. Detailed kinetic studies indicate that the effective catalytic agent is silver(II) ion, Ag^{2+}. The apparent oxide of divalent silver, AgO, actually contains a mixture of Ag^+ and Ag^{3+}. The Ag^{2+} ion, as the Cu^{2+} ion, is paramagnetic, having one unpaired electron. The most important and numerous compounds of silver(II) are various complexes normally prepared by persulfate oxidation of silver(I) solutions containing the required ligand. Nearly all silver(II) complexes have square coordination. A few compounds containing trivalent silver are known, such as the oxide, AgO, just mentioned and another black oxide with a composition approximating to Ag_2O_3, as well as a few complexes such as bis[hexaoxoiodato(VII)]argentate(III), $[Ag(IO_6)_2]^{7-}$, and tetrafluoroargentate(III), AgF_4^-.

Silver forms organometallic compounds exclusively in the oxidation state $+1$. The simple alkyl and aryl derivatives are very unstable and generally decompose below 0° C. The more important compounds are those derived from acetylenes, olefins, and aromatic compounds. The silver ion has the ability to interact with the pi electron systems of such substances, and the resulting complexes are often useful in the isolation and separation of substances, either purely organic or organometallic, that contain unsaturated organic moieties.

Gold compounds. The chemistry of gold in either of its oxidation states ($+1$ or $+3$) is mainly one of complex compounds. There is no evidence for gold(I) oxide but gold(III) oxide, Au_2O_3, is known as a brown powder obtained by dehydration of the brown precipitate of $Au(OH)_3$. The chloride and the bromide of trivalent gold are dimeric molecules, Au_2Cl_6 and Au_2Br_6, which form red crystals. They are made by direct reaction of gold with chlorine or bromine at about 200° C. On heating gold(III) chloride in absence of excess chlorine it is decomposed to form gold(I) chloride, AuCl. Gold(III) fluoride, AuF_3, can be made by fluorination of gold(III) chloride at 300° C (about 600° F).

The gold(I) ion, like the silver(I) ion, forms mainly linear complexes, of which the most important are dicyanoaurate(I), $Au(CN)_2^-$, dichloroaurate(I), $AuCl_2^-$, and chlorotrialkyl (or aryl) phosphinegold, R_3PAuCl, in which R represents an alkyl or aryl group. Gold also forms some curious compounds in which there are clusters of metal atoms, an example being one formulated $Au_{11}I_3[P(C_2H_5)_3]_7$, which contains a polyhedron of 10 gold atoms with the 11th gold atom in the centre and iodine and triethylphosphine ligands appended to the outer gold atoms. The full extent of this type of gold chemistry is still unknown. Gold mercaptides, $(AuSR)_n$, in which R is an alkyl group, are obtained from sulfurized terpenes; they are highly soluble in organic solvents and are used for decorating china and glass articles with gold film. They may contain clusters of gold atoms.

Complexes of trivalent gold are more numerous and important. When gold is dissolved in aqua regia or Au_2Cl_6, gold(III) chloride, is dissolved in hydrochloric acid and the solution evaporated a substance known as chloroauric acid is obtained as yellow crystals. It has the formula $H_3O^+(AuCl_4)^- \cdot 3H_2O$. Other water-soluble salts containing the tetrachloroaurate ion, such as potassium tetrachloroaurate(III), $KAuCl_4$, or sodium tetra-

chloroaurate(III) dihydrate, $NaAuCl_4 \cdot 2H_2O$, are readily obtainable. Other complex anions are tetracyanoaurate(III), $[Au(CN)_4]^-$, and tetranitratoaurate(III), $[Au(NO_3)_4]^-$. There are also a variety of complex cations in which the ligands are a mixed set of amine molecules, chloride ions, and water molecules, as for example dichlorodipyridineaurate(III), $[AuCl_2(pyridine)_2]^+$ in which the gold is four-coordinate.

Although organogold compounds are not of major importance, it is worth mentioning that alkyls of gold, formulated RAu, were among the first organometallic compounds of transition metals to be prepared.

BIBLIOGRAPHY. FRANK A. COTTON and GEOFFREY WILKINSON, *Advanced Inorganic Chemistry*, 3rd ed. (1972), presents a comprehensive discussion of fundamental descriptive chemistry and theory; EDWIN M. LARSEN, *Transitional Elements* (1965), gives a much briefer and more elementary topical discussion. S.F.A. KETTLE, *Coordination Compounds* (1969), is an excellent introduction to its subject. FRED BASOLO and RALPH G. PEARSON, *Mechanisms of Inorganic Reactions*, 2nd ed. (1967), presents much general information on coordination compounds. IRVING WENDER and PIERO PINO (eds.), *Organic Syntheses Via Metal Carbonyls* (1968), has excellent coverage of metal carbonyls; and M.L.H. GREEN, *Organometallic Compounds*, vol. 2, *The Transition Elements*, 3rd ed. (1967), deals with the organometallic compounds systematically and in detail. J.P. CANDLIN, K.A. TAYLOR, and D.T. THOMPSON, *Reactions of Transition-Metal Complexes* (1968), covers its subject matter in great detail. CHARLES L. THOMAS, *Catalytic Processes and Proven Catalysts* (1970), reviews the actual uses of industrial catalysts by process type. CARL J. BALLHAUSEN, *Introduction to Ligand Field Theory* (1962), gives a working account of how ligand field theory is applied to the *d*-block elements. WILLIAM P. GRIFFITH, *The Chemistry of the Rarer Platinum Metals* (1967); R.J.H. CLARK, *The Chemistry of Titanium and Vanadium* (1968); RAY COLTON, *The Chemistry of Rhenium and Technetium* (1965); FRED FAIRBROTHER, *The Chemistry of Niobium and Tantalum* (1967); and J.H. CANTERFORD and RAY COLTON, *Halides of the Second and Third Row Transition Metals* (1968), are encyclopaedic accounts of their respective subjects.

(F.A.C.)

Transplants, Organ and Tissue

A transplant, in the context of this article, is a section of tissue or a complete organ removed from its original natural site and transferred to a new position in the same or a separate individual. The term, like its synonym, graft, was borrowed by surgeons from horticulture. Both words imply that success will result in a healthy and flourishing graft or transplant, which will gain its nourishment from its new environment.

Historical background. Transplants of animal tissue have figured prominently in mythology since the legend of the creation of Eve from one of Adam's ribs. Historical accounts of surgical tissue grafting as part of the cure of patients date back to the early Hindu surgeons who, some 600 years before Christ, reconstructed noses from skin flaps taken from the arm. This method was introduced to Western medicine by the great Italian surgeon Gaspare Tagliacozzo in the 16th century. The flap was left attached to the arm for two to three weeks until new blood vessels had grown into it from the nose remnant. The arm was then freed from the new nose.

Purposes and sites of transplants. It was found that extremely thin pieces of skin could be cut free and would obtain enough nourishment from the serum in the graft bed to stay alive while new blood vessels were being formed. This free grafting of skin, together with the flap techniques already mentioned, have constituted the main therapeutic devices of the plastic surgeon in the correction of various types of defects. Skilled manipulations of such grafts can produce surprising improvements in the appearance of those born with malformed faces and in the disfigurements resulting from severe burns. Cornea, which structurally is a modified form of transparent skin, can also be free grafted, and corneal grafts have restored sight to countless blind eyes.

Structural implants of dead tissue, such as bone, cartilage, arteries, or heart valves, are not true grafts or transplants, but are more akin to the stick to which the rose is attached for support—they are perhaps essential to its welfare, but their function does not depend on biological processes; in fact, inert manufactured devices may often be equally suitable substitutes.

Blood transfusion can be regarded as a form of tissue graft. The blood-forming tissues—bone-marrow cells—can also be transplanted. If these cells are injected into the bloodstream, they home to the marrow cavities and can become established as a vital lifesaving graft in patients suffering from defective marrow.

Organ and limb grafts

The chief distinguishing feature of organ and limb grafts is that the tissues of the organ or limb can only survive if blood vessels are rapidly joined (anastomosed) to blood vessels of the recipient. This provides the graft with a blood supply before it dies from lack of oxygen and nourishment and from the accumulation of poisonous waste products.

As can be seen from the examples cited, living-tissue grafts may be performed for a variety of reasons. Skin grafts can save life in severe burns, can improve function by correcting deformity, or can improve appearances in a cosmetic sense, with valuable psychological benefits. Organ grafts can supply a missing function and save life in cases of fatal disease of vital organs, such as the kidney.

Types of transplant. A skin graft removed from one part of the body and transplanted to another site in the same individual is called an autograft. Autografts cannot be rejected. Similarly, grafts between identical twins or highly inbred animals—isografts—are accepted by the recipients indefinitely. Grafts from a donor to a recipient of the same species—allografts or homografts—are usually rejected unless special efforts are made to prevent this. Grafts between individuals of different species—xenografts or heterografts—are usually destroyed very quickly by the recipient.

Tissue or organ grafts may be transplanted to their normal situation in the recipient and are then known as orthotopic—for example, skin to the surface of the body. Alternatively, they may be transplanted to an abnormal situation and are then called heterotopic—for example, kidneys are usually grafted into the lower part of the abdomen instead of into the loin (the back between the ribs and the pelvis), as this is more convenient. If an extra organ is grafted, it is called auxiliary, or accessory —for example, a heterotopic liver graft may be inserted without removal of the recipient's own liver.

Grafts are usually performed for long-term effects. Occasionally, the limited acceptance of a skin allograft may be lifesaving, by preventing loss of fluid and protein from extensive burned surface in severely ill patients. The graft also provides a bacteria-proof covering, so that infection cannot occur. When the allograft is removed or rejected, the patient may be sufficiently recovered to receive permanent autografts (see BURNS).

Scope of this article. In this article the present state of organ and tissue transplantation is summarized. Specific instances are included, especially if these are of established or potential value. A short account is given of graft rejection, the central problem in tissue transplantation, and the methods by which rejection can be overcome, immunosuppression. Selection of donor, organ and tissue preservation, and the ethical and legal aspects of transplantation are considered. The article concludes with speculations on the future of transplants and the role of artificial organs.

TISSUE TRANSPLANTS

Skin. Most skin grafting practiced at present is with autografts; the special indication for skin allografts in severely burned patients has been mentioned. Skin allografts seem to be rejected more aggressively than any other tissue, and there are many experimental situations in which skin grafts between two inbred strains of animal fail, although kidney grafts between the same strains survive indefinitely. There can be no doubt that if rejection could be predictably and safely overcome, there would suddenly be a whole new field of surgery. With autografts, the donor skin is limited to what the patient has available, and sometimes in extensive burn cases this becomes a

matter of robbing Peter to pay Paul. If allografts were not rejected, skin from cadavers could be used for coverage of burned areas without the need for subsequent autografting, and many lives would be saved.

Flap grafts. Flap grafts as used by Tagliacozzo are particularly valuable if fat as well as skin has been lost. The procedure of raising a flap and keeping the donor site adjacent to the recipient bed can be complicated and uncomfortable for the patient. The cosmetic results are good, and the fat under the skin contained in the flap can be used to cover exposed bone or to allow movement in a contracted joint or to fashion a new nose.

Full-thickness free-skin grafts. Full-thickness free-skin grafts are the maximum thickness that can survive without a blood supply, and they are therefore in some danger of failure to survive. They produce good cosmetic appearances and are especially useful on the face. Their main defect is that, unless they are very small, the donor site from which they come is a defect that needs to be closed in its own right and may itself need skin grafting.

Split or partial-thickness skin grafts. Split, or partial-thickness, skin grafts are by far the most commonly used grafts in plastic surgery. Superficial slices of skin the thickness of tissue paper are cut with a hand or mechanical razor. The graft, which contains living cells, is so thin that it usually gains adequate nourishment directly from the raw surface to which it is applied, and the risk of failure to take (that is, to survive in the new location) is therefore much less than with full-thickness grafts. Another major advantage is that the donor site is not badly damaged. It is tender for only two or three weeks, and it resembles a superficial graze both in appearance and in the fact that healing takes place from the deep layer of the skin left behind. Split skin grafts can be taken quickly from large areas to cover big defects. They tend to have an abnormal shiny reddish appearance that is not as satisfactory cosmetically as the other types of skin graft.

Other tissue transplants. *Cornea.* There are certain forms of blindness in which the eye is entirely normal apart from opacity of the front window, or cornea. The opacity may be the result of disease or injury, but, if the clouded cornea is removed and replaced by a corneal transplant, normal vision can result. Since cells of the cornea remain viable for some 12 hours after death, a cornea can be grafted if it is removed within that period. Cooling will slow the process of deterioration, although the sooner the section of cornea is transplanted the better. The graft bed to which a cornea is transplanted has no blood supply. Nourishment comes directly by diffusion from the tissues. Because most rejection factors are carried in the bloodstream, the lack of blood vessels permits most corneal allografts to survive indefinitely without rejection, a circumstance that has been of great benefit to many patients.

Cornea, blood vessel, and heart valves

Blood vessels. By far the most satisfactory blood-vessel transplant is an autograft, similar in principle to skin autografts. One of the commonest and most serious blood diseases in the legs is caused by blockage of the main artery in the thigh by fatty deposits in the degenerative form of arteriosclerosis (hardening of the arteries), the disease that is responsible for most heart attacks and strokes. In the leg the result is, first, pain in the calves, and then gangrene of the foot, necessitating amputation of the leg. If dealt with early, the effects of the arterial blockage can often be overcome by removing a nonessential superficial vein from the leg, reversing it so that the valves will not obstruct blood flow, and then joining this graft to the thigh artery above and below the block—thus bypassing the obstruction.

Vein or arterial allografts are far less successful. In time the walls tend to degenerate, and the vessels either dilate, with the danger of bursting, or become obstructed.

Heart valves. Valvular diseases of the heart can be dangerous, since both a blocked valve and a valve that allows blood to leak backward create a strain on the heart that can lead to heart failure. If the valve is seriously damaged it can be replaced with an allograft valve or a manufactured mechanical valve. Neither is ideal. Allograft valves have a normal central blood flow, but after a few years they may become rigid and cease to function. Plastic valves—usually of ball valve type—allow blood to flow around the surface of the ball, and this tends to damage red blood cells and cause anemia.

Bone. When fractures fail to unite, autografts of bone can be extremely valuable in helping the bone to heal. Bone allografts can be used for similar purposes, but they are not as satisfactory, since the bone cells are either dead when grafted or are rejected. Thus, the graft is merely a structural scaffold that, although useful as such, cannot partake actively in healing.

Fascia. Fascia, sheets of strong connective tissue that surround muscle bundles, may be used as autografts to repair hernias. The principle of use is like that for skin.

Nerves. Nerves outside the brain and spinal cord can regenerate if damaged. If the delicate sheaths containing the nerves are cut, however, as must happen if a nerve is partially or completely severed, regeneration may not be possible. Even if regeneration occurs it is unlikely to be complete, since most nerves are mixed motor and sensory paths and there is no control ensuring that regenerating fibres take the correct path. Thus, there will always be some fibres that end in the wrong destination and are therefore unable to function. Defective nerve regeneration is the main reason why limb grafts usually are unsatisfactory. A mechanical artificial limb is likely to be of more value to the patient.

Blood and bone marrow. Mention has already been made of blood transfusion and of transplantation of bone marrow. Blood transfusion has been one of the most important factors in the development of modern surgery. There are many lifesaving surgical procedures that are possible only because the blood loss inevitable in the operation can be made up by transfusion. Blood transfusion is of value in saving life following major injury, bleeding ulcers, childbirth, and many other conditions involving dangerous loss of blood. Bone-marrow transplantation has only recently been used in man with success. The potential value will not be realized until allograft rejection can be more effectively controlled; then a variety of diseases of the blood-forming tissues might be treated by marrow transplantation.

Transfusions

ORGAN TRANSPLANTS

Organ transplantations are relatively new surgical procedures, and, in general, they are, for a variety of reasons, not all of which are surgical or medical, more difficult to perform successfully than are most other grafts.

It is justifiable to consider a new and dangerous form of treatment only when all conventional methods have been tried and failed and the patient is not well enough to lead an independent existence outside of the hospital in the interval before death. In such circumstances, most persons would prefer a chance to live, even if it were small, rather than the alternative of certain death.

Although new treatments are based on careful and prolonged investigations in animals, the results of certain operations in animals may not be the same in man. There can be no guarantee, therefore, that successful results of an operation in the laboratory will be equally successful in man. Careful and cautious trial in human beings is eventually undertaken of methods that seem to be promising in the laboratory. Often the first patients to be selected for a new and dangerous operation are desperately ill or even moribund and are unlikely to withstand the extensive surgery and live long enough to demonstrate whether the operation can have a long-term success. If the patient and his relatives wish the operation to be attempted, then it would seem to be morally justifiable to proceed. Many failures can be expected, but the occasional success represents a definite and valuable gain. There have been early disappointing results in many new operations, but eventually the operation has become standard practice. Operations on the stomach at the turn of the century had an extremely high mortality, but now they are routine and are often performed on patients at a relatively early stage in their disease. This has also been the pattern of development in organ transplantation. Approximately 10,000 kidney grafts had been performed in man prior to January 1, 1973. There have been more than 100 heart grafts, and liver grafts, but fewer than 30 lung grafts. Other organ grafts have not been performed in sufficient numbers to make any assessment of their possible value.

The kidney. The surgery of kidney transplantation is straightforward, and the patient can be kept fit by dialysis with an artificial kidney before and after the operation. The kidney was the first organ to be transplanted successfully in man, and experience is now considerable. Effective methods of preventing graft rejection have been available for only about a decade. It is, therefore, too early to predict how long a kidney might function. Fatal kidney disease is relatively common in young people. There are, for example, some 2,000–3,000 deaths from this cause each year in England and Wales out of a population of 50,000,000.

When there is deterioration of kidney function, eventually, despite all conventional treatment, the patient becomes extremely weak and anemic. Fluid collects in the tissues, producing swelling, known as dropsy or edema, because the kidneys cannot remove excess water. Fluid in the lungs may cause difficulty in breathing and puts an excessive strain on the heart, which may already be suffering from the effects of high blood pressure as a result of kidney failure.

Effects of kidney disease

Waste products that cannot be removed from the body can cause inflammation of the coverings of the heart and the linings of the stomach and colon. As a result, there may be pain in the chest, inflammation of the stomach leading to distressing vomiting, and diarrhea from the colitis. The nerves running to the limbs may be damaged, resulting in paralysis. Kidney failure is, therefore, exceedingly unpleasant for the patient and a source of great distress for his relatives. Treatment with the artificial kidney followed by kidney grafting can eliminate all these symptoms and has a good chance of permitting the dying person to return to a normal existence. Unfortunately, only a minority of patients receive this treatment because of a shortage of donor kidneys.

Artificial kidney treatment for about 12 hours, two to three times a week, removes all the features of kidney failure in one to two months, and the patient is able to leave the hospital. He then can be assessed as to his suitability for receiving a kidney transplant. It is customary to remove both diseased kidneys, as the presence of one that is diseased may interfere with the patient's future health after a successful kidney transplant.

Transplantation and postoperative care. The patient may receive a kidney from a live donor or a dead person. Such cadaver kidneys may not function immediately after transplantation, and further treatment with the artificial kidney may be required for two to three weeks while damage in the kidney is repaired. The patient is given drugs that depress his immune responses and prevent the graft from being rejected. Immediately after the operation, for the first week or two, every effort is made to keep the patient from contact with bacteria that might cause infection. He is usually nursed in a separate room, and doctors and nurses entering the room take care to wear masks and wash their hands before touching the patient. The air of the room is purified by filtration. Close relatives are allowed to visit the patient, but they are required to take the same precautions. When stitches have been removed the patient is encouraged to get up as much as possible and to be active, but in the first four months after operation careful surveillance is necessary to make sure that the patient is not rejecting the graft or developing an infection. He may be discharged from the hospital within a few weeks of the operation, but he will need to make frequent visits to the hospital for medical examination and biochemical estimations of the blood constituents to determine the state of function of the graft and to make sure that the drugs are not damaging the blood-forming cells in the bone marrow. Each patient requires a carefully adjusted dose of the immunosuppressive drugs that prevent transplant rejection.

Once the dosage of immunosuppressive drugs is stabilized, the patient is encouraged to go back to a normal

Maintenance of health after transplantation

existence and return to work. The only restrictions are that he must continue to take his drugs and make frequent visits to the outpatient department for surveillance. Restrictions are rather similar to those for patients with diabetes but perhaps less rigorous, since diabetics need a special diet and insulin has to be injected, while the immunosuppressive drugs can be taken by mouth. Patients can return even to heavy work, such as driving a bulldozer, but more often a relatively light job is preferable. Women can certainly bear normal children after a transplant, and men can become fathers. The course of events is not always so happy, unfortunately. If the patient rejects the kidney or develops a serious infection, it may be necessary to remove the graft and stop administration of the immunosuppressive drugs. The patient must then return to regular maintenance treatment with an artificial kidney.

Data on kidney transplant results. In Boston, a kidney transplantation registry was set up to collect the results of transplants throughout the world. This was later moved to Chicago, where the registry, under the joint auspices of the American College of Surgeons and the National Institutes of Health, follows the results of the transplants of all organs. The pooled results of the first 10,000 kidney patients are encouraging and compare favourably with the results of treatment for many common forms of cancer. Kidney grafting has not been practiced long enough to provide knowledge of the eventual outcome. It is not known, for example, whether a kidney graft in a young person will last for his full life span. Even though the outcome is not known, restoration from an unpleasant illness, which would certainly lead to death, to a normal life with a functioning transplant is worthwhile, and nearly all patients are well aware of the benefits even after as short a period as six months. A few years of full and enjoyable life resulting from kidney transplantation entirely justify the procedure. It is now possible to offer nearly an 80 percent chance of a two-year survival with a kidney graft from a close blood relative, but the figure drops to around 50 percent when the graft comes from an unrelated cadaver donor. Even if the graft fails, it is common practice to return the patient to artificial kidney treatment and then provide him with a second transplant or even a third or fourth.

The heart. A group of American investigators perfected the technique of heart transplantation in the late 1950s. They showed that a transplanted dog's heart can keep the animal with a normal circulation until the heart is rejected. The features of rejection of the heart are similar to those of the kidney. The cells that produce immune reactions, the lymphocytes, migrate into the muscle cells of the heart, damage it, and also block the coronary arteries, depriving the heart of its own circulation. In most experiments it has been more difficult to prevent rejection of the heart than of the kidney. Despite this, rejection has been prevented for long periods in animals. The liver and the heart are both more sensitive to lack of blood supply than the kidney. They need to be removed from the donor more quickly and can be preserved without damage for only a short period.

The heart is a pump with a built-in power supply; it has a delicate regulatory mechanism that permits it to perform efficiently when excessive demands are not made on it. During moments of fear, passion, or violent exercise, the heart rate increases greatly, and the contractions become more forceful, so that the pumping of the blood intrudes on the consciousness; this is experienced by the individual as palpitations. Activity in the bowels may also produce alarming physical symptoms at moments of fear and stress, and the ancient biblical scribes made reference to these sensations in their sacred texts. Prudish medieval translators substituted the word heart for bowel. Cessation of the heartbeat has also been, throughout the ages, the cardinal sign of death. Thus, it is perhaps not so surprising that there was a pathological public interest when the first attempts were made at grafting a heart in man. The objectives of heart transplantation, nevertheless, are the same as those of other organ grafts.

One of the most important advances in surgery after World War II was in direct operations on the heart. Heart valves are repaired or replaced with artificial valves, and techniques have been developed so that the heart can be stopped and its function taken over by an electrical pump. If, however, the muscle of the heart is destroyed, as occurs in certain diseases, the only operation that could cure the patient would be to replace the heart with a graft or possibly, someday, an artificial heart, since the temporary artificial substitutes presently available cannot be implanted safely within the chest. Blockage of the coronary arteries and certain other heart muscle diseases can kill the patient because the muscle of the heart cannot contract properly. A patient with one of these diseases who is close to dying is, therefore, a possible recipient for a heart transplant. Since the experimental work has been done in animals, it would seem to be perfectly justified for a cautious approach to be made with clinical heart grafting. To transplant a heart in man was a logical step forward, and the South African surgical team in Cape Town showed that the results of animal investigations could be applied to man. A number of patients have now lived more than four years after heart transplantation.

Appropriate circumstances for a heart transplant

The liver. Many of the functions of the liver are not known. It is a complicated organ producing many vital substances in the blood and is in effect a chemical factory. The two categories of fatal liver disease that may be treated by liver grafting are nonmalignant destructive diseases of the liver cells—for example, cirrhosis—and primary cancer of the liver affecting either the main liver cells or the bile ducts. The liver is extremely sensitive to lack of blood supply and must be cooled within 15 minutes of the death of the donor. The operation can be difficult, since the liver is rather large and of complex structure. Both its removal from the corpse and its grafting into the recipient are major surgical operations. In man, the operation is more difficult than in animals; particularly, the removal of the diseased liver from the recipient. This may be much enlarged and adherent to surrounding structures so that its removal may result in serious bleeding. Once transplanted, the liver must function immediately or the patient will die. There is no treatment available that is comparable to the use of the artificial kidney for kidney disease. If the liver functions well immediately after transplantation, the rest of the management is similar to that followed in kidney operations, and the same drugs are given. Many liver transplantation operations have failed, but the procedure is certainly possible and capable of restoring dying patients to normal existence. The longest survival is now more than four years after grafting. Of the 102 liver grafts performed so far, eight patients have survived a year or more and two for more than two years.

The lung. Chronic fatal disease of the lung is common, but the progress of the disease is usually slow, and the patient may be ill for a long time; when the lung eventually fails he is likely to be unfit for a general anesthetic and an operation. The function of the lung is to allow exchange of gases between the blood and the air. The gas passes through an extremely fine membrane lining the air spaces. This exposure to air makes the lungs susceptible to infection, more so than any other organs that have been grafted. Lung infection is one of the commonest causes of death after grafting of other organs, and it is consequently not surprising that infection has caused failure of many lung transplants. Even a mild rejection reaction can severely damage the gas-exchange membrane, and the patient may die before the rejection is reversed. The actual ventilation of the lungs with air produced by a rhythmic breathing is a complicated movement controlled by nerves connecting the lungs to the brain, and the muscles that produce the breathing to the brain. Cutting the nerves can interfere with the rhythmicity of breathing, and this may be an important cause of the difficulties of successfully transplanting both lungs. Nevertheless, these difficulties have been overcome. If only one lung is transplanted, however, the patient's own diseased lung may interfere with the function of the graft by robbing it of air and directing too much blood into the graft. The longest survivor with a lung transplant was a

Failure of lung transplants from infection

Belgian who lived for ten months after receiving a cadaver lung transplant. Instead of being bedridden and continually using an oxygen mask, he was able to leave the hospital and return to activity, but eventually rejection and infection caused function of the new lung to deteriorate. Further progress in lung transplantation may depend on a safer, more perfect control of rejection.

Special legal and ethical problems. *Legal aspects.* In most countries, the law on organ transplantation is poorly defined, as legislation has not yet been created to cope with this advance in surgery. The existing framework relating to physical assault and care of the dead has no provision for organ transplantation. It is customary to ask the permission of the relatives, but, because organ removal must take place immediately after death, it may be impossible to reach the relatives in time. It has been suggested that there should be a widespread campaign to encourage persons to provide in their wills that their organs be used for transplantation. An alternative is to provide by law that permission is assumed unless removal has been forbidden by the individual in his lifetime. Such laws have been passed in Denmark, France, Sweden, Italy, and Israel. Compulsory postmortem examination, a far more extensive procedure than organ removal for grafting, is required in most countries after unexpected death, and this compulsion is not a matter of public concern and debate.

There would seem to be no reason why organ removal for transplantation purposes should not also be acceptable to public opinion, provided there is a mechanism by which individuals in their lifetime can refuse this permission. This, of course, requires an efficient register of those who indicate their refusal; the register would be consulted before any organs would be removed. It is important that there be public reassurance that considerations of transplantation would not impair normal resuscitative efforts of the potential donor.

Ethical considerations. Transplantation has obviously raised important ethical considerations concerning the diagnosis of death, and, particularly, how far resuscitation should be continued. Every effort must be made to restore the heartbeat to someone who has had a sudden cardiac arrest or breathing to someone who cannot breathe. Artificial respiration and massage of the heart, the standard methods of resuscitation, are continued until it is clear that the brain is dead. Most physicians consider that beyond this point efforts at resuscitation are useless.

REJECTION

Transplantation research is focussed on the tendency of the body to destroy the lifesaving graft. It would be an immense advance if this process could be predictably controlled in a safe manner, but there are other difficulties to be overcome, particularly in providing undamaged organs of suitable size in sufficient numbers for those requiring such grafts.

As a result of evolution, there are in human beings complex defense mechanisms against bacterial and viral invaders. One attack of viral disease, such as measles, usually results in specific immunity to a further attack. The artificial utilization of immunity to provide immunization against smallpox and poliomyelitis represents one of the greatest contributions to modern medicine. Unfortunately, this life-protecting defense mechanism cannot differentiate between infective micro-organisms and potentially lifesaving organ grafts.

Selection of donor and tissue matching. The factors that provoke graft rejection are called transplantation, or histocompatibility, antigens. If donor and recipient have the same antigens, as do identical twins, there can be no rejection. All cells in the body have transplantation antigens except the red cells, which have their own type of red-blood-group antigen. Tissue typing involves the identification of an individual's transplantation antigens. The typing is done with lymphocytes, which are one of the main types of white blood cell. It is important also that the red blood cells be grouped, since red-cell-group antigens are present in other tissues and can cause graft rejection.

Tissue and blood-cell typing

Although transplantation antigens are numerous and complicated, the principles of tissue typing are the same as for red-cell grouping. Incompatibility results in agglutination or death of the lymphocytes tested. Persons who have rejected grafts or have had multiple blood transfusions or multiple pregnancies may develop antibodies to transplantation antigens in their blood. The serum that results when the cells are removed from the blood taken from such a patient can be used as a typing serum.

If the lymphocytes of both donor and recipient are killed by a given serum, then, as far as that typing serum is concerned, the individuals have antigens in common. If neither donor nor recipient lymphocytes are affected, then donor and recipient lack antigens in common. If the donor lymphocytes are killed but not those of the recipient, then an antigen is present in the donor and is missing from the recipient. Much careful work has been done on tissue typing between related and unrelated people, and the results of the typing have been tested by skin grafting.

There is now considerable knowledge concerning the inheritance of transplantation antigens, but, even so, tissue typing is not sufficiently advanced to give an accurate prediction of the outcome of a graft in an individual case, particularly when the donor and recipient are not related to one another.

Immunosuppression. The aim of transplantation research is to allow the recipient to accept the graft permanently with no unpleasant side effects. With current drugs that are used for this purpose, after some months the dosage can often be reduced and sometimes even stopped without the graft's being rejected. In such a case, the patient is no longer susceptible to infections. There would appear to be adaptation of the recipient toward the graft and the graft toward the recipient. The adaptation is probably akin to desensitization, a process used sometimes to cure patients suffering from asthma by giving them repeated injections of small doses of the pollen to which they are sensitive.

There are many agents that prolong graft survival, but the two most effective and widely used are the anticancer drug azathioprine and the corticosteroids.

Azathioprine. Azathioprine, which has been used to treat leukemia and also protects animals from the rejection of kidney grafts, can be given by mouth, but the dose must be carefully adjusted so that the blood-cell-forming tissues in the bone marrow are not damaged, which could lead to infections and bleeding. The white-blood-cell and platelet counts need to be determined frequently to make sure that azathioprine is not being given in too large a dose. It is an extremely valuable drug and has been the basis of most immunosuppressive regimens in patients with organ grafts. At first high doses are given, but eventually the doses may be reduced. Even years after transplantation, small doses of azathioprine may still be needed to maintain coexistence between graft and host. The exact action of the drug is not known.

Adrenocorticosteroids. Cortisone and its relatives, prednisone and prednisolone, are very useful in patients with organ grafts. They can also be given by mouth, but although not damaging to the blood-forming cells, they do predispose the body to infection and have other injurious effects. Persons receiving these substances may develop bloated complexions with swollen faces, may tend to gain weight and become diabetic, and their bones may become brittle. Few recipients of organ transplants, however, can do without corticosteroids, particularly when there is an acute rejection crisis.

Antilymphocyte serum. If rabbits receive repeated injections of mouse lymphocytes, they become immunized and develop antibodies against the mouse cells. The serum from the rabbits' blood after it is clotted can be injected into mice and will often prevent them from rejecting grafts, both from other mice and even, sometimes, from other species. Such antilymphocyte serums can be produced between a variety of species, but in higher mammals, particularly man, it has been difficult to obtain a powerful immunosuppressive serum without side effects of toxicity.

Most of the activity of the serum lies in its gamma

Ill effects
of
antilym-
phocyte
serum

globulin, which contains most of the antibody proteins. Antilymphocyte globulin is used in man but still contains many proteins that are ineffective and may be harmful. It can be added to standard azathioprine and cortisone treatment without adding to the toxicity of these agents, but antilymphocyte serum has its own disadvantages. It can cause severe pain at the point at which it is injected, or, if injected into the circulation, it can cause unpleasant allergic responses. Sometimes, the serum can form compounds that damage the kidney, a particularly unfortunate sequel for an agent used to prevent kidney graft rejection. Antilymphocyte globulin destroys lymphocytes but may have other actions that are important but are not well understood. It has been difficult to obtain a consistently effective product, and there are not good methods of assaying the potency of one serum compared with another. Even when they are prepared by exactly the same methods and the same species, one batch may differ greatly from another. The horse has usually been used to produce antilymphocyte serum for the treatment of human patients, but some persons are sensitive to horse proteins and can become extremely ill when treated with horse serum. It is expected that many of these difficulties will be overcome and that an effective, safe product will be available in the future.

It is clear that none of the agents so far used to prevent rejection is ideal. No one would use such dangerous agents except as a last resort in a desperate situation. This, unfortunately, is the exact plight of a person in need of a vital organ transplant. For the present, azathioprine, cortisone, and antilymphocyte globulin must be utilized.

ORGAN AND TISSUE BANKS

Without a blood supply organs deteriorate rapidly. Cooling can slow down the process but cannot stop it. Organs differ in their susceptibility to damage. At body temperature, irreversible destruction of the brain occurs after more than three to five minutes; of the liver, after 15 to 20 minutes; of the heart and lung, after 30 to 40 minutes; of the kidney after 50 to 100 minutes; and of the skin and cornea, after 6–12 hours. Although the shorter the time the organ is deprived of its blood supply the better, the cornea can be removed for grafting at relative leisure, but every minute is of vital importance for a liver transplant.

Preserva-
tion of
kidneys for
transplan-
tation

When a kidney is removed from a living donor, it is not necessary to use elaborate preservation techniques. The operations on the donor and recipient are performed at the same time, and the recipient is prepared to receive the graft by the time that the donor organ is removed. Kidneys are removed from cadavers as soon as possible after death, and, preferably within an hour, cool solutions are infused into the blood vessels of the kidney, which is then kept at 4° C (39° F) in a refrigerator or surrounded by ice in a vacuum flask. At the same time, the recipient is prepared for operation. Kidneys can be conserved in this simple way for eight to 12 hours with little deterioration, and during this time they can be moved for long distances. For a kidney to be preserved from 12 to 72 hours, a complicated machine is required to provide artificial circulation. Cool, oxygenated, physiological solutions, solutions with the same osmotic pressure as blood, are passed through the blood vessels of the kidney. The imperfections of the machinery mean that there is a slow deterioration of the organ that does not occur normally in the body. To keep a kidney undamaged for longer than 72 hours is difficult. Blood cells, spermatozoa, and certain other dissociated tissue cells can be frozen to subzero temperatures and kept alive indefinitely. Special preserving fluids will prevent cell destruction by ice crystals, but these fluids have damaging effects if introduced into whole organs such as the kidney.

Long-term storage and banking of organs seem unlikely in the near future. Preservation techniques for the heart, lung, and liver have not been so extensively studied as the kidney. The principles are the same, although these other organs will not tolerate such long periods without a blood supply. Much research will be necessary before it is possible to keep organs banked in the way that blood can be stored.

THE FUTURE OF TRANSPLANTS

It is likely that better immunosuppressive drugs that are less harmful and more certain in their actions will be discovered, but biological control of rejection in a manner akin to desensitization is the ideal method of retaining a graft. There are reasons to be hopeful that production of biological tolerance in mature animals may be possible if transplantation antigens can be prepared in a form that would cause desensitization. It is possible that the tolerance effect could be produced by treatment with antigen at the time of transplantation, but, if a course of pretreatment should be required, antigen from the donor could not be used in the case of cadaver transplants. It might be possible, however, to use antigen of an identical specificity from other sources. Antigen might be prepared from a large number of tissue-typed cadavers, and material of known specificity could be stored and subsequently used to desensitize recipients requiring organ transplants. There is a great deal of work going on in this field, and new knowledge is rapidly becoming available.

Artificial
cornea

The functions of the cornea are to transmit light and protect the eye. Corneal grafts fulfill these functions, and it is possible to construct inert synthetic materials that are equally effective. In cases in which corneal grafts have failed, these inert preparations may be preferable to attempting a second graft. Mechanical substitutes for the heart are used routinely in operations on the heart. They are effective for only a few hours. Like a normal heart, the mechanical substitute has pumping chambers, valves, and a supply of energy, but, despite much effort, there has been no success in devising an artificial built-in rhythmic energy supply that is similar in its main characteristic to normal heart muscle. Artificial hearts are cumbersome and cannot be used as long-term heart substitutes. They do not compare at present with heart transplants, which function well, provided that they are not rejected by the recipients.

The difficulties of devising artificial substitutes for the lung are similar to those mentioned with the heart. Artificial devices are excellent for oxygenation of the blood over short periods of time, but the process requires cumbersome machinery.

Much more successful is the artificial kidney, because intermittent treatment with a machine can keep patients in good health indefinitely. The principle depends on a cellophane membrane, on one side of which is the blood and on the other, the so-called dialyzing fluid. There is a tendency for dissolved substances to pass back and forth across the membrane until their concentrations are the same on each side. The patient's blood containing waste products is dialyzed against a fluid containing normal body salts. Protein and blood cells cannot get through the cellophane membrane, but waste products can. To maintain reasonable health, the patient needs to be treated by dialysis for approximately 14 hours two to three times a week. His bloodstream is joined to a large and complicated machine that can develop faults either electrical or mechanical. The points of attachment for the body to the machine have limited lives and, eventually, dialysis may become extremely difficult for an individual patient. Most patients would prefer to have a well-functioning kidney transplant, even though the risks of rejection are greater than those of death on the artificial kidney.

Most of the vital synthetic processes of the liver are not understood and certainly cannot be artificially reproduced. There are many functions of the liver that are not even known. There is, therefore, no basis on which to construct a satisfactory artificial substitute for the liver. Significant progress cannot occur until more is known of normal liver function.

BIBLIOGRAPHY. F.D. MOORE, *Give and Take* (1965), an account of the history of organ transplantation; *Ethics in Medical Progress* (1966), proceedings of a symposium sponsored by the Ciba Foundation, discussing the ethical aspects of transplantation; R.Y. CALNE, *Renal Transplantation* (1967), a technical account of kidney grafting with a discussion of immunological aspects; *A Gift of Life* (1970), a book for the nonspecialist, covering the immunological and clinical aspects and the ethics of organ grafting.

(R.Y.C.)

Transportation, Air

Air transportation includes the design and operation of airports, air-traffic control (ATC), and the operation of passenger and cargo aircraft. For most of its history the great bulk of traffic consisted of scheduled airliners, but in the 1960s tremendous growth took place in the two other types of air transportation: unscheduled or chartered airline and private business air transport.

Overall growth of air transportation has been spectacular throughout the world since the late 1940s, with steady increases in numbers, speed, and, probably most significantly, carrying capacity of aircraft. The trend toward increased size was continued in the 1970s with the introduction of the "jumbo" jets. One result was chronic congestion, sometimes of crisis proportions, at nearly all of the world's major airports. New airports planned for Paris, London, New York, Chicago, and elsewhere may take up to 12,000 acres (5,000 hectares) of land, further complicating problems of moving passengers and cargo within the airport. Noise is another continuing problem of airports near large cities.

A high degree of international and national organization has always been required of air transportation. Problems of international traffic rights and freedom of passage, and questions of air safety, health, and commercial competition had to be dealt with in the decade after World War I, but these did not receive comprehensive treatment until the immense expansion of air transportation after World War II.

By 1970 a massive body of international regulations, based largely upon bilateral agreements between governments on traffic rights and upon international operating practices recommended by the International Civil Aviation Organization (ICAO)—the aviation agency of the United Nations—and backed up by national air navigational regulations and international airline agreements, had been accumulated to guide the operation of worldwide air services. (The history of aviation in general may be found under FLIGHT, HISTORY OF.)

This article is divided into the following sections:

I. History of commercial aviation
    The origin of commercial airline operations
    Post-World War II developments
II. Airport design and operation
    Evolution of airports from early landing fields
    Modern airports
III. Air-traffic control
    General considerations
    Control in different types of airspace
    Navigational aids and procedures
    Operation of air-traffic control
    The future of air-traffic control
IV. Air-transport industry
    The structure of a modern airline
    General aviation
    Air cargo
    Economic significance

I. History of commercial aviation

The immense stimulus that World War I gave to aviation in general paved the way for the immediate development of commercial operations. Twin-engine bombers were converted for passenger use, and a scattering of commercial flights was recorded in the United Kingdom, the United States, the Soviet Union, and India. Almost at once the idea of sustained, scheduled operations came into being.

THE ORIGIN OF COMMERCIAL AIRLINE OPERATIONS

In 1919 sustained daily schedules were begun on three routes in Europe: Berlin to Weimar, Paris to Brussels, and London to Paris. These operations were rapidly extended or superseded as experience was gained in the regular operation of aircraft on domestic and international routes. The economic problems of air transport were met in a variety of ways in different countries. During the 1920s major efforts were made to produce transport aircraft that would be economical to operate, reliable in service, attractive to passengers, safe, and reasonably comfortable. The range of aircraft with an economic

payload was strictly limited, and refuelling at intermediate points was required on trips of more than 300–400 miles (500–650 kilometres). Aircraft could be designed with seating for 12 to 15 persons or more, but it was not until the mid-1930s that the associated technology of engines, propellers, general structures, movable wing surfaces (flaps), and retractable undercarriages (landing gear) had progressed to a stage that resulted in the availability of the first economically viable transport aircraft to meet the various requirements. In the United States, United Kingdom, Germany, and France, 30- to 40-seat aircraft were introduced, and a worldwide network of air services had come into operation by the outbreak of World War II.

Pre-World War II developments. In the United States, the major concentration was on the domestic routes. It was for these routes that the most famous of the prewar transport aircraft, the Douglas DC-3, was developed. The DC-3 was flown from New York to Los Angeles, with three or four stops, in about 24 hours (18 flying hours). In Europe, the colonial empires of Great Britain and France and the ambitions of Germany and Italy encouraged the development of long-distance overwater operations. The Soviet Union developed long-distance airlines to link distant regions with Moscow.

In 1937 flying-boat service was inaugurated by British Imperial Airways Ltd. between Southampton and the Far East, with a preliminary flight to New Zealand. Flying-boat services, however, involved specialized handling facilities. Route planning at this stage of airline growth was restricted by the limitations of aircraft range and capability, and by the limited ground navigational and landing aids available. The Imperial Airways service to Cape Town, South Africa, involved three landplane sectors (London–Paris, Cairo–Khartoum, and Kisumu–Cape Town), two flying-boat sectors (Brindisi–Alexandria and Khartoum–Kisumu), and two rail journeys (Paris–Brindisi and Alexandria–Cairo).

Stiff competition developed between Royal Dutch Airlines (KLM), operating the DC-3, and Imperial Airways, operating flying boats; and by mid-1938 both lines were operating an eight-day service from western Europe to Sydney. In 1934, Imperial Airways and Qantas, the Australian airline, had formed Qantas Empire Airways, which operated that part of the U.K.–Australia route between Singapore and the Australian east coast. Other routes developed from Europe before World War II were the Air France routes from Paris, through Tangier and Dakar in Africa to Natal, Rio de Janeiro, Montevideo, and Santiago in South America, and in the East to Cairo, Beirut, Calcutta, and Hong Kong. The German airline Deutsche Lufthansa had routes to South America via Lisbon, and to Bangkok via Baghdad and Karāchi.

Airship services. Airship (dirigible) services also were inaugurated in Germany at an early stage. Between 1932 and 1937 paying passengers were carried on the "Graf Zeppelin" and the "Hindenburg" on transatlantic flights from Frankfurt am Main to Lakehurst, New Jersey, and to Pernambuco (Recife) in South America. With the destruction by fire of the "Hindenburg" at Lakehurst in 1937, transatlantic service came to an end. Britain also planned to develop airship services, and successful flights were made by the airships R-100 and R-101 to India and Canada, but the loss of the R-101 in a crash at Beauvais, France, in 1929 ended the venture.

Air transport in World War II. Immensely important contributions to the development of long-haul air transport occurred during the years of World War II. Following pioneer Pan American World Airways and Imperial Airways flying-boat flights in 1937, inaugural airmail services between Britain and North America took place in August 1939 with the aid of in-flight refuelling. Tanker aircraft were based at Foynes, Ireland, and Botwood, Newfoundland. Both British and U.S. flying-boat services were in operation when war broke out. After a series of U.S. neutrality acts were passed in the late 1930s, the Pan American Clippers could fly only to Ireland. Early in the war, however, another service, known as the North Atlantic Return Ferry, was introduced and

The first successful air transport

The "Hindenburg" disaster

eventually maintained a year-round service; it was taken over completely by British Overseas Airways Corporation (BOAC). Because of its good weather record in winter months, Prestwick, Ayrshire, was chosen at an early stage as the U.K. terminal for the transatlantic ferry.

The Far Eastern routes from Europe were cut at an early stage in the war (1940) when Italy began hostilities. In due course the famous horseshoe route was established, linking 16 countries, from Durban, South Africa, to Sydney, Australia, via Khartoum, Cairo, Karāchi, Bangkok, and Singapore. Landplane and flying-boat routes linked West Africa and the Far East.

In the Pacific, the services of the flying boat and landplane also expanded steadily throughout the war. Thus, at the end of hostilities in 1945, the world was extensively provided with military air-transport services, equipped predominantly by flying boats that were to provide the capacity for many scheduled long-haul services in the immediate postwar era.

POST-WORLD WAR II DEVELOPMENTS

International agreements. The new pattern of air-transport organization emerged in the post-World War II era as a result of international conferences at Chicago (1944) and at Bermuda (1946). The Chicago conference established a form for international organization of air transport on lines more restrictive than that sought by the United States, but it established a permanent International Civil Aviation Organization (ICAO), which still exists and has proved highly effective. The problems of air-traffic regulations between the U.S. and the U.K. were effectively resolved at the Bermuda conference when a bilateral agreement was reached that proved of lasting significance as a standard. One of the features of the Bermuda agreement was that fares and rates were to be regulated by governments after agreement by the International Air Transport Association (IATA), a private association formed by the principal international world airlines. The traffic, financial, and technical conferences of IATA have notably aided the advance of the air-transport industry through the postwar era. By 1969 membership exceeded 100, and collaboration, encouraged through operation of common types of aircraft and equipment, promoted a steadily increasing level of professional work.

The immediate postwar period. World War II had the effect of establishing the United States as the world leader in the civil-aircraft manufacturing and airline industries. While Europe was at war and concentrating on building fighting aircraft, U.S. airlines were re-equipping with the ubiquitous Douglas DC-3. During the war years, U.S. airlines took advantage of the better economics of the DC-3 to meet a new surge in demand for air transport. More than 800 DC-3s had been produced directly for commercial use when production ceased in 1944. By the end of the war, U.S. airlines were preparing to put the newly developed four-engine DC-4 and Lockheed L.049 Constellation into sustained scheduled service. The scheduled routes with the largest passenger volume in the United States at the end of the war were the New York to San Francisco and Los Angeles, and the New York to Chicago routes. Transcontinental and Western Air (currently Trans World Airlines, TWA) introduced Constellations on the New York to Los Angeles route in February 1946, a few weeks ahead of American Airlines' introduction of the DC-4. In the same month American introduced the DC-4 onto the high density New York to Chicago route, and National Airlines Inc., also used the DC-4 on the direct overwater route from New York to Miami. The postwar availability of large numbers of former military-transport aircraft (particularly the DC-3 and DC-4), together with a rapidly rising demand for air transport, furthered the expansion of airline activity. This rapid U.S. expansion was not confined to the trunk airlines (*i.e.*, the airlines operating on the main domestic routes), and in the period up to 1950 some 20 local service airlines emerged, mainly operating the DC-3, to develop feeder services connecting with the principal points on the trunk airlines route networks.

The end of World War II also left the U.S. airlines in a

dominant position on the most important of the international routes, the North Atlantic. U.S. airlines started the postwar era with 90 percent of the North Atlantic traffic and achieved two significant firsts. American Overseas Airlines (later acquired by Pan American World Airways) was the first airline to operate scheduled transatlantic flights with a landplane (the DC-4); and TWA, in February 1946, introduced the long-range pressurized Constellation in the New York–London flights.

The revival of postwar civil air transport in Europe was led by Great Britain. British European Airways Corporation (BEA) was formed in 1946 to take over the European services previously operated by BOAC and the domestic services of the small British independent airlines. BEA was soon established as the leading airline in Europe, and its route network was rapidly extended to the North African coast and to the eastern Mediterranean. By 1970 BEA was the eighth largest passenger-carrying airline in the world. With the exception of Aeroflot, the Russian state airline, all the others above it were American.

BEA's expansion was aided by the introduction of Britain's first successful postwar civil aircraft, the Vickers Viking, which was significantly faster than the DC-3, and entered BEA service in September 1946 initially on the Scandinavian routes. The Viking was the first of a series of British aircraft launched by BEA. British Overseas Airways Corporation, Britain's principal long-haul airline, was not able to support the British manufacturers as was BEA, so BOAC had to put Constellations into service in 1946 to remain competitive as it developed an extensive intercontinental route network.

Air France, the French national airline, was re-formed at the beginning of 1946 and quickly established a European network and transatlantic services. The French airline was second only to BEA in European air transport. An international cooperative airline emerged in the third position, Scandinavian Airlines System (SAS), formed as a consortium of the principal airlines of Sweden, Denmark, and Norway in July 1946. Sweden held three-sevenths of the airline's capital shareholding and the remainder was shared equally between Denmark and Norway. This consortium enabled the three Scandinavian countries to play a major part in the development of civil air transport.

It is not possible to summarize the development of all the world's airlines during this important postwar period, but it should be noted that there was considerable growth in airline service in the less developed areas of the world, as well as in the United States and Europe.

The transition to turbine-powered aircraft. The period between 1946 and the mid-1950s was one of maturation for many of the world's leading airlines. Douglas and Lockheed four-engined aircraft offered the airlines more range, better standards of comfort, and better economics. The immediate postwar stalwarts, the DC-4 and Constellation, were gradually replaced on the trunk routes by the Douglas DC-6 and DC-7 and the Lockheed Super Constellation series, and on the short-haul routes the DC-3 gave way to the twin-engined Convair series and the Martin 404. During this period, the U.S. manufacturers, supported by a booming domestic market, consolidated the lead they had held at the end of the war. In Britain, the postwar adaptation to peacetime production had prevented the aircraft industry from competing with the U.S. to any significant extent in developing large piston-engined civil aircraft. British thoughts turned instead to the development of turbine-engined aircraft (see also AIRCRAFT).

The Vickers Viscount. The British Vickers Viscount was the first propeller-turbine (turboprop) civil aircraft to go into production, and BEA played an important part in the definition and early development of this very successful short-haul aircraft, powered by Rolls-Royce Dart turbine engines. BEA ordered 20 Viscount Series 701 in August 1950, and the aircraft was put into service in April 1953 on the London–Cyprus route. The Viscount attracted the interest of the world's airlines, and within two years, Air France, Aer Lingus (Ireland), and Trans-Australia Airlines (TAA) all ordered Viscounts. Trans-Canada Airlines (TCA) introduced the Viscount onto

Viscounts in U.S.

North American scheduled services on the Montreal–Toronto–Lakehead–Winnipeg and the Montreal–New York routes in April 1955. In 1954 Capital Airlines of the U.S. ordered 60 Viscounts. The turboprop Viscount brought new standards in airline comfort and speed and boosted air traffic and airline profits throughout the world. Approximately 440 Viscounts of all variants eventually were sold.

The Bristol Britannia. While the Viscount was making its impact on the short-haul networks, the medium- and long-haul routes were still dependent on the U.S. piston-engined aircraft; and it was not until some four years after the introduction of the Viscount that the first large turboprop aircraft, the Bristol Britannia, was put into service. Following a number of delays during its development, the Britannia 100 finally entered service with BOAC in February 1957 on the London–Johannesburg route. The following month it was introduced on BOAC's Australian routes, taking over from the Constellation and reducing the time to Sydney from 56 to 47½ hours. The longer range Britannia 300 Series entered service on the London–New York route in December 1957, offering for the first time a reliable nonstop service in each direction.

The Britannia was sold to only nine airlines, and apart from BOAC the largest order was for five aircraft from Canadian Pacific Airlines. The U.S. Lockheed Electra was the only large turboprop aircraft produced in the U.S. for the civilian market, and both the Electra and its British counterpart, the Vickers Vanguard, were too late (1959–60) to be widely adopted by the airlines, which were at that time already converting to jet equipment.

Introduction of the jet. The commercial jet era started in May 1952, when BOAC put the British de Havilland Comet 1 onto the London–Johannesburg route. By 1953, BOAC, UAT (French), and Air France were operating the Comet 1 on routes to the Far East, India, and Africa. In 1954, however, disaster struck; there were two serious accidents, and the Comet 1 was withdrawn from service. Investigations revealed the cause of the Comet 1 disaster as the previously unknown problem of metal fatigue; that is, the gradual weakening of metal under continued stress and vibration. De Havilland retained faith in the Comet and modified the basic design to produce the larger and longer range Comet 4, which entered service with BOAC in 1958.

On October 13, 1955, Pan American ordered 20 Boeing 707 and 25 Douglas DC-8 jet airliners. These orders heralded the rush of orders from the world's long-haul airlines for the big jets. The Soviet Tupolev Tu-104, however, was the first jet to enter sustained commercial service, in September 1956. The Soviet state airline had previously operated only twin-piston-engined aircraft, and the Tu-104 had a dramatic impact in developing communications across the U.S.S.R.

Tupolev Tu-104 introduced

Transatlantic jet services began in October 1958 with BOAC operating the first scheduled London–New York service with the Comet 4, just three weeks before Pan American introduced the Boeing 707–120 on the route. Pan American consolidated its leading position on the North Atlantic route ten months later by introducing the long-range Boeing 707–320; BOAC, with the Comet, was its only jet competitor. The 707–320 was the first commercial jet specifically intended for intercontinental service, and most of the transatlantic operators used this aircraft. Another competitor, the DC-8-30, was first operated on the North Atlantic in April 1960 by the Dutch KLM (Royal Dutch Airlines).

The wider use of jet aircraft. Throughout 1960 and 1961 most of the world's leading airlines operating on the ten major trunk routes took delivery of 707 and DC-8 aircraft. The others chose either the Comet 4, the Convair CV880 or CV990, or the Boeing 720, the smaller version of the 707.

The Caravelle. It was left to the French to counteract the jet's high operating costs on short- and medium-haul operations. The twin jet Sud-Est (later Sud-Aviation, and then Aérospatiale France) Caravelle was unique in that it was the first aircraft to adopt the rear-engined design philosophy. Air France gave strong support to the development of the Caravelle, giving the manufacturer its first order for 12 aircraft in February 1956, nine months after the first test flight.

When the Caravelle entered service with Air France in May 1959, more than 50 Caravelles were on order, mainly from the European scheduled airlines. By February 1961 nine airlines were operating Caravelles on services in Europe. Air France and SAS, the second airline to order the Caravelle, rapidly established extensive short-haul jet services. United Air Lines was the only U.S. airline to order the Caravelle, first putting it into service on the New York–Chicago route in July 1961.

Only three of the more important European airlines did not buy the Caravelle. BEA chose a short-range version of the Comet called the Comet 4B, while KLM and Lufthansa continued with short-range turboprop equipment until the second generation short-haul jets became available.

Other jets. The medium-range, medium-capacity jet requirement brought about the Comet 4C, which was operated by Mexicana, East African Airways Corporation, and some of the Arab airlines, and the Boeing 720/720B series. The Boeings were widely adopted in the United States because of their flexibility of operation and similarity to the Boeing 707, from which the 720 was derived. The success of the 707 and 720 established Boeing as the leading commercial jet company, and this success was followed by the even greater success of the Boeing 727 series. The 727 design incorporated a T-tail configuration that permitted the installation of three engines, an integral aft (rear) boarding stairway, and an auxiliary power unit to provide power and air conditioning on the ground without running the main engines. These aircraft and the stretched 727–200, developed from the earlier 727–100, offered the world's airlines an extremely flexible and economic aircraft with which to meet the air-traffic boom brought about by the wider development of jet travel in the 1960s. United Air Lines alone was operating more than 150 727s during 1970.

Three-engine design

The de Havilland (Hawker Siddeley) Trident and the Vickers (BAC) VC10, attempts by British manufacturers to compete with Boeing and Douglas, were designed to meet BEA and BOAC specifications, respectively, and because they were not as large or as economic as their U.S. alternatives, neither aircraft sold well abroad.

Development of regional and feeder routes. By the early 1960s the Caravelle and the Viscount were being introduced on those principal secondary routes that had sufficient traffic to warrant their operation. There was, however, a further airline demand for a twin-turbined aircraft to replace the DC-3 on the low traffic-density routes that had been initiated throughout the world during the 1950s.

The most successful DC-3 replacement came from The Netherlands, the Fokker F.27, which first entered airline service in 1958 with Aer Lingus Teoranta (Irish International) in Europe, and West Coast Airlines in the U.S. Both the F.27 and its British equivalent, the Hawker Siddeley HS 748, were widely used to extend regular air-service networks to remote locations previously not served by air, often utilizing unprepared runway strips.

Short-haul jets. The mid-1960s saw the beginning of one of the most competitive aircraft sales campaigns in commercial aviation history as the airlines prepared to replace the Viscounts and F.27s operating on the more important regional routes with short-haul jets. The British BAC One-Eleven was the first short-haul jet to enter service, being first operated by British United Airways and Braniff International Airways in April, 1965. The Douglas DC-9-10 entered service eight months later, and by offering a developed stretched DC-9-30 for early delivery, Douglas captured the largest part of the market.

The roles to which the short-haul twin-jets were applied varied considerably. In the Hawaiian Islands, Aloha and Hawaiian Airlines operated these aircraft over an average distance of 118 miles (190 kilometres), whereas in Europe a number of tourist airlines operated them over distances of more than 800 miles (1,300 kilometres). From 1967 Eastern Air Lines in the U.S. operated DC-9s on the air shuttle—an hourly departure, no reservation,

Air shuttle service

guaranteed-seat commuter service from New York to Boston and Washington. The unique service carried 3,272,000 passengers in 1969.

A much lower level of service was offered in many parts of the world by small operators using small aircraft on feeder routes. The third-level airlines, or commuter carriers as they were called in the United States, developed rapidly in the late 1960s, although the number of commuter carriers in the U.S. fell from 240 in 1968 to 150 in 1969.

Helicopter services. In 1971 there were still only a small number of operators providing limited scheduled helicopter services. Experimental helicopter services began in Britain, the United States, and Belgium after World War II. A few of these services developed into more sustained scheduled services during the 1950s and early 1960s. SABENA, the Belgian airline, started the only international scheduled helicopter service in 1953, linking Brussels with Paris, Rotterdam, Cologne, and six other cities in France, The Netherlands, and Germany. The SABENA service ceased in 1965 because the operation was uneconomical. At the beginning of 1971 the principal scheduled helicopter services remaining in operation were New York Airways, Inc., in the U.S., which had 64 flights daily among the three New York airports, and BEA Helicopters, which connected Penzance in the southwest of England with the Scilly Isles. Both of these airlines were using Sikorsky S-61 helicopters.

Growth of nonscheduled passenger services. Nonscheduled passenger services grew largely from the efforts of the postwar private airlines in the United States and Europe to expand their limited operations to an economic level. On both sides of the Atlantic, postwar troop transport and military freight contracts allowed the supplemental, or charter, airlines to expand while the growth of nonscheduled commercial traffic gained momentum.

By the early 1950s commercial charter traffic was beginning to exploit tourism to a significant degree. Because the scheduled airlines feared a fall in their rate of traffic growth, a new tourist-fare class was introduced in 1952 to compete with the lower rates of the charter airlines. These scheduled fare reductions had an immediate effect. On the North Atlantic route 63 percent of the passengers travelled at tourist fares in the first full year, and the tourist proportion rose to 71 percent by 1957. A further scheduled fare reduction occurred in 1958 with the introduction of the economy class, which eventually replaced the tourist fare.

The new scheduled fares came at a time when, in the United States, the military contract rates were being reduced, and in Great Britain a large number of small independent airlines were being grouped into larger operating units. The result in the U.S. was that the charter airline industry experienced a setback and a number of airlines failed. In Great Britain, British United Airways Ltd., (BUA) and British Eagle International Airlines became established as the leading independent (privately owned) airlines.

By the mid-1960s the U.S. supplemental (nonscheduled) airlines were acquiring long-haul jets, and with the help of a revised system of awarding military contracts, this addition set a firm base for expansion. The supplementals began to concentrate on developing nonmilitary charter work and specialized in Affinity Group Charters, in which an aircraft's capacity was chartered to a club or organization for its own members, who shared the costs of the flight equally. Two other types of commercial charter were also developed—single entity charters, where a person or corporation chartered an aircraft for his or its own use, and Inclusive Tour Charters (ITC). In ITC's the aircraft was chartered to a tour promoter who sold the aircraft's seating capacity as one part of a travel package.

In the United States, the booming demand for affinity charters was the main commercial attraction to the supplementals. The ITC market in the U.S. had been exploited only to a small extent by the beginning of the 1970s. The principal ITC operations were to Hawaii and

the Orient. In Europe, however, the inclusive tour led to the development of a vast new type of air traffic in the late 1960s.

The British independent charter operators led the development of ITC's in Europe with the promotion, through travel agents, of Mediterranean summer-holiday packages, principally to Spain and Italy. By the early 1960s Scandinavian and German charter airlines were also offering inclusive tour arrangements, and by 1965 the Europe–Mediterranean ITC business was booming. Until 1965 the charter airlines had been using such turbo-prop aircraft as the Viscount, but in that year BUA introduced new BAC One-Eleven jets on inclusive tour services. The European tour promoters were able to offer inexpensive holidays by obtaining large contract booking rates with both the charter airlines and the hotels at the destination points.

In 1969 more than 10,000,000 passengers were carried on inclusive tour flights in the Europe–Mediterranean area. The Danish charter carrier Sterling Airways was Europe's largest ITC airline. One of the main problems for the European charter airlines was the highly seasonal variation in ITC traffic. To overcome the difficulties of low aircraft use during the winter months, the airlines negotiated long-term contracts (often five years) with the tour promoters, who guaranteed sufficient aircraft use to warrant the purchase of new jets. Thus, the charter airlines obtained jets as modern as those operated by the national scheduled airlines.

The growth of charter operations during the 1960s gave the independent charter lines a new status and contributed significantly to the growth of world tourism. By 1970 it was estimated that in Europe nonscheduled passenger traffic would exceed the scheduled traffic by the mid-1970s.

The world airline industry in the 1970s. *Jumbo jets.* A most significant stage in the development of air transportation was reached in 1970 with the introduction of the Boeing 747 into airline service. The Boeing 747 was the first of the wide-bodied, or "jumbo," jets as they were commonly called; they could seat as many as 500 tourist-class passengers. Their first competitors, the Lockheed 10–11s and McDonnell Douglas DC-10s, could seat up to 400 passengers.

Supersonic transports. In 1970 the world's airlines also had placed optional orders for two new supersonic transports (SST's), the Anglo-French BAC Aérospatiale Concorde and the Boeing 2707. In the Soviet Union, the Tu-144, the first SST to fly, was also being developed. But while the Boeing was still in the preliminary design stage, public debate developed in the United States over the cost and over the environmental problems; that is, the noise generated in the airport environment and the sonic boom that would result from the supersonic speed of the plane. The possible pollution of the upper atmosphere was largely discounted. In March 1971, the U.S. Senate voted to end further funding of the aircraft, and financing from private sources seemed unlikely. The economic operation of the SST's would depend to a large extent on whether they would be allowed to fly at supersonic speeds over land.

Financial status. The 1970s did not begin with high profitability for the airlines. As an economy measure, early in 1971 United Air Lines and American Airlines took the step of reducing the frequency of scheduled flights on some U.S. transcontinental routes. The financial position of the world's scheduled airlines in 1970 began to show an increase in operating profit after a two-year decline. Scheduled passenger traffic, which accounted for 80 percent of revenue, had increased to 307,-000,000 passengers.

While the growth of total scheduled air traffic over the decade up to 1970 had averaged about 15 percent per year, traffic forecasts in 1970 were for a rate of growth up to 1980 of 12 percent per year. This increase compared with estimates for the growth of charter traffic at rates of more than 16 percent. This significant rate of growth of charter traffic and the introduction of high-capacity jets was influencing the major scheduled airlines to concen-

Inclusive
Tour
Charters

The SST
debate in
the U.S.

trate more effort on marketing charter services and inclusive tour holidays based on reduced scheduled service fares. As part of this expansion into the tourist field, the major international airlines also began to invest in the development of hotels, often through consortiums of several international airlines and hotel organizations.

Pollution problems. One effect of growth of commercial jet transportation during the 1960s was the increased public reaction against aircraft noise and exhaust pollution. To combat the problem of noise, engine and aircraft manufacturers intensified research into reducing noise at the source by developing quieter engines. Another possible solution was development of short take-off and landing (STOL) and vertical take-off and landing (VTOL) aircraft. The high angles of approach and "climb out" of these aircraft would lessen the surface area affected by the aircraft's noise. The airlines, however, were cool toward STOL and VTOL, which could not be placed in extensive commercial operation for several years; besides this, the airlines, in the midst of heavy investment for the wide-bodied jets, were looking toward the late 1970s and early 1980s to recoup. With the technology available it was possible that limited STOL services could be started by the mid-1970s, using 30- to 50-passenger propeller-driven STOL aircraft on short-range high-density services, but the commercial impact would probably not be significant before the mid-1980s, when 80- to 100-passenger V/STOL aircraft might be available.

STOL and VTOL

II. Airport design and operation

An aerodrome is described by the International Civil Aviation Organization as a defined area on land or water (including any buildings, installations, and equipment) intended to be used either wholly or in part for the arrival, departure, and movement of aircraft. The term airport has, however, come into common use and refers particularly to those aerodromes where air-transport movements occur on a considerable scale, and especially in the United Kingdom where full-time customs facilities are available. Airfield is used in reference to small aerodromes, generally without hard runways or facilities for handling large transport aircraft or their passengers and cargo.

EVOLUTION OF AIRPORTS FROM EARLY LANDING FIELDS

The essential requirements for a landing field have expanded steadily since the earliest days of flying. Just before World War II, the landing and takeoff distance required was a maximum of 650 yards (600 metres), and the additional demands that could result from an engine failure were not clearly defined. In these terms the airfields at New York, London, Paris, and Berlin were laid down, the area involved rarely exceeding 500 acres. London's airport at Croydon had no runway. Hard runways were rare. Tempelhof (Berlin), constructed in 1929, was one of the busiest airfields in prewar Europe; it became a major social centre with restaurants and rooftop observational areas. More than 750,000 visitors were recorded during its first year of operation. Le Bourget (Paris), Croydon (London), and La Guardia (New York) likewise attracted many visitors. The aircraft and the air passenger at that time had made little impact upon the design of airfields or air terminals. Such a situation, in fact, still exists in the great majority of airfields throughout the world. In the overall world pattern, the small grass airfield with simple terminal building, rudimentary control tower, and negligible landing aids is still dominant.

A wide variety of airports and airfields has developed to accommodate the great range of modern aircraft types and the different kinds of facilities needed for passenger and cargo handling.

The increasing demand for air travel has created the need for the large transport aircraft, now almost exclusively of multijet design. The demands such aircraft make upon all kinds of ground facilities, runways and taxiways, fire fighting and safety services, passenger and cargo-handling facilities, car parking, and lighting, navigational, and approach aids, are the principal determinants in the design of the large, sophisticated airports adjacent to the main centres of world population.

Of the 13 airports handling more than 8,000,000 passenger movements in 1969, ten were located in the United States, a reflection of the fact that about 60 percent of the world's air transport occurs there. Chicago (O'Hare) heads the list. Of the non-U.S. airports, London (Heathrow) was sixth, Paris (Orly) was 12th, and Frankfurt (Rhine-Main) was 13th.

It should be noted that it is primarily at these large airports that the problems of noise, congestion in the air and on the ground, and conflicts in land use with other regional planning objectives have arisen. The difficulties of smaller airports have been largely those of economics.

MODERN AIRPORTS

The elements of a major airport. The four principal elements of a major airport are airport management and control; passenger and cargo terminals; the runway, taxiway, and apron systems; and airport services.

The airport management and control function embraces the day-to-day operation and long-term planning of the airport; the terminal; runway and taxiway system; local air-traffic control; the lighting, navigational, and aircraft approach guidance system; as well as fire fighting, fuel supply, and all ancillary services, including customs facilities.

The passenger and cargo terminals provide for handling passengers, baggage, and cargo and the related activities.

The runway, taxiway, and apron systems are required to meet the needs of the aircraft for landing and takeoff, for positioning correctly for these manoeuvres, for aircraft location to receive and discharge loads, and for the operating and servicing crews to work.

Airport services related to the aircraft comprise the apron (the part of the airport surface adjacent to the terminal), the handling of aircraft, passengers' baggage, cargo, aircraft fuel supply, aircraft catering, cabin cleaning, and engineering services. Ground-related services include passenger-terminal catering and the concessionary facilities within the terminal (such as car rental), and the car parking and garage arrangements in the airport-terminal area for the travelling public and the airport staff.

Airport planning. There is no uniform pattern of airport layout and design. In the hierarchy from the great metropolitan airport to the small-town field with a single landing strip of tarmac, an immense variety of layouts has proved successful. The site itself is a critical factor. Runway orientation is the starting point for design, site selection being generally determined by its suitability for an appropriate runway system. Particularly important elements are the availability of level, well-drained land without approach-path obstruction or possible conflict with roads and urban development and access to existing major road systems. As in all exercises in technical development, conflicts arise at every stage in decision making, the most significant being that between noise and access to the urban community.

Site selection

It is important to note that airport layout and operation are keyed to development. The industry is dynamic and there are two sources of change: traffic growth and technological change. Most airports are in a period of dramatic growth, with passenger movements doubling every four to five years. In the major city airports such conditions are almost universal, but the small-town airport is often in a less favourable position. Technological change in aviation, however, is worldwide, being based on advanced aircraft and avionics industries in the United States, United Kingdom, France, Germany, Italy, The Netherlands, and Japan. These industries are steadily promoting new types of aircraft, usually of increased size and performance, forcing modifications in airport design virtually each decade.

Runway, taxiway, and apron systems. The essentials of a runway and taxiway system for a given airport are related to the types of aircraft, the scale of traffic, and the prevailing meteorological conditions.

Modern types of jet aircraft can accept higher crosswinds than the aircraft of the immediate postwar years.

Thus, in the mid-1970s fewer runways were needed than formerly. Light aircraft may need to land and take off at an angle to the main runway because of limited handling capability in strong crosswinds, but the operation of such aircraft would not be sanctioned at major international airports. Indeed, considerable controversy exists concerning the use of large airports by executive and private aircraft.

Meteorological information is fully recorded and analyzed to determine the most desirable orientation for the principal runway(s), subject always to the suitability of the weather (visibility, cloud base, etc.) for an airport development in any region.

Experience in air operations has encouraged the International Civil Aviation Organization (ICAO) of the United Nations to establish standards of practice for the design and layout of airports and runway systems. These complex requirements have been incorporated in the Air Navigational and Air Terminal Regulations of most member governments of ICAO. Certain of these relate to the length, strength, and width of runways and taxiways, the limiting position of obstructions, and the lighting, navigational, communications, and approach aids.

Safety
standards

Airworthiness standards are promulgated by the governments of aircraft-manufacturing nations to safeguard the operating standards, performance, and weight of aircraft in the various stages of flight, including takeoff and landing. Air-navigational regulations (based predominantly upon ICAO recommended practices) set down the runway specifications essential to allow the safe operation of transport aircraft.

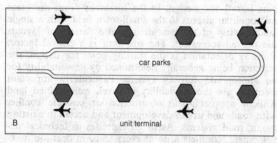

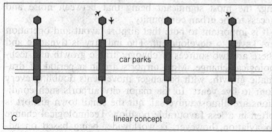

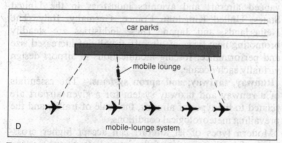

Typical airport terminal layouts.

Detailed requirements specify the many other critical design factors in runways, taxiways, and aprons. Runway length has probably reached a limit that is unlikely to be exceeded even with the development in the next decade of larger jets and SST's. More stringent standards in design of equipment and layout for airfields are, however, gradually being incorporated by the licensing authorities.

Airport layout and terminal design. Different styles of airport layout and terminal design have developed since 1960 to meet the demands of the jet transport and the massive traffic increases.

The principal characteristic types of layout that have developed in this period are shown in the illustration. The essential need is to deploy a large number of aircraft into positions for unloading and loading so that passengers can embark and disembark with minimum expenditure of time and effort and so that the other essential apron services can be performed. The essential terminal services must be provided and a high order of access, especially for road traffic, must be arranged. Provision for expansion of all such facilities, with full retention of efficiency, must be built into the system.

The finger system (A), extensively developed through the 1960s, is entirely suitable for medium-sized terminals with twin-jet aircraft and also the four-jet Boeing 707 and McDonnell Douglas DC-8. A major problem has been the long distances the passengers must travel from the reception room to the aircraft.

Breaking the passenger flow into a number of units is effectively achieved in the unit terminal (B), which has the merits of shortening the passenger walk, allowing more space for expansion, and providing a convenient geometrical arrangement for the "nosing in" of large transports; the design has proved especially effective with the jumbo jets.

The linear concept (C) is also under active development and incorporates many of the basic features of the unit terminal. A new airport planned for Louisville, Kentucky, is based on the linear concept. The British Airport Authority has described plans for the third London airport based on the linear concept. A decision has been made by the British government (1971) that this should be built on the coast at Foulness.

The mobile-lounge system (D) has been applied at Dulles International Airport outside Washington, D.C. Mobile lounges transfer passengers between aircraft and terminal. This method offers a more intensive and flexible use of the apron space for the aircraft but at a high cost in motorized transfer and some congestion of vehicles on the apron when aircraft are being serviced at peak times.

Apron servicing. Terminals and aprons must be designed so that the aircraft is held for the shortest possible time in the turn-around phase on the apron. This is most important in handling short-haul aircraft, for which ground time is a high percentage of operating time. A typical transit turn-around time for a modern airbus type of aircraft is 25 minutes. A large number of vehicles are in circulation on the apron during the turn-around, and marshalling of aircraft and vehicles is critical to the smooth operation of a large airport. During peak periods at O'Hare International Airport (Chicago), for example, an aircraft comes on the apron or taxis out every 20 seconds.

Passenger and cargo terminals. The principal passenger and cargo areas should be related to the expected traffic flows. The limit of traffic through an airport may be determined by several factors, including aircraft landing and takeoff movements, congestion on the apron, or congestion in the air-traffic-control system. Limits may also arise in the passenger terminal or, less frequently, through congestion in the road or rail approaches to the airport buildings and parking areas.

The terminal areas may be self-contained and restricted, as originally on the central island site at Heathrow, or they may develop on the satellite principle, as at John F. Kennedy International Airport (New York City). More recent designs for large city airports have concentrated, however, on the linear concept, in which a continuous process of development and growth can be provided.

Factors in
terminal
size

The determining factors that fix the scale of the buildings are the standard busy rates of aircraft and passenger and cargo movements in the different categories of arrival, departure, domestic, and international movements. Standard busy rates are defined as submaximum movement rates, likely to be exceeded on about 20 occasions a year. With growth rates in passenger traffic in some cases exceeding 20 percent per annum, the need to make provision for the growth of all facilities becomes apparent.

Air-cargo movement on the apron is conducted in a variety of ways. At major airports, automated systems can be justified by the high use achieved and the reduced manpower required. Lack of flexibility is inherent in such systems. Labour problems beset the early introduction of such arrangements (e.g., at Heathrow). In smaller airports, truck transport from warehouse or freight shed to and from the aircraft is all that is required. Special accommodations for freight forwarders and bonded stores are provided at major international airports.

The airlines normally provide their own cargo handling and storage facilities at the airport. Cargo is delivered to the terminal by the freight forwarder, agent, or shipper and is documented and located for loading or consolidating on a pallet or in a container for the next flight departure. Cargo aircraft tend to operate during the latter part of the day and at night; thus, it is generally true that cargo flights do not contribute greatly to congestion in the air or on the ground at major airports.

Congestion. At major airports, congestion has reached a high level both in the air and on the ground. Takeoff delays sometimes reach a point at which aircraft must return to the apron to refuel because of depletion of fuel while waiting to take off. It is largely because of the cost of such delays that an immense program of airport building is underway throughout the world.

Some cities in the United States and Europe have sought to encourage general aviation use of the smaller aerodromes rather than the main air hub. Congestion in the air space, on aprons, and on runways becomes a matter for air-traffic control; it also arises in the terminal, in the car parking spaces, and on the access routes to and from the airport. Space at congested airports, such as Kennedy International (New York City) and Heathrow (London), is at such a premium that ancillary services such as car parking, restaurants, and sales stands may need to be moved from the airport precincts. Off-airport parking has become a feature at London airport; rates, including the transport of passengers by bus to the airport terminal, are considerably lower than on the airport. Passenger and freight processing may eventually be carried out only at central city points or at peripheral sites, airport space being reserved exclusively for loading and unloading aircraft and essential ground vehicles.

Proposals to situate airports away from congested zones have found favour with some regional planners and with most conservationists. Air transport, however, must be accessible to its markets, and the offshore sites proposed for a London airport at Foulness as well as the Seadrome ten miles (16 kilometres) west of Los Angeles in Santa Monica Bay have been strongly resisted by the airlines.

Airport noise problem. A serious threat may exist to the development of aviation if action to curtail aircraft noise is not effective. In the early 1970s, action took a number of forms. Restrictions on jet-aircraft movements were introduced, especially at night (e.g., at London and New York City). Restraints on urban (particularly residential) development were imposed by many planning authorities within the zones having high-noise ratings. Control of the flight path of aircraft (especially after takeoff) and in the use of runways (for landings and takeoff) was exercised to minimize noise nuisance in the airport environment and over a wider area. Airport development and new site selection were directed to minimize deterioration in the environment. Aircraft noise certification standards for new types of jet transport aircraft were introduced, and intensive research was under way to produce quieter engines.

Airport links to local ground transportation. One aspect of an airport is that of a transport hub where different transport modes connect. Passenger and cargo consignments change between ground and air. Thus, access for surface vehicles is as critical a factor in airport design as in site selection.

The road traffic generated by the large air terminals is already on a scale that demands special consideration of the layout and width of roads and access routes to the city centres.

The peak traffic in the airport approach roads tends to occur in the morning and evening, coinciding with other peaks of suburban traffic, so that journey times to and from an airport from the downtown areas are difficult to forecast in the rush periods. Because major airports have gradually moved farther away from the city centres, journey times to airports have increased. Road traffic congestion has accentuated the problem, and the cost of idle time has become critical in the economic comparison of air and surface transport. A major argument for vertical takeoff and short takeoff aircraft lies in their lesser requirements for airport space, promising sites close to the central city.

Highway
congestion

III. Air-traffic control

GENERAL CONSIDERATIONS

If aircraft flew in a random fashion across the surface of the earth and within its atmosphere, the chances of collisions would be remote. The greatest number of aircraft, however, fly on the most popular routes and converge on the most frequently used destinations. With the growing popularity of air transport in the 1920s and 1930s, it became necessary to mark the most frequently used aircraft routes, first by aerial navigational lights at airfields and at strategic points on the ground beneath the intended routes. Later, with the introduction of radio aids, came rules to help aircraft traversing the same route to avoid one another, particularly at night or in conditions of low visibility.

An alerting service was provided to confirm aircraft arrivals and to initiate a search for overdue planes. Air-to-ground radio communication introduced such other services as up-to-date weather forecasts and warnings of major atmospheric disturbances.

International standards. During World War II the need for international standards was recognized by the International Civil Aviation Organization at its 1944 Convention in Chicago. ICAO set up a Rules of the Air and Air Traffic Control (RAC) Division to make recommendations for standards, practices and procedures for air-traffic control. This action produced an annex to the convention—Annex 11—the title of which was later changed to "International Standards and Recommended Practices—Air Traffic Services," to include other functions besides that of control. Annex 11 defines the various types of airspace and procedures and gives recommendations for an Air Traffic Services (ATS) organization. It is then the responsibility of each contracting state to implement, as it sees fit, these recommendations and to notify ICAO of deviations from them. Each state has sovereign rights applicable to the airspace above its own territory, and each determines which portion of that airspace will be provided with an air-traffic service and defines the various areas (geographically and by altitude) that will comprise the various types of controlled airspace. Parts of the world where large stretches of airspace exist and over which no state has sovereign rights, such as the oceans, are allocated by ICAO to such states as are willing to provide a service for them.

There are naturally quite wide variations among states as to the degree of compliance with these publicized practices. The ICAO has to make careful compromises when deciding on standards. A standard involving the introduction of the latest, most sophisticated navigational aids, for example, might be implemented by the prosperous countries of the world, but if it is beyond the budgets of other countries its adoption as an international standard can have only limited value.

Air-traffic control—definition and purposes. The term air traffic is used to describe movement of passengers, cargo, and aircraft, depending on the context. In the term air-traffic control, however, it refers solely to the movement of the aircraft itself, and it covers movement and manoeuvring both on the ground and in the air.

The four main purposes of air-traffic control (ATC) are to prevent collisions between aircraft; to prevent collisions between aircraft and obstructions on the ground; to provide for a fast, orderly flow of traffic; and to provide advice and information useful in planning and executing flights.

Divisions of airspace

To fulfill these ends, the air above all countries of the world is divided into various areas, zones, and routes, each with its own set of rules for flying. The various areas are explained later in this article, but the two main divisions are controlled airspace and uncontrolled airspace. As the names imply, controlled airspace refers to areas where air-traffic control is exercised in a positive manner for some types of flights. In uncontrolled airspace the air-traffic-control services offer only a minimum advisory and information service.

Visual- and instrument-flight rules. There are two sets of rules under which a flight may be carried out, and the use made of air-traffic control depends on which set of rules is being applied to a particular flight. The differences between these sets of rules must be appreciated before the regulations applying to the various kinds of airspace are examined.

The first set of rules is referred to as visual-flight rules (VFR), and an aircraft being flown under these rules is referred to as being on a VFR flight, or flying under VFR. To operate under VFR, the pilot must be capable of avoiding collision with other aircraft or with obstructions on the ground by visual observation of the hazards and by taking necessary action. For these rules to apply, therefore, the pilot must have adequate vision; the rules specify that he must remain away from all clouds, separated from them by at least one nautical mile horizontally and at least 1,000 feet (300 metres) vertically. Visibility itself must be at least five nautical miles. Outside controlled airspace these rules are relaxed slightly by specifying that if the aircraft is flown at a 3,000-foot altitude or below, then so long as the pilot remains clear of clouds and in sight of the ground, he may fly under visual-flight rules. It is the pilot's responsibility to ensure that his flight is conducted under VFR and that weather conditions permit him to continue to fly under these rules.

If aircraft are unable to comply with visual-flight rules, they must be flown under instrument-flight rules (IFR). An aircraft being operated under these conditions is said to be on an IFR flight, or flying under IFR. While the words "instrument flight" are derived from the weather conditions when a pilot has to rely on his instruments to maintain his altitude and course, without reference to the ground, it is important to understand that instrument-flight rules do not apply solely to aircraft flying in poor weather conditions or low visibility. While the term visual-flight rules is to some extent self-explanatory within the conditions laid down above, the term instrument-flight rules should be regarded as a set of regulations that can apply to the flight of an aircraft quite independently of what the weather conditions may be.

CONTROL IN DIFFERENT TYPES OF AIRSPACE

The basic zone of airspace as defined for air-traffic-control purposes is the flight information region (FIR). Within this region, as geographically defined, are provided air-traffic-control services, the services provided being dependent on the types of airspace within the FIR. It is common practice to name each FIR by the name of the centre providing the ATC service, thus Paris FIR, London FIR, etc. These centres are termed air traffic control centres (ATCC's). Within the FIR the airspace is divided into the two basic areas mentioned earlier, controlled and uncontrolled airspace, and a third termed advisory airspace.

Uncontrolled airspace. Even within uncontrolled airspace the ATCC's will provide a minimum service for aircraft within their FIR. It is not, however, compulsory for aircraft flying in uncontrolled airspace to make use of this service. Aircraft whose pilots do choose to partici-

ATC service

pate in the service provided are given proximity warnings of other aircraft that the FIR controller knows to be in its vicinity. This information is strictly limited because aircraft in uncontrolled airspace are not required to communicate with Air Traffic Control. Indeed, some may not have the radio equipment necessary to do so. Hence, the FIR controller does not know the position, or even the presence, of all aircraft in his area. To participating aircraft, the FIR controller also provides an alerting and flight-information service.

Advisory airspace. As a kind of halfway step between uncontrolled and controlled airspace, some of the FIR is divided into advisory routes and areas. As in the case of uncontrolled airspace, the advisory service provided by ATC is not obligatory. Aircraft that do choose to use the advisory airspace service, however, are required to comply with the ATC instructions given. Separation is not provided by ATC between all aircraft using advisory airspace.

Controlled airspace. Within each FIR and outside uncontrolled and advisory airspace each country establishes controlled airspace. This area takes the form of control zones, which normally surround airfields and airports; control areas providing a larger area of control surrounding major hubs of aviation activity; and control areas in the shape of corridors, termed airways, that connect these major hubs with each other. Within all these types of controlled airspace, aircraft are required to conform to air-traffic-control procedures and regulations. Separation is provided by the air-traffic-control service, and all aircraft are required to remain in communication with the air-traffic controller. To maintain separation between aircraft the controller obviously must be aware of the position of each aircraft under his control, both in terms of geographical location and in terms of height. He obtains this data and exercises control by two distinctly different methods: procedural control and radar control.

Procedural control. Each airway and route within control areas is defined by radio beacons. The beacons are of different types, which will be described later, but basically they provide heading information for the pilot of a suitably equipped aircraft. This information tells him which course to take to fly to the beacon, and it is presented to the pilot in the form of a pointer on his instrument panel. It tells him also when he is over a beacon, since the pointer swings around as the aircraft passes overhead, continuing to point to the beacon, which by this time is behind the aircraft. Some beacons have an associated facility for indicating the aircraft's distance from them known as distance-measuring equipment (DME).

The pilot keeps the controller informed of his progress along the airway and of his altitude by radio-telephonic communication. The controller has a board in front of him on which he places "flight progress strips." These small rectangular pieces of paper identify the aircraft with its call sign, type, and other information, so that the controller has a ready visual reference of the traffic proceeding down the airway for which he is responsible. He is thus able to space aircraft out along the airway and provide minimum separations. Should this minimum separation become endangered (for example, if a faster aircraft is catching up to a slower one), he can regain adequate separation by ordering a change of altitude on the part of one of the aircraft; or if another altitude is not available, he can "hold" one aircraft over one of the reporting points. Holding is a procedure whereby an aircraft circles over a given location, and it is much more common in a control area, where aircraft are queueing to land on a runway, than along the airways. It is, however, an acceptable way of providing separation.

Radar control. Procedural control as described above has certain limitations, especially when traffic is heavy. First, it depends on two-way radio transmissions between the pilot and the controller; even if reception conditions are good, the actual transmission and receipt of messages takes time. Second, the controller is often unaware of the precise geographical position of the aircraft. With the advent of surveillance radar, the controller can be presented with a cathode-ray tube display of each aircraft's

"Blips"

position. The aircraft reflect the radar beam, and each aircraft shows up as a spot, or "blip," on the tube. Thus, the controller has an indication of all the aircraft within the range of his radar, and the necessity for frequent voice communication between pilot and controller is reduced. On this primary radar, however, the controller still does not know the height of individual aircraft; and, all blips being essentially identical, he cannot make positive identification. He can, by radiotelephone, ask an aircraft to make a turn—which is known as turning for identification—and so identify that particular aircraft on his tube. Such a procedure is time-consuming and undesirable, and modern techniques are being introduced to overcome this deficiency of primary radar.

Transponders and secondary radar. The aircraft itself acts as a "reflector" for the radar beam associated with primary radar. This is why the air-traffic controller cannot distinguish between the blips on his radar screen. To overcome this disadvantage of primary radar and to provide the controller with routine information to reduce voice transmission between pilot and controller, secondary surveillance radar (SSR) is being progressively introduced into the air-transport (ATC) system.

This radar system requires that the aircraft themselves carry a special transmitter and responder called a transponder. On a request from the controller, the pilot activates his transponder, which provides a second blip alongside the original blip representing his aircraft. The second blip eliminates the need for identification turns. Also being introduced are two extra facilities provided by the transponder—the transmission of the aircraft identification, in the form of letters and numbers, and its altitude. These data are displayed on the controller's radar screen alongside the aircraft blip. With this system, the radar controller has full, immediate information on the aircraft's geographical position and its identification and altitude.

NAVIGATIONAL AIDS AND PROCEDURES

Airways and routes within controlled areas are marked by radio beacons of various types.

Route aids. *The nondirectional beacon.* The nondirectional beacon (NDB) provides a radio station for use by aircraft. The equipment in the aircraft consists of an automatic direction finder (ADF, or radio compass), which gives the pilot information in the form of a pointer indicating the bearing of the NDB transmitter. The pilot can thus fly courses to or from the NDB. If dual ADF equipment is provided on an aircraft, it is possible to fix position by combining the information provided by two NDB's. The term nondirectional is derived from, and indicates the insensitivity of, the transmitted radio beam to direction; that is, it transmits indiscriminately in all directions. There are still many NDB's throughout the world, providing navigational aids to aircraft. The tendency, however, is to replace them with the VOR (see below).

The VHF omnidirectional radio range (VOR). The VHF (very-high-frequency) omnidirectional radio range (VOR) is the radio aid selected by the International Civil Aviation Organization as the recommended standard short-distance aid for aerial navigation. It operates in the very-high-frequency wave band. Like the NDB, the VOR transmits in all directions but has two separate transmitting signals—one stationary and one rotating. The second signal alters phase as it rotates, the two signals together providing distinct "radials," which are identifiable on the aircraft receiving equipment. The radials can be visualized as 360 lines radiating from the VOR station, representing the 360 degrees of a circle. (In practice, there are an infinite number of radials.) The 90-degree radial radiating outward from the VOR represents magnetic east, the 180-degree radial represents magnetic south, and so on. The pilot can select any of the 360-degree radials and fly toward or away from the VOR station. A simple "fly right, fly left" indicator on his instrument panel indicates when he is on the radial. An alternative instrumentation is a radio magnetic indicator (RMI), similar to that used in the NDB instrument, with a pointer mounted above a compass card, the pointer indicating the direction of the

VOR transmitting signals

VOR station. With the pointer at the "top" of the instrument, a direct course to the VOR station is indicated. The advantage of the VOR over the NDB lies in the relatively static-free VHF band operation, simplicity of use, and identification of precise radials to and from the VOR.

Distance-measuring equipment. Distance-measuring equipment (DME) is often used in conjunction with VOR. Used in combination, the system is designated VOR/DME. An interrogator carried on DME-equipped aircraft transmits radio pulses, triggering a reply from one ground-based DME responder. The time between transmitting and reply is electronically measured, giving an indication of aircraft distance from the ground station. This distance is given the pilot in nautical miles in a form similar to the mileage meter in an automobile. Without DME, the only time the pilot knows his precise position is when he is directly over the NDB or VOR transmitting antenna. At other times he only knows his bearing from the station. The VOR/DME enables the pilot to fix his position precisely once he knows his bearing from a point on the ground and his distance from it. Such position-fixing systems are known as rho-theta systems (distance-bearing).

Tactical air-navigation (Tacan) system is basically a military navigation rho-theta aid, but it is the distance-measuring element of Tacan that provides the DME element for VOR/DME. The original ICAO intention was to recommend VOR as the standard short-range navigational aid, associated with co-located distance measuring equipment. With the widespread introduction of the military Tacan system, however, this intention was modified on economic grounds and use is made by civil aircraft of the Tacan distance-measuring element.

Fan markers. Fan markers are also used to mark specific points along the airways and in control zones. A fan marker transmits identification signals in the form of dots and dashes, but the transmission is arranged by means of the aerial design to radiate a narrow fan-shaped beam vertically upward. The "length" of fan extends across the airway, while its width is limited so that an aircraft flying through the beam receives the transmission for a relatively brief period. The pilot in the cockpit is given the data by a flashing light, and the signal is also transmitted through the pilot's headset. Fan markers are also used in conjunction with the instrument-landing system discussed later.

Area-coverage aids. The most commonly used area-coverage aids are based on a master ground transmitting station and two or more subordinate, or "slave," stations. The master and slave stations, separated from each other in some cases by hundreds of miles, are synchronized so that the transmissions from each can be identified and used as position lines in the shape of hyperbolas surrounding the stations. Such area-coverage systems are also referred to as hyperbolic systems (see also NAVIGATION). In the long-range navigational aid loran, for example, the master station transmits a series of pulses, the slave transmitters retransmitting these pulses after a measured delay. If a line is drawn representing a constant delay between the two signals, it takes the form of two hyperbolas, one focussed on the master station and one on the slave station. Identification of two position lines, one associated with each master–slave pair, provides the aircraft position.

A short-range hyperbolic aid more applicable to airways flying is the decca navigation system. Decca consists of a master station surrounded by three slaves, but it uses continuous waves, as opposed to the pulses used in loran. Decca can be used in conjunction with a flight log, which consists of a moving map display on which the aircraft track is continuously traced by an ink pen. The accuracy and simplicity of the decca flight log combination have resulted in its increasing use.

Long-range aids. The radio navigation aids discussed earlier have been mainly those used for flying along airways and within control areas, with the exception of loran, which introduced the basis of hyperbolic aids. Other aids are available for long-range navigation, the most important being the Doppler system and the inertial navigation system (see also NAVIGATION).

Hyperbolic systems of navigation

The Doppler system is a self-contained airborne system using transmissions from the aircraft and measuring the time taken for their return from the earth's surface. The system provides a measurement of ground speed and of drift caused by wind.

The inertial navigation system is also completely self-contained within the aircraft and uses gyroscopes to measure aircraft acceleration in three planes and integrates the accelerations to obtain aircraft speed. As in the Doppler system, these data must be used in conjunction with some known datum in the form of a precise starting position (see also GYROSCOPE).

Instrument-landing system. The radio aids described above allow the pilot to fly precise tracks along the airways and within control areas. Having reached the terminal area surrounding his destination, he needs some form of aid, especially in adverse weather, to allow him to descend from a safe altitude and land on the runway. Runways equipped with such aids are termed instrument runways, and the standard approach aid is the instrument-landing system (ILS).

The ILS is not strictly a landing system at all but rather a means of giving the pilot guidance so that he can make his final approach to the runway and arrive at some point that gives him sufficient visual reference to the ground to enable him to land the aircraft. The ILS system consists of two radio transmitters, called the localizer and the glide slope. The localizer antenna is situated in line with the runway but beyond the far end; that is, the end remote from the touch-down end and toward which the aircraft lands. The antenna transmits a thin horizontal beam divided into two. These two transmissions overlap by an angle of five degrees, the centre of this overlap being accurately aligned with the centre line of the runway. If the approaching aircraft is within the five-degree overlap, a pointer on the pilot's instrument hangs vertically from its hinge at the top of the instrument, telling the pilot he is approaching in line with the runway. Should the pilot fly to his left outside the overlap, the vertical pointer will swing to the right, indicating "fly right" to regain the centre line; if the aircraft deviates to the right, the pointer will indicate "fly left" by moving to the left. The amount of deviation of the pointer from the vertical indicates the distance of the aircraft from the localizer (and hence runway) centre line.

This system gives the pilot accurate guidance in azimuth, or track. Altitude and rate of change of altitude information is provided by the glide slope transmitter, located to the side of the runway and at the opposite end from the localizer; that is, near the point of touch-down. Like the localizer, the glide slope transmitter provides a pattern of two interlocking radiations, but in this case they are in a vertical plane. The upper and lower signals overlap by about one degree, and this overlap slopes up from the glide slope antenna at approximately three degrees to the horizontal, corresponding to a generally acceptable angle of approach. A horizontal pointer is incorporated in the same instrument as the vertical localizer pointer on the pilot's instrument panel. If the aircraft is above the three-degree glide slope this pointer indicates "fly down" by moving down; if the aircraft descent is below the glide slope it moves up, indicating "fly up."

By reference to both localizer and glide slope pointers in the one ILS meter instrument, the pilot can fly an accurate approach path to near the end of the runway. Standard ILS, however, is not accurate enough to permit him to descend all the way to runway level, and landing of the aircraft is accomplished visually.

To complete the instrument landing system, it is common practice to provide two fan markers along the ILS approach path. These fan markers, described earlier, allow the pilot to determine his precise position on the final approach path and enable him to check his actual altitude against the glide-slope indication.

OPERATION OF AIR-TRAFFIC CONTROL

Outlined above are the basic practices and instruments that form a framework on which air-traffic control can work. This section describes how it works in practice.

The flight plan. When flying within any part of a flight-information region (FIR), a pilot can file a flight plan. This flight plan, on an internationally standardized form, gives details of the pilot's intention: his expected time of takeoff; the route and altitudes at which he intends to fly; his estimated time at various points along the route; his destination airfield; and his expected landing time. The flight plan also specifies an alternate destination, to be used if he is unable to land at his chosen first destination. In addition, the flight plan includes information that would be useful in case the aircraft makes a forced landing, such as the number of people aboard and the nature of the emergency equipment carried.

Flight plans must be filed if the pilot intends to fly within controlled airspace under instrument flight rules or if he wants to use the Air Traffic Advisory Service in controlled or advisory airspace. In some countries, it is necessary to submit a flight plan if the flight is to be undertaken in controlled airspace at night, regardless of weather conditions.

Flight plans are usually filed with the Air Traffic Service Office at the departure airfield. If the aircraft is outside controlled airspace, they can be filed in flight by radio, normally with the FIR controller. A copy of the flight plan is sent to the destination airfield and to all air traffic control centres responsible for the areas through which the flight will pass.

Air Traffic Control personnel consider the flight plan in conjunction with other flight plans that have been filed that refer to the use of the same airspace at the same time. A clearance is then given that will, where possible, clear the pilot to use the route, altitudes, and timing as shown on the flight plan. If there is conflicting traffic, however, the clearance may alter the flight plan.

From all these filed flight plans, the controller at the ATCC prepares the flight progress strips mentioned earlier, which contain the aircraft identities and radio call signs. These strips of paper are inserted on a board viewed by the executive controller who, if the flight is in controlled airspace, moves the strips along the board as the aircraft passes each reporting point. The reporting points, geographically marked by radio aids, are mandatory if the flight is taking place under IFR in controlled airspace; the pilot must report to the controller when he reaches them. He then indicates his estimated time of arrival at the next reporting point. The ground controller is thus enabled to record the progress of aircraft under his control and to provide each with adequate separation from other flights.

Separation standards. Aircraft are considered to be adequately separated if the distance between them, both vertically and horizontally, allows for inaccuracies in position fixes, errors in instruments such as altimeters, and other variables. The actual distance depends on a number of factors and is not constant. Up to an altitude of about 29,000 feet (8,800 metres) vertical separation is considered adequate if there is at least 1,000 feet (300 metres) between aircraft; that is, up to this altitude aircraft can fly over the same geographical point at the same time if their altitude differs by at least 1,000 feet. Above 29,000 feet, separation is increased to 2,000 feet (600 metres). If aircraft are at the same altitude, a succeeding aircraft flying in the same direction may not pass over a reporting point within ten minutes of the first aircraft overflying it. (This time may be reduced to five minutes, if the first aircraft is flying at a speed 20 knots faster than the succeeding aircraft, or to two minutes if it is 40 knots faster). Similarly, aircraft on converging tracks at the same altitude, and aircraft climbing or descending through other aircraft's tracks, are separated by ten minutes.

The controller progresses all aircraft with filed flight plans in controlled or advisory airspace by using these separation standards. He clears aircraft from point to point, ensuring adequate time separations at each reporting point. He issues clearances to each aircraft to continue to the next reporting point when he is satisfied that adequate separation exists. For climbing or descending aircraft, he issues clearance to change altitude only when he is sure that the new altitude, or the altitudes through which the aircraft will fly to reach it, are clear of other aircraft or that other aircraft are adequately separated in time as the cleared aircraft passes through their altitudes. If one aircraft is climbing and another descending on opposite courses, for example, vertical separation of at least 1,000 feet must exist ten minutes before the aircraft pass each other and for ten minutes afterward.

As the aircraft moves from one controller's area to the next, responsibility is handed over to the adjacent area controller by telephone, with relevant information on the aircraft, intended route, altitude, and identity. The pilot is instructed to contact the adjacent controller by radio.

On approaching his destination airfield, the pilot is given clearance to leave his airway altitude and begin descent.

Aerodrome approach procedures. If aircraft are queued up, waiting to land on the airfield, an arriving aircraft joins the holding pattern, located over the final reporting position. All aircraft in the pattern are separated by 1,000 feet in altitude and are flying a "racetrack" pattern, turning over the beacon to fly outbound for one or two minutes before reversing direction again and flying inbound toward the beacon, each circuit taking four or six minutes. Aircraft are taken from the lowest altitude of this "stack" to begin intermediate approach procedures. As one aircraft leaves, the aircraft above it is cleared down by 1,000-foot steps to the vacant altitude and so on up the stack—the aircraft descending in 1,000-foot steps as cleared, until the lowest altitude (normally 5,000 feet) is reached. Usually the intermediate approach—that is, from the final beacon until the aircraft is lined up with the runway—is conducted by radar control. The radar controller accepts responsibility from the procedural controller and gives the pilot a course to steer—known as "vectoring"—so that he approaches the extended centre line of the runway. The radar controller uses vectoring to provide the final spacing between aircraft as they turn onto final approach. This spacing is normally four to five miles (six to eight kilometres). Leaving the beacon, the aircraft is vectored until instructed to turn onto the final approach usually at eight to 15 miles (13 to 24 kilometres) from the runway end. During vectoring, the aircraft is also let down from the lowest altitude in the stack to 2,000 or 3,000 feet (600 or 900 metres), at which height it turns onto the final, straight run in toward the runway and picks up the instrument-landing system radio beams described earlier. When the preceding aircraft has turned off the runway, the approaching aircraft is given clearance to land, and control is handed over to the aerodrome controller, whose responsibility it is to direct the aircraft after landing to its position at the terminal. For this purpose, at larger airports, he is assisted by ground radar, which shows the position of all moving vehicles on the airfield surface.

Precision approach and ground-controlled approach

At some airfields an additional, very accurate radar provides a service similar to the ILS. This is called PAR (precision-approach radar) or GCA (ground-controlled approach). In this system voice transmission to the pilot enables the PAR controller to pass on instructions regarding the aircraft heading and glide path as shown to him on two radar screens (one shown in the horizontal plane, the other in the vertical plane). This system has been largely superseded by the more accurate and readily used ILS, although some units are still operated for monitoring approaches.

The procedures and techniques of procedural control and the use of radar in the terminal area have been described in some detail to provide an appreciation of the practicalities and theory of ATC. In principle, these are used throughout the world wherever there is sufficient traffic density to warrant formal control and the provision of controlled airspace. All centres, of course, are not equipped to the same standards, although the International Civil Aviation Organization lays down certain standards and recommendations to ensure uniformity of techniques and equipment and to provide assistance to those countries that need help in implementing them.

Air-traffic control is itself becoming more sophisticated and automation is being introduced. In the United States

and Europe, the air-traffic controller is becoming part of an integrated system aimed at exploiting both the advances in radar and the availability of computers. Flight plans are submitted directly to the computer, which carries out a more thorough check for traffic conflicts than is possible using manual means. In addition, meteorological information can be combined in the computer with flight-plan information, and the whole can be displayed on cathode-ray tubes to the controller, who thus has more accurate and more detailed information available to help him make his decisions.

Another development is one in which adjacent ATCCs will have computer connections, and ATC will become better integrated in an international sense. Steps in this direction have already been taken in Europe, where the many national boundaries make the need greatest. This situation has led to the formation of Eurocontrol, a supranational authority contributed to by the United Kingdom, Ireland, France, West Germany, and the Benelux countries, which will finally provide a truly international ATC system, eliminating the present discontinuities experienced at national boundaries.

Meteorological services. It is of prime importance that pilots be provided with first-class weather information. The majority of airfields have their own observation stations and send reports to a central meteorological office, which provides weather forecasting and advisory services for all purposes.

Each air traffic control centre has a main meteorological office that services a number of subsidiary offices. Weather charts are prepared every three hours, and reports on existing weather conditions and forecasts are supplied as requested.

Supplementary to the international teleprint methods over which meteorological information is transmitted for general purposes are special telecommunications links for purely aviation purposes. In Europe, the Meteorological Operational Telecommunications Network Europe (MOTNE) collects and distributes airfield weather reports and forecasts for most large airfields. The ATCCs and major airfields are connected to this network, and weather reports are issued at half-hourly intervals. Aerodrome forecasts are prepared every three hours and cover a period of nine hours.

The pilot has ready access to up-to-date weather information at all stages of flight. During the critical last few miles of his approach, approach control provides him with continual information on wind strength and direction and, in marginal weather, on the visibility along the runway. Enroute he has a number of sources of information.

Automatic weather printout

Receiving and copying weather information over the radiotelephone link is time-consuming, however, and often distracting for a pilot, who is usually engaged in other activities. The trend is to install in aircraft data-recording equipment that automatically prints out the weather information. This printout, rather like an ordinary telex printout, is then available for the pilot to consult at his convenience. Such a system also eliminates the difficulties in receiving voice transmission when radio reception is bad.

Ocean station vessels located in the North Atlantic also provide services for air navigation. These are maintained under international agreements and provide weather information to aircraft in flight, on request.

THE FUTURE OF AIR-TRAFFIC CONTROL

Although the new techniques and equipment are providing better safety standards and improved traffic flow, the rapidly expanding volume of traffic is beginning to impose many strains on the system.

Some of the world's major airports are becoming congested at peak periods. Uneconomic "flow control" methods have had to be used at New York City's Kennedy International. This involves "queueing" arrivals as far back as the airport of origination, allowing an aircraft to take off only when it can be assured of a "slot" of time during which to land at Kennedy. Such methods are patently undesirable.

In addition to the high rate of traffic growth, new types of aircraft are being introduced which impose their own problems on ATC. Air turbulence behind the Boeing 747 during its introduction led to the imposition of increased separation of other aircraft following it down on the approach path, thus compounding the problems of congestion.

The supersonic transport will require larger areas of airspace in which to manoeuvre. It will impose additional constraints on the ATC system because it will not be allowed to operate supersonically over some landmasses. In addition, wide-ranging changes in altitude and in speed will become necessary, larger holding areas may prove desirable, and certainly better landing aids will be essential.

ATC has, since 1946, developed into an advanced and sophisticated service that generally has been adequate. Safety in the air is the cornerstone of ATC policy, both long-term and short-term, and no major development in equipment or in procedures can be introduced until it has been thoroughly tested and proved adequate. Consequently, ATC must plan well ahead of the growth in air traffic itself, matching each new generation of aircraft and each surge of growth as it emerges. Thus ATC and ATC planning have become one of the most dynamic sectors of the aviation industry.

IV. Air-transport industry

THE STRUCTURE OF A MODERN AIRLINE

The air-transport industry has been built up on a framework of scheduled and charter services provided by short-, medium-, and long-haul air carriers. Many large airlines operate both short- and long-haul routes in the domestic, continental, and intercontinental fields. Such operators are TWA (U.S.), Air France, Lufthansa (West Germany), and KLM (The Netherlands). On the other hand, Pan American, BOAC, Qantas, Air Canada, and Japan Air Lines have little freedom to operate on domestic or short-haul regional sectors. Air-route licensing in the U.S., Europe, and in many other countries elsewhere has firmly defined the region of individual airline activity and has determined the pattern of competition.

The pattern of airline organization. The organization of a major airline has become highly complex, more especially since the introduction of jet fleets in the early 1960s. The increased scale of operations and the intense competition have increased the need for rapid decision making. Frequent reorganization has become characteristic of the industry. Although this section of the article deals primarily with the major airlines, a wide range of airlines exists, down to the small commuter airlines or operators who provide feeder services on a small number of sectors in one region.

Factors used in rating airlines

There are many measures of airline achievement, and the list of the top airlines varies slightly depending on whether passenger miles, passengers carried, or freight ton miles is the selected criterion. On the basis of passenger kilometres flown in 1969, the top ten airlines of the world are listed in Table 1. Although the Soviet airline Aeroflot is certainly the largest in terms of passenger kilometres, passengers, and staff, it is not included in the table because the appropriate statistical information is not available. It is clear that size of staff is not directly related to the passenger kilometres travelled. The field of

operations, the spread and intensity of services, and the length of the average flight sector may strongly affect the staff complement. The most powerful factors determining staff required per unit of traffic carried are the intensity of traffic per route mile and the number of airport arrivals and departures per unit of traffic generated.

Many small nations have considered it politically expedient to operate their own airlines. As a mode of national publicity this is probably effective. Such objectives will not lead, however, to outstanding records for airline operating efficiency. Nations in strategic global situations (e.g., Greece, Italy, and India) are well placed to obtain reciprocal traffic rights from nations with strong air operating industries, namely, the United States, Great Britain, Germany, and France. Traffic, however, has tended to support the airlines with a long and trusted record of operation.

Organization of some major airlines. Numerous studies undertaken in the 1960s sought without success to establish the optimum size for an airline. Increased potential for efficiency with growth in scale of operations has proved difficult to realize in practice.

For a consideration of airline organization four major airlines have been chosen: Pan American, United, BEA, and Lufthansa.

Figures on the number of staff members of these airlines were broken down in 1970 as shown in Table 2.

Table 2: Staff Makeup of Four Major Airlines (1970)

	U.S.		Europe	
	Pan Am	United	Lufthansa	BEA
Pilots and copilots	2,201	4,034	869	1,347
Other cockpit crew	977	2,118	365	0
Cabin attendants	4,195	6,007	1,694	1,757
Maintenance and overhaul	10,125	10,447	6,323	7,257
Traffic and sales	10,440	13,746	8,751	7,585
All other staff	11,341	15,327	3,946	6,986
Total	39,279	51,679	21,948	24,932
Ton-kilometres carried (millions)	4,018	4,561	1,284	506
Average flight sector (miles)	1,295	635	585	357

Source: *World Air Transport Statistics*, I.A.T.A., Number Fifteen, 1970.

Pan American World Airways. Pan American is the largest of the intercontinental airlines. In 1970 it operated a fleet of 175 aircraft (all jets) with a staff of 39,279 and carried a total of 4,018,267,000 ton-kilometres of passenger and cargo transportation in that period. As in the great majority of modern airlines, the operations, technical, and marketing or traffic/sales departments are run as three separate units under vice presidents.

The pattern in Pan American, as in BOAC and in Air France (also long-established companies with a tradition of delegation of responsibility to trusted and experienced middle management), is to decentralize where possible and control when essential through clearly defined instructions and manuals.

United Air Lines. United, the second largest airline in the world (28 million passengers in 1970) and still largely confined to operations in the United States, is organized on a slightly different basis, with two major departments, marketing and services, and operations, the latter including the engineering/maintenance and flight operations departments.

The major staff concentrations are in San Francisco, Chicago, New York, Los Angeles, Washington, D.C., and Denver. More than 80 cities are served.

Education and training form an important part of the organization of an airline the size of United. At a centre near O'Hare International Airport 4,000 stewardesses and management employees are trained annually. Flight-deck training is also given on a large scale, a $30,000,000 centre at Denver's Stapleton International Airport training more than 6,000 pilots annually, including flight crews of other airlines. United Air Lines's engineering and maintenance base at San Francisco is the largest of its kind in the Western world.

British European Airways. One of the two British corporations (the other being BOAC), BEA is unique in that it

Table 1: Leading Airlines of the World (1970)

	passenger kilometres (000,000)	staff numbers
United	38.2	51,679
TWA	29.9	38,555
American	26.8	35,919
Pan Am	26.4	39,279
Eastern	23.6	32,129
Delta	15.6	20,943
Air Canada	10.6	17,447
BOAC	10.5	24,086
Air France	10.2	27,593
Northwest	7.3	12,695

is the only major airline to operate exclusively within the confines of Europe. The high staffing ratio per unit of transport generated is clearly a reflection of the short-haul characteristic of BEA. A reorganization in 1967 confirmed the most common executive management framework of three departments, traffic and sales, engineering, and operations, with the first of these reorganized to give considerable autonomy to the regional general managers. In 1971 another reorganization further decentralized the corporation by setting up divisions based in Manchester, Scotland, and the Channel Islands.

A significant achievement of BEA and one stimulated by the problems of the short-haul airline has been the introduction of integrated management planning and control technique (known as IMPACT), a concept of management control based on the use of advanced computer technology. A group of interrelated computer models has been developed to aid planning and decision making at both the corporate and divisional levels. Computerized control systems are also available for regulating seat reservations, passenger and cargo acceptance and load control, and flight information and control. In addition, an extensive set of largely independent information and accounting systems is under development to support the control of aircraft maintenance servicing. Such developments are typical of the current activity of major international airlines in setting the computer to work for increased airline productivity.

Lufthansa. Following early recognition of the significance of the North Atlantic route, Lufthansa by 1968 had outpaced Air France to become fourth (after Pan American, TWA, and BOAC) of the North Atlantic air carriers. Since 1967 Lufthansa has extended its interests to include the hotel business in developing countries as well as in major cities in Germany and overseas. The company also owns a number of subsidiaries, of which the most important are Condor Flugdienst, a Frankfurt-based charter company active in the holiday-tour business, and Lufthansa Service GmbH, a catering company.

The three main departments are: (1) operations, including flight operations, maintenance, and engineering, based primarily at Hamburg; long-haul aircraft, however, are maintained at Frankfurt, where the flight operations department is also located; (2) administration and commercial, based at Cologne; and (3) sales and traffic, based at Frankfurt.

The integration of airline organization on an international basis in the interests of overall operating economy is illustrated by the Atlas Group project, whereby five airlines—Lufthansa, Air France, UTA, Alitalia, and SABENA—will cooperate in the maintenance and stocking of spares for the Boeing 747. Lufthansa is to cover engines and simulator training at the Frankfurt base.

A characteristic of the Lufthansa system is that international air services are operated from nine airports in West Germany. This considerable choice for departure from the country reflects the regional pattern of government in the republic.

GENERAL AVIATION

The category of air transport known as general aviation covers business aircraft and private aircraft used for business and pleasure. Aircraft belonging to industrial or financial concerns are usually classified as business aircraft and vary in size from converted airliners to small single-engined machines; they may also include rotorcraft such as helicopters and autogiros (rotorcraft in which the rotor is not powered). Private aircraft cover the whole range of smaller types, including in many countries a number of former military aircraft.

By far the largest number of business and private general aviation aircraft are found in the United States, where, by 1970, the total had for several years exceeded 100,000. It is estimated that 60–70 percent of these aircraft are used for business purposes. Other nations with sizable numbers of business and private aircraft in 1969 were Canada (7,130), France (5,400), Australia (3,550), Germany (3,000), Great Britain (2,070), South Africa (1,850), and Italy (1,050).

In France, government grants and subsidies encourage private flying as is shown in the number of business and private aircraft. Because of the large domestic demand, U.S. manufacturers dominate the general aviation market and in total can produce over 14,000 aircraft per year, considerably more than the rest of the world combined.

Business aircraft. The largest general aviation aircraft are those operated by international companies, which frequently use them for transoceanic flights. The aircraft employed may be current medium-range jet airliners, costing over $4,000,000, which have been equipped with special interiors and fuel tanks for intercontinental range. Alternatively, they may be special-purpose business jet aircraft intended for as many as 15 passengers. Such aircraft are operated to airline standards in terms of flight crew, navigational equipment, all-weather capability and performance, and licensing standards. The next category consists of the smaller special-purpose jets capable of carrying six to ten passengers in comfort at 450 miles (725 kilometres) per hour for distances of up to 1,200 miles (1,900 kilometres). In general, these aircraft are able to operate from hard runways of about 4,000 feet (1,200 metres). Next in size and performance are turboprop executive aircraft, which cruise at about 300 miles (480 kilometres) per hour over distances of at least 1,000 miles (1,600 kilometres), carrying up to 10 passengers. As might be expected from their lower speed, they are significantly cheaper than the pure jets in purchase cost and in operating costs. Aircraft in the above categories are invariably operated by full-time professional flight crews; for long hauls a relief crew may also be carried.

International use. Transatlantic flights by business aircraft are commonplace, and at least one type of business aircraft can fly from New York to London nonstop. A small number of international corporations use such aircraft extensively for long-distance overseas flights of 2,000–3,000 miles (3,200 to 4,800 kilometres). Special high-frequency radio communication equipment is fitted in these aircraft as well as Doppler or inertial navigation systems. Special arrangements are often required for their servicing and maintenance if their stay abroad is lengthy. Flight planning, customs, and proof of airworthiness may necessitate special arrangements when planes visit foreign countries for the first time.

Advantages of business aircraft. Despite the costs, a large corporation can achieve considerable savings in executive staff time, and even in travel costs by operating its own aircraft, if scheduled flights to necessary destinations are infrequent or nonexistent. Where plants are far apart, a company aircraft is almost essential for staff mobility and shipment of critical materials. Investment grants, depreciation, and tax allowances can often be used to reduce the funding and operating costs.

Smaller business aircraft. Smaller aircraft, usually below 6,500 pounds (2,950 kilograms) gross weight, are used extensively by smaller businesses and by larger firms to fill in for the bigger corporate aircraft on short flights. Planes of smaller firms are often flown by the owner or by company staff. With the advent of the small, supercharged piston engine, these aircraft may have pressurized cabins and be capable of ranges up to 1,200 miles at altitudes of over 20,000 feet. They will have full radio and navigation systems, autopilots, and often anti-icing.

Further down the scale are the lighter, unpressurized twin- and single-piston-engined aircraft, with seating for four or more. These represent the minimum investment and, though usually fully equipped with radio and navigation aids, may lack full all-weather capability because of limited altitude performance. Typically, this category flies below 10,000 feet (3,000 metres) at between 160 and 230 miles per hour (260 and 370 kilometres) over ranges from 500 to 600 miles (up to 1,000 kilometres).

Rotorcraft. The use of rotorcraft in general aviation showed a marked growth in the 1960s because of the availability of small, fast helicopters with small, lightweight gas turbines and improved rotor aerodynamics. Since 1960 their cruise speed has increased from 90 to 135 miles (140 to 220 kilometres) per hour, and at the same time passenger seating has increased from two to

IMPACT concept

Use of airline standards in business aircraft

five. As a result, they now offer excellent average speeds over short distances and can land in areas only 100 feet (30 metres) square. The capital and operating costs are high because of the requirement for complete integrity of the rotor system, which propels, lifts, and controls the flight path of the machine; this complex system requires frequent inspection and component replacement. Twin-engined helicopters are becoming available in the smaller sizes, and the additional security of a second engine may make them more acceptable as corporate aircraft in the future.

The problem of helicopter complexity

Business aviation costs. Capital cost is a major factor in purchasing a business aircraft, and it is reflected in depreciation, insurance, hangar costs, and, to some extent, crew salaries. Operating costs include these factors, together with fuel and oil, maintenance, landing, parking and navigation fees, handling charges, customs charges, and license fees. Some costs, such as fuel and oil, are directly related to the annual aircraft use (*i.e.,* the number of aircraft flying hours in a year). The greater the use, the lower the cost per flying hour, a common cost criterion for this class of aircraft. Utilizations of over 400 hours are desirable to make economic use of the capital cost of a large business aircraft.

Private aircraft. This category includes aircraft that may be used for business and for private travel and are usually flown by the owner or by nonprofessional pilots. Many different aircraft types are involved, some dating from the 1930s. Though perhaps not strictly in the air transportation category, many pre-1930 aircraft are still flying, and the building of replicas of World War I aircraft is popular.

"Home builts"

The smallest aircraft in the private category are the "home builts" or "ultralights." Many of these are superb examples of ingenuity, workmanship, and aerodynamic efficiency. Design, construction standards, and licensing are usually controlled by national bodies, such as the Experimental Aircraft Association in the United States and the Popular Flying Association in the United Kingdom, which have the approval of the national aviation regulatory body. Home builts, often powered by automobile engines, have been produced for as little as $2,000.

Since the 1960s, motorized gliders have been produced commercially, particularly in Europe (140 in West Germany alone), and these represent a halfway step between the ultralights and the more conventional light aircraft. One- and two-seat versions are available, fully certificated, and because of their inherent aerodynamic efficiency, they offer excellent fuel economy at a cruise speed of about 100 miles (160 kilometres) per hour. Some private rotorcraft exist, the majority of which are autogiros. These are usually single-seat kit-built aircraft, with cruising speeds of 60 to 70 miles (95 to 110 kilometres) per hour and limited range. Landing and takeoff runs required are only about 50 feet (15 metres).

The next large category, one- to four-seat single-engined aircraft, is by far the most popular in every country, representing, for example, 83 percent of general aviation aircraft in the United States in 1968. These aircraft are fitted with engines of from 90 to 250 horsepower and cruise between 100 and 200 miles (160 and 320 kilometres) per hour over distances up to 1,000 miles (1,600 kilometres). This class of aircraft is manufactured principally in the United States, France, and Germany. Metal construction is almost universal, though reinforced plastic has also been used. Equipment varies enormously and may be extensive in the larger aircraft; the cost of equipment may well add 50 percent to the bare aircraft cost. A number of types can be fitted with floats for water operation or with skis for snow landing and takeoff. A few true amphibians, capable of landing on land or water, are also available. Aircraft in this size category are capable of operating from 2,000-foot (600-metre) strips, many requiring less than half this distance. Their unsupercharged engines, however, reduce their effective use in areas where the ground is 5,000 to 10,000 feet (1,500 to 3,000 metres) above sea level.

Private balloons

One minor category of private air transportation is the free balloon. A number are registered in Europe, particularly in Switzerland, and are normally of the hot-air type. Small private airships also exist, classified as business aircraft.

Use in sparsely populated areas. In less populous parts of the world, where distances are large, as in Australia, Africa, South America, and Canada, light aircraft have been a vital method of transportation for as long as 40 years. Casualty evacuation, transport of doctors, and freighting of vital supplies are among the uses remote regions make of such aircraft. In Canada, extensive use is made of the country's thousands of lakes to operate float planes.

Where landing is impossible, ingenious methods of air dropping and picking up are used. In most remote-area operations, funds, and consequently facilities, are at a minimum; the use of rotorcraft has not so far made a great impact except for exploration and survey work.

Regulation. The regulation of private flying, both in terms of pilot licensing and aircraft certification, is similar to that employed for commercial aircraft. Efforts usually are made to simplify the procedures to reflect the less sophisticated requirements of the majority of lighter aircraft.

Nations with sizable general aviation fleets have at least one national body to represent this sector of aviation. Each nation is represented also at the International Council of Aircraft Owners and Pilots Association (IAOPA), the general aviation equivalent to ICAO, which represents more than 300,000 members worldwide.

Activity and growth. Worldwide figures for the activity of all general aviation are difficult to obtain, but in 1967 there were 98,000,000 general aviation movements in the United States and 383,000 in Great Britain. In 1968 there were, respectively, 282,000 and 12,000 pilots holding private licenses in each country. The economic value of general aviation shipments in the U.S. was estimated at $596,300,000 in 1968, with the probability that this figure would be nearly doubled by 1975.

AIR CARGO

Air cargo is an essential part of the air transport industry, with all-cargo airlines and all-cargo aircraft offering specialized facilities and services, supported by the freight-forwarding industry, in all parts of the world.

Increasing importance of cargo

Some observers forecast that air cargo will be the dominant element in air transport well before 1990. It is receiving increasing attention by the airline industry, if only because the integration of cargo, passenger, and combined services is economic and encourages the provision of cargo and passenger services that complement each other. Although freight and mail revenues for nearly all air carriers are a small proportion, seldom more than 10 percent, of total revenue, such revenues play an important part in the overall financial position of the airlines. The major world airlines make full use of the increased capacity and improved performance of modern jet aircraft. All-cargo jets now provide the greater part of the capacity on the North Atlantic routes. Air cargo may be defined as the load carried by air-transport companies, excluding passengers and their baggage allowance. Thus air cargo includes revenue-earning freight, mail, and excess passenger baggage.

Air-cargo growth. The air transport of cargo has developed into an industry with a growth rate higher than any other field of transportation. On the most favourable sectors, such as the North Atlantic where aircraft have a great time advantage, the carriers recorded traffic increases of well over 30 percent per annum in 1969 and 1970. On the intra-European routes development has been less rapid, but traffic doubled in the 1965–1970 period.

Even in the United States, the domestic air-cargo growth has not compared with that on the North Atlantic. International trade acts as the vital stimulus to air cargo, and 40 percent of all cargo moving in the United States has its origin or destination in an overseas territory. Domestic air freight in the United Kingdom and in Europe is of small significance. The historic trading links between the western European states and the Middle and Far Eastern countries, as well as with Africa, have formed a basis for the developing pattern of world air-cargo business. Restrictions on imports still affect the air trade of more than 50 nations, and all-cargo flights are restricted on a number of transatlantic routes even within the framework of bilateral agreements.

During the 1965–69 period, the freight revenue carried by the world's scheduled airlines increased to approximately three times the mail revenue. Cargo traffic carried by the scheduled airlines grew by 106 percent in this five-year period. On the North Atlantic routes the growth in the total carrier cargo traffic of members of the International Air Transport Association (IATA), including charter flights, has been increasing at a greater rate, and from 1965 to 1969 grew by 152 percent. It should be noted that in this period a dominant factor in the development of traffic was the increasing number of all-cargo aircraft flights.

The private operation of cargo aircraft, on the same lines that some companies operate their own executive aircraft, is generally ruled out by cost considerations. The economics of cargo aircraft require high minimum flight loads on a regular basis of at least 3,000 hours per year per aircraft. Few organizations can provide such traffic single-handedly on a routine basis.

Necessity of high minimum loads

New transport aircraft and containers. The introduction of the wide-fuselage "super-jet" passenger aircraft of very large capacity (350–550 seat) with large under-floor capacity may modify this trend toward all-cargo services.

The Boeing 747 passenger aircraft offers more than 6,000 cubic feet (170 cubic metres) and approximately 45,000 pounds (20,400 kilograms) of under-floor cargo and mail capacity. There is also an all-cargo version (747F), whose payload may exceed 200,000 pounds (90,000 kilograms) on the North Atlantic. Containerization, whereby loads are prepacked in large consignments at the individual production plant, the premises of a freight forwarder, or the airline cargo centre, should reduce costs. Air-shipper associations and co-operatives are active in the promotion of consolidation services for container loads. Greater security against loss and pilferage are important advantages claimed for the unitized and containerized load. Lack of standardization of container sizes, the rental cost of containers, and the low-load factors are restraining the greater use of these methods of handling and transport. Moreover, a deterrent to the use of containers is the time lost in waiting for shipment until a complete container load has built up. Ship containers may offer considerable cost competition to air containers on routes where a reasonably good ship frequency is achieved, as is the case on the North Atlantic. Ship frequencies from Europe to West Africa, on the other hand, cannot yet offer competitive service.

In most cases air shipment costs more than surface shipment; its advantage lies in the reduction of ancillary costs and in the generation of new business. A wider market in extent and time can be reached by faster transport modes. Thus, the speed of air transport has been found to be significant in generating business, presuming always that delays are small at the air terminals, and that the loading, unloading, and surface-delivery times are related to the time saved in the air.

Air-cargo commodities. A pattern of commodities most suitable for air transport is apparent in most countries. High-value goods naturally predominate. Few really low-value commodities are candidates for air freight. Engineering goods, chemical and pharmaceutical products, textiles, paper products, livestock, and samples of all kinds form the bulk of air freight shipments into most markets. Automotive spare parts are at the top of the list of scheduled airline cargo commodities in the United States. Automotive spares ranked sixth in import tonnage and ninth in export tonnage through New York airports in 1969. Air freight is also used extensively by European automobile manufacturers. The international trade in such commodities is increasing more rapidly than that of other industrial goods. Thus, air cargo is in a favourable growth position. It seems reasonable to expect that the air-cargo trade will grow throughout the 1970s

and that there will be a greater range of goods airlifted. Manufacturers have increasing reluctance to carry large quantities of high-value goods in inventory. Moreover, technological obsolescence is becoming a critical factor in advanced industries such as avionics (electrical and electronic devices for use in aviation). Air delivery can be helpful in both cases.

Shipping services. The air-cargo business must not be considered as the province only of airline and shipper. A complex pattern of operations and procedures has developed that is the concern of manufacturers of aircraft and equipment, groups providing ground facilities at airports and at cargo terminals, and worldwide freight-forwarding agencies. The air-freight forwarder provides an increasingly important service to both airline and shipper. He consolidates small packages into a large consignment to take advantage of the improved economy of handling by pallet or container. He can provide complete pickup and door-to-door delivery service. He provides a single responsible agent for the forwarding and accounting process from origin to destination. As the air-freight business moves into the lower value commodity groups, the functions of the agent or forwarder become more significant. The pattern is worldwide, and approximately 20 percent of air cargo is now handled internationally by the agent.

Regional variations in air cargo. The use of aircraft for the transport of goods has regional variations. Aircraft are extensively used for access to the frozen wastes of Northern Canada and the Soviet Union, and in such cases the costs per ton-mile may be far lower than alternative surface transport.

In South America, air-freight service to mountainous areas has maintained communities that otherwise might have vanished. Thus Avianca, the Colombian airline, had over 33 percent of its total air traffic in 1969 in the form of air cargo (freight and mail). Aircraft of older types, such as the piston-engined DC-3 (Douglas), are still in operation in such areas.

Use of older aircraft

Africa provides special opportunities for air cargo, since heat causes spoilage and a lack of refrigerated cars and trucks from seaports restricts onward surface shipment for a wide range of goods. Such a situation arises also in the Middle East and the Persian Gulf, in Central America, and in parts of South America.

Air-cargo traffic on domestic services in most countries has grown at a moderate rate. On sectors of less than 350 to 400 miles (560 to 640 kilometres), especially when no natural barrier exists, the lower costs of road and rail transport are decisive and air is used mainly in emergencies. Such traffic can rarely support all-cargo flights except on special charters.

ECONOMIC SIGNIFICANCE

While the volume of air-transport business trebled during the 1960s, net profit as a percentage of revenue fell steadily from the middle of the decade. Operating revenues and expenses of the world's scheduled airlines (1965 and 1970) are given in Table 3. Where private resources support the air-transport industry, major efforts have been made to find answers to its widespread unprofitability. Wage increases and capital investments, including costs of introducing the new jet fleets, have escalated operating costs. Moreover, airline capacity has continually grown in anticipation of higher levels of traffic. Serious problems can be expected if the anticipated traffic growth does not materialize. A similar situation arose in the early 1960s at the time of the acquisition of the first turbojet fleets.

The impact of air transport upon the economy of nations is far wider than the traffic growth itself would indicate. The air-transport manufacturing industries themselves have become important national assets in a number of countries.

The purchase and operation of home-built aircraft and the export of aircraft to foreign governments and airlines can be an important factor in the balance of payments of nations with aircraft industries. It may be an argument for retaining such capability if prospects for export sales

Table 3: Operating Revenues and Expenses of the World's Scheduled Airlines ($000,000)

	1965	1970*
Operating revenues		
Scheduled services		
Passengers	7,378	16,825
Freight	904	1,694
Mail	404	619
Nonscheduled services	469	709
Incidental	217	487
Total operating revenues	9,372	18,015
Operating expenses		
Flight operations	2,177	4,610
Maintenance and overhaul	1,462	2,448
Flight-equipment depreciation	950	1,954
Station and ground	1,317	2,789
Passenger services	714	1,619
Ticketing sales and promotion	1,343	2,621
General and administrative	509	985
Total operating expenses	8,472	17,026

*Preliminary.
Source: International Civil Aviation Organization.

The balance-of-payments argument for the SST

are also adequate. The potential advantage to the United States and to the United Kingdom and France, respectively, in international monetary balance has been used as an argument by the protagonists of supersonic aircraft.

A national airline can provide a saving in foreign exchange, and this advantage has given many small states an incentive to operate their own airlines. Moreover, receipts from foreign travellers, export freight, and airport expenditures by foreign airlines provide revenues of great value in the balance of foreign exchange for many airline-operating states. In the United States, for example, the expenditure by foreign visitors reaches approximately one-half of the U.S. overall travel expenditure abroad, and on the air-transportation ledger the account is far more evenly balanced.

Further economic gains are achieved by the use of air transport as a stimulant to trade and industry. No adequate measure of this benefit has yet been evolved, but it is evident that it greatly exceeds the expenditure on passenger and cargo transport. The location of one or more great airport terminals in the vicinity of a capital city is a factor critical to national growth.

As noted earlier, air cargo has created new markets and has contributed notably to the development of international trade in certain high-cost commodities.

In travel and tourism, airlines are finding an even more expansive field. The wide-ranging opportunities offered by long-haul aircraft are already bringing tourists and related economic benefits to smaller and less-developed countries where scenery, climate, or historical associations may be outstanding. The airlines are themselves taking part in providing new ground facilities, such as hotels. In helping to redress the imbalance in the wealth of nations, air transport may thus play a far-reaching role in the 1970s.

BIBLIOGRAPHY

General: Merchant Airmen (HMSO 1946), a British government publication with historical accounts, photographs, and maps of World War II civil aviation, emphasis on U.K., British Commonwealth, and Europe; CHARLES GIBBS-SMITH, *The Invention of the Aeroplane* (1966), a classic in the history of aircraft; R.E.G. DAVIES, *A History of the World's Airlines* (1964), a detailed history; PETER W. BROOKS, *The Modern Airliner* (1961), an early but perceptive treatment of the origins and development of the modern airliner; J.E. ALLEN and J. BRUCE (eds.), *The Future of Aeronautics* (1970), papers reprinted from the *Journal of the Royal Aeronautical Society* on the next 100 years in aviation; K.R. SEALY, *The Geography of Air Transport*, rev. ed. (1966), a brief but sound early work on essentials.

Specialized: (*Edwards Committee Report*), *British Air Transport in the Seventies*, Cmnd. 4018 (HMSO 1969), an essential report on U.K. aviation, air transport, manufacturing, and political issues; R.F. HANSFORD, *Radio Aids to Civil Aviation* (1960), the fundamentals of air-transport radio aids; INTERNATIONAL CIVIL AVIATION ORGANIZATION, *Review of the Economic Situation of Air Transport 1957-67* (1968), a report giving essential background to the study of international air-transport trends; H.M. SAMUELSON, *The Executive Aircraft* (1963), on the principles of operation and selection of aircraft; R.E. CAVES, *Air Transport and Its Regulators* (1962), for advanced readers; *Janes All the World's Aircraft* (annual), accounts, photographs, and drawings of all types of transport aircraft; ALAN STRATFORD, *Air Transport in the Supersonic Era*, 2nd ed. (1972), summary of the economics and state of the art; S.E.T. TAYLOR, *Ground Studies for Pilots* (1970), essential for a full understanding of air-traffic control and aircraft navigational equipment. The major airlines publish annual reports that contain useful statistical information.

(A.H.St.)

Transportation, History of

From earliest times the conditions in which man lives have been powerfully influenced by the ease and speed with which he has been able to move himself and his materials from point to point on the earth's surface. By harnessing nature directly and indirectly, man has been able to explore and exploit the earth's resources. The chief landmarks in the history of transportation—the wheel, the sail, the steam engine, the internal-combustion engine, the electric motor, and the great technological breakthrough of flight—promise, as the 21st century approaches, to be capped by the rocket engine, which frees man from dependence on earth's atmosphere and permits him to visualize travelling to other planets. (E.A.J.D.)

PRIMITIVE TRANSPORTATION

Early man was a wanderer—of necessity rather than choice. Food was scarce and hard to come by; enemies abounded. Techniques were invented for carrying loads, on the end of a stick on one shoulder, on the single yoke, or on both ends of a pole carried across the shoulders, the double yoke. A slain deer or buffalo could be carried on a pole borne by two men; a 5,000-year-old alabaster relief from Sumer shows a large vessel carried thus between two bearers.

The travois. The earliest agricultural workers probably shifted hay on the forked branch of a tree. From this developed the Y-shaped sledge, or travois, used in more recent times by North American Indians. The travois was two poles tied together, with the inverted V resting on the back of a man or animal. Between the poles was slung a wooden or net frame. The Y-sledge was widely used in northern Europe and throughout the cattle regions of Africa.

The slide car. Whereas the travois can be put together and taken apart as necessary, the slide car is permanent. In the slide car, two shafts are harnessed to a horse or other draft animal; their ends drag along the ground and the shafts are kept apart by crossbars. The very wide geographical distribution of the slide car is proof of its antiquity, and it held its own in some mountainous districts of Europe until recent times.

Sledges and skis. By 5000 BC the sledge was in common use in northern Europe, North America, Egypt, Assyria, and the Middle East. Originally a simple rectangular platform that could be either hauled or pushed, it was soon improved by the addition of runners. Sledges can travel well over snow, marsh, clay, or grass, and to this day are used in Lapland, northern Asia, and British Columbia. The Egyptians and Assyrians used them to move the materials required for their pyramids, obelisks, and huge river statues, and they constructed some of the earliest known roads to enhance the capabilities of the sledge. The use of runners in the form of skis is also very old. A carving on a rock-face in northern Norway dating to about 2000 BC is clearly identifiable as a man on skis.

Use of sledges for hauling

Animal transport. The ass, native to northeastern Africa, was almost certainly the first draft animal and was in common use in northeast Africa, upper Egypt, the Mediterranean Basin, and the Near and Far East well before 3000 BC. By that date pack animals were in regular service on the caravan routes stretching from eastern Europe and North Africa to India and China. A graphic presentation of convoys of pack asses regularly crossing the Syrian Desert and the Taurus Mountains (Turkey) is obtained from the surviving business letters of a group of Assyrian merchants established at the court of a Hittite prince in central Asia Minor about 2000 BC. An Egyptian relief from Bari Hasan, dated around 1900 BC, shows the arrival of the Canaanites with their pack asses laden with children and tribute. The ox, the reindeer, the elephant, the yak, the buffalo, and the llama were also used in earlier times. The camel, both the one-hump (Arabian) and the two-hump (Bactrian) varieties, was uniquely fitted by nature for long overland journeys because of its extraordinary capacity to store food and water and its ability to walk on soft sand. The camel could carry up to 600 pounds (270 kilograms) in weight. The most important draft animal for the future, the horse, was a relative latecomer. When or where horses were first domesticated is not known; they were introduced to Egypt by the Hyksos about 1675 BC.

Early water transport. Before ships and even boats, man must have had recourse to a wide variety of rafts and similar craft. The type varied according to environment; in Egypt, where the Nile was once flanked by masses of papyrus, and timber was scarce, the first floats consisted of bundles of rushes tied together. While the small models that have survived are not sufficiently detailed to indicate their mode of construction, a close parallel can be seen in modern Peru, where coastal fishermen use reed rafts, known as caballitos. Basically, the caballito consists of two or three conical bunches of reeds, cut off square at their bases and lashed side by side, with the pointed end turned up to form a prow. Caballitos have a considerable history; an extant pottery vase made in the form of such a boat is dated around 1200 BC.

In Mesopotamia and the eastern Mediterranean development proceeded on different lines. On the Tigris and Euphrates, where papyrus was lacking, an early skin float inflated with air provided a vehicle on which a man could lie and kick or paddle himself across a river. From the single or double float there evolved the wooden raft to which were attached a number of inflated skin floats, producing a platform capable of supporting a substantial load. One of the earliest pictorial records of these rafts comes from Nineveh. At destination, after disposal of the cargo, the timbers of the raft were sold and the skins deflated and transported by pack animal back to their place of origin for future use. Similar craft were used until recently on downstream journeys on the Tigris.

Closely allied to the skin float, which is kept buoyant by air pressure, is the skin boat, which consists of a flexible leather cover stretched around an internal frame. Such craft survive today in the kayaks of the Eskimo, the curraghs of the west coast of Ireland, the coracles of Wales, the modern canvas canoe, and other counterparts scattered widely over Asia and America.

There is strong evidence that the coracle type was first developed in Asia. Coracles were in common use for carrying cargo on the Tigris and Euphrates as early as the 9th century BC.

The dugout. As Neolithic man acquired better tools, dugouts superseded bark canoes. Dugouts are found wherever there are suitable forests, the limiting factor being the tree diameter. Dugouts constructed in North Africa often had beams of no more than 18 inches (46 centimetres). The ancient British canoe of the Bronze Age was 35 feet (11 metres) long with a depth of two feet (0.6 metre) and a beam of nearly five feet (1.5 metres).

The development of larger craft from the primitive dugout involved more complex construction. From the remains of two boats, probably of the Iron Age, found in the river Humber in England, one possible line of advance can be deduced. The hull was roughly pontoon-shaped, with five thick floor planks bevelled and grooved to fit each other and sewn together with withies (willows). A more promising line of development may be inferred from various types of canoe hulls in the Pacific. In the Maori type of canoe, the tree trunk was hollowed out, and additional freeboard was provided by lashing beams to either side, thus providing bulwarks, which did not quite reach stem or stern. Where the available timber did not have a diameter large enough to provide sufficient

stability, outrigger floats were fitted. To secure the necessary freeboard for any carrying capacity required, additional planks were fitted at each side, as in the canoes of the Marshall Bennett Islands today. As time went on and the craft became more and more complex, the dugout part of the hull made a smaller and smaller contribution to buoyancy, and in the end survived only as the keel.

Of the earliest forms of water transportation, the raft, the coracle-type craft, and the dugout, there can be no doubt that the dugout is the most primitive; yet the line of descent to the cargo ships and passenger liners of today is clear and direct from the dugout.

THE WHEEL AND THE ROAD

Development of vehicle wheel. Archaeological evidence is insufficient to enable us to say whether the wheel as used in transport was an outgrowth of the potter's wheel or contemporaneous with it. On logical grounds it might be possible to argue that horizontal rotatory motion seems likely to have preceded vertical rotatory motion, but in the absence of evidence any conclusion must be tentative. All that can be said with reasonable certainty is that the revolution in transport caused by the introduction of the wheel occurred very soon after, if not at the same time as, the transformation of the ceramic industry brought about by the potter's wheel.

The earliest indication of the use of wheeled vehicles is the representation of a sledge on four solid wheels. It is a conventionalized symbol used as a pictographic character in the oldest extant written documents, the tablets of the Inanna Temple at Erech in lower Mesopotamia, inscribed not long after 3500 BC. The royal tombs at Kish, Sura, and Ur (3000 to 2000 BC) contained actual vehicles, while works of art and clay models of vehicles are found not only in Mesopotamia but in northern Syria and the Indus Valley and provide detailed information about their design and use. The archaic vehicles known from the archaeological record in Mesopotamia and the Indus River Basin before 2000 BC have parallels in China, Sindh, the Balkans, Sardinia, Spain, Scandinavia, and the British Isles.

All the oldest vehicles known to archaeology (and the types most widespread in the nonindustrialized countries of today) are distinguished by two peculiarities, solid wheels and provision for paired draft animals. Solid wheels have another distinguishing feature of their own. Most wheels before 2000 BC are constructed in the form of tripartite disks, consisting of three planks carved to fit segments of a circle and clamped together by transverse struts, with a raised area in the middle of the central plank forming a hub around the axle. The rims of these wheels were sometimes bound with heavily studded metal hoops. The axle was constructed independently and projected beyond the hub; the evidence is insufficient to determine whether the wheels revolved freely or turned with the axle.

The tripartite disk is demonstrably the oldest as well as the most widespread form of wheel, but it is by no means the only conceivable form, nor is it theoretically the simplest. The wide distribution of this particular form of wheel throughout the Near East and prehistoric Europe accordingly argues strongly for its diffusion from a single Mesopotamian or other west Asian source. Spoke wheels, some 1,500 years later, appear on clay models in northern Mesopotamia, eastern Turkey, and northeast Iran. By the 15th century BC, spoke wheels were in common use on chariots in Syria, Egypt, and the eastern Mediterranean generally, and it is a safe inference that the spoke wheel rapidly supplanted its solid predecessor for all the purposes for which wheeled transport could then be used.

The roads of the ancient world. In the central and eastern Mediterranean areas, and particularly in Greece and Asia Minor, wheeled vehicles were in more common use than elsewhere, and some progress was made in primitive road construction. The deliberately made rut, characteristic of the central and eastern Mediterranean, makes its first and most prominent appearance in Malta, in association with a society in the Late Neolithic and

Boats of inflated skins

Tripartite disk wheels

Early Bronze ages. These ruts were more or less uniform in their depth (three to six inches, or eight to 15 centimetres), width (eight inches, or 20 centimetres), and gauge (44–57 inches, or 112–145 centimetres). That they were deliberately constructed is shown by the fact that in some cases ruts occupy the centres of specially hollowed stone blocks placed in paved roads. Though they are of course a different type of construction, these roads foreshadowed the wooden and stone railways used in the mining industries of central Europe and Great Britain before the Industrial Revolution. Their likeness to modern railways is emphasized by the provision of sidings and passing places.

The roads of China. China developed the oldest known network of roads for everyday use; centuries before the Persian Empire, and over 2,000 years before the Incas, the Chinese had a fully developed system. Even before the Chou dynasty (*c.* 1122–221 BC) communications were controlled and roads maintained by a highways commissioner, with a separate budget of his own. During the Chou dynasty the volume of traffic necessitated the establishment of a uniform scale of size for wheeled vehicles, the prohibition of reckless driving, and traffic regulations for busy intersections. Roads were classified in five grades: pathways for men and pack animals; roads capable of taking narrow-gauge vehicles; roads that could accommodate larger vehicles; roads on which single vehicles could pass each other; and highways taking three wagons abreast.

Roads of the Persian Empire. The ruling dynasty in Persia, masters in their day (559–330 BC) of the entire Middle East, in order to maintain speedy communications with their provincial administrators, were forced to construct a road system. More accurately described as levelled and partly paved tracks, these roads were policed by guards posted at rest houses every 15 miles (24 kilometres). A continuous line of stations linked Sardis, on the Aegean shore, with Susa, the capital, 1,600 miles (2,600 kilometres) away; special messengers could cover the distance between Susa and Babylon (200 miles) in two days.

The Roman road system. It was the Romans who brought the art of road building in antiquity to its highest pitch. The Romans may have taken their road-building techniques from the Etruscans. The roads built by the Greek colonists in southern Italy may also have had some influence.

The first of the great Roman highways was the Via Appia, begun in 312 BC by the censor Appius Claudius. Built to link Rome with the military centre of Capua, it was later extended southeast to Tarentum (Taranto). The Via Flaminia, completed in 220 BC, gave Rome direct communications with the Po Valley.

By AD 200 the Roman system stretched from Hadrian's Wall in north Britain to the edge of the Sahara, and from Morocco to the Euphrates. Its primary purpose was to provide for speedy and safe military and civil contacts between the central seat of government and the capital cities of the imperial provinces. Horses that drew the two- or four-wheeled vehicles could be changed at stations along the road at intervals of six to 16 Roman miles. Rest houses were spaced at intervals of 20 to 30 Roman miles.

Medieval roads. The disintegration of the Roman Empire had disastrous effects on the imperial road system. The decline in security reduced trade and commerce, and the fragmentation of political authority brought a neglect of maintenance. One should, however, note the introduction of the iron horseshoe and horse collar which permitted horses to pull heavy loads long distances.

The Inca civilization. No account of the history of transportation would be complete without some mention of the astonishing achievements of the Incas in north and central South America. The Inca Empire reached its zenith under Pachacuti and Topa Inca (Tupac; 1438–93), when it stretched from the present Colombia–Ecuador border to central Chile, a coastal distance of over 2,500 miles and covering an area of approximately 380,000 square miles. From the capital, Cuzco, well constructed roads ran to all parts of the empire. Staging

posts were frequent, and relay runners were stationed at them to carry messages and parcels quickly. The Incas knew something about bridging, and where necessary they carried their roads over canyons, using suspension bridges.

The beginnings of modern roads. The revival of commerce in Europe and the Near East brought advances in water transport in the High Middle Ages, but land transportation developed more slowly. Four-wheeled wagons gradually came into commercial use; the four-ton carrier's wagon was a common sight in Shakespeare's England. In the mining industries of central and northern Europe, wooden and stone rails were used to facilitate the haulage of heavily laden ore trucks.

Though medieval people travelled extensively on pilgrimages, such journeys were either by water or on foot or pack animal. Two prerequisites were necessary for the expansion of travel for pleasure, a reasonably efficient and comfortable vehicle and a reasonably efficient and safe system of roads. It is a fair presumption that the invention of the former gave impetus to the development of the latter, although the needs of commerce and government of course played a large role.

Introduction of the coach. Legend has it that the coach was first introduced into England in 1564 by a Dutchman, who later became chief coachman to Queen Elizabeth I. The name, found in most European languages, derives from the reputed place of origin of the coach, the village of Kocs in Hungary, though what specific features of the coach are Hungarian will never be known. The covered wagon had been in use in the Far East, the Middle East, and Europe in the Middle Ages and probably much earlier, but the distinguishing feature of the coach that made the traveller's journey more comfortable was that its body was suspended by straps from the chassis. Another feature was that the front axle was attached to the chassis through a pivot, providing a turning train.

The introduction of iron rims on coach wheels meant severe wear and tear on the roads, and there was a period in the England of Charles I (1625–49) when stagecoaches were actually banned in order to protect the highways for other traffic. For the same reason the minimum width of these iron tires was for many years regulated in England by law, being at one time 18 inches (46 centimetres). The stagecoach grew to a considerable size, weighing in some instances as much as eight tons and being driven by teams of up to 12 horses. The introduction of springs, which supported the body of the coach on C-shaped straps of tempered steel, can be dated to approximately 1665.

To earn their keep, coaches had to travel considerable distances at a time, which meant the introduction of staging posts where the horses could be fed, watered, and changed. This made for a marked increase in the speed of travel, up to ten miles (16 kilometres) an hour being frequently recorded in good conditions (by contrast, when the King of Scotland's ransom had to be brought to London "with all speed" in 1375 it travelled no more than 30 miles per day).

The revival of road building. During the medieval period responsibility for making and repairing the roads rested as a rule on the parishes and landowners through whose land the road passed; those employed on road work were usually farmers and forced labourers. The widespread use of bundles of faggots, erroneously supposed to improve the drainage of the subsoil and the carrying quality of the road, was harmful. But in the 16th century Italian architects and engineers gave attention to the scientific study of road building; a Reims lawyer, Nicholas Bergier, studied the remains of a Roman road that he found in his garden and with the aid of material collected from classical texts and archaeological data compiled a book, *Histoire des grands chemins de l'empire romain*, which attracted wide attention.

The emergence of the nation states of western and central Europe made possible the gradual development of strong, centralized administrative and technical bodies to train engineers and impose uniform standards of road

The Appian and Flaminian ways

Introduction of staging posts

building. The change began to take place at the end of the 16th century, in the France of Henry IV. In 1599 Henry created the post of chief road engineer, with local lieutenants in the provinces. Royal grants were made for new roads. By 1664 the state of the road system allowed for the establishment of a stagecoach service. Many country roads were paved with stone blocks (the *pavés du roi*).

After a decline in road building caused by the demands of the wars of Louis XIV (1643–1715), progress was resumed under Louis XV. The Corps des Ponts et Chaussées, created in 1716, was the first body of road and bridge experts and engineers in Europe to be financed by a government. The method of construction employed was, in general, to trench the road and then lay successive layers of smaller and smaller stones until a smooth surface was reached. By 1776 France had no fewer than 25,000 miles of highway completed or under construction, of which half were being reconstructed or aligned as avenues.

Another factor contributing powerfully to the pressure for more and better roads was the expansion of trade and commerce and the constant pressure of merchants and manufacturers for improved communications. The process was most marked in Britain, where the presence of large quantities of easily mined coal and iron ore gave that country a head start in the Industrial Revolution. Indeed, the rapid growth of industrial production from the middle of the 18th century onward made better communications not so much a desirable objective as a pressing and immediate necessity. Initially, priority was given to canals, known in those days as navigations; cheap labour imported from Ireland in large quantities dug these canals, and the workmen were known as "navigators," hence the modern use of "navvies" to cover any type of unskilled heavy labourers. Canals, however, could not possibly be built on a sufficient scale to meet the demands of industry; thus, the crying need for more and better roads. John Loudon McAdam was the best known of a number of self-taught engineers, of whom John Metcalf and Thomas Telford were also outstanding. They were fully aware of the necessity for a proper drainage system, and McAdam invented an inexpensive, self-sealing road surface, consisting of small stones, chips, or gravel, which could be applied directly to the soil or subsoil of a properly made roadbed. His first experiments in Bristol in 1815 were so successful that they set in motion a road-building explosion that has continued with increasing momentum for 150 years.

John Loudon McAdam's new road

SAILS AND OARS

Early Egyptian, Greek, and Arab vessels. As early as 4000 BC the boats or rafts in use on the Nile had advanced a long way from the primitive bundles of reeds from which they derived. The Egyptian vessel was by now essentially a built-up dugout consisting of a massive outer shell formed of many pieces of timber dowelled and dovetailed together. It lacked stem, stern, and keel; the sail, when fitted, was a simple rectangular affair slung amidships.

By 1500 BC Crete had become the dominant sea power in the eastern and central Mediterranean. Little is known of the Cretans or of the Phoenicians, who inherited maritime supremacy after the eclipse of Crete in about 1200 BC. The Phoenicians were primarily traders, and, in search of fresh markets, carried their wares through the Straits of Gibraltar as far as Britain in the west and down the west coast of Africa. The Cretans and Phoenicians worked from the beginning on a ship design basically different from that used by the predynastic Egyptians. Stem, stern, and keel all formed an integral part of this design, and both Crete and Phoenicia had begun to differentiate between the fighting vessel and the merchantman and between the rowing galley and the sailing ship. Phoenician vessels (*c.* 700 BC) illustrate two further striking developments: the arrangement of oars in two banks at different levels, and the fitting of a ram in the bows of a fighting galley.

Athens, the dominant sea power in the eastern and central Mediterranean in the 5th century BC, had shipyards at Piraeus and neighbouring towns that could handle hundreds of vessels at a time. Their galleys carried mast and sail but were primarily rowing vessels, whereas the merchantman of this and later periods was a sailing vessel pure and simple. Its draft and beam were much greater than those of the galley, it did not carry a ram, and had stem- and sternposts curving down to a comparatively short keel. The mainsail was square, set on a yard slung horizontally from a mast erected amidships and carried more or less at right angles to the ship's fore and aft line. At first there was only one mast and one sail, but by the beginning of the Christian Era Mediterranean merchantmen carried a second, much smaller sail on a mast projecting from the bows and could also set a triangular sail or topsails from the mainsail. The steering gear (an inheritance from Egypt) consisted of two large paddle-shaped rudders, or steering oars, one on each quarter.

Chinese shipping and shipbuilding. In the other principal cradle of ancient civilization, China, shipbuilding followed an entirely different course. In Europe and eastern and southern Asia the keel was joined at each end to beams that slanted upward to form the stem- and sternposts, respectively. The planks of the hull that connected them were held apart, and the hull was given its strength and stability, by an internal framework. But the design of Chinese junks, from the earliest times to the epoch of the great voyages as far as the coasts of East Africa between AD 1405 and 1433, lacked all the three components—keel and stem- and sternposts—regarded elsewhere as essential. The ship's bottom was flat and slightly rounded, and the hull did not close in toward the stern but ended abruptly, leaving a space that was filled by a solid transom of planking. In most classical types there was no stem either but a similar rectangular transom bow. There was no true framework or ribbing; what took its place was a system of solid transverse bulkheads, of which the stem and stern transoms may be regarded as the outward units. Dr. J. Needham has suggested that the basic features of a Chinese ship may have derived from the structure of the bamboo used by the Chinese for a thousand purposes. A split section of bamboo, with transverse dividing walls, has clear affinities with Chinese ship design.

Design of Chinese junks

The lateen sail. If the first revolution in the history of shipping was the transformation of a river or seagoing craft from a simple dugout or raft to a more functional artifact with stem, stern, keel, and molded hull, the second was undoubtedly the adoption of the lateen sail. The lateen is triangular in shape and trimmed so as to take the wind on either side. It is set on a long yard coming down nearly to the deck forward and rising to well above the masthead at the other end. It is known to have been in use in the eastern Mediterranean as early as the 2nd century AD, and while its place of origin is not precisely known, the probabilities point to Egypt or the Persian Gulf. In any case, it is clear that Arab and Muslim conquest did much to extend its use. By the 10th century the lateen sail was in common use in the Mediterranean and on all European coasts, spreading to the East by way of the Red Sea, the Persian Gulf, and the Indian Ocean.

With the invention of gunpowder and the carrying of guns on ships soon after 1350, two processes were under way—one consisting of the gradual increase in dimensions and complexity of the masts and rigging of all ships, the other the increasing differentiation between the sailing man-of-war and the merchantman. In 1400, ships still had one mast and one sail; by 1450 some had three masts and three sails; by the end of the century the largest had four masts and eight sails.

Toward the end of the 12th century there came another of the great advances in the history of sailing ships—the supersession of the single-side starboard (steering board) rudder by the sternpost rudder. When or where this type of rudder first appeared in the Western world is uncertain, but it must have been about 1200, and its place of origin was in all probability the Netherlands or thereabouts. It had been in use in China more than 1,000 years earlier. The introduction of the sternpost rudder was important not only because of the improvement in navigation that it brought about but also because it forced a

The sternpost rudder

differentiation between bow and stern and in consequence the transformation of the double-ended ships of the Baltic and northern Europe into something far more like their Mediterranean contemporaries. When, about 1300, the maritime nations of southern Europe recognized the superiority of the sternpost rudder and incorporated it into their vessels, the standard European ship was not far off.

The magnetic compass was first carried on ships in the Western world around 1000 and was in common use by the 12th century. Originally the magnetized needle floated on straw, but by the latter half of the 13th century it was mounted on a pivot. The use of charts for maritime navigation developed at the same time; the first recorded use of a chart aboard ship (c. 1280) relates to the Mediterranean and Black Sea area.

The combination of the sternpost rudder and lateen sail made it possible to sail closer to the wind, and thus made for greater accuracy and safety of navigation; it is from this period that the development of many new sea routes is dated. Notable pioneers were the Genoese, who in the early 1300s began to undertake regular winter sailings and by the end of the century had established a defined sea route between Italy and the ports of the North Sea and the Baltic.

The opening of the oceans. The higher standards of navigation made possible by the use of such instruments as the magnetic compass and the astrolabe, for angle measurement, extended the field of exploration. This in turn led to a sharp increase in the size of cargo vessels. Beginning about 1418 with Prince Henry the Navigator (inaccurately so named, as he apparently never voyaged personally farther afield than Tangier), a succession of captains probed farther and farther down the west coast of Africa to the Cape of Good Hope, opening the sea route to India and China. At the same time Columbus sailed from Spain to make his accidental but history-making discovery of the New World. The discovery of the extent of the Pacific Ocean by Magellan in 1519–21 completed a generation of titanic achievements in ocean exploration, though major details remained to be filled in. The most notable of the later explorers was Capt. James Cook, who in the 18th century explored the Pacific and Antarctic oceans and was the first of the truly scientific navigators.

Jetties and harbour improvements. There is no conclusive evidence as to the dates of the first artificial harbour constructions, but it is known that the Phoenicians built harbours at Tyre and Sidon as early as the 13th century BC. Many other Mediterranean harbours, both natural and artificial, were of considerable commercial and military importance in Greek and Roman times.

In medieval times the prosperity of such cities as Venice, Genoa, and Alexandria (already a famous port in antiquity) required the building of harbour works for the protection and accommodation of their seaborne trade. The Pharos (lighthouse) of Alexandria was one of the seven wonders of the ancient world. Some of the early works at Venice and Genoa remain to this day. Natural harbours are more numerous in north Europe than in the Mediterranean. For many centuries these natural facilities, combined in some cases with rudimentary artificial harbour works, sufficed. From the late Middle Ages, Britain gave special prominence to the development of its port facilities. Artificial harbour works existed at Hartlepool (on the northeast coast) from about 1250 and at Arbroath in Scotland from about 1390. Dover lacked natural facilities but, because of its favourable situation on the English Channel, was a busy military and commercial port from the reign of Henry VIII (1509–47) onward, and a stone and timber breakwater was built there in his reign. Across the English Channel, Le Havre, Dieppe, La Rochelle, and Dunkerque were among the early ports to embark on harbour construction.

The history of ports on the American continent followed the Mediterranean and northern European pattern. In the early days, natural havens offering protective anchorages were sufficient, but as the North American economy developed, ships became larger and of deeper

Harbour-building on the English Channel

draft, demanding larger and deeper harbours. Both natural and artificial harbours had to be dredged to maintain and increase the depth of water at quayside. All the great natural harbours in the world today have seen their native facilities improved, and in some cases transformed, by dredging, by the construction of breakwaters to enclose an area of protected water, and by running jetties into deep water to accommodate the giant tankers and bulk carriers that dominate their trades today.

Worldwide seaborne trade and the discovery of the New World brought new traffic to ancient ports but above all created a number of entirely new ones. Gorée (the predecessor of Dakar, on the West African coast) came into being before 1450. In the 16th century such famous ports as Havana (c. 1514), Lima (c. 1535), and Manila (c. 1750) were founded, to be followed in the next century by New Amsterdam (New York), Cape Town, and Calcutta, among many others.

This multiplication of ports was the outstanding feature of world port development in the period up to 1800. The chief engineering works on these "new" ports were devoted to fortifications against attack, particularly from the sea. Ships could be beached or worked at anchor within a defensible natural harbour. In the late 16th century the then small port of Rotterdam built an artificial harbour that served for two centuries. More typical, and certainly more expensive and elaborate, were the works of military engineering such as the late-16th-century fortifications of Valletta (Malta) or, on a smaller scale, the Morro Castle of Havana (1590–1640).

Military engineering rapidly developed, and by the late 17th century the lagoon-harbour of Dunkerque had been enclosed within the complex fortifications of the town and was approached from the sea between timber jetties armed with timber forts.

By the 18th century the increasing number of ships and quantities of cargo justified more expensive commercial facilities, at major ports at least. The earliest commercial wet docks (for example, Liverpool) date from the early 18th century. Near the end of the century there came the most remarkable work of harbour engineering of the century: the breakwater at Brest, constructed between 1783 and 1795. Over 9,800 feet (3,000 metres) long and built of stone and prefabricated timber units floated into position, it was built partly as a fortification.

All this activity, widely spread though it was, only faintly foreshadowed the spectacular development of port facilities that gathered momentum throughout the 19th century and matched in its complexity the equally spectacular growth in trade and industry. (D.O'N.)

The breakwater at Brest

Growth of inland waterways. Throughout the centuries rivers have provided an obvious means of transport, but natural obstacles in the riverbeds and changes in water levels have hampered movement. With the invention of the lock, these could be overcome by lifting vehicles from one level to another and bypassing such hazards. Following the development of the lock in the 13th century, river navigation was improved and many artificial waterways were built.

To meet the demand for transport resulting from trade expansion, from the 16th century onward a network of canals was established linking Europe's navigable rivers. With technical improvements, and with further development of the mitre lock (see CANALS AND INLAND WATERWAYS), many canals incorporated unique engineering features including lock staircases, hydraulic lifts, and inclined planes that raised and lowered craft from one level to another. The expansion of trade created a need for the transport of raw materials and manufactured products that could not have been met by slow and hazardous road transport; as a result, canal construction was embarked upon on a grand scale. In the United Kingdom a series of canals joined the industrial Midlands to London and the ports, and links in the waterway system were forged in France to provide through navigation from the English Channel and the Atlantic to the Mediterranean. In Belgium and The Netherlands industrial expansion also led to the extension of canals that were more closely integrated with the French and German waterways. Russia provided through waterways from the Baltic to the Caspian Sea and interconnected its great rivers. In Greece, the Corinth Canal, abortively started by Nero to connect the Aegean and Ionian seas, was built. In the United States construction of canals contributed to the opening up of the West, with the Erie Canal, 363 miles (584 kilometres) long, joining the Hudson to Lake Erie and resulting in the establishment of New York as the predominant port on the Atlantic seaboard. Thus it was that apart from seagoing trade the main means for the transport of goods throughout the period of great industrial development of the late 18th and early 19th centuries was the river and canal.

Drawbacks in barge transportation Transport by inland waterways did have some serious handicaps: goods were transported in dumb barges, drawn mostly by horse along towpaths, and the canal boats often had to be manually handled through the numerous locks and tunnels. Because of the large number of locks, transport was slow and the volume carried per unit was small. The railways, with their larger volumes, greater carrying power, and higher speeds, inevitably encroached upon the canals and brought the canal era to an end. In many countries, however, navigable rivers and canals continued to be used as a major means of transport; and with the coming of steam, tugboats supplanted the horse. Heavier loads could be carried at increased speeds. Heavy investment in ocean canals became worthwhile; the Suez Canal, joining the Mediterranean Sea to the Red Sea and thereby considerably reducing the voyage to India and the Far East, was opened in 1869, and the Panama Canal, connecting the Atlantic and Pacific, was completed in 1914. Meanwhile in North America navigation on the Mississippi was improved with the construction of link canals that joined this system with the St. Lawrence and the Great Lakes; thus an extensive and combined network of inland waterways was established. Development of this system continued, climaxed by the St. Lawrence Seaway, opened in 1959, providing a continuous deep waterway for oceangoing ships from the Atlantic to the Great Lakes. In Europe and the Soviet Union also, after World War II the inland waterway networks of canalized rivers and artificial waterways were being brought up to modern standards, and with the application of the latest technological skills larger loads were capable of being carried at increased speeds.

(E.A.J.D.)

STEAM TRANSPORTATION

The railroad. *The first locomotives.* The first reported self-propelled steam vehicle was created in Peking about 1681 by a Jesuit missionary named Ferdinand Verbiest. Nicolas-Joseph Cugnot, a French artillery officer, built a full-sized steam car in Paris in 1769. He intended it to haul army cannon or munitions, but it was demonstrated as a passenger carrier. Richard Trevithick, a Cornish engineer, demonstrated a steam car on hilly roads near Camborne, Cornwall, in 1801 and his second, bigger version in London in 1803, attaining a speed of six miles (ten kilometres) per hour. In 1804 Trevithick created a four-wheeled tramway locomotive that hauled a five-wagon load of ten tons of iron and 70 men at a speed of five miles per hour. The locomotive set several trends for the future; besides justifying Trevithick's preference for high-pressure instead of low-pressure steam used in stationary steam engines of the period, its single large cylinder was set horizontally and had a sliding crosshead, and exhaust steam was adapted for drafting the boiler to improve thermal efficiency.

In 1805 Trevithick's second locomotive was built at Gateshead, Northumberland, and in 1808 he laid down a circular track in London to demonstrate a third, "Catch-Me-Who-Can." The ten-ton machine achieved ten miles per hour with an open coachload of passengers, but like its two predecessors it was eventually derailed by the flimsy track of the period, and Trevithick, discouraged, directed his talents elsewhere.

Others pursued the concept. John Blenkinsop, superintendent of a colliery near Leeds, strengthened the track and sought to improve traction by laying a toothed rack rail outside one running rail. In 1812 a Leeds engineer

named Matthew Murray designed two locomotives, each with a pair of double-acting cylinders connected by crankshafts to cogwheels that engaged the rack. These were the world's first commercially successful steam locomotives.

Meantime, the Northumberland colliery that had employed Trevithick rebuilt his track with cast-iron plates. The colliery's superintendent, William Hedley, designed two locomotives, "Puffing Billy" and "Wylam Dilly," that were successfully employed on coal haulage from 1814 until the colliery closed in 1862. Built as four-wheelers, they broke the plate rails and were soon rebuilt as eight-wheelers, to spread the axle loading, but in 1830 they were again reconstructed with four flanged wheels after the colliery line had been relaid with edge rails. A notable feature of Hedley's engines was their return flue boiler, with rear-end exhaust chimney; this was a first step to improved steam locomotives. The next was George Stephenson's adoption of a multitubed boiler in the "Rocket" of 1829.

George Stephenson and the "Rocket" George Stephenson, born at Wylam, followed his father's profession as colliery fireman but rapidly graduated to supervision of all machinery at Killingworth Colliery, north of Newcastle. In 1814 the owners allowed him to build for their wagonway his first locomotive, "Blücher." In its original form "Blücher" represented little advance, but in subsequent locomotive construction Stephenson perfected the direct drive from cylinders to flanged wheels via a sliding crosshead and connecting rods.

In 1826 George Stephenson was appointed engineer of a new passenger and freight railway between Liverpool and Manchester. The Newcastle works were taken over by his son Robert, who revolutionized much of the design; he was largely responsible for the multitube boiler that distinguished the "Rocket" of 1829 and set the pattern of future steam locomotive construction. Such a boiler had been pioneered also by the French engineer Marc Séguin. To be assured of steam's reliability for passenger haulage over a 30-mile route, the Liverpool and Manchester Railway directors organized the Rainhill Trials of October 1829, to assess the performance of several contending designs. "Rocket" alone passed the tests set; it touched 29 miles per hour on its own and maintained an average of 13.8 miles per hour with a load of nearly 13 tons. The railway era had started.

Meanwhile experiments were taking place with engines for use on the roads.

Spread of railways. The railway era had started in earnest. In 1830 the Liverpool and Manchester Railway became the first railway to seek primarily passenger traffic. It obtained at least half its income from passengers at the outset, building up an average daily traffic of more than 1,000 passengers, double the previous business of road coaches between the two cities. The 30 miles were covered in 90 minutes at an average fare of five shillings, about half the cost in time and money of the coaches. By 1843 fast trains in Britain were travelling 30–35 miles per hour, and by 1850 the best surpassed 40. Coach operators and canal owners were forced to give up the struggle.

Social impact of railways The same story was repeated in France and elsewhere on the European continent and in the United States. Everywhere the railway had tremendous social and economic impact, perhaps best illustrated by a statistic of population growth in Britain; in the first half of the 19th century the number of towns in England and Wales with populations of over 20,000 increased from 15 to 63, an increase for which the steam railroad was given substantial credit. (G.F.A.)

Railroad bridges and tunnels. Virtually the only important development in bridge building since Roman times had been the development of the elliptical masonry arch in place of the unnecessarily heavy and obstructive Roman circular arch. The advent of the railroad suddenly brought a demand for a vast number of bridges, many of great length, capable of carrying heavy loadings. The Stephensons were among the important pioneers of railroad bridges in Britain; Robert Stephenson's unique box girder, the Britannia Bridge (over the Menai Strait, in Wales), through which trains ran completely enclosed, became a national landmark. Capt. James B. Eads built the powerful triple-arch bridge over the Mississippi at St. Louis that inaugurated steel construction (1867–73). John and Washington Roebling built a number of suspension bridges that were capable of taking railroad loadings, notably over the gorge at Niagara Falls (1851–55) and over the East River between New York and Brooklyn (1869–83) (see also BRIDGES, CONSTRUCTION AND HISTORY OF).

The timber-truss bridge, pioneered principally by a number of American inventors in the early 19th century, was adapted for railroad loadings in iron, in a number of designs.

The invention of the tunnelling shield by Marc Brunel for his tunnel under the Thames, the world's first subaqueous tunnel (1828–42), made it possible to carry railroad traffic conveniently into major cities. The Mont Cenis Tunnel in the Alps, driven by Germain Sommeiller with the aid of dynamite and compressed-air drills (1857–71), similarly pioneered long-distance rock tunnelling, indispensable to the crossing of mountain ranges by railroad lines.   (H.N.G.)

Steam-powered road vehicles. In somewhat surprising contrast to the success of steam power on rails is its failure on roads. Many experiments were made, of which the most extensive were those of the English inventor Sir Goldsworthy Gurney, who produced a number of steam carriages that in his words resembled "common stage carriages but without the horses." Several regular services were started, some averaging between ten and 20 miles per hour with 20 or more passengers, but many difficulties were encountered, particularly regarding delays due to refuelling every few miles. By 1840 the first generation of steam carriages had come to a halt. Not until the end of the 19th century were further experiments successful, following which a number of steam buses were put on British roads, a few running in London up to World War I.
                                                           (G.F.A.)

Steam navigation. *The first steamships.* As early as 1685 a French physicist, Denis Papin, had asserted that steam propulsion could be utilized to drive a ship's paddle wheel. Credit for the first steamship to take the water also goes to France; in 1783 the "Pyroscaphe" managed to move upstream on the Saône River near Lyon for some 15 minutes. Two years later Joseph Bramah, an Englishman, took out a patent for a propeller; his patent application says, in part,

> instead of the paddlewheel may be introduced a wheel with inclined fans or wings . . . This wheel . . . may be . . . wholly under water, when it would . . . cause the ship to be forced backwards or forwards. . . .

It was many years, however, before the superiority of the propeller over the paddle wheel was recognized.

The first steamship to be put to practical use was the "Charlotte Dundas." She was built to replace the horses that hauled barges on the Forth and Clyde Canal in southern Scotland. In March 1802 she towed two 70-ton barges 19½ miles along the canal in about six hours against a strong wind. Horses continued to be preferred for canal work because of the damage caused to the canal banks by the action of the paddle-wheel blades; the "Charlotte Dundas" was laid up, and her builder, William Symington, died in poverty.

Robert Fulton's "Clermont"

Robert Fulton of the United States saw his first steamboat, after an initial disaster, successfully tested on the Seine in August 1804. He took his talents back to the United States, and the first steamship to go into commission was the "Clermont," built by him in 1807 and operating on the Hudson River. By travelling from New York, where she was built, to Philadelphia, the "Phoenix," built in 1807, can claim the distinction of being the first seagoing steamship.

The "Comet," launched on the Clyde in 1812, was the first merchant steamship in Europe. With a speed of 6.7 knots, she operated between Glasgow and the ports of Greenock and Helensburgh on the Clyde. The largest steamship of the day, 141.8 feet (43.2 metres) long and 47 feet (14 metres) wide at the paddle boxes, was the "James Watt," which plied on the coastal service between

London and Leith, in southeast Scotland. The first iron steamship was the "Aaron Manby," built in England but put into service on the Seine.

The first crossing of the Atlantic by a steamship was made by the "Sirius," built for the run between London and Cork but in fact chartered for traffic to the United States in 1838. This honour is sometimes claimed for the United States ship "Savannah." But the "Savannah" was in fact a fully rigged ship, with an accessory engine and collapsible paddle wheel, and when she made the crossing from the United States to Liverpool, during the summer of 1819, she very seldom used her machinery. The "Sirius" carried sail on two masts but relied much more on her paddle wheels, and they were in almost continuous use as she battled her way westward against strong winds.

The first propeller-driven ship to cross the Atlantic was the "Great Britain," in 1843. Designed by Isambard Kingdom Brunel, she was built wholly of iron. Her length was 322 feet (98 metres), her beam 50.5 feet (15.4 metres), and her draft 32.5 feet (9.9 metres), with a displacement of 3,618 tons. Confidence in steam was not yet firm, however, and the "Great Britain" carried, in addition to her engines, a total of 15,000 square feet (1,400 square metres) of sail on six masts.

In 1845 the British Admiralty, in an attempt to settle the propeller versus paddle wheel argument, arranged a tug-of-war between two steam sloops, the propeller-driven "Rattler," 888 tons with a 200-horsepower engine, and the paddle-driven "Alecto," 800 tons and also with a 200-horsepower engine. On a completely calm day the "Rattler" triumphed over the "Alecto" and succeeded in towing her stern-first at a speed of 2.8 knots.

From timber to iron. Iron took considerable time to oust timber as the principal component of a ship's hull. It was argued that ships built of iron would sink and that in the event of damage an iron hull would be more difficult to repair. Even when these and other fallacies had been disproved by experience, the shift to iron, and later to steel, was slow. The first iron ship was a barge launched on the Severn in 1787, but the first iron ship to cross the English Channel did not take the water until 1822; what was to become the great firm of Cammell Laird in Birkenhead, England, did not begin constructing iron ships until 1829, and Clydeside not until 1839.

Iron (and later steel) had the major advantages over wood of strength and economy of production; potentially, too, iron ships could be built to a greater length, 300 feet (90 metres) being reckoned the maximum safe length for a wooden ship. But what finally ensured the triumph of iron was the parallel development of steam power. Wooden ships were indeed built with paddle wheel or propeller, but as engines grew more powerful it was found that only an iron frame and an iron hull could withstand the vibration set up.

Brunel's "Great Eastern"

Built by Isambard Kingdom Brunel, and perhaps the most costly economic failure in the history of shipping, the "Great Eastern" was divided into ten watertight compartments, and the iron plating was double from keel to waterline. She was the only vessel in the world to carry two paddle wheels as well as a propeller. Her dimensions were: length 692 feet (211 metres), beam 82.7 feet (25.2 metres), draft 35 feet (11 metres), and her fully loaded displacement was 27,400 tons. Her speed was about 15 knots. Her six masts could spread a sail area of 58,000 square feet (5,400 square metres). She had passenger accommodations for 800 (first class), 2,000 (second), and 1,200 (third), a crew of 400, and a cargo-carrying capacity of about 6,000 tons. The "Great Eastern" was expected to cope successfully with the pitching and rolling experienced on the North Atlantic in bad weather; she did not, and the ship was unpopular with her passengers from the beginning. She turned out to be under-engined; few ports were large enough to handle her. She was an enormous economic liability and was sold for scrap in 1888. She did have one great achievement to her credit: the first telegraph cable between the United States and Europe was laid by her in 1865.

Sail held its own for many years and in many fields. The continuous expansion of seaborne trade throughout the

19th century called for more and more large and swift merchantmen of all kinds. These demands were met in part by the U.S. and British clipper ships, such as the "Flying Cloud" (U.S., 1851) and the "Cutty Sark" (U.K., 1869). The most famous of all clippers, the "Cutty Sark," was expressly designed to capture the China tea trade. But though oceangoing sailing ships were still being built in the early years of the 20th century, the battle for the means of propulsion of the long-distance oceangoing passenger liners, tramps, and bulk carriers had been effectively won before the turn of the century by steam, and the great fully rigged ships, with their graceful lines and their vast spread of sail, were a thing of memory.

Decline of the sailing fleets. The ascendancy that steam and motor vessels had established over sailing ships by the time of the outbreak of World War I is best illustrated by a comparison between the tonnages of the registered fleets of the principal maritime nations in 1886 and 1914. In the earlier year, vessels registered at ports in the British Empire totalled 11,166,000, of which 4,626,000 were sailing ships. In 1914 the gross figure was 21,046,000, of which only 522,000 represented sailing ships. Similar figures for the other leading maritime countries are (sailing ships in parentheses): France 1886, 1,057,000 (319,000), 1914, 2,319,000 (397,000); Germany 1886, 1,410,000 (806,000), 1914, 5,460,000 (325,000); United States 1886, 2,053,000 (1,587,000), 1914, 5,368,000 (1,038,000); Spain 1886, 521,000 (159,000), 1914, 899,000 (15,000); The Netherlands 1886, 419,000 (229,000), 1914, 1,497,000 (25,000). (Figures taken from *Lloyd's Register of Shipping.*)

(D.O'N.)

DEVELOPMENT OF MODERN TRANSPORTATION

The automobile. Although for two decades before the close of the 19th century there was much experimentation in the construction of road vehicles powered by the internal-combustion engine, not until the motorcar was mass-produced was the full impact felt by other forms of transport. Road transport, which had begun to encroach on rail and water transport before World War I, made great strides between the wars and challenged rail as the chief carrier of both passengers and goods in the two decades following World War II.

Although the automobile was pioneered in France, England, and Germany, it remained a novelty and a luxury until Henry Ford's Model T took to the road in the United States in 1908. A transport revolution followed, comparable in scale and effect to the Industrial Revolution of the previous century. The internal-combustion engine made a tremendous impact on the economic and social development of all developed countries and stimulated the advancement of underdeveloped countries by facilitating the opening up of previously inaccessible areas. Socially, by providing the individual with means of rapid personal travel, it provided a far wider choice of living space and consequently influenced urban environment. By generating a new volume of travel, the motor vehicle changed the relative importance of the different forms of transport and created a need for new and improved highways, resulting in expenditures on road networks comparable to that on the railways during the 19th century.

By the end of 1970 the United States had over 98,-000,000 motor vehicles on the roads. Two or three cars per family became common. In the United States there was one car for 2.5 persons, in Sweden one for 3.7 persons, in France one for 4.3 persons and in the United Kingdom one for every 4.8 persons. Japan had one car for every 14.3 persons, with the ratio rapidly increasing. The more densely populated countries had the greatest congestion problem with relatively more cars per road mile.

The impact of motorization on freight transport was equally significant, with the railways suffering a major encroachment. This trend continued at an accelerated rate through the 1960s and into the 1970s. In the U.S. between 1958 and 1968 ton-miles of intercity freight carried by motor trucks increased over 60 percent and in

1969 accounted for 21.5 percent of the total ton-miles of all such traffic. The trend in other countries was similar: in the United Kingdom in the same ten years the total ton-miles of freight carried by road nearly doubled while rail declined about 20 percent. Of the combined total of freight measured in ton-miles carried by road and rail, the former's share increased from 55.8 percent to 75 percent and rail's fell from 44.4 percent to 25 percent between 1958 and 1969.

To counter this encroachment on their traffic the railways streamlined their systems, closed uneconomical lines, consolidated freight depots, and reduced track mileage. Whereas U.S. railroads were operating 106,000 miles of passenger service track in 1958, the network totalled only 51,000 miles in 1970; in Europe, excluding the Soviet Union and eastern European countries, track mileage was reduced from 122,000 miles in 1953 to 110,000 miles in 1968. The railways also sought more efficient forms of traction, and by the 1970s steam had been eliminated from most of the major systems and replaced by diesel and electric traction. In Europe, steam traction, in terms of train-miles, in 1969 was less than 13 percent of the 1955 level, while electric traction more than doubled, and diesel traction more than quadrupled. Advanced forms of traction capable of higher speeds were being developed with gas-turbine locomotives hauling high-speed trains in France and North America.

By the 1970s the motor car was the accepted form of transport for the vast majority of families, and in many countries motor vehicles were carrying the larger proportion of freight. The passenger traffic of the railways was largely limited to commuter service and intercity travel up to the distances where air travel becomes practical. The role of the railroad in freight shipment was in the bulk shipment of goods and shipment of containers for transshipment by road or ship. (E.A.J.D.)

Roads, bridges, and tunnels. Modern road builders still use traditional materials, but quality is now closely controlled by scientific testing. Since World War II, machines have largely replaced hand labour; powerful diggers, scrapers, bulldozers, and graders handle the massive excavations needed in the cuttings and embankments of high-speed roads, and paving machines lay and surface both macadam and concrete roads. Modern pavers, guided by electronic sensors and preset alignment wires, can lay a mile of highway in a day. Firm foundations, efficient drainage, adequate thickness of base or slab, and strong antiskid surfaces are essential in good road building, as are adequate signs, markings, and lighting for the safe use of the finished road.

Bridge improvements during the past century stem from improved materials, new design concepts, more refined calculations, and better construction techniques. High strengths of concrete and steel, the development of steels resistant to brittle fracture at low temperatures, and, recently, the introduction of self-protecting steels to reduce maintenance costs have all helped to advance design. Computers have enabled engineers to save structural costs by quickly obtaining precise data. Wind effects on large structures are now better understood and can be confirmed by wind-tunnel tests.

Eugène Freyssinet's pioneer work in France on pre-stressed concrete, dating from 1928, marked a major advance in concrete construction, used in many notable bridges throughout the world. For the longest spans, steel suspension bridges are still favoured. This method was pioneered in the United States by John A. Roebling, whose greatest achievement, Brooklyn Bridge in New York City, was completed by his son in 1883. This was the first of many long suspension bridges constructed in the United States.

British engineers advanced the design of suspension bridges by substituting a shallow-plated box girder for the stiffening trusses and by inclining the suspenders for extra stability in the Severn Bridge linking England and Wales (1966). Steel box girders, acting on their own or compositely with concrete, have advanced the design of medium-span bridges (Tinsley Viaduct, Sheffield, England, 1968; and Europa Bridge, Austria), while box girders with cable stays can be used to attain spans of about 1,475 feet, or 450 metres (Severin, Cologne, West Germany, 1959).

The design of small bridges has been stimulated by their frequency on freeways, and, as more urban roads are built, refinements in elevated viaducts can be expected. In construction, rivetting has been almost entirely superseded by shop welding, and high-strength friction grip bolts are now used for site bolting. Foundation construction methods, especially in deepwater, continue to be improved.

Alpine tunnels for roads derive from the many 19th-century railway tunnels built throughout the world, but because tunnelling is very expensive and because motor vehicles can climb steep grades, there are as yet few major mountain-road tunnels. However, road traffic is now beginning to justify their cost on important routes as at Mont Blanc (7.8 miles, 1965) between Italy and France and Great St. Bernard (four miles, 1964) in the Swiss Alps and Straight Creek (1.6 miles, 1971) in the Colorado Rockies (see also TUNNELLING AND UNDERGROUND EXCAVATION).

Underwater tunnels for pedestrians, trains, and motor vehicles are to be found in many parts of the world. They avoid the use of high-level bridges over navigable waterways; and in populated areas, where they are usually found, they make less demand on surface space than bridges do. Since 1950 the trend has been toward the use of immersed tube tunnels, especially for estuarial crossings. Large prefabricated sections are built on shore, either of concrete or steel, then floated out and sunk into a trench in the riverbed. Urban tunnels, mostly short underpasses, are being built in many major cities to reduce traffic congestion.   (H.N.G.)

Mass urban transport. A phenomenon of the 19th century was the development of vehicle systems for movement in urban areas. Following introduction of the horse bus in Paris (1819), the word "omnibus" was coined and services were started in New York (1825) and London (1829). Increasing street traffic congestion brought the underground steam railway. London's first subway was completed in 1863. The first electric deep-level line, in London in 1890, was followed by lines in Budapest, Boston, Paris, New York, and eventually most of the world's great cities. Electric street tramways appeared in Berlin in 1881 and became general in many large cities. The electric trolleybus originated in France in 1901 and reached a peak of popularity 40 years later. High investment and fixed route characteristics were disadvantages, and it was progressively disappearing with the streetcar (tramway) after World War II. Streetcars are retained in some European cities.

The bus was motorized about the turn of the century, and after 1930 it became the most widely used form of public transport in urban areas. Outside urban areas a close mesh of rural and interurban services grew up. Routes and services were generally allocated by franchise and were subject to public service requirements and, frequently, fare control. Bus sizes expanded from the 34-passenger double-decker bus of 1910 to the 53-seat single-decker and 80-passenger double-decker bus of the 1970s.

With the great rise in automobile ownership after World War II, most developed countries shared the experience of a decline in patronage of urban public transport. Resultant traffic congestion led to deterioration in services, which declined even further with fares raised to meet growing deficits. Traffic management measures taken to meet the problem included priority treatment for buses, exemption from directional traffic regulations (one-way streets, turn bans, etc.), provision of segregated bus lanes and reserved rights of way, and priority at traffic signals. Electronic devices were also used to monitor vehicles and adjust headways and frequencies. To maintain uneconomic but socially desirable services in some countries, subsidies were granted from public funds and capital grants made to enable fleets to be modernized and new systems built or improved or extended. New rapid-transit systems were being constructed, as in Toronto, San Fran-

The
growth of
traffic
congestion

cisco, and Washington, D.C., and others were extended and improved, as in London and Paris. In the 1970s there was a growing realization of the need to maintain mass transportation to control automobile usage in city centres. The resultant trend was the consolidation of operators, to provide better integrated and organized services of all transport modes as in New York, Paris, and London. In Britain, Passenger Transport Authorities were made responsible for integrating all public transport services in four areas, while interurban bus services were merged into a publicly owned National Bus Company. Looking to the future, new forms of transport were being sought to provide services competitive with the automobile and thereby to attract patronage. But in the 1970s urban mass transportation had made no major technological advance comparable to those made by other forms of transportation.

For the most part mass transportation continued to be provided by the bus, streetcar, or rapid rail transit, as it had been since the 1920s. This accounted in part for its failure to meet the challenge of the automobile and for its subsequent decline.   (Ed.)

Traffic networks. The form of each road and traffic network is dictated by geographical, historic, and traffic factors; today, the traffic factor is perhaps the most important.

Networks emerged with the development and expansion of successful early settlements at harbours, river crossings, or mountain passes, or where minerals existed. The roads linking the settlements, large and small, formed the rural road networks. These sufficed for private and commercial travel until the 20th century, when the motor vehicle and road systems generally proved unfitted in alignment, construction, and safety for the new motor vehicle. Carrying heavy loads over long distances at high speeds, motor vehicles required new national highways, and in urban areas, which were the destinations of the majority of the journeys, traffic congestion made the replanning of road systems essential.

The growth of road networks can be followed especially well in the United States. The American road network gradually spread as settlers pushed westward. In the East, harbours, rivers, and mountains established road patterns, as did similar features in the far West, and the Mississippi River–Great Lakes system. In the Midwestern plains, land development based on surveys produced a grid network that was absorbed into the primary road system.

Before World War I, most countries had realized the need for improving existing rural networks. Existing roads were widened and straightened, new bypasses built around congested towns, old bridges realigned and strengthened. Only three countries, however, embarked at that time on the building of new long-distance national routes to supplement existing networks: the United States and Italy, where tolls were charged, and Germany, where the new autobahns were toll-free.

Since World War II, most advanced countries have modernized their rural networks with new road construction patterned for modern traffic. The United States led the way with its nationwide system of interstate highways, mainly freeways without tolls, all of which are dual carriageways (divided highways) with controlled access. When completed in 1972 the total system will comprise 42,500 miles (68,400 kilometres), and all large towns, harbours, and strategic sites will be served (see also ROADS AND HIGHWAYS).

Germany, with its 3,000 miles of autobahns, is building a further 8,000 miles due for completion in 1985. Italy is rapidly extending its prewar *autostrada* system, and in Britain 1,200 miles of motorway were in use during the early 1970s. France and Belgium are also constructing new national routes, and Japan had 600 miles in use in 1971 out of a total projected 4,700 miles. The United Nations through its various economic commissions sponsored the building of such intercontinental routes as the Asian Highway, while the Pan-American Highway system was initiated by the Organization of American States.

The adaptation of urban networks to modern needs is

difficult and expensive. Long-distance traffic can be removed from town centres by the provision of new routes, generally urban motorways, although in large towns and cities this through traffic is only a small proportion of all the total traffic movements.

Traffic engineering

Traffic engineering measures, including centralized regulation of traffic flow over wide areas by electronic computer, are now applied in many large urban areas to ensure the effective use of road space, while parking restrictions are used to deter journeys to city centres. A common pattern of the urban road system is a hierarchy of roads: primary roads, ring or tangential, coping with through traffic or bringing it to the periphery; radial roads bringing it to the city centre; and distributory roads serving it. The spacious layout of many American cities aided the containing of traffic, but construction of new urban expressway systems, of which Los Angeles has the most extensive, was general in the postwar period. More recently the trend has been to limit such construction and to consider the provision of mass transportation systems, especially rapid transit, with a view to restricting the use of the automobile, particularly for commuting to work.

(H.N.G.)

Air transportation. The rapid development of air transport might not have been possible but for military requirements and direct government aid, which, in some form, was made available almost universally until the 1950s, when the United States and United Kingdom terminated their subsidies or grants, but many other countries still continued to assist their national airlines and were doing so in the 1970s. Airlines were pioneered from 1919 onward by Britain and by European countries with relatively advanced aircraft industries and subsidies justified by the need for better communications, especially with overseas territories. Services followed in areas of Latin America, Canada, Africa, and Australia, where surface communications were slow, difficult, or nonexistent.

By contrast, airline progress in the United States was slow until 1930, though the Post Office had been operating coast-to-coast mail services from 1920 to 1927. Under the Air Mail Act of 1925 these services were taken over by the airlines themselves under contract. The mergers that resulted produced, by the mid-1930s, a pattern of internal trunk airlines that was to remain effectively unchanged for more than 35 years, while overseas routes were being continuously developed. The bigger airlines were capable of ordering fleets of specialized aircraft, such as the Boeing 247 and the Douglas DC-2 and, later, the highly successful DC-3. With a monopoly of overseas services and with ample government aid, Pan American World Airways advanced in the 1930s through Latin America and across the Pacific. Earlier, the European airlines had been extending their route networks through the continents of Asia and Africa.

In 1940 a system of controlled competition was introduced in the United States through the formation of the Civil Aeronautics Board (CAB), which was given the responsibility for route licensing. Elsewhere, competition had been limited by governments, by the sharing out of international traffic rights, and by tariff and other agreements reached by the then International Air Traffic Association.

The U.S. airlines, essentially unaffected by World War II and backed by a strong aircraft industry, were in a good position to advance rapidly after 1946. Further route expansion followed the CAB's decision in 1943 to encourage new airlines to operate subsidized feeder services over local networks connecting with the trunk routes.

The DC-4 and the Lockheed Constellation, which, with the DC-3, made worldwide postwar airline recovery possible, were the result of civil requirements, but war production meant that they were available quickly and in quantity. The more positive influences of the war were in progress with equipment such as navigation aids and radar, the ready acceptance of flying, and the availability of more and better airfields.

The requirements of war also provided the turbine (jet) engine, but air transport was already a major industry when this came into airline use in the late 1950s. Its most important effect was to reduce operating costs. These were reaching a practical minimum by the mid-1960s. Further reductions were possible only with big increases in payload capacity. The early 1970s saw the entry of the 300–450-seat "wide-body" jets, led by the Boeing 747. Whether the next generation of aircraft would be supersonic remained unresolved in the early 1970s, with the Anglo-French and Soviet projects well advanced. Vertical takeoff and landing (VTOL) aircraft were also being developed and could well have a considerable impact on the future pattern of civil aviation. Already, however, there was excess capacity, which arose when jet aircraft were first introduced; and the situation was repeated when the big jets were entering service in 1970. Nonetheless, new air routes were being continually developed, including those from Europe to the Far East over the North Pole.

The coming of the jets

Excluding figures for the Soviet Union and for non-scheduled carriers, world passenger traffic increased from 18,000,000 in 1946 to 310,000,000 in 1970. Practically every part of the world became accessible by air transport. By 1958 more passengers were travelling over the North Atlantic by air than by sea, and by 1970, 97 percent were travelling by air and only 3 percent by sea.

(H.A.T.)

TRANSPORTATION TRENDS

New forms of transportation have always evoked new problems, not least because each new mode has required an increasing amount of land space for its tracks and vehicles both in movement and at rest.

The universal availability of present automobile transport has not only made a vast demand for land use but also has created ecological and environmental problems. Transportation and land-use studies and the drawing of development and transport and traffic plans have become essential to contain uncontrolled use of both land and transport and to ensure the availability of suitable transport facilities. But their implementation would be of little value without the application of the latest technologies to the transport modes needed. Technology is being exploited to produce transportation systems that make the least demand on land use and cause the minimum of congestion in urban areas but maximize the return on capital already invested in existing forms and new capital investments.

On the railways, replacement of steam by electric and diesel traction has made possible far higher overall average speeds, and many scheduled services now run at over 100 miles per hour on existing tracks and faster in Japan on such specially constructed tracks as those of the New Tōkaidō Line. New forms of traction are being developed: turbo trains are in service in Canada and France and on the Metroliner in the "northeast corridor" between Washington and Boston in the U.S. Other new forms of traction being developed include the tracked hovertrain, an air-cushion vehicle propelled by linear induction motors, which is being studied in Britain, France, and the United States. In addition, the advanced passenger train (APT) being built in Britain represents an entirely new approach by applying aeronautical principles to the conventional train to raise its speed to 150 miles per hour and eventually to 250 or more, on existing tracks.

On the road a major thrust of effort is certain to be the application of electronics to increase traffic control. Centralized computer control of signals over a wide area is already in use in many cities, and its effectiveness is being continuously improved. Another approach is to bring automation to the vehicle on the highway. Experiments are being conducted on systems for guiding vehicles and controlling their progress by electronic impulses transmitted from circuits in or outside the road and received by the vehicle. Many other new concepts of transport systems and vehicles for urban transportation are being considered, while others have reached the development stage. One concept in a variety of forms is for driverless vehicles to be routed by computer to a destination preselected by the passengers. One variety would link the

The driverless car

vehicles on guideways after the passengers had driven them there. Other systems are based on the conveyor belt that travels continuously, with passengers boarding and leaving from moving walkways. Many types of electric cars are being tried out to combat air pollution but are waiting for a breakthrough in battery development, while the mounting traffic-accident rate has led to a search for new designs to produce safer cars.

Another possibility for future travel is the gravity-vacuum train, consisting of wheeled trains in tubes rolling downhill at great speed and then being propelled by a combination of the acquired momentum and vacuum pressure for the uphill section of the journey.

At sea the supertanker of up to 1,000,000 tons' capacity, the giant container ship, and the barge-carrying ship are among foreseen developments. The air-cushion principle, mentioned earlier in connection with advanced rail designs, has been successfully applied to water craft, and many types are in civilian and military service. In the air, supersonic liners and vertical takeoff and landing aircraft may serve the airlines of the future.

Another form of transport being developed is the pipeline, through which an increasing variety of products may be carried. While some of these concepts may prove impracticable, others not yet conceived may be evolved and radical changes in transport, not yet imagined, may take place in the last decades of the 20th century.

(E.A.J.D.)

BIBLIOGRAPHY

General: CHARLES SINGER et al. (eds.), *A History of Technology,* vol. 1–5 (1954–58), an authoritative and standard work containing much material on the history of transportation; JOSEPH NEEDHAM, *Science and Civilisation in China,* vol. 1–2 (1954), a history of the discovery, invention, and technological development in China through the centuries; EDWIN A. PRATT, *A History of Inland Transport and Communication in England* (1912); C.I. SAVAGE, *An Economic History of Transport,* rev. ed. (1966).

Ships: JAMES HORNELL, *Water Transport: Origins and Early Evolution* (1969), a general and comprehensive account of the development of seagoing vessels; BJORN LANDSTROM, *Das Schiff* (Eng. trans., *The Ship,* 1961), an authoritative, readable, and even romantic history of ships.

Railways: C.F. DENDY MARSHALL, *A History of Railway Locomotives Down to the End of the Year 1831* (1953); J.G. WARREN, *A Century of Locomotive Building by Robert Stephenson & Co., 1823–1923* (1923); and ANGUS SINCLAIR, *Development of the Locomotive Engine* (1907), three well-documented histories of the steam locomotive; C.B. ANDREWS, *The Railway Age* (1937), an introduction to the study of early British railways and the various social and political reactions to their development; H. PERKING, *The Age of the Railway* (1970), a later account of railway development; R.M. HAYWOOD, *The Beginnings of Railway Development in Russia in the Reign of Nicholas I, 1835–1842* (1969); O.S. NOCK, *Railways at the Turn of the Century: 1895–1905* (1969), the first volume of a projected six-volume set that will cover the history of the major world lines from the early 19th century to the present.

Roads: JOHN COPELAND, *Roads and Their Traffic, 1750–1850* (1968), the story of the construction and use of Britain's roads and of the carriage of goods, passengers, and mail on them; R.S. PILCHER, *Road Passenger Transport* (1937), a general study of the evolution, administration, and operation of road public transport, covering bus, tram, and trolleybus in Britain, up to World War II; HERMANN SCHREIBER, *Merchants, Pilgrims, and Highwaymen: A History of Roads Through the Ages* (1962).

Air: R.E.G. DAVIES, *A History of the World's Airlines* (1964), the definitive record of the development of airline structures, aircraft, and their operations from infancy to the jet age; ROBIN HIGHAM, *Britain's Imperial Air Routes, 1918–1939* (1960), a detailed account of the early history of Britain's air communications with its Commonwealth and Empire.

(H.A.T./G.F.A./H.N.G./D.O'N./E.A.J.D.)

Transportation, Urban

Urban transportation includes the movement of people and materials within any town or city but particularly within large metropolitan areas. In the last third of the 20th century, such movement was primarily by automo-

bile and truck powered by internal-combustion engines, despite the fact that mass transit had long been recognized in all developed countries as desirable and necessary.

Before taking up the problems and possible solutions within the framework of urban transportation itself, it should be observed that solutions may come from technological advances outside the system. The picturephone, facsimile transmission, and other developments in communications may reduce the need for person-to-person contacts and eliminate many trips now considered necessary. Energy presently transported by railroads or trucks in the form of coal or oil can also be moved by pipelines. Generating plants can be built at mine mouths or other nonurban areas, and electricity can be transmitted by buried, high-voltage power lines to the urban area. Advances in building construction may also have large impact on transportation by facilitating development of more efficiently organized urban agglomerations.

HISTORY

While freight movement by water determined the location of many cities, major local transportation has rarely been by boat. Wheels have been paramount from the horse-drawn buggy and omnibus to the bicycle, streetcar, subway, and automobile. The first successful omnibus service was inaugurated in Paris in 1819; within a dozen years, London, New York, and other major cities had copied the idea. Electric traction was tried out in Richmond, Virginia, in 1888, followed by a rapid spread of electric transit first in the U.S. and then in Europe.

Meanwhile, London had pioneered the subway, or underground, as early as 1862 with a line of about four miles connecting the principal railroad terminals. The line was so successful that it was rapidly expanded, taking advantage of a tunnel driven under the Thames River a generation earlier by Marc Brunel; the tunnel had been intended for vehicular use, but suitable approaches had not been constructed. From this beginning the City and South London Railway grew, at first using steam traction and later (1890) electricity. Budapest, Boston, Paris, Berlin, New York, and other cities followed in rapid succession; within a few years hundreds of miles of subway were built, mostly by trenching streets and covering over (cut-and-cover method). A parallel development was the interurban system of electric surface traction, widely used in suburban areas and between small, neighbouring cities.

First subway

Like the subway the elevated railroad was conceived and built before electric traction, the first operating with a cable drive on Ninth Avenue, New York City, in 1867, and shifting in 1871 to steam locomotives. The first elevated to be equipped with electric power was the West Side Metropolitan Elevated Railroad in Chicago in 1895, soon followed by all other such railroads. The first use of multiple-unit cars, in which most units are powered but controlled from a single location, also came in Chicago, on the South Side Elevated, in 1897.

The last major component of the modern urban transportation system to arrive on the scene, but the one with the largest impact of all, was the automobile. As early as World War I, the automobile was an important user of city streets, especially in the U.S. but also in Europe; taxicabs were numerous enough in Paris in 1914 to be commandeered for a critical troop movement in the Battle of the Marne. Motor buses began to make a significant impact in the 1920s, especially in the U.S., where by mid-century they had nearly replaced electric streetcars. Buses received favoured treatment from government in the belief that they provided advantages, some of which, such as routing flexibility, subsequently proved illusory. Britain and France followed the U.S. lead, but other European countries generally retained their streetcars. In the U.S., the expectation that bus service could be upgraded through such devices as reserved lanes on freeways or preferential access at intersections was not widely borne out. In Detroit an experiment with operation of buses on freeways showed rider resistance and preference for the old surface-street routes. In Europe, efforts were made to separate tramlines from automobile traffic by placing them at the side of highways or on elevated tracks, by building grade separations at main intersections, and, especially in West Germany, by using special vehicles with high manoeuvrability.

The automobile's relationship to mass-transit systems proved complicated. As soon as commuter railroads developed in the late 19th century, isolated suburban clusters began to form. Streetcars and interurbans extended the reach of the railroads and filled in gaps in the system. The automobile, however, played the principal role both in extension and filling in, thus becoming indispensable to suburban living. The automobile thus created further demand for highways and expressways, both around and into the central business district. Expressway development both in the U.S. and Europe so accelerated growth in city and suburban areas that the word megalopolis was coined (or, more precisely, revived) to describe such areas as the chain of metropolitan regions along the northeast U.S. coast. The density of traffic in such areas had the effect of reducing the value of the automobile; by the 1960s, technologically innovative transportation modes were under consideration.

Possibly even more important in the changes in transportation thinking in the 1960s and 1970s was the growing conviction that land use must be planned. This concept was much more widely accepted in Europe than in the U.S., where the multiplicity of local and regional political units created a chaotic situation. In some small countries such as Sweden, it appeared possible to predict future land use, to design construction as transit lines were extended, to build roads to complement the transit lines, and thus to have appropriate facilities available when the suburb was developed rather than setting in motion an uncontrolled cycle of growth.

Planning land use

PROBLEMS OF URBAN TRANSPORTATION

The automobile's readiness and versatility has been the catalyst of spectacular suburban growth in almost all developed countries, making possible the exploitation of unused land areas farther out from the central city. The experience of Japan, Europe, and the U.S. has been the same; those who can afford new houses can afford automobiles to reach them.

Yet even apart from the inevitable pattern of overgrowth and congestion, public transit systems are indispensable for the large groups of persons who cannot drive autos, such as the poor, the very young or very old, and the disabled. In recent years a need for public transit has been shown in cities as small as 30,000.

Traditionally, transportation problems have been considered under the headings of cost and convenience, meaning primarily speed of travel. To these aspects have now been added such questions as pollution abatement and safety, the latter a question of increasing complexity.

High costs. In most countries the history of mass transit has been a history of maintenance problems versus rising fares. Lengthened trips combined with popular resistance to fare increases create maintenance problems; when these become acute, fares rise, often sharply. Flat fares discourage the short-distance rider, who may pay two or three times as much per mile as the long tripper. Zone fares are difficult and expensive to collect. Too often the result is a cycle of rising flat fares that discourages short-distance passengers and reduces revenue gains.

Another aspect of rising costs in mass transit is the substitution of subways for surface lines; a system such as the Montreal subway built in the 1960s cost 1,000 or 2,000 times as much per mile or kilometre as did the surface transportation that served the city at the turn of the 20th century.

While costs of both automobiles and highways have likewise risen steadily, apparent in Europe, the U.S., and Japan has been the willingness of the public to pay more for automobiles and to support highway construction through bond issues and toll collections while exhibiting marked resistance to paying more for improved mass transit. Signs of this public attitude have even become discernible in the Communist countries.

Social effects. The high cost of urban transportation has invariably fallen most heavily on the poorest classes, who pay a higher proportion of family income for transportation, and often cannot find adequate means of reaching employment. In modern industrial centres new jobs tend to be located away from the congested districts where the poor traditionally live.

Speed of travel. Normal walking speed for a man has remained at about 3.1 miles (4.9 kilometres) per hour since the beginning of recorded history. Horses and horse-drawn omnibuses raised the speed of travel to approximately 6 miles (10 kilometres) per hour. Buses and trolleys provide average speeds of 5 to 6 miles per hour in rush-hour traffic to 12–14 miles per hour on most city streets in other time periods. Speeds of up to 50 miles (80 kilometres) per hour are often reached by buses in outlying streets of large cities, but schedule speeds, which include stopping times, are much lower.

Studies of relative speeds of principal mid-20th-century urban-transit modes showed average automobile speeds of up to 19 miles per hour, compared with 16 miles per hour for suburban railroads, and substantially less for other mass transit. While doubtless valid statistically, such studies are misleading because of the different functions of the different types of transit. To gain a real picture of urban transit speeds in a city like Paris or New York would require a rationale that included the number of persons moved per mile, how near the centre of the city the movement took place, and also station spacing. Broadly speaking, it may be said that while speed of movement, especially during rush hours, still leaves something to be desired in most cities, it is not as critical a problem as that of costs.

Pollution. The relationship between air pollution and health began to be investigated in the 1950s, with London pioneering in research and abatement. The importance of automobile emissions in air pollution in urban centres was well established by 1970. The diesel engine, widely used in freight movement by truck and railroad both in Europe and the U.S., has been found to contribute a relatively minor amount as compared with the gasoline engine almost universally used on passenger vehicles. Because urban travel is largely start and stop and emissions are generally higher when vehicles are idling, it can probably be assumed that more than half of the motor-vehicle pollutants are concentrated in urban areas. Efforts were underway in the 1970s to eliminate lead from gasoline and otherwise reduce emissions.

Another side effect of urban transportation is noise pollution, which takes the form of rumbling elevated railroads, aircraft takeoffs and landings, and trucks and autos in heavy concentrations on freeways and downtown streets. Such European cities as Rome, Florence, Genoa, Marseilles, and Dijon, with ancient or medieval street layouts, are especially noisy.

So-called visual pollution by the urban transport system is another cause of urban blight. The abandoned automobile, for example, stripped of useful parts and not valuable enough as scrap to pay for removal, is a growing problem in the U.S. Another form of visual pollution is actually hazardous; many municipalities have done a poor job in maintenance of street hardware, permitting saturation of intersections with confusing directional signs that fight for space with commercial signs. Long delays in repairing broken street lights and even broken traffic signals are also dangerous as well as unsightly.

Many U.S. cities fail to keep streets adequately clean. Some European and Japanese cities set a better standard, despite high concentrations of vehicles and people.

Finally, the automobile has produced what might be termed space pollution, simply through its ubiquity. Parking lots now occupy squares and open spaces; in many cities, sidewalks have been reduced in width to accommodate extra traffic lanes for automobiles. In such European cities as Naples, and throughout the tropics, people normally overflow the sidewalks into the streets.

Several interesting experiments have been carried out to restrict or eliminate automobile traffic from certain sections or streets. Rome barred motor vehicles from one of

Space pollution

its principal squares, the spacious Piazza Navona. Other Italian cities, such as Pisa, closed streets to auto traffic at certain hours. New York and other cities have temporarily or permanently closed some of their main avenues for the benefit of shoppers and strollers. Side streets may be closed for the benefit of children. These measures, however, have hardly counteracted the prevailing trend toward greater and greater domination of the city by the automobile.

Safety hazards. Though transportation in all ages has involved hazards to life and limb, the appalling toll in deaths and injuries brought by the automobile in the 20th century raises entirely new questions. Even if private automobiles can be shown to provide a substantially greater convenience, it is uncertain that a rationale can be supplied for their use in competition with safer public transit. The London underground, for example, had only one serious accident, in which 12 were killed, throughout the 1950s and 1960s. The Paris Metro had no deaths between 1930 and the late 1960s. The Tokyo subway had no deaths during the 1960s. The Toronto subway had no accidents in the 15 years following its opening in 1954.

Other types of urban mass transit, such as buses, have much less dramatic records but are still far ahead of the private automobile in safety.

Planning problems. Attempts by government agencies and others to plan systems to meet urban transit needs encounter chronic problems. The type and quality of transit systems that may be technically feasible a few years hence are difficult to predict safely; in addition, the public response even to improved versions of existing systems is difficult to determine. That people want a substantially improved urban-transit system in Tokyo, New York, and London cannot be doubted; how much they are willing to pay for what degree of improvement is uncertain. When the long lead time involved in planning a new or radically altered transportation system is taken into account, it becomes evident that considerable courage is needed on the part of planning authorities. In countries where public ownership or substantial government control over land use exists, some of the more obvious problems can be mitigated.

ELEMENTS OF URBAN TRANSPORTATION

Streets, expressways, and associated facilities. Since cities first developed, the construction and maintenance of urban streets have been almost exclusively a governmental function. Many methods of classification have been used in attempts to define street networks in a systematic way to provide for maintenance and expansion. One widely used method is based on volume of through traffic; those with nearly 100 percent through traffic are classed in the highest category, with high speeds and maximum traffic control required; those with the lowest percent of through traffic are placed in the lowest category. The classification is complicated by the obvious fact that most urban streets are in an intermediate role, carrying several kinds of traffic. This necessitates an attempt to classify on the basis of the predominant role of a given street, which may vary at different times of day and may change over a period of time.

Street planning

Street planning has always been a complex process, involving local commissions, intermediate agencies, and national governmental authorities. Land-use problems in metropolitan areas are particularly troublesome. Political agencies that let design contracts for new highways in urban areas permitted wide latitude to the engineers in determining location as well as design and construction details; this is done because intruding an expressway into the tightly congested metropolitan area involves major technological problems. A good illustration is furnished *by the Arch of Triumph tunnel in Paris. The rotary traffic pattern, without traffic lights, at the twelve-way intersection that circles this famous monument was established in the early years of the century and served very well until the congestion of the 1950s and 1960s. The problem was defined as finding a route that would keep through traffic out of the rotary pattern. The solution undertaken in

1968 was an underpass of almost one-quarter mile capable of passing 200,000 vehicles a day under the Arch of Triumph. The presence of five subway (Metro) tunnels, various pedestrian walkways and utility lines, and a large parking garage complicated the work, which also had to be carried out with minimum disturbance of existing traffic patterns. The crowns of three of the subway tunnels had to be removed to make room for the two-lane roadway.

Many other ingenious devices have served engineers attempting to reduce congestion and facilitate through traffic in cities. In several cities waterways have been used as sites, with a new expressway occupying the bed of a disused canal, or with an expressway built out over one side of a river. But for most expressway projects demolition and removal of residences and businesses is necessary, which creates problems much broader than the merely technological. Not only engineers, but sociologists, city planners, political scientists, and architects are commonly involved in the decision making.

Even after an urban expressway is completed, problems arise because of the difficulty of performing maintenance work on a road surface in constant use.

Parking. In recent years urban parking has gone increasingly underground, though above-ground, multilevel structures are still being built. In Europe and the U.S. it is becoming more and more common to integrate parking with new office and residential buildings by utilizing the lower several floors. Another trend is to reserve the surface above the underground structure for park space.

Traffic control. A complex traffic-control system embracing several transportation modes is inseparable from modern urban movement. Auto-traffic devices range from parking meters and signal lights to automatic scanners that measure traffic flow and adjust lane entrances. One problem is uniformity; a present goal is to establish worldwide sign standards. Western Europe has long employed an ingenious system of wordless signs, on which symbols indicate "no entrance," "one-way street," "stop," and other directives, thus overcoming the language barrier (see also TRAFFIC CONTROL).

Surface transit. Many European and American cities abandoned electric trolley systems in favour of buses, which were believed to have certain advantages. Some of the advantages have proven illusory—for example, the greater flexibility of routing possible with buses. In addition, buses are contributors to air pollution, albeit primarily disagreeable odours. In the 1960s San Francisco, Philadelphia, and Boston, in the U.S., and Hamburg, Frankfurt, and other cities in Europe were maintaining and expanding their limited surface transit lines (tramlines). In some European cities, limited tramlines are being built in parkways or moved to one side of expressways or other through road arteries.

Interurban transit lines have also largely been abandoned in the U.S., despite remnants in Chicago, Philadelphia, and elsewhere. In Europe and Japan, several such lines survive, some in private ownership, most government operated. In the 1970s, however, the gasoline or diesel-powered bus has become the most ubiquitous form of mass transit for the whole world.

Interurban lines

Subway and elevated transit. Subways are best adapted for carrying large numbers of people over short and medium distances into and through the central business district. The money savings achieved by building elevated lines has been shown to represent false economy in the long run because of the damaging effects of elevated structures on business and residential streets. Though arguments have been advanced that aesthetically pleasing and quiet monorail lines could be built in city streets, present experience is not favourable. Though most world fairs of recent years have had monorail systems, and Dallas has a short line connecting the airport parking area to one passenger terminal, no successful system has been built for a central business district.

Subways have continued to be built despite mounting costs and engineering problems because they are the most satisfactory solution to moving large numbers of people inside a city. They do no damage to streets and neigh-

Proposed Rail Transit Service Standards

service standards	subway-elevated	supersubway	suburban rapid transit	suburban railroad
Service territory (distance from Manhattan)	0–11 m	9–17 m	15–35 m	25–50 m
Average service speed	22 mph	35 mph	45 mph	45 mph
Peak-hour period passenger loading				
Passengers per track	48,000	40,000	30,000	30,000
Percent seated	30%	60%	100%	100%
Service frequency (outlying lines)				
Peak period	4 min	6 min	8 min	15 min
Off peak	8 min	12 min	15 min	30 min
Night-weekend	12 min	20 min	30 min	60 min
Fare level	$.15	$.25–$.45	$.50–$1.00	$.75–$1.40
Train characteristics				
Car type	standard rapid transit	modified rapid transit	modified rapid transit	standard suburban
Seats per car	50	80	100	125
Hourly trains per track	30	30	30	20
Hourly cars per track	300	300	300	240
Manhattan distribution	subway	subway	subway or terminal	terminal

Source: The City of New York, *Metropolitan Mobility*.

bourhoods overhead; and on the contrary they usually contribute to rising land values. The Toronto subway is a good example of the common effect of increasing population density along a new line.

The stations on the newest subway lines are much improved over those built early in the century; in some, as the Moscow and Rome subways, serious efforts have been made to create aesthetically pleasing as well as comfortable and convenient station facilities. The newer aluminum and stainless steel subway cars are also much improved, with easily cleaned plastic or plastic-covered seats, and increasingly, with air conditioning. Recorded vocal announcements and visual displays assist strangers and speed passenger loading and unloading. Higher rates of acceleration in the all-powered-car trains further increase overall speeds.

Automatic systems control has been installed in some subways, including a variety of automatic fare collection devices. Television monitoring of stations by central observers is increasingly provided, along with radio communications, also widely used for bus spacing.

Commuter rail service. Suburban or commuter railroads grew out of the desire of 19th-century railroad management to increase the number of collection and distribution points in metropolitan areas for its long-range passenger service. With long-range rail service undergoing radical modification in most of the world and facing abandonment in some areas, notably in the U.S., this concept is far out of date, yet suburban rail service has become an increasingly indispensable component of metropolitan transit. The situation has led toward increasing participation in suburban rail management of governments and commuter groups, with ultimate results yet to be seen. In the U.S., public agencies formed for the purpose in various metropolitan areas have sought operational control of suburban lines (see also RAILROADS AND LOCOMOTIVES).

The supersubway. One increasingly discernible tendency of the early 1970s, worldwide, was a blurring of distinction between rapid-transit lines and suburban railroads. In some cities, such as Philadelphia and Boston, in the U.S., standard subways have been extended over suburban railroad lines. In some cases the suburban rail lines have been abandoned by the former operators, and in some the subway trains are being integrated into an ongoing operation. In 1965 the New York City Planning Commission outlined what may be the shape of metropolitan rapid transit in the world's large cities in the later years of the century. The commission proposed that rail transit be differentiated by service standards only and suggested the plan shown in the Table for the differentiation.

The supersubway would have a higher fare than present subway–elevateds in New York, but would provide seating for 60 percent of the riders instead of 30 percent, thus giving better service for those more able to pay. Better service includes higher speeds, more seats, and transverse seats giving better support during acceleration and deceleration. The service would not operate as frequently, but its quality would be upgraded.

People movers. The moving stairway, or escalator, is one of the earliest examples of a people mover. Although initially provided inside retail establishments to replace the elevator, today such stairways facilitate the movement of people in railroad or subway stations as they move upstairs or down in the station or from station to street. Although fewer have been constructed, the moving sidewalk is similar to the moving stairway in concept. Generally, a moving sidewalk is a rubber belt approximately 30 inches (76 centimetres) wide, carried on rollers, and is equipped with a moving handrail. The belt is rigid enough to carry the load between rollers but flexible enough to turn around drums at each end. Other designs use a belt that is rigid in the centre with rollers at the edge. Entering and leaving requires some agility, so that people with slow reflexes, particularly the elderly, often find it difficult to utilize these facilities. Consequently, though speeds of 10 miles (16 kilometres) per hour are possible, present units rarely operate at more than one-fifth this speed.

Moving sidewalks

Mixed modes. In its broad sense, the term mixed modes simply refers to the use of more than one technology for a single trip; thus the Japanese and western European combination of bicycle and commuter railroad is a mixed mode. A narrower form of mixed mode is two kinds of public transportation, such as railroad or subway train and city bus. A possibility under discussion on the 1970s is a cross of taxicab and bus to provide an on-call form of public transportation from suburban or metropolitan home to railroad or subway terminal. A computer would be programmed with appropriate data, and when a telephone call activated the system the computer would assign an available vehicle to pick up the passenger. The computer would further optimize the route of the vehicle for origins and destinations.

Another possibility is that small vehicles or buses could be designed to operate on both railroad tracks, or other types of guideways, and on city streets. These vehicles would pick up passengers along the street system, move to a guideway and travel off-street and out of congestion to their destination. Railroads have equipment permitting track supervisors to drive on-street to a section of track, drop steel-flanged wheels onto the track structure, and drive along the track for inspection purposes. Similarly, buses have been equipped with retractable flanged wheels and axles to permit operation on either streets or rails. Technical problems with this type of vehicle will require substantial sums of money and time to resolve, relating primarily to the truck design and quality of the ride. The vehicle must be light enough to travel easily over the roads but heavy enough to function on track or structure

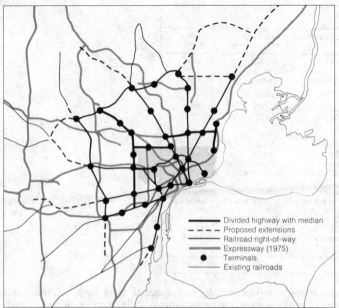

Figure 1: Artist's conception of a dual-mode guideway network superimposed on Detroit and its suburbs utilizing rail, air rights, and expressway median strips. The dots illustrate the location of local stations where ingress and egress can be made. In most cases, these are near shopping centres, airports, the central business district, as well as residential areas.
By courtesy of Ford Motor Company

in moderate snow. Inadequate maintenance of lightly used track is a problem, and proponents of this system have rarely estimated the cost of upgrading and signalizing track for frequent use by small vehicles. Union conflicts can also be anticipated as the technique bridges transit and rail modes where different labour unions have contracts.

Just as trucks are being moved on flatcars, or containers on trucks and flatcars or both, it has been suggested that passenger containers be loaded in key sectors of a city and flown to airports by helicopter. When this proposal was evaluated in Los Angeles, investigators concluded that it was not feasible at the time. Special vehicles designed to move passengers from terminal to airplace, however, are being utilized at major airports in such cities as London and Washington, D.C.

NEW CONCEPTS AND NEW TECHNOLOGY

Increasing efforts are being put forward on many levels in all of the developed countries to untangle the urban transportation problem. These include both modes of conceptualization and technological innovations (Figure 1).

The systems concept. The systems approach, which has been used successfully in solving many complex engineering problems, has an obvious application to urban transportation. The systems engineer seeks to analyze a large problem by identifying its components and calculating the approximate effects of the trade offs that can be made among them. In viewing urban transportation, he asks such questions as these:

Is a cardinal aim the reduction of congestion in the central business district? Must congestion also be reduced on all links of the system or is there a tolerable level that can be permitted on some? Are these radial or circumferential to the central business district? How important is safety? Must the present automobile accident rate be radically reduced? How important are the transportation requirements of nondrivers? Must air and noise pollution be reduced? By how much?

Once the list of factors is determined and put in reasonable order of importance, engineers synthesize a design and analyze its performance, estimated cost, and socioeconomic attributes. The engineer can easily state the performance anticipated from the design in factors like acceleration and deceleration, overall speed, noise levels, and amount of pollutants from the engine. Cost of facilities can readily be estimated, especially for subsystems or components that have already been built. It is more dif-

ficult to evaluate the socioeconomic attributes and to weigh the costs of externalities to the system. Externalities are those factors that affect third parties who have no direct connection with the system. How important is it to soundproof the track of a transit line that goes through a densely populated neighbourhood? What is it worth to reduce air pollution if emission meets the present public health standards but still has an adverse impact on health or increases the cost of laundry for citizens living nearby? As difficult as such evaluations are, they must be attempted.

After making his evaluation, the engineer attempts to correct the deficiencies where the design falls below the established goals or the ranking of the criteria. Correcting the deficiencies may increase the cost, so cost estimates must be changed. When the new design is completed it is evaluated by the same process. Reiteration continues until the design is acceptable in terms of performance, cost, and socioeconomic effects.

Correcting design deficiencies

Unfortunately, the decision-making process in respect to urban transportation is fraught with so many complications that the systems approach at present promises only limited benefits. Government authorities overlap; pressure groups abound. A small town or village may block the development of an off-street transit line that would benefit a whole region. This is especially a problem in the U.S., but there are serious difficulties in applying the systems approach to metropolitan transit everywhere.

Technological innovations. Of the many directions of research on road transportation under active pursuit in the 1970s, perhaps that of most immediate interest for urban transportation is the automatically controlled vehicle. One imaginative concept involves completely relieving the driver of responsibility, substituting an electronic roadway control connected to a central computer system. The principal aim would be to increase safety. Cost estimates, however, run very high. Another possibility is to have the vehicle operate under its own power and driver on local streets but move onto a guideway with central power and control for longer distances. Among the many problems of such a system is the prospective overloading of ramps leading to and from guideways.

Another version, designed to eliminate the downtown parking problem, would provide an army of small vehicles that would be automatically controlled once the destination was identified. So ambitious a system probably will have applicability, even when technical problems are solved, only within a "new city," which can be designed with the system in mind or reconstruction of a very large area.

In mass transit, several intriguing ideas have been put forward. One, the gravity-vacuum tube system (Figure 2), is a new model of a concept dating to the 19th century; a train that would be accelerated and braked by a combination of gravity and atmospheric pressure. The

Gravity-vacuum tube system

After a painting by Pierre Mion © 1969 National Geographic Society

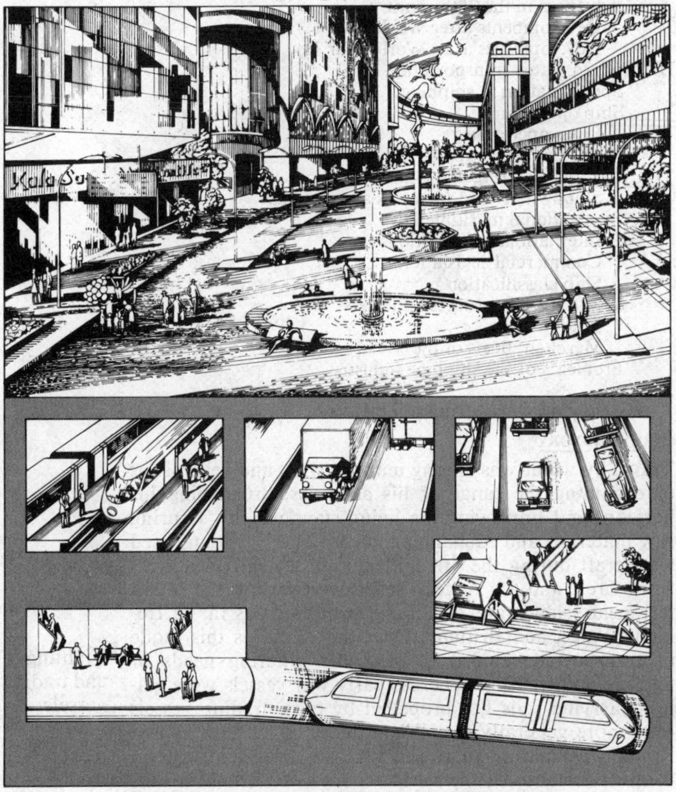

Figure 2: *Possible urban transportation system of the future.* In this system, streets are for pedestrian use. Underground, starting at left, is space for trains, truck traffic, automobile traffic, and special capsules directed by computer and capable of carrying four persons. At the lowest level is a pneumatic train, which travels between stations by means of gravity and air pressure (see text).

train would be circular in cross section and considerably longer than most trains, with the wheels located between the cars and inset so that the train could act as a seal while in the tunnel. The tube would descend from each station and rise toward the next. Gravity would reinforce the pressure from the atmosphere, exerted as air was evacuated from the portion of the tube in front of the train. The economy of power makes the idea attractive, but several problems remain, among which is the cost of the tunnel construction and the difficulty of precise braking.

Another old concept that has been tried with success in France and elsewhere is the linear-induction electric motor, in which the stator (magnetic coil) is attached to the vehicle while the "rotor" is stretched out flat to become the rail along which the train runs. High speeds have been attained; costs and reliability appear favourable. The possibility of combining linear induction with air-cushion support is promising (see also ELECTRIC MOTOR).

Less innovative in detail is the Japanese National Railroad's new lines; the New Tokaido, opened between Tokyo and Osaka in the mid-1960s, has proved that conventional railroad technology, when fully exploited, can produce a highly satisfactory high-speed system.

In the air helicopters have a growing potential for many roles, and vertical takeoff and short takeoff aircraft (VTOL and STOL) may be useful within metropolitan regions as well as between cities, though existing forms present noise problems.

Research and development programs are under way in

Europe, the U.S., Japan, and other countries on these and many other possibilities. The Railway Technical Research Institute of Japan, the British Railways Board, the French National Railways, and other national railroad systems, though concerned with the problem of rail transportation generally, produce valuable information for urban transit. Such national railroad systems have usually found government research grants easier to obtain than is the case with privately owned railroads.

Despite the efforts of these and many other agencies, public and private, the most important requirement of urban transportation in the 1970s remains funds for research and development. The cost of developing a system capable of meeting the needs of today's congested, pollution-plagued metropolis is fully comparable to that of a major space program. Only a public and government commitment on such a scale can produce favourable results.

BIBLIOGRAPHY. Surveys of the current status of urban transportation, including its economics, problems, and some proposed solutions, are presented in W. OWEN, *The Metropolitan Transportation Problem*, rev. ed. (1966); J.R. MEYER *et al.*, *The Urban Transportation Problem* (1965); and G.M. SMERK (ed.), *Readings in Urban Transportation* (1968). R.L. CREIGHTON, *Urban Transportation Planning* (1970), outlines the planning process, drawing on the author's experience with the Chicago and Niagara Frontier studies. Origin-destination techniques, trip generation, and travel expeditures are discussed in W.Y. OI and P.W. SHULDINER, *An Analysis of Urban Travel Demands* (1962). E.N. THOMAS and J.L. SCHOFER, *Strategies for the Evaluation of Alternative Transportation Plans*, a report prepared for the National Cooperative Highway Research Program (1970), applies systems analysis to transportation decision making.

Additional materials useful for review of urban transportation planning are UNIVERSITY OF CALIFORNIA INSTITUTE OF TRANSPORTATION AND TRAFFIC ENGINEERING, *Fundamentals of Traffic Engineering*, 7th ed. (1969), *Urban Mass Transit Planning* (1967); and WILBUR SMITH AND ASSOCIATES, *Transportation and Parking for Tomorrow's Cities* (1966), *Parking in the City Center* (1965). Pricing of streets, rather than the limitation of street use by congestion, is explored in G.J. ROTH, *Paying for Roads: The Economics of Traffic Congestion* (1967). C.D. FOSTER, *The Transport Problem* (1963), covers the economic criteria for transport investment.

Rail and bus transit are discussed in A. SCHEFFER LANG and R.M. SOBERMAN, *Urban Rail Transit: Its Economics and Technology* (1964); ORGANIZATION FOR ECONOMIC COOPERATION AND DEVELOPMENT, *Improvements and Innovations in Urban Bus Systems* (1969); WILBUR SMITH AND ASSOCIATES, *The Potential for Bus Rapid Transit* (1970), and *Motor Trucks in the Metropolis* (1969).

Concern for system environment and amenity is expressed in the BRITISH MINISTRY OF TRANSPORT, *Traffic in Towns: A Study of the Long Term Problems of Traffic in Urban Areas* (1963); L. HALPRIN, *Freeways* (1966); H. BLUMENFELD, "Criteria for Judging the Quality of the Urban Environment," in H.J. SCHMANDT and W. BLOOMBERG, JR. (eds.), *The Quality of Urban Life* (1969); G.R. TAYLOR, "The Beginnings of Mass Transportation in Urban America," *Smithsonian Journal of History*, vol. 1, no. 2 pp. 35–50 and vol. 1, no. 3, pp. 31–54 (1966), traces the growth of urban transportation in Boston, New York, and Philadelphia between 1820 and 1860. B. RUDOFSKY, *Streets for People: A Primer for Americans* (1969); and D.N. LEWIS (ed.), *The Pedestrian in the City* (1965), consider city planning and pedestrian circulation.

Conclusions of a study on new concepts for urban transportation are presented in U.S. DEPARTMENT OF HOUSING AND URBAN DEVELOPMENT, URBAN TRANSPORTATION ADMINISTRATION, *Tomorrow's Transportation: New Systems for the Urban Future* (1968). Other studies on this subject include: R.A. WOLF, *Metrotran 2000: A Study of Future Concepts in Metropolitan Transportation for the Year 2000* (1967); and the MPC CORPORATION, *Report on Testing and Evaluation of the Transit Expressway* (1967).

(J.A.Ba.)

Transportation, Water

The movement of goods and persons by water dates back to the earliest times. Over the centuries the discovery of new lands by seagoing adventurers and the continuing exploitation of technological advances by the shipping industry have steadily expanded the role of water transportation in the growth of international trade and the world economy. Despite the invention of new and faster forms of movement, technological progress within the shipping industry has enabled it to remain a provider of facilities for international trade on a scale unsurpassed by any other transport mode. Carryings more than doubled in the 1960s alone, reaching a total of 2,570,000,000 tons in 1970. The world's merchant fleet continues to increase both in types and size of ships and in total tonnage: ships of 100 gross registered tons or more in 1970 totalled 227,490,000, or 338,838,000 deadweight tons. (For an explanation of the methods by which ship weight is computed, see *Tonnage measurement* below.)

Beginning of the modern shipping industry

The shipping industry as it exists today dates from the invention of the marine steam engine, screw propulsion, the construction of ships of iron and steel, and the opening of the Suez Canal in 1869. This event triggered an enormous expansion of seaborne trade, which in turn led to the building of larger and faster ships, their more efficient handling in ports developed for the purpose, and the growth of large steamship companies serving every continent along defined, internationally organized routes. There is no limit to the type of cargo modern ships move, but the greater part has always consisted of basic raw materials, such as coal, oil, minerals, and fertilizers, and foodstuffs, such as grain, sugar, rice, vegetable oils, fruit, meat, and dairy produce. But over a period, as technological discoveries are made and new demands arise from them and as sources of supply are exhausted and others developed, the proportions of given commodities within the overall total steadily change, and directional flows are altered. Since World War II, oil has to a considerable extent replaced coal as the chief source of power; fresh territories have been developed, and new countries are emerging, adding to the volume of international trade and influencing its pattern.

To cope with the expansion of trade, the shipping industry has had to grow and develop new techniques and methods. The broad aim of carrying larger bulk loads more speedily has involved the speeding of loading methods. One way of achieving this has been by the construction of cellular container ships designed to carry cargoes in sealed boxes of standard size that can be transported from their point of origin, loaded, shipborne, unloaded, and transported to their final destination by other transport modes with the load unbroken. Faster and larger than the conventional cargo liner and with far faster turnaround, container ships greatly increase efficiency and economy. Roll-on, roll-off vessels, transporting trucks, trailers, and automobiles, serve a similar purpose. Tankers and other bulk carriers have increased both in size and in the list of goods they carry in unbroken loads. The traffic of the orthodox tramps and scheduled cargo-liner services has been eroded by the growing fleets of specialized ships. Only in the range of small and high-priced goods has air transport successfully competed with sea, though passenger traffic has largely passed to the air.

With vessels expensive to construct and requiring special handling equipment, the so-called container revolution has brought in its train changes in the organization of the shipping industry. Many of the long-established liner shipping companies have cooperated among themselves to form consortia to operate long-distance routes across the Atlantic, to the Far East, and to Australia, while the oil companies have built their own tanker fleets, which they supplement by chartering. This trend toward larger ships carrying greater loads of cargoes in ever growing variety seems likely to characterize water transportation in the 1970s.

The sections that follow do little more than outline the history of the movement of people and goods by water and trace the development of the shipping industry through sail to steam and down to the shape of the industry today. The history of ships themselves is dealt with in the article SHIP. Inland waterways are treated in CANALS AND INLAND WATERWAYS (see also such articles as HARBOURS AND SEA WORKS; SAILS AND SAILING SHIPS; MARITIME LAW; and MATERIALS HANDLING). The article is divided into the following sections:

I. History of water transportation

EARLY HISTORY

Travel by water was among man's earliest and best means of extending the range of his activities, broadening his horizon, and improving his living standards by securing raw materials and exchanging goods. The Egyptians used watercraft during the 4th millennium BC; early seafarers from Crete and the Aegean sailed westward to the Mediterranean islands and Spain and penetrated as far as Ireland, Wales, and Brittany. Over the centuries this mode of transport developed to meet the differing needs of fighting and trading. Whereas early war vessels were galleys carrying sails but propelled by oars, trading vessels took more generally to sail, and those of the Greeks and Romans carried a square sail that was deep and wide in contrast to those of the narrower men-of-war. With sailing ships, trade routes were opened up, among the earliest known being one from Elath at the head of the Gulf of Aqaba through the Red Sea to Ophir on the Arabian Sea. Because ships were able to carry only small quantities of goods and journeys were long and slow, water transport was expensive, and only luxury goods were carried. Cargoes of precious metals were brought by water in Solomon's day, while from Palestine shipping moved by established routes to southern and western Europe.

Fighting and trading vessels

Considerable trade was carried over water by the Romans between the Mediterranean and their northern territories; by the end of their occupation of Britain (5th century AD) some 800 ships were in service carrying cereals between Britain and Gaul, and large quantities of wool were being exported to the south. In northern waters ships developed more slowly, but in the Middle Ages Viking trading vessels were venturing far from their Scandinavian homelands to pioneer sea routes to Greenland and Iceland, to trade in cloth between Flanders and the Baltic, and to trade with Constantinople through Russia by the river Dnepr to the Black Sea. The timber products, furs, and slaves of the North were exchanged for the spices, textiles, and wines of the southern and eastern Mediterranean.

In the 10th and 11th centuries the Venetians were responsible for a great trade expansion along the routes they developed through the southern seas to Constantinople and the Middle East. Wheat, wine, timber, and salt were carried from the north Adriatic to exchange for the products of the East carried from Indian ports to the Persian Gulf and through the Red Sea. Sailing through the Bay of Biscay, the Mediterranean traders also established themselves in Flanders, leading to the growth of the Dutch carrying trade. Wool was transported from Britain by sea to the Mediterranean. The Genoese pioneered sea routes to the North Sea and the Baltic, where the Hanseatic League flourished in the 13th century. Centred on Lübeck, the league was a federation of north German trading cities engaged in general trade along the river routes to southern Germany, Poland, and central Europe and from the Baltic to Britain, to trade northern products for wool and metals.

The Age of Discovery

The great Age of Discovery, with its voyages of exploration, was largely motivated by the search for gold and silver to pay for goods imported to Europe from the Middle and Far East. The sea route to India and the Far East was established, America discovered, and the Pacific reached. The seas were infested with buccaneers, however, and faster ships were wanted to outsail them. Larger vessels able to carry bigger cargoes were also needed to make the long voyages worthwhile. With the opening of the sea route to India, the Portuguese built merchantmen as large as men-of-war and took full advantage of the great new trade route. Portugal established trading posts in India, South China, and East Africa, thereby creating a monopoly of trade with India and the East that it held for nearly a century. In 1592, however, Britain founded the Levant Company, with a monopoly of eastern Mediterranean trade, and established the East India Company in 1600. Fierce competition followed, with the French and Dutch helping to break Portugal's monopoly. The Dutch established trading posts in the East Indies, whereas Britain opened up trade with northern Europe as far as the White Sea.

With colonization of the Americas, trade flowed across the Atlantic. Routes sailed in order to take advantage of the prevailing winds were necessarily long and often involved triangular or even quadrangular voyages; *i.e.*, by way of Africa and the West Indies, thence to North America or the Caribbean, and back by the North Atlantic route. As a result, cargoes were collected and exchanged en route, metalware being traded in Africa for slaves and ivory to be left in the West Indies for sugar, rum, and cotton, with return cargoes from America of tobacco and skins. There were many routes, varying according to cargoes and seasons. In addition to the European countries, especially Britain and The Netherlands, the American colonies built up their own merchant fleet, at first principally to carry fish.

The British East India Company

The British East India Company's trade influenced ship design throughout the 16th and 17th centuries. Ships of heavy construction were built by the East India Company similar to men-of-war, the largest being 1,200 tons, 165 feet (50 metres) long and 42 feet (13 metres) wide, built for maximum capacity rather than speed. Reduction of the British tea duty at the end of the 18th century greatly increased trade and stimulated the construction of even larger and more efficient vessels. With the ending of the company's monopoly in trade with India in 1813, competition was renewed, and speed became important. The Americans, who had always built for speed, made the fastest time on the Far East runs. The great trade revival that followed the ending of the Napoleonic Wars and the American War of 1812 made faster speeds and prompter deliveries necessary to ensure profitable operations. Atlantic packets were thus built for speed to facilitate regularly scheduled services; these achieved surprising results despite their dependence on weather. On the China run, especially in shipping opium to evade both pirates and government junks, speed was of the essence; this led to the development of the clipper with its raking stern and stern posts. When the East India Company's monopoly of the China trade ended in 1833, intense rivalry followed; the Americans took full advantage, attaining remarkable speeds from China to New York and Boston. These were the days of the great tea races, with the American clippers outpacing the British. In mid-19th century, America quit the China trade for the more lucrative one of carrying passengers to San Francisco for the gold rush.

LATER DEVELOPMENTS

From sail to steam. Technological advances in the late 18th and early 19th century, particularly the coming of steam and the building of ships of iron and, later, of steel, brought about changes in propulsion and construction that were to lead to the emergence of the world's merchant fleets as they existed up to World War II. Early in the 19th century the successful harnessing of steam to ship propulsion was exploited by traders, who were quick to realize the advantages of speed provided by steam over sail; one trade followed the other in turning to this new power unit. Yet the advantages of sail for long voyages, on which steamships had to be able to carry large amounts of fuel, kept a considerable sailing cargo fleet alive into the 20th century. World War I was the final blow to sail.

Steam power

Initially, steam was used mainly for passengers and mails. One of the earliest passenger steamship services was in Russia between St. Petersburg (now Leningrad) and the Kronstadt fortress; a regular service also operated on the River Neva. In Britain steam packets were used for postal services to Ireland in the 1820s. In the United States large and speedy steamboats operated on the Hudson River; a 1,000-ton vessel accommodated 600 passengers and made 20 knots (nautical miles) per hour. Steamships also carried thousands of immigrants from Europe to the New World. Claims for the first regular crossings under steam across the Atlantic are disputed between the "Savannah" and the "Sirius." The "Savannah," built in New York, crossed in 1819, but because it was under steam for only 80 hours of its 25 days at sea, the "Sirius" claims the honour with her voyage in 1838 using a paddle wheel most of the way. The "Sirius" voyage stimulated interest in regular steam passenger service. The "British Queen," of 2,400 tons, inaugurated an Atlantic passenger service for the British and American Steam Navigation Company in April 1839, carrying 500 passengers and 80 tons of cargo. The first truly regular service, however, was operated by the Cunard Steam-Ship Company, Ltd., which obtained the British contract for mails and built four sister ships, paddle steamers with 740-horsepower engines raising 8½ knots. Inaugurating the service, the "Britannia," starting from Liverpool on its maiden voyage, made Boston in 14 days and eight hours, including a 12-hour stop at Halifax, Nova Scotia, to unload mails and take on coal. Several steamship lines were soon established to exploit the profitable Atlantic routes.

First Atlantic steamship crossings

Concurrently, the shipping companies turned to steam on the India and Far East routes, the first voyage from England to India being completed by a 470-ton paddle steamer in 113 days, including coaling en route. Regular services began in 1834, starting in England, stopping at Spanish and Portuguese ports, Malta, and Alexandria, then shipping cargo and passengers overland to Suez to connect with the East India Company steamers to Madras, Calcutta, and later, Hong Kong and Shanghai. The first steam mail services to Australia were established in 1852 by the Royal Mail Steam Packet Company, which, with the aid of a government mail subsidy, also operated services via Mexico to the Caribbean, Rio de Janeiro, and the Río de la Plata. Services to Australia via the Atlantic were inaugurated with overland connections across the Isthmus of Panama. The importance of the coastal trade within the United States led to high-speed steamers carrying mails, passengers, and cargo from New England to the southern states. Finally, in 1875, Japan turned to steam for trade among her islands.

The steamship, combined with the Industrial Revolution, vastly extended world commerce, with the main emphasis on exchange of manufactured goods for raw materials and foodstuffs; at the same time the development of steam power caused a worldwide demand for coal, of which Britain was the chief exporter. Steamship companies rapidly increased in number and size.

Technological progress. The great increase in world trade contributed to the development in ship construction, design, and propulsion. Despite fears of the skeptics that iron would not float, that ships hulls would become fouled, and that metal would render the magnetic compass inaccurate, experiments in the construction of iron ships were carried on from the late 18th century. By the early 19th century the endurance of iron vessels had been proved, a surface composition had been developed for protecting the hull, and means had been found for correcting the compass. Cunard introduced its first iron ship, the "China," on its North Atlantic service in 1862, and from then on iron progressively replaced wood. Early steamboats were all paddle vessels, but the inefficient engines not only took up much space themselves but also required huge bunkers to feed their furnaces. This led to problems of payload and the operation of refuelling points. One early solution to the problem was a small auxiliary engine and collapsible paddles for use only when there was no wind to fill the sail. For better propulsion, screw propellers were developed to replace the paddle wheel. One of the earliest screw-propeller vessels, the British engineer Isambard K. Brunel's "Great Britain," completed in 1843, was of iron construction, had a four-cylinder steam engine supplemented by sail on six masts, and achieved 11 knots.

The screw propeller

Savings in space and the opportunity to move the engines to the stern so that the more comfortable midships section could be used for passengers brought an end to a quarter of a century of paddle-liner operation. During that time the paddle vessels had not only grown larger and faster but more elegant as well. Cunard's last ocean paddle steamer was a handsome two-masted brig, the "Scotia," an iron vessel of 3,871 gross tons, which cost the company £170,000 and broke both the eastbound and westbound speed records. In addition to accommodations for 240 passengers, the "Scotia" could carry 1,400 tons of cargo and earn about £6,000 from freight on each voyage.

With the screw replacing the paddle and the fitting of water tanks for ballast and the great increase in coal-bunkering stations along the trade routes, the type of services provided by shipowners underwent a change. Heretofore the steamship had been built for definite, regular scheduled services operating on defined sea routes, whereas bulk cargoes were mainly carried by ships chartered for the purpose. To these liner and chartered services a third was now added—tramping. The tramp cargo ship became available to transport cargoes between ports as required on a negotiated contract basis. Though engine development in response to demands for economy on long voyages to the Far East, Australia, and New Zealand was rapid, ship operators responded rather slowly to other innovations until the last part of the 19th century. Increased carrying capacity was achieved by replacing iron with steel in ship hulls, strengthening them and reducing their weight. Though some steel-hulled ships were built in the 1870s, it was not until shortages of the metal were overcome in the 1880s that steel successfully supplanted iron.

The first tramp ships

Specialization of carriers. With changes in the types and quantities of goods carried, there arose a need for ships specially adapted to different purposes, of which the chief types were refrigerated vessels for perishable foodstuffs and bulk carriers for oil and grain. Although the importance of refrigeration was realized only slowly, early trials were initiated in the 1870s; and the first refrigerated ship was the French "Frigorifique," in which ammonia was used to produce low temperatures. Shortly afterward compressed air was employed on the British "Strathleven"; in 1880 this ship delivered a sound cargo of frozen meat from Australia to London. Compressed-air machines were latter replaced by carbon dioxide and ammonia systems. Refrigeration was now generally accepted and by the end of the 19th century a number of refrigerated ships were entered in *Lloyd's Register of Shipping.*

Though oil had previously been transported in barrels aboard ships, it became advantageous to carry it in bulk as demand grew, thereby lowering handling costs. Accordingly, in 1886, three British vessels, forerunners of the modern tanker, commenced operation. Two of these employed the outer shell of the ship as the skin of the tank, and the third carried oil up the underside on the weather deck.

Oil tankers

Improvements in ports and harbours. The changing conditions in ship operation necessitated the provision of new facilities at the world's ports and harbours to accommodate the greatly increased size and variety of shipping. Efficient services for docking, loading, discharging cargoes, warehousing, and transit of goods from ports were developed. With increases in their draft, steamships required deeper channels and better docking arrangements.

The traditional quay wall berth, parallel to the shore, was not easy to adapt to large vessels. The lineal quay, built perpendicular to the shore, overcame this disadvantage; additional length of quay could always be added and the berths thus adapted to accommodate larger ships. In the 19th century considerable port construction was undertaken; docks were dredged deeper, wharves extended outward, and quays lengthened. There were new developments in construction technology, often aided by new materials, such as portland cement, which replaced stone in seawalls (see HARBOURS AND SEA WORKS).

Influence of Suez and Panama canals. With the opening of the Suez Canal in 1869 and the shortening of the sea route to India and the Far East by some 3,500 miles (5,600 kilometres), a great stimulus was given to world trade. Shorter voyages, combined wtih the reduction in distance between bunkering stations, enabled more of a ship's capacity to be given over to cargo. Consequently, one-third more traffic could be carried by the same vessels. As their coal-bunkering costs fell, steamers were able to challenge the clipper successfully.

Shipowners were slow at first to take advantage of this new route, but by the 1880s the Suez Canal had a substantial impact; by shortening the route to India and thereby lowering transport costs, it made Indian cotton competitive with American cotton in the markets of Europe. Britain, with the world's largest merchant fleet and with readily available coal for export (which ensured return cargoes), predominated in the use of the canal. During 1870, Suez' first full year of operation, 437,000 shipping tons traversed the canal, of which 66.25 percent was British. By 1880 this total had risen to more than 3,000,000 tons (2,700,000,000 kilograms), of which 79.33 percent was British. In 1913, 20,000,000 tons, 7.5 percent of the world's total, passed through Suez, of which 60.16 percent was British. In 1892 the first oil tanker passed through the canal. In 1966, the last full year before the canal was closed by the Arab-Israeli War, total transits were 241,900,000 tons, of which 175,800,000 tons were oil and 66,100,000 tons dry cargo.

Britain and the Suez Canal

The Panama Canal, opened in 1914, shortened the distance from the Atlantic to Pacific by 7,000 to 9,000 miles (11,000 to 14,000 kilometres) and had as great an effect as Suez on world trade routes. The average annual traffic during the Panama's first five years was 1,691 ship transits and 5,900,000 tons of cargo. After World War I, transits and cargo rose, averaging in the ten years 1920–29, 4,443 transits and 21,600,000 tons of cargo. During the decade up to World War II traffic continued to rise, averaging 5,253 transits and 25,300,000 tons. By 1960 they had nearly doubled to 5,448 transits and 48,100,000 tons. The traffic flow through the Panama Canal is greater from the Atlantic to the Pacific than in the reverse direction, and the cargoes differ. The closing of the Suez Canal greatly increased traffic through Panama to the Far East; in the United States fiscal year 1971, 74,344,000 tons of cargo were transported through the canal to the Pacific, of which half was petroleum products, coal, and coke. Of the 44,283,000 tons traversing the canal in the other direction, ores and lumber constituted about one-quarter of the total, with a great miscellany of commodities making up the other three-quarters. Asia-bound traffic accounted for the greater part, with Japan the predominant destination, whereas the second largest tonnage was carried from the west coast of South America to the east coast of the United States and the third largest amount was destined for Europe from South America.

Safety at sea. With the expansion of steam navigation, the greater variety of cargo carried, the growth in size of merchant fleets, and the increase in number of countries taking part in shipping, rules for ensuring safety at sea have needed frequent adaptation. The earliest steps to establish international standards were taken by a London group of marine underwriters who in 1760 cooperated to establish, assess, and classify ships' conditions. From this beginning, the Lloyd's Register of Shipping was to evolve and its classification to be accepted the world over.

Lloyd's Register of Shipping

Lloyd's took the lead in seeking rules for safety at sea; when in the mid-19th century unscrupulous operators bought old ships, insured them, and sent them to sea speculating on their loss, public opinion was aroused, and a Merchant Shipping Act was enacted by the British Parliament. As revised in 1876, it defined proper methods of dealing with different types of cargo and required every ship to carry on her sides a mark showing the maximum depth to which she might be loaded in saltwater. This "Plimsoll line," named for Samuel Plimsoll, the promoter of the bill, was accepted internationally. The British rules on navigation at sea of ships in relation to one another were also adopted internationally, and a series of international conventions were negotiated and adopted by most seafaring countries (see the section *Maritime law* below).

ADVANCES IN THE 20TH CENTURY

Developments after World War I. At the beginning of the 20th century the world steamer merchant fleet was less than 25,000,000 tons; 6,500,000 tons of sail were still engaged in trading. During the 14 years before World War I, steamship tonnage doubled and subsequent wartime losses were replaced by new building, largely by United States Liberty ships. During the interwar years world seaborne trade rose by 1929 to 35 percent above 1913 but declined during the Depression of the early 1930s. Seaborne trade did not recover to the 1929 level until 1937. During the period, important technological changes had taken place, including conversion from coal to oil burning and the development of diesel motor ships. Despite much experimentation in the late 19th and early 20th century the use of oil as fuel did not come into use on a large scale until after World War I. Conversion was then rapid. Whereas in 1914, 96.6% of the world merchant fleet tonnage was coal burning and only 2.9% oil, the balance being internal-combustion-powered motor ships, by 1939, 45.3% used coal, 30% burned oil for steam, and 24.7% were motor ships. The first oceangoing, diesel-engined ship, the "Selandia," was built in 1912; by 1939 one out of four ships was motor driven; the turbine and the diesel engine competed for speed and economy. Turbines were favoured for greater speed for long voyages, but diesel was preferred for intermediate and short distances. Other substantial economies and improvements contributed to greater shipping efficiency, including increases in size of ships, new bow designs reducing wave formation and water resistance, and better safety equipment, with radar an outstanding innovation.

Developments after World War II. After World War II shipping underwent several major changes resulting from rapid technological progress in ship construction and port handling and in the greater development of specialized ships, including the cellular vessel, built or adapted to carry cargo in standard containers. World trade expanded and with it the volume of goods and the variety shipped, accompanied by changes in their directional flow. Shipping routes were altered to meet the new requirements. With competition from the air, passenger traffic declined sharply, particularly on the North Atlantic and on the long voyages to the Far East. Of all these changes, the most significant were the strides made in the construction of special-purpose vessels for specialized trades to handle the widening range of commodities often carried in entire shiploads. The multipurpose dry bulk carrier was developed to transport new cargoes, such as iron and steel products, forest products, fertilizers, and automobiles, in addition to the traditional bulk commodities, such as grains, coal, phosphate, sugar, and timber. Specially designed combination vessels carried dry and liquid bulk cargoes in either the same or adjacent holds, the basic combinations being crude oil and mineral ores or other bulk solids. A major change in general cargo carriage was the development of cellular bulk cargo ships, which rapidly eroded the traffic of conventional liners. The first container ships were converted cargo ships or tankers, but the great economies offered by containerization led to the building of special-purpose cellular ships. The United States built the first such vessels with special handling equipment, employing them on do-

Decline of passenger traffic

mestic routes and to offshore islands, but the introduction in 1966 of the first successful international deep-sea container service across the North Atlantic heralded the container revolution. Other countries entered the container trade, and by the 1970s services were operating on most of the long-distance routes serving Europe, North and South America, Japan, Africa, and Australia, with feeder lines serving minor peripheral ports from transshipment points. One advantage of containerization is that it provides through-transit of containers from point of origin to final destination, the continuous process being facilitated by the establishment of inland clearance centres with customs facilities enabling containers to be shipped direct to the vessel. Because of the ease and speed of loading and unloading, the time ships spend in port is reduced up to 75 percent. Fewer ships are needed to offer the same frequency of service, up to 70 percent less, for example, on the North Atlantic run. A further development in special-purpose vessels was the so-called roll-on, roll-off ship designed to carry trucks, trailers, and automobiles driven onto the ship through side or interdeck ramps in the bow or the stern. Another unit load system involved loading cargo on pallets (small, light frameworks, usually of wood), to be lowered into the hold or carried on deck and offloaded on the pallets at their destination. Roll-on, roll-off services were first developed in the United Kingdom for short sea routes to Ireland and nearby European ports but have become so numerous that many goods are carried overland in this way rather than being sent by sea. Oceangoing roll-on, roll-off ships for general cargo on the longer sea routes were coming into service in the early 1970s on the North Atlantic route. With these developments, the proportion of goods shipped by bulk carriers increased greatly in the 1960s and was continuing to increase into the 1970s. In 1960 bulk carriers took only 16% of the five major bulk commodities and 7% of total dry cargo, but by 1969 the figures were 74% and 36%, respectively.

Roll-on, roll-off ship

The economies obtainable through large-scale operation also brought increases in the size of ships, limited only by draft and available port facilities. During the 1960s the average size of tankers rose from 23,000 tons to 38,000 tons, that of bulk carriers from 18,000 tons to 30,000 tons. In the dry-cargo field, tramps ranged from 8,000 to 15,000 tons deadweight, but the specialized bulk carriers capturing much of their cargoes weighed 100,000 tons or more. Tankers of over 300,000 tons deadweight were coming into service in the early 1970s.

Before World War II, Britain, the United States, Japan, and the nations of western Europe collectively owned 90 percent of the world's fleet; by the end of the 1960s total fleets had trebled in tonnage, and these countries owned only 60 percent, although through flags of convenience (see below) they owned another 20 percent. The fleet of the Soviet Union has grown fastest; tonnage rose from 1,200,000 to approximately 15,000,000 between 1945 and 1970. Ship registration under the flags of convenience of such countries as Liberia, Panama, Cyprus, Singapore, Somalia, and Lebanon has also grown quickly. These countries, whose combined gross tonnage totalled over 41,000,000 in 1970, or one-fifth of the world fleet, allow ownership or control of vessels by noncitizens, permit easy transfer, give taxation exemption, and have few or no governmental or international regulations.

Government subsidies or requirements regarding use of national vessels represent another influence on ownership. Few countries subsidize their shipping directly, an exception being the United States, which pays subsidies to operators up to the level of costs of competitors on all routes of national importance. Furthermore, government-financed cargo is reserved to national flag vessels. Japan also subsidizes shipping operators, and Italy, France, and Spain grant payments for specific purposes. Government assistance is also given by some countries for new ship construction.

After World War II, shortages in countries devastated by war influenced seaborne trade, but by the end of the 1950s definite trends had emerged resulting from the growth of the world population, expansion of industriali-

Changing trade patterns

zation, changes in sources of supply for raw materials, and the demands of the developing nations. The main sources of power shifted from coal to oil, for example, and some nations such as Britain began to import iron ore for steelmaking. The net result of the postwar changes in trade was more than a doubling of world international seaborne trade between 1960 and 1969, from 1,110,000,000 tons to 2,280,000,000 tons. Oil transport grew rather faster than dry-cargo shipments during this period, increasing from 49 to 54 percent of total world trade. The three principal bulk dry commodities—iron, coal, and grain—accounted for about 35 percent of all movements. Generally speaking, more manufactured goods were imported by the three important regions of North America, western Europe, and Japan during this period, while fuel and raw materials imports to Europe and North America fell, rising slightly in Japan. In the early 1970s Japan was becoming the second most important region in terms of seaborne import tonnages, although its total imports by value were far behind those of North America.

II. Modern water transportation

SPECIALIZATION IN SHIPPING

The liner and the tramp ship. The two main types of ships are the liner, operating regular, scheduled services on a predetermined trade route, charging advertised rates, and the tramp ship, prepared to carry any suitable cargo from any port to any other on a negotiated contract basis. Liner services are of particular value for passengers and mails and for traders not dealing in entire shiploads of commodities. The bulk shipper finds it more economical to purchase transport services on the open market, offering his business to the lowest bidder. Thus tramp ships usually carry homogeneous cargoes, whereas liners transport small consignments of many different kinds of goods.

The principal bulk cargoes have varying characteristics. Liquids, for example, require specially designed ships and are considered as a separate branch of the industry. The normal dry-cargo tramp ship is designed for flexibility so that it can carry, as the occasion arises, commodities as different as iron ore, coal, grain, sugar, cotton, or copra. Because of the difference in stowage factors (cubic capacity required per ton of cargo), for example, a ship large enough to carry 10,000 tons of coal might be loaded to its maximum draft with less than 5,000 tons of ore; and if it were to carry grain, interior partitions would be necessary to prevent the cargo from upsetting the stability of the ship by shifting when the ship rolled.

Loading and unloading

Different methods are used for loading and discharging different types of cargo. Cargoes shipped in cases, bales, or bags must be handled by the ship's derricks or by shore cranes, and the same applies to cargoes of commodities like timber, steel, or scrap. Iron ore and coal are discharged by grab and grain by elevators or suction pipes. Bulk solids are gravity loaded by conveyers and chutes. Oil is often pumped from tankers directly into pipelines connected to storage tanks and refineries. With the trend toward larger bulk carriers, the installation of self-discharging gear has increased. A number of systems are in use, including various forms of conveyers and elevators.

Specialized carriers. Specialized ships such as ore carriers may still be divided into the two categories of liner and tramp. Some are constructed by tramp shipping companies to be hired out or chartered on a long-term basis to shippers or importers of ore, whereas others are built and operated by the shippers or consumers of ore themselves, mainly the large steelworks. Several other industrial consumers of raw materials in bulk, such as major importers of sugar, newsprint, molasses, gypsum, and chemicals, operate their own fleets of bulk carriers in a similar fashion and also hire ships from tramp shipowners on the open market.

Barge tows and barge carriers. Barges towed by high-powered tugs are another recent development; some of the units now being built are high-capacity carriers of around 10,000 tons. The tug and barge concept is mainly valuable when voyages are short; one tug can sometimes serve three barges—one loading, one discharging, and one in transit—providing the best possible utilization of the high-cost power unit and the labour required to man it.

Lighter aboard ship system

Even further advances in utilization have been made with the adoption of a so-called lighter aboard ship (LASH) system, which involves a mother ship carrying nests of lighters that are loaded and discharged by powerful stern cranes. This system permits the preloading and assembling of the cargo in the lighters and can be a particular advantage if the point of origin or destination of the cargo is not approachable by a larger vessel. Such ships now operate across the North Atlantic.

Tankers. The transport of petroleum products by sea has vastly expanded in the 20th century, particularly since World War II. In 1939 the world tanker fleet totalled 11,568,000 tons gross, comprising 16.9 percent of the total tonnage of all merchant ships. By 1970 the tanker fleet had reached a total of 86,140,000 tons gross, representing as much as 37.9 percent of the total world fleet. Accompanying this growth of total tonnage was a remarkable advance in the size of individual tankers, up to 300,000 tons deadweight, over 1,000 feet (300 metres) in length, 130 feet (40 metres) in breadth, and drawing up to 64 feet (20 metres) of water.

Tankers must be subdivided into compartments in order to restrict the movement of the cargo by the motion of the ship. No shipborne cargo-handling facilities are required; the oil is pumped on board and off.

Before World War II the greater part of the world tanker fleet was owned and operated by the major oil companies, operating as industrial carriers. Tramp tankers occasionally supplemented these vessels. After World War II, however, and despite the expansion of their own fleets, the oil companies came to rely also on tramp tankers. A particular feature of the tanker trade is that it is almost entirely a one-way traffic; since tankers are not suitable for carrying any other type of cargo without structural alterations, the outward journey must be made in ballast. An exception to this rule is made for iron ore. Sweden, an ore-exporting and oil-importing country, has evolved ships capable of carrying an inward cargo of oil and an outward cargo of ore. As a result of the exploitation of the Labrador ore fields, this combined oil and ore carrier was increasingly built after World War II. In the winter season, when the ore-loading ports of Labrador are closed by ice, these specially designed ships find alternative employment as oil carriers. Other liquid cargoes, such as molasses, caustic soda, asphalt, and wine, are also carried in bulk at sea.

Coastal and short-sea shipping. Most oceangoing ships have their smaller scale counterparts in coastal shipping, the function and extent of which varies in different parts of the world according to geographical conditions. Coastal shipping, sometimes referred to as cabotage, is a separate branch of the shipping industry, generally confined to the coastal waters of a particular country. In those with continental coastlines, such as the United States, Australia, and India, coastal shipping differs little operationally from oceangoing shipping; and in the United States the term is even extended to include the intercoastal trade between the Pacific and Atlantic coasts via the Panama Canal and the noncontiguous trade between continental America and outlying areas such as Hawaii. In Europe, where national coastlines are comparatively short, coastal shipping has a more international character.

British coastal trade

In the United Kingdom there can be distinguished the purely coasting trade, plying among the islands and along the coast of Great Britain; the home trades, which ply between the United Kingdom and the continent of Europe within the limits of Brest, France, and Hamburg; and the short-sea trade, between the United Kingdom and Scandinavia, the Baltic Sea, and the Mediterranean. Some shipping companies operate liners, tramps, or tankers in all of these trades, while others may specialize in any one.

In the coasting and short-sea trades there are also many specialized vessels, such as cross-channel passenger ships, train ferries, ramp-loading or roll-on, roll-off motor vehicle transport ships specially designed for container traffic, as well as colliers and tankers. These tend to be operated by companies specializing in particular routes over which traffic is heavy but localized. As these services often form sea links between, or extensions of, railway systems, the railway companies often operate them. Indeed, the coastal shipping industry may be regarded as complementary to the inland system of transport communications as well as a link with neighbouring countries; a useful characteristic of the coastal ship is its ability to load cargo directly from the oceangoing vessel for transshipment along the coast and distribution to smaller ports whose depth of water or lack of facilities precludes the direct approach of the larger ship.

Ancillary services.   At the port, where the sea transport and inland transport systems meet, many ancillary services must be provided for ships. These include towage, stevedoring, warehousing, replenishment of stores, repair, and maintenance. Practice varies widely among different ports, the various services being provided by independent contractors, by the port authority, or by the shipping companies. In many ports, particularly those in which large liner companies operate, the companies have their own subsidiary organizations to provide such services not only for their own ships but also for others. Some of the larger shipping groups operate or control fleets of tugs, loading and discharging facilities and labour, warehouses and refrigerated stores, lighterage and land transport, and even provide for the building, repairing, equipment, and maintenance of ships for themselves and for other shipowners.

SHIP OPERATION

As the carrying performances of liners and tramps differ, so do the operational organization and methods of the companies that run them.

Liner operation.   The operator of a liner service has special interests in the particular trade route on which he travels. The design and performance of his ships is directed toward fulfilling the requirements of shippers using his services in the most economical way possible. Since a liner may carry cargo from dozens or even hundreds of individual consignees, the company must maintain extensive facilities and staff, both at the loading port and at the port of discharge. In less active ports these functions may be carried out by agents acting for one or more liner companies. Furthermore, passengers and cargo must be solicited from inland centres often quite distant from the ports of shipment, and it must always be possible to arrange for the transshipment or onward movement of cargo and passengers from terminal ports to ultimate destinations.

The conference system.   Liner companies provide regular and frequent carriage of all kinds of cargo in consignments large and small, at advertised fixed charges. They are enabled to do this by the liner conference system, which was first tried out on the Britain–Calcutta trade in 1875. The object of the conference system is to regulate uneconomic competition. Shipping companies of different ownership and nationality that service the same range of ports form a conference agreement to regulate rates for each type of freight; in some cases the agreement also allocates a specified number of sailings to each company. Coupled with this agreement there is generally a deferred-rebate system, by which regular shippers of goods by conference vessels receive a rebate of a percentage of the tariff freight rate, payable after a period of proved loyalty, provided they use conference vessels exclusively.

The shipping conference system has sometimes come under attack as tending to create a monopoly and to restrain competition against the public interest. It is, however, generally agreed that evidence is in favour of this system: it has been concluded that no realistically possible combination of shipping companies can force unreasonable rates and that shipping companies that provide regular sailings with good ships and maintain staffs and organizations in ports to handle and dispatch cargoes, irrespective of whether trade is good or bad, are entitled to some protection against the casual vessel that picks up an occasional cargo at cut rates. Advocates agree that through the system, the shipper can rely on a well-managed service, running vessels that will carry any desired quantities of his goods at predetermined rates.

Ship brokering and chartering.   As mentioned above, tramp-ship sailings and rates are determined by negotiation. Most of the world's tramp-ship chartering business is carried out in the Baltic Mercantile and Shipping Exchange in London, commonly known as the Baltic Exchange. This exhange had its origins in the 17th century, when merchants and ships' captains were accustomed to meet in coffeehouses to arrange cargoes for ships. The Baltic and the Jerusalem were the two coffeehouses chiefly patronized by merchants and captains until the business was concentrated in the Baltic tavern in 1810. In 1823 the first rules and regulations of a "Baltic Club" were drawn up, limiting membership to 300 and providing for accommodations and refreshments. At that time tallow was the principal commodity in the Baltic trades, but with the repeal of the British protectionist Corn Laws in 1846, the buying and selling of grain cargoes became one of the chief activities.

The Baltic Exchange

On the floor of the Baltic Exchange brokers circulate daily, some of them representing the shippers of cargoes, such as grain, coal, or ores, who require shipping space for their movement, and others representing the owners of tramp ships wanting employment. When seeking a ship for the carriage of a cargo, the broker naturally looks for a ship of the right size and specifications, ready at the right time and in the right port and prepared to carry the cargo at the cheapest possible rate. Conversely, the owner's broker must attempt to anticipate the charterer's requirements by having his ship at the right place at the right time but must also try to obtain the highest freight rate possible without running the risk of losing the contract to a competitor. This constant interplay of supply and demand, of ships as well as of cargoes, has the effect of reducing sea transport costs to a minimum, although tramp rates fluctuate frequently and widely at times.

These fluctuating rates also offer opportunities for speculation, as on a stock exchange. The shipper of grain, for example, may decide to charter a ship at what he considers to be a cheap rate even before he has sold the cargo, which he attempts to dispose of in the best market while it is still afloat. In this case the ship is chartered for a voyage from, say, the Río de la Plata to the English Channel "for orders," freight rates having been previously arranged to cover a variety of alternative destinations. Again, a shipper or owner may agree to charter a ship for a period of time at a certain rate, in the hope that he will later be able to "rent it" to another owner or shipper at a higher rate if the market improves. A good deal of "forward" chartering may also occur, in which a contract is entered into for performance at some specified time at a predetermined rate that both owner and hirer hope will prove favourable, according to their estimate of future market conditions.

The four principal methods of chartering a tramp ship are voyage charter, time charter, bareboat charter, or on a contract or "lump sum" basis. The voyage charter, in which a ship is chartered for a one-way voyage between specified ports, with a specified cargo at a negotiated rate of freight, is most common. The charterer agrees to provide the cargo for loading within an agreed range of dates. Once the cargo has been delivered at the port or ports of destination, the ship is free to further employment at the owners' discretion. Sometimes, however, the arrangement is for a series of consecutive voyages, generally for similar cargoes over the same route. The freight rate is expressed in terms of so much per ton of cargo delivered.

On time charter, the charterer undertakes to hire the ship for a stated period of time or for a specified round-trip voyage or, occasionally, for a stated one-way voyage, the rate of hire being expressed in terms of so much per ton deadweight per month. Whereas on a voyage charter the owner bears all the expenses of the voyage (subject to agreement about costs of loading and discharging), on time charter the charterer bears the cost of bunkers and stores consumed. On bareboat charter, which is less frequently used in ordinary commercial practice, the owner of the ship delivers it up to the charterer for the agreed period without crew, stores, insurance, or any other provision, and the charterer is responsible for running the ship as if it were his own for the period of the contract.

Contracts can also be arranged on a lump-sum basis, when an owner agrees to ship a given quantity of a stated cargo from one port to another for a stated sum. Sometimes large quantities of cargoes such as coal are arranged for on a contract basis. The shipowner agrees to undertake the shipment of a given quantity over a given period at a fixed price per ton of cargo, but not necessarily in any specified ship, although he generally uses his own ships if they are available. The question of substituted ships, however, often leads to disputes, and the terms of the contract may make special provisions for this eventuality. Once the owner's broker and the charterer's broker have agreed on the terms of contract, the ship is "fixed," although by word of mouth alone. The motto of the Baltic Exchange is "our word is our bond," and that code of ethics is observed by ship brokers throughout the world, whether they are members of the Baltic or not, for the simple reason that any ship broker who does not abide by it would be unable to transact further business. Legal-

"Charter party"

ly, however, the final contract is the written "charter party," which for most transactions is accepted as a standard document and is agreed to by all parties normally concerned in a tramp-ship "fixture" for a particular trade. The standard form of a charter party covers all the main points that experience has shown might lead later to misunderstanding or disputes about the liabilities of each party, while the variable details, such as the particulars of the voyage, cargo, ship, loading and discharging conditions, ports, and rate of freight, can be inserted in accordance with the prior verbal agreement. The charter-party document is subject to scrutiny and interpretation by a court of law in the event of dispute, but in practice most disputes are submitted to arbiters (generally independent ship brokers appointed by each participant) for settlement, unless an important legal precedent is involved.

Among the most important clauses in any charter party are those that lay down the number of days allowed for loading or unloading and those that determine who is to bear the expense involved. Normally a certain number of days are allowed for loading, and if the charterer fails to finish loading in the time specified, the shipowner is entitled to compensation. Quite often, on the other hand, the charterer receives dispatch money if the cargo is loaded in less than the time agreed in the charter party. Similar conditions usually apply in the port of discharge.

Many tankers, ore carriers, or other specialized bulk-cargo carriers are operated by an oil company or a steel company or an ore exporter exclusively on company business, whether on a regular schedule or not, or they are owned by an independent tramp shipowner and taken on charter by an oil or steel company to fulfill its marginal transport requirements on terms similar to those employed in the dry-cargo tramp shipping market.

Shipowners' and seamen's associations. Shipowners are organized on a national and a regional basis, generally in Chambers of Shipping or their equivalent. The chambers deal with policy issues, recruitment, and training of seafarers and the supply of crews. Such associations have sections to look after the special interest of subgroups in the industry, such as tankers, liners, tramps, and bulk carriers. Chambers consult governments on matters of high policy and are concerned with a wide range of issues affecting the industry as a whole, such as port organization, international relations, technical research, marine safety, radio and navigation questions, marine pollution, maritime law, marine insurance, information, and fiscal policy. The chambers are the voice of the industry and the forum for discussing and deciding policy on whatever (except labour relations) affects the well-being of shipping.

On the international level, the chief shipowning organizations include the International Chamber of Shipping

and the International Shipping Federation, whose offices and secretariats are housed in London. Formed in 1921, the International Chamber of Shipping excluded state shipping organizations of any kind. The ownership of the national fleet or of a substantial part of it had to be vested in private individuals or companies. Though the International Chamber of Shipping was suspended during World War II, shipowners representing 14 nations met in London in 1946 to reconstitute it, and in 1970 it had 19 member countries. To avoid the overlap of its functions with those of other organizations and to preserve the principles of private enterprise, it drew up a broad definition of its own purpose: to promote internationally the interests of the shipping industry; to coordinate expert advice on technical questions, in particular, with standards of safety and technical and scientific progress; and to provide a medium for the exchange of views and information on questions affecting the industry internationally.

To deal with more routine matters, other international shipping organizations exist. Prominent among these is the Baltic and International Maritime Conference, started in Copenhagen in 1905 as the Baltic and White Sea Conference to curtail cutthroat competition among tramp shipowners engaged in the Baltic and White Sea trades. The conference was organized primarily to secure minimum freight rates and negotiate uniform chartering terms between shipowners of different flags and the charterers. By 1969 the Baltic and International Maritime Conference consisted of shipowner and ship broker members from 75 different countries representing some 71,000,000 tons gross of shipping. The conference now embraces many kinds of trades in all parts of the world, and one of its principal functions is to inform members of changes in port expenses, in costs of loading and discharging cargoes, and in port labour conditions; but perhaps the most valuable part of its work consists of the drawing up of standard forms of charter party for use in a wide variety of tramp-shipping trades. There is also an International Committee of Passenger Lines and a Comité Maritime International and, on a regional basis, a Committee of European Shipowners, Committee of European National Shipowners' Association, and a Committee of Liner Operators: South America.

On the governmental level, in the United States the Federal Maritime Commission carries out regulatory activities, as do government departments in most countries. Of the international governmental organizations, the United Nations' specialized agency, the Inter-Governmental Maritime Consultative Organization, is one of the most important and in the early 1970s was very much concerned with problems of oil pollution. Other bodies include the United Nations Conference on Trade and Development–Committee of Shipping and the Maritime Transport Committee of the Organization for Economic Cooperation and Development.

Government regulation agencies

INTERNATIONAL MARITIME LAW

International conventions. Ships operate in an international field, the high seas, and are subject not only to the laws of the country in which they are registered and to the laws of the country in whose territorial waters they may be but also to a series of international conventions, the principles of which are incorporated into the domestic legislation of most maritime. countries. There has grown up, particularly in the years since the expansion of steam navigation, a body of international maritime law —"the common law of the sea"—that has been developed through international agreement. Nearly all the world's maritime nations, for example, have adopted the International Regulations for Preventing Collisions at Sea, originally based on British rules formulated in 1862 and made internationally effective after a series of international meetings culminating in a conference at Washington, D.C., in 1889. These rules specify in great detail how ships must navigate in respect of each other, what lights must be shown and what signals must be given in accordance with circumstances; any infringement of this international code of conduct is accepted in all maritime courts of law as prima facie evidence of liability in case of collision.

Similarly, the internationally accepted requirements for the protection and safety of life at sea, as far as the ship and its equipment are concerned, are embodied in the International Convention for Safety of Life at Sea. The sinking of the liner "Titanic" in 1912 gave rise to a general desire to raise the standards of safety of life at sea. Although a convention was drawn up in 1914 requiring certain minimum standards for passenger ships, it did not become fully operative because of the outbreak of World War I. A second Safety of Life at Sea Convention, drawn up in 1929, determined minimum standards for the construction of passenger ships engaged in international voyages and for the provision of lifesaving appliances and extended its rules for the safety of navigation to all ships on all voyages. The provisions regarding radio equipment were extended to cover cargo ships of more than 1,600 tons gross.

Improved techniques led to the convening of a third Safety of Life at Sea Conference in London in 1948, after which a third International Convention for Safety of Life at Sea was adopted. This convention came into force on November 19, 1952, having been ratified one year previously by the following countries in order of acceptance: United Kingdom, New Zealand, the United States, France, The Netherlands, Sweden, Norway, South Africa, Iceland, Portugal, Canada, Pakistan, Denmark, Yugoslavia, Italy, Belgium, Israel, Japan, and the Philippines. The scope of the 1929 convention was again extended to include, in several matters, cargo ships of 500 tons gross and above. Minimum requirements were laid down for construction of ships, provision of watertight bulkheads, closing of openings in hulls, lifesaving appliances, fire appliances, radio equipment and direction finders, grain divisions in ships carrying grain cargoes, precautions in carriage of dangerous goods, and emergency musters and drills. The 1948 convention also embodied the recommendations of governments associated with the World Meteorological Organization and provided for the continuance of the International Ice Patrol maintained by the United States Coast Guard in the North Atlantic. This convention was again revised in 1960. Whereas the Safety of Life at Sea Convention deals with the construction of ships from the safety point of view, particularly in respect of passengers and crews, the International Load Line Convention deals with the strength and seaworthiness of ships in normal operating conditions. This convention emerged from the British Merchant Shipping Act, 1875, providing the Plimsoll load line on the ship's side, indicating the maximum depth to which a ship could legally be loaded. In order to protect the competitive position of British ships, the Merchant Shipping Act of 1890 required all foreign ships leaving British ports to comply with the load-line regulations. This led to the adoption of load-line rules by most maritime countries, and the International Load Line Convention of 1930 was ratified by 54 nations. A new International Convention on Load Lines, drawn up in 1966, came into force in July 1968 and allowed for a smaller freeboard (vertical distance between the water and the deck) for large ships while calling for more stringent protection of openings in decks and superstructures.

In 1958 the Inter-Governmental Maritime Consultative Organization, a specialized agency of the United Nations, came into existence. The purpose of this advisory organization is to promote international cooperation in maritime navigation. By mid-1971, membership had grown to 73 nations.

Commercial legislation. International agreements and international law are also concerned with the business dealings between maritime countries. In this connection, the International Maritime Committee (Comité Maritime International) and the International Law Association did invaluable work. Delegates to the International Conference on Maritime Law held at Brussels in 1922 recommended to their respective governments the adoption of a set of rules, known as The Hague Rules, which establish the responsibilities, rights, and immunities of carriers under bills of lading (documents acknowledging receipt of cargo for shipment and proving entitlement to

the goods). The Hague Rules, which are generally also incorporated into the terms of a charter party, were given widespread legislative sanction by maritime countries.

Legislative sanction is not necessary to secure international agreement or observance. The York-Antwerp Rules of General Average, for example, differ in some respects from English law relating to marine insurance and contracts of affreightment. They were formulated by delegates from various maritime countries meeting at York, England, in 1864 and at Antwerp in 1877 and were revised at Stockholm in 1924 and at Amsterdam in 1950. They were so widely adopted by the maritime nations that for all practical purposes they have the force of law.

Ship classification.   To ensure compliance with the various international safety and load-line and other maritime conventions as well as with the requirements of national legislation concerning the registry and construction of merchant ships, most maritime nations require ships to be built under the supervision of government surveyors or of surveyors belonging to recognized classification societies and in accordance with their standards.

Lloyd's Register of Shipping.   The leading classification society, operating in almost every country in the world, is Lloyd's Register of Shipping, which began its work long before any national legislation existed for the performance of its purposes. The history of Lloyd's Register of Shipping can be traced back to 1760. The society was reconstituted in 1834 and again in 1914. The shipping community maintains it voluntarily, and its principal work is to supervise the survey and classification of merchant ships of all nationalities according to rigid standards. Through a worldwide organization of surveyors, initial classifications are made when ships are built, and maintenance surveys of such items as the hull, machinery, boilers, and refrigerating plant are carried out periodically or whenever the ship has suffered damage from collision or from any other cause. Lloyd's Register surveyors test and approve, during its manufacture, the steel intended for use in the ship's structure or in its engines and boilers; survey refrigerating machinery at sea or on land; supervise the testing of chains, anchors, and pressure vessels; and are competent authorities for the assignment of freeboard to all classes of ship in accordance with the provisions of merchant shipping acts or the load-line regulations.

The society publishes an annual multi-volume register book, which contains full details of all merchant ships in the world of more than 100 tons gross; this is kept up-to-date by means of regular supplements. Separate registers are kept of British and American yachts. The society also publishes annual and quarterly statistical summaries of shipping registered or under construction in the world.

Lloyd's Register of Shipping operates in most maritime countries, often in cooperation with classification societies established by other nations. These include the American Bureau of Shipping, originally established in 1867 and resuscitated as a result of the large volume of merchant ships built in the United States during World Wars I and II; the Bureau Veritas, which was founded in Antwerp in 1828 but moved its headquarters to Paris in 1832; the Norske Veritas, established in Norway in 1894; Germanischer Lloyd, founded in Germany in 1867; and Registro Italiano Navale, founded in Italy in 1861. Most of these and other national classification societies work in close conjunction with Lloyd's Register of Shipping.

Tonnage measurement.   Classification societies largely agree on the strength requirements of different types of ship; the technical, legal, or commercial enactments of the conventions are almost universally accepted. On the other hand, complete international agreement on methods of interpreting the term tonnage measurement was slow to develop. The two chief reasons for this were, first, the possibility of interpreting the term tonnage itself in several senses and, second, the fact that a ship's tonnage is calculated by one of several methods, according to the standard of measurement required. In speaking of shipping, the term ton may be used not only to name a unit of weight in the usually accepted sense but also to name a unit of volumetric capacity.

International Load Line Convention

The Hague Rules

Displace-
ment
tonnage
and
dead-
weight
tonnage

As far as weight is concerned, the ton is the long ton of 2,240 pounds avoirdupois (1,016 kilograms, almost identical with the metric ton); this is used to measure the weight of the ship and its contents. According to Archimedes' law, the weight of a floating vessel and its contents is equal to the weight of water that it displaces. This weight is known as the displacement tonnage, and the term is used most commonly in comparing the size of warships. In a cargo-carrying ship it is obvious that the displacement varies according to the amount of cargo, bunkers, and stores that are in the ship; and as it is important to determine the amount of cargo that can be carried, the ship's displacement must be calculated both when it is in light condition and when it is loaded to find the difference, which represents the weight of cargo that can be carried. The lightweight displacement tonnage is equivalent to the weight of water displaced by the ship's hull, machinery, and equipment plus the weight of the crew and their effects, when no cargo or bunkers are carried. When the maximum admissible weight of bunkers and cargo is added, the ship has reached its full displacement tonnage. The difference between the full displacement tonnage and the lightweight displacement tonnage is called the deadweight tonnage, and this corresponds to the maximum weight of cargo and bunkers the ship can safely carry. Deadweight tonnage is the measurement ordinarily used to describe and compare the sizes of dry-cargo ships and tankers.

In many procedures, such as the assessment of harbour dues and canal transit dues, a different system of tonnage measurement, based on the volumetric ton, is required. The volumetric ton is a measure of the capacity of the enclosed space in a ship, one ton equalling 100 cubic feet (about three cubic metres) of enclosed space. The volume of the ship up to the tonnage deck (which is generally the uppermost continuous deck), excluding certain exempted spaces, such as the double-bottom tanks, the steering-gear compartments, the galley, and other spaces not used for the carriage of cargo, is called the underdeck tonnage and is expressed in terms of tons of 100 cubic feet. The internal volume of between-deck spaces and deck erections used for the carriage of cargo is added to the underdeck tonnage to give what is called the gross tonnage, again in terms of tons of 100 cubic feet. In merchant shipping statistics the gross registered tonnage is usually given. It is also given for passenger ships, whose deadweight tonnage is relatively unimportant as a means of comparing them in size. For the purpose of assessing dues payable for port, canal, pilotage, lighthouse, and other services, the freight-earning capacity of the ship is usually accepted as the criterion of measurement; this is commonly computed by deducting the space devoted exclusively to such items as machinery, bunkers, crew accommodation, and navigating quarters from gross tonnage, in order to calculate the net registered tonnage. It is apparent that the final tonnage measurement of a ship according to the volumetric reckoning depends much on the definition of the spaces exempted from computation.

The British system of tonnage measurement is the one most used by maritime nations, but in certain areas, notably the Suez and Panama canals, there are different systems of measurement for the assessment of tonnage on which dues are payable, and all ships have to be specially measured for the assessment of their dues when passing through these areas.

The
measure-
ment
ton

For purpose of assessing freight rates on cargo, yet another form of volumetric tonnage is employed, known as the measurement ton, which is equivalent to 40 cubic feet (about one cubic metre) of capacity. This term has no connection with the tonnage measurements used for registration and for the assessment of dues. It derives from the fact that the charge made for carrying cargo is normally based either on the weight of the cargo or on the amount of space it occupies. Freight rates cannot all be fairly assessed by weight alone; a ton of feathers would occupy a far greater amount of the ship's hold than a ton of coal. Similarly, heavy machinery, although occupying much less space than coal, would prevent the extra space being used for the carriage of more cargo, for

such a deadweight cargo would bring a ship down to its load-line limits with much of the cubic capacity of its holds still unfilled. Hence liner freight-rate tariffs are generally expressed in terms of so much per ton weight or measurement, the measurement ton being the equivalent of 40 cubic feet of capacity and the rate paid being the higher of the two.

WORLD SHIPPING ROUTES AND FLEETS

Trade routes. Over the years a comprehensive pattern of worldwide liner services has been built up for both passengers and freight, linking all continents and countries, supplemented by the random movement of goods from one part of the world to another as occasion and demand has arisen. Despite the directional changes in world trade with the development of new areas, exploitation of new sources of supply, and different demands arising, these major routes have remained largely the same for the last century. An outstanding addition of new routes has been those served by the modern tankers, including those from the Persian Gulf to the United Kingdom and Europe; from the Persian Gulf to Japan; from the Caribbean to the United Kingdom and Europe; from the Caribbean to North Africa and Europe; from the Middle East to Japan; and from the Middle East to Europe and North America. While the worldwide trade routes are operated by liners and tramps, in the 1970s container services were extending further into the major deep-sea trade routes. Apart from the North Atlantic routes, which experienced the greatest expansion of capacity and hence intense competition, container services were operating between Japan and Australia and New Zealand; from the United Kingdom to Australia and New Zealand, the United States, and the Far East; between the United States and Australia; and on many short sea routes, such as between the United Kingdom and Ireland; the United Kingdom and near continental and Scandinavian ports; between Scandinavian and Baltic ports; and in United States coastal waters.

Merchant fleets of the world. By 1939, before the outbreak of World War II, world merchant shipping totalled 69,404,000 tons gross. Despite the enormous war losses, the world fleet reached 80,292,000 tons by 1948 and by 1955 exceeded 100,000,000 tons gross for the first time. In 1971 the world merchant fleet totalled 247,203,000 gross registered tons, over one-third (96,141,000 tons) of which consisted of tankers. Ore and bulk carriers totalled 53,797,000 tons and the fully cellular container tonnage 2,780,000 tons gross.

A significant feature of the development of the world merchant fleet after 1920 was the growth of the number of ships propelled by diesel engines. A simultaneous development was the replacement of coal by oil as fuel for steamships, a movement that reached its peak just after World War II. Motor ships totalled 145,425,000 gross registered tons and steamships 82,065,000 tons, of which only a negligible part was coal burning.

British Commonwealth. Among the merchant fleets of the world, the world's largest, that of the British Commonwealth, has declined steadily in importance in percentage terms. In 1886 the Commonwealth owned 63.6 percent of the mechanically propelled fleet of the world, but by 1939 this share had fallen to 30.7 percent. By 1970, though total tonnage amounted to more than 36,000,000 tons gross, making combined British and Commonwealth shipping still the largest fleet in the world, its proportion of world tonnage had fallen to about 16 percent.

Though most of the British-registered tonnage is owned and operated by the United Kingdom, significant numbers of vessels are owned in such Commonwealth countries as Australia, Canada, Hong Kong, India, Malaysia, New Zealand, and the West Indies. A general movement toward flags of convenience began in 1956, with a consequent increase in ships registered in Bermuda and the Bahamas. Of the privately owned United Kingdom merchant fleet, about half the vessels are oil tankers and whaling factory ships, while an additional third consists of passenger and cargo liners, the largest fleet of passenger ships in the world. Of special interest are the refrigerator cargo liners that carry agricultural products from Commonwealth nations, such as Australia, and New Zealand, and to Britain.

Western Europe. Among western European nations, Denmark, France, Germany, Greece, Italy, The Netherlands, Norway, and Sweden have important merchant fleets. Though Danish shipping suffered severe losses during World War II, by 1950 its strength had more than recovered. By 1971, over 1,200 ships flew the Danish flag, comprising over 3,500,000 tons gross, of which about 36 percent (in terms of tonnage) were tankers. Most Danish ships were propelled by diesel engines; there is substantial ferry traffic between Denmark and neighbouring countries.

French shipping

The principal activity of the French mercantile marine is the carrying of trade from metropolitan France to parts of the French Union and its former members, notably to North Africa, West Africa, and the West Indies, and to former French-controlled territories in Southeast Asia. By 1971 the French flag fleet amounted to over 7,000,000 tons gross, including a high proportion of specially designed banana carriers and fruit ships and a significant number of passenger liners.

German shipping suffered heavily in World Wars I and II but recovered rapidly; the West German fleet totalled over 2,800 vessels of 8,678,000 tons gross by 1971. Roughly similar tonnage groups are employed for tramping and bulk cargoes, amounting in each case to about one-fifth of total tonnage, while regular shipping services account for about one-third. The German merchant fleet also runs a passenger service. The transportation activities of the German merchant fleet take the form mainly of import and export via German ports and in so-called cross trade between foreign ports, which in 1971 accounted for 40 percent of carryings. Tankers account for about one-fifth of German sea transportation; Germany's refrigerated shipping, with over 70 units, is the most efficient of its kind. German firms have also entered the container trade, carrying cargoes between Bremerhaven and Australia.

After World War II, Greek shipowners purchased large numbers of war-built United States Liberty ships to replace vessels lost during the conflict. Thereafter, a decline set in, with many Greek owners preferring to register their ships under flags of convenience. In the 1950s more favourable Greek maritime legislation brought about a large-scale repatriation of Greek-owned tonnage to the national flag, and in 1971 the Greek flag fleet totalled 2,056 vessels of just over 13,000,000 tons gross. Owners of Greek nationality achieved a predominant position in world dry-cargo and tanker tramping after World War II, operating mainly from London and New York.

Though Italy lost an enormous percentage of its merchant fleet during World War II, by 1953 the prewar total was exceeded, and by 1970 the Italian flag fleet exceeded 8,100,000 tons gross. A state-owned liner group built several large passenger liners, fast cargo liners, and specialized ships, while private firms engaged in liner, tramping, and tanker operations.

The Netherlands' shipping industry consists of oceangoing passenger and cargo liners, tankers owned by the major oil companies, and coasting and short-sea vessels engaged mainly in trade with the United Kingdom and neighbouring and Baltic Sea countries. The granting of independence to Indonesia caused the Dutch liner companies to lose much of their traditional network of services, but they established themselves in other trades, notably to the Great Lakes in North America, to Australia, and to the Far East. In 1971 the fleet totalled over 5,200,000 tons gross.

Although the overseas trade of Norway itself is not sufficient to maintain a large merchant fleet, Norwegian shipping grew to large proportions through the enterprise of Norwegian shipowners in the worldwide tramping trades. A number of liner groups developed, operating worldwide services, but the recovery and expansion of the fleet after World War II to 21,720,000 tons gross in 1971 (almost half being tankers) was again due to the enterprise of tramp-tanker owners.

In 1971 the Swedish merchant fleet amounted to almost 5,000,000 tons gross, of which about 35 percent were tankers. In addition to a substantial coasting and short-sea traffic and a fair-sized oceangoing tramp fleet, Sweden has a number of well-established liner groups. Iron ore is a major Swedish export; a large fleet of ore carriers exists to carry this trade, many of the larger units being able to carry iron-ore exports on the outward voyage and cargoes of imported oil products on the return trip.

Japan. The geographical situation of Japan is favourable to the natural development of a large shipping industry; in 1971 that nation's fleet was the second largest in the world, totalling over 30,000,000 tons gross, and was expected to double by 1975. Though 60 to 70 percent of shipping is in the liner trades, the tramper side was expanding more rapidly, and Japan's world share of the three most important raw materials carried by tramps— iron ores, coking coals, and cereals—increased from 18 percent in 1963 to 40 percent in 1969. Japan has entered the container trade with the formation of five shipping firm groups operating services in the Pacific between Japan and the Pacific coast of the United States and between Japan and Australia.

Japanese tramping

Liberia and Panama. Liberia and Panama are both flags of convenience; in 1971 the Liberian fleet was the largest single-flag fleet in the world, totalling 38,552,000 tons gross. The Panamanian flag flew over 6,260,000 gross tons. Of the Liberian fleet, nearly 55 percent consists of tankers, with the remainder dry-cargo ships or bulk carriers engaged in international tramping. Nearly 60 percent of the Panamanian fleet is also tankers.

Eastern Europe. Poland and the Soviet Union have the largest merchant fleets in eastern Europe, with the Polish fleet comprising 606 ships, with a total of 1,760,000 tons gross in 1971. Container ships were being operated by the Polish Ocean Lines between Polish and British ports, and services were planned on the Baltic and North Atlantic and Far East routes to start in 1974, when a large number of container ships under construction would be in service. During 1971 East Germany's merchant fleet topped 1,000,000 tons gross for the first time.

The merchant fleet of the Soviet Union registered a phenomenal growth after World War II, amounting in 1971 to 16,194,000 gross tons, of which over one-quarter was tankers. Though the Soviet fleet included no container ships, some 600,000 tons were transported in containers on conventional ships in 1970, and a program was announced in 1971 for construction of container ships for both international and coastal trade. The Soviet Union is experimenting with gas-turbine-engine ships; one, the 11,800-horsepower "Paris Commune," built in 1968, had by 1971 successfully sailed more than 70,000 miles (110,000 kilometres) and carried 150,000 tons of cargo across the Atlantic.

Soviet gas-turbine ships

People's Republic of China. The fleet of China exceeded 1,000,000 tons gross for the first time in 1971.

United States. By mid-1971 the total seagoing merchant fleet of the United States comprised over 3,300 ships, totalling 16,265,000 tons gross. Of the oceangoing fleet, 345 vessels, totalling 4,644,000 tons gross, were tankers, container ships totalling over 1,000,000 tons. One of the largest container shipping lines operated 45 vessels in 1971, carrying containers to 48 ports in 23 countries around the world. Another specialized container line operates across the North Atlantic with especially fast ships including two gas-turbine models capable of 28 knots. United States shipping on the Great Lakes reached a peak in 1934 and nearly matched that total in 1956. Thereafter, prospects began to decline with the decrease of iron-ore deposits in the area and with the completion of the St. Lawrence Seaway, which opened the Great Lakes to intense competition from oceangoing foreign flag vessels.

PROBLEMS OF THE SHIPPING INDUSTRY

As shipping entered the 1970s it faced a number of new problems, largely caused by the changing pattern and continual growth of world trade and the technological advances that brought larger, speedier, and otherwise improved vessels. The volume of cargo moving in international trade doubled between 1900 and 1950 and quadrupled between 1950 and 1970, from 500,000,000 tons to 2,000,000,000. During the same period—1900 to 1970—the merchant fleet increased sevenfold, most of it in the last 20 years. If past rates of increase in population, trade, and shipping are maintained, by the year 2000 the world fleet required to carry the seaborne proportion could be six times the level of today, or about 1,200,000,000 tons. Faced with this prospect, shipowners have striven for greater size, efficiency, and diversification. Shipping has become more specialized and more capital intensive. In the bulk trades, the trend has been increasingly away from spot charter of general-purpose ships toward long-term contracts, in which owners undertake to carry large volumes of a particular cargo over a period of years. This has led to owners cooperating in consortia to accumulate the necessary finance, tonnage, and management resources and to building specialized ships to meet the requirements of shippers. Between 1960 and 1970 the typical bulk-carrier size shot up from about 15,000 to 20,000 tons. For oil tankers the growth has been even greater, with the typical supertanker rising from about 50,000 tons in the late 1950s to 250,000 tons in the 1970s, with vessels up to 3,500,000 being constructed and vessels of 500,000 to 1,000,000 tons planned. Specialization in the carriage of liquid cargoes, such as chemicals and liquefied gas, to meet the growing demand has also required more costly and sophisticated ships. In general cargo, the major change has been in the development of containerization, with its certain advantages of speed, reliability, and control. But all these developments create new technical problems for the industry—in handling at sea and in port, in threatened pollution of the oceans and seacoasts, in an imbalance between the conventional liner and tramps and the bulk, unit load, container, and roll-on, roll-off ships. New international regulations are required, including those on pollution. This imbalance was particularly noticeable at the beginning of the 1970s, with an overcapacity of container ships, particularly on the North Atlantic routes, where container capacity exceeded cargo availability by some 50 percent. This led to withdrawal of some of the consortia from the trade. Equally, the ports of the world competing for the container trade were constructing the necessary facilities far in excess of requirements. At the same time the industry faced rising costs both in ship construction and operation. To help to meet these higher operating costs, automatic controls are being applied at every stage of a journey and the randomness of operation is being eliminated at the same time as the ratio of manpower to vessel size is being reduced.

Over-capacity problems

The passenger trade faced a more serious and longer lasting problem. Competition from air, particularly on the longer sea voyages, had drastically reduced demand for passenger accommodations. On the North Atlantic routes, in 1970, scheduled and chartered flights carried 2,202,000 passengers between North America and Europe, while ships carried only 249,000. To meet this challenge, growing with the advent of the jumbo jet, the passenger shipping companies were turning to car ferries and cruises. Their future appears to lie in the leisure and holiday field.

Meanwhile, many of the older problems of the shipping industry remain. Despite the large measure of international agreement and cooperation achieved in the shipping industry, competition among merchant fleets persists. Current problems and developments have driven several major lines to merge nationally or to cooperate through consortia at the international level.

The shipping industry is unique in that it has an economic and strategic as well as a commercial importance and is rarely free from political or strategic interference by governments. For internal political reasons, some states consider shipping services as a state monopoly. In practice, however, this is difficult to achieve since a state's jurisdiction does not extend beyond territorial waters. Nevertheless, various practices are observed from time to time to protect the domestic shipping industry and to discriminate against other flags. Higher port dues may be charged to foreign ships, or national flag ships may be favoured. In bilateral trade agreements it is sometimes stipulated that a fixed proportion of the cargoes must be carried in ships of the national flag. A common method of assisting the domestic shipping industry is to reserve coastal shipping to ships of the national flag, a policy that greatly assisted the expansion of the British mercantile marine until the policy was abandoned with the repeal of the Navigation Acts in 1849, except for the coastal trades, which were not brought into line until 1854. Several other nations, notably the United States, still follow this practice and strictly reserve their coastal trade for their own vessels. Assistance in the form of tax exemptions, preferential credit terms, direct subsidy of shipbuilding, or operating costs is often given to protect national fleets.

Although operating costs are much the same for ships of all flags, the rates of taxation vary, and after World War II heavy taxes, combined with a sharp rise in shipbuilding prices, caused the registration of more and more shipping companies under flags of convenience. Some 40,000,000 gross tons, over one-fifth of world tonnage, were so registered in the early 1970s.

Despite problems, the shipping industry has always proved itself resilient and, particularly in recent years, ready to adopt new technological aids to efficiency. Thus, it can be expected to meet the challenge of competition and changes in economic conditions. Its adaptation may be less through the increase of vessel sizes and the resultant economy of scale than through even greater specialization, rationalization of existing structures, and innovations through new types of vessels and services.

BIBLIOGRAPHY. CHARLES SINGER *et al.* (eds.), *A History of Technology*, 5 vol. (1954–58), an authoritative and standard work containing much material on the history and development of ships and shipping; GUNNAR ALEXANDERSSON and GORAN NORSTROM, *World Shipping* (1963), an economic geography of ports and seaborne trade that gives a general survey of international trade and shipping and covers all branches of cargo traffic from World War I onward—the most comprehensive work on the subject; DANIEL MARX, JR., *International Shipping Cartels* (1953), a study of industrial self-help regulation of shipping conferences that describes and analyzes the functions of these organizations and provides detailed data on their operations; E.F. STEVENS, *Shipping Practice*, 9th ed. (1970), a concise technical manual on procedures, practices, and relevant law of all aspects of the shipping industry that is periodically revised and brought up to date together with the current forms and documentation employed; *Lloyd's Register of Shipping Annual Reports and Statistical Tables*, the *Chamber of Commerce of the United Kingdom Annual Reports and British Shipping Statistics*, and the *American Bureau of Shipping Annual Reports and Statistics*, standard reference works with detailed statistics on world shipping; GEORGE BLAKE, *Lloyd's Register of Shipping, 1760–1960* (1960), the romantic history of Lloyd's Register of Shipping from its foundation to the world role it holds in the classification and vetting of ships; ORGANIZATION FOR ECONOMIC COOPERATION AND DEVELOPMENT, *Annual Reports of Its Maritime Committee*, contains international shipping developments during the year in the OECD countries and much data on the supply and demand in the shipping industry and the freight markets with statistical tables; the 1970 report includes a review of seaborne trade in the 1960s.

(E.A.J.D.)

Transport Phenomena

The subject of transport phenomena in physics is generally understood to deal with the movement of various entities, such as mass, momentum, or energy, through a medium, fluid or solid, by virtue of nonuniform conditions existing within the medium. Variations of concentration in a medium, for example, lead to the relative motion of the various chemical species present, and this mass transport is generally referred to as diffusion. Variations of velocity within a fluid result in the transport of momentum, which is normally referred to as viscous flow. Variations in temperature result in the transport of energy, a process usually called heat conduction. There are many similarities in the mathematical description of these three phenomena, and, hence, it is advantageous to group them together as one subject. Furthermore, the three phenomena often occur together physically, as in combustion, where a flowing, viscous, fluid mixture is undergoing chemical reactions that produce heat, which is conducted away, and that produce various chemical species that interdiffuse with one another.

Transport phenomena include not only the transport of mass, momentum, and energy but also the transport of angular momentum, electrical charge, entropy, and other quantities. The mechanism for transport of the various entities can involve neutrons, ions, photons, colloidal particles, macromolecules, and other particles. This article is restricted for the most part to transport of mass, momentum, and energy in fluids composed of molecules.

Varieties of transport phenomena

Transport phenomena can be studied at various levels of description, all the way from the molecule level, where one deals with the transport occurring by virtue of molecular collisions, to the industrial-equipment level, where one is concerned with mass, momentum, and energy relations for large pieces of apparatus.

Kinetic molecular theory of transport properties. The transport properties to be considered are viscosity (a measure of the resistance to flow), thermal conductivity (a measure of the ability to conduct heat), and diffusivity (a measure of the tendency to interdiffuse); these properties are characteristic for each substance, and they depend in general on the temperature, pressure, and composition of the substance. Fluids that flow sluggishly (*i.e.*, fluids with high viscosity), such as molasses, are more difficult to shear or distort than are fluids with low viscosity; or, to phrase it differently, momentum is transferred more rapidly in fluids of high viscosity than in fluids of low viscosity. Thermal conductivity is a measure of the ability of a material to conduct heat; copper has a high thermal conductivity and transfers energy by conduction quickly, whereas wood has a low thermal conductivity and transports energy by conduction slowly. The diffusivity of a two-component mixture is a measure of the tendency of the two species to intermingle or diffuse into one another; a high diffusivity indicates that the mass of one species is transported quickly relative to the motion of the mixture, whereas a low diffusivity indicates that the mass will be transported slowly. Viscosity, thermal conductivity, and diffusivity, therefore, are associated with the transport of momentum, energy, and mass, respectively.

Theoretical physics has developed kinetic theories (that is, theories based on the motion of the molecules and the dynamics of their collisions) that enable the prediction of transport properties from the properties of the individual molecules making up the material. Although the theories are highly mathematical and the details quite tedious, the final results are simple and easy to use.

Idealized molecular models

Because of the complexity of these theories it is necessary to introduce some kind of idealization (or model) for the molecules that make up the matter under consideration; for example, nonpolar molecules (*i.e.*, molecules with negligible dipole moment—the dipole moment being defined as the product of the distance between two poles and the charge on one pole; examples of nonpolar molecules are methane and nitrogen) are sometimes approximated as rigid spheres; polar molecules (molecules with a non-negligible dipole moment such as water and ammonia) are considered to be rigid spheres with an embedded dipole (*i.e.*, they have a positive and negative pole built in). Very long molecules may be approximated as ellipsoids, and macromolecules or polymers may be pictured as beads interconnected with springs. These idealizations or simplifications are generally referred to as models. The reason such models are needed when, in fact, so much is known today about molecular structure is twofold: first, most transport properties are not terribly sensitive to details of molecular structure, and, second, the kinetic-theory calculations would be prohibitively difficult if they were to include all of the information about molecular structure. In the molecular model, therefore, only such information is included as seems intuitively to be essential for describing the properties that are to be calculated.

Gases. In calculations for gases consisting of nonpolar molecules, the idealization that they are rigid spheres is

often useful. For viscosity of a pure gas, thermal conductivity of a pure gas, and diffusivity of a binary mixture of gases equations can be developed that show how the transport properties depend on the absolute temperature, the pressure, the molecular weight, and the diameter of the rigid sphere. Based on the rather crude rigid-spherical model, these equations give the essential behaviour of the transport properties of gases: the increase of viscosity, thermal conductivity, and diffusivity with temperature; the fact that viscosity and thermal conductivity are independent of pressure; and the fact that diffusivity is inversely proportional to pressure. These results also show that the transport properties are all inversely proportional to the square of the diameter of the molecules; *i.e.*, the larger the molecule, the smaller the value of the transport property. The formulas have been considerably refined by using more realistic molecular models that take into account the attractive and repulsive forces between molecules, their shape, and their dipole moments. With these equations, the transport properties of gases can often be estimated within 1 or 2 percent of the experimental values over rather wide ranges of temperature and pressure.

Realistic molecular models

Liquids. For liquids, the kinetic theory has not yet been developed to as high a degree of utility as it has been for gases; the problem with liquids is orders of magnitude more difficult because the molecules are in a continual state of multiple collision, whereas for dilute gases only binary, or two-body, collisions have to be considered. Although considerable work has been done, the most useful formulations at present employ a very rough picture of the liquid state. These rough theories lead to the following widely used results: the Eyring equation for viscosity, the Bridgman equation for thermal conductivity, and the Stokes-Einstein equation for diffusivity; these equations relate the transport properties to Avogadro's number (number of molecules in one mole of the substance), Planck's constant, Boltzmann's constant, the molar volume, the absolute temperature, the boiling point, the velocity of sound, the radius of the diffusing species, and the viscosity of the solvent. Until rigorous theories have been worked out and the concomitant numerical analysis completed, the above-mentioned equations are useful as rough approximations.

Suspensions. For suspensions and other kinds of two-phase materials (consisting of any two phases of matter; *e.g.*, gas–liquid or liquid–solid), the transport properties of the composite, or mixture, can sometimes be computed in terms of the properties of the individual phases. The most famous of these is Einstein's formula for the viscosity of a dilute suspension of rigid spheres in a viscous liquid, obtained by methods of classical hydrodynamics; this gives the suspension viscosity in terms of the viscosity of the solvent, the radius of the suspended spheres, and the concentration of the spheres. Einstein's work has been extended to emulsions (suspensions of liquid droplets in a liquid), suspensions of deformable spheres, suspensions of ellipsoids, and other, more complicated kinds of two-phase fluids.

Polymers. For polymer solutions (a polymer is a macromolecule formed by joining together chemically thousands of small molecules called monomers), various bead–spring or bead–rod models have been used. These models consist of many beads joined together by rods or springs, with freely rotating joints. These pearl necklaces, as they are sometimes called, are imagined to be suspended in a solvent in which they are subjected to hydrodynamic drag forces and Brownian-motion forces (the movement imparted to particles of larger than molecular size by bombardment of the liquid molecules). The simplest model of this type is the rigid dumbbell—two beads connected by a rigid rod. For this model it is possible to obtain an expression for the viscosity in terms of the concentration (number of dumbbells per unit volume), solvent viscosity, temperature, and a time constant which depends on the drag coefficient of the bead and the length of the dumbbell. The result is interesting because it shows that the viscosity decreases with increasing velocity gradient (or, to put it another

Models for polymeric molecules

way, with rate of shear), a phenomenon that is well-known in polymer solutions (often called non-Newtonian viscosity or shear thinning). The time constant that appears in the expression is also interesting because it is related to the rate at which stress relaxation, recoil, and other time-dependent phenomena occur in polymer solutions. Many more complicated models have been used for polymer kinetic theory, and the theory is highly developed and mathematically rather complicated.

Phenomenological expressions of transport. *Rate equations in simplified cases.* To make the connection between the transport properties and the rates at which momentum, energy, and mass are transported, equations for the fluxes (flow per unit area per unit time) are introduced. These mathematical expressions, which define the transport properties can be discussed in terms of three simple "thought," or imaginary, experiments.

"Thought" experiments

To understand viscosity and momentum transport, a fluid is imagined to be placed in the region between two parallel plane surfaces separated by a known distance, and the lower plane, or plate, is imagined to be moving with a constant velocity while the other remains stationary. The force per unit area that has to be supplied to the lower plate is postulated to be directly proportional to the velocity of the plate and inversely proportional to the distance between the plates (that is, the farther apart the plates, the smaller the force). This is Newton's law of viscosity, and the proportionality coefficient, found by measurement of the other factors, is called the viscosity of that particular fluid.

For describing thermal conductivity and energy transport, a material is imagined to be placed in the region between two parallel plates with a known separation, as before. The top plate is held at a fixed temperature, whereas the bottom plate is maintained at a higher temperature. It is reasonable to expect, then, that the rate of heat flow upward will be proportional to the temperature difference and inversely proportional to the plate separation. This is Fourier's law of heat conduction, and the proportionality constant in the equation that relates the various quantities is called the thermal conductivity of the substance.

For describing diffusivity and mass transport, a mixture of two substances, A and B, is imagined to be placed between the two parallel plates, again as before. The concentration of A at the upper plate may be expressed as the mass fraction (the mass of A per unit volume, divided by the mass of the mixture AB per unit volume), and the concentration at the lower plate is at a higher concentration. It would be expected that the rate of movement of A would be proportional to the difference between the two concentrations and inversely proportional to the distance between the plates. This is to a good approximation Fick's (first) law of diffusion, and the proportionality constant is conventionally taken to be the product of the density and the diffusivity.

Similarity of three formulations

The description above shows that the elementary experiments used to relate the transport properties and the fluxes, or rate of transport, are quite similar and that the three formulations that describe the fluxes have a similar mathematical form that may be written: (flux) = (transport property) × (driving force).

These laws of Newton, Fourier, and Fick are generally written as differential expressions that give linear relationships between the fluxes and the gradients. The laws written in this way are valid for unidirectional transport. When one considers the more general situation that the velocity, temperature, and concentration depend on all three directions in space and on the time, then the phenomenological relations have to be generalized. The generalizations for the energy and mass fluxes (which are vectors, quantities that associate a scalar with each coordinate direction) are straightforward; but the generalization for the momentum flux (which is a tensor, a quantity that associates a scalar with each ordered pair of coordinate directions) is somewhat more complicated. In fact, in the process of generalizing Newton's law, which contains the viscosity, one obtains an expression with two physical properties: the viscosity and the dilatational viscosity. The latter property is much less well-known; it describes the resistance to flow in which an expansion or contraction of the fluid occurs.

Exceptions and qualifications. There are further generalizations: (1) For multicomponent mixtures the generalization of Fick's law is rather complicated; if the number of chemical species present is designated by N, then there will be N times N–1 diffusivities required to describe the diffusional processes occurring. (2) Even for binary mixtures, Fick's law is incomplete; if there is a thermal gradient in the system, there may be a flow of matter (*i.e.,* a mass flux) associated with this gradient, known as thermal diffusion, or the Soret effect; the effect has been exploited for separating isotopic mixtures (isotopes of an element are atoms with identical chemical properties but different mass) in a device called the Clusius–Dickel column. If there is a pressure gradient in the system, there will be a flux of mass, and such a phenomenon is called pressure diffusion. The effect is used in centrifugation, the technique of whirling or spinning mixtures at enormously fast speeds, causing the heavier components to concentrate in the container farthest from the axis of rotation. In addition, if the diffusing mixture contains ions, then an electric field can bring about an ionic flux, and such a phenomenon is termed forced diffusion. (3) Fourier's law is valid only for a pure substance. For mixtures there may be flow of energy, or an energy flux, associated with a variation in concentration; this is termed the diffusion-thermo effect, or the Dufour effect. The Dufour and Soret effects and other "cross effects" have been studied from the viewpoint of the thermodynamics of irreversible processes. (4) The various phenomenological laws discussed above embody the idea that the fluxes are directly proportional to the gradients. For energy and mass transport this kind of relationship has been found to be satisfactory, and for momentum transport in gases and chemically simple liquids the linear relationship is also satisfactory. For structurally complex fluids, however, notably polymers, it is found that Newton's law of viscosity is totally inadequate; such fluids are termed non-Newtonian fluids, and they exhibit some remarkable flow properties. Not only does the viscosity become dependent on the velocity gradient (*i.e.,* the viscosity changes as the rate of shear is increased) but, in addition, even in steady shear flow the normal stresses are not zero, and they, too, depend on the velocity gradient. Furthermore, in generalizing from steady-state to unsteady-state flows, additional information about the time-response properties of the fluids (*i.e.,* the time it takes for the fluid to respond to changes imposed on it) have to be included. This requirement leads to the construction of rather complex mathematical expressions for the momentum flux needed to describe such nonlinear effects of viscosity and elasticity. The subject is generally treated under rheology, the science of deformation and flow.

Energy transport by radiation. All the fluxes discussed so far have been associated with molecular phenomena. For energy transport an important additional mechanism must be discussed; namely, energy transport by radiation, a type of transport that can occur through a vacuum. The simplest case deals with the energy emitted from what is called a black body, and it is given by the celebrated Stefan–Boltzmann law, an equation that relates the energy flux to the absolute temperature, the Boltzmann constant, the speed of light, and Planck's constant. This formula is extremely useful in physics, but it applies only to energy transport across a vacuum. The problems of radiant-energy transport through moving, absorbing fluids are exceedingly difficult to deal with.

Hydrodynamic aspects of transport. *Equations of change.* In many situations one wishes to obtain what are called the profiles or distributions of velocity, temperature, and concentration—*i.e.,* the dependence of these quantities on position and time. This problem is solved by combining the equations for the fluxes given in the previous section with the equations of change or conservation equations, which express the laws of conservation of mass, momentum, and energy for a continuous medium. The equations for conservation of mass for the

The
momen-
tum-
conserva-
tion
equations

various species are often called the equations of continuity. The three momentum-conservation equations, usually called the equations of motion, result from applying Newton's second law of motion to the fluid (*i.e.*, mass times acceleration equals the sum of the pressure and of viscous and gravity forces). The energy equation is the statement of the first law of thermodynamics applied to the flowing fluid (that is, the energy increase is equated to the heat added minus the work done). These equations form the starting point for theoretical hydrodynamics, the rheology of viscoelastic fluids, heat transfer, diffusion, and the fluid dynamics of reacting fluids. In order to use the equations of change for calculating the velocity, temperature, concentration, and pressure distributions, one must insert the expressions for the fluxes in terms of the transport coefficients.

The solution to the equations of change is no easy task. Considerable attention has been given to the analytical and numerical solutions since their formulation in the middle of the 19th century. Thousands of solutions for appropriately simplified boundary and initial conditions have been tabulated in the literature and are widely used in science and engineering. Furthermore, the equations are the starting point for many fields of study, including hydrodynamics, heat transfer, diffusion, acoustics, aerodynamics, lubrication theory, viscoelastic flow, boundary-layer, turbulence, and reactive-gas dynamics.

Transfer coefficients at boundary surfaces. For many applications there is no need for detailed velocity, temperature, and concentration profiles—only for the rate at which momentum, energy, and mass are transferred at some bounding surface. This situation leads to the definition of transfer coefficients that can be calculated if the profiles are known. For very complex situations the transfer coefficients are often obtained experimentally and then correlated by means of dimensional analysis, a practical method for summarizing the results of many experiments.

First the transfer of momentum is considered at solid surfaces, leading to the definition of the friction factor, or drag coefficient. A fluid flowing through a duct or around a submerged object will exert a force on the duct or object. This force will contain two parts: the force that would be exerted even if the fluid were stationary and the additional force associated with the fluid motion. (The discussion is restricted to flows that result in a simple force on the solid but with no torque, or twisting effect.) It is then customary to define the friction factor as the proportionality constant between the force associate with the fluid motion and the product of a characteristic area and a characteristic kinetic energy per unit volume. For flow in conduits, the area is taken to be the wetted inside surface area, and the kinetic energy is taken to be the average velocity inside the conduit. For flow around submerged objects, the area is taken to be the area obtained by projecting the solid onto a plane perpendicular to the velocity of approach of the fluid, and the kinetic energy is taken to be the approach velocity of the fluid at large distances. For flow in circular tubes, for example, the friction factor is given separately for laminar flow and for turbulent flow. The laminar-flow equation is merely a restatement of the Hagen-Poiseuille law for laminar flow in circular tubes, and it may be derived by solving the equations of motion and continuity for an incompressible fluid. The turbulent-flow-friction-factor equation is only approximate and is obtained essentially from experimental data.

For flow around spheres, the friction factor (drag coefficient) can be obtained for creeping flow and for noncreeping flow. The creeping-flow equation, or expression, is merely a restatement of the Stokes law for creeping (*i.e.*, very slow) flow around a sphere; the second expression, for noncreeping flow, is empirical and designed to fit the experimental data over a wide range.

The transfer of energy at solid–fluid boundaries is usually discussed in terms of the heat-transfer coefficient. It is defined as the proportionality coefficient between the wall heat flow and the product of the heat transfer area and the temperature differences. The expression obtained for the heat loss from a heated object shows that the heat loss increases as the velocity of the surrounding fluid increases. An equation of this type is the basis for the wind-chill temperature, which accounts for the heat loss from the human body in a cold wind.

Finally, the transfer of mass at solid-fluid boundaries is usually expressed in terms of a mass-transfer coefficient. The mass-transfer coefficient (for small concentrations and small mass-transfer rates) is defined as the proportionality constant between the molar flow of one species into the fluid across the solid surface and the mass-transfer area and the concentration difference. The results for the heat transfer may be taken over for isothermal mass transfer simply by changing the nomenclature. The great similarity between the results for heat and mass transfer stems basically from the fact that, when the proper assumptions are made, the differential equations describing the two processes are identical. Considerable use is made in engineering of this analogous behaviour.

Transport in macrosystems. For the description of pieces of industrial equipment or portions thereof, it is customary to use integrals of the equations of change known as the macroscopic balances. These are relations among the input quantities (that is, various quantities pertaining to fluid streams entering the equipment), the output quantities, and the quantities describing the interaction of the system with its surroundings; the various transfer coefficients discussed in the preceding section are used.

The general results of the integration of equations for multicomponent reacting mixtures are too complicated to present here, but for pure fluids the integration of the equations of change over the volume of the system may be described schematically thus (the integration of an equation is designed by $\int$):

$\int$ (equation of continuity) $\rightarrow$ macroscopic mass balance
$\int$ (equation of motion) $\rightarrow$ macroscopic momentum balance
$\int$ (velocity times equation of motion) $\rightarrow$ macroscopic mechanical energy balance
$\int$ (position vector times equation of motion) $\rightarrow$ macroscopic angular momentum balance
$\int$ (equation of energy) $\rightarrow$ macroscopic energy balance

The resulting balances are rather simple in form if one makes the following assumptions concerning the whole system: (1) it is in a steady state, (2) it has flat velocity profiles at input and output, and (3) it has no swirling of the fluid at input and output.

BIBLIOGRAPHY. For general background, see R.B. BIRD, W.E. STEWART, and E.N. LIGHTFOOT, *Transport Phenomena* (1960, 10th corr. ptg. 1970), an elementary textbook on viscous flow, heat conduction, and diffusion. For mathematical and theoretical reference, see S. CHAPMAN and T.G. COWLING, *Mathematical Theory of Non-Uniform Gases*, 3rd ed. (1970), the modern mathematical treatise on the transport properties of dilute and ionized gases; and J.O. HIRSCHFELDER, C.F. CURTISS, and R.B. BIRD, *Molecular Theory of Gases and Liquids*, 2nd corr. ptg. (1964), a compendium of theories and formularies for the thermodynamic and transport properties with emphasis on intermolecular forces. For applications of transport theory, see L. LANDAU and E.M. LIFSHITZ, *Fluid Mechanics*, trans. by J.B. SYKES and W.H. REID (1959; orig. pub. in Russian, 1954), an advanced textbook dealing with the continuum theory of transport phenomena, including applications to detonations, sound propagation, shock waves, and liquid helium; W. JOST, *Diffusion in Solids, Liquids and Gases* (1952), a survey of the kinetic theory and experimental methods in diffusion; and H.S. CARSLAW and J.C. JAEGER, *Conduction of Heat in Solids*, 2nd ed. (1959), the classic work on heat conduction, containing thousands of solutions to the heat conduction equations. Of historical interest is L. BOLTZMANN, *Vorlesungen über Gastheorie*, 2 vol. (1896–98; Eng. trans., *Lectures on Gas Theory*, 1964), the pioneering book on the kinetic theory of transport phenomena in dilute gases.

(R.B.Bi.)

Transuranium Elements

The transuranium elements are so called because they all lie beyond uranium; that is, they are elements with atomic numbers higher than 92 in the periodic table (see Figure 1). Thirteen elements, up to and including atomic number 105, have been discovered. All are unstable, decaying

The
heat-
transfer
and
mass-
transfer
coefficients

The
friction
factor

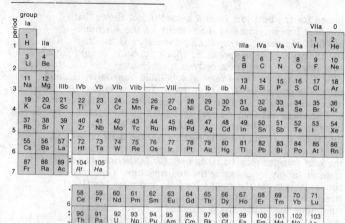

Figure 1: Transuranium elements in the periodic table.

radioactively, with half-lives that range from tens of millions of years to fractions of a second. Since only two of the 13 have been found in nature, and those only in trace amounts, the synthesis of these elements through nuclear reactions is an important source of man's knowledge about them. That knowledge has expanded man's understanding of the fundamental structure of matter and makes it possible to predict the existence and basic properties of elements much heavier than element number 105; i.e., the "superheavy" elements with atomic numbers from around 110 to 126. Since it is predicted that these should have significant nuclear stability and, therefore, may exist in nature, some of them are being sought. Elements with atomic numbers even higher, around 164, are also predicted, but with lesser stability; and present theory suggests that the maximum atomic number will be found to lie somewhere between 170 and 210. All these still unknown elements belong to the transuranium group.

Although the first transuranium element was found only in 1940, some have already become useful, for example as fuel in the generation of electricity from nuclear fission. Isotopes (see below) of transuranium elements are used in the diagnosis and treatment of disease and in control methods in industrial processes. They may also become useful in cancer therapy and in chemical analysis.

DISCOVERY OF THE FIRST TRANSURANIUM ELEMENTS

General atomic structure. To understand the subject of transuranium elements, a knowledge of atomic structure is necessary. Here, only a brief and very general summary of atomic structure can be given. The basic structure of atoms was understood by the early 1930s. Every atom consists of a massive nucleus surrounded by electrons, each with negligible mass. The nucleus is composed of two particles (called nucleons and bonded together), the neutron and the proton, of about equal mass, but with a positive electrical charge on the proton. All the atomic nuclei of a particular element have a fixed number of protons and, therefore, a fixed positive charge (e.g., uranium has 92), and this is called its atomic number, symbolized as Z. The number of neutrons bonded to any Z, however, is not fixed. In fact, every element has several species of atoms each with the same number of protons with different numbers of neutrons. The sum of neutrons and protons, called the atomic mass number, is symbolized as A. All the species of an element are called its isotopes. Some nuclei are unstable and decay in any of several ways, the process producing other nuclei with different Z and A. A nucleus bombarded by neutrons may absorb one and become another isotope of that element—the A having changed, but the Z remaining the same—and become unstable (that is, radioactive), so that it will decay into the isotope of a different element. If large enough, the nucleus that captured the neutron may split (fission) into two more or less equal parts, each being an isotope of an element. Since the bonding forces in a nucleus involve extremely high concentrations of energy, any sort of nuclear change produces exceedingly large energy changes, relative to the energy changes that

accompany chemical reactions; the latter involve only the orbiting electrons, and their energy changes are ignored when nuclear reactions are discussed.

First synthesis. The first attempt to prepare a transuranium element was made in 1934 in Rome where a team of Italian physicists headed by Enrico Fermi and Emilio Segrè bombarded uranium nuclei with free neutrons. Although transuranium species may have been produced, the results of the experiment were ultimately interpreted by the German physical chemists Otto Hahn and Fritz Strussman in terms of nuclear fission. Not until 1940 was a transuranium element first positively produced and identified by two American physicists, Edwin Mattison McMillan and Philip Hauge Abelson, who, in California, exposed uranium oxide to neutrons from a cyclotron target. The resulting element was found to have an atomic number of 93. It was named neptunium.

Transformations in atomic nuclei are represented by equations that balance all the particles of matter and the energy involved before and after the reaction. The above transformation of uranium into neptunium may be written as follows:

$$^{238}_{92}U(n,\gamma)^{239}_{92}U \xrightarrow{\beta^-} \, ^{239}_{93}Np$$

In this equation, the atomic symbol of the particular isotope reacted upon, in this case U for uranium, is given with its mass number (sum of neutrons and protons, or A) at upper left and its atomic number (protons, or Z) at lower left: $^{238}_{92}U$. The symbols within the parentheses indicate, first, the species of matter or of energy (here n for neutron) reacting with the nucleus and, second, the species (here γ, for a quantum of energy called a gamma ray) emitted by the nucleus during the reaction. The resulting isotope is shown next, with its changed mass at the upper left ($^{239}_{92}U$). Together, these symbols represent the transformation of a single uranium-238 nucleus, reacting with a neutron and releasing gamma radiation, to produce the isotope uranium-239. The next event is represented by an arrow showing a spontaneous loss of a beta particle (symbolized β), an electron with very high velocity, from the nucleus of uranium-239. What has happened is that a neutron within the nucleus has been transformed into a proton, with the emission of a beta particle which carries off a single negative charge; the nucleus, therefore, now has one more positive charge than it had before the event, when its atomic number was 92. The resulting isotope, as a result, has an atomic number of 93 but, because the beta particle has negligible mass, the mass number of the nucleus has not changed. It is still 239. The nucleus resulting from these events is an isotope of the element neptunium, atomic number 93, and mass number 239. The above is called negative beta-particle decay; a nucleus may also emit a positron, or positive electron, resulting in beta-particle decay. (In another type of decay the nucleus, instead of emitting a β-particle, "captures" or absorbs one of the electrons orbiting the nucleus, thus reducing the positive charge by one.)

The usual manner of writing nuclear reactions drops the atomic number from the symbol for the element and this rule will be followed in the rest of this article.

The discovery of the next element after neptunium followed rapidly. Early in 1941 three American chemists, Glenn T. Seaborg, J.W. Kennedy, and Arthur C. Wahl, first produced and chemically identified element 94, named plutonium (Pu). In 1944 after further discoveries, Seaborg hypothesized that a new series of elements called the actinide series, akin to the lanthanide series (elements with atomic numbers 58–71) was being produced, and that this new series began with thorium (Th), atomic number 90. Thereafter, discoveries were sought, and made, in accordance with this hypothesis.

For further information on discoveries of transuranium elements, see Table 1.

SYNTHESIS OF TRANSURANIUM ELEMENTS

The most abundant isotope of neptunium is neptunium-237 that, with a half-life of approximately 2×10^6 years for decay by the emission of alpha particles (composed of two neutrons and two protons, actually the very stable

Margin notes:
Atomic structure in the 1930s

Equations for nuclear transformations

Table 1: The Transuranium Elements

atomic number	element	symbol	atomic weight	discoverers and date of discovery	source of first preparation	first isolation in weighable amount—(half-life)
93	neptunium	Np	237*†	E.M. McMillan and P.H. Abelson 1940	irradiation of uranium with neutrons $^{238}U(n, \gamma)$ $^{239}U \xrightarrow{\beta^-} {}^{239}Np$	1944, ^{237}Np (2.14 × 10⁶ years) L.B. Magnusson and T.J. La-Chapelle
94	plutonium	Pu	239† 244*	G.T. Seaborg, E.M. McMillan, J.W. Kennedy, and A.C. Wahl 1940–41	bombardment of uranium with deuterons $^{238}U(^2H, 2n)$ $^{238}Np \xrightarrow{\beta^-} {}^{238}Pu$	1942, ^{239}Pu (24,400 years) B.B. Cunningham and L.B. Werner
95	americium	Am	241† 243*	G.T. Seaborg, R.A. James, L.O. Morgan, and A. Ghiorso 1944–45	irradiation of plutonium with neutrons $^{239}Pu(2n, \gamma)$ $^{241}Pu \xrightarrow{\beta^-} {}^{241}Am$	1945, ^{241}Am (433 years) B.B. Cunningham
96	curium	Cm	244† 247*	G.T. Seaborg, R.A. James, and A. Ghiorso 1944	bombardment of plutonium with helium ions $^{239}Pu(^4He, n)$ ^{242}Cm	1947, ^{242}Cm (162.5 days) L.B. Werner and I. Perlman
97	berkelium	Bk	247* 249†	S.G. Thompson, A. Ghiorso, and G.T. Seaborg 1949	bombardment of americium with helium ions $^{241}Am(^4He, 2n)$ ^{243}Bk	1958, ^{249}Bk (314 days) S.G. Thompson and B.B. Cunningham
98	californium	Cf	251* 252†	S.G. Thompson, K. Street, Jr., A. Ghiorso, and G.T. Seaborg 1950	bombardment of curium with helium ions $^{242}Cm(^4He, n)$ ^{245}Cf	1958, $^{249-252}Cf$ B.B. Cunningham and S.G. Thompson
99	einsteinium	Es	253† 254*	A. Ghiorso, S.G. Thompson, G.H. Higgins, G.T. Seaborg, M.H. Studier, P.R. Fields, S.M. Fried, H. Diamond, J.F. Mech, G.L. Pyle, J.R. Huizenga, A. Hirsch, W.M. Manning, C.I. Browne, H.L. Smith, and R.W. Spence 1952	irradiation of uranium with neutrons in first thermo-nuclear explosion $^{238}U(15n, \gamma)$ $^{253}U \xrightarrow{7\beta^-} {}^{253}Es$	1961, ^{253}Es (20 days) B.B. Cunningham, J.C. Wallmann, L. Phillips, R.C. Gatti
100	fermium	Fm	257*†	A. Ghiorso, S.G. Thompson, G.H. Higgins, G.T. Seaborg, M.H. Studier, P.R. Fields, S.M. Fried, H. Diamond, J.F. Mech, G.L. Pyle, J.R. Huizenga, A. Hirsch, W.M. Manning, C.I. Browne, H.L. Smith, and R.W. Spence 1953	in first thermonuclear explosion $^{238}U(17n, \gamma)$ $^{255}U \xrightarrow{8\beta^-} {}^{255}Fm$	…
101	mendelevium	Md	258*	A. Ghiorso, B.G. Harvey, G.R. Choppin, S.G. Thompson, and G.T. Seaborg 1955	bombardment of einsteinium with helium ions $^{253}Es(^4He, n)$ ^{256}Md	…
102	nobelium	No	259*	A. Ghiorso, T. Sikkeland, J.R. Walton, and G.T. Seaborg 1958	bombardment of curium with carbon ions $^{246}Cm(^{12}C, 4n)$ ^{254}No	…
103	lawrencium	Lr	260*	A. Ghiorso, T. Sikkeland, A.E. Larsh, and R.M. Latimer 1961	bombardment of californium with boron ions $\left.\begin{matrix}{}^{250}Cf\\{}^{251}Cf\\{}^{252}Cf\end{matrix}\right\} + \begin{matrix}{}^{11}B\\{}^{10}B\end{matrix} \longrightarrow {}^{258}Lr + \left\{\begin{matrix}2n\\3n\\4n\\5n\end{matrix}\right.$	…
104	rutherfordium‡	Rf	261*	A. Ghiorso, M. Nurmia, J. Harris, K. Eskola, and P. Eskola 1969	bombardment of californium with carbon ions $^{249}Cf(^{12}C, 4n)$ $^{257}104$ $^{249}Cf(^{12}C, 3n)$ $^{259}104$	…
	kurchatovium§	Ku		G.N. Flerov, Yu. Ts. Oganesyan, Yu. V. Lobanov, V.I. Kuznetsov, V.A. Druin, V.P. Perelygin, K.A. Gavrilov, S.P. Tretyakova, and V.M. Plotko 1964	bombardment of plutonium with neon ions $^{242}Pu(^{22}Ne, 4n)$ $^{260}104$	…
105	hahnium‡	Ha	262*	A. Ghiorso, M. Nurmia, K. Eskola, J. Harris, and P. Eskola 1970	bombardment of californium with nitrogen ions $^{249}Cf(^{15}N, 4n)$ $^{260}105$	…
	nielsbohrium§	Ns		G.N. Flerov, V.A. Druin, A.G. Demin, Yu. V. Lobanov, N.K. Skobelev, G.N. Akapev, B.V. Fefilov, I.V. Kolesov, K.A. Gavrilov, Yu. P. Kharitonov, and L.P. Chelnokov 1968	bombardment of americium with neon ions $^{243}Am(^{22}Ne, 5n)$ $^{260}105$ $^{243}Am(^{22}Ne, 4n)$ $^{261}105$	

*Mass number of longest-lived isotope.   †Mass number of more available isotope.   ‡Proposed by U.S. scientists, not yet approved by Commission on Atomic Weights of International Union of Pure and Applied Chemistry.   §Proposed by U.S.S.R. scientists, not yet approved by Commission on Atomic Weights of International Union of Pure and Applied Chemistry.

nucleus of helium), is formed in kilogram quantities as a by-product of the large-scale production of plutonium in nuclear reactors. This isotope is synthesized from the reactor fuels, uranium-235 and uranium-238, by the following reactions:

$$^{238}U(n, 2n)^{237}U \xrightarrow{\beta^-} {}^{237}Np$$

$$^{235}U(n, \gamma)^{236}U(n, \gamma)^{237}U \xrightarrow{\beta^-} {}^{237}Np$$

In the first reaction, uranium-238 captures one neutron but emits two, reducing the mass number by one. Plutonium, as the isotope plutonium-239, is produced in ton quantities in nuclear reactors by the reaction:

$$^{238}U(n, \gamma)^{239}U \xrightarrow{\beta^-} {}^{239}Np \xrightarrow{\beta^-} {}^{239}Pu$$

The plutonium isotope plutonium-238, which is of sec-

ondary importance, is produced in kilogram quantities by the reaction:

$$^{237}Np(n, \gamma)^{238}Np \xrightarrow{\beta^-} {}^{238}Pu$$

The production of transuranium elements by a process of continuous, intensive irradiation with slow neutrons is illustrated in Figure 2, in which the heavy line indicates the principal path of neutron capture and negative beta-particle decay that results in successively heavier elements and higher atomic numbers. The lighter lines show subsidiary paths that augment the major path. The major path terminates at an isotope of fermium (fermium-257), because the short half-life of the next fermium isotope (fermium-258), for radioactive decay by spontaneous fission (360 microseconds), precludes its production and the production of isotopes of elements beyond fermium

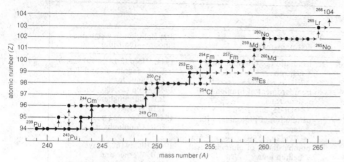

Figure 2: Nuclear reactions for the production of heavy elements by intensive slow neutron irradiation (see text).
From G. Seaborg, "Elements Beyond 100, Present Status and Future Prospects," *Annual Review of Nuclear Science*, vol. 18, p. 119 (1968)

by this means. The lighter lines beyond indicate predictions only.

Heavy isotopes of some transuranium elements are produced in nuclear explosions. Since 1965, underground detonations of nuclear explosive devices have resulted in the production of significant quantities of einsteinium and fermium isotopes, which are separated from rock debris by mining techniques and chemical processing. Again, the heaviest isotope found is that of fermium-257. Why this is the case is not yet completely understood.

An important method of synthesizing transuranium isotopes, currently as well as historically, is by bombarding heavy element targets with charged particles, rather than neutrons, from accelerators. For the synthesis of elements with atomic numbers of 101 or greater, so-called heavy ions (*i.e.*, charged particles heavier than the helium nuclei, mentioned above as alpha particles) have been used.

Accelerators for superheavy elements

New accelerators, or modifications of existing ones, are necessary in order to accelerate the heavy ions needed to produce the superheavy elements. Targets and projectiles relatively rich in neutrons are required so that the resulting superheavy nuclei will have sufficiently high neutron numbers; too low a neutron number renders the nucleus extremely unstable and unobservable because of its resultingly short half-life.

NUCLEAR PROPERTIES OF TRANSURANIUM ELEMENTS

Isotopes of the transuranium elements are radioactive in the usual ways: they decay by emitting alpha particles, beta particles, gamma rays; and they also fission, or break up, spontaneously. In Table 2, significant nuclear properties of certain important isotopes are listed. Only the principal mode of decay is given, though in many cases other modes of decay also are exhibited by the isotope. In particular, with the isotope californium-252, alpha-parti-

cle decay is important because it determines the half-life, but the expected applications of the isotope exploit its spontaneous fission decay that produces an enormous neutron output. Other isotopes, such as plutonium-238, are useful because of their relatively large thermal power output during decay (given in Table 2 in watts per gram). Research on the chemical and solid-state properties of these elements and their compounds obviously requires that isotopes with long half-lives be used. Isotopes of plutonium and curium, for example, are particularly desirable from this point of view. The discovery of the mendelevium isotope, with a half-life of 54 days (for the emission of alpha particles), has raised hopes that all elements, at least through atomic number 101, will have some isotopes with half-lives long enough so that some of their macroscopic properties can be measured. In Table 2, the specific activities, such as disintegrations per minute per unit weight, are given for those elements that can be produced in nuclear reactors (formerly called atomic piles). Beyond element 100 the isotopes must be produced by charged-particle reactions using particle accelerators, with the result that only relatively few atoms can be made at any one time.

Nuclear structure and stability. Although the decay properties of the transuranium elements are important with regard to the potential application of the elements, these elements have been studied largely to develop a fundamental understanding of nuclear reactions and nuclear and atomic structure. Study of the known transuranium elements also helps in predicting the properties of yet undiscovered isotopes and elements as a guide to the researcher who can then design experiments to prepare and identify them. As shown in the allegorical Figure 3,

From G. Seaborg, *Proceedings of The Robert A. Welch Foundation Conference XIII: Transuranium Elements* (November 17, 1969)

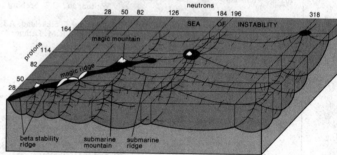

Figure 3: Known and predicted regions of nuclear stability, surrounded by a "sea" of instability.

the known isotopes of the elements can be represented graphically with the number of protons in the nucleus along the left-hand axis and the number of neutrons plotted on the axis along the bottom. The relative stabilities of the isotopes are indicated by their relative heights. In such representation, the known isotopes resemble a peninsula rising above a sea of instability. The most stable isotopes, appearing as mountain tops, occur at specific values called magic numbers.

The magic numbers derive from calculations of the energy distribution based on the theoretical structure of the nucleus. According to theory, neutrons and protons (collectively, nucleons) are arranged within the nucleus in shells that are able to accommodate only fixed maximum numbers of them; when the shells are closed (*i.e.*, unable to accept any more nucleons) the nucleus is much more stable than when the shells are only partially filled. The number of nucleons in the closed shells yields the magic numbers. As the proton and neutron numbers depart further and further from the magic numbers, the nuclei are relatively less stable.

Magic numbers

As the highest atomic numbers are reached, decay by alpha-particle emission and spontaneous fission sets in (see below). At some point the peninsula is terminated. With experimental methods available in the early 1970s, it appeared that the point at which the peninsula of stability disappeared lay in the vicinity of the element with atomic number 108. There was, however, considerable speculation, based on a number of theoretical cal-

name and mass	principal decay mode	half-life	specific activity	
			d/m/μg*	watts/gram
Neptunium-237	alpha	2.14×10^6 years	1.56×10^3	2.07×10^{-5}
Plutonium-238	alpha	86 years	3.86×10^7	0.570
Plutonium-239	alpha	2.44×10^4 years	1.36×10^5	$\sim 1.91 \times 10^{-3}$
Plutonium-242	alpha	3.8×10^5 years	8.63×10^3	1.13×10^{-4}
Plutonium-244	alpha	8×10^7 years	39.7	4.93×10^{-7}
Americium-241	alpha	433 years	7.59×10^6	0.114
Americium-243	alpha	7.4×10^3 years	4.24×10^5	6.45×10^{-3}
Curium-242	alpha	163 days	7.30×10^9	122
Curium-244	alpha	17.6 days	1.79×10^8	2.83
Curium-247	alpha	1.6×10^7 years	1.96×10^2	$\sim 2.8 \times 10^{-6}$
Curium-248	alpha	4.7×10^5 years	8.34×10^3	5.32×10^{-4}
Berkelium-249	beta (minus)	314 days	3.71×10^9	0.358
Californium-249	alpha	360 years	9.06×10^6	0.152
Californium-252	alpha	2.65 years	1.19×10^9	39
Einsteinium-253	alpha	20 days	5.7×10^{10}	1,000
Fermium-257	alpha	80 days	1.2×10^{10}	~ 200
Mendelevium-256	electron capture	1.5 hours		
Mendelevium-258	alpha	54 days		
Nobelium-259	alpha	1.5 hours		
Lawrencium-260	alpha	180 seconds		
Element 104-261	alpha	70 seconds		
Element 105-262	alpha	40 seconds		

*Disintegrations per minute per microgram.

culations, that two islands of stability might also exist. The first was expected to extend from about element 110 to element 126, while the second would be centred on element 164. With heavy-ion accelerators, experimenters might be expected to find such islands, especially the first.

Processes of nuclear decay. The correlation and prediction of nuclear properties in the transuranium region are based on systematics (that is, extensions of observed relationships) and on the development of theoretical models of nuclear structure. The development of structural theories of the nucleus has proceeded rather rapidly, in part because valid parallels with atomic and molecular theory can be drawn. At the same time, systematics has been successfully used in the case of alpha-particle decay by noting regularities in experimental alpha-particle decay energies and half-lives as a function of mass and atomic number. Similarly, for beta-particle decay, nuclear thermodynamics gives useful results. Half-lives for spontaneous fission also can be predicted by the application of systematics.

Alpha-particle decay. A nucleus can decay to an alpha particle (helium nucleus) plus a daughter product if the mass of the nucleus is greater than the sum of the mass of the daughter product and the mass of the alpha particle; *i.e.*, if some mass is lost during the transformation. The amount of matter defined by the difference between reacting mass and product mass is transformed into energy and is released with the alpha particle. The relationship is given by Einstein's equation: $E = mc^2$, in which the product of the mass (m) and the square of the velocity of light (c) equals the energy (E) produced by the transformation of that mass into energy. It can be shown that because of the inequality between the mass of a nucleus and the masses of the products, most nuclei beyond about the middle of the periodic table are likely to be unstable because of the emission of alpha particles. In practice, however, because of the reaction rate (*i.e.*, speed of reaction), decay by ejection of an alpha particle is important only with the heavier elements. Indeed, beyond bismuth (element 83) the predominant mode of decay is by alpha-particle emission, although at californium (element 98) an alternate process, called spontaneous fission, becomes possible (as a result of changes in energy balances) and begins to compete favourably with alpha-particle emission. In addition, with a number of transuranium nuclei, a third process, beta-particle decay (emission of a negative electron by the nucleus or the capture by the nucleus of an orbital electron) is of considerable importance.

The regularities in the alpha-particle-decay process that have been noted from experimental data have been used to predict half-lives of as yet undiscovered isotopes. Such predicted half-lives are essential for experiments designed to discover new elements and new isotopes, because the experiment must take the expected half-life into account. The regularities in alpha-particle-decay energies can be plotted in a graph and, since the alpha-particle-decay half-life depends in a regular way on the alpha-particle-decay energy, the graph can be used to obtain the estimated half-lives of undiscovered elements and isotopes.

Beta-particle decay. In elements lighter than lead, beta-particle decay—emission of either negative electrons (usually called simply electrons) or positive electrons (positrons)—is the main type of decay observed. In the transuranium elements, alpha-particle decay and spontaneous fission occur, in addition to decay, by emission of negative electrons or by capture of orbital electrons. (Positron emission has not been observed in transuranium elements.) When the beta-particle decay processes are absent in transuranium isotopes, the isotopes are said to be stable to beta decay.

Decay by spontaneous fission. Regularities also are observed for spontaneous fission in the very heavy element region. If the half-life of spontaneous fission is plotted against the ratio of the square of the number of protons in the nucleus (symbolized by Z) divided by the mass of the nucleus (symbolized by A)—*i.e.*, the ratio Z^2/A—then a regular pattern results for nuclei with even numbers of both neutrons and protons (even–even nuclei). Although this uniformity allows very rough predictions of half-lives for undiscovered isotopes, the methods actually employed are considerably more sophisticated. Nuclei with odd numbers of neutrons or protons exhibit longer half-lives for spontaneous fission than those shown in the figure.

The results of study of half-life systematics for alpha-particle, negative beta-particle, and spontaneous-fission decay in the near region of undiscovered transuranium elements can be plotted in graphs for even–even nuclei, and for nuclei with an odd number of protons or neutrons, and for odd–odd nuclei (those with odd numbers for both protons and neutrons). These predicted values are in the general range of experimentally determined half-lives and correctly indicate trends, but individual points may differ appreciably from known experimental data. Such graphs show that isotopes with odd numbers of neutrons or protons have longer half-lives for alpha-particle decay than do neighbouring even–even isotopes.

Nuclear structure and shape. *Liquid-drop models.* From the theoretical point of view, spontaneous-fission half-lives are generally treated by assuming that the nucleus has the properties of a liquid drop whose interior is inhomogeneous. The inhomogeneity arises from the fact that the neutrons and protons within the nucleus are more likely to be found inside rather than outside certain regions of the nucleus, called shells. This circumstance requires that a shell correction be applied to the ordinary homogeneous liquid-drop model of the exact nucleus. Nuclei with the exact number (or close to the exact number) of neutrons and protons dictated by closed shells (magic numbers, see above) have spherical shapes.

Since many transuranium nuclei have numbers of neutrons and protons different from the magic numbers and thus are nonspherical, considerable theoretical work has been done to describe the motions of the nucleons in their orbitals outside the spherical closed shells. These orbitals are important in explaining and predicting some of the nuclear properties of the transuranium and superheavy elements.

Nuclear-shape isomers. The mutual interaction of fission theory and experiment brought about the discovery and interpretation of fission isomers. At Dubna, U.S.S.R., in 1962, americium-242 was produced in a new form that decayed with a spontaneous-fission half-life of 14 milliseconds, or about 10^{21} times shorter than the half-life of the ordinary form of that isotope. Subsequently, more than 50 other examples of this type of behaviour were found in the transuranium region. The nature of these new forms of spontaneously fissioning nuclei was believed, in the early 1970s, to be explainable, in general terms at least, by the idea that the nuclei possess greatly distorted but quasi-stable nuclear shapes. The greatly distorted shapes are called isomeric states, and these new forms of nuclear matter are consequently called shape isomers. As mentioned earlier, calculations relating to spontaneous fission involve treating the nucleus as though it were an inhomogeneous liquid drop, and in practice this is done by incorporating a correction for shells in the homogeneous liquid-drop model. The theorist found an apparently reasonable way to amalgamate the shell and liquid-drop energies. The remarkable result obtained through the use of this method reveals that nuclei in the region of thorium through curium possess two energetically stable states with two different nuclear shapes. This theoretical result furnished a most natural explanation for the new form of fission, first discovered in americium-242.

This interpretation of a new nuclear structure is of great importance, but it has significance far beyond itself because the theoretical method and other novel approaches to calculation of nuclear stability have been used to predict islands of stability beyond the point at which the peninsula of Figure 3 disappears into the sea of instability.

EXTENSION OF THE PERIODIC TABLE: THE SUPERHEAVY ELEMENTS

Possible existence of superheavy elements. According to these calculations, islands of stability will occur over the region of atomic numbers from approximately 110 to

Marginal notes:

Predicted half-lives

Odd–odd and even–even isotopes

Two stable states for each nucleus

126 and also at around 164. The so-called superheavy elements that exist at these islands of stability are predicted to have neutron numbers ranging from about 184 to 318. The nucleus most stable against all forms of decay is thought by many to be element 110, of mass 294, although the assignment of a specific atomic number and mass number is speculative. This particular nuclide (isotopic species) may have an overall half-life (although unlikely) of 10^8 years. Other hypothetical nuclides that are predicted to have exceptional stability are those with atomic numbers 114 and 124; when the neutron number of 184 is added to these numbers of protons, mass numbers of 294 and 308, respectively, are obtained. If these projections are correct, it is considered possible that superheavy elements exist in nature and many scientific groups were looking for such elements.

The possibility of natural occurrence depends not only on the length of the half-life, but also on whether they were created in the first place. The discussion of the possible manufacture of these elements is as difficult and speculative as the discussion of their half-lives. At any rate, in the late 1960s, astronomers first observed a new kind of celestial object called a pulsar. It was thought that the most reasonable model for a pulsar was a rapidly rotating neutron star. The rapidly rotating electromagnetic and electrostatic fields associated with such a star should be able to accelerate charged particles to the velocities found in cosmic rays. If cosmic rays should originate in neutron stars, their composition might include superheavy elements. Unconfirmed evidence suggesting that elements in the atomic number range of 105 to 110 exist in cosmic rays was reported in 1968.

The existence of superheavy elements in meteorites or in terrestrial minerals depends on the probability of their having been formed by the same fundamental processes that created the other elements. Consequently, it is worthwhile to look for superheavy elements in meteorites and terrestrial minerals, since their presence or absence may tell something about the origin of the universe. In the early 1970s, searches had uncovered certain anomalies that might be attributed to superheavy elements, but the results could not be said to furnish proof of their existence.

Superheavy elements and their predicted properties. The postulated nuclear islands of stability are important to chemistry. The periodic table of the elements classifies a wealth of physical and chemical properties, and study of the chemical properties of the superheavy elements would show how far the classification scheme of the table could be extended on the basis of nuclear islands of stability. Such studies would shed new light on the underlying properties of electrons orbiting the nucleus because it is these properties that produce the periodic system. The positions of superheavy elements in the periodic table ultimately would be determined by the characteristic energies of the electrons of their atoms, especially those called the valence electrons, which are involved in chemical reactions. In all known atoms these valence electrons can be considered to be arranged around the nucleus in a variety of orbit-like paths that are designated as s, p, d, f, and g orbitals. The orbitals are arranged in shells numbered 1 to 8, each shell having s orbitals, and the larger also p, d, f, and g orbitals. Thus, an electron is identified by the position it has taken up (*e.g.*, 1s, 2s, 4p, 7s). Complex calculations have predicted meaningful distribution of electrons in orbitals for a number of superheavy elements. Results for elements 104–121 are given in Table 3, the configurations being those that the atoms have when they are at their lowest energy level, called the ground state.

Elements 113 and 114. These calculations of electronic structure permit predictions of detailed physical and chemical properties of some superheavy elements. If, for example, the structure of the periodic system (Figure 4) remains predictable to higher atomic numbers, then element 113 will be in the same group of elements as boron, aluminum, gallium, indium, and thallium; and element 114 will be in the group with carbon, silicon, germanium, tin, and lead. Element 113 usually is called

Electronic structure of atoms (margin)

Table 3: Calculated Electronic Ground States for Some Superheavy Elements

atomic number	electronic structure of two outermost shells*	atomic number	electronic structure of outermost shells†
104	$6d^27s^2$	113	$7s^27p^1$
105	$6d^37s^2$	114	$7s^27p^2$
106	$6d^47s^2$	115	$7s^27p^3$
107	$6d^57s^2$	116	$7s^27p^4$
108	$6d^67s^2$	117	$7s^27p^5$
109	$6d^77s^2$	118	$7s^27p^6$
110	$6d^87s^2$	119	$7s^27p^68s^1$
111	$6d^97s^2$	120	$7s^27p^68s^2$
112	$6d^{10}7s^2$	121	$7s^27p^68s^28p^1$

*Added to the structure of radon, element 86, plus orbitals $5f^{14}$.
†Added to the structure of radon, element 86, plus orbitals $5f^{14}6d^{10}$.

ekathallium, and element 114 is called ekalead. If they ever are discovered, of course, these elements will be given proper names of their own. Computer calculations of the character and energy levels of possible valence electrons in the atoms of these two superheavy elements have substantiated the placement of the elements in their expected positions. Extrapolations of properties from elements with lower numbers to elements 113 and 114 can then be made within the usual limitations of the periodic table. In Table 4, the results of such extrapolations are given. Although, in many cases, theoretical calculations are combined with extrapolation, the fundamental method involved is to plot the value of a given property of each member of the group against the appropriate row of the periodic table. The property is then extrapolated to the

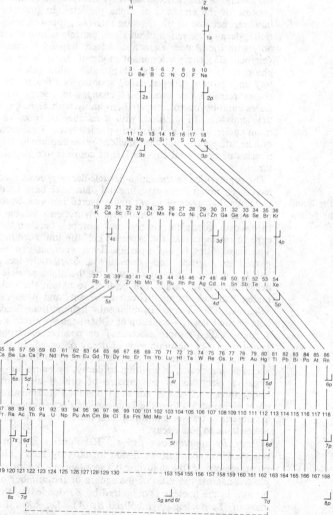

From G. Seaborg, *Proceedings of The Robert A. Welch Foundation Conference XIII: Transuranium Elements* (November 17, 1969)

Figure 4: Modified form of a periodic table showing known and predicted electron shells.

Table 4: Some Predicted Properties of Elements 113 and 114		
	element 113 (ekathallium)	element 114 (ekalead)
Chemical group	III	IV
Atomic weight	297	298
Most stable oxidation state	+1	+2
Oxidation potential, V	−0.6	−0.8
	$M \rightarrow M^{+} + e^{-}$	$M \rightarrow M^{2+} + 2e^{-}$
Metallic radius, Å	1.75	1.85
Ionic radius, Å	1.48	1.31
First ionization potential, eV	7.4	8.5
Second ionization potential, eV	...	16.8
Density, g/cm³	16	14
Atomic volume, cm³/mole	18	21
Boiling point, °C	1,100	150
Melting point, °C	430	70
Heat of sublimation, kcal/mole	34	10
Heat of vaporization, kcal/mole	31	9
Debye temperature, °K	70	46
Entropy, eu/mole (25° C)	17	20

seventh row, the row containing elements 113 and 114. The method is illustrated in Figure 5 for estimating the melting point of element 113.

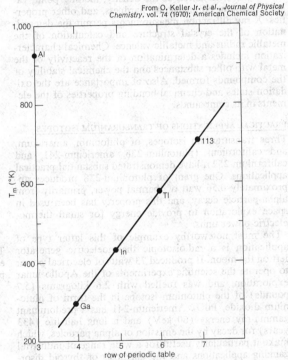

From O. Keller Jr. et al., *Journal of Physical Chemistry*, vol. 74 (1970); American Chemical Society

Figure 5: Melting points (Tm) in degrees Kelvin (°K) of Group III elements extrapolated to element 113 (see text).

Bonding properties

The bonding property of an element can be expressed by the energy required to shift a bonding, or valence, electron. This energy can be expressed in various ways, one of which is a relative value called the oxidation potential. The relative stabilities of possible oxidation states of an element represent what is probably that element's most important chemical property. The oxidation number of the atom of an element indicates the number of its orbiting electrons available for chemical bonds or actually involved in bonds with other atoms, as in a molecule or in a crystal. When an atom is capable of several kinds of bonding arrangement, using a different number of electrons for each kind, it has that many oxidation numbers, or oxidation states. The number is indicated in roman numerals following the name or symbol of the element, as copper (II), meaning copper in its oxidation state of two, and copper (I), oxidation state of one. Oxidation states may be positive or negative to indicate that the electrons involved may be considered as lost or gained, respectively. The prediction of oxidation states can be illustrated with element 114, ekalead, which occurs in Group IVa of the periodic table. The outstanding periodic characteristic of the Group IVa elements is their tendency to go from a +4, or tetrapositive, oxidation state, to a +2, or diposi-

tive state, as the atomic number increases. Thus, carbon and silicon are very stable in the tetrapositive state, whereas germanium shows a weak dipositive state in addition to its strong tetrapositive state. Tin chemistry is characterized by about equal stability in the tetrapositive and dipositive states, and lead chemistry is dominated by the dipositive state—the element showing only weak tetrapositive properties. Extrapolation in the periodic table to the seventh row, then, results in a predicted most stable dipositive oxidation state for element 114. This result is supported by valence bond theory and by extrapolations of thermodynamic data.

Other superheavy elements. Less detailed predictions have been made for other superheavy elements. Element 117, for example, is expected to be a member of the halogen series, the group composed of fluorine, chlorine, bromine, iodine, and astatine. Solid elemental 117 should be metallic in appearance, as is astatine, but it is expected that instead of the minus one (−1) oxidation-state characteristic of the natural halogens, it will show +3, +5, and +7 oxidation states. It should also form stable interhalogen compounds with fluorine, chlorine, and bromine.

Computer calculations suggest that element 118 should have the closed-shell electronic configuration of the noble gas elements helium, neon, argon, krypton, xenon, and radon. The element should be the most electropositive of the noble gases and, therefore, the existence of a (partially ionized) difluoride of the element 118 is predicted. A tetrafluoride and an oxide of the type formed by xenon (XeO₄) are also expected.

Although detailed predictions of the chemistry of element 119 have not as yet been completed, it is expected to be a typical alkali metal with a plus one (+1) oxidation state. The energetic properties of its valence electron, the 8s electron, suggest that its first ionization potential will be higher than the oxidation potential predicted by simple extrapolation, so that the element may be more like potassium than cesium in its chemistry. This higher energy will cause the metallic and ionic radii to be smaller than simple extrapolation would indicate.

Element 120 would be expected to be a typical alkaline-earth element. As with element 119, the ionization potentials should be raised to higher level than the normal family trend would indicate and, also, should make the metallic and ionic radii smaller. These changes should make the chemistry of element 120 similar to that of calcium and strontium.

Element 121 should be similar in its chemical properties to lanthanum and actinium, but detailed properties have not been predicted.

Superactinide series. It is probable, in a formal sense at least, that element 122 will begin another series of elements in which each successive electron is added to a deep inner orbital, in a manner similar (see Figure 4) to that found in the lanthanide and actinide series (see RARE-EARTH ELEMENTS AND THEIR COMPOUNDS; ACTINIDE ELEMENTS AND THEIR COMPOUNDS). Such a series, which would be listed under the actinide series in the periodic table, should consist of 32 elements, ending in the neighbourhood of element 153 and resulting primarily from the filling of the 5g and 6f inner electron shells (shell 5 orbital g, and shell 6 orbital f). Since the number of elements proposed for this series is much greater than the number of elements in the actinide series, the new series might be called the "superactinide" series. This nomenclature is equivalent to suggesting for element 121 the name "superactinium" in recognition of the prediction that it would be the approximate prototype for the 32 elements that follow it.

Not every element of this new series would correspond to an actinide (or lanthanide) element on a 1:1 basis, and prediction of the chemistry of the members of the series is a very complex problem. The difficulty arises partly because of uncertainty of the exact point at which the energetically similar 5g and 6f orbitals begin to fill, and partly because calculations indicate that the 8p and 7d orbitals may be very close in energy to the 5g and 6f orbitals. (The number 8 shell is outermost from the nucleus and in each shell the s orbital is the innermost.) These orbitals

Computer calculations of element 118

Bonding properties

may all be filled, then, in a commingling fashion, resulting in a series of elements that show multiple, barely distinguishable oxidation states. The electronic basis for the periodicity shown in Figure 4 will then no longer be present.

As shown, element 153 will be the last member of the superactinide series, at least in a formal sense. The prediction of properties on the basis of an orderly extrapolation appears to be of doubtful validity, however, in this heavy-element region of the periodic table. In still higher elements, the closely spaced energy levels are expected to make multiple oxidation states the rule. The placement of the elements in the heaviest portion of the periodic table as shown in Figure 4 is, therefore, probably also of only formal significance.

End of the periodic table. At some point the stability of the orbital electrons in the ordinary sense must be destroyed as more and more protons are added to the nucleus. There is, therefore, in the ordinary chemical sense, a critical atomic number, or range of atomic numbers, which represents the end of the periodic table. This end, it should be noted, is separate, at least philosophically, from the question of stability of the nucleus itself; *i.e.*, nuclear stability is not the same as stability of the electron shells. The maximum atomic number, according to current theories, lies somewhere between elements 170 and 210, as indicated above.

Maximum atomic number

CHARACTERIZATION AND IDENTIFICATION OF THE TRANSURANIUM ELEMENTS

Two important factors provided the key to the discovery and identification of many of the transuranium elements: one was knowledge of the lanthanide series coupled with the concept that it could be paralleled in the actinide series, and the other was the technique of separating elements with similar properties from a mixture by using the principle of ion exchange (see ION-EXCHANGE REACTIONS). Ion-exchange reactions depend on the fact that some complex molecules have a charge that will attract ions of the opposite charge, hold them, and then exchange them for other ions of the same charge when brought in contact with them. The actinide concept, proposed in 1944, stated that the transuranium elements were part of a series of elements that started at thorium and that the chemistry of the series would be similar to that of an earlier transition-element series, the lanthanides. By the use of ion-exchange reactions that are highly specific, many of the transuranium elements have been separated and identified. The tripositive ions of the lanthanides and actinides are eluted (washed) from a cation-exchange resin (a resin that has a negative charge and will hold positive ions or cations) using a particular organic ion, alpha-hydroxyisobutyrate. The striking similarity between elution patterns of the two groups constitutes strong support for the actinide concept. A certain measure of stability of the dipositive state for nobelium was predicted by the actinide concept. A position was predicted for lawrencium (Lr), but for this element the yields have been so small and the half-lives so short that its positive identification by ion exchange has not been achieved. The tripositive state of lawrencium has been confirmed by a very rapid solvent-exchange experiment in which the lawrencium displayed the behaviour of the tripositive actinides and not that of the dipositive nobelium or radium, again in accord with the predictions of the actinide concept.

Non-chemical identification and separation

When the yields of a new element are small and its half-life is short, chemical identification and characterization are frequently not possible. In such cases the atomic number is deduced from the method of production through nuclear reactions, from the parent-daughter relationship of the new element to known elements of lower atomic number resulting from its nuclear decay, and from its nuclear-decay systematics that cannot be attributed to any known nuclides. Additionally, the variation in the yield of the new element is noted when the bombarding energy is changed or when the target or projectile or both are changed.

Separation of the product nuclide from the target has been accomplished in the discoveries of elements 101

through 105 by a recoil collection method. When the target nucleus is struck by a heavy ion projectile, the product nucleus recoils out of the very thin target and is either attracted to a substrate by an electrostatic potential or is swept onto a substrate by a jet of helium gas. The new element is then in a position to be observed and characterized by suitable detection techniques, essentially free of the parent isotope.

It is desirable, though not essential, that the mass number of the new element be established by evidence related to its mode of production, or to its parent-daughter relationship through radioactive decay to a radioactive isotope of known mass number. When weighable quantities of a transuranium element are available, more extensive characterization experiments can be performed. The most important of these experiments is the preparation of the metal, frequently done by high-temperature reduction of the fluoride of the transuranium element with an alkali or alkaline-earth metal. Another method used for preparation of larger (gram) quantities of high purity is electrolytic reduction of the chloride of the transuranium element. Physical characterization of these metal samples includes determination of the density, melting point, vapour pressure, boiling point, hardness, and other properties. X-ray diffraction measurements permit the determination of the crystal structure and calculation of the metallic radius and metallic valence. Chemical characterization includes a determination of the reactivity of the metal with other substances and the chemical stability of the compounds formed. Also of importance are the oxidation states and chemical-bonding properties of the elements in its compounds.

PRACTICAL APPLICATIONS OF TRANSURANIUM ISOTOPES

Three transuranium isotopes, of plutonium, americium, and californium (plutonium-238, americium-241, and californium-252), have demonstrated substantial practical applications. One gram of plutonium-238 produces approximately 0.56 watt of thermal power, primarily from alpha-particle decay, and this property has been used in space exploration to provide energy for small thermo-electric-power units.

The most noteworthy example of this latter type of application is a radioisotopic thermoelectric generator left on the moon. It produced 73 watts of electrical power to operate the scientific experiments of the Apollo lunar exploration, and was fuelled with 2.6 kilograms (5.7 pounds) of the plutonium isotope in the form of plutonium dioxide, PuO_2. Americium-241 has a predominant gamma-ray energy (60 keV) and a long half-life (433 years) for decay by the emission of alpha particles, which make it particularly useful for a wide range of industrial gauging applications and the diagnosis of thyroid disorders. When mixed with beryllium it generates neutrons at the rate of 1.0×10^7 neutrons per second per gram of americium-241. The mixture is designated ^{241}Am–Be and a large number of such sources are in worldwide daily use in oil-well logging operations; *i.e.*, to find how much oil a well is producing in a given time span, as a day. Californium-252 is an intense neutron source: one gram emits 2.4×10^{12} neutrons per second. This isotope is being tested for applications in neutron activation analysis, neutron radiography, and portable sources for field use in mineral prospecting and oil-well logging. Both plutonium-238 and californium-252 are being studied for possible medical applications: as a heat source for use in heart pacemakers and heart pumps and as a neutron source for irradiation of certain tumours for which gamma-ray treatment is relatively ineffective.

Thermo-electric power

BIBLIOGRAPHY. G.T. SEABORG and J.L. BLOOM, "The Synthetic Elements: IV," *Scient. Am.*, 220:57–67 (1969), a popular article for the lay reader, fourth in a series that covers the field from its inception; G.T. SEABORG, *Man-Made Transuranium Elements* (1963), a semitechnical book suitable for scientifically inclined high school students and for college students; E.K. HYDE, *Synthetic Transuranium Elements* (1964), an Atomic Energy Commission booklet for the layman; C. KELLER, *The Chemistry of the Transuranium Elements* (1971), a comprehensive, more technical book.

(G.T.S.)

Transvaal

The Transvaal is the northernmost and second largest province of the Republic of South Africa. With an area of 109,621 square miles (283,917 square kilometres), it is bordered by Botswana and Rhodesia to the north, Mozambique and Swaziland to the east, the provinces of Natal and the Orange Free State to the south, and Cape Province to the west. Almost 76 percent of its 8,744,000 population is black, and about 22 percent is white. Many of the whites are descendants of the Afrikaners who in the earlier 19th century migrated north over the Vaal River, which now forms part of the province's southern boundary, thus giving the province its present name—Transvaal, "across the Vaal."

Rich in mineral resources, including gold and uranium, as well as in power resources, the Transvaal is South Africa's industrial heartland and also an important agricultural region in its own right. Pretoria, the provincial capital, is also the administrative centre of the republic. The province also contains Johannesburg, the largest city in South Africa. (For a related physical feature article, see VELD; see also the city article JOHANNESBURG; for general historical background, see SOUTHERN AFRICA, HISTORY OF.)

History. In the early 19th century the land between the Vaal River in the south and the Limpopo River, which today forms the northern border, was inhabited by agricultural Bantu tribes who were skilled in metalworking. They became unsettled in the 1820s and 1830s by invasions of refugee Bantu tribes fleeing south and west from the warring Zulu. Between 1837 and 1838 seminomadic pastoral Afrikaner farmers, the voortrekkers, moving northward to avoid British rule, crossed the Vaal River and entered the area, where they settled in isolated farms. More white settlers arrived when the United Kingdom annexed both Natal and the Orange River Sovereignty in the 1840s. In 1852 the independence of the Afrikaners in the Transvaal was recognized by the United Kingdom with the conclusion of the Sand River Convention. In 1857 the new Transvaal state was formally proclaimed as the South African Republic; its authority, however, was virtually limited to the southwest of the present Transvaal. In 1877 the republic was annexed by the United Kingdom, but the Afrikaners resorted to arms to maintain their independence, which they regained—subject to certain provisos—in 1881 after the British forces had been overwhelmed at the Battle of Majuba Hill. The discovery of gold in the Witwatersrand area in 1886 resulted in a tremendous influx of fortune seekers, primarily English and Germans, which caused new problems for the Afrikaner republic. Tension with the United Kingdom increased when an English adventurer, Leander Starr Jameson, led an abortive raid across the frontier of the South African Republic in an attempt to provoke an internal uprising. War between the republic and the United Kingdom subsequently broke out in 1899. Defeated by superior arms and numbers, the republic, together with its ally the Orange Free State, lost its independence when peace was concluded in 1902, after which the Transvaal became a British crown colony. In 1907 it regained self-government, and in 1910 became a province of the Union of South Africa, a status that was maintained when the Union became the Republic of South Africa in 1961.

Landscape. *Physiography.* There are six distinct physiographic regions in the province—the Highveld, the Bushveld Basin, the Waterberg Plateau, the Pietersburg Plain, the Limpopo Valley, and the Lowveld. In the south, the altitude of the Highveld ranges between 4,000 and 6,000 feet, declining slightly from east to west. The eastern area is covered by horizontal sandstones and shales (laminated clays) that produce gray, claylike acidic prairie soils with a leached upper layer that merges into lateritic (leached, reddish, iron-bearing) soils farther to the north and west. The relief is undulating but changes into a rugged landscape in the vicinity of the Witwatersrand Ridge, where older rocks have been bared. To the west of Johannesburg, the Highveld is monotonously even, being composed of water-bearing limestone and lavas. The region is drained by the Vaal River and its tributaries.

The central part of the province is occupied by the Bushveld Basin, formed by a large substratum of rock that has been solidified from the molten state. The peripheral ridge-and-valley landscape is composed of quartzites and intervening shales that dip toward the centre. These ridges are known as the Western Bankeveld around Pretoria and the Eastern Bankeveld near the Drakensberg Mountains. North of Pilgrimsrest, water erosion on the Eastern Bankeveld has created the spectacular canyon of the Blyde River. The black clays of the basin are associated with norite (a granular, mineral-bearing rock solidified from the molten state) and basalt, and are of exceptionally high fertility, as they are at the Springbok Flats.

The Waterberg Plateau rises from 3,500 to nearly 7,000 feet in altitude to the northwest of the basin. Few of its grass- and bush-covered sandstone areas are suitable for cultivation. To the northeast the Pietersburg Plain is almost entirely composed of a granite surface. It is bounded by the Strydpoort Mountains in the south and the Soutpansberg Mountains in the north.

The Limpopo Valley forms the northern border with Rhodesia. It cuts mainly into old granite in a bushy area covered by the sandy soil of the nearby Kalahari, and a red-brown unleached subtropical sandy soil to the east. Farther east, this sandy soil extends into the Lowveld, a bush-clad plain, generally below 2,000 feet in altitude, that gently slopes towards the Lebombo Mountains on the Mozambique boundary. On the slopes of the Great Escarpment—the ridge that separates the plateau from the Lowveld—thick, red, iron-bearing earths support dense plantation growth. The whole of the northern, and most of the eastern, Transvaal is drained by the Limpopo River and its tributaries, which include the Crocodile, Mogalakwena, Letaba, and Olifants rivers.

Climate. Temperatures are directly related to the altitudes of the region. Rainfall is unreliable and varies from year to year. Almost exclusively a summer phenomenon, it normally arrives as thunderstorms and showers. Hailstorms that frequently are destructive may be expected about five times a year, while the great amount of sunshine results in extensive evaporation.

The Highveld is warm and temperate, with mean annual surface temperatures of 57° F (14° C) in the east and 65° F (18° C) in the southwest. Rainfall varies from 40 inches in the east to 18 inches in the west. Frost is common from mid-May to mid-September, but its duration decreases to the north and east. North of Pretoria, the climate becomes subtropical and semi-arid, with an annual average rainfall ranging from 28 inches on the Waterberg Plateau to 16 inches in the Sand River Valley, which is the driest part of the Transvaal. The subtropical Lowveld is warm and oppressive except during the winter. The mean annual surface temperature is 74° F (23° C), and rainfall increases from 19 inches in the northeast to more than 72 inches on the Drakensberg slopes, where mist and drizzle are frequent.

Vegetation and animal life. The natural vegetation of the Highveld and part of the Bankeveld consists of successive sweet, mixed, and sour grassland toward the east, the extent of each zone depending upon the climate and type of soil. The whole of the Lowveld and the greater part of the country to the north of the Bankeveld carries a parkland type of vegetation, with acacia types predominating and tall grasses and scrubs forming the undergrowth. Where rainfall is high in the mist belt, true timber forests with dense undergrowth are found, but they have suffered severely from the hand of man.

Animal life has been severely decimated, except in conservation areas. Kruger National Park—covering some 8,000 square miles in the eastern Lowveld—supports a wide variety of primates such as monkeys and baboons; insect-eaters such as hedgehogs and ant bears; carnivores such as lions, cheetahs, jackals, and hyenas; and hoofed animals such as rhinoceroses, hippopotamuses, giraffes, buffalo, koodoos, blue wildebeests, and impalas. There are many species of birds. Crocodiles and several species of snakes are found, as well as freshwater fish.

Population. *Ethnic composition.* There are four main population groups in the Transvaal, which in 1970 to-

Settlement by the voortrekkers

The six regions

Kruger National Park

gether totalled 8,744,000. The whites number 1,892,000; the Coloureds (racially mixed), 152,000; the Asians, 81,000; and the Bantu, 6,619,000. In terms of simple densities, the total averages about 80 persons per square mile. More than 55 percent of the population is urbanized.

About 61 percent of the white population is Afrikaans-speaking and 33 percent is English-speaking. The balance are of German, Dutch, and other European origin. Approximately 80 percent of the whites are urban-centred, being concentrated in the Pretoria–Witwatersrand–Vereeniging metropolitan complex. The adjacent rural areas have a density of roughly 12 whites per square mile, the remainder of the province less than 4. The Afrikaners, once overwhelmingly engaged in farming, live increasingly in the cities; by 1960, 80 percent were urbanized.

The Bantu population, in spite of a broad cultural solidarity, is diversely grouped in numerous tribes and clans. The main groups are the Sotho, Nguni, Tsonga, and Venda. Since few members of the main groups can understand each other's language, a lingua franca called Fanagalo has developed, especially among the Bantu gold miners. The majority of the Bantu still live in rural areas, where the average density normally exceeds 20 persons per square mile, and reaches more than 60 per square mile in the Tswanaland area northwest of Pretoria.

The Coloureds are about 92 percent urbanized and are concentrated mainly in the Witwatersrand area and in the larger towns. They speak both Afrikaans and English. The Asians are also predominately urban; they consist mainly of Indians, although there is also a Chinese minority.

Religion. More than half of the white population are members of the three Afrikaans churches—the Nederduits Gereformeerde and the Nederduits Hervormde (both Dutch Reformed churches), and the Gereformeerde (Reformed Church of South Africa)—and 25 percent are members of the three main English churches—Anglican, Methodist, and Presbyterian. There is also a small Jewish community. Because of strong missionary activity, almost 90 percent of the Coloureds are Christian. Many of the Bantu have accepted Christianity, but they tend to form independent sects; 20 percent of the Bantu belong to more than 1,000 separatist churches. The Asian community has retained its affiliation with Hinduism and Islām.

Rural and urban settlement. Because of large, individually owned farms, rural settlement among whites is dispersed, with long distances separating neighbours. The pattern in the Bantu areas differs totally because their communal ownership and communal land use results in the appearance of rural villages separated by open stretches of cultivated and grazing lands.

Towns are generally small and few in number, having evolved as mining, marketing, or administrative centres. Over 130 of them have a population of less than 10,000, while 37 of them have between 10,000 and 200,000 inhabitants, and only Johannesburg, Pretoria, and Germiston exceed 200,000. Although the towns were founded by whites, they are numerically dominated by the Bantu. The highly built-up Witwatersrand region covers about 200 square miles, and supports more than 2,000,000 people. Johannesburg, Pretoria, and the Vereeniging–Vanderbijlpark complex—in fact, the whole of the southern Transvaal—forms the mining, industrial, commercial, and financial heart of South Africa. In the west, the gold-mining complex of Klerksdorp–Stilfontein–Orkney, and in the east the Witbank–Middelburg coalfields and industrial area, are important. Other important centres are Pietersburg, Nelspruit, Ermelo, and Lichtenburg, all with populations of between 10,000 and 50,000.

South Africa's urban heartland

Administration and social conditions. *Administration.* Provincial authority is delegated by the Parliament of the Republic of South Africa to the Provincial Council, the 73 members of which are elected every five years. Taxation for provincial purposes is under provincial control, and local administration is provided by some 50 city or town councils, various local boards, village councils, health committees, and a peri-urban area health board. There are 62 magisterial districts with responsibility for the administration of justice as well as for some functions of other government departments. Bantu Territorial Authorities function under the control of the Bantu affairs commissioner in internal matters of administration and finance.

Social conditions. There are some 57 provincial hospitals; together with private hospitals, they provide about 13,000 beds for whites, and about 20,000 for nonwhites. There are also mine hospitals and hospitals for leprosy, mental illness, and tuberculosis. The provincial authority maintains field services to combat malaria, plague, typhus, tuberculosis, trachoma, and other diseases. Indigent whites and most nonwhites receive free medical attention from the provincial hospitals. The biggest hospital on the African continent, and one of the biggest hospitals in the world specializing in the treatment of a wide range of diseases, is Baragwanath, a hospital for nonwhites near Johannesburg.

Elementary and secondary education and the training of teachers are administered by the provincial government. Schooling is compulsory for whites between the ages of 7 and 16, and for Coloureds and Asians between 7 and 14 where the demand justifies the establishment of facilities. School attendance for the Bantu is not yet compulsory, but Bantu literacy has risen to 85 percent for the group between 7 and 20 years old. Six universities—the universities of South Africa, Pretoria, the Witwatersrand, Potchefstroom, Rand Afrikaans University, and the University of the North for the Bantu—are subsidized by the federal government but remain autonomous. They provide a wide range of teaching and research facilities. Welfare activities are undertaken by voluntary organizations and by the Ministry of Social Welfare. From 1960 onward, in order to clear the so-called squatters' camps that resulted from a rapid industrialization that was accompanied by an unprecedented influx of Bantu into urban areas in the southern Transvaal, more than 100,000 houses were built; provision was also made for schools, parks, community halls, and other facilities.

Economy. The Transvaal contains one of the greatest known concentrations of mineral deposits, both in variety and quantity. Employing 280,000 nonwhites and 31,000 whites, and producing large quantities of gold and uranium, the mines of the Witwatersrand, Klerksdorp, and eastern Transvaal have stimulated the growth of a large complex of industries and economic activities. Gold purchased for industrial purposes had by 1968 reached the level of total world output of newly mined gold. Diamond output amounted to 2,550,000 metric carats in 1968. Enormous reserves of platinum, as well as of chromite, tin, and nickel, are associated with the Bushveld. Reserves of coal are estimated at 75,000,000,000 tons. Other mineral deposits include iron ore at Thabazimbi, copper at Messina and Phalaborwa, asbestos, vermiculite (a micaceous mineral), antimony, corundum (crystals used industrially as abrasives), and limestone. An ever-growing need for explosives for mining has resulted in the development of a large chemical industry.

Gold, uranium, and diamonds

Agriculture is productive, having adopted modern methods of conservation, irrigation, and fertilization. Products include maize, wheat, peanuts (groundnuts), sunflower seeds, cotton, sugar, tobacco, and potatoes and other vegetables, as well as a wide variety of fruits. Beef and dairy cattle are important, and there is some sheep ranching. Huge plantations of eucalyptus and coniferous trees in the mist belt comprise 37 percent of South Africa's total acreage of plantations.

The demand for water for mining, industry, power stations, and irrigation has exceeded the supply available from the Vaal River, 97 percent of which is already in use. Planners are seeking supplementary supplies from the Tugela River of Natal, and from the desalinization of seawater.

Transportation and communications. Total railway track mileage amounted to about 3,604 miles in 1969, of which almost 2400 miles were electrified. An underground pipeline from the port of Durban in Natal Province conveys petroleum products to the Witwatersrand over a distance of 450 miles. There were 7,000 miles of bituminous-surfaced national and provincial roads in 1969. South Africa's main international airport, Jan Smuts, is situated near Johannesburg. Post office services and the telecommunication system have expanded steadily to cope with increasing demands. There are national radio broadcasting stations at Johannesburg, Pretoria, and Pietersburg. The Voice of South Africa transmits to other countries from Bloemendal in ten languages for 182 hours weekly. Radio Highveld broadcasts continuously in Afrikaans and English. Television is to be installed in 1974.

Cultural life. The Transvaal's population diversity has resulted in a variety of different cultures. "White" Transvaal is culturally comparable to any Western country. Its well-known hospitality can be traced back to the rough environment and hard life of past decades, which stimulated mutual dependence and a close family life. There is a strong desire to preserve objects of historical significance; Afrikaner attachment to national tradition is symbolized by the Voortrekker Monument near Pretoria, which honours the first pioneers.

The Transvaal has attained international recognition for its contributions to art, music, and ballet. Opera is presented regularly, and the Aula at Pretoria and Johannesburg Civic Theatre are well-known cultural centres. A wealth of literature and folk song has accumulated, but there is little if any traditional architecture.

Bantu tribes are normally comprised of a number of clans whose members are related. A strong recognition of the power of the tribe's chief prevails, and traditional medicine has considerable influence. The Bantu are renowned for their music and dancing, of which the "Domba," or snake dance, of the Venda is an example.

The climate lends itself to outdoor living, and sports are extremely popular. Motoring vacations over large distances are common, and an exodus to the beaches of Natal is a holiday phenomenon at all seasons.

BIBLIOGRAPHY. W. ALBERTYN (ed.), *Official South African Municipal Yearbook* (annual); BUREAU OF STATISTICS, REPUBLIC OF SOUTH AFRICA, *Population Census 1960*; T. CAMPBELL, R. FINDLAY, and J. VAN DER MERWE, *Birds of the Kruger and Other National Parks*, 4 vol. (1957–65), illustrated; M.M. COLE, *South Africa*, 2nd ed. (1966), physical and human geographical coverage; DEPARTMENT OF PLANNING, REPUBLIC OF SOUTH AFRICA, *Development Atlas* (1966), contains maps and descriptions of the physical background, social aspects, water resources, minerals and mines, agriculture, communications, and economic aspects; A.K. HAAGNER, *South African Mammals* (1920), still a descriptive classic, illustrated; A.C. HARRISON et al., *Fresh-Water Fish and Fishing in South Africa*, ch. 3 (1963), deals with species in the Vaal and Limpopo river systems; D.H. HOUGHTON, *The South African Economy*, 2nd ed. (1967), a general survey; L.C. KING, *South African Scenery*, 3rd ed. rev. (1963), geomorphology, including chapters on topography; E. PALMER and N. PITMAN, *Trees of South Africa* (1961), a description of 51 families and their distribution, illustrated; J.N. SCHEEPERS, *A Cartographic Analysis of the Man-Land Ratio: An Adventure into the Population Geography of the Transvaal* (1967), contains analysis of the man–land ratio and chapters on distributional patterns, illustrated; J.H. WELLINGTON, *Southern Africa*, vol. 1 (1955), physical geography.

(J.N.S.)

Tree

Although the concept of a tree as a growth form is useful and generally well understood, it is not possible to provide a precisely delimiting definition of a tree. There is an imperceptible merging of plants that obviously are trees into shrubs and of woody plants into herbaceous plants. To qualify as a tree a plant must be a perennial (*i.e.*, a plant that renews its growth each year); in addition, trees usually have a single self-supporting trunk that contains woody tissues. The trunk generally is dominant for some distance above the ground and commonly produces secondary limbs, called branches; in some species, however, the trunk divides at a low, sometimes even at ground, level into two or more trunks. Most palms have no branches. Although height is often considered a factor in defining trees—minimum limits of 15 or 20 feet (five to

seven metres) being most commonly accepted—limits are an arbitrary measure of convenience; woody plants, like all others, are greatly influenced by environment, and the same species, and even specimens propagated by cuttings or some other means from the same stock of one species, may vary tremendously in size depending upon where they grow and the treatment they receive. Pines, spruces, birches, and many other trees, although reduced in size—in some cases to no more than a few inches tall—at the northernmost limits and the highest altitudes of their occurrence, may still have single woody trunks. Specimens of many species grown under adverse conditions of soil, moisture, exposure to wind, and other environmental factors may be similarly dwarfed. The Japanese, by manipulating natural factors that affect growth and by skillful pruning, practice the art of bonsai, in which species that would be forest trees in nature are so dwarfed that they never exceed a few inches to three feet or so in height; such trees develop the proportions and appearance of their fully developed counterparts, however.

TREE TYPES AND DISTRIBUTIONS

Botanical classification of trees. In 1948 the British botanist John Hutchinson, following a trend that had been gaining acceptance for several years, divided the traditionally recognized flowering plant class Dicotyledoneae into two classes: the Lignosae (containing all trees and shrubs as well as clearly related herbaceous plants) and the Herbaceae (all herbaceous plants in addition to some obviously related woody ones). This system stresses the woody characteristic of trees and shrubs more than do other modern systems of plant classification but is still very different from the arrangement put forward by the Greeks about 300 BC and accepted for 1,000 years; they separated plants according to their forms into such major groups as trees, shrubs, and vines.

Ancient system of classifying plants

An important objective of modern botanical classification has been to arrange species, genera, and other recognized groups phylogenetically; that is, according to their probable evolutionary lines of development and genetic relationships. In attempting such a classification, many factors are considered other than those concerned with plant form and gross morphology; *e.g.*, evidence from cytology, genetics, ecological behaviour, and indications of probable population migrations. Because of vast gaps in the knowledge of the actual evolutionary development that led to the Earth's present flora, phylogenetic systems of plant classification are based to a considerable degree on conjecture; in none of these systems, however, are trees treated as a discrete group.

Trees are represented in the major divisions and subdivisions of the plant kingdom called pteridophytes, gymnosperms, and angiosperms. To the first belong the tree ferns; to the second the cycads, the ginkgo, and the conifers; and to the third all flowering plants.

Tree ferns, which belong to the fern families Dicksoniaceae and Cyatheaceae, account for more than 300 of the approximately 10,000 species of ferns. Many attain heights of 20 to 30 feet (seven to ten metres); some are 50, 60, or occasionally 80 feet in height. These graceful trees, which are natives of humid mountain forests in the tropics and subtropics and of warm-temperate regions of the Southern Hemisphere, have huge lacy leaves; they are the remnants of a vastly more numerous flora that populated much of the Earth 280,000,000 to 345,000,000 years ago (the Carboniferous Period).

Cycads compose the Cycadaceae, a family consisting of nine genera and approximately 100 species. Natives of warm regions of the Eastern and Western Hemispheres, they also are remnants of a much larger number of species that in past geologic ages dominated the Earth's flora.

Ginkgo is the only living representative of the family Ginkgoaceae (order Ginkgoales). It is a relic that has been preserved in cultivation around Buddhist temples in China and elsewhere since the mid-18th century; the tree probably no longer exists in a wild state. It is believed to represent the last of a group of related genera that were most abundant in the Jurassic Period, some 165,000,000 years ago.

Conifers include trees and shrubs in seven families and more than 500 species. Familiar representatives are araucarias, cedars, cypresses, Douglas firs, firs, hemlocks, junipers, larches, pines, podocarpuses, redwoods, spruces, and yews.

Angiosperms, or flowering plants, dominate the Earth's present flora; they are divided into about 300 families and approximately 220,000 species, among which are the majority of the world's trees. Angiosperms are divided on the basis of a group of characteristics into two classes: the Monocotyledoneae, or monocotyledons, and the Dicotyledoneae, or dicotyledons. The most numerous of the monocotyledonous trees are palms; others include agaves, aloes, dracaenas, screw pines (*Pandanus*), and yuccas. By far the greatest number of tree species are dicotyledons; they are represented by such familiar groups as apples, birches, elms, hollies, magnolias, maples, oaks, poplars, willows, and a host of others.

Popular tree classification systems. For nonscientific usage, trees have been grouped in various ways, some of which more or less parallel their scientific classification; *e.g.*, softwoods are conifers and hardwoods are dicotyledons. Hardwoods are also known as broadleaf trees. It is important to note, however, that the designations softwood, hardwood, and broadleaf do not indicate with precision the characteristics they imply. The wood of some hardwoods—for example, certain willows and poplars, and the softest of all woods, balsa—is softer than that of some softwoods; *e.g.*, the longleaf pine (*Pinus palustris*). Similarly, some broadleaf trees (tree heaths, *Erica*, and some kinds of *Tamarix*) have narrower leaves than do those of certain conifers (*Podocarpus*).

Evergreen and deciduous trees

A popular and convenient grouping of trees is evergreens and deciduous. This is most useful at the local rather than the worldwide level: whether a particular species retains its foliage throughout the year and thus qualifies as evergreen may depend on climate. At the northern limits or, in the Southern Hemisphere, the southern limits of their occurrence and at high elevations, species that under more favourable circumstances retain their foliage may become leafless for a period. Many tropical and subtropical species that in uniformly humid climates are never without foliage are deciduous in regions in which dry and wet seasons alternate. In northern North America the term evergreen is often used as a synonym for conifer and thus excludes foliage-retaining angiosperms. But five coniferous genera—*Larix* (larch), *Metasequoia* (dawn redwood), *Pseudolarix* (golden larch), *Taxodium* (swamp cypress), and *Glyptostrobus*—are composed of or include deciduous species.

Other tree groups are popularly recognized: tree ferns as tree ferns, palms as palms, and, among desert plants, the tree forms of agaves, aloes, cactuses, euphorbias, and yuccas. Sometimes the layman includes as trees plants that botanists cannot accept as such; for example, the banana. Such confusion arises from the fact that what appears to be the trunk of the "banana tree" is actually leafstalks rolled tightly around each other. The banana plant is entirely herbaceous, has no true trunk, and thus is not a tree.

The distribution of trees. The occurrence of trees in nature is largely determined by the length of the growing season and the availability of water. In areas in which the time between the thawing of the ground in spring and its freezing in fall is insufficient for woody plants to develop and mature their season's growth and to produce seeds, trees are not part of the natural vegetation. Except for a few desert and semidesert species, trees are less successful than many other plants in regions in which rainfall is scanty. In such regions, trees, for the most part, give way to grasses and other herbaceous plants or to low shrubs (chaparral), succulents (fleshy plants such as the cactuses), and other desert-adapted plants. Factors such as inhospitable soils, persistent winds, agricultural practices, and repeated burning of vegetation may also be responsible for the absence of trees. Trees usually inhabit regions in which the annual rainfall exceeds 30 inches.

Northern cold-region evergreen forests consisting chiefly of conifers occupy a broad belt, occasionally extending northward to latitude 72° north, across North America, Europe, and Asia and with southward extensions in mountainous areas into the tropics. A moist temperate forest of chiefly conifers extends from central California to Alaska. In comparison with northern cold-region evergreen forests, this western North American forest experiences higher average temperatures and less violent seasonal changes. Temperate deciduous forests occupy or once occupied vast areas with marked seasonal changes of temperature in eastern North America, Europe, Australia, and southern South America. In parts of the Northern Hemisphere in which winter and summer temperatures are less extreme, subtropical broadleaf evergreen forests are found; they merge, wherever rainfall is adequate, into tropical rain forests, such as those that occupy vast areas in the Amazon and Orinoco drainage systems in South America; those of the Congo, Niger, and Zambezi rivers in Africa; and those in Madagascar, the Indo-Malayan region, Borneo, and New Guinea. Trees also occur as scattered individuals and groups in the savannas of South America, Africa, Australia, and elsewhere.

Forests of broadleaf evergreen trees

THE IMPORTANCE OF TREES TO MAN

Forests are of immense importance in soil stabilization and erosion control, especially in mountainous and hilly regions; they also protect and conserve water supplies and prevent floods. Small groups of trees and even single trees have a similar role locally in preventing washouts and in holding stream banks. Trees can be considered guardians of soil and water; where they predominate, loss by erosion is compensated by the production of new soil resulting from the weathering of rocks and the accumulation of organic debris. Trees not only provide shelter, homes, and food for many animals but also, like all green plants, help to purify the atmosphere by absorbing carbon dioxide and releasing oxygen.

Economic importance. Without trees the world would be bleak, and life as it is known impossible. Carbonized and fossilized wood (coal) supplies fuel for the energy needs of man; other fossilized products of trees include amber, which is formed from the gum of pines, and kauri gum, the product of *Agathis australis*. From earliest times man employed wood for such purposes as homes, rafts, canoes, fuel, and weapons. Too often, however, so-called advanced civilizations have wantonly destroyed trees; great forests of cedars of Lebanon, for example, were virtually eliminated in lumbering operations during early historic times for such purposes as the construction of King Solomon's great temple and palace. Forests that covered much of the Mediterranean region and Middle East were extravagantly exploited by the Assyrians, Babylonians, Greeks, and Romans. Primitive peoples were dependent on trees for many materials in addition to wood. Fruits and nuts of many kinds were important foods for both man and animals. Leaves of palms and other trees were used for thatching roofs. Tapa cloth and woven fabrics made from bark, leaves, and other tree parts were used for clothing. Utensils were fashioned from calabashes, coconuts, and other fruits. Medicines, including quinine, the properties of which were long known to South American Indians, were obtained from trees, as were dyes, tanning materials, and spices. Seeds and other tree parts were used as charms and ornaments.

Modern man is no less dependent upon trees. Although substitutes now are commonly used for some tree products—concrete, steel, glass, and plastics; synthetic drugs and dyes; and synthetic substitutes for natural rubber—the demand for tree products has vastly increased in the manufacture of newsprint, for example, and in the manufacture of other papers as well as cardboard and similar packagings. The modern plywood industry converts immense numbers of trees into useful building materials and, in so doing, makes more complete use of good lumber than can be done by other means.

Wood products

Many products other than wood and its derivatives are important to modern man. Edible fruits produced by trees include apples, cherries, peaches, pears, and others in temperate climates; avocados, figs, persimmons, and

Bristlecone pine *(Pinus aristata)*, among the oldest known trees.

General Grant tree, a giant sequoia, or big tree *(Sequoiadendron giganteum)*, among the largest trees in total bulk.

Cedars of Lebanon *(Cedrus libani)*, known throughout ancient art and literature as symbols of power and longevity.

Leaves and fruit of the female ginkgo, or maidenhair tree *(Ginkgo biloba)*.

Tree ferns *(Alsophila australis)*, the largest of all ferns.

Cycas media, a treelike cycad that produces large terminal seed cones.

Plate 1: (Top left) Lola B. Graham—National Audubon Society, (top right, centre left) Bruce Coleman Inc., (top right) Gene Ahrens, (centre left) S. Wilhelm, (centre right) John Kohout from Root Resources—EB Inc., (bottom left) Walter Chandoha, (bottom right) G.R. Roberts

Plate 2 Tree

Bald cypress (*Taxodium distichum*), showing emergent roots, or knees.

Joshua tree (*Yucca brevifolia*), tallest of the yuccas, occasionally reaching 35 feet.

Screw pine (*Pandanus*), showing prop roots.

Branches of the European larch (*Larix decidua*), one of the few conifers that loses its leaves in autumn.

Talipot palm (*Corypha umbraculifera*) in bloom.

Washington palm (*Washingtonia filifera*), the only palm native to California.

Plate 2: (Top left) Rudolf Schmid, (top right) Bucky Reeves—National Audubon Society, (centre right) Jim Annan—Annan Photo Features, (bottom left) D. Muench—Shostal, (bottom centre) Ingmar Holmasen, (bottom right) W.H. Hodge

Baobab *(Adansonia digitata)*, the trunks of which occasionally reach 30 feet in diameter and are often excavated as houses.

Strangler fig *(Ficus)* on host live oak *(Quercus virginiana)*.

Live oak *(Quercus virginiana)* draped with Spanish moss, a lichen that uses the tree for support.

Mangrove *(Rhizophora)*, showing (above) viviparous (germinating on parent) seedlings and (right) a thicket of tangled roots and stems spreading over a tidal estuary.

Plate 3: (Top left) Tierbilder Okapia, (top right) Dr. G.J. Chafaris—EB Inc., (centre left) Louise K. Broman from Root Resources—EB Inc., (bottom left) Rudolf Schmid, (bottom right) G.R. Roberts

Plate 4   Tree

White birch *(Betula alba).*

Weeping willow *(Salix babylonica).*

Bonsai of a Japanese maple *(Acer palmatum).*

Australian gum tree *(Eucalyptus).*

Deciduous forest in fall coloration, Wasatch Mountains, Utah.

Magnolia denudata in flower.

Plate 4: (Top left) G. Lord—Shostal, (top right) J.L. Watcham, (centre left) W.H. Hodge, (centre right) Ron Dorman—Bruce Coleman Inc., (bottom left) Dorothea W. Woodruff—EB Inc., (bottom right) Sven Samelius

citrus fruits in warm-temperate and subtropical regions; breadfruit, coconuts, jackfruit, mangoes, and mangosteens in tropical regions; and the important fruit of desert regions—the date. The coconut (*Cocos nucifera*), the oil palm (*Elaeis guineensis*), and the olive (*Olea europaea*) are important sources of oils and fats used as food and for other purposes. From trees come such spices as cinnamon, cloves, and nutmeg; substances used in beverages, such as chocolate, coffee, and kola nuts; and chicle, the basis of chewing gum. Nonedible tree products exploited commercially include rosin, turpentine, tanbark, creosote, cork, and kapok fibre.

The aesthetic values of trees are generally appreciated. They are admired in their natural settings in forests, savannas, and along river courses; they are planted and cared for in gardens, parks, parkways, cemeteries, and city streets. They serve as screens to secure privacy and to reduce noise levels, and they provide shade.

Unusual trees of special interest. Mangroves, which consist not of one genus or species of tree but several, colonize tidal shores and brackish waters in the tropics and subtropics. In so doing they not only stabilize shore lines but also create new land by trapping debris, silt, and mud among their interlacing roots. Mangroves spread out into the water by sending from their branches roots that reach into the mud and develop into sturdy supporting props. A distinctive feature of mangroves is their large fruits, the seeds of which germinate and grow into sturdy seedlings before they leave the parent plant. When the seedlings fall, they either become fixed in the mud or float away, to be washed up at some site at which the opportunity to become established may occur.

Mangroves are not the only trees that spread by dropping prop roots from their branches. The habit is well developed in several tropical figs (*Ficus*), including one popular in small sizes as a houseplant—the rubber plant (*F. elastica*). Most noteworthy of the group is the banyan tree (*F. benghalensis*) of India; its numerous prop roots develop into secondary trunks that support the widespreading head of massive, constantly extending branches. One specimen 2,000 feet (600 metres) in circumference has been estimated as being capable of sheltering 20,000 people. The wonderboom (*F. pretoriae*) of Africa grows in a similar manner; a specimen at Pretoria has a spread of 165 feet. Because of their unusual growth habits these tropical ficuses are called strangler figs. Often they begin life high in a palm or some other tree in which a monkey, bat, or bird that has fed on the fruits deposits seeds that have passed through its alimentary tract. The seeds germinate, the roots growing into organic matter collected in crotches or crevices of the host tree. Under humid conditions the seedlings grow rapidly, sending roots down along the trunk of the host tree. Upon reaching the ground the roots branch and establish themselves. Above the ground the roots thicken until they form an interlacing cylinder around the trunk of the host.

The ombu (*Phytolacca dioica*) is a remarkable South American relative of the pokeweed. A tree capable of attaining heights of 60 feet (20 metres) and a spread of 100 feet, it has a wide trunk; the branches contain as much as 80 percent water and very little wood tissue. From its base radiates a circle of rootlike outgrowths wide enough for a man to sit upon.

The traveller's tree of Madagascar (*Ravenala madagascariensis*) has a palmlike trunk up to 30 feet tall topped by a huge, symmetrical fan of long-stalked, paddle-shaped leaves often much shredded by wind. The vernacular name alludes to the leaves having hollow bases from which, it has been reported, travellers could obtain potable water.

The talipot palm (*Corypha umbraculifera*) of tropical Asia may live as long as 75 years before it flowers and fruits just one time, then dies. The huge panicle (many-branched cluster) of creamy white blooms arises from the centre of the cluster of fan-shaped leaves topping the trunk, which may be 80 feet tall and three to four feet in diameter. Another palm of special interest is the double coconut (*Lodoicea maldivica*); a native of two tiny islands of the Seychelles group in the Indian Ocean, it has

fruits that require about ten years to mature, weigh up to 50 pounds (20 kilograms), and have the appearance of a pair of coconuts joined together. Long before their source was known, these fruits were washed up by the sea in India, and magical properties were ascribed to them.

The tallest trees are Pacific Coast redwoods (*Sequoia sempervirens*) specimens of which exceed 350 feet (105 metres) in height in an impressive grove in Redwood Creek Valley, California. The species is confined to a narrow coastal belt extending from southern Oregon to California. The next tallest trees are the Australian mountain ash (*Eucalyptus regnans*), specimens of which in Victoria, Australia, exceed 300 feet (90 metres), the greatest heights known for nonconiferous trees. A close relative of the redwood, the giant sequoia (*Sequoiadendron giganteum*) develops the greatest total bulk of wood, but not the biggest girth, among trees. This tree, which attains heights in excess of 300 feet and may have a trunk diameter of about 25 feet some distance above its flaring base, is restricted to a strip about 280 miles long and less than 20 miles wide in the region of the Sierra Nevadas, in California.

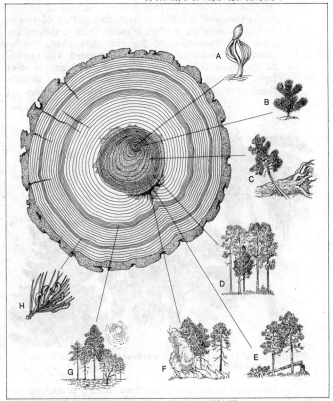

Figure 1: *Cross section of a tree trunk with events of its life indicated by growth patterns in wood.*
(A) A loblolly pine is born; (B) growth is rapid forming relatively broad, even rings; (C) "reaction wood" is formed to help support tree after something fell against it; (D) growth is straight but crowded by other trees; (E) competing trees are removed and growth is again rapid; (F) fire scars the tree; (G) narrow rings probably caused by prolonged dry spell; (H) narrow rings that may have been caused by an insect.

Records for tree girth are held by the baobab (*Adansonia digitata*) of Africa and the Mexican swamp cypress (*Taxodium mucronatum*). The baobab attains a maximum height of about 75 feet; its barrel-shaped trunk may be more than 25 feet in diameter a few feet above the ground. The most famous specimen of Mexican swamp cypress is "El Gigante," located at Tule, Oaxaca. The trunk of this massive tree is buttressed and not circular; if the bays and promontories of the buttresses are followed, the basal circumference is 150 feet.

The oldest living tree is a bristlecone pine (*Pinus aristata*) in Nevada; it has been reliably reported to be about 4,600 years of age. The species rarely exceeds a height of 35 feet.

Strangler figs

Trees have been worshipped as gods, accepted as the dwellings of good and evil spirits, and revered. In some parts of the world some of these practices still exist. Sacred trees and holy groves have existed and still exist. The Bible makes early reference to the tree of knowledge, and the pomegranate was long held in reverence by Jews and Persians as the biblical forbidden fruit. The name of the Druid priests of ancient Britain is derived from that of the oak tree they venerated. The use of holly, the leaves of *Ilex* trees, is traceable to the pre-Christian practice of the Druids, who decorated altars with it in winter. The asoka, or sorrowless tree (*Saraca indica*), and the bo tree (*Ficus religiosa*) are held sacred by Buddhists, the first as the tree under which Gautama Buddha was born, the other as the one under which he meditated and received enlightenment. The Hindu divinity Viṣṇu is also said to have been born under the bo tree. The banyan tree (*Ficus benghalensis*) is held sacred by Hindus, who believe that Brahmā was transformed into a banyan.

THE STRUCTURE AND GROWTH OF TREES

External growth forms. In outward form trees vary greatly according to species, and individuals sometimes differ in response to the environment. Because of inherent similarities within related groups, recognition of species and even varieties is often possible from distances too great for observation of the distinctive characteristics upon which botanical separations are based. The method of branching, for example, is highly significant. In some trees, including most conifers, the trunk forms a well-defined, dominant main axis, and the lateral branches are

Drawing by M. Pahl

Figure 2: Principal growth forms of trees. Left to right: columnar, deliquescent, and excurrent.

secondary in size and importance. Such a branching pattern, called excurrent, is characteristic of firs, spruces, larches, and most pines. In contrast is the decurrent, or deliquescent, branching pattern characteristic of many angiosperms, in which the trunk forms a well-defined central axis for the lesser part of the height of the tree and then divides and redivides as it forms a head of branches, or crown, of approximately equal dimensions. The decurrent pattern is characteristic of many oaks, the honey locust (*Gleditsia triacanthos*), the silver linden (*Tilia tomentosa*), and the American elm (*Ulmus americana*).

The angle from the horizontal assumed by branches can usually be strongly associated with species or variety and, together with the pattern of branching and comparative length of branches to trunk, is chiefly responsible for the form of the crown. The crown is usually strongly modified in trees growing in the forest as compared with those growing in open areas and thus not impeded by neighbours. In the consideration of tree forms presented here, specimens growing in the open are described. The Lombardy poplar (*Populus nigra* variety *italica*) is an upright form of strikingly columnar outline, very different from

the vase-shaped American elm (*Ulmus americana*). The heads of both are shaped differently from that of the pin oak (*Quercus palustris*), which typically has a well-defined central trunk with downsweeping lower branches, horizontal middle branches, and upward-angling high branches. Globular or billowy globular heads are characteristic of many trees, including the Chinese scholartree (*Sophora japonica*), the horse chestnut (*Aesculus hippocastanum*), the London plane (*Platanus acerifolia*), the Norway maple (*Acer platanoides*), the saucer magnolia (*Magnolia soulangeana*), and the white oak (*Quercus alba*). Others, such as the sugar maple (*Acer saccharum*), have more oval heads. A very common form, usually called pyramidal, is more correctly described as conical; it is characteristic of the various types of conifers.

Distinctive landscape patterns are provided by "weeping" trees, the best known of which is the weeping willow (*Salix babylonica*). In weeping trees the younger and often the older branches are pendulous or markedly downsweeping. There are many others, however, most of which are horticultural varieties of species that typically are more upright in their branching, such as the weeping beech (*Fagus sylvatica* variety *pendula*).

A characteristic feature, useful in the identification of many trees, is the protective layer of bark covering the trunks and branches. Bark varies from smooth, copper-coloured covering of the gumbo-limbo (*Bursera simaruba*) to the thick, soft, spongy bark of the punk tree (*Melaleuca leucadendron*). Other types of bark include the commercial cork of the cork oak (*Quercus suber*) and the rugged, fissured outer coat of many other oaks; the flaking, patchy-coloured barks of sycamores (*Platanus*) and the lacebark pine (*Pinus bungeana*); and the rough shingle-like outer covering of shagbark hickory (*Carya ovata*).

The trunks of some tropical trees, such as the silk-cotton tree (*Ceiba pentandra*), are supported by great flange-like buttresses. The presence of thorns is often an identifying characteristic of trees, as are the arrangement, form, shape, texture, and colour of leaves, flowers, and fruits.

Growth and internal structure. The life-spans of trees, like those of all organisms, are limited. They originate in the fertilization of a female egg cell (ovule) by a male reproductive cell (pollen grain), and eventually they die. During their life-spans trees respire and carry on photosynthesis and other physiological processes, including growth. Except in their early years, trees usually produce reproductive bodies (seeds or, in the case of ferns, spores). Growth, which includes elongation throughout life, is commonly most rapid in young trees; it slows markedly after maturity and in old age may be almost infinitesimal. Nevertheless, as long as a tree lives, its stems lengthen each year, and those of conifers and angiosperms increase in diameter.

Structurally, trees consist of three systems of vegetative organs—roots, stems, and leaves—and, in addition, reproductive organs. The latter include flowers, fruits, seeds, and spores. Roots (except for small feeder roots) and stems are permanent for the life of the tree. The other organs are transient, remaining for periods ranging from a few hours to a few years. Even leaves of evergreens fall and are replaced.

Roots provide firm anchorage for the aboveground parts and absorb practically all water and essentially all of the required nutrients except carbon dioxide, which is obtained from the air. The stems (trunks, branches, and branchlets) serve as a framework to support and dispose the leaves advantageously to the light needed in the process of photosynthesis; they also dispose and expose the reproductive parts to wind, insects, and other pollinating and dispersing agents. Also important is the pipeline function of stems by which water containing dissolved nutrients is moved from the roots to other parts, usually the leaves but sometimes leafless stems, in which photosynthesis takes place. Foods elaborated as a result of photosynthesis are translocated, or moved, to growing and storage tissues. The upward flow of water and solutes in conifers and angiosperms is almost exclusively through

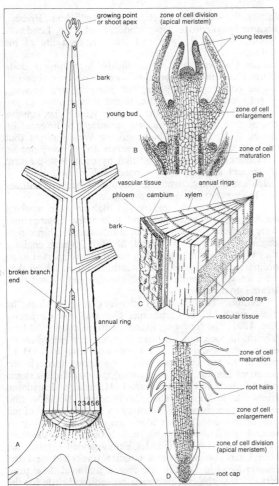

growing point
or shoot apex

zone of cell division
(apical meristem)

young leaves

bark

young bud

zone of cell
enlargement

B

zone of cell
maturation

vascular tissue

annual rings

pith

phloem   cambium   xylem

bark

broken branch
end

C

wood rays

vascular tissue

annual ring

zone of cell
maturation

root hairs

123456

zone of cell
enlargement

A

zone of cell division
(apical meristem)

D

root cap

Figure 3: *Growth regions of a tree.*
(A) Longitudinal section of a young tree showing how the
annual growth rings are produced in successive conical layers.
(B) Shoot apex, the extreme tip of which is the apical meristem,
or primary meristem, a region of new cell division that
contributes to primary growth, or increase in length, and which
is the ultimate source of all the cells in the above-ground
parts of the tree. (C) Segment of a tree trunk showing the
location of the cambium layer, a secondary meristem that
contributes to secondary growth, or increase in thickness.
(D) Root tip, the apex of which is also an apical meristem and
the ultimate source of all the cells of the root system.
From (A) W.W. Robbins and T.E. Weier, *Botany: An Introduction to Plant Science,*
©1950 by John Wiley & Sons, Inc.; (B, D) *Biological Science: An Inquiry into Life,*
2nd ed. (1968); Harcourt Brace Jovanovich, Inc., New York; by permission of the
Biological Sciences Curriculum Study; (C) E.W. Sinnott, *Botany: Principles and
Problems,* 4th ed., copyright 1946; used with permission of McGraw-Hill Book Co.

the tubular cells of the living xylem, or sapwood; the
downward movement is through the phloem, or bast,
which is a tissue layer that lies just beneath the bark.

Increase in the size of trees results from the production of new cells, the enlargement of old ones, and sometimes
the enlargement of the spaces between cells. New cells are
formed by meristem tissues, regions of rapid cell division,
which are located at the tips of stems and roots, and in
secondary meristems, called cambium layers, which form
a thin cylinder between the wood and the bark in conifers
and dicotyledons; cambium occurs to a lesser extent in
some monocotyledons and cycads. The meristems at the
tips of stems and roots are responsible for increases in
length and height, the secondary meristems for thickening. Tree ferns have no cambium; hence, no secondary
thickening of the trunk takes place. In conifers and dicotyledons, the successive layers of wood, usually one each
year, that are laid in concentric rings around previously
developed wood comprise the annual rings so clearly seen
when a trunk or branch of a tree is cut. The cells of the
annual rings usually live for several years. During the
time the cells are alive, the tissues they compose are
called sapwood. As the tree ages, the older, inner portions
of the sapwood undergo chemical changes and are infil-

**Growth
regions in
trees**

trated by oils, gums, resins, tannins, and other compounds. When the cells die, the sapwood has been converted to heartwood. Heartwood is often much darker in
colour, denser, and contains less moisture than sapwood.
Heartwood, although dead, persists for the life of the tree
and affords structural strength unless invaded by disease
organisms.

Trees that inhabit arid regions employ various devices
to conserve moisture. Thick, succulent, water-storage tissues form a large bulk of the leaves of tree aloes and
agaves and of the stems of tree cactuses. As additional
protection from desiccation these parts are often coated
with wax. Yuccas, including the Joshua tree (*Yucca brevifolia*), have tough, leathery foliage that transpires (loses
water by evaporation) only to a limited extent. Some
desert inhabitants, such as the tree euphorbias of Africa,
the great columnar cactuses of North and South America,
the boojum tree (*Idria columnaris*) of Baja California, and
the paloverde (*Cercidium torreyanum*) of western North
America, either have such meagre foliage—often in evidence only for short periods—or none, that it is not sufficient to photosynthesize the food they need. This deficiency
of leaves is met in part or entirely by the chlorophyll-con-
taining outer layers of the trunks and stems, which
carry on photosynthesis. The roots of a few trees, notably
the swamp cypress (*Taxodium distichum*) and mangroves,
which live in watery habitats, produce pneumatophores, or
"knees," that rise above the water level. It has been postulated that they are devices that ensure a supply of air to
the cells of the roots, but this is by no means certain.

THE ORIGIN AND EVOLUTION OF TREES

After the initial invasion of land by plants, perhaps 500,-
000,000 years ago, the evolution of the first trees began;
not until the Devonian Period (345,000,000 to 395,-
000,000 years ago) did the first vascular plants, including
some treelike forms, appear. The Devonian was succeeded by the Carboniferous Period (280,000,000 to 345,-
000,000 years ago), during which the climate of most of
the world was uniformly warm and moist. It favoured the
growth of trees, and numerous kinds, many of gigantic
size, evolved and populated the vast forests characteristic
of that period. These trees formed the great accumulations of decaying organic matter that, after being inundated, buried under mud and silt, and subjected to immense pressures, were transformed into coal. The extent
and thickness of the coal deposits of the world, some
covering thousands of square miles, give silent evidence
of the almost unbelievable lushness, extent, and persistence of the Carboniferous forests. It has been estimated
that 1½ inches (four centimetres) in the thickness of a
seam of coal represent on the average 1,000 years of
forest growth; some coal seams are hundreds of feet
thick. A change in climate ended the vast Carboniferous
forests and most of its plant forms, with the exception of
a few descendants now called horsetails, club mosses, and
ferns. The Permian Period (225,000,000 to 280,000,000
years ago) that succeeded the Carboniferous was by comparison cold, dry, and unfavourable to tree growth over
much of the Earth.

None of the early trees had flowers or seeds. They reproduced, as ferns and other lower plants still do, by
spores. Toward the end of the Devonian Period seed
plants appeared. They were the seed ferns, which are now
extinct; contemporary seed-producing plants now constitute by far the greatest portion of the vegetation of Earth.
Seeds in effect are embryonic plants packaged with starter
supplies of food. They enabled trees to colonize areas less
moist and humid than those essential for the development
of plants from spores. Seed ferns of tree dimensions became abundant during the Carboniferous Period. But
they, too, vanished and were replaced, about 200,000,000
years ago, by a new breed of trees now called gymnosperms. Of the 750 species that survive, some—the cycads, ginkgo, and conifers—are abundant. None has
flowers as that term is commonly accepted. Not until the
latter part of the Cretaceous Period (65,000,000 to 136,-
000,000 years ago) did the first flowering plants appear,
but their development and rise to ascendancy was re-

**Coal-age
forests**

markably rapid. The first flowering trees, having many of the characteristics of magnolias, appeared about the time the dinosaurs were becoming extinct.

BIBLIOGRAPHY. B.K. BOOM and H. KLEIJN, *The Glory of the Tree* (1966), on the beauty of trees, their uses, history, and folklore with 194 colour illustrations; ARTHUR CRONQUIST, *Introductory Botany*, 2nd ed. (1971), botanical facts and interpretation are stressed and new findings evaluated; THOMAS H. EVERETT, *Living Trees of the World* (1968), text and illustrations (many in colour) cover a wide range of tree subjects; ANDREAS FEININGER, *Trees* (1968), important facts on the history, structure, and uses of trees with magnificent photographs (many in colour); HILDERIC FRIEND, *Flowers and Flower-Lore*, 3rd ed., 2 vol. (1884), a plant lore classic; ALBERT F. HILL, *Economic Botany: A Textbook of Useful Plants and Plant Products*, 2nd ed. (1952), a concise, reference handbook on industrial, medicinal, and edible plants; PAUL J. KRAMER and THEODORE T. KOZLOWSKI, *Physiology of Trees* (1960), covers the role of physiological processes in tree growth; EDWIN A. MENNINGER, *Fantastic Trees* (1967), a popular treatment of unusual trees of the world; EUGENE P. ODUM, *Fundamentals of Ecology*, 3rd ed. (1971), concerned with interrelationships between plants and other organisms and the physical environment in which they exist; A.R. PENFOLD and J.L. WILLIS, *The Eucalypts: Botany, Cultivation, Chemistry, and Utilization* (1961), a simple, lucid survey of an important genus of trees; CARL L. WILSON, WALTER E. LOOMIS, and TAYLOR A. STEEVES, *Botany*, 5th ed. (1971), emphasis is placed upon plant diversity and the relation of plants to human affairs; ROBERT L. ZION, *Trees for Architecture and the Landscape* (1968), a well-illustrated work on landscaping with trees.

(T.H.E./L.M.W.)

Trevithick, Richard

Richard Trevithick, English mechanical engineer and inventor, was one of the major contributors to the development of the steam engine. By successfully harnessing high-pressure steam, he reduced the size and weight of engines and so made steam locomotion possible. His technical achievements were an important factor in the rise of the Industrial Revolution.

Trevithick, oil painting by John Linnell, 1816. In the Science Museum, London.

Early life in Cornwall's tin-mining district

Born on April 13, 1771, at Illogan in the tin-mining district of Cornwall, Trevithick attended the village school, where the master described him as "disobedient, slow and obstinate." His father, a mine manager, considered him a loafer, and throughout his career, Trevithick remained scarcely literate. Early in life, however, he displayed an extraordinary talent in engineering. Because of his intuitive ability to solve problems that perplexed educated engineers, he obtained his first job as engineer to several Cornish ore mines in 1790 at the age of 19. In 1797 he married Jane Harvey of a prominent engineering family. She bore him six children, one of whom, Francis, became locomotive superintendent of the London & North Western Railway and later wrote a life of his father.

Since Cornwall has no coalfields, high import costs obliged the ore-mine operators to exercise rigid economy in the consumption of fuel for pumping and hoisting. Cornish engineers, therefore, found it imperative to improve the efficiency of the steam engine. The massive engine then in use was the low-pressure type invented by James Watt. Inventive but cautious, Watt thought that "strong steam" was too dangerous to harness; not so Trevithick. He soon realized that by using high-pressure steam and allowing it to expand within the cylinder, a much smaller and lighter engine could be built without any less power than in the low-pressure type.

In 1797 Trevithick constructed high-pressure working models of both stationary and locomotive engines that were so successful that he built a full-scale, high-pressure engine for hoisting ore. In all, he built 30 such engines; they were so compact that they could be transported in an ordinary farm wagon to the Cornish mines, where they were known as "puffer whims" because they vented their steam into the atmosphere.

Trevithick built his first steam carriage, which he drove up a hill in Camborne, Cornwall, on Christmas Eve, 1801. The following March, with his cousin, Andrew Vivian, he took out his historic patent for high-pressure engines for stationary and locomotive use. In 1803 he built a second carriage, which he drove through the streets of London, and constructed the world's first steam railway locomotive at Samuel Homfray's Penydaren Ironworks in South Wales. On February 21, 1804, that engine won a wager for Homfray by hauling a load of ten tons of iron and 70 men along ten miles of tramway. A second, similar locomotive was built at Gateshead in 1805, and in 1808 Trevithick demonstrated a third, the "Catch-me-who-can," on a circular track laid near the Euston Road in London. He then abandoned these projects, because the cast-iron rails proved too brittle for the weight of his engines.

In 1805 Trevithick adapted his high-pressure engine to driving an iron-rolling mill and propelling a barge with the aid of paddle wheels. His engine also powered the world's first steam dredgers (1806) and drove a threshing machine on a farm (1812). Such engines could not have succeeded without the improvements Trevithick made in the design and construction of boilers. For his small engines, he built a boiler and engine as a single unit, but he also designed a large wrought-iron boiler with a single internal flue, which became known throughout the world as the Cornish type. It was used in conjunction with the equally famous Cornish pumping engine, which Trevithick perfected with the aid of local engineers. The latter was twice as economic as the Watt type, which it rapidly replaced.

Successful applications of steam engines

Trevithick, a quick-tempered and impulsive man, was entirely lacking in business sense. An untrustworthy partner caused the failure of a London business he started in 1808 for the manufacture of a type of iron tank Trevithick had patented—bankruptcy followed in 1811. Three years later, nine of Trevithick's engines were ordered for the Peruvian silver mines, and, dreaming of unlimited mineral wealth in the Andes, he sailed to South America in 1816. After many adventures, he returned to England in 1827, penniless, to find that in his absence other engineers, notably George Stephenson, had profited from his inventions.

Shortly before his death, he wrote:

Mr. James Watt said . . . that I deserved hanging for bringing into use the high pressure engine; this so far has been my reward from the public: but should this be all, I shall be satisfied by the great secret pleasure and laudable pride that I feel in my breast from having been the instrument of bringing forward and maturing new principles and new arrangements, to construct machines of boundless value to my country.

He died in poverty at Dartford, Kent, on April 22, 1833, and was buried in an unmarked grave.

BIBLIOGRAPHY. H.W. DICKINSON and A. TITLEY, *Richard Trevithick: The Engineer and the Man* (1934), the definitive book on its subject, including many drawings and sketches by Trevithick, a complete list of his patents, and a very complete bibliography; L.T.C. ROLT, *The Cornish Giant: The Story of Richard Trevithick, Father of the Steam Locomotive* (1960), a brief biography for the nontechnical reader; FRANCIS TREVITHICK, *Life of Richard Trevithick*, 2 vol. (1872), a work of filial piety (some of the drawings reproduced are reconstructions based, like parts of the text, on hearsay and are not accurate).

(L.T.C.R.)

Triassic Period

Triassic Period is the name given to that interval of geological time from about 190,000,000 to 225,000,000 years ago, during which the rocks of the so-called Triassic System were formed. It is the earliest period of the Mesozoic Era (65,000,000 to 225,000,000 years ago).

The term Trias, later modified to Triassic, was proposed in 1834 for a sequence of strata in central Germany lying above Permian (Zechstein) and below Jurassic (Lias) rocks of marine origin. The name refers to a threefold division of the strata into a lower unit of nomarine red-coloured sediments (Bunter, or Bundsandstein), a middle unit of marine limestone, sandstone, and shale (Muschelkalk), and an upper unit of nonmarine rocks (Keuper) that are similar to the lower division. This sequence is typical of Triassic strata of northern Europe, France, Spain, and north Africa; it is commonly known as the Germanic facies (the term facies refers to all aspects of the rocks involved, particularly to any lateral gradations or changes in characteristics that may occur). In contrast to the predominantly continental Germanic facies, there is in the Alps a complete marine fossiliferous sequence covering all of Triassic time that is commonly called the Alpine facies and that, with the addition of units in the lower beds from southern Asia, forms the primary standard sequence of stages and zones.

The standard divisions and correlation of the Germanic and Alpine units (descending from the most recent) plus the main zones, identified by ammonites (a type of cephalopod, a marine invertebrate animal), are shown in the Table. It should be noted that French geologists define the term Keuper in more restricted fashion than do the German geologists; the French apply the name Keuper to the middle part of the German sequence (Gipskeuper) and refer the Rhaetian (Rhät) to the Jurassic and the Lettenkohle to the Middle Triassic (Muschelkalk). In the French literature the German terms have been translated in ascending order, as *Grès bigarré* (Bunter), *Calcaire conchylien* (Muschelkalk), and *Marnes irisées* (Keuper restricted). An additional but minor variation is the use of Virglorian for Anisian and Werferian for Scythian.

Research in recent years on rock sequences and ammonoid faunas indicates that the zonal scheme shown in the Table is far from final. A new proposal of ammonoid zones for North America has illustrated some of the inconsistencies involved in the Alpine sequence. The stage names for the Middle and Upper Triassic have remained unchanged since their introduction; that for the Lower Triassic (Scythian) is under attack. Provincial stage names for this segment of time have been introduced in New Zealand and Japan. In the Soviet Union a two-name nomenclature for this segment of time has been adopted, the Induan below and the Olenekian above. On the basis of ammonoid sequences known from Arctic Canada, a fourfold nomenclature has been introduced, namely (from bottom to top) the Griesbachian, Dienerian, Smithian, and Spathian. These proposals reflect greatly increased study of this segment of geological time, but no consensus has yet been reached.

The Triassic Period is of special interest in Earth history because fundamental changes took place in the evolutionary pattern of the continents and of life. The preceding Permian Period was a time of great extinctions, especially among marine invertebrate life. During the Triassic, however, greatly renewed evolutionary radiation occurred. Among land animals the great radiation of the reptiles that so characterizes the subsequent Jurassic and Cretaceous periods became well established, and the first mammals made their appearance. The Triassic was also a period of great continentality (large areas of land emerged from beneath shallow seas), and most advocates of continental drift consider it to have been the period of initial breakup of the original supercontinent. Unlike most other geologic periods, it is not a time of formation of significant economic deposits. Triassic coal deposits are known in the Arctic islands of Canada, in various localities in Siberia, China, and Japan, in Queensland, and in Antarctica, but none of these is large or of economic importance. The same generalization applies to petroleum.

Dealt with in this article are the rocks, life forms, and environments of the Triassic Period. For comparable information on the prior and subsequent intervals of geological time see PERMIAN PERIOD and JURASSIC PERIOD, respectively. See also MESOZOIC ERA for an overview of Earth history that began in Triassic time and the articles FOSSIL RECORD; STRATIGRAPHIC BOUNDARIES; and PALEOGRAPHY for relevant information on stratigraphy and paleontology and the principles that underlie determination of ancient environments.

Major features of the Triassic

TRIASSIC ROCKS

Geosynclinal and shelf sea deposits. Triassic rocks are widely distributed in former geosynclinal belts (major depositional troughs in the Earth's crust) and on continental platforms and, to a much lesser extent, in former shallow marine shelf areas. The geosynclines are those of Tethys (an east–west belt extending from Spain to Indonesia) and the circum-Pacific region. In the Tethys belt a wide assortment of thick sequences of Triassic rocks occurs in the Alpine region, Turkey, Iran, Afghanistan, West Pakistan, and the Himalayas. In the western Pacific geosynclinal belt, extremely thick sequences of Triassic rocks are present in New Zealand and are well represented in Japan. In the eastern Pacific belt Triassic rocks of great thickness are known from Alaska, British Columbia, and the western United States and in Colombia, Ecuador, Peru, and Chile.

Sediments laid down in shelf seas, on the other hand, are

Triassic System Correlation Table

Germanic facies			series	stage	Alpine facies zones*
Keuper	Rhät	Rhaetian	Rhaetian	Rhaetian	*Choristoceras marshi*
	Gypskeuper	Keuper of French geologists (*Marnes irisées*)	Upper Triassic	Norian	*Sirenites argonautae* *Pinacoceras metternichi* *Cyrtopleurites bicrenatus* *Cladiscites ruber* *Sagenites giebeli* *Discophyllites patens*
				Karnian	*Tropites subbullatus* *Carnites floridus* *Trachyceras aonoides* *Trachyceras aon*
	Letten-kohle			Ladinian	*Protrachyceras archelaus* *Protrachyceras reitzi*
Muschelkalk (*Calcaire conchylien*)			Middle Triassic	Anisian (Virglorian)	*Paraceratites trinodosus* *Paraceratites binodosus* *Nicomedites osmani* *Neopopanoceras haugi*
Bunter or Bundsandstein (*Grès bigarré*)			Lower Triassic	Scythian (Werferian)	*Prohungariks–Subcolumbites* *Owenites–Anasibirites* *Gyronites–Prionolobus* *Otoceras–Ophiceras*

*Indexed by the ammonite fossils.

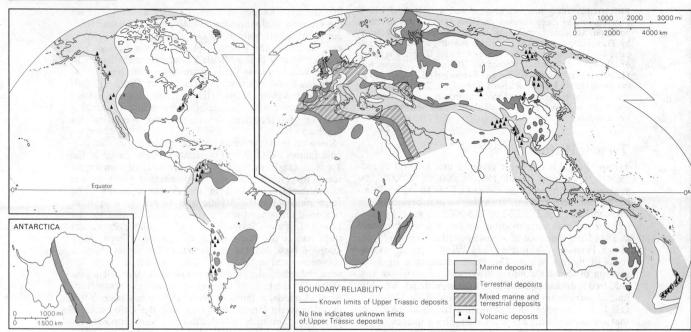

Distrbution of land, sea, and volcanic areas during Upper Triassic time.

BOUNDARY RELIABILITY
—— Known limits of Upper Triassic deposits
No line indicates unknown limits
of Upper Triassic deposits

Marine deposits
Terrestrial deposits
Mixed marine and
terrestrial deposits
Volcanic deposits

of more limited distribution. Along the northern margin of central and western Tethys, two conspicuous, large embayed regions were periodically occupied by shelf seas that spread outward. One is east of the Alps, occupying much of the Balkan region; another covered much of the area of the present Caspian Sea. Part of South China was also occupied by a shelf sea during Early Triassic time; this sea merged into Tethys. Deposits of shelf seas are also known along the southern margin of Tethys in Algeria, Libya, the Dead Sea region, Saudi Arabia, and in the Salt Range of West Pakistan. Shallow seas occupied a few very limited embayments along the west coast of Australia and a single area along the east coast of Australia in Queensland. The northwestern part of Madagascar was also occupied by shelf seas at least during Early Triassic time. Vladivostok, in eastern Siberia, was at the approximate centre of an embayment of shallow sea during parts of Early and Middle Triassic time. In the western United States shallow seas spread eastward over parts of Utah and Wyoming from the adjoining geosyncline only briefly during Early Triassic time. Much of the circum-Arctic region was occupied by shelf seas during the Triassic. Fairly thick deposits of primary clastic facies (sandstones and shales, in contrast to chemically precipitated sedimentary rocks) are present along northern Siberia from the Sea of Okhotsk to the Lena River. Similar kinds of rocks are a conspicuous part of the geologic record of Spitsbergen. Along the coast of eastern Greenland, Lower Triassic rocks of marine origin were laid down in a north–south embayment that opened to the Arctic Ocean but was closed at about 70° north latitude. The Canadian Arctic has very thick sequences of Triassic rocks in the Sverdrup Basin, and similar but much less well-known sequences are present in northern Alaska.

Red beds and evaporites   **Continental deposits.**   Continental sediments, especially of red-bed facies often associated with evaporite deposits, are especially widespread and characteristic of the Triassic. Throughout Eurasia north of Tethys, such rocks are a conspicuous part of the rock record. In northwest Europe these are the strata of the Germanic facies previously mentioned, and they include the New Red Sandstone of Great Britain. Vast areas of these continental sediments are present west of the Urals and in many scattered areas eastward across the remainder of Eurasia. South of Tethys continental sediments are the predominate sediment type. In peninsular India very thick deposits of Triassic age, all of nonmarine origin, are known. In Australia, as already noted, marine strata are very greatly restricted, but nonmarine red-bed formations representing stream, lake, and playa deposits are widely distributed

in Queensland and New South Wales. In South Africa the major part of the Karroo System is composed of Triassic formations, all of continental origin. Only a few of these formations are of red-bed facies; the variety of depositional environments represented by the Karroo includes streams, lakes, and deserts. East of the Andes in South America, there are several vast basins containing continental sediments of Triassic age. One is in the northwest over much of Colombia and Venezuela, and two are in northeastern Brazil; the largest, however, is in the Paraná Basin of southern Brazil, northern Argentina, and parts of Uruguay and Paraguay. In Antarctica no marine Triassic rocks have yet been identified, but in the Transantarctic Mountains there are extensive deposits of nonmarine sandstones of that age containing fossil plants, amphibians, and reptiles. Finally, in western North America, Triassic continental rocks compose much of the spectacular scenery of Utah, Wyoming, and Colorado. Many of these formations are stream, lake, and playa deposits and are red in colour. Others are vast sand dune deposits.

Overview of rock types.   The Triassic is represented by a great variety of sedimentary rocks. Limestone is confined mainly to the middle latitudes (including Tethys and western United States) and is represented by a great variety of carbonate facies, including reefs. One of the more interesting aspects is that no true reefs of Early Triassic age have yet been recognized; in fact, no corals are known from Lower Triassic formations. Scleractinian corals (a type that comprises the Mesozoic to Recent coral reef faunas) do not appear until the Middle Triassic and did not form true reefs but lived on banks. True reefs appeared in the Upper Triassic, and Triassic limestone formations are widely distributed in Tethys. Such formations are extremely thick in the Alps, Iran, and the Himalayas.

In the circum-Pacific geosyncline, graywacke (a type of sandstone containing a muddy matrix and a high proportion of rock fragments), sandstone, shale, and volcanic rocks predominate. In New Zealand the whole Triassic is made up of such facies, and the sequences are extremely thick. In the shelf areas of the circum-Arctic region, the Triassic formations are almost entirely sandstone, siltstone, and shale.

Volcanic activity   Extrusive and intrusive igneous rocks are not conspicuous in Triassic history. The eugeosynclinal belts (deepsea depositional troughs) of the circum-Pacific region include varying amounts of volcanic deposits, as is usual for such depositional regions. Large areas of Siberia were covered by basalt flows during the Triassic. The coastal region of Queensland was also a centre of active volcanic activity at this time. Such activity was also conspicuous in the Chilean Andes and adjoining regions of Argentina. In the downfaulted grabens (blocks that subside between fracture zones in the Earth's crust) that formed in the Appalachian Mountain region during the Upper Triassic, there were several phases of outpourings of basalt.

TRIASSIC LIFE

The geologic eras were first recognized by differences in the total fossil life. The Triassic Period is the harbinger of the Mesozoic Era, and its fossil record contrasts markedly with that of the preceding periods and sets the stage for the remainder of Mesozoic time. The evolution of life during earth history is punctuated by episodes of large-scale extinctions. That which took place toward the end of the Permian Period around 225,000,000 years ago was the most severe and widespread. Thus, the whole aspect of the Lower Triassic fossil record largely reflects this phase of Late Permian extinctions.

Invertebrate faunas.   Paleozoic marine strata are generally characterized by an abundant and very diverse fauna of invertebrate animals. Even to the nonspecialist this is evident on examination of these strata in the field, because the fossil record of the Lower Triassic strata has an impoverished aspect. The predominant invertebrate fossils are ammonites. These are not only abundant and diverse but extremely widespread. Bivalves and brachiopods are second and third in abundance but much less abundant than the ammonites. All other major invertebrate groups are rare, extremely rare, or absent in the Lower Triassic fossil record. It is worthwhile to document these points. Foraminifera are an extremely abundant and common fossil group from the Late Paleozoic to the Recent (the Holocene Epoch, or last 10,000 years). In the Lower Triassic, however, only 28 genera have been recorded to date. No corals have yet been recorded from Lower Triassic strata, and there is only a single record of a Bryozoa, a new genus of Trepostomata from Lower Triassic strata on Ellesmere Island, Arctic Canada. Though brachiopods are fairly well represented in the Lower Triassic record, they are difficult to interpret because there has been no study of the group in the 20th century. The latest compilations show 34 genera as being present in the Lower Triassic. According to the American paleontologist G. Arthur Cooper, the foremost authority on brachiopods, "The whole Triassic is a critical time in brachiopod history but a kind of never-never land between the Permian and the Jurassic." Among the most interesting new discoveries are Permian-type brachiopods in strata believed to be lowermost Triassic in the Salt Range of West Pakistan and at Guryul Ravine near Srinagar, West Pakistan. These are believed to be short-lived survivors of Permian-type brachiopods into Triassic time, but there is some disagreement on this interpretation. Bivalves are a fairly common element in Lower Triassic formations, but well-preserved specimens are rare. Some of the genera are worldwide in distribution. The relationship of Lower Triassic bivalves to Permian forms is poorly understood. The gastropods are exceedingly poorly represented in the Lower Triassic fossil record. For both the bivalves and gastropods there are relatively few genera recorded from the Lower Triassic. In each group greatly increased evolutionary radiation does not take place until the Late Triassic.

Remains of Echinodermata are important components in the composition of some Lower Triassic formations, but reasonably complete fossils are extremely rare. Among echinoids the only known is *Miocidaris*, a survivor from the Permian, whose fragmental remains are important in the composition of the lowest Triassic beds in the Salt Range of West Pakistan; ophiuroids and stelleroids are likewise extremely rare. Crinoids are only known from isolated columnals, which are abundant locally. Nautiloids are present in Lower Triassic formations but cannot by any means be considered as common. What is of particular interest in the nautiloids is that there is no change in pattern or mode of evolution of this group across the Permian–Triassic boundary.

The ammonites are the most conspicuous and prominent of all Lower Triassic faunal groups. In the Lower Triassic Scythian Stage, 136 genera of ammonites are known, ample testimony to the evolutionary vitality of this group.

Expansion of ammonites

There is no general consensus as to the cause of the Late Paleozoic phase of extinction. There has, however, been a great number of suggested causes, including changes in ocean salinity, climatic change, changes in geomagnetic polarity, cosmic radiation, changes in supply of nutrients, orogenies (mountain building), and regression of the seas off the continents. Whatever the cause or combination of causes, the result was a strange and impoverished Lower Triassic fauna. It has been tempting to examine the sedimentary facies as a corollary factor to explain the particular composition of Lower Triassic faunas. On careful analysis of the rock record, this explanation is not tenable. Lower Triassic formations include nearly a complete spectrum of marine rock types; the only major facies that is not present are true reefs.

In the Middle and Upper Triassic the ammonites maintained their predominance in the composition of marine invertebrate faunas. The bivalves increased, but nearly all other invertebrate groups were generally uncommon except in exceptional circumstances. The close of the Triassic was marked by the near extinction of the ammonites.

Vertebrate faunas.   The history of vertebrate life during the Triassic contrasts greatly with that of invertebrate life. In the first place, the phase of extinction toward the close of the Permian is not nearly as marked. Permian tetrapod faunas included labyrinthodont amphibians; cotylosaurs, primitive reptiles not far removed from their labyrinthodont ancestors; the eosuchians, a restricted group of small reptiles; the thecodonts (derived from an eosuchian ancestry); the araeoscelids or proterosaurs, another restricted but rather persistent group of reptiles; and the therapsids, or mammal-like reptiles. Of this group of tetrapods, only the labyrinthodonts, cotylosaurs, and therapsids are abundantly represented in sediments of Late Permian age. At the close of the Permian, one order of labyrinthodonts came to the end of its evolutionary line; all the remaining groups suffered great reduction in numbers of families at the close of the Permian, but others did survive into Triassic time. Tetrapod faunas of the earliest Triassic are dominated by these surviving groups from the Permian. Very soon, however, and progressively through the remainder of the Triassic, a number of new tetrapod orders appeared. The new orders were the proanurans (ancestors of the frogs), the chelonians or turtles, the lizards, the rhynchocephalians, the crocodilians, the saurischian dinosaurs, the ornithischian dinosaurs, the marine sauropterygians, placodonts, and ichthyosaurs, and the first mammals. The first lizards appeared in the Late Triassic, as did the first crocodilians and two orders of dinosaurs, the latter three groups being derived from thecodont ancestors. Turtles, arising from cotylosaurian forebears, evolved during Middle and Late Triassic time; and the rhynchocephalians, having arisen in the Early Triassic, went through a considerable range of evolutionary development during the Middle and Late Triassic. In the Late Triassic the first mammals appeared, as descendants from certain therapsid reptiles. The tetrapod invasion of the seas by the sauropterygians or nothosaurs and plesiosaurs, by the mollusc-eating placodonts, and by the fishlike or porpoise-like ichthyosaurs took place during Early and Middle Triassic time. There were 17 orders of tetrapods in the Triassic Period, as contrasted with seven orders in Late Permian time. Thus, as a result of evolutionary development following tetrapod extinctions that marked the end of Paleozoic history, the air-breathing vertebrates of Triassic time became more varied and, what is especially important, attained greater potentialities for future evolution along widely diverse lines than had been the case among tetrapods of Late Permian time. By the close of Triassic time, the whole character of tetrapod faunas had changed, and the stage was set for the even greater evolutionary radiation of the group in the following periods.

Dominant tetrapod faunas

Late Permian extinctions had little significance in the

evolutionary history of fish. The two or three families of sharks that existed in the Late Permian continued into the Triassic. The same is true for one family of coelacanths and one of lungfishes. Among the 18 genera of chondrostean families, eight persisted into the Triassic.

The floral record. Triassic floras are distinctive because they are dominated by gymnospermous types and thus contrast with the preceding Permian floras. Ferns, conifers, cycads, and ginkgos are the most common forms. The fossil floral record for the Triassic is not well documented, and this in part may be a reflection of widespread aridity for the period. At the same time large forests did exist, as illustrated by the Petrified Forest of Arizona. In the Gondwana areas, mainly the southern continents, Permian floras were dominated by *Glossopteris-Gangamopteris* elements. These were abruptly replaced by a new assemblage dominated by the pteriodosperm genus *Dicroidium*.

STRATIGRAPHIC-BOUNDARY PROBLEMS

In the type area of the Triassic, in Germany, most of the system comprises clastic formations of continental origin that are very poorly fossiliferous. The lower division, the Bunter, rests unconformably on the underlying Upper Permian Zechstein. The upper division, the Keuper, is unconformably overlain by marine shales of earliest Jurassic age.

The Permian–Triassic boundary. The first sequence of zones for the marine Triassic "pelagic facies" was proposed in 1895; the term pelagic refers to floating or freely swimming marine organisms, and the rocks in this facies are characterized by the fossil remains of such organisms. The sequence of zones for the Middle and Upper Triassic was based on Alpine data, whereas that for the Lower Triassic was based on Salt Range and Himalayan faunas. The lowest Triassic zone was named *Otoceras woodwardi*. It was soon recognized that in Tethys, wherever the lowest Triassic strata were present, the ammonite genus *Ophiceras* was associated with *Otoceras* and in much greater abundance. This lowest zone is now generally called that of *Otoceras-Ophiceras*. In the circum-Arctic region *Otoceras* appears first in the record, followed later by *Ophiceras*. The presence of Permian-type brachiopods with these index fossils in the Salt Range of West Pakistan and at Guryul Ravine, near Srīnagar, Kashmir, has prompted some specialists to consider this zone as of Permian age. This viewpoint, however, has received little support.

The nature of the Permian–Triassic boundary has been a subject of intense debate for a century. There are few places in the world where latest Permian strata are overlain conformably by youngest Triassic strata: there are the regions of Kap Stosch, eastern Greenland; Soviet Armenia and Azerbaijan and adjacent areas of northwest Iran; central Iran; the Salt Range of Pakistan; Kashmir; and Kwangsi Province, South China. At all of these localities there are small thicknesses of strata at the Permian–Triassic boundary that contain a mixture of Permian-type and Triassic-type faunal elements. The interpretation of these strata has been the crux of the problem. Much study has been concentrated on these areas in recent years. The Permian-type faunal elements associated with Triassic-type faunal elements in the Salt Range of Pakistan and in Kashmir are believed to be true survivors for a short period into Triassic time. In Soviet Armenia and Azerbaijan and adjacent northwestern Iran, the strata with the so-called mixed fauna have been conclusively shown to be of Late Permian age. The immediately overlying strata in Soviet Azerbaijan contain a rich and diverse *Ophiceras* fauna. In eastern Greenland the Permian-type faunal elements found in strata with *Otoceras* have been shown to be derived from outcrops of Permian rocks. The primary problem in definition of the Permian–Triassic boundary is not so much recognition of what is earliest Triassic but what represents latest Permian time.

The Triassic–Jurassic boundary. Definition of the upper boundary of the Triassic System has not been without difficulties. In the mid-19th century when the geological

time scale was being established, marine strata were recognized in England and in Europe north of the Alps containing the bivalve *Rhaetavicula contorta* resting on the nonmarine New Red Sandstone and the Keuper. These strata were overlain by very fossiliferous shales and limestones of the Lias. Because these strata represented an abrupt change from continental to marine deposition, it was natural to recognize this contact as the Triassic–Jurassic boundary. In the Alps, however, these same strata with *Rhaetavicula contorta* later yielded a small fauna of ammonites of Triassic affinity. These beds were given the name Rhaetic. The lowest zone of the overlying Lias beds is identified by the appearance of the ammonite *Psiloceras planorbis*, which is of nearly worldwide occurrence, with an accompanying molluscan fauna. At the present time stratigraphers in most countries except France include the Rhaetic in the Triassic.

TRIASSIC PALEOGEOGRAPHY

Distribution of land and sea. The Triassic Period was characterized by general emergence of land areas as a consequence of long continuing orogeny (uplift and mountain building) during the Late Paleozoic. In this process the Uralian Geosyncline, a north–south mobile zone separating Eurasia into two distinct areas of greater stability, underwent its final orogenic episode. The mobile belt of the geosynclinal region in eastern and southern North America also underwent its final orogenic phase. The same applies to the Tasman geosynclinal belt of eastern Australia.

Geosynclinal areas are confined to Tethys and to the circum-Pacific region. Shelf seas bordered the circum-Arctic region. Probably at no other time during the Paleozoic and Mesozoic were the world continents in such an emergent state.

At the same time, diastrophism (mountain-making movements) was areally restricted. During the Late Triassic the Appalachian Mountain region from Nova Scotia south to the Carolinas underwent faulting, forming deep subsiding grabens wherein many thousands of feet of terrestrial clastic sediments accumulated. In Nevada orogenic activity (thrust faulting) continued along the Antler orogenic belt in a north–south trend through central Nevada. Along the Pacific coastal margin from California to southern Alaska, no Lower or Middle Triassic formations are found. In fact, Upper Triassic formations are very widespread and tend to overlie Permian and older formations. It is believed that in the intervening time the area was emergent and undergoing orogeny. On the opposite side of the Pacific, a pronounced orogeny took place in late Middle Triassic time (Ladinian) in the inner zone of southwestern Japan. Throughout the Paleozoic, China had been subjected to periodic marine transgressions, northward out of Tethys, and these continued until Middle Triassic time. In the Late Triassic much of China underwent orogeny, ending all further marine transgressions. Triassic sediments in eastern Australia are primarily nonmarine intermountain-basin deposits, and these were gently folded at the close of Triassic time.

The hypothesis of continental drift (*q.v.*) is advocated by the majority of earth scientists and is strongly supported by evidence from the ocean floors (see ROCK MAGNETISM; SEA-FLOOR SPREADING). The problem is much too complex to be discussed here, but a few general comments, insofar as they pertain to the Triassic, are in order. One of the strongest arguments for drift is the geological fit of the opposing coasts of South America and Africa and the fact that there are no marine deposits of Triassic age on either side of the South or North Atlantic south of Spitsbergen. A great many different reconstructions of the continents have been proposed, and more can be expected in the future. There is considerable difference of opinion as to when the supercontinent began to break up, but Triassic time is favoured by a number of specialists. Most of the proposed continental reconstructions are based on physical criteria, such as fit of continental margins, similarity of rock facies and sequence, and paleomagnetic data from the ocean floor. The distribution of

Otoceras and Ophiceras as index fossils

Geosynclines and mountain building

fossil animals, especially amphibians and reptiles, is also used to support the hypothesis. Specialists on these groups, however, do not agree on the interpretation of the data. Among marine invertebrates there does appear to be a pronounced north–south faunal gradient, but lack of marine deposits along the Atlantic inhibits any statement on east–west movements that is based on paleontological evidence.

Indications of warm temperatures

Triassic climates. Beginning in mid-Permian time, approximately, widespread aridity became a major factor in world climatic patterns. This tendency increased through Late Permian time and set the pattern for Triassic climates. The fossil and rock record for Triassic time suggests highly homogeneous climatic conditions lacking extremes. For instance, there are no known continental glacial deposits of Triassic age. This contrasts greatly with pre-Triassic conditions. The most widespread continental deposits are red beds of sandstone and shale, in many places associated with evaporite deposits. There is no simple explanation for the origin of all these continental red-bed deposits, but most were probably not products of deposition in a fully arid climate. Many contain abundant fossil plants, fish, and tetrapods. These deposits were most likely formed in warm areas of seasonal rainfall and periods of drought.

Climatic interpretations on the basis of lithologic character of marine rocks are more difficult to make. The fact that there are essentially no limestones of Triassic age in the circum-Arctic region probably has some climatic significance, but the precise nature is difficult to establish. The absence of limestones may be a result of nothing more than an abundance of clastic sediments in the shelf seas adjoining the circum-Arctic region throughout much of Triassic time.

Geographic distribution of animal and plant life adds significant insight to the problem. Modern amphibians and reptiles are ectothermic, or "cold-blooded," animals having no internal-temperature-regulation mechanisms and are therefore more or less controlled by the temperature of the environments in which they live. It is assumed that the same factors existed in the past. The great majority of modern amphibians, for example, are inhabitants of the tropics or subtropics. Some have adapted to live in higher and lower latitudes, but these are small forms with very special habits. Caution, of course, is required in application of this principle, but plots of distribution of Triassic amphibians and reptiles yield provocative data. Lower Triassic amphibians and reptiles are known from as far north as 80° north latitude to about 30° south latitude. Of special interest is that the faunas of the higher and lower latitudes are made up of individuals of smaller size than those from the intervening zone. This is interpreted by some authorities as reflecting the influence of lower temperatures. In contrast to this pattern, Upper Triassic amphibians and reptiles have the same approximate latitudinal distribution, but large-size forms are found throughout the range. Again, this is interpreted as a reflection of equitable climatic conditions over much of the globe.

Temperature appears to be one of the most important factors controlling the distribution of marine invertebrates. Among modern shelf faunas, there are larger numbers of genera and species in tropical seas than in the Arctic seas. Much work in recent years has involved assembling data on faunal diversity for various periods of geologic time. One example for the Triassic illustrates the method. In one zone (the uppermost) of the Lower Triassic, 73 genera of ammonites are known, 64 of which lived in Tethys and only 22 in the circum-Arctic region; the intermediate zone has 32 genera. This is interpreted as a clear-cut faunal diversity gradient that probably reflects some temperature difference between the low and high latitudes. Although there is no reason to believe that the differences were great, they were probably sufficient to control the distribution of these marine invertebrates.

BIBLIOGRAPHY. R.C. MOORE (ed.), *Treatise on Invertebrate Paleontology*, pt. L by W.J. ARKELL *et al.* (1957), a comprehensive summary of Triassic ammonoid genera, the main fossil group used for zonation of the Triassic; C. DIENER, "Die Marinen Reihe der Trias Periode," *Denkschr. Akad. Wiss., Wien*, 92:405–549 (1916), the only complete synthesis of marine Triassic history, out of date in many aspects but still a valuable source; E.D. MCKEE *et al., Paleotectonic Maps, Triassic System*, U.S. Geol. Surv. Misc. Geol. Inv. Map 1–300 (1959), a fine summary of the character and time and space relations of Triassic strata in the United States; F.H. MCLEARN, "Correlation of the Triassic Formations of Canada," *Bull. Geol. Soc. Am.*, 64:1205–1228 (1953), a standard compilation of stratigraphic data for Triassic formations cropping out in Canada; J.B. REESIDE, JR. *et al.*, "Correlation of the Triassic Formations of North America Exclusive of Canada," *Bull. Geol. Soc. Am.*, 68:1451–1514 (1957), part of the same series as preceding reference; N.J. SILBERLING and E.T. TOZER, "Biostratigraphic Classification of the Marine Triassic in North America," *Spec. Pap. Geol. Soc. Am.*, 110: 1–63 (1968), the latest compilation of data on fossil zonation schemes for North America; E.T. TOZER, "A Standard for Triassic Time," *Bull. Geol. Surv. Can.*, 156:1–103 (1967), a comprehensive report summarizing relations of Triassic formations of Canada.

(B.Ku.)

Tribal Religious Movements, New

In the last five centuries, the tribal peoples of the world have had more extensive and disturbing encounters with the religions and cultures of highly sophisticated and powerful civilizations than ever before. Such encounters have been brought about by the expansion of the European peoples across the world, except in Asia and the Islāmic areas of North Africa and the Middle East. On a much smaller scale, the tribal peoples marginal to the Hindu and Buddhist societies in India and Southeast Asia have experienced the renewed impact of these dominant cultures and religions (*e.g.*, the reform movements among the Bhil tribes of western India under the influence of Hinduism and the cults among the Karen tribes of Burma under the influence of Buddhism).

Encounters between tribal peoples and higher civilizations

In the encounters between large, powerful, highly organized, and literate societies and small, weak, and nonliterate tribal peoples, the latter have responded by developing a vast proliferation of religious movements. These movements owe something to the religions of both their own and the newly introduced cultures, without being completely identified with either the old tribal or the new invasive religions. They are, in this sense, new religious creations, and the similarity of the situations in which they arise, of their characteristic features, and of the variety of their forms makes it possible to consider them in the aggregate as a new development in the history of religions.

NATURE AND SIGNIFICANCE

The problem of descriptive terminology. During the middle and latter part of the 20th century many different terms have been used to designate these movements. Those concerned with their political implications, especially in colonial situations, have spoken of revolutionary cults, rebellious prophets, or protonationalist movements. Their psychological aspects have been stressed in such terms as crisis or deprivation cults and reformative or revitalization movements. Sociologists may refer to separatist or independent sects or to voluntary religious societies and popular movements; and cultural anthropologists speak of adjustment or acculturation or of nativistic, perpetuative, revivalistic, or transformative movements. Their religious features appear when they are called, on the basis of certain distinguishing characteristics, heretical, syncretistic, or prophet movements; eschatological (with an emphasis on the end time), millennial (with an emphasis on a final reign of the saved elect), or messianic (with an emphasis on a salvatory figure or group) cults; or pentecostal (spiritual or charismatic) or visionary sects. This wide range of terms indicates the rich variety of the phenomena as well as the many disciplines interested in their study.

Only a few of these terms might apply to all such movements; they could perhaps be identified as independent syncretist adjustment movements. These terms, however, like all the others mentioned above, also apply to movements outside the phenomena being examined and thus do not provide a distinguishing description. Certain widely used terms would seem to be better avoided. "Nativistic," a term from the early 1940s, is suggestive of the tribal reference; but its regressive suggestions exclude many dynamic and creative movements, and it may be used elsewhere for movements within Western or other societies. The terms millennial and messianic have been seriously overworked because comparatively few such movements are messianic in the strict sense; and many are no more millennial than are most religions with some conception of a blessed future (see MESSIAH AND MESSIANIC MOVEMENTS; MILLENNIALISM). The term revitalization movements, though it was widely adopted in the 1950s, remains useful but is rather redundant because the concern with the renewal of vitality from the divine source lies near the centre of most religions.

Differences from folk religions These movements should be distinguished from folk religions, which do not arise in an encounter situation of the kind described but occur among rural and urban masses as unsophisticated popular religions in a symbiotic relationship with a more sophisticated and classic form. Also excluded from consideration are most of the New World Negro religions, some of which are regarded as forms of folk religion.

General basic characteristics. *Religious nature.* The first basic characteristic of these new tribal movements is their religious nature. Because of the integration of the secular and the religious in these societies, they have often appeared as predominantly political, economic, or social movements. Colonial governments, therefore, frequently regarded their religious concerns as fronts for subversive activities. The religious dimension has, however, usually persisted and continued to develop after the more secular concerns and functions have declined or have been taken over by political parties, trade unions, cooperatives, or social and cultural societies.

Acculturative processes. The second basic feature is the rise of these movements in situations provided by encounters of tribal societies with the more powerful and complex cultures associated with one of the major religions—usually with Western culture and Christianity and in a colonial setting. The interaction between the two cultures changes them both; but the subordinate, or tribal, culture is usually much more drastically affected. This is known as the acculturation process, although the changes may be either towards assimilation of selected features from the dominant culture or toward rejection of this culture by reassertion of the weaker culture in new forms. In either case, the process commonly (but not always) issues in new religious movements as bearers and formulators of the acculturative response.

Mere contact, however, no matter how extended, is not necessarily sufficient. West Africans had long contact with Europeans before the first series of new movements began in the 1880s. The Aborigines of northern Australia had met the more sophisticated Indonesians, Japanese whalers, and the earlier Europeans; but it was only when they were caught up in the activities of World War II and in postwar tourist developments and new government policies that the syncretistic Elcho Island movement appeared in Arnhem Land about 1958. It was founded by Buramara, a mission-influenced Aborigine. The scale or the suddenness of the encounter, and especially the degree of pressure or interference from the dominant culture by way of control, exploitation, or colonialization, usually precipitates the acculturative religious response.

Sensitivity to contacts with more sophisticated cultures Some tribal peoples, on the other hand, have proved to be exceedingly sensitive to slight and indirect contacts that have contained features capable of being given important meanings in local cultural terms. Thus, isolated New Guinea highlanders, beyond the reach of government agents or missions, have developed incipient cargo cults (*e.g.*, Zona [Ghost] wind cults) after steel tools and cloth goods were filtered through their ordinary trading channels, along with stories of mysterious whites, who were probably first seen in connection with airplanes from about 1930 on. These whites were in-

terpreted to be the long-awaited spirits of the ancestors now returning with abundant material wealth according to the hopes expressed in the tribal myths. For the highlanders this was a sudden and dramatic development requiring a new religious response that went beyond the gradual changes normally occurring in religions.

The acculturative religious movements are new in relation to the religious traditions of both the local and the invasive cultures. Their followers tend to be rejected by and to reject both those who seek to conserve the old traditions without change and those who make a complete conversion to the new religion of the dominant culture. The sources of the new movement, however, lie in the local and the invasive religions; and by various degrees of syncretism there emerges a new pattern of cultic and social forms, a new symbolic system, and a reforming ethic and distinctive ethos. As a working definition, new tribal religious movements can be described as

a historically new development arising in the interaction between a tribal society and its religion and one of the higher cultures and its major religion, involving some substantial departure from the classical religious traditions of both the cultures concerned, in order to find renewal by reworking the rejected traditions into a different religious system.

The stages of the religious acculturative process The term new development includes all forms and stages of the religious acculturative process—the embryonic stage of new ideas, the incipient stage of an individual with a new religious formulation but without followers, and the more explicit identifiable movement whereby a whole group transforms the old religious system, whether in a short-lived or local manner or in a more permanent and widespread fashion.

General causative factors. Earlier studies tended to explain the origin of these movements in terms of one or two major causes, usually drawn from those dealt with in the discipline of the scholar concerned or by one single general cause—extreme psychological, social, or cultural strain. It is now recognized, however, that a large number of factors may be at work in complex situations that may vary considerably from one area to another. Four kinds of causal factors may conveniently be considered: the situational or acculturative; the contributing; the precipitative; and the enabling factors.

The situational or acculturative factor. The matrix, or the general situation within which the appearances of new religious movements occur, has already been described, including the disturbing effects on a tribal people of interaction with a dominant society. This is a necessary but not a sufficient cause because not all people in such situations react in this particular way.

Contributing factors. Several contributing factors are significant in the rise of the new religious movements. (1) The psychological stress and conflict felt by individuals in unfamiliar or rapidly changing situations may cause them to be confused, powerless, and frustrated, especially if they are able or ambitious. (2) Because of the cultural and social disintegration experienced in tribal life, the new movements provide members of new social groups with a strong sense of belonging and with new ways of life. (3) Moral conflicts between the traditional and invading systems, with their different values and codes, are often resolved by the formation of new moral systems drawn from both cultures and sanctioned by the new religions. (4) Political domination, whether oppressive or paternalistic, in which traditional political structures have been eroded or replaced, are often countered by new religious movements, which provide alternative opportunities for organization and leadership, and, on occasion, a basis for political action. (5) Economic deprivation or exploitation, such as the loss of land, has contributed to the emergence of new religious movements among the peoples of North America, South Africa, Rhodesia, and New Zealand. The change from subsistence to wage-labour economies, the use of forced or migrant labour, and the creation of a new range of wants have all added their disturbing effects. (6) The colonial situation as such, which usually contains most of the above features, has been regarded as a major contributing factor, whether or not it was oppressive or more enlightened.

No close correlation, however, exists between any or all of these contributing factors and the rise of new religious movements. Ghana, for instance, has been one of the most prosperous of black African nations, with no white settlers, and has been politically independent since 1957; yet new religious movements appeared there in the 1960s more extensively than ever before.

Precipitative factors. Precipitative factors, such as severe personal crises or the traumatic effects of sudden epidemics (*e.g.,* a worldwide influenza epidemic in 1918), have provoked the appearances of new movements in situations that are already affected by the operation of deeper causes. A crisis precipitating the rise of a new religious movement may derive from new taxes or from severe economic depression, both of which were operative in the later Aladura ("prayer" people), prophet-healing groups in West Africa, in the early 1930s. In Melanesia, contact with the affluence of American armed forces in World War II precipitated a number of cargo cults; *i.e.,* groups that thrived on expectations of arrivals of special cargoes from supernatural sources. Elsewhere a movement might be touched off by the disciplining of a mission agent; casual contact with a nonwhite visitor, such as a Negro from an independent church in the United States; a miracle of healing, or the emergence of a charismatic individual with some special religious experience.

Enabling factors. The features of the two cultures involved that finally determine whether or not a new religious movement will appear and what shape it will assume may be called enabling factors. Among the major religions, Christianity seems to possess a peculiar potentiality for arousing new tribal religious movements. This potentiality has been attributed to Christianity's traditional appeal to the poor and the oppressed. Tribal peoples throughout the world have identified themselves with the suffering peoples of the Old Testament and their leaders with its great figures, especially the prophets Moses and Elijah. Biblical eschatology (doctrine of the last times) has provided a framework for the hope of a better future or a new world; and the tension between the Christian religion and Western culture has enabled tribal movements to draw upon the former in its conflicts with the latter. The dominant religion must, therefore, possess features suitable for application to and reinterpretation by the tribal peoples; and the religion of the latter requires beliefs and practices that can be reworked in the light of the invasive religion.

VARIATIONS AND FORMS

Any of the factors noted above may help to explain why only some peoples in the acculturative situation produce new religious movements, why different types of movements appear to characterize certain areas, or why a new movement in one tribe is accepted or rejected when it seeks to spread to others. New movements have proliferated in the West African peoples of the Ivory Coast, Ghana, Dahomey, and Nigeria, for example, but they have been rare or late in appearing in Sierra Leone, Liberia and Cameroon. The Ghost Dance of 1890, a North American Indian messianic movement, spread rapidly to more than 30 tribes of the Plains Indians but was ignored by the Navajo and the Hopi of the Southwest. Though cargo cults are characteristic of Melanesia, they are absent from the Trobriand Islands and New Caledonia and are rare in Polynesia, where the social system has much in common with that of these two areas of Melanesia. In the case of the cargo cults, the more developed Polynesian-type societies, with ranked social classes and either hereditary chiefs or a centralized political authority, have been better able either to oppose the invasive culture or to deal with it in its own terms and accommodate to it. Again, a psychological rather than a sociological reason has been suggested for the contrast between the dramatic cargo cults of the Melanesians, with their alleged proneness to ecstasy and violent movement and their ready loss of conscious control, and the new movements of

the Plains Indians of the United States. The Plains Indians were marked by a striking degree of self-control; they had to struggle for unconsciousness and trance or visions; and when the vision was achieved there were no physical excesses but only peaceful receptions of the revelations.

Some scholars have suggested that Protestant rather than Roman Catholic Christian missions have contributed to the appearance of new movements; and there appears to be some truth in this, connected especially with the Protestant policy of providing vernacular translations of the Bible. On the other hand, in the earlier centuries (*e.g.,* 16th–18th) there were many such movements in Latin America; and notable movements (*e.g.,* Maria Legio, or Legion of Mary, an independent church that arose in the 1960s) have emerged in recent times from a Catholic milieu in Africa.

Variations of incidence and of form are more likely to be connected with the different ways in which the various tribes have had contact with Westerners and Christian missions, and especially with the sequence in which the various aspects of Western culture have been encountered. Much depended on whether the earliest or the major contact was with traders, miners, ranchers, or farmers, with missionaries, with government officials, or with the military or the police. The missionaries might have been authoritarian or egalitarian, hostile to indigenous culture or appreciative of it, confined to one major Christian tradition or divided among many Christian denominations, concerned more with secular development, as were the early Quakers in North America who influenced the Seneca Indians, or with the rescue of souls before the imminent return of Christ, as was the case with many early missionaries in the Pacific.

Many tribal peoples who had made an initial mass response to Christianity involving a dramatic rejection of tribal religion later experienced various kinds of disappointments, and therefore turned to their own attempts at a new religion. Reactions and attempts of this kind include various themes or forms: (1) Because the return of Christ, the resurrection of the dead, and the new age failed to occur, tribal peoples produced their own millennial, messianic, or cargo cults. (2) Because the Bible did not prove to be the revealer of all the secrets of Western power and knowledge, cults arose around a prophet with his own new revelation or even with no more than a piece of paper with marks or diagrams or an alleged new book that was never publicly produced. (3) When it was discovered that the denominational Christianity first encountered was the religion of only one nation or that it was no older than the 16th or some later century, there began a search for the true original Christian church (*e.g.,* the African Greek Orthodox Church) or an attempt to create such themselves, as among many Aladura in Nigeria. (4) When Western medicine introduced by missionaries failed to show that it dealt with the spirit causes of sickness and was inadequate in many sicknesses, especially in psychic disorders and in epidemics such as that of 1918 (influenza), healing by other and more spiritual means figured prominently in new religious movements all over the world. (5) When second-generation Christians, who lacked the psychological rewards of intimate relationships with missionaries and the dramatic break from the past enjoyed by their fathers, discovered that they had only the administrative and financial responsibilities of church membership as replacements, they turned to their own churches with more immediate spiritual rewards and simpler organizational demands.

CHARACTERISTIC FEATURES

In spite of the diversity of movements and tribal backgrounds, it is possible to identify a wide range of characteristic features.

Origin in mystical experiences. The usual origin of those movements is a mystical experience of some contact with the spirit world through a dream, trance, coma, or apparently fatal sickness. Prophets often report having died and met the supreme God, Jesus, or the angels, or

Types of crises that precipitate new religious movements

Geographical variations

Reactions to Christianity that led to new religious movements

the ancestors or culture hero in heaven. After being instructed in a new way of life and religion, they returned equipped with a new teaching, perhaps a new sacred book or its equivalent, special rituals, songs, and dances, or the power to work miracles, especially healing.

Emphasis on a supreme and personal God. The spirits and divinities that operated in the traditional religions are likely, in the new religions, to be ignored, demoted, or reinterpreted as angels or even as the devil; and the emphasis will be on a single supreme and personal God. This Being, or his agents, is viewed as being responsible for the call and commission of the founder and for the charter and sanctions of the new movement.

The nature of charismatic leaders

Charismatic leadership. An individual leader who has had some such experience often possesses charismatic qualities. His peculiar nature and experience place a distinctive stamp upon the movement, whether he be primarily a prophet, preacher, messiah, healer, wonderworker, remote mystic, or one with political gifts. Especially notable is the extent to which women have been founders and leaders (*e.g.,* the Lumpa Church in Zambia, the Aladura churches in West Africa, or the Maria Legio in East Africa).

Institutional leadership. The charismatic leader has often been balanced sooner or later by others with organizational gifts who have institutionalized the movement or even redirected it into more secular channels for political action. The husband of Alice Lenshina, the leader of the Lumpa ("higher") Church of Zambia, and elders of that church seem to have played some such role from an early stage.

Rejection of traditional ways. A selective but dramatic rejection of many of the traditional ways has been a prelude to a radically new order that comes to be expected. Members of cargo cults may kill the pigs, destroy the food stores, and cease gardening. Followers of Siberian religious movements have burnt the shaman's drums, and those of North American movements have thrown away the medicine bags. In most cases there is strong hostility to the continued employment of magic and a sustained attack on witchcraft. Other traditional practices, such as polygamy and reliance upon dreams, however, have been defended against Christian criticisms.

Missionary zeal. The new way may be confined to a single tribe but it often transcends ethnic boundaries and offers a universalistic faith. This is expressed in a remarkable missionary zeal that was quite unknown in the original tribal faith and may result in the religion spreading from contact areas to pre-contact areas, as was the case with new religions that were carried to the Nunamiut Eskimos in the Brooks Range in Alaska by traders who had met Quakers on the coast.

Moral reform. Prominence is given to moral reform in the face of the breakdown of traditional codes and sanctions. The moral teaching may reinforce tribal practices or borrow new elements from the invasive culture, such as an insistence upon monogamy. Common features are: a stress upon love, peaceableness, sexual discipline, and industry. There is often a strong ascetic aspect, with a prohibition against tobacco and, especially, alcohol.

New symbolic forms. New rituals, symbolisms, and forms of worship appear, drawing upon the resources of both of the religions involved and sometimes showing considerable liturgical creativity.

New voluntaristic organizations. New organizations of a voluntary type are developed, with new roles filled by many officials with titles, ranks, and uniforms or insignia. This new community replaces or transcends the old tribal groups and may range from amorphous, loosely associated groups, such as the Native American Church that uses peyote (a part of a cactus that produces hallucinogenic effects), to highly integrated Western-style bodies, like some of the larger African independent churches.

Promise of definite blessings. In the new religions there is an offer of definite concrete blessings—either here and now in the form of healing, revelations or "messages," personal success, and protection from evil powers, or else in the nearer future in a new order (promising plenty, health, peace, and freedom from oppres-

sion) that will appear through some cataclysmic event. This new order may be either a recovery of lost lands or resources, an earlier state of sinlessness and freedom, or the inauguration of a great improvement in which members of the new religion will share all of the blessings and powers of the invasive group or even transcend these in some future paradise.

The forms of rewards to those who participate

Dependence on a transcendent being and compliance with moral and ritual requirements. The securing of these new blessings depends upon the action of someone from the spirit world, ancestors or culture heroes, guardian angels, Jesus, the spirit, or the deceased founder returning from the dead. It also depends, however, on faithful observance of the moral and ritual requirements of the new religion.

Concern for renewal and acceptance. Throughout these movements there also runs a deep concern for personal and spiritual renewal and for the assumption of full spiritual autonomy, responsibility, and dignity in the eyes of the world. One strand in this may separate into political forms of rebellion or nationalism and into attitudes that are anti-white or anti-Christian; but another element looks to the contribution that the tribal peoples may make even to the sophisticated peoples of the dominant culture and thus to the whole world.

CLASSIFICATION AND TYPOLOGIES

Since the first classification of the new religious movements among tribal peoples as "nativistic movements" (in 1943), social scientists have endeavoured to improve on this term in their search for a general theory that would also include movements outside the kind of acculturative situation here described. In the 1960s this attempt was criticized as premature and somewhat artificial, and it was suggested that it is better for each discipline to classify the movements according to its own categories and for its own purposes and to include nontribal phenomena as it sees fit, without attempting a single all-purpose definitive system. Thus, sociology can explore the relation of the movements to tribal social and kinship systems, or to the sect-church classification, and endeavour to classify such various forms as inchoate prophet or mass movements, clienteles dealing with a specialist practitioner (such as a healer), congregational or churchlike organizations, or new communities and holy cities. Yet, some of the anthropologists' terms remain useful for descriptive purposes ("nativistic," "reformative," "revivalistic") in particular cases; other terms may be useful in a regional context (such as "cargo" in Oceania or "Zionist" and "Ethiopian" in southern Africa). One attempt to secure a working classification for a whole culture area, Africa, was forced to fall back on a mixed system of religious and historical categories.

The simplest classification may be derived from the relation of the new movement to the two religions concerned. Thus, it would be possible to envisage a continuum embracing various degrees of syncretism in the range of possible types between a traditional tribal religion and an indigenous church that, for example, represents some form of Christian orthodoxy. New movements would then fall between these two poles, with neo-traditional movements (new forms of traditional indigenous religions) at the tribal end of the spectrum, followed by various degrees of syncretism in moving toward so-called Hebraist bodies (identifying with Israel; *i.e.,* the Hebrews or the Jews, such as the Ras Tafarians, a Jamaican-based Negro group that believes that the blacks are the true Jews) and independent churches at the other end. As an alternative response, at the tribal end, in cases in which traditional religion has been eroded, there may be a revival of magical procedures or of new witch finding movements. At the church end of the spectrum, the alternative responses are to be seen in the separation of various secular organizations from the original matrix of the religious movement.

Forms of classification

Alongside this type of continuum and, in general, in step with it, there is another continuum representing the relation to the acculturative process. The two poles here are: total rejection, represented by complete indifference or withdrawal into isolation, and total acceptance, or complete assimilation. Pure forms of either polar situation probably do not occur; but approximations to such forms are found, for example, in the conservatism of the Tewa and Hopi Indians of New Mexico and Arizona and the Seri Indians of Baja California and, at the other extreme, the assimilation of individual Indians to Western culture or the *évolués* ("assimilated ones") in French-speaking Africa. Along the intervening spectrum there are stages that can be called contra-acculturative (also regressive, nativistic, or revivalistic), which correspond to neo-traditional religious movements, followed by various degrees of semi-acculturation corresponding to degrees of religious syncretism, and then examples of pro-acculturation (also progressive, acceptive, or assimilative) represented by Hebraist movements and independent churches.

This religio-cultural method of classification is for descriptive and comparative purposes only. New movements may commence at any point on these continua, may change gradually or by mutations of form, and may move toward either pole. The overall tendency, however, especially for those that continue for a generation or more, is to move from the traditional to the more fully acculturated and invasive religion's position, as may be noted, for example, in the later introduction of the Bible into some Indian Shaker churches of the U.S. Pacific Northwest and into peyote groups, and in the Ringatu, a New Zealand Maori tribal prophetic movement, and into moves toward leadership training and association with the older churches by the African independent churches and movements.

HISTORY OF NEW MOVEMENTS IN MAJOR CULTURAL AREAS

Latin America and the Caribbean. *Latin America.* Approximately 40 identifiable new religious movements have been recorded among the South American Indian population, and others probably have escaped notice. The figure does not include the millennial movements among the Tupí-Guaraní in the interior of eastern Brazil, who have travelled over vast distances in search of their mythological "land-without-evil"; these migrations have occurred periodically since before white contact and into the present century and are a traditional and not a new acculturative phenomenon, even though they may have been aggravated by the advent of the whites. The "land-without-evil" theme, however, was emphasized in many of the millennial, syncretistic, and anti-white movements that appeared in the 16th century among Indians in more continuous contact with Europeans as slaves, mine or plantation workers, or converts.

The "land-without-evil" theme

The earliest recorded new religious movement was in 1546 in Colombia, followed by others in 1576, 1603, and 1613, when a cult of Luiz Andrea combined the worship of Christ and John the Baptist with the local divinity Buciraco. Among the Chiriguano Indians in what is modern Bolivia a young man known as Santiago seems to have led a reforming movement about 1571–73. In nearby Paraguay there were large numbers of "man-gods" and messianic movements reported by the Jesuit missionaries of the 16th and 17th centuries. The most fully recorded movement was one led by Obera, a Guaraní chief much influenced by Christianity, who claimed to be the divine son of a virgin. He rebaptized his followers and exhorted them to sing and dance rather than work for future blessing and in 1579 led an unsuccessful revolt.

Similar movements are recorded as early as 1578 in the Bahia region of Brazil among the semi-Christianized Tupinambá Indians. A most remarkable early movement occurred around 1583, with a church organized in imitation of the Jesuit missions, complete with hierarchy under an Indian pope, priests hearing confessions and conducting mass, schools with imitation books made from bark, and missionaries spreading the movement to other tribes. Traditional millennial beliefs included the return of the ancestors by ship to destroy the Portuguese oppressors. There were few Brazilian movements in the 17th and 18th centuries, when Indian slaves had been replaced by Negro slaves and had subsequently retired beyond white contacts to the Amazonian forests. When white settlers began penetrating the Brazilian interior in the mid-19th century, further millennial movements appeared; the "Christs" were reincarnated culture heroes, the Christian features in the syncretism were slender, and all were eventually suppressed.

In contrast to the Santiago movement of the 16th century, later examples in Bolivia, especially among the Chiriguano, took the form of religiously inspired revolts with messianic (salvatory figure) features. The first was reported in 1778 and the last in 1892, when a young prophet named Apiawaiki assured his followers that the Bolivian soldiers' bullets were mere water. In Peru the earliest such movement precipitated a Quechua (Inca) revolt of 1565, but the most remarkable was one led in 1742 by Juan Santos Atahualpa, who was educated and had been to Angola (in Africa) and Spain. Returning to Peru, he called himself after the Inca emperor Atahualpa and declared that God had sent him to restore the Inca Empire and free the Indians from Spanish oppression; in the new era there would be an Indian Catholic Church with native clergy. The Spaniards failed to defeat the movement, which lived on for some time in the remote highlands.

The movement of Atahualpa

In Central America, somewhat similar movements of revolt inspired by a new religious formulation have occurred ever since a messiah arose among the Quiché of Guatemala in 1530. One of the most notable revolts was led by a young Tzeltal prophetess in Mexico, Maria Candelaria, as a result of her vision of the Virgin Mary in 1712; but after initial wide success the movement was crushed by the Spanish.

The Caribbean area. Since about 1846 the Cariban-speaking tribes in the hinterland of Guyana have produced a series of messiahs or prophets who have claimed to have visited heaven and returned with a new religion. One of these movements, the Hallelujah religion—first reported in 1884—can be traced to a certain Bichiwung, who had probably visited England. The religion continued in the 1970s as a syncretistic system with a strong moral discipline and has been treated by the Anglican mission in the area as an ally in facing social disruption and as a potential prayer tradition within the Anglican Church.

The complex acculturative and syncretistic religious history of the Caribbean culture area is perhaps better studied in terms of folk religion. Some movements are primarily survivals of African religious and magic systems, perhaps with occasional Caribbean Indian elements: the former Nyame cult in Jamaica and similar cults among the bush Negroes of Surinam, or current "Obeah" magic (based on the Ashanti *obi* ["priest"] practices of removing evil spirits from, or placing them on, people) in Jamaica, the Bahamas, and the Black Caribs of Honduras. Others are best described as Afro-Christian syncretisms: in Jamaica, the older spirit Myallism, now almost extinct, the Pocomania and Revival Zionism cults since the Great (Christian) Revival of 1861–62, the spirit-possession Convince and Kumina cults connected with the Maroons ("runaway slaves," from the Spanish *cimarrones,* living in the Blue Mountains of eastern Jamaica), and the more recent Ras Tafarians; the Shango cult of Trinidad and Grenada; and the Rada (Dahomean-Catholic) cult of Trinidad; voodoo in Haiti; and Santería in Cuba. Others again are somewhat Africanized forms of mission or revival Christianity, such as the Jamaica Native Baptist Free Church of Alexander Bedward, a 19th–20th-century nearly illiterate labourer, the so-called Jumpers of the Church of God in the Bahamas, or the many prophet and healing cults.

North America. *Eastern and central United States.* The tribal peoples of the North American continent have produced approximately 100 distinguishable religious movements since the advent of the whites, most of these being in what later became the United States. The first firm evidence of such movements shows a whole series of prophets among the Delawares after they had been thoroughly demoralized by the invasive culture. In 1745 David Brainerd, the first missionary among them, was impressed with what seemed to be "like true religion" in a nameless prophet who sought to stem alcoholism and reform his people on the basis of a new revelation from God. Other prophets followed: Papoonan, with a similar basis for his town in 1758; an old prophet at Assinisink in 1760 with some booklike equivalent of the Bible; and, in the Ohio country, Neolin, "The Enlightened," who won converts from many tribes and gave spiritual support to Pontiac, an Ottawa chief, in his attack on Detroit in 1763. After Pontiac's War, the Delaware Indian Wangomend claimed to be God's preacher to the Ohio Indians, from 1766 to the 1790s; he was influenced by the Moravians but rejected white religion and also white customs, such as rum drinking and enslavement of Negroes, in favour of his own movement. In the decade 1800–10, when the Delaware nation was attempting to restore its shattered life in Indiana, a former Moravian prophetess named Beade had a series of visions in 1805 and initiated religious reforms.

The Delaware were also involved in the widespread movement of tribes on the Midwest frontier when the great chief Tecumseh sought to unite them against the Americans in 1805–12, supported by his brother the Prophet, or Tenskwatawa, whose message included rejection of shamanism (a belief system centring on the psychic transformation and healing powers of certain religious personages), magic, and the old healing ways, and also of white religion and culture, in favour of a new strict morality. Tecumseh died and the end of the Prophet's influence occurred in the War of 1812.

At about the same time (i.e., the late 18th and the early 19th centuries) a Seneca prophet, Ganioda'yo (Handsome Lake), was establishing a revitalizing and modernizing religion that syncretized both old and Christian beliefs and encouraged limited adoption of white ways; this remains the religion of some 5,000 Iroquois. A similar adoption of animal husbandry and agriculture from the whites, together with a strong moral code rejecting alcohol, marked the syncretistic teaching of the Indian prophet Kennekuk, who transformed a section of his Kickapoo people in Illinois and Kansas from 1827 until his death in 1852; a small Kennekuk church still existed in Kansas in the 1950s.

As the frontier of white settlement moved west in the 19th century, other new movements appeared among the Winnebago in Iowa (those of Wabokieshiek in 1832 and of Patheske in 1852–53), the Potawatomi (1883–c. 1890), and the Crow of Montana (1887). The Ketoowa Society, an Oklahoma Cherokee movement, led by Redbird Smith from 1896 until he died in 1918, was remarkable as a nativistic religious movement with neither prophet nor visions.

Northwestern United States. In the plateau and coastal areas of the Northwest the background of many new movements was the indigenous "prophet dance," which waxed and waned as different leaders were inspired through visions. The central rite was a circular dance that, it was believed, would hasten the imminent return of the dead and renewal of the world. From the 1820s, Christianized forms appeared among the Flathead, the Nez Percé, and other tribes of the Pacific Northwest; and by the mid-19th century there arose cults such as that of Smohalla (the Preacher) and the prophet dance of the Umatilla prophet Luls. The latter's cult met on Sundays and advocated a strict morality and monotheistic faith without millennial features, in contrast to the shamanism and individual vision quests that were persistent features of the traditional indigenous religions. Millennial forms, however, appeared in the famous Ghost Dances that spread from the Northern Paiute in Nevada; the first instance of this phenomenon penetrated westward in 1860–73 and the second, inspired by Wovoka "the messiah" (who died in 1932), spread eastward through the Plains tribes in the late 1880s, culminating in the defeat of the Sioux Indians at the Battle of Wounded Knee in 1890.

Christian elements appear in differing degrees in the Indian Shaker Church (unconnected with the white Shakers) of the Northwest derived from John and Mary Slocum, Squaxon Indians, in 1881–82, and in the Native

American Church that has grown out of the peyote cults since the 1880s and is now the largest of the new movements ever to have appeared in North America (see also PHARMACOLOGICAL CULTS).

Southwestern United States. In the Southwest the Apache produced the cult of militaristic medicine man Nokadelklinny in 1881, the Dahgodiyah (They Will be Raised Up, i.e., the dead) movement of 1903–07 begun by the medicine man Oaslahdn, which was also millennial but not anti-white, and the Holy Ground Religion, founded by Silas John Edwards in 1921. This last movement blends traditional and Christian symbolism and ritual, emphasizes morality and monotheism, and has absorbed Jesus into one of the mythological figures (Naiyenesgani) of the Apache; it has also survived the imprisonment of its founder from 1924–54. In the 19th century the Papago of Arizona and northern Mexico developed their own cult of St. Francis, quite independently of the Catholic Church, and this spread widely between 1890–1910. In 1906 a Papago group inspired by Protestant evangelists called themselves "Israelites," and some of these waited for the expected end of the world.

Most of the above movements may be placed in terms of classification nearer to the nativistic or neo-traditional end of the spectrum; but the 20th century has witnessed the emergence of Indian independent churches akin to those common in Africa. In Oklahoma there are a number that are Baptist in type; in Arizona the Hopi Mission Church and the Pima Independent Church and, in Florida, the Miccosukee Independent Indian Church emerged from Baptist missions; in Arizona the Mohave Mission Church derived from Presbyterian work, and the San Carlos Apache Independent Church from that of the Lutherans. The only earlier example of this type is the independent church of the Narraganset Indians in Rhode Island, which has remained a force for tribal identity since the 1740s.

In general, movements in the United States have tended to move from resistance with violence towards peaceful co-existence, from millenarian to nonmillenarian forms, and from nativistic to more Christian forms as in the independent churches.

Canada, Alaska, and Greenland. In Canada there have been over 20 indigenous movements reported, beginning with imitations of Roman Catholic missions among the Micmac of the east in the late 17th and 18th centuries. Others, mostly in the west, appeared throughout the 19th century and into the 20th century and derived from prophets with some visionary experience who then introduced ideas of a single supreme God and a few Christian symbols or rituals. The best recorded is Bini, a medicine man of the Carrier people, who introduced the sabbath, public confession, the sign of the cross, and went about preaching until his death about 1870. Two movements have taken the form of independent churches: that of the shaman Albert Tritt among the Kutchin of Alaska, from about 1910 until the 1930s; and the Christian Band of Workers, early in the 20th century, at Fort Simpson, Canada. The major movements in the United States have spread into Canada—Handsome Lake, the Ghost Dance (minimally), the Shaker, and Native American churches; Canadian movements have mostly been local and more short-lived.

This has also been true of the movements among the Eskimo, starting from the "great revival" of the prophet Habbakuk in a south Greenland Christian community at Evighedsfjörd, in 1790. Another nativistic Greenland movement, that of Matthew "the great sage" at Fredericksdal in 1853, expected the end of the world. In Alaska new religious forms appeared in the 1890s and 1900s among the Nunamiut, and later in the Hudson Bay area there was a nativistic prophet, Uming, from 1919 to 1922, and the millennial movement on the Belcher Islands from 1941 to c. 1942, both of these being influenced by access to the Bible.

Africa. In 1968, according to one estimate, some 6,000 movements had arisen in Africa since the 1880s, even excluding the neo-traditional forms. The concentration of these movements in sub-Saharan Africa raises the question as to why there seems to be almost no corresponding effect in the tribal encounter with Islām, unless it be found in such West African movements as postwar Hamallism, founded by Ḥamāllāh (died 1943), which is anti-Arab and has translated the Qur'ān into an African vernacular—a noteworthy action. Yorubaland in Nigeria raises the question: there, Western Christian and Arab Islāmic cultures penetrated about the same time and with equal success; the only reported new Islāmic movement is a conservative attempt to restore orthodox Islāmic life with no signs of African syncretism, though the same area has proliferated with new Christian syncretisms or independent churches. Certain features of Christianity may explain this situation, but the question awaits fuller examination.

South Africa. The earliest movements go back to the Portuguese period in the old Kingdom of the Congo in the 17th century; of these, the best known is the Antonian sect of a prophetess, Béatrice, that sought to become the national church of a restored and independent Congo. Béatrice, however, was burned alive in 1706. White settlement in South Africa was responsible for the next developments: the millennial prophecies of the Xhosa prophets Ntsikana and Nxele in the first decades of the 19th century and those of the later prophet Mhlakaza, which led to the near extinction of the Ndhlambe tribes when they destroyed their cattle and cereals in anticipation of the millennium in 1857. In South West Africa, Hendrik Witbooi, a Christian convert, became a prophet for the Nama people and was killed in conflict with the Germans in 1905. A similar tragedy attended the South African prophet Enoch Mgijima's "Israelites" when they defied the South African government in 1921. In movements like these and others in Bechuanaland (now Botswana), there was a strong nativistic and millenarian and anti-white emphasis, but the movements were gradually replaced by the more churchlike and often more Christian Ethiopian (independent all-African) and Zionist (all-African pentecostal type) bodies that continue today. By 1970 there were probably about 3,000,000 members in some 3,000 bodies of this kind in South Africa, with smaller but substantial numbers in Rhodesia and the other southern territories.

West Africa. In West Africa the developments have been much more peaceful and less millennial or messianic, as well as more concerned with reforming and applying Christianity in African terms. Neo-traditional movements have been a minority, the most outstanding being the National Church of Nigeria, which sought to restore worship of "the God of Africa" from 1948 and, in 1964, united with a similar Edo National Church, or Aruosa cult, founded in 1945 by the *oba* ("king") of Benin City. Most movements, however, have been independent churches corresponding to the South African Ethiopian or Zionist types. The Ethiopian type appeared in 1888 in Ghana and especially in Nigeria, where churches of this kind form a well-established group known as "the African Churches," centred in Lagos. Since the 1920s, the main growth has been in the Zionist type, with emphasis on healing and revelations; these are known in Nigeria as the Aladura and in Ghana and elsewhere as the "spiritual churches"; in the Ivory Coast they are called Harriste (Harris) churches because most of these groups owe something to the influence of a mass movement aroused by the Liberian prophet William Wade Harris around 1913–15. The following estimates of numbers of distinct West African bodies applied early in the 1970s: a few in Sierra Leone but probably over 50 in Liberia, scores in the Ivory Coast, as many as 500 in Ghana, and some hundreds in Nigeria.

Central Africa. Considerable variation has developed in the incidence of movements in Central Africa: in the Cameroon a few fairly orthodox independent churches since the Native Baptist Church of 1888; in Chad and the Central African Republic some secessions—mostly small and short-lived—from Protestant missions since the 1950s; in Gabon the syncretistic Bwiti cult among the Fang, which has been moving to a more Christian content, since the 1890s; in Angola Simon Toco's Church of

Tendencies toward independent churches

Our Lord Jesus Christ (also known as the Red Star Church) has been a substantial body since 1949. In Zaire (formerly the Belgian Congo) the early movements were strongly nativistic, anti-white, and prone to violence, as was the case of the Epikilipikili cult of 1904. Later movements in Zaire generally arose under the influence of the prophet Simon Kimbangu and his healing revival of 1921 and, to a lesser degree, of the Salvation Army after its arrival in 1935, such as the Khaki Church, or Église des Noirs (Church of the Blacks), of Simon-Pierre Mpadi, founded in 1939. The least syncretistic and most organized groups are now gathered in the Kimbanguist Church that became a member of the World Council of Churches in 1970. A total of some 400 distinct groups has been estimated for Zaire. In the Congo (Brazzaville) the Amicale movement of André Matswa, a successor of Simon Kimbangu, began in the 1920s with social and political concerns but developed in a more religious and messianic direction after his death in prison in 1942. In Zambia there was the Ethiopian Church of Barotseland as early as 1900 and the Kitawala, or Watch Tower movement, from 1908. The Watch Tower movement stemmed from the American body of this name (also known as Jehovah's Witnesses) and has had an extensive influence through Central Africa ever since. Among over 20 other groups in Zambia, the most famous has been the Lumpa Church, founded by the charismatic leader Alice Lenshina (*i.e.,* "Queen"), which has been in conflict with the government since 1964.

Eastern Africa. Of the areas in eastern Africa, Malawi is notable for the complex interaction of foreign and indigenous influences: the white missionary Joseph Booth, American Negro churches, the Watch Tower Bible and Tract Society, and South African Ethiopianism. In the earlier nationalist phases, a 1915 uprising against the British was influenced by the evangelist John Chilembwe and Elliott Kamwana's Watch Tower movement, which had been initiated in 1908. New bodies in Uganda have been comparatively few, partly because of the influence of the indigenous evangelical revival movement within the Anglican Church. The largest was the Society of the One Almighty God, which opposed Western medicine and claimed over 100,000 adherents by 1921 but has now virtually disappeared; the other notable movement is the African Greek Orthodox Church founded in 1929 by Reuben Spartas, an Anglican influenced by an American black nationalist, Marcus Garvey. Kenya shared in the Uganda movements but has produced a large number of movements of its own since 1929. Some have been nativistic revivals mixed with political nationalism, such as Dini ya Msambwa (Religion of the Ancestors); many others have stressed healing, like the Maria Legio; others again resemble their parent churches, such as the African Brotherhood Church (60,000 members in 1970), derived from the Africa Inland Mission and the Salvation Army in 1945, or the Church of Christ in Africa (about 75,000 members), derived from the Anglican Church in 1957. New religious movements in Tanzania and Mozambique have been smaller and much less numerous, but in Madagascar, where a short-lived syncretistic movement founded by Rainitscandavaka (a Merina tribesman) arose in 1833–34, there have been some 20 movements of the independent church form since the first in 1894.

Europe and Asia. Only one clear example of a new religious movement among tribal peoples is reported from Europe; the "Big Candle," or Kuga Sorta, a nativistic and millenarian movement among the Cheremis (a Finno-Ugric people) of the Upper Volga area from the 1870s. The main instance from Asian Russia is the millennial Burkhan (from the Mongolian word for Buddha) movement among the Altai Mountains Kalmyks. Founded in 1904 by the prophet Chot Chelpan, the Burkhan movement was anti-Russian and anti-Christian but with Christian elements; members burned the shamans' drums and rejected animal sacrifices but preserved traditional taboos and an indigenous term for its single divinity. In India there have been many examples of new religious movements since the late 18th century, chiefly among the hill tribal peoples, in response to a closer encounter with

Interaction of foreign and indigenous influences

New
religious
movements
based on
contacts
with
Hinduism
or
Buddhism

Hindu culture and religion or to a Western Christian influence. These have usually begun from a reforming prophet and have moved away from the tribal religion towards a monolatrous (worship of a single deity) form with a strict morality; some have been messianic and have led to revolts and violence.

Similarly, the marginal hill tribal peoples of Southeast Asia have produced a number of new religious movements. Ten or more with a Buddhist background, and sometimes with Christian elements, also have been reported among the Karen (a variety of tribal peoples) of Burma since the 1820s; at least two, the Leke (a messianic cult), founded by an unnamed couple, and Telakhon (Fruit of Wisdom), founded by Con Yu, have continued since the 1860s, and another new religious movement from this period took the form of an independent Karen Baptist Church. Among the Chin (a group of Mongoloid tribes inhabiting the mountain ranges separating Burma from Assam, India), a new religion, named after its founder Pau Cin Hau, in the 19th and 20th centuries replaced *nat* (spirits) worship and its expensive feasts with a more Christian form. In the 1950s the alleged inferiority of the aborigine Khmu people to the Lao people and Westerners in Laos was expressed in an embryonic millennial and cargo cult in which it is believed that ritual acts, including the killing of livestock, would enable the culture hero, Cûang, to return with fabulous wealth.

In the past century, as colonial administrations and Christian missions have penetrated the more intact tribal cultures of the Indonesian areas, new religions have arisen. The Pormalin movement, continuing from the 1870s into the 1960s in Sumatra, is a syncretistic movement with Christian elements. The Mejapi ("to hide oneself," *i.e.*, withdraw from a village) movements, reported in 1902, 1908, and the 1960s in Sulawesi, have been millennial; and at one period members abandoned farms and animals in expectation of joining the ancestors in the spirit world. Other apocalyptic movements, based on a belief in an intervention of the divine in history with accompanying cataclysmic events, have been the Parhudamdam religion among the Bataks in Sumatra around 1915–20, the Samin cults (founded by a peasant named Samin) at various times in central Java since the turn of the century, and the Njuli (Resurrection from Death) movements in southeast Borneo after World War I. All these were millennial and most came into contact with the government; only in the Njuli cults were there any Islāmic influences, in this case combined with Christian elements; these were also evident in the reforming Bungan movement from 1948 in Borneo, with its trinity of God Almighty, a saviour son, and Bungan, a divine wife or mother.

New
religious
movements
in the
Philip-
pines

The Philippines exhibit all types of movements. There have been revised forms of traditional religion with a new moral emphasis, such as the Paluy cult founded by the prophet Angsui about 1896–98 among the Igorots ("non-Christian" mountain peoples of northern Luzon); syncretistic reform and accommodative movements, such as the Sapilada (founded by the reformer Pedro Degan), seeking economic improvement for the Igorots, from 1899 until the 1950s; and unsophisticated millenarianisms, especially the succession of such movements on Mindanao since the Tungud movement (founded by Mapakla, a Manobo tribesman) swept the area in 1908–10. A whole range of strongly nationalistic and often messianic movements opposed first to the Spanish and then to the American regimes: the Katipunan, or Highest and Most Respectable Society of the Sons of the People, founded by Andres Bonifacio (1892); Pulahan, a group of religio-political peoples who were identified by their red (*pula*) dress or turbans (1894); Colorum, a movement founded (1841) by Hermano Puli, also known as Apolinario de la Cruz, before the movement assumed its name (1897, with later revivals); Guardia de Honor, a peasant movement led by a certain Baltazar who founded a holy city known as Cabarvan (1897–*c.* 1919); and a host of messianic Rizalist cults (from 1897), based on a belief in the return of José Rizal, a hero martyred by the

Spanish in 1896. Independent churches, such as the Iglesia ni Kristo founded in 1914 by Felix Manalo and hundreds of smaller bodies of varying degrees of syncretism, have increased even faster after Philippine independence in 1946.

Oceania and Australia. In the Pacific area, the most distinctive form of the new religious movements is found in Melanesia, where scores of millennial cargo cults hold a belief that an imminent new order is to be inaugurated by the arrival of a cargo of goods from supernatural sources. Among the better known examples are the "Vailala Madness" (1919) in Papua, the anti-white John Frum and Naked cults of the 1940s in the New Hebrides, the Buka cult of the 1930s, founded by the prophet Pako and his successors, and the more modernizing Masinga (Brotherhood) Rule after World War II in the Solomon Islands, and the Tuka (cult of immortality) apocalyptic movement of the 1870–80s in Fiji, founded by the prophet Ndungumoi. Other movements have been millennial but non-cargo, such as that founded by the nativistic anti-white prophet Tokeriu of Milne Bay in the 1890s; or neither millennial nor cargo, such as transtribal Taro cults founded by the prophet Buninia after 1914 in Papua, who promised easier growing of taro, the staple food, and especially the movement of the Paliau in the Admiralty Islands. The Paliau cargo cult began in 1946 as a modernizing utopian independent Christian community and has moved toward economic and political concerns, with its leader, Paliau, a member of the House of Assembly by the 1970s and a member of the Order of the British Empire (OBE). The main independent church type is the Christian Fellowship Church, formed about 1959 by Silas Eto as a somewhat heretical secession from the Methodists in the Solomon Islands.

Cargo features have occasionally appeared in Polynesia, as in the Mamaia (Flock of God) movement of 1826–40s in Tahiti or the brief Kapuvai cult, founded by the prophetess-healer Kapuvai, of 1947 in the Cook Islands. Mamaia was primarily an example of a nativistic millennial reaction to the early mass Christian conversions, and influenced the similar cult of the prophet Joe Gimlet, or Siovili, in Samoa in the 1830–40s. Among the Maori people of New Zealand the best known movements include the 19th-century prophet Papahurihia, the reformative but nationalistic King movement from the 1850s, the nativistic Pai Marire (Good and Peaceful) or Hauhauism (based on the Maori battle cry "Hau! Hau!" when the movement became militant) during the Maori wars from 1862, in contrast to Te Whiti's (a minor chief of the Taranaki tribe) millennial but modernizing and peaceful Parihaka community from 1869, the Ringatu religion from 1867, and the Ratana independent church, founded by the Maori prophet and healer Tahupotiki Ratana, from 1919. In Hawaii there were nativistic reactions, such as the prophetess Hapu cult about 1825, and King Kalakaua's more sophisticated attempt to revive traditional religion in 1886; otherwise there has been a range of indigenous independent churches.

Australian aborigines have produced a few embryonic nativistic movements in the 20th century and several in more developed form, such as the transtribal Kurrangara cult since the 1900s, the anti-white millennial Worgaia (poison) movement, with Jesus as a culture-hero, since the 1950s, and the peaceful Elcho Island adjustment movement from about 1958.

NEW RELIGIOUS MOVEMENTS AMONG TRIBAL
PEOPLES TODAY AND FUTURE PROSPECTS

In some areas the main growth has passed or even ceased, but in others new movements continue to appear, especially in Africa and the Philippines. Their study is likely to increase and to become more systematically multidisciplinary and comparative across the cultural areas. More attention will be given to the historical setting and background, and to analysis and interpretation in terms of the phenomenology and history of religions. The movements themselves will inevitably learn more about one another and this will provide an inter-movement stimulus and critique.

Areas
in which
new
religious
movements
continue
to appear

Governments and development agencies may take a more positive interest in the potentiality of these popular and mass movements for modernization, for even the most nativistic movements have usually made some significant breach in the traditional order, and others have shown a capacity to operate transtribally and to initiate new social forms and economic projects as a religious voluntary society distinguished from politics and the state.

In areas where the dominant religion involved is Christianity, local older churches and missions have often changed since the 1950s from their traditional indifferent or hostile attitudes and now make serious attempts at understanding the new religious movements. In some cases the independent church forms have been admitted to Christian councils or are being assisted in training their leadership and in Bible study. Those concerned with mission policies have begun to learn from the successes and the failures of the new tribal movements, and there may be a growing interrelationship rendering Western theology less culturebound as it takes account of new modes of apprehension and forms of expression in other cultures. That many new nativistic or neo-traditional movements will appear does not seem likely, and those still at this end of the spectrum will probably either disappear or move towards the other more acculturated pole.

In general, the more sophisticated and developed societies no longer dismiss these movements as the fanatical mass hysterias of ignorant backward peoples. They are coming to appreciate such movements as signs of the dynamic, creative, and revitalizing capacities of tribal societies, which are able to produce their own leaders and reformers and their own transitional forms between the culture of the past and the invasive culture.

BIBLIOGRAPHY

General: V. LANTERNARI, *Movimenti religiosi di libertà e di salvezza dei popoli oppressi* (1960; Eng. trans; *The Religions of the Oppressed: A Study of Modern Messianic Cults,* 1963), the only general work in English, with good bibliography; R. LINTON, "Nativistic Movements," *Am. Anthrop.,* 45:230–243 (1943); A.F.C. WALLACE, "Revitalization Movements," *ibid.,* 58:264–281 (1956), two classic attempts by anthropologists to provide terminology and classification (now mainly of historic interest); S.L. THRUPP (ed.), *Millennial Dreams in Action* (1962); J. MIDDLETON (ed.), *Gods and Rituals,* ch. 13, 14, 16 (1967); K. BURRIDGE, *New Heaven, New Earth: A Study of Millenarian Activities* (1969).

Latin America: A. METRAUX, "Messiahs of South America," *Inter-American Quarterly,* 3:53–60 (1941), the only general survey of the earlier period in English; J.A. DABBS, "A Messiah Among the Chiriguanos," *SWest. J. Anthrop.,* 9:45–58 (1953), a full account of the first recorded movement in Bolivia; A.J. BUTT, "The Birth of a Religion," in J. MIDDLETON, *op. cit.,* ch. 16; D.G. BRINTON, *Maria Candelaria: An Historic Drama From American Aboriginal Life* (1897), a readable, detailed account; G.E. SIMPSON, "Jamaican Revivalist Cults," *Social and Economic Studies,* 5:320–321 (1956), and *The Shango Cult in Trinidad* (1965).

North America: A.F. CHAMBERLAIN, "New Religions Among North American Indians," *J. Religious Psychology,* 6:1–49 (1913), the first general survey, with extensive quotes from inaccessible sources (includes some Latin American movements also); W.C. MACLEOD, *The American Indian Frontier,* ch. 34–35 (1928); L. SPIER, *The Prophet Dance of the Northwest and Its Derivatives* (1935), standard work on earlier movements in the Northwest (U.S.); A.F.C. WALLACE, "New Religions Among the Delaware Indians, 1600–1900," *SWest. J. Anthrop.,* 12:1–21 (1956); E.H. SPICER, *Cycles of Conquest: The Impact of Spain, Mexico, and the United States on the Indians of the Southwest, 1533–1960* (1962), the only general survey of the Indians of the Southwest and of northern Mexico.

Africa: D.B. BARRETT, *Schism and Renewal in Africa: An Analysis of Six Thousand Contemporary Religious Movements* (1968); H.W. TURNER, "A Typology for African Religious Movements," *J. Religion in Africa,* 1:1–34 (1967); "The Place of Independent Religious Movements in the Modernization of Africa," *ibid.,* 2:45–63 (1969); R.C. MITCHELL and H.W. TURNER, *A Comprehensive Bibliography of Modern African Religious Movements* (1966).

Southern Africa: B.G.M. SUNDKLER, *Bantu Prophets in South Africa,* 2nd ed. (1961), a classic work on the Zulu; M.L. MARTIN, *The Biblical Concept of Messianism and Messianism in Southern Africa* (1964), a critical study from a theological viewpoint, with considerable detailed information on southern African movements; M.L. DANEEL, *Old and New in Southern Shona Churches,* vol. 1, *Background and Rise of the Major Movements* (1971).

West Africa: C.G. BAETA, *Prophetism in Ghana* (1962), a readable, informative survey; J.B. WEBSTER, *The African Churches Among the Yoruba, 1888–1922* (1964), a detailed historical work based on primary sources; H.W. TURNER, *African Independent Church,* 2 vol. (1967), the most comprehensive study of any single African body—historical, phenomenological, and theological; J.D.Y. PEEL, *Aladura: A Religious Movement Among the Yoruba* (1968), a very good account of two Nigerian movements, by a sociologist of religion; G.M. HALIBURTON, *The Prophet Harris* (1971), the definitive work on the Harriste movement.

Central Africa: E. ANDERSSON, *Messianic Popular Movements in the Lower Congo* (1958), a classic work, now dated; R.L. WISHLADE, *Sectarianism in Southern Nyasaland* (1965).

East Africa: F.B. WELBOURN, *East African Rebels: A Study of Some Independent Churches* (1961); F.B. WELBOURN and B.A. OGOT, *A Place to Feel at Home: A Study of Two Independent Churches in Western Kenya* (1966).

Europe and Asia: L. KRADER, "A Nativistic Movement in Western Siberia," *Am. Anthrop.,* 58:282–292 (1956), a good, detailed anthropological account of Burkhanism; T. STERN, "Ariya and the Golden Book: A Millenarian Buddhist Sect Among the Karen," *J. Asian Studies,* 27:297–327 (1968); S. FUCHS, *Rebellious Prophets* (1965), the only comprehensive book on Indian movements; E. JAY, "Revitalisation Movement in Tribal India," in L.P. VIDYARTHI (ed.), *Aspects of Religion in Indian Society* (1961), supplements Fuchs; J.M. VAN DER KROEF, "Racial Messiahs," in E.T. THOMPSON and E.C. HUGHES (eds.), *Race: Individual and Collective Behaviour* (1958), on messianic movements in Indonesia and Melanesia; D.J. ELWOOD, "Varieties of Christianity in the Philippines," in G.H. ANDERSON (ed.), *Studies in Philippine Church History* (1969).

Oceania and Australia: C.A. VALENTINE, "Social Status, Political Power, and Native Responses to European Influence in Oceania," *Anthrop. Forum,* 1:3–55 (1963); P. WORSLEY, *The Trumpet Shall Sound: A Study of "Cargo" Cults in Melanesia,* 2nd ed. (1968), a good popular work; J.M. VAN DER KROEF, "Patterns of Cultural Change in Three Primitive Societies," *Social Research,* 24:427–456 (1957), a very good detailed study of three Irian Barat movements; G. COCHRANE, *Big Men and Cargo Cults* (1970), another study on Melanesia—with less overall information than Worsley, but better on theory and interpretation; I.L.G. SUTHERLAND (ed.), *The Maori People Today,* ch. 10 (1940), a good popular survey of the important movements; R.M. BERNDT, *An Adjustment Movement in Arnhem Land, Northern Territory of Australia* (1962), the only extended account of an Australian movement in English; A.R. TIPPETT, *People Movements in Southern Polynesia* (1971).

(H.W.T.)

Tribological Phenomena

Tribology is the study of the interaction of sliding surfaces. It includes three subjects: friction, wear, and lubrication. There is a difficulty in that friction is generally characterized as a branch of physics or mechanical engineering, wear is part of material science or metallurgy, while lubrication is a branch of chemistry. Tribology is thus a complex interdisciplinary subject and has suffered the same neglect as have other such subjects.

Definitions. The phenomena considered in tribology are among the most fundamental and most common of those encountered by man in his interaction with his largely solid environment. Many manifestations of tribology are beneficial and, indeed, make life possible as we know it. Many other effects of tribology, however, constitute serious nuisances, and careful design is necessary to overcome the inconvenience arising from excessive friction or wear. On an overall basis friction uses up, or wastes, a substantial amount of the energy generated by mankind, while much of his productive capacity is devoted to replacing objects made useless by wear. It is this waste of resources that induced at least one government in the middle 1960s to undertake a systematic effort to increase research and education in this area. The term tribology was introduced to characterize this activity.

Friction
as a
factor

Friction is the resistance to sliding of a solid when the resistance is produced by a contacting body. It is, therefore, a vital factor in the operation of most mechanisms. High friction is needed for the satisfactory functioning of nuts and bolts, paper clips, and tongs, as well as in the familiar processes of walking, gripping objects manually, and building piles of sand or of apples. Low friction, however, is desired in objects that are designed to move continuously, like engines, skis, and the internal mechanism of watches. Constant friction is required in brakes and clutches, as otherwise unpleasant jerky movement would be produced.

Friction has been studied as a branch of mechanics for many hundreds of years and its laws, as well as satisfactory methods of estimating the magnitude of friction, have been known for nearly two centuries. The mechanism of friction, namely, the exact process by which energy is lost as two surfaces slip past each other, is understood only in an incomplete way.

Wear is the removal of material from a solid surface as a result of the mechanical action exerted by another solid. It is such a universal phenomenon that rarely do two solid bodies slide over each other or even touch each other without measurable material transfer or material loss. Thus, coins become worn as a result of continued contact with human fingers; pencils become worn after sliding over paper; and rails become worn as a result of the continued rolling of train wheels over them. Only living things (e.g., bone joints) are in general immune to the permanent damage caused by wear because only they have the property of healing through regrowth. And even a few living things do not heal themselves (e.g., teeth in humans).

The systematic study of wear has been severely hampered by two factors: first, the existence of a number of separate wear processes, which has led to much confusion, especially in terminology; second, the difficulties caused by the small amounts of material involved in wear processes. These difficulties were greatly alleviated when radioactive isotopes of the common engineering metals (iron, copper, chromium, etc.) became available in the 1940s; tracer techniques using these radioisotopes permit measurements of wear, even in small amounts, while it is occurring. This has made it possible to identify types of wear and discover the laws of wear.

The
use of
lubricants

The use of lubricants, namely, substances introduced into the interface between sliding surfaces to diminish friction, is an ancient practice, and Egyptian pictures dating back 4,000 years show the application of lubricants to reduce the friction involved in dragging heavy monuments. In modern lubrication practice, the main concern is to reduce the wear that accompanies sliding and, at the same time, to design lubrication systems that will operate for long periods without inspection or maintenance.

A large number of different lubricants are in use at any one time, (a single major oil company may market many hundreds of different varieties), and no aspect of tribology receives as much attention as the development and testing of improved lubricants.

Parameters that influence friction. In almost all cases the friction force F, defined as the force required to produce or maintain sliding, is proportional to a force L which is normal to the surface, so that if a force smaller than F is applied to stationary surfaces no sliding occurs. The constant of proportionality, equal to the ratio of the two forces F/L, is called the coefficient of friction f or μ. This coefficient is a convenient way of characterizing a sliding situation, and thus the effect of various variables on friction is best discussed in terms of their effect on the friction coefficient.

The friction coefficient is independent of the area or the shape of the interface, that is, of the apparent region of contact. Indeed, the real contact is made over only a few small patches or junctions whose extent is not determined by the size of the apparent contact area.

The friction coefficient is nearly independent of the sliding speed (see Figure 1). In some situations, it takes a larger coefficient to initiate sliding (the static coefficient) than to maintain sliding (the kinetic coefficient).

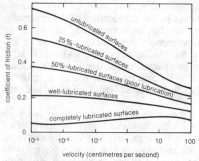

Figure 1: Plot of friction coefficient as a function of sliding velocity for low-carbon steel surfaces in various states of lubrication. Only for well-lubricated surfaces does the friction go up as the velocity goes up. In other cases the slopes are negative, thus allowing stick-slip to occur.

From E. Rabinowicz, *Friction and Wear of Materials* (©1965); John Wiley and Sons, Inc.

The friction coefficient is nearly independent of the surface roughness, although this fact might be hard to accept. The lowest friction is generally given by a surface with a fairly smooth but matte finish. Highly polished surfaces give somewhat higher friction because increased adhesion occurs, while very rough surfaces also give higher friction because there is some interlocking of surface high spots. Rough surfaces display relatively moderate friction because, while some of the contacts are sliding uphill, others are moving downhill.

Variation
of friction
with
materials

Typical clean, unlubricated surfaces give friction coefficients in the range of 0.3 to 0.4, and this is true for metals, for inorganic nonmetals, and for organic polymers. The exceptions consist of a number of miscellaneous categories: (1) high friction coefficients (0.8 to 1.5) are given by clean, soft metals (e.g., lead) and organic elastometers (e.g., rubber); (2) low friction coefficients of about 0.2 are given by hard nonmetals (e.g., diamond, tungsten carbide); (3) very low friction coefficients (0.1 to 0.05) are given by substances with layer lattice structures, (e.g., graphite), by substances with low adhesion properties (e.g., teflon), and by self-lubricating substances (e.g., ice near its melting point when it is lubricated by a film of water). When different clean surfaces are brought into contact, the friction coefficient is generally that of the softer one. When surfaces of different extent of lubrication are combined, the surface with the larger extent of lubrication controls the friction. For walking, friction coefficients of 0.2 or more are required. It will be seen from the above tabulation, and it is confirmed by experience, that rubber makes a good shoe material while ice makes a poor walking surface.

Lubricants
and con-
taminants

Lubricants often have a profound effect on the friction coefficient, surpassing other influences. Lubricants may be liquid or solid, but it has been found that a good liquid lubricant often forms a solid layer of molecular thickness on a sliding surface. Good lubricants in several categories (e.g., metallic soaps, graphite films) are able to reduce the friction coefficient to as low as 0.05, but no lower. More typical values for liquid lubricants are in the range of 0.08 to 0.15.

Contaminants are lubricants that are not deliberately applied to a surface but are already present as a result of the manufacturing process or of previous handling. Typically, they reduce the friction to about 0.2, and sliding surfaces must generally be carefully cleaned to give friction coefficients above the 0.2 level when lubrication is not desired.

Effect of
tempera-
ture

For unlubricated surfaces, friction is independent of temperature unless heating causes melting, oxidation, or other such drastic changes. Circumstances are far different, however, in the case of lubricated surfaces, since lubricants are generally effective only up to some definite limiting temperature (see Figure 2). Above that point they cease to function and the friction rises to the value applicable to unlubricated surfaces. This transition temperature is about 250° F for a bicycle oil, 350° F for an automobile engine oil, and 450° F for a jet engine lubricant.

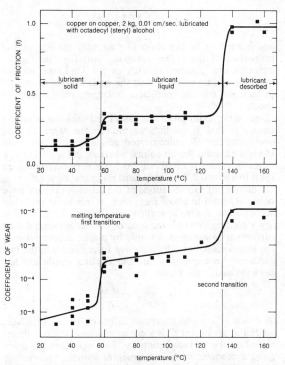

Figure 2: Plot of friction and wear as a function of temperature for copper surfaces lubricated by steryl alcohol (a long chain hydrocarbon with polar ending). There is an increase in friction and wear at the melting point of the lubricant (59° C); the lubricant completely loses its usefulness at a higher temperature (135° C). Above this temperature the friction and wear resemble those of unlubricated copper surfaces.

From E. Rabinowicz, *Friction and Wear of Materials* (© 1965); John Wiley and Sons, Inc.

Consequences of friction. A number of different phenomena occur as the results of frictional energy dissipation during sliding. Although some of these phenomena may have a limited degree of usefulness, they are classified essentially as nuisances.

The energy that must be applied in friction appears as a heat input to the sliding surfaces. Formerly, this frictional heat found use in the lighting of fires by rubbing sticks together, and the same mechanism is still encountered in the striking of matches. Most manifestations of frictional heat, however, constitute a severe nuisance since the sliding surfaces often become too hot if left unprotected, and cooling fluid must be circulated through the system to prevent surface damage.

Types of wear. Four types of material loss are associated with sliding surfaces. Each has different causes, proceeds in a different manner and, if not desired, is cured in a different fashion. They are listed here in order of diminishing importance.

Adhesive wear, the most common removal process, arises from the strong adhesive forces that are generated at the interface of two solid materials. It occasionally happens during sliding that the junctions at the interface are broken not at the original interface but inside one of the two bodies and, consequently, a wear particle is formed. The wear particle sticks initially to the surface to which it was transferred, later it may be retransferred to its original surface, but eventually it will come off in loose form and constitute a loss of material from the sliding system. A surface undergoing adhesive wear is easily characterized under high optical magnification by the irregular-appearing particles adhering to the surface.

The mathematical formulation for adhesive wear states that for any pair of sliding materials there is a probability that the breaking up of a junction will lead to formation of a wear particle, and the linear dimensions of the particle are assumed to be of the same magnitude as those of the junction. Thus, the volume (V) of wear particles formed on sliding a distance is derived by multiplying the distance moved (x), the applied load (L), and the probability factor (k), and dividing by the penetration hardness of the softer material (p):

$$V = \frac{kLx}{3p}.$$

The constant k is often referred to as the coefficient of adhesive wear. (It is found empirically for any two surfaces.)

Unfortunately, high accuracy in computing wear rates is not possible because adhesive wear depends greatly on the exact state of surface cleanliness and repeat experiments designed to produce exactly the same surface conditions often give wear rates that differ by factors of two or even three. Typical values of wear constant for a number of sliding situations are shown in Table 1. If two materials of

Table 1: Values of Wear

materials combination	value of k*
Carefully cleaned surfaces	
Metal on similar metal	5×10^{-3}
Metal on dissimilar metal	2×10^{-4}
Nonmetal on metal or on nonmetal	10^{-5}
Indifferently lubricated surfaces	
All categories	10^{-5}
Very well lubricated surfaces	
Metal on metal	10^{-7}
Nonmetal on metal or nonmetal	10^{-6}

*Value of the softer of two dissimilar metals.

different hardness are slid together, Table 1 gives the wear of the softer material. It is found that the harder material also undergoes wear, usually at a rate between one-tenth and one-hundredth that of the softer material.

Abrasive wear arises when a hard rough surface slides over a softer surface. The hard material penetrates below the surface and during sliding scratches a groove. Some of the material originally in the groove is pushed aside and the remainder is lifted by the cutting action above the surface and is removed in the form of a chip. A similar form of wear involves two soft surfaces and hard abrasive grains. The grains adhere momentarily to one of the surfaces and abrade material from the other. A surface that has undergone abrasive wear shows characteristic sharp scratches in the sliding direction.

Abrasive wear is governed by the same basic equation as that for adhesive wear: the volume worn away is directly proportional to the normal load, the distance slid, and the inverse of the hardness. The constant of proportionality k in this case is a function of the surface roughness and the roughest surfaces produce the highest abrasive wear rates. Typical values of k are shown in Table 2. If the file or abrasive paper is well worn, the abrasive wear drops by about a factor of ten.

Table 2: Typical Values During Abrasive Wear

process	value of k
Filing (sharp file)	2×10^{-1}
Lapping or sandpapering (fresh abrasive paper)	5×10^{-2}
Damage caused by loose abrasive grains	5×10^{-3}
Polishing	5×10^{-4}

Normally, when a surface corrodes, the products of corrosion tend to stay on the surface, thus slowing down further corrosion. But if sliding takes place, the sliding action removes the surface deposits continuously and corrosion takes place more rapidly. Thus, metal surfaces sliding at high temperatures in air are often subject to corrosive wear, because, as the oxide layer is removed during sliding, naked metal is exposed and further corrosion takes place. A surface that has experienced corrosive wear generally has a relatively smooth, matte appearance.

Surface-fatigue wear is observed during repeated sliding or rolling over the same surface. The repetition may cause surface or subsurface fatigue cracks to form. Eventually this leads to the breakup of the surface with the formation of large fragments, leaving large pits in the surface. A ball bearing, for example, may operate for some millions of revolutions without any external evidence of wear until, suddenly, a fragment separates from the surface. Soon other fragments are formed and the surface of the bearing and of the balls becomes completely destroyed.

Surface fatigue wear is the main form of wear for rolling elements, such as bearings and gears, since they are relatively immune to other forms of wear. For sliding surfaces, adhesive wear usually proceeds sufficiently rapidly so that there is no time for fatigue to occur.

Stick-slip oscillations. It has been pointed out that friction coefficients are nearly independent of sliding velocity and, in a typical case, increasing the sliding speed by a factor of 10 may raise or lower the friction coefficient by 5 or 10 percent. If the friction is reduced as the sliding speed increases (a so-called negative characteristic) then frictional oscillations, often called stick-slip, can arise. Musical instruments of the violin family produce their sound only by means of friction oscillations, and treatment of the violin bow with rosin is necessary to maintain the negative friction characteristic. Other manifestations of stick-slip are less tuneful, being the creaking, squeaking, and groaning noises often produced by sliding systems.

Well-lubricated systems do not squeak, while poorly lubricated ones frequently do. Thus, if the lubricant in a sliding system disappears or degrades, stick-slip will frequently set in, indicating that relubrication is in order.

Frictional electricity. The fact that two nonconducting surfaces become oppositely charged electrically during sliding has been known for a long time, and indeed this was the earliest method for generating electrical charge. Nowadays, frictional electricity exists mainly as a minor annoyance sometimes encountered by people walking on carpeted floors in winter, who generate a spark on touching a grounded object like a doorknob. Occasionally, sparks of this type are produced in chemical plants or in oil transportation facilities and have been known to start fires or even explosions.

Historical development of theories of friction. The first research study on friction was carried out by Leonardo da Vinci in the 15th century but his results were not published. Credit for discovering the laws of friction is given to G. Amontons (1699). His work was concerned only with static friction, or the friction of objects at rest, and it was only after Newton's laws of motion were enunciated that the friction of moving bodies was analyzed.

Early workers, most prominently Coulomb (1781), realized that there are two possible explanations of friction, that is, that it is due either to adhesion between the contacting surfaces or to the interlocking of surface protuberances. In fact, they wrongly chose the roughness theory because they felt that friction should be proportional to the area of the bodies in contact, which it is not. Widespread public belief in the roughness theory still persists even though the adhesion theory has been generally accepted by researchers in tribology since about 1945.

Adhesion theory

Modern research has adopted the adhesion theory because it explains why friction is largely independent of surface roughness, since even smooth surfaces often give very high friction, and because a mode of analysis published around 1940 by several groups of workers explains why friction is independent of the contact area. It is hypothesized that the interface between contacting solids consists of two types of region, one being a small number of highly stressed spots or junctions where the surfaces come into intimate contact (their atoms touch one another), the other being all the rest of the contacting area where there is no interaction between the surfaces. Friction originates only at the junctions, whose total area is independent of the apparent area of contact.

If two surfaces are pressed into contact, the pressure at the junctions is normally so high that deformation occurs and continues until the real area of contact A_r reaches a value given by L/p, in which L is the load and p the penetration hardness of the softer of the two materials in contact. In order to undertake sliding, the junction must be sheared, and the force F to do this is given by sA_r in which s is the shear stress of interface. In most unlubricated situations, s is the bulk shear stress of the softer material at the interface. The friction coefficient, f, is then derived by

$$f = \frac{F}{L} = \frac{sA_r}{pA_r} = \frac{s}{p}$$

and is seen to be the ratio of two quite similar plastic properties of the softer material. Not involved in the equation are parameters such as the load, the surface area, the sliding velocity, and the surface roughness and, in fact, the friction coefficient is largely independent of them.

One of the main problems associated with the adhesion theory is that it predicts essentially the same friction coefficient for all unlubricated solids because the ratio s/p is a constant for all solids, whereas, in fact, there is a range in values from about 2.0 for a very soft metal on itself to about 0.2 for a very hard nonmetal on itself.

Surface energy theory

A number of modifications of the adhesion theory have been suggested to allow facts such as this to be explicitly accommodated. One in particular is the surface energy theory according to which the area of contact between sliding surfaces is determined not only by plastic deformation at the junctions but also by adhesive forces between the two surfaces. An expression for the friction coefficient has been derived in the form

$$f = \frac{s}{p} + C\frac{W_{ab}}{p}$$

in which W_{ab} is the energy of adhesion of the interface, while the parameter C is a constant whose value is determined by the surface geometry. This equation has given good agreement with experimental values. The surface energy theory also gives a value for the diameter d of wear particles formed during adhesive wear, the relevant equation being

$$d = \frac{60,000\, W_{ab}}{p}$$

Lubrication, the reduction of friction. The lowest friction combined with an absence of wear occurs in cases of full fluid lubrication in which a thick, continuous film of fluid separates the sliding surfaces. To enable such a film to form, fresh lubricant has to be guided continually into the interface, the overall pressure has to be kept low, the sliding speed high, the lubricant should have a high viscosity, and the sliding surface should be smooth. In the bearings of rotating machinery, fluid lubrication is highly desirable because then the energy loss is small (typical friction coefficient values are as low as .001), and the only wear that takes place does so during start-up and slow-down. Occasionally, fluid lubrication occurs when it is unwanted, as between the tires and ground for an airplane landing on a smooth wet runway, so that a rough runway to prevent this is desirable.

For surfaces operating at high pressures, for example within a gear or a ball bearing, lubrication is often by a somewhat different mechanism, one in which sizeable elastic deformation of the sliding surfaces occurs, thus increasing the area of contact until a full fluid film can remain at the interface. This is known as elastohydrodynamic lubrication. The most important property of a lubricant that determines its ability to perform under hydrodynamic as well as elastohydrodynamic conditions is its viscosity, or resistance to shear.

In boundary lubrication, which takes place at high loads and low speeds, the lubricant layer is only one or two molecules thick and, in fact, there will generally be a few patches where solid–solid contact occurs. In this case, the adhesive bonds between the lubricant and the underlying surface become important. The earliest boundary lubricants were animal fats and vegetable oils. The molecules of these lubricants consist of a long hydrocarbon chain with one polar end that hooks firmly into the surface to form a structure like a carpet. Materials of this type are still used as lubricants for metal deformation processes such as wiredrawing, and as additives in mineral oil intended for light service, such as a bicycle lubricant. The two disadvantages of these lubricants are that they lose their effectiveness at relatively low temperatures and are readily oxidized and degraded by bacteria.

Boundary lubricants cannot reduce the friction coefficient below 0.05. If lower friction is required, then the system must be redesigned either to operate within the region of hydrodynamic lubrication or else rolling contact devices such as ball bearings must be used. These generally give friction coefficients of about .003.

Most modern lubricants are based on mineral oils derived from petroleum. The intrinsic lubricating ability of such oils is augmented by additives, which are frequently tailored to the intended application. For service under severe conditions, reliance is placed on synthetic lubricants, which give good performance even at very high temperatures.

Current research in tribology. Current research efforts are focussed in a number of areas. Some investigators are trying to improve the theoretical understanding so that tribology problems can be solved without resort to the present time-consuming empirical testing techniques. A second group is trying to overcome problems involving new applications, for instance, sliding systems to operate at the high temperature of a rocket engine or in the high vacuum of outer space. A third group is trying to devise new materials and new systems that will allow sliding to occur more cheaply, more effectively, and more reliably.

BIBLIOGRAPHY. F.P. BOWDEN and D. TABOR, *The Friction and Lubrication of Solids*, vol. 1 (1954), classic work on the adhesion theory of friction; E. RABINOWICZ, *The Friction and Wear of Materials* (1965), discussion of wear phenomena from the surface energy point of view; E.R. BRAITHWAITE (ed.), *Lubrication and Lubricants* (1967), a modern account of lubricants and bearing materials; INSTITUTION OF MECHANICAL ENGINEERS, *Lubrication and Wear: Fundamentals and Application to Design* (1968), a full review of the modern research literature on tribology.

(E.R.)

Trichoptera

Caddisflies are insects that comprise the order Trichoptera. The mothlike adult, attracted to light at night, often lives near lakes or rivers. Because fish feed on immature, aquatic stages and trout take flying adults, caddisflies are used as models for fishermen's "flies."

General features

Adult caddisflies are commonly 3 to 15 millimetres in length; their anterior wings range from 4 to 20 millimetres in length, providing wing spans of 8 to 40 millimetres. The wings at rest are folded rooflike over the body. One family (Hydroptilidae), commonly known as microcaddis, are only 1.5 millimetres in length, with anterior wings of 2 to 5 millimetres. Caddisfly wings are either covered with hairs or have hairs on the veins; the posterior pair are often broader than the anterior.

Caddisflies are widely distributed in freshwater habitats throughout the world. The larva of one marine species, *Philanisus plebeius*, occurs in intertidal zones of New Zealand and southern Australian coasts. The larva of one terrestrial European species, *Enoicyla pusilla*, lives in damp moss under trees, while one or two other species occur in brackish water. Approximately 7,000 species of caddisflies are known.

Natural history. *Life cycle.* Caddisflies undergo complete metamorphosis. Males generally have complicated external genitalia. Spermatozoa are transferred either directly or in spermatophores (capsules transferred to females). In the females of some species the terminal segments of the abdomen are modified to form a long ovipositor. Eggs, in masses numbering up to 800, are laid within a jelly that swells on contact with water. A female may wash off a partially extruded egg mass by dipping her abdomen into water during flight, or she may place the mass on stones in the water or on aquatic plants just above the water.

Young larvae, crawlers with strong legs, hatch within a few days and feed on vegetable material or algae. In some species the larvae form webs of debris for protection; others form a funnel-like web between stones in running water to catch food. Some protect their bodies with cases; others spin protective lairs or are free-living. Larvae may be herbivorous, carnivorous, or omnivorous. They produce silk from glands on the lower lip (labium), and many herbivorous species spin tubular protective cases, open at both ends, that enlarge as the larvae grow; sand grains or vegetable debris, added to cases, provide protection and

Larval cases

rigidity. In casebearing forms the head and thorax protrude from the case, which is pulled along by the abdomen. Larvae of one species (*Triaenodes bicolor*) swim by means of long, slender, hair-fringed posterior legs, dragging their cases through the water. Undulating movements of the enclosed larvae circulate water to provide oxygen for respiration.

Prior to the last molt before the pupal stage, the larva fixes the case to some solid object and closes both ends for further protection, leaving only water circulation holes. The larva pupates inside the larval case (which then becomes a cocoon) or inside a specially constructed cocoon. After two or three weeks the pupa bites its way out of the cocoon and swims or crawls to the water surface, using its hair-fringed middle pair of legs; then the winged caddisfly adult emerges and lives several weeks. Adults sometimes emerge in large numbers, often forming swarms. Caddisflies usually mate on vegetation or rocks surrounding water. There is generally one complete life cycle per year.

Ecology. Essentially, caddisflies are aquatic insects associated with a wide range of freshwater habitats. Oxygen concentration, associated with water velocity, is important to their larvae, as is the chemical content of the water. In fact, certain species have been used as indicators of pollution. Larvae feed on aquatic plants, algae, diatoms, or plant debris; a few are predatory on other aquatic insects, crustaceans, and mollusks; some are omnivorous. The larvae, often numerous, play an important role in the aquatic community, reducing plant growth and disposing of animal and plant debris; they use vegetation and debris in casemaking and for food. Most adult caddisflies, incapable of feeding on solids, imbibe liquids (*e.g.*, nectar) from flowers; one species pollinates an Alpine flower as it feeds.

Sponges and algae grow on the protective cases, and protozoans and mites grow on the larvae of some species. Two hymenopterans parasitize caddisflies; the parasitic wasp seeks its host underwater and lays it eggs inside the caddisfly larval case. The parasitic larva devours the caddisfly larva and remains inside the case to pupate; the adult parasite overwinters in the case and emerges in the early summer. Caddisflies are important as food for other animals. Freshwater fish, particularly trout, and eels feed on larvae and swimming pupae; trout, birds, lizards, frogs, spiders, dragonflies, and bats feed on adults. Day flight of caddisflies includes stationary swarming usually off some obvious object on the shore, or mobile swarming, in which the swarms move haphazardly. Most species fly at night, however, and are strongly attracted to light. Night flight may be bimodal, continuous, or intermittent. Warm moist nights are particularly conducive to caddisfly flight.

Form and function. Trichopteran adults are characterized by four wings that bear hairs on the membrane or prominent veins, or both. The head and thorax are also usually hairy. The many-jointed antennae, usually about the length of the anterior wing, may be longer than the wingspan. Mouthparts have nonfunctional mandibles but well-developed maxillary and labial palpi (or sensory appendages); the hypopharynx is modified to form a sucking tongue for imbibing fluids. Various sensory and scent organs may occur on the head or wings. Each of the three thoracic segments bears a pair of walking legs. Several of the ten abdominal segments may bear lateral filaments (or cerci), often with complicated external genitalia terminally in males, sometimes with prominent ovipositors in females.

Mouthparts

Evolution and paleontology. The caddisflies were long classified in the order Neuroptera; the two groups are now thought, however, to represent different evolutionary lines. Ancestral Mecoptera (scorpionflies) probably gave rise to the Neuroptera (lacewings), Trichoptera (caddisflies), and Lepidoptera (moths, butterflies). The closely related Trichoptera and Lepidoptera may have arisen from a common offshoot. Early aquatic trichopterans may have diverged from the terrestrial line in the Late Triassic Period (about 200,000,000 years ago). The earliest known trichopteran fossils are from the Early Jurassic Period

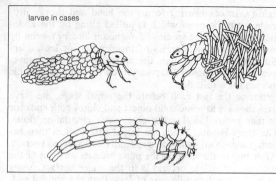

larvae in cases

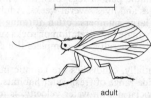

adult

General structure of caddisflies, larvae and adult; line indicates approximate size of adult.

From *Invertebrate Identification Manual* by Richard A. Pimental; © 1967 by Litton Educational Publishing, Inc. Reprinted by permission of Van Nostrand Reinhold Co.

(about 185,000,000 years ago). A few fossil wing prints from the Cretaceous Period (about 65,000,000 to 136,-000,000 years ago) are known; many fossils in Oligocene Baltic amber (about 26,000,000 to 38,000,000 years ago) belong to or are related to living genera. Later fossil wing prints occur in Miocene deposits.

Classification. *Distinguishing taxonomic features.* Caddisflies are mothlike insects with two pairs of hairy wings (sometimes a few scales) folded rooflike over the abdomen. Antennae are long and many jointed with a large basal joint. Large compound eyes are present; simple eyes (ocelli) number three or are absent. The number of maxillary palpal joints usually is five but varies between two and six. Posterior wings are broader than anterior; the pattern of veins is generalized and sometimes reduced. Legs are long and slender, tarsi five-jointed; tibial leg segments may bear variable numbers of spurs. Male genitalia, often complex, have been used for specific identification; female genitalia are of increasing taxonomic significance. Another system relies on the internal characters (*e.g.*, internal head skeletal structures, known collectively as the tentorium). Larvae are essentially aquatic. Campodeiform (elongated and flattened) larvae are free-living or net forming; eruciform (caterpillar-like) larvae are casebearing. In some groups head capsules, functional mandibles, thoracic shields, abdominal gills, abdominal prolegs or hooks, and types of nets or cases are distinct; in all groups antennae are short, and spiracles absent. Pupae have functional mandibles, free limbs, and hook-bearing dorsal plates.

Annotated classification. The number of living families has recently increased. Nineteen were listed in 1953 and 34 (based on a different method of classification) in 1967. The following is based on the later scheme.

ORDER TRICHOPTERA (caddisflies)
Insects with 2 pairs of wings held rooflike over the body in repose; the wing membrane or veins with hairs, or both; wing vein pattern generalized; tibiae usually with spurs, tarsi 5-jointed; larvae and pupae aquatic, with functional mandibles; larvae with terminal abdominal hooked prolegs or hooks, free-living, net spinning, or casemaking, pupate in larval case or cocoon.

Suborder Annulipalpia
Terminal segment of maxillary palpi annulate (with ringed appearance) or subdivided; larvae, net spinners.

Superfamily Hydropsychoidea. Antennae usually anterior wing length or less.
Family Philopotamidae. Ocelli medium to small; larval head elongated.
Family Stenopsychidae. Closely related to Philopotamidae; ocelli large or absent; larval head elongated.
Family Xiphocentronidae. Closely related to Psychomyiidae; ocelli absent.

Family Psychomyiidae. Ocelli absent.
Family Polycentropodidae. Ocelli absent.
Family Dipseudopsidae. Closely related to Polycentropodidae.
Family Hydropsychidae. Antennae mostly about anterior wing length or slightly longer; ocelli absent; larvae with many-branched ventral abdominal gills on most segments.

Suborder Integripalpia
Terminal segment of maxillary palpi undivided; larvae free-living or case makers.

Superfamily Rhyacophiloidea. Antennae shorter than anterior wing length.
Family Rhyacophilidae. Ocelli present; larvae free-living, produce a single line of silk.
Family Glossosomatidae. Adults similar to Rhyacophilidae; larvae, saddle case makers with modified terminal prolegs and hooks.
Family Hydroptilidae (microcaddis). Ocelli present or absent; wings reduced, narrow, with long hair fringes; larvae purse case makers or tube case makers in last larval stage; earlier stages free-living.

Superfamily Limnephiloidea. Larvae, tube case makers.
Limnephilid Branch
Antennae about anterior wing length; ocelli usually present; adult mandibles reduced or lost.
Family Limnocentropodidae. Primitive articulating mandibles.
Family Brachycentridae. Maxillary palpi 3-jointed in male.
Family Phryganeidae. Maxillary palpi usually 4-jointed in male.
Family Phryganopsychidae. Male maxillary palpi 4-jointed.
Family Goeridae. Ocelli absent; maxillary palpi of male 3-jointed.
Family Thremnidae. Closely related to Limnephilidae.
Family Limnephilidae. Maxillary palpi of male 3-jointed.
Family Plectrotarsidae. Closely related to Limnephilidae; specialized elongated mouthparts.
Family Lepidostomatidae. Ocelli absent; maxillary palpi 3-jointed in male.
Family Rhynchopsychidae. Closely related to Lepidostomatidae, but mouthparts elongated.

Leptocerid Branch
Antennae about anterior wing length or less, except Leptoceridae; ocelli absent.
Family Pisuliidae. Male maxillary palpi 3-jointed.
Family Calocidae. Maxillary palpi 5-jointed.
Family Pycnocentrellidae. Anterior arms of tentorium spread anteriorly; maxillary palpi 5-jointed.
Family Beraeidae. Corporotentorium atrophied; maxillary palpi 5-jointed.
Family Sericostomatidae. Male maxillary palpi 3-jointed or less.
Family Helicophidae. Maxillary palpi 5-jointed, both sexes.
Family Philanisidae. Maxillary palpi 5-jointed in both sexes; larvae only in marine littoral zone.
Family Antipodoeciidae. Apparently related to Odontoceridae; male maxillary palpi 3-jointed.
Family Odontoceridae. Maxillary palpi 5-jointed.
Family Molannidae. Maxillary palpi 5-jointed; claws specialized.
Family Philorheithridae. Maxillary palpi of males 5-, 4- and 3-jointed, basal joint with nodule.
Family Helicopsychidae. Maxillary palpi of male 2-jointed; larval cases look like small snail shells; very small in size, traditionally placed in Sericostomatidae; many adult characters reduced or absent; relationships uncertain.
Family Calamoceratidae. Maxillary palpi 5- or 6-jointed.
Family Leptoceridae. Antennae longer than wingspan; maxillary palpi 5-jointed; anterior wings elongated; vein pattern reduced.

Critical appraisal. Many species of caddisflies have been described from male characteristics, particularly genitalia, only, family characters being assumed. Work in recent years on female characters, internal adult characters, and larval characters has revealed new sources of taxonomic information. Further progress in classification depends upon these detailed studies. The classification used above reveals the extent of progress thus far.

BIBLIOGRAPHY. F.C.J. FISCHER, *Trichopterorum Catalogus* (1960–), a continuing checklist of world Trichoptera; N.E. HICKIN, *Caddis Larvae: Larvae of the British "Trichoptera"*

(1967), an excellent comprehensive work on caddis; M.E. MOSELY and D.E. KIMMINS, *The Trichoptera (Caddis-Flies) of Australia and New Zealand* (1953), a basic study, the fauna include species of importance in world classification; and H.H. ROSS, "The Evolution and Past Dispersal of the Trichoptera," *A. Rev. Ent.*, 12:169–206 (1967), brief work including a revolutionary reclassification of the group.

(K.A.J.W.)

Trinidad and Tobago

Trinidad and Tobago are two islands in the southernmost part of the Caribbean Sea that constitute an independent unitary state. Forming the two southernmost links in the Caribbean chain of islands, they lie close to the South American continent, northeast of Venezuela and northwest of Guyana. They have a combined area of 1,980 square miles (5,128 square kilometres).

Trinidad, the larger island, comprises 1,864 square miles (4,828 square kilometres). The island fits snugly into the South American coastline, its northwestern and southwestern peninsulas separated from Venezuela by two channels—the Dragon's Mouth (Boca del Dragon) and the Serpent's Mouth (Boca de la Sierpe)—12 and 9 miles wide, interspersed with small islands and rocks.

Tobago, the smaller island, with an area of about 116 square miles (301 square kilometres), lies in the Atlantic, 21 miles to the northeast of Trinidad, together with Little Tobago, also called Bird of Paradise Island. Little Tobago is noted for the bird by the name, originally introduced from the Pacific islands of New Guinea. Tobago, lying diagonally from southwest to northeast, is about 26 miles long and is more than 7 miles wide at its widest point; it is cigar shaped but has an indented coastline and tapers to the southwest.

The population of the islands was estimated at about 1,027,000 in 1970. The capital, Port-of-Spain, Trinidad, in the northwest, has an estimated 74,000 inhabitants.

Trinidad and Tobago achieved independence from the United Kingdom in 1962 and subsequently obtained membership in the British Commonwealth, the Organization of American States (OAS), and the Caribbean Free Trade Association (Carifta). The country has a Cabinet system of government, patterned on that of the United Kingdom. Exports include petroleum. The gross national product (GNP), which averaged about $890 per capita in 1969, was the highest of the Caribbean states (see also CARIBBEAN SEA). (A.N.R.R.)

History. Christopher Columbus reached Trinidad in 1498 on his third voyage. The island remained a Spanish possession for almost 300 years, until it surrendered to a British naval expedition in 1797. During most of these three centuries the island was neglected. Not until 1530 did Spain appoint a governor; no effective possession took place until the early 17th century and no effective development until the late 18th century. The right to trade with the Spanish colonies was restricted to the port of Seville, and in 1662 the complaint was made that no authorized Spanish ship had visited the island for 30 years, while trade was openly carried on with English, French, and Dutch vessels. The main commodity produced at this time was tobacco. In the 1720s, however, cocoa became important, though after a disastrous crop failure in 1727 cocoa did not again become of major importance until the 1820s.

The Spanish era

The original Amerindian population was worked to death on the Spanish plantations, and African slaves were brought in to replace them. As the Spanish had difficulty in populating the island, the King of Spain in 1783 encouraged Roman Catholic settlers to immigrate, bringing their slaves with them. This resulted in an influx, mainly of French planters, from neighbouring islands. In 1797 the last Spanish governor surrendered the island to a British naval force.

The British were reluctant to import more slaves from Africa to develop Trinidad as a sugar colony: there were objections from influential planters in Barbados and Jamaica who feared competition; there was growing opposition to slavery itself; and there had been a black uprising in Haiti in the 1790s. Early in the 19th century attempts were made to attract white settlement, and in 1802 Chinese immigration was tried; most of the Chinese, however, soon left the island.

Early in the 19th century, civil wars on the South American mainland brought an influx of Spanish immigrants. In 1845 a system of apprenticeship was introduced on the plantations, in order to try to compel workers to remain on the estates after the abolition of slavery, which was proclaimed in 1833, although full emancipation did not occur until 1838. In 1844, in order to provide labour needed by the plantations, the British began to subsidize Indian immigration, which continued until 1917.

While Trinidad experienced three centuries of Spanish rule, Tobago—also discovered by Columbus in 1498—was the subject of continual dispute between England, France, Spain, and Holland. Not until 1721 was there any attempt at settlement (by the British); development began only in 1781, after the French captured the island. Tobago was essentially a sugar colony, although nutmeg and cotton were also cultivated. England acquired the island in 1802, and Tobago subsequently had its own bicameral legislature, which it retained until 1874, though in 1833 Tobago, together with the other Caribbean islands of Grenada and St. Vincent, was put under the jurisdiction of the governor of Barbados. In 1889 the island was amalgamated with Trinidad, while retaining its own legal and fiscal systems; in 1899 it became a ward of Trinidad, uniting with it to form one colony.

Progress to independence

In 1923 a tentative move toward self-government occurred when seven elected members replaced seven nominated members in the colony's Legislative Council. From 1937 to 1938, a strike occurred in the Trinidad oil fields that ultimately affected labour relations throughout the Caribbean. Universal suffrage was introduced in 1945, and elected members of the Legislative Council began a gradual assumption of power. In 1956 Eric Williams, leader of the People's National Movement, won a victory at the polls. In 1962 the colony attained independence, while continuing to bear the marks and the burdens of a colonial economy. Popular mass demonstrations, resulting in part from widespread unemployment, led to the proclamation of a state of emergency, which was lifted in 1971. (C.L.R.J.)

The landscape. *Relief.* Physiographically, the islands represent an extension of the South American mainland. The outstanding physical feature of Trinidad is its Northern Range of hills (the counterpart of the Cadena Del Litoral Oriental in Venezuela), which runs from west to east at an average elevation of 1,500 feet rising to 3,085 feet (940 metres) at the Cerro Aripo, the nation's

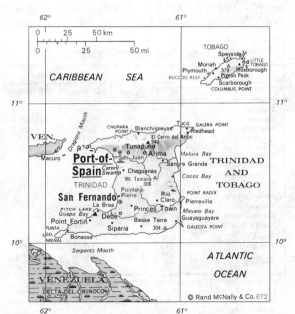

TRINIDAD AND TOBAGO

highest peak. The Northern Range is the site of many waterfalls, the most spectacular of which are the Blue Basin and the Maracas Falls, both 298 feet (91 metres) high. On the southern side of the range, foothills with an elevation of about 500 feet descend to the Northern Plain.

Running across the centre of the island, from southwest to northeast, is the Central Range, the highest point of which is Tamana Hill (1,009 feet, or 308 metres high). A third row of hills, the Southern Range, adds further variety to the mostly flat or undulating surface of Trinidad.

These three mountain ranges determine the island's drainage pattern. The average length of the rivers is about 21 miles; none exceeds 50 miles in length. About 13 swamps occupy parts of the low-lying areas, among them the Caroni Swamp in the northwest.

An oil-bearing belt occupies an area of about 800 square miles in the south of the island, extending from northwest to southeast. Gas and water seepages give rise to mud volcanoes of various types, the most famous of which is the Devil's Woodyard.

In the southwest of the island is the famous sedimentary volcano known as the Pitch Lake, which contains about 10,000,000 tons of asphalt.

Tobago's topography

Tobago is physiographically an extension of the Venezuelan or Caribbean coast range and the Northern Range of Trinidad. Its dominant feature is the Main Ridge, which runs from northeast to southwest, rising to a height of 1,899 feet (579 metres) at Pigeon Peak in the northeast. The ridge slopes more gently to the southwest onto a coral plain. The coral formation has given rise to a number of reefs, one of which, Buccoo Reef, is world famous for its marine life and sea bathing.

Climate, vegetation, and animal life. The climate of Trinidad and Tobago is tropical; there is a high degree of humidity. The coolest months are January and February, when the average minimum temperature is about 68° F (20° C). Warmest months are April, May, and October, which have an average maximum of about 89° F (32° C). In general, mean temperatures range between 77° F (25° C) in February and 85° F (29° C) in April. Temperatures vary significantly between day and night, and the climate is tempered by sea breezes.

There is a major dry season from January to May, and a short dry season (Petite Carême, or Indian Summer) in October. The prevailing winds are the northeast trades. The islands are outside the main hurricane zone, but Tobago has twice in a century—in 1867 and 1963—been struck by disastrous hurricanes.

Vegetation zones are well marked on both islands. In general, the highest areas coincide with the most luxuriant vegetation. Cultivated estates or small settlements are established in clearings on the hills. In the dry season, the hills are beautiful with the orange flowers of the mountain immortelle (a large flowering tree, growing to a height of about 80 feet) and the gold flowers of the poui.

Sugar, the main agricultural crop, is grown on the Central Plain. The Caroni Swamp is frequented by flocks of white flamingo and egret as well as the scarlet ibis—a national bird.

The forests on both islands are hunting grounds for small game, the most sought after being the lappe. Other kinds include agouti (a short-haired, short-eared, rabbit-like rodent), quenk or peccary (wild hog), tattoo (an armadillo), and iguana (a large lizard).

There are four main groups of reptiles: snakes, lizards, turtles, and crocodiles (one kind, the caiman, related to the alligator). Most of the 37 types of snake are harmless; the poisonous snakes include the fer de lance, common coral snake, and large coral snake.

The landscape under human settlement. Soils, climate, and vegetation have all influenced the pattern of local settlement. Villages stretch ribbon-like along the major roadways. In Trinidad, though not in Tobago, villages are so diverse that it would be difficult to call any typical.

Even in the sugar belt of the Central Plain, with its mainly, though not exclusively, East Indian population, patterns vary. Kinship tends to be the important structural element in the life of the East Indian villager; caste

may also have a localized influence, as may the Praja relationship (which implies a reciprocal obligation between one who needs and another who bestows a favour), in which a kind of boss exercises various kinds of influence. Religious festivals, such as Dīwālī (Festival of Lights) and various forms of Puja (ceremonial offering), are important events. Houses vary in size and architecture from the simple thatched hut to the well-built two-storied dwelling, brightly painted and ornamented, and roofed with corrugated iron.

The East Indian villages

A somewhat different life-style prevails in villages inhabited by people predominantly of African descent, though many villages have both Indian and African characteristics. Because of the conditioning of the slave system, traditional African culture has undergone considerable mutation or reinterpretation. The family unit is nuclear rather than extended and may be based upon marriage or upon a stable extralegal relationship. The main institution is the Christian Church, which may be Roman Catholic, Anglican, or Fundamentalist. Steel band and calypso music is heard everywhere in preparation for carnival, the national festival.

These different rural cultural streams converge on the capital, Port-of-Spain. This city, with its mixed population, its Spanish influence (particularly in architecture), and French Creole flavour, is one of the most cosmopolitan in the world. San Fernando, the second town, occupies the southwestern foothills of the Central Range in the heart of the oil belt. Arima, the smallest Trinidadian municipality, is the oldest and least opulent. Scarborough, the chief town in Tobago, is an administrative centre and market town.

People and population. The original inhabitants of Trinidad were chiefly Arawaks. Although there are inhabitants of the town of Arima who claim descent from Carib royalty, there is doubt that the land was also settled by Caribs. Tobago was frequently visited by Amerindians but was not settled before the arrival of Columbus. As described above, Spanish, French, African, English, East Indian, and Chinese have all contributed to the ethnic composition of the islands' population. The various immigrant groups brought with them their languages, culture, and religion.

Protestantism gained a foothold in its various forms (Anglican, Methodist, Moravian, and Baptist) with the advent of the British. Roman Catholicism, then the official religion, was strengthened by French immigration, which also introduced the patois dialect, while the East Indians brought with them their languages and their Hindu and Muslim religions. Further diversification followed with the immigration of Syrians and Lebanese.

Between 1901 and 1960, the population trebled, rising from 274,000 to 834,000. The annual rate of increase between 1946 and 1960 was 2.9 percent; this high rate was

Trinidad and Tobago, Area and Population				
	area		population	
	sq mi	sq km	1960 census	1970 census*
Counties				
Caroni	214	554	91,000	115,000
Mayaro	146	377	6,000	8,000
Nariva	206	534	17,000	21,000
Saint Andrew	283	732	33,000	39,000
Saint David	79	205	6,000	6,000
Saint George	354	917	256,000	319,000
Saint Patrick	261	676	108,000	117,000
Victoria	314	814	133,000	163,000
Municipalities				
Arima	3.7	9.6	11,000	12,000
Port-of-Spain	2.5	6.5	94,000	68,000
San Fernando	.9	2.4	39,000	37,000
Ward				
Tobago	116	301	33,000	39,000
Total Trinidad and Tobago	1,980	5,128†	828,000‡	945,000§

*Preliminary.   †Converted area figures do not add to total given because of rounding.   ‡Excluding adjustment for underenumeration. Adjusted total: 834,000.   §Figures do not add to total given because of rounding.
Source: Official government figures; UN.

Demographic trends

a result of an increasing birth rate, a declining death rate, and a sharp increase in immigration in 1958 and 1959, when Trinidad belonged to the now defunct Federation of the West Indies. The birth rate peaked in the mid-1950s at 4.2 percent but, by 1970, had declined to 2.4 percent. The death rate remained fairly constant. A sharp change in migration trends also occurred during the 1960s. There was an influx of 2,500 persons a year in 1962 and 1963, which changed to a net outflow of about 2,000 in 1964, rising to more than 15,000 in 1969. The rate of population increase for 1966 to 1970 was 1.1 percent.

The economy. *Components of the economy.* Principal features of the economy are a dependence on the petroleum industry and a high level of unemployment. In the period 1965–70, petroleum accounted for roughly 25 percent of gross domestic product, 30 percent of government recurrent revenues, and 83 percent of gross exports (or 60 percent of net exports). The petroleum industry, however, employed only 7 percent of the working population. By contrast, agriculture, while contributing only 8 percent of the gross domestic product, accounted for 22 percent of employment.

Oil production is both land and sea based and in 1969 was about equal from both sources, though the prospects for sea-based production are much better from 1972 onward because of new discoveries. Trinidad is also a major refining centre; crude petroleum is imported from Colombia and Saudi Arabia for refining.

After petroleum, agriculture accounts for the bulk of the country's traditional exports. Since 1964, however, the three major export crops—sugar, cocoa and coffee—encountered problems because of fluctuating export prices and difficulties in expanding supply. In addition, sugar may face loss of protection because of the entry of the United Kingdom into the European Common Market. Other agricultural products include citrus fruits, poultry, vegetables, and domestic food crops.

Manufacturing

Manufacturing output, apart from petroleum products, increased during the 1960s, partly as a result of the policy of encouraging local manufacturing to reduce dependence on imports and partly because of the stimulus of membership in the Caribbean Free Trade Association. Industrial plants are engaged in the assembly of consumer durables, (including motor vehicles) and in the manufacture of fertilizers, cement, furniture, garments, and processed foods.

Tourism, which is somewhat unstable owing to social and political conditions, is potentially the fastest growing industry; it is based particularly on Tobago and on Trinidad's northwest peninsula.

The principal instruments employed for management of the economy have been import duty and income-tax concessions; quota restrictions on imports; credit and subsidies to agriculture, manufacturing, and tourism; and budget deficits financed by internal and external loans.

Transportation and communications. The islands are served by a fairly well-developed network of main and local roads, but there is heavy congestion in urban areas. The traffic accident rate is high. Taxis are a prominent feature of traffic in Trinidad.

Two small ships and a domestic airline connect Tobago to Trinidad. Piarco International Airport on Trinidad has links with New York, North and South America, and the Caribbean. Crown Point Airport on Tobago is, so far, used almost exclusively for interisland travel.

Port-of-Spain is the chief commercial port, accommodating vessels with drafts of up to 32 feet; petroleum exports are handled in ports in the south, such as Pointe-à-Pierre and Brighton, while sugar is exported at Goodridge Bay and cement at Claxton Bay. There are proposals for the development of an industrial estate and extensive port facilities at Point Lisas on the west coast about 10 miles north of San Fernando. The islands are served with a dial-telephone system.

Administration and social conditions. *Governmental structure.* A constitution, promulgated as a British Order in Council (1962), provides for a governor general appointed by the queen; a Cabinet, consisting of the prime minister and not more than 11 other ministers appointed by the governor general on the advice of the prime minister; a bicameral legislature consisting of a Senate and a House of Representatives; an attorney general; a Supreme Court; and commissions dealing with judicial, public, and police services.

The country is divided into 11 local government areas including nine rural counties (one of which is Tobago), which have county councils, and the three municipalities of Port-of-Spain, San Fernando, and Arima, which have municipal councils.

A constitution reform commission was appointed in 1971 to review the entire structure of government.

Health, housing, and social welfare. Health conditions had deteriorated in the late 1960s and early 1970s; the death rate was about 7 per 1,000 and the infant mortality rate (1970) was about 40 per 1,000. In 1968, however, there was only about one doctor for every 2,320 people —one of the lowest such ratios in the Western Hemisphere. This low rate was principally a result of the emigration of doctors.

Health conditions

In housing, it was estimated in 1968 that some 3,000 more houses than provided per year are needed; the unemployment rate in the construction industry is 25 percent—well above the average rate of 15 percent for all industries. "Squatter" housing (erected on land that does not belong to the builders) has become a characteristic feature in and around the towns.

State provision for social security takes the form of noncontributory old-age-pension and public-assistance schemes, noncontributory government employee-pension schemes provided out of public revenues, and workmen's compensation compulsorily paid by employers. Proposals have been published to establish a national-insurance scheme.

Education. Education, the main requirement for upward social mobility, is free at primary and secondary levels. There has, however, been a growing disparity between school places and children of school age, particularly at the secondary school level. Three faculties of the University of the West Indies—engineering, agriculture, and liberal arts—are situated on the university campus at St. Augustine about 8 miles east of Port-of-Spain. There are two technical institutes, one in Port-of-Spain and the other in San Fernando.

A new education plan, which provides for a three-tier system—primary, junior secondary, and senior secondary schooling—would meet the deficiency in primary schools by providing 109,000 new places between 1969 and 1983; it faces, however, financial and other problems. The provision of physical facilities for junior secondary and vocational schools is assisted by loans from the Inter-American Development Bank (IADB).

Prospects for the future. Trinidad and Tobago as a unitary state occupies a position of major importance in the Caribbean. This is a result of its strategic location, its mixed population, its cultural diversity, and its underlying economic strength. The extraordinarily high rate of economic growth that the country experienced just before independence, from 1955 to 1961, however, levelled off sharply from 1962 to 1965; another period of growth from 1966 to 1968 also levelled off abruptly in 1969.

The principal task facing the country is the deployment of its human and natural resources to ameliorate growing social problems stemming mainly from a persistently high rate of unemployment, especially among the young. Civil disorders have periodically resulted in the proclamation of a state of emergency.

The causes lie deeper, however, in the structural weaknesses that are a feature of an inherited form of economic organization and in the tensions arising from attempts—or failures—to transform this structure. In this respect, Trinidad and Tobago share a common experience with many of their Western-Hemispheric neighbours, as well as a common need to participate in a closer form of regional cooperation. (A.N.R.R.)

BIBLIOGRAPHY

Physical features, vegetation, and animal life: H.H. SUTER, *The General and Economic Geology of Trinidad B.W.I.,* 2nd ed. (1960); MALCOLM BARCANT, *Butterflies of Trinidad and*

Tobago (1970); G.A.C. HERKLOTS, *The Birds of Trinidad and Tobago* (1961).

Sociology: MELVILLE J. and FRANCES S. HERSKOVITS, *Trinidad Village* (1947, reprinted 1964), a study on African influences; MORTON KLASS, *East Indians in Trinidad* (1961). Social commentaries can be found in: C.L.R. JAMES, *Beyond a Boundary* (1963), an anthology on cricket; VIDIADHAR NAIPAUL, *Miguel Street* (1959), a collection of stories and *A House for Mr. Biswas* (1961), a novel. See also DEREK WALCOTT, *In a Green Night* (1969), a collection of poems.

Politics and Economics: A.N.R. ROBINSON, *The Mechanics of Independence: Patterns of Political and Economic Transformation in Trinidad and Tobago* (1971); IVOR OXAAL, *Black Intellectuals Come to Power: The Rise of Creole Nationalism in Trinidad and Tobago* (1968); YOGENDRE K. MALIK, *East Indians in Trinidad* (1971); WILLIAM G. DEMAS, *Economics of Development in Small Countries* (1965), are all recent works with the first and last giving an inside view of the processes they describe.

General histories: GERTRUDE CARMICHAEL, *History of the West Indian Islands of Trinidad and Tobago, 1498–1900* (1961); ERIC WILLIAMS, *History of the People of Trinidad and Tobago* (1964); and DONALD WOOD, *Trinidad in Transition* (1968), the latter dealing with social conditions in the 18th and 19th centuries.

Pamphlets: HANS BOOS and VICTOR QUENSEL, *Reptiles of Trinidad and Tobago* (n. d.); C.B. BROWN, *et al.*, *Land Capability Survey of Trinidad and Tobago,* no. 1 (1965); J.A. BULLBROOK, *Aborigines of Trinidad* (1960), a work of original research; D.L. NIDDRIE, *Land Use and Settlement in Tobago* (1961), are all valuable official publications.

Government reports: MINISTRY OF PETROLEUM AND MINES, *Annual Administration Report;* CENTRAL STATISTICAL OFFICE, *Annual Statistical Digest; Draft Five Year Plan, 1969–1973* (1968); MINISTRY OF HEALTH AND HOUSING, *First National Health Plan for Trinidad and Tobago, 1967–1976* (1966); *Report of the Committee Appointed by Cabinet for the Purpose of Reappraising the Present System of Local Government in Trinidad and Tobago in the Context of Independence* (1966); COLONIAL DEVELOPMENT AND WELFARE, *Tobago Planning Team Report* (1957).

(A.N.R.R./C.L.R.J.)

Tripura

Tripura, the smallest of the five states of the northeastern arm of India, is bordered on the north, west, and south by Bangladesh, on the east by the union territory of Mizoram, and on the northeast by the Indian state of Assam. Its area of 4,035 square miles (10,451 square kilometres) is about equal to that of Lebanon but is half the size of nearby Manipur state, India. The population of some 1,557,000 early in the 1970s was less than one-fourth that of greater Calcutta. The capital city of Agartala is the only urban area in the state with more than 55,000 inhabitants. Tripura is basically an agricultural area in which rice is the major crop. Since the 1960s the Indian government has fostered the growth of small-scale industries.

History. Tripura was an independent Hindu kingdom for more than 1,000 years before it became part of the Mughal Empire in the 18th century. At the height of its power, its suzerainty extended over much of Bengal, Assam, and Burma. Tripura acceded to India in 1947 and was designated a union territory in 1956. Upon the administrative reorganization of India's northeastern territory in 1972, it acquired full status as a state.

The landscape and environment. The state can be divided physiographically into the four northern valleys—Dharmanagar, Kailāshahar, Kamalpur, and Khowai—and the southern plain of Agartala. The easternmost valley of Dharmanagar is bordered on the east by the long ranges of the Jamrai Tlang, which rise to between 2,000 and 3,000 feet (600 and 900 metres) above sea level, and on the west by the Sakhon Tlang, which rise to between 1,000 and 2,500 feet. It is drained by the northward-flowing Deo River in the south and the Juri River in the north.

West of the Sakhon Tlang is the Kailāshahar Valley, which, like the Dharmanagar Valley, runs the full length of the state. Its western limit is defined by the Langtarai Range, which rises to more than 1,500 feet above sea level. The northward-flowing Manu River and its tributaries drain the valley, which is much dissected and for-

The northern valleys

ested in its southern half. The northern half of the valley is more open and even marshy.

Between the Langtarai Range on the east and the Atharamura Range, which rises to more than 1,400 feet on the west, lies the Kamalpur Valley. The valley is drained by the northward-flowing Dhalai River; the south is covered with forests, and the north is largely marshy rice fields. West of the Atharamura Range lies the Khowai Valley, which is bordered on the west by the low Deotamura Range. The valley is drained by the northward-flowing Khowai River; its western hills do not rise much above 800 feet in elevation.

The southern half of Tripura is more open and contains an extensive plain to the west of the Deotamura Range. The region is drained by a number of rivers of which the Gumti is the largest. The Gumti receives several southward-flowing streams and cuts across the ranges in a steep-sided valley from east to west before emerging from the hills near Rādhākishorepur.

Over 80 in. (2,000 mm) of rainfall occurs during the monsoon season from June to September. Temperatures are hot in the valleys and cooler in the mountains. Climate

Natural vegetation consists largely of evergreen forests, much of which have been cleared for cultivation. The remaining forests contain valuable trees including the sal, an East Indian timber tree that yields hardwood, second in value only to teak. Animal life includes tigers, leopards, jackals, and wild dogs. The Asiatic elephant is fairly common, and there are wild boar, the gaur—the largest of the world's wild oxen—the gayal ox, and wild buffalo.

The people. Tripura had a population in 1971 of about 1,557,000, less than 10 percent of which could be classified as urban. The average population density was 386 persons per square mile (149 persons per square kilometre); the most densely populated areas were the Dharmanagar and Khowai valleys.

Of the total population, more than 246,000 persons belong to scheduled castes and scheduled tribes, groups outside the traditional Indian caste system. More than half the population speaks Bengali; other important languages are Tripuri and Manipuri. More than 50 percent of the population are Hindus. There are more than 121,-000 Muslims and more than 34,000 Buddhists.

Towns are concentrated on the southern plain, where the state capital of Agartala, Sonāmura, Udaipur, Amarpur, Belonia, and Sabrūm are located. The four towns for which the northern valleys are named all serve as local marketing centres.

Administration and social conditions. There is a common governor and high court for the five states and two union territories of northeastern India. In the early 1970s a Northeastern Council composed of representatives of the states and territories was proposed. The council would discuss common problems and coordinate development programs. Within the state, the government is headed by a chief minister and a Council of Ministers. There is also a unicameral 33-member Legislative Assembly.

Educational facilities in the late 1960s included 1,400 primary, 192 middle, and 81 higher secondary schools. There was one agricultural school, one nurses-training centre, and four industrial training centres, as well as seven professional and technical schools. The state's seven colleges offered general studies and curricula in music and engineering. To raise the literacy rate (only 31 percent), there were over 400 adult education centres.

Education and health services

Health services included 11 hospitals, 22 public health centres, and 124 dispensaries in the late 1960s. There were nine specialized clinics for the treatment of leprosy, venereal diseases, and diseases of the eyes, chest, and teeth. There were also 32 family-planning centres.

The economy. Tripura is primarily an agricultural area. The major crop is rice, which is chiefly grown in the northern marshy section of the Kailāshahar Valley. Other cash crops include jute (an East Indian plant that produces fibres used in the manufacture of sacking, burlap, and twine), cotton, tea, and fruit. Sugarcane, rape (a European herb of the mustard family that produces oilseeds), mustard, and potatoes are among the minor crops. Livestock includes cattle, buffalo, sheep and goats, horses, pigs, and poultry. Forestry activities produce timber, firewood, and charcoal. Manufacturing is largely on a small scale and includes many cottage industries, such as weaving, carpentry, basketry, and pottery manufacture. There are small units for the production of tea, sugar, sawn timber, bricks, tin articles, canned fruit, agricultural implements, and footwear; larger establishments include a spinning mill and plywood factory.

Financial services include one state cooperative bank and one land mortgage bank. There are also numerous service, agricultural, and marketing societies.

Power plants

Energy is provided by diesel-powered thermal power stations at Agartala, Ambāsā, Khowai, Dharmanagar, Kailāshahar, Udaipur, and Bogafa. The total installed capacity was 2,886 kilowatts in the late 1960s; power is also purchased from Assam. A hydroelectric power scheme was begun on the Gumti River in the late 1960s.

Transport. Tripura's topography has rendered communications difficult, and transport outside of the state is made difficult by the surrounding foreign territory of Bangladesh. There are about 1,000 miles (1,600 kilometres) of roads, of which more than 400 miles (700 kilometres) are paved. Two main roads link Agartala with Assam and with Sabrūm. There is also a railway link from Dharmanagar to Kalkalighat, Assam. Most of the rivers carry boat traffic, especially during the rainy season. Long-distance travel is most convenient by air, and there are three airstrips and one airport (in Agartala).

Cultural life. The major factor in Tripura's cultural life is its isolation from the nations around it. The members of the secluded tribes live in the hills and are divided into numerous groups speaking a variety of languages and dialects. Most of the population, adhering to Hinduism and speaking Bengali, seem to have cultural links to the rest of India, while the smaller Muslim population seems closer in culture to Bangladesh.

(S.P.C./Ed.)

Troeltsch, Ernst

Ernst Troeltsch was an influential German scholar (1865–1923) whose writings span the disciplines of theology, social history and theory, philosophy of religion, and the philosophy of history. His important contributions to the theory and methodology of sociology began to be recognized only long after his death, and in theology many now believe that his works prepared a kind of revolution in Protestant thought, anticipating what the 20th-century German theologian Dietrich Bonhoeffer (1906–45) was later to call "man's coming of age."

Troeltsch was born Feb. 17, 1865, near Augsburg in Bavaria (Germany). His father, a medical practitioner, early instilled in his son a passion for scientific observation and led him to see problems of history and civilization within a framework of the development of the sciences. After Troeltsch's school years at the Augsburg Gymnasium, where he acquired a solid grounding in classical languages and literature, he decided to study theology, which, according to an autobiographical sketch, seemed to him at that time the only study in which his historical, philosophical, and social interests could meet in the investigation of a worthwhile subject matter. He studied Protestant (Lutheran) theology at the universities of Erlangen, Göttingen, and Berlin, becoming in turn *Privatdocent* (lecturer) at Göttingen, extraordinary associate professor at Bonn (1892), and ordinary (full) professor in the chair of theology at Heidelberg (1894). He married in 1901, and an only son was born in 1913.

During 21 years at Heidelberg he published, besides his *Grundprobleme der Ethik* (1902; *Fundamental Problems of Ethics*), a large number of articles on a variety of subjects thematically linked with the development of the Christian Churches. Many of these were later integrated into his best known work, *Die Soziallehren der christlichen Kirchen und Gruppen* (1912; *The Social Teachings of the Christian Churches*, 1931). In that work he explored the relationships between and within social and cultural groups in the context of the social ethics of the Christian Churches, denominations, and sects. In 1915, realizing that his strength lay more in the philosophy of religion

Troeltsch, c. 1919.
By courtesy of the Archiv fur Kunst und Geschichte, Berlin

than in orthodox theology, he moved to a chair of philosophy at Berlin, a post he held until his death in 1923.

Troeltsch had a considerable influence on younger theologians of his time, especially through his insistence that the church must drastically rethink its attitude toward "absolutist" claims made for the truth of its doctrines. He was both fascinated and troubled by "historicism" (historical relativism): the view that whatever is valued, pursued, conceived, or achieved at any given time or place is relative to, and only understandable in the context of, the conditions of that time or place. Although the view seemed to him in important respects inescapable, he surmised that it applied inadequately to the norms—whether legal, religious, or ethical—that govern human conduct. If consistently applied, the historicist view would, he thought, make any present understanding of past ages impossible. The polymorphous, historically changing dogmas of the church had to be reconciled with the absolute aspects of revealed truth interpreted anew by every generation. Despite this, many theologians have seen in Troeltsch only a critic of the certainties of Christianity. Paul Tillich (1886–1965), a distinguished German philosopher and theologian, for example, accused him of sacrificing the absolute to the purely relative in religion (*Kant-Studien*, 1924).

The problem of "historicism"

Troeltsch's thought, never purely abstract, is always based on extensive knowledge of historical and factual data. His work has been influential precisely in those aspects that reveal his dislike of very general terms of reference—in its pioneering study of small social units or groups, such as the family, the guild, and the individual state, church, or sect, and also in its advocacy of the comparative approach to religious studies. Within Protestantism, he made important contributions to the study of the genesis of Lutheranism and Calvinism and their differing social ethics and social impact. Here he was in close sympathy concerning the nature of Protestant ethics with his friend the German sociologist and economist Max Weber (1864–1920). Troeltsch was familiar with the Marxist approach to sociology, and found its perspective on the socioeconomic substructure of civilization exciting and superior to the then current Hegelian view of history as the forward march of an inevitable dialectical process. Yet he rejected Marxism in favour of a more flexible conception of the interaction of cultural, social, and economic factors. This preoccupation with the problems of historical relativity and what he called the logic of historical development found expression in a late but important work, *Der Historismus und seine Probleme* (1922; *Historical Relativism and its Problems*).

Sociologist of culture and religion

Troeltsch had more than an academic interest in social and political affairs. He was a member of the Baden Upper House during his years in Heidelberg, and later, in Berlin, a member of the Prussian Landtag (the provincial legislature) and, for a number of years, undersecretary of state for religious affairs. Pondering the reasons, in the aftermath of World War I, for Germany's disastrous estrangement from the ethical, political, and social thought of the Western democracies, he put high on his list the glorification of the state at the expense of the rights and dignity of the individual.

A plan to visit England was frustrated by his death in 1923. The course of five lectures, which he was to have delivered in London and Oxford during March of that year, were published posthumously under a title that puts his work in perspective: *Der Historismus und seine Überwindung* ("Overcoming Historical Relativism"), a more revealing title than that of the English edition (*Christian Thought: Its History and Application*). Three volumes of Troeltsch's collected works appeared toward the end of his life, a fourth being published after his death (*Gesammelte Schriften*, Tübingen, 1922–25, 4 vol.). They do not contain all his published writings, but those for which Troeltsch himself would have wished to be remembered.

BIBLIOGRAPHY. A brief autobiography of Troeltsch, "Meine Bücher," is included in vol. 4 of his collected works, *Gesammelte Schriften* (1922–25); biographical material may be found in WALTER KOEHLER, *Ernst Troeltsch* (1941). A full bibliography and a list of Troeltsch's works with translations are contained in B.A. REIST, *Toward a Theology of Involvement: The Thought of Ernst Troeltsch* (1966). R.S. SLEIGH, *The Sufficiency of Christianity* (1923), is still a useful book for the theologically interested reader. Troeltsch's social philosophy is well presented in W.F. KASCH, *Die Sozialphilosophie von Ernst Troeltsch* (1963).

(Ev.S.)

Tromp, Maarten and Cornelis

Maarten and Cornelis Tromp, father and son, both famous Dutch admirals, played prominent roles in the Dutch wars of the 17th century. Maarten Tromp's victory over the Spanish in the Battle of the Downs, in 1639, signalled the passing of Spain's power at sea.

(Left) Maarten Tromp, engraving by Cornelis Danckerts de Ry (1603–56). (Right) Cornelis Tromp, detail of an oil painting by Sir Peter Lely (1618–80) and Willem van de Velde. In the Nederlandsch Historisch Scheepvaart Museum, Amsterdam.
By courtesy of the Nederlandsch Historisch Scheepvaart Museum, Amsterdam

Maarten Tromp. Maarten was born on April 23, 1598, at Den Briel (Brielle), the son of Harpert Maartenszoon. At the age of nine, he sailed with his father, the captain of a small man-of-war. When his father changed to the merchant fleet, Maarten accompanied him, but in 1609 the ship was taken by an English pirate, his father was killed, and Maarten was forced to serve the pirate captain for two years. After his return to Holland, he rejoined the navy in 1617. He took part in a successful expedition against Algerian pirates and was made helmsman. In 1619 he left the navy to sail with a merchant fleet to the Mediterranean, but in 1621 he fell once more into the hands of pirates. Set free after a year, he became a lieutenant in the Dutch navy. In 1621 the Twelve Years' Truce between the Netherlands and Spain expired, and it became necessary to prepare the fleet for war. In 1624 Tromp received his first commission as a captain, and five

years later he commanded the flagship of the new lieutenant admiral, Piet Heyn, who was killed on the first voyage in a fight with pirates from Ostend. After that Tromp operated successfully in the Flemish coastal waters, but his relations with Lieut. Adm. Philips van Dorp were strained, and this, combined with family circumstances, led him to resign from the navy in 1634. In 1636 he became a director of naval equipment at the Admiralty of the Maas. When van Dorp resigned, Tromp was appointed lieutenant admiral of Holland, at that time the highest post in the navy under the stadtholder, who was also the admiral general of the republic. Witte Corneliszn de With was nominated his vice admiral, which was to prove an unhappy combination. Nevertheless, de With and the vice admiral of Zeeland, Johan Evertsen, collaborated successfully with Tromp in February 1639, when he defeated a fleet of Dunkirk privateers; he then met a large Spanish armada that was transporting some 13,000 Spanish recruits to Flanders. Commanded by Adm. Antonio de Oquendo and several other experienced captains, the fleet consisted of 45 warships and 30 merchantmen hired as troopships. When Tromp spotted the armada off Beachy Head on September 15, 1639, he had only 13 vessels at his command; his other detachments were cruising in the Strait of Dover and off Dunkirk. De With arrived with five sail the next day, and the Dutch captains decided to give battle. After six hours of fighting, the armada—overcrowded with recruits who accounted for an extremely high number of casualties—withdrew to repair damages. The next day no action could take place for lack of wind, but the Dutch were reinforced by a Zeeland squadron, and, in the early morning of September 18, Tromp attacked the Spaniards in the Strait of Dover. In the afternoon Oquendo withdrew into the neutral roadstead of the Downs. Tromp, after taking in fresh supplies of gunpowder at Calais, soon followed him there, only separated by an English squadron under the command of Sir John Penington. Both fleets stayed on for weeks, and, while in Holland enthusiasm for Tromp's success led to a most unusual effort to strengthen the navy, the admiral showed himself a very tactful diplomatist in negotiating with the English. By October 10 the Dutch fleet was strong enough to challenge the Spaniards, and on October 21 Tromp attacked Oquendo, and Penington's efforts at protection were of little avail. In the Battle of the Downs, the armada was completely defeated, suffering severe losses both in ships and manpower. In 1640 Tromp was knighted by Louis XIII and in 1642 by Charles I when he visited Dover to escort Queen Henrietta Maria and Princess Mary to Holland.

Tromp's main task during the next years was action against the Dunkirk pirates who continued to attack the Dutch merchant fleet. In 1646 Tromp helped the French capture Dunkirk, after which the Order of St. Michael was conferred upon him. After the Peace of Westphalia in 1648, which concluded the Thirty Years' War, the activities of the Dutch navy diminished until, in 1651, growing privateering between Scandinavia and Gibraltar made it necessary to reinforce the neglected fleet and to protect maritime trade. Relations with England became increasingly strained after the Navigation Act (1651), which was passed to restrict Dutch trade with British possessions, while much resentment was also caused by the English claim to sovereignty over the seas.

A skirmish with Adm. Robert Blake off Dover in May 1652 resulted in the First Dutch War, which marked a crisis in the rivalry between England and the Netherlands as carriers of world trade. Although Tromp was unable to stir the English admirals to action later in the year—for which he was censured by the Dutch authorities, who even kept him from his command for some months—he defeated Blake off Dunge Ness in December. But the English fleet was superior to the Dutch; Tromp was unable to continue his successes and lost the three-day battle between Portland and Calais (March 1653), as well as the Battle of Gabbard in June. Tromp was killed in the battle off Terheijde near Scheveningen (on August 10, 1653). He was buried with great pomp in the Oude

Maarten's early career

Defeat of the Spanish

Outbreak of First Dutch War

Kerk (Old Church) at Delft. He combined great gifts as a sea commander with an amiable personality and an unusually considerate attitude toward his crews.

Cornelis Tromp. Cornelis Tromp, the second son of Maarten Tromp, was born on September 9, 1629. After serving as a lieutenant of his father's ship in 1645, he became a captain in 1649. He fought the North African pirates in the Mediterranean (1650) and, in the First Dutch War, the British. After taking part in the Battle of Leghorn (1653) against the English, he was made a rear admiral. He always showed a strong need for independent action and found pleasure in a fiery battle. In 1654, he fought the Algerians and, in 1656, sailed to the Baltic to take part in the First Northern War (1655–60) between Sweden and Poland. In 1663 he was appointed commander of the Dutch fleet in the Mediterranean. Some years of inactivity followed before he returned to the fleet as vice admiral (1665) during the Second Dutch War. In 1666 he was promoted to lieutenant admiral of the Admiralty of the Maas and made commander in chief of the Dutch fleet, but, when Adm. Michiel de Ruyter returned from the West Indies, the older and more experienced officer was given Tromp's commission, which caused understandable bitterness on Tromp's part. In 1666 he switched to the Admiralty of Amsterdam and soon came into conflict with de Ruyter. A more serious conflict arose in July 1666 after de Ruyter blamed his defeat by the English on the lack of assistance received from Tromp. This led to the withdrawal of Tromp's commission as lieutenant admiral, after which he left the navy. He then refused an invitation to enter French service. In 1673 Prince William III of Orange was able to reconcile de Ruyter with Tromp, who was a well-known sympathizer with the House of Orange. He was restored as lieutenant admiral of the Admiralty of Amsterdam and fought with de Ruyter in the battles of Schooneveld and Kijkduin in the same year. After the Treaty of Westminster (1674), between England and the Netherlands, he cruised the French coast and then, contrary to his instructions, sailed off to the Mediterranean on an expedition that was unsuccessful. He was censured by the admiralty. In 1676 Tromp became commander in chief of a combined Danish–Dutch fleet that operated against Sweden and stayed in Danish service until 1678. Afterwards he helped the Elector of Brandenburg to recover the island of Rügen from Sweden. He then returned to Holland and in 1691 received command of the fleet as lieutenant admiral general of the republic; but, being ill, he did not sail and died on May 29, 1691. He had been made a baronet by Charles II of England and a count by the King of Denmark.

margin: Cornelis' rivalry with de Ruyter

BIBLIOGRAPHY

Maarten Tromp: M.G. DE BOER, *Tromp en de Duinkerkers* (1949); C.R. BOXER (ed.), *The Journal of Maarten Harpertszoon Tromp Anno 1639* (1930), a translation of the original manuscript with introduction; "M.H. Tromp, 1598–1653," *The Mariner's Mirror*, 40:33–54 (1954), an excellent survey of Tromp's life with useful bibliography; F. GRAEFE, *De kapiteinsjaren van Maerten Harpertszoon Tromp. Bewerkt door M. Simon Thomas* (1938), treats the period from 1624 till 1634; J.K. OUDENDIJK, *Maerten Harpertszoon Tromp*, 2nd ed. (1952), the best biography available but without source indications.

Cornelis Tromp: A. HALLEMA, *Cornelis Maertenszoon Tromp, 1629–1691* (1942); J.C.M. WARNSINCK, *Twaalf doorluchtige zeehelden* (1941), contains a brief biography; *Van vlootvoogden en zeeslagen* (1940), treats Tromp's activities in the Mediterranean and in the Third Dutch War.

(E.H.K.)

Trotsky, Leon

Second only to Lenin, Leon Trotsky was the outstanding leader of the Russian Communist Revolution and, in many respects, the most colourful and controversial personality to emerge in its course. A gifted theorist and agitator, Trotsky was the principal leader of the October (November, new style) 1917 uprising and went on to serve the Soviet government as commissar of foreign affairs and commissar of war, before his ultimate political defeat and exile by Joseph Stalin.

Trotsky.
H. Roger-Viollet

Early life and education. Trotsky was born Lev Davidovich Bronstein in the village of Yanovka in the Ukraine on November 7 (October 26, old style), 1879. His father, David Bronstein, was an independent farmer of Russified Jewish background who had settled as a colonist in the steppe region. His mother, Anna, was middle class and educated. He had an older brother and sister, not counting two siblings who died in infancy.

At the age of eight, young Bronstein was sent to school in Odessa, where he spent the next eight years residing with the family of his mother's nephew, a liberal intellectual. He showed intellectual brilliance and a literary and linguistic gift. When he moved to Nikolayev in 1896 to complete his schooling, he was drawn into an underground Socialist circle and introduced to Marxism. After briefly attending the University of Odessa in 1897, he returned to Nikolayev to help organize the underground South Russian Workers' Union.

Revolutionary career. In January 1898, Bronstein was arrested for revolutionary activity and spent the next four and a half years in prison and in exile in Siberia (during which time he married his co-conspirator Aleksandra Sokolovskaya and fathered two daughters). He escaped from Siberia in 1902 with a forged passport bearing the name Trotsky, which he adopted as his revolutionary pseudonym. His wife remained behind, and the separation became permanent.

margin: Exile, imprisonment, and marriage

Following his escape, Trotsky made his way to London, where he joined the group of Russian Social-Democrats working with Vladimir Ulyanov (Lenin) on the revolutionary newspaper *Iskra* ("The Spark"). A remarkably articulate speaker and writer, Trotsky quickly assumed a leading role within the party.

At the Second Congress of the Russian Social-Democratic Workers' Party, held in Brussels and London in July 1903, Trotsky sided with the Menshevik faction—advocating a democratic approach to Socialism—against Lenin and the Bolsheviks, rejecting Lenin's dictatorial methods and organizational concepts aiming at immediate revolution. Shortly before this, in Paris, Trotsky had met and married Natalya Sedova, by whom he subsequently had two sons, Lev and Sergey (both of whom later used their mother's name, Sedov).

Upon the outbreak of revolutionary disturbances in 1905, Trotsky returned to Russia. He became a leading spokesman of the St. Petersburg Soviet (council) of Workers' Deputies when it organized a revolutionary strike movement and other measures of defiance against the Tsarist government. In the aftermath, Trotsky was arrested with the other leaders of the soviet, jailed, and brought to trial in 1906.

While in jail Trotsky wrote one of his major theoretical works, "Results and Prospects," setting forth his theory of permanent revolution. This was an effort to adjust Marxist theory to Russian conditions of a backward country in revolutionary ferment. A bourgeois revolution in Russia, Trotsky held, would lead to a continuous or permanent state of revolution during which the proletariat could take power in the urban centres. Even though Russia was a largely peasant country, this seizure of urban power would not prove temporary in Trotsky's view because the revolution in Russia would create a permanent state of revolution internationally as well. The Russian Revolution would inspire proletarian revolution in the West and assure the establishment of Socialist governments that could support the revolutionaries in Russia.

In 1907, after a second exile to Siberia, Trotsky once again escaped abroad. He settled in Vienna and supported himself as a journalist, serving as a war correspondent in the Balkan Wars of 1912–13. He remained active in Russian Social-Democratic émigré circles as a celebrated but isolated figure on the left wing of the Menshevik faction. As such, he engaged in intermittent polemics with Lenin and the Bolsheviks over organizational and tactical questions.

At the outbreak of World War I, Trotsky joined the majority of Russian Social-Democrats who condemned the war and refused to support the war effort of the Tsarist regime. He moved to Switzerland and thence to Paris, where he helped edit an anti-war Russian journal. In 1915 he participated in the international conference of anti-war Socialists at Zimmerwald in Switzerland. Trotsky's anti-war agitation led to his expulsion from France in 1916. He went to Spain, whence he was ordered out again, and arrived in New York in January 1917. There he joined the Bolshevik theoretician Nikolay Bukharin in editing the Russian-language paper *Novy Mir* ("The New World").

Leadership in the Revolution of 1917.   Trotsky hailed the outbreak of revolution in Russia in February (March, new style) as the opening of the permanent revolution he had predicted. Independently, he took a position similar to Lenin in calling for the overthrow of Prince Georgy Lvov's Provisional Government by the workers. Late in March, Trotsky and his family left the United States by ship for Russia but were detained by the British authorities when the vessel put in at Halifax, Nova Scotia. Released a month later at the behest of the Russian government, Trotsky reached Petrograd in mid-May and assumed the leadership of a left wing Menshevik faction, the Interdistrict Group, who were of one mind with the Bolsheviks in agitating for a new revolution.

Following the abortive July Days uprising, Trotsky was arrested in the crackdown on the Bolshevik leadership carried out by Aleksandr Kerensky's liberal government. In August, while still in jail, Trotsky was formally admitted to the Bolshevik Party at the party's Sixth Congress, along with the Interdistrict Group. He was also elected to membership on the Bolshevik Central Committee. Trotsky was released from prison in September, at the time of General Lavr Kornilov's abortive right wing coup against Kerensky, and shortly afterward he was elected chairman of the Petrograd Soviet of Workers' and Soldiers' Deputies when the Bolsheviks and their allies established a majority in it. Thenceforth, until the Bolshevik seizure of power, while Lenin was still in hiding, Trotsky was the principal leader of the Bolshevik Party in its preparations to take power.

In the debates among the Bolsheviks over whether to accede to Lenin's insistence on the violent seizure of power, Trotsky took a middle course. He agreed with Lenin's call for the overthrow of the Provisional Government but calculated that this could be done under the cloak of legitimacy provided by the forthcoming Second All-Russian Congress of Soviets, which the Bolsheviks expected to dominate. He threw himself into the work of winning control over the Petrograd garrison, particularly through the Military Revolutionary Committee of the Petrograd Soviet (which he inspired as chairman of the soviet, though he was not actually chairman of the committee). Trotsky's strategy was to mobilize enough force to protect the Congress of Soviets while it voted itself into power and to prevent a countercoup by the Kerensky government in the meantime.

When fighting was precipitated by an ineffectual government raid early on November 6 (October 24, old style), Trotsky took a leading role in directing countermeasures for the soviet, while reassuring the public that his Military Revolutionary Committee meant only to defend the

Congress of Soviets. Governmental authority crumbled quickly, and Petrograd was largely in Bolshevik hands by the time Lenin reappeared from the underground in the early hours of November 7 (October 25, O.S.) to take direct charge of the Revolution and present the Congress of Soviets with an accomplished fact when it convened 24 hours later.

Subsequently, the Bolshevik leaders, including Trotsky, were loath to admit that they had been waiting for action by the congress, and Trotsky went so far as to suggest that his speeches to that effect were prevarications to deceive the opposition. Official Soviet histories under Stalin and since have leaned heavily on Trotsky's reluctance to attack the Provisional Government prior to the congress, even alleging this as evidence of treason to the Revolution.

On the afternoon of November 7 (October 25, O.S.) Trotsky made one of his most impassioned speeches to the Petrograd Soviet, to proclaim the overthrow of the Provisional Government and to introduce Lenin in public. Addressing the Congress of Soviets that evening, Trotsky was uncompromising in his defense of the power now violently won. The congress was swiftly led to proclaim the Bolsheviks' program and to install the new Soviet government headed by the Council of People's Commissars, with Trotsky as commissar of foreign affairs.

Trotsky continued to function as the military leader of the Revolution when Kerensky vainly attempted to retake Petrograd with loyal troops. He organized and supervised the forces that broke Kerensky's efforts at the Battle of Pulkovo on November 13 (October 31, O.S.). Immediately afterwards, he joined Lenin in defeating proposals for a coalition government including Mensheviks and Socialist Revolutionaries.

Role in Soviet government.   As foreign commissar, Trotsky's first charge was to implement the Bolsheviks' program of peace by calling for immediate armistice negotiations among all the warring powers. Germany and its allies responded, a cease-fire was agreed on, and in mid-December peace talks were begun at Brest-Litovsk, though Trotsky continued vainly to invite support from the Allied governments. Early in January 1918, Trotsky entered into the peace negotiations personally and shocked his adversaries by turning the talks into a propaganda forum. He then recessed the talks and returned to Petrograd to argue against acceptance of Germany's annexationist terms, even though Lenin had meanwhile decided to pay the German price for peace and thus buy time for the Soviet state. Between Lenin's position and Bukharin's outright call for revolutionary war, Trotsky proposed the formula "no war, no peace." When the Germans resumed their offensive in mid-February, the Bolshevik Central Committee was compelled to make a decision; Trotsky and his followers abstained from the vote, and Lenin's acceptance of the German terms was narrowly endorsed.

Following the conclusion of the Treaty of Brest-Litovsk, Trotsky resigned as foreign commissar and turned the office over to Georgy Chicherin. He was immediately made commissar of war, theretofore a committee responsibility. As war commissar, Trotsky faced the formidable task of building a new Red Army out of the shambles of the old Russian Army and preparing to defend the Communist government against the imminent threats of civil war and foreign intervention. Trotsky chose to concentrate on developing a small but disciplined and professionally competent force. His abandonment of the revolutionary ideal of democratization and guerrilla tactics prompted much criticism of his methods among other Communists. He was particularly criticized for recruiting former tsarist officers ("military specialists") and putting them to work under the supervision of Communist military commissars. Trotsky's military policies were resisted unsuccessfully by a coalition of ultraleft purists and rival party leaders, notably Stalin, with whom Trotsky had an acrimonious clash over the defense of the city of Tsaritsyn (later Stalingrad, now Volgograd). Trotsky's approach was, however, vindicated by the success of the

Conversion to Bolshevism

Military leader of the Revolution

Red Army in turning back attacks by the anti-Communist White armies in 1918 and 1919, with Trotsky himself frequently in charge in the field.

With the triumph of the Communist forces and the end of the Russian Civil War in 1920, Trotsky, retaining his office as commissar of war, turned his attention to the economic reconstruction of Russia. He first proposed a relaxation of the stringent centralization of War Communism to allow market forces to operate. Rejected in this, he endeavoured to apply military discipline to the economy, using soldiers as labour armies rather than demobilizing them, and attempting to militarize the administration of the transportation system. Trotsky was one of the earliest Soviet thinkers to conceive of the coercive role of the state in accelerating the economic development of the country, a possibility neglected in Marxist theory but made the cornerstone of Soviet economic policy under Stalin later on.

During the Civil War and War Communism phase of the Soviet regime, Trotsky was clearly established as the number-two man next to Lenin. He was one of the initial five members of the Politburo when that top Communist Party policy-making body was created in 1919. In sheer intellectual power and administrative effectiveness, he was Lenin's superior and did not hesitate to disagree with Lenin on numerous occasions, but he lacked facility in political manipulation to win party decisions against Lenin. Trotsky took a prominent part in the launching of the Comintern (Communist International) in 1919 and wrote its initial manifesto calling for the overthrow of capitalism throughout the world.

As a relative newcomer, moving in abruptly to the top level of leadership in the Bolshevik Party, Trotsky incurred the personal enmity of a number of long-standing Bolsheviks, particularly Grigory Zinoviev, who had figured as Lenin's second in command for several years prior to 1917. Trotsky and Zinoviev were adversaries on every party issue from 1917 to 1924. Trotsky's later struggle with Stalin was less personal, although the two clashed more than once during the Civil War period.

In the winter of 1920–21 widespread dissension broke out over the policies of War Communism, not only among the populace but among the Communist Party leadership as well. The point at issue in the protracted controversy was the future role of the trade unions. The utopian left wing wanted the unions to administer industry; Lenin and the cautious wing wanted the unions confined to supervising working conditions; Trotsky and his supporters tried to reconcile radicalism and pragmatism by visualizing administration through "governmentalized" unions representing the central state authority.

The crisis came to a head in March 1921, with agitation for democracy within the party on the one hand and armed defiance represented by the naval garrison at Kronstadt on the other. At this point Trotsky sided completely with Lenin, commanding the forces that suppressed the Kronstadt Rebellion and backing the suppression of open factional activity in the party. As did virtually the entire party, Trotsky accepted Lenin's retreat from ideal communism in favour of the New Economic Policy, including his conventional view of the trade unions. This degree of accord, however, did not prevent Trotsky from losing a substantial degree of political influence at the Tenth Party Congress in March 1921. The party Secretariat, up to this time controlled by followers of Trotsky, was restaffed and put in the hands of supporters of Stalin.

The struggle for the succession. When Lenin was stricken with his first cerebral hemorrhage in May 1922, the question of eventual succession to the leadership of Russia became urgent. Trotsky, owing to his record and his charismatic qualities, was the obvious candidate in the eyes of the party rank and file, but jealousy among his colleagues on the Politburo prompted them to combine against him. As an alternative, the Politburo supported the informal leadership of the troika composed of Zinoviev, Lev Kamenev, and Stalin, with Stalin, as general secretary of the Communist Party, rapidly obtaining control of the organizational levers.

Economic reconstruction

Kronstadt Rebellion

In the winter of 1922–23 Lenin recovered partially and turned to Trotsky for assistance in correcting the errors of the troika, particularly in foreign trade policy, the handling of the national minorities, and reform of the bureaucracy. In December 1922, warning in his then-secret "Testament" of the danger of a split between Trotsky and Stalin, Lenin characterized Trotsky as a man of "exceptional abilities" but "too far-reaching self-confidence and a disposition to be too much attracted by the purely administrative side of affairs." Just before he was silenced by a final stroke in March 1923, Lenin invited Trotsky to open an attack on Stalin, but Trotsky chose to bide his time, possibly contemplating an alliance with Stalin against Zinoviev. Stalin then moved rapidly to consolidate his hold on the party organization and the Central Committee at the 12th Congress in April 1923. Trotsky had lost his most auspicious opportunity for establishing himself as Lenin's successor, partly, as he explained himself, out of a reluctance to assert himself while Lenin still lay dying.

By fall, alarmed by inroads of the secret police among party members and efforts to weaken his control of the war commissariat, Trotsky decided after all to strike out against the party leadership. In October he addressed a wide-ranging critique to the Central Committee, stressing especially the violation of democracy in the party and the failure to develop adequate economic planning. Reforms were promised, and Trotsky responded with an open letter, "The New Course," detailing the direction they should take. This, however, served only as the signal for a massive propaganda counterattack by the leadership against Trotsky and his supporters on grounds of factionalism and opportunism. At this critical moment Trotsky fell ill of an undiagnosed fever and could take no personal part in the struggle. Because of Stalin's organizational controls, the party leadership easily won, and the "New Course" controversy was terminated at the 13th Party Conference in January 1924 (the first substantially stage-managed party assembly) with the condemnation of the Trotskyist opposition as a petty bourgeois, Menshevik-like, illegal factional deviation. Lenin's death a week later only confirmed Trotsky's isolation. Convalescing on the Black Sea coast, Trotsky was deceived about the date of the funeral, failed to return to Moscow, and left the scene to Stalin.

Attacks on Trotsky did not cease. When the 13th Party Congress, in May 1924, repeated the denunciations of his violations of party discipline, Trotsky vainly professed his belief in the omnipotence of the party. The following fall he took a different tack in his essay *The Lessons of October 1917,* linking the opposition of Zinoviev and Kamenev to the October Revolution with the failure of the Soviet-inspired German Communist uprising in 1923. The party leadership replied with a wave of denunciation, counterposing Trotskyism to Leninism, denigrating Trotsky's role in the Revolution, and denouncing the theory of permanent revolution as a Menshevik heresy. This verbal abuse was followed in January 1925 with Trotsky's removal from the war commissariat.

Early in 1926, following the split between the Stalin–Bukharin leadership and Zinoviev–Kamenev group and the denunciation of the latter at the 14th Party Congress, Trotsky joined forces with his old adversaries Zinoviev and Kamenev to resume the political offensive. For a year and a half this "United Opposition" grasped at every opportunity to put its criticisms before the party membership, despite the increasingly severe curbs being placed on such discussion. Again they stressed the themes of party democracy and economic planning, condemned the leadership's concessions to bourgeois elements (especially the peasantry), and denounced Stalin's theory of "Socialism in one country" as a pretext for abandoning world revolution.

The response of the leadership to this campaign was a rising tide of official denunciation, supplemented by an anti-Semitic whispering campaign. In October 1926 Trotsky was ousted from the Politburo; just a year later he and Zinoviev were dropped from the Central Committee for printing their platform clandestinely. After an abor-

Struggle against Stalin

tive attempt at a demonstration on the tenth anniversary of the Revolution in November 1927, the two were expelled from the Communist Party. At the 15th Congress in December, the opposition was ritually condemned without a single voice represented in its favour, and the entire Trotskyist group was expelled from the party.

During this period of fruitless political struggle, Trotsky carried on an enormous intellectual activity. He produced books on a wide range of subjects from international politics to literature and the elevation of mass culture, as well as innumerable platforms, essays, and diatribes that were condemned to remain unpublished.

Exile and assassination. In January 1928, Trotsky and his principal followers were exiled to remote parts of the Soviet Union, Trotsky himself being assigned to Alma-Ata in Central Asia. There he kept up an active correspondence with his supporters, condemning Stalin's methods in initiating the new industrialization drive and endeavouring to keep his own men from making their peace with Stalin. In January 1929 Trotsky was banished from the territory of the U.S.S.R.

Trotsky was initially received by the government of Turkey and domiciled on the island of Prinkipo. He plunged into literary activity there and completed his autobiography and his history of the Russian Revolution, while simultaneously striving to organize and encourage the anti-Stalin factions that had been expelled from various Communist parties throughout the world. In 1933 Trotsky secured permission to move to France. After Hitler's victory in Germany, he gave up the hope of reforming the Communist International and called on his followers to establish their own revolutionary parties and form a Fourth International. This movement (whose American branch was the Socialist Workers' Party) proved to be little more than a shadow organization, although a small founding conference was officially held in France in 1938.

In 1935 Trotsky was compelled to move to Norway, and in 1936, under Soviet pressure, he was forced to seek asylum in Mexico, where he settled at Coyoacán, near Mexico City. He was represented as the principal conspirator, in absentia, in the treason trials of former Communist opposition leaders held in Moscow in 1936, 1937, and 1938. The evidence of treasonable plotting was, however, proven to be fictitious by an investigating commission chaired by the American philospher John Dewey.

Trotsky remained outspoken in his criticisms of the Stalin regime as a bureaucratic and "Bonapartist" perversion of the dictatorship of the proletariat. He came to the conclusion that the Russian Revolution had as early as 1923 entered the conservative phase of Thermidor (by analogy with the overthrow of the radical Jacobins in France in July 1794, in the month of Thermidor according to the Revolutionary calendar). This backsliding of the Revolution Trotsky explained with reference to his theory of permanent revolution: a Socialist regime under Russian conditions of backwardness, isolated by the failure of world revolution, was bound to degenerate. By 1937 he was calling for a new revolution in the U.S.S.R. to restore power to the workers.

Subsequent to Trotsky's political defeat in 1927, the official history of the Communist Party was rewritten to minimize and denigrate Trotsky's role in the Revolution and in the Soviet regime. After the Moscow Trials he was represented as having been a counterrevolutionary plotter ever since the Revolution. Following Premier Nikita Khrushchev's destalinization campaign in 1956, the treatment of Trotsky's role was moderated but not fundamentally re-examined. His widow was unsuccessful in petitioning for his rehabilitation by the Soviet authorities.

Trotsky was the object of two assassination attempts, presumably by Stalinist agents. The first, a machine gun attack on his house, failed. The second was successful when a Spanish Communist by the name of Ramon Mercader, who had won the confidence of the Trotsky household, fatally wounded Trotsky with an alpine axe on August 20, 1940. The Soviet government disclaimed any responsibility, and the murderer was sentenced to the maximum 20-year term under Mexican law.

Assessment. Trotsky was undoubtedly the most brilliant intellect brought to prominence by the Russian Revolution, outdistancing Lenin and other theoreticians such as Bukharin both in the range of his interests and in the imaginativeness of his perceptions. He was an indefatigable worker, a rousing public speaker, and a quick and decisive administrator. On the other hand, Trotsky was not successful as a leader of men, partly because he allowed his brilliance and arrogance to antagonize the lesser lights in the Communist movement, partly because of the intellectual's perception of subtleties that inhibited his decisiveness at such critical political moments as 1917 and 1923. Perhaps he fatally compromised himself when he became a Bolshevik in 1917, subordinating himself to Lenin's leaderhip and accepting the methods of dictatorship that he had previously condemned.

Had Trotsky won the struggle to succeed Lenin, the character of the Soviet regime would almost certainly have been substantially different, particularly in foreign policy, cultural policy, and the extent of terroristic repression. Trotsky's failure, however, seems almost inevitable considering his own qualities and the conditions of authoritarian rule by the Communist Party organization. Trotsky comes close to the archetype of the tragic hero, ultimately destroyed by the consequences of the steps he accepted in his pursuit of revolutionary greatness.

MAJOR WORKS

The Moscow edition of Trotsky's collected works, begun in 1924, was discontinued after 1927. English editions of individual writings include *Our Revolution: Essays on Working-class and International Revolution, 1904–1917* (1918); *Terrorizm i kommunizm* (1920; *The Defence of Terrorism: Terrorism and Communism*, 1921; new ed., 1935); *Mezhdu imperializmom i revolyutsiey: Osnovnye voprosy revolyutsii na chastom primere Gruzii* (1922; *Between Red and White: A Study of Some Fundamental Questions of Revolution, with Particular Reference to Georgia*, 1922); *Voprosy byta* (1923; *Problems of Life*, 1924); *Literatura i revolyutsiya* (1923; *Literature and Revolution*, 1925); *Uroki Oktyabrya* (1924; *The Lessons of October 1917*, 1925; new version, 1937); *O Lenine: Materialy dlya biografa* (1924; *Lenin*, 1925); *Kuda idet Angliya?* (1925; *Where Is Britain Going?*, 1926); *Ikh moral i nasha* (1925; *Their Morals and Ours*, 1939); *K sotsializmy ili k kapitalizmy?* (1926; *Towards Socialism or Capitalism?*, 1926); *The Real Situation in Russia* (1928); *Moya zhizn: Opyt avtobiografii* (1930; *My Life: An Attempt at an Autobiography*, 1930); *Permanentnaya revolyutsiya* (1930; *The Permanent Revolution*, 1931); *Istoriya russkoy revolyutsii*, 2 vol. (1931–33; *The History of the Russian Revolution*, 3 vol., 1932–33); *Problems of the Chinese Revolution* (1932); *What Next? Vital Questions for the German Proletariat* (1932); *Stalinskaya shkola falsifikatsii* (1932; *The Stalin School of Falsification*, 1937); *The Suppressed Testament of Lenin* (1935); *The Third International After Lenin* (1936); *The Revolution Betrayed: What Is the Soviet Union and Where Is It Going?* (1937); *Stalin: An Appraisal of the Man and His Influence* (1941); *Diary in Exile, 1935* (1958).

BIBLIOGRAPHY. ISAAC DEUTSCHER, *The Prophet Armed: Trotsky, 1879–1921; The Prophet Unarmed: Trotsky, 1921–1929; and The Prophet Outcast: Trotsky, 1929–1940* (1954–63), is the major biography of Trotsky from a sympathetic, neo-Marxist point of view. MAX EASTMAN, *Leon Trotsky: The Portrait of a Youth* (1925), provides a sympathetic treatment. See also BERTRAM D. WOLFE, *Three Who Made a Revolution* (1948), a triple biography of Lenin, Stalin, and Trotsky to 1914; and E.V. WOLFENSTEIN, *The Revolutionary Personality: Lenin, Trotsky, Gandhi* (1967), a psychoanalytic study. LEON TROTSKY, *The Case of Leon Trotsky* (1937), contains Trotsky's testimony to the Preliminary Commission of Inquiry headed by John Dewey, concerning the Moscow Trials. Trotsky's *History of the Russian Revolution*, 3 vol. (1932–33; orig. pub. in Russian, 1931–33), treats his own role in the third person, and *The Revolution Betrayed* (1937), is his major polemic against Stalin. ROBERT V. DANIELS, "Trotskyism," in MICHAEL T. FLORINSKY (ed.), *The McGraw-Hill Encyclopedia of Russia and the Soviet Union* (1961), and the same author's *Conscience of the Revolution: Communist Opposition in Soviet Russia* (1960), cover Trotsky's career from 1917 to 1929. JAN. M. MEIJER (ed.), *The Trotsky Papers, 1917–1922* (1964), contains documents from the Trotsky Archive, including the Lenin–Trotsky correspondence. Also of interest is IRVING HOWE (ed.), *The Basic Writings of Trotsky* (1963).

(R.V.D.)

Trucks and Buses

A bus is a road vehicle, usually driven by an internal-combustion engine; it is designed to carry a number of passengers, generally on a fixed route. In most cities buses have largely or entirely replaced electric streetcars, and they carry much intercity passenger traffic.

A truck, or lorry, is a motor vehicle designed to carry freight, or goods. Trucks are driven by gas, diesel, or gasoline engines, and they provide a fast and flexible transportation system for durable and perishable commodities of all kinds. In most countries they carry a substantial part of the long-distance cargoes and do most of the short-distance hauling.

In the early 1970s there were over 50,000,000 trucks and buses throughout the world, more than a fifth of all road vehicles. Annual world production of trucks and buses was about 7,000,000.

Buses. *Development.* In 1830 Sir Goldworthy Gurney of Great Britain designed a large stagecoach driven by a steam engine that may have been the first bus in operation. In 1895 an eight-passenger omnibus, driven by a four- to six-horsepower (hp) single-cylinder engine, was built in Germany. In 1903 the Austro-Daimler firm built an omnibus that had a four-cylinder, eight-horsepower engine with a four-speed transmission. In 1904 an experimental route in Germany from Wendeburg to Braunscherg was begun, using a Büssing-built vehicle. In 1905 buses in Berlin pulled trailers carrying passengers, a practice that continued until 1962.

Until the 1920s the technical history of the bus was that of the motor truck, since the early bus consisted of a bus body mounted on a truck chassis. The majority of present-day school buses are made in this way. In 1922 the *First vehicle designed as bus* first vehicle with a chassis specifically designed for bus service was made in the United States by Fageol Safety Coach Company of Oakland, California. Its frame was about one foot lower than a truck frame, and it also had an extra-long wheelbase, a wide tread, and an engine in front. In 1926 the Fageol organization developed the first integral-frame bus, with twin engines mounted amidships under the floor. The integral frame utilized the roof, floor, and sides of the bus as structural members.

Other early bus manufacturers were Mack and Yellow Coach in the United States, both of which built gasoline-electric models. In these buses, a gasoline engine drove a direct-current generator, and the output of the generator provided electrical power for the driving motors on the rear wheels. This electrical system performed the functions of a transmission; *i.e.*, it multiplied driving torque and provided a means of connecting and disconnecting the engine from the drive wheels. In 1928 the first transcontinental bus service was initiated in the United States.

In 1931 the first rear engine in an integral-frame bus was introduced. Two-stroke-cycle diesel engines were first used in buses in 1938 and were still used by most city and intercity models in the 1970s.

Advantage of air suspension In 1953 air suspension was first used in buses; in the 1960s most of the integral-frame models continued to employ this type of suspension; the others used conventional metal leaf springs. Air suspension, although first tried on automobiles and trucks, found more general acceptance on buses. It required an air compressor, and automobile manufacturers and consumers soon concluded that the improvement in riding comfort did not justify the expense of the equipment for passenger cars.

Air suspension consists of two or four air springs (heavy rubber bellows) per axle (Figure 1). The air springs are supplied with air from an air reservoir in which the pressure is maintained at about 100 pounds per square inch (7 kilograms per square centimetre). An advantage gained from this type of suspension is that as the load increases or decreases the level and height of the vehicle remain constant. This is accomplished by valves that are actuated by the vehicle height between the body and the axle; as the load is increased, the air pressure is increased in the air spring. The increased unit pressure multiplied by a nearly constant area gives a greater load capacity. As the load is removed, the air is released from the air spring, reducing the pressure and load capacity.

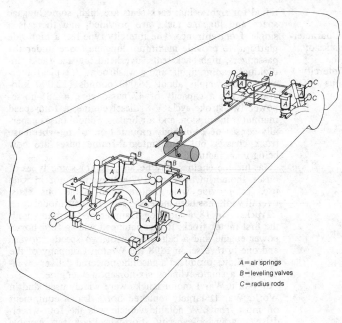

A = air springs
B = leveling valves
C = radius rods

Figure 1: Air suspension for a modern bus or motor coach. The shaded area indicates the air lines.

Unlike the leaf spring but like the coil spring, the air spring is capable of withstanding only vertical forces. Consequently, braking and cornering forces must be absorbed by links or arms with one end attached to the axle and the other to the body by pin or ball joints.

Another interesting development in motor-bus transportation was the Scenicruiser introduced in the United States in 1954 for transcontinental use. It utilizes air suspension and has six wheels, two singles in the front for the steering axle and four doubles in the rear in a tandem arrangement (one axle directly behind the other with an interconnection to allow the equalization of the load). Thus, the weight of this vehicle, about 30,000 pounds (14,000 kilograms) empty, is supported by ten tires, two on the front axle and four on each of the rear axles. The frame is of the integral type and provides two *Two-level* levels. The first level carries the driver, ten passengers, *design of* and sanitary facilities; the upper level carries 33 pas- *Sceni-* sengers and has a windshield so that passengers can *cruiser* see forward. The Scenicruiser is powered by two four-cylinder two-stroke-cycle diesel engines of 133 horsepower each. Only a limited number of these vehicles were built because of cost.

Modern buses. In Europe, especially in England, the double-decker bus is used to minimize the street space occupied and to take advantage of the greater manoeuvrability of the shorter wheelbase without loss of passenger capacity. A typical bus of this type carries 26 passengers on the lower deck and 30 on the upper. In Germany, double-decker and 1½-decker buses are operated, as are trolley buses and articulated buses. An articulated bus is one in which a single-deck bus pulls a trailer, using a flexible joint. Consequently, unless it is turning a corner, the vehicle appears to be one continuous unit. In most of the world, however, the trend is toward one-unit single-deck vehicles, usually of large size. In Japan as late as 1963, 21-passenger buses were used in Tokyo and Kyōto, often mounted on a truck chassis. The improvement of roads and the building of expressways have triggered the rapid expansion of the automotive industry in Japan, which, in 1970, included eight bus manufacturers building buses ranging in size from small gasoline-driven units to large diesel-driven units.

There are four main types of buses: city or transit, suburban, intercity, and school. The city bus operates within the city limits and is characterized by low maximum speed, low-ride platform, provision for standing passengers, two entrances on the curb side, low-back seats, and no luggage space or racks. The suburban bus is designed for short intercity runs, with roof windows optional for sightseeing; back seats are high, some luggage space and luggage racks are provided, and there is a single, front entrance. The intercity type has a high-ride platform to provide maximum luggage space under the passengers, high-back seats, overhead luggage racks, individual reading lights, and a washroom. A typical intercity coach weighs about 26,000 pounds (12,000 kilograms), has a capacity of 47 passengers, a 285-horsepower two-stroke-cycle V-8 diesel engine, a four-speed manual transmission, and air brakes. School buses generally consist of a bus body mounted on a long-wheelbase truck chassis, but some integral-frame buses are now being manufactured.

Gas-turbine engines may be adopted for some types of buses, though in the early 1970s they were not in wide use. To provide wider, more comfortable bus seats, overall width has been increased on some new models.

Trucks. In 1896 Gottlieb Daimler of Germany built the first motor truck. It was equipped with a four-horsepower engine and a belt drive with two speeds forward and one in reverse. In 1898 the Winton Company of the United States produced a gasoline-powered delivery wagon with a single-cylinder six-horsepower engine.

In World War I motor trucks were widely used and in World War II largely replaced horse-drawn equipment on most fronts. A notable vehicle was the four-wheel-drive, quarter-ton-capacity, short-wheelbase jeep, capable of performing a variety of military tasks.

Types and definitions. Trucks can be classified as either straight or articulated. A straight truck is one in which all axles are attached to a single frame. An articulated vehicle is one that consists of two or more separate frames connected by suitable couplings. A truck tractor is a motor vehicle designed primarily for drawing truck-trailers and constructed to carry part of the weight and load of a semitrailer, which is a truck-trailer equipped with one or more axles, so constructed that the end and a substantial part of its own weight and that of its load rests upon a truck tractor. In contrast, a full trailer is so constructed that all of its own weight and that of its load rests upon its own wheels.

A device called a fifth wheel is used to connect a truck tractor to a semitrailer and to permit articulation between the units. It generally includes a lower half, consisting of a trunnion (pivot assembly) plate and latching mechanism, mounted on the truck tractor for connection with a kingpin mounted on the semitrailer. A semitrailer may be converted to a full trailer by a trailer-converter dolly, an auxiliary axle assembly equipped with the lower half of a fifth wheel, a drawbar, and other special parts.

Axle assemblies of heavy trucks may be made up of two or more axles, any of which may be powered. Normally, they are so spaced that the distance between axle centres is not more than one and one-half times the overall diameter of the wheel and tire. If the axles are separated by a larger distance the assembly is called a spread tandem.

Shown in Figure 2 are several types of trucks and truck tractors in use, with a digit code to aid in identification of the vehicles. The first digit refers to the power unit and a second single digit refers to a full trailer. A digit with an S prefix refers to a semitrailer; for example, 2-S1 means a two-axle tractor and one-axle semitrailer; 3-2 means a three-axle truck with two-axle full trailer; 2-S1-2 means a two-axle tractor, one-axle semitrailer, and two-axle full trailer.

Frames. Truck and truck-tractor frames, except for the very small sizes, have remained separate from the cab and body. The frame is generally made of two channel sections of alloy steel with a standardized width of 34 inches (0.86 metre) overall. Semitrailers and tank trailers in many instances now employ the integral, or unitized, type of construction.

Suspensions. The most common form of front suspension is a drop-forged one-section front axle attached to the frame through leaf springs and shock absorbers. In 1960 individual front suspension was introduced.

The variations of rear suspensions for trucks and truck tractors are almost limitless. In the case of a truck with a single powered axle, the axle is generally attached to the

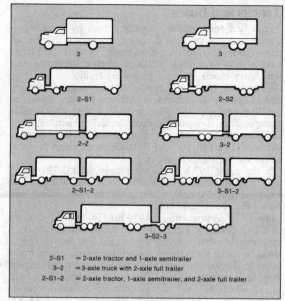

Figure 2: Truck types as designated by code based on axle arrangement.

frame by leaf springs. The axle is always full-floating; *i.e.*, all the weight is carried by the axle housing and none by the live or driving axle inside the housing. Thus, if a driving axle breaks, the load is still supported by the axle housing. The axle may be a single reduction type, meaning that it has one-gear reduction, or double reduction. A two-speed axle is one in which there is a gear change built into the axle. This makes it possible to have two speeds for each transmission speed. The tandem-drive axle has two powered axles. There may be two drive shafts, one to each axle. There is always a system of levers between the two axles to equalize the load. A powered axle may be either the Hotchkiss type, in which all of the driving and braking thrust is taken by the leaf springs, or the torque-arm type, in which the thrusts are taken by the rods. Because the vertical movement of the body is only one-half that of the wheels in a tandem axle, this axle is used successfully with solid rubber springs, reducing maintenance to a minimum.

Steering. Steering of trucks, with their relatively heavy loads, was a problem until power steering came into use in the early 1950s. Steering is always by the Ackermann system, which provides a kingpin for each front wheel. Maximum cramp angle of the front wheels is about 35 degrees. The minimum turning radius is dependent on the wheelbase. A few vehicles have been built with two steering axles in the front.

Engines and fuels. Until the 1930s the gasoline engine was widely used for trucks, especially in the United States, but since World War II the diesel engine has become increasingly favoured for trucks used for long-distance hauls. In 1950 the Boeing Company of the U.S. installed the first gas turbine in a truck; in the 1960s there was renewed interest in this type of engine. In 1952 an engine using liquid-propane gas was introduced. While the diesel engine has the disadvantage of high initial cost, the propane-burning engine has the disadvantage of lower output for a given engine displacement.

Tires. Although pneumatic tires appeared on automobiles as early as 1904, large trucks were equipped with hard rubber tires until World War I. Cotton was replaced by rayon in the carcass of truck tires in the 1930s, with wire and nylon appearing a decade later. Recent developments include the use of a single wide tire to carry the same load as a dual wheel. Tire chains first became available in 1904, knobby snow tires by 1936, and snow tires with embedded wire coils about 1950. One of the latest and most effective versions of this tire has curved tread ribs. To reduce costs, many trucks use recapped tires, extending the life of the carcass about two and a half times. In 1955 tubeless tires became available in large truck sizes.

Transmissions. Although automatic transmissions for trucks have been available since the 1950s, they have not received popular acceptance for large units. For some diesels it is necessary to operate the engine within a relatively narrow speed range, typically 1,500 to 2,200 revolutions per minute. This requires a large number of forward speeds. One of the most recent diesel-powered units has 16, obtained by combining two transmissions, each with four forward speeds. The single-plate dry-disk clutch is commonly used to connect and disconnect the engine from the transmission.

Brakes. The first truck brakes were brake shoes operating directly on the wheels. From this simple beginning has evolved one of the most complex braking systems found on any type of vehicle. The first air brakes were introduced in 1918. Seven years later four-wheel brakes were introduced on trucks, and the internally-expanding type was introduced by 1930. In the late 1930s the vacuum booster, or hydraulic brake, was introduced. This was the power brake available on the automobiles in the mid-1950s.

Another means of brake application is electrical. A floating armature contracts a rotating disk on the wheel when electric current is applied, and through a cam arrangement applies the shoes to the drums. Vacuum brakes working off the vacuum in the intake manifold of the spark-ignition gasoline engine have been used to apply the brakes on car carriers. Air-over-hydraulic brakes are also used in some vehicles.

Air, air-over-hydraulic, vacuum, and electrical brakes are all adaptable to articulated vehicles. Of these methods of application, air, or full air, as it is sometimes called, is the most widely used. The engine-driven compressor supplies air at a nominal pressure, regulated by an air governor. Air pressure is indicated by a pressure gauge and a low-pressure warning device, either audible or visual. Air is stored in the reservoirs and supplied to the brake valves; a foot valve supplies air to all brake chambers on the vehicle, including those being towed. Another brake valve is hand controlled and applies the brakes on the towed vehicle only. Both the foot pedal and hand valve supply air to the same service line, which extends back to the towed vehicles. The second, or emergency, line carries full air pressure when the vehicle is in operation. If this line is broken, the emergency brakes are applied on all towed vehicles from air reservoirs located on the towed vehicles. After reaching the brake chamber from the brake valves, the air acts on a diaphragm connected to a push rod, which in turn actuates a cam that moves the shoes against the brake drum. In the early 1970s the cam was being replaced by a wedge.

In recent years much attention has been given to the problem of brake failures that have resulted from loss of air pressure. The emergency system mentioned previously can be utilized in case of a failure in the service line by the use of the tractor protection valve and control valve. The driver can flip the lever of the control valve and apply all brakes on the towed vehicles.

There is another form of safety system that in normal use is a parking brake but in the event of loss of air can be used as an emergency system. It is known as a DD3 actuator. The driver has the option of using the axle on which the DD3 actuators are mounted as a parking system or as an emergency braking system by operating a push-pull button. Once this system is actuated, a mechanical lock holds the brake on, even if all air pressure is lost.

Another emergency system is the spring brake system, in which springs are used to apply the brakes if the air has been lost. As long as normal air pressure is available, the spring brake actuator is inactive and the normal brake chambers apply the brakes. The driver can place the emergency system in action at his option by means of a push-pull valve.

Although air-cooled, disk-type hand brakes on the drive shafts of heavy-duty trucks have been used for some time, it was not until recent years that experimental models for the wheels were available. In the early 1970s there was rather strong interest in antilocking brakes for articulated vehicles in order to reduce the possibility of jackknifing.

BIBLIOGRAPHY. J.H. WHERRY, *Automobiles of the World* (1968), the story of the development of the automobile, with many rare illustrations; RICHARD CRABB, *Birth of a Giant* (1969), a detailed history of the development of the United States automobile industry.

Journals: Motor Truck Facts, an annual bulletin published by the Automobile Manufacturers Association, Washington, D.C.; *Bus Facts,* an annual bulletin published by the National Association of Motor Bus Operators, Washington, D.C.; *Automobile Quarterly,* the connoisseur's magazine of motoring; *Society of Automotive Engineers Handbook* (annual). Each year annual statistical data are published in the March 15 issue of *Automotive Industries.*

(A.H.E.)

Truffaut, François

When his film *The 400 Blows* won the "best direction" prize at the 1959 Cannes Festival, François Truffaut established himself as a leader of the French cinema's *nouvelle vague* ("new wave")—a term for the simultaneous presentation of first feature films by a number of French directors—a tendency that profoundly influenced the rising generation of film makers around the world. The New Wave marked a reaction against the commercial production system: the well-constructed plot, the limitations of a merely craftsmanlike approach, and the French tradition of quality with its heavy reliance on literary sources. Its aesthetic theory required every detail of a film's style to reflect its director's sensibility as intimately as a novelist's prose style retraces the workings in depth of his mind—hence the phrase *le camera-stylo* ("camera-pen"). The emphasis lay on visual nuance, for, in keeping with a general denigration of the preconceived and the literary, the script was often treated less as a ground plan for a dramatic structure than as merely a theme for alfresco improvisation. Improvised scenes were filmed, deploying the visual flexibility of newly developed television equipment (*e.g.*, the hand-held camera) and techniques (*e.g.*, extensive postsynchronization of dialogue). The minimization of costs encouraged producers to gamble on unknown talents, and the simplicity of means gave the director close control over every aspect of the creative process, hence Truffaut's term *auteur,* or film author.

Truffaut was born in Paris on February 6, 1932, into a working-class home. His own troubled childhood provides the inspiration for *The 400 Blows,* a semi-autobiographical study of a working-class delinquent. It is the first of the Antoine Doinel trilogy, tracing its hero's evolution from an antisocial anguish to a happy and settled

By courtesy of Les Films du Carrosse

Truffaut (right) directing Jean-Pierre Léaud in *Les Deux Anglaises et le Continent,* 1971.

---

domesticity. Outside his art, Truffaut is reticent about his private life, although it is known that he was sent to a reformatory before leaving school at 14 to work in a factory. But his interest in the cinema brought him to the attention of the critic André Bazin, doyen of the monthly avant-garde film magazine *Cahiers du Cinéma*, who incorporated him into the staff. For eight years Truffaut asserted himself as the most truculent critic of the contemporary French cinema, which he considered stale and conventional, and advocated a cinema that would allow the director to write dialogue, invent stories, and, in general, produce a film as an artistic whole in his own style. Thus, he was influential in the cinema world before he actually made a film. Like his leading character in *Stolen Kisses*, another film in the Doinel series, he deserted from his military service, being committed to various prisons until he was able to resume his journalistic career and, eventually, put his ideas into creative practice. Again like Doinel in *Domicile conjugale* (*Bed and Board*), he married and became the father of two daughters.

His initial creative effort was a short slapstick comedy *Une Histoire d'eau* (1958), for which he felt unable to evolve a suitable conclusion and which he turned over to his unfailingly ingenious contemporary Jean-Luc Godard. His second short, *Les Mistons* (1958), depicting a gang of boys who thoughtlessly persecute two young lovers, met with sufficient appreciation to facilitate his first feature-length film, *The 400 Blows*. An evocation of the adolescent's pursuit of independence from a staid adult world of conformity and protocol, for which Truffaut evinced a romantic sympathy, the film proved to be one of the most popular New Wave films, especially in England and the United States. Two tenderly pessimistic studies in sexual tragedy followed, *Jules and Jim* (1961) and *Shoot the Piano Player* (1960), the latter adapted from the American thriller *Down There* by David Goodis, a genre for which Truffaut has evinced great admiration. After these three films he seems to have had a period of hestitation. His films since then, however, have all been intensely personal and are divided between two themes: studies in forlorn childhoods—*e.g.*, The Doinel trilogy and *The Wild Child* (1970), the chronicle of an 18th-century doctor who attempts to domesticate an uncivilized child; and sensitive melodramas sadly celebrating disastrous confrontations between shy heroes and boldly emancipated or possessive women. The first theme shows the influence of film maker Jean Vigo, in its uncompromising stance against authority of any kind, and of Jean Renoir, in its feeling for place and atmosphere and its mingling of the nostalgic with sudden outbursts of blatant humour, as well as of Truffaut's personal experience. The second owes much to the American *roman noir*, or "black novel," the diverse manifestations of which, from the morally disintegrated heroes of William Faulkner to the sadistic gangsters of Mickey Spillane, have fascinated French novelists from Sartre to the present. One senses a certain hero worship, also, in Truffaut's long, published conversations with the veteran American film maker Alfred Hitchcock, whose work he admires in complete defiance of his earlier theories. Of Truffaut's features only *Fahrenheit 451*, a film version of Ray Bradbury's science-fiction novel, falls outside these categories, though it relates to the American style and the poetic-melodramatic form. Through his production company, Les Films du Carrosse, Truffaut coproduced, among other films, Godard's first feature and Jean Cocteau's last.

For Truffaut, now, the cinema must be, on the one hand, personal and, on the other, a splendid spectacle, like a circus. On the one hand, childhood's vulnerability; on the other, its joys. The style of his first three films, at once delicate, lyrical, and exceptionally fertile in cinematographic invention, has become, partly by choice, more prosaic and conventional. Controversy has centred on the extent to which his films involve a militant conservatism—whether, for example, Truffaut in *The Wild Child* deplores, documents, feels nostalgic for, or positively and without reservation, approves the narrow, strict rigidities with which its psychologist (played by Truffaut

himself) sets about civilizing the abandoned, autistic child. It may be that Truffaut's inspiration is rooted in the nostalgias and despairs of his childhood, and as with success he has matured into adult and father, so his films have lost in lyricism, while maintaining their fidelity to life's prosaic side. But life's grayness and flatness are recorded with a sense of resignation and quiet achievement quite distinct from platitude or petulant nihilism.

MAJOR WORKS
Les Mistons (1958, *The Mischief-Makers*); *Les Quatre Cents Coups* (1959, *The 400 Blows*); *Tirez sur le pianiste* (1960, *Shoot the Piano Player*); *Jules et Jim* (1961, *Jules and Jim*); *La Peau douce* (1964, *Silken Skin, The Soft Skin*); *Fahrenheit 451* (1966); *La Mariée était en noir* (1968, *The Bride Wore Black*); *Baisers volés* (1968, *Stolen Kisses*); *La Sirène du Mississippi* (1969, *The Mississippi Mermaid*); *L'Enfant sauvage* (1970, *The Wild Child*); *Domicile conjugale* (1970, *Bed and Board*).

BIBLIOGRAPHY. GRAHAM PETRIE, *The Cinema of François Truffaut* (1970); and C.G. CRISP, *François Truffaut* (1972), are two useful book-length studies. In addition to TRUFFAUT's *Hitchcock* (1967), the scripts of *Les Quatre Cents Coups* (1969) and *Jules et Jim* (1968) have been translated into English.

(R.Du.)

Truman, Harry S.

In a comparison of U.S. presidents, Harry S. Truman, the 33rd president of the United States (served 1945–53), must be judged one of the strongest. Yet during his term of office his reputation was that of a man far too small for his job. Compared unfavourably by Northern Democrats with his popular predecessor, Franklin D. Roosevelt, condemned by Southern Democrats for his liberal civil rights program, and at war with Republican isolationists and economic conservatives, Truman spent a turbulent period in office. But after his term the significance of his efforts slowly became evident, especially his foreign policy goal of containing Communist expansion and his largely unsuccessful programs of social and economic reforms to raise standards of living for workers and farmers and to broaden civil rights for minorities; his continual pursuit of these goals kept them viable for future action.

The keys to Harry Truman's outlook were a Midwestern agrarianism, a suspicion of big business, and an inordinate interest in history and battles. In personality he was characterized by a low boiling point, a loyalty to his friends, an inoffensive cockiness, and native shrewdness and wariness.

Truman was born in Lamar, Missouri, on May 8, 1884, the son of a mule trader and farmer. His paternal forebears were English and first came to America in 1666. Truman attended school in Independence, Missouri. He completed high school in 1901; but he could not go to college because of family financial reverses, nor could he attend West Point because of his vision. He became a bank clerk in Kansas City; then in 1906 he took over management of his maternal grandmother's farm at Grandview. He also served as local postmaster, town road overseer, and national guardsman. He became a partner in a lead mine in 1915 and in an oil-prospecting business a year later, but both failed.

Truman distinguished himself in heavy action as a captain in World War I, showing bravery and other qualities of leadership. On June 28, 1919, he married Elizabeth Bess Wallace, an Independence girl he had known since childhood. He became a partner in a Kansas City haberdashery store; and when the business failed, he entered politics with the help of Thomas Pendergast, a Democratic boss of Jackson County.

With support of Pendergast's machine and of World War I veterans, Truman won a seat as county judge in 1922. But despite excellent work, in 1924 (the same year his daughter Margaret was born) non-Pendergast Democrats combined with the Ku Klux Klan to defeat him. Truman then sold memberships in the Kansas City Automobile Club and attended night classes for two years at the Kansas City Law School. A state bank in Englewood in which he became a partner went into bankruptcy be-

Early life

Truman, 1945.
By courtesy of the U.S. Signal Corps

cause of the fraudulent activities of its former owner; but Truman enjoyed his first business success following his organization of the Community Savings & Loan Association in Independence.

With Tom Pendergast's backing, in 1926 he became presiding judge of the county court. As a two-term, eight-year county administrator, Truman's reputation for **Reputation** honesty and good management gained him Republican as **for honesty** well as Democratic support. Meanwhile, Pendergast was gaining dictatorial control over Jackson County; he achieved statewide power in the early 1930s, determining who would serve as Missouri's governor and as its members of the U.S. House of Representatives. That Truman was not in his inner circle was revealed in 1932 when Pendergast stifled his ambition to become governor and refused to name him to the Missouri delegation to the Democratic National Convention.

In 1934 Truman's political career seemed ended because of the two-term tradition attached to his job. But the machine's gangsterism in the March municipal election, in which four persons were killed at the polls, had a direct bearing on his future. After three individuals rejected Pendergast's subsequent offer of support in the coming U.S. Senate primary contest, Truman, his fourth choice, quickly accepted. Truman was elected with the help of a suspicious machine vote in Jackson County.

Truman entered the U.S. Senate in 1935 under the cloud of being the puppet of a crooked boss. But his attention to duties and his friendly personality soon won over his colleagues. He was the author of the Civil Aeronautics Act of 1938, and his two-year committee investigation led to the Transportation Act of 1940. The outlook for Truman's re-election in 1940, however, was gloomy; the Pendergast machine lay in shambles, with Tom Pendergast in prison for having taken bribes. President Roosevelt offered Truman a face-saving place on the Interstate Commerce Commission, but he stubbornly ran for another term even though newspapers rated him a distant third in a three-man primary race. Yet because of the last-minute support of Robert E. Hannegan, a young St. Louis Democratic subboss, Truman won by a slender margin.

The nation's growing defense and then war production programs soon launched Truman into his major senatorial endeavour. His Special Committee Investigating National Defense exposed a long list of graft, waste, and product deficiencies and brought him public praise. At the same time, he used his expanding patronage power to reward Hannegan with a series of appointments. The advancement of Hannegan to chairman of the Democratic National Committee in January 1944 led to a successful effort to have Roosevelt replace Vice Pres. Henry A. Wallace with Truman on the victorious 1944 presidential ticket. Truman's vice presidency lasted only 82 days, during which time he met with Roosevelt only twice and had little knowledge of the administration's programs and plans. Roosevelt died on April 12, 1945. Truman was a month away from his 61st birthday when he took the **Succession** presidential oath of office. Vital decisions had to be made **to the** at a relentless pace, despite his lack of tutelage. In swift **presidency** order he made final arrangements for the San Francisco charter-writing meeting of the United Nations, helped arrange Germany's unconditional surrender on May 8, and went in July to his first and only summit meeting, at Potsdam, Germany, for inconclusive talks about a peace settlement. The Pacific war ended officially on September 2, after atomic bombs had been dropped on the Japanese cities of Hiroshima and Nagasaki following Truman's orders. His justification for the bombings was a report from advisers that 500,000 Americans would be lost in an invasion of Japan.

Truman enjoyed a five-month honeymoon with Congress, which ended in September 1945 when he submitted his "Economic Bill of Rights," which included social reforms that he hoped would head off a return to economic depression. The developing vocal opposition, added to public weariness over meat shortages and inflation and the defection of Roosevelt admirers when Truman installed his own choices in his Cabinet, combined to give Republicans control of Congress in 1946. Two years later many Democratic leaders believed Truman could not win election and demanded that he retire. But the 1948 convention nominated him, with Sen. Alben W. Barkley as his running mate. All public opinion polls showed that the New York governor Thomas E. Dewey, the Republican nominee, would be an easy winner. Undaunted, Truman carried out a "give 'em hell" campaign, repeatedly denouncing the "Republican do-nothing 80th Congress." In November he upset a complacent Dewey by a 114-electoral-vote margin.

In his State of the Union message in 1949, Truman proposed the Fair Deal, a liberal 24-plank domestic program. But despite his efforts, only a single plank was enacted into law—a low-cost public housing measure. He fared much better in foreign affairs, however, where he considered the Soviet Union the principal roadblock to world peace. To restrict Soviet territorial advances and spreading spheres of influence, he developed a "containment" policy, thus setting the course of U.S. foreign policy for decades to come. Among his Cold War moves were the Truman Doctrine of economic and military aid to Greece and Turkey in 1947 to reduce Communist pressures on their governments; the four-year $17,-000,000,000 Marshall Plan of 1948 for economic recovery in western Europe; and the North Atlantic Treaty Organization (NATO) pact of 1949, a collective security agreement with non-Communist European nations. When China came under Communist control in 1949, Truman's containment policies were extended to include that giant nation. He also established the Central Intelligence Agency (CIA) in 1947, initiated the Berlin airlift of 1948 to bring supplies into the former German capital when the Soviets blocked surface entrances, instituted the Point Four Program of 1949 to provide aid to underdeveloped countries, and decided in 1950 to construct the hydrogen bomb in order to maintain an arms lead over the Soviets, who had recently exploded an atomic bomb.

In June 1950 Communist North Korea crossed the 38th **Outbreak** parallel boundary and attempted to seize South Korea. **of the** Truman sent U.S. forces to Korea under Gen. Douglas **Korean** MacArthur with UN sanction. Once MacArthur had lib- **War** erated the south, the administration ordered the capture of North Korea; but MacArthur's advance to the Yalu River boundary with Manchuria brought hundreds of thousands of Chinese Communist troops into the fighting. MacArthur's insistence on attacking China as well forced Truman to fire him.

The unpopularity of the continuing war and the uncovering of unsavoury and fraudulent activities by several federal officials made Truman's last two years in office appear chaotic. A further decline of confidence in the government was brought on by the charges of Sen. Joseph R. McCarthy of Wisconsin that the State Department and other agencies were Communist-controlled.

After Truman left office in January 1953 and returned to Independence, his popularity soared. And with the perspective of passing years the haze surrounding his presidency lifted. What remained was a man who had generally succeeded in his foreign policy and a president who, as Harry Truman himself once put it, had "done his damndest." He died on December 26, 1972, in Kansas City, Missouri, and was buried at the Truman Library grounds in Independence, Missouri.

BIBLIOGRAPHY. ALFRED STEINBERG, *The Man from Missouri* (1962), covers Truman's life and activities through his presidency. Other biographies are JONATHAN DANIELS, *The Man of Independence* (1950), which contains a good account of Truman's early career; and CABELL PHILLIPS, *The Truman Presidency* (1966), a complete study. WILLIAM HILLMAN, *Mr. President* (1952), has letters and excerpts from Truman's diaries. WILLIAM M. REDDIG, *Tom's Town, Kansas City and the Pendergast Legend* (1947), is the best work on the Pendergast machine. DONALD H. RIDDLE, *The Truman Committee* (1964), deals with the Senate period; TRISTRAM COFFIN, *Missouri Compromise* (1947), presents a picture of the early Truman presidency; TOM CONNALLY and ALFRED STEINBERG, *My Name Is Tom Connally* (1954), relates aspects of the unfolding Cold War. See also HARRY S. TRUMAN, *Memoirs*, 2 vol. (1955–56); *Public Papers of the Presidents: Harry S. Truman, 1945–53*, 8 vol. (1961–66), the best collection of source materials; and MARGARET TRUMAN, *Harry S. Truman* (1973), a candid, readable account that was written by his daughter.

(A.Sg.)

Trusts, Law of

The trust is one of the most comprehensive institutions of modern law, being rivalled in scope and flexibility only by the limited company, or corporation. Although there are many different kinds of trusts, they all include the feature that a person who is called the trustee has vested in him property that he is bound by an equitable obligation to hold and, in many cases, to administer on behalf of other persons or institutions, who are termed beneficiaries, though the trustee himself may be one of them. There may be a trust of any property that is capable of being owned or transferred.

An increasing number of the world's legal systems now recognize, in a variety of forms, the institution of the trust; but for many centuries its development was one of the principal achievements of Anglo-American law.

HISTORICAL DEVELOPMENT

The "use" of medieval England

The predecessor of the modern trust was the medieval "use," the creation of which can be traced to the limitations and burdens imposed upon landowners of freehold land by the feudal common law in England. Until the 16th century there could not be a will of freeholds at common law, but the practice grew up of transferring the land to another, termed the feoffor to uses, who undertook to hold it for purposes declared by the feoffor (that is, the grantor). This transaction was employed not only as a legitimate method of providing for property management and for conveyancing, however, but also as a method of defrauding creditors, depriving feudal landlords of their dues, and permitting religious institutions to derive the benefit of land that they could not own directly. For about 150 years the carrying out of the use depended on the conscience of the person entrusted with the property, because there was no writ by which the common-law courts could enforce it. Toward the end of the 14th century, however, the chancellor who administered equity began to issue decrees for its enforcement, and the use changed from a merely honorary to an enforceable obligation.

The loss of feudal revenue to the feudal lords and, particularly, to the king as the ultimate overlord was the principal reason for the passing of the Statute of Uses (1535), which was intended to abolish the use. Through interpretations and court decisions, however, some types of use escaped the operation of the statute; and, in any event, the statute set in motion changes in the transfer of land. It came to pass that a greater variety of legal estates could be created than had previously been possible at law; and, although the statute destroyed the possibility of making a will to uses, the subsequent Statute of Wills (1540) for the first time permitted a legal will of freehold land. Furthermore, in the next 200 years all the main features of the modern trust were established by the decisions of the courts of equity.

The appearance of the modern trust

Although the modern trust is derived from the medieval use, there are important differences between the two institutions. The use was developed in respect to land. The trust is applicable to all forms of property and particularly to commercial securities of all kinds. Further, the great majority of uses were passive; that is, the feoffee was not expected to act in relation to the land but had to allow the beneficiary to administer it. The vast majority of modern trusts are active—the trustee administers the property—and in consequence the courts of equity have developed a body of equitable rules defining the administrative powers of the trustee. These relate to trustee investments—the power to sell, lease, or mortgage trust property; the powers of maintenance and advancement of beneficiaries; the power to appoint agents; and numerous other matters. During the last century many of these rules have been embodied in statutes in the United Kingdom, the United States, and the countries of the Commonwealth.

One of the most striking features of the law of trusts during the present century has been its progressive extension in some civil-law countries, such as Mexico and Cuba, as well as in all English-speaking countries that have adopted to some degree the common law.

THE CHARACTERISTICS OF TRUSTS

Elements involved in a trust. Certain features are always found in a trust.

Settlor. The settlor is so called because early trusts in England were created in marriage and other settlements. He is the person who owns property and goes through the acts necessary to create a trust of it.

Trust property. There can be no trust without identified property to which the trust is to attach, which is called the trust property or subject matter. It may consist, for example, of real property, stocks, bonds, mortgages, insurance policies, a bank account, or real estate.

Trustee. Although a trustee is not necessary in order that a trust be created (the court will supply one if none is named by the settlor), the trust cannot be carried out without some person in whom title to the trust property can be vested and who can perform the acts of trust administration. There may be two or more trustees. These are usually persons in whom the settlor has confidence (relatives, friends, or business associates) or corporations to whom the power to carry out trusts has been given by statute (banks and trust companies). A person who is named as trustee may decline or accept, as he chooses. After acceptance he may resign (usually by court permission, but in England, under statutory provisions, usually requiring consent of his co-trustees); he may be removed by the court if he has committed serious breaches of trust or if his continuance greatly endangers the welfare of the beneficiaries. In the United States, in most cases before a trustee can act, he must go through certain formalities called qualification—for example, filing a surety bond. Corporate trustees are generally excused by statute from giving a bond, but they are required to deposit a security fund with a public official to guarantee their responsibility.

The role of the trustee

In England, under the Public Trustee Act (1906), and in certain other jurisdictions, an official has been appointed to undertake the work of trustee. Fees are charged, but the settlors and beneficiaries are offered the advantage of a state guarantee against loss. The institution is useful in offering a trustee who can be appointed when there is no other suitable candidate.

Beneficiary. No private trust can exist without beneficiaries who are identifiable legal entities (natural persons or corporations) or a class of persons (such as children of the settlor). Although the beneficiaries must be described with certainty at the beginning of the trust, provision may be made for the addition of new beneficiaries as persons are born and other events happen; and so the group may shift in membership from time to time, as long as all are clearly identifiable at any particular time.

Trust instrument. The trust instrument is the document in which the settlor expresses his intent to have a trust and describes its provisions. It usually consists of a deed or a will.

The varieties of trust. *Express trusts.* An express trust arises as a result of the deliberate act of the creator of the trust. It is an equitable institution for which no particular form is generally required, so long as the intention to create a trust is plainly manifested. Particular statutes may nevertheless impose requirements for particular kinds of trust. Thus Section 53(1) of England's Law of Property Act (1925) provides that all declarations of trust of land or of any interest in land shall be "manifested and proved" by some writing signed by the declarer. It is not necessary that this writing should come into existence at the time when the trust is created. It is sufficient if it exists when steps are taken to enforce the trust. This statute relates primarily to trusts created inter vivos—that is, by a person during his lifetime. It is, however, a common practice for a testator to establish a trust by his will, usually for the benefit of his family. When this occurs, the creation of the trust must satisfy the requirements of the law of wills in the country where the testamentary disposition is made. In England, for example, the Wills Act (1837) requires all testamentary acts to be in writing, signed by the testator at the foot or end of the will, and attested by the signatures of two witnesses (neither of whom may receive a benefit under the will).

When the instrument establishing a trust sets out all the beneficial limitations that the settlor intends, or when it provides the machinery whereby these limitations can be determined (as, for example, when the settlor gives the trustees power to divide among a class of beneficiaries in such proportion as they should decide), the trust is said to be executed, and the court will construe its terms in accordance with the general rules applicable to documents of this kind. This situation means that if the settlor uses such technical terms as "heirs" or "next of kin," they will be given the meaning that the law of property attaches to these terms.

Executed, executory, and discretionary trusts

Contrasted with the executed trust is that which is executory. Executory trusts are created by more than one document. The first usually does no more than transfer property to trustees, indicating the general purposes for which they will hold it. At a later date a more elaborate trust instrument is prepared, setting out in detail the objects for which the trust is being created. An employer, for example, might transfer a block of shares to trustees for the purpose of establishing a pension fund for his employees; or the parents of two persons engaged to be married might transfer property to trustees for the benefit of the spouses and their issue. In the latter case, a trust instrument would normally come into existence only after the marriage was celebrated. In both cases the transfer of property would be sufficient to establish the trust, and the court, in construing it, would seek to give effect to the general intention of the settlor.

Modern trust instruments frequently create discretionary trusts. In these the trustees have complete discretion to apply trust funds within a specified class of persons—the shares that each member of the class takes being determined from time to time by the trustees. If the class is within a family, the discretion will enable the trustees to take into account the needs of the family at times after the trust has come into existence and also to accommodate the effects of changing taxation upon the shares taken by beneficiaries.

Implied trusts. A number of trusts come into existence as a consequence of the operation of equitable presumptions. They are, therefore, trusts implied by law. Thus, if A provides the purchase money for a house and the conveyance is taken in the name of B, then in the absence of any expressed intention, the law implies that B holds as a trustee for A (unless A is the father or husband of B, in which case there is a presumption that A wished to confer a benefit on B). One special variety of an implied trust is a resulting trust. This situation arises whenever there is a disposition of the whole interest in the property at law to trustees without a complete disposition of the beneficial interest in equity. If property is transferred to A, for example, on trust to pay the income to B for life, with no instruction about what is to happen on B's death, then on B's death A will hold the property on a resulting trust for the settlor. A similar presumption will operate when property is transferred to A with a direction to pay specified amounts of the income to various beneficiaries and, after these payments have been made, there is surplus income. This again will be held on trust for the settlor.

Constructive trusts. The term constructive trust is applied to a wide variety of relationships, the common element in which is the imposition by courts of equity of an obligation to hold property for the benefit of another, independently of the wishes of the person in whom the property is vested. Thus, for example, if a trustee (who is legally forbidden from making a profit from his trust unless expressly permitted to do so by the settlor) profits by misuse of trust property, the courts will direct that he hold that profit on a constructive trust for the beneficiary. In general, anyone who stands in a fiduciary relationship to another (such as a guardian, a solicitor, or other confidential agent) will become a constructive trustee of any property acquired by misuse of his position. In England a constructive trust is regarded as a special variety of trust—that is, a relationship between trustee and beneficiary. In the United States, a constructive trust is generally applicable to anyone who is found in possession of property that he is not entitled to retain, and the remedy is available to any person who is entitled to its recovery.

Remedies against the trustee profitting from the trust

Statutory trusts. Modern statutes have in some cases created trusts as a means of facilitating the holding or devolution of property. Thus, on the death of a person intestate, his personal representatives may hold his estate on a statutory trust for his issue and certain other classes of relatives. Or if there should be a conveyance of a legal estate to an infant jointly with one or more adults, the adults will serve as trustees for themselves and the infant (because the infant himself cannot hold a legal estate in land). Also, when there is a conveyance of land to a number of persons as joint tenants or tenants in common, four out of the total may act as trustees for all.

Public and private trusts. As the name suggests, public trusts are trusts that benefit the public or some general class within it, such as the members of a profession or the inhabitants of a locality. The most numerous and important trusts within this class are charitable trusts, but there are others that are not charitable, such as a trust for a golf club or a trade association.

Because charitable trusts are allowed to continue indefinitely and are granted many other privileges (such as freedom from taxation), it often becomes important to decide whether a trust purpose involves substantial social advantages and is therefore technically charitable or is a private trust. Certain purposes are admittedly charitable, as, for example, the advancement of education and scientific research, the prevention or cure of disease, the relief of poverty, and the support of religion. According to Lord Macnaughten (in the Pemsel case, 1891) there is another class of charitable gifts "for other purposes beneficial to the community." In this class may be cited gifts to furnish governmental services and to beautify towns and cities. Among borderline cases may be placed gifts for cemeteries and monuments, generally not charitable at common law but made so by many statutes, though not in England; the furnishing of recreation and amusement, not charitable in England until the enactment of the Recreational Charities Act, 1958, but approved in the

Charitable trusts

United States; and the protection and care of animals, charitable if for domestic animals in general but not if for particular animals or for wild animals that are hostile to man. Trusts to aid a political party are not charitable.

The social benefit involved in a charity must be substantial. Hence the aid of a business enterprise that has small incidental public advantages is not charitable. The views of the courts as to what is charity are controlling and not the opinion of the settlor. At one time in England religious trusts were not charitable unless for the benefit of the established church, but toleration acts have changed the law, and now the advancement of any religion not contrary to current morality is charitable. In the United States the support of any religion would probably be sustained as charitable.

THE FUNCTIONS OF TRUSTS

Family provision. One of the main objects of the development of the law of trusts has been to provide machinery whereby a settlor may make provision for the successive members of his family to the extent that the law will permit. This purpose is emphasized by the fact that trusts may be made either during life or by will to take effect on death and frequently involve strict settlement of land.

One form of trust that is often executed by a living donor is the marriage settlement, either on his own marriage or on the marriage of a member of his family. By such a settlement, property is usually given to trustees for the benefit of the husband and wife during their joint lives; thereafter for the survivor for his or her life; and finally for division among their children or remote issue upon attainment of a specified age.

Trusts arising by will are exceedingly common and often take the form of a trust for sale. By such a trust, the trustees are directed to sell all the testator's assets to pay his debts and to invest the proceeds in income-bearing trustee securities for the beneficiaries. These will usually be the surviving spouse for the remainder of his or her life, and thereafter for the children or remoter issue of the testator in equal shares. In default of children, there may be other trusts for remoter relatives.

The dominating motive in establishing a family trust is to give financial security to one's close relatives. At various times, therefore, there have evolved a number of devices for their protection. These may be inserted by the settlor, but in some systems of law they are now recognized by statute. In general, for instance, an infant beneficiary under trust may not directly touch his interest because he lacks legal capacity. The trustees thus have discretionary powers to use his income for his maintenance, education, and benefit, irrespective of whether he has parents bound by law to support him. If, at any time, there is an excess of income after the infant has been maintained, this is used as capital and is invested.

All modern systems of law make special provision for the protection of persons of unsound mind; but most of them also make it possible for the property to be protected by means of a trust, in which the trustees enjoy wide discretionary powers to employ income and, if necessary, capital for the maintenance and benefit of such persons. The property of irresponsible persons may also be protected in a similar way. In England this is achieved through the establishment of a protective trust, by means of which the interest of the beneficiary vests in the trustees on a discretionary trust for his benefit. In the United States most jurisdictions permit the same end to be achieved by means of a spendthrift trust or spendthrift clause, which often confines the beneficiary to the enjoyment of the income of his property only as it falls due.

The high incidence of modern taxation has given a new importance to the trust, as it has become the chief instrument of estate planning. Moreover, in England the Variation of Trusts Act (1958) has given beneficiaries and trustees the right to apply to the courts for the modification of trust dispositions; one reason for such an application is the desire to frame new limitations making taxation (possibly introduced after the settlement was made) less severe.

Social functions. A very wide variety of social and public purposes may be achieved by way of trusts. Social clubs, trade unions, and philanthropic organizations of all kinds commonly hold their property in this way, the trustees representing the institution so far as the outside world is concerned. Possibly the most important trusts within this class are the charitable trusts mentioned earlier. In these cases the beneficiaries are not identifiable persons because society as a whole is presumed to be the beneficiary of such a trust, and any human beings who are involved are merely conduits through whom the advantages flow to the state. Thus in the case of a trust to aid the poor, the impoverished individuals chosen yearly by the trustees to receive trust income are not the beneficiaries; rather society, which is benefitted by the relief of poverty, is considered the beneficiary.

Charity in the legal sense is a technical concept that has proved difficult to define with precision. The Statute of Charitable Uses (1601) enumerated a number of purposes considered charitable at that date, but even that was not exhaustive. In *Commissioners of Income Tax* v. *Pemsel*, decided by the British House of Lords in 1891, charitable trusts were classified as (1) trusts for the advancement of education, (2) trusts for the advancement of religion, (3) trusts for the relief of poverty, and (4) trusts for other purposes beneficial to the community, not falling under any of the other three heads. This decision has been generally followed, but it should be added that not all purposes beneficial to the community are charitable and that words such as philanthropic or benevolent are wider than charitable, and, accordingly, trusts established for such purposes may not stand up.

There are many trusts for social purposes that cannot take effect as charities, either because they do not benefit the public generally, or some public section of it, or because their trust deeds include both charitable and noncharitable objects. Such trusts must therefore conform to the law governing private trusts, and in particular the objects for which they exist must be certain.

Commercial functions. In modern times trusts have been used increasingly in a variety of ways in commercial life. A principal service of trust companies for business corporations, for example, is to act as trustees for their bond issues. As trustee under a corporate bond indenture, a trust company takes title to or a lien upon any property that may be put up as security, certifies the genuineness of each bond, observes whether or not the corporation continues to fulfill its obligations as set forth in the indenture, and takes action to protect the bondholders should the corporation default upon these obligations. Usually, it also manages whatever sinking fund the corporation provides for the redemption of the bonds and makes the interest and principal payments to the bondholders out of funds supplied by the corporation. In a comparable capacity, trust companies serve as trustees for equipment-trust certificates issued on behalf of railroad companies to acquire locomotives and cars.

Another important service of trust companies for business corporations is to act as trustees for their employee profit-sharing and pension plans. Depending upon the terms of these plans, the trust companies invest the funds in securities or use them to buy annuity contracts from life insurance companies.

Another complicated modern development has been the business-insurance trust, evolved for the purposes of minimizing taxation and at the same time ensuring the transmission of a business enterprise, or a major holding in such an enterprise, to one or more persons (possibly a relative or an associate) on death of the settlor.

TRUSTS IN CIVIL-LAW SYSTEMS

Neither Roman law nor modern legal systems directly or remotely derived from it have evolved the trust with its highly developed operation; that is, they have not determined the trustee's right to administer property distinct from the beneficiary's right to enjoy it. This situation is partly a carry over of the Roman concept of property, which did not readily lend itself to this conception of dual ownership; but it is also a reflection of the fact that

Trusts in marital settlements and in wills

Protective and spendthrift trusts

Corporate trusts

Roman law systems have developed fiduciary institutions for somewhat similar purposes in a different way.

In old Germanic law, the absence of the capacity to make a will was supplied by the practice of conveying property to an individual called a *Salmann*, who undertook to comply with the donor's instructions with regard to its disposition. Normally there would be a reservation of a life interest to the donor. By this transaction the *Salmann* became the legal owner of the property, subject to a fiduciary obligation to carry out the donor's instructions. (In this institution it is possible to discover the origin of the executor and the administrator in English law.) When the influence of Roman law was revived in Germany in the 19th century, however, the functions of the testamentary executor were limited, and there developed the concept of the *Treuhänd* as an institution not necessarily connected with the law of succession. By this institution property is once again transferred to the ownership of the *Treuhänder* for a declared purpose. If he seeks to act contrary to that purpose he will not succeed in transferring the property, and the settlor has a personal right against him for any loss. Some legal writers have argued that the *Treuhänd* is a conveyance of property subject to resolutive conditions. Thus if the *Treuhänder* commits a breach of trust, or the purposes for which the trust was created fail, the settlor can recover the property. So far as the beneficiary is concerned, his right is limited to seeking the performance of the *Treuhänder*'s obligation in his favour. Unlike the beneficiary under a trust, he has no right against the trust property itself.

In Roman law systems, primary obligations on behalf of others were imposed by what was called a *fiducia*—a two-stage transaction in which (1) ownership of the property was conveyed to the fiduciary, and (2) the fiduciary agreed to use his right only for the attainment of the purpose for which the conveyance had been made, with a further undertaking to reconvey when the purpose had been fulfilled. In the later Roman law and in modern systems there has been extensive development of this fideicommissum, as it came to be called. It was originally a means of circumventing the rule that only Roman citizens could be established as heirs, but it became widely used to settle property on death. It differs from the trust on several counts: (1) Whereas the trustee's legal ownership and the beneficiary's equitable ownership are concurrent, the fideicommissary's ownership commences only when that of the fiduciary ends, and vice versa. (2) Thus the fideicommissum does not distinguish between legal and equitable estate, as does the trust. (3) The rights of the fideicommissary, once vested, are good against the whole world, and another fiduciary cannot destroy or burden it by alienation or charge—which is not always true under trusts. (4) The fideicommissum almost always arises by testamentary act, though in some Roman law systems, such as that of The Netherlands, there does seem a trend toward creating them inter vivos in marriage settlements.

Another civil-law concept sometimes compared with the trust is the hypothec. This is a charge of one person over the property of another. Hypothecs exist for a wide variety of purposes, such as security for a debt, but they are also used to protect a person's rights over property in fiduciary or quasi-fiduciary situations. Thus in French civil law, a married woman has a hypothec over the property of a husband to protect her marital right of property; and a ward has a similar hypothec on the property of the guardian.

Charitable purposes in the civil law. Gifts for charitable purposes have been treated in the civil law in a way quite distinct from that of Anglo-American law. In the latter, the prospective benefactor may (1) give the property to an existing institution or foundation, relying on the terms of the latter's trust deed or character of incorporation to secure fulfillment of his wishes; or (2) he may transfer the property to trustees to apply it to the organization; or (3) he may find it necessary to establish a trust for a new institution, founded directly to carry out his instructions. In the civil law there is a close analogy to the first method; property may be transferred to an exist-

The
concept of
Treuhänd

The
concept of
fideicommissum

ing foundation that will become subject to a charge to carry out the donor's instructions. This was in fact the sole means of making gifts to charity in classical Roman law.

Other ways of making charitable gifts have been devised in systems derived from, or influenced by, Roman law. German law took advantage of the concept of the *Treuhänd*, making the church itself the *Treuhänder*. In more recent German law and in some other systems, the donor achieves his object frequently by creating a new foundation as an alternative to presenting an existing institution with a gift that may be subject to charge. Under modern German law there are provisions regulating the creation of a *Stiftung*, or charitable foundation, which has corporate personality. Every *Stiftung* must have a board of directors (*Vorstand*) through which it acts; but while the membership of the board may change, the *Stiftung* itself is unaffected. In Anglo-American law there has been development of a similar kind in the creation of a corporate trusteeship for some large charities.

The
German
Stiftung

The reception of the trust in civil-law countries. Some civil-law writers have raised objections to the idea of introducing the trust itself; basically, they feel that the civil law of property does not lend itself readily to the concept of dual ownership, which is fundamental to the trust, with its division of rights over the property between trustee and beneficiary. Laymen, too, seem particularly disturbed by the separation of the trustee's right to administer property from the beneficiary's right to enjoy it. From the point of view of the civil law, whoever has the beneficial enjoyment of property is its owner and has the right to freely dispose of it. Taking the right of property disposal away from an owner (as thus conceived) would appear to violate civil-law rules. These difficulties appear more plainly in French law than in many other civil-law systems, some of which have even given statutory definitions to the rights that are enjoyed specifically by trustee and beneficiary.

One striking feature of modern legal development has nevertheless been the reception of the trusts in numerous countries with a civil-law background. It has been introduced into Sri Lanka (formerly Ceylon) and South Africa, which have basically the Roman–Dutch system of law, and it has been adopted in the civil-law systems of Quebec, Liechtenstein, Panama, Puerto Rico, Mexico, and Venezuela. The reception has been influenced especially in Mexico by the works of the French writer P. Lepaulle, whose treatise *Traité théorique et practique des trusts*, published in 1932, did much to explain to lawyers trained in the civil law the nature of the institution and of the rights and duties that it gave.

BIBLIOGRAPHY. An account of the historical development of uses and trusts is contained in SIR W. HOLDSWORTH, *History of English Law*, vol. 4 and 6. The most complete accounts of the modern law of trusts in England, written primarily for practitioners, may be found in T. LEWIN, *Lewin on Trusts*, 16th ed. (1964); and SIR A. UNDERHILL, *Law Relating to Trusts and Trustees*, 12th ed. (1970). The two leading American treatises are: A.W. SCOTT, *The Law of Trusts*, 3rd ed. (1967); and G.G. BOGERT, *Handbook of the Law of Trusts*, 4th ed. (1963). D.W. WATERS, *The Constructive Trust* (1964), is a valuable comparison of English and American views of this institution.

The trust in Scotland is traced in T.B. SMITH, *The Trust in the Civil Law* (1962). The trust was introduced by statute into India and Ceylon (now Sri Lanka) during British rule; the *Indian Trust Act 1882* is discussed by AGGARWAL (2nd ed., 1954); and L.J.M. COORAY, *Reception in Ceylon of the English Trust* (1971), is a valuable discussion of the trust in Ceylon (now Sri Lanka), in comparison with the fideicommissum, which was derived from Roman-Dutch law. Similarly, in South Africa, where Roman-Dutch law is again the basic law, the English trust was introduced during British rule; it is acutely discussed by A.M. HONORE, *The South African Law of Trusts* (1966). The only modern work on the trust in New Zealand is that by P. NEVILL, *Concise Law of Trusts, Wills and Administration in New Zealand*, 2nd ed. (1957).

Many articles on the trust in civil-law countries are scattered through legal journals, but among major works, P.G. LEPAULLE, *Traité théorique et practique des trusts . . .* (1932), is essential first reading. Two Swiss discussions are: MAX BRUNNER, *Wesen und Bedeutung der englisch–amerikanischen Treu-*

händ (1931); and CLAUDE RAYMOND, *Le trust et le droit Suisse* (1954). Generally, for civil-law countries, two important works are: F. WEISER, *Trusts on the Continent of Europe* (1936); and K.W. RYAN, "The Law of Trusts," in *An Introduction to the Civil Law* (1962).

(G.W.K.)

Tseng Kuo-fan

The official most responsible for suppressing the Taiping Rebellion (1850–64), and hence, the saviour of the Ch'ing dynasty (1644–1911), Tseng Kuo-fan was a follower of Confucius, China's most famous teacher and philosopher, and actually applied the Master's principles.

Early career in civil service. Tseng Kuo-fan was born on November 26, 1811, in Hsiang-hsiang, in eastern Hunan Province, some 200 miles inland from China's south coast. His prosperous family was dominated by his grandfather, Tseng Yü-p'ing, a farmer with social ambitions. Tseng Kuo-fan passed the prefectural examination in 1833, one year after his father had succeeded at his 17th attempt. The next year, he passed the provincial examination and, after failing the metropolitan examination at the capital in 1835, finally passed in 1838.

By courtesy of the National Palace Museum, Taipei, Taiwan, Republic of China

Tseng Kuo-fan, portrait by an unknown artist. In the National Palace Museum, Taipei, Taiwan.

The *chin-shih* ("doctorate degree") led to appointment to the Hanlin Academy, a body of the most outstanding scholars in the country, which performed literary tasks for the court, and Tseng served continuously in the capital for over 13 years. He was introduced to the writings of such philosophers of the Sung dynasty as Ch'eng Hao, Ch'eng I, and Chu Hsi, and he always remained devoted to interpreting the Confucian Classics.

Tseng's intellectual progress helped his political career. He was soon appointed junior vice president of the Board of Ceremonies, serving later as vice president of the Boards of Defense, Works, Justice, and Finance. Tseng was, nevertheless, bored with his routine life and wanted to help the people more substantially. In 1850, 1851, and early in 1852, he repeatedly submitted memorials criticizing the Emperor's personal behaviour, the government's financial policy, and Imperial treatment of an outspoken official.

Military exploits. In 1852, Tseng Kuo-fan's mother died, and, in accordance with prevailing custom, he asked permission to observe the three-year mourning period at home. This granted, he was soon called into service again when the Taiping rebels, who had taken up arms in 1850, had by 1852 reached the fertile Yangtze River Valley in

south central China, seriously threatening the Ch'ing dynasty's survival. The rebellion, a great religious–political upheaval, eventually caused the loss of some 20,000,000 lives and was the greatest threat the Ch'ing dynasty had ever faced. Tseng joined the local defense forces in Hunan early in 1853, gradually shouldering more and more responsibility for the rebellion's suppression.

This was accomplished in 1864, owing largely to the intense conflicts among the Taiping leadership but also partly to Tseng's own leadership and perseverance. He had suffered two serious naval defeats in 1854, had been surrounded by enemy troops at Ch'i-men (some 130 miles west of the coast at Hang-chou) in 1861, and had frequently lacked adequate finance and staff, but, nonetheless, he fought on for 12 years.

During his campaign Tseng concluded that ethics alone were insufficient for politics and that leadership necessitated compromise with subordinates' vainglorious greed. Thus, on resuming military responsibilities in July 1858, having stayed at home for a mere one and one-half years —this time to mourn his father—he conscientiously answered letters, received petitioners, and magnanimously, though selectively, recommended subordinates for promotion. Consequently, he became very popular with his army, though still maintaining discipline.

Compromise with lobbying

Later administrative activity. Victory over the Taiping rebels in 1864 was the climax of his career. Thereafter, he was mainly an administrator, serving twice as governor general of Chiang-nan and Chiang-hsi (about 100 miles inland from the southeast coast) and once as governor of Chihli. Between May 1865 and October 1866 he again assumed military command in order to quell the Nien Rebellion that took place in northern China, but was compelled to resign after criticism by government censors.

Tseng never had an opportunity to work at the capital again after 1864, but his prestige, power, and open-mindedness enabled him to make important changes. Li Hung-chang, his protégé, gained tremendous power in the government, power that few other Chinese officials ever held and that, when passed on to the official Yüan Shih-k'ai, finally led to the collapse of the Ch'ing dynasty. (When the dynasty fell, Yüan Shih-k'ai served as president of the Republic of China.) With Tseng's support, Jung Hung, a graduate of Yale University in the United States, established an ironwork in Shanghai that later became the Chiang-nan Arsenal and is still a shipbuilding centre. It was upon Tseng's recommendation, too, that the government introduced student education overseas.

Tseng had four younger brothers, four sisters, two sons and five daughters. He treated them affectionately and frequently wrote them letters relating his experiences. Despite his contributions to the modernization of China, his views toward women were rather old-fashioned: family harmony was to be achieved by women's tolerance of masculine supremacy.

Tseng died in Nanking (some 100 miles upriver from the Yangtze's mouth on China's east coast) on March 12, 1872, and was given the posthumous title of Wen-Cheng, the highest title given to civil officials under the Ch'ing dynasty.

Since the 1920s, Tseng's role in history has caused controversy. Conservatives, such as the Kuomintang (KMT), or Nationalist Chinese, leaders, after 1928, hailed him as a symbol of Confucianism and a model of moral cultivation, while revolutionaries, including several founders of the Kuomintang and most of the Communist leaders, bitterly criticized him for nationalist reasons. He was essentially a Confucian without being dogmatically conservative in policy, and it was with the philosophy of the ancient reformer that his deepest loyalties lay.

BIBLIOGRAPHY. WILLIAM JAMES HAIL, *Tseng Kuo-fan and the Taiping Rebellion* (1927), helpful in understanding Tseng Kuo-fan's career as the supreme commander of the Hsiang braves who suppressed the Taiping Rebellion—very critical toward the rebels (outdated in many respects); TENG SSU-YU, "Tseng Kuo-fan," in ARTHUR W. HUMMEL (ed.), *Eminent Chinese of the Ch'ing Period (1644–1912),* vol. 2, pp. 751–756 (1944), a succinct but very useful biography of Tseng

Confucian influences

Kuo-fan, describing the most important events in Tseng's life; SHEN CHEN HAN-YIN, "Tseng Kuo-fan in Peking, 1840–1852: His Ideas on Statecraft and Reform," *Journal of Asian Studies*, 27:61–80 (1967), a detailed description and analysis of Tseng Kuo-fan's political career in Peking and the development of his thought during that period; WILHELM HELLMUT, "The Background of Tseng Kuo-fan's Ideology," *Asiatische Studien*, 3:90–100 (1949), a succinct analysis of Tseng Kuo-fan's political ideas.

(S.Y.H.)

Tsinghai

Tsinghai (Ching-hai in Pin-yin romanization), a province of northwestern China in the Tibetan Highlands, has an average elevation of 13,000 feet (4,000 metres). It is bounded on the north and east by Kansu, on the southeast by Szechwan, on the south and west by the Tibetan Autonomous Region, and on the west and north by the Sinkiang Uighur Autonomous Region. The province, a historic home of nomadic herdsmen, is noted for its horse breeding; recent geological surveys have given it new prominence as a source of both oil and coal.

The province derives its name from a large lake, the Ch'ing Hai (Blue Lake), which is conventionally known as Koko Nor, in the northeast. Tsinghai has an area of about 278,400 square miles (721,100 square kilometres), and its population in 1970 was 2,100,000. The capital is Hsi-ning (Sining), which is 120 miles west of Lan-chou, Kansu Province.

History. Tsinghai was a remote region of China, lying to the west of the historic provinces that made up China proper. Parts of it came under Chinese control in the 3rd century BC. For centuries it was sparsely occupied by nomadic herdsmen, chiefly Tibetans and Mongols, plus a few Chinese settlers on farms around the northeastern corner of Koko Nor. The Chinese population increased over the years, and Tsinghai was made a province of China in 1928.

Physical geography. Most (about 90 percent) of the province consists of mountains and high plateaus. In the north are the Ch'i-lien Shan-mo (Ch'i-lien Mountains), which form the divide between the interior and exterior drainage systems of China. Through the central part of the plateau extend the Pa-yen-k'a-la Shan (Gory Bayankhara-ula; a spur of the Kunlun Mountains), which serve as the watershed of the headwaters of both the Yangtze and Huang (Yellow) rivers. In the southern part of the plateau, the Tsinghai–Tibetan boundary parallels the T'ang-ku-la Shan-mo. Between these high mountains are broad valleys, rolling hilly areas, and extensive flat tableland.

In the northwestern part of the plateau lies the Tsaidam Basin, an immense, low-lying area between the Pa-yen-k'a-la and the Ch'i-lien ranges, which is surrounded by high mountains. The basin proper is vast and flat, its lowest point about 8,700 feet above sea level. There are many fertile spots in the piedmont and lakeside areas of the basin. The southeastern part of the basin is a broad swamp formed by a number of rivers flowing from the snowcapped T'ang-ku-la Shan-mo.

Climate

The extensiveness and the complex terrain of the region result in great variations in climate, soil, and vegetation. On the whole, the climate is typically continental, being influenced by the region's remoteness from the sea and by the mountain ranges in the south and east that bar maritime winds. The average annual precipitation in most places is less than four inches, most of which occurs during the summer. Winter is dry, cold, and windy; summer is hot. Strong winds from the Mongolian Plateau blanket the region with a sea of sand, which presents a serious menace to local agriculture. Grass thrives on the vast plateau, however, and the region possesses some of China's best pasturelands for sheep, horses, and yaks. Antelope, wild horses, wolves, foxes, and bears occur, and exotic birds are found in many places.

Population. There are many national minorities in Tsinghai, including Tibetan, Han (Chinese), Mongol, and Hui (Chinese Muslims). The Tibetans comprise about 35 percent of the total population, the Han about 30 percent, the Hui about 20 percent, and the Mongols

10 percent, with various other nationalities comprising about 5 percent of the total.

The Tibetans speak Tibetan and the Mongols Mongolian; both follow Tibetan Buddhism (Lamaism). The Han are Chinese in language, culture, and religion. Hui (T'ung-kan) speak Chinese but are Muslims.

The national minorities

Although Tsinghai is the third-largest political unit in China, it is thinly populated, having about eight persons per square mile (2.9 persons per square kilometre).

Administration. The provincial capital is Hsi-ning. The province is subdivided for administrative and governmental purposes into six autonomous nationality areas (*tzu-chih-chou*) and one municipality (*shih*). The special status of the Tsaidam Basin was reflected administratively in late 1956 by the establishment of a separate Tsaidam Administrative District, with its headquarters at Ta-ch'ai-tan, a new settlement situated on the northern edge of a salt swamp and at the junction of east–west and north–south roads. In 1964 the Tsaidam district was reincorporated into the Hai-hsi Mongol-Tibetan-Kazakh Autonomous District.

Education. The educational system of the province consists of elementary schools, high schools, and temple schools. There are two types of elementary schools, comprehensive (for six years) and junior (for four years). For the whole province, there are about 60 comprehensive elementary schools and 600 junior elementary schools, for male students only. The number of students ranges from 35 to 65 for each school. There are five elementary schools for girls. Among the ethnic groups, the Hui have the highest percentage of attendance. There are eight high schools that have about 200 students each and one, Kunlun High School, that has more than 3,000 students. Temple education plays an important role in the province. Among the Tibetan Buddhists, a child who becomes a lama begins his studies at the age of ten and continues for more than ten years. A Muslim child's studies begin when he is six years old and continue for 15 years.

Economy. Economically, Tsinghai is divided into two parts by the Jihyneh Mountains. On the eastern side is the Huang Ho drainage, consisting of large tracts of farmland crisscrossed by irrigation canals and dotted with settlements. Spring wheat, barley, and Irish potatoes are the principal crops. On the western side is the plateau basin, where herds of cattle, yaks, horses, and sheep graze on vast stretches of grassland. Most of the Tibetan and Mongol minorities have long engaged in herding there. The output of sheep and yak wool is high and of good quality. Vast areas of land in the pastoral areas have been opened up for cultivation, introducing a mixed farming–livestock economy. The Kunlun and Ch'i-lien mountains are well forested, and in the farming areas there are peach, apricot, pear, apple, and walnut orchards. Among the timber products are spruce, birch, Chinese pine, and Chinese juniper.

Agricultural products and livestock

The development of the Tsaidam Basin oilfield began in the late 1950s, and a considerable quantity of crude oil is now produced there. The basin also has deposits of coal, iron ore, and other minerals, including potassium, which supplies a large fertilizer plant located in the basin. The big salt lakes offer large reserves of borax and especially of salt—so much that blocks of salt are used to pave roads, build bridges, and construct houses.

In older days, Tsinghai had only a few small and poorly equipped tanneries and match factories, all located in Hsi-ning. Today, a number of industrial enterprises have been established, most notably in woolen textiles and dairy products.

Transportation and communications. The opening of the Lan-chou–Hsi-ning section of the Lan-chou–Tsinghai railway in 1959 provided the province's first rail link with the rest of China. Truck transportation is important, and main highways lead from Hsi-ning to Lan-chou, Chang-yeh in Kansu, Tibet, Sinkiang, and Kan-te in Tsinghai. Several highways, including the Tsinghai–Tibet highway, intersect at the southern margin of the Tsaidam Basin at Ko-erh-mu (Golmo), making it a communications centre.

Cultural life. Urban cultural institutions such as museums, theatres, universities, and libraries are few. Life is largely rural, strongly influenced by the traditional culture of the several ethnic and nationality groups that make up the population. Among the Mongols and Tibetans, for example, one son from every family is supposed to enter a lamasery. This custom imposes a limitation on population growth. The chief monastery in Tsinghai is about 20 miles from Hsi-ning. It is a centre of Tibetan Buddhism (Lamaism), to which thousands of believers make pilgrimages from the Mongolia region, Tibet, Sinkiang, and Szechwan.

BIBLIOGRAPHY. GEORGE B. CRESSEY, *Land of the 500 Million: A Geography of China* (1955), a standard geography text; *Asia's Lands and Peoples*, 3rd ed. (1963), a widely-used college text; THEODORE SHABAD, *China's Changing Map*, 2nd ed. (1972), an up-to-date book on the geography of China; T.R. TREGEAR, *A Geography of China* (1965), a general geography text; CHIAO-MIN HSIEH, *China: Ageless Land and Countless People* (1967), a political geography; KEITH M. BUCHANAN, *The Chinese People and the Chinese Earth* (1966), a geography text using Communist information; OWEN LATTIMORE, *Inner Asian Frontiers of China* (1940), a classic study of Asian frontiers; SIR AUREL STEIN, "Innermost Asia: Its Geography As a Factor in History," *Geogrl. J.*, 65:377–403, 473–501 (1925); section on Tsinghai in the HUMAN RELATIONS AREA FILES, *A Regional Handbook for Northwest China* (1956), a useful collection.

(C.-M.H.)

Tsiolkovsky, Konstantin Eduardovich

Konstantin Eduardovich Tsiolkovsky, Russian research scientist in aeronautics and astronautics, pioneered the development of rocket and space research. He was among the first to study the aerodynamics of airfoils with a wind tunnel and to work out the theoretical problems of rocket travel in space.

Tass—Sovfoto

Tsiolkovsky.

Tsiolkovsky was born on September 17, 1857, in Izhevskoye, Ryazan Province, into a family of modest means. His father, Eduard Ignatyevich Tsiolkovsky, a provincial forestry official, was a Polish noble by birth; and his mother, Mariya Ivanovna Yumasheva, was Russian and Tatar. The boy lost his hearing at age nine as a result of scarlet fever; four years later his mother died. These two events had an important bearing on his early life in that, being obliged to study at home, he became withdrawn and lonely, yet self-reliant. Books became his friends. He developed an interest in mathematics and physics, and, while still a teen-ager, began to speculate on space travel.

At 16 Tsiolkovsky went to Moscow, where he stayed for three years, studying chemistry, mathematics, astronomy, and mechanics, attending lectures with the aid of an ear trumpet, and expanding his grasp of the problems of flight. But the elder Tsiolkovsky understandably wanted

Two major influences

his deaf son, notwithstanding his growing ability to deal with abstruse questions in physics, to achieve financial independence. After discovering that the youth was going hungry and overworking himself in Moscow, his father called him home to Vyatka in 1876.

The future scientist soon passed the teachers examination and was assigned to a school in Borovsk, about 100 kilometres from Moscow, where he began his teaching career, married Varvara Yevgrafovna Sokolovaya, and renewed his deep interest in science. Isolated from scientific centres, the deaf teacher made discoveries on his own. Thus, in Borovsk, he worked out equations on the kinetic theory of gases. He sent the manuscript of this work to the Russian Physico-Chemical Society in St. Petersburg, but was informed by the chemist Dmitry Ivanovich Mendeleyev that it already had been done a quarter century before. Undaunted and encouraged by Mendeleyev, he continued his research. Impressed by the intellectual independence of this young provincial school teacher, the Russian Physico-Chemical Society invited him to become a member.

In 1892 Tsiolkovsky was transferred to another teaching post in Kaluga, where he continued his research in astronautics and aeronautics. At that time he took up the problem that occupied almost all his life: the problem of constructing an all-metal dirigible with an adjustable envelope. In order to demonstrate the validity of his experiment, he built a wind tunnel, the first in Russia, incorporating into it features that would permit testing the aerodynamic merits of various aircraft designs. Since he did not receive any financial support from the Russian Physico-Chemical Society, he was obliged to dip into his family's household budget in order to build the tunnel; he investigated about 100 models of quite diverse designs.

Building a wind tunnel

Tsiolkovsky's experiments were subtle and extremely clever. He studied the effects of air friction and surface area on the speed of the air current over a streamlined body. The Academy of Sciences learned of his work and granted him modest financial aid of 470 rubles, with which he built a larger wind tunnel. Tsiolkovsky then compared the feasibility of dirigibles and airplanes, which led him to develop advanced aircraft designs.

While investigating aerodynamics, however, Tsiolkovsky began to devote more attention to space problems. In 1895 his book *Gryozy o zemle i nebe* (*Dreams of Earth and Sky*) was published, and in 1896 he published an article on communication with inhabitants of other planets. That same year he also began to write his largest and most serious work on astronautics, "Exploration of Cosmic Space by Means of Reaction Devices," which dealt with theoretical problems of using rocket engines in space, including heat transfer, a navigating mechanism, heating resulting from air friction, and maintenance of fuel supply.

Problems of space travel

The first 15 years of the 20th century undoubtedly were the saddest time of Tsiolkovsky's life. In 1902 his son Ignaty committed suicide. In 1908 a flood of the Oka River inundated his home and destroyed many of his accumulated scientific materials. In 1911, after participating in a revolutionary movement, his oldest daughter Lyubov Konstantinovna was arrested. The Academy of Sciences did not recognize the value of his aerodynamic experiments, and, in 1914, at the Aeronautics Congress in St. Petersburg, his models of an all-metal dirigible met with complete indifference. Depressed by these events, Tsiolkovsky turned to the problems of alleviating poverty; they occupied his attention until the revolution in 1917, when he was 60 years old.

In the final 18 years of his life, Tsiolkovsky continued his research, with the support of the Soviet state, on a wide variety of scientific problems. His contributions on stratospheric exploration and interplanetary flight were particularly noteworthy and played a significant role in contemporary astronautics. The German scientist Hermann Oberth wrote, "You have lighted the flame and we will not permit it to go out, but will try to accomplish the greatest dream of mankind." In 1919 Tsiolkovsky was elected to the Socialist Academy (later the Academy of Sciences of the U.S.S.R.). On November 9, 1921, the council of the People's Commissars granted him a pension for life in recognition of his services in education and aviation. Before his death in Kaluga, after surgery for stomach cancer, on September 19, 1935, Tsiolkovsky bequeathed his entire lifework to the Soviet state.

BIBLIOGRAPHY. A.A. KOSMODEMYANSKYI, *Konstantin Tsiolkovsky: His Life and Work* (1956; orig. pub. in Russian, 1954), is the only book-length study of the subject in English. In Russian, see M.S. ARLAZAROV, Циолковской (1967), a biography with a preface by YURI GAGARIN.

(M.S.A.)

Tundra

The Finns called their treeless northern reaches the *tunturi*, but the concept of a vast frozen plain as a special ecological realm was developed by the Russians and called by them the tundra. Dotted by lakes and bogs and crossed by streams, the tundra supports a patchy mantle of low vegetation, mainly grasses, sedges, and dwarf shrubs. A meagre variety of animals inhabits the tundra, although in surprisingly large numbers. Characteristic rock fields (fell-fields) and windswept earthen mounds (hummocks) may be barren except for seemingly painted-on lichen growth and scant mossy crevices. Alternate freezing and thawing, the constant factor shaping the tundra, and the presence of a permanently frozen subsoil layer, the permafrost, are unique features that set the tundra apart from the polar vastness of ice and snow, on the one hand, and the evergreen forest belt, on the other. Essentially, there are two kinds of tundra: the Arctic tundra, lying north of the coniferous forest and encircling the North Pole, and the Alpine tundra, clothing the mountain slopes above the treeline in temperate regions. The Antarctic, virtually covered with ice, lacks a well-developed tundra, though lichens, mosses, and at least three species of flowering plants occur in more favourable habitats.

THE ENVIRONMENTAL SETTING

The global extent of tundras is considerable. The southern limit of Arctic tundra, an area roughly one-tenth of the earth's land surface, follows the northern edge of the coniferous forest belt (see map). In North America most of the tundra lies above 60° N, while in Eurasia most of it occurs north of 70° N, except in eastern Siberia where it extends to 60° N in Kamchatka. This bulge northward in Eurasia results from warmer summers over a large land mass.

Patterned ground

Patterned ground, a conspicuous feature of most tundras, results from differential movement of soil, stone, and rock on slopes and level land, plus a downward creep (solifluction) of the soil mantle. These phenomena result from freeze-thaw cycles, especially in spring and fall. Such features as rock rings, stripes, and polygons in alpine regions are usually 6 to 12 inches (15 to 30 centimetres) across. In the Arctic tundra, rock slabs may be found standing on end. Solifluction terraces and lobes are common in many Alpine tundras where there is adequate moisture for soil lubrication.

While permafrost is an ever-present feature of the Arctic and Antarctic, it is seldom encountered in Alpine tundra. The southern limit of continuous permafrost is within the northern forest belt of North America and Eurasia. Its southern boundary can be correlated with average annual air temperatures of 20° F (−7° C), south of which the permafrost exists in patches. Over much of the Arctic, permafrost extends to a depth of 300 to 1,500 feet (90 to 456 metres) to 2,000 feet (610 metres) in a few areas of Siberia. The summer thaw penetrates to a depth of 6 to 12 inches (15 to 30 centimetres) in the higher latitudes of the Arctic and from 1.5 to 10 feet (0.5 to 3 metres) in lower latitude sites with a complete plant cover and well-drained soils. Most biological activity is limited to this thawable area, in terms of root depth, burrowing of animals, and decomposition of organic matter (see PERMAFROST).

Tundra climates are variable and range from the severe polar deserts, with temperatures averaging 40° F (5° C) in midsummer and about −25° F (−32° C) in mid-winter, to Alpine conditions of cool summers and moderate winters with temperatures seldom falling below 0° F (−18° C). Precipitation, measured as water, is less than 15 in. (38 cm) annually over most of the Arctic tundra; roughly two-thirds of it falls as summer rain, the remainder falling in expanded form as snow, from 25 in. (64 cm) to rarely more than 75 in. (191 cm).

The Arctic tundra is more characterized by low summer temperatures than by low winter temperatures. The coastal tundra is cooler and foggier than inland tundra. Late summer and early fall are the cloudiest seasons because of the availability of groundwater for evaporation. With the first winter freeze, the clear skies return.

The presence of permafrost retards drainage, and lowlands of the Arctic tundra become saturated and boggy during the summer thaw. Alpine tundra is generally drier, even though precipitation, especially as snow, is higher than in Arctic tundra. The lack of a continuous permafrost and the steep topography result in rapid drainage, except in certain Alpine meadows.

Although winds are not so strong in the Arctic as in Alpine tundras, their influence on snowdrift patterns and whiteouts (blowing snow) is an important climatic factor. Blizzard conditions may reduce visibility to 30 feet (about nine metres) and cause snow crystals to penetrate any tiny opening in clothing and buildings. Winds in the Alpine tundras are often quite strong; they may average five to ten miles per hour only two feet (60 centimetres) above ground level, and they quite frequently reach 75 to 125 miles per hour in high reaches of the Rockies and the Alps.

Important differences between Arctic and Alpine tundras include day length and carbon dioxide levels. Plants and animals of Alpine tundras are subjected to the same day–night regime as are other organisms at lower elevations in temperate regions. Numerous activities of these organisms are controlled by the length of the night. Over most of the Arctic, light prevails continuously for one to four months, and biological rhythms are induced by variables other than a daily dark period. Many tundra plants flower abundantly only when exposed to continuous or near continuous light. Insects' rhythms of feeding, flight, and swarming, normally controlled by light–dark cycles, respond rather to prevailing temperature or sunlight. Birds and large mammals appear to observe a "quiet period" in early morning, though not as pronounced as in animals in temperate region Alpine tundras. Carbon dioxide levels are lower in Alpine tundras because of thinner air at higher altitudes. Alpine plants are more efficient in utilizing these lower levels of carbon dioxide in photosynthesis than are their Arctic counterparts.

THE BIOTIC COMPONENT

In Arctic and Alpine tundras, the number of species of plants and animals is usually small compared with temperate regions, yet the number of individuals per species is often high. As a result, food and feeder relationships are simple and more subject to upset if a critical species decreases in numbers or is eliminated.

Plant life. In many Alpine tundras and over much of the Arctic tundra, the general appearance of the vegetation is that of a greenish-brown, low grassland. While plants do not remain in flower for more than a few days or weeks, the blossoms are generally large in relation to plant size and are rather colourful, especially in Alpine habitats.

Species variation

Change in species composition with time (succession), which leads to a more stable, or climax, community, is, as in deserts and other severe environments, often very slow. In many instances, vegetational changes are cyclic rather than directional, with the erosion of soil and plants by wind and needle ice being an important factor. Succession along lake and pond shores, river floodplains, animal burrows, etc. does occur with the replacement of one group of species by another group. In many cases, succession is mainly the shift in the relative numbers of a species rather than a total replacement.

Across the southerly Arctic tundra, with vast areas of low relief, boggy peat soils with an abundance of lakes

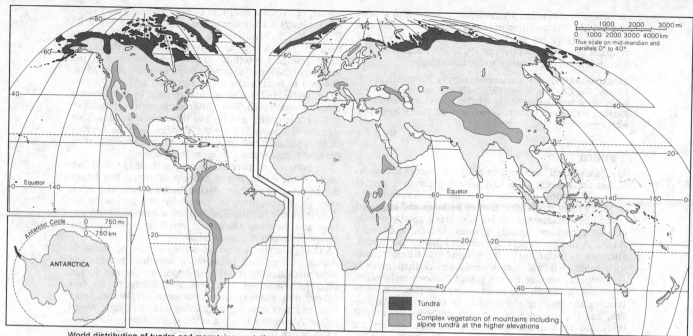

World distribution of tundra and mountain vegetation.

Adapted from *Biological Sciences Curriculum Study Green Version High School Biology*, 2nd ed.; Chicago: Rand McNally & Co., 1968

and meandering rivers prevail. These coastal plain areas are dominated by sedges and cotton grass, and mosses including *Sphagnum* are common. On slightly elevated sites, often only 6 to 24 in. (15 to 60 cm) above the wet peaty soils, low willows, grasses, and rushes occur. Taller willows, grasses, and plants in the sunflower and legume families are common on the sands and gravels of river-banks.

On higher lands, foothills, and Arctic mountains, the vegetation is quite sparce.

Transitions from mountain forest to the shrub- and herb-dominated Alpine tundra at higher altitudes is very similar to the transition from coniferous forest belt to Arctic tundra. The Alpine transition, however, occurs over only a few hundred feet of vertical rise. Timberline trees are mostly spruce, fir, and pine, with very few deciduous tree species. Willow clumps less than 2 ft (60 cm) tall are common among the scattered clumps of stunted trees (*Krummholz*) and beyond, where snowdrifts are extensive. Willows are also common along streams, in the lee of rocks, and in basins or the lee side of ridges, where winter snow is deeper.

On gentle slopes where soil has developed, extensive meadows occur. On wind swept ridges, cushion plants dominate. On rocky slopes and peaks, plants are found in scattered patches where there is a bit of soil and some snow cover in winter.

In higher mountains, having much snow, ice, and exposed rock, lichens and mosses manage to grow on rocks. Vascular plants usually end at or just below the line of permanent snow.

In Alpine tundra, as in the Arctic tundra, the plant communities are influenced by soil drainage; snow cover and time of melt; and localized microclimates with their differences in temperature, wind, soil moisture, and nutrients.

Animal life. Organisms of the northern Alpine tundra probably evolved before those of the Arctic tundra in the Mongolo-Tibetan Plateau. Few Alpine animals contributed to the evolution of Arctic tundra species because of physical barriers and animal specialization. Alpine plants, however, and some animals migrated east and west via mountain ranges to Europe and North America. Lowland tundra animals appear to have evolved in Central Eurasia when tundra replaced the cold temperate steppe. These animals then migrated to Europe in mid-Pleistocene times (about 1,000,000 years ago) and to North America later.

Warm interglacial periods eliminated many tundra species and were probably detrimental to the reinvasion of

truly Alpine animals. Thus the Alps, Rocky Mountains, and other ranges have a restricted Alpine fauna today, with the larger animals spending only the more favourable seasons above timberline, grazing in the lowlands in winter.

As a product of east–west migration routes from Central Asia, many of the common Arctic animals are circumpolar. These include polar bear, Arctic fox, Arctic wolf, Arctic hare, Arctic weasel, several species of lemming, ptarmigan, snowy owl, and also a number of species of waterfowl.

With plant growth and many aspects of animal activity confined to two to four months of the year, when temperatures are above freezing, evolution has favoured a rapid completion of life cycles. Tundra organisms are opportunistic. Many species of plants are perennials that flower within a few days after the snow begins to melt, and some produce ripe seed within four to six weeks. Very few species are annuals. Plants one to 3 in. (2.5 to 7.5 cm) tall typically flower first because they are in the warmer air layers near the soil surface. Some plants frozen while in flower when sudden storms hit continue to develop and produce seed upon thawing. Many plants set few seeds but depend mostly upon runners or underground stems for increasing their numbers. A few species produce bulblets that develop roots and shoots on the parent plant before they drop to the ground. The hairy flower stalks of cottongrass (*Eriophorum*), lousewort (*Pedicularis*), and willows (*Salix*) retain warm air, raising the temperature near the stalks 5° to 15° F (3° to 9° C); this ability is an important adaptation for flowering in areas where air temperatures may approach the freezing point.

During cloudy periods, in shade, and at night, flower temperature is very similar to that of the surrounding air, but in sunlight flowers may be to 4° to 18° F warmer than the air around them.

Although the number of species of Arctic insects is small compared with that of temperate regions, those that are present are quite successful. Arctic insects resist freezing winter temperatures. In some species a high glycerol content acts as an "antifreeze" to lower the temperature at which freezing occurs. Many tundra insects and spiders are dark in colour, as a result of which they absorb more sunlight and maintain higher body temperatures. Some of the tundra species of black flies and mosquitoes do not require a blood meal before depositing their eggs, in contrast to their temperate-region counterparts.

Most tundra birds are migratory, staying long enough to

nest and molt. An exception is the ptarmigan, which feeds upon willow buds and other exposed plant parts in winter and upon leaves, buds, and flowers in summer. Ptarmigan have heavily feathered feet, which provide some insulation against the winter snow and ice. Several migratory birds feed upon seeds and fruits until the emergence of insects and spiders in summer.

Small mammals of the tundra have high reproductive rates; most notable in this regard are the lemmings, which reach a population peak every three to five years in some regions. Lemmings remain active all winter, living under the snow where they feed upon roots of grasses and sedges; they may even reproduce under the thin yet insulative snow layer. When the lemming population increases, many plants are harvested and there is a large accumulation of feces. The manuring around animal burrows adds nitrogen and other nutrients, which stimulate plant growth.

With environmental extremes as pronounced as they are in the Arctic and with the number of species so limited, there are often considerable oscillations in animal populations. The populations of lemming predators, such as jaegers, snowy owls, and foxes, closely follow the rise and fall of lemming numbers. Snowy owls migrate to the coniferous forest belt during lemming "lows," and the number of foxes drops significantly. When lemming peaks are reached, vegetation becomes scarce and large number of lemmings move into less densely populated areas.

Characteristic large herbivores in the Arctic are caribou in North America, both domestic and wild reindeer in Eurasia, and musk oxen on Greenland and some of the Canadian Arctic islands. These animals are rather large, considering the severe environments in which they live. **Adaptive advantage of size** Such size confers an adaptive advantage: there is less surface area relative to volume and therefore less opportunity for heat to dissipate to the outside. Musk oxen are especially well equipped for surviving in cold climates because of their exceptionally thick coats. Caribou and reindeer are equipped with sharp hooves and antlers, which enable them to cut through snow for winter foraging on lichens and flowering plants.

Leonard Lee Rue III

Caribou feeding on mosses, lichens, and dwarf trees common to the tundra.

Geese often denude areas of cotton grass, leaving behind mostly mosses and indirectly promoting deep thaws that may result in soil creep on slopes.

Important birds of prey are the jaegers, which are summer visitors, and the snowy owls, permanent residents, though the latter move southward into the forest in winters when food supply is scarce. The several species of jaegers and the owls feed upon small birds and insects, although lemmings are the most important item of their diet.

Polar bear are as much a part of the marine environment as they are of the tundra. In winter they spend much of their time hunting seal. Foxes and wolves often follow

bear to feed on leftovers. In summer, foxes and wolves are found mostly on land, where they raise their young and feed on birds and small mammals.

Alpine tundras are similarly limited in the number of animal species and diversity. Accumulating evidence indicates that Alpine animal life in the Northern Hemisphere evolved in the Central Asian highlands and spread to Europe via mountain systems and to North America via the Bering Straits.

Many animals found in Alpine tundras are not especially adapted for year-round Alpine life and undergo vertical migrations, descending into the less severe forest environments in winter and returning to the heights in summer. Such mammals include the mountain sheep, ibex, chamois, several wildcats, and many birds. Mountain goats spend more time in winter at higher elevations than do ptarmigan.

In contrast with Arctic tundra mammals, some Alpine ones hibernate, such as marmots, ground squirrels, and zapodids. These animals consume large amounts of vegetation in summer and early fall before hibernation begins. Other small mammals, such as the pika and voles, cache hay in the fall for winter feeding, while rabbits and others forage as they can in winter. Foxes range over large areas of Alpine habitats in winter.

Many tundra animals sport white coats in winter, among them the foxes, wolves, ptarmigan, and polar bears. This camouflage helps both predator and prey: predators can steal up without detection and prey can hide easily in the snow.

BIOLOGICAL PRODUCTIVITY

The biological production of plants and animals is an important measure of natural ecological systems or ecosystems. A five-year international program (1967–72) dealing with an assessment of marine, freshwater, and terrestrial ecosystems is being conducted in more than 50 countries. As a part of the International Biological Program (IBP), tundra ecosystem studies are designed to determine the total production, rates of production, and the general functioning of these little-known systems. Major studies are underway in Alaska, Canada, England, Finland, Ireland, Norway, Sweden, and the U.S.S.R. While few data are available, there is enough to show some patterns.

In polar regions the greatest biological production occurs in marine waters rather than on land, with higher production occurring in the Antarctic than in the Arctic Ocean (see POLAR BIOMES).

Production studies of Arctic tundra lakes indicate that there are many species of algae and even aquatic mosses living in the higher latitudes of the Arctic. These support a limited number of small crustaceans, worms, and insect larvae, which in turn support the Arctic char, a fish related to salmon.

Plant production Plant production in the tundra appears to range from three to ten grams of vegetable matter per square metre of area (g/m^2), in willow–dryas barrens of the higher latitudes of the Arctic to values of 100 to 250 g/m^2, in lower latitude sedge-dominated wet sites. The widespread cotton-grass–dwarf-shrub heath communities produce about 50 to 75 g/m^2 in new shoots per year. Values for temperate region grasslands and forests are about four to six times as great as the maximum rates for the Arctic tundra.

The accumulating data for Alpine tundras show 50 to 100 g/m^2 in windswept habitats, 100 to 200 g/m^2 in meadows, and values of 250 to 300 g/m^2 in dwarf-shrub heath communities. These values are higher than those in the Arctic because the growing season is often longer by several weeks.

These data do not tell the entire story, for the amount of plant material (standing crop) is often 10 to 25 times greater below ground than above ground, which indicates that the soil environment may be more favourable for growth than is the air.

In many tundras, the harvest by plant-eating animals is no more than 0.1 to 2.0 percent of the live plants per year. This means that most of the plants produced fall to decay and are decomposed by micro-organisms.

With Alpine and Arctic vegetation so sparse, it is no accident that man has harvested herbivorous animals, including caribou, reindeer, ducks, and geese, rather than harvesting native or cultivated plants as he does in other major vegetation types (forests, grasslands, deserts).

BIBLIOGRAPHY. W.D. BILLINGS and H.A. MOONEY, "The Ecology of Arctic and Alpine Plants," *Biol. Rev.*, 43:481–529 (1968), a review of the physiological ecology of tundra flowering plants; L.C. BLISS, "Adaptations of Arctic and Alpine Plants to Environmental Conditions," *Arctic*, 15:117–144 (1962), a review of environmental factors in relation to plant growth; J.A. DOWNES, "Adaptations of Insects in the Arctic," *A. Rev. Ent.*, 10:257–274 (1965), a review of the ecological and physiological adaptation of insects; M.J. DUNBAR, *Ecological Development in Polar Regions: A Study in Evolution* (1968), on the adaptations of polar organisms, especially marine, to low temperatures, and also the evolution of polar ecosystems; A.W. FULLER and P.G. KEVAN (eds.), "Productivity and Conservation in Northern Circumpolar Lands," *International Union for Conservation of Nature and Natural Resources (IUCN) Pub. New Series No. 16* (1970), 36 articles on the production and conservation of Arctic animals and plants, oil development, and the role of human resources in the north; G.H.T. KIMBLE and D. GOOD (eds.), *Geography of the Northlands* (1955), a general work on the physical geography, transportation, people, and economic and biological aspects of the north; W.H. OSBURN and H.E. WRIGHT, JR. (eds.), *Arctic and Alpine Environments* (1968), a collection of papers dealing with the climatology, geology, and ecology of tundras.

(L.C.B.)

Tungsten Products and Production

Tungsten, in its various forms, is a widely used industrial material. It is particularly important as an alloying element in the production of high-speed steel and, as cemented tungsten carbide, in cutting tools and other applications requiring hardness. The pure metal retains its strength at high temperatures, and additions of tungsten to other metals may improve their high-temperature strength.

The word tungsten (derived from the Swedish words *tung*, "heavy," and *sten*, "stone") was first used in 1755 by Baron Axel Fredrick Cronstedt, who applied it to the mineral later known as scheelite because of its high density. Other researchers identified the ore as a compound of lime and a previously unknown substance and discovered the same mysterious substance, which they named "wolfram," in a mineral that contained iron and manganese. Today the metal is known as tungsten in British and American usage and as wolfram in European. The mineral is known as either wolfram or wolframite.

Tungsten was a rare metal until 1847 when industrial development was started under a British patent for the manufacture of sodium tungstate and tungstic acid. A later patent (1857) described the manufacture of iron-tungsten alloys, which were to form the basis of modern high-speed steels. Industrial development followed an exhibition of tungsten tool-steels by Bethlehem Steel Corporation at Paris in 1900.

The first application of unalloyed tungsten was as filaments in electric incandescent lamps, following the production of ductile filaments by a powder metallurgical process patented in 1909, a process that remains the basis of modern production methods.

Tungsten carbide in cast form was produced in Germany in 1914, but was too brittle to be useful. Not until 1927 did the Krupp laboratory in Essen discover that when tungsten carbide powder is mixed with a bonding, or cementing, material such as cobalt, the product is much less brittle and retains its hardness. Cemented carbide found an immediate application in metallurgy in dies and tools requiring great hardness.

MINING

Tungsten minerals are widely distributed. The commercially important ones are wolframite and scheelite. Wolframite is iron and manganese tungstate (Fe, Mn)WO_4, a mixed crystal of huebnerite, $MnWO_4$, and ferberite, $FeWO_4$. Scheelite is calcium tungstate, $CaWO_4$.

In 1970 it was estimated that the free world reserve was 253,000 tons (226,000 metric tons) of tungsten metal content. Reserves in China, North Korea, and the U.S.S.R. may be about four times as great.

Every tungsten deposit must be examined critically to determine the most suitable and economic method of concentration. The method chosen will depend upon the type of mineral, associated minerals, and the identity of the gangue (worthless material in which the mineral occurs).

Gravity methods of concentrating the relatively heavy tungsten minerals are used frequently, though most large-scale mills use a combination of flotation and gravity methods.

If calcite and apatite are the principal contaminants, acid leaching can be used to upgrade the concentrate. Low-grade concentrate is also converted to synthetic scheelite by chemical treatment. Roasting, magnetic separation, or electrostatic separation may also be used to improve the quality.

Molybdenum, tin, and bismuth may be present in the ore in sufficient quantities to warrant their recovery, a circumstance that can complicate the process.

The aim of most mills is to produce a concentrate containing a minimum of 60 percent tungsten trioxide, WO_3. A range of 60 to 70 percent is normal.

METAL RECOVERY

The first step in the recovery of tungsten from wolframite is to fuse it with sodium carbonate under oxidizing conditions or by digestion with a concentrated sodium hydroxide solution. Scheelite is usually decomposed by digestion with concentrated hydrochloric acid.

The reaction between wolframite and sodium carbonate may be carried out in a gas-fired reverberatory furnace at 800° C with constant rabbling (stirring) or in a gas-fired rotary furnace at a slightly higher temperature sufficient to cause the charge to flow down the kiln. In the case of digestion with a sodium hydroxide solution, the reaction is best carried out in a steam-heated autoclave.

The resulting product is leached with water to produce sodium tungstate liquor, which can be treated with calcium chloride solution to produce insoluble calcium tungstate (synthetic scheelite).

Hydrochloric acid is added, while stirring, to a slurry of the calcium tungstate to produce insoluble tungstic acid (H_2WO_4) and soluble calcium chloride. The tungstic acid is recovered by filtering, washing, and drying.

The digestion of scheelite with concentrated hydrochloric acid yields a crude tungstic acid. After the calcium chloride is washed out, the dried acid contains 80 to 98 percent WO_3. Purification is achieved by dissolving the tungstic-acid sludge in concentrated ammonia solution, filtering and evaporating to produce ammonium paratungstate crystals, $5(NH_4)_2O \cdot 12WO_3 \cdot xH_2O$. Further purification is obtained by decomposing the crystals with hydrochloric acid and redissolving the precipitated tungstic acid in ammonia solution and crystallizing again as ammonium paratungstate.

Most tungsten powder is produced by hydrogen reduction of tungstic acid, tungstic oxide, or ammonium paratungstate.

Particle size. The particle size of the powder is important in determining the success of the subsequent operations and it is necessary to produce different types of powder for various applications. Tungsten powder for the production of massive metal (sheet, rod, and wire) has a wide range of particle size to produce maximum compaction, whereas the particle size of powder for conversion to carbide for hard metal production should be tightly controlled around the size specified, which size will vary from less than one micron to several microns, depending on the application. The reduction procedure must be carefully controlled to produce the required type of powder.

Reduction. The basic reduction process is to pass metal boats charged with tungstic acid or oxide through a heated tube with a counterflow of hydrogen. The acid or oxide is reduced to metal, and water vapour is removed in the flow of hydrogen. The temperature of reduction varies from 700° to 1,100° C; the higher the temperature, the coarser

[margin note: Lamp filaments]

[margin note: Wolframite reaction]

the powder. For the finest powder it is necessary to use a shallow charge of oxide with a high flow of dry hydrogen and carry out reduction at a low temperature, preferably in two stages. For coarser metal with a wide range of particle size, deep charges are reduced at high temperatures.

Some tungsten powder is produced by carbon reduction of the oxide, but this powder is less pure than hydrogen-reduced metal and is used mainly for alloy production.

High-purity tungsten powder is produced by the hydrogen reduction of tungsten hexafluoride in a fluidized bed at 550° C.

THE METAL AND ITS ALLOYS

Powder metallurgy

Tungsten powder is converted to massive metal by a powder metallurgy process. The powder is pressed into a bar shape that is presintered in hydrogen to give it enough strength to be handled. The bar is then clamped vertically between electrical contacts in a hydrogen-filled chamber, and a current of several thousand amperes is passed directly through it. The temperature of the bar is raised to about 3,000° C and held at that temperature for about 30 minutes.

The sintered bar (93–95 percent of the density of solid tungsten) is too brittle to be worked at ordinary temperatures; it can, however, be forged and rolled at about 1,500° C.

Production of rod and wire is accomplished by swaging (passing the metal while hammering through a die). The first pass is made at 1,500° C and the temperature gradually lowered to about 1,200° C. As the metal is worked it becomes more dense and more ductile.

Plate and sheet are produced from sintered bar by forging at 1,500° C followed by rolling first at 1,400° C, and later down to 700° C as the ductility increases.

Small additions of nickel (about 1 percent) result in lower sintering temperatures, but the resulting product cannot be worked.

The difficulties in melting tungsten (melting point about 3,400° C) have been overcome with the development of melting by means of an electric arc or by electron-beam melting techniques, but the resulting product in both cases is an ingot with coarse columnar grains unsuitable for working.

Tungsten components have been made by other methods than powder metallurgy; e.g., by centrifugally casting arc-melted tungsten, usually with a little added molybdenum; by building up shapes on formers by plasma-spraying tungsten powder; and by slip casting followed by sintering.

Depositing tungsten in vapour form from tungsten hexafluoride is used to produce coatings of tungsten.

Hot isostatic compaction is a recently developed means of consolidating tungsten powder. The tungsten powder is sealed in a metal container and heated in a high-pressure, inert gas. Full-density tungsten is produced at pressures of 10,000 to 20,000 pounds per square inch, at temperatures between 1,500° and 1,600° C.

Applications of tungsten metal. The applications are based on tungsten's high melting point, excellent high-temperature strength, and good heat and electrical conductivity. It is used for lamp filaments, electrical contacts, X-ray cathodes, heating elements, and equipment (including thermocouples) for high-temperature furnaces.

Aerospace applications. Aerospace applications have been investigated, but the good high-temperature mechanical properties of tungsten are marred by a lack of resistance to oxidation. Alloying has failed to overcome this fault. Protective coatings have achieved some improvement, but none is completely satisfactory in providing resistance to oxidation, abrasion, alternate heat and cold, and impact. Tungsten nozzles have been used in some types of rocket motors. The material is usually in the form of porous sintered tungsten infiltrated with silver.

Important alloys and their uses. Stellite is the name of an important series of alloys containing cobalt (30 to 56 percent), chromium (30 percent) and tungsten (10 to 20 percent), and small additions of carbon. These alloys combine excellent hot-hardness with good corrosion and

World Production of Tungsten Ore and Concentrate, by Countries* (Thousand pounds of contained tungsten)†		
country	1964	1970‡
North and Central America		
Canada	840	2,956
Guatemala	…	…
Mexico	8	586
United States	8,798	8,105
South America		
Argentina	64	260§
Bolivia	2,106	4,068
Brazil	402	2,557
Peru	676	1,823
Europe		
Austria	110	350§
Italy	1	3§
Portugal	1,854	3,935
Spain	35	430
U.S.S.R.	11,400§	14,800§
Africa		
Zaire	244	…
Rwanda	156	400§
South Africa	4	7
South West Africa‖	198	139
Tanzania	…	…
Uganda	…	152
Asia		
Burma	600	419
China (mainland)	21,400§	17,600§
India	10	40
Japan	910	1,493
Malaysia	9	300
North Korea	4,200§	4,720§
South Korea	5,698	4,564
Thailand	452	1,567
Oceania: Australia	1,768	2,743
Total¶	61,928	74,017

*In addition to the countries listed, the following also produced tungsten, but reliable data are not available: Hong Kong, New Zealand, Nigeria, and Rhodesia.   †Conversion factors: WO₃ to W, multiply by 0.7931; 60 percent WO₃ concentrate to W, multiply by 0.4758.   ‡Preliminary.   §Estimate.   ‖Data are for the South-West Africa Co., Ltd. only, and are for the year ended June 30 of the year stated.   ¶Total of listed figures only. Source: U.S. Department of the Interior. Bureau of Mines, *Minerals Yearbook 1965* and *1970*.

oxidation resistance at high temperatures. The alloys can be used as solid tool bits or hard-facing rods for deposition as abrasion-resisting coatings on ferrous metals. Cast shapes are also used for surgical implants.

Additions of rhenium (35 atomic percent; that is, 35 percent of the atoms in the alloy are rhenium) greatly improve low-temperature ductility of tungsten. Aerospace and nuclear applications are considered possible, but the high cost of rhenium is a deterrent. Tungsten containing 26 percent rhenium is used in thermocouples for temperatures up to 3,000° C.

Heavy metal, an alloy of tungsten (93 percent), copper (2 percent), and nickel (5 percent), is used because of its high density for machine-balancing weights and for containers for radioactive substances.

Composites of "alloys" of tungsten and copper or silver, produced by infiltrating porous sintered tungsten with copper or silver, are used for electrical contacts for switch gear.

Small amounts of thoria (about 1 percent) are incorporated in tungsten to improve its high-temperature properties, particularly its resistance to sagging.

Cutting steels. An important use for tungsten is in making high-speed cutting steels that retain their hardness at high temperatures. These steels contain 6 to 20 percent tungsten with molybdenum, chromium, vanadium, or niobium. Tungsten can be added to steel in various forms, such as ferrotungsten (about 78 percent tungsten), melting base alloy (about 35 percent tungsten), scrap that is high in tungsten, and high-purity scheelite (natural or synthetic). Metal powder, pellets, and certain proprietary compositions are also used.

Most ferrotungsten is produced by carbon reduction of the concentrate in an electric furnace. A metallothermic process uses aluminum and silicon reducing agents.

Chemical compounds—preparation and uses. The most important compound is tungsten carbide (WC). It is used in the production of cemented carbides (hard metal) because of its great hardness, which it retains at high temperatures.

The carbide is prepared by heating an intimate mixture of tungsten powder with the required amount of carbon, in a nonoxidizing atmosphere, at about 1,400° to 1,500° C. The product is crushed and milled to a fine powder and intimately mixed with the requisite amount of fine cobalt powder by prolonged ball-milling.

The normal procedure is to press the mixed powder to the shape required. Usually a lubricant such as paraffin wax is incorporated in the powder to aid pressing and to reduce wear on the dies. The wax is removed by heat treatment before sintering at about 1,400° C. Originally, sintering was performed in a hydrogen atmosphere; but vacuum sintering, particularly when titanium and tantalum carbides are present, has largely replaced this technique. Large pieces of cemented carbide are produced by hot-pressing to shape in carbon dies.

The main use for cemented carbides is as cutting tools. The tool is brazed or mechanically fixed to a steel shank. Additions of titanium and tantalum carbides improve the cutting qualities. The application of a thin deposit of titanium carbide on the surface of the cemented carbide tools has, it is claimed, produced a very large increase in the cutting life.

The cobalt content of cemented carbides usually varies between 6 and 15 percent, the strength increasing and the hardness decreasing as the cobalt increases.

Other important applications for cemented carbides include drawing dies, rock drills, wear-resisting parts for machinery, automobile tire studs for use on icy roads, and deposits on other metals to reduce wear.

When tungsten is melted in a carbon crucible with an addition of carbon, the alloy $WC-W_2C$ is produced. It may be cast—*e.g.*, in the form of sleeves—and used as sand-blast nozzles, or crushed and incorporated in hard-facing welding rods.

Economic importance. The Table gives the world production of tungsten ore and concentrates.

BIBLIOGRAPHY. K.C. LI and C.Y. WANG, *Tungsten*, 3rd ed. (1955), a comprehensive textbook covering history, geology, ore dressing, metallurgy, chemistry, analysis, applications, and economics; C.J. SMITHELLS, *Tungsten*, 3rd rev. ed. (1952), covers the metallurgy, properties, and applications, with particular reference to production; G.D. RIECK, *Tungsten and Its Compounds* (1967), useful for latest data; C. AGTE and J. VACEK, *Wolfram und Molybdän* (1959; Eng. trans., *Tungsten and Molybdenum*, 1963), all aspects of the metals are included, most useful in detailing conditions for sintering and working; T.E. TIETZ and J.W. WILSON, *Behavior and Properties of Refractory Metals* (1965), detailed descriptions of mechanical, oxidation, and thermal properties of tungsten and its alloys; N.E. PROMISEL (ed.), *The Science and Technology of Tungsten, Tantalum, Molybdenum and Niobium and Their Alloys* (1964), report of a conference on the positions of the metallurgy of tungsten and other metals, with information on alloying, properties, protection, and fabrication; LOS ALAMOS SCIENTIFIC LABORATORY, *Bibliography on Tungsten, its Alloys and Compounds*, LAMS-2401, 2 vol. (1960), very detailed listing; P. SCHWARZKOPF and R. KIEFFER, *Refractory Hard Metals* (1953), deals with the preparation and properties of tungsten carbide, nitride, and silicide; and *Cemented Carbides* (1960), details the preparation, composition, properties, and application of composites formed by sintering refractory materials with a binder metal.

(G.L.M.)

Tunicata

The Tunicata, a subphylum of the Chordata, are a diverse group of about 2,100 species of marine organisms that includes forms that are sessile (*i.e.*, fixed to the sea floor or to some other surface) and pelagic (*i.e.*, drifting in the open sea). Tunicates are distinguished by the presence of a soft outer protective covering—the test, or tunic —and by the occurrence in the larvae (and in the adults of one group) of a notochord, or stiffening rod, which supports a muscular tail. The presence of a notochord is of evolutionary significance; it is possible that the tunicate larva represents the ancestral type of chordate organism.

General features. *Economic importance.* Tunicates are of economic importance because they grow on submerged man-made structures and in some cases—as on ships' hulls—affect their performance. Some species yield substances useful in the treatment of leukemia and other diseases. Pelagic forms are important as successful herbivores (*i.e.*, plant-eating animals), thus forming a link in ecological food chains.

Size range and distribution. Larvacea, the smallest tunicates, are often scarcely visible unless parts of the body are pigmented. Ascidiacea vary in length from a few millimetres to about 30 centimetres (about one foot). The Thaliaceae are usually organized into colonies, some of which may attain a length of four metres.

Tunicates are almost universally distributed throughout the seas of the world, from the intertidal zones down to the deepest regions (abyss). Pelagic forms occur in the vast expanse of open ocean. The sessile ascidians, or sea squirts, are often found on the sea bottom, along or near the shores of all oceans; they also grow on seaweeds, on or under rocks, in submerged sand flats, on coral reefs, on submarine cables, on ship bottoms, on wharf piles, and on the shells of lobsters and mollusks. They abound from polar regions to the tropics. Some species are cosmopolitan; others are distributed only locally.

Appearance. Externally tunicates are enclosed by the test, except for two apertures, or siphons. A water current for feeding and respiration is drawn in through a so-called branchial siphon; after filtration the water is discharged through an atrial siphon. Sessile forms, the Ascidiacea, have the two apertures close together near the anterior, or front, end and are attached posteriorly to the sea floor or to the surface of an object.

Natural history. *Solitary and colonial forms.* Ascidians may be solitary or live in colonies. In colonial forms the individuals, called zooids, may be separate or fused so that they share a common atrial siphon. Each zooid, however, has its own branchial siphon; this arrangement occurs in one pelagic group, Pyrosomida, which forms thimble-shaped colonies. Zooids are arranged around the body wall in such a way that the branchial siphons open to the exterior and the atrial siphons open internally. The common effluent from the atrial siphons is discharged through the open end of the "thimble" to propel the organism forward. In Salpida and Doliolida (both pelagic groups), the zooids have apertures at opposite ends of the body; the discharge of water from the atrial siphon propels the organism forward. Both groups may, nevertheless, form complicated colonies in the course of their life cycle. The pelagic Larvacea bear a superficial resemblance to the ascidian larva and probably represent a neotenic development (*i.e.*, the organism achieves sexual maturity even though otherwise not fully developed).

Reproduction and life cycle. Tunicates are usually dioecious—*i.e.*, male and female reproductive systems usually occur in different individuals. In most forms, fertilization and embryonic development take place in the surrounding water; in a few species, however, embryos are retained in the atrial cavity during development. Embryonic development is rapid and may be completed in nine hours, producing a tadpole-like larva about one millimetre (0.04 inch) long. Two-thirds of each larva consists of a muscular tail supported by a notochord and containing a hollow dorsal (*i.e.*, along the back) nerve cord. In the anterior trunk region the branchial sac and the alimentary canal are forming. A dorsal sensory vesicle, or organ, is sensitive to light and gravity, and the larva has three anterior adhesive papillae, or fingerlike projections.

Ascidian larvae are free-swimming for a period of six hours to several days, after which they settle on a surface, attaching themselves to it with the papillae. Immediately after attachment the tissues of the tail are resorbed into the trunk and form food reserves, which are utilized dur-

Separate
or fused
zooids in
colonies

Budding and other types of asexual reproduction

ing metamorphosis into an adult ascidian; metamorphosis takes from 42 hours to several days. In pelagic tunicates, metamorphosis occurs without attachment.

In colonial forms, budding (*i.e.*, the development of a new individual from an outgrowth of the parent that usually breaks off) or some other type of asexual reproduction occurs. Four types of budding occur in Ascidiacea. Stolons, or rootlike processes, may grow out from the posterior end of the ascidian zooid, giving rise to new buds; the resulting zooids may either separate (as in Clavelinidae) or remain in functional continuity with one another (Perophoridae). In the family Didemnidae, two small buds appear on the esophagus; one bud grows into a new thorax (branchial sac), the other into a new abdomen; the new thorax subsequently attaches to the old abdomen, and the new abdomen attaches to the old thorax to form two new zooids. In Polyclinidae and related families, the thorax and abdomen are resorbed into a postabdomen, which subsequently develops into several buds, each of which grows into a new zooid. In Botryllidae new buds arise from outgrowths of the body wall.

Ventral stolonic (rootlike) outgrowths are the characteristic type of bud formation in pelagic tunicates, but complicated life cycles occur in both Doliolida and Salpida. In Doliolida the solitary form is a gonozooid, a sexually reproducing organism. The larva gives rise to an oozoid, or asexually reproducing form. Buds formed by the stolon migrate to a dorsal outgrowth of the oozoid, where they are arranged in several series, some as feeding zooids, some as supporting zooids onto which the young gonozooid bud attaches and grows. When fully grown, the gonozooid breaks free to complete the life cycle. In Salpida the oozoid forms chains of zooids from the ventral stolon. Each zooid in a chain is a sexually reproducing gonozooid; the entire chain lives a colonial existence.

In temperate latitudes, tunicates usually spawn in spring and summer and may produce several generations each year. Many colonial forms regress in the autumn, overwintering as dormant buds. In the tropics, reproduction goes on throughout the year. Growth is rapid: in solitary forms sexually mature adults may develop in two months; in colonial forms the process is even faster.

Ecological adaptations. The fact that larval tunicates do not feed necessitates that the larval period be brief and that metamorphosis be rapid. Adult pelagic forms utilize phytoplankton, or microscopic plants, as their primary source of food. Larvacea feed exclusively on nannoplankton (*i.e.*, plankton smaller than 0.04 millimetre [0.002 inch] in diameter). The sessile ascidians utilize a variety of suspended materials. Differences in the branchial structure of tunicates are probably functional adaptations to the type of material ingested. Most ascidian species live on hard surfaces such as rock faces and piers; a few species, however, have adapted to living in sand and mud. Ascidians apparently are poor competitors; in sessile communities they often appear to die off as more successful forms such as sponges displace them. The lifespan of colonial forms is often short and in some instances may not exceed six months. Solitary forms usually live 18 to 24 months.

Habitat and life-span of the ascidians

Form and function. *Structural features.* The structure of tunicates is best studied in the ascidian zooid. The branchial siphon is anterior, and the atrial siphon is dorsal. The test surrounding the animal is a living structure supplied with blood vessels. The true body wall, or mantle, is in direct contact with the inner surface of the test and is supplied with muscles for opening and closing the siphons and for contracting the whole body. The branchial siphon leads into a large sac, or pharynx, which occupies much of the interior of the animal; a space, the atrial cavity, remains between the pharynx and the mantle and connects with the exterior through the atrial siphon. The walls of the branchial sac, the main food-collecting structure, are pierced by many apertures, or stigmata, giving it the appearance of a fragile latticework.

Cilia (*i.e.*, tiny hairlike structures) around the margins of the stigmata drive water from the branchial sac into the atrial cavity and provide the main water current through the animal. Mucus secreted from a groove, the

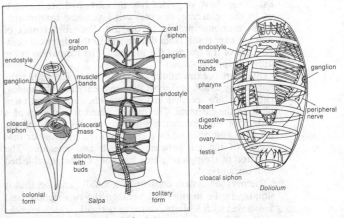

Body plans of representative tunicates.
From P.A. Meglitsch, *Invertebrate Zoology*, copyright © 1967 by Oxford University Press, Inc.; reprinted by permission

endostyle, on the ventral side of the branchial sac is transferred by cilia across the inner side of the sac trapping food from the water. The food-laden mucus is rolled into a cord on the dorsal side of the sac and carried backward to the esophagus along a fold, the dorsal lamina. Tentacles surrounding the base of the branchial siphon prevent large particles from entering the sac and ensure that only finely divided, suspended particles are utilized as food. The esophagus leads posteriorly to the alimentary canal, which loops so that the anus opens into the atrial cavity just below the atrial siphon. This arrangement ensures that waste material is carried away in the outgoing stream of water. Posterior to the intestine lies the heart, which supplies blood vessels to the test, alimentary canal, branchial sac, and to the mantle. The gonads lie in the loop of the intestine, and the gonoducts, or tubes that carry sperm or eggs to the outside, open posteriorly to the anus.

In primitive ascidians (*e.g.*, *Ciona*) the alimentary canal, heart, and gonads are enclosed by two membranous sacs, the epicardia, which grow backward from the branchial sac. Epicardia probably correspond to coelomic sacs (the body cavities of higher forms). In more highly evolved ascidians the epicardia lose their connection with the pharynx and take on new functions. In some they become storage sacs for insoluble body wastes; in others they become involved in the growth of new tissue during asexual reproduction.

Within ascidians the above organization may be modified in two ways. In one evolutionary line the viscera descend behind the thorax to form a distinct abdomen; in some species a further extension forms a postabdomen in which the gonads descend posterior to the alimentary canal. In the second line of development, the viscera fold forward and lie beside the branchial sac between it and the mantle.

Variations in the ascidian visceral system

Physiology and biochemistry. Tunicates exhibit a number of interesting physiological and biochemical features. The direction of blood flow is reversible. The heart normally beats between 50 and 100 times in one direction before stopping and then resuming its beat in the opposite direction. This activity is controlled by so-called pacemakers at either end of the heart, but the functional significance of such reversal is obscure. The nature of the pacemakers is also uncertain, but it is generally believed that they are myogenic (centred in the heart muscle itself) and not neurogenic (*i.e.*, nervously controlled).

The blood contains a number of different cell types, the most important of which are amoebocytes, macrophages, morula cells, and nephrocytes. Amoebocytes and macrophages are concerned with routine metabolic processes; *e.g.*, gas exchange, nutrition. Morula cells are usually pigmented and contain vanadium or iron compounds that in some way have to do with the secretion and deposition of material for the test; the precise role of these cells is not yet fully understood. Some authorities believe that morula cells deposit carbohydrate (*e.g.*, sugars, starches); others have suggested that the carbohydrate is secreted by the epidermis, or outer cell layer, and that morula cells contribute protein to the test. Such differences of opinion may result from differences in the chemical composition of the test and the manner of its formation in the different species studied.

Digestion is extracellular; *i.e.*, it takes place within the alimentary canal, and most digestive enzymes (biological catalysts) are secreted in the stomach. Absorption takes place in the intestine. The pyloric gland is made up of a system of fine tubules ramifying over the walls of the intestine and opening by a duct into the pylorus, or that region of the gut between stomach and intestine. The function of the pyloric gland has not yet been established with certainty.

The nervous system consists of a small ganglion that is situated in the mantle wall between the two siphons and associated with a plexus, or nerve network, which branches throughout the mantle wall and siphonal muscles. Closely associated with the nerve ganglion is the neural gland, which opens immediately anterior to the dorsal wall of the branchial sac. Its proximity to the nerve ganglion has led to the suggestion that it may have a regulatory function comparable with that of the pituitary gland in higher chordates. It has also been suggested that the neural gland may have a sensory function in testing incoming water or in detecting the presence of eggs or sperm of other members of the species and initiating spawning. It is possible that the neural gland has several functions; it remains one of the most enigmatic structures in ascidian biology.

Theories of neural-gland function

Classification.   *Distinguishing taxonomic features.* Within the class Ascidiacea, the position of the gonad and the structure of the branchial sac are considered the most important taxonomic characters. In Thaliacea, the organization of the colony, the nature of the transverse muscles, and the form of the branchial sac are of significance. In Larvacea, the form of the endostyle (ventral groove), spiracles (respiratory holes), and tail are diagnostic characters.

Annotated classification.

SUBPHYLUM TUNICATA
Larval forms with many chordate features absent in adult. In the adult the pharynx is perforated with ciliated apertures for filter feeding and respiration; the circulatory system is open, with tubular heart; dioecious (sexes separate), with well-differentiated gonads and ducts; found worldwide in seas; about 2,100 species described.

Class Ascidiacea (sea squirts)
Sessile (fixed to sea floor); outlet siphon located dorsally; branchial region (pharynx) with transverse rows of ciliated apertures or stigmata; larvae free-swimming; solitary or colonial forms.

Order Enterogona
Body divided into thorax and abdomen or undivided; impaired gonad lies within loop of intestine.

Suborder Aplousobranchiata.   Branchial sac simple without internal longitudinal bars or vessels; intestinal loop always posterior to branchial sac.

Suborder Phlebobranchiata.   Branchial sac has internal anteroposteriorly directed tubular vessels.

Order Pleurogona
Body never divided into thorax and abdomen; gonads in lateral body wall.

Suborder Stolidobranchiata (Ptychobranchiata).   With internal anteroposteriorly directed vessels; wall of pharynx folded to increase surface area.

Class Thaliacea
Wholly pelagic (open-sea dwelling) forms with alternating cycles of sexual and asexual reproduction; asexual buds form from a ventral vessel.

Order Pyrosomida
Colonies of hollow floating tubes open at one end only, individuals being imbedded in the wall of the tube; intake siphons extend from the outer surface; outflow siphons open into the hollow interior of the colony.

Order Doliolida
Primary individuals reproduce by budding; budded individuals become sexually mature; recognizable, but temporary, tadpole stage.

Order Salpida
Primary individuals reproduce by budding; buds form a long chain; eggs attached to parent; no tadpole stage.

Class Larvacea
Minute forms with trunk and tail resembling ascidian larva; anterior epidermis secretes complex structure around animal that acts as food-collecting device.

Critical appraisal.   The Tunicata have left no fossil record; their origin and affinities with groups other than chordates are obscure. The view that they represent a degenerate offshoot of the Chordata is no longer accepted. It is now believed that the tailed larva with a notochord was evolved by the ascidians either to improve the orientation of the larva at the time of attachment or in response to production of the test and consequent loss of cilia for locomotion. The ancestral form was probably similar to *Ciona*, with the gut loop lying immediately posterior to a simple branchial sac and with open epicardia. Some authorities believe that this was a solitary form and that asexual reproduction arose independently at different times during the evolution of the group. Other authorities believe that asexual reproduction was an ancestral character and that all forms of budding have a common origin. These viewpoints have not yet been resolved, but it is agreed by most authorities that further evolution of the ascidians resulted, on the one hand, in descent of the viscera and simplification of the branchial sac to form the Aplousobranchiata and, on the other hand, in a turning forward of the viscera and internal folding of the branchial sac to form the Stolidobranchiata. The Thaliacea have in common their asexual mode of reproduction from a ventral stolon as well as their pelagic habit. The Pyrosomida probably arose from a sessile ascidian stock. The organization of the branchial sac suggests that this occurred very early in tunicate evolution. Doliolida and Salpida are considered to have evolved successively from the Pyrosomida. The origin of the Larvacea is still uncertain, but they may represent the neotenic larva of either an ascidian or a doliolid.

BIBLIOGRAPHY.   E.J.W. BARRINGTON, *The Biology of Hemichordata and Protochordata* (1965), a college textbook, with 43 pages devoted to tunicates; N.J. BERRILL, *The Tunicata* (1950), a taxonomic account of British species with a useful section on tunicate biology; *The Origin of Vertebrates* (1955), an evolutionary study mostly devoted to tunicates; P.P. GRASSE (ed.), "Echinoderms-stomocordés-procordés," in *Traité de zoologie* (1948), an advanced zoological treatise (in French) devoted to tunicates; W.A. HERDMAN, *The Cambridge Natural History*, vol. 7, *Ascidians and Amphioxus* (1904), a general account at the college-textbook level; R.H. MILLAR, *Ciona* (1953), a detailed morphological account of a single species of ascidian; "Evolution in Ascidians," in H. BARNES (ed.), *Some Contemporary Studies in Marine Science* (1966), a brief paper; "The Biology of Ascidians," *Adv. Mar. Biol.*, 9:1–100 (1971), a detailed account of ascidian biology but does not include physiology; W.G. VAN NAME, "The North and South American Ascidians," *Bull. Am. Mus. Nat. Hist.*, vol. 84 (1945), a taxonomic account.

(I.M.G.)

Tuning and Temperament, Musical

Musical sound largely depends on the organization of pitch, the high or low quality of sound; and the determination of acceptable pitch plays a large part in both the theory and practice of music. The adjustment of one sound source—such as a voice, a string, or a column of air enclosed in a wind instrument—to produce a desired pitch in relation to a given pitch is called tuning. Two concepts fundamental to the theory of tuning are those of frequency ratio and of consonance and dissonance. A given musical pitch is determined by the frequency of vibration of the sound wave that produces it, as $a' = 440$ cycles per second. An interval, or distance between two pitches, can thus be mathematically described as the ratio of the frequency of the first pitch to the frequency of the second. Various frequency ratios can be reduced to the same basic relationship; for example, 440:220 and 30:15 and 750:375 can all be reduced to the ratio 2:1.

Conso-nance and dissonance When two tones are sounded together the subjective reaction may be anything from one of perfect consonance (concord, harmony, repose) to one of extreme dissonance (harshness, clashing, tension). Dissonance is produced by beats (interference between pulsations of sound waves), and it is found that maximum dissonance occurs when the rate of beats between the two tones is about 33 per second. Consonance results from the absence of beats, which occurs only when the ratio between the frequencies of the two tones is numerically simple. When the two tones are tuned to the same pitch, they are said to be in unison (ratio 1:1) and their consonance is absolute. Next in order of consonance comes the octave (2:1), the interval between c and c' (encompassing eight notes of the piano keyboard); another highly consonant interval is the fifth (3:2, as from c to g). When a unison, octave, or fifth is slightly mistuned, the resulting combination is markedly dissonant and is judged "out of tune." The slight mistunings that occur in systems of tempered tuning are necessary for reasons that will be discussed later in this article.

The problems of tuning. So long as music consists of melody without harmony, consonance plays little part in the determination of successive pitches in a scale. Many primitive scales are sung, not played, and are variable in the exact pitches of their notes. When instruments are made, it is often necessary to determine precise pitches. The tendency is either to make the steps in the scale sound equal in size or to place them in simple arithmetic relationship to one another. The fundamental unit is the octave, which has the unique property that its two notes are felt in some indefinable way to be the same, though in pitch level they are recognizably different. For this reason, high and low voices naturally sing the same tune an octave apart. In nearly all musical cultures the octave is subdivided into a number of steps, each a simple fraction of an octave. In the diatonic, or seven-note scale, for example, which is the basis of Western music and is represented by the white notes on the piano keyboard, there are five steps of one-sixth of an octave and two of one-twelfth. In contrast to these uncomplicated fractions, the frequency ratios of these intervals are actually *Conflict of scale and conso-nance* the irrational numbers: $\sqrt[6]{2}{:}1$ and $\sqrt[12]{2}{:}1$. As has been noted, consonance is related to simple frequency ratios such as 2:1. Consequently, the arithmetic subdivision of the octave can never produce perfectly consonant intervals. This unavoidable fact underlies many of the problems in the history of tuning. Insignificant when notes are heard melodically, it becomes highly important when notes of different pitch are heard simultaneously. The complex development of harmony has been the most striking peculiarity of Western music, and it has brought with it a host of tuning problems.

Apart from the octave, which presents no problem, there are really only three distinct intervals in the diatonic scale the consonance of which is important. These are the fifth (3:2), the major third (5:4, as C–E), and the major sixth (5:3, as C–A). The other three consonant intervals are the fourth (4:3), the minor sixth (8:5, one-twelfth of an octave smaller than a major sixth, as D–B), and the

minor third (6:5, as D–F). The intervals of this second group are not truly distinct, for they can be derived from the first three by inversion—*i.e.*, by transposing *Inversion of intervals* the lower note of the interval up an octave. Thus, inverting the fifth c–g yields the fourth g–c'. Inverting the major third c–e yields the minor sixth e–c', and inverting the major sixth c–a yields the minor third a–c'. Because of the phenomenon of inversion, if the fifths in a scale are in tune, the fourths also will be in tune. For each of these six intervals the tuning expressed by the above simple frequency ratios sounds "right"; if modified slightly in either direction it sounds seriously out of tune. The same cannot be said of other intervals of the diatonic scale. The major and minor seventh (as c–b and d–c') and the diminished fifth (as b–f'), with their inversions, sound dissonant in any case; they have no one tuning that is clearly more acceptable than another. Hence the harmonic merits of any tuning system depend on the way fifths, major thirds, and major sixths are tuned. In the diatonic scale (indefinitely extended through several octaves) there are six perfect fifths (F–C, C–G, G–D, D–A, A–E, E–B), three major thirds (F–A, C–E, G–B), and four major sixths (F–D, C–A, G–E, D–B). It is impossible to tune the seven notes of the scale so that each of these 13 intervals is maximally consonant. This is the second inescapable obstacle to perfection in the tuning of the diatonic scale.

Classic tuning systems. Of the two ancient Greek systems that were chiefly used in the Middle Ages, one, *The Pythagorean tuning*, makes all the fifths perfectly consonant. As a result, all the major thirds and major sixths are *Pythag-orean system* sharp (too wide) by 22 cents (a cent is 1/1200 of an octave) or by the ratio of 81:80. This amount is called a comma of Didymus, and it makes intervals severely dissonant when their notes are sounded simultaneously. Within the gamut, the pitch range in use during the Middle Ages, a major third or sixth mistuned by a comma beats between 6 and 32 times a second. Melodically, the Pythagorean system is satisfactory. (Table 1 compares whole tone and semitone sizes in the four main tuning systems.) Pythagorean tuning makes all five whole tones (the larger steps in the diatonic scale) equal at 9:8 (204 cents), and the two semitones (the smaller steps) equal at 256:243 (90 cents). The semitones are considerably less than half the whole tones in size, but this is not particularly objectionable in a melody.

Ptolemaic tuning, often misleadingly named just intona- *Just* tion, sacrifices one of the fifths (D–A), which is altered *intona-* to 40:27 from the simpler ratio 3:2, making it flat (too *tion* narrow) by a comma. The advantage of this system is that all the major thirds are true, or "in tune," as are all the major sixths except F–D, which is tuned to the ratio 27:16, as in the Pythagorean tuning (instead of to 5:3). The triad D–F–A is quite unusable, although the other triads used are perfectly in tune. (A triad is a chord built of two thirds.) For melody the system has the drawback of employing two different sizes of whole tones: C–D, F–G, and A–B are major tones (9:8 or 204 cents), and D–E and G–A are minor tones (10:9 or 182 cents). The difference is noticeable without being great enough to suggest that they are two purposely distinct intervals. To sing the first phrase of "Three Blind Mice" with the middle note perceptibly too high can hardly have seemed satisfactory at any period.

Although just intonation occupied the attention of many theorists, its disadvantages are so great that it is doubtful whether the system was ever strictly applied to harmonized music. Some kind of temperament may have been practiced empirically long before it was described in writing. The addition over several centuries of the five chromatic notes (the black notes of the piano), giving the full chromatic scale, certainly does nothing to improve either the Pythagorean or the Ptolemaic tuning (see Table 2, which shows the deviation of the four main tuning systems from the ideal tuning of the principal intervals). To either system the use of the chromatic notes adds more true fifths but also more untrue thirds and sixths. The advantages of just intonation over Pythagorean tuning are experienced only in chords made up of white notes.

Table 1: Melodic Comparison of the Four Principal Tuning Systems*

	diatonic scale					chromatic scale			
	Pythagorean tuning	"just intonation"	mean-tone temperament	equal temperament		Pythagorean tuning	"just intonation"	mean-tone temperament	equal temperament
C					**C**				
semitone	90	112	117	100		90	112	117	100
B					**B**				
whole tone	204	204	193	200		114	92	76	100
A					**Bb**				
whole tone	204	182	193	200		90	112	117	100
G					**A**				
whole tone	204	204	193	200		90	90	117	100
F					**G#**				
semitone	90	112	117	100		114	92	76	100
E					**G**				
whole tone	204	182	193	200		90	112	117	100
D					**F#**				
whole tone	204	204	193	200		114	92	76	100
C					**F**				
						90	112	117	100
					E				
						114	92	76	100
					Eb				
						90	90	117	100
					D				
						90	112	117	100
					C#				
						114	92	76	100
					C				

*The sizes of successive steps in the diatonic and chromatic scales are shown for each of the four systems, in cents. Black notes of the chromatic scale are indicated by bold lines.

With the development of harmony and the increased use of chromatic notes, both tuning systems became increasingly unsatisfactory.

Temperament. The first mention of temperament is found in 1496 in the treatise *Practica musica* by the Italian theorist Franchino Gafori, who stated that organists flatten fifths by a small, indefinite amount. This practice tends to spread out the mistuning of the fifth D–A over several fifths, so that all are tolerable although none is perfect. This principle was systematized as mean-tone temperament, first described in 1523. Under this scheme, all the major thirds of the scale are made perfect (*i.e.*, are tuned in the simple ratio 5:4); it results in an imperfection in the tuning of fifths that is spread out evenly over the entire cycle. Specifically, the interval of two octaves and a major third is tuned perfectly and divided into four fifths (C–G–d–a–e′), each of which has the ratio $\sqrt[4]{5}:1$ (compared to 3:2 for a perfectly tuned fifth). The fifths are flat by a quarter of a comma, which is much less dissonant than a comma: it gives a beat rate of 0.9 to 4 per second for fifths that fall within the compass of the medieval gamut. All major sixths are sharp by the same amount. Melodically, the scale resulting from mean-tone temperament is superior to the Ptolemaic (just intonation) scale, for all the whole tones are equal in size, being exactly half a true major third, or 193 cents. This is the source of the system's name: the mean, or average, whole tone. The semitones of the diatonic scale are relatively large, at 117 cents.

Mean-tone temperament, specifically designed for keyboard instruments, was an acceptable compromise so long as the black notes used in a composition did not extend beyond Eb and G#. As soon as D# was needed as well as Eb, the system collapsed. The keyboard provided only one key for Eb and D#. This key was tuned as Eb and with no reference to the G# below it. The enharmonic fifth G#–Eb (in which Eb is treated as equal to D#) is nearly two commas out of tune in the mean-tone system. Worse even than the mistuned fifth of just intonation, it was often given the name "the wolf." Organs were occasionally built with split black keys so that Eb and D# could be differently tuned and also Ab and G#. This expedient slightly extended the range of usable harmonies, but a more drastic remedy was soon needed. By spreading out the mistuning of the "wolf" fifth among its neighbours, in the same way that their predecessors had spread out the mistuning of the fifth D–A, musicians of the 17th century moved imperceptibly away from mean-tone temperament, in which the fifths are tuned unequal-

ly, toward the system of equal temperament, in which all fifths are equally flat.

In equal temperament, all intervals are made up of semitone units, each of which is set exactly at a 12th of an octave, or 100 cents. A fifth is built of seven semitones; in relation to a pure fifth, it is 2 cents flat. A major third is four semitones and is 14 cents sharp; a major sixth is nine semitones and is 16 cents sharp. Because in equal temperament the intervals are identical in all parts of the chromatic scale, the system is the only one that can accommodate the expanded range of harmonies of 19th- and 20th-century music. Melodically, it fulfills the ideal of equal steps. The price for these great advantages is the total disappearance of perfectly tuned intervals, save only the octave. For the piano and the harpsichord this is scarcely a drawback: the characteristic tone of these instruments is, in any case, rich in dissonant components. Indeed, it has been found that piano tuners systematically set octaves and even unison strings out of tune. But on the organ, with its purer and more sustained tone, the disadvantages of equal temperament are considered by many to outweigh its blessings. In England such musicians as the organist and composer Samuel Sebastian Wesley continued to oppose it even as late as the mid-19th century.

On fretted instruments, such as lutes, guitars and viols, the frets extend across the fingerboard, producing at any one point divisions of equal lengths on strings of different pitch. Unless equal temperament is used, the positioning of the frets results in mistuned octaves and unisons when the same note is played on different strings. For this reason equal temperament was applied at least as early as the 16th century in the construction of fretted instruments.

It has often been stated that singers and players on instruments of undetermined tuning, such as violins and trombones, naturally use just intonation when performing together. Experimental evidence does not support this theory. In such circumstances musicians tend either to play in equal temperament, or, if anything, to distort intervals away from perfect consonance. Most probably this is the result of generations of conditioning. Moreover, it has been found that few musicians can distinguish melodically between just intonation and equal temperament and that those who can do so prefer the latter.

Other tuning systems. An enormous number of systems of tuning have been proposed and experimented with at different times, many involving subdivision of the octave into other than 12 equal units. None of them has passed into general use.

(margin notes) Mean-tone temperament

(margin notes) Equal-tempered tuning

Table 2: Harmonic Comparison of the Four Principal Tuning Systems*

	diatonic scale						added black notes					enharmonic intervals			
Perfect fifths	F-C	C-G	G-D	D-A	A-E	E-B	E♭-B♭	B♭-F	B-F♯	F♯-C♯	C♯-G♯	G♯-E♭			
Pythagorean tuning	0	0	0	0	0	0	0	0	0	0	0	−24			
"just intonation"	0	0	0	−22	0	0	0	0	0	0	0	−2			
mean-tone temperament	−5	−5	−5	−5	−5	−5	−5	−5	−5	−5	−5	+35			
equal temperament	−2	−2	−2	−2	−2	−2	−2	−2	−2	−2	−2	−2			
Major thirds	F-A	C-E	G-B				E♭-G	B♭-D	D-F♯	A-C♯	E-G♯	B-E♭	F♯-B♭	C♯-F	G♯-C
Pythagorean tuning	+22	+22	+22				+22	+22	+22	+22	+22	−2	−2	−2	−2
"just intonation"	0	0	0				+22	+22	+22	+22	+22	+20	+20	+20	+20
mean-tone temperament	0	0	0				0	0	0	0	0	+42	+42	+42	+42
equal temperament	+14	+14	+14				+14	+14	+14	+14	+14	+14	+14	+14	+14
Major sixths	F-D	C-A	G-E	D-B			E♭-C	B♭-G	A-F♯	E-C♯	B-G♯	F♯-E♭	C♯-B♭	G♯-F	
Pythagorean tuning	+22	+22	+22	+22			+22	+22	+22	+22	+22	−2	−2	−2	
"just intonation"	+22	0	0	0			+22	+22	+22	+22	+22	+20	+20	+20	
mean-tone temperament	+6	+6	+6	+6			+6	+6	+6	+6	+6	+49	+49	+49	
equal temperament	+16	+16	+16	+16			+16	+16	+16	+16	+16	+16	+16	+16	

*The tuning of each of the three basic intervals is analyzed for each system. Deviations from the "true" intervals are given in cents. 100 cents = 1 equal-tempered semitone. The sizes of the "true" intervals are as follows: perfect fifth, 702 cents; major third, 386 cents; major sixth, 884 cents.

Tuning and musical history. It is seldom realized what an important effect tuning practices have had on the development of harmony and tonality. From the 10th to the 13th centuries thirds and sixths—now considered consonant—were treated as dissonances simply because, according to then-current tuning methods, they *were* dissonances. In Pythagorean tuning, only the bare fifth and octave could provide a tolerable point of repose in music accompanied by the organ. Although just intonation permitted some harmony based on triads, the use of sharpened leading notes (the last note of the scale, leading upward into the first), which by the 16th century had caused the older system of modes to disintegrate, was made acceptable only by the use of some kind of temperament. At a later date it was the existence of lutes tuned in equal temperament that made possible the more extreme experiments in chromaticism of composers such as Luca Marenzio (1553–99) and Carlo Gesualdo (c. 1560–1613). The formation of a unified orchestra was probably delayed by the simultaneous practice of two incompatible tuning systems—mean-tone for keyboard instruments, equal temperament for lutes and viols. The decline of viols and their replacement by the violin family may have been hastened by the inability of viols to play with the organ. The modern orchestra began with the Vingt-quatre Violons du Roi (Twenty-four Violins of the King) of Louis XIV, and most later Baroque music is based on a keyboard instrument with from one to 30 members of the violin family, playing in mean-tone temperament. The cycle of six related keys, established in the operas of Alessandro Scarlatti (1660–1725) and the sonatas of Arcangelo Corelli (1653–1713) and followed closely in most of the music of J.S. Bach (1685–1750) and George Frideric Handel (1685–1759), is probably a direct outcome of mean-tone temperament. Within the limits of mean-tone temperament, the six keys exhaust the chromatic compass available. On the other hand, "wolf" chords may have been deliberately introduced by Domenico Scarlatti (1685–1757), François Couperin (1668–1733), and other composers to give an added piquancy to certain harpsichord passages. Many harpsichord players, including Bach, would retune a few notes of their instruments to prepare to play a piece in a new key, shifting the "wolf" fifth to part of the scale where it would do no harm. But in organ works such temporary retuning was hardly possible. Bach's organ tuning must have been as close to equal temperament as modern instruments are, although it is known that he was opposed to a strictly mathematical equality of intervals. By his title *Well-Tempered Clavier* he probably meant a kind of modified mean-tone temperament.

Enharmonic modulation, in which one note (say B♭) is treated as identical to another (say A♯) that actually has the same pitch only in equal temperament, was an exceptional device in Baroque music. But as orchestras became free of keyboard instruments and as keyboard instruments increasingly adopted equal temperament, it became a normal stock-in-trade, allowing the use of a series of key changes in one direction that eventually returns to the original key. Thus, it is not unusual for Mozart to complete the cycle of 12 keys in the course of a movement. Equal temperament permitted 19th-century composers to use the 12 notes of the chromatic scale with the utmost freedom. It also fixed those 12 notes so immutably in the Western musical consciousness that the revolutionary developments of 20th-century music, far from undermining them, have tended to perpetuate them.

BIBLIOGRAPHY. L.F. HERMANN HELMHOLTZ, *Die Lehre von den Tonempfindungen als physiologische Grundlage für die Theorie der Musik* (1862; Eng. trans. by ALEXANDER J. ELLIS, *On the Sensations of Tone*, 1875), still the classic treatment of the subject, with useful additional observations by the translator; J. MURRAY BARBOUR, *Tuning and Temperament: A Historical Survey* (1951), a comprehensive study of the theoretical aspects of the subject, with a good bibliography; LLEWELYN S. LLOYD and HUGH BOYLE, *Intervals, Scales and Temperaments* (1963), designed for the musician; PAUL C. GREENE, "Violin Intonation," *Journal of the Acoustical Society of America*, 9:43–44 (1937), disposes of the theory that violinists naturally play in just intonation; ROGER E. KIRK, "Tuning Preferences for Piano Unison Groups," *ibid.*, 31:1644–48 (1959), shows that musicians prefer groups of unison strings on the piano to be mistuned; D.W. MARTIN and W.D. WARD, "Subjective Evaluation of Musical Scale Temperament in Pianos," *ibid.*, 33:582–585 (1961), shows that musicians do not prefer just intonation to equal temperament; FRITZ A. KUTTNER and J. MURRAY BARBOUR, *The Theory of Classical Greek Music; Meantone Temperament in Theory and Practice*; and *The Theory and Practice of Just Intonation*, Musurgia Records, Theory Series A, No. 1–3, an opportunity to hear the three major tuning systems that preceded equal temperament, both in scales and chords and in actual music.

(N.T.)

Tunis

Tunis (Arabic: Tūnus or Tūnis), the capital and largest city of the Republic of Tunisia and of the *wilāyat* (governorate) of Tunis, is one of the oldest of Mediterranean cities. It is situated to the southwest of the Gulf of Tunis, six miles inland from its ancient outport of Ḥalq al-Wādī (La Goulette). Located near the site of ancient Carthage, now a suburb of the city, it occupies a key position on the Barbary Coast of North Africa, between the western and eastern basins of the Mediterranean Sea. Its mixture of medieval and modern architecture, its exotic covered markets, and other historic and scenic sights have long appealed to visitors, and tourism, in fact, is Tunis' fastest growing industry. A steady and increasing influx of population from rural areas presents it with long-term employment, housing, and other urban problems. The *wilāyat* of Tunis has an area of 803 square miles (2,080 square kilometres).

History. Nothing certain is known about the origins of the city of Tunis, which is mentioned in Greek and Latin texts under the name Tynes, or Tunes. It was undoubtedly founded by the Libyans, the earliest occupants of the area, and it was probably these Libyans who, in about 800 BC, surrendered the site of Carthage to a colony of

Enharmonic modulation

Phoenicians from Tyre. Tunis soon gravitated into the orbit of Carthage, sharing its fortunes—and misfortunes. In 146 BC, during the Third Punic War, between Carthage and Rome, Tunis, like Carthage, was destroyed. But it arose from its ruins and even flourished under the rule of the Roman emperor Augustus, although there is not much record of it during Roman, Vandal, and Byzantine times.

When Carthage was destroyed a second time by the Arab conqueror Ḥassān ibn an-Nuʿmān in 698, Tunis was no more than a poor, small town. Ḥassān established an arsenal at Tunis, bringing in a thousand Coptic families from Egypt; among them were specialists in shipbuilding.

Rebuilding of the city by the Arabs

The new city was at first the seat of a governor; from the time of the reign of the Aghlabids (800–909), however, it shared with al-Qayrawān the role of capital city. Its oldest and most venerated monument, the mosque of az-Zaytūnah, had been built around 734 and remained until 1958 the seat of the country's oldest university. The local Banū Khurāsān dynasty (1059–1159) did a great deal to expand and beautify the city. The suburbs of Bāb as-Suwayqah on the north and Bāb al-Jazīrah on the south date from this period. The Almohad caliphs of Morocco, however, reduced Tunis to the role of a provincial seat (1160–1236). Under the Ḥafṣid dynasty (1236–1574), however, it regained its position as the capital, which it has held since. It was the Ḥafṣids who organized the specialized covered markets (suqs) so that each trade had its own separate quarter. In around 1300 the old city assumed its definitive form which it still retains.

Tunis has endured many trials in its history. King Louis IX (*q.v.*) of France (St. Louis), on the Eighth Crusade in 1270, besieged it and met his death from plague beneath its walls. In the middle of the 14th century, the Marīnids of Morocco took it twice. In 1534 it was the turn of famous Barbary corsair Barbarossa (Khayr ad-Dīn) to capture it, though he had to surrender it almost at once to Charles V, Holy Roman emperor (1535). The city then passed into the hands of the Turks (1539). It was retaken by the Spaniards, who held it from 1573 to 1574 but who were obliged to yield it to the Ottoman Empire, under whose rule it remained until the French protectorate (1881–1956). It was occupied by the Germans in 1942 and liberated by British forces and Allied troops in 1943. It became the national capital of Tunisia when independence was achieved in 1956.

The contemporary city. *City plan.* Tunis occupies a slightly elevated isthmus separating two salt lakes—the Buḥayrat Tūnis (Lake of Tunis) on the east and the marshy Subkhat as-Sījūmī on the southwest. The old city, al-Madīnah (227 acres), together with the suburbs of Bāb as-Suwayqah and Bāb al-Jazīrah (428 acres) comprise the ancient nucleus of Tunis. This old city, lying on the side of hills sloping down from the old fort (Qaṣabah), on a high point in the west, is oval in shape and is encircled by boulevards that have replaced the ancient walls. Of the old gates, only Bāb Manārah and Bāb al-Baḥr (Gate of the Sea) still stand. The old city's colourful az-Zaytūnah Street leads to Bāb al-Baḥr, from which the Avenue de France and its extension the Avenue Habib Bourguiba, the capital's largest (nearly 200 feet wide) artery sweeps into the modern, European-style city. The modern city began to develop on the flat, low-lying land between the old city and the Lake of Tunis to the east especially after 1830, when the European presence and interest became more manifest with the occupation of Algiers.

Transportation. A canal connecting the port of Ḥalq al-Wādī (La Goulette) with the shallow Lake of Tunis was cut in 1893. The new harbour complex of Tunis–Ḥalq al-Wādī, inaugurated in 1967, greatly increased the capacity of the port to handle both passengers and merchandise. Al-ʿUwaynah International Airport is a few miles northeast of the city; the increase in air traffic in the 1960s and 1970s necessitated the creation of a second airport (at Tunis–Carthage) equipped with runways for large jet aircraft. The city is the eastern terminus of the railroad from Morocco and has rail and road links with the interior and with coastal towns.

A street in a section of al-Madīnah, the old city of Tunis.
Andy Bernhaut—Photo Researchers

Demography. The population of Tunis, 186,000 at the time of the 1926 census, stood at 685,000 by the time of the 1966 census; of that number, 352,000 were males. The population of the *wilāyat* of Tunis, including the city, was 790,000. It is estimated that by the early 1970s the population of the *wilāyat* had reached 1,127,000 inhabitants, 950,000 of whom were in the city of Tunis. Of this population, 52 percent are under 20 years of age, and many are unable to find employment. To relieve that situation, emigration was being organized and encouraged. In addition to a high birth rate, an exodus from the rural areas that the authorities have been unable to stem has brought about the fast rise in the city's population. A quarter of the entire population of Tunisia is concentrated in an area of only 89 square miles. This trend appears to be intensifying, and it is estimated that by 1980 Greater Tunis will contain 1,500,000 inhabitants.

Population

Housing and architectural features. Out of a total of approximately 144,000 dwellings in the *wilāyat* of Tunis, 63,000 were individual houses, 26,000 apartments, 33,000 collective houses (rented lodgings, with rooms grouped around an interior courtyard), and 18,000 shacks (*gourbis*); the remainder consisted of tents or other temporary shelters. Of these dwellings, about 70,000 had running water, 90,000 had electricity, and 40,000 were supplied with gas.

The buildings give the city the appearance of being low and white. The cathedral, the municipal theatre and handicrafts centre, the banks, and the principal hotels and cafes are on the Avenue Habib Bourguiba. In 1971 the sky-blue silhouette of the 21-story Africa Hotel rose up, towering over the avenue. In general, the buildings of the modern city are never more than six or seven stories tall, while the tortuous alleys of the old medieval city thread among one-story cubes of ancient, windowless houses. To move from one section of Tunis to another is seemingly to travel back several centuries in time. There is a sharp contrast between the hovels of Mellassine, located amid the muddy marshes of Sabkhat as-Sījūmī, and the gleam-

Appearance of the city

ing villas of the new residential quarters on higher ground, some of which overlook the Gulf of Tunis. Great efforts have been made to create healthful working-class quarters at a moderate price, but there is resistance to change.

Industrial activity and tourism

Economic life. Agriculture remains the chief source of wealth, olives and cereals being the principal crops grown in the surrounding farmlands. Manufactures include foodstuffs, olive oil, textiles, carpets, and cement and metal building structures; there are also chemical (superphosphate), metallurgical, machine, and electrical industries and railways workshops. There are two thermoelectric plants, at Ḥalq al-Wādī, and a lead smelter, at Maqrīn. Tourism is of particular economic importance; tourist accommodations, which could house about 3,500 at a time in 1966, had increased to over 5,000 by 1970.

Government. The *wilāyat* (governorate) of Tunis is composed of nine administrative units, called delegations, and 22 communes. It has at its head a governor, appointed by the government, who presides over the municipal council of the city of Tunis. There are 30 councillors who are elected to the municipality for three-year terms by direct universal suffrage and who are eligible for re-election.

Public health and education. Within the *wilāyat* there were, early in the present decade, ten hospitals, two auxiliary hospitals, 25 local dispensaries, and 21 rural dispensaries.

The city's water is supplied from an artificial lake and various wells, springs, and subterranean sources from as far away as 60 miles to the south in the catchment of the Wādī al-Kabīr-Milyān. It is carried by pipeline to a reservoir in the Bāb al-Jazīrah quarter.

In the late 1960s there were about 110,000 pupils in the primary schools, of whom 50,000 were girls. The University of Tunis (founded in 1960) had a student body of 11,000 in the early 1970s.

Cultural life and entertainment. Tunis has two cultural centres, as well as a theatre that is used by international theatre groups. The summer festival—the Festival of Carthage, held in July—has achieved a certain renown. Among the city's attractions are its thermal baths, dating from the time of Rome's Antonine emperors (who ruled in the 2nd century), the heights of Sīdī-Bū Saʿīd, and the exoticism of its markets (suqs); in addition, several parks and green areas have been established. Nearby, southeast of the city along the valley of the Wādī Milyān, are magnificent remains of the aqueduct (originally Roman) from Jabal Zaghwān to Carthage.

Thermal baths and exotic markets

Projects intended to improve the already difficult traffic situation, to save the character of al-Madīnah, and to modernize the city are envisaged. The most important of these is perhaps the project to transform the 7,000 acres of the Lake of Tunis, now a source of pollution, into a vacation spot.

BIBLIOGRAPHY. On the history of Tunis, see CHARLES R. DESSORT, *Histoire de la ville de Tunis* (1924), now somewhat out of date; and HENRI SALADIN, *Tunis et Kairouan* (1908), which should be used with caution. For the contemporary situation, the following are suggested: J.B. DARDEL and C. KLIBI, "Un Faubourg clandestin de Tunis: le Djebel Lahmar," *Cahiers de Tunisie (CT)* 3:211–224 (1955); P. SEBAG, "Le Bidonville de Borgel," *CT*, 6:267–309 (1958); *L'évolution d'un ghetto nord-africain: la hara de Tunis* (1959); "Le Faubourg de Sîdî Fathallâh," *CT*, 8:75–136 (1960); and *et al., Un Faubourg de Tunis: Saida Manoubia* (1960).

(M.Ta.)

Tunisia

The Republic of Tunisia (in Arabic al-Jumhūrīyah at-Tūnisīyah) is a small country with an area of 63,378 square miles (164,150 square kilometres) and an estimated population of 5,194,000 in 1971. It occupies a central position of primary strategic importance in the Mediterranean, where its situation has kept it open to virtually every historic influence in the region. It is bounded by Algeria to the west and southwest, Libya to the southeast, and the Mediterranean Sea to the east and north. The capital is Tunis.

With its 750 miles of coastline, Tunisia has often been

compared to the hull of a ship, solidly moored on the continent but also freely washed by the waves; in consequence, its destiny, as its leaders never tire of repeating, is at once Mediterranean and Maghribian (the Maghrib, or the "Arab West," consists of the northwest African countries of Morocco, Algeria, Tunisia, and Libya). As North Africa constitutes a single geographic entity, the lines separating Tunisia from Libya and from Algeria do not assume the form of any natural barrier but, rather, have been shaped by the vicissitudes of human history. As a result, there have been many attempts, so far unproductive, to restore natural frontiers; Maghrib Arab unity is one of the political goals of every North African country.

Tunisia's strategic situation

Unlike its immediate neighbours, who are potentially rich, Tunisia has somewhat meagre resources at its disposal. In addition, its usable territory is limited and its domestic market restricted, and the problem of promoting economic development is particularly difficult. Thus, after the stagnation that opened the way to the trials and changes of the colonial era, Tunisia is entering the modern world with determination, sometimes with imagination, but without decisive economic advantages. For associated physical features, see ATLAS MOUNTAINS; and SAHARA (DESERT); see also the city article TUNIS; for historical aspects, see NORTH AFRICA, HISTORY OF.

THE LANDSCAPE

Relief and drainage. Tunisia is characterized by its moderate relief. The Tunisian Dorsale, a southwest to northeast mountain range that is an extension of both the Atlas Saharien (Saharan Atlas) of Algeria and of the Haut Atlas of Morocco, tapers off in the direction of the Gulf of Tunis in the northeast, on which stands Tunis. The highest peak, Kāf ash-Shaʿnabī (Mt. Chambi), located near the centre of the Algerian border, rises to 5,066 feet (1,544 metres), while Jabal Zaghwān (Mt. Zaghouan), about 30 miles southwest of Tunis, reaches only 4,249 feet (1,295 metres). Between the limestone peaks of the central Tunisian Dorsale and the sandstone chains of the Kroumirie mountains in the northwest, which reach altitudes of 3,000 feet, and of the Mogods, which run along the deeply indented coastline to the north, lies the valley of the Majardah (Medjerda), which is formed by a series of ancient lake basins covered with alluvium. This valley was once the granary of ancient Rome and remains the richest grain-producing region of Tunisia.

The Majardah and its tributaries form the principal river system; the river crosses the northern part of the country, flowing northeastward to empty into the Gulf of Tunis.

To the south of the Tunisian Dorsale lies a region of high steppes (treeless plains), with altitudes ranging from about 600 to 1,500 feet, crossed by north–south secondary ranges. Further south begins a low–steppe zone, then a series of *shatt* (salty lake) depressions. Large plains border the eastern coasts, while the extreme south consists of desert.

Climate, vegetation, and animal life. Tunisia is situated in the hot temperate zone between the 37th and the 30th parallels. It has a Mediterranean climate characterized by mild, rainy winters and hot, dry summers. Prevailing winds are from the west most of the year, producing unsettled weather. In summer the prevailing wind is from the northeast, but Saharan influences also appear that give rise to the sirocco, a hot, blasting wind from the south that can have a seriously drying effect on vegetation.

Temperatures are affected by the sea, being less extreme at Sūsah (Sousse) on the coast, for example, than at al-Qayrawān inland. Temperatures at Sūsah over a 50-year period (1901–50) varied from an average daily low of 44° F (less than 7° C) for the month of January to an average daily high of 89° F (32° C) for the month of August. Comparable temperatures at al-Qayrawān were 40° F (4° C) in January and 99° F (37° C) in August.

Temperature and rainfall

The amount of rainfall is irregular. In 1968, 51 inches were recorded at al-Fayjah in northwest Tunisia, as opposed to four inches at Matmātah. Generally, from the middle of autumn to the middle of spring, northern Tu-

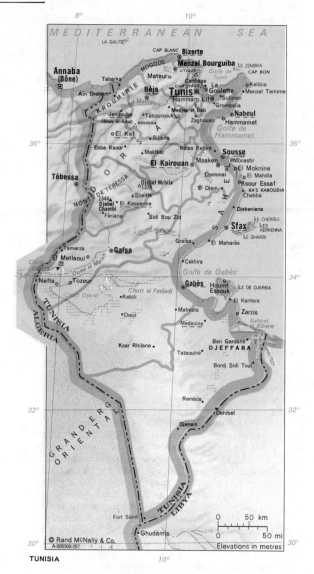

TUNISIA

nisia receives more than 16 inches of rainfall, and the steppe region receives from six to 16 inches. Amounts also vary considerably from one year to another; for example, 36 inches fell at Makthar in north central Tunisia in 1963–64, in contrast to 16 inches in 1966–67. Harvests vary as a result, being poor in dry years.

The vegetation and animal life of the country are affected by these climatic conditions. From north to south, the Kroumirie forest of cork oaks, with its fern undergrowth sheltering wild boars, gives way to steppes covered with esparto grass and populated with small game, and finally to the desert, where hunting is forbidden so as to preserve the remaining gazelles. Scorpions are found in all regions; among dangerous snakes are the horned viper and the cobra. Desert locusts sometimes damage crops in the southern part of the country.

Traditional regions. Tunisia is divided into four natural and demographic regions: the north, which is relatively fertile and well watered; the semi-arid central region; the Sāhil in the east central coastal region, which is pre-eminently olive-growing country; and the south, where, except in the oases, all vegetation disappears. In the central and southern regions, there are still tribes that have preserved a certain cohesion through following a quasi-nomadic way of life. Ethnic mixtures in these regions are rare. In the north, on the other hand, particularly along the coasts, the population is quite mixed, the life of the cultivator is more complex, the villages are more crowded, and the cities are larger. In the early 1970s the cities were continuing to expand at the expense of the countryside. In 1970, the estimated urban population numbered about 2,200,000 out of a total of 5,100,000.

Apart from Tunis (population about 944,000 in 1969), the largest towns (1966 population) are Ṣafāqis (Sfax), with 100,000 inhabitants; Sūsah (Sousse), with 75,000; Bizerte (Banzart), with 65,000; and al-Qayrawān (Kairouan), with 45,000.

THE PEOPLE

Groups historically associated with the contemporary country. The population of Tunisia is essentially Arab Berber. Throughout the centuries Tunisia has, however, received various waves of immigration; these have included Phoenicians, black Africans, Jews, Romans, Vandals, and Arabs, as well as Muslim refugees from Sicily, who settled in as-Sāḥil (Sahel) after their homeland was captured by the Norman kings in 1091. The most important immigration, however, was that of the Spanish Moors, which began after the fall of Seville, in Spain, in 1248 and turned into a veritable exodus in the early 17th century; 200,000 Spanish Muslims thus settled in the area of Tunis, in the Majardah Valley, and on Cape Bon in the north, bringing with them urban traditions and more advanced agricultural and irrigation techniques. Finally, from the 16th to the 19th centuries, the Turks brought in their wake different elements of Asiatic or European origin. This great ethnic diversity is still seen in the variety of Tunisian family names.

Languages　The cultural Arabization of the country can be considered to have been essentially completed by the end of the 12th century. Today less than 1 percent of the population, in the south, still speaks the Berber language. French, introduced during the protectorate (1881 to 1956), paradoxically came into wider use after independence because of the spread of education. Although Arabic is the official language of the country, French continues to play a dominant role in the press, education, and government, and Tunisia, significantly, was among the countries that in the 1950s and 1960s worked to organize the French Community.

Population density of Tunisia.

The last indigenous Christian communities in Tunisia, which were still sizable in the 12th century, disappeared as long ago as the end of the 14th century. Only the Jewish community has survived, but its membership, which in the early 1970s numbered approximately 85,000, was constantly decreasing as a result of emigration. Non-Muslim foreigners, who numbered about 250,000 in 1956, in the early 1970s scarcely exceeded 40,000.

Demography. Tunisia has a high birth rate. Despite the authorization or tolerance of all contraceptive methods, the present population growth rate is 2.5 percent. Forty-six percent of the population is less than 15 years of age. This high rate of growth has led to a policy of emigration; 130,000 Tunisians work abroad, 80,000 of

them in France, 30,000 in Libya, and 10,000 in Germany. The Tunisian population is very unevenly distributed. There are 180 inhabitants per square mile in the north and in as-Sāḥil (Sahel) compared with 25 on the steppes.

Tunisia, Area and Population				
	area		population	
	sq mi	sq km	1966 census	1970 estimate
Governorates (wilāyāts, gouvernorats)*				
al-Kāf (Le Kef)	3,110	8,060	311,000	339,000
al-Qaṣrayn (Kasserine)	3,490	9,040	212,000	229,000
al-Qayrawān (Kairouan)	2,710	7,030	278,000	302,000
Bājah (Béja)	2,590	6,710	321,000	296,000
Banzart (Bizerte)	1,650	4,280	330,000	316,000
Jundūbah (Jendouba)	1,180	3,050	255,000	276,000
Madanīyīn (Médenine)	22,130	57,320	242,000	266,000
Nābul (Nabeul)	1,600	4,150	324,000	329,000
Qābis (Gabes)	11,180	28,950	204,000	224,000
Qafṣah (Gafsa)	7,150	18,530	321,000	365,000
Safāqis (Sfax)	3,430	8,870	425,000	482,000
Sūsah (Sousse)	2,350	6,080	521,000	586,000
Tūnis wa al-Aḥwāz (Tunis)	800	2,080	790,000	1,127,000
Total Tunisia	63,380	164,150	4,533,000†	5,137,000

*In parenthesis the term is given in Arabic and French in the order named.
†Figures do not add to total given because of rounding.
Source: Official government figures; UN.

Despite the efforts at family planning, in the early 1970s the rate of population growth was not expected to drop in the near future, a fact that posed serious economic problems.

THE ECONOMY

Tunisia is a country with a low national income. Its gross national product per inhabitant increased from $147 U.S. a year in 1957 to $230 in 1969, as compared with more than $4,200 for the United States and $1,210 for the Soviet Union. Its annual growth rate for the period 1960 to 1971 was 3.7 percent overall and 1.5 percent per inhabitant. For 1970, the overall rate seemed to be between 6 and 7 percent. The rate of investment was between 10 and 15 percent. Tunisia is classed among the "developing" countries, its standard of living is about equal to that of Algeria but higher than that of Morocco.

Resources and resource exploitation. The Tunisian economy is characterized by the predominance of the agricultural over the manufacturing sector. In the early 1970s, about 60 percent of the population was engaged in agriculture, producing 19 percent of the national income. Yields are low and crops are, in addition, endangered by changes in the weather. The manufacturing sector, despite major efforts toward investment and acquisition of equipment in the 1960s, remained insufficiently developed. Another factor of imbalance arises from the difference in conditions between the north and the Sāḥil, on the one hand, which are more fertile and more economically developed, and the central and southern regions, on the other, which have fewer natural advantages.

Natural resources of the soil and subsoil are relatively　Natural meagre. The lumber industry is essentially confined to the　resources exploitation of oak and cork from the Kroumirie forest in the north. The esparto grass of the plains is used for the manufacture of quality paper. The principal mineral resource is phosphate. By the late 1960s, however, Tunisian phosphate production was encountering difficulties, largely because of United States and Moroccan competition, a circumstance that led to a fall in production.

Other mineral resources are iron, lead, zinc, and mercury. Petroleum, discovered in the extreme south in 1964 at the al-Borma field, by the early 1970s was beginning to play an important role in the Tunisian economy. Of the 4,150,000 tons extracted in 1970, 1,150,000 tons were sent to the Bizerte refinery, in operation since 1963, and 2,860,000 tons were for export. The constantly increasing petroleum revenues rose from 8,500,000 dinars (0.52 dinars = $1 U.S.; 1.25 dinars = £1 sterling in Dec. 1971) in 1969 to 15,000,000 dinars in 1970, when production exceeded 4,100,000 tons. Oil discoveries made in 1971 in the Ṣafāqis (Sfax) area will make it possible to double production, and other encouraging indications have been noted in the Gulf of Gabes (Qābis) on the east coast.

Tunisia's agriculture, which in the early 1970s accounted for 22 percent of its exports, remains its principal source of income. The low yields are primarily due to the division of the property into excessively small plots and the predominance of obsolete farming methods. The uncertainty of the rainfall often jeopardizes harvests; grain production is generally inadequate, and Tunisia has had to resort to imports. In addition to cereal grains, the principal products are citrus fruits, olive oil, and dates. Wine is also important, but output is decreasing. In order to improve agricultural production, dams and wells are being used to expand the irrigated area, but water resources nevertheless remain limited. The fishing industry is, however, fully developed. Sheep, goats, and cattle are raised to a limited extent.

The industrialization of Tunisia has encountered two major difficulties. Raw material and power supplies are inadequate, and the domestic market is limited. Notable and sometimes costly projects, such as the Manzil Bū Ruqaybah (Menzel-Bourguiba) iron-smelting complex, located near Bizerte, however, have been successfully established since independence was achieved in 1956. Existing industries produce foodstuffs, textiles, clothing, construction materials, household articles, and fertilizers. In the early 1970s efforts were being made to develop the south economically; for example, the Industries Chimiques Maghrébines (Maghreb Chemical Industries) complex, which produces phosphoric acid, was opened at Qābis in 1971. Tourism, however, remains Tunisia's leading industry. The number of tourists rose from 200,000 in 1966 to 400,000 in 1970.   (M.Ta.)

Trade, finance, and management of the economy. Tunisian overseas trade still reflects the importance of primary production. About three-fifths of the exports by value are foodstuffs and raw mineral products, including petroleum. About a third of all trade is with France, with which Tunisia reached an agreement on trade and tariffs following the abolition of a customs union in 1959. The balance of payments is frequently adverse, and in some years this has obliged the government to limit imports. In the late 1960s an increasing proportion of Tunisia's trade was being channelled to the countries of the European Economic Community, to which it had applied for associate membership in 1967 with a measure of success. At that time Kuwait, the United States, and West Germany were advancing generous capital aid loans.

The strength of the dinar and of the economy was helped in the late 1960s by international confidence in the political stability of Tunisia. The Banque Centrale de Tunisie performs the functions of an issuing bank.
                    (W.C.B.)

Economic doctrine
Tunisian economic doctrine consists of a flexible and undogmatic form of Socialism based on the existence of three sectors—private, cooperative, and parastate (comprising chiefly gas, electricity, and railway services). The attempt at collectivization, which was carried out in the 1960s through the forced spread of the cooperative system, finally resulted in failure, particularly in the agricultural sector, and was abandoned in 1969. There are three large professional organizations. The Union Générale des Travailleurs Tunisiens (General Union of Tunisian Workers; U.G.T.T.) is the principal trade union, and there are also associations grouping employers and farmers respectively.

Transportation and communications. The network of roads (about 10,000 miles) and of railways (about 1,420 miles) is sufficiently dense so that all metropolitan areas of any importance are linked with the interior regions. Tunisia is connected by both road and rail with Algeria and Morocco but only by road with Tripoli (Ṭarābulus), Libya, and with Cairo, since the railway ends at Qābis. Train service, however, is slow and uncomfortable, and except for the main routes, the roads are quite narrow.

The principal ports are Tunis-Ḥalq al-Wādī (La Goulette), which is the outpost of Tunis, Ṣafāqis (Sfax),

Bizerte (Banzart), and Sūsah (Sousse), as well as the port of Qābis, which was opened in 1970 and accommodates 50,000-ton ships. An oil pipeline runs from Edjeleh, Algeria, to the port of aṣ-Ṣukhayrah on the Gulf of Gabes.

Despite the creation of the Munastīr and Jarbah airports, which handle domestic or tourist (charter) flights, international air traffic is directed almost exclusively through al-ʿUwaynah airport near Tunis. Telecommunications have benefitted from an extensive modernization effort.

Tunisia is connected to Libya by microwave and to Algiers and Rabat by cable. In addition, the Qulaybīyah–Sicily and Bizerte–Marseilles cables give Tunisia access to the European automatic network. In 1971 there were over 76,000 telephone subscribers, of whom almost half were in Tunis.

ADMINISTRATION AND SOCIAL CONDITIONS

The structure of government. The Tunisian constitution, currently under revision, was promulgated in 1959; it defines Tunisia as a republic whose religion is Islām and whose official language is Arabic. Legislative power is exercised by the National Assembly, which consists of 90 delegates elected for five-year terms by universal suffrage. Executive power is in the hands of the president of the republic, who is both head of state and of government. He must be a Muslim and is elected for a five-year term by universal suffrage at the same time as the deputies; he is elegible for three consecutive terms.

The country is administered by the Cabinet, headed, since 1969, by a prime minister. The most important ministry is not that of defense, since the role and size of the armed forces has been somewhat reduced but rather that of national education, which in 1970 received almost one-quarter of the national budget. The 12 Cabinet ministers are responsible to the president rather than to the Assembly. Since 1957 the president has been Habib Bourguiba (q.v.).

Judicial power is exercised by judges whose independence is constitutionally guaranteed.

The Tunisian national army has a strength of about 24,000 men. The navy possesses two escort vessels and six patrol boats. There is a small air force.

The constitution guarantees "freedom of opinion, expression, press, publication, assembly, and association" ("under the conditions defined by law"), as well as the right to form trade unions. Tunisia in reality is governed under a one-party system, that of the Destour Socialist Party, generally called the Neo-Destour, to distinguish it from an older Destour Party founded in 1920 (*Destour* meaning "constitution"), which holds all the seats in the National Assembly. All Tunisians, including women, who are at least 20 years of age can vote. There is always a massive turnout for elections, with from 90 to 99.5 percent of the registered voters participating.

Local administration
The country is divided into 13 administrative areas called *gouvernorats* (*wilāyāt* in Arabic), which are headed by governors (*wālī*). Each *gouvernorat* is designated by the name of its chief town and is in turn subdivided into units called *délégations* (*muʿtamadīyāt*), whose number varies according to the *gouvernorat*'s size. *Muʿtamadīyāt* are administered by a *muʿtamad* and are in turn divided into varying numbers of districts called *cheikhats* (*mashyakhāt*).

Social conditions. *Education.* Education is free to all students, and scholarships in schools and universities are offered largely on the basis of merit and need. The number of students—and consequently the number of schools and teachers—has steadily increased since independence, at a rate that in the early 1970s was generally considered to be too high in relation to the rate of economic growth. Between the time of independence (1956) and the early 1970s, the number of students in primary schools rose from about 225,000 (of whom about 75,000 were girls) to more than 935,000 (of whom 370,000 were girls); in the secondary schools, from 30,000 to 195,000; and in higher education, from 2,000 to 10,000.

This growth has been accompanied by a certain drop in

educational standards; it has also posed problems of financing and of finding enough job opportunities for qualified people. A board of education was thus formed in 1971 to revise Tunisia's educational policy. A new tendency at this time was to place more emphasis on technical and agricultural training. Along with education, great efforts were being made in the early 1970s to improve housing, sanitation, and medical care. Significant results were being obtained, but these efforts were limited by problems of financing.

Social welfare. The living standards of the population in general are quite low. An improvement, recorded in 1971, brought the daily earnings of agricultural workers, who are at the bottom of the scale, up to 0.6 of a dinar. The monthly wage of a labourer is about 25 dinars, and that of a lower ranking government worker, about 35 dinars. Salaries are markedly higher in the private sector, varying from between 50 dinars for office workers to 250 dinars for managers. Rents range from a few dinars a month for a hovel, to 100 dinars for a comfortable house, rising to 200 dinars and more for luxurious lodgings. The advantages available to the less privileged consist, in addition to the distribution of milk to newborn babies and of school lunches, of free medical care for the destitute and of the extension of the social security system (providing medical benefits and hospitalization, etc.) to virtually all wage earners.

Cultural life. Tunisia is an Arab-speaking Muslim country that was deeply imbued with French culture during the 75 years of the protectorate, which ended in 1956. As in Algeria, but to a lesser extent, there was an attempt to establish a Tunisian literature written in French, but the trend apparently never took root. Although Tunisians generally use French in all scientific disciplines, they remain genuinely attached to Arabic in the literary sphere —in poetry, the novel, and the short story. Several literary reviews, the most important of which is *al-Fikr* ("Thought"), open their pages to youthful talents and stimulate literary output. Modern Tunisian literature, the subject of great debate on radio, television, and in the various government-sponsored Maisons de la Culture (Houses of Culture), has made remarkable progress, but it has not yet produced works of sufficient power to rival foreign and especially French literature, which is still preferred by the young. Tunisian literature continues to receive governmental encouragement, however, and an association of Tunisian writers was founded in 1971.

Although the Tunisian cinema is still in its infancy, having to its credit no more than a few successful short films, Tunisian painting can already lay claim to a certain tradition. Some of the artists enjoy a genuine local celebrity and have also exhibited abroad. The music conservatory, while devoting attention to developing national traditions, emphasizes the classical European heritage.

A major effort is in progress to diffuse and decentralize cultural benefits, although means are necessarily limited. Maisons de la Culture are being established in the chief towns, and travelling libraries bring films and books to the most remote corners. Television, which naturally plays an important role, likewise covers the entire country; its programs are in Arabic and French, and provide information and education as well as entertainment. Finally, mention may be made of the various scientific journals, connected with various research institutes and schools.

Prospects for the future. Geography has determined Tunisia's fate by making it a hyphen, thus giving it a calling always to seek a balance between different forces. The land of St. Augustine and of Ibn Khaldūn, a haven for the Arab Muslim tradition and at the same time a gateway to the West, Tunisia constitutes a melting pot for a multitude of cultural traditions.

The major problem now confronting Tunisia is that of economic development. Although Tunisia has benefitted from extensive foreign aid and has itself made considerable developmental investment, the laboriously launched enterprises frequently show deficits. Tunisia, moreover, is obliged to import not only industrial equipment and products but also large quantities of foodstuffs, particu-

larly cereal grains and meat, and its balance of trade constantly shows a deficit. The balance of payments, however, showed a surplus in the early 1970s, thanks to tourist revenues, to money sent by Tunisians working abroad to their families, and to influxes of capital in the form of investments or loans.

The current trend is toward granting priority to agriculture, improving crop yields, organizing emigration of workers, encouraging enterprises that require little capital and large amounts of labour, and reducing population pressure by making family planning more effective. Finally, it is hoped that wealth from new petroleum discoveries may help to finance Tunisia's future development.

(M.Ta.)

BIBLIOGRAPHY

Geography: PIERRE BIROT and JEAN DRESCH, *La Méditerranée et le Moyen-Orient,* 2 vol. (1953–56); JEAN DESPOIS, *Le Djebel Nefousa* (1935), *L'Afrique Blanche,* vol. 1, *L'Afrique du Nord,* 3rd ed. (1964), and *La Tunisie: ses régions* (1961); WILFRID KNAPP, *Tunisia* (1970).

Population: H.H. ABDUL-WAHAB, *Coup d'oeil général sur les apports éthniques étrangers en Tunisie* (1917, reprinted in *Cahiers de Tunisie,* 18:151–169, 1970); JEAN GANIAGE, *La Population européenne de Tunis au milieu du XIXᵉ siècle* (1960); R. LALUE and P. MARTHELOT, "La Répartition de la population tunisienne," *Annales—Economies, Sociétés, Civilisations,* 17:283–301 (1962); J.D. LATHAM, "Towards a Study of Andalusian Immigration and Its Place in Tunisian History," *Cahiers de Tunisie,* 5:209–252 (1957).

Social: ANDRE DEMEERSEMAN, *Tunisie, sève nouvelle* (1957) and *Lumière et Ombre au Maghreb* (1970).

Economy: MONCEF GUEN, *La Tunisie indépendante face à son économie* (1961); GHAZI DUWAJI, *Economic Development in Tunisia* (1967); E. MAKHLOUF, "Structures agraires et modernisation de l'agriculture dans les plaines du Kef," *Cahiers du C.E.R.E.S. (Série géographique),* no. 1 (1968); M.P. BRUGNES ROMIEU, "Investissements industriels et développement en Tunisie," *Cahiers du C.E.R.E.S. (Série economique),* no. 1 (1966); M. SEKLANI, "La Mortalité et le coût de la santé publique en Tunisie depuis l'après-guerre," *Cahiers du C.E.R.E.S. (Série démographique),* no. 1 and 2 (1967–68). See also *Revue Tunisienne des Sciences Sociales* (quarterly) and *Cahiers de Tunisie* (quarterly). The TUNISIAN SERVICE DE STATISTIQUES publishes a statistical annual, *Annuaire Statistique de la Tunisie,* a monthly statistical bulletin, *Bulletin Mensuel de Statistique,* and various other documents. Also see the TUNISIAN UNION OF INDUSTRY AND COMMERCE, *Economic Yearbook of Tunisia.*

Culture: The Institut des Belles Lettres Arabes journal, *IBLA,* provides a general view of cultural life, together with a bibliography.

(M.Ta./W.C.B.)

Tunnelling and Underground Excavation

A tunnel is an essentially horizontal underground passageway produced by excavation or occasionally by nature's action in dissolving a soluble rock, such as limestone. A vertical opening is usually called a shaft. Tunnels have many uses: for mining ores, for transportation—including road vehicles, trains, subways, and canals—and for conducting water and sewage. Underground chambers, often associated with a complex of connecting tunnels and shafts, increasingly are being used for such things as underground hydroelectric-power plants, ore-processing plants, pumping stations, vehicle parking, storage of oil and water, water-treatment plants, warehouses, and light manufacturing; also command centres and other special military needs.

True tunnels and chambers are excavated from the inside—with the overlying material left in place—and then lined as necessary to support the adjacent ground. A hillside tunnel entrance is called a portal; tunnels may also be started from the bottom of a vertical shaft or from the end of a horizontal tunnel driven principally for construction access and called an adit. So-called cut-and-cover tunnels (more correctly called conduits) are built by excavating from the surface, constructing the structure, and then covering with backfill. Tunnels underwater are now commonly built by the use of an immersed tube: long, prefabricated tube sections are floated to the site, sunk in a prepared trench, and covered with backfill. For all underground work, difficulties increase with the size of the opening and are greatly dependent upon weaknesses of the natural ground and the extent of the water inflow. This article is divided into the following sections:

I. History

ANCIENT TUNNELS

It is probable that the first tunnelling was done by prehistoric men seeking to enlarge their caves. All major ancient civilizations developed tunnelling methods. In Babylonia, tunnels were used extensively for irrigation; and a brick-lined pedestrian passage some 3,000 feet (900 metres) long was built 2180 to 2160 BC under the Euphrates River, to connect the royal palace with the temple. Construction was accomplished by diverting the river during the dry season. The Egyptians developed techniques for cutting soft rocks with copper saws and hollow reed drills, both surrounded by an abrasive, a technique probably used first for quarrying stone blocks and later in excavating temple rooms inside rock cliffs. Abu Simbel Temple on the Nile, for instance, was built in sandstone about 1250 BC for Ramses II (in the 1960s it was cut apart and moved to higher ground for preservation before flooding from the Aswān High Dam). Even more elaborate temples were later excavated within solid rock in Ethiopia and India.

The Greeks and Romans both made extensive use of tunnels: to reclaim marshes by drainage and for water aqueducts, such as the 6th-century-BC Greek water tunnel on the isle of Samos driven some 3,400 feet (one kilometre) through limestone with a cross section about six feet (two metres) square. Perhaps the largest tunnel in ancient times was a 4,800-foot-long, 25-foot-wide, 30-foot-high (1,500 × 8 × 9 metres) road tunnel (the Pausilippo) between Naples and Pozzuoli, executed in 36

Largest ancient tunnel

BC. By that time surveying methods (commonly by string line and plumb bobs) had been introduced, and tunnels were advanced from a succession of closely spaced shafts to provide ventilation. To save the need for a lining, most ancient tunnels were located in reasonably strong rock, which was broken off (spalled) by so-called fire quenching, a method involving heating the rock with fire and suddenly cooling it by dousing with water. Ventilation methods were primitive, often limited to waving a canvas at the mouth of the shaft, and most tunnels claimed the lives of hundreds or even thousands of the slaves used as workers. In AD 41, the Romans used some 30,000 men for ten years to push a 3.5 mile (six-kilometre) tunnel to drain Lake Fucinus. They worked from shafts 120 feet (37 metres) apart and up to 400 feet (120 metres) deep. Far more attention was paid to ventilation and safety measures when workers were freemen, as shown by archaeological diggings at Hallstatt, Austria, where salt-mine tunnels have been worked since 2500 BC.

FROM THE MIDDLE AGES TO THE PRESENT

Canal and railroad tunnels. Because the limited tunnelling in the Middle Ages was principally for mining and military engineering, the next major advance was to meet Europe's growing transportation needs in the 17th century. The first of many major canal tunnels was the Canal du Midi (also known as Languedoc) tunnel in France, built in 1666–81 by Pierre Riquet as part of the first canal linking the Atlantic and the Mediterranean. With a length of 515 feet and a cross section of 22 by 27 feet (157 × 7 × 8 metres), it involved what was probably the first major use of explosives in public-works tunnelling, gunpowder placed in holes drilled by hand-held iron drills. A notable canal tunnel in England was the Bridgewater Canal Tunnel, built in 1761 by James Brindley to carry coal to Manchester from the Worsley mine. Many more canal tunnels were dug in Europe and North America in the 18th and early 19th centuries. Though the canals fell into disuse with the introduction of railroads around 1830, the new form of transport produced a huge increase in tunnelling, which continued for nearly 100 years as railroads expanded over the world. Much pioneer railroad tunnelling developed in England. A 3.5-mile (six-kilometre) tunnel (the Woodhead) of the Manchester–Sheffield Railway (1839–45) was driven from five shafts up to 600 feet (180 metres) deep. In the United States, the first railroad tunnel was a 701-foot (214-metre) construction on the Allegheny Portage Railroad. Built in 1831–33, it was a combination of canal and railroad systems, carrying canal barges over a summit. Though plans for a transport link from Boston to the Hudson River had first called for a canal tunnel to pass under the Berkshire Mountains, by 1855, when the Hoosac Tunnel was started, railroads had already established their worth, and the plans were changed to a double-track railroad bore 24 by 22 feet and 4.5 miles long (7 × 7 metres by seven kilometres). Initial estimates contemplated completion in three years; 21 were actually required, partly because the rock proved too hard for either hand drilling or a primitive power saw. When the state of Massachusetts finally took over the project, it completed it in 1876 at five times the originally estimated cost. Despite frustrations, the Hoosac Tunnel contributed notable advances in tunnelling, including one of the first uses of dynamite, the first use of electric firing of explosives, and the introduction of power drills, initially steam and later air, from which there ultimately developed a compressed-air industry.

Simultaneously, more spectacular railroad tunnels were being started through the Alps. The first of these, the Mont Cenis Tunnel (also known as Fréjus), required 14 years (1857–71) to complete its 8.5-mile (14-kilometre) length. Its engineer, Germain Sommeiller, introduced many pioneering techniques, including rail-mounted drill carriages, hydraulic ram air compressors, and construction camps for workmen complete with dormitories, family housing, schools, hospitals, a recreation building, and repair shops. Sommeiller also designed an air drill that eventually made it possible to move the tunnel ahead at

First use of explosives

Tunnels in the Alps

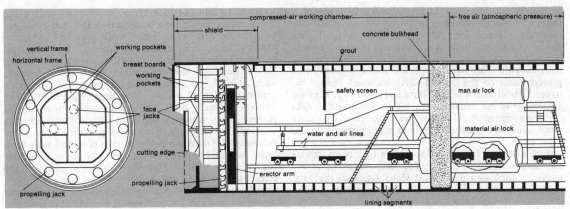

Figure 1: *Tunnelling shield, a basic engineering tool for underwater and soft-ground tunnelling.*
(Left) Front view, (Right) cross section, showing shield advancing, with lining being emplaced
behind it, and air locks for entry into compressed-air working chamber.
By courtesy of (right) Port of New York Authority; from (left) Richardson and Mayo, *Practical Tunnel Driving*
(copyright 1941); used with permission of McGraw-Hill Book Company

the rate of 15 feet (4.5 metres) per day and was used in
several later European tunnels until replaced by more
durable drills developed in the United States by Simon
Ingersoll and others on the Hoosac Tunnel. As this long
tunnel was driven from two headings separated by 7.5
miles (12 kilometres) of mountainous terrain, surveying
techniques had to be refined. Ventilation became a major
problem, which was solved by the use of forced air from
water-powered fans and a horizontal diaphragm at mid-
height, forming an exhaust duct at top of the tunnel.
Mont Cenis was soon followed by other notable Alpine
railroad tunnels: nine-mile (14-kilometre) St. Gotthard
(1872–82), which introduced compressed-air locomotives
and suffered major problems with water inflow, weak
rock, and bankrupt contractors; the 12-mile (19-kilo-
metre) Simplon (1898–1906); and the nine-mile (14-
kilometre) Lötschberg (1906–11), on a northern continuation of the Simplon railroad line.

Nearly 7,000 feet (2,100 metres) below the mountain
crest, Simplon encountered major problems from highly
stressed rock flying off the walls in rock bursts; high
pressure in weak schists and gypsum, requiring ten-foot-
(three-metre-) thick masonry lining to resist swelling tendencies in local areas; and from high-temperature water
(130° F [54° C]), which was partly treated by spraying
from cold springs. Driving Simplon as two parallel tunnels with frequent crosscut connections considerably aided ventilation and drainage.

Lötschberg
disaster
and its
effect
Lötschberg was the site of a major disaster in 1908.
When one heading was passing under the Kander
River Valley, a sudden inflow of water, gravel, and broken rock filled the tunnel for a length of 4,300 feet (1,300
metres), burying the entire crew of 25 men. Though a
geologic panel had predicted that the tunnel here would
be in solid bedrock far below the bottom of the valley fill,
subsequent investigation showed that bedrock lay at a
depth of 940 feet (290 metres), so that at 590 feet (180
metres) the tunnel tapped the Kander River, allowing it
and soil of the valley fill to pour into the tunnel, creating
a huge depression, or sink, at the surface. After this lesson
in the need for improved geological investigation, the
tunnel was rerouted about one mile (1.6 kilometres)
upstream, where it successfully crossed the Kander Valley in sound rock.

Most long-distance rock tunnels have encountered problems with water inflows. One of the most notorious was
the first Japanese Tanna Tunnel, driven through the Taki-
ji Peak in the 1920s. The engineers and crews had to cope
with a long succession of extremely large inflows, the first
of which killed 16 men and buried 17 others, who were
rescued after seven days of tunnelling through the debris.
Three years later another major inflow drowned several
workers. In the end, Japanese engineers hit on the expedient of digging a parallel drainage tunnel the entire
length of the main tunnel. In addition, they resorted to
compressed-air tunnelling with shield and air lock (see
below), a technique almost unheard of in mountain tunnelling.

Subaqueous tunnels. Tunnelling under rivers was considered impossible until the protective shield was developed in England by Marc Brunel, a French émigré
engineer. The first use of the shield, by Brunel and his son
Isambard, was in 1825 on the Wapping–Rotherhithe
Tunnel through clay under the Thames River. The tunnel was of horseshoe section 22¼ × 37½ feet (7 × 12
metres) and brick lined. After several floodings from
hitting sand pockets and a seven-year shutdown for re-
financing and building a second shield, the Brunels succeeded in completing the world's first true subaqueous
tunnel in 1841, essentially nine years' work for a 1,200-
foot- (370-metre-) long tunnel. In 1869 by reducing to
a small size (eight feet [2.4 metres]) and by changing to a
circular shield plus a lining of cast-iron segments, Peter
W. Barlow and his field engineer, James Henry Greathead, were able to complete a second Thames tunnel in
only one year as a pedestrian walkway from Tower Hill.
In 1874, Greathead made the subaqueous technique really practical by refinements and mechanization of the
Brunel–Barlow shield and by adding of compressed-air
pressure inside the tunnel to hold back the outside water
pressure. Compressed air alone was used to hold back the
water in 1880 in a first attempt to tunnel under New
York's Hudson River; major difficulties and the loss of
20 lives forced abandonment after only 1,600 feet (480
metres) had been excavated. The first major application
of the shield-plus-compressed-air technique occurred in
1886 on the London subway with an 11-foot (3.3-metre)
bore, where it accomplished the unheard-of record of
seven miles (11 kilometres) of tunnelling without a single
fatality. So thoroughly did Greathead develop his procedure that it was used successfully for the next 75 years
with no significant change. A modern Greathead shield
illustrates his original developments as pictured in Figure 1: miners working under a hood in individual small
pockets that can be quickly closed against inflow; shield
propelled forward by jacks; permanent lining segments
erected under protection of the shield tail; and the whole
tunnel pressurized to resist water inflow.

Greathead
technique

Once subaqueous tunnelling became practical, many
railroad and subway crossings were constructed with the
Greathead shield, and the technique later proved adaptable for the much larger tunnels required for automobiles.
A new problem, noxious gases from internal-combustion
engines, was successfully solved by Clifford Holland for
the world's first vehicular tunnel, completed in 1927 under the Hudson River and now bearing his name. Holland
and his chief engineer, Ole Singstad, solved the ventilation problem with huge-capacity fans in ventilating buildings at each end, forcing air through a supply duct below
the roadway, with an exhaust duct above the ceiling. Such
ventilation provisions significantly increased the tunnel
size, requiring about a 30-foot (nine-metre) diameter for
a two-lane vehicular tunnel.

Many similar vehicular tunnels were built by shield-
and-compressed-air methods—including Lincoln and
Queens tunnels in New York City, Sumner and Callahan

in Boston, and Mersey in Liverpool. Since 1950 however, most subaqueous tunnelers preferred the immersed-tube method, in which long tube sections are prefabricated, towed to the site, sunk in a previously dredged trench, connected to sections already in place, and then covered with backfill. This basic procedure was first used in its present form on the Detroit River Railroad Tunnel between Detroit and Windsor, Ontario (1906–10). A prime advantage is the avoidance of high costs and the risks of operating a shield under high air pressure, since work inside the sunken tube is at atmospheric pressure (free air).

Machine-mined tunnels. Sporadic attempts to realize the tunnel engineer's dream of a mechanical rotary excavator culminated in 1954 at Oahe Dam on the Missouri River near Pierre, South Dakota. With ground conditions being favourable (a readily cuttable clay–shale), success resulted from a team effort: Jerome O. Ackerman as chief engineer, F.K. Mittry as initial contractor, and James S. Robbins as builder of the first machine—the "Mittry Mole." Later contracts developed three other Oahe-type moles, so that all of the various tunnels here were machine-mined—totaling eight miles (13 kilometres) of 25- to 30-foot (eight- to nine-metre) diameter. These were the first of the modern moles that since 1960 have been rapidly adopted for many of the world's tunnels as a means of increasing speeds from the previous range of 25 to 50 feet (eight to 15 metres) per day to a range of several hundred feet per day. The Oahe mole was partly inspired by work on a pilot tunnel in chalk started under the English Channel for which an air-powered rotary cutting arm, the Beaumont borer, had been invented. A 1947 coal-mining version followed, and in 1949 a coal saw was used to cut a circumferential slot in chalk for 33-foot- (ten-metre-) diameter tunnels at Fort Randall Dam, South Dakota. In 1962 a comparable breakthrough for the more difficult excavation of vertical shafts was achieved in the U.S. development of the mechanical raise borer, profiting from earlier trials in Germany.

II. Tunnelling techniques

BASIC TUNNELLING SYSTEM

Four categories of tunnels

Tunnels are generally grouped in four broad categories, depending on the material through which they pass: soft ground, consisting of soil and very weak rock; hard rock; soft rock, such as shale, chalk, and friable sandstone; and subaqueous. While these four broad types of ground condition require very different methods of excavation and ground support, nevertheless, nearly all tunnelling operations involve certain basic procedures: investigation, excavation and materials transport, ground support, and environmental control. Similarly, tunnels for mining and for civil-engineering projects share the basic procedures but differ greatly in the design approach toward permanence, due to their differing purposes. Many mining tunnels have been planned only for minimum-cost temporary use during ore extraction, although the growing desire of surface owners for legal protection against subsequent tunnel collapse may cause this to change. By contrast, most civil-engineering or public-works tunnels involve continued human occupancy plus full protection of adjacent owners and are much more conservatively designed for permanent safety. In all tunnels, geological conditions play the dominant role in governing the acceptability of construction methods and the practicality of different designs. Indeed, tunnelling history is filled with instances in which a sudden encounter with unanticipated conditions caused long stoppages for changes in construction methods, in design, or in both, with resulting great increases in cost and time. At the Awali Tunnel in Lebanon in 1960, for example, a huge flow of water and sand filled over two miles (three kilometres) of the bore and more than doubled construction time to eight years for its ten-mile (16-kilometre) length.

Geological investigation. Thorough geological analysis is essential in order to assess the relative risks of different locations and to reduce the uncertainties of ground and water conditions at the location chosen. In addition to soil and rock types, key factors include the initial defects controlling behaviour of the rock mass; size of rock block between joints; weak beds and zones, including faults, shear zones, and altered areas weakened by weathering or thermal action; groundwater, including flow pattern and pressure; plus several special hazards, such as heat, gas, and earthquake risk. For mountain regions the large cost and long time required for deep borings generally limit their number; but much can be learned from thorough aerial and surface surveys, plus well-logging and geophysical techniques developed in the oil industry. Often the problem is approached with flexibility toward changes in design and in construction methods and with continuous exploration ahead of the tunnel face, done in older tunnels by mining a pilot bore ahead and now by drilling. Japanese engineers have pioneered methods for prelocating troublesome rock and water conditions.

Geologic problems in rock chambers

For large rock chambers and also particularly large tunnels, the problems increase so rapidly with increasing opening size that adverse geology can make the project impractical or at least tremendously costly. Hence, the concentrated opening areas of these projects are invariably investigated during the design stage by a series of small exploratory tunnels called drifts, which also provide for in-place field tests to investigate engineering properties of the rock mass and can often be located so their later enlargement affords access for construction.

Since shallow tunnels are more often in soft ground, borings become more practical. Hence, most subways involve borings at intervals of 100–500 feet (30–150 metres) to observe the water table and to obtain undisturbed samples for testing strength, permeability, and other engineering properties of the soil. Portals of rock tunnels are often in soil or in rock weakened by weathering. Being shallow, they are readily investigated by borings, but, unfortunately, portal problems have frequently been treated lightly. Often they are only marginally explored or the design is left to the contractor, with the result that a high percentage of tunnels, especially in the United States, have experienced portal failures. Failure to locate buried valleys has also caused a number of costly surprises. The five-mile (eight-kilometre) Oso Tunnel in New Mexico offers one example. There, in 1967, a mole had begun to progress well in hard shale, until 1,000 feet (300 metres) from the portal it hit a buried valley filled with water bearing sand and gravel, which buried the mole. After six months' delay for hand mining, the mole was repaired and soon set new world records for advance rate—averaging 240 feet (70 metres) per day with a maximum of 420 feet (130 metres) per day.

Excavation and materials handling. Excavation of the ground within the tunnel bore may be either semicontinuous, as by hand-held power tools or mining machine, or cyclic, as by drilling and blasting methods for harder rock. Here each cycle involves drilling, loading explosive, blasting, ventilating fumes, and excavation of the blasted rock (called mucking). Commonly, the mucker is a type of front-end loader that moves the broken rock onto a belt conveyor that dumps it into a hauling system of cars or trucks. As all operations are concentrated at the heading, congestion is chronic, and much ingenuity has gone into designing equipment able to work in a small space. Since progress depends on the rate of heading advance, it is often facilitated by mining several headings simultaneously, as opening up intermediate headings from shafts or from adits driven to provide extra points of access for longer tunnels.

Removing waste material

For smaller diameters and longer tunnels, a narrow-gauge railroad is commonly employed to take out the muck and bring in men and construction material. For larger size bores of short to moderate length, trucks are generally preferred. For underground use these require diesel engines with scrubbers to eliminate dangerous gases from the exhaust. While existing truck and rail systems are adequate for tunnels progressing in the range of 40–60 feet (12–18 metres) per day, their capacity is inadequate to keep up with fast-moving moles progressing at the rate of several hundred feet per day. Hence, considerable attention is being devoted to developing high-capacity transport systems—continuous-belt conveyors, pipelines, and innovative rail systems (high-capacity cars on high-speed trains). Muck disposal and its transport on the surface can also be a problem in congested urban areas. One solution successfully applied in Japan is to convey it by pipeline to sites where it can be used for reclamation by landfill.

For survey control, high-accuracy transit-level work (from base lines established by mountain-top triangulation) has generally been adequate; long tunnels from opposite sides of the mountain commonly meet with an error of one foot (30 centimetres) or less. Further improvements are likely from the recent introduction of the laser, the pencil-size light beam of which supplies a reference line readily interpreted by workmen. Most moles in the United States now use a laser beam to guide steering; and some machines are experimenting with electronic steering automated by the laser beam.

Ground support. The dominant factor in all phases of the tunnelling system is the extent of support needed to hold the surrounding ground safely. Engineers must consider the type of support, its strength, and how soon it must be installed after excavation. The key factor in timing support installation is so-called stand-up time; *i.e.*, how long the ground will safely stand by itself at the heading, thus providing a period for installing supports. In soft ground, stand-up time can vary from seconds in such soils as loose sand up to hours in such ground as cohesive clay and even drops to zero in flowing ground below the water table, where inward seepage moves loose sand into the tunnel. Stand-up time in rock may vary from minutes in ravelling ground (closely fractured rock where pieces gradually loosen and fall) up to days in moderately jointed rock (joint spacing in feet) and may even be measured in centuries in nearly intact rock, where the rock-block size (between joints) equals or exceeds size of the tunnel opening, thus requiring no support. While a miner generally prefers rock to soft ground, local occurrences of major defects within the rock can effectively produce a soft-ground situation and thus generally require radical changes to a soft-ground type of support in order to pass through such areas.

Under most conditions, tunnelling causes a transfer of the ground load by arching to sides of the opening, termed the ground-arch effect (Figure 2, top). At the heading the effect is three-dimensional, locally creating a ground dome in which the load is arched not only to the sides but also forward and back. If permanence of the

ground arch is completely assured, stand-up time is infinite, and no support is required. Ground-arch strength usually deteriorates with time, however, increasing the load on the support. Thus, the total load is shared between support and ground arch in proportion to their relative stiffness by a physical mechanism termed structure–medium interaction. The support load increases greatly when the inherent ground strength is much reduced by allowing excessive yield to loosen the rock mass. Because this may occur when installation of support is delayed too long, or because it may result from blast damage, good practice is based on the need to preserve the strength of the ground arch as the strongest load-carrying member of the system, by prompt installation of proper support and by preventing blast damage and movement from water inflow that has a tendency to loosen the ground.

Because stand-up time drops rapidly as size of the opening increases, the full-face method of advance (see Figure 2, centre), in which the entire diameter of the tunnel is excavated at one time, it is most suitable for strong ground or for smaller tunnels. The effect of weak ground can be offset by decreasing the size of opening initially mined and supported, as in the top heading and bench method of advance. For the extreme case of very soft ground, this approach results in the multiple-drift method of advance (Figure 3), in which the individual drifts

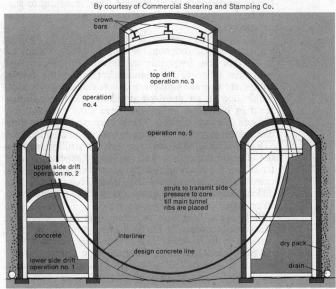

Figure 3: Multiple-drift method of excavation.

are reduced to a small size that is safe for excavation and portions of the support are placed in each drift and progressively connected as the drifts are expanded. The central core is left unexcavated until sides and crown are safely supported, thus providing a convenient central buttress for bracing the temporary support in each individual drift. While this obviously slow multidrift method is an old technique for very weak ground, such conditions still force its adoption as a last resort in some modern tunnels. In 1971, for example, on the Straight Creek interstate highway tunnel in Colorado, a very complex pattern of multiple drifts was found necessary to advance this large horseshoe-shaped tunnel 42 by 45 feet (13 by 14 metres) high through a weak shear zone over 1,000 feet (300 metres) wide, after unsuccessful trials with full-face operation of a shield.

In early tunnels, timber was used for the initial or temporary support, followed by a permanent lining of brick or stone masonry. Since steel became available, it has been widely used as the first temporary stage or primary support. For protection against corrosion, it is nearly always encased in concrete as a second stage or final lining. Steel-rib support with timber blocking outside has been widely employed in rock tunnels. The horseshoe shape is common for all but weakest rocks, since the flat bottom facilitates hauling. By contrast, the

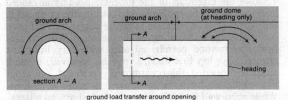

advance methods

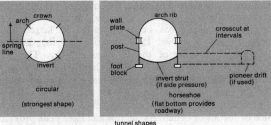

tunnel shapes
Figure 2: Tunnel terminology (see text).

Stand-up time

Multiple-drift method

stronger and more structurally efficient circular shape is generally required to support the greater loads from soft ground. Figure 2, bottom compares these two shapes and indicates a number of terms identifying various parts of the cross section and adjacent members for a steel-rib type of support. Here a wall plate is generally used only with a top heading method, where it serves to support arch ribs both in the top heading and also where the bench is being excavated by spanning over this length until posts can be inserted beneath. Newer types of supports are discussed below with more modern tunnel procedures, in which the trend is away from two stages of support toward a single support system, part installed early and gradually strengthened in increments for conversion to the final complete support system.

Environmental control. In all but the shortest tunnels, control of the environment is essential to provide safe working conditions. Ventilation is vital, both to provide fresh air and to remove explosive gases such as methane and noxious gases, including blast fumes. While the problem is reduced by using diesel engines with exhaust scrubbers and by selecting only low-fume explosives for underground use, long tunnels involve a major ventilating plant that employs a forced draft through lightweight pipes up to three feet (90 centimetres) in diameter and with booster fans at intervals. In smaller tunnels, the fans are frequently reversible, exhausting fumes immediately after blasting, then reversing to supply fresh air to the heading where the work is now concentrated.

High-level noise generated at the heading by drilling equipment and throughout the tunnel by high-velocity air in the vent lines frequently requires the use of ear plugs with sign language for communication. In the future, equipment operators may work in sealed cabs, but communication is an unsolved problem. Electronic equipment in tunnels is prohibited, since stray currents may activate blasting circuits. Thunderstorms may also produce stray currents and require special precautions.

Dust is controlled by water sprays, wet drilling, and the use of respirator masks. Since prolonged exposure to dust from rocks containing a high percentage of silica may cause a respiratory ailment known as silicosis, severe conditions require special precautions, such as a vacuum-exhaust hood for each drill.

While excess heat is more common in deep tunnels, it occasionally occurs in fairly shallow tunnels. In 1953, workers in the 6.4-mile (10.3-kilometre) Telecote Tunnel near Santa Barbara, California, were transported immersed in water-filled mine cars through the hot area (117° F [47° C]). In 1970 a complete refrigeration plant was required to progress through a huge inflow of hot water at 150° F (66° C) in the seven-mile (11-kilometre) Graton Tunnel, driven under the Andes to drain a copper mine in Peru.

MODERN SOFT-GROUND TUNNELLING

Settlement damage and lost ground. Soft-ground tunnels most commonly are used for urban services (subways, sewers, and other utilities) for which the need for quick access by passengers or maintenance staff favours a shallow depth. In many cities this means that the tunnels are above bedrock, making tunnelling easier but requiring continuous support. The tunnel structure in such cases is generally designed to support the entire load of the ground above it, in part because the ground arch in soil deteriorates with time and in part as an allowance for load changes resulting from future construction of buildings or tunnels. Soft-ground tunnels are typically circular in shape because of this shape's inherently greater strength and ability to readjust to future load changes. In locations within street rights-of-way, the dominant concern in urban tunnelling is the need to avoid intolerable settlement damage to adjoining buildings. While this is rarely a problem in the case of modern skyscrapers, which usually have foundations extending to rock and deep basements often extending below the tunnel, it can be a decisive consideration in the presence of moderate-height buildings, whose foundations are usually shallow.

In this case the tunnel engineer must choose between underpinning or employing a tunnelling method that is sufficiently foolproof that it will prevent settlement damage.

Surface settlement results from lost ground; *i.e.*, ground that moves into the tunnel in excess of the tunnel's actual volume. All soft-ground tunnelling methods result in a certain amount of lost ground. Some is inevitable, such as the slow lateral squeeze of plastic clay that occurs ahead of the tunnel face as new stresses from doming at the heading cause the clay to move toward the face before the tunnel even reaches its location. Most lost ground, however, results from improper construction methods and careless workmanship. Hence the following emphasizes reasonably conservative tunnelling methods, which offer the best chance for holding lost ground to an acceptable level of approximately 1 percent.

Hand-mined tunnels. The ancient practice of hand mining is still economical for some conditions (shorter and smaller tunnels) and may illustrate particular techniques better than its mechanized counterpart. Examples are forepoling and breasting techniques as developed for the hazardous case of running (unstable) ground. Figure

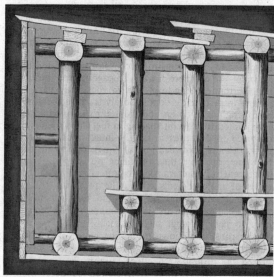

Figure 4: Heading advance by forepoling.

4 shows the essentials of the process: heading advanced under a roof of forepole planks that are driven ahead at the crown (and at the sides in severe cases) plus continuous planking or breasting at the heading. With careful work the method permits advance with very little lost ground. The top breastboard may be removed, a small advance excavated, this breastboard is replaced, and progress continued by working down one board at a time. While solid wall forepoling is nearly a lost art, an adaptation is termed spiling where the forepoles are intermittent with gaps between. Crown spiling is still resorted to for passing bad ground where spiles may consist of rails driven ahead, or even steel bars set in holes drilled into crushed rock.

In ground providing a reasonable stand-up time, a modern support system uses steel liner-plate sections placed against the soil and bolted into a solid sheeted complete circle and, in larger tunnels, strengthened inside by circular steel ribs. Individual liner plates are light in weight and are easily erected by hand. By employing small drifts (horizontal passageways), braced to a central core, liner-plate technique has been successful in larger tunnels—Figure 5 shows 1940 practice on the 20-foot (six-metre) tunnels of the Chicago subway. The top heading is carried ahead, preceded slightly by a "monkey drift" in which the wall plate is set and serves as a footing for the arch ribs, also to span over as the wall plate is underpinned by erecting posts in small notches at each side of the lower bench. As the ribs and liner plate provide only a light support, they are stiffened by installation of a

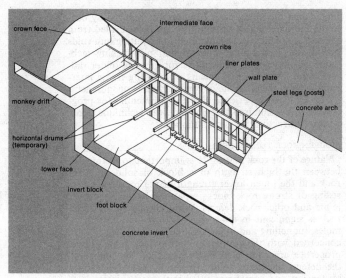

Figure 5: Soft-ground support by ribs and liner plates.

concrete lining about one day behind the mining. While liner-plate tunnels are more economical than shield tunnels, the risks of lost ground are somewhat greater and require not only very careful workmanship but also thorough soil-mechanics investigation in advance, pioneered in Chicago by Karl V. Terzaghi (founder of modern soil mechanics).

Shield tunnels. The risk of lost ground can also be reduced by using a shield with individual pockets from which men can mine ahead; these can quickly be closed to stop a run-in (Figure 1). In extremely soft ground the shield may be simply shoved ahead with all its pockets closed, completely displacing the soil ahead of it; or it may be shoved with some of the pockets open, through which the soft soil extrudes like a sausage, cut into chunks for removal by a belt conveyor. The first of these methods was used on the Lincoln Tunnel in Hudson River silt.

Internal support in shields — Support erected inside the tail of the shield consists of large segments, so heavy that they require a power erector arm for positioning while being bolted together. Because of its high resistance to corrosion, cast iron has been the most commonly used material for segments, thus eliminating the need for a secondary lining of concrete. Today, lighter segments are employed. In 1968, for example, the San Francisco subway used welded steel-plate segments, protected outside by a bituminous coating and galvanized inside. British engineers have developed precast concrete segments that are proving popular in Europe.

An inherent problem with the shield method is the existence of a two- to five-inch (five- to 13-centimetre) ring-shaped void left outside the segments as the result of the thickness of the skin plate and the clearance needed for segment erection. Movement of soil into this void could result in up to 5 percent lost ground, an amount intolerable in urban work. Lost ground is held to reasonable levels by promptly blowing small sized gravel into the void, then injecting cement grout (sand–cement–water mixture) into voids of the gravel.

Water control. A soft-ground tunnel below the water table involves a constant risk of a run-in; *i.e.*, soil and water flowing into the tunnel, which often results in complete loss of the heading. One solution is to lower the water table below the tunnel bottom before construction begins. This can be accomplished by pumping from deep wells ahead and from well points within the tunnel. While this benefits the tunnelling, dropping the water table increases the loading on deeper soil layers. If these are relatively compressible, the result can be a major settlement of adjacent buildings on shallow foundations, an extreme example being a 15- to 20-foot (five- to six-metre) subsidence in Mexico City due to over-pumping.

Dropping the water table

When soil conditions make it undesirable to drop the water table, compressed air inside the tunnel may offset the outside water pressure. In larger tunnels, air pressure is generally set to balance the water pressure in the lower part of the tunnel, with the result that it then exceeds the smaller water pressure at the crown (upper part). Since air tends to escape through the upper part of the tunnel, constant inspection and repair of leaks with straw and mud are required. Otherwise, a blowout could occur, depressurizing the tunnel and possibly losing the heading as soil enters. Compressed air greatly increases operating costs, partly because a large compressor plant is needed with standby equipment to insure against loss of pressure and partly because of the slow movement of men and muck trains through the air locks. The dominant factor, however, is the huge reduction in productive time and lengthy decompression time required for men working under air to prevent the crippling disease known as the bends (or caisson disease), also encountered by divers. Regulations stiffen as pressure increases up to usual maximum of 45 pounds per square inch (three atmospheres) where daily time is limited to one hour working and six hours for decompression. This plus higher hazard pay, makes tunnelling under high air pressure very costly. In consequence, many tunnelling operations attempt to lower the operating air pressure, either by partially dropping the water table or, especially in Europe, by strengthening the ground through the injection of solidifying chemical grouts. French and British grouting-specialist companies have developed a number of highly engineered chemical grouts, and these are achieving considerable success in advance cementing of weak soil, thus considerably reducing tunnelling difficulties.

Tunnel blowout

Soft-ground moles. Since their first success in 1954, moles (mining machines) have been rapidly adopted worldwide. Close copies of the Oahe moles were used for similar large-diameter tunnels in clay shale at Gardiner Dam in Canada and at Mangla Dam in Pakistan during the mid-1960s, and subsequent moles have succeeded at many other locations involving soft rocks. Of the several hundred moles built, most have been designed for the more easily excavated soil tunnel and are now beginning to divide into four broad types (all are similar in that they excavate the earth with drag teeth and discharge the muck onto a belt conveyor, and most operate inside a shield).

Four types of moles

The open-face-wheel type is probably the most common. In Figure 6 a scale model is used to illustrate the operation of the wheel within a shield and the lining of precast concrete segments that are conveyed forward for

Figure 6: Scale model of a tunnelling system (20 feet, two inches in diameter) for excavation in firm ground. The mechanism includes a wheel-type boring machine, electrohydraulic trailing power unit, 360° revolving drum-type segmented lining erector, segmented lining handling conveyor, and muck-removal conveyor.

erection within the tail of the shield. In the wheel in Figure 6 the cutter arm rotates in one direction; in a variant model it oscillates back and forth in a windshield-wiper action that is most suitable in wet, sticky ground. While suitable for firm ground, the open-face mole has sometimes been buried by running or loose ground.

The closed-faced-wheel partly offsets this problem, since it can be kept pressed against the face while taking in muck through slots. Since the cutters are changed from the face, changing must be done in firm ground. This kind of mole performed well on the 1968 San Francisco subway in soft to medium clay with some sand layers, averaging 30 feet (nine metres) per day. In this project, mole operation made it cheaper and safer to drive two single-track tunnels than one large double-track tunnel. When adjacent buildings had deep foundations, a partial lowering of the water table permitted operations under low pressure, which succeeded in limiting surface settlement to about one inch (25 millimetres). In areas of shallow building foundations, dewatering was not permitted; air pressure was doubled to 28 pounds per square inch (2 atmospheres), and settlements were slightly smaller.

A third type, still in the pioneering stage, is the pressure-on-face mole. Here, only the face and the tunnel proper operates in free air—thus avoiding the high costs of labour under pressure. In 1969 a first major attempt used air pressure on the face of a mole operating in sands and silts for the Paris Metro. A 1970 attempt in volcanic clays of Mexico City utilized a clay–water mixture as a pressurized slurry (liquid mixture); the technique was novel in that the slurry muck was removed by pipeline, a procedure simultaneously also used in Japan with a 23-foot- (seven-metre-) diameter pressure-on-face mole. The concept is being further developed in England, where an experimental mole of this type was constructed in 1971.

The digger-shield type of machine is essentially a hydraulic-powered digger arm excavating ahead of a shield, whose protection can be extended forward by hydraulically operated poling plates, acting as retractable spiles. In 1967–70 in the 26-foot- (eight-metre) diameter Saugus–Castaic Tunnel near Los Angeles, a mole of this type produced daily progress in clayey sandstone averaging 113 feet (34 metres) per day and 202 feet (62 metres) maximum, completing five miles (eight kilometres) of tunnel one-half year ahead of schedule. In 1968 an independently developed device of similar design also worked well in compacted silt for a 12-foot- (four-metre-) diameter sewer tunnel in Seattle.

Pipe jacking. For small tunnels in a five- to eight-foot (1.5- to 2.5-metre) size range, small moles of the open-face-wheel type have been effectively combined with an older technique known as pipe jacking, in which a final lining of precast concrete pipe is jacked forward in sections. Figure 7 illustrates the system as used in 1969 on two miles (three kilometres) of sewer in Chicago clay with jacking runs up to 1,400 feet (430 metres) between shafts. A laser-aligned wheel mole cut a bore slightly

From *Engineering News Record* (1969)

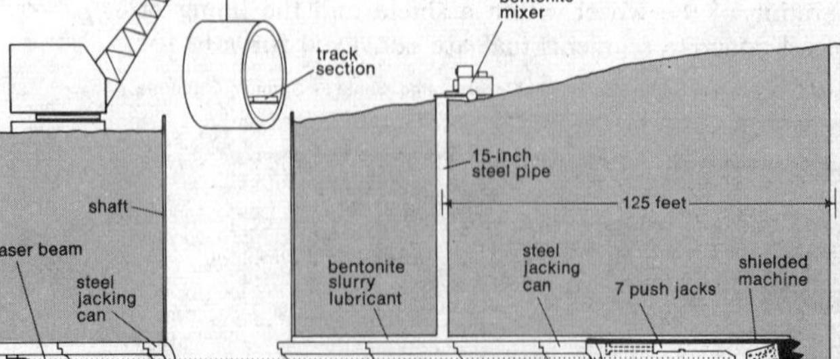

Figure 7: Pipe jacking within a tunnel (see text).

larger than the lining pipe. Friction was reduced by bentonite lubricant added outside through holes drilled from the surface, which were later used for grouting any voids outside the pipe lining. The original pipe-jacking technique was developed particularly for crossing under railroads and highways as a means of avoiding traffic interruption from the alternate of construction in open trench.

With Chicago experience showing a potential for progress of a few hundred feet per day, the technique is becoming attractive for small tunnels.

MODERN ROCK TUNNELLING

Nature of the rock mass. It is important to distinguish between the high strength of a block of solid or intact rock and the much lower strength of the rock mass consisting of strong rock blocks separated by much weaker joints and other rock defects. While the nature of intact rock is significant in quarrying, drilling, and cutting by moles, tunnelling and other areas of rock engineering are concerned with the properties of the rock mass. These properties are controlled by the spacing and nature of the defects, including joints (generally fractures caused by tension and sometimes filled with weaker material), faults (shear fractures frequently filled with claylike material called gouge), shear zones (crushed from shear displacement), altered zones (in which heat or chemical action have largely destroyed original bond cementing the rock crystals), bedding planes, and weak seams (in shale, often altered to clay). Since these geological details (or hazards) usually can only be generalized in advance predictions, rock-tunnelling methods require flexibility for handling conditions as they are encountered. Any of these defects can convert the rock to the more hazardous soft-ground case.

Also important is the geostress; *i.e.*, the state of stress existing *in situ* prior to tunnelling. Though conditions are fairly simple in soil, geostress in rock has a wide range because it is influenced by the stresses remaining from past geological events: mountain building, crustal movements, or load subsequently removed (melting of glacial ice or erosion of former sediment cover). Evaluation of the geostress effects and the rock mass properties are primary objectives of the relatively new field of rock mechanics and are dealt with below with underground chambers since their significance increases with opening size. Therefore, this section emphasizes the usual rock tunnel, in the size range of 15 to 25 feet (five to eight metres).

Geostress

Conventional blasting. Blasting is carried on in a cycle of drill, load, blast, ventilate fumes, and remove muck. Since only one of the five operations can be conducted at a time in the confined space at the heading, concentrated efforts to improve each have resulted in raising the rate of advance to a range of 40–60 feet (12–18 metres) per day, or probably near the limit for such a cyclic system. Drilling, which consumes a major part of the time cycle, has been intensely mechanized in the United States. High-speed drills with renewable bits of hard tungsten carbide are positioned by power-operated jib booms located at each platform level of the drilling jumbo (a mounted platform for carrying drills). Truck-mounted jumbos are used in larger tunnels. When rail-mounted, the drilling jumbo is arranged to straddle the mucker so that drilling can resume during the last phase of the mucking operation.

By experimenting with various drill-hole patterns and the sequence of firing explosives in the holes, Swedish engineers have been able to blast a nearly clean cylinder in each cycle, while minimizing use of explosives.

Dynamite, the usual explosive, is fired by electric blasting caps, energized from a separate firing circuit with locked switches. Cartridges are generally loaded individually and seated with a wooden tamping rod; Swedish efforts to expedite loading often employ a pneumatic cartridge loader. American efforts toward reduced loading time have tended to replace dynamite with a free-running blasting agent, such as a mixture of ammonium nitrate and fuel oil (called AN-FO), which in granular form (prills) can be blown into the drill hole by com-

Reducing explosive-loading time

pressed air. While AN-FO-type agents are cheaper, their lower power increases the quantity required, and their fumes usually increase ventilating requirements. For wet holes, the prills must be changed to a slurry requiring special processing and pumping equipment (see EXPLOSIVES).

Rock support.   Most common loading on the support of a tunnel in hard rock is due to the weight of loosened rock below the ground arch, where designers rely particularly on experience with Alpine tunnels as evaluated by two Austrians, Karl V. Terzaghi, the founder of soil mechanics, and Josef Stini, a pioneer in engineering geology. The support load is greatly increased by factors weakening the rock mass, particularly blasting damage. Furthermore, if a delay in placing support allows the zone of rock loosening to propagate upward (*i.e.*, rock falls from the tunnel roof), the rock-mass strength is reduced, and the ground arch is raised. Obviously, the loosened rock load can be greatly altered by a change in joint inclination (orientation of rock fractures) or by the presence of one or more of the rock defects previously mentioned. Less frequent but more severe is the case of high geostress, which in hard, brittle rock may result in dangerous rock bursts (explosive spalling off from the tunnel side) or, in a more plastic rock mass, may exhibit a slow squeezing into the tunnel. In extreme cases, squeezing ground has been handled by allowing the rock to yield while keeping the process under control, then remining and resetting initial support several times, plus deferring concrete lining until the ground arch becomes stabilized.

For many years steel rib sets were the usual first-stage support for rock tunnels, with close spacing of the wood blocking against the rock being important to reduce bending stress in the rib. Advantages are increased flexibility in changing rib spacing plus the ability to handle squeezing ground by resetting the ribs after remining. A disadvantage is that in many cases the system yields excessively, thus inviting weakening of the rock mass. Finally, the rib system serves only as a first-stage or temporary support, requiring a second-stage encasement in a concrete lining for corrosion protection.

Steel rib sets (margin note)

Concrete lining.   Concrete linings serve to aid fluid flow by providing a smooth surface and insure against rock fragment falling on vehicles using the tunnel. While shallow tunnels are often lined by dropping concrete down holes drilled from the surface, the greater depth of most rock tunnels requires concreting entirely within the tunnel. Operations in such congested space involve special equipment, including agitator cars for transport, pumps or compressed-air devices for placing the concrete, and telescoping arch forms that can be collapsed to move forward inside forms remaining in place. The invert is generally concreted first, followed by the arch where forms must be left in place from 14 to 18 hours for the concrete to gain necessary strength. Voids at the crown are minimized by keeping the discharge pipe buried in fresh concrete. The final operation consists of contact grouting, in which a sand–cement grout is injected to fill any voids and to establish full contact between lining and ground. The method usually produces progress in the range of 40 to 120 feet (12 to 36 metres) per day. In the 1960s there was a trend toward an advancing-slope method of continuous concreting, as originally devised for embedding the steel cylinder of a hydropower penstock. In this procedure, several hundred feet of forms are initially set, then collapsed in short sections and moved forward after the concrete has gained necessary strength, thus keeping ahead of the continuously advancing slope of fresh concrete. As a 1968 example, Libby Dam's Flathead Tunnel in Montana attained a concreting rate of 300 feet (90 metres) per day by using the advancing slope method.

Rock bolts.   Rock bolts are used to reinforce jointed rock much as reinforcing bars supply tensile resistance in reinforced concrete. After early trials around 1920, they were developed in the 1940s for strengthening laminated roof strata in mines (see MINING AND QUARRYING). For public works their use has increased rapidly since 1955,

as confidence has developed from two independent pioneering applications, both in the early 1950s. One was the successful change from steel rib sets to cheaper rock bolts on major portions of the 85 miles (135 kilometres) of tunnels forming New York City's Delaware River Aqueduct. The other was the success of such bolts as the sole rock support in large underground powerhouse chambers of Australia's Snowy Mountain Project. Since about 1960, rock bolts have had major success in providing the sole support for large tunnels and rock chambers with spans up to 100 feet (30 metres). Bolts are commonly sized from 0.75 to 1.5 inches (19–38 millimetres) and function to create a compression across rock fissures, both to prevent the joints opening and to create resistance to sliding along the joints. For this they are placed promptly after blasting, anchored at the end, tensioned, and then grouted to resist corrosion and to prevent anchor creep. Rock tendons (prestressed cables or bundled rods, providing higher capacity than rock bolts) up to 250 feet (75 metres) long and prestressed to several hundred tons each have succeeded in stabilizing many sliding rock masses in rock chambers, dam abutments, and high rock slopes. A noted example is their use in reinforcing the abutments of Vaiont Dam in Italy. In 1963 this project experienced disaster when a giant landslide filled the reservoir causing a huge wave to overtop the dam, with large loss of life. Remarkably, the 875-foot- (270-metre-) high arch dam survived this huge overloading; the rock tendons are believed to have supplied a major strengthening.

Pioneering uses of rock bolts (margin note)

Rock tendons (margin note)

Shotcrete.   Shotcrete is small-aggregate concrete conveyed through a hose and shot from an air gun onto a backup surface on which it is built up in thin layers. Though sand mixes had been so applied for many years, new equipment in the late 1940s made it possible to improve the product by including coarse aggregate up to one inch (25 millimetres); strengths of 6,000 to 10,000 pounds per square inch (400 to 700 kilograms per square centimetre) became common. Following initial success as rock-tunnel support in 1951–55 on the Maggia Hydro Project in Switzerland, the technique was further developed in Austria and Sweden. The remarkable ability of a thin shotcrete layer (one to three inches [25 to 75 millimetres]) to bond to and knit fissured rock into a strong arch and to stop ravelling of loose pieces soon led to shotcrete largely superseding steel rib support in many European rock tunnels. By 1962 the practice had spread to South America. From this experience plus limited trial at the Hecla Mine in Idaho, the first major use of coarse-aggregate shotcrete for tunnel support in North America, developed in 1967 on the Vancouver Railroad Tunnel, with its 20- by 29-foot- (six- by nine-metre-) high cross section and two-mile (three-kilometre) length. Here an initial two- to four-inch (five- to ten-centimetre) coat proved so successful in stabilizing hard, blocky shale and in preventing ravelling in friable (crumbly) conglomerate and sandstone that the shotcrete was thickened to six inches (15 centimetres) in the arch and four inches (ten centimetres) on the walls to form the permanent support, saving about 75 percent of the cost of the original steel ribs and concrete lining.

A key to shotcreting's success is its prompt application before loosening starts to reduce the strength of the rock mass. In Swedish practice this is accomplished by applying immediately after blasting and, while mucking is in progress, utilizing the "Swedish robot" shown in Figure 8,

Applying shotcrete (margin note)

From *Civil Engineering* (January 1970), A.S.C.E.

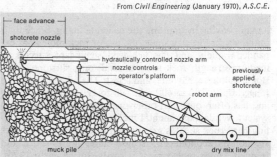

Figure 8: "Swedish robot" used for shotcreting.

which allows the operator to remain under the protection of the previously supported roof. On the Vancouver tunnel, shotcrete was applied from a platform extending forward from the jumbo while the mucking machine operated below. By taking advantage of several unique properties of shotcrete (flexibility, high bending strength, and ability to increase thickness by successive layers), Swedish practice has developed shotcreting into a single-support system that is strengthened progressively as needed for conversion into the final support.

Preserving rock strength. In rock tunnels, the requirements for support can be significantly decreased to the extent that the construction method can preserve the inherent strength of the rock mass. The opinion has been often expressed that a high percentage of support in United States rock tunnels (perhaps over half) has been needed to stabilize rock damaged by blasting rather than because of an inherently low strength of the rock. As a remedy, two techniques are currently available. First is the Swedish development of sound-wall blasting (to preserve rock strength), treated below under rock chambers, since its importance increases with size of the opening. The second is the American development of rock moles that cut a smooth surface in the tunnel (Figure 9), thus minimizing rock damage and support needs—here limited to rock bolts connected by steel straps for this sandstone tunnel. In stronger rocks (as the 1970 Chicago sewers in dolomite) mole excavation not only largely eliminated need for support but also produced a surface of adequate smoothness for sewer flow, which permitted

Rock moles

By courtesy of the U.S. Bureau of Reclamation

Figure 9: Workman tightening the nut on a rock bolt that holds a steel strap inside a mole-excavated tunnel. Laser beam target at left is used to guide steering of mole.

a major saving by omitting the concrete lining. Since their initial success in clay shale, the use of rock moles has expanded rapidly and has achieved significant success in medium-strength rock such as sandstone, siltstone, limestone, dolomite, rhyolite, and schist. The advance rate has ranged up to 300 to 400 feet (90 to 120 metres) per day and has often outpaced other operations in the tunnelling system. While experimental moles have succeeded in cutting hard rock such as granite and quartzite, such devices are not yet economical, because cutter life is short, and frequent cutter replacement is costly. In the early 1970s, this seemed likely to change, however, as mole manufac-

turers sought to extend the range of application. Improvement in cutters and progress in reducing the time lost from equipment breakages were producing consistent improvements.

American moles have developed two types of cutters: disk cutters that wedge out the rock between initial grooves cut by the hard-faced rolling disks and roller-bit cutters using bits initially developed for fast drilling of oil wells. As later entrants in the field, European manufacturers have generally tried a different approach—milling-type cutters that mill or plane away part of the rock, then shear off undercut areas. Attention is also focussing on broadening the moles' capabilities to function as the primary machine of the whole tunnelling system. Thus, future moles are expected to not only cut rock but also explore ahead for dangerous ground; handle and treat bad ground; provide a capability for prompt erection of support, rock bolting, or shotcreting; change cutters from the rear in loose ground; and produce rock fragments of a size appropriate to capability of the muck removal system. As these problems are solved, the continuous tunnelling system by mole is expected largely to replace the cyclic drilling and blasting system.

Water inflows. Exploring ahead of the path of a tunnel is particularly necessary for location of possible high water inflows and permitting their pretreatment by drainage or grouting. When high-pressure flows occur unexpectedly, they result in long stoppages. When huge flows are encountered, one approach is to drive parallel tunnels, advancing them alternately so that one relieves pressure in front of the other. This was done in 1898 in work on the Simplon Tunnel, and in 1969 on the Graton Tunnel in Peru where flow reached 60,000 gallons (230,000 litres) per minute. Another technique is to depressurize ahead by drain holes (or small drainage drifts on each side), an extreme example being the 1968 Japanese handling of extraordinarily difficult water and rock conditions on the Rokko Railroad Tunnel, using approximately three-quarters of a mile (1,200 metres) of drainage drifts and five miles (eight kilometres) of drain holes in a 0.25-mile (400-metre) length of the main tunnel.

Heavy ground. The miner's term for very weak or high geostress ground that causes repeated failures and replacement of support is heavy ground. Ingenuity, patience, and large increases of time and funds are invariably required to deal with it. Special techniques have generally been evolved on the job, as indicated by a few of the numerous examples. On the 7.2-mile (11.6-kilometre) Mont Blanc Vehicular Tunnel of 32-foot (ten-metre) size under the Alps in 1959–63, a pilot bore ahead helped greatly to reduce rock bursts by relieving the high geostress. The five-mile (eight-kilometre), 14-foot (four-metre) El Colegio Penstock Tunnel in Colombia was completed in 1965 in bituminous shale, requiring the replacement and resetting of over 2,000 rib sets, which buckled as the invert (bottom supports) and sides gradually squeezed in up to three feet (90 centimetres), and by deferring concreting until the ground arch stabilized.

While the ground arch eventually stabilized in these and numerous similar examples, knowledge is inadequate to establish the point between desirable deformation (to mobilize ground strength) and excessive deformation (which reduces its strength), and improvement is most likely to come from carefully planned and observed field-test sections at prototype scale, but these have been so costly that very few have actually been executed, notably the 1940 test sections in clay on the Chicago subway and the 1950 Garrison Dam test tunnel in the clay–shale of North Dakota. Such prototype field testing has resulted however, in substantial savings in eventual tunnel cost. For harder rock, reliable results are even more fragmentary; but test sections were scheduled to start in 1971 on four United States rock tunnels.

Unlined tunnels. Numerous modest-size conventionally blasted tunnels have been left unlined if human occupancy was to be rare and the rock was generally good. Initially, only weak zones are lined, and marginal areas are left for later maintenance. Most common is the case of a water tunnel that is built oversized to offset the

Continuous-tunnelling system

Desirable and excessive deformation

friction increase from the rough sides and, if a penstock tunnel, is equipped with a rock trap to catch loose rock pieces before they can enter the turbines. Most of these have been successful, particularly if operations could be scheduled for periodic shutdowns for maintenance repair of rockfalls; the Laramie–Poudre Irrigation Tunnel in northern Colorado experienced only two significant rockfalls in 60 years, each easily repaired during a nonirrigation period. In contrast, a progressive rockfall on the 14-mile (23-kilometre) Kemano penstock tunnel in Canada resulted in shutting down the whole town of Kitimat, British Columbia, and vacationing workers for nine months in 1961 since there were no other electric sources to operate the smelter. Thus, the choice of an unlined tunnel involves a compromise between initial saving and deferred maintenance plus evaluation of the consequences of a tunnel shutdown.

III. Underground excavations and structures

ROCK CHAMBERS

Swedish work on rock chambers

While chambers in 1971 were being excavated in rock to fulfill a wide variety of functions, the main stimulus to their development had come from hydroelectric-power-plant requirements. Though the basic concept originated in the United States, where the world's first underground hydroplants were built in enlarged tunnels at Snoqualme Falls near Seattle, Washington, in 1898 and at Fairfax Falls, Vermont, in 1904, Swedish engineers developed the idea into excavating large chambers to accommodate hydraulic machinery. After an initial trial in 1910–14 at the Porjus Plant north of the Arctic Circle, many underground power plants were subsequently built by the Swedish State Power Board. Swedish success soon popularized the idea through Europe and over the world, particularly to Australia, Scotland, Canada, Mexico, and Japan, where several hundred underground hydroplants have been built since 1950. Sweden, having a long experience with explosives and rock work, with generally favourable strong rock, and with energetic research and development, has even been able to lower the costs for underground work to approximate those for surface construction of such facilities as power plants, warehouses, pumping plants, oil-storage tanks, and water-treatment plants. With costs in the United States being five to ten times greater underground, new construction of underground chambers was not significantly resumed there until 1958, when the Haas underground hydroplant was built in California and the Norad underground airforce command centre in Colorado. By 1970, the United States had begun to adopt the Swedish concept and had completed three more hydroplants with several more under construction or being planned.

Advantages of underground location for a hydroplant

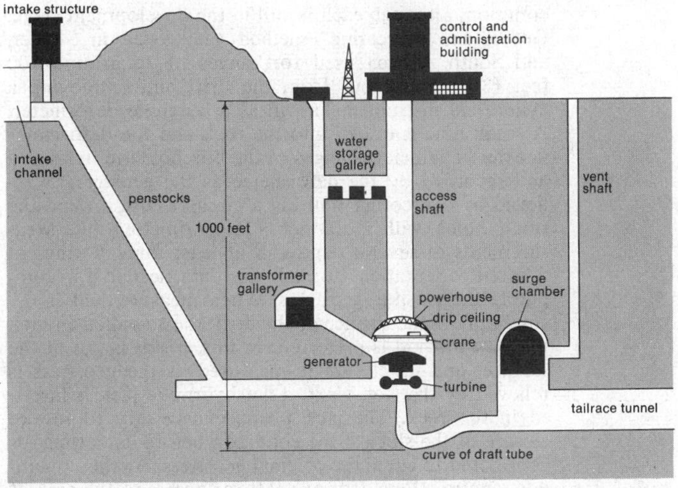

Favourably located, an underground hydroplant can have several advantages over a surface plant, including lower costs, because certain plant elements are built more simply underground: less risk from avalanches, earthquakes, and bombing; cheaper year-round construction and operation (in cold climates); and preservation of a scenic environment—a dominant factor in Scotland's tourist area and now receiving recognition worldwide. A typical layout involves a complex assembly of tunnels, chambers, and shafts. Figure 10 shows the world's largest underground powerhouse, Churchill Falls in the Labrador wilderness of Canada, with a capacity of 5,000,000 kilowats, under construction since 1967 at a total project cost of about $1,000,000,000. By building a dam of modest height well above the falls and by locating the powerhouse at 1,000 feet (300 metres) depth with a one-mile (1,600-metre) tunnel (the tailrace tunnel) to discharge water from the turbines below downstream rapids, the designers have been able to develop a head (water height) of 1,060 feet (320 metres) while at the same time preserving the scenic 250-foot- (75-metre-) high waterfall, expected to be a major tourist attraction once several hundred miles of wilderness-road improvement permits public access. Openings here are of impressive size: machine hall (powerhouse proper), 81-foot (25-metre) span by 154 feet (47 metres) high by 972 feet (296 metres) long; surge chamber, 60 feet (18

Figure 10. Churchill Falls underground powerhouse.
By courtesy of Churchill Falls Corp.

metres) by 148 feet (45 metres) high by 763 feet (234 metres); and two tailrace tunnels, 45 by 60 feet (14 by 18 metres) high.

Large rock chambers are economical only when the rock can essentially support itself through a durable ground arch with the addition of only a modest amount of artificial support. Otherwise, major structural support for a large opening in weak rock is very costly. The Norad project, for example, included an intersecting grid of chambers in granite 45 by 60 feet (14 by 18 metres) high, supported by rock bolts except in one local area. Here, one of the chamber intersections coincided with the intersection of two curving shear zones of fractured rock—a happening which added $3,500,000 extra cost for a perforated concrete dome 100 feet (30 metres) in diameter to secure this local area. In some Italian and Portuguese underground powerhouses, weak-rock areas have necessitated comparable costly lining. While significant rock defects are more manageable in the usual 10- to 20-foot (three- to six-metre) rock tunnel, the problem so increases with increasing size of opening that the presence of extensive weak rock can easily place a large-chamber project outside the range of economic practicality. Hence, geological conditions are very carefully investigated for rock-chamber projects, using many borings plus exploratory drifts to locate rock defects, with a three-dimensional geological model to aid in visualizing conditions. A chamber location is selected that offers the least risk of support problems. This objective was largely attained in the granite gneiss at Churchill Falls, where the location and chamber configuration were changed several times to avoid rock defects. Rock-chamber projects, furthermore, rely heavily on the relatively new field of rock mechanics to evaluate the engineering properties of the rock mass, in which exploratory drifts are particularly important in affording access for in-place field testing.

Rock-mechanics investigation. The young field of rock mechanics was beginning, early in the 1970s, to develop a rational basis of design for projects in rock; much is already developed for projects in soil by the older field of soil mechanics (see SOIL MECHANICS, APPLICATIONS OF). Initially, the discipline had been stimulated by such complex projects as arch dams and underground chambers and then increasingly with similar problems with tunnels, rock slopes, and building foundations. In treating the rock mass with its defects as an engineering material, rock mechanics utilizes numerous techniques such as theoretical analysis, laboratory testing, field testing on site, and instrumentation to monitor performance during construction and operation. Since rock mechanics is a discipline in itself, only the most common field tests are briefly outlined below to give some concept of its role in design, particularly for a rock-chamber project.

Techniques of rock mechanics

Geostress, which can be a significant factor in choice of chamber orientation, shape, and support design, is usually determined in exploratory drifts. Two methods are common, although each is still in the development stage. One is an "overcoring" method (developed in Sweden and South Africa) used for ranges up to around 100 feet (30 metres) out from the drift and employing a cylindrical instrument known as a borehole deformeter. A small hole is drilled into the rock and the deformeter inserted. Diameter changes of the borehole are measured and recorded by the deformeter as the geostress is relieved by overcoring (cutting a circular core around the small hole) with a six-inch (15-centimetre) bit. Measurements at several depths in at least three borings at different orientations furnish the data needed for computing the existing geostress. When measurement is desired only at the surface of the drift, the so-called French flat-jack method is preferred. In this, a slot is cut at the surface, and its closure is measured as the geostress is relieved by the slot. Next, a flat hydraulic jack is inserted in the rock. The jack pressure necessary to restore closure of the slot (to the condition before its cutting) is considered to equal the original geostress. As these methods require a long drift or shaft for access to the area of measurement, development is underway (particularly in the United States) to extend the range of depth to a few thousand feet. Such will aid in comparing geostress at alternate sites; and hopefully avoid locations with high geostress which has proven very troublesome in several past chamber projects.

Shear strength of a joint, fault, or other rock defect is a controlling factor in appraising strength of the rock mass in terms of its resistance to sliding along the defect. Although partly determinable in the laboratory, it is best investigated in the field by a direct shear test at the work site. While this test has long been used for soil and soft rock, its adaptation to hard rock is due largely to work performed in Portugal. Shear strength is important in all problems of sliding; at Morrow Point Dam, in Colorado, for example, a large rock wedge between two faults started to move into the underground powerhouse and was stabilized by large tendons anchored back in a drainage tunnel plus strut action provided by the concrete structure that supported the generator machinery.

The modulus of deformation (that is, the stiffness of the rock) is significant in problems involving movement under stress and in sharing of load between rock and structure, as in a tunnel lining, embedded steel penstock, or foundation of a dam or heavy building. The simplest field test is the plate-jacking method, in which the rock in a test drift is loaded by hydraulic jacks acting on a plate two to three feet (60 to 90 centimetres) in diameter. Larger areas can be tested either by radially loading the internal surface of a test tunnel or by pressurizing a membrane lined chamber.

Analysis methods in rock mechanics have helped in appraising stress conditions around openings—as at Churchill Falls—to identify and then correct zones of tension and stress concentration. Related work with rock block models is contributing to understanding the failure mechanism of the rock mass, notable work being underway in Austria, Yugoslavia, and the United States.

Chamber excavation and support. Excavation for rock chambers generally starts with a horizontal tunnel at the top of the area to be excavated and progresses down in steps. Rock is excavated by drilling and blasting, carried on simultaneously in several headings. This procedure may give way, however, as moles gain in their ability to cut hard rock economically and as a rock saw or other device is developed for squaring up the circular surface normally cut by the mole. High geostress can be a real problem (causing inward movement of the chamber walls) unless handled by a careful sequence of partial excavations designed to relieve it gradually.

Many of the earlier underground hydroplants were roofed with a concrete arch, often designed for a major load, as in some Italian projects in weak rocks or where blast damage was considerable, as at a few projects in Scotland. Since about 1960, however, most have relied solely on rock bolts for support (sometimes supplemented with shotcrete). That such a light support has been widely successful can be attributed to careful investiga-

Excavation methods for rock chambers

tion resulting in locations with strong rock, employment of techniques to relieve high geostress, and controlled blasting to preserve rock strength.

Sound-wall blasting. Sound-wall blasting is a technique, primarily developed in Sweden, that preserves the finished rock surfaces in sound condition by careful design of the blasting charges to fit the rock conditions. In underground work, Swedish practice has often produced remarkable results almost like rock sculpturing in which the excellent shaping and preservation of the rock surfaces often permits omitting concrete lining at savings greater than the extra cost of the engineered blasting. While Swedish success is due partly to the generally strong rock in that country, it is due even more to energetic research and development programs to develop (1) theoretical methods for blasting design plus field blast tests to determine pertinent rock properties, (2) special explosives for different rock conditions, and (3) institutes for the training of specialized blasting engineers to apply these procedures in the field construction.

Swedish work on sound-wall blasting

In the United States, sound-wall blasting has enjoyed only indifferent success underground. Reluctance of the blasting industry to change from its customary empirical approach and the lack of specialized blasting engineers trained in Swedish practices have led to a return to the more costly technique of mining an initial pilot bore to afford stress relief, followed by blasting successively thinner slabs toward the free face of the pilot bore.

For excavation from the ground surface, the requirements of sound-wall blasting largely have been met by the technique of presplitting, developed in the United States in the late 1950s. Basically, this technique consists of creating a continuous crack (or presplit) at a desired finished excavation line by initially firing a line of closely spaced, lightly loaded holes drilled there. Next, the interior rock mass is drilled and blasted by conventional means. If a high horizontal geostress is present, it is important that it first be relieved (as by an initial cut a modest distance from the presplit line); otherwise, the presplit crack is not likely to occur in the direction desired. Stockton Dam, in Missouri illustrates the benefit of presplitting. Here, vertical faces in dolomite up to 110 feet (34 metres) were successfully presplit and promptly rock bolted; this permitted a major reduction in thickness of the concrete facing, resulting in a net saving of about $2,500,000.

SHAFTS

The mining industry has been the primary constructor of shafts, because at many locations these are essential for access to ore, for ventilation, and for material transport. Depths of several thousand feet are common. In public-works projects, such as sewer tunnels, shafts are usually only a few hundred feet deep and because of their high cost are avoided in the design stage wherever practical. Shallower shafts find many uses, however, for penstocks and access to underground hydroplants, for dropping aqueduct tunnels beneath rivers, for missile silos, and for oil and liquefied-gas storage. Being essentially vertical tunnels, shafts involve the same problems of different types of ground and water conditions but on an aggravated scale, since vertical transport makes the operation slower, more costly, and even more congested than with horizontal tunneling. Except when there is a high horizontal geostress in rock, the loading on a shaft support is generally less than for a tunnel. Inflowing water, however, is far more dangerous during construction and generally intolerable during operation. Hence, most shafts are concrete lined and waterproofed, and the lining installation usually follows only a short distance' behind excavation. The shape is usually circular, although, before present mechanized excavation methods, mining shafts were frequently rectangular. Shafts may be sunk from the surface (or drilled in smaller sizes), or, if an existing tunnel provides access, they may be raised from below.

Shaft sinking and drilling. Mining downward, generally from the surface, although occasionally from an underground chamber, is called shaft sinking. In soil, shallow shafts are frequently supported with interlocking steel sheetpiling held by ring beams (circular rib sets); or a concrete caisson may be built on the surface and sunk by excavating inside as weight is added by extending its walls. More recently, large-diameter shallow shafts have been constructed by the "slurry trench method," in which a circular trench is excavated while filled with a heavy liquid (usually bentonite slurry), which supports its walls until finally displaced by filling the trench with concrete. For greater depth in soil, another method involves freezing a ring of soil around the shaft. In this method, a ring of closely spaced freezing holes is drilled outside the shaft. A refrigerated brine is circulated in double-wall pipes in the holes to freeze the soil before starting the shaft excavation. It is then kept frozen until the shaft is completed and lined with concrete. This freezing method was developed in Germany and The Netherlands, where it was used successfully to sink shafts through nearly 2,000 feet (600 metres) of alluvial soil to reach coal beds in the underlying rock. It has also been applied under similar conditions in Britain, Poland, and Belgium. Occasionally, the freezing technique has been used in soft rock to solidify a deep aquifer (layer of water-bearing rock). Due to the long time required for drilling the freezing holes and for freezing the ground (18 to 24 months for some deep shafts), the freezing method has not been popular on public-works projects except as a last resort, although it has been used in New York City for shallow shafts through soil to gain access for deep water tunnels.

More efficient methods for sinking deep shafts in rock were developed in South African gold-mining operations, in which shafts 5,000 to 8,000 feet (1,500 to 2,400 metres) deep are common and generally 20 to 30 feet (six to nine metres) in diameter. South African procedure has produced progress around 30 feet (nine metres) per day by utilizing a sinking stage of multiple platforms, which permits concurrent excavation and concrete lining. Excavation is by drilling and blasting with muck loaded into large buckets, with larger shafts operating four buckets alternately in hoisting wells extending through the platforms. Grouting is carried a few hundred feet ahead to seal out water. Best progress is achieved when the rock is pregrouted from two or three holes drilled from the surface before starting the shaft. Since the shallower shafts on public-works projects cannot justify the investment in the large plant needed to operate a sinking stage, their progress in rock is much slower—in the range of five to ten feet (1.5 to three metres) per day.

Occasionally, shafts have been sunk through soil by drilling methods. The technique was first used in British practice in 1930 and was subsequently further refined in The Netherlands and Germany. The procedure involves first advancing a pilot hole, then reaming in several stages of enlargement to final diameter, while the walls of the hole are supported by a heavy liquid (called drilling mud), with circulation of the mud serving to remove the cuttings. Then a double-wall steel casing is sunk by displacing the drilling mud, followed by injecting concrete outside the casing and within the annular space between its double walls. One use of this technique was in the 25-foot- (eight-metre-) diameter Statemine shaft in The Netherlands, 1,500 feet (460 metres) deep through soil that required one and one-half years before completion in 1959. For the 1962 construction of some 200 missile shafts in Wyoming in soft rock (clay shale and friable sandstone), a giant auger proved effective for sinking these 65-foot- (20-metre-) deep, 15-foot- (five-metre-) diameter shafts, generally at the rate of two to three days per shaft. Perhaps the largest drilled shaft is one in the Soviet Union: 2,674 feet (815 metres) deep, which was enlarged in four stages of reaming to a final diameter of 28.7 feet (about nine metres), progressing at a reported rate of 15 feet (five metres) per day.

More dramatic has been the adaptation in the United States of oil-well-drilling methods in a technique called big-hole drilling, used for constructing small shafts in the diameter range of three to six feet (90 to 180 centimetres). Big-hole drilling was developed for deep emplacement in underground testing of nuclear devices, with over 150 such big holes drilled in the 1960s up to 5,000 feet (1,500 metres) deep in Nevada in rocks ranging from soft tuff to granite. In big-hole drilling the hole is made in one pass only with an array of roller-bit cutters that are pressed against the rock by the weight of an assembly of lead-filled drill collars, sometimes totalling 300,000 pounds (135,000 kilograms). The drill rig must be huge in size to handle such loads. The greatest impediment controlling progress has been the removal of drill cuttings, where an air lift is showing promise.

Shaft raising. Handling cuttings is simplified when the shaft can be raised from an existing tunnel, since the cuttings then merely fall to the tunnel, where they are easily loaded into mine cars or trucks. This advantage has long been recognized in mining; where once an initial shaft has been sunk to provide access and an opportunity for horizontal tunnels, most subsequent shafts are then raised from these tunnels, often by upward mining with men working from a cage hung from a cable through a small pilot hole drilled downward from above. In 1957 this procedure was improved by Swedish development of the raise climber whose working cage climbs a rail fastened to the shaft wall and extends backward into the horizontal access tunnel into which the cage is retracted during a blast. Simultaneously in the 1950s Germans began experimenting with several mechanized reamers, including a motor-cutter unit pulled upward by a cable in a previously down-drilled pilot hole. A more significant step toward mechanized shaft raising occurred in 1962 when United States mole manufacturers developed a device called a raise borer, in which the cutting head is rotated and pulled upward by a drill shaft in a down-drilled pilot hole, with the power unit being located at top of the pilot hole. The capacity of this type of borer (or upward reamer) generally ranges from three- to eight-foot- (90- to 240-centimetre-) diameters in lifts up to 1,000 feet (300 metres) with progress ranging up to 300 feet (90 metres) per day. Furthermore, available cutters when operating on raise borers can cut through rock often almost twice as hard as rock moles can deal with. For larger shafts, bigger diameter reamers may be operated in an inverted position to ream downward, with the cuttings sluiced to the access tunnel below. A 12-foot- (four-metre-) diameter, 1,600-foot- (500-metre-) deep vent shaft was completed by this method in 1969 at the White Pine Copper Mine in Michigan. Starting from a ten-inch (25-centimetre) pilot hole, it was enlarged in three downreaming passes.

The introduction of a workable raise borer in the 1960s represented a breakthrough in shaft construction, cutting construction time to one-third and cost to less than one-half that for an upward-mined shaft. At the beginning of the 1970s, the procedure was being widely adopted for shaft raising, and some projects had been specifically designed to take advantage of this more efficient method. At a Northfield Mountain (Massachusetts) underground hydroplant (completed in 1971), the previously common large surge chamber was replaced by a series of horizontal tunnels at three levels, connected by vertical shafts. This layout permitted significant economy by the use of jumbos already available from other tunnels of the project and the use of a raise borer for starting the shafts. If very large shafts are involved, the raise borer is particularly useful in simplifying the so-called glory-hole method, (Figure 11), in which the main shaft is sunk by blasting; the muck is then dumped in the central glory-hole, previously constructed by a raise borer. The example is based on the construction of a 133-foot- (40-metre-) diameter surge shaft above the Angeles penstock tunnel near Los Angeles. The glory-hole technique was also used in 1944 in constructing a series of 20 underground fuel-oil chambers in Hawaii, working from access tunnels driven initially at both top and bottom of the chambers and later used to house oil and vent piping. The advent of the raise borer should now make this and similar construction more economically attractive. Recently, some deep sewer projects have been redesigned to utilize the raise borer for shaft connections.

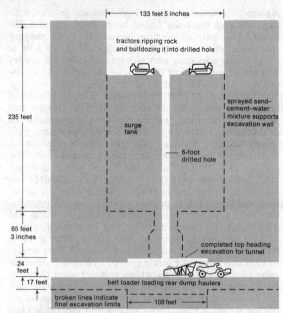

Figure 11: Shaft excavation by glory-hole method at the Angeles penstock tunnel near Los Angeles.
Adapted from A.D. Parker, *Planning and Estimating Underground Construction* (copyright 1970); used with permission of McGraw-Hill Book Co.

IMMERSED-TUBE TUNNELS

Development of method. The immersed-tube, or sunken-tube, method, used principally for underwater crossings, involves prefabricating long tube sections, floating them to the site, sinking each in a previously dredged trench, and then covering with backfill (Figure 13). While more correctly classified as a subaqueous adaptation of the dry-land cut-and-cover procedure often used for subways, the immersed-tube method warrants inclusion as a tunneling technique because it is becoming a preferred alternate to the older method of constructing a subaqueous tunnel under compressed air with a Greathead shield. A major advantage is that, once the new section has been connected, interior work is conducted in free air, thus avoiding the high cost and major risk of operating a large shield under high air pressure. Furthermore, the immersed-tube method is usable in water deeper than is possible with the shield method, which essentially is restricted to less than 100 feet (30 metres) of water by the maximum air pressure at which workmen can safely work.

The procedure was first developed by an American engineer, W.J. Wilgus, for the construction (1906–10) of the Detroit River twin-tube railroad tunnel between Detroit, Michigan, and Windsor, Ontario, where it was successfully used for the 2,665-foot (812-metre) river-crossing portion. A structural assembly of steel tubes was prefabricated in 262-foot- (80-metre-) long sections with both ends temporarily bulkheaded or closed. Each section was then towed out and sunk in 60 to 80 feet (18 to 24 metres) of water, onto a grillage of I-beams in sand at the bottom of a trench previously dredged in the river-bottom clay. After being connected to the previous section by locking pins driven by a diver, the section was weighted down by surrounding it with concrete. Next, after removal of the temporary bulkheads at the just-completed connection, the newly placed section was pumped out, permitting completion of an interior concrete lining in free air. These basic principles proved so practical that with subsequent refinements they still form the basis of the immersed-tube method.

After use on a four-tube New York subway crossing under the Harlem River in 1912–14, the method was tried for a vehicular tunnel in the 1925–28 construction of the 3,545-foot- (1,081-metre-) long, 37-foot- (11-metre-) diameter Posey tunnel at Oakland, California. Because these and other experiences have indicated that the problems encountered in building large vehicular tunnels could be better handled by the immersed-tube method, it

Advantages of immersed-tube method (margin note)

has been preferred for subaqueous vehicular tunnels since about 1940. While shield tunnelling continued in a transition period (1940–50), subsequently nearly all of the world's large vehicular tunnels have been constructed by the immersed-tube method, including such notable examples as the Bankhead tunnel at Mobile, Alabama; two Chesapeake Bay tunnels; the Fraser River tunnel at Vancouver, British Columbia; the Maas River tunnel in The Netherlands; Denmark's Limfjord tunnel; Sweden's Tingstad tunnel; and the Hong Kong Cross Harbor tunnel.

Modern practice. The world's longest and deepest application to date is the twin-tube subway crossing of San Francisco Bay, constructed between 1966 and 1971 with a length of 3.6 miles (5.8 kilometres) in a maximum water depth of 135 feet (41 metres) (Figure 12). The 330-foot- (100-metre-) long, 48-foot- (15-metre-) wide sections were constructed of steel plate and launched by shipbuilding procedures. Each section also had temporary end bulkheads and upper pockets for gravel ballast placed during sinking. After placement of the interior concrete lining at a fitting-out dock, each section was towed to the site and sunk in a trench previously dredged in the mud in the bottom of the bay. A tower mast at the forward end of each section was used for survey alignment. Before sinking each section, gravel bedding was placed at the bottom of the trench and carefully levelled. With diver guidance, the initial connection was accomplished by hydraulic-jack-powered couplers, similar to those that automatically join railroad cars. By relieving the water pressure within the short compartment between bulkheads at the new joint, the water pressure acting on the forward end of the new section provided a huge force that pushed it into intimate contact with the previously laid tube, compressing the rubber gaskets to provide a watertight seal. Following this, the temporary bulkheads were removed on each side of the new joint and interior concrete placed across the connection.

The San Francisco subway tunnel (margin note)

From *Civil Engineering* (December 1966)

Figure 12: Immersed-tube tunnel building procedure (see text).

Most applications of the immersed-tube procedure outside the United States have been by a Danish engineer–constructor firm, Christiani and Nielsen, starting in 1938 with a three-tube highway crossing of the Maas River in Rotterdam. While following United States technique in essence, European engineers have developed a number of innovations, including prestressed concrete in lieu of a steel structure (often consisting of a number of short sections tied together with prestressed tendons to form a single section 300 feet [90 metres] in length); the use of butyl rubber as the waterproofing membrane; and initial support on temporary piles while a sand fill is jetted beneath. An alternate to the last approach has been used in a Swedish experiment on the Tingstad tunnel, in which the precast sections were supported on water-filled nylon sacks and the water later replaced by grout injected into the sacks to form the permanent support. Also, the cross section has been greatly enlarged—the 1969 Schelde River tunnel in Antwerp, Belgium, used precast sections 328 feet (100 metres) long by 33 feet (10 metres) high by 157 feet (48 metres) wide. This unusually large width accommodates two highway tubes of three lanes each for a total of six lanes, one two-track railroad tube, and one bicycle tube. Particularly unusual was a 1963 use of the immersed-tube technique in subway construction in Rotterdam. Trenches were dug or, in some cases, made out of

European innovations (margin note)

abandoned canals and filled with water. The tube sections were then floated into position. This technique had been first tried in 1952 for one of the land approaches of the immersed-tube Elizabeth tunnel in Norfolk, Virginia; in low-elevation ground with the water table near the surface, it permits a considerable saving in bracing of the trench because keeping the trench filled eliminates the need for resisting external water pressure.

Thus, the immersed-tube method has become a frequent choice for subaqueous crossings, although some locations pose problems of interference with intensive navigation traffic or the possibility of displacement by severe storms (one tube section of the Chesapeake Bay tunnel was moved out of its trench by a severe storm during construction). The method is being actively considered for many of the world's most difficult underwater crossings, including the long-discussed English Channel Project.

IV. Future trends in underground construction

ENVIRONMENTAL AND ECONOMIC FACTORS

Improvement of surface environment.   Unexpectedly rapid increases in urbanization throughout the world, especially since World War II, have brought many problems, including congestion, air pollution, loss of scarce surface area for vehicular ways, and major traffic disruption during their construction. Some cities relying principally on auto transport have even found that nearly two-thirds of their central land area is devoted to vehicular service (freeways, streets, and parking facilities), leaving only one-third of the surface space for productive or recreational use. During the past decade there has been a growing awareness that this situation could be alleviated by underground placement of a large number of facilities that do not need to be on the surface, such as rapid transit, parking, utilities, sewage and water-treatment plants, fluid storage, warehouses, and light manufacturing. The overriding deterrent, however, has been the greater cost underground—except in Sweden where energetic research has reduced underground costs to nearly equal the surface alternates. Hence planners have rarely dared to propose underground construction except where the surface alternate was widely recognized as intolerable. Underground construction in urban areas has, thus, generally been limited to situations without a viable surface alternate; as a result, additional increases in surface construction have further aggravated the problem. At the same time, the low volume of underground construction has provided insufficient incentive for the development of innovative technology.

New approach to underground construction

A different approach for the United States was crystallized from a 1966–68 study by the National Academy of Sciences and the National Academy of Engineering, which proposed cost reduction from government stimulated technologic research plus broader evaluation of social impacts. This would often show the underground alternate as the better investment for society. A reduction of at least one-third in cost and one-half in construction time over the next two decades was foreseen, and it was proposed that social and environmental costs be included in estimates as well as construction costs. In 1970 an international meeting of some 20 countries was held in Washington, D. C., under the Organization for Economic Co-operation and Development (an assembly of NATO countries) to share views and develop recommendations on government policy in this area. The conference recommended that energetic stimulation of underground construction be adopted as national policy in each of the 20 countries represented and in effect visualized the underground as a largely undeveloped natural resource. This resource, it was pointed out, could be used to expand urban areas downward to help preserve the upper environment—for example, by tunnels for transport and interbasin water transfer, for recovery of minerals increasingly needed by the economy, and in developing presently unreachable resources under ocean areas adjoining the continents. Such international consensus suggests that this is indeed a powerful concept ready for acceptance.

Scope of the tunnelling market.   While informed people foresee a great increase in underground construction,

numerical estimates are crude at best, particularly since statistics have not been accumulated in the past for underground construction as a separate item either in the public-works or the mining sectors. The 1970 conference mentioned above included a survey suggesting an average annual volume in its 20 member countries of about $1,000,000,000 in public works for the 1960–69 decade ($3,000,000,000 including mining) and forecast that this volume should at least double for the 1970–79 decade. Such estimates assumed the continuation of the current rate of technological improvement and recognized that the increase would be far greater if stimulated by government support in an energetic research and development program to reduce cost. All estimates are alike in forecasting a huge increase in underground construction during the next two decades. Key factors affecting the actual increase are technological improvements reducing costs and an increasing awareness on the part of society and public-works planners of the many potential applications for better use of the underground.

POTENTIAL APPLICATIONS

Future applications are expected to range from expansion of existing uses to the introduction of entirely new concepts. Several of these are considered below; many others are likely to emerge as innovative planners turn their attention to utilizing the underground space. For the next decade, at least, the largest increase is likely to be in rock tunnelling: partly from the nature of the projects and partly from the expectation that improved moles will make rock tunnelling more attractive than soil tunnels, with their usual requirement for continuous temporary support plus a permanent concrete lining.

Intercity transit

Deep rock tunnels for rapid transit between cities are beginning to receive very serious consideration. These might include a 425-mile (680-kilometre) system to cover the nearly continuous urban area between Boston and Washington, D. C., probably with an entirely new type of conveyance at speeds of several hundred miles per hour. A forerunner system in Japan, the New Tōkai-dō Line, using standard railroad equipment at about 150 miles (about 250 kilometres) per hour, is currently undergoing expansion with many new tunnels. Highway tunnels are beginning to increase in number as well. Urban highway tunnels conceivably may offer a convenient opportunity to reduce pollution by treating the exhaust air that has already been collected by the ventilating system essential for longer vehicular tunnels.

There is increasing recognition that many more interbasin water transfers will be needed, involving systems of tunnels and canals. Notable current projects include the California Aqueduct, which transfers water from the northern mountains some 450 miles (725 kilometres) to the semi-arid Los Angeles area; the Orange–Fish Project in South Africa, which includes a 50-mile (80-kilometre) tunnel; and early studies for possible transfer of surplus Canadian water into the southwestern United States. Drainage can also be a problem, as in the old lakebed area occupied by Mexico City, where current expansion of the drainage system involves some 60 miles (100 kilometres) of tunnel.

Urban tunnels

Shallower tunnels for subways are bound to increase beyond those expansions currently under design or under construction in many cities, including San Francisco, Washington, D. C., Boston, Chicago, New York, London, Paris, Budapest, Munich, and Mexico City. Multiple use is likely to receive further consideration as communication agencies begin to show interest in adding space within the structures for the several types of utilities. Some merchants visualize mechanized movement of pedestrians between stores. One notable example is Montreal's extensive assembly of underground shopping malls, which interconnect most new downtown buildings as well as provide access to the subway and commuter railroads—a project that has relieved the streets from pedestrian traffic, particularly during severe weather. Another example involves utilization of space excavated above subway stations for parking facilities, as on the Toronto subway and more recently on the Paris

Metro, where the space above one of the stations in the Champs-Élysées area provides seven levels of parking.

Subaqueous crossings are becoming more ambitious. The world's longest railroad tunnel, for example, currently underway in Japan, is the 30-mile (50-kilometre) Seikan undersea rock tunnel between the islands of Honshu and Hokkaido, now being explored by a pilot tunnel that is also being utilized as a proving ground for several new types of moles. Of comparable scope is the more publicized projected English Channel tunnel for a rail connection between France and England, using special cars for auto transport. Studies early in the 1970s were concentrating on two alternatives: twin mole-excavated tunnels in chalk plus a service tunnel or an immersed-tube structure providing comparable space. The immersed-tube procedure is also being considered for a number of other difficult crossings; *e.g.*, from Denmark to Sweden and from Sicily to Italy. Immersed tubes are likely to become more attractive with improvement in methods for trench dredging in deeper water and for grading the trench bottom to support the tube structure. The Japanese are experimenting with an underwater bulldozer, robot-manned and television-monitored. One innovative proposal for supplying additional water to Southern California visualizes the immersed-tube method to construct a large pipeline for some 500 miles (800 kilometres) under the shallower ocean along the continental shelf. Subaqueous tunnelling also is likely to be involved as procedures are developed for utilizing the vast continental-shelf areas of the world; concepts are already being studied for tunnels to service oil wells and for extensive undersea mining such as has been pioneered in Britain and eastern Canada.

Fluid storage   Both Norway and Sweden have reduced the direct costs of fluid storage by storing petroleum products in underground chambers, thus eliminating the maintenance cost for frequent repainting of steel tanks in a surface facility. Locating these chambers below the permanent water table (and below any existing wells) ensures that seepage will be toward the chambers rather than outward; thus, the oil is prevented from leaking out of the chamber, and the lining may be omitted. Further economies may result from orienting the chambers vertically to take advantage of the raise borer and glory-hole techniques, previously mentioned. There are a number of underground installations for the storage of highly compressed gas cooled to a liquid state; these may increase once improved types of lining have been developed. Although the method involves only limited tunnelling for access, the United States Atomic Energy Commission has developed an ingenious method for disposal of nuclear waste by injecting it into fissured rock within a cement grout so that hardening of the grout reconverts the nuclear minerals into a stable rocklike state. Other disposal methods involve more tunnelling, such as within salt, which has particularly good ability for shielding against radiation.

A good example of an imaginative concept is Chicago's Underflow Tunnel and Reservoir Plan, which is intended to alleviate both pollution and flooding. Like most older cities, Chicago has a combined sewer system that carries both storm runoff and sanitary sewage during wet weather but only sanitary sewage during dry weather. The city's huge growth has so overtaxed older portions of the system that severe storms cause flooding in low areas. While sewage treatment has essentially eliminated sewage pollution of Lake Michigan, making Chicago virtually the only major city on the Great Lakes continuing wide recreational usage of its lake beaches, the treatment plants generally are sized to handle only the dry-weather flow. Thus, overflow during major storms is discharged into streams draining away from the lake as a mixture of sanitary sewage diluted by storm water. Conventional solutions adopted in the past, such as adding a second pipe system to collect only the storm water, discharging it into the streams, or adding plant capacity to treat all combined flow during severe storms, have proved tremendously expensive. An early version of a proposed solution of this problem is illustrated in Figure 13; a novel aspect of the plan is temporary storage of excess

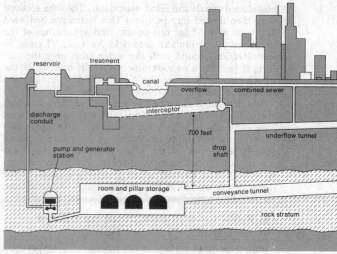

Figure 13: Potential water control plan for Chicago.
By courtesy of the Metropolitan Sanitary District of Greater Chicago

water in large underground caverns, which after each storm could be pumped out for gradual treatment by the existing sewage plants. Inclusion of the surface reservoir shown in Figure 13 makes practical the use of the diluted sewage in a pumped storage hydroplant; in this type of facility the fluid is pumped up during offpeak-electric-power night periods, when steam power is cheaply available, and then allowed to flow back to generate peak power when demand exceeds economic capacity of the steam plants. A second multiple use is the opportunity to reduce present surface quarrying for crushed stone aggregate by using the dolomitic limestone mined from the deep tunnels and caverns. Extension of the tunnel and reservoir plan to suburban areas was under consideration in the early 1970s; the enlarged project, requiring 120 miles of tunnels, would serve an area of 375 square miles. The concept is being studied by Boston and other cities.

The use of rock chambers for underground hydroplants seems certain to increase in most countries, particularly those in which until recently surface plants have been favoured because of their apparently lower cost. Scotland has been one of the first countries to recognize that extra construction cost can often be warranted to preserve the scenic environment, also recognized by choice of an underground location for recent U.S. pump–storage plants —Northfield Mt. in Massachusetts and Raccoon Mt. in Tennessee, plus others being planned. Sweden's use of the underground for plants treating sewage and water, for warehouses, and for light manufacturing is likely to find further application. The relatively small annual temperature range in the underground has made it a desirable environment for facilities requiring close atmospheric control. In the vicinity of Kansas City, Missouri, mined-out space in underground limestone quarries is being used effectively for laboratory space, for dehumidified storage of corrosion-sensitive equipment, and for refrigerated food storage, an application also favoured in Sweden.   *Temperature underground*

Similar environment factors plus the probability of less disturbance during earthquakes have made the underground desirable for a number of scientific installations, including atomic accelerators, earthquake research, nuclear research, and space telescopes. Since earthquake risk is a big factor in locating nuclear powerplants, the merits of an underground location are attracting interest in siting studies for future plants.

IMPROVED TECHNOLOGY

Worldwide efforts are under way to accelerate improvements in the technology of underground construction and are likely to be stimulated as a result of the 1970 OECD International Conference recommending improvement as government policy. The endeavour involves specialists such as geologists, soil- and rock-mechanics engineers, public-works designers, mining engineers, contractors, equipment and materials manufacturers, planners, and also lawyers, who aid in the search for more equitable contractual methods to share the risks of unknown geology and resulting extra costs. Many improvements and their early applications have been previously discussed; others are briefly mentioned here, including several that have not yet moved from the research stage to the pilot, or trial, stage. Projects in rock are emphasized, since the field of rock engineering is less developed than its older counterpart, soils engineering.

Geological prediction and evaluation

Geological prediction and evaluation are universally recognized as deserving a high priority for improvement. Since ground and water conditions are controlling factors in choosing both the design and construction method underground and seem destined to be even more so with greater use of moles, efforts are directed toward improving boring information (as with borehole cameras); faster borings (the Japanese are trying to bore one to three miles [about 1,600 to 4,800 metres] ahead of a tunnelling mole); geophysical methods to estimate rock-mass properties; and techniques to observe pattern of water flows. For evaluation, the new field of rock mechanics is concentrating on measuring geostress and rock-mass properties, failure mechanics of jointed rock, and analytical methods for applying results to design of underground openings.

For rock excavation, improved cutters are generally considered the key for expanding economic ability of moles to include harder rock. Much effort is being devoted to improving current mechanical cutters, including technical advances based upon space metallurgy, geometry of cutter shape and arrangement, mechanics of cutting action, and research in presoftening rock. Concur-

New rock-cutting methods

rently, there is an intensive search for entirely new rock-cutting methods (some nearing a pilot application), including high-pressure water jets, Russian water cannon (operated at high pressures), electron beam, and flame jet (often combined with abrasive powder). Other methods under research involve lasers and ultrasonics. Most of these have high power requirements and might increase ventilating needs from an already overtaxed system. Though some of these novel methods will eventually reach the stage of economic practicality, it is not possible to predict at present which ones will eventually succeed. Also needed is a means for testing rock in terms of mole drillability plus correlation with mole performance in different rocks, where promising work is under way at several locations.

A decided change in current materials-handling systems seems inevitable to keep up with fast-moving moles by matching the mole's rate of excavation and fragmentation sizing of the muck produced. Schemes now under study include long belt conveyors, high-speed rail with completely new types of equipment, and both hydraulic and pneumatic pipelines. Useful experience is being accumulated with pipeline transport of ore slurries, of coal, and even of such bulky material as canned goods.

For ground support, rock-mechanics engineers are working toward replacing past empirical methods with a more rational basis of design. One key factor is likely to be the tolerable deformation for mobilizing but not destroying the strength of the rock mass. There is wide agreement that progress will best be aided by field-test sections at prototype scale in selected ongoing projects.

Underground support

While several newer types of support have been discussed (rock bolts, shotcrete, and precast-concrete elements), developments are under way toward entirely new types, including lighter material plus yield-controllable types as a corollary to above tolerable deformation concept. For projects using concrete lining, major changes seem inevitable to keep pace with fast-moving moles, probably including some entirely new types of concretes. Current efforts include work with precast elements, plus research into stronger and faster set materials, which use resins and other polymers in lieu of portland cement.

Preservation of ground strength is beginning to win acceptance as vital for the safety of large rock chambers and also often a means of cost saving in tunnels. For preserving strength of the rock mass around tunnels, a

mole-cut surface provides a solution. For large chambers, consideration is being given to cutting a peripheral slot with a wire saw of the type used to quarry monument stone. Where chambers are blasted, engineered sound-wall blasting has provided a solution in Sweden.

Ground strengthening by precementation with chemical grouts is a technique notably developed in France and Britain through extensive research by specialized grouting firms. Figure 14 shows the world's outstanding appli-

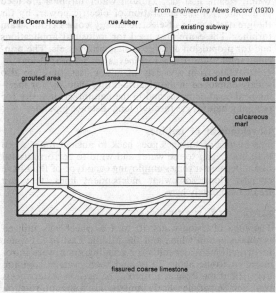

From *Engineering News Record* (1970)

Paris Opera House   rue Auber   existing subway

grouted area   sand and gravel

calcareous marl

fissured coarse limestone

Figure 14: Ground strengthening at Auber Station of the Paris Métro.

cation at the Auber Station of the Métro Express beneath the Place de L'Opéra traffic centre of Paris—a large chamber 130 feet (40 metres) wide by 60 feet (18 metres) high by 750 feet (230 metres) long in chalky marl below an existing subway, at a depth of 120 feet (40 metres), about 60 feet (18 metres) below water table. This was completed in 1970 without interrupting surface traffic and without underpinning the many old masonry buildings above (including the historic National Opera Building), a truly courageous undertaking made possible by surrounding the chamber with a pregrouted zone to seal out water and to precement the overlying sand and gravel. Different types of chemical grout were successively injected (totalling about 2,000,000,000 cubic feet [57,000,000 cubic metres]), working from crown and side drifts; then the chamber was mined and supported both top and bottom by prestressed arches of concrete elements. Similar procedure was also successful at the Étoile Station adjacent to the Arc de Triomphe. While this technique of ground strengthening by grout solidification requires highly skilled specialists, it is an instructive example of how a new technology is likely to make economically possible future projects previously considered beyond engineering ability.

BIBLIOGRAPHY. AGRICOLA, *De Re Metallica* (1556; Eng. trans. by H.C. and L.H. HOOVER, 1950), a classic work on early mining in Europe; F.W. SIMMS, *Practical Tunneling*, 3rd ed. rev. 1877), on early public works, with fascinating accounts of incredible difficulties overcome by pioneers; H.W. RICHARDSON and R.S. MAYO, *Practical Tunnel Driving* (1941), a history of U.S. practice to 1940, emphasizing tunnel equipment; C.A. PEQUIGNOT (ed.), *Tunnels and Tunnelling* (1963), on English practice, with comprehensive tables comparing noted tunnels of the world; G. E. SANDSTROM, *Tunnels* (British title, *The History of Tunneling*, 1963) an historical survey that summarizes Sweden's great contributions to underground engineering; K.G. STAGG and O.C. ZIENKIEWICZ, *Rock Mechanics in Engineering Practice* (1968), an introductory work, with each of its 12 chapters written by a noted authority; A.D. PARKER, *Planning and Estimating Underground Construction* (1970), on U.S. practice, emphasizing construction engineering and estimating. For comtemporary developments, see the periodicals, *Engineering News Record* (weekly); and *Tunnels and Tunnelling* (bimonthly).

(K.S.L.)

Turbine

The word turbine (Latin *turbo*, "a whirling object") designates a machine that converts the energy stored in a fluid into mechanical energy. Conversion is accomplished by passing the fluid through a system of fixed passages and moving finlike blades attached to a rotor, causing the latter to rotate. Turbines fall into three general classifications according to the most commonly used fluids—water, steam, and gas. Though water turbines are used principally for the generation of electric power, by far the greatest source of electric energy comes from steam turbines. These are also used for industrial applications and for propulsion of large oceangoing vessels. The principal application of gas turbines is for jet-propulsion aircraft. Aside from a variety of minor uses, they are also widely employed in the electric-utility industry for meeting peak-load demands and in the natural-gas industry for pumping natural gas through long-distance pipelines.

Development of turbines

The history of turbines goes back to ancient times when man first began to use water and wind to perform useful tasks. Because turbines employing each type of fluid have evolved along somewhat independent lines, they are treated separately here.

HISTORY OF WATER TURBINES

The idea of using water to turn a wheel was utilized centuries ago in China and the Middle East to lift water for irrigation. Water mills for grinding grain were introduced in Rome about 70 BC and soon became common throughout the Roman Empire. The earliest waterwheels were simple paddle wheels immersed in a stream; rotation was achieved by the impact of the current on the paddles. Later models confined the water in a channel, to prevent escape from around the edges of the vanes. Such wheels achieved efficiencies approaching 30 percent and were still in wide use until about 1800. A further development was the overshot wheel, in which water was introduced at the top of the wheel and carried down by gravity before being discharged near the bottom. Such wheels were capable of efficiencies between 70 and 90 percent, approaching that of present-day installations. They were used extensively until about 1850, when they began to be replaced by the more compact water turbines then coming into use (see WATERWHEEL).

The development of the modern water turbine began with experiments on the mechanics of reaction wheels by the Swiss mathematician Leonhard Euler and his son Albert, in the 1750s. These experiments led to further investigations, and the French engineer Benoît Fourneyron first achieved success in 1827 with a reaction turbine that could develop about six horsepower. This turbine used a radial outward flow, with water being directed through stationary guide vanes at the centre into curved blades of an outer runner (rotor, or rotating portion). The water discharging from the periphery of the runner created a reactive force causing the runner to rotate. By 1832 a turbine capable of developing about 50 horsepower had been perfected.

In 1838 an inward-flow turbine was patented by Samuel B. Howd of Geneva, New York, and about 1849 a fellow American, James B. Francis, designed a much improved version operating on the same general principle, which became universally known as the Francis turbine, one of the principal types in use today.

HISTORY OF STEAM TURBINES

The first device that could be classified as a steam turbine is generally attributed to Hero of Alexandria about the 1st century AD. Operating on the principle of reaction, this device achieved rotation through the action of steam issuing from curved tubes, or nozzles, in a manner similar to that of water issuing from a rotating lawn sprinkler. It consisted of a hollow sphere that was free to turn upon a horizontal axis above a caldron or boiler. Steam issuing from the caldron passed through two fixed tubes extending from the caldron to the sphere and escaped through two bent tubes attached to the sphere, causing rotation.

Another steam-driven machine, described about 1629, used a jet of steam impinging on blades projecting from a wheel, causing it to rotate. This machine, in contrast with that of Hero, operated on the impulse principle.

The first steam turbines having any commercial significance appear to have been those built in the United States by William Avery in 1831. These turbines consisted of two hollow arms, about two and one-half feet (750 millimetres) long, attached at right angles to a hollow shaft through which steam was supplied. At the extremity of each arm was a small opening through which the steam could issue. The openings were at the trailing edge of the arms, so that rotation was achieved by the reactive force of the steam. About 50 of these turbines were built for sawmills and woodworking shops, and at least one was tried on a locomotive. Although an efficiency approximately equal to that of contemporary steam engines was claimed, the turbines were abandoned because of their high noise level, difficult speed regulation, and frequent need of repair.

Not until the latter part of the 19th century were further significant contributions made. Probably the most prominent among a number of early inventors in the steam-turbine field was Sir Charles Parsons of England, who early recognized the advantage of employing a large number of stages in series so that the energy release by the expanding steam could take place in small steps. This principle opened the way for the development of the modern steam turbine. He also developed the reaction-stage principle, in which pressure drop and energy release are equal through both the stationary and moving blades. Turbines employing this principle are frequently called Parsons turbines.

Parsons' original ten-horsepower steam turbine was built in 1884 using a rotor and casing with attached multiple-stage blading (*i.e.*, several sets of blades in series rather than one), characteristic of modern turbines. Steam entered at the centre and flowed toward the ends.

Another prominent pioneer in the development of the steam turbine was Carl G.P. de Laval of Sweden, who built a small 42,000-revolutions-per-minute reaction turbine in the early 1880s. Although several of these were later employed for driving cream separators, he did not consider them practical for commercial application. De Laval turned to the development of reliable single-stage, simple-impulse turbines operating on the principle illustrated in Figure 1. He is credited with being the first

De Laval's simple impulse turbines

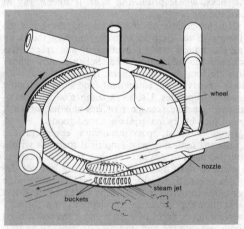

Figure 1: De Laval turbine, showing how the steam is formed into a jet by a specially shaped nozzle and is then deflected by the buckets or vanes on the wheel, causing the wheel to rotate.

to employ a convergent-divergent type of nozzle in a steam turbine in order to realize the full potential energy of the expanding steam in a single-stage machine. During the period from 1889 to 1897 de Laval built a large number of turbines ranging in size from about five horsepower to several hundred. In 1892 he built a 15-horsepower turbine for marine applications with two turbine wheels, one for forward motion and the other for astern operation. An early model similar to this was exhibited at the World's Columbian Exposition in Chicago in 1893.

Fourneyron's reaction turbine

In addition to Parsons and de Laval, two other pioneers in the field, C.-E.-A. Rateau of France and Charles G. Curtis of the United States, made important contributions during the 1890s. Rateau developed the multistage-impulse principle, now commonly known as pressure staging, in which pressure drop occurs only in the stationary nozzle elements and not in the moving blades. With this design, fewer stages are required than for a corresponding reaction-type turbine operating under the same steam conditions. Curtis is responsible for the development of the velocity-compounded impulse stage in which two rows of moving blades are employed. In his design, an intermediate row of stationary blading was inserted between the two moving rows in order to direct the steam from the first to the second moving row. He also developed the use of several velocity-compounded stages in series.

Shortly after the turn of the century, steam turbines began to replace steam engines as the principal prime mover in central-station power plants. As a result, developments were rapid and became associated chiefly with large companies rather than individuals. Improvements in both size and efficiency of units followed, leading to the commanding position now occupied by the steam turbine in the field of electric-power generation.

HISTORY OF GAS TURBINES

The smokejack

While the oldest type of gas turbine is undoubtedly the windmill, it can hardly be compared to the modern gas turbine, in which heated gas is used as the motivating force for rotating the turbine shaft. One of the earliest devices that might be classified as a gas turbine was the smokejack designed to operate with the aid of hot gases rising from a fireplace. The smokejack is believed to have first been sketched by Leonardo da Vinci but was later more fully described by John Wilkins, an English clergyman, in his *Mathematical Magick* (1648). The device consisted of a number of horizontal sails, similar to those of a modern windmill, attached to a vertical shaft and placed in a chimney. The hot gases rising past the sails caused the device to rotate. With the aid of a simple gearing system it was possible to employ the smokejack for turning a spit or for performing other simple tasks.

A somewhat similar device was later patented by John Dumbell of England. His device employed a large number of sails, one above the other, all attached to a hollow drum. In addition, he supplied his own furnace underneath, with means for supplying air and fuel and for keeping the component parts from melting.

The first patent for a gas turbine operating on a cycle resembling present-day units was issued to John Barber of England in 1791. The principle of operation was as follows: air and fuel from a gas producer, after being compressed in separate cylinders, were directed into a combustion chamber and burned. The products of combustion were released through a small nozzle onto a turbine wheel. The power thus produced was supposed to be sufficient to compress the air and fuel and to leave enough over for external work. From modern knowledge of the cycle and from the sketch supplied by Barber, it is known that his machine could not have operated successfully. It did, however, represent an ingenious invention and included most of the essential elements found in present-day gas turbines.

In the years following the issuance of John Barber's patent, many novel devices were proposed, but it was not until 1872 that a really significant advance was made. This came with the granting of a patent to F. Stolze of Germany for his fire turbine, which consisted of a separately fired combustion chamber, a heat exchanger, and a multistage axial-flow compressor directly coupled to a multistage reaction turbine. It operated as follows: compressed air was directed into the heat exchanger, where it was heated by means of combustion gases from a separately fired furnace. The heated compressed air passed into the turbine, through which it was expanded back to the atmosphere. Even though Stolze's gas turbine embodied almost every feature of a modern open-cycle gas turbine, it was unsuccessful, largely because the compressor

and turbine lacked the necessary efficiency to sustain operation with maximum turbine-inlet temperatures permissible at that time.

First successful gas turbine

The first successful gas turbine, built in Paris in 1903, consisted of a three-cylinder multistage compressor followed by a combustion chamber in which liquid fuel was burned with air supplied from the compressor. The hot gases issuing from the combustion chamber, after being cooled to some extent by the injection of water, were expanded through a two-row impulse turbine wheel. The unit was capable of operating with an efficiency of about 3 percent. Although by later standards this was an unimpressive performance, it was a significant achievement at the time. It is believed to have been the first gas turbine capable of delivering work on a scale suitable for commercial purposes.

Two other contributions should also be mentioned. In these, a different principle of operation was employed, that of exploding a mixture of air and fuel in constant-volume combustion chambers and then allowing the products of combustion to flow through nozzles onto a turbine wheel.

The first of these was a two-horsepower, 10,000-revolutions-per-minute unit built in Paris in 1908. It consisted of a simple de Laval impulse-type turbine wheel about six inches (150 millimetres) in diameter with four explosion chambers arranged around the periphery of the wheel, each leading to a nozzle directed against the wheel. The products of combustion from the four explosion chambers were released in sequence against the wheel. An ingenious method of drawing air and fuel into the chambers was provided. After explosion, the inertia of the gases leaving the chambers was employed to create a momentary partial vacuum inside the chambers that was capable of sucking in a new charge. During tests the device was reported to have a fuel consumption of about one pound (450 grams) of gasoline per horsepower-hour, corresponding to a thermal efficiency of about 2.5 percent.

The second and more important of the two contributions, historically, was the explosion-type turbine developed by Hans Holzwarth of Germany, who began a long series of experiments in 1905. His turbine consisted of a constant-volume combustion chamber into which a charge of fuel and air was introduced under pressure. Following ignition, the pressure was increased to approximately four and one-half times the original value, causing a spring-loaded valve to open, admitting the gases into nozzles directed against the blading of the turbine. The mechanism was so arranged that the valves remained open until the combustion chamber was emptied, after which a new charge was introduced. Although an air compressor was employed in the Holzwarth turbine, the efficiency of the compressor was not extremely important because the air could be supplied at a pressure of only about one-fourth that ultimately achieved during explosion and also because only enough air was required to furnish oxygen for combustion.

Over a period of about 30 years Holzwarth and various collaborators continued development of the turbine. Although now superseded, the Holzwarth explosion turbine represented a unique and important contribution.

The modern gas turbine is the result of the work of many individuals. Among the most prominent was Sir Frank Whittle of England, who early recognized its application to jet-propulsion aircraft. His efforts in this regard led to its development and use in military aircraft in the United Kingdom and the United States during World War II.

Basic principles and applications of turbines

Although turbine designs vary widely, depending on operating conditions and the type of working fluid, all operate on the same fundamental principle, namely, the conversion of energy stored in the fluid into mechanical energy. This transfer is accomplished by the conversion of the stored energy into kinetic energy and the release of this energy in a runner, or rotor, in the form of mechanical-power output.

In the case of a water turbine, the stored energy is in the form of potential energy of water stored in a reservoir at an elevation above the turbine outlet. This energy is measured in feet of head, H, and is based on the principle that to raise water through a difference in elevation of H feet would require an expenditure of energy equal to H foot-pounds per pound of water. Water in the reservoir, therefore, has a greater potential energy than at discharge, and the purpose of a water turbine is to make use of this difference in energy to produce mechanical work.

Enthalpy of steam

In the case of a steam turbine, the energy stored in the fluid is in the form of thermal or heat energy, called the enthalpy and designated by the letter h. The value of h depends upon the pressure and temperature of the steam and has been published in tables for ready use. Knowing the temperature and pressure of the steam at the turbine inlet and the pressure of the steam at the turbine exhaust, it is possible to find the energy available for the production of work. This energy, represented by the drop in enthalpy, is measured in British thermal units per pound and represents for a steam turbine essentially what the difference in head represents for a water turbine. A British thermal unit is the quantity of heat required to raise the temperature of one pound (454 grams) of water one degree Fahrenheit (0.555° C) at or near 63° F (17° C).

For a gas turbine, the energy stored in the fluid is also expressed in terms of the enthalpy. The treatment is similar to that of a steam turbine except that the working fluid usually consists of products of combustion, which, for practical purposes, can be treated as air. For a given temperature and pressure at the turbine inlet and a given exhaust pressure, the enthalpy drop available for conversion into work can readily be calculated by multiplying the specific heat at constant pressure of the air by its change in temperature. If greater accuracy is required, appropriate gas tables can be used instead.

Although water, steam, and gas turbines all operate on the same basic principle, they are sufficiently different to preclude a common treatment.

WATER TURBINES

Classification. Water turbines are divided into two classes: impulse turbines, generally used for high heads of water, and reaction turbines, generally used for heads ranging downward from 2,000 feet (600 metres). These two classes include six main types in common use—the Pelton and turgo impulse turbines and the propeller, Kaplan, Francis, and Deriaz reaction turbines—any of which can be arranged with either a horizontal or a vertical shaft. Wide variations are possible within each type to suit particular hydraulic conditions.

Each type of turbine can be further classified according to its specific speed, which is the revolutions per minute at which a scale model of the actual turbine should operate in order to develop one horsepower at one foot of head.

Impulse turbines. The impulse turbine extracts energy from water by first converting the head of water into kinetic energy by passing it through a carefully shaped nozzle that produces a free jet discharging in air. This jet is directed onto buckets that are fixed on the periphery of the runner and formed in such a way as to remove the maximum energy from the water.

Pelton turbine

Early designs of impulse turbines, using blades on the edge of the runner that caused substantial loss of energy because of impact, have been almost entirely supplanted by the Pelton type of turbine, patented in 1889 by the U.S. engineer Lester Allen Pelton. In this type a splitter edge in the centre of each bucket causes the jet of water impinging on it to divide into two divergent paths as it flows outward to fall clear of the runner (see Figure 2).

For maximum efficiency the speed of the runner of an impulse turbine should ideally be such that the buckets are moving with a velocity equal to about 50 percent of that of the impinging jet. The work produced will be equal to the potential energy surrendered by the water flowing through the turbine multiplied by the efficiency of its utilization by the turbine. The maximum efficiency of impulse turbines is about 91 percent when operating at 60–80 percent of full load.

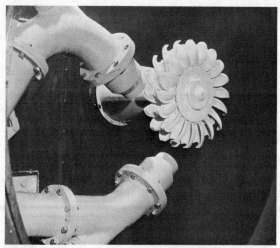

Figure 2: Pelton water turbine with twin jets.
Fox Photos Ltd.

The power of a given impulse wheel may be increased by using more than one jet, the two-jet arrangement being common for a horizontal shaft. With a vertical shaft there are usually four jets on a single runner, though occasionally there may be more. With a horizontal shaft it is also possible to mount two runners on the shaft driving a single electrical generator in order to produce a result equivalent to that of the multijet vertical arrangement.

The quantity of water flowing through each jet is controlled by a spear sliding inside the nozzle. This spear, operated by an automatically controlled oil-pressure motor (servomotor), can partially or completely close the nozzle orifice. The velocity of water leaving the nozzle will remain approximately constant over a wide range of openings; and because the runner will continue to turn at a fixed speed, the efficiency curve of a well-designed impulse turbine can be flat, but not as high as with other types.

It is not possible to reduce the water quantity flowing through the nozzle rapidly when a reduction in load is required, because there would be a large pressure rise in the pipeline. If a full quantity continues to be supplied to the runner after removal of the load, the motor would run too fast. To avoid this and to improve control, a second device in the form of a deflector, or diffuser, is inserted into the jet on load rejection, thus temporarily dissipating the energy of the water until the quantity is reduced by the spear closing off the flow from the nozzle.

Another type of impulse turbine is the turgo type, in which the jet impinges obliquely on the side of the runner and continues in a single path, discharging at the other side. This type of turbine is useful for medium-size units that use medium heads.

Reaction turbines. Reaction turbines achieve rotation mainly through the reactive force created by the acceleration of water in the runner, or rotor, rather than in the supply nozzles, as was the case for the impulse turbine. The basic principle employed is the same as that of a rotating lawn sprinkler, in which water enters the curved arms of the sprinkler at low velocity and leaves at high velocity. The exact manner in which the acceleration is achieved in water turbines, however, differs in accordance with whether the runner is of the propeller, Kaplan, Francis, or Deriaz type.

Runner geometry

Because of the great variety possible in the geometry of the runner, reaction turbines are far more widely used than impulse turbines. In all these types, a fraction of the hydraulic pressure is first converted into velocity in the passage of the water through the inlet structure, which is composed of a spiral casing and a gate apparatus leading to the runner. The power from the water associated with the pressure and velocity at this point is then converted to mechanical power in a single-stage runner that absorbs the full water energy down to a pressure usually below atmospheric pressure.

Of the four main types of reaction turbine, the propeller and the Kaplan turbines have axial-flow runners and are used for lower heads, while the Francis and the Deriaz turbines have mixed-flow runners; *i.e.*, flow is radial at the inlet and axial at the outlet. The runner blades on the propeller and Francis turbines are fixed, while those on the Kaplan and Deriaz turbines are movable.

Axial-flow turbines. A fixed-blade propeller turbine with a vertical shaft is almost invariably used for large units, because its higher specific speed permits a valuable saving in plant cost when compared with the Francis alternative. The running speed can be as much as twice that of the Francis at heads below about 35 feet (11 metres), and 50 percent greater at heads of 60 feet (18 metres). Even so, the running speed of high-output propeller turbines is often below 100 revolutions per minute. Though the components are very large, the form of the runner is such that it is possible to detach the blades for transport and to attach them by bolted flanges at the site so that the limiting item for transport becomes the runner hub.

At low heads (up to about 80 feet, or 24 metres) the turbine has a concrete spiral casing, which, for the larger machines, is provided with two or more rectangular inlets leading to the stay vanes. These vanes may be individually set in concrete, thus reducing one of the bulkier components for transport. The runner envelope, of cylindrical form, leads to the draft-tube cone and bend.

The propeller turbine has been used extensively in North America, where low head and large flow are common, thus requiring the installation of many units in one station. There are 32 propeller turbines in the St. Lawrence Power Station (where the St. Lawrence River forms part of the eastern boundary between Canada and the United States), 16 operated by Canada and 16 by the United States. With such power stations it is possible to run the turbine continually at or near its most efficient output by switching a complete unit in and out as the load fluctuates. If both the water quantity and the power required are such that only a few units are required to deal with a variable load, the efficiency of operation falls off very sharply below a 75 percent load. The same will apply if there is any marked variation in operating head, because an increase in head at a fixed load is equivalent to reduced load at a fixed head.

These limitations of the propeller turbine have been met by making the blade angle of the runner variable in order to match more accurately the correct angle for a given flow of water. This type is called the Kaplan turbine, after the Austrian inventor, Viktor Kaplan, who patented his design in 1920 (see Figure 3). The physical size and operating head for which the turbine can be used have increased markedly, and runner diameters of 30 feet (9 metres) have been employed. British manufacturers have developed designs operating at heads of 190 feet (58 metres), but it is likely that further progress in increased heads will be limited because of the advent of the Deriaz turbine (see *Mixed-flow turbines* below).

The runner-blade angle is varied by an oil-pressure-operated servomotor, which is usually mounted in the runner hub, with the oil being fed down tubes in the bore of the turbine and the alternator shafts. Runners having four to six blades are common, though more blades are used for high heads. The correct relationship of runner-blade angle to the water flow admitted by the turbine gate apparatus is ensured by a cam operated by a pilot servomotor in the governor system. When best performance is required over a wide range of operating heads, several cams may be used and brought into service to match the head at a given time. This flexibility is especially valuable when seasonal variations in head occur.

The Kaplan turbine in its traditional form has a vertical shaft, though one design uses a horizontal shaft and an electrical generator mounted in a nacelle, or metal shell, in the water flow. This design is particularly suitable for lower output machines operating on very low heads, in which case an almost straight water passage is possible. This type of turbine was designed for a French project on the Rance River Estuary, which employs tidal power.

Kaplan turbine

Figure 3: 131,000-horsepower Kaplan water-turbine runner.
By courtesy of The English Electric Co. Ltd.

Mixed-flow turbines. The Francis turbine is probably the most extensively used type of turbine because of the very wide head range for which it is suited—from the lowest economically usable (about ten feet, or three metres) to about 2,000 feet (600 metres). The turbines at the top range of heads must be of large output; otherwise the water quantities and the size of the water passages in the runner become too small for reasonable construction. At low heads the propeller turbine is usually more economical unless the output required is small. The Francis turbine, however, reigns supreme in the medium-head range of 400–1,000 feet (120–300 metres) and has a wide range of sizes.

Francis turbines can have either horizontal or vertical shafts, the latter being used for machines having runner diameters of six feet (two metres) or more. Each machine has certain advantages that affect the choice. Vertical-shaft machines usually occupy less space and also permit greater submergence of the runner, with a minimum of deep excavation. On the other hand, horizontal shafts provide a compact unit for small sizes and permit easier access to the turbine, though removal of the alternator rotor becomes difficult as the size increases.

The commonest form of Francis turbine has a fabricated, or cast-steel, spiral casing. This casing distributes water flow equally to the regulating gear, which consists of a number (about 24) of pivoted gates or guide vanes that when closed seal off the throat of the casing and are adjustable to any opening for the required output. The guide vanes are operated simultaneously by a regulating ring and are connected in such a way that if there is blockage no damage occurs. The regulating ring is driven by one or two oil-pressure servomotors controlled by the governor.

The design of the runner, or rotor, must recognize several factors in order to obtain the best efficiency at the required head and output. Its speed involves the correct choice of specific speed determined by experience and consideration of the generator design. The inlet and outlet diameters and the blade height at the inlet are then determined, after which the blade form is calculated to give smooth entry of water at the inlet and zero rotation at the outlet. The number of blades varies widely, normally from nine to 19. Construction is commonly cast steel or, for high heads, stainless steel. In the former case, stainless-steel protection is added to areas subject to cavitation (formation and collapse of vapour cavities in a turbulent liquid; this phenomenon can damage turbine parts severely). Runners of welded construction permit the formation of more accurate and more highly finished waterways for high-head turbines having long and narrow runner passages and also enable a runner to be made of an appropriate combination of steels.

Cavitation

The extent to which the runner is subject to cavitation depends on the amount of suction produced by the draft tube compared with the setting of the runner centreline relative to the tailwater level. Careful control of the blade form can reduce the tendency for cavitation, particularly on the back of the blades at exit.

Very large and high-output Francis turbines have been installed with outputs exceeding 600,000 horsepower from a single runner, though outputs of 800,000 horsepower were projected in the 1970s.

A form of mixed-flow turbine, named after its inventor (Paul Deriaz, a Swiss engineer), in 1956, has a variable pitch design that improves the efficiency under less than full load for medium-head machines (Figure 4). This

By courtesy of The English Electric Co. Ltd.

Figure 4: Runner for 108,000-horsepower Deriaz reversible pump turbine for Valdecañas Power Station, Spain.

design proved to be very useful for the higher heads and also for pumped-storage applications (see *Pumped storage* below). It also has the advantage of a lower runaway (no-load) speed than the Kaplan turbine, thus giving significant savings in the cost of the generator.

The first nonreversible Deriaz turbine, consisting of a 32,500-horsepower unit in an underground power station, was installed at Culligran in Scotland.

Control of speed and output. The control of the speed and output of water turbines involves the large forces necessary to operate the regulating gear and the high inertia of the water in the pipeline between the reservoir and the turbine inlet.

When a single turbine with governor is supplying an isolated load, any variation in load will initially produce a change in speed that is sensed by the governor. The turbine guide vanes, or the spears in the case of impulse turbines, are then opened or closed by the governor to restore the speed to its original value.

The rate at which the turbine guide vanes, or spears, may be opened or closed is determined by the relative inertia of the water in the supply pipe and the inertia of the rotating parts. If a long pipeline is provided, the closing time must be slow in order to keep the pressure

rise within reasonable limits, but, if it is too slow, instability will result. To assist regulation with long pipelines, a surge chamber is often connected to the pipeline as near as possible to the turbine, thus enabling part of the water in the pipeline to pass into the surge chamber as the turbine is closed. This operation also allows a faster opening time to be used. The spiral casings of medium-sized reaction turbines can be provided with pressure-relief valves through which surplus water is passed automatically as the governor closes. For difficult pipelines a combination of the two devices can be used.

Inertia factors in guide vane control

Water turbines supplying large, interconnected power systems are sometimes required to operate on a predetermined load program or to maintain system frequency control according to master clock directions. These requirements can be met by using an electronic governor in which the speed-sensitive pendulum is replaced by an electric actuator operating a hydraulic pilot valve.

Applications. *Generation of electric power.* Water turbines are used almost exclusively for the production of electric power that can be transmitted over high-voltage lines to existing load centres for distribution to surrounding communities. Countries leading in hydroelectric-power production are the United States, the Soviet Union, and Canada, but many other countries have extensive hydroelectric developments. Until the late 1950s the largest units in operation were less than 200,000 horsepower, but since then a number of larger units have been built and many more are projected for completion in the 1970s. Largest of the turbines in operation in the early 1970s were the 12 Francis turbines at Krasnoyarsk on the Yenisey River in Siberia, Soviet Union. These units each have a capacity of 685,000 horsepower, making an aggregate total of 8,220,000 horsepower, or about 6,000,000 kilowatts. Scheduled for completion in the early 1970s was the Sayano-Sushensk plant, also on the Yenisey River, with 12 units, each having a capacity of 740,000 horsepower, aggregating about 6,600,000 kilowatts. At Churchill Falls, Canada, a plant having 11 units, each with a capacity of 648,000 horsepower, was under construction, with completion expected about 1973. This plant employs Francis turbines under a head of 1,025 feet (312 metres). The largest projected plant in the world was at the Grand Coulee Dam on the Columbia River in the United States. There, 12 units, each having a capacity of 600,000 kilowatts, were to be added to the existing plant, which contains 18 units, each capable of 125,000 kilowatts, giving a grand total of about 9,200,000 kilowatts. The new units are Francis turbines operating under a head of 285 feet (87 metres), with a speed of 64.7 revolutions per minute.

Pumped storage. One method of utilizing water turbines for the generation of electricity is a system called pumped storage. With this system, two water reservoirs are used, one at a low level and the other at a higher level. The two reservoirs are connected to each other through a reversible pump-turbine capable of operating as a turbine-generator when rotating in one direction and as a pump when operating in the opposite direction. When the electrical load on the system falls below the desired base load value, the extra power available can be used to pump water from the lower reservoir into the upper reservoir, thus storing it for later use. During peak-load periods, when the power required by the system exceeds the base-load value, the water is allowed to flow back through the reversible-pump turbine unit into the lower reservoir, generating power in the process. Such a system provides a steady load at night and the needed additional power to meet peak demand during the day. Even though pumped storage systems have no inherent source of energy production, they are economical in capital cost compared with thermal plants and have high overall efficiency. The reversible-pump turbine has been developed extensively, and, in the late 1960s, about 60 such units were in operation, varying between 28,000 and 240,000 horsepower in capacity. At the same time, more than 50 additional units were planned or under construction, ranging up to 430,000 horsepower in capacity.

Reversible-pump turbine

The turbine runner for all but the lowest heads is of the

mixed-flow reaction type. Some of the most economical pumped-storage plants have heads exceeding 1,000 feet (300 metres), which in the past were generally considered to be too high for single-stage pumps, and, therefore, multistage nonreversible units were used. Satisfactory reversible-pump turbines have been developed for heads exceeding 1,000 feet.

For medium heads, the Deriaz pump turbine is ideal, because of the ease of adjusting the runner-blade angles to suit the differing requirements set by pumping and generating. The pumping load can also be varied, a change that cannot be made satisfactorily with a Francis runner, even when there are guide vanes, because of the hydraulic conditions when they are partly open. A further advantage of the Deriaz pump turbine is that, when starting up as a pump, the runner vanes can be closed to form a smooth cone, and thus it can be started with a minimum of load while submerged in water. Six 52,500 horsepower units of this type were operating at Niagara Falls, Canada, in the early 1970s, and there are reversible units of this type with outputs of more than 100,000 horsepower in Spain (Figure 4).

Future trends. Although hydroelectric sites relatively near to existing load centres are gradually dwindling, there is an increasing demand for pollution-free power generation. Though the hydroelectric plant meets these requirements to a high degree, it is not wholly free from criticism, because the necessity for scarring the landscape and creating a large impoundment of water often meets with resistance from conservationists.

It is believed that hydroelectric turbines of as high as 2,000,000 horsepower are feasible and that such units may eventually be installed in the more remote locations still available. The Fraser River in Canada is estimated to have a potential of 8,700 megawatts (one megawatt equals 1,000 kilowatts). Other rivers having potential hydroelectric sites are the Orinoco in Venezuela, 8,000 megawatts; the Inga in the Congo, 25,000 megawatts; and the Brahmaputra in India, 20,000 megawatts.

In the Soviet Union, the Yenisey–Angara River system is estimated to have a potential capacity of 64,000 megawatts. At the beginning of the 1970s there were three stations completed on this system, with a total capacity of 11,000 megawatts, and three more stations under construction with about the same total capacity. Plans for continued development of the system, running into the 21st century, call for the construction of seven more plants, bringing the ultimate developed capacity to about 52,000 megawatts. The above examples represent only a few of the world's promising hydroelectric resources remaining to be tapped.

STEAM TURBINES

A steam turbine is a machine for converting thermal energy stored as steam into work. It consists of a shaft or rotor resting in bearings and enclosed in a cylindrical casing. The rotor is made to turn smoothly by means of jets of steam issuing from nozzles located around the periphery of the turbine cylinder and impinging upon blades or buckets attached to the rotor. Thus a steam turbine is a prime mover that generates motive power in the same manner as a series of windmills mounted on a single shaft but on a vastly greater scale. Instead of a current of air being used to rotate the shaft, steam is employed as the working agent.

Because of its ability to develop tremendous power within a comparatively small space, the steam turbine has superseded all other prime movers, except hydraulic turbines, for the generation of large quantities of electric energy. The economic importance of the steam turbine has provided an incentive for continued development, resulting in units capable of generating as high as 1,200,000 kilowatts of power on a single shaft and even more in other combinations.

Classification. Steam turbines are complex machines and may be classified in many ways. One method is according to whether rotation is achieved by impulse or reaction forces. In modern turbines this distinction is somewhat blurred because most machines employ a com-

bination of the two methods. Nevertheless, certain manufacturers tend toward machines that are basically of the reaction type while others prefer the impulse type. Another method of classification is according to whether the entire machine is mounted on a single shaft with one electric generator or on two shafts, each with its own generator. The former are called tandem compound turbines and the latter cross-compound turbines.

Steam turbines may also be classified as condensing or noncondensing, depending upon whether or not the steam is exhausted to a condenser. Noncondensing turbines are those in which steam, after expanding through the turbine, is exhausted to the atmosphere, to a heating system, or to some other type of equipment. Their most frequent application is in industrial plants where steam is needed at low or intermediate pressures and where by-product power can be generated economically by inserting a noncondensing turbine between the steam generator and the equipment requiring steam.

In condensing turbines, condensation of the exhaust steam is effected by the circulation of large quantities of cold water through the tubes of the condenser. The circulating water absorbs the heat given up during condensation and carries it away. The process of continuous condensation maintains a low pressure in the condenser, thus increasing the expansion ratio of the steam (*i.e.*, the ratio of the expanded volume of the steam to its original volume) and the consequent efficiency and work output of the turbine. Because of the necessity of maintaining the highest possible efficiency, all central-station power plants employ condensing turbines, which are connected directly to large electrical generators capable of generating power at high voltage.

An additional classification of turbines may be made on the basis of whether or not a portion of the steam is extracted from the turbine during passage through the machine and in what manner the extraction takes place. On this basis turbines may be classified as follows: (1) straight-through turbines; (2) bleeder turbines; and (3) automatic-extraction turbines.

Straight-through turbines are those in which there are no extraction points, and all steam supplied to the input passes all the way through the turbine and out the exhaust. Bleeder turbines are those in which provisions are made for heating the water that is eventually converted to steam (feedwater). This end is accomplished by extracting steam at various locations along its path of flow through the turbine. In bleeder turbines no attempt is made to control the pressure of the steam extracted. Because of this, extraction pressure automatically varies in almost direct proportion to the load being carried by the turbine. The principal advantage of a bleeder turbine over a straight-through turbine is that steam bled from the turbine does not flow to the condenser; its latent heat (the heat required to vaporize water to steam), therefore, is retained in the cycle. Another advantage is that the exhaust area of the turbine can be smaller because less steam flows to the condenser.

The use of bleed-point steam for feedwater heating is universal in central-station power plants because it increases the thermal efficiency of a plant by 10–15 percent. In most cases, the fraction of steam withdrawn is about 30 percent of the steam initially supplied at the turbine inlet.

Automatic extraction turbines are machines designed for the withdrawal of variable quantities of constant-pressure steam from one or more extraction points along the path of flow, regardless of how much load is being carried by the turbine. Such turbines are widely used in industrial power plants where steam is needed at one or more pressures for process work. Because it is desirable to hold both extraction pressure and speed constant, regardless of power requirements, a complicated system of governing is required. This need makes the turbines more expensive than either bleeder or straight-through turbines. Automatic-extraction turbines may be designed for either condensing or noncondensing operation.

Principal components. The principal components of a steam turbine are: (1) the rotor that carries the blading

Hydro-electric potential of various rivers

Condensing and non-condensing steam turbines

employed for converting energy of the steam into rotary motion of the shaft; (2) the casing or cylinder, inside which the rotor turns and that carries fixed nozzle passages through which steam is accelerated before being directed against the rotor blading; (3) the speed-regulating mechanism by which the speed of rotation is governed; (4) the lubrication system for bearings and other apparatus associated with the turbine.

Blading design

Of the various elements of the turbine, perhaps the most difficult to design properly is the blading, because it must have adequate strength and the correct aerodynamic shape to convert the energy of the steam into shaft work efficiently. Various types of blading and blading arrangements have been proposed, but all are designed to take advantage of the principle that when a given mass of substance suddenly changes its velocity, a force is exerted by the mass in direct proportion to the rate of change of velocity.

Two types of blading have been developed to a high degree of perfection: impulse blading and reaction blading. The principle of impulse blading may best be illustrated by referring to Figure 1. This simplified diagram of a turbine rotor wheel shows four fixed nozzles directing high-velocity steam against blades mounted around the periphery of the wheel. If there were no blades in the path of the steam, it would proceed in a straight line. The blades catch the impinging steam, however, and turn it in the opposite direction, thus changing its velocity from a high value at entrance to a low value at exit. This decrease in velocity of the mass of steam produces a force on the rotor blading, causing the shaft, to which the disk and blading are attached, to turn.

Proper operation of an impulse wheel requires that the blading be of approximately symmetrical design and that it move past the nozzles with a speed approximately equal to one-half that of the steam issuing from the nozzles. Figure 5A shows an arrangement of nozzles and blading for a simple impulse-turbine stage.

When reaction blading is employed (Figure 5B), the

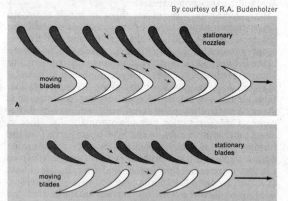

By courtesy of R.A. Budenholzer

Figure 5: Arrangement of nozzles and blading for (A) a simple impulse-turbine stage and (B) a reaction-turbine stage.

rotor is designed to turn at a speed approximately equal to that of the steam issuing from the nozzles, instead of half the velocity, as is the case in an impulse stage. The steam thus enters the moving blades with almost zero relative velocity. Also, the blades of the rotor of a reaction turbine are unsymmetrical and have a profile such that the space between blades forms nozzle passages. As the steam flows through these passages, it expands, thereby increasing its velocity relative to the blading. The acceleration of the steam creates a reactive force, turning the rotor in a direction opposite to that of the exit steam.

With either impulse blading or reaction blading, the overall principle is the same: the velocity of the steam is first built up in the stationary nozzles, after which it is decreased in the moving blades. Energy stored in the steam is thereby first converted into kinetic energy and then into rotational shaft work.

Turbine staging. In modern turbines a large number of nozzle and moving blade combinations similar to those

illustrated in either Figure 5A or 5B are required. Each of these combinations is called a turbine stage. If only one is employed the turbine is a single stage machine whereas if several are employed it is a multistage machine. There are several reasons for staging, the most important of which are the following: (1) steam, in expanding through a modern turbine, often enters under a pressure in excess of 3,000 pounds per square inch (200 kilograms per square centimetre) and exhausts under a pressure below one pound per square inch absolute. (Absolute pressure is the pressure above a vacuum, or zero pressure.) This situation means a several-hundredfold increase in volume of flow between entrance and exit. Such large expansions cannot be accommodated efficiently by a single stage, because the cross-sectional area perpendicular to the flow would have to increase several hundred times through a single row of nozzle passages and one or two rows of moving blades. (2) By breaking the expansion into small steps more efficient nozzle and blade passages can be designed, and thus a velocity relationship that best accommodates the conversion of energy in the steam into work can be realized. (3) Centrifugal and other forces acting on the blading limit its maximum velocity at the tip to values that will not permit the efficient use of only one stage, even when all of the other factors are favourable to such an arrangement.

Reasons for staging

In modern steam turbines, three types of staging are employed, either separately or in combination. These are pressure staging, reaction staging, and velocity compounded staging.

Pressure staging. Pressure staging is simply the use of a number of simple-impulse stages similar to the one illustrated in Figure 5A arranged in sequence. Turbines using this principle employ a large number of stages, each contributing a small fraction to the total power output. Turbines employing pressure staging range in size from a few kilowatts to 1,200,000 kilowatts, or even larger. A turbine with this type of staging is illustrated in Figure 6.

Reaction staging. Reaction staging is similar to pressure staging except that a number of reaction stages are employed in sequence. Turbines using this principle require about twice as many stages as corresponding machines employing pressure staging. The cost, however, is about the same, because blading for pressure staging must withstand greater forces and, therefore, be more rigidly constructed. Reaction turbines are built in the same size range as pressure-stage turbines.

Velocity-compounded staging. This type of staging employs the same type of blading as impulse staging except that two rows of moving blades instead of one are used, and a stationary row is inserted between the rows to redirect the steam from one moving row to another. With this arrangement, four times more power can be obtained from a single velocity compounded stage than from a single pressure stage with the same blade velocity. Velocity-compounded staging is well suited for small turbines in which the steam, after passing through the turbine, exhausts to a heating system or to some other use in which the pressure is atmospheric or higher. A velocity-compounded stage is also frequently employed as the first of a number of stages in large industrial and central-station type turbines. In this application, the velocity-compounded stage serves as a control stage and offers a powerful means of quickly changing the turbine output in response to the slightest change in steam flow as dictated by the governing mechanism. Such a velocity-compounded stage also permits a large drop in pressure and temperature before the steam enters the first moving blades of the turbine. This drop makes possible the use of higher initial temperatures and pressures without the use of special heat-resistant alloys that are expensive and difficult to machine. Also the specific volume of the steam flowing through the blading is greater, allowing the use of longer blades, which results in lower frictional losses.

Power development. The force of the steam acting on the blading of a single-impulse stage and the theoretical

Figure 6: Rendering of an installed 1,800 revolution-per-minute tandem-compound, six-flow, nuclear steam turbine–generator unit rated at over 1,000,000 kilowatts.
By courtesy of General Electric Company, Schenectady, N.Y.

horsepower obtainable can be calculated. These calculations are based on highly idealized conditions that cannot be realized in actual operation, however, and, thus, the true value of power produced will be somewhat less.

For the same blade velocity, pressure staging produces about twice as much power per stage as reaction staging, and velocity compounded staging about eight times as much. Thus, turbines employing reaction staging would require the greatest number of stages to produce a given power output while those employing velocity compounded stages would require the least. Pressure staged turbines would require a number somewhere between the two.

Stage efficiency. The efficiency of a turbine stage may be defined as the power output divided by the enthalpy drop that would occur if expansion of steam took place through the stage without friction, turbulence, or other losses.

The maximum ideal efficiency for all three types of turbines is theoretically the same. In actual turbine stages, numerous losses—such as wall friction, turbulence, and leakage losses—serve to reduce the efficiency to well below the theoretical maximum. Efficiency of turbine stages also varies with the ratio of blade velocity to steam-jet velocity. The maximum efficiency of the velocity-compounded stage with two rows of moving blades tends to be less than that of the simple-impulse stage, and both tend to have a lower maximum efficiency than the reaction-type stage. In general, velocity-compounded stages are avoided except for the first control stage of turbines.

Performance characteristics. The performance of a steam turbine is measured in terms of the turbine heat rate, a measure of the heat that must be supplied to the steam in order to produce a specified power output. For central-station applications the turbine is always connected directly to an electric generator, and the combination is called a turbogenerator. The turbine heat rate for this type of machine is defined as the number of British thermal units of heat that must be added to the steam in order to produce one kilowatt-hour of electric-power output. In the case of a turbine not connected to an electric generator, the heat rate is usually expressed in terms of British thermal units per horsepower-hour output.

The turbine heat rate depends upon many factors, the most important being: (1) pressure and temperature of the inlet steam; (2) exhaust pressure; (3) internal efficiency of the turbine, a measure of effectiveness with which the energy in the steam is converted into work; (4) exhaust loss, the kinetic energy loss associated with the high velocity of exhaust; (5) mechanical losses; (6) generator losses. With the exception of the first two factors, the above all depend to some extent upon the fraction of rated load being carried by the turbine.

In general, the turbine heat rate increases with decrease in load. This inverse relation means that more steam is required to generate a unit of output at low load than at high load. Because of various losses, the generator output is usually about 80 percent of the energy in the steam available for producing power.

Taking into account the efficiency of the turbine itself as well as the heat which must be discarded in the condenser, the overall thermal efficiency of the best steam power plants is about 40 percent for fossil fuel plants and about 30 percent for nuclear plants.

Future trends. Until the 1970s most electric energy was generated in fossil-fuel power plants. The soaring cost of such fuel stimulated the building of increasingly larger turbines with higher and higher efficiencies. To secure these efficiencies, it was necessary to raise the pressure and temperature of the turbine-inlet steam to very high values. These reached their peak in the decade 1950–60, which witnessed the introduction of supercritical pressure plants operating with initial pressures as high as 5,000 pounds per square inch (350 kilograms per square centimetre) and temperatures as high as 1,100° F (600° C). In the 1965–75 period, the ever-increasing demand for electric power and the necessity of generating this power with minimal air pollution caused a gradual movement toward the installation of nuclear plants. This trend is expected to continue in succeeding decades and to require even larger steam turbines, since nuclear plants are only economic in very large sizes. In the early 1970s nuclear plants had not reached the stage in development where they could provide the very high temperatures and pressures employed in fossil-fuel plants; consequently nuclear turbines had to be designed for operation at comparatively low pressures—approximately 1,000 pounds per square inch. To secure efficient operation under these conditions and to prevent blade erosion from moisture particles in the steam, provision for separating liquid moisture from the steam as it flows through the turbine must be made. Turbines for nuclear plants were expected to range up to 1,500,000 kilowatts in the 1970s and even larger thereafter. Figure 6 is a cutaway view of a 1,000,-000-kilowatt turbine designed for a nuclear-power installation in the early 1970s.

Power losses

Supercritical pressure plants

GAS TURBINES

A gas turbine is a form of heat engine for producing work with the aid of heated gases. It differs from the conventional internal-combustion engine in the manner in which the heated gases are employed.

The gas turbine achieves some of the advantages of internal-combustion engines without the complications associated with reciprocating, or up-and-down, motion of conventional piston engines. Its principle of operation is to direct a continuous stream of hot gases against the blading of a turbine rotor. In modern units, the air is first compressed in either an axial-flow or centrifugal compressor before being directed into combustion chambers. In these, fuel is mixed with a portion of the air and burned. Some of the air is bypassed around the burner and subsequently mixed again with the products of combustion to prevent excessive temperature of the gases leaving the combustion chambers. The emerging gases are directed through nozzles and against the blading of the turbine rotor, furnishing sufficient power to drive the compressor with enough left over for other useful purposes. The result is a relatively vibration free, smooth-running machine.

Idealized simple open-cycle gas turbine. Most gas turbines operate on the constant-pressure combustion cycle. Figure 7 is a sketch of a simple open-cycle unit with

By courtesy of Solar Division of International Harvester Company

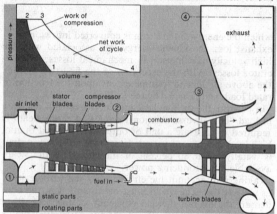

Figure 7: Open-cycle constant-pressure combustion-gas turbine. Circled numbers refer to points on the inset graph of the pressure–volume relationship during a working cycle (see text).

accompanying pressure-volume diagram indicating the sequence of processes to which the working substance is subjected as it flows through the various items of equipment. In the idealized cycle shown, air enters the axial-flow compressor at section 1 under atmospheric pressure and temperature. It is then compressed at constant entropy (no heat added or subtracted and without friction or other losses) to section 2. From section 2 the air flows into the combustion chamber, where fuel is added and burned at constant pressure, raising the temperature to its maximum value for the cycle. From the combustion chamber the heated gases enter the turbine, where expansion occurs to atmospheric pressure. The amount of work obtainable from the unit is the difference between that required to compress the gas and that obtained from the turbine. This difference may be represented by areas on the pressure-volume diagram in the insert. In the simple ideal cycle, the efficiency depends on the pressure ratio employed and increases rapidly with pressure ratio, at first, and then begins to level off slowly. Theoretically, if the pressure ratio were to approach infinity, the thermal efficiency would approach 100 percent.

Actual simple open-cycle gas turbine. The principal difference between the ideal cycle described above and the actual cycle obtainable in practice is that the compression and expansion processes cannot actually be carried out without friction or other losses as assumed. Instead, the work of compression is increased, and the work of expansion is decreased. The net result is a drastic reduction in the net-work output and thermal efficiency of

Ideal and actual cycles

the cycle. In typical actual cycles, the efficiency of the compressor is about 85 percent and that of the turbine about 87 percent. Maximum cycle temperatures ranging from 1,000° to 1,750° F, (540° to 950° C) are employed, the latter being about the maximum feasible temperature permissible with modern alloys without special arrangements for cooling the blades of the turbine.

Unlike the ideal cycle, where the efficiency depends only on the pressure ratio, the thermal efficiency of an actual cycle increases with maximum temperature of the cycle T_3, and there is an optimum value of pressure ratio for each value of T_3. The maximum temperature must be high if a satisfactory efficiency is to be obtained. The lower the efficiencies of the compressor and turbine, the lower will be the net work output of the cycle. These facts explain the failure of Stolze's turbine and of all similar early models in which high-compressor and turbine efficiencies were unattainable. They also explain the reason for Holzwarth's efforts to perfect the explosion-type turbine, in which the efficiency of compression is less important.

Reheating, intercooling, and regeneration. There are three basic ways in which the efficiency of the simple gas-turbine cycle can be increased. These are: (1) to increase the work output of the turbine; (2) to decrease work input to the compressor; (3) to decrease the amount of heat added by the fuel.

The first of the above objectives can be realized by dividing the expansion process into two or more steps. This division can be accomplished by employing a high-pressure and low-pressure turbine with a combustion chamber in between for reheating the air and combustion products. The effect is to increase the volume of the gas undergoing expansion, thus increasing the work of the turbine.

The second objective may be accomplished by compressing the air in a manner as near isothermal (constant temperature) as possible. The closest practical approach to this objective is to employ intercooling, a process in which the air is compressed in two or more steps and cooled back to inlet temperature between steps. The purpose of such a practice is to maintain the volume of air as low as possible in order to reduce the power required for compression.

To accomplish the third objective, it should be possible by means of a heat exchanger to warm the air on its way to the combustion chamber by transferring some of the heat from the turbine exhaust gases to the air. In practice this warming is accomplished by means of a regenerative heat exchanger in which the hot exhaust gases are passed in such a manner that the heat surrendered by these gases is absorbed by the compressed air before it enters the combustion chamber. This absorption reduces the amount of heat added by the fuel.

This particular type of cycle is advantageous insofar as thermal efficiency is concerned, but the disadvantages of added complexity and first cost often outweigh the advantages.

Design features. Although a detailed discussion of the many design features of gas turbines cannot be undertaken here, enough can be included to give the reader an idea of the arrangement of essential components. Figure 8 is a cross-section drawing of a 3,600-revolutions-per-minute, single-shaft gas turbine designed primarily for electric-power generation. It is rated at about 54,000 kilowatts for base-load service and 60,000 kilowatts for peak-load service when operating with air intake at sea level and 59° F (15° C). It incorporates a 19-stage axial-flow compressor in which air is compressed to several times atmospheric pressure before being discharged into a cavity at the compressor outlet. The air is next turned toward the left and flows through the annular (ring-shaped) space surrounding each of the ten combustion chambers before being fed through liner holes and louvers into the interior-combustion zones. The combustion products are discharged at about 1,600° F (900° C) into individual transition ducts that convey the gas to the three-stage, axial-flow turbine. From the turbine exhaust, the gas is directed through the annular diffuser and turn-

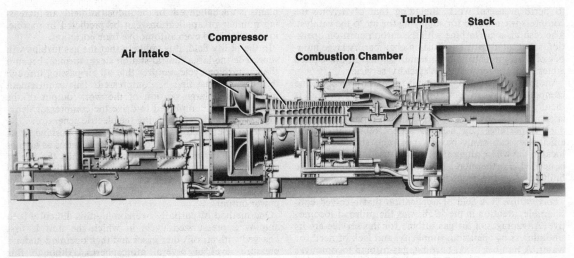

Figure 8: Cutaway view of simple-cycle, single-shaft gas turbine rated at about 54,000 kilowatts.
By courtesy of General Electric Company, Schenectady, N.Y.

ing-vanes into the stack. During expansion of the gas through the turbine, sufficient work is performed to drive an electric generator (not shown) capable of generating about 60,000 kilowatts. More complicated arrangements are available, including those with provisions for the intercooling, reheating, and regeneration processes mentioned previously.

Applications. The gas turbine is a versatile prime mover and has many applications, notably in aircraft, electric-power generation, industrial, locomotive, marine, and automotive uses.

Aircraft. By far the most important present-day application is in aviation, in which the gas turbine provides the motive power for jet propulsion (see JET ENGINE).

Jet-propulsion engines are most efficient at high altitudes and high airspeeds and are particularly suited for high-performance military aircraft. Modern military jet-propulsion engines are capable of producing tremendous power. In emergencies this can be augmented still further with the aid of an afterburner, which adds heat to the gases just before they enter the exhaust nozzle. This afterburning increases their velocity and adds to the forward thrust of the engine.

Turboprop application   Another gas-turbine application for aircraft is the turboprop. In this application the gas turbine has two purposes: it drives a conventional propeller, and it produces additional thrust by means of the reactive force of the jet leaving the exhaust nozzle of the engine. The advantage of short takeoff inherent in propeller-driven aircraft is thus combined with the faster and higher flying capabilities of the conventional jet-propulsion engine.

Intermediate between the conventional jet-propulsion engine and the turboprop is a later development called the turbofan engine. It differs from the ordinary jet-propulsion engine in that a fan is located at the inlet that takes in a great deal more air than actually passes through the core of the engine. The fan compresses this air slightly and then delivers most of it through a bypass duct around the engine, where it is accelerated and released with a higher velocity than it had at intake, thus adding to the thrust of the engine. The remainder of the air flows through the core of the engine, where it is compressed, heated, and expanded through the turbine and exhaust nozzle as in a conventional jet.

The ratio of air bypassed through the duct surrounding the core of the engine to that passing through the core is called the bypass ratio. This varies widely according to application. Bypass ratios as high as 8 to 1 are common in large turbofan engines. In general, high bypass ratios and high compression ratios result in improved fuel economy.

The turbofan engine has a number of advantages. The added thrust of the engine eliminates the need for carrying heavy additional loads of water sometimes employed for injection to increase the thrust of conventional engines during takeoff on warm days. When operating with-

in the proper speed and altitude range, fuel savings of the order of 20 percent can be realized. These advantages have made this type of engine the favourite for commercial use on very large jet aircraft.

Electric-power generation. In the field of electric-power generation, the gas turbine must compete with the diesel engine and steam turbine. Gas turbines are limited in capacity by the fact that the pressure involved is low, making it necessary to employ large turbines and compressors in order to handle the huge volumes of air required. For this reason no serious attempt has been made to design a gas-turbine power plant capable of competing with the modern central-station, steam power plant in which single units as large as 1,200,000 kilowatts have been built.

Three applications deserve special mention: (1) operation in combination with steam power plants as a means of increasing the overall efficiency; (2) for standby and peak-load service; and (3) for portable power plants. A promising combined steam-turbine–gas-turbine power plant is one in which high-temperature exhaust gases from a conventional gas turbine are employed to supply oxygen to the furnace of a steam boiler in place of preheated combustion air. This combination is feasible because the gases exhausted from a gas turbine still contain about 80 percent of the oxygen in the air supplied to the compressor inlet. Such an arrangement is capable of increasing substantially the overall efficiency of the plant. It also offers savings in size and weight of the boilers required, less building volume, quicker starting of the boiler, and elimination of the forced and induced draft fans normally required by the boiler.

Other ways in which the gas turbine can be employed to improve the efficiency of a steam power plant are to use the exhaust gases for feedwater heating or for the generation of steam in an exhaust-heat boiler.

The gas turbine offers an attractive means for providing additional peak-load and standby power. It can often be installed for this purpose at lower cost than additional steam or hydroelectric capacity. Furthermore, it offers the advantages of virtually automatic operation, simplicity, small space requirements, and minimum maintenance. Another similar application is for end-of-the-line voltage-booster service on long-distance transmission lines. A third application is for portable power plants. Here the gas turbine can be mounted on railroad cars or barges for emergency use.

Industry. An early and still important application of the gas turbine in industry is in connection with the Houdry process of refining oil. In this application, air under pressure must periodically be passed over a catalyst for the purpose of burning off carbon accumulated during the refining process. The air employed thus becomes heated in the same manner as it would in a combustion chamber and can, therefore, be passed through a turbine

Limitations of the gas turbine for electric-power generation

Houdry process

to perform useful work, including that of driving the compressor employed for supplying the air to the catalyst. The result is a gas turbine with the carbon burn-off operation substituted for a combustion chamber. A large number of these units have been manufactured in the United States and are rendering satisfactory service.

Another industrial application is for natural-gas pipeline compressor stations. For this purpose the gas turbine is ideally suited, because natural gas is an excellent fuel and is available at low cost, making fuel economy of secondary importance. By using a regenerator, satisfactory efficiencies can easily be obtained, and stations can be located anywhere along the line because no water supply is needed. Furthermore, fully automatic stations can be built that require practically no supervision and only a minimum of maintenance.

Locomotive. A field of application that received considerable attention in the 1950s was the railroad locomotive. Advantages of the gas turbine for this service are its smoothness of operation, simplicity, and lack of need for water. A number of oil-burning, gas-turbine locomotives built in the United States and Switzerland have provided satisfactory service. They have been unable to replace the diesel locomotive, however, because of lower thermal efficiency. Attempts were made to overcome this economic disadvantage by developing a coal-burning, gas-turbine locomotive, but the engineering difficulties were too great. Much work remains to be accomplished before a successful unit can be built.

Marine. In the field of ship propulsion, the gas turbine offers advantages of light weight and lower space requirements than a corresponding boiler and steam-turbine plant. In the early 1970s an all-gas, turbine-powered ship in the 20,000-horsepower class demonstrated its capability at sea with more than 5,000 engine hours of service. As a result, marine gas turbines were selected to power 30 new United States Navy destroyers, the Navy's first gas turbine-powered combat ships.

There is some indication that, with further development, a gas-turbine outboard motor may become competitive with conventional reciprocating motors. During the early 1960s, at least one model was successfully built and tested.

Automotive. There is much speculation as to the future of the gas turbine for automotive applications. Its principal advantages are its smooth, vibrationless operation, high power at low speeds, light weight, small space requirement, lack of need for a cooling system, and the possibility of burning a cheaper grade of fuel than gasoline. Its disadvantages are high cost of manufacture and materials, high fuel consumption, especially at part load, high noise level, and poor acceleration characteristics.

During the 1960s, work on small gas-turbine engines by automobile manufacturers offered hope that many of these disadvantages could be overcome. The development of new casting techniques made it possible to make satisfactory compressor and turbine wheels, thus eliminating the high cost of individually machining these components. Also, the improvement of rotary regenerators and the use of other schemes—such as adjustable turbine nozzles and two-shaft designs—greatly improved the fuel-consumption outlook for both full- and part-load operation. In addition, they have given the engines much better acceleration characteristics. Several test vehicles were built and operated on a variety of fuels and showed performance approaching that of conventional automobile engines.

The gas turbine also may provide an automotive power plant with cleaner exhaust, because it does not produce as much unburned hydrocarbons and carbon monoxide as reciprocating engines. The combustion process in the gas turbine also minimizes the formation of nitrogen oxides in the exhaust. These considerations became increasingly important with the imposition of higher standards of environmental quality.

Future trends. The many applications for which the gas turbine is especially well suited seem to assure an attractive future. In military and commercial aviation, its status as the leading contender among all types of power plants is unchallenged. In the industrial field, an increasing number of applications can be predicted in marine, locomotive, and even automotive transportation.

In the utility field, it is unlikely that the gas turbine will supersede the large central-station steam turbine, because the gas-turbine cycle requires that all air passing through the turbine must first be compressed. This requirement means that a large portion of the work output of the turbine must be employed to drive the compressor, leaving only a fraction for driving the electric generator.

Still another factor favouring the steam turbine is its ability to expand steam through pressure ratios as high as 10,000 to 1 or more, an ability that permits the use of very high initial pressures, resulting in relatively small turbine components. With the gas turbine, pressures are always low, making large components essential for high power output.

One method of partially overcoming this difficulty is to employ a pressurized cycle in which the unit is first charged with air or other gases and then operated under a pressure level of several atmospheres. Although this method has the advantage of reducing the size of the rotating machinery, it requires a cooling medium capable of lowering the temperature of the turbine exhaust gases back to compressor-inlet temperature before they can be reintroduced into the compressor. It is also necessary to add heat to the compressed gases in a separately fired furnace, or to continuously add sufficient new air and fuel to the cycle, under pressure, to maintain combustion.

A possible future application of the pressurized cycle is in conjunction with a steam cycle in nuclear power plants employing helium-cooled reactors. In such a system, a pressurized helium-gas turbine would be used with the reactor supplying heat in place of the combustion chamber used in conventional units. The helium exhausted from the turbine would first transfer some of its heat to a regenerator, after which it would be cooled back to the compressor-inlet temperature by transferring its remaining heat to the feedwater in the steam cycle. Heat in the gas-turbine portion of the cycle that is normally rejected to the atmosphere would be transferred to the feedwater, increasing the efficiency of the overall cycle.

BIBLIOGRAPHY

Water turbines: J.G. BROWN (ed.), *Hydro-electric Engineering Practice*, 3 vol. (1958), 2nd ed., vol. 1 (1964–); W.P. CREAGER and J.D. JUSTIN, *Hydroelectric Handbook*, 2nd ed. (1950); J.J. DOLAND, *Hydro Power Engineering* (1954); ROLT HAMMOND, *Water Power Engineering* (1958); PHILIP J. POTTER, *Power Plant Theory and Design*, 2nd ed. (1959).

Steam turbines: A. STODOLA, *Steam and Gas Turbines*, 2 vol., trans. from the 6th German ed. by L.C. LOEWENSTEIN (1927), a classic work; E.F. CHURCH, JR., *Steam Turbine*, 3rd ed. (1950); J.K. SALISBURY, *Steam Turbines and Their Cycles* (1950); JOHN F. LEE, *Theory and Design of Steam and Gas Turbines* (1954).

Gas turbines: B.H. JENNINGS and W.L. ROGERS, *Gas Turbine Analysis and Practice* (1953); H.R. COX (ed.), *Gas Turbine Principles and Practice* (1955); JAMES HODGE, *Cycles and Performance Estimation* (1955); I.H. DRIGGS and O.E. LANCASTER, *Gas Turbines for Aircraft* (1955); M.J. ZUCROW, *Aircraft and Missile Propulsion*, vol. 2 (1958); JOHN W. SAWYER (ed.), *Gas Turbine Engineering Handbook* (1966); C.W. SMITH, *Aircraft Gas Turbines* (1956); WALTER J. HESSE and N.V.S. MUMFORD, JR., *Jet Propulsion for Aerospace Applications*, 2nd ed. (1964); P.G. HILL and C.R. PETERSON, *Mechanics and Thermodynamics of Propulsion* (1965); W.H.T. LOH, *Jet, Rocket, Nuclear Ion and Electric Propulsion, Theory and Design* (1968).

(R.A.B.)

Turenne, Henri de

The victories of France's marshal-general Henri de la Tour d'Auvergne, vicomte de Turenne in the last years of the Thirty Years' War and his role in suppressing the rebellion known as the Fronde on behalf of the crown have earned him a foremost place in French military annals of the 17th century.

He was born on September 11, 1611, at Sedan, a son of the Protestant Henri, duc de Bouillon, by his second wife, Elizabeth of Nassau, daughter of William the Silent, the stadtholder of the Netherlands.

Turenne, portrait by Charles Le Brun (1619–90). In the Musée National de Versailles et des Trianons.
Cliche des Musees Nationaux, Paris

Victories in the Thirty Years' War. When his father died in 1623, Turenne was sent to learn soldiering with his mother's brothers, Maurice and Frederick Henry, the princes of Orange who were leading the Dutch against the Spaniards in the Netherlands. Though he was given command of an infantry regiment in the French service for the campaign of 1630, he was back with Frederick Henry in 1632. In 1635, however, when Louis XIII's minister Cardinal de Richelieu brought France into open war against the Habsburgs (see THIRTY YEARS' WAR), Turenne, with the rank of *maréchal de camp*, or brigadier, went to serve under Cardinal de La Valette (Louis de Nogaret) on the Rhine. He was a hero of a retreat from Mainz to Metz and was wounded in the assault on Saverne in July 1636. After a mission to Liège to hire troops for the French, he was sent to the Rhine again in 1638 to reinforce Bernhard of Saxe-Weimar at the siege of Breisach; he conducted the assault and won the respect of Bernhard's German troops. Two campaigns fought in Italy, culminating in the capture of Turin on September 17, 1640, confirmed his reputation.

In 1642, when the French army was besieging Spanish-held Perpignan, Turenne was second in command. The conspiracy of the King's favourite, the Marquis de Cinq-Mars, against Richelieu was then brought to light, and the Duc de Bouillon was arrested. Turenne remained loyal to Louis XIII and to Richelieu; but Bouillon had to surrender Sedan in order to obtain his freedom. When Louis XIII died in 1643, the queen, Anne of Austria, became regent for her infant son Louis XIV. She gave Turenne a command in Italy in the same year, but his brother's conduct made him suspect to Richelieu's successor, Cardinal Mazarin; and as no fresh troops were sent to him, Turenne could do nothing. Anne made Turenne a marshal of France, however, on May 16, 1643.

Command of the French forces in Germany

On December 3, 1643, news reached Paris that France's Army of Germany had been scattered in the Black Forest, and its commander was dead. The command was given to Turenne, who made an effective army from this broken force—mainly Germans who had followed Bernhard of Saxe-Weimar. But he had barely 10,000 men and remained weaker than his Bavarian opponents, a fact that dictated his conduct from 1644 to 1648. The Rhineland was devastated, and Turenne could act only by marching far into Germany to seize control of new forage lands. Unless he could join forces with another army, therefore, he could do nothing.

In 1644 Turenne watched the Bavarians take Freiburg in Breisgau, appealed for help, and was joined by the small army of the duc d'Enghien, Louis II de Bourbon, prince de Condé. The latter was younger by ten years than Turenne but took command of both armies because a French prince was senior to a French marshal; even so, they were good colleagues. Three fierce actions near Freiburg induced the Bavarians to leave the Rhine Valley; and Enghien and Turenne took Philippsburg in September and gained control of the Rhine towns as far north as Bingen.

In 1645 Turenne, intending to effect a junction with France's Swedish allies in Germany, marched through Württemberg. But in May the Bavarians made a surprise attack, and half of Turenne's army was lost in the Battle of Marienthal (Mergentheim). Turenne fell back, and Mazarin sent Enghien to rescue him. Their united forces met the Bavarians in the Battle of Nördlingen and reached the Danube, but with such heavy loss in infantry that they soon had to return to the Rhine.

In 1646 Turenne achieved his plan of joining the much stronger Swedish army, though Mazarin feared the Protestant supremacy in Germany that might be the result. Turenne crossed the Rhine at Wesel and met the Swedes under Field Marshal Carl Gustav Wrangel. The two commanders evaded the Austro-Bavarians on the Main, marched straight for the Danube, and threatened Augsburg and Munich. The elector Maximilian I of Bavaria then began negotiations with the French, and, by the Treaty of Ulm (March 14, 1647), abandoned his alliance with the Holy Roman emperor Ferdinand III. But Turenne was thwarted and Ferdinand's Austrians were saved when Mazarin ordered the Army of Germany to operate in Luxembourg. Then, when the army reached the Vosges, the German cavalry mutinied and turned back across the Rhine. For three months Turenne marched with them far into Germany. In the end his powerful personality brought most of them back to the French service.

When Bavaria returned to the Emperor's side in 1648, Turenne rejoined Wrangel and they reached the Danube, the Lech, and—after the Battle of Zusmarshausen—the Inn River, the nearest point to Austria yet attained by the French. Maximilian fled from Bavaria, and the Emperor agreed to the Peace of Westphalia, ending the Thirty Years' War.

Participation in the Fronde. The same year marked the beginning of the so-called Fronde, an aristocratic rebellion against Mazarin. Turenne's family's interests and the friendship of Condé's sister, the Duchesse de Longueville, led him to intervene on the side of the rebellion in the first war of the Fronde, precipitated by the unpopularity of Mazarin's fiscal measures. The Cardinal at once sent a new general and arrears of pay to the Army of Germany, and Turenne fled to Holland just when the compromise peace was being negotiated at Rueil. He returned to Paris in May 1649.

When Mazarin arrested the overbearing Condé on January 18, 1650, Turenne again fled, joining the Duchesse de Longueville at Stenay on the eastern border of Champagne. They tied themselves by treaty to the Spaniards, then at war with France, and waged war in Champagne until Turenne was completely defeated in the Battle of Rethel (December 15, 1650) by superior forces under Marshal du Plessis-Praslin (César, later Duc de Choiseul) and narrowly escaped capture.

Mazarin's voluntary exile from Paris and Condé's release brought Turenne back to Paris in May 1651, with his credit at a low point. In August 1651 he married the firmly Protestant Charlotte de Caumont. He stood aloof from politics without committing himself to Condé's faction. It was his brother, the duc de Bouillon, who came to terms with the Queen-Regent in March 1652, with the result that Turenne was promptly put in command of one of the two divisions of the royal army, each 4,000 strong, which had been assembled on the Loire to oppose Condé and his allies. A few days later his courageous and clear-sighted action in blocking the bridge at Jargeau saved the young King from capture by the rebels; and in April, at Bléneau, he checked Condé and rescued his defeated colleague, Marshal d'Hocquincourt (Charles de Monchy).

Suppression of the Fronde

His campaign of 1652–53, first on the Loire, then before Paris, and in Champagne, was Turenne's greatest service to the monarchy: his resources were small, and but for his great skill he might have been overwhelmed; yet he staunchly kept the Queen-Regent's court from taking refuge far from Paris and thus enabled the young Louis XIV at last to re-enter his capital.

Successes in the Franco-Spanish War. With the defeat of the rebellion, good troops from other parts of France could be brought to reinforce those in the northeast and to prosecute the struggle there against the Spaniards, with whom Condé was now serving. The turning point came in 1654, when Turenne and his colleagues stormed three lines of trenches and expelled the army that was besieging Arras. In 1658 Turenne surmounted the physical obstacles to investing Dunkirk and, when the Spaniards advanced, defeated them in the Battle of the Dunes (June 14), skillfully using the difficult ground into which his enemy had unwisely moved. His victory enabled him to hand Dunkirk over to France's English allies and allowed him to move freely in Flanders, taking Ypres and threatening Ghent and Brussels. The Franco-Spanish Peace of the Pyrenees followed in 1659. For the second time Turenne's operations had won an advantageous peace.

Last campaigns. On April 5, 1660, Turenne was appointed "marshal-general of the camps and armies of the King," an extraordinary honour that implied that he might have been constable of France if he abjured his Protestant faith. When he abjured in 1668, after his wife's death (1666), however, he was not made constable (ex officio commander in chief in war). The development of the Ministry of War by the Marquis de Louvois enabled Louis XIV to command in person, and in the War of Devolution (1667–68) and in the invasion of Holland (1672) Turenne marched at his side. Then, when the German allies of the Dutch menaced the lower Rhineland, Turenne was once more sent east of the Rhine, but with only 16,000 men, a secondary command.

Yet these campaigns of 1672–75 brought him enduring fame. He resented the detailed control of military affairs by the arrogant Marquis de Louvois, but the minister's supplies enabled him to maintain active operations into the winter. He had long been a master of "strategic chess moves," but he was bolder now; he offered battle more often and looked for opportunities when his more powerful adversaries were weakened by detachments. By January 1673 he had broken the German coalition for a time and by invading the County of Mark had forced the elector Frederick William of Brandenburg to negotiate; he had also prevented the enemy from crossing the Rhine. Later in the year his wider manoeuvring against the emperor Leopold I's army had such success that he could have reached Bohemia; but Louvois refused him reinforcement for a decisive operation, and when Turenne was called back to cover Alsace, the Emperor's forces struck at Bonn and so broke the French control of the lower Rhine.

Greatly superior German forces moved toward the Rhine in 1674. Turenne defeated a detached corps at Sinzheim, near Heidelberg, on June 16, and ravaged the Palatinate. But by September he was again west of the Rhine, with little hope of barring the advance of the main enemy forces. At Enzheim, near Strassburg, he attacked them on October 4, but he drew back before a decisive point was reached; and as the Brandenburgers also joined the Emperor's forces, their 57,000 men seemed in secure possession of Alsace. Turenne replied in December with the most famous of his marches. He turned south on the French side of the Vosges, reappeared at Belfort, and, at Turckheim on January 5, 1675, delivered so heavy a blow on the flank of the main army that the Germans decided to recross the Rhine. Alsace was saved.

In June 1675 Turenne was on the right bank of the Rhine manoeuvring against the Italian field marshal in imperial service Raimondo Montecuccoli for the control of the crossing near Strassburg. The armies were in contact at Sasbach, and Turenne was examining a position when he was killed by a cannon shot on July 27, 1675. He was buried with the kings of France at Saint-Denis. Later the emperor Napoleon had his remains transferred to the Invalides in Paris.

BIBLIOGRAPHY. C.G. PICAVET, *Les Dernières Années de Turenne, 1660–1675* (1919), still a standard work; M. WEYGARD, *Turenne: Marshall of France* (1929; Eng. trans., 1930); G. ZELLER, *L'Organisation défensive des frontières du Nord et de l'Est an XVIIᵉ siècle* (1928), a general survey of the defense of France's northern and eastern frontiers in the 17th century.

(I.D'O.E.)

Turgenev, Ivan

The first Russian writer of the 19th century to acquire an international reputation, Ivan Turgenev was a novelist, poet, and playwright whose works offer realistic, affectionate portrayals of the Russian peasantry and penetrating studies of the Russian intelligentsia who were attempting to move the country into a new age. The many years he lived in western Europe as virtually an unofficial cultural ambassador were due in part to his personal and artistic stand as a liberal between the reactionary tsarist rule and the spirit of revolutionary radicalism that held so great a sway in the contemporary artistic and intellectual circles in Russia. He poured into his writings not only a deep concern for the future of his native land but also an integrity of craft that has ensured his place in Russian literature.

Brown Brothers

Turgenev, oil painting by V.G. Peroff, 1872.

Ivan Sergeyevich Turgenev was born on November 9 (October 28, old style), 1818, in Orel, central Russia. He was the second son of a retired cavalry officer, Sergey Turgenev, and a wealthy mother, Varvara Petrovna, *née* Lutovinova, who owned the extensive estate of Spasskoye-Lutovinovo. Turgenev's father, who died in 1834, was a lesser influence in his life than his mother. His memory was to fascinate the author in later years, however, finding its most powerful embodiment in the portrait of the father in Turgenev's famous short story *First Love* (1860). The dominant figure of his mother throughout his boyhood and early manhood probably provided the example, if not the model, for the dominance exercised by the heroines in his major fiction. Her despotic temperament ruled over her son's life and the estate of Spasskoye with equal arbitrariness. Spasskoye itself came to have a twofold meaning for the young Turgenev, as an island of gentry civilization in rural Russia and as a symbol of the injustice he saw inherent in the servile state of the peasantry. On the other hand, Spasskoye, as the source of an idyll, was to be the context not only of many of his later works, particularly his novels, but also of his view of civilization as something that, like the human spirit, was essentially isolated and forever menaced by an outer darkness. Against the social system Turgenev was to take an oath of perpetual animosity, which was to be the source of his liberalism and the inspiration for his vision of the intelligentsia as people dedicated to their country's social and political betterment.

Turgenev's earliest memory was of nearly falling into the bear pit in Bern, Switzerland, during his family's grand tour of Europe in 1822. He was rescued by his father, but he was not saved from Europe. Turgenev was to

Role in the Dutch wars

Parental influences

First visit to Europe

be the only Russian writer with an avowedly European outlook and sympathies. Though he was given an education of sorts at home, in Moscow schools, at the universities of both Moscow and St. Petersburg, Turgenev tended to regard his education as having taken place chiefly during his plunge "into the German sea" when he spent the years 1838 to 1841 at the University of Berlin. Here he became friendly with leading figures of his own generation such as the anti-Marxist revolutionary Mikhail Bakunin. Through them his interest was aroused in the philosophy of G.W.F. Hegel, which underlay much revolutionary thought, and he was also inspired with the ideal of dedicating his life and talent to the future of Russia. He returned home as a confirmed believer in the superiority of the West and of the need for Russia to follow a course of Westernization.

Early works. Earlier, Turgenev had composed derivative verse and a poetic drama, *Steno* (1834), in the style of the English poet Lord Byron. The first of his works to attract attention was the long poem *Parasha,* published in 1843. The potential of the author was quickly appreciated by the critic Vissarion Belinsky, who soon became Turgenev's close friend and mentor. Belinsky's conviction that literature's primary aim was to reflect the truth of life and to adopt a critical attitude toward its observable injustices became an article of faith for Turgenev. He never believed, however, that social concerns should take precedence over art. Despite the influence of Belinsky, he remained a writer of remarkable detachment, of a cool and sometimes ironic objectivity that his enemies unfairly labelled disdain.

He was not a man of grand passions, although the love story was to provide the most common formula for his fiction, and a love for the renowned singer Pauline Viardot, whom he first met in 1843, was to dominate his entire life from that moment. His relation with Mme Viardot, like his love for Europe, usually has been considered platonic, yet some of his letters to her, often as brilliant in their observation and as felicitous in their manner as anything he wrote, suggest the existence of a greater intimacy. Generally, though, they reveal him as the fond and devoted admirer, in which role he was for the most part content. He never married, though in 1842 he had an illegitimate daughter by a peasant woman at Spasskoye; he later entrusted the upbringing of the child to Mme Viardot.

During the 1840s, Turgenev wrote more long poems, including *A Conversation* and *Andrey Kolosov, The Landowner,* and several pieces of criticism. Having failed in his attempt to obtain a professorship at St. Petersburg university and having abandoned work in the government service, he began to publish short works in prose. These were studies in the "intellectual-without-a-will" so typical of his generation. The most famous was "The Dairy of a Superfluous Man" (1850), which supplied the epithet "superfluous man" for so many similar weak-willed intellectual protagonists in Turgenev's work as well as in Russian literature generally.

Simultaneously, he tried his hand at writing plays, some, like *A Poor Gentleman* (1848), rather obviously imitative of the older Russian master Nikolay Gogol (1809–52). Of these, *The Bachelor* (1849) was the only one staged at this time, the others falling afoul of the official censors. Others of a more intimately penetrating character, such as *One May Spin a Thread Too Finely* (1848), led to the detailed psychological studies in his dramatic masterpiece, *A Month in the Country* (1855). This was not staged professionally until 1872. Without precedent in the Russian theatre, it required for its appreciation by critics and audiences the prior success after 1898 of the plays of Anton Chekhov at the Moscow Art Theatre. It was there in 1909, under the great director Konstantin Stanislavsky, that it was revealed as one of the major works of the Russian theatre.

Sketches of rural life. Before going abroad in 1847, Turgenev left in the editorial offices of the literary journal *Sovremennik* ("The Contemporary") a short study, "Khor and Kalinych," of two peasants whom he had met on a hunting trip in the Orel region. It was published with the subtitle "From a hunter's sketches," and it had an

instantaneous success. From it was to grow the cycle *Sportsman's Sketches,* first published in 1852, that brought him lasting fame. In all he wrote 25 such sketches. Many of them portrayed various types of landowners or episodes, drawn from his experience, of the life of the manorial, serf-owning Russian gentry. Of these, the most important are "Two Landowners," a study of two types of despotic serf-owners, and "Hamlet of Shchigrovsky Province," which contains one of the most profound and poignant analyses of the problem of the "superfluous man." Far more significant are the sketches that tell of Turgenev's encounters with peasants during his hunting trips. Amid evocative descriptions of the countryside, Turgenev's portraits suggest that, though the peasants may be "children of nature" who seek the freedom offered by the beauty of their surroundings, they are always circumscribed by the fact of serfdom.

He could never pretend to be much more than an understanding stranger toward the peasants about whom he wrote, yet through his compassionate, lucid observation, he created portraits of enormous vitality and wide impact. Not only did they make the predominantly upper class reading public aware of the human qualities of the peasantry but also they may have been influential in provoking the sentiment for reform that led eventually to the emancipation of the serfs in 1861. He added to the *Sketches* during the 1870s, including the moving study of the paralyzed Lukeriya in "A Living Relic" (1874).

When the first collected edition appeared, after appearing separately in various issues of the *Sovremennik,* Turgenev was arrested, detained for a month in St. Petersburg, then given 18 months of enforced residence at Spasskoye. The ostensible pretext for such official harrassment was an obituary of Gogol, which he had published against censorship regulations. But his criticism of serfdom in the *Sketches,* certainly muted in tone by any standards and explicit only in his references to the landowners' brutality toward their peasants, was sufficient to cause this temporary martyrdom for his art.

First novels. Although Turgenev wrote "Mumu," a remarkable exposure of the cruelties of serfdom, while detained in St. Petersburg, his work was evolving toward such extended character studies as *Yakov Pasynkov* (1855) and the subtle if pessimistic examinations of the contrariness of love found in "Faust" and "A Correspondence" (1856). Time and national events, moreover, were impinging upon him. With the defeat of Russia in the Crimean War (1854–56), Turgenev's own generation, "the men of the forties," began to belong to the past. The two novels that he published during the 1850s are permeated by a spirit of ironic nostalgia for the weaknesses and futilities so manifest in this generation of a decade earlier.

Turgenev's novels are "months in the country," which contain balanced contrasts such as those between youth and age, between the tragic ephemerality of love and the comic transcience of ideas, between Hamlet's concern with self and the ineptitudes of the quixotic pursuit of altruism. The last of these contrasts he amplified into a major essay, "Hamlet and Don Quixote" (1860). If he differed from his great contemporaries Fyodor Dostoyevsky and Leo Tolstoy in the scale of his work, he also differed from them in believing that literature should not provide answers to life's question marks. He constructed his novels according to a simple formula that had the sole purpose of illuminating the character and predicament of a single figure, whether hero or heroine. They are important chiefly as detailed and deft sociopsychological portraitures.

A major device of the novels is to examine the effect of a newcomer's arrival upon a small social circle. The circle, in its turn, subjects the newcomer to scrutiny through the relation that develops between the heroine, who always belongs to the "place" of the fiction, and the newcomer-hero. Promise of happiness is offered, but the ending of the relation is invariably calamitous.

The first of Turgenev's novels, *Rudin* (1856), tells of an eloquent intellectual, Dmitry Rudin, a character modelled partly on Bakunin, whose power of oratory and passionately held belief in the need for progress so affect the younger members of a provincial salon that the heroine,

Love for Pauline Viardot

Dramatic works

Themes in the novels

Natalya, falls in love with him. When she challenges him to live up to his words he fails her. The evocation of the world of the Russian country house and of the summer atmosphere that form the backdrop to the tragicomedy of this relationship is evidence of Turgenev's power of perceiving and recording the constancies of the natural scene. The vaster implications about Russian society as a whole and about the role of the Russian intelligentsia are present as shading at the edges of the picture rather than as colours or details in the foreground. Such suggestibility, so basic to Turgenev's mastery of his art, was fully present in this first long work of prose.

Turgenev's second novel, *Home of the Gentry* (1859), is an elegiac study of unrequited love in which the hero, Lavretsky, is not so much weak as the victim of his unbalanced upbringing. The work is notable for the delicacy of the love story, though it is a shade mawkish on occasion. More important in terms of the author's thought is the elaborate biography of the hero. In it is the suggestion that the influence of the West has inhibited Turgenev's generation from taking action, forcing them to acknowledge finally that they must leave the future of Russia to those younger and more radical than themselves.

The objectivity of Turgenev as a chronicler of the Russian intelligentsia now begins to become apparent. Unsympathetic though he may have been to some of the trends in the thinking of the younger, radical generation that emerged after the Crimean War, he endeavoured to portray the positive aspirations of these young men and women with scrupulous candour. Their attitude to him, particularly that of such leading figures as the radical critics Nikolay Chernyshevsky and Nikolay Dobrolyubov, was generally cold when it was not actively hostile. His own rather self-indulgent nature was challenged by the forcefulness of these younger contemporaries. He moved away from an emphasis on the fallibility of his heroes, who had been attacked as a type by Chernyshevsky, using the short story "Asya" (1858) as his point of departure. Instead, Turgenev focussed on their youthful ardour and their sense of moral purpose. These attributes had obvious revolutionary implications that were not shared by Turgenev, whose liberalism could accept gradual change but opposed anything more radical, especially the idea of an insurgent peasantry.

The novel *On the Eve* (1860) deals with the problem facing the younger intelligentsia on the eve of the Crimean War and refers also to the changes awaiting Russia on the eve of the emancipation of the serfs in 1861. It is an episodic work, further weakened by the shallow portrayal of its Bulgarian hero. Although it has several successful minor characters and some powerful scenes, its treatment of personal relations, particularly of love, demonstrates Turgenev's profound pessimism toward such matters. Such pessimism became increasingly marked in Turgenev's view of life. It may have sprung in part from his unusual relation with Mme Viardot and her husband, but it was undoubtedly aggravated by his own lack of self-confidence. When, in 1859, Chernyshevsky travelled to London to see Aleksandr Herzen, the liberal leader and Turgenev's friend, the confrontation between the older and younger generations of the Russian intelligentsia became an open split. It seems that there could be no real reconciliation between the liberalism of Turgenev's generation and the revolutionary aspirations of the younger intelligentsia. Turgenev himself could hardly fail to feel a sense of personal involvement in this rupture.

Fathers and Sons

Turgenev's greatest novel, *Fathers and Sons* (1862), grew from this sense of involvement and yet succeeded in illustrating, with remarkable balance and profundity, the issues that divided the generations. The hero, Bazarov, is the most powerful of Turgenev's creations. A nihilist, denying all laws save those of the natural sciences, uncouth and forthright in his opinions, he is nonetheless susceptible to love and by that token doomed to unhappiness. In sociopolitical terms he represents the victory of the nongentry revolutionary intelligentsia over the gentry intelligentsia to which Turgenev belonged. In artistic terms he is a triumphant example of objective portraiture, and in the poignancy of his death he approaches

tragic stature. The miracle of the novel as a whole is Turgenev's superb mastery of his theme, despite his personal hostility toward Bazarov's anti-aestheticism, and his success in endowing all the characters with a quality of spontaneous life. Yet at its first appearance the radical younger generation attacked it bitterly as a slander, and the conservatives condemned it as too lenient in its exposure of nihilism.

Self-exile and fame. Always touchy about his literary reputation, Turgenev reacted to the almost unanimously hostile reception by leaving Russia. He took up residence in Baden-Baden in southern Germany, to which resort Mme Viardot had retired. Quarrels with Tolstoy and Dostoyevsky and his general estrangement from the Russian literary scene made him an exile in a very real sense. Bitterness at the Russia that had seemed to reject him is discernible in the short pieces "Phantoms" (1864) and "Enough" (1865). His only novel of this period, *Smoke* (1867), set in Baden-Baden, is infused with a satirically embittered tone that makes caricatures of both the left and the right wings of the intelligentsia. The love story is deeply moving, but both this emotion and the political sentiments are made to seem ultimately no more lasting and real than the smoke of the title.

The Franco-Prussian War of 1870 to 1871 forced the Viardots to leave Baden-Baden, and Turgenev followed them, first to London and then to Paris. A similar reorientation occurred in Turgenev's views. The once ardent Germanophile became more sober and sadder. He now became an honoured ambassador of Russian culture in the Paris of the 1870s. The writers George Sand, Gustave Flaubert, the Goncourt brothers, the young Émile Zola, and Henry James were only a few of the many illustrious contemporaries with whom he corresponded and who sought his company. He was elected vice president of the Paris international literary congress in 1878, and in 1879 he was awarded an honorary degree by Oxford University. In Russia he was feted on his annual visits.

The literary work of this final period combined nostalgia for the past—eloquently displayed in such beautiful pieces as "A Lear of the Steppes" (1870), "Torrents of Spring" (1872), and "Punin and Baburin" (1874)—with stories of a quasi-fantastic character—"The Song of Triumphant Love" (1881) and "Klara Milich" (1883). Turgenev's final novel, *Virgin Soil* (1877), was designed to recoup his literary reputation in the eyes of the younger generation. Its aim was to portray the dedication and self-sacrifice of young populists who hoped to sow the seeds of revolution in the virgin soil of the Russian peasantry. Despite its realism and his efforts to give the work topicality, it is the least successful of his novels. His last major work, *Poems in Prose*, is remarkable chiefly for its wistfulness and for its famous eulogy to the Russian language. The first edition, in 1878, contained 50 poems; the entire collection of 83 was not published until 1930. He died at Bougival, near Paris, on September 3, (August 22, O.S.), 1883, and he was buried in St. Petersburg.

Last works

Evaluation. Turgenev's work is distinguished from that of his most famous contemporaries by its sophisticated lack of hyperbole, its balance, and its concern for artistic values. His greatest work was always topical, committed literature, having universal appeal in the elegance of the love story and the psychological acuity of the portraiture. He was similarly a letter writer of great charm, wit, and probity. His reputation may have become overshadowed by those of Dostoyevsky and Tolstoy, but his own qualities of lucidity and urbanity and, above all, his sense of the extreme preciousness of the beautiful in life endow his work with a magic that has lasting appeal. For Henry James he was reputedly "the only real beautiful genius." This estimate, for all its extravagance, has been largely endorsed by a century of readers.

MAJOR WORKS

VERSE: *Parasha* (1843); *Razgovor* (1845; *A Conversation*); *Pomeshchik* (1846; *The Landowner*); *Andrey* (1846).

PLAYS: *Neostorozhnost* (1843); *Bezdenezhe* (1846; *A Poor Gentleman*); *Gde tonko, tam i rvyotsya* (1848; *One May Spin a Thread Too Finely*); *Zavtrak u predvoditelya* (performed 1849, printed 1856); *Kholostyak* (1849; *The Bachelor,*

1953); *Razgovor na bolshoy doroge* (performed 1850, printed 1851); *Provintsialka* (1851; *A Provincial Lady*, 1934, 1950); *Mesyats v derevne* (printed 1855, performed 1872; *A Month in the Country*, 1933, 1934); *Nakhlebnik* (printed 1857, performed 1862; *Vecher v Sorrente* (performed 1884, printed 1891).

NOVELS: (works described by the author as *romany*)— *Rudin* (1856; *Dimitri Roudine*, a novel, 1873; *Rudin*, 1947, 1950, 1955); *Dvoryanskoye gnezdo* (1859; *Liza*, 2 vol., 1869; *A Nest of Gentlefolk*, 1959; *Home of the Gentry*, 1970); *Nakanune* (1860; *On the Eve*, 1871, 1950); *Otsy i deti* (1862; *Fathers and Sons*, 1867, 1921, 1950; *Fathers and Children*, 1928, 1947); *Dym* (1867; *Smoke*, 2 vol. 1868; 1 vol., 1928, 1949); *Nov* (1877; *Virgin Soil*, 1877, 1911, reissued 1955).

STORIES OR SHORTER NOVELS: (*razskazy* or *povesti*)—Twenty-two stories, dealing mainly with aspects of rural life, most of them published separately in periodicals from 1847 onward, were collected under the title *Zapiski okhotnika* (1852); and later editions included three more such stories, originally published 1872–74 (*Russian Life in the Interior*, 1855; *A Sportsman's Sketches*, 1932; *A Sportsman's Notebook*, 1950). Collected under the title *Povesti i razskazy*, 3 vol. (1856), were the following "tales" or "stories," which date from 1844 onward (undated English titles are those of the Hapgood translation, 1903–04): "Andrey Kolosov" ("Andrei Kolosoff"); "Bretyor" ("The Bully"); "Tri portreta" ("Three Portraits"); "Zhid" ("The Jew"); "Petushkov" ("Pyetushkoff"); "Dnevnik lishnyago cheloveka" ("The Diary of a Superfluous Man," with "Mumu," 1884); "Tri vstrechi" ("Three Meetings"); "Mumu" ("The Dumb Door Porter," 1862; "Mumu," 1884); "Postoyaly dvor" ("The Inn"); "Dva priyatelya" ("The Two Friends"); "Zatishe" ("The Region of Dead Calm"); "Perepiska" ("A Correspondence"); "Yakov Pasynkov" ("Yákoff Pásynkov"); "Faust." Later short novels and tales (with Hapgood titles as above unless otherwise indicated) include: *Asya* (1858; *Annouchka*, 1884); *Pervaya lyubov* (1860; *First Love*, 1884, 1950); "Prizraki" (1864; "Phantoms"); "Dovolno" (1865; "It Is Enough"); "Istoriya leytenanta Ergunova" (1868; "The Story of Lieutenant Ergúnoff"; *Neschastnaya* (1869; *An Unfortunate Woman*, 1886; *The Unfortunate One*, 1888); *Stepnoy korol Lir* (1870; *A Lear of the Steppe*, 1874); *Veshniye vody* (1872; *Spring Floods*, 1874, 1895); "Punin i Baburin" (1874; "Púnin and Babúrin," 1884); "Son" (1877; "The Dream"); "Pesn torzhestvuyushchey lyubvi" (1881; "The Song of Love Triumphant"); *Klara Milich* (1883).

MISCELLANEOUS WRITINGS OF SPECIAL INTEREST: Obituary article on "Gogol" in *Sovremennik* (1852); essay "Gamlet i Don Kikhot" (1860; *Hamlet and Don Quixote*, 1930); *Literaturnya i zhiteyskiya vospominaniya* (1880; *Literary Reminiscences and Autobiographical Fragments*, 1958); *Stikhotvoreniya v proze*, originally entitled *Senilia* (1878, enlarged edition 1930; *Poems in Prose*, 1883, 1945, 1951).

The earlier Russian collections of Turgenev's works (10 vol., 1880; 12 vol., 1898; 12 vol., 1928–34; 11 vol., 1949; and 12 vol., 1954–58) are superseded by the edition of his complete works and correspondence in 28 volumes (1960–68, supplemented by collections of additional materials). English collections include: *The Novels of Ivan Turgenev*, trans. by Constance Garnett, 15 vol. (1894–99 and 17 vol. 1919–23, with new ed. 1951 ff.); *The Novels and Stories of Iván Turgénieff*, trans. by Isabel F. Hapgood, with introduction by Henry James, 13 vol. (1903–04); *The Plays of Ivan S. Turgenev*, trans. by M.S. Mandell (1924).

BIBLIOGRAPHY

Bibliographies: R.A. GETTMAN, *Turgenev in England and America* (1941); R. YACHNIN and D.H. STAM (comps.), *Turgenev in English* (1962).

Translations: Original translations by CONSTANCE GARNETT, ISABEL F. HAPGOOD, W.R.S. RALSTON *et al.* are seriously dated; many recent translations of major works are available. Useful new translations are: *Turgenev's Literary Reminiscences and Autobiographical Fragments*, trans. by DAVID MAGARSHACK, with an essay by EDMUND WILSON (1958); and *Turgenev's Letters: A Selection*, ed. and trans. by E.H. LEHRMAN (1961).

Biography and criticism: A. YARMOLINSKY, *Turgenev the Man: His Art and His Age* (1926, rev. ed. 1959); DAVID MAGARSHACK, *Turgenev: A Life* (1954), are useful complementary biographies. See also H. GRANJARD, *Ivan Tourguénev et les courants politiques et sociaux de son temps* (1954), a valuable study of Turgenev's political evolution; R.H. FREEBORN, *Turgenev: The Novelist's Novelist* (1960), a guide to Turgenev's novels; E. GARNETT, *Turgenev: A Study* (1917); and A. FITZLYON, *The Price of Genius: A Life of Pauline Viardot* (1964).

(R.H.Fr.)

Turgot, Anne-Robert-Jacques

A high functionary during the reign of Louis XV and, briefly, minister of finance under Louis XVI, Turgot attempted those fiscal, administrative, and political reforms by which the French monarchy might have been preserved. As a result of conflicts with certain of the privileged classes he lost his position and his career was ended. His reforms were subsequently abandoned.

He was born in Paris on May 10, 1727, into an old Norman family whose members had already held some important administrative posts. (His father, Michel-Étienne [1690–1751], was to be *prévôt des marchands*, the head of the Paris municipality, from 1729 to 1740.) Destined for the church, he entered the Seminaire de Saint-Sulpice (1743) and the Sorbonne (1749), exhibiting both as a schoolboy and as an advanced student a precocious but sound maturity of intellect. He was influenced from his adolescence by all the fashionable ideas of his day: scientific curiosity, liberalism, tolerance, and an interest in social evolution. In 1751, on the threshold of ordination, he drew back, explaining to his relatives that it would have been impossible for him always to have lived under false pretenses, being, in fact, a deist. His rare attendance at mass was necessitated by his rank.

From that time on, Turgot's friends comprised such Philosophes as the Marquis de Condorcet and Pierre-Samuel du Pont de Nemours, who were both attached to the famous Physiocratic school of thought, which generally has been regarded as the first scientific school of economics. Late in 1751 he announced his intention of seeking a career in the royal administration and entered the law, becoming a *substitut du procureur général* (deputy solicitor general) in January 1752 and later a *conseiller* (counsellor magistrate) to the Parlement (supreme court of law) in Paris (December 1752).

Early career. In 1753 he bought, as was the custom, the office of *maître des requêtes* (examiner of petitions), thus entering the branch of the magistracy that provided officials for the bureaucracy and that upheld the royal authority. With 39 other *maîtres des requêtes* he was called upon to serve in the Chambre Royale (Royal Chamber), which acted as a supreme court in 1753–54, when the Parlement was exiled for defying the crown. He combined his duties with other forms of intellectual activity. In 1753 he translated into French Josiah Tucker's *Reflections on the Expediency of a Law for the Naturalization of Foreign Protestants* (1752) and the following year published *Lettres sur la tolérance*. Between 1753 and 1756 Turgot accompanied J.-C.-M. Vincent de Gournay, the mentor of the Physiocratic school and an intendant of commerce, on his tours of inspection to various French provinces. By 1761 he had drawn enough attention to himself for Louis XV to accept his nomination as intendant to the province of Limoges. He occupied this post, then considered one of the

The influence of the Physiocratic school

Turgot, portrait by an unknown French artist, 18th century. In the Musée de Versailles.
Giraudon

least desirable available, for 13 years and there displayed his extraordinary capacities as an administrator, reformer, and economist. In 1766 he published his best known work, *Réflexions sur la formation et la distribution des richesses,* to which he was to add—among other famous works—*Lettres sur la liberté du commerce des grains* (1770; "Letters on the Freedom of the Grain Trade"). He introduced new methods to the peasant region he administered, substituting a small tax in money for the *corvée* (unpaid work required of peasants for the upkeep of roads); compiling a land register (*cadastre*) for tax purposes; and combatting the famine of 1770–71, during which—despite opposition—he maintained the free commerce in grain. He was appointed comptroller general by Louis XVI on August 24, 1774.

Ministry. Turgot was all that a successful courtier should not be. Large and fat, with regular and quite distinguished features, he was nevertheless a shy and awkward bachelor who blushed easily, spoke with hesitation, and was rarely convivially gay. Though his customary serious manner was tinged with humour, he was not persuasive and could irritate a questioner with the brusqueness of his statements, his theoretical cast of thought, and the suppressed irony of his half smile.

Realizing that the young king was inexperienced and wishing to avoid political storms, Turgot temporized during the first days of his ministry, but later, feeling himself threatened by his adversaries, a frenzy for public service drove him to accumulate reforms. He introduced his Six Edicts in 1776. Four of them (suppressing certain dues and offices) were of no great importance, and the fifth (suppressing the guilds of Paris) encountered no serious opposition. It was against the sixth edict, that abolishing the *corvée,* that his enemies, who defended privilege, concentrated their attack. Appealing in vain to the good sense and courage of the young king from whom he had been alienated by a coalition of financiers, place-holders, privileged classes, and the religious party at court, he saw his reforms abandoned and, after his dismissal on May 12, 1776, forgotten. Five years later, on March 18, 1781, having published nothing since his public disgrace, he died in Paris attended by a few friends.

The Six Edicts

BIBLIOGRAPHY. The best modern work on Turgot is by the French politician EDGAR FAURE, *La Disgrâce de Turgot,* 2 vol. (1961). Earlier but nevertheless useful works are w. WALKER STEPHENS (ed.), *The Life and Writings of Turgot* (1895); and DOUGLAS DAKIN, *Turgot and the Ancien Régime in France* (1939). Other significant works are the biography by Turgot's contemporary, P.S. DUPONT DE NEMOURS, *Mémoires sur la vie et les ouvrages de M. Turgot* (1782); H. HAUSER, "Turgot," in *La Grande Encyclopédie,* vol. 31; GUSTAVE SCHELLE, *Turgot* (1909); and F. ALENGRY, *Turgot (1727–1781) homme privé, homme d'État* (1942). The complete works of Turgot have been edited by GUSTAVE SCHELLE, 5 vol. (1913–33). B. CAZES has published extracts from his works under the title *Turgot, écrits économiques* (1970).

(Je.B.)

Turkey

Turkey (Türkiye) is a country of the Middle East lying partly in Asia and partly in Europe. Its location in two continents has been a central factor in its history, culture, and politics; Turkey has often been called a bridge between East and West. The country's area of 301,380 square miles (780,576 square kilometres) includes 9,158 square miles in European Turkey, known as Eastern Thrace (Turkish Trakya), and a larger area of 292,222 square miles in Asia, called Anatolia (Turkish Anadolu, derived from the Greek word *anatolē,* "sunrise"—*i.e.,* eastern land). İmroz (Imbros) and Bozca Ada (Tenedos) islands in the Aegean Sea also belong to Turkey.

Turkey is bounded on the east by Iran and the Soviet Union, on the south by Iraq and Syria, and on the west by Greece and Bulgaria. Turkey in Europe is separated from Anatolia by the Bosporus, the Sea of Marmara, and the Dardanelles Strait (anciently called the Hellespont), which form the only sea passage between the Black Sea and the Mediterranean. During the 17th century, when Turkish expansion was at its peak, the Ottoman Empire reached into central Europe to include

what is now Romania, Hungary, and most of present-day Yugoslavia. It also included what is now Syria, Iraq, Israel, Egypt, and North Africa as far west as Algeria.

THE LANDSCAPE

The natural environment. *Relief.* Turkey forms part of the belt of young mountain ranges that run from the Balkan Peninsula to Iran. The mean altitude of the country is over 3,600 feet, and it increases eastward to above 6,560 feet. Lofty mountains are interspersed with depressions surrounded by steep slopes and high plateaus. Less than 9 percent of Turkey's area consists of level or gently sloping lands. Lowlands are mainly in the coastal areas. Turkey acquired its rugged relief in relatively recent geological times, and it is still a very active region of the Earth's crust, as is shown by frequent tremors in some areas and occasional destructive earthquakes.

The mountainous relief is dominated in the north and south by ranges of over 10,000 feet that encircle the Central Anatolian Plateau and separate it from the narrow coastal lowlands. North of the central plateau the Pontic Mountains follow the contour of the southern shore of the Black Sea, their altitude increasing eastward to the highest peak in Kaçkar Dağı (12,917 feet [3,937 metres]), where traces of Quaternary glaciation (occurring during the last 2,500,000 years) are extensive and where even today small glaciers are found. South of the central plateau are the Taurus Mountains, composed of several ranges that extend in broad arches along the Mediterranean coast and north of Syria. Their highest points are Mt. Aladag (12,250 feet [3,734 metres]), in the middle Taurus, and the intensely glaciated Cilo Dağı (13,675 feet [4,168 metres]), in the southeastern Taurus. The Taurus system is composed mainly of limestone and therefore is full of caves, potholes, and underground streams, all characteristic of limestone formations.

Central Anatolia is a semi-arid plateau with a core of older rocks overlain by horizontal or slightly tilted Tertiary deposits (from 65,000,000 to 2,500,000 years ago). It is divided into several basins, some of which were prehistoric lakes. Today the greater part of the region is an interior basin with a number of shallow salt lakes (*e.g.,* Tuz Gölü, covering 635 square miles with a depth of only one or two feet) and extensive eroded areas—as around Ürgüp, near the middle course of the Kızıl Irmak River, where there are cave dwellings, underground churches, and subterranean villages. The region is rich in young volcanic features, like the glacier-crowned Erciyes Dağı (12,848 feet [3,916 metres]), the highest point of central Anatolia; many volcanic cones, crater lakes, and explosion pits lie between Konya and Kayseri.

Central Anatolia

Eastern Anatolia is composed of lofty ranges and recent volcanic cones, such as Ağrı Dağı (Mt. Ararat, the highest peak in Turkey with an altitude of 16,945 feet [5,165 metres]—the legendary site where Noah's ark came to rest) and Süphan Dağı (14,547 feet [4,434 metres]). These rise above high plateaus often covered by extensive lava flows. The plateaus are interrupted by basins, one of which is occupied by Lake Van, a salt lake formed by the action of the now-extinct volcano of Nemrut Dağı, which last erupted in 1441.

Western Anatolia, known as the Aegean region, has elongated mountain ridges separated by depressed floors: a system of young, roughly parallel fault lines running east and west. It includes, from north to south, the valleys of Bakır Çayı (ancient Caicus); Gediz (Hermus); Küçükmenderes (Cayster), with the ruins of Ephesus; and Büyükmenderes Nehri (Maeander), where there are the remains of several ancient towns, including Miletus. These valleys form corridors leading from the Aegean up to the plateau.

The landforms of northwestern Turkey around the Sea of Marmara are simple. Thrace is a large basin bounded by mountains of moderate height on the north (Istranca Dağları) and south (Ganos Dağı) and by low plateaus 300 to 500 feet in altitude around the Bosporus on the east. The semi-arid central part of Thrace, filled by recent deposits, forms a rolling plain. The plateaus around Istanbul are deeply dissected by valleys. One of these, the

Bosporus, a former river valley drowned by the rising sea level after the last glaciers melted, is now the channel between the Sea of Marmara and the Black Sea. The Dardanelles, linking the Sea of Marmara at its other end to the Aegean, originated in the same way.

Drainage and soils. The water divide between the drainage basins of the Atlantic and Indian oceans runs obliquely through eastern Anatolia. The land east of the divide drains to the Caspian through the Kuruçay and Aras rivers and to the Persian Gulf through the Euphrates and Tigris rivers. The country west and north of the main divide drains to the Black Sea through the Kızıl Irmak (Halys) and Sakarya rivers. The Yeşil Irmak (Iris) also empties into the Black Sea. The western regions of the country drain to the Sea of Marmara through the Susurluk (Macestus) river and to the Aegean through the Gediz (Hermus) and the Büyükmenderes (Maeander) rivers. The principal rivers of the Mediterranean basin are the Göksu (Calycadnus), Seyhan (Sarus), Ceyhan (Pyramus), and the lower course of the Orontes (Asi). Approximately one-seventh of Turkey has no exterior drainage. Turkish rivers have generally irregular and shallow beds, and their seasonal changes in depth make them unsuitable for navigation.

The principal lakes of the country are Lake Van, 1,443 square miles, over 330 feet deep, and highly saline, in eastern Anatolia; Tuz Gölü (Salt Lake), 635 square miles and only one or two feet deep, in central Anatolia; and the freshwater lakes Beyşehir, Eğridir, and Burdur, northeast of the Gulf of Antalya.

Turkey has a variety of soil types, reflecting great differences in climate, geology, and vegetation. An outer belt of red and reddish-brown podzolic soils extends over the humid northern and southern marginal regions. The extremely humid eastern Black Sea coasts have strongly acid red soils, whereas the drier northwestern part of the country is covered by slightly acid brown and yellowish-brown podzolic soils. In the Mediterranean area, red and podzolic soil alternates frequently with patches of red clayey soil and in the northwest with rich limy soil. Most of the interior is covered by alkaline, brown and reddish-brown steppe soils. In the driest core of central Anatolia even patches of desertic gray soils occur, and saline soils cover considerable areas. The transitional regions between the dry interior and the humid margins are generally occupied by a belt of brown forest soils. Turkey faces a serious problem in soil erosion, resulting from extensive deforestation that began in the Hellenistic and Roman periods and continued in later times.

Climate. The climate is varied, depending largely on geographic factors. The coastal areas are generally humid, while the interior is semi-arid because it is cut off from the rain-bearing winds by mountain ranges. The northern slopes of the Black Sea mountains receive heavy rain even during summer. Annual rainfall in the coastal areas is more than 27 inches and as much as 96 inches in the eastern Black Sea region. In most of central Anatolia average annual precipitation varies between 10 and 14 inches. Areas of moderate rainfall (15 to 24 inches) include the Marmara and Aegean regions and southeastern and eastern Anatolia.

The low coastal areas have relatively high annual temperatures and warm winters. Along the Mediterranean coast frosts are rare, and snowfall is almost unknown. In the interior, on the other hand, winter temperatures are often below freezing, and in the northeastern plateaus the winters are very cold. Snow cover lasts 20 to 40 days in central Anatolia and more than 120 days in the northeast. The regional differences are much less marked in summer. Four climatic regions can be distinguished. The south and west coasts have a Mediterranean climate with hot, dry summers and mild, rainy winters; the mean annual temperature is about 68° F (20° C) and ranges from 53° F (11° C) in the coldest month to 84° F (29° C) in the warmest month. The Black Sea coast enjoys warm summers, mild winters, and a fair amount of rainfall throughout the year; the mean annual temperature is about 58° F (14° C), ranging from 44° F (7° C) in the coldest month to 73° F (23° C) in the warmest month.

The high northeastern plateaus have fairly warm summers but very severe winters, with maximum precipitation in the summer; the mean annual temperature is about 39° F (4° C), ranging from 10° F (−12° C) in the coldest month to 64° F (18° C) in the hottest. The semi-arid interior and southeast have cold, moist winters and hot, dry summers; the mean annual temperature is about 53° F (12° C), ranging from 32° F (0° C) in the coldest month to 74° F (23° C) in the warmest.

Plant and animal life. Large areas in the south, west, and northwest are covered by a Mediterranean vegetation, consisting mainly of thick, scrubby underbrush in the lowlands and deciduous or coniferous forests at higher altitudes up to the timberline (6,000 or 7,000 feet). The humid northern margins of the country are the most densely wooded region of Turkey. On the eastern Black Sea there are subtropical forests. The Anatolian interior is a region of steppes. Forests, mostly oak and coniferous trees, occur only on the elevated parts.

Turkey is fairly rich in wild animals and game birds. The wolf, fox, boar, wildcat, beaver, marten, jackal, hyena, bear, deer, gazelle, and mountain goat are among the animals still found in secluded and wooded regions. Domestic animals include the buffalo, Angora goat (on the Central Plateau), and camel. Major game birds are partridge, wild goose, quail, and bustard.

Geographic regions. *The Black Sea Coast.* Extending along the northern margins of the country from the Soviet frontier in the east to the lower course of the Sakarya River in the west is a mountainous area with abundant precipitation at all seasons. It is densely wooded, comprising more than one-fourth of Turkey's forested areas. It also has the highest rural population density, in some local areas exceeding 500 inhabitants per square mile. The region is mainly agricultural, corn (maize) being the dominant field crop and staple food. Tea is grown in the most eastern coastal strip, hazelnuts around Giresun and Ordu, and tobacco in Samsun and Trabzon. West of Sinop and south of the mountains, the transition toward the Marmara region and the Anatolian interior is marked by increasing acreage in wheat and fallow land. The principal mineral resources of the region are copper in the east (at Murgul) and coal in the west (the Ereğli-Zonguldak Basin). Samsun, Zonguldak, and Trabzon (site of a university) are the leading towns and ports.

The Marmara region. The areas adjacent to the Sea of Marmara, including Thrace, are the most heavily urbanized of the country. The principal cities are, in decreasing order of size, Istanbul (formerly Constantinople), Bursa, İzmit, Adapazarı, and Edirne. Istanbul, situated at the Bosporus, is Turkey's leading industrial, commercial, and cultural centre. The Marmara region is economically the most developed area of Turkey. Its agriculture is variegated, including tobacco, wheat, rice, sunflower, corn, olives, grapes, and natural silk. On the straits and coasts of the Sea of Marmara fishing is well developed. The leading manufacturing districts are around Istanbul and in a narrow coastal strip between Istanbul and İzmit.

The Aegean region. The coastal area from the Dardanelles on the north to the vicinity of Rhodes on the south is densely populated and economically one of the most advanced regions of the country. Its wealth rests on the production of several export crops, including tobacco (more than 50 percent of Turkey's total production), cotton (30 percent of the total), high-quality grapes suitable for drying, olives (more than 50 percent of the Turkish output), and figs. The main cities are İzmir (the leading export outlet of Turkey and site of a university), Manisa, and Aydın. The area draws many tourists with its beaches and historical sites (Pergamum, Ephesus, Miletus). Between the Aegean region and central Anatolia there is a high, thinly populated area specializing in grain and livestock production; in the 1960s it also produced much of the Western world's supply of opium.

Mediterranean region. Turkey's Mediterranean region extends from Rhodes to the Syrian frontier, and is occupied largely by the Taurus Mountains. Principal passes in the Taurus Mountains connecting the interior plateaus with the narrow coastal strip are the Külek Boğazı, lead-

The rivers of Turkey

Four climatic regions

The Taurus Mountains

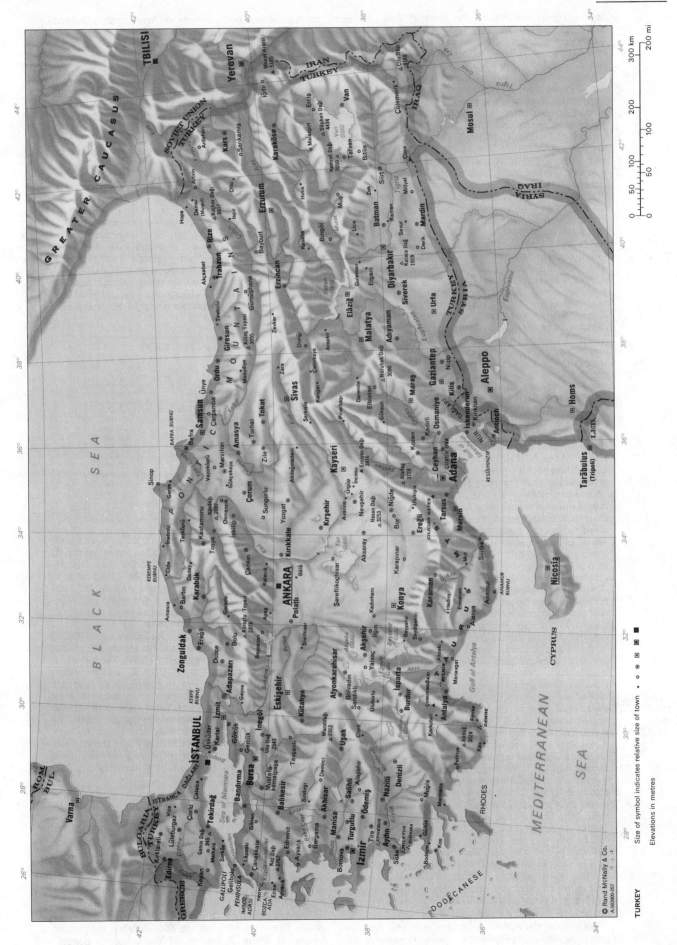

TBILISI

Yerevan

IRAN
TURKEY

GREATER CAUCASUS

SOVIET UNION
TURKEY

Mount Ararat
5185 △

Van

Kars

Karaköse

Erciş

Şiphan Dağı
4434

Malazgirt

IRAQ

Mosul

Ağrı

Sarıkamış

Ardahan

Artvin

Oltu

Hınıs

Nemrut Dağı
3050 △

Van
Gölü

Tatvan

Bitlis

Muş

Mosul

Damar
(Muş)

Kaçkar Dağı
3937 △

Erzurum

İspir

Bayburt

Kelkit

Bingöl

Lice

Siirt

Zok

Midyat

Cizre

Çölemerik

SYRIA
IRAQ

Hopa

Rize

Trabzon

Akçaabat

Tirebolu

Gümüşhane

PONTIC MOUNTAINS

Erzincan

Murat

Batman

Raman

Savur

Mardin

Derik

Karaca Dağı
1919 △

TURKEY
SYRIA

Euphrates

Giresun

Ordu

Ünye

Kılınç Tepesi
3095 △

Mesudiye

Zavker

Diyarbakır

Ergani

Güleman

Siverek

Urfa

Nizip

Euphrates

Samsun

Bafra

C. Çarşamba

Amasya

Turhal

Zile

Tokat

Kızıl

Sivas

Zara

Şarkışla

Kangal

Çetinkaya

Divriği

Darende

Malatya

3090 △
Nurhak Dağı

Elbistan

Adıyaman

Gaziantep

Kilis

Aleppo

BAFRA BURNU

Bafra

Sinop

Vezirköprü

Merzifon

Gökçeağaç

Çorum

Sungurlu

Yozgat

Aladağmadeni

Erciyes Dağı
3916 △

Kayseri

Ürgüp

İncesu

Pınarbaşı

Göksun

Kozan

Kadirli

Osmaniye

İskenderun

Kırıkhan

Antioch

NUR DAĞLARI

Homs

Tarābulus
(Tripoli)

KEREMPE
BURNU

Cide

İnebolu

Taşköprü

Kastamonu

Küradağı
2087 △

Osmancık

İskilip

Tosya

Çankırı

Kırşehir

Aksaray

Avanos

Nevşehir

Hasan Dağı
3253 △

Niğde

Bor

Ulukışla

Ereğli

Tarsus

Mersin

Ceyhan

Adana

ÇUKUR OVA

3724 △
Aladağ

Seyhan

CILICIAN GATES

Mut

Silifke

Nicosia

KERPE
BURNU

Amasra

Bartın

Karabük

Daday

Kalecik

ANKARA

Polatlı

Bala

Şereflikoçhisar

Tuz Gölü

Kadınhanı

Karapınar

Konya

Karaman

Hadim

Ermenek

ANAMUR
BURNU

Anamur

CYPRUS

Zonguldak

Ereğli

Bolu

Düzce

Gerede

Beypazarı

Ayaş

Küroğlu Tepesi
2378 △

Sivrihisar

Kırıkkale

Kızıl

Akşehir
Gölü

Akşehir

Ilgın

Beyşehir

Beyşehir
Gölü

Seydişehir

Alanya

TAURUS

Adapazarı

Geyve

Sakarya

Eskişehir

Kütahya

Afyonkarahisar

Bolvadin

Sandıklı

Yalvaç

Eğridir
Gölü

Burdur
Gölü

Isparta

Burdur

Manavgat

Gulf of Antalya

Antalya

İzmit

İnegöl

Gölcük

Uludağ
2543 △

Bursa

Muratdağı
2312 △

Uşak

Civril

Dinar

Uluborlu

Çivril

Gelibolu
PENINSULA

İSTANBUL

Üsküdar

Kartal

Boğazı

Gemlik

Mustafa-
kemalpaşa

Tavşanlı

Simav

Demirci

Akhisar

Salihli

Alaşehir

Nazilli

Denizli

Muğla

Korkuteli

Akdağ
3024 △

Finike

Kaş

DEMRE

İstranca Dağları

Tekirdağ

Çatalca

Bandırma

Balıkesir

Sındırgı

Simav

Manisa

Turgutlu

Ödemiş

Tire

Aydın

Söke

Gülük

ROM
BUL

Varna

BULGARIA
TURKEY

Kırklareli

Lüleburgaz

Vize

Çorlu

Sea of Marmara

GREECE
TURKEY

Edirne

Keşan

Ganos Dağı
945 △

Şarköy

Gören

Edremit

Bergama

Bornova

İzmir

EPHESUS

MILETUS

DIDYMA

Bodrum

Kos

RHODES

MEDITERRANEAN SEA

DODECANESE

Meriç

Enez

GALLIPOLI

İMROZ
ADASI

BOZCA
ADA

TROY

Küçük Menderes

Büyük Menderes

Aksu

Göksu

Seyhan

Ceyhan

Tigris

Great Zab

Lesser Zab

BLACK SEA

TURKEY

A-563900-257

Size of symbol indicates relative size of town • ∘ ⊙ ⊡ ■

Elevations in metres

200 km
300 km
200 mi
0 50 100 200

ing to Tarsus and Adana; the Sertavul Pass, between Karaman and Silifke; and the Çubukboğazı pass, between the lake district and Antalya in the west. The Amanus Dağları (mountains) bordering the Gulf of Iskenderun are crossed by the Belen Pass. The region has several subregions: the sparsely populated limestone plateaus of Taşeli in the middle; the lake district in the west with its continental climate, where grain is grown; and the intensively cultivated, densely populated coastal plains. Principal cities of the region include Adana, an important commercial and industrial centre; Mersin; İskenderun (Alexandretta); Antalya; and Gaziantep. The coastal areas produce crops such as cotton (60 percent of Turkey's output), sesame, citrus fruits (more than 90 percent of the country's production), early vegetables, and bananas. The higher parts of the region have relatively little arable land and much soil erosion; grain and livestock are produced, and there is pastoral nomadism among the Yürüks.

Central Anatolia. The middle of the Anatolian plain has a continental steppe climate and scanty rainfall. Grain occupies over 90 percent of the arable land (40 percent of the country's wheat production). More than one-third of Turkey's sheep and nearly all of its Angora goats are raised there. The chief commercial and industrial centres are Ankara (capital of Turkey), Eskişehir, Konya, Kayseri, and Sivas.

Eastern Anatolia. The eastern part of the interior is a high and extremely rugged region with coniferous forests and mountain pastures in the northeast and wooded steppes in the south. Eastern Anatolia is the most thinly populated region of the country, with population densities as low as 13 people per square mile in some areas. Farming is difficult because of the long, severe winters, steep slopes, and eroded soil. Grain, chiefly summer wheat and barley, is the dominant crop. In the humid northeast, beef and dairy cattle are raised; in the south there are pastoral nomads who raise sheep and goats. Eastern Anatolia is rich in mineral resources (iron ore at Divriği, copper at Ergani, chrome at Guleman). The principal cities are Erzurum, Malatya, Elâzığ, and Van.

Southeastern Anatolia. At the foot of the Taurus mountains is a barren plateau drained by the Tigris and Euphrates rivers. Agriculture is confined mainly to irrigated valleys and basins (wheat, rice, vegetables, grapes). Much of the population is nomadic or seminomadic. Turkey's only oil fields are at Raman and Garzan, linked by pipeline to the port of İskenderun. The principal urban centres are Gaziantep, Urfa, and Diyarbakır.

Cultural landscape. *Rural settlements.* Turkey is essentially an agricultural country, and more than 60 percent of its population live in rural areas. There are around 35,000 rural settlements. In physical form these differ from region to region: wooden houses are typical in the Black Sea area; sun-dried bricks and flat roofs prevail in the semi-arid interior, and stone is the dominant building material in the Taurus Mountains, the Aegean region, and parts of Eastern Anatolia.

Types of rural settlements

Rural settlement types range from single-residence units and several types of temporarily occupied settlements to agglomerated villages. The types correspond to different natural and economic conditions and to different stages in the evolution of land occupancy. Single rural settlement units and dispersed settlements occur in the eastern and western Black Sea regions, in eastern Anatolia, and in the Taurus Mountains. In eastern Anatolia they are associated with stock raising, while in the eastern Black Sea region they are small farmsteads, based on a subsistence agriculture. In the karst (limestone sink) regions of the Taurus area, the scattered distribution of soil in small depressions accounts for the occurrence of dispersed settlements and single-residence units. In the Mediterranean coastal strip, single rural settlement units usually consist of a two-story dwelling surrounded by a large field in which cash crops such as bananas, citrus fruits, and early vegetables are cultivated; the lower story of the house is used for storage.

Between the single rural settlement units and the more prevalent agglomerated villages, there are many transitional types. A *mahalle* consists of a group of single

rural settlement units. *Divan*s, occurring mainly in northern Anatolia, comprise a number of *mahalle*s organized into a single administrative unit. *Mezraa*s are settlements founded on agricultural lands that were originally inhabited only temporarily during plowing and harvesting but later became permanently settled villages or towns. Among temporary settlements, *kom*s are usually smaller than *mezraa*s. *Yayla*s are temporary summer rural settlements, associated with nomadism. Every nomadic group in southeastern Anatolia or in the Taurus Mountains has its own *yayla*, used solely for pasture. The practice of migrating between summer-dry lowlands and humid mountain pastures has resulted in most permanently inhabited villages in many regions of Turkey possessing one or more *yayla*s. *Kişla*s (literally, "winter quarters") are the sheltered winter quarters of nomads or former nomads. A considerable number of *yayla*s and *kişla*s have in time been transformed into permanent settlements.

Urban settlements. Approximately 40 percent of Turkey's population is located in municipalities of more than 10,000 inhabitants. The percentage of urban population is relatively high in the northwestern and western parts of the country, in northwestern central Anatolia, and around the Gulf of İskenderun. Most towns have fewer than 25,000 inhabitants. Only 20 had more than 100,000 inhabitants in 1970.

The growing towns

Table 1: Cities with More Than 100,000 Inhabitants (1970)			
	population		population
Ankara*	1,209,000	Erzurum	135,000
Istanbul	2,248,000	Samsun	134,000
İzmir	521,000	Sivas	133,000
Adana	356,000	Malatya	130,000
Bursa	276,000	İzmit	123,000
Gaziantep	226,000	Mersin	114,000
Eskişehir	216,000	Elâzığ	108,000
Konya	201,000	Maraş	105,000
Kayseri	168,000	Adapazarı	102,000
Diyarbakır	139,000	Urfa	100,000
*Capital city.			

More than half of the towns with more than 25,000 inhabitants are concentrated around the Sea of Marmara, in the western coastal region, and in the Adana subregion. Most are so old that they may be traced back to pre-Roman or Roman times. The great majority are commercial centres benefiting from a favourable location. Others are administrative, manufacturing, mining, or port centres, or a combination of these.

Istanbul, Ankara, and İzmir all had more than 500,000 inhabitants in the early 1970s, and the biggest city, Istanbul, had a population exceeding 2,200,000. The last was a conurbation extending 30 miles from the former village of Küçükçekmece on the west to Pendik on the east and 12 miles north along the Bosporus. Surrounding it is an industrial area that produces nearly one-third of the country's manufacturing output. Ankara, the capital of Turkey, was a flourishing trading centre and military base under Roman rule. Since World War I the city had grown very rapidly, and in 1970 it had more than 1,200,000 inhabitants. İzmir, a busy commercial city, had more than 520,000 inhabitants.

PEOPLE AND POPULATION

Languages, races, and religions. *Linguistic groups.* Turkish is the mother tongue of over 90 percent of the country's population. Modern Turkish, one of the southwestern groups of the Turkic family of languages, has been derived from Ottoman Turkish through a long nationalistic effort to purify it of the Arabic and Persian words and idioms that invaded the literary language during the Ottoman Empire. Turkish is written in Latin script.

The principal linguistic minority groups are Kurds and Arabs. Kurdish (including the Zaza dialect), the mother tongue of about 7 percent of the country's population, is widely spoken by a predominantly rural popula-

Table 2: Turkey, Area and Population

Regions (bölgeler)	area* sq mi	sq km	population 1965 census	1970 census†
Black Sea Coast				
Provinces (iller)				
Artvin	2,871	7,436	210,000	226,000
Bolu	4,267	11,051	384,000	403,000
Giresun	2,677	6,934	428,000	447,000
Kastamonu	5,061	13,108	442,000	447,000
Ordu	2,317	6,001	544,000	607,000
Rize	1,514	3,920	281,000	318,000
Sakarya	1,721	4,457	404,000	456,000
Samsun	3,698	9,579	756,000	822,000
Sinop	2,263	5,862	266,000	265,000
Trabzon	1,809	4,685	596,000	662,000
Zonguldak	3,332	8,629	650,000	742,000
Central Anatolia				
Provinces				
Adıyaman	2,940	7,614	267,000	305,000
Amasya	2,131	5,520	286,000	310,000
Ankara	11,859	30,715	1,644,000	2,023,000
Çankırı	3,263	8,451	251,000	263,000
Çorum	4,950	12,820	486,000	521,000
Kayseri	6,532	16,917	536,000	610,000
Kırşehir	2,537	6,570	197,000	212,000
Konya	18,309	47,420	1,123,000	1,290,000
Malatya	4,754	12,313	453,000	515,000
Maraş	5,532	14,327	438,000	523,000
Nevşehir	2,111	5,467	203,000	232,000
Niğde	5,519	14,294	362,000	409,000
Sivas	10,999	28,488	705,000	729,000
Tokat	3,845	9,958	495,000	544,000
Yozgat	5,453	14,123	438,000	470,000
East Anatolia				
Provinces				
Ağrı	4,392	11,376	247,000	293,000
Bingöl	3,137	8,125	151,000	178,000
Bitlis	2,590	6,707	154,000	185,000
Diyarbakır	5,928	15,354	476,000	575,000
Elâzığ	3,533	9,151	323,000	378,000
Erzincan	4,596	11,903	259,000	278,000
Erzurum	9,678	25,066	628,000	686,000
Gümüşhane	3,949	10,227	263,000	282,000
Hakkâri	3,676	9,521	84,000	103,000
Kars	7,165	18,557	606,000	663,000
Muş	3,164	8,196	199,000	234,000
Siirt	4,248	11,003	265,000	330,000
Tunceli	3,002	7,774	154,000	160,000
Van	7,363	19,069	267,000	326,000
Marmara and				
Aegean Coasts				
Provinces				
Aydın	3,092	8,007	525,000	567,000
Balıkesir	5,518	14,292	708,000	753,000
Bursa	4,268	11,053	756,000	848,000
Çanakkale‡	3,147	8,152	300,000	360,000 §
Istanbul ‖	896	2,320	537,000	¶
İzmir	4,623	11,973	1,235,000	1,430,000
Kocaeli	1,539	3,986	336,000	384,000
Manisa	5,332	13,810	749,000	793,000
Muğla	5,150	13,338	335,000	372,000
Mediterranean Coast				
Provinces				
Adana	6,661	17,253	903,000	1,035,000
Antalya	7,950	20,591	487,000	577,000
Hatay	2,086	5,403	506,000	596,000
İçel	6,121	15,853	511,000	596,000
South East Anatolia				
Provinces				
Gaziantep	2,951	7,642	511,000	605,000
Mardin	4,927	12,760	398,000	458,000
Urfa	7,175	18,584	451,000	542,000
Thrace				
Provinces				
Çanakkale♀	612	1,585	50,000	§
Edirne	2,419	6,266	303,000	318,000
Istanbulδ	1,310	3,392	1,756,000	2,995,000¶
Kırklareli	2,529	6,550	258,000	257,000
Tekirdağ	2,401	6,218	287,000	297,000
West Anatolia				
Provinces				
Afyonkarahisar	5,494	14,230	502,000	543,000
Bilecik	1,559	4,308	139,000	139,000
Burdur	2,659	6,887	195,000	211,000
Denizli	4,582	11,868	463,000	512,000
Eskişehir	5,271	13,652	415,000	463,000
İsparta	3,449	8,933	266,000	300,000
Kütahya	4,585	11,875	398,000	483,000
Uşak	2,062	5,341	191,000	208,000
Total Turkey	297,812	771,333	31,391,000▢	35,667,000▢
	301,380	780,576		

*Areas for provinces are 1965 census areas and purportedly exclude lakes. Of the two country total area figures, which are as of 1969, the first is the land area, the second the total area.   †Preliminary.   ‡Part of this province lies in the Thrace region; area and population figures for the part that lies in the Marmara and Aegean Coasts region are for the districts of Ayvacık, Bayramiç, Biga, Bozcaada, Çan, Ezine, Lâpseki, and Yenice.   §Population for the entire province is given under the Marmara and Aegean Coasts region because no breakdown for the province was available.   ‖Part of this province lies in the Thrace region; area and population figures for the part that lies in the Marmara and Aegean Coasts region are for the districts of Adalar, Beykoz, Kadiköy, Üsküdar, Kartal, Şile, and Yalova.   ¶Population for the entire province of Istanbul is given under the Thrace region because no breakdown for the province was available.   ♀Part of this province lies in the Marmara and Aegean Coasts region; area and population figures for the part that lies in the Thrace region are for the districts of Eceabat, Gelibolu, and İmroz.   δPart of this province lies in the Marmara and Aegean Coasts region; area and population figures for the part that lies in Thrace region are for the districts of Bakirköy, Beşiktaş, Beyoğlu, Eminönü, Eyüp, Fatih, Gaziosmanpaşa, Sarıyer, Şişli, Zeytinburnu, Çatalca, and Silivri.   ▢Figures do not add to total given because of rounding.
Source: Official government figures.

tion in the eastern and southeastern regions. Arabic is spoken by 1.2 percent of the population, principally in parts of southeastern Anatolia. Greek, Armenian, and Yiddish are spoken by small groups in the larger cities, mainly in Istanbul. Most Turkish Jews are descendants of Jews expelled from Spain and speak a kind of Spanish mingled with some Turkish words; others speak Yiddish.

Ethnic groups. Turkey has been a melting pot of racially and culturally distinct groups since early prehistoric times. It was penetrated, settled, or ruled by Hittites, Phrygians, and Gauls from the north and northwest; by Greeks and Macedonians from the west; and by Parthians and Mongols from the east. The most decisive influence was the incursion of Turks from the east, who introduced a new element of mixed Mediterranean-Mongoloid origin into the country's ethnic composition. The rise and decline of the Ottoman Empire contributed to the racial mixture, particularly during the empire's decline, when many Muslim groups living in former Turkish territories in southeastern Europe and in countries around the Black Sea migrated to the home country. It is at present almost impossible to define an average Turk ethnically. He may be blond and blue-eyed or even red haired; he may be of roundheaded alpine stock with dark hair and eyes; he

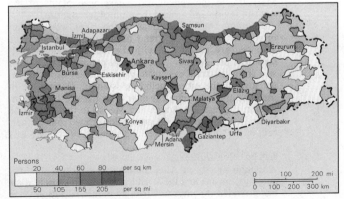

Population density of Turkey.

may be of longheaded Mediterranean stock; or he may be Mongoloid with high cheekbones. The dominant stock seems to be Mediterranean-Turkic, giving way to Mediterranean in western and southern coastal areas and mixed with Alpine stock in the interior and the east.

Religious groups. Over 99 percent of the country's

Population
growth

population are Muslims. The Sunnī rite is predominant, followed closely by the Shīʿite. Christians are few: in 1965 there were about 74,000 Orthodox Christians (mostly Greeks), 70,000 Gregorians (mostly Armenians), and 26,000 Roman Catholics. There were 18,000 Jews. The Christian and Jewish minorities live mainly in Istanbul, Ankara, and İzmir. In the *il* of Mardin in southeastern Anatolia a community of 22,000 Nestorians has survived. Religion and the state were strictly separated in Turkey after the foundation of the republic in 1923.

Demographic trends. Turkey has had one of the highest rates of population increase in the world. Total population, only 13,648,000 in 1927, almost tripled in the following 43 years to exceed 35,000,000 in 1970. Between 1950 and 1970 the annual average rate of population growth was approximately 27 per 1,000.

The rapid increase in Turkey's population is largely the consequence of a high birth rate, estimated at about 40 per 1,000 in recent decades. The average death rate, on the other hand, was believed to be around 15 per 1,000 in the same period and as low as 11 per 1,000 for the urban population. No detailed statistical data have been published for rural birth and death rates and their geographical distribution. It is known, however, that in rural regions of Turkey both the birth and death rates are considerably higher than in urban areas. The highest birth rates occur in underdeveloped eastern and southeastern Anatolia, where the average time interval between two successive births in the same family is only 22.7 months. The metropolitan areas of Istanbul, Ankara, and İzmir have the lowest birth rates in the country and the largest average time interval (33.2 months) between successive births in the same family.

As in other countries with high rates of natural increase, Turkey's population is young. About 66 percent of the population were under 30 years of age in 1970, and only 7.2 percent were 60 and over. Males outnumbered females by 455,000, but females predominated in rural areas because of migration of males to the cities.

In the 1960s and 1970s large numbers of Turks emigrated to western Europe as workers. In 1970, 300,000 were living in West Germany, and 100,000 in Switzerland, Belgium, and The Netherlands. Emigration is regulated by mutual agreement among the countries concerned.

Although the population density rose from 45 per square mile in 1927 to 118 in 1970, Turkey was not heavily populated in comparison with other countries. There were striking differences between the sparsely populated areas of Anatolia and the dense agglomerations in the northern and western parts of the country, in which over 40 percent of the population lived. The most densely inhabited area was the eastern Black Sea coastal strip, averaging over 260 people per square mile. Relatively high population densities also occurred around the Sea of Marmara, in the agriculturally developed plains of the Aegean region and around the Gulf of İskenderun.

Migration from rural areas to the cities was another important demographic trend of the second half of the 20th century, associated with the increasing industrialization of the country. The general pattern of migration was from the rural eastern *iller* (provinces) of the country toward the cities, including Istanbul, Zonguldak in the coal and metallurgical district in the northwest, Ankara in the interior, Adana and Mersin in the south, and İzmir in the west. Urban population grew from 24 percent of the total in 1927 to 38.7 percent in 1970.   (S.Er.)

THE NATIONAL ECONOMY

Although mostly in Asia, the country's economy is oriented to Europe and the Western world. This orientation has provided the impetus for rapid industrialization since 1950. At the same time, Turkey has close economic links with Iran and Pakistan within the framework of Regional Cooperation for Development (RCD), with other countries in the Middle East, and with eastern Europe.

Gross national product (GNP) rose by an average of about 6.5 percent per annum in real terms in the 1960s. Because the population continued to increase by 2.5 percent per annum, the net improvement in GNP per capita

was just under 4 percent per annum. Turkey's exports, which increased in value by 139 percent (to 6,909,000,000 lire) between 1960 and 1970, are represented chiefly by agricultural produce, mainly cotton, fruit, nuts, and tobacco. Imports increased in the same period by 117 percent (to 9,161,000,000 lire), and the cost of importing development capital brought about a chronic payments deficit. The lire was devalued by two-thirds in August 1970.

National resources.   *Mineral resources.* Turkey is believed to be rich in a wide variety of mineral deposits, but relatively few of these have been exploited on a large scale because of a lack of domestic capital for exploration and exploitation, political pressures that have discouraged wide-scale investment from abroad, a preponderance of large but inefficient state mining concerns, and inadequate processing facilities.

State enterprises dominate the production of hard coal, lignite, copper, sulfur, mercury, iron ore, lead, salt, and chrome; while private producers are the principal exploiters of asbestos, antimony, barites, boron minerals, zinc, meerschaum, manganese, emery, magnesite, marble, sodium sulfate, dolomite, and other minerals. Bauxite deposits were being tapped on a big scale in the early 1970s by an aluminum-manufacturing centre near Konya. Crude oil production began on a regular basis in 1961.

Turkey's hard coal is of poor quality, and only negligible quantities are exported. The marketable annual output late in the 1960s was 4,700,000 tons. Lignite was becoming an increasingly important fuel, its annual output increasing from 4,000,000 tons early in the 1960s to 9,000,000 tons in the early 1970s. Iron-ore production, formerly exported, was barely keeping pace with the rising home demand in the early 1970s; annual production in the early 1970s was 3,000,000 tons. Chrome ore reserves are widespread; annual output approached 750,000 tons in the early 1970s. The output of blister copper averaged around 24,000 tons per annum but was expected to rise to over 60,000 tons per annum with the completion of a new plant on the Black Sea coast. Crude oil output quintupled after 1962, reaching 3,600,000 tons annually early in the 1970s. Exploration for oil was continuing over a wide area in the 1970s.

Biological resources. Turkey has a wide diversity of climate and ecology. The total area used for field crops increased by nearly 60 percent in the 1950s, reaching what appears to be its maximum feasible extent. Further increases will require greater use of fertilizers and irrigation and more efforts to combat soil erosion.

Vineyards, gardens, and orchards cover 9,000 square miles. A gradual extension of this area in the 1970s, especially in the Çukurova and Aegean regions, was probable in the light of the government's plans to develop fruit and vegetable production. About one-fourth of Turkey is covered with forests, which are predominantly coniferous but also include deciduous beech, poplar, oak, and walnut. Virtually all forest land is state owned, but only a fraction has been made productive, and much is completely virgin; untold damage has been done by the large peasant population in the forest areas. In the 1970s serious steps were being taken to implement a long-term forestry development plan; lumber and timber production were expected to reach 240,000,000 cubic feet in 1972, compared with 95,000,000 in 1962.

Hydroelectric power. Turkey has many rivers and mountain watercourses, but much remains to be done in harnessing these resources. Hydroelectric power rose from only 3.8 percent of the electricity output of 790,000,000 kilowatt-hours in 1950 to 27 percent of the 9,624,000,000 kilowatt-hours produced in 1971. The percentage was to rise sharply in 1973 with the coming into production of the 620-megawatt Keban (Euphrates) and the 300-megawatt Gökçekaya power stations (a megawatt equalling 1,000,000 watts). At least two more Euphrates hydroelectric schemes were planned for the 1970s. Although, like Keban, these were to be linked into the national grid, they would help to open up the sparsely populated eastern regions of the country.

Sources of national income.   *Agriculture, forestry, and fishing.* The livelihood of 70 percent of the population and

Unexploited mineral wealth

31 percent of the national income came from agriculture, forestry, and fishing in the late 1960s. The 1963 census of agriculture showed that of 3,500,000 agricultural holdings only 491 were of more than 1,200 acres, while 1,600,000 were of seven acres or less and a further 1,100,000 of between 7.7 and 25 acres. The situation in the early 1970s was basically the same, although the government intended to introduce legislation to prevent or at least to inhibit the further fractionalization of land used for farming.

Major crops

Cereals—predominantly wheat and barley—are the largest crop, covering 32,000,000 acres in 1970; industrial crops—principally cotton, tobacco, sugar beets, and oilseeds—were sown over 4,200,000 acres. Other major agricultural products included pulses, potatoes, grapes, citrus and soft fruits, olives, hazelnuts, and tea. In the 1970s the government was attempting to guarantee minimum prices for the main crops without inducing the large surpluses of low-grade tobacco and tea and sugar beet that accumulated during the 1960s. It was also encouraging farmers to adopt improved methods by subsidizing credit, fertilizers, and improved seeds.

Livestock holdings totalled 84,000,000 head early in the 1970s, including 14,000,000 cattle, 36,000,000 sheep, and 6,000,000 Angora goats. The fishing industry contributes only 0.3 percent of the national income. Better organization, modern equipment, and an appreciation of the potential of deep-sea fishing are all urgently needed.

Forestry development was given a high priority in the early 1970s, at which time it provided less than 0.5 percent of the national income.

Very substantial sums of foreign aid capital have been invested in coal, lignite, copper, and bauxite mining and processing, along with government funds. State and foreign investment in the oil industry has been high. Mining and quarrying nevertheless accounted for only about 1.7 percent of the national income in the late 1960s.

Manufacturing. The manufacturing industries provided approximately 18.5 percent of the national income annually late in the 1960s, compared with 13 percent early in the decade. Manufacturing attracted about 20 percent of all investment in the late 1960s. The textile industry was the most important and had been considerably modernized in preceding years. Motor-vehicle production (assembly and parts manufacturing) had grown in importance, along with chemicals, petroleum products, rubber and plastics, and iron and steel products. Other dynamic manufacturing industries included processed foodstuffs, paper, nonferrous metals, domestic appliances, beverages, and cement and building materials. State-run firms accounted for about one-third of the overall output of manufacturing. The state had a monopoly only in cigarettes, tea, spirits, and newsprint; in other fields it competed with private industry.

Turkey's balance-of-payments problems in the early 1950s caused the government to favour industries that would reduce the need for imports. After 1968, however, when the State Planning Organization was made responsible for approving many investment projects, greater attention was paid to the earning rather than the saving of currency. Industrial growth in the 1970s was expected to be dictated largely by the needs of export markets.

Output in manufacturing was still generally well below capacity; and the labour force, especially in the state sector, was above the optimum level for economic production. By international standards, therefore, productivity was rather low.

Energy consumption

Between 1962 and 1967 Turkey's energy consumption increased by almost 50 percent, to the equivalent of 30,-600,000 tons of coal. Consumption in 1972 was expected to be 42,600,000 tons, double the 1962 total. But consumption per capita remained extremely low. In the mid-1960s about 29 percent of the energy consumed was provided by petroleum products (approximately half of which were imported), 22 percent by wood, 18 percent by dried dung, 28 percent by hard coal and lignite, and only 3 percent by hydroelectric power.

Financial services. The Central Bank of the Republic of Turkey, set up in 1931, effectively controls the banking system. It is the only note-issuing bank, is the sole channel for the issue of import licenses (on behalf of the Ministry of Commerce), provides access to foreign currency, and plays a key role in the administration of the government's credit policies. There are 33 commercial banks, a state-run Agriculture Bank, and a number of special-purpose, state-owned institutions, such as the Sümerbank (concerned with industrial enterprises), the Etibank (mining and electric power), and the Turkish Maritime Bank (Denizçilik Bankası).

The main source of new finance for the numerous state enterprises is the State Investments Bank. The private sector was depending increasingly in the 1970s for its development funds upon the Industrial Development Bank of Turkey (established with World Bank assistance in 1950) and to a lesser extent upon the Industrial Investment and Credit Bank. Turkey in the 1970s did not yet have an organized capital market. The true public company that raises capital by selling its securities to the public was still practically unknown, and the vast majority of the many joint-stock companies were family-owned or family-controlled enterprises. The stock exchange at Istanbul dealt mainly in government securities.

Foreign trade. Between 1960 and 1970 export earnings increased by 139 percent to 6,909,000,000 lire, or at a slightly lower average annual rate of growth than that of the economy as a whole. During this period cotton displaced tobacco as the largest single currency earner. By 1971 agricultural products still accounted for 73 percent, minerals for 6 percent, and industrial and processed goods for only 21 percent of total earnings. The limitations of world demand for such traditional exports as cotton, tobacco, dried fruit, and nuts made imperative the development of exports of manufactures and other items, such as fresh fruit and vegetables.

The countries of the European Economic Community (EEC), or Common Market, accounted for more than 40 percent of all exports. The countries of the European Free Trade Association (EFTA) took 18 percent of all exports in 1970. The U.S., Japan, and Canada took 18 percent. Exports to eastern Europe, Yugoslavia, and Egypt averaged 18 percent of the total.

Imports rose by an average of 12 percent annually in the 1960s, an increase not enough to meet industrial requirements; in the late 1960s there were serious shortages of raw materials, capital equipment, and spare parts. In the early 1970s, however, the balance of payments account showed much improvement; all shortages of essential imported goods were eradicated. The chief suppliers of Turkey's imports in 1970 were West Germany, the United States, the United Kingdom, Italy, Switzerland, the Soviet Union, and France.

Management of the economy. *The role of government.* Turkey's first ventures into industry were made in the 1930s, in the early years of the republic, when the state was of necessity the principal investor. Although the state still owned nearly half of the country's economic resources in 1970, increasing importance was being given to private industry, which provided almost 50 percent of the new fixed capital investment. The state sector was concerned mainly with investment in fields in which the capital requirement was too large or the expected returns too low to attract private enterprise.

The State Planning Organization, set up in 1960, became the arbiter of all foreign investment, as well as of all major Turkish private and state investment. Its five-year plans and annual programs set the guidelines for economic development. Through the Central Bank, the Agriculture Bank, and other state banking institutions, the government maintained a firm hold on all financial and investment operations. The railways, post office, airways, and internal sea passenger services were operated as government enterprises.

The State Planning Organization

Taxation. Annual treasury revenue in the late 1960s totalled 24,028,000,000 lire. Direct taxation accounted for 6,798,000,000 lire, indirect taxation for 12,343,000,000 lire, foreign aid counterpart funds for 1,019,000,000 lire, and nontaxation revenues for 1,560,000,000 lire. The net revenues from state monopolies, the universities, and the State Farms Administration amounted to 836,000,000 lire; treasury bonds raised 600,000,000 lire, and savings bonds, which are compulsorily purchasable at the rate of 3 percent of taxable income, raised 727,000,000 lire. Direct taxation consisted mainly of an income tax on private individuals and companies and a corporation tax. There was widespread tax evasion, largely resulting from a shortage of qualified inspectors and also from the absence of a recognized body of professional accountants. The government continued to rely heavily on indirect taxation, such as sales and excise taxes. Banking, insurance, and other transactions were also subject to indirect taxation.

Trade unions. The trade union movement was relatively unimportant until the 1960s. Before July 1963, when the Strikes, Lockouts and Collective Agreements Law came into force, strikes and lockouts had been illegal. In the early 1970s there were about 1,000 unions, the majority affiliated to the moderate Turkish Trade Union Confederation and a few to the left-wing Confederation of Reformist Workers' Unions. Union membership totalled about 4,000,000.

The government fixes minimum wages by geographical areas, but these bear little relationship to actual rates, which in most establishments are determined by collective agreements. The agreements also cover a wide variety of such fringe benefits as holiday pay, performance bonuses, and food allowances. Social insurance and fringe benefits are equal to more than 60 percent of basic wages. The Confederation of Employers' Associations of Turkey grew rapidly in the 1960s.

Balance of payments. Since the inception of the First Five-Year Plan in 1962–63, the government has tried to achieve a 7 percent annual increase in national output. The deterioration of the balance of payments in the later 1960s led to a two-thirds devaluation of the lira and to the adoption of austerity measures in August 1970. Short- and medium-term policies called for greater emphasis on investment in currency-earning enterprises, for the curbing of internal demand and of price increases, and for an overall improvement in productivity.   (E.I.U.)

Transportation. The Turkish Republic began very early to improve the transportation system as a means of integrating isolated regions and of developing the national economy. The length of railway tracks increased from about 2,500 miles in 1924 to around 6,000 in 1970. After World War II more emphasis was placed on road and harbour construction. The result was to give Turkey the best developed road and rail network in the Middle East. In 1970 the highways carried 43 percent of the freight traffic and 70 percent of the passenger traffic; the railroads carried 55 percent of the freight traffic and only 28 percent of the passenger traffic.

Passenger and freight traffic

The heaviest traffic is between Istanbul and Ankara, followed by that of the Aegean region, with İzmir as its centre, the area around the Gulf of Iskenderun, with Adana as its centre, and the Ankara–Zonguldak route. Istanbul is the chief harbour; there are heavy flows of passengers and freight by sea between İzmir and Istanbul through the Aegean, between the southern coasts of the Sea of Marmara and Istanbul, and between Istanbul and the Black Sea ports of Zonguldak, Samsun, and Trabzon.

Roads. All-weather highways totalled 37,000 miles in 1971, of which over 13,000 miles were paved, the rest consisting of stabilized gravel or macadam. The main highways radiate from Ankara, in central Anatolia, from Istanbul and İzmir, in the west, from Adana, in the south, and from Erzurum and Diyarbakır, in the east.

Railways. The railroad pattern consists of a ring around the central Anatolian Plateau, from which branches radiate to the peripheral regions: two to Zonguldak and Samsun, on the Black Sea; three to the western ports of Istanbul, İzmir, and Bandırma; three to the east; and one to the south (via Adana to Syria and Iraq).

Port facilities. Turkey's merchant shipping fleet is relatively small, consisting in 1971 of 714,000 gross tons, of which 80 percent were oil tankers or cargo carriers. The port of Istanbul handles more than 50 percent of the country's imports and 11 percent of its exports. İzmir ranks second, handling 35 percent of the exports. Other principal ports, in decreasing order, are Mersin and İskenderun in the south and Zonguldak, Samsun, and Trabzon, in the north; all of these ports are located at the end of rail or land routes serving large hinterlands. Inland water transportation does not exist in Turkey except on Lake Van.

Air transport. The state-owned Turkish Airlines (Türk Hava Yolları) flies from Ankara to Istanbul, İzmir, Adana, Erzurum, Van, Samsun, and Trabzon. While Ankara is the major junction of the domestic air routes, Istanbul is the busiest airport and the principal terminus of international lines. İzmir ranks third in traffic volume.
                                                                (S.Er.)

ADMINISTRATION AND SOCIAL CONDITIONS

Government. Turkey is a republic, with its capital at Ankara. Under the constitution of 1961, political authority is centred in the Grand National Assembly, which has a lower chamber, the National Assembly, composed of 450 elected members, and a Senate made up of 165 members, 150 elected and 15 nominated by the president of the republic. There are also a few senators for life: army officers who carried out the 1960 revolution.

The head of state is the president of the republic, elected by the Grand National Assembly for a term of seven years. He is not eligible for a second consecutive term. The president selects a prime minister, who forms a government subject to approval by the National Assembly.

The country is divided into 67 provinces. Each province (*il* or *vilâyet*) is subdivided into districts and each district (*ilçe* or *kaza*) into communes. The highest administrative official in each is, respectively, the *vali* (governor), the *kaymakam* (prefect), and the *nahiye müdürü* (district official). The *vali*, who is appointed by the president on the recommendation of the minister of the interior, is the chief administrative officer of the province, representing all the national departments (except those of war and justice) and coordinating their work in his province. He corresponds directly with each ministry and has a staff of advisers, who also form an administrative council under his chairmanship. The organization of the district under the *kaymakam* and of the commune under the *nahiye müdürü* follows the same pattern. The commune comprises a number of villages, each of which has a headman (*muhtar*) and a council of elders (*ihtiyarlar meclisi*) numbering from 5 to 12 according to the size of the village. A provincial council, elected for four years, debates questions of local administration, and its resolutions have legal effect; the *vali*, who is president of the council, may, however, refer proposals to the Council of State. In every headquarters town of a province or district and in all other towns of 2,000 inhabitants or more, there is a municipality (*belediye*). At its head is the mayor (*belediye reisi*), assisted by an elected council and a committee composed of officials and of persons chosen by the council for a year's term.

The provinces and districts

All citizens over 21 are entitled to vote unless they have been legally deprived of their rights. Deputies to the National Assembly are elected every four years, and a third of the senators are elected every two years. The constitution prescribes a secret ballot. Actual voting procedures are determined by legislation. Before 1961 a party securing a majority in a province was given all the deputies from that province. The electoral law of 1961 introduced a form of proportional representation by which the deputies of a province were apportioned among the parties according to the size of each party's vote.

Turkey was a one-party state until 1946. Since then a number of parties have contested elections, and in October 1971 eight had deputies in the National Assembly.

The judicial system is entirely independent of the assembly and the government. The old Muslim legal and judicial system was swept away in the early years of the republic, and a new Western system was adopted that was based on the Swiss civil code, the Italian penal code, and German commercial law. The highest court, the Constitutional Court, was created in 1961 to review the legislation of the Grand National Assembly; it has 15 regular and 5 alternate members. The highest administrative court is the Council of State, with 31 judges, which serves as the final court of appeals for the decisions of lower administrative courts. There is a Court of Cassation that serves as a court of last resort for reviewing the decisions of other courts. A system of courts run by the Ministry of Justice handles ordinary civil and criminal cases.

The military forces had a total strength of about 508,-500 men in 1971, of which 420,000 were in the army, 50,000 in the air force, and 38,500 in the navy. Young men are subject to two years of compulsory service at the age of 20. Turkey is a member of the North Atlantic Treaty Organization (NATO) and of the Central Treaty Organization (Cento). United States influence has been strong, exercised by a military mission in Ankara that directs the delivery of arms from the U.S. and supervises training programs in the three services. In 1971 land forces included 12 infantry divisions, one armoured division, four armoured brigades, and two parachute battalions. The navy had 12 submarines and ten destroyers. There were three tactical air forces. Headquarters of the Southeastern Command of NATO is at İzmir.

Education, health, and welfare. At the time the Turkish Republic was formed, the population was estimated to be only 10 percent literate. By the start of the 1970s, primary education was compulsory for all children from seven to 12, but a considerable number of children, particularly in the provinces, did not attend school. Although the educational system underwent great expansion after World War II, many peasants were reluctant to send their children to school or could not afford to keep them there during planting and harvesting seasons. The literacy rate in 1970 was estimated at 55 percent of the population of six years and over. Over 5,000,000 children attended primary school early in the 1970s, while the number in secondary schools and lycées was a little over 1,100,000. There were 245,000 in technical and vocational schools and colleges and 155,000 in various institutes of higher education. Religious instruction, forbidden in the early years of the republic, was permitted in primary schools and in the schools training religious personnel.

The Ministry of Health and Social Welfare carried out public health programs and operated a large number of hospitals and dispensaries. Others were run by the Ministry of Labour. State medical services are provided free to the poor. There are also private medical institutions run by philanthropic organizations and large business enterprises. In 1969 there was one hospital bed for every 495 persons and one doctor for every 2,267 persons.

Successful public health campaigns have been conducted against tuberculosis, trachoma, malaria, and syphillis, but in the late 1960s trachoma and tuberculosis were still endemic. Infant mortality, which stood at 160 per 1,000 live births in 1960, was 153 per 1,000 in 1970.

A basic law concerning labour and social insurance and regulating conditions of employment, passed in 1936, established the 48-hour week with paid holidays of 12 to 24 working days, depending upon length of service. Later legislation provided health and accident insurance and old-age pensions. In the late 1960s approximately 1,000,000 workers were covered by social insurance.

Housing standards in general have been low, and overcrowded conditions in the cities have given rise to shantytowns (*gecekondu*) on the outskirts, put up by peasants migrating from the countryside. The Ministry of Reconstruction and Resettlement was established in 1958 to organize and direct this migration. In the mid-1960s it was estimated that persons living in shantytowns comprised 45 percent of the population of Ankara, 21 percent of that of Istanbul, and 18 percent of that of İzmir. On the other hand, all of the larger cities contain modern, middle-class residential areas that have expanded at a rapid rate and in which people live by Western standards.

The maintenance of internal security is the responsibility of the police, the gendarmerie, and the army. The police are organized on a national basis under the Ministry of the Interior but carry out their duties at the command of local civil authorities. In each province there is a directorate of security, divided into administrative, judi-

cial, and political sections. The gendarmerie is a paramilitary force drawn from military conscripts and assigned to sectors not under police jurisdiction, notably rural frontier areas. It is attached to the Ministry of the Interior and subject to the same local authorities as the police.

CULTURAL LIFE AND INSTITUTIONS

Turkey has a long and various cultural heritage. When the Turks arrived in Anatolia in the 11th century they had already adopted Islām, and they soon fell under the influence of the highly developed Iranian and Arab civilizations. Another part of the Turkish inheritance came from the Byzantine civilization that had developed in the Eastern Roman Empire. As the Ottoman Empire expanded into Europe, it received cultural influences from the West, and, when the empire entered on its downward course in the 19th century, the cultural pressure of Europe became stronger. At the same time, European interest in Turkish language, history, and art inspired many educated persons in Turkey with a desire to strengthen and preserve the national culture. Among the most important of the reforms carried out after the national revolution were those aimed at reviving the Turkish language and breaking the hold of Islām upon the nation.

Modern Turkish culture has been dominated by nationalism. Writers, artists, and musicians have abandoned the long tradition of Islām and returned to the vernacular in literature, village scenes in painting, and folk ballads in music. The theatre has become popular, and innumerable Turkish or foreign plays are performed. The Ankara State Opera was founded in 1940 and the Istanbul Opera in 1950; both perform classical Western works.

The popular arts flourish and are encouraged. Popular literature takes the form of narrative (*hikâye*) and poetry (*siir*), recited by minstrels known as *âşiks*. There are many popular dances and games, varying according to region. Folk instruments include drums, trumpets, flutes, pipes, tambourines, viols, and cymbals, along with some modern instruments. Popular drama includes shadow plays, performed by dolls reflected on a linen screen, and the *orta oyunu*, a type of improvized comedy.

Formal cultural institutions begin with the Ministry of Culture, set up in 1971. Various organizations are devoted to the sciences and arts, including three music conservatories, in Ankara, İzmir, and Istanbul; the Academy of Fine Arts, in Istanbul; the National Folklore Institute, in Ankara; the Turkish Folklore Society, in Istanbul; and a number of scientific and professional societies. Every province has its museums. There are archaeological museums in Ankara, Istanbul, and İzmir and a Museum of Turkish and Islāmic Art in Istanbul. The National Library (Milli Kütüphane) in Ankara had over 500,000 volumes at the beginning of the 1970s.

Ankara early in the 1970s had 18 daily newspapers and ten weeklies; Istanbul had 24 dailies and 24 weeklies. There were six dailies in İzmir, three each in Adana and Bursa, and two in Eskişehir. Radio and television broadcasting are carried on by the government. In the early 1970s Radio Ankara had three domestic services and three to foreign listeners. Radio Istanbul had two domestic services. Television broadcasting began in Ankara in 1965 and by 1971 was carried on four days a week. A station in Istanbul began operating in 1971.   (A.Te.)

BIBLIOGRAPHY. A general introduction that contains a useful bibliography is THOMAS D. ROBERTS et al., *Area Handbook for the Republic of Turkey* (1970). Another recent work is BERNARD LEWIS, *The Emergence of Modern Turkey*, 2nd ed. (1968). For geography, see W.C. BRICE, *South–West Asia* (1966); and GEORGE B. CRESSEY, *Crossroads: Land and Life in Southwest Asia* (1960). For the economy, see Z.Y. HERSHLAG, *Turkey: The Challenge of Growth* (1968); UNION OF CHAMBERS OF COMMERCE, INDUSTRY, AND COMMODITY EXCHANGES OF TURKEY, *Investment Guide to Turkey* (1964); ORGANIZATION FOR ECONOMIC COOPERATION AND DEVELOPMENT, *Annual Survey of the Turkish Economy;* and the annual publications of the Economic Research Department, Ankara, and of the Industrial Development Bank of Turkey, Istanbul. The State Planning Organization, Ankara, has issued three five-year development plans (1964, 1969, and 1972).

(S.Er./A.Te.)

The military

Housing conditions

Turkistan, History of

Turkistan, an area of Central Asia, lies partly in the Soviet Union and partly in the People's Republic of China. Historically, it can be divided into three broad geographic zones, each possessing quite distinct features. The first of these, known in Islāmic times as Mā Warā' an-Nahr, is the area lying between the Rivers Amu Darya (called Oxus by the Greeks and Jayḥūn by the Arabs) and Syr Darya (the Jaxartes to the Greeks and the Sayḥūn to the Arabs). This is an arid, semidesert region where, prior to the recent development of irrigation projects, the sedentary population maintained itself by intensive cultivation of the oases or of the riparian tracts bordering the Amu Darya, the Syr Darya, and the Zarafshan—the river of Samarkand.

The second zone is the steppe region, extending northeast of the Syr Darya and north of the Tien Shan as far as the foothills of the Altai—an expanse of fertile grazing lands ideally suited for pastoral nomadism. On the south this region is bounded by the Tien Shan and on the north by the Siberian forest zone; on the west it passes unbroken into the great Eurasian steppe zone, stretching as far as the Ukraine; while on the east it is confined by the foothills of the ranges lying between the Altai and the Tien Shan. To the Turks the area to the south and east of Lake Balkhash was known as the Yeti Su (Land of the Seven Rivers), and from this is derived the Russian name of Semirechiye.

The third zone, Kashgaria, possesses characteristics different from both Mā Warā' an-Nahr and Semirechiye. This region is dominated by the Takla Makan desert, one of the most forbidding tracts on the face of the earth, bounded on the north by the Tien Shan, on the west by the Pamirs, and on the south by the Kunlun Range. There human settlement is restricted to the higher land ringing the desert or to oasis settlements watered by the streams that lose themselves in the Takla Makan—the Tarim and its main tributaries, the Khotan and Yarkand rivers.

Neither the Pamirs nor the Tien Shan, although both climb to impressive altitudes, have ever restricted movement into or out of Kashgaria, either in the direction of Mā Warā' an-Nahr or of Semirechiye. Indeed, one striking characteristic of the Turkistan region—notwithstanding the prevailing aridity, the expanse of desert, and the barriers presented by lofty ranges—has been the comparative ease with which it has been traversed at all times, especially by nomadic tribes acting as a catalyst upon the sedentary civilizations—Iranian, Indian, and Chinese—on its peripheries. Paradoxically, although the inhospitality of so much of the terrain has served as a check to extensive contacts between the Far East, India, the Middle East, and the Mediterranean world, the caravan routes that straddled it have provided the means for varied cultural and commercial interchange.

WEST TURKISTAN

The early empires. The recorded history of West Turkistan begins with its inclusion in the Achaemenid Empire of Cyrus the Great in the 6th century BC. The rock inscription of Darius I (Achaemenid king, 522–486 BC) at Bīsitūn (Behistun) lists three Persian satrapies beyond the Amu Darya, the historic frontier of Iran—Suguda, the Sogdiana of the Greeks, between the Amu Darya and the Syr Darya; Uvarazmish, the Chorasmia of the Greeks, on the lower Amu Darya southeast of the Aral Sea; and Saka, the steppes beyond the Syr Darya. The Sogdians and the Chorasmians were mainly sedentary cultivators, while the Sakas were nomadic pastoralists related to the Scythians of the steppes north of the Black Sea; but all were of Iranian stock and spoke Iranian languages. The Sogdians, assisted by Saka auxiliaries, proved resourceful foes of Alexander the Great during his extended campaign in the eastern satrapies of the defunct Achaemenid Empire (4th century BC). Only with great difficulty did Alexander succeed in overcoming them, and at the close of the campaign he made an overt gesture of conciliation: he himself married Roxana, daughter of the Bactrian Oxyartes, defender of the unidentified stronghold known as the Rock of Sogdiana,

Inclusion in the Achaemenid Empire

while his general Seleucus married Apama, daughter of the Sogdian Spitamenes and his most intrepid opponent.

From the second half of the 3rd century BC both the newly founded Parthian Empire of the Arsacids and the Greco-Bactrian kingdom of Diodotus I and his successors faced ever increasing pressure from Saka nomads who had penetrated Sogdiana and were pressing southward along the line of the Amu Darya. By the second half of the 2nd century BC they had crossed the river and established a foothold in Bactria. The southward movement of the Sakas was part of a chain reaction resulting, in the first instance, from the expanding power of a tribal confederacy—known as the Hsiung-nu and identified with the ancestors of the later Huns—poised upon the Mongolian frontiers of China. The Hsiung-nu attacked and dispersed another tribal confederacy centred in Kansu, the Yüeh-chih, who fled westward down the valley of the Ili and onto the steppes north of the Syr Darya, where they met with the Saka tribes, who, threatened now from the east, began to press southward with renewed vigour, first into Sogdiana and then across the Amu Darya into Bactria. By the close of the 1st century BC the Yüeh-chih had driven the Sakas deep into what is now Afghanistan and even across the Indus into the Punjab.

The Yüeh-chih are probably to be identified with the Tochari of Western documents, among whom the dominant clan or clans consisted of the group later known as Kushans. Under Kujūla Kadphises, early in the 1st century AD, the Kushans controlled a vast area that included Sogdiana between the Amu Darya and the Syr Darya, as well as Bactria and Gandhāra on the upper Indus, stepping-stone to future conquests in India. This area remained under Kushan rule for about two centuries, and during that time Sogdiana participated fully in the syncretistic culture of the Kushan Empire, exposed both to Mahāyāna ("Greater Vehicle") Buddhism and to the Buddhist art of Gandhāra. It was finally lost to the Kushans as a result of the eastward drive of Ardashīr I, founder of the Sāsānid Empire in Iran, perhaps in AD 227, the last known regnal year of the Kushan emperor Vasudeva I.

Under the Sāsānids, Sogdiana was administered, together with Bactria and Gandhāra, by governors of the Sāsānid royal house. Holding the title of *kushanshāh*, these continued down to the middle decades of the 4th century, when the region was invaded by the Huns, probably the northern wing of the former Hsiung-nu confederacy. Advancing from the steppes beyond the Syr Darya, the Huns penetrated Sogdiana in successive waves, which have been tentatively classified as three distinct groups —Chionites, Kidarites, and Hephthalites, of whom the last became a great scourge in northern India during the 5th and 6th centuries. For nearly 200 years the Huns were to threaten the frontiers of the Sāsānid Empire, but in about AD 559 they were crushed by the Sāsānid ruler Khosrow Anūshīrvān (reigned 531–579), in alliance with new invaders from beyond the Syr Darya—the Western Turks under a khan known as Sinjibu or Silzibul. For the next 100 years Sogdiana continued under the rule of the Western Turks, although it is unlikely that their overlordship greatly reduced the influence of the indigenous Sogdian chieftains or disturbed the basic social and economic organization of the sedentary population. The life-style of the Sogdian ruling elite was an impressive one, if judged by the striking series of wall paintings discovered by Soviet archaeologists at Pyanjikent, on the upper Zarafshan. The culture of the region, in any case, had long been highly syncretistic, influenced by Zoroastrianism, Nestorian Christianity, Judaism, Manichaeism, and Buddhism; and to this welter of faiths the Turks added the characteristic shamanism of the Central Asian steppe zone.

Muslim rule. The decline of the Western Turks in the second half of the 7th century tempted the Muslim Arabs, advancing from the southwest, to embark upon the conquest of Sogdiana, to which they gave the name Mā Warā' an-Nahr, meaning "that which lies beyond the river" (equivalent to the Latin name of Transoxania). The annexation of Sogdiana to the Umayyad caliphate

Under the Sāsānids

proved a difficult task; and although it began shortly after the appointment of 'Ubayd Allāh ibn Ziyād to the governorship of Khorāsān in 674, it was not until the governorship of the famous Qutaybah ibn Muslim (who was killed in Farghana, the valley of the upper Syr Darya, in 715) that any substantial progress was made in the task of pacification. Even so, the death of Qutaybah produced an immediate reaction. While the Arab tribes in Khorāsān, which provided the troops for the garrisons in Sogdiana, indulged themselves in reckless tribal feuds, the Sogdian chieftains revolted against the Arab yoke and sought the assistance of the Türgesh Turks, whose entry into Sogdiana temporarily ended Arab rule. Shortly afterward, however, the Türgesh were defeated in battle by the governor of Khorāsān, Asad ibn 'Abd Allāh al-Qaṣrī, whose successor, Naṣr ibn Sayyār—a dexterous and conciliatory administrator appointed in 737—was able to place the Arab administration upon a sound and stable footing. Even then, however, the new province of the caliphate was still exposed to danger. Within a year of the revolution that substituted the rule of the 'Abbāsids for that of the Umayyads, a Chinese army invaded the valley of the upper Syr Darya (751), where it was defeated by the troops of Ziyād ibn Ṣāliḥ, a general of Abū Muslim.

Under the 'Abbāsids, Sogdiana (or Mā Warā' an-Nahr, as it will henceforth be called) was gradually drawn into the Islāmic culture zone, to be celebrated in later centuries for the scholars and saints it gave to the Muslim world, especially from Bukhara, the *quṭb al-Islām* ("Pillar of Islām"). The late 9th century, which saw 'Abbāsid control in the eastern provinces disintegrating with the de facto independence of the Ṭāhirids in Khorāsān and of the Ṣaffārids in Seistan, witnessed the rise in Mā Warā' an-Nahr of the Sāmānid dynasty, under whose comparatively mild rule the region enjoyed a substantial degree of peace and prosperity. The Sāmānids (ruled *c.* 874–*c.* 999), natives of Balkh in Khorāsān who claimed a probably spurious descent from the famous Sāsānid general Bahrām Chūbīn, were of Iranian stock and stood out as generous patrons of the so-called New Persian Renaissance of the 10th century. Under their rule Bukhara became a brilliant centre of Irano-Islāmic culture, while the stability of the regime rested on the support of an extensive class of small landholders (*dehqān*s) and a professional army of pagan Turkish slaves (*mamlūk*s), recruited from beyond the Syr Darya.

Rise of the Sāmānid dynasty

From P. Holt, A. Lambton, and B. Lewis (eds.), *Cambridge History of Islam*, vol. 1 (1970); Cambridge University Press

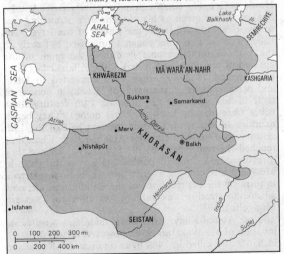

Territories controlled by the Sāmānid dynasty in the 10th century.

For all their wealth, their extensive military power, and their identification with traditional Iranian culture values, the Sāmānids remained unswervingly loyal to the Sunnī 'Abbāsid caliph in Baghdad. By the close of the 10th century, however, their possessions south of the Amu Darya had passed into the hands of the Turkish Ghaznavids, while Mā Warā' an-Nahr itself was occupied by the

Turkish Qarakhanids (Karakhanids), who finally took Bukhara in 999. Although the origin of the Qarakhanids is uncertain, they were probably a branch of the Qarluq tribe, which by the mid-10th century occupied an extensive territory to the north and south of the Tien Shan, with the centres of their power at Balāsāghūn on the River Chu, Talas (now Dzhambul) to the west, and Kashgar across the mountains.

The Qarakhanids exercised a loose control over the whole of Mā Warā' an-Nahr, though they were prevented from advancing south of the Amu Darya by the Ghaznavids, who also seized Khwārezm south of the Aral Sea (the ancient Chorasmia). Nor did Qarakhanid rule endure for long, though its end is confused and uncertain since, by the middle of the 11th century, both Mā Warā' an-Nahr and Khorāsān, as well as an extensive area to the west, had passed into the hands of the Seljuqs, a branch of the Oğuz Turks that appeared in Mā Warā' an-Nahr at the close of the Sāmānid period as auxiliaries of the ruling house in its struggle with the Qarakhanids. For a century Mā Warā' an-Nahr was part of the farflung Seljuq Empire, but even before the death, in 1157, of Sanjar, the last effective sultan, Seljuq rule had ceased to be anything but a name in the lands beyond the Amu Darya. Meanwhile, Khwārezm had become the seat of an independent Turkish dynasty, that of the Khwārezm-Shāhs, descended from a *mamlūk* officer in the service of the Seljuq sultans. Takash, the ablest of the line, ruled one of the most extensive Muslim states of the 12th century, adding Khorāsān and much of the Iranian plateau to his possessions on the Amu Darya; yet he remained a tribute-paying vassal of the Qarakhitans (Karakhitans), remnants of the Khitan or Liao dynasty of China (947–1125) who, driven out of China by the Juchen or Chin dynasty (1122–1234), had moved westward to occupy the former territories of the Qarakhanids. Takash died in 1200, and his successor, Muḥammad ibn Takash, galled by his dependence upon the Qarakhitans, whose power he rightly judged to be in decline, threw off his allegiance and made himself master of Mā Warā' an-Nahr and of virtually the entire Muslim East.

The Chagatai khans and the Timurids. In striking at the power of the Qarakhitans, the Khwārezm-Shāh had unwittingly weakened the only buffer protecting his frontiers from perhaps the greatest scourge Islām was ever to experience, the Mongols of Genghis Khan, who in the spring of 1220 crossed the Syr Darya and overran Mā Warā' an-Nahr, leaving a trail of devastation—cities sacked, populations massacred, and irrigation works destroyed or abandoned. The view is widely held that the region did not recover its former prosperity until the Russian occupation in the second half of the 19th century.

Mongol invasions

Before his death in 1227, Genghis Khan divided his vast empire among his sons. Turkistan (consisting of Mā Warā' an-Nahr, the steppes northeast of the Syr Darya, and Kashgaria, which had escaped the initial Mongol visitation) passed to his second son, Chagatai, whose descendants ruled this extensive *ulus* (appanage) down to the early 14th century, when the khanate divided into two successor states: an eastern khanate beyond the Syr Darya and the Pamirs, where the Chagatai khans continued to exercise a nominal suzerainty down to the 17th century, and a western khanate, consisting of Mā Warā' an-Nahr, which eventually passed into the hands of the celebrated conqueror Timur. His descendants ruled there until the close of the 15th century, when they were dispossessed by the invading Uzbeks.

The Chagatai khanate. The history of the Chagatai khanate is both confused and obscure, the only relatively detailed chronicle relating to this area being the *Tārīkh-e Rashīdī*, written in Persian by Mīrzā Muḥammad Ḥaydar Dūghlāt, cousin of the Mughal emperor Bābur and ruler of Kashmir between 1541 and 1551; it has been translated into English by N. Elias and E. Denison Ross (London, 1895).

As rulers whose power rested solely upon the support of their tribal followers, the Chagatai khans at first located their headquarters on the steppes close to Lake Balkhash, where there was rich grazing for the flocks and herds of the nomads. Chagatai himself made his capital at Bish-baliq, an old Uighur centre. It was later transferred to Almaliq between Lake Balkhash and the Tien Shan—whereas his main *orda* (encampment) was generally sited close to the Ili River. The administration of Mā Warā' an-Nahr and its predominantly Muslim population he left to a series of Muslim governors: the first was Maḥmūd Yalavach, a merchant from Khwārezm, who was succeeded by his son Mas'ūd Beg. The Mongols required collaborators of this kind—men of business accustomed to Irano-Islāmic bureaucratic methods and capable of squeezing the maximum revenue out of the khan's subjects. Even under these comparatively enlightened governors the Muslim population of Mā Warā' an-Nahr only slowly recovered from the destruction wrought by the initial Mongol conquest. Urban life in particular was slow to revive, and it received little assistance from such rulers as Barak Khan (reigned 1264–70), who, en route to invade Khorāsān, allowed his troops to plunder his own cities of Bukhara and Samarkand. When the Moroccan traveller Ibn Baṭṭūṭah visited Mā Warā' an-Nahr during the second quarter of the 14th century, he was appalled by the decay of urban life: much of Samarkand was still in ruins, Tirmiz had been rebuilt on a new site, and across the Amu Darya in Khorāsān both Merv and Balkh were utterly desolate.

Like the Mongol elite in the contemporary khanates of Kipchak and Iran, the Chagatai khans and their followers found themselves drawn inexorably toward an Irano-Islāmic life-style such as was still to be found in the cities of Mā Warā' an-Nahr and, to a lesser degree, in those of Kashgaria. This, in turn, involved the adoption of Islām in place of Mongolian shamanism and of the Sharī'ah, the law of Islām, in place of the Yāsa of Genghis Khan and tended to alienate their pagan nomad followers, concentrated mainly on the steppes beyond the Syr Darya. As early as 1264 an imprudent great-grandson of Chagatai became a Muslim, calling himself Mubārak Shāh, but he rapidly disappeared from the scene. More significant of changing times, Kebek Khan (reigned c. 1318–26) a half century later transferred the seat of government from Almaliq to Qarshi in Mā Warā' an-Nahr. One of Kebek's younger brothers, Tarmashirin, openly proclaimed himself a Muslim and was driven from his throne (c. 1334), but by then the conflict of interests was too deep to be healed. Shortly afterward the unified khanate disintegrated: in Mā Warā' an-Nahr a line of Chagatai khans openly espoused Islām and the Muslim way of life, as did perhaps the majority of their followers, while across the Syr Darya a rival line endeavoured to maintain the traditions of their Genghiskhanid ancestors, though with steadily diminishing success. This latter eastern khanate was known in Mā Warā' an-Nahr and Iran as Mughalistān and its inhabitants as Jāṭs (literally, "robbers").

The Timurids. During the second half of the 14th century, Mā Warā' an-Nahr was the scene of the spectacular rise of Timur Lenk (Tamerlane), a Barlas Turk from Shahr-e Sabz, who first united under his command the dominant Turko-Mongol tribes of Mā Warā' an-Nahr, Khwārezm, and Mughalistān, as well as Khorāsān and Seistan in eastern Iran. Between 1384 and 1395 Timur added to his conquests a vast area consisting of what are now Iran and Iraq, eastern Turkey, and the Caucasus region. In addition, he launched two successful attacks upon the Mongol khanate of Kipchak on the Volga. Moreover, he also invaded northern India (1398–99) and sacked Delhi before turning westward again, between 1399 and 1402, to harry the Egyptian Mamlūks in Syria and the Ottoman sultan, whom he captured in battle at Ankara. At the time of his death at Otrar on the Syr Darya, in 1405, Timur was already bound for the invasion of China.

The extent to which Mā Warā' an-Nahr benefitted from Timur's conquests is open to debate, but much of the plunder acquired on his campaigns was expended upon his capital, Samarkand. On capturing enemy cities he followed the Genghiskhanid precedent of sparing the lives of artisans and craftsmen, who were transferred to Mā Warā' an-Nahr; and it is recorded that after the sack

of Delhi, in particular, large numbers of Indian workmen were taken to Samarkand. The city was visited by Ruy González de Clavijo, ambassador of Henry III of Castile, who left an impressive description of the metropolis in the last years of Timur's life. Timur never assumed the full attributes of sovereignty, contenting himself with the title of emir while upholding the fictional authority of a series of puppet khans of the line of Chagatai, to whom he claimed kinship by marriage, in consequence of which he was styled *gurkhan* ("son-in-law").

Timur appears to have lacked the administrative capacity or the foresight of Genghis Khan; and following his death his empire became a bone of contention among a numerous progeny of sons, grandsons, and great-grandsons because there existed among the Timurids no fixed law of primogeniture and because, as with other Turko-Mongol dynasties, it was held that sovereignty was invested in the entire ruling house rather than in a single individual. In the ensuing struggle Timur's youngest son, Shāh Rokh, emerged victorious; but he withdrew to Herāt in Khorāsān, which he made his capital, leaving his eldest son, Ulugh Beg, as his deputy in Mā Warā' an-Nahr. Ulugh Beg's rule in Samarkand, from 1409 to 1446, probably brought a considerable measure of tranquillity to the region. An enthusiastic amateur astronomer and the builder of a celebrated observatory, he ensured that during his lifetime Samarkand would be a major centre of scientific learning, especially in astronomy and mathematics.

Throughout the second half of the 15th century, Mā Warā' an-Nahr was divided into a number of separate principalities, ruled by various descendants of Timur, of which Bukhara and Samarkand were the most important. Together with other Timurid principalities in the Farghana valley and at Balkh and Herāt in Khorāsān, these petty courts patronized Persian literature and also writing in Chagatai, an eastern Turkish language derived partly from the Khaqani spoken at the Qarakhanid court, which now emerged as a flexible vehicle for sophisticated literary expression. These Timurid princelings, however, were locked in unceasing rivalry with each other, and their inability to combine, even temporarily, against intruders from beyond their frontiers was to prove their undoing. By the close of the century the whole of Mā Warā' an-Nahr had passed into the hands of the Uzbeks.

The Uzbek khanates. The early history of the Uzbek people is wrapped in obscurity; but at the time of the establishment of the khanate of Kipchak (the Golden Horde), Genghis Khan's grandson Shibaqan (Arabic: Shaybān) was given as his *ulus* the area stretching east of the Urals toward the upper waters of the Irtysh. His tribes were at that time pagan shamanists; but early in the 14th century, presumably during the reign of the greatest of the rulers of Kipchak, 'Abd Allah Özbeg (Uzbek; reigned 1313–40), they were converted to Islām and perhaps assumed the name of Uzbeks in honour of their distant sovereign (by the late 14th century these tribes were already known by that name). They began to move southeastward during the first half of the 15th century; and under their ruler Abū al-Khayr Khan they reached the north bank of the Syr Darya, whence they threatened the Timurid possessions across the river in Mā Warā' an-Nahr but whence they were also threatened, in turn, by the depredations of the Buddhist Oirats, now advancing steadily westward out of Jungaria (western Mongolia).

Before Abū al-Khayr Khan could undertake a full-scale invasion of Mā Warā' an-Nahr, however, he was defeated in battle and killed in 1468 by two kinsmen—Karay and Jani Beg—who, refusing to recognize Abū al-Khayr's paramount position, had defected, together with their tribal followers, and had placed themselves under the nominal suzerainty of the Chagatai khan of Mughalistān. Their descendants were to become the Kazakh hordes of later centuries.

With the death of Abū al-Khayr Khan, the fortunes of the Uzbeks declined, only to revive under the leadership of his grandson Muḥammad Shaybānī, who was an empire builder cast in the ancestral Genghiskhanid mold.

By 1500 he had seized the whole of Mā Warā' an-Nahr, including the metropolis of Samarkand, and was threatening the remaining Timurid rulers in Khorāsān. Although he himself was killed at Merv (1510), fighting Shāh Esmā'īl I the Ṣafavid, he had changed the course of Central Asian history. By the time of his death all the lands between the Syr Darya and the Amu Darya were in Uzbek hands, and so they were to remain.

The Shaybānid dynasty (it should perhaps more correctly be styled the Abū al-Khayrid, since none of the later Shaybānids were lineal descendants of Muḥammad Shaybānī) ruled Mā Warā' an-Nahr down to 1598, with a separate line reigning in Khwārezm. Like the Timurids, the Shaybānids followed Turko-Mongol tradition in selecting as their paramount chieftain the senior member of the ruling family and in dividing their territory into separate appanages for the brothers, sons, and nephews of the khan—a practice tending toward instability. Mā Warā' an-Nahr under the Shaybānids appears to have declined in prosperity by comparison with the preceding century of Timurid rule, due partly to a falling off in the importance of the transcontinental caravan trade. In other respects the Shaybānids followed the precedents set by the Timurids, especially in regard to their patronage of literature and the arts, although neither in architecture nor in miniature painting did the output of the Shaybānid period compare favourably with the best Timurid work. Unlike the Timurids, however, the Shaybānids strove to establish a reputation for impeccable orthodoxy. This was especially the case with the greatest of Shaybānid rulers, 'Abd Allāh Khan II (reigned 1583–98).

On the extinction of the Shaybānid line, Mā Warā' an-Nahr passed into the hands of a family related by marriage to the preceding dynasty, the Janids or Astrakhanids (descended from the former khans of Astrakhan on the Volga). Under the Janids there was a marked decline in material prosperity and in the general level of cultural life; and such pretensions to sovereignty as the dynasty still possessed by the early 18th century vanished with the invasion of Mā Warā' an-Nahr by the Iranian warlord Nāder Shāh, who, in 1740, entered Bukhara as a conqueror before passing on to attack the khanate of Khiva, the name used hereafter for Khwārezm. During the second half of the 18th century the last Janid ruler, Abū al-Ghāzī Khan (reigned 1758–85), lost much of his power to chieftains of the Mangit tribe, who, in the person of Shāh Mūrad (reigned 1785–1800), eventually usurped the throne.

Dominance of the Bukhara, Khiva, and Kokand khanates

At the beginning of the 19th century the area between the Amu Darya and the Syr Darya was dominated by three khanates—Bukhara, Khiva, and Kokand. Not one of these states had defined frontiers with its neighbours; not one was able to keep recalcitrant chieftains permanently in check; and not one could trust its neighbour not to intervene in times of difficulty or crisis. In addition, the emir of Bukhara and the khan of Khiva exercised a nominal suzerainty over the Turkmen tribes of the Karakum Desert, whose slave-raiding proclivities in the direction of Iran they encouraged—to provide labour in the oases of Khiva and Bukhara—but over whose movements they exercised not the slightest control. Paradoxically, however, all three khanates were probably better administered in the first half of the 19th century than at any time during the preceding century: in Kokand both Muḥammad 'Umar Shaykh (died 1822) and his son Muḥammad 'Ali (died 1842) were talented rulers, while in Bukhara the ferocious Naṣr Allāh (Nasrullah; reigned 1827–60) aspired to the role of a second Timur.

Yet nowhere in the Muslim world during the 19th century were there regimes less prepared to face the challenge of European expansion than the khanates of Central Asia; and it was their geographical isolation alone that impeded the otherwise inexorable advance of Russia, especially in the case of Khiva, ringed by desert, against which Russia mounted unsuccessful expeditions in 1717 and 1839. The Russian conquest began in earnest, however, with the acquisition from Kokand in 1855 of the fort of Ak-Mechet on the Syr Darya. Kokand was attacked in 1864–65, Chimkent and Tashkent taken, and a treaty

extracted from Khudāyār Khan in 1866. In 1868 Bukhara was invaded, and the emir was compelled to accept the status of a Russian vassal. The same happened with Khiva in 1873. In 1875 there was an uprising in Kokand, which was swiftly suppressed, and the khanate was formally annexed in 1876. Meanwhile, the occupation of the Turkmen country had begun in 1873. The Turkmens, however, put up a more strenuous resistance than did any of the khanates, and it was not until after the massacre at Geok-Tepe in 1881 and the occupation of the Merv Oasis in 1884 that all opposition was overcome.

The Kazakh khanate. The pattern of Uzbek history in Mā Warā' an-Nahr down to the Russian conquest of the late 19th century was shaped largely by the fact that these former nomadic pastoralists had established themselves in a region where favourable conditions for a pastoral economy were limited and where much of the country's wealth consisted of the revenue derived from taxing the sedentary agriculturist and the urban artisan and merchant. In these circumstances, the Uzbeks gradually adapted themselves to the role of landowners in the oases or became, in some cases, wholly urbanized. Very different was the case of their Kazakh kinsmen, who remained on the steppes north of the Syr Darya after the Uzbeks had crossed into Mā Warā' an-Nahr. In this vast area, perfectly suited to a nomadic pastoral economy and devoid of sedentary agriculture or urban life except along the northern bank of the Syr Darya, the Kazakhs were able to preserve intact all the nomadic traditions of their forebears. Unlike the Uzbeks, whose rulers, in taking possession of such ancient centres of Islāmic culture as Bukhara, had assumed the role of orthodox Muslim potentates, the Kazakhs—and to an even greater extent the Kirgiz of the Tien Shan—remained indifferent Muslims, possessing a rich oral literature but no written language before the coming of the Russians and being altogether without the traditional Irano-Islāmic apparatus of administration, which the Uzbeks had inherited in Mā Warā' an-Nahr.

During the late 15th century and throughout the 16th century the Kazakhs were able to consolidate a nomadic empire stretching across the steppes east of the Caspian and north of the Aral Sea as far as the upper Irtysh and the western approaches to the Altai. The time was peculiarly favourable: the Oyrat (Oirat) Empire, formidable during the 14th and early 15th centuries, had passed into temporary eclipse; the Chagatai khanate bestriding the Tien Shan was moribund; the Noghay Horde between the mouths of the Volga and the Ural rivers was in a similar condition; and the Uzbeks were preoccupied with the conquest of Mā Warā' an-Nahr and with raiding Khorāsān. Under Burunduk Khan (reigned 1488–1509) and Kasym Khan (reigned 1509–18) the Kazakhs were the masters of virtually the entire steppe region, reputedly able to bring 200,000 horsemen into the field and feared by all of their neighbours. Under Kasym Khan's sons—Mamash (reigned 1518–23), Tagir (reigned 1523–33), and Buydash (reigned 1533–38)—there was, however, a partial weakening of the khan's authority, accompanied by a trend, later to become more pronounced, for the khanate to disintegrate into three separate "hordes." These were, from east to west: the Great Horde, in the Semirechiye north of the Tien Shan; the Middle Horde, in the central steppe region east of the Aral Sea; and the Little Horde, between the Aral Sea and the Ural River. In each horde the authority of the khan, invariably a Genghiskhanid, tended to be curtailed by the de facto power exercised by tribal chieftains known as sultans and perhaps even more by the beys and batyrs (the heads of the clans that were the components of each tribe). Nominally, the khans commanded a formidable force of mounted warriors, but, in reality, they depended upon the loyalty of the sultans, who, in turn, were dependent upon the loyalty of the beys and batyrs. The last son of Kasym Khan to rule the Kazakh steppes, Ḥaqq Naẓar (reigned 1538–80), overcame these obstacles and, having succeeded in reuniting the three hordes, embarked upon systematic raiding into Mā Warā' an-Nahr, a trend that continued under his immediate successors down to the reign of

Kazakh consolidation

Tevkkel Khan (1586–98), who even temporarily occupied Samarkand.

During the 17th century the Kazakhs lost ground, although even in the last quarter of the century Tauke Khan (reigned 1680–1718) was still able to hold the tribes together in a single confederacy. By then, however, the Kazakhs were already in decline, having suffered from the ceaseless depredations of the revived Oyrat Empire in Jungaria. These Oyrat raids began as early as 1643 but reached their peak during the reign of the Oyrat ruler Cevang Rabtan (1697–1727), when the Kazakh steppes were ravaged again and again without the Kazakhs being able to offer any effective resistance. Not until the Oyrats were finally overthrown by the Manchu rulers of China in 1757 were the Kazakhs released from this scourge, which had for so long decimated their man-power and appropriated their livestock.

The reverses experienced by the Kazakhs at the hands of the Oyrats undoubtedly retarded the emergence of a unified Kazakh state and further depressed the prevailing level of Kazakh cultural life. It also rendered the Kazakhs even less able to resist the encroachments of Russia from the north. The Russian advance onto the Kazakh steppe began with the construction of a line of forts—Omsk in 1716, Semipalatinsk in 1718, Ust-Kamenogorsk in 1719, and Orsk in 1735—which was then steadily advanced southward. Some Kazakhs believed that the Russian presence might at least provide some security against Oyrat raids, and in 1731 the Little Horde accepted Russian protection, followed by the Middle Horde in 1740 and by part of the Great Horde in 1742, although its effect upon the Oyrats was to prove minimal. During the second half of the 18th century the Kazakhs found themselves threatened not only by Russian encroachments from the north but also by the Manchus from the east, who considered themselves the heirs of the Oyrats in Jungaria and who, in 1771, demanded the submission of the khan of the Great Horde. But, in reality, the Manchu Empire was too remote to intervene effectively; it was the Russians alone who were in a position to exert severe pressure on the Kazakhs. Finally, after a series of ineffectual uprisings, of which the most extensive was that of Batyr Srym in 1792–97, Russia resolved to suppress such autonomy as the Kazakh khans still possessed. In 1822 the khanate of the Middle Horde was abolished; in 1824, the Little Horde; and in 1848, the Great Horde.

Under Russian rule. The Russian conquests in Central Asia had given the tsars control of a vast area of striking geographical and human diversity, acquired at relatively little effort in terms of men and money. The motives for the conquest had not been primarily economic; peasant colonization of the virgin steppes and the systematic cultivation of cotton were later developments. The factors that determined the Russian advance into the area were both complex and interrelated. They included the historic pull of the frontier, the thirst for military glory on the part of the officer corps, and the fear of further British penetration into Central Asia from across the Indus, as well as the infectious rhetoric of imperialism common to the age. From the outset, Russia's objectives as a colonial power were strictly limited: to maintain "law and order" at minimum cost and to disturb as little as possible the traditional way of life of its new subjects. Such an approach was favoured by the remoteness of the area and its isolation even from the rest of the Muslim world. It was improbable that an almost wholly illiterate population, its prejudices formed by a venal and obscurantist 'ulamā' (class of Muslim theologians and scholars), could offer any concerted resistance to the Russian presence; and such, indeed, proved to be the case. The Russians, like other colonial powers, did experience an occasional uprising, generally of a very localized character, but the overwhelming military superiority displayed by the Russians at the time of the initial conquest, the inability of the inhabitants of the khanates to offer effective resistance, and the heavy-handedness with which subsequent insurrection or insubordination was dealt with ensured minimal opposition. Finally, by preserving the titular sovereignty of the emir of Bukhara and the khan of Khiva, they left a substantial part of the population, especially the urban classes, most deeply devoted to the Islāmic way of life, under traditionally minded Muslim rulers.

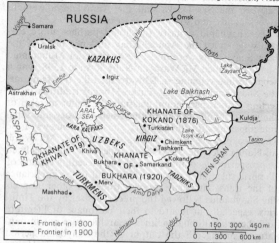

From P. Holt, A. Lambton, and B. Lewis (eds.), *Cambridge History of Islam*, vol. 1 (1970); Cambridge University Press

Russian penetration of Turkistan in the 19th and 20th centuries.

West Turkistan under tsarist rule. Yet the Russians, whether intentionally or not, became agents of change throughout the area in much the same way as any other colonial power. The economy was gradually realigned to meet the Russian need for raw materials and new markets. This required the construction of railroads: by 1888 the Trans-Caspian Railroad had reached Samarkand; between 1899 and 1905 the Orenburg-Tashkent Railroad was completed; the Turkistan-Siberian Railroad came later, begun just before World War I and not completed until 1930. In Tashkent and Samarkand new European suburbs were laid out at a distance from the walled native cities, but as in the case of the newly established garrison towns, such islands of European life required local services and supplies. Nor did the Russians wholly ignore the welfare of their new subjects. An effort was made, halfheartedly at first, to put down the indigenous slave trade; irrigation projects were initiated; and bilingual elementary education was cautiously introduced. As elsewhere in colonial Asia, the work of Russian scholars studying the literature, history, and antiquities of the Central Asian peoples aroused upon the part of a numerically small but influential Russian-educated elite, especially among the Kazakhs, nostalgic awareness of a colourful past and a sense of national, or cultural, identity.

Of the major racial groups in Central Asia—Uzbeks, Kazakhs, Turkmens, Tadzhiks, and Kirgiz—the Kazakhs were the first to respond to the impact of Russian culture. Their early contacts with their new masters had in the main been carried out through intermediaries—Kazan Tatars, who, paradoxically, had contributed to strengthening the Kazakhs' awareness of being part of a greater Muslim world community and their sense of being a "nation" rather than a welter of tribes and clans. Moreover, through the Tatars they were exposed to current Pan-Turkish and Pan-Islāmic propaganda. In the 1870s the Russians countered Tatar influence by establishing bilingual Russian-Kazakh schools, from which emerged a westernized elite of considerable distinction. The time seemed ripe for a meaningful process of cultural interchange, made more credible by the fact that, despite the growing sense of Kazakh national identity, the Kazakhs were too much on the peripheries of the Islāmic world to feel strongly the pull of Pan-Islāmic or even Pan-Turkish sentiment.

This Russo-Kazakh "dialogue" was, however, doomed to founder on the rock of the government's policy of settling peasants from European Russia and the Ukraine on the Kazakh steppe, where agricultural settlement on an extensive scale could be undertaken only by curtailing the area available for grazing by the nomads' livestock

Left margin notes:

Russian advance onto the Kazakh steppe

Kazakh response to Russian rule

and by restricting their seasonal migrations. As early as 1867–68 the northwestern fringes of the Kazakh steppe had been the scene of violent protests at the presence of colonists; but it was not until the last decade of the century that the movement got fully under way with the arrival of upward of 1,000,000 peasants, resulting in the inevitable expropriation of Kazakh grazing grounds and in savage conflict between the Kazakhs and the intruders. Finally, in 1916, during World War I, the Kazakhs, driven to desperation by the loss of their lands and by the ruthlessness of the wartime administration, rose up in protest against a decree conscripting the non-Russian subjects of the empire for forced labour. The rebellion assumed the character of a popular uprising, in which many colonists and many more Kazakhs and Kirgiz were massacred. The revolt was put down with the utmost savagery, and more than 300,000 Kazakhs are said to have sought refuge across the Chinese frontier.

With the collapse of tsarist rule, the westernized Kazakh elite formed a party, the Alash-Orda, as a vehicle through which to express their aspirations for regional autonomy. Having found during the Russian civil war that the anti-Communist "Whites" were implacably opposed to their aspirations, the Kazakhs cast in their lot with the "Reds."

After the war the Kazakhs were granted their own republic, in which, for the first few years, the leaders of the Alash-Orda maintained a fairly dominant position and were active in protecting Kazakh interests; after 1924, however, direct confrontation with the Communist Party became more intense, and in 1927–28 they were liquidated as "bourgeois nationalists."

The history of the Kazakhs in the first half of the 20th century has been bleak indeed—expropriation of their grazing lands under the tsars, the bloody uprising and reprisals of 1916, the losses in the civil war and in the famine in 1921, purges of the intelligentsia in 1927–28, collectivization during the 1930s, and further peasant colonization after World War II.

In Mā Warā' an-Nahr, divided between the administration of the Russian governor general of Turkistan, based on Tashkent, and that of the emir of Bukhara and the khan of Khiva, opposition to colonial domination was centred in the most conservative elements of a profoundly Islāmic society—the 'ulamā' and the inhabitants of the bazaar. Nonetheless, the Russian favoured, for reasons of expediency, the preservation of the traditional social framework and endeavoured, with only partial success, to insulate the inhabitants of the region from contact with the more "advanced" Muslims of the empire—the Volga and Crimean Tatars. In this they were aided by the fact that the virtual absence of European colonization provided no fuel for popular resentment comparable to that felt by the Kazakhs; and, in consequence, the westernized products of the bilingual Russian–Uzbek educational system, primarily concerned with reform of the Islāmic way of life, regarded the Muslim "ultras" as their most dangerous opponents.

If the main influence in shaping the outlook of the Kazakh intelligentsia was the educational system imported from European Russia, the catalyst in the case of the Uzbeks was knowledge of the educational reforms and the Pan-Turkish ideology of the Crimean Tatar renaissance of the late 19th century. The Uzbek reformers, known as Jadidists, advocated the introduction of a modern educational system as a prerequisite for social change and cultural revitalization; and despite intense opposition from the clerical classes, they opened their first school in Tashkent in 1901 and by 1914 had established more than 100. After 1908, influenced by the Young Turks of the Ottoman Empire, the Young Bukharans and the Young Khivans worked for a program of radical institutional change in the ramshackle governments of the khanates. By 1917, however, it may be doubted whether the Uzbek intelligentsia had made any substantial impact outside a fairly narrow circle of like-minded persons.

West Turkistan under Soviet rule. Neither before nor after the Russian Revolution were the nationalist aspirations of the Muslims of Central Asia compatible with the interests of the Russian state or those of the European population of the region. This was demonstrated once and for all when the troops of the Tashkent Soviet crushed a short-lived Muslim government established in Kokand in January 1918. Indeed, the Soviet authorities in Central Asia regarded the native intelligentsia, even the most "progressive" of them, with lively and (from their point of view) justifiable apprehension. At the same time there was the problem of an active resistance on the part of conservative elements, which was anti-Russian as much as anti-Communist. Having extinguished the khanate of Khiva in 1919 and that of Bukhara in 1920, local Red Army units found themselves engaged in a protracted struggle with the Basmachis—guerrillas operating in the mountains in the eastern part of the former khanate of Bukhara. Not until 1925 did the Red Army gain the upper hand.

In time, however, the Soviet Union came to realize that armed insurrection was far less dangerous to the new regime than the adherence to local Communist parties of members of the Muslim intelligentsia—former Nationalists turned Marxists but suspected of harbouring separatist and Pan-Turkish designs. This indigenous leadership was therefore systematically liquidated during the 1930s. Thereafter, the Soviets continued to reinforce the administrative and cultural autonomy of Kazakhstan, Uzbekistan, Turkmenistan, Tadzhikistan, and Kirgizia with a view to eliminating Pan-Turkish or Pan-Islāmic sentiment through a policy of "divide and rule." It would be unwise, however, not to recognize the positive advantages accruing to the inhabitants of Russian Central Asia as a result of the Soviet Union's federal structure or to underestimate the scope that it has allowed for the cultural development of each individual republic.

EAST TURKISTAN

Kashgaria, unlike Mā Warā' an-Nahr and Semirechiye, did not offer favourable conditions for pastoral nomadism except on the slopes of the Tien Shan, where the Kirgiz pasture their flocks, and, in consequence, the area remained somewhat outside the main course of the invasions and migrations that dominated so much of the early history of Central Asia. The importance of Kashgaria was due primarily to the caravan routes that traversed it, coming down to Kashgar and Yarkand from the passes over the Pamirs, either from the watershed of the Amu Darya and Badakhshan or from the watershed of the Syr Darya and Farghana. From Kashgar and Yarkand two ancient roads led toward the Kansu Corridor, a southern road, via Khotan, and a northern one, via Kucha, Turfan, and Hami; part of the famous "Silk Road," it was along this route that Buddhism made its way from India to China, its stages marked by sites—excavated (1900–30) by the Hungarian-British archaeologist Sir Aurel Stein and others—revealing the syncretistic art that flourished in the oases from Kushan times.

The early history of Kashgaria was the scene of recurring conflicts between successive Chinese rulers, claiming suzerainty over the region, and the nomad tribal confederacies to the north, ever seeking to throw off a distant and largely nominal Chinese yoke. With the fall of the khanate of the Uighur Turks of the Orkhon in the 9th century, a number of Uighur tribes moved southwestward, first into the Tien Shan and then into the oases of the Tarim Basin. There they remained the dominant racial component. The Uighurs were in the main Manichaeans, followers of a religion founded by the 3rd-century Persian prophet Mani, but they tolerated both Buddhist and Nestorian Christian communities in their midst. Under the Qarakhanids in the 10th century the process of Islāmization began, though even at the time when the area was incorporated into the Mongol Empire in the early 13th century, the cultural pattern was still extremely diverse. Kashgaria, together with Mā Warā' an-Nahr and Semirechiye, was part of the *ulus* of Chagatai; and, following the breakup of the khanate in the middle decades of the 14th century, the Muslim cities south of the Tien Shan—Kashgar, Uch Turfan, Aksu, Kucha, Yangi Hissar, and Yarkand—acted as a magnet to the infidel khans of the East and their retainers in the same way that the cities of Mā Warā' an-Nahr had already lured the khans of the West.

By the second half of the 15th century the rulers of the eastern Chagatai khanate were wholly Islāmicized; but already their power was waning, assaulted by the Oyrats in Jungaria, the Kazakhs in Semirechiye, and the Kirgiz in the Tien Shan. Throughout the 16th century this decline continued, although it was temporarily halted during the reign of Sa'id Khan (reigned 1514–c. 1533). By the beginning of the 17th century, however, the khan had become a mere figurehead, the cities having passed into the hands of a quasi-theocratic dynasty of Khwājahs from Bukhara while the countryside was dominated by rival Kirgiz confederacies. In the late 17th century the whole Tarim Basin became part of the Oyrat Empire of the khan Galdan, who, nevertheless, left the Khwājahs as de facto rulers in Kashgar and Yarkand. In 1758–59 the area was occupied by the Manchus, following their defeat of the Oyrats, and it was finally incorporated into the Chinese Empire under the Manchu (Ch'ing) dynasty.

Manchu rule

The new administration, supervised by Manchus, left the inhabitants of the area very much to themselves, disturbing neither their religion nor their traditional way of life. Manchu rule was bitterly unpopular, however, and the exiled Khwājahs frequently attempted to foment insurrection from Kokand, across the mountains. In 1867 Kashgaria passed into the hands of a Kokandī adventurer, Ya'qūb Beg, who proclaimed his independence and established diplomatic contacts with British India and the Ottoman Empire. Not until 1878 were the Manchus able to reassert control. From that time the administration of the region, now known as Sinkiang (New Dominion), was somewhat more closely regulated from Peking, especially because the period witnessed a dangerous growth of Russian influence in the area. Following the 1911 Revolution in China, Sinkiang became the "fief" of a Yunnanese (Chinese) warlord, Yang Tseng-hsin, who ruled with an iron hand until 1928, at a time when the disturbances across the Russian frontier made the region peculiarly vulnerable. After 1933 Sinkiang was ruled by another formidable warlord, Shang Shih-ts'ai, who was nonetheless compelled to surrender it to the Kuomintang (Chinese Nationalists) in 1941. In 1949 it passed into Communist hands, and in 1955 the Sinkiang Uighur (*q.v.*) Autonomous Region was set up. In none of these events, at least after 1878, had the indigenous Turkish inhabitants of the region played any active part.

BIBLIOGRAPHY

General: G.R.G. HAMBLY (ed.), *Central Asia* (1970).

West Turkistan (the early empires): V.V. BARTHOLD, *Turkestan Down to the Mongol Invasion*, 3rd ed. (1968; Eng. trans. from the 1963 Russian edition); J.A. BOYLE (ed.), *The Cambridge History of Iran*, vol. 5 (1968); R.N. FRYE, *Bukhara: The Medieval Achievement* (1965); H.A.R. GIBB, *The Arab Conquests in Central Asia* (1923); O. PRITSAK, "Die Karachaniden," *Der Islam*, 31:17–68 (1953–54). (*The Mongol-Timurid periods: Uzbek and Kazakh khanates*): V.V. BARTHOLD, *Four Studies on the History of Central Asia*, 3 vol. (Eng. trans. 1956–62); J.A. BOYLE, *The History of the World-Conqueror*, 2 vol. (Eng. trans. 1958); N. ELIAS and E. DENISON ROSS, *A History of the Moghuls of Central Asia* (1895); M. HOLDSWORTH, *Turkestan in the Nineteenth Century* (1959). (*West Turkistan under Russian rule*): E. ALLWORTH (ed.), *Central Asia: A Century of Russian Rule* (1967); S. BECKER, *Russia's Protectorates in Central Asia: Bukhara and Khiva, 1865–1924* (1968); A. BENNIGSEN and C. LEMERCIER-QUELQUEJAY, *Islam in the Soviet Union* (1967); H. CARRERE D'ENCAUSSE, *Réforme et Révolution chez les Musulmans de l'Empire Russe, Bukhara, 1867–1924* (1966); G.N. CURZON, *Russia in Central Asia in 1889, and the Anglo-Russian Question* (1889); K.K. PAHLEN, *Mission to Turkestan* (1964); A.G. PARK, *Bolshevism in Turkestan, 1917–1927* (1957); R.A. PIERCE, *Russian Central Asia, 1867–1917* (1960); G. WHEELER, *The Modern History of Soviet Central Asia* (1964); S.A. ZENKOVSKY, *Pan-Turkism and Islam in Russia* (1960).

East Turkistan: H.W. BELLEW, *The History of Kashgharia* (1875); M. BUSSAGLI, *Painting of Central Asia* (Eng. trans. 1963); M. COURANT, *L'Asie Centrale aux XVIIe et XVIIIe siècles: empire Kalmouk ou empire Mantchou?* (1912); M. HARTMANN, *Der islamische Orient*, 3 vol. (1899–1910); I.C.Y. HSU, *The Ili Crisis: A Study of Sino-Russian Diplomacy, 1871–1881* (1965); A.N. KUROPATKIN, *Kashgaria* (1882); O. LATTIMORE, *Inner Asian Frontiers of China* (1940 and 1962); W. SAMOLIN, *East Turkestan to the Twelfth Century* (1964); M.A. STEIN, *On Ancient Central-Asian Tracks* (1933). BIBLIOGRAPHIES: R.A. PIERCE, *Russian Central Asia, 1867–1917: A Selected Bibliography* (1960); D. SINOR, *Introduction à l'étude de l'Eurasie Centrale* (1963).

(G.R.G.H.)

Turkmen Soviet Socialist Republic

A sun-beaten land of deserts and oases, the Turkmen Soviet Socialist Republic (also known as Turkmeniya, or Turkmenistan) is situated on the same latitude as the Mediterranean but deep in the heart of the Asian continent, the southernmost Soviet territory. With 188,500 square miles (488,100 square kilometres), it was the home of 2,495,000 persons by the mid-1970s. It was formed on October 27, 1924, and on May 13, 1925, formally became one of the constituent republics of the Soviet Union; its capital is at Ashkhabad. Its Central Asian neighbours are the Kazakh S.S.R. to the north, the Uzbek S.S.R. to the east, and Iran and Afghanistan to the south, while the Caspian Sea forms its western boundary.

For related information, see SOVIET UNION; AMU DARYA (RIVER); KARA-KUM DESERT; CENTRAL ASIAN PEOPLES, ARTS OF; ALTAIC LANGUAGES; INNER ASIA, HISTORY OF; TURKISTAN, HISTORY OF.

THE LANDSCAPE

Deserts occupy 90 percent of Turkmenistan's territory. The Kara-Kum (Black Sand) is one of the world's largest sand deserts, taking up the entire central part of Turkmenistan and extending into Kazakhstan. Topographically, four-fifths of Turkmenistan is plains—the southern part of the Turan Plain. Mountains and foothills rise mainly in the southern part of the republic, the Kugitangtau and Kopet-Dag ranges being spurs of the Pamir-Alay mountain ranges. The Kopet-Dag is geologically young, its instability indicated—as in 1929 and 1948—by intermittent earthquakes of great destructive force.

Climate. Turkmenistan's position deep inside Asia, the resultant unique air-mass circulation, and the character of the relief are responsible for a strongly continental climate, which exhibits great fluctuations in temperatures during the day and the year. The average annual temperature is 57°–61° F (14°–16° C), but this figure masks an extremely wide range. The temperature is seldom lower than 95° F (35° C) during summer days, and the absolute maximum high temperature in the southeast Kara-Kum reaches 122° F (50° C) in the shade. By contrast, in winter, the temperature in Kushka drops to −27° F (−33° C). Humidity is very low and rainfall meagre. Precipitation occurs mainly in the spring and ranges from about 3 inches (80 millimetres) per year in the northwest desert to as much as 12 inches (300 millimetres) in the mountains.

Water resources and irrigation. Turkmenistan's main rivers are the Amu Darya (the Oxus of classical times), flowing along its northeastern border toward the Aral Sea, and the Tedzhen, Murgab, and Atrek; there are also numerous small mountain rivers. The annual total of water transported by the republic's rivers reaches 2,100,-000,000–2,300,000,000 cubic feet (60,000,000–65,000,-000 cubic metres). Unfortunately, however, the geographical position of the rivers and the direction of their flow do not coincide with the location of cultivable lands; the most fertile—and still insufficiently used—lands lie chiefly in the south, northeast, and west, whereas the principal rivers run mostly in the east. A great number of canals and reservoirs has been built. The construction, across the Kara-Kum, of the world's largest irrigation and shipping canal, the Karakumsky Kanal (Kara-Kum Canal), began in the mid-1950s; when completed it will be 870 miles (1,400 kilometres) long. By the mid-1970s the canal was irrigating about 300,000 hectares, and construction was proceeding in the direction of Krasnovodsk, on the shores of the Caspian.

The Kara-kumsky Kanal

Soils and plant and animal life. Turkmenistan's soils are varied. A unique feature is that there is no definitely formed soil layer in most of the desert region. In the northern and western Kara-Kum, on raised areas, the sand gives way to sandy loam and sandy and clay soils, sometimes mixed with broken rock. In the oases, a layer suitable for irrigated cultivation has formed.

The biological resources are varied but not abundant. Except in the oases and mountain valleys and plateaus, vegetation is of a pronounced desert character. In the mountain valleys of the Kopet-Dag, wild grape, almond, fig, and walnut are found, while juniper and pistachio trees grow on the open slopes. On the riverbanks and islands, chiefly in and along the Amu Darya, stand *tugai* forests of black poplar, willow, reed, and cane.

The animal world is represented mainly by desert creatures: steppe and Persian fox, wildcat, Kara-Kum gazelle, and tortoise. The wildlife of the mountains includes mountain rams and goats; such wild cats as the cheetah, lynx, and snow leopard; and the porcupine. Jackals, wild boars, and birds frequent the *tugai*. Rare pink deer are also found along the Amu Darya, and wild donkeys roam the Badkhyz and Karabil plateaus in the southwest. The eastern coast of the Caspian Sea is the winter home of vast flocks of ducks, geese, and swans.

In the waters of the eastern Caspian, various kinds of herring, sprat, roach, and sturgeon (including the beluga, prized for caviar) are widespread; the Amu Darya and its lakes, and other rivers, contain carp, barbel, and pike.

The human imprint. There is much variety in the different regions of Turkmenistan, but two broad divisions may be seen: an oasis region—characterized by adequate water supply, cultivated lands, and developed industry—composed of the Kopet-Dag, Tedzhen, Murgab, Middle Amu Darya, and Lower Amu Darya oases; and a desert region, subdivided into Western Turkmenistan, with a well-developed industry, and the Kara-Kum, with cattle raising and resources of natural gas and petroleum under the sands.

The oases. The Kopet-Dag Oasis stretches along the northern foothills of the Kopet-Dag Range, the slopes of which offer large areas for nonirrigated farming; both the mountains and foothills are also rich in mineral resources. The economic and cultural centre of the oasis is Ashkhabad, the republic's capital, with about 290,000 inhabitants. The development of the capital has stimulated industry, turning an agrarian oasis into the industrial-agrarian core of the republic. The Central Asian Railway, linking Tashkent, in the Uzbek S.S.R., with Krasnovodsk, via Ashkhabad and other cities of Turkmenistan, runs between the foothills and the Kara-Kum. The Firyuza and Chuli mountain valleys, rich in water and with a mild climate, have become known as health resorts.

The Murgab Oasis is famous for its fine-staple cotton, silk, handmade carpets and rugs, and Karakul sheep. The Murgab River, now that its lower reaches are crossed by the Karakumsky Kanal, can supply more water for irrigation. Mary (formerly Merv), with some 70,000 inhabitants, is the centre of the oasis and the surrounding region, and one of the most attractive towns in the republic.

Separated from the Murgab by a stretch of the Kara-Kum, the Tedzhen Oasis formed along the Tedzhen River. Because of the scarcity of water, only small areas of wheat, barley, and melons could be cultivated. After the oasis was crossed by the Karakumsky Kanal, however, and the Khauz-Khan Reservoir was built, large areas were irrigated, thus making possible the cultivation of long-staple cotton and the construction of cotton-processing plants. The economic and cultural centre is the town of Tedzhen, with 25,000 inhabitants. South of the oasis lies the Badkhyz National Reserve, with unique pistachio tree woodlands strongly resembling African savanna.

The Middle Amu Darya Oasis, in contrast to other oases, stretches almost without interruption for hundreds of miles and is almost entirely cultivated. The Amu Darya waters are very rich in silt, an excellent natural fertilizer. Raising of cotton and silkworms has long been widespread in that area. It is an important producer of kenaf and other fibre crops and the only supplier of wild

The Kopet-Dag Oasis (margin)

licorice in the Soviet Union. The adjoining deserts provide fodder for Karakul sheep. Industries processing agricultural products and mineral raw materials have been developed in the oasis and the adjoining Gaurdak-Kugitang district. The Soviet Union's largest deposits of sulfur as well as deposits of potassium and other salts are found here, together with building materials. The economic and administrative centre of the oasis and the region is Chardzhou (with about 104,000 inhabitants), the second largest city and industrial centre in Turkmenistan.

The Lower Amu Darya Oasis lies in the ancient delta of the Amu Darya; Turkmenistan's northernmost oasis, it is one of the most important agricultural regions of the republic. The oasis is cut by a dense network of old riverbeds as well as by irrigation channels and ditches beginning in the neighbouring Uzbek S.S.R. The climate is more continental than that of other oases, but it is warm enough to grow medium-staple cotton and alfalfa. Rice, sweet sorghum, beans, kenaf, sesame, grapes, vegetables, and melons are also grown, and cattle and silkworms are raised. Most industrial enterprises are concentrated in the regional centre, the town of Tashauz (population about 75,000).

The deserts. The desert of Western Turkmenistan is an enormous and almost waterless expanse, with only a small oasis irrigated by the Atrek River in the extreme southwest. The mountainous part of Western Turkmenistan, a continuation of the Caucasus Mountains, has mineral and fuel resources. The unique deposits of mirabilite in the Kara-Bogaz-Gol Gulf of the Caspian Sea, petroleum (with natural gas and iodine- and bromine-containing waters), and rock salt and common lake salt are of great importance.

Western Turkmenistan (margin)

Western Turkmenistan is one of the most developed regions of the republic industrially, emphasizing oil extraction and refining, chemical and mining industries, and fisheries and fish processing. The rural population in Western Turkmenistan is less dense than that in the east. People are mostly engaged in raising sheep, goats, and camels and, to a lesser extent, grains and melons.

In the southern part of the Krasnovodsk Plateau, overlooking a bay of the Caspian Sea, stands the city of Krasnovodsk (53,000 inhabitants). Nebit-Dag (62,000) lies inland, east of Krasnovodsk.

The three parts of the Kara-Kum and the other featureless deserts—occupying the greater portion of the republic—enter, in part, all of the above-mentioned areas. They are distinguished by the same desert landscape, lack of surface water, exceptionally meagre precipitation, and high summer temperatures. At the same time, the desert is a zone of fuel and mineral resources, and its richest pastures can be used all the year round for sheep, goats, and camels.

THE PEOPLE

Demographic trends. The population of Turkmenistan had reached 2,495,000 by January 1975. The republic has a high natural population increase because of a high birth rate (34 per 1,000 population) and low mortality rate (seven per 1,000).

It is a multinational republic with Turkmens (66 percent of the total in 1970, compared with 61 percent in 1959) the predominant nationality, followed by Russians (14.5 percent), Uzbeks (8.3 percent), Kazakhs (3.2 percent), and small numbers of Tatars, Ukrainians, Armenians, Azerbaijanis, and Kara-Kalpaks. The 1,417,000 Turkmens living in the republic at the census of 1970 made up almost 93 percent of all Turkmens in the Soviet Union; the remaining 7 percent live mainly in Uzbekistan, Tadzhikistan, and the Northern Caucasus and the Astrakhan *oblast* of the Russian S.F.S.R.

The population is distributed unevenly, the average density in 1970 being about 11.4 persons per square mile (4.4 per square kilometre), only 40 percent of the overall Soviet average; in the Kara-Kum and mountain regions, there are fewer than three persons per square mile, but in the oases the figure reaches 780 per square mile (300 per square kilometre). With the development

Population distribution (margin)

of the Turkmenistan economy, numbers of non-Turkmen skilled workers and scientific and technical intelligentsia —with a large proportion of youth and women—immigrated to the republic.

There is a large urban population (48 percent of the total) inhabiting 15 major and more than 70 minor settlements. The rest of the people live in rural settlements and villages. Since the 1950s, the number of towns has been growing, while that of the traditional rural settlements has been diminishing, although the size of individual settlements is on the increase. Turkmens made up only 31.7 percent of the republic's town and city dwellers in 1970. The urban population consisted mainly of outsiders, those from the Soviet west and the Russian S.F.S.R. being concentrated in the principal centres: 95.7 percent of the republic's 313,079 Russians lived in towns, as did 83.3 percent of Ukrainians, 91.8 percent of Tatars, 97.4 percent of Armenians, and 96.8 percent of Azerbaijanis. In the capital city, Ashkhabad, those same five ethnic groups accounted for 56.1 percent of the residents, while Turkmens constituted 38.2 percent.

Ethnic characteristics. For centuries the Turkmens were divided into numerous tribes and clans, the largest being the Tekke, Ersari, and Yomut, whose total number exceeded 500,000. The number of people in other tribes (the Salor, Sarïq, Goklan, and Chaudar) fluctuated between 20,000 and 40,000.

Up to the time of the Russian Revolution (they had come under Russian domination in the 19th century) most of the Turkmens were pastoral nomads, though during the 18th and 19th centuries many had settled in the oases and become agriculturalists. Their tribal organizations and loyalties were strong. They had always been warlike and had commonly hired themselves out as mercenaries to various rulers in Central Asia. The establishment of the Turkmen S.S.R.—which was not done without a struggle, in which Turkmens joined with Bukharan Uzbeks and others in a protracted battle to throw off Russian domination—had the effect of bringing greater unity to the Turkmen tribes and of giving them the beginning of a sense of nationhood.

THE ECONOMY

By 1970, 450,000 factory and office workers and 230,000 collective farmers were employed in the Turkmenistan economy. The republic now specializes in cotton growing and in oil and gas extraction. Although it occupies a relatively small place in overall Soviet industrial and agricultural output, the republic turns out considerable quantities of certain products: 24–28 percent of iodine and bromine, and about 40 percent of the Soviet Union's sodium sulfate total.

Resources. Turkmenistan is rich in various minerals and in petroleum and natural gas. The potential reserves of the latter, occupying second place (in the Soviet Union) after the Russian S.F.S.R., are estimated at 210,000,000,000,000 cubic feet (6,000,000,000,000 cubic metres). Chemical resources are also extensive, especially those of mirabilite and other similar salts in the Kara-Bogaz-Gol area of the Caspian. Deposits of sulfur, potassium, and sodium chloride and oil-field waters containing iodine and bromine are also considerable. Dolomites, limestone, and marl are found in the mountains and foothills, and the Kara-Kum supplies sands used in making glass and bricks.

Reserves of natural gas

Industrial development. The radical reconstruction of the economy was finished by 1930. Old branches (cotton ginning, oil pressing, and carpet making) were retained, and new ones (heavy and light industry, and food processing) made their appearance. The net result has been a 40-fold increase in gross industrial output during the Soviet period.

Petroleum deposits and the associated oil industry are centred in the Caspian plain in Western Turkmenistan and in the offshore oil fields to the west of the Cheleken Peninsula in the Caspian Sea. In oil extraction Turkmenistan holds third place among the Soviet republics, after the Russian S.F.S.R. and Azerbaijan. Turkmenistan oil is of a very high grade, both as a fuel and as a chemical

raw material, and its production reached nearly 16,000,000 tons annually by the mid-1970s. The prospects for the gas industry are good, 22 deposits having been discovered between 1950 and 1975. These include the Shakhetli deposit, with estimated reserves of 35,000,000,000,000 cubic feet (1,000,000,000,000 cubic metres). A network of gas pipelines links gas deposits in Western Turkmenistan with Ashkhabad, Krasnovodsk, Cheleken, and the central regions of the republic.

Significant in the chemical industry are the Chardzhou superphosphate plant, mirabilite from the vicinity of the Kara-Bogaz-Gol, sulfur from Gaurdak, iodine and bromine factories on the Cheleken Peninsula, and sulfanole production at the Krasnovodsk oil refinery.

Turkmenistan has a number of thermal power stations, using liquid fuel, at Nebit-Dag, Ashkhabad, Bezmein, Krasnovodsk, and elsewhere; a station near the town of Mary uses natural gas. Hydropower stations include the Hindu Kush plant, as well as plants at Kaushtubent and at the Tashkeprin Reservoir on the Murgab River.

Electrical power

Engineering and metal-processing enterprises include repair shops for diesel locomotives, railway cars, and agricultural machinery. In Ashkhabad and in Mary there are plants producing, among other products, equipment for extracting and refining oil. Textile and cotton-ginning industries are also important; there are silk-winding and silk-weaving mills, as well as cotton, cotton-wool, and worsted mills. Textile production amounted to more than 26,700,000 linear metres (87,700,000 linear feet) in 1974. Artificial furs, leather footwear, and sewn goods are also produced.

The most important branches of the food industry are vegetable oil, fish, meat, and flour production and wine making. The republic exports oil, butter, wine, fish, and salt to other parts of the Soviet Union.

Domestic industries, especially carpet and rug making, occupy an important place in the republic's economy. Turkmen carpets and rugs, long renowned for their durability and unique designs, are exported to more than 50 countries. Among Turkmen carpets well known in the West are those made by the Tekke, Yomut, Salor, and Ersari Turkmens and called by those names.

Agriculture. The growing of cotton and the raising of Karakul sheep, horses, and camels (see Table) are the most important branches of agriculture. Turkmenistan is the largest producer of fine-staple cotton in the Soviet Union.

Agricultural enterprises are large; there were in 1975 about 330 large collective farms (*kolkhozy*) and 55 state farms (*sovkhozy*). The average collective farm has 458 households, 3,535 acres of sown land, and about 8,000 sheep and goats.

Kenaf is a new industrial crop, and sesame is important among oil-bearing plants. Wheat and barley account for much of the area sown in grain crops; areas under millet and rice are as yet insignificant. Fodder crops (maize, alfalfa, and others) occupy one-sixth of the sown area. Turkmenistan melons have long been famous, and the republic's grapes are also well known.

Main Indexes of Agricultural Development in Turkmenistan*					
item	1913	1940	1960	1970	1974
Sown area					
(000 ac)	786	1,016	1,103	1,440	1,978
(000 ha)	318	411	446	600	801
Cattle (000 head)	...	268	365	444	486
Meat cattle, including cows	...	96	143	188	197
Sheep and goats (000 head)	...	2,596	4,928	4,489	4,337
Of which, sheep	...	1,999	4,647	4,291	...
Output of agricultural products					
Raw cotton (000 tons)	69	211	363	869	1,117
Grain crops (000 tons)	159	124	40	69	181
Vegetables (000 tons)	...	32	68	136	195
Fruit and berries (000 tons)	...	21	28	57	...
Of which, grapes	...	16	24	36	50
Meat (000 tons)	58	22	51	51	64
Milk (000 tons)	63	107	126	192	232
Wool (000 tons)	9.7	4.9	15.9	14	14.9
Eggs (000,000)	18	37	56	122	169

*Metric tons unless otherwise indicated.

The republic produces Karakul pelts, including black *arabi*, golden *sur*, and silver-gray *shirazi*, all very beautiful, durable, and in great demand in the world market; indeed, Karakul sheep account for more than 70 percent of all sheep in the republic.

Over the centuries, Turkmens have also evolved the horses of the Akhal Tekke and Yomut breeds, valued for their physical endurance, speed, and beauty. Camels—mainly Arabian, and indispensable in the desert as a means of transport for sheep herders, for getting water from desert wells, and as a source of meat, wool, and milk—are also traditional Turkmen livestock. Turkmenistan leads the Soviet Union in the production of silkworm cocoons.

Horse-breeding traditions

Transportation. The basic means of transport is the railways, though the density of the rail network (1,310 miles, or 2,110 kilometres, of track in 1970) is much below the Soviet average. The main trunk line is between Krasnovodsk and Tashkent (in the Uzbek S.S.R.), with branch lines from Mary to Kushka and from Nebit-Dag to Vyshka. In the 1950s a line was built to link Chardzhou, and areas as far northwest along the Amu Darya as Kungrad, to the central regions.

Motor transport is developing more rapidly than rail, and trucks handle most freight traffic within the republic (1,289,000,000 ton-miles, or 1,882,000,000 ton-kilometres in 1970). The main highways pass near railway lines and supplement them, especially in short-distance deliveries, but roads are also being constructed in more remote regions.

There is a merchant fleet, and the Krasnovodsk–Baku ferry provides a 210-mile link across the Caspian Sea; the electrically powered ferries are each capable of handling a freight train and making two trips daily. River transport, in seasonal operation on the Amu Darya and the Karakumsky Kanal, is of local importance.

Passenger planes and helicopters connect Ashkhabad, the capital, with many towns in the republic and elsewhere in the Soviet Union, as well as with remote geological prospectors' camps.

A network of pipelines connects the oil fields and gas deposits with transportation or consumption points. Natural gas is taken to central regions of the Russian S.F.S.R. and to the Urals through a two-pipe line, each pipe being up to five feet in diameter.

ADMINISTRATION AND SOCIAL CONDITIONS

Constitutional framework. The republic has its own flag, emblem, and anthem; its official languages are Turkmen and Russian. According to the 1937 constitution, all power in Turkmenistan derives from the workers; however, there are no democratic elections, hence no effective channels for exercising the will of an electorate.

The Supreme Soviet

The highest body of republic government is the one-chamber Supreme Soviet of the Turkmen S.S.R., which is elected for a four-year term. The great majority of its 300 deputies are Turkmens, and about a third are women. All citizens of the republic reaching the age of 18 are eligible to vote, and those over 23 years of age can be elected deputies. The Supreme Soviet of the Turkmen S.S.R., however, exercises no real power. It meets for only a short time at six-month intervals, and deputies are selected from a single list of persons provided by the authorities without primary contests. The ethnic makeup of the Supreme Soviet is mixed, though there are no specifically stated protections for the various nationalities, nor are selections for the single list of candidates organized ethnically. Rather, candidates appear as designees from precincts, though often they are neither residents of the given precinct nor even permanent residents of the Turkmen S.S.R. (high-ranking Russian generals of the Soviet Army, for example, often emerge from the list as deputies to both the republic and union-wide supreme soviets). The Turkmen S.S.R., along with all other constituent republics, is represented in the national Supreme Soviet, the country's highest organ of state power. The Presidium of the Supreme Soviet consists of a chairman, two vice chairmen, a secretary, and 11 members.

The highest executive and administrative body in the republic is the Council of Ministers, formed by the republican Supreme Soviet; it organizes and supervises the activity of all ministries and other accountable departments. The chairman of the Council of Ministers of the republic is ex officio a member of the Council of Ministers of the Soviet Union.

Local government is carried out through district, town, rural settlement, and village soviets, elected for terms of two years.

The highest judicial body is the Supreme Court of the republic; in districts and in cities there are people's courts, with judges and people's assessors elected from one list of candidates provided by the authorities.

The Communist Party in Turkmenistan (there is no Turkmen Communist Party or party division) is a branch of the Communist Party of the Soviet Union (CPSU) and the real centre of organized power in the republic. In 1967 Turkmens were vastly under-represented in the party, with only 53 percent of the 62,679 members within Turkmenistan.

Communist Party

Though Russians made up less than 15 percent (1970) of the republic's population, they supplied nearly 25 percent of this privileged organization's membership (1967). These proportions represented a gain for Turkmens from 50 percent, and a comparable decline for Russians from 27 percent, in 1959. However, between 1969 and 1972, union-wide Turkmen membership, despite an advance from 38,963 card carriers to 43,111, failed to move relatively from 0.3 percent of the overall CPSU total, and Turkmens generally lacked a powerful voice in higher party councils.

Public health. The public health system has undergone radical changes. In pre-Revolutionary Turkmenistan there were fewer than one doctor and three hospital beds for every 10,000 of the population; present-day figures are more than 23 and about 100, respectively. Medical service is free.

Education. Until the collapse of the Khanate of Bukhara in 1920, Turkmens not attending schools in the Khanate of Khiva (also terminated the same year) largely received their education from the *mekteb*s (primary schools) and *medrese*s (seminaries) of Bukhara, that ancient, multi-ethnic Muslim centre, as well as in a scattering of New Method (Jadid) schools established by Muslim reformers in the early 20th century in towns such as Kerki and Chardzhou. A great extension of Turkmenistan's educational facilities has occurred since 1924, though the beginnings were relatively ineffective, compared with the best years of the late 19th-century revival in the Muslim educational system.

There were in the mid-1970s about 1,800 general primary and secondary schools serving more than 600,000 pupils of all ethnic groups. The six institutions of higher learning—the Turkmen State University (located in Ashkhabad), a teachers' training college, and medical, agricultural, and polytechnical institutes—together with 30 specialized secondary schools enroll an additional 58,000 students.

Education is supported from turnover taxes affecting most employees and from levies upon factories and other firms. It is provided tuition-free to students, and those selected for higher education receive stipends from the republic budget.

In the scientific field, the major institution is the Academy of Sciences of the Turkmen S.S.R., set up in 1951. It incorporates 16 research institutes of various kinds employing highly qualified staffs.

Cultural life. The intellectual and cultural life of Soviet Turkmenistan, led initially by the outstanding graduates of Bukharan seminaries such as Abdulhekim Qulmuhammed-oghli (died about 1937)—once active in the resistance movement, later a Communist, and influential as writer, editor, researcher, and cultural organizer—passed into the hands of Soviet-educated persons after the Stalinist purges of the 1930s "liquidated" men such as Qulmuhammed-oghli.

The widespread Turkmen traditional practice of composing poetry orally gave way, after printing became well established in Turkmen centres in the 1920s, to writing and to the dissemination of verse and prose in book form. Though written Turkmen literature dates back at least to the 18th-century poet Mahtum Quli (Magtim Guli), it underwent a burst of growth when the literary publications of the new republic began to appear in the late 1920s and '30s.

Publishing
In 1973, volumes of literature in all languages published in Turkmenistan numbered 545, with 5,300,000 copies. In general, publishing of books in the Turkmen language declined sharply between 1958–61 and 1968–71 (from 423 titles annually, on the average, to 266), and though the number of copies was increased substantially, books available to readers dropped from 2.7 per person per year to 2.3, in the same period.

There are about 1,200 libraries in the republic (containing some 7,100,000 volumes), about 800 trade-union and collective-farm clubs, eight museums, and six theatres, with 700,000 visits annually. A film studio in the capital produces features and documentaries, and Ashkhabad and Krasnovodsk have television stations. Films, television, radio, and theatre, however, are largely carried on in the Russian language and for Russian constituents rather than in Turkmen for the eponymous nationality. In 1970, for example, Ashkhabad television devoted less than 18 percent of its time to offerings in Turkmen; 82.3 percent of the transmissions, in terms of time, were in Russian; further, Turkmen-language programs included many devoted to translations from Russian or about Russian subjects and themes.

PROSPECTS FOR THE FUTURE

The Turkmen S.S.R. has great prospects for development as more natural wealth is utilized and, in particular, as more thermal power stations are built and connected to the Central Asian power grid. A unique feature is the republic's potential resources of solar (it has nearly 300 days of sunshine per year) and wind energy, which can be transformed into electrical energy. Thermoelectric, photoelectric, and other generators may well produce cheap electricity that can be used for desalinization of water and also for consumer use in sparsely populated areas where it is unprofitable to build electric-power transmission lines.

The chemical, mining, oil, and consumer-goods industries are likely to witness development in coming decades, whereas desert territories in the outlying and central regions of the Kara-Kum will be used more productively. A vital role will be played by the completed Karakumsky Kanal and by irrigation projects using the waters of the Amu Darya.

Possessing considerable natural wealth in petroleum and mineral resources as well as large land areas available for development, the Turkmens nevertheless do not seem to be benefitting as much, proportionately, as do the large numbers of immigrant workers and specialists who have populated the urban and industrial centres in the republic.

Overwhelming predominance of Russians and Russian-language use in the educational, journalistic, and cultural establishment and networks, concentrated in the towns, has relegated most Turkmens, in their own republic, to a secondary position in high-level employment and thus in economic achievement. The coming years will be crucial for the maintenance and growth of a genuine Turkmen-oriented society.

BIBLIOGRAPHY. For further information on Turkmen life, see EDWARD ALLWORTH, *Central Asian Publishing and the Rise of Nationalism* (1965); EDWARD ALLWORTH (ed.), *Central Asia: A Century of Russian Rule* (1967); ZEV KATZ et al. (eds.), *Handbook of Major Soviet Nationalities* (1975); *Canadian Slavonic Papers* (*Russian and Soviet Central Asia*), vol. 17, no. 2 and 3 (1975).

(V.B.Z./E.Al.)

Turner, J.M.W.

The English Romantic painter J.M.W. Turner was perhaps the greatest landscapist of the 19th century. Al-though brought up in the academic traditions of the 18th century, he became a pioneer in the study of light, colour, and atmosphere that, despite his lack of any real formal education, was based on considerable scientific inquiry. He anticipated the French Impressionists in breaking down conventional formulas of representation; but, unlike them, he believed that his works must always express significant themes. A line of development can be traced from his early ambitious "historical landscapes" in the manner of the French painters Nicolas Poussin and Claude Lorrain—landscapes given significance as the setting for important human subjects, such as the plagues of Egypt or the story of Dido and Aeneas—to his later studies of sea and sky. Even without figures, these late works were expressions of important subjects: the relationship of man to his environment, to the power of nature as manifested in the terror of the storm or the beneficence of the sun. Unmatched in his time and beyond in the range of his development, he was also unrivalled in the breadth of his subject matter and stylistic treatment.

Turner, self-portrait, oil painting, 1798. In the Tate Gallery, London.

Early life and works. Joseph Mallord William Turner was born on April 23, 1775, in London, the son of a barber. Nothing is known about Turner's mother except that she died insane in 1804. At the age of ten Turner was sent to live with an uncle at Brentford, Middlesex, where he attended school. Several drawings (British Museum) are dated as early as 1787. These are sufficiently professional to corroborate the tradition that his father used to sell the boy's work to his customers. After some instruction under Thomas Malton, a topographical watercolorist, Turner entered the Royal Academy schools in 1789 and exhibited a watercolour the following year, when he was only 15. He used to spend the summer holidays touring the country in search of subjects and visited Oxford in 1789, Bristol in 1791, and Wales in 1792. His sketchbooks, filled with drawings to be worked up later into finished watercolours for commissions or for exhibition, are preserved in the British Museum. His early work is topographical (concerned with accurate depiction of places) in character, imitating the best masters of the day —Thomas Malton, Edward Dayes, and Paul Sandby. In 1794 he began working for engravers, supplying designs for the *Copper Plate Magazine* and the *Pocket Magazine*. Engraved views of picturesque ruins of castles and abbeys were much in demand at the time. In the winters he attended the evening sessions at the house of Thomas Monro, the doctor and connoisseur who had treated John Robert Cozens, an English landscape painter in watercolours, during his last illness and who owned a number of his drawings. Turner, Thomas Girtin, and other young artists were employed at making copies or elaborations of his unfinished drawings. The influence of Cozens and of the Welsh landscape painter Richard Wilson helped broaden Turner's outlook and revealed to him a more poetic and imaginative approach to landscape, which he pursued to the end of his career with ever increasing brilliance.

From 1796 Turner began to exhibit oil paintings as well as watercolours at the Royal Academy. The first one, "Fishermen at Sea," is a moonlight scene and was acclaimed by a contemporary critic as the work "of an original mind."

Professional success

In 1799, at the youngest permitted age (24), Turner was elected an associate of the Royal Academy, and in 1802 he became a full Academician, a dignity he marked by a series of large pictures in which he emulated the achievements of the old masters, especially the 17th-century painters Poussin, Claude, Aelbert Cuyp, and the Van de Veldes. He took his duties seriously, attending academic functions regularly, filling various offices, and bequeathing £20,000 to the Academy. He was helpful and encouraging to other artists insofar as his shyness and brusque manner allowed. In 1807 he was appointed professor of perspective. His infrequent lectures were said to have been difficult to follow but worth it for his diagrams (now in the British Museum). In about 1800 Turner took a studio at 64 Harley Street, London, and in 1804 opened a private gallery, where he continued to show his latest work for many seasons. He was by this time overwhelmed with commissions, and the success of his career was assured.

In the midst of professional success came personal grief. In 1800 Turner's mother became hopelessly ill and was committed to a mental hospital. His father came to live with him and devoted the rest of his life to serving as a studio assistant and general agent. Turner's private life, such as it was, was secretive, unsociable, and somewhat eccentric. In 1798 he entered into an affair, which was to last about ten years, with Sarah Danby, a widow who bore him two children. As he never married, was very close with money, and devoted his time almost entirely to his art, he was able to amass a considerable fortune.

He continued to travel in search of inspiration. His travels in 1797 took him to Yorkshire and the Lake District, in 1798 to Wales again, in 1801 to Scotland, and in 1802 to the Continent for the first time. The crossing to Calais was rough, and in his picture "Calais Pier" he has left a vivid record of his experience on arrival. From Paris he proceeded to Lyons, Grenoble, Geneva, around Mont Blanc to Courmayeur and Aosta, over the St. Bernard Pass to Vevey, then to Interlaken, the St. Gotthard Pass, Zürich, Schaffhausen, and back to Paris through Strasbourg and Nancy. He made more than 400 drawings during the tour and continued for many years after to paint pictures of scenes that had impressed him on the tour, the most important being three pictures of Bonneville, Savoy (1803 and 1812); "The Festival upon the Opening of the Vintage at Macon" (1803; Graves Art Gallery, Sheffield); the watercolours "Devil's Bridge" and "The Great Falls of the Reichenbach" (1804; Cecil Higgins Museum, Bedford); "Falls of the Rhine at Schaffhausen" (1806; Museum of Fine Arts, Boston); and "Snowstorm: Hannibal and His Army Crossing the Alps" (1812; Tate Gallery, London). In Paris he made detailed notes in the Louvre, where all the paintings brought from Italy by Napoleon were then displayed. He filled a sketchbook with copies and criticism of the paintings, showing that his taste was for the great Venetians of the 16th century and for Poussin but not for Rubens, whose landscapes struck him as "one continual glare of colour." Turner's figure compositions "Venus and Adonis" and "Holy Family" (1803; Tate Gallery) show that he tried his hand in the Venetian manner. These pictures and the many early seapieces, in which he surpasses the Dutch 17th-century marine painters, reveal his methodic attempt to master every style he admired and the ease with which he accomplished this. The rivalry he felt with painters who had influenced his style—Poussin, Wilson, and Claude, for example—is suggested by his bequest to the National Gallery of his "Dido Building Carthage, or the Rise of the Carthaginian Empire" (1815) and "Sun Rising Through Vapour: Fishermen Cleaning and Selling Fish" (1807) on condition that they be hung beside his two favourite Claudes.

In 1807 Turner began his great enterprise of publishing a series of 100 plates known as the *Liber Studiorum*. His aim was to perpetuate the great variety and range of his work; some of the subjects were taken from existing paintings and watercolours; others were specially designed for the *Liber*. He employed several engravers, although he supervised the work at every stage, etched some of the plates himself, and made innumerable preparatory drawings. The publication was issued in parts consisting of five plates each, covering all the styles of landscape composition, such as historical, architectural, mountainous, pastoral, and marine. The first part appeared in June 1807 and the last in 1819, when Turner evidently lost interest in the project and abandoned it after the publication of 71 plates.

Development of an original style

The treatment of landscape in the oil Thames sketches of about 1807 and "The Shipwreck" (1805; Tate Gallery) suggests that at this time Turner was also developing an original approach to landscape—emphasizing luminosity, atmosphere, and romantic, dramatic subjects. "The Shipwreck" was the first of many works to be engraved. A list of subscribers to the engraving of "The Shipwreck" shows that by this time Turner had a wide public among the nobility and collectors as well as among fellow artists.

Middle years. During the second decade of the 1800s, Turner's painting became increasingly luminous and atmospheric in quality. Even in paintings of actual places, as "St. Mawes at the Pilchard Season" (1812; Tate Gallery) and the two pictures of Oxford painted between 1809 and 1812 (exhibited in 1812), the hard facts of topography are diffused behind pearly films of colour; other pictures, such as "Frosty Morning," are based entirely on effects of light.

Turner was much in demand as a painter of castles and countryseats for their owners. Two examples of such paintings are "Somer Hill, Tunbridge" and "Linlithgow Palace" (1810; Walker Art Gallery, Liverpool). He continued to excel in marine painting, one of the most ambitious works being "Wreck of a Transport Ship" (1810; Gulbenkian Foundation, Lisbon).

The Earl of Egremont, who had bought a seapiece in 1802, became a regular patron and close friend. Turner probably paid his first visit to his other great friend and patron, Walter Fawkes, at Farnley Hall, Yorkshire, in 1810 and subsequently spent some weeks there nearly every summer until the death of Fawkes in 1825.

Turner continued to make extensive tours, between 1811 and 1813 of Devonshire, Cornwall, and Somerset, and in 1815 and 1816 of Yorkshire for the purpose of supplying 20 watercolours to illustrate T.D. Whitaker's *History of Richmondshire*. The following year he went to the Continent, primarily to visit the battlefield of Waterloo, of which he afterward painted a dark and romantic picture, "The Field of Waterloo" (1818; Tate Gallery).

With "Dido and Aeneas, Leaving Carthage on the Morning of the Chase" (1814; Tate Gallery), Turner began a series of Carthaginian subjects, in which he presaged the decline of Britain as a great power. The last exhibits of his life, at the Academy in 1850, included four works on the same theme. By appending long poetic quotations either from James Thomson's *Seasons*, Byron, Milton, Shakespeare, Pope, or from his own composition, *Fallacies of Hope*, he showed that he regarded the poetic interpretation as of paramount importance. Among the most ethereal dreams of this period are "Lake of Geneva" (1810; Los Angeles County Museum), "Crossing the Brook," and "England; Richmond Hill, on the Prince Regent's Birthday," one of his largest and most ambitious pictures.

Advance of style in Italy

As if he felt that he had done all he could with the beauty of his native country, he set out in the summer of 1819 on his first visit to Italy. He spent three months in Rome, visited Naples, Florence, and Venice, and returned home in midwinter. During his journey he made about 1,500 drawings, and in the next few years he painted a series of pictures inspired by what he had seen. They show a great advance in Turner's style, particularly in the matter of colour, which becomes purer, more prismatic, with general heightening of key. A comparison of "The Bay of Baiae, with Apollo and the Sibyl" with any of the earlier pictures reveals a far more iridescent treatment resembling the transparency of a watercolour. The shadows are as colourful as the lights, and he achieves contrasts by setting off cold and warm colours instead of dark and light tones.

During the 1820s, tours of the Continent alternated with visits to various parts of England and Scotland. In 1821 Turner painted a series of delicate watercolours of the Seine on blue paper; in 1825 he revisited The Netherlands and Belgium and the following year the Meuse, Moselle, and the Loire. Notable among the pictures of this period are such views as "The Harbor of Dieppe," "Cologne: The Arrival of a Packet Boat: Evening," and "Mortlake Terrace: Early Summer Morning" (Frick Collection, New York). In 1827 he stayed with John Nash, the architect, at Cowes and painted the brilliant sketches of the regatta now at the Tate Gallery. In 1828 he went to Italy again and held an exhibition of some of his pictures in Rome. After his father's death in 1829, Turner often visited the Earl of Egremont at Petworth, Sussex. The splendid sketches of Petworth probably belong to the early 1830s.

Later life and works. In the last years of his life, Turner was more famous, richer, and more secretive than ever. After several years of inactivity as professor of perspective at the Royal Academy, he resigned in 1838. In 1839 he bought a cottage in Chelsea, where he lived incognito under the assumed name of Booth. He was looked after by his old housekeeper, who guarded his privacy so zealously that she made it difficult for people to gain admission to his gallery.

Turner continued to travel, however. In the last 15 years of his life, he revisited Italy, Switzerland, Germany, and France. Observers have recorded the untiring energy with which he sketched while abroad, and the drawings, numbering about 19,000 in the Turner Bequest, bear witness to this labour.

Characteristics of later works

While his earlier paintings and drawings show the most accurate observation of architectural and natural detail, in his later work this is sacrificed to general effects of colour and light with the barest indication of mass. His composition tends to become more fluid, suggesting movement and space; some of his paintings are mere colour notations, barely tinted on a white ground, such as "Norham Castle, Sunrise" and "Sunrise, with a Boat Between Headlands" (1835–45; Tate Gallery). Contemporary accounts describe how Turner used to send canvases in this state to the Academy and add the detail, and perhaps the specific subjects that Turner felt to be necessary before his art was worthy to be shown to the public, on the three or more varnishing days allowed to academicians before the exhibition was formally opened, so that they could make last-minute adjustments to allow for the particular circumstances of the placing and lighting of the work. Turner's extreme exploitation of this opportunity served as a demonstration of his extraordinary virtuosity and, on occasion, of his consideration—or lack of it —for the paintings of his neighbours; Constable, for example, was the victim of an enlarged red buoy in Turner's seapiece "Helvoetsluys," which completely eclipsed the reds in his own "Opening of Waterloo Bridge" at the Royal Academy in 1832. This practice may account for the large number of slightly brushed-in canvases found in Turner's studio at the time of his death. These colourful abstractions are far more appreciated now than the romantic subjects he exhibited.

Apart from fanciful reconstructions of ancient Rome and the scintillating Venetian subjects, which found ready purchasers in his day, the outstanding examples of his late work are "The Parting of Hero and Leander" (1837; National Gallery, London), a daring composition of sunset and moonlight with visions of spirits rising from the waters; "The 'Fighting Téméraire' Tugged to Her Last Berth to be Broken Up, 1838," a tribute to the passing age of sail; and "Rain, Steam, and Speed—the Great Western Railway." Actually, the first picture to be hung in the National Gallery was the opalescent "Venice from the Steps of the Europa" (1842), presented in 1847, while Turner was still alive. Turner's preoccupation with the elements of fire and water appears in the two pictures "Burning of

the Houses of Parliament," in the large sketch "A Fire at Sea" (Tate Gallery), and in "Rockets and Blue Lights" (1840; Sterling and Francine Clark Art Institute, Williamstown, Massachusetts). The "Snow Storm" was painted from observations made when Turner crossed from Harwich in such a wild storm that he had to be lashed to the mast for four hours and did not expect to survive. The last pictures he exhibited in 1850 show some falling off of his artistic powers, though the colour is still radiant.

The Turner Bequest

Turner died in London on December 19, 1851, and was buried in St. Paul's Cathedral. By his will he intended to leave his fortune of £140,000 to found a charity for "decayed artists" and his pictures to the nation, on condition that a gallery be built to exhibit them. As a result of protracted litigation with his rather distant relatives, the money reverted to them, while the pictures and drawings of the Turner Bequest became national property. It was not until 1908 that a special gallery was built by Sir Joseph Duveen to house them at the Tate Gallery. All the drawings and watercolours were transferred to the British Museum for safety after the Thames flood of 1928, when the storerooms at the Tate Gallery were inundated. At the time of his death, Turner's own gallery was in such a state of neglect that many of his paintings were said to be mere shadows of what they had been originally. The sketches, not then considered worthy of exhibition, escaped the hands of unskilled restorers and have retained their original freshness and spontaneity.

Reputation. Even in the early years of the 19th century, Turner was strongly criticized by the more conservative critics and connoisseurs, such as Sir George Beaumont, for his forcefulness and high-keyed colour. By the end of his life, although his Venetian subjects and more finished watercolours still appealed to some purchasers, mainly from the newly rich merchant or manufacturing classes, and imitations of his works were beginning to be made, his style was developing along lines totally different from the contemporary taste for realism and high finish typified by such artists as William Powell Frith and the Pre-Raphaelite movement, founded in 1848. Turner's immense reputation in the second half of the 19th century was due largely to the enthusiastic if sometimes misguided championship of the most influential English art critic of the time, John Ruskin, who published the first part of *Modern Painters* in 1843 to prove Turner's superiority to all previous landscape painters and to extol his accurate rendering of natural appearance.

In his pursuit of light and pure colour Turner had anticipated the achievements of the French Impressionists; and when Monet and Pissarro saw his work in London in 1870, they were greatly interested, although few of his truly impressionist sketches were shown at that time. In the 1920s, when the Postimpressionist cult was at its height through the writings of the English art critic Roger Fry, Turner's reputation suffered a temporary eclipse. In 1948 a representative collection of his work was shown at the Venice Biennale and afterward in the principal capitals of Europe, and abstract painters began to find a common purpose with their own work in some of Turner's late colour compositions. Subsequent major exhibitions have further strengthened his status.

MAJOR WORKS

"Fishermen at Sea" (1796; F.W.A. Fairfax-Cholmeley Collection, on loan to Tate Gallery, London); "Buttermere Lake, with Part of Cromack Water, Cumberland, a Shower" (1798; Tate Gallery, London); "Self-Portrait" (*c.* 1798; Tate Gallery, London); "The Fifth Plague of Egypt" (1800; Indianapolis Museum of Art, Indianapolis, Indiana); "Calais Pier: An English Packet Arriving" (1802–03; National Gallery, London); "Venus and Adonis" (1803–05; Huntington Hartford Collection, New York); "Sun Rising Through Vapour: Fishermen Cleaning and Selling Fish" (1807; National Gallery, London); Thames sketches (*c.* 1807; Tate Gallery, London); "Somer Hill, Tunbridge" (1811; National Gallery of Scotland, Edinburgh); "Snowstorm: Hannibal and His Army Crossing the Alps" (1812; Tate Gallery, London); "Frosty Morning" (1813; Tate Gallery, London); "Crossing the Brook" (1815; Tate Gallery, London); "Dort or Dordrecht" (1818; Mr. and Mrs. Paul Mellon Collection); "England; Richmond Hill, on the Prince Regent's Birthday" (1819; Tate Gallery, London); "Rome, from the Vatican" (1820; Tate Gallery, London);

"The Bay of Baiae, with Apollo and the Sibyl" (1823; Tate Gallery, London); "The Regatta at Cowes" (1828; Victoria and Albert Museum, London); "Ulysses Deriding Polyphemus" (1829; National Gallery, London); Petworth landscapes (*c.* 1830; Tate Gallery and Petworth House, Suffolk, London); "The Evening Star" (*c.* 1830; National Gallery, London); "Childe Harold's Pilgrimage: Italy" (1832; Tate Gallery, London); "Burning of the Houses of Parliament" (1835; Philadelphia Museum of Art and Cleveland Museum of Art); "Keelmen Heaving in Coals by Moonlight" (1835; National Gallery of Art, Washington, D.C.); "Norham Castle, Sunrise" (*c.* 1835–45; Tate Gallery, London); "Juliet and Her Nurse" (1836; the late Mrs. G. Macculloch Miller Collection, New York); "Interior at Petworth" (*c.* 1837; Tate Gallery, London); "The 'Fighting Téméraire' Tugged to Her Last Berth to be Broken Up, 1838" (1839; National Gallery, London); "The Slave Ship" (1840; Museum of Fine Arts, Boston); "Peace: Burial at Sea" (1841–42; Tate Gallery, London); "Snow Storm—Steam-Boat Off a Harbour's Mouth Making Signals in Shallow Water, and Going by the Lead" (1842; Tate Gallery, London); "Shade and Darkness: The Evening of the Deluge" (1843; Tate Gallery, London); "Light and Colour" (1843; Tate Gallery, London); "Rain, Steam, and Speed—the Great Western Railway" (1844; National Gallery, London).

Turner also produced thousands of watercolour sketches and drawings, the majority of which are in the British Museum, London.

BIBLIOGRAPHY

JOHN RUSKIN, *Modern Painters* (1843–60) and *Works*, library edition, 39 vol. (1903–12), the greatest 19th-century British critic on the greatest 19th-century British artist; G.W. THORNBURY, *The Life of J.M.W. Turner, R.A.*, 2 vol. (1862–77), the first full-length life, undocumented and unreliable; C.F. BELL, *The Exhibited Works of Turner* (1901), with catalog; W. ARMSTRONG, *Turner* (1902), with partial catalog; W.G. RAWLINSON, *The Engraved Work of Turner, R.A.*, 2 vol. (1908–13), still the only catalog of Turner's engravings; A.J. FINBERG, *Complete Inventory of the Drawings in the Turner Bequest*, 2 vol. (1909), includes sketchbooks and watercolours; *Turner's Water-Colours at Farnley Hall* (1909); *A History of Turner's Liber Studiorum* (1924), fully illustrated with preparatory drawings and all states; T. ASHBY, *Turner's Visions of Rome* (1925); *In Venice with Turner* (1930); and *The Life of J.M.W. Turner, R.A.*, 2nd ed. (1961), the standard life but badly documented and excluding any reference to Turner's personal life, with full list of Turner's exhibited works; M. BUTLIN, *Turner Watercolours* (1962); A. STOKES, *Painting and the Inner World*, pt. 3 (1963), a psychological (Kleinian) approach to Turner's art; J. ROTHENSTEIN and M. BUTLIN, *Turner* (1964), a general introduction, well illustrated; M. KITSON, *J.M.W. Turner* (1964), a good survey of Turner's art; L. GOWING, *Turner: Imagination and Reality* (1966), a stimulating account of Turner's later style that accompanied the 1966 Museum of Modern Art exhibition; J. LINDSAY, *J.M.W. Turner: A Critical Biography* (1966), the best approach to Turner the man, though overstressing the sociological, political, and psychological aspect, with full bibliography; L. HERRMANN, *Ruskin and Turner* (1968), an account of Ruskin's Turner collection with a catalog of the watercolours and drawings in the Ashmolean Museum; J. GAGE, *Color in Turner: Poetry and Truth* (1969), an analytical treatment of Turner's colour theory, exploring a completely new level of Turner research; GRAHAM REYNOLDS, *Turner* (1969), a sound introduction to Turner's work.

(Ma.Bu./M.Ch.)

Twain, Mark

Writing under the pseudonym Mark Twain, Samuel Langhorne Clemens, still the United States' most famous humorist, won a worldwide audience for stories of boy adventure and brusque observations on the fallibility and mendacity of the "damn'd human race."

Youth in Hannibal. Clemens was born on November 30, 1835, in Florida, Monroe County, Missouri, the sixth child of John Marshall and Jane Lampton Clemens. He was four when the family moved to Hannibal, in nearby Marion County, on the west bank of the Mississippi, where his father kept a dry-goods and grocery store, practiced law, and entered local politics. There Samuel spent his boyhood, enchanted by the romance and awed by the violence of river life—the steamboats, keelboats, and giant lumber rafts and also the human flotsam washed up by the river, professional gamblers and confidence men, itinerate stevedores and indigent raftsmen,

Mark Twain.
By courtesy of the Mark Twain Home

quick with fist, knife, or derringer. Away from its boisterous waterfront, Hannibal was an ideal place for a boy to grow up. Nearby Holliday's Hill was just right for picnics or playing pirate or Robin Hood, and the cave near its summit tempted exploration. Glasscock's Island, just a long swim away, invited truant days of fishing or simply watching the river, perhaps with Tom Blankenship, the village drunkard's son, who was to be immortalized years later as Huckleberry Finn. To a boy, the village graveyard was ominous and foreboding, for death was no stranger to a frontier village. Young Samuel saw death on the wharves and in his own home. One of his sisters died when he was four, his ten-year-old brother died when he was seven, and his father died in 1847 when he was 11. From that time on, it became necessary for Samuel to contribute to the family's support. He became —"fretfully," he later remembered, "lazily, repiningly, complainingly"—a delivery boy, grocery clerk, and blacksmith's helper during summers or after school. At the age of 13, with school finally behind him, he became a full-time apprentice to a local printer. When his brother Orion, ten years older than he, established the *Hannibal Journal*, Samuel became a compositor for that paper and soon a contributor who signed himself "Rambler." At 17, a humorous sketch, "The Dandy Frightening the Squatter," appeared over his initials in the *Carpet-Bag*, published in Boston. **First published work**

Early travels. At 18 he became in truth a rambler. He left Hannibal for St. Louis, becoming a journeyman printer for a short time, but set out for New York, where he found brief employment printing and then went on to Philadelphia and Washington, then westward again to Muscatine, Iowa, to set type again for his almost equally peripatetic older brother. Soon he was back in St. Louis, until he left again to join his brother, now in Keokuk, Iowa, where Samuel remained uneasily for almost two years.

But the rambler seemed unhappy when too long in one place. At 22 he set out again, this time to discover whether a young man might find his fortune in South America along the lush banks of the Amazon. Clemens achieved some measure of stability when he agreed to furnish the Keokuk *Daily Post* with letters describing his travels. Only five letters, signed "Thomas Jefferson Snodgrass," appeared, for on the way down the Mississippi toward New Orleans, Clemens met a steamboat pilot named Horace Bixby who agreed to take him on as an apprentice and teach him the perils and possibilities for profit provided by the great and treacherous river. For almost four years, Clemens plied the Mississippi; he later remembered these years as the most carefree of his life. He never met a man later anywhere whose kind he had not known on the river. After 1859 he was a licensed pilot in his own right, but two years later the Civil War cut across the river, bringing an end to traffic from north to south. Clemens probably remained briefly in New Orleans, where evidence supplied in a series of letters in the *Cres-* **Experiences on the Mississippi River** *cent* signed "Quintius Curtius Snodgrass" suggests that he may have had connections with the local militia there; but in general, Clemens' attitude toward and participation in the war is clouded. Years later as Mark Twain, he delighted readers of the *Century* magazine with a "Private History of a Campaign That Failed" (1885), which told of forming a company in Hannibal that tried to attach itself to the Confederate army but disbanded after two weeks when it could not find the main army. Mark Twain's testimony about Samuel Clemens, however, is not always reliable.

Journey west. Meanwhile, Orion Clemens, as a reward for his activities in Abraham Lincoln's presidential campaign, had been appointed secretary to the Nevada Territory. In the summer of 1861, Samuel accompanied his brother on a 21-day journey by stagecoach to the west. In Nevada, after unsuccessful stock speculation in mining and timberlands, and equally unsuccessful prospecting for gold and silver, he became a writer for the Virginia City *Territorial Enterprise*. He signed his contributions "Josh" and delighted in perpetrating such journalistic hoaxes as an account of "The Petrified Man" and "The Empire City Massacre," preposterous tall tales told so plausibly that other newspapers reprinted them as true.

Birth of
"Mark
Twain"

It was in Virginia City on February 3, 1863, that "Mark Twain" was born when Clemens, then 27, signed a humorous travel account with that pseudonym. The new name was appropriate, for it was a riverman's term for water that was just barely safe for navigation, and, as Huck Finn would later testify, "Mr. Mark Twain . . . he told the truth, mainly." In the spring of 1864, Clemens' redheaded temper and biting pen involved him in a quarrel with a rival editor, which made it advisable for him to leave Nevada for California. In San Francisco he met and was encouraged by the author Bret Harte and spent convivial evenings with Charles Farrar Browne, who, under the pseudonym Artemus Ward, was then one of the most popular American humorists and platform lecturers and who encouraged him to contribute to a collection of western sketches that he planned to publish. Clemens, however, had run afoul of the police because of articles he had written about political corruption in San Francisco, and he retreated once again to the Tuolumne Hills, where he did pocket mining at Angels Camp. With friends at nearby Jackass Hill, he heard the story that Mark Twain would make famous as "The Celebrated Jumping Frog of Calaveras County." He wrote it down as he had heard it and sent it to Artemus Ward for his collection, but it arrived too late and was printed instead in the New York *Evening Press*. Mark Twain, known in California as the "Washoe Giant, the Wild Humorist of the Sage Brush Hills," had now reached the East, and his fame soon spread.

Trips abroad. When, in 1866, the Pacific Steamboat Company inaugurated passenger service between San Francisco and Honolulu, Mark Twain took the trip as a correspondent for the *Sacramento Union*. His letters and the lectures that he later gave in California and Nevada about the trip were immediately popular. Since he enjoyed going places and talking about them, he set out again as "travelling correspondent" for California's largest paper, the *Alta California*; it was advertised that he would "circle the globe and write letters" as he went. The first leg of the journey was to New York by way of the Isthmus of Panama, and in June 1867 he took the excursion steamship "Quaker City" for a voyage to Europe and the Holy Land. The letters that he wrote during the next five months, for the *Alta California* and Horace Greeley's *New York Tribune*, caught the public fancy and, when revised for publication in 1869 as *The Innocents Abroad; or, The New Pilgrim's Progress*, established Mark Twain as a popular favourite. His seemed to be a new voice, authentically American in attitude and tone.

Career
as a
journalist

Family life and mature writing. But Clemens was restless still. He served briefly as secretary to a senator in Washington and then resumed his career as a public lecturer who charmed audiences with laconic recitations of incredible comic incidents. Meanwhile, he had met Olivia Langdon, the daughter of an established family in El-

mira, New York. On February 2, 1870, they were married, and with money advanced by his father-in-law, Clemens purchased a partnership in the *Buffalo Express*. But sedentary work seemed confining and dull, so in September 1871 Clemens moved to Hartford, Connecticut, where he built a large and elaborate house in which he and his family would live for the next 20 years—the happiest and most productive period of his life.

Three daughters were born to the Clemenses. Hartford neighbours, at first aloof, proved finally charming. Authoress Harriet Beecher Stowe was among them, and Joseph Twichell, a clergyman for whom Clemens was to write a few years later the mildly scatological *Conversation, As It Was by the Social Fireside, in the Time of the Tudors* (c. 1880). The distinguished novelist and critic William Dean Howells was a frequent visitor from Boston and became a lifelong friend. In 1872 *Roughing It* appeared, a chronicle of Clemens' overland stagecoach journey more than ten years before and of his adventures among the Pacific islands. Meanwhile, he collaborated with his neighbour Charles Dudley Warner on *The Gilded Age*, a satire on financial and political malfeasance that, when published in 1873, gave name to the expansive post-Civil War era.

Using the pseudonym Mark Twain, he continued to lecture with great success in this country and, in 1872 and 1873, in England, holding audiences spellbound with his comic-coated satire, drawling cadences, and outlandish exaggerations. As a writer, however, his imagination temporarily flagged. At Twichell's suggestion, he recorded his experiences as a pilot in "Old Times on the Mississippi" for the *Atlantic Monthly* (1875), expanded eight years later in *Life on the Mississippi*, an authentic and compelling description of a way of life that was, even then, long past. After having written boyhood friends, asking them to send their recollections of old days in Hannibal, he published *The Adventures of Tom Sawyer* in 1876, a narrative of youthful escapades that became an immediate and continuing favourite. In 1878 and 1879 the Clemens family again travelled abroad. A walking tour through the Black Forest with Twichell provided much of the material for *A Tramp Abroad* (1880). A year later, in *The Prince and the Pauper* (1881), Mark Twain again captured popular fancy as he spoke once more of boyhood adventures, this time in old England, but with an undertone of social criticism that ridiculed the pretensions and achievements of monarchy.

Immediate
success
of *The
Adventures
of Tom
Sawyer*

Mark Twain's books were handsomely made, profusely illustrated subscription books, sold by agents who circulated all through the country. They helped sell Mark Twain's lectures, and his lectures helped sell the books, earning for Clemens more money than any previous American author. Clemens, however, did not trust publishers. They were, he complained, scoundrels, intent on defrauding him, so in 1884, he established his own publishing firm, Charles L. Webster and Company, with a nephew titularly in charge. Webster's published the *Memoirs* of Ulysses S. Grant with great success in 1885 and in the same year published the American edition of Mark Twain's *Adventures of Huckleberry Finn*, the book on which his fame largely rests, although at the time it was considered by many to be vulgar and unfit for young readers. He followed *Huckleberry Finn* in 1889 with *A Connecticut Yankee in King Arthur's Court*, which celebrated American homespun ingenuity in contrast to the superstitious ineptitude of even a chivalric monarchy.

The popular image of Mark Twain was by now well established. He was a gruff, but a knowledgeable, unaffected man who had been places and seen things and was not fooled by pretense. He talked and wrote with contagious human charm, in the language of ordinary people. His prejudices, even his publicly exploited minor shortcomings—like smoking or swearing too much or staying too long in bed—were theirs. At the same time, he scornfully berated man as a poor creature who "begins as dirt and departs as stench," created for no purpose except the entertainment of microbes. Evolution failed, he said, when man appeared, for he has the only evil heart in the entire animal kingdom. Yet Mark Twain was one with those he scorned: what any man sees in the human race, he admitted, "is merely himself in the deep and private honesty of his own heart." Perceptive, comic, but also bitter, Mark Twain seemed to be the mirror of all men. Samuel Clemens had made him well.

Financial difficulties. Clemens, who had speculated unsuccessfully in Nevada and California, began speculating again. In the late 1880s he had become an enthusiastic supporter of an inventor in Hartford named James W. Paige, who was developing a typesetting machine. For several years he gave large sums, sometimes as much as $3,000 a month, for its construction and improvement. By 1891 he began to feel the effects of his long-term investments and, in order to economize, closed the large Hartford house and moved with his family to Europe. In 1892 the Webster company published *The American Claimant* and in 1894 *Tom Sawyer Abroad*, neither of which was spectacularly successful. The company became more embroiled in financial difficulties. Leaving his family in Italy, Clemens made several trips to America in attempts to rectify his affairs and stave off what now seemed the inevitable failure of the Paige typesetting machines. In 1894 the Webster company filed assignment papers, and the typesetter, though ingeniously devised, failed to stand up in competition against another machine. Clemens was bankrupt and deeply in debt.

Friend-
ship with
Henry H.
Rogers

Meanwhile, Samuel had met Henry Huttleston Rogers, a major executive of the Standard Oil Company, and an immediate friendship had sprung up between them. Though reputedly harsh in business dealing, in private Rogers was a kindly man, fond of horseplay, billiards, and yachting. He took over the management of Clemens' affairs, stood as a buffer between him and his creditors, and encouraged him to announce that Mark Twain would embark on a worldwide lecture tour, the receipts of which would be used to pay all his debts. He arranged to have Mark Twain's writings assigned to Mrs. Clemens so that income from them could not be attached. He managed Clemens' financial affairs, dissuading him from speculative investments, and put whatever money was available into solid stocks. He saw to the publication of *The Tragedy of Pudd'nhead Wilson* (1894), which is sometimes remembered as Mark Twain's second best novel, and *Personal Recollections of Joan of Arc* (1895), a book that Clemens thought so serious a revelation of what idealistic rectitude might accomplish that he refused to allow the name Mark Twain to appear on the title page, lest readers think it another comic narrative.

In the summer of 1895, Mark Twain set out on the lecture tour that took him as far as Australia and then back to London, where he received news of the death of his oldest daughter, Susy, the only member of the family who had not accompanied him. Grief stricken, the Clemenses remained abroad for five more years. Jean, the youngest daughter, was discovered to be incurably ill; Mrs. Clemens, never robust, was failing. Clemens himself became increasingly bitter. He described his lecture tour in *Following the Equator* (1897), dedicated to Rogers' son. Finally, in 1898, the investments made by Rogers and his management of Mark Twain's publications made Clemens financially solvent again. *The Man That Corrupted Hadleyburg and Other Stories and Sketches* was issued in 1900 by Harper & Brothers, soon to become the exclusive publishers of Mark Twain.

Last years. Late in that year, Clemens and his family returned to the United States. He was widely acclaimed as a man who had refused to bow to bankruptcy but had laboured diligently to pay every creditor every dollar he was owed. The Clemenses lived then in New York, where Mark Twain was greatly in demand as a speaker and where he associated on an intimate basis with Rogers and other wealthy magnates such as Andrew Carnegie, Henry M. Flagler, and William Rockefeller. Yale University conferred an honorary degree on him in 1901, the University of Missouri did the same in 1902, and Oxford University in 1907. In his mid-60s, he was a public hero, lauded and applauded. He spoke out frankly and bitterly on public issues. *To the Person Sitting in Darkness* in 1901 was a scathing indictment of imperialism. *King Leo-*

pold's Soliloquy, published four years later, denounced the baseness of the white man's conduct in subduing the Congo.

In the fall of 1903, the Clemenses again left the United States and, because of Mrs. Clemens' health, settled near Florence, Italy. When she died six months later, Clemens was stricken with grief. *Extracts from Adam's Diary* (1904) and *Eve's Diary* (1906) are whimsical accounts of man's dependency on woman's superior management, and the books speak feelings of the loneliness of life when a man must lead it alone. In *What Is Man?* in 1906, he fulminated desperately on what fate did to bungling man. Many of his later thoughts on human cupidity were, he thought, so severe that he speculated they could not be published until 100 years after his death. When most of them appeared in 1962 as *Letters from the Earth*, they did not seem as caustic or reprehensible as Clemens seems to have thought them to be.

Last
works

In 1906 Clemens began to dictate his autobiography. Portions of it were selected for periodical publication, for enough money to allow Clemens in 1908 to build a new house in Redding, Connecticut, which he called Stormfield. This autobiographical material has been compiled by different editors and published in various volumes over the years to the present time. *Extract from Captain Stormfield's Visit to Heaven* in 1909 was a book over which Clemens had puttered for many years. Its rollicking burlesque humour barely disguised the author's tired despair of the "damn'd human race" of which he was an irrevocable part. He worked over drafts of *The Mysterious Stranger*, which was published in a somewhat garbled form six years after Clemens' death. Increasingly bitter, tired, a pampered public favourite, but in private a wounded lion whose growl grew fainter though not less menacing, he made several trips to Bermuda to bolster his waning health. He died at Stormfield on April 21, 1910.

MAJOR WORKS

NOVELS: *The Gilded Age*, with Charles Dudley Warner (1873); *The Adventures of Tom Sawyer* (1876); *The Prince and the Pauper* (1881); *The Adventures of Huckleberry Finn* (1884); *A Connecticut Yankee in King Arthur's Court* (1889); *The American Claimant* (1892); *Tom Sawyer Abroad* (1894); *The Tragedy of Pudd'nhead Wilson* (1894); *Personal Recollections of Joan of Arc* (1895); *Tom Sawyer, Detective* (1896); *The Mysterious Stranger* (1916, posthumously published from the incomplete manuscript; re-edited more accurately, 1969).

TALES AND SKETCHES: *The Celebrated Jumping Frog of Calaveras County, and Other Sketches* (1867); *Mark Twain's Sketches, New and Old* (1875); *The Stolen White Elephant and Other Stories* (1882); *The £1,000,000 Bank-Note and Other New Stories* (1893); *The Man That Corrupted Hadleyburg and Other Stories and Sketches* (1900); *A Double Barrelled Detective Story* (1902); *The $30,000 Bequest, and Other Stories* (1906).

TRAVEL SKETCHES: *The Innocents Abroad; or, The New Pilgrim's Progress* (1869); *A Tramp Abroad* (1880); *Following the Equator* (1897).

REMINISCENCES: *Roughing It* (1872); *Life on the Mississippi* (1883).

AUTOBIOGRAPHY: *Mark Twain's Autobiography* (incomplete upon his death, published in 1924 with additional fragments appearing in later editions).

PHILOSOPHICAL DIALOGUE: *What Is Man?* (1906).

OTHER WORKS: *Mark Twain's (Burlesque) Autobiography* (1871); *How to Tell a Story and Other Essays* (1897); *Extracts from Adam's Diary* (1904); *King Leopold's Soliloquy* (1905); *Eve's Diary* (1906); *Christian Science* (1907); *Is Shakespeare Dead?* (1909); *Extract from Captain Stormfield's Visit to Heaven* (1909).

BIBLIOGRAPHY. The authorized biography, ALBERT B. PAINE, *Mark Twain, a Biography: The Personal and Literary Life of Samuel Langhorne Clemens*, 3 vol. (1912), though often corrected by later writers, is still important; as are such reminiscent accounts as WILLIAM DEAN HOWELLS, *My Mark Twain* (1910, reprinted 1967); MARY LAWTON, *A Lifetime with Mark Twain* (1925); and CLARA CLEMENS, *My Father, Mark Twain* (1931). DIXON WECTER details early years in *Sam Clemens of Hannibal* (1952); as does M.M. BRASHEAR in *Mark Twain: Son of Missouri* (1934). IVAN BENSON writes of *Mark Twain's Western Years* (1938); EDGAR M. BRANCH of *The Literary Apprenticeship of Mark Twain* (1950); KENNETH R. ANDREWS of *Nook Farm: Mark Twain's Hartford*

Circle (1950); SAMUEL C. WEBSTER of *Mark Twain: Business Man* (1946); LOUIS J. BUDD of *Mark Twain: Social Philosopher* (1962); and HOWARD G. BAETZHOLD of *Mark Twain and John Bull* (1970). EDWARD C. WAGENKNECHT, *Mark Twain: The Man and His Work*, 3rd ed. (1967), contains valuable bibliographical material; but see also MERLE JOHNSON, *A Bibliography of the Works of Mark Twain* (1935). More complete modern biographies are J. DeLANCEY FERGUSON, *Mark Twain: Man and Legend* (1943); and JUSTIN KAPLAN, *Mister Clemens and Mark Twain* (1966). VAN WYCK BROOKS, *The Ordeal of Mark Twain*, rev. ed. (1923), answered by BERNARD DEVOTO, *Mark Twain's America* (1932), created a controversy about Clemens' literary integrity; for details, see LEWIS LEARY (ed.), *A Casebook on Mark Twain's Wound* (1962). Critical studies include: WALTER BLAIR, *Mark Twain and Huck Finn* (1960); HENRY NASH SMITH, *Mark Twain: The Development of a Writer* (1962); and JAMES M. COX, *Mark Twain: The Fate of Humor* (1966).

(L.Le.)

Tylor, Sir Edward Burnett

Edward Burnett Tylor, one of the first and most eminent British anthropologists, is regarded as the founder of cultural anthropology. He was the first anthropologist to study man's cultural growth rather than merely his physical evolution, and the influence of his method is, in one form or another, felt to this day.

By courtesy of the National Portrait Gallery, London

Tylor, chalk drawing by G. Bonavia (fl. 1851–76). In the National Portrait Gallery, London.

Tylor was born at Camberwell, London, on October 2, 1832, the son of a prosperous Quaker brass founder. He attended a Quaker school until he was 16, when, barred by his faith from entering a university, he became a clerk in the family business. In 1855, at the age of 23, symptoms of tuberculosis led him to travel to America in search of health. He made his way to Cuba in 1856, where, on a bus in Havana, by one of those chance occurrences that can determine the course of a man's life, he entered into conversation with a fellow Quaker, who turned out to be the archaeologist and ethnologist Henry Christy. Christy was on his way to Mexico to study remnants of the ancient Toltec culture in the Valley of Mexico. The two became friends, and Christy persuaded Tylor to accompany him on his expedition.

Travelling in arduous and sometimes dangerous circumstances, they searched for the Toltec remains, Tylor under Christy's experienced direction gaining practical knowledge of archaeological and anthropological fieldwork. The expedition lasted for six months, and after its conclusion Tylor, now firmly set on the course of his life's work, returned to England. In 1858 he married and spent some time travelling in Europe before publishing the experiences of his Mexican expedition in his first book, *Anahuac: or Mexico and the Mexicans Ancient and Modern* (1861). Although mainly a well-conceived travelogue, *Anahuac* contains elements that characterize Tylor's later work when he had become a full-fledged anthropologist: a firm grasp on factual data, a sense of cultural differences, and a curious combination of em-

pirical methods with occasional hints of the superiority of a 19th-century Englishman in judging other cultures.

After *Anahuac,* Tylor published three major works. *Researches into the Early History of Mankind and the Development of Civilization* (1865), which immediately established his reputation as a leading anthropologist, elaborated the thesis that cultures past and present, civilized and primitive, must be studied as parts of a single history of human thought. "The past," he wrote, " is continually needed to explain the present, and the whole to explain the part." Tylor's fame, however, is based chiefly upon the publication of *Primitive Culture* (1871). In it he again traced a progressive development from a savage to a civilized state and pictured primitive man as an early philosopher applying his reason to explain events in the human and natural world that were beyond his control, even though his scientific ignorance produced erroneous explanations. Tylor identified, for example, the earliest form of religious belief as "animism," a belief in spiritual beings, arrived at, he assumed, by primitive attempts to explain the difference between the living body and the corpse and the separation of soul and body in dreams.

Primitive Culture also elaborates upon a theme that became a central concept in his work: the relation of the life of primitive to that of modern populations.

> By long experience of the course of human society, the principle of development in culture has become so ingrained in our philosophy that ethnologists, of whatever school, hardly doubt but that, whether by progress or degradation, savagery and civilization are connected as lower and higher stages of one formation.

Thus, "culture" should be studied not only in the artistic and spiritual achievements of civilizations but in man's technological and moral accomplishments made at all stages of his development. Tylor noted how customs and beliefs from a distant, primitive past seemed to have lived on into the modern world, and he became well known for his examination of such "survivals," a concept that he introduced. His evolutionary view of human development was endorsed by most of his colleagues and, of course, by Charles Darwin, who had established biological evolution as the key to human development. "It is wonderful," he wrote to Tylor,

> how you trace animism from the lower races up to the religious beliefs of the highest races. . . . How curious, also, are the survivals or rudiments of old customs.

In the late-19th-century political and theological controversy over the question whether mankind belonged physically and mentally to a single species, Tylor was a powerful advocate of the physical and psychological unity of all mankind. "There seems to be no human thought so primitive as to have lost its bearing on our own thought," he wrote in *Primitive Culture,* "nor so ancient as to have broken its connection with our own life." But in this question, as in all anthropological disputes, he based his position on respect for empirical evidence, which he hoped would bring the standards and procedures of the natural sciences, including elementary statistical investigations, to the study of humanity.

His last book, *Anthropology, an Introduction to the Study of Man and Civilization* (1881), is an excellent summary of what was then known and thought in that field and, like all Tylor's work, conveys a vast quantity of information in a lucid and energetic style.

Tylor was made a fellow of the Royal Society in 1871 and given a doctorate of civil law at Oxford in 1875. Eight years later he returned to Oxford to give lectures and stayed there as keeper of the university's museum, becoming reader in anthropology in 1884 and the first professor of anthropology in 1896. He was also elected the first Gifford lecturer, a position created by the endowments of the Scottish judge Adam Gifford, at Aberdeen University in 1888. He retired from active life in 1909 and was knighted in 1912. He died at Wellington, Somerset, on January 2, 1917.

BIBLIOGRAPHY. R.R. MARETT, *Tylor* (1936), is the only biography that contains an account of Tylor's contribution to anthropology. G. ELLIOT SMITH, "Edward Burnett Tylor,"

Publication
of
*Primitive
Culture*

Assessment

in H.J. and HUGH MASSINGHAM (eds.), *The Great Victorians* (1932), contains a biographical essay and critical assessment, particularly of Tylor's ideas on invention and the diffusion of culture. GODFREY LIENHARDT, "Edward Tylor," in TIMOTHY RAISON (ed.), *The Founding Fathers of Social Science* (1969), is a short essay on Tylor's life and work that attempts to assess his influence in contemporary social anthropology. *Anthropological Essays Presented to Edward Burnett Tylor in Honour of His 75th Birthday, Oct. 2nd 1907*, with a bibliography by BARBARA W. FREIRE MARRECO (1907), is a *Festschrift* with essays on ethnological themes by a number of Tylor's contemporaries; the bibliography is indispensable for students of Tylor's work.

(B.V.S.)

Typewriter

A typewriter is a machine for writing characters like those made by printer's type; when no more than a few copies are needed, it has the advantages of economy over typeset printing and of clarity and speed over handwriting. The typewriter consists of a keyboard that controls impressions made in any sequence from type arranged on separate rods or on the periphery of a disc, cylinder, or sphere. In the machine's early days the term typewriter was also applied to the operator; later the operator became known as a typist.

The typewriter was one of the great transforming factors of modern business. It also has had impact on education, communication, and even the arts, and it first opened to women the doors of business life.

History. The first recorded attempt to invent a typewriter may have been covered by a 1714 British patent for "an Artificial Machine or Method for the Impressing or Transcribing of Letters Singly or Progressively one after another, as in Writing, whereby all Writing whatever may be Engrossed in Paper or Parchment so Neat and Exact as not to be distinguished from Print." No drawings of this machine exist, and its construction is not known. The only other attempt recorded in the 18th century was a machine invented in France in 1784 for embossing characters for the blind. In 1829 a machine called a typographer was patented in the United States; it consisted of type mounted on a semicircular frame that was turned to bring the desired letter to the printing point and was then depressed against the paper by means of a lever.

The first practical typewriter. Several typewriter models followed, but, despite some improvements, such as the introduction of the cylinder, or platen, for holding the paper, none achieved practical success. Most were large and cumbersome, some resembling pianos in size and shape. All were much slower than handwriting in operation. Finally in 1867 the American inventor Christopher Latham Sholes read an article in the journal *Scientific American* describing a new British-invented machine and was inspired to construct what became the first practical typewriter. His second model, patented in 1868, wrote at a speed far exceeding that of a pen. It was a

crude machine, but Sholes added many improvements in the next few years, and in 1873 he signed a contract with E. Remington and Sons, gunsmiths, of Ilion, New York, for manufacture. The first typewriters were placed on the market in 1874, and the machine was soon renamed the Remington. Among its original features that were still standard in machines built a century later were the cylinder, with its line-spacing and carriage-return mechanism; the escapement, which causes the letter spacing by carriage movement; the arrangement of the typebars so as to strike the paper at a common centre; the actuation of the typebars by means of key levers and connecting wires; printing through an inked ribbon; and the positions of the different characters on the keyboard, which conform almost exactly to the arrangement that is now universal. Mark Twain purchased a Remington and became the first author to submit a typewritten book manuscript.

Christopher Sholes's first machines

The first typewriter had no shift-key mechanism—it wrote capital letters only. The problem of printing both capitals and small letters without increasing the number of keys was solved by placing two types, a capital and lowercase of the same letter, on each bar, in combination with a cylinder-shifting mechanism. The first shift-key typewriter—the Remington Model 2—appeared on the market in 1878. Soon after appeared the so-called double-keyboard machines, which contained twice the number of keys—one for every character, whether capital or small letter. For many years the double keyboard and the shift-key machines competed for popular favour, but the development of the so-called touch method of typing, for which the compact keyboard of the shift-key machines was far better suited, decided the contest.

Another early issue concerned the relative merits of the typebar and the type wheel, first used on the typographer of 1829 and applied in cylinder models brought out in the 1880s and later.

In modern machines of this variety the type faces are mounted on a circle or segment, the operation of the keys brings each type to correct printing position, and the imprint of type on paper is produced by a trigger action. The type-wheel machines offer an advantage in the ease with which the type segments may be changed, thus extending the range and versatility of the machine.

Following the first shift-key typewriter of 1878, the next great advance was visible writing. On all the early typebar machines the bars were arranged in a circular basket, located underneath the carriage, and the type printed at a common point on the underside of the cylinder. This construction compelled the operator to raise the carriage in order to see the writing line.

Introduction of visible writing

The first visible-writing machine appeared in 1883. The early machines employed the downstroke principle, the type striking on top of the cylinder. Later, the front-stroke machines took the lead in the general-business field; the first machine of this kind to attain prominence resulted from the work of John N. Williams, an American, in 1890. In front-stroke machines the typebars are placed in a segment in front of the carriage, and the type prints on the front of the cylinder. This solved the problem of visible writing, and all writing machines of the leading standard makes are of this type.

On nearly all typewriters the printing is done through an inked ribbon, which is fitted on spools, travels with the operation of the machine, and reverses automatically when one spool becomes completely unwound. On other machines an inking pad is used, the type contacting the pad prior to printing.

Noiseless typewriters. The noiseless linkage is a variation of the conventional typebar linkage causing the typebar to strike the platen at a lower velocity but with the same momentum. Although it produces less noise than the conventional typewriter, the noiseless typewriter cannot produce as fine an impression or as many carbon copies.

Electric typewriters. A significant advance in the typewriter field was the development of the electric typewriter, basically a mechanical typewriter with the typing stroke powered by an electric-motor drive. The typist

Early typewriter, the Sholes and Glidden model of 1873.

initiates the key stroke, the carriage motion, and other controls by touching the proper key. The actuation is performed by the proper linkage clutching to a constantly rotating drive shaft. Advantages of this system include lighter touch, faster and more uniform typing, more legible and numerous carbon copies, and less operator fatigue. Especially valuable as an office machine capable of a high volume of output, electric typewriters are produced by all major typewriter manufacturers.

The first electrically operated typewriter, consisting of a printing wheel, was invented by Thomas A. Edison in 1872 and later developed into the ticker-tape machine. The electric typewriter as an office writing machine was pioneered by James Smathers in 1920.

Spherical type carriers

In 1961 the first commercially successful typewriter based on a spherical type-carrier design was introduced by the International Business Machines Corporation. The sphere-shaped typing element moves across the paper, tilting and rotating as the desired character or symbol is selected. The motion of the element from left to right eliminates the need for a movable paper carriage.

Portable typewriters. The early portables of the late 19th century were slow, awkward, type-wheel machines. In 1909 the first successful portables appeared on the market. By the 1950s practically every typewriter manufacturer produced a portable typewriter; all of them were typebar machines similar in operation to the office machines. Designed with lighter parts than those of standard models, portables are more compact but less sturdy. Electrical operation of portable typewriters was introduced in 1956.

Modern developments. The inherent versatility of the typewriter, particularly the electric typewriter, has led to its application to many tasks once considered beyond its scope. One example is the accounting machine, which evolved from the typewriter; another is the adding machine. This office machine is capable of tabulating in vertical columns, performing arithmetic functions concurrently, as well as typing horizontal rows, thus performing complete bookkeeping functions. Its development served as a natural bridge for the entry of the typewriter industry into the data-processing, or computer, field. A typical device illustrating this outgrowth from typewriters to data processing is the paper-tape punch and reader. This machine is connected to a specially modified typewriter so that it may control the printing of the typewriter or may produce punched tape under control of the typewriter.

Typewriter composing machines. Special-purpose typewriting machines have been developed for use as composing machines; that is, to prepare originals that look as if they had been set in printer's type (or at least more so than ordinary typewriting does), from which additional copies can be printed. Ordinary typewriting cannot compare in quality, style, and versatility with printing from type produced directly on metal slugs by standard composing machines, but the high cost of skilled typesetting labour prompted the development of composing typewriters that require far less operator training. Since the fundamental requirement of a composing typewriter is the ability to supply different styles and sizes of type, the type-wheel machine is far more suitable than the typebar. Other major requirements of a typing machine whose output must resemble print are the proportional spacing of characters in a word (rather than centring every character within the same width, as in ordinary typewriting) and justification, or alignment of the right-hand margin. An electric typebar machine was developed that provided proportional spacing—assigning space for each character in proportion to its width. The other requirement, margin justification, proved more difficult to attain. Most of these machines provided for preliminary typing of a line, determining the necessary compensation for the line length, and retyping to the exact length. A more complicated machine was introduced that would automatically justify a line of type with one keyboarding. This was accomplished by a system in which the operator typed manually into a storage unit, from which a computer first automatically compensated for line length and then operated a second typing mechanism. By mid-20th century the type-

Proportional spacing

writer had begun to be used as a composing machine in spite of its limitations, and it became more popular as improvements were developed.

Automatically controlled machines. One of the most important advances in the field of typewriters and office machines was the development of automatic controls that allow typing from remote electrical signals rather than from manual control. This technique enabled office-machine manufacturers to develop an integrated system of business communication utilizing remote-control typewriters and computer techniques. With such a system, machines handling all the different office-machine functions, such as the typewriter, calculating machine, and printing telegraph, together with mass data-processing computers and electronic storage systems, are tied together by the use of a "common language" in the form of coded electrical signals. This coded information, coming into an office via appropriate communication channels, can be automatically recorded and printed. Component machines produced by any manufacturer can be connected to any other without the use of special code converters. Other automatic typewriter devices also have become available. A vacuum-operated system, for example, controls and operates any number of standard typewriters from a perforated roll of paper tape, much like the player piano, making possible rapid production of form letters and other papers.

High-speed printers. The need for high-speed printing machines to convert the output of computers to readable form prompted the introduction of a specialized high-speed form of "typewriter" in 1953. In this class of machines, the paper is fed between a continuously rotating type wheel and a bank of electrically actuated printing hammers. At the instant the proper character on the face of the type wheel is opposite the proper hammer, the hammer strikes the paper and prints the character, while the type wheel continues to rotate. By this means, speeds up to 100,000 characters per minute have been attained, as compared with about 1,000 characters per minute attainable with conventional typebar mechanisms. A number of different models operating on this principle were developed; all of them required elaborate electronic controls to solve the complex synchronization problem. Many other high-speed-output devices for computers were developed. Most of them utilize techniques that are remote from the typewriter field, in some cases using printing mediums other than paper. Speeds of up to 10,-000 characters per second were attained by certain non-mechanical systems, which, although not actually typewriters, compete with typewriters as computer-output devices (see also COMPUTERS).

BIBLIOGRAPHY. BRUCE BLIVEN, JR., *The Wonderful Writing Machine* (1954); and RICHARD N. CURRENT, *The Typewriter and the Men Who Made It* (1954), are readable and entertaining accounts with considerable detail. JOHN A. ZELLERS, "The Typewriter: A Short History on Its 75th Anniversary, 1873–1948" (1948), is a short pamphlet, published by the Business Equipment Manufacturing Association, with a tabulation of important developments.

(I.S.L.)

Typography

Typography as an art is concerned with the design, or selection, of letter forms to be organized into words and sentences to be disposed in blocks of type as printing upon a page. Typography and the typographer who practices it may also be concerned with other, related matters —the selection of paper, the choice of ink, the method of printing, the design of the binding if the product at hand is a book—but the word without modifier is most usually taken to refer to the activities and concerns of those most involved in and concerned with the determination of the appearance of the printed page.

Thus understood, there was by definition almost—but not quite—no typography before the invention of printing from movable type in the mid-15th century; and, thus understood, it is only by analogical extension that the term can be applied, if ever it can be, to "reading" in which the material at hand is something other than words that remain stationary on flat firm surfaces. The electronically created letter that lives out its brief life while moving across the face of a signboard or a cathode-ray tube is not a typographic item. Typography, then, exists somewhere between the extreme of manuscript writing, on the one hand, and the transient image on the electronic device, on the other hand. Whether the letter be made by metal type or photographic image is no longer important in defining the subject; whether the finished item is a book or a page influences its inclusion as typographic not one bit.

The nature of typography

TYPOGRAPHY AS A USEFUL ART

An overview of typography suggests that a number of generalized observations may be reasonable:

First and most important, typography and printing, the mechanical processes by which the plans of the typographer are realized, are useful arts. Though there is indeed fine typography, typography is not a fine art. Books, the primary source of typographic examples, are written in the main by people with something to say; they are selected for printing in the main by publishers who see merit and hope for profit in disseminating the statements of the writers to an audience; properly they are edited and designed and printed in the main by craftsmen whose boundaries are fixed for them by considerations germane to the needs of the writers to communicate and the needs of the readers to understand and appreciate. The typographer exists not to express his own design preferences, his own aesthetic needs, but to provide a useful (because usable) connection between someone with something to say and someone to say it to.

Relationship between typography and communication

But to say—as did the late Beatrice Warde, one of England's great typographic authorities—that printing ought to be invisible is not to say that the typographer has no contribution to make; to say that typography is a functional art and as such ought not to get between the writer and the reader is not to say that there is only one solution to every typographical problem, that aesthetics, taste, personal judgments, and imagination cannot find room for expression in the typographic studio.

Nonetheless, there are limitations to what the typographer may and may not do; for, in addition to being a useful art with the generally accepted first use of transmitting information, typography for at least three reasons is a secondary art.

First, it is secondary in that its basic materials, the alphabets or other similar notational systems with which it works, are not of its own invention. The impact of this fact on the art form is obvious. Generally speaking, Western writing, or printing, is accomplished by the use of a relatively small number of individual letters capable of being grouped in almost infinite numbers of meaningful permutations. Even in the face of language differences, there is a wide carry-over of letter shapes and typefaces from one language to another. Because the number of images (letters) to be designed is limited and entirely manageable, the type designer's job is made less difficult. The language carry-over makes possible the establishment of meaningful typologies, the evolution of international styles and conventions, and the development of criteria and traditions of taste by which typographers improve their work. As the result, it is fairly certain that in a little more than 500 years of printing history since Gutenberg, at least 8,000 and very probably 10,000 or 11,000 typefaces have been designed. The practicing typographer has, then, a vast number of types to choose from, and, because the best of those types have evolved within cosmopolitan traditions and have stood the test of judgment by many people in many places over many years, there are, within the several thousands of types available, many that are of unquestioned excellence.

By way of contrast, the Japanese method of writing and printing involves a combination of three systems—some 3,000 kanji (symbols based on Chinese characters) and two groups of phonetic symbols (hiragana and katakana) each of which consists of 48 separate symbols. The problem of individually designing some 3,000 symbols, some of them of incredible complexity, is not one that many designers are able to surmount in a lifetime. As a result, to all intents and purposes, Japanese typographers have had only two typefaces to choose from—*mincho*, roughly equivalent to the West's roman (see below), and Gothic, functionally a Japanese sans serif (see below). In the 1960s a group of Japanese designers produced a third typeface called Typos.

By courtesy of *Visible Language, c/o* The Cleveland Museum of Art, Ohio

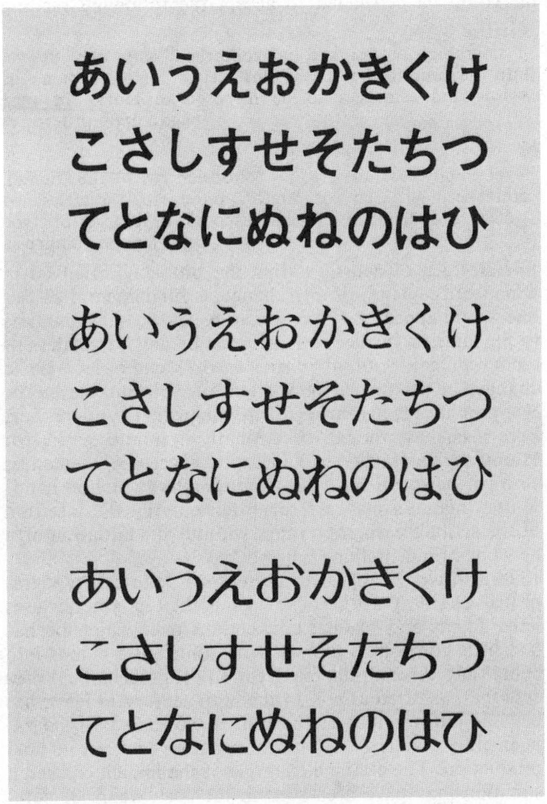

あいうえおかきくけ
こさしすせそたちつ
てとなにぬねのはひ

あいうえおかきくけ
こさしすせそたちつ
てとなにぬねのはひ

あいうえおかきくけ
こさしすせそたちつ
てとなにぬねのはひ

Figure 1: *The three Japanese typefaces.* (Top) Gothic, (centre) *mincho,* and (bottom) the new Typos.

Second, the typographer is limited by reading conventions over which he has little or no effective control. The appearance of a book page, whether well or badly designed, is governed more by the fact that Western readers begin at the top left of a page and read right, a line at a time until they get to the bottom, than it is by the aesthetic desiderata of the designer. Many typographers have long been attracted to the clean and uncluttered look of so-called sans serif type (the two little bases on which the vertical elements of the lower case "n" rest are serifs, as are the backward pointing slab atop the lower case "i" or "l," and sans serif types are those in which such embellishments are lacking [*T l*]). But the difficulty is that

Reading conventions and typography

By courtesy of The Monotype Corporation Ltd.

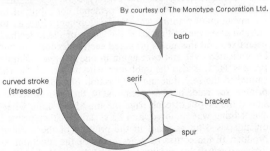

Figure 2: Typeface nomenclature.

almost every study ever completed has indicated that sans serif type is less easy to read in text than is type with the serif. It may well be that if Western texts were printed vertically, from the bottom of a page to the top and read upward so that each letter occupied a separate line with no horizontal connection to those before and after it, the apparent advantage of serif types in this regard might disappear.

To consider another example of the restrictions put on the typographer by the necessity of working with the reading conventions, it is arguable that the appearance of the printed page would be changed and one of the petty annoyances of reading—"doubling," in which the eyes finish a line and then return to the left margin and begin the same line all over again—could be eliminated if people could be persuaded to accept the following reading pattern:

Typography as an art is concerned with the design, into organized be to forms letter of ,selection or words and sentences to be disposed in blocks of type .page a upon printing as

or

Typography as an art is concerned with the design, otni dezinagro eb ot smrof rettel fo ,noitceles ro words and sentences to be disposed in blocks of type .egap a nopu gnitnirp sa

But the fact, of course, is that the problems involved in winning acceptance of any change as fundamental as this one would appear to be so numerous and so substantial as to preclude its further consideration by any but writers of typographical journal articles or textbooks. Basic changes in the format of written text attributable to the typographer or, his earlier form, the printer-typographer, have been few, though occasionally dramatic, as in, for example, the practice of separating succeeding sentences with periods or of separating paragraphs (which in hand-written manuscripts were separated only by the insertion of the scribe's paragraph mark without the initiation of a new line or indentation).

Third, it would appear to be reasonable to call typography a secondary art because, just as the typographer uses letter forms and reading conventions over which he has had little control, so too what he contributes comes into being only through the intervention of a mechanical process that, as often as not, in the 20th century at least, has become the province of the printer, so that the typographer practices his art at least once removed from its final production. The extreme example of the impact of such a situation may have been seen in the early years of computer-generated typefaces in which, many felt, most faces revealed quite clearly that they had been developed by specialists whose first capabilities were not in the field of typography. And when typographers were later introduced into the process, they found that they had to work through the electronics expert, even as, for many years, those unable to cut their own type had been forced to work through typefoundries.

Dependence upon a mechanical process

It will already have become apparent that there is, at the worst, some confusion and, at the least, some lack of uniformity involved in talking about typographers and typography. The words themselves are of relatively recent origin and have been used self-consciously in their contemporary sense only from about the mid-20th century. The difficulty is, of course, the matter of the process involved. Gutenberg was his own typographer. It may well be, in fact, that his major personal contribution to the invention of printing was the development of a way to cut and cast type so that after the shape of the letter had been fixed and the molds prepared each letter form might be replicated over and over again in one relatively simple process. He was also the publisher, who undertook to risk capital in the selection and preparation of material to be printed for sale; he was presumably the man who designed the layout of each page; he may have done whatever editing was required, and he certainly either printed or supervised an assistant in the printing of the finished product. In the course of years many of the functions at first performed by one man came to be divided among several. Quite early, some printers employed men to cut type to their design; others employed men to design and cut the type; some held their services out for hire to others who became publishers; editors were separated from the process, though not always from decision-making roles in the appearance of the final product. After the introduction of bound volumes, trends were initiated that led eventually to the creation of binding designers as separate artists; it became not uncommon to find persons performing services as book designers and, as such, responsible for coordinating and leading the work of type designers, layout artists, binding designers—all who were in any way responsible for the appearance of the book as a whole. The situation became further clouded by the great variety of practice as to the status of each of the persons who perform one or more or, in some cases, all of these functions. They may be professionals retained by printing concerns for a single project; they may be full-time members of a corporate printing staff; in some very few cases they may be a single artist-craftsman-patron carrying out all of the functions in operations (usually necessarily small) devoted self-consciously to the production of "fine books."

Function of the book designer

Parenthetically, it is significant to note that, in general, the major examples of really fine typography—the significant developments that have raised the possibilities for the improvement of the typographic arts and, in fact, a preponderance of the typographic examples held up as outstanding—have been produced by publisher, printer, and typographer all working within the normal day-to-day requirements of their regular operations. Such a statement must not, however, be taken as dismissing the outstanding services rendered by the best work of the so-called private presses and by the valued demonstration volumes produced in limited numbers by major presses such as the Cambridge University Press in England, in holding up to view the best that the craft is capable of and thus serving as models for the craft itself.

AESTHETIC QUALITIES OF THE TYPOGRAPHIC PAGE

Confusion notwithstanding, the typographer as he is most generally understood is responsible—whether or not he does all of the work himself—for the appearance of the printed page, and his work is best seen in the several examples of the printed page that are used to illustrate the present article.

The typographic page may be considered in terms of two aesthetic qualities. The first of these has been called "atmosphere," "feel," "impress," "sense," and other similar terms. It is easier felt than defined, and it depends in large measure on such things as the size of the block of type, its placement on the page, the kinds of display letters used for titles, running heads, and subheads, and the size of the margins—all elements that in the hands of a competent typographer create an expectation regarding the contents (possibly even the purpose) of the page and lead to a sense of the time of its production, its seriousness, and its function.

The second aesthetic quality is that of colour, the darkness or lightness of the block of type sensed somehow as a whole rather than as a collection of individual letter forms with substantive meanings. Colour is the result of letter shapes, distances between letters and between words, the amount of space left between lines, the inking of the type, the printing process employed in making the impression on paper, and the paper itself.

Of all elements the design of the letters is, in the dominant view, the most important. It is important that early typography was in fact overtly engaged in the explicit search for typefaces that would mechanically reproduce the written scripts in which, before the invention of printing, books had been prepared. For most of its life since the invention of printing with movable type in the mid-15th century, typography in the West has been dominated by three type families—roman, italic, and black letter (see below). All are easily recognizable as refined and regularized versions of letter styles first developed and standardized by scribes. The debt of sans serif, more a subclass than a family, is apparent but less unequivocal.

Design of the letters

To divide the several thousand typefaces that have existed since Gutenberg into three major families is only the grossest type of classification, and historians of typography, like teachers of typography, have found it useful to set up other classifications. Unfortunately, but not unexpectedly, they have not found it possible to agree on a system of classification. The variety of proposals has been so bewildering as to defeat one of the first purposes of classification. Some have concentrated on the influence of seminal workers in the field and talk of "Caslon's," "Bodoni's," etc. Others have concentrated on the major uses or types of literature from which various dominant types have come and talk, for example, of Humanistic faces. Other systems have employed nomenclatures that emphasize the early manuscript models from which a face evolved or a national influence. In attempts to meet a growing need for standards that can be applied more rigorously in legal and commercial and technical bibliographical uses, some countries and some craft associations have tried to develop classification schemes based on precise, in some cases almost mathematical, descriptions of the various elements of letter shapes. These schemes are not as yet worked out to the satisfaction of all concerned and are matters of some controversy, even among those who applaud the aims.

The system that has enjoyed the longest general favour and seems to be about as useful as any other divides typefaces into four classifications. Unfortunately, though the classifications are based as much on differences in letter styles as on chronology, the names given each suggest a temporal alignment and one that is, at first glance, confusing.

The first of these is called in most places old face—though Americans sometimes call it old style. In general, old faces were largely those types developed from *c.* 1722 to *c.* 1763 (dates of William Caslon and John Baskerville). Their letter forms had marked affinities with the penned letter styles of the scribes: they tended to squareness, there was little contrast between the thick and thin strokes, the stresses (the thickest part of the curves in a letter) were heavy and tilted or slanted, and the serifs tended to be full or thick and had brackets—gracefully rounded curves where they joined the letter body proper.

The second classification is usually described as transitional and, as its name suggests, came more or less between—and had letter styling midway between—old face and modern.

So-called modern types were produced between *c.* 1788 (date of Giambattista Bodoni) and approximately 1820, when type design almost everywhere went into a major decline. Modern faces in general share characteristics resulting from the engraver's tool rather than the pen. There is a marked contrast between the thick and thin strokes of the letter, the thins in particular being almost exaggeratedly thin, and the change from thick to thin is sudden and pronounced; serifs tend to be thinner and somewhat longer, and the stresses are less pronounced and are vertical rather than tilted. The effect is that of a letter less square, more up and down, than old-face letters, with lines more sharply defined.

Old style faces — The classification called old style or, in America, modernized old style is reserved for revivals of old faces undertaken by contemporary type designers, a practice typified by the important work of one of England's truly prestigious type designers, Stanley Morison. It is necessary to establish a special classification for such types because in each case the modern reworking, while it owed much to the original, was in fact sufficiently different to be a new creation in its own right.

It is worth pointing out once more that typefaces are assigned to one or the other classification on the basis of the style in which their letters are drawn and not—despite their time-oriented designations—by the year of their creation.

Finally, and although this is not the place for a detailed history of the evolution of the written letter forms on which printing depends, it is significant that models for all three major type families were in use before the invention of printing by movable type: in England and Germany, a handwriting that was symmetrical, elongated, spiky, magnificently decorative, and difficult to read, not unlike certain parts of letters called today Old English, German script, and Gothic, was to be the origin of black type; in Italy and Spain, a free, open, square, uncluttered writing, not too far from the letter forms regularized by a decree of Charlemagne in the late 8th century, is recog-

nizable today as the seed source of roman type; and a slanted, cursive, more hurried form of the same—from which it evolved by chancery scribes whose work required speed in handwriting—is easily seen to be the origin of italic.

Figure 3: *Traditional and modern typefaces.*
(A) Black face, line of type from the Gutenberg 42-line Bible, 1456. (B) "Old style" italic, pre-1700. (C) Roman by P.S. Fournier, revised as Monotype Fournier, 1925. (D) Gill Sans, E. Gill, 1928.

The ready availability of serviceable letter models freed typography from the necessity of creating its own prototypes and left it able to spend its creative impulses in other ways. So well did it succeed that, within the first few decades after Gutenberg, it had brought forth almost every major development that it was to contribute and, in fact, had established itself so well that it may be fair to say that, until the 20th century, the art was a static one for all but the first 50 years of its existence. Further, the fact that the art form could take its basic ingredients from existing sources gave it a stability that it would not otherwise have had. Since it was unnecessary to wait while various producers in various countries came to agreement on which letter shapes to adopt or what reading conventions to employ, the typographer was enabled to get on with the work of overseeing the printing of books for distribution on a scale never before envisioned. The impact on the Renaissance was of incalculable importance if, indeed, it was not one of a cause and effect relationship.

History of typography

TYPE, FROM GUTENBERG TO THE 18TH CENTURY

Whatever else the typographer works with, he works with type, the letter that is the basic element of his trade. It has already been said that there have been but three major type families in the history of Western printing: (1) black letter, commonly and not quite rightly called Gothic by the English; (2) roman, in Germany still called by its historical name of Antiqua; and (3) italic. All had their origin in the scripts of the calligraphers whose work printing came ultimately to replace.

Calligraphy is dealt with at length in other articles (see further CALLIGRAPHY: *Paleography*). It is necessary here only to provide a context for the evolution of the typefaces of the printer's font. The basic letter forms of the Latin alphabet were established by the classical imperial capital letters of 1st-century Rome. Lowercase letters emerged only slowly, with their most vigorous development coming between the 6th and 8th centuries.

Charlemagne, in order to encourage standardization and discourage further experimentation, ordered his educational program for the Holy Roman Empire to be written in a script consisting of roman capitals and a specific form of minuscules (lowercase letters) known as Caroline. The uniformity thus achieved was short-lived. Under the impact of the national and regional styles of the scribes who worked with the alphabet, the letters—clear, simple, and somewhat broad by today's standards—were gradually compressed laterally, until, by the 11th century, the curves had been converted to points and angles, and the body of the letter had been made thinner while the strokes of which it was composed had been made thicker. This was black letter. By the 15th century it had completed its evolution into the formal, square-text Gothic letter.

It was this formal black letter that provided the first model for printer's type when printing was invented. It served well in Germany, but when printers in Italy, in part under the influence of the Humanist movement, turned to the printing of Latin texts, they found the pointed elegance of the Gothic letter out of keeping with the spirit of Humanism. For these works, they went back in calligraphic history to a time when the text had been less open than the first Caroline alphabet but more rounded than the narrowed, blackened, and pointed Gothic that it had become. When the printers Konrad Sweynheim and Arnold Pannartz in Subiaco, Italy, brought out an edition of Cicero in 1465, they used a typeface that was explicitly intended to be, but was not, a printed copy of the text of Cicero's own time. To distinguish this type from the Gothic that was more "modern" in the 15th century, the Italians called it Antiqua. Known today as roman, it spread rapidly throughout western Europe except in Germany, where the Humanist movement was blocked by the counter-impulses of the Reformation. There, Gothic type was accepted almost as a national typeface until 1940, when its discontinuance was ordered.

It is notable that most early printers continued for many years to use the Gothic type for non-Humanist texts, ecclesiastical writings, and works on law. In Spain, Jacob Cromberger printed books in which the text was set in roman and commentary on the text in Gothic.

Like the Gothic and roman, the third great family of types had its origins in the writings of the scribes. The italic and the Gothic Schwabacher, which serves as a kind of italic to Fraktur (as black letter is known in Germany), both had their genesis in the fast, informal, cursive, generally ligatured letters developed by chancellery clerks to speed their work.

The early years. *Germany: Gutenberg.* The 11th edition (1910–11) of *Encyclopædia Britannica,* not uniquely in its day, gave the honour of inventing the printing press to Laurens Coster of Haarlem. Later research and more or less common consent today give it to Johannes Gutenberg (*q.v.*), a Mainz goldsmith. Actually, the amount of invention involved in the development is open to argument. Certainly, there was in the air at the time much interest in an artificial method of reproducing calligraphic scripts, and books had already been printed from blocks; the techniques necessary to the punching of type and the making of matrices from which to cast it were known to the metalsmiths; paper was replacing vellum; and wine, oil, and cheese presses were well available as adaptable models. It remained only for someone to combine what was in existence or clearly capable of creation.

Gutenberg began his experiments around 1440 and was ready to put his method to commercial use by 1450. In that year, facing the need (not unknown to later printers) for financing, he borrowed from Johann Fust. About 1452 he borrowed once more from Fust, who at that time became his partner. The only extant printing known for certain to be Gutenberg's is the so-called 42-line (the number of lines in each column) Bible, completed in 1456, the year after Fust had foreclosed on his partner and turned the business over to his own future son-in-law, Peter Schöffer. Experts are generally agreed that the Bible displays a technical efficiency that was not substantially bettered before the 19th century. The Gothic type is majestic in appearance, medieval in feeling, and slightly less compressed and less pointed than other examples to appear shortly.

The 42-line Bible, like the other works of its day, had no title page, no page numbers, no innovations to distinguish it from the work of a manuscript copyist—this was presumably the way both Gutenberg and his customers wanted it.

Some five years later, also in Mainz and quite possibly from the re-established printshop of a refinanced Gutenberg, there appeared the *Catholicon,* notable among other reasons for its early use of a colophon, a tailpiece identifying the printer and place of printing, and for the slight condensation of its type—a move toward more economic use of space on the page and greater type variety in printing.

While not all early results of the printer's art were accepted in all quarters (in 1479 the cardinal who later became Pope Julius II ordered scribes to copy by hand a printed edition of Appian's *Civil Wars* as printed in 1472), they were generally well received by a basically conservative literate public that wanted reading matter in clear, legible, compact forms and in quantities greater than, and at prices less than, would have been possible for the copyists of the day. Within 15 years of the 42-line Bible, the printing press had been established in all of western Europe except Scandinavia.

Italy. When printing moved outward from Germany, it established itself first in Italy, where it was nurtured by German and German-trained craftsmen. Sweynheim and Pannartz (mentioned above) were the first printers in Italy. They opened their press in Subiaco in 1465 and almost immediately produced a Cicero (*De oratore*) printed in an early and interesting Antiqua type that would with time become roman. (This, rather than a type cut by another German, Adolf Rusch, in Strassburg in 1464, is generally credited with being the initial roman simply because to most modern eyes its connection with the later face seems more clearly demonstrable, less tenuous. Indeed, more conservative theorists are not entirely convinced that even the Subiaco type was close enough to roman to be so called, except in the light of very informed hindsight.)

The brothers Johann and Wendelin von Speyer (sometimes called da Spira and sometimes of Spire) opened the first press in Venice in 1469 and, until Johann died in 1470, had a one-year monopoly on all printing in that city. They used a clear and legible typeface that represented another step toward the contemporary roman. Whether or not these earlier types were really roman, there would seem to be no reason for putting the production of the first clearly recognizable roman any later than the work of a Frenchman, Nicolas Jenson, who had learned printing in Germany and set up business in Venice at about the time the von Speyer monopoly ran out. An excellent idealization of the roman typeform, Jenson's type was cut for an edition of Cicero's *Epistolae ad Brutum,* printed in 1470. It has been described by most modern critics as an elegant cutting, and one—Stanley Morison—called it perhaps the most perfect roman face ever cut. The expertness of the work may be attributed to Jenson's training as a medalist before becoming a printer. It is notable that Jenson never used his roman type for the printing of ecclesiastical or legal works—for which various versions of black letter were to remain standard.

By all measurement the commanding figure in late-15th-century typography was Aldus Manutius, also in Venice. Manutius established his business around 1490 and, by 1495, was issuing a series of Greek texts, notable more for their editorial authority than for their typographical excellence. Manutius was his own editor. His type designer and cutter was Francesco Griffo of Bologna, who made two major contributions: he drew on pre-Caroline scripts as the inspiration for a more authentic roman type that soon displaced the Jenson version; and, for what was to become the most important series of books in its time, he cut the first example of the cursive type now known as italic. It was, in the opinion of some critics, not a very good italic face, and it has been described as more a slanted roman than an italic. Nevertheless, it was the first of a new family of typefaces. Interestingly, it was at first a combination of new-face lowercase letters with roman uppercases. Equally interesting, the entire text of the Aldine books for which it was used were set in the new type. Not until 1550 did it become what it is today, a special-function type.

The books for which this new type—based on a chancellery (*cancellaresca*) cursive—was first cut consisted of a spectacularly successful series of Latin texts initiated in 1501, with Virgil's works as the initial release. The series was planned deliberately to interest a market of new readers—Renaissance men who were hardly interested in liturgical writings or Greek classics but who had instead the Humanist's passion for the Latin writers, with whom, somehow, they associated themselves. To fill that market,

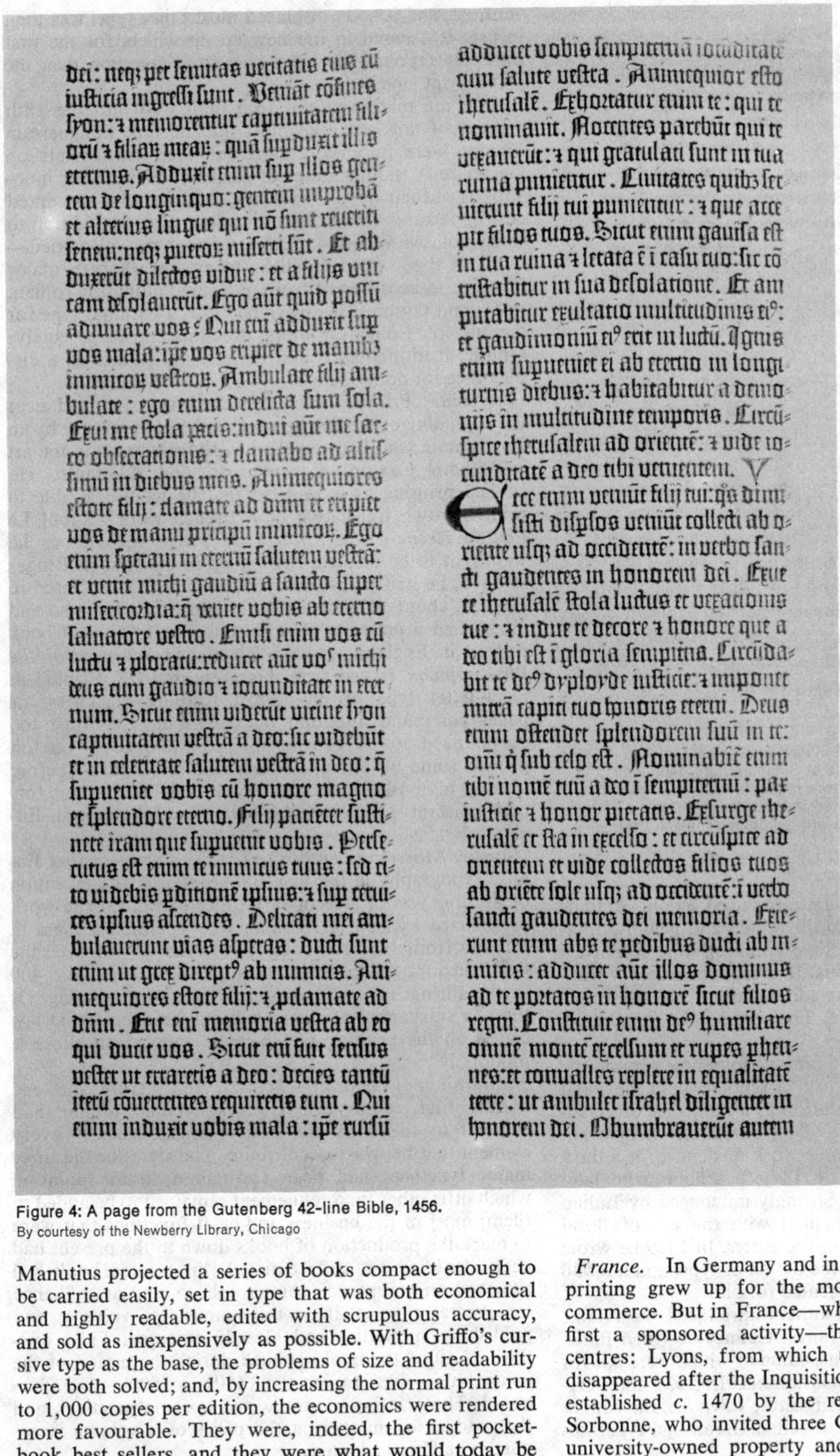
dei: neq; per semitas veritatis eius cū
iusticia ingressi sunt. Veniāt cōfines
syon: et memorentur captiuitatem fili-
orū et filiarū mearū: quā supduxit illis
eternus. Adduxit enim sup illos gentem de longinquo: gentem improbā
et alterius lingue qui nō sunt reueriti
senem: neq; puerorū miserti sūt. Et ab-
duxerūt dilectos vidue: et a filijs uni-
cam desolauerūt. Ego aūt quid possū
adiuuare vos? Qui eni adduxit sup
vos mala: ipē vos eripiet de manib3
inimicorū vestrorū. Ambulate filij ambulate: ego enim derelicta sum sola.
Exui me stola pacis: indui aūt me sac-
co obsecrationis: et clamabo ad altis-
simū in diebus meis. Animequiores
estote filij: clamate ad dnm et eripiet
vos de manu principū inimicorū. Ego
enim speraui in eternū salutem vestrā:
et venit michi gaudiū a sancto super
misericordia: q veniet vobis ab eterno
salvatore vestro. Emisi enim vos cū
luctu et ploratu: reducet aūt vos michi
deus cum gaudio et iocunditate in eter-
num. Sicut enim viderūt vicine syon
captiuitatem vestrā a deo: sic videbūt
et in celeritate salutem vestrā in deo: q
superueniet vobis cū honore magno
et splendore eterno. Filij pacienter susti-
nete iram que superuenit vobis. Perse-
cutus est enim te inimicus tuus: sed ci-
to videbis pditionē ipsius: et sup ceruī-
ces ipsius ascendes. Delicati mei am-
bulauerunt vias asperas: ducti sunt
enim ut grex direpti ab inimicis. Animequiores estote filij: et pclamate ad
dnm. Erit eni memoria vestra ab eo
qui ducit vos. Sicut eni fuit sensus
vester ut erraretis a deo: decies tantū
iterū cōuertentes requiretis eum. Qui
enim induxit vobis mala: ipē rursū
adducet vobis sempiternā iocunditatē
cum salute vestra. Animequior esto
iherusalē. Exhortatur enim te: qui te
nominauit. Nocentes peribūt qui te
vexauerūt: et qui gratulati sunt in tua
ruina punientur. Ciuitates quib3 ser-
uierunt filij tui punientur: et que acce-
pit filios tuos. Sicut enim gauisa est
in tua ruina et letata ē i casu tuo: sic cō-
tristabitur in sua desolatione. Et am-
putabitur exultatio multitudinis ei9:
et gaudimoniū ei9 erit in luctū. Ignis
enim superueniet ei ab eterno in longi-
turnis diebus: et habitabitur a demo-
nijs in multitudine temporis. Circūspice iherusalem ad orientē: et vide iocunditatē a deo tibi venientem. V
Ecce enim veniūt filij tui: qs dimi-
sisti dispsos veniūt collecti ab o-
riente usq; ad occidentē: in verbo sancti gaudentes in honorem dei. Exue
te iherusalē stola luctus et vexacionis
tue: et indue te decore et honore que a
deo tibi est i gloria sempitna. Circūda-
bit te de9 dyploide iusticie: et impone
mitrā capiti tuo honoris eterni. Deus
enim ostendet splendorem suū in te:
omī q sub celo est. Nominabit enim
tibi nomē tuū a deo i sempiternū: pax
iusticie et honor pietatis. Exsurge iherusalē et sta in excelso: et circūspice ad
orientem et vide collectos filios tuos
ab oriēte sole usq; ad occidentē: i verbo
sancti gaudentes dei memoria. Exie-
runt enim abs te pedibus ducti ab inimicis: adducet aūt illos dominus
ad te portatos in honorē sicut filios
regni. Constituit enim de9 humiliare
omnē montē excelsum et rupes phen-
nes: et conualles replere in equalitatē
terre: ut ambulet israhel diligenter in
honorem dei. Obumbrauerūt autem

Figure 4: A page from the Gutenberg 42-line Bible, 1456.
By courtesy of the Newberry Library, Chicago

Manutius projected a series of books compact enough to be carried easily, set in type that was both economical and highly readable, edited with scrupulous accuracy, and sold as inexpensively as possible. With Griffo's cursive type as the base, the problems of size and readability were both solved; and, by increasing the normal print run to 1,000 copies per edition, the economics were rendered more favourable. They were, indeed, the first pocket-book best sellers, and they were what would today be called an instant success. The volumes were sought after throughout Europe, as much or more for their scholarly authority as for the excellence of their typography. New volumes were issued every two months for the next five years, and Manutius early had the honour, but dubious pleasure, of being pirated.

First pocket-book best sellers

The continuity implicit in the work of Manutius and others during this period destroys the value of that older approach to the history of typography that isolated everything printed from 1455 to 1500 as incunabula. The year 1500 did not provide a genuine dividing point, and later historians have generally marked the end of the first valid "period" in typographic history at around 1540, after which the importance of experiments with typefaces tended to be ignored, if not disapproved of.

France. In Germany and in Italy, the many centres of printing grew up for the most part in the centres of commerce. But in France—where printing was from the first a sponsored activity—there were only two such centres: Lyons, from which significant printing largely disappeared after the Inquisition; and Paris, where it was established *c.* 1470 by the rector and librarian of the Sorbonne, who invited three German printers to occupy university-owned property and who later supervised all of their work. The first book printed in France—a manual of instruction in Latin composition—was printed in an Antiqua type, and, though there is some history of the use of a mixed Gothic until about 1520, France from the start led the way to the victory of roman and italic. Important influences in effecting the almost exclusive use of roman type were the printers Simon de Colines, Henri and Robert Estienne, Geoffroy Tory, and the man who was the world's first commercial typefounder, Claude Garamond.

Perhaps because of the quasi-official nature of printing in France, French publishers early established and long maintained a reputation for careful and elegant work. Their volumes, sumptuous more often than not, were characterized by minute attention to almost extravagant

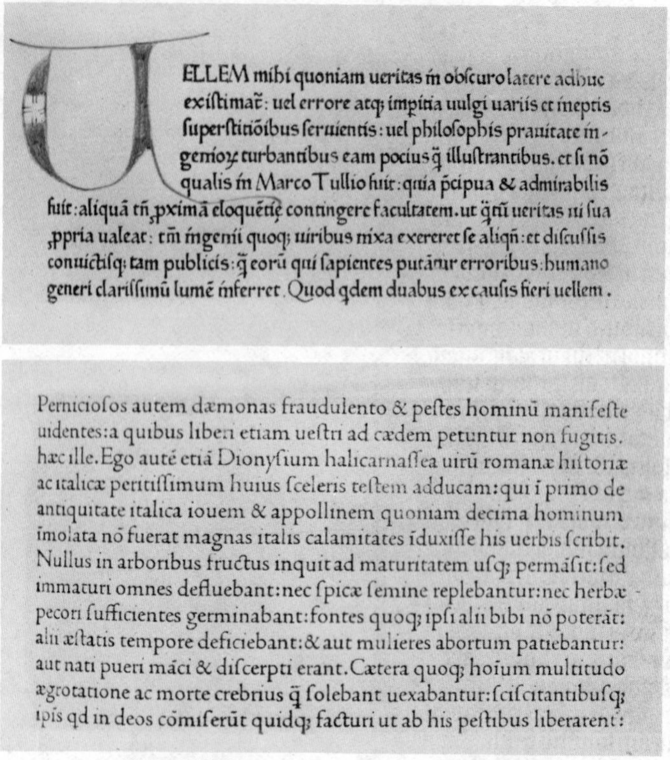

ELLEM mihi quoniam ueritas in obscuro latere adhuc
exiſtimař: uel errore atq; impitia uulgi uariis et ineptis
ſuperſtiōibus ſeruientis: uel philoſophis prauitate in-
genioȝ turbantibus eam pocius q̃ illuſtrantibus. et ſi nō
qualis in Marco Tullio fuit: quia pcipua & admirabilis
fuit: aliquâ tñ, pximâ eloquētiẽ contingere facultatem. ut q̃tū ueritas ni ſua
, ppria ualeat: tñ ingenii quoq; uiribus mixa exereret ſe aliqñ: et diſcuſſis
contuicĥiſq; tam publicis: q̃ eorū qui ſapientes putāur erroribus. humano
generi clariſſimū lumē inferret. Quod qdem duabus ex cauſis fieri uellem .

Perniciofos autem dæmonas fraudulento & peſtes hominū manifeſte
uidentes: a quibus liberi etiam ueſtri ad cædem petuntur non fugitis.
hæc ille. Ego autē etiã Dionyſium halicarnaſſea uirū romanæ hiſtoriæ
ac italicæ peritiſſimum huius ſceleris teſtem adducam: qui i primo de
antiquitate italica iouem & appollinem quoniam decima hominum
imolata nō fuerat magnas italis calamitates iduxiſſe his uerbis ſcribit.
Nullus in arboribus fructus inquit ad maturitatem uſq; permãſit: ſed
immaturi omnes defluebant: nec ſpicæ ſemine replebantur: nec herbæ
pecori ſufficientes germinabant: fontes quoq; ipſi alii bibi nō poterāt:
alii æſtatis tempore deficiebant: & aut mulieres abortum patiebantur:
aut nati pueri mãci & diſcerpti erant. Cætera quoq; hoium multitudo
ægrotatione ac morte crebrius q̃ ſolebant uexabantur: ſciſcitantibuſq;
ipis qd in deos cōmiſerūt quidq; facturi ut ab his peſtibus liberarent:

Figure 5: *Early roman face types.*
(Top) Paragraph from the Lactantius printed by Konrad
Sweynheim and Arnold Pannartz at Subiaco, Italy, 1465, one
of the earliest attempts to create a roman face type. (Bottom)
A section of the Eusebius, printed in Venice in 1470 by
Nicolas Jenson, who is credited with producing the first true
roman type form.
By courtesy of the Newberry Library, Chicago

detailing. Books of the hours, introduced by one Antoine
Vérard, whose tastes ran to illustrated and heavily ornamented pages bound in deluxe editions, were important
influences in these directions. It is estimated that Vérard
published over 200 of these editions in a little more than
25 years, beginning in 1485. They are precise, mannered,
delicate, and elegant.

The work of Henri Estienne

Henri Estienne established himself sometime around the
beginning of the 16th century. A scholar, publisher, and
printer, he gained his reputation as a publisher of classical literature. His edition of Galen's *De sectis medicorum*
is an interesting early scientific work. Estienne, for a time,
had as his adviser Geoffroy Tory, a scholar who later
became a printer himself. Strongly influenced by Italian
typography, Tory experimented with the use of floral
ornamentation and ornate initial letters. In 1529 he wrote
the first known treatise on the design of type, and in 1530
the title king's printer was created for him.

Tory, Colines, and a few others introduced the Aldine
publishing methods into France. Colines designed italic,
roman, and Greek type fonts, some of which were cut for
him by his punch cutter, Garamond. In 1531 they created, for an edition of St. Augustine's *Sylvius*, the roman
typeface to which all later so-called Garamond typefaces
are traced.

As the first commercial typefounder, Claude Garamond
was a major force in making well-designed and superbly
cut types available to printers, including those who could
not have afforded the services of capable cutters. Though
Garamond's efforts with a Greek font were not notably
successful, his French versions of the roman type of Manutius and an italic type of Ludovico degli Arrighi (an
official in the apostolic chancellery who soon after 1522
had produced specimen pages of a type based on the
cursive letters of the chancellery clerks) were of commanding importance in European typography until the
end of the 16th century. In 1540 Garamond perfected a
roman type that, though it had affinities with the lettering
of scribes, was designed unmistakably for mechanical
reproduction. It was sharply drawn, graceful and of good

contrast, and it soon displaced most other typefaces then
in use. It ushered in the new era in which, for the first
time, the typographic book was more common than the
manuscript one.

From the middle of the 16th until well into the 18th
century, if not later, the most notable type designers in
Europe were important more for their refinements on
Garamond's modifications of earlier faces than for innovations of their own. One of the very few who attempted
new departures was Robert Granjon, who, in addition to
some notable versions of Garamond types, also tried—
with his type called Civilité—to create a fourth major
typeface to be different from and stand alongside roman,
italic, and Gothic. He envisioned it as a national type for
the use of French printers. Reminiscent of a cursive
Gothic, it ultimately found its only acceptance as a display face for nonbook use.

England. Printing was introduced into England near
the beginning of the last quarter of the 15th century by an
Englishman who had travelled to Europe to study the art
—William Caxton, a gentleman and dilettante. He
studied printing, it is said, so that he would be able to
print his own translation of a French work—Raoul Le
Fèvre's *Recueil des histoires de Troye*—exactly as he
wanted it to be printed. Setting up in business in Bruges
in 1473, he issued the *Recuyell*, the first book printed in
English, about 1475; in 1476 he returned to England and
established a press in Westminster. The first dated book
printed in England was the *Dictes and Sayenges of the
Phylosophers*, issued from his press in 1477. Printed in
black-letter type of an almost startling blackness, its
pages command attention by means of a contrast too
pronounced to be comfortable to the reader. Caxton
printed some 90 books—70 of them in English—before
turning his business over to Wynkyn de Worde, his former assistant. De Worde used the first italic type in England in 1524.

Introduction of printing to England by William Caxton

Stanley Morison is authority for the statement that English typography in the first 100 years after the invention
of printing was of a secondary order except for the work
of Richard Pynson, a Norman who operated a press in
London from 1490 to about 1530. Pynson, who used the
first roman type in England in 1518, issued over 400
works during his approximately 40 years of printing. Of
these, a substantial number are legal handbooks and law
codes, on the printing of which he enjoyed an effective
monopoly.

Maturation of the printed book. Well before the end
of the first century of typography, the printer had
brought to the book the basic forms of nearly every
element that he was to contribute. The styles of the three
major typefaces had been formalized to the point at
which little other than refinement remained to be added to
them; most of the business and craft functions that were
to mark the production of books down to the present had
been identified and differentiated; the printed book had
achieved an acceptance comparable to, and an audience
far greater than, that of the manuscript volume; and
publishing specialties had already emerged. Fully one-
third of all of the books printed during the period of the
incunabula—that is from the 1450s to 1500—were illustrated. The printing of music had become practical, and
the practice of numbering the pages of a volume in sequence had been adopted.

The printer's mark, an identifying device, was used—
though only briefly at first—in the typographic book
from the very beginning. Almost as early, and probably
more important, was the typographer's addition of the
colophon, in which the printer-publisher recorded the
place and date of publication, asserted his claim to credit
for his role in the production of the work, advertised the
merits of the enterprise, and, on occasion, attempted to
protect his property from the depredations of rival print-
er-publishers. Indeed, Caxton turned the colophon into a
short essay in which he included, in addition to the
normal elements, an editor's preface and a dedication.
Whether or not it is accurate to assert that the title page
—the major nonmanuscript feature of the typographic
book—emerged from the colophon, it is a fact that the

The printer's mark

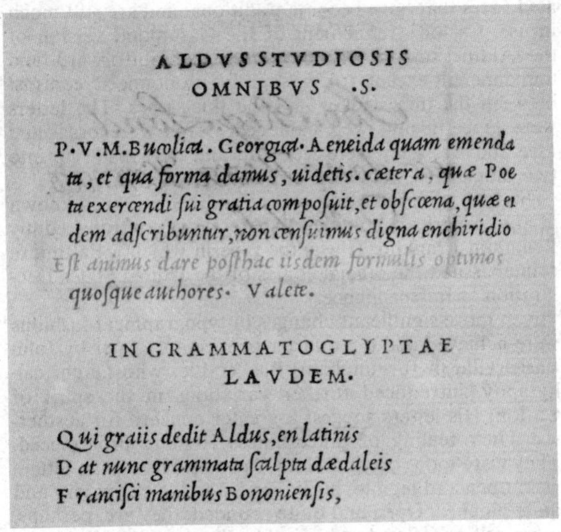

ALDVS STVDIOSIS
OMNIBVS ·S·

P·V·M·Bucolica·Georgica·Aeneida quam emenda
ta, et qua forma damus, uidetis. cætera, quæ Poe
ta exercendi sui gratia composuit, et obscœna, quæ ei
dem adscribuntur, non cœnsuimus digna enchiridio
Est animus dare posthac iisdem formulis optimos
quosque authores· Valete·

INGRAMMATOGLYPTAE
LAVDEM·

Qui graiis dedit Aldus, en latinis
Dat nunc grammata sculpta dædaleis
Francisci manibus Bononiensis,

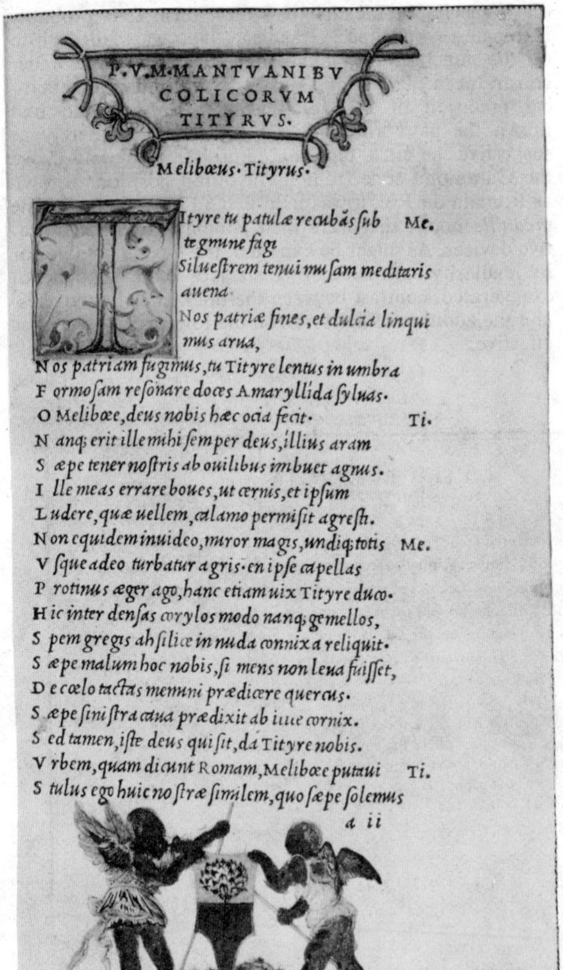

P·V·M·MANTVANIEV
COLICORVM
TITYRVS·

Melibœus· Tityrus·

Tityre tu patulæ recubás sub   Me.
te gmune fagi
Siluestrem tenui musam meditaris
auena
Nos patriæ fines, et dulcia linqui
mus arua.
Nos patriam fugimus, tu Tityre lentus in umbra
Formosam resonare doces Amaryllida syluas.
O Melibœe, deus nobis hæc ocia fecit.   Ti.
Nanq; erit ille mhi semper deus, illius aram
Sæpe tener nostris ab ouilibus imbuet agnus.
Ille meas errare boues, ut cernis, et ipsum
Ludere, quæ uellem, calamo permisit agresti.
Non equidem inuideo, miror magis, undiq; totis   Me.
Vsque adeo turbatur agris. en ipse capellas
Protinus æger ago, hanc etiam uix Tityre duco·
Hic inter densas corylos modo nanq; gemellos,
Spem gregis ah silice in nuda connixa reliquit·
Sæpe malum hoc nobis, si mens non leua fuisset,
De cœlo tactas memini prædicere quercus.
Sæpe sinistra caua prædixit ab ilice cornix.
Sed tamen, iste deus qui sit, da Tityre nobis.
Vrbem, quam dicunt Romam, Melibœe putaui   Ti.
Stulus ego huic nostræ similem, quo sæpe solemus
                                          a ii

Figure 6: *Pages from the first book to incorporate italic
typeface.*
(Left) Dedication and (right) first page from Virgil's *Opera,*
printed by Aldus Manutius in Venice in 1501.

title page took over some of the content of the colophon, which, however, continued to exist.

The first title page was probably used by Gutenberg's successor, Peter Schöffer, in 1463 on a papal bull. It was Schöffer's only known use of the device, and, like the other early versions that followed, it was really—in today's terms—a half title. The full title page did not appear until 1476, when one Erhard Ratdolt in Venice used it on an astronomical and astrological calendar. The device was well established by the end of the incunabula period. Continuing the tradition of relative anonymity of authorship of the manuscript books, the earliest pages never, and later ones only seldom, revealed the author of the work. The title page, apparently, was meant to provide, first, a protective cover for the text within and, second, an opportunity for advertising for the publisher-printer.

The middle years. The first really notable roman type had been cut by Jenson for a text by Cicero in 1470. It had been replaced in popularity and importance by the romans that Francesco Griffo cut for Manutius in the late 15th century. The first italic had been a Griffo design introduced by Manutius in his pocket editions early in the 16th century. These two faces had, in turn, been displaced in European typography by letters designed in the mid-16th century by Garamond in France: a roman based on Griffo's cutting and an italic based on a form put forth by Ludovico degli Arrighi. The Garamond versions of these faces were to be of prime importance in European typographical work until the end of the 16th century, during which time so many adaptations of them were produced that "Garamond type" came to be used as a generic term.

Romain du Roi. By the end of the 16th century, typography in Europe had, generally speaking, deteriorated in vigour and quality. In France, the first comeback step was taken in 1640 by Louis XIII, who, under the influence of Cardinal de Richelieu, established the Imprimerie Royale at the Louvre. In 1692 Louis XIV ordered the creation of a commission charged with developing the design of a new type to be composed of letters arrived at on "scientific" principles. The commission, whose deliberations were fully recorded, worked mathematically, drawing and redrawing each letter on squares divided into 2,304 equal parts. The approach was far removed from the style of the calligraphers, whose work had provided models for

The 17th century revival of typography

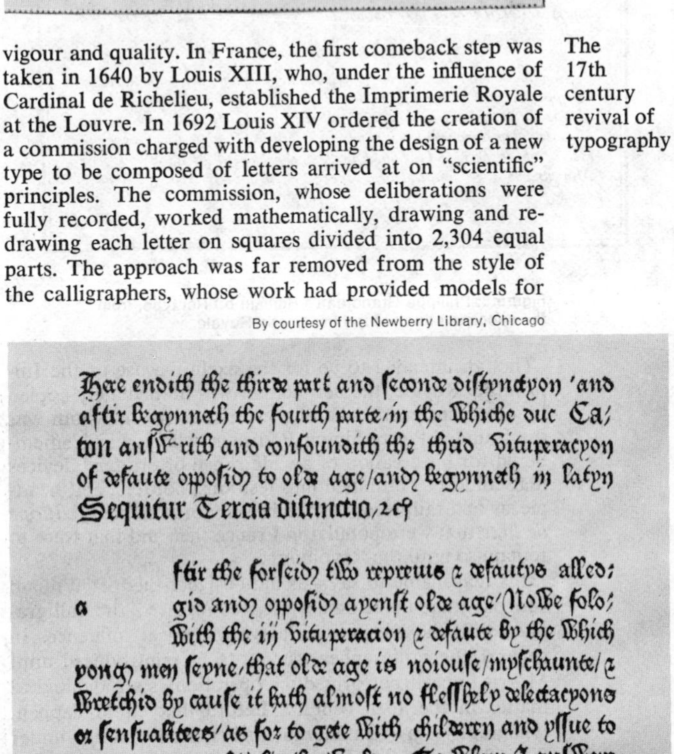

Here endith the thirde part and seconde distynccyon 'and
aftir begynneth the fourth partee in the Whiche due Cay
ton ansWrith and confoundith the thrid Vituperacyon
of defaute opposid to olde age/ and begynneth in latyn
Sequitur Tercia distinctio, &c

After the forseid tWo reproues & defautes alled
gid and opposid ayenst olde age/ NoWe folo
With the iij Vituperacion & defaute by the Which
yong men seyne, that olde age is noiouse/ myschaunte/ &
Wretchid by cause it hath almost no flesshely delectacyono
or sensualitees/ as for to gete With children and yssue to
encrece and multiplie the World. To Whom I ansWere
forWith/ that it is right a noble gyfte reWard & the right

Figure 7: Portion of a page from William Caxton's edition of
Cicero's *De senectute,* printed at Westminster in 1481.

all of the important alphabets until then. It is probably fortunate that Philippe Grandjean, who was called on to do the punch cutting, did not feel himself to be under constraint to carry out his own work with the mathematical precision of the commission members who had drawn the patterns. Using the basic designs merely as suggestive, he cut a type that almost immediately drove the Garamond style from its favoured position. Known as Romain du Roi, it was used first (1702) in one of the *médaille* books that were then popular as commemorative devices. As might be expected, the type is notable for its regularity and precision; there is a good, though not exaggerated, contrast between the thick and thin strokes, and the addition of flat serifs on the lowercase letters was effective.

By courtesy of the Newberry Library, Chicago

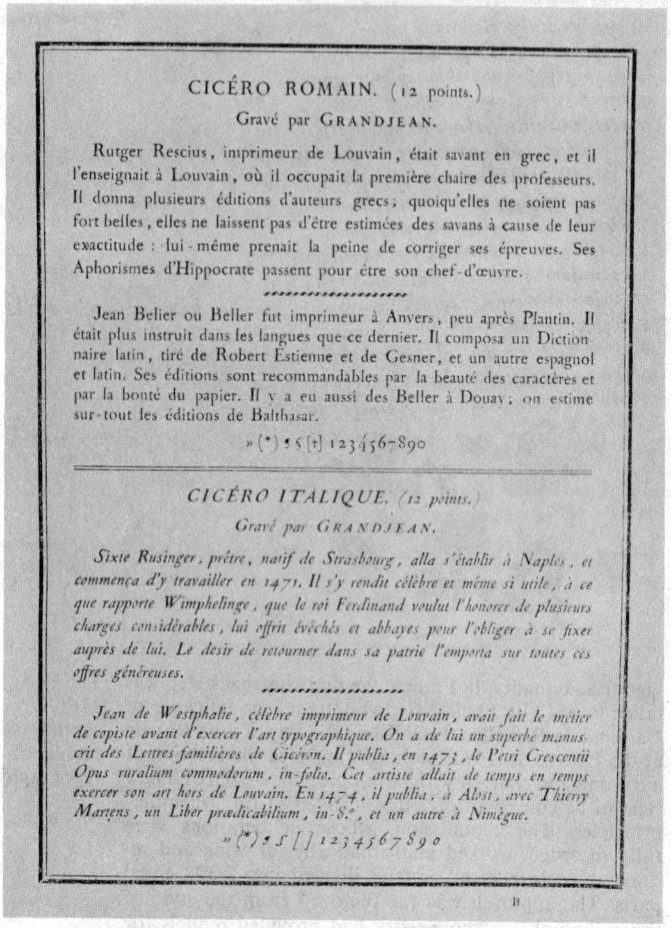

CICÉRO ROMAIN. (12 points.)

Gravé par GRANDJEAN.

Rutger Rescius, imprimeur de Louvain, était savant en grec, et il l'enseignait à Louvain, où il occupait la première chaire des professeurs. Il donna plusieurs éditions d'auteurs grecs; quoiqu'elles ne soient pas fort belles, elles ne laissent pas d'être estimées des savans à cause de leur exactitude : lui-même prenait la peine de corriger ses épreuves. Ses Aphorismes d'Hippocrate passent pour être son chef-d'œuvre.

Jean Belier ou Beller fut imprimeur à Anvers, peu après Plantin. Il était plus instruit dans les langues que ce dernier. Il composa un Dictionnaire latin, tiré de Robert Estienne et de Gesner, et un autre espagnol et latin. Ses éditions sont recommandables par la beauté des caractères et par la bonté du papier. Il y a eu aussi des Beller à Douay; on estime sur-tout les éditions de Balthasar.

» (*) ſ ſ [†] 1234567890

CICÉRO ITALIQUE. (12 points.)

Gravé par GRANDJEAN.

Sixte Rusinger, prêtre, natif de Strasbourg, alla s'établir à Naples, et commença d'y travailler en 1471. Il s'y rendit célèbre et même si utile, à ce que rapporte Wimphelinge, que le roi Ferdinand voulut l'honorer de plusieurs charges considérables, lui offrit évêchés et abbayes pour l'obliger à se fixer auprès de lui. Le desir de retourner dans sa patrie l'emporta sur toutes ces offres généreuses.

Jean de Westphalie, célèbre imprimeur de Louvain, avait fait le métier de copiste avant d'exercer l'art typographique. On a de lui un superbe manuscrit des Lettres familières de Cicéron. Il publia, en 1473, le Petri Crescentii Opus ruralium commodorum, in-folio. Cet artiste allait de temps en temps exercer son art hors de Louvain. En 1474, il publia, à Alost, avec Thierry Martens, un Liber prædicabilium, in-8.°, et un autre à Nimègue.

» (*) ſ ſ [ ] 1234567890

B

Figure 8: Philippe Grandjean's Romain du Roi type, from the specimen book of the Imprimerie Royale.

Though intended to be for the exclusive use of the Imprimerie Royale, the new roman was immediately copied by other designers, one of the most active of whom was the founder Pierre-Simon Fournier, who is also remembered for his creation of a wide range of printers' devices that could be combined into festoons, borders, and headpieces and tailpieces for the heavily ornamented *éditions de luxe* that were popular in France then and that were to remain so until the Revolution.

It is reasonable to say—as did designer-theorist William Morris—that the Romain du Roi replaced the calligrapher with the engineer as a typographical influence. In general, the calligrapher was not to be reintroduced until Morris himself performed the operation as an ideological matter in the 19th century. Before that could happen, typography was to undergo further modifications under the influence of three great designers, two in England and one in Italy.

Caslon, Baskerville, and Bodoni. William Caslon, who issued his first type-specimen sheet in 1734, made a number of refinements of the Garamond style and created faces that have become traditional and are still much in use. Caslon's refinement of the Garamond version of the Aldine roman was essentially straightforward and unmannered except for a slightly pronounced contrast between the thin strokes and the thick ones. The letters were graceful and well balanced. Serifs were bracketed (see above). They were well cut, and they made up into type blocks that were comfortable to read.

The type won wide acceptance and became well-known in the American colonies, where it was introduced by Benjamin Franklin. It was the type in which a Baltimore printer issued the official copies of the United States Declaration of Independence.

Even more significant changes in typographical fashions were achieved about a quarter of a century later by John Baskerville in Birmingham. Baskerville, who taught calligraphy, introduced further variations in the spirit of Caslon. His letters suggest a greater concern for aesthetics. Their feeling of gracefulness is more pronounced. They were more original than Caslon's. His roman letters were open and legible; his italics tended to be spidery and quite pinched. Open and quite rounded, they are, perhaps, more self-consciously pleasing to the eye. As a book designer, Baskerville combined his new faces with exaggerated page margins and relatively wide spacings between letters to suggest new directions in style. By the use of special papers, improved press methods, and special inks, he achieved an effect of almost glaring contrast, an effect heightened by his preference for emphasizing the typographer rather than the illustrator or the engraver. Though his acknowledged masterpiece, a Cambridge Bible, was not printed until 1763, he was an important influence on English and European typography almost from the first printing of his Virgil in 1757.

The Bodoni type faces

In Italy, Giambattista Bodoni enthusiastically took up the principle of page design as worked out by Baskerville, though not his typefaces. Further modifying the Aldine roman of Garamond, he mechanically varied the difference between the thick and thin strokes of his letters to achieve the ultimate contrast possible in that direction. His letters are rather narrower than those of either Caslon or Baskerville. He exaggerated his thick lines and reduced the thin ones almost—it seems at times—to the point of disappearance. Like Baskerville, he used opulent papers and inks blended for special brilliance. His pages were not easy to read, but he became, in the words of Stanley Morison, the typographical idol of the man of taste, and his "plain"—though deliberately and artfully contrived—designs were an important factor in the decline in importance of the *édition de luxe* and its replacement by works more austere in feeling, more modern even to today's eyes. He set what was, in general, to be the standard book style of the world until the appearance of William Morris. (W.E.P.)

TYPE AND BOOK DESIGN SINCE THE 19TH CENTURY

Two late-19th-century developments—one technological, the other aesthetic—profoundly changed the course of book typography and design. The advent of mechanical type composition in the 1880s (the so-called Linotype machine was patented by Ottmar Mergenthaler, a German inventor, in 1884; the Monotype, by an American, Tolbert Lanston, in 1887) had much to do with the look of the 20th century book. The Arts and Crafts Movement, whose leader in typography as in other aspects was William Morris, had an equally great influence on the quality of modern book printing.

The private-press movement. The Industrial Revolution changed the course of printing not only by mechanizing a handicraft but also by greatly increasing the market for its wares. Inventors of the 19th century, in order to produce enough reading matter for a constantly growing and ever more literate population, had to solve a series of problems in paper production, composition, printing, and binding. The solution that most affected the appearance of the book was mechanical composition; the new composing machines imposed new limitations not only on type design but also on the number and kinds of faces available, since the money required to buy a new typeface

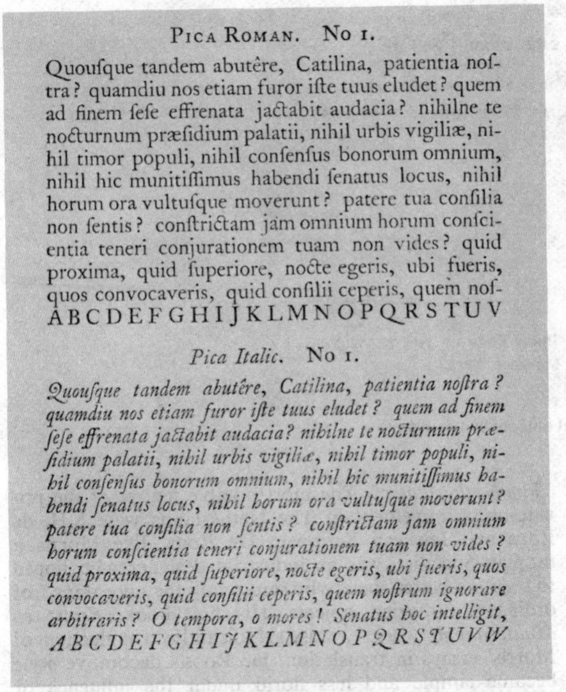

PICA ROMAN. No 1.

Quoufque tandem abutère, Catilina, patientia noftra? quamdiu nos etiam furor ifte tuus eludet? quem
ad finem fefe effrenata jactabit audacia? nihilne te
nocturnum præfidium palatii, nihil urbis vigiliæ, nihil timor populi, nihil confenfus bonorum omnium,
nihil hic munitiffimus habendi fenatus locus, nihil
horum ora vultufque moverunt? patere tua confilia
non fentis? conftrictam jam omnium horum confcientia teneri conjurationem tuam non vides? quid
proxima, quid fuperiore, nocte egeris, ubi fueris,
quos convocaveris, quid confilii ceperis, quem nof-
ABCDEFGHIJKLMNOPQRSTUV

Pica Italic. No 1.

Quoufque tandem abutère, Catilina, patientia noftra?
quamdiu nos etiam furor ifte tuus eludet? quem ad finem
fefe effrenata jactabit audacia? nihilne te nocturnum præ-
fidium palatii, nihil urbis vigiliæ, nihil timor populi, ni-
hil confenfus bonorum omnium, nihil hic munitiffimus ha-
bendi fenatus locus, nihil horum ora vultufque moverunt?
patere tua confilia non fentis? conftrictam jam omnium
horum confcientia teneri conjurationem tuam non vides?
quid proxima, quid fuperiore, nocte egeris, ubi fueris, quos
convocaveris, quid confilii ceperis, quem noftrum ignorare
arbitraris? O tempora, o mores! Senatus hoc intelligit,
ABCDEFGHIJKLMNOPQRSTUVW

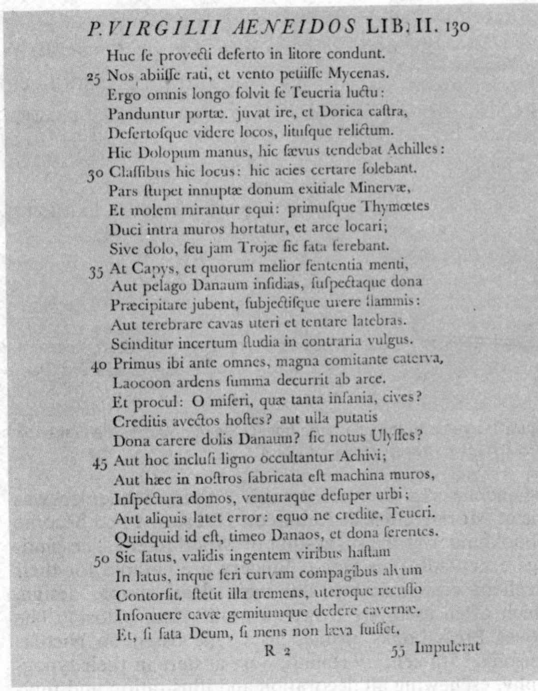

P. VIRGILII AENEIDOS LIB. II. 130

Huc fe provecti deferto in litore condunt.
25 Nos abiiffe rati, et vento petiiffe Mycenas.
Ergo omnis longo folvit fe Teucria luctu:
Panduntur portæ. juvat ire, et Dorica caftra,
Defertofque videre locos, litufque relictum.
Hic Dolopum manus, hic fævus tendebat Achilles:
30 Claffibus hic locus: hic acies certare folebant.
Pars ftupet innuptæ donum exitiale Minervæ,
Et molem mirantur equi: primufque Thymœtes
Duci intra muros hortatur, et arce locari;
Sive dolo, feu jam Trojæ fic fata ferebant.
35 At Capys, et quorum melior fententia menti,
Aut pelago Danaum infidias, fufpectaque dona
Præcipitare jubent, fubjectifque urere flammis;
Aut terebrare cavas uteri et tentare latebras.
Scinditur incertum ftudia in contraria vulgus.
40 Primus ibi ante omnes, magna comitante caterva,
Laocoon ardens fumma decurrit ab arce.
Et procul: O miferi, quæ tanta infania, cives?
Creditis avectos hoftes? aut ulla putatis
Dona carere dolis Danaum? fic notus Ulyffes?
45 Aut hoc inclufi ligno occultantur Achivi,
Aut hæc in noftros fabricata eft machina muros,
Infpectura domos, venturaque defuper urbi;
Aut aliquis latet error: equo ne credite, Teucri.
Quidquid id eft, timeo Danaos, et dona ferentes.
50 Sic fatus, validis ingentem viribus haftam
In latus, inque feri curvam compagibus alvum
Contorfit. ftetit illa tremens, uteroque recuffo
Infonuere cavæ gemitumque dedere cavernæ.
Et, fi fata Deum, fi mens non læva fuiffet,

R 2   55 Impulerat

Figure 9: *English typography, 18th century.*
(Left) Portion of a page from William Caslon's specimen book, 1785, (Right) A page from John
Baskerville's Virgil, printed in Cambridge in 1757.

was enough to inhibit printers from stocking faces of
slight utility. As a result, Victorian exuberance of design,
which might use a dozen or more typefaces within a
single book, was effectively curbed.

William Morris. It is paradoxical that what became
Influence
of the
Arts and
Crafts
Movement known as the Arts and Crafts Movement, with its roots in
the romantic Gothicism propounded by the critic John
Ruskin and by Morris, should have had a considerable
influence on modern industrial design, including that of
the book. An Englishman, William Morris was a fervent
Socialist who believed that the Industrial Revolution had
killed man's joy in his work and that mechanization, by
destroying handicraft, had brought ugliness with it. Morris was above all a decorator; his work in the decorative
arts had added great lustre to the fame he had already
achieved as a writer when, partly as a result of dissatisfaction with the editions of his own works, he decided to
establish a press. In 1888 Morris attended a lecture given
by the printer Emery (later Sir Emery) Walker and was
entranced by Walker's lantern slides of early types, greatly enlarged. He proposed to Walker that they cut a new
font of type that would recapture the strength and beauty
of the early letters, based upon medieval calligraphy. The
Kelmscott Press, in its brief life (1891–96), printed 52
books that exemplified Morris' standards of perfect workmanship. A firm believer that a return to the past would
produce a better society, he commissioned handmade paper like that used in the 15th century, had new, blacker
inks made, and used the handpress and hand binding
exclusively; a few copies of each title were also printed on
vellum. With Walker, he designed three types: a roman,
based upon that of Nicolas Jenson, and two Gothics after
German models; all were cut and cast by hand. Woodcut
initials and borders were engraved to his own design, and
wood-block illustrations were cut from drawings by Edward Burne-Jones and other of his friends. The Kelmscott Press's major book was its *Chaucer*, finished in 1896,
a sumptuous folio whose rich decorations and strong
black pages are reminiscent of the German incunabula
Morris admired. A table book, meant to be looked at
rather than read, it is one of the most influential books in
the history of printing—a revolutionary book, despite its
anachronisms, which caused a whole generation of printers and designers to be dissatisfied with the books they
saw about them and to attempt to improve the badly
made, weakly designed books of the late Victorian age.

Private presses on the Morris model proliferated in England, on the Continent—especially in Germany and the
Scandinavian countries—and in the United States. The
best of these, notably the Doves and Ashendene presses in
England and the Bremer and Cranach presses in Germany, published books of great style and strength. There
were also poorer imitations, as the Roycroft Press in the
United States. Prolifera-
tion of
private
presses

Doves Press. The most influential of the private presses was the Doves Press, established in 1900 by T.J. Cob-

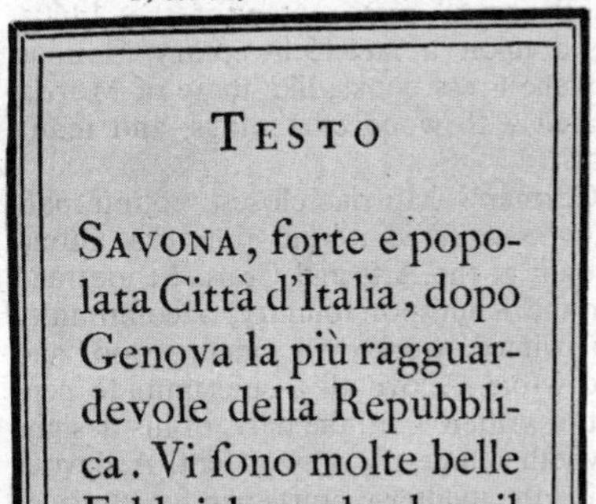

TESTO

SAVONA, forte e popo-
lata Città d'Italia, dopo
Genova la più ragguar-
devole della Repubbli-
ca. Vi fono molte belle
Fabbriche, e ha dato il
natale al famofo Chia-
brera. Venne efpugna-
ta dal Re di Sardegna
nell' ultima guerra. El-
la giace in riva del ma-
re con porto chiufo dal-
le fabbie, in territorio
abbondante di agrumi.

Figure 10: Proof sheet for an apparently
unpublished specimen book by Giambattista
Bodoni.

den-Sanderson and Emery Walker. Walker, who was one
of the prime movers in fine printing for over half a century, also played an important role in creating type for the

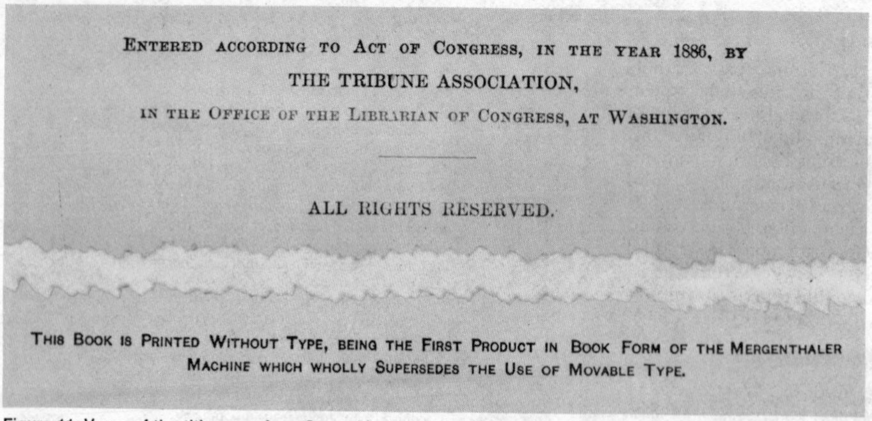
ENTERED ACCORDING TO ACT OF CONGRESS, IN THE YEAR 1886, BY
THE TRIBUNE ASSOCIATION,
IN THE OFFICE OF THE LIBRARIAN OF CONGRESS, AT WASHINGTON.

ALL RIGHTS RESERVED.

THIS BOOK IS PRINTED WITHOUT TYPE, BEING THE FIRST PRODUCT IN BOOK FORM OF THE MERGENTHALER MACHINE WHICH WHOLLY SUPERSEDES THE USE OF MOVABLE TYPE.

Figure 11: Verso of the title page from *Open-Air Sports*, the first book set entirely by Linotype.
By courtesy of the Newberry Library, Chicago

Ashendene and Cranach presses. Cobden-Sanderson was one of Morris' circle at Kelmscott House and had become a bookbinder at the suggestion of Mrs. Morris. The bindings executed at his Doves Bindery are notable for their excellent craftsmanship and their clear, simple design, which often used Art Nouveau motifs (see below). The Doves Press books, printed in a type based on Nicolas Jenson's 15th-century roman, were austere in their typography, eschewing all decoration and illustration and relying for their effect on the beauty of their type, spacing, and presswork. Occasionally a second colour, a splendid red, was used, and superbly drawn initials adorned many of the 50-odd books. A five-volume Doves Bible, issued between 1903 and 1905, is among the monuments of fine bookmaking, as well as one of the most influential modern books, a result of its virility, purity of design, and perfection in craftsmanship.

Ashendene Press. The third great English private press, the Ashendene, was conducted by C.H. St. John Hornby, a partner in the English booksellers W.H. Smith and Son. Hornby in 1900 met Emery Walker and Sydney Cockerell (Morris' secretary at the Kelmscott Press), who encouraged and instructed him and helped in devising two types for his own use: Subiaco, based upon Sweynheim's and Pannartz' semi-roman of the 1460s, and Ptolemy, based upon a late-15th-century German model. The Ashendene Press books, like those of Morris, were often illustrated with wood engravings, and many had coloured initials.

Germany. In Germany Morris' closest counterpart was Rudolf Koch, who gathered around himself at Offenbach, where he taught at the Arts and Crafts School and designed types for the Klingspor foundry, a community of craftsmen who painted, worked in metal, wood, and stone, printed, and wrote. Above all a consummate penman, Koch made the written word the basis of his designs in any medium, whether tapestry or woodcut. A devout Christian, Koch, like the medieval craftsmen he admired, saw the Gothic style as a supreme manifestation of religious spirit; he was no mere imitator but an artist who freely reinterpreted in his types and books the traditional Fraktur type of Germany. Koch also created a number of modern types, among them sans serifs and romans.

Influence of Cobden-Sanderson

Cobden-Sanderson's influence, however, far exceeded that of Morris in Germany. The most important of the German private presses, the Bremer Presse (1911–39), conducted by Willy Wiegand, like the Doves Press, rejected ornament (except for initials) and relied upon carefully chosen types and painstaking presswork to make its effect. The most cosmopolitan of the German presses was the Cranach, conducted at Weimar by Count Harry Kessler. It produced editions of the classics and of German and English literature illustrated by artists such as Aristide Maillol, Eric Gill, and Gordon Craig and printed with types by Emery Walker and Edward Johnston on paper made by hand in France. Kessler's book did not attempt to imitate medieval or Renaissance models; they sought to create—using the same methods as the early printers—books modern—or, rather, timeless, in spirit.

The Netherlands. The most notable figures of the private-press movement in The Netherlands were S.H. de Roos and Jan van Krimpen. De Roos, like Morris a utopian Socialist, was an industrial designer who hoped to create a better society by improving the appearance of ordinary utilitarian objects. His first book, *Kunst en Maatschappij* (1903), was, significantly, a collection of Morris' essays in translation. De Roos's decorative style became simple and less florid under the influence of Cobden-Sanderson, whose work he greatly admired, although his ideals remained those of the Arts and Crafts Movement. Unlike Morris and Cobden-Sanderson, de Roos was a book designer, designing books for others, rather than a printer—one of the earliest of the new school of typographers, who provided layouts for the publisher or printer, specifying type, format, and overall design. Increasingly, as technology became more complex and shops more highly specialized and automated, design became more a profession; the typographer, trained in industrial design or graphic arts, succeeded the printer or the publisher in deciding how a book should look. De Roos, who drew a number of typefaces for the Typefoundry Amsterdam, designed books for the Zilverdistel, the Meidoorn, and other private presses, as well as for trade publishers.

Jan van Krimpen used little decoration in his work, which achieved its effect through a classic clarity of style and impeccable printing. His books, for the Enschedé firm for which he worked, for private presses, or for trade publishers, attempted always to interpret the author's meaning as clearly as possible, to reflect it rather than to enhance it. Krimpen also designed a number of typefaces, all of which show his earlier study of calligraphy. Among them are Lutetia, a modern roman and italic of great distinction; Romulus, a family of text types that includes a sloped roman letter instead of the conventional italic; and Cancellaresca Bastarda, an italic notable for its great number of attractive decorative capitals, ligatures, and other swash (*i.e.*, with strokes ending in flourishes) letters, elegant in appearance.

Krimpen's typefaces

Italy. Another typographer working in the classic mode, Giovanni Mardersteig, spent most of his creative life in Italy, though he was born and trained in Germany. His Officina Bodoni utilized Bodoni's types to print the collected works of D'Annunzio. Mardersteig not only used the handpress for limited editions (usually on handmade Italian papers), which rival 15th-century printing in their beauty of spacing and presswork, but also supervised at the Stamperia Valdònega in Verona long-run editions on high-speed presses, which are likewise remarkable for their craftsmanship. In addition he designed several typefaces, among them Pacioli, Griffo, Zeno, and Dante.

Art Nouveau. The Art Nouveau movement was an international style, expressed in the consciously archaic types of Grasset in France; in posters and magazine covers by artist Will Bradley in the United States; and in initials and decorations by Henry van de Velde in Belgium and Germany. Van de Velde, the leading spokes-

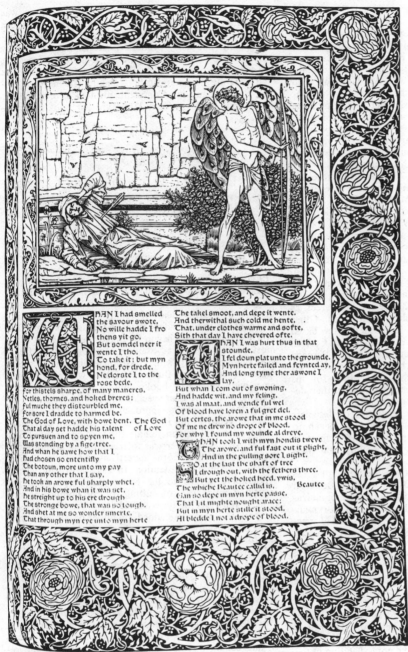

Figure 12: A page from the *Chaucer* printed by the Kelmscott Press, with illustration by Edward Burne-Jones and type and decorations by William Morris.

man for the movement as well as one of its most skilled practitioners, in his essay "Déblaiement d'art" (1892) advocated the development of a new art, one that would be both vital and moral, like the great decorative arts of the past, but that would use contemporary modes. For a reprint of the essay, he designed a series of initials and typographic ornaments that express the characteristics of the style: decoration based upon natural forms; pages whose typography and decoration blend to make overall patterns; and a richness of texture reminiscent of illuminated manuscripts. Van de Velde's most important book was an edition of Nietzsche's *Also sprach Zarathustra*, which he designed for the Insel Verlag and had printed by the Drugulin-Presse of Leipzig and for which he created a series of ornaments printed in gold, as well as endpapers, title page, and binding; a small folio, conceived as an architectonic whole rather than a series of unrelated openings, it is a striking, if dated, volume.

Mechanical composition. The private-press movement did much to raise the standards of the ordinary trade book. Small, independent publishers who wished to make

a mark not only through the distinction of their titles but also through the distinctiveness of their house styles acted as a bridge between the deluxe bibliophilic editions and ordinary books. Companies such as those of John

l'heure dont nous nous souvenons tous, le Bourgeois vivait dans un décor voulu de vertu apparente et solide, d'austérité laide, revêtue de housses blanches. Le revêtement blanc des églises s'était étenduaux maisons. Les meubles n'étaient pas plus provoquants que les lits où s'appendaient des rideaux ingénus et l'on put croire que la vertu s'était installée parmi les hommes.

Mais les juifs aussi s'étaient installés parmi nous qu'une révolution bénévole combla en leur facilitant la brocante, par le fait d'une extension

13

Figure 13: Art Nouveau initial decoration from Henry van de Velde's essay "Déblaiement d'art."

Lane and Elkin Mathews, who published Oscar Wilde and the periodical *The Yellow Book;* J.M. Dent, who commissioned Aubrey Beardsley to illustrate Malory and who used Kelmscott-inspired endpapers for his Everyman's Library; Stone and Kimball of Chicago and Thomas Mosher of Maine, who issued small, readable editions of avant-garde writers with Art Nouveau bindings and decorated title pages; the Insel Verlag in Germany, with millions of inexpensive yet well-printed and designed pocket books—these and their many colleagues brought within the reach of the ordinary book buyer mass-produced books whose appearance, if not their method of manufacture, had been profoundly altered and improved by the Arts and Crafts Movement.

During the early years of the 20th century, more and more printers installed composing machines (see PRINTING). The early Linotype and Monotype faces, like the foundry faces they imitated, were weak and poor. The first significant face cut especially for mechanical composition appeared in 1912, when a new face based upon the old-style types of Caslon was produced for *The Imprint,* a short-lived periodical for the printing trade published by Gerard Meynell of the Westminster Press in London. Its contributors included Edward Johnston, who not only wrote for the magazine but designed its calligraphic masthead; and Stanley Morison, who began his career as printing historian and typographer on its staff. Other Monotype faces cut at this time included Plantin, based upon the types of the great Antwerp printer, and Caslon; the latter was made at the instigation of George Bernard Shaw's publishers, since Shaw, who had strong views on typography, would not allow any other face for his books. World War I, however, stopped any further development of types for the composing machines.

United States. In America the generation of designers who had begun as disciples of Morris soon began to develop their own styles. Among the most important were D.B. Updike, Bruce Rogers, F.W. Goudy, and W.A. Dwiggins.

Daniel Berkeley Updike opened the Merrymount Press in Boston in 1893. His books, most of which he designed himself, are noteworthy for the clarity of their organization, their easy readability, and their excellent workmanship, based upon the use of a few carefully selected typefaces and immaculate presswork. Updike stocked only types that met the twin criteria of economy in use and beauty of design. His books, whether a complex folio such as the *Book of Common Prayer* (1930), considered by many to be his masterpiece, or the small and amiable *Compleat Angler* (1928), are both functional and pleasing to the eye.

Bruce Rogers was a typographer, trained as an artist, who had the faculty of drawing the best from the printers with whom he worked. His greatest book, a monumental Oxford Lectern Bible of 1935; is the noblest edition of the Bible ever issued in English; his smaller and less ambitious efforts, often decorated with the typographic ornament at which he was a master, possess enormous wit and charm. His one type design, Centaur, based upon Jenson, is among the most successful modern adaptations of an early roman, although too elegant for frequent use.

Frederic William Goudy, the most prolific American type designer, created more than 100 faces during a long career as printer, editor, and typographer. In 1908 he began a long association with the Lanston Monotype Corporation, for which he did much of his best work. Among his types were Forum and Trajan, based upon the roman capital letters inscribed on Trajan's Column; Goudy Modern, his most successful text page; and a number of black-letter and display faces. Goudy edited two journals, *Typographica* and *Ars Typographica,* in which he expounded his theories of design; he also wrote a number of books, among them *Elements of Lettering* and *The Alphabet.*

William Addison Dwiggins, a student of Goudy's, was long associated with the publishing firm of Alfred A. Knopf, whose house style he helped to establish. In hundreds of volumes of trade books he designed, typography was taken seriously (each book carried a brief

colophon on the history of the type employed); there was an attempt to use contemporary typographic decoration; and the bindings, using designs made up of repeated decorative units like early printers' fleurons, were extremely successful. Dwiggins designed a number of typefaces for the Linotype, two of which, Electra and Caledonia, have had wide use in American bookmaking. In the U.S., unlike England and the Continent, printers have relied far more upon Linotype than Monotype for book composition.

Education: To prepare us for complete on which education has to discharge. H on is properly to draw forth, and implie

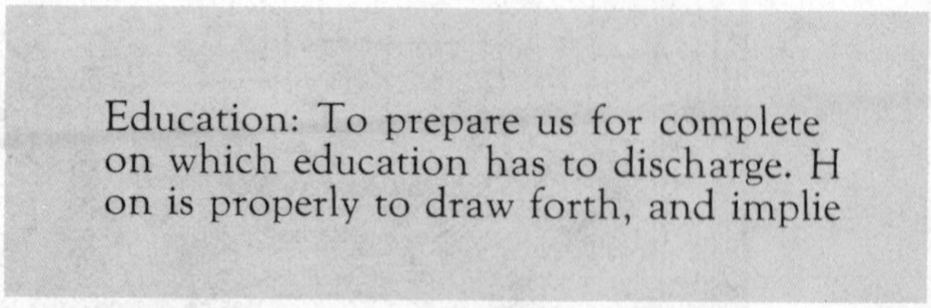

Figure 14: Goudy's Old Style typeface.

England. English typography, like that everywhere, marked time during World War I but made remarkable progress soon after. A new generation of typographers, inspired by Morris' ideals of quality but at the same time aware of the need to adapt them to the new mass-production techniques, had begun to make their names. Foremost among these was Stanley Morison, who, after a year's apprenticeship with *The Imprint,* became a typographer on the staff of Burns and Oates, where he worked on a wide variety of books, among them the liturgical texts in which the firm specialized; here he began to develop the rationalistic approach to typographic design that characterizes the English school. Morison demanded that typography be functional: the task of the book and the newspaper designer was to transmit the author's text clearly, and the task of the advertising and display designer was to command attention. In 1922 Morison became typographic adviser to the Monotype Corporation and instituted a program of cutting for the composing machine a repertory of types culled from the best faces of the past, to which were added a number of contemporary faces designed for modern needs. He had prepared himself for the task by a strenuous course of self-education in paleography and calligraphy, in order to understand the written hands that the early types imitated, and in the history of printing design itself. In 1923 he joined Oliver Simon in publishing *The Fleuron,* a journal of printing history and design in which he published a number of important articles on calligraphy and typography.

In 1925 Morison was made typographic adviser to the Cambridge University Press, whose printer, Walter Lewis, had begun a complete reform of its typographic resources. Cambridge stocked most of the types Morison commissioned for Monotype and demonstrated by their intelligent use that mechanical composition could be used to produce books at once handsome and functional. Among these types were Garamond, based upon a 17th-century French letter (see above); Bembo, after an Aldine roman; Centaur, an adaption of Rogers' foundry face; and Baskerville and Bell, based upon English models. Italics included Arrighi, a version of the letter used by the 16th-century papal writing master and printer (see above). Among the modern faces whose design Morison supervised were Eric Gill's Sans Serif, which enjoyed a wide vogue in advertising and avant-garde book typography; Gill's Perpetua, based upon his stone-cut letters; and Times New Roman, designed by Morison himself for *The Times* (London), whose staff he joined in 1930. The last has been called the most successful type design of the 20th century, a result of its economy and legibility when used on high-speed presses.

Francis Meynell was another who demonstrated that mechanical composition and printing, properly used, could produce aesthetically satisfying books. The books of Meynell's Nonesuch Press, usually limited editions of the classics reflecting his own catholic and excellent literary taste, are marked by restrained design, fine papers,

Margin notes: Early Linotype and Monotype faces · Goudy's type faces · Morison's work for Cambridge University Press

ADVERTISEMENT

This pamphlet is the announcement of a new Lino-
type face to be called "Electra," cut from designs
drawn for The Mergenthaler Linotype Company by
W. A. Dwiggins. The face—at this stage completed
in twelve point, roman and italic—provides a new
type texture for book-page composition. In the larger
sizes now in preparation it will furnish the printer
with a new note in advertising typography.

The face, as may be seen from this specimen, falls
within the "modern" family of type styles, but is

Golo Mann, professor and writer of his-
tory, was born in 1909 in Munich,
Germany, the son of the famous novel-
ist, Thomas Mann. He received his
Ph.D. from Heidelberg University in
1932 and, leaving Germany the follow-
ing year, lectured at French universities
until 1937. He then edited the literary
review "Mass und Wert" in Zurich,
Switzerland, and in the early 1940's
moved to the United States. He re-
mained in this country until 1958 and
during this time taught at Olivet Col-

Figure 15: *Linotype typefaces designed by W.A. Dwiggins.*
(Left) Page from *A Baker's Dozen of Emblems* set in Electra,
1935. (Right) Caledonia italic.
By courtesy of (left) the Newberry Library, Chicago, (right) EB Inc.

and careful presswork. More varied and original than
those of the earlier private presses, they were printed not
by the proprietor but by large, mechanized shops. Meynell's trade books, published under the same imprint,
demonstrated that well-designed and manufactured
books need not be costly; the Nonesuch one-volume editions of English classical authors were inexpensive, handsome, and readable.

The most influential modern publisher of English low-
priced books, however, was Allen Lane, whose Penguin
books, established in 1935 and inspired by such continental publishers as Insel Verlag and Albatross, proved that
a well-designed series of inexpensive paperbacks, both
worthwhile reprints and new titles, could succeed both
commercially and intellectually. They did much to bring
about the paperback revolution that swept both the Continent and the United States in the period that followed
World War II.

International styles. German typography from World
War I until the advent of Hitler was greatly influenced by
the Bauhaus, which stressed the graphic arts; its books,
heavily illustrated, broke away from traditionally symmetrical layouts, in which pictures were inserted into a
rigid framework of text, and strove instead for freer arrangements, usually asymmetrical, in which the type supported the dominant illustrations. The attempt was to
create graphic patterns on the page and to enhance the
reader's consciousness of the illustrations. Many of the
Bauhaus faculty were architects and industrial designers,
whose principles demanded that the types they used, like
the buildings and machines they designed, be sharp and
unornamented, symbolic of a machine-dominated society. Their favourite types were sans serifs, such as Gill's
Sans Serif and Paul Renner's Futura. With the Nazi dispersal of the Bauhaus group, its style became truly international. It has since lost favour among book designers,
except for art and architectural books, partly because
sans serif types and asymmetrical layout proved less legible than traditional modes and partly because typographers grew tired of its rigid limitations.

Other between-war styles, closely linked to literary or
artistic movements that affected book design, were Dada-
ism and Surrealism. The Dadaists' pamphlets, posters,

Influence
of the
Bauhaus

and books employed free, abstract layout, a great mixture
of type sizes and faces, and an attempt to create mood
through typography. Surrealist writers such as Guillaume
Apollinaire and André Breton often collaborated in the
design of their own books, attempting to make the typography of their works reflect its mood.

In France, especially, the production of books intended
to be works of art in their own right was dominated by
painters and sculptors. Publishers such as Ambroise Vol-
lard commissioned members of the School of Paris,
among them Braque, Matisse, Bonnard, and Picasso, to
illustrate books in which the illustrator worked closely
with highly skilled craftsmen to create colourful, original, limited editions, which, while they sometimes may
fail as readable books, achieve admirable success as visual decoration.

By courtesy of the Newberry Library, Chicago

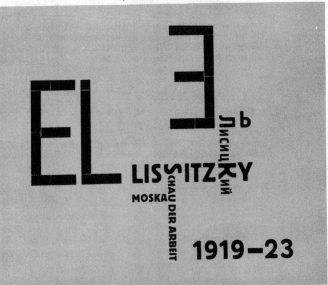

Figure 16: Catalog cover by El Lissitzky, in the Bauhaus
Asymmetric style.

During the 20th century, styles in book design, as in all the arts, fine or applied, have become increasingly international. Styles born in one country spread throughout the world and die through overuse at a dizzying rate. As a consequence it has become increasingly difficult to distinguish truly individual or national styles—books, magazines, clothes, paintings, music, regardless of country of origin, all resemble one another far more than they differ. (See further CALLIGRAPHY; PRINTING.) (J.M.Ws.)

BIBLIOGRAPHY. There is a vast literature on typography and printing history. *A Bibliography of Printing*, comp. by EDWARD C. BIGMORE and C.W.H. WYMAN, 2nd ed., 2 vol. (1880–86), was still useful enough to merit reprinting in 1945. Several learned and technical journals print annual bibliographies. See especially *Studies in Bibliography* and *Publications of the Modern Language Association*, which emphasize articles dealing with analytic bibliography and printing history. The best brief history in English is SIGFRID H. STEINBERG, *Five Hundred Years of Printing*, rev. ed. (1962). CURT BUHLER, *The Fifteenth-Century Book* (1960), is an excellent survey of early printing and publishing practice. JOSEPH MOXON, *Mechanick Exercises on the Whole Art of Printing* (1683–84), is the earliest comprehensive manual on printing, typography, and type making. The 1962 edition of HERBERT DAVIS and HARRY CARTER, with an excellent introduction and full annotation, gives considerable insight into the typography and printing of the day; there were no significant changes from the invention, c. 1450, until the early-19th century. DANIEL B. UPDIKE, *Printing Types*, 3rd ed., 2 vol. (1962), is a thorough and interesting history of the development of type design from the beginnings to about 1930 —highly personal, highly dogmatic, but the classic work on the subject. Of the many books and articles by STANLEY MORISON, three are especially noteworthy to the non-professional reader: *First Principles of Typography*, 2nd ed., with postscript (1967), is an expanded version of his Britannica article on "Typography," which became the definitive statement of his views on the subject, and has been translated into several languages. *The Typographic Arts* (1950), contains two essays on *inter alia*, the interrelationship between calligraphy, engraving, and type design. *The Typographic Book*, ed. by KENNETH DAY (1962), is an expanded version of an earlier work entitled *Four Centuries of Fine Printing*. It contains good reproductions of specimen titles and text pages spanning 1450–1953. HELLMUT LEHMANN-HAUPT (ed.), *The Book in America*, 2nd ed. (1951), is an historical survey of American printing and publishing from the beginning to the present. KENNETH DAY (ed.), *Book Typography, 1815–1965, in Europe and the United States of America* (1966), contains uneven but generally good articles on its subject. JOHN CARTER and PERCY MUIR (eds.), *Printing and the Mind of Man* (1967), the catalog of two major exhibitions held in London for an International Printing Exhibition, contains much technical information on the technological development of printing and type founding from the invention to today, as well as notes on books important for their intellectual or aesthetic impact. HENRI J. MARTIN and LUCIEN FEBVRE, *L'Apparition du livre* (1958), while heavily French in its emphasis, is a stimulating and original history of the social, economic, cultural, and technical evolution of the book trades from the manuscript period to the 19th century. Of the many modern manuals on typography, mainly reflecting the Bauhaus school, two that are representative and better than average are JAN TSCHICHOLD, *Typographische Gestaltung* (1935; Eng. trans., *Asymmetric Typography*, 1967); and EMIL RUDER, *Typographie* (1967). The latter has text in German, French, and English, and also shows Dadaist and other modern schools. Tschichold became converted to traditional typography, and in *Designing Books* (1951), gives an excellent exposition of his later views. HUGH WILLIAMSON, *Methods of Book Design*, 2nd ed. (1966), is a full and good survey of modern book design and production methods. *The Penrose Annual*, published in London, has technical articles on new developments in design and processes as well as good essays on the history and aesthetics of printing. The *Gutenberg Jahrbuch*, emanating from Mainz, the cradle of printing, emphasizes incunabula but includes articles on later printing, publishing, and binding.

(W.E.P./J.M.Ws.)

Uccello, Paolo

A painter of early 15th-century Florence whose work represented an original attempt to reconcile two distinct artistic styles—the lingering Gothic tradition, which was essentially decorative, and the new, heroic style of the early Renaissance—Paolo Uccello was long thought to be significant primarily for his role in establishing new means of rendering perspective that became a major component of the Renaissance style. The 16th-century biographer Giorgio Vasari said that Uccello was "intoxicated" by the subject of perspective. Later historians have found the unique charm and the decorative genius evinced by his compositions to be an even more important contribution. Though in ruinous condition, they indicate the immense difficulties faced by artists of his time in taking advantage of new developments without giving up what was best in traditional art.

Paolo di Dono, known as Paolo Uccello, was born in 1397 in Pratovecchio, just outside Florence. By the time he was 10, he was already an apprentice in the workshop of the sculptor Lorenzo Ghiberti, who was then at work on what became one of the supreme masterpieces of the history of art—the bronze doors for the Baptistery of the Florence cathedral, which consisted of 28 panels illustrating New Testament scenes of the life of Christ. In 1414 Uccello joined the confraternity of painters (Compagnia di S. Luca), and in the following year he became a member of the Arte dei Medici e degli Speziale, the official guild to which painters belonged. Though Uccello must by then have been established as an independent painter, nothing of his work from this time remains, and there is no definite indication of his early training as a painter, except that he was a member of the workshop of Ghiberti, where many of the outstanding artists of the time were trained.

Apprenticeship with Ghiberti

Uccello's earliest, and now badly damaged, frescoes are in the Chiostro Verde (the Green Cloister, so called because of the green cast of the frescoes that covered its walls) of Sta. Maria Novella; they represent episodes from the creation. These frescoes, marked with a pervasive concern for elegant linear forms and insistent, stylized patterning of landscape features, are consistent with the late Gothic tradition that was still predominant at the beginning of the 15th century in Florentine studios and have given rise to the hope that Uccello's artistic origins may yet be found in some of these studios.

From 1425 to 1431, Uccello worked in Venice as a master mosaicist. All his work in Venice has been lost, and plans to reconstruct it have been unsuccessful. Uccello may have been induced to return to Florence by the commission for a series of frescoes in the cloister of S. Miniato al Monte depicting scenes from monastic legends. While the figural formulations of these ruinous frescoes still closely approximate the Sta. Maria Novella cycle, there is also a fascination with the novel perspective schemes that had appeared in Florence during Uccello's Venetian sojourn and with a simplified and more monumental treatment of forms deriving from the recent sculpture of Donatello and Nanni di Banco.

In 1436 in the Florence cathedral, Uccello completed a monochrome fresco of an equestrian monument to Sir John Hawkwood, an English mercenary who had commanded Florentine troops at the end of the 14th century. In the Hawkwood fresco, a single-point perspective scheme, a fully sculptural treatment of the horse and rider, and a sense of controlled potential energy within the figure all indicate Uccello's desire to assimilate the new style of the Renaissance that had blossomed in Florence since his birth. Following the Hawkwood monument, in 1443 Uccello completed four heads of prophets around a colossal clock on the interior of the west facade of the cathedral; between 1443 and 1445 he contributed the designs for two stained-glass windows in the cupola.

Completion of the Hawkwood fresco

After a brief trip to Padua in 1447, Uccello returned to the Chiostro Verde of Sta. Maria Novella. In a fresco illustrating the Flood and the recession, Uccello presented two separate scenes united by a rapidly receding perspective scheme that reflected the influence of Donatello's contemporary reliefs in Padua. Human forms in "The Flood," especially the nudes, were reminiscent of figures in Masaccio's frescoes in the Brancacci Chapel (c. 1425), perhaps the most influential of all paintings of the early Renaissance, but the explosion of details throughout the narrative again suggests Uccello's Gothic training. More than any other painting by Uccello, "The Flood"

"The Flood," fresco by Paolo Uccello, *c.* 1447–48. In the Chiostro Verde, Sta. Maria Novella, Florence.
By courtesy of the Soprintendenza alle Gallerie, Florence

indicates the difficulties that he and his contemporaries faced in attempting to graft the rapidly developing heroic style of the Renaissance onto an older, more decorative mode of painting.

Perhaps Uccello's most famous paintings are three panels representing the rout of San Romano, now in the Louvre, Paris; the National Gallery, London; and the Uffizi, Florence. These panels represent the victory in 1432 of Florentine forces under Niccolò da Tolentino over the troops of their arch rival, Siena. There are Renaissance elements, such as a sculpturesque treatment of forms and fragments of a broken perspective scheme in this work, but the bright handling of colour and the elaborate decorative patterns of the figures and landscape are indebted to the Gothic style, which continued to be used through the 15th century in Florence to enrich the environments of the new princes of the day, such as the Medici, who acquired all three of the panels representing the rout of San Romano.

Most famous paintings and perspective studies

Uccello is justly famous for his careful and sophisticated perspective studies, most clearly visible in "The Flood," in the underdrawing (sinopia) for his last fresco, "The Nativity," formerly in S. Martino della Scala in Florence, and in three drawings universally attributed to him that are now in the Uffizi. These drawings indicate a meticulous, analytic mind, keenly interested in the application of scientific laws to the reconstruction of objects in a three-dimensional space. In these studies he was probably assisted by a noted mathematician, Paolo Toscanelli. Uccello's perspective studies were to influence the Renaissance art treatises of artists such as Piero della Francesca, Leonardo da Vinci, and Albrecht Dürer.

Uccello apparently led an increasingly reclusive existence during his last years. He died in Florence on December 10, 1475.

Uccello's modern reputation as a painter and theoretician has suffered because of the bad state of preservation of his work and, more significantly, because of his naïve attempt to reconcile the two distinct styles of the Gothic and the Renaissance. Although any union of these two styles was destined to be an uneasy one, Uccello's attempt, nevertheless, documents the powerful impact of the new style of the Renaissance on older traditions.

MAJOR WORKS
"The Creation of the Animals"; "The Creation of Adam"; "The Creation of Eve"; "The Fall" (frescoes, early 1430s; Sta. Maria Novella, Florence); "Sir John Hawkwood" (fresco, 1436; cathedral, Florence); "Scenes from Monastic Legends" (frescoes, *c.* 1440; S. Miniato al Monte, Florence); "The Flood," "The Recession of the Flood," "The Sacrifice of Noah," and "The Drunkenness of Noah" (1447–48; Sta. Maria Novella, Florence); "The Rout of San Romano" (mid-1450s; panels in the National Gallery, London; Uffizi, Florence; and the Louvre, Paris); "St. George and the Dragon" (1455–?60; Musée Jacquemart-André, Paris); "St. George and the Dragon" (*c.* 1460; National Gallery, London); "The Profanation of the Host" (*c.* 1466–69; Galleria Nazionale delle Marche, Urbino, Italy); "A Hunt in a Forest" (after 1460; Ashmolean Museum, Oxford, England); "The Founders of Florentine Art" (after 1460?; Louvre).

BIBLIOGRAPHY. The standard and most readable and complete work on Uccello (and his followers) in English is JOHN POPE-HENNESSY, *Paolo Uccello*, 2nd ed. (1969). EVE BORSOOK discusses Uccello's Florentine frescoes in *The Mural Painters of Tuscany, from Cimabue to Andrea del Sarto* (1960). Uccello's role in the investigation of perspective is mentioned by JOHN WHITE in *The Birth and Rebirth of Pictorial Space*, 2nd ed. (1967); and this subject is treated more fully by ALESSANDRO PARRONCHI in *Studi su la dolce Pospettiva* (1964).

(J.T.Pa.)

Uganda

Uganda is a landlocked republic of East Africa. At least 500 miles from the Indian Ocean, it is bounded by Kenya to the east. The Sudan to the north, Zaire to the west, Rwanda and Burundi to the southwest, and Tanzania to the south. Not a large country, it covers an area of 91,452 square miles (236,860 square kilometres). By the early 1970s it had a population of over 10,000,000. The national capital is at Kampala.

Uganda is a member of the Commonwealth of Nations, has been in the forefront of the Pan-African movement, was a founder member of the Organization of African Unity, and, together with Kenya and Tanzania, belongs to the East African Community. Since 1962, when Uganda achieved independence, increasing emphasis has been placed on state participation in its economy. Every effort has been made to create an industrial base, but the economy remains basically agricultural and subject to world price fluctuations. Coffee and cotton are the main cash crops. (For history, see EAST AFRICA, HISTORY OF. For physical features, see EAST AFRICAN LAKES; EAST AFRICAN MOUNTAINS; NILE RIVER; and VIRUNGA MOUNTAINS.)

THE LANDSCAPE

The natural environment. *Relief.* Most of the country is situated on part of the Central African Plateau. A great, monotonous expanse, it drops gently from about 5,000 feet in the south to 3,000 feet in the north. The limits of Uganda's plateau region are marked by mountains and valleys.

To the west, this natural boundary is composed of the Virunga (Mufumbiro) Mountains, the Ruwenzori Range, and part of the Great Rift Valley System. The volcanic Virunga Mountains rise to 13,541 feet (4,127 metres) at Mt. Muhavura and include Mt. Sabinio, where the borders of Uganda, Zaire, and Rwanda meet. Further north, the Ruwenzori Range—popularly believed to be Ptolemy's Mountains of the Moon—rise to 16,763 feet (5,109 metres) at Margherita Peak; their heights are often hidden by clouds, and their peaks are capped by snow and glaciers. Between the Virunga and Ruwenzori mountains lie Lakes Edward and George. The rest of the boundary is composed of the western Rift Valley, which contains Lake Albert and the Albert Nile.

The Mountains of the Moon

The northeastern border of the plateau is defined by a string of volcanic mountains, including Mounts Zulia (7,048 feet [2,148 metres]), Morungole (9,022 feet [2,750 metres]), Moroto (10,116 feet [3,083 metres]),

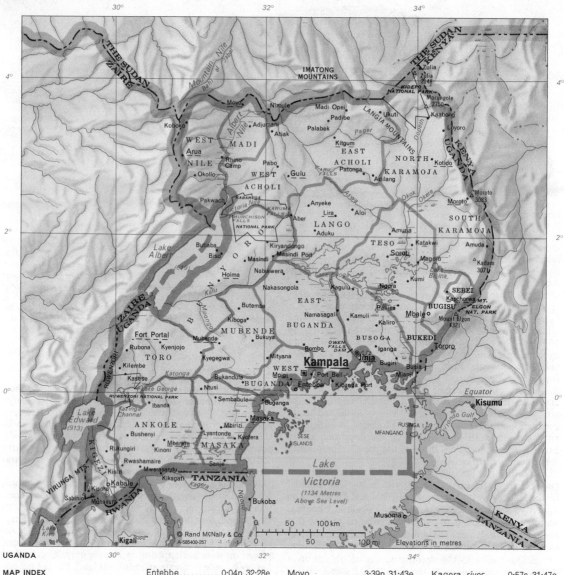

and Kadam (Debasien; 10,074 feet [3,071 metres]). The southernmost mountain—Mt. Elgon—is also the highest of the chain, reaching 14,178 feet (4,321 metres). South and west of these mountains are an eastern extension of the Rift Valley, as well as Lake Victoria. To the north, the plateau is marked on the Sudanese border by the Imatong Mountains, with an altitude of about 6,000 feet.

Drainage. The country's drainage system is dominated by six major lakes—Victoria (26,418 square miles), the world's second largest inland freshwater lake (after Lake Superior in the United States) to the southeast; Edward and George to the southwest; Albert to the west; and Kyoga and Bisina (Salisbury) in the east. Together with the lakes, there are eight major rivers. These are the Victoria Nile in central Uganda; the Aswa, Dopeth-Okok, and Pager in the north; the Albert Nile in the northwest; and the Kafu, Katonga, and Mpongo in the west.

The Victoria Nile

The southern rivers empty into Lake Victoria, the waters of which escape through Owen Falls near Jinja and form the Victoria Nile. The river flows northward through the eastern extension of Lake Kyoga. It then turns west and north to drop over Karuma Falls and Murchison Falls before emptying into Lake Albert.

Lake Albert is drained to the north by the Albert Nile, which is known as the Baḥr al-Jabal, or White Nile, after it enters The Sudan at Nimule. Rivers that rise to the north of Lake Victoria flow into Lake Kyoga, while those that rise north of Kyoga tend to flow into the Albert Nile. The rivers of the southwest flow into Lakes George and Edward.

Except for the Victoria and Albert Niles, the rivers are sluggish and often swampy. Clear streams are found only in the mountains and on the slopes of the Rift Valley. Most of the rivers are seasonal and flow only during the wet season. The few permanent rivers are also subject to seasonal changes in their rates of flow.

Soils and climate. The soils are predominantly ferralites (soils containing iron and aluminum). Interspersed with these are the waterlogged clays characteristic of the northwest and of the western shores of Lake Victoria. In general the soils are fertile, although they are of poorer quality in the north than in the south.

The climate is characteristically tropical—the Equator passing through southern Uganda. Temperatures are modified, however, by altitude and by the presence of the lakes. The major air currents are northeasterly and southwesterly. There is little variation in the height of the sun at midday, and the length of daylight is nearly always 12 hours. All of these factors, combined with an equatorial cloud cover, ensure an equable climate throughout the year.

Most parts of Uganda receive adequate rainfall; amounts range from a low of less than 15 inches a year in the northeast to a high of 80 inches in the Sese Islands of Lake Victoria. In the south there are two wet seasons, that occur in April and May and in October and November and that are separated by dry periods broken by tropical thunderstorms. In the north, the climate is roughly divided into a wet season from the months of April to October and a dry season that lasts from November to March.

Vegetation. Wooded savanna (grassy parkland) is typical of central and northern Uganda. Under less favourable conditions, dry acacia woodland, dotted with the occasional candelabra (tropical African shrubs or trees with huge spreading heads of foliage), euphorbia (plants often resembling cacti and containing a milky juice), and interspersed with grassland, occurs in the south. Similar components are found in the vegetation of the Rift Valley floors. The steppes (treeless plains) and thickets of the northeast represent the driest regions of Uganda. In the Lake Victoria region and the western highlands, the mosaic of elephant grass and forest remnants appears to have resulted from human incursions affecting the former forest covering. The medium-altitude forests contain a rich variety of species, with many representatives of West African vegetation. The high-altitude forests of Mt. Elgon and the Ruwenzori Range

occur above 6,000 feet; on their upper margins they give way, through transitional zones of mixed bamboo and tree heath, to high mountain moorland. Uganda's 5,600 square miles of swamp include both papyrus swamp and seasonal, grassy swamp.

Animal life and national parks. Lions and leopards are widely distributed but are seen only infrequently. Hippopotamuses and crocodiles inhabit most lakes and rivers, although the latter are not found in Lakes Edward and George. Mountain gorillas, chimpanzees, and small, forest elephants occur only in the extreme west. Elephants, buffalo, and the Uganda kob (an antelope) are found in the west and north, while the black rhinoceros, white rhinoceros, and giraffe are confined to the north. Zebras, topis, elands, and roan antelopes occur both in the northeastern and southern grasslands, but other kinds of antelopes, such as the oryx, greater and lesser kudu, and Grant's gazelle, live only in the northeastern area. The varied fish life includes ngege (a freshwater, nest-building fish of the tilapia species) and Nile perch. Insects comprise a significant element in the biological environment. The female anopheles mosquito may transmit malaria anywhere below 5,000 feet. Extensive areas of good grazing are closed to cattle because of the presence of deadly tsetse flies.

The three national parks contain an interesting variety of animal life. The Kabarega National Park, with an area of 1,500 square miles, stretches on either side of the Victoria Nile. Paraa and Chobe lodges cater to tourists. The Ruwenzori National Park occupies some 760 square miles in the Lake Edward–Lake George Basin and contains the Mweya Lodge. The Kidepo National Park consists of 500 square miles of magnificent country adjacent to the Sudan frontier.

The landscape under human settlement. The traditional regions of Uganda can be divided into two groups on the basis of their past governmental structures. Those areas that had centralized hierarchical governments include the southern regions of the kingdoms of Ankole, Buganda, Bunyoro, Toro, Koki, and the Busoga states. The second group consists of the less centralized state systems of eastern and northern Uganda and of Kigezi district in the extreme southwest. In most of the centralized states government was headed by a king. The king was known as the *kabaka* in Buganda, the *omugabe* in Ankole, and the *omukama* in Toro and Bunyoro.

Uganda's kingdoms

Rural settlement. Rural settlement has been greatly affected by the socio-economic changes that have taken place since 1900. Traditional life in the segmented societies of northern and eastern Uganda revolved around the clan, and people tended to live in clans or communities in particular areas. In the area of the kingdoms, society was more individualistic, although in Ankole society it was—and still is—divided into two groups represented by the ruling pastoralist Hima people and the agricultural Bairu. The Bunyoro and Toro kingdoms were divided along caste lines, while Buganda's society was without caste, if not without class.

The economic differences between the regions of Uganda tend greatly to influence life styles. In Buganda cultivation is left almost entirely to women, while in the north and east both men and women engage in agricultural activities. In the pastoral regions of Ankole, Toro, and Bunyoro, cattle herding is done by men. The introduction of cash crops and modern ranching and the spread of education have greatly affected rural attitudes and expectations.

Urban settlement. One of the major characteristics of the socio-economic change that has occurred has been the growth of towns and cities. As a heritage from the colonial period, every district has at least one township in which government offices and markets are found. Kampala, near Lake Victoria, is the national commercial and administrative capital; before independence, nearby Entebbe was the administrative capital and most of the government offices were located there. Jinja, the industrial capital, was steadily growing in the early 1970s. Mbale is an important centre of the eastern region. Increasing urbanization has led to the depopulation of the villages, especially in Buganda, because young people are reluctant to adhere to what they often regard as the dull and unexciting life of the countryside. This trend has resulted in an increase in the number of unemployed youths in the towns.

THE PEOPLE

Population groups. *Linguistic groups.* For more than 1,000 years Uganda has been a meeting place of different peoples. The three main linguistic groups are the Bantu, the Nilotics, and the Nilo-Hamitic. As in other parts of East and Central Africa, the Bantu groups are the most numerous, comprising about 70 percent of the population in the south, west, and east. The Nilotics—who are of Sudanic origin—are found in the north, northwest, and north central regions. The Nilo-Hamitic speakers are found in the northeast. English and Swahili serve as common languages. The most widely spoken African language is Luganda.

Ethnic groups. The major Bantu ethnic groups are the Ganda (the largest group), Soga, Nyoro, Nkole (Banyankole), Toro, Chiga (Kiga), Gisu, Gwere, and Nyole (Banyuri). The Acholi, Lango, Karamojong (Bakaramoja), Teso (Iteso), Madi, and Kakwa are the larger Nilotic groups. (To these names the prefix "ba-" is habitually added to denote "people.") Although there has been much admixture of these groups over the centuries, there are still clear linguistic, cultural, and traditional occupational divisions between them. Before the European invasion at the end of the 19th century, the Bantu were largely agricultural, although some districts of the southwest were occupied by a pastoral people called the Hima. The Bunyoro kingdom and northern and northeastern Uganda were partly pastoral and partly agricultural.

About 6 percent of the present African population is composed of recent immigrants from Rwanda, Burundi, Kenya, Zaire, The Sudan, and Tanzania. Since about 1870, foreigners of non-African origin—Arabs, Indians, and Europeans—have settled in the country. Until the 1972 deportation the Indian population, though small, occupied a strategic economic position that has often led to racial tensions in the past.

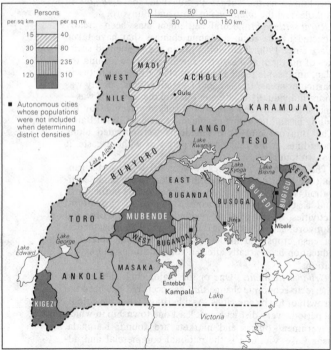

Population density of Uganda.

English, the official language, is understood by 25 to 30 percent of the population. Luganda, the language of the Ganda people, is understood everywhere but in the non-Bantu areas of the north.

Religious groups. Islām and Christianity were introduced during the 19th century. In 1968 about 60 percent of the population was Christian, 33 percent was animist, and about 5 percent was Muslim. Until the deportation of Asians began in 1972, there were also sizable numbers of Hindus and Sikhs.

Demography. The average population density is about 133 people per square mile, but densities vary from district to district. Areas of heavy concentration are the Bugisu and Bukedi districts in the eastern region and the Kigezi District in the southwest. Density in these areas varies between 350 and 470 persons per square mile of land area. Buganda and Busoga, which stretch along Lake Victoria and contain the principal urban areas, are also densely populated. The lowest density—32 persons per square mile—occurs in North and South Karamoja Districts. The total population numbered 10,127,000 in 1971.

Uganda, Area and Population

	area		population	
	sq mi	sq km	1969 census*	1971 estimate
Regions				
Buganda				
Districts				
East Buganda	9,050	23,440	844,000	902,000
Masaka	8,224	21,300	641,000	683,000
Mubende	3,981	10,310	336,000	357,000
West Buganda	2,532	6,559	847,000	912,000
Eastern				
Districts				
Bugisu	983	2,546	422,000	441,000
Bukedi	1,758	4,553	519,000	545,000
Busoga	5,424	14,047	945,000	1,005,000
North Karamoja†	10,507	27,213	283,000	296,000
Sebei	671	1,738	64,000	68,000
South Karamoja†	...	...	...	...
Teso	4,989	12,921	568,000	590,000
Northern				
Districts				
East Acholi‡	10,754	27,853	465,000	493,000
Lango	5,305	13,740	505,000	528,000
Madi	1,933	5,006	90,000	96,000
West Acholi‡	...	...	...	...
West Nile	4,139	10,721	579,000	593,000
Western				
Districts				
Ankole	6,248	16,182	855,000	932,000
Bunyoro	7,571	19,609	348,000	391,000
Kigezi	2,015	5,218	642,000	672,000
Toro	5,368	13,904	571,000	624,000
Total Uganda	91,452	236,860	9,526,000§	10,127,000§

*Preliminary. †North Karamoja includes the area and population of South Karamoja. The former Karamoja Province was divided in April, 1971. Separate figures are not available. ‡East Acholi includes the area and population of West Acholi. The former Acholi Province was divided in April, 1971. Separate figures are not available. §Figures do not add to total given because of rounding.
Source: Official government figures.

The level of fertility in Uganda is estimated to be 50 per 1,000 females of child-bearing age. The African birth rate is high—between 30 and 40 per 1,000 females. The highest birth rates are recorded among the Chiga (Kiga), Ankole, Karamojong, and Acholi peoples. Low birth rates are recorded among the Teso (Iteso). The Asian population birth rate is also high, being 35 per 1,000. There are signs, however, of a decline in family size among the African and Asian middle-income groups. The adult death rate is about 20 per 1,000, and infant mortality is about 160 per 1,000. The average life expectancy of the inhabitants of these areas is only between 45 and 50 years of age.

The population growth rate of about 3 percent a year is partially due to immigration from Rwanda, Burundi, Kenya, and The Sudan. There is, however, little African emigration. Between the years 1965 and 1972, large numbers of Asians left the country, as did many Africans from Kenya, The Sudan, and Zaire. In the early 1970s the population of Uganda was expected to continue to grow; the birth rate remained high and the death rate decreased.

Important economic regions in Uganda.
(Left) Rural village in the central Karamoja district, where raising cattle is the chief source of income. (Right) Industrial village in the Ruwenzori Range at the Kilembe mine, important for its copper extraction.
By courtesy of (left) the Uganda Government Ministry of Information and Broadcasting, (right) UNESCO; photograph (right) J H. Blower

THE NATIONAL ECONOMY

Uganda is basically an agricultural country. In the past, there was a lack of crop diversification, and the country relied on two major cash crops—coffee and cotton. Fluctuations in the prices of these crops on the world market led to attempts to diversify the cash crops grown. By the late 1960s the economy was fairly healthy, and trade within the East African Community—Uganda, Kenya, and Tanzania—had greatly increased.

The extent and distribution of resources. *Mineral resources.* Uganda is not rich in minerals. Copper and tin ores are the most important minerals, with copper constituting three-quarters of the total minerals produced in 1969. Prospects for finding iron ore are encouraging, but there are no workable coal deposits. Small amounts of tungsten and salt are available. Beryllium ore, used as an alloy and as a source of nuclear energy, is found in large deposits. Small quantities of gold are scattered about, and there are deposits of bismuth, a mineral used in medicines and cosmetics. Industrial and nonmetallic minerals include sand, stone, clay, mica, and phosphate.

Biological resources. Grasslands prevail in dry areas where perennial agriculture is not possible. There are 3,980,000 acres of forest reserves, including stands of mountain bamboo and poor thicket. The government has begun an extensive program of afforestation that includes the introduction of soft woods such as pines.

By 1970 there were 4,400,000 head of cattle, 1,900,000 goats, 900,000 sheep, 10,200,000 poultry, and 74,000 pigs. Cattle, goats, and sheep are concentrated largely in the Districts of North and South Karamoja and Teso in the northeast and of Ankole in the southwest.

 Hydro-electric potential

Power resources. There are no known deposits of coal or oil, but many of the rivers are potential sources of hydroelectric power. By 1970 there were three power plants—located on the Victoria Nile, Kagera, and Kiruruma rivers—and plans had been drawn up for additional installations on the Victoria Nile and others.

Sources of national income. *Agriculture, forestry, and fishing.* About two-thirds of the national income is derived from agriculture, and the country is able to meet most of its domestic demand for food. Staple food crops include bananas in the south and west; finger millet (a cereal grass) in the grain belt that stretches across the country from southeast to northwest; sorghum in the extreme northeast and southwest; cassava (manioc) west of the Albert Nile; peanuts (groundnuts) in the southeast; and sesame in the north. Coffee is the most valuable cash crop; the robusta type is grown in the Lake Victoria region and arabica coffee is grown in the east. Most of the cotton crop is grown in the southeast and the northwest. Sugar and tea are grown as cash crops on estates, but

tobacco is cultivated by individual farmers. Forestry products include timber, poles, and firewood.

Most fishing on Lakes Victoria, Albert, and George is carried out by canoes on the inshore waters and by motor-powered boats in the deeper waters. Domestic fish ponds are becoming widespread. In 1970 the annual catch was about 130,000 tons, most of which supplied the domestic market. Dried fish is exported to Zaire, and frozen fish fillets are sold to Kenya.

Mining and quarrying. The most important mining operation is the extraction of copper from the Kilembe mine on the eastern flank of the Ruwenzori Range. Other minerals that are mined include tin, tungsten, and beryl. Rock and sand are produced to support the cement industry, while clay is extracted for the production of ceramics.

Manufacturing. Industry has greatly expanded since independence in 1962. Agricultural processing plants—such as cotton gins, coffee works, tea factories, tobacco curing barns, and sugar mills—tend to be situated in their respective crop areas. Jinja has developed as a centre of heavy industry and contains installations for copper smelting, steel rolling, plywood and match manufacture, papermaking, textile production, cigarette manufacture, grain milling, and brewing. Other industries include those producing cement, asbestos, and fertilizer.

Energy. Because of its hydroelectric production, Uganda has not had to rely heavily on imported fuel; gasoline and diesel fuel are, however, imported. The Uganda Electricity Board supplies electricity throughout the country and also exports power to Kenya. More than 90 percent of the country's power in 1970 was produced by the Owen Falls power station. Located near Jinja on the Victoria Nile, its installed capacity is 170,000 megawatts of electricity. There are also two smaller stations—one at Maziba Gorge on the Kagera River, near Kabale, and the other at Kikagati on the Kiruruma River in Ankole District. There are plans to erect another power station at Aru Falls in eastern Acholi District.

Financial services and foreign trade. The Bank of Uganda issues the national currency, acts as banker to the government, and controls the country's commercial banks. In 1970 there were six commercial banks, several of which were branches of banking institutions in the United Kingdom, India, The Netherlands, and Turkey. The Commercial Bank of Africa is represented in Kampala, and the Uganda Commercial Bank has branches throughout the country. Savings may be deposited with cooperative societies, rural thrift and loan societies, and insurance companies.

A distinction may be made between external trade and that within the common market and customs union of the East African Community. The most important external exports are coffee, cotton, copper, tea, fodder, and hides and skins. The main markets are those of the United States, the United Kingdom, Japan, West Germany, and India. The major imports are machinery, vehicles, and fabrics from the United Kingdom, Japan, West Germany, the United States, and Italy.

Imports from the East African Community include petroleum products, soaps, unmilled wheat, paper and paperboard, and sacks. Exports comprise cotton fabrics, iron and steel bars, and processed foods.

Management of the economy. *The private sector.* The private sector includes all foreign-owned businesses, such as oil companies, banks, insurance companies, and breweries. Since 1970 the government has played a role in this sector and now holds between 40 and 49 percent of these businesses. Many of the originally foreign-owned businesses are now incorporated in Uganda and must retain a specified amount of capital within the country.

The public sector. The government plays an increasingly important economic role in the management of the economy. The government contributes two-thirds of the expenditure in the public sector; the balance is contributed by local authorities, government corporations, and the East African Community. Government corporations include the Uganda Development Corporation, the Uganda Electricity Board, the Coffee Marketing Board, the Lint Marketing Board, the National Trading Corporation, and the Export and Import Corporation.

Taxation. Uganda has one of the highest rates of both direct and indirect taxation in East Africa. Direct taxes include a graduated personal tax, an income tax, and a development tax. Indirect taxes are levied on foodstuffs and contribute to the high cost of living. Customs and excise duties are the responsibility of the East African Community, and their derived revenue is used to run such common services as the railways, postal services, and telecommunications.

Trade unions. Few workers are landless labourers dependent upon wages. Most of them do not identify their long-term interests with wages, and trade unions have consequently been slow to develop. The unions were active in the liberation movement and were closely associated with the urbanization process; they are, therefore, supratribal. An Industrial Relations Charter of 1967—drawn up between the government, the Federation of Uganda Employers, and the Trade Union Congress—established procedures for settling industrial disputes. The government largely established procedures for conciliation and arbitration and has maintained control of the union movement.

Contemporary economic policies. A rapid growth of exports is essential to the attainment of the overall growth-rate target of 6 percent per annum. To help attain this goal, the government has established the Export Promotions Council. The government controls the level of imports by the need to maintain a favourable balance of trade and to keep external reserves at an adequate level. In the industrial sector, steel production using imported iron ore is expected to be greatly expanded by 1974.

Problems and prospects. Contemporary economic policy concentrates on the attraction of foreign capital while encouraging Ugandans to play an increasing role in the management of the economy. The aim is to diversify the range of national resources by such projects as the introduction of a vigorous dairy and ranching industry. Officials hope that by the late 1970s Uganda will not only meet all its beef and dairy needs but will be able to export these products to neighbouring countries. The main economic problems are those of limited capital and the falling or fluctuating of coffee and cotton prices. There is also a relative lack of skilled labour and of highly trained technical personnel.

TRANSPORTATION

Because Uganda is landlocked, the maintenance of an effective line of external communication is essential. An internal transportation system radiates from Kampala, while links with the outside world are maintained by railway, water, and air.

Roads. Uganda's roads are among the best in Africa. Murram, or lateritic (leached, iron-bearing) soil, which is suitable for road construction and hard gravel surfaces, is found everywhere but in the Toro and Kigezi districts. Before World War II such gravel-surfaced roads stood up to the light traffic of that era; the policy in the 1970s is to rebuild old roads while constructing new ones.

The road network

There are four main road systems—radial networks around Kampala and Masaka, across the Nile in Busoga District, and in the eastern region in the Teso, Bukedi, and Bugisu districts. There are also mountainous roads in Kigezi District.

Railways. In 1901 the Uganda Railway (later the Kenya–Uganda Railway and now the East African Railway run by the East African Community) was completed. It ran across Kenya from Mombasa on the Indian Ocean to the eastern shores of Lake Victoria, thus linking the country to the sea. In 1912 another line was opened between Jinja and Namasagali on the Victoria Nile, and in 1928 a line joined Jinja to the Uganda Railway at Nakuru, Kenya, creating a direct railway link to the Indian Ocean. In 1931 a further extension connected Jinja to Kampala, another section from Tororo to Soroti was constructed in the late 1940s, and a line from Kampala to Kasese and the Kilembe copper mines was completed in 1957.

Water transport. Lakes Victoria, Albert, and Kyoga and the Albert Nile are navigable. Before the expansion of road and rail transport, steamship services were of vital importance. Since the late 1940s, however, the importance of water transport has declined. A modern passenger vessel maintains a biweekly service round the lake.

Air services. The international airport at Entebbe—capable of handling large jets—lies on one of the main air routes between Europe and South Africa. Several daily flights to Europe are operated by either East African Airways or various European air lines. American and other African air services operate flights between Uganda and West Africa, and there are regular scheduled flights to the Middle East, Pakistan, and India. There are about a dozen domestic airfields, including the field used by the Ugandan air force at Gulu.

ADMINISTRATION AND SOCIAL CONDITIONS

The structure of government. *Constitutional framework.* According to the constitution of 1967, Uganda is a sovereign republic within the Commonwealth of Nations. An executive president is the head of state, head of government, and commander in chief of the armed forces. The president is assisted by a cabinet of ministers who are appointed from among the members of the unicameral National Assembly. In theory the National Assembly consists of 82 elected members and such number of specially elected members as may be required to give the party having the greatest numerical strength in the assembly an overall majority of not more than ten. The president takes an active part in the deliberations of the assembly, which sits under the chairmanship of a speaker. The statutory life of the National Assembly was fixed at five years.

Local government. Under the 1962 constitution, the four kingdoms of Ankole, Buganda, Bunyoro, and Toro and the territory of Busoga were in a federal relationship with the central government. The kingdoms were ruled by their traditional hereditary kings, and Busoga was governed by a district council. In 1967 all the kingdoms were abolished and the country was divided into districts. Each district is headed by a commissioner who is officially appointed by the president. The districts are divided into counties, subcounties, and parishes. Kampala, Jinja, Mbale, and Masaka are governed by urban authorities. Responsibility for the whole structure of local government lies with the Ministry of Public Service and Local Administration.

The political process. In 1971 Uganda's one-party government was overthrown by the armed forces. After the coup d'etat, the National Assembly and district and city councils were dissolved and all political activities were banned. A return to civilian rule was promised as soon as an investigation into the activities of the previous government had been concluded.

Justice. The system of justice was modelled on that of the United Kingdom. The High Court of Uganda, with jurisdiction throughout the republic, consists of a Ugandan chief justice, at least six puisne (associate) judges, and registrars and magistrates. All judges are appointed by the president with the advice of the cabinet. Judges of the High Court can be removed by the president for "bad behaviour or for reasons of infirmity." There is a Judicial Service Commission composed of the chief justice as chairman, the attorney general, and such puisne judges as may be designated with the advice of the chairman. There are also district courts throughout the country. Because of its membership in the East African Community, Uganda is also a member of the Court of Appeal for East Africa, a judicial body which sits in the various national capitals and is presided over by an appeal judge that is appointed by the three presidents of the Community.

The armed forces. The Uganda armed forces evolved out of the colonial King's African Rifles; they are now completely Africanized. The 12,000-man Army consists of battalions, paratrooper units, and an air force. Many of the high-ranking officers have been trained abroad, especially in the United Kingdom and Israel.

Administration. *Education.* Since independence, the role of the missionaries in education has remained prominent, although the government has overall responsibility for educational services at all levels. In 1970 there were about 2,700 public primary schools with about 1,000 private ones. There are relatively few secondary schools. Postprimary-school enrollment is strictly controlled and linked closely to manpower needs. At the beginning of the 1970s, Uganda was spending nearly one-fifth of its revenue budget on education, and there had been rapid expansion of the educational services since independence. In spite of these efforts, less than 45 percent of the children of primary school age attended school. In the early 1970s plans included the expansion of technical and vocational schools.

Until the early 1960s, Makerere University College in Kampala was the only institution of higher education in East and Central Africa. For a time it became part of the University of East Africa, before becoming an independent university in 1970. It has faculties of arts, social sciences, science, law, engineering, veterinary science, agriculture, and education. Its medical school, founded in 1924, is one of the best in Africa, as is its Institute of Social Research.

Health and welfare services. Health and welfare services are the responsibility of the Ministry of Health and the Ministry of Community Development and Culture. Since 1955 emphasis has been placed on preventive medicine. Health personnel include doctors, nurses, midwives, and health inspectors. There are schools for nursing and midwifery at all major hospitals, the largest of which is in Kampala. Medical facilities include a school of hygiene at Mbale, a department of preventive medicine at Makerere, a vector control unit, and a number of rural health centres. Despite the expansion of health services at all levels, there is still only one doctor for about 8,690 of the population.

Pensions are granted to high civil servants after 25 years of service. Wage earners participate in a contributory social security system, and companies offer contributory pension plans.

Housing. In the early 1970s more than 90 percent of Uganda's population lived in rural areas and provided their own housing. Rural buildings are largely of rectangular design and are constructed of woven branches plastered with mud, roofed with corrugated iron. The urban population was expanding rapidly, especially around Kampala and Jinja, where there was a scarcity of housing for middle-income groups. The National Housing Corporation and private builders had built houses for different income groups, but a tremendous shortage of housing for the low-income group still remained. In urban centres houses are built of concrete blocks or burnt bricks and are roofed with corrugated iron or tiles. Buildings in urban fringe areas are of traditional structure. Various employers, such as the oil companies, the East African Community, and the government, house their employees at nominal or free rents. Outside the urban areas of Uganda, housing is unplanned, and there are no services such as street lighting, waste disposal, or telephones.

Police services. The Ugandan police force numbers between 7,000 and 8,000 men but is understaffed. There are also paramilitary units that assist the armed forces in border patrol and riot control. Police stations are located in all the towns, and there is a police training school in Kampala.

Social conditions. *Wages and the cost of living.* The wages of unskilled workers remain low, a problem that has been aggravated because the growth of employment opportunities has not kept pace with the increase of the labour force. One of the legacies of the colonial period is a salary structure that contains enormous disparities between the highest and the lowest incomes. There is also a difference in wage structure between the urban and the rural areas and between the different urban centres.

Health conditions. The health situation is generally better than that in many other African countries. A number of diseases such as malaria, hookworm, venereal disease, and intestinal disorders are, however, common. Adults do not generally suffer from malnutrition, but the low-protein content of most foodstuffs results in the occurrence of kwashiorkor (a food-deficiency disease) among infants and children.

Social and economic divisions. People in Uganda comprise three groups—the Africans, Asians, and Europeans—among which there is little social contact except at formal gatherings. Most of the Africans comprise the agricultural population; the urban African is a wage earner, salaried civil servant, or university professor. Prior to 1972 the Asians dominated the nation's commerce and provided the largest source of skilled labour. The Europeans are professionals, civil servants, or owners of industry.

CULTURAL LIFE AND INSTITUTIONS

Uganda's varied ethnic groups have each contributed to the general cultural environment. Traditional cultures have generally survived the colonial impact, but not without modifications. Christianity in its various forms, Islām, and other world religions have been influential and seem to be the cultural focus for a fairly large section of the population. Institutions such as the cinema and the theatre are integral components of urban life. In order to promote the performing arts of dance, music, and drama, the government created a Ministry of Community Development and Culture.

The state of the arts. The practice and appreciation of fine arts are limited to a small but expanding section of the population. The Makerere School of Fine Art has trained some of East Africa's leading painters, sculptors, and art teachers; the school also teaches industrial art and design. In order to strengthen the performing arts, the Ministry of Community Development and Culture established the "Heart Beat of Africa," a dancing group consisting of representatives of major ethnic groups. Among the dances traditionally performed only by women are the *bakisimba* and *nankasa* dances of the Ganda, the *bwola* and *jing ding* dances of the Acholi, and the *lunyege* dance of the Anyoro and Toro.

On the academic level, historians, musicologists, anthropologists, and theologians delve into oral traditions in order to reconstruct aspects of Ugandan culture. There seems to be an attempt among middle-income groups to reaffirm the cultural heritage; in the dance halls, popular music is frequently interrupted by traditional tunes.

Cultural institutions. Churches, mosques, schools, theatres, and museums are the new repositories of national culture. There is the National Theatre and the Uganda Museum, in Kampala. In Buganda, Bunyoro, and Ankole the royal jawbone (relics of kings) shrines and tombs

Primary and secondary schools

Traditional art forms

recall the historic power of the kingdoms. The Entebbe Botanical Gardens contain local and exotic plants. The Forest Department maintains a library, herbarium, and museum, and there are a game and fisheries museum, zoo, aquarium, and library. There are also museums at the Ruwenzori and Kabarega national parks. Makerere University maintains two libraries.

The press. The press traces its origin to the weekly newspapers published by missionaries. The major Ugandan dailies are *Argus* (published in English) and *Taifa Empya* and *Munno* (both published in Luganda). Kenyan newspapers such as the *Nation* and the *East African Standard* are widely read, as are some British newspapers.

Radio and television. Radio Uganda maintains broadcasting stations in all the major towns and transmits the same program throughout the country. Nearly all of the vernacular languages are used along with Swahili and English. There were plans for an external service in the early 1970s. Television was introduced in 1963. Programs are transmitted as far as Bukoba, Tanzania. Through the services of Radio Uganda and Uganda Television, plays and traditional music are broadcast and drama festivals are organized periodically. A number of educational programs are also broadcast.

PROSPECTS FOR THE FUTURE

The military regime established by the coup d'etat of 1971 may be followed with a return to parliamentary government by 1980. Rural economic development is likely to receive greater attention than it has hitherto. Efforts are being made to increase employment opportunities and to place trained Africans in managerial positions. Uganda has suffered from a long-term drain on capital transfers; there is a need for stricter exchange controls. Despite governmental efforts to diversify the economy, there is still an excessive dependence upon coffee and cotton.

BIBLIOGRAPHY. SIR H.H. JOHNSTON, *The Uganda Protectorate*, 2 vol. (1902), excellent on animal life but outdated on ethnology; H.B. THOMAS and R. SCOTT, *Uganda* (1935), the best handbook on colonial administration up to 1940; K. INGHAM, *The Making of Modern Uganda* (1958), and D.A. LOW and R.C. PRATT, *Buganda and British Overrule, 1900–1955* (1960), good accounts of British rule and the growth of the Legislative Council; J. ROSCOE, *The Baganda: An Account of Their Native Customs and Beliefs* (1911), *The Banyankole* (1923), *The Bagesu, and Other Tribes of the Uganda Protectorate* (1924), and *The Bakitara or Banyoro* (1923), detailed anthropological studies of which *The Baganda* is best; J. GORJU, *Entre le Victoria, l'Albert et l'Edouard* (1920), a study of the clan system in southern Uganda; KIWANUKA SEMAKULA, *The Kings of Buganda* (1971) and *A History of Buganda from the Foundation of the Kingdom to 1900* (1971), the most up-to-date accounts of Buganda.

There is no single text covering the economic and political developments in Uganda since independence; the following cover various aspects of these subjects: D.E. APTER, *The Political Kingdom in Uganda* (1961); D.A. LOW, *Political Parties in Uganda, 1949–62* (1962); F.B. WELBOURN, *Religion and Politics in Uganda, 1952–1962* (1965). Apart from government reports and development plans, the following economic studies are quite useful: W.T.W. MORGAN, *East Africa: Its Peoples and Resources* (1969); A.M. O'CONNOR, *Railways and Development in Uganda: A Study in Economic Geography* (1965); ROGER SCOTT, *The Development of Trade Unions in Uganda* (1966), a detailed study of the trade union movement; F.G. BURKE, *Local Government and Politics in Uganda* (1964). Factual accounts of political and economic developments may be found in the Uganda constitutions of 1961, 1966, and 1967, and in the Uganda Development Plans of 1961–66, 1966–71, and 1971–76 (all issued by the Uganda government printer). The political and economic organization of the peoples of northern Uganda may be found in J.H. DRIBERG, *The Lango* (1923); and J.C.D. LAWRANCE, *The Iteso: Fifty Years of Change in a Nilo-Hamitic Tribe of Uganda* (1957). The two best accounts of the land system are those by A.B. MUKWAYA, *Land Tenure in Buganda* (1953); and H.W. WEST, *The Mailo System in Buganda* (1965). *The Economic Development of Uganda* (1962), a report of the International Bank for Reconstruction and Development, is a concise account, with useful statistics, though slightly out of date.

(M.S.Ki.)

Ugarit

Ugarit was an ancient city lying in a large artificial mound called Ra's Shamrah six miles (ten kilometres) north of al-Lādhiqīyah (Latakia) on the Mediterranean coast of northern Syria. Its ruins, about half a mile from the shore, were first uncovered by the plow of a peasant at Mīnat al-Baydā. Excavations were begun in 1929 by a French archaeological mission under the direction of Claude F.A. Schaeffer.

The golden age of Ugarit. The most prosperous and the best documented age in Ugarit's history, dated from c. 1450 to c. 1200 BC, produced great royal palaces and temples and shrines, with a high priests' library and other libraries on the acropolis. Some of the family vaults built under the stone houses show strong Mycenaean influence. Mycenaean and Cypriot pottery has also been found.

After the discovery of the temple library, which revealed a hitherto unknown cuneiform alphabetic script as well as an entirely new mythological and religious literature, several other palatial as well as private libraries were found, along with archives dealing with all aspects of the city's political, social, economic, and cultural life.

The art of Ugarit in its golden age is best illustrated by a golden cup and patera (bowl) ornamented with incised Ugaritic scenes; by carved stone stele and bronze statuettes and ceremonial axes; by carved ivory panels depicting royal activities; and by other fine-carved ivories. Despite Egyptian influence, Ugaritic art exhibits a Syrian style of its own.

Hirmer Fotoarchiv, Munchen

Golden bowl from Ugarit, 14th century BC. In the Musée National, Aleppo, Syria.

Soon after 1200 BC Ugarit came to an end. Its fall coincided with the invasion of the Northern and Sea Peoples, and probably with earthquakes and famines. In the Iron Age and during the 6th–4th centuries BC there were small settlements on the site.

The excavators of the site were fortunate in the number and variety of finds of ancient records in cuneiform script. The excavations continue and each season throws some new and often unexpected light on the ancient north Canaanite civilization. The texts are written on clay tablets either in the Babylonian cuneiform script or in the special alphabetic cuneiform script invented in Ugarit. Several copies of this alphabet, with its 30 signs, were found in 1949 and later. A shorter alphabet with 25, or even 22, signs seems to have been used by 13th-century traders.

Scribes used four languages: Ugaritic, Akkadian, Sumerian, and Hurrian, and seven different scripts were used in Ugarit in this period: Egyptian and Hittite hieroglyphic and Cypro-Minoan, Sumerian, Akkadian, Hurrian, and Ugaritic cuneiform. These show clearly the cosmopolitan character of the city.

The Middle Bronze Age period. A carnelian bead identified with the pharaoh Sesostris I (reigned 1971–1928 BC) and a stela and statuettes, gifts to the kings of Ugarit from other Middle Kingdom pharaohs (*e.g.*, Sesostris II, 1897–1878, and Amenemhet III, 1842–1797), provided the first exact dating in the history of Ugarit. Eggshell ware from Crete (Middle Minoan period) and Babylonian cylinder seals found in the tombs of level II also provided cross datings. During the 18th and 17th centuries BC Ugarit was apparently under the control of new tribes related to the Hyksos, probably mainly Hurrians or Mitannians, who mutilated the Egyptian monuments.

Ras Shamra texts and the Bible. Many texts discovered at Ugarit, including the "Legend of Keret," the "Legend of Aghat" (or "of Danel"), the "Myth of Baal-Aliyan," and the "Death of Baal," reveal an Old Canaanite mythology. A tablet names the Ugaritic pantheon with Babylonian equivalents; El, Asherah of the Sea, and Baal were the main deities. These texts not only constitute a literature of high standing and great originality but also have an important bearing on Old Testament studies. It is now evident that the patriarchal stories in the Old Testament were not merely transmitted orally, but were based on written documents of Canaanite origin, the discovery of which at Ugarit has led to a new appraisal of the Old Testament.

The Ras Shamra mound. Soundings through the Ras Shamra mound revealed a reliable stratigraphic sequence of settlements from the beginning of the Neolithic period. Above the ground level, five main upper levels (levels V to I) were identified. The three lowest levels have been subdivided into smaller layers. The earliest settlement on level V—already a small fortified town in the 7th millennium BC—shows a prepottery stage with flint industries. Also on level V, but in a later layer, light, sun-dried pottery appears. Level IV and part of level III date back to the Chalcolithic, or Copper–Stone, Age, when new ethnic groups arrived from the northeast and the east. This stage shows Mediterranean as well as strong Mesopotamian influence. During the Early Chalcolithic Age, painted pottery of the Hassunan and Halafian cultures of northern Iraq is very common. The Late Chalcolithic shows fresh Mesopotamian influence with its monochromatic, Ubaidian, geometrical painted pottery. The flint industry was then in competition with the first metal tools, made of copper. The Early Bronze Age (3rd millennium) layers, immediately above, in level III, yielded no more painted ware but various monochromatic burnished wares and some red polished ware of Anatolian origin. With Early Bronze Age III, metallurgy quickly developed. In the Middle Bronze Age newcomers, so-called Torque-Bearers, expert in bronze metallurgy, arrived (*c.* 2000–1900 BC). Levels II and I correspond to historical periods within the 2nd millennium BC.

BIBLIOGRAPHY. C.F.A. SCHAEFFER, *Ugaritica*, 1–6 (1939–69), *The Cuneiform Texts of Ras Shamra-Ugarit* (1939), and preliminary reports in *Syria* (since 1929); *Stratigraphie comparée et chronologie de l'Asie occidentale IIIᵉ et IIᵉ millénaires . . . Syrie, Palestine, Asie Mineure, Chypre, Perse et Caucase*, vol. 1 (1948); C.F.A. SCHAEFFER, JEAN NOUGAYROL, and CHARLES VIROLLEAUD, *Le Palais royal d'Ugarit*, vol. 2–6 (1955–70); CHARLES VIROLLEAUD, "Les Inscriptions cunéiformes de Ras Shamra," *Syria* (1929–53), *La Légende phénicienne de Danel* (1936), and *La Légende de Keret, roi des Sidoniens* (1936); RENE DUSSAUD, *Les Découvertes de Ras Shamra (Ugarit) et l'Ancien Testament*, 2nd ed. (1941); ROBERT DE LANGHE, *Les Textes de Ras Shamra-Ugarit et leurs rapports avec le milieu biblique de l'Ancien Testament* (1945); G.R. DRIVER, *Canaanite Myths and Legends* (1956).

(C.F.A.S.)

Ukrainian Soviet Socialist Republic

The Ukrainian Soviet Socialist Republic (or Ukrainian S.S.R., also called the Ukraine) lies in the southwest of the European Soviet Union, bordered by the Belorussian S.S.R. on the north; the Russian S.F.S.R. on the east; the Sea of Azov, the Black Sea, the Moldavian S.S.R., and Romania on the south; and Hungary, Czech-oslovakia, and Poland on the west. With an area of 233,100 square miles (603,700 square kilometres), it is one of the largest geographical entities in Europe, third in size after the Soviet Union and the Russian S.F.S.R. Nonetheless, it constitutes only 2.7 percent of Soviet territory, though it produces more than 20 percent of the Soviet industrial and agricultural output and one-fourth of its grain. It became a union republic of the Soviet Union in 1924.

In 1975 the population of the Ukraine was estimated at 48,830,000, of whom 74.9 percent were Ukrainians (formerly also called Ruthenians, or Little Russians). The Ukrainian language belongs to the East Slavic group, of which Russian and Belorussian are also members.

The following article describes the land, people, economy, and society of the contemporary Ukraine. For history, see RUSSIA AND THE SOVIET UNION, HISTORY OF; for a description of the capital city, see KIEV; for related physical features, see DNEPR RIVER; DNESTR RIVER; AZOV, SEA OF; BLACK SEA; CARPATHIAN MOUNTAINS; and PRIPET MARSHES; see also SLAVIC LANGUAGES; SOVIET UNION.

THE LAND

Topography. The Ukraine, consisting almost entirely of level plains at an average elevation of 574 feet (175 metres) above sea level, occupies a considerable portion of the East European Plain. Such mountainous areas as the Ukrainian Carpathians and Crimean Mountains occur only on the borders and account for barely 5 percent of the area. The landscape is nevertheless diverse, and the plains are broken by highlands—running in a continuous belt from northwest to southeast—as well as lowlands. The rolling plain of the Dnepr Plateau, which lies between the middle reaches of the Dnepr (Dnipro; alternative spellings given in parentheses are Ukrainian) and Yuzhny (Southern) Bug (Boh, or Buh) rivers, is the largest highland area, broken up by many river valleys, ravines, and gorges, some more than 1,000 feet deep. From the west, the plateau is abutted by the characteristically rugged Volyn–Podolsk (Podilian) Upland, which rises to 1,549 feet (472 metres) at its highest point, Mt. Kamul. On the left bank of the Dnepr the Azov Upland, the highest point of which is Mt. Mogila-Belmak (1,070 feet), stretches gently away from the mountains to the Donets Ridge on its northeastern edge, which is surmounted by Mt. Mogila-Mechetnaya (1,204 feet). The northeastern portion of the Ukraine is a spur of the Central Russian Upland, but it reaches an elevation of only 774 feet (236 metres) at its highest point.

In the northern part of the republic lie the Pripet Marshes, crossed by numerous river valleys. In the central Ukraine is the Dnepr Lowland, flat in the west and gently rolling in the east. The Black Sea Lowland extends along the shores of the Black and Azov seas, its level surface, broken only by low rises and shallow depressions, sloping gradually toward the Black Sea. In the Crimean Peninsula it becomes the North Crimean Lowland. In the Transcarpathian region of the western Ukraine, the Tisa Lowland lies in the valley of the Tisa (Tysa) River and its tributaries. Toward the south it becomes the Pannonian Basin. In the west the parallel ranges of the Carpathian Mountains—one of the most picturesque areas in the Ukraine—extend for more than 150 miles. Easily accessible, the mountains range in height from about 2,000 to 6,500 feet, rising to 6,762 feet (2,061 metres) in Mt. Hoverla, the highest point. A number of passes through the mountains provide routes for both highways and railroads.

About 90 miles long and 30 miles wide, the Crimean Mountains lie in three low, parallel ranges, with fertile valleys between them. They form the southern coast of the Crimean Peninsula, the belt of land between the Black Sea and the Sea of Azov; Mt. Roman-Kosh, at 5,069 feet (1,545 metres), is their highest point. The shores of the two seas are low, characterized by narrow, sandy spits of land that jut out into the water.

Climate. The Ukraine lies in a temperate climatic zone, influenced by moderately warm, humid air from the Atlantic Ocean. Winters in the west are considerably

Chalcolithic and Bronze ages

The Carpathian Mountains

milder than those in the east, which is strongly affected by the northern high-pressure belts, or anticyclones. In summer, on the other hand, the east often experiences higher temperatures than the west. Average annual temperature ranges from 42°–45° F (5.5°–7° C) in the north to 52°–55° F (11°–13° C) in the south. The average temperature in January, the coldest month, is 26° F (−3° C) in the southwest and 18° F (−8° C) in the northeast. The average in July, the hottest month, is 73° F (23° C) in the southwest and 66° F (19° C) in the northeast.

Precipitation is uneven, with two to three times as much rainfall in the warmer seasons as in the cold. Maximum rainfall generally occurs in June and July, minimum in February. Snow falls mainly in late November and early December, varying in depth from a few inches in the Steppe region to several feet in the Carpathians.

Precipitation

The southern shore of the Crimea has a warm, gentle, Mediterranean-type climate. Winters are mild and rainy, with little snow, and the average January temperature is 39° F (4° C). Summers are dry and hot, with an average July temperature of 75° F (24° C). Precipitation totals 16 to 24 inches (400 to 600 millimetres) per year.

River systems and drainage. Inland waters of the Ukraine include rivers, lakes, reservoirs, ponds, and marshes, as well as underground water sources. Almost all of the major rivers flow through the plains toward the Azov–Black Sea Basin; only 3 percent of drainage enters the Baltic Sea Basin. Nearly 23,000 rivers and streams are found within the republic's borders; some 3,000 of these are at least six miles long, and 116 exceed 60 miles in length. Of the total course of the Dnepr, 748 miles (1,204 kilometres) is in the Ukraine, making it by far the longest river in the republic, of which it drains more than half. Like the Dnepr, the Yuzhny Bug, with its major tributary, the Ingul, flows into the Black Sea. To the west and southwest, partly draining Ukrainian territory, the Dnestr (Dnister) also flows into the Black Sea; among its numerous tributaries, the largest in the Ukraine are the Stry and the Zbruch. The Danube River flows along the southwestern frontier of the Ukraine, and one of its tributaries, the Tisa, flows through Transcarpathia. The middle course of the Donets River, a tributary of the Don, flows through the Ukraine and is an important source of water for the Donets Basin. The largest river in the Crimea, the Salgir (Salhyr), flows into the Sea of Azov.

The rivers are most important as a water supply, and for this purpose a series of canals has been built, such as the Donets–Donets Basin, the Dnepr–Krivoy Rog, and the Kakhovka Reservoir–Crimea. Several of the larger rivers are navigable, including the Dnepr, Danube, Dnestr, Pripyat (Prypiat), Donets, and Yuzhny Bug (in its lower course). Mountain rivers are also used for rafting timber, and hydroelectric plants are situated on all of the larger ones.

The Ukraine has a few lakes, all of them small and most of them very old, scattered over the river floodlands. One of the largest is Lake Svityaz (Svytiaz), 11 square miles (28 square kilometres) in area, in the northwest. Small saltwater lakes occur in the Don Basin and the Black Sea Upland. Lakes in the Carpathians are of the small, deep, alpine type. Some artificial lakes have been formed, the largest of which are reservoirs at hydroelectric dams. The Lenin Reservoir of the Lenin hydroelectric station on the Dnepr near Zaporozhye (Zaporizhia) is the best example, but other large reservoirs are found in the Donets and Krivoy Rog (Kryvyi Rih) basins near Zhdanov, Kharkov (Kharkiv), and other industrial centres. Almost 3 percent of the Ukraine is marshland, primarily in the northern river valleys and in the lower reaches of the Dnepr, Danube, and other rivers. Underground water is exceptionally important for agriculture, especially in three large artesian basins: the Volyn–Podolsk (Lvov), the Dnepr–Donets, and the Black Sea.

Lakes and reservoirs

Soils and vegetation. From northwest to southeast, the soils of the Ukraine may be divided into three major aggregations—a zone of sandy podzolized soils (a podzol is a soil having an acidic surface of forest humus, a light gray zone of leaching beneath it, and a bottom layer of

accumulation); a central belt consisting of the famous Ukrainian chernozems (black-earth soils); and in the southeast a zone of chestnut and salinized soils surrounding the Black Sea.

The podzolized soils of the forested steppe, occupying about 21 percent of the republic's area, mostly in the northwest, were formed by the extension of postglacial forests into regions of grassy steppe; most of these soils may be farmed, although they require the addition of nutrients leached by the podzolizing process to obtain good harvests.

The chernozems of the centre are among the most fertile soils in the world, occupying about 65 percent of the republic's area; they may be divided into three broad groups: in the north a belt of the so-called deep, or thick, chernozems (the most fertile; about 5–6½ feet [1.5–2 metres] thick and rich in humus); south and east of the former, a zone of degraded (podzolized) chernozems, lean (eroded) chernozems, and podzolized mountain soils; the southernmost of these southwest–northeast-trending belts consists of ordinary steppe, or prairie, chernozems and the southern chernozems (both of the latter types are thinner than the deep chernozems, about 3 feet [1 metre], and high in humus, the southern less so than the ordinary). About 9 percent of the republic is covered by mixed gray and black-earth soils. Almost all soils in this belt are very fertile when enough water is available.

The remaining 5 percent of the soil cover consists of the chestnut soils of the south and east, similar in chemistry to the chernozems but lower in calcium and higher in sodium; they become increasingly salinized as they approach the Black Sea, where highly saline solonets and solonchak soils are found.

Plant life exists in great variety. In the north the abundant rainfall and moderate temperatures provide favourable conditions for forest vegetation. Woodlands alternate with areas of steppe in the central region. Forest usually covers river valleys and the slopes of ravines and gorges. The total area of forested land, however, is only about 19,800,000 acres (8,000,000 hectares), and nearly one-third of this has been planted by man. Most of the rich forest lands are in the Transcarpathian region, with very little woodland in the south.

Three natural zones of vegetation are distinguishable: the Polesye (woodland and marsh), the Lesostep (woodland–steppe), and the Steppe.

Polesye, Lesostep, and Steppe

The Polesye zone lies in the northwest and north, with an area of about 44,000 square miles (114,000 square kilometres), of which 35 percent is arable land. Nearly one-quarter of this land is covered with mixed woodland, including oak, elm, birch, hornbeam, ash, maple, pine, linden, alder, poplar, willow, and beech. About 5 percent is peat bog, a substantial portion is marshland, and the river valleys are floodplains. Swamp drainage is a primary project in the Ukraine's program of land reclamation; in the 1970s about 7,500 square miles of marshland were being reclaimed annually, most of it in the Polesye.

The 78,000-square-mile (202,000-square-kilometre) Lesostep extends south from the Polesye. Arable land covers about 67 percent of this agricultural region, forests only about 12 percent. Farther south, near the Black and Azov seas and the Crimean Mountains, the Lesostep joins the Steppe zone (92,500 square miles, or 240,000 square kilometres). The natural vegetation of the Steppe is protected in nature reserves, the largest being the Askaniya-Nova reserve in Kherson *oblast*. The lack of moisture makes necessary widespread irrigation, which in the mid-1970s was carried out on about 5,000 square miles of the Ukraine's arid land, mostly in the Steppe zone.

Three other natural regions are found near the borders of the republic: the Carpathians, the Crimean Mountains, and the southern coast of the Crimean Peninsula. In the mountainous areas the lower slopes are covered with mixed forests, the intermediate slopes (4,000–5,000 feet, or 1,200–1,500 metres) with pine forests; these give way to grassland and alpine meadows at higher altitudes. A narrow strip of land, only six miles wide, along the southern coast of the Crimea constitutes a unique natural region where both deciduous and evergreen grasses and shrubs grow. Near the city of Yalta is located the Nikitsky Botanical Garden, in which plants from almost every country in the world are found. An exceptionally beautiful environment, a warm climate, and the sea make the southern shore of the Crimea one of the finest vacation areas in the world.

Animal life. The animal life of the Ukraine is diverse, with more than 350 species of birds, about 100 of mammals, and more than 200 of fish. The commonest predators are wolf, fox, wildcat, and marten, while hoofed animals include the roe deer, wild pig, and sometimes elk and mouflon (a wild sheep). The wide variety of rodents includes gophers, hamsters, jerboas, and field mice. The major bird species are black and hazel grouse, owl, gull, and partridge, as well as many migrating birds, such as wild goose, duck, and stork. Among the fish are pike, carp, bream, perch, sturgeon, and sterlet. Introduced and well-acclimatized wildlife includes muskrat, raccoon, beaver, nutria, and silver fox. Common insect pests are the meadow butterfly, sugar beet weevil, and cabbage butterfly.

Nature reserves. The conservation of the biological heritage of the republic is given high priority, and considerable manpower is expended on it. The republic established its first nature reserve, Askaniya-Nova, in 1921, three years before it entered the Soviet Union. This reserve, occupying about 25,900 acres (10,500 hectares), preserves a portion of virgin steppe, with characteristic fescue and feather grasses. Some 40 different mammals, including the onager and Przewalski's horse, have been introduced as part of a successful program of breeding endangered species; even ostriches have been successfully introduced.

Among the other important reserves is the Black Sea (established 1927; area 90,400 acres [36,600 hectares]), including protected areas of the sea. It is among the most visited reserves in the Ukraine, the attractions including many species of waterfowl, and is the only breeding ground in the Soviet Union of the gull *Larus melanocephalus*.

The Ukrainian Steppe reserve is discontinuous, comprising four separate sections, each of which preserves a special type of steppe: the Mikhaylovsk (Mykhailiv; virgin meadow steppe), the Strelets (Striletsky; a *stipa*, or grass steppe), the Khomutovsky (chernozem, or blackearth, steppe), and Kammeniye Mogily (Kamiani Mohyly, "Stone Tombs"; a stony steppe). This reserve was established in the period 1925–37. Other major reserves include the Crimean (established 1923, area 65,700 acres), the Azov-Sivash (established 1927, area 21,000 acres), and the Kanev (Kaniv; established 1931, area 2,570 acres).

THE PEOPLE

With 48,830,000 persons in 1975, the Ukraine ranks as the second most populous Soviet republic, after the Russian S.F.S.R., with about 19 percent of the Soviet Union's total population. The annual rate of growth in the mid-1970s was 5.7 per thousand, with a birth rate of 15.1 and a death rate of 9.4. The majority are Ukrainians, who are the second most numerous ethnic group in the Soviet Union, after Russians. Although more than 100 different nationalities live in the Ukraine, 96 percent of the people are linguistically classified as Slavs, including Ukrainians (74.9 percent), Russians (19.4 percent), Poles (0.6 percent), Belorussians (0.8 percent), and Bulgarians (0.5 percent). Jews account for 1.6 percent of the total, and there are small numbers of Greeks, Romanians, Armenians, Gypsies, Hungarians, Tatars, Chuvash, Lithuanians, Bashkirs, and Kazakhs.

Population density The population density is among the highest in the Soviet Union, with an average of almost 210 persons per square mile (81 per square kilometre) and in some areas, particularly in the highly industrialized Donets Basin and Dnepr Lowland, many more. These two regions also account for 76 to 87 percent of the total urban population.

In the Ukraine as a whole, 58 percent of the people live in cities. In 1975 there were 393 cities, 897 towns, and 9,657 rural settlements. At the 1970 census, about 150 cities had populations ranging from 10,000 to 20,000, 130 from 20,000 to 100,000, and 40 or so with more than 100,000 inhabitants. Odessa, Donetsk, Dnepropetrovsk, Zaporozhye, Krivoy Rog, and Lvov (in Ukrainian, Odessa, Donetske, Dnipropetrovske, Zaporizhia, Kryvyi Rih, and Lviv) each had more than 500,000 inhabitants. The only cities with populations of more than 1,000,000 at that time were Kiev and Kharkov (Kharkiv), but in 1974 Odessa also passed the 1,000,000 mark. The rural population is distributed among the villages and the more than 9,600 other settlements, such as *sovkhozy* (state farms), collective farms (*kolkhozy*), and so on. More than 50 percent of the rural population lives in large villages (1,000 to 5,000 inhabitants), most of them located in the Lesostep area.

THE ECONOMY

The complex industrial–agrarian economic structure of the Ukraine is integrally related to that of the entire Soviet Union. In its rate of economic development it ranks second among the Soviet republics (after the Russian S.F.S.R.). The effects of the devastation of the Nazi invasion in World War II have been completely overcome.

Mineral resources. The Ukraine has about 72 kinds of mineral resources. Iron ore reserves, equalling nearly 19,400,000,000 tons, are located in the Krivoy Rog, Kerch, Belozyorka, Kremenchug, and Mariupol regions. The Ukraine is one of the richest areas in the world in manganese-bearing ores. Anthracite and bituminous coal reserves, largely in the Donets Basin (called Donbass), total 39,000,000,000 tons, and reserves of brown coal are estimated at about 6,000,000,000 tons, mostly in the Dnepr Basin.

The three major petroleum-producing areas in the Ukraine are the Ciscarpathian, Dnepr–Donets, and Crimean regions, where nearly 100 separate oil and gas deposits are known. The developed gas reserves at the beginning of 1969 amounted to 24,200,000,000,000 cubic feet (684,000,000,000 cubic metres).

Among the most important deposits of other minerals are the Irsha titanium ores, the Smela and Vysokopolye bauxite deposits, nephelites from the Oktyabrskoye and Yelanchitsa deposits near the Sea of Azov, the Beregovo and Began deposits of alunites, and the Nikitovka mercury (cinnabar, or mercuric sulfide) ores in the Donets Basin. The largest deposit of ozokerite (a natural paraffin wax) in the Soviet Union is near the city of Borislav. Ciscarpathia possesses potassium salt deposits with strata 170–180 feet (50–55 metres) thick. That region and the Donets Basin have very large resources of rock salt. Some phosphorites exist, notably in the Izyum and Krolevets deposits, as well as natural sulfur in the Ciscarpathian and Dnepr regions and in the Crimea. In Transcarpathia and near the cities of Lvov, Kiev, Vinnitsa (Vinnytsia), Poltava, Khmelnitsky (Khmelnytsky), and Kharkov are health spas noted for their mineral springs; spas near the Black Sea and the Sea of Azov specialize in mud baths.

Health spas and mineral springs

Industry. The Ukrainian S.S.R. has a major ferrousmetal industry, producing nearly half of the Soviet Union's cast iron, more than 40 percent of its steel and rolled steel, and about a quarter of its steel pipe. Mining output is also a very high proportion of the Soviet total, the main products being coal, natural gas, and iron ore. Manufactured goods include metallurgical equipment, diesel locomotives, tractors, and television sets. The Ukrainian chemical industry accounts for half of all the coke, 21 percent of the mineral fertilizers, and 18 percent of the sulfuric acid produced in the Soviet Union. The food industry accounts for 60 percent of the national output of granulated sugar, and Ukrainian agriculture produces nearly a quarter of the gross national grain yield, roughly half of the sugar beets and sunflower seeds, and approximately a quarter of all potatoes, vegetables, meat, eggs, and milk. One-tenth of the world's cast iron, 9 percent of its steel, and 8.5 percent of its coal are produced in the Ukraine. Diversified industry, in more than 150 fields, is the most important sector in the economy in terms of productivity and revenue earned.

Extractive industries. The major product of Ukrainian mining is coal. During the Five-Year Plan covering 1971–75, more than 1,000,000,000 tons of coal were mined, about 90 percent in the Donets Basin. Petroleum is far less significant, only about 14,100,000 tons being extracted in 1975, mainly in the Ciscarpathian region. In this same region, however, the exploitation of natural gas deposits, which began during the postwar period, reached production of almost 2,426,000,000,000 cubic feet (68,700,000,000 cubic metres) in 1975. A new high-capacity field, the Vostochny, is in operation in Kharkov *oblast*.

In 1974, 134,000,000 tons of iron ore were mined. The Ukraine also produces limited amounts of titanium, bauxite, and mercury and ranks first in world production of manganese-bearing ores, which have been mined in the Nikopol area since 1886. Raw materials for the chemical industry are likewise significant, and building materials, ranging from granite to the components of cement (marl and chalk), are extracted from Ukrainian quarries. In the south are found reserves of limestone, graphite, sand, and clay.

Manufacturing industries. The Ukraine is the major Soviet centre for the production of ferrous metals. The Dnepr region accounts for 70 percent of the republic's cast-iron production, much of it coming from mills in Dnepropetrovsk. Railway locomotives and freight cars, seagoing vessels, hydroelectric and thermal steam and gas turbines, electrical generators, and automobiles are also made in Ukrainian factories. Expanded residential and industrial construction demands hoisting and transportation equipment and other machinery for the building trades. The Ukraine is also the principal centre of production of the giant airliner Antey, which can carry up to 720 passengers.

Plants for the production of equipment for food-processing and other light industries are scattered throughout the republic. The Ukraine, one of the great agricultural regions of the world, also has more than 50 factories engaged in the production of a wide range of agricultural equipment, the chief centres of production being Kharkov, Odessa, Lvov, and Kherson. Machine-tool and instrument-manufacturing industries are being developed. The growing importance of consumer goods is reflected in the increasing output of, among other items, cameras, television sets, refrigerators, and washing machines.

The Ukrainian chemical-equipment industry, accounting for one-third of Soviet production, is mainly concentrated in Kiev, Sumy, Fastov (Fastiv), and Korosten. The chemical industry includes coking and the manufacture of coke products, as well as the manufacture of mineral fertilizers, sulfuric acid, synthetic fibres, caustic soda, petrochemicals, photographic chemicals, and pesticides.

Food processing. The larger divisions of the Ukrainian food-processing industry—sugar refining, processing of meat, fruit, and dairy products, wine making, and distilling—are important to the entire Soviet Union. Of the approximately 2,000 products, one of the most important is sugar. Production of vegetable oil, mainly from sunflower seeds, is also significant. Nearly 30 percent of all the wine made in the Soviet Union comes from the Ukraine—in the south, in the Transcarpathian region, and in the Crimea, where the vintners of the Massandra group are established near Yalta. In the coastal cities, such as Odessa, are found local industries processing fish.

Some of the principal products of light industry are textiles, both knitted and woven, ready-to-wear garments, and shoes.

Energy. About 99 percent of the energy for industrial processes in the Ukraine is provided by fossil fuels, hydroelectricity accounting for only 1 percent. Producing 194,400,000,000 kilowatt-hours of electric power in 1975, the Ukraine provided about 19 percent of the Soviet Union's total electricity. Thermal power stations are found in all parts of the republic, though

the largest are in the Donets Basin and along the Dnepr. A third electric energy-producing area is in the vicinity of the Lvov–Volyn coal basin, and in the Ciscarpathian region there is a group of six hydropower stations. The major hydroelectric plant, in the Dnepr cascade region near Zaporozhye, the Lenin station, underwent a program of renovation and expansion in the 1970s; the combined capacity of the Lenin station and its sister station, called Dnepr II, nearby, eventually will reach 1,478,000 kilowatts. Two thermal power stations of similar design, one near Zaporozhye and the other at Uglegorsk, in the Donets Basin, were designed for 3,600,000 kilowatts output when completed; by 1975 the installed capacity of both had reached 2,000,000 kilowatts.

The Lenin hydro-electric plant

Agriculture. Although the German occupation in World War II almost completely destroyed Ukrainian agriculture, recovery was achieved by 1955. The Ukraine today accounts for more than 20 percent of the Soviet Union's agricultural produce and, in particular, for more than 23 percent of its grain. Agriculture generates 18 percent of the gross national product of the republic.

Crops. Four-fifths of Ukrainian agricultural production is represented by grain, potatoes, vegetables, fodder crops, fruit, and grapes. Out of a total land area of approximately 150,000,000 acres (60,000,000 hectares), 105,000,000 acres, or 70 percent, are devoted to agriculture. Of these, 84,200,000 acres are under crops, almost half grain. In 1950 the average annual yield of cereals was about 0.38 metric ton per acre; the figure rose to 0.58 in 1960 and to 1.04 during 1971–74, a significant increase.

Cereals

About 10,000,000 acres are allocated to industrial crops. Sugar beets, the most important, occupy 4,200,000 acres, primarily in the Lesostep region. Sunflower seeds, the principal oil crop, are grown on 4,300,000 acres. In the northwest a considerable acreage is allotted to flax. Potatoes occupy about 4,700,000 acres in the northern and central regions. In the southern steppes, especially where irrigation is practiced, vegetables are grown on almost 1,225,000 acres. Truck farming, or market gardening, takes place in the Donets Basin and along the Dnepr River and on the outskirts of the cities of Kiev, Kharkov, and Lvov. Fruit is grown throughout the Ukraine but especially in the Crimea, Transcarpathia and Ciscarpathia, and the Lesostep. About 3,000,000 acres yield almost half of the fruit grown in the Soviet Union. Vineyards in the Crimea and in Transcarpathia cover 659,000 acres.

Stock raising. There are about 23,600,000 head of cattle in the Ukraine, of which 9,000,000 are in dairy herds. Pigs, raised throughout the republic, number at least 20,800,000. Sheep and goats together number 9,500,000 head. Bees are kept chiefly in the Lesostep and the Polesye, and silkworms are raised in Transcarpathia.

Collective farming. Almost 8,000 collective farms (*kolkhozy*) and 1,700 or so state farms (*sovkhozy*) farm 93 percent of the cultivated land and raise 78 percent of the cattle. They also produce 96 percent of the cereal harvest, all of the sugar beets, 65 percent of the meat, and 66 percent of the milk. These highly mechanized enterprises employ about 200,000 agronomists, zoologists, veterinarians, engineers, and other specialists.

Fishing. The Black Sea estuaries are the main fishing grounds, although the Sea of Azov, rivers, lakes, ponds, and reservoirs also contribute to the fish catch. Among the major rivers for fishing are the Dnepr, Danube, Dnestr, Yuzhny Bug, and Donets. There are about 21,000 ponds in the country, covering more than 370,000 acres (148,000 hectares). In the early 1970s Ukrainian fishermen caught about 900,000 tons annually, or 12 percent of the total Soviet catch.

TRANSPORTATION

The flat relief of most of the Ukraine presents few obstacles to transportation, and the republic thus utilizes almost every means of modern transport.

Railroads. The Ukraine's 13,810 miles (22,230 kilometres) of track represents an average of 59 miles of track for every 1,000 square miles (37 kilometres per

1,000 square kilometres) served and 16 percent of the total trackage in the Soviet Union. Freight carried by rail in 1974 amounted to 305,000,000,000 ton-miles (445,-000,000,000 ton-kilometres), about 90 percent of total freight carried in the republic. The heaviest concentration of trackage is in the Donets Basin and near the Dnepr River, especially its right bank; the largest railroad centres are Kharkov, Kiev, Dnepropetrovsk, Bakhmach, Yasinovataya, Debaltsevo, Kovel, and Kupyansk.

Waterways. Ukrainian docks on the Black Sea and the Sea of Azov handle more than a fifth of the Soviet Union's ocean freight, mainly at the ports of Odessa, Ilyichevsk (Illichevske), Nikolayev (Mikolayiv), Kherson, Feodosiya (Feodosia), Kerch, and Zhdanov. Ships of the whaling fleet Sovetskaya Ukraina (Soviet Ukraine) sail from Odessa to the Antarctic. River shipping is conducted primarily on the Dnepr and its tributaries (the Pripyat and Desna), on the Yuzhny Bug, and on the Danube, important in trade with other European countries. Ships on the Danube call at the port of Izmail, which is accessible to oceangoing freighters and passenger liners. Through the Dneprovsko–Bugsky (Dnepr–Bug) Kanal, in Belorussia, the inland waterways of the Ukraine are joined to the Vistula Basin of Poland and to the Baltic. Efforts to transform the Dnepr into a continuous, deep waterway have been furthered by the creation of large reservoirs at hydroelectric stations. The largest ports on the Dnepr are Kiev, Dnepropetrovsk, Zaporozhye, and Kherson.

River shipping (margin note)

Road transportation. The republic has 120,050 miles of roads, of which some 70,090 miles are hard-surfaced. A network of good highways connects all the regions and large industrial centres. The links between Kiev and Moscow, Kiev and Leningrad, Moscow–Kharkov–Simferopol (Symferopol), and Kharkov and Rostov-na-Donu are of importance to the whole Soviet Union. Freight carried by truck within the Ukraine amounts to some 37,800,000,000 ton-miles (55,200,000,000 ton-kilometres) annually, or 17.7 percent of the Soviet total.

Air transportation. Kiev is connected by air with all the regional centres of the republic and with major cities throughout the Soviet Union. Annual air traffic totals some 11,000,000 passengers and 62,000,000 ton-miles of freight. Major airports include Borispol (Boryspil), near Kiev, and those at Kharkov and Odessa.

Pipelines. The exploitation of petroleum and natural gas has brought about the creation of a pipeline transport system, the total length of which is about 6,200 miles (10,000 kilometres). The major natural gas lines connect Mukachevo and Kiev; Shebelinka (Shebelynka) and Kharkov; Shebelinka, Poltava, and Kiev; Shebelinka, Dnepropetrovsk, Krivoy Rog, and Odessa; and Shebelinka and Slavyansk. The chief petroleum pipelines are the Dolina–Drogobych (Dolyna–Drohobych) and Gnedintsy–Priluki lines and a 420-mile segment of the trans-European Druzhba (Friendship) line, which supplies Soviet oil to other eastern European countries.

Distribution patterns. The Ukrainian transportation system makes industrial and agricultural products available to the entire Soviet Union. By this same network, the Ukraine receives petroleum and petroleum products from the Trans-Volga region, nonferrous metals from Kazakhstan and the Urals, and several types of machinery, fabric, footwear, and printed material from the central Soviet regions. By sea, bread, sugar, iron ore, coal, manganese, and machinery are exported to about 70 countries, and coffee, tea, cocoa, fruit, jute, machinery, and equipment are imported from more than 60 countries.

ADMINISTRATION AND SOCIAL CONDITIONS

Government and constitution. The government of the Ukrainian Soviet Socialist Republic is organized according to the 1937 constitution. As amended in 1944, the constitution (like the constitutions of the other union republics, as well as that of the Soviet Union) gives the Ukraine the right to "enter into direct relations with foreign states, to conclude agreements, and to exchange diplomatic and consular representatives with them" and to maintain its own military forces. The only real expression of these constitutional prerogatives in international affairs is the Ukraine's membership in the United Nations (it was one of the founding members), a distinction it shares with Belorussia, the two being the only UN members that are not fully sovereign countries. It is also a member of some 70 other international organizations.

These international contacts are more direct and of longer historical standing than those of most Soviet republics, and, because there are large communities of Ukrainians in Europe and North America, official institutions display considerable nationalism. There is, for example, a society specifically created to maintain cultural relations with foreign organizations and individuals, and two weekly newspapers on events in the Ukraine are published for distribution overseas.

Ukrainians abroad (margin note)

In the main, however, contacts permitted by the central authorities of the Soviet Union between the Ukraine and foreign countries are not of great importance. While the Ukrainian Ministry of Trade is permitted to establish agreements (especially exchanges) overseas, usually these are limited to the Socialist countries of eastern Europe and are not of great enough value or volume to affect the promulgation of national policy either domestically or internationally.

The highest legislative unit is the unicameral Supreme Soviet of the Ukrainian S.S.R., whose members are elected for four years from a single slate of candidates. The Supreme Soviet meets twice a year for a few days to approve, generally unanimously, budgetary and other proposals made by the central government in Moscow and legislation passed by its Presidium and Council of Ministers. The Presidium of the Supreme Soviet, selected by that body and composed of a chairman, two vice chairmen, a secretary, and 15 members, acts for the Supreme Soviet between sessions, exercising both executive and legislative powers.

The Supreme Soviet (margin note)

The highest executive and administrative organ is the Council of Ministers, which is equivalent to a cabinet; its chairman is the counterpart of a premier in the West. Most legislation introduced to the Supreme Soviet comes from the Council of Ministers, which is responsible for carrying out policy decisions made in Moscow.

The administrative divisions of the Ukraine include 25 *oblasti* (regions) divided into 477 *rayony* (districts), with 393 cities, 897 towns, and 9,657 rural settlements. In all of these, the unit of government is a Soviet of Workers' Deputies, whose members are nominated by the local Communist Party organization and voted for locally. The soviets elect executive bodies.

Justice. The highest court in the judicial system is the Supreme Court of the Ukrainian S.S.R., consisting of five judges elected for five-year terms by the Supreme Soviet. The court's function is to supervise judicial activities; it does not rule on constitutional questions (a function of the Presidium). On the local level, justice is dispensed by "people's courts."

Political organizations. The only political party is the Communist Party of the Ukraine (CPU), a branch of the Communist Party of the Soviet Union (CPSU) formed in 1918. Most of the major legislation approved by the Supreme Soviet originates in, or is approved by, the CPU. In the mid-1970s it had nearly 2,500,000 members and 80,000 candidates for membership. More than 5,670,000 young persons are members of the Communist Youth League (Komsomol). Under the guidance of the CPSU, the Komsomol administers the Pioneers, of which about 4,000,000 schoolchildren are members.

Sporting organizations. Various sporting clubs are concerned with physical culture, among them the Dinamo (Dynamo), Spartak (Spartacus), and Trudovye Reservy (Labour Reserves), set up by the army, air force, and navy.

Education. In 1917 more than 70 percent of the population was illiterate. Within the next half century, illiteracy was practically wiped out, and 99 percent of the population can now read and write. Universal education is now required for 10 years, and in the 1974–75 school year, 8,300,000 pupils were being taught in 27,000 schools for general education. In more than 80 percent of

Further
education
for
workers

the schools, Ukrainian is the main language of instruction, although there are schools in which Russian, Moldavian, Polish, Bulgarian, Hungarian, French, German, Spanish, or English is dominant.

Great emphasis is placed on general and correspondence schools to allow young industrial and agricultural workers to receive an education without interrupting their work. About 900,000 students are enrolled in these schools. A network of vocational schools trains young persons, about 250,000 annually, for work in industry, transportation, and agriculture. About 730 specialized secondary schools enrolled 780,000 students in the mid-1970s. There were 142 institutions of higher education in the republic, serving 818,000 students, of whom 6,000 came from more than 100 other countries. More than 100,000 students attend the state universities at Kiev, Kharkov, Odessa, Dnepropetrovsk, Lvov, Chernovtsy (Chernivtsi), Uzhgorod (Uzhhorod), and Donetsk (Donetske). The various forms of instruction involve nearly 16,000,000 persons, almost one-third of the population.

Science and research. There are about 162,100 scientific workers in the republic, including some 4,100 doctors of science and 45,000 advanced students and candidates. The largest single scientific organization is the Academy of Sciences of the Ukrainian S.S.R. Founded in 1919, the academy received the Order of Lenin in 1969 for its contributions to science and Soviet life. In the mid-1970s it comprised 76 institutions, staffed by about 11,600 scientific workers, whose work is published in 35 Ukrainian scientific journals and some 440 monographs annually as well as in numerous publications originating elsewhere in the Soviet Union.

After the Academy of Sciences, the largest concentration of scientific and technical workers is in the universities. Among the specialized scientific facilities available in the republic are a half dozen oceanographic research vessels, which are the basis of a substantial concentration of scientific manpower in the areas of mineral resources, biology, and, with the cooperation of schools of chemistry and technology, desalination of seawater.

Elsewhere in the republic can be found one of the finest experimental nuclear reactors in the world, five computer centres, four astronomical observatories, and seven major botanical gardens. Ukrainian scientists and technicians have made important discoveries and advances in the fields of cybernetics; nuclear and plasma physics; foundry, blast furnace, and powder metallurgy technology; and welding methods. In medicine they have made contributions in the areas of tissue therapy and brain biochemistry.

Social welfare, health, and housing. Some 4,200 hospitals with 565,000 beds, staffed by 151,000 doctors and specialists and more than 470,000 general medical personnel, serve the Ukrainian people. Medical help also is available at about 6,000 medical centres in such places as factories and schools. There are also some 235 sanitation-epidemiological centres, 18,000 institutions staffed by paramedical personnel and midwives, about 4,700 gynecological outpatient clinics, 2,500 children's clinics, and more than 580 sanatoriums and rest homes. More than 2,500,000 workers are sent annually to sanatoriums, rest homes, resorts, camps, and boardinghouses. Many workers get accommodations at one-third of the cost or free of charge. The residue is paid by trade unions from social consumption funds at their disposal. All the funds originally derived from a turnover tax, from various taxes levied on individuals, collective farms, etc., and others.

The death rate has decreased to one-third the level of 1917, and the average life expectancy now stands at 72 years.

Standard
of living

The standard of living of the Ukrainian people is rising. More than three-quarters of the republic's income is used for individual workers' funds and collective benefits, such as public health, education, and pension funds. Between 1965 and 1970, the republic's income rose 39 percent and real wages 23 percent. The major supplements to wages from public funds included free medical care and education, pension and stipend payments, vacation benefits, and the maintenance of kindergarten and child-care facilities. The 9,463,000 pensioners in the Ukraine collect between 50 and 100 percent of their former salaries.

During World War II, 714 cities and towns and 26,000 villages were devastated, and reconstruction is still going on. Almost 400,000 apartments are constructed annually, and in 1966–70 new housing was provided for 40 percent of the republic's population.

CULTURAL LIFE AND INSTITUTIONS

Visual arts. Over the centuries Ukrainians have evolved a varied folk art. Embroidery, wood carving, ceramics, and weaving are highly developed, with stylized ornamentation in many regional styles. Intricately designed Easter eggs (*pysanky*) have become popular in many countries that have Ukrainian immigrant populations.

With the introduction of Christianity in the 10th century, the various forms of Byzantine art (architecture, mosaics, frescoes, manuscript illumination, icon painting) spread rapidly and remained the dominant art forms through the 16th century. The mosaics and frescoes of the churches of Kiev, notably the Cathedral of St. Sophia (11th–12th century), and the icons of the more distinctively Ukrainian school in Galicia (15th–16th century) are particularly noteworthy. Western European influences in the 17th and 18th centuries affected iconography and stimulated portrait painting, engraving, and sculpture. From the Ukraine the Western trends penetrated into Russia, where many Ukrainian artists worked, especially after the Ukraine lost its autonomy to Russia in the 18th century. During the late 18th and early 19th centuries the portraitists Dmytro Levytsky and Volodymyr Borovykovsky were among the leading figures of the St. Petersburg Classical school of painting.

The Classicism and the emergent Realism of the 19th century are best exemplified by the poet–painter Taras Shevchenko. New movements—Impressionism, Expressionism, Futurism—affected the work of such 19th-century painters as Ivan Trush and Oleksandr Novakivsky. Modernism and experimentation ended in the Soviet Ukraine in the 1930s, however, when Socialist Realism became the only officially sanctioned method in the arts.

A number of Ukrainian artists have won considerable renown in the West, among them the painter Alexis Gritchenko (Hryshchenko). The sculptor Alexander Archipenko, one of the pioneers of Cubism, who later experimented in Constructivism, Expressionism, and Surrealism, was a major figure of 20th-century European art.

Music. Folk music in the Ukraine retains great vitality to this day. Ritual songs, ballads, and historical songs (*dumy*) were sung *a cappella* or accompanied by folk instruments, of which the multi-stringed *bandura* is the most popular. Church music was patterned on Byzantine and Bulgarian models with local variations evolving in Kiev in the early period. Polyphonic singing developed by the 16th century and was subsequently in the 17th transmitted to Russia, where Ukrainian singers and musical culture soon won a dominant position. Ukrainian choral music reached its peak in the 18th and early 19th centuries in the works of Maksym Berezovsky, Dmytro Bortnyansky, and Artem Vedel.

Choral
music

Secular music became ascendant in the 19th century. The opera *Zaporozhets za Dunayem* ("A Cossack Beyond the Danube"; 1863) by Semen Hulak-Artemovsky gained great popularity, as did *Kateryna* by Mykola Arkas and the compositions of Petro Nishchynsky. At the turn of the century, Ukrainian musical life was dominated by Mykola Lysenko, whose output encompassed vocal and choral settings, piano compositions, and operas, including *Natalka Poltavka* (1889), *Utoplena* ("The Drowned Girl"), and *Taras Bulba*. Other major composers of the period were Kyrylo Stetsenko and Mykola Leontovych.

In the early years of the Soviet period several composers produced works of high artistic merit, particularly Lev Revutsky and Borys Lyatoshynsky and their contemporary in Polish-occupied Galicia, Stanyslav Lyudkevych. From the mid-1930s, however, political regimentation dampened individual expression and innovation in musical language. Typical among contemporary composers of the Soviet Ukraine are Kostyantyn Dankevych, Yuliy Meytus, and the brothers Yuriy and Platon Maiboroda.

The Ukraine has six opera theatres, numerous symphony orchestras, academic and folk choirs, and other performing ensembles.

Theatre and motion pictures. The theatre originated in the Ukraine under Western influence in the 17th century. Verse dialogue (*intermedia*) rapidly developed into a specific genre, the school theatre, whose repertory expanded to encompass dramatization of Christian legends, historical drama, and a puppet play (*vertep*) performed on a stage of two levels. The best example of the Cossack Baroque theatre was Feofan Prokopovich's historical play *Vladimir* (1705). After a period of decline, a Ukrainian ethnographic theatre developed in the 19th century. Folk plays and vaudeville were raised to a high level of artistry by such actors as Mykola Sadovsky and Maria Zankovetska in the late 19th and early 20th centuries. The lifting of censorship in 1905 permitted a significant expansion of the repertory to include modern dramas by Lesya Ukrainka, Volodymyr Vynnychenko, and Oleksandr Oles, as well as translated plays.

The real flowering of the Ukrainian theatre occurred between 1917 and 1933. The Berezil Theatre (1922–33) in Kharkov, under the artistic director Les Kurbas, was the most distinguished troupe. Pre-eminent among the playwrights was Mykola Kulish, whose *Patetychna Sonata* ("Sonata Pathétique") combined Expressionist techniques with the forms of the Ukrainian *vertep*. Since the mid-1930s, however, the theatre in the Ukraine has been dominated by Socialist Realism. Oleksandr Korniichuk has been the most favoured of the playwrights writing in the approved manner.

There are about 60 professional theatres in the Ukraine, notably the Ivan Franko Theatre in Kiev and the Maria Zankovetska Theatre in Lvov.

Ukrainian film has achieved some marked successes. The director and scenarist Aleksandr (Ukrainian Oleksandr) Dovzhenko (who died in 1956) was an important innovator in world cinematography. His *Zvenyhora* (1927), *Arsenal* (1929), and especially *Zemlya* (1930; "The Earth") have become classics of the silent film era. More recently *Tini zabutykh predkiv* ("Shadows of Forgotten Ancestors"), directed by Serhii Paradzhanov, won critical acclaim in the West. The motion-picture industry is centred on the O. Dovzhenko Studio in Kiev and on the Odessa studio.

Literature. Oral literature in the Ukraine can be traced back to pre-Christian times. Pagan ritual songs were subsequently much modified by association with various church feasts (*e.g.*, *koliadky* with the Christmas cycle). The heroic epics of the early medieval period (*byliny*) may have survived in the Ukraine until the 16th century, but they were then wholly superseded by historical songs (*dumy*) based on events in the 16th and 17th centuries in the Cossack Ukraine.

Written literature began with Christianization and the introduction of Church Slavonic as a liturgical and literary language, later increasingly influenced by vernacular Ukrainian. Only with the school theatre of the 17th–18th century and with Ivan Kotlyarevsky's *Eneida* (1798) did vernacular Ukrainian begin to develop as an independent literary language.

The earliest works of the Kievan period (10th century and following) were the historical annals: *Povest vremennykh let* ("Tale of Bygone Years"), the Hypatian (Kievan) chronicle, and the Galician–Volhynian chronicle. The 12th-century *Slovo o polku Igoreve* ("Lay of Igor's Campaign") is a unique historical epic, written in the ornamental style. Sermons, tales, and lives of the saints comprised the major genres.

After the Mongol invasions (13th century), literature suffered a period of decline. Revival began in the late 16th century with the introduction of printing, the Reformation ferment, and the advance of the Counter-

Reformation into Polish-dominated Ukrainian lands. The Union of Brest-Litovsk (1596), which united several million Ukrainian and Belorussian Orthodox with Rome, stimulated an exceedingly rich polemical literature, with the *Apocrisis* ("Reply"; 1598) of the pseudonymous Khrystofor Filalet and the anonymous *Perestoroha* ("Warning"; 1605) on the Orthodox side and the *Antirizis* ("Refutation"; 1599) of Ipatii Potii in the Uniat camp. The most distinguished and prolific polemicist was the Orthodox Ivan Vyshensky, whose ornate style combines Church Slavonic with vernacular elements.

The major current in Ukrainian literature of the 17th and 18th centuries, as in all of Europe, was the Baroque, with its love of adornment and originality. Among the major figures of this age were Kassian Sakovych and Ivan Velychkovsky in verse, Yoannikiy Galyatovsky in homiletics, and Feofan Prokopovich in the drama. Historical writing is best represented by the Cossack chronicle of Samoil Velychko (*c.* 1720). Of interest for their content and their literary qualities were the 18th-century writings of the philosopher Hryhoriy Skovoroda, styled the "Ukrainian Socrates." (For Ukrainian literature of the 19th and 20th centuries, see LITERATURE, WESTERN.)

Publishing and broadcasting. In the mid-1970s about 2,053 newspapers were being published in the republic (1,600 in the Ukrainian language), totalling about 23,-900,000 copies. There were also more than 500 magazines and journals, with total circulations of about 218,200,000 copies. In 1974 about 8,800 book titles were published, a total printing of 153,500,000 copies, of which 104,800,000 were in Ukrainian. Not only the works of Ukrainian and Russian authors are included in this total but a number of foreign writers as well. The works of Ukrainian authors are published in many languages of the Soviet Union and are translated into more than 40 other languages. There are around 30 large publishing houses in the Ukraine, and book dealers in 80 countries buy Ukrainian-produced books.

In the early 1970s there were some 85 radio stations, and about 100 radio relays operating in the republic, as well as 20 television centres and many television relays. Some 8,000,000 radio receivers and 7,000,000 television sets were in use. The Kiev television centre is connected to Moscow, Leningrad, the regional centres of the republic, and television studios in several foreign countries.

Cultural institutions. The Ukraine supports numerous houses and palaces of culture which include libraries, museums, theatres, cinemas, parks, and concert halls. Almost 26,000 such institutions are active in addition to some 27,000 public libraries, 151 museums, 74 theatres, about 28,200 cinemas, and some 500 schools of music, painting, and choreography. The public libraries contain almost 317,000,000 books; the largest single collection is that of the Central Scientific Library of the Academy of Sciences, with more than 7,000,000 volumes.

Creative workers are gathered in unions, including the writers (with about 800 members), the painters (about 1,500), the composers (more than 150), the architects (more than 1,500), and the journalists (about 5,000); there are also organizations of film workers, theatre people, and singers.

THE OUTLOOK

Plans for the future call for expansion in all branches of industry. The major problem for agriculture is to increase the grain yield, and land reclamation has high priority. Great official emphasis will continue to be placed on capital growth and the further improvement of the material and cultural situation of the Ukrainian people.

BIBLIOGRAPHY. M.P. BAZHAN (ed.), *Ukrainska radianska entsyklopediya*, 18 vol. (1959–68), is the most complete Soviet reference work; vol. 17 of that work, *Ukrainska RSR*, includes topical articles about the Ukraine, and an English-language edition of this volume appeared as *Soviet Ukraine* (1969). The most extensive Western reference work is v. KUBIJOVYC (ed.), *Entsyklopediya ukrainoznavstva*, of which Part 1, 3 vol. (1949–52), has appeared, extensively revised and updated, as *Ukraine: A Concise Encyclopaedia*, 2 vol. (1963–71); Part 2, 7 vol. (1955–), contains alphabetical headings on Ukrainian topics. Physical geography is treated in K.I. HERENCHUK (ed.), *Heohrafichni landshafty Ukrainy* (1966), and V.P. POPOV *et al.* (eds.), *Fiziko-geograficheskoye raionirovaniye Ukrainskoy S.S.R.* (1968), both of which contain extensive bibliography. The economic life of the republic is examined in M.M. PALAMARCHUK, *Ukrainskaya S.S.R. (ekonomiko-geograficheskaya kharakteristika)* (1970), and in the numerous "national economy" volumes on the individual *oblasti* of the Ukraine issued by the central statistical office in Kiev, as well as the corresponding volume for the Ukraine itself (annually). Details of the demographic and ethnic characteristics of the Ukrainian people may be found in the reports of the 1970 census of the Soviet Union, including information on ethnic makeup, households, education, and so on. For political, administrative, and cultural affairs in contemporary Soviet Ukraine, *see* R.S. SULLIVANT, *Soviet Politics and the Ukraine, 1917–1957* (1962); Y. BILINSKY, *The Second Soviet Republic: The Ukraine after World War II* (1964); J.A. ARMSTRONG, *Ukrainian Nationalism*, 2nd ed. (1963); and R. SZPORLUK, "The Ukraine and the Ukrainians," in Z. KATZ *et al.* (ed.), *Handbook of Major Soviet Nationalities* (1975). K. SAWCZUK, *The Ukraine in the United Nations: A Study in Soviet Foreign Policy* (1975), treats the Ukrainian S.S.R's role in international affairs. The most comprehensive study of Ukrainian art is M.P. BAZHAN (ed.), *Istoriya ukrainskoho mystetstva*, 6 vol. (1966–68). S. HORDYNSKY, *The Ukrainian Icon: The Twelfth to the Eighteenth Centuries* (1973), covers Ukrainian schools of icon painting. The most exhaustive surveys of early Ukrainian literature are M. VOZNYAK, *Istoriya ukrainskoi literatury*, 3 vol. (1920), and M. HRUSHEVSKY, *Istoriya ukrainskoi literatury*, 5 vol. (1923–27; facsimile ed. 1959–60). In English, *see* D. CYZEVS'KYJ, *A History of Ukrainian Literature* (1975), C.A. MANNING, *Ukrainian Literature: Studies of the Leading Authors* (1944; facsimile ed. 1970), and YE. SHABLIOVSKY, *Ukrainian Literature Through the Ages* (1970).

(I.A.Y.; Ed.)

Ultrasonics and Infrasonics

In physics, ultrasonics is the term applied to periodic stress waves, often loosely referred to as either sound or acoustical waves, that occur at frequencies above the limit of human hearing. Stress waves are called thus because they create a stress or deformation of the medium through which they are passing. Ultrasonic waves exist in frequency ranges over 20,000 hertz (cycles per second), the upper limit of human hearing. At their upper extreme, ultrasonic frequencies are so high that their extremely short wavelengths are comparable to the agitation of molecules caused by heat; these very high waves are called hypersonic waves. Infrasonic waves are those the wavelengths of which are so long and frequency so low that they exist below the level of human hearing; their principal natural source is earthquakes.

Early applications

Until about 1910 ultrasonic waves were little more than a scientific curiosity. Following the successful development of the piezoelectric transducer (described later), they were used in an early form of sonar to detect the presence of submerged submarines. Other attempted early applications were as a means of communication, and as light modulators in early experiments with television. Following the development of radar during World War II, ultrasonic techniques were used in such wide-ranging fields as the study of molecular properties of materials, detection of flaws in metals, ultrasonic cleaning, industrial and dental drills, measuring the thickness of the heart walls in man, and determining the presence of fluid in the sac around the heart.

GENERAL PRINCIPLES

Properties of stress waves. Stress waves exist in three principal forms: longitudinal, transverse, and shear. Longitudinal waves stress the medium through which they travel in the direction in which they propagate. Ordinary sound waves in air are longitudinal; the molecules of air vibrate back and forth in the direction the sound wave is travelling. Transverse waves produce stress at right angles to the direction of propagation, such as occurs with a vibrating string, whereas shear waves are a form of transverse wave travelling through the bulk of a medium. They are accompanied by a time-varying shear of the medium such as may be produced by a torsionally vibrat-

ing cylinder immersed in a fluid. Two other types of waves can be generated by special techniques. So-called Rayleigh waves are a special type of shear wave in which the wave is confined to a thin layer at the surface of a solid; earthquakes are an example. Lamb waves are a combination of longitudinal and shear waves travelling inside a very thin medium such as the wall of a thin-walled tube.

Applications of ultrasonics can be divided roughly into two classes: low energy and high energy. In the former, the amplitude (that is, the height of the wave from its highest point to its lowest point) is sufficiently low so that the wave is not distorted in passing through the medium, and the medium is left unchanged except for a slight rise in temperature. High-energy waves, on the other hand, modify the medium in some irreversible manner, either by the generation of large stresses or high temperatures, which induces physical or chemical changes.

When a low-energy ultrasonic wave travels through a medium, its energy decreases rapidly because of a characteristic of the medium known as its absorption coefficient. Absorption is caused by a medium's viscosity and thermal conductivity, though recently it has been found that the absorption coefficient is often much higher than calculations based on viscosity and thermal conductivity alone would indicate. Much information about the molecular properties of materials has been obtained from studies of the variation of this excess absorption with frequency.

Relaxation effect

Another important factor in dealing with the passage of an ultrasonic wave through a material is the relaxation time, or relaxation effect, a measure of how rapidly the material changes its volume as a result of the pressure changes caused by the passage of the ultrasonic wave. If an appreciable lag takes place between the wave's passage and the completion of deformation, a relaxation effect is said to occur. Whenever the relaxation effect exists, the wave velocity through the material depends on the frequency of the wave.

Transducers. An ultrasonic transducer (a device for converting energy from one form to another) generates ultrasonic waves by converting electrical, mechanical, or hydraulic energy into ultrasonic energy. In many cases these devices work both ways, and, for example, by converting ultrasonic energy back into electrical energy, can be used as receivers.

Piezoelectric transducers. A piezoelectric material, such as a quartz crystal, generates an electric voltage in response to mechanical pressure, or oscillates mechanically when an oscillating voltage is applied to it. Transducers made from piezoelectric materials are the commonest form of ultrasonic generator, and, depending upon how they are made, can generate either longitudinal or shear waves. By use of piezoelectric ceramic materials, it is possible to produce transducers that can be molded to any desired shape, such as a section of a sphere, enabling their radiated energy to be focussed into a small volume to give a localized region of very high ultrasonic intensity. For more discussion, see PIEZOELECTRIC DEVICES.

Magnetostrictive transducers. A magnetostrictive material is a material that alters its dimensions parallel to the direction of an applied magnetic field. The variation in the length of a magnetostrictive rod under the influence of an alternating magnetic field is exactly analogous to the thickness variation of a piezoelectric disk under the influence of an alternating voltage. Thus, the rod can be used to generate ultrasonic waves.

The typical magnetostrictive transducer shown in Figure 1 is composed of a laminated core of nickel or nickel–cobalt alloy stampings, with coils wound around the core. A steady current passed through the coils produces an initial elongation of the core. An alternating current of the desired frequency is then superimposed on this steady current. The core is bonded to a tapering cone, the function of which is to force the energy radiated from the core through a smaller area than that of the core, thereby increasing its intensity. The core-plus-cone unit will exhibit a resonance at which frequency the opposing ends of the unit will be moving in opposite directions at any given time. Thus, at some point along the unit there

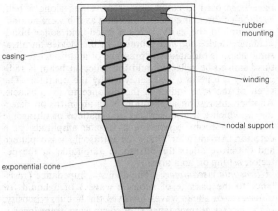

Figure 1: Cross section through typical magnetostrictive transducer.

rubber mounting

casing

winding

nodal support

exponential cone

will be no motion. The unit is mounted at this position, known as a node, since with no motion, no energy will be extracted by the mounting. Magnetostrictive transducers are less efficient than piezoelectric types because of the losses of the core. They are, however, capable of generating intense waves at frequencies up to around 20 kilohertz (20,000 cycles per second).

Mechanical transducers. Mechanical transducers convert mechanical into ultrasonic energy, either by rhythmically interrupting the flow of a gas through a series of holes by means of a toothed disk rotating in front of the holes, as in a siren, or by using the kinetic energy of a stream of gas or liquid to set a cavity or thin wedge into vibration, as in a whistle. Sirens are relatively efficient (70 percent) and can generate several hundred watts of ultrasonic energy at frequencies up to 20 kilohertz. Whistles have much lower efficiencies but can generate a few watts of power at frequencies up to 40 kilohertz.

Electromagnetic and electrostatic transducers. Devices similar to the microphones and loudspeakers of conventional sound systems can also be used to generate and detect ultrasonic waves. These devices are considered in greater detail in the article SOUND RECORDING AND REPRODUCING.

Ultrahigh-frequency transducers. Semiconductor materials (relatively poor conductors of electricity) have been used in recent years in the development of very thin piezoelectric transducers capable of resonating at extremely high frequencies. A very thin insulating layer is formed within the bulk of a semiconducting piezoelectric material, such as cadmium sulfide, by the use of semiconductor device (*q.v.*) techniques. This layer will act as a piezoelectric transducer. A high-frequency transducer can also be made by condensing a thin layer of cadmium sulfide onto a suitable base material.

Ultrasonic detectors. Many transducers not only convert electrical into ultrasonic energy but also work in reverse and can, therefore, be used to detect the presence of ultrasonic waves. Whereas a piezoelectric transducer acting as a receiver will have its maximum response at a resonant frequency (*i.e.,* the frequency at which it vibrates naturally), it nevertheless still gives a useful output at frequencies below resonance. In fact, over a range of frequencies from about 0.1 to 0.6 times the fundamental resonant frequency, the response will be reasonably flat.

The detector being used to probe an ultrasonic field must be physically small so that it will disturb the field as little as possible. For this reason very thin-walled ceramic tubes are used as detectors, with electrodes fired onto the inner and outer walls. A thin wire of nickel with a coil wound on one end will also act as a detector.

Propagation of stress waves. The manner in which ultrasonic waves propagate, or spread, through different media determines their applications. Ultrasonic waves are absorbed in a gas because of its viscosity (resistance to flow) and thermal conductivity (the ability to conduct heat). Relaxation effects, defined above as the measure of how rapidly a material changes its volume as a result

of the pressure changes caused by passage of an ultrasonic wave, are also significant. Though liquids absorb for the same reasons as gases, measured values in many cases are greater than would be predicted on the basis of their viscosity and thermal conductivity, indicating that relaxation effects predominate. The thermal conductivity of a solid, like that of liquids and gases, also causes absorption. Thermal conductivity is enhanced in a solid composed of a large number of crystals of microscopic size (microcrystals). In addition, the microcrystals tend to scatter the wave as it passes through. The relation between the fraction of incident energy thus scattered and microcrystal grain sizes is a function of the frequency of the ultrasonic wave, and measurements of scattered energy versus frequency can be employed to determine grain sizes.

An ultrasonic wave produces strains in a medium as it passes through; if the medium is piezoelectric, the strains generate an electrical field. If the piezoelectric medium is also a semiconductor, the current carriers (if negative) are accelerated by a positive electrical field and decelerated by a negative field. In the presence of the ultrasonic wave the current carriers bunch together and drift through the medium with a velocity dependent upon an applied electrostatic field (voltage). If these bunches drift more slowly than the ultrasonic wave, the latter tends to accelerate the bunches. The energy required for this to happen comes from the ultrasonic wave, which is, therefore, absorbed. If the drift velocity of the bunches exceeds the ultrasonic wave velocity, the opposite occurs and energy flows from the current carriers into the ultrasonic wave, which is therefore amplified. Although amplification factors of 30 have been obtained in cadmium sulfide crystals, there have, as yet, been no practical applications of this amplifying technique.

LOWER POWER APPLICATIONS

Flaw detection and thickness gauging. Ultrasonic waves are scattered when they meet an acoustical impedance mismatch—*i.e.,* a point at which the resistance to the passage of ultrasonic waves changes abruptly. This mismatch can occur at a flaw, such as a hole or a crack in a metal casting. The detection of such flaws, vital in metallurgy, can therefore be performed by using an ultrasonic version of radar. In this application, the pulses of the ultrasonic waves are scattered when they strike a flaw in, for example, a metal casting, with some energy returning either to the same or another transducer. By measuring the time required for the ultrasonic wave to pass through the material, be deflected, and return, it is possible to determine the location of the flaw; thickness can be gauged by similar techniques.

Ultrasonic delay line. In certain electronic systems, such as that in the colour separation section of a colour television receiver, it is necessary to delay the passage of an electrical signal from one point to another. This time delay must be precisely controllable, appreciable (that is, greater than a few millionths of a second, or microseconds), and reproducible. One form of delay unit employs two quartz transducers cemented to the sides of a glass polyhedron. Ultrasonic waves emitted by one transducer bounce from side to side of the polyhedron until they reach the other transducer where they are converted back into electrical signals.

Measurement of mechanical stresses. The presence of a stress in a body rotates the plane of polarization of polarized shear waves (a situation in which the particles that propagate the wave are all vibrating in the same direction or plane), and some correlation has been found between the amount of rotation and the magnitude, or physical size, of the stress. In the early 1970s work in this field was still in its early stages.

When a material is stressed it emits bursts of ultrasonic waves at frequencies up to about 40 kilohertz (40,000 cycles per second) for ductile materials and up to 400 kilohertz for brittle materials. Materials undergoing plastic deformation emit signals of a lower amplitude than when the deformation is such as to produce cracks. The repetition rate of the bursts increases with increasing

Amplification of an ultrasonic wave

Ultrasonic bursts

Sirens and whistles

rates of stain. It is anticipated that the detection of these bursts of ultrasonic waves can provide an early-warning system for incipient mechanical failure.

Ultrasonic image converters. The data presented by the type of flaw detector considered above is essentially one-dimensional; interpretation is difficult and somewhat subjective. For this reason much effort has been devoted to developing an ultrasonic camera equivalent to the X-ray machine.

In the ultrasonic camera a transducer generates an ultrasonic wave in a liquid. This wave passes through the object to be investigated and then strikes the metallized surface of a quartz disk that forms the front plate of a cathode-ray tube. The variation in ultrasonic intensity across the surface of the disk produces a corresponding variation in the alternating charge pattern appearing at the rear surface of the disk. This rear surface is scanned by an electronic beam that converts the charge pattern into a visible image on the face of a television picture tube. The picture on the television tube will then be an ultrasonic "X-ray" of the object.

A hologram is a three-dimensional picture made (without a camera) on photographic film by the pattern of interference formed by laser light reflected from the object; the picture is viewed by passing laser light through the film (see also LASER AND MASER). In recent years optical holography (see HOLOGRAPHY) has appeared as a powerful tool for optical imaging. Some work is being carried out to develop an ultrasonic hologram. In one

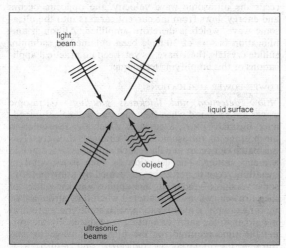

Figure 2: System for production of ultrasonic hologram (see text).

system, illustrated in Figure 2, two beams of ultrasonic waves at identical frequencies are directed at an angle to the underside of a liquid surface. One of these beams passes through the object to be investigated. At the surface, the two beams interfere to produce an ultrasonic wave pattern containing, effectively, an ultrasonic hologram of the object. This wave pattern is visualized by shining monochromatic (single-frequency) light at an oblique angle onto the liquid surface. The liquid wave pattern behaves like a diffraction grating and the first order diffraction image contains a picture of the ultrasonic cross section. In fact, the light beam is behaving in the same way as the beam used to reconstruct a picture from an optical hologram.

Ultrasonic holography, as so far developed, has a much higher resolving power than the ultrasonic camera.

Underwater applications. Underwater applications of ultrasonic waves are basically flaw-detection systems, in which an object such as a submarine, shoal of fish, or the seabed acts as the flaw. Such systems are treated in the article SONAR. Ultrasonic waves have been used for short-range underwater communication but most transducers are so highly directive that their use is of limited value.

Applications in air. The applications of ultrasonic waves in air are similar to those in liquids and solids and are essentially forms of flaw detection. Ultrasonic waves

have been used to count objects travelling along a belt, each object breaking the sound beam as if it were an optical beam. In the early 1970s a hand-held sonar blind-guidance device showed promise. In this device an ultrasonic beam is radiated; the presence of an obstacle causes this beam to be reflected, and the reflected beam is indicated by a tone in a headset worn by the operator. The pitch of the tone indicates the distance to the obstacle. Another interesting application is as an intrusion detector, in which a transducer sets up a pattern of ultrasonic waves in a room, producing a specific amplitude at a detector. An intruder alters the ultrasonic wave pattern and therefore alters the ultrasonic amplitude at the detector, setting off an alarm.

Ultrasonic viscometer. The acoustic impedance (resistance to the passage of acoustic waves) of a liquid for transverse or shear waves involves the liquid's viscosity. If the electrical impedance of a shear wave transducer is measured in air (which presents negligible resistance) and then in a liquid, the impedance difference can be related to the liquid's viscosity, enabling the latter to be determined conveniently.

Ultrasonic flowmeter. The apparent frequency of an utrasonic wave travelling in a medium moving relative to the transducer in a direction parallel to that of the wave, differs from the vibration frequency of the transducer because of the Doppler effect (see RADAR). The frequency shift is directly related to the medium's velocity, and hence, if the frequency shift can be measured, the medium's velocity can be calculated. This principle has been applied to the measurement of fluid flow rates.

Medical applications. The use of X-rays has been well-established for many years for medical investigations (see DIAGNOSIS). X-rays, however, suffer from two defects—it is difficult to delineate soft tissues of the human body with them, and their use is not advisable in the early stages of pregnancy. Ultrasonic waves, however, are reflected by some soft tissues and, as far as is known, cause no harmful effects if the ultrasonic intensity is sufficiently low. In medicine, the main application of ultrasonics has been as a flaw detector in such applications as detecting shifts in the midline of the brain and investigations of the fetus. Fetal echoes are obtainable many weeks before the fetal skeleton is visible by radiography (see also THERAPEUTICS).

HIGH-POWER APPLICATIONS

The effects produced by high-energy ultrasonic waves are normally irreversible and arise from cavitation (see below), intense mechanical stresses, or intense localized heating.

If the ultrasonic pressure exceeds the ambient (normal average) pressure in a liquid, the pressure in the liquid will fall below zero at the ultrasonic wave pressure trough, or point of minimum pressure. If this occurs, a process known as cavitation takes place; the liquid ruptures and forms small cavities, which—if they have a suitable radius—will expand as the pressure rises and then, as the pressure starts to fall, will become unstable and collapse very rapidly. At the end of the collapse, the gas within the cavity will be highly compressed (measurements indicate pressures of several hundreds of atmospheres); these high pressures will be relieved by the radiation of shock waves. These intense shock waves can cause liquids to mix that normally would not do so—such as oil and water; they can break up giant molecules such as polymers, proteins, and viruses; force dirt and grease off surfaces for cleaning purposes; break up cells; and initiate chemical reactions. The violent agitation caused by cavitation has also been used to improve the quality of electrodeposited copperplate and the quality of optical glass by irradiating the glass, when melted, with high-power ultrasonic energy.

The rapid vibration of a gas or liquid under the influence of intense ultrasonic waves causes a net attractive force to develop between particles suspended in the fluid. In addition, small, light particles will take up more of the fluid's motion than large, heavier ones. This difference in motion will increase the chance of collisions between the

Measuring
fluid flow
rates

particles. If the particles coalesce (adhere) on collision, irradiation by ultrasonic waves provides a means of coagulating the suspended particles. This has found applications in the removal of suspended particulate matter, as in the cleaning of factory exhaust gases.

Another useful application of intense ultrasonic waves is the ultrasonic soldering iron. The iron is designed to be a magnetostrictive transducer. The rapid vibration at its tip removes oxide layers from the surface of the metal to be soldered and not only improves the quality of the soldering but also permits the soldering of materials otherwise difficult to solder, such as aluminum.

Ultrasonics in brain surgery Intense ultrasonic waves have also found an application in medicine, particularly in brain surgery. Four beams of ultrasonic energy are beamed into the brain through holes cut in the skull. The intensity of each beam is insufficient to cause damage, but when combined at some point within the brain the total intensity is sufficient to heat a small region to a high enough temperature to destroy the tissue that the surgeon wants destroyed. This technique has been used successfully in the treatment of Parkinson's disease.

INFRASONICS

Infrasonic waves are those whose frequencies are nominally below the lower limit of human hearing. In recent years, however, evidence has been accumulating that waves with frequencies down to one cycle per second can be detected by human beings, provided the intensity is sufficiently high. The detection process, not yet fully understood, is believed to be a disturbance of the inner ear leading to dizziness. These waves are generated wherever a large high-speed flow of air occurs into, or around, an enclosed box or room. Of particular current interest is their effect on automobile drivers driving with open windows. Some microphones operate down to these frequencies and can be used to detect the presence of infrasonic waves.

Other sources of infrasonic waves of even much lower frequency (sometimes below one cycle per second) are earthquakes and tidal motion. Earthquakes require special detectors that usually consist of a large, well-sprung mass acting as an inertial element, the movement of which relative to the Earth is monitored, either by a pen drawing onto a chart mounted on the Earth or by a light beam falling onto photographically sensitive paper. When the Earth moves, the chart moves with it, but the inertial mass remains stationary and, therefore, the deflection of the trace on the chart indicates the motion of the Earth relative to the stationary mass. For portable use in seismographic surveys, the inertial mass is formed by a well-sprung magnet, between whose poles is situated a coil connected to the Earth. The motion of the Earth relative to the magnet induces a voltage in the coil proportional to the speed of relative motion (see also SEISMOGRAPH).

Use in underground exploration Underground explosions are used to generate infrasonic waves. From the traces provided by several seismometers of the paths traversed by the waves, the properties of the underlying rocks can be evaluated. This technique is used extensively in mineral and oil surveys. Recently, extremely sensitive seismometers have been employed to monitor infrasonic waves produced by underground nuclear explosions as part of the implementation of the nuclear test ban treaty.

Earthquakes are the main source of naturally occurring infrasonic waves. The main shock is often preceded by smaller shocks; by detecting these preliminary waves it may be possible to develop an early-warning system for large earthquakes. A similar early-warning system has been suggested for volcanic eruptions, which are usually preceded by seismological activity.

BIBLIOGRAPHY. W.P. MASON (ed.), *Physical Acoustics*, 6 vol. (1964–70), the most comprehensive survey of the whole field of ultrasonics ever published; G.L. GOOBERMAN, *Ultrasonics Theory and Practice* (1968), a short comprehensive textbook covering most of the theory of ultrasonics with some typical applications; L. BERGMANN, *Der Ultraschall und seine Anwendung in Wissenschaft und Technik* (1954), the classical text (in German) with only an elementary treatment of theory but an encyclopaedic coverage of applications and a complete list of references (two additional lists of references published); T.F. HUETER and R.H. BOLT, *Sonics: Technique for the Use of Sound and Ultrasound in Engineering and Science* (1955), a useful book particularly good on the design of transducers; K.F. HERZFELD and T.A. LITOVITZ, *Absorption and Dispersion of Ultrasonic Waves* (1959), an excellent book although limited to gases and liquids; B. BROWN and J.E. GOODMAN, *High-Intensity Ultrasonics: Industrial Applications* (1965), a good text covering most of the relevant industrial applications of ultrasonics; B. BROWN and D. GORDON (eds.), *Ultrasonic Techniques in Biology and Medicine* (1967), a useful collection of papers dealing with mainly diagnostic applications of ultrasonics in medicine.

(G.L.G.)

Undersea Exploration

Ocean exploration is a scientific pursuit involving numerous disciplines. The efforts of oceanographers, who go to sea regularly to expand man's knowledge, have been supported by innovative engineering and technology. The pace of discovery is, to a certain degree, regulated by the rate of scientific innovation (see also the article OCEANS AND SEAS).

The practical value of ocean exploration has long been established by those countries that exploit the sea's natural resources, transport goods and people across its surface, or maintain their national security by controlling its lanes. Investigations of the sea are expanding both in scientific scope and total effort.

By the 1970s ocean-exploration achievements were strongly dependent on new platforms and instruments, and included manned descent to the deepest undersea point (35,800 feet [10,740 metres]); a submerged circumnavigation of the world; transits beneath the North Pole and the Arctic ice cap; discovery of major new features of the sea floor, including a 40,000-mile-long (60,000-kilometre) mountain-range system under the Atlantic, Indian, and Pacific oceans; observation of major ocean-current systems; and evidence of major historical changes in the sea and the basins that contain them. All of these accomplishments can be traced to new instruments and vehicles with capabilities not available to earlier investigators. Sixty ships from 40 nations were combined during the International Geophysical Year in 1957–58, demonstrating the feasibility of carrying out oceanographic studies on a massive scale.

This article is divided into the following sections:

History of undersea exploration
  The 19th century
  The 20th century
Types of programs and research bodies
  National institutions, universities, and private industry
  International organizations
Research and exploration vessels
  Surface vessels
  Fixed platforms
  Submersibles
  Aircraft and satellites
  Buoys and other unmanned units
Techniques and equipment
  Basic methods and equipment of oceanographic measurement
  Techniques and equipment of physical oceanography
  Techniques and equipment of chemical oceanography
  Techniques and equipment of marine geology
  Techniques and equipment of biological oceanography
Recent advances and future trends

HISTORY OF UNDERSEA EXPLORATION

The 19th century. *Beginnings of oceanography.* Modern oceanography began in the mid-1800s when Matthew Fontaine Maury, an American naval officer, assembled and analyzed the qualitative observations and simple measurements of waves, winds, and currents gathered routinely by 19th-century mariners. He spent a lifetime compiling charts of major currents, prevailing winds, and storm tracks. Updating these valuable charts continues to be a regular routine for modern mariners and oceanographers. Primitive measuring devices and simple estimates have been replaced by accurate instruments on special ships and buoys; they provide continuous records that relate all data to specific geographical positions.

Marine biology exploration got its initial impetus at about the same time. The Englishman Edward Forbes was one of the first to make combined use of the related sciences now called oceanography. Using a naturalist's dredge, he discovered that ocean-bottom geology and marine life were closely related. His dredging revealed that the shape of the bottom was varied and as complex as that known on the continents. He noted too that the chemistry and physics of the sea influenced the type and quantity of animals and plants in a given locality. Though recognized by most as the father of modern marine biology, Forbes also introduced a fundamental interdisciplinary approach to oceanography.

One of Forbes's best known hypotheses, however, was later refuted. Reasoning that sunlight was necessary for plant photosynthesis and that animals needed plants for food, he suggested that no life could exist more than 1,800 feet below the ocean surface. Though contrary evidence, based on retrieval of lines and cables from great depths with plant and animal life clinging to them, appeared many times through the years, Forbes's theory was not everywhere discarded until 1960. In that year, Jacques Piccard of Switzerland and the United States navy lieutenant Don Walsh, from within the protective shell of the bathyscaphe "Trieste," at a depth of 35,800 feet, witnessed life in the form of a flat fish, a medusa, and a shrimp.

HMS "Challenger" expedition and subsequent research. The general lack of knowledge of the deep sea and the practical need for the successful laying of expensive transoceanic cables led a British professor, William B. Carpenter, to initiate the greatest oceanographic project of the 19th century, one that marked the beginning of oceanography as an integrated science. A committee established by the Royal Society wrote out a comprehensive deep-sea exploration program, and the Admiralty made HMS "Challenger" available for a four-year around-the-world expedition.

Oceanographers, until recent years, have had to make do with ships and platforms constructed originally for purposes other than ocean research. The "Challenger" was such a vessel, but was also one of the most substantial of its time. A fully-rigged corvette of 2,306 tons with auxiliary steam power, she compared favourably with modern vessels in oceanographic service. Her crew and scientists sailed around the globe, logged 68,890 nautical miles through all the major oceans, and gathered data and samples from waters of all depths and at almost all latitudes. From December 7, 1872, to May 24, 1876, she amassed a wealth of information requiring 20 years for compilation in 50 thick quarto volumes.

The success of the "Challenger" led to a series of other national oceanographic expeditions during the rest of the century. Each added valuable information to the fundamental discoveries of the British. The American marine zoologist Alexander Agassiz, for example, amassed an unprecedented 10,000 miles (16,000 kilometres) in tropical seas to map more lines across deep-sea basins and make more deep soundings than had all other scientific expeditions combined. Agassiz' proficiency as an engineer provided solutions to the problems associated with cable tensioning and winding. He designed a double-edged bottom trawl that worked equally well regardless of which edge hit the bottom. He invented remote opening and closing devices for tow nets to eliminate any uncertainty of the depth at which specimens were captured.

Oceanography in Monaco

Prince Albert of Monaco sent his own fleet of yachts on numerous expeditions. Each ship was fully equipped for deep-sea research; many of the devices deployed were on display in the early 1970s at the Musée Océanographique de Monaco. Among the Prince's engineering contributions were huge baited traps, special nets and trawls for use at various depths, and a system of underwater electric lights to attract fish. His most famous innovation (in 1885 and still in use) was the mass use of copper floats, with instructions in nine languages, to track major currents in the Atlantic.

The 20th century. By the beginning of the 20th century, oceanography was firmly established, but primarily within institutions devoted to the biological sciences. By the 1930s, small seashore laboratories were established by virtually every European country.

The practical value of oceanographical techniques was demonstrated in World War II. Acoustical devices, for example, were successfully employed in locating submarines. They were also used for wave forecasting and reconnoitring beaches in advance of landings. During the immediate postwar period, theoretical studies enabled oceanographers to translate water-temperature and salinity data into water-flow data (speed and direction), thereby providing subsurface water movement tracking. The currents could not be observed directly, however, until the 1950s, when improved technology appeared in two forms: a special marker buoy to identify deepwater currents, and the modern echo sounder to provide a continuous silhouette of the sea floor over which a ship is passing (see also SONAR; HYDROGRAPHIC CHARTING).

The echo sounder, however, at times would show a sea-floor depth of a few hundred feet when the true bottom was actually several thousand feet below. No physical explanation seemed plausible for this newly discovered phenomenon until a zoologist surmised that the echoes might come from vast populations of marine organisms—a hypothesis that is now universally accepted. Evidence indicating the specific organisms causing the echoes had to await development of deep-submersible technology. In the 1960s the deep-diving platform bathyscaphe "Trieste" and the submersible "Alvin" viewed and photographed large concentrations of these organisms.

TYPES OF PROGRAMS AND RESEARCH BODIES

National institutions, universities, and private industry. The national oceanographic program in most countries is a combined effort by government laboratories and academic institutions, with the government providing most of the funds and general coordination. The benefits of such exploration are shared by many segments of the national economy: natural-resources exploitation, transportation, national defense, and recreation. Nations on all continents have oceanographic programs. Some examples are the Zoological Station of Algeria; the Argentine Antarctic Institute; the Institute of Fisheries Research in Varna, Bulgaria; the Korea Central Fisheries Experimental Station; and the Oceanographic Laboratory of the Institute of French Oceania. The United States government has numerous laboratories, including the important station at Woods Hole, Massachusetts. Many universities maintain laboratories; an example is the Scripps Institution of Oceanography of the University of California, San Diego.

Private enterprise, particularly the petroleum industry, has become a significant participant in oceanographic exploration. Since the late 1940s, petroleum firms have developed their own oceanographic fleets and specialized instruments. The industry's special requirements have been fulfilled by innovative platform designs, sampling and measuring techniques, and handling facilities. The disciplines of geology and geophysics have benefitted most from the industry's activities. Markedly improved seismic techniques for acquiring, compiling, and processing data, from which three-dimensional models of sub-bottom geological features could be made, have significantly aided geologists. Improved ship designs, open-sea anchoring techniques, ship control, navigation aids, and new tools and techniques have been adopted by the scientific oceanographer.

Marine fisheries have been closely allied to oceanography for many decades, and the industry has turned to the biological oceanographers for information about the marine environment. In contrast to the petroleum industry, the fishing industry has not established a significant private research capability, but has adopted engineering advances developed for other purposes.

Involvement of marine fisheries

International organizations. *United Nations.* The principal international oceanographic organization is the Inter-governmental Oceanographic Commission of the

United Nations Educational, Scientific and Cultural Organization (UNESCO), founded in 1961. UNESCO also operates an Office of Oceanography that provides staff support to the commission and conducts some activities of its own. Such activities as the recent International Indian Ocean Expedition and the International Tropical Atlantic Expedition were sponsored by the commission. The International Hydrographic Bureau, Monaco, assists in the standardization and dissemination of ocean survey data. The World Meteorological Organization and the Food and Agriculture Organization are also concerned with oceanographic problems that relate to meteorology and fisheries.

In the early 1970s the integrated Global Ocean Station System was being planned by the Inter-governmental Oceanographic Commission to monitor and predict the state of the oceans, a project that included many elements of the World Weather Watch of the World Meteorological Organization; coordination procedures were established. The commission also had international coordinating responsibility for the Pacific Tsunami Warning System, a system that was designed to warn of extraordinarily high waves created by seismic disturbances or underground volcanoes. Other international organizations had the responsibility for such additional activities as the Ocean Station Vessel Program and the International Ice Patrol.

International Council of Scientific Unions. The principal nongovernmental world body providing a forum for all sciences is the International Council of Scientific Unions, whose marine-science groups are the Scientific Committee on Oceanic Research and the former International Union of Geodesy and Geophysics, now called the International Association for the Physical Sciences of the Ocean (IAPSO). The council established the World Data Center (WDC) system in 1957 to assemble and make available the data collected by the observational programs of the International Geophysical Year (see below). That network of data centres was continued on a permanent basis by international agreement. One group, or subcentre, of offices is located in the United States; another in the Soviet Union; and still others are located in Australia, Japan, and various countries in western Europe. Establishing WDCs at several locations ensures against catastrophic destruction of a single centre, is convenient geographically and provides easy communication for workers in different parts of the world. Each country in which a component of the system is located is responsible for its financial support.

International Geophysical Year. A major international scientific effort that included many oceanographic disciplines was the International Geophysical Year in 1957–58. Its principal fields of study were aurora and airglow, cosmic rays, geomagnetism, glaciology, gravity, ionospheric physics, longitudes and latitudes, meteorology, oceanography, seismology, solar activity, and nuclear radiation, all of which are global in nature. The project involved organizing ocean expeditions; collecting, reducing, and tabulating data; and exchanging this information among data centres and making it available to the scientific community.

In addition to the establishment of the World Data Centers, the effort also contributed to the organization of such continuing programs as those of the Scientific Committee for Antarctic Research and the Scientific Committee on Oceanic Research. The oceanographic and other findings of the International Geophysical Year were published in 48 volumes entitled *Annals of the International Geophysical Year.*

Deep-Sea Drilling Project. The Deep-Sea Drilling Project, sponsored by the United States National Science Foundation, began in the summer of 1968 with the objective of learning about the origin and history of the Earth through the study of samples obtained from previously inaccessible sites. Sediment and rock cores were obtained from the ocean floor at depths of 20,000 feet, and holes were drilled in the bottom to depths of thousands of feet. Ocean-bottom sediments from land erosion and from the remains of microscopic marine organisms provided fresh

insights into the origin and movement of the Earth's crust (see also MARINE SEDIMENTS).

Barbados Oceanographic and Meteorological Experiment (Bomex). The point of contact between the atmosphere and the sea is the scene of a complex and continuous exchange of energy, water, gases, and particulates. Most of the heat received from the Sun is stored in the tropical ocean between 30° south and 30° north latitude. Since the Earth loses heat by radiation almost uniformly at all latitudes, heat must be transported from equatorial regions to higher latitudes. Though scientists know that the atmosphere, not the ocean, carries this heat, very little more is known about the process. For that reason, the Barbados Oceanographic and Meteorological Experiment (Bomex) was set up.

Bomex involved 12 ships, 28 aircraft, and 1,500 men from the United States, Canada, and Barbados. The project focussed on the exchange of energy between the ocean and the atmosphere and on the vertical and horizontal spreading of the energies within each medium. One goal was to broaden scientific understanding of basic processes of energy exchange at low altitudes. The site selected was a 300-mile square just east of Barbados, an area where energy exchange between the atmosphere and the ocean is particularly significant. Extensive and detailed measurements were taken of temperature structures, turbulent stresses, wind stresses, growth and dissipation of kinetic energy, radiant energy exchange, chemical exchange, and other phenomena. Instruments were deployed from ships, aircraft, buoys, rockets, and stable platforms. Much new information was obtained suggesting considerable revision of theories concerning the sea-to-air interface.

International Decade of Ocean Exploration (1970–80). In recognition of the rapidly growing significance of ocean resources and the increasing importance of an understanding of ocean processes, Pres. Lyndon Johnson of the United States proposed on March 8, 1968, that the nations of the world join together in a concerted, long-term cooperative program of ocean exploration. He proposed an initial ten-year period of expanded collaborative effort to be designated the International Decade of Ocean Exploration.

The decade 1970 to 1980 was conceived to be a period of intensified collaborative planning, development of national capabilities, and execution of worldwide programs of oceanic research and resource exploration. Because of the size, complexity, and variability of the marine environment, scientific investigations of vast scope are necessary if the limited knowledge of this environment is to increase within a reasonably short interval. At the same time, excellence, experience, and capabilities in marine science and technology are shared by many nations. Hence, a broad program of ocean exploration can best be carried out through a cooperative effort by many nations.

In the early 1970s most nations gave most of their financial support to programs close to their own shores, such as exploration of the continental shelf and of their coastal fishery stocks. Even though nations are moving farther out to sea every year, much of the world's ocean exploration activity will probably continue to be this type of coastal activity.

Advances in marine science and technology depend critically upon the effective flow of information from data collectors to data consumers. As more sophisticated data-processing equipment comes into use, particular attention will be given to the compatibility of national data systems. Standardization of data collection techniques and common procedures for calibrating oceanographic instruments may also help make data useful on a broad basis.

RESEARCH AND EXPLORATION VESSELS

Surface vessels. The traditional platform for oceanographic research has, until recent years, been described as any sturdy, seaworthy vessel capable of carrying oceanographic winches and a variety of measuring and sampling devices. In the 1950s a fleet of research ships designed

World
Data
Center
system

Data
exchange
and
compatibility

specifically for oceanography began appearing. Their varied characteristics reflected the design requirements of their respective owners. The international listing exceeded 500 in the early 1970s. All ocean vessels, usually over 70 metres (230 feet) in length, are operated by large academic institutions or government agencies. Smaller vessels are used for coastal work and are operated by virtually all oceanographic groups.

Shipboard equipment and facilities. The fundamental requirement for an oceanographic vessel is stability. The more stable the platform, the greater is the number of working days possible under adverse weather and sea conditions. In addition to stability, the ability to remain on station with a minimum amount of drift is necessary. Thus, a deep-draft vessel, with a minimum height above water level (freeboard) to avoid excessive wind forces, is desirable. Other basic requirements include adequate deck working space and machinery, laboratory facilities, cruising range, and living accommodations for the scientists and crew. Other desirable features include control of the ship's direction at very slow speeds and while stopped, and the ability to proceed silently (by use of batteries) for periods up to 12 hours.

Deck space and machinery. Open and uncluttered deck space facilitates handling the numerous pieces of large oceanographic equipment. Essential deck machinery includes winches, booms, and cranes, usually of special design. The largest winch is used for anchoring at great depths for periods ranging from a few hours to a month; its steel-wire rope is from 20,000 to 35,000 feet long. This winch may also assist in bottom dredging, towing large midwater trawls, taking large bottom cores, and obtaining samples of seawater for radioactive carbon analysis.

Deep-sea anchoring winch

The most commonly used oceanographic winch is of medium size, with 20,000- to 30,000-foot lengths of stainless-steel-wire rope. It operates at high speeds and has a variety of uses: for water-sampling bottles, current meters, underwater cameras, small coring devices, small dredges, plankton nets, various temperature-measuring instruments, and other equipment. One of the smallest is the bathythermograph winch. It is used to lower the bathythermograph, a recording thermometer capable of registering temperature against depth down to 900 feet. In shallow water the winch, with a specially designed device called a "scoopfish," takes small bottom samples. Mechanical current meters and vertical hand plankton nets are lowered from the bathythermograph winch.

Laboratory facilities. An oceanographic ship requires several laboratory spaces. A deck laboratory, for instrument preparation and operation and some analyses, is usually located near the oceanographic winch. Other laboratory spaces are needed for performing chemical, biological, and geological analyses, installing electronic recording equipment, and for photographic developing and printing. In addition, of course, space for offices and drafting rooms and for dry storage of oceanographic equipment and samples must be provided. Laboratory spaces are, by design, flexible. As one surface ship may serve a variety of scientists or disciplines within a short period of time, a vessel needs to be available for multipurpose missions. Portable laboratories that can be deck-loaded offer the convenience of being available for outfitting on shore, precluding losses of valuable ship time.

Portable laboratories

Fixed platforms. The need for long-term investigations with fixed equipment has led to the construction and installation of fixed towers in moderate depths of water (Figure 1). Three such towers are actively used: the Naval Undersea Research and Development Center tower near San Diego, California, and two Naval Ship Research and Development Laboratory towers near Panama City, Florida.

Moored platform. For long-term measurements at selected sites, platforms that support instruments at desired depths are moored to the ocean floor. Large oceanographic buoys and their associated sensors are classified as platforms. The largest is a moored, 40-foot-diameter platform that can measure and record 100 separate channels of data, sending the data on command by radio to shore stations thousands of miles away. Both short-term and long-term memory devices store collected data, the long-term for periods of up to one year. This buoy was used, for example, as a master in an array of buoys moored between Hawaii and Alaska in the North Pacific, collecting their measurements and transmitting them to shore.

Figure 1: Shallow-water oceanographic research tower. Vertical tracks on three sides of the structure permit instrument carts to be positioned at any water depth. Other instrument mountings include subsurface tripods and extendible booms.
By courtesy of the Naval Undersea Center, San Diego, California

Sea Spider is a submerged buoy intended to provide stable support for underwater instruments at depths up to 20,000 feet. A model experimentally placed in 2,600 feet (800 metres) of water by the Woods Hole (Massachusetts) Oceanographic Institution exhibited movements of less than three feet, essentially equal to or better than the accuracy of its position. A system of installation in 19,000 feet of water was under way in the early 1970s.

The United States Naval Arctic Research Laboratory at Point Barrow, Alaska, operates numerous field stations, including research platform stations on ice islands. Temporary stations are located on ice floes. One such ice-island station drifted approximately 5,000 miles in four years from near Point Barrow, through the Arctic Ocean, almost over the North Pole, and through the Greenland Sea to a point near Iceland, where it was evacuated. A permanent station has been occupied for many years on Fletcher's Ice Island. Research conducted from ice stations covers nearly every aspect of oceanography. Airborne observations, including the distribution and dynamics of pack ice, have supplemented their findings.

Ice floe stations

Floating instrument platform (FLIP). Developed under sponsorship of the United States Navy, FLIP (Figure 2) is an unusual vessel, the first of its kind. Built in 1962 to fulfill a need for an extremely stable and yet mobile platform from which accurate acoustical measurements could be made at sea, FLIP is a long pole-shaped platform towed in the horizontal position to the research area. On station, ballast tanks in the after two-thirds of the 355-foot vessel are flooded. As the stern gradually sinks, the prow rises. Ultimately the vessel is completely vertical with approximately 55 feet of prow above water and pointed skyward. As the hull is only 12½ feet in diameter some distance above and below the waterline, the rise and fall of the waves cause a very small percentage change in the displacement. Consequently, the vertical motions that do occur are extremely small compared with those of a conventional ship.

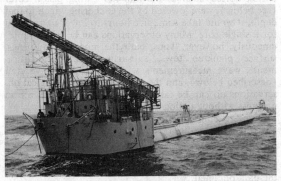

Figure 2: *Floating Instrument platform (FLIP).*
The platform has no motive power of its own but is towed in the horizontal position (top) to the research area, then "flipped" (centre) to the vertical position by flooding its ballast tanks. Fifty-five feet (16.5 metres) of prow show above water in the vertical position (bottom), affording scientists a stable platform from which to carry out oceanographic research.

Stability, coupled with the unusually deep draft in the vertical position, makes FLIP an ideal platform for many sea experiments. Oceanographic instruments may be mounted anywhere along the submerged hull. By use of precision equipment, the location, depth, and orientation of the instruments may be determined and controlled to a higher precision than can be achieved with any other platform. Although first developed for acoustical experiments, FLIP has found many other uses since it was placed in operation on August 15, 1962. Operations have included experiments or studies of wave attenuation, sound propagation, sound-scattering or sound-reverberation measurements, seismic wave recording, wave-pressure and wave-acceleration measurements, meteorological work, and measurement of internal waves.

FLIP has no propulsion power of its own other than two small orientation propellers that rotate the vessel about its vertical axis. Three diesel generators supply electrical power for all ship and scientific needs. Practical tow speeds for FLIP vary up to about ten knots (nautical miles per hour) in the horizontal position. It is sometimes towed slowly in the vertical position for station keeping or small changes in position.

Submersibles. The descent of the bathyscaphe "Trieste" to 35,800 feet (10,740 metres) in 1960 was a major event in the deep-submersible field. The family of vehicles that has evolved since ranges in size from small one-man submarines for exploration of the continental shelf to vehicles capable of routine operation at great depths. In the continuing development of deep-sea research vehicles, the goal is to operate safely at any depth. In the early 1970s materials were being fabricated and tested, and techniques of life support, navigation, communications, bottom mapping, photography, direct viewing, and in-place measuring were being studied to improve vehicle capability. New methods of providing power for propulsion and life support at great depths were also under investigation.

A major advance in the evolution of deep submersibles was "Alvin," a vehicle built for ocean science and operated by the Woods Hole Oceanographic Institution. It has been successful in working at depths down to 6,000 feet (see SUBMARINE).

Aircraft and satellites. Major advances have been made in the use of aircraft for obtaining operational oceanographic information. With the development of air-dropped bathythermographs, aircraft can obtain information on subsurface layers as well as on the surface. Lasers as airborne remote sensors can take profiles of polar sea ice and of the ocean surface. In the North Pacific, expendable bathythermographs were dropped from planes every 25 miles along a great circle line approximately 1,800 miles long in 12 monthly transits to study temperature as a function of depth, position, and time. Because each transit was completed in about eight hours, records of the temperature profile and approximate sound-velocity structure (*i.e.*, the rate at which sound would pass through ocean water at different temperatures) were provided for a vast area of the Pacific at monthly intervals.

Many acoustical and seismological measurements, including those of propagation loss, ambient noise, and sediment sound speed and thickness, have been made successfully by employing sonobuoys (buoys incorporating sonar equipment) from aircraft. Use of aircraft is a logical step toward use of satellites to obtain oceanographic observations globally; satellite navigation systems, with their accurate positioning devices, have already influenced ocean science research. Current measurements made from an ice platform, itself in motion, have been improved by accurate position data, permitting determination of rate of drift.

The use of satellites for telemetering oceanographic data from buoy systems has been successfully demonstrated. Sound signals from hydrophones deep in the Pacific Ocean and depth measurements from a research ship were transmitted continuously for several hours via satellite to the United States Navy Underwater Sound Laboratory in New London, Connecticut, where the data were processed for frequency content and amplitude one-fourth second after being transmitted. Such a system is ideally suited for transmitting underwater acoustic signals used for a variety of scientific purposes: subbottom profiling, depth readings necessary for charting the ocean bottom, and measurements of the Earth's gravitational and magnetic fields. A dramatic development has been the possibility of collecting useful ocean data from remote platforms in space. Earth-orbiting satellites have demonstrated a capability for collecting and transmitting oceanographic data and acting as data communications relays. The TIROS, NIMBUS, and ESSA series of

Telemetering data by satellite

satellites, for example, have demonstrated operational capability for providing useful global photographs showing clouds and limited indications of sea ice; other applications were under development in the early 1970s.

Buoys and other unmanned units. Buoys serve as effective instrument platforms that can remain unattended at a given location for extended periods. Buoy design was still under active development in the early 1970s. Simple can and spar buoys, decked-over skiffs, boat-shaped hulls, and giant saucer-shaped buoys are a few examples of unmanned buoys. Extra large spar buoys with excellent vertical stability have been created to serve oceanographers.

Remote underwater manipulator (RUM). The remote underwater manipulator (RUM) is a remotely controlled, tracked, sea-floor work vehicle with mechanical arms and pincers developed as a research tool. Areas of particular interest are remote manipulation, navigation, cable telemetry systems, ambient-pressure-exposed electronics, and environmental and mechanical design considerations. Design depth for the RUM vehicle is 10,000 feet. Its hull, tracks, and suspension system are those of a surplus United States Marine Corps vehicle rifle platform. Equipment includes two television cameras, a scanning sonar, an acoustic transponder navigation system, and numerous other instruments to monitor operational conditions. The manipulator can work off either side or to the rear of the vehicle and is capable of exerting 50 pounds (20 kilograms) of force in any direction at full arm's length. Two tethered swimming platforms called CURV and RUWS offer similar features.

Towed instrument platforms. To explore the details of sea-floor topography and related characteristics, instrumented vehicles commonly called FISH (fully instrumented submersible housing) are towed by a research ship. A network of bottom-mounted acoustic transponders (two-way sonars) is used to provide precise navigational information. The FISH usually consists of a pressure resistant enclosure to protect the electronic gear. Instrument sensors are mounted in various locations on the outside.

Communication between the vehicle and the ship's laboratory is provided by a single coaxial electrical conductor in the core of the tow cable, even while the winch is running. The cable is also used to transmit power to the vehicle.

Precise navigation in a survey area is aided by acoustic transponders dropped from the ship at random locations at the beginning of the operation. With the transponders, some of which are recoverable, the towed vehicle and the ship can be located in relation to the network to an accuracy of 30 feet. Their usable range is from five to ten miles.

A FISH system is a powerful research tool for studying details of the sea floor. By virtue of its complex of instruments and the precision of its acoustic transponder navigation system, magnetic, topographic, subsurface sediment, and photographic data may be closely correlated to identify features of special interest and to increase understanding of the processes of formation of the sea floor.

TECHNIQUES AND EQUIPMENT

Basic methods and equipment of oceanographic measurement. Oceanographic observations are made from a surface ship while either under way or on station or at anchor. Those taken while under way are generally limited to meteorological and bathythermographic observations with occasional shallow-water bottom sampling. For special surveys, hull-mounted recording devices for obtaining continuous data of water temperature, salinity, and conductivity are used. The greater portion of oceanographic work at sea is carried out while lying to on an oceanographic station.

Outboard from most oceanographic winches is a platform, with an A-frame over it. From the A-frame a metre wheel is usually suspended as well as a special block that will quickly receive a cable. The amount of oceanographic wire that passes over the metre wheel in or out is registered on dials, indicating the depths to which the lead-weighted wire has been lowered. The wire is used,

variously, for carrying water-sampling bottles with attached thermometers to desired depths or to make a series of plankton tows, or for a lowering of an underwater camera or a coring device to the bottom.

The time needed to take a series of observations in water about 13,000 feet deep is about seven hours. If a large coring device, such as the half-ton Ewing piston corer (see below), were lowered by the anchoring winch to that depth, it would take some five hours to lower and raise it for a single core. Many observations can be taken simultaneously, however. Thus, bathythermograph lowerings, surface plankton tows, subsurface-visibility measurements, wave measurements with the electric wave staff (described below), and the associated meteorological observations all can be taken while other lowerings are in progress without adding to the time on station.

While steaming to the next station, measurements of currents and sea-floor echo soundings may be taken. Equipment and instruments are cleaned, the samples stored, preparations for operations at the next station made, and work is started on computing and analyzing the data obtained.

Water-sampling bottles. Seawater is collected from various depths by means of specially adapted water-sampling bottles, the first of which was invented by the English chemist Robert Hooke in 1611. More than 50 types have been developed since. The types of bottles in general use, however, have been reduced to those few proved capable of withstanding rigorous working conditions. The most universal water sampler, the Nansen bottle, is a modification of one developed in the latter part of the 19th century by the Norwegian Arctic explorer and oceanographer Fridtjof Nansen. It is a metal water sampler with a 1.25-litre capacity, intended to bring an uncontaminated water sample from a desired depth to the surface. Nansen bottles are made of brass, with the exterior parts chromium plated and the interior silver or tin plated to provide resistance to seawater. The exterior is painted yellow to increase visibility.

In 1936 the International Association of Physical Oceanography proposed the following standard depths at which observations should either be taken directly or the data adjusted by interpolation from the distribution at other levels. The standard depths, in metres below the sea surface, are: 10, 20, 30, 50, 75, 100, 150, 200, (250), 300, 400, 500, 600, (700), 800, 1,000, 1,200, 1,500, 2,000, 2,500, 3,000, 4,000, and thence every 1,000-metre interval to the bottom. The depths in parentheses are optional. (One metre equals about 3.3 feet.) — Standard observation depths

Other temperature-measuring devices and seawater samplers have been developed. A few such instruments are the bathythermograph, the salinity–temperature-depth recorder, the conductivity–temperature-indicator recorder, and the microthermal depth recorder. The Nansen bottle still maintains a high level of usage, as all of these other instruments are limited to relatively shallow-depth operations.

The bathythermograph. The bathythermograph is an instrument for obtaining a permanent, graphic record of water temperature at various depths as it is lowered and raised in the ocean. It can be used while the ship is under way. A depth element in the instrument drives a smoked-glass slide at right angles to a stylus, which in turn is driven by a thermal element consisting of copper tubing filled with an organic liquid, xylene, that expands and contracts, transmitting pressure to a stylus. Thus, a continuous record of both temperature and pressure (or depth) is charted. The trace, or record, scribed by the stylus, is read by comparing it with a grid individually calibrated for each instrument.

Techniques and equipment of physical oceanography. Physical oceanography includes the study of tides, currents, sea and swell, temperatures, densities, origin and circulation, sound propagation, optical transparency, sea ice, and other physical properties of seawater (see also OCEANS AND SEAS).

Of major importance is the acquisition of knowledge on surface and subsurface currents: whence they originate, their speed and direction, and their influence on other oceanic factors. Determinations of subsurface currents may be made by direct measurements with current meters (see below) or by mathematical computations from the densities of the masses of water under study. Density is a function of the temperature and salinity of water under a given pressure; these two variables provide basic information required to determine sound propagation and patterns, both vertically and horizontally, in seawater.

Depth information is an essential part of every oceanographic expedition and is a fundamental reference for all sampling. The echo sounder is an electronic instrument that automatically and continuously measures ocean depth by transmitting and receiving acoustic sound pulses. Echo sounders that can generate strong acoustic pulses can penetrate not only large water columns but also sedimentary sea-floor deposits and record layering to depths of several tens of metres.

The use of high-energy electrical discharges underwater has directly augmented the echo sounder. Acoustic energy generated in this manner, sufficient to produce strong echoes from well below the bottom of the sea, extends the oceanographer's capacity for identifying sub-bottom structures, such as salt domes and potential oil-producing geologic structures, hundreds of metres below the sea floor. Models constructed from seismic profile surveys provide three-dimensional information about the sea floor. Deep-sea drilling sites are most often selected on the basis of seismic surveys. Drilling cores provide confirming evidence for the conjectured forecasts of what would be discovered by drilling in a given location.

Temperature. Oceanographers require thousands of temperature readings. The measure of seawater temperature both vertically and horizontally continues to be of great importance to oceanographers exploring the subtleties of ocean currents and physical forces related to them. For measuring the temperature of surface water, a conventional, highly accurate mercury thermometer is used.

For measuring temperatures below the surface to all depths in the sea, a simple mechanical scheme was devised in 1874 for capturing and maintaining the temperature reading taken at depth. Two thermometers, one pressure protected and one unprotected, are mounted in a frame that can be inverted on demand. The design is such that when the thermometers are inverted, the mercury column breaks at a certain point. The amount of mercury remaining in a graduated capillary portion of the thermometer is then read to indicate temperature at the point of inversion. Traditionally, the reversing thermometers are cable lowered to approximate depth, and the unprotected thermometer used to provide precise depth. The probable depth error for such measurements is about 0.5 percent. Reversing thermometers continue to be a standard device for oceanographers throughout the world.

Exploratory activities of physical oceanography profit from temperature–salinity measurements. Water masses can be classified on the basis of their temperature–salinity characteristics. A series sample of water, plus an accurate temperature measurement for each, provides one of the most valuable tools in physical oceanography. A temperature–salinity diagram can be constructed and anomalies easily recognized. Water masses so characterized are traceable over great distances and at varying depths, providing information on currents and water mass mixing.

Measuring waves. Internal waves are similar to the commonly observed surface waves but occur at the point of contact between layers of water of different densities rather than at the sea–air boundary. Until recently, observations of deepwater waves were limited to visual data. Recently developed electrical wave staffs and pressure-operated wave indicators now provide recorded data for analyses. The success of long- and short-range wave forecasting is dependent upon the number of observers reporting and the accuracy of the observations.

The electric wave staff records wave heights and periods at sea. It consists of three lengths of watertight aluminum tubing, a circular steel damping disk, a recorder, a transformer–rectifier circuit, electrical cables, floats, retrieving lines, and balancing weights. The upper section of tubing, called the step-resistance gauge, has 36 contact points and

a connection for the electrical cable at the top. The remaining two sections of tubing provide proper buoyancy to the gauge so that it will float vertically with one-half of its length exposed. Below the end of the lower tube is suspended the damping disk, the function of which is to provide weight to keep the staff vertical and to damp the tendency of the staff to rise and fall with the passing waves. The wave water rising and falling along the step-resistance gauge increases and decreases the resistance in the gauge at successive contact points. This variation in resistance is transmitted to the recorder aboard ship and a record of the wave height and period is made. Observations are made when the ship is lying to; the wave-staff assembly is put overboard to windward so that the drift of the ship will be away from the staff.

Observations of transparency, light penetration, scattering, and colour are aided by the use of photoelectric cells that are lowered to various depths. Such studies assist in the determination of currents and provide clues to biological conditions.

Meteorological oceanography. The interaction of sea and air and the influence of one medium upon the other make up another important part of oceanographic studies. Prevailing winds in certain areas affect ocean currents, while in other areas the air temperatures are tempered by the sea surface. Solar radiation affects the heat budget (the sum of all Earth heat gains and losses) and influences biological conditions. Thus, the types of meteorological information that must accompany all oceanographic observations include air temperatures, humidity, wind direction and speed, atmospheric pressure, cloud types and amount, and visibility, along with the oceanographic variables of sea-surface temperature, wind waves, and swell.

Currents. Surface ocean currents are a portion of a thin veneer overlying other currents that do not usually match the surface currents in any way. Probably more types of instruments are used for measuring currents than for any other single oceanographic operation. Although many types have been developed, most are limited in use either by cost or design. A simple, rugged, and accurate instrument that can indicate weak as well as strong current speed, direction, and depth is still one of the most important needs of oceanographic instrumentation. The types may be divided into three broad categories: free floating, shallow water, and shipboard. The free-floating category includes drift bottles, dye marks, and floats that can be observed from ship, shore, or aircraft. Shallow-water instruments include those attached to piers, buoys, or beacons or placed on the bottom in nearshore areas at more or less set depths. Shipboard types include instruments that can be operated when the ship is under way and those used when the ship is anchored. Representative instruments of the shallow-water and shipboard categories are described below.

Surface-current measurements when under way are often taken by the geomagnetic electrokinetograph, which records the electrical potential developed by the movement of an electrolyte (ocean current) through a magnetic field (the Earth's) at depths of more than 100 fathoms (600 feet). A matched pair of electrodes mounted 300 feet apart on a two-conductor cable is trailed about three ship lengths behind the stern, and thus away from the magnetic influences of the ship. The geomagnetic electrokinetograph makes observations of the potential difference between the electrodes along the ship's course and at right angles to it. These potential differences are caused by the motion of the water through the Earth's magnetic field and are mathematically related to the set and drift of the ship and to the electrodes.

Another device that gives the speed and direction of ocean current at any depth is the Ekman current meter, developed by Vagn Walfrid Ekman, a Swedish scientist. This meter consists of an impeller, or screw, and shaft connected to a set of dials. The number of shaft revolutions per unit of time is read from the dials on the main body of the meter. A reservoir of bronze balls is connected by a narrow tube to a compass box containing a compass needle. Below the needle is the compass-ball recepta-

Depth information

Temperature–salinity measurements

Current-measuring devices

cle, which is divided into 36 chambers, each representing 10° of azimuth. As the impeller rotates, the balls fall, one at a time, onto the top of the compass needle, which guides them into one or another of the chambers, depending on the heading of the current meter. This gives the direction toward which the current is flowing.

The current meter is lowered on either the oceanographic or bathythermograph wire. The impeller is locked while lowering or hoisting. A small metal device known as a messenger is sent down the wire, unlocks the impeller, and sets the meter in operation. A second messenger is sent down later to lock the impeller and stop the meter before hoisting. Valid measurements cannot be made with an Ekman current meter unless the ship or buoy from which it is suspended is anchored.

The Roberts radio current meter, an instrument designed specifically to record subsurface current speeds accurately while simultaneously indicating the direction of the flow, consists of a buoy from which one to three meters may be suspended; an automatic radio-transmitting system within the buoy; and a ship- or shore-based radio-receiving monitoring system that can monitor up to 15 meters. The buoys usually are anchored in bays, rivers, channels, or other relatively shallow areas. Meters have been operated successfully at depths as great as 8,000 feet from anchored ships.

Water transparency and light absorption. The physical relationships governing the penetration and absorption of light, the colour, and the transparency of the sea are of prime importance to physical and biological oceanography. Such measurements are taken with three general types of instruments: the submarine photometer, the hydrophotometer, and the Secchi disk.

The submarine photometer detects and records directly, in footcandles, the light at the surface and at all depths down to approximately 500 feet. Through the use of filters, observations are made in the infrared and ultraviolet ranges of the spectrum. The hydrophotometer has a self-contained constant light source that allows greater latitude in observation. It may be used at any time of day or night and will measure finer graduations of transparency. The Secchi disk, designed to measure water transparency, is dependent upon the available illumination, which varies with the time of day, cloud formation, and amount of cloud cover. To a circular plate, or disk, usually of wood painted a flat white, a graduated line is secured, and the disk is lowered into the water from the shaded side of the ship until it is just visible. Then the depth in metres is noted, and lowering is continued until the disk can no longer be seen. At that point the disk is slowly raised until it is barely visible. The depth reading of this point is then averaged with the reading obtained on lowering and is recorded. The greater the depth reading, the more transparent is the water.

Techniques and equipment of chemical oceanography. Chemical oceanography is concerned with determining the various constituents of seawater and their distribution. The salinity of seawater is of major importance in computing its density and determining currents as well as sound velocities. Analyses of nutrient concentration (*e.g.*, phosphate, nitrate, silicate), the pH (acidity), and the content of dissolved gases (oxygen and carbon dioxide) provide information that aids in determining age, origin, and movement of water masses and their influences upon marine life. One of the more rapidly expanding areas of interest in chemical oceanography is the study of dissolved gases in seawater. New, very sensitive analytical methods that can be used aboard ship permit rapid accumulation of data on the distribution of dissolved gases. Analysis of such data is useful in tracing ocean-mixing processes, in studying the production of gases in the ocean, and in elucidating the natural cycles of atmospheric pollutants.

New and improved methods of trace-element analysis are being developed for use on shipboard. An electrochemical technique, for example, provides a means of investigating unexplained fluoride concentration anomalies in certain parts of the deep ocean, the possible influence of submarine volcanism in causing such anomalies,

Studying dissolved gases in seawater

and the physical chemistry of fluoride ions in seawater involving complex formation by elements such as magnesium. It is now possible to detect 25 parts per 1,000,000,000 of fluoride in seawater.

The utilization of seawater trace constituents has enabled scientists to identify water masses and to trace currents. By using characteristic chemical tags of water masses, water in the Caribbean Sea has been identified as of South Atlantic origin.

Chlorinity and salinity of seawater. Determining the chlorinity of seawater is of fundamental importance to oceanography. The ratios of concentrations of several major constituents of seawater are virtually constant with the concentration of chlorinity. Of these, salinity is probably the most important.

Chlorinity is briefly defined as the number of grams of chlorine, bromine, and iodine contained in one kilogram of seawater, assuming that the bromine and iodine are replaced by chlorine. Salinity is the total weight of dissolved solids, in grams, found in one kilogram of seawater, and may be determined from the concentration of chlorinity.

Titration of chloride, the basic process for nearly all measurements of salinity in oceanographic work, is used extensively around the world, both ashore and at sea. Chlorinity is determined by adding a solution of silver nitrate of a known strength to a sample of seawater until enough is added to produce the same reaction as with standard seawater. The difference in the amounts added gives the degree of salinity. To ensure worldwide uniformity in chlorinity and salinity determinations, the International Council for the Exploration of the Sea prepared a universal reference, *Eau de Mer Normale* ("standard seawater"), in 1902. A new primary standard, prepared in 1937 and having a chlorinity of 19.381 parts per 1,000, is used to determine the chlorinities of all batches of standard seawater.

Oxygen content of seawater. The concentration of dissolved oxygen in seawater may vary from supersaturation near the surface, where photosynthetic activity by the phytoplankton is very high, to no oxygen in stagnant basins or deep fjords. The values, therefore, may be anything from zero to ten millilitres or more per litre of seawater.

The analysis for dissolved oxygen in seawater is important for numerous reasons: it aids in the interpretation of biological processes taking place in the ocean; it is finding increased use in studies of oceanic currents and mixing processes; and it is sometimes used as an index for detecting malfunctional sampling equipment and erroneous values.

Techniques and equipment of marine geology. The ocean floor has the same general character as the land areas of the world: mountains, plains, channels, canyons, exposed rocks, and sediment-covered areas. Because sound propagation is markedly affected by the ocean bottom and subbottom, extensive measurements have been made by means of an evolving series of geological or geophysical instruments of increasing precision and discrimination. These methods are providing increasingly accurate data on bottom topography and roughness that aid in understanding reflection loss at the bottom as a function of composition, roughness, frequency, and grazing angle. Investigators are using deep-ocean photography in conjunction with precision echo soundings to make detailed studies of bottom roughness and sediment structure.

Analysis and classification of marine sediments. Marine sedimentation embraces that phase of oceanography that is related to the deposition, composition, and classification of organic and inorganic material found on the ocean floor. Various sampling devices are utilized to obtain bottom sediments. Once obtained, samples are packed and shipped to a sedimentation laboratory to be analyzed and classified. Analysis of marine sediments generally includes the determination of size, shape, and percentage of component particles; identification of minerals and ratio of light to heavy minerals; wet density; pH (acidity–alkalinity); and calcium carbonate content.

The concept of standard seawater

Biological and ecological studies emphasize the animal population as well as the environmental factors determined by temperature, depth, type of sediment, and geographic location.

Bottom sediments are classified according to composition. Samples may be composed of terrigenous material (formed by the erosive action of rivers, tides, and currents), material from surface or submarine volcanoes, organic matter, inorganic material, and extraterrestrial matter. Size of the component materials may range widely, and it is used as a further, more detailed classification characteristic. From thousands of reported classifications and collected samples, bottom sediment charts are prepared (see also MARINE SEDIMENTS).

Bottom sediment charts

Geological sampling: coring devices. Marine sediments are collected by means of three basic categories of bottom samplers: coring tubes, snappers, and dredges. Coring devices are essentially steel tubes that are driven into the ocean floor. A typical coring device consists of interchangeable core tubes, a main body of streamlined lead weights, and a tailfin assembly that directs the corer in a vertical line normal to the bottom; all three components are referred to as the main weight. The amount of sediment collected by coring devices depends upon the length of the corer, size of the main weight, and penetrability of the bottom.

Designed to obtain cores up to about four feet in length, the small, lightweight Phleger corer takes only samples of the upper layers of the sea bottom. Coring tubes 12 and 36 inches in length, plus a main body weight, an upper tube, check valve, and tailfin assembly, account for an overall length of three to five feet for the Phleger corer.

Kullenberg and Ewing corers are representative of the piston corer. A closely-fitting piston attached to the end of the lowering cable is installed inside the coring tube just above the core catcher. When the coring tube is driven into the ocean floor, friction will exercise a downward pull on the core sample. The hydrostatic pressure on the ocean bottom, however, exerts an upward pressure on the core that will work against a vacuum being created between the piston and the top of the core. The piston, in effect, provides a suction that overcomes the frictional forces acting between the sediment sample and the inside wall of the coring tube. The complete assembly of the Kullenberg corer and releaser gear weighs about 400 pounds. The Ewing piston core is even larger, with coring tubes approximately 20 feet in length; one, two, or three lengths may be coupled together by connecting sleeves to obtain cores up to about 60 feet.

Small bottom samplers. Bottom samplers of the second category, clamshell snappers, are used to obtain small samples of the superficial layers of bottom sediments. They are of two general types: one, about 30 inches long and weighing about 60 pounds, is ruggedly constructed of stainless steel. The cast stainless steel snapper jaws, closed by heavy arms actuated by a strong spring and lead weight, trap about a pint of bottom material. The other type is smaller; it is called a mud snapper and is about 11 inches long and weighs three pounds. The jaws are cast bronze and are actuated by a spring.

Orange peel bucket samplers are for collecting bottom materials in shallow waters. A small hook attached to the end of the lowering wire supports the sampler as it is lowered and also holds the jaws in the open position. When contact is made with the bottom, the sampler jaws sink into the sediment and the wire tension is released, allowing the hook to swing free of the sampler. Upon hoisting, the wire takes a strain on the closing line, which closes the jaws and traps a sample.

The underway bottom sampler, or scoopfish, is designed to sample rapidly without stopping the ship. It is lowered from the bathythermograph winch in depths less than 100 fathoms (600 feet) from a ship under way at speeds not over 15 knots. The sampler weighs 11 pounds (five kilograms) and can capture samples ranging from mud to coral.

Dredges. The third major category of bottom sampler is the dredge. Bottom dredging operations require very sturdy gear, particularly when dredging for rock samples. A dredge is constructed of steel plate and is one foot deep, two feet wide, and three feet long. The forward end is open, but the aft end has a heavy grill of round steel bars that is designed to retain large rock samples. When finer sized material is sought, a screen of heavy hardware cloth is placed over the grill.

Techniques and equipment of biological oceanography. Biological oceanography is concerned with both plant and animal life in the sea. Animal life is divided into three general groups—the benthos (bottom living), the nekton (swimming), and the plankton (wanderers—the floating and drifting life). The plankton are further divided into phytoplankton (plant forms) and zooplankton (animal forms). Little is known of the life cycles of most marine life. Oceanographers are interested in the distribution of plankton populations, from both quantitative and qualitative points of view (see also PLANKTON).

Underwater sea life

Some of the most commonly used of oceanographers' samplers are plankton nets and midwater trawls. Nets have a mesh size capable of sieving micro-organisms such as zooplankton and phytoplankton from water; the trawls have a net-mesh size that permits plankton to pass through but filters out larger forms. Some nets can be used only when a ship is stopped or at anchor, while others take samples while a ship is under way. Plankton nets are further diversified in construction to allow sampling at one or several depths.

Plankton nets can be subdivided into qualitative and quantitative samplers. A qualitative sampler sieves organisms from the water without measuring the volume of water that has passed through it. A quantitative sampler does measure the volume, and hence the concentration of the organisms in a unit volume of water can be determined.

The midwater trawl is a specially designed net for rapid trawling at great ocean depths and at such a speed that active, fast-swimming fish are unable to swim out of the net once caught. Ships towing a certain type of trawl can travel as fast as five knots.

Clarke-Bumpus quantitative plankton sampler. The Clarke-Bumpus sampler is unique in that it can take an uncontaminated sample from any desired depth while simultaneously estimating the filtered volume of the seawater. The device is equipped with a flow meter to which an impeller is geared so that the number of revolutions made by the impeller can be recorded by a counter. By reading the counter, the volume of water that has passed through the sampler can be determined. A shutter opens and closes on command, admitting water and spinning the impeller while filtering out zooplankton and phytoplankton. When the impeller is stopped by closing the shutter, the sample can be raised without contamination from plankton in the overlying water strata.

The midwater trawl. To counteract the tendency of an ordinary net to surface behind the towing vessel, the Isaacs-Kidd midwater trawl (Figure 3) utilizes an inclined-plane surface rigged in front of the net entrance to act as a depressor. In form it is essentially an asymmetrical cone with a pentagonal mouth opening and a round, closed end. Within the net, an additional netting is attached as a lining. A steel ring (or rings) is fastened in the end of the net to maintain the tubular shape. A large perforated can is fastened by draw strings on the end of the net to retain the sample in a relatively undamaged condition.

Biological sound recordings. Major studies are under way on the acoustical properties and behaviour of marine organisms. Some organisms contribute to the background noise by their own acoustic signal emissions. Organisms that passively affect various electronic systems are the large mammals, schools of fish, and plankton that scatter sound and thus appear as false targets or background reverberation or that attenuate the acoustic signal.

Oceanic biologists record and analyze sounds produced by marine animals, their geographic and temporal distribution, and their behaviour as it relates to sound production. Concentrated effort has been made to identify sounds of biological origin. Some fish and invertebrates make up layers of acoustic-scattering material that may exhibit daily vertical movement related to diurnal changes in light. The acoustical and biological properties of these layers have been studied for many years by

By courtesy of Scripps Institution of
Oceanography, University of California, San Diego

Figure 3: The Isaacs–Kidd midwater trawl, designed for collecting marine specimens from waters a mile or more below the surface. The wide metal vane keeps the trawl level and at the required depth during towing.

scientists of several nations, partly because of their military importance in interfering with underwater target detection. They have made repeated examinations of the same regions of the oceans in order to discover, for example, seasonal rhythms and evidence of the geographic range of the scatterers.

Marine biology in the laboratory. The description and classification of marine organisms continues to be an active field as hundreds of new species are collected each year. Advances in biochemistry, physiology, animal be-

haviour, and other fundamentally shore-based investigations are being emphasized as new equipment and techniques evolve.

Laboratory experiments involving biochemical studies on marine plants and animals have resulted in the isolation of chemicals that have antiviral, antimicrobial, cancer-inhibiting, nerve-blocking, or heart-stimulating properties. Some of these chemicals have potential pharmacological value, as shown by biotoxins from poisonous shellfish and pufferfish that are 200,000 times more powerful in blocking nervous activity than are drugs such as curare currently used for this purpose. Recent investigations of sponges have unexpectedly revealed a unique material, an arabinosyl nucleoside, that is apparently highly effective in the treatment of certain virus infections and leukemia in laboratory animals. Other products from sponges also show a broad spectrum of antimicrobial effects.

Many sea cucumbers, starfish, and their relatives produce highly toxic mixtures of steroid glycosides, a group of chemicals that includes the powerful cardiac drug digitalis, which is obtained from a terrestrial plant. Steroid glycosides from these marine organisms have suppressed growth of several different kinds of tumour in experimental animals and may provide leads toward the chemotherapy of malignant tumours.

Potential new drugs from the sea

RECENT ADVANCES AND FUTURE TRENDS

Important oceanographic prospects lie in increased drilling and core-sampling capabilities provided by improved technology. The "Glomar Challenger" (Figure 4), a 10,500-ton vessel built on the basis of the technology available in the 1960s, can maintain an exact position for days and weeks at a time by means of an acoustical beacon dropped to the sea floor, hydrophone reception of the beacon's signals, shipboard computer calculations, and four special propulsion units. The ship is stabilized against roll by a gyroscopically controlled system, so that drillers can effectively control, even in heavy seas, the 23,000 feet of drill pipe carried. A powerful drilling derrick operates through the bottom of the ship, extracting cores of extraordinary length from depths of thousands of metres, thus making available for study clues to the

By courtesy of Scripps Institution of Oceanography, University of California, San Diego

Figure 4: "Glomar Challenger," a vessel designed for drilling and coring in the open ocean, using dynamic positioning to maintain position over the hole. Visible amidship is the drilling derrick. Below it, not visible, is the centre well, through which the bit, drill pipe, and other tools are lowered (see text).

history of oceans, climates, mountain building, volcanic eruptions, life and evolution, and the movements of sea floor and continents.

The "Glomar Challenger" used the latest navigation aids, including satellite observations and the various electro-magnetic systems such as shoran and Lorac. These have made possible the positioning of oceanographic vessels with a precision heretofore impossible.

Among the important practical benefits that promise to accumulate from more sophisticated oceanographic research are more efficient use of the potential marine food supply, new sources of pharmacological materials, and mineral resources, including not only oil and gas but hard minerals. Salt, bromine, and magnesium are already being economically extracted, and submerged placer deposits on the inner edge of the continental shelf may presently be exploited. The seabed may also yield coal, potash, phosphatic rock, iron ore, bauxite, and possibly metallic vein deposits. Coal has already been mined from onshore shafts or artificial islands off the coasts of Canada, the United Kingdom, Japan, and Taiwan. The nodules and crusts that rise in certain places in the deep ocean contain manganese, copper, cobalt, and nickel. Rich brines have been discovered on the floor of the Red Sea.

Electronic sensors, communications systems, and data storage and analysis systems are in the forefront of the new instrumentation becoming available to oceanography. Far from replacing men, however, such aids only increase man's capabilities and therefore value. Manned habitats and diver-transport systems will permit scientists to work routinely at great depths; operations at 2,000 feet appear feasible. Undersea tunnel drilling and a new technology for mating submersibles to a sea-floor shaft entrance may provide a completely independent sub-sea-floor installation for extended geophysical studies.

The immense efforts involved in the design of such submersibles as "Aluminaut," "Alvin," "Trieste," and "Deepstar" in the 1950s and 1960s demonstrated the problems and the promise of such vessels. As obstacles are overcome, the oceanographer will have increased mobility to go where he wishes, at many depths, and with greater convenience and safety.

BIBLIOGRAPHY. The classical tools of the oceanographer for probing the depths of the sea are described by H.U. SVERDRUP, M.W. JOHNSON, and R.H. FLEMING in *The Oceans* (1942). This single treatise continues to serve as the fundamental reference to which others offer supplemental material. An introduction to oceanography and marine biology is provided by R.E. COKER, *This Great and Wide Sea* (1947, reprinted 1962); CORD-CHRISTIAN TROEBST, *Der Griff nach dem Meer* (1960; Eng. trans., *Conquest of the Sea*, 1962); R.C. COWEN, *Frontiers of the Sea* (1960); JOHN LYMAN in E.J. LONG (ed.), *Ocean Sciences*, ch. 2 (1964); and HAROLD BARNES, *Apparatus and Methods of Oceanography* (1959). Exploration and discovery references are PETER FREUCHEN, *Peter Freuchen's Book of the Seven Seas* (1957); T.F. GASKELL, *World Beneath the Oceans* (1964); G.E.R. DEACON (ed.), *Seas, Maps, and Men* (1962); RACHEL L. CARSON, *The Sea Around Us*, rev. ed. (1966); JAMES DUGAN and RICHARD VAHAN (eds.), *Men Under Water* (1965); JACQUES COUSTEAU, *Le Monde du silence* (1953; Eng. trans., *The Silent World*, 1953); HARRIS B. STEWART, JR., *Deep Challenge* (1966); and the documentary of famous explorers such as C.W. BEEBE, *Half Mile Down* (1934); HANS HASS, *Wir Kommen aus dem Meer* (1957; Eng. trans., *We Come from the Sea*, 1958); OTIS BARTON, *The World Beneath the Sea* (1953); GEORGES HOUOT and PIERRE WILLM, *Le Bathyscaphe à 4.050m. au fond de l'océan* (1954; Eng. trans., *Two Thousand Fathoms Down*, 1955); JACQUES PICCARD and ROBERT DIETZ, *Seven Miles Down: The Story of the Bathyscaph Trieste* (1961); JACQUES PICCARD, *The Sun Beneath the Sea* (1971); GEORGE RITCHIE, *Challenger: The Life of a Survey Ship* (1958); A.F. BRUUN, *The Galathea Deep Sea Expedition, 1950–52* (1956); HELEN RAITT, *Exploring the Deep Pacific* (1956); JOHN STEINBECK and EDWARD RICKETTS, *Sea of Cortez* (1941; reprinted as *The Log from the Sea of Cortez*, 1963); G.F. GASKELL, *Under the Deep Oceans* (1960); and WILLARD BASCOM, *A Hole in the Bottom of the Sea: The Story of the Mohole Project* (1961). The major national and international institutions and organizations involved in undersea exploration are listed in compilations by R.C. VETTER, *International and National Organizations of Oceanographic Activities* (1959, and subsequent editions) and *An International Directory of Oceanographers*

(1964). Exploration and survey vessels in operation today may be found in a catalog updated annually by the UNITED STATES NAVAL OCEANOGRAPHIC OFFICE, *Oceanographic Vessels of the World*, and many are included in *Jane's Fighting Ships* (annual); a complete history of United States vessels used for oceanographic exploration is given in S.B. NELSON, *Oceanographic Ships Fore and Aft* (1971). The sciences of the sea are treated in detail by ALISTAR HARDY, *The Open Sea*, 2 pt. (1956), on plankton of the sea and other marine organisms; F.P. SHEPARD, *Submarine Geology* (1963); W.S. VON ARX, *An Introduction to Physical Oceanography* (1962); GUNTER DIETRICH and KURT KALLE, *Allgemeine Meereskunde* (1957); SVEN P. EKMAN, *Tiergeographie des Meeres* (1935; Eng. trans., *Zoogeography of the Sea*, 1953); C.E. ZOBELL, *Marine Microbiology* (1964); ALBERT DEFANT, *Physical Oceanography* (1961); and HILARY B. MOORE, *Marine Ecology* (1958). Modern undersea explorers are strongly dependent on innovative engineering and technology such as that treated in J.J. MYERS *et al.*, *Handbook of Ocean and Underwater Engineering* (1969); JOHN F. BRAHTZ (ed.), *Ocean Engineering* (1968); and R.L. WIEGEL, *Oceanographical Engineering* (1964). See also J.B. HERSEY (ed.), *Deep-Sea Photography* (1967). A report of the U.S. COMMISSION ON MARINE SCIENCE, ENGINEERING, AND RESOURCES, *Our Nation and the Sea* (1969), covers virtually all aspects of undersea exploration and serves as a forecast of undersea exploration for the 1970s. The UNITED STATES NAVAL OCEANOGRAPHIC OFFICE, *Science and the Sea* (1970); and periodicals, such as the following, are good sources of current events: *Sea Frontiers; Science; Undersea Technology; Offshore; Scientific American; National Geographic Magazine; Oceanology;* and *Ocean Industry.*

(A.B.R.)

Unidentified Flying Objects

Although sightings of unusual phenomena in the sky have been reported since ancient times, an extraordinary outburst of such sightings in the late 1940s and over the next two decades created a sharp scientific controversy, centred in the U.S., but extending around the globe. The term UFO, short for "unidentified flying object," was introduced in 1953 by the U.S. Air Force. An earlier term, "flying saucer," is still widely used in Australia, South America, and Europe, while in the Soviet Union the Russian equivalent of "flying sickle" is used. The term UFO is not restricted to saucer-shaped objects nor even to objects in the sky, and in general refers simply to any sighting the observer could not understand, even though it may have been later identified.

History. A series of radar detections coincident with visual sightings near the National Airport in Washington, D.C., in July, 1952, led the U.S. government to establish a panel of scientists headed by H.P. Robertson, a physicist of the California Institute of Technology, and including engineers, meteorologists, physicists, and an astronomer. The thrust of public and governmental concern was indicated by the fact that the panel was organized by the Central Intelligence Agency (CIA) and was briefed on U.S. military activities and intelligence, and that its report was originally classified Secret. Later declassified, the report revealed that 90 percent of UFO sightings could be readily identified with astronomical and meteorological phenomena (bright planets, meteors, auroras, ion clouds) or with aircraft, birds, balloons, searchlights, hot gases, and other terrestrial phenomena, sometimes complicated by unusual meterological conditions.

The publicity given to early sightings in the press doubtless helped stimulate further sightings not only in the U.S. but in western Europe, the Soviet Union, Australia, and elsewhere. A second panel organized in February 1966 reached conclusions similar to those of its predecessor. This left a number of sightings admittedly unexplained, and in the mid-1960s a few scientists and engineers, notably James E. McDonald, a University of Arizona meteorologist, and J. Allen Hynek, a Northwestern University astronomer, concluded that a small percentage of the most reliable UFO reports gave definite indications of the presence of extraterrestrial visitors.

This sensational hypothesis, already promoted in newspaper and magazine articles, met with prompt resistance from other scientists. The continuing controversy led in 1968 to the sponsorship by the U.S. Air Force of a study at the University of Colorado under the direction of

Lenticular clouds over São Paulo, Brazil, exemplify natural phenomena that can be easily mistaken for "flying saucers."
By courtesy of the Aerial Phenomena Research Organization, Inc., Tucson, Arizona

E.U. Condon, a renowned physicist. The Condon Report, "A Scientific Study of UFO's," was reviewed by a special committee of the National Academy of Sciences and released in early 1969. A total of 37 scientists wrote chapters or parts of chapters for the report, which covered investigations of 59 UFO sightings in detail, analyzed public-opinion polls, and reviewed the capabilities of radar and photography. Condon's own "Conclusions and Recommendations" firmly rejected "ETH"—the extraterrestrial hypothesis—and declared that no further investigation was needed.

This left a wide variety of opinions on UFOs. A large fraction of the U.S. public, and a few scientists and engineers, continued to support ETH. A middle group of scientists felt that the possibility of extraterrestrial visitation, however slight, justified continued investigation, and still another group favoured continuing investigation on the grounds that UFO reports are useful in sociopsychological studies. These varying views and attitudes were expressed at a symposium held by the American Association for the Advancement of Science, in December 1969.

REPORTED UFO SIGHTINGS AND EVENTS

Official records. In 1948 the U.S. Air Force began to maintain a file of UFO reports called Project Blue Book. By 1969 the project had recorded reports of 12,618 sightings or events, each of which was ultimately classified as "identified" with a known astronomical, atmospheric, or artificial phenomenon, or as "unidentified," including cases in which information was insufficient. In 1969, following the Condon Report, Project Blue Book was discontinued. The only other official and fairly complete records of UFO sightings were maintained in Canada, where they were transferred in 1968 from the Canadian Department of National Defense to the Canadian National Research Council and placed under the supervision of Peter Millman, a meteoriticist. The Canadian records totalled about 750 in 1969. Less complete records were maintained in Britain, Sweden, Denmark, Australia, and Greece, and were usually destroyed after five years.

Press reports. Press reports have been worldwide, including a number from the Soviet Union. But though such reports reflect a general public concern, they tend to emphasize the sensational and are not properly evaluated. No comprehensive summary of press reports has yet been made, but they seem to have followed an eastward-moving geographic trend starting with the first widely publicized "flying saucer" sighting in the western U.S. in 1947. Many press reports of sightings on the U.S. East Coast in the early 1950s were followed by reports from Britain, France, the Soviet Union, Australia, and on to the U.S. West Coast in the 1960s. In the 1960s there were many sightings of UFOs "taking off" from the ground,

a shift from saucer shapes to cigar shapes in the images reported, and a number of reports of effects on the electrical systems of automobiles. Many authorities believe that mass-media coverage of UFOs both stimulated more reports of sightings and encouraged a change to more dramatic events and differently shaped images. A series of feature articles in an Argentine newspaper in 1968 was promptly followed by a number of sightings in Buenos Aires and other cities.

Types of UFO reports. UFO reports varied widely in reliability, as judged by the number of witnesses, whether the witnesses were independent of each other, by the observing conditions (fog, haze, illumination, etc.), and by the direction of sighting. Typically, the witness who reported a sighting considered the object extraterrestrial in origin, or possibly a military vehicle, but certainly under intelligent control, a conclusion usually based on apparent formation-flying of multiple objects, unnatural motions seemingly centred on a target, or arbitrary alterations in direction, brightness, and motion.

That the unaided human eye plays tricks bordering on hallucinations is well known. A bright light, such as the planet Venus, often appears to move, although a clamped telescope or a sighting bar shows it to be fixed. Visual impressions of distance are also highly unreliable, being based on assumed size. Reflections from windows and eyeglasses can provide superimposed views. Optical defects can turn point sources of light into apparently saucer-shaped objects. Such optical illusions, and the psychological desire to interpret visual images, are known to account for many visual UFO reports. Radar sightings, while more reliable in certain respects, fail to discriminate between physical objects and meteor trails, tracks of ionized gas, rain, or thermal discontinuities. Even "contact events"—in which activities besides sighting were reported—have been found most frequently to involve dreams or hallucinations; the reliability of such reports depended heavily on whether there were two or more independent witnesses.

Sightings and reports may be conveniently classified in four broad categories, for each of which selected examples are given below:
1. Visual sightings in daytime (some photographed);
2. Visual sightings at night (a few photographed);
3. Radar sightings;
4. Close encounters or physical evidence.

The absence of a given explanation does not necessarily mean that the example constitutes evidence favouring the ETH. It merely means that no explanation is known.

Examples of daytime sightings. Many of these sightings have been identified with the planet Venus, from its known position in the sky.

Louisville, Kentucky, Jan. 7, 1948. At 1:15 PM the State Highway Patrol reported a flying saucer to the Godman Air Force Base, where the base commander and several other persons saw the object. A group of four USAF F-51 aircraft arrived at the base and three were directed by the control tower toward the UFO. One pilot saw it and started a rapid climb toward it; the other two fighter pilots remained behind and lost radio contact with the first just after he reported that he would climb to 20,000 feet altitude. He had no oxygen equipment and was killed when his plane crashed without further communication half an hour later. The first USAF investigation concluded that the pilot saw Venus, which was in the direction of his sighting, but later discussion suggests that it was a 100-foot "Skyhook" balloon being tested by the U.S. Navy. (This uncertainty is typical of early UFO identifications, and led to greater USAF effort in Blue Book.)

Newton, Illinois, Oct. 10, 1966, 5:20 PM CST. A woman and five children witnessed the slow passage of a metallic object past their farm home. Observing conditions were excellent, with clear, dry weather. The object was first seen by the children, ages four through nine years. The mother responded to the children's call and joined them in the yard, walking parallel with the object's motion. The object moved slowly and uniformly in a westerly direction, at walking speed, approximately 50 feet

U.S. Air Force Project

Radar sightings

above the ground. Abruptly turning its nose up and moving rapidly upward, it disappeared from sight in one or two seconds. An analysis of the reported sighting suggested a cigar-shaped spheroid approximately 20 feet long and eight feet in diameter, possibly of aluminum, with longitudinal seams, a small dorsal fin at the rear, and a rectangular, black aperture near the front. A brownish-gold design was observed on the lower rear portion. The object was surrounded by a bluish haze that contained luminous bubbles or sparks. No sound was heard except for an unusual vibrating noise perceived for a few seconds when the object was nearest.

Seventy minutes later, under dark-sky conditions, an elliptical blue light of the same colour and shape was seen moving in the same general direction by a witness seven miles from the first sighting.

Tremonton, Utah, July 2, 1952. At 11:10 AM, a Navy Chief Warrant Officer with his wife and two children was driving along State Highway 30 when they saw a group of strange white objects above the eastern horizon. The officer stopped the car, estimated that there were 12 to 14 of the objects, and photographed them for several minutes, using a 16-mm movie camera. He was sure that the UFOS were large objects at high altitude. Analysis of the film showed that they might have been sea gulls at 2,000 feet distance; at 50,000 feet they would have been moving at 300 miles per hour, executing maneuvers impossible for aircraft known in 1952.

Socorro, New Mexico, April 24, 1964. A patrolman reported that at 6 PM he sighted a "blue flame" about 2,000 feet off Highway 7A. He drove along a ranch road to within 200 feet of a 20-foot hemispherical object standing on four legs near an abandoned shack where he earlier thought he had seen two people dressed in white. As he approached, the UFO took off with a loud roar, apparently emitting a blue jet flame, and climbed in a southwesterly direction away from the highway. There were no other witnesses, although the observer had radioed another patrolman for assistance when he left the highway. After recovering from his fright, the observer located four deep impressions in the soft ground where he said the UFO stood. There were two smaller impressions where a ladder had led to a door seen by the observer.

Examples of nighttime sightings. Many of these sightings have been identified with planets, bright stars, meteors, and airplanes. Some may be explained by the refraction of light in layers of warm air hundreds of feet above the observer, allowing him to see surface lights high in the sky.

Montgomery, Alabama, July 24, 1948, 2:45 AM. A pilot and copilot in the cockpit of an airline passenger plane at 5,000 feet altitude, en route from Houston to Boston, saw a dull-red object approaching on a collision course. During the next ten seconds it veered slightly to the right, passed the plane on the right at high speed, then seemed to pull up, and disappeared in the clouds overhead. One passenger on the right side of the plane glimpsed the bright light as it flashed by. There was no disturbance of the plane. The pilots described the object as cigar-shaped, about 100 feet long, with two rows of lighted windows, a dark blue glow underneath, and a red-orange jet flame about 50 feet long behind it. They estimated the closest approach to be less than a mile. Authorities concluded that the object was probably a distant meteor.

Dexter, Michigan, March 21–22, 1966. A farmer and several of his friends reported coloured lights that landed in a swamp, where they later saw a "pyramid-shaped object" with lights rippling eerily across its surface in the dark. The next night, several girls at a nearby college reported three large coloured lights moving up and down in a "synchronized" way, and two other co-eds reported a glowing disc in the swamp.

The lights have been interpreted as glowing marsh gas, or will-o'-the-wisp. The faint, fingerlike, glowing methane is often seen low on the ground on damp nights, and is well known to result from decaying vegetation, but its appearance did not fit the large coloured balls seen "landing" in the swamp. This case was lampooned extensively by the U.S. press.

Examples of radar sightings. Radar measures the distance to a UFO and the direction, which may be affected by refraction of the radio beam in the atmosphere. Several effects can give false radar echoes: electronic interference, reflections from ionized layers or clouds, and reflections from regions of higher temperature or humidity, as in a cumulus cloud. A simultaneous radar detection and visual sighting in the same direction is the most reliable—but not certain—evidence of a physical object.

Lakenheath, England, Aug. 13, 1956, 11:00 PM–3:30 AM. Two RAF ground radar stations detected several objects moving at high speed on a clear moonlit night. One was tracked by the first radar as going at about 3,000 miles per hour westward at 4,000 feet altitude; simultaneously, tower operators reported a bright light passing overhead toward the west, and the pilot of an aircraft at 4,000 feet over the airfield saw the bright light streak westward underneath him. The second radar station, alerted by the first, detected a stationary target at about 20,000 feet altitude that suddenly went north at 600 miles per hour. It made several sudden stops and turns. After 30 minutes an RAF fighter was called in and made airborne-radar contacts with the object over Bedford (just north of Cambridge, England). Suddenly the object moved around behind the fighter plane, both being tracked by ground radar. The fighter pilot could not "shake" the object. A second plane was called in but never made contact, and all radar contacts were then lost. Several other radar targets were tracked in the same area and several other small moving lights were seen, but all disappeared at 3:30 AM.

This is believed to be one of the best established and most puzzling of the unexplained cases.

Colorado Springs, Colorado, May 13, 1967, 3:40 PM. The weather was overcast with scattered rain and sleet showers and gusty winds. As an airliner came in for a landing, the ground radar detected an object beyond it at about twice the range. As the plane landed, the object pulled to the east and passed low over the airport (at 200 feet altitude, about 1.5 miles from the control tower). The tower operators, alerted by the radar operation, saw and heard nothing. The pilot of another aircraft, three miles behind the first, saw nothing when asked to look.

Examples of close encounters or physical evidence. These include foot impressions described above in Socorro, New Mexico, circular burned patches in fields, and melted patches in road pavement, possibly due to jet take-off. It is barely possible that strong magnetic fields or plasma clouds of ions produced by a UFO could affect the electrical components of an automobile.

Methuen, Massachusetts, Jan. 20, 1967, after dark. Three people were driving northeast on a street bordered by woods, fields, and a few houses. They reported that on reaching the top of a hill they suddenly came upon a straight string of bright red lights moving along the roadside at an altitude of 500–600 feet. When they were almost broadside to the lights, which then were hovering, the object to which they were apparently attached swung around to reveal four distinct lights in a perfect trapezoid. Two red lights formed the top and two white lights formed the base. The red lights resembled a hot electric-stove burner. A reflecting metal was seen about the lights. The centre of the trapezoid was dark. When the driver pulled over to the side of the road directly broadside to the object, his car engine, lights, and radio failed completely. The driver tried to start the car again, but was unsuccessful. No noise was heard as the object began moving slowly and then shot away at great speed in a southwest direction. The driver was then able to start the car, and the lights and radio worked perfectly.

Ubatuba, São Paulo, Brazil, Sept. 10, 1957, 12 noon. Three fishermen saw a flying saucer diving into the sea at high speed. Just before reaching the water, it turned sharply upward and exploded into "thousands of fiery fragments." The fishermen picked up several of these fragments, which fell on the beach, and sent them in an anonymous letter to a Rio de Janeiro newspaper. A Brazilian government laboratory did a chemical analysis and announced that the metal was "magnesium of higher purity than attainable in purification techniques known to man." The impurities detected were zinc, strontium, and other trace metals totalling about 0.15 percent. Analysis, however, soon showed that industrial magnesium in the U.S. is a good deal purer (less than 0.002 percent impurities). The abundance of strontium was unusual, however, and may lend some weight to the claim that the Ubatuba fragments were from an extraterrestrial space vehicle.

Southern New Hampshire, Sept. 19, 1961, 11 PM to 2 AM. A couple returning to Boston via Lancaster and Concord saw a large disk-shaped object and felt obliged to stop and walk over to it. Their stories, recorded separately under hypnosis by a psychiatrist in Boston in 1964, were consistent and told of their being taken aboard the flying saucer, undressed, and examined by a group of humanoids. Later, psychologists concluded that this widely publicized case was a hallucination by the woman, transmitted to her husband so thoroughly that he "remembered" it as real, even under hypnosis.

Role of hallucination

CONTINUING ACTIVITIES

In accordance with the conclusions and recommendations from the 1969 Condon Report, the U.S. Air Force terminated its Project Blue Book study of UFOs in December 1969. Several groups of American scientists claim, nevertheless, that the UFO phenomenon warrants further study; and groups in other countries are continuing their studies of UFOs. These studies are of three types:

1. Detailed analysis of reported cases similar to the examples cited above, often called "soft data" because they depend on the reliability of witnesses. The goal is to identify new physical phenomena or to confirm the extraterrestrial hypothesis.

2. Systematic collection of "hard data" by networks of cameras, or radar sets or other instruments that cover a broad area nearly 100 percent of the time without the questionable reliability of eyewitnesses. The goal is often associated with studies of meteors, auroras, or other atmospheric phenomena.

3. Statistical studies of past reports to establish definite psychological and sociological patterns. The duration of the UFO phenomenon—over 20 years—puzzles psychologists because mass hysteria has never been so long enduring or so widespread.

It is claimed by many experts that type 1, detailed analyses of soft data, will not produce new information, although some scientists hold that an exceptionally good sighting may occur and lead to significant conclusions.

Instrumental developments. There are at least two new instrumental developments than can provide hard data for type 2 studies: "all-sky" camera networks and TV cameras in artificial satellites. The first of these is typified by the Prairie Meteorite Network of 64 automated cameras in groups of four at 16 stations spaced about 140 miles (225 kilometres) apart to cover about 500,000 square miles (1,500,000 square kilometres) of the U.S. Midwest centred on Steinauer, Nebraska. This network is operated by the Smithsonian Astrophysical Observatory in Cambridge, Massachusetts, for the purpose of observing meteors and locating meteorites soon after impact. Each camera is programmed to make four three-hour exposures each night, and the 9x9-inch film (totalling 3.6 acres per year) is quickly scanned for nearly straight meteor tracks. Except for about 200 films used in connection with the Condon Report to check UFO reports, the Prairie Network films have not been scanned for irregular UFO tracks or images, a job that would require at least 30 persons working full time.

Single all-sky cameras, photographing about 80° down from the zenith on all sides, are used for broad sky-brightness measures but do not have sufficient resolution to detect UFOs. A large number were operated by international cooperation during 1957–58, and two or three are operated continuously in Czechoslovakia. The Canadians started operating a meteorite network similar to the Prairie Network in 1970, but their films have not been scanned for UFOs.

The National Aeronautics and Space Administration operates several artificial satellites equipped with optical TV cameras that radio image-data to ground-based receivers.

Prairie Meteorite Network

Two sets of satellites record cloud patterns for weather prediction, and they might detect bright, high UFOs. Other optical satellites used for astronomical observations look outward and have a very small chance of detecting small objects. Similarly, the telescopes used by astronomers at observatories all around the world have little chance of photographing a passing UFO.

Two radar networks covering most of the United States and Canada are operated jointly by the U.S. and Canadian (civilian) Aviation Administrations and by the North American (military) Air Defense Command. Together, they track every airplane, balloon, rocket, satellite, or other moving object; but the task of sorting out UFOs from full-time records of the millions of other objects tracked each day would require an expensive and very special computer. It is probable that most of the radar targets not associated with scheduled aircraft, known balloon launches, and known rocket firings would be thunderstorms, air currents, and other complex meteorological phenomena; and a systematic search for UFOs would require hundreds of weather specialists.

Statistical studies. The statistical studies of type 3 could be undertaken by psychologists if the UFO reports filed by Project Blue Book or other groups are systematized and recorded on punch cards or tape for use in an electronic computer. The difficulty here lies in the wide variety and incomplete nature of UFO soft data. None of the files contains *all* sightings, and the record of any one sighting usually omits several points of significance to sociological or psychological studies.

The sample of over 12,000 sightings is, however, large enough so that in the early 1970s psychologists were planning to sort the records into broad categories that could be statistically corrected for incompleteness and used to study mass hysteria, hysterical contagion, and possible causes of hallucination. Some of the hallucinations associated with UFO reports may be related to the so-called Isakower syndrome, wherein a drowsy person visualizes scenes of his remote past, which would account for apparitions and misidentifications.

Response of the public. Psychologists are also interested in the strong emotions aroused by UFOs among the witnesses who sighted them, the public who read about them, and the scientists who evaluate reports. In addition to defending the validity of their reports, witnesses are usually somewhat "shaken" by their sightings, a reaction similar to that of religious experiences. The witnesses, however, are seldom active in organizing UFO study groups or in writing books and articles.

Public reaction ranges from excited curiosity to ridicule. The excitement is probably related to the extraterrestrial hypothesis, exemplified by the strong public interest since 1900 in possible intelligent life on Mars. Some of the emotion may derive from religious beliefs about terrestrial man's place in the universe or from ancient myths about the supremacy of angels over ordinary men. It often involves fear of extraterrestrial visitors.

The evidence for these psychological reactions is displayed in the 50 books and over 250 magazine articles written in the U.S. about UFOs since the first flying saucer was reported in 1947. U.S. public interest was indicated by some 30 UFO clubs and societies that sprang up in the 1950s and '60s. There were signs that this public interest was diminishing following publication of the Condon Report and the termination of Project Blue Book in 1969. The number of newspaper articles on UFOs significantly declined to a fraction of its peak of 1966.

The reaction of physical scientists has been centred on reluctance to change their systems of belief based on current physics and astronomy. The basic philosophical question raised by UFO reports is one of reality. Because of the confusing variety of evidence and the doubtful reliability of most reports, it has been difficult to apply accepted criteria of physical reality to UFOs themselves, but the psychological UFO phenomenon is certainly real.

BIBLIOGRAPHY. L.E. CATOE, *UFOs and Related Subjects: An Annotated Bibliography* (1969), a very complete list of books and magazine articles published since 1950, with descriptive comments on each; E.U. CONDON, *Scientific Study of Unidentified Flying Objects*, ed. by D.S. GILLMOR (1969), a lengthy and poorly organized collection of chapters written by 36 members of the University of Colorado project, including detailed studies of 59 cases and reviews of 32 others, plus appendices reprinting earlier governmental reports and private studies; J. JASTROW, *Error and Eccentricity in Human Belief* (1963), a historical summary of popular misconceptions; CARL JUNG, *Ein moderner Mythus* (1958; Eng. trans., *Flying Saucers: A Modern Myth of Things Seen in the Sky*, 1959), a sociopsychological analysis; D.H. MENZEL and L.G. BOYD, *The World of Flying Saucers* (1963), an attempt to explain the wide variety of reports in terms of astronomical and meteorological phenomena, including many case descriptions and some physiological explanations; T. PAGE and C. SAGAN, *Physics and Psychology of UFO's; Proceedings of the AAAS Symposium, Boston, 1969* (1970), a collection of 15 speeches on various aspects of UFOs, including expert analyses of photographs, radar detections, hallucinations, meteorological effects, extraterrestrial life, press reporting, and many unexplained cases; E.J. RUPPELT, *The Report on Unidentified Flying Objects* (1956), a summary of unexplained reports received by the U.S. Air Force over eight years; JULES and J. VALLEE, *Challenge to Science: The UFO Enigma* (1966), a survey of reports that are difficult to explain in terms of natural phenomena.

(T.L.P.)

Uniformitarianism

Uniformitarianism is a point of view held by scholars who accept the principle of the uniformity of nature as a basis for their investigations. This principle has been stated in many ways, most commonly in the form, "The present is the key to the past." In the context of the history of science, uniformitarianism is the name of a geological doctrine that developed in opposition to the doctrine of catastrophism during the late 18th century and thereafter. The meaning and usefulness of the principle of uniformity, no less than the identification and analysis of points at issue during the debate between the uniformitarians and the catastrophists of the 19th century, are matters on which no consensus has yet been reached.

Sir Charles Lyell (1797–1875) was the leader of the uniformitarian school of geological thought in the last century. His monumental *Principles of Geology* (3 vol., 1830–33) was based upon the hypothesis that "the ancient changes of the animate and inanimate world, of which we find memorials in the Earth's crust, may be similar both in kind and degree to those which are now in progress." William Whewell (1794–1866), reviewing the second volume of the *Principles* in 1832, conceded that the same *kinds* of geological changes now in action, namely those related to erosion and deposition of sediment and to dislocations attending earthquakes, apparently have operated in the distant past. But he questioned the assumption of uniformity in the average *rates* of changes past and present. "Have the changes which have led us from one geological state to another been, on a long average, uniform in their intensity," Whewell asked, "or have they consisted of paroxysmal and catastrophic action, interposed between periods of comparative tranquility? These two opinions will probably for some time divide the geological world into two sects, which may perhaps be designated as the Uniformitarians and the Catastrophists." Because catastrophism was the more popular view in the 1830s, it is useful to examine that doctrine first, in order to identify the issues that the uniformitarians were attacking.

The doctrine of catastrophism. The catastrophism of the early 19th century gained much of its authority and respectability from the writings of the French scientist and statesman Georges Cuvier (1769–1832). A master of vertebrate paleontology and comparative anatomy, Cuvier made detailed studies of the large quadrupeds whose bones are preserved in strata of Cenozoic age around Paris. In the younger alluvial deposits he found remains of rhinoceros, hippopotamus, tapir, elephant, and mastodon. With the exception of the mastodons, Cuvier could classify most of these fossils as exinct species of modern genera. The underlying and older strata of Tertiary age, however, yielded remains of pachyderms and other vertebrate animals that belong to extinct genera. In the alternating deposits of marine and freshwater origin, which are characteristic of the Tertiary System in the Paris Basin, Cuvier found, moreover, that each forma-

The views of Cuvier and Buckland

tion has its distinctive suite of vertebrate fossils. To explain these discontinuities in the record of ancient life, Cuvier invoked the agency of recurrent catastrophies.

As envisioned by Cuvier, the catastrophic episodes that divided the history of the Earth into chapters were brief, convulsive, and lethal. Sudden changes in the level of land and sea were attended by the upheaval and dislocation of strata to form ranges of mountains, by the flooding of continents, and by abrupt changes of climate. Whole races of organisms were supposedly wiped out; terrestrial animals drowned, and marine life was left stranded as parts of the ocean's floor were uplifted. Following each convulsion, the normal order of nature was restored and the Earth was repopulated by organisms that had somehow survived the ordeal. Cuvier estimated that the last catastrophe took place 5,000 to 6,000 years ago when a deluge covered all areas previously inhabited by man. The few surviving men and other animals then propagated and spread over the lands left dry after this flood subsided.

In England William Buckland (1784–1856) was the leading geologist of the 1820s and the chief advocate of catastrophism. Buckland's investigations concentrated upon the vertebrate fossils which he collected from the Kirkdale Cave of Yorkshire and more than 20 other caves in England and on the Continent. Buckland collected a Quaternary fauna that included bones of hyenas, lions, tigers, elephants, and hippopotamuses. He interpreted the layers of clastic sediment covering the uppermost bone beds as aqueous deposits laid down by Noah's flood. This most recent catastrophe was but one example in Buckland's mind of many such convulsions that left their records in the rocks and that offer "proofs of an overruling Intelligence continuing to superintend, direct, modify, and control the operations of the agents which He originally ordained." The belief that the normal operations of nature have been repeatedly suspended by direct intervention of a supernatural agency was one of the tenets of catastrophism that the uniformitarians specifically rejected.

A second point at issue revolved around the doctrine of progressive development of organic species. This doctrine was based on the paleontological evidence that lower orders of life are preserved as fossils in the oldest strata and are followed by progressively higher orders in successively younger rocks. Invertebrate animals evidently appeared on the Earth long before the vertebrates; in the vertebrate succession the oldest were fishes, after which came in turn the amphibians, reptiles, mammals and birds, and finally man. Many catastrophists interpreted this record as the unfolding of a divine plan. Following the destruction of numerous species during catastrophic episodes they held that the Earth was replenished with new and higher forms of life. The doctrine of progressive development was supported by many outstanding geologists of the 19th century, including W.D. Conybeare, Hugh Miller, Roderick Murchison, and Adam Sedgwick. To the extent that successive creations implied supernatural interventions, the uniformitarians rejected the doctrine on principle, but for many years Lyell also denied the evidence that the doctrine was intended to explain.

In the catastrophist view, the folded and fractured strata of mountain chains, in which former marine sediments now stand thousands of metres above sea level, seemed to call for forces greater by many orders of magnitude than any manifest in nature today. "Do not vertical strata prove rapid elevation?" Whewell asked. Great thicknesses of coarse sandstone, conglomerates, and breccias, which occur at intervals throughout the stratigraphic column, were taken as evidence for ages of violent aqueous action. Beds in which the fossilized remains of marine animals and terrestrial plants were mingled seemed to attest the destructiveness and confusion of paroxysmal events. Whole mountains of igneous rock exist, and the magma that formed these masses must have burst through the Earth's crust. The widespread veneer of alluvium upon the continents was thought to record the force of the last great deluge, which also excavated gorges and canyons as the waters subsided.

Uniformitarianism according to Hutton, Playfair, and Lyell. The initial thrust of Lyell's attack upon catastrophist geology, beginning in 1830, was directed against the proposition that the natural course of events that followed the creation of the Earth has been interrupted time and again by supernatural causes. Lyell was willing to concede that the earth was divinely created, but he insisted that the subject of "first causes" lay beyond the reach of geology. If the reconstruction of the Earth's history is to be pursued on scientific grounds, geologists are constrained to invoke only secondary and naturalistic causes: the causes presently in operation.

One of the prejudices that has persistently retarded the progress of geology, Lyell contended, is the tendency to undervalue greatly the duration of geologic time. Compressing a lengthy sequence of geological events into a span of time that is unreasonably short can indeed cause these to unfold in a manner that might seem miraculous.

We should be warranted in ascribing the erection of the great pyramid to superhuman power, if we were convinced that it was raised in one day; and if we imagine, in the same manner, a mountain chain to have been elevated, during an equally small fraction of the time which was really occupied in upheaving it, we might be justified in inferring that the subterranean movements were once far more energetic than in our own times. We know that one earthquake may raise the coast of Chile a hundred miles to the average height of about five feet. A repetition of two thousand shocks of equal violence might produce a mountain chain one hundred miles long and ten thousand feet high. Now, should only one of these convulsions happen in a century, it would be consistent with the order of events experienced by the Chileans from the earliest times; but if the whole of them were to occur in the next hundred years, the entire district must be depopulated, scarcely any animals or plants could survive, and the surface would be one confused heap of ruin and desolation.

The above quotation well illustrates Lyell's method. To account for the origin of some geological phenomenon or some feature of the landscape he appealed to processes now operating in a modern geographic setting. By assuming that these same processes will operate over long intervals of time, he showed how these might produce results similar to the phenomena under investigation.

For example, it is not uncommon to find in Mesozoic and younger strata certain sequences in which fossilized parts of terrestrial animals and plants are mingled with the remains of marine organisms. Those sequences were sometimes interpreted by the catastrophists as evidence of supranatural convulsions. As a more reasonable if less spectacular alternative, Lyell suggested that strata of this kind must today be forming off the delta of the Mississippi River. He described how this great river, during its stages of flood, annually sweeps into the sea:

sand and finer matter . . . together with the wreck of countless forests and the bones of animals which perish in the inundations. When these materials reach the Gulf of Mexico, they do not render the waters unfit for aquatic animals; but on the contrary, the ocean here swarms with life. . . . Yet many geologists, when they behold the spoils of the land heaped in successive strata, and blended confusedly with the remains of fishes, or interspersed with broken shells and corals . . . . they read in such phenomena the proof of chaotic disorder, and reiterated catastrophes, instead of indications of a surface as habitable as the most delicious and fertile districts now tenanted by man.

Deep valleys excavated in solid rock were often cited by the catastrophists as evidence of the torrential scouring action exerted upon the land by the retiring waters of the Noahian Deluge. Lacking any evidence to the contrary, Lyell assumed that these valleys had been cut by the long-continued erosive action of the streams that now occupy them. Thus, to explain the gorge below Niagara Falls, Lyell appealed to the recurrent undermining of the limestone lip and the sweeping away of the fallen debris by the river below. Historical reports indicated that the falls had receded upstream by about 50 yards (46 metres) during a period of 40 years. At this rate of recession, he argued, nearly 10,000 years would have been required for the excavation of the gorge above Queenstown, seven miles (13 kilometres) downstream. Lyell later increased his earliest estimate of the age of the gorge more than threefold but regarded all figures for age as no more than

approximations, subordinate to the general proposition that "the river supplies an adequate cause for executing the whole task thus assigned to it, provided we grant sufficient time for its completion."

Lyell's uniformitarian method owed much to the writings of his predecessors, James Hutton (1726–97) and John Playfair (1748–1819) in particular. Hutton's *Theory of the Earth*, published first as an essay in 1788 and expanded to a two-volume work in 1795, developed the idea that the Earth functions essentially as a heat machine. The agents of erosion, particularly streams, wear down the continents over long periods of time. The sediments spread from the wasting continents are periodically upheaved to form new continents by the expansive force of subterranean heat. These new or rejuvenated continents in turn waste away until the next cycle of uplift and deformation. In the record of the rocks, Hutton saw an apparently endless sequence of such cycles that afforded "no vestige of a beginning, no prospect of an end." Although he was willing to concede that the Earth was divinely created as an abode suitable for man and other organisms, he invoked no supernatural causes to explain the workings of the terrestrial heat machine once it had been set in motion. As for the length of time that has elapsed since the world was formed, Hutton was only certain that it must be vast beyond human comprehension. "Time," he wrote, "is to nature endless and as nothing." Playfair, in his *Illustrations of the Huttonian Theory of the Earth* (1802), summarized, elaborated upon, and defended Hutton's views in a work of grace and clarity.

Lyell incorporated into his synthesis Hutton's views on the immensity of geologic time, the idea that past changes in the configuration of the Earth can be explained in terms of natural causes now in action, and the idea that great changes in the Earth's configurational aspects may be accomplished by a series of small changes operating over long periods of time. Unlike Hutton, Lyell held that the elevation of continents and the formation of folded mountain chains were accomplished no less gradually than the wearing down of the continents by erosion.

19th-century debate. Lyell's uniformitarian synthesis was attacked on theological, philosophical, and scientific grounds. Most of the counterarguments are summarized in Whewell's *Philosophy of the Inductive Sciences* (2nd ed., 1847). Whewell insisted that there must be "a Providential as well as a Natural Course of Things." The assumption that known causes have always operated at their present rates is philosophically unsound and scientifically suspect.

Whether the causes of change do act uniformly;—whether they oscillate only within narrow limits;—whether their intensity in former times was nearly the same as it now is;—these are precisely the questions which we wish Science to answer to us impartially and truly. . . .

The theory of constant change through virtually infinite time is untenable because the Earth cannot be a perpetual motion machine, regardless of whether the motive power be mechanical or chemical. The paleontological record unequivocally shows that in the course of geological history hosts of new species have appeared in an orderly succession, but nothing in the Lyellian theory can explain the creation of new species by "causes now in action."

Despite these and other criticisms, Lyell did not yield. In two successive presidential addresses delivered before the Geological Society of London in 1850 and 1851, he defended the position that he had set forth 20 years earlier in the first edition of his *Principles*. Granting that the deformation of strata in the Alps is spectacular, he argued that it is no more intense, nor more extended geographically, than may be observed in mountain chains that were deformed far earlier in geologic time. There is no evidence to be drawn from folded mountains, therefore, that the Earth's orogenic energy has diminished with time. Granted that deposits of rounded pebbles measuring more than one kilometre in thickness have been found in the Alps, do not deposits of this kind require long periods of time for their accumulation if each pebble is to be rounded by attrition before its burial? As for the "theory of successive development of organisms," Lyell questioned both the adequacy of the empirical evidence offered in support of it and the progressionist interpretation of this evidence. The fossil record is so incomplete and so little known that it affords no conclusive evidence as to the time when the major groups of plants and animals first appeared on the Earth, he argued. Fossilized remains of birds, for example, are paleontological rarities in general; for this reason it cannot be deemed impossible to find birds in strata as old as the Carboniferous. Even accepting the record as it stands, there is no evidence of progressive development: the conifers of the Carboniferous were as highly organized as any in the plant kingdom; the marine invertebrate animals of the Silurian were as perfect as their counterparts in existing seas; and the record of mammals during the Tertiary Period shows no advance from earliest Tertiary times to the present.

Significance of organic evolution
As the debate between the uniformitarians and catastrophists developed, the question as to the progressive development of organisms through time became the central issue. Lyell's position, as originally stated in the early 1830s and long maintained thereafter, was that organic species are stable, susceptible to extinction, but incapable of alteration. This viewpoint was shaken when, in April of 1856, Charles Darwin first outlined his hypothesis of natural selection to Lyell in a private conversation. Four years later, following the publication of the Darwin-Wallace papers on natural selection in 1858 and Darwin's *Origin of Species* in 1859, Lyell confessed in his private journal that Darwin's hypothesis seemed more probable than the theory of miraculous creation. But nine more years were to pass before Lyell would become a confessed convert, at the age of 72, to Darwin's theory of evolution.

Much has been written about Darwin's indebtedness to Lyell and the doctrine of uniformitarianism, but it is important to recognize that strict Lyellian uniformitarianism was at the outset anti-evolutionary. Naturalism, gradualism, and the long scale of geological time were the ingredients of uniformitarianism that were essential to Darwin's synthesis. The evolution of organic species through the mechanism of natural selection substituted causes now in action for supernatural causes. Darwin denied great and sudden changes in the modification of organic species, preferring to believe that major changes in the organic world are the summation of a host of minute mutations. This gradualism, in turn, required a very long, if indefinite, span of geological time.

Against the catastrophists and the uniformitarians, who were prodigal of time despite their doctrinal differences, William Thomson (Lord Kelvin, 1824–1907) launched an attack beginning in 1862. Kelvin revived, this time in formidable mathematical terms, Whewell's contention that the Earth could not be a perpetual motion machine. Kelvin's argument rested upon two interrelated assumptions: the heat of the Earth is residual from its original molten state, and the matter of the Earth is chemically inert. Reasoning from the laws of thermodynamics, Kelvin concluded in 1899 that the Earth is probably no older than 24,000,000 years. Kelvin's estimates were soon discredited by the discovery of radioactivity, which in turn led to the dating of terrestrial events as ancient as 3.5×10^9 years.

Modern status of uniformitarianism. The guiding principle of uniformitarianism, the principle of the uniformity of nature, is somewhat ambiguous. As S.J. Gould has pointed out, most of the many and diverse formulations of the uniformity principle fall into two classes: those *Substantive versus methodological uniformity* descriptive of the history of nature (substantive uniformity) and those descriptive of the procedures by which scientists investigate the history of nature (methodologic uniformity). Lyell's assumption that the laws of nature are unchanging through time and space is procedural or methodologic. On the other hand, his assertion that the rates of geologic change through time also are invariant over the long term is a substantive statement, subject to testing like any other scientific hypothesis.

Certain critics maintain that substantive uniformitarianism is disproved: theoretically on the ground that the terrestrial heat machine cannot have maintained a steady state throughout the 4.6×10^9 years or so during which the Earth presumably has been in operation, and empirically on the ground that the paleontological record shows wide variations in the rate of extinction and generation of species through time. Methodologic uniformitarianism, it has been asserted, is no more than the logical principle of simplicity applied to the causes of geologic change: naturalistic causes of change, other than those in operation at present, should not be invented without necessity. In other words, substantive uniformitarianism is outmoded and methodologic uniformitarianism is common to all scientific investigation and not unique to geology.

It is unlikely that these criticisms will be acceptable to all scientists and philosophers of science. Substantive uniformitarianism can no longer be entertained in any authoritarian sense but will probably continue to serve as a point of departure in arriving at first approximations of the time required for the deposition of sedimentary formations, the development of landforms, and the origination of other geological features. Methodologic uniformitarianism, in G.G. Simpson's terms, is the proposition that the inherent properties of matter and energy throughout the universe remain constant through time and space. So stated, this principle seems basic to the historical sciences: astrohistory, geohistory, and biohistory.

BIBLIOGRAPHY. R. HOOYKAAS, *The Principle of Uniformity in Geology, Biology, and Theology* (1963); C.C. ALBRITTON (ed.), *The Fabric of Geology* (1963). See especially the essays, "Theory of Geology," by D.B. KITTS and "Historical Science," by G.G. SIMPSON. The indexed and annotated bibliography by the editor includes most of the basic references on uniformitarianism. C.C. ALBRITTON (ed.), "Uniformity and Simplicity: A Symposium on the Principle of the Uniformity of Nature," *Spec. Pap. Geol. Soc. Am. 89* (1967); C.C. GILLISPIE, *Genesis and Geology: A Study in the Relations of Scientific Thought, Natural Theology, and Social Opinion in Great Britain, 1790–1850* (1951); CHARLES LYELL, *Scientific Journals on the Species Question*, ed. by L.G. WILSON (1970); G.G. SIMPSON, "Uniformitarianism: An Enquiry into Principle, Theory, and Method in Geohistory and Biohistory," in M.K. HECHT and W.C. STEERE (eds.), *Essays in Evolution and Genetics in Honor of Theodosius Dobzhansky* (1970); S.J. GOULD, "Is Uniformitarianism Necessary?", *Am. J. Sci.*, 263:223–28 (1965). Classical references include: JAMES HUTTON, *Theory of the Earth*, 2 vol. (1795); JOHN PLAYFAIR, *Illustrations of the Huttonian Theory of the Earth* (1802); CHARLES LYELL, *Principles of Geology*, 3 vol. (1830-33); and WILLIAM WHEWELL, *Philosophy of the Inductive Sciences*, 2nd ed., vol. 1, pp. 665–700 (1847), a summary of the catastrophist counterattack against uniformitarianism.

(C.C.A.)

Unitarians and Universalists

Unitarians and Universalists are religious groups who trace their heritage to certain unorthodox theological views in the early church and the Reformation period. They formed their respective churches in Hungary, Romania, and Poland in the 16th century and in England, the United States, and other countries in the 18th and 19th centuries. Believing that God is One, they deny the deity of Christ and the doctrine of the Trinity.

Unitarian or Unitarian-Universalist churches exist today in three regions: North America, Britain, and central Europe, with only a few small groups elsewhere. The International Association for Liberal Christianity and Religious Freedom (founded in 1900) links them with liberal churches and with liberal groups within other churches, notably in Holland, Switzerland, West Germany, Czechoslovakia, India, and Japan. Universalist churches are found mainly in the United States; in 1961 they merged with the Unitarians to form the American Unitarian Universalist Association.

There are about 1,100 Unitarian-Universalist congregations in the United States, Canada, and Iceland; about 300 in the British Isles, including the allied Non-Subscribing Presbyterian Church of Ireland; 250 in Hungary, Romania, Czechoslovakia, and West Germany; and about 100 elsewhere. Membership totals perhaps 300,000, but like-minded groups, in the International Association, bring the number to over 2,000,000. Unitarians assert that there are many members of orthodox churches who are "Unitarian without knowing it."

Though their views have been influenced by past development and change, modern American Unitarians see themselves as freed from tradition and committed to open inquiry and to advancing scientific truth, rather than to Christian origins. Unitarians in other lands view themselves similarly, but are more attached to a liberal Protestant tradition. They believe that religion is universal rather than specifically Christian, and their International Association includes liberal non-Christians in India and Japan.

Historical development. *Unitarian and Universalist views in the early church.* The New Testament contains a variety of doctrines about the status of Jesus Christ. One of them is that he was a man adopted by God to proclaim the coming kingdom. The Ebionites, an early Jewish-Christian sect that called Jesus the Son of man and the true prophet, believed that he was a man who was miraculously endowed and who became the Messiah ("annointed one") because he obeyed the Jewish law. Several early Christian theologians (*e.g.*, Clement of Alexandria and Origen) of the 2nd and 3rd centuries—who were influenced by Middle Platonism with its concern (mainly religious) for the problem of the one and the many; *i.e.*, what is really one—viewed God as the Eternal One and Christ as the divine Logos ("Word") who was the image of God and who enabled man to become one with God. Arius, a 4th-century priest of Alexandria, in teaching that Christ was the Son of God only as a created being and not coequal or coeternal with God, precipitated the Arian controversy; his views (declared heretical at the Council of Nicaea in 325) became, for a time, the official theology in the eastern Roman Empire and among the Goths. But Athanasius, the orthodox opponent of Arius, said that a subordinate Christ could not save man. The ecumenical councils of Nicaea and Chalcedon (451) firmly established the doctrine of the Trinity and the doctrine that Christ was the God-man. Thus, Arianism, an early form of Unitarianism, was anathematized (formally denounced) by the orthodox bishops.

Origen, the great Alexandrian theologian of the 3rd century, taught that all would be restored to God on the Last Day, a prefiguring of Universalism. But orthodoxy eventually affirmed the finality of heaven and hell, and the concept of the universal restoration (or the *apokatastasis pantōn*) was held to be heretical, though other early Christian theologians as individuals taught that there would be a universal salvation.

Unitarianism in the Reformation period. Most Reformers (*e.g.*, Luther, Calvin, Zwingli) reaffirmed Christian orthodoxy, but there were also liberal, radical, and rationalist Reformers who extended their ideas. Devout Italians, in a revival of Platonism (a Greek philosophical system), exalted reason (the *logos*) as the divine spark in man. Declared heretics, they fled from the Roman Catholic Inquisition to Calvin's Geneva, but there found a Protestant orthodoxy that was equally strict. Michael Servetus, a Neoplatonic Unitarian—*i.e.*, one who denied the Trinity because of an acceptance of the ineffable One as the basis of reality—was burned at Geneva in 1553. His death caused Sebastian Castellio, a liberal humanist, to plead for religious toleration. Others who denied the Trinity were burned or exiled. Some Anabaptists (radical Reformers) also were anti-Trinitarian. In the midst of these controversies, such Reformers as Kaspar Schwenckfeld urged latitude in religion.

Some Italians found refuge in Poland, then a land of toleration, where the Minor Reformed Church (Polish Brethren) with a Unitarian theology was founded in 1565. Inspired by Faustus Socinus, an Italian exile who arrived at Cracow in 1579, the minor church flourished for half a century. The Polish Socinian Church was destroyed in the 17th century by the Counter-Reformation. Its exiled ministers and nobility and its publications (*Bibliotheca Fratrum Polonorum*, 8 folio vols., Amsterdam 1656/1665–69) influenced radical thought in Holland and England.

Unitarianism (or anti-Trinitarianism) became influen-

tial in Transylvania, the eastern portion of the old Kingdom of Hungary, under the encouragement of Georgius Blandrata (or Giorgio Biandrata), an Italian court physician to the Polish-Italian bride of the king, John Sigismund (died 1571). He encouraged Ferenc Dávid, bishop of the Reformed Church in Transylvania and court preacher—who had been successively Catholic, Lutheran, and Calvinist—to preach anti-Trinitarian sermons. In 1568, at the Diet of Torda, the king granted wide religious toleration, one of the earliest such toleration decrees in Christian history, and Dávid became head of the Unitarian churches. Three years later the Unitarians were granted legal recognition. In opposition to Blandrata, however, Dávid denied that prayers could be addressed to Christ, and after a trial and conviction as an innovator, he died (1579) in prison. His church still exists. It is the world's oldest Unitarian Church. Its congregations were divided after World War I into two separate organizations—one in Hungary and the other in Romania—as a result of the Treaty of Trianon (1920) that divided the old Austro-Hungarian Empire.

Unitarianism in the British Isles. An English translation of the Polish Socinian catechism was publicly burned in London in 1614 and 1652, and John Biddle, an English Socinian, was exiled to the Scilly Isles. Under the English monarchs Elizabeth and James I some Unitarian Anabaptists were burned, and later General Baptists adopted unorthodox views of Christ that were similar to those of Unitarians. Also, some Anglican clergy published Unitarian pamphlets, arousing controversy within the Anglican Church, leading to the Arian theology of Samuel Clarke, who denied the essential divinity of Christ.

The mainstream of British Unitarianism, as of American, however, grew out of Calvinist Puritanism. Calvin's doctrine of the absolute providential rule of God, the scientist Isaac Newton's picture of a mathematically regular universe, and the philosopher John Locke's plea for common sense and open discussion greatly influenced the Presbyterian, or "moderate," party among the Dissenters in the English Church. They preached God as the sole creator and ruler of the world, best worshipped by a moral life, with Christ as his messenger, whose authority was authenticated by his miracles and resurrection—the so-called Arian scheme. Many Dissenting preachers, challenged to define their faith in orthodox terms, would use only the words of Scripture, which gave them greater freedom. But the evangelical revival, led by John Wesley, caused a renewal of orthodoxy, and the Dissenters split into orthodox and liberal factions.

Joseph Priestley, a scientist and Dissenting minister, began to preach overt "Unitarian Christianity": Jesus as man, though unique in his miracles and resurrection; God as all-powerful and all-knowing; the primacy of reason and morals; and scientific determinism, materialism, and political reform. Many old Presbyterian congregations, diminished in number by the success of the evangelical (or Methodist) revival initiated by John Wesley, became Unitarian. Other groups joined them: Anglican reformers at Cambridge University, vainly petitioning Parliament to relax "subscription" in the Church of England—including Theophilus Lindsey, who in 1774 opened a Unitarian chapel in London with a modified Anglican liturgy modelled on that of Samuel Clarke; some General Baptists, resisting an evangelical revival in 1770; and some early 19th-century seceders from Methodism. The English Unitarians—by the early 19th century a small body struggling against penal laws that were enacted against heresy and nonconformity—were strong in Parliament, local government, the professions, and social reform. In 1825 they established the British & Foreign Unitarian Association. Their tenure of Puritan chapels and endowments was challenged in the courts. Though some were lost, the rest were saved by the Dissenters' Chapels Act (1844), which recognized tenure and change.

In Scotland in the 18th century, leaders of the national (Presbyterian) church were liberal, encouraging the English Arians; later, however, came an orthodox revival. The few Scottish Unitarian churches were of radical

Margin notes:

Arius and Arianism

Unitarianism in eastern Europe

The rise of English "Unitarian Christianity"

origin. In Ireland the former Presbyterian clergyman Thomas Emlyn suffered persecution as a Socinian; and in 1725 and 1828 trouble over "subscription," or acceptance of the Westminster Confession of faith (of 1646) in the Presbyterian Church led to the founding of the Non-Subscribing Presbyterian Church of Ireland, with an Arian doctrine.

Crisis in English Unitarianism

About 1840 a crisis arose among English Unitarians; Priestley's rationalism was challenged by a new leader, James Martineau, who pleaded for deeper feeling, and for a faith based on intuition rather than on argument and the Bible. He opposed the name "Unitarian" as sectarian and divisive, preferring "Free Christian," or even "Presbyterian." He wanted comprehension within a liberal national church, not denominational propaganda. Partly as a result of Unitarian efforts, penal laws were repealed, and many Unitarians became prominent in commerce and public life. The latter half of the 19th and early part of the 20th centuries was, for Unitarians, an age of church building, large congregations, and social idealism. In 1928 the two English Unitarian groups (the denominationalists and the liberals) were united in the General Assembly of Unitarian and Free Christian Churches.

Unitarianism in the United States. American Unitarianism developed more slowly out of the Congregational churches of eastern Massachusetts, which rejected the revivalism of the 18th-century preachers George Whitefield and Jonathan Edwards. Over against the revivalists, some Congregational ministers preached moderation, stressing reason and morals, and were protected from controversy by congregational autonomy. Charles Chauncy, for 60 years minister of the First Church, Boston, led in deprecating controversy. In 1783 King's Chapel, Boston (Episcopal), became Unitarian, with a modified Anglican liturgy like Lindsey's in London. Unitarian congregations were organized at Portland and Saco (Maine) in 1792. In 1803 conflict arose between liberals and conservatives over the appointment of a professor of theology at Harvard University, and unwillingly the moderates found themselves labelled Unitarian. Legal battles over church property left the Unitarians in possession of churches founded by their Puritan ancestors in and around Boston. In 1825, on the same day as its

The founding of the American Unitarian Association

British counterpart, the American Unitarian Association was founded, with headquarters in Boston. The American Unitarian Church thus founded claims five presidents of the United States and many leading figures in literature, education, social reform, and public life.

As in England, there was a theological crisis about 1840. William Ellery Channing of Boston challenged the orthodox doctrine of the atonement and taught the loving fatherhood of God. Sparked by the "Divinity School Address" (1838) of Ralph Waldo Emerson, the Transcendentalist Movement, the so-called flowering of New England, shook American Unitarianism and exploded beyond it. It shattered rationalist, biblical Unitarianism— now grown conservative—and replaced it with intuitional religion and social idealism. When Unitarianism spread to the newly opened Middle West, its religious fundamentals changed to human aspiration and scientific truth, rather than Christianity and the Bible. In 1866 a Free Religious Association was founded to assert free thought over against the conservative Boston tradition. In 1900 the Americans took the lead in founding the International Association for Liberal Christianity and Religious Freedom. In the 1920s "humanism"—a nontheistic, antisupernatural Unitarianism—arose and influenced even those Unitarians who did not accept it. Fellowships, informal groups with lay leadership, were founded in almost every American state and among Americans abroad. In 1961 Unitarians merged with Universalists in a new united church, the American Unitarian Universalist Association.

Universalism in America and in Britain. Universalism (a belief in the final restoration of all things to God, and a denial of everlasting hell) was first preached in America by George de Benneville, a French mystic who came to America in 1741, and his disciple Elhanan Winchester, and by the former English Methodist John Murray,

who founded the first Universalist Church in 1779. Murray was a follower of the Welsh revivalist preacher James Relly, who taught that all men will be saved because they share the holiness of Christ. The teaching was partly Calvinist, partly mystical. Hosea Ballou gave American Universalism its definitive form: belief in the fatherhood of God, the brotherhood of man, the moral authority of Jesus, and earthly life as a time of perfecting man for heaven. In 1830-60 Universalism had much popular success, challenging the hellfire preaching of orthodox revivalism. Universalist churches were founded in many states, and also in Scotland and Japan. Elhanan Winchester founded a Universalist Church in London in 1793, and made missionary journeys in southern England. He was succeeded by William Vidler, who allied with the Unitarians. Another English Universalist group, the Freethinking Christians, also was Unitarian. Universalist ideas spread among British Unitarians. There was also an unsuccessful revolt against "eternal punishment" in the Church of England in the mid-19th century.

The Unitarian-Universalist merger, 1961. In the 19th century, U.S. Unitarians and Universalists shunned one another; they used different religious terminologies, and appealed to different social groups. As viewed by one another, Unitarians were "insufficiently Christian," and Universalists "made light of sin." But they came to have similar ideas about God, Christ, man, and social reform, and learned to cooperate. After negotiation, a merger took place in 1961 establishing the American Unitarian Universalist Association. The Universalists were legally organized on a state basis and the Unitarians in geographical regions that did not coincide, but this difficulty was solved. It was soon overshadowed by the demands of black militant Unitarians for radical social change in the U.S., appealing with some success to the liberal idealism of Unitarians and Universalists.

Beliefs, practices, and organization. Among Universalists and Unitarians there is no official formula of belief, and much variety. Development of beliefs, as already noted, went through several stages—Neoplatonic mysticism, Socinianism, moderate Calvinism, the Arian scheme, Priestley's moralistic determinism, and Martineau's intuitionism. In America there was a development from liberal Congregationalism to Channing's optimism, and on to Transcendentalism, to the Unitarianism of the Middle West, based on moral idealism rather than solely upon the Bible, and then to humanism. A great change came in the 19th century when, in Martineau's words, Unitarians came to see God "not as First Cause prefixed to the scheme of things, but as Indwelling Life pervading it" (his preface to the 2nd ed. of J.J. Taylor, *A Retrospect of the Religious Life of England*, 1876); one result of this view is the Unitarian concept of humanism, which is agnostic about God and emphasizes the human condition and scientific progress. According to the U.S. Unitarian historian E.M. Wilbur, Unitarian history shows a steady drive toward freedom, reason, and tolerance. Unitarians have been especially responsive to the spirit of the age in which they live, and have been leaders and transmitters of current thought. They vary from liberal-traditional to extreme modernist. Though humanism is widely accepted, many Unitarians and Universalists, especially outside the U.S., are theistic and Christian. Most German Unitarians are humanists.

Stages of Unitarian and Universalist belief

All have inherited Protestant (Calvinist and Anglican) forms of worship, but some experiment considerably. Transcendentalism, as a movement within U.S. Unitarianism, produced many fine hymns, now in many English-language Christian hymnbooks. Of the Christian sacraments, Baptism is usually practiced as a simple dedication of infants, and the Lord's Supper is celebrated by the more traditional Unitarians and Universalists as a memorial. Preaching is especially important, and in some groups a lecture is the dominant part of the meeting. Besides the Bible, the sacred scriptures of other religions and other inspiring writings are often used.

In polity, most Unitarians and Universalists are congregational; each congregation is self-governing, uniting with others in district and national assemblies on a voluntary basis. The Irish churches follow a presbyterian form of church government under a general synod, and the churches in Hungary and Romania are headed by bishops, each with a lay curator. The International Association for Religious Freedom (so named since 1969) is purely consultative.

BIBLIOGRAPHY. The literature on this subject is quite extensive. See N.R. BURR, *A Critical Bibliography of Religion in America*, 2 vol. (1961), which also refers to Britain. Standard works are: E.M. WILBUR, *A History of Unitarianism*, 2 vol. (1946–52), covering all countries; R. EDDY, *Universalism in America*, 2 vol. (1884–86); and s. KOT, *Socinianism in Poland* (1957; orig. pub. in Polish, 1932). C.W. REESE (ed.), *Humanist Sermons* (1927), should also be consulted. Recent English works include: C.G. BOLAM *et al.*, *The English Presbyterians, from Elizabethan Puritanism to Modern Unitarianism* (1968); and K. TWINN (ed.), *Essays in Unitarian Theology* (1959). See also current denominational yearbooks, national and international.

(H.L.S.)

United Arab Emirates

Seven tiny emirates strung out along the eastern Persian Gulf coast of the Arabian Peninsula together form the United Arab Emirates (Ittiḥād al-Imārāt al-ʿArabīyah). Formerly known as the Trucial States, Trucial Oman, or the Trucial Sheikhdoms, they are bordered by Qatar on the northwest, Saudi Arabia on the west and south, and Oman on the east and northeast. Most of the union's area of 32,300 square miles (83,650 square kilometres) is occupied by Abu Dhabi, which lies along the mainland coast. The six other emirates are clustered on the Ruʾus al-Jibāl that separates the Persian Gulf from the Gulf of Oman; they are Dubai, Ajman, Sharjah, Umm al-Qaiwain, Ras al-Khaimah, and Fujairah. The total population of some 197,000 is concentrated on the peninsula and along the coast. Upon formation of the union, in 1971, the town of Abu Dhabi was chosen as the national capital for a period of five years, after which a new capital would be built on the border between Abu Dhabi and Dubai emirates.

Physical features
The landscape and environment. Nearly the entire union is desert, containing broad patches of sand and numerous salt flats. Along the eastern portion of the peninsula, the northern extension of the al-Ḥajar mountains offers the only other major relief feature. Steep on all sides, the mountains rise to 10,000 feet (3,000 metres) in some places. The Persian Gulf coast is broken by shoals and dotted with islands that offer shelter to small vessels. There are, however, no natural deepwater harbours. The coast of the Gulf of Oman is more regular, and there are three natural harbours: Dibbah, Khawr al-Fakkān, and Kalbāʾ.

The climate is hot and dry. Rainfall averages only three to four inches annually, and the summer heat may reach 114° F (46° C) in some places. The mean January temperature is 65° F (18° C), while in July it reaches 92° F (33° C). In midwinter and early summer seasonal winds known as the *shamāl* blow from the north and northwest, bearing dust and sand.

Because of the desert climate, vegetation is scanty and largely limited to the low shrubs that offer forage to nomadic herds. In the oases, date palms are raised together with alfalfa. Food grains include wheat, barley, and millet. Fruits are popular, and al-Buraymī oasis in Abu Dhabi is famous for its mangoes. Animal life is mostly restricted to domesticated camels, sheep, and goats. The gulf waters offer schools of mackerel, groupers, tuna, and porgies, as well as sharks and occasional whales.

The people. Most of the union's 185,000 inhabitants are Arabs who adhere to the Sunnī and Shīʿah sects of Islām. Many of the Bedouins who once roamed the interior in search of pasturage for their flocks have migrated to the towns. In the al-Ḥajar mountains are several groups of isolated peoples, including the Shiḥūḥ. A blue-eyed people of unknown origin, the Shiḥūḥ live in caves, practice subsistence agriculture, and are nominal adherents of Islām. The national language of the United

Arab Emirates is Arabic. The towns contain immigrant populations from India, Pakistan, and Iran.

Most of the population is concentrated in the towns of the peninsula. They include Dubayy (Dubai town), ash-

Settlements

United Arab Emirates, Area and Population				
	area		population*	
	sq mi	sq km	1968 census	1971 estimate
States (*emirates*)				
Abu Dhabi	26,000	67,350	46,000	...
Ajman	100	250	4,000	...
Dubai	1,500	3,900	59,000	...
Fujairah	450	1,200	10,000	...
Ras al-Khaimah	650	1,700	24,000	...
Sharjah	1,000	2,600	31,000	...
Umm al-Qaiwain	300	800	4,000	...
Total	32,300	83,650†	180,000†	197,000

*De jure. Total area includes 2,300 sq mi (5,957 sq km) not accounted for in state areas.   †Figures do not add to total given because of rounding.
Source: Official government figures; UN.

Shāriqah (Sharjah town), ʿUjmān (Ajman town), and Umm al-Qaywayn (Umm al-Qaiwain town) on the Persian Gulf and Dibbah, Khawr al-Fakkān, and Kalbāʾ on the Gulf of Oman. Towns in Abu Dhabi include Abū Ẓaby (Abu Dhabi town) on an island off the coast, aṭ-Ṭarīf on the coast, and al-Buraymī oasis near the border with Oman. A new group of towns known as al-ʿAyn was constructed in the oasis in the late 1960s.

The economy. The union's economy is dominated by the oil boom in the Abu Dhabi and Dubai emirates. The richest of the emirates is Abu Dhabi, which is also the richest political unit per capita in the world. With a population of about 70,000, it had an income in 1972 of $420,000,000.

Oil was first discovered in Abu Dhabi in 1958. The largest concessions are held by the Abu Dhabi Marine Areas Ltd. (ADMA), which is owned by British and French interests. One of the main offshore fields is located in Umm Shaif, 80 miles (130 kilometres) into the Persian Gulf and 20 miles from Dās island. The field is connected by a submarine pipeline to the separating facilities, storage tanks, and tanker berths on the island. The field at Zakhum (Zakum), 40 miles southeast of Umm Shaif, is also joined by pipeline to Dās. Al-Bunduq offshore field is shared with neighbouring Qatar but is operated by ADMA. A Japanese company has struck oil at Mubarraz, 70 miles west of Abu Dhabi town, and other offshore concessions are held by United States companies.

Oil reserves

Onshore oil concessions are held by the Abu Dhabi Petroleum Company, which is owned by Iraqi, United States, and Canadian interests. Bab Dome field at Murban, 60 miles southwest of Abū Ẓaby, and the Bū Ḥassah field, 25 miles southwest of Murban, are connected by pipeline to aẓ-Ẓannah on the coast. Other onshore concessions are held by Japanese companies.

In the early 1970s Dubai had one offshore oil field at Fateh. Operated by a United States company and its subsidiary, the Dubai Petroleum Company, it is known as the Three Pyramids of Dubai. The oil is pumped into three steel storage tanks placed on the seabed that are shaped like inverted champagne glasses. By the early 1970s, oil had not been discovered in the other emirates.

A national oil company was proposed in the early 1970s. It would be funded by the union government and public subscription and would distribute oil products, run a proposed petrochemical complex, and attain oil concessions of its own.

Agriculture is concentrated in the two mountain enclaves of Ajman and in the mountains of Fujairah. The Arid Lands Research Centre at Saʿdīyāt, Abu Dhabi, experiments with the raising of vegetables in the desert with water obtained from a desalinization plant. There are also agricultural projects at al-Buraymī oasis and in Ras al-Khaimah. Marine fishing at Umm al-Qaiwain is fairly extensive; it is proposed that the fisheries be developed on an industrial level.

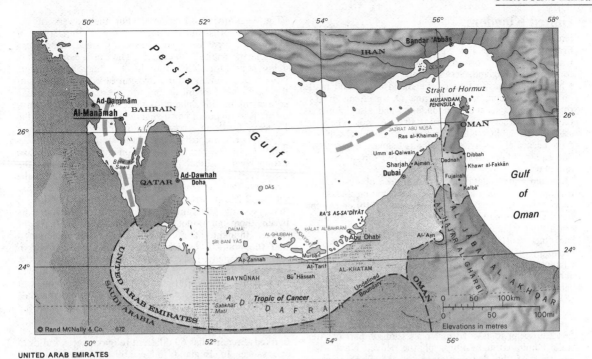

UNITED ARAB EMIRATES

There is little industry in the union. The five oilless states, especially Ajman, produce stamps mainly for philatelists. Boats and fish traps are built in Ajman, and there are ship-repair facilities at ash-Shāriqah; but plans existed in the early 1970s to develop Dubayy industrially with factories, assembly plants, and a possible dry dock for oil tankers.

Upon formation of the union there were two currencies in circulation—the Bahrain dinar in Abu Dhabi and the Qatar-Dubai rial elsewhere. In the early 1970s the creation of a Gulf dinar, at par with the Bahrain dinar, was proposed. There is no central bank, and numerous banks, mostly foreign-owned, were licensed by the individual emirates.

Trade
patterns

Trade is important in Dubai and Sharjah. Dubayy is a free port on the Persian Gulf. Its creek has been dredged, and a modern harbour has been built nearby at Port Rashīd that is equipped with 15 berths and 12 transit sheds. Sharjah's trade centres upon the port of Khawr al-Fakkān on the Gulf of Oman. It is a centre for the smuggling of gold from the United Kingdom to India and Pakistan.

Exports are dominated by oil, more than 40 percent of which is sold to western Europe and 20 percent to Japan. Imports include foodstuffs and beverages, machinery, building materials, fuel and oil, arms and ammunition, drilling materials, and consumer goods. Major trading partners are Japan, the United Kingdom, Switzerland, the United States, India, West Germany, Pakistan, China, The Netherlands, and Hong Kong.

Transportation. There are no railways in the union, and the developing road system is concentratred along the coast. Abū Ẓaby is linked to the mainland by a bridge that is then connected to al-ʿAyn and al-Buraymī oasis by a four-lane highway. In the early 1970s construction was under way to connect Abū Ẓaby to Dubayy with an 80-mile road and to connect the capital to Qatar. There were also proposals for a road that would run across the mountains from the Gulf of Oman to the Persian Gulf and for a 40-mile coastal road on the east to Oman. Air services are provided by the airports at Abū Ẓaby, Dubayy, and ash-Shāriqah.

Govern-
ment
structure

Administration and social conditions. The union government was still developing in the early 1970s. The highest governmental authority is the Supreme Council, which is composed of the rulers of the seven emirates. The president, vice president, and premier of the union are appointed by the Supreme Council. A proposed Cabinet is to serve as the executive branch of the govern-

ment; it also is to be appointed by the Supreme Council. The proposed legislature will be composed of eight members each for Abu Dhabi and Dubai, six members for Sharjah and Ras al-Khaimah and four members for each of the remaining emirates. Abu Dhabi's armed forces are to form the nucleus of the union's army.

Education is free, and facilities are to be developed by the former Abu Dhabi Education Ministry. Medical services are concentrated in Dubai, which contains four hospitals and four child-welfare clinics. Hospital services are free; there is little private medical practice, and most people are treated in hospital out-patient clinics. The union set a goal of one doctor for every 1,000 people, to be reached by the mid-1970s; most of the doctors will be expatriates. There are also two small hospitals in Ajman and a medical mission in Sharjah.

Cultural life. The union has declared itself part of the greater Arab world, and its culture is that of Islām. The people are divided into tribal groups united under the patriarchal emirates of each of the union members.

The news media are concentrated in Dubayy. There is one Arabic weekly newspaper and two daily news bulletins printed in English. The Ṣawt as-Sāḥil (Voice of the Coast) broadcasts daily radio programs from Dubai in Arabic and English. Television programs are received in Dubai from Kuwait and are rebroadcast to the other union members.

Prospects for the future. A group of poor, separate emirates in the 1950s, the union members are now joined together for both administrative and development purposes. The wealth of Abu Dhabi and Dubai is to be shared among all the emirates, and the continued flow of oil promises a rapid entry into the 20th century. Long-range problems centre about current economic planning: the union intends to develop trade and industry, rather than continuing its reliance on a diminishing resource. Along with economic development, the Supreme Council was working out plans in the early 1970s that would also encompass progress in health, education, and welfare services. If controlled economic planning continues, it is hoped that the union will present the world with a model of cooperation toward the advancement of all.

BIBLIOGRAPHY. For general works, see DONALD HAWLEY, *The Trucial States* (1970); and JOHN G. LORIMER, *Gazetteer of the Persian Gulf, Omān, and Central Arabia,* 2 vol. (1908–15, reprinted 1970). CLARENCE MANN, *Abu Dhabi: Birth of an Oil Sheikhdom* (1964), reveals the impact of petroleum on the economy of the region.

(Ed.)

United Kingdom

Situated in northwestern Europe, lying to the north of France and west of The Netherlands and Denmark, the United Kingdom comprises Great Britain (the island consisting of England, Scotland, and Wales) and Northern Ireland (that portion of the island of Ireland made up of the six counties of Antrim, Down, Armagh, Tyrone, Fermanagh, and Londonderry, and also known as Ulster), together with numerous small islands. The total area of the United Kingdom (known popularly, if not quite accurately, as Britain) is 94,512 square miles (244,-786 square kilometres), including 1,190 square miles of inland water.

England and Scotland, it has often been observed, were fortunate in being ruled by centralized monarchies from very early times; and the United Kingdom still enjoys the benefits attributed to a constitutional monarchy. In modern history what Shakespeare described as "this scept'red isle" has resisted invasion by Spain, France, and the Germany of Adolf Hitler. Its "moat" is the English Channel. As islanders, none of whom lives more than about 75 miles from the coast, the British have, over the centuries, taken naturally to the sea. This circumstance has made of them a nation of overseas venturers who, in their time, have held in fee India and the Spice Islands. An English navigator, James Cook, was the first European to take formal possession of part of Australia, and Arthur Phillip, of the Royal Navy, was governor of the first settlements there. English-speaking peoples now control the vast resources of North America, and in the 19th and early 20th centuries large parts of Africa were within the British colonial system.

The British Empire and Commonwealth

During the 20th century the British Empire has been converted into a self-governing Commonwealth, and the Commonwealth finally into independent political units. One of the greatest imperial experiments in the history of the world has thus been changed into a free association of peoples. Britain stood alone again as an island off the northwest of Europe until 1971, when the decision of its Parliament to join the European Economic Community seemed to many to open for it a new destiny.

Britain's economy is remarkable for the fact that it has to import the vast majority of its raw materials. Coal, agricultural products, and traces of iron ore are its only indigenous wealth, for the value of gas and oil from North Sea drilling is still uncertain. Since its population (some 55,000,000 in the early 1970s) constitutes one of the biggest import markets for food and other essentials, there is a perpetual struggle to export sufficient goods to balance the external-payments account. In the 18th and 19th centuries Britain was among the first of the European countries to undergo an industrial revolution, which brought with it a leadership in the field of commerce and industry. It also brought a train of social problems, to the solution of which a state sickness- and unemployment-insurance system, first introduced by the Liberal statesman David Lloyd George in 1911, and a free health service and education system are contributing.

Apart from the events surrounding the political separation of Ireland in the early 20th century, Britain, since the Middle Ages, has had one major civil war, that of the mid-17th century in the time of Charles I and Oliver Cromwell. This, with the subsequent settlement made when William III replaced James II in 1689, decided that the British monarchy should be constitutional and not dictatorial.

The British constitution is largely unwritten. Also, there is no separation of the powers (that is, of the legislature and executive), a concept that the United States Constitution, for example, derived from the 18th-century French philosopher Charles-Louis de Montesquieu. The British legislature and the executive mix freely together, ministers sitting and answering for their policy in both Houses of Parliament. The government can be overturned by an adverse vote in the House of Commons. The judiciary remains independent, the judges being irremovable except through age. One exception is the Lord Chancellor, who sits as chairman of the House of Lords and speaks on behalf of the government, of which he is a member.

The legislature is bicameral, but the powers of the House of Lords, once equal to those of the House of Commons, have been cut drastically since the controversies early in the 20th century. The Lords can now only delay a bill for a few months, but they have unique powers of amendment and revision of bills. Members of the Lords are hereditary and life peers, the latter being equivalent in this sphere to aldermen in local government. Recent attempts further to reform or abolish the House of Lords have come to naught.

The unwritten constitution of the United Kingdom depends for its proper functioning on the existence of two strong rival political parties. These are at present the Conservative and Labour parties. Earlier in history, the Conservatives, or Tories, and the Whigs, later to develop into the Liberal Party, were in rivalry. It has been proved that a strong government and a strong opposition between them guarantee the preservation of liberty of speech, thought, action, and worship. It is understood that the political parties have certain fundamentals in common, namely, respect for the monarchy, care for the defense of the realm, the maintenance of personal liberty through the system of habeas corpus, whereby no one can be kept in prison without trial, and the principle of equality before the law. There is also broad agreement on the main aspects of social policy.

Two-party government

As the Neapolitan admiral Francesco Caracciolo remarked, England has 60 different religious sects, but only one sauce. In England the established church is the Church of England, of which the Queen is head; in Scotland the established church is the Presbyterian Church of Scotland. In Wales and Northern Ireland there is no established church. The Roman Catholics are well represented numerically, and there is a variety of free churches: Congregational, Baptist, Unitarian, and Quaker. The only specific clerical representatives in Parliament are the bishops of the Anglican Church, who sit in the House of Lords.

The characteristics of the British constitution derive primarily from England, because historically England conquered and to some extent imposed its institutions on Wales and Ireland. Scotland, united with England under one monarchy from 1603 and joined in full constitutional union since 1707, has kept certain of its own distinctive practices, especially in the field of law. All of its four component countries have brought to the United Kingdom traditions of vigorous independence of thought, speech, and worship. Scotland's sons have made a vast contribution to the island's history, and Edinburgh, the Scottish capital, called the Athens of the North, was, in the 18th and early 19th centuries, particularly prominent as a centre of literature and the arts. Britain's long association with Ireland has provided the larger country with a series of great statesmen and soldiers, such as Viscount Castlereagh, foreign secretary after the Napoleonic Wars, and the Duke of Wellington, victor of Waterloo. When the Irish Free State became independent in 1921, the majority of the peoples of the six northern counties wished to remain as part of the United Kingdom and were provided with their own government at Stormont. The Welsh have contributed much to British artistic life, especially in connection with music; and their coal helped to further the Industrial Revolution and Britain's economic power.   (Bu.)

(The article that follows provides sections on the landscape of the United Kingdom, the people, the economy, transportation systems, administrative and social conditions, and on cultural life. There are also separate articles under the titles ENGLAND; NORTHERN IRELAND; SCOTLAND; and WALES concerned with characteristics peculiar to those component parts of the United Kingdom. There are also articles on the major cities of the United Kingdom. History is covered in the article BRITAIN AND IRELAND, HISTORY OF.)   (Ed.)

The land

Great Britain, the island comprising England, Scotland, and Wales, forms, together with numerous smaller islands, an archipelago that is as irregular in shape as it is diverse in its natural heritage. This latter circumstance stems largely from the nature and disposition of the underlying rocks, which are westward extensions of European structures, with the shallow waters of the Strait of Dover and the North Sea concealing former land links. Northern Ireland—which politically completes the United Kingdom—is a westward extension of the rock structures of Scotland, breached by the narrow North Channel. Northern Ireland, too, has a very diverse natural environment.

On a global scale, this natural endowment covers a small area—approximating that of Oregon, in the United States, or the African nation of Guinea—and its internal diversity, accompanied by rapid changes of often beautiful scenery, may perhaps convey to visitors from larger countries a striking sense of compactness and consolidation. The peoples who, over the centuries, have made their way to, and hewed an existence from, this Atlantic extremity of Eurasia have put their own imprint on the environment, with the ancient and distinctive palimpsest of their field patterns and settlements complementing the natural diversity.

THE NATURAL ENVIRONMENT

Topography. The traditional division of Great Britain into a Highland and Lowland zone is still meaningful. A line running from the mouth of the River Exe, in the southwest, to that of the Tees, in the northeast, is a crude expression of this division. The course of the 700-foot contour, or of the boundary separating the generally older rocks of the north and west from the younger southeastern strata, provide more appropriate indications of the extent of the Highlands.

The Highland zone. Even in terms of geological time, the creation of the Highlands was a long process, yet altitudes, compared with European equivalents, are low, with the highest summit, Ben Nevis, only 4,406 feet (1,342 metres) above sea level. In addition, the really mountainous areas above 2,000 feet often lie in smooth profiles against the changing skies, reminders of the effects of former periods of erosion.

Scotland's three main topographic regions follow the northeast to southwest trend of the ancient underlying rocks. The northern Highlands and the Southern Uplands are separated by the intervening rift valley, or subsided structural block, of the Central Lowlands. The core of the Highlands is the elevated, worn-down surface of the Grampians, 2,000–3,000 feet above sea level, with the Cairngorm Mountains rising to over 4,000 feet. This majestic mountain landscape is furrowed by numerous wide valleys, or straths, and occasional large areas of lowland, often fringed with long lines of sand dunes, add variety to the east. The Buchan peninsula, the Moray Firth estuarine flats, and the plain of Caithness—all low-lying areas—contrast sharply with the mountain scenery and show more mellow outlines than do the glacier-scoured landscapes of the west, where northeasterly-facing hollows, or corries, separated by knife-edge ridges and deep glens, sculpture the surfaces left by erosion. The many freshwater lochs further enhance a landscape of wild beauty. The linear Glen More, where the Caledonian Ship Canal now threads a chain of lakes, is the result of a vast structural sideways tear in the whole mass of the Northwest Highlands. To the northwest of Glen More stretch most of the counties given over to agricultural small holdings, or crofts; settlement is intermittent and mostly coastal, a pattern clearly reflecting the pronounced dissection of a highland massif that has been scored and plucked by the Ice Age glaciers. Many sea-drowned, glacier-widened, river valleys (fjords) penetrate deeply into the mountains, the outliers of which rise from the sea in stately, elongated peninsulas or emerge in hundreds of offshore islands.

In comparison with the northern Highlands of Scotland, the Southern Uplands present a more subdued relief, the land nowhere rising above 2,790 feet. The main hill masses are the Cheviots, which rise to 2,676 feet, while Merrick and Broad Law reach just above the 2,700-foot contour line. Broad plateau surfaces, separated by numerous dales, are again characteristic of these uplands, and in the west most of the rivers flow across the prevailing northeast-southwest trend, following the general slope of the plateau, toward the Solway Firth. Bold masses of granite and the rugged imprint of former glaciers occasionally impart a mountainous quality to the scenery. In the east, the valley network of the Tweed and its many tributaries forms a broad lowland expanse between the Lammermuir and Cheviot Hills.

The Central Lowlands are bounded by great regular structural faults. The northern boundary with the Highlands is a wall-like feature, but the boundary with the Southern Uplands exhibits a linear topographic form only near the coast. This vast trench is by no means a continuous plain, for high ground—often formed of sturdy, resistant masses of volcanic rock—meets the eye in all directions, rising above the low-lying areas that flank the rivers and the deeply penetrating estuaries of the Firth of Clyde and the Firth of Forth.

In Northern Ireland, structural extensions of the Scottish Highlands reappear in the generally rugged mountain scenery and in the peat-covered summits of the 2,240-foot Sperrin Mountains. The uplands of County Down and County Armagh are the western continuation of the Southern Uplands but rise only in limited areas over 500 feet, the one important exception being the Mourne Mountains, a lovely cluster of granite summits, the loftiest of which, Slieve Donard, rises to 2,796 feet within two miles of the sea. Compared with that of the Scottish Central Lowlands, Northern Ireland's structure has been complicated by the outpouring of basaltic lavas to form a huge plateau, much of which is occupied by the shallow Lough Neagh, the largest freshwater lake in the British Isles.

The Highland zone of England and of Wales consists, from north to south, of four broad upland masses: the Pennines, the Lake District, Wales, and the South West Peninsula. The Pennines are usually considered to end in the north along the River Tyne gap, but the surface features of the Northumberland Fells are in many ways similar to those of the northern Pennines. The general surface of the asymmetrically arched backbone (anticline) of the Pennines is remarkably smooth, because many of the valleys, though deep, occupy such a small portion within the total area that the windswept moorland between them appears almost featureless. This is particularly true of the landscape around Alston, in Cumberland, which, cut off by faults on its north, west, and south sides, stands out as an almost rectangular block of high moorland plateau with isolated peaks (known to geographers as monadnocks), rising up above it. Farther south, the Pennine plateau is cut into by deep and scenic dales, their craggy sides formed of Millstone Grit, beneath which lie streams stepped by waterfalls. The most southerly part of the Pennines is a grassy upland, in places over 2,000 feet above sea level, but it is characterized by the dry valleys, steep-sided gorges, and underground streams and caverns of a limestone-drainage system rather than the bleak moorland that might be expected at this altitude. At lower levels, the larger dales are more richly wooded, the trees standing out against a background of rugged cliffs of white-gray rocks. On both Pennine flanks, older rocks disappear beneath younger layers, and the uplands merge into flanking coastal lowlands.

The famous Lake District, celebrated in poetry by William Wordsworth and the other "Lake poets," is an isolated, compact mountain group to the west of the Pennines. The tough slate rocks of the northern portion have been cut into many deep gorges, separated by narrow ridges and sharp peaks. Greater expanses of level upland, formed from thick beds of lava and the ash thrown out by ancient volcanoes, are found to the south. Although Scafell Pike, at 3,210 feet, and Helvellyn, at 3,117 feet, are high for Britain, the volcanic belt is largely an irregular upland, traversed by deep, narrow valleys. Nine rivers, flowing out in all directions from the centre of this uplifted dome, form a classic radial drainage pattern. The valleys, often occupied by long, narrow lakes, have been

---

The Tees–Exe Line

Landscapes of the Scottish Highlands

Northern Ireland extensions of the Scottish Highlands

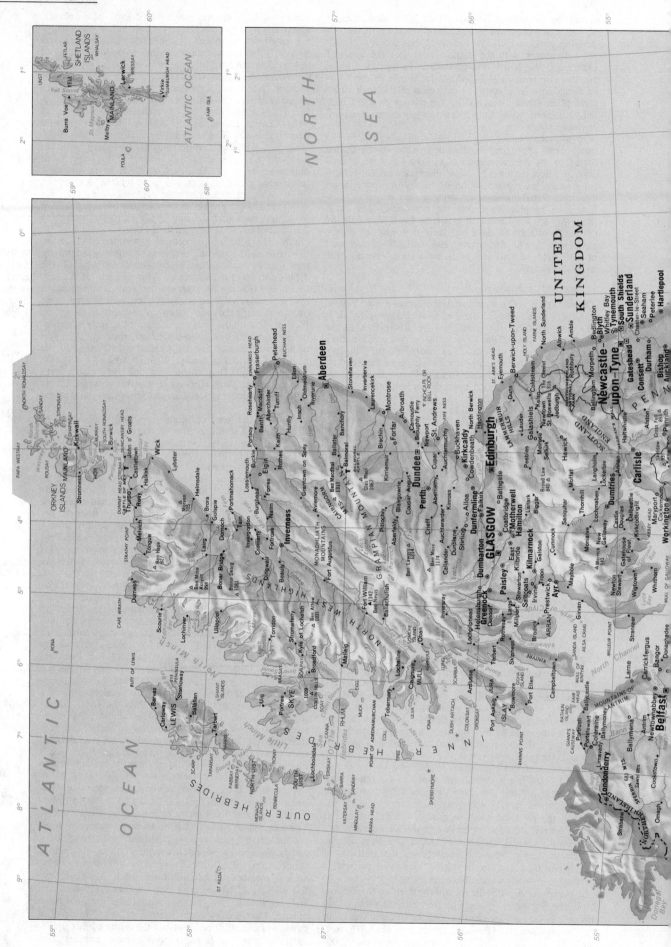

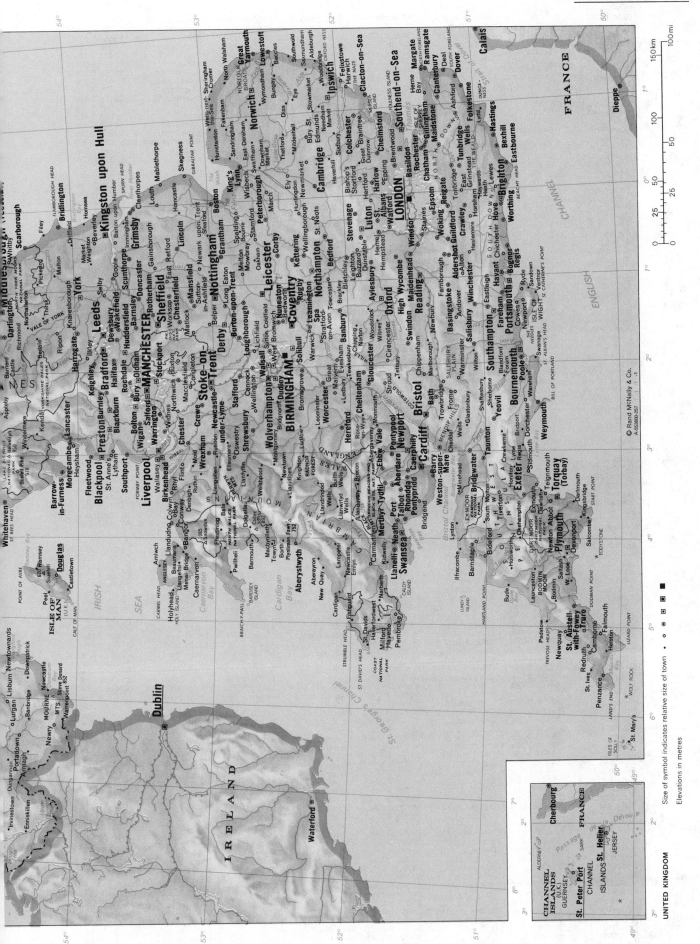

Size of symbol indicates relative size of town

Elevations in metres

UNITED KINGDOM

CHANNEL
ISLANDS (U.K.)
GUERNSEY,
St. Peter Port
CHANNEL
ISLANDS St. Helier

MAP INDEX (continued)

Melton Mowbray..52·46n 0·53w
Melvich..........58·33n 3·55w
Menai Bridge.....53·14n 4·10w
Merthyr Tydfil.....51·46n 3·23w
Middlesbrough (Teesside).......54·35n 1·14w
Mildenhall........52·21n 0·30e
Milford Haven.....51·40n 5·02w
Millport...........55·46n 4·55w
Minehead........51·13n 3·29w
Moffat.............55·20n 3·27w
Mold.............53·10n 3·08w
Moniaive.........55·12n 3·55w
Monmouth........51·50n 2·43w
Montgomery......52·33n 3·03w
Montrose.........56·43n 2·29w
Morecambe.......54·04n 2·53w
Morpeth..........55·10n 1·41w
Motherwell.......55·48n 4·00w
Nairn.............57·35n 3·53w
Narberth..........51·48n 4·45w
Neath.............51·40n 3·48w
Needham Market..........52·09n 1·03e
Newark upon Trent............53·05n 0·49w
Newbury..........51·25n 1·20w
Newcastle........54·12n 5·54w
Newcastle Emlyn...........52·02n 4·28w
Newcastle-under-Lyme............53·00n 2·14w
Newcastle-upon-Tyne............54·59n 1·35w
New Galloway....55·05n 4·10w
Newmarket.......52·15n 0·25e
Newport, Eng.....50·42n 1·18w
Newport, Scot....56·27n 2·56w
Newport, Wales...52·01n 4·51w
Newquay, Eng....50·25n 5·05w
New Quay, Wales.52·13n 4·22w
Newry............54·11n 6·20w
Newton Abbot.....50·32n 3·36w
Newton Stewart...54·57n 4·29w
Newtown..........52·32n 3·19w
Newtownabby.....54·42n 5·54w
Newtownards.....54·36n 5·41w
Newtown Saint Boswells.........55·34n 2·40w
Northallerton.....54·20n 1·26w
North Berwick.....56·04n 2·44w
Northampton.....52·14n 0·54w
North Sunderland......55·34n 1·39w
North Walsham...52·50n 1·24e
Northwich........53·16n 2·32w
Nottingham.......52·58n 1·10w
Nuneaton.........52·32n 1·28w
Oakham...........52·40n 0·43w
Oban.............56·25n 5·29w
Okehampton......50·44n 4·00w
Oldham...........53·33n 2·07w
Oldmeldrum......57·20n 2·20w
Omagh...........54·36n 7·18w
Oswestry.........52·52n 3·04w
Oxford............51·46n 1·15w
Padstow..........50·33n 4·56w
Paignton..........50·26n 3·34w
Paisley...........55·50n 4·26w
Peebles...........55·39n 3·12w
Peel..............54·13n 4·40w
Pembroke.........51·41n 4·55w
Penrith...........54·40n 2·44w
Penzance.........50·07n 5·33w
Perth.............56·24n 3·28w
Peterborough.....52·35n 0·15w
Peterhead........57·30n 1·49w
Peterlee..........54·46n 1·19w
Pickering.........54·14n 0·46w
Pitlochry..........56·43n 3·45w
Plymouth..........50·23n 4·10w
Pontypool.........51·43n 3·02w
Pontypridd........51·37n 3·22w
Poole.............50·43n 1·59w
Portadown........54·26n 6·27w
Port Askaig.......55·51n 6·07w
Port Ellen.........55·39n 6·12w
Portmahomack....57·49n 3·50w
Portree...........57·24n 6·12w
Portrush..........55·12n 6·40w
Portsmouth.......50·48n 1·05w
Portsoy...........57·41n 2·41w
Portstewart.......55·11n 6·43w
Port Talbot.......51·36n 3·47w
Preston...........53·46n 2·42w
Prestwick.........55·30n 4·37w
Pwllheli..........52·53n 4·25w
Ramsey...........54·20n 4·21w
Ramsgate.........51·20n 1·25e
Reading..........51·28n 0·59w
Reay.............58·33n 3·47w
Redruth..........50·13n 5·14w
Reigate..........51·14n 0·13w
Rhondda..........51·40n 3·27w
Rhyl..............53·19n 3·29w
Richmond........54·24n 1·44w
Ripon............54·08n 1·31w
Rochdale.........53·38n 2·09w
Rochester.........51·24n 0·30e
Rosehearty.......57·42n 2·07w
Ross-on-Wye......51·55n 2·35w
Rothbury..........55·19n 1·55w
Rotherham.......53·26n 1·20w
Rothes...........57·31n 3·13w
Rothesay.........55·51n 5·03w
Ruabon...........52·59n 3·02w
Rugby............52·23n 1·15w
Ruthin............53·07n 3·18w
Ryde.............50·44n 1·10w
St. Albans.......51·46n 0·21w
St. Andrews......56·20n 2·48w
St. Anne's.......53·45n 3·02w
St. Austell-with-Fowey...........50·20n 4·48w
St. Davids........51·54n 5·16w
St. Helier.........49·13n 2·07w
St. Ives...........50·12n 5·29w
St. Mary's.........49·55n 6·17w
St. Neots.........52·14n 0·17w
St. Peter Port.....49·27n 2·32w
Salcombe.........50·13n 3·47w
Salford............53·28n 2·18w
Salisbury.........51·05n 1·48w
Saltash...........50·24n 4·12w
Saltcoats.........55·38n 4·47w
Sandown..........50·39n 1·09w
Sandringham.....52·50n 0·30e
Sanquhar.........55·22n 3·56w
Saxmundham.....52·13n 1·29e
Scarborough.....54·17n 0·24w
Scourie...........58·20n 5·08w
Scunthorpe.......53·36n 0·38w
Seaham..........54·52n 1·21w
Selby.............53·48n 1·04w
Selkirk............55·33n 2·50w
Shaftesbury.......51·01n 2·12w
Sheffield..........53·23n 1·30w
Sherborne........50·57n 2·31w
Sheringham......52·57n 1·12e
Shrewsbury.......52·43n 2·45w
Sidmouth..........50·41n 3·15w
Skegness..........53·10n 0·21e
Skipness..........55·46n 5·22w
Sleaford..........53·00n 0·24w
Solihull...........52·25n 1·45w
Southampton.....50·55n 1·25w
Southend-on-Sea 51·33n 0·43e
South Molton.....51·01n 3·50w
Southport.........53·39n 3·01w
South Shields.....55·00n 1·25w
Southwold.........52·20n 1·40e
Spalding..........52·47n 0·10w
Stafford...........52·48n 2·07w
Staines...........51·26n 0·31w
Stamford..........52·39n 0·29w
Stevenage.........51·55n 0·14w
Stewarton.........55·41n 4·31w
Stirling...........56·07n 3·57w
Stockport..........53·25n 2·10w
Stoke-on-Trent....53·00n 2·10w
Stonehaven.......56·38n 2·13w
Stornoway........58·12n 6·23w
Stowmarket.......52·11n 1·00e
Stranraer.........54·55n 5·02w
Stratford-on-Avon............52·12n 1·41w
Stromeferry.......57·21n 5·34w
Stromness........58·57n 3·18w
Stroud............51·45n 2·12w
Sudbury..........52·02n 0·44e
Sunderland.......54·55n 1·23w
Sutton Coldfield...52·34n 1·49w
Sutton-in-Ashfield.........53·08n 1·15w
Swaffham.........52·39n 0·41e
Swanage.........50·37n 1·58w
Swansea.........51·38n 3·57w
Swindon..........51·34n 1·47w
Tain..............57·48n 4·04w
Tarbert...........55·52n 5·26w
Tarbert...........57·54n 6·49w
Taunton..........51·01n 3·06w
Teesside, see Middlesbrough
Teignmouth......50·33n 3·30w
Tetbury...........51·39n 2·10w
Tewkesbury.......51·59n 2·09w
Thetford..........52·25n 0·45e
Thirsk............54·14n 1·20w
Thornhill..........55·15n 3·46w
Thurso............58·35n 3·32w
Tiverton..........50·55n 3·29w
Tobermory........56·37n 6·05w
Tonbridge.........51·12n 0·16e
Tongue...........58·28n 4·25w
Torquay (Torbay).50·28n 3·30w
Torridon..........57·33n 5·31w
Towcester........52·08n 1·00w
Towyn............52·35n 4·05w
Troon.............55·32n 4·40w
Trowbridge.......51·20n 2·13w
Truro.............50·16n 5·03w
Tunbridge Wells..51·08n 0·16e
Turriff............57·32n 2·28w
Tynemouth.......55·01n 1·24w
Uig...............57·35n 6·23w
Ullapool..........57·54n 5·10w
Ventnor..........50·36n 1·11w
Virkie............59·53n 1·18w
Wakefield.........53·42n 1·29w
Wallasey..........53·26n 3·03w
Walsall...........52·35n 1·58w
Wareham.........50·41n 2·07w
Warminster.......51·13n 2·12w
Warrenpoint......54·06n 6·15w
Warrington.......53·24n 2·37w
Warwick..........52·17n 1·34w
Watford...........51·40n 0·25w
Wellingborough ..52·19n 0·42w
Wellington........52·43n 2·31w
Wells.............51·13n 2·39w
Wells-next-the-Sea..............52·58n 0·51e
Welshpool.........52·40n 3·09w
West Bromwich...52·31n 1·56w
West Looe........50·21n 4·28w
Weston-super-Mare............51·21n 2·59w
Weymouth........50·36n 2·28w
Whitby............54·29n 0·37w
Whitehaven.......54·33n 3·35w
Whithorn.........54·44n 4·25w
Whitley Bay.......55·03n 1·25w
Wick..............58·26n 3·06w
Widnes............53·22n 2·44w
Wigan.............53·33n 2·38w
Wigtown..........54·52n 4·26w
Wilton............51·05n 1·52w
Winchester.......51·04n 1·19w
Windermere......54·23n 2·54w
Windsor...........51·29n 0·38w
Wisbech..........52·40n 0·10e
Witney............51·48n 1·29w
Woking...........51·20n 0·34w
Wolverhampton...52·36n 2·08w
Woodbridge......52·06n 1·19e
Woodstock.......51·52n 1·21w
Worcester.........52·11n 2·13w
Workington.......54·39n 3·35w
Worksop..........53·18n 1·07w
Worthing.........50·48n 0·23w
Wrexham.........53·03n 3·00w
Wymondham......52·34n 1·07e
Yeovil............50·57n 2·39w
York.............53·58n 1·05w

Physical features and points of interest

Abbey Head, *headland*.........54·46n 3·58w
Adrdnamurchan, Point of..........56·44n 6·12w
Ailsa Craig, *island*............55·16n 5·07w
Alde, *river*........52·03n 1·28w
Anglesey, *island*..53·27n 4·22w
Antrim, Mountains of.....55·00n 6·10w
Arran, *island*......55·35n 5·15w
Atlantic Ocean...59·00n 7·30w
Attow, Ben, *mountain*........57·14n 5·17w
Avon, *river*........50·43n 1·46w
Avon, *river*........52·25n 1·31w
Awe, Loch, *lake*...56·15n 5·15w
Ayre, Point of.....54·26n 4·22w
Balmoral Castle...57·02n 3·15w
Bann, *river*.........55·10n 6·46w
Bardsey Island.....52·45n 4·45w
Barra, *island*......57·00n 7·30w
Barra Head, *headland*..........56·46n 7·36w
Beachy Head, *headland*.........50·44n 0·16e
Beauly, *river*......57·29n 4·29w
Belfast Lough, *bay*..............54·40n 5·50w
Benbecula, *island*.57·27n 7·20w
Berneray, *island*..57·43n 7·15w
Berwyn Mountains.........52·52n 3·24w
Black Mountains..51·51n 3·35w
Bodmin Moor.....50·33n 4·33w
Bonar Bridge, *mountain*........57·53n 4·21w
Braich-y-Pwll, *cape*..............52·48n 4·36w
Brecon Beacons and Black Mountains National Park....51·52n 3·25w
Bressay, *island*....60·08n 1·05w
Bridgewater Bay..51·16n 3·12w
Bridlington Bay...54·04n 0·08w
Bristol Channel...51·20n 4·00w
Broad Bay........58·15n 6·15w
Broad Law, *mountain*........55·30n 3·22w
Brora, *river*.......58·01n 3·51w
Buchan Ness, *headland*.........57·32n 1·48w
Bude Bay.........50·50n 4·37w
Burray, *island*.....58·51n 2·48w
Butt of Lewis, *promontory*.......58·31n 6·15w
Cader Idris, *mountain*........52·42n 3·54w
Caernarvon Bay...53·05n 4·30w
Cairngorm Mountains.......57·06n 3·30w
Caldy Island......51·38n 4·41w
Cam, *river*........51·48n 0·25e
Cambrian Mountains.......52·35n 3·35w
Canna, *island*.....57·03n 6·33w
Cardigan Bay.....52·30n 4·20w
Carmel Head, *headland*.........53·24n 4·34w
Channel Islands..49·20n 2·20w
Cheviot, The, *mountain*........55·28n 2·09w
Clyde, *river*.......55·56n 4·29w
Clyde, Firth of, *estuary*..........55·42n 5·00w
Coast National Park.............51·47n 5·06w
Coll, *island*........56·40n 6·35w
Colonsay, *island*..56·05n 6·10w
Cotswold Hills....51·45n 2·10w
Cross Fell, *mountain*........54·42n 2·29w
Cuillin Hills.......57·14n 6·15w
Cuillin Sound.....57·04n 6·20w
Dartmoor, *moor*...50·35n 4·00w
Dartmoor National Park.............50·37n 3·52w
Dee, *river*.........57·08n 2·04w
Déroute, Passage de la............49·12n 1·51w
Derwent, *river*....53·45n 0·57w
Dodman Point....50·13n 4·48w
Don, *river*.........57·10n 2·04w
Dornoch Firth, *fjord*.............57·52n 4·02w
Dover, Strait of...51·00n 1·30e
Dubh Artach, *reef*.56·08n 6·42w
Duncansby Head, *headland*.........58·39n 3·01w
Dundrum Bay....54·13n 5·45w
Dungeness, *point*.50·55n 0·58e
Dunnet Head, *headland*.........58·39n 3·23w
Eday, *island*.......59·11n 2·47w
Eddrachillis Bay..58·19n 5·15w
Eddystone, *rocks*..50·12n 4·15w
Eden, *river*........54·57n 3·01w
Eigg, *island*.......56·54n 6·10w
Enard Bay........58·06n 5·20w
English Channel..50·30n 0·30w
Ericht, Loch, *lake*..56·50n 4·25w
Eriskay, *island*....57·05n 7·17w
Erne, Lough, *lake*..54·10n 7·30w
Exe, *river*.........50·37n 3·25w
Exmoor, *moor*.....51·10n 3·45w
Exmoor National Park.............51·12n 3·46w
Eye Peninsula....58·13n 6·05w
Fair Head, *headland*.........55·13n 6·09w
Fair Isle, *island*....59·30n 1·40w
Farne Islands.....55·38n 1·38w
Fens, The, *marsh*..52·38n 0·02e
Fetlar, *island*......60·37n 0·52w
Fife Ness, *promontory*.......56·17n 2·36w
Flamborough Head, *headland*.........54·07n 0·04w
Formby Point.....53·33n 3·06w
Forth, Firth of, *estuary*..........56·05n 2·55w
Foula, *island*......60·10n 2·05w
Foulness Island...51·36n 0·55e
Foyle, Lough, *lake*.55·07n 7·08w
Fyne, Loch, *inlet*..56·00n 5·20w
Galloway, Mull of, *headland*.........54·38n 4·50w
Giants Causeway, *scenic area*.......55·14n 6·30w
Gibralter Point....53·05n 0·19e
Gigha Island......55·41n 5·44w
Glas Maol, *mountain*........56·52n 3·22w
Grampian Mountains.......56·45n 4·00w
Guernsey, *island*..49·28n 2·35w
Hadrian's Wall, *historic site*......54·59n 2·26w
Harris, *island*.....57·53n 6·55w
Harris, Sound of..57·45n 7·08w
Hartland Point....51·02n 4·31w
Hebrides, Sea of the.......57·00n 7·00w
Helvellyn, *peak*....54·32n 3·01w
Holy Island, Eng..55·41n 1·48w
Holy Island, Wales............53·18n 4·37w
Hope, Ben, *mountain*........58·24n 4·36w
Hoy, *island*........58·52n 3·18w
Humber, River....53·40n 0·10w
Inchcape or Bell Rock, *rocks*.......56·55n 2·50w
Inner Hebrides, *islands*..........57·00n 6·45w

widened to a U-shape by glacial action, which has also etched corries from the mountainsides and deposited the heaps of debris known as moraines.

The Welsh Massif

The core of the principality of Wales is formed by a highland block, clearly defined by the sea except on its eastern side, where a sharp break of slope often marks the transition to the English plain. Cycles of erosion have several times worn down its ancient and austere surfaces; many topographic features may be attributed to glacial processes; some of the most striking scenery owes much to former vulcanism. The mountain areas above 2,000 feet are most extensive in North Wales, in Snowdonia and its southward extensions, Cader Idris and the Berwyn mass. With the exception of Plynlimon and the Forest of Radnor, central Wales lacks similar high areas, but the monadnocks of South Wales—notably the Black Mountains and the Brecon (Brecknock) Beacons—again stand out in solitary splendour above the upland surfaces. Three of these are distinguishable: a high plateau of 1,700 to 1,800 feet; a middle peneplain, or worn-down surface, of 1,200 to 1,600 feet; and a low peneplain of 700 to 1,100 feet. These smooth, rounded, grass-covered moorlands present a remarkably even skyline. Below 700 feet lies a further series of former wave-cut surfaces. Several valleys radiate from the highland core to the coastal regions. In the west these lowlands have provided a haven for traditional Welsh culture, but the deeply penetrating eastern valleys have channelled anglicizing influences into the highland. A more extensive lowland—physically and structurally an extension of the English plain—in the southeast borders the Bristol Channel. The irregularities of the 600-mile Welsh coast exhibit differing adjustments to the pounding attack of the sea.

The South West peninsula

The South West—England's largest peninsula—has six locally conspicuous uplands: Exmoor, where Dunkery Beacon reaches 1,707 feet; the wild, granite uplands of Dartmoor (High Willhays; 2,039 feet); Bodmin Moor; St. Austell (Hensbarrow); Carnmenellis; and the spectacular extremity of Land's End. Granite reappears above the sea in the Isles of Scilly, 28 miles further southwest. Despite this variation in general elevation, the landscape, like that of so many other parts of the United Kingdom, has a quite marked uniformity of summit heights, with a high series occurring between 1,000 and 1,400 feet; a middle group between 700 and 1,000 feet; and coastal plateaus ranging between about 200 and 400 feet. A network of deep, narrow valleys alternates with flat-topped, steplike areas rising inland. The South West derives much of its renowned physical attraction from its peninsular nature, for, in addition to magnificent drowned estuaries created by sea-level changes, the coastline is unsurpassed for its diversity.

The Lowland zone. Gauged by the 700-foot contour, the Lowland zone starts around the Solway Firth in the northwest, with a strip of low-lying ground extending up the fault-directed Vale of Eden. Southward, the narrow coastal plain bordering the Lake District broadens into the flat, glacial-drift-covered Lancastrian lowlands, with their slow-flowing rivers. East of the Pennine ridge, the lowlands are continuous, save for the limestone plateau north of the River Tees and, to the south, the North York Moors, with large, exposed tracts over 1,400 feet. South again lies the wide Vale of York, which the broad lower Trent Valley links to the younger rocks of the Midland Plain, terminating against the Welsh Massif on the west. The lowland continues southward along the flat landscapes bordering the lower River Severn, becomes constricted by the complex Bristol–Mendip upland, and opens out once more into the extensive and flat plain of Somerset. The eastern horizon of much of the Midland Plain is the scarp face of the Cotswolds, part of the discontinuous outcrop of limestones and sandstones that arcs from the Dorset coast across the heart of England, continuing in the Cleveland Hills as far as the north Yorkshire coast. The more massive limestones and sandstones give rise to noble, 1,000-foot-high escarpments, yet the dip slope is frequently of such a low angle that the countryside resembles a dissected plateau, passing gradually on to the clay vales of Oxford, White Horse, Lincoln, and Pickering. The flat, often reclaimed landscapes of the Fenlands are also underlain by these clays, and the next scarp, the western-facing chalk outcrop (cuesta), undergoes several marked directional changes in the vicinity of the Wash, a shallow arm of the North Sea.

Eastern chalklands and vales

The chalk outcrop is a more conspicuous and continuous feature than its sandstone and limestone predecessor: it begins in the north with the open rolling country known as the Yorkshire Wolds, where heights of 750 feet are reached; is breached by the River Humber; and then continues in the Lincolnshire Wolds. East of the Fens the outcrop, or cuesta, is very low, barely attaining 150 feet, but it then rises gradually to the 807 feet reached in the attractive Chilterns, a ridge interrupted by several wind gaps, or former river courses; the Thames alone actually cuts through it, in the Goring Gap. Where the dip slope of the chalk is almost horizontal, as is the case in the open Salisbury Plain, the landscape is that of a large dissected plateau, of 350 to 500 feet. Only the main valleys contain rivers, and most of the tributary valleys are dry.

The chalk outcrop continues into Dorset, but in the south the chalk has been folded along west-to-east lines. Downfolds, subsequently filled in by geologically recent sands and clays, now floor the London and Hampshire basins. The former, an asymmetrical synclinal, or structurally downwarped, lowland rimmed by chalk, is occupied mainly by gravel terraces and valley-side benches and has relatively little floodplain; the latter is similarly cradled by a girdle of chalk, but the southern rim, or monocline, has been cut by the sea in two places to form the scenic Isle of Wight.

Between these two synclinal areas rises the anticlinal, or structurally upwarped, dome of the Weald region of Kent and Sussex. The arch of this vast geological upfold has long since been eroded away, and the bounding chalk escarpments of the North and South Downs (uplands so named because of their open, rolling, treeless grassland) are therefore inward facing and enclose a concentric series of exposed clay vales and sandstone ridges. Eaten into by the waters of the English Channel, a dazzling succession of chalk cliffs faces the European mainland, 21 miles distant at the narrowest point.

The main watershed

Drainage. The main water parting in Great Britain runs from north to south, keeping well to the west until the basin of the River Severn. Westward-flowing streams attain the Atlantic in relatively short reaches, and the Clyde in Scotland, the Eden and Mersey in northwest England, and the Welsh Dee, Teifi, and Tywi are the only significant rivers. The drainage complex that debouches into the Severn Estuary covers a large area in central and eastern Wales and the greater part of seven English counties. Thereafter, the Bristol Avon and the Parret catchments take the water parting somewhat to the east, but subsequently, with the exception of the Taw–Torridge valleys, it runs very close to the west coast in Devon and Cornwall.

The rivers draining east from the main water parting are longer, several coalescing into wide estuaries. The fast-flowing Spey, Don, Tay, Forth, and Tweed of eastern Scotland run generally across impermeable rocks, and their discharges increase rapidly after rain. From the northern Pennines, the Tyne, Wear, and Tees flow independently to the North Sea, but thereafter significant estuary groupings occur. A number of rivers drain into the Humber, including, after it leaves the Pennines, the important Trent. To the south, another group of rivers enters the Wash after sluggishly draining a large flat countryside. The big drainage complex of the Thames dominates South East England; its source is in the Cotswolds, and, after being joined by many tributaries as it flows over the Oxford Clay, the mainstream breaches the chalk escarpment in the Goring Gap. A number of tributaries add their discharges farther downstream, and the total drainage converging on the Thames Estuary exceeds 4,000 square miles. The rivers flowing into the English Channel are mainly short, as are those in Northern Ireland, with the exceptions of the Erne, Foyle, and Bann.

Soils. The regional pattern of soil formation can be correlated usefully with local variations of relief and climate. Although changes are gradual and can be complicated by local factors, a division of Britain into four climatic regimes (see below *Climate*) goes far to explain the distribution of soils.

On those loftier parts of the Highland zone, particularly in Scotland, experiencing a cold, wet regime of more than 40 inches (1,000 millimetres) rainfall and less than 47° F (8° C) mean temperature annually, blanket peat and peaty podzol soils, the organic surface layer of which rests on a gray, leached base, are found. A similarly wet regime, but with a mean annual temperature exceeding 47° F, obtains over most of the remainder of the Highland zone, particularly on the lower parts of the Southern Uplands, the Solway Firth–Lake District area, the peripheral plateaus of Wales, and most of South West England. These areas are covered by acid brown soils and weakly podzolized associates. On the lower lying areas within the Highland zone, more particularly in eastern Scotland and the eastern flanks of the Pennines, a relatively cold, dry regime gives rise to soils intermediate between the richer brown earths and the podzols.

Over the whole of the Lowland zone, which also has a mean annual temperature above 47° F (8° C) but less than 40 inches of rain, leached brown soils are characteristic. Calcareous, and thus alkaline, parent materials are widespread, particularly in the southeast, and so acid soils and podzols are confined to the most quartz-laden parent materials. In Northern Ireland, above about 460 feet, brown earths are replaced by semipodzols, and these grade upslope into more intensively leached podzols. This is particularly the case in the Sperrins and the Mournes, but, between them in the Lough Neagh lowland, rich brown earth soils are extensively developed.

Climate. The climate of the United Kingdom, a perennial topic of conversation within the country, is broadly determined by its setting within the pattern of the atmosphere's general circulation and its position in relation to the form and distribution of land and sea. Regional diversity does exist, but the boundaries of major world climatic systems do not pass through the country. Britain's marginal position between the European landmass to the east, and the ever-present, relatively warm Atlantic waters to the west, ensures the modification of both the thermal and moisture characteristics of the principal types of air reaching British shores. These, according to their source regions, are Arctic, polar, and tropical, and, by their route of travel, may in each case be maritime or continental. For much of the year the weather is dominated by the sequence of disturbances within the midlatitude Westerlies that bring in mostly polar-maritime, and, occasionally, tropical-maritime air.

Air-mass characteristics

In winter, occasional high-pressure areas to the east allow biting Arctic or polar-continental air to sweep over Britain. All these atmospheric systems tend to fluctuate rapidly in their paths and to vary both in frequency and intensity throughout the seasons of the year and also from year to year for any given season. Variability contributes much to the character of British weather, and extreme conditions, though rare, can be very important for the life of the country.

The westerly maritime derivation of so much of the air reaching the country in winter creates a temperature distribution that does not reflect latitudinal differences. Thus the north-to-south run of the 40° F (4° C) January isotherm, or line of equal temperature, from the coast in northwest Scotland right down to the Isle of Wight betrays the moderating influence of the winds blowing off the Atlantic Ocean. In summer, polar-maritime air is less common, and a nine-degree difference of latitude and distance from the sea assume more importance, with temperatures increasing from north to south and from the coast inland. Above-average temperatures are usually associated with tropical-continental air, particularly in anticyclonic, or high-pressure, conditions. These southerly or southeasterly airstreams can bring to southern England heat waves with temperatures of more than 90° F (32° C). In spring and autumn a variety of airstreams and temperature conditions may be experienced, and changing patterns of sun and shadow enhance the natural seasonal beauty of the landscape.

Rainfall patterns

Rain-producing atmospheric systems arrive from a westerly direction, and some of the bleak highest summits of the Highland zone can receive as much as 200 inches (5,100 millimetres) of driving rainfall a year. East Anglia and the Thames Estuary, in contrast, can expect as little as 20 inches (500 millimetres). Rain is fairly well distributed throughout the year: June, on the whole, is the driest month all over Britain; May is the next driest in the east and centre of England, but April is drier in parts of the west and north. The wettest months are usually October, December, and August, but in any particular year almost any month can prove to be the wettest, and the association of Britain with seemingly perpetual rainfall (a concept popular among foreigners) is based on a germ of truth. Some precipitation falls as snow, and the average number of days with snow falling can vary from as many as 30 in blizzard-prone northeast Scotland to as few as five in South West England.

Vegetation and animal life. Except for northern Scotland, the highest hills of the north and west, the saturated fens and marshes, and the seacoast fringes, the natural vegetation of the British Isles was deciduous summer forest dominated by oak. The hand of man has, however, lain long and heavy on this heritage, and only scattered woodlands and the areas of wild or seminatural vegetation lie outside the enclosed cultivated fields. Few of these fine moorlands and heathlands, wild though they may appear, can lay claim to any truly natural plant communities: nearly all show varying degrees of adjustment to grazing, swaling (controlled burning), or other activities. Woodland now covers a little less than 7 percent of the country, and, though the State Forestry Commission has been most active since its creation in 1919, by far the greater part of this woodland remains in private hands. The largest areas of woodland are now to be found in northeast Scotland; Kielder in Northumberland; South East England; Monmouthshire; and Breckland in Norfolk.

Flora of the moorlands and heathlands

The moorlands and heathlands occupy about a third of the total area of the United Kingdom. They consist of the possibly true Arctic–Alpine vegetation on some mountain summits in Scotland and the much more extensive peat moss, heather, bilberry, and the thin *Molinia* and *Nardus* grass moors of the Highland zone. A similar vegetation exists on high ground in eastern Northern Ireland and on the Mournes, with considerable areas of peat moss vegetation on the mountains of Antrim. In the Lowland zone, where light sandy soils are found, the vegetation is dominated typically by the common heather—the deep purple of which adds a splash of colour to the

autumn countryside—but sometimes by bilberry or bell heather. A strip of land immediately bordering the coastline has also largely escaped the attention of man and his animals, so that patches of maritime vegetation can frequently be found in approximately their natural state.

The survival of the wild mammals, amphibians, and reptiles of the United Kingdom depends on their ability to come to terms with the changing environment and to protect themselves from the attacks by their enemies—the most dangerous being man. British mammals survive in a greater range of habitats than do amphibians and reptiles. Most of the former larger mammals have become extinct, but red deer survive in the Scottish Highlands and on Exmoor, and roe deer in the wooded areas of Scotland and southern England. The carnivore mammals (badgers, otters, foxes, stoats, and weasels) thrive in most rural areas; also widely distributed are the rodents (rats, squirrels, mice) and the insectivores (hedgehogs, moles, shrews). Rabbits are widespread and their numbers are again increasing in spite of the outbreak, in the 1950s, of the disease known as myxomatosis. The other nocturnal vegetarian, the brown hare, is found in open lowland country, while the mountain hare is native to Scotland. The amphibians are represented by three species of newt and five species of frogs and toads, while reptiles consist of three species of snakes, of which only the adder is venomous, and three species of lizard. There are no snakes in Northern Ireland.

THE HUMAN IMPRINT ON THE LAND

Traditional regions. When a long view is taken of the slow possession of Britain by its peoples, it seems an inescapable conclusion that the man–land relationship probably reached its greatest intimacy late in the 18th century: communications at this time were good enough to bind the community into a unity but were not yet so good as to destroy the sense of belonging to a specific locality, as well as to a particular nation, Scotland, England, Wales, or Ireland. Generations of toiling hands had won the necessities of life from the landscape, and generations of tongues had shaped the national languages and dialects for the expression of local things. The regional character of British life is still recognizable, but its heyday has passed. The consciousness of being a Northern Irelander, a Scot, a Welshman, or a Cornishman—to say nothing of the rivalry between a North and South Walian, or a Highland and Lowland Scot—is as marked as is the obvious geographical identity of these parts of the Highland zone.

The conditions of regional awareness

Within England nine traditional regions are to be distinguished. The North Country province, including the present counties of Durham, Northumberland, Cumberland, and northern Westmorland, formed, after the Anglo-Saxon settlement of the mid-5th to late 6th century AD, the central part of the Anglian Kingdom of Northumbria. Later, it became an area whose life, over a period of centuries, was dominated by border warfare with Scotland; this strengthened its regional traditions and folklore. With the coming of the Industrial Revolution, the region's wealth in coal and iron gave it great advantages that later were to enhance its traditions of independence and initiative. The county of Yorkshire, finally dismembered in the administrative reorganization of the 1970s, has existed as a northern unit in varying degrees since Roman times, and the cohesion given to it when it became the Danish Kingdom of York was maintained until the Council of the North—a prerogative court established in Tudor times to ensure the fair administration of English common law—was abolished in 1641. The growth of the wool-textile industry in the West Riding wrought major changes in the rural economy, but, in spite of this and the variety in the landscape, the sense of being a Yorkshireman is still a reality. Across the Pennines, on the other hand, it would be difficult to find a time before the Industrial Revolution when Lancaster formed a unit, yet there now exists a Lancastrian tradition and dialect, as well as a provincial entity. These stem from a certain physical unity and from the cohesion imposed by the long dominion of the cotton industry. The English Midlands are really divisible into two regions: a West Midland province, which has become conscious of its identity since the emergence of Birmingham as a regional capital, and, in contrast, the East Midland province, with a greater physical and historic—but much less economic—unity.

Norfolk, Suffolk, and Cambridgeshire and Isle of Ely make up the ancient Kingdom of East Anglia. This is an agricultural province. In this respect it forms a marked contrast with its London-dominated neighbour, South East England, which in size and density of population is the largest English region. The Hampshire Downs form the core of Wessex, a province with that well-marked regional consciousness and patriotism that is so vividly depicted in the writings of the novelist Thomas Hardy. The eastern side of the Severn Estuary, together with the Somerset Levels, has become known as the West of England, a province which looks to the old city of Bristol as its centre. The completion of the elegant Severn Bridge, as part of the motorway system, is tending to unify both sides of the Severn Estuary into a Severnside region.

Patterns of rural settlement. The forms and patterns of settlement are remarkably varied in the United Kingdom and reflect not only the physical variety of the landscape but also the successive movements of peoples arriving as settlers, refugees, conquerors, or traders from continental Europe. The social and economic advantages that led folk to cluster and, on the other hand, the equally strong desire for separateness on the part of some individuals are apparent in settlement forms from very early times, and so regional contrasts in the degree of dispersion and nucleation are frequent.

Highland-zone hamlets

The single farmstead, together with many survivals of the old clachan (cluster or hamlet), interspersed with the occasional village and small town, is still characteristic of much of the Highland zone. Radical alteration has nevertheless occurred in some nucleated settlement patterns: in Wales the breakup of hamlets began in the later Middle Ages as a result of the related processes of consolidation and enclosure that accompanied the late medieval decline in the numerical strength of the bond (feudally tied) population. This trend was reinforced by the Black Death of 1349, which spread quickly among the inhabitants of lowly status. Many surviving bondsmen took advantage of the turmoil caused by the nationalistic uprising led by Owen Glendower (Welsh Owain Glyndŵr) to escape their servile obligations by flight, and thus many Welsh hamlets fell into decay by 1410, when the rebellion was crushed. In Scotland great changes accompanied the Highland clearances in the mid-18th century; in Northern Ireland, as late as the 1880s, many clachans disappeared as part of a deliberate policy of reallocating land to new dispersed farmsteads. Great changes are also to be seen in the Lowland zone, where the swing to individual ownership or tenancy from the medieval custom of landholding in common brought about not only dispersion and deserted villages but also the enclosure of fields by hedges and walls. Nucleations remain remarkably stable features of the rural landscape of Britain, and linear, round, oval, and ring-shaped villages survive, many with their ancient greens still held in common by the community.

Urban settlement. By any standards Britain must be regarded as the most urbanized of countries, for towns are not only particularly expressive of the national way of life but are also unusually significant elements in the geography of the country. The greatest overall change in settlement was, in fact, the massive urbanization that accompanied Britain's early industrial development. The increasing percentage of employees in offices and service industries ensures continued contemporary urban growth. Of every ten people in the United Kingdom, almost eight now live in towns, four of them in one of the eight major urban groups, or conurbations. The Greater London conurbation, the greatest port, the largest centre of industry, the most important centre of office employment, and the capital city, is by far the largest of these. The need for accommodating business premises has involved the displacement of population from inner London, and this, in

The role of Greater London

part, has led to the designation of nine New Towns outside the ten-mile-wide Green Belt, which surrounds London's built-up area, and two more distant "overspill" towns.

Large conurbations have also formed on or near the exposed coalfields. The extensive built-up area of the West Midlands conurbation (with a population of almost 2,800,000) is dominated by Birmingham, but the industrial Black Country—named for its formerly polluted skies and grimy buildings—has also several large and flourishing towns. In the Manchester conurbation, with an equivalent number of inhabitants, urbanization accompanied the mechanization of the cotton-textile industry. Across the Pennines, similar mechanization of wool textiles created the West Yorkshire conurbation, the home of over 2,000,000 people, with Leeds and Bradford as its twin centres. Tyneside and the Central Clydeside conurbation are also located on coalfields, the latter housing about one-third of Scotland's 5,000,000 people. Merseyside is not on the Lancashire coalfield, but it has close economic links with it. In Northern Ireland, only Belfast may be considered a major conurbation.

In addition to these large metropolitan areas, there are many minor conurbations and large towns, a large number of which are strung out along the coast.

With so much urban and suburban concentration, the problems of air, water, and noise pollution have become subjects of much concern in the United Kingdom. Considerable progress has been made with the air-pollution question as a result of changes in fuel usage and the operation of clean-air legislation, which has led to the establishment of smoke-control areas in most cities and towns. Pollution of the rivers remains a large problem, particularly in the highly industrialized parts of the United Kingdom, but vigilance and control on the part of the river authorities, research done by the Water Pollution Research Laboratory, and general public concern for the environment are encouraging features of contemporary Britain. Several statutory and voluntary organizations support measures to protect the environment; they have as their aim the conservation not only of the countryside's natural amenity and beauty but that of the towns and cities also.

The people

LINGUISTIC AND ETHNIC GROUPS

All the traditional languages spoken in the United Kingdom are descended from a common Aryan, or Indo-European, original, a tongue so ancient that, over the centuries, it has split into a variety of languages, each with its own peculiarities in sounds, grammar, and vocabulary. A separate idiom in what became the United Kingdom was initiated when peoples from the Continent were cut off, in their new homes, from regular intercourse with their continental kindred.

Of the surviving languages the earliest to arrive were the two forms of Celtic: the Goidelic (from which Irish Gaelic, Manx, and Scottish Gaelic are derived) and Brythonic, from which are descended the old Cornish language and modern Welsh. Among the contemporary Celtic languages Welsh is the strongest: more than a quarter of the total population of the principality are able to speak it, but there are still extensive interior upland areas and regions facing the Irish Sea where the percentage rises to 70 percent and more. Scottish Gaelic is at its strongest among the inhabitants of the Islands and is still heard in the nearby Northwest Highlands. As only about 1.6 percent of Scotsmen are able to speak it, it has long since ceased to be a national language, and even in the northwest, where it remains the language of religion, business, and social activity, Gaelic is losing ground. In Northern Ireland very little Gaelic is spoken; similarly Manx is now used by very few individuals indeed, although as late as 1870 it was spoken by about half the people of the Isle of Man. Cornish became extinct in the early 18th century.

The second link with Indo-European is through the ancient Germanic group of languages, two branches of which, North Germanic and West Germanic, were des-

Germanic language links

tined to make contributions to the English language. Modern English is derived mainly from the four Germanic dialects spoken by the Angles, Saxons, and Jutes (who all arrived in Britain in the 5th century AD) and by the Danes, whose long series of raids began about 790. The Humber became an important linguistic as well as geographical boundary, and the English-speaking portion of what became England was divided into a Northumbrian and a Southumbrian province (in which the most important kingdoms were Mercia, Wessex, and Kent). In the 8th century, Northumbria was foremost in literature and culture, followed, for a short time, by Mercia; finally Wessex remained the linguistic centre until the time of King Edward the Confessor. The Normans, although also of Viking stock, were at first regarded as much more of an alien race than the Danes. Under the Norman and Angevin kings, England formed part of a continental empire; and the prolonged connection with France retained by its new rulers and landlords made a deep impression on the English language. An Anglo-French hybrid speech developed and remained the official language, sometimes even displacing Latin in public documents, until the mid-14th century. Many additions to English have been made since that date, but the Normans were the last important linguistic group to enter Britain.

RELIGIOUS GROUPS

The various Christian denominations in the United Kingdom have emerged from the schisms that divided the church. The greatest of these occurred in England in the 16th century, when Henry VIII rejected the absolute supremacy of the pope. This break with Rome facilitated the adoption of some Protestant tenets and was the foundation of the Anglican Church, still the established church of England. In Scotland, the Reformation gave rise to a church governed by a presbytery—a body composed of ministers and laymen—rather than by bishops, as was the case in England. Roman Catholicism in Ireland as a whole was almost undisturbed by these events, but what became Northern Ireland came strongly under the influence of the Anglican and Presbyterian churches. In the 17th century further schisms divided the Church of England; these were associated with the rise of the Puritan movement, which, with its desire for simpler forms of worship and government, led to a proliferation of nonconformist churches, such as those of the Baptists and the Congregationalists; the Society of Friends (Quakers) also originated at that time. Religious revivals of the mid-18th century gave to Wales a form of Protestantism closely linked with the Welsh language; Calvinistic Methodism is still the most powerful religious influence in the principality. The great evangelical revivals of the 18th century, associated with John Wesley and others, led to the foundation of Methodist churches, particularly in the industrial areas; northeastern England and Cornwall still have the largest percentages of adherents to this denomination. In the 19th century the Salvation Army and various fundamentalist sects grew from minor schisms. That century also saw the introduction of sects from the United States as well as a marked increase in the number of Jews in Britain. The first Jewish community to be established in Britain since their expulsion in 1290 had been created in London during the 17th century, and in the 19th century they also settled in many of the large provincial cities. Over half the number of British Jews live in London and the rest are essentially members of urban communities. In the 20th century, immigrants from India and Pakistan have introduced various Eastern religions into the United Kingdom, but their places of worship are, for the most part, found only in the largest cities.

The Judaic and Eastern traditions

It is difficult to characterize and describe this variety of beliefs and their distribution in the United Kingdom, since the statistics for the various denominations are collected separately and on widely differing bases. The generalized description of England as Anglican, Scotland as Presbyterian, Wales as Calvinistic Methodist, and Northern Ireland as Protestant remains useful so long as it is remembered that each country contains large minority groups adhering to other Christian denominations and that a large proportion of the population is, in effect, agnostic.

DEMOGRAPHIC TRENDS

General factors. At any time, the basic factors governing population changes are the relation of births to deaths and of immigration to emigration. Since the making, in 1086, of the Domesday Survey, a detailed compilation that enables the earliest reasonable estimate of population to be made, at least of England's population (the survey did not cover other areas), the number of people has been increasing. This has been in spite of some setbacks, by far the most serious of which was the Black Death in the mid-14th century, in which it is estimated that about one-third of the population died. There is little concrete data, however, concerning variation in these rates until 1801, when the first official census was taken. The assumption is that a population of about 2,000,000 lived in what became the United Kingdom during the 11th century and that this figure increased to about 12,000,000 by 1801. This slow growth rate, in contrast with that of more modern times, resulted mainly from the fact that a high birth rate was accompanied by an almost equally high death rate. Family monuments in old churches show many examples of men whose "quivers were full" but whose hearths were not crowded. It is estimated that, in the first half of the 18th century, three-quarters of the children born in London died before they reached puberty. Despite the appalling living conditions it produced, the Industrial Revolution resulted in an acceleration of the birth rate; gradually the greater medical knowledge, improved nutrition, and concern for public health that characterized the 19th century bore fruit in a lessened mortality rate. The birth rate also continued to rise, until it reached 35.5 per thousand in 1871; since that time, except during the years immediately following World Wars I and II, it declined and, throughout the 1950s, steadied at around 16 per thousand. During the 1960s it rose again, to 18.5 and fell back to about 16.2 per thousand by the early 1970s. This marked decline in the birth rate since the late 19th century was due in part to the spread of deliberate methods of family planning. Over the same period the death rate declined from 22.3 per thousand in 1871 to a steady 11.6 per thousand 100 years later. When the birth and death rates are considered together, the margin of births over deaths shows an overall increase in population. While the death rates remained high, a population of low average age was being formed; but, as the death rates fell, each successive census showed a gradual increase in the proportion of elderly people.

First official census

In the contemporary United Kingdom, death rates differ between the sexes and also show variations from region to region, reflecting the response of people to the totality of their cultural and physical environments. As men are likely to follow more dangerous pursuits than women do and adjust less well to retirement, male death rates are normally higher. The principal regional difference is between the generally low death rates in southeastern and eastern counties and the high rates in northern and western Britain. Rates for males are distinctly high in parts of Lancashire, West Yorkshire, Lowland Scotland, northeastern England, South Wales, the West Midlands, and London, while for females the five major areas of high-mortality experience are southern Scotland, northern and northwestern England, Wales, and parts of Northern Ireland. For both sexes Cambridgeshire and the Isle of Ely, Rutland, Huntingdonshire, Oxfordshire, West Sussex, and Hampshire are the counties, and Canterbury, Oxford, and Bath the towns, with the most favourable mortality experience.

Regional variations in death rates

Immigration and emigration. Although historical records make reference to emigration to North America in the 17th and 18th centuries, there is little quantitative information about such movements before the middle of the following century. The greatest numbers appear to have left Great Britain in the 1880s and between 1900 and the outbreak of World War I. Emigration, particular-

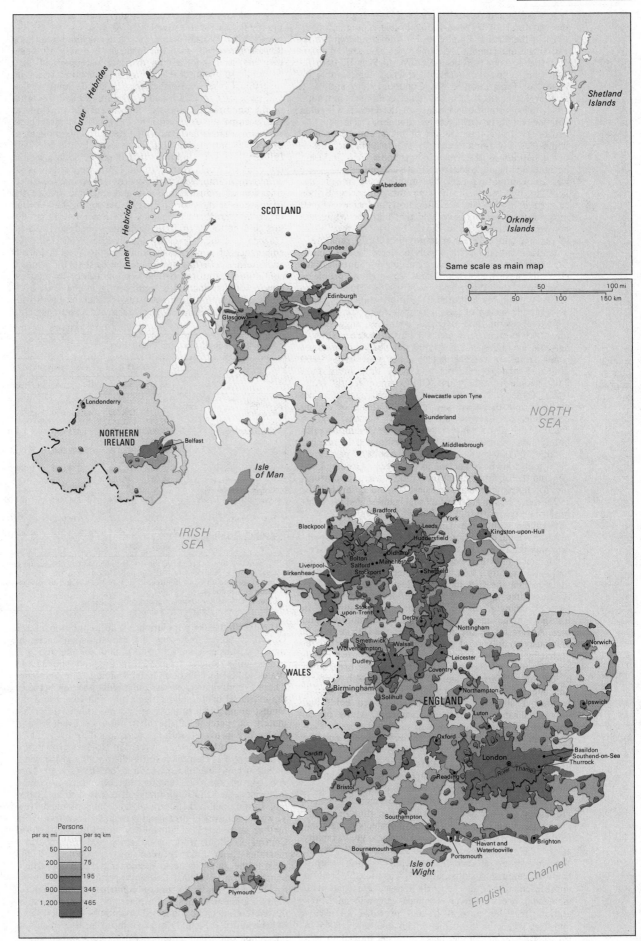

Outer Hebrides

Inner Hebrides

SCOTLAND

Aberdeen

Dundee

Edinburgh

Glasgow

Londonderry

NORTHERN
IRELAND

Belfast

Isle
of Man

Newcastle upon Tyne

Sunderland

Middlesbrough

NORTH
SEA

IRISH
SEA

Bradford

Blackpool

Leeds   York

Huddersfield

Kingston-upon-Hull

Liverpool

Bolton
Salford Manchester
Stockport

Oldham

Sheffield

Birkenhead

Stoke-
upon-Trent

Derby

Nottingham

Norwich

WALES

Smethwick
Wolverhampton
Dudley

Walsall

Leicester

Coventry

Birmingham

Solihull

Northampton

ENGLAND

Ipswich

Luton

Oxford

Basildon
Southend-on-Sea
Thurrock

Cardiff

London

River Thames

Bristol

Reading

Southampton

Brighton

Bournemouth

Havant and
Waterlooville

Portsmouth

Isle of
Wight

English Channel

Plymouth

Shetland
Islands

Orkney
Islands

Same scale as main map

0		50		100 mi
0	50	100	150 km	

Persons

per sq mi		per sq km
50		20
200		75
500		195
900		345
1,200		465

Population density of the United Kingdom.

ly to Canada and Australia, continued at a high rate after the war until 1930, when unfavourable economic conditions in the British Empire and in the United States reversed the movement. The same years also saw an influx of refugees from Europe. After World War II, both inward and outward movements reached considerable dimensions. Emigration to the Commonwealth and, to a smaller degree, to the United States continued, but, until 1951, the net migration balance of the United Kingdom with the rest of the world was not thought to be large.

After 1957 the immigration of black and other non-white ("New Commonwealth") people from such developing nations as the West Indies, India, and Pakistan became significant, and, from that year until 1962, there was a net migration gain. The immigrants came, it was held, to find work in the buoyant prosperity Britain enjoyed in the 1960s. Despite efforts to achieve racial integration, observers have held that both the white and non-white communities in Britain tend to see themselves as distinct and different, but not necessarily separate— a neutral relationship for which the term "social pluralism" has been coined. As in many other countries, race relations nevertheless continued to present problems throughout the 1960s and early 1970s. During fiscal 1965–70, suitably adjusted migration statistics, based on a sample survey of passenger movements between the United Kingdom and overseas countries, suggest that the gross migrant movements from all sources show a net loss averaging about 44,500 per year. These losses
Racial factors in migrant movements
result from an average net loss per year of 145,000 United Kingdom residents and of a little more than 2,000 people from the white "Old Commonwealth" (Australia, Canada, New Zealand), balanced against a net gain per year of an average of 24,000 aliens, of 52,000 non-white, or "New Commonwealth" citizens, and of 26,000 Irish. Non-white ("coloured") Commonwealth immigrants and their families were estimated to number about 1,300,000 by the early 1970s. About 60 percent of the immigrants have flocked to the areas—Greater London and the Birmingham conurbation—where opportunities for employment are greatest. In the latter half of 1972, there was a great influx of Ugandan Asians holding British passports into the United Kingdom.

Migration within the United Kingdom has at times reached sizable dimensions. Until 1700, the small population was thinly distributed and largely rural and agricultural, much as it had been in medieval times. From the mid-18th century, scientific and technological innovations created the first modern industrial state, while, at the same time, agriculture was experiencing technical and tenurial changes, and revolutionary improvements in transport made easier the movement of materials and men. As a result, by the first decade of the 19th century, a previously mainly rural population had been largely replaced by a nation of industrial workers and town dwellers. The rural exodus was a long process; the breakdown of communal farming started before the 14th century; and, subsequently, enclosures advanced steadily, especially after 1740, until, a century later, open fields had virtually disappeared from the landscape. Many of the landless agricultural labourers so displaced were attracted to the better opportunities for employment and the higher wage levels existing in the growing industries; their movements, together with those of the surplus population produced by the contemporary rapid rise in the birth rate, resulted in a high volume of internal migration, taking the form of a townward movement.

Industry, as well as the urban centres that inevitably grew up around it, was increasingly located on the coalfields, while the railway network, which grew rapidly after 1830, enchanced the nodality of many towns. The migration of people, especially young people, from the country to industrialized towns took place at an unprecedented rate in the early railway age, and such movements were relatively confined geographically. Migration from agricultural Ireland provided an exception, for, when the disastrous potato disease of 1845-46 led to widespread famine, large numbers moved to Britain to become the urban workers of Lancashire, Clyde-

side, and London. The rural exodus continued, but on a greatly reduced scale, after 1901.

Soon after World War I, new interregional migration flows commenced when the formerly booming 19th-century industrial and mining districts lost much of their economic momentum. Declining or stagnating heavy industry in Clydeside, northeastern England, South Wales, and parts of Lancashire and Yorkshire swelled the ranks of the unemployed, and the consequent outward migration became the drift south to the relatively more prosperous Midlands and south of England. This movement of people continued until it was arrested by the relatively full employment conditions that obtained soon after the outbreak of World War II. In the 1950s, opportunities for employment improved with government-sponsored diversification of industry, and this did much to reduce the magnitude of the prewar drift to the south. The decline of certain northern industries—coal mining, shipbuilding, and cotton textiles in particular—had nevertheless reached a critical level by the middle 1960s, and the emergence of new growth points in the West Midlands and southeastern England made the drift to the south a continuing feature of British economic life. In addition population has increased significantly in the East Midlands and around the great estuaries such as the Bristol Channel, Southampton Water, Merseyside, and Teesside.
The drift south

United Kingdom, Area and Population				
	area*		population	
	sq mi	sq km	1961 census	1971 census†
Countries				
England	50,053	129,637	43,461,000	45,870,000
	50,333	130,362		
Northern Ireland	5,206	13,484	1,425,000	1,525,000
	5,452	14,129		
Scotland	29,799	77,179	5,179,000	5,228,000
	30,414	78,772		
Wales	7,969	20,640	2,644,000	2,724,000
	8,017	20,764		
Crown dependencies				
Guernsey and Jersey	75	194	111,000	125,000
	75	194		
Isle of Man	221	572	48,000	50,000‡
	221	572		
Total United Kingdom	93,323	241,705§	52,868,000	55,522,000‖
	94,512	244,785§		

*Where two figures are given, the first is the land area, the second the total area.   †Preliminary.   ‡Estimate.   §Converted area figures do not add to total because of rounding.   ‖Figures do not add to total given because of rounding.
Source: Official government figures; UN.

The distribution of population. The population of the United Kingdom including the crown dependencies at the 1971 census was about 55,522,000, the densities per square mile ranging from 935 in England and 339 in Wales to 280 in Northern Ireland, and 172 in Scotland. These overall figures express the middle position between the extremes of densely settled cities and towns and the almost uninhabited mountains and moorlands. Approximately 80 percent of the population of England and Wales live in towns, with the corresponding figure at 70 percent in Scotland and 55 percent in Northern Ireland.

Urban areas. Dominant in the distribution is the widespread urban development centred on the Greater London conurbation (7,379,000), but strong metropolitan influences extend to large marginal towns such as Chatham, Luton, Bedford, Southend, and nine planned New Towns. Railway electrification has encouraged a further movement of dormitory areas outward from Central London, while good road and rail communications foster links between the metropolis and the coast to the south: as far as passenger traffic is concerned, Southampton (215,000) has long operated as an outport for London, while the minor conurbation of Brighton offers seaside amenities and a place for the retirement of the more affluent Londoners. Portsmouth (197,000) and Bournemouth (153,000) are two more large elements in the complex of urban settlements along the south coast.

All the other large concentrations of population are

found in the great industrial conurbations, and all are located on or near the coalfields. Placed in the centre of England and Wales, a few miles to the south of what was the Roman Watling Street but is now the central "grand thoroughfare" for road and rail traffic is the West Midland conurbation of Birmingham and the Black Country. Nearly half of the almost 2,800,000 people in the conurbation live in Birmingham and its two satellites, Solihull and Sutton Coldfield, and the remainder live in 21 other small and medium-sized towns. The official name for the northern conurbation, which has Manchester as its centre, was South East Lancashire, an inappropriate title, since the continuous built-up area spreads deep into Cheshire. By the early 1970s, the conurbation (renamed Greater Manchester) was the home of over 2,700,000 people, with Manchester (541,000), Salford (over 131,000), and Bolton (154,000) the largest elements within it. Only a few miles to the southwest is the Merseyside conurbation (1,659,000), but it is unlike the other provincial conurbations in that its expansion is due mainly to the enlargment of its large centre, Liverpool (607,000), and Birkenhead (138,000) on the south bank of the Mersey Estuary. On the eastern flanks of the Pennines, the high-density West Yorkshire conurbation of over 2,050,000 people consists of a large number of industrial settlements, with Leeds (495,000) and Bradford (294,000) dominant. Many settlements are strung out over the countryside in a southerly direction, making an almost continuous belt of high population density all the way round the Pennines as far as its junction with the West Midland conurbation. Within this belt lie the large and important cities of Sheffield (520,000), Rotherham (85,000), Chesterfield (70,000), Nottingham (almost 300,000), Derby (nearly 220,000), and Leicester (284,000).

Two further major population groupings, those of Northeast England and South Wales–Bristol, are located on coalfields with their own independent access to the sea. The main urban concentrations in northeastern England lie alongside the Tyne, Tees, and Wear rivers, while in South Wales–Bristol the population is concentrated in the striking, long, terraced rows in the many narrow mining valleys and on the coast of Swansea Bay and Severnside. In both areas the port cities of Bristol (over 425,-000), Cardiff (278,000), and Swansea (173,000) dominate the scene. Third in rank numerically among the cities of Britain is Glasgow, with a population of almost 900,000; together with seven other large burghs it forms the Central Clydeside conurbation of almost 2,000,000 people. High densities, however, continue northeastward toward the Firth of Forth, on the shores of which lies Edinburgh, with nearly 450,000 inhabitants. Aberdeen (about 180,000) is the only really large settlement outside the Central Lowlands. In Northern Ireland the only area with a high density of population extends from the southeast corner of Lough Neagh to the shores of Belfast Lough, where Belfast and its vicinity house nearly half a million people.

Rural patterns. Outside these urban groupings lie the rural areas of the United Kingdom in which about 23 percent of the population reside. The pattern of high relief bears a very close relationship to the low density of population, particularly in the Highland zone, where there are extensive areas of very thin rural population.

These uplands have for a long time been losing people by migration, especially of young people, and this can produce a difficult situation culturally, socially, and economically, when an increasingly elderly population is thinly spread in scattered farms. Hydroelectric schemes, afforestation, and the development of the tourist industry have improved the economy of some of these upland areas, while rural electrification and better roads, together with the increase in car ownership, have all helped to mitigate the rigours and isolation of life in these remote parts. The attractiveness of town life is still great, however, and the downward trend in the population of upland zones continues.

In the Lowland zone, on the good agricultural land, a pattern of country towns, villages, hamlets, and dispersed farms can give a dense rural population, but densities rise even higher as the distinction between urban and rural settlement becomes blurred. This is particularly the case where the homes of a motorized people fill in the spaces between the old nuclei, so that long-distance commuters become the neighbours of local rural workers.

The demographic outlook. Tentative projections of the future peopling of the United Kingdom forecast a population of about 57,700,000 in 1981, rising to over 63,000,000 in the year 2001. Population is likely to continue to grow around many of the conurbations, although increasing emphasis on the rehabilitation of their centres, particularly inner London, may help to avert the current downward spiral in social conditions that seems to afflict the large city centres of the Western world. Attempts to reduce the nationwide trend toward an ever increasing concentration of population in South East England now seem to have met with some success, for there was, in 1970, a very small net outward migration from the region, while the projected natural increase in the area's population, though it remains high up to the year 1999, has nevertheless been revised downward. (W.Ra.)

The national economy

The United Kingdom occupies a unique position in the world economy. The dominant industrial nation of the 19th century, it has, during the 20th century, seen its markets and its position in the world whittled away by other developed countries, especially by the United States, the nations of western Europe, and, more recently, Japan. Part of this relative decline has been due to the increasing industrialization of other countries, but a more fundamental reason has been the maintenance of the national role as sterling-area banker, necessitating restrictions on any domestic growth that might precipitate balance-of-payments deficits, loss of confidence in sterling, and consequent outflows of currency. The United Kingdom growth rate has thus compared poorly with that of other industrial countries, and, at the start of the 1970s, annual growth in gross national productivity, at just under 3 percent, was the lowest among comparable members of the Organisation for Economic Co-operation and Development (OECD). This slow growth rate has, in turn, retarded the British standard of living, as measured in terms of disposable income per head, to a level considerably lower than those in the United States, Canada, Sweden, and the Federal Republic of Germany and slightly lower than those in Italy and France.

Given favourable conditions, the potential for United Kingdom growth, relative to that of other countries, is nevertheless large. An increasing proportion of world trade is in manufactured goods, and thus the British industrial sector, already providing a larger proportion of such trade relative to its population size than any other country except Japan, is in a favourable position to take advantage of increased growth in world trade. By the beginning of the 1970s, exports to other countries of western Europe already exceeded those to the Commonwealth, even before Britain joined the European Economic Community (EEC) in January 1972. The extent to which the country would remain the focal point of Commonwealth trade also remained uncertain, for Australia, among other countries, was loosening its old ties with the former imperial homeland and turning to new trading partners such as Japan.

THE EXTENT AND DISTRIBUTION OF NATURAL RESOURCES

Mineral resources. Unlike most developed countries, the United Kingdom has very few natural mineral resources. With the exception of iron ore, virtually all metallic ores have to be imported, and even the proportion of home-produced iron ore, mined mainly in eastern England, and with an average 27 percent iron content, is decreasing. There are also small quantities of west coast ore with 48 percent average iron content. Annual consumption exceeded 30,000,000 tons, of which about a third was home produced, by the 1970s. Minerals in which the nation is self-sufficient are sand and gravel, chalk, limestone, salt, slate, china clay, and, most important, coal. Production of coal, however, has been decreasing rapidly since the early 1950s, mainly because competition from other energy sources, such as oil, has increased, and also because easily worked seams have been exhausted. In 1961, 180,000,000 tons of coal were produced; a decade later the figure was 147,000,000, of which nearly 3,000,000 tons were exported. Government policy has been to close the many small, uneconomical pits and to hold production at about 120,000,000 tons by the mid-1970s, using only the most efficient pits.

Of the more than 90,000,000,000 tons of crude oil consumed annually, only a tiny fraction, coming mainly from small fields in the Midlands, is home produced. The 1960s search for natural gas in the North Sea revealed large reserves of oil, and production of oil from the continental shelf was likely to begin in 1975. It remains to be seen whether large-scale extraction could be economical, a situation that would certainly improve the balance of payments and the economy as a whole. Natural gas from the North Sea has been entering the country since 1962. A controlled licensing system over the 100,000 square miles of the British claim area is operated by the Ministry of Power. The gas comes from West Sole and Leman Bank, which produced just under 1,400,000,000 cubic feet per day in 1971. Exploration continues, and larger quantities might be available by the late 1970s.

Natural gas (margin note)

Hydroelectric resources. Although rainfall in the mountainous areas is high, the topography does not provide ideal conditions for hydroelectric schemes, and by the 1970s power from such schemes accounted for only about 2 percent of all electric power generated. The majority of hydroelectric stations are found in the north of Scotland, where more than 1,000 megawatts are generated by some 54 stations, most of which use high-level water storage and have their own catchment areas. A pumped storage plant with a capacity of 400 megawatts operates at Cruachan, Loch Awe, and a further 300-megawatt plant at Foyers, Loch Ness, was to be completed in 1974. Other stations operate in the south of Scotland (122 megawatts) and in Wales (469 megawatts), the latter group including a 360-megawatt station at Ffestiniog.

SOURCES OF NATIONAL INCOME

Agriculture. The two main features that distinguish British agriculture from that of other western European and industrialized countries are, first, the small proportion of the total population (2 percent of those in civil employment) engaged in the industry and, second, its advanced degree of mechanization. With one tractor for every 35 acres of arable land, Britain has one of the heaviest tractor densities in the world. Agriculture accounts for about 3 percent of the total gross national product (GNP) and utilizes about 47,000,000 acres, with arable and rough grazing land accounting for about 18,000,000 and 16,000,000 acres respectively, and permanent grass accounting for the remainder. The arable area is decreasing slightly, while that under permanent grass is increasing, changes brought about mainly by government-support policies. Individual holdings numbered about 422,000 in the early 1970s, slightly more than half of which were operated part-time. Half of the total agriculture output was then attributable to about 42,000 large holdings, while, of the remainder, about 66,000 were thought to be commercially viable. Some 112,000 holdings were too small to operate profitably; the government policy is to encourage amalgamations. The average size of a full-time farm is about 160 acres. In Northern Ireland there are about 63,000 holdings, almost all of which are owner occupied, but some 40 percent of these are either very small or let on a seasonal basis, so that the number of agricultural businesses is around 37,000, half of which are part-time, with an average size of from 40 to 70 acres.

Total British agricultural output by the early 1970s was just over £2,000,000,000, the main contribution being from crops (19 percent), livestock (36 percent), livestock products (31 percent), and horticulutral products (12 percent). Of the farm crops, wheat and potatoes each accounted for almost a quarter, barley for about a third, and sugar beet for about 11 percent. Cattle and calves accounted for 40 percent of livestock output, pigs for over 30 percent, poultry for just under 20 percent, and sheep and lambs for 10 percent. Milk and milk products comprised over two-thirds, and eggs nearly one-third, of livestock products.

The British government is intimately concerned with agriculture, since it has been considered a matter of national interest to maintain a stable, efficient food-producing industry, with the lowest possible prices consistent with reasonable incomes for those involved. An agricultural-support policy, required by the Agricultural Act of 1947, enabled the government to provide guaranteed prices for the main agricultural products and, if necessary, to impose minimum prices for imports. Annual reviews determined guaranteed prices over a 12-month period, and deficiency payments, related to the difference between the market price and the guaranteed price, were made to producers. The government also gave extensive production grants for improvements to land, crops, livestock, and equipment and was also empowered to meet up to 50 percent of the approved costs of voluntary amalgamation of small farms into commercial units. By the early 1970s this system was in the process of being changed to one whereby import duties would be levied on temperate-zone foodstuffs coming into the country, thus raising the internal-market prices for similar British food and so stimulating further home production. The funds collected from the levies were to be used to provide price-deficiency payments on those home products whose prices fall below the guaranteed minimum. This change would bring agricultural policy in the United Kingdom closer into line with that of the EEC. The difference between the old farm-support system and the policy of maintaining high market prices followed in the EEC was nevertheless a major problem in the United Kingdom's application to join the Common Market. It was thought that adoption by the United Kingdom of the EEC's common agricultural policy would increase farm incomes and agricultural output by between 3 and 10 percent, but, at the same time, security and a basis for forward planning would be lost.

Government support for agriculture (margin note)

Forestry. Productive woodland occupies about 6.5 percent of the total United Kingdom land area; scrubs and old felled areas increase this to nearly 8 percent, the large area of unproductive woodland being largely the result of neglect of work during World Wars I and II. Ownership is divided about evenly between the Forestry Commission and private landlords. Replanting progresses at the annual rate of about 87,000 trees, most of which are Sitka spruce, lodgepole pine, Scotch pine, and Norway spruce. The home timber industry provides for only about 10 percent of the country's needs, and most of its produce is low-grade when compared with that imported from Scandinavia and elsewhere.

Fishing. In 1971 over £93,000,000 worth of fish was landed in the United Kingdom, of which nearly 92 percent was wet (*i.e.*, nonshell) fish. Of this total, about 47 percent were cod, 20 percent haddock, 8 percent plaice, and 6 percent herring; the 8 percent shellfish were mainly mussels and oysters. The industry is especially important to Scotland, the fishing fleet of which numbered over 2,600 ships in 1971, while that of England and Wales numbered about 3,200. Over the previous decade the size of the Scottish fleet had declined by over 15 percent and that of the English and Welsh by 13 percent. This is in part due to rationalization—bigger vessels are being used for freezing the catch.

The weight of landed fish by the early 1970s was over 1,100,000 tons annually, an increase of 43 percent over the figure for ten years earlier. Exports of fish are a minor, but rapidly increasing, factor in the industry's economy, having doubled over the 1960s. The white fish industry covers three areas: distant water, near and middle water, and inshore fisheries. There are over 160 distant water vessels, operating from Hull, Grimsby, and Fleetwood, while near and middle water vessels number about 350. The industry employs about 18,000 people.

Government aid to the fishing industry consists of grants and loans toward purchase and improvement of vessels and equipment. Subsidies are given according to the class of vessel used, with the white fish trade receiving the most support. There are no subsidies for shellfish. There is also a subsidy related to the operating efficiency of vessels.

Mining and quarrying. This is a rapidly declining sector of the national economy, its output having dropped by more than 20 percent during the 1960s. During the same period, output per head nevertheless increased by almost the same proportion. The decline is due mainly to the running down of the coal industry (see below *Energy*). Mining and quarrying of other materials predominantly concerns sand and gravel (over 100,000,000 tons annually by the early 1970s), limestone (over 85,000,000 tons), and clays, shale, and igneous rock (about 35,000,000 tons each).

Principal mining and quarrying products

Manufacturing. The manufacturing sector is a vital element in the economy, employing nearly 9,000,000 people; that is, 35 percent of the total labour force. It contributes nearly 35 percent of the total GNP and its production rose by over a quarter during the 1960s. Industries with the highest growth rates tend to be those involved in advanced technology; examples are the chemical industries, instrument and electrical engineering, and those concerned with the by-products of coal and petroleum. Declining sectors are shipbuilding and leatherwork, falling, respectively, by 15 percent and 6 percent in the same period. This decline occurred because other countries were more competitive, mainly through the availability of cheaper labour. In terms of output and work force, the engineering and electrical-goods industry was, in the early 1970s, the largest manufacturing industry, employing 26 percent of the total manufacturing labour force of 8,900,000 and contributing 18 percent of the gross manufacturing output. The textile, leather, and clothing industries employed 14 percent of the labour force, and contributed 1 percent of its total output, while the vehicle industry employed well over 9 percent of the sector total and contributed more than 10 percent of gross output.

Iron and steel industry

A key supply industry to the manufacturing sector is the iron and steel industry. Re-nationalized in 1967, the British Steel Corporation combines 13 major steel companies producing over 90 percent of the country's total crude-steel output, which in 1971 was 26,600,000 tons. Capital expenditure, which up to the early 1960s was concentrated on increasing capacity, especially in strip-mill expansion, was in the early 1970s aimed at improving efficiency. As a result, the country now has some of the most modern converter- and electric-furnace plants in Europe.

Investment in manufacturing industry is vital to economic growth, and it increased a third, to over £1,800,000, during the 1960s. Of the total investment in the manufacturing sector, over two-thirds is spent on new plants and machinery. In the early 1970s the low level of industrial investment was a matter of serious concern.

Energy. The structure of national energy production has altered radically since the early 1950s. At that time, indigenous coal provided nearly 90 percent of total power requirements. Since then, the coal industry has contracted dramatically, and its competitors have become much more important; so much so that, by the early 1970s, little more than 39,200,000,000 therms, or 47 percent of total gross energy consumption, was provided by coal itself. Oil provided the bulk of the remainder, dwarfing the contributions of nuclear energy, gas, and hydroelectric power. Electricity-generating capacity in the early 1970s was nearly 62,000 megawatts, an increase of over 80 percent on the figure a decade earlier. The most significant recent change has been the increase in the use of oil power, the production of which doubled between 1955 and 1960 and virtually doubled again during the 1960s. The most radical change, in terms of future impact, has been the switch to nuclear energy. The United Kingdom has been a pioneer in this field, its use of electricity generated by nuclear plants exceeding, by 1970, that of the rest of the world put together. It was expected that, by the mid-1970s, as much as 25 percent of the total public electricity supply would come from nu-

Nuclear energy

clear sources. The electricity authorities themselves operate nine nuclear-powered "magnox" stations, with total output of 4,500 megawatts. These stations, using early, less sophisticated reactors were developed between 1955 and 1970; a second expansion with advanced gas-cooled reactors, began production in 1970 and was expected to contribute 8,000 megawatts by 1976. These latest plants were to use enriched uranium dioxide fuel encased in stainless steel, a development of the magnox system. The Atomic Energy Authority, which directs nuclear research, has three stations producing electricity, with a total capacity of 128 megawatts. The former AEA stations at Calder Hall, in Cumberland, and Chapelcross, Dumfriesshire (both 198 megawatts), are now owned and operated by British Nuclear Fuels Ltd.

The use of gas as a source of energy has also greatly increased, the total available at gasworks increasing by over two-thirds in the 1960s, to 6,300,000,000 therms. Most is now oil-based, the proportion of coal-based gas having declined rapidly during the 1960s. The remainder of available gas comes from privately owned coke ovens and oil refineries. Annual growth rates in overall consumption stood at around 12 percent in the early 1970s, when the gas industry was engaged in a major transformation of its equipment in order to cope with expanded production of natural gas, expected to reach 3,000,000,000 cubic feet per day by 1975. This transformation took place especially in the domestic market, which accounted for three-fifths of total demand.

Finance. The United Kingdom has one of the globe's oldest, most extensive, and most highly developed financial systems, and for many purposes London is still the financial centre of the Western world, sharing in the convulsions and crises that afflicted the international monetary system in the late 1960s and early 1970s. The hub of this system is the Bank of England, established in 1694 and nationalized in 1946. Its main function is to act as banker to the government, to the private banks, and to overseas central banks. Externally, it administers exchange control and operates the Exchange Equalisation Account, which is used to maintain within certain set limits the exchange rate of sterling against other currencies. Internally, the bank acts as the sole note-issuing authority in England and Wales (Scottish and Northern Ireland banks have their own limited issuing right), the issue being virtually all fiduciary (*i.e.*, dependent for its value on public confidence or securities) since almost all the gold backing for issue has been transferred to the Exchange Equalisation Account. The bank works in close contact with the government, especially over the control of monetary policy, in which it acts as the government's executive arm in giving directives to the commercial banks. The major policy instrument is control of bank rate, which is the rate at which the bank will lend money as lender of last resort to the discount houses. The country's whole interest-rate structure is based either on a fixed relationship to bank rate or on expectations about its possible movements. In many circumstances movements in bank rate can in fact have considerable effect on the money supply and on the cost of borrowing. The bank also manipulates the supply of money by open-market operations on the money and gilt-edged (government stock) markets. It can affect the policy of the commercial banks by issuing directives on the level of lending and credit regarded as permissible, and it can extract from them special deposits over and above those already held at the bank as liquid assets.

The Bank of England

The commercial bank group consists of six London clearing banks, which carry on virtually all commercial banking in England and Wales, three Scottish clearing banks, and two Northern Ireland banks. All have numerous branches. Certain Bank of England regulations affect the operation of the commercial banks; their holdings of coin, notes, and balances at the Bank of England must be kept at 8 percent of total deposits, and the minimum ratio for liquid assets is 28 percent. Between 1951 and 1958 advances varied between 26 and 30 percent of total deposits, but since then they have averaged 40 to 50 percent.

This comprehensive banking system is integrated with complex and sophisticated capital and discount markets, which are based in the City of London, a small area of old London that retains its global pre-eminence as a commercial and financial centre. The importance of the City has been based on the United Kingdom's position as banker for the sterling area; this has meant that substantial funds are held in the City for overseas sterling countries and are utilized, together with funds from many nonsterling countries, in various financial transactions to the City's and its customers' advantage. A major recent trend has been for London banks to receive large deposits of dollars, which are then re-lent, creating the Eurodollar market.

Many other important institutions operate in the City; among them the Stock Exchange, the largest of the eight in the nation. About 9,000 securities with an enormous total value were quoted on the London Stock Exchange by the early 1970s. There are numerous insurance companies, dominated by the international insurance market of Lloyds; shipping companies; the merchant banks and discount houses; foreign banks; life assurance offices; building societies; and many of the world's major commodity markets. The various activities of the City make a large contribution to the United Kingdom's favourable balance on invisible trade transactions.

Foreign trade. With less than 2 percent of the world's population, the United Kingdom entered the 1970s as the world's third largest trading nation, taking over 11 percent of the total trade and 8 percent of the export trade in manufactured goods. With few natural resources of its own, the country relies on imports for nearly half of its food and for most of its raw materials. In order to earn the foreign exchange needed to pay for these, exports value about one-fifth of the total national GNP. Although the terms of trade with the rest of the world have tended, since the late 1950s, to be favourable to the United Kingdom, adverse movements in 1963 and 1964 were repeated in the late 1960s, prompting a pessimistic interpretation of the ultimate effects of the devaluation of the pound carried out in 1967.

The rate of growth of imports has been erratic compared with that of exports, mainly because of their changing composition. Over the 1960s, imports increased in volume by almost a half. The proportion of foodstuffs, drink, and tobacco decreased, although the absolute amounts imported increased. Imports of basic raw materials, including fuels, exhibited a similar decline, falling from over a third of the total in the early 1950s to barely a quarter in 1971, while imports of semimanufactures have tended to increase, as developing countries turn to processing their raw materials before exporting them. Crude petroleum and lubricants are the largest single commodity import, accounting for more than 10 percent of total import value. Finished manufactured goods have shown the greatest percentage rise in recent years, from 7 percent in 1957 to 23 percent in 1971, the steepest rise being in capital goods. Exports have also risen rapidly, at a steady rate of about 5 percent per annum in the early 1960s and fluctuating greatly in the latter part of the decade between 10 and 25 percent. More than five-sixths of total exports are in manufactured goods, and, by 1971, 45 percent of the total was engineering goods. Machinery, both electrical and mechanical, vehicles, tractors, and scientific instruments are the major components of this sector, while chemicals are a rapidly growing export. Sectors in relative decline include textiles and metal manufactures other than machinery.

The sources and destinations of United Kingdom trade include every country in the world, but the trend is for a relatively larger percentage of all trade to be carried out with western Europe. Just prior to British entry to the EEC, exports to western Europe were almost 40 percent of total exports; those to EEC countries accounted for 21 percent, and those to the European Free Trade Association (EFTA) for 15 percent. Conversely, trade with the sterling area and the Commonwealth has relatively declined, exports reaching only 28 percent of the total in 1971. Imports from these areas have similarly declined.

Despite the increased importance of western Europe in the country's trade, the U.S. remains its major single customer, the source in 1971 of 11 percent of imports and the recipient of 12 percent of exports.

Considered year by year, visible imports are greater than visible exports, although the gap has, until recently, been largely covered by such invisible exports as shipping, civil aviation, financial services, travel, and tourism. During the 1960s, however, a continuous balance-of-payments deficit grew up, eventually leading to the devaluation of the pound in 1967. The consequent government-sponsored export drive achieved considerable success, and by mid-year 1971 pressure on sterling had eased. There was some uncertainty in 1970 and 1971 as to whether the favourable trade situation could be maintained in the face of continuing domestic and international inflation.

MANAGEMENT OF THE ECONOMY

The private sector. The British economy is a good example of a mixed economic system, for the public and private sectors claim almost equal shares of the GNP. The relationship between government and the private sector varies to some extent, according to whether a Conservative or a Labour government is in power; the former tends to allow the private sector to succeed or fail according to its own resources and energy, while the latter usually intervenes more actively, bolstering up failing sectors and also initiating new projects. Within such a system, and given an international situation beyond its control, a government can clearly impose no overall plan, but it is able to indicate to private industry the lines of expansion that it believes necessary and, to some extent, force it along them. The main ways in which a government influences industry are by its fiscal and monetary policies, by its control of the level of public expenditure, and by provision of government contracts, services, information, and advice. These operate mainly to affect aggregate demand, supply, investment, and savings. Equally effective is the two-pronged policy of encouraging investment and counteracting relatively high unemployment in the more depressed areas, forcing development away from the prosperous and congested areas of the Midlands and the South East. Under the Labour government of 1964–70, investment incentives took the form of grants of varying sizes. The Conservative government of the early 1970s operated a system of investment allowances, by which 60 percent of capital expenditure could be written off in the first year and 25 percent of the remainder in succeeding years. In development areas free depreciation was allowed. Other development inducements included the provision of ready-built factories, building grants, and assistance with planning. For manufacturing industries in development areas, a selective employment tax, introduced by the Labour government in 1966 and originally scheduled to be abolished by the Conservatives in 1974, was refunded; firms were also granted a 37.5 percent premium and a regional employment premium of £1.50 per head on their employees. Among the government bodies concerned with the private sector is the National Economic Development Council, which runs committees to study and promote productivity in some 21 separate industries. The Monopolies Commission and the Restrictive Practices Court (Department of Employment and Productivity) operate to ensure that agreements entered into by companies do not jeopardize the public interest.

The public sector and the role of government. About 10 percent of the total British labour force works for statutory bodies directly controlling public corporations, which operate major industries and services in the public interest. These include the Bank of England, the Post Office, the British Broadcasting Corporation (BBC), the major airlines, the Atomic Energy Authority, the coal, gas, electricity, and steel industries, and the railway, docks, waterway, and freight services. Although not part of government departments, these bodies are under varying degrees of control by them. Responsibility for management nevertheless lies with the boards and staff of each public corporation, not with the minister of the government department concerned. Some bodies are self-supporting, while others receive Exchequer grants. The minister appoints the chairman and members of the board and can direct the general running of the corporation; but he does not interfere in day-to-day operations. In the early 1970s it was the aim to achieve a higher degree of financial self-support than that of the 1960s. Capital expenditure is met by loans from the Exchequer if it cannot be met from internal funds. Financial targets vary from 12.4 percent gross return to a mere break-even, the test discount rate applied for investment being 8 percent.

Con-sumers' councils

Consumer interests are usually looked after by consumers' councils, which deal with complaints and suggestions and can make representations to the boards of the ministers concerned.

Between 1956 and 1966 the public sector accounted for around 40 percent of fixed investment, reaching some 48 percent in the early 1970s. This was divided between public corporations, the central government, and local authorities. The share taken by local government has recently increased, while that of the central government has diminished.

Taxation.   Total national taxation receipts for the financial year April 6, 1971, to April 5, 1972, an average example for the early 1970s, were estimated at £16,217,000,000 and were produced by three major forms of taxation: on income, on capital, and on expenditure. Considerable reform of the structure of taxation, outlined in the 1971 budget, is due to come into effect in subsequent years.

Taxes on income.   Although accurate comparisons are not feasible because of differences in taxation methods, costs of living, and social security benefits and payments, it is generally thought that personal taxation in the United Kingdom is among the highest in the world. On a single person's earned income of £30,000, for example, the effective total rate of income tax and surtax was 60.7 percent before, and 60.5 percent after, the 1971 budget. Income taxes include personal income tax, surtax, and corporation tax. In 1972 the standard rate of personal income tax, estimated to produce 41 percent of total tax receipts, was 38.75 pence in the pound sterling; this was applied to an individual's total income after deduction of personal, earned-income, marriage, children's, and various other allowances or reliefs. Until April 1, 1972, a married couple's income was aggregated and treated as the husband's income, but thereafter the wife was free to choose either aggregation or a separate tax evaluation. Surtax, estimated to produce 2.17 percent of total tax receipts in 1972–73, is an additional graduated tax payable on personal incomes, which, after certain allowable deductions have been made, including earned-income relief and a further deduction of up to £2,000 on earned income, exceeds £3,000. Reforms of personal taxation planned to come into effect in 1973 were to include the replacement of income tax and surtax by a single, graduated tax. This would be constructed in terms of earned income, a broad band of which would be charged at a provisional rate of 30 percent; higher rates would apply to higher income groups, rising to a top rate of 75 percent on an earned income over £20,000. Higher rates would also be applied to unearned income above a certain level, but, as one of the major aims of the reform is to ease the burden on this income, its lower levels will attract only the new earned-income rate.

Corporation tax, estimated to produce 8.06 percent of total tax receipts in 1972–73, is a company income tax on profits. The 1972 budget proposed that, effective April 1973, an imputation system should be introduced.

Taxes on capital.   Taxes on capital are estate duties, popularly called death duties, and capital gains tax, estimated to account, respectively, for 2.5 percent and 1.2 percent of total tax receipts in 1972–73. The former is applicable at death on estates of over £15,000; above this sum the rate ranges from 25 to 75 percent. Capital gains tax is payable on disposal of assets; with companies the profits occurring from such disposals are liable to corporation tax, while for individuals the rate is generally 30 percent. The sale of a person's principal private residence,

Capital gains tax

chattels worth less than £1,000, goods with a predictable life of shorter than 50 years, gifts to charities, and certain securities are not subject to the tax.

Taxes on expenditure.   Taxes on expenditure include customs and excise duties, applying mainly to tobacco, hydrocarbon oil, and alcoholic drinks, estimated to account, respectively, for 7, 9, and 6.5 percent of total 1972–73 tax receipts. Another tax on expenditure is purchase tax, which is applied to a wide range of goods, usually consumer goods, at two different rates which can be varied by the Chancellor of the Exchequer for up to a year at a time, under the so-called regulator system. It was estimated to account for 8.1 percent of total 1972–73 receipts. Other taxes on expenditure are betting taxes and motor-vehicle-license charges.

A selective employment tax (SET), was introduced in 1966 that fell into none of the three major tax categories noted above. Designed mainly to encourage the transfer of labour from service to manufacturing industries, it was, from July 1971, charged on employers at a rate of £1.20 pence per week for every man employed, and £0.60 pence for every woman. Manufacturing employers in developing areas got a refund, together with two premiums, while those not in developing areas and employers in nationalized industries, in transport and communications, agriculture, and the extractive industries receive the refund but no premiums. From April 1, 1973, SET was to be replaced by a value-added tax at the rate of 10 percent on the supply of goods and services and on importation of goods subject to certain exceptions. From that date, a tax on new and imported cars would be levied at 10 percent of the wholesale value.

Employers' associations and trade unions.   The main employers' organization is the Confederation of British Industry (CBI), which deals with all industrial matters affecting employers. In close contact with the government, the public, and other interested parties, it includes more than 1,400 different employers' organizations, of which about 90 are nationwide. These are the bodies that negotiate most of the important collective agreements with trade unions.

Labour in nearly all industries and occupations is organized, to a varying extent, into trade unions. Total membership by the early 1970s exceeded 10,000,000 divided among over 500 unions, of which some two dozen accounted for almost three-quarters of all members. Just over half the total number of trade union members were in the nine unions with a membership of more than 250,000. Membership at the beginning of the 1970s was increasing most rapidly among white-collar workers, largely because manual labourers, skilled and unskilled, were earlier organized into unions. Most unions belong to the Trades Union Congress (TUC), the central body of the movement. The TUC is empowered to mediate between unions, to comment on wage claims, and to deal with unauthorized or unconstitutional strikes. It is nonpolitical, but unions may set up a political fund financed by a membership levy, from which anyone may opt out. Most unions have such a fund, used to support the Labour Party.

Trades Union Congress

Industrial relations in the United Kingdom were going through fundamental changes in the early 1970s. For many years previously, agreements between employers and unions had been only exceptionally enforceable by law, and the conditions surrounding such agreements were often archaic, complex, and liable to considerable misunderstanding. As a result, although the official figures for strikes were not as bad as those in many countries, enormous harm was done in the late 1960s and early 1970s by numerous unrecorded unofficial strikes. The Conservative government, in 1971, passed an Industrial Relations Act, aimed at modernizing the structure of industrial relations. By it the registrar of trade unions was given additional powers, and a National Industrial Relations Court was set up to adjudicate on "unfair" industrial practice, both on the unions' and on the employers' side. Registered unions were obliged to define precisely who is entitled to call a strike against employment contracts, which are, under the act, legally enforceable unless

The changing context of industrial relations

the signatories specifically state that they shall not be so. Those not legally entitled to strike are liable for damages. Registered unions are held responsible for the activities of their members; if the National Industrial Relations Court decides that a union has helped or condoned the activities of an unregistered group, that union's funds will be put at risk, and the ultimate sanction is the threat of deregistration. The act is expected to eliminate the closed shop, by which unionists demand that nonunion workers be excluded from the factory or work group.

Contemporary economic problems and policies.   The period since World War II has witnessed continuous expansion in the British economy, rising standards of living, high industrial production, and generally low unemployment. There has also been a fundamental disequilibrium in the balance-of-payments situation, whereby imports have tended to rise faster with national income than have exports. The situation has been aggravated by the United Kingdom's position as banker to the sterling area, which meant that any loss of confidence in the strength of sterling vis-à-vis other currencies, such as might be prompted by a continual balance-of-payments deficit, immediately led to outflows of sterling with consequent further loss of confidence. In such circumstances it would be impossible to maintain the exchange rate without further reducing gold reserves. Until 1967, it had been the policy of successive governments to attack this problem by reducing the rate of growth of demand through restrictive fiscal and monetary policies whenever the balance-of-payments deficit seemed seriously increasing. Thus, interest rates would rise and foreign currencies be attracted back to the United Kingdom. Such action restricted growth rates and increased unemployment, however, and the potential of the economy remained seriously unexploited.

In 1967 the government finally recognized that the prolonged overvaluation of sterling created a fundamental flaw in the economy, and the pound was devalued. In order to benefit from this action, resources had to be diverted from the domestic to the export market as quickly as possible, and the measure of success achieved is shown by the fact that between 1967 and 1971 the balance of exports over imports changed from a deficit of £225,000,000 to a surplus of £299,000,000. The price paid in this achievement was high; the increase in domestic output was extremely small, and unemployment soared to a 1971 level of 3.6 percent (excluding Northern Ireland) compared with an average level of 1.7 percent in the 1960s.

The problem inherited by the Conservative government in 1970 was thus that of maintaining progress in the balance of payments while at the same time encouraging growth rates commensurate with the productive potential of the economy as a whole. Its task was made more difficult by a rapid rise in the number of damaging strikes in many key export industries, which inevitably gave Britain the reputation of an unreliable provider of goods. At the same time industrialists, both British and foreign, showed a marked reluctance to invest in the United Kingdom at anything like the rate required to parallel the growth in demand and to maintain production at a level high enough to keep unemployment at an acceptable level. Inflation, a problem throughout the world, became particularly serious in the United Kingdom, where, in the year 1971, it was in the region of 13 percent. It was aggravated by many wage claims put in by unions in order to meet and anticipate an ever-increasing cost of living. Although the balance-of-payments problem had, by the early 1970s, been solved for at least the short term, this had thus been achieved only at the cost of a high rate of inflation, combined with serious stagnation and rising unemployment. In this period wage and price increases were so high that it seemed possible that a disastrous form of hyperinflation could develop. This sort of inflation had never occurred in Britain, although it was common in many countries between World Wars I and II and in some developing countries in the 1950s and 1960s. The various methods used by the government to restrict or counter wage claims, all of which depended for success on voluntary union agreement to conform to wage-rise

Inflation

norms strictly related to productivity growth, had met with little real success by mid-1971; it remained to be seen what could be achieved by means of the controversial Industrial Relations Act. This was expected to produce a slow but sure change in the high rate of wage increases, reducing them from the 10–15 percent level typical of 1971 to something around 5–7 percent or more, where productivity deals could be made. The act also provides for any wage contracts made to remain legally binding for a longer period of time; although, therefore, official strikes may occur when the time limit runs out, the United Kingdom's liability to damaging unofficial strikes should, hopefully, be reduced, thus encouraging investment. Provided that such renewed investment in fact takes place, the growth rate in the GNP for the early 1970s might reach nearly 4 percent, reducing unemployment to less than 2 percent. In such a situation the government would be in a much stronger position to deal with more peripheral economic problems such as those of the traditionally depressed areas. Attention could also be given to the restructuring of several older industries and to improving equipment for the social and educational services. Such an outcome was rendered even more vital by Britain's joining the EEC, in which the rewards could be spectacular for a prosperous United Kingdom with a sound economic growth rate but in which difficulties would be multiplied if the economy remained stagnant and inflationary.   (E.I.U.)

Transportation

THE OVERALL SYSTEM

Main transportation routes.   Most of the heaviest British passenger and freight loads travel along the main English commercial axis running from London, through Birmingham, to Liverpool and Manchester. Along this route, that of the Roman Watling Street and the famous Scottish civil engineer Thomas Telford's London to Holyhead Road, now lie the principal electrified trunk rail line, the M.1 and M.6 motorways, the Grand Union Canal, the principal internal air corridor, and the main natural-gas and petroleum pipelines. This axis has extensions: northward as the west coast route to Scotland; westward through North Wales to Holyhead, the principal port for travel to Dublin; and southward from London to the south coast and the prospective Channel Tunnel. London and Liverpool–Manchester are by far the largest freight ports, as well as the largest centres of population and industry. Major transport arteries have developed linking them with other cities and regions in Britain.

The English commercial transport axis

The role of public transportation.   Apart from traffic covering the main intercity routes, most urban and interurban public transportation of both people and freight is in decline. Despite the growing population and the consequent increase of production and consumption, the amount of freight moved by railways fell from an annual 500,000,000 tons before 1914 to little more than 200,000,000 tons in the early 1970s. In the same period the number of passengers carried fell from 1,300,000,000 to nearly 824,000,000. Although urban populations have steadily increased, public passenger traffic in towns and cities had been declining by a few percent per annum for many years even before the 1960s, when spiralling fare increases and diminished services accelerated the annual falloff rate to between 3 and 5 percent. Ownership of private cars has been increasing consistently since the 1920s, except during World War II and periods of economic depression, at a little under 10 percent per annum. By 1971 about 225 private cars were registered for every 1,000 persons; this was estimated to be about half the anticipated saturation level for private car ownership, a status that, unless checked by changes in taste or policy, would be reached by the end of the 20th century. By 1971 more than 75 percent of total passenger mileage was made in privately owned vehicles.

Transportation policy.   The near-crisis conditions that have developed for the publicly owned road, rail, and waterways transportation systems and the seriously congested state of most main roads have brought the problem of transportation under closer public scrutiny in recent years. In the face of the need to maintain some form of passenger-transport services despite declining demand and consequent increasing losses, some practical attempts to cut costs, especially labour costs, have been made. Some one-man buses have been introduced into service; in London the new Underground Victoria Line has automated trains, and automated ticket collection is being introduced in underground stations.

Automation in urban transport

Government policy for the national transport undertakings has varied according to whether the government is Conservative or Labour. The Conservatives practice a fairly strict commercialism: they closed uneconomical services in the early 1960s and proposed, in the early 1970s, to end the subsidization of commuter rail travel. Labour has tended to recognize the social value of many of the country's public transport services and, in the late 1960s, was paying considerable subsidies to the British Railways Board.

A policy statement that preceded the 1968 Transport Act showed government acceptance of the movement away from rail traffic and from public transport in general. It cleared the way for the railways to concentrate on providing the services for which they are best suited; that is to say, intercity passenger trains, city commuter services, and trainload freight. By the terms of the act, previously competing bus and rail passenger services in many city regions were placed under the operational control of unified passenger transport authorities, which were required to coordinate services and balance operating costs against revenues supplemented by local taxation. The act incorporated most of the bus undertakings that were not municipally owned into a National Bus Company, operating in ten areas, and, in 1969, control of London Transport (buses and underground railways) was vested in the Greater London Council. In 1970 the Conservatives decided to strengthen the main private airline by the transfer to it of some routes previously served by the state airlines.

INTERNAL COMPONENTS

Roads. Since 1914, the importance of roads for freight and passenger movement has been growing steadily, and, in the early 1970s, road travel accounted for 90 percent of all passenger movement within the United Kingdom. Roads provide excellent coverage of most of the country, except in the thinly populated areas of the Highland zone. Most roads are of minor status, however, and less than 5 percent of total United Kingdom road mileage consists of trunk roads—the major routes—that are the financial responsibility of the central government. These trunk roads, together with principal roads, a classification embracing a further 10 percent of the total, carry the major intercity and intertown flows in the regions.

Despite the reconstruction, sometimes to high standards, of many roads, serious traffic congestion and low travel speeds, to say nothing of pollution problems, are normal on most of the principal roads that carry two-directional traffic. Motorways and other roads that carry the two opposing streams of traffic on separated (dual) roadways are usually less congested, but in some areas, particularly near cities, these too are becoming overloaded. The United Kingdom, containing more than 70 registered vehicles per mile of road, has a higher vehicle density than any other country.

Motorways

The United Kingdom's motorway, or freeway, building program got under way only in the 1950s. The first substantial length of motorway in Britain, the M.1, came into service in 1959, and the first 1,000 miles of such roads were due to be completed in the early 1970s. By the early 1970s motorways linked London with the Midlands, the northwest, and the Scottish border by the west coast route; with the West Yorkshire cities; and with Bristol and South Wales. An east–west trans-Pennine motorway, linking Liverpool and Manchester with Leeds and Hull, was under construction, and further motorways were planned to serve the south coast of England. In Scotland there was a Glasgow–Edinburgh–Stirling triangle of motorways, and in Northern Ireland some 40 miles of motorway radiated from Belfast. The motor-

ways relieve pressure on other roads, creating a better environment for local traffic.

Most of the motorways in existence in the early 1970s were national routes, connecting London with the regions and the regions with one another. A second group of motorways, more regional in character and designed to duplicate and relieve existing heavily loaded interurban routes, was also taking shape: some were urban motorways, created to ease the acute problems of traffic congestion in the nation's older cities.

Capital expenditure on new roads and major reconstructions, amounting to about three-fifths of total central and local government roadwork expenditure, was expected to rise with the increasing use of road transport. In 1970 the Ministry of Transport, shortly before its merger into the Department of the Environment, published a strategy for a 20-year development of a national, interurban network of main roads with dual roadways but not necessarily motorways, or even new routes. The program was to be correlated with plans for the economic development of the regions.

Railways. The 1960s and early 1970s have seen changes in Britain's railway system perhaps unequalled since the first 20 years of railway development in the early 19th century. At its peak in 1914 the railway system had about 20,000 miles of routes and carried nearly 1,300,000,000 passengers and more than 500,000,000 tons of freight annually. It was controlled by some 120 competing companies, which had, between them, a virtual monopoly of inland traffic. Passenger traffic remained stable between World Wars I and II, but there was a steady loss of freight traffic to road transport. Nationalized in 1947 by the Railway Executive established under the British Transport Commission, the railways were run in much the same way as before. Steam, replaced by diesel power in the 1950s and by electric power in the 1960s, disappeared entirely in 1968.

Rail nationalization

A major investigation into the commercial viability of the system, undertaken in 1962, showed that a large number of routes, services, and stations were uneconomical, half the route mileage carrying insignificant freight and passenger traffic and half the stations handling only 2 percent of traffic. By the end of 1970, route mileage had been reduced to almost 12,000 and the number of stations from 7,000 in 1961 to fewer than 2,900, less than one-quarter of which handled freight. Specialization of services, undertaken as a result of the 1968 Transport Act, resulted in an increase of trunk trainload freight, of intercity express passenger trains, and the suburban commuter services. Unprofitable miscellaneous traffic was transferred to a new National Freight Corporation, and technological improvements were also made. Track reconstruction, the introduction of long, continuously welded rails, and new signalling all combined to improve comfort, safety, and speeds. Following main-line electrification and track reconstruction between, for example, London (Euston) and Liverpool–Manchester, many daily trains have scheduled journey speeds of 80 miles (130 kilometres) per hour, with top speeds of 100 miles per hour, which reduce the pre-electrification journey time by one-third. In 1971 the decision was taken to extend the electrification of the London to Liverpool–Manchester line to the whole of the main west coast line to Glasgow. For specialized freights, liner trains have been introduced: these function as indivisible units and operate on regular schedules at express-passenger-train speeds. Inland container bases are connected by liner train to the port container berths, and the use of these sealed, easily handled bulk containers is having an increasing impact on the carriage of goods to and from ports.

In their development of high-speed track, signalling, and rolling stock, British railways are among the most modern in the world. By the early 1970s, the railway's research division had an advanced passenger train, planned for speeds of 125-150 miles per hour, in the development stage. This project has aroused considerable international interest; because of these speeds railways can compete with air travel for journeys of up to about 350 miles.

The
Cale-
donian
Canal

The
London
and
Manchester
pipeline

Inland waterways. Most of Britain's canals are 18th- or early 19th-century narrow-boat canals. Though not without scenic attraction, except in the grimy industrial regions, canals have been at a commercial disadvantage ever since railways were first built, and their traffic has so dwindled that, by the early 1970s, they were carrying less than 0.5 percent of the total inland freight tonnage.

One of Britain's more interesting canals is the Caledonian, another early-19th-century engineering feat by Telford. Linking Loch Ness to Loch Linnhe and the Moray Firth, it allows small vessels to traverse the "waist" of Scotland and so avoid the Pentland Firth passage.

Almost the whole of the 2,000 miles of navigable rivers and canals in Britain, together with their small estuarine ports, were nationalized in 1947 and came under the control of the British Waterways Board. One exception is the Manchester Ship Canal, open to deep-sea vessels, which allows ships of up to 10,000 tons to travel 30 miles inland from the Mersey Estuary to Manchester.

The 1968 Transport Act introduced a new function for many of the noncommercial canals. They were to become amenity waterways for cruising and recreation and thus take on a new and important role in a more leisure-oriented society. Service facilities and amenity clubs are increasing, and some attempt is being made to include canal frontages in urban redevelopment.

In the early 1970s more than half the board's revenue came from the sale of water, a function of canals that had scarcely begun to be exploited adequately. This, with their importance for land drainage and their new leisure role, constitutes the foreseeable future use of the canals.

Pipelines. The increasing demand for oil and oil products, coupled with the growing congestion in road transport and the discovery of natural gas in the North Sea, led during the 1960s to a development of pipelines for the transport of oil and gas. Two major systems are operated: one by the Gas Council for the distribution of natural gas and the other by the petroleum industry for that of oil and oil products.

Gas. The first high-pressure gas pipeline was commissioned in 1964 to distribute imported liquefied natural gas from the port terminal at Canvey Island, near London, to the industrial Midlands. Discovery of the major North Sea natural-gas fields in 1965–66, which according to a 1971 report could hold gas reserves of 50,000,000,000,000 cubic feet, meant that very large indigenous supplies of natural gas would become available, and it was decided to supply this form of gas to all parts of Britain as quickly as possible, to replace coal gas. The Gas Council constructed a large-diameter high-pressure pipeline between London and Manchester, together with feeders from the natural-gas-field landing points on the east coast. This link was to be connected eventually to Bristol and South Wales, and, through West Yorkshire, to Newcastle and Glasgow. In the early 1970s the system could supply an annual total of 2,000,000,000 cubic feet, at a pressure of 1,000 pounds per square inch, to the 12 existing area gas boards. These could regulate the pressure to feed their supergrids, high-pressure grids, and local grids for industrial and domestic supplies.

Oil. The history of oil pipelines is rather longer, dating from the wartime oil supply lines of the 1940s. These were subsequently extended with the commission of new refineries on the River Thames, Southampton Water, and the River Humber. In the early 1970s pipelines for the transmission of petroleum interconnected the major refineries on the Thames, Merseyside, Southampton, the Severn, and the Humber, also supplying inland distribution terminals. The building of further lines from the refineries to new deepwater-tanker terminals at Milford Haven and Anglesey was under consideration. Some of the pipelines transport crude oil from port to refinery; most are used to convey refined white oils to inland distribution centres, but some move other oil products between refineries and centres of the petrochemical industries.

Other materials. Pipelines have been used to a limited extent for conveying material other than liquid hydrocarbons. A 57-mile pipeline carries chalk slurry from quarries at Dunstable, in Bedfordshire, to a cement works at Rugby, in the Midlands, while, in the early 1970s, experiments were being made in the moving of coal by pipeline. The development of pipelines as an important form of transport is likely to continue as experience in this area increases and industries become more integrated.

EXTERNAL FUNCTIONS

Seaports. Ownership of the majority of commercial seaports in Britain was vested in the British Transport Docks Board by the 1962 Transport Act. Half of Britain's imports and exports are nevertheless handled by the major independent ports, particularly those on the Rivers Mersey and Thames. The traffic of the docks of the British Transport Docks Board is mainly of the cross-Channel, short-haul variety, serving Ireland, the offshore islands, and the closer continental ports, as well as British coastwise traffic.

The association of shipping lines with individual ports has led to a tendency for traffic with particular parts of the world to become associated with one particular port. Thus, Tilbury, part of the Port of London, is associated with the Australasian passenger trade, Liverpool with that to Canada, West Africa, and the Far East, and Southampton with the North and South American and South African trades. During the 1960s, however, much of the deep-sea passenger-liner traffic was transferred to Southampton, which is exceptional among ports of the British Transport Docks Board in that it is developing a major traffic role comparable with that of Liverpool and London. Much of its success is due to its geographical location, its peculiar double-crested tide, which obviates the need for enclosed water docks, and to a history of good labour relations. Although other major ports have made considerable investments to equip themselves to handle container-freight traffic, it appears that much of this trade will also go through Southampton.

The role
of
South-
ampton

Of the total annual traffic through Britain's seaports (332,000,000 tons at the beginning of the 1970s), more than two-thirds are fuels, mainly petroleum. The combined ports of the British Transport Docks Board handled a total of over 86,000,000 tons, about 30 percent of which was in coastwise traffic. Of the independent ports, the Port of London Authority and other ports on the Thames, the major sea gateway to Britain, carry about 80,000,000 tons of traffic annually, three-quarters of which is fuels, but also with major imports of cereals, sugar, wood, wood pulp, and paper. The ports on the River Mersey (Liverpool, Manchester, and Garston) together handle 25,000,000 tons of petroleum and about 20,000,000 tons of nonfuel traffic, with cereals, sugar, and iron ore as the most important commodities imported.

A National Ports Council was set up in 1964 to control major port investment and to produce a national ports plan. Impending changes in world trade and methods of sea transportation are likely to effect radical structural changes in the United Kingdom port system, some berths or docks becoming redundant or inadequate to handle the new-style, mainly container, traffic and larger vessels.

Airways. Britain is linked with the rest of Europe and other continents by state-owned airlines. A number of subsidiary and independent companies also operate airlines. Most world airlines use London's Heathrow Airport, making it one of the busiest in the world; in 1970 it dealt with more than 270,000 aircraft movements and 15,700,000 passengers. It is, in fact, the world's busiest airport for international passengers, carrying some 12,600,000 in 1970. It is supported by the smaller subsidiary airports of Gatwick to the South, Southend on the east, and Luton and Stanstead to the north. In 1970 Heathrow and Gatwick together handled over 50 percent of the 32,000,000 international passengers passing through the seaports and airports of the United Kingdom, as well as 10 percent by value of the country's visible imports and exports. By far the greatest passenger traffic at Heathrow is with the European continent, just over 50 percent in 1970, compared with some 18 percent domestic traffic and 15 percent with North America. Traffic with other continents was much smaller.

The role
of
Heathrow
Airport

Domestic air traffic is comparatively light, since distances between the principal cities are small, and air travel offers scant saving in travel time. Each major city region, nevertheless, has its airport, with passenger services to London accounting for about 18 percent of the traffic. Special networks serve the offshore islands and some cross-country routes. Few of the provincial airports have significant international links other than cross-Channel, the exceptions being Manchester and Prestwick (Glasgow), which both have a moderate level of traffic services to North America.

The British Airport Authority administers Heathrow, Gatwick, Stanstead, Edinburgh, and Prestwick. Since 1967 it has been investing more than £9,000,000 per annum in Heathrow and increasingly large amounts in Gatwick. By the early 1970s Heathrow had almost reached its capacity limit for aircraft movements. Although Gatwick was being expanded, the high rate of increase of air traffic, generally exceeding 10 percent per annum and usually doubling over about a seven-year period, made a third major airport for London, to be located at Foulness, an urgent necessity. (J.Pro.)

Administration and social conditions

THE STRUCTURE OF GOVERNMENT

Constitutional framework. Britain is a constitutional monarchy and a parliamentary democracy. Its permanent head of state is the reigning king or queen, and the head of government is the prime minister, who derives his position from the fact that he is leader of the political party that currently possesses, or can command, a majority in the House of Commons.

Sources of the constitution

The British constitution is partly unwritten and wholly flexible. Its basic sources are legislative enactments of Parliament, such as the Act of Settlement, 1701, and decisions made by courts of law. Matters for which there is no formal law, as, for instance, the resignation of office by a government, are determined by important conventions of the constitution, based on precedent, but always open to development or modification. The main elements in the constitution are the legislature, the executive, and the judiciary; and government, in the most general sense, involves all three, with many functions overlapping, since there is no separation of powers. Sovereignty resides in Parliament, which comprises the monarch, referred to as the Crown, the hereditary and appointive House of Lords, and the elected House of Commons acting in concert, and is expressed in its legislative enactments. These are therefore binding on all, although the liberty of the individual subject, secured in essence by the rule of law, is, in practice, exemplified by the right of the private individual to contest in the courts the legality of any action under a specific statute.

All political power is concentrated in the prime minister and his Cabinet, and the monarch must act on their advice. Members of the Cabinet are chosen by the prime minister from among his own political party in Parliament. Most Cabinet ministers are heads of such government departments as the Home Office or the Foreign Office. The prime minister's authority over his Cabinet colleagues has tended to increase, and some decisions previously within the competence of the Cabinet as a whole are now made by the prime minister alone. A clear example of this development occurred in 1918, when the right to dissolve Parliament and fix the date of an election passed by tacit consent from Cabinet to prime minister. The prime minister can also, on occasion, alone or with one or two colleagues, make decisions without consulting the Cabinet. A prime minister has nevertheless been overruled by his Cabinet on many occasions, right up to the present day; and, in order to exercise fully his enhanced powers, he must, as a rule, carry his Cabinet with him. The prime minister also appoints about 25 ministers not in the Cabinet, and about 50 junior ministers.

Powers of the Cabinet

The Cabinet exercises the sovereignty of Parliament because, as it is drawn from, and supported by, the party that has a majority in the House of Commons, it can effectively control legislation. The royal right of veto has not been exercised since the early 18th century, and the once coequal legislative power of the hereditary House of Lords was reduced in 1911 to a mere right of temporary delay. The Cabinet plans, drafts, and lays before Parliament all important bills, including the budget, using its majority to get them through Parliament with reasonable dispatch. While the Cabinet thus controls the lawmaking machinery, it is also subject to Parliament, in the sense that it must expound and defend its policy in debate.

Administrative decisions of the Cabinet are implicitly and immediately obeyed and carried out by the entire executive apparatus, both civil and military. The mechanism by which its decisions, always in exercise of already existing statutory powers or of the reserve powers of the Crown or, exceptionally, requiring retrospective parliamentary authorization, are converted into executive action is the Cabinet secretariat, which grew up after World War I. Besides preparing the agenda of the Cabinet and circulating all relevant papers to members, the secretariat records the conclusions of the Cabinet in such a form that the government departments concerned can speedily carry them into effect.

Within the United Kingdom, Scotland has a distinct legal system based on Roman law; much of Wales is bilingual, and in some parts Welsh is the first language. Both regard themselves as nations on a par with England. England itself is divided by dialect and sentiment into regions that are in varying degree conscious of their own identity. Northern Ireland has a Parliament (located at Stormont) and a Cabinet that (under a United Kingdom act in 1920) have autonomy in purely domestic affairs. The powers of the Stormont Parliament were suspended for a year by the United Kingdom government in London in March 1971, a step necessitated by the continuing crisis in Northern Ireland.

Compared with other countries, the United Kingdom is, to a high degree, homogeneous. Practically everyone speaks English; the electoral system is uniform; the same legal system prevails throughout England, Wales and Northern Ireland; three-quarters of the population live within daily travelling distance of the centres of six conurbations.

Local government. Local government is also homogeneous. Although its roots stretch back to a period before the Norman Conquest in 1066, it was established on its present uniform basis between the years 1835 and 1888. Local authorities are subordinate corporations formed by acts of Parliament or charters. Their powers, which are executive as well as legislative and which include the levying and appropriating of financial rates, derive from statute and from judicial interpretation. Local government bodies in England, Wales, Northern Ireland, and Scotland include county (shire) councils, whose area of jurisdiction in the main follows that of the corresponding geographical counties but excludes county-borough areas; county borough councils, established in some large boroughs having a population of 100,000 upward; ordinary borough (or, in Scotland, burgh) councils; and urban district or rural district councils (in Scotland, district councils). County councils and county borough councils consist of a chairman, aldermen, and councillors; borough councils of a mayor, aldermen, and councillors; and urban and rural district councils of a chairman and councillors. In Scotland burgh councils consist of a provost, bailies, and councillors.

Local government officials

Many local-government responsibilities are subsidized, and to some extent supervised, by the central government, but local authorities are proud and careful of their independence. They are organized into national associations capable of making potent representations to the government of the day.

A royal commission was set up in 1966 to examine the system of local government; its report in 1969 formed the basis of government proposals, issued in February 1971, for a reorganization of local government planned to take effect in England and Wales in April 1974 and in Scotland in 1975. An almost uniform two-tier system is envisaged, which will largely extinguish the existing extensive powers wielded by borough councils. A large reduction in the number of local government authorities will be effected, and there are to be 59 new larger areas, called counties in England and Wales and called regions in Scotland. These, in turn, will be subdivided into districts. The new English county areas will, in the main, follow the historic county boundaries, but each new Scottish region will take in two or more of the original shires. Both counties and districts will have separate elected councils, and proposals for representation at parish or community levels within both rural and urban districts are under consideration.

London government
Districts will be responsible for local services, such as housing and refuse collection, the larger areas for major services such as police, education, and social works; but, in six new English metropolitan counties to be formed in areas of extensive urban development, responsibility for education and social services will be given to the district councils. This follows the practice already current in London. The government of London, reformed in 1963, when its boundaries were enlarged to include 610 square miles and a population of about 7,750,000 and responsibilities were divided between the Greater London Council and 32 London borough councils, will not be further altered. Many existing boroughs or burghs, including the Scottish cities of Edinburgh, Glasgow, Aberdeen, and Dundee, often with a long history of civic autonomy, will thus lose to their respective county or region control of services such as education.

The final form of British local government may be affected by the report of another royal commission, on the constitution, set up in 1969 and reported in 1971. The Conservative Government's proposals provided for a two-tier structure in which there would be two distinct forms of local authority—county councils, and district or borough councils—each with its own statutory duties and obligations.

Government proposals for reform of local government in Northern Ireland, including a reduction to 17 of the number of local authorities and abolition of the plural "company" vote, (i.e., the right of an elector to vote in respect to business premises owned by him) were made in December 1967 and July 1969.

The political process. *Elections.* Voters in Britain vote in parliamentary and local government elections. The former are either general elections, in which a whole new House of Commons is chosen, or by-elections, which occur when a sitting member has died or has resigned. All other public posts are filled by appointment.

Each member of the House of Commons represents one parliamentary constituency. Constituency boundaries are drawn so that they are all roughly the same size in population—about 50,000 people. They are divided into wards and other units for the election of local government councillors. Periodically, a commission recommends to Parliament any boundary changes that may seem necessary because of shifts of population.

Registration of electors is compulsory and is carried out annually by the state. Candidates for election to Parliament or a council are chosen by the local parties. There is no primary system, on the United States model, and there could not well be any, since the timing of general elections is unpredictable.

Duration of Parliament
The House of Commons is elected, not for a fixed, but for a maximum term—reduced in 1911 from seven to five years. At any time during this five years, the prime minister has the right to dissolve Parliament and call a general election. The use of this power for party advantage is checked by the probability of public resentment at such a manoeuvre. A government returned with a majority is expected to govern for the major part of the five-year life of Parliament. It is accepted that Parliament may be dissolved at any time in about the last year and a half of its life, and it rarely runs its full five years.

An early election is, however, acceptable if the prime minister and Cabinet emerge from a general election with less than a working majority—that is, one of about 20 seats—in which case the paramount need for effective government justifies an election. This is especially so if the government majority is so slim that it might be lost altogether should a handful of by-elections run against the government.

Only three weeks' notice of a general election need by law be given, and expenses of parliamentary candidates are strictly limited by law. These provisions and the uncertainty about the timing of an election produce campaigns of unusual brevity and inexpensiveness.

Political parties. A two-party political system has existed in Britain since the late 17th century, and the two rival groups have always respectively embodied, in some form related to the main issues of the day, the conservative and radical elements in human character. This two-party system, which predominates despite the existence of minority parties such as the extremely small Communist Party, or the rump of the historic Liberal Party, is one of the most outstanding features of British politics and has done much to produce a history of firm and decisive government.

The two-party system

The political system and the nature of the great parties themselves have been shaped by the special role of the Cabinet as the centre of political authority. Control of the Cabinet has long been the prize and object of British politics, fought for from the early 18th century by Whigs against Tories, later by Liberals against Conservatives, and now by Labour against Conservatives. The practice of simple majority voting, which had always prevailed, and the final establishment of single member constituencies of uniform population size have tended to exaggerate the majority of the winning party and thus to eliminate third parties. On occasions when the two-party system has been disturbed, these factors have helped to restore it. If one of the giant parties has been, temporarily, in abeyance, two rival groups have thus usually developed among members of the predominant party and have contended for control of the Cabinet. A new party only rises to power by displacing another, as happened when Labour superseded the Liberals in the first half of the 20th century.

Progressive widening of the franchise from the early 19th century (the vote is now given to all at the age of 18) made it increasingly necessary to organize mass parties in the country in order to win a clear and firm majority of parliamentary seats in a general election. But, equally, the parties in the country depended on their representatives in Parliament and, in particular, on those who, as members of the Cabinet, drafted and introduced bills to carry through the parties' legislative programs. Thus the parliamentary parties not only became indissolubly linked with the national parties but inevitably dominated them. There grew up in the 20th century one of the most distinctive features of the British party system, namely the choice by the parliamentary parties of leaders who were then automatically accepted as leaders of the national parties.

The growth and maintenance of a mass two-party system, together with the uncertainty of the timing of a general election, produced the British phenomenon of the Opposition. Each party when out of office has to organize and conduct itself so as, if possible, to win the next general election. The decisive characteristic of the Opposition is that it is a viable alternative government, ready at any time to take office. The leader of the Opposition is paid an official salary as such.

The Opposition

Government and Opposition are ranged against each other in daily battle in Parliament. The perpetual conflict between them has caused national political issues to dominate, increasingly, local elections, while ensuring that the two main parties themselves remain continuously alert and disciplined. In the last resort the two-party system depends upon its acceptance by the British voters and upon their readiness to find satisfaction in and through one of the two major parties and to reject independent candidates or those of third parties.

The participation of the citizen. Fundamentally, the right of the citizen to participate in public affairs is exercised when he casts his vote in parliamentary or local elections. He can also participate in the political field by becoming a paid-up member or a voluntary worker for the party of his choice. Further participation in affairs of state can take the form of support of particular causes and attempts to urge Parliament to further them; **or,** more often effectively, of protest outside the field of electoral politics against actions or proposed actions of the government. Vested interests and pressure groups nevertheless play a relatively small part in British parliamentary life. The disciplined two-party system means that a member's loyalty to a party normally transcends loyalty to an interest and that he is more conscious of the authority of the party whips than of the influence of pressure groups or vocal minorities. Members are not subjected to massive campaigns of letters and telegrams.

Political protest movements

Movements of protest have been endemic in British history and have been associated with many major reforms. In the 20th century, although no less frequent in occurrence, they have perhaps been more fragmented and less likely to be effective. Movements of protest against nuclear weapons and against the war in Vietnam were organized in the 1960s. Students also staged sit-ins in universities and committed some acts of violence; but, in comparison with student demonstrations in other like countries, their activities were on a small scale. Nationalist movements exist in Scotland and Wales. Supporters of the Welsh movement have organized protests to further the use of the Welsh language, and have on rare occasions resorted to sabotage, such as the blowing up of pipelines carrying water from Welsh lakes to English cities. Each of these movements secured the election of a member of Parliament in the 1966–70 Parliament, but both of these men lost their seats. In Northern Ireland a civil rights movement has in recent years worked for the ending of discrimination against the Roman Catholic minority. The result of civil violence led to the dispatch of troops from Britain. Since 1970 a number of British soldiers have been killed by snipers. Northern Ireland is the only part of the United Kingdom where tear gas has ever been used by the authorities. Violence—with many civilian casualties—continued in the early 1970s.

Trade unions directly challenged the authority of the state in the general strike of 1926. That experience convinced them that strikes for political ends would always be defeated by the government, backed by considerable popular support. They also realized that such strikes were incompatible with parliamentary democracy, in that they would usurp or frustrate the electoral processes that make possible the constant criticism and ultimate replacement of a government. Since 1926, the trade unions, which participate in politics by supporting the Labour Party by their funds, have thus used industrial action solely in furtherance of the economic interests of their members. Strikes in 1971 against the Conservative government's Industrial Relations Bill were "in token" only; the stated determination of some unions to refuse to register, as would be required when the bill became law, came close to political action but was within their legal rights under the law.

Britain has a long history of participation by the private citizen in voluntary work outside party politics. Unpaid justices of the peace, besides hearing cases, discharge many administrative functions such as the annual licensing of public houses (bars) and betting shops. The welfare services run by central and local government are reinforced by a great deal of voluntary help.

JUSTICE

Judges are irremovable and appointed. There is no election to judicial office. The Bench, as it is known, is recruited from practicing lawyers and never from people in public or elected office. The courts alone declare the law; but any act of Parliament is accepted by them as part of the law. No court can declare a statute invalid.

An accused person is presumed innocent until proved guilty. The courts strictly enforce the law of contempt to prevent newspapers or television from prejudicing by comment the trial of the accused before a jury. Accused persons and litigants in civil actions are entitled to legal aid paid by the state on a scale varying with their income. Two-thirds or more of persons in criminal cases are granted legal aid.

Legal aid

Criminal and civil cases. About 90 percent of criminal cases are tried and determined by justices of the peace, who act as unpaid magistrates, or in towns and some other places by stipendiary (paid) magistrates who are trained lawyers. Magistrates' courts sit in about 1,000 places in England and Wales and are therefore within comparatively easy reach of everyone. The remaining 10 percent of more serious crimes also come in the first place before a magistrate's court. The police must bring an arrested person within 24 hours before a magistrate, who alone decides whether he shall be remanded on bail or in custody. If they so find, they commit him for trial by a judge and jury. In 1967 an act of Parliament enabled jurors to give a majority verdict in criminal cases; the majority must be at least 10–2. Hanging for murder was abolished in 1965.

The vast majority of civil actions are tried in local county courts before paid judges. Their jurisdiction is limited by the nature of the action and by the amount of money at stake. In both these respects the jurisdiction of the courts has been steadily widened. County courts sit in over 370 places.

Higher courts. Partly in an effort to reduce delays in the hearing of criminal cases, which had been running at about four and one-half months, the higher courts were radically reorganized by an act of Parliament in 1971. As a result, the Supreme Court of Judicature now consists of the Appeal Court; the High Court of Justice with civil jurisdiction; and the Crown Court, for criminal work above the level handled by the magistrates' courts. High Court and Crown Court move between the major centres of population. The High Court hears the most important and difficult criminal and civil cases; criminal cases of less importance are tried by the Crown Court.

Appeals in both civil and criminal matters lie from the High and Crown Courts to the Appeal Court. This court can give leave, in cases of great legal importance, for a final appeal to the judges in the House of Lords.

Appeals

THE ARMED FORCES

Supreme responsibility for national defense rests with the prime minister and the Cabinet. The secretary of state for defense formulates and proposes defense policy. His ministry, created in 1970 by a merger of the three original service ministries, has responsibility for all the armed forces. The secretary of state is advised by the chief of defense staff aided by the three service chiefs.

Both the cost and strength of the forces have been reduced. Between 1966 and 1971 the proportion of the gross national product devoted to defense fell from 6.6 to 5.8 percent. At the beginning of the 1970s the Defence Budget ran over £2,850,000,000 and service manpower at 372,000 (Army, 180,000; Royal Air Force, 110,000; Royal Navy, 82,000). The armed forces are wholly raised by voluntary recruitment.

In the late 1960s military commitments east of Suez were drastically reduced, and the defense effort was concentrated in and around Europe. The prime function of the armed forces became participation in the North Atlantic Treaty Organization (NATO). At the beginning of the 1970s, more than 60,000 men were deployed in Germany and nearly 25,000 in the Mediterranean area; 37,000 were at sea with the navy, mainly in European or Atlantic waters; 259,000 were stationed in Britain, including major units in Northern Ireland acting in aid of the civil authorities. The British contribution to the Western nuclear deterrent rests with the four Polaris submarines of the Royal Navy.

Forces with NATO

SERVICES

Educational services. The government operates no schools, employs no teachers, prescribes no textbooks or curricula; nor does it control universities. There is, however, a central Department of Education and Science headed by a minister who is responsible to Parliament and who is usually in the Cabinet.

Prime responsibility for managing schools is in the hands of elected local education authorities, which allocate children among schools and appoint and pay teachers. Head teachers (principals) enjoy a high measure of independence; they cannot be given instructions on textbooks or teaching methods. Local education authorities plan and build schools, of which there were about 19,000 at the beginning of the 1970s. They also meet the greater part of the cost of some 10,000 voluntary schools—those maintained by religious bodies. The authorities receive a central-government grant of 60 percent of their expenditure.

Secondary schools. The Education Act of 1944 established free and compulsory secondary education from 11 to 15 years old. In 1972 the school-leaving age was raised to 16.

By the terms of the act, children were allocated by examination at the age of 11 either to grammar schools, which prepared them for universities, or to secondary modern schools, from which they generally went into industry. In November 1964 the Labour government announced a reorganization of secondary education on comprehensive lines to end this segregation. All children were to go to comprehensive schools.

Compre-
hensive
schools

Independent schools exist outside the public system. Chief of these are about 300 free-paying public schools, half of which are for girls.

Universities. Some 30 percent of the United Kingdom's 18–20-year-olds go on to some form of higher education. Britain has 44 universities, 16 of which were founded after World War II. Almost the whole cost is met by the government. The money is given to the University Grants Committee, an independent body that deals directly with the universities.

Universities are wholly independent, arrange their own courses of study and research, and appoint their own staff. They also decide about the admission of students. Recently students in some universities have achieved some measure of representation on the governing councils. Universities are relatively small: none except London has over 15,000 students; many have fewer. Although the number of places has risen rapidly, at the beginning of the 1970s, of about 120,000 annual applicants, fewer than 65,000 were admitted; some 7,000 of these were non-British, 2,000 coming from the United States.

The staff–student ratio is under 1:10—the lowest in the world. The failure rate in British universities is 13 percent (compared with 40 percent in France and the United States).

Most of those who fail to gain entry to a university go to some other form of higher education. Local education authorities maintain about 700 colleges providing mainly technical and commercial courses: some of these institutions award degrees of university level. There are also nearly 170 colleges of education for the training of teachers, who can also gain degrees.

All students are entitled to grants varying with the income of their parents: 260,000 were in receipt of grants at the end of the 1960s.

The Open
University

In January 1971 the Open University—something unique of its kind in the world—was launched. It provides for adults who missed the chance of university education, and it uses television, radio, and local study and lecture courses. Applicants have to be accepted for a number of places limited at any one time by the availability of teachers. Degrees are awarded as at any university.

Health and welfare services. *The National Health Service.* A complete national health service began to operate on July 5, 1948. Every man, woman, and child is entitled to medical treatment of every kind, free at the moment of need. The only exceptions are a number of charges that meet part of the cost of dental work, spectacles, and prescribed medicines. All these charges are remitted for children, old-age pensioners, and people below a certain income level. The charges meet 4 percent of the cost of the National Health Service. The service is voluntary: doctors may, if they wish, take only fee-paying patients, but 98 percent of general practitioners (numbering 24,000 in England and Wales at the beginning of the 1970s) were in the service, as were almost all the 10,000 or so dentists. Some 2,500 hospitals provided entirely free treatment. A small number have opted out of the service—most of them run by religious orders or maintained for special groups, as in the case of the Ital-

ian, Jewish, and trade-union hospitals. Private nursing homes are permitted, but they must be registered.

The normal doctor–patient relationship is maintained. A patient can freely choose or change the doctor with whom he is registered, and a doctor may decline to have a patient on his list. A doctor receives from the state a basic practice allowance, payments for ancillary staff, and a capitation grant for each patient on his list, limited to a maximum of 3,500. He receives a higher fee for every patient over 65, for night visits, and for practicing in an underdoctored area. He can also take private patients.

Some of the total cost of the National Health Service comes from central or local government.

General management and discipline of the family practitioner service is exercised by about 150 local bodies, half of the members of which are appointed by doctors, dentists, and pharmacists. Hospitals are supervised by 20 regional boards, which receive government grants and are responsible for planning and building hospitals.

The local authorities have a legal obligation to provide maternity and child-welfare services, home nursing, health visiting, domestic help for those in need, and the care and aftercare of illness, including mental disorder. They organize ambulance services and build and maintain health centres.

Social security. The social security system makes up a vital part of the welfare services. It, too, was established in 1948 and is based on compulsory insurance. Some 25,000,000 employees pay, by law, a weekly contribution, which is supplemented by a charge upon the employer. The state meets the balance of the cost.

In return for his contribution, every employee is entitled to a retirement pension (at 65 for men and at 60 for women) and to cash benefits in unemployment or sickness. The duration of these benefits depends on the number of contributions paid.

Retire-
ment
pension

Should these be exhausted, the employee can draw supplementary benefit, as can anyone whose income falls below a certain level, even if in work. Supplementary benefit depends upon a means test, and the cost is borne wholly by the state. It also meets the entire cost of family allowances for all children after the first so long as they remain in full-time education.

The total cost of the social services to central and local government was £9,750,000,000 for the year 1971–72 alone.

A beginning has been made in changing this system of flat contributions and flat benefits to one based on a percentage of wages.

In 1965 a statutory system of redundancy or severance pay was introduced. An employee who loses his job through no fault of his own receives a lump-sum payment. The cost is met in part by his employer and in part out of a fund made up by a levy on all employers.

Housing. Local authorities have a legal obligation to see that housing in their area is adequate. This they fulfill mainly by building houses and apartments (flats) for rent. The central government lays down mandatory minimum standards, and local authorities maintain waiting lists and allocate houses according to need. The cost is met in part by government subsidies, in part by rents collected from the tenants, and in part by contributions from local taxation. Since 1971 local authorities have had a statutory duty to operate rent rebates. They must charge their tenants the true economic rent and make rebates to those whose income falls below a certain level. Local authorities can make grants up to 50 percent of the cost, up to a certain limit, of improving privately owned houses, for instance by the installation of a bathroom.

Local authorities own and administer about one-third of the 19,000,000 houses in the country; half that total are owner occupied, and the remainder are rented from private landlords. In the quarter century since the end of World War II, some 7,000,000 dwellings have been built by private and public enterprise. It is estimated that almost another 4,000,000 must be put up before Britons are properly housed. Since the war, 200,000 new dwellings have been constructed in 32 New Towns that have been built or are being built. They are at a considerable dis-

New
Towns

tance from the conurbations and are carefully planned with separate industrial areas and traffic-free precincts.

The whole country is now subject to town and country planning by eight regional boards, which control where new building or the substantial alteration of existing structures may be undertaken.

Police services. There is in Britain no national police force nor any minister exclusively responsible for the police. Each provincial police force is maintained by a police authority—a committee elected by a number of local authorities—which determines the establishment of the force and provides and maintains buildings, vehicles, and other equipment. It also appoints and dismisses the chief constable, who, however, has sole right of appointment, promotion, discipline, and deployment of his force and who alone decides police action in individual cases.

The home secretary is the police authority for the Metropolitan Police in London. Broadly, the commissioner in charge of the Metropolitan Police has status similar to that of a chief constable. The famous Scotland Yard (the criminal investigation department of the Metropolitan Police) helps other police forces on request and handles the British business of the International Criminal Police Organization (Interpol).

The supervisory powers of the home secretary over the police forces of the country have been steadily extended by acts of Parliament. In 1856 he was empowered to appoint officials to inspect all police forces; those forces certified by the Home Office to be efficient received a government grant, which now amounts to 50 percent. In 1919 the home secretary was given the right to make regulations dealing with pay, pensions, and conditions of service. In 1964 he was further empowered to compel the amalgamation of police forces, and, by 1970, the number of police forces had been reduced by one-third, to 67. These are further grouped into eight regions for the provision of forensic-science laboratories, wireless services, criminal records, and crime squads.

The total strength of the police force in the United Kingdom was about 107,000 in the early 1970s. In addition, chief constables appoint special constables, unpaid volunteers who can be called upon to act as auxiliaries to the police. Police authorities appoint and pay 5,000 traffic wardens, who have limited powers in relation to parking offenses and the direction of traffic.

Traffic wardens

The British police wear a uniform that is nonmilitary in appearance. Their only regular weapon is a short wooden truncheon, which they keep out of sight and which may not be employed except in self-defense or to restore order. Police engaged on dangerous missions may carry firearms for that specific occasion.

SOCIAL CONDITIONS

Wages and cost of living. By 1970 weekly earnings of full-time manual workers averaged £28 a week, and, over the previous five years, earnings of all workers increased by almost a half, and the retail-price index by over a quarter, giving, over this period, a 20 percent rise in the standard of living.

The best measure of the cost of living is a combination of the general index of retail prices with the consumer price index. For the economically troubled 1960–70 period, this indicated a nearly 50 percent rise in the cost of living, and, on these figures, the average real standard of living rose in that decade by about 17 percent.

Averages of these kinds are significant, but they conceal many important variations. Workers in the most powerful trade unions tended to do better than the average, while those on fixed incomes, for example, found them eroded by an inflation not far short of 50 percent in ten years. All social security benefits, including retirement pensions, are reviewed about every second year and increased in an attempt to make good any increase in the cost of living.

Health conditions. Improved standards of living and the steady extension of free medical services till they covered the whole population are reflected in the vital statistics for England and Wales.

Deaths from tuberculosis, for example, fell by 90 per-

cent between 1938 and the mid-1960s, while deaths from diphtheria have virtually disappeared as a result of free and nearly universal vaccination of children. Between 1947 (the year before the introduction of the National Health Service) and 1970, infant mortality fell by 57 percent to 18.5 per 1,000. Over the same period maternal mortality fell by 86 percent, to 0.18 per 1,000. Decreases in mortality rates are due, in part, to lengthened life expectancy—itself an index of a nation's health conditions.

Britain is one of the few countries that is free from rabies. This is partly because it is an island. Wildlife cannot invade it from other countries, and all cats and dogs brought into the country are compulsorily quarantined for a period of nine months.

The Clean Air Act of 1956 enables local authorities to establish smokeless zones in which the emission of smoke from all chimneys is prohibited. By 1968 smoke-control orders affected 3,500,000 premises, including 1,700,000 in London, which can now claim to be the cleanest great city in the world, almost entirely free from smog.

Smokeless zones

Social and economic division. By 1971 total personal income before tax was about £47,000,000,000, equivalent to £855 a year to every man, woman, and child in the land. In 1969 the actual distribution of income before tax was as follows: 7,000 people had incomes of over £20,000 a year; 16,600,000 had incomes under £1,000 a year; 2,250,000 had incomes under £250 a year. These extreme inequalities were mitigated by direct taxation, which reduced the total income of all those earning £20,000 a year gross from £221,000,000 to £56,000,000 a year.

The distribution of the ownership of wealth (that is, of property and capital) remains unequal: 14,000,000 people owned net wealth of over £1,000, and their total net wealth was £89,000,000,000; some 20,000 individuals, or about 0.15 percent of all these wealth owners, owned almost 8 percent of this total.

Educational divisions tend to accentuate the social divisions caused by the distribution of net income and wealth. Their original economic class still to a considerable extent determines the chances of access of young people to higher education, and this in turn is the main avenue to socially approved and better rewarded careers.

Educational divisions

Reform and reorganization is, nevertheless, steadily mitigating, indeed reversing, the divisive effects of the educational system. The introduction of grants for all students and the spread of comprehensive schools have markedly increased the proportion of students of working class origin in higher education. These educational changes, together with the rise in the real incomes of workers, has carried much farther the social fluidity that, in varying degree, has for centuries characterized British society.
(P.G.W.)

Cultural life and institutions

Widespread changes in the United Kingdom's cultural life have occurred since 1945. The most remarkable was perhaps the emergence first of Liverpool, then of London in the 1960s as a world centre of popular culture. The capital soon became a mecca for pleasure-seekers of all varieties, replacing, for many of them, the perennial popularity of Paris. The Beatles were only the first and best known of the many British rock-music groups to bring new dimensions to the musical tastes of Europe and the Americas. British designers for a time led the world as innovators of new styles of dress for both men and women, and the brightly coloured, often extreme, outfits sold in Carnaby Street and King's Road shops perhaps became more symbolic of Britain than the traditionally staid tailoring of Savile Row and neighbouring streets, while flea markets as sources of bizarre clothing flourished in many large towns, particularly London. The long-established addiction of the British to betting and gambling was recognized in the easing of legal restrictions during the 1960s, which led to the establishment of casino-style gambling in London and other large cities, as well as to a boom in horse-racing betting shops.

The new cultural milieu

More traditional fields also have experienced renewed vigour. In the decade after World War II, the British film industry came of age and set a standard of excellence that, by and large, it has maintained. The steady stream of productions on London and provincial stages includes many new works by a large group of dramatists who are nearly as well represented on stages from New York to Melbourne, Australia. Beginning in the 1930s, Britain has enjoyed an eminence as well in the visual arts, most notably in sculpture, in which a sense of the organic unity of form and material asserted itself.

The social settings of the arts

Underlying these changes were several important social developments. Most evident was the rising standard of education, the school-leaving age having been extended from 15 to 16. Increasingly large numbers of pupils were going on to higher education with a major expansion in the number of universities and other institutions of higher education. By the early 1970s, Britain had 44 universities as compared with 17 in 1945. Within the schools, especially since the early 1960s, new emphasis was placed on creative activity and play. In society in general there was an increase in leisure, and, until the late 1960s, steady employment and improved wages for younger workers markedly increased people's capacity to take part in all kinds of culture and recreation.

During this same period, successive governments have shifted their policies toward the arts. The Arts Council, formed in 1946, provides widespread support for many kinds of contemporary creative and performing arts. This has coincided with a great expansion of the cultural market, mainly commercial, and of audiences and viewers for the arts generally. The ordinary person's life was greatly changed by the more sophisticated standards of design in domestic equipment and home furnishing and decoration—as well as the impact of television and radio. These changes have been accompanied by continuous argument about their nature and bearings and about the effects on the arts of an expanded audience. A clash of tastes and values between generations and, to some extent, between social classes has been sharp, and the quality of the national life increasingly has been judged —favourably and unfavourably—in terms of current work in the arts. By comparison with any earlier period, this is a unique situation in Britain.

DEVELOPMENTS IN THE ARTS

A notable postwar development has been proliferation of festivals involving one or several of the arts, of which the Edinburgh International Festival of Music and Drama is only the most ambitious. In the late 1960s the popular arts began to follow suit, and in 1970 a huge three-day "pop festival" took place on the Isle of Wight.

Literature. Books reached a majority public in Britain for the first time during the 1950s, and well over 30,000 new titles were appearing annually by the 1970s. Paperbacks, introduced in the 1930s, transformed all previous ideas of the extent of the reading public. Since World War II, the novel, social reporting, and criticism have attracted major attention. The several new movements in poetry have included vigorous revival of live readings for audiences, a movement perhaps sparked largely by the Welshman Dylan Thomas. Commercially, however, the many new little magazines often have had difficulty in surviving, and the financial situation of all but a few best selling authors has not improved in the proportion that might be expected from an enlarged readership.

The performing arts

Theatre. During the 20th century, the number of theatres in Britain has fallen to less than one-half of those existing in 1900, and the financial situation of the living theatre has been and remains precarious. At the same time, there has been continuous dramatic experiment, principally in the "little theatres" and in independent experimental companies, from the revival of verse drama in the 1930s and 1940s, through Joan Littlewood's Theatre Workshop in the 1950s and early 1960s, and to the English Stage Company at the Royal Court Theatre, London, from the 1950s onward. Many writers have turned back to the theatre or have developed through it: the work of John Arden, Arnold Wesker, John Osborne, and Harold Pinter is only the best known. In the 1950s a number of writers—playwrights, novelists, and critics—

who were dubbed collectively as "the angry young men" brought a new thrust of social criticism to British letters, perhaps most clearly evident in Osborne's *Look Back in Anger* (performed 1956). In 1968, after theatre censorship by the lord chamberlain ended, for a time the most obvious beneficiary of the new freedom was eroticism, though the resulting wave of staged nudity, often gratuitous, often proved unarousing. The National Theatre Company began in 1963, and a National Theatre is being built on the south bank of the Thames in Central London. The Royal Shakespeare Company, based at Stratford-on-Avon and in London, has been vigorous and generally successful and, like other new developments, is supported by the Arts Council. Such avant-garde ventures as theatre clubs of the restaurant cellar type and London's short-lived Arts Laboratory helped to ferment a counter-West End climate that, however, often shared orthodox theatre's preoccupation with sex and politics as subject matter, while breaking some new ground in the development of often anarchic, experimental, theatre techniques. The many provincial theatres and companies—some of them new, such as those at Coventry and Nottingham—provide further assurances of the continued vitality of this traditionally richest of British arts.

Music. Music has gained a vast new public in Britain since the 1930s, at first through the influence of radio and, more recently, through the great expansion of record buying. Concerts draw substantial audiences in many of the larger towns, but the financial situation of orchestras has remained precarious and requires regular subsidy. There is also a continuing shortage of adequate concert halls in many towns. In the same period, there has been a remarkable expansion of popular music. In the 1960s, British rock groups acquired international fame, providing models for similar groups in virtually every city of the world.

Opera. Before 1945 it had proved very difficult to establish a permanent English opera company, and most singers and even choruses had come from abroad. New arrangements for a national opera theatre were developed at Covent Garden in London, between 1945 and 1947, and there is now a world-renowned resident company. In addition to the international repertory, new English-language operas by such composers as Benjamin Britten, Sir William Walton, and Michael Tippett have been performed. Though audiences are substantial, the heavy deficit has to be met partly by an Arts Council grant. Standards of performance and production have made Covent Garden one of the world's great opera houses. The Sadler's Wells Company, performing usually in English and undertaking more extensive tours in Britain and abroad, in 1968 moved to a larger London theatre, the Coliseum. The English Opera Group, associated with the Royal Opera Company, presents works of smaller scale, a number of them new and experimental.

Covent Garden

Ballet. English ballet enjoys a high international esteem both for its direction and dancing. In 1956 the Sadler's Wells Ballet, formed in 1931 under Ninette de Valois, became the Royal Ballet. From 1945 it was based at Covent Garden, where it is backed up by a Theatre Ballet and the Royal Ballet School. The company has won the highest reputation, both in the classical repertory and in the production of new works by English choreographers and composers. London's Festival Ballet has a mainly classical repertory, while the Ballet Rambert, a leading pioneer in English ballet since 1930, has returned to the experimental role of its earlier years. In spite of a shortage of suitable provincial theatres, a limited touring program is maintained by most companies.

Film. British film art has been affected radically by the decline in attendances, by its exposure to the climate of the American market, and by what is widely regarded as a restrictive distribution system. In the late 1940s a series of social comedies made by Ealing Studios, such as *Kind Hearts and Coronets* and *Passport To Pimlico*, brought international acclaim to the British film industry. The most valuable new work has come, however, from relatively short-lived independent companies. Among important directors are Tony Richardson, Lindsay Anderson,

Joseph Losey, Karel Reisz, Ken Loach, and Ken Russell. The nearness of film studios to the London stages has allowed directors and actors to pursue careers in both mediums to an extent unknown in the United States. A new school of actors emerged in the production of genre films based on working class and provincial life. It was at its finest in the late 1950s and early 1960s. Important films have been made in Britain by major foreign directors, including the Italian Michelangelo Antonioni and the Frenchman Jean-Luc Godard. Organizational difficulties have severely restricted British film makers, and many of the younger generation have turned to the experimental work of the underground cinema, which is exhibited mainly by the many thriving film societies or on television.

Painting and sculpture. The revival of the visual arts in Britain that began in the 1930s was effected largely through the work of the generation of painters born between 1890 and 1910: Ben Nicholson, Ivon Hitchens, Victor Pasmore, Sir Stanley Spencer, John Piper, and Graham Sutherland. They have been followed by such artists as Francis Bacon, John Minton, John Craxton, John Bratby, David Hockney, and Bridget Riley. Among sculptors, Henry Moore and Barbara Hepworth were followed by Reg Butler, Kenneth Armitage, Lynn Chadwick, Elisabeth Frink, and Anthony Caro. Public interest was stimulated by sponsored exhibitions both in the national galleries and throughout the country and by the acquisition of new works of art for many public buildings and developments. Public sponsorship of individual artists has been undertaken, but commissions and purchases are now more common. Experiment among the younger generation has been not only in the pop-art field and in the use of new materials but also in the interaction between art and industrial design.

Design. A wide field of design, ranging from architecture to dress fashions, has experienced a remarkable growth of confidence and experiment. Though most apparent in inexpensive everyday objects—gaily coloured paper bags, for example—it shows up as well in furniture, textiles, pottery, toys, and, above all, clothes. Many young artist-designers now choose to work not only in the industrial field but in that part of it producing for the mass market. Since the late 1950s, the look of Britain, not only in the capital but very widely in the provinces, has been changed quite remarkably by their efforts, though a heavy legacy of bleak and dull industrial townscape still survives. Glass and steel skyscrapers owing their genesis to the modern international style of architecture have risen virtually alongside buildings echoing a centuries-older Britain.

Much of the excitement of this new work has been reflected in the art colleges, where controversies about the relations between art and design and about the proper place of art and design in the educational complex date at least from the 19th century. Public interest in design is fostered by the Council of Industrial Design, a government-grant-aided body established in 1944, which runs selective and changing displays of well-designed domestic products in London and Glasgow, maintains a Design Index of more than 10,000 well-designed products, and promotes good design standards in industrial equipment.

THE MASS MEDIA

The communications media—press, publishing, broadcasting, and entertainment—provide mass coverage in Great Britain, but their scale varies from the multi-million audiences for television, radio, and national newspapers to the small minority audiences for local papers, specialist periodicals, or experimental theatre and film that may count their following in a few thousands or even hundreds. Though the mass media have been subject to the economic trends toward concentration in large single-ownership groups, variety has been preserved in the expression of political views and the satisfaction of cultural tastes. A tradition of editorial independence is recognized in newspaper groups, which give substantial freedom to the running of each of their newspapers and periodicals. This philosophy of independence extends to the state-owned British Broadcasting Corporation (BBC)

and also to the Independent Television News (ITN), the news service that supplies the commercial television companies. It is well understood that broadcasting and the press, whether publicly or privately owned, will resist political pressures from government. The BBC, with a monopoly of radio until 1972, and with two out of three television channels, has been in practice as critically independent of government as has privately owned broadcasting media. A similar philosophy animates the work of the Arts Council, to which the government allocates a flat sum to cover all its work—with no strings attached. The Arts Council chooses its beneficiaries and distributes funds to a large number of organizations and individuals, so that creative independence may be preserved.

The press. The structure of the British newspaper industry is derived from the dense population and the availability of a closely knit rail network, which has enabled newspapers published in London to sell all over the country the next morning. Hence a sharp division has emerged between national newspapers and the regional and local press. Both in sales and reputation, the national papers dominate. Within the national-newspaper business, a distinction has grown up between popular papers with multi-million circulation, and quality papers with relatively small sales. Four populars account for about 85 percent of the total morning paper circulation. In both groups, competition for circulation and advertising has been acute in a market in which total sales have been declining since the late 1950s, and some advertising has been diverted to television. With continuously escalating labour costs in the printing industry, the financial viability of some of the most prestigious papers, such as *The Times, The Guardian,* and *The Observer* has been precarious. Both *The Times* and *The Guardian* have been run at a heavy loss, covered by the profits of other papers in their respective companies.

Though many national papers have been in difficulties and some have disappeared in recent years, the British remain among the world's most avid newspaper readers, buying more than 460 copies for every 1,000 population in the early 1970s. There are more than 130 regional daily papers, most of them evening papers and almost all of them benefiting from a monopoly situation in their own area. There are more than 1,000 weekly magazines, ranging from some popular women's magazines with circulations around the 2,000,000 mark down to a host of small specialist magazines. A loss in sales of mass-circulation women's weeklies has been accompanied by gains in some monthly magazines.

The financial insecurity of many newspapers was to some extent aggravated by excessive dependence on advertising revenue. From 1970, however, the sale price of most newspapers was substantially increased, in some cases doubling within a period of two years. Dependence on advertising, however, did not in general make newspapers subservient to advertisers. Competition among the populars, already tending to concentrate on entertaining news such as sports, crime, and human interest at the expense of the less compelling serious news, led, however, to an aggressive exploitation of sex interest. The standards of the British press were watched over by the Press Council, which had little influence in matters of taste but helped to secure the basic traditions of factual accuracy and fairness.

The variety of the newspaper and periodical press was sustained by some of the newer and relatively cheap printing techniques, which made it possible for fringe interests to publish their own papers cheaply and provided scope for the "underground press," which was probably rather more successful in outraging conventional opinion than influential in spreading its views of a "dropout," or alternative, society.

Broadcasting. A monopoly of both radio and television broadcasting was in the hands of the BBC, established as an independent public corporation in 1927, until the establishment of the Independent Television Authority (ITA) in 1954 to provide the facilities for a number of commercial television program companies. In 1972 the ITA became the Independent Broadcasting Authority (IBA) with responsibility also for commercial radio. The

Marginal notes:

Industrial and commercial arts

The tradition of editorial independence

The BBC and ITA

BBC draws its revenue from license fees (on a scale fixed by the government) from persons owning receiving sets. The IBA owns transmitters that it leases to the commercial program companies, which obtain their revenue from selling advertising time. The BBC operates two television channels and the IBA one (with a second projected). Since 1970 all three have been in colour. Until 1972 the BBC had a monopoly of radio, operating national radio programs and a number of local stations. From 1972 Parliament authorized the creation of local commercial radio stations financed by advertising. The BBC's four programs were Radio 1 (mostly popular music), Radio 2 (mostly light music), Radio 3 (mostly classical music, and some programs of an intellectual content in the tradition of the BBC's famous Third Programme), and Radio 4 (mostly news, current affairs, and speech programs). In its second television channel the BBC has tended to put programs of above-average intellectual and cultural interest—competition that the IBA commercial channel meets with its own cultural programs. The BBC also operates a comprehensive external service, broadcasting around the world in 40 languages, as well as a world service in English 24 hours a day.

The BBC has won an international reputation for the impartiality and objectivity of its news services. The concept of public-service broadcasting requires the BBC to inform, to educate, and to entertain. As a public service, the BBC must maintain a fair balance in political argument and must not express political views of its own. Similar requirements have been placed on the IBA. Both the BBC and the IBA supply educational programs for schools and for adult studies. The Open University, offering degree courses to people without formal academic qualifications who work at home, is based on educational programs broadcast by the BBC backed by correspondence courses.

Both the BBC and IBA are public bodies that in the last resort can be controlled by the government, and Parliament can alter the terms of their authority. The government has the statutory power to veto a broadcast, but this power has never been exercised, and the BBC and the IBA program companies are not interfered with in the day-to-day management of their affairs. Furthermore, on such rare occasions as the Suez crisis of 1956, when governmental pressure has been brought to bear on the BBC, the broadcasters successfully have asserted their independence. There have been complaints by politicians, however, that individual broadcasting producers sometimes have misused their power, and objections by politicians partly account for the disappearance of political satire, which floundered during the mid-1960s, from the BBC. Some viewers have complained persistently about what they consider to be the BBC's "permissive" attitude to sex.

POPULAR PURSUITS

Statistically it could be argued that the British have become a nation of television watchers. Almost every family has a television set. Viewing is said to average about four hours a day, and audiences for the most popular programs exceed 20,000,000. Nevertheless, a good many British pursuits are what they used to be. With most people working a five-day week and an eight-hour day, or thereabouts, there is time for gardening, going round to the pub for a drink and gossip, fishing, walking, looking after the pets (dogs, cats, rabbits, white mice, what-have-you), filling in the football pools in the hope of winning a fortune, fixing this and that in the home with a do-it-yourself kit, playing the latest pop records, and so on—predominantly, it is safe to say, home-based pursuits. An outing in the car is a growing weekend habit, and the British have been learning to eat out more than they did, but most of the time (when they are not at work) they are to be found at home.   (Ed.)

Prospects for the future

The period following World War II saw the final dissolution of the British Empire; one by one, former colonies were granted independence until Britain stood more really alone even than it had been in the short period in 1940, when it was the only power effectively at war with Hitler's Germany. The resultant loss of control of a vast network of ports and airports of strategic and military value across the world drastically reduced Britain's weight in international deliberations, while the transfer to some new nations of ownership of the production of raw materials in their countries, as in the case of Zambia copper and Ceylon (now Sri Lanka) tea, contributed to Britain's endemic economic troubles. Thus, the history of Britain as a world power seemed almost to be ended. Its membership in the European Economic Community (EEC), made effective by its formal adherence (on January 22, 1972) to the Treaty of Rome, did open to the country a new sphere of influence and provide the chance for the development of a new role in the world. The world is divided into large economic and political blocs: the Soviet Union, the United States, the EEC, Japan, and China; as part of one of these blocs, Britain should be both more secure and more able to make worthwhile contributions to world developments than if it had contributed alone.

Significance of EEC membership

It is important that Britain's leaders expect that, after joining the EEC, Britain's links with its independent Commonwealth of Nations will be no less close and intimate than in the past. This applies particularly to its family relationship with the former dominions of Canada, Australia, and New Zealand. Britain will also maintain its ties with the countries of the Indian subcontinent, with countries in Africa that were formerly British colonies, and with other countries, such as Singapore and Malaysia. Its "special relationship" with the United States is expected to continue. All these ties will continue to enhance Britain's reputation as a world power, but increases in its real influence are likely to derive primarily from the opportunities for increased commerce and industrial strength from which it is hoped the country will be able to profit as a member of the EEC.

It is hoped by its leaders that the economic benefits occurring to Britain from membership in the EEC will favourably affect its investment and employment position and create a better economic growth rate. As a member of the EEC, Britain is more likely to attract international investment, particularly in advanced industrial and technological concerns, which generate the greatest expansion of exports. Such expansion should help employment, and it was hoped that, in time, the high rate of unemployment (about 1,000,000 persons were out of work early in 1972) would be reduced to the level generally prevailing in the countries of western Europe. Although Britain at the time of joining the EEC had a strong balance-of-payments position, its membership should ease the general problems of sterling as an international currency, and currency support may well be developed in a European as well as in a world context.

Britain also has every reason to hope for a better growth rate as a member of the EEC; and it is from such an increase that the country's immense social-service budget and its unrivalled National Health Service must be financed. It is, therefore, not only hoped that the level of prosperity will rise but that continued and improved help for the aged and infirm may be guaranteed. Britain is proud of—and determined to maintain—its social services and its educational record. In 1972 considerable extra financial support was being given to the primary-school range of education, and, in due course, with planned expansion of higher education, the proportion attending courses at universities, institutes of technology, or technical colleges is expected to approach a little more closely that of students receiving higher education in the United States.

Prospects in education

In joining the EEC, Britain will have the opportunity to take part in a unique political experiment. With its long history of parliamentary democracy and its record of tolerance, ability to compromise, and ingenuity, Britain has much to offer, and the experience of its excellent civil service should enable it to assist in solving the EEC's administrative problems. In facing the future, whether of a confederation of nations or of the more remote possibility of a European federal state, Britain will presumably be unwilling to prejudice the existence of its monarchy or the independence of its Parliament. All treaties involve some degrees of abrogation of sovereignty, but Britain will be ready to sign conventions and treaties in the confidence that its island sovereignty will not be essentially impaired.

In the future, Britain will lend the aid of its armed forces to European as well as to North Atlantic Treaty Organization (NATO) defenses. With France it will continue to possess nuclear energy and weapons.

By widening its boundaries under the Treaty of Rome, Britain will have unique opportunities to mingle its culture with that of Europe. A strong and more homogeneous Europe will be to the advantage of the developing countries. There is probably no problem in the world more severe or poignant than that of the wide discrepancy in wealth and well-being between the rich and poor nations. An increased investment and growth rate will give Britain the opportunity to maintain and, if possible, increase its overseas-aid programs. (Bu.)

BIBLIOGRAPHY

The land and the people: The *British Association Handbooks* prepared for the annual meetings constitute an important source of local and regional scientific information. E.H. BROWN, *The Relief and Drainage of Wales* (1960), is one of the classics of landscape interpretation. W.G. EAST, (ed.), *Regions of the British Isles* (1961–), is a series that presents complete, well-illustrated surveys of the major regions. C.B. FAWCETT, *Provinces of England*, rev. ed. (1960), presents familiar material from a novel standpoint. T.W. FREEMAN, *The Conurbations of Great Britain* (1959), gives emphasis to the growth and character of the administrative units within Britain's cities. G.M. HOWE, *National Atlas of Disease Mortality in the United Kingdom* (1963), shows for males and females separately, and for the country's administrative units, a number of interesting distributions of mortality from certain specific causes. The *Registrar General's Annual Estimates of the Population of England and Wales* are important sources of data for between-census years. L.D. STAMP, *The Land of Britain: Its Use and Misuse*, 3rd ed. (1962), is a basic reference work that provides a view of the human ecology of the whole of Britain. J.A. STEERS (ed.), *Field Studies in the British Isles* (1964), are narratives of the itineraries and regions covered on the field-study tours arranged for the 20th International Geographical Congress. A.G. TANSLEY, *The British Islands and Their Vegetation*, 2 vol. (1949), is a monumental work that demonstrates the vast extension of ecological knowledge of British vegetation. J.W. WATSON and J.B. SISSONS (eds.), *The British Isles: A Systematic Geography* (1964), is an inventory of British geography written by 20 leading authorities.

The economy: Particularly recommended are the following studies—RICHARD E. CAVES et al., *Britain's Economic Prospects* (1968); PHYLLIS DEANE and W.A. COLE, *British Economic Growth, 1688–1959: Trends and Structure*, 2nd ed. (1967); ELY DEVONS, *An Introduction to British Economic Statistics* (1956); J.H. DUNNING and C.J. THOMAS, *British Industry: Change and Development in the Twentieth Century*, 2nd ed. (1963); ROY F. HARROD, *The British Economy* (1963); GRAHAM TURNER, *Business in Britain* (1969); G.D.N. WORSWICK and P.H. ADY (eds.), *The British Economy in the Nineteen-Fifties* (1962); and A.J. YOUNGSON, *The British Economy, 1920–1957* (1960).

Transportation: MINISTRY OF TRANSPORT, *Transport Policy*, Cmnd. 3057 (1966–67), the White Paper in which the Government first outlined its proposals that led to the 1968 Transport Act; *Passenger Transport in Great Britain 1968* (HMSO 1970), an abstract of statistics relating to travel by road, rail, and domestic airline for 1968, with summaries for years from 1952; *The Atlas of Britain and Northern Ireland* (1963), includes sections on transport, population, and industry; A.W.J. THOMSON and L.C. HUNTER, *The Nationalized Transport Industries* (1973), examines the history, rationale, and interaction of all the nationalized transport industries, their performances and prospects. (*Roads*): BRITISH ROAD FEDERATION, *Basic Road Statistics* (annual), an abstract of motor-vehicle registrations and road construction in the United Kingdom, with comparisons between Britain and other countries; *Motorway Progress*, a broadsheet issued periodically to review the current state of motorway construction and planning; MINISTRY OF TRANSPORT, *Traffic in Towns: A Study of the Long Term Problems of Traffic in Urban Areas* (1963), a study that considers the effects of the increase in private car use on the urban environment and examines a number of possibilities for dealing with the problem. (*Railways*): D.H. ALDCROFT, *British Railways in Transition* (1968), a review of the economic problems of Britain's railways since 1914, tracing the patterns of ownership and investment, traffic and operating policies, and government involvement over this period that followed the great heyday of railways; E.F. CARTER, *An Historical Geography of the Railways of the British Isles* (1959), a very detailed report on the proposals, construction, and fortunes of railway companies in the British Isles during the 19th and 20th centuries; O.S. NOCK, *Britain's New Railway* (1965), a description of the reconstruction, resignalling, and re-equipping of the main line between London and the northwest for electrification and high-speed running. (*Ports and inland waterways*): E.C.R. HADFIELD, *Introducing Canals: A Guide to British Waterways Today* (1955); MINISTRY OF TRANSPORT, *Report of the Committee of Inquiry into the Major Ports of Great Britain*, Cmnd. 1842 (1962), the Rochdale committee report into the adequacy of Britain's ports to meet future traffic needs; PORT OF LONDON AUTHORITY, *Britain's Foreign Trade*, 2nd ed. (1967), statistics of the trade handled by the major ports in the United Kingdom, by commodity type and by region of origin; J.A. BIRD, *The Major Seaports of the United Kingdom*, 2nd ed. (1969), a descriptive treatise on the history, development, and present trade of the more important seaports of the United Kingdom. (*Airways*): BRITISH AIRPORT AUTHORITY, *Annual Report and Accounts for the Year Ended . . .* (HMSO), annual report on the operation of the principal British airports, including a useful section of comparative statistics relating all British airport traffic flows to those at the most important airports in other countries; COMMISSION ON THE THIRD LONDON AIRPORT, *Papers and proceedings* (HMSO 1969–70), many volumes of research papers and proceedings of public enquiries into the needs and siting of London's third airport.

Administration and social conditions: On the constitutional framework of the structure of government, see I.H.J. GILMOUR, *The Body Politic* (1969); P.C. GORDON WALKER *The Cabinet: Political Authority in Britain* (1970); SIR W.I. JENNINGS, *Cabinet Government*, 3rd ed. (1959); J.P. MACKINTOSH, *The British Cabinet*, 2nd ed. (1968); and H.S. MORRISON, *Government and Parliament* (1954). On regional variations and local government, see R.M. JACKSON, *The Machinery of Local Government*, 2nd ed. (1965); R.E.C. JEWELL, *Central and Local Government* (1966); and the *Royal Commission Report on Local Government in England*, Cmnd. 4040 (1969). Information on the political process may be found in D.E. BUTLER, *The Electoral System in Britain, 1918–1951* (1953); and R. ROSE, *Politics in England* (1964), two works on elections in Britain; R.T. MACKENZIE, *British Political Parties* (1955); and on participation of the citizen in A.M. POTTER, *Organized Groups in British National Politics* (1961). (*Justice*): *Royal Commission Report on Assizes and Quarter Sessions*, Cmnd. 4153 (1969); H.G. HANBURY, *English Courts of Law*, 4th ed. prepared by D.C.M. YARDLEY (1967). (*Armed forces*): *Annual Defence White Papers* and information from the Ministry of Defence. (*Educational services*): *Royal Commission Report on Higher Education*, Cmnd. 2154 (1963); TYRRELL BURGESS, *Guide to English Schools* (1964). (*Health and welfare services*): P. GREGG, *The Welfare State: An Economic and Social History of Great Britain from 1945 to the Present Day* (1967); R.M. TITMUSS, *Essays on "the Welfare State,"* 2nd ed. (1963). (*Housing*): J.B. CULLINGWORTH, *Housing and Local Government in England and Wales* (1966); *Town and Country Planning in England and Wales* (1964). (*Police services*): T.A. CRITCHLEY, *A History of Police in England and Wales, 900–1966* (1967). (*Wages and cost of living*): CENTRAL STATISTICAL OFFICE, *Annual Abstract of Statistics* and the *Monthly Digest of Statistics.* (*Health conditions*): C.F. BROCKINGTON, *A Short History of Public Health*, 2nd ed. (1966); J. MOSS, *Health and Welfare Services Handbook*, 3rd ed. rev. (1962).

Cultural life: JOHN S. HARRIS, *Government Patronage of the Arts in Great Britain* (1970), is the most general and authoritative work of reference. On particular media, see P.E.P., *The British Film Industry, 1958* (1958); and FRANCIS WILLIAMS, *Dangerous Estate: The Anatomy of Newspapers* (1957). For independent accounts, see STUART HALL and PADDY WHANNEL, *The Popular Arts* (1964); and RICHARD BOSTON (ed.), *The Press We Deserve* (1970). On effects, see JAMES HALLORAN (ed.), *The Effects of Television* (1970). For general cultural analysis, see RICHARD HOGGART, *The Uses of Literacy* (1957). For history, see RAYMOND WILLIAMS, *The Long Revolution* (1961), especially ch. 2; and for origin of institutions in the media, see the same author's *Communications*, rev. ed. (1967).

(W.Ra./J.Pro./P.G.W.)

United Nations

The name United Nations was adopted during World War II to denote the nations allied in opposition to the so-called Axis powers—Germany, Italy, and Japan—and later adopted as the name of the postwar world organization. The term first achieved worldwide prominence when the Declaration of the United Nations was signed by 26 states on January 1, 1942, setting forth the war aims of the Allied powers.

The first major step toward the formulation of a permanent organization was taken at the Dumbarton Oaks Conference, a meeting of diplomatic experts of the Big Four powers (U.S., U.K., U.S.S.R., China) held August 21–October 7, 1944, at Dumbarton Oaks, an estate in Washington, D.C. The proposals developed at the meeting did not represent a complete plan of organization. Furthermore, the United States and the United Kingdom became stalemated with the Soviet Union on two essential issues: (1) on the voting system of the proposed Security Council, which later became famous as the "veto problem"; (2) on membership because the Soviet Union demanded seats in the General Assembly for all of its constituent republics. Roosevelt, Churchill, and Stalin finally resolved these two issues at the Yalta Conference and also agreed that the new agency would include a trusteeship system to succeed the League of Nations mandate system.

The Dumbarton Oaks proposals, as modified at the Yalta Conference, thus formed the basis of negotiations at the United Nations Conference on International Organization (UNCIO), which convened at San Francisco on April 25, 1945, and drafted the Charter of the United Nations (UN). The Charter was signed on June 26 and entered into force on October 24, 1945, by which time the Big Four, France, and a majority of the other signatories had deposited their ratifications.

San Francisco Conference   The San Francisco Conference was attended by representatives of the 46 states that had signed the Declaration of the United Nations. Four other states (Ukrainian S.S.R., Belorussian S.S.R., Argentina, and Denmark) were admitted during the conference. Poland, not present at the conference, was permitted to become an original member of the UN, which thus began with 51 members.

The San Francisco Conference was the first major international conference for two millenniums not dominated by Europe. Not only was it remote from Europe geographically but only nine continental European states west of the U.S.S.R. were represented. The 21 American republics, seven Near Eastern states, six Commonwealth nations, three Soviet republics, two Far Eastern, and two African states represented all parts of the world. Nine enemy states (Germany, Italy, Japan, Hungary, Austria, Romania, Bulgaria, Finland, and Thailand), eight neutral states (Switzerland, Spain, Portugal, Sweden, Ireland, Afghanistan, Iceland, and Yemen), and Poland, which was unable to organize a government until the conference was over, were not represented.

The international Secretariat provided interpreters and translators and distributed documents and speeches daily in the five official languages (English, French, Spanish, Russian, and Chinese). The chairmanship of the plenary sessions rotated among the Big Four. The private consultations of the Big Four, to which France was later added, exerted a great deal of influence. The rule of unanimity, usually adopted by political conferences, was abandoned. Measures could be carried in committees, commissions, and plenary sessions by a two-thirds vote.

Political issues arose, especially between the Western powers and the U.S.S.R., over the admission of Ukrainian S.S.R., Belorussian S.S.R., and Argentina; the recognition of a government of Poland; and the extension of the great-power veto in the Security Council to discussion as well as to recommendations and decisions. These controversies were settled by compromises. The issues concerning domestic jurisdiction versus international competence for the protection of human rights and the promotion of economic and social welfare, the status of colonial areas and of regional and defense arrangements, and great-power dominance versus the equality of states involved other groupings. In these matters the small states, the

Oriental states, and the Latin American states succeeded in obtaining modifications of the Dumbarton Oaks proposals.
(Q.W.)

This article is organized as follows:

PURPOSES AND MEMBERSHIP

The first article of the Charter outlines the purposes of the organization, declaring that the primary objective of the United Nations is the maintenance of international peace and security. The organization is also dedicated to the development of friendly relations among nations, based on the principle of equal rights and self-determination of peoples; to the achievement of international cooperation in solving international economic, social, cultural, or humanitarian problems; and to serving as a centre for harmonizing the actions of nations in the attainment of these common ends. Some of the basic principles of the United Nations, as outlined in Article 2 of the Charter, are the following: the United Nations is based on the sovereign equality of its members; disputes are to be settled by peaceful means; members undertake not to use force or the threat of force in contravention of the purposes of the United Nations; each member must assist the organization in any action it takes under the Charter; and states that are not members of the United Nations are required to act in accordance with these principles insofar as necessary for the maintenance of international peace and security. Article 2 also stipulates that, except to take enforcement measures, the organization shall not intervene in matters within the domestic jurisidiction of any state.

The original members of the United Nations were Argentina, Australia, Belgium, Belorussian S.S.R., Bolivia, Brazil, Canada, Chile, China, Colombia, Costa Rica, Cuba, Czechoslovakia, Denmark, Dominican Republic, Ecuador, Egypt, El Salvador, Ethiopia, France, Greece, Guatemala, Haïti, Honduras, India, Iran, Iraq, Lebanon, Liberia, Luxembourg, Mexico, The Netherlands, New Zealand, Nicaragua, Norway, Panama, Paraguay, Peru, the Philippines, Poland, Saudi Arabia, South Africa, Syria, Turkey, Ukrainian S.S.R., Union of Soviet Socialist Republics, United Kingdom, United States, Uruguay, Venezuela, and Yugoslavia.

Original members

New members are admitted to the United Nations on recommendation of the Security Council and by a two-thirds vote of the General Assembly. They must be peace-loving states that accept the obligations contained in the Charter and be able and willing to carry out these obligations. The requirement of concurrence of the permanent members of the Security Council was for many years a serious obstacle to the admission of new members. By 1950 only nine of 31 applicants had been admitted: Afghanistan, Iceland, Sweden, Thailand (all in 1946);

Pakistan, Yemen (1947); Burma (1948); Israel (1949); and Indonesia (1950).

A number of efforts had been made by the General Assembly to break the deadlock. In the tenth assembly session (1955) there was wide support for a "package deal" sponsored by 29 members under the leadership of Canada. Though it became necessary to drop Japan and Mongolia from the package, the proposal was approved by the Security Council in modified form, and the General Assembly voted to admit 16 new members: Albania, Austria, Bulgaria, Cambodia, Ceylon, Finland, Hungary, Ireland, Italy, Jordan, Laos, Libya, Nepal, Portugal, Romania, and Spain.

In its 11th session (1956–57) the General Assembly voted to admit Ghana, Japan, Morocco, The Sudan, and Tunisia. The Federation of Malaya (later Malaysia) was admitted in 1957. In 1958 the Egyptian and Syrian delegations consolidated into one, representing the United Arab Republic (U.A.R.); in December 1958 Guinea became a member.

In September 1960, 16 nations were admitted: Cameroon, Central African Republic, Chad, Cyprus, Dahomey, Gabon, Ivory Coast, Malagasy Republic, Mali, Niger, Republic of Congo, Democratic Republic of the Congo (former Belgian Congo), Senegal, Somalia, Togo, and Upper Volta. Nigeria was admitted in October 1960 and Sierra Leone in September 1961. In October 1961 Syria, having seceded from the U.A.R., resumed its separate membership; Mongolia and Mauritania were admitted in October 1961 and Tanganyika in December. Rwanda, Burundi, Jamaica, and Trinidad and Tobago were admitted in September 1962, followed by Algeria and Uganda in October. Kuwait was admitted in May 1963 and Zanzibar and Kenya in December, bringing the membership to 113. When Tanganyika and Zanzibar in April 1964 signed an agreement to unite under the name of Tanzania, the total was reduced to 112. With the admission of Malawi, Zambia, and Malta in December 1964, the total membership reached 115.

Indonesia, by letter of January 21, 1965, informed the United Nations that it was withdrawing from the organization, but on September 19, 1966, it sent another letter stating that it was resuming "full cooperation." Without formalities Indonesia resumed participation in the activities of the UN as if it had never been absent.

Singapore, The Gambia, and Maldives were admitted to membership in September 1965. In 1966 Guyana, Botswana, Lesotho, and Barbados were admitted. Southern Yemen was admitted in 1967; Mauritius, Swaziland, and Equatorial Guinea in 1968; Fiji in 1970; and Bahrain, Bhutan, Oman, Qatar, and the United Arab Emirates in 1971. At the end of 1971 the membership was 132.

With UN membership approaching universality, another problem confronted the organization: that of the large number of leftover fragments of empire. If all of these small territories, of which there were more than 50, should become members of the UN, the effectiveness of the organization would be seriously diminished. With the preponderant voting or political power in the General Assembly resting with the small states, the big states may be tempted to ignore the United Nations and resort to big-power politics. Secretary General U Thant in his 1967 annual report drew attention to the difficult problem of the role that "microstates" should attempt to play in world politics. Some of them find it a strain to maintain representations at the headquarters of the United Nations. Thant suggested the desirability of limiting membership on the basis of ability to carry out the responsibilities of membership and raised the question of some form of associate membership in the organization for these very small states.

The question of Chinese representation

The question of China's representation in the UN was before the General Assembly at every session since 1950, when India introduced a resolution declaring that the Communist regime was entitled to representation in the assembly. This resolution failed by a vote of 33 to 16, with ten abstentions—largely because of the opposition led by the United States. For twenty years, efforts to bring the People's Republic of China into the organiza-

tion and, concurrently, to expel the representatives of Nationalist China on Taiwan were consistently frustrated. Finally, in 1971, the United States acquiesced to the idea of admitting Communist China to the Security Council and General Assembly if, at the same time, Nationalist China could retain a seat in the General Assembly. This compromise failed. The General Assembly on October 25, 1971, voted 76 to 35, with 17 abstentions and three members absent, to admit the representatives of the People's Republic and to wholly remove the Nationalist representatives. Nationalist China's permanent Security Council seat was also given to Communist China.

PRINCIPAL ORGANS

The United Nations has six principal organs: General Assembly, Security Council, Economic and Social Council, Trusteeship Council, International Court of Justice, and Secretariat.

General Assembly.   This is the only body in which all of the UN members are represented. A member may send as many as five representatives, but each member has only one vote. Decisions on substantive questions are taken by a majority or by a two-thirds vote, depending on the importance of the matters involved. Procedural questions are decided by majority vote.

Article 10 and the role of the General Assembly

Through its deliberative, supervisory, financial, and elective functions the General Assembly occupies a central position in the functioning of the United Nations. Its role as a deliberative organ is based in articles 10–14 of the Charter. Article 10 states that the General Assembly may discuss and make recommendations on "any questions or any matters within the scope of the present Charter or relating to the powers and functions of any organs provided for in the present Charter."

In performing its supervisory functions, the General Assembly exercises control over the activities of UN organs in the economic and social fields and in dealing with the problems of non-self-governing territories. It receives annual reports from the secretary general, Security Council, Economic and Social Council, and Trusteeship Council and may make recommendations to these organs. The Economic and Social Council and the Trusteeship Council operate under the authority of the General Assembly. The assembly approves trust agreements and through the Trusteeship Council supervises the administration of trust territories. It exercises general supervision and control over the operations of the Secretariat. The financial power of the assembly is exercised through its control over the budget of the United Nations and the scale of assessments levied on members.

In its elective capacity, the General Assembly chooses all the members of the Economic and Social Council and the elective members of the Security Council and Trusteeship Council. Along with the Security Council, it also participates in the election of judges of the International Court of Justice and the appointment of the secretary general. The assembly shares with the Security Council the power to propose amendments to the Charter as well as the right to convene a conference for the purpose of revising the charter.

During its first ten years the General Assembly progressively increased in importance as an organ of deliberation and political influence. At the same time the influence and the effectiveness of the Security Council declined because of the inability of the permanent members to cooperate. The broad language of articles 10, 11, and 14 of the Charter permitted the role of the General Assembly to increase far beyond what was originally envisaged, and most of its members encouraged this increase. Members consequently became more and more concerned with ways and means of strengthening the assembly, in organization and procedure, so that it could more effectively handle its growing responsibilities.

The assembly convenes annually, but its rules also permit the calling of special sessions on short notice. It works through a complex structure of main committees, procedural committees, standing committees, and subsidiary and ad hoc bodies.

Security Council. The Charter assigns the Security Council primary responsibility for maintenance of international peace and security. The council consisted originally of 11 members—five permanent members (Nationalist China, France, the United Kingdom, the U.S.S.R., and the United States) and six nonpermanent members elected by the assembly for two-year terms. In 1965, when an amendment to the Charter was ratified, the council became a 15-member body consisting of the original five permanent members and ten nonpermanent members. The latter were to be chosen as follows: five from African and Asian states, one from eastern European states, two from Latin-American states, and two from western European and other states. The presidency is held by each member in turn for one month. In selecting nonpermanent members the assembly must not only strive for an equitable geographical distribution but must also consider the contribution of members to the maintenance of international peace and security. From the beginning, nonpermanent members of the Security Council were elected with a view to giving representation to certain regions or groups of states. This practice ran into increasing difficulty as the number of UN members increased, and there were not enough seats on the Security Council to distribute among the groups and regions desiring representation.

Under the Charter, members of the UN agreed to carry out the decisions of the Security Council. This agreement refers primarily to decisions pertaining to the maintenance of international peace and security under Chapter VII of the Charter. The council may investigate any dispute that might threaten international peace and security, but it can make recommendations only for its peaceful settlement. The council may, however, require members of the UN to apply various sanctions against any state that the council has found guilty of a threat to the peace, breach of the peace, or act of aggression (Article 39), or of failing to "perform the obligations incumbent upon it under a judgment" of the International Court of Justice (Article 94). Recommendations for the regulations of national armaments may also be made by the council (Article 26).

On procedural matters, decisions by the council are made by an affirmative vote of any nine (seven until 1965) of its members. On substantive matters, including the investigation of a dispute and the application of sanctions, nine (seven until 1965) affirmative votes (including those of the five permanent members) are required, but in practice a permanent member may abstain without impairing the validity of the decision. A vote on whether a matter is procedural or substantive is itself a substantive question. Because the council is required to function continuously, each member is represented at all times at UN headquarters.

Economic and Social Council. The Economic and Social Council is charged with directing and coordinating the complex system of economic, social, humanitarian, and cultural activities of the United Nations. Its 27 members (18 before 1965) are elected by the General Assembly for three-year terms with the possibility of re-election. Although the Economic and Social Council has no permanent members, states the participation of which is considered necessary to the work of the council have been regularly re-elected. When the membership of the council was increased in 1965 it was provided that seven of the additional members would represent African and Asian states, one would represent a Latin-American state, and one a western European or other state.

The Economic and Social Council meets at least twice a year; it is directed by the Charter to carry on studies and make recommendations for the promotion of international cooperation in economic and social matters. It may prepare draft conventions for submission to the assembly and call international conferences.

The council is assisted in its work by commissions organized on functional or geographical bases. The functional commissions, including an economic, a social, and a human rights commission, carry out studies in their fields and otherwise assist the council in the performance of its duties. They formulate resolutions, recommendations,

Procedural and substantive voting in the Security Council

and international conventions on which the council and General Assembly take action. Four regional commissions—for Europe, Asia and the Far East, Latin America, and Africa—that were established to deal with specific regional economic problems assumed roles of considerable importance both as advisory organs and as organs with important operational responsibilities.

Trusteeship Council. Acting under the authority of the General Assembly, the Trusteeship Council supervises the administration of trust territories by the administering states. The council is composed of UN members who administer trust territories; the permanent members of the Security Council not administering trust territories; and as many other nonadministering members elected by the assembly for three-year terms as are necessary to ensure an equal number of administering and nonadministering members in the total membership of the council. The Trusteeship Council is authorized to send visiting inspection missions into the trust territories, to receive and examine petitions, to consider reports submitted to it annually by the administering authorities, and to make recommendations with respect to all the matters coming within its purview. The council is required to submit annual reports on its activities to the General Assembly.

International Court of Justice. The court, popularly known as the World Court, is the principal judicial organ of the United Nations, and its statute is an integral part of the Charter. The 15 judges of the court are elected by the General Assembly and the Security Council voting independently. No two judges may be nationals of the same state. The main forms of civilization and the major legal systems of the world are to be represented on the court. Judges serve for nine years and are eligible for re-election. The seat of the court is The Hague, The Netherlands.

The jurisdiction of the court comprises "all cases which parties refer to it and all matters specially provided for in the Charter of the United Nations or in treaties and conventions in force." By formal declaration, states may accept the compulsory jurisdiction of the court in specified categories of disputes. The court may give advisory opinions at the request of the General Assembly or the Security Council or at the request of other organs and specialized agencies authorized by the General Assembly (see INTERNATIONAL COURT OF JUSTICE).

Secretariat. The Secretariat is headed by the secretary general, who is appointed by the General Assembly upon the recommendation of the Security Council. At the beginning of its first session in 1946, the General Assembly chose Trygve Lie of Norway for a term of five years, which was extended in 1950 for three more years. This extension was bitterly opposed by the U.S.S.R., and in November 1952 Lie resigned. In April 1953 Dag Hammarskjöld of Sweden succeeded him and was re-elected in 1957. In September 1961 Hammarskjöld was killed in an airplane crash in Northern Rhodesia. After a period of controversy, during which the U.S.S.R. proposed that the Secretariat be headed by a three-member committee, the powers agreed upon the choice of U Thant of Burma. In December 1966 Thant was unanimously elected to a second term. When he resigned at the end of 1971, Dr. Kurt Waldheim of Austria was elected to succeed him for a five-year term.

In addition to being the chief administrative officer of the United Nations, the secretary general also has important political functions, being specifically charged with bringing before the organization any matter that threatens international peace and security (see also below, *Administration*).

The UN secretary general

MAINTENANCE OF INTERNATIONAL PEACE AND SECURITY

Settlement of disputes. The preamble to the Charter begins with the declaration that the peoples of the United Nations are determined "to save succeeding generations from the scourge of war"; and Article 1 places the maintenance of international peace and security first among the purposes of the organization, followed by the development of "friendly relations among nations" and the achievement of "international cooperation in solving international problems of an economic, social, cultural, or humanitarian character." In the long run the secondary purposes may be more important than the first, but it is only in peace that the United Nations can function to achieve the secondary purposes.

The primary responsibility for the maintenance of international peace and security is placed on the Security Council. The founders realized that without basic agreement among the great powers on important international issues there could be no effective cooperation in the maintenance of peace or the application of sanctions against an aggressor. For this reason the Charter provided that substantive decisions would require the unanimous vote of the five permanent members of the Security Council. But this requirement means that when there is disagreement on substantive matters among the big powers the Security Council is unable to act. It was assumed by those who drafted the Charter that the five great powers who were given permanent membership in the council would cooperate in security matters. This assumption proved false. Almost immediately there developed a sharp rift between the Soviet Union and the Western powers; and the Soviet Union, being in a minority, resorted to frequent use of the veto to prevent what it considered adverse action by the council.

Articles 11–12 and the role of the General Assembly

With a stalemate in the Security Council, members of the United Nations began to look to the General Assembly. Article 11, paragraph 2, of the Charter authorizes the General Assembly to "discuss any questions relating to the maintenance of international peace and security" and to "make recommendations with regard to any such questions to the state or states concerned or to the Security Council or to both." This broad authorization is restricted somewhat by the provision of Article 12, that, "while the Security Council is exercising in respect of any dispute or situation the functions assigned to it in the present Charter, the General Assembly shall not make any recommendations with regard to that dispute or situation unless the Security Council so requests." Whereas these provisions grant the assembly a broad secondary role, there exists a very important difference between the two bodies. The Security Council can make decisions that bind all the members, whereas the General Assembly can only make recommendations.

Because the Soviet representative was absent from the Security Council in protest against the allegedly illegal representation of China on that body by the Nationalist government, the Security Council was able to take prompt action against the North Korean forces when they attacked South Korea in June 1950. After a few weeks, however, the Soviet representative returned to the council, and further action by that body to deal with the Korean situation was blocked by Russian vetoes. To enable it to carry out its peace-keeping function more effectively, the General Assembly in November 1950 adopted the Uniting for Peace Resolution proposed by the United States. It provided for immediate consideration by the General Assembly of a threat to the peace, breach of the peace, or act of aggression, with a view to recommending collective measures, including the use of armed force when necessary, "if the Security Council, because of lack of unanimity of the permanent members, fails to exercise its primary responsibility." The resolution established a Peace Observation Commission to "observe and report on the situation in any area where there exists international tension the continuance of which is likely to endanger the maintenance of international peace and security." It also established a Collective Measures Committee to "study and report on methods which the Assembly might use in strengthening international peace and security."

1950 Uniting for Peace Resolution

In carrying out its responsibility the Security Council must first seek to bring about a pacific settlement of disputes, in accordance with Chapter VI of the Charter. If the parties to a dispute that threatens the peace fail to settle it by peaceful means of their own choice, the Security Council must call upon them to settle it. The council may investigate any dispute or situation in order to determine whether its continuance is likely to endanger international peace and security. Any state, whether it is a member of the UN or not, may bring any such dispute or situation to the attention of the Security Council or the General Assembly. At any stage of the dispute or situation the Security Council may recommend appropriate procedures or methods of adjustment, and if the parties fail to settle the dispute by peaceful means the Security Council may recommend terms of settlement.

Whenever the Security Council determines that a threat to the peace exists or that a breach of the peace or act of aggression has taken place, it may decide upon measures to be taken to meet the situation. The Charter envisages the application of graduated measures, from economic and diplomatic sanctions to action by air, sea, and land forces. By subscribing to the Charter, all the members undertook to place at the disposal of the Security Council armed forces and facilities for military sanctions against aggressors or disturbers of the peace; but this provision did not become operative because no agreements to give it effect were concluded.

During the first 20 years of its life, a large number of disputes and situations involving the maintenance of peace came before the Security Council and the General Assembly, reflecting the unsettled conditions in the world after World War II. The United Nations succeeded in helping to settle some of them, such as the removal of Soviet troops from northern Iran in 1946; others remained unsolved and were a continuing concern of the Security Council and the General Assembly. Because most of these disputes have involved actions taken by nations acting outside, as well as within, the United Nations, the detailed histories of each will not be found in the present article. For references to these disputes, see RELATED ENTRIES under UNITED NATIONS in the *Ready Reference and Index*.

Regulation of armaments. The Charter places responsibility on the Security Council for preparing and submitting plans for the regulation of armaments. The General Assembly may discuss and recommend principles governing "disarmament and the regulation of armaments." The word regulation has been interpreted to include making armaments available for United Nations purposes as well as limiting or reducing armaments used for national purposes. The development of the atomic bomb during World War II created a situation in which it seemed to the United States and other governments that the international control of atomic energy demanded consideration even in advance of any perfection of collective security arrangements. Consequently, the first act of the United Nations was to establish the Atomic Energy Commission in January 1946 to prepare plans for the control of atomic energy. In December 1946 the General Assembly adopted a resolution providing for the urgent consideration of the control of atomic weapons and other weapons of mass destruction and for the regulation and reduction of all armaments and armed forces.

Atomic Energy Commission

The Atomic Energy Commission began its deliberations in June 1946. It soon became apparent that there was complete disagreement between the United States and the U.S.S.R. The commission submitted reports to the Security Council in 1946, 1947, and 1948. The majority of the members of the commission called for international managerial control or ownership of atomic-energy facilities, international inspection by a proposed international atomic development authority, and the elimination of the veto from enforcement provisions of the agreement. The majority also insisted that the control system should be in operation before the existing stockpile of atomic bombs was destroyed. The Soviet Union, however, took an opposite view. It refused to agree to international ownership and to the kind of international inspection demanded by the majority; it demanded that the veto be applicable to enforcement measures under the plan and that the destruction of atomic stockpiles accompany the establishment of a control system. The commission recorded an impasse in negotiations in its 1948 report, though some agreement had been reached on matters of detail.

To deal with armaments other than weapons of mass destruction, the Security Council organized the Commission for Conventional Armaments, but progress in this field was also blocked by disagreement between the U.S.S.R. and the Western powers. Although the commission and the General Assembly in 1949 approved a plan whereby each state would submit full information to the commission on its conventional armaments and armed forces, the refusal of the U.S.S.R. to accept the plan prevented any implementation. By early 1950 it was clear that a hopeless deadlock had been reached.

Disarmament Commission

In January 1952 the assembly voted to merge the Atomic Energy Commission and the Conventional Armaments Commission into a Disarmament Commission, thus recognizing the interdependence of the various elements of the problem. The Disarmament Commission, which consisted of the members of the Security Council and Canada, was directed to prepare proposals for the regulation, limitation, and balanced reduction of all the armed forces and armaments; for the elimination of major weapons adaptable to mass destruction; and for the effective international control of atomic energy to ensure its use for peaceful purposes only. The development of atomic and hydrogen weapons by the U.S.S.R. fundamentally altered the terms of the problem of the regulation and reduction of armaments and resulted in important changes in national positions. In spite of vigorous efforts to achieve constructive results through the commission and the General Assembly itself, little progress was made.

In his annual report to the 12th General Assembly, which convened in 1957, Secretary General Hammarskjöld stated that the year had witnessed "most sustained and intensive efforts by the members of the disarmament subcommittee to find common ground." Instead of attempting to work out a comprehensive, detailed, general disarmament plan there was a shift toward efforts to obtain a limited "first step" agreement. After over a decade of stalemate there was some hope that a limited agreement might be possible. Much attention was devoted to means of preventing surprise attacks; the United States urged acceptance of the Eisenhower "open skies" proposal for aerial inspection and exchange of military blueprints; the U.S.S.R. supported the Bulganin plan of ground observation posts at strategic centres. No agreement resulted. In 1957, however, the International Atomic Energy Agency was established to promote the peaceful uses of atomic energy.

World public opinion, as expressed in the General Assembly, continued to exert pressure on the great powers to resume negotiations for disarmament. A Ten-Nation Disarmament Committee, composed of five members from eastern Europe and an equal number from the West, began deliberations in March 1959, but negotiations soon reached an impasse. The committee was enlarged to 18 members by the addition of neutral countries, but one member, France, did not participate. Both the U.S.S.R. and the Western powers declared that general and complete disarmament was their goal, but little agreement was reached on how to achieve that goal. The Western approach was primarily military: a step-by-step movement toward a carefully inspected and controlled system of disarmament. The Soviet approach was primarily political: an agreement for complete and total disarmament within a few years. The General Assembly in 1961 adopted a resolution declaring the use of nuclear or thermonuclear weapons to be contrary to international law, to the UN Charter, and to the laws of humanity.

An important step toward disarmament was achieved by the Nuclear Test-Ban Treaty signed on August 5, 1963, by the Soviet Union, the United Kingdom, and the United States. This agreement—to which over 100 states later adhered—prohibited nuclear tests or explosions in the atmosphere, in outer space, and under water, but not underground. (China and France, both atomic powers, did not sign the treaty.)

Treaty on the Peaceful Uses of Outer Space

In June 1966 the Soviet Union and the U.S. submitted draft space treaties to the UN. The legal subcommittee of the UN Committee on the Peaceful Uses of Outer Space, assigned to reconcile the two drafts, on December 8 produced a historic document: it prohibited countries that ratified it from placing nuclear arms or other weapons of mass destruction in orbit, on the moon, or on other bodies in space and required nations to use the moon and other celestial bodies for peaceful purposes only. The General

Assembly approved the treaty unanimously. Signature and ratification by UN members and nonmembers were to follow. After more than six years of negotiation, the Soviet Union and the United States reached an agreement on a draft of a treaty to ban the further spread of nuclear weapons. By resolution of June 12, 1968, the General Assembly commended the draft and urged members to ratify it.

Revision of the Charter. In accordance with Article 109, a proposal to call a conference to review the Charter was placed on the agenda of the General Assembly at its tenth session in 1955. The assembly decided that such a conference should be held at some appropriate time in the future, but no date was set. Three specific proposals for Charter amendment were urged by a number of Latin American states as early as 1956: to increase the number of nonpermanent members of the Security Council, to increase the membership of the Economic and Social Council, and to increase the number of judges on the International Court of Justice. As the membership of the United Nations rose to more than 100, the demand for enlargement of the councils became more insistent; some regions, particularly Africa, felt they were not given adequate representation.

The General Assembly adopted, on December 17, 1963, a resolution proposing an amendment to the Charter to enlarge the Security Council to 15 (by increasing the number of nonpermanent members to ten) and to raise the membership of the Economic and Social Council to 27. Under the proposed revision, decisions of the Security Council on procedural matters would require an affirmative vote of any nine members, and decisions on all other matters would require nine affirmative votes, including those of the five permanent members. The proposed amendment provided for the geographic distribution of the seats of the nonpermanent members as follows: Africa and Asia, five; eastern Europe, one; Latin America, two; western Europe and other regions, two. The Soviet Union, which previously had opposed any amendment to the Charter so long as China was barred from the United Nations, changed its position and was the first of the permanent members of the Security Council to ratify the proposed revision. By September 1965 the two amendments had been ratified.

DEVELOPMENT OF INTERNATIONAL LAW

International Law Commission

In November 1947 the General Assembly established the International Law Commission of 15 members to make recommendations for the progressive development and codification of international law. In setting up the commission, the General Assembly directed it to formulate the principles of international law recognized at the Nuremberg trial of Nazi war criminals and to prepare a draft code of offenses against the peace and security of mankind.

In 1950 the commission submitted its formulation of the Nuremberg principles, which covered crimes against the peace, war crimes, and crimes against humanity. The commission presented to the assembly in 1951 draft articles on offenses against the peace and security of mankind, which enumerated 12 crimes against international law, including any act of aggression, threat of or preparation for aggression, annexation of territory, and genocide. The commission also prepared a draft declaration on the rights and duties of states.

The commission made studies of the possibility of codifying certain branches of international law, giving priority to the law of treaties and the law of the sea (see INTERNATIONAL LAW). It also prepared a study on the legal aspects of reservations to multilateral conventions. Draft conventions were prepared on statelessness, the peaceful settlement of disputes, the law of the sea, diplomatic relations, consular relations, and the law of treaties. The commission was also concerned about the subjects of arbitral procedure and international criminal jurisdiction. After the commission has completed a draft convention it submits it to the General Assembly, which may either convene an international conference to draw up formal conventions based on the draft or merely commend the text to the states. A conference to consider the draft convention on the law of the sea was held at Geneva in 1958; conferences held at Vienna in 1961 and 1963 completed conventions on diplomatic relations and optional protocols on the acquisition of nationality and the compulsory settlement of disputes and on consular relations. The commission in 1966 completed a draft convention on the law of treaties, which was placed before a conference meeting in split sessions in 1968 and 1969.

During its first two decades the UN made considerable effort to arrive at an acceptable definition of aggression. The San Francisco Conference, the International Law Commission, and special committees set up by the assembly all sought an agreement on such a definition but failed. Failure to reach agreement on the definition of aggression delayed progress on the drafting of certain conventions. The commission was engaged in preparing draft conventions on special diplomatic missions, relations between states and intergovernmental organizations, state responsibility, and succession of states and governments.

The General Assembly also set up two special committees to promote the development and codification of international law—one on the principles of international law concerning friendly relations of states and another on international trade law.

ECONOMIC AND SOCIAL COOPERATION

A major purpose of the United Nations is "to achieve international cooperation in solving international problems of an economic, social, cultural, or humanitarian character, and in promoting and encouraging respect for human rights and for fundamental freedoms for all without distinction as to race, sex, language, or religion." The General Assembly, the Economic and Social Council, the Secretariat, and the specialized agencies are the organs primarily responsible for action in this field. An important part of this aspect of UN activity consists of research, publication of reports, and rendering technical assistance to governments. The United Nations has no authority to legislate or to enforce measures of economic and social cooperation; it can only make recommendations, which the member governments may or may not follow.

Major UN annual publications

The United Nations has rendered a valuable service by publishing carefully prepared statistical data and surveys of economic and social developments. Among the more significant of its yearly publications are the *World Economic Report*, the *Statistical Yearbook*, the *Demographic Yearbook*, and the *Yearbook on Human Rights*.

Economic reconstruction. The devastation of large areas of the world and the dislocation of normal economic relations during World War II resulted in the need for concerted measures of relief, rehabilitation, and reconstruction. The United Nations Relief and Rehabilitation Administration, established in 1943, did much to alleviate the situation. To assist in dealing with regional problems the Economic and Social Council in 1947 established the Economic Commission for Europe and the Economic Commission for Asia and the Far East. Similar commissions were established for Latin America in 1948 and for Africa in 1958.

Technical assistance. A modest program of technical assistance to the less developed countries was undertaken in 1946 when the General Assembly passed a resolution calling for the establishment of machinery in the Secretariat for giving such aid. The Expanded Program of Technical Assistance was approved by the General Assembly in 1949. It is financed by voluntary contributions from members. Pledges are made at an annual conference.

Financing economic development. The United Nations gave a great deal of consideration to ways and means of making capital available to less developed countries for financing projects that were not self-liquidating or that did not meet the International Bank's requirements for loans. In 1954 the General Assembly recommended that both capital-importing and capital-exporting countries examine their policies and practices with a view to encouraging the flow of private capital. In April 1955 the Bank submitted to its members the draft charter of the International Finance Corporation, to come into operation as soon as ratified by 30 states and as soon as 75 percent of $100,000,000 capital had been subscribed. The corporation was to make direct loans to private enterprises without government guarantees and was to be allowed to make loans for other than fixed returns. The charter entered into force on July 20, 1956.

In 1960 the International Development Association was established as an affiliate of the International Bank. It was created to make loans to less developed countries on terms that were more flexible than bank loans. It was authorized to finance any project "which will make an important contribution to the development of an area or areas concerned, whether or not the project is revenue producing or directly productive."

International Development Association

To assist in the financing of non-self-liquidating development projects a proposal was submitted to the General Assembly for a Special United Nations Fund for Economic Development (SUNFED). The General Assembly in 1957 unanimously adopted a resolution to set up a separate fund to provide systematic assistance in fields essential to technical, economic, and social development of less developed countries. The Special Fund began operations in 1959 with Paul G. Hoffman as the managing director. The Expanded Program and the Special Fund had similar goals, but they were different in structure and operation. The Special Fund put greater emphasis on the preevaluation of projects; about one-third of its expenditures were allocated for surveys and feasibility studies. Nevertheless, because of the similarity of functions there was a growing demand for a merger of the Expanded Program and the Special Fund. This merger was effected in 1965 under the name United Nations Development Programme.

Trade and development. The less developed countries contended that the terms of international trade were against them. They complained that the prices of the manufactured goods they had to import from industrialized countries were high, whereas the prices of the primary commodities that they produced for export were low, thus frustrating their efforts to obtain more rapid growth. Although they became parties to the General Agreement on Tariffs and Trade (GATT), they were critical of it, insisting that more was required than the application of the most-favoured-nation principle and the mere reduction of tariffs. They demanded a conference to consider means for the removal of obstacles to the trade of developing countries.

A United Nations Conference on Trade and Development (UNCTAD) met in Geneva in the early months of 1964, chiefly to consider the trade needs of the developing countries, and established the following items: a continual United Nations Conference on Trade and Development to promote international trade, especially with a view to accelerating economic development; a Trade and Development Board composed of 55 members elected by the conference; a permanent and full-time Secretariat; and a secretary general to be appointed by the UN secretary general with the confirmation of the General Assembly. This UNCTAD has proposed a variety of means, such as agreements on commodity trade and tariff rates favouring exports of developing countries.

UNCTAD

Refugees. The International Refugee Organization (IRO) was established in 1946 to take over the refugee functions of the United Nations Relief and Rehabilitation Administration, which expired in 1947. The IRO was successful in resettling, repatriating, transporting, and maintaining more than 1,000,000 European refugees. Because the IRO was conceived as a short-term emergency organization, it was abolished in 1952 and replaced by a new refugee structure. A United Nations High Commissioner for Refugees was appointed and was directed to act under the Convention Relating to the Status of Refugees, drawn up by the Economic and Social Council and approved by the General Assembly in 1951. An Advisory Committee on Refugees was appointed by the council in 1951 to assist the high commissioner. The assembly in 1957 voted to continue the office of UN high commissioner for refugees for five years from January 1959, and in 1963 and

1968 voted to extend it for five-year periods (to 1974). The assembly appealed to member governments to aid Chinese refugees in Hong Kong and urged them to meet the critical need for funds for Arab refugees.

Human rights. The General Assembly in 1948 adopted the Universal Declaration of Human Rights, which was prepared by the Commission on Human Rights. In 1948 the commission began to draft a Covenant of Human Rights that, upon ratification by governments, would become legally binding upon them. Wide differences in economic and social philosophies hampered efforts to achieve agreement on a common text, but finally a Draft Covenant on Economic, Social, and Cultural Rights and a Draft Covenant on Civil and Political Rights were completed in 1954 and submitted to the General Assembly for its consideration. The years of work by the Commission on Human Rights culminated in the adoption in 1966 by the General Assembly of the International Covenant on Civil and Political Rights, the International Covenant on Economic, Social and Cultural Rights, and the Optional Protocol to the Covenant on Civil and Political Rights, but by the middle of 1972 neither covenant had been ratified or acceded to by the 35 states necessary for its entry into force. In the general field of human rights, the assembly also concerned itself with discrimination against citizens of India, the policy of apartheid in South Africa, and violations of the civil-rights provisions of peace treaties by Hungary, Romania, and Bulgaria. The General Assembly in 1962 established a Special Committee on Apartheid and recommended that member states break off diplomatic relations with South Africa and apply economic sanctions against it. In 1963 the General Assembly adopted a Declaration on the Elimination of all Forms of Racial Discrimination, and in 1965 it approved an international convention on the same subject, which then went before the member states for signature and ratification.

Control of narcotics. The Commission on Narcotic Drugs was authorized by the assembly in 1946 to carry out the functions entrusted by international conventions to the League of Nations Advisory Committee on Traffic in Opium and Other Dangerous Drugs. The agreements, conventions, and protocols on the control of narcotic drugs concluded in 1912, 1925, 1931, and 1936 were amended in a draft protocol approved by the assembly in November 1946 and subsequently came into force among its signatories. In addition to re-establishing the pre-World War II system of narcotics control, which had suffered from the dislocations of the war, the UN concerned itself with new problems resulting from the development of synthetic drugs. Efforts were made to simplify the system of control by drafting one convention incorporating all the agreements in force.   (L.M.G./A.Va.)

Specialized agencies. The League of Nations provided a focal point for intergovernmental organizations and also for the growing network of nongovernmental agencies. Following World War II, the United Nations became a kind of "roof organization" for the major enterprises in systematic international cooperation. In accordance with its Charter, the UN entered into coordinating agreements with intergovernmental agencies operating in economic, social, cultural, educational, health, and related fields. In the second half of the 20th century the roster of specialized agencies affiliated with the United Nations included the following: Inter-Governmental Maritime Consultative Organization (IMCO); International Labour Organisation (ILO); United Nations Educational, Scientific and Cultural Organization (UNESCO); Food and Agriculture Organization (FAO); International Civil Aviation Organization (ICAO); International Bank for Reconstruction and Development (World Bank); World Health Organization (WHO); International Telecommunication Union (ITU); Universal Postal Union (UPU); World Meteorological Organization (WMO); International Atomic Energy Agency (IAEA); International Development Association (IDA); and the International Finance Corporation (IFC). The Economic and Social Council, acting under the Charter of the United Nations, endeavoured to maintain a consultative relationship with practically 300

nongovernmental organizations, virtually every one of them international in scope.

The general structure of each specialized agency follows a common pattern. Each agency has a general conference in which all the members are represented, and the conference elects an executive body that is charged with initiating proposals and carrying out decisions of the general conference. Each agency also has a permanent secretariat headed by a director. Many agencies have regional subcommissions operating in various parts of the world. Some of the specialized agencies were in existence before the United Nations was organized; some were in the process of establishment during World War II; and some agencies were organized under the auspices of the United Nations.   (Ed.)

International Labour Organisation. The ILO is an example of an official international institution now affiliated with the UN but existing before World War II. In 1919, the Peace Conference of Paris, fearful of social revolution, set up a commission for international labour legislation headed by Samuel Gompers, president of the American Federation of Labor. The commission put aside the more ambitious claims for a body with legislative authority and proposed a body with powers of recommendation to national governments for action by them, in composition a tripartite body in which half the representation would be by governments, and one-fourth each by labour and by employers. The peace conference adopted these proposals and, by inserting them in the Treaty of Versailles, thereby set up the ILO.

In its first decade the ILO was concerned primarily with its research efforts; with the definition and promotion of proper minimum standards of labour legislation for adoption by member states; and with "mutual education" and some forms of collaboration among worker, employer, and government delegates and the office professional staff. During the 1930s the ILO sought ways to combat worldwide unemployment and economic depression. Its proposals of extensive international public works never influenced national decision makers.

After 1945, the "Cold War," the breakup of European colonial empires, and the claims of the developing nations placed new tasks in the foreground for an organization the membership of which was no longer chiefly that of European, economically developed states but increasingly that of the less developed states. The ILO's major emphases shifted therefore to the area of human rights and to technical assistance and other work of an operating character in the interest of the less developed countries of Asia, Africa, Latin America, and Europe itself. The ILO's ideal has been universality of membership. It admitted Germany in 1919, long before the League of Nations did. Some nations—Brazil and, for a time, Japan—remained in the ILO after resigning from the League. Others became members of the ILO without joining the League or the UN. The United States, aloof from the League, joined the ILO in 1934. After World War II the ILO admitted the German Federal Republic and Japan in 1951. But South Africa was practically forced out of the organization because of its racial policies. Post-World War II amendments made it easier to join the ILO. Members of the UN do not have automatic membership in the ILO, as did League members, but they may become members simply by filing a declaration accepting the obligations of the ILO constitution. Nonmembers of the UN must be accepted by a vote of two-thirds of the conference, including that of two-thirds of the government delegates. By the end of 1971 the ILO had 119 members.

The International Labour Office is the secretariat of the organization and its research staff. By 1970 it had international civil servants from more than 90 nations, including technical-assistance experts on temporary missions, working in Geneva, or in the field, all over the world. Their work was made possible by the ILO's own budget plus funds from other sources, chiefly UN Development Program funds. Some idea of the ILO's manifold activities may be gleaned from its current *Catalogue of Publications;* most widely used are the monthly *International Labour Review* and the *Year Book of Labour Statistics.*

Marginal notes:

Commission on Human Rights

Commission on Narcotic Drugs

General structure of UN agencies

Membership of the ILO

In 1962 there opened under ILO auspices—but with its own endowment fund—an International Institute for Labour Studies at Geneva, concerned with leadership training, especially for the developing countries, and with long-range research (in contrast to the ILO's own service-oriented research). Three years later the ILO, in cooperation with the Italian government, opened an International Centre for Technical and Vocational Training in Turin, which began to emphasize management training for different types of enterprises, including cooperatives, in the developing nations. (V.R.L.)

International Bank for Reconstruction and Development and International Monetary Fund. Two complementary, but separate, organizations, the International Bank (better known as the World Bank) and the International Monetary Fund (IMF), had their origin in wartime preparations for postwar international financial and economic cooperation that culminated in the United Nations Monetary and Financial Conference held in July 1944 at Bretton Woods, New Hampshire, and attended by 44 nations. The principal purposes of the World Bank, set forth in its articles of agreement (charter), may be summarized as follows: (1) To assist in the reconstruction and development of its member countries by facilitating the investment of capital for productive purposes, thereby promoting the long-range growth of international trade and improvement of standards of living. (2) To promote private foreign investment by guarantees of and participations in loans and other investments made by private investors. (3) When private capital is not available on reasonable terms, to make loans for productive purposes out of its own resources or funds borrowed by it.

The World Bank came into existence on December 27, 1945, when its articles of agreement were signed by 29 governments. The Bank officially began operations at its headquarters in Washington, D.C., in June 1946. By 1972 the Bank had 119 member countries. The largest of these, in terms of capital subscribed, were the United States, the United Kingdom, West Germany, France, India, Canada, and Japan. Also among the Bank's members were many other countries such as Iceland, Israel, Lebanon, Ceylon (now Sri Lanka), Indonesia, Afghanistan, Libya, Lesotho, Somalia, Ghana, Yugoslavia, and all the Latin-American republics except Cuba.

The World Bank's charter authorized it to engage in the following types of financing: it may lend funds directly, either from its capital funds or from funds that it borrows in private investment markets; it may guarantee loans made by others; or it may participate in such loans. Loans may be made to member countries directly or to any of their political subdivisions or to private business or agricultural enterprises in the territories of members. When the member government in whose territory the project is located is not itself the borrower, however, this member government must guarantee the loan.

The World Bank obtains its funds for loans from paid-in capital subscription, from borrowings in the capital markets of the world, and from net earnings. Sales to investors of portions of the Bank's loan portfolio and repayments of loans to the Bank, while representing only a recovery of funds originally derived from one of the above sources, have the same effect as new capital in that they reduce the amount the Bank would otherwise have to obtain from other sources. The capital markets of the world provide the largest amount of funds for loans. By the late 1960s the Bank's outstanding funded debt amounted to over $4,000,000,000. Loan funds available from other sources were $2,000,000,000 from paid-in capital subscriptions, about $1,000,000,000 from operations, and about $4,000,000,000 from repayments and sales of loans.

Because the World Bank is primarily a source of long-term loan capital, its resources have been used largely to assist in the financing of investments for which large amounts of long-term loan capital are required and for which this method of financing is appropriate. For this reason, a large part of the Bank's portfolio consists of loans to publicly and privately owned utilities, such as undertakings for the generation and distribution of electric power, railroads, ports and inland waterways, airlines and airports, telecommunications, and pipelines.

The International Monetary Fund was designed to stabilize international monetary rates. It came into existence in March 1946 after the ratification and appropriation of funds by national governments had been completed, but the Fund was not actually opened until March 1947, and the first transactions were made in May of that year. Operating funds of the IMF are subscribed by member governments. Each member has a quota, of which an amount equal either to 25 percent of the quota or 10 percent of the member's holdings of gold and U.S. dollars, whichever is smaller, is subscribed in gold and the remainder in national currency. The IMF was designed to stabilize exchange rates by assisting members over temporary difficulties in their international balance of payments. It does so partly by consultation and technical advice, but also by allowing members to purchase from it with their own national currencies the gold or foreign exchange they need. In principle not more than 25 percent of the member's quota may be purchased in any one year, but in an emergency this limit may be, and often is, waived. Not more than 125% of the quota may be purchased in all. Charges begin at ½% for the first 25% for the first year, rising by ½% for each additional year, with a limit of 5%. Members may arrange standby credits to use as and if necessary. If demands for any currency outrun the IMF's resources it may be declared scarce and rationed. Members may then impose discriminatory exchange controls against it. Members are required to repurchase the excess of their own currencies over their quotas within an agreed period (three to five years) as their balances improve. Members agree not to alter the exchange value of their currencies (except once by no more than 10 percent) without prior IMF agreement.

The expansion of world trade, however, coupled with a succession of international financial crises, created a demand for additional reserves that could be used in settlement of international balances. In October 1969 the IMF voted to distribute a total of $9,500,000,000 in Special Drawing Rights. These served, in effect, to enlarge members' quotas without any additional subscription either in gold or in national currencies, and thus to create a base for new credit expansion. But demands upon international liquidity continued to increase. A realignment of currencies agreed upon in December 1971 included an effective 11 percent devaluation of the U.S. dollar and the upvaluation of other major currencies. Another realignment came after the U.S. announced a new devaluation of 10 percent in February 1973. A number of countries allowed their currencies to "float"—*i.e.*, to change in value according to market conditions and without formal announcement. (J.H.A./J.B.C./Ed.)

Food and Agriculture Organization. The FAO, first of the permanent specialized agencies of the United Nations to be founded after World War II, came into formal being in October 1945 with the signing of its constitution at a conference held in Quebec City. The immediate factor leading to its foundation was the Conference on Food and Agriculture convened at the request of Pres. Franklin D. Roosevelt at Hot Springs, Virginia, in 1943. In 1951 the organization was transferred from its temporary headquarters in Washington, D.C., to a permanent seat in Rome.

The ideas underlying foundation of the new organization came from two sources. First was the International Institute of Agriculture founded in Rome in 1905. The IIA had been designed to protect farmers against the effects of sudden slumps and gluts and was, therefore, concerned with information about market trends and agricultural statistics. Second was the League of Nations, which in the period immediately before World War II had been interested in problems of nutrition and their relationship to health. Both the IIA and the League, however, had been principally concerned with the more advanced countries, whereas in the foundation of the FAO several of the new and developing countries took great interest and played an active part.

Because FAO was in part an answer to the question of

World Bank

International Monetary Fund

Basis of FAO

feeding vast populations in the countries the economics of which had been seriously disrupted by World War II, it was natural that the first few years should be devoted to trying to help bring about a rapid increase in the world's overall supplies of food. At the same time the member countries had an eye on the possible emergence of surpluses of some commodities in certain countries should the distribution system break down or should needy governments not be able to pay for the food they required. Finally, an appreciation of the rapid rise in population in virtually all the parts of the world in the immediate postwar period added urgency to the organization's work.

With the creation of the United Nations Expanded Program of Technical Assistance, further extrabudgetary sums became available for FAO's field operations and from 1950 onward an increasing number of countries received technical assistance from FAO under the terms of that fund. The range of projects covered all of the FAO's activities in agriculture, nutrition, forestry, fisheries, and economics.

Most of the experts working under the technical-assistance program were on individual assignments, advising governments concerned on specific problems. FAO also helped its member governments through regional projects, including widespread plant and animal disease control schemes, such as the desert locust-control program in the Arabian Peninsula; projects for the eradication of rinderpest; and creation of a European commission for the control of foot-and-mouth disease. A broad educational program was also in continual operation, with training centres and seminars in many subjects and a fellowship program run in connection with the assignment of technical-assistance experts.

These programs were implemented by various publications and reports of a technical nature, including the *Plant Protection Bulletin*, comprising the work of a worldwide reporting service on plant diseases and quarantine regulations. A parallel informational service for animal diseases included an annual overall summary of developments in the subject field as well as periodical reports. The FAO-sponsored monthly bulletin of agricultural statistics and allied yearbooks on production and trade in agriculture, fisheries, and forest products were standard works in their fields.

United Nations Educational, Scientific and Cultural Organization.   The historical roots of UNESCO lie in the intellectual cooperation efforts of the League of Nations and in the 1945 UN founding conferences at San Francisco and London, at which scholars who wanted to help increase the flow and exchange of knowledge drafted the organization's program.

UNESCO's activities were intended to be facilitative; through conferences, seminars, and publications, through the promotion of research and exchange of information and knowledge, and through technical advisory services, it was to assist, support, and seek to complement national efforts of member states. The significance of its activities in the life of any individual nation is limited. Even the allocation of the total budget among the neediest members would provide small amounts compared to what is spent by the countries themselves. The real effect is to be measured by the influence of internationally formulated standards of excellence, by the effectiveness of scholarly communication and exchanges, and by the quality of technical assistance provided.

Administration of UNESCO

UNESCO is administered by a director general and an international civil service of about 1,500 persons, subject to advice and direction from an executive board of 30 (originally 18) elected by the General Conference and designated by individual member states. Its permanent headquarters are in Paris. The constitution provides for national citizen advisory commissions in member states. The activities of UNESCO are coordinated with those of other UN agencies by the UN Economic and Social Council and by the policies of their respective member states. UNESCO's membership, 44 in 1945, had reached 127 by 1972.

Emphasis has been placed upon strengthening interna-

tional professional (nongovernmental) organizations in education, science, and culture; establishing clearing-houses for the exchange of information; and promoting international professional conferences, symposia and seminars, and publication of scholarly abstracts. A Universal Copyright Convention and an Agreement on the Importation of Educational, Scientific, and Cultural Materials were drafted and submitted for ratification by member states. The necessity of extending communication, within the fields of UNESCO's interest, to include relatively less developed areas of the world produced at first only modest projects. Among these were in the Science Cooperation Offices in Montevideo, Uruguay, Cairo, New Delhi, and Djakartar, Indonesia; assistance for developing public library resources in certain emerging countries; fellowships for study in more highly developed areas of the world; studies and conferences on illiteracy; and some pilot projects in so-called fundamental education.

Although UNESCO's contributions have been mainly indirect, exceptions have been the annual *Study Abroad*, a comprehensive index to foreign study opportunities; a few seminars for teachers on methods to increase international understanding; the multivolume *Scientific and Cultural History of Mankind* (1963–   ); some modest promotion of social science research into national character and the nature of race; a project urging member states to increase understanding between Asia and the West; and some efforts to promote international exchanges in the arts.

United Nations Children's Fund.   The General Assembly established the United Nations International Children's Emergency Fund (later styled the UN Children's Fund but still officially called UNICEF) in December 1946 to provide for the emergency needs of children in devastated areas. Financed by contributions from member states, UNICEF was effective in helping to feed destitute children in more than 50 countries; preventing such diseases as tuberculosis, whooping cough, and diphtheria; and providing for children's clothing and other needs. In 1953 it was made a permanent UN organization.   (Ed.)

UNICEF

World Health Organization.   WHO, established in 1948, is a specialized agency of the United Nations designed to further international cooperation for improved health conditions. WHO inherited from the Health Organization of the former League of Nations, set up in 1923, and from the International Office of Public Health at Paris, established in 1909, various international duties relative to epidemic control, quarantine measures, and the standardization of drugs. Under its constitution, however, WHO is given a much broader mandate—to promote the attainment of "the highest possible level of health" by all peoples. Health is defined positively as "a state of complete physical, mental, and social well-being and not merely the absence of disease or infirmity," and good health is held to be fundamental to world peace and security.

The membership of WHO consists of sovereign states and non-self-governing territories, their number growing from 26 in 1948 to 133 in 1972. The organization is financed primarily from annual contributions made by member governments on the basis of relative capacity to pay. The regular annual budget expanded in the first decade from $5,000,000 to more than $30,-000,000, the largest contributor being the United States, which provided approximately one-third. In addition, after 1951 WHO was allocated substantial resources from the expanded technical-assistance program of the UN. Grants for special purposes have been also made to WHO from time to time by private foundations and individual governments.

The work of WHO embraces three fairly distinct categories of activities:

1. The provision of central clearinghouse and research services. As an example, information about the occurrence of pestilential disease anywhere in the world is broadcast over an international radio network to national health authorities, seaports, airports, and ships at sea. In 1952, 13 outdated international sanitary agreements were

Activities of WHO

replaced by a codified set of international sanitary regulations designed to standardize quarantine measures without interfering unnecessarily with trade and air travel across national boundaries. The central WHO Secretariat also issues numerous publications, sets statistical standards, and keeps member countries informed of the latest developments in use of vaccines, cancer research, nutritional discoveries, control of drug addiction, and health hazards of nuclear radiation.

2. Measures for the control of epidemic and endemic disease. This category consists chiefly of mass campaigns promoted by WHO against communicable diseases. These campaigns, some of them conducted with the cooperation of the United Nations Children's Fund, have been dramatically successful in reducing the incidence of tuberculosis, malaria, and venereal disease in the more backward regions of the globe. The organization launched a worldwide campaign for the complete eradication of malaria. Considerable progress was also made by WHO in attacking such diseases as cholera, yellow fever, yaws, and trachoma. Among the techniques employed in these campaigns are nationwide vaccination programs, instruction in the use of antibiotics and insecticides, the improvement of laboratory and clinical facilities for early diagnosis and prevention, assistance in providing pure water supplies and sanitation systems, and health education for rural communities. In 1963 WHO established an Expert Advisory Panel on Air Pollution to study methods of measuring and analyzing atmospheric pollutants.

3. Efforts to strengthen and expand the public health administrations of member nations. As its program developed, WHO set as its most important task the strengthening of national and local health services, especially in Africa, Asia, and Latin America. In furthering this vital objective, a wide variety of devices are utilized. The organization provides technical advice to governments on request in the preparation of long-term national health plans; sends out to the field international teams of experts to conduct surveys and demonstration projects; helps set up local health centres; offers aid in the development of national training institutions for medical and nursing personnel; makes available teachers for on-the-spot short-course training experiments; and makes travelling fellowship awards to doctors, public health administrators, nurses, sanitary inspectors, and laboratory technicians.   (W.R.S.)

DEPENDENT AREAS

The United Nations maintained concern for people residing in non-self-governing territories on two different levels: (1) under principles and procedures developed for making administering states internationally accountable for the treatment of their non-self-governing territories and (2) under the United Nations trusteeship system.

Non-self-governing territories. Under Article 73 of the Charter, members of the United Nations responsible for administering non-self-governing territories agreed to ensure the people of such territories just treatment, protection against abuses, and advancement toward self-government. They also agreed to transmit to the secretary general technical information concerning the economic, social, and educational conditions in their territories. In 1947 the General Assembly created a special committee to receive and analyze information on these territories and to make recommendations to the administering authorities on the basis of information received. Attempts of the committee to obtain political information on territories from the administering states met with resistance. Only Australia, The Netherlands, New Zealand, and the United States transmitted such information, the other administering states contending that the Charter did not require the transmission of political information.

There was considerable controversy over the question as to which territories were non-self-governing and when they ceased to be non-self-governing. France soon stopped transmitting information on a number of territories on the ground that they had either become self-governing or had become an integral part of France. Later

Great Britain ceased to send information on Malta and Ghana, the United States on the Panama Canal Zone and Puerto Rico, Denmark on Greenland, and The Netherlands on Surinam and the Antilles. Administering states claimed the sole right to decide whether Article 73 (e) did or did not apply to one of their territories, but this position was challenged by the assembly, which in 1952 adopted a resolution containing a list of factors to serve as a guide in deciding whether a territory had obtained a full measure of self-government. In 1947 the committee received information on 74 territories with about 215,-000,000 inhabitants; by 1956 this had declined to 55 territories with 115,000,000 inhabitants. In 1963 the committee was dissolved, and its functions were transferred to a Special Committee on Colonialism that had been created in 1961.

The anticolonial movement in the United Nations reached a high point in 1960 when the General Assembly adopted a resolution sponsored by 43 Afro-Asian states. This resolution, called the Declaration on the Granting of Independence to Colonial Countries and Peoples, condemned "the subjection of peoples to alien subjugation, domination, and exploitation" and declared that "immediate steps shall be taken ... to transfer all powers" to the peoples in the colonies "without any conditions or reservations, in accordance with their freely expressed will and desire . . . in order to enable them to enjoy complete independence and freedom. . . ." The declaration was adopted 89–0 (with 9 abstentions).

Spain, Portugal, South Africa, and Southern Rhodesia were the chief targets of the anticolonial drive. Spain and Portugal had refused to transmit information on their overseas territories on the ground that they were not dependencies but provinces enjoying constitutional equality with the provinces in the homeland. Southern Rhodesia was a peculiar case; the situation in South Africa was somewhat similar, except that South Africa was completely independent. Hostility toward South Africa, Southern Rhodesia, and Portugal on the part of the other African countries became intense. By 1965 the age of colonialism was about over. There remained a number of dependent territories, some of them isolated islands, that seemed too poor or too small to stand alone as political entities. How the principles of the declaration were to be applied to them became a difficult question. In many colonial areas to which self-government had been granted the basic social and economic problems remained unsolved, and all of them looked to the UN for help in gaining the strength needed to make them truly independent countries. The breakup of the colonial empires and the greatly enlarged membership of the UN modified the political structure of that organization and enabled the small states to play an important role in world politics.   (L.M.G./A.Va.)

Trusteeship system. The trusteeship system of the UN, the successor to the mandates system of the League of Nations, was established on the principle that colonial territories wrested from defeated enemies should not be annexed by any victorious nation but should be administered by mandatory or trust power under international supervision until they were able to determine their own future status.

Eleven such territories taken from Germany, Italy, and Japan were brought under the trusteeship system after 1945. Other colonial territories could have been voluntarily brought under the system by Article 77 of the UN Charter, but no such action was taken. With the attainment of independence by Togo, British Cameroons, French Cameroun, Somalia, Tanganyika, Western Samoa, Ruanda-Urundi, and Nauru, only the trust territories in the Pacific area—New Guinea and the Pacific Islands—remained under trusteeship. Failure to utilize the trusteeship system for other colonial areas has been attributed to two principal developments: (1) after 1945 many colonies attained independence without being made subject to the trusteeship system, and (2) the colonial powers were reluctant to bring their colonial territories under the system because of the critical and even hostile attitude shown in the debates of the United Nations toward any form of colonial relationship.

Declaration on the Granting of Independence to Colonial Countries and Peoples (1960)

The UN trusteeship system differed in two important respects from the mandates system of the League of Nations. The first difference was the provision that facilitated the submission of petitions from inhabitants of the trust territory or from any other source. In addition, the Charter provided that a petitioner might appear in person to present his case orally before the Trusteeship Council or the General Assembly. Tens of thousands of written petitions were submitted to the United Nations. Indeed, the flood of petitions was sometimes so great that it was difficult to work out a procedure for handling them efficiently and expeditiously. The second basic innovation that differentiated the trusteeship system from the mandates system was the Charter provision for periodic visits by UN missions to the trust territories. In practice, each territory was visited by such a mission every three years. The purpose of the missions was to supplement information provided in the annual reports of the administering authorities and to provide what were regarded as objective and impartial evaluations of the conditions in each territory. Each visiting mission was composed of two persons drawn from administering countries and two from nonadministering countries, accompanied by five or six members of the UN Secretariat. The two members from administering countries were not drawn from among the nationals of the country administering the territory to be visited.

A Trusteeship Council was established by the Charter under the authority of the UN General Assembly. The council was empowered to consider reports made to it by the administering authorities, accept and examine petitions in consultation with the appropriate administering authority, provide for periodic visiting missions to the respective trust territories, and take such other actions as might be in conformity with the terms of trusteeship agreements between each administering authority and the General Assembly or, in the case of a strategic trust territory, with the Security Council.

The Trusteeship Council was to consist of an equal number of members administering trust territories and members not administering such territories, provided all of the permanent members of the Security Council were also to be members of the Trusteeship Council. To keep the council in balance there were to be as many nonadministering members elected for three-year terms as would be necessary to ensure that the council was equally divided between the administering and nonadministering members.

All of the former mandatory powers entered into UN trusteeship agreements after 1945 except South Africa, which refused to enter into such an agreement for the mandated territory of South West Africa. The United States became a member of the Trusteeship Council both by virtue of the fact that it was a permanent member of the Security Council and because it negotiated an agreement with the UN regarding the Pacific Islands, which it had taken from Japan in World War II. In 1950 Italy became a member of the Trusteeship Council by assuming responsibility for the administration of Somalia for a period of ten years and accordingly ceased to be a member of the council in 1960 when Somalia became an independent member of the United Nations. In 1960 France ceased to be an administering power when the trust territory of French Cameroun became independent, but France retained its membership on the Trusteeship Council as a nonadministering member because it was a permanent member of the Security Council.

The UN Charter (Article 82) provided that certain areas, which might include part or all of a trust territory, could be designated as strategic areas. This provision was placed in the Charter in 1945 on the initiative of the United States, and in 1947 a strategic trusteeship agreement was concluded between the United States and the United Nations that placed the Pacific Islands (the Marshalls, Marianas, and Carolines) under the trusteeship system. All of the other trust agreements were made between the administering authority and the General Assembly but that for the Pacific Islands was made with the Security Council. In practice, however, there was no appreciable difference in the way the two types of territories were handled within the system. In the agreement with the Security Council the United States provided that it might close off any area for security reasons. This provision was never put into effect, and the United States freely permitted UN visiting missions to go through the territory and agreed that the Trusteeship Council should examine the annual reports on political, economic, and social conditions in the territory.   (O.B.G.)

ADMINISTRATION

Finances. The secretary general must submit an annual budget including estimated expenditures to the General Assembly for approval. The Charter stipulates that the expenses of the organization shall be borne by members as apportioned by the General Assembly. The Committee on Contributions prepares a scale of assessments for each member, based on the general economic level and capacity of each state, and this scale is submitted to the General Assembly for approval. The United States is the largest contributor, but a few members make a larger per capita contribution. The U.S. assessment began at 49 percent of the total but, at the request of the United States government, this figure was steadily reduced until in 1963 it was 32 percent.

The normal operating expenses of the United Nations increased from $19,000,000 in 1946 to over $200,000,000 for 1972. When the cost of the special programs, specialized agencies, and peace-keeping operations was added to the regular budget, the total annual cost of the United Nations system became much greater. The special programs are financed by voluntary contributions of the members of the United Nations, and the specialized agencies have their own budgets. The rapid increase in membership after 1955 did not help UN finances, for most of the new members were economically weak. Nearly all of them needed help, and their financial contributions to the UN were minimal.

Personnel. The Secretariat of the United Nations, serving under the secretary general, influences the day-to-day work of the organization to a degree that is not indicated by the words of the Charter. This influence is largely a result of the fact that the members of the Secretariat are permanent expert officials. The staff is recruited on a merit basis, with regard to equitable geographical distribution. Members of the organization are required to take an oath of loyalty to the United Nations and are not permitted to receive instructions from member governments.

A United Nations Field Service and a United Nations Panel of Field Observers were organized by the assembly in 1949. The Field Service looks after the safety of UN missions in many parts of the world, and the Panel of Field Observers assists the various missions in supervising truces and observing plebiscites. Both are under the supervision of the secretary general.

Privileges and immunities. A General Convention on Privileges and Immunities of the United Nations, approved by the General Assembly in February 1946 and accepted by most of the members except the United States, asserted that the UN possesses juridical personality. The convention also provided for such matters as immunity from legal process of the property and officials of the United Nations. An agreement between the UN and the U.S., signed in June 1947, defined the privileges and immunities of the UN headquarters in New York.

Headquarters. The General Assembly decided during the second part of its first session in New York to locate its permanent headquarters in that city. John D. Rockefeller, Jr., gave land for a building site in Manhattan. Temporary headquarters was established at Lake Success on Long Island, New York. The permanent Secretariat building was completed and occupied in 1951. The building providing accommodations for the General Assembly and the councils was completed and occupied in early 1952.

The design of the UN flag, adopted in 1947, consists of the official emblem of the UN in white centred on a light-blue background. The Assembly designated October 24 as United Nations Day.   (L.M.G./A.Va.)

Differences between the mandate and trusteeship systems

Strategic areas

BIBLIOGRAPHY. ROBERT E. ASHER *et al., The United Nations and Promotion of General Welfare* (1957), a scholarly, comprehensive analysis of the operation and development of the United Nations during its first decade; INIS L. CLAUDE, *The Changing United Nations* (1967), a collection of essays on fundamental changes in the UN from its founding to the publication date, with an annotated bibliography; E.A. GROSS, *The United Nations: Structure for Peace* (1962), an account of the organizational structure and the means of operation in maintaining peace; H.G. NICHOLAS, *The United Nations As a Political Institution,* 2nd ed. (1962), a perceptive analysis, with an extensive suggested reading list; MAURICE WATERS (ed.), *The United Nations: Institutional Organization and Administration* (1967), an authoritative collection of articles on all aspects of the UN.

Current information may be found in the *United Nations Yearbook* (published annually since 1946–47); the *United Nations Bulletin* (monthly); and the *Annual Report of the Secretary-General on the Work of the Organization.*

United States of America

The foremost nation in the Western Hemisphere in population and economic development, the United States of America is in form a federal republic comprising 50 states. It is often referred to simply as the United States and, colloquially, as America. The 48 conterminous states occupy the central one-third of the North American continent, bounded on the west by the Pacific Ocean, on the north by Canada, on the east by the Atlantic Ocean, on the south by Mexico and arms of the Atlantic and Pacific. The newest states, Alaska and Hawaii, lie at the northwestern extremity of the continent and in the mid-Pacific, respectively.

The total area of the nation is 3,615,122 square miles (9,363,123 square kilometres), making it the fourth largest nation in the world in area (after the Soviet Union, Canada, and China), while its de facto 1972 population of some 208,837,000 made it the fourth most populous (after China, India, and the Soviet Union). Such outlying possessions as the Virgin Islands and the U.S. trust territories in the Pacific, and such politically related entities as the Commonwealth of Puerto Rico added 12,940 square miles (33,514 square kilometres) and 3,026,690 persons (1970) to these figures.

The major characteristic of the United States is probably its great variety. Its physical environment ranges from the Arctic to the subtropical, from the moist rain forest to the arid desert, from the bald mountain peak to the flat prairie stretching beyond all horizons. Its people probably comprise a wider range of racial, ethnic, and cultural types than any other nation. Quite apart from the presence of surviving American Indians and the descendants of slaves brought from Africa, the nation shows the effects of having taken in some 35,000,000 immigrants from around the world between the declaration of national identity in 1776 and the imposition of immigration quotas in 1921. Its natural resources, though becoming depleted or seriously polluted in some areas, continued to sustain an economic life that is more diversified than any other on Earth, providing the majority of its people with an unrivalled standard of living and richness of material choice. And, although it seemed still to offer its people opportunities for unparalleled personal advancement and wealth in the second half of the 20th century, it contained areas of poverty and blight in both urban and rural areas that were becoming an increasing threat to the social and political fabric of the nation.

The article is divided into the following main sections:

For more detailed information, see the articles on each of the 50 states, in addition to PUERTO RICO; UNITED STATES OUTLYING TERRITORIES; and VIRGIN ISLANDS. The nation's history is covered in UNITED STATES, HISTORY OF THE, while NORTH AMERICA places the United States in the larger geological, climatic, historical, demographic, economic, and cultural contexts of the continent. Contributions to the arts are covered in such articles as LITERATURE, WESTERN; THEATRE, WESTERN; and VISUAL ARTS, WESTERN, as well as in AMERICAN INDIAN PEOPLES, ARTS OF. (Ed.)

I. The natural landscape

The two great sets of elements that mold the physical environment of the United States are, first, the geological, which determines the main patterns of landforms, drainage, and mineral resources and influences soils to a lesser degree; and, second, the atmospheric, which dictates not only climate and weather but also in large part the geographic distribution of soils, plants, and animals. Although climatic and geologic processes are not wholly independent of one another, each produces on a map patterns that are so profoundly different that essentially they comprise two separate geographies. Since this portion of the article covers only the conterminous United States, see also ALASKA; HAWAII; and PUERTO RICO.

LANDFORMS AND MINERALS

The centre of the conterminous United States is a great sprawling interior lowland, reaching from the ancient shield of central Canada on the north to the Gulf of Mexico on the south. To east and west, this lowland rises first gradually, then abruptly, to mountain ranges that divide it from the sea on both sides. The two mountain systems differ drastically. The Appalachians on the east are low, almost unbroken, and in the main set well back from the Atlantic. From New York City to the Mexican border stretches a low Coastal Plain, whose swampy and convoluted shoreline merges almost imperceptibly with the ocean. Southward, the plain grows wider, swinging westward in Georgia and Alabama to truncate the Appalachians along their southern extremity and separate the interior lowland from the Gulf.

West of the Central Lowlands is the mighty Cordillera, part of the global mountain system that entirely rings the Pacific Basin. The Cordillera encompasses fully one-third of the United States, with an internal variety commensurate with its size. At its eastern margin lie the Rocky Mountains, a high, diverse, and discontinuous chain that stretches from New Mexico to the Canadian border. The Cordillera's western edge is a Pacific coastal chain of rugged mountains and inland valleys, the whole rising spectacularly from the sea without benefit of a coastal plain.

Finally, pent between the Rockies and the Pacific chain is a vast intermontane complex of basins, plateaus, and isolated ranges, so large and remarkable that they merit recognition as a region separate from the Cordillera itself. These regions—the Interior Lowlands and their upland fringes, the Appalachian Mountain system, the Atlantic Plain, the Western Cordillera, and the Western Intermontane Region—contain so much variety that they require further division into 24 major subregions (see accompanying map).

The Interior Lowlands and their upland fringes. Andrew Jackson is supposed to have remarked that the United States begins at the Alleghenies, implying that only west of the mountains, in the isolation and freedom

Location and general character of the nation

The grand geological pattern

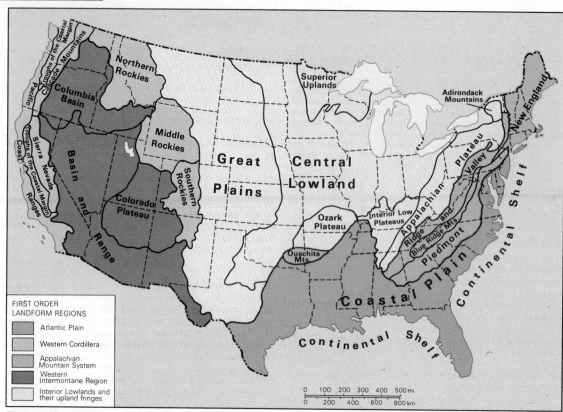

FIRST ORDER
LANDFORM REGIONS

- Atlantic Plain
- Western Cordillera
- Appalachian Mountain System
- Western Intermontane Region
- Interior Lowlands and their upland fringes

Physiographic regions of the United States.

The midcontinent of the nation

of the great Interior Lowlands, could people finally escape Old World influences and become truly American. Whether or not the lowlands constitute the cultural core of the nation is debatable; there can be no doubt, however, that they comprise the geological core and in many ways the geographical core as well.

This enormous region rests upon an ancient, much-eroded platform of complex crystalline rocks that have lain undisturbed by major orogenic (mountain-building) activity for over 600,000,000 years. Over much of central Canada, these old rocks are exposed at the surface and form the continent's single largest topographic region, the formidable and ice-scoured Canadian Shield.

In the United States, most of the crystalline platform is concealed under a deep blanket of sedimentary rocks. In the far north, however, the naked shield extends into the United States far enough to form two small but distinctive landform regions: the rugged and occasionally spectacular Adirondack Mountains of northern New York; and the more subdued but austere Superior Uplands, of northern Minnesota, Wisconsin, and Michigan. As in the rest of the shield, glaciers have stripped soils away, strewn the surface with boulders and other debris, and obliterated preglacial drainage systems. Most attempts at farming in this region have been abandoned, but the combination of a comparative wilderness in a northern climate, clear lakes, and white-water streams have turned both areas into seasonal vacationlands.

Mineral wealth in the Superior Uplands is legendary. Iron lies near the surface and close to the deepwater ports of the lower Great Lakes. Iron is mined both north and south of Lake Superior, but most famous are the colossal deposits of Minnesota's Mesabi Range, known for more than a century as one of the world's richest and a vital element in America's rise to industrial power. In spite of recent depletion, the Minnesota and Michigan mines still yield 80 percent in value of the nation's iron and about 10 percent of the world's supply.

South of the Adirondacks and Superior Upland lies the boundary between crystalline and sedimentary rocks; abruptly, everything is different. The core of this sedimentary region—quite literally the heartland of the United States—is the great Central Lowland, which stretches for 1,500 miles from New York state to central Texas

and north another 1,000 miles to the Canadian province of Saskatchewan. To some, the landscape may seem dull, for heights over 2,000 feet are unusual, and truly rough terrain is almost unknown. Landscapes are varied, however, largely as the result of glaciation that directly or indirectly affected most of the region. North of the Missouri–Ohio river line, the advance and readvance of continental ice left an intricate mosaic of boulders, sand, gravel, silt, and clay and a complex pattern of lakes and drainage channels, some abandoned, some still in use. The southern part of the Central Lowlands is quite different, covered mostly with wind-borne loess that subdued the already low relief to nearly billiard-table flatness. Elsewhere, especially near major rivers, postglacial streams carved the loess into rounded hills, and visitors have aptly compared their billowing shapes to the waves of the sea. Above all, the loess produces soil of extraordinary fertility. As the Mesabi iron is the foundation of the United States' industrial wealth, the nation's agricultural prosperity is rooted in Middle Western loess.

The Central Lowlands resemble a vast saucer, rising gradually to higher lands on all sides. Southward and eastward, the land climbs gradually to three major plateaus. Beyond the reach of glaciation to the south, the sedimentary rocks have been raised into two broad upwarps, separated from one another by the great valley of the Mississippi River. The Ozark Plateau lies west of the river and occupies most of southern Missouri and northern Arkansas; on the east, the Interior Low Plateaus dominate central Kentucky and Tennessee. Except for two nearly circular patches of rich limestone country—the Nashville Basin of Tennessee and the fabled racehorse country of the Kentucky Bluegrass—most of both plateau regions is sandstone uplands, intricately dissected by streams. Local relief runs to several hundreds of feet in most places, and visitors to the region must travel winding roads along narrow stream valleys. Not many take the trouble, however, for soils are poor and mineral resources scanty.

Eastward from the Central Lowlands, the Appalachian Plateau—a narrow band of dissected uplands that strongly resembles the Ozark Plateau and Interior Low Plateaus in steep slopes, wretched soils, and endemic poverty—forms a transition between the interior plains

The plateaus surrounding the midcontinent

and the Appalachian Mountains. Usually, however, the Appalachian Plateau is considered a subregion of the Appalachian Mountains, partly on grounds of location, partly because of geologic structure. Unlike the other plateaus, where rocks are warped upward, the rocks here form a long narrow basin, wherein bituminous coal has been preserved from erosion. This Appalachian coal, like the Mesabi iron that it complements in American industry, is extraordinary. Extensive, thick, and close to the surface, it has stoked the furnaces of northeastern steel mills for decades and helps explain the huge concentration of heavy industry along the lower Great Lakes.

The
Great
Plains

The western flanks of the Interior Lowlands are the Great Plains, a region of awesome bulk that spans the full distance between Canada and Mexico in a swath nearly 500 miles wide. The Great Plains were built by successive layers of poorly cemented sand, silt, and gravel—debris laid down by parallel east-flowing streams from the Rocky Mountains. Seen from the east, the surface rises inexorably from about 2,000 feet near Omaha, Nebraska, to over 6,000 feet at Cheyenne, Wyoming, but the climb is so gradual that popular legend holds the Great Plains to be flat. True flatness is rare, although the High Plains of west Texas, Oklahoma, Kansas, and eastern Colorado come very close. More commonly, the land is broadly rolling, and parts of the northern plains are sharply dissected into "badlands."

The main mineral wealth of the Interior Lowlands derives from fossil fuels, scarcely surprising in a region underlain by sedimentary rocks. Coal occurs in structural basins protected from erosion—high-quality bituminous in the Appalachian, Illinois, and west Kentucky basins; and poorer bituminous and lignite in the eastern and northwestern Great Plains. Petroleum and natural gas have been found in nearly every state between the Appalachians and the Rockies, but the Midcontinent Fields of west Texas, the Texas Panhandle, Oklahoma, and Kansas surpass all others in the Interior Lowlands. Aside from small deposits of lead and zinc, metallic minerals are of little importance.

The Appalachian Mountain system. The Appalachians dominate the eastern United States and separate the Eastern Seaboard from the interior with a belt of subdued uplands that extends 1,500 miles from northeastern Alabama to the Canadian border. They are old and very complex mountains, the eroded stumps of much greater ranges. Present topography results from prolonged erosion that has differentially carved weak rocks away, leaving a skeleton of resistant rocks behind as highlands. Geologic differences are thus faithfully reflected in topography. In the Appalachians, these differences are sharply demarcated and elegantly arranged, so that all the major subdivisions except New England lie in strips parallel to the Atlantic and to one another.

The core of the Appalachians, both geologically and geographically, is a belt of complex metamorphic and igneous rocks that stretches from Alabama to New Hampshire. The west side of this belt forms the long slender rampart of the Blue Ridge Mountains, containing the highest elevations in the Appalachians (Mt. Mitchell, North Carolina, 6,684 feet [2,037 metres]) and some of its most handsome mountain scenery. On its seaward side, the Blue Ridge descends in an abrupt and sometimes spectacular escarpment to the Piedmont, a well-drained, rolling land—never quite hills, never quite a plain. Before the settlement of the Middle West, the Piedmont was the most productive agricultural region in the United States, and several Pennsylvania counties still consistently report some of the highest farm yields per acre in the nation.

West of the crystalline zone, away from the axis of geologic deformation, sedimentary rocks have escaped metamorphism but are compressed into tight folds, like a rug that has slid and crumpled on a slippery floor. Erosion has carved the upturned edges of these folded rocks into the remarkable Ridge and Valley country of the western Appalachians. Seen from the air, this region looks as if some cosmic rake had been dragged 1,000 miles the length of the Appalachian system. Long

linear ridges characteristically stand about 1,000 feet from base to crest and run for tens of miles, paralleled by broad open valleys of comparable length. In Pennsylvania, ridges run unbroken for great distances, occasionally turning abruptly in a zigzag pattern; by contrast, the southern ridges are broken by faults and form short parallel segments that are lined up like magnetized iron filings. By far the largest valley—and one of the most important routes in North America—is the Great Valley, an extraordinary trench of shale and limestone that runs nearly the entire length of the Appalachians. It provides a lowland passage from the middle Hudson Valley to Harrisburg, Pennsylvania and on southward where it forms the Cumberland and Shenandoah valleys, one of the main paths through the Appalachians since pioneer times. In New England it is floored with slates and marbles and forms the Valley of Vermont, one of the few fertile areas in an otherwise mountainous region.

Topography very much like that of the Ridge and Valley occurs in the Ouachita Mountains of western Arkansas and eastern Oklahoma, an area generally thought to be a detached continuation of Appalachian geologic structure, the intervening section buried beneath the sediments of the lower Mississippi Valley.

The
New
England
mountain
systems

The glaciated New England section of the Appalachians is divided from the rest of the chain by an indentation of the Atlantic. Although almost completely underlain by crystalline rocks, New England is laid out in north–south bands, reminiscent of the southern Appalachians. The rolling, rocky hills of southeastern New England are not dissimilar to the Piedmont, while, farther northwest, the rugged and lofty White Mountains are an obvious New England analogue to the Blue Ridge. (Mt. Washington, New Hampshire, at 6,288 feet [1,917 metres] is the highest peak in the northeastern United States.) And the westernmost ranges—the Taconics, Berkshires, and Green Mountains—exhibit a strong north–south lineation like the Ridge and Valley. Unlike the rest of the Appalachians, however, glaciation has scoured the crystalline rocks much like those of the Canadian Shield, so that New England is best known for its picturesque landscape, not its fertile soil.

Typical of diverse geologic regions, the Appalachians contain a great variety of minerals. Only a few occur in quantities large enough for sustained exploitation, notably iron in Pennsylvania's Blue Ridge and Piedmont and the famous granites, marbles, and slates of northern New England. In Pennsylvania, the Ridge and Valley region contains one of the world's largest deposits of anthracite coal, once the basis of a thriving mining economy; now most of the mines are shut, oil and gas having replaced anthracite as the major fuel for heating U.S. homes.

The Atlantic Plain. The eastern and southeastern fringes of the United States are part of the outermost margins of the continental platform, repeatedly invaded by the sea and veneered with layer after layer of young, poorly consolidated sediments. Part of this platform now lies slightly above sea level and forms a nearly flat and often swampy Coastal Plain, which stretches from Cape Cod to and beyond the Mexican border. Most of the platform, however, is still submerged, so that a band of shallow water, the Continental Shelf, parallels the whole Atlantic and Gulf coasts of the United States, in some places reaching 250 miles out to sea.

Coastal
uplifts and
depressions

The Atlantic Plain slopes so gently that even slight crustal upwarping can shift the coastline far out to sea at the expense of the Continental Shelf. The peninsula of Florida is just such an upwarp; nowhere in its 400-mile length does the land rise more than 350 feet above sea level; much of the southern and coastal areas rise less than ten feet and are poorly drained and dangerously exposed to Atlantic storms. Correspondingly, downwarps can result in extensive flooding. North of New York City, for example, the weight of glacial ice depressed most of the Coastal Plain beneath the sea, and the Atlantic now beats directly against New England's rock-ribbed coasts. Cape Cod, Long Island, and a few offshore islands are all that remain of New England's drowned Coastal Plain.

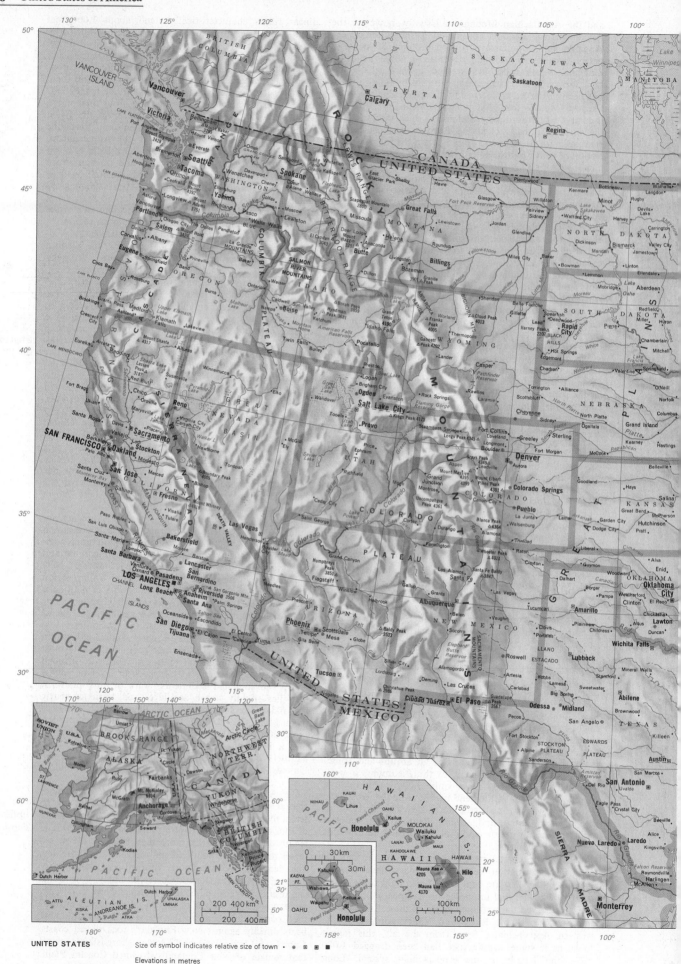

PACIFIC OCEAN

UNITED STATES

Size of symbol indicates relative size of town • ⊙ ⊡ ▣ ■

Elevations in metres

MAP INDEX

MAP INDEX (continued)

Price.........39·36n 110·48w
Prineville....44·18n 120·51w
Providence....41·50n 71·25w
Provo.........40·14n 111·39w
Pueblo........38·16n 104·37w
Pullman.......46·44n 117·10w
Quincy........39·56n 91·23w
Racine........42·43n 87·48w
Raleigh.......35·47n 78·39w
Rantoul.......40·19n 88·09w
Rapid City....44·05n 103·14w
Raton.........36·54n 104·24w
Rawlins.......41·47n 107·14w
Raymondville..26·29n 97·47w
Reading.......40·20n 75·56w
Red Bluff.....40·11n 122·15w
Redding.......40·35n 122·24w
Redfield......44·53n 98·31w
Red Wing......44·34n 92·31w
Reidsville....36·21n 79·40w
Reno..........39·31n 119·48w
Rhinelander...45·38n 89·25w
Richfield.....38·46n 112·05w
Richland......46·17n 119·18w
Richmond, Ind..39·50n 84·54w
Richmond, Ky..37·45n 84·18w
Richmond, Va..37·30n 77·28w
Riverside.....33·59n 117·22w
Roanoke.......37·16n 79·57w
Rochester,
  Minn........44·02n 92·29w
Rochester, N.Y..43·10n 77·36w
Rockford......42·17n 89·06w
Rock Hill.....34·56n 81·01w
Rock Island...41·30n 90·34w
Rockland......44·06n 69·06w
Rock Springs..41·35n 109·13w
Rocky Mount...35·56n 77·48w
Rolla.........37·57n 91·46w
Rome, Ga......34·16n 85·11w
Rome, N.Y.....43·13n 75·27w
Roseburg......43·13n 123·20w
Roswell.......33·24n 104·32w
Roundup.......46·27n 108·33w
Ruby..........64·44n 155·30w
Rugby.........48·22n 99·60w
Russellville..35·17n 93·08w
Ruston........32·32n 92·38w
Rutland.......43·36n 72·59w
Sacramento....28·35n 121·30w
Saginaw.......43·25n 83·58w
Saint
  Augustine...29·54n 81·19w
Saint Charles...38·47n 90·29w
Saint Cloud...45·33n 94·10w
Saint George...37·06n 113·35w
Saint Joseph...39·46n 94·51w
Saint Louis...38·38n 90·11w
Saint Paul....44·58n 93·07w
Saint
  Petersburg....27·46n 82·38w
Salem.........44·57n 123·01w
Salina........38·50n 93·73w
Salinas.......36·40n 121·38w
Salisbury, Md..38·22n 75·36w
Salisbury, N.C..35·40n 80·29w
Salt Lake City..40·46n 111·53w
San Angelo....31·28n 100·26w
San Antonio...29·28n 98·31w
San Bernardino.34·06n 117·17w
Sanderson.....30·09n 102·24w
San Diego.....32·43n 117·09w
Sandpoint.....48·16n 116·33w
Sandusky......41·27n 82·42w
Sanford.......28·48n 81·16w
San Francisco..37·48n 122·24w
San Jose......37·20n 121·53w
San Luis
  Obispo......35·17n 120·40w
San Marcos....29·53n 97·57w
Santa Ana.....33·43n 117·54w
Santa Barbara..34·25n 119·42w
Santa Cruz....37·21n 121·57w
Santa Fe......35·36n 106·20w
Santa Maria...34·57n 120·26w
Santa Rosa....38·26n 122·43w
Sapulpa.......35·60n 96·06w
Sarasota......27·20n 82·34w
Sault Sainte
  Marie.......46·30n 84·21w
Savannah......32·04n 81·05w
Schenectady...42·47n 73·53w
Scottsbluff...41·52n 103·40w
Scottsdale....33·30n 111·56w
Scranton......41·24n 75·40w
Searcy........35·15n 91·44w
Seattle.......47·36n 122·20w
Sedalia.......38·42n 93·14w
Selma.........32·25n 87·01w
Seward, Alaska.60·06n 149·26w
Seward, Nebr..40·55n 97·06w
Shawnee.......35·20n 96·55w
Sheboygan.....43·46n 87·44w
Sheffield.....34·46n 87·40w
Shelby........48·30n 111·51w
Shenandoah....40·46n 95·22w
Sheridan......44·48n 106·58w

Sherman.......33·38n 96·36w
Shreveport....32·30n 93·45w
Sidney, Mont..47·43n 104·09w
Sidney, Nebr..41·09n 102·59w
Sikeston......36·53n 89·35w
Silver City...32·46n 108·17w
Sioux City....42·30n 96·23w
Sioux Falls...43·32n 96·44w
Sitka.........39·03n 135·14w
Skagway.......59·28n 135·19w
Socorro.......34·04n 106·54w
Somerset......37·05n 84·36w
South Bend....41·41n 86·15w
Spartanburg...34·57n 81·55w
Spearfish.....44·30n 103·52w
Spencer.......43·09n 95·09w
Spokane.......47·40n 117·23w
Springfield, Ill..39·47n 89·40w
Springfield,
  Mass.......42·07n 72·36w
Springfield, Mo.37·14n 93·17w
Springfield,
  Ohio........39·56n 83·49w
Springfield,
  Oreg.......44·03n 123·01w
Springfield,
  S. Dak.....42·49n 97·54w
Stamford......32·57n 99·48w
Staunton......38·09n 79·04w
Steamboat
  Springs....40·29n 106·50w
Sterling, Colo..40·37n 103·13w
Sterling, Ill..41·48n 89·42w
Steubenville..40·22n 80·37w
Stevens Point..44·31n 89·34w
Stillwater, Minn.45·04n 92·49w
Stillwater, Okla..36·07n 97·04w
Stockton......37·57n 121·17w
Storm Lake....42·39n 95·13w
Stuttgart.....34·30n 91·33w
Suffolk.......36·44n 76·35w
Sumter........33·55n 80·20w
Sun Valley....43·42n 114·21w
Superior......46·44n 92·05w
Susanville....40·25n 120·39w
Sweetwater....32·28n 100·25w
Syracuse......43·03n 76·09w
Tacoma........47·15n 122·27w
Tahlequah.....35·55n 94·58w
Talladega.....33·26n 86·06w
Tallahassee...30·25n 84·16w
Tampa.........27·57n 82·27w
Tempe.........33·25n 111·56w
Temple........31·06n 97·21w
Terre Haute...39·28n 87·24w
Texarkana, Ark..33·26n 94·02w
Texarkana, Tex..33·26n 94·03w
Texas City....29·23n 94·54w
The Dalles....45·36n 121·10w
Thermopolis...43·39n 108·13w
Thief River
  Falls.......48·07n 96·10w
Thomasville...30·50n 83·59w
Tiffin........41·07n 83·11w
Tifton........31·27n 83·31w
Titusville....38·37n 80·49w
Toledo........41·39n 83·32w
Tonopah.......38·04n 117·14w
Tooele........40·32n 112·18w
Topeka........39·03n 95·41w
Torrington....42·04n 104·11w
Traverse City..44·46n 85·37w
Trenton.......40·13n 74·45w
Trinidad......37·10n 104·31w
Troy, Ala.....31·48n 85·58w
Troy, N.Y.....42·43n 73·40w
Tucson........32·13n 110·58w
Tucumcari.....35·10n 103·44w
Tulare........36·13n 119·21w
Tullahoma.....35·22n 86·11w
Tulsa.........36·09n 95·58w
Tupelo........34·16n 88·43w
Tuscaloosa....33·13n 87·33w
Twin Falls....42·34n 114·28w
Two Harbors...47·01n 91·40w
Tyler.........32·21n 95·18w
Ukiah.........39·09n 123·13w
Umiat.........69·22n 152·08w
Union.........34·43n 81·37w
Union City....36·26n 89·03w
Uniontown.....39·54n 79·44w
Utica.........43·05n 75·14w
Uvalde........29·13n 99·47w
Valdosta......30·50n 83·17w
Valentine.....42·52n 100·33w
Vallejo.......38·07n 122·14w
Valley City...46·55n 97·59w
Van Buren.....35·26n 94·21w
Vancouver.....45·39n 122·40w
Vaughn........34·36n 105·13w
Ventura.......34·17n 119·18w
Vermillion....42·47n 96·56w
Vero Beach....27·38n 80·24w
Vicksburg.....32·14n 90·56w
Victoria......28·48n 97·00w
Vincennes.....38·41n 87·32w
Virginia......47·31n 92·32w
Virginia Beach.36·51n 75·58w
Virginia City..39·19n 119·39w

Visalia.......36·20n 119·18w
Waco..........31·55n 97·08w
Wahiawa.......21·30n 158·01w
Wahpeton......46·16n 96·36w
Wailuku.......20·53n 156·30w
Waipahu.......21·23n 158·01w
Walhalla......48·55n 97·55w
Wallace.......47·28n 115·56w
Walla Walla...46·08n 118·20w
Walsenburg....37·37n 104·47w
Warren........42·28n 83·01w
Warrensburg...38·46n 93·44w
Washington,
  D.C.........38·54n 77·01w
Waterloo......42·30n 92·20w
Watertown, N.Y.43·59n 75·55w
Watertown,
  S. Dak......44·54n 97·07w
Waterville....44·33n 69·38w
Watford City..47·48n 103·17w
Waukegan......42·22n 87·50w
Wausau........44·60n 89·39w
Waycross......31·13n 82·21w
Wayne.........42·14n 97·01w
Weatherford...35·32n 98·42w
Weiser........44·15n 116·58w
Wenatchee.....47·25n 120·19w
Wendover......40·44n 114·02w
West Palm
  Beach.......26·43n 80·04w
West Point....33·36n 88·39w
Wheeling......40·05n 80·42w
Whitefish.....48·25n 114·20w
Wichita.......37·41n 97·20w
Wichita Falls..33·54n 98·30w
Wilkes-Barre..41·14n 75·53w
Williamson....37·41n 82·17w
Williamsport..41·14n 77·00w
Williston.....48·09n 103·37w
Wilmington,
  Del.........39·44n 75·33w
Wilmington,
  N.C.........34·13n 77·55w
Wilson........35·44n 77·55w
Winchester, Ky.37·60n 84·11w
Winchester, Va..39·11n 78·10w
Winfield......37·15n 96·59w
Winnemucca....40·58n 117·44w
Winona........44·03n 91·39w
Winslow.......35·01n 110·42w
Winston-Salem.36·06n 80·15w
Winter Haven..28·01n 81·44w
Wisconsin
  Rapids......44·23n 89·49w
Woodward......36·26n 99·24w
Worcester.....42·16n 71·48w
Worland.......44·01n 107·57w
Worthington...43·37n 95·36w
Wrangell......56·28n 132·23w
Yakima........46·36n 120·31w
Yankton.......42·53n 97·23w
York..........39·58n 76·44w
Youngstown....41·06n 80·39w
Yuma..........32·43n 114·37w
Zanesville....39·56n 82·01w

**Physical features
and points of interest**

Absaroka
  Range,
  *mountain
  range*........44·45n 109·50w
Adams, Mount,
  mountain...46·12n 121·28w
Adirondack
  Mountains....44·00n 74·00w
Alabama, *river*.31·08n 87·57w
Albemarle
  Sound........36·03n 76·12w
Aleutian
  Islands......52·00n 176·00w
Altamaha, *river*.31·19n 81·17w
American Falls
  Reservoir....43·00n 113·00w
Amistad
  Reservoir....29·34n 101·15w
Andreanof
  Islands......52·00n 176·00w
Apalachee Bay.30·00n 84·13w
Apalachicola,
  river......29·44n 84·59w
Apostle Islands.46·50n 90·30w
Appalachian
  Mountains....41·00n 77·00w
Arctic Ocean..71·00n 140·00w
Arkansas, *river*.33·48n 91·04w
Aroostook, *river*.46·48n 67·45w
Atka, *island*..52·15n 174·30w
Atlantic Ocean.32·00n 74·00w
Attu, *island*..52·55n 173·00e
Bear Lake.....42·00n 111·20w
Baker, Mount,
  mountain...48·47n 121·49w
Baldy Peak....33·55n 109·35w
Basswood Lake.48·05n 91·40w
Bering Strait..65·30n 169·00w
Bighorn, *river*.46·09n 107·28w
Bighorn
  Mountains....44·00n 107·30w

Bitterroot
  Range........47·06n 115·10w
Black Hills,
  mountains..44·00n 104·00w
Blanca Peak...37·35n 105·29w
Blanco, Cape..42·50n 124·34w
Blue
  Mountains....44·35n 118·25w
Blue Ridge,
  mountains..37·00n 82·00w
Borah Peak....44·08n 113·48w
Boston
  Mountains....35·50n 93·20w
Boundary Peak.37·51n 118·21w
Brazos, *river*..28·53n 95·23w
Brooks Range..68·00n 154·00w
Bull Shoals
  Lake.........36·30n 92·50w
Canadian, *river*.35·27n 95·03w
Cascade Range,
  *mountain
  range*........45·00n 121·30w
Champlain,
  Lake.........44·45n 73·15w
Channel
  Islands......34·00n 120·00w
Chattahoochee,
  river......30·52n 84·57w
Chesapeake
  Bay..........38·40n 76·25w
Cheyenne, *river*.44·40n 101·15w
Chippewa, *river*.44·25n 92·10w
Chiricahua
  Peak.........31·52n 109·20w
Cimarron, *river*.36·10n 96·17w
Clark Hill
  Reservoir....33·50n 82·20w
Clingmans
  Dome,
  mountain...35·35n 83·30w
Cloud Peak....44·25n 107·10w
Coast Ranges,
  *mountain
  range*........41·00n 123·30w
Cod, Cape.....41·42n 70·15w
Colorado, *river*.32·30n 114·45w
Colorado
  Plateau......36·30n 108·00w
Columbia, *river*.46·15n 124·05w
Columbia
  Plateau......44·00n 117·30w
Connecticut,
  river......41·17n 72·21w
Cumberland,
  river......37·09n 88·25w
Death Valley..36·30n 117·00w
Delaware Bay..39·05n 75·15w
Deschutes,
  river......45·38n 120·54w
Des Moines,
  river......40·22n 91·26w
Disappointment,
  Cape.........46·18n 124·03w
Edwards
  Plateau......31·20n 101·00w
Eel, *river*....40·40n 124·20w
Elbert, Mount,
  mountain...39·07n 106·27w
El Capitan,
  mountain...46·01n 114·23w
Elephant Butte
  Reservoir....33·19n 107·10w
Erie, Lake....42·15n 81·00w
Everglades,
  swamp......26·00n 81·00w
Falcon
  Reservoir....26·37n 99·11w
Fear, Cape....33·50n 77·58w
Flaming Gorge
  Reservoir....41·15n 109·30w
Flathead Lake.47·52n 114·08w
Flattery, Cape.48·23n 124·43w
Flint, *river*...30·52n 84·38w
Florida,
  straits of....24·00n 81·00w
Florida Keys,
  islands.........24·45n 81·00w
Fort Peck
  Reservoir....47·45n 106·50w
Francis Case,
  Lake.........43·15n 99·00w
Franks Peak...43·58n 109·20w
Gannett Peak..43·10n 109·40w
Gila, *river*......32·43n 114·33w
Goose Lake,
  salt lake......41·57n 120·25w
Grand Coulee
  Dam..........47·57n 118·59w
Grande, Rio,
  river.........25·57n 97·09w
Grand Teton,
  mountain......43·44n 110·48w
Granite Peak..45·10n 109·48w
Grays Peak....39·37n 105·45w
Great Basin...40·00n 117·00w
Great Plains..42·00n 100·00w
Great Salt Lake.41·10n 112·30w
Green, *river*....38·11n 109·53w
Green Bay.....45·00n 87·30w

Another downwarp lies perpendicular to the Gulf coast and guides the course of the Lower Mississippi. The river, however, has filled with alluvium what otherwise would be an arm of the Gulf, forming a great inland salient of the Coastal Plain called the Mississippi Embayment.

South of New York, the Coastal Plain gradually widens, but ocean water has invaded the lower valleys of most coastal rivers and turned them into estuaries. The greatest is Chesapeake Bay, merely the flooded lower valley of the Susquehanna and its tributaries, but there are literally hundreds of others. Offshore a line of sandbars and barrier beaches stretches intermittently the length of the Coastal Plain, hampering entry of shipping into the estuaries but providing the crowded eastern United States with a marine playground over 1,000 miles long.

Poor soils are the rule on the Coastal Plain, though rare exceptions have formed some of America's most famous agricultural regions—for example, the citrus country of central Florida's limestone uplands and the Cotton Belt of the Old South, once centred on the alluvial plain of the Mississippi and belts of chalky black soils of east Texas, Alabama, and Mississippi. The Atlantic Plain's greatest natural wealth derives from petroleum and natural gas trapped in domal structures that dot the Gulf coast of east Texas and Louisiana. Onshore and offshore drilling have revealed colossal reserves, and Louisiana alone produces one-fourth of the nation's crude oil and one-fifth of the natural gas in the world.

The Western Cordillera. West of the Great Plains, the United States seems to become another world, a craggy land whose skyline is rarely without mountains—totally different from the open plains and rounded hills of the East. On a map, the alignment of the two main chains—the Rockies on the east, the Pacific ranges on the west—tempts one to assume a certain geological and hence topographic homogeneity. Nothing could be further from the truth, for each chain is divided into widely disparate sections.

The Rockies are typically diverse. The Southern Rockies comprise a disconnected series of lofty elongated upwarps, their cores made of granitic basement rocks, stripped of sediments, and heavily glaciated at high elevations. In New Mexico and along the western flanks of the Colorado ranges, widespread volcanism and deformation of colourful sedimentary rocks have produced rugged and picturesque country, but the characteristic central Colorado or southern Wyoming range is impressively austere rather than spectacular. The Front Range west of Denver is prototypical, rising abruptly from its base to rolling alpine meadows between 11,000 and 12,000 feet. Peaks appear as low hills perched on this high-level surface, so that Colorado, for example, boasts 53 mountains over 14,000 feet but not one over 14,500.

Diversity of the Rocky Mountain chains

The Middle Rockies occupy most of west central Wyoming. Most of the ranges resemble the granitic upwarps of Colorado, but thrust faulting and volcanism have produced varied and spectacular country to the west, some of which is included in Grand Teton and Yellowstone national parks. Much of the region, however, is not mountainous at all but consists of extensive intermontane basins and plains—largely floored with enormous volumes of sedimentary waste eroded from the mountains themselves. Whole ranges have been buried, producing the greatest gap in the whole Cordilleran system, the Wyoming Basin—which is, in fact, an intermontane peninsula of the Great Plains. As a result, the Rockies have never posed an important barrier to east–west transportation in the United States; all major routes, from the Oregon Trail to interstate highways, funnel through the basin, essentially circumventing the Rockies.

The Northern Rockies contain the most varied mountain landscapes of the Cordillera, reflecting a corresponding geologic complexity. The region's backbone is a mighty series of batholiths—huge masses of molten rock that slowly cooled below the surface and were later uplifted. The batholiths are eroded into rugged granitic ranges, which, in central Idaho, compose the most extensive wilderness country in the conterminous United States. East of the batholiths and facing the Great Plains, sediments have been folded and thrust-faulted into a series of linear north–south ranges, a southern extension of the spectacular Canadian Rockies. Although elevations run 2,000 to 3,000 feet lower than the Colorado Rockies (most of the Idaho Rockies lie well below 10,000 feet), increased rainfall and northern latitude have encouraged glaciation—here as elsewhere a sculptor of handsome alpine landscape.

The western branch of the Cordillera directly abuts the Pacific Ocean. This coastal chain, like its Rocky Mountain cousins on the east flank of the Cordillera, conceals bewildering complexity behind a facade of apparent simplicity. At first glance, the chain consists merely of two lines of mountains with a discontinuous trough between. Immediately behind the coast is a line of hills and low mountains—the Pacific Coast Ranges. Farther inland, averaging 150 miles from the coast, the line of the Sierra Nevada and the Cascade Range includes the highest elevations in the conterminous United States. Between these two unequal mountain lines is a discontinuous trench, the Troughs of the Coastal Margin.

The apparent simplicity disappears under the most cursory examination. The Pacific Coast Ranges actually contain five distinct sections, each of different geologic origin, each with distinctive topography. The Transverse Ranges of Southern California are a crowded assemblage of barren island-like ranges, with peak elevations over 10,000 feet but sufficiently separated by plains and low passes that travel through them is easy. From Point Conception to the Oregon border, however, the main California Coast Ranges are entirely different, resembling the Appalachian Ridge and Valley region, with low linear ranges that result from erosion of faulted and folded rocks. Major faults run parallel to the low ridges, and the greatest—the notorious San Andreas Fault—was responsible for the earthquake that destroyed San Francisco in 1906. Along the California–Oregon line, everything changes again. There, the wildly rugged Klamath Mountains represent a western salient of interior structure reminiscent of the Idaho Rockies and the northern Sierra Nevada. In western Oregon and southwestern Washington, the Coast Ranges are also different—a gentle, hilly land carved by streams from a broad arch of marine deposits interbedded with tabular lavas. Finally, in the northernmost part of the Coast Ranges and the remote northwesternmost corner of the conterminous United States, a domal upwarp has produced the Olympic Mountains, whose serrated peaks tower nearly 8,000 feet above Puget Sound and the Pacific and whose upper slopes still support the largest active glaciers in the United States outside Alaska.

East of the Coast Ranges, the Troughs of the Coastal Margin contain the only extensive lowland plains of the Pacific margin—California's Central Valley, Oregon's Willamette Valley, and the half-drowned basin of Puget Sound in Washington state. Parts of an inland trench that extends great distances along the east coast of the Pacific, similar valleys occur in such diverse areas as Chile and the Alaska Panhandle. Blessed with better than average soils, easily irrigated, and freely accessible from the Pacific, these valleys have enticed settlers for over a century and have become the main centres of population and economic activity for much of the West Coast.

Still farther east rise the two highest mountain chains in the conterminous United States—the Cascades and the Sierra Nevada. Aside from elevation, geographical continuity, and spectacular scenery, however, the two ranges differ in almost every important respect. Except for its northern section, where sedimentary and metamorphic rocks occur, the Sierra Nevada is largely made of granite, part of the same batholithic chain that creates the Idaho Rockies. The range is grossly asymmetrical, the result of massive faulting that has gently tilted the western slopes toward the Central Valley but has uplifted the eastern side to confront the interior with an awesome escarpment nearly two miles high. At high elevation, glaciers have scoured the granites to an astonishing gleaming white, while on the west the ice has carved spectacular valleys such as the Yosemite. The loftiest peak in the Sierras is Mt. Whitney, which, at 14,494 feet (4,418 metres), is the highest mountain in the contiguous 48 states. The upfaulting that produced Mt. Whitney is accompanied by downfaulting that formed nearby Death Valley, at 282 feet (86 metres) below sea level the lowest point on the North American continent.

The Cascades as well are made of volcanic rock, in northern Washington granitic like the Sierras, but for the rest, formed from relatively recent lava outpourings of dun-coloured basalt and andesite. The Cascades are in effect two ranges. The lower, older range is a long belt of upwarped lava, rising unspectacularly to elevations between 6,000 and 8,000 feet. Perched above the "low Cascades" is a chain of lofty quiescent volcanoes that punctuate the horizon with magnificent glacier-clad peaks. The highest is Mt. Rainier, whose 14,410 feet (4,392 metres) are all the more dramatic for rising from near sea level.

The Western Intermontane Region. The Cordillera's two main chains enclose a vast intermontane region of arid basins, plateaus, and isolated mountain ranges that stretches from the Mexican border nearly to Canada and extends 600 miles from east to west. This enormous territory contains three huge subregions, each with a distinctive geologic history and its own striking topographic personality.

Nestled against the west flanks of the Southern Rockies, the Colorado Plateau comprises an extraordinary island of geologic stability set in the turbulent sea of Cordilleran tectonic activity. Stability was not absolute, of course, so that parts of the plateau are warped and injected with volcanics, but in general the landscape results from the erosion by streams of nearly flat-lying sedimentary rocks. The result is a mosaic of angular mesas, buttes, and steplike canyons intricately cut from rocks that often are vividly coloured. Large areas of the plateau are so improbably picturesque that they have been set aside as national preserves. The Grand Canyon of the Colorado River is merely the most famous of several dozen such areas.

West of the plateau and abutting the Sierra Nevada's eastern escarpment lies the barren, arid Basin and Range, among the most remarkable topographic provinces of the United States. Rocks of great complexity have been broken by faulting, and the resulting blocks have tumbled, eroded, and been partly buried by alluvial debris that has accumulated in the desert basins at their feet. The eroded blocks form mountain ranges that are characteristically several tens of miles long, several thousand feet from base to crest, with peak elevations only occasionally much over 10,000 feet, and almost always aligned roughly north–south. The basins are typically floored with alluvium and sometimes salt.

The Pacific mountain chains

The Cascades and Sierras

The third intermontane region, the Columbia Basin, is literally the last, for in some parts its rocks are still being formed. Its entire area is underlain by innumerable tabular lava flows that have flooded the basin between the Cascades and Northern Rockies to undetermined depths. The volume of lava must be measured in thousands of cubic miles, for the flows blanket large parts of Washington, Oregon, and Idaho and in southern Idaho have drowned the Northern Rocky Mountains in a basaltic sea. Where the lavas are fresh, as in southern Idaho, the surface is often nearly flat, but more often the floors have been trenched by rivers—conspicuously the Columbia and the Snake—or by glacial floodwaters that have carved an intricate system of braided canyons in the remarkable Channeled Scablands of eastern Washington. In surface form, the eroded lava often resembles the topography of the Colorado Plateau, but the gaudy colours of the Colorado are replaced here by the sombre black and rusty brown of weathered basalt.

Minerals of the cordillera Most large mountain systems are sources of varied mineral wealth, and the American Cordillera is no exception. Metallic minerals have been taken from most crystalline regions and have furnished the United States with both romance and wealth—the Sierra gold that provoked the 1849 Gold Rush, the fabulous silver lodes of western Nevada's Basin and Range, and gold strikes all along the Rocky Mountain chain. Today, however, industrial metals are far more important, copper and lead among the base metals and the more exotic molybdenum, vanadium, and cadmium, mainly useful in alloys.

In the Cordillera, as elsewhere, the greatest wealth stems from fuels. Most major basins contain oil and natural gas, conspicuously the Wyoming Basin, the Central Valley of California, and the Los Angeles Basin. The Colorado Plateau, however, has yielded some of the most interesting discoveries of recent years—considerable deposits of uranium and colossal occurrences of oil shale. Oil from the shale, however, probably could not be economically removed without widespread strip mining, and correspondingly large-scale damage to environment. Finally, and still more recently, wide exploitation of low-sulfur bituminous coal has been initiated in the Four Corners area of the Colorado Plateau, and open-pit mining has already devastated parts of this once pristine country as completely as it has in the ravaged Appalachian Plateau of West Virginia.

WATERWAYS

As befits a nation of continental proportions, the United States possesses an extraordinary network of rivers and lakes, including some of the largest and most useful in the world. In the humid East, they provide an enormous mileage of cheap inland transportation; westward, most rivers and streams are unnavigable but are heavily used for irrigation and power generation. Both East and West, unfortunately, have traditionally used lakes and streams as public sewers, and most large U.S. waterways are laden with vast poisonous volumes of industrial, agricultural, and human wastes.

The Eastern systems. Chief among U.S. rivers is the Mississippi, which, with its great tributaries, the Ohio and the Missouri, drains most of the midcontinent. It is one of the world's great inland waterways, navigable The Mississippi and Great Lakes waters to Minneapolis nearly 1,200 airline miles from the Gulf of Mexico. Its eastern branches, chiefly the Ohio and the Tennessee, are also navigable for great distances. From the west, however, many of its numerous Great Plains tributaries are too seasonal and choked with sandbars to be used for shipping. The Missouri, for example, though longer than the Mississippi itself, was essentially without navigation until recently, when a combination of large dams, locks, and continual dredging has opened the river to considerable barge traffic.

The Great Lakes–St. Lawrence system comprises the second half of the world's greatest network of inland waterways, for it is connected to the Mississippi–Ohio by canals. No description of the Great Lakes is possible without superlatives, for the five lakes (four of which are shared with Canada) constitute by far the largest freshwater lake group in the world and carry a larger tonnage of shipping than any other. The three main barriers to navigation—the St. Marys Rapids, at Sault Ste. Marie; Niagara Falls; and the rapids of the St. Lawrence—are all bypassed by locks, whose 27-foot draft lets ocean vessels penetrate 1,300 miles into the continent, to Duluth and Chicago.

The third group of Eastern rivers drains the coastal strip along the Atlantic and Gulf of Mexico. Except for the Rio Grande, which rises west of the Rockies and flows 1,900 circuitous miles to the Gulf, few of these coastal rivers measure more than 300 miles, and most flow in an almost straight line to the sea. Except in glaciated New England and in arid southwest Texas, most of the larger coastal streams are navigable for some distance.

The Pacific systems. West of the Rockies, nearly all of United States' rivers are strongly influenced by aridity. In the deserts and steppes of the intermontane basins, most of the scanty runoff disappears into interior basins only one of which, the Great Salt Lake, holds any substantial volume of water. Aside from a few minor coastal streams, only three large river systems manage to reach the sea—the Columbia, the Colorado, and the San Joaquin–Sacramento system of California's Central Valley. All three are exotic: that is, they flow for considerable distances across dry lands from which they receive no water. Both the Columbia and Colorado have carved awesome gorges, the former through the sombre lavas of the Cascades and the Columbia Basin, the latter through the brilliantly coloured rocks of the Colorado Plateau. These gorges lend themselves to easy damming, and the once wild Columbia has been turned into a stairway of placid lakes whose waters irrigate the arid plateaus of eastern Washington and power one of the world's largest hydroelectric networks. The Colorado is less extensively developed, and recent proposals for new dam construction have met fierce opposition from those who want to preserve the spectacular beauty of the river's canyon lands.

CLIMATE AND ITS EFFECTS

Climate affects human habitats both directly and through its influence on vegetation, soils, and wildlife. In the United States, however, the natural environment has been altered drastically by nearly four centuries of European settlement, not to mention many thousand years of Indian occupancy.

But, wherever land is abandoned, "wild" conditions return rapidly, achieving over the long run a dynamic equilibrium among soils, vegetation, and the inexorable strictures of climate. Thus, though Americans have created an artificial environment of continental proportions, the United States, in fact, can be divided into a mosaic of bioclimatic regions, each distinguished by peculiar climatic conditions and each with a potential vegetation and soil that eventually would return in the absence of man. The main exception to this generalization applies to fauna, so grossly altered that it is almost impossible to know what sort of animal geography would redevelop in a United States if man were removed from the scene.

Climatic controls. The pattern of U.S. climates is largely set by three primary geographic controls: (1) the location of the conterminous United States almost entirely in the middle latitudes; (2) its position with respect to the continental landmass and its fringing oceans; and (3) the nation's gross pattern of mountains and lowlands. Each of these operates to determine the character of air masses and their changing behaviour from season to season.

The conterminous United States lies entirely between the Tropic of Cancer and 50° N latitude, a position that Climatic impact of latitude, landforms, and oceans confines Arctic climates to the high mountaintops and genuine tropics to a small part of southern Florida. By no means, however, is the climate literally temperate, for the middle latitudes are notorious for extreme variations of temperature and precipitation.

The great size of the North American landmass tends to reinforce these extremes. Since land heats and cools more rapidly than water, places distant from an ocean tend to exhibit "continental" climates; that is, they alternate between extremes of hot summers and cold winters, in contrast to the "marine" climates, which are more equable. Most U.S. climates are markedly continental, the more so because the Cordillera effectively confines the moderating Pacific influence to a narrow strip along the West Coast. Extremes of continentality occur near the centre of the continent, and North Dakota has seen ranges between a summer high temperature record of 121° F (49° C) and a winter low of −60° F (−51° C). Moreover, the general eastward drift of air over the United States carries continental temperatures all the way to the Atlantic coast. Bismarck, North Dakota, for example, exhibits a great annual temperature range; Boston, on the Atlantic but largely exempt from its influence, has a lesser but still continental range; but San Francisco, which is under strong Pacific influence, has only a small summer–winter differential.

The Western Cordillera confines not only Pacific temperatures to the coastal margin but also the Pacific rainfall. The Coast Ranges are high enough to make a local rain shadow in their lee, but the main barrier is the great rampart of the Sierra Nevada and Cascades. Rainy on their western slopes, barren on the east, this mountain crest forms one of the sharpest climatic divides in the United States.

The rain shadow continues east to the Rockies, leaving the entire Intermontane Region either arid or semi-arid, except where isolated ranges manage to capture leftover moisture at high altitudes. East of the Rockies, the westerly drift brings mainly dry air, and as a result the Great Plains are semi-arid. Still farther east, humidity increases owing to the frequent incursion from the south of warm, moist, and unstable air from the Gulf of Mexico, which produces more precipitation in the United States than the Pacific and Atlantic oceans combined.

Although the landforms of the Interior Lowlands have been termed dull, there is nothing dull about their weather conditions. Gulf air can flow northward across the Great Plains, uninterrupted by topographic barriers, but continental Canadian air flows south by the same route, and, since these two air masses differ in every important respect, the collisions often produce disturbances of monumental violence. Plainsmen and Middle Westerners grow accustomed to unexpected displays of furious weather—tornadoes, blizzards, hailstorms, precipitous drops and rises in temperature, and a host of other spectacular meteorological displays, sometimes dangerous but seldom boring.

The march of the seasons.   Most of the United States is marked by sharp differences between winter and summer. In winter, when temperature contrasts between land and water are greatest, a huge mass of frigid, dry Canadian air spreads far south over the midcontinent, bringing cold, sparkling weather to the interior and generating great cyclonic storms where its leading edge confronts a shrunken mass of warm Gulf air to the south. Although such cyclonic activity occurs throughout the year, it is most frequent and intense during the winter, parading eastward out of the Great Plains to bring the Eastern states practically all their winter precipitation. Temperatures differ widely, depending largely on latitude. Thus, New Orleans, at 30° N latitude, and International Falls, Minnesota, at 49° N, have respective January temperature averages of 55° F (13° C) and 3° F (−16° C). In the north, therefore, precipitation comes as snow, often driven by furious winds; farther south, cold rain alternates with sleet and occasional snow. Southern Florida is the only dependably warm part of the East, though "polar outbursts" have been known to bring temperatures below 0° F (−18° C) as far south as Tallahassee. The main uniformity of Eastern weather in wintertime is the expectation of continual change.

Winter climate on the West Coast is very different. A great spiralling mass of relatively warm, moist air spreads south from the Aleutian Islands of Alaska, its semipermanent front producing gloomy overcast and drizzles that hang over the Pacific Northwest all winter long, occasionally reaching Southern California, which re-

Nationwide seasonal variations

ceives nearly all of its rain at this time of year. This Pacific air brings mild temperatures along the whole coast; the average January day in Seattle ranges between 33° and 44° F (1° and 7° C), in Los Angeles between 45° and 64° F (7° and 18° C). In Southern California, however, rains are separated by long spells of fine weather, and the whole region is a winter haven for those seeking refuge from less agreeable weather patterns. The Intermontane Region is similar to the Pacific coast, but with much less rainfall and a somewhat wider range of temperatures.

Summer sees a reversal of the air masses, and east of the Rockies the change resembles the summer monsoon of Southeast Asia. As the midcontinent heats up, the cold Canadian air mass weakens and retreats, pushed north by an aggressive mass of warm, moist air from the Gulf. The great winter temperature differential between North and South disappears as the hot, soggy blanket spreads from the Gulf coast to the Canadian border. Heat and humidity are naturally most oppressive in the South, but northern latitude brings small comfort. Houston expects its normal July day to reach 92° F (33° C), with relative humidity averaging near 75 percent, but Minneapolis, over 1,000 miles north, is only slightly cooler and less humid.

Since the Gulf air is unstable as well as wet, convectional and frontal summer thunderstorms are endemic east of the Rockies, accounting for a majority of total summer rain. These storms usually drench small areas with short-lived, sometimes violent downpours, so that crops in one Middle Western county may prosper, those in another shrivel in drought, and those in yet another are flattened by hailstones. Relief from the humid heat comes in the north from occasional outbursts of cool Canadian air; small, but more consistent relief is found through influences from the Great Lakes and high elevations in the Appalachians. East of the Rockies, however, U.S. summers are distinctly uncomfortable, and air conditioning is viewed today as a desirable amenity in any Eastern city.

Again, the Pacific regime is different. The moist Aleutian air retreats northward, to be replaced by mild, stable air from over the cool subtropical Pacific, and except in the mountains the Pacific coast is nearly rainless, though often foggy. Meanwhile, a small but potent mass of dry hot air raises temperatures to blistering levels over much of the intermontane Southwest. In Yuma, Arizona, for example, the normal July day reaches 108° F (42° C), while nearby Death Valley, California, holds the national record, 134° F (57° C). During its summer peak, this scorching air mass spreads from the Pacific margin as far as Texas on the east and Idaho to the north, turning the whole interior basin into a summer desert.

Over most of the United States, as in most continental climates, spring and autumn are agreeable but disappointingly brief. Autumn is particularly idyllic in the East, the romantic Indian summer of ripening corn and brilliantly coloured foliage, of mild days and frosty nights. The shift in dominance between marine and continental air masses, however, spawns furious weather in some regions. Along the Atlantic and Gulf coasts, for example, autumn is the season for hurricanes—the American equivalent of Southeast Asian typhoons—which rage northward from the Gulf and Caribbean to visit havoc along the Coast as far north as New England. The Mississippi Valley holds the dubious distinction of recording more tornadoes than any other area on Earth. These violent storms are usually focussed on relatively small areas and are confined largely to springtime.

The bioclimatic regions.   Three first-order bioclimatic zones encompass most of the conterminous United States —regions in which climatic conditions are similar enough to dictate similar conditions of mature (zonal) soil and potential climax vegetation (*i.e.*, the assemblage of plants that would grow and reproduce indefinitely given stable climate and average conditions of soil and drainage). These are the Humid East, the Humid Pacific Coast, and the Dry West. In addition, the boundary zone between the Humid East and the Dry West is so large and important that it constitutes a separate region, the Humid-Arid Transition. Finally, because the Western Cordillera contains an intricate mosaic of climatic types, largely determined by local elevation and exposure, it is useful to distinguish the Western Mountain Climate. The first three zones, however, are very diverse and require further breakdown, producing a total of ten main bioclimatic regions. For two reasons, the boundaries of these bioclimatic regions are much less distinct than boundaries of landform regions. First, climate obviously varies from year to year, especially in boundary zones, whereas landforms do not. Second, regions of climate, vegetation, and soils coincide generally but sometimes not precisely. Boundaries, therefore, should be interpreted as zonal and transitional, rarely as sharp lines in the landscape.

For all of their indistinct boundaries, however, these bioclimatic regions have strong and easily recognized identities. Such regional identity is strongly reinforced when a particular area falls entirely within a single bioclimatic region and at the same time a single landform region. The result—as in the Piedmont South, the central Middle West, or the western Great Plains—is a landscape with an unmistakable regional personality.

The Humid East. The largest and in some ways the most important of the bioclimatic zones, the Humid East was where the Europeans first settled, tamed the land, and learned the new ways that were to make them American. In aboriginal times, nearly all this territory was forested, a fact of central importance in American history that profoundly influenced both soils and wildlife. As in most of the world's humid lands, soluble minerals have been leached from the earth, leaving a great family of soils called pedalfers, rich in relatively insoluble iron and aluminum compounds.

Both forests and soils, however, differ considerably within this vast region. Since rainfall is ample and summers warm everywhere, the main differences result from the length and severity of winters, which determine the length of growing season. Winter, obviously, differs according to latitude, so that the Humid East is sliced into four great east–west bands of soils and vegetation, with progressively more amenable winters as one travels southward. These changes occur very gradually, however, and the boundaries therefore are extremely subtle.

A Sub-Boreal Forest Region is the northernmost of these bands. Only a small and discontinuous part of the United States, it represents the tattered southern fringe of the vast Canadian taiga—a scrubby forest dominated by evergreen needle-leaf species that can endure the ferocious winters and reproduce during the short, erratic summers. Average growing seasons are below 120 days, though Newberry, Michigan, has recorded frost-free periods lasting as long as 161 days and as short as 76. What soils survived the scour of glaciation are miserably thin podzols—heavily leached, highly acid, and often interrupted by extensive stretches of bog. Most attempts at farming in the region long since have been abandoned.

Farther south lies a Humid Microthermal Zone of milder winters and longer summers. Large broadleaf trees begin to crowd out the evergreens, producing a mixed forest of greater floristic variety and economic value and famous for its brilliant autumn colours. As the forest grows richer in species, sterile podzols give way to more productive gray-brown podzolic soils, stained and fertilized with humus. Although winters are warmer than the Sub-Boreal zone, and although the Great Lakes help temper the bitterest cold, January temperatures ordinarily average below freezing, and a winter without a few sub-zero days is uncommon. Everywhere, the ground is solidly frozen and snow covered for several months of the year.

Still farther south are the Humid Subtropics. The region's northern boundary is one of the United States' most portentous climatic lines, the approximate northern limit of a 180–200-day growing season, the outer margin of cotton growing, and, hence, of the Old South. Most of the South lies in the Piedmont and Coastal Plain, for higher elevations in the Appalachians cause

a peninsula of Northern mixed forest to extend as far south as northern Georgia. The red-brown podzolic soil, once moderately fertile, has been severely damaged by overcropping and burning. Thus much of the region that ordinarily sustains a rich, broadleaf-forest flora in fact supports poor pinewoods. Throughout the South, summers are hot, muggy, long, and disagreeable; Dixie's "frosty mornings" bring a welcome respite in winter.

The southern margins of Florida contain the conterminous United States' only real tropics, an area in which frost is almost unknown. Hot, rainy summers alternate with warm and somewhat drier winters, with a secondary rainfall peak during the autumn hurricane season—altogether a typical monsoonal regime. Soils and vegetation are mostly immature, however, since southern Florida rises so slightly above sea level that substantial areas, such as the Everglades (*q.v.*), are swampy and often brackish. Peat and sand frequently masquerade as soil, and much of the vegetation is either salt-loving mangrove or sawgrass prairie.

The Humid Pacific Coast. The western humid region differs from its eastern counterpart in so many ways as to be a world apart. Much smaller, it is crammed into a narrow littoral belt to the windward of the Sierra–Cascade summit, dominated by mild Pacific air, and chopped by irregular topography into an intricate mosaic of climatic and biotic habitats. Throughout the region, rainfall is extremely seasonal, falling mostly in the winter half of the year. Summers are droughty everywhere, but the main regional differences come from the length of drought—from two months in humid Seattle to nearly five months in semi-arid San Diego.

Western Washington, Oregon, and Northern California lie within a zone that climatologists call Marine West Coast. Winters are raw, overcast, and drizzly—not unlike northwestern Europe—with subfreezing temperatures restricted mainly to the mountains, upon which enormous snow accumulations produce local alpine glaciers. Summers, by contrast, are brilliantly cloudless, cool, and with frequent foggy intervals along the Coast and somewhat warmer in the inland valleys. This mild marine climate produces some of the world's greatest forests, enormous straight-boled evergreen trees that furnish the United States with much of its commercial timber. Mature soils are typical of humid midlatitude forest lands, a moderately leached gray-brown podzol.

Toward the south, with diminishing coastal rain the moist marine climate gradually gives way to California's tiny but much publicized Mediterranean regime. Although mountainous topography introduces a bewildering variety of local environments, scanty winter rains are quite inadequate to compensate for the long summer drought, and much of the region has a distinctly arid flavour. For much of the year, cool, stable Pacific air dominates the Coast, bringing San Francisco its famous fogs and Los Angeles its infamous smoggy temperature inversions. Inland, however, summer temperatures reach blistering levels, so that in July, while Los Angeles expects a normal daily maximum of 76° F (24° C), Fresno expects 100° F (38° C) and is climatically a desert. As might be expected, Mediterranean California contains a huge variety of vegetal habitats, but the commonest perhaps is the chaparral, a drought-resistant, scrubby woodland of twisted hard-leafed trees, picturesque but of little economic value. Soils are similarly varied, but most are light in colour and rich in soluble minerals, qualities typical of subarid soils.

The Dry West. In the United States, to speak of dry areas is to speak of the West. It covers an enormous region beyond the dependable reach of moist oceanic air, occupying the entire Intermontane area and sprawling from Canada to Mexico across the western part of the Great Plains. To Americans nurtured in the Humid East, this vast territory across the path of all transcontinental travellers has been harder to tame than any other—and no region has so gripped the national imagination as this fierce and dangerous land.

In the Dry West, nothing matters more than water. Thus, though temperatures may differ radically from

Indistinctness of climatic boundaries

Climatic subregions of the Eastern U.S.

The United States' Mediterranean-like climes

place to place, the really important regional differences depend overwhelmingly on the degree of aridity, whether an area is extremely dry and hence desert or whether it is semi-arid and therefore steppe.

Americans of the 19th century were preoccupied by the myth of a Great American Desert, which supposedly occupied more than one-third of the nation. True desert in fact is confined to the Southwest, with patchy outliers elsewhere, all without exception located in the lowland rain shadows of the Cordillera. Vegetation varies between nothing at all (a rare circumstance confined mainly to salt flats and sand dunes) to a low cover of scattered woody scrub and short-lived annuals that burst into flamboyant bloom after rains. Soils are usually thin, light coloured, and overrich with mineral salts. In some areas, wind erosion has removed fine-grained material, leaving behind desert pavement, a barren veneer of broken rock.

Most of the West, however, lies in the semi-arid region, in which rainfall is scanty but adequate to support a thin cover of short bunchgrass, commonly alternating with scrubby sagebrush. As in the desert, soils fall into the large family of the pedocals, rich in calcium and other soluble minerals, but here, in a slightly wetter environment, enriched with humus from decomposed grass roots. Under proper management, these chestnut-coloured steppe soils can prove very fertile.

Weather in the West resembles that of other dry regions of the world, often extreme, violent, and reliably unreliable. Rainfall, for example, obeys a cruel natural law: as total precipitation decreases, it becomes more undependable. John Steinbeck's novel *The Grapes of Wrath* describes a family enticed to the arid frontier of Oklahoma during a wet period, only to be driven out by the savage drought of the 1930s that turned the western Great Plains into the great American Dust Bowl. Temperatures also fluctuate convulsively within short periods, and high winds are infamous throughout the region.

The Humid-Arid Transition. East of the Rockies, all climatic boundaries are gradational. None, however, is so important nor so imperceptibly subtle as the boundary zone that separates the Humid East from the Dry West and that alternates unpredictably between arid and humid conditions from year to year. Stretching from Texas to North Dakota in an ill-defined band between the 95th and 100th meridians, this transitional region deserves separate recognition, partly because of its great size, partly because the fine balance between surplus and deficit rainfall produces a unique and valuable combination of soils, flora, and fauna. The native vegetation, insofar as it can be reconstructed, was prairie, the legendary sea of tall, deep-rooted grass now almost entirely tilled and planted to grains. Soils, often of loessial derivation, include the enormously productive chernozem ("black earth") in the north, with reddish prairie soils of nearly equal fertility in the south. Throughout the region, temperatures are severely continental, with bitterly cold winters in the north and scorching summers everywhere.

The western edge of the prairie fades gradually into the shortgrass steppe of the High Plains, the change a function of diminishing rainfall. The eastern edge, however, represents one of the few major discordances between a climatic and biotic boundary in the United States, for the grassland penetrates the eastern forest in a great salient across humid Illinois and Indiana. Many scholars believe this part of the U.S. prairie was artificially induced by repeated Indian burning and consequent destruction of the forest margins.

The Western Mountain climates. Throughout the Cordillera and Intermontane regions, irregular topography shatters the grand bioclimatic pattern into an intricate mosaic of tiny regions that differ drastically according to elevation and exposure. No small- or medium-scale map can accurately record such complexity, and mountainous parts of the West are said, noncommittally, to have a "mountain climate." Lowlands are usually dry, but increasing elevation brings lower temperature, decreased evaporation, and—if a slope faces prevailing winds—greater precipitation. Soils vary wildly from place to

place, but vegetation is fairly predictable. From the desert or steppe of intermontane valleys, a climber typically ascends into parklike savanna, then through an orderly sequence of increasingly humid and boreal forests until, if the range is high enough, he reaches timberline and Arctic tundra. The very highest peaks are snowcapped, although permanent glaciers rarely occur outside the cool humid highlands of the Pacific Northwest.

Animal life. With most of North America, the United States lies in the Nearctic faunistic realm, a region containing an assemblage of species similar to Eurasia and North Africa but sharply different from the tropical and subtropical zones to the south. Main regional differences correspond roughly with primary climatic and vegetal patterns. Thus, for example, the animal communities of the Dry West differ sharply from those of the Humid East and from those of the Pacific coast. Because animals tend to range over wider areas than plants and because they migrate, faunal regions are generally coarser than vegetal regions and harder to delineate sharply.

The animal geography of the United States, however, is far from a natural pattern, for European settlement produced a series of environmental changes that grossly altered the distribution of animal communities. First, many species were hunted to extinction or near extinction, most conspicuously, perhaps, the American bison, which ranged by the millions nearly from coast to coast but now lives only in zoos and wildlife preserves. Second, habitats were upset or destroyed throughout most of the country —forests cut, grasslands plowed and overgrazed, and migration paths interrupted by fences, railroads, and highways. Third, certain introduced species found hospitable niches and, like the English sparrow, spread over huge areas, often pre-empting the habitats of native animals. Fourth, though their effects are not well understood, chemical biocides such as DDT were used for so long and in such volume that they are believed at least partly responsible for catastrophic mortality rates among large mammals and birds, especially predators high on the food chain. In consequence, many native animals have been reduced to tiny fractions of their former ranges or exterminated completely, while other animals, both native and introduced, have found the new anthropocentric environment well suited to their needs, with explosive effects on their populations. The coyote and several species of deer are among the animals that now occupy much larger ranges than they once did.   (P.F.L.)

II. Patterns of settlement and cultural development

Although the land was occupied and much affected by diverse Indian cultures over many millennia, these pre-European settlement patterns have had virtually no impact upon the contemporary nation—except locally, as in parts of New Mexico. A benign habitat permitted a huge contiguous tract of settled land to materialize across nearly all the eastern half of the United States and within lesser, but still substantial, patches of the West. Climate, physiography, soils, plant cover, and drainage were such that access or occupance was difficult only locally—with the result that reasonably pure wilderness is a rare phenomenon in the United States today. The vastness of the land, the scarcity of labour, and the abundance of migratory opportunities in a land replete with raw physical resources contributed to exceptional human mobility and a quick succession of ephemeral forms of land use and settlement. Although the handiwork of man is everywhere visible in the grossly altered environments, human endeavour has been largely exploitative and destructive. Most of the pre-European landscape in the United States was so swiftly and radically altered that it is difficult to conjecture intelligently about its earlier appearance.

For further details on settlement and cultural patterns, see the articles on the individual U.S. states and on the major cities.

RURAL AND URBAN AMERICA

The overall impression of the settled portion of the U.S. landscape, rural or urban, is one of disorder, of lack of coherence, even in areas of strict geometric survey. Indeed, the individual landscape unit is seldom in visual harmony with its neighbour, so that, however sound in design or construction the single structure may be, the general effect is untidy. These attributes have been intensified by the acute individualism of the American, vigorous speculation in land and other commodities, a strongly utilitarian attitude toward the land and the treasures above and below it, and government policy and law. Further, the landscape is remarkable for its emphasis upon transportation facilities, which are often critical in determining both form and function.

Another special characteristic of U.S. settlement, one that became obvious only by the mid-20th century, is the convergence of rural and urban modes of life. The farmsteads—and rural folk in general—have become increasingly citified, and agricultural operations have become ever more factory-like, while the metropolis grows more and more gelatinous, unfocussed, and pseudo-bucolic along its vague but rapidly spreading margins.

Rural settlement. Patterns of rural settlement everywhere and always tell much about the history, economy, society, and minds of those who create them as well as about the land itself. The essential design of rural activity in the United States bears a strong family resemblance to that of other neo-European lands, such as Canada, Australia, New Zealand, South Africa, Argentina, or Siberia —places that have undergone rapid occupation and exploitation during recent times by vigorous immigrants intent upon short-term development and enrichment. In all such areas, under novel social and political conditions and with a relative abundance of territory and physical resources, ideas and institutions derived from a relatively stable medieval or early-modern Europe have undergone major transformation. Further, these are nonpeasant countrysides, alike in thus far having failed to achieve the intimate symbiosis of man and habitat, the humanized rural landscapes characteristic of many relatively dense, stable, earthbound communities in parts of Asia, Africa, Europe, and aboriginal Latin America.

Early models of land allocation. From the beginning, the prevalent official policy of the British (except between 1763 and 1776) and then of the new U.S. government was to promote agricultural and other settlement, to push the frontier westward as fast as physical and economic conditions permitted. The British crown's grants of large, often vaguely specified tracts to individual proprietors or companies enabled the grantees, in turn, to draw settlers by the sale or lease of land at attractive prices or even by outright gift.

Of the numerous attempts at group colonization, the most notable effort was the theocratic yet collectivist New England town that flourished, especially in Massachusetts, Connecticut, and New Hampshire, during the first century of settlement. The town, the basic unit of government and comparable in area to townships in other states, allotted both rural and village parcels to single families by group decision. The residences of farmers and all others were concentrated in a central village. This quasi-communal system broke down before the end of the colonial era, although the village persisted as an amoeba-shaped entity straggling along converging roads, neither fully rural nor agglomerated in form. The only latter-day settlement experiment of notable magnitude to achieve enduring success was a series of Mormon settlements in the Great Basin region of Utah and adjacent states, with their tightly concentrated farm villages reminiscent of the New England model. Many other efforts were, or are being, made along ethnic, religious, or political lines, but success has been at best brief and fragile.

Creating the national domain. With the coming of independence and after complex negotiations, the original 13 states surrendered to a new national government nearly all their claims to the unsettled western lands beyond their boundaries. Some tracts, however, were reserved for disposal to particular groups. Thus the Western Reserve of northeastern Ohio gave preferential treatment to natives of Connecticut, while the military tracts in Ohio and Indiana were used as bonus payments to veterans of the Revolution.

A federally administered national domain was created, to which the great bulk of the territory acquired in the 1803 Louisiana Purchase and later beyond the Mississippi and in 1819 in Florida was consigned. The only major exceptions were the public lands of Texas, which were left within that state's jurisdiction, such earlier French and Spanish land grants as were confirmed, often after tortuous litigation, and some Indian lands. In sharp contrast to the slipshod methods of colonial land survey and disposal, the federal land managers expeditiously surveyed, numbered, and mapped their territory in advance of settlement, beginning with Ohio in the 1780s, then sold or deeded it to settlers under inviting terms at a number of regional land offices.

The design universally followed in the new survey system (except within the French, Spanish, and Indian grants) was a simple, efficient rectangular scheme. Townships were laid out as square blocks, six by six miles in size, oriented with the compass directions. Thirty-six sections, each one square mile, or 640 acres, in size, were designated within each township; and public roads were established along section lines and, where needed, along half-section lines. At irregular intervals, offsets in survey lines and roads were introduced to allow for the Earth's curvature. Individual property lines were coincident with, or parallel to, survey lines, and this pervasive rectangularity generally carried over into the geometry of fields and fences or the townsites later superimposed upon the basic rural survey.

This all-encompassing checkerboard pattern is best appreciated from an airplane window over Iowa or Kansas. There, one sees few streams or other natural features or few diagonal highways or railroads interrupting the triumphant squareness of the landscape. A systematic rectangular layout, rather less rigorous in form, also appears in much of Texas and those portions of Maine, western New York and Pennsylvania, and southern Georgia pioneered from the 1780s onward.

Distribution of rural lands. Over the past two centuries, Congress has enacted a series of complex schemes for distribution of the national domain: the Homestead Act of 1862, which offered title to 160 acres to individual settlers, subject only to residence for a certain period and the making of minimal improvements, is only the most famous of these. The legal provisions have varied with time as the nature of farming technology and the remaining lands have changed, but their clear intention has been to flesh out the Jeffersonian ideal of a republic peopled by yeoman farmers owning and tilling economically self-sufficient properties.

The program succeeded well in providing private owners with almost all choice lands, aside from parcels reserved for schools and various township and municipal uses. Just over one-third of the national territory is still owned by the federal government, about one-half of this in Alaska. Nearly all, however, aside from that used by government agencies, is in the West and is unsuited for intensive agriculture or grazing because of the roughness, dryness, or salinity of the terrain, but much federal land is leased out for light grazing or for timber cutting.

Patterns of farm life. During the classic period of U.S. rural life, around 1900, the typical American lived or worked on a farm or was economically dependent upon farmers. In contrast to rural life in many other parts of the world, the farm family lived on an isolated farmstead some distance from town and often from farm neighbours; its property averaged less than one-quarter square mile. This farmstead would vary in form and content with local tradition and economy. In particular, barn types were localized—for example, the tobacco barns of the South, the great dairy barns of Wisconsin, or the general-purpose forebay barns of southeast Pennsylvania —as were modes of fencing. In general, however, the farmstead contained dwelling, barn, storage and sheds for small livestock and equipment, a small orchard, and kitchen garden. A woodlot might be found in the least accessible or least fertile part of the farm.

Successions of such farms were connected with one another and with the towns by means of a dense, usually

Comparative rural patterns: U.S. and elsewhere

The establishment of townships

The U.S. farm around 1900

rectangular lattice of roads, largely unimproved at the time. The hamlets, villages, and smaller cities were arrayed at relatively regular intervals, with size and affluence determined in large part by presence and quality of rail service or status as county seat. But, among a population that has been historically rural, individualistic, and anti-urban in bias, many a service normally located in urban places might be found in a rustic setting. Thus much retail business was transacted by means of itinerant peddlers; the post office and many small shops for the fabrication, distribution, or repair of some basic items were often located in isolated farmsteads.

Social activity also tended to be widely dispersed among numerous rural churches, schools, or grange halls; and the climactic event of the year might well be the county fair, political rally, or religious encampment—again on a rural site. Not the least symptomatic sign of the strong tendency toward spatial isolation are the countless family burial plots or community cemeteries so liberally distributed across the countryside.

Town morphologies in the rural U.S.

Regional small-town patterns. There has been and still is much regional variation among smaller villages and hamlets. Unfortunately, such phenomena have received relatively little attention from students of U.S. culture or geography. The distinctive New England village, of course, is generally recognized and cherished: a loose clustering of white frame buildings, including a church (more often than not Congregationalist or Unitarian), town hall, shops, and stately homes with tall shade trees around the central green or commons, a grassy expanse that may contain a bandstand and monuments or a flower bed. Derivative village forms were carried westward to several sections of the northern Middle West.

Less widely known but equally distinctive is the town morphology characteristic of the Midland, or Pennsylvanian, culture area and most fully developed in southeastern and central Pennsylvania and Piedmont Maryland. It differs totally from the New England model in density, building materials, and general appearance. Closely packed, often contiguous buildings—mostly brick, but sometimes stone, frame, or stucco, which may be either shops or residences or both—abut directly on a sidewalk, often paved with brick and usually thickly planted with maple, sycamore, or other shade trees. Characteristically, such towns are linear in plan, have only one or two principal streets, and may radiate outward from a central square lined with commercial and governmental structures.

The most characteristic U.S. small town was the one whose pattern was evolved in the Middle West. Its simple scheme was usually platted on the grid plan. Functions are rigidly segregated spatially, with the central business district, consisting of closely packed two- or three-story brick buildings, limited exclusively to commercial and administrative activity and usually quite desolate in the evenings. The residences, generally set well back within spacious lots, are peripheral in location, as are most rail facilities, factories, or warehousing.

Even the modest urbanization represented by the small town came late to the South. Most usual urban functions long were spatially dispersed—almost totally so in early Chesapeake Bay country or North Carolina—or were performed entirely by the larger plantations dominating the economic life of much of the region. When city and town began to materialize in the 19th and 20th centuries, they tended to follow the Middle Western model in layout.

Although quite limited in geographical area, the characteristic villages of the Mormon and Hispanic-American districts contain much of interest. The former uncompromisingly followed the ecclesiastically imposed pattern of a grid plan composed of perfectly square blocks, each with perhaps only four very large house lots, and the block surrounded by extremely wide streets. Those villages in New Mexico whose population and culture were derived from Old Mexico were often built according to the standard Latin American plan. The distinctive feature is a central plaza dominated by a Roman Catholic church and encircled by low stone or adobe buildings.

The rural–urban transition. *Weakening of the agrarian ideal.* The United States has had little success in achieving or maintaining the family-farm ideal. Through purchase, inheritance, leasing, and other means of dubious legality, smaller properties have been merged into much larger entities. In 1964, when average farm size had grown to 352 acres, those farms containing 2,000 or more acres accounted for about 42 percent of all farmland and 12 percent of cropland harvested, although comprising less than 2 percent of all farms. At the other extreme were those 63 percent of all farms containing less than 180 acres and reporting less than 19 percent of cropland harvested. Succeeding years have intensified this trend toward fewer but larger farms.

The huge, heavily capitalized "neoplantation," essentially a factory in the field, is especially conspicuous in parts of California, Arizona, and the Mississippi Delta, but examples can be found in any state. There are also many smaller but intensive operations calling for large investments and advanced managerial skills. This trend toward large-scale, capital-intensive farm enterprise has been paralleled, of course, by a sharp drop in rural farm population—a slump from the all-time maximum of around 32,000,000 in the early 20th century to 9,400,000 in 1971; but even in 1940, when farm folk still numbered more than 30,000,000, nearly 40 percent of farm operators were tenants, and another 10 percent were only part owners.

The mythology of small-town America

As the absolute, as well as the relative, size of the truly agrarian open-country and small-town population of the United States has dwindled in recent years, so too has its immediate impact lessened, though less swiftly, in economic and political matters. The real strength of the rural United States, however, remains in the realm of image and myth rather than in mundane material fact. Although the United States has become a highly urbanized, technologically advanced society far removed in daily life from cracker barrel, barnyard, corral, or logging camp, Americans have gravitated, sometimes reluctantly, to the big city; and in the deeply internalized daydreams and mythological assumptions that guide basic sociopolitical decisions, the lingering memory of a rapidly vanishing agrarian small-town America glows brightly. This is revealed not only in the works of some of the better contemporary novelists, poets, and painters but also throughout the popular arts: in movies, television, soap opera, folklore, country-and-western music, political oratory, and in much leisure-time activity.

Highways and human settlement

Impact of the motor vehicle. Since about 1920, more genuine change has occurred in U.S. rural life than during the preceding three centuries of European experience in North America. Although the basic explanation is the profound social and technological transformation engulfing most of the world, the most immediate agent of change has been the internal-combustion engine. The auto, truck, bus, and paved highway have more than supplanted a moribund passenger-railroad system. While many a local rail depot has been boarded up and scores of secondary lines have been abandoned, hundreds of thousands of miles of old dirt roads have been paved, and a vast system of multiple-lane, limited-access interstate highways is under construction to connect all sizable cities in a single nonstop network. The net result has been a shrinking of the mile, a great extension of effective circulatory space for the individual driver, rural or urban. In balance, the total population of small towns has remained about the same. Those towns with strategic locations with respect to highways and urban opportunity have prospered; the less fortunate are wounded or dying, and, if the residents linger on for the sake of relatively cheap housing, the downtown businesses are often extinct.

As the United States has become increasingly wheel borne, the visual aspect of the rural U.S. has altered drastically. The highway has become the central physical fact, and many of the functions once confined to town or city now stretch mile after mile along major roads (see below).

Reversal of the classic rural dominance. The metropolitanization of U.S. life has not been limited to city, suburb, or exurb; it has now involved nearly the entirety of the inhabited rural United States and its people. The result has been the decline of local crafts and regional peculiarities, quite visibly in terms of such items as farm implements, fencing, silos, and housing and in many everyday commodities such as clothing or bread. In other ways, to an extent not yet fully realized, the countryside is now economically at the mercy of the city.

The city dweller is a dominant patron for products other than those of field, quarry, or lumber mill; and city location now determines patterns of rural economy rather than the reverse. During weekends and the vacation seasons, swarms of city folk stream out to second homes in the countryside, to campgrounds, ski trails, beaches, boating areas, or hunting and fishing tracts. For many large rural tracts, recreation is the principal source of income and employment; and such areas as northern New England and Upstate New York are now in essence playgrounds and sylvan refuges for the more affluent citizens of the multiple metropolises.

The larger cities reach far into the countryside for their vital supplies of water and energy; there is an increasing reliance upon distant mine-mouth power plants for electrical power; and they have gone far afield in seeking out rural dumps for their evergrowing excretion of garbage and trash.

The greater part of the rural population of the nation now lives within daily commuting range of a sizable city. This enables many a farm resident to stick to the farm while working part- or full-time at a city job and prevents the drastic decline in rural-farm population that has occurred in remoter parts of the country. Similarly, many a small town within the shadow of the metropolis, with fewer and fewer farmers to service, has stabilized or even increased its wealth and population and preserved its outward appearance while actually undergoing a drastic shift in function by becoming a dormitory satellite whose residents—some natives; others, migrants from the city in quest of a placid, simpler environment—work within accessible cities or suburbs.

Urban settlement.   The United States has moved rapidly from an emphatically rural past into an overwhelmingly urban present. In so doing, it has followed the same general path that other advanced nations have travelled and one along which the contemporary developing nations have begun to hasten. Three-quarters of the population live clustered within officially designated urban places and "urbanized areas" (which account for less than 2 percent of the national territory), and at least another 15 percent in dispersed residences are actually urban in economic or social orientation.

Classic patterns of siting and growth.   Although at least 95 percent of the population was rural throughout the colonial period and for the first few years of independence, cities were crucial elements in the settlement system from the earliest days. Boston, New Amsterdam (New York City), Jamestown, Charleston, and Philadelphia were founded at the same time as the colonies they served. Like nearly all other North American colonial towns of consequence, they were ocean ports. Until at least the beginning of the 20th century, the historical geography of U.S. cities has been intimately related with that of successive transportation systems. The location of successful cities with respect to the areas they served, as well as their internal structure, was determined largely by the nature of these systems.

The colonial cities acted as funnels for the collection and shipment of farm and forest products and other raw materials from the interior to trading partners in Europe, the Caribbean, or Africa and for the return flow of manufactured goods, immigrants, and other locally scarce items. Essentially marts and warehouses, they gave only minimal attention to social, military, educational, or religious functions. The inadequacy and costliness of overland traffic dictated sites along major ocean embayments or river estuaries; the only pre-1800 non-ports worthy of notice were Lancaster and York, Pennsylvania, and Williamsburg, Virginia. With the populating of the interior

and the spread of a system of canals and improved roads, such new cities as Pittsburgh, Cincinnati, Buffalo, and St. Louis mushroomed at junctures between various routes or at which modes of transport were changed. Older ocean ports, such as New Castle, Delaware; Newport, Rhode Island; Charleston, South Carolina; Savannah, Georgia; and Portland, Maine, whose locations prevented them from serving large hinterlands tended to stagnate.

From about 1850 to 1920, the success of new cities and the further growth of older ones were related critically to their location within the totally triumphant new steam railroad system and to how effectively they could dominate a large tributary territory. Such waterside rail hubs as Buffalo, Toledo, Chicago, and San Francisco gained population and wealth rapidly, while such new offspring of the rail era as Atlanta; Indianapolis; Minneapolis; Fort Worth, Texas; and Tacoma, Washington, also grew lustily. Much of the rapid industrialization of the 19th and early 20th centuries occurred in places already favoured as to water or rail transport systems; but in some instances, such as in the cities of northeastern Pennsylvania's anthracite region, some New England mill towns, and the textile centres of the Carolina and Virginia Piedmont, manufacturing was the principal cause of rapid urbanization and the consequent attraction of transport facilities. The mining of gold, silver, copper, coal, iron, and, more recently, gas or oil led to rather ephemeral centres—unless these places were able to capitalize on local or regional advantages other than minerals.

A strong early start, whatever the initial economic base may have been, was often the key factor in interurban competition. With sufficient early momentum, urban capital and population would tend to expand almost automatically in a circular and cumulative process. The point is illustrated perfectly by the larger cities of the northeastern seaboard, from Portland (Maine) through Baltimore. The nearby physical wealth is poor to mediocre, and they are now far off-centre on the national map; but a prosperous mercantile beginning, good land and sea connections with distant places, and a rich local accumulation of talent, capital, and initiative were sufficient to bring about the growth of the world's largest concentration of industry, commerce, and people.

New factors in municipal development.   The pre-1900 development of the U.S. city was almost completely a chronicle of the economics of the production, collection, and distribution of physical commodities and basic services in relation to geography, but recent decades have seen striking deviations from this pattern. The physical determinants of urban location and growth have given way to social factors. Increasingly, those older cities faring best and the more successful newer ones are oriented toward the more advanced modes for the production and consumption of services, specifically the knowledge, managerial, and pleasure industries. The largest cities are becoming more dependent upon corporate headquarters, communications, and the manipulation of information for their sustenance. Washington, D.C., is the most obvious example of a metropolis in which government and ancillary activities have been the spur for vigorous growth; but almost all the state capitals have displayed a similar demographic and economic vitality. Further, those urban centres containing a major college or university have enjoyed remarkable expansion during the past generation.

With the coming of relative affluence and abundant leisure among the masses and a decrease of labour input in industrial processes, an entirely new breed of cities has sprouted across the land: those that cater to the pleasure-seeker, vacationer, and the retired—for example, the young, flourishing cities of Florida or Nevada and many a place in California, Arizona, Colorado, and other states.

With the coming of the automobile as a means of personal transportation, about the time of World War I, the U.S. city was catapulted into a radically new period, both quantitatively and qualitatively, in the further evo-

Evolving functions of U.S. cities

lution of physical form and function. Previously, the size, density, and internal structure of the city were constrained by the limitations of the pedestrian and early mass-transit systems. Only the well-to-do could afford horse and carriage or a secluded villa in the countryside. Cities were relatively small and compact, with a single clearly defined centre, and grew by accretion along their edges, without any significant spatial hiatuses, except where commuter railroads linked outlying towns and suburbs to the largest of metropolises. Workers living beyond the immediate vicinity of their place of work had no choice but to locate within reach of the few horse-drawn omnibuses or the later electric street railways.

Effect of the automobile on urban development

The universality of the automobile, even among the less affluent, and the parallel proliferation of service facilities and highways greatly loosened and fragmented the U.S. city, almost literally exploding and splattering it over surrounding rural lands. Older, formerly autonomous towns were swallowed up, grew swiftly, and became satellites of the larger city. Multitudes of new suburbs and subdivisions arose with single-family homes on lots much larger than had been possible for the ordinary householder in the city. These were almost totally dependent on the highway for the flow of commuters, goods, and services, and many were located in open country in splendid isolation, separated by tracts of farmland, brush, or forest from other such developments. At the major interchanges of the limited-access highways, a new form of agglomerated settlement has sprung up: the service station, motel, restaurant, and other establishments for a mobile clientele. Such satellite communities are especially noteworthy in the environs of such larger cities as Philadelphia, New York, Detroit, and Chicago.

The new look of "the metropolitan area." The outcome has been a broad, ragged, semi-urbanized belt of land surrounding each city, large or small, and quite often melting imperceptibly into the suburban–exurban halo encircling a neighbouring metropolitan centre. A great sameness exists in the makeup and general appearance of all such tracts: the planless intermixture of scraps of the old rural landscape with the fragments of the scattered metropolis; the randomly distributed subdivisions or single homes; the vast shopping centres, the large commercial cemeteries, drive-in theatres, junkyards, and golf courses and other recreational enterprises; and the regional or metropolitan airport, often with its own cluster of factories, warehouses, or travel-oriented businesses. The traditional city—unitary, concentric in form, with a single well-defined middle—was replaced by a relatively amorphous, polycentric metropolitan sprawl.

Present-day inner cities

The inner city of the larger U.S. metropolitan area, now as in the past, displays the basic traits common to the larger centres of all advanced nations. A central business district, almost always the oldest section of the city, is surrounded by a succession of roughly circular zones, each distinctive as to economic and social–ethnic character. The symmetry of this scheme is distorted by the irregularities of surface and drainage or the effects of radial highways and railroads. Land is most costly and hence land use most intensive, toward the centre. Major business, financial and governmental offices, department stores, and specialty shops dominate the downtown, which is usually fringed by a band of factories and warehouses. The outer parts of the city, like the suburbs, are mainly residential.

With some exceptions—*e.g.,* new, large apartment complexes in downtown Chicago—people do not reside in the downtown areas, and there is a steady downward gradient in population density per unit area (and more open land and single-family residences) as one moves from city centre toward open country. Conversely (again with some exceptions), there is a rise in income and social status with increasing distance from the core. The sharply defined immigrant neighbourhoods of the 19th century generally persist in somewhat diluted form, though specific ethnic groups may have shifted their location. Recent migrant groups, notably Southern blacks and Latin Americans, often dominate the more decrepit of the inner-city residential districts.

Individual and collective character of U.S. cities. U.S. cities, more so than the small-town or agrarian landscape, are more the product of period than of place. The relatively venerable centres of the Atlantic Seaboard—Boston; Philadelphia; Baltimore; Albany, New York; Chester, Pennsylvania; Alexandria, Virginia; or Georgetown (a district of Washington, D.C.), for example—are virtual replicas of the fashionable European models of their youth rather than the fruition of a regional culture—as New Orleans and Santa Fe, New Mexico, reflect other times and regions. The townscapes of Pittsburgh, Detroit, Chicago, and Denver speak of national modes of thought and the technologies of their formative years, just as Dallas, Texas; Las Vegas, Nevada; San Diego; Tucson, Arizona; and Albuquerque, New Mexico, proclaim the values and gadgetry of the present, rather than any local distinctiveness. Only when strong-minded city founders instituted a highly individual plan and their successors managed to preserve it—as, for example, in Savannah, Georgia; Washington, D.C.; and Salt Lake City—or when there is a happy match of a spectacular site with an appreciative populace—as in San Francisco or Seattle, Washington—does a genuine individuality seem to emerge. Some such identity may also be developing where immigration has been highly selective, as appears to be happening in such places as Miami; Phoenix, Arizona; and Los Angeles.

As a group, U.S. cities differ from others in both kind and degree. The political structure of the nation, the social inclinations of the people, and the strong outward surge of urban development have led to an unparalleled political fragmentation of metropolises that socially and economically are relatively cohesive units of their own. The fact that a single metropolitan area may sprawl across numerous incorporated towns and cities, several townships, and two or more counties and states has a major impact upon both its appearance and the way it functions. Not the least of these effects is a dearth of overall physical and social planning (or its ineffectuality when attempted), and the rather chaotic, inharmonious appearance of both inner-city and peripheral zones painfully reflects the absence of any strong collective conscience concerning such matters.

Political fragmentation and lack of planning

The U.S. city is a place of sharp transitions in both time and space. Construction, demolition, and reconstruction go on almost ceaselessly, with little thought given to preserving traces of the past. From present evidence, it would be impossible to guess that New York City and Albany date from the 1620s or that Detroit was founded in 1701. Preservation and restoration do occur, but generally only when it makes sense in terms of tourist revenue. Physical and social blight has reached epidemic proportions in the older slum areas of the inner city; but, despite the recent wholesale razing of such areas and the subsequent urban-renewal projects (often as apartment or commercial developments for the affluent), the belief is becoming widespread that the ills of the U.S. city are, in fact, incurable, especially with the increasing flight of capital, tax revenue, and the more highly educated, affluent elements of the population to suburban sanctuaries and the spatial and political polarization of whites and non-whites.

In the central sections of U.S. cities, physical evidence abounds of the weakness of any sense of history, of the dominance of the engineering mentality, and of the credo that the business of the city is business. Commercial and administrative activities are paramount, and usually there is little room for the church buildings or for parks or other nonprofit enterprises. The role of the cathedral, so central in the medieval European city, is filled by a U.S. invention serving both utilitarian and symbolic purposes, the skyscraper. Some cities have felt the need for other bold secular monuments; hence the Jefferson Memorial Arch looming over St. Louis, Seattle's Space Needle, and Houston's Astrodome. Future archaeologists may well conclude from their excavations that American society was ruled by an oligarchy of highway engineers and bulldozer operators. The great expressways converging upon, or looping, the downtown area and the huge amount of space devoted to parking lots and garages are even more impressive than the massive surgery executed upon the vitals of U.S. cities a century ago to hack out room for railroad terminals and marshalling yards.

Altered landforms and landscapes of the city

Within many an urban site, there has been such gross physical transformation of shoreline, drainage systems, and land surface as would be difficult to match elsewhere in the world. Thus, in their physical lineaments, Manhattan and inner Boston bear scant resemblance to the landscapes seen by their initial settlers; the surface of downtown Chicago has been raised several feet above its former swamp level, the city's lakefront extensively reshaped, and the flow of the Chicago River reversed; and present-day Los Angeles, which has become a byword for environmental vandalism, has its concrete arroyo bottoms, terraced hillsides and landslides, and its own man-induced microclimate.

The super-cities of the United States. In the unprecedented outward sprawl of urban settlement, the United States has created some novel settlement forms, for the quantitative change has been so great as to induce qualitative transformation. The conurbation—a territorial coalescence of two or more good-sized cities whose peripheral zones have grown together—may have first appeared in early-19th-century Europe. There are major examples in Great Britain, the Low Countries, and West Germany, as well as in Japan.

Megalopolis: concept and forms

Nothing elsewhere, however, rivals in sheer size and complexity the aptly named megalopolis, that super-city of more than 30,000,000 inhabitants stretching along the Atlantic Seaboard from southern Maine to central Virginia. Other large conurbations include, in the Great Lakes region, one centred on Chicago and containing large slices of Illinois, Wisconsin, and Indiana; another based in Detroit, embracing large parts of Michigan and Ohio and reaching into Canada; and a third stretching from Buffalo through Cleveland and back to Pittsburgh. All three are reaching out toward one another and will shortly form another megalopolis, one that, in turn, may soon be grafted onto the seaboard megalopolis by way of a corridor through central New York state.

Also worthy of note is the huge Southern California conurbation reaching from Santa Barbara, through a dominating Los Angeles, to the Mexican border. A lesser counterpart exists as a solid strip of urban territory lining the eastern shore of Puget Sound. Quite exceptional in form is the slender linear multi-city occupying Florida's Atlantic coastline, from Jacksonville to Miami, and the loose swarm of medium-sized cities clustering along the Southern Piedmont, from south central Virginia to Atlanta.

One of the few predictions that seem safe in so dynamic and innovative a land as the United States is that, unless some severe and painful controls are placed on land use by powerful governmental agencies, the shape of the urban environment will be increasingly megalopolitan: a small set of great constellations of polycentric urban zones, each complexly interlocked socially and physically with its neighbours.

TRADITIONAL REGIONS OF THE UNITED STATES

The differences among U.S. "traditional regions," or "culture areas," tend to be slight and shallow as compared with such areas in most older, more stable countries. The muted, often subtle nature of interregional differences can be ascribed to the relative newness of U.S. settlement, a perpetually high degree of mobility, a superb communication system, and the galloping centralization of economy and government. It might even be argued that some of these regions are quaint vestiges of a vanishing past, of interest only to antiquarians.

Yet, in spite of the nationwide standardization in many departments of U.S. thought and behaviour, the lingering effects of the older culture areas do remain potent. Indeed, in one instance, that of the South, the differences helped to precipitate the gravest political crisis and bloodiest military conflict in the nation's history. And more than a century after the Civil War, the South remains a powerful entity in political and social terms, and its peculiar status is formally recognized in religious, educational, athletic, and literary circles.

Even more intriguing is the appearance of a series of essentially 20th-century regions. The Southern Californian is the largest and most distinctive, and its quite special culture has yet to reach full bloom. Similar trends are visible in southern Florida, in the burgeoning Texas identity, and probably in the more ebullient segments of New Mexico and Arizona as well. At the metropolitan level, it is difficult to believe that such aggressively narcissistic cities as San Francisco, Las Vegas, Dallas, Tucson, and Seattle are becoming like all other American cities. In any event, a detailed examination would show significant if sometimes subtle interregional differences in terms of language, religion, diet, folklore, folk architecture and handicrafts, political behaviour, social etiquette, and any number of other cultural categories.

The hierarchy of culture areas. A multi-tiered hierarchy of culture areas might be postulated for the United States; but the most interesting levels are, first, the nation as a whole and, second, the five to ten large subnational regions, each comprising parts or the entirety of several states. A remarkably close coincidence exists between the political United States and the cultural United States. Crossing into Mexico, the traveller negotiates a passage across a cultural chasm. If the contrasts are less dramatic between the two sides of the U.S.–Canadian boundary, they are nonetheless real, especially to the Canadian. The cultural barrier has been eroded along only a single major segment of the international frontiers: that reaching from northern New York state to Aroostook County, Maine. There, a vigorous demographic and cultural invasion by French-Canadians has gone far toward eradicating international differences.

Relation of political and cultural boundaries

If the international boundaries act as a cultural container, the interstate boundaries are curiously irrelevant. Even when the state enjoyed a strong autonomous early existence—as happened with Massachusetts, Virginia, or Pennsylvania—subsequent economic and political forces have tended to wash away such initial identities. Actually, it could be argued that the existence of 48 conterminous states is anachronistic in the context of contemporary socio-economic realities, not to mention cultural forces. Partially convincing cases might be built for equating Utah and Texas with their respective culture areas because of exceptional historical and physical circumstances or perhaps Oklahoma, given its very tardy European occupation and unique status as dumping ground for the relict Indian tribes of the East. In most instances, however, the states either contain two or more distinctly different culture areas or fragments thereof or are part of a much larger single culture area. Thus sharp North–South dichotomies characterize California, Missouri, Illinois, Indiana, Ohio, and Florida, while Tennessee advertises that, in fact, there are really three Tennessees. In Virginia, the opposing cultural forces were so strong that actual fission took place in 1863 (with the admission to the Union of West Virginia) along one of those rare interstate boundaries that approximate a genuine cultural divide.

Indefinite relation of cultures and economies

Much remains to be learned about the cause and effect relations between economic and culture areas in the U.S. If the South or New England could at one time be correlated with a specific economic system, this is no longer easy to do. Cultural systems appear to respond more slowly to agents of change than do economic or urban systems. Thus the American Manufacturing Belt, a core region for many social and economic activities, now spans major parts of three traditional culture areas—New England, the Midland, and the Middle West—and the northern fringes of a fourth, the South. And the great urban sprawl, from southern Maine to central Virginia, blithely ignores the steep relict cultural slopes still visible in its more bucolic tracts.

The cultural hearths. The culture areas of the modern United States are European in origin, the result of importing European colonists and ways of life and the subsequent interactions among and within social groups and with a novel set of habitats. In the large picture, the aboriginal cultures remain territorially insignificant. In the Southwestern and the indistinct Oklahoman subregions, the Indian element merits consideration only as one of several ingredients making up the regional mosaic. With minor exceptions, the map of contemporary U.S. culture areas can be explained in terms of the genesis, development, and expansion of the three principal colonial cultural hearths along the Atlantic Seaboard. Each was basically British in character, but their personalities remain distinct because of, first, different sets of social and political conditions during the critical period of first effective settlement and, second, localized physical and economic circumstances. The cultural gradients between them tend to be much steeper and the boundaries more distinct than is true for the remainder of the continent.

New England. New England was clearly the dominant region during the century of national expansion following the American Revolution and not merely in terms of demographic or economic expansion. In social and cultural life—in education, politics, theology, literature, science, architecture, and the more advanced forms of mechanical and social technology—the area exercised its primacy. New England was the leading source of ideas and styles for the nation from about 1780 to 1880; it furnishes an impressive example of the capacity of strongly motivated communities for rising above the constraints of a parsimonious environment.

During the first two centuries of its existence, New England was unusually homogeneous in its population characteristics. With rare exceptions, the British immigrant stock shared the same religion (Congregationalist), language, social organization, and general outlook. Over the years a distinctive regional culture took form, most noticeably in terms of dialect, town morphology, and folk architecture. The personality of the people also took on a regional coloration both in folklore and in actuality: there is a sound basis for the belief that the New England Yankee is self-reliant, thrifty, inventive, and highly enterprising. The massive influx of the foreign-born that began in the 1830s diluted and altered the New England identity, but much of its early personality survived.

By virtue of location, wealth, and seniority, the Boston metropolitan area has acted as the functional hub for all of New England both culturally and economically. This sovereignty is shared to some degree, however, with two other old centres, the lower Connecticut Valley and the Narragansett Bay region of Rhode Island.

The early westward demographic and ideological expansion of New England was so persistent that it is justifiable to call New York, northern New Jersey, northern Pennsylvania, and much of the Upper Middle West "New England Extended." Further, the energetic endeavours of New England whalers, merchants, and missionaries resulted in a perceptible imprinting of population or culture or both in Hawaii, various other Pacific isles, and scattered points in the Caribbean. New Englanders were also active in the Americanization of early Oregon and Washington, with results visible to this day. Later, the overland diffusion of New England natives and practices meant a recognizable New England flavour not only for the Upper Midwest, from Ohio to the Dakotas, but also more dilutely in the Pacific Northwest in general.

The South. By far the largest of the three primordial Anglo-American culture areas, the South is also the most aberrant with respect to national norms—or slowest to accept them. Indeed, the South has been so distinct from the non-South in almost every observable or quantifiable feature and so fiercely jealous of its peculiarities that for some years the question of whether it could maintain political and social unity with the non-South was in serious doubt. These differences are observable in almost every realm of human activity, including rural economy, dialect, diet, costume, folklore, politics, architecture, social customs, and recreation. Only during the 20th century can an argument be made that it has achieved a decisive convergence with the rest of the nation, at least in terms of economic behaviour and material culture.

Southern deviation from the U.S. mainstream

An early, persistent deviation from the national mainstream probably commenced during the first years of settlement. The settlers of the South were almost purely British, not outwardly different from the British, Welsh, or Scots-Irish who flocked to New England or the Midland but almost certainly distinct in terms of motives and social values and more conservative in retaining the rurality and the family and social structure of premodern Europe. The vast importation of African slaves was surely a factor, as was a degree of interaction with the aborigines that was missing farther north. And certainly the unusual (for northwest Europeans) pattern of economy, settlement, and social organization, in part a matter of a starkly unfamiliar physical habitat, may have prompted a deviation from other culture areas.

In both origin and spatial structure, the South has been characterized by diffuseness. In the search for a single cultural hearth, the most plausible choice is the Chesapeake Bay area and the northeastern corner of North Carolina, the earliest area of recognizably Southern character. Early components of Southern population and culture also arrived from other sources. A narrow coastal strip from North Carolina to the Georgia–Florida border and including the Sea Islands is decidedly Southern in flavour, yet it stands apart self-consciously from other parts of the South. Though colonized directly from Great Britain, it had also significant connections with the West Indies, in which relation the African cultural contribution was strongest and purest. The cities of Charleston and Savannah, which nurtured their own quite special civilizations, dominated this subregion in every sense. Similarly, French Louisiana received elements of culture and population—to be stirred into the special Creole mixture—not only from a putative Chesapeake Bay hearth area but also indirectly from France, French Nova Scotia, the French West Indies, and Africa. In the case of south central Texas, the Teutonic influx was so heavy that a special subregion can quite properly be designated.

It would seem, then, that the Southern culture area may be an example of convergent, or parallel, evolution of a variety of elements arriving along several paths but subject to some single general process that could mold one larger regional consciousness and way of life.

Because of its slowness in joining the national technological mainstream, the South can be subdivided into a much greater number of subregions than is possible for any of the other older traditional regions. Those described above are of lesser order than the two principal Souths, variously called Upper and Lower (or Deep) South, Upland and Lowland South, or Yeoman and Plantation South.

The former, which comprises the southern Appalachians, the upper Appalachian Piedmont, the Cumberland and other low interior plateaus, and the Ozarks and Ouachitas, was colonized culturally and demographically from two sources—the Chesapeake Bay hearth area and the early Midland; it is most emphatically white Anglo-Saxon Protestant in character. The latter area, which contains a large Afro-American population, includes the greater part of the South Atlantic and Gulf coastal plains and the lower Appalachian Piedmont. Its early major influences came principally from the Chesapeake Bay area, with only minor elements from the coastal Carolina–Georgia belt, Louisiana, or elsewhere. The division between the two subregions remains distinct from Virginia to Texas, but each region can be further broken down. Within the Upland South, the Ozark segment might legitimately be detached from the Appalachian; and, within the latter, the proud and prosperous Kentucky Bluegrass, with its emphasis on tobacco and thoroughbreds, certainly merits special recognition.

Toward the margins of the South, the difficulties in delimiting subregions become greater. The outer limits themselves are a topic of special interest. There seems to be more than an accidental relation between these limits and various climate factors. The fuzzy northern boundary, definitely not associated with the conventional Mason and Dixon Line or the Ohio River, seems most closely associated with length of frost-free season or with temperature during the winter months. As the Southern cultural complex was carried to the West, it not only retained its strength but became even more intense, in contrast to the experience of New England and the Midland. But the South finally fades away as one approaches the 100th meridian, with its critical decline in annual precipitation. The apparent correlation of the cultural South with a humid subtropical climatic regime is an old but provocative one.

The Texas subregion is so large, unmistakable, vigorous, and self-assertive that it presents some vexing classificatory questions. Is Texas simply a subordinate fraction of the Greater South, or has it now acquired so strong and divergent an identity that it can be denoted a new first-order region? It is conceivable that a major region is being born in a frontier zone in which several distinct cultural communities confront one another and in which the mixture has bred the vigorous, extroverted, aggressive Texas personality so widely celebrated in song and story. Similarly, peninsular Florida is either within or juxtaposed to the South but without being unequivocally part of it. In this case, an almost empty territory began to receive significant settlement only after about 1890; and, if like Texas, most of it came from the older South, there were also vigorous infusions from elsewhere.

The Midland. The significance of this region has not been slighter than that of New England or the South, but its characteristics are the least conspicuous to outsiders as well as to its own inhabitants—reflecting, perhaps, its centrality in the course of U.S. development. The Midland (a term not to be confused with Middle West) comprises portions of the following Middle Atlantic and Upper Southern states: Pennsylvania, New Jersey, Maryland, and Delaware. Serious European settlement of the Midland began a generation or more after that of the other major cultural nodes and after several earlier, relatively ineffectual trials by the Dutch, Swedes, Finns, and British. But once begun late in the 17th century by William Penn and associates, the colonization of the area was an instant success. Within southeastern Pennsylvania this culture area first assumed its distinctive form: a prosperous, sober, industrious agricultural society that quickly became a mixed economy as mercantile and later industrial functions came to the fore. By the middle of the 18th century, much of the region had acquired a markedly urban character, resembling in many ways the more advanced portions of the North Sea countries. In this respect, at least, the Midland was well ahead of neighbouring areas to the north and south.

It differed also in its polyglot ethnicity. From almost the very beginning, the various ethnic and religious groups of the British Isles were joined by immigrants from the European mainland. This diversity has, if anything, grown through the years—and promises to persevere indefinitely. The mosaic of colonial ethnic groups has persisted in much of Pennsylvania, New York, New Jersey, and Maryland, as has the remarkable variety of more recent nationalities and churches in coalfields, company towns, cities large and small, and many a rural tract. Much the same sort of ethnic heterogeneity is to be seen in New England, the Middle West, and a few other areas, but the Midland still stands out as perhaps the most polyglot region of the nation.

The Teutonic element has always been notably strong, if irregularly distributed, in the Midland, accounting for more than 70 percent of the population of many townships. Had not the Anglo-American culture finally proved supreme, the area might well be designated as Pennsylvania German.

Considerations of physiography and migrational history carried the Midland culture area into the Maryland Piedmont; and, although its width tapers quickly below the Potomac, it reaches into parts of Virginia and West Virginia, with traces legible far down the Appalachian zone and into the South in general.

The northern half of the greater Midland region (the New York subregion, or New England Extended) cannot be assigned unequivocally to either New England

Polyglot nature of the Midland culture

or this Midland. Essentially it is a hybrid formed mainly from two parental strains of almost equal potency: New England and the post-1660 British element moving up the Hudson Valley and beyond. In addition, there has been a persistent, if slight, residue of early Dutch culture and some subtle filtering northward of Pennsylvania influences. Within the New York subregion apparently occurred the first major intra-American blending and fusion of regional cultures, especially within the early-19th-century "Burned-Over District," in and near the Finger Lakes and Genesee areas of central and western New York state. This locality, the seedbed for a number of important social innovations, was a major staging area for westward migration and quite possibly a chief source for the people and notions that were to build the Middle Western culture area.

Toward the west, the Midland retains its integrity for only a short distance—certainly no further than eastern Ohio—as it becomes submerged within the Middle West. Still, its significance in the genesis of the Middle West or of the national culture cannot be belittled. Its very success in projecting its image upon so much of the country may have rendered the source area less visible. As both name and location suggest, the Midland is intermediate in character in many respects, as between New England and the South. Moreover, its residents are much less concerned with, or conscious of, its existence (excepting the "Pennsylvania Dutch" caricatures) than is true for the other regions, and, in addition, the Midland lacks their strong political and literary traditions, though it is unmistakable in its distinctive townscapes and farmsteads.

The newer culture areas. *The Middle West.* No such self-effacement exists in the Middle West, that large triangular region justly regarded as the most nearly representative of the national average. Everyone within or outside the Middle West knows of its existence, but no one is certain where it begins or ends. The older apex of the eastward-pointing triangle appears to rest around Pittsburgh, while the two western corners melt away somewhere in the Great Plains, possibly in southern Manitoba in the north and southern Kansas in the south. The eastern terminus and the southern and western borders are broad, indistinct transitional zones.

This historical geography of the Middle West remains largely unstudied, but it seems plausible that this culture region was the progeny of all three colonial regions and that the fertile union took place in the upper Ohio Valley. The early routes of travel—the Ohio and its tributaries, the Great Lakes, and the low, level corridor along the Mohawk and the Lake Ontario and Lake Erie coastal plains—converge upon Ohio. There, the people and cultural traits from New England, the Midland, and the South were first funnelled together. Thence there would seem to have been a fanlike widening of the new hybrid area into the West as pioneer settlers worked their way frontierward.

Two major subregions are readily discerned, the Upper and Lower Middle West. They are separated by a line roughly approximating the 41st parallel, one that persists as far west as Colorado in terms of speech patterns and indicates differences in regional provenance in ethnic and religious terms as well. Much of the Upper Middle West retains a faint New England bouquet, although Midland influences are probably as important. A rich mixture of German, Scandinavian, Slavic, and other non-WASP elements has greatly diversified a stock in which the British element usually remains dominant and the range of church denominations is great. The Lower Middle West, except for the relative scarcity of Negroes, tends to resemble the South in its predominantly Protestant and British makeup. Local exceptions include areas of Catholic and non-WASP strength, but on the whole the subregion tends to be more nativistic in inclination than most other parts of the nation.

The problem of "the West." The foregoing culture areas account for roughly the eastern half of the conterminous United States. A genuine dilemma exists in classifying the remaining half. The concept of an "American West," strong in the popular imagination, is reinforced constant-

Contrasts of Upper and Lower Middle West

ly by romanticized cinematic and TV images of the cowboy. It is tempting to accept the widespread Western livestock complex as somehow epitomizing the full gamut of Western life, but, although the cattle industry may have accounted for more than one-half of the active Western domain as measured in acres, it employed only a relatively small fraction of the total population. As a single subculture, it cannot bear the burden of representing the total regional culture.

It is not clear whether a genuine, single, grand Western culture region exists. Unlike the East, in which settlement is virtually continuous through space and in which culture areas and subregions abut and overlap in splendid confusion, the eight major and many lesser nodes of population in the western United States are all oasis-like, separated from one another by wide expanses of nearly uninhabited mountain or arid desert. The only obvious properties these isolated clusters have in common are, first, the recent intermixture of several strains of culture, primarily from the East but with additions from Europe, Mexico and East Asia, and, second, except for one subregion, a general modernity, having been settled in a serious way no earlier than the 1840s. Some may be viewed as inchoate, partially formed cultural entities; the others have acquired definite personalities but are difficult to classify as first-order or lesser order culture areas at this time.

There are three (or, possibly, four) major tracts in the western United States that reveal a genuine cultural identity: the Upper Rio Grande region; the Mormon region; Southern California; and Northern California. (To this group one might add the anomalous Texan and Oklahoman subregions, which may adhere to the South, to the West, or to both).

Upper Rio Grande and Mormon regions

The term Upper Rio Grande region was coined to denote the oldest and strongest of the three sectors of Hispanic-American activity in the U.S. Southwest, the others having been Southern California and portions of Texas. Although focussed upon the valley of the Upper Rio Grande, the region also embraces segments of Arizona and Colorado as well as other parts of New Mexico. European communities and culture have been present there in strength, with only one interruption, since the late 16th century. The initial sources were Spain and Mexico, but after 1848 at least three distinct strains of Anglo-American culture were increasingly well represented—the Southern, Mormon, and a general undifferentiated northeastern U.S. culture—plus a distinct Texan subcategory. For once, this has occurred without obliterating the aboriginal folk, whose culture endures in various stages of dilution, from the strongly Americanized or Hispanicized to the almost undisturbed.

The general mosaic is a fabric of aboriginal, Anglo, and Hispanic elements, and all three major groups, furthermore, are complex in character. The aboriginal component embraces the Navajo, Pueblos, and several smaller groups, each of which is quite distinct from the others. The Hispanic element is also diverse—modally Mexican mestizo, but ranging from pure Spanish to nearly pure pre-Spanish aboriginal.

The Mormon region is expansive in the religious and demographic realms, though it has ceased to expand territorially as it did in the decades after Utah's settlement in 1847. Despite its Great Basin location and an exemplary adaptation to environmental constraints, this cultural complex appears somewhat non-Western in spirit: the Mormons may be in the West, but they are not entirely of it. Their historical derivation from the Middle West and from ultimate sources in New York and New England is still apparent, along with the generous admixture of European converts to their religion.

Here again, as in New England, the power of the human will and an intensely cherished abstract design have triumphed over an unfriendly habitat. The Mormon way of life is expressed in many recognizable ways in the settlement landscape and economic activities within a region more homogeneous internally than any other U.S. culture area.

In contrast, the Northern California region has yet to gain its own strong cultural coloration. From the beginning of the great 1849 Gold Rush, the area drew a thoroughly diverse population from Europe and Asia as well as the older portions of the United States. Whether the greater part of the Northern California region has produced a culture amounting to more than the sum of the contributions brought by immigrants is questionable. San Francisco, the regional metropolis, may have crossed the qualitative threshold. An unusually cosmopolitan outlook that includes an awareness of the Orient stronger than that of any other U.S. city, a fierce self-esteem, and a unique townscape may be symptomatic of a genuinely new, emergent local culture.

Northern and Southern California regions

The Southern California region is the most spectacular of the Western regions, not only in terms of economic and population growth but also for the luxuriance, regional particularism, and general avant-garde character of its swiftly evolving cultural pattern. Until the coming of a direct transcontinental rail connection in 1885, the region was remote, rural, and largely inconsequential. Since then, the invasion by persons from virtually every corner of North America and by the foreign-born has been massive and, until the late 1960s, apparently ceaseless. A loosely articulated series of conurbations has encroached upon what little is left of arable or habitable land in the Coast Ranges and valleys from Santa Barbara to the Mexican border.

Although every significant ethnic and racial group and every other U.S. culture area is amply represented, there is reason to suspect that a process of selection for certain kinds of people, attitudes, and personality traits may have been at work at both source and destination. Certainly the region is aberrant from, or perhaps in the vanguard of, the remainder of the nation. One might view Southern California as the super-American region or the outpost of a rapidly approaching postindustrial future; but, in any event, its cultural distinctiveness, in visible landscape and social behaviour, is evident to all. Southern California in no way approaches being a "traditional region," or even the smudged facsimile of such, but rather the largest, boldest experiment in creating a "voluntary region," one built through the self-selection of immigrants and their subsequent interaction.

The remaining identifiable Western regions—the Willamette Valley of Oregon, the Puget Sound region, the Inland Empire of eastern Washington and adjacent tracts of Idaho and Oregon, central Arizona, and the Colorado Piedmont—can be treated jointly as potential, or emergent, culture areas, still too close to the national mean to display any cultural distinctiveness. In all are evident the arrival of a cross section of the national population and the growth of regional life around one or more major metropolises. A New England element is noteworthy in the Willamette Valley and Puget Sound regions, while a Hispanic-American component appears in the Colorado Piedmont and central Arizona. Only time and further study will reveal whether any of these regions, so distant from the historic sources of U.S. population and culture, can engender the capacity or will for an independent cultural existence.   (W.Ze.)

Emergent culture areas of the West

III. The people of the United States

As they entered the 1970s, a majority of the people of the United States had achieved a relatively high level of material comfort, prosperity, and security. They appear to be, however, in a bad and divided mood. They were worried about crime, racial injustice, urban decay, the war in Vietnam, environmental pollution, narcotics, alienation among the young, and the high cost of living. Moreover, they were unhappy: to a public-opinion-poll question that asked "Do you believe that life is getting better or worse in terms of happiness?" nearly half (49 percent) of the respondents, who live in the country in which the standard of living is the highest in the world, glumly answered "worse."

Social unrest and tensions and divisions among its citizens were, such attitude surveys showed, the major causes of this general malaise. Many Americans perceived these as caused by the failure of U.S. society to extend

Table 1: United States, Area and Population

Divisions	area* sq mi	area* sq km	population 1960 census	population 1970 census	Divisions	area* sq mi	area* sq km	population 1960 census	population 1970 census
Divisions					**Divisions**				
East North Central	244,366	632,905†	36,225,000	40,253,000	Pacific	892,266	2,310,958	21,198,000	26,522,000
	248,283	643,050				916,728	2,374,315		
States					**States**				
Illinois	55,877	144,721	10,081,000	11,114,000	Alaska	566,432	1,467,052	226,000	300,000
	56,400	146,075				586,412	1,518,800		
Indiana	36,189	93,729	4,662,000	5,194,000	California	156,537	405,429	15,717,000	19,953,000
	36,291	93,993				158,693	411,013		
Michigan	56,818	147,158	7,823,000	8,875,000	Hawaii	6,425	16,641	633,000	769,000
	58,216	150,779				6,450	16,705		
Ohio	41,018	106,236	9,706,000	10,652,000	Oregon	96,209	249,180	1,769,000	2,091,000
	41,222	106,764				96,981	251,180		
Wisconsin	54,464	141,061	3,952,000	4,418,000	Washington	66,663	172,656	2,853,000	3,409,000
	56,154	145,438				68,192	176,616		
East South Central	179,427	464,714	12,050,000	12,804,000					
	181,964	471,285†			South Atlantic	267,352	692,438†	25,972,000	30,671,000
States						278,776	722,027		
Alabama	50,851	131,703	3,267,000	3,444,000	**States**				
	51,609	133,667			Delaware	1,982	5,133	446,000	548,000
Kentucky	39,851	103,214	3,038,000	3,219,000		2,057	5,328		
	40,395	104,623			District of	61	158	764,000	757,000
Mississippi	47,358	122,657	2,178,000	2,217,000	Columbia‡	67	174		
	47,716	123,584			Florida	54,136	140,212	4,952,000	6,789,000
Tennessee	41,367	107,140	3,567,000	3,924,000		58,560	151,670		
	42,244	109,411			Georgia	58,197	150,730	3,943,000	4,590,000
Middle Atlantic	100,426	260,102†	34,168,000	37,199,000		58,876	152,488		
	102,745	266,108†			Maryland	9,891	25,618	3,101,000	3,922,000
States						10,577	27,394		
New Jersey	7,532	19,508	6,067,000	7,168,000	North Carolina	48,880	126,599	4,556,000	5,082,000
	7,836	20,295				52,586	136,197		
New York	47,869	123,980	16,782,000	18,237,000	South Carolina	30,280	78,425	2,383,000	2,591,000
	49,576	128,401				31,055	80,432		
Pennsylvania	45,025	116,614	11,319,000	11,794,000	Virginia	39,841	103,188	3,967,000	4,648,000
	45,333	117,412				40,817	105,716		
Mountain	856,633	2,218,669†	6,855,000	8,281,000	West Virginia	24,084	62,377	1,860,000	1,744,000
	863,887	2,237,457†				24,181	62,629		
States									
Arizona	113,563	294,127	1,302,000	1,771,000	West North Central	508,192	1,316,211	15,394,000	16,320,000
	113,909	295,023				517,247	1,339,664		
Colorado	103,794	268,825	1,754,000	2,207,000	**States**				
	104,247	270,000			Iowa	56,043	145,151	2,758,000	2,824,000
Idaho	82,677	214,107	667,000	713,000		56,290	145,790		
	83,557	216,412			Kansas	82,056	212,524	2,179,000	2,247,000
Montana	145,603	377,110	675,000	694,000		82,264	213,063		
	147,138	381,086			Minnesota	79,289	205,356	3,414,000	3,805,000
Nevada	109,889	284,611	285,000	489,000		84,068	217,735		
	110,540	286,297			Missouri	69,046	178,828	4,320,000	4,677,000
New Mexico	121,445	314,541	951,000	1,016,000		69,686	180,486		
	121,666	315,113			Nebraska	76,522	198,191	1,411,000	1,483,000
Utah	82,381	213,366	891,000	1,059,000		77,227	200,017		
	84,916	219,931			North Dakota	69,280	179,434	632,000	618,000
Wyoming	97,281	251,957	330,000	332,000		70,665	183,022		
	97,914	253,596			South Dakota	75,956	196,725	681,000	666,000
New England	62,992	163,149†	10,509,000	11,842,000		77,047	199,551		
	66,608	172,514†							
States					West South Central	429,284	1,111,840†	16,951,000	19,320,000
Connecticut	4,870	12,613	2,535,000	3,032,000		438,884	1,136,704		
	5,009	12,973			**States**				
Maine	30,933	80,116	969,000	992,000	Arkansas	52,175	135,133	1,786,000	1,923,000
	33,215	86,026				53,104	137,539		
Massachusetts	7,833	20,287	5,149,000	5,689,000	Louisiana	45,155	116,951	3,257,000	3,641,000
	8,257	21,386				48,523	125,674		
New Hampshire	9,033	23,395	607,000	738,000	Oklahoma	68,984	178,668	2,328,000	2,559,000
	9,304	24,097				69,919	181,089		
Rhode Island	1,049	2,717	859,000	947,000	Texas	262,970	681,089	9,580,000	11,197,000
	1,214	3,144				267,338	692,402		
Vermont	9,274	24,020	390,000	444,000	Total United States	3,540,938	9,170,987	179,323,000§	203,212,000§
	9,609	24,887				3,615,122	9,363,123†		

*Where two figures are given, the first is the land area, the second the total area.   †Converted area figures do not add to total given because of rounding.   ‡District of Columbia is a federal district.   §Figures do not add to total given because of rounding.
Source: Official government figures.

what is traditionally called the "American dream" equally to all its people, particularly to those who were members of minority groups. The traditional spirit of U.S. society had characterized the nation as a democratic "land of opportunity," in which social, political, economic, and religious freedom prevail, one man is as good as another, and every man can achieve if only he will.

A shared belief in such egalitarian ideals is often seen as being perhaps the strongest bond that has united Americans, and the fact that the nation has not achieved equality for all troubles the American soul. More than half of all Americans say, according to opinion polls, that they "often feel bad" about the poverty and hunger that exist in the United States. One in three says he "often feels bad" about the treatment of Negroes and the American Indian. Nearly two out of three agree that "Until there is justice for minorities, there will not be law and order" in the United States.

The population of the United States is the most widely diverse of any nation in the world. It is possible to create pictures of statistically "typical" Americans—the average U.S. voter, for example, is a 47-year-old housewife who lives in the outskirts of Dayton, Ohio, and whose husband works as a machinist. Far more typical, however, is the fact that, on a recent summer Sunday in Chicago, three queens were being crowned: one by the Polish National Alliance, another by the Scandinavian Midsummer Night Festival, and a third to lead the annual Puerto Rican Independence Day parade. The United States is not homogeneous; it is a pluralistic

Social pluralism and the "melting-pot" myth

society, a nation of groups. The long cherished belief that the United States has been a great "melting pot" in which people from all nations and cultures have blended into what are called "Americans" is a myth. In the early 1970s a strong trend among United States minorities, black and white, to organize groups to press for social change made the American people increasingly conscious of the characteristics of the various ethnic and racial groups that make up the population of the United States.

THE MIX OF PEOPLES

The "old-stock" Americans. Until about 1860, the population of the United States was relatively homogeneous. It was overwhelmingly white, Anglo-Saxon (the majority had come originally from the British Isles), and Protestant. Of the 5,000,000 European immigrants who had entered the United States between 1820 and 1860, nine out of ten were from England, Ireland, or Germany. With the exception of some of the Irish Catholics, these early immigrants, many of whom were barely distinguishable from the native stock, were easily assimilated by the English Protestant United States.

After the Civil War, however, ever larger numbers of immigrants began to arrive from the countries of central and southeastern Europe: Italy, the Balkans, Poland, and Russia. This vast group of newcomers, some 30,000,000 of them from 1860 to 1920, flooded the U.S. cities. Most were non-English, non-Protestant, and markedly different in culture and language from the older Americans. The immigrants established their own neighbourhoods and rapidly developed ethnic societies, clubs, newspapers, and theatres; and their living areas became distinctive cultural and social enclaves within the larger U.S. society.

The immigrants, however separate, were not denied access to the mainstreams of U.S. life. It was an open society, and those with ability and intelligence usually achieved success—and some achieved greatness.

The old-stock English Protestants who remained the dominant U.S. cultural group came, in time, to be defined by the fact that they were not immigrants or the descendants of recent immigrants. Today, the term WASP (for White Anglo-Saxon Protestant) is frequently used to describe all those—including such groups as the Dutch and Scots-Irish—whose assimilation has become so complete that the national origins of their families have become merely a memory. They comprise about 45 percent of the U.S. population.

The "Yankee Patricians" among them still retain a firm grip on the U.S. social order. They are predominant in the headquarters of large corporations, banks, insurance companies, law offices, and educational, cultural, and philanthropic institutions. Many other less affluent old-stock white Protestants are concentrated in the rural areas of the United States and in the South.

The "ethnics." The term ethnics was coined in the early 1970s to describe the 40,000,000 Americans of Polish, Italian, Lithuanian, Bohemian, Slovakian, and other extraction, most of whom live in the northern and Middle Western cities. They are Catholic, middle-class (with incomes ranging from $7,000 to $11,000 per year), and most are workers, either part of the blue-collar labour force or holders of low-level white-collar jobs.

Group identity of the white "ethnics"

The neighbourhoods in which most of them still live have their roots in the many "Little Italys" and "Polish Hills" established by the immigrants. Their strong ethnic ties are apparent in the pattern of their lives: spouses, friends, neighbours, fellow churchmembers, and even co-workers are usually also Polish or Italian or Slovakian.

Their ethnic group identity is not, however, merely a holdover from the era of mass immigration. It is based not only upon a common cultural heritage but also on the fact that the group has common interests, needs, and problems in present-day United States. Concentrated in the inner cities, the white ethnics are intimately affected by high crime rates, deteriorating municipal services, inferior schools, and urban unrest. They fear

losing their jobs and neighbourhoods to blacks. Neither rich nor poor, they anxiously watch their purchasing power being diminished by inflation and rising taxes.

As the children and grandchildren of immigrants, they have been taught to believe that the road to success in the United States is achieved through individual effort. They believe in equality of opportunity and self-improvement, and they attribute poverty to the failing of the individual and not to inequities in society. This attitude makes them largely unsympathetic to the demands of Negro groups, to student protest (which they tend to view as the antics of spoiled children of the rich), and to the peace movement, which they regard as un-American, especially since their own sons, who did not attend college, made up a large percentage of the fighting force in Vietnam.

As the ethnics became more vocal in the early 1970s, the public became aware of the problems and concerns of the urban ethnic minorities and stopped dismissing them as merely "racist" or "uneducated." Ethnic groups began to be included in the planning and administration of social-welfare programs of government or foundations, and an ethnic identity was no longer looked upon as somehow un-American and vaguely shameful. It had become legitimate to be an "ethnic."

The blacks. The civil-rights movement that gained momentum in the early 1960s awakened the nation's conscience to the fact that black Americans, who constitute 11 percent of the population, had long been denied first-class citizenship. By 1970, despite government poverty programs and equal-opportunity laws that outlawed discrimination in education, housing and employment, blacks remained clearly unequal partners in U.S. society. Their median family income was only 64 percent that of whites. Half of all white families had incomes over $10,000, while only 24 percent of black families had reached that income level. About one in three black persons had an income below the poverty line, as compared to one in ten whites. Although 62 percent of the whites had completed high school, only 40 percent of the adult blacks had done so. Blacks represented 11 percent of the labour force, yet held only 5 percent of the better paying jobs. Two out of five black men remained in low-paid service, labouring, or farm occupations. The black population nonetheless had made important advances between 1960 and 1970. Their share of the higher paying jobs had increased by 72 percent. Median income had increased 100 percent. Black college enrollment had almost doubled.

Militancy among the blacks

The civil-rights movement prior to the mid-1960s was largely middle-class and interracial; it had used nonviolence and passive resistance to change discriminatory laws and practices, primarily in the South. It aimed for an integration of blacks into U.S. life. For the militants who later arose from the urban poor in the North and West, separatism replaced integration as the primary objective. The militants rejected the U.S. cultural mainstream and spoke instead of black pride, of "soul," of Afro-American history and culture. Instead of attempting to bring change through the moral persuasion of white governmental bodies and institutions, the militants aimed for black autonomy and community control. They turned their attention to developing black political organizations that would give them a position of bargaining strength and political control over their own communities. Most frightening to whites, the militants rejected nonviolence and proclaimed the need for self-defense to protect themselves from police harassment in the city ghetto. The militant movement was strongest among the young; and, as the nation moved into the 1970s, urban high schools had become centres of black protest, with students demanding community control of the schools and the development of educational programs relevant to black history and black needs.

There were strong indications that the majority of blacks generally support the more militant posture. The militants' concern with the daily problems of ghetto living speaks directly to the three out of five blacks who live in inner-city areas. Moreover, sociological studies and public-opinion polls made subsequent to riots and demonstrations indicate that, though deploring violence and destruction, blacks generally view militant-type activities as useful and legitimate forms of protest.

The Spanish-Americans. Persons with Spanish surnames make up about 5 percent of the American population. About half of them are of Mexican origin, the descendants of ancestors who settled in areas that were once part of Mexico. A majority of these still live in Arizona, California, Colorado, New Mexico, and Texas. Another 16 percent of the Spanish-Americans are of Puerto Rican origin; they are concentrated in New York City. Six percent are fairly recent immigrants of Cuban origin who have settled in or near Miami.

Although the Spanish-Americans have experienced less outright discrimination than the blacks, they, like the blacks, have a generally lower economic and educational level than the rest of the population. Family income is only 70 percent that of white families. They are only half as likely to hold white-collar jobs as the rest of the population and are twice as likely to be unemployed, and they have about 3½ years less education than the average American. Although four out of five Spanish-Americans were born in the United States or the Commonwealth of Puerto Rico, Spanish is the main language in about half of the homes. The continued use of Spanish indicates the strength of the bonds that tie Spanish-Americans together.

After generations of quiet acceptance and near-invisibility, Mexican-Americans began to organize in the 1960s. Following the example of black activism, Mexican-Americans formed groups in the barrios of such large cities as Los Angeles and Denver and in the southern Texas towns in which they often constituted a majority. Their major goals were greater political representation through which they might gain better health, housing, and municipal services, bilingual school programs, and a better education for their children.

The Indians. The 800,000 Indians, the only Americans who can truly be called native, are the group that has been least integrated into U.S. society. The Indian population is concentrated in Oklahoma, Arizona, New Mexico, California, and North Carolina.

Cultural isolation of the American Indian

The Indian reservations, on which more than 40 percent of all Indians still live, are enclaves of deep poverty and social distress. In 1971 the median Indian family income was about $4,000 compared with the national figure of $9,867; since Indian families tend to be large, most lived near destitution. Four out of ten Indian children do not finish high school, and many of those who do lag behind the national educational norms by several years. Substandard, unsanitary, and overcrowded housing conditions are reflected in the fact that their death rates from tuberculosis and from dysentery are, respectively, four and five times that of the nation as a whole. Their infant mortality rate is more than 40 percent higher than the overall U.S. rate; their average age at death is about 20 years younger than the rest of the population.

The physical and social isolation of the reservation has caused a cultural hiatus that has left Indians unprepared educationally and culturally to take part in the urbanized, technical United States. The poverty and frustration of life on the reservation prompted sizable numbers of Indians to migrate to large cities, especially Los Angeles and Chicago. In such environments they possessed neither the occupational skills nor the cultural background necessary to sustain themselves, and social workers reported a high percentage of family disintegration, alcoholism, and suicide among them. By 1972, a few "red-power" Indian groups had begun to organize to call attention to their condition and press for change.

The Oriental Americans. The Oriental population of the United States consists of Japanese, Chinese, and Filipinos, the great majority of whom live in the cities of California and in Hawaii. Like other ethnic groups, the Oriental Americans have established their own urban neighbourhoods, the most famous of which is San Francisco's Chinatown. The Oriental Americans are not "problem minorities": strong family ties, cultural pride,

respect for authority, and an emphasis on education have brought them extraordinary success in the United States. Despite severe discrimination and internment during World War II, the Japanese Americans have achieved educational and employment levels that are substantially higher than those of the white population.

Religious groups. Churches and synagogues in the United States claimed 131,000,000 members in 1970. Of these, more than 48,000,000, nearly 24 percent of the population, were Roman Catholics, and about 5,900,000 were Jews. The Protestant sects reported membership of about 72,000,000; unlike the Catholics and Jews, however, they count children as members only after they are confirmed. Nine out of ten churches in the United States are Protestant, with the largest groups being the Baptists, Methodists, Lutherans, and Episcopalians.

Catholics are, by and large, members of the working class. Jews are predominantly white-collar workers (75 percent), followed in percentage terms by Episcopalians (57) and Baptists (26). Two-thirds of all Methodists are farm workers or labourers.

Religious intermarriage is still not common: Protestants marry other Protestants 80 percent of the time; Catholics marry other Catholics 80 percent of the time; and Jews marry other Jews 95 percent of the time.

DEMOGRAPHIC FIGURES AND TRENDS

Population growth. The 203,211,926 citizens of the United States counted in the 1970 census represented a 13.3 percent increase over the 1960 population, but it was the second lowest percentage increase of any decade in U.S. history. Only in the 1930s, the decade of the Great Depression, when the increase was 7.3 percent, had the nation grown at a slower rate.

Population projections for the year 2000

Projections of the population in the year 2000 range from 251,000,000 to 300,000,000. National surveys of birth expectations suggest that, on the average, families are settling on the two-child family as most desirable. If women continue to have children at about the rate of the early 1970s, the population in the year 2000 will be 280,000,000. If environmental concerns, more effective contraceptive methods, legalized abortion, and other factors have the result of permanently reducing the birth rate to 2.11 children per woman—the rate, reached in 1972, at which population exactly replaces itself—the population in the year 2000 will be only 271,000,000 and will level off at 276,000,000 in 2037.

Mortality rates. Americans can expect to live until about age 71. This average life expectancy is nearly double that of many underdeveloped countries. The death rate per 1,000 population is about 9.3, about half the world death rate of 18.

Death rates have remained stable in the United States since 1950. The dramatic decreases of the first half of the 20th century, during which the death rate dropped from 17.2 in 1900 to 9.6 in 1950, were the result of medical discoveries in the area of immunology and the antibiotic drugs. Currently, the major causes of death are the chronic diseases of old age, such as heart disease, and cancer. Barring a major medical breakthrough in curing or preventing such diseases, substantial decreases in overall death rate are unlikely.

Death, however, does not strike all Americans equally. On the average, the life expectancy of blacks is seven years shorter than that of whites. Comparative mortality rates at various ages for non-white males are consistently 30 to 50 percent higher than those of white males. Such differences have narrowed considerably in recent years as blacks have experienced increases in their general standard of living and of medical care.

Infant mortality rates—the number of deaths under one year of age per 1,000 live births—reached a low of 19.2 in 1971, due largely to advances in prenatal and infant health care. Infant mortality rates as low as 11.7 and 12.7 have been achieved in Sweden and The Netherlands, respectively, indicating that U.S. rates remain far from an irreducible minimum. Despite narrowing racial differentials, the non-white infant mortality rate remains one-half higher than the white.

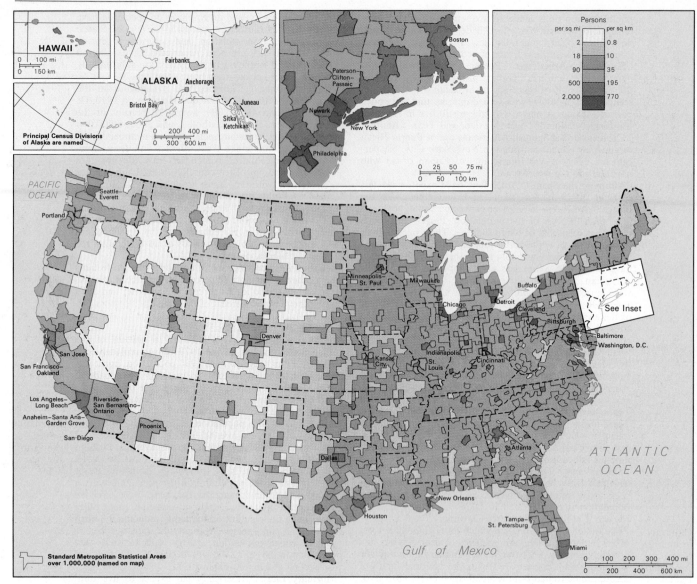

Population density of the United States.

Birth and fertility rates.   The United States entered the 1970s with the lowest birth rate in its history, a decline that was not anticipated by demographers. In 1970 the number of births per 1,000 population was 18.2; in October 1972, however, it was down to 15.6. In the 1970s, the children who were born during the post-World War II "baby boom" from 1947 to 1957 were reaching child-bearing age; it was not expected that this increase in the size of the childbearing population would result in an increase in the birth rate.

Declining
birth rates

That the birth rate showed a decline instead of the predicted increase was attributed mainly to such factors as a rise in the knowledge of contraception and its use and the legalization of abortion by the United States Supreme Court. Several sociocultural factors may also have combined to cause a decline in the willingness or desire to have children, among them an increasing concern with the effect of overpopulation on the quality of the environment; the women's liberation movement, which led more women into the work force; and the increasing emphasis placed by young people on humanistic values, which may have begun a movement toward more carefully planned childbearing than in previous generations.

Birth rates are not uniform for all groups. The nonwhite birth rate is about 50 percent higher than the white, and the highest birth rate occurs for women between the ages of 20 and 29. Socio-economic level is also a factor: in general, as family income and educational levels rise,

the number of children declines. Religion also influences fertility, with the Roman Catholics and the more fundamentalist Protestant sects, notably the Baptists, having the highest birth rates and averaging about 50 percent more children than the Jews and more liberal Protestant groups.

Migratory trends.   Few populations are as mobile as that of the United States, where 20 percent of the people move every year. Westward expansion continued: between 1960 and 1970, the Western states grew by 24.1 percent, the largest increase of any region in the nation. The Negro migration from the South, which began after World War I, had by 1970 so altered the distribution of the black population that only slightly more than half of all American Negroes were living in the South. The proportion had been two-thirds as recently as 1950.

Immigration of blacks accounted for one-third of the growth of inner-city populations between 1960 and 1970. Blacks represented one-fifth of the population of central cities by 1970 and were in the majority in four major cities—Washington, D.C.; Newark, New Jersey; Gary, Indiana; and Atlanta, Georgia. The population of seven other major cities was more than 40 percent black.

The United States became a suburban nation in 1970, with 75,600,000 people living in the suburbs, 63,800,000 in the central cities, and 63,200,000 in rural areas. During the 1960s the suburban rings about the cities increased in population by 27 percent, whereas the cities themselves grew by only 6 percent. Although 762,000 blacks had moved to the suburbs during the decade, along with 12,-500,000 whites, the suburbs remained 95.5 percent white in 1970. The farm population was down to 10,000,000 persons (less than five percent of the total population), the lowest percentage in the history of the nation.

Immigration. The era of mass immigration came to an abrupt end soon after World War I, when the Immigration Act of 1924 established an annual quota, later fixed at 150,000 immigrants (1929). The act also established the national origins system, which was to characterize national immigration policy until 1968. Under it, quotas were established for each country based on the number of persons of that national origin who were living in the United States in 1920. The quotas had the effect of reducing drastically the flow of immigrants from southeastern Europe—who, since they were still relatively recent arrivals in the United States, formed only a small percentage of the population in 1920—and of discriminating in favour of the countries of northwestern Europe. Under this system Great Britain, Ireland, and Germany were allotted more than 70 percent of the quota, an allotment that rarely was filled.

The quota system was liberalized in December 1965, and in 1968 it was finally abolished in favor of a first-come, first-served policy. An annual ceiling of 170,000 immigrant visas for nations outside the Western Hemisphere was established, with 20,000 the maximum allowed to any one nation. A ceiling of 120,000 was set for persons from the Western Hemisphere.

The new policy radically changed the pattern of immigration. In 1965, the last year during which the old national-origins system was still in effect, Mexico, Canada, and Great Britain topped the list of countries sending immigrants to the United States. By 1971, the last two had been displaced by nine other countries. The number of Philippine immigrants was nine times larger in 1971 than in 1965; the number of Chinese, nearly four times larger; the number of Koreans, almost seven times larger; and the number of persons from India, 25 times larger. Of the 3,300,000 immigrants who entered the United States between 1960 and 1970, nearly 14 percent were non-white. (Jo.N./T.K.F.)

IV. The national economy

By a very wide margin, the United States is the world's greatest economic power, measured in terms both of Gross National Product (GNP) and of GNP per capita. While precise comparisons among countries are difficult, in 1969 GNP per capita in the U.S. was more than twice that of the industrialized countries of western Europe.

This position of the United States is partly a reflection of its richness in natural resources. In 1970, the U.S., with less than 6 percent of the world's population, produced 25 percent of the world's output of coal, 21 percent of its crude petroleum, 25 percent of its copper, and 12 percent of its iron ore. In 1970 the agricultural sector produced 46 percent of the world's maize, 21 percent of its beef, pork, mutton, and lamb, and 13 percent of its wheat. The U.S. owes much more, however, to its developed industry. In the 1960s U.S. industrial production was still increasing more rapidly than that of most other countries. Between 1965 and 1970 it grew by 18 percent; this represented an average annual growth rate in gross domestic product of 3.3 percent, and a per capita growth rate of 2.3 percent. (Gross domestic product [GDP] is the total of goods and services produced in a country. GNP is GDP plus net factor income from abroad, which can be a minus quantity.) The latter rate may be compared with a rate of 4.0 percent in the Federal Republic of Germany, 4.9 percent in France, 1.9 percent in the United Kingdom, 2.6 percent in Canada, and 11.5 percent in Japan.

Despite its relative self-sufficiency, the U.S. is the most important single factor in world trade by virtue of the sheer size of its economy. In 1971 its exports represented about 14.0 percent of the world total, while those of West Germany, United Kingdom, and Japan were, respectively, about 12.5 percent, 7.2 percent, and 7.7 percent. The

U.S. market also accounted for 13.9 percent of world imports in 1971, compared with West Germany's 10.5 percent, the U.K.'s 7.3 percent, France's 6.5 percent, and Japan's 6.0 percent.

The United States impinges on the economy of the rest of the world not only as a trading power but also as a source of investment capital. The book value of direct investments abroad by U.S. firms amounted to $78,100,000,000 at the end of 1970. This investment was a dominant factor in the economies of Canada and many Latin American countries; $22,800,000,000 in Canada and $12,200,000,000 in Latin America (predominantly Venezuela, Brazil, and Mexico). U.S. investments in Europe, valued at $24,500,000,000 at the end of 1969 ($8,000,000,000 in the U.K.), were concentrated in high-technology growth areas.

NATURAL RESOURCES

Mineral resources. The U.S. is the world's major petroleum-producing nation, accounting for about one-fifth of world output. Its proved petroleum reserves at the end of 1971 amounted to 38,063,000,000 barrels, including reserves offshore from Texas, Louisiana, and California. This represented 10.9 times the amount extracted in 1971, whereas at the end of 1960, proved reserves, at 31,613,000,000 barrels, had been equivalent to 12.3 times annual production. But, while the ratio of production to reserves worsened throughout most of the 1960s, it seemed likely to be improved by major oil discoveries in Alaska. In 1971 Texas accounted for 35.2 percent of U.S. production (1,220,000,000 barrels), and its proved reserves represented over 34 percent of the national total. Next most important in terms of 1971 production was Louisiana (948,000,000 barrels), followed by California (359,000,000 barrels).

Important reserves of natural gas exist, estimated to amount to 290,746,000,000,000 cubic feet of recoverable gas at the end of 1970, an increase of 10.2 percent over the figure for 1960 despite a large increase in annual off-take throughout the 1960s. Proved recoverable reserves represented 13.3 times production at the end of 1970, compared with 20.7 times at the end of 1960. The state producing the most natural gas in 1970 was Texas, with over 38 percent of national output and nearly 37 percent of proved recoverable reserves. Its output of 8,358,000,000,000 cubic feet was followed by those of Louisiana (7,788,000,000,000), Oklahoma (1,595,000,-000,000), and New Mexico (1,139,000,000,000).

Coal deposits are concentrated largely in eastern parts of the country. Total production of bituminous coal and lignite in 1970 was 602,932,000 tons, of which 349,868,000 tons were mined in West Virginia, Kentucky, and Pennsylvania—the last-named state also producing the country's only anthracite (9,729,000 tons in 1970). Illinois produced 65,119,000 tons of coal in 1970 and Ohio 55,351,000 tons. Iron ore is mined predominantly in the Great Lakes region; there has been a long-term shift away from the mining of hematite, which accounted for 89 percent of output in 1950 but only 46 percent in 1970, toward the mining of magnetite. Iron-ore production declined marginally in the 1950s and 1960s, while demand for it grew, with the result that in 1970 over 40 percent of demand was met by imports.

The U.S. also has important reserves of copper, lead, and zinc. Copper production is concentrated in the mountainous states of the West. In 1971, nearly 54 percent of copper-mining output came from Arizona and 17 percent from Utah; most of the rest was mined in Montana, Nevada, and New Mexico. In the 1950s and 1960s the grade of the ore mined became lower. Zinc mining is more scattered than that of copper; just over 22 percent of production in 1971 came from Tennessee, nearly 13 percent from New York, and 12 and 8 percent from Idaho and Colorado, respectively. Lead mining is concentrated in Missouri, which accounted for 75 percent of the output in 1971. Other metals mined in the U.S. are gold, silver, molybdenum, manganese, tungsten, bauxite, uranium, vanadium, and nickel. Important nonmetallic minerals produced are phosphates, potash, and sulfur.

Quota system of immigration

Economic power of the U.S.

Oil and gas reserves

Biological resources. Of a total land area of 2,264,000,000 acres, about 47 percent were devoted to farming in 1969. Cropland, including fallow, comprised 17.1 percent of the land area in 1969 and grassland pasture 23.8 percent. Tobacco is produced in the Southeast and cotton in the South and Southwest; California is noted for its vineyards and citrus groves; the Middle West is the centre of corn (maize) and wheat farming, while dairy herds are concentrated in the Northern states; and the Southwestern and Rocky Mountain states support large herds of livestock.

Total forest land amounted to 753,549,000 acres at the beginning of 1970. Of this, 499,697,000 acres were in commercial forest land, defined as economically available land producing or capable of producing industrial timber. The area with most forest land was the West, with 355,169,000 acres, including 119,051,000 acres in Alaska, but the total commercial area was only 129,254,000 acres. The South had 211,885,000 acres of forest land, 192,542,000 of them commercial, and the North 186,495,000 of which 177,901,000 were commercial. The nation's growing stock of timber, excluding cull trees, amounted, at the beginning of 1970, to 431,874,000,000 cubic feet of softwood and 217,005,000,000 cubic feet of hardwood. Over half of the hardwood was located in the North. Of total commercial forest land, 73 percent was in private ownership, and 21 percent was owned or controlled by the federal government, the remainder being under the control of state and local administrations.

Hydroelectric resources. The U.S. had 1,176 hydroelectric power stations in 1971. Although this was fewer than in 1950 (1,458) and 1960 (1,331), installed hydroelectric capacity had grown from 18,000,000 kilowatts in 1950 to 32,000,000 kilowatts in 1960 and 56,000,000 in 1971, an annual average growth rate of almost 6 percent. Much unused potential remained. In 1967 the Federal Power Commission estimated that only one-quarter of the potential waterpower was being used. Hydroelectric resources are heavily concentrated in the Pacific and Mountain regions, which together accounted for 57 percent of the installed capacity in 1970. Alaska, where installed hydroelectric capacity was only 77,000 kilowatts in 1970, is estimated to have nearly one-quarter of the nation's unrealized potential capacity.

SOURCES OF NATIONAL INCOME

Agriculture, forestry, and fishing. Despite the enormous output of U.S. agriculture, the sector of agriculture, forestry, and fishing produced altogether only 3.0 percent of the net national income in 1971 and 4.1 percent in 1960. Farm productivity grew at a very rapid rate, enabling a smaller labour force to produce more than ever before. Farm manpower fell from 7,485,000 in 1960 to 4,708,000 in 1970, a drop of 37.1 percent, but over the same period the index of farm output (1967 = 100) rose from 90 to 111, a gain of 23.3 percent. This was made possible by an improvement of 82.1 percent in farm output per man-hour. The high rate of growth in farm productivity was important to the overall growth of the economy, in that over a decade it released 2,800,000 people for employment in other sectors. It was accompanied and to a large extent made possible by a marked concentration of farm holdings. While in 1960 there were 3,962,000 farms, with an average 297 acres per farm, in 1971 there were about 2,876,000 farms with an average of 389 acres. Thus, the average size of farms had increased by nearly one-third in a decade, while the number had decreased by more than one-quarter. Farms of more than 1,000 acres accounted for 54.4 percent of all farmland in 1969 and for 48.7 percent of all cropland harvested.

The 1960s saw a considerable increase in the yields of most important crops. The 1961–65 average for maize, at 66.3 bushels per acre, was nearly 30 percent higher than that for 1956–60, and the yield rose further to 86.8 bushels in 1971. For the same periods—1956–60, 1961–65, and 1971—the yields per acre for other crops were as follows: wheat 23.4 bushels, 25.3 bushels, and 33.8 bushels; oats, 39.7 bushels, 45.2, and 55.7; grain sorghums

32.4 bushels, 45.0, and 53.9; cotton, 434 pounds, 491, and 442; rice, 3,265 pounds, 3,892, and 4,638; soybeans, 23.2 bushels, 24.2, and 27.6; tobacco, 1,591 pounds, 1,921, and 2,078. The general improvement in yields was accompanied by an increase in the use of commercial fertilizers of more than 50 percent in seven years.

The U.S. is second only to the Soviet Union as a producer of timber. Production amounted to 36,639,000,000 board feet in 1971, made up of 30,283,000,000 board feet of softwoods and 6,356,000,000 board feet of hardwoods; the principal trees cut in the first category were Douglas fir and southern yellow pine, and, in the second category, oak. Domestic consumption of timber products has been growing faster than national production; imports rose from less than 4,000,000,000 board feet in 1960 to more than 7,000,000,000 in 1971.

In terms of the weight of its fishing catch, the U.S. was the fourth most important country in the world in 1970, after Peru, Japan, and Norway. Fish for human consumption accounted for 50.5 percent of the tonnage landed in 1960, but this proportion had dropped to 48.3 percent in 1970. Nearly half the 1970 catch, in terms of value, consisted of shellfish.

Mining and quarrying. Less than 2 percent of the national income now comes from mining and quarrying, despite the fact that the U.S. is a major world producer of a number of metals and of coal and petroleum. Mineral production showed a modest rise of 3.7 percent a year throughout the 1960s, being faster for fuels (3.6 percent a year) than for metals (2.7 percent a year).

Coal. The late 1960s saw something of a recovery in coal production, which had fallen from an average of 616,000,000 tons in the 1940s to an average of 483,000,000 tons in the 1950s and to 474,000,000 in 1961–65 but averaged 574,000,000 in the five years 1966–70. The recovery owed something to the rise in exports of coal, from 36,500,000 tons in 1960 to 71,000,000 by 1970. The main source of demand for coal, however, remained the electricity-generating industry, where consumption rose by 9.7 percent a year between 1950 and 1960 and by 7.6 percent in the period 1960–70. This helped to offset the stagnation of sales to the manufacturing sector and the really drastic fall in household deliveries (from 84,400,000 tons in 1950 to 12,000,000 in 1970). Total domestic consumption rose by 3.3 percent a year in the period 1960–70. The coal industry underwent a massive increase in productivity: output per man almost doubled in the 1950s, from 1,239 tons a year in 1950 to 2,453 in 1960, and subsequently rose to a level of 4,296 tons a year in 1970.

Petroleum. The output of crude petroleum in 1971 was 3,478,000,000 barrels, compared with 1,974,000,000 in 1950 and 2,575,000,000 in 1960. The number of wells producing natural gas rose rapidly in the late 1950s and early 1960s, from 64,900 at the end of 1950 to 90,761 at the end of 1960 and 117,496 at the end of 1970. Total consumption of natural gas reached 22,046,000,000,000 cubic feet in 1970, having risen since 1960 at an average annual rate of 6.9 percent.

Iron, copper, zinc, lead. Production of iron ore amounted to 82,298,000 tons in 1971, a level below that of 1950. Copper mining, by contrast, expanded considerably in the 1960s, the 1971 output being 41.9 percent higher than that of 1960. Zinc-mine output fluctuated considerably from year to year, but the 1971 figure of 492,000 tons (recoverable content) was 19.5 percent below that of 1965 and 21.0 percent below that of 1950. The statistics for mine production of recoverable lead showed a clearer trend, declining between 1950 and 1960 from 431,000 tons to 247,000 and recovering in the early 1970s to 573,000 tons. Domestic mine production is not, however, the principal source of supply of lead, since even in 1971 it was outstripped by recovery of lead from scrap (587,000 tons), while lead imports, in the form of both ore and metal, amounted to 265,000 tons.

Manufacturing. Manufacturing output grew in the 1960s at roughly the same rate as the economy as a whole. Between 1960 and 1971 the index of manufacturing production increased by 60.6 percent, at an average

2,500 SQ MI
AREA

0   50

Elevations and depressions are given in feet

B-520502-26 -4-4-5"
COPYRIGHT BY
RAND McNALLY & COMPANY
MADE IN U.S.A.

Longitude West of Greenwich

©RMCN   Longitude East of Greenwich   Longitude West of Greenwich   Same scale as main map

0   50   100   200   300   400 Miles
0   100   200   300   400   500   600 Kilometers

Plate 2   United States of America

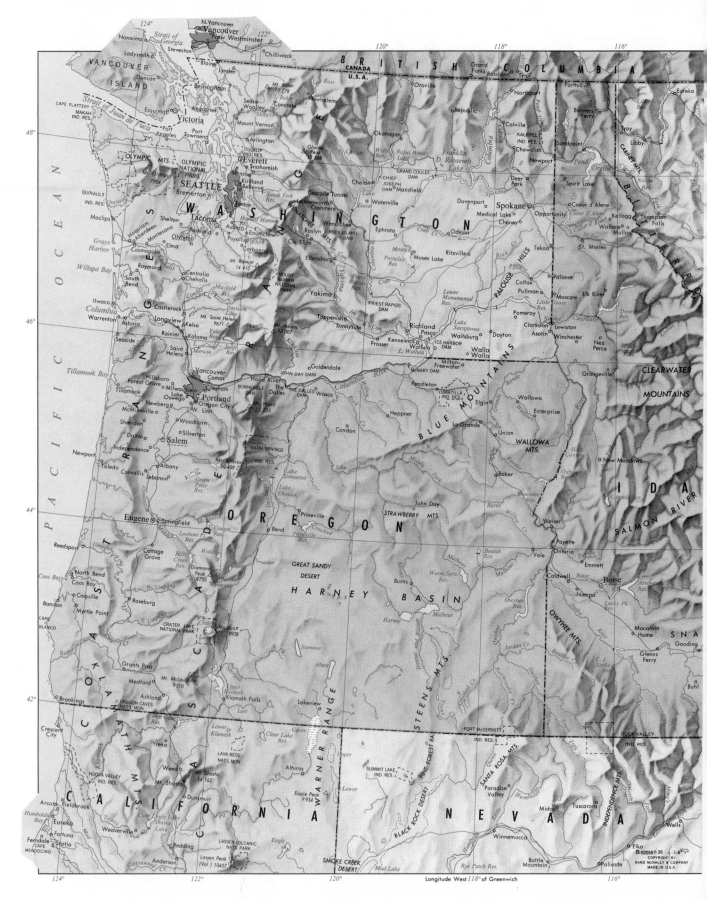

Elevations and depressions are given in feet

Plate 4   United States of America

2,500 SQ MI
AREA

0   50
Miles

NEVADA

CALIFORNIA

BAJA CALIFORNIA NORTE

122°   120°   118°   116°

40°
38°
36°
34°
32°

COAST RANGES
SIERRA NEVADA
SAN JOAQUIN VALLEY
COAST RANGES
MOJAVE DESERT
DEATH VALLEY
DEATH VALLEY NATL. MON.
SPRING MTS.

PACIFIC OCEAN

Anderson
Red Bluff
Cottonwood
Mill Cr.
Lassen Peak (Vol.) 10 457
LASSEN VOLCANIC NATL. PARK
Susanville
Westwood
SMOKE CREEK DESERT
Mud
Battle Mountain
Palisade
Franklin
RUBY MTS.
Ruby
McGill
Chico
Oroville
Willows
Oroville Res.
Black Butte Res.
Portola
Dawnieville
PYRAMID LAKE
Pyramid
INDIAN RESERVATION
Lovelock
Humboldt Sink
Winnemucca
HUMBOLDT RA.
Humboldt R.
Ely
Ruth
Eureka
Gridley
Colusa
Yuba City
Marysville
Nevada City
Grass Valley
Truckee
Reno
Sparks
Wadsworth
Fallon
Carson Sink
Humboldt Salt Marsh
STILLWATER RA.
Austin
Ukiah
Lakeport
Cloverdale
Healdsburg
Cache Cr.
Woodland
Lincoln
Auburn
Roseville
Placerville
Folsom Lake
Folsom City
Virginia City
Carson City
Yerington
WALKER RIVER IND. RES.
Arc Dome 11 775
TOIYABE RANGE
Duckwater Pk. 11 493
POINT ARENA
Santa Rosa
Sebastopol
Petaluma
Napa
Vallejo
Benicia
Berryessa
Sacramento
Jackson
San Andreas
Angels Camp
Sonora
Hawthorne
WASUK RANGE
Walker Lake
POINT REYES
MUIR WOODS NATL. MON.
San Rafael
Richmond
Berkeley
Oakland
Alameda
San Francisco
Daly City
Burlingame
San Mateo
Redwood City
Palo Alto
Santa Clara
Sausalito
Pittsburg
Lodi
Stockton
Oakdale
Modesto
Turlock
YOSEMITE NATIONAL PARK
Mt. Lyell 13 095
Dana Mtn. 13 055
DEVILS POSTPILE NAT. MON.
Benton
Boundary Peak 13 145
Coaldale
Tonopah
Goldfield
Alamo
Tracy
Livermore
San Jose
Los Gatos
Santa Cruz
Watsonville
Gilroy
Hollister
Merced
Mariposa
Madera
White Mt. 14 246
Bishop
Monterey Bay
Pacific Grove
Monterey
Salinas
PINNACLES NATL. MON.
King City
Fresno
Sanger
Reedley
Selma
Dinuba
Visalia
KINGS CANYON NATL. PARK
SEQUOIA NATL. PARK
Lone Pine
Mt. Whitney 14 494
Owens Lake
Beatty
FRENCHMAN FLAT
MOAPA RIVER IND. RES.
Las Vegas
Coalinga
Hanford
Tulare
Exeter
Porterville
TULE RIVER IND. RES.
Telescope Peak 11 045
Death Valley Jct.
Henderson
HOOVER DAM
Boulder City
Paso Robles
Atascadero
Estero Bay
San Luis Obispo
San Antonio R.
Nacimiento R.
Coalinga
Delano
Tulare Basin
Trona
Searles
Inyokern
SPRING MTS.
San Luis Obispo Bay
Santa Maria
Buena Vista Lake Reservoir
Taft
Bakersfield
Aqueduct
Mojave R.
Mojave
Barstow
Daggett
MOJAVE DESERT
Cadiz
Lompoc
POINT ARGUELLO
POINT CONCEPTION
Santa Barbara
Ventura
Oxnard
Santa Paula
TEHACHAPI MTS.
Los Angeles Aqueduct
FORT MOHAVE IND. RES.
Goffs
Needles
Santa Barbara Channel
SAN MIGUEL
SANTA CRUZ
SANTA ROSA
SANTA BARBARA ISLANDS
LOS ANGELES
Santa Monica
Inglewood
Redondo Beach
SAN PEDRO
Long Beach
Burbank
Glendale
Pasadena
Monrovia
Alhambra
Huntington Park
Compton
Santa Ana
Newport Beach
Huntington Beach
Orange
Pomona
Riverside
San Bernardino
Redlands
Palm Springs
MORONGO IND. RES.
SAN BERNARDINO MTS.
JOSHUA TREE NATL. MON.
Aqueducts
Rice
Colorado River
Blythe
SANTA BARBARA CHANNEL ISLANDS NAT'L. MON.
SANTA CATALINA
Avalon
SAN NICOLAS
Elsinore
AGUA CALIENTE IND. RES.
SANTA ROSA IND. RES.
TORRES MARTINEZ IND. RES.
Salton Sea
Bottom 235 Ft. below sea level
IMPERIAL VALLEY
Brawley
Calipatria
Holtville
FT. YUMA IND. RES.
SAN CLEMENTE
Santa Catalina
Gulf of Santa Catalina
Oceanside
Escondido
SANTA YSABEL IND. RES.
LA JOLLA IND. RES.
INAJA IND. RES.
CUYAPAIPE IND. RES.
CAMP IND.
El Centro
Calexico
Mexicali
SAN DIEGO
Coronado
National City
Chula Vista
Tijuana
Somerton
Laguna Salada
Colorado R.
All American Canal

Death Valley 282 Ft. below sea level

B-520599-26°-65°-10°
COPYRIGHT BY
RAND McNALLY & COMPANY
MADE IN U.S.A.

Longitude West of Greenwich

Elevations and depressions are given in feet

Plate 6   United States of America

106°   104°   102°   100°   98°   96°

CANADA
U.S.A.
S A S K.   M A N I T O B A

Opheim Scobey Plentywood Crosby Estevan Whitewater Boissevain Morris Whitemouth
Grenora Bowbells Mohall Bottineau Upper des Lacs TURTLE MTS. St. John Mordon Emerson
FORT PECK IND. RES. Poplar Wolf Point Kenmare Souris Rolla TURTLE MOUNTAIN IND. RES. Hannah Pembina Roseau
Medicine Williston Darling Langdon Cavaliero Hallock Roseau

48° Missouri Stanley Minot Towner Rugby Leeds Cando Grafton Argyle Thief RED LAKE IND. RES.
Sidney Newtown Lake Sakakawea Harvey New Rockford DEVILS LAKE IND. RES. Larimore Grand Forks East Grand Forks Red Lake Falls
Brockway FORT BERTHOLD IND. RES. Garrison Sweetwater Devils Northwood Crookston Fosston Bagle
MONTANA Glendive THEODORE ROOSEVELT NAT'L MEM. PARK Killdeer N O R T H   D A K O T A Fessenden Carrington Cooperstown Mayville Fertile Ada Mahnomen WHITE EARTH IND. RES.
Terry Beach Dickinson Hebron Wilton Hope Hillsboro
Miles City Glen Ullin Mandan Bismarck Jamestown Res. Valley City Casselton Fargo Hawley Detroit Lakes
46° Bake Marmarth BADLANDS Long Jamestown Enderlin Moorhead Frazee Perha
Bowman Streeter Marion Lisbon Barnesville Pelican Rapids Lida
Hettinger Lemmon Linton Wishek Edgeley La Moure Milnor Wahpeton Breckenridge Fergus Falls MIN
STANDING ROCK IND. RES. McIntosh McLaughlin Ashley Ellendale Oakes Lidgerwood Hankinson Elbow Lake Alexandria
Eureka Longlake Leola Britton SISSETON Wheaton Glenwood
Mobridge Bowdle Aberdeen Groton Sisseton IND. RES. Morris Graceville
Faith CHEYENNE RIVER IND. RES. Ipswich Columbia Road Res. Webster Waubay Ortonville Benson
S O U T H   D A K O T A Gettysburg Conde Milbank Madison Appleton
Redfield Clark Watertown Dawson Mounteview
DEVILS TOWER NAT'L MON. Belle Fourche Res. Newell Canby Granite Falls
Gillette Moorcroft Sundance Spearfish Lead Deadwood Sturgis OAHE DAM Highmore Miller Bryant Minneota Marshall
44° BLACK HILLS Rapid City Pierre Arlington Brookings Tyler
Newcastle Custer JEWEL CAVE NAT'L MON. Philip LOWER BRULE IND. RES. CROW CREEK IND. RES. De Smet Lake Preston Elkton PIPESTONE NAT'L MON. Slayton
WIND CAVE NAT'L PARK Hot Springs BADLANDS NAT'L MON. Presho BIG BEND DAM Wessington Springs Woonsocket Madison Dell Rapids Pipestone Jasper Heron Lake
Edgemont BADLANDS Murdo Chamberlain Kimball Mitchell Howard Salem Flandreau Adrian Worthington
WYOMING PINE RIDGE Wood Winner Lake Francis Case Alexandria Sioux Falls Luverne Rock Rapids Sibley
INDIAN RESERVATION ROSEBUD IND. RES. Dallas Gregory Platte Parkston Parker Lennox Rock Valley Sheldon Hartley
42° Lusk Chadron Gordon Rushville Valentine Armour FORT RANDALL DAM Tripp Scotland Menno Canton Beresford Orange City Le Mars Cherokee
Wheatland Crawford Box Butte Res. Niobrara Tyndall Centerville Hawarden
Torrington Alliance Antioch Merritt Res. Ainsworth Long Pine Atkinson O'Neill GAVINS POINT DAM Crofton Yankton Vermillion Sioux City Idagrove
Morrill Mitchell Scottsbluff Gering Bayard SAND HILLS Bloomfield Hartington Elk Point WINNEBAGO IND. RES. Odebo
SCOTTS BLUFF NAT'L MON. Bridgeport N E B R A S K A Creighton South Sioux City Ponca OMAHA IND. RES. Onawa Denison
Plainview Randolph Wakefield Pender
Cheyenne Kimball Oshkosh Hemingford Nelish Wayne Dunlap Woodbine
Sidney Chappell Lake McConaughy North Platte Burwell Spalding Albion Norfolk Stanton Wisner Lyons Oakland Westpoint Tekamah
COLORADO Ogallala Broken Bow Loup City Ord Sargent Madison Missouri Valley
Fort Collins Julesburg Gothenburg St. Paul Ravenna Fullerton Columbus Schuyler Fremont Blair
Eaton Sterling Cozad Lexington Shelton Grand Island Central City David City Wahoo Omaha Council Bluffs Glenwood
Greeley Haxtun Holyoke Curtis Kearney Aurora York Osceola Ashland Plattsmouth Red Oak
40° Fort Lupton Frenchman Harvard Friend Lincoln Nebraska City Hamburg
Brighton DENVER

AB-511005-26 7 8-41
COPYRIGHT BY
RAND McNALLY & COMPANY
MADE IN U.S.A.

Longitude West 102° of Greenwich   100°   98°   96°

Elevations and depressions are given in feet.

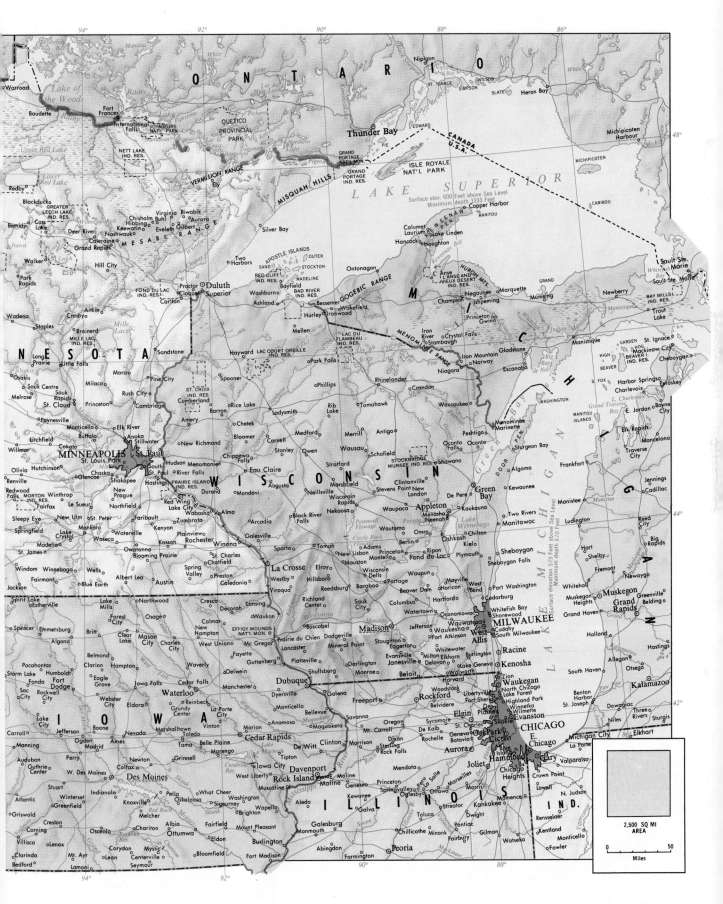

Plate 8   United States of America

WYO.   Cheyenne

NEBRASKA

COLORADO

KANSAS

NEW MEXICO

ROCKY MOUNTAINS

OKLA

TEXAS

Oshkosh
Lake McConaughy
North Platte
Ord
Sherman Res.
N. Loop
Loop City
St. Paul
Fullerton
Central City
Kimball
Sidney
Chappell
Ogallala
North Platte
Broken Bow
Gothenburg
Cozad
Lexington
Grand Island
Aurora
Harvard
Julesburg
Sterling
Haxtun
Holyoke
Brush
Akron
Yuma
Wray
Fort Morgan
Curtis
Cambridge
Mc Cook
Holdrege
Minden
Hastings
Benkelman
Beaver City
Alma
Red Cloud
Franklin
Superior
Harlan Co. Res.
Fort Collins
Windsor
Eaton
Greeley
Loveland
Longmont
Boulder
Golden
Louisville
Brighton
Littleton
DENVER
Englewood
Idaho Springs
Moffat Tunnel
Steamboat Springs
Oak Creek
Glenwood Springs
Berg
Aspen
Leadville
Mt. Massive 14,418
Mt. Elbert 14,431
La Plata Pk. 14,340
Hagerman Pass
Mt. Lincoln 14,286
Castle Peak 14,265
Crested Butte
Gunnison
Buena Vista
Salida
Manitou Springs
Colorado Springs
Cripple Creek
Canon City
Florence
Pueblo
Ordway
Sugar City
Rocky Ford
Fowler
La Junta
Las Animas
Wiley
Lamar
Syracuse
Atwood
Oberlin
Norton
Phillipsburg
Smith Center
Mankato
Lovewell Res.
Goodland
Colby
Hill City
Stockton
Kirwin Res.
Downs
Beloit
Oakley
Wa Keeney
Ellis
Hays
Russell
Wilson Res.
Lincoln
Sharon Springs
Scott City
Ness City
La Crosse
Great Bend
Hoisington
Lyons
Sterling
Ellsworth
Kanopolis Res.
Kit Carson
Cheyenne Wells
Garden City
Dodge City
Kinsley
Larned
St. John
Hutchinson
Stafford
Ulysses
Greensburg
Pratt
Kingman
Cheney Res.
Springfield
Meade
Coldwater
Medicine Lodge
Harper
Anthony
Kiowa
Elkhart
Hugoton
Liberal
Ashland
Great Salt Plains Res.
Alva
Cherokee
Medford
Hooker
Guymon
Beaver
Waynoka
Woodward
Enid
Perryton
Fairview
Hennessey
Okeene
Watonga
Kingfisher
Shattuck
Seiling
Roy
Dalhart
Dumas
Borger
Pampa
Miami
Canadian
Thomas
Clinton
Geary
El Reno
Elk City
Weatherford
Foss Res.
Sayre
Erick
Shamrock
Cordell
Anadarko
Chickasha
Carnegie
Cement
Hobart
Lindsay
Amarillo
Canyon
Hereford
Clarendon
Wellington
Memphis
Mangum
Altus
Snyder
Fort Sill
Lawton
WICHITA MTS.
Duncan
Marlow
Frederick
Comanche
Grandfield
Waurika
Tulia
Hollis
Childress
Quanah
Vernon
Electra
Burkburnett
Iowa Park
Wichita Falls
Henrietta
Plainview
Floydada
Paducah
Bowie
Littlefield
Muleshoe
Clovis
Farwell
Portales
Lubbock
Slaton
Spur
Seymour
Olney
Jacksboro
Graham
Bridgeport
Decatur
Possum Kingdom Eagle Mt.
Brownfield
Post
O'Donnell
Haskell
Stamford
Anson
Seagraves
Lamesa
Snyder
Rotan
Hamlin
Hobbs
Roswell
Artesia
Dayton
McMillan
Carrizozo
GRAN QUIVIRA NAT'L MON.
Fort Sumner
Vaughn
Santa Rosa
Puerto de Luna
Tucumcari
Santa Fe
Las Vegas
Galisteo
Albuquerque
Bernalillo
PUEBLO IND. RES.
Las Cruces
North Truchas Pk.
La Mesa
Wagon Mound
FT. UNION NAT'L MON.
Springer
Clayton
Boise City
Folsom
Des Moines
Raton
CAPULIN MOUNTAIN NAT'L MON.
Taos
Park View
SANGRE DE CRISTO RANGE
GREAT SAND DUNES NAT'L MON.
Del Norte
Monte Vista
Alamosa
Saguache
Antonito
Starkville
Trinidad
Aguilar
Delagua
Walsenburg
Cimarron
Guymon
LLANO ESTACADO

2,500 SQ MI
AREA
0   50
Miles

A B-511006-26   6-7-9
COPYRIGHT BY
RAND McNALLY & COMPANY
MADE IN U.S.A.

Longitude West 98° of Greenwich

Elevations and depressions are given in feet.

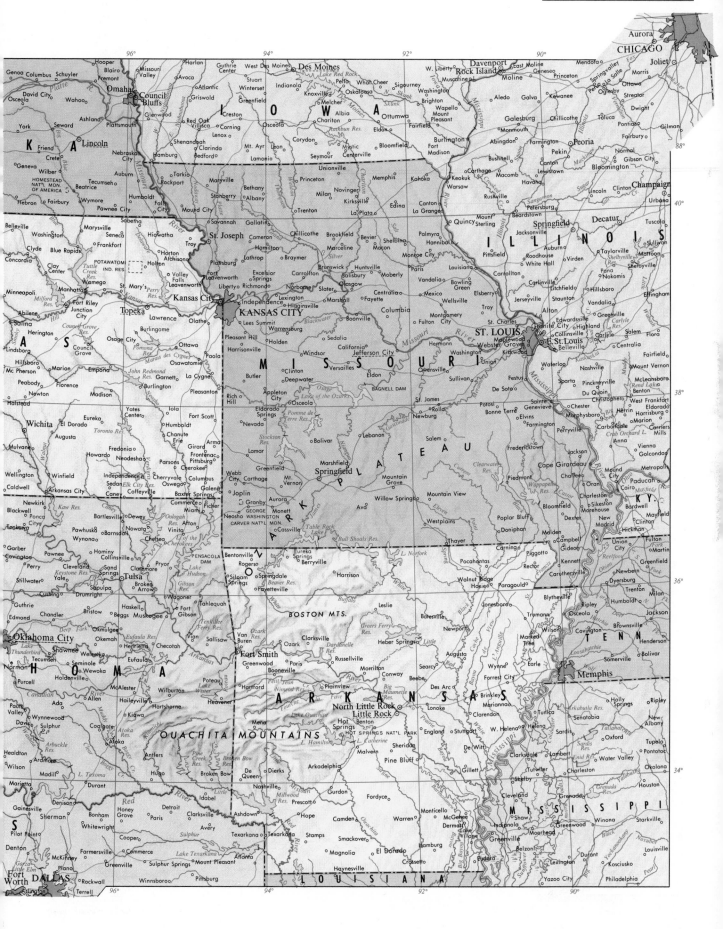

Plate 10   United States of America

NEW MEXICO
TEXAS
CHIHUAHUA
COAHUILA
MEXICO
DURANGO
NUEVO LEON
TAMAULIPAS
ZACATECAS

EDWARDS PLATEAU
STOCKTON PLATEAU
DAVIS MTS.
GUADALUPE MTS.
SANTIAGO MTS.
SIERRA MADRE DE ORIENTAL
BOLSÓN DE MAPIMÍ
SERRANÍAS DEL BURRO

WHITE SANDS NAT'L MON.
CARLSBAD CAVERNS NAT'L PARK
BIG BEND NAT'L PARK

Alamogordo, Alamo Pk 7820, Artesia, Dayton, McMillan, Hobbs, Seagraves, Seminole, O'Donnell, Lamesa, Snyder, Rotan, Hamlin, Stamford, Haskell, Newcastle, Graham, Possum Kingdom Res., Mineral Wells, Breckenridge, Hubbard Creek Res., Strawn, Albany, Anson, Merkel, Sweetwater, Roscoe, Colorado City, Big Spring, Stanton, Midland, Wink, Odessa, Abilene, Baird, Cisco, Eastland, Ranger, Thurber, Desdemona, Gorman, De Leon, Stephenville, Dublin, Hico, Winters, Ballinger, Coleman, Brownwood, Santa Anna, Comanche, Hamilton, Goldthwaite, Sterling City, McCamey, Fort Stockton, Sanderson, San Angelo, Eden, Brady, San Saba, Lometa, Lampasas, Burnet, Menard, Mason, Llano, Sonora, Junction, Rocksprings, Fredericksburg, Kerrville, San Marcos, Boerne, New Braunfels, Seguin, San Antonio, Camp Wood, Del Rio, Brackettville, Uvalde, Hondo, Sabinal, Floresville, Pleasanton, Poteet, Pearsall, Kenedy, Crystal City, Carrizo Springs, Asherton, Cotulla, Fowlerton, George West, Corpus Christi, Encinal, San Diego, Alice, Laredo, Mirando City, Kingsville, Premont, Hebbronville, Falfurrias, Edinburg, McAllen, Mission, Weslaco, Riogrande, Reynosa

El Paso, Ysleta, Ciudad Juárez, Fabens, Guadalupe, Villa Ahumada, Sierra Blanca, Van Horn, Eagle Pk 7496, Pecos, Toyah, Marfa, Alpine, Ojinaga, Presidio, Coyame, Cuchillo Parado, Aldama, Chihuahua, Meoqui, Naica, Ciudad Camargo (Santa Rosalía), Jiménez, Hidalgo del Parral, Santa Barbara, Rosario, Indé, Santa Cruz, Villa Ocampo, Villa López, Valle de Allende, Escalón, Villa Coronado, Mapimí, San Pedro de las Colonias, Gómez Palacio, Torreón, Lerdo, Matamoros, Viesca, San Luis del Cordero, Rodeo, Nazas, Cuencamé, San Juan del Río, Santa Clara, San Bartolo, San Juan de Guadalupe, Juan Aldama, Cañatlán, Pánuco de Coronado, Durango

Sierra Mojada, Cuatro Ciénegas, Sacramento, San Buenaventura, Nadadores, Monclova, Abasolo, Muzquiz, San Juan de Sabinas, Progreso, Villa Acuña, Jiménez, Piedras Negras, Fuente, Zaragoza, Morelos, Nava, Allende, Guerrero, Rosales, Eagle Pass, Hidalgo, Dolores, Nuevo Laredo, Zapata, Guerrero, Camargo, Mier, Bustamante, Villaldama, Sabinas Hidalgo, Lampazos, Agualeguas, Cerralvo, China, Paredon, Salinas Victoria, General Zuazua, Los Herreras, García, Monterrey, Santa Catarina, Cadereyta Jiménez, Montemorelos, Villa de Allende, Ramos Arizpe, General Cepeda, Arteaga, Saltillo, Gómez Farías, Galeana, Linares, Burgos, San Fernando, Cruillas, San Carlos, Villagrán, Mazapil, Concepción del Oro

N. Franklin Mtn 7176, Wind Mtn 7278, Guadalupe Pk 8751, Baldy Peak 8382, Cathedral Mt 6860, Chinati Pk 7730, Emory Pk 7835

Rio Grande, Pecos, Concho, Nueces, Falcon Res., Presa de D. Martin, Presa de Azucar, Amistad Res., Red Bluff Res., Laguna de Mayrán, Laguna de Viesca

2,500 SQ MI AREA
0 — 50 Miles

Longitude West of Greenwich

Elevations and depressions are given in feet.

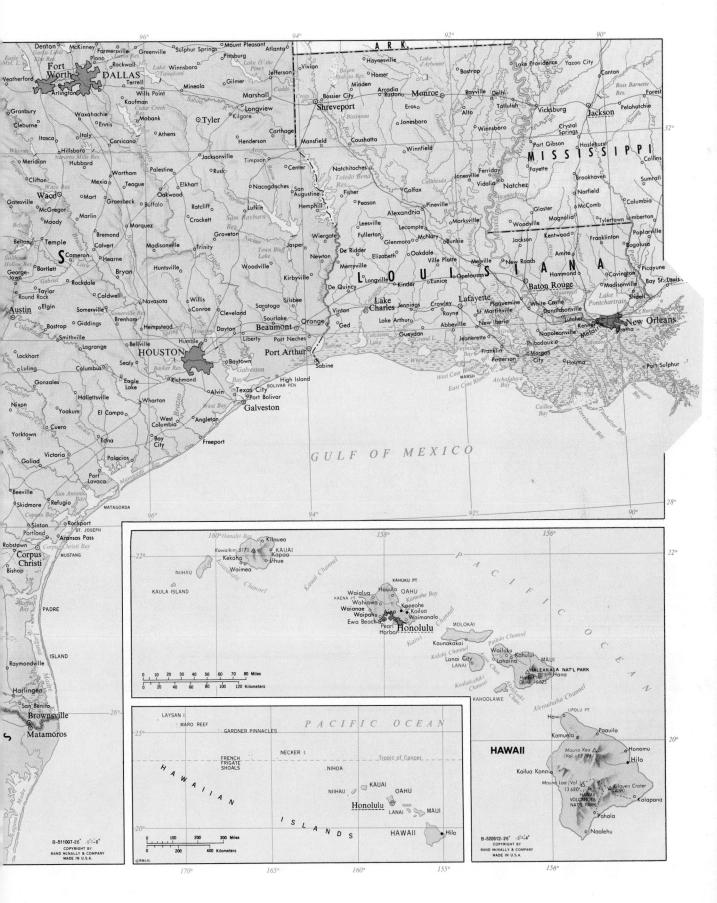

ARK.

DALLAS
Fort Worth
Arlington

Denton McKinney Farmersville Greenville Sulphur Springs Mount Pleasant Atlanta
Plano Rockwall Pittsburg Haynesville Lake Providence Yazoo City Canton
Weatherford Terrell Lake Winnsboro Jefferson Vivian Homer Bastrop Ross Barnette Res. Forest
Granbury Waxahachie Wills Point Gilmer Marshall Bossier City Minden Arcadia Monroe Rayville Delhi Vicksburg Jackson Pelahotchie
Cleburne Ennis Kaufman Mineola Longview Shreveport Rustone Eros Winnsboro Crystal Springs Collins
Itasca Italy Corsicana Tyler Kilgore Carthage Jonesboro Alto Tatlulah Port Gibson Hazlehurst
Hillsboro Athens Henderson Mansfield Coushatta Winnfield Natchez MISSISSIPPI Brookhaven Sumrall
Meridian Hubbard Jacksonville Center Natchitoches Jonesville Ferriday Fayette Gloster McComb Columbia
Clifton Wortham Palestine Rusk Colfax Vidalia Magnolia Norfield Tylertown Lumberton
Gatesville Mexia Teague Elkhart Nacogdoches Fisher Pineville Marksville Woodville Kentwood Poplarville
Waco Groesbeck Oakwood San Augustine Peason Alexandria Jackson Franklinton Bogalusa
McGregor Mart Buffalo Ratcliff Lufkin Hemphill Leesville Lecompte New Roads Amite Picayune
Moody Crockett Groveton Wiergate Fullerton McNary Bunkie Hammond Covington Bay St. Louis
Temple Calvert Madisonville Trinity De Ridder Glenmora Melville Opelousas Baton Rouge Madisonville Slidell
Bartlett Hearne Jasper Newton Elizabeth Oakdale Ville Platte New Orleans
Cameron Bryan Huntsville Woodville Merryville Longville Kinder Eunice Plaquemine White Castle Lutcher Kenner
Rockdale Caldwell Kirbyville De Quincy LOUISIANA St. Martinville Donaldsonville Metairie
Taylor Navasota Willis Saratoga Silsbee Vinton Lake Charles Jennings Crowley Lafayette Rayne New Iberia Napoleonville Thibodaux
Austin Elgin Somerville Conroe Cleveland Ged Lake Arthur Abbeville Jeanerette Franklin Morgan City Houma Port Sulphur
Smithville Lagrange Brenham Hempstead Dayton Beaumont Orange Gueydan Patterson
Lockhart Bellville Humble Liberty Port Neches Sabine
Luling Columbus Sealy HOUSTON Baytown Port Arthur
Gonzales Hallettsville Wharton Richmond Alvin Texas City High Island
Nixon Eagle Lake West Columbia Angleton Galveston
Yoakum El Campo Bay City Freeport
Cuero Edna
Yorktown Victoria Palacios
Goliad Port Lavaca

GULF OF MEXICO

Beeville
Skidmore Refugio
Sinton Rockport
Portland Aransas Pass
Corpus Christi
Bishop

PADRE

Raymondville

Harlingen
San Benito
Brownsville
Matamoros

PACIFIC OCEAN

KAUAI
Kawaikini 5170 Kapaa
Kekaha Lihue
Waimea
NIIHAU
KAULA ISLAND

Hanalei Bay Kilauea

KAHUKU PT.
Haleiwa OAHU
Waialua Kaneohe Bay
KAENA PT. Wahiawa Kaneohe
Waianae Kailua
Waipahu Aiea Waimanalo
Ewa Beach Honolulu
Pearl Harbor
MOLOKAI
Kaunakakai
Wailuku Kahului
Lanai City Lahaina MAUI
LANAI HALEAKALA NAT'L PARK
Hana
KAHOOLAWE

0 10 20 30 40 50 60 70 80 Miles
0 20 40 60 80 100 120 Kilometers

PACIFIC OCEAN

LAYSAN I.
MARO REEF
GARDNER PINNACLES
NECKER I.
FRENCH FRIGATE SHOALS
NIHOA Tropic of Cancer
KAUAI
NIIHAU OAHU
Honolulu
LANAI MAUI
HAWAII Hilo

HAWAIIAN ISLANDS

0 100 200 300 Miles
0 200 400 Kilometers

©RMcN.

HAWAII

UPOLU PT.
Hawi Paauilo
Kamuela Honomu
Mauna Kea △ Hilo
(Vol.) 13 796
Kailua Kona Kalapana
Mauna Loa (Vol.) Kilauea Crater
13 680 4090
HAWAII VOLCANOES NAT'L PARK
Pahala
Naalehu

0 20 40 60 80 100 120 Miles
0 20 40 60 80 100 120 140 160 180 200 Kilometers

Plate 12   United States of America

MISSOURI

ILL.

KENTUCKY

ARKANSAS

TENNESSEE

CUMBERLAND PLATEAU

APPALACHIAN

BLUE

MISSISSIPPI

ALABAMA

GEORGIA

LOUISIANA

FLORIDA

GULF OF MEXICO

Memphis

Nashville

Knoxville

Chattanooga

Birmingham

Tuscaloosa

Montgomery

ATLANTA

Columbus

Macon

Albany

Baton Rouge

New Orleans

Mobile

Pensacola

Panama City

Tallahassee

Jackson

Meridian

Vicksburg

Natchez

Hattiesburg

Gulfport

Biloxi

GREAT SMOKY MOUNTAINS NAT'L PARK

MAMMOTH CAVE NAT'L PARK

CHEROKEE INDIAN RES.

CHANDELEUR ISLANDS

OCMULGEE NAT'L MON.

MERIWETHER LEWIS NAT'L MON.

ACKIA BATTLEGROUND NAT'L MON.

CAPE SAN BLAS

CAPE ST. GEORGE

B-520598-26   COPYRIGHT BY   RAND McNALLY & COMPANY   MADE IN U.S.A.

Longitude West 84° of Greenwich

Elevations and depressions are given in feet.

Plate 14   United States of America

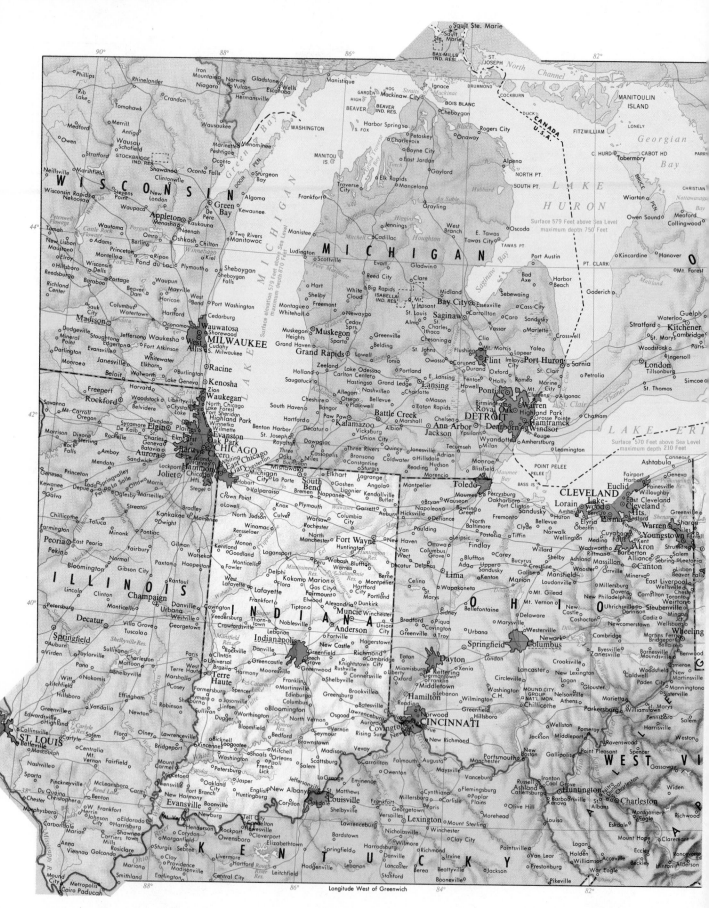

Elevations and depressions are given in feet

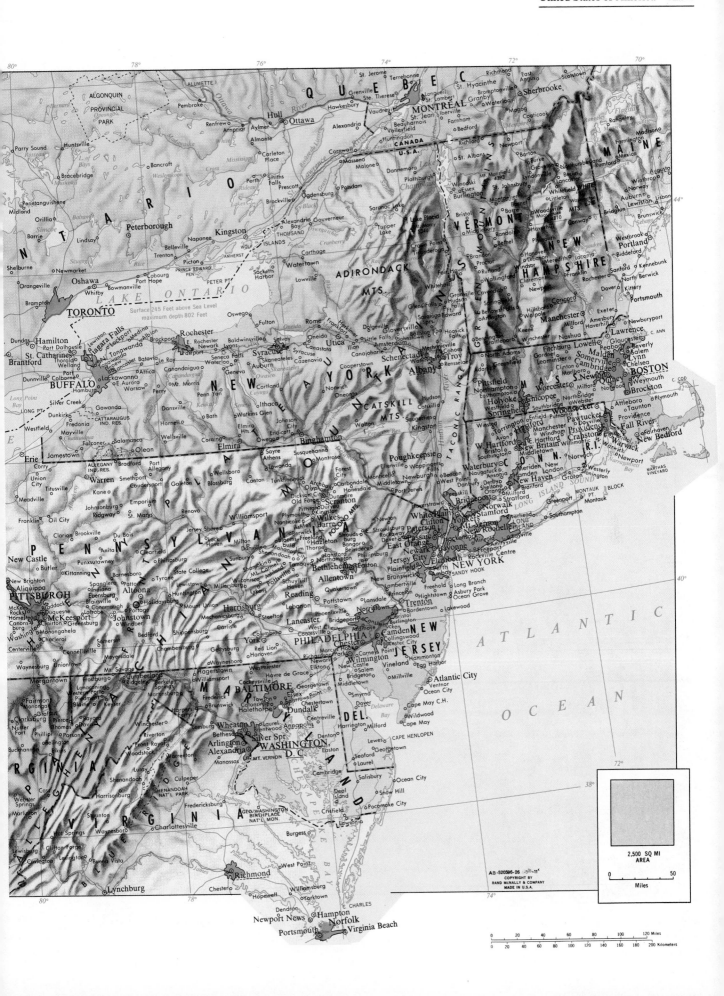

2,500 SQ MI
AREA

0   50
Miles

AB-520596-26
COPYRIGHT BY
RAND MCNALLY & COMPANY
MADE IN U.S.A.

0   20   40   60   80   100   120 Miles
0 20 40 60 80 100 120 140 160 180 200 Kilometers

Plate 16   United States of America

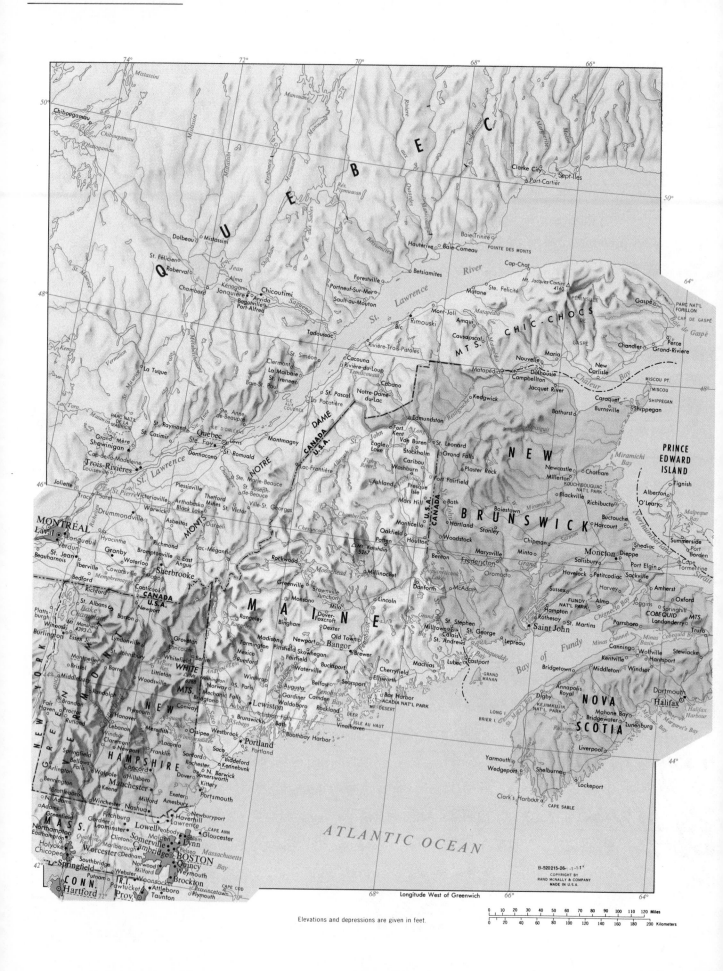

ATLANTIC OCEAN

B-520215-26- -1-1"
COPYRIGHT BY
RAND MCNALLY & COMPANY
MADE IN U.S.A.

Longitude West of Greenwich

Elevations and depressions are given in feet.

0 10 20 30 40 50 60 70 80 90 100 110 120 Miles
0 20 40 60 80 100 120 140 160 180 200 Kilometers

annual rate of 5.1 percent, compared with 3.7 percent between 1950 and 1960. The increase was slightly higher for durable manufactures, slightly lower for nondurables. This rate of growth was made possible by two factors: an average annual increase of 3.2 percent in output per man-hour in manufacturing (compared with 2.2 percent during the 1950s) and an increase of just over 2 percent a year in the manufacturing labour force (compared with an increase of only 1 percent a year in the 1950s). The increase in output per man-hour was in part a function of the increased level of capital investment in the 1960s. Manufacturing accounted for 26.6 percent of the net national income in 1971.

Leading
sectors
in
manufac-
turing The total value added by manufacturing (*i.e.*, the value of production less the cost of materials, supplies, and overhead) was $298,000,000,000 in 1970. One of the most important sectors in terms of value added was the manufacture of transportation equipment ($28,900,000,-000 or 9.7 percent of the total in 1970). Of this, motor vehicles and equipment accounted for roughly half. Sales of passenger cars from U.S. factories amounted to 6,547,000 in 1970 and 8,585,000 in 1971, while the corresponding figures for trucks and buses were 1,692,000 in 1970 and 2,053,000 in 1971. The nonelectrical machinery industry accounted for 10.6 percent of value added by manufacturing in 1970 and the output of electrical machinery for 9.3 percent. These two sectors enjoyed a high growth rate in the 1960s, averaging 9.4 percent annually (1960–70), compared with 7.6 percent for fabricated metal products, 4.8 percent for primary metals, and 5.2 percent for motor vehicles and parts.

Steel production was 120,443,000 tons in 1971, compared with 99,282,000 in 1960; nearly 20 percent of all shipments of steel-mill products in 1970 went to the automotive industry and another 11 percent to the construction industry. The chemical industry showed rapid growth during the 1960s, its production increasing at an average annual rate of 11.5 percent between 1960 and 1971. Against these high-flying industries must be set several the growth of which was below average; in textiles, the average was 4.5 percent a year; in food and beverages, only 4.0 percent a year; and in apparel, 4.6 percent a year.

The ownership of many industries in the U.S., as in other countries, is highly concentrated. In the production of motor vehicles and parts, 79 percent of the value added by the industry in 1966 was accounted for by the largest 4 producers and 83 percent by the largest 8. In aircraft, 67 percent of the value added was accounted for by the largest 4 companies in the industry and 88 percent by the largest 8. In terms of value of shipments, the corresponding figures for the aircraft engines and parts industry were 58 and 77 percent, respectively; for oil refining, 32 and 57 percent; for paper mills, 28 and 40 percent; radio and TV receivers, 48 and 68 percent; cigarette production, 81 and 100 percent; pharmaceuticals, 24 and 41 percent. Litigation by the federal government under the antitrust laws may have helped to prevent significant increases in concentration in many individual industries, but the rise of "conglomerates"—corporations with interests in diverse industries—increased the concentration of ownership overall. Thus, the largest 50 companies accounted for 25 percent of the total value added in manufacturing in 1966, compared with 17 percent in 1947; the largest 200 companies accounted for 42 percent of value added, compared with 30 percent in 1947.

Military orders were of considerable importance to industry in the 1960s. According to the U.S. Department of Labor, 8.7 percent of all those working in private manufacturing industry in 1970 were in employment generated by the Department of Defense. This meant that certain industries and geographic areas were particularly sensitive to reductions in defense spending. In 1968, for example, 6.2 percent of the total labour force in California was in defense-generated employment.

Energy. Energy consumption in the U.S. reached 68,810,000,000,000 British thermal units (BTU) in 1970, rising by an annual average of 4.7 percent in the period 1960–70. (The growth rate over the period 1950–70

was 4.4 percent a year.) Expressed in terms of an equivalent amount of coal, the 1970 figure represented a per capita consumption of 11.1 tons. The corresponding figure for the world as a whole was 1.9 tons; for Japan, it was 3.2 tons; for western Europe, 3.8; for the Soviet Union, 4.4; and for Canada, 9.1. U.S. energy consumption was equal to 33.3 percent of total world energy production in 1970.

Changes
in the
composi-
tion of
energy
supplies Major changes occurred in the composition of energy supplies in the 1950s, when the share of soft coal and anthracite dropped from 37.8 to 23.2 percent, while that of natural gas rose from 20.3 to 31.6 percent and that of crude petroleum from 37.2 to 41.6 percent. Change in the 1960s was slower; the share of soft coal and anthracite continued to decline, falling to 18.2 percent in 1971, while that of natural gas rose to 36.5 percent. Electricity from water power and nuclear fission accounted for 2 percent of total energy consumption in 1971.

Oil and gas. Petroleum production rose on the average by 2.7 percent a year throughout the 1950s and by 3.3 percent a year between 1960 and 1971. In the latter year it was 3,478,000,000 barrels, compared with total domestic consumption of 5,041,000,000 barrels. The balance was made up by natural-gas-plant liquids (291,000,000) and imports (1,247,000,000). The U.S. had become slightly less self-sufficient in petroleum production since 1950, when domestic supplies of crude oil accounted for 91.9 percent of the total, as compared with 87.8 percent in 1970. The oil industry is protected from foreign competition by a quota system.

Natural-gas production rose much more rapidly than that of crude petroleum, by an average of 9.4 percent in the 1950s and by 6.5 percent a year between 1960 and 1970. The number of residential consumers of natural gas rose from 16,900,000 in 1950 to 31,100,000 in 1960, reaching 38,600,000 in 1970, while industrial and commercial consumers increased from 1,300,000 in 1950 to 2,600,000 in 1960 and 3,300,000 in 1970.

Coal. Although coal lost ground relatively to petroleum and natural gas in the steadily expanding energy market, its use increased in absolute terms: its 22.9 percent share of the domestic energy market in 1970 represented 613,000,000 tons, compared with 454,200,000 tons in 1950 and 330,400,000 tons in 1960. Consumption rose further in 1970 to 517,000,000 tons, of which electric-power utilities took 320,000,000 tons.

Electricity. The output of electricity reached 1,718,-000,000,000 kilowatt-hours in 1971, compared with 842,000,000,000 in 1960, representing an average rate of increase of 8.7 percent a year. The sources of electric energy changed considerably in the 1950s and 1960s. In 1950, coal provided 47.1 percent of the electric energy, increasing its share to 53.6 percent in 1960 and decreasing to 44.3 percent in 1971. The importance of hydroelectric power fell sharply, from 29.2 percent in 1950 to 19.3 percent in 1960 and only 16.5 percent in 1971. Oil provided 10.3 percent of the electricity in 1950 and 13.5 percent in 1971, while natural gas, which provided only 13.5 percent of the energy in 1950, provided 23 percent in 1970. Total installed capacity was 367,400,000 kilowatts in 1971, compared with 186,000,000 in 1960. About three-quarters of the electricity sold to the public was produced by privately-owned companies. The rest came from facilities owned cooperatively, municipally, and by the federal government.

Financial services. Under the Federal Reserve System, central banking functions are exercised by 12 Federal Reserve banks, each serving an important area of the country, supervised by a Board of Governors in Washington, D.C. The governors are appointed by the president, subject to confirmation by the Senate, but are by no means invariably in accord with the administration's views on economic policy—in contrast to the formal dependence of the Bank of England on the treasury in the United Kingdom. The Federal Reserve System regulates bank credit and the money supply by changes in the rediscount rate charged on loans to member banks, by changes in the reserve requirements imposed on commercial banks, and by open-market operations in government The
capital
market securities. The Treasury is not, however, without influence on the working of the monetary system; it influences market interest rates through its management of the national debt, while, by changing its own deposits with the Federal Reserve banks, it can affect the volume of credit.

Laws hindering the formation of branch banks have led to a proliferation of individual commercial banks, of which there were 13,687 at the end of 1971. Of these, 5,727 accounting for nearly 80 percent of total deposits with commercial banks, were members of the Federal Reserve System. Banks incorporated under national charter—4,599 at the end of 1971—must be members of the system, while banks incorporated under state charters may become members, though only about 14 percent of them have done so. Member banks must maintain minimum legal reserves with a Federal Reserve bank, ranging from 10 to 22 percent of their net demand deposits in the case of banks in reserve cities and from 7 to 14 percent in the case of country banks. Member banks must also deposit between 3 and 10 percent of their time (savings) deposits with a Federal Reserve bank.

In addition to commercial banks, there are 490 mutual savings banks and 5,500 savings and loan associations or building societies. Other financial intermediaries include insurance companies, with enormous assets, and finance companies dealing mainly in consumer credit. The federal government sponsors other credit agencies in the fields of housing and farming.

Security ownership is widespread; in the 1960s the number of shareholders rose from 13,000,000 to 31,000,000 in 1970. The market value of listed shares held by private individuals at the beginning of 1970 was almost two-thirds of the estimated total; the other third was held by institutions—pension funds, insurance companies, bank trust departments, mutual funds, etc.—which accounted for about half of the trading on the New York exchanges. New York has two organized stock exchanges, the New York Stock Exchange and the American Stock Exchange. The former trades in 1,830 of the most important securities and the latter in 1,200 other securities. There are, however, subsidiary New York markets: one in which members of the two exchanges sell unlisted stocks across the counter; another in which firms that are not members sell listed stocks across the counter without commission, taking a jobber's profit rather than a broker's; and a third in which institutions bypass the exchanges and deal directly with one another. The latter has been a cause of growing concern to the two exchanges.

A total of $105,200,000,000 was raised on the domestic capital market in 1971. Corporations raised $12,961,-000,000 with issues of preferred and common stock, and $32,100,000,000 with bond issues. The U.S. government raised $17,300,000,000 (compared with a record amount of $19,400,000,000 four years earlier) and other noncorporate borrowers, principally government agencies and state and local governments, raised $43,-000,000,000.

Foreign trade. International trade plays a relatively small part in the U.S. economy, as compared with the foreign trade of other major industrial countries. In 1971 imports of goods and services were equivalent to 7.0 percent of Gross National Product, while exports of goods and services represented 7.1 percent. Nevertheless, the sheer size of the economy makes the U.S. a major factor in world trade: in 1971 the U.S. absorbed 14 percent of total world imports and contributed 14 percent of total world exports, making it in both respects the most important single trading country.

Changes in imports and exports

U.S. imports rose at an average annual rate of 15.7 percent throughout the 1960s, reaching $40,000,000,000 by 1970. In 1970 nearly three-quarters of the imports were drawn from the developed countries of the world, compared with less than 60 percent in 1960, an illustration of the extent to which the growth in world trade in the 1960s was predominantly among the industrialized countries. The same point emerges from a consideration of the commodity composition of U.S. imports. In 1970, 60 percent of U.S. imports consisted of manufactures, compared with only 40 percent at the beginning of the

decade. Imports of food and raw materials grew much more slowly in the 1960s than total imports. This is partly explained by the increased use of domestically produced substitutes for imports of natural rubber and textile fibres. At the same time, there were dramatic increases in imports of manufactures, particularly of machinery and transport equipment.

While U.S. imports grew faster than world imports in the 1960s, U.S. exports rose more slowly than world exports. They totalled $42,600,000,000 in 1970. This represented a sharp drop in the massive trade surpluses that had been recorded in the early 1960s and was one reason for the growing difficulties in the balance of payments. The proportion of exports going to the developed nations rose during the 1960s, from 64 percent in 1960 to 69 percent in 1970. The largest single export market in 1970 was Canada ($9,100,000,000, or nearly one-fifth of total exports), followed by Japan ($4,700,000,000), West Germany ($2,700,000,000), and the U.K. ($2,500,000,000).

The compositon of exports changed during the 1960s to give greater weight to manufactures, in particular to machinery and transport equipment. In 1970 manufactured exports accounted for over 59 percent of the total, compared with 53 percent in 1960. Exports of food and raw materials remained of some importance, however.

One factor assisting the U.S. balance of trade in the 1960s was a shift in the terms of trade. Taking the years 1957–59 as a baseline, the unit value of U.S. exports had risen 16.5 percent by 1969, while the unit value of its imports had risen only 7.2 percent—representing an 8.7 percent improvement in the terms of trade over that period.

MANAGEMENT OF THE ECONOMY

Government and private enterprise. Government plays only a small direct part in economic activity in the U.S., where it is restricted to the United States Postal Service, the uranium enrichment facilities of the U.S. Atomic Energy Commission, and market activities such as those of the Tennessee Valley Authority. Enterprises that are often in public hands in other countries, such as railways, airlines, and telephone systems, are run privately in the U.S.

A principal effort of the government has been the fostering of competition through enforcement of the antitrust laws. These are designed to combat collusion among companies with respect to prices, output levels, or market shares and, where feasible, to prevent mergers that significantly reduce competition. The 1969 merger between The Standard Oil Co. (Ohio) (Sohio) and a subsidiary of The British Petroleum Co. Ltd., for example, was challenged by the Department of Justice and allowed to go through only when Sohio agreed to exchange stations in Ohio for others elsewhere in the country, thus fostering competition in gasoline retailing. So-called conglomerate mergers, between corporations in unrelated industries, which accounted for 82 percent of all combinations in the period 1966–68, had not come within the purview of the antitrust laws. There was strong sentiment at the end of the 1960s for opposing such mergers among the 200 largest manufacturing companies or any merger by one of them with a leading producer in a highly concentrated industry, on the ground that conglomerates were able to switch the profits of one market to subsidize price wars in others, thus reducing competition in the long run, and were also able to require suppliers of one industry in the group to buy from others, on the principle of reciprocity, thus again potentially excluding competitors.

Fiscal and monetary policy

The major area of government regulation of economic activity is through fiscal and monetary policy. The small-scale recession of 1970–71, for example, was the result of a decision to restrict the growth of the money supply in an effort to control inflation. Reductions in federal income tax rates played an important part in initiating the boom of the 1960s. The government also exerts considerable leverage on certain sectors of the economy as a purchaser of goods, notably in the aircraft and aerospace industries.

Proposals for governmental controls of prices and incomes were a source of much controversy in the 1960s and early 1970s. Between 1962 and 1966 the Kennedy and Johnson administrations established so-called guideposts for wages and prices in an effort to prevent the economic upswing from leading to inflation. These were to be followed voluntarily rather than enforced by regulation, but there were instances in the 1960s when the prospect of major price increases in important industries brought down on the manufacturers concerned a heavy weight of what was euphemistically called "moral persuasion" on the part of the President. The strong inflationary trend of the late 1960s and early 1970s led the Nixon administration to more radical intervention in the summer of 1971. A three-month freeze on wages and prices was imposed in August, followed in November by the establishment of a Pay Board and a Price Commission that were to set limits on subsequent increases.

Another field in which the government regulates private economic activity is farming. It endeavours to support farm incomes through direct payments to farmers, controls on output, price supports, and the provision of storage and marketing facilities. In 1971 direct payment to farmers cost $3,200,000,000. One disadvantage of the system is that payments are related to farm output, so that the benefit has often gone to the larger commercial farms rather than to those the income level of which was the main object of governmental concern.

Taxation. Nearly all of the federal government's revenues come from taxes. By far the most important source of tax revenue is the personal income tax, which yielded 42.5 percent of total federal receipts in the fiscal year 1972–73. The effective rate of tax in 1972 on the income of a married couple with two dependents varied from 2.0 percent if they had an income of $5,000 a year to 17.0 percent if their income was $25,000—at which income level a single person without dependents paid an effective rate of 18.8 percent. The 17.0 percent rate in 1972 would have been 19.0 percent in 1964 and 21.3 percent in the period between 1954 and 1963, while the 2.0 percent rate would have been 6.5 in 1964 and 8.4 percent between 1954 and 1963. Marginal tax rates in 1966 in the various income brackets—*i.e.*, the rate applicable to the top dollar of income taxable at normal and surtax rates—were 18.4 percent in the $5,000–$10,000-a-year bracket, 32.8 percent in the $20,000–$50,000 bracket, and 57.3 percent in the $100,000–$500,000 bracket; the marginal rate on incomes of over $1,000,000 was 58.2 percent.

Corporate income taxes yielded 16.2 percent of total federal receipts in the 1972/73 fiscal year. The tax was levied at a rate of 48 percent. Excise duties yielded only 7.4 percent of the total federal revenue, but this was offset by the fact that the individual states levy their own excise and sales taxes. Federal excises rest heavily on alcohol, gasoline, and tobacco. Another major source of revenue in the 1972/73 fiscal year was social-insurance taxes and contributions, which yielded 28.8 percent of total revenue. There are also estate and gift duties, yielding 1.9 percent of the total in 1972/73.

Federal tax receipts rose rapidly in the later years of the 1960s, partly because the prevailing inflation brought compensatory wage and salary increases that resulted in higher marginal rates of taxation. Total federal revenue rose in the five years from fiscal 1967 to fiscal 1972 by 32.2 percent, but the net yield of individual income taxes rose by nearly 41 percent. In contrast, the net yield of the corporation income tax declined by 13 percent over the same period—an indication of how severely the monetary squeeze of 1969 and the ensuing fall in demand had affected corporate profits.

Trade unions. The labour force in the U.S. is not highly organized. Total union membership in 1970 (excluding Canadians who are members of U.S. unions) was 19,381,000, of whom 15,978,000 belonged to unions affiliated with the American Federation of Labor-Congress of Industrial Organizations (AFL-CIO), the nationwide federation of unions. Of the total nonagricultural labour force, 27.9 percent in 1968 belonged to unions; in 1960 the comparable figure had been 31.4 percent. About 46

percent of wage and salary earners in manufacturing belonged to unions in 1966. The unionized proportion in mining and quarrying was over 50 percent, in contract construction just over 75 percent; but, in wholesale and retail trade and the service industries, it reached only about 10 percent. The biggest unions in 1970 were the International Brotherhood of Teamsters, Chauffeurs, Warehousemen, and Helpers of America, with 1,829,000 members, the United Automobile Workers (1,486,000), and the United Steel Workers of America (1,200,000). Most unions in manufacturing bargain on a plant- or company-wide scale, although the older unions, such as those of the carpenters and the electricians, bargain by crafts. Settlements negotiated by the unions do not necessarily set the pattern for the movement of wage rates in general. There have been periods when negotiated settlements secured wage increases rather lower than the rate at which wage rates were rising overall.

Although the freedom to strike is hedged about with legislative provisions for "cooling-off" periods and in some cases compulsory arbitration, the major unions are able and willing to embark on long strikes. In 1971 there were 5,100 stoppages causing the loss of 47,400,000 man-days, of which 2,598 stoppages were about general wage claims. Some 1,473 stoppages lasted for longer than 30 days.

Contemporary economic policies. The first economic concern of President Nixon's administration was to bring under control the inflation it inherited from the previous administration; the inflation had been caused in large measure by rapidly increasing military expenditures from the war in Vietnam, coupled with a reluctance to forgo higher expenditures on domestic programs. The problem, in the government's view, was not simply that the economy had veered briefly into excessive expansion, but rather that it was entering its fourth successive year of inflation, which itself served to generate expectations of further inflation that would make the reattainment of reasonable price stability difficult. President Johnson's administration had imposed a 10 percent surcharge on income taxes at the end of June 1968, swinging from a budget deficit of $25,000,000,000 in the fiscal year ending that month to an estimated surplus of $3,200,000,000 in the 1968/69 fiscal year. The Nixon administration began by adopting a policy of balanced budgets and a tight money supply, hoping that a decline in economic activity would put a stop to inflation. The resulting recession, however, was accompanied by continued increases in prices. In response to mounting criticism of its economic policies, the administration decided in mid-1971 to swing over to direct controls on prices and wages (see above), while at the same time attempting to stimulate the economy by giving tax concessions to business and consumers and allowing the federal budget to remain in deficit.

The summer of 1971 also saw a major shift in foreign-trade policy. In previous years, under the Trade Expansion Act of 1962, the government had taken part in a series of tariff negotiations with other industrialized countries known as the Kennedy Round. In exchange for tariff concessions by its main trading partners, the U.S. had agreed to tariff cuts averaging 35 percent, to be made in five annual installments beginning on January 1, 1968. Subsequently, strong pressures developed in some industrial circles and in Congress for a more protectionist stance. President Nixon, for example, gave an election pledge in 1968 to restrict entry of Japanese textiles to the U.S. market if Japan proved unwilling to limit them voluntarily. Proposals were made in Congress to impose quota restrictions on the entry of other products that were underselling domestically produced goods. Other tensions arose with the countries of the European Economic Community (EEC; Common Market) over the more protectionist aspects of the EEC's common agricultural policy, which hindered U.S. exports, and over the EEC's policy of signing preferential agreements with Mediterranean countries. Impatience was also expressed at the protectionist policies of Japan. To the difficulties in trade was added a severe international financial crisis resulting from continued deficits in the U.S. balance of payments.

In August 1971 President Nixon called upon the major trading partners of the U.S. to revalue their currencies upward, on the ground that the dollar, as the currency in terms of which all others were expressed, could not be unilaterally devalued. He also announced that the U.S. was suspending the free convertibility of the dollar into gold and imposing restrictions on imports—including a 10 percent surcharge on those covered by tariff legislation.

In December 1971 a realignment of currency rates was agreed in Washington, D.C., involving an 8.57 percent increase in the dollar price of gold and a further revaluation of the Deutsche Mark, yen, guilder, Belgian franc, and Swiss franc. During 1972, continuing (and increasing) balance of trade deficits, combined with other monetary pressures, led to a second devaluation of the dollar (by 10 percent) in February 1973.

Problems and prospects. The problems facing the U.S. economy in the early 1970s were similar to those of other highly industrialized countries. One of them was the question whether high levels of employment could be maintained without inflation or whether the quest for price stability would require damping down economic growth and incurring unacceptable amounts of unemployment—a course that the congressional elections of 1970 indicated would be dangerous to the party in power.

Public concern with environmental pollution also increased at the beginning of the 1970s, leading many to question whether economic growth could continue at previous rates without disastrous consequences to plant and animal life, including human life. It became apparent that serious efforts to deal with the side effects of industrial development would require new economic and social policies. Any slowing in the rate of economic growth, however, would in itself create problems. As the *Economic Report of the President* for 1970 pointed out, the probable increase in federal expenditure arising from existing commitments and policies would be sufficient in coming years to absorb virtually all the additional revenues the government would receive even if growth resumed at a rate of 4.3 percent per annum by 1973. A slower rate of growth would therefore mean reducing the claims on the federal budget, most likely in the area of social policy.

(E.I.U.)

TRANSPORTATION

The economic and social complexion of life in the United States mirrors the nation's extraordinary mobility. It may be that no other people on Earth allocate so many resources and so much of their time and attention to moving and getting things moved. A pervasive transportation network has helped bring together in the vast geographic expanse of the country a surprisingly homogeneous and close-knit social and economic environment. This freedom to move explains in large measure the dynamism of the U.S. economy. Mobility has made possible vast metropolises, spreading suburbs, a lengthening radius of commuter travel, the dispersal of shops and industry, and the growing millions of nonfarm rural residents who constitute a new kind of urbanization without community. Mobility has also had destructive effects. It has accelerated the decay of the old urban areas, multiplied traffic congestion, intensified the pollution of the environment, undermined the public-transportation systems, and made recluses of those who lack automobiles.

A view of the continental United States from a spacecraft would show 3,000,000 square miles (8,000,000 square kilometres) of land etched by 3,700,000 miles (6,000,000 kilometres) of roads and streets. The network of roads is thickest on the eastern seaboard, along the Mississippi and Ohio valleys, and on the Pacific coast. Over this network in 1971 moved 111,000,000 motor vehicles—92,000,000 passenger cars and 19,000,000 trucks and buses. In addition, there are 344,000 miles of railway track, 176,000 miles of intercity pipelines, 142,000 miles of airways, and 25,000 miles of navigable waterways on the rivers and Great Lakes. Together these systems make it possible to provide 9,000 ton-miles of

freight transportation per year for each inhabitant. The number of persons employed in the transportation services and in their supporting equipment and supply industries exceeds the combined population of Norway and Sweden.

Methods of passenger travel. The overriding factor in the nation's mobility is the automobile. Eighty-three percent of all families own at least one car, and 28 percent own two or more. It is possible to eat a meal, attend the theatre, or make a bank deposit without getting out of one's car, and only slightly more effort is required to spend the night at a motel or to visit a shopping centre where business caters to a wheeled clientele. Millions work in suburban factories far from any means of public transportation, where getting the job requires having a car.

The increase in car ownership has exceeded the rising output of goods and services and far outstripped the growth of population. Taking 1950 as 100, the index of gross national product in 1969 was 205, the index of population 133, and the index of auto registration 213. At the same time, the city transit systems have undergone a sharp decline: between 1950 and 1971 the number of bus and subway rides taken annually dropped from 17,000,000,000 to 7,000,000,000, despite a great increase in urban population.

Table 2: Motor Vehicles
Registered in the United States
(000,000 vehicles)

year	total motor vehicles	passenger automobiles
1940	32	27
1950	49	40
1960	74	62
1970	108	89

Source: Automobile Manufacturers Association, *Automobile Facts and Figures*.

The purposes of automobile riding were revealed in a survey of the Baltimore metropolitan area in the early 1960s. It showed that 38 percent of all trips were for the purpose of getting to work, and 9 percent were for personal business. Shopping accounted for 16 percent of the total trips and social or recreational travel for an equal proportion. Another 10 percent of the riding was to school (Wilbur Smith and Associates, *Baltimore Metropolitan Area Transportation Study* [1964]).

While seven out of ten trips in metropolitan areas are made by car, public transit and rail commuter lines play an important role in the most populous cities. From 70 to 90 percent of home-to-work travel in the rush hours is by public carrier in such large centres as Boston, Philadelphia, Chicago, and New York. On an average day 26,000,000 people in the United States patronize local buses and subways. Only 15 percent of U.S. workers walk to their jobs.

The automobile also dominates intercity travel patterns. According to a Census Bureau survey in 1967, of those making trips of 100 miles or more, 86 percent go by car. Of the remainder, 3 percent go by bus, 8 percent by air, and 1 percent by railway. When intercity travel by public carrier is measured in terms of passenger miles, however, the figure for air travel is three times the total of rail and bus transportation combined, because trips by air are much longer than by bus or rail.

Household budgets reflect the travel picture. Out of every consumer dollar spent for travel in 1968, 93 cents went for automobiles and their upkeep. The remaining seven cents was spent on public carriers, divided almost equally between intercity transportation and carriers serving urban areas. In other words, only 3.2 cents out of the transportation dollar was spent on non-automobile transportation in cities. Since nearly one-third of this amount was taxi fares, the urban public transportation systems, including the commuter railroads, received only 2.2 cents of the transportation dollar.

Table 3: Personal Consumption Expenditures for Transportation in the United States, 1968
(in $000,000)

	expenditures	percentage
User-operated transportation	73,035	93.6
Purchased local transportation	2,322	2.9
Streetcars and local bus	1,401	1.79
Taxi	759	0.9
Railway	162	0.2
Purchased intercity transportation	2,645	3.39
Railway	164	0.2
Intercity bus	362	0.46
Airline	2,086	2.67
Other	33	*
Total	78,002	100.0

*Less than 0.1 percent.
Source: U.S. Department of Commerce, Office of Business Economics, *Survey of Current Business* (July 1970).

Rail-roads as bulk carriers

Freight transportation. Railroads still play an important part in freight transportation between cities. In 1970 they carried 41 percent of the total domestic ton-miles of freight, compared with 22 percent carried by pipelines, 21 percent by truck, and 16 percent by the inland waterways and on the Great Lakes. The railways carry a preponderance of heavy bulk materials, while trucks carry the lighter and more valuable goods. The result is that trucks get the lion's share of the intercity freight dollar: 73 cents, compared with only 14 cents for the railways. Altogether, the volume of freight traffic in the United States in 1970 amounted to 1,900,000,000,000 ton-miles, or about two ton-miles for every dollar of gross national product.

The transportation bill. The total freight bill paid by Americans in 1968 amounted to $75,000,000,000, of which $55,000,000,000 was for trucking. Outlays for passenger travel totalled $97,000,000,000 of which $83,000,000,000 was spent on private automobiles.

Government expenditures for basic transport facilities in 1970 totalled nearly $23,000,000,000, about one-third supplied through the federal government and two-thirds by the states and localities. The major outlay was for roads, on which nearly $20,000,000,000 was spent; the remaining $3,000,000,000 was shared by all other transportation media. A little less than $2,000,000,000 was spent on airways and airports. The most spectacular part of the government program was the ongoing 42,000-mile Interstate Highway System, a national network of multiple-lane dual expressways connecting 48 states and 90 percent of all cities of 50,000 population or more. This $50,000,000,000 system, begun in the 1950s, was to be completed by 1974, when it would carry 20 per cent of the nation's motor traffic. It would be possible to drive from coast to coast on the Interstate network without stopping for a traffic light.

Policy issues. The automobile age has brought some unpleasant consequences, including traffic congestion and air pollution. Some efforts were being made at various governmental levels in the early 1970s to adapt the transportation system to the changing needs of society. These included a new program of aid for urban transit in hope of providing an attractive alternative for automobile commuters. New federal safety requirements for passenger cars were aimed at reducing the highway death toll (nearing 60,000 per year), and new engines and fuels were being developed to reduce air pollution. Efforts were directed to making transportation investment decisions more responsive to community desires. Bans were beginning to be imposed on cars on the downtown streets in some large cities.

The U.S. Congress gave recognition to the urgency of transportation problems in 1965 by establishing a Department of Transportation in the federal government. The country was entering a new era of jumbo jets, vertical- and steep-take off airplanes, high-speed ground transport, computerized freight systems, automated highways, and new power sources. Many believed that the central question was how to arrive at a compromise between the desire to be urbanized and motorized and the desire to remain civilized. (W.O.)

V. Administration and social conditions

THE STRUCTURE OF GOVERNMENT

The national government. The United States Constitution sets up and defines a federal system of government in which certain powers are delegated to the national government and all other powers fall to the states. The national government consists of executive, legislative, and judicial branches designed to check and balance each other, all interrelated and overlapping yet each quite distinct.

Since the Constitution came into effect in 1788, there have been 26 amendments to it. The first ten, known as the Bill of Rights, established certain individual liberties. Notable among the other amendments are the 13th, 14th, and 15th, which abolished slavery and declared former slaves citizens with the right to vote; the 19th, which effected female suffrage; and the 17th, which provided for the direct election of United States senators. Amending the Constitution requires a proposal by a two-thirds vote in Congress or by a national convention, followed by ratification by three-fourths of the state legislatures or state conventions.

The executive branch of the government is headed by the president, whose formal responsibilities include those of chief executive, treaty maker, commander in chief of the army, and head of state. In practice, they have grown to include the drafting of legislation, the formulation of foreign policy, personal diplomacy, and leadership of his political party. The members of the president's Cabinet —the secretaries of State; Treasury; Defense; Interior; Agriculture; Commerce; Labor; Health, Education and Welfare; Housing and Urban Development; Transportation; and the Attorney General—are defined in the 25th amendment as "the principal officers of the executive departments," but much power has come to be exercised by presidential aides who are not in the Cabinet. Thus, the president's Executive Office includes the Office of Management and Budget, the National Security Resources Board, the Council of Economic Advisers, the National Security Council, and the Office of Defense Mobilization.

The executive and legislative branches

The legislative branch of the government is the Congress, which has two houses: the Senate and the House of Representatives. Powers granted Congress under the Constitution include the power to levy taxes, borrow money, regulate interstate commerce, declare war, seat members, discipline its own membership, and determine its rules of procedure.

The House of Representatives is chosen by direct vote of the electorate in each state, the number of representatives allotted to each state being based on population. Members must be 25 years old, inhabitants of the states from which they are elected, and previously citizens of the United States for at least seven years. It has become practically imperative, though not constitutionally required, that they be inhabitants of the districts that elect them. They serve for a two-year period. The speaker of the House, who is chosen by the majority party, presides over debate, appoints members of select conference committees, and performs other leading duties. The parliamentary leaders of the two parties are the majority floor leader and the minority floor leader; they are helped by party whips who maintain contact between the leadership and the members of the House. Bills introduced by members in the House of Representatives are received by the standing committees, which meet in private executive session and can amend, expedite, delay, or kill the bills. The committee chairmen attain their positions on the basis of seniority, a criterion that is increasingly challenged. Among the most important committees are those on Appropriations, Ways and Means, and Rules. The Rules Committee, traditionally conservative, has great power to determine which bills will be brought to the floor of the House for consideration.

Each state elects two senators. Senators must be at least 30 years old, inhabitants of the state from which they are elected, and previously citizens of the United States for at least nine years. Each term of service is for six years, and terms are so arranged that one-third of the members are elected every two years.

The Senate has 16 standing committees, among which the most prominent are those on Foreign Relations, Finance, Appropriations, and Government Operations. Debate is almost unlimited and may be used to delay the vote on a bill indefinitely. Such a delay is known as a filibuster and can be brought to an end only if two-thirds of the Senate agree. Treaties made by the president with other governments must be ratified by a two-thirds vote of the Senate.

The judicial branch

The United States Supreme Court, the third, or judicial, branch of the government, interprets the meaning of the Constitution and of federal laws. It consists of nine justices (including the chief justice) appointed for life by the president with the consent of the Senate. It has appellate jurisdiction for the lower courts and from state courts of last resort if a federal question is involved. It has original jurisdiction over cases involving foreign ambassadors, ministers, consuls, and cases to which a state is a party.

Three types of cases commonly reach the Supreme Court: cases involving litigants of different states, cases involving the interpretation of federal law, and cases involving the interpretation of the Constitution. Six judges consider each case, and a majority vote of the whole court is decisive; a tie vote sustains a lower-court decision. Often the minority judges will write a dissenting report.

The Supreme Court has often been criticized for its decisions. In the 1930s a conservative court overturned much of Pres. Franklin D. Roosevelt's New Deal legislation. In the area of civil rights it has received criticism from various groups at different times. After a 1954 ruling against school segregation, Southern political leaders attacked it harshly. Later, they were joined by Northern conservatives. During the 1960s a number of decisions involving the pretrial rights of prisoners came under attack on the ground that the court had made it difficult to convict criminals.

Below the Supreme Court is the U.S. Court of Appeals. Special courts handle property and contract damage suits against the United States (U.S. Court of Claims), review customs rulings (U.S. Customs Court), and apply the uniform Code of Military Justice (U.S. Court of Military Appeals). Each state has at least one federal district court and at least one federal judge. District judges are appointed for life by the president with Senate consent. Appeals from district-court decisions are carried to the Court of Appeals.

State and municipal governments. The governments of the 50 states have structures closely paralleling those of the federal government. Each state has a governor, a legislature, and a judiciary. Each state has its own constitution.

All state legislatures but one have two houses, Nebraska's being unicameral. Traditionally, state legislatures have been dominated by rural representatives who are not always sympathetic to the needs of growing urban areas. State judicial systems are based upon elected justices of the peace, above whom come the major trial courts, often called district courts, and appellate courts. In addition, there are probate courts concerned with wills, estates, and guardianships. Most state judges are elected

State governments have a wide array of functions, encompassing agriculture and conservation, highway and motor-vehicle supervision, public safety and correction, professional licensing, regulation of intrastate business and industry, and certain aspects of education, public health, and welfare. These activities require a large administrative organization, headed by the governor. In most states there is also a lieutenant governor, not always of the same party as the governor, who serves as the presiding officer of the Senate. Other elected officials include the secretary of state, state treasurer, state auditor, attorney general, and superintendent of public instruction.

Municipal governments are more diverse in structure than state governments. There are three basic types: mayor–council governments, commission governments, and council–manager governments. In the first type, the mayor and the council are elected; the council is nominally responsible for formulating city ordinances, which the mayor enforces; often the mayor controls the actions of the council. Boston, New York, Philadelphia, Chicago, and Seattle have the mayor–council type of city government. In the commission type, voters elect a number of commissioners each of whom serves as head of a city department; the presiding commissioner is generally the mayor. Des Moines and New Orleans have commission governments. In the council–manager type, an elected council hires a city manager to administer the city departments. The mayor, elected by the council, simply chairs it and officiates at important functions. Over 2,200 cities had adopted the manager plan by 1968.

The three types of municipal government

Political parties. There are two major political parties in the U.S., the Democratic Party and the Republican Party. Other parties have occasionally challenged these two but without permanent success. One reason for their failure is that to win a national election, a party must appeal to a broad base of voters and a wide spectrum of interests. The two major parties tend to be moderate in their programs, and, in fact, there is usually little difference between them. Each has a conservative wing, and each has a wing that is considered liberal. The conservative Democrats are more conservative on racial issues than their Republican counterparts; the liberal Democrats are more radical on economic issues than the liberal Republicans. The national parties exist mainly to contest presidential elections every four years, and, in between their quadrennial national conventions, they are little more than loose alliances of state and local party organizations.

The political process

In elections for president, voters actually choose among electors committed to the support of a particular candidate. Each state is allotted one electoral vote for each senator and representative in Congress. This is called the electoral-college system.

At the state level, political parties reflect the diversity of the population. Large urban centres are likely to support a Democratic ticket, whereas rural areas, small cities, and suburban areas tend to vote Republican. In many states the rural areas and smaller towns control the state legislatures, even though the more populous city areas provide the greater proportion of tax revenue. A Supreme Court ruling in 1964 sought to remedy this situation by ordering states to reapportion their legislatures more according to population. Some states have traditionally given majorities to one particular party. The 11 Southern states of the old Confederacy have until recently voted almost solidly for Democratic candidates; in Maine and South Dakota the Republicans more often won.

Municipal political parties have a pyramidal structure based, at the lowest level, on districts or precincts. The leaders of these units are responsible to ward leaders, who form the governing body of the municipal party. All of these party functionaries are responsible for getting their voters to the polls at election time, often on the basis of a return for services rendered. It is to them after all, that voters have gone with requests for better municipal services, jobs, and assistance in minor difficulties. One route to political office for the ordinary citizen has been through the organization: belonging to a neighbourhood party club, helping to raise funds, getting out the vote, watching the polls, and gradually rising through the system to committeeman, city councilman, representative to the state legislature, or—depending on chance, talent, political expediency, and a host of other factors—to higher positions.

As society has become increasingly urban, politics and government have become more and more complex. Many problems of the cities, including the problems of transportation, housing, education, health, and welfare, can no longer be handled entirely on the local level. Since even the states do not have the necessary resources, the cities have been forced to turn to the federal government for assistance.

Decline of local autonomy

Armed forces. The military forces of the U.S. consist of the army, navy, marines, air force, and coast guard, under the umbrella of the Department of Defense with its headquarters in the Pentagon building in Arlington, Virginia. Military personnel numbered over 3,600,000 in 1971, and the military budget exceeded $78,000,000,000. Since a large part of it is spent on matériel and research and development, military programs may have considerable economic and political impact.

The influence of the military also extends to other countries through various multilateral and bilateral treaties for mutual defense and military assistance. In the early 1970s the U.S. had military bases in Africa, Asia, Europe, and Latin America.

The armed forces in the early 1970s were made up of conscripts as well as career personnel and volunteers. Under the Military Selective Service Act of 1967 (Public Law 90–40), all men between 18 and 26 years of age were required to register for service, although provisions were made for the physically handicapped, conscientious objectors, and others in special circumstances. The equity of the draft provisions was increasingly questioned, however, and in the early 1970s a completely volunteer service began to be created. The four armed services also maintain reserve forces that may be called upon in time of war. Each state has a National Guard consisting of reserve groups subject to call at any time by the governor of the state.

THE SOCIAL SECTOR

Education. The interplay of local, state, and national programs and policies is nowhere more evident than in the field of education. Historically, education has been considered the province of the state and local governments. Of the more than 2,500 colleges and universities, only one—Howard University in Washington, D.C.—is considered a federal institution. (The U.S. also administers the College of the Virgin Islands.) For years, however, the federal government has been involved in education at all levels, beginning in 1872 with the grant of public lands to the states for the purpose of establishing agricultural and mechanical arts colleges. There are 68 of these land-grant colleges. Additionally, the federal government supports school lunch programs, administers Indian education, makes research grants to universities, underwrites loans to college students, finances education for veterans, and prepares teaching materials. In 1971 the Office of Education administered $11,400,000,000 in federal school aid. Whether the government should also give assistance to private and parochial (religious) schools has been widely debated. The Supreme Court has ruled that direct assistance to parochial schools is barred by the First Amendment to the Constitution, which states that "Congress shall make no law respecting an establishment of religion," although this has not been extended to the use of textbooks and so-called "supplementary educational centres."

Entry to colleges and universities in the U.S. is still closely correlated with family income. In the 1968–69 academic year about 20 percent of college-age children of families with incomes up to $3,000 attended college. The figure was about 30 percent in the case of families with incomes of $3,000 to $4,000, 50 percent for families with incomes between $7,500 and $10,000, and 85 percent for those with incomes of $15,000 and over.

The amount of education received by the general population has increased over the years. In 1940, among persons 25 years of age and older, only 24.5 percent had completed high school; in 1960, 41.1 percent; and in 1970, 55.2 percent had completed high school. The figure was higher for whites (57.5 percent in 1970) than for blacks (33.8). Of the general population in 1970, only 13.4 percent had completed fewer than eight years of school and only 5.3 percent fewer than five years.

Although responsibility for elementary education still rests primarily with local government; it is increasingly affected by state and national policies. The 1964 Civil Rights Act, for example, required federal agencies to cut off financial aid to school districts that are not racially integrated. This raised difficult problems for the school systems of some Northern cities where blacks were living in largely segregated enclaves, requiring children to be transported long distances to nonsegregated schools.

Current trends in education are toward meeting the needs of a complex society: preschool programs; nongraded, multilevel classrooms; classes in the community; summer and night schools; increased facilities for exceptional children; and a general restructuring of traditional mores to improve education of the culturally deprived and the disaffected student.

Welfare and health services. For all its wealth, poverty remains a reality for many persons in the United States. In 1960 an estimated 28,300,000 whites and 11,500,000 non-whites were at or below what was considered the poverty level by government statisticians. In 1971 the total was 25,600,000, of whom 4,300,000 were 65 or older, and 8,400,000 were children under 14. About 60 percent of the poor were in homes in which there was a full or part-time wage earner. Of the others, 80 percent were too old or handicapped to work, while 15 percent were mothers of young children. The states provide assistance to the poor in varying amounts. In the late 1960s, state assistance ranged from approximately $2,400 a year for a family of four to as low as $600. The U.S. Department of Agriculture subsidizes the distribution of low-cost food to the poor through the state and local governments.

Increasing public concern with poverty and welfare led to new federal legislation in the 1960s. Work, training, and rehabilitation programs were established in 1962 for welfare recipients. Between 1965 and 1969 the Office of Economic Opportunity set in motion a host of programs: the Head Start program for preschool children, the Neighborhood Youth Corps, the Teacher Corps, and the Manpower Training and Development program for unemployed workers. In 1969 the Nixon administration proposed among other measures, a sliding scale of payments for workers earning less than the poverty level. The plan would require all able adult family members to accept work or training when possible and would provide day-care centres to free mothers for work.

Persons who have been employed are eligible for retirement pensions under the federal social security program established in the 1930s. Many employers also provide additional retirement benefits, as well as health insurance and life insurance, usually based on contributions by both the employer and the worker. In 1970 about 90 percent of those employed, or 80,600,000 persons, were covered by Social Security. In addition, 29,700,000 persons were covered by private pension plans.

The provision of medical and health care is the second largest industry in the United States. In 1970 about 7 percent of the gross national product, amounting to over $300 per person, was spent in this field. There were, nevertheless, many inadequacies in medical services, particularly in rural and poor areas. The number of practicing physicians for every 100,000 persons was about 164 in 1970, ranging from 78 in Mississippi to 234 in New York State.

About one-sixth of the population, including members of the armed forces and their families, receive medical care paid for or subsidized by the federal government. Many people are not covered by any form of health insurance. In 1965 some medical care was provided for the aged under the federal Social Security program, but most health insurance is on a private basis.

Of the total amount spent on medical and health care in 1970, 37 percent or $26,724,000,000 came from government sources. The federal Department of Health, Education and Welfare through its National Institutes of Health supports over 40 percent of the biomedical research in the U.S. Grants are made also to researchers in clinics and medical schools.

Infant mortality was 19.8 per thousand in 1970. Life expectancy at birth was 74.0 years for females and 66.6 for males.

Housing. About 68,627,000 housing units existed in the United States in 1970, of which more than 64,000,000

Colleges and universities

Elementary and secondary education

The poor

Financing of health care

Quality
of housing

were occupied. For the country as a whole, there were about 2.7 persons per occupied unit, as compared with 3.4 in 1960 and 3.8 in 1940. Over 90 percent of the occupied housing units had hot running water, flush toilets, and bathing facilities inside. About 70 percent of them were single-family houses, and a majority of the remainder were in structures containing two, three, or four units. Most houses in the United States are of wood construction, though often covered with shingles or brick veneer.

Housing, like health, was long considered a private rather than public concern. The growth of urban slums led many municipal governments to enact stricter building codes and sanitary regulations. In 1934 the Federal Housing Administration was established to make loans to institutions that would build low-rent dwellings. In 1945, Congress authorized the building of 810,000 housing units by public housing authorities. In 1949 it provided large sums in loans and grants to local communities for slum clearance and redevelopment. The continued deterioration of housing conditions in large cities led in 1968 to new federal legislation to subsidize the building of 26,000,000 new units in ten years, 6,000,000 of which were to be low-cost.

Efforts to reduce the slums in large cities by developing low-cost housing in other areas have been resisted by property owners. For many years the restrictive covenant, by which property owners pledged not to sell to certain racial or religious groups, served to bar those groups from many communities. A 1948 Supreme Court decision declared covenants unenforceable; a 1962 executive order by President Kennedy prohibited discrimination in housing built with federal aid; and many states and cities have adopted fair-housing laws and set up fair-housing commissions. All these efforts, however, have had little effect upon the black ghettos in large cities.

Law enforcement. The enforcement of law in the United States has traditionally been centred in the hands of local police officials. The bulk of the work is done by patrolmen, detectives, and policewomen in the cities and by sheriffs and constables in rural areas. Many of the state governments also have law-enforcement agencies, and all of them have highway-patrol systems for traffic-law enforcement. Crimes that come under federal jurisdiction (for example, those committed in more than one state) are the responsibility of the Federal Bureau of Investigation (FBI), which also provides assistance through fingerprint identification and technical laboratory services to state and local law-enforcement agencies.

Crime rates rose in the 1960s, and law enforcement became a major political issue in the early 1970s. In 1966 the federal government began encouraging state coordinating councils composed of local police, prosecutors, courts, and corrective officers—a trend that was strengthened by the omnibus Crime Control and Safe Streets Act (Public Law 90–351). Other measures taken to combat crime included enlarging police departments and raising the level of competence in police work.

Living levels. The decade of the 1960s saw a continued improvement in the level of living of much of the U.S. population. Average family incomes in 1970 dollars rose from $6,962 in 1960 to $9,867 in 1970. The incomes of Negro families in the latter year averaged about 63 percent of the incomes of white families, as compared with 55 percent in 1960. Food consumption, although accounting for a smaller part of the consumer's dollar than formerly, continued to increase. Daily per capita food consumption was about 3,290 calories in 1970, one of the highest levels in the world. The consumption of wheat flour and fluid milk declined; the consumption of meat increased from about 161 pounds per person (73 kilograms) in 1960 to 185 pounds in 1970.

The latter part of the 1960s and the beginning of the 1970s were shadowed by price inflation that approached a rate of 6 percent a year—considered high in the U.S.— and also by increased unemployment. The latter fell more heavily upon blacks than upon whites and was especially severe among young people under 20 years of age.

(J.T.H.)

VI. Cultural life and institutions

THE CULTURAL MILIEU

The dominant fact of cultural life in the United States during the 20th century has been rapid and continual change brought about by such factors as population growth, technological development, urbanization, and the press of world events. By the middle decades of the 20th century, the principal question was whether change was producing a more unified, homogeneous, and standardized culture or a culture increasingly divided and fragmented into sometimes conflicting parts.

Trends toward uniformity. With the advent of commercial television at midcentury, it was generally believed that cultural life would be increasingly shaped by the techniques and requirements of mass cultural institutions. According to this view, the major media of communications—television, radio, motion pictures, national magazines, and phonograph-record companies, operating principally in New York City and Los Angeles—would produce an overwhelming proportion of the entertainment and information available to the public. Such cultural production, it was argued, would inevitably be controlled by the commercial need to appeal to the largest possible audience and to sell advertised goods and services. The result would be a growing cultural uniformity throughout the country at a level of lowest-common-denominator mediocrity, wiping out ethnic and regional differences and confining the creation and preservation of "high culture"—literature, the fine arts, classical music and opera, philosophy and social thought—to a small, educated elite.

Homogenizing influences of mass communications and institutions

Certainly, some part of these pessimistic predictions came true in U.S. cultural life at midcentury. In a period of rapid communications and nationwide consolidation of corporate industry, regional variations in such facets of cultural life as architecture, language, popular entertainment, and style of dress unquestionably diminished. It was possible to travel west across the country in a few hours and find in Arizona or Oregon shops and restaurants with the same names, buildings, and products, as well as television channels and movie theatres with the same programs, that had been left behind in Virginia or Connecticut. Few other countries had attained such unity of cultural life over so vast a territory and so large a population.

The counter-cultures. In this period of increasing standardization of cultural life, however, a countertrend began that opposed the process of unification with a process of fragmentation. In its origins, this countermovement consisted very little in a conscious effort to resist the development of mass culture, in the form, for example, of a bohemian colony of nonconformists. Rather, its sources came from movements of social change and political opposition, the renewed civil-rights movement of the early 1960s, and the opposition to the growing United States' military involvement in Vietnam in the latter half of that decade. As groups formed around issues and developed identities through the struggles, a consciousness emerged not merely of political disagreement but also of cultural difference. The movement for civil rights became a movement for black power, dividing rather than uniting black and white people. Middle class college and university students, shifting their concern from civil rights to the antiwar movement as the United States became more deeply involved in Southeast Asia, developed a sense of youth culture and adopted the phrase generation gap and the slogan "never trust anyone over 30." By the end of the 1960s, the term counter-culture was commonly used as a loose umbrella covering a variety of alternatives to the traditional norms of cultural life.

The counter-culture differed significantly from the alternative cultures of other eras. Past alternative cultures had accepted high culture as their standard against the alleged mediocrity or commercialism of the mass. They were minority cultures founded on appreciation and creation of literature and other fine arts. This facet of cultural alternative was not entirely missing from the counter-culture that began in the 1960s, but it was not its central aspect. The new focus was on opposing the norms of conventional culture, including the class and aesthetic distinctions reflected in the idea of high culture. Its most publicized symbols were "hippies," long-haired young people who popularized the use of marijuana and hallucinogenic drugs, rock music, and communal life-styles.

The fragmentation of cultural life continued to take new forms. Black power for Negroes became red power for American Indians, brown power for Chicanos and other Spanish-speaking people, women's liberation as a new form of feminism, gay liberation for homosexuals. In all these cases the rhetoric of "power" and "liberation" implied a pride and self-confidence in racial, ethnic, sexual, and ultimately cultural differences. It marked a new form of consciousness among minority groups in the cultural life of the United States, a militancy arising from the assertion of group solidarity and the distinctive traits and appearances of the group. Only a few years before, members of minority groups had been striving to adapt themselves as much as possible to a unified mode of cultural behaviour in grooming, dress, work habits, and recreation. By the early 1970s such efforts at acculturation had proven so effective that many of the old ethnic, nationality, and religious distinctions among white Americans had lost their emotional force. White Americans of the middle classes, whatever their country of origin or form of worship, were described as a "silent majority" of "middle Americans," marked by an increasing resistance to social and cultural change. But it remained to be seen how much cohesion this group possessed, whether political or economic differences would take on growing importance as cultural differences waned. There were signs, moreover, that the new minority consciousness was also affecting the older European ethnic allegiances, causing a revival of ethnic awareness and assertion among groups nominally part of the undifferentiated "middle Americans."

The roots of the startling and unexpected trend toward cultural differentiation have been traced to several causes. One useful explanation centres on the practical impossibility of attaining a single standardized cultural life in the United States. This viewpoint holds that differences in ethnic and racial background and in sexual and cultural experience are real and that the effort to deny them led to social and cultural tensions that exploded in cultural conflict and self-assertion. It would be better, according to this view, to foster cultural pluralism in the United States and encourage groups and individuals to create their own cultural lives based on their differences and also their inevitable relation within the shared activities of national life.

Another explanation finds the cause of cultural divergence paradoxically in the very technologies that make a unified culture possible. This view asserts that the new electronic technologies of computers, artificial Earth satellites, and television have created a revolution in communications and in culture. They make possible an instantaneous transmission of information to any part of the world. Instant communications thereby pose a double challenge to traditional centralized and large-scale organizations. People are learning to think in global terms, as part of a single Earth system. At the same time, transnational technologies encourage people to re-examine their cultural identities. One result has been the desire to reformulate cultural life in smaller, more distinctive units.

Such theories may help to explain many of the contradictory features of the new cultural movements in the United States. Although the counter-culture has an explicitly anti-technological ideology, its members often extol the products of mass-technological culture, including movies, television, records, and tapes. The distinctive styles and languages of the minority cultures are projected across the nation through the media and are adopted, imitated, or commercialized for mass cultural use. Information made available by the new technologies has convinced many that technological growth is leading the society to ecological disaster. An ecology movement has developed that opposes further technological expansion and fosters the trend toward smaller cultural units. In the

early 1970s cultural life in the United States continued to be marked by rapid change, emphasizing new relationships among people and between people and their environment.

New forces and forms. The technological, economic, social, and intellectual factors underlying cultural change obviously affect the work of artists and entertainers in the United States, as well as the audiences and status of the various arts. But the relationship of the arts to the structure of culture has always been an ambiguous one, with artists sometimes anticipating or prefiguring cultural change in their works and at other times reflecting or documenting such changes. In either case, the arts in recent years have been deeply involved with the transformations shaping cultural life in the United States.

Literature. This involvement may be readily seen in literature, the form of artistic expression in which U.S. artists first received worldwide recognition. Fiction and poetry have traditionally been mediums that members of minority groups have used to express their sense of life in the United States. Burdened and blessed with a double consciousness, at once insider and outsider to the mainstream of cultural life in the United States, the minority-group writer has a special perspective that can illuminate aspects of the national culture inaccessible to others. After World War II, writers from regional and ethnic minorities thus played significant roles in sensing and interpreting U.S. life through fiction and poetry. Southerners were prominent among U.S. writers, including William Faulkner, Eudora Welty, Robert Penn Warren, Katherine Anne Porter, Flannery O'Connor, and Walker Percy; in the 1950s, Jewish writers came to the fore in literary life, among them Saul Bellow, Norman Mailer, Bernard Malamud, Philip Roth, and Allen Ginsberg.

In the mid-1960s, as a counterpart to the civil-rights movement, it appeared that blacks would become the latest minority to take a leading part in U.S. literature. Black novelists such as James Baldwin and Ralph Ellison had already become prominent, and Ellison's *Invisible Man* (1952) was considered by many critics the outstanding U.S. novel of the quarter century following World War II. But, as the civil-rights movement turned to black power, the writers who expressed the black perspective on U.S. culture were not novelists but militant activists who wrote essays, memoirs, and polemics. Such works as *The Autobiography of Malcolm X* (1965), Eldridge Cleaver's *Soul on Ice* (1968), and George Jackson's *Soledad Brother* (1970) claimed for nonfiction the imaginative force and depth that the literary public had been accustomed to finding only in poetry and fiction.

The predominance of nonfiction among black writers was one part of a general movement in the U.S. literary community to reassess the traditions and future of literature. Many of the functions of literature as a source of description and information seemed to have been taken over by the communications media and the social sciences. The question was asked, "Is the novel dead as an art form?" Some writers responded to the challenge by proclaiming a new form, the "nonfiction novel," and at least one masterwork was produced in this form, Norman Mailer's *The Armies of the Night* (1968). Other writers, such as John Barth and Donald Barthelme, experimented with new forms, emphasizing fiction as a source of fantasy rather than fact. Such genre forms as the science-fiction novels of Kurt Vonnegut, Jr., were taken more seriously, but so too were novels of social realism such as those of Joyce Carol Oates. Literature, like other aspects of cultural life, was in a state of change.

The visual arts. While the perspectives of minority groups helped to shape the development of U.S. literature, the advance of technology played a similar role for painting and sculpture. Until around 1960, however, trends in general cultural life, technological or otherwise, seemed to bear little relation to the practice of the visual arts in the United States. In the aftermath of World War II, U.S. painting came for the first time to take a dominant position in the world art scene in the style of abstract expressionism, which took as its subject matter not a rendering of natural forms but rather the formal properties of the artistic mediums—line and colour; the textures of paint, wood, or stone; purely geometric form; and the like—and the subjectivity of the artist. In the early 1960s, however, a sudden shift occurred in the climate of the New York art world, in which most of the leading U.S. artists lived and exhibited. Amid considerable publicity and controversy, a new style came to the fore called Pop art, a style that seemed to celebrate—at least to present—the banal objects of U.S. commercial, technological, and popular culture: comic strips, advertisements, soda bottles, soup cans, trademarks, billboards, hamburgers, automobiles, telephones, and much more.

When the furor over Pop art subsided, it became apparent that the new style was a continuation of abstract expression in a new form, stressing the abstract and formalist qualities of the old and discarding the subjective and psychological expressionism. Instead of taking the self as subjects, Pop artists such as Andy Warhol, Roy Lichtenstein, or Claes Oldenburg turned to everyday life and the objects around them, abstracting such objects from their environment and presenting them almost as icons. The motives and goals of the Pop artists varied widely, some aiming toward satire or parody, others professing admiration for the culture from which they drew their subjects. The central tendency, however, was formalist, asserting the impersonality of the artist and his or her indifference to the subject except as a form to enable viewers to see in ways they had not before.

The abstract tradition was carried forward more directly into the 1960s in Minimal art, a style of stark geometric forms, shapes, and colours practiced by such older artists of the New York school as Barnett Newman and Mark Rothko and carried forward by younger painters such as Frank Stella. Later in the decade, as the fashion of Pop art began to wane, many artists became increasingly interested not only in the products of modern technology as subject matter but also in technology itself as a medium for artistic creation. An exhibition at the Museum of Modern Art in New York, "The Machine as Seen at the End of the Mechanical Age," publicized the ways in which 20th-century artists depicted and used technology in their work. The Los Angeles County Museum of Art—one of the many newer museums around the country that were becoming increasingly active participants in art rather than passive repositories—carried the process a step further, developing collaboration between artists and business firms specializing in advanced technology; in 1971, it exhibited the art works that were created in this program.

The theatre.   Much of the expressionism and subjectivity that was excluded from painting and sculpture in the 1960s was channelled into new forms of theatre, sometimes called "happenings" or "assemblages." These were performances involving several mediums, including music, film, sound and light effects, materials, live acting, and often the audience as well. Arising from the works and teachings of the composer John Cage, the new theatre practiced an aesthetic of chance and indeterminacy, aiming at times toward the elimination of distinctions between art and life. One composition by Cage called for musicians to maintain 4 minutes and 33 seconds of silence, allowing incidental sounds, coughing in the audience, or outdoor noises to become the "music."

Similar innovations occurred in the drama, though not quite such extreme breaks with traditional forms. The dominance of Broadway over conventional theatrical production of drama, comedy, and musicals continued to give way to regional theatre as well as to Off-Broadway theatre in New York, a development of the 1950s, and Off-Off-Broadway, a more experimental theatre that emerged in the 1960s. Many of the new playwrights expressed the same fascination as the Pop artists with the artifacts and myths of popular culture and the U.S. past, and they tried to infuse them with a similar iconographic objectivity and mystery. Two plays presenting such themes, Arthur Kopit's *Indians* and Howard Sackler's

The Great White Hope, were first produced at the Arena Stage in Washington, D.C., and later moved to Broadway; other works, such as Jean-Claude van Italie's *America Hurrah* and the short plays of Sam Shepard, originated Off-Off-Broadway under the auspices of the La Mama Experimental Theatre Company and other small theatres. The coming together of high culture and popular culture in the theatre reached a new level in the late 1960s with *Hair,* the first rock musical, followed in 1971 by *Jesus Christ Superstar,* a rock musical based on a rock-opera record album.

Musical activity.   No other art form was more popular in the 1960s than rock music. Its origins, as with so much of the art of mid-20th-century U.S. culture, lay both in popular and folk cultures and in technology. Rock music drew on the traditions of country folk songs, black urban blues, and the rhythm-and-blues and rock-and-roll popular music of black performers such as Little Richard and whites such as Elvis Presley in the 1950s. It adapted its roots to the new technology of electric instruments. Rock evolved from similar American sources both in the United States and Great Britain and first made its impact felt in the mid-1960s through a group from Liverpool, the Beatles, and the U.S. performer Bob Dylan.

Rock grew in popularity in the latter years of the 1960s as a counterpart to the emergence of the youth and counter-cultures. The rock sound was often music of social and political protest, and the youthful culture that grew up around rock musicians was in the vanguard of unorthodox hairstyles and dress styles, communal living, and drug use. The high point of the rock-music culture perhaps occurred in the summer of 1969, when the Woodstock Music and Art Fair, an outdoor rock concert in Bethel, New York, featuring many of the leading musical groups, attracted several hundred thousand young spectators who lived together and listened to music in harmonious mass community for two or three days. Many young people for a time called themselves the "Woodstock generation" or citizens of "Woodstock nation."

In the early 1970s, however, some of the bloom had come off the rock generation. The murder of a spectator by Hell's Angels at a Rolling Stones concert, the deaths of leading rock musicians Jimi Hendrix and Janis Joplin, the latter from a drug overdose, the virtual retirement of Bob Dylan, and the breakup of the Beatles marked a more somber end to the possibility of a utopian community through rock culture. But the quality of musical inventiveness and performance remained high among other groups and individuals, continuing one of the most remarkable periods of innovation in the history of U.S. popular music.

Motion pictures.   The popularity of rock music and the celebrity of rock musicians began in the late 1960s to rival the appeal of motion pictures and their stars in earlier decades of mass popular culture. The movies had dominated the popular arts and entertainment from the 1920s until shortly after World War II, when the advent of television and new uses of leisure time for sports and recreation began to cut down their audience. Rapidly increasing production costs, the breakup of the studio system, with its emphasis on star performers and its virtual control of production and distribution of films, and the retirement of important creative workers continued to weaken the Hollywood-based U.S. motion-picture industry in the 1950s and 1960s, although the work of a new generation of foreign film makers developed an audience for movies as a form of high culture. In 1967, however, two striking critical and commercial successes seemed to revive the fortunes of U.S. motion pictures—director Arthur Penn's *Bonnie and Clyde,* a film that skillfully fashioned a myth of the U.S. past, and Mike Nichols' *The Graduate,* a satire on contemporary youth and the "generation gap."

Both films appealed particularly to young people, and the motion-picture industry discovered the importance of "youth culture" for consumption of entertainment products. Proclaiming that youth were a "film generation" as well as a "rock generation," the industry began making

Deification of technology and the banal

Theatrical investigations of U.S. mythologies

The "rock generation": Woodstock and afterward

films aimed specifically at the youth market. The strategy paid off handsomely with Dennis Hopper's *Easy Rider* (1969), a film featuring drugs, motorcycles, and conflict between long-haired youth and rural red-necks, backed by a soundtrack of popular rock songs. But neither the youth market nor "youth culture" as a subject halted the decline of motion-picture attendance. In 1971, one of Hollywood's worst years at the box office, the one subject above all others that seemed to draw audiences to movies was nostalgia for the U.S. past, expressed in such films as Peter Bogdanovich's *The Last Picture Show*.

Audiences. If the arts and entertainment were deeply implicated in forms of cultural change, perhaps nowhere was this more apparent than in the way culture was disseminated to the general population. In the long run, it may be recognized that the mid-20th-century decades in the United States were years of cultural revolution brought about by communications technology. Beginning with television around 1950, followed rapidly by paperbound books, long-playing records, multiple reproductions of art works, transistors, tape recorders, and other innovations, technology made possible an unprecedented inexpensive mass production of art and entertainment products. A steadily increasing enrollment in colleges and universities during these years brought a far greater proportion of the U.S. population into contact with instruction in the history, criticism, and techniques of the arts and also, for the first time, with professional performances of music, dance, and drama and exhibitions of painting and sculpture.

The democratization of the arts

The consequences of such a historic democratization of culture remained a subject of much debate. Some critics saw largely negative results, pointing to the commercialization of "high culture" and a concomitant turning of artists into celebrities and art styles into fads and fashions that change before they can develop; to continuing weaknesses in the educational system, suggesting that culture has not penetrated much beyond its usual minority audience; and to the precarious survival of many cultural institutions. Others, recognizing such criticisms, nevertheless contended that democratization of culture, spreading information about society and the arts to new sectors of the population, belied the prediction that mediocrity and homogeneity would be the result and led to the dramatic transformation of attitude and expectation affecting U.S. society at all its levels.

Mass culture, with its opposing tendencies toward standardization and differentiation, remained in the early 1970s the central fact of artistic life in the United States. Some artists and entertainers were directly employed in mass-culture industries—motion pictures, recording, and television. Others used the technology of mass culture—audiotape and videotape, film, and electronics—in their artistic creation. And, in all fields, the artifacts and myths of mass popular culture were a major subject of artistic exploration and treatment. Historically, the boundary between folk traditions and commercial culture had always been ambiguous in the United States. Artists born in the 20th-century urban United States, re-creating their own roots, found a new modern folklore emerging from older manifestations of commercial mass culture. The notion grew that rapid social and cultural change makes today's new thing tomorrow's antique, an icon to enshrine as art and probe as a subject for cultural self-understanding.

CULTURAL INSTITUTIONS

Leadership and support for such cultural institutions as museums, symphony orchestras, and theatres in the United States has come traditionally from individual and private sources. In the 1950s and 1960s, however, local, state, and federal government began to play a larger role in the planning and financing of cultural institutions. Nowhere was this public expenditure more significant for cultural life than in the expansion and transformation of colleges and universities.

Educational–cultural complexes. In response to the growing need for a skilled work force, state legislatures and the federal government contributed to a swift development of higher education in the United States. Older public universities added new departments and schools; teacher-training colleges became full-scale universities; and two-year junior colleges became four-year institutions. Hundreds of new junior colleges were founded and many new four-year and graduate institutions as well. States such as New York and Massachusetts developed almost entirely new systems of public higher education and states such as California, with a traditionally strong system, vastly expanded their institutions and resources. The number of students attending degree-granting institutions more than doubled.

Expanding role of the university in the arts

Universities continue to function as institutions in which the cultural heritage of the past is preserved and transmitted to a new generation, but, in this period of growth, many universities also took on new roles as centres in which the arts were performed, exhibited, and created. As part of their task of teaching skills as well as knowledge, universities added active writers, composers, musicians, painters, sculptors, and other artists and performers to their staffs. A number of schools established or expanded museum, music, and theatre programs as the means of training students and also improving the cultural environments of their cities and states. Among the most notable examples of such programs was the Tyrone Guthrie Theater associated with the University of Minnesota, which became nationally known for the quality of its stagings and performances. The new cultural activities of universities served in important ways to decentralize cultural production in the United States and make live performances of the arts available to a far wider audience.

Government support for the arts also took the form of aid and planning for new cultural centres in the nation's cities. During the period of extensive urban renewal in the 1950s and 1960s, many cities sought to concentrate or revive their cultural institutions by constructing centres for cultural activity in inner-city locations. New York established the Lincoln Center for the Performing Arts, with facilities for opera, theatre, music, film, and other arts, and Los Angeles developed its Music Center. In 1971 the federally sponsored John F. Kennedy Center for the Performing Arts was opened, to mixed critical reception, in Washington, D.C.

Declining financial support for the arts

Areas of friction and instability. In the late 1960s, both privately and publicly supported cultural institutions became increasingly involved in the cultural and social issues of the larger society. Although the cultural activities of universities were not directly affected by the political controversies and turmoil on many college campuses, the resulting cutbacks in state aid and private donations placed a strain on the financing of higher education that curtailed the growth or even threatened the survival of many cultural programs. Museums and cultural centres in inner cities suffered declines in attendance and revenues because patrons became reluctant to enter high-crime areas in which they were located.

At the same time, a number of groups made demands directly on cultural institutions. In several cities, symphony-orchestra musicians and museum employees organized labour unions to press demands for better wages and working conditions. Some painters and sculptors in New York, recognizing the major role museums play in developing cultural tastes, fashioning reputations and critical judgments of artists, and influencing the prices of their works, demanded a share in setting museums' policies. Minority groups protested land acquisition by cultural institutions, their indifference to minority cultures and artists, high prices, and their isolation from minority patrons. The Metropolitan Museum of Art's unprecedented photographic show in New York, Harlem on My Mind, was one effort to respond to such protests.

Above all, the problem for cultural institutions was one of finding continued financial support. The recession of the early 1970s caused both governments and private donors to reduce their assistance. Museums and libraries were forced to lay off employees and cut back their acquisitions and hours of service, and in some cases there seemed little alternative to closing entirely. At a time when the resources of cultural institutions had reached their highest levels of quality and breadth in the history of the United States, many such institutions were plagued by financial difficulties that could only be solved by changes in national economic conditions that were beyond their control.

THE COMMUNICATIONS MEDIA

The development of media for communicating news, entertainment, and commercial advertising since midcentury has been primarily shaped by the two dominant factors of contemporary cultural life: technological change and the emergence of minority cultures. Television has become the major medium, surpassing newspapers, magazines, and radio and profoundly influencing the structure of their institutions. With its production centralized in three commercial networks, television has been less affected by minority interests than the other mediums, but technological innovations within television itself may provide more opportunities for minority expression.

Printed media and radio. The impact of television struck newspapers at the same time that the growth of suburbs and satellite cities around urban centres began to reshape the needs and desires of newspaper readers. With the loss of advertising revenue to television and of readership to suburban newspapers, the big-city dailies were seriously hurt. During the 1950s and 1960s, scores of major urban newspapers ceased operation, leaving most large U.S. cities with no more than one morning and one afternoon newspaper. Since the ownership is often in one company, a diversity in editorial point of view or content was usually lacking. At the same time, the growing number of suburban papers led to a small net gain in the number of newspapers in the United States. Most of these, however, were smaller and often less ambitious, and observers noted a trend toward less independent reporting and an increasing reliance on nationwide press services for national and international news.

When the counter-culture and minority cultures emerged in the mid-1960s, their members perceived that the national press was indifferent or hostile to their activities. They responded by founding newspapers and magazines of their own, an "underground press" that rapidly attained a solid place in the communicatons field, appealing to youth and minority audiences and aided by advertising revenues from record companies. *Ramparts* and *Rolling Stone*, two San Francisco-based magazines, emerged from the "underground press" and gained readerships of several hundred thousand persons.

Television had similar effects on general magazines and radio. Those magazines edited for a broad common denominator of readers tended to suffer from competition with television, and *Collier's*, *The Saturday Evening Post*, *Life*, and *Look* were among the major general-readership periodicals that ceased publication. At the same time, smaller magazines, edited for a specialized audience, thrived by reaching audiences and providing services that competing media could not offer. Radio was most directly affected by television, giving up almost entirely its variety programming and concentrating on music for teen-age audiences. A new trend in radio broadcasting in the late 1960s was the "talk shows," featuring conversations between listeners and announcers or guests in the studio. Thus, the development of television had the long-range effect of loosening the structure of other media and permitting increasing diversity of communications—although increases in printing costs and postal rates in the early 1970s were causing difficulties for periodical publishers and threatening to reduce the number of specialized and minority magazines.

The television industry. Within the television industry itself, however, just the opposite development occurred. Television production rapidly became concentrated in three major networks, whose uniformity of programming seemed to bear out the fears of the critics of mass culture that standardization and the lowest common denominator of cultural communication would result from the growth of mass media.

By the early 1970s, about 95 percent of U.S. homes had television receivers, and the very size of the potential audience—virtually the entire U.S. population—made

television a medium different from any other in U.S. history. Commercial advertisers paid large sums of money to advertise their products in the evening "prime-viewing" time, and a one-half-hour network entertainment show cost several hundred thousand dollars to produce. These high costs of production and advertising time led the television industry to place great emphasis on national ratings of audiences, the number of persons believed to be watching a show. Shows that did not get high ratings were dropped after a few weeks or a season, and successful shows were widely copied. Original and innovative programming gave way to a standard television schedule featuring movies, sports, celebrity talk shows, and genre programs adapted from other media—soap operas, comedies, westerns, and mysteries.

Efforts were made to increase the variety and quality of programming through the National Educational Television network, broadcast largely on ultrahigh-frequency (UHF) wavelengths, and a federally financed Public Broadcast Laboratory. The potentially most important trend of the 1970s, however, was cable television, carried to homes on wires rather than through the atmosphere. Cable TV was expected to increase vastly the number of channels available to viewers and, according to regulations of the Federal Communications Commission, to provide opportunities for community-controlled channels and programming.

VII. Problems and prospects

As the United States entered its third century as an independent republic, the problems and challenges of the future occupied its citizens more deeply than the celebration of 200 years of national history. Many Americans expressed the belief that the social and environmental foundations not only of the United States but of the entire world were endangered unless fundamental changes could be made in institutions, policies, and attitudes. Others decried such pessimism, as they called it, and predicted a future of continued national power and growth in harmony with the development of the nation in the past. This future orientation, of course, had been a characteristic of U.S. values and perspectives from the earliest colonial settlements. But, in the last third of the 20th century, the future seemed more problematic and troubling than at almost any other time in the nation's history. The United States at its bicentennial faced at least two principal concerns that were unique in its experience: it was forced to seek a new conception, a new ideology for its role and purpose as a major national power in world affairs, and it had to decide how to limit the destruction and preserve the quality of its human and natural environment.

Throughout its history, operating on a partly religious and partly secular foundation, the United States has proclaimed its mission to improve the world, its Manifest Destiny to expand in territory and power and to bring to less fortunate nations the benefits of U.S. political and economic systems and moral values. Although the policies generated by this impulse have often been controversial, not until the undeclared counterinsurgency war in Indochina, the longest military conflict on foreign soil in U.S. history, was the validity of this basic U.S. world view widely questioned. It became clear that many of the world's peoples, particularly in the largely non-white and underdeveloped nations of Africa, Asia, and Latin America, did not want to adopt U.S. systems and, above all, did not want to be forced to conform to U.S. world-power objectives, which they considered merely a 20th-century version of traditional Western imperialism. Although it seemed improbable that the United States would (or could) withdraw from its role as a world power, it began to appear more and more likely that the country might have to choose between (1) a world role based purely on self-interest, without the justification of a moral mission and with the prospect of continuing internal dissent, or (2) the forging of a new relationship of cooperation rather than conflict with the aspirations of peoples throughout the world.

Similarly, the dream of U.S. destiny was an expectation

of expansion in territory, in resources, in population, and in material well-being. It was perhaps no coincidence that the questioning of U.S. destiny as a world power was accompanied by an increasing awareness of the threat of unlimited growth. For the first time in U.S. history, a considerable part of the population came to recognize that irreplaceable land, water, and mineral resources were being used up at rapid rates, that uncontrolled development had deteriorated the environment, and that continued unplanned growth could lead to social crisis and personal suffering. The United States began to tackle the difficult problems of how to conserve and improve its natural resources, how to protect and enhance the lives of human beings, and, above all, how to plan and make choices without the sustaining ideology of continued growth and expansion in all facets of national life.

More than most nations in world history, the United States justified its development, its acquisition of land and power, and its treatment of its citizens by reference to an overriding purpose that was larger than mere national concerns—a universal moral purpose to transform the world into its own image. In the last third of the 20th century, the nation was learning that there were limits to its power and its growth. How the people of the United States, their leaders, and their institutions would respond to that knowledge was the great question for the third century of national existence. The country had grown more organized and bureaucratized at its higher levels, at the same time becoming more disordered in its cities and communities, more fragmented in its values and group allegiances. Few people were able to say whether further organization, on the one hand, or decentralization and fragmentation, on the other, would prove the more effective means of forging a just and humane internal order, world role, and system of values for the United States.

(R.Sk.)

Necessity for revising national values

BIBLIOGRAPHY

The land: Although no treatment of the contemporary American landscape has yet appeared that is comprehensive and adequate for both town and countryside, several items do provide useful introductions to the topic. DAVID LOWENTHAL, "The American Scene," *Geogrl. Rev.,* 58:61–88 (1968), skillfully sets forth several basic themes apparent in the visual landscape and the American's attitude toward it. A serviceable description of many current landscape features and a manual for their improvement is available in CHRISTOPHER TUNNARD and BORIS PUSHKAREV, *Man-Made America: Chaos or Control?* (1963); while a more pessimistic assessment of the situation is given in IAN NAIRN, *The American Landscape: A Critical View* (1965). Rural land use is treated in terms of both historical development and modern physical pattern in FRANCIS J. MARSCHNER, *Land Use and Its Patterns in the United States* (1959). The historical geography of open-country and village settlement in the early Atlantic Seaboard is discussed in GLENN T. TREWARTHA, "Types of Rural Settlement in Colonial America," *Geogrl. Rev.,* 36: 569–596 (1946); and the same area and topic, along with much else, is dealt with in HENRY GLASSIE, *Pattern in the Material Folk Culture of the Eastern United States* (1968). Both these publications are also valuable in the study of traditional regions. For a concise but substantial survey of the townscapes of the nation and their evolution, see CHRISTOPHER TUNNARD and HENRY HOPE REED, *American Skyline* (1955). JOHN W. REPS, *The Making of Urban America: A History of City Planning in the United States* (1965), is a masterly account in word and map of the development of urban street patterns and related matters. Two exemplary presentations of the geography and history of specific metropolitan areas may be found in JEAN GOTTMANN, *Megalopolis: The Urbanized Northeastern Seaboard of the United States* (1961); and HAROLD M. MAYER and RICHARD C. WADE, *Chicago: Growth of a Metropolis* (1969). The only general discussion of the traditional regions of the country and related subjects is WILBUR ZELINSKY, *The Cultural Geography of the United States* (1973). Of the several general texts covering the human geography of the continent, perhaps the most stimulating and informative is J. WREFORD WATSON, *North America, Its Countries and Regions* (1967). Two atlases that are indispensable for the serious study of any aspect of the American human or physical scene are CHARLES O. PAULLIN and JOHN K. WRIGHT, *Atlas of the Historical Geography of the United States* (1932); and the UNITED STATES GEOLOGICAL SURVEY, *The National*

Atlas of the United States of America (1970). Although several sections of the country lack adequate monographic treatment, there are commendable volumes for a few areas, notably: RUPERT B. VANCE, *Human Geography of the South,* 2nd ed. (1968); HANS KURATH (ed.), *Linguistic Atlas of New England,* 3 vol. (1939–43); D.W. MEINIG, *Imperial Texas* (1969) and *Southwest: Three Peoples in Geographical Change, 1600–1900* (1971).

General physical geography: CHARLES B. HUNT, *Physiography of the United States* (1967), is solid and well illustrated, though geology receives disproportionate attention. An excellent brief summary comprises the first three chapters of J. WREFORD WATSON's lucid and authoritative *North America, Its Countries and Regions* (1967), which includes a useful bibliography. (*Landforms and geology*): The standard work on American landforms is W.D. THORNBURY, *Regional Geomorphology of the United States* (1965), superbly illustrated with maps, diagrams, and air photos, an excellent bibliography, and balanced discussions of controversial questions. NEVIN FENNEMAN, *Physiography of Western United States* (1931) and *Physiography of Eastern United States* (1938), are exhaustive and still standard references. An authoritative treatment of American tectonics is PHILIP B. KING, *The Evolution of North America* (1959). The effects of Pleistocene glaciation are exhaustively analyzed in a collection of scholarly essays, H.E. WRIGHT, JR., and D.G. FREY (eds.), *The Quaternary of the United States* (1965). (*Maps of landforms*): Overwhelmingly the best depiction of American landforms is ERWIN RAISZ, *Landforms of the United States,* 6th rev. ed. (1957). The UNITED STATES GEOLOGICAL SURVEY, *Tectonic Map of the United States Exclusive of Alaska and Hawaii* (1962), is invaluable. Essential for understanding Northeastern landscapes are the *Glacial Map of the United States East of the Rocky Mountains* (1959), showing the main deposits of continental ice; and *Pleistocene Eolian Deposits of the United States, Alaska, and Parts of Canada* (1952), which maps the location of glacially-derived loess and sand; both are published by the Geological Society of America. For small areas, excellent large topographic maps and air photos are available for most of the country from the United States Geological Survey. (*Mineral resources*): Basic data on mineral deposits, production, exports, and imports are collected by the United States Bureau of Mines and published annually in the *Minerals Yearbook.* (*Climate*): U.S. climate and its role in human affairs is intelligently treated in the classic *Climate and Man,* the *1941 Yearbook of Agriculture,* which contains numerous maps and statistical data. Excellent atlases of American climate include C.W. THORNTHWAITE, *Atlas of Climatic Types in the United States, 1900–1939* (1941), including detailed maps that show the annual variations over 40 years; STEPHEN S. VISHER, *Climatic Atlas of the United States* (1954), with more than 1,000 maps showing every aspect of American weather and climate; and the UNITED STATES DEPARTMENT OF COMMERCE, ENVIRONMENTAL DATA SERVICE, *Climatic Atlas of the United States* (1968), a careful and authoritative assemblage of maps and selected statistics in paperback. (*Vegetation and animal life*): HENRY A. GLEASON and ARTHUR CRONQUIST, *The Natural Geography of Plants* (1964), is a highly readable and beautifully illustrated introduction to plant ecology and geography, with heavy emphasis on North America. An authoritative regional treatment of U.S. plant and animal ecology is VICTOR E. SHELFORD, *The Ecology of North America* (1963). The most honoured treatment of American forests is E. LUCY BRAUN, *Deciduous Forests of Eastern North America* (1950). The best medium-scale map of U.S. vegetation patterns is A.W. KUCHLER's authoritative "Natural Vegetation," in E.B. ESPENSHADE (ed.), *Goode's World Atlas,* 13th ed. (1970). (*Soils*): C.F. MARBUT, "Soils of the United States," pt. 3 of the *Atlas of American Agriculture* (1935), remains an authoritative description of American soil geography. *Soils and Men* (1938) and *Soil* (1957), contain a wide variety of useful information. All three works are issued by the United States Department of Agriculture.

The people: *The Statistical Abstract of the United States,* published annually by the BUREAU OF THE CENSUS, is the standard summary of statistics on the social, political, and economic organization of the United States. The Census Bureau also published *Historical Statistics of the United States,* 2 vol. (1960–65), which contain similar data from colonial times to 1962. For interpretation of demographic data, see EDWARD G. STOCKWELL, *Population and People* (1968); and RICHARD M. SCAMMON and BEN J. WATTENBERG, *The Real Majority* (1970); for analysis of national values and their historical development, D.W. BROGAN, *The American Character* (1944); and SEYMOUR MARTIN LIPSET, *The First New Nation* (1963); for contemporary attitudes and opinions, ALBERT H. CANTRIL and CHARLES W. ROLL, JR., *Hopes and Fears of the American People* (1971); for history of the era of mass immigration, 1860–1920, OSCAR HANDLIN, *The Uprooted* (1951); and for an examination of contemporary American minority groups, NATHAN GLAZER and DANIEL P. MOYNIHAN, *Beyond the Melting Pot*, 2nd ed. (1970).

The Economy: General surveys of the U.S. economy include SHEPHARD B. CLOUGH and THEODORE F. MARBURY, *The Economic Basis of American Civilization* (1968); EDWARD F. DENISON, *The Sources of Economic Growth in the United States and the Alternatives Before Us* (1962); CHARLES H. HESSION, *The Dynamics of the American Economy* (1956); UNITED STATES ECONOMIC DEVELOPMENT ADMINISTRATION, *Regional Economic Development in the United States* (1967); EMMA WOYTINSKY, *Profile of the U.S. Economy: A Survey of Growth and Change* (1967). Trends in production and employment are analyzed in CLOPPER ALMON, *The American Economy to 1975: An Interindustry Forecast* (1966); EDITORS OF FORTUNE, *Markets of the Seventies: The Unwinding U.S. Economy* (1968); NATIONAL INDUSTRIAL CONFERENCE BOARD, *The Consumer of the Seventies* (1969); UNITED STATES BUREAU OF LABOR STATISTICS, *Patterns of U.S. Economic Growth: 1980 Projections of Final Demand, Interindustry Relationships, Output, Productivity, and Employment* (1970); and the UNITED STATES NATIONAL GOALS RESEARCH STAFF, *Toward Balanced Growth: Quantity with Quality* (1970). Issues of economic policy are treated in GEORGE L. BACH, *Making Monetary and Fiscal Policy* (1971); COMMITTEE FOR ECONOMIC DEVELOPMENT, *Fiscal and Monetary Policies for Steady Economic Growth* (1969); WALTER W. HELLER, *New Dimensions of Political Economy* (1966); ARTHUR M. OKUN, *The Political Economy of Prosperity* (1970); MELVILLE J. ULMER, *The Welfare State, U.S.A.: An Exploration in and Beyond the New Economics* (1969); and the PRESIDENT'S TASK FORCE ON ECONOMIC GROWTH, *Policies for American Economic Progress in the Seventies* (1970). Various points of view are in NEIL W. CHAMBERLAIN (ed.), *Contemporary Economic Issues* (1969); and WALTER W. HELLER (ed.), *Perspectives on Economic Growth* (1968).

Transportation: WILFRED OWEN, EZRA BOWEN, and the EDITORS OF LIFE, *Wheels* (1967), a book on the technological development of transport throughout history and on proposed scientific innovations to help solve future problems; WILFRED OWEN, *The Metropolitan Transportation Problem*, rev. ed. (1966), an analysis of the transportation problems and traffic congestion of American cities concluding that future solutions lie to a major degree in the design of the city and urban region; GEORGE M. SMERK (ed.), *Readings in Urban Transportation* (1968), a varied collection of essays by widely known authors in the field.

Administration and social conditions: The contemporary political and social milieus are analyzed in an avalanche of publications expressing every conceivable philosophy of government and social management; few have yet been able to achieve the necessary distance, in time or sentiment, for unaffected analysis of the structure or functioning of U.S. government, politics, or social dynamics. A few, however, can provide a valuable beginning. In government and politics, the *United States Government Organization Manual* (annual), offers a broad overview of the federal structure; while the *Congressional Record* and the *Congressional Quarterly* provide closer views of the public record of the federal legislature. Other basic books on government include AARON WILDAVSKY and NELSON W. POLSBY (eds.), *American Governmental Institutions* (1968); PETER WOLL, *American Government: Readings and Cases*, 2nd ed. (1965); and ROBERT A. GOLDWIN (ed.), *A Nation of States* (1963). Among the more penetrating insights into the complexities of politics are JOSEPH R. FISZMAN (ed.), *The American Political Arena*, 2nd ed. (1966); FRED I. GREENSTEIN, *The American Party System and the American People* (1963); the series by THEODORE WHITE begun with *The Making of the President, 1960* (1961) and continued to cover subsequent presidential elections; RICHARD M. SCAMMON and BEN. J. WATTENBERG, *The Real Majority: How the Silent Center of the American Electorate Chooses Its President* (1970), based on studies of voting behaviour in 1968; and SHIRLEY CHISHOLM, *Unbought and Unbossed* (1970). The U.S. military is studied in terms of its politics in ADAM YARMOLINSKY, *The Military Establishment* (1971). The political and social structures are bridged in C. WRIGHT MILLS, *Power Elite* (1956); while other studies probing special areas of politico-social concern include BARBARA and JOHN EHRENREICH, *American Health Empire: Power, Profits, and Politics* (1970); MICHAEL HARRINGTON, *The Other America* (1962), a study of poverty in the U.S.; JANE JACOBS, *The Death and Life of Great American Cities* (1961), an inquiry into the structuring and destruction of the city;

HARRY M. CAUDILL, *Night Comes to the Cumberlands* (1963), a historical survey of the development of poverty in the southern Appalachians; and ROBERT C. COLES on rural poor and effects of their migrations to the city. For social statistics see the *Statistical Abstracts of the United States* (annual).

Cultural life: A good way to begin the study of cultural life and institutions in the United States is through MARSHALL MCLUHAN, *Understanding Media: The Extensions of Man* (1964). Although McLuhan's works have been highly controversial, no writer has done more to stimulate awareness of the role of media in modern culture. A broad introduction to the "counter culture" is THEODORE ROSZAK, *The Making of a Counter Culture: Reflections on the Technocratic Society and Its Youthful Opposition* (1969). Information about minority cultures and movements must be found primarily in their polemical writings. Interesting discussions of all phases of contemporary literature, including nonfiction, journalism, and the theatre, as well as poetry and fiction, appear in ELIZABETH JANEWAY (ed.), *The Writer's World* (1969). A useful survey of Pop art is LUCY R. LIPPARD *et al.*, *Pop Art* (1966); while two books by MICHAEL KIRBY cover multimedia experiments, *Happenings* (1965) and *The Art of Time: Essays on the Avante-Garde* (1969). Rock music is explored in CARL BELZ, *The Story of Rock* (1969). A valuable study of the television industry is LES BROWN, *Television: The Business Behind the Box* (1971); while a more historical treatment of radio and television is ERIK BARNOUW, *A History of Broadcasting in the United States*, 3 vol. (1966–70). The magazine *Saturday Review* (weekly), provides a broad survey of social and cultural aspects of American life.

(W.Ze./P.F.L./T.K.F./Jo.N./W.O./J.T.H./R.Sk.)

United States, History of the

The United States of America grew from a group of English colonies established along the east coast of North America in the 17th and early 18th centuries. This article begins with the history of those colonies and is divided into the following sections:

I. Colonial America to 1763

THE EUROPEAN BACKGROUND

The English colonization of North America was but one

chapter in the larger story of European expansion throughout the globe. The Portuguese, beginning with a voyage to Porto Santo off the coast of West Africa in 1418, were the first Europeans to promote overseas exploration and colonization. By 1487 the Portuguese had travelled all the way to the southern tip of Africa, establishing trading stations at Arguin, Sierra Leone, and El Mina. In 1497 Vasco da Gama rounded the Cape of Good Hope and sailed up the eastern coast of Africa, laying the groundwork for Portugal's later commercial control of India. By 1500, when Pedro Álvares Cabral stumbled across the coast of Brazil en route to India, Portuguese influence had expanded to the New World as well.

Though initially lagging behind the Portuguese in the arts of navigation and exploration, the Spanish quickly closed that gap in the decades following Columbus' (see COLUMBUS, CHRISTOPHER) voyages to America. First in the Caribbean and then in spectacular conquests of New Spain and Peru, they captured the imagination, and the envy, of the European world.

French settlement

France, occupied with wars in Europe to preserve its own territorial integrity, was not able to devote as much time or effort to overseas expansion as Spain and Portugal. Beginning in the early 16th century, however, French fishermen established an outpost in Newfoundland, and in 1534 Jacques Cartier began exploring the Gulf of St. Lawrence. By 1543 the French had ceased their efforts to colonize the northwest portion of the New World. In the last half of the 16th century, France attempted to found colonies in Florida and Brazil; but each of these efforts failed, and by the end of the century Spain and Portugal remained the only two European nations to have established successful colonies in America.

The English, although anxious to duplicate the Spanish and Portuguese successes, nevertheless lagged far behind in their colonization efforts. The English possessed a theoretical claim to the North American mainland by dint of the 1497 voyage of John Cabot off the coast of Nova Scotia, but in fact they had neither the means nor the desire to back up that claim during the 16th century. Thus it was that England relied instead on private trading companies, which were interested principally in commercial rather than territorial expansion, to defend its interests in the expanding European world. The first of these commercial ventures began with the formation of the Muscovy Company in 1554. In 1576–78 the English mariner Martin Frobisher undertook three voyages in search of a Northwest Passage to the East. In 1577 Sir Francis Drake made his famous voyage around the world, plundering the western coast of South America en route. A year later Sir Humphrey Gilbert, one of the most dedicated of Elizabethan imperialists, began a series of ventures aimed at establishing permanent colonies in North America. All of his efforts met with what was, at best, limited success. Finally, in September 1583, on what would prove to be his final voyage, Gilbert, with five vessels and 260 men, disappeared in the North Atlantic. With the failure of Gilbert's voyage, the English turned to a new man, Sir Walter Raleigh, and a new strategy—a southern rather than a northern route to North America—to advance England's fortunes in the New World. Raleigh's efforts to found a permanent colony off the coast of Virginia, although they did finally fail with the mysterious destruction of the Roanoke Island colony in 1587, awakened popular interest in a permanent colonizing venture.

The voyages of Sir Humphrey Gilbert

During the years separating the failure of the Roanoke colony and the establishment in 1607 of the English settlement in Jamestown, English propagandists worked hard to convince the public that a colony in America would yield instant and easily exploitable wealth. Even men like the English geographer Richard Hakluyt were not certain that the Spanish colonization experience could or should be imitated but hoped nevertheless that the English colonies in the New World would prove to be a source of immediate commercial gain. There were, of course, other motives for colonization. Some hoped to discover the much sought after route to the Orient in North America. English imperialists thought it necessary to settle in the New World in order to limit Spanish expansion. Once it was proven that America was a suitable place for settlement, some Englishmen would travel to those particular colonies that promised to free them from religious persecution. There were also Englishmen, primarily of lower and middle class origin, who hoped the New World would provide them with increased economic opportunity in the form of free or inexpensive land. These last two motives, while they have been given considerable attention by historians, appear not to have been so much original motives for English colonization as they were shifts of attitude once colonization had begun.

SETTLEMENT

Virginia. The leaders of the Virginia Company of London, a joint-stock company in charge of the Jamestown enterprise, were for the most part wealthy and well-born commercial and military adventurers eager to find new outlets for investment. During the first two years of its existence, the Virginia colony, under the Charter of 1607, proved an extraordinarily bad investment. This was principally due to the unwillingness of the early colonizers to do the necessary work of providing for themselves and to the chronic shortage of capital for supply of the venture.

A new charter in 1609 significantly broadened membership in the Virginia Company, thereby increasing temporarily the supply of capital at the disposal of its directors; but most of the settlers continued to act as though they expected the Indians to provide for their existence, a notion that the Indians fiercely rejected. As a result, the enterprise still failed to yield any profits and the number of investors again declined.

The crown issued a third charter in 1612 authorizing the company to institute a lottery to raise more capital for the floundering enterprise. In that same year John Rolfe harvested the first crop of a high-grade and therefore potentially profitable strain of tobacco. At about the same time, with the arrival of Sir Thomas Dale in the colony as governor in 1611, the settlers gradually began to practice the discipline necessary for their survival, though at an enormous personal cost.

The administration of Sir Thomas Dale

Dale carried with him the "Laws Divine, Morall and Martial," which were intended to supervise nearly every aspect of the settlers' lives. Each person in Virginia, including women and children, was given a military rank, and his duties were spelled out in minute detail. Penalties imposed for violating these rules were severe: those who failed to obey the work regulations were to be forced to lie neck and heels together all night for the first offense, whipped for the second, and sent to a year's service in the galleys for the third. The settlers could hardly protest against the harshness of the code, for that might be deemed slander against the company—an offense punishable by service in the galleys or by death.

Dale's Code brought order to the Virginia experiment, but it hardly served to attract new settlers. To increase incentive the company, beginning in 1618, offered 50 acres of land to those settlers who could pay their transportation to Virginia and a promise of 50 acres after seven years of service to those who could not pay their passage. Concurrently, the new governor of Virginia, Sir George Yeardley, issued a call for the election of representatives to a House of Burgesses, which was to convene in Jamestown in July 1619. In its original form, the House of Burgesses was little more than an agency of the governing board of the Virginia Company, but it would later expand its powers and prerogatives and become an important force for colonial self-government.

Despite the introduction of these reforms, the years from 1619 to 1624 proved fatal to the future of the Virginia Company. Epidemics, an Indian massacre in 1622, and internal disputes took a heavy toll on the colony. In 1624 the crown finally revoked the charter of the company and placed the colony under royal control. The introduction of royal government into Virginia, while it was to have important long-range consequences, did not produce an immediate change in the character of the col-

Virginia made a crown colony

ony. The economic and political life of the colony continued as it had in the past. The House of Burgesses, though its future under the royal commission of 1624 was uncertain, continued to meet on an informal basis; by 1629 it was officially re-established. The crown also grudgingly acquiesced to the decision of the Virginia settlers to continue to direct most of their energies to the growth and exportation of tobacco. By 1630 the Virginia colony, while not prosperous, at least showed signs that it was capable of surviving without royal subsidy.

Maryland. Maryland, Virginia's neighbour to the north, was the first English colony to be controlled by a single proprietor rather than by a joint-stock company. George Calvert (Lord Baltimore) had been an investor in a number of colonizing schemes before being given a grant of land from the crown in 1632. Baltimore was given a sizable grant of power to go along with his grant of land; he had control over the trade and political system of the colony so long as he did nothing to deviate from the laws of England. Baltimore's son Cecilius Calvert took over the project at his father's death and promoted a settlement at St. Mary's on the Potomac. Supplied in part by Virginia and buoyed by their own crop of corn in the very first year, the Maryland colonists managed to prosper from the beginning.

The colony was intended to serve at least two purposes. Lord Baltimore, a Roman Catholic, was anxious to found a colony where Catholics could live in peace, but he was also eager to see his colony yield him as large a profit as possible. From the outset Protestants outnumbered Catholics, although a few prominent Catholics tended to own an inordinate share of the land in the colony. Despite this favouritism in the area of land policy, Lord Baltimore was for the most part a good and fair administrator.

Following the accession of William and Mary to the English throne, however, control of the colony was taken away from the Calvert family and entrusted to the royal government. Shortly thereafter the crown decreed that Anglicanism would be the established religion of the colony. In 1715, after the Calvert family had renounced Catholicism and embraced Anglicanism, the colony reverted back to a proprietary form of government.

The New England Colonies. Although lacking a charter, the founders of Plymouth in Massachusetts were, like their counterparts in Virginia, dependent upon private investments from profit-minded backers to finance their colony. The nucleus of that settlement was drawn from an enclave of English émigrés in Leyden, Holland. These religious "Separatists" believed that the true church was a voluntary company of the faithful under the "guidance" of a pastor and tended to be exceedingly individualistic in matters of church doctrine. Unlike the settlers of Massachusetts Bay, the Pilgrims chose to "separate" from the Church of England rather than to reform it from within.

In 1620, the first year of settlement, nearly half the settlers died of disease. From that time forward, however, and despite decreasing support from English investors, the health and the economic position of the colonists improved. The Pilgrims soon secured peace treaties with most of the Indians around them, enabling them to devote their time to building a strong, stable economic base rather than diverting their efforts toward costly and time-consuming problems of defending the colony from attack. Although none of their principal economic pursuits—farming, fishing, and trading—promised them lavish wealth, the Pilgrims in America were, after only five years, self-sufficient.

Although the Pilgrims were always a minority in Plymouth, they nevertheless controlled the entire governmental structure of their colony during the first four decades of settlement. Before disembarking from the "Mayflower" in 1620, the Pilgrim founders, led by William Bradford, demanded that all 41 adults aboard sign a compact promising obedience to the laws and ordinances drafted by the leaders of the enterprise. Although the Mayflower Compact has been interpreted as an important step in the evolution of democratic government in Ameri-

Mayflower Compact

ca, it is a fact that the compact represented a one-sided arrangement, with the settlers promising obedience and the Pilgrim founders promising very little. Although nearly all the male inhabitants were permitted to vote for deputies to a provincial assembly and for a governor, the colony, for at least the first 40 years of its existence, remained in the tight control of a few men. After 1660 the people of Plymouth gradually gained a greater voice in both their church and civic affairs, and by 1691, when Plymouth colony was annexed to Massachusetts Bay, the Plymouth settlers had distinguished themselves by their quiet, orderly ways.

The Puritans of Massachusetts Bay, like the Pilgrims, sailed to America principally to free themselves from religious restraints. Unlike the Pilgrims, the Puritans did not desire to "separate" themselves from the Church of England but, rather, hoped by their example, to reform it. Nonetheless, one of the recurring problems facing the leaders of the Massachusetts Bay Colony was to be the tendency of some, in their desire to free themselves from the alleged corruption of the Church of England, to espouse "separatist" doctrine. When these tendencies or any other hinting of deviation from orthodox Puritan doctrine developed, those holding them were either quickly corrected or expelled from the colony. The leaders of the Massachusetts Bay enterprise never intended their colony to be an outpost of toleration in the New World; rather, they intended it to be a "Zion in the wilderness," a model of purity and orthodoxy, with all backsliders subject to immediate correction.

The civil government of the colony was guided by a similar authoritarian spirit. Men like John Winthrop, the first governor of Massachusetts Bay, believed that it was not the duty of the governors of society to act as the direct representatives of their constituents but rather to decide, independently, what measures were in the best interests of the total society. The original charter of 1629 gave all power in the colony to a General Court composed of only a small number of shareholders in the company. On arriving in Massachusetts, many disenfranchised settlers immediately protested against this provision and caused the franchise to be widened to include all church members. These "freemen" were given the right to vote in the General Court once each year for a governor and a Council of Assistants. Although the Charter of 1629 technically gave the General Court the power to decide on all matters affecting the colony, the members of the ruling elite initially refused to allow the freemen in the General Court to take part in the lawmaking process on the grounds that their numbers would render the court inefficient.

John Winthrop and Massachusetts Bay

In 1634 the General Court adopted a new plan of representation whereby the freemen of each town would be permitted to select two or three delegates and assistants, elected separately but sitting together in the General Court, who would be responsible for all legislation. There was always tension existing between the smaller, more prestigious group of assistants and the larger group of deputies. In 1644, as a result of this continuing tension, the two groups were officially lodged in separate houses of the General Court, with each house reserving a veto power over the other.

Despite the authoritarian tendencies of the Massachusetts Bay Colony, a spirit of community developed there as perhaps in no other colony. The same spirit that caused the residents of Massachusetts to report on their neighbours for deviation from the true principles of Puritan morality also prompted them to be extraordinarily solicitous about their neighbours' needs. Although life in Massachusetts was made difficult for those who dissented from the prevailing orthodoxy, it was marked by a feeling of attachment and community for those who lived within the enforced consensus of the society.

Many New Englanders, however, refused to live within the orthodoxy imposed by the ruling elite of Massachusetts, and both Connecticut and Rhode Island were founded as a by-product of their discontent. The Rev. Thomas Hooker, who had arrived in Massachusetts Bay in 1633, soon found himself in opposition to the colony's restric-

Connecticut and Rhode Island

tive policy regarding the admission of church members and to the oligarchic power of the leaders of the colony. Motivated both by a distaste for the religious and political structure of Massachusetts and by a desire to open up new land, Hooker and his followers began moving into the Connecticut Valley in 1635. By 1636 they had succeeded in founding three towns—Hartford, Windsor, and Wethersford. In 1638 the separate colony of New Haven was founded, and in 1662 Connecticut and Rhode Island merged under one charter.

Roger Williams, the man closely associated with the founding of Rhode Island, also fled Massachusetts because of his objections to the arbitrary nature of Massachusetts government. Williams, however, was in some ways more rigid in his approach to religious polity than those Puritans he criticized. His own strict criteria for determining who was regenerate, and therefore eligible for church membership, finally led him to deny any practical way to admit anyone into the church. Once he recognized that no church could insure the purity of its congregation, he ceased using purity as a criterion for membership. Though this train of logic ultimately led him to adopt a position that subsequent generations labelled "democratic," the fact is that the principal source of Williams' policy of religious libertarianism was his very extremism in Calvinist orthodoxy.

The unpopularity of Williams' views forced him to flee Massachusetts Bay for Providence in 1636. In 1639 William Coddington, another dissenter in Massachusetts, settled his congregation in Newport. Four years later Samuel Gorton, another minister banished from Massachusetts Bay because of his differences with the ruling oligarchy, settled in Shawomet (later renamed Warwick). In 1644 these three communities joined with a fourth in Portsmouth under one charter to become one colony called Providence Plantation in Narragansett Bay. The early settlers of New Hampshire and Maine were also ruled by the government of Massachusetts Bay. New Hampshire was permanently separated from Massachusetts in 1692, although it was not until 1741 that it was given its own royal governor. Maine remained under the jurisdiction of Massachusetts until 1820.

The Middle Colonies. New Netherland, founded in 1624 on Manhattan Island by the Dutch West India Company, was but one element in a wider program of Dutch expansion in the first half of the 17th century. The English captured New Netherland in 1664; it was renamed New York, after James, duke of York, brother of Charles II, and was placed under the proprietary control of the Duke. In return for an annual gift to the King of 40 beaver skins, the Duke of York and his resident Board of Governors were given extraordinary discretion in the ruling of the colony. Although the grant to the Duke of York made mention of a representative assembly, the Duke was not legally obliged to summon it and in fact did not summon it until 1683. The Duke's interest in the colony was chiefly economic, not political, but most of his efforts to derive economic gain from New York proved futile. Indians, foreign interlopers (the Dutch actually recaptured New York in 1673 and held it for more than a year), and the success of the colonists in evading taxes made the proprietor's job a frustrating one.

Dominion of New England

In February 1685 the Duke of York found himself not only proprietor of New York but also king of England, a fact that changed the status of New York from that of a proprietary to a royal colony. The process of royal consolidation was accelerated when, in 1688, the colony was made part of the ill-fated Dominion of New England. In 1691, Jacob Leisler, a German merchant living on Long Island, led a successful revolt against the rule of the deputy governor, Francis Nicholson. The revolt, which was a product of dissatisfaction with a small aristocratic ruling elite and a more general dislike of the consolidated scheme of government of the Dominion of New England, served to hasten the demise of the dominion.

Pennsylvania, in part because of the liberal policies of its founder, William Penn, was destined to become the most diverse, dynamic, and prosperous of all the North American Colonies. Penn himself was a liberal, but by no means radical, English Whig. His Quaker faith was marked not by the religious extremism of some Quaker leaders of the day but rather by an adherence to certain dominant tenets of the faith—liberty of conscience and pacifism—and by an attachment to some of the basic tenets of Whig doctrine. William Penn sought to implement these ideals in his "holy experiment" in the New World.

Penn received his grant of land along the Delaware River in 1681 from Charles II. The "first frame of government" proposed by Penn in 1682 provided for a council and an assembly, each to be elected by the freeholders of the colony. The council was to have the sole power of initiating legislation; the lower house could only approve or veto bills submitted by the council. After numerous objections about the "oligarchic" nature of this form of government, Penn issued a second "frame of government" in 1682 and then a third in 1696, but even these did not wholly satisfy the residents of the colony. Finally, in 1701, a Charter of Privileges, giving the lower house all legislative power and transforming the council into an appointive body with advisory functions only, was approved by the citizens. The Charter of Privileges, like the other three frames of government, continued to guarantee the principle of religious toleration to all Protestants.

Pennsylvania prospered from the outset. Although there was some jealousy between the original settlers (who had received the best land and important commercial privileges) and the later arrivals, economic opportunity in Pennsylvania was on the whole greater than in any other colony. Beginning in 1683 with the immigration of Germans into the Delaware Valley and continuing with an enormous influx of Irish and Scots-Irish in the 1720s and 1730s, the population of Pennsylvania increased and diversified. The fertile soil of the countryside, in conjunction with a generous government land policy, kept immigration at high levels throughout the 18th century. William Penn's sons, John, Richard, and Thomas, although they ultimately converted back to Anglicanism, continued their father's policies of religious toleration after his death in 1718.

New Jersey

New Jersey remained in the shadow of both New York and Pennsylvania throughout most of the colonial period. Part of the territory ceded to the Duke of York by the English crown in 1664 lay in what would later become the colony of New Jersey. The Duke of York in turn granted that portion of his lands to John Berkeley and George Carteret, two close friends and allies of the King. In 1665 Berkeley and Carteret established a proprietary government under their own direction. Constant clashes, however, developed between the New Jersey and the New York proprietors over the precise nature of the New Jersey grant. The legal status of New Jersey became even more tangled when Berkeley sold his half interest in the colony to two Quakers, who in turn placed the management of the colony in the hands of three trustees, one of whom was William Penn. The area was then divided into East Jersey, controlled by Carteret, and West Jersey, controlled by Penn and the other Quaker trustees. In 1682 the Quakers bought East Jersey. A multiplicity of owners and an uncertainty of administration caused both colonists and colonizers to feel dissatisfied with the proprietary arrangement, and in 1702 the crown united the two Jerseys into a single royal province.

When the Quakers purchased East Jersey, they also acquired the tract of land that was to become Delaware, in order to protect their water route to Pennsylvania. That territory remained part of the Pennsylvania colony until 1704, when it was given an assembly of its own. It remained under the Pennsylvania governor, however, until the Revolution.

The Carolinas and Georgia. The English crown had issued grants to the Carolina territory as early as 1629, but it was not until 1663 that a group of eight proprietors —most of them men of extraordinary wealth and power even by English standards—actually began colonizing the area. The proprietors hoped to grow silk in the warm climate of the Carolinas, but all efforts to produce that valuable commodity failed. Moreover, it proved difficult to attract settlers to the Carolinas; it was not until 1718, after a series of violent Indian wars had subsided, that the population began to increase substantially. The pattern of settlement, once begun, followed two paths. North Carolina, which was largely cut off from the European and Caribbean trade by its unpromising coastline, developed into a colony of small to medium farms. South Carolina, with close ties to both the Caribbean and Europe, produced rice and, after 1742, indigo for a world market. The early settlers in both areas came primarily from the West Indian colonies. This pattern of migration was not, however, as distinctive in North Carolina, where many of the residents were part of the spillover from the natural expansion of Virginians southward.

The Fundamental Constitutions
The original frame of government for the Carolinas, the Fundamental Constitutions, drafted in 1669 by Anthony Ashley Cooper (Lord Shaftesbury) with the help of the philosopher John Locke, was largely ineffective because of its restrictive and feudal nature. The Fundamental Constitutions was abandoned in 1693 and replaced by a frame of government diminishing the powers of the proprietors and increasing the prerogatives of the provincial assembly. In 1729, primarily because of the proprietors' inability to meet the pressing problems of defense, the Carolinas were converted into the two separate royal colonies of North and South Carolina.

The proprietors of Georgia, led by James Oglethorpe, were wealthy philanthropic English gentlemen. It was Oglethorpe's plan to transport imprisoned debtors to Georgia where they could rehabilitate themselves by profitable labour and make money for the proprietors in the process. Those who actually settled in Georgia—and by no means all of them were impoverished debtors—encountered a highly restrictive economic and social system. Oglethorpe and his partners limited the size of individual landholdings to 500 acres, prohibited slavery, forbade the drinking of rum, and instituted a system of inheritance that further restricted the accumulation of large estates. The regulations, though noble in intention, created considerable tension between some of the more enterprising settlers and the proprietors. Moreover, the economy did not live up to the expectations of the colony's promoters. The silk industry in Georgia, like that in the Carolinas, failed to produce even one profitable crop.

The settlers were also dissatisfied with the political structure of the colony; the proprietors, concerned primarily with keeping close control over their utopian experiment, failed to provide for local institutions of self-government. As protests against the proprietors' policies mounted, the crown in 1753 assumed control over the colony; subsequently, many of the restrictions that the settlers had complained about, notably that prohibiting slavery, were lifted.

IMPERIAL ORGANIZATION
British policy toward the American Colonies was inevitably affected by the domestic politics of England; since the politics of England in the 17th and 18th centuries were never wholly stable, it is not surprising that British colonial policy during those years never developed along clear and consistent lines. During the first half century of colonization, it was even more difficult for England to establish an intelligent colonial policy because of the very disorganization of the Colonies themselves. It was nearly impossible for England to predict what role Virginia, Maryland, Massachusetts, Connecticut, and Rhode Island would play in the overall scheme of empire because of the diversity of the aims and governmental structures of those colonies. By 1660, however, England had taken the first steps in reorganizing her empire in a more profitable manner. The Navigation Act of 1660, a modification and amplification of a temporary series of acts passed in 1651, provided that goods bound to England or to English colonies, regardless of origin, must be shipped only in English vessels; that three-fourths of the personnel of those ships be Englishmen; and that certain "enumerated articles," such as sugar, cotton, and tobacco, be shipped

Navigation Acts

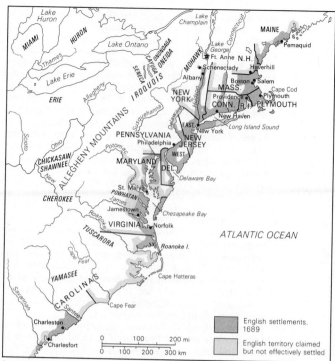

Seventeenth-century English colonies in North America.
Adapted from R. Treharne and H. Fullard (eds.), *Muir's Historical Atlas: Medieval and Modern*, 9th ed. (1962); George Philip and Son, Ltd., London

only to England, with trade in those items with other nations prohibited. This last provision hit Virginia and Maryland particularly hard; although those two colonies were awarded a monopoly over the English tobacco market at the same time that they were prohibited from marketing their tobacco elsewhere, there was no way that England alone could absorb their tobacco production.

The 1660 act proved inadequate to safeguard the entire British commercial empire and in subsequent years other navigation acts were passed strengthening the system. In 1663 Parliament passed an act requiring all vessels with European goods bound for the Colonies to pass first through English ports to pay customs duties. In 1673 Parliament, in order to prevent merchants from shipping the enumerated articles from colony to colony in the coastal trade and then taking them to a foreign country, required that merchants post bond guaranteeing that those goods be taken only to England. Finally, in 1696 Parliament established a Board of Trade to oversee Britain's commercial empire, instituted mechanisms to insure that the colonial governors aided in the enforcement of trade regulations, and set up vice admiralty courts in America for the prosecution of those who violated the Navigation Acts. The effectiveness of Britain's commercial policy is not altogether clear. It is certain that a significant amount of trade occurred in violation of that policy. The most recent investigations suggest, however, that by the end of the 17th century the Navigation Acts were being enforced successfully and that these acts did, in fact, constitute a significant economic burden for the American colonists.

In addition to the agencies of royal control in England, there were a number of royal officials in America responsible not only for aiding in the regulation of England's commercial empire but also for overseeing the internal affairs of the Colonies. The weaknesses of royal authority in the politics of provincial America were striking. In some areas, particularly in the corporate colonies of New England during the 17th century and in the proprietary colonies throughout their entire existence, direct royal authority in the person of a governor responsible to the crown was nonexistent. The absence of a royal governor in those colonies had a particularly deleterious effect on the enforcement of trade regulations. In fact, the lack of royal control over the political and commercial activities of New England prompted the Board of Trade to overturn the Massachusetts Bay Charter in 1684 and to consolidate Massachusetts, along with the other New England colonies and New York, into the Dominion of New England. After the colonists, aided by the turmoil of the Revolution of 1688 in England, succeeded in overthrowing the dominion scheme, the crown installed a royal governor in Massachusetts to protect its interests.

Powers of the royal governors

In those colonies with royal governors—the number of those colonies grew from one in 1650 to eight in 1760—the crown possessed a mechanism by which to insure that royal policy was enforced. The Privy Council issued each royal governor in America a set of instructions carefully defining the limits of provincial authority. The royal governors were to have the power to decide when to call the provincial assemblies together, to prorogue, or dissolve, the assemblies, and to veto any legislation passed by those assemblies. The governor's power over other aspects of the political structure of the colony was just as great. In most royal colonies he was the one official primarily responsible for the composition of the upper houses of the colonial legislatures and for the appointment of important provincial officials, such as the treasurer, attorney general, and all colonial judges. Moreover, the governor had enormous patronage powers over the local agencies of government. The officials of the county court, who were the principal agents of local government, were appointed by the governor in most of the royal colonies. Thus, the governor had direct or indirect control over every agency of government in America.

THE GROWTH OF PROVINCIAL POWER

Political growth. The distance separating England and America, the powerful pressures exerted on royal officials by Americans, and the inevitable inefficiency of any large bureaucracy all served to weaken royal power and to strengthen the hold of provincial leaders on the affairs of their respective colonies. During the 18th century, the colonial legislatures gained control over their own parliamentary prerogatives, achieved primary responsibility for legislation affecting taxation and defense, and ultimately took control over the salaries paid to royal officials. Provincial leaders also made significant inroads into the governor's patronage powers. Although theoretically the governor continued to control the appointments of local officials, in reality he most often automatically followed the recommendations of the provincial leaders in the localities in question. Similarly, the Governor's Councils, theoretically agents of royal authority, came to be dominated by prominent provincial leaders who tended to reflect the interests of the leadership of the lower house of assembly rather than those of the royal government in London.

Thus, by the mid-18th century most political power in America was concentrated in the hands of provincial rather than royal officials. These provincial leaders undoubtedly represented the interests of their constituents more faithfully than any royal official, but it is clear that the politics of provincial America were hardly democratic by modern standards. In general, both social prestige and political power tended to be determined by economic standing; and the economic resources of colonial America, though not as unevenly distributed as in Europe, were nevertheless controlled by relatively few men.

In the Chesapeake societies of Virginia and Maryland, and particularly in the regions east of the Blue Ridge Mountains, a planter class came to dominate nearly every aspect of those colonies' economic life. These same planters, joined by a few prominent merchants and lawyers, dominated the two most important agencies of local government—the county courts and the provincial assemblies. This extraordinary concentration of power in the hands of a wealthy few occurred in spite of the fact that a large percentage of the free adult male population (some have estimated as high as 80 to 90 percent) was able to participate in the political process. The ordinary citizens of the Chesapeake society, and those of most colonies, nevertheless continued to defer to those whom they considered to be their "betters." Although the societal ethic that enabled power to be concentrated in the hands of a few was hardly a democratic one, there is little evidence, at least for Virginia and Maryland, that the people of those societies were dissatisfied with their rulers. For the most part they believed that their local officials ruled responsively.

In the Carolinas a small group of rice and indigo planters monopolized much of the wealth. As in Virginia and Maryland, the planter class came to constitute a social elite. As a rule the planter class of the Carolinas did not have the same long tradition of responsible government as did the ruling oligarchies of Virginia and Maryland, and, as a consequence, they tended to be absentee landlords and governors, often passing much of their time in Charleston, away from their plantations and their political responsibilities.

The western regions

The western regions of both the Chesapeake and Carolina societies displayed distinctive characteristics of their own. Ruling traditions were fewer, accumulations of land and wealth less striking, and the social hierarchy less rigid in the west. In fact, in some western areas antagonism toward the restrictiveness of the east and toward eastern control of the political structure led to actual conflict. In both North and South Carolina armed risings of varying intensity erupted against the unresponsive nature of the eastern ruling elite. As the 18th century progressed, however, and as men accumulated more wealth and social prestige, the societies of the west came more closely to resemble those of the east.

New England society was more diverse and the political system less oligarchic than that of the South. In New England the mechanisms of town government served to broaden popular participation in government beyond the narrow base of the county courts.

New England town meetings

The town meetings, which elected the members of the provincial assemblies, were open to nearly all free adult males. Despite this, a relatively small group of men dominated the provincial governments of New England. As in the South, men of high occupational status and social prestige were closely concentrated in leadership positions in their respective colonies; in New England, merchants, lawyers, and to a lesser extent clergymen made up the bulk of the social and political elite.

The social and political structure of the Middle Colonies was more diverse than any region in America. New York, with its extensive system of manors and manor lords, often displayed genuinely feudal characteristics. The tenants on large manors often found it impossible to escape the influence of their manor lords. The administration of justice, the election of representatives, and the collection of taxes often took place on the manor itself. As a consequence, the large land-owning families exercised an inordinate amount of economic and political power.

The "Great Rebellion of 1766"

The "Great Rebellion of 1766," a short-lived outburst directed against the manor lords, was a symptom of the widespread discontent among the lower and middle classes. By contrast, Pennsylvania's governmental system was more open and responsive than that of any other colony in America. A unicameral legislature, free from the restraints imposed by a powerful governor's council, allowed Pennsylvania to be relatively independent of the influence of both the crown and the proprietor. This fact, in combination with the tolerant and relatively egalitarian bent of the early Quaker settlers and the subsequent immigration of large numbers of Europeans, made the social and political structure of Pennsylvania more democratic but more faction ridden than that of any other colony.

Population growth. The increasing political autonomy of the American Colonies was a natural reflection of their increased stature in the overall scheme of the British Empire. In 1650 the population of the Colonies had been 52,000; in 1700 it was 250,000 and by 1760 it was approaching 1,700,000. Virginia had increased from 54,000 in 1700 to approximately 340,000 in 1760. Pennsylvania had begun with 500 settlers in 1681 and had attracted at least 250,000 people by 1760. And America's cities were beginning to grow as well. By 1765 Boston had reached 15,000; New York City, 16,000–17,000; and Philadelphia, the largest city in the Colonies, 20,000.

African
slaves

Part of that population growth was the result of the involuntary immigration of African slaves. During the 17th century, slaves remained a tiny minority of the population. By the mid–18th century, after Southern colonists discovered that the profits generated by their plantations could support the relatively large initial investments needed for slave labour, the volume of the slave trade increased markedly. In Virginia the slave population leaped from 2,000 in 1670 to 23,000 in 1715 and reached 150,000 on the eve of the Revolution. In South Carolina it was even more dramatic. In 1700 there were probably no more than 2,500 blacks in the population; by 1765 there were 80,000–90,000, with blacks outnumbering whites by about two to one.

One of the principal attractions to the immigrants who moved to America voluntarily was the availability of inexpensive arable land. The westward migration to America's frontier—in the early 17th century all of America was a frontier, and by the 18th century the frontier ranged anywhere from 10 to 200 miles from the coastline—was to become one of the distinctive elements in American history. English Puritans, beginning in 1629 and continuing through 1640, were the first to immigrate in large numbers to America. Throughout the 17th century most of the migrants remained English; but beginning in the second decade of the 18th century, a wave of Germans, principally from the Rhineland Palatinate, arrived in America: by 1770 some 225,000–250,000 Germans had emigrated to America, more than 70 percent of them settling in the Middle Colonies, where generous land policies and religious toleration made life more comfortable for them. The Scots-Irish and Irish immigration, which began on a large scale after 1713 and continued past the Revolution, was more evenly distributed. By 1750 both Scots-Irish and Irish could be found in the western portions of nearly every colony. The French Huguenots, unlike most other groups immigrating to America, tended to be skilled and reasonably affluent when they first arrived.

Economic growth. Provincial America came to be less dependent upon subsistence agriculture and more on the cultivation and manufacture of products for the world market. Land, which initially served only individual needs, came to be the fundamental source of economic enterprise. The independent yeoman farmer continued to exist, particularly in New England and the Middle Colonies, but most settled land in North America by 1750 was devoted to the cultivation of a cash crop. New England turned its land over to the raising of meat products for export. The Middle Colonies were the principal producers of grains. By 1700 Philadelphia exported more than 350,000 bushels of wheat and over 18,000 tons of flour annually. The Southern Colonies were, of course, even more closely tied to the cash crop system. South Carolina, aided by British incentives, turned to the production of rice and indigo. North Carolina, although less oriented toward the market economy than South Carolina, was nevertheless one of the principal suppliers of naval stores. Virginia and Maryland steadily increased their economic dependence on tobacco and on the London merchants who purchased that tobacco; and for the most part they ignored those who recommended that they diversify their economies by turning part of their land over to the cultivation of wheat. Their near-total dependence upon the world tobacco price would ultimately prove disastrous, but for most of the 18th century Virginia and Maryland soil remained productive enough to make a single-crop system reasonably profitable.

As America evolved from subsistence to commercial agriculture, an influential commercial class increased its power in nearly every colony. Boston was the centre of the merchant elite of New England, who not only dominated economic life but also wielded social and political power as well. Merchants like James De Lancey and Philip Livingston in New York and Joseph Galloway, Robert Morris, and Thomas Wharton in Philadelphia exerted an influence far beyond the confines of their occupations. In Charleston the Pinckney, Rutledge, and Lowndes families controlled much of the trade that

Predom-
inance of
cash crops

passed through that port. Even in Virginia, where a strong merchant class was nonexistent, those people with the most economic and political power were those commercial farmers who best combined the occupations of merchant and farmer. And it is clear that the commercial importance of the Colonies was increasing. During the years 1700–10, approximately £265,000 sterling was exported annually to Great Britain from the Colonies, with roughly the same amount being imported by the Americans from Great Britain. By the decade 1760–70, that figure had risen to more than £1,000,000 sterling of goods exported annually to Great Britain and £1,760,000 annually imported from Great Britain.

CULTURAL AND RELIGIOUS DEVELOPMENT

Colonial culture. America's intellectual attainments during the 17th and 18th centuries, while not inferior to those of the nations of Europe, were nevertheless of a decidedly different character. It was the techniques of applied science that most excited the minds of Americans, who, faced with the problem of subduing an often wild and unruly land, saw in science the best way to explain, and eventually to harness, those forces around them. Ultimately this scientific mode of thought might be applied to the problems of civil society as well, but for the most part the emphasis in colonial America remained on science and technology, not politics or metaphysics. Typical of America's peculiar scientific genius was John Bartram of Pennsylvania, who collected and classified important botanical data from the New World. The American Philosophical Society, founded in 1744, is justly remembered as the focus of intellectual life in America. Men like David Rittenhouse, an astronomer who built the first planetarium in America; Cadwallader Colden, the lieutenant governor of New York, whose accomplishments as a botanist and as an anthropologist probably outmatched his achievements as a politician; and Benjamin Rush, a pioneer in numerous areas of social reform as well as one of colonial America's foremost physicians, were among the many active members of the Society. At the centre of the American Philosophical Society was one of its founders, Benjamin Franklin, who (in his experiments concerning the flow of electricity) proved to be one of the few American scientists to achieve a major theoretical breakthrough but who was more adept at the kinds of applied research that resulted in the manufacture of more efficient fireplaces and the development of the lightning rod.

American cultural achievements in nonscientific fields were less impressive. American literature, at least in the traditional European forms, was nearly nonexistent. The most important American contribution to literature was neither in fiction nor in metaphysics but rather in such histories as Robert Beverley's *History and Present State of Virginia* (1705) or William Byrd's *History of the Dividing Line* (1728–29, but not published until 1841). The most important cultural medium in America was not the book but the newspaper. The high cost of printing tended to eliminate all but the most vital news, and thus local gossip or extended speculative efforts were sacrificed so that more important material such as classified advertisements and reports of crop prices, could be included. Next to newspapers, almanacs were the most popular literary form in America, Franklin's *Poor Richard's* being only the most famous among scores of similar projects. Not until 1741 and the first installment of Franklin's *General Magazine* did literary magazines begin to make their first appearance in America. Most of the 18th-century magazines, however, failed to attract subscribers, and nearly all of them collapsed after only a few years of operation.

Art and drama, though flourishing somewhat more than literature, were nevertheless slow to achieve real distinction in America. America did produce one good historical painter in Benjamin West and two excellent portrait painters in John Copley and Gilbert Stuart; but it is not without significance that all three men passed much of their lives in London, where they received more attention and higher fees.

The Southern Colonies, particularly Charleston, seemed

American
Philo-
sophical
Society

Art and
drama

to be more interested in providing good theatre for their residents than did other regions, but in no colony did the theatre approach the excellence of that of Europe. In New England, Puritan influence was a roadblock to the performance of plays, and even in cosmopolitan Philadelphia the Quakers for a long time discouraged the development of the dramatic arts.

If Americans in the colonial period did not excel in achieving a high level of traditional cultural attainment, they did manage at least to disseminate what culture they had in a manner slightly more equitable than that of most nations of the world. Newspapers and almanacs, though hardly on the same intellectual level as the Encyclopédie produced by the European Philosophes, probably had a wider audience than any European cultural medium. The New England Colonies, although they did not always *Public* manage to keep pace with population growth, pioneered *education* in the field of public education. Outside of New England, education remained the preserve of those who could afford to send their children to private schools. The existence of privately supported but tuition-free charity schools and of some of the more inexpensive "academies" made it possible for the children of the American middle class to receive at least some education. The principal institutions of higher learning—Harvard (1636), William and Mary (1693), Yale (1701), Princeton (1747), Pennsylvania (a college since 1755), King's College (1754, now Columbia), Rhode Island College (1764, now Brown), Queen's College (1766, now Rutgers), and Dartmouth (1769)—served the upper class almost exclusively.

The "Great Awakening."   A series of religious revivals known collectively as the "Great Awakening" swept over the Colonies in the 1730s and the 1740s. Its impact was first felt in the Middle Colonies, where Theodore J. Frelinghuysen, a minister of the Dutch Reformed Church, began preaching in the 1720s. In New England, in the early 1730s, men such as Jonathan Edwards, perhaps the most learned theologian of the 18th century, were responsible for a reawakening of religious fervour. By the late 1740s the movement had extended into the Southern Colonies, where itinerant preachers such as Samuel Davies and George Whitefield exerted considerable influence, particularly in the backcountry.

The Great Awakening represented a reaction against the increasing secularization of society and against the corporate and materialistic nature of the principal churches of American society. By making conversion the initial step on the road to salvation and by opening up the conversion experience to all who recognized their own sinfulness, the ministers of the Great Awakening, some intentionally and others unwittingly, democratized Calvinist theology. The technique of many of the preachers of the Great Awakening was to inspire in their listeners a fear of the consequences of their sinful lives and a respect for the omnipotence of God. This sense of the ferocity of God was often tempered by the implied promise that a rejection of worldliness and a return to faith would result in a return to grace and an avoidance of the horrible punishments of an angry God. There was a certain contradictory quality about these two strains of Great Awakening theology, however. Predestination, one of the principal tenets of the Calvinist theology of most of the ministers of the Great Awakening, was ultimately incompatible with the promise that man could, by a voluntary act of faith, achieve salvation by his own efforts. Furthermore, the call for a return to complete faith and the emphasis on the omnipotence of God was the very antithesis of Enlightenment thought, which called for a greater questioning of faith and a diminishing role for God in the daily affairs of man. On the other hand, Jonathan Edwards, one of the principal figures of the Great Awakening in America, explicitly drew on the thought of men like John Locke and Isaac Newton in an attempt to make religion rational. Moreover, in attacking the leadership of the prevailing religious sects of the time, the ministers of the Great Awakening fostered a questioning of many forms of institutional authority and helped break up the oligarchic control of a few wealthy, traditionalist-minded men on organized religion in America.

AMERICA, ENGLAND, AND THE WIDER WORLD

The American Colonies, though in many ways isolated from the nations of Europe, were nevertheless continually subject to diplomatic and military pressures from abroad. In particular, Spain and France were always nearby, waiting to exploit any signs of English weakness in America to increase their commercial and territorial designs on the North American mainland. The Great War for the Empire, or the French and Indian War as the Americans termed it (see SEVEN YEARS' WAR), was but another round in a century of warfare between the major European powers. First in King William's War (1689–97), then in Queen Anne's War (1702–13), and in King George's War (1744–48; the American phase of the War of the Austrian Succession), Englishmen and Frenchmen had vied for control over the Indians, for possession of the territory lying to the north of the North American Colonies, for access to the trade in the Northwest, and for commercial superiority in the West Indies. In most of these encounters France had been aided by her ally, Spain. Because of its own holdings immediately south and west of the British colonies and in the Caribbean, Spain realized that it was in its own interest to join with the French in limiting British expansion. The culmination of these struggles came in 1754 with the Great War for the Empire. Whereas previous contests between Great Britain and France in America had been mostly provincial affairs, with American colonists doing most of the fighting for the British, the Great War for the Empire saw sizable commitments of English troops to America. The strategy of the English under William Pitt was to allow their ally, Prussia, to carry the brunt of the fighting in Europe, thus freeing the English to concentrate their troops in America.

The French, despite the fact that they were outnumbered 15 to one by the English colonial population in America, were nevertheless well-equipped to hold their own against the British. They had a larger military organization in America than did the English, their troops were better trained, and they were more successful than the British in forming military alliances with the Indians. The early engagements of the war went to the French; the surrender of George Washington to a superior French force at Ft. Necessity, the annihilation of Gen. Edward Braddock at the Monongahela River, and French victories at Oswego and Ft. William Henry all made it seem as if the war would be a short and unsuccessful one for the British. Even as these defeats took place, however, the English were able to increase their supplies of both men and material in America. By 1758, with its strength finally up to a satisfactory level, England began to implement its larger strategy, which involved sending a combined land and sea force to gain control of the St. Lawrence and a large land force aimed at Ft. Ticonderoga to eliminate French control of Lake Champlain. The first expedition against the French at Ticonderoga was a disaster, as Gen. James Abercrombie led 15,000 British and colonial troops in an attack against the French before his forces were adequately prepared. The English assault on Louisburg, the key to the St. Lawrence, was more successful. In July 1758 Lord Jeffrey Amherst led a naval attack in which his troops landed on the shores from small boats, established beachheads, and then captured the fort at Louisburg.

In 1759, after several months of sporadic fighting, the forces of James Wolfe captured Quebec from the French *The* army led by the Marquis de Montcalm. This was proba- *capture of* bly the turning point of the war. By the fall of 1760 the *Quebec* British had taken Montreal, and England possessed practical control of all of the North American continent. It took another two years for England to defeat her rivals in other parts of the world, but the contest for control of North America had been settled.

In the Treaty of Paris of 1763, England took possession of all of Canada, East and West Florida, all territory east of the Mississippi in North America, and St. Vincent, Tobago, and Dominica in the Caribbean. The British victory had not come cheaply, however. British government expenditures, which had amounted to £6,500,000 annually before the war, rose to £14,500,000 annually during the war. The cost of winning the war, and of maintaining the spoils of war, would be very high indeed —so high, in fact, that most Englishmen thought that the American Colonies should help pay the costs. The American colonists in 1763, freed for the first time in the 18th century from the threat posed by the French and the Indians, were more reluctant than ever before to be taxed to pay for a burdensome military establishment. The British, at least in part to pay the costs of the Great War for the Empire, would institute a program reorganizing the structure of the empire and imposing taxes on the Colonies to pay for that reorganization. The American Colonies, now economically powerful, culturally distinct, and steadily becoming more independent politically, would ultimately rebel before submitting to the English plan of empire. (R.R.B.)

II. The establishment of the nation

THE AMERICAN REVOLUTION

AND THE FORMATIVE PERIOD, 1763–89

Effects of the French and Indian War. Although the immediate results of the war had been to secure and greatly expand Britain's empire in North America, the longer range results were to achieve just the opposite; for in winning the war, Britain had dissolved the empire's most potent material adhesives. What had held the empire together were common interests and common enemies, along with a common reverence for the "rights of Englishmen" and for an imperial constitution that all parties had scrupulously avoided defining. Subjects in the parent country and in the Colonies alike had profitted from the maintenance of a vast enclosed common market; and, when colonials had wanted or needed to trade outside the empire, lax law enforcement usually made illicit trade possible. Similarly, the presence of Spanish and French colonies to the south, west, and north of the British colonies had produced interdependence of military and political interests between England and America. Removal of the French after 1760 destroyed Anglo-American strategic interdependence and (though this was slower to become visible) thoroughly disrupted the community of economic interests. Assorted conflicts between Britain and the various colonies began to arise; and, as they arose, spokesmen for all sides arose also, demanding their "rights" and defining the imperial constitution as they understood it. For 13 years definition followed conflict and conflict followed definition until the only thing remaining clear was that the empire could no longer be held together in peace.

Even before the end of the war, two ominous developments had indicated that Americans and Englishmen were not of one mind in their understanding of the consti-

Constitutional differences with Britain

tution. These were the celebrated Writs of Assistance case in Massachusetts (1761), protesting general search warrants, and the case of the Parson's Cause in Virginia (1763), in which James Otis and Patrick Henry successfully challenged, on "constitutional" grounds, the authority of both Parliament and royal officials. Otis argued in terms of John Locke's (see LOCKE, JOHN) concept of a higher law, and Henry in terms of Viscount Bolingbroke's (see BOLINGBROKE, HENRY ST. JOHN, 1ST VISCOUNT) concept of the king as father to his subjects; but the significance of their arguments was that they won the support of the local populace and jury and were worlds away from attitudes current in London.

But the warning implicit in these cases was lost in the wave of euphoria and myopia that swept Britain and the Colonies at the war's end. Military victory and the Peace of Paris seemed an unmixed blessing; indeed, a large part of what went wrong in the 1760s was that everyone behaved as if only his own circumstances and opportunities had been altered and failed to perceive that anything fundamental had gone wrong or even changed.

Officers of the government in London, to the extent that they concerned themselves with America at all, were interested primarily from a military point of view. They proposed to make various minor reforms in the adminis-

tration of the old empire, to require the colonials to bear a share of the cost of running the expanded territory that was acquired for their own protection, to ignore as much as possible the civil administration of the former French colonies, and to devote careful attention only to the changed military situation in America.

The most important part of the latter involved relations with the Indians, who had long been taught by the French to fear and despise the English. Prudently, in the Proclamation of 1763, London ordered that Anglo-Americans remain east of the crest of the Appalachians and allowed dealings with the Indians for land or goods only through London-appointed commissioners. Rather less prudently, the British refused to pacify the Indians with either an overwhelming show of force or a systematic program of bribes, both of which the French had long found necessary to comfortable and profitable relations with the red men. The immediate consequence was that in 1763 the Indians, under the Ottawa chief Pontiac, rose in a series of "guerrilla" attacks. The professional British military men were helpless until Col. Henry Bouquet—borrowing a technique that Anglo-Americans had earlier discovered —learned to wipe out the home bases of the Indians by burning their villages and fields and killing their women and children. By 1765 the Indians were willing to acknowledge defeat, and most British officials expected relations between England and America to reach a state of harmony.

Proclamation of 1763

Local grievances. Local activities, however, sometimes in interplay with actions in London, produced turbulence instead. In the Middle Colonies—Pennsylvania, New York, New Jersey, and Delaware—there was general economic prosperity but also social and political friction and disagreement with the mother country. Production of wheat and flour boomed, bringing good times for farmers and merchants; and the output of the area's second major product, ironware, expanded steadily. But the arrival of hordes of immigrants—especially New Englanders, Ulstermen, and Highland Scots—created social tensions in each of the Middle Colonies. Each, moreover, was rent by the efforts of land speculators to gain political power so as to profit from the immigration.

In New York this took the form of rivalry between aristocratic family connections, the De Lanceys and the Livingstons, and was purely local until a new issue intruded: Parliament's Sugar Act of 1764, imposing taxes and new commercial regulations, squeezed New York's West Indies merchants and their artisan adjuncts; the De Lanceys gained popular support and power by assuming a stance as defenders of American liberties against parliamentary encroachments. (Their most important defiance of Parliament was their refusal to obey the Quartering Act, requiring colonies to support the imperial soldiers stationed in America.) In Pennsylvania a clique headed by Joseph Galloway and Benjamin Franklin made a popular issue out of efforts to secure revocation of the Penn family's proprietary charter, secretly expecting that under a royal charter they could gain for themselves the vast tracts of land they sought; their opponents, led by John Dickinson, opposed a royal charter and, by logical extension, assumed a stance comparable to that of the De Lanceys in New York.

Aristocratic factions in New York

In the lower South—the Carolinas and Georgia—the situation was somewhat similar to that in the Middle Colonies. The economy, based on the production of rice, indigo, and naval stores, was booming; but the social order was strained. Indians were strong and hostile in South Carolina and Georgia, and in the backcountry of both Carolinas the frontiersmen, mainly Scots-Irish immigrants, were demanding overhaul of local government. In the middle and late 1760s, when so-called frontier Regulators rose in armed defiance of the authority of the low-country aristocrats, they sought imperial intervention; the aristocrats for that and other reasons opposed the extension of imperial authority.

In the upper South, in the tobacco colonies of Virginia and Maryland, everything was awry. Tobacco prices were erratically downward and crop failures were common. One faction of tidewater planters, led by the speaker of the House of Burgesses, remained afloat through fraudulent manipulations of paper currency, in violation of Parliament's Currency Act of 1764, requiring the extinction of such currency. Another pair of factions, one southwestern and the other Potomac-based, hoped to survive by land speculation that could succeed only through circumvention of the Proclamation of 1763.

Finally, there was New England, socially more or less calm and politically harmonious, except in Massachusetts, but economically depressed and afoul of the mother country and the other colonies in various ways. With rare exceptions, the complex New England economy failed to perform well after 1763. The Yankees blamed their troubles variously on the Sugar Act and other tightened commercial regulations, the Currency Act, the Proclamation of 1763, and malice in London. Meanwhile, settlers from overcrowded Connecticut, backed by the colony's government, invaded Pennsylvania; and, less officially but more numerously, colonials from Massachusetts invaded upper New York.

The Stamp Act and Townshend Duties. In sum, by the mid-1760s the colonists were sharply divided against one another, and objection to several parliamentary acts was strong though diffuse. Then, in 1765, Parliament passed the Stamp Act, designed to produce colonial revenues and thus reduce the heavy tax burden in England—which many Englishmen thought stemmed from the cost of maintaining the enlarged colonial establishment. In several American ports (notably Boston, where Samuel Adams formed and led a widely copied organization called the Sons of Liberty), opposition to collecting the Stamp Tax was violent; in Virginia legislative opposition (under Patrick Henry) was based on a radical constitutional position; and in many places colonists refused to import any British goods until the tax should be repealed. For the most part, however, the resistance, though firm, was more moderate. In October 1765, nine colonies sent delegates to New York for an extralegal congress that protested the Stamp Act mainly on the ground that it violated the ancient principle that taxes were a voluntary gift from the people to the sovereign.

The Stamp Act Congress

Much misunderstanding ensued. Parliament repealed the act, largely at the behest of London merchants suffering from the American boycott, but it saved face by pretending to bow to a distinction between acceptable "external" taxes and unacceptable "internal" taxes—a distinction suggested by Franklin, then pursuing his land schemes in London, but actually held by virtually no colonists. Colonial spokesmen cheered the repeal and failed, almost unanimously, to notice the Declaratory Act —passed along with the Stamp Act's repeal—asserting Parliament's right to legislate for the Colonies "in all cases whatsoever." Fifteen months later (June 1767) Parliament passed the Townshend Duties (Acts), imposing external taxes on lead, glass, paint, paper, and tea imported into America. Disregarding Franklin's misleading distinctions, John Dickinson penned a series of articles (*Letters from a farmer in Pennsylvania*), that galvanized a new colonial resistance. Dickinson's position was quickly adopted as the majority position in America; Parliament could tax the Colonies, but only incidentally to the power to regulate trade and other relations within the empire— and not at all for purposes of revenue.

Repeal of Townshend Duties

Though all the Townshend Duties except that on tea were shortly repealed, partly in response to a new colonial nonimportation policy and partly in response to political pressures inside England, three positions besides Dickinson's soon became manifest. Britain's position, apart from what was based on practical political considerations, was one of bewilderment; for, since the Glorious Revolution of 1688, chasing James II from the throne, the only limitation on the power of Parliament, as most Englishmen understood things, was Parliament's own self-restraint. Rather to the right of this position was that held by the Virginia Burgesses, who professed allegiance only to the crown, felt not even that, and regarded Parliament as being at best co-equal with the assembly of Virginia. Far to the left were the Yankees, especially those of Massachusetts, who regarded themselves as the heirs of 17th-century Puritanism, beyond the reach of crown and the corrupt 18th-century Parliament.

After the repeal of the Townshend Duties, however, everything cooled for awhile. A tide of credit-based prosperity, engendered by fraudulent banking activities in Scotland, swept the empire. Swollen revenues lulled royal government officials, and in New England and Virginia the more dissident elements succumbed to the lure of unexpected credit and prosperity. In Pennsylvania and in the lower South, the sudden and unexpected boom was enough to create the illusion that internal strains (from frontiersmen and Indians) were not so potent as had been imagined. In New York the De Lanceyites, given special exemption from the Currency Act and favourable treatment with regard to Indian land titles, abandoned all opposition to Parliament. In Massachusetts, Sam Adams found himself a radical leader virtually without a following.

The Tea Act and "Intolerable Acts." But late in 1772 the bubble burst. The effects of the collapse were slow to be felt, but in the spring of 1773 the most volatile groups in the Colonies felt them severely: radicals in Boston suddenly found themselves supported by the normally conservative farmers of the interior of Massachusetts, who had gotten themselves deeply into debt during the credit boom; the tobacco planters of Virginia, long trembling on the brink of insolvency, suddenly found themselves deeper in debt than farmers in New England could possibly imagine. Operators in Parliament, lately encouraged by speculative profits to ignore colonial problems, suddenly found themselves with a colonial problem in an unexpected area. The East India Company, the grandest speculation of them all, was tottering on the verge of bankruptcy. To save the company, Parliament passed (May 10, 1773) a complicated act giving it various new privileges, including a refund of import duties already paid on tea stored in London if it were reshipped to America. Consequently, high-quality English-India tea could, despite the Townshend Duties, be sold in America cheaper than inferior Dutch tea, which Americans habitually consumed because of its lower price.

The Tea Act reunited dissident elements in America. Merchants in New York, Philadelphia, and the New England outports, long accustomed to profits from illicit tea trade and now doubly squeezed by the financial collapse, financed and supported a new resistance. Propagandists, both opportunistic and idealistic, denounced the act as a dangerous "innovation" by Parliament and as an insidious plot to subvert American liberties by bribery—that is, by inducing Americans to buy taxed tea because it was cheaper. Radicals in Boston and Charleston capitalized on the furore, the former (in the Boston Tea Party) destroying and the latter confiscating cargoes of tea; tea consignments were turned back elsewhere. Virginia land speculators and planters sought any advantage they could find in the confusion.

The Boston Tea Party

Parliament, succumbing to an almost paranoid fear that the Americans were plotting independence, responded by cracking down on what most Englishmen regarded as the main source of trouble. In a series of acts passed in 1774, Parliament imposed a strangulating set of commercial restrictions on the port of Boston. Coincidentally, Parliament also passed an act, long in the making, providing for the government of the recently acquired French province of Quebec. The act provided, among other things, for retaining French law and the Roman Catholic establishment in the province and extended the province's jurisdiction to the trans-Appalachian area north of the Ohio River—thereby convincing New Englanders that the whole affair was a Catholic conspiracy aimed against Yankee Puritans along with the Boston Port Act and incidentally cutting Virginians off from the possibility of profitable land dealings in the Ohio country. Thus New England Yankees and Virginia plantation aristocrats, distrustful of one another since the Roundhead–Cavalier struggles of the English Civil War more than a century earlier, were thrust into the same radical camp in 1774.

General American response to the "Intolerable Acts"— as the restrictive parliamentary legislation was promptly

dubbed in America—resulted in the calling of a Continental Congress in October. Despite the radicalism of the
Yankees and Virginians, the dominant voice in the Congress was that of John Dickinson, a thoroughgoing conservative in the sense later identified with Edmund Burke.
Dickinson, steeped in British history and law but obliv-
ious to constitutional developments since 1689, insisted
that recent acts of Parliament were innovations that, if
persisted in, could destroy the excellent British constitution and insisted also that colonial resistance was justified
by history and tradition. He was supported by most delegates from the Middle Colonies and the lower South,
where, despite inner tensions, imperial regulation had
been advantageous, at least to the dominant groups.

The struggle for independence. Radical voices were
distinctly in the minority, and that fact did not change
much though violence was soon forthcoming. In April of
1775 British troops clashed with colonial militiamen in
Lexington and Concord, Massachusetts, and at the suggestion of Congress the several colonial militias prepared themselves for more conflict. Brilliant young propagandists—notably Thomas Jefferson, John Adams,
James Wilson, and Alexander Hamilton—penned persuasive tracts that essentially denied all power of Parliament over the Colonies, placed the burden of conflict
upon the crown, and came perilously close to advocating
independence; but still, despite everything, anger on neither side was sufficient to cause many to contemplate
seriously the dismemberment of the empire. Then in December Thomas Paine wrote "Common Sense," a masterpiece of sledge-hammer logic couched in the near-poetry
of the King James Bible, dissolving every claim that had
been advanced for loyalty to kings.

Thomas
Paine's
"Common
Sense"

Early in 1776 resistance hardened into war, and advocates of independence grew in numbers. Until the very
end, however, congressional delegates and popular majorities in the Middle Colonies and the lower South opposed independence, for the empire had been good to
them and revolution could unleash a host of troubles
from Indians, slaves, and frontiersmen. New England and
Virginia, less blessed by the fruits of empire and socially
far more stable—and also, unlike the other colonies, having matured in the 17th century, when rebellion and even
regicide were common—were willing to take the risk. On
July 2, 1776, Congress voted for independence. Two days
later it published the Declaration of Independence, written by Jefferson and addressed "to the opinions of mankind." (For the military history of the war, see WAR OF
INDEPENDENCE, U.S.)

**The Confederation and the framing of state constitu-
tions.** As the debate on independence moved toward a
climax, the internal political alignments of the various
colonies began to harden around that issue. In New
England, minority groups were overridden, royalists
fleeing for Nova Scotia or England, while Baptists and
other religious minorities were vigorously suppressed;
south of the Potomac, backcountry dissenters were subdued by force, though Loyalism remained endemic in the
area. In the Middle Colonies, Galloway broke with
Franklin and remained Loyalist as a matter of conscience;
Pennsylvania's Quakers became nonmilitantly Loyalist;
New York's De Lanceyites became militantly so out of
fear of the social turmoil that seemed in store; the Livingston connection became reluctant rebels.

"Repub-
licans"
versus
centralists

Among those who supported independence, two broad
divisions soon became manifest. The reluctant rebels of
the Middle Colonies and the lower South insisted, at the
last minute, that if independence was to come, it should
be preceded by the creation of a strong national government. The more ardent rebels of New England and Virginia became hard-shelled "republicans"—by which they
meant opponents of monarchy, central government, executive authority, and all other forms of restraint upon the
power of dominant local groups. The republicans prevailed from 1776 until 1780, almost preventing victory by
their hostility to central authority and ensuring the adoption of the Articles of Confederation (a "league of
friendship" rather than the strong national government
proposed by Dickinson and supported by nationalists).

Predictably, few internal reforms were brought about
by the prevalence of republicanism: all colony-states except Rhode Island and Connecticut, which had long governed themselves under colonial charters, did adopt new
constitutions, but none save those of Pennsylvania and
Georgia were especially radical. The latter two established unicameral legislatures virtually unchecked by executive or judicial branches and experienced considerable
political turbulence. The other nine were relatively conservative and were designed to freeze political power
where it was in the summer of 1776; all emasculated the
executive branch and expanded legislative authority, but
few broadened the franchise, only seven provided bills of
rights (none of which had the force of law), and several
provided elaborate checks on direct popular rule.

Problems under the Articles of Confederation. Government under the Articles of Confederation and the
new state constitutions was adequate to see the United
States through to independence, but only after republicanism had been discredited by corruption and incompetence in 1781, after nationalists had seized unconstitutional powers under Superintendant of Finance
Robert Morris, after Gen. George Washington's army
acquired military discipline and a most unrepublican
spirit, and after various British generals, notoriously the
commander of the southern army, Lord Cornwallis,
committed blunders that bordered on the preposterous.
At Yorktown, Virginia, in October of 1781, Cornwallis
was forced to surrender to Washington. A year later, a
definitive treaty of peace, recognizing American independence and placing the western boundary of the
United States at the Mississippi, had been signed.
Britain retained Canada, Spain received Florida to the
Mississippi, and everything west of the river remained
Spanish. France, allied with the United States after
1778, got nothing for all its troubles. End of
the war

The Americans suddenly found themselves in an unfriendly world. Britain closed its West Indies to American
shipping, Spain closed its colonies entirely and also, by
closing New Orleans, deterred development of the West,
though frontiersmen spilled over the mountains in great
numbers. Even France imposed commercial restrictions,
cutting New England fish and Virginia tobacco from
profitable markets. In short, the tangible gains many expected from independence were simply not forthcoming.

Domestic tensions aggravated the difficulties of the new
republic. Congress, nearly impotent under the Articles of
Confederation and weakened further by the resurgence
of republicans after the peace, was unable to cope with
either national or local problems. The most pressing of
all domestic problems was the public debt, national and
state, of about $60,000,000, incurred to finance the war.
The vast domain of public lands might have been used to
retire these debts—trans-Appalachia north of the Ohio
River had come, by circuitous means, to be vested in
Congress by 1784—but local and private greed, Spanish
obstructionism, and efforts of nationalists to use public
debts and lands as cements of a stronger union combined
to thwart such action.

In default of effective national action, the several states
attempted to service the public debts, with varying results. Most of the Southern states virtually repudiated
their debts, alienating public creditors and straining the
private economy. Even so, Georgia and North Carolina
thrived for special local reasons, South Carolina might
have flourished but for a freakish succession of crop failures, Virginia did well until 1786, and only Maryland was
torn by internal political and financial problems. In the
Middle states, New York and Pennsylvania handled
their public affairs well, with the result that New York
drifted away from nationalism, though internal dissension kept Pennsylvania divided. New Jersey and Delaware and two New England states, Connecticut and
New Hampshire, were entirely unable to manage
alone. Massachusetts, sorely depressed economically
in the postimperial world and burdened by high taxes
imposed to pay war debts, was torn in civil war
(Shays' Rebellion) in 1786. In all of New England,
only Rhode Island flourished, and it did so only through Shays'
Rebellion

the kind of brigandage that Americans had come to expect from the "otherwise-minded" colony-state.

The Constitutional Convention. In sum, by the winter of 1786–87 America was in crisis. In Massachusetts, Capt. Daniel Shays, a Revolutionary War veteran, led a band of embattled farmers against the state court to prevent foreclosures on tax delinquent farmers; and in New York the state legislature defeated an amendment to the Articles of Confederation giving Congress an independent source of revenue from import duties. In desperation, Congress and all the states except Rhode Island acceded to a call—issued by nationalists at a commercial convention in Annapolis the preceding September—for a general convention to meet in Philadelphia in May 1787 and "consider the exigencies of the Union."

The Philadelphia Convention has been described, and not without merit, as the most gifted collection of statesmen ever assembled (even though Jefferson, Sam and John Adams, Richard Henry Lee, John Hancock, Patrick Henry, and other heroes of 1776 were absent). Well-versed in political theory, the delegates were nonetheless practical men of business and public affairs who addressed themselves less to the theoretical problem of what kind of national government America should have (which, given everything, could only be answered republican and federal) than to the more basic question, whether the United States would have a national government at all. On that crucial question, the 55 delegates lined up in four general camps.

Alignment of the delegates

A majority of delegates were strong nationalists; an unconditional nationalist group of eight or ten, led by Washington and Franklin, who preferred a limited national authority based on a separation of powers but who would have accepted almost any form approved by the other delegates; two monarchists, Dickinson and Hamilton; six or eight aristocrats, led by Gouverneur Morris of Pennsylvania and John Rutledge of South Carolina, who would accept almost any energetic national government but preferred one as "high-toned" as possible; and seven or eight rather "democratic" nationalists, led by James Wilson of Pennsylvania and James Madison of Virginia, who wanted a strong national government founded on a broad popular base.

Next came two groups of conditional nationalists. The first of these—consisting of Elbridge Gerry of Massachusetts, George Wythe, Edmund Randolph, and George Mason of Virginia, and Luther Martin and John Francis Mercer of Maryland—were ideologues, who would support a national government only if it were founded on narrowly defined republican principles. The other group, which included most of the delegates from Maryland, New Hampshire, Connecticut, New Jersey, and Delaware, shared a more tangible concern. As representatives of states without viable claims to western lands, they insisted that the lands become the common property of all the states; but, given that condition, they were willing to support an extremely strong central authority. Finally, a few delegates, notably two of the three from New York, were flatly opposed to increased national authority.

In reconciling the ideological differences, Madison and Wilson were the most important delegates; in managing the political and economic differences, Rutledge, together with Roger Sherman and Oliver Ellsworth of Connecticut, towered over the rest.

The main business began with Washington presiding and Governor Randolph of Virginia presenting 15 resolutions, probably authored by Madison. The idea of creating a national authority was quickly approved, along with the principle that the new government should be divided into executive, legislative, and judicial branches. The most heated debate concerned the makeup of the legislative branch, the "landless" states insisting on equal representation by states and their opponents demanding that representation be apportioned according to population. A compromise was reached with a bicameral legislature, one house representing population and the other representing the states equally and the latter having control over questions of public lands. This arrangement was agreed upon by mid-July, but the constitution of the

other branches was left vague and unsettled. The work of the convention was then turned over to a five-man Committee of Detail, which produced (August 6) a rough draft of a constitution, retaining the compromise legislature and making executive and judiciary subordinate to it. Early in September, however, after several weeks spent mainly in haggling over special interest features, the cumbersome electoral college was proposed (probably by Franklin), making the presidency independent of the proposed Congress. That feature made the Constitution awkward but also built into it the principle of separation of powers. Following a few more days of discussion, the convention's various resolutions were turned over to a Committee on Style, under Gouverneur Morris, which drafted the final document. Morris took several liberties with the text, introducing ambiguity at key points to make the Constitution flexible and also (without the delegates noticing) injecting various features, notably on "contract clause," which had been voted down. On September 17, 1787, the Constitution was approved by 39 of the 42 delegates remaining in the convention.

Proposal of the electoral college

Struggle for ratification. The Constitution stipulated that it should become effective when specially elected conventions in nine states ratified, despite the requirement in the Articles of Confederation that amendments be ratified by the legislatures of every state. The smallest and weakest states, most pleased with the new system, ratified quickly: Delaware, New Jersey, and Georgia all unanimously and before year's end and Connecticut early in 1788 by a majority of three to one. Meanwhile, Pennsylvania, one of the states expected to be reluctant, responded to political manipulation and high-pressure campaign techniques and ratified in December 1787 by a convention vote of 46 delegates to 23. Massachusetts, another "swing" state, ratified early in 1787 in response to clever politicking by Federalists, as proponents of the Constitution called themselves, though "Anti-Federalists" may well have been in a majority in the state.

With six states having approved and three to go, the contest came to a climax in the spring of 1788. Maryland and South Carolina (both being extremely aristocratic states that had been lukewarm toward the democratic trends implicit in independence and both being landless states that stood to gain from the pooling of the domain of public lands) ratified by sizable majorities early in the year. But New Hampshire, populated mainly by backcountrymen who were loathe to accept any change, postponed a decision; and the dominant groups in Virginia, New York, North Carolina, and Rhode Island were opposed to ratification. After considerable debate and political jockeying, however, the first three had ratified by July of 1788, despite the probable opposition of popular majorities. North Carolina finally ratified in November of 1789, several months after the new government had begun to operate, and Rhode Island ratified in May 1790.

Attitudes toward the Constitution can be accounted for on four major sets of grounds, apart from considerations already mentioned: (1) proximity to regular commerce and communication, those Americans having the broadest world view, deriving from regular contact with other places, being more favourable to national authority than those in more isolated places; (2) military vulnerability, those areas that had suffered most from the wartime fighting being the most nationalist (a striking number of the ablest pieces in favour of the Constitution, *The Federalist Papers* by Jay, Hamilton, and Madison, were concerned with the advantages for national defense that would result from ratification); (3) relative success under the Confederation, those states that had fared best as sovereign entities being least favourable toward the Constitution; and (4) ideology, the more doctrinaire republicans being cool toward the Constitution because of its ambiguity and lack of a bill of rights. Economic interests also entered the contest over ratification but won about as many enemies as friends for the new system.

NATIONAL POLITICS, 1789–1816

The first elections under the Constitution were held late in 1788. Federalists, mainly old nationalists, swept to

The United States, 1783–1803.

power: Washington received every electoral vote and became president, John Adams became vice president, and only a handful of Anti-Federalists were elected to Congress. The new government wasted some time on precedents and protocol, but by early summer of 1789 it had plunged earnestly into serious business. One such concerned an issue raised during the conflict over ratification: Anti-Federalists had demanded a second convention to add a bill of rights to the Constitution, some hoping that a second convention might undo the work of the first. Madison, fighting for his political life in predominantly Anti-Federalist Virginia, sought to please his constituents by proposing a number of amendments; he was supported, for reasons of political expediency, by some Federalists who actually opposed a bill of rights and was opposed, for similar reasons, by some Anti-Federalists who favoured such amendments. Twelve amendments were finally approved by Congress and submitted to the states for ratification. Ten, which became the Bill of Rights, were ratified in December 1791. Together the amendments restricted national authority against states and individuals and guaranteed various procedural rights, but the restrictions did not apply to state governments.

The Bill of Rights

Meanwhile, Congress was resolving two other major problems in 1789. It levied a tariff on imports, and though supplementary internal taxes were enacted from time to time, import duties would remain the major

source of national revenue for more than a century. The first Congress also passed the Judiciary Act, filling a void in the Constitution by establishing a hierarchical system of appellate courts. For practical purposes this act became part of the Constitution itself.

In dealing with its remaining major tasks, Congress went only part of the way in 1789. Instead of creating new executive departments, it adopted and modified the machinery of the Confederation. The Department of Foreign Affairs became State (to head which Washington appointed Thomas Jefferson, after incumbent John Jay indicated his preference for the chief justiceship); the War Department was retained intact, including the incumbent head, Henry Knox. The Confederation's three-man Board of the Treasury was replaced by a department headed by a single secretary. Washington wanted Robert Morris, Philadelphia merchant and erstwhile "financier of the Revolution," for the post, but Morris declined and Washington appointed instead his own former aide-de-camp, the brilliant young New Yorker Alexander Hamilton. Congress promptly instructed Hamilton to produce, by the time it reconvened at year's end, a plan for retiring the public debts.

Hamilton's fiscal system. The following January, Hamilton presented his First Report on the Public Credit, a comprehensive plan modelled after the system evolved in England between the 1690s and 1730s. Instead of attempting to retire the public debt, which imposed crippling tax burdens on the nascent American economy, Hamilton proposed to "fund" it and transform it into currency. Toward that end, all obligations of the old Confederacy as well as the war debts of the states would be made exchangeable for bonds of the new national government; the new bonds would receive regular interest payments and be supported by open-market purchases by Treasury Department agents, using a "sinking fund" created for the purpose. With public bonds thus stabilized and "pegged," government obligations could form the basis of a paper currency: a national bank, quasi-public and patterned after the Bank of England, could issue notes based on the public debt.

"Funding" the debt

Most Congressmen from the tobacco-growing states opposed Hamilton's plan, partly because the planters were major importers who had largely repudiated their own debts and thus stood to pay heavily for a scheme that would directly profit them little. In part, however, their antagonism arose from much deeper roots, the so-called agrarian mentality. The aristocratic republicans of the tobacco belt were by no means opposed to making profit; indeed they were so avid for profit that they were willing to enslave blacks and slaughter Indians to obtain it; but they fiercely opposed the monetization of American life, much as the Bolingbroke Tories (whom the Virginians regularly read and quoted) had opposed the monetization of England by the Walpole Whigs.

Accordingly, Hamilton's proposals met stiff resistance from the "republican interest" in Congress, led by Madison, but the plan for assuming the state debts and funding all the debts was passed in August 1790. The act creating the Bank of the United States was passed in February 1791. Washington's cabinet split on this issue, Jefferson arguing, as a "strict constructionist," that the bank was unconstitutional and Hamilton defending its constitutionality with the doctrine of implied powers. Other portions of Hamilton's program, notably his proposal for protective tariffs to promote infant American industries, were defeated.

Formation of political parties. Mainly as a result of these disputes, something resembling political parties had begun to crystallize by 1792. Republicans, led by Madison and Jefferson, founded an anti-administration newspaper, built local organizations through private clubs called Democratic-Republican societies, and tried to coordinate electioneering activities; they were strong in the upper South, on the western frontier, and among erstwhile Anti-Federalists in the Middle states. Federalists, led by Hamilton, also founded a newspaper, but for the most part their political organization consisted of Treasury Department employees. The prosperity attending Hamilton's program and the immense popularity of President Washington won Federalist supporters everywhere, though the "party" was strongest in New England, South Carolina, and the environs of New York City and Philadelphia.

Effects of the French Revolution. In 1793 a new issue arose, one that would dominate American affairs for 22 years: the wars of the French Revolution. American involvement began with the arrival of Citizen Edmond Genet as minister from France, claiming that the Franco-American Alliance of 1778 bound the United States in the current French war against England, Spain, and other European nations. Hamilton, recognizing that war with England would dry up revenues from imports (most of which came from Britain) and thus destroy the financial system that bound the nation together, insisted on neutrality. Republicans warmly favoured France, partly out of ideological kinship, partly because of opposition to Hamilton's system, partly because the alliance would justify seizure of Spanish territory on the southern and western frontiers. Washington followed Hamilton's advice and issued a neutrality proclamation, and Jefferson soon resigned as secretary of state.

The Republicans gained popular support in the winter of 1793–94, when the British Navy seized many American commercial vessels and impressed into its service a number of American seamen. To prevent a break with England, Washington sent John Jay to London. The resulting treaty ensured cordial Anglo-American relations, provided for the evacuation of British posts in the American Northwest, and (in conjunction with Orders in Council issued at the same time) afforded great opportunities for American commerce as the neutral carrier of belligerent goods. Meanwhile, when Jay was in London the so-called Whiskey Rebellion (actually only a limited opposition to the federal excise tax on liquor) was crushed in western Pennsylvania; and because the "rebels" were associated with Democratic-Republican societies, such societies were widely discredited. Even so, Republicans were able to organize a spirited opposition to Jay's Treaty; but its obvious advantages, together with the loss of enthusiasm for France during and as a result of the Reign of Terror (1793–94), were enough to secure senatorial ratification by the necessary two-thirds majority. A year later the Federalists scored another diplomatic gain with Pinckney's Treaty, whereby Spain opened the Mississippi, allowing Americans the right of deposit at Spanish New Orleans.

The Jay Treaty

On that note, and largely because the tenor of domestic politics had grown so scurrilous, Washington decided to retire at the end of his second term (March 3, 1797). Federalist vice president John Adams was elected president, but the Republican Jefferson became vice president. Adams' administration was marked throughout by strained relations with a France that was angry over Jay's Treaty and arrogant after defeating the best armies of Europe, a France that demanded bribes and tribute as a condition to recognizing American diplomats. Incensed, the United States prepared for war. What followed was complex. There was some naval fighting in 1798–99 at a time when the infant U.S. Navy consisted mainly of a new class of super-frigates designed by Joshua Humphreys. Hamilton, retired from the Treasury but still dominating the Federalist Party, demanded a large army also, partly for conquest of Spanish territory in the Southwest (Spain having become an ally of France) and partly to suppress a pro-French insurrection he feared was brewing in the South. Virginia, North Carolina, and Kentucky did contemplate insurrection and armed their militias to fight if Hamilton's "invasion" materialized. Moreover, in opposition to the Alien and Sedition Acts, restrictive measures passed as part of the war preparations, Madison and Jefferson penned the so-called Virginia and Kentucky Resolutions, defying Congress and postulating the classical states-sovereignty constitutional position. (Actually, the Alien and Sedition Acts were the mildest restrictions on civil liberties ever imposed by the United States in time of war.)

Alien and Sedition Acts

In 1799, France, suddenly jeopardized by the formation of a new coalition in Europe, signified its willingness to negotiate. Adams then sent a new minister, William Vans Murray, who agreed to the Convention of 1800, terminating the quasi-war. France continued to have designs on America; the secret Treaty of San Ildefonso, whereby Napoleon (now ruling France) obtained Spanish Louisiana, was signed on October 1, 1800, the day after Murray's convention was signed. But Adams had avoided war and gained considerable popularity in so doing. He had also split his party by his open break with Hamilton, however, and thereby prevented his re-election in 1800. Jefferson and Aaron Burr tied for the lead in the electoral college, and only after an acrimonious contest in Congress did Jefferson become president.

Jefferson's presidency. The "Revolution of 1800," as Jefferson later described his election, reflected no popular mandate—most electors were chosen by state legislatures —and did not, in fact, bring sweeping changes to the national government. To the disappointment of Republican ideologues, Jefferson neither purged the government of Federalist employees nor destroyed the Hamiltonian system, and he abandoned the principles of strict construction and a weak executive branch. Albert Gallatin, as secretary of the treasury, introduced various administrative reforms; but otherwise the Jeffersonians, in domestic affairs, concentrated mainly on trying to rid the federal courts of Federalist judges. The President and his intimates shared a distrust of the judicial branch, were incensed by Adams' "midnight appointments" (several new judgeships created in February of 1801 and filled by Adams just before he left office in March), and were outraged when one of the late appointees, Chief Justice John Marshall, established the principle of judicial review by declaring an act of Congress unconstitutional (*Marbury* v. *Madison,* 1803). Attempts to clear the bench by impeachment reached a climax early in 1805, with the trial of Justice Samuel Chase. When Chase was acquitted, the Jeffersonians abandoned the effort.

*Establish-
ment of
judicial
review*

Jefferson's main concern was with foreign affairs and especially with territorial expansion. The most successful action in that direction was the purchase of the vast Louisiana territory from France in 1803 for $15,000,000. Jefferson also sought diligently to obtain Spanish Florida, which was needed for a southern outlet to the sea. Toward that end he played up to Napoleon, who could have forced Spain to cede Florida to the United States—and who tantalized the President by hinting he might do so. Jefferson also flirted with the idea of secretly backing a private expedition against Spanish territory. One such expedition was that of Aaron Burr, who in 1804 had been dumped by the Jeffersonians, ran unsuccessfully for governor of New York, and killed Hamilton in a duel and who in 1805–06 was engaged in various western conspiracies. Arrested late in 1806, he was tried for treason and acquitted in 1807.

Meanwhile, the United States had again become entangled in the European wars. In 1805 Britain reversed the orders that enabled Americans to grow rich as neutral carriers to belligerents, and the next year Britain and France imposed various orders and decrees that sorely limited American trade with Europe and confiscated hundreds of American ships for violating the new rules. As a countermeasure, Jefferson requested and Congress authorized an embargo on all American exports. This was the darkest hour in Jefferson's presidency. In the enforcement of the embargo, civil liberties were ruthlessly suppressed; the embargo's main effect was to starve slaves in the West Indies—which the Jeffersonians expected and even welcomed because it had the incidental advantage, from their point of view as slaveowners, of punishing the blacks who had fought a successful revolution in Santo Domingo; and the effect on the European belligerents was nil. When his second term ended, Jefferson retired and never participated in public affairs again.

*Jefferson's
embargo
on exports*

Madison's presidency. Jefferson's secretary of state, James Madison, succeeded him as president in 1809. Madison had been skillful in politics, both as theoretician and as practical operator, but he lacked the qualities of leadership that Jefferson had brought to the presidency. Slavishly adhering to his narrow understanding of Jefferson's policies, Madison tried with a succession of commercial restrictions to force Britain and France to respect freedom of the seas. The efforts were futile, and Britain, master of the oceans since Nelson's victory over the combined French and Spanish fleets at Trafalgar in 1805, seized American ships and seamen at will and periodically insulted the small American navy. Meanwhile, the navy was considerably reduced, out of ideological opposition to standing armed forces, and the national government was drastically weakened when the charter of the national bank expired and Republicans in Congress refused to renew it.

Thus, as 1812 approached, American relations with both Britain and France degenerated, as did America's ability to wage war. But just then a popular clamour for war began to mount. In part the clamour was born of frustration and a desire to redeem the national honour. In part it was triggered by the private conquest of a portion of Spanish Florida (Spain having rejoined Britain against France), which convinced many expansionists that the rest of Florida and all of Canada would be easy prey for American militiamen. Madison himself inched toward war, seeking no conquests but determined to win freedom of the seas. These mounting forces, compounded by bungling diplomacy, resulted in a declaration of war against England on June 18, 1812. The vote was close, 79-49 in the House and 19–13 in the Senate. North and east of the Delaware River the vote was almost unanimous for peace.

THE WAR OF 1812

The American strategy in the War of 1812 was to fight for freedom of the seas by staying ashore. The navy was to be ordered to port, to defend the major cities; Canada was to be invaded at Detroit, Ft. Niagara, and Lake Champlain by a large militia force (100,000 were authorized for six months' service) and the small regular army. British strategy was to bottle the American navy in port, blockade the coast, and ignore the militia threat as so much braggadocio.

In the first year of the war, British thinking proved eminently the sounder. American militiamen under Gen. William Hull, instead of invading Canada, made a series of blunders and on August 16 surrendered Detroit to a small detachment of British. At Ft. Niagara the militiamen, first under Gen. Stephen Van Rensselaer and then under Alexander Smyth, refused to cross the frontier into Canada. At Lake Champlain the same thing happened with the largest American force, under Henry Dearborn.

Luckily for the Americans, naval captains William Bainbridge and Charles Stewart persuaded Madison, at the last moment, to allow the small U.S. Navy (12 ships fit for sea duty, versus more than 600 in the Royal Navy) to go to sea. There the Americans distinguished themselves. Capt. John Rodgers sailed with five ships on a cruise that, though disappointing in its haul of prizes, diverted the British for months. The Humphreys frigate USS "Constitution," first under Isaac Hull and then under Bainbridge, destroyed HMS "Guerrière" and "Java," two frigates of her own class; and the Humphreys frigate "United States," under Stephen Decatur, captured HMS "Macedonian." In smaller ship actions, USS "Wasp" took HMS "Frolic," and USS "Hornet" defeated HMS "Peacock." It had been years since an enemy had defeated a British naval vessel of its own class in single combat, and yet the Americans did so five times in succession during the first eight months of the war.

Early in 1813, however, the Royal Navy bottled the United States Navy in port, and it was ineffectual on the high seas thereafter. Then, having neutralized the Americans' fleet and being contemptuous of their fighting ability on land, the British in Canada were emboldened to attempt the conquest of the American Northwest, with a

Louisiana Purchase.

combined force of regulars and Indians. Success depended on control of the Great Lakes, however, and once again the U.S. Navy performed admirably. A naval building race on Lake Ontario was more or less a stalemate. On Lake Erie, a motley fleet under Oliver Hazard Perry defeated a similar British fleet under R.H. Barclay (September 10, 1813). That victory enabled the American western commander, Gen. William Henry Harrison, to move a force of 4,500 across the lake and, at the Battle of the Thames (October 5), rout the British and their Indian allies, killing the chief Tecumseh. Efforts to follow up this victory were futile, but at least the western frontier was secure.

Perry's victory

Elsewhere, however, the United States was nearing calamity. The British, victorious over Napoleon (March–April 1814), prepared a massive blow to destroy the United States: diversionary naval raids on coastal cities, followed by invasions at Ft. Niagara, Lake Champlain, and New Orleans. Moreover, American public finances were chaotic, and popular morale was even worse. Having destroyed the Bank of the United States and alienated almost every merchant north of New York, the Republican administration had neither money nor credit. New Yorkers and New Englanders openly opposed the war, traded with the enemy, and talked of rejoining Britain (though at the Hartford Convention in December, secessionist proposals were rejected).

Yet in the actual fighting of 1814, the Americans were surprisingly successful. The only part of the British plan that worked was that for coastal raids: great destruction was wrought on the Connecticut River, Buzzard's Bay (Massachusetts), and Alexandria, Virginia; and Royal Marines took Washington and burned the public buildings there and then bombarded Baltimore (August–September). At Ft. Niagara, however, American militiamen and regulars repulsed the invasion attempt (July–September); and on Lake Champlain Capt. Thomas Macdonough, USN, assembled a fleet that, for the second time in the war, defeated a British fleet (September 11)—thus precluding invasion by that route. Finally, at the Battle of New Orleans (fought January 8, 1815, two weeks after the peace treaty had been signed), Americans under Andrew Jackson slaughtered the invading British army.

Meanwhile, the British government had heeded the sage advice of the Duke of Wellington. The hero of the Peninsular Campaign maintained that, in an unorganized frontier country like the United States, fighting could go on endlessly without either side "winning," despite the superiority of British resources. Accordingly, British negotiators at Ghent, Belgium (where talks with an American commission had been underway for several months), agreed to peace on December 24, 1814. The terms were status quo antebellum. The illusion of victory in the U.S. plus the re-establishment of peace, strengthened Madison's administration. His handpicked successor, James Monroe—former secretary of state and war—easily won the presidential election of 1816. (F.McD.)

III. The United States from 1816 to 1850

THE ERA OF MIXED FEELINGS

The years between the election to the presidency of James Monroe in 1816 and of John Quincy Adams in 1824 have long been known in American history as the "Era of Good Feelings." The phrase was conceived by a Boston editor during Monroe's visit to New England early in his first term. That a representative of the heartland of Federalism could speak in such positive terms of the visit by a Southern president whose decisive election had marked not only a sweeping Republican victory but also the demise of the national Federalist Party was dramatic testimony that former foes were inclined to put aside the sectional and political differences of the past.

Effects of the War of 1812. Later scholars have questioned the strategy and tactics of the United States in the War of 1812, the war's tangible results, and even the wisdom of commencing it in the first place. To contemporary Americans, however, the striking naval victories and Andrew Jackson's victory over the British at New Orleans created a reservoir of "good feeling" on which Monroe was able to draw.

Abetting the mood of nationalism was the foreign policy of the United States after the war. Florida was acquired from Spain (1819) in negotiations the success of which owed more to Andrew Jackson's indifference to such niceties as the inviolability of foreign borders and the nation's evident readiness to back him up than it did to diplomatic finesse. The Monroe Doctrine (1823) was actually a few phrases inserted in a long presidential message; its immediate effect on other nations was slight, and that on its own citizenry was impossible to gauge, yet its self-assured tone in warning off the Old World from the New reflected well the nationalist mood that swept the nation. Internally, the decisions of the Supreme Court under Chief Justice John Marshall in such cases as *McCulloch* v. *Maryland* (1819) and *Gibbons* v. *Ogden* (1824) promoted nationalism by strengthening Congress and national, or federal, power at the expense of the states. The congressional decision to charter the second Bank of the United States (1816) was explained in part by the nation's financial weaknesses, exposed by the War of 1812 and in part by the intrigues of financial interests. The readiness of Southern Jeffersonians—former strict constructionists—to support such a measure indicates, too, an amazing degree of national feeling. Perhaps the clearest sign of a new sense of national unity was the victorious Republican Party, standing in solitary splendour on the national political horizon, its long-time foes the Federalists vanished without a trace (on the national level), the Republican standard bearer elected so overwhelmingly in 1820 that it was long believed that the one electoral vote denied him had been held back only in order to preserve George Washington's record of unanimous selection.

Foreign policy

National disunity. For all the signs of national unity and feelings of oneness, equally convincing evidence points in the opposite direction. The very Supreme Court decisions that delighted friends of strong national government infuriated its opponents, while Marshall's defense of the rights of private property was construed by critics as betraying a predilection for one kind of property over another. The growth of the West was by no means regarded as an unmixed blessing. Eastern conservatives sought to keep land prices high, speculative interests opposed a policy that would be advantageous to poor squatters, politicians feared a change in the sectional balance of power, businessmen were wary of a new section with interests unlike their own. European visitors testified that, even during the so-called Era of Good Feelings, Americans characteristically expressed scorn for their countrymen in sections other than their own.

Opponents of nationalism

The causes of the financial panic in 1819 are complex. Far clearer was the tendency of its victims to blame it on one or another hostile or malevolent interest—whether the second Bank of the United States, Eastern capitalists, selfish speculators, or perfidious politicians—each charge expressing the bad feeling that existed side by side with the good. If harmony seemed to reign on the level of national political parties, disharmony prevailed within the states. In the early-19th-century United States, local and state politics were typically waged less on behalf of great issues than for petty gain. That the goals of politics were often sordid did not mean that political contests were bland. In every section, state factions led by shrewd men waged bitter political warfare to attain or entrench themselves in power.

The most dramatic manifestation of national division was the political struggle over slavery, particularly over its spread into new territories. The Missouri Compromise of 1820 eased the threat of further disunity, at least for the time being—the sectional balance between the states was preserved; in the Louisiana Purchase, with the exception of the Territory of Missouri, slavery was to be confined to the area south of the 36°30′ line. Yet astute men knew that this compromise did not end the crisis but only postponed it. The determination by Northern and Southern senators not to be outnumbered by one

The United States, 1812–22.

another suggests that the people continued to believe in the conflicting interests of the various great geographical sections. The weight of evidence indicates that the decade after the Battle of New Orleans was an era not of good feelings so much as it was one of mixed feelings.

THE ECONOMY

Economic growth and maturation

The American economy expanded and matured at a remarkable rate in the decades after the War of 1812. The rapid growth of the West created a great new centre for the production of grains and pork, permitting the nation's older sections to specialize in other crops. New processes of manufacture, particularly in textiles, not only accelerated an "industrial revolution" in the Northeast but, by drastically enlarging the Northern market for raw materials, helped account for a boom in Southern cotton production. If by midcentury the white South had come to regard slavery as a "positive good" rather than the "necessary evil" it had earlier held the system to be, it was due largely to the increasingly central role played by cotton in earning profits for the section; the cotton economy relied on slavery. Industrial workers organized the nation's first trade unions and even workingmen's political parties early in the period. The corporate form thrived in an era the booming capital requirements of which made older and simpler forms of attracting investment capital obsolete. Commerce became increasingly specialized, the division of labour in the disposal of goods for sale matching the increasingly sophisticated division of labour that had come to characterize production. Banks were created in unprecedented numbers, turning out quantities of paper money to meet the thriving economy's need for additional exchange. The fact that little coin or specie was actually kept in vaults to back up this paper explains both why many bank notes were discounted severely and why the state of the economy was typically unstable. A rage for speculation was widely noted by contemporaries, encouraged by an almost frighteningly rapid rise in real-estate values and in the production by state banks of large quantities of paper money on demand. Probably the most important changes occurred in the nation's system for moving people and goods. According to a number of later scholars, a "transportation revolution" was the key to almost all other economic changes in the period.

Transportation revolution. The controversial political issue of "internal improvements" focussed on a simple question: would national government finance local and state transportation projects? That some presidents hesitated, in the absence of explicit language in the Constitution urging federal support, had little effect in dampening the near-mania for such projects. More federal moneys were expended on them under Pres. Andrew Jackson (served 1829–37), who on this issue was a strict constructionist, than in the administrations of all previous presidents combined. Actually, most of the capital was raised by state governments, by private citizens, and from abroad. In their turn, turnpikes (or tollroads), canals, steamboats, and railroads inspired booms, typically featured by lack of planning, business failures, shoddy construction, profits that fell far short of expectations largely because costs exceeded anticipations, rampant corruption, and, withal, an improved transportation system that was the wonder of the world. The system did well the basic job that transportation was called on to do for a swiftly expanding region.

Waterways. Steamboats replaced rafts on the Mississippi and sharply reduced the price of Latin-American coffee in ports upstream by drastically cutting shipping time and expense. The Erie Canal, the most publicized as well as the most successful individual project constructed during the era, enabled efficient Western grain producers ultimately to undersell Eastern farmers in the distant New York City market for similar reasons. Imitators of the Erie in Pennsylvania and throughout the South and West discovered, however, that canals were poor business propositions unless cheaply and efficiently built, heavily used, and spared from drought or flooding.

Railroads. A controversy has developed among scholars over the significance of railroads in antebellum America—one interpretation regards their development as the key to the era's industrialization, while another viewpoint holds that the West would have been developed as quickly and goods moved as cheaply without them. In any case, the speed and reliability of the "iron horse" attracted investors and, at first, passengers, seeking comfort in travel, rather than freight. By midcentury, however, the advantages of the new form, for all its expense, were luring shippers of industrial and agricultural products to use the nation's thousands of miles of railroad network.

Beginnings of industrialization. Agriculture remained an important industry in all sections, although a sectional division of labour became increasingly discernible at the era's end, spurred on by transportation and mechanical developments that permitted more productive areas to undersell their competitors even in the home markets of the latter. Nevertheless, New York and Pennsylvania in the Northeast and Kentucky and Tennessee in the South remained important producers of corn, wheat, and livestock even in the 1840s. The trend, however, was in the the direction of specialization. Cotton became king, not only in the South but in the nation as a whole, because its sale overseas brought in more money than the sale of all other products combined. Slavery accordingly became more entrenched, despite the sharp rise in the price of slaves that marked the era. Econometricians have used detailed statistical evidence to challenge the ideas that slavery was unprofitable and that the South's overcommitment to cash crops was ruinous to its economy in the long run. Contemporary Southerners put ever more capital into the system that promised quick profits and a "social harmony" based on the total subordination of the slaves. Slavery was a complex system, particularly in cities, marked by the hiring out of tens of thousands of skilled slave artisans and by an amazing degree of free physical movement and personal behaviour displayed by slaves in such a city as New Orleans. When most of the country referred to slavery, however, they appeared to mean the plantation system based on the labour of hundreds of field hands, though, actually, a minority of Southern whites owned slaves.

By midcentury, factories accounted for most textile production in the northeastern states, while the factory system was beginning to spread across the states of the Ohio Valley. The labour organizations that sprang up in the nation's cities were composed not of machine hands but primarily of skilled mechanics. A major purpose of this movement was to enable their membership to withstand the spread of a system associated by labour spokesmen with speedup, the devaluation of skill, low wages, child and female labour, and a general debasement of the working class. The spread of the factory system was not to be deflected, however, not even by a movement that at its height claimed a membership of 300,000 (a claim that was undocumented and undoubtedly exaggerated). The labour movement was crushed not by industrialization but rather by a depression that followed financial panics in 1837 and 1839.

These panics, like the earlier crisis in 1819, illustrate well the erratic course of the American economy during the era. Growth was not unbroken. Overspeculation, inflation, governmental inaction in some instances or chicanery in others created an atmosphere of instability that was as characteristic of the era as were its tangible achievements. Hundreds of bank and business failures, large-scale unemployment, and hard times followed in the wake of these debacles, lasting in the latter case to the middle 1840s before the economy again moved forward, more productive than ever, to resume its upward thrust.

SOCIAL DEVELOPMENTS

In the decades before the Civil War (1861–65), the civilization of the United States exerted an irresistible pull on visitors, hundreds of whom were assigned to report back to European audiences that were fascinated by the new society and insatiable for information on every facet of the "fabled republic." What appeared to intrigue the travellers above all was the uniqueness of American society. In contrast to the relatively static and well-ordered civilization of the Old World, America seemed turbulent, dynamic, and in constant flux, its people crude but vital, awesomely ambitious, optimistic, and independent. Many well-bred Europeans were evidently taken aback by the self-assurance of lightly educated American common folk. Ordinary Americans seemed unwilling to defer to anyone on the basis of rank or status.

The people. American society was rapidly changing. Population grew at what to Europeans was an amazing rate—although it was the normal pace of American population growth for the antebellum decades—of between three-tenths and one-third a decade. After 1820 the rate of growth was not uniform throughout the country. New England and the Southern Atlantic states languished—the former region because it was losing settlers to the superior farmlands of the Western Reserve, the latter because its economy offered too few places to newcomers.

The special feature of the population increase of the 1830s and 1840s was the extent to which it was composed of immigrants. Whereas about 250,000 Europeans had come in the first three decades of the 19th century, ten times as many arrived between 1830 and 1850. The newcomers were overwhelmingly Irish and German. Travelling in family groups rather than as individuals, they were attracted by the dazzling opportunities of American life: abundant work, land, food, and freedom, on the one hand, and the absence of compulsory military service, on the other.

The German contingent did well, settling mostly on semi-improved farms and towns in the Ohio Valley, their success promoted by their relatively prosperous state on arrival and by the solid aid given newcomers by the efficient network of economic and cultural organizations founded by earlier German settlers. Irish immigrants, however, fared poorly; too poor to buy land, lacking in skills, disorganized, members of a faith considered alien and even dangerous by many native Americans, the Irish suffered various forms of ostracism and discrimination in the cities, where they tended to congregate. They provided the menial and unskilled labour needed by the expanding economy. Their low wages forced them to live in tightly packed slums, whose chief features were filth, disease, rowdyism, prostitution, drunkenness, crime, a high mortality rate, and the absence of even rudimentary toilet facilities. Adding to the woes of the first generation of Irish immigrants was the tendency of many disgruntled natives to treat the newcomers as scapegoats who allegedly threatened the future of American life and religion. In the North, only free blacks were treated worse.

Most Northern blacks possessed theoretical freedom and little else. Confined to menial occupations for the most part, they fought a losing battle against the inroads of Irish competition in northeastern cities. The struggle between the two groups erupted spasmodically into ugly street riots. The hostility shown free blacks by the general community was less violent but equally unremitting. Discrimination in politics, employment, education, housing, religion, and even in cemeteries, resulted in a cruelly oppressive system. Unlike a slave, the free Northern Negro could criticize and petition against his subjugation, but this proved fruitless in preventing the continued deterioration of his situation.

Most Americans continued to live in the country. Although improved machinery had resulted in expanded farm production and had given further impetus to the commercialization of agriculture, the way of life of independent agriculturists had changed little by midcentury. The public journals put out by some farmers insisted that their efforts were unappreciated by the larger community. Private accounts kept by farmers pointed to lives marked by unremitting toil, little cash, and little leisure. To own land was an achievement beyond the expectations of their European counterparts; but in all sections of the country, much land and agricultural wealth was concentrated in the hands of a few farmers.

Cities. Cities thrived during the era, their growth in population outstripping the spectacular growth rate of the nation as a whole. Urban expansion was not confined to New York City, Philadelphia, Charleston, or New Orleans; towns such as Syracuse, Natchez, St. Louis, Lexington, Pittsburgh, Chicago, and Cincinnati also flourished. And their importance and influence far transcended the relatively small proportions of citizens living in them. Whether on the "urban frontier" or in the older seaboard region, antebellum cities were the centres of wealth and political influence of their outlying hinterlands. New York City, with a population approaching 500,000 by midcentury, faced problems of a different

Trend toward industrial specialization

European interest in American life

German and Irish immigrants

Urban expansion

order of magnitude from those confronting such cities as Poughkeepsie or Newark. Yet the pattern of change during the era was amazingly similar for eastern cities or western, old cities or new, great cities or small. The lifeblood of them all was commerce. Old ideals of economy in town government were grudgingly abandoned by the merchant, professional, and landowning elites that typically ruled. Taxes were increased in order to deal with pressing new problems and to enable the urban community of midcentury to realize new opportunities. Harbours were improved, police forces professionalized, services expanded, waste more reliably removed, streets improved, welfare activities broadened, all as the result of the statesmanship and the self-interest of property owners who were convinced that amelioration was socially beneficial.

Education and religion. Cities were also centres of educational and intellectual progress. The emergence of a relatively well-financed public educational system, free of the stigma of "pauper" or "charity" schools, and of a lively "penny press," made possible by a technological revolution, were among the most important developments. An evangelical movement that swept the Northeast and West before 1840 was largely an urban phenomenon. Cutting across Protestant denominational lines, the movement was regarded by many of its leaders as a struggle against satanic influences that thrived best in the secular atmosphere of cities. Influential merchants made generous contributions to this great "revival," which combined detailed, fiery exhortations against sin and the devil with a social message of unabashed conservatism. The urban wealthy had reason to find such a message useful.

Wealth. The brilliant French visitor Alexis de Tocqueville, in common with most contemporary observers, believed American society to be remarkably egalitarian. Most rich American men were thought to have been born poor; "self-made" was the term Henry Clay popularized for them. The society was allegedly a very fluid one, marked by the rapid rise and fall of fortunes, with room at the top accessible to all but the most humble; opportunity for success seemed freely available to all, and although material possessions were not distributed perfectly equally they were, in theory, dispersed so fairly that only a few poor and a few rich men existed at either end of the social spectrum.

The actuality, however, was far different. While the rich were inevitably not numerous, America by 1850 had more millionaires than all of Europe. New York, Boston, and Philadelphia had 1,000 individuals, each admitting to $100,000 or more, at a time when wealthy taxpayers kept secret from assessors the bulk of their wealth. Because an annual income of $4,000 or $5,000 enabled a man to live luxuriously, these were great fortunes indeed. Typically, the wealthiest 1 percent of urban citizens owned approximately one-half the wealth of the great cities of the Northeast, while the great bulk of their populations were worth little or nothing. In what has long been called the "Age of the Common Man," rich men were almost invariably born not into humble or poor families but into wealthy and prestigious ones. In western cities, too, class lines increasingly hardened after 1830. The common man lived in the age, but he did not dominate it. It appears that contemporaries, overimpressed with the absence of a titled aristocracy and with the democratic tone and manner of American life, failed to see the extent to which money, family, and status exerted power in the New World even as they did in the Old.

JACKSONIAN DEMOCRACY

The democratization of politics. American politics became increasingly democratic during the 1820s and 1830s. Local and state offices that had earlier been appointive became elective. The suffrage was expanded as property and other restrictions on voting were reduced or abandoned in most states. The free-hold requirement that had denied voting to all but holders of real estate was almost everywhere discarded before 1820, while the taxpaying qualification was also re-

moved, if more slowly and gradually. In many states a printed ballot replaced the earlier system of voice voting, while the secret ballot also grew in favour. Whereas in 1800 only two states provided for the popular choice of presidential electors, by 1832 only South Carolina still left the decision to the legislature. Conventions of elected delegates increasingly replaced legislative or congressional caucuses as the agencies for making party nominations. By the latter change, a system for nominating candidates by self-appointed cliques meeting in secret was replaced by a system of open selection of candidates by democratically elected bodies.

Extension of voting rights

These democratic changes were not engineered by Andrew Jackson and his followers, as was once believed. Most of them antedated the emergence of Jackson's Democratic Party, and in New York, Mississippi, and other states some of the reforms were accomplished over the objections of the Jacksonians. There were men in all sections who feared the spread of political democracy, but by the 1830s few were willing publicly to voice such misgivings. Jacksonians effectively sought to fix the impression that they alone were champions of democracy, engaged in mortal struggle against aristocratic opponents. The accuracy of such propaganda varied according to local circumstances. The great political reforms of the early 19th century in actuality were conceived by no one faction or party. The real question about these reforms concerns the extent to which they truly represented the victory of democracy in the United States.

Small cliques or entrenched "machines" dominated democratically elected nominating conventions as earlier they had controlled caucuses. While by the 1830s the common man—of white if not of black or red skin—had come into possession of the vote in most states, the nomination process continued to be outside his control. More importantly, the policies adopted by competing factions and parties in the states owed little to ordinary voters. The legislative programs of the "regencies" and juntos that effectively ran state politics were designed primarily to reward the party faithful and to keep them in power. State parties extolled the common people in grandiloquent terms but characteristically focussed on prosaic legislation that awarded bank charters or monopoly rights to construct transportation projects to favoured insiders. That American parties would be pragmatic vote-getting coalitions, rather than organizations devoted to high political principles, was due largely to another series of reforms enacted during the era. Electoral changes that rewarded winners or plurality gatherers in small districts, in contrast to a previous system that divided a state's offices among the several leading vote getters, worked against the chances of "single issue" or "ideological" parties while strengthening parties that tried to be many things to many men.

The status of the common man

The Jacksonians. To his army of followers, Andrew Jackson was the embodiment of popular democracy. A truly self-made man of will and courage, he personified for many citizens the vast power of nature and providence, on the one hand, and the majesty of the people, on the other. His very weaknesses, such as a nearly uncontrollable temper, were political strengths. Opponents who branded him enemy to property and order only gave credence to the claim of Jackson's supporters that he stood for the poor against the rich, the plain people against the interests.

Jackson, like most of his leading antagonists, was in fact a wealthy man of conservative social beliefs. In his many volumes of correspondence he rarely referred to labour. As a lawyer and man of affairs in Tennessee prior to his accession to the presidency, he aligned himself not with have-nots but with the influential, not with the debtor but with the creditor. His reputation was created largely by astute men who propagated the belief that his party was the people's party and that the policies of his administrations were in the popular interest. Savage attacks on those policies by some wealthy critics only fortified the belief that the Jacksonian movement was radical as well as democratic.

Illusions about American wealth

At its birth in the middle 1820s, the Jacksonian, or Democratic Party was a loose coalition of diverse men and interests united primarily by a practical vision. They held to the twin beliefs that "Old Hickory," as Jackson was known, was a magnificent candidate and that his election to the presidency would benefit those who helped bring it about. His excellence as candidate derived in part from the fact that he appeared to have no known political principles of any sort. In this period there were no distinct parties on the national level. Jackson, Henry Clay, John C. Calhoun, John Quincy Adams, and William H. Crawford—the leading presidential aspirants—all portrayed themselves as "Republicans," followers of the party of the revered Jefferson. The National Republicans were the followers of Adams and Clay; the Whigs, who emerged in 1834, were, above all else, the party dedicated to the defeat of Jackson.

The major parties. The great parties of the era were thus created to attain victory for men rather than measures. Once in being, their leaders understandably sought to persuade the electorate of the primacy of principles. It is noteworthy, however, that former Federalists at first flocked to the new parties in largely equal numbers and that men on opposite sides of such issues as internal improvements or a national bank could unite behind Jackson. With the passage of time, the parties did come increasingly to be identified with distinctive, and opposing, political policies.

By the 1840s, Whig and Democratic congressmen voted as rival blocs. Whigs supported and Democrats opposed a weak executive, a new Bank of the United States, a high tariff, distribution of land revenues to the states, relief legislation to mitigate the effects of the depression, and federal reapportionment of House seats. Whigs voted against and Democrats approved an independent treasury, an aggressive foreign policy, and expansionism. These were important issues, capable of dividing the electorate just as they divided the major parties in Congress. Certainly it was significant that Jacksonians were more ready than their opponents to banish and use other forceful measures against the southern Indian tribes or to take punitive measures against blacks or abolitionists. But these differences do not substantiate the belief that the Democrats and Whigs were divided ideologically, with only the former somehow representing the interests of the propertyless.

Party lines earlier had been more easily broken. Jackson's firm opposition to Calhoun's policy of Nullification (*i.e.*, the right of a state to nullify a federal law) in 1828 had commanded wide support within and outside the Democratic Party. Clay's compromise solution to the crisis represented not an ideological split with Jackson but Clay's ability to conciliate and to draw political advantage from astute tactical manoeuvring.

The Jacksonians depicted their war on the second Bank of the United States as a struggle against an alleged aristocratic monster that oppressed the West, debtor farmers, and poor people generally. Jackson's decisive re-election in 1832 was once interpreted as a sign of popular agreement with the Democratic interpretation of the bank war, but recent evidence discloses that Jackson's margin was hardly unprecedented and that Democratic success may have been due to other considerations. The second bank was evidently well thought of by many Westerners, many farmers, and even by Democratic politicians who admitted to opposing it primarily not to incur the wrath of Andrew Jackson.

Jackson's reasons for detesting the bank and Nicholas Biddle, its president, were complex. Anticapitalist ideology would not explain a Jacksonian policy that replaced a quasi-national bank as repository of government funds with dozens of state and private banks, equally controlled by capitalists and even more dedicated than was Biddle to profit making. The saving virtue of these "pet banks" appeared to be the Democratic political affiliations of their directors. Perhaps the pragmatism as well as the large degree of similarity between the Democrats and Whigs is best indicated by their frank adoption of the "spoils system." The Whigs, while out of office, de-nounced the vile Democratic policy for turning lucrative custom-house and other posts over to supporters; but once in office they resorted to similar practices. It is of interest that the Jacksonian appointees were hardly more plebeian than were their so-called aristocratic predecessors.

Minor parties. The politics of principle was represented during the era not by the major parties but by the minor ones. The Anti-Masons aimed to stamp out an alleged aristocratic conspiracy. The Workingmen's Party called for "social justice." The Locofocos (so named after the matches they used to light up their first meeting in a hall darkened by their opponents) denounced monopolists in the Democratic Party and out. The variously named nativist parties accused the Roman Catholic Church of all manner of evil. The Liberty Party opposed the spread of slavery. All of these parties were ephemeral since they proved incapable of mounting a broad appeal that attracted masses of voters in addition to their original constituencies. The Democratic and Whig parties thrived not in spite of their opportunism but because of it, reflecting well the practical spirit that animated most American voters.

AN "AGE OF REFORM"

Historians have labelled the period 1830–50 an "age of reform." At the same time that the pursuit of the dollar was becoming so frenzied that some observers called it the nation's true religion, tens of thousands of Americans joined an array of movements dedicated to spiritual and secular uplift. There is not yet agreement as to why a rage for reform erupted in the antebellum decades. A few of the explanations cited, none of them conclusive, include an outburst of Protestant evangelicalism, a reform spirit that swept across the Anglo-American community, and a delayed reaction to the perfectionist teachings of the Enlightenment.

What is not in question is the amazing variety of reform movements that flourished simultaneously in the northern states—women's rights, pacifism, temperance, prison reform, abolition of imprisonment for debt, an end to capital punishment, improving the conditions of the working classes, a system of universal education, the organization of communities that discarded private property, improving the condition of the insane and the congenitally enfeebled, and the regeneration of the individual were among the causes that inspired zealots during the era.

Abolitionism. There can be no doubt that antislavery, or "Abolition" as it came to be called, was the nonpareil reform. Abolition was a diverse phenomenon. At one end of its spectrum was William Lloyd Garrison, an "immediatist," who denounced not only slavery but the Constitution of the United States for tolerating the evil. His newspaper, *The Liberator,* lived up to its promise that it would not equivocate in its war against slavery. Garrison's uncompromising tone infuriated not only the South but many Northerners as well and was long treated as though it were typical of Abolitionism in general. Actually it was not. At the other end of the Abolitionist spectrum and in between stood such men and women as Theodore Weld, James Birney, Gerrit Smith, Theodore Parker, Julia Ward Howe, Lewis Tappan, Salmon P. Chase, and Lydia Maria Child, all of whom represented a variety of stances, all more conciliatory than Garrison's. James Russell Lowell, whose emotional balance has been cited by a recent biographer as proof that Abolitionists need not have been unstable, urged in contrast to Garrison that "the world must be healed by degrees."

Whether they were Garrisonians or not, Abolitionist leaders were scorned as cranks who were either working out their own personal maladjustments or as people using the slavery issue to restore a status that as an alleged New England elite they feared they were losing. The truth may be simpler. Few neurotics and few members of the northern socio-economic elite became Abolitionists. For all the movement's zeal and propagandistic successes, it was bitterly resented by many Northerners, and the masses of free whites were indifferent to its message. In the 1830s,

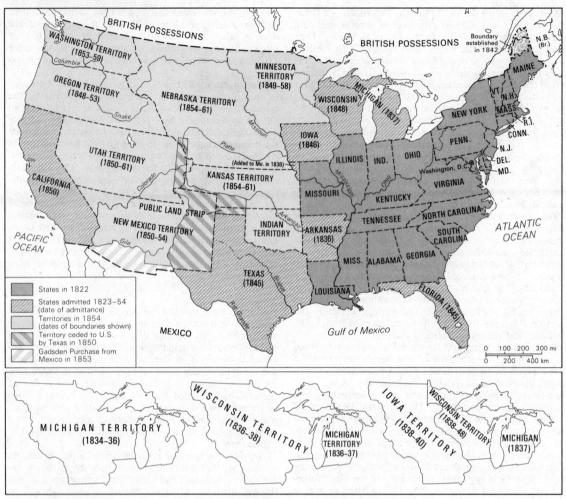

The United States, 1822–54.

Resentment of Abolitionists

urban mobs, typically led by "gentlemen of property and standing," stormed Abolitionist meetings, wreaking violence on the property and persons of blacks and their white sympathizers, evidently indifferent to the niceties distinguishing one Abolitionist theorist from another. It is a good question as to who betrayed greater emotional imbalance, men who attacked slavery with words or those whose hatred of such verbal attacks drove them to murder. That Abolition leaders were remarkably similar in their New England backgrounds, their Calvinist self-righteousness, their high social status, and the relative excellence of their educations are hardly evidence that their cause was either snobbish or elitist. Ordinary men were more inclined to loathe Negroes and to preoccupy themselves with personal advance within the system.

Support of reform movements. The existence of many reform movements did not mean that a vast number of Americans supported them. Abolition did poorly at the polls. Some reforms were more popular than others, but by and large none of the major movements had mass followings. The evidence indicates that few persons actually participated in these activities. Utopian communities such as Brook Farm and those in New Harmony, Indiana, and Oneida, New York, did not quite succeed in winning over many followers or in inspiring many other groups to imitate their example. The importance of these and the other movements derived neither from their size nor their achievements. Reform reflected the sensitivity of a small number of persons to imperfections in American life. In a sense, the reformers were "voices of conscience," reminding their materialistic countrymen that the American Dream was not yet a reality, pointing to the gulf between the ideal and the actuality.

Religious-inspired reform. A unique feature of antebellum reform was its religious character. Unlike European social critics of the same era, who were not only

secular but often anti-religious, American perfectionists were largely inspired by religious zeal. Not that religious enthusiasm was invariably identified with social uplift; many reformers were more concerned with saving souls than with curing social ills. The merchant princes who played active roles in, and donated large sums of money to, the Sunday school unions, home missionary societies, and Bible and tract societies did so in part because the latter organizations stressed spiritual rather than social improvement while teaching the doctrine of the "contented poor." In effect, conservatives who were strongly religious found no difficulty in using religious institutions to fortify their social predilections. Radicals, on the other hand, interpreted Christianity as a call to social action, convinced that true Christian rectitude could be achieved only in struggles that infuriated the smug and the greedy. Ralph Waldo Emerson was a nice example of the American reformer's insistence on the primacy of the individual. The great goal according to him was regeneration of the human spirit rather than a mere improvement in material conditions. But Emerson and reformers like him acted on the premise that consistency was indeed a hobgoblin of small minds. For they saw no contradiction in uniting with like-minded idealists to act out or argue for a new social model. The spirit was to be revived and strengthened through forthright social action undertaken by similarly independent individuals.

Conservative religion

EXPANSIONISM AND POLITICAL CRISIS AT MIDCENTURY

Throughout the 19th century, eastern settlers kept spilling over into the Mississippi Valley and beyond, pushing the frontier farther westward. (The American historian Frederick Jackson Turner in 1893 was to say that this ever-moving frontier was the most decisive influence on American civilization and values.) The Louisiana Purchase territory offered ample room to pioneers and those who came after. American wanderlust, however, was not confined to that area. Throughout the era Americans in varying numbers moved into regions south, west, and north of the Louisiana Territory. Because Mexico and Great Britain held or claimed most of these outlying lands, dispute inevitably broke out between these governments and the United States.

Westward expansion. The growing nationalism of the American people was effectively engaged by Democratic presidents Jackson and James K. Polk (served 1845–49) and the expansionist Whig president John Tyler (served 1841–45) to promote their goal of enlarging the "empire for liberty." Each of these presidents performed shrewdly. Jackson waited until his last day in office to establish formal relations with the Republic of Texas, one year after his friend Sam Houston had succeeded in dissolving the ties between Mexico and the newly independent state of Texas. On the Senate's overwhelming repudiation of his proposed treaty of annexation, Tyler resorted to the use of a joint resolution so that each house could vote by a narrow margin for incorporation of Texas into the Union. In the northwest, Polk succeeded in getting the British to negotiate a treaty (1846) whereby the Oregon Country south of the 49th latitude would revert to the United States. These were precisely the terms of his earlier proposal, which had been rejected by the British. Intent on securing the Mexican territories of New Mexico and upper California and ready to resort to almost any means to do so, Polk used a border incident as a pretext for commencing a war with Mexico that the Congress did not declare and that many congressmen disliked, but appropriations for which few dared oppose.

Although there is no evidence that these actions had anything like a public mandate, clearly they did not evoke widespread opposition. Nonetheless, the expansionists' assertion that Polk's election in 1844 could be construed as a popular clamour for the annexation of Texas was hardly a solid claim; Clay was narrowly defeated and would have won but for the defection from Whig ranks of small numbers of Liberty Party and nativist voters. The nationalistic idea, conceived in the 1840s by a Democratic editor, that it was the "manifest destiny" of the United States to expand westward to the Pacific undoubtedly prepared public opinion for the militant policies shortly after undertaken by Polk. It has been said that this notion represented the mood of the American people; it is safer to say that it reflected the feelings of many of the people.

Attitudes toward expansionism. Public attitudes toward expansion into Mexican territories were very much affected by the issue of slavery. Men opposed to the spread of slavery or simply not in favour of the institution joined Abolitionists in discerning a proslavery policy in the Mexican War. The great political issue of the postwar years concerned slavery in the territories. Calhoun and spokesmen for the slaveowning South argued that slavery could not be constitutionally prohibited in the Mexican cession. "Free Soilers" supported the Wilmot Proviso idea—that slavery should not be permitted in the new territory. Others supported the proposal that "squatter sovereignty" should prevail—settlers in the territories should decide the issue. Still others called for the extension westward of the 36°30′ line of demarcation for slavery that had resolved the Missouri controversy in 1820. Now, 30 years later, Henry Clay again pressed a compromise on the nation, supported dramatically by the aging Daniel Webster and by moderates in and out of the Congress. As the events in the California gold fields showed (beginning in 1849), many men had things other than political principles on their minds. The Compromise of 1850, as the separate resolutions resolving the controversy came to be known, infuriated men of high principle on both sides of the issue—Southerners resented California being admitted as a free state and the theoretical right given territories to deny existence to their "peculiar institution," while antislavery men deplored the same theoretical right of territories to permit the institution and abhorred the new, more stringent federal fugitive slave law. That Southern political leaders ceased talking seces-

sion shortly after the enactment of the compromise, indicates who truly won the political skirmish. The people probably approved the settlement—but as subsequent events were to show, the issues in controversy had not been met; they had only been deferred.   (E.Pe.)

IV. Civil War, Reconstruction, and the New South, 1850–1900

PROLOGUE TO WAR, 1850–60

Before the Civil War, the United States experienced a whole generation of nearly unremitting political crisis. Underlying the problem was the fact that America in the early 19th century had been a country, not a nation. The major functions of government—those relating to education, transportation, health, and public order—were performed on the state or local level, and little more than a loose allegiance to the government in Washington, a few national institutions such as churches and political parties, and a shared memory of the Founding Fathers of the republic tied the country together. Within this loosely structured society every section, every state, every locality, every group could pretty much go its own way.

Gradually, however, changes in technology and in the economy were bringing all the elements of the country into steady and close contact. Improvements in transportation—first canals, then toll roads, and especially railroads—broke down isolation and encouraged the boy from the country to wander to the city, the farmer from New Hampshire to migrate to Iowa. Improvements in the printing press, which permitted the publication of penny newspapers, and the development of the telegraph system broke through the barriers of intellectual provincialism and made everybody almost instantaneously aware of what was going on throughout the country. As the railroad network proliferated, it had to have central direction and control; and national railroad corporations—the first true "big businesses" in the United States—emerged to provide order and stability.

For many Americans the wrench from a largely rural, slow-moving, fragmented society in the early 1800s to a bustling, integrated, national social order in the midcentury was an abrupt and painful one; and they often resisted it. Sometimes resentment against change manifested itself in harsh attacks upon those who appeared to be the agents of change—especially the newly arrived immigrants, who seemed to personify the forces that were altering the older America. Vigorous nativist movements appeared in most cities during the 1840s; but not until the 1850s, when the huge numbers of Irish and German immigrants of the previous decade became eligible to vote, did the antiforeign fever reach its peak. Directed both against immigrants and against the Catholic Church, to which so many of them belonged, the so-called Know-Nothing movement emerged as a powerful political force in 1854 and increased the resistance to change.

Sectionalism and slavery. A more enduring manifestation of hostility toward the nationalizing tendencies in American life was the reassertion of strong feelings of sectional loyalty. New Englanders felt themselves threatened by the rising West, which drained off the ablest and most vigorous members of the labour force and also, once the railroad network was complete, produced grain crops that undersold the products of the poor New England hill country. The West, too, developed a strong sectional feeling, blending its sense of its own uniqueness, its feeling of being looked down on as raw and uncultured, and its feeling that it was being exploited by the businessmen of the East.

The most conspicuous and distinctive section, however, was the South—an area set apart by climate; by a plantation system designed for the production of such staple crops as cotton, tobacco, and sugar; and, especially, by the persistence of Negro slavery, which had been abolished or prohibited in all other parts of the United States. It should not be thought that all or even most white Southerners were directly involved in the section's "peculiar institution." Indeed, in 1850 there were only 347,525 slaveholders out of a total white population of about 6,000,000 in the slave states. Half of these owned four

(margin notes)

The Mexican War

Pre-Civil War changes that linked the states more closely

Reassertion of sectional loyalty

slaves or less and could not be considered planters. In the entire South there were fewer than 1,800 persons who owned more than 100 slaves.

Nevertheless, slavery did give a distinctive tone to the whole pattern of Southern life. If the large planters were few, they were also wealthy, prestigious, and powerful; often they were the political as well as the economic leaders of their section; and their values pervaded every stratum of Southern society. Far from opposing slavery, small farmers thought only of the possibility that they too might, with hard work and good fortune, some day join the ranks of the planter class—to which they were closely connected by ties of blood, marriage, and friendship. Behind this virtually unanimous support of slavery lay the universal belief—shared by many whites in the North and West as well—that blacks were an innately inferior people who had risen only to a state of barbarism in their native Africa and who could live in a civilized society only if disciplined through slavery. Though by 1860 there were in fact about 250,000 free blacks in the South, most Southern whites resolutely refused to believe that the slaves, if freed, could ever coexist peacefully with their former masters. With shuddering horror they pointed to an insurrection of blacks that had occurred in Santo Domingo, to a brief slave rebellion led by the Negro Gabriel in Virginia in 1800, to a plot of Charleston, South Carolina, blacks headed by Denmark Vesey in 1822, and, especially, to a bloody and determined Virginia insurrection led by Nat Turner in 1831 as evidence that black persons had to be kept under iron control. Facing increasing opposition to slavery outside their section, Southerners developed an elaborate "proslavery argument," defending the institution on biblical, economic, and sociological grounds.

A decade of political crises. In the early years of the republic, sectional differences had existed, but it had been possible to reconcile or ignore them because distances were great, communication was difficult, and the powerless national government had almost nothing to do. The revolution in transportation and communication, however, eliminated much of the isolation, and the victory of the United States in its brief war with Mexico left the national government with problems that required action.

Popular sovereignty. The Compromise of 1850 was an uneasy patchwork of concessions to all sides that began to fall apart as soon as it was enacted. Most unsatisfactory of all in the long run would be the principle of popular sovereignty, which was bound to make of each territory a battleground where the supporters of the South would contend with the defenders of the North and West.

The seriousness of those conflicts became clear in 1854, when Stephen A. Douglas introduced his Kansas–Nebraska bill in Congress. Unconcerned over the moral issue of slavery and desiring only to get on with the settling of the West and the construction of a transcontinental railroad, Douglas knew that the Southern senators would block the organization of Kansas as a free territory, as had been provided by the Missouri Compromise. Recognizing that the North and West had outstripped their section in population and hence in the House of Representatives, the Southerners clung desperately to an equality of votes in the Senate and were not disposed to welcome any new free states. Accordingly, Douglas thought that the doctrine of popular sovereignty, which had been applied to the territories gained from Mexico, might provide an escape from this impasse; and with the backing of Pres. Franklin Pierce (served 1853–57), he bullied, wheedled, and bluffed congressmen into passing his bill.

Polarization over slavery. Northern sensibilities were outraged. Disliking slavery, Northerners had made few efforts to change the South's "peculiar institution" so long as the republic was loosely articulated. (Indeed, when William Lloyd Garrison began his *Liberator* in 1831, urging the immediate and unconditional emancipation of all slaves, he had only a tiny following; and a few years later he had actually been mobbed in Boston.)

Black insurrections

The Kansas–Nebraska bill

MISSOURI COMPROMISE, 1820

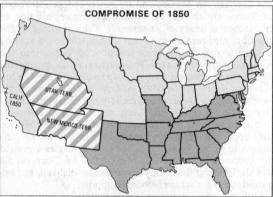

COMPROMISE OF 1850

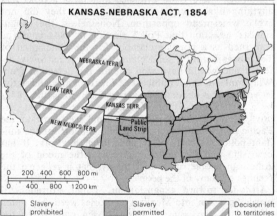

KANSAS-NEBRASKA ACT, 1854

| Slavery prohibited | Slavery permitted | Decision left to territories |

Compromises over extension of slavery into the territories.
By courtesy of Carnegie Institution

But with the sections, perforce, being drawn closely together, Northerners could no longer profess indifference to the South and its institutions. Sectional differences, centring on the issue of slavery, began to appear in every American institution. During the 1840s the major national religious denominations, such as the Methodists and the Presbyterians, split over the slavery question. The Whig Party, which had once allied the conservative businessmen of the North and West with the planters of the South, divided and virtually disappeared after the election of 1852. When Douglas' bill opened up to slavery Kansas and Nebraska—land that had long been reserved for the westward expansion of the free states—Northerners began to organize into an antislavery political party, called in some states the Anti-Nebraska Democratic Party, in others the People's Party, but in most places, the Republican Party.

Events of 1855 and 1856 further exacerbated relations between the sections and strengthened this new party. Kansas, once organized by Congress, became the field of battle between the free and the slave states in a contest in which concern over slavery was mixed with land speculation and office seeking. A virtual civil war broke out, with rival free- and slave-state legislatures both claiming legitimacy. During the turmoil, John Brown, a free-state partisan, on May 24–25, 1856, led a small party in a

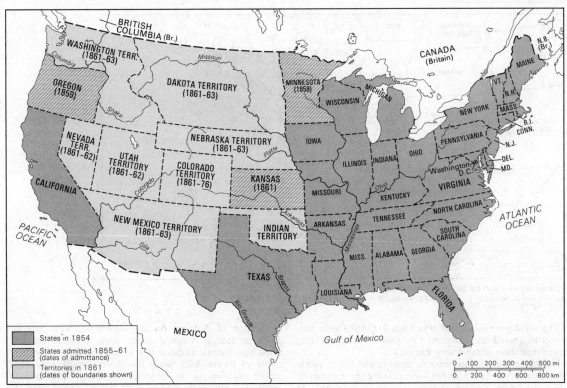

The United States, 1854–61.

Legend:
- States in 1854
- States admitted 1855–61 (dates of admittance)
- Territories in 1861 (dates of boundaries shown)

raid upon some proslavery settlers on Pottawatomie Creek, murdered five men in cold blood, and left their gashed and mutilated bodies as a warning to the slaveholders. As if to show that atrocities could be committed by both sides, almost simultaneously (May 22) a South Carolina congressman brutally attacked Sen. Charles Sumner of Massachusetts at his desk in the Senate chamber because of a speech he had given that presumably insulted the Carolinian's "honour." The 1856 presidential election made it clear that voting was becoming polarized along sectional lines. Though James Buchanan, the Democratic nominee, was elected, John C. Frémont, the Republican candidate, received a majority of the votes in the free states.

The Dred Scott case

The following year the Supreme Court of the United States tried to solve the sectional conflicts that had baffled both the Congress and the President. Hearing the case of Dred Scott, a Missouri slave who claimed freedom on the ground that his master had taken him to live in free territory, the majority of the court, headed by Chief Justice Roger B. Taney, found that Negroes were not citizens of the United States and that Scott hence had no right to bring suit before the court. Taney also concluded that the U.S. laws prohibiting slavery in the territory were unconstitutional. Two Northern antislavery judges on the court bitterly attacked Taney's logic and his conclusions. Acclaimed in the South, the Dred Scott decision was condemned and repudiated throughout the North.

By this point many Americans, North and South, had come to the conclusion that slavery and freedom could not much longer coexist in the United States. For Southerners the answer was withdrawal from a Union that no longer protected their rights and interests; they had talked of it as early as the Nashville Convention of 1850, when the compromise measures were under consideration, and now more and more Southerners favoured secession. For Northerners the remedy was to change the social institutions of the South; few advocated immediate or complete emancipation of the slaves, but many felt that the South's "peculiar institution" must be contained. In 1858 William H. Seward, the leading Republican of New York, spoke of an "irrepressible conflict" between freedom and slavery; and in Illinois a rising Republican politician, Abraham Lincoln, who unsuccessfully contested Douglas for a seat in the Senate, announced that

"this government cannot endure, permanently half *slave* and half *free*."

That it was not possible to end the agitation over slavery became further apparent in 1859 when John Brown, fresh from his crimes in Kansas, on the night of October 16, staged a raid on Harpers Ferry, Virginia (now in West Virginia), designed to free the slaves and, apparently, to help them begin a guerrilla war against the Southern whites. Though Brown was promptly captured and Virginia slaves gave no heed to his appeals, Southerners feared that this was the beginning of organized Northern efforts to undermine their social system. The fact that Brown, who may have been partially insane, was an inept strategist did not lessen Northern admiration for him.

The presidential election of 1860 occurred, therefore, in an atmosphere of great tension. Southerners, determined that their rights should be guaranteed by law, insisted upon a Democratic candidate willing to protect slavery in the territories; and they rejected Stephen A. Douglas, whose popular-sovereignty doctrine left the question in doubt, in favour of John C. Breckinridge. Douglas, backed by most of the Northern and border-state Democrats, ran on a separate Democratic ticket. Elderly conservatives, who deplored all agitation of the sectional questions but advanced no solutions, offered John Bell as candidate of the Constitutional Union Party. Republicans, confident of success, passed over the claims of Seward, who had accumulated too many liabilities in his long public career, and nominated Lincoln instead. Voting in the subsequent election was along markedly sectional patterns, with Republican strength confined almost completely to the North and West. Though Lincoln received only a plurality of the popular vote, he was an easy winner in the electoral college.

Election of 1860

SECESSION AND CIVIL WAR, 1860–65

The coming of the war. In the South, Lincoln's election was taken as the signal for secession, and on December 20 South Carolina became the first state to withdraw from the Union. Promptly the other states of the lower South followed. Feeble efforts on the part of Buchanan's administration to check secession failed, and one by one most of the federal forts in the Southern states were taken over by secessionists. Meanwhile, strenuous efforts in Washington to work out another compromise failed.

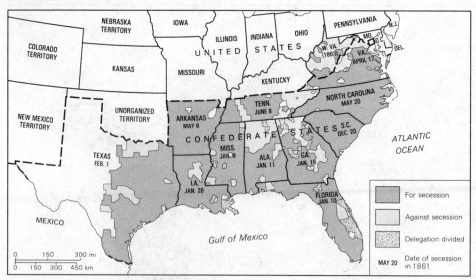

Vote on secession in the South by counties.
Adapted from R. Hofstadter, W. Miller, and D. Aaron, *The American Republic*, vol. 1, to 1865 (© 1959); by permission of Prentice-Hall, Inc.

Formation
of the
Confed-
eracy

(The most promising plan was John J. Crittenden's proposal to extend the Missouri Compromise line, dividing free from slave states, to the Pacific.)

Neither extreme Southerners, now intent upon secession, nor Republicans, intent upon reaping the rewards of their hard-won election victory, was really interested in compromise. On February 4, 1861—a month before Lincoln could be inaugurated in Washington—six Southern states (South Carolina, Georgia, Alabama, Florida, Mississippi, Louisiana) sent representatives to Montgomery, Alabama, to set up a new independent government. Delegates from Texas soon joined them. With Jefferson Davis of Mississippi at its head, the Confederate States of America came into being, set up its own bureaus and offices, issued its own money, raised its own taxes, and flew its own flag. Not until May 1861, after hostilities had broken out and Virginia had seceded, did the new government transfer its capital to Richmond.

Faced with a *fait accompli*, Lincoln when inaugurated was prepared to conciliate the South in every way but one; he would not recognize that the Union could be divided. The test of his determination came early in his administration, when he learned that the Federal troops under Maj. Robert Anderson in Ft. Sumter, South Carolina—then one of the few military installations in the South still in Federal hands—had to be promptly supplied or withdrawn. After agonized consultation with his cabinet, Lincoln determined that supplies must be sent even if doing so provoked the Confederates into firing the first shot. On April 12, 1861, just before Federal supply ships could reach the beleaguered Anderson, Confederate guns in Charleston opened fire upon Fort Sumter, and the war began.

The course of the war. For the next four years the Union and the Confederacy were locked in conflict—by far the most titanic waged in the Western Hemisphere. (The military engagements of the struggle are traced in the article CIVIL WAR, U.S.; here it is enough to suggest the general course of the war.)

Relative strengths. The Union clearly had the advantage in manpower and economic resources. It had 23 states as against 11 in the Confederacy (the states of the upper South—Virginia, Arkansas, Tennessee, North Carolina—having seceded promptly after the firing on Ft. Sumter and Lincoln's call for troops). Omitting Kentucky and Missouri, which were divided in loyalty between North and South, the Union had 20,700,000 inhabitants; the Confederacy, 9,105,000. The North in 1860 had 110,000 manufacturing establishments with 1,300,000 industrial workers, to the South's 18,000 factories with 110,000 workers. Of the 31,256 miles of railroad in the United States in 1861, only 9,283, or less than 30 percent, were in the South. Yet the Confederacy had the

advantage of fighting on the defensive, with interior lines, so that it required fewer men; it began the war with high morale because it was fighting for the positive cause of its freedom, while the North usually saw itself in the negative role of subjector. Infused with a military tradition, Southern young men were accustomed to handling firearms, and Southern generals were among the finest products of West Point.

Northern and Southern policies. The policies pursued by the governments of Abraham Lincoln and Jefferson Davis were astonishingly similar. Both presidents at first relied upon volunteers to man the armies, and both administrations were poorly prepared to arm and equip the hordes of young men who flocked to the colours in the initial stages of the war. As the fighting progressed, both governments reluctantly resorted to conscription—the Confederates first, in early 1862, and the Federal government more slowly, with an ineffective measure of late 1862 followed by a more stringent law in 1863. Both governments pursued an essentially laissez-faire policy in economic matters, with little effort to control prices, wages, or profits. Only the railroads were subject to close government regulation in both regions; and the Confederacy, in constructing some of its own powder mills, made a few experiments in "state socialism." Neither Lincoln's nor Davis' administrations knew how to cope with financing the war; neither developed an effective system of taxation until late in the conflict, and both relied heavily upon borrowing. Faced with a shortage of funds, both governments were obliged to turn to the printing press and to issue fiat money; the United States government issued $432,000,000 in "greenbacks" (as this irredeemable, non-interest-bearing paper money was called), while the Confederacy printed over $1,554,-000,000 in such paper currency. In consequence, both sections experienced runaway inflation, which was much more drastic in the South, where, by the end of the war, flour sold at $1,000 a barrel.

Even toward slavery, the root cause of the war, the policies of the two warring governments were surprisingly similar. The Confederate Constitution, which was in most other ways similar to that of the United States, expressly guaranteed the institution of Negro slavery. Despite pressure from Abolitionists, Lincoln's administration was not disposed to disturb the "peculiar institution," if only because any move toward emancipation would upset the loyalty of Delaware, Maryland, Kentucky, and Missouri—the four slave states that remained in the Union.

Moves toward emancipation. Gradually, however, under the pressure of war, both governments moved to end slavery. Lincoln came to see that emancipation of the blacks would favourably influence European opinion

Manning
and
financing
the armies

toward the Northern cause, would deprive the Confederates of their productive labour force on the farms, and would add much-needed recruits to the Federal armies. In September 1862 he issued his preliminary proclamation of emancipation, promising to free all slaves in rebel territory by January 1, 1863, unless those states returned to the Union; and when the Confederates remained obdurate, he followed it with his promised final proclamation. A natural accompaniment of emancipation was the use of black troops, and by the end of the war the number of blacks who served in the Federal armies totalled 178,895. Uncertain of the constitutionality of his Emancipation Proclamation, Lincoln urged Congress to abolish slavery by constitutional amendment; but this was not done until January 31, 1865, and the actual ratification did not take place until after the war.

Lincoln's Emancipation Proclamation

Meanwhile the Confederacy, though much more slowly, was also inevitably drifting in the direction of emancipation. The South's desperate need for troops caused many military men, including Robert E. Lee, to demand the recruitment of blacks; finally, in March 1865 the Confederate congress authorized the raising of Negro regiments. Though a few blacks were recruited for the Confederate armies, none actually served in battle because surrender was at hand. In yet another way Davis' government showed its awareness of slavery's inevitable end, when, in a belated diplomatic mission to seek assistance from Europe, the Confederacy in March 1865 promised to emancipate the slaves in return for diplomatic recognition. Nothing came of the proposal, but it is further evidence that by the end of the war both North and South realized that slavery was doomed.

Sectional dissatisfaction. As war leaders, both Lincoln and Davis came under severe attack in their own sections. Both had to face problems of disloyalty. In Lincoln's case, the Irish immigrants in the Eastern cities and the Southern-born settlers of the Northwestern states were especially hostile to the Negro and, therefore, to emancipation, while many other Northerners became tired and disaffected as the war dragged on interminably. Residents of the Southern hill country, where slavery never had much of a foothold, were similarly hostile toward Davis. In order to wage war, both presidents had to strengthen the powers of central government, thus further accelerating the process of national integration that had brought on the war. Both administrations were, in consequence, vigorously attacked by state governors, who resented the encroachment upon their authority and who strongly favoured local autonomy.

Disloyalty to both presidents

The extent of Northern dissatisfaction was indicated in the congressional elections of 1862, when Lincoln and his party sustained a severe rebuff at the polls and the Republican majority in the House of Representatives was drastically reduced. Similarly in the Confederacy the congressional elections of 1863 went so strongly against the administration that Davis was able to command a majority for his measures only through the continued support of representatives and senators from the states of the upper South, which were under control of the Federal Army and consequently unable to hold new elections.

As late as August 1864, Lincoln despaired of his re-election to the presidency and fully expected that the Democratic candidate, Gen. George B. McClellan, would defeat him. Davis, at about the same time, was openly attacked by Alexander H. Stephens, the vice president of the Confederacy. But Federal military victories, especially William T. Sherman's capture of Atlanta, greatly strengthened Lincoln; and as the war came to a triumphant close for the North, he attained new heights of popularity. Davis' administration, on the other hand, lost support with each successive defeat, and in January 1865 the Confederate Congress insisted that he make Robert E. Lee the supreme commander of all Southern forces. (Some, it is clear, would have preferred to make the general dictator.)

RECONSTRUCTION, 1865–77

Reconstruction under Lincoln. The original Northern objective in the Civil War was the preservation of the Union—a war aim with which virtually everybody in the free states agreed. As the fighting progressed, the Lincoln government concluded that emancipation of the slaves was necessary in order to secure military victory; and thereafter freedom became a second war aim for the members of the Republican Party. The more radical members of that party—men like Charles Sumner and Thaddeus Stevens—believed that emancipation would prove a sham unless the government guaranteed the civil and political rights of the freedmen; and equality of all citizens before the law became a third war aim for this powerful faction. The fierce controversies of the Reconstruction era raged over which of these objectives should be insisted upon and how these goals should be secured.

Northern war aims

Lincoln's plan. Lincoln himself had a flexible and pragmatic approach to Reconstruction, insisting only that the Southerners, when defeated, pledge future loyalty to the Union and emancipate their slaves. As the Southern states were subdued, he appointed military governors to supervise their restoration. The most vigorous and effective of these appointees was Andrew Johnson, whose success in reconstituting a loyal government in Tennessee led to his nomination as vice president on the Republican ticket with Lincoln in 1864. In December 1863 Lincoln announced a general plan for the orderly reconstruction of the Southern states, promising to recognize the government of any state that pledged to support the Constitution and the Union and to emancipate the slaves if it was backed by at least 10 percent of the number of voters in the 1860 presidential election. In both Arkansas and Tennessee loyal governments were formed under Lincoln's plan; and they sought readmission to the Union with the seating of their senators and representatives in Congress.

The Radicals' plan. Radical Republicans were outraged at these procedures, which savoured of executive usurpation of Congressional powers, which required only minimal changes in the Southern social system and which left political power essentially in the hands of the same Southerners who had led their states out of the Union. The Radicals put forth their own plan of Reconstruction in the Wade–Davis bill, which Congress passed on July 2, 1864; it required not 10 percent but a majority of the white male citizens in each Southern state to participate in the reconstruction process, and it insisted upon an oath of past, not just of future, loyalty. Finding the bill too rigorous and inflexible, Lincoln pocket-vetoed it; and the Radicals bitterly denounced him. During the 1864–65 session of Congress, they in turn defeated the president's proposal to recognize the Louisiana government organized under his 10 percent plan. At the time of Lincoln's assassination, therefore, the President and the Congress were at loggerheads over Reconstruction.

Reconstruction under Johnson. At first it seemed that Andrew Johnson might be able to work more cooperatively with Congress in the process of Reconstruction. A former representative and a former senator, he understood congressmen. A loyal Unionist who had stood by his country even at the risk of his life when Tennessee seceded, he was certain not to compromise with secession; and his experience as military governor of that state showed him to be politically shrewd and tough toward the slaveholders. "Johnson, we have faith in you," Radical Benjamin F. Wade assured the new president on the day he took the oath of office. "By the gods, there will be no trouble running the government."

Johnson's policy. Such Radical trust in Johnson proved misplaced. The new president was, first of all, himself a Southerner. He was a Democrat who looked for the restoration of his old party partly as a step toward his own re-election to the presidency in 1868. And, most important of all, Johnson shared the white Southerners' attitude toward the Negro, considering black men innately inferior and unready for equal civil or political rights. On May 29, 1865, Johnson made his policy clear when he issued a general proclamation of pardon and amnesty for most Confederates and authorized the provisional governor of North Carolina to proceed with the reorganization of that state. Shortly afterward he issued similar proclamations for the other former Confederate states. In each case a state constitutional convention was to be chosen by the voters who pledged future loyalty to the U.S. Constitution. The conventions were expected to repeal the ordinances of secession, to repudiate the Confederate debt, and to accept the Thirteenth Amendment, abolishing slavery. The President did not, however, require them to enfranchise the blacks.

"Black Codes." Given little guidance from Washington, Southern whites turned to the traditional political leaders of their section for guidance in reorganizing their governments; and the new regimes in the South were suspiciously like those of the antebellum period. To be sure, slavery was abolished; but each reconstructed Southern state government proceeded to adopt a "Black Code," regulating the rights and privileges of freedmen. Varying from state to state, these codes in general treated blacks as inferiors, relegated to a secondary and subordinate position in society. Their right to own land was restricted, they could not bear arms, and they might be bound out in servitude for vagrancy and other offenses. The conduct of white Southerners indicated that they were not prepared to guarantee even minimal protection of Negro rights. In riots in Memphis (May 1866) and New Orleans (July 1866), black persons were brutally assaulted and promiscuously killed.

Civil rights legislation. Watching these developments with forebodings, Northern Republicans during the Congressional session of 1865–66 inevitably drifted into conflict with the President. Congress attempted to protect the rights of blacks by extending the life of the Freedmen's Bureau; but Johnson vetoed the bill. An act to define and guarantee the blacks' basic civil rights met a similar fate, but Republicans succeeded in passing it over the President's veto. While the President, from the porch of the White House, denounced the leaders of the Republican Party as "traitors," Republicans in Congress tried to formulate their own plan to reconstruct the South. Their first effort was the Fourteenth Amendment, which guaranteed the basic civil rights of all citizens, regardless of colour, and which tried to persuade the Southern states to enfranchise blacks by threatening to reduce their representation in Congress.

The President, the Northern Democrats, and the Southern whites spurned this Republican plan of Reconstruction. Johnson tried to organize his own political party in the National Union Convention, which met in Philadelphia in August 1866; and in August and September he visited many Northern and Western cities in order to defend his policies and to attack the Republican leaders. At the President's urging, every Southern state except Tennessee overwhelmingly rejected the Fourteenth Amendment.

Victorious in the fall elections, Congressional Republicans moved during the 1866–67 session to devise a second, more stringent program for reconstructing the South. After long and acrimonious quarrels between Radical and moderate Republicans, the party leaders finally produced a compromise plan in the First Reconstruction Act of 1867. Expanded and clarified in three supplementary Reconstruction acts, this legislation swept away the regimes the President had set up in the South, put the former Confederacy back under military control, called for the election of new constitutional conventions, and required the constitutions adopted by these bodies to include both Negro suffrage and the disqualification of former Confederate leaders from officeholding. Under this legislation, new governments were established in all the former Confederate states (except Tennessee, which had already been readmitted); and by July 1868 Congress agreed to seat senators and representatives from Alabama, Arkansas, Florida, Louisiana, North Carolina, and South Carolina. By July 1870 the remaining Southern states had been similarly reorganized and readmitted.

Suspicious of Andrew Johnson, Republicans in Congress did not trust the President to enforce the Reconstruction legislation they passed over his repeated vetoes,

and they tried to deprive him of as much power as possible. Congress limited the President's control over the army by requiring that all his military orders be issued through the general of the army, Ulysses S. Grant, who was believed loyal to the Radical cause; and in the Tenure of Office Act (1867) they limited the President's right to remove appointive officers. When Johnson continued to do all he could to block the enforcement of Radical legislation in the South, the more extreme members of the Republican Party demanded his impeachment. The President's decision in February 1868 to remove the Radical secretary of war Edwin M. Stanton from the Cabinet, in apparent defiance of the Tenure of Office Act, provided a pretext for impeachment proceedings. The House of Representatives voted to impeach the President, and after a protracted trial the Senate acquitted him by the margin of only one vote.

The South during Reconstruction. Contrary to conventional stereotypes, the Southern states were relatively tranquil during the Reconstruction period. Exhausted and bankrupt after four years of war, most Southern whites wanted nothing more than to return to their farms and try to make a living. Most of the former slaves also settled down to quiet lives of labour on the farms after some initial wandering about to test their freedom. Indeed, the most important developments of the Reconstruction era were not the highly publicized political contests but the slow, almost imperceptible changes that occurred in Southern society. Blacks could now legally marry, and they set up conventional and usually stable family units; they quietly seceded from the white churches and formed their own religious organizations, which became centres for the black community. Without land or money, most freedmen had to continue working for white masters; but they were now unwilling to labour in gangs or to live in the old slave quarters under the eye of the plantation owner.

Sharecropping gradually became the accepted labour system in most of the South—planters, short of capital, favoured the system because it did not require them to pay cash wages; blacks preferred it because they could live in individual cabins on the tracts they rented and because they had a degree of independence in choosing what to plant and how to cultivate. The section as a whole, however, was desperately poor throughout the Reconstruction era; and a series of disastrously bad crops in the late 1860s, followed by the general agricultural depression of the 1870s, hurt both whites and blacks.

The governments set up in the Southern states under the congressional program of Reconstruction were, contrary to traditional clichés, fairly honest and effective. Though the period has sometimes been labelled "Black Reconstruction," the Radical governments in the South were never dominated by blacks. There were no black governors, only two black senators and a handful of congressmen, and only one legislature controlled by blacks. Those blacks who did hold office appear to have been about equal in competence and honesty to the whites. It is true that these Radical governments were expensive, but large state expenditures were necessary to rebuild after the war and to establish—for the first time in most Southern states—a system of common schools. Corruption there certainly was, though nowhere on the scale of the Tweed Ring, which was simultaneously looting New York City; but it is not possible to show that Republicans were more guilty than Democrats, or blacks than whites, in the scandals that did occur.

Though some Southern whites in the mountainous regions and some planters in the rich bottomlands were willing to cooperate with the blacks and their Northern-born "carpetbagger" allies in these new governments, there were relatively few such "scalawags"; the mass of Southern whites remained fiercely opposed to Negro political, civil, and social equality. Sometimes their hostility was expressed through such terrorist organizations as the Ku Klux Klan, which sought to punish so-called uppity Negroes and to drive their white collaborators from the South. More frequently it was manifested through support of the Democratic Party, which gradually regained

Conflict between Republicans and Johnson

Impeachment of Johnson

Southern Reconstruction governments

its strength in the South and waited for the time when the North would tire of supporting the Radical regimes and would withdraw federal troops from the South.

The Grant administrations, 1869–77. During the two administrations of President Grant there was a gradual attrition of Republican strength. As a politician the President was passive, exhibiting none of the brilliance he had shown on the battlefield. His administration was tarnished by the dishonesty of his subordinates, whom he loyally defended. As the older Radical leaders—men like Sumner, Wade, and Stevens—died, leadership in the Republican Party fell into the hands of technicians like Roscoe Conkling and James G. Blaine, men devoid of the idealistic fervour that had marked the early Republicans. At the same time, many Northerners were growing tired of the whole Reconstruction issue and were weary of the annual outbreaks of violence in the South that required repeated use of federal force.

Weakening of the Radicals

Efforts to shore up the Radical regimes in the South grew increasingly unsuccessful. The adoption of the Fifteenth Amendment (1870), prohibiting discrimination in voting on account of race, had little effect in the South, where terrorist organizations and economic pressure from planters kept blacks from the polls. Nor were three Force Acts passed by the Republicans (1870–71), giving the President the power to suspend the writ of habeas corpus and imposing heavy penalties upon terroristic organizations, in the long run more successful. If they succeeded in dispersing the Ku Klux Klan as an organization, they also drove its members, and their tactics, more than ever into the Democratic camp.

Growing Northern disillusionment with Radical Reconstruction and with the Grant administration became evident in the Liberal Republican movement of 1872, which resulted in the nomination of the erratic Horace Greeley for president. Though Grant was overwhelmingly reelected, the true temper of the country was demonstrated in the congressional elections of 1874, which gave the Democrats control of the House of Representatives for the first time since the outbreak of the Civil War. Despite Grant's hope for a third term in office, most Republicans recognized by 1876 that it was time to change both the candidate and his Reconstruction program, and the nomination of Rutherford B. Hayes of Ohio, a moderate Republican of high principles and of deep sympathy for the South, marked the end of the Radical domination of the Republican Party.

The circumstances surrounding the disputed election of 1876 strengthened Hayes's intention to work with the Southern whites, even if it meant abandoning the few Radical regimes that remained in the South. In an election marked by widespread fraud and many irregularities, the Democratic candidate, Samuel J. Tilden, received the majority of the popular vote; but the vote in the electoral college was long in doubt. In order to resolve the impasse, Hayes's lieutenants had to enter into agreement with Southern Democratic congressmen, promising to withdraw the remaining federal troops from the South, to share the Southern patronage with Democrats, and to favour that section's demands for federal subsidies in the building of levees and railroads. Hayes's inauguration marked, for practical purposes, the restoration of "home rule" for the South—*i.e.,* that the North would no longer interfere in Southern elections to protect the blacks and that the Southern whites would again take control of their state governments.

Restoration of Southern "home rule"

THE NEW SOUTH, 1877–90

The era of conservative domination, 1877–90. The Republican regimes in the Southern states began to fall as early as 1870; by 1877 they had all collapsed. For the next 13 years the South was under the leadership of white Democrats whom their critics called "Bourbons" because, like the French royal family, they supposedly had learned nothing and forgotten nothing from the revolution they had experienced. For the South as a whole, the characterization is neither quite accurate nor quite fair. To be sure, Democrats in South Carolina, led by former Confederate general Wade Hampton, seemed to desire nothing so much as the restoration of the antebellum plantation way of life. But in most Southern states the new political leaders represented less the planters than the rising Southern business community, interested in railroads, cotton textiles, and urban land speculation.

Even on racial questions the new Southern political leaders were not so reactionary as the label Bourbon might suggest. Though whites were in the majority in all but two of the Southern states, the conservative regimes did not attempt to disfranchise the Negroes. Partly their restraint was caused by fear of further federal intervention; chiefly, however, it stemmed from a conviction on the part of conservative leaders that they could control the black voters.

Indeed, Negro votes were sometimes of great value to these regimes, which favoured the businessmen and planters of the South at the expense of the small white farmers. These "Redeemer" governments sharply reduced or even eliminated the programs of the state governments that benefitted poor people. The public school system was starved for money; in 1890 the per capita expenditure in the South for public education was only 97 cents, as compared with $2.24 in the country as a whole. The care of state prisoners, the insane, and the blind was also neglected; and measures to safeguard the public health were rejected. At the same time these conservative regimes were often astonishingly corrupt, and embezzlement and defalcation on the part of public officials were even greater than during the Reconstruction years.

Reduced benefits for the poor

The small white farmers resentful of planter dominance, residents of the hill country outvoted by Black Belt constituencies, and politicians excluded from the ruling cabals tried repeatedly to overthrow the conservative regimes in the South. During the 1870s they supported Independent or Greenback Labour candidates, but without notable success. In 1879 the Readjuster Party in Virginia—so named because its supporters sought to readjust the huge funded debt of that state so as to lessen the tax burden on small farmers—gained control of the legislature and secured in 1880 the election of its leader, Gen. William Mahone, to the United States Senate. Not until 1890, however, when the powerful Farmers' Alliance, hitherto devoted exclusively to the promotion of agricultural reforms, dropped its ban on politics, was there an effective challenge to conservative hegemony. In that year, with Alliance backing, Benjamin R. Tillman was chosen governor of South Carolina and James S. Hogg was elected governor of Texas; the heyday of Southern Populism was at hand.

Jim Crow legislation. Negro voting in the South was a casualty of the conflict between Redeemers and Populists. Though some Populist leaders, such as Tom Watson in Georgia, saw that poor whites and poor blacks in the South had a community of interest in the struggle against the planters and the businessmen, most small white farmers exhibited vindictive hatred toward the blacks, whose votes had so often been instrumental in upholding conservative regimes. Beginning in 1890, when Mississippi held a new constitutional convention, and continuing through 1908, when Georgia amended its constitution, every state of the former Confederacy moved to disfranchise blacks. Because the United States Constitution forbade outright racial discrimination, the Southern states excluded Negroes by requiring that potential voters be able to read or to interpret any section of the Constitution—a requirement that local registrars waived for whites but rigorously insisted upon when an audacious black wanted to vote. Louisiana, more ingenious, added the "grandfather clause" to its constitution, which exempted from this literacy test all of those who had been entitled to vote on January 1, 1867—*i.e.,* before Congress imposed Negro suffrage upon the South—together with their sons and grandsons. Other states imposed stringent property qualifications for voting or enacted complex poll taxes.

Discrimination in voting

Socially as well as politically, race relations in the South deteriorated as farmers' movements rose to challenge the conservative regimes. By 1890, with the triumph of Southern Populism, the black's place was clearly defined by law; he was relegated to a subordinate and entirely segregated position. And while legal sanctions were being imposed upon the Negro, informal, extralegal, and often brutal steps were being taken to keep him in his "place." From 1889 to 1899 lynchings in the South averaged 187.5 per year.

Booker T. Washington and the "Atlanta Compromise." Faced with implacable and growing hostility from Southern whites, many blacks during the 1880s and 1890s felt that their only sensible course was to avoid open conflict and to work out some pattern of accommodation. The most influential black spokesman for this policy was Booker T. Washington, the head of Tuskegee Institute in Alabama, who urged his fellow Negroes to forget about politics and college education in the classical languages and to learn how to be better farmers and artisans. With thrift, industry, and abstention from politics, he thought that Negroes could gradually win the respect of their white neighbours. In 1895, in a speech at the opening of the Atlanta Cotton States and International Exposition, Washington most fully elaborated his position, which became known as the "Atlanta Compromise." Abjuring hopes of federal intervention in behalf of the Negro, Washington argued that reform in the South would have to come from within. Change could best be brought about if blacks and whites recognized that "the agitation of questions of social equality is the extremist folly"; in the social life the races in the South could be as separate as the fingers, but in economic progress as united as the hand.

Enthusiastically received by Southern whites, Washington's program also found many adherents among Southern blacks, who saw in his doctrine a way to avoid head-on, disastrous confrontations with overwhelming white force. Whether or not Washington's plan would have produced a generation of orderly, industrious, frugal blacks slowly working themselves into middle class status is not known because of the intervention of a profound economic depression throughout the South during most of the post-Reconstruction period. Neither poor white nor poor black had much opportunity to rise in a region that was desperately impoverished. By 1890 the South ranked lowest in every index that compared the sections of the United States—lowest in per capita income, lowest in public health, lowest in education. In short, by the 1890s the South, a poor and backward region, had yet to recover from the ravages of the Civil War or to reconcile itself to the readjustments required by the Reconstruction era.   (D.H.D.)

Economic depression in the South (margin)

V. The transformation of U.S. society, 1865–1900

NATIONAL EXPANSION

Growth of the nation. The population of the continental United States in 1880 was slightly above 50,000,000. In 1900 it was just under 76,000,000, a gain in 20 years of over 50 percent. Despite the arrival of more than 9,000,000 immigrants between 1880 and 1900, the rate of population increase was the lowest for any 20-year period of the 19th century. The rate of increase was unevenly distributed, ranging from less than 10 percent in northern New England to more than 125 percent in the 11 states and territories of the Far West. Most of the states east of the Mississippi reported gains slightly below the national average.

Immigration. The 9,000,000 immigrants who entered the United States in the last 20 years of the century were the largest number to arrive in any comparable period up to that time. From the earliest days of the republic until 1895, the majority of immigrants had always come from northern or western Europe. Beginning in 1896, however, the great majority of the immigrants were from southern or eastern Europe. Nervous Americans, already convinced that immigrants wielded too much political power or were responsible for violence and industrial strife, found new cause for alarm, fearing that the new immigrants could not easily be assimilated into U.S. society. Those fears gave added stimulus to agitation for legislation to limit the number of immigrants eligible for admission to the United States.

Westward migration. In 1880 about 22 percent of the American people lived west of the Mississippi. By 1900 that figure had increased to 27 percent. The development of the West continued to add new states to the Union. Nebraska became a state in 1867 and Colorado in 1876; they were followed by North and South Dakota, Washington, and Montana in 1889, by Wyoming and Idaho in 1890, and by Utah in 1896. In 1900 there were only three territories still awaiting statehood in the continental United States: Oklahoma, Arizona, and New Mexico.

New states 1867–96 (margin)

Urban growth. In 1890 the Bureau of the Census discovered that a continuous line could no longer be drawn across the West to define the farthest advance of settlement. Despite the continuing westward movement of population, the frontier had become a symbol of the past. The movement of people from farms to cities more accurately predicted the trends of the future. In 1880 about 28 percent of the American people lived in communities designated by the Bureau of the Census as urban; by 1900 that figure had risen to 40 percent. In those statistics could be read the beginning of the decline of rural power in America and the emergence of a society built upon a burgeoning industrial complex.

The West. Abraham Lincoln once described the West as the "treasure house of the nation." In the 30 years after the discovery of gold in California, prospectors found gold or silver in every state and territory of the Far West.

The mineral empire. There were few truly rich "strikes" in the post-Civil War years. Of those few, the most important were the fabulously rich Comstock Lode of silver in western Nevada (first discovered in 1859 but developed more extensively later) and the discovery of gold in the Black Hills of South Dakota (1874) and at Cripple Creek, Colorado (1891).

Each new discovery of gold or silver produced an instant mining town to supply the needs and pleasures of the prospectors. If most of the ore was close to the surface, the prospectors would soon extract it and depart, leaving behind a ghost town—empty of people but a reminder of a romantic moment in the past. If the veins ran deep, organized groups with the capital to buy the needed machinery would move in to mine the subsoil wealth, and the mining town would gain some stability as the centre of a local industry. In a few instances, those towns gained permanent status as the commercial centres of agricultural areas that first developed to meet the needs of the miners but later expanded to produce a surplus that they exported to other parts of the West.

The open range. At the close of the Civil War, the price of beef in the Northern states was abnormally high. At the same time, millions of cattle grazed aimlessly on the plains of Texas. A few shrewd Texans concluded that there might be greater profits in cattle than in cotton, especially because it required little capital to enter the cattle business—only enough to employ a few cowboys to tend the cattle during the year and to drive them to market in the spring. No one owned the cattle, and they grazed without charge upon the public domain.

The one serious problem was the shipment of the cattle to market. The Kansas Pacific resolved that problem when it completed a rail line that ran as far west as Abilene, Kansas, in 1867. Abilene was 200 miles (300 kilometres) from the nearest point in Texas where the cattle grazed during the year, but Texas cattlemen almost immediately instituted the annual practice of driving that portion of their herds that was ready for market overland to Abilene in the spring. There they met representatives of Eastern packinghouses, to whom they sold their cattle.

The problem of cattle shipment (margin)

The open-range cattle industry prospered beyond expectations and even attracted capital from conservative investors in the British Isles. By the 1880s the industry had expanded along the plains as far north as the Dakotas. In the meantime, a new menace had appeared in the form of the advancing frontier of population; but the construction of the Santa Fe Railway through Dodge City, Kansas, to La Junta, Colorado, permitted the cattlemen to move their operations westward ahead of the frontier; Dodge City replaced Abilene as the principal centre for the annual meeting of cattlemen and buyers. Despite sporadic conflicts with settlers encroaching upon the high plains, the open range survived until a series of savage blizzards struck the plains with unprecedented fury in the winter of 1886–87, killing hundreds of thousands of cattle and forcing many owners into bankruptcy. Those who still had some cattle and some capital abandoned the open range, gained title to lands farther west, where they could provide shelter for their livestock, and revived a cattle industry on land that would be immune to further advances of the frontier of settlement. Their removal to these new lands had been made possible in part by the construction of other railroads connecting the region with Chicago and the Pacific Coast.

Completion of the first transcontinental railroad

The expansion of the railroads. In 1862 Congress authorized the construction of two railroads that together would provide the first railroad link between the Mississippi Valley and the Pacific coast. One was the Union Pacific, to run westward from Council Bluffs, Iowa; the other was the Central Pacific, to run eastward from Sacramento, California. To encourage the rapid completion of those roads, Congress provided generous subsidies in the form of land grants and loans. Construction was slower than Congress had anticipated, but the two lines met, with elaborate ceremonies, on May 10, 1869, at Promontory Point, Utah.

In the meantime, other railroads had begun construction westward, but the Panic of 1873 and the ensuing depression halted or delayed construction of many of those lines. With the return of prosperity after 1877, some of those railroads resumed or accelerated construction; by 1883 three more rail connections between the Mississippi Valley and the West Coast had been completed—the Northern Pacific, from St. Paul to Portland; the Santa Fe, from Chicago to Los Angeles; and the Southern Pacific, from New Orleans to Los Angeles. The Southern Pacific had also acquired, by purchase or construction, lines from Portland to San Francisco and from San Francisco to Los Angeles.

The construction of the railroads from the Middle West to the Pacific coast was the railroad builders' most spectacular achievement in the quarter century after the Civil War. No less important, in terms of the national economy, was the development in the same period of an adequate rail network in the southern states and the building of other railroads that connected virtually every important community west of the Mississippi with Chicago.

The West developed simultaneously with the building of the Western railroads, and in no part of the nation was the importance of railroads more generally recognized. The railroad gave vitality to the regions it served, but, by withholding service, it could doom a community to stagnation. The railroads appeared to be ruthless in exploiting their powerful position: they fixed prices to suit their convenience; they discriminated among their customers; they attempted to gain a monopoly of transportation wherever possible; and they interfered in state and local politics to elect favourites to office, to block unfriendly legislation, and even to influence the decisions of the courts.

Indian policy. Large tracts of land in the West were reserved by law for the exclusive use of specified Indian tribes. By 1870, however, the pressure of the frontier and the outbreak of a series of Indian wars had raised serious questions about the government's Indian policies. Many agents of the Bureau of Indian Affairs, charged with responsibility for dealing directly with the tribes, were lax, and some were corrupt in the discharge of their duties. Most Westerners and some army officers contended that the only satisfactory resolution of the Indian question was the removal of the tribes from all lands coveted by the whites.

Programs for assimilation of Indians

In the immediate postwar years, reformers advocated adoption of programs designed to prepare the Indians for ultimate assimilation into American society. In 1869 the reformers persuaded Pres. Ulysses S. Grant and Congress to establish a nonpolitical Board of Indian Commissioners to supervise the administration of relations between the government and the Indians. The board, however, encountered so much political opposition that it accomplished little. The reformers then proposed legislation to grant title for specific acreages of land to the head of each family in those tribes thought to be ready to adopt a sedentary life as farmers. Congress resisted that proposal until land-hungry Westerners discovered that, if the land were thus distributed, a surplus of land would result that could be added to the public domain. When land speculators joined the reformers in support of the proposed legislation, Congress in 1887 enacted the Dawes Act, which empowered the President to grant title to 160 acres (65 hectares) to the head of each family, with smaller allotments to single members of the tribe, in those tribes believed ready to accept a new way of life as farmers. With the grant of land, which could not be alienated by the Indians for 25 years, they were to be granted United States citizenship. Reformers rejoiced that they had finally given the Indians an opportunity to have a dignified role in U.S. society, overlooking the possibility that there might be values in Indian culture worthy of preservation. Meanwhile, the land promoters placed successive presidents under great pressure to accelerate the application of the Dawes Act in order to open more land for occupation or speculation.

INDUSTRIALIZATION OF THE U.S. ECONOMY

The growth of industry. By 1878 the United States had re-entered a period of prosperity after the long depression of the mid-1870s. In the ensuing 20 years the volume of industrial production, the number of workers employed in industry, and the number of manufacturing plants all more than doubled. A more accurate index to the scope of this industrial advance may be found in the aggregate annual value of all manufactured goods, which increased from $5,400,000,000 in 1879 to $13,000,000,000 in 1899. The expansion of the iron and steel industry, always a key factor in any industrial economy, was even more impressive; in 20 years, from 1880 to 1900, the annual production of steel in the United States went from 1,400,000 to 11,000,000 tons. Before the end of the century, the United States surpassed Great Britain in the production of iron and steel and was providing more than one-quarter of the world's supply of pig iron.

Many factors combined to produce this burst of industrial activity. The exploitation of Western resources, including mines and lumber, stimulated a demand for improved transportation, while the gold and silver mines provided new sources of capital for investment in the East. The construction of railroads, especially in the West and South, with the resulting demand for steel rails, was a major force in the expansion of the steel industry and increased the railroad mileage in the United States from less than 93,262 miles (150,151 kilometres) in 1880 to about 190,000 miles (310,000 kilometres) in 1900. Technological advances, including the utilization of the Bessemer and open-hearth processes in the manufacture of steel, resulted in improved products and lower production costs. A series of major inventions, including the telephone, typewriter, linotype, phonograph, electric light, cash register, air brake, refrigerator car, and the automobile, became the bases for new industries, while many of them facilitated the conduct of business. The use of petroleum products in industry as well as for domestic heating and lighting became the cornerstone of the most powerful of the new industries of the period, while the trolley car, the increased use of gas and electric power, and the telephone led to the establishment of important public utilities that were natural monopolies and could operate only on the basis of franchises granted by state or municipal governments. The widespread employment of the corporate form of business organization offered new opportunities for large-scale financing of business enterprise and attracted new capital, much of it furnished by European investors. Over all this industrial activity, there presided a colourful and energetic group of entrepreneurs, who gained the attention, if not always the commendation, of the public and who appeared to symbolize for the public the new class of leadership in the United States. Of this numerous group the best known were John D. Rockefeller in oil, Andrew Carnegie in

New class of leadership

steel, and such railroad builders and promoters as Cornelius Vanderbilt, Leland Stanford, Collis P. Huntington, Henry Villard, and James J. Hill.

The dispersion of industry.   The period was notable also for the wide geographical distribution of industry. The Eastern seaboard from Massachusetts to Pennsylvania continued to be the most heavily industrialized section of the United States, but there was a substantial development of manufacturing in the states adjacent to the Great Lakes and in certain sections of the South.

The experience of the steel industry reflected this new pattern of diffusion. Two-thirds of the iron and steel industry was concentrated in the area of western Pennsylvania and eastern Ohio. After 1880, however, the development of iron mines in northern Minnesota (the Vermilion Range in 1884 and the Mesabi Range in 1892) and in Tennessee and northern Alabama was followed by the expansion of the iron and steel industry in the Chicago area and by the establishment of steel mills in northern Alabama and in Tennessee.

Most manufacturing in the Middle West was in enterprises closely associated with agriculture and represented expansion of industries that had first been established before 1860. Meat-packing, which in the years after 1875 became one of the major industries of the nation in terms of the value of its products, was almost a Middle Western monopoly, with a large part of the industry concentrated in Chicago. Flour milling, brewing, and the manufacture of farm machinery and lumber products were other important Middle Western industries.

The industrial invasion of the South was spearheaded by textiles. Cotton mills became the symbol of the New South, and mills and mill towns sprang up in the Piedmont region from Virginia to Georgia and into Alabama. By 1900 almost one-quarter of all the cotton spindles in the United States were in the South, and Southern mills were expanding their operations more rapidly than were their well-established competitors in New England. The development of lumbering in the South was even more impressive, though less publicized; by the end of the century the South led the nation in lumber production, contributing almost one-third of the annual supply.

Industrial combinations.   The geographical dispersal of industry was part of a movement that was converting the United States into an industrial nation. It attracted less attention, however, than the trend toward the consolidation of competing firms into large units capable of dominating an entire industry. The movement toward consolidation received special attention in 1882 when John D. Rockefeller and his associates organized the Standard Oil Trust under the laws of Ohio. A trust was a new type of industrial organization, in which the voting rights of a controlling number of shares of competing firms were entrusted to a small group of men, or trustees, who thus were able to prevent competition among the companies they controlled. The stockholders presumably benefitted through the larger dividends they received. For a few years the trust was a popular vehicle for the creation of monopolies, and by 1890 there were trusts in whiskey, lead, cottonseed oil, and salt.

In 1892 the courts of Ohio ruled that the trust violated that state's antimonopoly laws. Standard Oil then reincorporated as a holding company under the more hospitable laws of New Jersey. Thereafter, holding companies or outright mergers became the favourite forms for the creation of monopolies, though the term trust remained in the popular vocabulary as a common description of any monopoly. The best known mergers of the period were those leading to the formation of the American Tobacco Company (1890) and the American Sugar Refining Company (1891). The latter was especially successful in stifling competition, for it quickly gained control of most of the sugar refined in the United States.

Foreign commerce.   The foreign trade of the United States, if judged by the value of exports, kept pace with the growth of domestic industry. Exclusive of gold, silver, and re-exports, the annual value of exports from the United States in 1877 was $590,000,000; by 1900 it had increased to $1,371,000,000. The value of imports also

The margin note: Trusts, mergers, and holding companies

rose, though at a slower rate. When gold and silver are included, there was only one year in the entire period in which the United States had an unfavourable balance of trade; and, as the century drew to a close, the excess of exports over imports increased perceptibly.

Agriculture continued to furnish the bulk of U.S. exports. Cotton, wheat, flour, and meat products were consistently the items with the greatest annual value among exports. Of the nonagricultural products sent abroad, petroleum was the most important, though by the end of the century its position on the list of exports was being challenged by machinery.

Despite the expansion of foreign trade, the U.S. merchant marine was a major casualty of the period. While the aggregate tonnage of all shipping flying the U.S. flag remained remarkably constant, the tonnage engaged in foreign trade declined sharply. On the eve of the Civil War, the tonnage in overseas trade had exceeded 2,400,000 tons; by 1877 it had dropped to 1,571,000 tons, and, thereafter, it continued to decline until it reached a low point in 1898 of only 726,000 tons. In 1900 only about 10 percent of the exports of the United States were sent abroad in ships of U.S. registry.

Labour.   The expansion of industry was accompanied by increased tensions between employers and workers and by the appearance, for the first time in the United States, of national labour unions.

Formation of unions.   The first effective labour organization that was more than regional in membership and influence was the Knights of Labor, organized in 1869. The Knights believed in the unity of the interests of all producing groups and sought to enlist in their ranks not only all labourers but everyone who could be truly classified as a producer. They championed a variety of causes, many of them more political than industrial, and they hoped to gain their ends through politics and education rather than through economic coercion.

The margin note: The Knights of Labor

The hardships suffered by many workers during the depression of 1873–78 and the failure of a nationwide railroad strike, which was broken when Pres. Rutherford B. Hayes sent federal troops to suppress disorders in Pittsburgh and St. Louis, caused much discontent in the ranks of the Knights. In 1879 Terence V. Powderly, a railroad worker and mayor of Scranton, Pennsylvania, was elected grand master workman of the national organization. Powderly supposedly favoured a program of aggressive action on behalf of labour. In practice, however, he hesitated to endorse strikes, and the effective control of the Knights shifted to regional leaders who were willing to initiate strikes or other forms of economic pressure to gain their objectives. The Knights reached the peak of their influence in 1885, when they claimed a national membership of nearly 700,000. In that year a much-publicized strike against the Wabash Railroad attracted substantial public sympathy and succeeded in preventing a reduction in wages. In that year also Congress took note of the apparently increasing power of labour and prohibited the entry into the United States of immigrants who had signed contracts to work for specific employers.

The year 1886 was a troubled one in labour relations. There were nearly 1,600 strikes, involving about 600,000 workers, with the eight-hour day the most prominent item in the demands of labour. About half of these strikes were called for May Day; some of them were successful, but the concerted action by workers on a nationwide basis turned public opinion against labour and deprived it of much of the sympathy it had enjoyed in the preceding year.

The Haymarket Riot.   The most serious blow to the unions came from a tragic occurrence with which they were only indirectly associated. One of the strikes called for May Day in 1886 was against the McCormick Harvesting Machine Company in Chicago. Fighting broke out along the picket lines, and, when police intervened to restore order, several strikers were injured. Union leaders called a protest meeting at Haymarket Square for the evening of May 4; but, as the meeting was breaking up, a group of anarchists took over and began to make inflammatory speeches. The police quickly intervened, and a bomb exploded, killing seven policemen and injuring many others. Eight of the anarchists were arrested, tried, and convicted of murder. Four of them were hanged, and one committed suicide. The remaining three were pardoned in 1893 by Gov. John P. Altgeld, who was persuaded that they had been convicted in such an atmosphere of prejudice that it was impossible to be certain that they were guilty.

The public tended to blame organized labour for the Haymarket tragedy, and many persons had become convinced that the activities of unions were likely to be attended by violence. The Knights never regained the ground they lost in 1886, and, until after the turn of the century, organized labour seldom gained any measure of public sympathy. Aggregate union membership did not again reach its 1885–86 figure until 1900. Unions, however, continued to be active; and in each year from 1889 through the end of the century there were more than 1,000 strikes.

The American Federation of Labor

As the power of the Knights declined, the leadership in the trade union movement passed to the American Federation of Labor (AFL). This was a loose federation of local and craft unions, organized first in 1881 and reorganized in 1886. For a few years there was some nominal cooperation between the Knights and the AFL, but the basic organization and philosophy of the two groups made cooperation difficult. The AFL appealed only to skilled workers, and its objectives were those of immediate concern to its members: hours, wages, working conditions, and the recognition of the union. It relied on economic weapons, chiefly the strike and boycott, and it eschewed political activity, except for state and local election campaigns. The central figure in the AFL was Samuel Gompers, a New York cigar maker, who was its president from 1886 to his death in 1924.

NATIONAL POLITICS

The dominant forces in U.S. life in the last quarter of the 19th century were economic and not political. This fact was reflected in the ineffectiveness of political leadership and in the absence of deeply divisive issues in politics, except perhaps for the continuing agrarian agitation for inflation. There were colourful political personalities, but they gained their following on a personal basis rather than as spokesmen for a program of political action. No president of the period was truly the leader of his party, and none apparently aspired to that status except Grover Cleveland during his second term (1893–97). Such shrewd observers of U.S. politics as Woodrow Wilson and James Bryce agreed that great men did not become presidents; and it was evident that the nominating conventions of both major parties commonly selected presidential candidates who were "available" in the sense that they had few enemies.

In the absence of leadership from the White House, public policy was largely formulated in Congress. As a result, public policy commonly represented a compromise among the views of many congressional leaders—a situation made the more essential because of the fact that in only four of the 20 years from 1877 to 1897 did the same party control the White House, the Senate, and the House.

The Republicans appeared to be the majority party in national politics. From the Civil War to the end of the century, they won every presidential election save those of 1884 and 1892, and they had a majority in the Senate in all but three Congresses during that same period. The Democrats, however, won a majority in the House in eight of the ten Congresses from 1875 to 1895. The success of the Republicans was achieved in the face of bitter intraparty schisms that plagued Republican leaders from 1870 until after 1890 and despite the fact that, in every election campaign after 1876, they were forced to concede the entire South to the opposition. The Republicans had the advantage of having been the party that had defended the Union against secession and had freed the slaves. When all other appeals failed, Republican leaders could salvage votes in the North and West by reviving memories of the war. A less tangible but equally

Regional political differences

valuable advantage was the widespread belief that the continued industrial development of the nation would be more secure under a Republican than under a Democratic administration. Except in years of economic adversity, the memory of the war and confidence in the economic program of the Republican Party were normally enough to ensure Republican success in most of the northern and western states.

The administration of Rutherford B. Hayes. President Hayes (served 1877–81) willingly carried out the commitments made by his friends to reconcile Southerners to the decisions of the electoral commission that had awarded him the disputed electoral votes in three key Southern states needed for his election. He withdrew the federal troops still in the South, and he appointed former senator David M. Key of Tennessee to his Cabinet as postmaster general. Hayes hoped that these conciliatory gestures would encourage many Southern conservatives to support the Republican Party in the future. But the Southerners' primary concern was the maintenance of white supremacy; this, they believed, required a monopoly of political power in the South by the Democratic Party. As a result, the policies of Hayes led to the virtual extinction rather than the revival of the Republican Party in the South.

Hayes's efforts to woo the South irritated some Republicans, but his attitude toward the federal civil service was a more immediate challenge to his party. In June 1877 he issued an executive order prohibiting political activity by those who held federal appointments. When two friends of Sen. Roscoe Conkling defied this order, Hayes removed them from their posts in the administration of the Port of New York. Conkling and his associates showed their contempt for Hayes by bringing about the election of one of the men (Alonzo B. Cornell) as governor of New York in 1879 and nominating the other (Chester A. Arthur) as Republican candidate for the vice presidency in 1880.

One of the most serious issues facing Hayes was that of inflation. Hayes and many other Republicans were staunch supporters of a sound-money policy, but the issues were sectional rather than partisan. In general, sentiment in the agricultural South and West was favourable to inflation, while industrial and financial groups in the Northeast opposed any move to inflate the currency, holding that this would benefit debtors at the expense of creditors.

In 1873 Congress had discontinued the minting of silver dollars, an action later stigmatized by friends of silver as the Crime of '73. As the depression deepened, inflationists began campaigns to persuade Congress to resume coinage of silver dollars and to repeal the act providing for the redemption of Civil War greenbacks in gold after January 1, 1879. By 1878 the sentiment for silver and inflation was so strong that Congress passed, over the President's veto, the Bland–Allison Act, which renewed the coinage of silver dollars and, more significantly, included a mandate to the Secretary of the Treasury to purchase silver bullion at the market price in amounts of not less than $2,000,000 and not more than $4,000,000 each month.

The silver controversy

Opponents of inflation were somewhat reassured by the care with which Secretary of the Treasury John Sherman was making preparation to have an adequate gold reserve to meet any demands on the Treasury for the redemption of greenbacks. Equally reassuring were indications that the nation had at last recovered from the long period of depression. These factors re-established confidence in the financial stability of the government; and, when the date for the redemption of greenbacks arrived, there was no appreciable demand upon the Treasury to exchange them for gold.

Hayes chose not to be a candidate for re-election. Had he sought a second term, he would almost certainly have been denied renomination by the Republican leaders, with whom he had never been popular. His tolerant disposition and quiet dignity had won the respect of millions of his fellow countrymen, and he appeared to symbolize the amelioration of the economic and sectional tensions that had gripped the country in 1877. But the forces that molded national destiny during his administration and for 20 years thereafter were economic and social rather than political.

The election of 1880. Three prominent candidates contended for the Republican presidential nomination in 1880: Grant, James G. Blaine, and John Sherman. Grant had a substantial and loyal bloc of delegates in the convention, but their number was short of a majority. Neither of the other candidates could command a majority, and on the 36th ballot the weary delegates nominated a compromise candidate, Congressman James A. Garfield of Ohio. To placate the "Stalwart," or pro-Grant, faction, the convention nominated Chester A. Arthur of New York for vice president.

The Democrats probably would have renominated Samuel J. Tilden in 1880, hoping thereby to gain votes from those who believed Tilden had lost in 1876 through fraud. But Tilden declined to become a candidate again, and the Democratic convention nominated Gen. Winfield S. Hancock. Hancock had been a Federal general during the Civil War, but he had no political record and little familiarity with questions of public policy.

The campaign failed to generate any unusual excitement and produced no novel issues. As in every national election of the period, the Republicans stressed their role as the party of the protective tariff and asserted that Democratic opposition to the tariff would impede the growth of domestic industry. Actually, the Democrats were badly divided on the tariff, and Hancock surprised political leaders of both parties by declaring that the tariff was an issue of only local interest.

Garfield won the election with an electoral margin of 214 to 155, but his plurality in the popular vote was a slim 9,644. The election revealed the existence of a new "solid South," for Hancock carried all the former Confederate states and three of the former slave states that had remained loyal to the Union.

The administrations of James A. Garfield and Chester A. Arthur. Garfield had not been closely identified with either of the two major factions within the Republican Party—the "Stalwarts" and the "Half-Breeds." Upon becoming president, he named James G. Blaine, the leader of the "Half-Breeds," as secretary of state. He gave even more serious offense to the pro-Grant "Stalwart" faction by appointing as collector of customs at New York a man who was unacceptable to the two senators from that state, Roscoe Conkling and Thomas Platt, who showed their displeasure by resigning their Senate seats, expecting to be re-elected triumphantly by the legislature of New York; but in this they were disappointed.

The tragic climax to this intraparty strife came on July 2, 1881, when Garfield was shot, in Washington, D.C., by a disappointed and mentally deranged office seeker. For two months the President lingered between life and death. He died on September 19 and was succeeded by Vice Pres. Chester A. Arthur.

The accession of Arthur to the presidency caused widespread concern. He had held no elective office before becoming vice president, and he had been closely associated with the Grant wing of the party. It was assumed that like others in that group he would be hostile to reform of the civil service, and his nomination for the vice presidency had been generally regarded as a deliberate rebuke to President Hayes. The members of Garfield's Cabinet immediately tendered their resignations, but Arthur asked them to continue in office for a time. By mid-April 1882, however, all but one of the Cabinet officers had been replaced. Among those replaced was Secretary of State Blaine.

Arthur soon surprised his critics and the country by demonstrating an unexpected independence of his former political friends. In his first annual message to Congress, in December 1881, he announced his qualified approval of legislation that would remove appointments to the federal civil service from partisan control. In January 1883 Congress passed and Arthur signed the Pendleton Civil Service Act, which established the Civil Service Commission and provided that appointments to certain categories of offices should be made on the basis of exam-

The assassination of Garfield

inations and the appointees given an indefinite tenure in their positions.

In May 1882 Congress enacted the Chinese Exclusion Act, prohibiting for a period of ten years the immigration of Chinese labourers into the United States. This act was both the culmination of more than ten years of agitation on the West Coast for the exclusion of the Chinese and an early sign of some modification of the traditional U.S. philosophy of welcoming virtually all immigrants. In response to pressure from California, Congress had passed an exclusion act in 1879, but it had been vetoed by Hayes on the ground that it abrogated rights guaranteed to the Chinese by the Burlingame Treaty of 1868. In 1880 these treaty provisions were revised to permit the United States to suspend the immigration of Chinese. The Chinese Exclusion Act was renewed in 1892 for another ten-year period, and in 1902 the suspension of Chinese immigration was made indefinite.

The Chinese Exclusion Act

The election of 1884. President Arthur hoped to be the presidential nominee of the Republicans in 1884. His administration had won the respect of many who had viewed his accession to office with misgivings. It had not, however, gained him any powerful following among the leaders of his party. The strongest candidate for the Republican nomination was James G. Blaine. Despite opposition from those who believed he was too partisan in spirit or that he was vulnerable to charges of corrupt actions while speaker of the house many years before, Blaine was nominated on the fourth ballot.

The Democratic candidate, Gov. Grover Cleveland of New York, was in many respects the antithesis of Blaine. He was a relative newcomer to politics. He had been elected mayor of Buffalo in 1881 and governor of New York in 1882. In both positions he had earned a reputation for political independence, inflexible honesty, and an industrious and conservative administration. His record made him an attractive candidate for persons who accepted the dictum that "a public office is a public trust." This was, in 1884, a valuable asset; and it won for Cleveland the support of a few outstanding Republicans and some journals of national circulation that usually favoured Republican nominees for office.

As in 1880, the campaign was almost devoid of issues of public policy: only the perennial question of the tariff appeared to separate the two parties. Cleveland had not served in the army during the Civil War, and Republicans made an effort to use this fact, together with the power of the South in the Democratic Party, to arouse sectional prejudices against Cleveland. During the campaign it was revealed that Cleveland, a bachelor, was the father of an illegitimate son, an indiscretion that gave the Republicans a moral issue with which to counteract charges of corruption against their own candidate.

The election was very close. On the evening of the voting it was apparent that the result depended upon the vote in New York State, but not until the end of the week was it certain that Cleveland had carried New York by the narrow margin of 1,149 votes and been elected president. In the electoral college, Cleveland received 219 votes to 182 for Blaine.

Grover Cleveland's first term. Cleveland was the first Democratic president since James Buchanan a quarter of a century earlier. More than two-thirds of the electoral votes he received came from southern or border states, so that it appeared that his election marked the close of one epoch and the beginning of a new political era in which the South could again hope to have a major voice in the conduct of national affairs. Because of his brief career in politics, Cleveland had only a limited acquaintance with leaders of his own party. He accepted literally the constitutional principle of the separation of powers, and he opened his first annual message to Congress, in December 1885, with an affirmation of his devotion to "the partitions of power between our respective departments." This appeared to be a disavowal of presidential leadership, but it quickly became apparent that Cleveland intended to defend vigorously the prerogatives that he believed belonged to the executive.

During his first term (1885–89) Cleveland was con-

Cleveland's relations with his party and politics

fronted with a divided Congress—a Republican Senate
and a Democratic House. This added to the complexities
of administration, especially in the matter of appointments. Cleveland was a firm believer in a civil service
based on merit rather than on partisan considerations,
but, as the first Democratic president in a quarter of a
century, he was under great pressure to replace Republicans in appointive offices with Democrats. He followed a
line of compromise. In his first two years he removed the
incumbents from about two-thirds of the offices subject to
his control, but he scrutinized the qualifications of Democrats recommended for appointment and in a number of
instances refused to abide by the recommendations of his
party leaders. He thus offended both the reformers, who
wished no partisan removals, and his fellow Democrats,
whose nominees he rejected. Although his handling of the
patronage alienated some powerful Democrats, he scored
a personal triumph when he persuaded Congress to repeal the obsolete Tenure of Office Act of 1867, which
Republican senators had threatened to revive in order to
embarrass him.

Cleveland was a conservative on all matters relating to
money, and he was inflexibly opposed to wasteful expenditure of public funds. This caused him to investigate as
many as possible of the hundreds of private bills passed
by Congress to compensate private individuals, usually
Federal veterans, for claims against the federal government. When, as was frequently the case, he judged these
claims to be ill founded, he vetoed the bill. He was the
first president to use the veto power extensively to block
the enactment of this type of private legislation.

The surplus and the tariff. The flurry of private pension bills had been stimulated, in part, by a growing
surplus in the Treasury. In every year since the Civil War,
there had been an excess of revenue over expenditures,
a circumstance that encouraged suggestions for appropriations of public funds for a variety of purposes. The surplus also focussed attention upon the tariff, which was the
principal source of this excess revenue. In 1883 Congress
had reviewed the tariff and made numerous changes in
the rates, increasing the tariff on some items and reducing
it on others, without materially decreasing the revenue
received. Cleveland believed that the surplus presented a
very real problem. It hoarded in the Treasury money that
could have been in circulation, and it encouraged reckless
spending by the government. Like many other Democrats, he disliked the high protective tariff. After waiting
in vain for two years for Congress to meet this issue
boldly, Cleveland adopted the extraordinary tactic of devoting his entire annual message in 1887 to a discussion
of this question and to an appeal for a lowering of the
tariff. The House then passed a bill generally conforming
to Cleveland's views on the tariff; but the Senate rejected
it, and the tariff became a leading issue in the presidential
campaign of 1888.

The public domain. After 1877 hundreds of thousands
of agricultural settlers went westward to the plains, where
they came into competition for control of the land with
the cattlemen, who hitherto had dominated the open
range. The pressure of population as it moved into the
plains called attention to the diminishing supply of good
arable land still open to settlement, thus presaging the
day when there would no longer be a vast reservoir of
land in the West awaiting the farmer. It also focussed
attention on the fact that millions of acres of Western
land were being held for speculative purposes and that
other millions of acres had been acquired by questionable
means or were still in the possession of railroads that had
failed to fulfill the obligations they assumed when the
land was granted to them. Upon assuming office, Cleveland was confronted with evidence that some of these
claims had been fraudulently obtained by railroads, speculators, cattlemen, or lumbering interests. He ordered an
investigation, and for more than a year agents of the
Land Office roamed over the West uncovering evidence
of irregularities and neglected obligations. Cleveland
acted firmly. By executive orders and court action he
succeeded in restoring more than 81,000,000 acres
(33,000,000 hectares) to the public domain.

The Interstate Commerce Act. The railroads were vital to the economy of the nation, but because in so many
regions a single company enjoyed a monopoly of rail
transportation, many of the railroads adopted policies
that large numbers of their customers believed to be unfair and discriminatory. Before 1884 it was clear that the
Granger laws of the preceding decade (state laws prohibiting various abuses by the railroads) were ineffective,
and pressure groups turned to the federal government for
relief. In this, Western farm organizations were joined by
influential Eastern businessmen who believed that they,
too, were the victims of discrimination by the railroads.
This powerful political alliance persuaded both parties to
include regulation of the railroads in their national platforms in 1884 and induced Congress to enact the Interstate Commerce Act in 1887.

This law, designed to prevent unjust discrimination by
the railroads, prohibited the pooling of traffic and profits,
made it illegal for a railroad to charge more for a short
haul than for a longer one, required that the roads publicize their rates, and established the Interstate Commerce
Commission to supervise the enforcement of the law. The
rulings of the commission were subject to review by the
federal courts, the decisions of which tended to narrow
the scope of the act. The commission was less effective
than the sponsors of the act had hoped, but the act in
itself was an indication of the growing realization that
only the federal government could cope with the new
economic problems of the day.

The election of 1888. Cleveland's plea for a reduction
of the tariff in his annual message of 1887 made it certain
that the tariff would be the central issue in the presidential campaign of 1888. The Democrats renominated
Cleveland, although it was thought that he had endangered his chances of re-election by his outspoken advocacy of tariff reduction. The Republicans had their usual
difficulty in selecting a candidate. Blaine refused to enter
the race, and no other person in the party commanded
substantial support. From among the many who were
willing to accept the nomination, the Republicans selected Benjamin Harrison of Indiana, a Federal general in
the Civil War and the grandson of Pres. William Henry
Harrison.

Cleveland had won respect as a man of integrity and
courage, but neither he nor Harrison aroused any great
enthusiasm among the voters. One feature of the campaign noted by observers was the extensive use of money
to influence the outcome; this was not a new phenomenon, but the spending of money to carry doubtful states
and the apparent alliance between business and political
bosses had never before been so open.

The results were again close. Cleveland had a plurality
of 100,000 popular votes, but the Republicans carried
two states, New York and Indiana, which they had lost in
1884, and in the electoral college Harrison won by a
margin of 233 to 168.

The administration of Benjamin Harrison. The Republicans also gained control of both houses of the 51st
Congress. Their margin in the House of Representatives,
however, was so small that it seemed uncertain whether
they could carry controversial legislation through it. This
obstacle was overcome by the speaker of the House,
Thomas B. Reed of Maine. Reed refused to recognize
dilatory motions, and, contrary to precedent, he counted
as present all members who were in the chamber. Using
that tactic, he ruled, on occasion, that a quorum was
present even though fewer than a majority had actually
answered a roll call. His iron rule of the House earned
him the sobriquet Czar Reed, but only through his firm
control of the House could the Republicans pass three
controversial bills in the summer and early autumn of
1890. One dealt with monopolies, another with silver,
and the third with the tariff.

The Sherman Anti-Trust Act. The first of these major measures declared illegal all combinations that restrained trade between states or with foreign nations. This
law, known as the Sherman Anti-Trust Act, was passed
by Congress early in July. It was the congressional response to evidence of growing public dissatisfaction with

Cleveland's use of veto powers

Diminishing supply of land

Interstate Commerce Act

Public dissatisfaction with monopolies

the development of industrial monopolies, which had been so notable a feature of the preceding decade.

More than ten years passed before the Sherman Act was used to break up any industrial monopoly. It was invoked by the federal government in 1894 to obtain an injunction against a striking railroad union accused of restraint of interstate commerce, and the use of the injunction was upheld by the Supreme Court in 1895. Indeed, it is unlikely that the Senate would have passed the bill in 1890 had not the chairman of the Senate Judiciary Committee, George F. Edmunds of Vermont, felt certain that unions were combinations in restraint of trade within the meaning of the law. To those who hoped that the Sherman Act would inhibit the growth of monopoly, the results were disappointing. The passage of the act only three years after the Interstate Commerce Act was, however, another sign that the public was turning from state capitals to Washington for effective regulation of industrial giants.

The silver issue. Less than two weeks after Congress passed the antitrust law, it enacted the Sherman Silver Purchase Act, which required the secretary of the treasury to purchase each month 4,500,000 ounces (130,000 kilograms) of silver at the market price. This superseded the Bland–Allison Act of 1878 and had the effect of increasing the government's monthly purchase of silver by more than 50 percent. The act was adopted in response to pressure from mineowners, who were alarmed by the falling price of silver, and from Western farmers, who were always favourable to inflationary measures and who, in 1890, were also suffering from the depressed prices of their products.

The McKinley Tariff. Most Republican leaders had been lukewarm to the proposal to increase the purchase of silver and had accepted it only to assure Western votes for the measure in which they were most interested—upward revision of the protective tariff. This was accomplished in the McKinley Tariff Act of October 1890, passed by Congress one month before the midterm elections of that year. The tariff was designed to appeal to the farmers because some agricultural products were added to the protected list. A few items, notably sugar, were placed on the free list, and domestic sugar planters were to be compensated by a subsidy of two cents a pound. The central feature of the act, however, was a general increase in tariff schedules, with many of these increases applying to items of general consumption.

The new tariff immediately became an issue in the congressional elections. It failed to halt the downward spiral of farm prices, but there was an almost immediate increase in the cost of many items purchased by the farmers. With discontent already rife in the agricultural regions of the West and South, the McKinley Tariff added to the agrarian resentment. The outcome of the elections was a major defeat for the Republicans, whose strength in the House of Representatives was reduced by almost half.

The agrarian revolt. Political disaster befell the Republicans in the trans-Mississippi West, resulting from an economic and psychological depression that enveloped the region after widespread crop failures and the collapse of inflated land prices in the summer of 1887. The Western boom had begun in the late 1870s, when the tide of migration into the unoccupied farmlands beyond the Mississippi quickly led to the settlement of hitherto unoccupied parts of Iowa and Minnesota and to the pushing of the frontier westward across the plains almost literally to the shadows of the Rocky Mountains.

Westward expansion was encouraged by the railroads that served the region. It was supported by the satisfactory price and encouraging foreign market for wheat, the money crop of the plains. For ten years, from 1877 through 1886, the farmers on the plains had the benefit of an abnormally generous rainfall, leading many to assume that climatic conditions had changed and that the rain belt had moved westward to provide adequate rainfall for the plains. Confidence was followed by unrestrained optimism that engendered wild speculation and a rise in land prices. Lured on by these illusions, the settlers went into debt to make improvements on their farms while small-

Farmers' resentment of the tariff

town leaders dreamed of prodigious growth and authorized bond issues to construct the public improvements they felt certain would soon be needed.

The collapse of these dreams came in 1887. The year opened ominously when the plains were swept by a catastrophic blizzard in January that killed thousands of head of cattle and virtually destroyed the cattle industry of the open range. The following summer was dry and hot; crops were poor; and, to compound the woes of the farmers, the price of wheat began to slide downward. The dry summer of 1887 was the beginning of a ten-year cycle of little rainfall and searingly hot summers. By the autumn of 1887 the exodus from the plains had begun; five years later, areas of western Kansas and Nebraska that had once been thriving agricultural centres were almost depopulated. The agricultural regions east of the plains were less directly affected, though there the farmers suffered from the general decline in farm prices.

Although the disaster on the plains bred a sense of distress and frustration, the lure of good land was still strong. When the central portion of the present state of Oklahoma was opened to settlement in April 1889, an army of eager settlers, estimated to have numbered 100,000, rushed into the district to claim homesteads and build homes.

Settlement of Oklahoma

The Populists. The collapse of the boom and the falling prices of agricultural products forced many farmers to seek relief through political action. In 1888 and again in 1890 this discontent was expressed through local political groups, commonly known as Farmers' Alliances, which quickly spread through parts of the West and South. The alliances won some local victories and contributed to the discomfiture of the Republicans in 1890. They were not, however, an effective vehicle for concerted political action; and in 1891 the leaders of the alliances organized the Populist (People's) Party.

The Populists aspired to become a national party and hoped to attract support from labour and from reform groups generally. In practice they continued through their brief career to be almost wholly a party of farmers, with a platform tailored to meet the wishes of Western farmers. They demanded an increase in the circulating currency, to be achieved by the unlimited coinage of silver, a graduated income tax, government ownership of the railroads, a tariff for revenue only, the direct election of United States senators, and other measures designed to strengthen political democracy and give the farmers economic parity with business and industry. In 1892 the Populists nominated Gen. James B. Weaver of Iowa for president.

The election of 1892. The nominees of the two major parties for president in 1892 were the same as in the election of 1888. The Republicans reluctantly renominated Harrison, whose personal relations with many party leaders were distinctly cool. Before the Democratic convention there was a spirited struggle for the nomination between Cleveland and Gov. David Hill of New York, but Cleveland had far greater support among rank-and-file Democrats and was nominated on the first ballot.

The unpopularity of the McKinley Tariff gave Cleveland an advantage, as did the discontent in the West, which was directed largely against the Republican Party. From the beginning of the campaign it appeared probable that the Democrats would be successful, and Cleveland carried not only the southern states but such key northern states as New York and Illinois. His electoral vote was 277 to 145 for Harrison. Weaver carried four Western states, three of them states with important silver mines, and received 22 electoral votes.

Cleveland's second term. When Cleveland was inaugurated for his second term in March 1893, the country hovered on the brink of financial panic. Six years of depression in the trans-Mississippi West, the decline of foreign trade after the enactment of the McKinley Tariff, and an abnormally high burden of private debt were disquieting features of the situation. Most attention was centred, however, on the gold reserve in the federal Treasury. It was assumed that a minimum reserve of $100,000,000 was necessary to assure redemption of gov-

The Panic of 1893

ernment obligations in gold. When, on April 21, 1893, the reserve fell below that amount, the psychological impact was far-reaching. Investors hastened to convert their holdings into gold; banks and brokerage houses were hard pressed; and many business houses and financial institutions failed. Prices dropped, employment was curtailed, and the nation entered a period of severe economic depression that continued for more than three years.

The causes of this disaster were numerous and complex, but the attention that focussed on the gold reserve tended to concentrate concern upon a single factor—the restoration of the Treasury's supply of gold. It was widely believed that the principal cause of the drain on the Treasury was the obligation to purchase large amounts of silver. To those who held this view, the obvious remedy was the repeal of the Sherman Silver Purchase Act.

The issue was political as well as economic. It divided both major parties, but most of the leading advocates of existing silver policies were Democrats. Cleveland, however, had long been opposed to the silver purchase policy and in the crisis he resolved upon repeal as an essential step in protecting the Treasury. He therefore called Congress to meet in special session on August 7, 1893.

The new Congress had Democratic majorities in both houses, and, if it had any mandate, it was to repeal the McKinley Tariff. It had no mandate on the silver issue, and more than half of its Democratic members came from constituencies that favoured an increase in the coinage of silver. Cleveland faced a herculean task in forcing repeal through Congress, but, by the use of every power at his command, he gained his objective. The Sherman Silver Purchase Act was repealed at the end of October by a bill that made no compensating provision for the coinage of silver. Cleveland had won a personal triumph, but he had irrevocably divided his party; and in some sections of the nation he had become the most unpopular president of his generation.

Cleveland's splitting of the Democratic Party

The extent to which Cleveland had lost control of his party became apparent when Congress turned from silver to the tariff. The House passed a bill that would have revised tariff rates downward in accordance with the President's views. In the Senate, however, the bill was so altered that it bore little resemblance to the original measure, and on some items it imposed higher duties than had the McKinley Act. It was finally passed in August 1894, but Cleveland was so dissatisfied that he refused to sign it; and it became law without his signature. The act contained a provision for an income tax, but this feature was declared unconstitutional by the Supreme Court in 1895.

In the midterm elections of 1894 the Republicans recaptured control of both houses of Congress. This indicated the discontent produced by the continuing depression. It also guaranteed that, with a Democratic president and Republican Congress, there would be inaction in domestic legislation while both parties looked forward to the election of 1896.

The election of 1896. At their convention in St. Louis the Republicans selected Gov. William McKinley of Ohio as their presidential nominee. He had served in the Federal Army during the Civil War, and his record as governor of Ohio tended to offset his association with the unpopular tariff of 1890. His most effective support in winning the nomination, however, was provided by Mark Hanna, a wealthy Cleveland businessman who was McKinley's closest friend.

The Democratic convention in Chicago was unusually exciting. It was controlled by groups hostile to Cleveland's financial policies, and it took the unprecedented step of rejecting a resolution commending the administration of a president of its own party. The debate on the party platform featured an eloquent defense of agrarian interests by William Jennings Bryan, which won him not only a prolonged ovation but also his party's presidential nomination. Bryan was a former congressman from Nebraska, and at 36 he was the youngest man ever to be the nominee for president of a major party. By experience and conviction he shared the outlook of the agrarian elements that dominated the convention and whose principal spokesman he became.

Bryan conducted a vigorous campaign. For the first time a presidential candidate carried his case to the people in all parts of the country, and for a time it appeared that he might win. The worried conservatives charged that Bryan was a dangerous demagogue, and they interpreted the campaign as a conflict between defenders of a sound economic system that would produce prosperity and dishonest radicals who championed reckless innovations that would undermine the financial security of the nation. On this interpretation they succeeded in raising large campaign funds from industrialists who feared their interests were threatened. With this money, the Republicans were able to turn the tide and win a decisive victory. Outside the South, Bryan carried only the Western silver states and Kansas and Nebraska.

Economic recovery. Soon after taking office on March 4, 1897, McKinley called Congress into special session to revise the tariff once again. Congress responded by passing the Dingley Tariff Act, which eliminated many items from the free list and generally raised duties on imports to the highest level they had yet reached.

Although the preservation of the gold standard had been the chief appeal of the Republicans in 1896, it was not until March 1900 that Congress enacted the Gold Standard Act, which required the Treasury to maintain a minimum gold reserve of $150,000,000 and authorized the issuance of bonds, if necessary, to protect that minimum. In 1900 such a measure was almost anticlimactic, for an adequate gold supply had ceased to be a practical problem. Beginning in 1893, the production of gold in the United States had increased steadily; by 1899 the annual value of gold added to the American supply was double that of any year between 1881 and 1892. The chief source of the new supply of gold was the Klondike, where important deposits of gold had been discovered during the summer of 1896.

Increase in gold production

By 1898 the depression had run its course; farm prices and the volume of farm exports were again rising steadily, and Western farmers appeared to forget their recent troubles and to regain confidence in their economic prospects. In industry, the return of prosperity was marked by a resumption of the move toward more industrial combinations, despite the antitrust law; and great banking houses, such as J.P. Morgan and Company of New York, played a key role in many of the most important of these combinations by providing the necessary capital and receiving, in return, an influential voice in the management of the companies created by this capital.   (H.W.Br.)

VI. Imperialism, the Progressive Era, and the rise to world power, 1896–1920

AMERICAN IMPERIALISM

The Spanish–American War. Militarily speaking, the Spanish–American War of 1898 was so brief and relatively bloodless as to have been a mere passing episode in the history of modern warfare. Its political and diplomatic consequences, however, were enormous: it catapulted the United States into the arena of world politics and set it, at least briefly, on the new road of imperialism. To be sure, specific events drove the United States to hostilities in 1898; but the stage had already been set by profound changes in thought about the nation's mission and its destiny.

The United States in world politics

Before the 1890s, roughly speaking, most Americans had adhered stubbornly to the belief, as old as the Revolution itself, that their country should remain aloof from European affairs and offer an example of democracy and peace to the rest of the world; but slowly in the 1880s, and more rapidly in the 1890s, new currents of thought eroded this historic conviction. The United States had become a great power by virtue of its prodigious economic growth since the Civil War; numerous publicists said that it ought to begin to act like one. Propagandists of sea power argued that future national security and greatness depended upon a large navy supported by bases throughout the world. After the disappearance of the American frontier in 1890, the conviction grew that the United States would have to find new outlets for an ever-increasing population and agricultural and industrial production; this belief was particularly rife among farmers in dire distress in the 1890s. Social Darwinists said that the world is a jungle, with international rivalries inevitable, and that only strong nations could survive. Added to these arguments were those of idealists and religious leaders that Americans had a duty to "take up the white man's burden" and carry their assertedly superior culture and the blessings of Christianity to backward peoples of the world.

It was against this background that the events of 1898 propelled the United States along the road to war and empire. Cuban rebels had begun a violent revolution against Spanish rule in 1895, set off by a depression caused by a decline in U.S. sugar purchases from Cuba. Rebel violence led progressively to more repressive Spanish countermeasures. Cuban refugees in the United States spread exaggerated tales of Spanish atrocities, and these and numerous others were reprinted widely (particularly by William Randolph Hearst's New York *American* and Joseph Pulitzer's New York *World*, then engaged in a fierce battle for circulation). Pres. Grover Cleveland resisted the rising public demand for intervention, until by early 1898 the pressure, now on his successor, William McKinley, was too great to be defied. When an explosion —caused by a submarine mine, according to a U.S. naval court of inquiry—sank the USS "Maine" with large loss of life in Havana Harbour on February 15, 1898, events moved beyond the President's control. Though Spain was willing to make large concessions to avoid war, it adamantly resisted what had become the minimum public and official U.S. demand—complete Spanish withdrawal from Cuba and recognition of the island's independence. Hence Congress in mid-April authorized the President to use the armed forces to expel the Spanish from Cuba.

War with Spain

For Americans it was, as Theodore Roosevelt, lieutenant colonel of a volunteer regiment called the "Rough Riders," put it, "a splendid little war." An American expeditionary force, after quickly overcoming the Spaniards in Cuba, turned next against Spain's last island in the Caribbean, Puerto Rico. Meanwhile, on May 1, 1898, the American commodore George Dewey, with his Asiatic squadron, destroyed a decrepit Spanish flotilla in the Harbour of Manila in the Philippine Islands.

The fighting was over by August 12, when the United States and Spain signed a preliminary peace treaty in Washington, D.C. Negotiators met in Paris in October to draw up a definitive agreement. Spain recognized the independence of Cuba and ceded Puerto Rico to the United States, but the disposition of the Philippines was another matter. Business interests in the United States, which had been noticeably cool about a war over Cuba, demanded the acquisition of the entire Philippine Archipelago in the hope that Manila would become the base for a great Far Eastern trade; chauvinists declaimed against lowering the flag under Spanish pressure. Concluding that he had no alternative, McKinley forced the Spanish to "sell" the Philippines to the United States for $20,000,000.

But a strong reaction in the United States against acquisition of the Philippines had already set in by the time the Treaty of Paris was signed on December 10, 1898; and anti-imperialists declared that the control and governance of distant alien peoples violated all American traditions of self-determination and would even threaten the very fabric of the republic. Though there were more than enough votes in the Senate to defeat the treaty, that body gave its consent to ratification largely because William Jennings Bryan, the Democratic leader, wanted Democrats to approve the treaty and then make imperialism the chief issue of the 1900 presidential campaign.

The new American empire. McKinley easily defeated Bryan in 1900. The victory, however, was hardly a mandate for imperialism, and, as events were soon to disclose, the American people were perhaps the most reluctant imperialists in history. No sooner had they acquired an overseas empire than they set in motion the processes of its dissolution or transformation.

By the so-called Teller Amendment to the war resolution, Congress had declared that the United States would not annex Cuba. This pledge was kept, although Cuba was forced in 1903 to sign a treaty making it virtually a protectorate of the United States. The Hawaiian Islands, annexed by Congress on July 7, 1898, were made a territory in 1900 and were hence, technically, only briefly part of the American empire. Puerto Rico was given limited self-government in 1900; and the Jones Act of 1917 conferred full territorial status on the island, gave American citizenship to its inhabitants, and limited its self-government only by the veto of a governor appointed by the president of the United States. Establishing any kind of government in the Philippines was much more difficult because a large band of Filipinos resisted American rule as bravely as they had fought the Spanish. The Philippine insurrection was over by 1901, however, and the Philippine Government Act of 1902 inaugurated the beginning of partial self-government, which was transformed into almost complete home rule by the Jones Act of 1916.

The Open Door in the Far East. Although Americans were reluctant imperialists, the United States was an important Pacific power after 1898, and American businessmen had inflated ambitions to tap what they thought was the enormous Chinese market. The doors to that market were being rapidly closed in the 1890s, however, as Britain, France, Russia, and Japan carved out large so-called spheres of influence all the way from Manchuria to southern China. With Britain's support (the British stood to gain the most from equal trade opportunities), on September 6, 1899, Secretary of State John Hay addressed the first so-called Open Door note to the powers with interests in China; it asked them to accord equal trade and investment opportunities to all nationals in their spheres of interest and leased territories. With considerable bravado, Hay announced that all the powers had agreed to respect the Open Door, even though the Russians had declined to give any pledges. On July 3, 1900, after the Boxer Rebellion—an uprising in China against foreign influence—Hay circulated a second Open Door note announcing that it was American policy to preserve Chinese territorial and political integrity.

Such pronouncements had little effect because the United States was not prepared to support the Open Door Policy with force; successive administrations to the 1940s, however, considered it the cornerstone of their Far Eastern policy. Pres. Theodore Roosevelt reluctantly mediated the Russo-Japanese War in 1905 in part to protect the Open Door as well as to maintain a balance of power in the Far East. When Japan attempted in 1915 to force a virtual protectorate on China, Pres. Woodrow Wilson intervened sternly and in large measure successfully to protect Chinese independence. Victory for American policy seemed to come with the Nine-Power Treaty of Washington of 1922, when all nations with interests in China promised to respect the Open Door.

Building the Panama Canal and American domination of the Caribbean area. Strategic necessity and the desire of eastern businessmen to have easy access to Pacific markets combined in the late 1890s to convince the President, Congress, and a vast majority of Americans that an isthmian canal linking the Atlantic and Pacific oceans was vital to national security and prosperity. In the Hay–Pauncefote Treaty of 1901, the British government gave up the rights to joint construction with the United States that it had gained under the Clayton–Bulwer Treaty of 1850. A French company, which had tried unsuccessfully to dig a canal across the Isthmus of Panama, was eager to sell its right of way to the United States. Thus, the only obstacle to the project was the government of Colombia, which owned Panama. When Colombia refused to cooperate, Roosevelt, in 1903, covertly supported a Panamanian revolution engineered by officials of the French company. A treaty was quickly negotiated between the United States and the new Republic of Panama; construction began, and the canal was opened to shipping in January 1914.

Acquisition of Panama

Concern over what Americans regarded increasingly as their "lifeline" increased in proportion to progress in the construction of the canal. An early manifestation of that concern came in 1902–03, when Britain, Germany, and Italy blockaded Venezuela to force the payment of debts, and particularly when the Germans bombarded and destroyed a Venezuelan town; so agitated was American opinion that Roosevelt used a veiled threat to force Germany to accept arbitration of the debt question by the Hague Court. When the Dominican Republic defaulted on its foreign debt to several European countries in 1904, Roosevelt quickly established an American receivership of the Dominican customs in order to collect the revenues to meet the country's debt payments. Moreover, in his annual message to Congress of 1904, the President announced a new Latin American policy, soon called the Roosevelt Corollary to the Monroe Doctrine—because the Monroe Doctrine forbade European use of force in the New World, the United States would itself take whatever action necessary to guarantee that Latin American states gave no cause for such European intervention. It was, in fact, a considerable extension of the Monroe Doctrine, not a correct historical interpretation of it; but it remained the cornerstone of American policy in the Caribbean at least until 1928.

Actually, Roosevelt was reluctant to interfere in the domestic affairs of neighbouring states; his one significant intervention after 1904—the administration of the Cuban government from 1906 to 1909—was undertaken in order to prevent civil war and at the insistence of Cuban authorities. Roosevelt's successor, however, William Howard Taft, had more ambitious plans to guarantee American hegemony in the approaches to the Panama Canal. Adopting a policy called Dollar Diplomacy, Taft hoped to persuade American private bankers to displace European creditors in the Caribbean area and thereby to increase American influence and encourage stability in countries prone to revolution. Dollar Diplomacy was a total failure; its one result was to involve the United States in a civil war in Nicaragua with the effect of perpetuating a reactionary and unpopular regime.

Dollar Diplomacy

The accession of Woodrow Wilson in 1913 seemed to augur the beginning of a new era in Latin American relations; the new president and his secretary of state, William J. Bryan, were idealists who had strongly condemned interventions and Dollar Diplomacy. But although Wilson did negotiate a treaty with Colombia to make reparation for U.S. complicity in the Panamanian revolution, it was defeated by the Senate. Moreover, Wilson tried hard to promote a Pan-American nonaggression pact; but it foundered on the opposition of certain Latin American governments.

When crises threatened the domestic stability of the Caribbean area, however, Wilson revealed that he was just as determined to protect American security as Roosevelt and Taft had been and that he was perhaps even more willing to use force. Frequent revolutions and the fear of European intervention led Wilson to impose a protectorate and a puppet government upon Haiti in 1915 and a military occupation of the Dominican Republic in 1916. He concluded a treaty with Nicaragua making that country a protectorate of the United States. Moreover, he purchased the Danish Virgin Islands in 1916 at the inflated price of $25,000,000 in order to prevent their possible transfer from Denmark to Germany.

THE PROGRESSIVE ERA

The character and variety of the Progressive movement. The inauguration of Pres. William McKinley in 1897 had seemed to mark the end of an era of domestic turmoil and the beginning of a new period of unparalleled tranquility. Prosperity was returning after the devastating Panic of 1893. The agrarian uprising led by Bryan in the election of 1896 had been turned back, and the national government was securely in the hands of friends of big business. The Dingley Tariff of 1897 greatly increased tariff rates; the Gold Standard Act of 1897 dashed the hopes of advocates of the free coinage of silver; and McKinley did nothing to stop a series of industrial combinations in defiance of the Sherman Anti-Trust Act.

Origins of Progressivism. Never were superficial signs more deceiving than during McKinley's first term. Actually, the United States already was in the first stages of what historians came to call the Progressive Movement.

Generally speaking, Progressivism was the response of various groups to problems raised by the rapid industrialization and urbanization that followed the Civil War. These problems included the spread of slums and poverty; the exploitation of labour; the breakdown of democratic government in the cities and states caused by the emergence of political organizations, or machines, allied with business interests; and a rapid movement toward financial and industrial concentration. Many Americans feared that their historic traditions of responsible democratic government and free economic opportunity for all were being destroyed by gigantic combinations of economic and political power.

Problems of industrialization and urbanization

Actually there was not, either in the 1890s or later, any one Progressive movement. There were numerous movements for reform and reconstruction on the local, state, and national levels that were too diverse, and sometimes too mutually antagonistic, ever to coalesce into a national crusade. But they were generally motivated by common assumptions and goals—*e.g.*, the repudiation of individualism and laissez-faire, concern for the underprivileged and downtrodden, the restoration of government to the rank and file, and the enlargement of governmental power in order to bring industry and finance under a measure of popular control.

The origins of Progressivism were as complex and are as difficult to describe as the movement itself. In the vanguard were various agrarian crusades, such as the Grangers and the Populists and Democrats under Bryan, with their demands for stringent railroad regulation and national control of banks and the money supply. At the same time a new generation of economists, sociologists, and political scientists was undermining the philosophical foundations of the laissez-faire state and constructing a new ideology to justify democratic collectivism; and a new school of social workers was establishing settlement houses and going into the slums to discover the extent of human degradation. Allied with them was a growing body of ministers, priests, and rabbis—proponents of what was called the Social Gospel—who struggled to arouse the social concerns and consciences of their parishioners. Finally, journalists called "muckrakers" probed into all the dark corners of American life and carried their message of reform through mass-circulation newspapers and magazines.

Two specific catalytic agents set off the Progressive movement—the agrarian depression of the early 1890s and the financial and industrial depression that began in 1893. Low prices drove farmers by the hundreds of thousands into the radical People's Party of 1892. Widespread suffering in the cities beginning in 1893 caused a breakdown of many social services and dramatized for the increasing number of urban middle class Americans the wide contrast between rich and poor.

Depressions of the early 1890s

Urban reforms. A movement already begun, to wrest control of city governments from corrupt political machines, was given tremendous impetus by the Panic of 1893. The National Municipal League, organized in 1894, united various city reform groups throughout the country; corrupt local governments were overthrown in such cities as New York in 1894, Baltimore in 1895, and Chicago in 1896–97. And so it went all over the country well into the 20th century.

Despite differences among urban reformers at the beginning of their movement, by the early 1900s the vast majority of them were fighting for and winning much the same objectives—more equitable taxation of railroad and corporate property, tenement house reform, better schools, and expanded social services for the poor. Even big-city machines like Tammany Hall became increasingly sensitive to the social and economic needs of their constituents. Reformers also devised new forms of city government to replace the old mayor–city-council arrangement that had proved to be so susceptible to corrupt influences. One was the commission form, which vested all responsibility in a small group of commissioners, each responsible for a single department; another was the city-manager form, which provided administration by a professionally trained expert, responsible to a popularly elected council (these two forms were in widespread use in small and medium-sized cities by 1916).

Reform in state governments. The reform movement spread almost at once to the state level, for it was in state capitals that important decisions affecting the cities were made. Entrenched and very professional political organizations, generously financed by officeholders and businessmen wanting special privileges, controlled most state governments in the late 1890s; everywhere, these organizations were challenged by a rising generation of young and idealistic anti-organization leaders, ambitious for power. They were most successful in the Middle West, under such leaders as Robert M. La Follette of Wisconsin; but they had counterparts all over the country—*e.g.*, Charles Evans Hughes of New York, Woodrow Wilson of New Jersey, Andrew J. Montague of Virginia, and Hiram W. Johnson of California.

Anti-organizational leaders

These young leaders revolutionized the art and practice of politics in the United States, not only by exercising strong leadership but also by effecting institutional changes such as the direct primary, direct election of senators (rather than by state legislatures), the initiative, referendum, and recall—which helped restore and revitalized political democracy. More important, perhaps, progressives to a large degree achieved their economic and social objectives—among them, strict regulation of intrastate railroads and public utilities, legislation to prevent child labour and to protect women workers, penal reform, expanded charitable services to the poor, and accident insurance systems to provide compensation to workers and their families.

Theodore Roosevelt and the Progressive movement. By 1901 the reform upheaval was too strong to be contained within state boundaries. Moreover, certain problems cried out for solution, with which only the federal government was apparently competent to deal. McKinley might have succeeded in ignoring the rising tide of public opinion, had he served out his second term. But McKinley's assassination in September 1901 brought to the presidency an entirely different kind of man—Theodore Roosevelt, at age 42 the youngest man yet to enter the White House. Roosevelt had broad democratic sympathies; moreover, thanks to his experience as police commissioner of New York City and governor of New York State, he was the first president to have an intimate knowledge of modern urban problems. Because Congress was securely controlled by a group of archconservative Republicans, the new president had to feel his way cautiously in legislative matters; but he emerged full-grown as a tribune of the people after his triumph in the presidential election of 1904. By 1906 he was the undisputed spokesman of national Progressivism and by far its best publicity agent. (The White House was, he said, "a bully pulpit.") Meanwhile, by his leadership of public opinion and by acting as a spur on Congress, he had revived the presidency and made it incomparably the most powerful force in national politics.

In 1901 Americans were perhaps most alarmed about the spread of so-called trusts, or industrial combinations, which they thought were responsible for the steady price increases that had occurred each year since 1897. Ever alert to the winds of public opinion, Roosevelt responded by activating the Sherman Anti-Trust Act of 1890, which had lain dormant because of Cleveland's and McKinley's refusal to enforce it and also because of the Supreme Court's ruling of 1895 that the measure did not apply to combinations in manufacturing. Beginning in 1902 with a suit to dissolve a northwestern railroad monopoly, Roosevelt moved next against the so-called Beef Trust, then against the oil, tobacco, and other monopolies. In every case the Supreme Court supported the administration, going so far in the oil and tobacco decisions of 1911 as to reverse its 1895 decision. In addition, in 1903 Roosevelt persuaded a reluctant Congress to establish a Bureau of Corporations with sweeping power to investigate business practices; the bureau's thoroughgoing reports were of immense assistance in antitrust cases. While establishing the supremacy of the federal government in the industrial field, Roosevelt, in 1902, also took action unprecedented in the history of the presidency by intervening on labour's behalf to force the arbitration of a strike by the United Mine Workers of America against the Pennsylvania anthracite coal operators.

The breaking of the trusts

Roosevelt moved much more aggressively after his 1904 election. Public demand for effective national regulation of interstate railroad rates had been growing since the Supreme Court had emasculated the Interstate Commerce Commission's (ICC) rate-making authority in the 1880s. Determined to bring the railroads—the country's single greatest private economic interest—under effective national control, Roosevelt waged an unrelenting battle with Congress in 1905–06. The outcome—the Hepburn Act of 1906—was his own personal triumph; it greatly enlarged the ICC's jurisdiction and forbade railroads to increase rates without its approval. By using the same tactics of aggressive leadership, Roosevelt in 1906 also obtained passage of a Meat Inspection Act and a Pure Food and Drug Act. Passage of the former was aided by the publication of Upton Sinclair's famous novel, *The Jungle* (1906), which revealed in gory detail the insanitary conditions of the Chicago stockyards and packing plants.

Meanwhile, almost from his accession to the presidency, Roosevelt had been carrying on a crusade, often independent of Congress, to conserve the nation's fast-dwindling natural resources and to make them available for exploitation under rigorous national supervision. He withdrew from the public domain some 148,000,000 acres of forest lands, 80,000,000 acres of mineral lands, and 1,500,000 acres of water-power sites. Moreover, adoption of the National Reclamation Act of 1902 made possible the beginning of an ambitious federal program of irrigation and hydroelectric development in the West.

Republican troubles under Taft. Roosevelt was so much the idol of the masses of 1908 that he could have easily gained the Republican nomination in that year. After his election in 1904, however, he had announced that he would not be a candidate four years later; adhering stubbornly to his pledge, he arranged the nomination of his secretary of war, William Howard Taft of Ohio, who easily defeated Bryan.

Taft might have made an ideal president during a time of domestic tranquility, but his tenure in the White House was far from peaceful. National progressivism was nearly at high tide; and a large group of Republican progressives, called "insurgents," sat in both houses of Congress.

The high tide of Progressivism

The Republican insurgents. These Republicans, like a majority of Americans, demanded such reforms as tariff reductions, an income tax, the direct election of senators, and even stricter railroad and corporation regulations. Taft, who had strongly supported Roosevelt's policies, thought of himself as a progressive. Actually he was temperamentally and philosophically a conservative; moreover, he lacked the qualities of a dynamic popular leader. In the circumstances, his ineptness, indecision, and failure to lead could only spell disaster for his party.

Taft's troubles began when he called Congress into special session in 1909 to take up the first item on his agenda—tariff reform. The measure that emerged from Congress actually increased rates. Republican insurgents and a majority of Americans were outraged, but Taft signed the bill and called it the best tariff law that the Republican Party had ever enacted.

By 1910 the Republican insurgents were clearly in the ascendancy in the Congress. Taking control of the President's railroad-regulation measure they added new provisions that greatly enlarged the ICC's authority. The following year they bitterly opposed Taft's measure for tariff reciprocity with Canada; it passed with Democratic support in Congress, only to go down to defeat at the hands of the Canadian electorate.

The 1912 election. Republican insurgents were determined to prevent Taft's renomination in 1912. They found their leader in Roosevelt, who had become increasingly alienated from Taft and who made a whirlwind campaign for the presidential nomination in the winter and spring of 1912. Roosevelt swept the presidential primaries, even in Taft's own state of Ohio; but

Taft and conservative Republicans controlled the powerful state organizations and the Republican National Committee and were able to nominate Taft by a narrow margin. Convinced that the bosses had stolen the nomination from him, Roosevelt led his followers out of the Republican convention. In August they organized the Progressive Party at Chicago and named Roosevelt to lead the third-party cause.

Democrats had swept the 1910 congressional and gubernatorial elections; and after the disruption of the Republican Party in the spring of 1912, it was obvious that almost any passable Democrat could win the presidency in that year. Woodrow Wilson, former president of Princeton University, who had made a brilliant progressive record as governor of New Jersey, was nominated by the Democrats on the 46th ballot.

Taft's single objective in the 1912 campaign was to defeat Roosevelt. The real contest was between Roosevelt and Wilson for control of the progressive majority. Campaigning strenuously on a platform that he called the New Nationalism, Roosevelt demanded effective control of big business through a strong federal commission, radical tax reform, and a whole series of measures to put the federal government squarely into the business of social and economic reform. By contrast Wilson seemed conservative with a program he called the New Freedom; it envisaged a concerted effort to destroy monopoly and to open the doors of economic opportunity to small businessmen through drastic tariff reduction, banking reform, and severe tightening of the antitrust laws. Roosevelt outpolled Taft in the election, but he failed to win many Democratic progressives away from Wilson, who won by a huge majority of electoral votes, though receiving only about 42 percent of the popular vote.

The New Freedom and its transformation. A trained political scientist and historian, Wilson believed that the president should be the leader of public opinion, the chief formulator of legislative policy, and virtually sovereign in the conduct of foreign relations. With the support of an aroused public opinion and a compliant Democratic majority, he was able to put his theories of leadership into effect with spectacular success.

Wilson's domestic program

The first item in Wilson's program was tariff reform, a perennial Democratic objective since the Civil War; the President's measure, the Underwood Tariff Act of 1913, reduced average rates from 40 percent to 25 percent, greatly enlarged the free list, and included a modest income tax. Next came adoption of the President's measure for banking and monetary reform, the Federal Reserve Act of 1913, which created a federal reserve system to mobilize banking reserves and issue a flexible new currency—federal reserve notes—based on gold and commercial paper; uniting and supervising the entire system was a federal reserve board of presidential appointees.

The third, and Wilson thought the last, part of the New Freedom program was antitrust reform. In his first significant movement toward Roosevelt's New Nationalism, Wilson reversed his position that merely strengthening the Sherman Anti-Trust Act would suffice to prevent monopoly. Instead, he took up and pushed through Congress the Progressive-sponsored Federal Trade Commission Act of 1914. It established an agency—the Federal Trade Commission (FTC)—with sweeping authority to prevent business practices that would lead to monopoly. Meanwhile, Wilson had abandoned his original measure, the Clayton Anti-Trust Bill passed by Congress in 1914; its severe provisions against interlocking directorates and practices tending toward monopoly had been gravely weakened by the time the President signed it. The Clayton Bill included a declaration that labour unions, as such, were not to be construed as conspiracies in restraint of trade in violation of the antitrust laws; but what organized labour wanted, and did not get, was immunity from prosecution for such measures as the sympathetic strike and the secondary boycott, which the courts had proscribed as violations of the Sherman Act.

In a public letter in November 1914, the President announced that his reform program was complete. But various groups were still demanding the advanced kind of social and economic legislation that Roosevelt had advocated in 1912; also, by early 1916 the Progressive Party had largely disintegrated, and Wilson knew that he could win re-election only with the support of a substantial minority of Roosevelt's former followers. Consequently —and also because his own political thinking had been moving toward a more advanced progressive position— Wilson struck out upon a new political course in 1916. He began by appointing Louis D. Brandeis, the leading critic of big business and finance, to the Supreme Court. Then in quick succession he obtained passage of a rural-credits measure to supply cheap long-term credit to farmers; anti-child-labour and federal workmen's-compensation legislation; the Adamson Act, establishing the eight-hour day for interstate railroad workers; and measures for federal aid to education and highway construction. With such a program behind him, Wilson was able to rally a new coalition of Democrats, former Progressives, independents, social workers, and a large minority of Socialists; and he narrowly defeated his Republican opponent, Charles Evans Hughes, in the 1916 presidential election.

THE RISE TO WORLD POWER

Wilson and the Mexican revolution. Although Wilson's consuming interest was in domestic politics, he had to deal primarily with foreign affairs while in the White House; and before the end of his presidency he had developed into a diplomatist of great skill as well as one of the commanding figures in world affairs. He was a "strong" president in the conduct of foreign policy, writing most of the important diplomatic correspondence of his government and making all important decisions himself. He usually worked well with his secretaries of state, Bryan and Robert Lansing, and often relied for advice upon his confidential counsellor, Col. Edward M. House of Texas.

Wilson's conduct of foreign affairs

Wilson served his apprenticeship by having to deal at the outset of his administration with an uprising in Mexico, set off when a military usurper, Victoriano Huerta, murdered liberal president Francisco Madero and seized the executive power in February 1913. It was difficult for the United States to remain aloof because Americans had invested heavily in Mexico and 40,000 American citizens resided there.

If Wilson had followed conventional policy and the urgings of Americans with interests in Mexico, he would have recognized Huerta (as most European governments did), who promised to respect and protect all foreign investments and concessions. But Wilson was revolted by Huerta's bloody rise to power; moreover, he believed that the revolution begun by Madero in 1910 was a glorious episode in the history of human liberty. Wilson thus not only refused to recognize Huerta but also tried to persuade the dictator to step down from office and permit the holding of free elections for a new democratic government. When Huerta refused to cooperate, Wilson gave open support to the Constitutionalists—Huerta's opponents under Madero's successor, Venustiano Carranza— and when it seemed that the Constitutionalists could not themselves drive Huerta from power, Wilson seized the port of Veracruz in April 1914 to cut off Huerta's supplies and revenues. This stratagem succeeded, and Carranza and his army occupied Mexico City in August.

The revolutionary forces then divided between Carranza's followers and those of his chief rival and most colorful general, Pancho Villa; and civil war raged for another year. Wilson refused to interfere; Carranza emerged victoriously by the summer of 1915, and Wilson accorded him de facto recognition in October. But Villa, seeking to provoke war between the United States and Mexico, raided Columbus, New Mexico, on March 9, 1916, burning the town and killing 19 inhabitants. Wilson sent a punitive expedition under Gen. John J. Pershing into Mexico in hot pursuit of Villa; but the wily bandit eluded Pershing, and the deeper the Americans penetrated into Mexican territory, the more agitated the Carranza government became. There were two serious skirmishes between regular Mexican and American troops in the spring, and full-scale war was averted only when Wilson withdrew Pershing's column some months later. Relations between the two governments were greatly improved when Wilson extended de jure recognition to Carranza's new constitutional regime in April 1917. Thereafter, Wilson adamantly rejected all further foreign and American suggestions for intervention in Mexico.

The struggle for neutrality. The outbreak of general war in Europe in August 1914 raised grave challenges to Wilson's skill and leadership in foreign affairs. In spite of the appeals of propagandists for the rival Allies and Central Powers, the great majority of Americans were doggedly neutral and determined to avoid involvement unless American rights and interests were violated. This, too, was Wilson's own feeling, and in August he issued an official proclamation of neutrality and two weeks later appealed to Americans to be "impartial in thought as well as in action."

Loans and supplies for the Allies. Difficulties arose first with the British government, which at once used its vast fleet to establish a long-range blockade of Germany. The U.S. State Department sent several strong protests to London, particularly against British suppression of American exports of food and raw materials to Germany. Anglo-American blockade controversies were not acute, however, because the British put their blockade controls into effect gradually, always paid for goods seized, argued persuasively that in a total war food and raw materials were as essential as guns and ammunition, and pointed out that they, the British, were simply following blockade precedents established by the United States itself during the Civil War. As a result of a tacit Anglo-American agreement, the United States soon became the chief external source of supply for the food, raw materials, and munitions that fed the British and French war machines. In addition, and in accordance with the strict rules of neutrality, the Wilson administration permitted the Allied governments to borrow more than $2,000,000,000 in the United States in order to finance the war trade. At the same time, the President resisted all efforts by German Americans for an arms embargo on the ground that such a measure would be grossly unneutral toward the Allies.

German submarine warfare. There was no possibility of conflict between Germany and the United States so long as the former confined its warfare to the continent of Europe; a new situation full of potential danger arose, however, when the German authorities decided to use a new weapon, the submarine, to challenge British control of the seas. The German admiralty announced in February 1915 that all Allied vessels would be torpedoed without warning in a broad area and that even neutral vessels were not safe. Wilson replied at once that he would hold Germany to "strict accountability" if submarines destroyed American ships and lives without warning. The Germans soon gave broad guarantees concerning American ships, and their safety against illegal submarine attacks was not an issue between the two countries before 1917.

An issue much more fraught with danger was the safety of Americans travelling and working on Allied ships. A German submarine sank the unarmed British liner "Lusitania" without warning on May 7, 1915, killing, among others, 128 Americans. Wilson at first appealed to the Germans on broad grounds of humanity to abandon submarine warfare, but in the subsequent negotiations he narrowed the issue to one of safety for unarmed passenger liners against violent underseas attack. Momentary resolution came when a submarine sank the unarmed British liner "Arabic" in August. Wilson warned that he would break diplomatic relations if such attacks continued, and the Germans grudgingly promised not to attack unarmed passenger ships without warning. The controversy escalated to a more dangerous level when a submarine torpedoed the packet steamer "Sussex" in the English Channel with heavy loss of life in March 1916. In an ultimatum to Berlin, Wilson threatened to break diplomatic relations if the Germans did not cease attacking liners and merchantmen without warning; once again the Germans capitulated, but they threatened to resume unrestricted submarine warfare if the United States failed to force the British to observe international law in their blockade practices.

The Allies complicated the submarine controversy in late 1915 by arming many of their liners and merchantmen sailing to American ports. Wilson tried to arrange a compromise by which the Allies would disarm their ships in return for a German promise not to sink them without warning. When the British rejected the proposal, the President gave the impression that he would hold Germany accountable for American lives lost on armed ships, setting off a rebellion in Congress and the near passage of resolutions forbidding American citizens to travel on armed ships. Actually, the President had no intention of permitting armed ships to become a serious issue; their status was never a subject of serious controversy between the United States and Germany.

Arming for war. Meanwhile, the increasingly perilous state of relations with Germany had prompted Wilson, in December 1915, to call for a considerable expansion in the nation's armed forces. A violent controversy over preparedness ensued, both in Congress and in the country at large. The army legislation of 1916 was a compromise, with Wilson obtaining only a modest increase in the army and a strengthening of the National Guard; but the Naval Appropriations Act of 1916 provided for more ships than the administration had requested.

The United States enters the war. Wilson's most passionate desire, aside from avoiding belligerency, was to bring an end to the war through his personal mediation. He sent Colonel House to Europe in early 1915 to explore the possibilities of peace and again early in 1916 to press for a plan of Anglo-American cooperation for peace. The British refused to cooperate, and the President, more than ever eager to avoid a final confrontation with Germany on the submarine issue, decided to press forward with independent mediation. He was by this time also irritated by the intensification of British blockade practices and convinced that both sides were fighting for domination and spoils. On December 18, 1916, Wilson asked the belligerents to state the terms upon which they would be willing to make peace. Soon afterward, in secret, high-level negotiations, he appealed to Britain and Germany to hold an early peace conference under his direction.

Break with Germany. Chances for peace were blasted by a decision of the German leaders, made at an imperial conference on January 9, 1917, to inaugurate an all-out submarine war against all commerce, neutral as well as belligerent. The Germans knew that such a campaign would almost certainly bring the United States into the war; but they were confident that their augmented submarine fleet could starve Britain into submission before the U.S. could mobilize and participate effectively.

The announcement of the new submarine blockade in January left the President no alternative but to break diplomatic relations with Germany, which he did on February 3. At the same time, and in subsequent addresses, the President made it clear that he would accept unrestricted submarine warfare against belligerent merchantmen and would act only if American ships were sunk. In early March he put arms on American ships in the hope that this would deter submarine attacks. The Germans began to sink American ships indiscriminately in mid-March; and Wilson, on April 2, asked Congress to recognize that a state of war existed between the United States and the German empire. Congress approved the war resolution quickly, and Wilson signed it on April 6.

Mobilization. Generally speaking, the efforts at mobilization went through two stages. During the first, lasting roughly from April to December 1917, the administration relied mainly on voluntary and cooperative efforts. During the second stage, after December 1917, the government moved rapidly to establish complete control over every important phase of economic life. Railroads were nationalized; a war industries board established ironclad controls over industry; food and fuel were strictly rationed; an emergency-fleet corporation began construction of a vast merchant fleet; and a war labour board used coercive measures to prevent strikes. Opposition to

Margin notes:

Outbreak of World War I

The sinking of unarmed ships

Wilson's attempts to achieve peace

Government controls during the war

the war was sternly suppressed under the Espionage Act of 1917 and the even severer Sedition Act of 1918. By the spring of 1918, the American people and their economy had been harnessed for total war (a near miracle, considering the lack of preparedness only a year before).

America's role in the war.   The American military contribution, while small compared to that of the Allies during the entire war, was in two respects decisive in the outcome. The United States Navy, fully prepared at the outset, provided the ships that helped the British overcome the submarine threat by the autumn of 1917. The United States Army, some 4,000,000 men strong, was raised mainly by conscription under the Selective Service Act of 1917; the American Expeditionary Force of more than 1,200,000 men under General Pershing reached France by September 1918, and this huge infusion of manpower tipped the balance on the western front and helped to end the war in November 1918, a year earlier than military planners had anticipated.

Wilson's vision of a new world order.   In one of the most ambitious rhetorical efforts in modern history, President Wilson attempted to rally the people of the world in a movement for a peace settlement that would remove the causes of future wars and establish machinery to maintain peace. In an address to the Senate on January 22, 1917, he called for a "peace without victory" to be enforced by a league of nations that the United States would join and strongly support. He reiterated this program in his war message, adding that the United States wanted above all else to "make the world safe for democracy." And when he failed to persuade the British and French leaders to join him in issuing a common statement of war aims, he went to Congress on January 8, 1918, to make, in his Fourteen Points Address, his definitive avowal to the American people and the world.

Wilson's Fourteen Points

In his general points Wilson demanded an end to the old diplomacy that had led to wars in the past. He proposed open diplomacy instead of entangling alliances, and he called for freedom of the seas, an impartial settlement of colonial claims, general disarmament, removal of artificial trade barriers, and, most important, a league of nations to promote peace and protect the territorial integrity and independence of its members. On specific issues he demanded, among other things, the restoration of a Belgium ravaged by the Germans; sympathetic treatment of the Russians, then involved in a civil war; establishment of an independent Poland; the return of Alsace-Lorraine to France; and autonomy or self-determination for the subject peoples of the Austro-Hungarian and Ottoman empires. A breathtaking pronouncement, the Fourteen Points gave new hope to millions of liberals and moderate socialists who were fighting for a new international order based upon peace and justice.

The Paris Peace Conference and the Versailles Treaty.   With their armies reeling under the weight of a combined allied and American assault, the Germans appealed to Wilson in October 1918 for an armistice based on the Fourteen Points and other presidential pronouncements. The Allies agreed to conclude peace on this basis, except that the British entered a reservation about freedom of the seas, and Wilson agreed to an Anglo-French demand that the Germans be required to make reparation for damages to civilian property.

Wilson led the American delegation and a large group of experts to the peace conference, which opened in Paris in January 1919. He fought heroically for his Fourteen Points against the Allied leaders—David Lloyd George of Britain, Georges Clemenceau of France, and Vittorio Orlando of Italy—who, under heavy pressure from their own constituencies, were determined to divide the territories of the vanquished and make Germany pay the full cost of the war. Wilson made a number of compromises that violated the spirit if not the letter of the Fourteen Points, including the imposition of a potentially astronomical reparations bill upon Germany. Moreover, the Allies had intervened in the Russian Civil War against the dominant revolutionary Socialist faction, the Bolsheviks; and Wilson had halfheartedly cooperated with the Allies by dispatching small numbers of troops to northern Rus-

sia, to protect military supplies against the advancing Germans, and to Siberia, mainly to keep an eye on the Japanese, who had sent a large force there. But Wilson won many more of his Fourteen Points than he lost; his greatest victories were to prevent the dismemberment of Germany in the west and further intervention in Russia and, most important, to obtain the incorporation of the Covenant of the League of Nations into the Versailles Treaty. He was confident that the League, under American leadership, would soon rectify the injustices of the treaty.

The League of Nations

The fight over the treaty and the election of 1920.   Public opinion in the United States seemed strongly in favour of quick ratification of the Versailles Treaty when the President presented that document to the Senate in July 1919. But traditional isolationist sentiment was beginning to revive, and a group of 16 senators, irreconcilably opposed to American membership in the League, vowed to oppose the treaty to the bitter end; but they were a small minority, helpless by themselves. A crucial controversy developed between the President and a majority of the Republican senators, led by Henry Cabot Lodge of Massachusetts. Lodge insisted upon adding 14 reservations to the treaty; the second reservation declared that the United States assumed no obligations under Article X of the Covenant, which guaranteed the integrity and independence of members of the League, and moreover it said that the president could not use the armed forces to support the Covenant without the explicit consent of Congress in every instance.

Calling this reservation a nullification of the treaty, Wilson in September made a long speaking tour of the West to build up public support for unconditional ratification. He suffered a breakdown at the end of his tour and a serious stroke on October 2. The President's illness, which incapacitated him for several months, may have increased his intransigence against the Lodge reservations; with equal stubbornness, the Massachusetts senator refused to consent to any compromise. The result was failure to obtain the necessary two-thirds majority for ratification, with or without reservations, when the Senate voted on November 19, 1919, and again on March 19, 1920.

Wilson had suggested that the ensuing presidential campaign and election should be a "great and solemn referendum" on the League. The Democratic candidate, James M. Cox of Ohio, fought hard to make it the leading issue; but the Republican candidate, Warren G. Harding of Ohio, was evasive on the subject, and a group of 31 leading Republican internationalists assured the country that Harding's election would be the best guarantee of American membership in the League of Nations. Harding swamped Cox, and his victory ended all hopes for American membership. In his inaugural Harding announced that the United States would not be entangled in European affairs; he emphasized this determination by concluding a separate peace with Germany in 1921.   (A.S.L.)

VII. The United States from 1920 to 1945

THE CHARACTER OF THE POSTWAR
REPUBLICAN ADMINISTRATIONS

Politics and economics.   Harding assumed the presidency pledged to return to normalcy a nation suffering postwar dislocation and depression. He and his Republican administration put into effect his campaign slogan, "Less government in business and more business in government." They reversed the progressive and wartime trend toward business regulation but tried through a number of measures to foster business both large and small.

Harding's administration

Harding's cabinet, together with Republican congressional leaders, helped establish probusiness policies. Harding wanted to put the best qualified men in the cabinet and was partly successful. The distinguished secretary of state, Charles Evans Hughes, was a well-known New York lawyer who fostered American economic interests overseas. The secretary of the treasury Andrew W. Mellon, one of the nation's wealthiest men, tried to stimulate business expansion by persuading Congress to cut drastically the taxes of those with large incomes; Mellon also promoted economy within the government and sharply reduced the national debt. The secretary of commerce Herbert Hoover, the defender of small enterprise, promoted foreign trade and, through the National Bureau of Standards, improved business efficiency; Hoover also encouraged the formation of trade associations. The secretary of agriculture Henry C. Wallace obtained for Midwest farmers (with progressive Republican support) legislation regulating commodity exchanges and stockyards, providing credit for distressed farmers, and encouraging farm cooperatives. The secretary of the interior Albert B. Fall was one of the most outspoken opponents of conservationist interference with western development. The attorney general Harry M. Daugherty aided railroads and mining companies by obtaining injunctions against strikes.

Capping this program to aid businessmen and farmers was a tariff act in 1922, which, although it placed a 42¢ a bushel duty on wheat, gave farmers little protection. By raising duties to cover the differential between the cost of production within the United States and that abroad, it helped manufacturers. Its effect upon other countries was to stimulate them to raise their own tariffs.

The government itself became more businesslike. The Budget and Accounting Act of 1921 established the Bureau of the Budget, which prepared a single unified budget, and also the General Accounting Office, an auditing agency.

Legislation restricting immigration reversed traditional American policy and stemmed the flow from Europe. In 1920, the year before enactment of emergency legislation, 800,000 immigrants had arrived. Added to the protests of organized labour were the objections of business leaders and patriotic organizations, who feared that some of the immigrants might be radicals. Legislation in 1924 set small quotas totalling 164,000 people yearly; it favoured immigrants from northwestern Europe and outraged the Japanese by banning all immigration from east Asia. Immigration from within the Western Hemisphere continued—900,000 Canadians (mostly French-speaking) and 500,000 Mexicans entered the United States during the 1920s.

The return of prosperity

By 1923, with the return of prosperity, Harding was enjoying widespread popularity but was heartsick over evidence of scandal within his administration. He died of a heart attack in the summer of 1923, and in subsequent months the public learned of the corruption. The most publicized was the illegal leasing of naval oil reserves at Teapot Dome, Wyoming, which led to the conviction of Secretary Fall for accepting a bribe.

Calvin Coolidge and the progress of business. Calvin Coolidge, Harding's successor, was so impeccably honest and frugal that his administration suffered none of the stigma of the Harding scandals. "Keep cool with Coolidge," was the campaign slogan when he ran in 1924 against the conservative Democrat John W. Davis. The Republicans directed more of their campaign oratory against the third-party Progressive candidate, Sen. Robert La Follette. Coolidge received more popular votes than his opponents combined.

Through essentially negative policies, the President presided over what came to be known as the years of "Coolidge prosperity." He was considerably more conservative than Harding, and through exercise of the veto and appointment power he prevented restrictions upon business. Like his predecessor, he appointed judges and members of regulatory commissions whom he felt would not interfere with the nation's economic life, and regulation did slacken (he did not always succeed, however; Harlan F. Stone, whom he appointed to the Supreme Court, became one of its most liberal members). Toward the end of his administration, Coolidge refused to use his influence to tighten credit or to make stock market speculation more difficult. In 1927 he vetoed a bill that would have raised prices of basic farm commodities because he considered it contrary to laissez-faire; the same day he authorized a 50 percent increase in the tariff on pig iron. In 1928 he pocket-vetoed Sen. George W. Norris' bill for the development of the federally owned dam at Muscle Shoals on the Tennessee River. On the other hand, Norris led the senators in blocking Coolidge's recommendation to sell Muscle Shoals to the industrialist Henry Ford.

Overall, the national economy was booming during the 1920s. Improvements in machinery and management brought an increase of 50 percent in industrial productivity, while labour costs dropped 9.5 percent. Production of automobiles and consumer durable goods rose dramatically; although the wealthy benefitted most, living standards of middle class and working people rose. Between 1922 and 1929 salaries increased 42%; wages, 33%; and consumer purchases, 23%. Corporate net profits rose 76%; dividends to stockholders, 108%. On the other hand, agriculture and several industries, such as textiles and bituminous coal mining, were seriously depressed, and after 1926 construction declined; thus the prosperity was not solidly based.

New social trends and the growth of organized crime. For millions of Americans, the sober-minded Coolidge was a more appropriate symbol for the era than the journalistic term "jazz age." Although there was stock market speculation and a real estate boom in Florida, and though there were emancipated young women with short skirts and bobbed hair—the "flappers"—dancing the Charleston to the music of jazz orchestras, playing in speakeasies, where liquor was sold illegally, most people shared in the excitement only vicariously, through several innovations of these years—through tabloid newspapers or radio or through silent motion pictures, which drew an audience of 50,000,000 a week (all these were novel, as was the automobile, in which the family went out on freshly paved highways for a Sunday outing or to spend an afternoon at the country club). They also read the novels of Sinclair Lewis, which satirized the age, and those of F. Scott Fitzgerald, which made it glamourous.

The "jazz age"

Many of the nation's writers and intellectuals were sharply critical of the mass culture of the period. Nevertheless the 1920s brought improved communications, erasing differences between urban and country life; the building of highways, parkways, and parks; and spectacular improvement in education, from kindergarten through universities.

On the darker side, the 1920s were years of mass lawbreaking and the rise of organized crime. The Volstead Act, providing for the federal enforcement of the Prohibition (Eighteenth) Amendment (which prohibited the manufacture, sale, or transportation of intoxicating liquors), went into effect in January 1920. But enforcement machinery was so slight that gangsters were soon engaged in large-scale smuggling, manufacture, and sale of alcoholic beverages. Millions of otherwise law-abiding citizens drank the prohibited liquor. On the other hand, millions of mostly Protestant churchgoers hailed prohibition as a moral advance, and the liquor consumption of working people seemed to have dropped.

The presidential campaign of 1928 between the Republican nominee, Herbert Hoover, and the Democrat, Gov. Alfred E. Smith of New York, involved the twin issues of prohibition and religion. Smith was an opponent of prohibition and a Roman Catholic. His candidacy brought enthusiasm and a heavy Democratic vote in the large cities and a landslide against him in the dry and Protestant hinterlands. Some of the opposition to Smith was marshalled by the Ku Klux Klan, anti-Catholic as well as anti-Negro, which had flourished in the early 1920s. A national law enforcement commission, formed to study the flouting of prohibition and the activities of gangsters, was to report in 1931 that prohibition was virtually unenforceable; and with the coming of the Great Depression, prohibition ceased to be a key political issue. In 1933 the Twenty-first Amendment brought its repeal.

Herbert Hoover and the Great Depression. Hoover won an overwhelming victory in 1928, in part because his opponent was a "wet" Catholic but in larger part because Hoover, as the "Great Engineer," seemed best qualified to continue the prosperity of the 1920s. Yet within a few months of his inauguration in 1929, the stock market crashed and the Great Depression began; ironically Hoover had to devote his administration to trying to regain a vanished prosperity.

In the stock market crash of October 1929, stocks in a few weeks lost 40 percent of their value; the market continued an intermittent downward course through 1932. The crash had come in response to declines in industrial production, construction, and retail sales. It helped trigger a deflationary spiral that became difficult to stop as businessmen were gradually forced to curtail their activities.

Anti-Depression measures. In trying to end the Depression, Hoover went further than any of his predecessors in utilizing government powers in a positive, although limited way; his administration created many of the precedents for later measures. At first he tried to restore public confidence by obtaining the voluntary cooperation of business and labour leaders, who pledged to maintain production, employment, and existing pay scales. Hoover also tried to stem deflation by liberalizing Federal Reserve credit, cutting taxes, and obtaining from Congress an unprecedented increase of $423,000,000 in the public works appropriation. Before the crash, he had already signed the Agricultural Marketing Act of 1929, creating the Federal Farm Board to bolster farm prices by purchasing surpluses. In 1930 he signed the Hawley–Smoot Tariff Bill, which raised the average ad valorem duty from 26 to 50 percent and brought retaliation from other countries.

Into 1931 these mild expedients seemed sufficient, and the Depression appeared no worse than that of 1921. Then, the threatened financial collapse of western Europe brought a new wave of deflation to the United States. In order to save the financial system of Germany, whose collapse might well take under that of other nations, Hoover agreed in June 1931 to a one-year moratorium on reparations and war debt payments. This was of relatively little help. The financial systems of England and other western European nations survived, but by September most of them had gone off the gold standard and had devalued their currency. European gold was withdrawn from the United States, and European-held securities were dumped on the U.S. stock markets. Devaluation of currency further cut the already declining foreign trade. These disasters, heightening difficulties at home, caused the Depression to become steadily worse from May 1931 to July 1932.

Democratic control of Congress. Worsening conditions forced Hoover to propose more drastic expedients to bring recovery; but as much as possible, he still wished the recovery program to be voluntary. In the 1930 elections the Democrats had won control of the House by a narrow margin and had almost won the Senate. Through a coalition with 12 Republican progressive senators, the Democrats were able to muster a majority of votes against administration measures when the 72nd Congress assembled in December 1931. Congress thus attacked many of Hoover's proposals and called for still more drastic action.

Nevertheless Congress did, as Hoover requested, in January 1932 establish a federal loan agency—the Reconstruction Finance Corporation (RFC)—with a capitalization of $2,000,000,000, empowered to make loans to banks, insurance companies, agricultural associations, railroads, and other industries. The RFC loaned $1,500,000,000 to banks and businesses during its first year. In July 1932 Hoover signed a measure allowing it to lend an additional $1,500,000,000 for self-liquidating public works and $300,000,000 for relief purposes. The RFC did much to keep the Depression from becoming even worse than it eventually became.

Despite the efforts of President Hoover and Congress, the Depression continued to deepen. By 1932 banks had failed by the hundreds; mills and factories were shut down or operating only part-time. Estimates of the unemployed ranged as high as 13,000,000 (one worker in four); many of those employed received only subsistence wages. A quarter of the farmers had lost their farms. In the 1932 election, voters by a wide margin rejected Hoover and voted for the Democratic candidate, Gov. Franklin D. Roosevelt of New York, who promised them a New Deal.

THE NEW DEAL

The first New Deal. The nation was in a state of acute banking crisis when Roosevelt took office. Beginning in Michigan in mid-February 1933, runs on banks had forced state after state to close or limit the activities of its banks. This was the setting in which the new President delivered his inaugural address on March 4. Above all he tried to dispel the fright in peoples' minds; he emphatically stated, "the only thing we have to fear is fear itself."

Roosevelt's first 100 days. In the next several days Roosevelt acted quickly, and rather conservatively, to restore business confidence. In March he submitted to Congress the Emergency Banking Bill, empowering the administration to strengthen and reopen sound banks; Congress enacted the bill in four hours. Within three days three-fourths of the banks within the Federal Reserve system had reopened. There followed an economy act reducing federal salaries and veterans' pensions and legislation legalizing the sale of beer of 3.2 percent alcoholic content. The stock market went up 15 percent.

With the country enthusiastically behind him, Roosevelt kept Congress in special session and piece by piece sent it recommendations that formed the basic recovery program of his first 100 days in office. He expected later to submit to Congress proposals for long-range reform legislation to eliminate maladjustments responsible for the Depression and likely to cause future depressions. Between March 16 and May 17, 1933, he sent messages and draft bills to Congress proposing an agricultural recovery program, unemployment relief, federal supervision of investment securities, creation of a Tennessee Valley Authority, prevention of mortgage foreclosures on homes, railroad recovery legislation, and an industrial recovery program. From March 9 to mid-June 1933, Congress enacted all of Roosevelt's proposals—an unprecedented legislative achievement.

Farm recovery. The passage of the Agricultural Adjustment Act in May 1933 marked the beginning of an era in which the American farmer received aid from the Federal government to improve his economic status. It was an omnibus farm-relief bill embodying the schemes of the major farm organizations to limit crops and of agrarian radicals to inflate the currency. The Agricultural Adjustment Administration (AAA) established by the act put into effect a "domestic allotment" plan to make benefit payments to producers of seven basic commodities, including wheat, cotton, and corn, in return for cutting their output. At first a processing tax upon the commodities provided funds for the benefit payments; but after an adverse Supreme Court decision in 1936, Congress appropriated funds for crop reduction coupled with soil conservation. The AAA program was of only limited help to farmers. Drought in 1933–36 did more than production quotas to cut farm surpluses and increase commodity prices, but most farmers nonetheless favoured the early program. The cash income of farmers nearly doubled between 1932 and 1936 but did not again reach the 1929 level until 1941.

Business recovery. The New Deal sought to bring business recovery through the omnibus National Industrial Recovery Act (NIRA) of June 1933. This act, administered by the National Recovery Administration (NRA), granted businessmen government backing for agreements to stabilize production and prevent price slashing. Labour was to receive wages-and-hours protection and the right to bargain collectively. A large-scale public-works appropriation, administered through the Public Works Administration (PWA), was intended to pour sufficient money into the economy to increase consumer buying power while prices and wages went up.

In practice, the NRA program went awry. While codes were being negotiated, in the summer of 1933, manufacturers increased production in anticipation of higher prices and greater demand. Buying power did not keep pace, and in the fall of 1933 the boomlet collapsed. The NRA then became too complicated; by February 1934 it had negotiated far too many codes with even minor industries, covering vast intricacies of regulations—a total

Margin notes: The stock market crash of 1929 · The Reconstruction Finance Corporation · Roosevelt's recovery program · Failure of the NRA

of 557 basic codes and 208 supplementary ones. Such a mass of detail proved almost unenforceable. Workingmen felt they obtained little from the codes, although in a few industries, like textiles, child labour was ended and working conditions were improved. The collective bargaining provision in the act led to a strong unionization movement and to numerous strikes against nonunion employers. The National Labor Board in 1933 and its successor, the National Labor Relations Board, dealt with labour disputes but had little power.

The NRA was a failure, despite some achievements in improving wages and hours and in bringing order to chaotic large industries. It was too complicated to be enforceable, it tended to create monopoly conditions, and because public works expenditures were too slow it raised prices without a comparable increase in consumer buying power. When the Supreme Court invalidated the NRA code system in 1935, Congress enacted new laws salvaging parts of it, but the experiment was basically over.

Relief. Relief programs were urgent in the New Deal to provide aid to millions of hungry people for whom states and cities were able to provide only a pittance. The Federal Emergency Relief Administration provided grants to state relief agencies; in return the state agencies had to meet federal standards. The Civilian Conservation Corps (CCC), which employed young men from families on relief in reforestation and similar projects, became one of the most popular New Deal agencies. Several laws aided farmers and homeowners threatened by mortgage foreclosures. The Farm Credit Administration (FCA) was a consolidation of several earlier federal agencies; in 1933–34 it refinanced one-fifth of all farm mortgages. A farm bankruptcy act of June 1934 enabled farmers who had lost their farms to regain them. For homeowners, the Home Owners Loan Corporation refinanced about one-sixth of the mortgages on homes. In 1934 the Federal Housing Administration (FHA), more a recovery than a relief agency, began to insure mortgages upon new construction and home repairs. The Reconstruction Finance Corporation continued to make large recovery loans.

The economic downturn in the fall of 1933 led to new relief and recovery devices. During the winter of 1933–34, the Civil Works Administration (CWA) employed 4,000,000 people on emergency projects. Roosevelt also experimented with mild currency inflation, devaluating the gold content of the dollar to 59.06 percent of what it had been formerly and beginning in 1934 a silver purchase program (these were the beginnings of America's government management of the currency).

Reform. Early in the New Deal there was some reform legislation. The Glass–Steagall Act of 1933 created the Federal Deposit Insurance Corporation (FDIC), guaranteeing small bank deposits. Later, the Banking Act of 1935 altered and strengthened the Federal Reserve System. Two measures regulated stock exchange: the Truth-in-Securities Act of 1933, requiring corporations to file data on new securities, and the Securities Exchange Act of 1934, establishing a commission to check new securities and to police the stock markets. The most spectacular piece of conservation legislation was the establishment in 1933 of the Tennessee Valley Authority (TVA), which took over the dam at Muscle Shoals and four other existing dams; it also built 20 new dams in the next two decades, regulating floods in an area previously devastated by them, generating cheap electricity, and undertaking the general rehabilitation of a poverty-stricken area. Other power development and irrigation projects were built in the West. The Taylor Grazing Act of 1934 regulated public rangeland; the Indian Reorganization Act of 1934 protected the Indians and their lands.

The second New Deal and the Supreme Court. In reaction to pressures from the left and hostility from the right, the New Deal shifted more toward reform in 1935–36. Popular leaders, promising more than Roosevelt, threatened to pull sufficient votes from him in the 1936 election to bring Republican victory. Sen. Huey P. Long of Louisiana was building a national following with a "Share the Wealth" program. The poor in northern cities were attracted to the Roman Catholic priest the

The
shift
toward
reform

Rev. Charles E. Coughlin, who later switched from a program of nationalization and currency inflation to an antidemocratic, anti-Semitic emphasis. Many older people supported Dr. Francis E. Townsend's plan to provide $200 per month for everyone over age 60. At the same time, conservatives, including such groups as the American Liberty League, founded in 1934, attacked the New Deal as a threat to states' rights, free enterprise, and the open shop.

Roosevelt's response in 1935 was to propose greater aid to the underprivileged and extensive reforms. Congress created the Works Progress Administration (WPA), which replaced direct relief with work relief; between 1935 and 1941 an annual average of 2,100,000 workers were carried on WPA rolls. For younger people there was the National Youth Administration (NYA). Of long-range significance was the Social Security Act of 1935, which provided federal aid for the aged, retirement annuities, unemployment insurance, aid for persons who were blind or crippled, and aid to dependent children; the original act suffered from various inadequacies, but it was the beginning of a permanent, expanding national program. A tax reform law, labelled by newspapers as the "soak the rich tax," fell heavily upon corporations and well-to-do people. The National Labor Relations Act, or Wagner Act, reluctantly accepted by Roosevelt, gave organized labour federal protection in collective bargaining; it prohibited a number of "unfair practices" on the part of employers and created the strong National Labor Relations Board (NLRB) to enforce the law.

While the New Deal was moving toward reform in 1935, the Supreme Court was invalidating several of its earlier key measures. In *Schechter Poultry Corp.* v. *U.S.* the Court invalidated the NIRA, creating a national sensation; Roosevelt charged the justices with taking a "horse-and-buggy age view" of federal regulatory power. In 1936 Roosevelt, aided by his reform program, defeated the Republican nominee for president, Gov. Alfred ("Alf") M. Landon of Kansas, receiving over 60 percent of the popular vote and the electoral votes of every state except Maine and Vermont.

Viewing his decisive victory as an electoral mandate for continued reform, Roosevelt sought to remove the impediment the Supreme Court seemed to be placing in his way. He felt that the powers involved in such reform legislation as the Wagner Act and Social Security Act, both being challenged before the Supreme Court, were to be found in the Constitution and that the court had been interpreting it too narrowly. In February 1937 he proposed to Congress a reorganization of the court system, which would have included giving him the power to appoint one new justice for each justice who was 70 years of age or older, but not exceeding six new justices in all. Roosevelt's proposal created a furor, especially because he did not state frankly the obvious fact that he wished the court to interpret the Constitution more broadly. Some Democrats and a few liberal Republicans in Congress supported the proposal, but a strong coalition of Republicans and conservative Democrats, backed by much public support, fought the so-called court-packing plan.

Meanwhile the court itself in a new series of decisions began upholding as constitutional measures involving both state and federal economic regulation. In April 1937 it approved the National Labor Relations Act. These decisions, which began an extensive revision of constitutional law concerning governmental regulation, made the reorganization plan unnecessary; the Senate defeated it in July 1937 by a vote of 70 to 22. Roosevelt had suffered a stinging political defeat, even though he no longer had to fear the court. Turnover on the court was rapid as older members retired or died; by 1942 all but two of the justices were Roosevelt appointees.

The culmination of the New Deal. Roosevelt lost further prestige in the summer of 1937, when the nation plunged into a sharp recession. Economists had feared an inflationary boom as industrial production moved up to within 7.5 percent of 1929. Other indices were high except for a lag in capital investment and continued heavy

Roosevelt's
court-
packing
plan

unemployment. Roosevelt, fearing a boom and eager to balance the budget, cut government spending, which most economists felt had brought the recovery. Between August 1937 and May 1938 the index of production fell from 117 to 76 (on a 1929 base of 100) and unemployment increased by 4,000,000 persons. Congress voted an emergency appropriation of $5,000,000,000 for work relief and public works, and by June 1938 recovery once more was under way.

Considerable legislation augmenting and consolidating earlier New Deal measures was passed during the second Roosevelt administration. There was further legislation to reduce farm production and raise crop prices and to alleviate rural poverty. For workers the Fair Labor Standards Act of 1938 established a minimum wage and maximum work week (in later years the minimum wage was repeatedly raised and coverage was broadened). Substantial construction of public housing began with establishment of the U.S. Housing Authority in 1937. Altogether this was a considerable array of legislation; but it had been vigorously opposed by many conservative Democrats in Congress, allied with the Republicans. During the congressional campaign of 1938, Roosevelt intervened in primaries, mostly in the South, trying to defeat conservative Democratic congressional leaders. For the most part he failed; throughout the country the tide of support for the New Deal was ebbing, and the Republicans gained 80 seats in the House and seven in the Senate. Nevertheless, the Democrats still controlled each house by a heavy margin.

Spectacular violence accompanying union organization drives was another factor in the New Deal's waning popularity among middle class Americans. Aided by the Wagner Act, unions had begun organizing vigorously early in the New Deal. A few months after the passage of the Wagner Act, John L. Lewis, president of the United Mine Workers of America, led in forming the Committee for Industrial Organization (CIO) to organize the great mass-production industries, which for the most part had never been unionized. The CIO came into conflict with the American Federation of Labor (AFL), which mounted its own unionization drives. The result was struggle between organizers and industrialists and at times between rival organizers. In bitter fights with the automobile companies the CIO used the sit-down strike, in which the strikers entrenched themselves in the factories and refused to work or to let others in to work; in February 1947 General Motors Corporation recognized the United Automobile Workers, and gradually other manufacturers did the same. The United States Steel Corporation signed union contracts in the spring of 1937 rather than risk strikes, but three "little steel" companies resisted vigorously before finally signing contracts with the CIO. Roosevelt, declining to take sides during the struggle, called down "a plague on both your houses." The organizing drives continued to make headway; union membership, which had been about 3,000,000 in 1932, was 9,500,000 by 1941.

An assessment of the New Deal. The New Deal established federal responsibility for the welfare of the economy and the American people. At the time, conservative critics, among whom the most notable was former President Hoover, charged it was bringing statism or even socialism. Left-wing critics of a later generation have charged just the reverse—that it bolstered the old order and prevented significant reform. Others have suggested that the New Deal was no more than the extension and culmination of Progressivism.

In its early stages, the New Deal did begin where Progressivism left off and built upon the Hoover program for fighting the Depression. But Roosevelt soon took the New Deal well beyond Hoover and Progressivism, programs came to have more of an element of compulsion in them and were larger in scale. For the first time the federal government assumed responsibility for the social security of the nation's citizens. The Wagner Act fostered unionism, and organized labour became a vital part of the Democratic coalition, contributing both votes and campaign dollars.

New Deal efforts to stimulate prosperity resulted in a trial-and-error approach to economic regulation. National planning failed in the NRA yet continued for decades as a means of reducing production of major farm crops. Management of currency and credit, beginning in 1933, slowly became more sophisticated and came to be a key means by which the government could control inflation or prevent deflation. Government spending, undertaken at first as a means primarily of relief, became the prime device for stimulating the economy. Social Security through automatically providing benefits in time of unemployment became another countercyclical economic stabilizer.

Roosevelt himself, though he adopted some of his proposals, never became a disciple of J.M. Keynes, the contemporary British economic theorist, who advocated spending during reunion; but many of the young New Deal economists were Keynesians by the late 1930s. The New Deal did not achieve complete economic recovery before war intervened, but it had taken the nation well in that direction. (It was also evolving economic devices which after 1945 further developed in both Democratic and Republican administrations as the means of preventing runaway inflation and depression.)

THE IMPACT OF WORLD WAR II

Isolation, neutrality, and the U.S. entry into the war. During the New Deal years the American response to threats of war in other parts of the world was to seek security through isolation. Congress, with the approval of Roosevelt and Secretary of State Cordell Hull, enacted a series of neutrality laws; in order to keep the nation out of a new conflict, these legislated against the factors that supposedly had taken the United States into World War I. As Italy prepared to invade Ethiopia, Congress passed the Neutrality Act of 1935, embargoing shipment of arms to either aggressor or victim. Stronger legislation followed the outbreak of the Spanish Civil War in 1936, even relinquishing the traditional American claim to freedom of seas in wartime.

Threats to American security. The gravest threat seemed to come from Japan. Roosevelt followed the doctrine of nonrecognition of Japan's conquests on the Asiatic mainland, and in 1934, began rebuilding the navy toward treaty strength. When Japan in 1937 began a large-scale drive into north China, Roosevelt did not proclaim neutrality; thus munitions could be sold to both sides. But in October, when Roosevelt suggested that war, like disease, was a contagion that peace-loving nations should quarantine, he created a furor and had to retreat. In December, when Japanese aviators sank the U.S. gunboat "Panay" in the Yangtze River, the United States accepted Japanese apologies and indemnities.

As war continued in Asia and threatened to break out in Europe as a result of German aggressions, Roosevelt tried to develop a policy of collective security. He encountered little opposition as long as he confined himself to working agreements for mutual defense among the nations of the Western Hemisphere—at Buenos Aires in 1936, at Lima in 1938, and with Canada in 1938.

When Germany's invasion of Poland in 1939 touched off World War II, Roosevelt called Congress into special session to revise the Neutrality Act to allow belligerents (in reality only Great Britain and France both on the Allied side) to purchase munitions on a "cash-and-carry" basis. With the fall of France to Germany in 1940, Roosevelt, with heavy public support, threw the resources of the United States behind the British, including the spectacular exchange of 50 overage U.S. destroyers in return for 99-year leases on bases stretching from Newfoundland to British Guiana. In the fall of 1940 Roosevelt also conducted a political campaign for a tradition-breaking third term, running against the Republican Wendell L. Willkie, and was re-elected with over 54 percent of the popular vote.

From the fall of France until the Japanese bombing of the American naval base at Pearl Harbor, Hawaii (December 1941), a great debate stirred the nation as isolationists, especially through a group called the America First Committee, charged that Roosevelt was taking the nation into war, and interventionists complained that he was not moving rapidly enough. While the debate went on, the United States built its defenses and sent supplies to the British. The Burke–Wadsworth Act of 1940 established the first peacetime selective service, or conscription, act in the nation's history. The Lend-Lease Act of 1941, passed after vehement debate, provided the British and their allies with munitions, which could be repaid after the crisis was over. In August 1941 Roosevelt met with British prime minister Winston Churchill off the coast of Newfoundland and then announced a set of war aims known as the Atlantic Charter. It called for national self-determination, larger economic opportunities, freedom from fear and want, freedom of the seas, and disarmament.

American military involvement. In September a German submarine attacked an American destroyer, and Roosevelt issued orders to "shoot on sight." In October another destroyer was sunk, and the United States embarked on an undeclared naval war against Germany.

For a decade the relations of the United States with Japan had grown less friendly. In January 1940 the United States abrogated its commercial treaty of 1911 with Japan, yet Americans continued to sell Japan materials used in its war against China. When Japanese armies invaded French Indochina in September 1940 with the apparent purpose of establishing bases for an attack on the East Indies, the United States placed an embargo on scrap iron and steel. Japan retaliated by signing a triple alliance agreement with Germany and Italy (September 1940). Japan was close to war with the United States, but it entered into negotiations in the spring of 1941, which continued into December. The United States, to try to thwart an expected Japanese thrust into the East Indies, placed tight economic sanctions upon Japan in July. The Japanese reaction was to prepare for war in case negotiations failed. Neither nation would make serious concessions over China, and by the end of November the United States (through intercepted Japanese messages) knew that a military attack was likely. Roosevelt and his military advisers, expecting it to be against the East Indies and possibly the Philippines, were caught by surprise when Japanese planes struck at Pearl Harbor on December 7, 1941. They destroyed or damaged 15 ships and 188 airplanes and inflicted 3,435 casualties.

Declaration of war

On December 8, 1941, Congress with only one dissenting vote declared war against Japan. Three days later Germany and Italy declared war against the United States; and Congress, voting unanimously, reciprocated. As a result of the attack on Pearl Harbor, the previously divided nation entered into the global struggle with virtual unanimity.

The conduct of the war and its domestic effects. Within the United States during World War II, the American people had to produce the enormous quantities of every sort of material of war, clothing, and food with which to defeat the enemies. The war also meant great dislocations as 15,000,000 men and women went into uniform and many additional millions moved to jobs in war plants. The war brought an enormous increase in productivity and a higher living standard than ever before; it also brought continued debates among the American people over the way in which the war was to be conducted and what national policies should be afterward.

Congressional controls. Congress moved to the right during the war. In the 1942 election Republicans gained 47 seats in the House and 10 in the Senate. Democrats still controlled Congress, but conservatives of both parties were able to force dismantling of several New Deal agencies. Congress used its investigatory power to keep a check on war agencies and military expenditures, especially through the Senate War Investigating Committee, headed by Harry S. Truman of Missouri. Congress also became committed to the policy of postwar American cooperation with other nations to preserve the peace.

War production. As the government tried to control war production, government agencies were organized and reorganized repeatedly. In January 1942 the War Production Board replaced an earlier agency, and in 1943 it became subsidiary to the Office of War Mobilization. Agencies established priorities to channel scarce raw materials into the most essential types of production, controlled prices (through the Office of Price Administration), and allocated war supplies to the various branches of the armed forces and to the Allies. After initial snarls and never-ending disputes, by the beginning of 1944 production was reaching astronomical totals—double those of all the enemy countries combined. The output of American factories almost doubled between 1939 and 1945. (By the end of the war the United States had produced, for example, 6,500 naval vessels, 296,400 airplanes, and 86,330 tanks.)

Much of the production was in new types of weapons, as U.S. engineers and scientists matched their ingenuity against the Germans. The Office of Scientific Research and Development directed scientists in the development of superior radar and sonar, radio-directed proximity fuses, and countless other devices. The most dramatic race was the secret one to try to build an atomic bomb more quickly than the enemy. Through the Manhattan Project, $2,000,000,000 was expended upon plants and laboratories; and on July 6, 1945, the first workable atomic bomb was tested.

Development of the atomic bomb

The use of manpower. The War put manpower suddenly at a premium after years of heavy unemployment. Selective Service draft boards registered 31,000,000 men; including volunteers, more than 15,000,000 men and women served in the armed forces during the war. At the same time, the working force at home increased from 46,500,000 to 53,000,000, and 6,600,000 persons moved from rural poverty to cities. Some 2,000,000 blacks obtained work in war industries, protected by the Fair Employment Practices Committee (FEPC), established in 1941. Although 2,000,000 families still suffered from substandard incomes, most families benefitted economically from the war; gross weekly wages increased from $25.20 to $43.39. Most workers were better off, although the cost-of-living index (1935–39 = 100) went up to 128.4 by 1945, and most workers for the first time had to pay a federal income tax. Personal incomes were a third greater than available goods and services; much of the excess buying power was drained off into purchases of war bonds and stamps.

Financing the war. Through taxes the government raised 41 percent of the cost of the war (compared with 33 percent in World War I). The Revenue Act of 1942 levied 94 percent on the largest incomes; a withholding-tax measure passed in 1943 provided for deducting tax payments from workers' pay as it was earned. The total cost of the war to the Federal government between 1941 and 1945 was $321,000,000,000 (ten times as much as World War I), and the national debt mounted from $49,000,000,000 in 1941 to $259,000,000,000 in 1945.

Labour. Unions agreed not to strike during the war and submitted disputes to the strong National War Labor Board. Nevertheless, there were 15,000 work stoppages during the war, which created much resentment among the public and in Congress (they accounted for only one-ninth of 1 percent of total hours worked). Congress in 1943 passed over the President's veto the Smith–Connally, or War Labor Disputes, Act, requiring unions to wait 30 days before striking and giving the president the right to seize a struck war plant.

Farmers. Congress was relatively generous with farmers, granting them less than they wanted but nevertheless setting price ceilings at 100 percent of parity. Produce prices more than doubled. In good-crop years during the war, agricultural production set new records, increasing from an index figure of 108 to 123.

Japanese Americans. During the war most Americans were undisturbed in the exercise of their civil liberties. But Japanese Americans felt the brunt of public anger. In February 1942 Roosevelt authorized the removal of 117,000 of them, two thirds of whom were United States citizens, from the Pacific Coast to ten interior relocation centres. Some 17,600 Japanese Americans fought in the armed forces; some of their units established notable records for bravery.

The 1944 election. In 1944 the United States underwent the first wartime presidential election since the Civil War. Roosevelt was nominated for a fourth term; the vice presidential nominee was Sen. Harry S. Truman. The Republican party nominated the governor of New York, Thomas E. Dewey. Roosevelt was again elected.

The end of isolation and the new U.S. role in world affairs. The United States entry into World War II brought an end to isolation. The United States as a result of conferences between President Roosevelt and Prime Minister Churchill in December 1941 formed a grand wartime alliance, the United Nations, which 46 nations ultimately joined.

International conferences

In 1943 six major conferences took place. At Casablanca, Morocco, in January the Allies decided to invade Italy and declared the need for "unconditional surrender." In May, in Washington, D.C., they decided to increase the bombing of Germany. From Quebec in August came the decision to invade German-occupied France in a "second front." In October Secretary Hull in Moscow reached agreements on establishment of a United Nations organization after the war. At Cairo in November Roosevelt and Churchill, meeting with Pres. Chiang Kai-shek of the Republic of China, affirmed a postwar settlement for east Asia. Later that month at Teheran, Iran, Roosevelt, Prime Minister Joseph Stalin of the Soviet Union, and Churchill agreed upon plans for launching a second front in Europe.

In June 1944 a cross-channel Allied landing took place on the coast of German-occupied Normandy. By the end of August, Allied forces occupied most of France. In August, at Dumbarton Oaks in Washington, D.C., representatives of the United States, Great Britain, the Soviet Union, and China met and agreed upon a charter for a permanent international organization. In mid-September in Quebec, Roosevelt again met with Churchill, and they tentatively agreed upon plans for dealing with Germany after the war.

The year 1945 brought an end to the war. Roosevelt, in February, met with Stalin and Churchill at Yalta in the Crimea. There policies were agreed upon to enforce the unconditional surrender of Germany, to divide it into zones for occupation and policing by the respective Allied forces, and to provide democratic regimes in eastern European nations. A series of secret agreements were also made at Yalta; chief among these was the Soviet pledge to enter the war against Japan after the German surrender, in return for concessions in east Asia.

Roosevelt died on April 12 and was succeeded by Truman. In the following months, the German armed forces collapsed; and on May 7, all German forces surrendered. In the Pacific, the invasions of Iwo Jima and Okinawa in early 1945 brought Japan under a state of siege. In the summer, before an invasion could take place, the United States dropped atomic bombs on Hiroshima and Nagasaki. On September 2 the surrender of Japan was signed in Tokyo Harbour on the battleship "Missouri." (F.Fr.)

VIII. The United States since 1945

THE PEAK COLD WAR YEARS, 1945–60

The death of Roosevelt

The Truman administration. Upon the sudden death of President Roosevelt on April 12, 1945, Harry S. Truman became president of the United States. Truman was aware of the nation's problems only in a general way, for he had not had close association with the administration. The conference to establish the United Nations took place as planned, opening on April 25 in San Francisco. In May the German forces surrendered, and in July Truman conferred at Potsdam, Germany, with Stalin and Churchill (later succeeded by Clement Richard Attlee) to discuss future operations against Japan and a peace settlement for Europe. The Soviets had been ignoring many of their Yalta pledges concerning eastern Europe; at Potsdam they refused to make satisfactory arrangements with Truman. These difficulties did not seem serious, because the United States held a monopoly of atomic secrets and it was thought that the Soviet Union would need U.S. help to reconstruct its vast devastated areas.

In September the war with Japan ended and extensive demobilization of United States forces began. By the end of 1946 the army was down to 1,500,000 men and the navy to 700,000; by the spring of 1950 the army numbered 500,000 men, and the United States was relying mainly on air power and atomic weapons.

In June 1946 the United States proposed a plan for international control of atomic energy through the United Nations, but the Soviet Union would not agree to such control, insisting that the United States unilaterally destroy its atomic arsenal. Meanwhile, Soviet scientists were engaged in nuclear research; in 1949 they exploded their first atomic bomb. The U.S. continued research and development in atomic energy under the control of a five-man Atomic Energy Commission (AEC), created in 1946. The U.S. armed forces were reorganized and brought under a secretary of defense by the National Security Act of 1947, which created the U.S. Air Force as an independent service. In 1949 a Department of Defense was established, and greater unification of the services took place.

The Cold War and containment. In 1946 and early 1947 the Soviet Union supported Communist guerrillas in Greece and brought pressure upon Turkey in a way that seemed to foreshadow Soviet expansion to the Mediterranean. In March 1947, after the British government declared that it could no longer afford to continue its aid to Greece and Turkey, Truman asked Congress to appropriate funds for military aid to help these two countries resist Communist aggression. "It must be the policy of the United States," he declared, "to support free peoples who are resisting attempted subjugation by armed minorities or by outside pressures." This policy came to be known as the Truman Doctrine. Congress appropriated $400,000,000, and by 1949 the Communist threat had diminished.

The Truman Doctrine

In June 1947 Secretary of State George C. Marshall proposed a plan for economic rehabilitation of Europe to meet the growing Communist threat. Despite Communist harassment, 16 nations (plus western Germany) participated, and in the next three years the United States spent $12,000,000,000 through the Economic Cooperation Administration. The Marshall Plan (or European Recovery Program) revitalized the economy of western Europe and cut the strength of western European Communist parties. In his inaugural address in 1949, following re-election, Truman proposed extending the same sort of aid to underdeveloped nations throughout the world. The fourth of his proposals called for giving technical assistance to underdeveloped countries and came to be known as the Point Four Program.

The U.S. and Great Britain set out to rebuild western Germany as an economically strong area with sovereignty over its domestic affairs. When the U.S.S.R. retaliated in June 1948 by blockading the land and waterway routes leading from eastern Germany into the western-occupied sectors of Berlin, Truman ordered military planes to fly food and supplies into the city. In the spring of 1949 the Soviet Union ended the blockade.

In June 1948 the U.S. Senate passed the Vandenburg Resolution, authorizing negotiations that led to the signing of the North Atlantic Treaty of April 1949 by 12 nations (and later also by Greece and Turkey). The treaty created a new defense force to resist Soviet aggression, the North Atlantic Treaty Organization (NATO). Its first supreme commander was Gen. Dwight D. Eisenhower.

On the other side of the world, Truman had sent General Marshall to China as early as December 1945 to prevent warfare between Nationalist and Communist forces and to form a coalition government. In the summer of 1947, after the Communists had made rapid advances, the President sent Gen. A.C. Wedemeyer to study the situation; Wedemeyer recommended sending military personnel and large quantities of supplies. The President, who was concentrating upon containment in Europe, asked for only $570,000,000 to aid Chiang Kai-shek; Congress in April 1948 voted $400,000,000, of which only $125,000,000 could be spent for military supplies. By the end of 1949 the Nationalist government had fallen and had retreated to Taiwan. The response of the United States was to inaugurate a policy of strengthening occupied Japan.

The Fair Deal. In September 1945 Truman sent a message to Congress outlining a 21-point domestic program, which later came to be known as the Fair Deal. It called for expanded social security, new wages-and-hours and public-housing legislation, and a permanent Fair Employment Practices Act to prevent racial or religious discrimination in hiring. Congress and the country were so preoccupied with problems of reconversion and the threat of inflation, however, that Truman was unable to get his proposals enacted; one significant exception was the Employment Act of 1946, which clearly stated the government's responsibility for maintaining full employment and established a three-man Council of Economic Advisers to advise the President and issue an annual economic report.

Truman's 21-point domestic program

Reconversion went smoothly and rapidly: war contracts were cancelled and settled; war agencies were curtailed; and surplus factories and property were sold. The Serviceman's Readjustment Act of 1944 (the G.I. Bill of Rights) provided aid to former members of the armed forces. Consumer buying power, including almost unlimited credit, was far greater than the output of consumer goods and put pressure on prices to rise. In addition, labour unions, no longer bound by their wartime no-strike pledge, began to strike for higher wages. Settlement of a steel strike early in 1946 allowed a large wage increase and a resulting rise in steel prices. This "bulge in the line," justified on the basis that living costs had gone up by more than 30 percent since 1941, led to a spiral of increased wages and prices throughout industry. Farmers and businessmen tried to end price controls entirely, but Congress in June 1946 passed a bill preserving limited controls; Truman vetoed the bill because it did not go far enough. Controls expired, the prices of 28 basic commodities jumped 25 percent in the first 16 days of July, and Congress passed a new price-control bill, which Truman signed. Because of price increases, real earnings dropped 12 percent below what they had been in July 1945. In 1946 Republicans won control of both houses of Congress. Truman, regarding the election as a mandate against controls, dropped most of them. Retail prices rose at the rate of 3 percent a month, leading to a second round of strikes and higher wages and prices.

The 80th Congress, dominated by conservative Republicans, ignored the Fair Deal program. It authorized a commission on the reorganization of executive departments, and Truman appointed former president Herbert Hoover as chairman. It also enacted a new basic labour law, the Taft-Hartley Labor Management Relations Act of 1947, over Truman's veto, which removed some restrictions on management and added several on labour unions.

In the 1948 campaign the Republican presidential candidate, Gov. Thomas E. Dewey of New York, seemed almost certain of victory over Truman. A third party, the Progressive Party, calling for a more conciliatory policy toward the Soviet Union, nominated former vice president Henry A. Wallace; a fourth party, the States' Rights Democrats (Dixiecrats), protesting civil-rights provisions in the Democratic platform, nominated Gov. Strom Thurmond of South Carolina. Truman embarked upon a vigorous campaign directed against the conservative congressional Republicans. Mustering the support of labour, discontented farmers, and Northern Negroes, Truman defeated Dewey by a popular vote of 24,106,000 to 21,-970,000 and an electoral vote of 303 to 189. Thurmond received 1,169,000 votes and 39 electoral votes; Wallace, 1,157,000 votes. The Democrats recaptured the House (263 to 171) and the Senate (54 to 42).

In his inaugural address on January 20, 1949, Truman called for a vigorous advancement of his Fair Deal program to aid the underprivileged. Except for the Social Security Act of 1950, which added almost 10,000,000 persons to the beneficiaries of old-age insurance, only a small part of the Fair Deal was enacted into law.

During the postwar years public attention focussed more and more on charges that the federal government was infiltrated with Communists. In 1946 a Soviet spy ring was uncovered in Canada, and Truman set up a Temporary Commission on Employee Loyalty, which recommended the establishment of loyalty review boards. By 1951 these boards had dismissed 212 government employees, and more than 2,000 others had resigned; 3,000,000 had been cleared. Over the President's veto, Congress in 1950 passed the McCarran Internal Security Act, which placed numerous restrictions upon Communists throughout the nation. In 1949, under the Smith Act of 1940, which prohibited conspiring to teach the violent overthrow of the government, 11 Communist leaders were convicted and sentenced to prison. In 1951 two Communist agents, Julius and Ethel Rosenberg, were convicted of transmitting atomic secrets to the U.S.S.R.; they were executed in 1953. In 1950 Alger Hiss, formerly an employee of the Department of State, was convicted of perjury. Capitalizing upon the resulting furor, Sen. Joseph R. McCarthy of Wisconsin charged in February 1950 that he had a list of 57 (some listeners said 205) men loyal to Communism still in the State Department. A subcommittee of the Senate Foreign Relations Committee could not find even one, but McCarthy, going on rapidly to other sensational charges, built a national following. (F.Fr.)

Charges of Communists in government

With the victory of the Communists in China in 1949 and the announcement that September of a Soviet atomic explosion, fear of Communist expansion and a determination to contain it became the dominant theme in U.S. foreign policy. Truman's Point Four program was motivated in large part by a desire to persuade impoverished nations to cast their lot with the United States rather than with the Soviet Union. It was matched by the announcement in January 1950 that the President had directed the U.S. Atomic Energy Commission to proceed with work on a hydrogen bomb that would be vastly more powerful than the atomic bombs used in World War II.

The Korean War. On June 25, 1950, armed forces of the Democratic People's Republic of Korea (North Korea), supported by the Soviet Union, advanced south of the 38th parallel separating the northern Communist state from the Republic of Korea (South Korea). The U.S. government immediately presented the matter to the UN Security Council, urging that military forces under UN auspices be sent to Korea to resist Communist aggression. The Security Council, acting during a Soviet boycott, adopted a resolution calling upon UN members to resist the North Korean invasion.

Under the command of Gen. Douglas MacArthur, UN forces drove the North Koreans north of the 38th parallel. As the year ended, however, the UN troops were forced into a costly and precarious retreat by overwhelming numbers of Chinese Communists, whose entrance into the struggle had been foreseen as a possibility but was not expected. The situation for the United States, as the leader against Communist aggression, now became critical, and Congress supported the President in a gigantic program for defense. On December 16, 1950, Truman declared a national emergency and outlined plans for placing the nation on a war basis.

Truman's defense program

MacArthur, whose view of the conduct of the war contrasted with the policy of the administration, was recalled by Truman on April 11, 1951, and was succeeded by Gen. Matthew B. Ridgway. Armistice talks began on July 10, 1951, but not until July 27, 1953, was an armistice signed. After further negotiations, an exchange of prisoners was completed by September 6, 1953. Efforts to negotiate the unification of Korea ended in failure at Geneva in June 1954.

Peace treaties. The United States had meanwhile taken the lead in concluding a peace treaty with Japan; the treaty was signed in San Francisco on September 8, 1951, by 49 nations. Japan and the U.S. also agreed upon a bilateral security treaty, which provided that U.S. troops could be stationed in Japan for an indefinite period; the U.S. signed separate defense pacts with the Philippines, Australia, and New Zealand.

On July 1, 1952, the Senate approved a peace agreement

between western Germany and the western Allies. The U.S.S.R. retained control of all territory it occupied at the end of World War II and drew an "iron curtain" between eastern and western Europe.

The election of 1952. In 1952 General Eisenhower's name was entered in Republican state presidential primaries, a number of which he won. After he retired from his military post, Eisenhower's supporters campaigned actively for his nomination, and the Republican convention nominated him on the first ballot. Sen. Richard M. Nixon of California was named Republican vice presidential candidate. The Democratic national convention nominated Gov. Adlai E. Stevenson of Illinois as its presidential candidate.

Eisenhower charged the Truman administration with responsibility for events leading to the Korean War and promised that, if elected, he would visit Korea before his inauguration. Republican campaigners continued to make accusations of Communist infiltration in government offices. Truman supported Stevenson.

Eisen-
hower's
landslide
victory

In November the popular vote of more than 61,000,000 was the largest in the nation's history. Eisenhower carried 39 states (442 electoral votes); Stevenson carried 9 (89 electoral votes). Republicans gained control of the House and won a narrow 48-to-47 margin in the Senate, not including one independent Republican. Gubernatorial contests in 30 states resulted in 20 Republican victories.

The Eisenhower administration. The new president had run far ahead of his party ticket, attracting portions of the labour vote that had been consistently Democratic for 20 years, as well as a substantial Negro city vote and a widespread Middle Western farm vote.

Domestic policies. Eisenhower's middle-of-the-road policy in domestic affairs weakened the influence of labour elements in the Democratic Party and strengthened liberal elements in the Republican Party. Among his appointments were those of Gov. Earl Warren of California as Supreme Court chief justice and John Foster Dulles as secretary of state. Eisenhower was not supported by the united action of his party members in House and Senate. His differences with the right-wing elements were most marked. The President won important victories in legislation only because of Democratic support.

The Eisenhower administration was plagued throughout its first two years by the activities of the Senate subcommittee charged with investigation under the loyalty-security program. Eisenhower took the position that loyalty and security maintenance were the responsibility of the executive branch of the government; yet he did not interfere with the activities of the subcommittee, the chairman of which, Senator McCarthy, was later condemned by the Senate for conduct "contrary to Senate traditions."

The years 1953–56 were characterized by general prosperity. Confidence on the part of investment capital contributed to business development, but the Federal Reserve Board checked expansion of bank credit by adopting a tight-money policy intended to prevent inflation. The national budget was balanced, despite huge expenditures for national defense, because taxes were maintained at the necessary level and employment and earnings were moderately high.

The
Supreme
Court
decision
on racial
segrega-
tion

On May 17, 1954, the Supreme Court unanimously ruled, in effect, that racial segregation in elementary and secondary public schools was unconstitutional. This decision resulted in a division of sentiment in both political parties, especially the Democratic Party. Some immediate progress toward integration of schools was made in the North and in the border states, but in the South change was less immediate.

Foreign policy. Eisenhower's attempts to improve international relations were seconded by John Foster Dulles, who travelled widely on diplomatic missions; but the administration suffered a series of defeats in promoting U.S. objectives. Following the prolonged Korean armistice discussions, a stalemate ensued in the Far East and Communist strength in that area continued to grow.

Eisenhower's Atoms for Peace plan, proposed in 1953, was a step toward using nuclear science for the welfare of the world. His proposals for international control of at-

omic armaments and his suggestion for open-sky inspection of military installations were not adopted, but they conferred an important initiative on the democracies in the controversy with the Soviet Union over arms limitation. The leaders of the Big Four powers met in Geneva in 1955 in the hope of lessening Cold War tensions, but the results were inconclusive.

Eisenhower's illness and re-election. The President's personal role in government was basically altered in the months following a heart attack on September 24, 1955. Although he gradually resumed the responsibilities of the presidency, the temporary disability raised concern over the increasing burden placed upon a president of the United States and the calibre of men nominated for the vice presidency. The President's gradual return to health was interrupted by a severe attack of ileitis and a surgical operation on June 9, 1956. He resumed his duties and, well in advance of the Republican convention, let it be known that he would accept the nomination for re-election. He and Vice President Nixon were nominated unanimously. Adlai E. Stevenson was again nominated by the Democrats.

World
crises in
1956

The outcome of the election was largely determined by external events. Late in October eastern Europe and the Middle East burst into flames. Protest against Soviet Communist Party domination raged in Poland and brought the Soviet army into Hungary. An invasion of Egyptian territory by Israel, claiming self-defense against border depredations, and the swift attack of Great Britain and France upon Egypt to regain control of the Suez Canal, which Egypt had seized in July, dominated the final days of the presidential campaign. The electorate voted overwhelmingly for the President, who carried all but seven states. It was more a personal than a party victory, however, for the Democrats won control of both houses of Congress.

The Democratic majority in House and Senate was divided, especially on civil rights, and there was also a wide division among the Republican minority. Eisenhower's vetoes defeated Democratic plans on public housing, enlarged social security, and deficit spending.

In the midterm elections an economic recession in 1957–58 and a continuing increase in unemployment were determinning influences. The Democrats won a widespread national victory, including 32 governorships. Alaska was formally admitted to the Union on January 3, 1959. The resolution admitting Hawaii as the 50th state was signed by the President on March 18.

Racial and labour problems increased in intensity; public-school integration was contested by Southern states, and peaceful sit-in demonstrations by blacks seeking service at "white" lunch counters led to police action. In July 1959 some 500,000 steelworkers went on strike. The strike lasted 116 days before the government obtained an injunction forcing the workers back while efforts were made for government arbitration. No decision completely satisfactory to either side was reached, but work was resumed. Investigation of union leadership by committees of Congress led to passage in 1959 of the Landrum–Griffin Act, aimed at fighting corruption in labour unions and at the establishment of procedures to maintain democratic elections within unions.

The United States in world affairs. On October 4, 1957, the Soviet Union launched the first artificial Earth satellite. This achievement seemed to shift the world balance of power to the Soviet Union until, on January 31, 1958, the U.S. Army launched an Earth satellite. Within the United States the space age brought increased attention to the long-range program of education necessary for scientists and the increased costs of experimental programs.

Beginning
of the
space race

Several crises in 1958 brought the U.S. to the brink of war. In July Eisenhower ordered U.S. troops to Lebanon to prevent the overthrow of the Lebanese government by elements unfriendly to the Western powers. In August, the bombardment, by Communist China, of the offshore islands of Quemoy and Matsu brought the administration face to face with its treaty commitment to Nationalist China. In November, the Soviet Union again threatened to isolate Berlin. On December 31 rebels led by Fidel Castro seized control of the government of Cuba.

The illness of Secretary of State Dulles in March 1959 led the President to increase his own activity in foreign affairs. On April 15 Eisenhower announced Dulles' resignation, and on April 18 he named Undersecretary of State Christian Herter to replace him. Dulles died on May 24.

Eisenhower's personal diplomacy. Eisenhower accepted personal diplomacy by heads of states as desirable in the Cold War. The President on August 26, 1959, flew to Europe, where he conferred with British prime minister Harold Macmillan, French president Charles de Gaulle, and West German chancellor Konrad Adenauer. On September 15 Soviet premier Nikita Khrushchev, at Eisenhower's invitation, began a tour of the United States. In December Eisenhower travelled 22,000 miles (35,000 kilometres) in 19 days, visiting 11 countries; early in 1960 he visited five countries in Latin America.

Khrushchev proposed that a summit conference be held in May 1960 at Paris to discuss a relaxation of world tensions. But, when the heads of state met in Paris, the conference was broken up by Khrushchev, who angrily announced that a high-altitude U.S. reconnaissance plane (U-2) had been shot down over Soviet territory on May 1. Eisenhower still pursued his plan to visit the Far East that summer. He visited Alaska, Hawaii, the Philippines, Okinawa, Taiwan, and Korea. Violent anti-American outbursts in Japan brought about cancellation of a visit to Tokyo. On his return, he restated his belief in the efficacy of personal diplomacy.

Anti-American outbursts in Japan

Growth and prosperity. The decade 1950–60 was marked by a steady increase in population, which passed 179,000,000 in 1960. The shift of population from east to west continued, with a new emphasis upon movement from urban to suburban areas. Widespread prosperity, increased productivity, and higher incomes gave impetus to construction activities of all kinds. Recessions in 1953–54 and 1957–58 did not alter the generally prosperous character of the period, although agricultural income continued to lag and unemployment persisted. (E.E.R.)

The election of 1960. The two major U.S. political parties nominated comparatively young presidential candidates at their 1960 national conventions. The Republican nominee, Vice Pres. Richard M. Nixon of California, was 47; the Democrat, Sen. John F. Kennedy of Massachusetts, was 43. A dramatic feature of the campaign was a series of television appearances (publicized as debates), during which the two candidates stated their positions and answered questions from newsmen. Kennedy defeated Nixon in the most closely contested election of the century; Kennedy won 303 electoral votes to Nixon's 219, but, in the popular vote of more than 68,000,000, Kennedy's margin was only 118,000. The Democrats retained control of both houses of Congress but with a somewhat smaller majority than before.

The Kennedy-Nixon debates

THE 1960S AND 1970S

The Kennedy administration. The population growth and westward movement continued into the 1960s, with the total U.S. population passing the 200,000,000 mark and California replacing New York as the most populous state. The nation's economy was fairly stable and buoyant, as production, employment, and corporate profits reached new high levels. U.S. scientists and engineers made remarkable progress in space exploration in the 1960s. But numerous problems remained. In domestic affairs, racial tensions mounted, urban problems multiplied, poverty remained widespread, and air and water pollution reached alarming proportions. The predicted long-term effects of automation on employment posed fundamental questions as to the future of the nation's economy and of its educational system. In Southeast Asia a controversial war in Vietnam continued year after year with increasing U.S. involvement. In Europe, NATO, a key element in U.S. military strategy of the 1950s, suffered a severe setback in 1966 when France declared its intention of withdrawing its forces and requested the removal of all NATO installations from French soil. The proliferation of

nuclear weapons, with both France and China setting off nuclear explosions during the decade, greatly complicated the prospects for disarmament and world peace.

Kennedy was inaugurated as the 35th president of the United States on January 20, 1961, the first Roman Catholic and the youngest man ever to be elected to that office. His vice president was Lyndon B. Johnson of Texas, who had been majority leader of the Senate during the Eisenhower administration. The new President set the tone of his administration in an eloquent inaugural address that called for national dedication to a worldwide struggle against tyranny, poverty, disease, and war. His Cabinet included Dean Rusk as secretary of state, Robert F. Kennedy, the President's brother, as attorney general, and Robert S. McNamara as secretary of defense.

Foreign affairs. President Kennedy's first year in office saw an abortive invasion of Cuba, aimed at overthrowing the Castro regime by forces that had been secretly trained and supplied by the United States, a personal meeting of the President with Soviet premier Khrushchev in Vienna, and a continuation of Cold War tensions. In October 1962 the Cuban problem reached a critical point, when U.S. intelligence agencies learned that the Soviet Union had installed in Cuba ballistic missiles capable of attacking the United States. The President ordered a naval quarantine of Cuba to prevent Soviet ships from delivering additional missiles to the island. After five tense days during which the U.S. and the U.S.S.R. seemed on the verge of war, the U.S.S.R. agreed to dismantle its missile bases and to withdraw its troops.

The Cuban missile crisis

On August 5, 1963, diplomats representing the U.S., the U.S.S.R., and the U.K. signed a nuclear test-ban treaty in Moscow. The signatories agreed to stop all testing of nuclear weapons in the atmosphere, in outer space, and under water, thus permitting only underground tests, which did not contaminate the atmosphere. Within a few months, more than 100 other nations signed the treaty. France, the only other nation then possessing a nuclear capability, did not sign, nor did China, which was soon to detonate its first nuclear device and become the world's fifth nuclear power.

Domestic affairs. President Kennedy appealed to Congress for legislation to stimulate international trade, reduce unemployment, provide medical care for the aged under social security, reduce federal income taxes, and protect the civil rights of blacks. The latter issue, which had aroused national concern in 1962 when federal troops were employed to assure the admission of a Negro at the University of Mississippi, caused further concern in 1963, when similar action was taken at the University of Alabama. Although the Democrats controlled both houses of Congress, the administration's proposals encountered strong opposition from a coalition of Republicans and Southern Democrats. Enactment of the Trade Expansion Act and a tax-reform law were the only important administration victories in 1962. The two most important bills before Congress in 1963 called for reduction of income taxes and the strengthening of civil-rights legislation.

On November 22 President Kennedy was assassinated in Dallas, Texas. Lyndon Johnson took the oath of office as 36th president of the United States at the Dallas airport and flew to Washington. Hours after the assassination, the Dallas police arrested 24-year-old Lee Harvey Oswald. While the Dallas police were transferring the suspected assassin from one jail to another on November 24, Jack Ruby, owner of a Dallas nightclub, shot and killed Oswald in full view of millions of persons watching the events on television.

Kennedy's assassination

The Johnson administration. During his first days in office, Johnson conferred with scores of leaders from other countries, who were in Washington for the funeral of President Kennedy, and assured them that there would be no basic change in U.S. foreign policy. He also appointed a commission, headed by Chief Justice Earl Warren, to investigate the events surrounding the assassination.

Domestic affairs. On November 27, before a joint session of Congress, Johnson paid tribute to his predecessor and called for prompt enactment of measures Kennedy had proposed. Johnson's skill as a parliamentary strategist helped push the tax-reduction bill through Congress, but the civil-rights bill encountered opposition from Southern Democrats in the Senate, finally passing in June 1964.

Johnson's Great Society

In his state-of-the-union message of 1964, Johnson declared "an unconditional war on poverty," and in 1965 he outlined a program for a "Great Society." Many of his proposals were enacted by Congress, among them the antipoverty bill; Medicare, providing hospital and nursing-home care for persons over 65 under the Social Security Act; a strong right-to-vote bill that abolished literacy tests and other voting restrictions; two new executive departments, of housing and urban development and of transportation; and a measure to aid cities to rebuild their blighted areas.

In 1964 Johnson won a landslide victory over his Republican opponent, Sen. Barry Goldwater of Arizona, losing only six states. The Democrats also strengthened their majority in Congress; in 1966, while retaining a comfortable majority, they lost 47 seats in the House and three in the Senate.

Shortly after the 1966 election, Johnson underwent surgery—the second time in 13 months—focussing attention on the proposed 25th Amendment to the Constitution that provided procedures by which the vice president could become acting president and for filling the office of vice president if it became vacant. The amendment became a part of the Constitution in February 1967.

Riots in the Negro slums of many large cities during the mid-1960s caused extensive property damage. After the riots of 1967 President Johnson appointed a commission to investigate the causes and to recommend a course of action. The commission's report in February 1968 placed most of the blame on "white racism" and recommended action by all levels of government to provide employment, better housing, improved education, and more adequate police protection for black ghetto residents.

In April the nation was shocked by the assassination in Memphis of the black civil-rights leader Martin Luther King, Jr. Congress passed a civil-rights bill forbidding discrimination in the sale or rental of houses and apartments because of race, religion, or national origin.

Foreign affairs. President Johnson soon gave American foreign policy his own emphasis. It was directed chiefly toward Southeast Asia, where the U.S. had for several years been helping South Vietnam defend itself against the Viet Cong, who were being aided by North Vietnam. During 1964 U.S. aid, initially military supplies and advisers, rapidly increased. When U.S. warships patrolling the Gulf of Tonkin were allegedly attacked by torpedo boats, Johnson ordered retaliatory air strikes against North Vietnamese torpedo-boat bases. Congress approved a resolution authorizing "all necessary measures to repel any armed attack" against U.S. forces and "to prevent further aggression." Beginning in 1965 the President sent more and more troops to Vietnam, the total reaching more than 500,000 by 1968. He also ordered the bombing of North Vietnamese military targets, while repeatedly announcing a willingness to negotiate peace.

Expansion of the war in Vietnam

Opposition to the Vietnam War rose sharply in the winter of 1967–68 as casualties mounted and victory for either side seemed impossible. In March 1968 Johnson declared that he would not seek or accept the Democratic nomination for another term. He restricted the U.S. bombing of North Vietnam and again called upon Hanoi to negotiate. A discussion between the U.S. and North Vietnam began at Paris in May 1968. On November 1 all bombing of North Vietnam ceased.

The election of 1968. The Vietnam War was the major issue in 1968. The chief contenders for the Democratic presidential nomination were Sen. Eugene J. McCarthy of Minnesota, a champion of the antiwar faction; Sen. Robert F. Kennedy of New York; and Vice Pres. Hubert H. Humphrey. On June 5 Kennedy was shot by an assassin; he died the following day. Humphrey was nominated at Chicago in August, with Sen. Edmund S. Muskie of Maine as his running mate. Violent disorders, arising from opposition to the war as well as to party positions

and procedures, marred the convention. Earlier in August, the Republicans had nominated former Vice President Nixon for president and Gov. Spiro T. Agnew of Maryland for vice president. In the election the popular vote was close, but Nixon won most of the electoral votes, 301 to 191 for Humphrey and 46 for the former governor of Alabama, George Wallace, who led a third party. The Democrats, however, retained substantial majorities in both houses of Congress.

The Nixon administration. *Foreign affairs.* Nixon in 1969 enunciated what some observers called the "Nixon Doctrine," to the effect that the United States would maintain a presence in the Far East but that Asian nations would have to carry the main burden of their own defense. Strategic Arms Limitation Talks (SALT) between the U.S. and the Soviet Union were initiated in Helsinki in November 1969; on November 24 the Treaty on the Nonproliferation of Nuclear Weapons was signed.

The Vietnam War

The pace of the Vietnam War slackened in 1969, but in April 1970 the fighting spread to Cambodia. Nixon continued his policy of "Vietnamization" and reduced U.S. ground forces to fewer than 70,000 by early 1972; air power, however, remained heavily employed. The long-stalled peace negotiations in Paris concluded a cease-fire agreement in January 1973, providing for the exchange of prisoners of war and for U.S. withdrawal from South Vietnam. Thus ended 12 years of U.S. military effort that had taken nearly 46,000 American lives.

In March 1972 Nixon completely reversed U.S. policy by accepting an invitation from the People's Republic of China and visiting Peking. Long-term tensions between the two nations were markedly lessened by the journey, which included several days of discussion with the Chinese leaders Mao Tse-tung and Chou En-lai. Similarly Nixon travelled to Moscow in May for discussions with Soviet leaders; several accords were signed, including agreements aimed at limiting the production of strategic armaments. In July Nixon announced an agreement for the sale of large quantities of grain to the Soviet Union over a period of three years.

In June 1973 a visit to the U.S. by Leonid I. Brezhnev, general secretary of the Soviet Communist Party, appeared to strengthen the détente of the previous year, but the Arab–Israeli war that broke out in October brought some strain to the relationship. Secretary of State Henry A. Kissinger was active in negotiations that brought about a cease-fire between Israel and Egypt in November and between Israel and Syria in mid-1974.

Domestic affairs. Nixon's domestic policies made slow progress, partly because of opposition from the Democratic Congress. On May 21, 1969, the President nominated Warren E. Burger to succeed Earl Warren as chief justice of the United States, and the nomination was quickly approved. He also nominated, successively, two Southern judges for associate justice, but both were rejected by the Senate. The President's third nominee was confirmed in May 1970.

Supreme Court appointments

As a political issue the Vietnam War had subsided until the announcement in April 1970 of the U.S. military involvement in Cambodia. This aroused strong protest, especially on university and college campuses. Student demonstrations at Kent State University in Ohio led (May 4) to a confrontation with troops of the Ohio National Guard, who fired on the students, killing four and wounding several others.

The fight for minority rights continued as a major domestic issue, and the 12 black members of the U.S. House of Representatives charged the administration with reneging on past promises and with refusing to listen to minority groups. In 1972 Congress, with the support of the President, adopted (49 years after it was first introduced) a proposed constitutional amendment guaranteeing equal rights for women and submitted it to the states for ratification.

Nixon gave high priority to the control of inflation and the reduction of military expenditures. But the cost of living continued to rise, until by June 1970 it was 30 percent above the level of 1960; industrial production declined, as did the stock market. By mid-1971 unemployment had reached a 10-year peak of 6 percent, and inflation continued. Wage and price controls were instituted in various phases, the dollar was devalued twice, and the limitation on the national debt was raised three times in 1972 alone. The U.S. trade deficit improved, but inflation continued.

The 1972 election and the Watergate scandal. Sen. George McGovern of South Dakota, an early and earnest opponent of the Vietnam War who called for drastic reforms in welfare programs and cuts in military spending, won the Democratic nomination for president in 1972. The primary campaign had been marred by an assassination attempt on George Wallace that left him disabled. Sen. Thomas Eagleton of Missouri was the vice-presidential candidate but was soon replaced by R. Sargent Shriver after unfavourable publicity about the Senator's earlier psychiatric treatment. Nixon and Agnew, who were renominated by the Republicans, won a landslide victory in November, capturing every state except Massachusetts and the District of Columbia. The Democrats retained majorities in both the Senate and the House.

Watergate

The scandal that was to haunt Nixon's second term, and lead to its premature end, first surfaced in June 1972, when five men were arrested for breaking into the Democratic national headquarters at the Watergate office–apartment building in Washington. It was revealed that the men were in the hire of the Committee for the Re-election of the President (CRP). The director of security and a counsel of CRP were discharged and later convicted on charges of burglary and wiretapping; John N. Mitchell, former U.S. attorney general and the campaign director of CRP, resigned.

The events had no effect on the election and roused no national attention until 1973, when it was revealed that an attempt to suppress knowledge of the connection between the Watergate affair and CRP involved highly placed members of the White House staff. In response, a Senate select committee was formed and opened hearings on May 17, 1973; Nixon appointed a special prosecutor on May 25 to investigate the scandal.

The Watergate affair itself was further complicated by the revelation of other irregularities. It became known that a security unit in the White House had engaged in illegal activities under the cloak of national security. Nixon's personal finances were questioned, and Vice President Agnew resigned after pleading no contest to charges of income-tax evasion. On December 6, 1973, Nixon's nominee, Congressman Gerald R. Ford of Michigan, was approved by Congress as the new vice president.

The resignation. By late 1973, both Democratic and Republican leaders were beginning to talk of Nixon's resignation or impeachment. His popularity in the country, as indicated by public-opinion polls, declined steadily. On July 24, 1974, the Supreme Court ruled unanimously that Nixon must provide potential evidence (including, in this case, tapes of recorded conversations) for the criminal trial of his former subordinates, rejecting flatly his contention that he had authority to withhold such material. The Judiciary Committee of the House of Representatives, which since May 9 had been hearing evidence relating to a possible impeachment proceeding, voted on July 27–30 to recommend that Nixon be impeached on three charges. When, on August 5, Nixon released transcripts of three of the tape recordings previously sought by the Supreme Court, he admitted to having taken steps to direct the FBI away from the White House during its Watergate inquiries.

The admission created a storm, and Nixon's support in Congress vanished. On the evening of August 8, in a television address, Nixon announced his resignation, effective the next day. He was the first man to resign the presidency. At noon on August 9, Vice President Ford was sworn in as his successor, the first president not elected to the office or to the vice presidency.

The Ford administration. *Domestic affairs.* Ford saw as his first duty the binding of the nation's wounds and the restoration of confidence in the presidency. His nomination on August 20 of Nelson A. Rockefeller to be vice president was widely acclaimed, although extensive congressional hearings delayed confirmation until De-

cember 19. But Ford's pardon of Nixon on September 8 undermined his base of support so seriously that he volunteered to appear before a subcommittee of the House of Representatives to explain his action. Watergate reappeared in the headlines in October at the beginning of the trial of five of Nixon's aides on charges of obstructing justice (four were subsequently convicted). Ford took an active part in the autumn election campaigns, but the Democrats gained 43 seats in the House, three in the Senate, and the governorships of four states. The new Congress took action that reduced the powers of its firmly entrenched seniority system.

Ford presented an anti-inflation program to Congress on October 8. His "Whip Inflation Now" (WIN) proposals contained little mandatory action and were received coolly. As unemployment overtook inflation as a serious problem, a recession began, and the WIN program quietly disappeared. The pace of inflation rose to 10.2 percent for 1974 but declined to a "manageable" 5 to 6 percent in 1976; the unemployment rate reached a peak of 8.9 percent in April 1975 and remained high. The administration was criticized for inaction, but it was generally agreed that the economy was improving by the end of 1975. In the post-Watergate mood of assertiveness, the Congress passed a bill that established procedures for greater involvement of Congress in the budget-making process, and in September 1976 an extensive revision of the tax structure was enacted.

Inflation and unemployment

The growing financial plight of U.S. cities reached crisis proportions in 1975. In New York City expenses had exceeded tax revenues over the previous 10 years, and the city was unable to pay its maturing debt obligations. In June 1975 the state legislature created the Municipal Assistance Corporation (MAC), which virtually took control of the city's fiscal affairs. President Ford repeatedly refused federal help, but he changed his position after the state approved still more aid and the city showed signs of making major economies. Congress authorized restricted loans and a revision of municipal bankruptcy laws.

Allegations made during the Watergate scandal led separate subcommittees of the Senate and House in 1975–76 to scrutinize the Central Intelligence Agency (CIA) and the Federal Bureau of Investigation (FBI), as well as the Internal Revenue Service and the army intelligence staff. The inquiries revealed numerous illegal activities, both at home and overseas, that dated back through several administrations. Tighter controls were urged; actions included the dismissal of the CIA director and the FBI associate director, issuance of an executive order outlining a new command structure and restricting activities, and selection of a Senate committee to oversee all intelligence gathering.

Additional scandal emerged in 1976, when it was revealed that the Lockheed Aircraft Corporation had paid $24,400,000 in bribes to members of foreign governments to facilitate sales of its planes. Repercussions were felt in Japan, The Netherlands, and Italy.

Foreign affairs. Soon after assuming the presidency, Ford began a series of trips that included two visits to the Orient and three to Europe by the end of 1975.

The Vietnam War came to an end in April 1975. Just a few weeks earlier the President had requested nearly $1,000,000,000 in military and humanitarian aid for South Vietnam but had been rebuffed by Congress. Only hours before the end he ordered an airlift of refugees from Indochina, and Congress later authorized expenditure of $455,000,000 for assistance to refugees. In May Ford sent the Marines to rescue a cargo ship from illegal seizure by Cambodia.

End of the Vietnam War

The policy of détente continued as the basis of relations between the U.S. and the Soviet Union, but not without incidents of strain. A five-year trade agreement was signed in October 1975, under which the U.S. would supply grain to the Soviet Union in return for petroleum; this was followed two months later by a six-year shipping agreement. The Soviet government had cancelled (January 1975) a trade agreement made in 1972, claiming internal interference in Congress' stipulation that Moscow must permit freer emigration of Jews. A treaty limiting underground nuclear explosions for peaceful purposes, signed in May 1976, complemented a treaty of July 1974. The Strategic Arms Limitation Talks (SALT) continued, but produced only limited agreements.

Henry A. Kissinger was retained as secretary of state from the Nixon Cabinet (one of only three holdovers remaining by the end of 1975), and he dominated foreign policy in the Ford administration even more thoroughly than he had under Nixon. He accompanied Ford on his travels and undertook many missions of his own, continuing his "shuttle diplomacy" in the Middle East and in 1976 adding Africa to his areas of activity. He was responsible for a five-year treaty of friendship and cooperation (January 1976) between Spain and the U.S. and for Iran's plans (August 1976) to purchase U.S. arms worth $10,000,000,000.

Bicentennial celebration. July 4, 1976, marked the 200th anniversary of the Declaration of Independence, the birth of the nation. A celebration began in July 1975 and continued to the end of 1976 with projects, exhibits, and activities in almost every institution and community of the country. The bicentennial inspired many varieties of commemoration, including restoration and conservation projects, such as refurbishing and restoring parts of Independence Historical National Park in Philadelphia, the site of the original event; and the British Parliament's loan of one of the four first copies of Magna Carta, escorted from London by 25 members of Congress and displayed in the rotunda of the Capitol in Washington. In perhaps the most spectacular observance of all, more than 225 high-masted sailing ships under 31 flags entered New York Harbor on the historic day, followed by 53 warships from 22 nations and an estimated 30,000 small craft.

The election of 1976. The election of 1976 was the first to be held under provisions of a law regulating the financing of political campaigns, passed in 1974 and amended in 1976. Ford announced his candidacy for the Republican nomination in July 1975 and in November said that he would enter all of the 30 primaries. Though he was seriously challenged by Ronald Reagan, the former governor of California, Ford had secured slightly more votes by the beginning of the nominating convention in August 1976. The President retained his lead and won the nomination, choosing Sen. Robert J. Dole of Kansas as his running mate (Vice President Rockefeller had removed himself from consideration in November 1975).

Reagan challenge of Ford nomination

In the Democratic contest there were, at the beginning, 10 major contenders. By June 1976, however, more than a month before the Democratic National Convention, Jimmy Carter, a former governor of Georgia, had won enough delegates to be assured of the nomination. He chose Walter F. Mondale, senator from Minnesota, as his running mate.

The most notable feature of the autumn campaign was a series of debates on television (the first in 16 years) between the two major presidential candidates and one between the vice-presidential opponents. Both Ford and Carter seemed to stand solidly in the traditions of their respective parties. Though stumbling badly in the first weeks of the campaign, Carter maintained his early lead and was elected president in November.

The Carter administration. *Foreign affairs.* During his first year in office, Carter introduced his policy of tying the guarantee of human rights to the conduct of foreign affairs. This policy was echoed by Andrew Young, the U.S. ambassador to the United Nations, despite protests by the Soviet Union. To protest racial policies, the U.S. voted for a UN embargo of arms sales to South Africa and ended the importation of chromium from Rhodesia. In May restrictions on arms sales to all nations not linked to the U.S. in defense treaties were announced.

In February 1977 the U.S. extended its control of fishing rights to 200 miles offshore, giving priority to U.S. fishermen, placing restrictions on the kinds of fish caught, and limiting foreign fishing permits. This action led to the first direct formal negotiations in 16 years with Cuba, which lies only 90 miles off the U.S. coast.

On September 7, 1977, the U.S. and Panama signed two treaties giving control of the Panama Canal to Panama at the end of 1999 and guaranteeing the neutrality of the waterway thereafter. Ratification of the treaties by the U.S. Senate, however, was resisted.

A change in U.S. policy in the Middle East was indicated by a joint U.S.–Soviet communiqué issued on October 1 and calling for a guarantee of "the legitimate rights of the Palestinian people," the "withdrawal of Israeli armed forces from territories occupied in the October 1967 conflict," and the presence of Palestinians at the Geneva Conference. This was balanced, however, by U.S. support for the negotiations between Egypt and Israel begun by Pres. Anwar as-Sadat and Prime Minister Menahem Begin in November 1977. On December 29, Carter began a foreign tour to Poland, Iran, India, Saudi Arabia, France, and Belgium.

Domestic affairs. The day after his inauguration on January 20, 1977, Carter granted a pardon to those who evaded the armed services draft between August 1964 and March 1973; *i.e.,* during the period of the war in Indochina. He also ordered a review of the cases of deserters and of those who received qualified discharges during the same period. This swift fulfillment of a campaign promise was followed by three months of intense activity that produced numerous proposals for reform. Congress was presented with programs including reform of the government bureaucracy and of the electoral, federal welfare, and Social Security systems.

Energy program

Carter stressed his energy program, which met with great resistance in Congress. Aimed at reducing domestic consumption of energy and promoting the search for alternatives to foreign petroleum products, the program included a gasoline tax, taxes on domestic oil, and tax incentives for the purchase of automobiles of low gasoline consumption and for the discovery of new domestic natural gas deposits. Although the House passed all but the gasoline tax, the Senate blocked or greatly modified the entire program.

U.S. economic growth was slower than expected in 1977 and continued to be obstructed by the large deficit in foreign trade caused by petroleum imports. Inflation continued at an annual rate of 6 percent, and unemployment hovered at just under 7 percent of the work force. The adverse effects of a second successive severe winter were exacerbated by a nation-wide coal strike that began in December and led to Carter's implementation of the Taft–Hartley Labor Relations Act in March 1978.

In August 1977 Tongsun Park, a Korean businessman living in Washington, D.C., was indicted on charges of attempting to bribe government officials on behalf of the South Korean government. The action further cooled U.S. relations with South Korea, which had been strained in February by the U.S. decision to withdraw its troops from Korea over a five-year period. (Ed.)

BIBLIOGRAPHY

Colonial Development to 1763: CHARLES M. ANDREWS, *The Colonial Period of American History,* 4 vol. (1934–38, reprinted 1964), the starting point for any study of colonial America; LAWRENCE H. GIPSON, *The British Empire Before the American Revolution,* 15 vol. (1936–70), the culmination of the "British Imperial school" of interpretation; CLARENCE VER STEEG, *The Formative Years, 1607–1763* (1964), the best one-volume synthesis of the colonial period written to date; DANIEL J. BOORSTIN, *The Americans: The Colonial Experience* (1958), a brilliant, but perhaps overstated interpretation of American cultural and intellectual development during the colonial period; CURTIS NETTELS, *The Roots of American Civilization,* 2nd ed. (1963), one of several competent textbook histories of the colonial period. (*Settlement*): PERRY MILLER, *The New England Mind* (1939) and *The New England Mind: From Colony to Province* (1953), together these comprise perhaps the finest work of intellectual history ever written by an American historian; EDMUND MORGAN, *The Puritan Dilemma: The Story of John Winthrop* (1958), an accurate, readable account of the early years of the Massachusetts Bay settlement; WESLEY F. CRAVEN, *The Southern Colonies in the Seventeenth Century, 1607–1689* (1949), a competent survey of the early development of the Southern colonies; GARY NASH, *Quakers and Politics: Pennsylvania 1681–1726* (1968), the most recent account of the founding of Pennsylvania; JOHN POMFRET, *The Province of West New Jersey, 1609–1702* (1956) and *The Province of East New*

Jersey, 1609–1702 (1962), standard accounts; LAWRENCE LEDER, *Robert Livingston, 1654–1728 and the Politics of Colonial New York* (1961). (*Imperial organization*): CHARLES M. ANDREWS (*op. cit.*); GEORGE L. BEER, *The Old Colonial System, 1660–1754,* 2 vol. (1912, reprinted 1958), an old, but still reliable history of British colonial policy; LEONARD W. LABAREE, *Royal Government in America* (1930), still the classic work on the subject of the royal governors of America. (*The growth of provincial power*): CARL BRIDEN-BAUGH, *Myths and Realities: Societies of the Colonial South* (1952), a persuasive argument that the colonial South consisted of not one, but three separate sections; CHARLES SYD-NOR, *Gentlemen Freeholders: Political Practices in Washington's Virginia* (1952), still the most reliable account of political behaviour in 18th-century Virginia; JACK P. GREENE, *The Quest for Power: The Lower Houses of Assembly in the Southern Royal Colonies, 1689–1776* (1963), details the process by which provincial leaders acquired power at the expense of royal officials; VIOLA BARNES, *The Dominion of New England: A Study in British Colonial Policy* (1923), still the standard work on the subject; RAY A. BILLINGTON, *Westward Expansion,* 3rd ed. (1967), the best general survey of the movement of Americans westward; LEWIS C. GRAY and E.K. THOMPSON, *History of Agriculture in the Southern United States to 1860,* 2 vol. (1933, reprinted 1969), indispensable source for an understanding of Southern economic life during the colonial period; WILLIAM B. WEEDEN, *Economic and Social History of New England, 1620–1789,* 2 vol. (1890, reprinted 1963); FREDERICK B. TOLLES, *Meeting House and Counting House: The Quaker Merchants of Colonial Philadelphia* (1948), a good survey of economic and social life in colonial Philadelphia; LAWRENCE HARPER, *The English Navigation Laws* (1939, reprinted 1964), an important source on the effect of British legislation on the colonial economy. (*Cultural and religious development*): DANIEL J. BOORSTIN (*op. cit.*); LOUIS B. WRIGHT, *The Cultural Life of the American Colonies, 1607–1763* (1957), a general survey of American cultural achievement in the colonial period; VERNON L. PARRINGTON, *Main Currents in American Thought,* 3 vol. (1927–30; reprinted in 1 vol., 1958), a provocative, if often polemical interpretation of the development of liberal America; WILLIAM W. SWEET, *Religion in Colonial America* (1942), one of the standard surveys of religious development in colonial America; ALAN HEIMERT, *Religion and the American Mind: From the Great Awakening to the Revolution* (1966), an important new contribution to our understanding of the Great Awakening. (*America, England, and the wider world*): LAWRENCE H. GIPSON (*op. cit.*); FRANCIS PARKMAN, *A Half-Century of Conflict,* 5th ed., 2 vol. (1893, reprinted 1965); HOWARD PECKHAM, *The Colonial Wars, 1689–1762* (1964), an excellent overview of the balance of power struggles in America; MAX SAVELLE, "The American Balance of Power and European Diplomacy, 1713–78," in RICHARD B. MORRIS (ed.), *The Era of the American Revolution* (1939), an important interpretation of the place of the American continent in the balance of power struggles of Europe.

From 1763–1815: The classical work on the coming of the Revolution is LAWRENCE H. GIPSON (*op. cit.*); Gipson's one-volume summary, *The Coming of the Revolution, 1763–1775* (1954), is less valuable. Far better is MERRILL JENSEN, *The Founding of a Nation* (1968); for a good brief treatment see EDMUND S. MORGAN, *The Birth of the Republic, 1763–1789* (1956). A provocative and controversial view is CHARLES H. MCILWAINE, *The American Revolution: A Constitutional Interpretation* (1923, reprinted 1958). American arguments are set forth in RANDOLPH G. ADAMS, *The Political Ideas of the American Revolution,* 3rd ed. (1958). An excellent account of the development of American ideology, suffering only by inattention to the importance of Bolingbroke and his circle in shaping thinking of American radicals, is BERNARD BAILYN, *Ideological Origins of the American Revolution* (1967). On British politics during the period, the indispensable work is LOUIS NAMIER, *England in the Age of the American Revolution,* 2nd ed. (1961). CARL BECKER, *The Declaration of Independence* (1922, reprinted 1942), is a masterpiece of historical literature, though it and Becker's other works on the Revolution are no longer highly regarded. On the Confederation and Constitution, Jensen's *Articles of Confederation* (1940) is extremely valuable, his *New Nation . . . 1781–1789* (1950) is less so. E. JAMES FERGUSON, *The Power of the Purse* (1961), is excellent on the crucial matter of public finance in the wartime and postwar years. ALLAN NEVINS, *The American States During and After the Revolution, 1775–1789* (1924), is a standard work but contains many inaccuracies and other shortcomings. CHARLES A. BEARD, *An Economic Interpretation of the Constitution of the United States* (1913), was for decades the most influential work on the making of the Constitution, but the consensus of his-

torians is that his work was effectively disproved by ROBERT E. BROWN, *Charles Beard and the Constitution* (1956); and FORREST MCDONALD, *We the People* (1958). McDonald's own interpretation of the event, followed in the present account, is *E Pluribus Unum: The Formation of the American Republic, 1776–1790* (1965). On the 1790s the best one-volume narrative is JOHN C. MILLER, *The Federalist Era, 1789–1801* (1960). For a provocative essay from the Republican point of view, see JOSEPH CHARLES, *Origins of the American Party System* (1956). Adams' presidency is covered—adequately, if one discounts the bias against both Hamilton and Jefferson—by STEPHEN KURTZ, *The Presidency of John Adams* (1957); and MANNING J. DAUER, *The Adams Federalists* (1953). More useful than either, perhaps, is CHARLES PAGE SMITH, *John Adams,* 2 vol. (1962). On politics in general, see WILLIAM N. CHAMBERS, *Political Parties in a New Nation: The American Experience, 1776–1809* (1963). On the years after 1800 the classical work, still towering over everything written since, is HENRY ADAMS, *The History of the United States of America During the Presidencies of Thomas Jefferson and James Madison, 1801–1817,* 9 vol. (1889–91). Also useful are JULIUS PRATT, *The Expansionists of 1812* (1925); and ROGER H. BROWN, *The Republic in Peril: 1812* (1964).

From 1816 to 1850: (*The era of mixed feelings*): GEORGE DANGERFIELD's two books, *The Era of Good Feelings* (1952) and *The Awakening of American Nationalism, 1815–1828* (1965), are highly readable and comprehensive works, particularly useful on foreign affairs. SHAW LIVERMORE, JR., *The Twilight of Federalism: The Disintegration of the Federalist Party, 1815–1830* (1962), is a detailed study of what became of the Federalist Party after the War of 1812.

Books, the topics of which are clearly stated by their titles, are MURRAY N. ROTHBARD, *The Panic of 1819* (1962); DEXTER PERKINS, *The Monroe Doctrine, 1823–1826* (1927, reprinted 1966); F. LEE BENNS, *The American Struggle for the British West Indies Carrying Trade, 1815–1830* (1923); GLOVER MOORE, *The Missouri Controversy, 1819–1821* (1953); and BRAY HAMMOND, *Banks and Politics in America: From the Revolution to the Civil War* (1957). (*The transportation revolution and the beginnings of industrialism*): GEORGE R. TAYLOR, *The Transportation Revolution, 1815–1860* (1951), is a survey of other than agricultural economic developments during the entire period. Also useful as surveys are DOUGLASS C. NORTH, *The Economic Growth of the United States, 1790–1860* (1961); and STUART BRUCHEY, *The Roots of Economic Growth, 1607–1861* (1965). An example of the "new economic history," with its stress on econometric interpretations of quantitative data is PETER TEMIN, *The Jacksonian Economy* (1969). (*Social developments*): Many European visitors wrote accounts of America. Among the most valuable are ALEXIS DE TOCQUEVILLE, *De la démocratie en Amérique,* 3rd ed., 2 vol. (1838; Eng. trans., *Democracy in America,* 2 vol., 1898, reprinted 1964); FRANCIS TROLLOPE, *Domestic Manners of the Americans,* 2 vol. (1832, reprinted 1969); HARRIET MARTINEAU, *Society in America,* 3 vol. (1837); and MICHEL CHEVALIER, *Lettres sur l'Amérique du Nord,* 3rd ed., 2 vol. (1838; Eng. trans., *Society, Manners, and Politics in the United States,* 1839, reprinted 1969). Useful scholarly studies are FREDERICK JACKSON TURNER, *The Frontier in American History* (1920, reprinted 1962); CARL R. FISH, *The Rise of the Common Man, 1830–1850* (1937); ROBERT RIEGEL, *Young America, 1830–1840* (1949); and EDWARD PESSEN, *Jacksonian America: Society, Personality, and Politics* (1969). For discussions of immigration and immigrant life during the era, see OSCAR HANDLIN, *Boston's Immigrants, 1790–1865* (1941); MARCUS LEE HANSEN, *The Atlantic Migration, 1607–1860* (1940); and ROBERT ERNST, *Immigrant Life in New York City, 1825–1863* (1949). LEON LITWACK, *North of Slavery, The Negro in the Free States, 1790–1860* (1961), is comprehensive. Modern studies of urban developments are RICHARD C. WADE, *The Urban Frontier: The Rise of Western Cities, 1790–1830* (1959); D. CLAYTON JAMES, *Antebellum Natchez* (1968); ROBERT A. DAHL, *Who Governs? Democracy and Power in an American City* (1961); and JEFFREY G. WILLIAMSON and JOSEPH A. SWANSON, "The Growth of Cities in the American Northeast, 1820–1870," *Explorations in Entrepreneurial History,* 2nd Series, vol. 4, pp. 3–101 (1966). EDWARD PESSEN, "The Tocqueville Myth and the American Social Reality: Wealth, Mobility, and Equality in the 'Age of Egalitarianism,' " a paper read before the American Historical Association (December 1970), is a detailed, factual refutation of the thesis that antebellum America was egalitarian. Making a similar point are DOUGLAS T. MILLER, *Jacksonian Aristocracy: Class and Democracy in New York, 1830–1860* (1967); and GARY B. NASH, "The Philadelphia Bench and Bar, 1800–1861," *Comparative Studies in Society and History*, 7:203–220 (1965). (*Jacksonian democracy*): Comprehensive studies whose interpretations are diametrically opposed are ARTHUR M. SCHLESINGER, JR., *The Age of Jackson* (1945), which sees the Jacksonian movement as radical and dedicated to the interests of have-nots; and EDWARD PESSEN (*op. cit.*), which disagrees. GLYNDON G. VAN DEUSEN, *The Jacksonian Era, 1828–1848* (1959), is a brief survey of national politics. JOHN W. WARD, *Andrew Jackson, Symbol for an Age* (1955), is an interpretation of Jackson's popular appeal; and MARVIN MEYERS, *The Jacksonian Persuasion* (1957), discerns tensions and ambivalence in the movement's political beliefs. For the "new politics" of the era, see RICHARD P. MCCORMICK, *The Second American Party System: Party Formation in the Jacksonian Era* (1966); CHILTON WILLIAMSON, *American Suffrage: From Property to Democracy, 1760–1860* (1960); ROBERT V. REMINI, *Martin Van Buren and the Making of the Democratic Party* (1959) and *The Election of Andrew Jackson* (1963); SIDNEY H. ARONSON, *Status and Kinship in the Higher Civil Service* (1964); and LEONARD D. WHITE, *The Jacksonians: A Study in Administrative History, 1829–1861* (1954). For national issues see ROBERT V. REMINI, *Andrew Jackson and the Bank War* (1967); JOEL H. SILBEY, *The Shrine of Party: Congressional Voting Behavior, 1841–1852* (1967); and an old but still important study, ARTHUR C. COLE, *The Whig Party in the South* (1914, reprinted 1962). A useful collection of newer viewpoints is EDWARD PESSEN, *New Perspectives on Jacksonian Parties and Politics* (1969). ALFRED A. CAVE, *Jacksonian Democracy and the Historians* (1964), contains summaries of the various interpretations of Jacksonian Democracy. (*An age of reform*): The most comprehensive single treatment of reforms is ALICE FELT TYLER, *Freedom's Ferment: Phases of American Social History to 1860* (1944), a book more descriptive than analytical. LOUIS FILLER, *The Crusade Against Slavery, 1830–1860* (1960), covers its subject thoroughly. Useful collections are edited by MARTIN DUBERMAN, *The Antislavery Vanguard: New Essays on the Abolitionists* (1965); RICHARD O. CURRY, *The Abolitionists: Reformers or Fanatics?* (1965); GEORGE F. WHICHER, *The Transcendentalist Revolt Against Materialism* (1949; rev. by GAIL KENNEDY, *The Transcendentalist Revolt*, 1968); and DAVID BRION DAVIS, *Ante-Bellum Reform* (1967). Studies that explore the connection between religious enthusiasm and reform are WHITNEY R. CROSS, *The Burned-Over District: The Social and Intellectual History of Enthusiastic Religion in Western New York, 1800–1850* (1950); DAVID M. LUDLUM, *Social Ferment in Vermont, 1791–1850* (1939); JOHN HUMPHREY NOYES, *A History of American Socialisms* (1870, reprinted 1961); HENRY STEELE COMMAGER, *Theodore Parker* (1936, reprinted 1960); CLIFFORD S. GRIFFIN, *Their Brothers' Keepers: Moral Stewardship in the United States, 1800–1865* (1960); and TIMOTHY L. SMITH, *Revivalism and Social Reform in Mid-Nineteenth-Century America* (1957). (*Expansionism and political crisis at midcentury*): Valuable discussions of the ideology of expansionism are conducted by ALBERT K. WEINBERG, *Manifest Destiny: A Study of Nationalist Expansionism in American History* (1935, reprinted 1958); FREDERICK MERK, *Manifest Destiny and Mission in American History* (1963); and NORMAN A. GRAEBNER, *Empire in the Pacific: A Study in American Continental Expansion* (1955). Useful studies of the process of expansionism include RAY A. BILLINGTON, *The Far Western Frontier, 1830–1860* (1956); FRANCIS PARKMAN's classic, *The California and Oregon Trail* (1849, reprinted 1964); BERNARD DEVOTO, *Across the Wide Missouri* (1947) and *The Year of Decision, 1846* (1943); FREDERICK MERK, *The Oregon Question: Essays in Anglo-American Diplomacy and Politics* (1967); WILLIAM C. BINKLEY, *The Texas Revolution* (1952); ALLAN NEVINS, *Fremont, Pathmaker of the West*, new ed. (1955); A.H. BILL, *Rehearsal for Conflict: The War with Mexico, 1846–1848* (1947); and OTIS A. SINGLETARY, *The Mexican War* (1960). For the political conflicts stemming from expansionism and the war with Mexico, informed coverage is provided by HOLMAN HAMILTON, *Prologue to Conflict: The Crisis and Compromise of 1850* (1964); and ERIC FONER, *Free Soil, Free Labor, Free Men: The Ideology of the Republican Party Before the Civil War* (1970).

From 1850 to 1877: The best general synthesis of modern scholarship, covering the entire era, is J.G. RANDALL and DAVID DONALD, *The Civil War and Reconstruction*, 2nd ed. rev. (1969), which contains an extensive annotated bibliography. Though outdated at many points, JAMES FORD RHODES, *History of the United States from the Compromise of 1850 . . . to 1877*, 8 vol. (1893–1906; abridged ed., 1966), gives sweeping coverage. More recent scholarly interpretations are incorporated in ALLAN NEVIN, *Ordeal of the Union*, 2 vol. (1947); *The Emergence of Lincoln*, 2 vol. (1950); and *The War for the Union*, 4 vol. (1959–71), which cover the period from 1848 to 1865. CLEMENT EATON, *A History of the Old South*, 2nd ed. (1966), is the best general history of the region. ULRICH B. PHILLIPS, *American Negro Slavery* (1918, reprinted 1966), depicts the peculiar institution as essentially kindly, while KENNETH M. STAMPP, *The Peculiar Institution* (1956), sharply criticizes it from an abolitionist point of view. AVERY CRAVEN, *The Coming of the Civil War*, 2nd ed. (1957), is a provocative work, which stresses the possibility that the war could have been averted. The most perceptive account of the political conflicts of the late 1850s is ROY F. NICHOLS, *The Disruption of American Democracy* (1948). THOMAS J. PRESSLY, *Americans Interpret Their Civil War* (1954), offers a thorough review of the literature on the causes of the conflict. BRUCE CATTON, *The Centennial History of the Civil War*, 3 vol. (1961–65), is an eloquent and moving treatment, which stresses military developments. The best accounts of Lincoln's presidency are CARL SANDBURG, *Abraham Lincoln: The War Years*, 4 vol. (1939); and J.G. RANDALL and RICHARD N. CURRENT, *Lincoln the President*, 4 vol. (1945–55). Two comprehensive general histories of the South at war are CLEMENT EATON, *A History of the Southern Confederacy* (1954); and CHARLES P. ROLAND, *The Confederacy* (1960). HUDSON STRODE, *Jefferson Davis*, 3 vol. (1955–64), is the most ambitious account of the Confederate President. Three excellent syntheses of recent scholarship on the Reconstruction period are REMBERT W. PATRICK, *The Reconstruction of the Nation* (1967); JOHN HOPE FRANKLIN, *Reconstruction: After the Civil War* (1961); and KENNETH M. STAMPP, *The Era of Reconstruction, 1865–1877* (1965). Though old, W.E.B. DU BOIS, *Black Reconstruction* (1935, reprinted 1956), remains an invaluable account of the part played by blacks. The best account of Grant as President is WILLIAM BEST HESSELTINE, *Ulysses S. Grant, Politician* (1935, reprinted 1957), which, however, should be supplemented with ALLAN NEVINS, *Hamilton Fish: The Inner History of the Grant Administration*, rev. ed., 2 vol. (1957). DAVID DONALD, *Charles Sumner and the Rights of Man* (1970), offers a full account of one of Grant's principal critics. PAUL L. HAWORTH, *The Hayes-Tilden Disputed Presidential Election of 1876*, new ed. (1927, reprinted 1966), is the standard account of the political compromises that ended Reconstruction, but C. VANN WOODWARD, *Reunion and Reaction* (1951), tells more about behind-the-scenes political and economic negotiations. The definitive account of the South in the post-Reconstruction era is C. VANN WOODWARD, *Origins of the New South, 1877–1913* (1951).

The late-19th century: (*The West*): The one comprehensive study of the several "frontiers" of the period is HAROLD E. BRIGGS, *Frontiers of the Northwest* (1940). WALTER PRESCOTT WEBB, *The Great Plains* (1931, reprinted 1957), is a scholarly classic by a man who knew and loved the Plains. Important works dealing with special aspects of the post-Civil War West include RODMAN W. PAUL, *Mining Frontiers of the Far West 1848–1880* (1963); E.S. OSGOOD, *The Day of the Cattleman* (1929); J.B. FRANTZ and J.E. CHOATE, *The American Cowboy: The Myth and Reality* (1955); and ROBERT E. RIEGEL, *The Story of the Western Railroads* (1926). HENRY E. FRITZ in *The Movement for Indian Assimilation 1860–1890* (1963), traces the development of Indian policy after the Civil War. Two excellent studies of the occupation of the Plains by the farmers are FRED A. SHANNON, *The Farmer's Last Frontier: Agriculture 1860–1897* (1945, reprinted 1968); and GILBERT C. FITE, *The Farmers' Frontier, 1865–1900* (1966). EVERETT DICK presents a scholarly and interesting treatment of phases of frontier life unique to the Plains in *The Sod-House Frontier, 1854–1890* (1937, reprinted 1954). (*Industrial development*): Among many accounts of the development of industry after the Civil War, see EDWARD C. KIRKLAND, *Industry Comes of Age: Business, Labor, and Public Policy, 1860–1897* (1961). SAMUEL P. HAYS in *The Response to Industrialism, 1885–1914* (1957), offers a perceptive appraisal of the impact of industry upon many aspects of American life. Among many biographies of individual industrialists, two are noteworthy: ALLAN NEVINS, *John D. Rockefeller*, 2 vol. (1940, reprinted 1969), which is generally sympathetic with its subject; and JOSEPH WALL, *Andrew Carnegie* (1970), which is scholarly and unusually well balanced. The best brief summary of the role of the trade unions during the period is NORMAN J. WARE, *The Labor Movement in the United States, 1860–1895* (1929, reprinted 1964). (*Politics*): The literature dealing with the politics of the period is extensive, both in monographs and biographies. One contemporary study that is still invaluable for an understanding of the politics of the time is JAMES BRYCE, *The American Commonwealth*, 2 vol. (1888; new rev. ed., 1931–33), by a distinguished British scholar and public servant. LEONARD D. WHITE, *The Republican Era, 1869–1901* (1958), presents a careful and useful analysis of political and administrative policies of the period. Two valuable books that cover all or part of the period are H. WAYNE MORGAN, *From Hayes to McKinley* (1969); and HAROLD U. FAULKNER, *Politics, Reform and Expansion, 1890–1900* (1959). Books dealing with major parties include H.S. MERRILL, *Bourbon Democracy of the Middle West, 1865–1896* (1953); and ROBERT D. MARCUS, *Grand Old Party: Political Structure in the Gilded Age, 1880–1896* (1971). The standard study of Populism, regarded by some as too sympathetic with the Populists, is JOHN D. HICKS, *The Populist Revolt* (1931, reprinted 1961). Two works dealing with major political issues of the period are GABRIEL KOLKO, *Railroads and Regulation, 1877–1916* (1965), which attributes much of the support for regulation to railroad management rather than to reform groups; and H.B. THORELLI, *Federal Antitrust Policy* (1954). Among the numerous biographies of political leaders of the time, a few of the most important are HARRY BARNARD, *Rutherford B. Hayes, and His America* (1954); ALLAN NEVINS, *Grover Cleveland: A Study in Courage* (1932); H.J. SIEVERS, *Benjamin Harrison: Hoosier Statesman* (1959); LOUIS W. KOENIG, *Bryan: A Political Biography of William Jennings Bryan* (1971); MARGARET LEECH, *In the Days of McKinley* (1959); and HERBERT CROLY, *Marcus Alonzo Hanna: His Life and Work* (1912, reprinted 1965), which is still the only satisfactory biography of the man who was the chief architect of Republican policy at the end of the century.

Imperialism, Progressivism, and America's rise to power in the world, 1869–1920: ERNEST R. MAY, *Imperial Democracy* (1961) and *American Imperialism* (1968); WALTER LAFEBER, *The New Empire: An Interpretation of American Expansion, 1860–1898* (1963); WILLIAM APPLEMAN WILLIAMS, *The Roots of the Modern American Empire* (1969); and JULIUS W. PRATT, *Expansionists of 1898* (1936, reprinted 1964), present varying interpretations of imperialism. FRANK FREIDEL, *The Splendid Little War* (1958), is the best account of the Spanish-American War, while JULIUS W. PRATT, *America's Colonial Experiment* (1950), is nearly definitive on the administration of the American overseas empire. A. WHITNEY GRISWOLD, *The Far Eastern Policy of the United States* (1938, reprinted 1962), remains the standard work on this subject, but for the Open Door policy and relations with China, see also TYLER DENNETT, *John Hay* (1933) and *Roosevelt and the Russo-Japanese War* (1925); and CHARLES VEVIER, *The United States and China, 1906–1913* (1955). The story of American penetration and domination of the Caribbean is well recounted in SAMUEL F. BEMIS, *The Latin American Policy of the United States* (1943, reprinted 1967); DEXTER PERKINS, *The Monroe Doctrine, 1867–1907* (1937, reprinted 1966); and, most authoritatively, DANA G. MUNRO, *Intervention and Dollar Diplomacy in the Caribbean, 1900–1921* (1964). The best introduction to the United States during the progressive era is ROBERT H. WIEBE, *The Search for Order, 1877–1920* (1967). Still the standard work on Populism and its continuing contributions is JOHN D. HICKS, *The Populist Revolt* (1931). For the contributions of intellectuals to progressivism, see HENRY S. COMMAGER, *The American Mind* (1950); for the muckrakers, LOUIS FILLER, *Crusaders for American Liberalism*, new ed. (1964); for the social workers, ROBERT H. BREMNER, *From the Depths: The Discovery of Poverty in the United States* (1956); and ALLEN F. DAVIS, *Spearheads for Reform* (1967); and for the Social Gospel, CHARLES H. HOPKINS, *The Rise of the Social Gospel in American Protestantism, 1865–1915* (1940); HENRY F. MAY, *Protestant Churches and Industrial America* (1949); and AARON I. ABELL, *American Catholicism and Social Action* (1960). Excellent examples of the growing literature on urban and state progressivism are JAMES B. CROOKS, *Politics and Progress: The Rise of Urban Progressivism in Baltimore, 1895 to 1911* (1968); ZANE L. MILLER, *Boss Cox's Cincinnati* (1968); HOYT L. WARNER, *Progressivism in Ohio, 1897–1917* (1964); and SPENCER C. OLIN, JR., *California's Prodigal Sons: Hiram Johnson and the Progressives, 1911–1917* (1968). The best surveys of American national politics from Roosevelt through Wilson are GEORGE E. MOWRY, *The Era of Theodore Roosevelt, 1900–1912* (1958); and ARTHUR S. LINK, *Woodrow Wilson and the Progressive Era, 1910–1917* (1954). Biographical studies are particularly important for this period. Some of the best are WILLIAM H. HARBAUGH, *Power and Responsibility: The Life and Times of Theodore Roosevelt* (1961); HOWARD K. BEALE, *Theodore Roosevelt and the Rise of America to World Power* (1962); HENRY F. PRINGLE, *The Life and Times of William Howard Taft*, 2 vol. (1939, reprinted 1964); and ARTHUR S. LINK, *Wilson*, 5 vol. (1947–65), which concentrates on Wilson's public career from 1910 to 1917 and gives as much attention to foreign affairs as to domestic politics. The last three volumes of Link's *Wilson* contain the most

definitive account of the struggle for neutrality and American entrance into World War I, but see also ERNEST R. MAY, *The World War and American Isolation, 1914–1917* (1959); and CHARLES SEYMOUR (ed.), *The Intimate Papers of Colonel House*, 4 vol. (1926–28, reprinted 1971). American mobilization is well covered by BERNARD M. BARUCH, *American Industry in the War* (1941); and DANIEL R. BEAVER, *Newton D. Baker and the American War Effort, 1917–1919* (1966). For special aspects, see SEWARD W. LIVERMORE, *Politics Is Adjourned: Woodrow Wilson and the War Congress, 1916–1918* (1966); ZECHARIAH CHAFEE, JR., *Free Speech in the United States* (1941); and HORACE C. PETERSON and GILBERT C. FITE, *Opponents of War, 1917–1918* (1957). On Wilson and the Russian Revolution, see GEORGE F. KENNAN'S magisterial *Russia Leaves the War* (1956) and *The Decision to Intervene* (1958), published together as *Soviet-American Relations, 1917–1920* (1967); and the more compact monograph, BETTY M. UNTERBERGER, *America's Siberian Expedition, 1918–20* (1956). ARNO J. MAYER, *Political Origins of the New Diplomacy, 1917–1918* (1959), is a brilliant account of the development of Wilson's peace program in its worldwide context. Still the best studies on Wilsonian and American participation in the Paris Peace Conference are PAUL BIRDSALL, *Versailles Twenty Years After* (1941); and RAY STANNARD BAKER, *Woodrow Wilson and World Settlement*, 3 vol. (1922); but see also THOMAS A. BAILEY, *Woodrow Wilson and the Lost Peace* (1944); ARNO J. MAYER, *The Politics and Diplomacy of Peacemaking* (1967); and N. GORDON LEVIN, JR., *Woodrow Wilson and World Politics: America's Response to War and Revolution* (1968). The fight over the treaty is amply covered by THOMAS A. BAILEY, *Woodrow Wilson and the Great Betrayal* (1945); DENNA F. FLEMING, *The United States and the League of Nations, 1918–1920* (1932); JOHN A. GARRATY, *Henry Cabot Lodge* (1953); and RALPH STONE, *The Irreconcilables: The Fight Against the League of Nations* (1970). Nearly definitive is WESLEY M. BAGBY, *The Road to Normalcy: The Presidential Campaign and Election of 1920* (1962).

From 1920 to 1945: FRANK FREIDEL, *America in the Twentieth Century*, 3rd ed. (1970), a textbook, provides a good survey of the period. A comprehensive political review of the twenties is JOHN D. HICKS, *Republican Ascendancy, 1921–1933* (1960); while WILLIAM E. LEUCHTENBURG, *The Perils of Prosperity, 1914–32* (1958), is a lively and enterprising short account. A second volume by Leuchtenburg provides a balanced examination of the New Deal: *Franklin D. Roosevelt and the New Deal, 1932–1940* (1963). Three vividly written and richly detailed volumes by ARTHUR M. SCHLESINGER, JR., *The Age of Roosevelt* (1957–60), cover the New Deal through the 1936 election. See also FRANK FREIDEL, *Franklin D. Roosevelt*, 3 vol. (1952–56), covering down to the 1932 election. Companion volumes providing the standard economic view for this period are GEORGE H. SOULE, *Prosperity Decade: From War to Depression, 1917–1929* (1947); and BROADUS MITCHELL, *Depression Decade: From New Era Through New Deal, 1929–1941* (1947). FREDERICK L. ALLEN'S two engaging contemporary studies of the social history of this era are *Only Yesterday: An Informal History of the Nineteen-twenties* (1931, reprinted 1957) and *Since Yesterday* (1940); while ARTHUR A. EKIRCH, *Ideologies and Utopias: The Impact of the New Deal on American Thought* (1969), offers a fine study of the intellectual milieu. Two solid summaries of diplomatic developments are FOSTER R. DULLES, *America's Rise to World Power, 1848–1954* (1955); and SELIG ADLER, *The Uncertain Giant, 1921–1941: American Foreign Policy Between the Wars* (1965). Roosevelt's wartime years are accurately portrayed in JAMES MacGREGOR BURNS, *Roosevelt: The Soldier of Freedom, 1940–1945* (1970); while A. RUSSELL BUCHANAN emphasizes military and administrative matters in *The United States and World War II*, 2 vol. (1964).

From 1945 to the present: The diplomatic history of the period after 1945 has attracted broad attention and interpretation. Among these, especially valuable are surveys of American foreign policy by WALTER LAFEBER, *America, Russia, and the Cold War, 1945–1966* (1967); and JOHN SPANIER, *American Foreign Policy Since World War II*, 2nd rev. ed. (1965). The difficulty of adjustment to world responsibility in foreign affairs is emphasized by HERBERT AGAR in *The Price of Power: America Since 1945* (1957); and by JOYCE and GABRIEL KOLKO in their *The Limits of Power: The World and United States Foreign Policy, 1945–1954* (1972). Important insights on presidential elections in the sixties can be gained from THEODORE H. WHITE, *The Making of the President*, 3 vol. (1960–68). Among the valuable works on individual presidents are CABELL PHILLIPS, *The Truman Presidency* (1966); BARTON J. BERNSTEIN and A.J. MATUSOW (eds.), *The Truman Administration* (1966); and ROBERT J. DONAVAN, *Eisenhower: The Inside Story* (1956). Two authors close to the Kennedy administration produced court studies of his presidential years that are important because of their inside knowledge of events. ARTHUR M. SCHLESINGER, JR., *A Thousand Days: John F. Kennedy in the White House* (1965); and THEODORE C. SORENSEN, *Kennedy* (1965). The Johnson years are examined in detail in ERIC F. GOLDMAN, *The Tragedy of Lyndon Johnson* (1969). Several studies of American society deserve mention. ERIC F. GOLDMAN, *The Crucial Decade* (1959), catches the tone of the immediate postwar years, 1945–55; while JOHN KENNETH GALBRAITH, *The Affluent Society*, 2nd ed. rev. (1969), emphasized the wealth and complacency of America in the 50s. WILLIAM O'NEILL, *Coming Apart: An Informal History of America in the 1960's* (1971), is a lively study of the quality of American life under the impact of changing social values. RONALD BERMAN writes of *America in the Sixties: An Intellectual History* (1968). WALT W. ROSTOW, *Politics and the Stages of Growth* (1971), offers an insightful commentary on national and international economic forces.

(R.R.B./F.McD./E.Pe./D.H.D./H.W.Br./F.Fr.)

United States Outlying Territories

The so-called United States Outlying Territories consist of about 2,360 islands, islets, atolls, and cays (small low islands), plus the Canal Zone. They reach almost halfway around the world from east to west, and are spread over nearly half the distance between the north and south poles. Their total area (excluding disputed islands in the Pacific Ocean) amounts to 5,142 square miles (13,318 square kilometres), or a little less than two thirds the size of Massachusetts. In 1970 their population totalled approximately 3,000,000.

Scattered through the Caribbean Sea and the Pacific Ocean, the outlying territories consist of areas that have United States sovereignty or are otherwise under U.S. jurisdiction or administration. These far-flung locations are most extensive in the Pacific where they penetrate the Eastern Hemisphere and extend south of the Equator into the Southern Hemisphere.

The term United States may be interpreted in two ways. In a narrow sense it identifies the 50 states and the District of Columbia. The U.S. Board on Geographic Names approves this usage and further defines continental United States as comprising the 49 states and the District of Columbia located on the North American Continent. A third approved term, conterminous United States, refers to 48 states and the District of Columbia and excludes both Hawaii and Alaska. In a broad sense the term United States can encompass territory beyond that of these definitions. In most instances the inhabitants of the outlying areas are United States citizens or nationals, thus giving some validity to the broader concept of national territory.

The various outlying territories conveniently break down into two major regional categories, those associated with the Caribbean and those lying in the Pacific. The groupings for the two regions may be listed as follows: (1) Caribbean: Canal Zone; Commonwealth of Puerto Rico; Navassa Island; Quita Sueño Bank, Roncador Cay, and Serrana Bank; Swan Islands; Serranilla Bank; and Virgin Islands of the United States; (2) Pacific: American Samoa; Disputed Islands in the Pacific; Guam; Howland, Baker, and Jarvis Islands; Islands under U.S. administration; Johnston and Sand Islands; Kingman Reef; Midway Islands; Palmyra Island; Trust Territory of the Pacific; and Wake Island. Both Colombia and Honduras claim Quita Sueño Bank and Roncador Cay. In addition, Colombia has claimed Serrana Bank.

The relatively small land surface of the territories is equal to only 0.14 percent of that within the 50 states. Likewise, any comparison of population statistics is highly disproportionate. In 1970 the 3,000,000 inhabitants of the territories represented only 1.48 percent of the population of 203,000,000 in the 50 states. For coverage of individual outlying territories, see PANAMA; PANAMA CANAL; PUERTO RICO; SAMOA (AMERICAN AND WESTERN); PACIFIC ISLANDS, TRUST TERRITORY OF THE; and VIRGIN ISLANDS. For historical aspects, see OCEANIA, HIS-TORY OF. For coverage of associated physical features, see CARIBBEAN SEA; PACIFIC ISLANDS; and PACIFIC OCEAN.

The status of the territories. The statuses of the various outlying territories are by no means uniform. Those in which the United States has residual sovereignty include the Commonwealth of Puerto Rico and the organized unincorporated territories of the Virgin Islands of the United States, America Samoa, and Guam. Before they became states in 1959, Alaska and Hawaii each had the status of incorporated territories—that is, areas that the U.S. Congress had "incorporated" into the United States by making the Constitution applicable to them. In addition, a number of smaller islands, including the Swan Islands, Navassa Island, Midway Islands, and Wake Island, are unincorporated territories. In all cases these small islands are uninhabited or have only a few residents, thus making an organized governmental structure impractical. Beyond these fragments of sovereign territory belonging to the United States, several others are included as outlying territories by virtue of other types of jurisdiction or for purposes of administrative control. The Canal Zone is under U.S. jurisdiction according to the provisions of a treaty with Panama and enjoys full sovereign rights granted in perpetuity. The Trust Territory of the Pacific Islands, consisting of the Caroline, Mariana (except Guam), and Marshall islands, in 1947 was placed under the international trusteeship system established by the Charter of the United Nations. The Bonin, Volcano, and Daito island groups and Marcus Island were formerly under U.S. administration. These islands, located some hundreds of miles south and southeast of Tokyo, were returned to Japan in 1968; the southern Ryukyu Islands, also formerly under United States administration, were returned to Japanese jurisdiction in 1972.

In the western Caribbean, several low-lying islands and banks have special jurisdictional association with the United States. The United States maintains control under an arrangement whereby the claims of these countries are not prejudiced.

The outlying territories of the United States are no longer considered to be colonies, nor are those with significant populations generally referred to as possessions. The decline of colonialism throughout the world has brought about this change in terminology. In each instance the status accorded America's populated outlying territories permits a degree of autonomy commensurate with the capacity of the inhabitants to assume responsibilities of self-government. Puerto Rico, its rank as a commonwealth interpreted as a "free associated state," is in some ways similar to an independent country. It is sometimes considered "semi-independent" or "quasi-independent," being free to govern itself but conforming to U.S. policies in matters of postage, currency, customs, and in international relations and defense. Organized unincorporated territories have limited self-government, though within their borders the Constitution has not been expressly and fully extended.

The Pacific territories. In the Pacific area the United States claims 25 islands that are in dispute, 18 of them also being claimed by the United Kingdom, and seven by New Zealand. In the case of two, Canton and Enderbury Islands, the United States and the United Kingdom have by agreement established joint control. In all instances the disputes entail no ill feelings or tensions, for populations are small and no strategic significance is attached to their locations.

The Caribbean territories. In the Caribbean area the outlying territories are extended in a 1,500-mile (2,400-kilometre) arc, extending from the Canal Zone through the western segment of the Caribbean to Puerto Rico, and to the Virgin Islands at the eastern extremity of the Greater Antilles. By far the largest, and most important, unit is Puerto Rico, making up well over half of the total area of all U.S. outlying territories and accounting for nearly 90 percent of the total population. In striking contrast, Quita Sueño Bank, Roncador Cay, and Serrana Bank must be measured in acres rather than square miles and are uninhabited. They represent formations that are

Variations in status

Degrees of autonomy

largely underwater, with only a few small surfaces emerging above the high water level to form true islands.

Locations and sizes. In the Pacific the outlying territories are far more scattered, though they tend to be concentrated in the Southwest Pacific region. The area of all the islands totals 1,604 square miles (2,580 square kilometres); the area of those directly under undisputed U.S. sovereignty amounts to only 293 square miles (470 square kilometres). Among the latter Guam is the largest with an area of 209 square miles (341 square kilometres) followed by American Samoa with 76 square miles (122 square kilometres). Population of the Pacific islands is unimpressive in size, totalling only about 200,000; about half of these live in the Trust Territory of the Pacific Islands. The Trust Territory of the Pacific Islands is widely scattered, encompassing 2,141 islands of which 96 have residents. Though occupying only 687 square miles (1,100 square kilometres) of land surface, the islands extend over an oceanic area of 3,000,000 square miles (4,800,000 square kilometres), nearly as large as the 48 conterminous states.

In both the Caribbean and Pacific, many of the United States outlying territories lie near or among territories of other countries and in some instances within actual sight of them. Seventeen national flags fly over lands in the Caribbean region, including those of the United Kingdom, France, and The Netherlands. The Virgin Islands of the United States make up only the western part of an archipelagic cluster, the remainder forming the British Virgin Islands. In the Pacific the United Kingdom, France, New Zealand, and Australia also have widely scattered island realms, while Japan's offshore islands extend as far as 1,500 miles (2,400 kilometres) east of continental Asia.

Administration. Each of the United States outlying territories has a civil government closely associated with, or under the direct control of, some federal agency in Washington. An exception is Puerto Rico, but even in this instance the Commonwealth maintains an office in the U.S. capital. The remainder of the islands stand in relationship to one or another of the U.S. executive departments, and thus have U.S. cabinet members as chief officials. The U.S. Departments of the Interior and of the Navy have the greatest responsibilities, while the U.S. Department of State is responsible for all affairs pertaining to islands in dispute. The Canal Zone has two administering agencies, one responsible for various civil services, and the other responsible for the operation of the canal. Four of the outlying territories have governors and legislatures. In Puerto Rico elections are held for the governorship and for the Senate and House of Representatives. American Samoa, Guam, and the Virgin Islands have appointed governors, but the local inhabitants are endeavouring to effect legislation for elected governorships. The inhabitants of the Trust Territory of the Pacific Islands are striving to increase the degree of self-government, although the U.S. Department of the Interior currently has administrative control.

History of their acquisition. All of the United States outlying territories were officially acquired or claimed between 1856 and the end of World War II. Each acquisition was made in conjunction with some advantage thought to accrue to the country, whether economic, political, or strategic. The first insular possessions came under the American flag through an Act of Congress (Guano Act of 1856) in order to secure rich deposits of natural fertilizer made up of bird droppings that had accumulated. As a result of the Treaty of Paris of 1898 that ended the Spanish–American War, Puerto Rico and Guam became U.S. possessions, as also did the Philippines, which remained as a U.S. Commonwealth until 1946 when it became independent. In 1917 the United States purchased the Virgin Islands from Denmark as a measure of protection against German submarines. From a strategic viewpoint, the Canal Zone is a centre of U.S. interest in the Caribbean, with Puerto Rico and the Virgin Islands serving as sentinels to guard its approaches. Following World War II it proved expedient to maintain control over the Caroline, Mariana, and Marshall is-

Marginal notes:
2,141 Pacific islands

Acquisition as the aftermath of wars

MAP INDEX

Political subdivisions

Baker Island....	0·15n	176·27w
Canton and Enderbury.....	2·50s	171·40w
Guam..........	13·30n	144·40e
Howland Island.	0·48n	176·38w
Jarvis Island....	0·23s	160·02w
Johnston Island.	16·45n	169·32w
Kingman Reef..	6·24n	162·22w
Midway Islands.	28·13n	177·26w
Palmyra Island..	5·52n	162·06w
Trust Territory of the Pacific Islands........	10·00n	155·00e
Wake Island....	19·17n	166·36e

Cities and towns

Agana (Guam)..	13·28n	144·45e
Agat (Guam)....	13·24n	144·39e
Barrigada (Guam)........	13·28n	144·48e
Dededo (Guam).	13·31n	144·49e
Fafalog (Guam).	13·37n	144·51e
Inarajan (Guam)........	13·16n	144·45e
Malolos (Guam).	13·18n	144·46e
Merizo (Guam).	13·16n	144·40e
Piti (Guam).....	13·28n	144·41e
Sinajana (Guam)........	13·28n	144·45e
Talofofo (Guam)........	13·21n	144·45e
Timoneng (Guam)........	13·29n	144·46e
Umatac (Guam).	13·18n	144·39e
Yona (Guam)...	13·25n	144·47e

Physical features and points of interest

Agana Naval Air Station (Guam)........	13·29n	144·48e
Agat Bay (Guam)........	13·24n	144·39e
Andersen Air Force Base (Guam)........	13·35n	144·56e
Apra Harbor (Guam)........	13·27n	144·38e
Bikar, *atoll* (T.P.I.)......	12·15n	170·06e
Bikini, *atoll* (T.T.P.I.).....	11·35n	165·23e
Cabras Island (Guam).......	13·27n	144·40e
Canton, *island* (C.&E.).......	2·50s	171·40w
Caroline Islands (T.T.P.I.).......	8·00n	147·00e
Cetti Bay (Guam)........	13·19n	144·39e
Christmas Island........	10·32s	105·40e
Cocos Island (Guam)........	13·14n	144·39e
Danger Islands.	10·50s	165·50w
Eastern Island (Midway).....	28·12n	177·20w
Eauripik, *atoll* (T.T.P.I.)......	6·42n	143·03e
Ebon, *atoll* (T.T.P.I.)......	4·38n	168·43e
Ellice Islands...	8·00s	178·00e
Eniwetok, *atoll* (T.T.P.I.)......	11·30n	162·15e
Facpi Point (Guam)........	13·20n	144·38e
Fadian Point (Guam)........	13·26n	144·49e
Fena Valley Reservoir (Guam)........	13·21n	144·42e
Flint, *island*.....	11·26s	151·48w
Flipper Point (Wake)........	19·18n	166·35e
Gaferut, *island* (T.T.P.I.)......	9·14n	145·23e
Gilbert Islands..	0·30s	174·00e
Hall Islands (T.T.P.I.)......	8·37n	152·00e
Heel Point (Wake)........	19·19n	166·37e
Janum Point (Guam)........	13·31n	144·55e
Kapinga-marangi, *atoll* (T.T.P.I.)......	1·04n	154·46e
Kuku Point (Wake)........	19·18n	166·34e
Kusaie, *island* (T.T.P.I.)......	5·19n	162·59e
Lam Lam, Mount, *mountain* (Guam)........	13·20n	144·40e
Line Islands....	0·05n	157·00w
Maldon Island..	4·03s	154·59w

Malilog Point (Guam)........	13·15n	144·43e
Manahiki, *atoll*.	10·24s	161·01w
Mariana Islands (T.T.P.I.)......	16·00n	145·30e
Marshall Islands (T.T.P.I.)......	9·00n	168·00e
Micronesia, *islands*........	11·00n	159·00e
Middle Ground, *reef* (Midway)..	28·15n	177·25w
Mili, *atoll* (T.T.P.I.)......	6·08n	171·55e
Midway Naval Station (Midway).....	28·13n	177·26w
North Breakers, *reef* (Midway)..	28·14n	177·25w
Orote Peninsula (Guam)........	13·26n	144·38e
Pacific Ocean...	5·00s	170·00w
Pago Bay (Guam)........	13·25n	144·48e
Palau Islands (T.T.P.I.)......	7·30n	134·30e
Pati Point (Guam)........	13·36n	144·57e
Peacock Point (Wake)........	19·16n	166·37e
Peale Island (Wake)........	19·19n	166·35e
Philippine Sea.	13·35n	144·40e
Phoenix Islands.	3·43s	170·43w
Polynesia, *islands*........	4·00s	156·00w
Ponape, *island* (T.T.P.I.)......	6·55n	158·15e
Rakahanga, *atoll*............	10·02s	161·05w
Ritidian Point (Guam)........	13·39n	144·51e
Sand Island (Midway)......	28·12n	177·23w
Sand Islet, *island* (Midway)......	28·16n	177·23w
Santa Rosa, Mount, *hill* (Guam)........	13·32n	144·55e
Seaward Roads, *channel* (Midway)......	28·13n	177·25w
Senyavin Islands (T.T.P.I.)......	6·55n	158·00e
Talofofo Bay (Guam)........	13·20n	144·46e
Tanguisson Point (Guam).	13·33n	144·49e
Taongi, *atoll* (T.T.P.I.)......	14·37n	168·58e
Tenjo, Mount, *mountain* (Guam)........	13·25n	144·42e
Tokelau Islands.	9·00s	171·45w
Toki Point (Wake)........	19·19n	166·35e
Truk Islands (T.T.P.I.)......	7·23n	151·46e
Tumon Bay (Guam)........	13·31n	144·48e
Vostok Island.	10·06s	152·23w
Wake Airport (Wake)........	19·17n	166·37e
Welles Harbor (Midway)......	28·12n	177·26w
Wilkes Island (Wake)........	19·18n	166·34e
Yap, *island* (T.T.P.I.)......	9·31n	138·06e
Ylig Bay (Guam)........	13·24n	144·46e

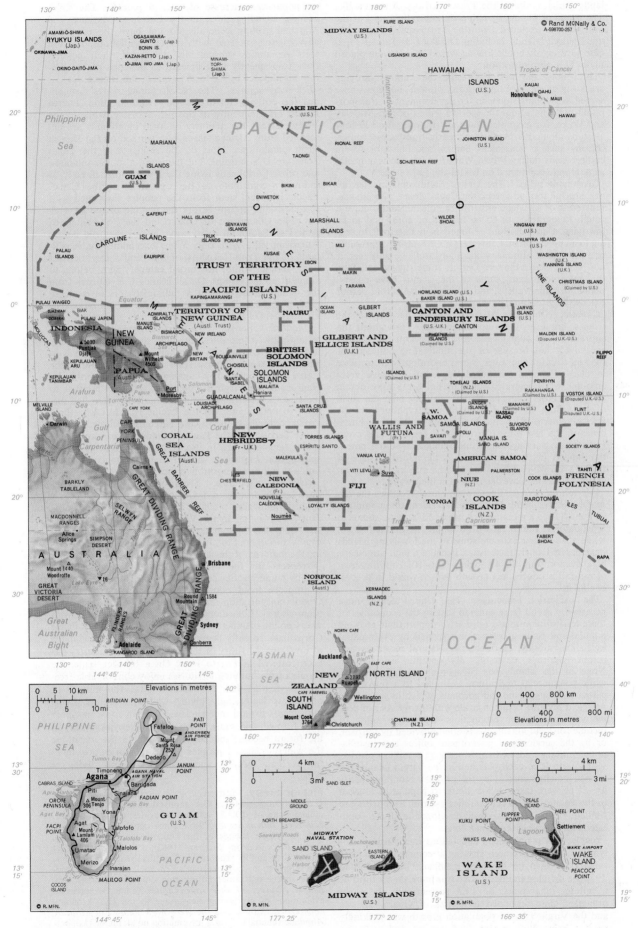

U.S. OUTLYING TERRITORIES IN THE PACIFIC OCEAN

lands, which make up the Trust Territory of the Pacific. The island of Guam, though geographically a part of the Marianas, is excluded from the Trusteeship. The southern Ryukyu Islands, including Okinawa, are under Japanese sovereignty but following World War II were placed under U.S. administration.

Throughout the western Pacific the various outlying areas—outposts over America's western horizon—have served as stepping stones in the development of transportation patterns across the world's widest ocean. Midway and Wake, for example, made air transportation history as stops along Pan American's early transpacific routes. Others—such as Kwajalein, Saipan, and Eniwetok—were battlegrounds during World War II. After the war nuclear tests were conducted on Bikini and Eniwetok.

Geographic relief. The United States outlying territories are all insular except the Canal Zone. The islands, regardless of size, tend either to be volcanic and to have a rough topography, or to be formed of coral and to be low-lying. Cerro de Punta Mountain in Puerto Rico, rising to an elevation of 4,389 feet (1,338 metres), represents one extreme of altitude, while many atolls lie only feet, if not inches, above the sea. Despite some rugged relief on the volcanic islands, some of the islands have coastal plains, streams, valleys, and rolling hill lands that permit extensive agricultural development.

Climate. Only the Midway Islands lie outside the tropics, but even these are subtropical. Throughout the entire area the climate is consistently warm but seldom excessively hot because of the moderating influence of the sea. Rainfall, however, varies enormously from place to place. Exposed windward slopes may receive great amounts while leeward slopes or flat areas may obtain relatively little. Climatic hazards usually take the form of hurricanes in the Caribbean and typhoons in the Pacific. Puerto Rico has had three destructive hurricanes in the last three quarters of a century, and every year storm warnings constitute reminders of the potential danger. In the Pacific there is the added menace of tidal waves, which from time to time may sweep over an entire island and leave destruction in their wake.

Hurricanes and typhoons (margin note)

Vegetation. Vegetative growth closely follows the climatic pattern, being primarily dependent upon rainfall. In Puerto Rico a mountain known as El Yunque stands in an equatorial rainforest with dripping, luxuriant foliage, while at the other extreme some of the low-lying islands have desert-like characteristics. Because a high sun means high evaporation, 30–40 inches (750–1000 millimetres) of rainfall produces less growth than it would in a cooler climate.

The territorial economies. The United States must necessarily spend large sums to sustain the economies of these territorial entities in order to support their growing populations. Such assistance is provided by preferential legislation, subsidy, or direct aid. Natural resources that permit vigorous economic development are lacking. None of the islands has substantial mineral deposits, while commercial agriculture is limited to a few crops, particularly sugarcane and coconuts, which in general do not yield revenue commensurate with the number of people employed in their production. A principle source of income for local inhabitants is often provided by tourism, or by the servicing of government offices and installations, military and civilian. More than a million tourists visit Puerto Rico each year and in the Virgin Islands the tourist industry constitutes the primary economic activity. Steps were taken in the 1960s to popularize tourism in the Pacific, but so far facilities catering to tourists are limited. Transportation is well developed in all the populated islands and in the Canal Zone.

Peoples and population. Populations in the major outlying territories have been growing at comparable or more rapid rates than on the U.S. mainland. From 1960 to 1970 the increase in Puerto Rico was more than a third of a million inhabitants, or 14.5 percent. On the three organized unincorporated territories of Guam, Samoa, and the Virgin Islands, population growth was strikingly greater, being 29.7 percent, 38.5 percent, and 96.9 percent respectively. The Canal Zone, however, had a mod-

est population increase of only 6 percent. The small islands, including those in the Caroline, Mariana, and Marshall groups, generally do not have the economic advantages associated with major installations, nor are their economies substantially developed; their populations consequently inch upward in defiance of the limitations imposed by the local means of subsistence.

Ethnic groupings. The racial characteristics throughout the outlying territories vary with location. Puerto Ricans are frequently of Spanish ancestry, while in the Virgin Islands the majority of local inhabitants are descended from African slaves who worked on the Danish sugar plantations. Most of the residents of the Canal Zone are U.S. citizens, but there are also Panamanians and other Caribbeans living there who either directly or indirectly contribute to the operation of the Canal. Pacific islanders stem from the peoples associated with specific island groups before the coming of the Europeans. The Chamorros of Guam and the Polynesians of American Samoa in many ways live as they did before American rule. With only a few exceptions the inhabitants of the Trust Territory of the Pacific are Micronesians, though within this broad category they belong to different ethnic groups. On all islands U.S. citizens from the mainland are present as administrators or as technical personnel. Others represent U.S. organizations or are members of the armed forces.

Linguistic patterns. To a marked degree linguistic patterns follow ethnic lines, although the English language has made great inroads on other tongues. Spanish is in wide local use in Puerto Rico and also penetrates the Canal Zone from nearby Panama. The English spoken by Negroes in the Virgin Islands is of a dialect peculiar to the eastern West Indies, which Americans often find difficult to understand. On the Pacific islands each ethnic group continues to use its own language or dialect. In the Trust Territory of the Pacific Islands, for example, nine major languages are in use, though Japanese is widely spoken and English is official. In all instances English holds an important position in the educational system.

Religious affiliations. Traditional religious practices have largely disappeared. Catholicism, traceable to early Spanish influence, prevails in Puerto Rico, the Canal Zone, and Guam. In the Virgin Islands churches represent Catholic, Protestant, and Jewish faiths. Missionary groups throughout the Pacific have succeeded in converting the majority of the islanders to Christianity.

Prospects for the future. Through various agencies and by numerous devices, the U.S. government is striving to improve living conditions in its outlying territories. Good transportation and communication facilities have been assured. Educational systems are said to rank with many on the mainland. Representatives of the U.S. Peace Corps have recently begun work to help the inhabitants of the Trust Territory of the Pacific Islands. Industry has been fostered in Puerto Rico. On a broader scale, the people of the outlying territories enjoy considerable freedom in running their own local affairs. Appointment of officials is increasingly giving way to elections. Local movements toward independence have in some instances been formed, and some of the outlying territories may in the future become independent states. In the meantime the widely scattered peoples of the territories are, in as far as their location and traditions permit, living as Americans.

BIBLIOGRAPHY. UNITED STATES DEPARTMENT OF STATE, *U.S. and Outlying Areas,* Geographical Bulletin No. 5 (1965), official status of all U.S. outlying territories; G. ETZEL PEARCY, *The West Indian Scene* (1965), some detail on Puerto Rico and the Virgin Islands of the United States; E.P. HANSON, *Puerto Rico: Ally for Progress* (1962), a thorough survey of Puerto Rico and its economy and political structure. For current information, see *Statesman's Yearbook* (annual), a dependable source of factual information on political areas; *Statistical Abstract of the United States* (annual), statistical evaluations of everything measurable in the U.S. economy and related matters; and the *New York Times Encyclopedic Almanac* (annual), factual information on all major U.S. outlying territories.

(G.E.P.)

Universe, Origin and Evolution of

Man's present knowledge of the origin and evolution of planets, stars, stellar systems, galactic systems, and the universe as a whole is pitifully small, and the French scientist Henri Poincaré's words (*Leçons sur les Hypothéses Cosmogoniques*) are as appropriate today as in 1913:

> It is impossible to contemplate the spectacle of the starry universe without wondering how it was formed: perhaps we ought to wait to look for a solution until we have patiently assembled the elements, . . . but if we were so reasonable, if we were curious without impatience, it is probable we would never have created Science and that we would always have been content with a trivial existence. Thus the mind has imperiously laid claim to this solution long before it was ripe, even while perceived in only faint glimmers—allowing us to guess a solution rather than wait for it.

Early views

In ancient Greece, the Milesian school of pre-Socratic thinkers, including Thales, Anaximander, and Anaximenes of the 6th century BC, developed the view that the formation of the world occurred as a natural, rather than supernatural, sequence of events. This view was elaborated by the Pythagorean school of that era, which stressed the concept of an ordered cosmos governed by mathematical relations, and which culminated in the work of Leucippus and Democritus of the Atomist school. The Atomist view is expressed by the Roman poet Lucretius in *De rerum natura*. He describes a boundless universe in which the interplay of atoms creates endless worlds in various stages of development and decay. These early pictures of the physical world were supplanted by the geocentric, finite cosmologies of Plato, Aristotle, and Ptolemy, which later were embodied in medieval theology. From the 16th century, the Copernican theory that the Sun is the centre of the universe, the meticulous celestial measurements of Tycho Brahe, the mathematical discoveries of Kepler, the observations and arguments of Galileo, and the theories of Newton, in a period of about 200 years, opened minds to the possibility of an apparently infinite universe whose centre has no specific location. The realization that stars may be arranged into a system of "island universes," now known as galaxies, emerged in the middle of the 18th century as a result of suggestions by the Swedish scientist and philosopher Emanuel Swedenborg, the British scientist Thomas Wright, the German philosopher Immanuel Kant, and the German scientist Johann Heinrich Lambert. Such conjectures were supported by the observations of the English astronomer William Herschel. Herschel's studies of the "structure of the heavens" were extended by his son, the astronomer John Herschel, and many others, who developed the view that the Milky Way is a single galaxy. Not, however, until after considerable dispute among astronomers was it finally established, in 1924 by the U.S. astronomer Edwin Hubble, that the majority of observed "nebulae" are at great distances outside the Galaxy and that most likely they, too, are galaxies. Hubble's discovery, in 1929, that the distant galaxies are apparently receding at speeds increasing with distance and Albert Einstein's theory of general relativity together established modern cosmology. Cosmology is the study of the universe as a unified whole, cosmogony is the study of the origin and evolution of the principal constituents of the universe. It is not always easy to strike a balance between the two, and nowadays it is recognized that cosmogony overlaps the separate sciences of cosmology and astrophysics. Thus subjects such as galaxy formation belong naturally to cosmology, whereas other subjects such as star formation and evolution are well-established areas of research in astrophysics. This article is concerned with the large-scale evolutionary processes operating in the universe, particularly the origin, evolution, and age of planets, stars, stellar systems (astrophysics), and galactic systems and the universe as a whole (cosmology), which together established modern cosmology.

EVOLUTION OF THE UNIVERSE

Alternative theories of evolution. The recession of distant galaxies implies that the universe is expanding. The expansion is isotropic—that is, the same in all directions —and, for objects not too distant, obeys Hubble's law, which states that the velocity of expansion equals distance over T ($V = \text{distance}/T$) where $1/T$ is called Hubble's constant. According to present estimates, the value of T lies between 10^{10} and 2×10^{10} years. Observations support the belief that, on a large scale, the universe is homogeneous; that is, it appears similar at all locations in space. This is the famous "cosmological postulate" whose origins can be traced back to Nicholas of Cusa (1401–64) and even earlier. The large-scale isotropy and homogeneity of the universe is independent of the small-scale irregularities due to galaxies and clusters of galaxies.

Because of the complexity of the universe, the usual procedure in cosmological studies is to construct simple representations known as cosmological models. In these models everything in the universe is smoothed out into a uniform fluid whose density is somewhere between 10^{-29} and 10^{-31} gram per cubic centimetre (g/cm³). Most cosmological models have these same kinematic properties: they are isotropic, homogeneous, and are expanding.

Models of the universe

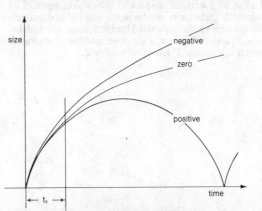

Figure 1: *Changes in the universe according to the Friedmann big-bang models.*
The present age of the universe is t_0. The negative and zero curvature models always expand; the positive curvature model, however, stops expanding at some time in the future and then collapses.

In the majority of models, it is assumed that gravity or some modification of gravity determines dynamic behaviour. Einstein's first model (1917), prior to Hubble's great discovery of the expanding universe, was static and of infinite age ($T = \text{infinity}$). It was assumed that a repulsive force exists, represented by a "cosmological term," that exactly balances the large-scale gravitational attraction. The more realistic evolutionary models of the Soviet mathematician Alexander Friedmann (1922, 1924) and later Einstein and the Dutch astronomer Willem de Sitter (1932) are of the big-bang kind (the universe began at high density, and it is still expanding; see below), and the

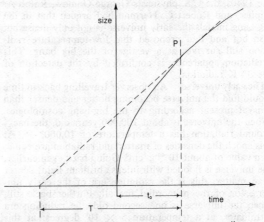

Figure 2: The relation of t_0, the age of the universe according to the Friedmann model, to time, T, with a measured value of between 10,000,000,000 and 20,000,000,000 years.

behaviour of these models is shown in Figure 1. The relation of T and the age t_0 of the universe is illustrated in Figure 2 for a model of this type. It is seen that with the Friedmann models the age t_0 is always less than T.

It was thought for many years that T had a value of only 2×10^9 years and, in the 1930s and 1940s, cosmologists were greatly concerned with the problem of reconciling this value with, for example, an age of the Earth of 5×10^9 years. One solution was the model proposed by the Belgian astronomer Georges Lemaître, about 1930, in which it is supposed that the cosmological term is even greater than in the Einstein static model. It is then possible for the age t_0 of the universe to be greater than T, as shown in Figure 3. A second solution was the steady-state model of the English astronomers Hermann Bondi, Thomas Gold, and Fred Hoyle, which is based on the theory that matter is continuously created at a rate sufficient to maintain a constant mean density in an expanding universe. According to this theory, the universe is of infinite age and obeys a "perfect cosmological postulate" such that it appears the same at all instants of time as well as at all locations in space. The revision upward of extragalactic distance estimates in the late 1950s drastically altered the value assigned Hubble's constant and increased T, and consequently the desperate need for models in which t_0 exceeds T has now vanished.

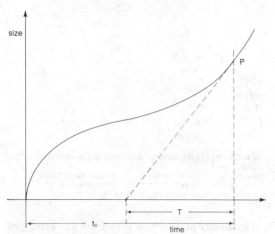

Figure 3: *Lemaître model of a universe containing a repulsive force.*
In this great model the age of the universe is at the present moment, *P*, greater than *T*.

The background radiation

Arguments in favour of the steady-state model were further weakened by the momentous discovery of the background blackbody radiation. This radiation, discovered by the U.S. physicists Arno A. Penzias and Robert W. Wilson in 1965, and identified by Robert Dicke and his colleagues, is distributed throughout the universe and has a temperature of 3° K. It is generally regarded as evidence supporting a big-bang origin of the universe. In the 1940s, the U.S. physicists George Gamow, Ralph A. Alpher, and Robert C. Herman had argued that in the big-bang models the early universe is not only dense but also hot and had proposed that low-temperature radiation still survives as a vestige of the big bang. This prediction apparently is confirmed by the detection of the 3° K radiation.

The early universe.   An observer travelling back in time would find the universe becoming hotter and denser than it is at present according to the big-bang cosmologies. When the universe is about 100,000 years old, the background radiation has a temperature of 10,000° K. At this epoch the densities of matter and radiation are equal, at a value of about 10^{-20} g/cm³. Going back even earlier, the universe is flooded with intense brilliant light, denser than matter; this is the radiation era of the early universe, or of the primordial fireball. Further back still, when the universe is one second old, the radiation era terminates, at a temperature 5×10^9 degrees; at this stage the universe is filled with electrons, positrons, and neutrinos, formed from the energetic photons of the

high-temperature radiation. At a time earlier than $\frac{1}{10,000}$ second when the temperature is thousands of times higher still, the universe consists mainly of strongly interacting particles (the hadrons) and antiparticles. The difference in the amounts of matter and antimatter can be calculated and is about one part in 10^9.

As the universe expands and cools, equal amounts of primordial matter and antimatter annihilate each other, leaving a slight residue of ordinary matter. The energy released by this annihilation is eventually transformed into the radiation of the radiation era, which survives and ultimately becomes the 3° K background radiation detected in 1965. The small amount of residual matter is not destroyed, and it therefore survives to become the present matter that occupies the universe. Thus the very early and present universes exhibit contrary properties: the small residual difference of matter and antimatter ultimately becomes the predominant constituent; whereas the 3° K radiation, which is now a minor ingredient, was once the immense energy of the big bang. It is possible, but by no means certain, that in some regions of the universe antimatter was originally in slight excess compared with matter. These regions would now consist entirely of antimatter. As yet there are no means of determining whether or not distant "antigalaxies" exist (see MATTER AND ANTIMATTER). At the beginning of the radiation era, the universe consists of photons, neutrinos, and relatively few protons, neutrons and electrons. The protons and neutrons continuously combine to form deuterium, which is then immediately dissociated by the energetic photons. But because of the expansion of the universe, the temperature is dropping, and the deuterium forms more rapidly than it is dissociated. The deuterium is now free to interact to form helium. The production of deuterium, and then helium, however, is possible for only a short period of time, principally because neutrons decay into protons and electrons. Calculations show that approximately 25 percent of the mass in the universe is converted to helium, so that the primordial matter from which the galaxies and earliest stars were formed consisted of 25 percent helium and 75 percent hydrogen by mass, with a negligible amount of other elements. There is uncertainty concerning this important result. Some blue stars in the halo of the Galaxy have apparently little or no helium in their atmospheres. One possibility is that the helium exists in these stars but so far has not been detected. Another possibility is that the helium abundance varies from place to place in the Galaxy owing to variations in the density of matter during the radiation era. Yet a third possibility depends on modifying the general theory of relativity to alter the expansion rate of the big-bang models in the manner proposed by Robert Dicke. Early work on element building was based on the hope that nuclear reactions in the primordial universe could account for the cosmic abundances of most elements that exist today. There is, however, a serious difficulty in building up elements beyond helium because of the absence of stable nuclei of atomic weights five and eight. One method is to combine three helium nuclei to form C^{12}, as in stellar nucleosynthesis. But the rate at which carbon is formed under the conditions prevailing is far too slow, and it is now thought that elements with atoms heavier than those of helium are produced only in stars (see CHEMICAL ELEMENTS, ORIGIN OF; STAR).

Production of the chemical elements

GALAXIES

Origin of galaxies.   One of the chief problems in cosmology is to explain why in an expanding universe matter becomes aggregated into galaxies. Since the time of Isaac Newton, most theories have invoked gravity as the basic cause. Newton himself stated, in some correspondence with the English classics scholar Richard Bentley: "But if the matter were evenly distributed throughout an infinite space some of it would convene into one mass and some into another, so as to make an infinite number of great masses, scattered great distances from one another throughout all that infinite space. And thus might the Sun and fixed stars be formed. . . ." And so began a long history of astrophysical investigation, of which the early pioneers were Wright, Kant, and P. de Laplace. In *Astronomy and Cosmogony*, 1928, the English physicist and astronomer Sir James H. Jeans wrote: "We have found that, as Newton first conjectured, a chaotic mass of gas of approximately uniform density and of very great extent would be dynamically unstable: nuclei would tend to form in it, around which the whole of matter would ultimately condense." On the basis of this theory he proposed that all celestial objects originate by a process of fragmentation: "of nebulae out of chaos, of stars out of nebulae, of planets out of stars and of satellites out of planets." The results of Jeans's mathematical analysis of a uniform and initially stationary gas cloud can be expressed rather simply as follows. A spherical region is considered in a uniform distribution of gas. If the escape velocity (the speed necessary for a particle to escape the gravitational attraction of the cloud), estimated from the mass within this region, is greater than the velocity of sound in the gas, then the region is unstable, and it commences to collapse. Thus there is a critical radius of the spherical region, known as the Jeans length, such that regions of greater radius are unstable, and those of lesser radius are stable and do not collapse. The gas cloud therefore breaks up into collapsing fragments, and the smallest fragments have a radius close to the Jeans length. But as these fragments collapse it is possible, as shown by Hoyle, for the Jeans length to contract even faster than the radius. Hence the fragments themselves divide into smaller fragments, which in turn subdivide, and so on.

In the formation of stars and even planets, it is possible that Jeans's basic idea is still largely true. But in the case of galaxies, the initial state probably consists of an expanding universe of gas and not the stationary distribution as conceived by Newton and Jeans. A spherical region that is part of an expanding gas cloud will become unstable when the expansion velocity at its surface is greater than the velocity of sound. When the region becomes unstable, its density increases as compared to the mean density. But the rate of this increase is extremely slow. An expanding universe in fact is not dramatically unstable; and this has led to an impasse in the study of galaxy formation. An initial state having density variations large enough to develop into galaxies in roughly 10^9 years will hopefully also explain why most galaxies are grouped in clusters.

Protogalaxies. According to the model of the U.S. astronomers R. Bruce Partridge and Phillip J.E. Peebles (1967) protogalaxies emerge from the radiation era with a density 1 percent greater than the average density in the universe. They continue to expand, but more slowly than the universe, and reach a maximum size a few times their present radius. Thereafter they collapse and attain their present size in a few hundred million years. During this early stage, gas clouds within the protogalaxy become gravitationally bound and evolve into globular clusters of stars (see STAR CLUSTERS AND STELLAR ASSOCIATIONS). Also there is widespread formation of the first generation of Population II stars (see STAR). The surviving gas, heated by stars and contaminated with elements produced in the rapidly evolving stars, settles slowly to the central region in the case of elliptical galaxies or to the equatorial plane (because of rotation) in the case of spiral galaxies. Formation of Population I stars (such as the Sun) in the disk of a spiral galaxy is delayed to a later stage because of turbulence, rotation, and the magnetic fields of the interstellar medium. Consistent with this model is the idea that galaxies acquire their rotation rather rapidly by the interplay of tidal forces. (In a somewhat analogous way, the rate at which the Earth rotates about its axis changes because of the tides produced by the Moon.) The tidal theory of the origin of galactic rotation is not yet entirely convincing, and an alternative view is that the initial fluctuations already possess rotation before they develop into galaxies, as in the vortex cosmogonies (particularly that of the German scientist Carl F. von Weizsäcker, 1951). If this is indeed true, then current ideas of galaxy formation must suffer drastic modification. Furthermore, the present model does not explain the origin of galactic magnetic

fields and leaves astronomers in the unhappy state of of having to suppose that the magnetic field in the Galaxy is a fossil remnant of a primordial field created with the universe. One of the attractions of the model is its simplicity; but perhaps it is too simple, for it gives no clue concerning the obscure nature of galactic nuclei, the large-scale energetic phenomena of exploding galaxies and radio galaxies, and the extraordinary quasistellar objects.

Evolution of galaxies. Hubble's classification of galaxies led to the belief that elliptical galaxies gradually flatten and evolve ultimately into spiral galaxies. It has also been suggested that irregularly shaped galaxies might evolve into spirals, and when the dust and gas has completely condensed into stars, they in turn become ellipticals. But nowadays it seems less certain that the different morphological types are linked by an evolutionary sequence. The oldest stars in the various galaxies of the Local Group are all of similar age. This suggests that most if not all galaxies formed at about the same time. Also, spirals rotate more rapidly than ellipticals, and it is difficult to see how massive systems like galaxies can change their rate of rotation. At present, rapid progress is being made in the study of galactic structure and evolution, although a glance at the *Atlas of Peculiar Galaxies* (1966) by the U.S. astronomer Halton Arp reveals an amazing assortment of complex structures for which so far there is no explanation whatever.

STARS

Formation and evolution of stars. The evolution of a given star cannot be directly observed. Stars such as the Sun evolve extremely slowly and their properties change significantly in a characteristic time of several times 10^9 years. Even stars that are much more massive have a characteristic time of several times 10^6 years. Stellar evolution tends therefore to be a theoretical subject, and the results are checked with the observed properties of stars thought to be at different stages in their evolution. The main-sequence stage, which occupies a long period of time during which the star converts hydrogen to helium, is well understood. But even these main-sequence studies are limited to the simplest configurations and exclude stars that rotate rapidly, that have strong magnetic fields, or are members of close binary systems. The protostellar or pre-main-sequence stages are by no means well understood, and the post-main-sequence evolution has been followed in detail only to the helium- and carbon-burning stages.

At present there is no general agreement concerning the formative stages of stars. The Soviet astronomer Viktor Amazaspovich Ambartsumian proposed (1955) that stars formed from prestellar matter at high density in the early universe. But the more common theory is that stars form from the low-density interstellar medium. Available information strongly suggests that stars have been forming for several times 10^9 years and are still being born. For example, stars in groups often recede from each other with speeds indicating that the groups were formed only a few times 10^9 years ago. Also, very luminous stars evolve so rapidly that ages of only millions of years are possible. Stars apparently form in those regions where the interstellar medium is rich in gas and dust, and the presence of stars in these regions indicates that they are still young and have not had time to leave their birthplaces.

The various stages in the formation of a star are possibly as follows: (1) A cloud or region of enhanced density in the interstellar medium becomes unstable and starts contracting under the influence of its gravitational field. The cloud has a radius of roughly a Jeans length and a mass of hundreds or thousands of times that of the Sun. (2) As the density increases, the gravitational attraction becomes stronger, and the cloud commences to collapse. But because it is transparent and radiation escapes, the cloud remains cool. The Jeans length therefore gets progressively smaller than the cloud radius and the cloud breaks up into separate collapsing fragments. Eventually, radiation fails to escape, and the temperature begins to rise. Fragmentation now ceases and the cloud has become a

Stability of gas clouds

Stages of star formation

cluster of protostars. (3) The pressure inside the protostars is now sufficient to halt collapse and a period of relatively slow contraction commences. The internal temperature slowly rises during the contraction and eventually reaches 2,000°–3,000° Kelvin. (4) At this stage energy is required to dissociate and ionize hydrogen. To supply this energy, the protostar enters a second phase of rapid collapse, and again fragmentation can occur. When the hydrogen and helium are ionized, and the protostar has a radius roughly equal to that of the Earth's orbit, collapse ceases and slow contraction recommences. (5) In the last stage the contracting protostar approaches the main sequence and reaches it when its central temperature has risen to several million degrees Kelvin and nuclear energy becomes available by the conversion of hydrogen into helium. For a star such as the Sun, the five stages (1) to (5) take a total time of approximately 10^7 years. If the mass of the star is less than 9 percent that of the Sun, the internal temperature is never high enough to convert hydrogen to helium. These stars continue to contract until the electron pressure is sufficient to stop contraction; they then cool down and become "black dwarfs."

Advanced stages of evolution. In stars of low mass (less than that of the Sun), the hydrogen in the central regions is converted into helium, which in turn is consumed and transformed into carbon. But the temperature is never sufficient to convert carbon into heavier elements. At the end of their active life, these stars contract and become white dwarfs with a radius of about 0.01 that of the Sun.

Collapse of massive stars

The fate of massive stars is apparently far more spectacular. As these stars approach the end of their life, their interiors consist largely of iron and other elements of similar atomic weight. Their nuclear fuel is almost exhausted, and yet the loss of energy by radiation and neutrino emission is thousands of times greater than the energy radiated by the Sun. There is only one solution: such a star must collapse; and as a result the temperature rises and the heavy elements are dissociated into helium and neutrons. Confronted with this ruinous situation, the star goes bankrupt and embarks on a career of catastrophic collapse. But the worst has yet to come: the helium begins to dissociate, and the star must pay back in seconds all the energy it has radiated in its main-sequence lifetime. At the same time, the rise of temperature in the outer layers causes the unconsumed nuclear fuel there to explode. The neutrino flux streaming outward from the central region has increased and become an intense blast that expels the exploding envelope.

This ejected mass then becomes a supernova remnant such as the Crab Nebula. Only one slender chance can save the imploding core. If its mass is less than the Chandrasekhar limit of approximately 1.4 solar masses, it may survive as a neutron star. But if its mass is greater than this critical value, it continues to collapse, and its ultimate fate is a challenge to the imagination. A massive supernova has momentarily a luminosity comparable with that of all the stars in the Galaxy taken together.

Neutron stars are extremely dense and have radii of only a few miles. The discovery of pulsars has awakened renewed interest in such objects, and one possibility suggested by the British astronomer Thomas Gold is that pulsars are rotating neutron stars emitting intense searchlight beams of radio waves.

THE SOLAR SYSTEM

The origin of the planetary system is the oldest problem in cosmogony and is still unsolved. A satisfactory theory must explain at least the following facts: (1) All planetary orbits are almost circular and in the same plane. The planets move around the Sun in the same direction as the Sun itself rotates. (2) The satellites move about the planets in almost circular orbits, mostly in the same plane; they have a mass roughly one-thousandth of the planets, whereas the planets have a mass approximately one-thousandth of the Sun. (3) The terrestrial planets (Mercury, Venus, Earth, Mars) are small, dense, and near the Sun, but the giant planets (Jupiter, Saturn, Uranus, Neptune) are large, of low density, and are further from the Sun. (4)

Elements essential to a theory of origin

The planetary distances from the Sun are in approximate agreement with the Titius-Bode law. This states that, in terms of the Earth's distance, the planetary distances are given by adding 0.4 to each term of the series 0, 0.3, 0.6, 1.2, 2.4, 4.8. . . . The asteroids, or minor planets, together are counted as one planet. (5) The Sun rotates slowly and its angular momentum is only ½ percent that of the planetary system (see SOLAR SYSTEM).

The various theories proposed to explain these and other facts can be characterized as either dualist or monistic.

Theories of origin through a chance encounter of stars. According to the dualistic theories, planetary systems are relatively rare and are created by the chance encounter of stars. The first known theory of this kind is due to Georges-Louis Leclerc, Comte de Buffon, who proposed in 1745 that the impact of a massive "comet" tore material from the Sun, which dispersed and condensed into planets. More than a century later, the English astronomer Alexander William Bickerton modified this idea into an encounter of the Sun with a second star, and in the early decades of the 20th century the idea was developed by the U.S. geologist Thomas Chrowder Chamberlin, the U.S. astronomer Forest Ray Moulton, the Swedish chemist Svante August Arrhenius, and others. In the work of the English astronomer Harold Jeffreys and Jeans the tidal effect of a close encounter produces a gaseous filament extending from the Sun, which then breaks up into planetary fragments. The U.S. astronomer Lyman Spitzer, Jr., has shown, however, that in all these theories the gas is dispersed long before it cools sufficiently to form condensations. More recently Hoyle has suggested that the Sun was once a member of a binary system, and the companion star evolved into a supernova. It is proposed that some of the material from the supernova outburst formed a gas cloud about the Sun and then condensed into planets. This theory is subject to objections of the kind raised by Spitzer.

Theories of origin from a single star. In these monistic-type theories a planetary system forms within a gas cloud that is part of the original star. The formation of planetary systems is thus an integral part of the subject of star formation, and it is therefore possible that large numbers of stars have planetary systems. In the nebular hypothesis of Kant (1755), developed by Laplace (1796), a rotating gas cloud contracts; the outer region of the cloud develops into a cool gaseous disk in which the planets condense, while the inner region contracts to form the Sun. According to this theory, the Sun should rotate much more rapidly than is observed. The Swedish astrophysicist Hannes Alfvèn and Hoyle have shown it is possible that the Sun transferred its original angular momentum to the planetary disk with the aid of magnetic fields. The U.S. astronomer Gerard P. Kuiper has suggested that the protoplanets were much more massive than the present planets and had a composition similar to that of the Sun. The inner planets, heated by the Sun, subsequently lost their volatile elements. The problem of how protoplanets condense in a Laplacean disk of gas and dust is still not understood. All theories so far are of a qualitative nature, and there is no generally accepted doctrine.

The Earth–Moon system is at present under intensive study stimulated by the scientific data from the space programs. In relation to its primary, the Moon is an unusually large satellite. Initial analyses of Moon rocks are disclosing differences in chemical abundances that suggest the Moon did not originate from the Earth, as proposed in the tidal resonance theories. It is generally agreed that the lunar craters and maria—some of which resemble in certain respects the surface features of Mars —were formed by a combination of volcanism and the explosive impact of incident bodies of all sizes. In its earlier stages, the solar system apparently contained a widespread distribution of aggregated material such as meteoroids and minor planets that were the remnants of the birth processes of the planets. Some of this material still survives, notably the minor planets, meteoroids, comets, and the finely divided dust in the ecliptic plane responsible for the zodiacal light—a diffuse glow seen in the

Analysis of Moon rocks

West after twilight and in the East before dawn. The minor planets, of which the majority have diameters less than a few tens of miles, are either fragments of a disrupted planet or are material aggregations that failed to coalesce into a single planet.

TIME-SCALE OF THE UNIVERSE

In most cosmologies, events are arranged in the following order: beginning of the universe; creation of hydrogen atoms; formation of the first galaxies; formation of the oldest stars in the Galaxy; origin of the heavy elements; formation of the solar system; and formation of the Earth's crust. Some adjacent steps in the sequence may have occurred simultaneously.

The age of the Earth's oldest surface rocks is estimated from the decay processes of the radioactive elements they contain. Uranium and thorium decay slowly at a known rate and produce other elements such as radium and lead. From the measured abundance of the radioactive elements and their decay products, it is possible to determine the age of the rocks. From the results of various investigations, it is found that the oldest surface rocks have an age of 3.5×10^9 years. From the abundances of lead isotopes, it is estimated that meteorites, the Moon, and the Earth itself have an age of 4.7×10^9 years. The age of the solar system, from the time it first began to form from the interstellar medium, is no more than about 5×10^9 years.

From the chemical composition of stars of various ages, it is known that the heavy elements were produced mainly during the early history of the Galaxy, 7 to 8×10^9 years ago. The production of heavy elements in stars since that period has not greatly affected their abundance. The determination of the age of the elements from the cosmic abundances depends on the theory of nucleogenesis (see above *The early universe*) in highly evolved stars and supernovae. The best estimates at the present time give an age of 6.2 to 7.7×10^9 years. The stars in globular clusters are among the oldest in the Galaxy. For a given cluster the stars have the same age and similar original composition. Initially, all the stars in the cluster belong to the main sequence. The massive stars evolve rapidly and are therefore the first to leave the main sequence; in the course of time stars of lesser mass also begin to evolve away from the main sequence. Thus by knowing the mass of the stars that are leaving the main sequence (the "turn-off point" in the Hertzsprung-Russell Diagram in which stellar brightness in magnitudes is plotted against the stellar temperatures), it is possible to calculate the age of the stars in the cluster. For the globular clusters a U.S. astronomer, Allan R. Sandage, finds (1968) an age of 10^{10} years, with a maximum uncertainty of 5×10^9 years.

Evolution of stars in clusters

According to current theories, the first galaxies were born after the radiation era at a time when the universe was a few hundred times 10^6 years old. The reciprocal of the Hubble constant is close to 10^{10} years, and for the simplest big-bang models the age of the universe is slightly less than this value. Although the various dating procedures mentioned above are still inexact, it is remarkable that the errors involved are generally not greater than a factor of 2. The results are consistent with a rational cosmology in which structure originates and evolves as an ordered sequence of events.

POSSIBLE FATE OF THE UNIVERSE

The remote future may be considered in the same spirit of speculation as the early universe. In some 10^{10} years, the Sun will have evolved into a luminous red giant and have a radius much greater than at present, perhaps reaching the orbit of Mercury. The oceans will have disappeared and the Earth lost much of its present atmosphere, and life as it is now known will have become impossible if only because of the intense heat. The gas and dust in the Galaxy must slowly disappear as it forms into new stars, and in 10^{10} years most stars will be old and only a very few will be young. Inevitably, in the course of time, the Milky Way will become faint and dark and the Galaxy a graveyard of stars that have reached the end point of stellar evolution, and similarly with other galaxies. Man, if he

has survived, in a form beyond the wildest dreams of the 20th century, will have embarked on his last and perhaps greatest adventure.

According to the steady-state theory, dying systems are forever superseded by new-born systems, and the general appearance of the universe will remain unchanged. But in the evolutionary cosmologies, the present dark and relatively empty universe is doomed to greater darkness and emptiness. If the cosmos must forever expand, the glory of the early universe has departed forever, and an eternal future lies gripped in a frozen state of meaningless death. But if expansion is followed eventually by collapse, the future is obscured by an eschatological shroud; in some tens of times 10^9 years the recession of neighbouring galactic systems will cease, and the process will start to reverse. Distant systems will still appear to recede because the observer will see them as they were in the past when the universe was still expanding. But as time passes more and more galaxies will be seen to be approaching, and eventually, either dying or dead, they will be back where they are now, but in a universe that is catastrophically collapsing. As the end approaches, first the galaxies, and then the stars, are crushed into each other in an overwhelming cataclysmic inferno, in which ultimately the collapsing cosmos reverts to the primeval chaos of the big bang. Whether the universe rises again phoenix-like is not known, and it depends perhaps on whether it can preserve identifying qualities as it passes through an inchoate quantum cosmological state of a nearly infinite density.

The Abbé Lemaître, in *The Primeval Atom* (1931), has written: "Standing on a cooled cinder, we see the slow fading of the suns, and we try to recall the vanished brilliance of the origin of the worlds." The brilliance has gone; the suns are doomed; but the vanished brilliance, and with it new worlds, may once again return.

BIBLIOGRAPHY. J.D. NORTH, *Measure of the Universe* (1965), gives a clear account of the developments in cosmology in this century. Some elements of the history of the subject may also be found in M.K. MUNITZ (ed.), *Theories of the Universe* (1957). R.B. PARTRIDGE, "Primeval Fireball Today," *Am. Scient.*, 57:37–74 (Spring 1969), discusses the discovery and meaning of the background radiation; see also E.R. HARRISON, "The Early Universe," *Physics Today*, 21:31–39 (June 1968). For information on galaxy and star formation see D. LAYZER, "Formation of Stars and Galaxies: Unified Hypothesis," *A. Rev. Astr. Astrophys.*, 2:341–362 (1964); and L. SPITZER, "Formation of Stars," in B.M. MIDDLEHURST and L.H. ALLER (eds.), *Nebulae and Interstellar Matter* (1968). More elementary treatments are out-of-date and generally unreliable. R.J. TAYLOR gives a recent and readable account of the "Origin of the Elements," *Rep. Prog. Phys.*, vol. 29, pt. 2, pp. 489–538 (1966). The best historical and critical review of solar-system cosmogony is still that of R. JASTROW and A.G.W. CAMERON (eds.), *Origin of the Solar System* (1963). Useful but rather technical information may be found in A. SANDAGE, "Time Scale of Creation," in L. WOLTJER (ed.), *Galaxies and the Universe*, pp. 75–112 (1968).

(E.R.H.)

Universe, Structure and Properties of

The physical universe as a whole is the universe that concerns astronomers, but only a part of that universe can be observed directly. The observed universe is composed basically of galaxies, vast star systems comparable to the Galaxy (see Table 1) of which Earth's solar system is a vanishingly small component.

Most of the objects to be seen in the sky without the use

Table 1: Properties of the Milky Way Galaxy
(approximate values)

Mass	10^{11} solar masses
Diameter	10^5 light-years
Overall density of main part*	10^{-23} g cm^{-3}
Total luminosity	10^{10} solar luminosities
Average energy-density of starlight	7×10^{-13} erg cm$^{-3} \approx 0.5$ eV cm^{-3}
Typical interstellar magnetic field	10^{-5} gauss giving energy density $\approx 4 \times 10^{-12}$ erg cm$^{-3} \approx$ 2 eV cm^{-3}

*Mostly in stars with about 2 percent in interstellar gas and dust.

Table 2: Features of the Universe
(approximate values)

Galaxies	
Average distance between neighbouring galaxies	10,000,000 light-years
Average density of galactic material	3×10^{-31} g cm^{-3}
Energy equivalent of this density	3×10^{-10} erg cm$^{-3} \approx 200$ eV cm^{-3}
Average number of galaxies per cluster	100
Expansion of the universe	25 km s^{-1} per million light-years giving "Hubble time" $\approx 1.3 \times 10^{10}$ years
Intergalactic matter	
Directly confirmed	none
In clusters	possibly exceeding material in galaxies
Average density through space (highest commonly estimated)	2×10^{-29} g cm$^{-3} \approx 2 \times 10^{-8}$ erg cm$^{-3} \approx 10^4$ eV cm^{-3}
Temperature of such material	10^5 °K
Cosmic rays	
Average energy-density in intergalactic space	less than about 0.6 eV cm^{-3}, possibly about 0.1 eV cm^{-3}
Microwave background radiation	
Temperature	3° K
Energy-density implied	6×10^{-13} erg cm$^{-3} \approx 0.4$ eV cm^{-3}
Intergalactic radiation from galaxies	
Average energy-density	10^{-14} erg cm$^{-3} \approx 0.008$ eV cm^{-3}
X-ray background	
Average energy-density	0.0005 eV cm^{-3}
Intergalactic magnetic field	none confirmed; almost no evidence
Gravitational waves	may be important carriers of information, but firm evidence still awaited

of a large telescope are stars and interstellar clouds that comprise the Milky Way Galaxy. Exceptions are the Andromeda Nebula in the northern sky and the Magellanic Clouds in the south, systems outside the Galaxy but generally similar to it; were the Andromeda Nebula and the Galaxy viewed from the same distance, they would probably look nearly like twin objects. With a large telescope an astronomer can observe millions of such systems, and it is evident that they are scattered through the depths of space. Whereas they differ much in size, shape, structure, and physical activity (see GALAXIES, EXTERNAL), the astronomer seems justified in regarding them all as members of a single class, the galaxies. A crucial problem for astronomy is to determine whether there is also sufficient intergalactic matter to form a significant constituent of the universe. Many astrophysicists believe that the most energetic cosmic-ray protons (see COSMIC RAYS) reach the Earth from remote galaxies. If so, they are the only known radiation, other than electromagnetic radiation, to reach Earth from these sources. At present there is no direct check because cosmic rays, being charged particles traversing magnetic fields, travel along paths that are not straight, so there is no simple way of knowing where they come from. If they do come from other galaxies, intergalactic space must be permeated by them, but their contribution to the total mass in any large region would be negligible.

Cosmology

Cosmology, in the broadest sense, is the branch of learning that treats of the universe as an ordered system. The name is derived from two Greek words, *kosmos* ("order," "harmony," "the world") and *logos* ("word," "discourse"). Almost all of the astronomical observations upon which modern cosmology depends depend in turn upon electromagnetic radiation sent out by the object observed. This includes visible light, but during the second half of the 20th century the astronomer has also become able to detect, as transmissions from celestial objects, radio radiation of wavelengths from metres down to millimetres and infrared radiation from the submillimetre range down to the red end of the optical spectrum; at the other end, using instruments in rockets and satellites, he can detect far ultraviolet radiation, X-radiation, and gamma radiation.

Every type of discrete source of any such radiation appears to be associated with some galaxy. Classification, however, is in relative terms rather than absolute distinctions. For example, whereas normal optical galaxies (those known chiefly by their emission of visible light) are relatively weak radio sources, galaxies that are strong radio sources are identified with optical galaxies in some disturbed state. The main sources of radio emission in such objects are often detached from the optical part.

While intergalactic space is traversed by electromagnetic radiations from the galaxies, these produce only a minute energy-density at a typical point in it—an astronomer there would have a darker sky than ever he has on Earth. Radio astronomers, however, have detected a microwave background radiation that, they infer, an observer anywhere in intergalactic space would also observe. The flux of this radiation—*i.e.*, the amount of it arriving anywhere in unit time—is extremely feeble; nevertheless, at a typical point it is about 100 times the estimated flux from all the galaxies. Thus, intergalactic space apparently contains a significant measure of radiations that have not come from observed sources.

Background radiation

Space scientists have discovered also an unexpected background of X-rays, but its energy contribution is relatively small. The energy contribution of intergalactic cosmic-ray particles is probably also small. There might be intergalactic magnetic fields, of intensity not exceeding perhaps 10^{-8} gauss (the strength of Earth's magnetic field at the surface is a little less than one gauss), pervading intergalactic space generally; but there is as yet no direct evidence of such fields. Another possibility is that space may be continually traversed by gravitational waves that may originate in matter collapsing into "black holes," the postulated terminal states of certain stars, too massive to allow the escape of light.

The astronomical universe consists then of all of the matter and radiation and gravitational fields that form the galaxies or that occupy the space around them. Table 2 gives some properties of that universe. The study of the universe as a whole is concerned with processes within any galaxy only to the extent to which they affect phenomena outside that particular galaxy; it leaves to astrophysics the study of such processes for their own sakes.

HISTORY OF MAN'S IDEAS ABOUT THE UNIVERSE

In ancient times and through the Middle Ages, people regarded everything outside the solar system as an unchanging background of "fixed stars." In the view of a few enlightened individuals, the Earth rotated about its axis relative to this background; but almost everybody held that the Sun, Moon, and the five known planets revolved around the Earth past the background of unchanging stars, and that the Earth was the centre of the universe. There were occasional new or guest stars, as the novae and supernovae (stars that suddenly brighten enormously) were then called, and sometimes comets moved swiftly through the system. Otherwise the heavens appeared to be eternally the same.

Astronomers inevitably took the Earth, from which they made their observations, as the origin of their system of reference; they described the apparent position of any other member of the solar system by its projection onto the celestial sphere of the fixed stars. With refinements, this is what observers still do. The earliest observers inferred that the Sun and the Moon move relative to the Earth

The Ptolemaic universe

approximately in circles centred on the Earth and described with uniform speed. More refined observations showed that the account could be improved by using epicyclic motion, complex systems of perfect circles, instead of simple circular motion, and that this method could be applied also to the motions of the planets. This scheme was elaborated between the 2nd century BC and the 2nd century AD, culminating in the work of Ptolemy about AD 140. It provided a kinematic model—*i.e.*, a model dealing with motion without consideration of mass or force—corresponding to the observations. Its most lasting concept was that the physical universe is not capricious but behaves with regularity in a fashion that man can discover and utilize to predict future experience.

The scheme became the victim of its own success. Thus, since all motions in it were compounded of uniform circular motions, such motion came to be regarded as having unique significance. It was then only a short and unfortunate step to treating this as the perfect motion from which the motion of all heavenly bodies must be derived. The apparent success of the notion that the "fixed" stars are in fact fixed in some sort of celestial sphere was even more unfortunate. For, so long as it served its purpose, it implied a special status for the Earth—*i.e.*, that it is permanently at the centre of the universe. What had begun as a descriptive convenience thus became a matter of singular significance. There was no further scope for cosmology in the model, which continued to be taught and used almost everywhere until the 17th century.

Aristarchus of Samos in the 3rd century BC had indeed taught that pride of place should be given to the Sun, not to the Earth. While the idea had had little lasting direct effect on ancient and medieval thought, it appears that in certain quarters the heliocentric hypothesis did come to be debated again during the century or so before Copernicus completed his own version in the early 16th century. Actually, there seems to have been no official or dogmatic view until after the disputes almost a century later, in which Galileo was concerned. About the time of Copernicus, the implicit attitude seems to have been the following: in principle, perhaps it does not matter what is used as a standard of rest, but in practice no one knows whether it is feasible to work out a scheme based on a standard other than the Earth or, if so, whether anything would be gained by doing this.

Significance of Copernicus

The significance of the work of Copernicus, finally published in 1543, was that he did work out and exhibit a system different from that of Ptolemy that was as good as, and even better than, the Ptolemaic system that had endured with little change for some 13 centuries. Although Copernicus took the Sun as providing the standard of rest, it played no particular physical role in his system. But he prepared the way for Johannes Kepler, who assigned to the Sun a physically unique position when, early in the 17th century, he formulated his simple rules of planetary motion. Isaac Newton, later in the same century, derived these rules, and much else, from far more powerful general laws of motion and gravitation. Conceptually, the great advance in all this was to remove the Earth from the centre of the cosmos to a rank as one of a half-dozen planets in modest attendance upon the Sun. It was not long before astronomers gave up the requirement for any preferred centre of the universe.

The change of outlook became complete in Newton's lifetime, largely as a result of his work. The idea that the fixed stars are bodies generally similar to the Sun, with its implication that the stars are at very great and diverse distances, came to be accepted. But the measurement of even a few of the shortest of these distances had to wait until the middle of the 19th century. Since then astronomers have patiently proceeded step by step to the measurement of greater and greater distances until, as will be seen, the concept of distance itself has had to be revised.

The greatest contribution made by Newton to cosmology was the concept of the universality of the laws of physics. Newton postulated that the behaviour of material systems may be inferred mathematically from certain simple general laws, and that these laws hold good at all times and at all places in the universe. While such laws have been modified and extended since the time of Newton, there has scarcely been any serious doubt that they could be formulated in such a way as to have the same validity throughout the universe. All progress has depended upon assuming this, and it has never led to any inconsistency.

Another great advance was the discovery of the universality of the composition of the universe. From the development of spectrum analysis in the 19th century, through all the applications of atomic physics and nuclear physics, to the latest work on quasi-stellar objects, all the evidence is that matter is everywhere made of the same particles and that the universal constants of physics are indeed universal. It is hoped that cosmology will sometime account for this situation in terms of some more fundamental concepts.

Universality of the laws of physics and of the composition of the universe

To return to the development of astronomy, in the late 18th and early 19th centuries the astronomer William Herschel, in England, followed by his son John Herschel and some contemporaries, inaugurated the study of stellar astronomy. This was partly the cause, and partly the result, of William Herschel's making better reflecting telescopes than had ever been made before. In far greater numbers than previously, stars could be resolved and apparent brightnesses assigned to them. On the principle that faintness is a statistical measure of distance, it was then possible to infer how the stars are distributed with respect to relative distance, in various directions in space. A qualitative picture of the Galaxy as a flattened system of stars and nebulae, isolated in space, emerged about 1785. But it was not until about 1918 that the United States astronomer Harlow Shapley and his contemporaries could assign reliable dimensions to the system and estimate the location of the Sun (some 30,000 light-years from the centre). In 1927 the Netherlands astronomer Jan Oort accounted for the motions of the stars as orbital motions in the gravitational field of the Galaxy. This led to the most direct way of estimating the mass of the Galaxy (about 100,000 million solar masses).

The conclusion that the observed stellar system is an island in boundless space suggested to William Herschel and his successors that there might be other such "island universes" beyond its boundaries, and that certain nebulae might in fact be such systems. Later in the 19th century astronomers discovered the spiral structure of some of these and the first observational indication that they are composed of stellar aggregates. Only about 1924 did astronomers derive reliable estimates of their distances and thence establish that they are indeed systems comparable with the Galaxy. The distance scale has ever since been under review, and even now the best that astronomers can claim is to know the distances of the nearer galaxies and clusters of galaxies within a factor of about two.

From 1925 astronomers had the quantitative knowledge necessary to embark upon large-scale observational exploration of the universe; it is now possible to survey the outcome of nearly half a century of observational and theoretical study.

BASIC PROPERTIES OF THE UNIVERSE

Structure of the universe. Galaxies are distributed through space in a patchy fashion; the Milky Way belongs to a Local Group of 20-odd members; there are single galaxies, galaxy pairs, large galaxies attended by a few satellite galaxies; there are clusters of galaxies of anything up to 1,000 members or more. Some of the nearer groupings seem to belong to a supercluster, and it seems possible to recognize other such systems; but evidence for a general hierarchical arrangement is not convincing.

The astronomer sees no significant difference in the general appearance of the universe looked at in different directions. Looking at his overall picture, he sees no reason to suppose that another astronomer anywhere else in the whole system would have a significantly different overall picture. So he tentatively infers that the universe in the large is homogeneous and isotropic.

Behaviour of the universe. Perhaps the most exciting observation about the universe in the large is that, seemingly, it is expanding. In 1929, following earlier fragmentary evidence, the U.S. astronomer Edwin Hubble published his finding that the lines in the spectra of remote galaxies show a red shift that, statistically, is systematically greater, the fainter the galaxy. The red shift is a change to longer wavelengths of recognizable lines in the spectrum and could be caused by a movement of the emitting object away from the observer. This is an instance of the Doppler effect that may be noticed, in the case of sound waves, in the change in pitch of a train whistle or automobile horn as the vehicle approaches or moves away, resulting in higher or lower pitch. Hubble interpreted his measurements as showing that every other galaxy is receding from the Milky Way with speed proportional to its distance; *i.e.*, recession speed equals distance divided by a quantity τ the same for all galaxies. This is called Hubble's law, and τ, which has the dimension of time, is the "Hubble time." The latest estimate is that it is about 1.9×10^{10} years. If the law applies to the galaxies as seen from one of them, it clearly applies to them as seen from any other. Had each galaxy always possessed the same speed, taken literally the law would mean that all galaxies were in the same place τ years ago.

The red shift, usually denoted by z, is such that $1 + z$ is the ratio of the wavelength of a line in the observed spectrum to the laboratory wavelength of the same line, which is assumed to be the wavelength that would be seen in a spectrum taken at the source. Hubble's law is derived from observing galaxies showing red shifts with z values up to about 0.2; *i.e.*, receding with speeds up to one-fifth that of light. Cases of much larger red shifts and the question of alternative interpretations are mentioned below. But the Hubble red shift is generally interpreted as a Doppler effect denoting the general recession of the galaxies; this is called the cosmological red shift.

Age of the universe. The Sun and the other stars are continually emitting energy into surrounding space and so, presumably, they have not been shining forever. On the other hand, astronomical and geophysical evidence demands certain minimum ages. Modern astrophysical theory has provided progressively more reliable inferences about physical conditions throughout a star, and physics has shown what nuclear reactions must proceed under these conditions to supply the star's energy output. Such work shows the oldest stars in the Galaxy to be about 10^{10} years old. Apparently, existing stars are survivors belonging to two or three generations. Astrophysicists commonly believe that the matter that forms the Galaxy was brought together in some diffuse state into about the volume now occupied by the Galaxy, and it was not long, astronomically speaking, before the matter formed itself into stars. The first-generation stars might have been on the average 10 to 100 times more massive than present typical stars. The time since their formation is calculated to be between 10^{10} and 2×10^{10} years—the so-called age of the Galaxy. During that time, it seems that it cannot have been appreciably influenced by any other material system. Accumulating evidence tends to show that all the galaxies in any cluster are of approximately the same age. But how the raw material of the galaxies was originally gathered together in appropriate quantities is a major unsolved problem.

Hubble's law implies some sort of a start to the expansion of the universe at a time of the order 10^{10} years ago. On totally different evidence, the estimated age of the Galaxy is also of this order. Even without the cosmological theories discussed below, a picture is thus formed of an evolving universe in which, somewhat over 10^{10} years ago, matter had a much higher average density than at present and was not yet resolved into galaxies and stars.

If an astronomer observes part of the universe a thousand million (10^9) light-years away, say, he sees it as it was 10^9 years ago when the light set out. If the whole universe is evolving, he sees that part as it was when 10^9 years younger than his own part. In particular, if there were no galaxies, say, 2×10^{10} years ago, the astronomer could see no galaxy more than 2×10^{10} light-years distant. Thus he does not see a background of galaxies that extends indefinitely into the distance (as "distance" is here understood). Estimates are that the background light from all other galaxies is only about 1 percent of the background light at the Earth from the Milky Way (excluding sunlight)—the cosmic sky is black indeed.

Structure of galaxies. Cosmology is bound to be somewhat concerned about the constitution of galaxies because: (1) a description of the universe should include that of its stock of galaxies; (2) recognition of the type of a galaxy aids in estimating its distance; (3) knowledge of the structure and evolution of galaxies aids in the interpretation of large-scale surveys—*e.g.*, counts of radio sources; (4) galaxies are the only sources of radiation that are observed (if, as mentioned above, the quasi-stellar sources are included) and it is necessary to take account of every kind of radiation transmitted by them. Although galaxies are described in greater detail elsewhere (see GALAXIES, EXTERNAL), brief descriptions of the main types are needed here and are given in the next few paragraphs.

An elliptical galaxy appears to contain very little interstellar gas or dust and to be composed almost entirely of stars distributed in a very regular fashion. In spiral galaxies, most of the stars occupy a lens-shaped volume; spirals also contain large amounts of gas and dust mostly concentrated, along with the brightest stars, into a structure of spiral arms or bars or both, which may exhibit remarkable regularity or much irregularity of form. Most galaxies have a marked concentration of material in their central regions; many possess a well-defined nucleus characterized by a sharp peak in the number-density of stars, there being between 10^7 and 10^9 stars in a volume probably no more than a few tens of light-years across. In 1 or 2 percent of spirals the nucleus is the dominant feature, making the rest of the object difficult to observe (the so-called Seyfert galaxies). In recent times, astronomers have been surprised to find that apparently every nucleus is to a greater or lesser extent the scene of some sort of activity revealed by the outflow of material and/or the variability of some component of its radiation. A galactic nucleus evidently may also experience a violent event, when material of millions of stellar masses is ejected to distances comparable to the whole extent of the galaxy concerned. Such an event may indeed denote a stage in the original formation of the nucleus and is possibly concerned in the genesis of spiral arms. Also, it has generally been considered that such an event may have something to do with a galaxy becoming a radio galaxy. More recently, however, astronomers have begun to question whether the material of the radio-source part of a radio galaxy has necessarily been ejected from the optical part; a galaxy as a whole may well be a more complex and extended object than hitherto envisaged.

The mass of a particular galaxy may be inferred from the motions of stars and gas contained in it and, to some extent, from its surface brightness; but the methods are such as to leave the integrated mass uncertain by a factor of perhaps two. Giant ellipticals and great spirals have masses up to almost one million million (10^{12}) solar masses, while some dwarf galaxies are estimated to have less than 1,000,000 solar masses.

Clusters of galaxies. Clusters differ greatly in the number of galaxies in them and in the space-density of these galaxies. Any sizable cluster includes members in a wide range of shapes and sizes. The study of clusters at known relative distances has led some astronomers to conclude that the brightest galaxy in a cluster is a rather standard object. If valid, this provides astronomers with "standard candles" that have, for instance, facilitated an apparently improved investigation of Hubble's law. It seems nearer the truth, however, to say that the luminosity distribution of galaxies has a rather abrupt cutoff on the high-luminosity side so in any sample, such as a cluster, the brightest member is apt to be fairly near this cutoff. Consequently, even the most recent determinations of Hubble's constant are less secure than had been hoped.

The study of the dynamics of groupings of apparently physically associated galaxies usually leads to masses 10

Formation of stars [left margin]

The centres, or nuclei, of galaxies [right margin]

The problem of "missing mass"

to 100 times the value obtained by totalling the estimated masses of the member galaxies. This produces the notorious problem of the "missing mass." Almost certainly, the explanation is that the groupings concerned may not be treated as independent permanent gravitating systems. The problem is mentioned here because it emphasizes the great difficulty in determining how much matter there is in even a relatively small tract of the universe. At the same time, the expansion of the universe should be described in terms of the mutual recession of clusters rather than of individual galaxies.

Counts of galaxies. Were all galaxies of the same intrinsic brightness, the radiation flux S from a galaxy would be inversely proportional to the square of its distance. Were all galaxies at rest and distributed uniformly through ordinary space, the number n within any distance would be proportional to the cube of the distance. Thus the number n of galaxies producing flux not less than S would be inversely proportional to the power $3/2$ of S. The rule is not affected even if the galaxies are not all of the same intrinsic brightness, provided the other assumptions hold good. In principle, it is, then, a simple matter to take some particular part of the sky and, for various values of S, to count the number N of actual galaxies giving a flux S or more. Comparing the observed values of N with the values of n calculated from the rule tells something about how the actual galaxies are distributed in depth; doing this for different parts of the sky shows how they are distributed in different directions in space.

In practice, this task is prohibitively difficult for optical astronomy. It is different for radio astronomy. This is because radio galaxies are much fewer than optical galaxies; using existing instruments, radio galaxies can apparently be detected out to considerably greater distances than optical galaxies; there is less difficulty with foreground objects; the radio records may be analyzed by statistical methods not applicable to optical observations.

Radio astronomers in Cambridge, England, have done the most extensive work in this field; some surveys have been made in a few other observatories and, taking account of the character of the radio spectrum when comparing observations at different wavelengths, the various counts are in satisfactory agreement. Radio observers claim that there cannot be any significant source category overlooked by the counts; for these counts, along with a plausible extrapolation allowing for unresolved sources, account for all the measured resultant flux at the wavelengths concerned—a test of completeness not available to optical astronomers. If N and n (as defined above) agree for the strongest sources, the counts show that N increases more steeply than n with decreasing radiation-flux S, until N reaches a value about 100 times the corresponding value of n: going to still smaller S, N increases less rapidly, ultimately reaching values below the corresponding n-values. The results for different parts of the sky are similar, thus confirming that what are being studied are genuine cosmical properties.

All objects that show a particular cosmological red shift z being at the same distance from the observer, they are seen as they were at a particular past cosmic epoch— "epoch z." While optical identifications and red shift measurements are not available for most of the sources concerned, a long chain of extrapolation from cases of known red shifts shows a possible interpretation of the counts to be that at about epoch $z = 3$ the ratio of radio sources to ordinary galaxies was about 100 times its present value, while before about $z = 4$ there were almost no sources.

Infrequency of radio sources beyond $z = 4$

This result is a major discovery about the structure and evolution of the universe. It confirms that the universe is evolving and is certainly not in a steady state on the scale concerned here. The result has frustrating implications, too, for it shows that evolutionary effects have a predominant influence on the counts, which are thus of little help in discriminating between different cosmological models.

Space-time. A 20th-century man describing the flight of a golf ball or a space vehicle employs the same notions of space and time as did Newton and all his followers. Obviously, these notions serve such purposes with great accuracy. But Newton and his followers assumed that space and time have an existence unaffected by anything else. Actually, however, times and distances are just the names given to the results of certain operations performed with pieces of material equipment. Ideally, therefore, matter and space and time ought to be treated as aspects of one entity, or "field," that cannot strictly be separated into independent parts. The realization of such a treatment was the great achievement of Einstein in his theory of general relativity. Einstein described everything within the scope of the theory by a single field; certain aspects of the field specify the density, momentum, and stress of the material present; certain other aspects describe the temporal and spatial interrelationships of the material; and still other aspects represent its gravitational interactions.

General relativity, as distinct from special relativity, is not important for laboratory physics, but it is essential for cosmology because: (1) it provides the best treatment of gravitation known, and gravitation appears to be the only interaction of matter that affects the behaviour of the universe in the large; (2) it shows (apparently correctly) that the field affects what is usually called the geometry of space-time in ways that are all-important for the structure of the universe in the large; (3) precisely because it treats space-time and matter as interdependent, it can treat the universe as a whole, which all previous theories had failed to do; (4) it makes predictions only in terms of quantities that are observable by means admitted by the theory; i.e., the theoretical results are directly testable by the astronomer's observations.

COSMOLOGICAL MODELS

Procedures for model construction. The aim of cosmological theory is to construct a theoretical model universe, in strict accordance with well-formulated physical theory, that adequately reproduces the broad features of the actual universe. In particular, the model universe is supposed to be filled with some continuous fluid, which is intended to represent a smoothed-out version of the contents of the actual universe.

In the model, an observer who moves along with the "fluid" where he happens to be is called a fundamental observer; he represents any typical observer in the actual universe. It is postulated that (1) each fundamental observer sees the (model) universe as isotropic (i.e., with its properties having the same values in all directions) about himself, and (2) the history of the universe seen by one fundamental observer is identical with that seen by any other. The time kept by a fundamental observer is called cosmic time t: it may be calibrated so that any two fundamental observers record the same t when they see the same cosmic state; i.e., fundamental observers may treat the universe as its own cosmic clock. The postulate that the model must admit these properties is called the cosmological principle. It is found to cause the model to depend essentially on only one unknown function of t, the expansion factor, symbolized as $R(t)$, say. General relativity then expresses the density and pressure of the material present in terms of $R(t)$. The nature of this material is specified by the appropriate relation between its density and pressure. This yields a single differential equation for $R(t)$. The Russian meteorologist Alexander Friedmann (1922) and the Belgian mathematician Georges Lemaître (1927), independently, were the first to formulate this mathematics; it is customary to speak of the Friedmann–Lemaître equation leading to the F–L model universes.

Fundamental observers

If a fundamental observer sees his universe to be expanding, he may estimate that every part has sufficient energy to escape from the gravitational pull of the rest so that the model will go on expanding forever; or he may estimate that no part has sufficient energy to escape from the gravitational pull of the rest so that the model must ultimately fall back upon itself. Clearly one parameter is needed to cover these possibilities. Further, in ordinary mechanics an arbitrary constant may be added to the pressure and energy without changing the equations of motion. If all fundamental observers are to be treated alike, it is found that just one constant arises in this way. It is the analogue of Einstein's "cosmical constant" in the relativistic treatment. Thus two parameters are needed to determine a model universe of the sort under discussion, including, of course, its expansion factor $R(t)$. The mathematical treatment would be needed, naturally, in order to give a full explanation. In order to compare the predicted observations of a fundamental observer with observations of the actual universe, the cosmic time at which he observes must be assigned additionally.

It is a major advance upon classical theory to obtain any self-consistent model of an entire universe. The mathematics shows that there is no stable static model; *i.e.*, the model has to be expanding (or contracting). Using the observational estimate of the Hubble time, almost all models predict a present mean density of the order 10^{-29} gram per cubic centimetre. So if the actual universe behaves in accordance with the theory, it must be expanding (or contracting); and the density is almost certainly about 10^{-29} gram per cubic centimetre. Now astronomers do find that the actual universe is apparently expanding and that the density of luminous matter in it is nearly 10^{-30} gram per cubic centimetre. Since there must be some other matter, the situation is entirely plausible. Consequently, most astronomers believe that the interpretation of the red shift in terms of the expansion of the universe is valid, and that the motion proceeds under the gravitational interaction of its parts and none other. Were any other interaction concerned, then some different universal constant would enter, and the calculations would presumably lead to some altogether different (and implausible) value of the density. This position was reached as early as 1930, and it is encouraging so far as it goes. Ever since, astronomers have tried strenuously to find whether some particular Friedmann–Lemaître model can be selected to give satisfactory overall agreement with all the relevant observations. The work has led to many discoveries about galaxies. Unfortunately, however, the main problem remains unsolved. Attempts to derive higher approximations to the Hubble magnitude-red shift relation are largely frustrated by the scatter in the intrinsic properties of the galaxies and by selection effects; attempts to use source-counts are defeated by evolutionary effects; attempts to set bounds to the amount of intergalactic matter would have to be about ten times more accurate than hitherto in order to be significant; hopes of using other properties—*e.g.*, some measure of the angular size of galaxies or of clusters—have not yet been fulfilled.

Cosmologists may claim that, were the search for a model basically misdirected, then 40 years of trying would have produced some absurdity. But such has not been the outcome, although it has sometimes seemed as if it might be. For instance, the early measures of the Hubble time led to an age of the universe that was less than the accepted age of the Earth. But in 1952 a well-known German-American astronomer, Walter Baade, showed how the intrinsic brightness of the stars known as Cepheid variables had been underestimated. This is a key quantity in constructing the scale of distances: so these stars and everything more remote must be farther away than had been supposed, whence the Hubble time and the inferred age of the universe are greater. The revisions due to Baade and his successors have greatly reduced the age difficulty, although, because of the uncertainty in the determination of all the quantities involved, it cannot yet be said to have been finally resolved.

The steady-state model. In its original form, the age difficulty played a crucial part in a dramatic phase of the subject—the emergence in 1948 of a steady-state cosmology.

The models thus far considered are derived on the hypothesis that there is nothing special about any particular place in the universe. It was argued by some, however, that scientists should also contemplate the possibility that there is nothing special about any particular epoch in the universe. The problem then became one of constructing a model of the expanding universe that is everywhere and always the same; and it was urged that if such could be

The true brightness of distance indicators

done, this steady-state universe might be regarded as the simplest possible universe and, if only for this reason, its model ought to be the first one studied. Crudely stated, this was the starting point in 1948 of Hermann Bondi and Thomas Gold, and of Fred Hoyle, all working in Cambridge (England).

Such a model calls for no new concept of space-time, and so the relativistic outlook is accepted. But not unnaturally, it is found that there is a unique geometry of space-time that can admit a steady-state behaviour. The matter in the model has to be always dispersing (so as to depict the expansion of the universe), but always of the same density (so as to preserve a steady state). Clearly, this requires that new matter be continually created at a fixed rate throughout the universe; this is a new concept of the behaviour of matter. It means that in any large region there is matter of all ages, and calculation gives the mean age of the matter as $\frac{1}{3} \tau$; there are galaxies of all ages, and the mean age of the galaxies is $\frac{1}{3} \tau$, and so on, where τ is again the Hubble time defined above (see above *Behaviour of the universe*). A consequence is that most of the material in any region must be renewed in a time of the order of τ.

If this is applied to the actual universe, the rate of creation would be utterly beyond the possibility of direct detection. The simplest interpretation would be that in any large region of space new matter is created at a statistically uniform rate in time and space, and that this material is continually condensing into new galaxies that replace those leaving the region by virtue of the continual recession of the galaxies. It can be estimated that it would require something of the order of the Hubble time for diffuse matter to condense into a galaxy, and that consequently, in any region at any time, there is between 10 and 100 times as much intergalactic matter as luminous matter in the form of galaxies. Further, the age difficulty is resolved because, even if it is found that the age of the Galaxy is greater than, for instance, the Hubble time itself, this means simply that the Galaxy happens to be older than the average. All such features are plausible and, to some minds, aesthetically satisfying.

As was pointed out above, however, an observer who looks into the distance looks into the past. But in a steady-state universe the past is the same as the present. In such a universe, therefore, no intrinsic feature can depend upon distance from the observer. In the actual universe, on the other hand, the occurrence of radio galaxies is evidently very different at different distances. This is a direct contradiction of the steady-state. It seems certain that simple steady-state cosmology cannot be accepted—in spite of its undoubtedly attractive features.

The concept of the continuous creation of matter

Differences between the actual universe and the steady-state universe

HISTORY OF THE UNIVERSE

It is necessary to return to models without continual creation, technically models in which the baryon number is conserved in accordance with standard physics (a baryon being an actual or potential proton). For simplicity, the cosmical constant (see above *Procedures for model construction*) is ignored here. All relevant F–L universes start explosively with a "big bang" at what may be called the zero of cosmic time t. They all give qualitatively about the same history of the universe, but they differ in the cosmic dating of developments.

The expansion factor for a model gives the rate of expansion at any epoch. Because of the homogeneity and isotropy of the model, the material in the vicinity of any fundamental observer behaves as though it were enclosed within an enclosure that expands with the expansion of the universe and whose bounding surface is perfectly reflecting for all forms of radiation present. So the behaviour can be inferred from ordinary physical theory.

As the universe expands, the density and temperature of the contents will diminish. The process starts explosively with the big bang. Up to some early epoch t_0, the density and temperature are so great that interactions between atomic nuclei are fast enough, compared with the rate of expansion, for the nuclear composition of the material to be determined by instantaneous conditions only, independently of what the composition was at any pre-

Table 3: Big-Bang Cosmology: History of the Universe

epoch	illustrative model (approximate estimates)		occurrence
	time	temperature (absolute)	
Primordial fireball			big bang: expansion of universe begins:
0	0		radiation and matter uniformly distributed and all constituents in thermal equilibrium
Radiation era			
t_0	$t_0 = 10$ seconds	5×10^9 °K	nearly all energy in form of photons
t_1	$t_1 = 100$ seconds	10^9 °K	helium formation: nuclear reactions die out
t_2	$t_2 = 1,000$ years	10^5 °K	changeover from radiation-dominated to matter-dominated universe
Matter era			
t_3	$t_3 = 10^5$ years	$5,000°$ K	matter becomes transparent to background radiation: matter temperature starts falling below radiation temperature
t_4	$t_4 = 10^8$ years	radiation $100°$ K matter $1°$ K	galaxy formation sets in
t_5	$t_5 = 5 \times 10^9$ years	radiation $12°$ K	occurrence of earliest known quasi-
Present	2×10^{10} years	radiation $3°$ K intergalactic matter 10^5 °K	stellar objects

vious instant. Thus there is no significance in an "initial chemical composition" of the universe. Following epoch t_0, there is a short interval t_0 to t_1 during which nuclear interactions continue to operate, but at a decreasing rate, so that they have effectively ceased at epoch t_1. Consequently, at t_1 a certain nuclear composition is "frozen into" the material. Until some subsequent epoch t_2, the energy in the form of radiation (photons) is large compared with that in the form of matter, while from soon after t_2 the reverse is the case. Up to some further epoch t_3 the radiation and matter are in thermal balance; but this circumstance has little effect upon the radiation field because, during this phase, the amount of energy that could be emitted or absorbed by the matter is small compared with the total energy that already resides in the radiation. After t_3 the radiation and the matter become "de-coupled"; *i.e.*, the material becomes highly transparent to the radiation. There is then a phase during which the temperature of the matter decreases more steeply than that of the radiation; the subsequent career of the matter is discussed below.

The "frozen in" chemical composition can be calculated only by following all the nuclear reactions through the interval t_0 to t_1 using a computer. Workers who did this in 1967 found that, for any plausible model, from t_1 onward the material consists effectively of hydrogen, helium, and small fractions of "heavy" hydrogen and lithium. For a wide range of models, helium constitutes between 25 and 35 percent of the mass, the rest being nearly all hydrogen.

On the picture here described, most of the photons in the universe at large have not interacted with matter since before t_3, at which time the universe was radiation-dominated anyhow. Thus most of the photons that compose cosmic background radiation have not come out of stars and galaxies. They are left from stages of the universe long before such sources existed; hence the term remanent radiation, which is sometimes used. Since a typical photon has travelled uninterruptedly through the universe from a very early stage, it has come a very long way and undergone an enormous red shift. This is why the radiation is so feeble at the present epoch. But if scientists can measure the present energy-density of this radiation and the present smoothed-out density of matter, it ought to be possible to work backward in time to construct a quantitative history of the actual universe—assuming that it behaves like a model of the present sort.

This program is usually illustrated by the case: Hubble time, 10^{10} years; present density of smoothed-out matter, 2×10^{-29} gram per cubic centimetre; present temperature of background radiation, $3°$ Kelvin (some few degrees above absolute zero). Table 3 shows some of the main results; these are not particularly sensitive to the choice of model.

As was remarked, after epoch t_3 the temperature of the matter begins to fall steeply. In the example, it could

Source of the background radiation (margin note)

reach about $1°$ K at cosmic epoch t_4 between 10^8 and 10^9 years, the density being then of order one-tenth the overall mean density of the Galaxy; if astronomers could see back to that stage it would correspond to a red shift z of about 20. Given that galaxies did form with the masses and sizes they are known to possess (although it is not yet known what determines these quantities), the conditions would be favourable to the formation of such condensations. It is usually reckoned that the formation of a condensation, or of the resulting galaxy, would occupy some few times 10^8 years, so that galaxies could not have formed before about t_4. On the other hand, source-counts are interpreted as implying the existence of radio galaxies, at any rate as far back as z about 4. Thus the stage in the history of the universe when conditions were suitable for the occurrence of condensations lies within the bounds set by these further considerations. After galaxies were formed, the various radiations from them would heat up the remaining intergalactic matter; its present temperature is estimated as between 10^5 and 10^6 degrees Kelvin ($180,000°$–$1,800,000°$ F). The rising temperature and falling density make conditions unfavourable for the formation of further condensations; in this picture, all galaxies would have been formed at about the same stage in the evolution of the universe. These conditions would also make intergalactic matter difficult to detect; *e.g.*, it could not interact appreciably with cosmic background radiation.

The first stars in the newly formed galaxies would be composed of the raw material already mentioned, consisting chiefly of hydrogen and helium. Heavier elements —which still compose only 1 or 2 percent of the mass of a galaxy—would be formed by nucleosynthesis in this and succeeding generations of stars. Calculations concerning this synthesis are based on accurate laboratory investigations of the properties of the relevant nuclei, and by about 1960 astrophysicists seemed to have reached substantial agreement about the course that events had taken. By 1970 the situation had changed. Evidence was being found that many of the first-generation stars were in the mass range of about 10 to 50 solar masses, and that these had ended their careers in explosions in which much of the production of heavy elements occurred.

Composition of stars in newly formed galaxies (margin note)

Before the possible importance of explosive nucleosynthesis was appreciated, astrophysicists had shown that helium synthesized in ordinary stars would be no more than about 2 percent of the mass of a galaxy like the Milky Way, whereas helium evidently forms 25 to 30 percent of the mass. The discrepancy presented the so-called helium problem. It is now seen that almost any hot big bang must ensure that the raw material of the galaxies contained over 25 percent helium. Whether a much larger fraction of the helium now in a galaxy could have been formed in explosions than the 2 percent or so formed in nonviolent evolution is not yet known.

Thus it apparently may be claimed that big-bang cosmology has correctly predicted the background radiation, solved the helium problem, and provided an overall history of the universe that accommodates various evolutionary developments in a plausible manner. Such positive claims have caused the hot big bang ("universal fireball") to be given serious scientific attention as possibly accounting for the main physical features of the cosmic environment (see Table 3).

QUASI-STELLAR OBJECTS

A few hundred quasi-stellar objects, or quasars, have been observed individually; it is estimated that about a million are accessible to the largest telescopes. The quasars have starlike optical images and characteristic optical spectra showing emission lines and sometimes absorption lines. Sometimes they are radio sources, and possibly they contribute largely to source-counts. Sometimes they emit strongly in the infrared, sometimes also in X-rays. The emission lines of a quasar show a unique red shift z, regarded as the red shift of the object; the status of absorption red shifts is complex. Whereas optical galaxies show red shifts up to about $z = 0.2$, and one or two radio galaxies have z values near 0.5, quasar red shifts range up to about $z = 2.9$.

If the red shifts are cosmological, a quasar is typically about 100 times brighter intrinsically than a bright optical galaxy. Quasars should thus enable astronomers to explore a volume of the universe about 1,000 times greater than they can by observing ordinary galaxies. Unfortunately, observations of quasars have hitherto made little contribution to cosmology. Apparently this is because the spread of intrinsic properties is so great that it obscures all other statistical properties. Some astronomers have doubted the cosmological interpretation of the red shifts, but have not succeeded in proposing an acceptable alternative. An understanding of the physics of quasi-stellar objects must precede progress in other directions.

PRESENT PROBLEMS OF COSMOLOGY

Originally, Friedmann–Lemaître models were intentionally the simplest ones possible that would illustrate the essentials of nonstatic relativistic cosmology. After nearly 50 years, it appears that little would be gained by using more general models; some of the most significant recent progress has been in discovering why this should be so. Relativists have shown that, under very general conditions, theory demands at least one happening that would be interpreted as a big bang. If, in fact, there has been just one—so that everything was once much closer together and has been dispersing ever since—to a first approximation the dispersal is bound to obey Hubble's law. If the universe is homogeneous, the discovery of neutrino viscosity shows it must have been isotropic from a very early stage, almost independently of what it was like before that. As already mentioned, study of the hot big bang shows that the broad features of the chemical composition of the universe could scarcely be other than as observed and that there must be background radiation like that which seems to be observed. Thus, it may be claimed that all the resources of physical theory are tending to show that the actual universe is the only universe permitted by the theory. If so, this is a discovery about physics just as much as about the universe.

In an evolving universe, the astronomer looks into the past by looking into the distance. But the further back he looks, the less precise the information he gets, and he certainly cannot see the actual beginning. He ought not to expect theory to tell him more than he can check by observation; this, too, seems to be how the subject is unfolding. On the observational side, there are foreseeable needs for more extensive work in all departments, and much is expected of observations made from space vehicles. But there are bound to be unforeseen developments like the discoveries about quasars in the 1960s. On the theoretical side, a proper understanding of these objects should lead to many advances. The central problem is perhaps that of the formation of galaxies. This is the study of the origin and evolution of inhomogeneities on a cosmically small scale. But there are also problems for observation and theory about the large-scale homogeneity. As ever larger tracts of the universe are considered, it is not yet known whether it should be treated as more nearly homogeneous, or whether the notion of homogeneity becomes ever less meaningful.

BIBLIOGRAPHY. Comprehensive surveys of modern astronomy are: W.M. SMART, *The Riddle of the Universe* (1968); and A. UNSOLD, *Der neue Kosmos* (1967; Eng. trans., *The New Cosmos*, 1969). A recent account of the astronomy of the Milky Way Galaxy is D. MIHALAS and P.M. ROUTLY, *Galactic Astronomy* (1968). Readable books on the universe of galaxies include: P.W. HODGE, *Galaxies and Cosmology* (1966); J. LEQUEUX, *Physique et évolution des galaxies* (1967; Eng. trans., *Structure and Evolution of Galaxies*, 1969); THORNTON PAGE (ed.), *Stars and Galaxies* (1962); and V.C. REDDISH, *Evolution of the Galaxies* (1967). The standard general work on quasars is G.R. and E.M. BURBIDGE, *Quasi-Stellar Objects* (1967). A fairly simple systematic account of cosmological theory is H. BONDI, *Cosmology*, 2nd ed. (1960); and a critical historical account of modern cosmology is J.D. NORTH, *The Measure of the Universe* (1965); examples of readable books on certain aspects are: G. GAMOW, *The Creation of the Universe* (1952); and G.J. WHITROW, *The Structure and Evolution of the Universe* (1959). The *Annual Review of Astronomy and Astrophysics* (1963–) has concise surveys of recent progress in the subject, with excellent bibliographies.

(W.H.McC.)

Upper Volta

The Republic of Upper Volta (République de Haute-Volta) is a landlocked West African state, with an area of 105,792 square miles (274,000 square kilometres). A former French colony, it gained independence in 1960. It is bounded to the north and west by Mali, to the south by the Ivory Coast, Ghana, and Togo, and to the east by Dahomey and Niger. The population numbers nearly 6,000,000. The capital, Ouagadougou, is about 500 miles by road from the sea.

Upper Volta's economy is based primarily on agriculture and livestock raising. About half the population belong to the Mossi tribe, and the former Mossi Empire is included within the borders of the present state. After a military coup in 1966, led by Gen. Sangoulé Lamizana, who was to become president, a new constitution was approved by referendum in 1970. (For an associated physical feature, see VOLTA RIVER; for historical aspects, see WEST AFRICA, HISTORY OF.)

The landscape. *Physiography.* Upper Volta consists of an extensive plateau, slightly inclined toward the south. The lateritic (red, leached, iron-bearing) layer of rock that covers the underlying crystalline rocks is cut into by the three principal rivers—the Volta Noire, Volta Rouge, and Volta Blanche—all of which converge in Ghanaian territory to the south to form the Volta River. The Oti, another tributary of the Volta, rises in southeastern Upper Volta. In the southwest there are sandstone plateaus, bordered by the Falaise de Banfora (Banfora Cliffs), which is about 500 feet high and faces southeast. The country is generally dry and infertile. Great seasonal variation occurs in the flow of the rivers.

Climate. The climate is generally sunny, hot, and dry. In the north it is of the Sahelian type (Arabic *sāḥil*, "shore"; in this instance it refers to the region bordering the Sahara [*q.v.*]), characterized by three to five months of rainfall, which is often erratic. To the south it becomes increasingly of the tropical savanna (grassy parkland) type, sometimes called Sudanic, characterized by greater variability of temperature and rainfall.

Four seasons may be distinguished: a dry and cool season from mid-November to mid-February, with temperatures dropping to about 50° F (10° C); a hot season from mid-February to June, when maximum temperatures rise to about 104° F (40° C) in the shade; a rainy season, which lasts from June to September; and an intermediate season, which lasts until mid-November.

Vegetation and animal life. The northern part of the country consists of savanna, with prickly shrubs and stunted trees that come to life during the rainy season. In the south the prickly shrubs give way to scattered forests, which become more dense along the banks of the perennial rivers. While tree growth in the north is dis-

The river system

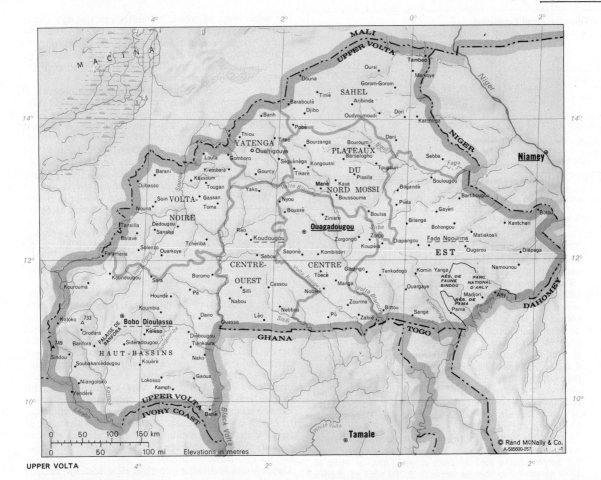

UPPER VOLTA

couraged by the climate, farmers in the south often permit only useful trees, such as the karite (shea tree) or the baobab, to survive.

Animal life in the eastern region includes buffalo, antelope, lions, hippopotamuses, elephants, and crocodiles. Elephants, buffalo, and antelope are also found in the southeast and on the banks of the Black Volta, while herds of hippopotamuses are to be seen some 40 miles from the city of Bobo Dioulasso. Animal life also includes monkeys. Bird and insect life is rich and varied, and there are many fish in the rivers.

The landscape under human settlement. Most of the population lives in villages, which tend to be grouped toward the centre of the country. For several miles on either side of the Volta rivers the land is uninhabited because of flooding and the prevalence of the deadly tsetse fly, carrier of sleeping sickness.

Ouagadougou, the administrative capital and the seat of government, is a modern town, in which several commercial companies have their headquarters. It is also the residence of the Moro Naba, emperor of the Mossi. The suburbs have shade trees and artificial lakes.

Bobo Dioulasso, in the west, was the economic and business capital of the country when it formed the terminus of the railroad running to Abidjan, Ivory Coast, on the coast; since 1955, however, when the railroad was extended to Ouagadougou, it has lost some of its former importance, although it remains a commercial centre.

The people. *Ethnic, linguistic, and religious groups.* Two principal ethnic groupings may be distinguished. The first of these is the Voltaic grouping, which may be subdivided into four groups—the Mossi, who numbered about 3,700,000 in the early 1970s including the Gurma and the Yarse; the Grunshis (Crurunsi) (310,000); the Bobo (300,000); and the Lobi (130,000). The second grouping is the Mande family, which is divided into five subgroups; the Samo (100,000), the Marka (80,000), the Busansi (50,000), the Senufo (50,000), and the Dyula (Diouala) (30,000). In addition, there are Hausa (Haoussa) traders, about 300,000 Fulani herds-

men, and the Tuareg, or rather their settled servants, the Bella, who number 250,000.

Each of the ethnic groups possesses its own language, although Moré, the language of the Mossi, is spoken by a great majority of the population, and Diula is the language of commerce. French, the official language, is used for all communication with other countries. About three-quarters of the population is animist in religion, attaching great importance to ancestor worship. Islām exerts an increasing influence upon customs; about 1,200,000 people, or 20 percent of the population, were Muslims in 1970; in the same period, Catholicism was the religion of about 5 percent, or 220,000 people. The seat of the Catholic archbishopric is Ouagadougou, and there are eight bishoprics. There are few Protestants.

Demography. Compared to most of the neighbouring countries, Upper Volta, with nearly 6,000,000 inhabitants in 1971, is populous, with an average population density of 55 persons per square mile. The total population figure does not include approximately 500,000 people from Upper Volta who live in the Ivory Coast, Ghana, or Mali. According to a survey conducted in 1968, the rate of population increase is about 2 percent a year and the birth rate about 5 percent a year. An alien population of about 20,000 persons is mostly composed of Yorubas from Nigeria and of citizens of Mali and other neighbouring countries. The European colony numbers about 4,000, most of whom are French.

The population as a whole is unequally distributed among the different regions. The Mossi country is densely settled, with an average population density of between 91 and 130 persons per square mile. Situated in the eastern and central regions, it contains about two-thirds of the total population. In the remaining regions the population is scattered, with an average density of between 13 and 39 persons per square mile.

About 95 percent of the population is rural, living in about 7,000 villages. Apart from Ouagadougou, the capital, which had a 1970 population of over 110,000, the principal towns are Bobo Dioulasso, with a population of

The two major ethnic groupings

The principal towns

Upper Volta, Area and Population

Départements	area sq mi	area sq km	population 1960–61 census	population 1971 estimate
Centre	9,336	24,179	...	995,776
Centre-Ouest	10,164	26,324	...	837,221
Est	22,792	59,031	...	666,907
Hauts-Bassins	24,764	64,138	...	945,754
Plateaux du Nord-Mossi	8,331	21,578	...	652,077
Sahel	14,235	36,869	...	288,832
Volta-Noire	11,424	29,588	...	536,168
Yatenga	4,746	12,293	...	563,246
Total Upper Volta	105,792	274,000	4,300,000*	5,845,981

*Estimate based on results of a sample survey of 226 villages and 10 urban centres surveyed on a 10 percent basis; excludes an estimated 100,000 persons in towns of Ouagadougou (numbering 59,000 at 1961 census) and Bobo Dioulassou (estimated at 52,000 in 1959) not covered by survey.
Source: Official government figures; UN.

77,000; Koudougou (25,000); Ouahigouya (13,000); and the towns of Kaya, Fada Ngourma, and Banfora, each with a population of about 10,000.

The national economy. About 95 percent of the population is engaged in agriculture or stock raising. This sector of the population produces peanuts (groundnuts), cotton, livestock, and sesame seeds for export. There is, however, considerable unemployment in rural districts, and every year about 150,000 people leave their villages to seek work in such neighbouring states as the Ivory Coast or Ghana. The development of industry is hampered by the small size of the market economy and by the absence of a direct outlet to the sea. The gross national product averages 14,000 francs CFA (CFA Fr. 277.71 = $1 U.S.; CFA Fr. 666.50 = £1 sterling on December 1, 1970) a head.

Agriculture. Agricultural production consists of foodstuffs, which are primarily grown for subsistence, with the surplus being sold as cash crops. Thus, in 1969 to 1970 about 7,000 tons of peanuts, 2,700 tons of sesame seeds, 15,000 tons (1968–69) of shea butter (oil), and 8,300 tons of cottonseed were grown for export, while 550,000 tons of sorghum, 120,000 tons of corn (maize), 93,000 tons of peanuts, and 40,000 tons of rice were grown for local consumption. Fonio (a crabgrass with seeds that are used as cereal), yams, sweet potatoes, and beans are also grown. Stock raising is one of the principal sources of revenue. Livestock is estimated to amount to 2,800,000 cattle, 4,500,000 sheep and goats, 139,000 pigs, 180,000 donkeys, 71,000 horses, and 6,000 camels. Chickens, ducks, and guinea fowl are also raised.

Industry. Industry is limited to a number of plants mainly in rural areas producing processed rice, vegetable oil, and hides, and manufactured soap and textiles.

Trade, aid, and development. External commerce, both in imports and in exports, is primarily with the franc zone in general and with neighbouring African countries in particular. Many cattle are exported to the Ivory Coast as well as to Ghana. There is a deficit in the balance of payments, largely due to the relatively small amounts of exports, which are not of sufficient value to equal the value of imported materials required for promoting further development.

Aid from abroad　Foreign aid is extended primarily by France, which finances a number of economic and social projects. Further financial aid and technical assistance is also supplied by the Federal Republic of Germany, the United States, the Republic of China, and Israel. United Nations assistance is supplied through the International Development Association and other United Nations agencies.

Developmental policy, outlined in the Second Five-Year Plan (1972–76), aims at increasing agricultural output. While mineral resources are little developed, copper, marble, bauxite, and manganese (the most significant) deposits have been located.

Transportation. In addition to the rail line, which links Ouagadougou to the port of Abidjan in the Ivory Coast, the capital is also linked by road to the principal administrative centres in the country and to the capitals of neighbouring countries. The railroad to Abidjan is

712 miles long, of which 341 miles run through Upper Volta. Running from east to west before crossing the border, the line serves Koudougou, Bobo Dioulasso, and Banfora. A proposed 220-mile extension to the manganese, chrome, and nickel deposits of Tambao in the northeast is being studied.

Upper Volta has the most extensive road network in proportion to its size of any of the French-speaking African states. Out of about 9,000 miles of roads, about 2,750 are usable year round. The remainder consist of rural roads. Three recently completed road-building projects were financed by the European Development Fund. The first of these roads runs from Bobo Dioulasso to Faramana to the Mali frontier. The second runs from Ouagadougou to Pô to the Ghanaian frontier. The third runs from Ouagadougou to Koupéla. Road transport is supplied by the Compagnie Transafricaine, as well as by individual enterprises.

International airports are located at Ouagadougou and Bobo Dioulasso. Internal air service, linking almost 50 smaller airstrips, is supplied by the national airline.

Administration and social conditions. *Administration.* Although the constitution adopted by referendum in 1970 provides that the people shall exercise sovereignty through regularly elected political representatives, the role of the army is nevertheless preponderant in political life. The constitution provided that, during a four-year transitional period, the presidency was entrusted to the highest ranking military officer with the longest term of service and that one-third of the members of the government were to be military men. The president of the republic is elected for five years by direct universal suffrage and may be re-elected only once. The prime minister establishes and conducts national policy, presiding over a council of ministers and directing the work of the government. A national assembly, elected for five years by universal suffrage, drafts legislation and regulates governmental initiatives.

Upper Volta is divided into eight *départements*, headed by prefects. These, together with their administrative centres, are the Centre (Ouagadougou), Volta-Noire (Dédougou), Hauts-Bassins (Bobo Dioulasso), the Est (Fada Ngourma), Yatenga (Ouahigouya), Centre-Ouest (Koudougou), Sahel (Doni), and Plateaux du Nord-Mossi (Kaya). The *départements* are grouped into 44 administrative areas called *cercles*, which in turn are divided into 39 subdivisions and 54 administrative posts. In addition there are six *communes* administered by mayors and elected municipal councillors.

Local government

Labour conditions. Labour conditions are governed by a labour code, adopted in 1962. Unemployment is endemic, however, and the industrial sector weak. The economically active population, numbering about 3,000,000, is for the most part intermittently employed in agriculture. There are about 27,000 wage earners, of whom about 15,000 are in public service. There are three trade unions.

Health. There are five hospitals—at Ouagadougou, Bobo Dioulasso, Ouahigouya, Pô, and Fada Ngourma —as well as 30 medical centres, about 250 dispensaries, and about 70 maternity centres. There are about 68 doctors—about one for every 74,000 people.

Education. School enrollment is one of the lowest in Africa. In 1960, at the time of independence, it amounted to only 8 percent of the school age population, and by 1970 it had risen to only 10 percent, even though the government devotes a quarter of the national budget to education. There are about 600 primary schools, with a total enrollment of about 100,000 pupils, as well as about 40 secondary schools, with an attendance of about 9,000 pupils. A program to promote education in rural areas is being financed by the European Development Fund. Students seeking higher education usually attend universities in France; in Dakar, Senegal; or in Abidjan, Ivory Coast. There is a teacher-training school at Ouagadougou, as well as a school of national administration.

Cultural life. Folklore is rich, reflecting the country's ethnic diversity. On national occasions, each region is represented in the capital by its own folkloric group.

Houses of Youth and Culture, where young people play cards, read, or watch films or theatrical performances, are located in the main administrative centres.

Press, radio, and television

Press and information services are provided by government agencies under the supervision of the Ministry of Information. Daily bulletins disseminate news and business information, and there are weekly and bimonthly newspapers, as well as an official journal, a monthly statistical bulletin, and a national press agency, the Agence de Press Voltaïque.

There are radio transmitters at Ouagadougou and at Bobo Dioulasso. A television transmitter provides two programs a week to the Ouagadougou area, where television receivers are available for public viewing.

Prospects for the future. Upper Volta, with an average annual per capita income of CFA Fr. 12,000, is one of the poorest countries in Africa. During the colonial period, development took place primarily in coastal countries endowed with rich natural resources; relatively little attention was paid to Upper Volta, where difficulty of access was added to a difficult climate. After independence, therefore, in addition to the problems faced by other newly independent states, Upper Volta was confronted with the necessity of constructing the infrastructure of a modern state—the necessary public buildings, a developed road network and communications system, and other services. It is symbolic of the change of direction that Ouagadougou, which for long was known as a "swish capital" (swish is a hard mud, made from West Africa's red iron-bearing laterite soil), today has a more modern aspect, characterized by a varied architecture, gardens, and paved streets.

Since the previous government, whose scale of expenditure had provoked public discontent, was overthrown in 1966 by the army and the trade unions, strict economic measures have been enforced, which have resulted in the reduction of the long-standing burden of debt. While there is still a foreign-trade deficit, this is also being reduced. With the return in 1970 to a type of civilian rule —in which the military will continue to play a transitional role for a further four years—there is hope that the progress already achieved will be consolidated and further progress made.

BIBLIOGRAPHY. *Afrique 1969* (annual), a special issue (June) that reports the principal developments of the year in Africa; EUROPE FRANCE OUTREMER, *L'Afrique d'expression française et Madagascar*, a special issue (June) of the monthly publication devoted to the political, economic, and social problems of African states of French expression; REPUBLIQUE DE HAUTE-VOLTA, MINISTERE DU DEVELOPPEMENT ET DU TOURISME, *Situation économique actuelle de la Haute-Volta* (1966), on the economic situation after the fall of the first post-independence administration; FRANCOIS D. BASSOLET, *Evolution de la Haute-Volta de 1898 au 3 janvier 1966* (1968), a historical account including a critique of the various political organizations of the country, to be read with certain reservations; REPUBLIQUE DE HAUTE-VOLTA, MINISTERE DES FINANCES ET DU COMMERCE, *Commerce extérieure et balance commerciale* (1968), a technical work, useful for businessmen and investors; BANQUE CENTRALE DES ETATS DE L'AFRIQUE DE L'OUEST, *Notes d'Information et Statistiques*, "Indicateurs économiques voltaïques," no. 166 (1969), and no. 170 (1970), informative notes on the economic and monetary situation.

(P.H.Gu.)

Ur

Ur (biblical Ur of the Chaldees) was an important city of ancient southern Mesopotamia (Sumer), reputed to have been the early home of Abraham. The site (now called Tall al-Muqayyar) lies about 140 miles (225 kilometres) southeast of the site of Babylon and about 10 miles (16 kilometres) west of the present bed of the Euphrates River, a mile and a half from the modern Ur Maḥaṭṭah (Junction) of the Iraqi Republican Railway in southern Iraq. In antiquity the river ran much closer to the city; the change in its course has left the ruins in a desert that once was irrigated and fertile land. The first serious excavations there were made after World War I by H.R. Hall of the British Museum, and as a result a joint expedition was formed by the British Mu-

seum and the University of Pennsylvania that carried on the excavations under Leonard Woolley's directorship from 1922 until 1934. Almost every period of the city's lifetime has been illustrated by discoveries made, and knowledge of Mesopotamian history has been greatly enlarged.

Foundation of the city. At some time in the 4th millennium BC, the city was founded by settlers thought to have been from northern Mesopotamia, farmers still in the Chalcolithic phase of culture. There is evidence that their occupation was ended by a flood, formerly thought to be the one described in Genesis. From the succeeding "Jamdat Nasr" (Late Protoliterate) phase a large cemetery produced valuable remains allied to more sensational discoveries made at Erech.

Ur in the early dynastic period, 29th–24th centuries BC. In the next (Early Dynastic) period Ur became the capital of the whole of southern Mesopotamia under the Sumerian kings of the 1st dynasty of Ur (25th century BC). Excavation of a vast cemetery from the period preceding that dynasty (26th century) produced royal tombs containing almost incredible treasures in gold, silver, bronze, and semiprecious stones, showing not only the wealth of the people of Ur but also their highly developed civilization and art. Not the least remarkable discovery was that of the custom whereby kings were buried along with a whole retinue of their court officials, servants, and women, privileged to continue their service in the next world. Musical instruments from the royal tombs, golden weapons, engraved shell plaques and mosaic pictures, statuary and carved cylinder seals, all are a collection of unique importance, illustrating a civilization previously unknown to the historian. A further development of it, or perhaps a different aspect, was shown by the excavation at al-'Ubaid, a suburb of Ur, of a small temple also of a type previously unsuspected, richly decorated with statuary, mosaics, and metal reliefs and having columns sheathed with coloured mosaic or polished copper. The inscribed foundation tablet of the temple, stating that it was the work of a king of the 1st dynasty of Ur, dated the building and proved the historical character of a dynasty that had been mentioned by ancient Sumerian historians but that modern scholars had previously dismissed as fictitious.

A few personal inscriptions confirmed the real existence of the almost legendary ruler Sargon I, king of Akkad, who reigned in the 24th century BC, and a cemetery illustrated the material culture of his time.

Third dynasty of Ur, 22nd–21st centuries BC. To the next period, that of the 3rd dynasty of Ur, when Ur was again the capital of an empire, belong some of the most important architectural monuments preserved on the site. Foremost among these is the ziggurat, a three-storied structure of burnt bricks set in bitumen, rather like a stepped pyramid, a solid mass of brickwork on the summit of which was a small shrine, the bedchamber of the moon god Nanna (Sin), the patron deity and divine king of Ur. The lowest stage measures at its foot some 210

The ziggurat

Hirmer Fotoarchiv, Munchen

The great ziggurat of the moon god Nanna at Ur, built during the 3rd dynasty of Ur (22nd-21st centuries BC). The northeastern facade is shown with the ascents partly restored.

by 150 feet (64 by 46 metres), and its height was about 40 feet (12 metres). On three sides the walls, relieved by shallow buttresses, rose sheer. On the northeast face were three great staircases, each of 100 steps, one projecting at right angles from the centre of the building, two leaning against its wall, and all three converging in a gateway between the first and the second terrace. From this a single flight of steps led upward to the top terrace and to the door of the god's little shrine. The lower part of the ziggurat, built by Ur-Nammu, the founder of the dynasty, was astonishingly well preserved; enough of the upper part survived to make the restoration certain.

The excavations showed that by the 3rd millennium BC Sumerian architects were acquainted with the column, the arch, the vault, and the dome—*i.e.*, with all the basic forms of architecture. The ziggurat exhibited its refinements. The walls all sloped inward, and their angle, together with the carefully calculated heights of the successive stages, leads the eye inward and upward; the sharper slope of the stairways accentuates that effect and fixes attention on the shrine, the religious focus of the whole huge structure. Surprisingly, there is not a single straight line in the structure. Each wall, from base to top and horizontally from corner to corner, is a convex curve, a curve so slight as not to be apparent but giving to the eye of the observer an illusion of strength where a straight line might have seemed to sag under the weight of the superstructure. The architect thus employed the principle of entasis, which was to be rediscovered by the builders of the Parthenon at Athens.

Succeeding dynasties, 21st–6th centuries BC. The great brick mausoleums of the 3rd-dynasty kings and the temples they built were sacked and destroyed by the Elamites, but the temples at least were restored by the kings of the succeeding dynasties of Isin and Larsa; and Ur, though it ceased to be the capital, retained its religious and its commercial importance. Having access by river and canal to the Persian Gulf, it was the natural headquarters of foreign trade. As early as the reign of Sargon of Akkad it had been in touch with India, at least indirectly. Personal seals of the Indus Valley type from the 3rd dynasty and the Larsa period have been found at Ur, while many hundreds of clay tablets show how the foreign trade was organized. The "sea kings" of Ur carried goods for export to the entrepôt at Dilmun (Bahrain) and there picked up the copper and ivory that came from the east.

Eastern trade

The clay tablets were found in the residential quarter of the city, of which a considerable area was excavated. The houses of private citizens in the Larsa period and under Hammurabi of Babylon (*c.* 18th century BC, in which period Abraham is supposed to have lived at Ur) were comfortable and well built two-story houses with ample accommodation for the family, for servants, and for guests, of a type that ensured privacy and was suited to the climate. In some houses was a kind of chapel in which the family god was worshipped and under the pavement of which the members of the family were buried. Many large state temples were excavated as were also some small wayside shrines dedicated by private persons to minor deities, the latter throwing a new light upon Babylonian religious practices; but the domestic chapels with their provision for the worship of the nameless family gods are yet more interesting and have a possible relation to the religion of the Hebrew patriarchs.

After a long period of relative neglect, Ur experienced a revival in the Neo-Babylonian period, under Nebuchadrezzar II (604–562 BC), who practically rebuilt the city. Scarcely less active was Nabonidus, the last king of Babylon (556–539 BC), whose great work was the remodelling of the ziggurat, increasing its height to seven stages.

The Neo-Babylonian city

The last phase, 6th–4th centuries BC. The last king to build at Ur was the Achaemenian Cyrus the Great, the inscription on whose bricks is similar to the "edict" quoted by the scribe Ezra regarding the restoration of the Temple at Jerusalem. The conqueror was clearly anxious to placate his new subjects by honouring their gods, whatever those gods might be. But Ur was now thoroughly decadent; it survived into the reign of Artaxerxes II, but only a single tablet (of Philip Arrhidaeus, 317 BC) carries on the story. It was perhaps at this time that the Euphrates changed its course; and with the breakdown of the whole irrigation system, Ur, its fields reduced to desert, was finally abandoned.

Discoveries made on other sites have supplemented the unusually full record obtained from the Ur excavations. Knowledge of the city's history and of the manner of life of its inhabitants, of their business, and of their art is now fairly complete and remarkably detailed (see also MESOPOTAMIA AND IRAQ, HISTORY OF).

BIBLIOGRAPHY. J.E. TAYLOR, "Notes on the Ruins of Muqeyer," *Jl. R. Asiat. Soc.*, 15:260–276 (1855)—the ruins of Muqeyer (Tall al-Muqayyar) were later identified as the site of Ur of the Chaldees. H.R. HALL, *A Season's Work at Ur* (1930); C.J. GADD, *History and Monuments of Ur* (1929); C. LEONARD WOOLLEY, *Excavations at Ur* (1954 and 1964) and *Ur of the Chaldees* (1938); C. LEONARD WOOLLEY et al., *Ur Excavations*, vol. 1–5 and 8–10 (1927–65); C.J. GADD and L. LEGRAIN et al., *Ur Excavations: Texts*, vol. 1–5 (1928–53). The Ur excavation volumes include reports on the excavations at al-'Ubayd (near Ur), the Royal Cemetery (the predynastic and Sargonid graves excavated between 1926 and 1931), archaic seal impressions, the sites and objects prior in date to the 3rd dynasty of Ur, the ziggurat and its surroundings, the Kassite period and the period of the Assyrian kings, the Neo-Babylonian and Persian periods, and seal cylinders.

(L.Wy./Ed.)

Uralic Languages

The Uralic language family consists of two related groups of languages, the Finno-Ugric and the Samoyedic, both of which are thought to have developed from a common ancestor, called Proto-Uralic, that was spoken 7,000 to 10,000 years ago in the general area of the northern Ural Mountain Range. Over the millennia, both Finno-Ugric and Samoyedic have given rise to more or less divergent subgroups of languages, which nonetheless have retained certain traits from their common source. For example, the degree of similarity between two of the least closely related members of the Finno-Ugric group, Hungarian and Finnish, is comparable to that between English and Russian (which belong to the Indo-European family of languages). The difference between any Finno-Ugric language and any Samoyedic tongue would be even greater. On the other hand, more closely related members of Finno-Ugric, such as Finnish and Estonian, differ in much the same manner as greatly diverse dialects of the same language.

The Finno-Ugric languages are represented today by some 15 languages scattered over an immense Eurasian territory. In the west they include the European national languages—Hungarian, Finnish, and Estonian—as well as Lapp, the westernmost member of the group, spoken by numerous separate groups across the northern Scandinavian Peninsula from central Norway to the White Sea. The remaining Finno-Ugric languages are located within the Soviet Union, with one major concentration—including Estonian, Livonian, Votic, Karelian, and Veps—along a broad zone extending from the Gulf of Riga to the Kola Peninsula. The Mordvin and Mari (or Cheremis) languages are found in the region of the central Volga; from there extending northward along the river courses west of the Urals are the Permic languages—Udmurt (Votyak) and Komi (Zyryan). East of the Urals, along the Ob River and its tributaries are the easternmost representatives of the Finno-Ugric group—Mansi (Vogul) and Khanty (Ostyak).

Finno-Ugric languages

The largely nomadic Samoyeds are sparsely distributed over an enormous area extending inward from the Arctic shores of the Soviet Union from the White Sea in the west to Khatangsky (Khatanga) Bay in central Siberia in the east. Nenets (Yurak), the westernmost of these languages, reaches eastward to the mouth of the Yenisey River and includes a small insular group on Novaya Zemlya. Speakers of Enets (Yenisey) are located in the region of the upper Yenisey. The lower half of the Taymyr Peninsula is the habitat of the Nganasan (Tavgi), the easternmost of the Uralic groups. The fourth language, Selkup, lies to the south in a region between the central Ob and central Yenisey; its major representation is located between Turukhansk and the Taz River. A fifth Samoyedic language, Kamas (Sayan), originally spoken in the vicinity of the Sayan Mountains, was spoken in the

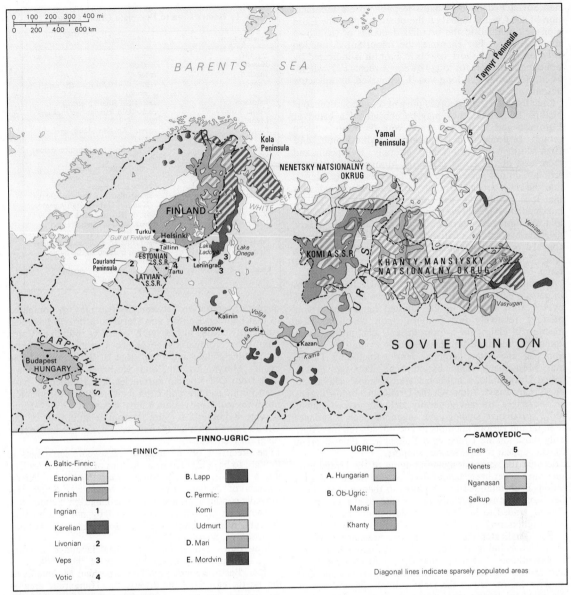

Distribution of the Uralic languages.

early 1970s by one elderly speaker, then residing in Estonia.

In general, the westernmost members of the Uralic family are spoken by the greatest numbers of speakers. The largest groups are Hungarian, with some 14,000,000 speakers; Finnish, with 5,000,000; and Estonian, with approximately 1,000,000. Among the lesser known Uralic languages of the Soviet Union, several have rather substantial representation: Mordvin, nearly 1,000,000 speakers; Mari, over 500,000; Udmurt, close to 500,000; Komi, almost 400,000; and Karelian, with just under 100,000 (estimates based on the 1970 Soviet census). The approximately 35,000 Lapps are distributed over four countries: Norway, 20,000; Sweden, 10,000; Finland, 3,000; and the Soviet Union, 1,500. Other Finno-Ugric languages with more than 1,000 speakers are Khanty (about 15,000), Veps (about 8,000) and Mansi (about 4,000). In the mid-20th century, Votic and Livonian were still maintained by small communities of speakers, but they appeared to be facing extinction in future generations. The entire Samoyedic group consists of only 25,000 to 30,000 speakers. Of these, Nenets claims over 24,000 speakers; Selkup, roughly 3,000; Nganasan, fewer than 1,000; and Enets, about 300.

The political history of the various Uralic groups largely has been one of resisting encroachment from adjacent European (especially Germanic and Slavic) and Turkic groups and from other Uralic neighbours. Only three

Numbers of speakers

groups have succeeded in achieving political independence—Hungary, Finland, and Estonia (the latter is now, however, one of the 15 republics of the U.S.S.R.). Five of the minority groups in the Soviet Union have the status of autonomous republics: Mordovskaya (Mordvin) A.S.S.R., Mari A.S.S.R., Udmurt A.S.S.R., Komi A.S.S.R., and the Karelian A.S.S.R. (formerly a republic of the U.S.S.R.). Four more groups are recognized at the level of local administration under their own *natsionalny okruga* (national areas): Khanty and Mansi (under one area), the Permyak dialect of Komi, and Nenets (under three *okruga*).

The earliest known manuscript in a Uralic language is a Hungarian funeral oration (*Halotti Beszéd*), a short, free translation from Latin, which stems from the turn of the 13th century AD. A 12-word Karelian fragment also dates from the 13th century. Old Permic, the earliest attested form of Komi, received its own alphabet (based on the Greek and Old Slavic symbols) in the 14th century through the missionary efforts of St. Stephen, bishop of Perm. The first Finnish and Estonian texts date from the 16th century, and are in printed form. Lapp was first written in the 17th century. Since then, nearly all the more populous Uralic languages have some kind of written form, but at present there is a native literature only for the above-mentioned languages and for those groups in the Soviet Union that have their own administrative regions. Currently, the Uralic languages within the Rus-

Alphabets
used for
the Uralic
languages

sian Soviet Federated Socialist Republic use a modification of the Cyrillic alphabet; the others employ the Latin alphabet, adapted to the peculiar demands of their own sound systems. For example, the important distinction between long and short vowels in Finnish is indicated by doubling the letters for long vowels (*a* versus *aa*), whereas in Hungarian the long vowel is marked by an acute accent (*a* versus *á*).

Racially, the Uralic peoples present an unhomogeneous picture. In general, they may be considered a blend of European and Mongoloid types, with the more western groups (especially the Hungarian, Baltic-Finnic, and Erza-Mordvin groups) being strongly European and those east of the Urals primarily Mongoloid. Although scholars do not agree as to what features, if any, constitute the most archaic Uralic type, recent study indicates that it is possible to speak of a Uralic racial type, an intermediate stage between the European and the Mongoloid, the basic features of which are medium-dark to dark hair and eye colour, relatively small stature, and often a concave bridge of the nose. According to this view, the more archaic Uralic type is best preserved among the Lapp, Mari, and Permic groups.

Attempts to trace the genealogy of the Uralic languages to periods earlier than Proto-Uralic have been hampered by the great changes in the attested languages, which preserve relatively few features upon which to base meaningful claims for a more distant relationship. Most commonly mentioned in this respect is a putative connection with the Altaic language family (including Turkic and Mongolian). This hypothetical language group, called Ural-Altaic, is not considered by most scholars to be soundly based. Although the Uralic and Indo-European languages are not generally thought to be related, more speculative studies have suggested such a connection. Of the various attempts to find outside relationships, only those linking Uralic with Yukaghir, a Paleosiberian tongue, appear to have serious support.

Because the names designating many of the Uralic peoples have never been standardized, a wide range of appellations is encountered in references to these groups. Earlier designations, especially in the case of the groups in Russia, tended to be taken from derogatory names used by neighbouring peoples; *e.g.*, Cheremis—now Mari. Table 1 indicates the names in use. Standard usage is in the left column, and earlier, Russian-based forms are in parentheses. The name that the group uses for itself and certain other information, such as Russian and Old Russian forms, are in the right column. Several names are identical to the word for man in these languages. (Finnish *mies* "man" has also been etymologically related to the names Magyar and Mansi.) It is important that Ostyak (Khanty) not be confused with Ostyak Samoyed (Selkup) nor with Yenisey Ostyak (Ket, a non-Uralic, Paleosiberian tongue), which should also not be confused with Yenisey (Enets).

LANGUAGES OF THE URALIC FAMILY

The two major branches of Uralic are themselves composed of numerous subgroupings of member languages on the basis of closeness of linguistic relationship. Finno-Ugric can first be divided into the most distantly related Ugric and Finnic (sometimes called Volga-Finnic) groups, which may have separated as long ago as five millennia. Within these, three relatively closely related groups of languages are found: the Baltic-Finnic, the Permic, and the Ob-Ugric. The largest of these, the Baltic-Finnic group, is composed of Finnish, Estonian, Livonian, Votic, Ingrian, Karelian, and Veps. The Permic group consists of Komi and Udmurt; the Ob-Ugric group includes Mansi and Khanty.

Divisions
within
Finno-
Ugric

The Ugric group comprises the geographically most distant members of the family—the Hungarian and Ob-Ugric languages. Finnic contains the remaining languages: the Baltic-Finnic languages, Lapp, Mordvin, Mari, and the Permic tongues. There is little accord on the further subclassification of the Finnic languages, although the fairly close relationship between Baltic-Finnic and Lapp is generally recognized (and is called North Finnic); the

Table 1: Names Used to Designate Uralic Groups

English form	native form
Finnish	*suomi*
Karelian	*karjala*
Ingrian	*izhor*
Veps	*vepsä, lüüd* (Old Russian *vesj, chudj*)
Estonian	*eesti* (Old Russian *chudj*)
Votic, Vote	*vadja* (Old Russian *vodj; chudj*)
Livonian	*liiv*
Lapp	*sabme* (Russian *saami;* earlier *lopj*)
Mordvin	*erza, moksha* (no common name)
Mari (Cheremis)	*mari* ("man")
Udmurt (Votyak)	*ud-murt* (*murt* = "man")
Komi (Zyryan)	*komi* (Old Russian *permj*)
Khanty (Ostyak)	*khanty* (Old Russian *jugra*)
Mansi (Vogul)	*manshi* (also used to designate the Khanty; Old Russian *jugra*)
Hungarian	*magyar* (Russian *vengr*)
Nenets (Yurak)	*nenets, hasawa* ("man"; Old Russian *samojadj*)
Enets (Yenisey)	*enet* (related to the name *nenets*)
Nganasan (Tavgi, Avam)	*ŋanasan* (related to the name *nenets*)
Selkup (Ostyak Samoyed)	*shöl-qup* (*shö[l]* = "earth," *qup* = "man")

degree of separation between the two may be compared to that between English and German. Mordvin has most frequently been linked with Mari (a putative Volga group), but comparative evidence also suggests a bond with Baltic-Finnic and Lapp (that is, West Finnic). The extinct Merya, Murom, and Meshcher groups, known only from Old Russian chronicles, are assumed to have been Finnic peoples and from their geographical location northwest of Mordvin must have belonged to West Finnic. One hypothesis for the internal relationships of the Uralic family as a whole is given in the accompanying diagram (see below).

The precursor of the modern Samoyedic languages is thought to have divided near the turn of the Christian Era into a northern and a southern group. North Samoyedic consists of Nenets, Enets, and Nganasan. South Samoyedic contains but a single living language, Selkup, but is known to have been represented by numerous other dialects, now extinct: Kamas, Motor, Koibal, Tofalar (Karagasy), Soyot, and Taigi.

Hungarian. Hungarian, the official language of Hungary, remains the primary language of the fertile Carpathian Basin. Bounded by the Carpathian Mountains to the north, east, and southwest, the Hungarian area is represented by over 2,000,000 speakers outside the boundaries of Hungary—in Czechoslovakia, the Ukranian S.S.R., and Romanian Transylvania (some 1,600,-000). To the south, a substantial Hungarian population (over 500,000) extends into central Yugoslavia. Hungarian emigrant communities are found in many parts of the world, especially in North America and Australia.

The ancestors of the Hungarians, following their separation from the other Ugric tribes, moved south into the steppe region below the Urals. As mounted nomads, in contact with and often in alliance with Turkic tribes, they moved westward, reaching and conquering the sparsely settled Carpathian Basin in the period 895–896. The Hungarians came under the influence of Rome through their first Christian king, Stephen (István), in 1001, and the use of Latin for official purposes continued into the 19th century. Following a Hungarian defeat at the Battle of Mohács in 1526, Hungary was occupied by Turkish forces, who were replaced by German Habsburg domination in the late 17th century. Concern for a common literary medium, closely tied with Hungarian nationalism, began in the late 18th century. More recent foreign influences on the language were suppressed and replaced by native words and constructions. The literary form received a broad dialect base, facilitating its use as a national language.

Modern Hungarian has eight major dialects, which permit a high degree of mutual intelligibility. Budapest, the nation's capital, is located near the junction of three dia-

Dialects
of
Hungarian

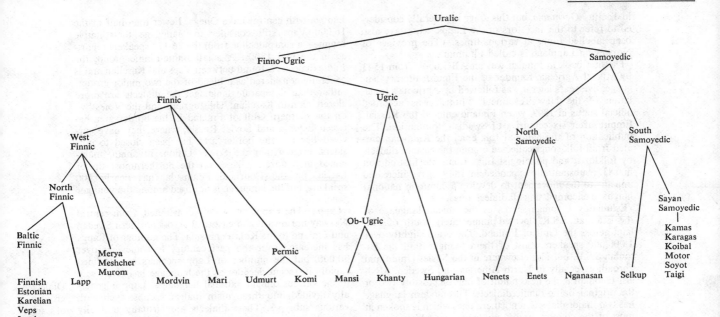

Family tree diagram of the Uralic languages (see text).

Uralic
- **Finno-Ugric**
  - **Finnic**
    - **West Finnic**
      - **North Finnic**
        - **Baltic Finnic**
          - Finnish
          - Estonian
          - Karelian
          - Veps
          - Ingrian
          - Votic
          - Livonian
        - Lapp
      - Merya Meshcher Murom
      - Mordvin
    - Mari
    - **Permic**
      - Udmurt
      - Komi
  - **Ugric**
    - **Ob-Ugric**
      - Mansi
      - Khanty
    - Hungarian
- **Samoyedic**
  - **North Samoyedic**
    - Nenets
    - Enets
    - Nganasan
  - **South Samoyedic**
    - Selkup
    - **Sayan Samoyedic**
      - Kamas
      - Karagas
      - Koibal
      - Motor
      - Soyot
      - Taigi

lect areas: the South, Transdanubian, and Palóc (Northwestern). As a result of unfavourable treaties following both world wars, especially the Treaty of Trianon, two dialects (Central Transylvanian and Székely) lie almost entirely within Romania, and the remaining six dialects radiate outward into neighbouring countries.

The Hungarians' own name for themselves is *magyar*. Other Western appelations, such as the French *hongrois*, German *Ungar*, and Russian *vengr*, all stem from the name of an early Turkic tribal confederation, the *on-ogur* (meaning "ten tribes"), which the Hungarians joined in their wanderings toward the west, and does not indicate relationship with the ancient Huns, a Turkic tribe. One of the earliest recorded references to the Hungarians, a Byzantine geographical survey of Constantine Porphyrogenitus (died 959) entitled *De administrando imperio*, lists the *megyer* as one of the Hungarian tribes, but, as was typical in early reports, the Hungarians were not distinguished from their Turkish allies.

Ob-Ugric: Khanty and Mansi. The Ob-Ugric peoples, the Khanty and the Mansi, are among the smallest Finno-Ugric groups. Although their numbers have declined over recent centuries, Khanty is still maintained by almost 15,000 speakers, and, according to the 1970 Soviet census, 52 percent of the 7,700 Mansi still claim it as their mother tongue. To a large extent they have been assimilated by their Russian and Tatar neighbours. These two peoples are widely dispersed along the Ob River and its tributaries, for the most part within the Khanty-Mansiysky *natsionalny okrug*, which has its administrative centre in Khanty-Mansiysk at the junction of the Ob and the Irtysh. The Mansi are found along the western tributaries primarily north of the Irtysh and just east of the Urals; a few speakers are also found in the Arctic lands west of the Urals. The Khanty live along both the Ob itself and its tributaries.

Because of the great distances between the various groups, the dialects of both languages show considerable divergence. They are usually designated by the name of the river on which they are spoken. Mansi has four main dialect groups, of which one (Tavda) is practically extinct and another (Konda) is no longer spoken by the youth of the area. The largest dialect group (Northern) is centred on the Sosva and serves as the basis for the literary language. Khanty is divided into three main dialects: a northern dialect in the general area of the mouth of the Ob, an eastern dialect extending from east of the Irtysh to the Vakh and Vasyugan tributaries, and a southern dialect lying between the other two. Literary Khanty has

been based primarily on the northern group, but standardization remains weak, and in recent decades other dialects have also been used.

After the division of the Proto-Ugric language into separate languages, it is likely that the precursors of the Ob-Ugric tribes were still centred west of the Urals well within historic times. The Old Russian Chronicles of Nestor, which assigned them the common name *jugra*, places them in the vicinity of the Pechora River in 1092; they did not shift to the Ob waterways until several centuries later. Both of the Ob-Ugric languages first appeared in printed form in 1868 as a result of gospel translations published in London, but it was not until after the formation of their *natsionalny okrug* in 1930 that any sort of literary form of Khanty and Mansi really existed. Until 1937 numerous books were published using a modified Latin (roman) alphabet; since then Cyrillic has been used. To a certain extent, elementary education is conducted in the native languages within the *natsionalny okrug*.

Finnish. Finnish, together with Swedish (an unrelated North Germanic language), serves as the official language of Finland. It is now spoken by over 5,000,000 people, including 92.4 percent of the inhabitants of Finland plus nearly 1,000,000 Finns in North America, Sweden, and the Soviet Union. It is also recognized as an official language in the Karelian A.S.S.R., alongside Russian.

Finnish as the common language of the Finns is not the direct descendant of one of the original Baltic-Finnic dialects; rather, it arose through the interaction of several separate groups in the territory of modern Finland. These included the Häme; the southwestern Finns (originally called Suomi), who appear to be close relatives to the Estonians, because they arrived directly from across the Gulf of Finland; and the Karelians, perhaps themselves a blend of Veps and more western Finnic groups. Early Russian chronicles refer to these as *jemj*, *sumj*, and *korela*. The intermixture of the three groups is still reflected in the distribution of the five main modern dialects, which form a western and an eastern area. The western area contains the southwest dialect (near Turku), Häme (south central), and a northern dialect subgroup (largely a mixture of the other two plus eastern traits). The eastern area consists of the Savo dialect (perhaps a blend of the original Karelian and Häme dialects) and a southeastern dialect, which strongly resembles Karelian. The Finnish word for their land and their language is *suomi*, the original meaning of which is uncertain. The first use of the term Finn (*fenni*) is found in the 1st century AD

(margin, left) Khanty and Mansi dialects

(margin, right) Modern Finnish dialects

in Tacitus' *Germania*, but this usage is generally considered to refer to the ancestors of the Lapps, who have also been labelled Finns at various times. (The province of Norwegian Lappland is called Finnmark.)

The first book in Finnish was an ABC book from 1543 by Mikael Agricola, founder of the Finnish literary language; five years later it was followed by Agricola's translation of the New Testament. Finnish was accorded official status in 1809, when Finland entered the Russian Empire after six centuries of Swedish domination. The publication of the national folk epic, the *Kalevala*, created from folk songs collected among the eastern dialects by folklorist and philologist Elias Lönnrot (first edition in 1835; substantially expanded in 1849), gave increased impetus to the movement to develop a common national language encompassing all dialect areas.

Estonian. Estonian serves as the official language of the Estonian S.S.R., located immediately south of Finland across the Gulf of Finland. There are slightly over 1,000,000 speakers, most of them living within the Estonian S.S.R. but also elsewhere in the Soviet Union and abroad, especially in North America and Sweden. Modern Estonian is the descendant of one or possibly two of the original Baltic-Finnic dialects. The modern language has two major dialects, a northern one, which is spoken in most of the country, and a southern one, which extends from Tartu to the south. The northernmost dialects share many features with the southwestern Finnish dialect. The Estonians' own name *eesti* came into general use only in the 19th century. The name *aestii* is first encountered in Tacitus, but it is likely that it referred to neighbouring Baltic-Finnic peoples.

The first connected texts in Estonian are religious translations from 1524; the *Wanradt-Koell Catechism*, the first book, was printed in Wittenberg in 1535. Two centres of culture developed—Tallinn (formerly Reval) in the north and Tartu (Dorpat) in the south; in the 17th century they gave rise to two literary languages. Influenced by the Finnish *Kalevala*, the Estonian author Friedrich Reinhold Kreutzwald fashioned a national epic, the *Kalevipoeg* ("Son of Kalevi"), which appeared in 20 songs between 1857 and 1861. As with the *Kalevala*, this was instrumental in kindling renewed interest in a common national literary form in the late 19th century.

Smaller Baltic-Finnic groups. The five less numerous Baltic-Finnic groups—Karelian, Veps, Ingrian, Votic, and Livonian—lie within the territory of the Soviet Union, largely in the general vicinity of the Gulf of Finland. The Karelians, Veps, and Livonians were among the original Baltic-Finnic tribes; Votic is considered to be an offshoot of Estonian, and Ingrian, a remote branch of Karelian. None of these languages currently has a literary form, although unsuccessful initial attempts to establish one have been made for all but Votic (for Livonian as early as the 19th century, for the others during the 1930s). Since the beginning of the 20th century the numbers of these Baltic-Finnic speakers have been drastically reduced, and, with the exception of Karelian and Veps, their extinction within several generations seems certain. Votic and Livonian, both with fewer than 1,000 speakers, were not included in the 1959 census, and of the 1,100 Ingrians recorded at that time only 34 percent still considered themselves native Ingrian speakers.

Karelian, the largest of these groups, with nearly 120,000 speakers—not counting those Karelians who emigrated into Finland following World War II—lies along a broad zone just east of the Finnish border from just north of Leningrad to the White Sea. A separate group of Karelians is found far to the south near Kalinin (formerly Tver) on the upper Volga. Karelian has two major dialects, Karelian proper and Olonets (*aunus* in Finnish), which is spoken northeast of Lake Ladoga. One of the first historical mentions of the Karelians is found in a report of the Viking Ohthere to King Alfred of England at the end of the 9th century; this indicates that they were already on the southern Kola Peninsula as neighbours of the Lapps and gives their name as *beorma*.

The language of one of the original Baltic-Finnic tribes, Veps, is spoken southeast on a line connecting lower Lake Ladoga with central Lake Onega. Fewer than half of the 16,000 Veps still consider the language their native tongue—a sharp decline from the 26,172 speakers reported in the mid 1800s. A small Baltic-Finnic group, the Ludic dialects, is found between Veps and Karelian and is generally considered as a blend of the two major groups, rather than a separate language; the dialects are more closely akin to Karelian. The Ingrians and the Votes live on the southern Gulf of Finland in the border area between Estonia and Soviet Russia, where they have survived because the border area has been closed to outsiders, even within the Soviet Union. Livonian, maintained in a dozen villages on the northernmost tip of Latvia, on the Courland Peninsula, has nearly 500 speakers, but the language is not used among the younger generation.

Lapp. The Lapps are widely distributed, from central Norway northward and eastward across northern Sweden and Finland to the Kola Peninsula. The number of Lapps has increased over the past century to somewhat over 30,000, but the number of Lapp speakers has declined rapidly in recent decades as the language has given way to the various official national languages. Lapp is generally divided into three main dialect groups, each with various subtypes. These dialects are virtually mutually unintelligible, so that when speakers of different Lapp groups meet, they generally converse in Finnish, Swedish, or Norwegian. To speak of a single Lapp language is thus misleading. Lapp represents a group of at least four or five languages at least as diverse as the separate Baltic-Finnic languages. The largest group, North Lapp (with roughly two-thirds of all speakers), is centred in northern Norway, Sweden, and Finland. East Lapp consists of two small groups in eastern Finland—Inari and Skolt—plus Kola Lapp in the Soviet Union. South Lapp is still represented by a few speakers scattered from central Norway to north central Sweden.

North Lapp has had a literary tradition that began with the 17th-century Swedish Lapp Bible and other religious translations; in the mid-20th century elementary schools that used Lapp as the language of instruction were found in many larger North Lapp communities. Two basic variants of the literary language are in use. One, in Norway and Sweden, employs a special Lapp orthographic system devised to accommodate a wide range of dialectal variation; a second, in Finland, is based on a more narrow adaptation of Finnish orthography. Each of the two types has numerous local variants, and progress toward a common Lapp orthography has been slow.

A wide range of theories has been posited to reconcile the apparent conflict between the different racial features of the Lapps and the Baltic-Finnic peoples and their strong linguistic similarities. The Lapps have been said to represent a non-Uralic people (the so-called Proto-Lapps) or perhaps a Samoyed tribe that abandoned its own language for a late stage of Finnic, perhaps early Baltic-Finnic. Another view is that the Lapps are one of the original Finnic tribes and not linguistically more closely related to Baltic-Finnic. In the absence of any compelling evidence, no conclusive answer can be provided. On the other hand, the fact that the non-Uralic origin of the Baltic Finns is rarely considered, despite recent evidence suggesting that the Lapps best represent the racial characteristics of the Finno-Ugric peoples, leads to the possibility of a certain degree of chauvinism in the earlier hypotheses suggesting outside origins for the Lapps. In any case, it is clear that the Lapps were already present north of the Gulf of Finland prior to the arrival of the first Baltic-Finnic tribes, and from there they may have extended over much of the Scandinavian Peninsula. They have been mentioned as the northern neighbours of the north Germanic tribes in numerous historical sources of the 1st millennium of the Christian Era. The Lapps were taxed by the Norwegians in the 9th century and by the Karelians in the 13th century and since that time have continually retreated northward under pressure from their southern neighbours. The Lapps' own name for themselves, *sabme*, is etymologically related to the Finnish dialect name, *häme*.

Karelian, Veps, Ingrian, Votic, Livonian

Dialect groups of Lapp

Other Finnic languages. Mordvin, Mari, and the Permic languages—Udmurt and Komi—are each recognized by autonomous republics within the Russian Soviet Federated Socialist Republic, where they share official status with Russian. Mordvin, Mari, and Udmurt are centred on the middle Volga River, in roughly the area considered to have been the original home of Proto-Finno-Ugric. Because of their location, the history of these groups over the past millennium has been closely tied to that of the Turkic Bulgars, the Tatars (until 1552), and then the Russians. The Komi, having moved far to the north, eventually reaching into the Arctic tundra, did not come under Bulgar or Tatar influence. A written form of early Komi, Old Permic, was used in religious manuscripts in the 14th century, and a native Komi literary tradition stems from the 19th century. Grammars of Mari and Udmurt prepared by Russian linguists appeared in 1775, but native literary development in these languages, as well as in Mordvin, is of recent origin. Although these groups currently enjoy the status of large minorities, even in their respective autonomous areas, their numbers have increased over the past century, and they have maintained ethnic consciousness.

Mordvin. Mordvin, with nearly 1,000,000 speakers (78 percent of the 1,263,000 Mordvinians reported in 1970), is the third-largest Uralic group. The Mordvinians are widely scattered over an area between the Oka and Volga rivers, some 200 miles southwest of Moscow. Less than half of their number live within the Mordovskaya Autonomous Soviet Socialist Republic. Mordvin has two main dialects, Moksha and Erza, which are sometimes considered separate languages. Both have literary status. Although the Mordvinians do not have a common designation for themselves beyond the two dialect names, the name *mordens* appears in the 6th-century *Getica* of Jordanes and is no doubt related to the Permic word for "man," *murt/mort.*

Mari. Mari is currently maintained by over 500,000 speakers (91 percent of 599,000 in 1970), primarily in an area north of the Volga between Kazan and Gorki, northeast of the Mordvin area, especially within the Mariyskaya A.S.S.R. Mari's three main dialects are: the Meadow dialect, used by the largest group north of the Volga and the basic dialect of the Mariyskaya A.S.S.R.; Eastern Mari, used by a small group near Ufa, originally speakers of the Meadow dialect who emigrated in the late 18th century; and the Mountain dialect, to the west and on the south bank of the Volga. The Mountain and Meadow dialects both serve as literary languages and differ from each other only in minor details.

The Permic languages. Speakers of the two closely related Permic languages number close to 1,000,000— roughly 581,500 Udmurts and 397,500 Komi. Udmurt is concentrated largely in the vicinity of the lower Kama River just east of the Mariyskaya A.S.S.R., in the Udmurtskaya A.S.S.R. Only very minor dialectal differences are found within Udmurt. The Komi language area extends into the Nenetskaya *natsionalny okrug* far to the north. Lesser groups of Komi are found as far west as the Kola Peninsula and east of the Urals. Three major dialects are recognized, although the differences are not great: Komi Zyryan, the largest group, which serves as the literary basis within the Komi A.S.S.R.; Komi-Permyak, the dialect of the Komi-Permyatsky *natsionalny okrug*, where it has literary status; and Komi-Yazva, spoken by some 4,000 Komi to the east of the Komi-Permyatsky *okrug* and south of the Komi A.S.S.R.

The Samoyed languages. Nenets, with the largest number of speakers of all the Samoyed languages, has added a substantial increase in the number of its speakers over the past century, from 9,245 in 1897 to over 24,000 in the mid-1900s. Two distinct groups of Nenets differ in dialect as well as in cultural traditions: the Forest Nenets, a smaller, more concentrated group in the wooded area north of the central Ob; and the Tundra Nenets, a group whose territory stretches roughly 1,000 miles eastward from the White Sea. These are the "Samoyadj" of Nestor's chronicles, but little is known of the history of any of the Samoyed peoples until recent centuries. Nenets

alone among the Samoyed languages can claim a native literature, although both it and Selkup have been in written form since the 1930s. Evidence of the cultural prestige of certain Nenets tribes is seen in the adoption of a Samoyed language by Khanty speakers on the Yamal Peninsula. Enets is spoken by a dwindling group of several hundred Samoyeds near the mouth of the Yenisey, just east of the Nenets. Nganasan, spoken by the northernmost Eurasian people, is found north and east of the Enets-speaking group, centring on the Taymir Peninsula. The number of Nganasans has remained fairly constant, and they seem to have a high degree of ethnic identity (93.4 percent of 1,000 Nganasans still claimed Nganasan as their mother tongue in 1970).

Selkup, the last of the southern Samoyed languages, is represented by scattered groups of speakers who live on the central West Siberian Plain between the Ob and the Yenisey. Only half of the 4,300 Selkup speakers counted in 1970 still consider the language their mother tongue.

EARLY HISTORY OF THE URALIC LANGUAGES

Determining the geographical location, material culture, and linguistic characteristics of the earliest stages of Uralic at a period thousands of years prior to any historical records is a problem beset with enormous difficulties; consensus among Uralic scholars is limited to a handful of general hypotheses.

The original homeland of Proto-Uralic is considered to have been in the vicinity of the central Urals, possibly centred west of the mountains. Following the dissolution of Uralic, the precursors of the Samoyeds gradually moved northward and eastward into Siberia. The Finno-Ugrians moved to the south and west, to an area close to the junction of the Kama and Volga rivers.

Knowledge of the location of these early groups is based on several kinds of indirect evidence. One approach attempts to reconstruct their natural environment on the basis of shared cognate words for plants, animals, and minerals and on the distribution of these words in the modern languages. For example, cognates (related words) designating certain types of spruce are found in all the Uralic languages except Hungarian (Finnish *kuusi*, Lapp *guossâ*, Mordvin *kuz*, Komi *koz*, Khanty *kol*, Nenets *xādy*, Selkup *kūt*). Because the range of this type of fir tree is restricted to more northern climates, it is generally assumed that the widespread consistent association of the name and the tree suggests a period in which Proto-Uralic was spoken within that zone. Several other terms for plants (*e.g.,* Finnish *muurain* "cloudberry" [*Rubus arcticus*]), a term for metal (Estonian *vask* "copper," Hungarian *vas* "iron," Nganasan *basa* "iron"), and a word for "reindeer" (Lapp *boaзo*) are also consistent with a northern Ural location. Great caution is necessary in such matters, because the association of words and objects can also result from borrowing, perhaps long after the period of Uralic unity; especially such culturally mobile items as "metal" and "reindeer" cannot with certainty be traced to a Proto-Uralic community. The central Volga location of Proto-Finno-Ugric is rather strongly supported by an abundance of shared terminology dealing with beekeeping, which forms an important part of the culture of this region.

A second approach to determining the location of Proto-Uralic is based on contacts with other, unrelated languages as evidenced by loanwords from one group to the other. Early Finno-Ugric borrowed numerous terms from very early dialects of Indo-European. Though these words are entirely lacking from the Samoyed languages, within the Finno-Ugric division they are shared by the most remotely related members and show the same phonetic relationships as the native Finno-Ugric vocabulary. Examples include agricultural and bee-culture terminology (*e.g.,* "honey": Finnish *mete*, Komi *ma*, Hungarian *méz* [compare Indo-European **medhu*-]; "pig": Finnish *porsas*, Komi *porś*); several numerals ("hundred": Finnish *sata*, Hungarian *száz*); mineral words ("salt": Finnish *suola*, Komi *sol*); and the word for orphan (Finnish *orpo*, Hungarian *árva*). The nature of these borrowings, together with the linguist's relatively richer knowledge of

(margin notes) Mordvin, Mari, and the Permic languages · Udmurt and Komi · Hypotheses concerning early Uralic cultures and languages · Loanwords from unrelated languages

Table 2: Representative Cognates in Selected Uralic Languages

English translation	Finnish	Estonian	Lapp	Mari	Komi	Khanty	Hungarian	Nenets	Proto-Uralic
head; end	*pää*	*pea*	—	—	*pom*	—	*fej*	*pä-*	* *päŋe*
tree	*puu*	*puu*	—	*pu*	*pu*	—	*fa*	*på*	* *puve*
fish	*kala*	*kala*	*guolle*	*kol*	*kul*	—	*hal*	*xal'ä*	* *kala*
house, hut	*kota*	*koda*	*goatte*	*kuðo*	*-ka*	*kat*	*ház*	—	* *kota*
who	*ken*	*ke(s)*	*gi*	*ke*	*kin*	—	*ki*	*x̂ib'ä*	* *ken*
hand	*käte-*	*kät-*	*giettä*	*kö*	*ki*	*köt*	*kéz*	—	* *käte*
louse	*täi*	*täi*	*dik'ke*	*ti*	*toj*	*tögtəm*	*tetü*	—	* *täjka*
know	*tunte-*	*tunde-*	*dow'dâ-*	—	*təd*		*tud*	*tumda-*	* *tumte-*
give	*anta-*	*anda-*	*vuow'de-*	*omta-*	*ud-*	*öntas*	*ad*	—	* *amta-*
eye	*silmä*	*silm*	*čal'bme*	*šinča*	*šin*	*sem*	*szem*	*sew*	* *silmä*
heart	*sydäm-*	*südam-*	*čâððam-*	*šüm*	*šaləm*	*səm*	*szív*	*sēj*	* *šüðam-*
lap	*syli*	*süli*	*sâllâ*	*šəl*	*syl*	*jöl*	*öl*	—	* *süle*
vein	*suoni*	*soon*	*suodnâ*	*šön*	*sən*	*jan*	*ín*	*tēn-*	* *sōne*
mouse	*hiiri*	*hiir*	—	—	*šyr*	*junkər*	*egér*	—	* *šiŋer*
ice	*jää*	*jää*	*jiegŋâ*	*ij*	*ji*	*jöŋk*	*jég*	—	* *jäŋe*
blood	*veri*	*veri*	*vârrâ*	*vür*	—	—	*vér*	—	* *vere*
water	*vete-*	*vet-*	—	*vüt*	*va*	—	*víz*	*jīd-*	* *vete*
go	*men-*	*min-*	*mânnâ-*	*mija-*	*mun-*	*mən-*	*men-*	*min-*	* *mene-*
one	*yhte-*	*üht-*	*ok'tâ*	*ikte*	*ət'ik*	*ït*	*?egy*	—	* *ükte*
two	*kahte-*	*kaht-*	*guok'te*	*kok*	*kyk*	*kät*	*két*	—	* *kakte*
three	*kolme*	*kolm*	*gol'bmâ*	*kum*	*kujim*	*koləm*	*három*	—	* *kolm-*
four	*neljä*	*neli*	*njæl'lje*	*nyl*	*ńol*	*ńalä*	*négy*	—	* *neljä*
five	*viite-*	*viit-*	*vit'tâ*	*vič*	*vit*	*vet*	*öt*	—	* *vit(t)e*
six	*kuute-*	*kuut-*	*gut'tâ*	*kut*	*kvajt*	*kut*	*hat*	—	* *kut(t)e*

*Unattested, reconstructed form.

early Indo-European, supports a southward movement of Proto-Finno-Ugric and also provides some insight into the culture of the Finno-Ugrians.

The central Volga location is also supported by the geographical distribution of the daughter languages. Except for Hungarian, which moved westward across the steppe, the Finno-Ugric languages form two chains distributed along major waterways, with the junction of the Kama and Volga at their centre. One chain extends northward along the Kama, across the northern tip of the Urals into the Ob watershed, then south along the Ob and its tributaries. The second extends northeast along the Volga to the Gulf of Finland. The extinct Merya, Murom, and Meshcher languages were once links in this chain. Finally, assumptions about the more distant relationships of Uralic have influenced views concerning its original location. Earlier, proponents of the Ural-Altaic hypothesis tended to place the Uralic homeland in south central Siberia, near the sources of the Ob and Yenisey, but there is no support for this view.

LINGUISTIC CHARACTERISTICS OF THE URALIC LANGUAGES

The linguistic structure of Proto-Uralic has been partially reconstructed by a comparison of the similarities and differences among the known Uralic tongues. Not all existing similarities can be attributed to a common Uralic origin; some may also reflect universal pressures and limitations on language structure (*e.g.*, the tendency to weaken stopped consonants between vowels, the modifying of a sound to become more similar to a preceding or following sound) or the influence of neighbouring, even genetically unrelated language structures (*e.g.*, the various types of vowel harmony [see below] in Finno-Ugric probably reflect such areal pressure).

Phonological characteristics. The correspondences of sounds in cognate Uralic words are illustrated in Table 2. Thus, a *p* in the beginning of a Finnish word corresponds to *f* in Hungarian (*puu* : *fa*); a Finnish *k* is matched by Hungarian *h* before a back vowel (*a, o*), otherwise by *k*; within the word, Finnish *t* is matched by Hungarian *z* and *nt* by *d*; Finnish initial *s* sometimes corresponds to Hungarian *s* (spelled *sz*) and sometimes to no consonant at all (*syli* : *öl*). In most of these instances, Finnish has retained the consonants of the Proto-Uralic consonant system. One exception is *nt*, which was originally **mt*; the *m* has become *n*, matching the position of articulation of the adjacent *t*. (An asterisk marks a form that is not found in any document or living dialect but is reconstructed as having once existed in an earlier stage of a language.) A second Finnish innovation is the loss of the distinction between the two original *s* sounds, **s* and palatalized **ś*. (Palatalization is the modification of a sound by simul-

taneous raising of the tongue to or toward the hard palate.) Hungarian maintains a distinction, but the original **s* words have lost this sound. By careful examination of such systematic relationships it is possible to sketch out much of the phonological structure of early Uralic. The reconstructions of Table 2 (last column) are based on the view that the vowel system of Baltic-Finnic is relatively more conservative, whereas the consonant contrasts have been best preserved in Lapp.

Consonants. The following consonant sounds are generally posited for the early stages of Uralic: **p*, **t*, **č*, **k*, **s*, **š*, **ð*, **l*, **r*, **m*, **n*, **ŋ*, **j*, **v* (*č* is pronounced as the *ch* in "chip," *š* as the *sh* in "ship," *ð* as the *th* in "then," *ŋ* as the *ng* in "sing," *j* as the *y* in "yet"), and the palatalized alveolar sounds **t'*, *ś*, *ð'*, *l'*, *ń*, plus a few others less well established. Modern Finnish has a much smaller inventory of consonants, having lost the palatalized alveolar sounds **č*, **š*, **ð*, and **ŋ*. Hungarian, on the other hand, has a larger number of consonants by virtue of a newly introduced distinction between sounds made with and without vibration of the vocal cords (voicing), such as voiceless *p*, *t*, *s* as opposed to voiced *b*, *d*, *z*; *e.g.*, *dél* "noon" : *tél* "winter." Other Uralic languages, such as Komi, have also acquired a voicing contrast (*e.g.*, *doj* "pain" : *toj* "louse"), but the geographical distribution of those languages in which the voicing contrast plays an active role leaves little doubt as to its areal (regional) origin under the influence of Indo-European and Turkic languages.

Vowels. Essentially nothing is known of the Proto-Uralic vowels, and there is little agreement about the nature of the Proto-Finno-Ugric vowel system. It is clear, however, that, in contrast to a relatively limited number of consonants, Finno-Ugric must have had a fairly large number of vowels (nine to 11 are usually posited). One hypothesis is that the original vowel system was essentially like that of Finnish, which has eight vowel sounds: *i, ü, u, e, ö, o, ä, a* (*ü*—spelled *y* in the standard orthography —and *ö* are front rounded vowels, as in German; *ä* is a low front vowel, as *a* in "cat"). Hungarian has a similar system, although not all dialects have a separate *ä* sound, which is not distinguished from *e* in the orthography. A second approach posits a Proto-Uralic vowel structure closely resembling that of Khanty, with seven full vowels and three reduced vowels.

The early Finno-Ugric system of vowels most likely possessed quantitative vowel contrasts (long versus short, or full versus reduced). Such contrasts are present in Baltic-Finnic, Lapp, and Ugric and within Samoyedic; *e.g.*, Finnish *tulen* "of fire" and *tuulen* "of wind," *tuleen* "into fire," and *tuuleen* "into wind"; Hungarian *szel* "slice" and *szél* "wind," *szelet* "wind" (accusative case),

Finnish and Hungarian sound correspondences

Proto-Uralic vowels

and *szelét* "its wind" (accusative). The possibility of influence by neighbouring languages cannot be ruled out in the case of vowel length, because western Finno-Ugric languages have been in close contact with Slavic and Germanic languages with similar vowel contrasts, and the eastern languages form an areal group among themselves. The remaining languages lack vowel quantity and are in intimate contact with Russian, which has lost the original contrastive vowel quantity of Indo-European. The Izhma dialect of Komi, adjacent to Nenets, has superficial contrasts such as *pi* "son" versus *pī* "cloud," but this vowel length is the result of a change of an *l* at the end of the syllable to a vowel.

Stress. In numerous Uralic languages—including Finnish, Estonian, Hungarian, and Komi—stress is automatically on the first syllable of the word; it is likely that Proto-Uralic also had word-initial stress. Closely related to this initial stress is the apparent severe limitation on early Finno-Ugric noninitial vowels; the full range of contrasts was permitted only in the first syllable. In certain languages, such as Eastern Mari and the Yazva Komi dialect, stress is not bound to a given syllable, and determining the place of stress requires information concerning vowel quality as well; *e.g.,* Yazva *śibdinə* "to bind," *liććinə* "to descend," *l'iśina* "wood" (the two stressed *i*'s are phonologically tense; *ś, ć, l'* are palatalized consonants). Stress at the end of a word is also found; *e.g.,* in Eastern Mari and Udmurt. Nganasan has a mora-counting stress, falling on the third unit of vowel length from the end of the word (where short vowels count as one unit, long vowels as two).

Vowel harmony. Vowel harmony is among the more familiar traits of the modern Uralic languages. Although most Uralic scholars trace this feature back to Proto-Uralic, there is good reason to question this view.

Conditions for vowel harmony

Vowel harmony is said to exist when certain vowels cannot occur with other specific vowels within some wider domain, generally within a word. For example, of the eight vowels of Finnish, within a simple word, any member of the set *ü, ö, ä* prohibits the use of any member of the set *u, o, a*, but *i* and *e* may occur with either set. That is, within a word, vowels that are either rounded, such as *ü, ö, u, o*, or low, such as *ä, a*, must agree with each other in frontness or backness. (The distinction is marked phonetically by putting two dots over the front vowels.) The unrounded front vowels, *i* and *e*, may occur with any of the other vowels. Thus, from *talo* "house" one may form *talossa* "in (the) house," but for *kynä* "pen" the comparable form is *kynässä* "in (the) pen"; similarly, *talossansa* "in his house" contrasts with *kynässänsä* "in his pen" and *talossansako* "in his house?" with *kynässänsäkö* "in his pen?", whereas *taloni* "my house" and *kynäni* "my pen" have the same ending because *i* can occur with either of the two sets of vowel classes. Hungarian has essentially the same system, differing only in certain minor details (short *e* is the front vowel counterpart of *a*); *e.g., asztal* "table," *asztalok* "tables," *asztalokban* "in the tables," but *föld* "land," *földök* "lands," *földökben* "in the lands." Similar though less general front–back vowel-harmony systems are found in given dialects of Mordvin, Mari, Mansi, Khanty, and Kamas.

Frequently confused with the true harmony situations above are partial and total assimilations of vowels in adjacent syllables. These assimilations illustrate a universal tendency of vowel interaction and are of relatively recent origin; they are best held apart from the question of vowel harmony. Examples of vowel assimilations abound. In Finnish an unstressed *e* in the illative case ("place into") is totally assimilated to a preceding vowel, even across an intervening *h*: *talo + hen* becomes *taloon* "into the house," *talo + i + hen* yields *taloihin* "into the houses," *työ + hen* becomes *työhön* "into the work." The Hungarian allative case ("place to or toward which") shows an assimilation of the phonetic feature of lip rounding with front vowels in addition to the standard vowel harmony; thus, *ház-hoz* "to the house," *kéz-hez* "to the hand," *betü-höz* "to the letter." Apart from such nonharmony alternations, no support for rounding harmony is found in Uralic.

Considered from an areal viewpoint, two aspects of Uralic vowel harmony must be considered. First, those languages that show productive or active vowel harmony, with the exception of Baltic-Finnic, have had recent Turkic neighbours whose languages exhibited vowel harmony. For languages such as Mansi and Khanty, dialects with vowel harmony are located closer to Tatar groups. Second, the original homeland of Uralic lies in the centre of an enormous hypothetical areal grouping, labelled by some as the "Eurasian language union." The languages of this "union" are said to be characterized by two features: (1) the absence of a tonal accent (changes in pitch that change meaning, as is found in Chinese, Swedish, or Serbian) and (2) the contrast of plain and palatalized consonants (as in Russian). The phonetic basis for the consonantal contrast between nonpalatalized and palatalized is acoustically the same as the contrast of front and back vowels (*i.e.,* it involves the timbre of the second formant). Indeed, in Erza-Mordvin, vowel harmony and palatalization appear to be conditioned by essentially the same rules. Instead of seeking a genetic explanation of vowel harmony in Uralic, a somewhat more recent areal origin—in part under Turkic influence—must be considered. Of significance is the further consideration that, among the northwestern languages far from Turkic influence, it is precisely Lapp and the Baltic-Finnic Estonian and Livonian that do not have vowel harmony and that have developed special syllable-accent systems (thus, they lack both traits of the Eurasian union).

Possible influence of Turkic and other languages

Consonant gradation. The alternation of consonants known as consonant gradation (or lenition) is sometimes thought to be of Uralic origin. In Baltic-Finnic, excluding Veps and Livonian, earlier single stops were typically replaced by voiced and fricative consonantal variants, and geminate (double) stops were weakened following a stressed vowel when the next syllable was closed; that is, $*p$ alternated with $*v$ and $*b$; $*t$, with $*ð$ and $*d$; $*k$, with $*ɤ$ and $*g$; $*pp$ with $*p$; and so on. Finnish thus shows pairs such as *mato* "worm" and *madon* "of the worm," *matto* "rug" and *maton* "of the rug," *poika* "boy" and *pojan* "of the boy," *lintu* "bird" and *linnun* "of the bird," *selkä* "back" and *selän* "of the back." Estonian shows the same type of alternations, with considerable difference in detail; *e.g., sada* "hundred" and *saja* "of a hundred," *madu* "snake" and *mao* "of the snake," *lind* "bird" and *linnu* "of the bird," and *selg* "back" and *selja* "of the back." Most of the Lapp languages exhibit similar alternations, but the process applies to all consonants and, moreover, works in reverse—single consonants are doubled in open syllables; *e.g., čuotte* "hundred" and *čuoðe* "of a hundred," *borra* "eats" and *borâm* "I eat." The change of *t* to *ð*, however, is not a part of Lapp gradation but rather a general process that voices and weakens all single stops between voiced sounds (in this case, vowels).

Despite their essential differences, the Baltic-Finnic and Lapp gradations appear to be areally related. The Baltic-Finnic type, which represents a more plausible phonetic change, indicates that early Lapp may have acquired its gradation under Baltic-Finnic influence. The evidence within Baltic-Finnic points to a relatively late, post-Proto-Baltic-Finnic origin. The existence of analogous consonant weakening in various Samoyedic languages (Nganasan, Selkup) is the result of independent innovation.

Syllable-accent structures. Closely related to the gradation phenomena is the development of syllable-accent structures in Estonian, Livonian, and Lapp. Estonian is known for its unique quantity alternations of three contrastive vowel and consonant lengths—thus, *vara* "early" versus *vaara* "of the hillock" (*aa* = long *ā*) versus *vaara* "hillock (partitive)" (here *aa* = extra-long *â*); *lina* "linen" versus *linna* "of the city" (*nn* is pronounced as two short *n*'s) versus *linna* "into the city" (here *nn* is pronounced as long *n̄* plus short *n*; the contrast with the previous *nn* is not shown in the standard orthography). The extra-quantity contrast is in fact found with all stressed syllable types containing at least one vowel or consonant following its first vowel; thus, *taevas* "sky" (with short *e*) versus *taevas* "in the sky" (with long *ē*);

Length variations in Estonian sounds

osta "buy!" (with short *s*) versus *osta* "to buy" (with long *s̄*), whereas a two-syllable form such as *osa* "part" (*o/sa*) with only a single vowel in the first syllable is incapable of such a quantity contrast. A multitude of analyses of Estonian quantity have been proposed, although not all have recognized the phenomenon as a function of whole syllables bound to stress—in other words, that it is an accent phenomenon. One orthographic dictionary (by E. Muuk), for example, utilizes this principle, placing a grave accent mark before syllables with extra quantity. Otherwise, Estonian orthography marks the three degrees of duration only for stops: *b, d, g* indicate single short (voiceless lenis) stops (*tuba* "room"); *p, t, k* are plain geminates, or double consonants (*tupe* "of the sheath"); and *pp, tt, kk* mark extralong geminates (*tuppa* "into the room," *tuppe* "into the sheath"). Because the extra quantity is in part tied to an original open next syllable, it frequently operates together with gradation alternations; *e.g.*, *linnu* "of the bird" versus *lindu* "bird (partitive)," with extra quantity.

The syllable quantity accent in Lapp superficially resembles that in Estonian and, like the former, occurs only under stress and is in part conditioned by the openness of the next syllable. In North Lapp (Utsjoki), alternations in paradigms involve three grades of quantity shaping: *mânâm* "I go" (*â* is a Lapp letter for a somewhat rounded *a*) versus *mânna* "he goes" versus *mân'ne* "goer"; *dieðam* "I know" versus *dietta* "he knows" versus *diet'te* "knower"; *juol'ge* "leg" versus *juolge* "of the leg." This series of contrasts shows a three-stage decrease in initial-vowel duration and a three-stage increase in the duration of the first consonant after the first vowel or vowels. The other northern and eastern Lapp languages display similar alterations, but there is considerable diversity in the phonetic details.

Grammatical characteristics. The grammatical structures of the various Uralic languages, despite numerous superficial differences, generally indicate a basic Proto-Uralic sentence structure of (subject) + (object) + main verb + (auxiliary verb)—the parenthesized elements are optional, and the last element is the finite (inflected) verb, which is suffixed to agree with the subject in person and number. This pattern has been best preserved in the more eastern languages, especially Samoyed and Ob-Ugric; *e.g.*, Nenets *tiky pevśumd'o-m saravna t'eńe-va°* "we well remember that evening" (literally, "that evening-[accusative] well remember-we"); Mari *joltaš-em-blak lum tol-mə-m buč-aš tüŋal-ət* "my friends begin to wait for the coming of snow" (literally, "friend-my-[plural] snow coming-[accusative] wait-to begin-they"). This order is common but optional in the languages of central Russia. Lapp, Baltic-Finnic, and Hungarian now show the typical European subject–verb–object order; *e.g.*, Finnish *isä osti talo-n* "father bought a house (-genitive)," Hungarian *János keres egy ház-at* "John seeks a house (-accusative)." Although these more western languages have relatively "free" word order, the object precedes the verb only for special emphasis; *e.g.*, Hungarian *János egy házat keres* "John is looking for a *house* (and not something else)," Estonian *ma ta-lle nuia ei anna* "I won't give *him* a *club*" (literally, "I him-to club not give"). Estonian sentence structure somewhat resembles that of German, with its tendency to place the finite verb in second position while the rest of the verb complex remains at the end of the sentence; *e.g.*, *mehe-d ol-i-d ammu koju jõud-nud* "the men had got home long ago" (literally, "man-[plural] be-[past]-they long-ago home get-[past participle]").

In place of a verb "have," the Uralic languages use the verb "be," expressing the agent in an adverbial (locative or dative) case; *e.g.*, Finnish *isä-llä on talo* "father has a house" (literally, "father-at is house"), Hungarian *János-nak van egy ház-a* "John has a house" (literally, "John-to is one house-his"). In Proto-Uralic the copula verb "be" was lacking in simple predicate adjective or noun sentences, although the predicate was probably marked to agree with the subject. The following Hungarian sentences reflect this situation: *a ház fehér* "the house [is] white," *a ház-ak fehér-ek* "the houses [are] white."

In Nenets and Mordvin such nonverbal predicates are conjugated for subject agreement and tense in the manner of intransitive verbs; *e.g.*, Nenets *mań xańenadm°* "I am a hunter," *pydari° xańenadi°* "you two are hunters," *mań xańenadamź* "I was a hunter," *pydara° xańenadać* "You (plural) were hunters." Otherwise, a wide range of grammatical usage is found. In Baltic-Finnic and Lapp the use of a copula verb is obligatory, in Permic it is optional, and in Hungarian the copula is absent only in the 3rd person ("he, she") in a nonpast tense.

Use of negative sentences

Negative sentences in Proto-Uralic were indicated by means of a marker known as an auxiliary of negation, which preceded the main verb and was marked with suffixes that agreed with the subject, and perhaps tense. This is best reflected in the Finnic and Samoyedic languages; *e.g.*, Finnish *mene-n* "I go," *e-n mene* "I don't go," *mene-t* "you go," *e-t mene* "you don't go." Ugric employs undeclined negative particles (*e.g.*, Hungarian *nem*), and in Estonian only negative imperative forms are still conjugated, although colloquial Estonian has initiated a tense distinction; *e.g.*, *ma/sa ei tule* "I/you don't come" and *ma/sa e-s tule* "I/you didn't come."

In Proto-Uralic questions were formed with interrogative pronouns, beginning with **k-* and **m-*, illustrated by Finnish *kuka* "who," *mikä* "what" and Hungarian *ki* "who," *mi* "what." Yes–no questions were formed by attaching an interrogative particle to the verb, as in Finnish *mene-n-kö* "am I going?", *e-n-kö minä mene* "am I not going?" (in Finnish, the verb also shifts to initial position). The use of intonation (changes in pitch) in interrogative sentences is currently widespread. In Hungarian it is the only way to form direct yes–no questions, although in indirect questions a particle *-e* is used; *e.g.*, *a házak fehérek?* (with sharply rising intonation of the next to the last syllable, dropping again on the final syllable) "are the houses white?", *nem tudom, fehérek-e a házak* "I don't know whether the houses are white."

Conjunction, the connecting of clauses, phrases, or words, was formerly without the aid of specialized conjunctions. In the modern languages the conjunctions are largely borrowings from Germanic (Finnish *ja* "and") and Russian (Mari *da* "and; in order to," *a* "but," *ńi . . . ni* "neither . . . nor," *jesle* "if"). Both coordination and subordination in sentences are marked by a wide range of constructions, especially by means of infinitive verbs, participles, and gerunds; e.g., Mari *keče peš purgəžan poranan ulmaš* "the weather was very stormy and snowy" (literally, "weather very stormy snowy was"), *ača-ž aba-št* "their father and mother" (literally, "father-his mother-their"), *nuno batə-ž-den* "he and his wife" (literally, "they wife-his with"); Finnish *kirja-n lue-ttu-a-ni* "when I had read the book, . . ." (literally, "book-[genitive] read-[past passive participle-partitive case]-my"), *luke-akse-ni kirja-n* "in order for me to read the book" (literally, "read-to-[translative case] my book-[genitive]").

Case suffixes and postpositions are and are used to show the function of words in a sentence. Prefixes and prepositions were unknown in Proto-Uralic. Adjectives, demonstrative pronouns, and numerals originally did not show agreement in case and number with the noun, as is still the case in Hungarian; *e.g.*, *a négy nagy ház-ban* "in the four large houses." Finnish, however, has initiated a case–number agreement system much like that in neighbouring Indo-European languages; *e.g.*, *neljä-ssä iso-ssa talo-ssa* "in the four large houses." The case system of the Proto-Uralic language contained an unmarked nominative case, an accusative, a case of separation (ablative), a locative (essive) case, and a case of direction (lative), plus possibly several others. The modern languages show a range of from three cases in Khanty, six in Lapp, 14 in Finnish, up to 16 to 21 for Hungarian (the case status of several suffixes is debatable). The average number of cases is around 12. For the most part, these cases are the same for all nouns (nouns are not classified for gender; and 3rd person pronouns generally do not distinguish between "he, she"), singular and plural, and many are similar in function to English prepositions.

Cases in the modern Uralic languages

The distinction between a case and a preposition is often based on arbitrary and superficial criteria. Postposi-

Proto-Uralic sentence structure

Table 3: Case Endings in Several Uralic Languages

Finnish	Komi	Hungarian	Nenets	English translation
talo-ssa	kerka-yn	ház-ban	xarda-xa-na	"in (the) house"
talo-i-ssa	kerka-jas-yn	ház-ak-ban	xarda-xa-ʔ-na	"in (the) houses"
talo-sta	kerka-ýś	ház-ból	xarda-xa-d	"from (the) house"
talo-i-sta	kerka-jas-ýś	ház-ak-ból	xarda-xa-t	"from (the) houses"
			(from xa-ʔ-d)	

tions, preposition-like elements placed at the end of words, are generally more independent, and also function as adverbs. They often resemble inflected nouns (e.g., Finnish takana "behind": talo-n takana "[at] behind the house [-genitive]," talo-n taka-a "from behind the house," taka-osa "back part").

The original case relationships of essive–lative–ablative form a three-way set of contrasts that has been extended into several parallel series of cases in the modern languages—perhaps under areal influence. For example, Finnish uses essentially the original three in relatively abstract functions (essive, a state of being, -na; translative, a change of state, -ksi; partitive, a case of separation, [-t]a), and also adds an -s- element to indicate internal relationship (-ssa from *s + na "in"; -hen, or a vowel + n, etc. from *s + ń "into"; -sta "out of"), and an -l- element to indicate external relationship (-lla from *l + na "on, at," -lle from *l + k "onto, to," -lta "off of, from"). Hungarian has nine cases similarly organized into three series of three, the internal set of three (-ben "in," -be "into," -ből "out of") has recently developed from a noun with the meaning "intestines" (bél). In Finnish the personal pronouns are declined throughout on a pronoun stem; e.g., minä "I," minu-ssa "in me," minu-n "me (genitive)," and so on. In Hungarian, however, only the nominative and accusative forms are formed this way, and the remaining cases are formed by adding the possessive suffixes to a form of the case marker (sometimes expanded); e.g., te "you (singular)," teged-et "you (accusative)," benn-ed "in you," belé-d "into you," belő l-ed "out of you."

The inflection of nouns for number (singular and plural) in the Uralic languages is much looser than in the Indo-European languages. Suffixes for the plural in the various Uralic languages are so diverse as to suggest that early stages of Uralic did not possess a specialized number marker; e.g., Finnish -t and -i-, Mari -blak, Komi -jas. A dual-plural distinction ("two" as opposed to "more than two") is found in Lapp, Ob-Ugric, and Samoyedic, but here again the specific elements cannot be traced to a common source. If Proto-Uralic had plural and dual suffixes, they were probably used only with the personal pronouns. In the modern languages personal pronouns often take a plural marker different from that of the nouns, and in Lapp the dual formation is restricted to pronouns and personal affixes.

The category of definiteness (like English "the") is marked in numerous ways in the modern languages and originally appears to have been tied to the manner of number marking in Uralic (plural being reflected by indefiniteness). Hungarian alone has a definite article, a(z), a demonstrative in origin; Mordvin has three sets of inflectional endings: indefinite, definite singular, and definite plural (kudo-so "in a house," kudo-so-ńt' "in the house," kudo-t'ńe-sə "in the houses"). Nearly all the more eastern members have a definite marker that is identical with the 3rd or 2nd person possessive suffix (Komi kerka-ys/yd "the house" or "his/your house").

In possessive constructions the possessor noun precedes the possessed noun, or in the case of a personal pronoun possessor, possessive suffixes are used; e.g., Finnish isä-n talo "father's house" (-n = genitive, talo-ni/si "my/your house"; Hungarian János ház-a "John's house" (-a = possessive construction marker), ház-am/ad "my/your house." Although in earlier stages the possessive suffixes followed the case suffixes, more recent case formations (especially from original postpositions) have led to a restructuring of this order; e.g., Finnish talo-i-ssa-ni "in my houses," but Hungarian ház-a-i-m-ban "in my houses" (-i- = plural); Komi kerka-yd-ly "for your house" (-yd-

= "your"), kerka-ś-yd "from your house," where two fixed orders coexist. The Proto-Uralic comparative construction was similar to the Finnish talo-a iso-mpi "house-from larg-er" (= "larger than a house"); cf. Hungarian egy ház-nál nagy-obb "house-by larg-er" (in dialects also ház-tól "house-from"); Komi kerka dor-yś yǐyd-ǐyk "house by-from larg-er." Parallel "than" type conjunctions are now common in the more western languages; e.g., "larger than a house" in Finnish can also be expressed as isompi kuin talo (kuin = "than"), and in Hungarian nagyobb mint egy ház (mint = "than").

The formation of nouns in Proto-Uralic included compounding (adding two or more words together) as well as derivation by the use of suffixes (word endings). In noun + noun constructions, including titles of address, the qualifying noun came first; cf. Hungarian házhely "house site," Szabó János úr "Mr. John Szabó"; Finnish taloryhmä "group of houses," Sirpa täti "Aunt Sirpa." The rich system of derived words in Uralic together with the various inflectional suffixes led to relatively long words; cf. Finnish talo-ttom-uude-ssa-ni-kin "even in my houselessness" (literally, "house-less-ness-in-my-even"), Hungarian ház-atlan-ság-om-ban "in my houselessness."

The Proto-Uralic verb was inflected for tense-aspect (*-pa indicated "nonpast," *-ka indicated "perfect nonpast; imperative," *-ja indicated "past") and mood (*-ne indicated "conditional-potential"). The use of auxiliary verbs to indicate tenses was unknown, although Lapp, Baltic-Finnic, and Hungarian now have essentially a Germanic-type tense system, with perfect formations based on the "be" verb; e.g., Finnish mene-n "I go," ole-n men-nyt "I have gone" ("be-I go-[past participle]"), men-i-n "I went," ol-i-n men-nyt "I had gone," men-isi-n "I would go," ol-isi-n men-nyt "I would have gone." Under Germanic and Slavic influence both Estonian and Hungarian have developed separable verbal prefixes with adverbial and aspectual meanings; e.g., Estonian ära söö- "eat (perfective)" and ta sõ-i kala ära "he ate the fish" versus ta sõi kala "he was eating fish," ta hakkas kala ära söö-ma "he began to eat (up) the fish"; Hungarian meg-tanul "learn" (perfective) and János megtanul-t magyar-ul "John learned Hungarian" versus János tanult magyarul "John was learning Hungarian," János tanult meg angolul "John learned English," János németül tanult meg "John learned German" (with special emphasis as indicated).

Proto-Uralic did not have specialized voice markers, such as the Indo-European passive; rather, the function of voice was interwoven with topicalization (a way of indicating the main subject of a sentence), emphasis, and definiteness of the subject and object as well as with verbal aspect. An indefinite subject of an intransitive verb or an indefinite object were marked with the ablative case (*-ta), but a definite object took the accusative marker (*-m) and other subject situations were unmarked (nominative). This system is best preserved in Finnish: vesi (-nominative) juoksee "the water is running" versus vettä juoksee "there is water running," juon vede-n "I will drink the water" (-n is from older *-m) versus juon vettä "I drink water," (Note that aspect as well as tense is affected by these case distinctions.)

The widespread use of separate subjective and objective conjugations among the Uralic languages (as in Mordvin, Ugric, and Samoyedic) are the result of an original system for singling out the subject or object for emphasis (focus), and not simply a device for object–verb agreement (similar to subject agreement). For example, Nenets tymʔ xada-v "I killed a deer (focus on the agent)" versus tymʔ xada-dmʔ "I killed a deer (focus on the object)," in which -v signifies "I . . . it" (the objective conjugation) and -dmʔ signifies "I" (the subjective conjugation). Note also the objective forms xada-n "I killed [them]," xada-r "you (singular) killed [it]," xada-d "you (singular) killed [them]," and so on for nine possible subjects (three persons times singular, dual, plural) times two object numbers (singular and nonsingular [not actually distinguished with 3rd-person subjects]); and the subjective forms xad-n "you (singular) killed" and so on, for nine subject agreements. Hungarian similarly opposes definite and indefinite conjugations: two

Number in Uralic nouns

Compounding and derivation in word formation

Subjective and objective conjugations

different sets of personal endings are used—one with transitive verbs with definite objects and the other elsewhere; *e.g.*, *olvas-om/od a level-et* "I/you read the letter" versus *olvas-ok/ol egy level-et* "I/you read a letter." Along with its subjective and objective conjugations Khanty has added a so-called passive conjugation (*cf. kitta-j-m* "I am being sent," *-j-* = "passive") as an extension of the earlier focus-topicalization system. Mari and Komi have two past tense formations with related function. Again, the westernmost languages have passive constructions similar to those in Slavic and Germanic.

Verbal derivation was richly developed already in Proto-Uralic with a wide variety of verbal nouns, infinitives, and participles. Each of the three tense-aspect markers was apparently used as a participial formative (*cf.* Finnish *lähde* from **läkte-k* "source," *lähtijä* "one who leaves," *lähte-vä* from **-pa* "leaving"). Several of the modern languages have made extensive use of their native derivational processes to eliminate foreign loanwords; *e.g.*, for "telephone" Finnish has *puhelin*, which is derived from *puhel-* "talk," just as *soitin* "musical instrument" comes from *soitta-* "to play." The Uralic finite verb originally may have been based on participial constructions parallel to the noun plus predicate adjective sentences (like Hungarian *a ház fehér* "the house [is] white"). Thus, one may reconstruct sentences like **ema tumte-pa* "mother [is] knowing," **ema tumte-pa-ta* "mothers [are] knowing" (with subject number expressed only in the predicate [agreement]) to explain the close similarity of participial and finite verb constructions such as Estonian *tundev ema* "knowing mother," *tundvad emad* "knowing mothers," *ema tunneb* "mother knows," *emad tunnevad* "mothers know."

BIBLIOGRAPHY

General works: The following manuals primarily reflect the views of their authors, but should serve as a basis for further study (especially in the numerous grammars of Uralic languages and articles on problems of Uralic linguistics—few of which are available in English). BJORN COLLINDER, *Fenno-Ugric Vocabulary: An Etymological Dictionary of the Uralic Languages* (1955), presents comparative Uralic word lists; *An Introduction to the Uralic Languages* (1965); and *Survey of the Uralic Languages* (1957), give short sketches of all but a few of the Uralic languages, with the lesser languages receiving only superficial treatment; LAURI HAKULINEN, *The Structure and Development of the Finnish Language* (Eng. trans. from the Finnish, 1961), an excellent presentation of Finnish from its earliest stages; TOIVO VUORELA, *The Finno-Ugric Peoples* (Eng. trans. from the Finnish, 1964), an anthropological survey.

Works dealing with specific languages: PETER HAJDU, *The Samoyed Peoples and Languages* (Eng. trans from the Hungarian, 1963); ROBERT T. HARMS, *Estonian Grammar* (1962), with an appendix that surveys numerous approaches to the problem of quantity in Estonian; THOMAS A. SEBEOK and FRANCES J. INGEMANN, *An Eastern Cheremis Manual* (1961), a clear, concise description of one of the lesser languages; JOHN ATKINSON, *Finnish Grammar* (1956); and ZOLTAN BANHIDI, ZOLTAN JOKAY, and DENES SZABO, *Learn Hungarian* (1965), two basic grammars.

(R.T.H.)

Ural Mountains

The major part of the traditional boundary between Europe and Asia, the Ural Mountains are a rugged spine running more than 1,250 miles (2,000 kilometres) from the fringe of the Arctic in the north to the Ural River Valley, at the same latitude as Paris, in the south. The low, severely eroded Pay-Khoy Ridge forms a fingerlike extension to the northern tip of the Urals proper, with the long curve of Novaya Zemlya forming an insular extension separating the Barents and Kara seas. The Mugodzhar Hills form a broad, arrowhead-shaped southerly extension beyond the Ural Valley. The Urals are the first mountains to be reached by the traveller journeying eastward across the huge expanses of the eastern European plain, a factor that adds to their significance, for the maximum elevation at Mt. Narodnaya is but 6,214 feet (1,894 metres), a relatively low figure for great mountain ranges. The north–south course of the Urals cuts across the vast latitudinal landscape regions of the Eurasian

landmass, from Arctic waste to semidesert; the Urals also separate the developed and populous western portion of the Soviet Union from the developing, mineral-rich Siberian region and are themselves the home of peoples with roots reaching deep into history. (For related information, see SOVIET UNION; and RUSSIAN SOVIET FEDERATED SOCIALIST REPUBLIC.)

The natural environment. *Physical features.* The Urals divide into five sections. The northernmost Polar Urals, extending 240 miles from northeast to southeast, are typically Alpine. Their highest peak is Mt. Pay-Er, 4,918 feet (1,499 metres). The next stretch, the Nether-Polar Urals, is on a larger scale, boasting, in addition to Mt. Narodnaya itself, Mt. Karpinsk, at 6,161 feet (1,878 metres) the second highest peak of the whole range. These first two sections are strewn with glaciers and heavily marked by permafrost (a permanently frozen layer of soil). Farther south come the Northern Urals, with most mountains topping 3,300 feet, the highest, Mt. Telpos-Iz, rising to 5,305 feet (1,617 metres). Many of the summits are flattened, the remnants of ancient peneplains (eroded surfaces of large area and slight relief) uplifted by recent tectonic (relating to deformation of the Earth's crust) movements. In the north, intensive weathering results in vast "seas of stone" on mountain slopes and summits. The lower Central Urals rarely exceed 1,600 feet, though the highest peak, Mt. Kachkanar, rises to almost twice the average. The summits are smooth, with isolated residual outcrops. The last portion, the Southern Urals, follows a north-northeast to south-southwest direction and consists of several parallel ridges rising to 3,900 feet, culminating in Mt. Yamantau, 5,374 feet (1,638 metres).

The rock composition helps shape the topography: the high ranges and low, broad-topped ridges consist of quartzites (compact rock composed of quartz), schists (crystalline rocks separable into thin plates), and gabbro (another type of rock), all weather-resistant. Buttes (isolated hills with steep sides) are frequent, and there are north–south troughs of limestone, nearly all containing river valleys.

Geological structure and mineral resources. The Urals date from the structural upheavals of the Hercynian orogeny (about 250,000,000 years ago). In the Upper Carboniferous and Permian periods (280,000,000 years ago) arose a high mountainous region, which, at the end of the Paleozoic and during the Mesozoic eras (about 200,000,000 years ago), was eroded to a peneplain. Alpine folding resulted in new mountains, the most marked upheaval being that of the Nether-Polar Urals. This slow uplifting still continues. In the watershed region lies the Ural-Tau Anticlinorium (a rock formation of arches and troughs, itself forming an arch), the largest in the Urals, and in the Southern Urals, west of it, is the Bashkir Anticlinorium. Both are composed of layers (sometimes four miles thick) of metamorphic (heat-altered) Precambrian and Lower Paleozoic rocks (from 570,000,000 to 395,000,000 years old), gneisses (metamorphic rocks separable into thin plates), quartzites, and schists.

The western slope of the Urals is composed of Middle Paleozoic (about 340,000,000 years ago) sedimentary rocks (sandstones and limestones). In many places it descends in terraces to the Cis-Ural region (west of the Urals), to which much of the eroded matter was carried during the Upper Paleozoic Era (about 300,000,000 years ago). Here there are widespread karst (a starkly eroded limestone region) and gypsum, with large caverns and subterranean streams. On the eastern slope, volcanic lavers alternate with sedimentary strata, all dating from Middle Paleozoic times (roughly 350,000,000 years ago). These rocks compose the Tagil-Magnitogorsk Synclinorium (a group of rock arches and troughs, itself forming a trough), the largest in the Urals. In the Central and Southern Urals, the eastern slope blends into broad peneplained foothills, where there are frequent outcrops of granite and often fantastically shaped buttes. To the north the peneplain is buried under the loose, easily pulverized deposits of the West Siberian Plain.

The Urals are extremely rich in mineral resources, with variations on the eastern and western slopes according to

The Urals' five sections

Sedimentary rocks of western slopes

geological structure. Ore deposits, for example, notably magnetite, predominate on the eastern slope, where contact (the surface where two different rock types join) deposits are found, as at Magnitogorsk, Vysokogorsk, and Mt. Blagodat, as well as magmatic deposits (formed from liquid rock), as at Kachkanar. Sedimentary deposits are of less importance. Some ores contain alloying metals —vanadium, a gray-white, resistant element, and titanium—as impurities. The largest copper-ore deposits are at Gay, Gumeshki, and Turinsk, and nickel ores are known in the regions of Orsk, Ufaley, and Rezh. There are also large deposits of bauxite, chromite, gold, and platinum. Among the nonmetallic mineral resources of the eastern slope are asbestos, talc, fireclay, and abrasives. Gems and semiprecious stones have been known for a long time: they include amethyst, topaz, and emerald. Among the western deposits are beds of potassium salts on the upper Kama River and petroleum and natural-gas deposits in the Ishimbay and Krasnokamsk areas. Bituminous coal and lignite are mined on both slopes. The largest deposit is the Pechora bituminous coalfield, located far to the north, where transport connections with the industries of the Urals are lacking.

Climate. The climate is of the continental type, marked by temperature extremes whose presence becomes increasingly evident both from north to south and from west to east. The Pay-Khoy Range and the Polar Urals enjoy the moderating influence of the Arctic and the North Atlantic oceans, particularly in winter. In the Mugodzhar Hills and the Southern Urals, there are summer breaths of hot, dry air from Central Asia. Winds are for the most part westerly and bring precipitation from the Atlantic Ocean. In spite of their low elevation, the mountains exert a considerable influence on the moisture distribution, and the western slope receives more moisture than the eastern. Precipitation is particularly heavy on the western slope of the Nether-Polar and Northern Urals, as high as 40 inches. Northward and southward precipitation diminishes to about 14 inches. On the eastern slope there is less moisture (about ten inches) and snow: the depth on the western slope averages 30 inches and, on the eastern, 18 inches. Maximum precipitation occurs in the summer, for the cold, dry air of the Siberian anticyclone is powerful in winter. The eastern slope is particularly chilled, and winter lasts longer than summer throughout the Urals. In January the average temperature in the north is −5.8° F (−21° C), and in the south the average is 5° F (−15° C). Average temperatures in July vary more, between 50° F (10° C) in the north and 72° F (22° C) in the south.

Drainage. The rivers flowing down from the Urals drain into the Barents, Kara (two gulfs of the Arctic Ocean), and Caspian seas. The Pechora River, which drains the western slope of the Polar, Nether-Polar, and part of the Central Urals, empties into the Barents Sea. Its largest tributaries are the Ilych, Shugor, and Usa. Almost all the rivers of the eastern slope belong to the Ob River system (*q.v.*), emptying into the Kara Sea. The largest are the Tobol, the Iset, the Tura, the Tavda, the Severnaya Sosva (Northern Sosva), and the Lyapin. The Kama (a tributary of the Volga) and the Ural rivers belong to the drainage basin of the Caspian Sea. The Kama collects water from a large area of the western slope: the Vishera, Chusovaya, and Belaya all empty into it. The Ural River, with its tributary the Sakmara, flows along the Southern Urals.

The location and character of the Urals' rivers and lakes are closely connected with the topography and climate. In their upper reaches many rivers flow slowly through the mountains in wide, longitudinal troughs. Later they change to a latitudinal direction, cut through the ridges in narrow valleys, and descend to the plains, particularly in the Northern and Southern Urals. The main watershed does not correspond with the highest ridges everywhere. The Chusovaya and Ufa rivers of the Central and Southern Urals, which later join the Volga drainage basin, have their sources on the eastern slope.

The rivers on the western slope carry more water than those of the east, particularly in the Northern and Neth-

er-Polar Urals; the slowest rate of flow is on the eastern slope of the Southern Urals, reflecting intense evaporation as well as low precipitation. In winter the rivers freeze for five months in the south and for seven months in the north.

There are many lakes, especially on the eastern slope of the Southern and Central Urals. The largest ones are Uvildy, Itkul, Turgoyak, and Tavatuy. On the western slope are many small karst lakes. In the far north, lakes occur in glacial valleys, the deepest of them being Lake Bolshoye Shchuchye, at 446 feet deep. Medicinal muds are common in a number of the lakes, such as Moltayevo, and spas and sanatoriums have been established.

Vegetation. The Urals pass through several vegetation zones, with the northern tundra giving way to vast mixed forests, while still farther south is the steppe, culminating in semidesert around the Mugodzhar Hills. Small nooks of mountain tundra still occur in the Southern Urals, where the foothills merge with steppe, especially in the east. Feather grass and meadows predominate on the chernozems (black earth) and dark-chestnut soils (a characteristic steppe soil). Other characteristic growths are clover, feather grass, fescue (a pasture grass), and timothy (a grass grown for hay). South of the Ural River the steppes give way to wormwood and semidesert growths on light-chestnut soils (again typical steppe soil), highly saline in places. Many steppe regions of the Southern Urals have been plowed up and converted to arable lands, and large areas grow wheat, buckwheat, millet, potatoes, and vegetables.

Forests appear about 100 feet up in the Southern Urals. Lindens, oaks, maples, birches, and pines grow on the western slope, and undergrowth consists of reed grass, ferns, and other plants. The predominant soils are of the gray mountain-forest type, loamy and clayey. The broadleaf forests extend to 2,100 feet, above which conifers appear. On the eastern slope there are no broadleaf trees except the linden, and magnificent pine forests with some larches are widespread.

Farther northward forests of spruce, fir, pine, and larch grow on mountain-taiga (a vast, swampy, coniferous region of Siberia), podsolic (type of soil developing in temperate or cold, moist climate) soils. In the more northerly regions, dark coniferous species are common, and, in the Northern Urals, the Siberian cedar is widespread. Here, forests climb to 2,800 feet or so, above which is a narrow belt of thin larch and birch, trailing off to mountain tundra. In the Nether-Polar and Polar Urals, the forest yields to mountain tundra as low as 1,400 feet up. North of the Arctic Circle there is only brushwood and moss-lichen tundra on the Pay-Khoy Ridge. The forests of the Urals are of great economic importance: they yield valuable wood, regulate the flow of the rivers, and shelter many valuable animals.

Animal life. There are no specifically mountain animals, primarily because of the low elevations and easy accessibility, and fauna differs little from that of eastern Europe and Western Siberia. In the last few centuries, valuable animals such as the Arctic fox, sable, and beaver have become scarcer, but the Soviet period has witnessed conservation measures, especially in the Ilmen and Bashkir national preserves in the Southern Urals and the Pechoro-Ilych National Preserve in the Northern Urals. New species have been introduced, for example, the spotted deer and muskrat. The most valuable animal of the tundra is the Arctic fox, and trade in its fur is flourishing. The lemming, the tundra partridge, and the reindeer are other inhabitants, though the latter are few. Many wild ducks, geese, and swans breed there in summer. But the richest and most varied fauna in the Urals, such as the brown bear, lynx, wolverine, and elk, are found in the forested zones. Some have valuable furs: the sable, ermine, fox, Siberian weasel, and squirrel. In the taiga forests there are such birds as the wood grouse and the hazel hen (a woodland grouse). Down in the mixed, broadleaf forests of the Southern Urals' western slopes live roe deer, badgers, and polecats, as well as many birds typical of the European part of the Soviet Union, such as the nightingale and oriole. The commonest animals of the steppes

[margin left] Precipitation

[margin right] Economic importance of the Ural forests

and semideserts are rodents, including susliks (a type of ground squirrel), jerboas (a social, nocturnal, jumping rodent), and other agricultural pests. Predators include the Siberian polecat and Afghan fox. The rivers and lakes of the Northern Urals abound in fish, the most valuable being the nelma (related to the whitefish), common salmon, grayling, and sea trout. Farther south, in the densely populated and industrial regions, animal life is less abundant.

The human imprint. *Population.* Human habitation of the Urals dates from the distant past. The Nentsy (Samoyeds—a Finno-Ugrian people) are natives of the Pay-Khoy region, and their language belongs to the Samoyedic group of languages, which is widespread throughout Northern Siberia. Farther south live the Komi, Mansi (Voguls), and Khants (Ostyaks), who speak a tongue belonging to the Ugric group of the Finno-Ugric languages (a family of languages spoken in Hungary, Finland, and parts of Russia). Another group, the Bashkirs, long settled in the Southern Urals, speak a tongue related to the Turkic group. Most of these formerly nomadic peoples are now settled. The majority of the population centres are concentrated in river valleys and on the lower slopes. The Nentsy, Komi, Mansi, and Khants are virtually the only inhabitants in the highest parts of the Urals, especially in the north, where they have preserved their traditional ways of life, raising reindeer, hunting, and fishing. The Bashkirs are excellent horse breeders. These people are nevertheless being drawn increasingly both to industries and to agriculture, part of a vigorous economic development of the Urals that has attracted large numbers of people (mostly Russians) from other parts of the country. The total population of the entire Ural region approached 20,000,000 in the early 1970s, while that of the Ural Economic Region, an administrative unit, exceeded 15,000,000. The Russian population is concentrated primarily in the Central and Southern Urals, and most people live in cities (notably Sverdlovsk, Chelyabinsk, Perm, and Ufa) and work in industries. The population of the central and southern Cis-Ural and Trans-Ural regions is primarily agricultural, where conditions are very favourable for wheat, potatoes, and other crops.

History, discovery, and exploration. The existence of the Riphean and Hyperborean mountains at the eastern fringe of Europe in antiquity was regarded as being more mythical than real. Not until the 10th century AD does the first mention of the Urals occur, in Arabic sources. At the end of the 11th century, the Russians discovered the northernmost part of the Urals, but they did not complete the discovery of the entire range until the beginning of the 17th century, when the mineral wealth of the Urals was discovered. Systematic extraction of iron and copper ore began early in the 18th century, and the Urals rapidly became one of the largest industrial regions of Russia. The first serious scientific study of the Urals was made in 1770–71. Scholars studying the Urals during the 19th century included several Russian geologists and also such prominent foreign scholars as the German naturalist Alexander von Humboldt. Much work has been done in the Soviet period on geological structure and associated mineral resources, while topographical research has discovered recent glaciation in the Polar and Circumpolar Urals.

Future prospects. With their rich natural resources, the Urals have become one of the foremost Soviet industrial regions. Mineral reserves are sufficient to allow increasing production of various metals. With the continuing eastward shift of the Soviet population, the whole region is likely to continue to be of major importance, though traces of traditional ways of life will doubtless remain.

BIBLIOGRAPHY. IVAN ARAMILEV, *Beyond the Ural Mountains: The Adventures of a Siberian Hunter,* trans. by MICHAEL HERON (1961), is mainly concerned with hunting, but contains fine pictures and descriptions of the mountains. An excellent work on the physical geography is A.M. Оленев, *Урал и Новая Земля: очерк природы* (1965).

(Y.V.Y.)

Scientific studies of the Urals (margin note)

Uranium Products and Production

Uranium—a dense, hard, radioactive nickel-white metal with the heaviest atomic weight of any naturally occurring element—was known for 150 years before any serious application could be found for it. The discovery in 1938 that the uranium nucleus could be made to fission, or split, when bombarded with neutrons suddenly opened the dramatic possibility that the uranium atom could be made to give up its energy in a sustained chain reaction. One pound of uranium—in size, about 1 cubic inch—can, in such a reaction, yield as much energy as 3,000,000 pounds of coal. As a consequence, intense study of the element was launched together with extensive exploration for its ores. The first nonlaboratory application of the 1938 discovery was military, in the form of the original atomic bomb dropped on Hiroshima in 1945. After World War II, exploitation of atomic energy as a power source and for other peaceful purposes was developed in the United States, Great Britain, the U.S.S.R., France, and other countries. By the 1970s uranium had become a metal of vast economic significance.

History. The discovery of uranium is usually attributed to Martin Heinrich Klaproth, a Berlin apothecary and an outstanding analytical chemist, who described it in a lecture to the Royal Prussian Academy of Science in 1789. Mineralogists had tended to classify the mineral pitchblende, found in Joachimsthal (now Jáchymov, Czechoslovakia) and in the Erzgebirge (Germany), as an ore of zinc. Klaproth processed the mineral to produce specks of a black substance, which he termed uranit, a new metal, but which in fact must still have been an oxide or mixture of oxides of uranium. A year later Klaproth changed the name from uranit to uranium, after the planet Uranus, which had been discovered in 1781. He continued to work with this substance and by the end of the 18th century had prepared nitrate, sulfate, formate, and acetate compounds of uranium.

A French chemist, Eugène-Melchior Peligot, was the first man to succeed in extracting the metal (1841). He passed chlorine over heated "uranium," studied the products of the reaction, and found that the "uranium" he used was an oxide. Peligot then tried to reduce uranium tetrachloride with potassium in a heated platinum crucible. The potassium chloride dissolved away, leaving a black powder that was truly the element uranium.

First extraction (margin note)

This new metal had an atomic weight of 120 ascribed to it, but Dmitry Ivanovich Mendeleyev, who developed the periodic table of the elements, found that that value did not accord with the properties expected on the basis of his table; he suggested that the correct value was 240. This hypothesis was subsequently confirmed, and the exact weight of 238.03 assigned. Scientific interest in the metal and its compounds was temporarily stimulated by French physicist Henri Becquerel's discovery of the radioactivity of uranium salts in 1896. In spite of this interest, however, in the early 20th century uranium found only very minor practical applications (as an occasional substitute for tungsten or as a colouring agent in glasses and glazes). But with the demonstration of uranium fission in the late 1930s and the harnessing of nuclear energy in the 1940s, scientific and technological study of uranium and its compounds was accelerated. It culminated in a massive release of information at the First International Conference on the Peaceful Uses of Atomic Energy (Geneva, 1955).

Occurrence. Uranium is estimated to be present in the earth's crust to the extent of about four parts per 1,000,000. It is thus considerably more abundant than gold and silver, ranking closer to tungsten and tantalum. Its presence in seawater amounts to 0.000001 to 0.000002 gram per litre. It is highly reactive and forms many compounds, some of which are water soluble.

Compounds of uranium are present in rocks of varying composition and origin. The actual concentration of uranium in most of these ores is low, however, and ore bodies suitable for economic mining are rare. Local concentrations of suitable ores may have occurred when uranium-rich compounds were exuded into rock faults after the molten uranium silicates in the earth's crust had crystallized. Later the rock weathered, leaving deposits of the more chemically unreactive uranium minerals; other uranium minerals may have been taken into aqueous solution, transported, and subsequently precipitated as oxides after reacting with other materials.

Uranium ore is found in Africa, in Zaire, and in the Witwatersrand region of South Africa; in France and Czechoslovakia; in Australia; in South America; in Canada, in the Great Bear Lake area and the province of Ontario; and in the western U.S. The U.S.S.R. and China are also believed to hold substantial deposits.

Primary, relatively unoxidized uranium minerals of particular importance are uraninite (a crystalline uranium form that is 45 to 85 percent uranium) and its black friable or massive variety, pitchblende; coffinite (hydrated uranium silicate; black, friable; 60 percent uranium); brannerite (uranium, thorium, calcium titanate; black; 30 to 40 percent uranium); davidite (rare earth, uranium, iron titanate; black; 7 to 10 percent uranium). Important secondary, oxidized uranium minerals are carnotite, autunite, and torbernite. Carnotite is a complex compound of uranium, potassium, vanadium, and oxygen; autunite is a calcium uranyl phosphate; and torbernite is a copper uranyl phosphate.

Mining. Ore deposits may be deep or shallow, regular or irregular, and may be found in association with a variety of other minerals. Most of the customary metal mining techniques are used, many quite technically advanced because of the relatively recent commercial interest in uranium.

For the period 1955–70, the United States was the largest producer of uranium in the Western world, followed in order by Canada and the Republic of South Africa.

Surface mining. The methods of mining uranium at the surface are similar to those for mining other minerals and coal. The Lucky Mc Mine in Wyoming produces ore at the rate of 400,000 dry tons per year and in the process must remove at least 13,500,000 cubic yards of waste. Earth-removing vehicles with capacities of 1.5–2.5 cubic yards follow the narrow, winding lodes, mining out 2-foot-thick slices of ore, while scrapers remove the surrounding waste. Pit design is dictated largely by the stability of the rock; at the Lucky Mc, the slopes of the pit walls average 50 to 57 degrees with bench heights (the distance from one horizontal surface to another) of 70 to 90 feet and widths of 20 to 40 feet. Keeping the wall angle as steep as possible reduces the total volume of waste material, or overburden, that must be removed.

To set up a surface-mining program, engineers must determine the pit limits and ore reserves, as well as uranium content of the ore. Radiometric surveys to determine the extent and amount of the ore's radioactivity both prior to and during working may provide the first two sets of data; rapid spectrographic analysis measures content. This information must then be coupled with other relevant data in scheduling production. Computer systems are widely used in this process.

Underground mining. Techniques of underground mining vary somewhat with the nature of the ore body. Deposits that lie at depths of 1,000 to 4,000 feet, in thicknesses of up to 100 feet, and in strata sloping at angles of up to 45 degrees are extracted by the usual underground mining methods.

Basically, the ore is released from the main body of rock by blasting and then transported to collection points for transmission to the surface through vertical shafts. For a more detailed description of these and other mining techniques, see MINING AND QUARRYING; COAL MINING.

Control of ore grade quality is important and, again, radiometric assessment methods are widely used underground. Ventilation is of particular importance in underground uranium mining because of the presence of radon gas, one of the products of the radioactive disintegration of uranium. Radon also is radioactive and must be kept at a strictly regulated low level, to protect miners from overexposure to radiation.

In South Africa, where uranium is a by-product of gold-ore processing, mining practice is determined by gold-mining requirements.

Refining and recovery. The chemical inertness of uranium minerals makes recovery difficult, but because of their relatively high density and hardness, mechanical enrichment of the ore is possible (see illustration). Such enrichment, or concentration, is necessary, since the bulk of uranium in most regions comes from ores that contain fewer than six pounds of uranium per ton of ore; the uranium mineral is finely distributed throughout a quartz-containing matrix.

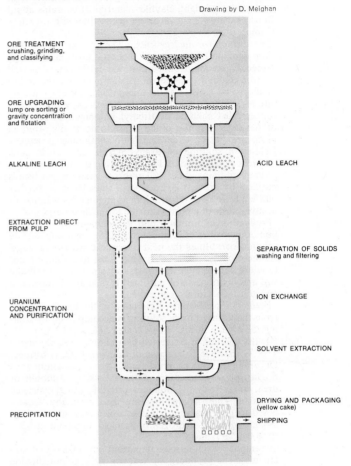

Drawing by D. Meighan

ORE TREATMENT
crushing, grinding,
and classifying

ORE UPGRADING
lump ore sorting or
gravity concentration
and flotation

ALKALINE LEACH

ACID LEACH

EXTRACTION DIRECT
FROM PULP

SEPARATION OF SOLIDS
washing and filtering

ION EXCHANGE

URANIUM
CONCENTRATION
AND PURIFICATION

SOLVENT EXTRACTION

DRYING AND PACKAGING
(yellow cake)

PRECIPITATION

SHIPPING

Steps involved in the recovery of uranium.

Mechanical separation. The mined ore is first coarse-crushed, sometimes separated on the basis of its radioactivity, and then fine-ground and mixed with water to produce a slurry. The fine grinding exposes the uranium mineral for subsequent chemical attack. Mechanical concentration of the ore slurry is accomplished in a series of steps. First, the water is drained off; then the use of thickeners or filters, or both, creates a product suitable for leaching (dissolving out the uranium). Either acid or alkali agents are used in such leaching processes.

Leaching and purifying. In the most common leaching process dilute sulfuric acid is added to the pulverized ore in a pachuca, a vessel in which the mixture is agitated with compressed air. Mechanical stirring may also be used, along with high pressures and temperatures. Such leaching produces a rather crude solution of uranyl sulfate. Some ores, particularly those rich in carbonates and alkaline earths that would be expensive to acid-leach, can be alkali-leached by sodium carbonate, yielding sodium uranyl carbonate. The alkali-leach solution is generally more concentrated than that for the acid process, but, because the chemical reaction is specific in nature, finer initial grinding is necessary to ensure efficient breakdown of the uranium mineral in the alkali method.

After leaching, the crude solution is separated from the ore pulp by filtration or settling, with the raw mineral solution gradually concentrated as it moves along the processing line; the solution is then purified by various chemical techniques. Precipitation from the purified solution, separation, and drying constitute the final stages of the extraction of uranium concentrates. The solution is neutralized with caustic soda, ammonia, or magnesia. By controlling the acidity, the iron is precipitated out first and then the uranium, as a uranate, usually sodium diuranate, the principal component of yellow cake. After thickening, the uranium precipitate passes through automatic filter presses or vacuum filter drums and is allowed to dry. This crude uranium compound concentrate is in the form of a bright, claylike material. It contains about 60 percent by weight of uranium together with a variety of impurities.

Preparation for nuclear uses. The nuclear uses of uranium demand high purity in general, particularly a high degree of freedom from certain rare-earth metals, as well as from cadmium and boron, all of which have the ability to absorb neutrons. For the final purification stage uranyl nitrate solution is extracted in a process employing a concentrated solution of tributyl phosphate in kerosene or hexane. First the crude concentrate is dissolved in nitric acid, using either batch or continuous processes, yielding a solution of uranyl nitrate and silicic acid, which is separated out. The remaining uranyl nitrate solution containing about 200 grams of uranium per litre is purified by solvent extraction. The solvent is further purified to recover the uranium as an aqueous solution of uranyl nitrate of a purity suitable for nuclear purposes.

Production of uranium and its compounds. Preparation of the oxides of uranium from the pure uranyl nitrate solution constitutes the next important processing stage. As these oxides are used in solid form to produce other uranium compounds, their physical state (particularly the size and distribution of particles) is of major importance and must be closely controlled.

Extraction processes. Extraction of the uranium oxide from the uranyl nitrate solution is accomplished by heating the nitrate in air. When heated below 300° C (570° F), the solution is converted to uranium trioxide; above 430° C (810° F), the oxide of uranium U_3O_8 is formed. Or uranium may be precipitated from the solution as bright yellow ammonium diuranate using ammonia or urea, or as hydrated uranium peroxide using hydrogen peroxide. These compounds are then thermally decomposed to give uranium trioxide, which is reduced to the dioxide by using hydrogen or cracked ammonia at 600° C (1,100° F), and above.

Uranium tetrafluoride, important in making uranium metal, is produced by reaction of uranium dioxide with anhydrous hydrofluoric acid at 450°–600° C (840°–1,100° F). The higher the temperature the more rapid the reaction rate, but a practical upper limit is imposed by the availability of structural materials and equipment able to withstand attack by hydrofluoric acid and the ability to control the reaction, which produces considerable heat. In all these refining methods the trend has been away from batch to continuous processes, which generally result in a more uniform product.

Preparation of uranium metal. Of the many processes for the preparation of uranium metal, the one in almost universal use employs uranium tetrafluoride with magnesium as the reducing agent. The compound is mixed with magnesium chips, compacted, loaded into a refractory container, and placed inside an electric resistance furnace in an argon atmosphere. The mixture is then heated; the reaction generates sufficient heat to melt both the resulting uranium and the magnesium fluoride. Because of the large differences in their specific gravities, the molten magnesium fluoride forms a slag on the uranium surface. Uranium ingots weighing about 3,000 pounds (1,360 kilograms) have been produced by this method.

Uranium oxides can also be reduced to a metal using calcium and magnesium in a similar manner, but of the reaction products only uranium is melted by the heat of reaction and is thus produced as a powder in a lime or magnesia matrix.

Uranium hexafluoride used in the gaseous diffusion enrichment process (see below) can be prepared by fluorinating the metal, an oxide, uranium tetrafluoride, or other compounds with fluorine, hydrogen fluoride, or halogen fluorides. The least amount of fluorine is needed for the fluorination of uranium tetrafluoride. This reaction, the basis of methods for industrial preparation of uranium hexafluoride, occurs at high temperatures (above 400° C, 750° F). Fluorination of the tetrafluoride with chlorine trifluoride, which requires lower temperatures (50°–150° C, 120°–300° F), is also used to produce uranium hexafluoride on an industrial scale. The hexafluoride may be handled as gas, solid, or liquid. Because this process, like much of the industrial chemistry of uranium compounds, entails major usage of highly corrosive fluorine and fluorine compounds, highly sophisticated chemical engineering techniques, standards, and equipment are required.

Applications of uranium and its compounds. *Fuelling nuclear reactors.* Uranium in elemental or compound form fuels nuclear reactors, principally for the generation of electricity. In practice, when the uranium is used in reactors, it is alloyed with minor amounts of aluminum and iron, which serve to minimize dimensional changes resulting from fission. Uranium alloyed with molybdenum also is used as fuel in some reactors.

Many different compounds of uranium have been explored as nuclear fuels. Uranium dioxide has so far proved the most economically attractive fuel for reactors in the production of electricity. Its use was being built into the systems of the majority of nuclear power stations being installed in the early 1970s. The fuel consists of pellets of uranium dioxide of about 95 percent theoretical density packed into a can of stainless steel or zirconium alloy. The dioxide has a low thermal conductivity and tends to fragment in the can under the thermal stresses imposed in service. The can protects the fissionable material from contamination from coolants, and prevents contamination of the coolant and hence the remainder of the reactor by fission products from the uranium.

Uranium monocarbide, in contrast with uranium dioxide, is more metallic in nature, more chemically reactive, has a much higher thermal conductivity, and is better able to withstand thermal stresses. Its behaviour in a nuclear reactor is acceptable, but since its chemical reactivity is more akin to that of uranium metal, the choice of coolants for use with it is limited largely to molten sodium. Uranium carbide, therefore, is likely to find major application in sodium-cooled fast reactors.

Natural uranium contains only 0.7 percent of the fissionable isotope, uranium-235. In many reactor applications, this percentage must be increased, a process called enrichment. This is accomplished by a gaseous diffusion technique in which the lighter isotope uranium-235 diffuses through a membrane more rapidly than the heavier uranium-238. With a sufficient number of diffusion stages, enrichment can be carried out to any desired degree. Uranium hexafluoride, being gaseous at moderate temperatures and pressures, is the main feed material for this process. The by-product from such enrichment is uranium with most of its uranium-235 removed (primarily the isotope uranium-238), called depleted uranium.

Other uses. Efforts to find outlets for uranium outside nuclear technology have met with little success. Because it is more dense than lead, it has replaced that metal for some X-ray and gamma-ray shielding in which there is a need to minimize the volume of material, as in apparatus for medical therapy or as screening for remote-handling of radioactive material. As an oxide it can be used for catalytic purposes but has proved beneficial only in minor applications.

Economic importance. The needs of the nuclear power industry will probably determine the economic importance of uranium during the remainder of the century. By 1970 capacity for nuclear electrical generation exceeded 5,000,000 kilowatts in Britain, 3,000,000 kilowatts in the United States, and smaller but substantial amounts in France, Germany, Italy, Japan, the Soviet Union, and in some of the developing countries. Worldwide installations on order in 1970 totalled nearly 100,000,000 kilowatts, with capacities near 200,000,000 kilowatts projected for 1980.

Within national power programs the balance among the

Final purification

Reactor fuel for power production

Nuclear electrical generation

various methods of power generation is determined by social and political pressures as well as by economics. Within the industry, technological advances in reactor design are aimed at increasingly efficient use of uranium. These advances will culminate in the introduction of a new class of reactors called fast-breeder reactors, which produce more fissionable material than they use. In such reactors, uranium-235 will be supplanted by plutonium-239 as the important fissile material, thereby greatly reducing uranium demand.

It has been estimated that by the end of the century world demand for the basic raw material, the uranium oxide U_3O_8, will reach 165,000 tons per year, against a 1970 production of 23,707 tons and a peak of about 44,000 tons in 1959. Known mineral reserves recoverable within reasonable cost limits stood at a little less than 1,000,000 tons in 1970 and estimated reserves at an equivalent amount. If the demand reaches the expected level, a further reserve of 1,000,000 tons will be required by the year 2000. New ore discoveries are being reported continuously. A number of discoveries of the magnitude of the Queensland, Australia, ore body discovered in 1970, would help to remove any concern over supply. Other possible sources are low-grade deposits, expensive to mine, but economically feasible at a higher price; and the oceans, which have been estimated to contain 1,000,000,000 tons of uranium.

BIBLIOGRAPHY. J.H. GITTUS, *Uranium* (1963); N.P. GALKIN and B.N. SUDARIKOV et al., *Technology of Uranium* (1966; orig. pub. in Russian, 1964); R.G. BELLAMY and N.A. HILL, *Extraction and Metallurgy of Uranium, Thorium and Beryllium* (1963); E.H.P. CORDFUNKE, *The Chemistry of Uranium* (1969); and W.D. WILKINSON, *Uranium Metallurgy*, 2 vol. (1962), are comprehensive texts in which the emphasis varies slightly from book to book. The text by the Russian authors together with any one of the other books will provide very good coverage.

F.S. PATTON, J.M. GOOGIN, and W.L. GRIFFITH, *Enriched Uranium Processing* (1963), is a general introduction to processes capable of uranium enrichment, of historical as well as technical interest.

Together with the texts on uranium metallurgy the following books provide a general background to those fuels currently being used in nuclear reactors, or likely to be used in quantity over the next decade: J. SAUTERON, *Les combustibles nucléaires* (1965); J. BELLE (ed.), *Uranium Dioxide* (1961); R.B. HOLDEN, *Ceramic Fuel Elements* (1966); and L.E. RUSSELL et al. (eds.), *Carbides in Nuclear Energy*, 2 vol. (1964).

(J.Wi.)

Uranus

Seventh in order of distance from the Sun, Uranus is the third largest of the planets of the solar system. Less than half the size of Jupiter, it has a diameter still four times that of the Earth. Although faintly visible to the naked eye, Uranus has been known as a planet for less than 200 years. It has five known satellites, a number exceeded only by the 12 of Jupiter and the ten of Saturn. Physically, Uranus is almost a twin of Neptune. These two, with Jupiter and Saturn, constitute the family of Jovian planets characterized by large size, low density, and compositions consisting primarily of the very light chemical elements. Hence, they are radically different from the terrestrial planets.

Discovery, naming, and early observations. The planets out through Saturn have been known since antiquity; Uranus was the first major solar-system body to be discovered after the invention of the telescope. The outstanding astronomer of the 18th century, William Herschel of England, undertook a survey of all stars down to the eighth magnitude—*i.e.*, those about ten times fainter than are visible to the naked eye—using a six-inch telescope of his own manufacture at his private observatory in Bath. On March 13, 1781, he found "a curious either nebulous star or perhaps a comet," distinguished from the stars by its clearly visible disk. Its lack of any trace of tail and its slow motion led almost immediately to the suggestion that the observations were consistent with a planet moving in a nearly circular orbit. Within a year, independent studies established that the orbit was planetary, with a radius exceeding 18 astronomical units (one astronomical unit is the mean Earth–Sun distance, 149,700,000 kilometres [93,000,000 miles]). The object was thus twice as far from the Sun as Saturn, and its discovery at once doubled the size of the known solar system.

Three names were seriously considered for the new planet. Herschel proposed first to call his discovery Georgium Sidus (in English, Georgian Planet) after his sovereign patron, King George III of England. The name Georgian appeared intermittently in England for more than 50 years, especially in the *Nautical Almanac*. In France the name Herschel was also used occasionally until the middle of the 19th century. But already in the year of discovery the German astronomer Johann Elert Bode had suggested Uranus, as the father of Saturn in Roman mythology, who was, in turn, the father of Jupiter; and this name was eventually universally accepted.

Progressive improvements in knowledge of the motion made possible the projection of the orbit farther into the past, in a search for prediscovery observations for which accurate coordinates had been noted by observers who assumed the planet to be a star. The earliest of 22 such prediscovery observations proved to have been made in 1690, nearly a century before Herschel's discovery.

The orbit. The orbit of Uranus departs only slightly from a circle, the deviation corresponding to an elliptical orbit with eccentricity of 0.047. The mean distance from the Sun is 19.18 astronomical units; the eccentricity brings Uranus to a perihelion (or point nearest the Sun) of 18.3 astronomical units and an aphelion (point farthest from the Sun) of 20.1 astronomical units, corresponding to an extreme difference of about 10 percent. The orbit is very slightly inclined, by 0.73°, to the ecliptic plane (the Earth's orbit).

Uranus completes one revolution about the Sun in 84.01 years. In the nearly 300-year span over which at least some observations exist, the planet has thus completed about three and one-half revolutions. This is sufficient to test rigorously any proposed orbit of Uranus, including a careful accounting for the perturbations (gravitational influences) exerted by the other known planets of the solar system. But determinations of precise orbits for Uranus proved vexing from the beginning. By 1830 the observed motion departed from a best-fitting ellipse by an intolerable 15″ of arc. Several astronomers suggested that perturbations by a hitherto unknown planet, lying outside the orbit of Uranus, might explain the anomalies. Computations, first in 1845 by an English mathematician and astronomer, John Couch Adams, and in 1846 by a French astronomer, Urbain-Jean-Joseph Le Verrier, led to precise predictions of the position of the hypothetical planet. The resulting discovery of Neptune in 1846 provided a stunning vindication of gravitational theory.

Appearance and spectrum. Under good conditions, Uranus shows a perceptible blue-green disk, through even a four-inch telescope. The astronomically unusual colour is caused by absorption of red light in its atmosphere. Experienced visual observers report faint markings on the disk, in particular, grayish belts; but such features are far less conspicuous than the latitudinal cloud belts on Jupiter. Elusive faint spots plus darkening of the disk toward the limbs, or edges, of the planet are also reported. Such observations are difficult, since the disk of the planet subtends an angle less than 4″ of arc in the sky; and atmospheric conditions on Earth seldom permit features smaller than about 0.5″ of arc to be resolved. A fine series of pictures taken in 1971, resolving 0.1″ of arc, showed pronounced limb darkening but no clearly discernible surface markings with contrast as great as 5 percent.

On the visual stellar-magnitude scale, Uranus over the past century had an average brightness at mean opposition (that is, when closest to the Earth) of about 5.8 magnitudes (the faintest stars visible to the naked eye on a very clear, totally dark night are about 6.5). The observed brightness can change by half a magnitude from the mean, depending on the Earth–Uranus and Uranus–Sun distances and also possibly on real change of reflectivity. Recent accurate photoelectric measures give a mean-opposition (photoelectric–visual) magnitude of about 5.5.

Proposed names for the new planet

Reports of faint markings

Possible brightness changes. Some 3,000 visual observations made during 1916 showed a regular 15 percent variation of brightness with a period of 10 hours 49.4 minutes. This was taken to be the rotation period, but the large diffuse spots or areas presumably responsible for hemispheric differences in brightness apparently change with time, since observations of 1917–18 were not consistent with those of 1916. Other visual and photographic observers have found transient intervals in which a period very close to the 1916 value appears to be present in their data. But more accurate photoelectric observations, beginning in 1927 and including half a dozen series up through the 1950s, showed no detectable (1 to 2 percent) change in brightness with rotation. If the visual observations of variations are correct, either the spottedness is rare and transient, or the variation may be present only in red light, to which the eye is somewhat sensitive but which was generally excluded in the photoelectric observations so far reported.

In 1933 a summary of most of the observations for the previous 50 years contained evidence for two additional variations, each of about 30 percent, in the brightness of Uranus, with eight-year and 42-year periods, respectively. The longer interval coincides with half the orbital period of Uranus. If real, it probably arises from effects connected with the alternate presentation of equatorial and polar hemispheres to the Earth and Sun as a consequence of the planet's rotational axis lying nearly in its orbital plane; Uranus appears brightest when seen pole-on. A careful series of photoelectric observations in blue light at the Lowell Observatory beginning in 1949 failed to detect any eight-year variation exceeding the 1 percent level.

Effect
of rapid
rotation

The rapid rotation of Uranus on its axis leads to an appreciable reduction in the effective force of gravity at the equator, hence to a substantial oblateness (equatorial bulging). Direct micrometer measures give an equatorial diameter about 6 to 8 percent greater than the polar diameter, consistent with the amount of flattening expected theoretically.

For a rotating planet, spectral lines from the approaching limb are shifted to shorter wavelengths and from the receding limb to longer wavelengths (according to the phenomenon known as the Doppler effect) in a uniform progression across the planet. The tilt of the resulting spectral lines allows direct determination of the rotational velocity of the planet. Measures of this type made in the decades 1910–30 give for Uranus a rotation period about 10.75 hours, consistent with the photometric value.

Uranus' atmosphere. Since the 1860s the spectrum of Uranus has been known to contain deep absorption bands toward the red. In 1932 these were shown theoretically to be almost certainly due to methane (CH_4). Laboratory and high-resolution spectroscopic studies confirmed this. The photographic spectrum of Uranus is dominated by methane, corresponding to about 3.5 kilometre atmospheres of the gas. Like those of Jupiter and Saturn, the atmosphere must, nevertheless, consist primarily of hydrogen and helium; but, because both these gases are nearly invisible spectroscopically at low temperatures, the methane dominates. Weak hydrogen quadrupole lines are found in the spectrum of Uranus, in amounts consistent with some 480 kilometre atmospheres of this gas in the visible part of the atmosphere. Other common gases, such as water and ammonia, would be frozen out of the upper atmosphere and be present only at depths to which the line of sight from Earth cannot penetrate.

The temperature of a planet can be determined either by direct measurement of the infrared and radio radiation that it emits or by detailed spectroscopic studies of relative strengths of temperature-sensitive spectral features. Both techniques indicate that temperatures in the visible outer atmosphere of Uranus are in the range −150° to −200° C (−250° to −350° F).

Mass, radius, density, and composition. The orbital period and orbital radius of any satellite suffice to establish the mass of its primary, a result first derived by Newton. Determinations in 1950, using all five satellites, give Uranus a mass that is $\frac{1}{22.934}$ times that of the Sun,

or about 14.5 times that of the Earth. The mass has also been determined from perturbations by Uranus on the orbit of Saturn, and in 1970 this method gave $\frac{1}{22.692}$.

The actual size of any object may be calculated from its distance and apparent angular size. For Uranus the best results for equatorial diameter are probably those made in 1902, 56,100 kilometres (34,900 miles), and 1949, 47,400 kilometres (29,500 miles). Several indirect arguments suggest adoption of the intermediate value 52,700 kilometres (32,800 miles), uncertain by 5 percent; this corresponds to 4.1 times the diameter of the Earth.

With the mass and diameter of Uranus given above, the average density is about 1.15 times the density of water; for comparison, that of Saturn is 0.71 and that of the Earth is 5.52. So low a mean density requires Uranus to be composed of materials far lighter than those that make up the Earth; otherwise, its greater mass would lead to compression producing greater central pressures and densities than the Earth's. By the same reasoning, its average composition must be somewhat heavier than that of Saturn. Theoretical models of Jupiter and Saturn are consistent with a total composition similar to the basic solar chemical abundance (roughly 70 percent hydrogen, most of the remainder helium). But in Uranus these two lightest elements must be accompanied by appreciable amounts of the next heavier common elements, especially carbon, nitrogen, and oxygen. Since comets are rich in these elements, preferential accretion of comet-like bodies in cool outer regions of the early solar nebula may have contributed greatly to the formation of Uranus.

The satellites. In 1787 William Herschel found two faint Uranus satellites, later called Oberon and Titania. The next two satellites, Ariel and Umbriel, were discovered in 1851 at Liverpool. The names for these first four satellites were apparently proposed by the English scientist and astronomer Sir John Herschel, the son of William Herschel. The last known satellite, Miranda, less than 10″ of arc from the planet, was first photographed in 1948 at the McDonald Observatory in Texas. There are probably no other satellites of Uranus brighter than 20th magnitude within a radius of 0.5° from Uranus.

Uranus's satellite system is compact and closely coplanar with the planet's equator. But, whereas the equators and satellite orbits of all the other planets of the solar system have only modest inclinations to the plane of the ecliptic, in the case of Uranus these are all curiously tilted, by an extreme 98°. Thus, the rotation of the planet and revolution of its satellites are essentially perpendicular to the orbital revolution of Uranus about the Sun. Further satellite data are shown in the Table.

Satellites of Uranus

name	date discovered	discoverer	telescope size (in.)	satellite diameter (km)	orbit period (days)	magnitude
Oberon	1787	W. Herschel	19	950	13.5	14.1
Titania	1787	W. Herschel	19	1,100	8.7	14.0
Ariel	1851	W. Lassell	24	800	2.5	13.9
Umbriel	1851	W. Lassell	24	650	4.1	14.8
Miranda	1948	G.P. Kuiper	82	300	1.4	16.5

BIBLIOGRAPHY. A comprehensive and detailed summary of essentially all the serious work done on Uranus from its discovery through the early 1960s is ARTHUR F.O.'D. ALEXANDER, *The Planet Uranus* (1965). More technical treatments, setting Uranus in the context of other planets, especially in terms of its fundamental properties, interior structure, and satellite system, are found in the articles by Brouwer and Clemence, Wildt, and Harris in *Planets and Satellites*, ed. by G.P. KUIPER and B.M. MIDDLEHURST (1961). The mass of Uranus may be determined by its perturbations on the orbit of Saturn, resulting in a value somewhat in conflict with that derived from the satellite; this work is summarized by W.J. KLEPCZYNSKI, P.K. SEIDELMANN, and R.L. DUNCOMBE in "The Masses of Jupiter and Saturn," *Astr. J.*, 75:739–742 (1970). Details of the atmosphere of Uranus may be found in the papers by M. BELTON, M.B. McELROY, and M.J. PRICE, "The Atmosphere of Uranus," *Astrophys. J.*, 164:191–209 (1971); and by M.B. McELROY, "Atmospheric Composition of the Jovian Planets," *J. Atmos. Sci.*, 26:798–812 (1969).

(H.Sm.)

Urartu and Armenia, History of

Urartu and Armenia are the names given to two ancient countries of southwest Asia centred in the mountainous region southeast of the Black Sea and southwest of the Caspian. Urartu, mentioned in Assyrian sources from the early 13th century BC, enjoyed considerable political power in the Near East in the 9th and 8th centuries BC. The Urartians were succeeded in the area in the 6th century BC by the Armenians, who, by the late 1st century AD had built a state that briefly contested the hegemony of the Roman Empire in the East. Thereafter the region was dominated by powerful neighbouring empires, but its people retained a fiercely independent spirit. Armenian nationalism nettled international diplomacy even in the late 19th century. The geographical boundaries of both kingdoms varied greatly with their political vicissitudes, and today the region is divided among eastern Turkey, northwest Iran, and the Armenian Soviet Socialist Republic of the U.S.S.R.

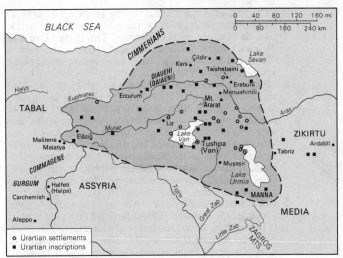

Ancient Urartu.
Adapted from B. Piotrovsky, *Urartu*, Coll. Archaeologia Mundi; Nagel Publishers, Geneva, Paris, Munich

URARTU

Urartian territory, c. 1275–840 BC. Shalmaneser I, king of Assyria, marched through the country of "Uruatri" as early as 1275 BC. It then denoted a region close to Arina (Ardini) in the land of Musri (Muṣaṣir) in the upper valley of the Great Zab River. By 860 BC the Assyrians came to use the name Urartu specifically for the kingdom that had newly arisen around Lake Van, Turkey, and the Urartian kingdom is sometimes called the Kingdom of Van. The Urartians themselves called their country Biainili and their capital, located at modern Van, Tushpa (Turushpa). Most Urartian settlements are found between the four lakes Çildir and Van in Turkey, Urmia in Iran, and Sevan in Soviet Armenia, with a sparser extension toward the Euphrates.

Hurrian background

The Urartians had a number of traits in common with the Hurrians, an earlier Near Eastern people. Both nations spoke closely related languages and must have sprung from a common ancestor nation (perhaps 3000 BC or earlier). Both people worshipped certain gods in common, which they may have inherited from the ancestor nation: the principal Hurrian god, Teshub ("the Destroyer"), corresponds to the second-ranking Urartian god, Teisheba, while the Hurrian sun god Shimegi corresponds to the Urartian Shiwini (Shiuini). Common features in Hurrian and Urartian religious imagery, such as the animals that served as mounts for the gods and the minor deities that were depicted holding up the sky, must have been derived from a common ethnic background, or the Urartians may have borrowed wholesale from the Hurrians, who surrounded Urartu on the west, south, and east. In Hittite sources of the 2nd millennium BC, Hurrian geographical and personal names are widely attested in the Euphrates Valley near the Taurus Mountains, to the west of Lake Van. In Assyrian sources of the 1st millennium BC, Hurrian names, among others, also appear in the south, on the Upper Tigris and its tributaries.

The Assyrians used the term Nairi for the area later to become the territory of the Urartian state. In a general sense, it denoted the headwaters of the Tigris and Euphrates, together with lakes Van and Urmia. In a narrower sense, King Shalmaneser III of Assyria used the term as an equivalent of Urartu, with its capital at Arzashku, somewhere north of Lake Van. (Arzashku may possibly have been located at Mollakent, near Liz, the site of a large Urartian town.) Early in his reign Shalmaneser III (858–824 BC) fought and overcame an Urartian king named Arramu, or Arame, who resided at Arzashku.

Rise of the Urartian kingdom. It was probably the complete destruction of this capital by Shalmaneser in 856 and the destruction of additional Urartian settlements in 844 that made possible the rise to power of a new and more formidable dynasty founded by Sarduri I (c. 840–830) that was to rule Urartu for two and a half centuries. Sarduri I's descendants were usually designated ruler of Tushpa as part of their title, and it is natural to assume that the city was in Urartu's domain before Sarduri I extended his power over most of Nairi. The link between the country of Nairi and the kings of Urartu at

Van is established by an inscription of Sarduri I on the building blocks of a fortress at the foot of the citadel of Van. There he styled himself "great king, mighty king, king of the universe, king of (the country of) Nairi." This title was obviously copied after those of the Assyrian kings, and the inscription is in Assyrian, unlike those of his descendants, which are in Urartian, transcribed in 9th-century Assyrian script.

The inscription suggests that Sarduri I had founded his kingdom on the Assyrian pattern. There is good reason to believe that his family came from the bilingual buffer zone of Muṣaṣir, and the chief god of the Urartian state was to be Haldi (Khaldi, god of the heavens and war), whose holy city Ardini (Muṣaṣir) was the capital of that zone.

Assyrian influences

If the Urartians owed much of their cultural heritage to the Hurrians, they were to a much greater degree indebted to the Assyrians, from whom they borrowed script and literary forms, military and diplomatic practices, and artistic motifs and styles.

The Assyrian influence was manifested in two phases: first, from c. 1275 BC to 840, when the Assyrians campaigned in Urartian territory and met only scattered resistance; second, from 840–612, during the heyday of the Urartian kingdom. In the first phase Assyrian influence was felt directly, and the local inhabitants were helplessly exposed to ruthless depredation at the hands of the Assyrians. But they seem also to have eagerly absorbed or imitated the amenities of Assyria's higher civilization. In the second phase, Urartu produced its own distinctive counterparts to all Assyrian achievements.

The first century of the new kingdom seems to have emphasized military operations in imitation of Assyria, and Urartu waged relentless warfare on its neighbours to the east, west, and north.

For the reign of Sarduri I there remain only the inscriptions at Van mentioned above. But for the reigns of his son Ishpuini (c. 830–810) and especially of Ishpuini's son Meinua (c. 810–781) Urartian conquests can be measured indirectly from widespread inscriptions ranging from the lower Murat basin (around Elâzığ) in the west, to the Aras (Araks, Araxes River; from Erzurum to Mount Ararat) in the north, and to the south shore of Lake Urmia in the southeast. Ardini, or Muṣaṣir, once conquered by Tiglath-pileser I of Assyria c. 1100, now became part of the Urartian sphere of influence, although technically neutral under its own dynasty of priest-rulers. The temple of Haldi at Ardini was richly endowed by the Urartian kings, but was open to Assyrian worshippers.

A number of Urartian inscriptions dealing with religious subjects date to the end of Ishpuini's reign, when Meinua acted as co-regent. It seems that the state religion received its established form under these kings, and the hierarchy of the many gods in the Urartian pantheon is expressed by a list of sacrifices due them.

The first evidence of engineering projects, designed to increase the productivity of the home country by irrigation, dates to the reign of Meinua. This is the "Canal of Meinua," which led and still leads fresh water over a distance of about 46 miles from an abundant spring to the southern edge of Van.

From the reigns of Meinua's son Argishti I (c. 780–756) and grandson Sarduri II (c. 755–735) there is, in addition to inscriptions, a direct historical source in the form of annals carved into the rock of Van and into stelae that were displaced in later times to other locations in the vicinity. Under these kings Urartu thrust out westward to the great bend of the Euphrates and intermittently beyond, toward Melitene (modern Malatya) and the ancient Syrian district of Commagene, thus cutting off one of the main supply roads by which Assyria obtained essential iron from the western Taurus Mountains. Argishti I subdued the Melitene Hilaruada (c. 777), as did Sarduri II in the 750s. King Kushtashpi of Commagene was subjected by Sarduri II around 745. Part of the domain of King Tuate of Tabal in the Taurus had also fallen to Argishti I about 777. For a short time Urartu thus had a bridgehead west of the Euphrates from Malatya to Halfeti (ancient Halpa) in Commagene, and its empire reached to within 20 miles of Aleppo in northern Syria.

Argishti and Sarduri also embarked on what was in the end to prove the most fruitful of all Urartian ventures: the conquest and subsequent agricultural exploitation of the regions across the Aras: under Argishti I, Diauehi ("the Land of the Sons of Diau"; Assyrian Daiaeni) was finally defeated, and the upper and middle Aras Valley became a major centre of building, irrigation, and agricultural activity. Sarduri added lakes Çildir and Sevan. Further advance to the northwest was checked by a new adversary, the kingdom of Qulha (Greek Colchis). The tens of thousands of prisoners taken on the yearly military campaigns (in one year as many as 39,000) provided the manpower for intensive cultivation of the royal estates and processing of their crops.

Agricultural organization

Armenian legend attributed much of the surviving Urartian construction to Queen Semiramis. The historical queen Sammu-ramat, however, Babylonia-born regent of Assyria from 810 to 806, did not intervene at all in the affairs of Urartu. On the contrary, the reigns of her husband, son, and elder grandsons (823–745) marked a period of Assyrian military decline, during which the Urartians extended their frontiers.

Several times the Urartian kings of this period claimed, probably with justification, to have defeated Assyrian armies: Argishti reported victories over the Assyrians in his sixth and seventh regnal years, when he operated in the Zab and Lake Urmia areas; and Sarduri II defeated the Assyrian king Ashur-nirari V in the upper basin of the Tigris c. 753.

Destruction of the Urartian kingdom. The period c. 744–715 saw the renewal of Assyrian expansion. In spite of the support of a number of south Anatolian and north Syrian vassals, Sarduri II lost ground steadily, and in 743 Tiglath-pileser III of Assyria (744–727) defeated him and his allies in Commagene near Halfeti. When Tiglath-pileser in 735 advanced all the way to the gates of Tushpa, a palace revolt may have placed Sarduri's son Rusas I (c. 735–713) at the head of the state.

Tiglath-pileser's son, king Sargon II of Assyria (721–705) completed the elimination of Urartu as a rival for hegemony in the Near East. Urartu's hopes of help from the north Syrian principalities were dashed by their swift subjection, ending with the incorporation of Carchemish into the Assyrian Empire in 717. In the metal-rich Taurus Mountains, the kingdom of Tabal remained a potential ally of Rusas I, as well as of the Phrygian king Midas of the legendary golden touch. After the latter's defeat, Tabal was annihilated and annexed to Assyria.

In the same year Sargon began to close in on Urartu from the east. For two years operations were mostly limited to western Iran. There Assyria championed the interests of the kingdom of Manna, while Urartu aided and abetted Iranian tribes encroaching upon Manna from east and north. But behind the Urartian lines Assyrian intelligence officers were collecting information with a view to a much more ambitious military undertaking against Urartu.

What finally tipped the scales in favour of Assyria was the opening up of a second front: the Cimmerians, a nomadic people from the Caucasus, invaded Urartu shortly before 714. Perhaps Rusas I (c. 735–713) himself provoked the onslaught by unwisely destroying several buffer states to the north. In any case, Rusas soon found the Cimmerians at his borders. Undaunted, he proceeded to the attack but suffered a major disaster: the Assyrian crown prince Sennacherib, sent north by King Sargon II (721–705) to gather intelligence about Urartian affairs, reported to his father that Rusas' whole army had been defeated in Cimmerian territory and that Rusas himself had fled back to Urartu, having lost contact with his commanders. This encouraged Sargon to undertake the ambitious campaign of 714 that put an end to the aspirations of the Urartian kings outside of their mountain homeland. After unsuccessfully heading a coalition of his allies against Assyria, Rusas hastened back to Tuspha, which Sargon wisely did not try to besiege. Sargon avoided a clash with the Cimmerians and instead plundered the main sanctuary of the Urartians at Ardini and carried off the statue of Haldi. Hearing of this third calamity, Rusas committed suicide.

Cimmerian invasion

The military setbacks of Rusas I ended Urartu's political power. Nevertheless, his son Argishti II (c. 712–685) and successors continued the royal tradition of developing the country's natural resources, and Urartian culture not only survived but continued to flourish, despite its political impotence. Inscriptions of Argishti II have been found near Erzincan, 100 miles from the Black Sea, and on the way from Tabriz to Ardabīl, 60 miles from the Caspian Sea.

Under Rusas II (c. 685–645) Urartu witnessed a renaissance, based on a further shift away from military exploits and toward economic and administrative activity.

It was probably Rusas II (not Rusas I, as earlier scholars believed) who created the artificial "Lake of Rusas" about 25 miles to the east of Van and the "Canal of Rusas" that carries fresh water to the vineyards, forests, and barley fields at the foot of Toprakkale (ancient Rusahinili), which must have been founded at the same time. This huge irrigation project still waters this garden area that has become the new city of Van.

Raids on neighbouring countries are mentioned by Rusas II, but these were conducted only as a means to populate newly built cities: women were forcibly imported from Kurdistan and men from the Anatolian districts Halitu (Pontus), Mushki (Phrygia), and Hate (Cappadocia). Possibly Rusas II allowed the Cimmerians to raid these neighbouring countries from a base in Urartu. By 672 he had also come to an understanding with the Assyrians under Esarhaddon, who in turn was negotiating with the Scythians and certain Median chieftains. Ashurbanipal re-established Assyrian sovereignty over Manna in 660 or 659. In or shortly after 654 Rusas II sent a diplomatic mission to the court of Ashurbanipal, presumably still on the basis of an equal. In Rusas II's later years his son Sarduri III served as co-regent. After c. 650 Urartu and Assyria felt the pressure of a new and more formidable power in the east: the Medes. In 644, probably at the beginning of his sole kingship, Sarduri III (c. 644–640) sent an embassy to Ashurbanipal acknowledging the latter as sovereign. Three more kings reigned Urartu between 640 and 609: Sarduri IV, son of Sarduri; Erimena, son of Ar . . . (Argishti?); and Rusas III, son of Erimena.

In the last days of the Assyrian Empire, Urartu allied with Manna and Assyria against Media and Babylonia, but to no avail, as the latter put an end to the Assyrian empire, between 612 and 609. A change of allegiance by the Scythians is said to have tipped the scales in favor of Media and Babylonia.

Similarly, the cast-bronze arrowheads found both in and outside the citadel of Teishebaini (Karmirblur, near Yerevan, Soviet Armenia) indicate the presence of Scythians among both defenders and attackers of this Urartian stronghold. According to the Babylonian chronicle, the

Scythian attack

Scythians in 609 marched "as far as the district of the city of Urartu," stayed there for some time and plundered it. This would seem to indicate the conquest and sack of Van itself and surroundings, especially as the Babylonians then proceeeded to annex the mountainous parts of Urartu south of the Taurus range in 608–607. In an alternate view, based on Jeremiah 51:27, Urartu (biblical Ararat) existed as an independent country as late as 593 BC.

Influence of the Urartian state. Gold scabbards found in the Kelermes and Melgunov barrows in southern Russia clearly show that goldsmiths steeped in the traditions of the Urartian court worked for Scythian chieftains in the time shortly after 600 BC. After a new war (590–585), in which the western Anatolian kingdom of Lydia unsuccessfully championed the cause of the Scythians, eastern Anatolia, up to the river Halys (Kizil Irmak), was incorporated into the Median empire.

There are indications that some Urartian sites, such as the citadel of Erebuni (Arin-berd above Yerevan, Soviet Armenia), were not destroyed but continued through the Median and into the Persian period. This would explain how certain characteristics of Urartian statecraft, literature, architecture, and artistic representation were inherited by the Persian Empire. Urartian settlements are distingushed from those of the Assyrians by vast irrigated and drained royal estates, worked largely by resettled captives. At their centre stood well-watered hilltop fortresses, where the agricultural produce was processed and stored, where a garrison was stationed, and where the king could reside and worship. From the material remains Urartu appears largely as the creation of one single-minded dynasty imposing a uniform life-style over a wide area. In this respect it resembled, and probably served as a prototype for, the Median and Persian empires.

In addition to the speakers of the Urartian language (written in cuneiform script) there was in the kingdom of Urartu a second ethnic group that wrote in hieroglyphs. It is not known if this was the language later called Armenian. In the enumeration of countries subjected by the Persian king Darius I (520), Armina is given as the Old Persian name for Urartu.   (M.N.v.L.)

ARMENIA

The Armenians, an Indo-European people, first appear in history shortly after the collapse of Urartu toward the end of the 7th century BC. Driving some of the ancient population to the east of Mount Ararat, where they were known to the Greeks as Alarodioi ("Araratians"; *i.e.*, Urartians), the invaders imposed their leadership over regions which, although suffering much from Scythian and Cimmerian depredations, must still have retained elements of a high degree of civilization (*e.g.*, walled towns, irrigation works, arable fields, and vineyards) upon which the more primitive newcomers might build. The Hayk, as the Armenians name themselves (the term Armenian is probably due to an Iranian or Greek confusion of them with the Aramaeans), were not able to achieve the power and independence of their predecessors and were rapidly incorporated first by Cyaxares into the Median Empire and then annexed with Media by Cyrus II the Great to form part of the Achaemenian Empire of Persia (*c.* 550). The country is mentioned as Armina and Armaniya in the Bīsitūn inscription of Darius I the Great and, according to the 5th-century Greek historian Herodotus, formed part of the 13th satrapy (province) of Persia, the Alarodians forming part of the 18th. Xenophon's *Anabasis*, recounting the adventures of Greek mercenaries in Persia, shows the local government *c.* 400 BC to have been in the hands of village headmen, part of whose tribute to the Persian king consisted of horses. Armenia continued to be governed by Persian or native satraps until its absorption into the Macedonian empire of Alexander the Great (331) and its successor, the Seleucid Empire (301).

The Artaxiads. After the defeat of the Seleucid king Antiochus the Great by Rome at the Battle of Magnesia (winter 190–189), his two Armenian satraps, Artashes (Artaxias) and Zareh (Zariadres), established them-

selves, with Roman consent, as kings of Greater Armenia and Sophene, respectively, thus becoming the creators of an independent Armenia. Artashes built his capital Artashat (Artaxata) on the Aras River near modern Yerevan. The Greek geographer Strabo names the capital of Sophene as Carcathiocerta. An attempt to end the division of Armenia into an eastern and a western part was made about 165 BC when the Artaxiad ruler sought to suppress his rival, but it was left to his descendant Tigran II the Great (*c.* 94-*c.* 56 BC) to establish, by his conquest of Sophene, a unity that was to last almost 500 years. Under Tigran, Armenia ascended to a pinnacle of power unique in its history and became, albeit briefly, the strongest state in the Roman east. Extensive territories were taken from the kingdom of Parthia in Iran, which was compelled to sign a treaty of alliance. Iberia (Georgia), Albania, and Atropatene had already accepted Tigran's suzerainty when the Syrians, tired of anarchy, offered him their crown (83 BC). Tigran penetrated as far south as Ptolemais (Acre). Deeming Artaxata too far north to serve as the capital of his new empire, he founded a new one, Tigranakert (Tell Armen/Kızıl Tepe? or Silvan?), nearer the centre. Although Armenian culture at the time of Tigran was Iranian, as it had been and as it was fundamentally to remain for many centuries, Hellenic scholars and actors found a welcome at the Armenian court. The Armenian Empire lasted until Tigran became involved in the struggle between his father-in-law, Mithradates VI of Pontus, and Rome. The Roman general Lucullus, capturing Tigranakert in 69 BC, failed to reach Artashat, but in 66 the legions of Pompey, aided by one of Tigran's sons, succeeded, compelling the King to renounce Syria and other conquests in the south and to become an ally of Rome. It has been the fate of Armenia throughout a long and turbulent history to be a small state struggling to preserve its independence between two poweful neighbours; it now became a buffer state, and often a battlefield, between Rome and Parthia. Their natural self-interest gave the Armenians a reputation for deviousness; the Roman historian Tacitus called them an *ambigua gens*.

The Arsacids. Both Rome and Parthia strove to establish their own candidates on the Armenian throne until a lasting measure of equilibrium was secured by the treaty of Rhandeia, concluded in AD 63 between the Roman general Corbulo and Tiridates (Trdat), whereby an Arsacid occupied the throne of Armenia, but as a Roman vassal. A dispute with Parthia led to the country's annexation by the emperor Trajan in 114, but his successor, Hadrian, withdrew the frontier of the Roman Empire to the Euphrates. A similar dispute resulted in the destruction of Artashat by Marcus Aurelius' general Priscus in 163 and in the building of a new capital, Kainepolis (Vagharshapat, modern Echmiadzin). After Caracalla's capture of King Vagharshak and his attempt to annex the country in 216, his successor, Macrinus, recognized Vagharshak's son Tiridates II (Khosrow the Great in Armenian sources) as king of Armenia (217). Tiridates II's resistance to the Sāsānids after the fall of the Arsacid dynasty in Persia (224) ended in his assassination by their agent Anak the Parthian (*c.* 238) and in the conquest of Armenia by Shāpūr I, who placed his vassal Artavazd on the throne (252). Under Diocletian, the Persians were forced to relinquish Armenia, and Tiridates III, the son of Tiridates II, was restored to the throne under Roman protection (*c.* 287). The reign of Tiridates III determined the course of much of Armenia's subsequent history. His ultimate conversion by St. Gregory the Illuminator and the adoption of Christianity as the state religion (*c.* 300) created a permanent gulf between Armenia and Persia, and the Armenian patriarchate became one of the surest stays of the Arsacid monarchy while it lasted and the guardian of national unity after its fall. The Mamikonian family, which played a similar role, came to the fore in his reign. Tiridates' assassination by his own chamberlain in league with the *nakharar*s (clan chiefs, barons; Parthian *n.ḥwd.r*, "Nohodares") of Siuniq underlines the disloyalty of many of the local nobles, whose revolts and jealous quarrels fill the pages of Armenian historians.

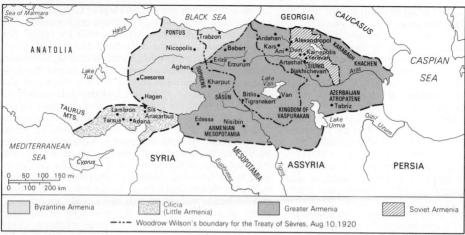

Historical divisions of Armenia.

The dissatisfaction of the *nakharar*s with Arshak II led to the division of Armenia into two sections, Byzantine Armenia and Persarmenia (*c.* 390). The former, comprising about one-fifth of Armenia, was rapidly absorbed into the Byzantine state, to which the Armenians came to contribute many emperors and generals. The latter continued to be ruled by an Arsacid in Dvin, the capital after the reign of Khosrow II (330–339), until the deposition of Artashes IV and his replacement by a Persian *marzpan* (governor) at the request of the *nakharar*s (428). Although the Armenian nobles had thus destroyed their country's sovereignty, the cause of national unity was furthered by the development of a national Christian literature; culturally, if not politically, the 5th century was a golden age.

The marzpans. The Persians were not as successful as the Byzantines in their efforts to assimilate the strongly individualistic Armenian people. The misjudged attempt of Yazdegerd II to impose the Zoroastrian religion upon his Armenian subjects did much to reunite them as a nation. In the war of 451, which resulted from this policy, the Armenian commander St. Vardan Mamikonian and his companions were slain at the Battle of Avarayr (June 2?, 451), but the Persians renounced their plans to convert Armenia by force and deposed their *marzpan* Vasak of Siuniq, the archtraitor of Armenian history. The revolt of 481–484 led by Vahan Mamikonian secured religious and political freedom for Armenia in return for military aid to Persia, and with the appointment of Vahan as *marzpan* the Armenians were again largely the arbiters of their own affairs. Their independence was further asserted in 554, when the second Council of Dvin rejected the dyophysite formula of the Council of Chalcedon (451), a decisive step that cut them off from the West as surely as they were already ideologically severed from the East.

Byzantine Armenia

In 536 Justinian I reorganized Byzantine Armenia into four provinces, and, by the suppression of the power of the Armenian nobles and by transfers of population, he completed the work of hellenizing the country. In 591 its territory was extended eastward by the emperor Maurice as the price of re-establishing Khosrow II on the throne of Persia. After transporting many Armenians to Thrace, Maurice (according to the Armenian historian Sebeos) advised the Persian King to follow his example and to send "this perverse and unruly nation, which stirs up trouble between us" to fight on his eastern front. During the war between the emperor Phocas and Khosrow, the Persians occupied Byzantine Armenia and appointed a series of *marzpan*s, only to be ousted by the emperor Heraclius in 623. In 628, after the fall of Khosrow, the Persians appointed an Armenian noble, Varaztirotz Bagratuni, as governor. He quickly brought Armenia under Byzantine rule but was exiled for plotting against Heraclius (635).

The Mamikonians and Bagratids. The first, unsuccessful, Arab raid into Armenia in 640 found the defense of the country in the hands of the Byzantine general Procopius and the *nakharar* Theodor Rshtuni. Unable to prevent the pillage of Dvin in 642, Theodor in 643 gained a victory over another Arab army and was named commander in chief of the Armenian army by Constans II. In 653, after the truce with Mu'āwiyah, then governor of Syria, Constans voluntarily surrendered Armenia to the Arabs, who granted it virtual autonomy and appointed Theodor as governor (*ostikan*).

Theodor's successor, Hamazasp Mamikonian, sided with Byzantium, but after 661 Arab suzerainty was re-established, although Byzantine-Arab rivalry, Armenian nationalism, and reluctance to pay the tribute made the region a difficult one to govern. An unsuccessful revolt led by Mushegh Mamikonian (771–772) resulted in the virtual extinction of the Mamikonians as a political force in Armenia and in the emergence of the Bagratunis and Artsrunis as the leading noble families. The Arabs' choice in 806 of Ashot Bagratuni the Carnivorous to be prince of Armenia marked the establishment of his family as the chief power in the land. The governor Smbat Ablabas Bagratuni remained loyal to the caliph al-Mutawakkil when he sent his general Bugha al-Kabir to bring the rebellious *nakharar*s to submission, although he too was dispatched in 855 with the rest of the captive nobles to Samarra. The election by the nobles of Smbat's son Ashot I the Great, who had been accepted as "prince of princes" by the Arabs in 862, to be king of Armenia in 885 was recognized by both Caliph and Emperor. Throughout the 10th century art and literature flourished. Ashot III the Merciful (952–977) transferred his capital to Ani and began to make it into one of the architectural gems of the Middle Ages.

The Bagratids of Ani, who bore the title of *shāhanshāh* ("king of kings"), first conferred upon Ashot II the Iron by the Caliph in 922, were not the sole rulers of Armenia. In 908 the Artsruni principate of Vaspurakan became a kingdom recognized by the Caliph; in 961 Mushegh, the brother of Ashot III, founded the Bagratid kingdom of Kars; and in 970 the Prince of East Siuniq declared himself a king.

By the time of the Seljuq invasions in the 11th century the Armenian kingdoms had already been destroyed from the west. The province of Taron had been annexed to the Byzantine Empire in 968, and the expansionist policy of Basil II finally extinguished Armenian independence. The possessions of David of Tayq were annexed in 1000 and the kingdom of Vaspurakan in 1022. In the latter year, the Bagratid king of Ani, Yovhannes-Smbat, was compelled to make the Emperor heir to his estates, and in 1045, despite the resistance of Gagik II, Ani was seized by Constantine IX Monomachus. The Byzantine conquest was short-lived: in 1048 Togrul led the first Seljuq raid into Armenia, and in 1064 Ani and Kars fell to Alp-Arslan, and after the Battle of Manzikert (1071) most of the country was in Turkish hands. In 1072 the Kurdish Shāddādids received Ani as a fief. A few native Armenian rulers survived for a time in the Kiurikian kingdom of Lori, the Siunian kingdom of Baghq or Kapan, and the principates of Khachen (Artzakh) and Sasun. In the 12th century

Byzantine conquest

many former Armenian regions became part of Georgia, and between 1236 and 1242 the whole of Armenia and Georgia fell into the hands of the Mongols. Armenian life and learning, centred around the church, continued as best it could.

Little Armenia. On the collapse of Greater Armenia many Armenians emigrated to Georgia, Poland, and Galicia, while others crossed into Cilicia, where some colonies had already settled at the end of the 10th century. One of Gagik II's lieutenants, a certain Ruben, established himself about 1080 at Bardzrberd in the Taurus, and another noble named Oshin at Lambron: the former became the founder of Rubenid dynasty of barons and kings who ruled Cilicia until 1226, and the latter was the ancestor of the Hethumid dynasty, which succeeded them and ruled until 1342. The barons Constantine I (1092–1100), Thoros I (1100–29), and Leo I (1129–39) enlarged their domains at the expense of the Byzantines, and by 1132 Vahka, Sis, Anazarbus, Mamistra, Adana, and Tarsus were under Rubenid rule. Although the Byzantine emperor John II Comnenus succeeded in annexing the whole of Cilicia during 1137–38, Thoros II (1145–68) and Mleh (1170–75) restored Armenian rule, with some Turkish aid. Leo II (I) the Great (1187–1219), an ally of the German emperor Frederick I Barbarossa, received the royal crown from the latter's son Henry VI and Pope Celestine III and was crowned king of Armenia in Tarsus in 1199 by the cardinal Conrad von Wittelsbach. The Byzantine Emperor lost no time in sending a crown also, but Little Armenia was now firmly allied to the West.

Influence of the crusaders

Intermarriage with Frankish crusading families from the West was common, and Frankish religious, political, and cultural influence, though resisted by the more nationalistic barons, was strong. Leo reformed his court and kingdom on Western models, and many French terms entered the language. Little Armenia played an important role in the trade of the Venetians and Genoese with the East, and the port of Lajazzo (on the Gulf of Iskenderun) rivalled Alexandria. Leo II left no son, and the throne passed to his daughter Zabel. Her first husband, Philip of Antioch, who refused to accept the Armenian faith—Leo II's lip service to Rome as the price of his coronation being largely ignored—was deposed by the barons, and the regent Constantine, baron of Lambron, a descendant of Oshin, arranged the marriage of Zabel to his son Hethum (Hayton) I (1226–69), the first of the Hethumid dynasty. Hethum conceived the idea of employing the Mongols against the growing menace of the Mamlūks of Egypt and was present with the Mongol army that entered the Syrian cities of Aleppo and Damascus in 1260. His successors followed the same policy, but the Mongols weakened and, after their defeat in 1303 near Damascus, were unable to protect Cilicia.

On the death, without heir, of Leo V, the crown passed to Guy de Lusignan, the eldest son of Hethum II's sister Zabel and her husband Amaury de Lusignan (Amalric of Cyprus). He was assassinated by the barons in 1344 for doctrinal reasons, and the next two kings, Constantine IV and V, were elected from their own ranks. On the assassination of Constantine V, the crown passed again to a Lusignan, to Guy's nephew Leo VI (V) (1374–75). By this time, as a result of the Mamlūk advance, little remained of Armenia except Sis and Anazarbus; Lajazzo had finally fallen in 1347, followed by Adana, Tarsus, and the Cilician plain in 1359. In 1375 the capital of Sis fell to the Mamlūks, and the last king of Armenia was captured; ransomed in 1382, he died in Paris in 1393. The title "king of Armenia" passed to the kings of Cyprus, thence to the Venetians, and was later claimed by the house of Savoy, but from the end of the 14th century the history of Armenia as a separate state is replaced by the history of Armenians under foreign domination.

The Turkish conquest. After the capture of Constantinople by the Ottoman Turks, the Armenian bishop of Bursa, transferred in 1461 to the capital, was appointed leader of the Armenian *millet* in the Ottoman Empire. Although as non-Muslims they were greatly disadvantaged, the Armenians of Turkey retained, as *zimmîs* (Arabic, *dhimmī*) or "people of the Book," the management

of their own affairs. Their numbers were increased at the beginning of the 16th century by the conquest of Cilicia and Greater Armenia.

On the death of Timur in 1405, the eastern Armenian regions had passed into the hands of the Turkmen rival confederacies, the Black Sheep and the White Sheep, until the defeat of the latter by the Persian Shāh Esma'īl I in 1502. Armenia again became the battlefield between two powerful neighbours, and in 1514–16 the Ottomans wrested it from Persian rule. During the war that broke out in 1602, Shah 'Abbās I strove to regain the lost territories, and in 1604–05, with the aim of stimulating trade in his dominions, he forcibly transferred thousands of Armenians from Julfa to Isfahan, where those who survived the march settled in the quarter named New Julfa. At the peace of 1620, while the greater part of Armenia remained in Ottoman hands, Persia regained the regions of Yerevan, Nakhichevan, and Karabagh. In the mountainous region of Karabagh a group of five Armenian *maliks* (princes) succeeded in conserving their autonomy and maintained a short period of independence (1722–30) during the struggle between Persia and Turkey at the beginning of the 18th century; despite the heroic resistance of David Beg, the Turks occupied the region but were driven out by the Persians under Nāder Qolī (the future Nāder Shāh) in 1735. In New Julfa the Armenian merchants served as links between Europe (including England, Spain, and Russia) and the East, exporting Persian silk and importing glass, clocks, spectacles, paintings, etc. In the course of the 17th century they amassed great wealth and built many magnificent churches and mansions, thereby attracting Persian envy, and from the beginning of the 18th century, when Nāder Shāh (1736–47) penalized them with excessive taxation, they began the gradual decline that continues at the present day.

Armenian settlement in New Julfa

Armenia and Europe. At the beginning of the 19th century the Russians advanced into the Caucasus. In 1813 the Persians were obliged to acknowledge Russia's authority over Georgia, northern Azerbaijan, and Karabagh, and in 1828 they ceded Yerevan and Nakhichevan. Contact with liberal thought in Russia and western Europe was a factor in the Armenian cultural renaissance of the 19th century. In Turkey, the Armenians benefitted with the rest of the population from what measures of reform there were, and in 1863 a special Armenian constitution was recognized by the Ottoman government. But social progress in Turkey was slow and the Armenians in Anatolia were subject to many abuses. After the Russo-Turkish War of 1877–78, in which Russian Armenians had taken part, Russia insisted in the Treaty of San Stefano that reforms be carried out among the Sultan's Armenian subjects and that their protection against the Kurds be guaranteed. This demand was reiterated at the Congress of Berlin, and the "Armenian question" became a factor in international politics in which Great Britain took a special interest.

The socialist Hènchak ("Handbell") party was founded in 1887 and the nationalist Dashnaktzutiun ("Confederacy") party, commonly called Dashnaks, in 1890, and in the face of increasing Armenian demands for much needed reforms both the Turkish and Russian governments grew more repressive. In 1895, after Abdülhamid II had felt compelled to promise Britain, France, and Russia to carry out reforms, large-scale systematic massacres took place in the provinces. In 1896, following the desperate occupation of the Ottoman Bank by 26 young Dashnaks, more massacres broke out in the capital. In 1897 Nicholas II closed hundreds of Armenian schools, libraries, and newspaper offices, and in 1903 he confiscated the property of the Armenian Church. The greatest single disaster in the history of the Armenians came with the outbreak of World War I. In 1915 the Young Turk government, regarding the Turkish Armenians, despite pledges of loyalty, as a dangerous foreign element with friends among the enemies who had launched the Dardanelles campaign and with cousins in the Russian army on their eastern front, resolved to deport the whole Armenian population of about 1,750,000 to Syria and Mesopotamia.

The chances of survival in these ill-prepared desert re-

Russian and Turkish atrocities

gions were slight: it was a death sentence, a "final solution" that Adolf Hitler was to emulate consciously in Germany. It is estimated that about 600,000 Armenians died or were massacred en route. Many of those who survived or escaped settled in Syria or emigrated to France and the United States.

The Republic of Armenia. In 1916 the Turkish Armenian regions fell to the Russian army, but in March 1918 Russia was forced by the Treaty of Brest-Litovsk to cede all Turkish Armenia and part of Russian Armenia to Turkey, though some Armenians continued to hold out against the advancing Turks. On April 22, 1918, Armenia, Georgia, and Azerbaijan formed the Transcaucasian Federal Republic, but their basic diversity caused them to split into separate republics on May 26, 1918. Though short-lived, this Armenian republic was the first independent Armenian state since the Middle Ages. On June 4, 1918, Armenia was forced to sign the Treaty of Batum with Turkey, acknowledging the pre-1878 Russo-Turkish frontier along the Arpa and Aras rivers as its boundary, but after the Allied victory the Armenians reoccupied Alexandropol (Leninakan) and Kars. A short war with Georgia ensued for the possession of Borchalu and Akhalkalaki, and with Azerbaijan for the Karabagh region; despite temporary military success, these regions were destined to remain outside Armenia. On January 15, 1920, the Allies recognized the de facto existence of the three Transcaucasian republics. Pres. Woodrow Wilson hoped to persuade the U.S. to accept a mandate for an independent Armenia, but the Senate refused the responsibility (June 1, 1920). On August 10, 1920, Armenia, now recognized de jure, signed the Treaty of Sèvres by which Turkey recognized Armenia as a free and independent state. On November 22, 1920, Wilson, as instructed, announced projected boundaries that ceded to Armenia most of the vilayets of Erzurum, Trabzon, Van, and Bitlis. Already in the summer of 1919, however, the Turkish government of Ankara, under Mustafa Kemal, had repudiated Constantinople's treaties with Armenia. In September 1920 the Turks attacked, seizing Kars and Alexandropol by November 7; at the treaty of Alexandropol on Dec. 2, 1920 Armenia renounced all pre-1914 Turkish territories and Kars and Ardahan, recognized that there were no Armenian minorities in Turkey, and accepted that the region of Nakhichevan should form an autonomous Turkish state. The next day a new Armenian government at Yerevan, a coalition of Communists and Dashnaks (nationalists), proclaimed Armenia a Soviet republic; the Dashnaks were quickly eliminated, provoking an abortive revolt in February 1921. In March 1922 Armenia joined Georgia and Azerbaijan to form the Transcaucasian Soviet Federated Socialist Republic, which became part of the U.S.S.R. on December 30, 1922. The Nakhichevan enclave was awarded to Azerbaijan, sandwiching the southern part of Armenia between Turks and remaining a constant cause of friction between Armenia and Azerbaijan. Irrigation and hydroelectrical work began immediately, and though industry developed slowly at first, by 1935 the value of the gross industrial product was six times that of 1928. Yerevan State University was founded in January 1921. Under the new Soviet constitution (December 5, 1936) Armenia, Georgia, and Azerbaijan became separate constituent republics of the Soviet Union (SEE ARMENIAN SOVIET SOCIALIST REPUBLIC).

(C.J.F.D.)

Proclamation of the Soviet republic

BIBLIOGRAPHY

Urartu: B.B. PIOTROVSKY, *The Ancient Civilization of Urartu* (1969; trans. from 2nd Russian ed., 1959), an illustrated political and cultural history; E. CASSIN, J. BOTTERO, and J. VERCOUTTER (eds.), *Die Altorientalischen Reiche*, vol. 3, *Die erste Halfte des 1. Jahrtausends*, pp. 44–127 (1967), a history of Assyrian-Urartian and Anatolian-Urartian politics; M.N. VAN LOON, *Urartian Art: Its Distinctive Traits in the Light of New Excavations*, pp. 1–28, 80–87 (1966), a summary of political and economic history.

Armenia: H.F.B. LYNCH, *Armenia: Travels and Studies*, vol. 1, *The Russian Provinces*, vol. 2, *The Turkish Provinces* (1901), an excellent account (with well-informed historical details) of two journeys to Armenia in 1893–94 and 1898, comprising scientific descriptions of geographical and archi-

tectural features, with numerous photographs of the monuments and inhabitants, many plans, large bibliography, and the best physical map of Armenia available; R. GROUSSET, *Histoire de l'Arménie des origines à 1071* (1947), an excellent general history of Armenia from prehistoric times to the Seljuq conquest, with chapters on the geographical background, a brief history of Urartu, full and up-to-date documentation, and historical maps; H. PASDERMADJIAN, *Histoire de l'Arménie depuis les origines jusqu'au traité de Lausanne*, 2nd rev. ed. (1964), a patriotic political history of Armenia, useful for the periods of Ottoman and tsarist domination; S. DER NERESSIAN, *The Armenians* (1969), a short cultural history of Armenia, with well-illustrated chapters on literature, architecture, sculpture, and painting.

(C.J.F.D./M.N.v.L.)

Urban II, Pope

Urban II, as pope during the last years of the 11th century—an epoch of profound historical change in the medieval world and an age of crisis and reform in the church, especially in its relations with temporal political powers—continued the ecclesiastical reform begun by his predecessors, particularly Gregory VII, one of the great reformers of the church in the Middle Ages. Urban defined the reform ideas of papacy, church, and Christian society more precisely, developed them further, and won recognition for them in large areas of Europe. Many of Urban's legal decisions were adopted in the church's legal code of the Middle Ages, the *Decretum* of Gratian, which was completed about 1140. Urban demonstrated the pope's leading position in Christendom by launching the Crusade movement, which greatly enhanced papal prestige and influence.

Urban II (left), attended by Abbot Hugh of Cluny (right) and cardinals and monks, consecrates the third abbey church at Cluny. Detail of a miniature from "Chronicon Cluniacense," late 12th century. In the Bibliothèque Nationale, Paris (lat. 17,716, fol. 91).

Urban, whose name was Odo, was born of noble parents about 1035 in Châtillon-sur-Marne or Lagery in the Champagne region of France. After studies in Soissons and Reims, he took the position of archdeacon in the diocese of Reims, at that time the most important metropolis in France. An archdeacon was an ordained cleric appointed by the bishop to assist him in administration; in the Middle Ages it was an office of considerable power. Odo held the position probably from 1055 to 1067. Subsequently he became a monk and then (c. 1070–74) prior superior at Cluny, the most important centre of reform monasticism in Europe in the 11th century. At Reims and Cluny, Odo gained experience in ecclesiastical policy and administration and made contacts with two important reform groups of his time: the canons regular—clergymen dedicated to the active service of the church, who live a strict life in community—and the monks of Cluny. In 1079 he went to Rome on a mission for his abbot, Hugh of Cluny. While in Rome he was created cardinal and bishop of Ostia (the seaport for Rome) by Gregory VII. In 1084 Gregory VII sent him as papal legate to Germany.

Early life and career

During the crisis of Gregory VII's struggle with Henry IV, the Holy Roman emperor, Odo remained loyal to the legitimate papacy. After Gregory VII's death in 1085, he also served his successor, Victor III, who died in September 1087. After a long delay during which the reform cardinals tried unsuccessfully to regain control of Rome from Guibert of Ravenna, who had been named Pope Clement III by Henry IV in 1080, Odo was elected pope in Terracina, south of Rome, on March 12, 1088.

As pope, Urban II found active support for his policies and reforms among several groups: the nobility, whose mentality and interests he knew; the monks; the canons regular, for whom he became patron and legislator; and also, increasingly, the bishops.

Urban felt that his most urgent immediate task was to secure his position against the antipope Clement III and to establish his authority as legitimate pope throughout Christendom. He attempted, with moderation and tolerance, to reconcile the church–state traditions of his age with ecclesiastical notions of reform. In practice he pushed the question of lay investiture—the act whereby a temporal ruler granted title and possession to a church office—more into the background while at the same time retaining reform legislation. He thus softened the conflict and permitted a more peaceful discussion of the problems at issue. At the Council of Clermont, France, in 1095, during which he eloquently called the First Crusade, Urban attempted, however, to prevent a further and complete feudalization of church–state relationships by prohibiting the clergy from taking an oath of fealty to the laymen.

Despite Urban's attempts at reconciliation, it did not prove possible to come to terms with Henry IV or with a large part of the church within the empire. England also remained closed to papal policies of reform and centralization, although Urban had been recognized there since 1095; a conflict between Anselm, the theologian who was named archbishop of Canterbury, and King William II particularly strained the relations between Urban and the King. On the other hand, despite a long standing conflict between Philip I of France and Urban (brought about by the King's scandalous marriage), France began under this French pope to become the most important support of the medieval papacy. Urban obtained special support in southern Europe: his particularly faithful allies were the Normans of southern Italy and Sicily. In Spain, Urban supported the Christian reconquest of the country from the Moors and carried out the ecclesiastical reorganization of the country. In southern Italy, southern France, and Spain, kings and princes became vassals of the Roman See and concluded treaties and concordats in feudal form with the pope: by this the temporal rulers sought to secure their independence from more powerful lords, and the pope for his part was able to carry out his reform aims in these territories.

From 1095 Urban was at the height of his success. From this time several important church councils took place: in 1095 at Piacenza, Italy, at which reform legislation was enacted; also in 1095 at Clermont, where Urban preached the First Crusade; in 1098 at Bari, Italy, where he worked for a reunion between Greek Christians and Rome; and in 1099 at Rome, where again reform legislation was passed. Urban's idea for a crusade and his attempt to reconcile the Latin and Greek churches sprang from his idea of the unity of all Christendom and from his experiences with the struggles against the Muslims in Spain and Sicily. He was, for a while, able to attract the Byzantine emperor Alexius I to his plans but never the Greek Church. Whereas the First Crusade led to military success with the conquest of Jerusalem in 1099, the project for union failed. Urban's pontificate not only led to a further centralization of the Roman Church but also to the expansion of papal administration; it contributed to the development of the Roman Curia, the administrative body of the papacy, and to the gradual formation of the College of Cardinals. The term Curia Romana first appeared in a bull written by Urban in 1089.

Urban died in Rome on July 29, 1099. Despite many problems that were still unsolved, the victory of medieval reform papacy was secured. Urban was beatified in 1881 by Pope Leo XIII, and his feast day is celebrated on July 29.

BIBLIOGRAPHY. The latest account of Urban II's life and pontificate is given by A. BECKER, *Papst Urban II*, vol. 1 (1964; vol. 2 in prep.). The chapters by F. KEMPF in H. JEDIN and J. DOLAN (eds.), *Handbuch der Kirchengeschichte*, vol. 3 (1966; Eng. trans., *Handbook of Church History*, vol. 3, 1969), present a good survey of Urban's history and offer a rich bibliography. The First Crusade and its connection with the history of Byzantium is related by S. RUNCIMAN in *A History of the Crusades*, vol. 1 (1951). Among the earlier biographies, the work of H.K. MANN, *The Lives of the Popes in the Early Middle Ages*, 2nd ed., vol. 7 (1925), still has value. The most important recent works are A. FLICHE in *Histoire de l'Église*, vol. 8 (1944), who tends to emphasize the Gregorian point of view; and J. HALLER, *Das Papsttum*, vol. 2 (1951), who brings the political aspects of the papacy more to the fore.

(Al.Be.)

Urban Climates

The climates of most large urban areas differ from those of their rural surroundings and, appropriately, are designated urban climates. High concentrations of such pollutants as sulfur oxides, nitrogen oxides, hydrocarbons, particulate matter, carbon monoxide, and oxidants are becoming more and more characteristic of the atmosphere over large cities throughout the world. Differences of air temperature, atmospheric humidity, wind speed and direction, precipitation, and visibility also distinguish urban climates from surrounding rural climates.

Man has changed his immediate climate from that of the natural state by the activity of industry and the populace, alterations in the physical features of the city terrain, and the introduction of foreign materials into the atmosphere. The heat generated by combustion for energy production, for example, is largely responsible for warmer urban temperatures. The presence of tall buildings, paved streets, and parking lots affects the wind flow and energy balance of a city, as well as precipitation runoff. Although they constitute only a fraction of the total land area of the earth, metropolitan areas nevertheless emit the bulk of all the air pollutants, and these pollutants can and do influence temperature, visibility, and precipitation, as well as other climatic elements.

Of increasing concern is the extent to which the urban atmosphere influences both the life within it and the larger scale climate with which it interacts. The warmer city temperatures can cause greater death rates for urban residents during summer heat waves; air pollution frequently causes eye irritation and respiratory illness, and other problems are known or suspected. Certain plants are susceptible to damage from ozone, a photochemically produced pollutant, for example, and such materials as house paint and fabrics are often damaged by air pollutants. The pollutants emitted into the atmosphere can also affect the environment on a global scale. Most prominent in this regard is the background concentration of carbon dioxide in the atmosphere; it directly influences world climate and has been increasing steadily during the past century as a result of the burning of fossil fuels.

This article treats the elements of urban climate and describes the various air pollutants. A discussion of possible ways in which man's activities may be affecting climate on a global scale also is presented. For an overview of climate and its meteorological basis in general, see CLIMATE; WINDS AND STORMS; see also MICROCLIMATES, which covers the climate near the ground, and the separate articles on climate elements (*e.g.*, HUMIDITY, ATMOSPHERIC; PRECIPITATION).

ELEMENTS OF URBAN CLIMATE

Air temperature. Of all the urban–rural meteorological differences, those of air temperature are probably the most documented. That the centre of a city is warmer than its environs, forming a "heat island," has been known for more than a hundred years; two main processes are involved in its formation, both of which depend on the season. In summer, the buildings, pavement, and con-

Formation of heat islands

Elected pope

crete of the city absorb and store larger amounts of solar radiation than do the vegetation and soil typical of rural areas. In addition, less of this energy is used for evaporation in the city than in the country because of the large amount of precipitation runoff from streets and buildings. During the night, both the city and countryside cool by radiative losses, but the urban construction material gradually gives off the additional heat accumulated during the day, keeping urban air warmer than that of the outlying areas.

In winter a different process dominates. Because the sun angle at midlatitudes is low, and lesser amounts of solar radiation reach the earth, man-made energy significantly augments the solar energy naturally received. This artificially produced heat results from such sources as combustion for home heating, power generation, industry, transportation, and human and animal metabolism. This energy reaches and warms the urban atmosphere directly, or indirectly by passing through imperfectly insulated homes and buildings.

Besides these primary seasonal causes of heat islands, another factor is important throughout the year. The "blanket" of pollutants over a city, including particles, water vapour, and carbon dioxide, absorbs a portion of the upward-directed thermal radiation emitted by the earth's surface. Part of this radiation is re-emitted by the pollutants; another part warms the ambient (surrounding) air, a process that tends to increase the low-level atmospheric stability over the city, enhancing the probability of higher pollutant concentrations. Thus, airborne pollutants not only can cause a more intense heat island but can alter the vertical temperature structure in a way that hinders their own dispersion.

Urban-rural temperature differences

Daily minimum temperatures at related rural and urban sites often show the urban site to be 6° C (10° F) warmer than the rural site, and occasionally this difference is as great as 11° C (20° F). These nighttime temperatures are dependent on the topography of the site and its surroundings, however, and some significant fraction of these differences can often be ascribed to terrain features.

The greatest mean-temperature differences occur in summer or early autumn, but the greatest extreme city-country difference usually occurs in winter. For large, relatively flat cities, such as London or Washington, D.C., the mean annual minimum temperature is about 2° C (about 3° to 4° F) warmer than that of the surrounding rural areas. This difference is less for smaller cities.

Diurnal and seasonal heat-island variations are illustrated by the hour by hour monthly average of temperatures at an urban and a suburban site in Vienna (Figure 1). The city's nighttime temperature is higher during both February and July, with the greatest urban–rural

difference in July. In the daytime, however, the city–suburban temperature differences are small during July and consistently small and positive during winter.

The heat island of a city can be detected during the day but much less readily than during the evening. The slight daytime temperature differences observed are often difficult to distinguish from those due to topographic differences. In some instances, daytime city temperatures may even be lower than those of the suburbs. City and airport observations at Lincoln, Nebraska, which is essentially free from complicating terrain factors, showed little difference between the cold-season daily maximum temperatures at the two sites. During the warm season, however, the airport was frequently warmer than the downtown site. Such results are not the rule, and data from such diverse cities as London, Toronto; San Jose, California; Dallas, Texas; Minneapolis, Minnesota; and Winnipeg, Manitoba, have shown that the city's warmest sector, near the downtown or central area, averages about 0.5° C (about 1° F) warmer than its environs.

A city's warmest temperatures at ground level often do not occur in the central section of tall buildings, but rather just outside the central area, near that part of downtown that frequently consists of parking lots and densely packed three- to five-story buildings. A map of daily maximum temperatures over a city frequently resembles a doughnut, with cooler temperatures in the hole and outside the doughnut.

As a general rule, the larger the city, the greater is the average difference between its temperature and that of the surrounding countryside. The annual urban–rural temperature difference for large cities such as Washington, D.C., Paris, Moscow, Berlin, and New York averages about 1° C (about 1.5° to 2.0° F). The relation between city size and urban–rural temperature difference is not linear, however; sizable nocturnal-temperature contrasts have been measured even in such relatively small cities as Palo Alto, California (population 33,000 at the time of survey), Corvallis, Oregon (population 21,000), and Ina, Japan (population 12,000). On the other hand, during daytime hours the magnitude of the heat island is small in such small communities. Effects of city size and population

General relationships have been developed between heat-island magnitude and some parameter representing city size, such as area, population, or building density. The heat-island magnitude at a given location often depends strongly on the local microclimatic conditions, however. Data from several English towns have shown that the strength of the local heat island strongly depends upon the density of urban development very near the observation point, sometimes within a radius of 500 metres (1,650 feet).

Rural nighttime temperatures, through the lowest several hundred feet of the atmosphere, are frequently coldest at the ground and warmest at the top of this layer, a "temperature inversion." When such an inversion occurs, this part of the atmosphere becomes very stable, and the dispersion of pollutants is inhibited. In large cities, however, the heat released by man's activities warms the air and retards the formation of surface-based inversions. In contrast to rural areas, air temperature usually decreases with height through the lowest few hundred feet over large cities. Vertical temperature distribution

The magnitude of an urban heat island depends on various meteorological parameters in addition to city size. The urban–rural nighttime-temperature contrasts, for example, are greatest when wind speeds are low and skies clear. The meteorological parameter most significantly related to heat-island magnitude, however, is the nearby rural, low-level, temperature lapse rate (vertical gradient). Heat islands tend to be greatest when pronounced ground-based inversions exist and least when air temperature decreases rapidly with height. This relationship results because the heat added to the atmosphere by the city serves to warm the atmosphere near the ground and, by convection, to warm higher layers of the atmosphere. For a given amount of heat added by the city, the greatest surface-temperature increase occurs when this added heat is distributed through a small layer of the atmo-

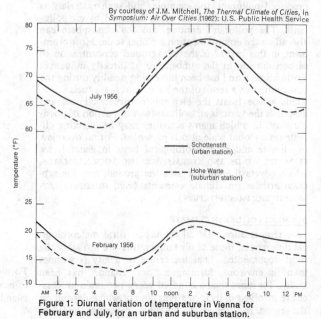

By courtesy of J.M. Mitchell, *The Thermal Climate of Cities*, in *Symposium: Air Over Cities* (1962); U.S. Public Health Service

Schottenstift (urban station)

Hohe Warte (suburban station)

July 1956

February 1956

temperature (°F)

AM 12   2   4   6   8   10 noon 2   4   6   8   10 12 PM

Figure 1: Diurnal variation of temperature in Vienna for February and July, for an urban and suburban station.

sphere (when a strong temperature inversion is present); the least urban-temperature increase occurs when air temperature decreases rapidly with height, so added heat is distributed through a large atmospheric layer.

Humidity. The average relative humidity in towns is usually several percent lower than that of nearby rural areas, whereas the average absolute humidity is only slightly lower in built-up regions. The main reason to expect differences in the humidity of urban and rural areas is that markedly different surfaces lead to a lower evaporation rate in a city than in the country. The countryside is covered with vegetation, which retains rainfall, whereas the floor of a city is coated with concrete, asphalt, and other impervious materials that cause rapid runoff of precipitation. Although the city's low evaporation rates result from the shortage of available water and the lack of vegetation for evapotranspiration, some moisture is added to urban atmospheres by the many combustion sources. Usually the addition is through chimneys at a height somewhat above ground level.

Variations of relative humidity within metropolitan areas resemble those of temperature because the temperature changes of a city are significantly greater than changes in vapour pressure. Thus, because of the heat island, relative humidities in a city are lower than in suburbs and outlying districts. The humidity differences are greatest at night and in summer, corresponding to the time of greatest heat-island intensity. Data from several cities, including Tokyo and London, have shown that a relative-humidity difference of about 5 percent is common between downtown and rural sites.

Wind. The flow of wind over a city differs in several aspects from that over the open countryside. Two features that represent deviations from the regional wind-flow patterns are the differences in wind speeds in city and country and the convergence of low-level wind over a city. These differences occur because the surface of a built-up city is much rougher than that of rural terrain—causing increased frictional drag on air flowing over it—and because the heat island of a city causes horizontal thermal gradients, especially near the city periphery. The excess heat and friction also produce more turbulence over the urban area. The annual mean surface wind speed over a city has been estimated to be 20 to 30 percent lower than that over the nearby countryside, the speed of extreme gusts to be 10 to 20 percent lower, and the calms to be 5 to 20 percent more frequent.

Turbulence over urban areas

A difficulty in estimating urban–rural wind differences is selecting representative sites within the city from which to take measurements. Most observations of urban wind flow have been made either from the roofs of downtown buildings, usually several stories high, or from parks or open spaces. Very few data have been obtained at street level in the city centre, the place where most human activity occurs. These measurements are generally representative, however, and can be useful for urban–rural comparisons.

The conventional measurements do not provide data on the fine-scale wind-flow patterns that are often important in the diffusion of pollutants very near their source. Even an isolated building increases turbulence in the atmosphere both in its lee and immediately upwind. The wind-flow direction near the ground for some distance in the lee of the building is actually opposite of that away from the building. Furthermore, wind direction in the "canyons" of the downtown section of most major cities usually parallels the street orientation, regardless of the direction of the natural wind flow. This channelling of the wind is also frequently observed naturally within straight, narrow valleys.

Past research on the direction of wind flow over urban areas has been primarily concerned with detecting and measuring a surface flow in toward the urban complex. It has been surmised that, if a city is warmer than its environs, the warm city air should rise and be displaced by cooler rural air. This inflow is weak, however, and occurs only in conjunction with well-developed heat islands, which in turn are dependent on certain meteorological conditions. Direct measurements of the inflow require a

coordinated set of accurate observations, and few such investigations have been made. One such study was made at Frankfurt am Main, Germany, where during clear, calm nights an inflow toward the city centre was detected. When the large-scale surface wind speed reached three to four metres (ten to 13 feet) per second, however, a local city-circulation was prevented.

Two indirect techniques have been used to investigate the low-level convergence of wind flow over a city: the observation of smoke plumes from household chimneys and measurement of rime ice, which forms on the windward side of tree trunks. The thickness of the rime ice has been found to be proportional to wind speed around the periphery of Asahikawa, Japan (Figure 2). Local

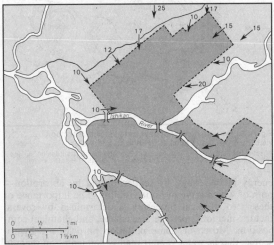

Adapted from T. Okita, "Estimation of Direction of Air Flow from Observation of Rime Ice," *Journal of the Meteorological Society of Japan*, vol. 38 (1960); Meteorological Society of Japan

Figure 2: The direction of wind flow around Asahikawa, Japan, February 26, 1956, as deduced from formation of rime ice on tree trunks. Arrows represent wind direction and numerical values refer to ice thickness.

wind-flow patterns can therefore be deduced; when the large-scale wind flow is weak, a convergence occurred.

Solar radiation. The blanket of particulates in the atmosphere over most large cities causes the solar energy that reaches urban areas to be significantly less than that observed in rural areas. The particles are most effective as attenuators of radiation when the sun angle is low because the path length of the radiation passing through the particulate material is dependent on sun elevation. Thus, for a given amount of particles, solar radiation will be reduced by the largest fraction at high-latitude cities and during winter. On the average, the largest cities annually receive 15 to 20 percent less total solar radiation than nearby rural areas. Measurements taken in and around Rotterdam, The Netherlands, show that the city centre received 3 to 6 percent less radiation than the urban fringe and 13 to 17 percent less than the country. Until recently, central London annually received about 270 hours less of bright sunshine than did the surrounding countryside because of the high concentration of atmospheric particles. Other examples of the pollution effect on solar radiation have been obtained by comparing records of radiation received on weekdays with those of Sundays, when man's activities are at a minimum.

Reduction of sunshine in cities

The introduction of smoke controls in London during the mid-1950s has afforded an opportunity to study the relationship between solar radiation and atmospheric particles. In general, the income of solar radiation and the frequency of bright sunshine in London have increased markedly in recent years, since implementation of the air-pollution laws. During the period 1958 to 1967, the average number of hours of bright sunshine from November through January was 50 percent greater than that observed from 1931 to 1960.

Visibility. Increased concentrations of particles usually characterize the atmosphere of metropolitan areas; consequently, visibilities are lower within a city than beyond its limits. These particles attenuate visible solar

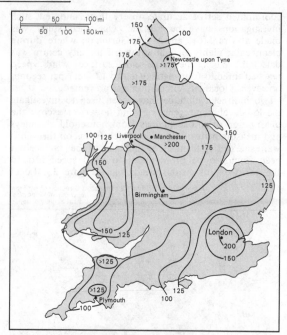

Figure 3: Average number of days per year with afternoon visibilities less than 6¼ miles in England and Wales.
Adapted from L.P. Smith, "Frequencies of Poor Afternoon Visibilities in England and Wales," 1923–51, *Meteorological Magazine*, vol. 90 (1961) HMSO; London

cause combustion sources add to the amount of water vapour in the atmosphere, higher temperatures intensify thermal convection, greater surface roughness increases mechanical turbulence, and the urban atmosphere contains greater concentrations of particles effective as ice nuclei. On the other hand, the higher concentrations of cloud condensation nuclei and very high concentrations of ice nuclei in a city's atmosphere may cause less precipitation. The relative significance of these parameters is not easy to establish because the few studies of urban precipitation have not included their continuous, quantitative measurement. Data from Europe and North America suggest, however, that the amount of precipitation over many large cities is about 5 to 10 percent greater than that over nearby country areas, with the greatest increases occurring downwind of the city centre.

An example of the distribution of precipitation around a Midwestern American city that is free of complicating topography is shown in Figure 4. The mean summer

Stanley A. Changnon, Jr., Illinois State Water Survey

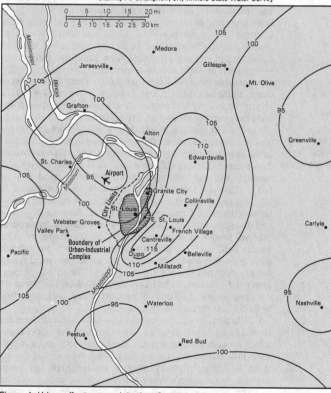

Figure 4: Urban effect on precipitation, St. Louis, Missouri. Contours represent relative values of annual rainfall; points that fall along the 110 contour line receive 10 percent more rainfall than points along the 100 contour line. Downwind (east) of the city the mean rainfall exceeds that of the built-up area by more than 15 percent.

Increase of fog frequency

energy in two ways, by scattering and by absorption—both of which serve to limit visibility. The importance of these two physical processes is determined by several factors, including particle size, shape, and chemical composition. Moreover, some pollution particles are hygroscopic; that is, water vapour readily condenses on them to form small water droplets, the ingredients of fog. By this process, a small dust particle becomes a much larger water droplet, which, because of its size, is a much more effective attenuator of solar energy. Water vapour condenses on some hygroscopic pollution particles at relative humidities as low as 70 percent; it condenses on many such particles at 90 percent relative humidity. Thus, urban visibilities are often less than those of nearby rural areas because of higher concentrations of dust particles and greater frequencies of fog. Industrial areas, such as those near London and in Manchester, Lancashire, report about twice as many days with low visibilities as occur in rural areas (Figure 3).

Fog generally occurs more frequently within metropolitan areas than the nearby countryside; this is not true for very dense fog, however. Apparently the extra warmth of a city often reduces the relative humidity and prevents the thickest fogs from reaching the densities reported in outlying districts. Table 1 shows the number of hours per year of the various-density fogs occurring in the vicinity of London.

Visibility in some communities has actually improved during the last two decades in response to local efforts at air-pollution abatement and the substitution of cleaner burning oil and gas for soft coal. London is notable in that respect, and several cities in the United States have shown similar improvement.

Precipitation. A city also influences the occurrence and amount of precipitation in its vicinity. An urban complex might be expected to increase precipitation be-

rainfall around St. Louis, Missouri, for the years 1949–68 is presented as a percentage of the mean amount for the built-up urban and industrial area. Immediately east, or downwind, of the city is a large region over which the mean rainfall exceeds that of the built-up area; the largest excess is more than 15 percent. Elsewhere around St. Louis, the summertime average precipitation is generally within 5 percent of that of the built-up region.

Table 1: Fog Frequencies in London

	hours per year with visibilities less than			
	130 feet (40 metres)	650 feet (200 metres)	1,300 feet (400 metres)	3,300 feet (1,000 metres)
Kingsway (central)	19	126	230	940
Kew (inner suburbs)	79	213	365	633
London Airport (outer suburbs)	46	209	304	562
Southeast England (mean of seven stations)	20	177	261	494

Urban air pollution photographed on two consecutive days in New York City.
By courtesy of the National Air Pollution Control Administration, Maryland; photographs, the *New York Daily News*

Factors
that
complicate
analysis
of urban
rainfall

Several difficulties have limited the number of detailed studies of the distribution of precipitation around metropolitan areas, such as that for St. Louis. Few rural areas remain undisturbed from their natural state, and many cities are associated with bodies of water or hilly terrain that affect the patterns of precipitation. Moreover, there are few urban areas that have many rain gauges with long-term records and uniform exposure throughout the period of record. Finally, the natural variability of rainfall, particularly the summer showers of mid-America, further complicates the analysis of urban–rural precipitation differences. The record from Central Park, New York City, illustrates the general difficulty of rainfall analysis. A statistically significant decreasing trend of precipitation of 0.3 inch per year was observed for this area from 1927 to 1965. Data from other nearby sites did not substantiate this trend, and, in fact, at Battery Place (the nearest measurement station) a small rainfall increase was observed during the same period.

Urban areas produce large amounts of heat that cause a warming of the atmosphere near the earth's surface and in turn may lead to increased vertical motions within the atmosphere. The buildings in a city, both large and small, present obstacles to a smooth flow of wind. This greater "surface roughness" causes greater turbulence of the urban wind flow and increases the likelihood of vertical atmospheric motions. The greater tendency for rising air over a city because of the added heat and roughness, together with the added possibility of atmospheric water vapour from combustion sources, increases the likelihood of precipitation in a metropolitan region.

Urban areas are a prolific source of cloud condensation nuclei, and these, theoretically, can lead to a decrease in rainfall. The concentration of continental condensation nuclei in the lower atmosphere is naturally only a few hundred per cubic centimetre of air. Consequently, when water vapour condenses within the atmosphere to form a cloud, the available water is shared by relatively few nuclei, and large waterdrops result. Downwind of and within urban areas, however, where cloud condensation nuclei concentrations often exceed 1,000 per cubic centimetre, the same amount of available water forms many small droplets. This inhibits the coalescence mechanism of rainfall development, which depends upon the presence of some large drops within a cloud. The large drops will fall by gravity, collect other drops as they do fall, and thereby grow large enough to fall to the ground.

Ice nuclei also are an important factor in cloud and precipitation development. If these nuclei are present at the right time and place within clouds that contain supercooled water droplets, they can augment the growth of the clouds and their ability to produce precipitation. Too great a concentration of these nuclei can result in too many ice crystals within a cloud, however, and, as in the case of condensation nuclei, inhibit the formation of raindrops large enough to fall from the cloud. Certain human activities produce ice nuclei; a particularly good source is steel mills. The lead particles in automobile exhaust also are effective ice nuclei when combined with atmospheric iodine to form lead iodide. Although the amount of iodine in the atmosphere is apparently quite small, this mechanism represents a great potential for the modification of metropolitan ice-nucleus counts and the corresponding precipitation patterns because of the large amount of automobile traffic.

Ice nuclei
produced
by
automo-
bile
exhaust

POLLUTION

The most common air pollutants of urban atmospheres are such substances as carbon dioxide, carbon monoxide, sulfur dioxide, hydrocarbons, nitrogen oxides, ozone, and particles that originate from such sources as automobile exhaust, industrial processes, fuel combustion for electrical-power generation, burning of wastes, and photochemical reactions. Nearly every urban area can attribute a significant monetary loss to the adverse effect of these pollutants on human health, vegetation, such materials as rubber and house paint, and visibility.

Two important factors that determine the concentration of a pollutant within an urban area are the magnitude of the local emission sources of that pollutant and prevailing meteorological conditions. The meteorological parameters that specify the "ventilation" of an area are the height of the atmospheric layer through which pollutants are being mixed and the average wind speed through that layer. These parameters are usually least favourable for pollutant dispersion from sunset, throughout the evening, until just after sunrise. The observed urban concentrations of pollutants the major source of which is automobile exhaust frequently have two maxima each 24 hours, during the early-morning and late-afternoon peak-traffic periods. In general, the morning concentrations are greater than those of the afternoon because of less favourable atmospheric dispersion at that time. At infrequent intervals, meteorological conditions conducive to the accumu-

Concentra-
tion of
pollutants
and fatal
episodes

lation of pollutants will persist over an area for several days. These episodes are usually characterized by temperature inversions (temperature increases with height), which strongly inhibit atmospheric mixing. Three of the worst such past episodes, resulting in loss of life, occurred at the Meuse Valley, Belgium (1930), Donora, Pennsylvania (1948), and London (1952). During the Donora incident, 43 percent of the local population reported illness; at London, about 4,000 people died as a result of several days of high pollutant concentrations.

Carbon dioxide. Carbon dioxide (CO_2) is an important constituent of the atmosphere because of its influence on global climate. The background concentration of this substance has been increasing for more than a century, mainly as a result of the burning of fossil fuels. It is now slightly over 320 parts per million (ppm) by volume. Concentrations are higher over urban areas, and they show a strong diurnal and seasonal dependence. During summer, green plants convert carbon dioxide to oxygen by photosynthesis during daytime, whereas decomposition and respiration of organic matter produces carbon dioxide continuously. During winter, plant growth and organic decomposition are minimal, and little diurnal variation occurs in near-surface atmospheric carbon dioxide concentrations.

Carbon monoxide. Carbon monoxide (CO) is a highly toxic, but nonirritating (colourless, odourless, tasteless) gas with a natural background concentration of about 0.1 part per million. A major source of pollutant carbon monoxide is the emissions from internal-combustion engines. In fact, vehicle exhaust accounts for about 60 percent of all the pollutant carbon monoxide released in the United States, and in many cities the mass of carbon monoxide annually emitted exceeds that of any other pollutant. The highest urban concentrations are usually found where automobile traffic is heaviest, and the daily concentration variations over most cities show a bimodal distribution, reflecting usual weekday traffic patterns. Typical urban concentrations for large cities range from five to ten parts per million; the maximum observed concentrations are about ten times as great. Although even the highest concentrations of carbon monoxide observed today appear to have no effect on vegetation or materials, this substance has a notably detrimental effect on human health. Large dosages of carbon monoxide can cause death, but even exposure to concentrations as small as ten to 15 parts per million for eight hours have been shown to affect time-interval discrimination in nonsmoking adults.

Sulfur dioxide. Sulfur dioxide (SO_2) is a common gaseous pollutant in nearly all cities. More than 75 percent of all the pollutant sulfur dioxide in the United States is caused by the combustion of coal and petroleum products; about 40 percent results from electrical-power generation alone. Sulfur dioxide is a relatively short-lived atmospheric pollutant because it is readily oxidized to sulfur trioxide (SO_3) and finally to sulfuric acid mist and sulfate particles. This characteristic oxidation, coupled with a very low natural background concentration and variable meteorological conditions, causes a wide range of sulfur dioxide concentrations to be observed over urban areas. Typical concentrations for large cities range from 0.01 to 0.1 part per million; only occasionally do observed concentrations exceed one part per million. High concentrations of sulfur dioxide can affect human health, visibility, materials, and vegetation. A mean concentration of 0.04 part per million for a year or 0.11 part per million for three to four days can be detrimental to human health; an annual mean concentration of 0.03 part per million can damage vegetation. As these adverse effects of sulfur dioxide have become documented and air-pollution regulations have been tightened many electric utility companies and other industries have begun using fuel with low sulfur content to reduce sulfur dioxide emissions. Reliable, economical techniques to control emissions of sulfur dioxide from smokestacks have not been available generally.

Hydrocarbons. A class of pollutants known as hydrocarbons is composed of hundreds of individual organic compounds made up of atoms of hydrogen and carbon. Methane is the most common hydrocarbon and usually represents more than 50 percent of the total. Other common constituents are such compounds as ethane, propane, acetylene, butane, and ethylene. Motor vehicles are the source of roughly one-half of all the hydrocarbon emissions, and consequently the diurnal variation of observed concentrations exhibits a morning and late-afternoon peak. Typical urban concentrations are a few parts per million. Hydrocarbons themselves apparently have no adverse effect on human health, but the nonmethane fraction is important in photochemical reactions. In the presence of sunlight, hydrocarbons will combine with oxides of nitrogen to produce photochemical oxidants, including ozone, which are harmful to human health.

Nitrogen oxides. Within the oxides of the nitrogen group of air pollutants, nitric oxide (NO) and nitrogen dioxide (NO_2) occur most frequently. Nitric oxide is commonly formed during high temperature combustion. In nearly every city, the source of at least 50 percent of all the nitric oxide emissions is automobile exhaust. Nitrogen dioxide is formed both by combustion and within the atmosphere when nitric oxide combines with oxygen. At low nitric oxide concentrations this atmospheric reaction proceeds slowly, but in the presence of sunlight and hydrocarbons nitrogen dioxide is formed rapidly. In the Los Angeles area, characterized by heavy automobile traffic and much sunlight, nitrogen dioxide is primarily responsible for the brownish colour of the local smog. Both nitric oxide and nitrogen dioxide are short-lived pollutants without any global accumulation because of their ability to participate in atmospheric reactions. In Los Angeles, concentrations of nitrogen dioxide occasionally have exceeded one part per million, but concentrations of 0.1 part per million to 0.3 part per million are more typical. Observed concentrations of nitric oxide apparently have no direct adverse effects, but concentrations of nitrogen dioxide greater than one part per million can affect both human health and sensitive plants. Furthermore, these pollutants play a vital role in the formation of photochemical oxidants.

Oxidants. The group of pollutants called photochemical oxidants is defined as that class of substances that will oxidize certain substances not readily oxidized by oxygen. Ozone (O_3) is the main constituent of the group, which also includes peroxyacetyl nitrate (PAN), and in terms of vegetation damage is the most harmful of all pollutants. Photochemical oxidants are the products of atmospheric reactions involving hydrocarbons, oxides of nitrogen, and sunlight. Because sunlight is necessary for these reactions, maximum oxidant concentrations usually occur around noon, whereas during nighttime, concentrations are quite low. In the Los Angeles area, the highest concentrations occur in late summer and fall; one-hour average values may then exceed 0.5 part per million during episodes of high air pollution. Average hourly concentrations exceeding 0.07 part per million have been shown to impair the performance of student athletes; instantaneous oxidant concentrations of about 0.1 part per million have been associated with eye irritation. Sensitive vegetation has been adversely affected by exposure to concentrations of 0.05 part per million for four hours.

Particles. In addition to the gaseous pollutants, large quantities of solid material, generally referred to as particulate matter, or particles, are emitted into the atmosphere over urban complexes. These man-made emissions are superimposed on a natural continental background concentration of about 20×10^{-6} gram of particles per cubic metre of air (one cubic metre equals 35.05 cubic feet). Natural particles are composed of such materials as sea salt, windblown dust from the earth's surface, and volcanic ejecta. The sources of atmospheric particulate matter resulting from man's activities include both particles directly emitted into the atmosphere and those formed within the atmosphere from conversion of gaseous pollutants to particles, including sulfur dioxide, oxides of nitrogen, and hydrocarbons. The main sources of directly emitted particles are internal-combustion engines (automobiles), industrial processes, refuse incineration,

Relation to automobile traffic *(margin note)*

Need for low-sulfur coal *(margin note)*

Role of sunlight in creation of smog *(margin note)*

Source and concentrations of particulate matter *(margin note)*

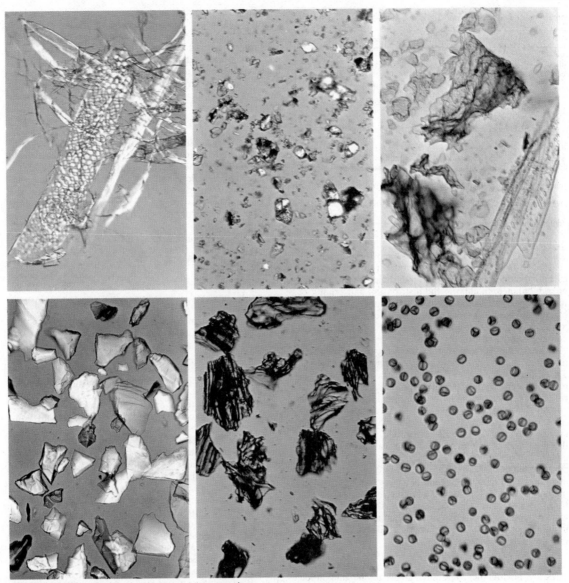

Photomicrographs of particulate pollutants of the atmosphere.
(Top left) Hardwood pulp (magnified 70 ×); (top centre) cement (magnified 70 ×); (top right)
coffee grounds (magnified 70 ×); (bottom left) quartz (magnified 35 ×); (bottom centre)
pumice (magnified 35 ×); (bottom right) ragweed pollen (magnified 60 ×).
From (top left and bottom left) W.C. McCrone, R.G. Draftz, and J.G. Delly, *The Particle Atlas*, reproduced by
permission of Ann Arbor Science Publishers, Inc.; photographs, Walter C. McCrone Associates, Inc.

and fuel combustion for electrical-energy production and heat. Typical concentrations of particulate matter in the centre of large cities are about 200×10^{-6} gram per cubic metre; higher concentrations are often found near heavy industrial areas. Particles collected over urban areas have a widely varied chemistry; nitrates, sulfates, organic material, and many elements, including iron, lead, zinc, manganese, copper, nickel, and carbon, have all been commonly identified. Both the natural and man-made particles are removed from the atmosphere primarily by sedimentation (large particles fall to the earth by gravitational attraction) and washout by rain and snow. The smaller ones may be carried many miles by the prevailing wind patterns, however. Natural dust blown from the surface of the Sahara during the summer, for example, is transported westward by the trade winds and can frequently be detected in the West Indies, several thousand miles away.

Both natural and man-made atmospheric particles near the earth's surface vary greatly in size. Particles will coexist with radii between about 10^{-7} to 10^{-2} centimetre (one inch equals 2.5 centimetres). Very few of the larger particles are present in the atmosphere, but the number increases rapidly at progressively smaller sizes. Most particles are usually about 10^{-6} to 10^{-5} centimetre in size. The smallest particles (10^{-6} centimetre and smaller) can

affect human health because this size will remain in the respiratory tract once it enters. Those with sizes between about 10^{-5} and 10^{-4} centimetre attenuate visible solar radiation most effectively and thus have a significant effect on visibility. The larger particles may act as cloud condensation nuclei and thereby influence fog formation.

Table 2 summarizes the principal atmospheric pollutants in terms of the characteristics of London and Los Angeles types of smog. London pollution features particulate matter, the presence of sulfur compounds from combustion of coal and petroleum, and very low visibilities. The major source of the Los Angeles type of pollution is automobile exhaust; through photochemical reactions, the exhaust products are transformed into oxidants, particularly ozone, which can cause eye irritation and damage to vegetation.

EFFECTS OF MAN'S ACTIVITIES ON GLOBAL CLIMATE

Man's ability to alter his environment is a recognized aspect of the modern world. Some of the local effects of atmospheric pollution, which have been previously discussed, are obvious to the inhabitants of urban areas. A more subtle aspect of air pollution may be the long-term modification of climate, particularly on a global scale, brought about by a worldwide buildup of pollutants. This section will indicate some of the ways in which man

Ways in
which man
may affect
climate

Table 2: Comparison of Los Angeles and London Smog

	Los Angeles	London
Air temperature	24° to 32° C	−1° to 4° C
Relative humidity	less than 70 percent	85 percent (plus fog)
Type of temperature inversion	subsidence	radiation (near ground)
Wind speed	less than 3 metres per second	calm
Visibility	less than 0.8 to 1.6 kilometres	less than 30 metres
Months of most frequent occurrence	August–September	December–January
Major fuels	petroleum	coal and petroleum products
Principal constituents	O_3, NO, NO_2, CO, organic matter	particulate matter, CO, S compounds
Type of chemical reactions	oxidative	reductive
Time of maximum occurrence	midday	early morning
Principal health effects	temporary eye irritation	bronchial irritation; coughing

may inadvertently be modifying his climate on a large scale as a result of his activities, most of which are centred in urban areas. These include: (1) the effects of carbon dioxide and atmospheric particles on the earth's energy balance, modifying the distribution and quality of radiant energy; (2) the effect of particles in the form of condensation and ice nuclei on the precipitation mechanisms; and (3) the effect of the heat produced by man's activities on the global energy balance.

No study has yet shown that the large-scale global climate has been significantly affected by man's activities. The climate within an urban area has been demonstrated to be different from that which would have existed naturally, but man's role in altering continental or larger scale climate has not been proved. This inconclusiveness results because the specific cause or causes of climatic change have not yet been determined. Although many theories have been presented, no one can definitively account, for example, for the origin of the glaciers that covered much of North America 10,000 to 15,000 years ago. Similarly, a cooling of the mean surface temperature of the earth by a fraction of a degree has been observed since World War II, but scientists cannot determine whether the cause of this climate change was natural or man-induced or what specific factor produced this change (see further CLIMATIC CHANGE).

Nonetheless, several mechanisms have been proposed to relate man-made pollution to climate. As yet, these theories are not detailed, and such items as the magnitude and specific nature of the change in climate resulting from a given amount of a pollutant remain to be determined. Several of these theories are mentioned below.

Increase of carbon dioxide. The global concentration of carbon dioxide (CO_2) has been steadily increasing since the mid-1800s, mainly as a result of the burning of such fossil fuels as coal and oil. At that time, the concentration of carbon dioxide in the atmosphere was about 290 ppm by volume, whereas in the early 1970s it averages slightly over 320 ppm. Through the mechanism known as the greenhouse effect, carbon dioxide in the atmosphere absorbs thermal infrared radiation emitted by the surface of the earth and re-radiates a portion of it back toward the earth. Thus, as the amount of atmospheric carbon dioxide increases, the average temperature of the earth's surface also increases. This fact—that changes in the amount of carbon dioxide can cause changes in climate—was first suggested in about 1900. Since then, a number of theoretical attempts have been made to relate quantitatively carbon dioxide concentration and the mean temperature of the earth. The conclusion drawn from one theoretical model is that a doubling of carbon dioxide would result in a 2° C (4° F) rise in mean surface temperature. Despite this model's sophistication, it is based on radiative processes alone and does not include the interactions between carbon dioxide and such factors as evaporation and condensation, cloudiness, and the oceans. Consequently, it cannot provide a definitive analysis of the relationship between carbon dioxide and climate. If these results are accepted as indicative of the true effect of carbon dioxide, then the 10

The greenhouse effect and temperature

percent carbon dioxide increase since the end of the 19th century has resulted in an increase of mean, worldwide temperature by only a fraction of a degree centigrade.

Beginning with the International Geophysical Year in 1957, accurate and systematic measurements of carbon dioxide have been made at several widely separated locations. The most frequent and continuous are those at the Hawaiian Volcano Observatory, at 11,150 feet elevation. These observations have shown that since 1958 the carbon dioxide concentration has been steadily increasing at an average rate of about 0.7 ppm (0.2 percent) per year. During this time the total amount of carbon dioxide produced from fossil-fuel consumption has been roughly double the amount that stayed in the atmosphere. The fraction not in the atmosphere has gone into the hydrosphere (the waters of the earth) and the biosphere (the mass of organic matter and living things in all earth environments), the largest component of which is the forests.

These nonatmospheric reservoirs are important in attempts to forecast future carbon dioxide concentrations because changes in the mass of the biosphere or the circulation and mean temperature of the oceans could affect the fraction of carbon dioxide remaining in the atmosphere. If, however, it is assumed that the annual growth rate in the global consumption of fossil fuel is 4 percent and that 50 percent of the released carbon dioxide remains in the atmosphere, a concentration of about 380 ppm can be forecast for the year 2000. This would be an increase of nearly 20 percent from the 1970 concentration. This carbon dioxide increase theoretically corresponds to an increase in mean air temperature of roughly 0.5° C.

Atmospheric particles and recent cooling. From the late 1800s until World War II the mean surface air temperature of the earth increased by about 0.5° C (about 1° F). Many scientists attributed this warming to the gradual increase in carbon dioxide. Since then, however, much of this temperature increase has been offset by a cooling trend. This reversal of the global temperature trend, coincident with increased industrial activity throughout the world, has led to suggestions that the recent cooling trend is a result of the attenuation of solar radiation by atmospheric aerosols. From measurements in large cities it is apparent that particle-laden air can cause a depletion in the amount of total solar radiation received at the city surface. Some of the greatest observed reductions of solar energy, as previously noted, occurred over London and other British cities about 1955, before any significant pollution-abatement actions were undertaken. At that time, attenuation of total solar radiation of 50 percent over the major cities during winter was not uncommon.

The theory that particulate matter in the atmosphere is responsible for the recent global cooling is supported by evidence that the background concentration of atmospheric particles has increased during this century. Measurements of direct solar radiation, which indirectly yield a measure of the atmospheric particle concentration, have shown a trend of decreasing solar intensity and atmospheric transparency at sites throughout the United States, Europe, and the Soviet Union. An upward trend in fine-particle pollution over the north Atlantic Ocean has been inferred from measurements of atmospheric electrical conductivity. These data have been confirmed by direct particle measurements at remote sites throughout the United States during the last decade. Whereas particle concentrations have been rising at remote United States locations, similar observations in urban areas have shown a slight decreasing trend, presumably the result of air-pollution-abatement activity.

Atmospheric particles are not uniform in composition or physical characteristics, and the absorptive and scattering properties of many of them are unknown. Consequently, scientists cannot determine whether the aggregate of particles being emitted into the atmosphere is causing a warming or cooling of the atmosphere. The solution to this problem requires more detailed knowledge of the characteristics of atmospheric particles and a sophisticated mathematical computer model that can accurately simulate the effect of particulate matter on global climate.

Another aspect of weather and climate that possibly can be modified on a large-space scale by man's activities is the distribution and amount of precipitation.

Modification of precipitation

An example of inadvertent precipitation modification was reported in which the smoke particles from the burning of sugarcane fields in Australia were found to be effective condensation nuclei. A subsequent analysis of local climatological records showed that, as the production of cane increased over the years, a 20 percent decrease in precipitation had occurred downwind of the cane-producing areas during the three months of the harvesting season. It was concluded that the local clouds had been stabilized by these smoke particles—the many condensation nuclei present inhibited the formation of large droplets that could fall as rain.

Perhaps the particles in automobile exhaust, particularly the lead particles, have the greatest potential for inadvertent modification of precipitation on a large scale. It has been suggested that, when these lead particles combine with iodine in the atmosphere, the resulting product, lead iodide, is very effective as an ice nucleus. Because of the proliferation of automobiles, this mechanism may be an important influence on both local and large-scale weather when sufficient quantities of iodine are present in the atmosphere.

Thermal energy. Man can also affect world climates when the artificial heat produced by his activities becomes a significant fraction of that received naturally from the sun. Unfortunately, present knowledge of the dynamic interactions between this thermal-energy release and climate is not sufficient to predict accurately just when and how climate will be significantly affected. Man-made heat is known to cause urban heat islands, however, and during winter, when the solar intensity is relatively small, energy produced by man's activities in large metropolitan areas can actually be greater than that naturally received from the sun. On a global scale, the artificially produced energy is an insignificant fraction of that received naturally. If the amount of worldwide waste thermal energy continues to increase at the current rate (about 5.5 to 6 percent per year), it will still not be of global climatic significance in the year 2000. But, if this growth in energy consumption continues indefinitely into the future, it undoubtedly will affect global climate eventually. Using a crude model and tenuous projections of future energy consumption, it has been concluded that climate could be significantly altered within several hundred years.

Effects of other activities of man. A number of man's other activities have been suggested as being responsible for or capable of causing global climatic change. First, man may be altering climate on a large scale by changing the surface characteristics of the land and oceans. Converting forests and prairies to agricultural fields, building cities, damming rivers to create lakes, and spilling oil at sea all affect the surface absorption of solar radiation and evaporation of water (see further PHYSIOGRAPHIC EFFECTS OF MAN). These activities can influence climate on a small scale, such as the city heat island, but apparently have a minor effect on global climate. Second, because the amount, type, and distribution of clouds are extremely important factors in regulating worldwide climate, when man significantly alters natural cloudiness, climate will probably also be altered. He can affect cloudiness by such processes as the emissions of cloud and ice nuclei, moisture, heat, and the condensation trails formed by high-flying jet aircraft. Third, the development of supersonic transport (SST) aircraft has been accompanied by controversy concerning the effect that the exhaust products may have on climate. These aircraft emit water vapour, soot particles, and other combustion products in the stratosphere at a height of about 20 kilometres (12 miles), where the diffusion of these substances will be slower—and their lifetime longer—than at lower altitudes. In sufficient quantity the water vapour could increase cloudiness and, through the greenhouse effect, change atmospheric temperatures. The particulate matter

Cloudiness and supersonic aircraft

also could affect climate by attenuation of solar radiation.

BIBLIOGRAPHY. T.J. CHANDLER, *The Climate of London* (1965), a detailed description of the climate of London and its variation with urban morphology; A.C. STERN (ed.), *Air Pollution*, 2nd ed., vol. 1 (1968), an up-to-date discussion of the physical properties, meteorological aspects, and effects of air pollution; STUDY OF CRITICAL ENVIRONMENTAL PROBLEMS (SCEP), *Man's Impact on the Global Environment: Assessment and Recommendations for Action* (1970), a current, comprehensive discussion of the global climatic and ecological effects of man's activities, including recommendations for future study; *Inadvertent Climate Modification, Report of the Study of Man's Impact on Climate* (SMIC), a sequel to the SCEP report, focussing solely on climatic aspects, that provides a very good discussion of basic climate theory and a current analysis of man's impact on climate; WORLD METEOROLOGICAL ORGANIZATION, *Urban Climates* (1970), proceedings of a symposium on urban climates and building climatology; P.A. KRATZER, *Das Stadtklima*, 2nd ed. (1956; Eng. trans., *The Climate of Cities*, 1956), a very thorough discussion of urban climates and a review of the literature to the mid-1950s; J.T. PETERSON, *The Climate of Cities: A Survey of Recent Literature* (1969), a technical survey of the literature on the meteorological aspects of city climate with emphasis on that written during the last decade; R. GEIGER, *Das Klima der bodennahen Luftschicht*, 4th ed. (1961; Eng. trans., *The Climate Near the Ground*, 1965), a thorough treatment of the broader subject of microclimatology, with a discussion of urban climates and references to other urban studies.

(J.T.P.)

Urban Design

Design is the imaginative creation of possible form intended to achieve some human purpose: social, economic, aesthetic, or technical. One can design a garden, the layout of a book, a fireworks display, a drainage channel. Urban design deals with the form of possible urban environments. Urban designers work on three different kinds of task: (1) Project design, which is concerned with the form of a definite geographic area in which there is a definite client, a concrete program, a foreseeable time of completion, and effective control over the significant aspects of the form; housing projects, shopping centres, and parks are examples. (2) System design, which considers the form of a functionally connected set of objects. These may be distributed over extensive areas, are built or managed by one agency, but do not make a complete environment. A highway network, a lighting system, and a set of standardized signs provide examples. (3) City or regional design, in which there are multiple clients, indeterminate programs, partial control, and constant change. Regional land-use policies, the formation of new towns, and the rehabilitation of older urban districts are examples of this kind of design. In emphasizing the direct human impact of the environment, it must be noted that design is not solely concerned with any single influence of form.

Three aspects of urban design

This article is outlined as follows:

I. Modern practice

FAILURES OF URBAN DESIGN

Many examples of magnificent buildings, gardens, or bridges may be cited. It is far harder to find cases of fine complete environments, particularly in the modern world. There are a few residential areas of moderate scale that are comfortable, workable, and handsome. There is an equally small number of well-designed urban centres.

Large planned settlements of distinguished form are quite rare; Tapiola in Finland and Vällingby in Sweden are among the few. But planned, ugly and inhuman places, formless suburbs, gray city districts, and industrial wastelands are endless.

Toni Schneiders

Pedestrian centre, Vällingby, Sweden.

Toni Schneiders

Distinguished historical, unplanned areas are much easier to find. Most texts on landscape or urban design are illustrated with views of historic cities, old farming regions, or primitive or wilderness areas. The apparently unplanned squatter settlement, or the old urban district, can have more visual warmth and interest than the newest designed suburb or apartment project.

Explanations of design failures

There are a number of possible explanations. One is that a fine landscape will only develop in time, as historical meaning accumulates, and form and culture come to a close rubbed fit. If so, the best that can be done is to conserve the past, while producing technically workable settings today in the hope that they will acquire character for later generations. If true, it is discouraging for a generation committed to building more urban environment than already exists.

The difficulty may be one of scale and control: that good environments are the direct products of their users, or of professionals who have an exact knowledge of user requirements and values. Superb houses are designed, but not superb housing projects, which are designed for people en masse. Or the true reason may be more profound—that environments reflect the state of society. The crisis of environmental quality arose with the Industrial Revolution, which looked on space and people as resources to be used. That crisis can only be surmounted by a radical change in society, and technical innovations will be of small account.

A possible solution may be the resolve to spend greater resources on quality, but while it is true that such efforts are often starved for funds, some very expensive projects are equally inhuman. And many areas of the world are too hard pressed to be able to allocate economic resources specifically to fine environment.

A final explanation for failure is the technical one: that large-scale environmental design is simply very new, and that urban designers have yet to learn their trade. Good environments were made piecemeal, because that was the only way in which they could be produced in the past. Good ones are not made now, because no one has mastered the new scale of intervention. There have been some successes in planned environments and there may be some hope in increased technical skill. But it will not be effective on any substantial scale unless it is linked to changes in values and in society.

Urban design is effected by many kinds of professionals and decision makers, sometimes consciously, often inadvertently. Those who call themselves urban designers are most likely to be men with architectural or landscape backgrounds, working as parts of much larger teams. For the most part they do project design: shopping centres, housing projects, parks, expositions, universities, medical or government centres, urban renewal sites, and large suburbs. Their employers are large investors and real estate developers, or public development authorities.

Urban designers tend to be found in one of three kinds of organizations. One is the large architectural planning and consulting firm which develops complete projects for their clients from market studies, through programming, financial and legal planning, physical design and engineering, to working drawings and field supervision. They are also employed within public or private agencies that are actually building and managing a piece of the environment. Finally, urban designers may be found in area governments, particularly at the city level, where they regulate the design of public and private projects.

The professional urban designer is distant from the ultimate user, and often at odds with the other actors in the decision-making process. The designer may only implement decisions already made, or may wield substantial power, because of his personal prestige and his ability to frame the terms of debate about spatial alternatives. But his concerns are usually seen as skills to be applied after a basic program is fixed and are thus rarely well meshed into the web of decision. Many other professionals and decision-makers shape the city environment, with far more aggregate effect, most often without conscious consideration for environmental quality. Engineers design roads, bridges, and other major features. Real estate developers create substantial districts. Economic planners set resource allocations. Lawyers and administrators frame tax regulations and municipal codes, or set the standards of eligibility for grants. Architects and builders erect single buildings; industrial designers create store fronts, signs, light fixtures, and street furniture. Government departments build and maintain the public ways and put up public buildings. Surveyors lay out subdivisions; utility companies design and install their systems. The manufacturers of standard products, such as light standards or wall panels, have a pervasive effect. Even in Socialist countries, the responsibility for developing and maintaining the city environment is widely fragmented. The man who ultimately suffers or enjoys the product is heard with difficulty.

Fragmentation of urban design

ELEMENTS AND MATERIALS OF URBAN DESIGN

The raw materials from which the urban designer creates his effects are numerous, but the more salient ones may be categorized as follows:

Space. The voids in a landscape are of primary importance, since man is a mobile animal. The urban designer deals with the spaces accessible to the public, both external (streets, parks, squares) and also internal (lobbies, arcades, tunnels, concourses), with their location, scale, and form, as well as the linkages between them. Large spaces, outdoor ones in particular, are often loose in form, and subject to many optical illusions of distance, visual masking, level change, and geometry. Spaces may be enclosed by opaque barriers, or by intermittent walls, or even by visual suggestions: colonnades, bollards, changes in group pattern, breaks in grade, and imaginary extensions. Buildings have been the traditional enclosures of urban space, but outdoor places are rarely completely enclosed, and contemporary spaces are increasingly open and complex.

Spatial character is affected by proportion, or the size of parts relative to each other, and also by scale, or the size in relation to surrounding objects and to the observer. Spaces vary in effect by the way one moves through them, and by the spaces that precede or follow them. Appearance is modified by activity, by the colour and texture of walls and floor, and by the objects with which they are furnished. A deserted square is quite different from a

Complex urban spatial types.
(Top) The Italian piazza. "Piazza Navona," etching by Giambattista Piranesi (1720–78).
(Bottom) The English residential square. "Belgrave Square," lithograph from *Cassell's Old & New London.*
(Top) By courtesy of the Metropolitan Museum of Art, New York; (bottom) The Mansell Collection

busy one. Light can be used effectively to emphasize texture, conceal or reveal a feature, contract or expand spatial dimensions.

Other senses than vision convey the shape of a space, hearing most notably, since echo location is an accurate cue. The smell of a place is part of its identity, and so is its microclimate: it will be remembered as cool and moist, or hot, bright, and windy. All of these can be modified by the design of a place. Spatial forms have symbolic connotations as well: the awesomeness of great size and the interest of diminutive scale; the protection of the cave and the freedom of the prairie.

There is a rich vocabulary of spatial types: the vista, the court, the slot, the maze, the tunnel, the avenue, the canopy, the glade, the meander, the park, the bowl, the crest, the valley, and many others. At a less abstract level, there are complex urban spatial types: the English residential square, the Italian piazza, the formal French place, the parkway, the avenue, the arcade, the waterfront promenade. New social requirements and the creative efforts of designers are evolving new types as well: freeway, subway station, shopping mall, superblock interior, and industrial estate.

Visible activity. While designers traditionally focus on visible space, it is not as prominent to most observers as is the sight and sound of other human beings. Seeing and being seen—observing who is there, what they are doing, and what they intend are permanent attractions. The designer can make activity visible; provide places for meetings, promenades, and celebrations; and can reinforce the conduct and mood of action. Light and distance determine whether faces can be read; sound levels make conversation easy or difficult. The movement of ships and trains, the workings of giant machinery, are as fascinating as fire and water.

Sequences. A landscape is also a network of sequences along the streets, walkways, and transit lines. Any single view is less important than the cumulative effect of a series of views. Coming out of a narrow slot into a broad expanse, for example, is a sure-fire effect. Questions of orientation become significant: the apparent direction toward a goal, the marking of the distance traversed, the clarity of entrance and exit. Each event should prepare for the next. Great cities are known for their walks—a pleasure now often denied. A basic step in urban design is to analyze the consequences of a setting seen, not flatwise or instantaneously, but as a form through which one moves.

Communications. A landscape communicates meanings to its users, whether by explicit symbols or by the observer's knowledge of the meaning of visible shapes and motions. These meanings are frequently embodied in

City patterns and textures.
(Left) Study of New York City walls. "Landscape Story,"
by Burk Uzzle. (Right and bottom) Studies of city floors:
trolley track in London and granite setts with puddle
reflecting St. Peter's in Rome.
(Left) Burk Uzzle—Magnum, (right) Rodger Birt—Photofind,
(bottom) Fritz Henle

Shapes
and
motions,
signs
and
symbols

intentional symbols: words, icons, or conventional refer-
ents like the barber pole or the marquee. These signs are
necessary and interesting, a flow of information to be
clarified and enhanced. They can be used, not simply to
sell or command, but to speak of history, ecology, the
presence of people, the flow of traffic, weather, time,
events to come, and basic values.

Surfaces. The texture of walls, roofs, and floors is a
very noticeable characteristic of the urban scene. The city
floor is most important: one touches it as well as sees it.
Its cleanliness is an emotional symbol; changes of level
force one's attention to it. Textural patterns guide and
express action patterns: curbs, runnels, footpaths, tan-

bark, sand. Textures neutralize or dramatize form. Asphalt is a metaphor for urbanization, but the range of
possible surfacing is much wider: cultivated and stabilized
earth, low shrubs and ground covers, tall weeds and grass,
thickets, tanbark, macadam, sand, gravel, concrete with
jointing or surface aggregates, wood blocks and decking,
terrazzos, mosaics, blocks, bricks, tiles, cobbles, setts, and
slabs. Short-run cost and mechanical maintenance lead to
the use of concrete or grass, but variety of use should lead
to variety of material.

Rock, earth, and water. Under the surface finish, the
environmental base is rock and earth. Cuts and fills, pits
and outcrops, cliffs, caves, and hills give one an intuition

of the planet whose surface one inhabits. Underlying rock is hidden, and bare earth seems indecent, yet they are expressive, and often welcome, materials.

Water is also elemental—simple in its nature but extremely varied in effect. The range of common terms is an index of its potential—ocean, pool, sheet, jet, torrent, rill, drop, spray, cascade, film—as are the kinds of liquid motion—trickle, splash, foam, flood, pour, spout, surge, ripple, run. This range of form and motion, this changeableness in unity, the play of light and sound, the intimate connection with life, all make water a superb outdoor material. Moving water gives a sense of life, still water unity and rest. Water plays with light, reflecting the changing sky or sunlit objects nearby. Water is technically troublesome, but hypnotically attractive.

Plants. Many great landscapes are treeless; there are handsome squares that do not include a visible plant of any description. Yet plants are one of the fundamental landscape materials, and the most widely enjoyed. But planting is the "extra" in development, the first item to be cut when the budget pinches.

Reasons for the choice of plants

Plant species are chosen for their hardiness, given the microclimate, soil condition, expected traffic, and level of maintenance. Texture and the general habit of growth are more predictable than individual shape, and more telling. Initial appearance, maturity, and decay must all be considered, since this is a living landscape. The aim is to so manage the landscape that it becomes a stable, self-replacing system as rapidly as possible.

Detail. A developed site includes many man-made details: fences, seats, signal boxes, poles, meters, trash cans, fireplugs, manholes, wires, lights, mailboxes, steps, curbs, and telephones. It is curious that most of this list evokes a sense of disharmony. This is the as yet unassimilated equipment of urban civilization whose presence cannot be banished. Alarms must be found; trash cans must be moved; tired people want to sit; fences mark off personal territory. Designers have often been concerned about site detail, but usually in order to hide it, or to "organize" it, or to give it stylish form. Less attention has been given to its actual use and the form appropriate to that use.

CRITERIA

Environmental stress. A place may be too hot, too noisy, too bright, too loaded with information, too odorous, too windy, too dirty or polluted, even too clean, too empty, or too silent. The physiological and perceptual stresses imposed by the physical environment are a common complaint of city life. Climate, noise, pollution, and the level of visual input are the factors most often referred to. Usually there is an acceptable range, with a threshold of tolerance at either end. The range has a biological basis, but it is affected by what is culturally acceptable, by the temperament of the person, and by the activity he is engaged in. For particular groups, engaged in similar behaviour, one can usually find substantial agreement about what is unpleasant or intolerable. Thus there is a commonly accepted Western standard for the maximum noise level in a sleeping area, while the standards for comfortable domestic indoor temperatures shift by as much as ten degrees from one European country to another.

Relation of environmental stress to health

Somewhat more objective than the sense of comfort is the relation of environmental stress to health and efficiency. There is information that links air pollution to lung disease, and noise to work output or to the health of pregnant mothers, for example. But the human organism is notoriously adaptable, and survives, sometimes without conscious difficulty, under conditions of loud noise or heavy pollution. The key issue is whether these adaptations may not be exacting a severe but hidden price. In any event, the complaints about city noise, city pollution, and city climate are widespread. There are known ways of ameliorating those effects, and no place should be designed without thought for the microclimate it will produce, how clean its air or water will be, and whether it will be well shielded from intrusive noise.

Behavioral support. It may seem obvious that a place should support the actions that people want to undertake in it, but this is normally disregarded. Doors cannot easily be opened, packages must be carried up steep stairs, paths are slippery or do not lead where people want to go, there is no place to sit or to talk in comfort, public toilets are lacking, there is no place to wash the car, or to dig, or to leave the baby. Outdoor spaces are conceived of as volumes having a visual or formal character, rather than as settings for people doing things. If behaviour is considered, it is usually of the most formal and stereotyped kind: playing baseball, admiring a view, or parking a car. The actions intended are reduced to a single class, to which the place is completely dedicated. Or the setting is used as a determinant to compel people to act in a certain way—an effort that normally and happily fails. No thought is given to the actual diversity and richness of human behaviour, nor to how different groups and actions often overlap with each other. This can in part be overcome by a specific program; *i.e.,* a careful and detailed statement of the human behaviour that is expected and desired, an account of how the environment should facilitate it, and to what extent it should be open to variant behaviour. This is quite different from the standard program, which is a simple list of spaces to be provided. The behavioral program must consider timing as well as location, so that conflicts and joint use can be provided for. Places can also be analyzed to see if they provide for the actions that men are always engaged in: the ability to move about easily, without confusion, and safely; the ability to use one's senses; the opportunity to communicate with others; the chance for privacy and security. A place should increase a user's competence in doing what he proposes to do and even more, make it possible for him to act in new ways. Thus the designer must consider the management of a place, as well as its initial form.

Identity. Particular places should have a clear perceptual identity: recognizable, memorable, vivid, engaging of attention, and differentiated from other locations. This is the objective basis for perception. It is a support for the sense of belonging to some place-attached group, as well as a way of marking a behavioral territory.

The test for site identity is not the novelty of its graphic presentation, but the degree to which it is vividly remembered and identified by its people. Thus an understanding of how a user looks at the world is critical to achieving identity. Since it is a function of the observer's mental image, identity can also be increased by educating the observer, and by training him to see significant differences that he never noticed before. If users are allowed to adapt a site to their particular purposes, and if these adaptations are allowed to accumulate over time, the identity of the site can be expected to increase.

Diversity. One of the commonly recognized delights of great cities is their diversity of people and places. A corresponding criticism of small towns, or suburbs, or central ghettoes, is the lack of access to varied opportunities. Diversity is an obvious prerequisite for choice, and corresponds to a widely felt pleasure in variety and change. Some variety of stimulus is an important condition for cognitive development, and indeed for the very maintenance of the human perceptual system, as experiments have demonstrated.

It is more difficult to determine what should be diversified, and the relative diversity between two different proposals is also difficult to measure. All objects are to some extent different from each other, and most differences are trivial. Equally puzzling is the measurement of "adequate" diversity. A range of choice exhilarating to one person may be threatening to another. One person may want choice of places in which to buy clothes, and another a choice of views.

An urban designer must therefore inquire into the diversity that people consider important. Much of the apparent variety in the environment—of commercial products, for example—is simply trivial and confusing. Some of the diversity that is desired will refer to the sensuous environment—to having choices between places that are calm or stimulating, lonely or crowded, artificial or natural, as well as some choice of behaviour settings. There

Legibility.
The legibility of the Piazza of St. Peter's (1656-67), Gian Lorenzo Bernini's memorable Baroque enclosure in Rome, was destroyed in the 20th century by the addition of a desolate and monumental approach from the Tiber River. View from St. Peter's basilica, (left) before and (right) after opening an avenue to the Tiber.
Alinari

is a common fantasy, for example, of living in a secluded garden, from which one may pass onto a lively street.

Perceived diversity is a function of actual variety, but also of how accessible that variety is, and of how capable or interested the residents are in being aware of that objective variety. Perceived diversity can therefore be changed by increasing objective diversity, but also by improving the access to it, or by educating the person to be interested in it. Building on present choices, a good environment also opens up new ones.

Legibility. There is a common, and more debatable, argument that the elements of an environment should be so arranged that the normal observer can understand their pattern in time and space. Under this rule, a city whose layout can be understood, or whose history is visible, is better than one that is chaotic or has destroyed its past.

Impor-
tance of
"legibility"
of structure Legible structure in the outside world has an obvious value in facilitating the practical tasks of way-finding and cognition. It improves access, and therefore opportunity. It can be a source of emotional security, and a basis for a sense of self in relation to society. It can support civic cohesion, and be a means of extending one's knowledge of the world. It also confers the aesthetic pleasure of perceiving the relatedness of a complex thing. There is a common pleasure in seeing a city from some high place. On the other hand, the structural chaos of the great urban regions is notorious.

Legibility must work for the anxious tourist, the knowledgeable inhabitant intent on his practical task, and the casual stroller. Different people look for different kinds of clues, yet most refer to certain basic elements, such as main circulation, basic functional areas, principal centres, the natural site, the big open spaces, perhaps the best-known "historic" points. Temporal legibility is as important as spatial legibility. The landscape can orient its inhabitants to the past, to the cyclical rhythms of the present and even to the hopes and dangers of the future.

Meaning. The environment is an enormous communications device. People read it constantly—they seek practical information, they are curious, they are moved by what they see.

The
symbolic
role of
landscape The symbolic role of landscape is interesting, but it is unfortunately little understood. Significance differs widely between various groups. Dominant values may be clearly expressed by the size of buildings devoted to large corporations and insurance companies, or by the multiplicity of signs that urge one to buy things. But these symbols are not correspondent to the values of the sub-

merged groups, or to values newly rising into prominence.

Regardless of this divergence, the identity and legibility of places provide a common visible base to which all people can give their own interpretations. A cluster of skyscrapers may signify exhilarating power to one and cruel oppression to the other, but both have a visible object for their feelings. Visible structure should be congruent with functional and social structure. Visual units, for example, should correspond with social units, such as the family. Landmarks should correspond to actual foci of activity or of social significance. Physically defined territories fitted to behavioral territories is another example of congruence between the visible and the social world.

City signs are often damned on aesthetic grounds, but they perform an important function. The flow of information must be regulated, so that priority signs (public control messages, for example) cannot be missed. At the same time, the observer must be able to tune out, which argues against various obtrusive devices: public broadcasts, flashing lights, or the pre-emption of key locations in vistas or at decision points. Signs may be used to expand what a man can learn of his city. Public information centres could become highly attractive.

It may also be desirable to increase the "transparency" of the city landscape, for economic and social processes are today increasingly hidden from sight. Indeed, construction sites are so interesting because they are one of the few industrial processes still left open to view. It might be public policy to encourage visual exposure, partly directly, and partly by remote sensing. Cities might regain, without impairment of function, some of the vitality and immediacy of the pre-industrial city, with its open workshops and markets. On the other hand, there is also the risk of invading privacy. A policy of visual exposure is intriguing but sensitive. The
"trans-
parency"
of the
city
landscape

As one goes deeper into the subject, numerous difficulties are encountered: diversity of values, the efforts of special interests to capture and to falsify the communications system, and even the embarrassments of revealing some features of society as they really are. And yet places and buildings evoke strong feelings in their observers, and these feelings should be an important concern for the designer; the seeming aloofness and impenetrability of a city hall, for example, the awesome frigidity of an office lobby, or the calm invitingness of a public park.

Development. Particularly in childhood, but to some extent in later years, environment plays its part in the intellectual, emotional, and physical growth of the individual. The negative effects of highly impoverished settings have been demonstrated. The role of rich sense perceptions in human maturation has some basis in laboratory experiment, but for the most part it remains speculative, although highly probable.

An educative environment would be full of available information, visibly encouraging attention and exploration, particularly when the observer is not task-oriented —as when he is at play, travelling, or just waiting. A learning environment alternates moments of high stimulus and quiet privacy. It would include opportunities to manipulate the world directly. The use of a city as a teaching device is a fascinating subject. Its connection to city design criteria is suggestive but uncertain.

Perceptual engagement. Beyond all these, there is the sheer delight of sensing the world: the play of light, the feel and smell of the wind, touches, sounds, colours, forms. It is difficult to impose such things, but the designer can prevent the blotting-out of sensation (as by featureless noise, or a bland facade). He can keep the environment open to the sky or the presence of people. Dynamic elements never fail to catch attention: moving water, living creatures, clouds, light and fire, moving machinery, or pennants, which make visible the currents of air.

Constraints. The power and purposes of clients and users will always be the key determinant in the urban design process. There are numerous other conditions, however, that also influence the outcome. One is the basic nature of the site itself: its topography, vegetative cover, climate, ecology. Seacoast and riverine sites, plains and mountains, marshes and deserts, each impose typical limitations and offer typical possibilities. Local accidents of ground, as well as basic site character, are also influential: a small rise of ground may determine a view, the orientation of a building, or the course of a street. The variations in the microclimate can be particularly important.

Influence of the nature of the site itself

Natural site conditions are perhaps less determining than in the past, because of the power of modern technology to change them: to fill in the sea, cut off a hill, or air condition large interior spaces. But as this power is exercised, it is often found that the secondary consequences are surprising: the buried river floods, heat islands build up over the cities, tidal water becomes stagnant, and the land slips and erodes.

The power to override the particularities of natural site has had still another effect. Cities begin to look like one another all over the world. Airports, as an extreme case, are almost indistinguishable, but so are many central areas, suburbs, or apartment districts. Closer attention to site conditions would help to prevent this. But close support and expression of cultural differences would do even more.

Urban designers must cope not only with natural, but with previous man-made conditions. There are existing structures, and an existing system of circulation. There is a network of utilities and of public services. Only occasionally can a society afford to sweep away all its previous environmental capital, and even then the unanticipated social and psychological costs are likely to be severe. Urban designs are most often complex remodellings, successive sets of changes that retain much of the previous pattern of development. An analysis of what previous elements must be retained and which can be cleared away is a typical early step.

Persistence of circulation patterns

Circulation patterns are particularly persistent, since they are reinforced by other patterns such as ownership lines and utility systems. The pattern of streets will last for centuries, while buildings come and go, and even the street itself is many times rebuilt. The invisible lot lines and buried utilities are extremely conservative in effect. There will be other legal or social rights, inclusive of mutually agreed-upon "territories" felt to be the proper domain of some special group. There will be persistent behaviour settings: places where people are accustomed to doing certain things, and which resist disruption. There are sacred places, old market locations, and meeting grounds; and any plan that displaces them will meet

resistance. Therefore, account must be taken of the images that people have about their environment: the territories they divide it into, how they link it up, what meanings they attach to it, what activities they are accustomed to carry out where. Like the ecological system, or the inherited physical setting, this existing social image must be understood before changes can be made. If not, the consequences may be unexpected: vandalism, bitterness, the failure of a new commercial facility, disorientation, or political opposition.

In planning, as in spatial economics, the environment is considered to be a set of activity locations and their linkages. Each activity has preferences for its site and for its connection to other activities. A plan seeks an optimum pattern of locations and linkages, considering the relative importance of each activity (which may be measured in social value, political power, or the ability to pay). This planned pattern, which includes a transportation network, can then become the framework of an urban design. How those activities were classified, linked, and weighted was critical in setting the pattern. Therefore, those assumptions cannot be accepted without demur. Circulation requirements, in particular, are a chief technical constraint in urban design. Requirements for moving and storing automobiles loom very large in most urban schemes: the demands of access, alignment, and sheer volume of space are substantial. That these demands are not iron laws, but rather the reflection of social decisions about the mode and speed of travel, is sometimes forgotten. But a high level of circulation and communication, whatever the mode, is likely to be a persistent feature of any new urban development, and so the techniques of arranging highways, vehicle storage, transit lines, airports, waterways, railways, and pedestrian paths turn out to be the most frequently used urban design skill. Utilities and communication nets are equally important features of the urban infrastructure, but their technical demands are less often determining in the spatial arrangement of a place.

Among other technical requirements, the demands of safety usually rank high; *i.e.*, safety from fire or earthquake, and individual safety from moving traffic or personal assault. Traffic fatalities are numerous, and the incidence of theft and assault is rising. Thus there will be much attention given to the safety of intersection designs, the spacing of buildings for fire retardation, or the ability of an area to be surveyed and controlled by police or local neighbours. Elsewhere, the dominant fear may be the likelihood of organized assault: aerial bombardment, ground attack, or organized sabotage. Historically, one of the chief technical skills of a city designer was his knowledge of defense fortifications.

Health requirements are another set of technical constraints. The greatest successes of 19th-century city planning were their improvements in local sanitation, improvements generally well assimilated into the urban design principles of today. The worst problems are now the large-scale pollution of ground, air, and water and its long-term consequences for human health. Preventing such pollution puts some special constraints on environmental design, of which planners are only now becoming aware. Of the effects of environmental form on mental health, however, there is still great ignorance.

Cost is a powerful constraint, as in any kind of capital investment, and urban designers must know how to make estimates of construction and maintenance costs. These costings are not only less detailed than typical architectural or engineering estimates, but are quite incomplete in other ways. The social and psychological costs of a change are often disregarded, a feature sadly so familiar in most economic decisions. But even the direct money costs of a proposal are incompletely analyzed due to the multiplicity of clients, the long time spans, and the way in which decisions are made. Political costs may dominate the outcome. Only the money costs to the initiating developer or agency may be computed, while the resulting costs to other actors—a transit agency, for example, or a dislocated business—are simply ignored. The effects of inflation over the long period of construction,

Costs of design decisions

or the costs of maintenance, are as often neglected. Urban developments thus typically cost substantially more to carry out than originally estimated. Since benefits are calculated even more carelessly, it sometimes happens that real benefits may inflate as rapidly as costs. Rational cost–benefit accounting of urban designs is just beginning and necessarily remains incomplete, since many costs and benefits are not to be translated into money units. More rational cost–benefit studies may, in fact, tend to submerge factors not easily quantifiable.

THE SOCIAL SETTING OF URBAN DESIGN

The visible form of a city reflects the social and economic setting in which it was created and maintained. This is quite apparent during the normal design process. When the designer enters that process, the solution has long been evolving. A problem has been recognized, a client organized, the economic resources to be allotted to the task are usually determined, and the political and administrative rules are set. Even the act of turning to an urban designer implies that a new spatial pattern should be a part of the solution. More often than not, a complete schedule of space requirements has been prepared.

Even within these limits, the designer has some room in which to manoeuvre. He can raise questions about elements of the program. He can communicate with others who have a stake in the outcome, or even help them to manoeuvre into a client position. He can propose other values and criteria, such as those outlined above, and suggest possibilities that resolve old conflicts or that create new values to be exploited. He may also sway decisions by his personal prestige, or by the way he formulates the complicated alternatives for decision, alternatives that are difficult for the nondesigner to pick apart and reformulate. Finally, he is often able to make decisions about form in areas independent of his client's major concerns, which may focus on profit, on a favourable political reaction, or on completion on time and within the budget. In this case, the client may be glad to leave to the designer features that do not compromise those central aims.

Decision-making in the design process

A number of groups are usually involved in any decision, and the designer is often motivated to bring in still more, so that ultimate users can also participate in the decision making. This implies complex and sometimes cumbersome communications, and causes frequent recycling of design. Usually it is necessary to impose arbitrary limits on the participating clients, if the decision process is to work at all. Deciding on the key clients—those with the greatest stake in the outcome or with the greatest real power to carry it out—and determining the balance between those clients is difficult. Enforcing it takes substantial political energy. The designer does not usually make such decisions, but he plays some role in the decision making, and is ethically implicated.

Since there are many decision makers, conflicts are to be expected. Progress is made by negotiation, and the negotiators who have a single functional goal in mind or are focussed on a small area and can therefore be flexible on all other issues, are those most likely to succeed. The private developer will accept all sorts of public rules that do not threaten his rate of profit. The transit agency is happy as long as it gets its routes and terminals. Quality, however, usually depends on the effect of a whole system. At the points of hard bargaining and over a long succession of decisions, quality gives ground to the thrust of quantifiable, bounded, functional goals or of narrow territorial interests.

On occasion, this typical situation is modified. Sometimes the designer is part of a constructing agency that has effective powers of decision and implementation—a new town authority, for example. The designer does not make the decisions, but he is linked directly to those who make and carry out decisions; and he is therefore in a much better position to help set up the problem and participate in its realization and management. In return, the decision makers and implementers penetrate more deeply into his own design process.

At other times, designers attach themselves directly to some client group, helping the group organize to influence the definition of the problem. Rather than creating some definite solution, the designer gathers technical information and sketches possibilities so that his group can influence a larger decision process. He is an advocate, whose loyalty is to his client group—which may be a comfortable position, or may entail sacrifices if the client is weak and poor.

The designer may become a champion rather than an advocate, attaching himself to some solution and pressing to assemble the client and the power to carry it through. This is uphill work, only rarely successful in the individual case, but often having a slow cumulative effect, as the possibilities of some new kind of design solution begin to enter the world of alternatives perceived by the decision makers. Thus new towns, parkways, adventure playgrounds, urban renewal, city parks, or downtown plazas have been successfully championed and picked up by other groups to carry through. In some cases, however, the motives of the implementing group may differ from those of the champion, and thus the nature of the solution will be distorted.

Controlling environmental form

The form of the environment can be influenced in a number of ways. The most obvious, to a designer trained in architecture, is simply to specify the environment in a set of drawings. This is rarely possible. It may be possible, however, to design the key localities in detail (major squares, main avenues) or some special elements or systems (bikeways, lighting, prototype housing, highways). The design of repeatable systems is an opportunity often neglected in urban design. One may choose to design some demonstration project as a stimulus to other actors.

Most urban designs are diagrammatic. They refer, not so much to the exact form of things, as to the character or spatial effect intended, the clusters of behaviour expected in the spaces provided, the image structure, the basic circulation and activity location, and the types of management of control. They may specify selected detail: lighting, signs, textures, sounds. A diagrammatic model, a control document, a series of slides, or a film, may be better than a plan, section, or elevation. Showing how a place will develop over time is more effective than drawing what its final form will be. Illustrative sketches, showing one possible outcome according to the principles proposed, are frequently used in place of definitive plans. The "hardline" drawings of engineering and architecture are too frequently used in circumstances in which there is no certainty, finality, or detailed control.

Without making specific designs, one may control the design process of others. This can be done by legal rules, or by specifying characteristics of the design process (imposing competitions or user consultation, for example), by design review, or by indirect economic controls (subsidies, tax rules). In the complexities of large-scale development, such indirect controls must be relied upon. Design review has often been successful, especially where it has been introduced early in the design process. Economic controls are a powerful means in an economy dependent upon private enterprise. Design controls, such as those that specify the character of facades or the shape of built volume, have had very uneven success, and are laborious to administer. All too often, they are a signal that urban designers are playing at designing a city as if it were a building.

Performance standards of environmental quality might be a more efficient and flexible means of control, although they are not often employed. They could be founded on a sensuous program that would specify desired visibility, spatial character, visible activity, texture, apparent motion, sign content, light, noise, or climate. Thus such a program might propose, at some particular junction, that there be a landmark identifiable day or night from a mile away, visibly displaying its internal activity, whose form distinguishes the various turns and approaches one from another. Such a program could be satisfied by many particular shapes, according to the motives of that structure's developer. In another case, the desired microclimate, noise level, sign content, and provision of seating and shelter along a public street might be the characteristics specified, just as one is as accustomed to specify lane width for

New settlements: romantic form and arid order.
(Left) Reston, Virginia; (right) Brasília, Brazil.
(Left) Stan Wayman—Life Magazine, © 1965 Time Inc., (right) Shostal Assoc.

traffic, or the allowable inflammability of building materials.

The principal aim of urban design is to improve the quality of the human spatial environment, and, by so doing, to improve the quality of human life. It does not directly attack underlying social problems, such as poverty, war, inequality, or alienation, nor is it usually a very efficient way of doing so. But since it deals with the setting of social life, it is necessarily influenced by those underlying problems, and in turn influences them. War can destroy a fine landscape, poverty can make it unbearable, and alienation can render it meaningless. The effect of a place cannot be judged without reference to social conditions; neither can the quality of life be deduced solely from social conditions without reference to the spatial setting. Environment can have specific effects of its own: its territorial division may serve to reinforce segregation; it may open up new opportunities to people; its form influences the personal growth of children. The process of building the environment may support self-reliance and new institutions among disadvantaged people. Environmental modification is always a possible element in any general strategy of social change. Most revolutionary societies devote some of their effort to the reorganization of their living space, even though purely perceptual effects may not have a high priority.

TYPICAL PROBLEMS IN URBAN DESIGN

A better understanding of urban design comes from looking at some of the typical situations in which it is involved, or might be involved.

Area policy. Only rarely has environmental quality been considered at the scale of the whole city or region, at which level recommendations have traditionally dealt with land use and open space patterns, housing supply, public facilities, and the technical systems of transport and utilities. Regional quality is the framework for local quality, however. Analyses of the visual form of a region or a city have been accomplished recently: as in the cities of Minneapolis, San Francisco, and Los Angeles in the United States. Large landscape elements have also been surveyed, such as the lower Thames and its banks in England, and part of the valley of the Ticino, in Italy. Regional plans have been made that incorporated visual criteria with ecological considerations, such as a plan for the Green Spring and Worthington valleys near Baltimore. The new agricultural greenbelt around Havana, the so-called Cordon, is a conscious attempt to create a

new visual scene, as well as to remold the economy of the city and the ideology of its citizens. Existing areas of strong character have plans for their preservation, as in the vicinity of Florence. Studies of the ability of small areas to absorb new development without visual damage are being used as one input for regional growth policy, notably around Helsinki. But the technical and political effort that will be required to control regional landscape quality and to think of humane conditions of existence at that reach of size, has still to be made.

New settlements. Where new settlements are being built by conscious plan, there is greater acceptance of the necessity for dealing with sensuous form, although the results have not been spectacular. The best work has been done in residential suburbs of moderate size, usually built for the well-to-do. Roland Park, Riverside, Chatham Village, and Radburn in the United States, and the earlier Bedford Park and Hampstead Garden Suburb in Great Britain, may be cited. Good suburbs are still being built, and the most recent phenomenon is the designed community of vacation homes, as at New Seabury, on Cape Cod. These are pleasant places, relying on a careful fit to the ground, ample space and greenery, good design of spatial form along the street, and close control of signs, lights, fences, street furniture, and other detail.

Designs for new towns have been more ambitious, and in general the earlier examples, such as England's Welwyn, seem to be the more successful ones. Reston, Virginia has a handsome, if rather unreal, central area and lake; and the recent Tapiola in Finland is outstanding for its landscaping and the variety and finesse of its detailed site planning. Most of the new towns, however, have been no better than moderately pleasant suburbs, at least in visual terms, and many are quite monotonous or raw. Thamesmead, upriver of London, displays a sophisticated use of industrialized components and a fine use of river bottom land, but the housing is expensive, and some of its formal brilliance is of doubtful use. Cumbernauld (Scotland), Chandīgarh (India), and Brasília (Brazil) are now widely criticized for their imposition of an alien form on a living community.

The difficulties in dealing with the form of new towns are quite similar to those in evolving areawide policies: the large scale, the complexity, the distance between designer and user, the inability to control or diversify rapid mass development. Thus the plans for one of the newest and technically most advanced of the British new towns —Milton Keynes—passes over questions of visual form

(margin left) Examples of plans for regions

(margin right) Problems of new town design

very lightly, except for policies on the retention of natural features. To these difficulties must be added the peculiar nature of the new towns—their rapid growth, their lack of a past, the dissociation of the planning from the future inhabitants. The visual richness deriving from a visible history, or from the diverse ways in which different people fit their environment to a local situation, are necessarily missing. Any successes have primarily depended on skillful local site planning. The vast mass of new urbanization throughout the world is monotonous and barren. Nor is this simply a matter of poverty, since some of the most interesting new places are the intricate self-help settlements of the underdeveloped nations.

The record in the denser housing project is equally poor, although the task is closer to the normal architectural one, and the techniques are better developed. It is quite possible to cite moderate- or high-density residential projects of good quality, but they are lost in a great wilderness of inhuman slabs and grim barracks. In Great Britain and Scandinavia, however, there are many more frequent examples of livable, pleasant housing projects.

Rehabilitation, redevelopment, conservation. Urban design received its strongest official impetus in the United States from the federally sponsored urban renewal program, in which moderately large sites were cleared for complex housing and commercial projects in the centre of the cities. Since this was a highly visible program under political attack and was backed by groups for whom visual quality was important, a substantial stress was put on good urban design. Opportunities for laying out complex projects were frequent, whereas previously they had been rare. Schools and firms specializing in this work appeared. The results were uneven. While some handsome projects resulted, mostly in central business districts, most work suffered from designer megalomania and administrative confusion. Operating agencies and large developers made the key decisions, while the future user (much less the existing one) was rarely consulted.

Even though these projects were concerned with city-centre areas, they were usually treated as isolated designs.
True renewal (*i.e.*, a restoration of the existing fabric for the use of existing occupants) was not accomplished. Urban design has little skill in enhancing existing social and built values, as one might enhance a natural landscape. Improvements have occurred in older areas attractive to higher income owners, but these improvements usually conceal social costs. In only a very few instances have public agencies been successful in helping local inhabitants to improve the appearance of their own local region, as in Wooster Square in New Haven. The key action has been the rendering of design services to the inhabitants, rather than designing for them. Rehabilitation and renewal remain among the most critical social tasks to be undertaken in urban design.

When the problem is not rehabilitation, but the preservation of quality already achieved, the technical task is relatively simple and familiar: to analyze the existing visual quality of the place, and to draw up guidelines for any remodelling or new construction. These guidelines may require strict replacement or copying, especially of exterior facades, or may only entail careful attention to mass, scale, spacing, fenestration, and materials. There are numerous successful and admired examples of this type of action: Boston's Beacon Hill, New Orleans' Vieux Carré, or the heart of Charleston, South Carolina spring to mind. At times, preservation of this kind may have a high political priority, and may absorb significant capital in a hard-pressed nation, as did the Stare Miasto in Warsaw. Preserving existing values is easier than creating new ones, yet preservation can play no more than a minor role in the general task of urban design.

Lines of movement. One perceives the city while walking or riding through it. Since roads, paths, and transit systems are normally built and maintained by public agencies, the design of these channels is an important branch of urban design. The design criteria focus on the functioning of the transportation line, the pleasure and information to be had while travelling along it, and the impact of the channel on the observer who is outside of

it. The latter concern introduces goals partially in conflict with the former ones.

Main avenues have been designed in the past, principally in terms of their cross section, and sometimes as slow monumental approaches. Designs that deal with sequence and dynamic experience are relatively new and scarce. A number of rural freeways in the United States are among the best examples of large-scale environmental design in the world today. The fit to ground, the use of landscaping, the variations of space and motion, are superb. On the other hand, although there are interesting urban highways whose form arose by exterior circumstance (the Schuylkill River Parkway in Philadelphia, for example), there are no examples of successful deliberate design, although there have been illustrative proposals.

While some thought has been given to highway visual design, almost no consideration has been given to mass transit design. Riding a bus or train is quite different in visibility and role from driving a car, and expectations are low. The view from the bus enters into no current designer calculations. The design of pedestrian ways in parks or tourist grounds is a more traditional concern, but the pedestrian on the ordinary city street is usually ignored. Bicycle paths are carefully designed in many European countries and are appearing in the United States, but again with little thought for the moving view. In Great Britain, some of the old industrial canals have been retained and refurbished for recreational voyages. The view from the airplane seems a ridiculous question and yet in the future may merit attention. Roads are often only one element of an entire linear environment. The highway commercial strip is notoriously ugly and confusing, but it has a strong functional justification. In order to create a handsome landscape, it might be feasible to combine a highway with linear uses in one integrated structure. The idea has been proposed intermittently, but never carried through, except in a few rather trivial uses of "air rights" by office or apartment buildings.

Commercial centres and central districts. Some of the most sophisticated work in urban design has occurred in commercial centres. This is hardly surprising, considering the large investments in those centres, the effective control of form that is possible, and the importance of attractive form for increasing profits. The urban renewal work most often admired for its quality has almost all occurred within central business districts. The projects are typically a mix of shops, offices, public buildings, and some luxury apartments. They are complex in form, using separate levels and specialized buildings to deal with use and traffic mixtures at high densities. Normally, they include a public plaza. Arcades, escalators, raised pedestrian decks and walkways, and underground parking are common features. They are expensive, handsome in detail, and often rather cold and inhuman in general effect because of the design focus on pure form and of economic pressures toward a narrow spectrum of high-paying uses. The complex sequences of interior public space set new problems for design. Artificial light and climate replace their natural counterparts. The public ways are the corridors and tunnels.

The regional shopping centre is now a successful and much imitated model, more closely based on behavioral knowledge than any other type of environmental design. Now rather artificial, specialized, and physically isolated, they could, nonetheless, be integrated with other functions to become true social centres.

Special areas. Urban design has had some success in the layout of large institutions, where centralized control of form has also been possible. Large urban hospitals have usually been an exercise in complex technical form at high intensity. Campus planning for universities and colleges has provided frequent opportunities to establish an integrated landscape. Not only are the existing schools growing, but new campuses are being set out. Many of them are barren affairs, but it is quite possible to produce a pleasant environment. Some of the outstanding successes provide complete living environments, usually with

Hötorgscity, Stockholm, a modern commercial centre consisting of five 18-story office blocks and a pedestrian mall with shops on two levels.
© Sven Samelius

enough space to allow for fine landscaping. Planning for rapid growth is a typical difficulty, as is maintaining a handsome landscape in the face of demands for parking and access. The traditional organization of higher education often results in some rather stereotyped buildings and unit organizations. The nature of an environment for learning has not yet been considered in any profound way. Yet university campuses are often, because of their visible life and landscaped setting, very attractive parts of cities. Too often, they are islands of culture, as shopping centres are islands of consumption.

Another special area that has received some design attention is the industrial park or estate. Extensive areas under single control are set aside for industry, often with accompanying services such as banks, restaurants, or maintenance and distribution facilities. Most often, the form of these estates has been determined by rail and road access, or by internal layout requirements. More recently, the visible aspect of these estates has come to be considered. Such estates or parks are regulated to keep factories simple in form, of good materials, and well set back and landscaped. At best, an innocuous green landscape of low buildings is the result. Little attention is given to making the work that goes on in these areas significant or pleasant, or to connect it with other life functions. Similarly, no advantage is taken of the potential drama of industry: there is no immediate vision of what goes on inside.

The great expositions are excellent occasions for innovation, and indeed many of the earlier ones were outstanding: the World's Columbian Exposition of 1893 in Chicago, the Paris Exposition of 1889, and the London Exposition of 1851. Recent fairs have produced little that is new amid much visual confusion. There have been innovations in structures, such as Montreal's Habitat, but not in the organization of the general environment. The modern fair is highly competitive, and the scattered developers, who are under extreme time pressure, are difficult to coordinate.

Large natural and man-made features. The design of large state and national parks has become a well-devel-

oped environmental specialty, closely related to landscape architecture and forestry. Handling big crowds, preventing ecological damage, preserving the appearance of a natural landscape, supplying a whole range of recreation for varied tastes without mutual interference—all of these are the central problems, and they are often competently handled. Details are simple, and maintenance is stressed. The landscape is used to teach the visitor about the structure of nature.

The smaller urban park was the problem on which landscape architecture cut its teeth, and some of the older city parks provide fine examples of environmental design. Recent city park design has been less successful, and suffers from a certain standardization and emptiness of appearance and function. New work in children's playgrounds has been more impressive: complex and challenging landscapes have been created, built of simple materials, and fitted to the actual behaviour and interests of the child. The "adventure playgrounds" in which children use space and raw materials to build their own surroundings and equipment, have been particularly interesting. Hopefully, this will lead into the design of true "learning environments."

Recent work with children's playgrounds

The enhancement of large natural features was an important aspect of earlier work in what was then called civic design. Seafronts, lakefronts, streams, and ponds were improved as promenades, or for boating, swimming, and picnicking. Waterfronts and river banks have been magnificently developed in many European cities. They have been generally neglected in the United States, although there are a few fine examples: the Chicago lakefront, the basin of the Charles River in Boston, the Golden Gate Park in San Francisco, and the river walk in San Antonio. But with the economic decline of the city waterfront as a port and industrial region, many cities in the United States are now slowly moving to reclaim those water edges: Boston, New York, Philadelphia, and St. Louis are but a few among the best-known American examples.

Mountains and great hills, less frequent within urban limits, are rarely used for their landscape qualities, although they may have a small park or panoramic view near their summit. A number of great cities have exceptional opportunities in the contrast of mountain and city: Caracas, San Salvador, Buenos Aires, and Los An-

Arvid Bengtsson

Children playing in Notting Hill Adventure Playground, London.

Habitat, Montreal, designed by Moshe Safdie, 1967.
Ewing Galloway

geles, to name a few. The great bridges are dramatic city elements, but few are designed as landscape to be walked over, climbed, passed under, and played upon. Dams and reservoirs are strong landscape elements, but the enormous spoil heaps of industry are classed as ugly and therefore ignored or camouflaged.

Special systems. Some work has been done on particular environmental systems: sets of things that are extended over large areas but do not make complete landscapes in themselves. In a time when urbanized areas will expand at unprecedented rates, using industrialized components in designing systems may be an excellent lever for the extensive improvement of quality. Planting plans are the most familiar example of environmental system design. Typical arrangements and species are prescribed for avenues, minor streets, walkways, paths, and front gardens. The designs are intended to ensure minimum quality and to fit tree types to typical demands and scales. They may also be used to give an identifiable character to particular districts or streets, or to mark out the main structure of the region. Although trees are not usually thought of as industrial products, in fact they are grown in quantity, on demand, by factory methods. Many fine urban areas are notable primarily for the way in which they are planted.

Signs have been given some attention. Most of the emphasis has been on immediate visual appearance, and very little on information content, which is a sign's reason for being. Public lighting has also been discussed, since many designers see the tremendous potentialities of artificial light. But lighting studies frequently come down to the form of the light pole, which is the least important aspect of the subject. Other products are rarely designed for their direct human impact. Various pieces of street furniture are obvious examples, as are the ubiquitous paving materials: asphalt, concrete, and the concrete curb.

System design might also be applied to larger chunks of the environment. One promising possibility is the design of mobile housing units and their immediate settings. While the houses themselves are meticulously designed as industrial products, the trailer settlements are not far from the quality of the original lots where they were first parked. Systematic design of typical units and their arrangement in housing neighbourhoods would be a strategic way of affecting the quality of a large sector of the moderate cost housing supply. The temporary settlements

of the Tennessee Valley Authority were pioneer successes whose results have been forgotten.

VISIONS

Most urban designers take no time to create new visions, in contrast to their reputations as imaginative men. Their visions are the historic plazas of Europe or the romantic site planning of Sir Raymond Unwin and Frederick Law Olmstead, or that combination of high density and high technology that is found in Le Corbusier's designs.

Perhaps the most famous recent demonstration of new environmental possibilities has been the Habitat of Expo 67, the Montreal World's Fair of 1967, in which residential units were piled one above the other in an irregular hill-like structure. The roofs of units below provided the open spaces for units above, and all parts were interconnected by pedestrian links at every level, as if the apartment building had become a three-dimensional village. Construction costs were high, but visitors were enchanted.

Recent visionary projects for large environments take up the theme of three-dimensional complexity and usually marry it with a very advanced technology of movement and climate control, coupled with an emphasis on rapid change, high density, and a display of startling, machine-made yet organic-looking forms. These ideas arise just at a time when most people in the world are hoping for lower densities and when there is a revulsion against high technology and centralized control. The visions seem to point where no one wants to go and ignore much of what has been learned about the impact of environment on behaviour.

Another strong idealistic current has as yet had less direct effect on urban design, although the current comes from deep historical sources, and most urban designers have a sympathy for it. This is the theme of ecological balance, which links up with the old ideas of a "return to nature," and to some extent with the Marxist ideal of the merging of city and country. The romantic, low-density suburb and the widespread American "second home in the country" have been a realistic working out of the same ideas. But while suburbs and vacation houses allow many people to enjoy a more pleasant and humane setting, they have also been one further step in the urbanization of the countryside. They make no true integration to rural pursuits.

In the United States the new "communes" are another expression of the longing for a rural return, as were many

Concern
for
ecological
balance

attempts at subsistence farming during the Great Depression. The communes combine radical social change with the old dream of agricultural simplicity and with a preference for handmade artifacts and environment. As yet all these currents have had little direct influence on the practice of urban design, except for the new use of ecological surveys to help determine the future use of undeveloped land. It is remarkable that no visions (with the exception of the "paradigms," which appeared in the 1940s in the Goodmans' "Communitas") deal with new social possibilities or with what we are learning about the interaction between man and environment.

The urban design field is in upheaval and conflict. Throughout the world, the architect is losing his unquestioned position of primacy and is becoming one member of a complex design team. Some attempts are being made to train men as designers able to analyze and deal with areawide spatial form, or with the coordinated management and design of environment, rather than as architects with an added knowledge of city problems. Research on the interaction of environment and behaviour is developing, and its findings are challenging many cherished ideas about civic form. New methods for large-scale design are evolving, relying on the computer in particular. Urban design is under attack for its preoccupation with visual form, and is accused of remoteness from basic social issues. Designers themselves are bewildered by the complicated politics and economics of large-scale decisions. Clients are no longer passive and mute, but demand a part in the design process.

Urban design as a separate profession arose in response to certain gaps between the older arts of environment, disturbing gaps which appeared, for example, when it became necessary to design large building complexes for multiple clients. The new profession aspired to the design of entire cities, under the misapprehension that they might be detailed in the same way that buildings are, as if constructed rapidly for a single client. It tended to stress the psychological and sensuous aspects of form, because these factors were generally disregarded at the scale of the community, region, or large engineering work. It blossomed in the wake of the city planning field, which is moving from purely physical concerns to a focus on economic and social policy, and is probably on the verge of breaking into various subdisciplines. It is instructive to note the areas of environmental success: the affluent suburb, the shopping centre, the historic district, the rural freeway, the campus, the large country park. It is even more instructive to see the areas of failure, or at least of nonperformance: the quality of large regions, the new towns and extensive new residential areas, localities in need of rehabilitation and renewal, the city streets, the working landscape of industry and agriculture, the mobile home park.

Where this turmoil may lead is hard to see. Hopefully, it would result in a profession competent to deal with community spatial form in all its social, political, economic, and psychological dimensions. This implies that the profession would focus its attention on those qualities in the environment that allow people to develop to their fullest potential. It would mean looking on the landscape as a changing, living system of which man is an integral part. Therefore, it would draw eagerly on knowledge from ecology, environmental psychology, and sociology. It would develop the design process into a recycling process of forethought, invention, experiment, and management, in which the ultimate user has an intimate role, so that the acts of planning and building and maintaining become joyful social arts. Its attention would turn to neglected areas: regions, rehabilitation, new settlements, environmental systems, and the small ordinary everyday places where people live and work and pass their lives. Necessarily, its course would parallel, and reinforce, changes in the organization of society. (K.L./Ed.)

II. Historical review

ORIGINS

For eons men lived as roaming hunters, now sheltering in caves or earth pits, in trees or in primitive tents, now moving on with the horde, following wandering herds of game. What the hunting range was to the hunter, the fishing range was to the fisherman. The latter, though, tended to keep to a "good ground." Fishermen were indeed the first to found settlements. These first settlements at the water's edge present three features: (1) a certain order in the relative positions of huts or tents, or in their subordination to external influences such as temperature, the sun's path, tides, and winds; (2) a tentative order of precedence of buildings; and (3) magical symbols, deterrent or propitiating, to avert harm or induce good. Frightened by the phenomena of disease and death, men sought the protection of supernatural powers and propitious signs.

A new era dawned when men learned to tame and domesticate animals; this led to livestock breeding and pasturing. Yet it still compelled man to keep moving, following good grazing and the seasons. Thence arose an extensive trade by which animal products were bartered for wares from far places. New symbols appear in textiles and in graves; winter quarters and summer pastures became fixed poles, as did good watering places. But still the need for mobility ruled out any fixed abodes for the summer. Nomadic life meant living in tents.

A third era began with crop growing. There appear increasing signs of integration of the human habitation into its environment (shelter from sun, cold, and wind), and observation of the cardinal points of the compass and their pleasant and unpleasant implications.

It is today hardly possible to locate the areas of the earliest village settlements. The only certain fact is that they arose in crop-growing areas, chief among which were the alluvial plains of the rivers Nile, Tigris, Euphrates, Indus, Yangtze, and Huang Ho. In Egypt, Palestine, Syria, Mesopotamia, and Iran settlements assumed village form about 5000 BC. And so mankind split for the second time. It had done so first when the livestock breeders dissociated from the hunters and fishermen, and it did so again when the cultivators dissociated from the breeders. This development seems to have been brought about by a brown-skinned race, perhaps related to the aboriginal population of South Arabia and the Dravidians of India, perhaps to the Hamites of North Africa. In Egypt, villages developed in the Badarian period (to about 4000 BC). In the Gerzean period (to about 3100 BC) there were already very small towns on the substratum of a rural culture. Villages, proto-urban settlements, and the first primitive towns appeared in Mesopotamia and Syria during the same period. **Earliest village settlements**

WESTERN ANTIQUITY

Urban culture began in antiquity in the regions of Egypt, Mesopotamia, Syria, Iran, and Asia Minor. These developments may be considered independent. Rarely are any influences recognizable between countries, even less so between regions. The natural conditions in each land largely determined the patterns of development—first of all, in the orientation of the towns. Thus, in ancient Egypt, the towns are largely oriented in a north–south axis, with the exception of Thebes and Tell el-Amarna, which followed the local course of the Nile. In Mesopotamia (Sumer, Babylonia, Assyria), however, the towns are oriented along the course of the rivers Euphrates and Tigris and at the same time on the preferred wind direction, so that their main axes run from northwest to southeast. In Palestine, Syria, and Anatolia the towns are variously oriented, depending on their situations on the coast, in valleys, or on hills. Rules also emerge from the plan of the town: in Egypt it is mostly square or rectangular, in Sumer oval, in Assyria rectangular. Yet all the town layouts follow geomantic (geographic divining) or religious notions.

Ancient Egypt. Among the most remarkable of the Early Dynastic sites is the town founded by King Djoser (3rd dynasty). He, with his adviser and architect Imhotep, built the town of Memphis and his own tomb at Ṣaqqārah. Town and tomb correspond in layout as the dwelling of the living king and that of the dead king. Djoser's necropolis covered an area of about 3,900 by **Memphis: town and tomb for kings**

Plan of Kahun, Egypt, Middle Kingdom (c. 2040–1786 BC). (A) Large mansions probably belonging to court officials. (B) Workmen's tenements.

From A. Badawy, *Ancient Egyptian Architectural Design: A Study of the Harmonic System*; originally published by the University of California Press; reprinted by permission of the Regents of the University of California

1,740 yards (3,600 by 1,600 metres), or about the same area as that occupied by the inner city of Memphis. Both town and necropolis were strictly oriented north and south. Imhotep obtained the town's presumed area of 4.1 by 8.2 miles (6.6 by 13.2 kilometres) by diverting the Nile into a new bed farther east and upstream of the site. The town, favoured by the 3rd to 6th dynasties, grew to megalopolitan proportions until 2263 BC when it was destroyed in a revolution.

The same planning skill is observable in the remains of the town of Kahun, founded about 2000 BC under the 12th dynasty. In layout it reveals divisions between the workmen's district in the west, with very small houses; the notables' district in the north, with big houses of several hundred rooms, courts, and corridors; the market in the east; and what is thought to be the temple area in the centre. The big houses of the notables face the pleasant north wind, while those of the workmen in the west are exposed to the hot desert wind. The remains of Thebes, located in Upper Egypt, are scattered in and around Luxor, Karnak, Birket Habu, and the area of mortuary temples on the west bank of the present Nile. Thebes became the country's capital under the 11th dynasty and, favoured by the succeeding dynasties, grew into the greatest and most monumental city of antiquity. It was destroyed first by the Assyrians in 661 BC, then by the Persian king Cambyses in 525 BC, and again by the Romans in 24 BC. Always encroached upon by the Nile, its original layout can only be tentatively traced out today. The terrain would permit a town to cover an area of 6 by 4 miles (9 by 6 kilometres) or, including Birket Habu, one of 8 by 4 miles (13 by 7 kilometres), with the long axis running southwest and northeast.

The capital at Amarna

The capital founded at Amarna by Amenophis IV (Ikhnaton) (1379–1362 BC), who seems to have been under the influence of his queen, Nefertiti, probably a foreigner, arose from an attempt to break with all the old traditions and to introduce an enlightened way of life. The cult of the sun, or light; a realistic art; equal rights for women; and naturalness of manner characterize the reign of that revolutionary monarch. Those traits also marked the layout of the new town, which extended in a narrow ribbon, slightly curved, along the Nile. It was more than 2.3 miles (3.7 kilometres) long and 0.9 mile (1.4 kilometres) wide. A street system flexibly adapted to the Nile's course connected the palace and temple district in the north with the dwelling quarters in the south. In these were courtyard houses for the lords' dwellings, surrounded by courts and outbuildings of all kinds, including farm buildings, servants' dwellings, cattle sheds, store houses, and gardens. The town seems to have been far removed from anything magical, mystical, dark, and sombre. The big houses of the residential quarters are interspersed with smaller houses, revealing that even social attitudes changed under Amenophis and his queen. It may be that the influence of Nefertiti was responsible for this short-lived bright Amarna period; it remained a refreshing oasis in the history of ancient Egypt. Then, cursed by the priests of Amon in Thebes, abandoned by all its people after the king's death, the sun city sank back into the sand and dust.

Iran. Only gradually did the Indo-European Medes who invaded Iran develop fixed dwellings with primitive markets from the existing settlements of peasants and cattle breeders. Rarely were there any suggestions of a town in connection with a feudal stronghold before whose walls an urban population of craftsmen and traders settled. Yet the very first Medo-Iranian capital, Ecbatana, had a citadel modelled on the universe. According to Herodotus, that citadel was girdled with seven walls in the colours of the planets. The innermost ring was golden (sun, Sunday), the second one silver (moon, Monday), the third scarlet (Mars, Tuesday), the fourth blue (Mercury, Wednesday), the fifth amber (Jupiter, Thursday), the sixth black (Venus, Friday), and the seventh ring white (Saturn, Saturday). This pattern points to the significance of the number seven, the star cult of the Medes, and the connection of the microcosm (citadel town) with the macrocosm of the universe.

Of Pasargadae, the early Persian capital, still less remains than of Ecbatana. More has been preserved of Persepolis, built by Darius in 520–515 BC. Its remains do not represent a town, however, but rather a magnificent palace complex. Sited on a terrace, Persepolis is essentially oriented toward the plain before it, parallel to the Zagros range. Nothing suggests any geomantic or magical notions, although the inscriptions set by Darius speak of the great supreme god Ahura-Mazdā, who bade Darius build the town and whom Darius requests to protect the land.

Influence of Zoroastrianism on Parthian towns

The spiritual successors of the Persians, the Parthians, or Arsacids, whose empire lasted from 247 BC to AD 224, were much influenced in their design of towns by Zoroastrianism. Of special interest is the old Parthian town of Phraaspa, allegedly Zoroaster's place of birth, which lay southeast of Lake Urmia. It was oval-elliptical in plan. From the south, along the northward main axis, lay an artificial lake, the fire temple, and a tower. It is possible to recognize in the ruins two parallel north–south main streets defining the central sacred area on the sides. It is also possible to visualize a quarter with small buildings in the northeast and the remains of a big complex of buildings in the west. In any case, Phraaspa is yet another example of a town designed to an overruling idea. Other Parthian towns, such as in Dārābgerd, a Parthian metropolis, are laid out in a perfectly concentric form, with circular outer and inner walls, eight main streets, eight gates, and a hill in the centre, the Meru.

It was the symbol of light and fire that the successors of the Parthians, the Sāsānids (AD 226–651), adopted as the basic idea for their towns. The first Sāsānid king, Ardashīr I, built his new capital of Gūr (Fīrūzābād) around that symbol—the disk of the sun. Gūr was laid out as a circular town with three ring walls. The innermost area comprised the palace and the government quarter, temples, fire tower, and priestly dwellings. The innermost wall had four gates, as did the outermost wall. The impression made by the town on its plain reveals successive ring streets and radial streets, forming two pairs of crossed axes. The whole town had the form of a shallow dish, surrounding the fire tower in its middle. The pattern seemed designed to symbolize the disk of the sun. It was also oriented on the cardinal points. The circles and rays symbolized the penetration of all earthly life, with its dark and evil aspects, by the light and the good.

Greece. Although Europe has a rich record of town developments, it is poor in models and rules of urban design. Pre-Hellenic and early Greek towns were laid out around strongholds or palaces on hills or terraces—as in Crete at Gourniá, Mallia, Phaestus, and Knossos, or in the Peloponnese at Mycenae and Tiryns. They were all laid out to serve practical and military needs, without a hint of a basic, symbolic idea of urban design, except that of building a stronghold protected against enemy attack. The plans of early towns of the Aegean are clearly influenced by Phoenicia in the layout of their harbours, both naval and commercial, and beyond that show the influence of the early Greek dwelling in the form of the megaron (a large, central hall). The houses face south, as does the town, but no geomantic notions are detectable.

The later development of the town in the Aegean islands, in Greece, and in western Asia Minor had a rich mythological accompaniment. Each town was linked with a city deity, yet without giving rise to any rules on layout. The Greeks were, in fact, for a long time reluctant to adopt rules for the layout of a town as a whole. The rebuilding of Miletus in 479 BC, after its destruction by the Persians, seems to mark the birth of a new style. It consisted in laying out a regular system of streets crossing at right angles within an arbitrary town plan determined by the local topography. The public and private buildings were then set within the squares of the grid. Priene—the third town of that name (350 BC), the two earlier ones having perished in the alluvial mud of the Meander—shows, within a plan freely adapted to the topography, a street system strictly oriented on the cardinal points, with all the buildings ordered into the grid. A similar pattern had already been adopted in 408 BC in the planning of Selinus on the south coast of Sicily, and at many other places. Generally, the new style preferred southward-sloping sites and south orientation.

The orientation of the Hellenistic town was freer. Doura-Europos (end of 4th century BC) follows the northwest–southeast orientation usual in Mesopotamia from olden times. In Laodicea, the position of the ruined buildings suggests a street system diagonal to the cardinal points; and the same applies to Pamukkale, ancient Hierapolis. The new style assumed a regularity that made it a classic model for later times. And so geomantic notions and mystical connections gave way to rational criteria.

The Roman town. Rome was bound by ideas of foundation ritual as well as formal town layout. In the foundation of a Roman town, Pierre Lavedan, a 20th-century French historian of architecture, distinguishes four phases: *inauguratio* (siting), *limitatio* (demarcation of area and subdivision thereof), *orientatio* (orientation of streets), and *consecratio* (consecration of the town). There were planning experts, the *gromatici*, and sacred formulas comparable to those of the geomancers of China and India. These formulas met the Roman bent for codification and deep religious sentiment, for the codified rule was both right and law.

The German Werner Müller gives a detailed description of the Roman *limitatio* and *orientatio*, which arose from Roman surveying practice and also harked back to very ancient notions. In the *limitatio*, the surveyors saw the earthly reflection of a heavenly model.

Mythological associations of Greek towns

Not only does the cardo (baseline) represent the world axis, but the quartering of the ground mirrors the cosmological model: the quartered terra in the Roman idea of the world.

Even in Roman antiquity, a whole literature, including textbooks and polemic treatises, arose on the subject. The origins of the *limitatio* go back to the Etruscans, but whether that Etruscan root really represents the earliest origin of the Roman idea of the world, the *mundus*, is an open question.

In their ideas on construction, however, the Romans followed Greek and Hellenistic models. Rome thus relied for urban design on a tradition that the Etruscans had brought from Asia, and for architecture on the concepts of the Greek feeling for nature. Even the form of the *castrum* (fortress) presumably has an Alexandrian origin, the Romans having followed the model of the camp of Pyrrhus, which they had captured in 275 BC. The application of the ancient rules to the *castrum* made this the prototype of Roman urban design. The model consist-

Fortress towns as prototypes of Roman urban design

By courtesy of the Herzog August Bibliothek, Wolfenbüttel, Germany

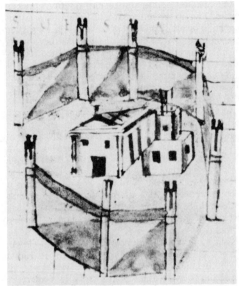

Representation of a Roman *castrum* from the Roman codex *Corpus agrimensorum romanorum*. In the Herzog August Bibliothek, Wolfenbüttel, Germany.

ed of a square plan, oriented on the cardinal points, with central crossroads leading to the four gates of the square on the north, south, east, and west. Even so, remains of *castra* show that the directions were not always and everywhere strictly adhered to. Instead of taking sights on the true cardinal points, the *gromatici* might work out some relation between the point of sunrise and the emperor's birthday or the day of foundation. And so the *orientatio* varied, for it seems that the *gromatici* followed fashions or practical needs and might on one occasion simply set the *porta praetoria* (main gate) opposite the enemy. Whether the lore of the *gromatici* came from Old Babylonia via Etruria, or, as some claim, from the north via the neighbouring Celts or Teutons, is still a matter for research.

EARLY ASIA

Indian region. The layout of the early towns of the Indus civilization (2600–1500 BC) has become known mainly through the excavations at Mohenjo-daro and Harappā. Mohenjo-daro, on the lower reach of the Indus River, now a field of ruins measuring about 1,100 by 1,100 yards (1,000 by 1,000 metres), was square in plan, probably with three north–south streets crossed by two east–west streets; thus, the town was oriented on the cardinal points. In the middle third of its western strip stood a citadel containing a *stupa* (cylindrical mound or tower), baths, assembly hall, and storehouses, while the other areas were occupied by dwellings (courtyard houses) of various size. It seems that part of the town was washed away by the Indus breaking its banks. Harappā, of about the same size and layout, also had its citadel in the middle of the west side, with storehouses and workmen's quarters to the north. It may thus be that locating the civic centre on the town's middle west side corresponded to the rules and concepts of urban design at the time. Streets and drainage systems as well as the house layouts reveal that the art of construction had reached a very high level and that nothing was left to chance.

Soon after the arrival of the Aryans in India, a new culture was founded. Beginning on a rural base, it gradually matured into an urban culture. Settlements with forts as power bases and for the protection of the peasantry were built. About 1000 BC certain settlements began to be fortified with girdling walls and rules started to be formulated for the layout of house and town. Those rules are laid down in the *Śilpa-śāstra* (compendium of science in 64 books), notably in the *Mānasāra* book of 58 chapters, containing rules on architecture and sculpture, and also in another book called *Bṛhat-Saṃhitā*. The first prerequisites of "good luck" in house and town were strict orientation on the cardinal points and certain divisions and endowments of area in the inner town. All measures, forms, and proportions were fixed. Every town had a long street running from east to west called *rāja-patha* (king's way), and a short street running north and south, called *mahākāla* (broad way), as well as a ring street within the walls, called *mangalavithi*, for religious processions. The centre of the town was to be occupied by a hill, later in tower form (the *stupa*).

Ancient towns of India

The struggle between the invading Aryans in India and the aboriginal population was reflected in the ancient Vedic traditions as the struggle of the Pandu sons with the Kuru sons. Named as their chief towns are Indraprastha (Pandu) and Hastinapura (Kuru), towns that the epic work of that time, the *Mahābhārata*, describes as splendid, glamorous cities. Nothing remains of them or of any contemporary cities of the Vedic or immediate post-Vedic periods, but they are described as having been modelled on the heavenly city. How is modern man to imagine them?

In Sanskrit literature, the identity of microcosm (town) and macrocosm (world) is taken for granted. In Indian religion (both Hindu and Buddhist), the world spreads out toward the four cardinal points from its centre, the world mountain, which is called Hinawat or Meru and commands the concentric bands of the world and the oceans. The town layout reflects the plan of the universe. Such a pattern is shown in particular by the towns of Indochina, such as Angkor Thom, the capital of the Khmer kingdom (modern Cambodia). Jayavarman II (*c.* 802–850) founded the first Angkor as one of his residences, and Jayavarman VII (1181–*c.* 1215, possibly as late as 1219) built the second Angkor Thom in 1201. In the centre of the earlier town of Angkor Thom stood the temple complex of Phnom Bakheng. In the southeast quadrant rose the huge structure of the Angkor Wat temple. Town and temple were quartered by crossroads, with the step pyramid (Bayon) in the centre. In the Bayon, the Buddhists set up an image of Bodhisattva Avalokiteśvara, the Lord of the World, while the Hindu kings set up the *linga*, the phallic symbol of Śiva, the supreme god. Angkor was thus the perfect uranopolis (heavenly city). Later, when rebuilt, Angkor Thom was considerably reduced in size. Phnom Bakheng remained outside the new town, south of the new south gate, and so did Angkor Wat, but yet farther to the south. The model becomes clear from the designation of the town walls as world mountain, the town moats as world ocean, the step temples as gold (sun) mountains, and the centre as the gods' abode. And so the notion of the heavenly city provided the model for the earthly city. Some cosmological layouts were followed in many early cities of Southeast Asia.

China. In China, as in India, a feudal form of society developed early, with protectors and clients, rulers and subjects. An urban system arose that was shaped partly by the need to ward off the continual raids of the nomads of the steppes on the settled population. The towns were thus laid out as refuges. The priests, augurs, and geoman-

Early Chinese towns

cers, on the other hand, wanted the towns laid out in keeping with the divine and natural laws. It was only by the time of the Chou dynasty (*c.* 1122–221 BC), however, that this deeper sense of law and regularity was felt. Later, the towns at the time of the barbarian raids were laid out square, usually with twin girdling walls, but with sufficient space between the two for crop-growing to sustain the population during a siege. The philosopher Mencius (*c.* 371–289 BC) describes such a town, and the chronicle *Shu-li* calls its general arrangement a rational and organic system. Soon, however, those towns seem to have been taken over by temples and the military, and the peasants, traders, and craftsmen told to settle outside the gates.

The geomantic rules on the construction of house, palace, temple, and town employed in later periods also probably arose during the Chou dynasty. The principles of town layout are laid down in the *Feng-shui* doctrine, which treats of the integration of human works into the pattern of the universe (*feng*—wind, floods of heaven; *shui*—water, floods of the earth). On *feng* and *shui* depends man's luck. It was the task of the geomancer to fix a propitious site for every structure (house, bridge, town, and so on). He used a compass disk divided into rings and sectors that indicated the site's relation both to the five elements (water, fire, metal, wood, and earth) and to the four cardinal points. The general rule governing the town is called *pei-shan-mien-shui* ("mountains to the north, water to the south"). Rules governing the design

Ernst Egli

Early Chinese drawing showing the principle *pei-shan-mien-shui* ("mountains to the north, water to the south"), which generally governed the establishment of a town.

of houses were concerned with spirits and forces within the house that could be controlled by arrangements relating to air, light, and shelter from the wind and cold.

Japan. The Japanese house and the Japanese town are primarily models of the integration of building into nature. It appears that the early Japanese did not regard the town as a desirable ideal. Towns in the real sense only arose after the adoption of Buddhism (about AD 550). They were founded by the emperors and laid out on Chinese models. Thus were founded Hesho Kio (south of Kyōto) after AD 710, Nagaoka after 784, and Kyōto ("the big city") after 792. They are laid out in a regular chessboard pattern. Kyōto measured 3.3 by 3.0 miles (5.3 by 4.8 kilometres) and was oriented on the cardinal points. The emperor's palace stood in the middle of the north side. It is likely that geomancers also had a hand in laying out other towns, as in China. From 1200 on, however, the Chinese model was discarded in favour of a picturesque, spatial composition. The Japanese were more given to a mystical feeling for nature that included both the remoter scenery and the close vicinity of the site. Streams, groves, bridges, rocks, pebble tracts, stones—all had their symbolic meaning. Thus, to the Japanese, all nature was pervaded with spiritual symbols, and to bring these into their right mutual relations was a great art—an art that consisted in a symbolic spiritualization of the details, yet without any geometry or axes.

ANCIENT AMERICA

Singularity of the towns of ancient America

When referring to towns in ancient America, it must be remembered that one cannot say whether they really were towns in the normal sense. Few remains of a complete town have been found that include all the usual sections: a commercial and industrial district and market, an administrative area with castle or palace, a religious compound with temples and places of worship, and an agricultural complex with storehouses. The existing remains are mostly confined to a monumental nucleus, the religious or ruling centre of a town. It is not known whether any dwelling quarters were associated with such centres. Sometimes the ruins comprise dwellings without any trace of a temple or sacrificial site or of a commercial section. This applies particularly to the pueblo settlements of the southwestern United States. As far as the apparently purely ceremonial centres are concerned, it is most unlikely that they did not employ numbers of servants, officials, and craftsmen. Their dwellings, however, apparently were not built of stone.

The choice of site seems to have been determined less by good communications than by the proximity of fertile land, suitable building material, water, and possibly by the geomantic aspects of the place. An important factor seems to have been the possibility of laying out terraces. In plan, the towns do not always follow geomantic notions, and in the mountains are often adapted to the terrain for defense.

Pueblo cultures. The chief sites are Betatakin (Arizona), Mesa Verde (Colorado), Aztec (New Mexico), Canyon de Chelly (Arizona), Pueblo Bonito, and Frijoles Canyon (both New Mexico). The population of the region between the Rio Grande and the Colorado River built cliff settlements either as clusters of cells in natural caves or as compact, uniform settlements in open country. Which form is the earlier is arguable. The pueblo form might be regarded as being based on an old cave settlement removed into a valley and subsequently transferred back again to a cave under the pressure of external enemies. Pueblos follow a comprehensive form, with structures curving or set at angles surrounding a court area.

The site at Aztec (New Mexico) obviously represents a later development, as it is regulated by a strict order. Both forms, however, are based on an ancient symbol, the mother's enclosing of a valuable fruit. The spaces enclosed by the pueblos are either rectangular rooms, which may have served as dwelling and store rooms, or circular ceremonial chambers called kivas, from 10 to 33 feet (3 to 10 metres) in diameter.

The cave form of pueblo structure is found at Mesa Verde, in Colorado. Carbon dating of the timber remains assigns it to the 12th century AD.

For an earlier example, reference might be made to Pueblo Bonito, one of the twelve pueblo ruins in the Chaco Canyon. The plan reveals an earlier building subsequently greatly extended. The ring of the structure rises rearward to form a high back surface, from which the approaching person descends toward the inner court. A second early example, at Aztec, has a rectangular plan of U-shape; the house encloses the rectangular court, with the main kiva in the centre. Smaller kivas inside the building were regularly distributed.

Middle America. The capital of the Toltecs, Teotihuacán, was a large-scale layout 28 kilometres northeast of

Cliff Palace, Mesa Verde National Park, Colo.
By courtesy of the Colorado Department of Public Relations

Mexico City. The ruins comprise a straight, monumental avenue running north and south, about two kilometres long; abutting it in the north is the Pyramid of the Moon and further groups of buildings. On its east side is the great Sun Pyramid, 200 feet (60 metres) high, and further groups of buildings on both sides of the avenue. To the south is found the so-called Citadel, and perhaps (though this is merely conjecture) the secular town, possibly with the ruler's seat. Around Teotihuacán, at a distance of a few miles, were big communal dwellings of 50 to 60 rooms. So the town may have been a combination of a monumental temple city serving priests and king, and rural communal villages.

Monumental layout of Teotihuacán

Tenochtitlán, the Aztec capital, sited on an island in

Plan of Tenochtitlán, from a woodcut in Ramusio's *Delle navigationi et viaggi*, 1550–59.

Lake Texcoco, much larger at the time, flourished after AD 1400. Canals were its main thoroughfares. Three main streets running south, north, and west from the central square gave access to the hinterland. The town was peopled by 20 different tribes, each of which had its own tribal house and which all jointly owned the big central square. Facing the square from the east was the great pyramid with the main temple on its top platform; beside it stood the palace of Montezuma; farther south rose a second pyramid. According to a contemporary account there was also a great market square surrounded by colonnades.

Similar in layout to Tenochtitlán was the town of Tlatelolco, which had a large and remarkable market place with shops arranged behind colonnades. Of special interest is Monte Albán, the town of the Zapotecs and later of the Mixtecs. To judge by its ruins, it measured about 19 square miles (50 square kilometres) and was exactly oriented on the cardinal points. The town centre was a big square, measuring 330 by 215 yards (300 by 195 metres), with a remarkable flight of steps, 121 feet (37 metres) wide and 39 feet (12 metres) high. A ball court with rows of stone seats at the sides occupied a corner of the square. Again, nowhere in this large-scale layout of well-planned proportions and classic style can any traces of ordinary dwelling districts be found.

Other towns of the period include Texcoco, Culhuacán, Tenayuca, Xochicalco, Malinalco, Calixtahuaca, Tajín, Cholula, and La Venta, which is assigned to the Olmecs. The remains of La Venta's religious quarter reveal an architecturally important cultural centre, oriented on the cardinal points, with pyramids, squares, cisterns, tombs and sarcophagi, altars, columns, and stelae, all overgrown by jungle.

Accomplishment of Mayan design— Copán and Tikal

The Maya towns, dating from an earlier period, are noted for their masterly grouping of temples, squares, pyramids, courts, and colonnades, interspersed with individual buildings. Outstanding examples are Copán (in present-day Honduras) and Tikal (in Guatemala); they are models of accomplished layout. The remains of the monumental centre of Tikal cover an area of 900 by 1,300 yards (800 by 1,200 metres); in Copán, part of the centre was washed away by the Copán River, but the remainder still measures more than 1,100 yards (1,000 metres) in length. The later Maya period saw the construction of the towns of Chichén-Itzá (not later than AD 450), Uxmal, Labná, Tula, Mayapán, Cobá, and others. They reveal a free, picturesque attitude in their layout and architectural detail and thus almost exactly correspond to the development that Chinese urban design took between Ch'ang-an or Ho-Yang and the later town of Tsien-fu. Typical of this second Maya period is the development of Chichén-Itzá, where three periods are discernible: the first from 534 to 987, the second from 987 to the arrival of the Spaniards in the 16th century, and the third marking the decline of the town. The town centre belongs to the first period; it comprises the so-called Nunnery, the Red House, and the House of the Three Lintels (about 889). Under the Toltecs, further typical units were added: squares, temples, courts, and also baths.

The Andes. In the Andes region, the towns on the coastal plain are quite different in character from those built in the Andes themselves. The towns on the plateau of the Andes are no doubt the earlier. Of special importance was Tiahuanaco, southeast of Lake Titicaca at an altitude of 12,546 feet (3,825 metres). The remains antedating AD 1000 comprise the Acapana, an artificial earth mound set broad on an area 690 by 690 feet (210 by 210 metres), presumably a kind of acropolis; the Calasasaya, a temple area of 425 by 440 feet (130 by 135 metres) surrounded by huge walls, which also served as a celestial observatory; and the Puma-Puncu (Lion Gate), the Tunka-Puncu (Gate of Ten), and the Umu-Puncu (Water Gate), surrounded by many pieces of architecture. The gates undoubtedly had symbolic value, but the riddles posed by the town have so far been neither solved nor plausibly interpreted.

In the coastal area of the Andes, various political enti-

ties from prehistoric times can be identified. The Chimú area was of paramount importance. Pacatnamú in the north was a large town of regular layout containing about 70 pyramids, the biggest measuring 65 by 65 yards (60 by 60 metres), as well as steps, terraces, and a palace. Huanca de Chira, seat of a Chimú ruler, had a three-stepped pyramid measuring 100 by 130 yards (90 by 120 metres) at the base. Chan Chan, probably the most important layout in the whole south, has a ruined area measuring 11 square miles (28 square kilometres). Sited between the sea and a river in the south, with mountains on the north and east, Chan Chan had a harbour before its west wall, with docks that could be closed by gates. It also had residential districts with gardens. Inside the town walls were the clan quarters, separated from each other by walls. Each was rectangular in plan, interspersed with pyramids, tumuli (grave mounds), and temples. Two special complexes attract attention: the so-called Great Palace, about 450 by 550 yards (400 by 500 metres), and the small, second palace. The former comprised courts, quadrangles, countless buildings with many rooms, and a large poundlike water reservoir. All the elements of the Great Palace are ruled by a rigorous order. This applies similarly to the small palace, comprising a large number of buildings similar to courtyard houses, large quadrangles, a pyramid, corridors, and courts. All sections of this admirably laid-out town are oriented strictly on the cardinal points, with the south–north direction dominating. Without a doubt, Chan Chan presented a splendid sight with its regular pattern, its wall alignments, its parks along the canals, its painted scenes, and the stucco ornamentation of the walls. It may be compared to Peking, the residence of Kublai Khan, and it is fair to ask whether the roots of those two towns had not at some time grown on common ground.

(margin: Layout of Chan Chan)

Chavín de Huántar is the second most important town in the Andes region south of the Chimú realm. It was a centre of religion and power, as evidenced by the ruins of temples and a palace. To the south are further complexes, palaces, forts, temple areas, pyramids, irrigation systems, water reservoirs, terraces, and remains of dwellings with scattered centres not concentrated within the framework of a comprehensive town. It is a town scattered within the confines of a valley community. Farther south lay Pachacamac, a large town within the realm of the Cuismancú rulers, with a large temple complex, which in the 9th century became the main centre of pilgrimage on the coast. The temple, measuring 133 by 60 yards (122 by 55 metres), formed the centre of a sacred enclosure and rose in five steps. Adjacent to the temple lay the old town, itself girdled by a wall. It was divided into four quarters by crossroads.

Pacatnamú, Chan Chan, and Pachacamac were all complete towns, places of both temporal and spiritual rule, with dwellings for the ordinary people. All three were the result of a social system that submitted to supernatural powers and infused its life with symbols. A glance at the layouts and the monumental ruins is sufficient to suggest how strongly those people felt committed to their ideas of order within the community. It was therefore easy for the urban designers of the time to embody that spiritual order in an artistic order.

EARLY AFRICA

There are various accounts of the feudal system prevailing in early African times, mainly by the Arabs al-Bakri (11th century), Yāqūt (12th century), Ibn Baṭṭūṭah and Ibn Khaldūn (both 14th century), and others.

According to one authority the population was divided into five classes: the knights (*horro*), the bards (*korrongo* or *djulli*), the serfs (also weavers), the smiths and other craftsmen (*numu*), and the domestic servants and captives (*ulussu*). The *horro* were the town founders. The disinherited sons of knights, they set out with bards and smiths to found a town. The site chosen was by a river, and was marked out as a circle or a rectangle in keeping with geomantic rites. Four gates were set up to the cardinal points, and a bull was ritually sacrificed. After three months, another bull was sacrificed together

(margin: Founding of an early African town)

Walled city of Kano, Nigeria.
Marilyn Silverstone—Magnum

with a virgin; only then was the town permitted to hold market. Then the *horro* set out on raiding expeditions, after which the newly built houses were occupied and life took its normal course.

The shape of the towns may be deduced from present-day Kano (Nigeria), Timbuktu (Republic of Mali), Benin (Nigeria), and Loandjili (Congo [Brazzaville]). In Kano there are compounds with cubic components set against the enclosure wall, and with huts of clay standing clear in the court. The huts are cylindrical, and not too high. The streets are mainly winding and often with dead ends. In Loandjili, the houses are quite different: they are built as a group around a free central space, which they face. These groups seem to be laid out as districts forming clan dwellings. Both Kano and Loandjili are complete with temple, palace, market place, and commercial section.

The towns of early Africa were oriented on the cardinal points; were related to the country, to water and rivers, certainly allowing for the influence of the environment on settlements; and followed geomantic rules governing layout. They varied in plan, being circular or rectangular or often compact, with the clan compound as the basic unit. They obviously formed neighbourhoods, and were built on hillsides, hilltops, and on plains.

MEDIEVAL ISLAM

Islām refashioned the urban concepts that had developed earlier in the Near and Middle East areas. The new urban concept was deeply rooted in Islām itself, which had arisen in the world of the nomads, in Arabia's steppes and deserts, and thence spread out over the Near and Middle East, North Africa, and neighbouring areas. And it was that world that conditioned the Muslim way of thinking and feeling. The people living in that dry, bare, and hazardous environment carried in them a dream image of paradise; in the Qur'ān it is described in terms of gardens and springs, shade-giving trees, and abundance of food and drink. But while that dream image inspired various Islāmic palace layouts, it never determined an Islāmic town layout. For the actual initiators of Islām, the Arabians, were nomads and as such were hostile to urban life. To them, and to most Muslims, the town was not essential; it was simply accepted as incidental. Nevertheless, the Muslims founded towns, partly for military necessity, partly from the wish of the Muslims to camp in quarters of their own, partly from the wish of their rulers to build protected palaces, and, above all, because of the worldwide trade of the Muslim empire and the tradition of peoples who had lived in urbanized areas before the rise of Islām.

Muslims as town founders

Istanbul, seat of the caliph, the Prophet's successor, was not called the holy city or the Prophet's city, but rather the seat of felicity, with a clear allusion to the idea of paradise. Islām knew practically no generally applicable rules for the layout of towns. The town consisted simply of so many quarters, without any plan ordering the whole. It was the Muslim quarter, the *mahalle*, the neighbourhood associated with a particular mosque, that constituted the real unit in the social life of the Islāmic town. Such a quarter, in its advanced phase, comprised the mosque, a library, baths, a hospital, a school, a religious college, and well-houses. In setting out his environment, the Muslim wavered between sheer neglect of the worldly city and lavish attention to the world of the hereafter, to the divine and the eternal.

And so the Islāmic town is conditioned by outlook, but also by climatic factors, being built as an enclosed town of the arid zone, with enclosed quarters and enclosed courtyard houses. Politically, it may be divided into two sections: the palace of the rulers and, surrounding it, the quarters of the faithful. It is further characterized by its peculiar street system. This comprises two types of street: winding streets, which turn in one direction and then another, as if searching for the way; and blind streets, which simply provide access to the interior of a quarter or dwelling group and come to an abrupt end. Thus, a district is usually skirted with winding streets, from which radiate the blind streets into the interior.

The early period of Islām saw the growth of cities from military camps, called *ḥīrah*. Kufa and Basra, founded in 638, provided examples. In 642 the Muslims founded Fusṭāṭ on the Nile; it developed rapidly from a military camp into a large town surrounding the 'Amr Mosque, on the site of present-day Cairo. Kairouan (modern al-Qayrawān) in Tunisia was founded as a military camp in the 7th century. None of these towns reveals any specific design, let alone a common one. Neither do Mecca, the city of pilgrimage, or Medina, originally a trading post, show any deliberate design or any development toward such. In Syria and Palestine, urban layouts had mostly been established before the rise of Islām—as in Damascus, Jerusalem, Jericho, Amman, Haifa, and other important centres.

In Mesopotamia, however, Islām founded new towns, such as Baghdad and Sāmarrā' on the Tigris. Baghdad in particular is of interest in terms of design. It was founded in 762 by the Abbāsid caliph Mansūr and was completed in 766. Mansūr, advised by a former Persian magus, Halit, undoubtedly followed the model of the Sāsānian town of Gūr, which was laid out in a circle as a symbol of the sun. The diameter of Baghdad was 3,100 yards (2,800 metres), so that the town covered 1,500 acres (600 hectares). It had four gates, the Syrian Gate in the north-

From S. Moholy-Nagy, *Matrix of Man* (1968); Praeger Publishers, Inc.

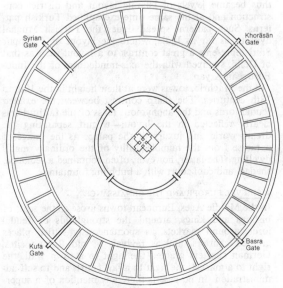

Plan of Baghdad, founded AD 762.

"Perspective of an Ideal City," panel painting designed by Luciano Laurana, third quarter of the 15th century. In the Galleria Nazionale delle Marche, Palazzo Ducale, Urbino.
SCALA, New York

west, the Khorāsān Gate in the northeast, the Basra Gate in the southeast, and the Kufa Gate in the southwest. The town's main axes were thus diagonal to the square of the cardinal points, as had been the practice in earlier times. Sāmarrā,' however, took the form of a ribbon town along the left bank of the Tigris, mainly because the caliphs at various times built their residences at that spot, with all their retainers, troops, craftsmen, and merchants settling around them.

Islāmic towns of Persia

The Persian towns of Tabrīz, Tūs, Isfahan, Mashad, Shīrāz, Hamadan, Kandehar, Neyshābūr, and Kermān are typical Islāmic towns. Isfahan, rebuilt in 903 on a circular plan, had four gates and a hundred towers on the Zoroastrian model. It reached its zenith with the buildings erected by 'Abbās (1587–1629). These included the palace and monumental avenues and bridges, all governed by geometrical regularity. But frequent dynastic changes and earthquakes make it difficult to trace the development of the town. Like Isfahan, Shīrāz seems to have originally been circular in plan, while Hamadan was laid out square. Besides the influences of Islāmic architecture and Sāsānian tradition, it is possible to detect a Turanian influence from Central Asia. These influences are mostly superimposed on one another.

In central Asia, the Turkish element is dominant. The layout of the Turkish town consisted of a casual grouping devoid of axes. The Turkish contribution to urban design consists in the picturesque arrangement of domes and pavilions. Thoroughfares stretching from gate to gate formed the trading and religious centres, while the buildings themselves, influenced by Persian architecture, presented geometrical crystalline perspectives of exceptional charm and imagination. The centres of the bigger towns thus became jewels of Islāmic layout and district construction and at the same time exemplified Turkish patterns. Such patterns spread under the Turkish Mughal dynasty as far as India, where the layout of Fatehpur Sikri represents a great contrast to a layout such as that of Delhi, stamped with the axis-mindedness of the Indo-European Aryans.

In the Maghrib, towns were at their height in the 10th to 13th centuries. The sharp contrast between the exalted feudal lords and the anonymous mass of the faithful was clearly reflected in the layout—a gulf separating the dream world and luxury of the palace as the image of paradise from the humble utility of the ordinary man's dwelling. The latter, however, often contained a secluded, shaded, and cool court with a bubbling fountain.

MEDIEVAL EUROPE AND THE RENAISSANCE

In the Middle Ages, European towns arose as the seats of bishops and kings, around the strongholds of feudal lords, around markets, as spontaneously settled places granted charters, and as revivals of old Roman sites. German charters granted the right to a town wall, the right to a market, the right to a law court, and to self-administration. In no case is there any mention of a supernatural order, of the town as the mirror image of a

heavenly city or of a universal order. Layouts were diverse, with parallel, radial, grid, triangular, and square plans. The main determinant of layout was topography.

Diverse layouts of medieval towns

A medieval town was hallowed not for having a cross in its plan, but for its associations with a saint; cathedrals were hallowed not because of their plan, but because they enshrined a holy relic. And this superseded the geomancy of the ancients and filled the people's need for mysticism.

The Renaissance introduced the rational element in the form of geometry, mathematics, and practical considerations as the factors determining urban design. The square, the octagon, polygons, and the circle are proposed as the plan, with the streets visualized as laid in regular chessboard patterns or radiating from a centre. Thus, a great many ideal towns were set out, on paper, but most of them were never built. The real towns were already there, creations of the Middle Ages, and with them all the institutions, laws, and patterns. Since adoption of the new trend would have required wholesale demolition, only in special cases was it possible to apply new concepts. All Renaissance theorists searched for new models for urban design. Vitruvius, the ancient Roman architect, provided the basis for Leon Battista Alberti (1404–72), who starts with the environment of the town, its topography, climate, and soil, and discusses the rational choice of site and the best form for a town and its streets from the military angle. His are the views of a thinker and architect who sees the town in the light of practical needs and who attempts to subordinate these needs to a rational order. The same applies to Antonio di Pietro Averlino Filarete, who intended to create a rational town with a planned place for each of its parts. Following him come several designers of ideal towns, such as Francesco di Giorgio, Francesco de Marchi, Pietro Cataneo, and others. They all visualize their towns set in fortifications. Alberti mentions two basic elements of design: *commoditas*, corresponding to the modern idea of functionality, and *voluptas*, or the pleasure taken in styling. In this context he speaks of beauty, which to him is the effect of rational design, geometrical relations, and numerical laws. His approach spread from Italy to Francė, Germany, Spain, and to the rest of Europe, including Russia. In all those countries arose theorists of urban design, and models passed from one hand to another, from one country to another.

Soon, however, there was a change of attitude, leading in the 16th century to the Baroque style. As it was impossible in practice to build a town as a whole, the urban designers lost out to the detail designer, the architect. And his thought proceeded not from the whole to the detail, but rather from his work to its surroundings, and his object was to make his work radiate into the surroundings. Urban design thus abandoned the comprehensive view and became the architecture of the individual building complex. As a consequence, the concerns of the ordinary citizens were neglected in favour of those of the princely builders of the period. Such was the background to Michelangelo's design for the Capitol in Rome, the

The Baroque style in architecture

rebuilding of Rome by Sixtus V, and the construction of St. Peter's in Rome. Everywhere in Europe the supremacy of perspective began. Axes of vision became axes of architecture. The influence of Baroque design extended even outside Europe, to Latin America. (E.A.E.)

BIBLIOGRAPHY. DONALD APPLEYARD, KEVIN LYNCH, and JOHN R. MYER, *The View from the Road* (1964), an early discussion of the possibilities of highway design for the pleasure of the observer in motion; EDMUND N. BACON, *Design of Cities* (1967), a discussion of city design with many historic examples by an experienced planner who takes a strong formalist stand; includes an interesting re-evaluation of Brasília; F. STUART CHAPIN, *Urban Land Use Planning*, 2nd ed. (1965), the standard text in the field; PHILIPPE BOUDON, *Pessac de Le Corbusier* (1969), an excellent analysis of an early housing project of Corbusier, and of how it is seen by its inhabitants; GORDON CULLEN, *Townscape* (1961), examples of visual effects in urban settings; FRANCOISE CHOAY, *The Modern City: Planning in the 19th Century* (1969), an excellent, well-illustrated, brief history of the city planning ideas that lead to our current dilemmas, with a clear analysis of the inadequacies; HERBERT J. GANS, *People and Plans* (1968), sharp essays by a sociologist who is skeptical of the importance of physical setting for social behaviour; PAUL GOODMAN and PERCIVAL, *Communitas* (1947), an interesting critique of planning ideas, with three examples of imaginary environments designed to support particular values and ways of living; WERNER HEGEMANN, *City Planning, Housing*, vol. 3, *A Graphic Review of Civic Art, 1922–1937* (1938), a classic pictorial review of examples of urban design through the early 20th century; KEVIN LYNCH, *The Image of the City* (1960), an early study of the perception and cognition of urban places by their inhabitants; *Site Planning*, rev. ed. (1971), a text on the basic principles and methods of arranging complex outdoor environments; IAN L. MCHARG, *Design with Nature* (1969), an impassioned plea for the use of ecological principles in environmental design; MARTIN MEYERSON, *The Face of the Metropolis* (1963), a pictorial summary of recent examples of urban design in the traditional sense; GREAT BRITAIN, MINISTRY OF HOUSING AND LOCAL GOVERNMENT, *Design in Town and Village* (1953), a solid discussion of well-accepted principles in the layout of building groups; IAN NAIRN, *The American Landscape* (1965), a personal and observant analysis of the U.S. visual scene with emphasis on identity, pedestrian sequences, and the picturesque view; AMOS RAPOPORT, "Observations Regarding Man-Environment Studies," *Man-Environment Systems* (January 1970), an excellent review article on the analysis of the impact of environment on behaviour and perception, with a full bibliography; STEEN EILER RASMUSSEN, *Towns and Buildings Described in Drawings and Words* (1951), delightful descriptions of several cities or city centres famous for their visual qualities; CAMILLO SITTE, *Der Stadtebau* (1889; Eng. trans., *City Planning According to Artistic Principles*, 1965), the classic statement of the romantic viewpoint in urban aesthetics; ROBERT SOMMER, *Personal Space: The Behavioral Basis of Design* (1969), an excellent summary of the best current work on the interaction of space and behaviour; PAUL D. SPREIREGEN, *Urban Design: The Architecture of Towns and Cities* (1965), a recent general review of the methods and aims of urban design; CLARENCE S. STEIN, *Toward New Towns for America* (1951), a clear description and analysis of a cluster of U.S. innovations in group-housing design; CHRISTOPHER TUNNARD and BORIS PUSHKAREV, *Man-Made America: Chaos or Control?* (1963), essays on the large-scale design of various elements in the environment.

History: PIERRE LAVEDAN, *Histoire de l'urbanisme*, 3 vol. (1926–52), an in-depth history, particularly of Greek and Roman urban design but including chapters on the Middle and modern ages; FREDERICK R. HIORNS, *Town-Building in History* (1956), a history of urban design, particularly from the English standpoint; ERNST EGLI, *Geschichte des Städtebaues*, vol. 1, *Die alte Welte* (1959), vol. 2, *Das Mittelalter* (1962), and vol. 3, *Die neue Zeit* (1967), a general history of urban design in all parts of the world in all periods; LE CORBUSIER, *Urbanisme* (1924), contains the early theories of architect and city designer Corbusier, which led to new directions in building; *La charte d'Athènes* (1957), a summary of the basic principles of modern urban design and construction; LUDWIG HILBERSEIMER, *The New City* (1944), Hilberseimer develops his ideas of a city and gives theoretical applications; FRANK LLOYD WRIGHT, *Broadacre City: When Democracy Builds* (1945), Wright's argument against "megalopolis-mania" and the importation of un-American urban designs into America.

(K.L./E.A.E./Ed.)

Urbanization

The term urbanization refers to the process by which a population becomes concentrated in cities or "urban places." The process may proceed in either of two distinct ways: (1) through an increase in the number of urban places or (2) through an increase in the size of the population resident in each urban place. Although the term is sometimes also used to refer to the consequences of living in urban places, scholars prefer, for that purpose, to use the word urbanism, as in "urbanism as a way of life."

An *urban place* or city may be defined in as many ways as there are ways of regarding it—architecturally, geographically, economically, politically, and so on. As a matter of convenience and in the interest of comparability, an urban place or city is generally defined in demographic terms—on the basis of some minimum number of inhabitants. The United Nations, for purposes of international comparability, has recommended that all nations in tabulating their censuses and other official statistics, regard all concentrated places of 20,000 or more inhabitants as urban. Currently and in the past, various countries have defined different cutting-off points ranging from under 1,000 to over 20,000 (the U.S. uses the figure 2,500), and some countries use no criterion of size at all.

Conventional terminology

The *place* element in "urban place" also poses problems of definition, for a city's boundaries may be subject to change through annexation or disannexation or may be ill defined or nonexistent. Prior to 1950 in the United States, for example, an urban place included only *incorporated* places of 2,500 persons or more, but beginning in 1950 *unincorporated* places of 2,500 or more were also included as "urban"—a practice that required census geographers to impose arbitrary boundaries around concentrations of population, usually around larger cities. The problem is compounded by the fact that in many countries (including the U.S.) incorporated urban boundaries may embrace open country or "rural" populations.

With continued urbanization, population agglomerations have often spilled over established city boundary lines, thus inspiring new areal concepts in an effort to capture the actual, as contrasted with the political, population unit. The U.S. census report for Chicago, for instance, has information on the City of Chicago (the area incorporated in a charter granted by the state of Illinois), the Urbanized Area of Chicago (the city plus all adjoining densely populated areas), the Standard Metropolitan Statistical Area (the central city together with the adjoining counties—six of them—that are socially and economically related to the central city), and the Chicago-Northwestern Indiana Standard Consolidated Area (consisting of two adjoining Standard Metropolitan Statistical Areas, the Chicago area and the Gary-Hammond-East Chicago area). Besides such official designations, another term that has appeared with increasing frequency is megalopolis, referring to metropolitan areas that coalesce to become one continuous clumping of peoples and economic activities. One such area in the United States stretches from metropolitan Boston to metropolitan Washington, D.C. The English use the term conurbation to refer to essentially the same thing around such areas as London and Manchester-Liverpool.

CHARACTERISTICS OF URBANIZATION

Urban population growth. In view of the complexities of definition and the absence of widespread census taking prior to 1800, one can readily understand the impossibility of tracing world urbanization with any precision prior to the beginning of the 19th century. But since 1800 the proportion of the world's population resident in cities of 20,000 or more (and 100,000 or more) has been reasonably summarized. In the accompanying table it can be seen that the proportion of the world's population that was urban increased between 1800 and 1950, from 2.4 percent to 20.9 percent. By 1970, according to the United Nations, about 28 percent of the world's population was resident in urban places (of 20,000 or more population).

The United States can be taken as an illustration of the process of urbanization. In 1790, when the first decennial census of the United States was taken, there were only 24 urban places (with 2,500 persons or more). By the 19th

Percentage of World's Population Living in Cities		
year	cities of 20,000 or more	cities of 100,000 or more
1800	2.4	1.7
1850	4.3	2.3
1900	9.2	5.5
1950	20.9	13.1
1970	27.8	24.0

Sources: Kingsley Davis, "The Origin and Growth of Urbanization in the World," *The American Journal of Sociology*, March 1955 and *World Urbanization 1950–1970*, 1969; United Nations, *Statistical Yearbook 1969*.

decennial census in 1970, the number had increased to 7,062. However, not only did the number of urban places increase but so did the average number of inhabitants in each place: in 1790 the average number of persons in an urban place was 8,400; by 1970 the average number had risen to 21,145. In consequence of both these increases, the urban proportion of the population rose from five percent in 1790 to 73.5 percent in 1970.

Population distribution. Man, in building his culture over his 2,000,000-to-4,000,000-year occupation of this planet, has precipitated three developments that have culminated in urbanization and urbanism as a way of life. The *population explosion* describes the remarkable acceleration in the rate of world population growth, especially during the past three centuries of the modern era. This phenomenon is highlighted by pointing out that it required almost all of the time man has been on the earth to produce a world population of 1,000,000,000, a number not attained until about 1830. It required but one additional century to produce a second billion persons, achieved in 1930. The third billion required only 30 years and was reached in 1960. By the century's end present patterns of fertility and continued mortality decline could result in a population of 7,500,000,000. Even with allowances for fertility declines, the population of the world is almost certain, short of castastrophe, to exceed 7,000,-000,000 by the year 2000.

The *population implosion* refers to the increased concentration of the world's peoples into relatively small portions of the earth's surface. This also is a relatively recent phenomenon. Fixed human settlement was not possible until as recently as the Neolithic Period, some 10,000 years ago. Human settlements in excess of 100,000 persons were as recent as Greco-Roman civilization, and the proliferation of cities of 1,000,000 or more was as recent as the beginning of the 19th century.

Population differentiation refers to the increasing heterogeneity of peoples sharing the same geographic locale and the same economic and political activities. Heterogeneity refers to diversity of population by culture, language, religion, value systems, ethnicity, and race. This, too, is a relatively recent phenomenon achieved on a global basis only with the shrinking of the world by means of modern communication and transportation. It is probably correct to say that the world has shrunk more during the course of this century, as measured by the interaction of diverse peoples, than in all previous human history.

Initial requirements for urban development. *The ecological base.* It was no accident that the earliest of man's fixed settlements are found in the rich subtropical valleys of the Nile, the Tigris, the Euphrates, the Indus, and the Yellow rivers or in such well-watered islands as Crete. Such areas provided favourable environmental factors making town living relatively easy: climate and soil favourable to plant and animal life, an adequate water supply, ready materials for providing shelter, and easy access to other peoples. Although man with ingenuity has been able to utilize almost any environment for town living, environments favourable to the production of food and shelter and ease and comfort of living clearly possessed advantages for the beginnings of urban life.

Psychological influences. A distinguished historian, Ralph E. Turner, has suggested that various preurban de-

velopments made possible the technology and organization permitting city life. These included psychological elements such as recognition of "in-group" versus "out-group" interests; the notion of a universe, even if mysterious, that could be controlled; and belief in the existence of a soul. The in-group and out-group differentiation provided a basis for respect for the rights of others and for life, property, and family values. The notion that man could control the world in which he lived was of great importance, even if the methods of control were primitively based on magic and religion. The belief in a soul helped make life on earth more acceptable, even if hard, for life was just an incident in a long journey.

Sociological influences. Preurban developments that paved the way for urban life also included such factors as traditionalism, a power structure, and a form of economic as well as social organization. Traditionalism lay in the acceptance and transmission of what had worked in the life of the group and was therefore "right" and to be retained. Some form of power structure involving subordination was necessary, for leadership was a vital element in urban living in that it was essential to the performance of such vital functions as sustenance, religious practices, social life, and defense. Also prerequisite to group life were new economic and social institutions and groupings such as property, work, the family, a system for distribution of commodities and services, record keeping, police for internal security, and armed forces for defense.

New value orientations and ideologies may also have affected the course of urbanization, though their importance is still highly conjectural. There are those who have felt that urbanization depended on a new outlook; it meant that people had become more rationalistic (and less mystical); it meant that, for purposes of building, they were more willing and able to defer immediate for more desirable later gratification; it meant more emphasis on achievement and success as distinguished from status and prestige; it meant a cosmopolitan as distinguished from a parochial outlook; and it meant that relations between people were more ordered, impersonal, and utilitarian, rather than only personal and sentimental.

PATTERNS OF URBANIZATION BEFORE THE MODERN ERA

Ancient world. *Technological developments.* About 10,000 years ago in the Neolithic Period, man achieved relatively fixed settlement, but for perhaps 5,000 years such living was confined to the semipermanent peasant village—semipermanent because, when the soil had been exhausted by the relatively primitive methods of cultivation, the entire village was usually compelled to pick up and move elsewhere. Even when the village prospered in one place and the population grew relatively large, the village usually had to split in two, so that all cultivators would have ready access to the soil.

The evolution of the Neolithic village into a city took at least 1,500 years—in the Old World from 5000 to 3500 BC. The technological developments making it possible for man to live in urban places were, at first, mainly advances in agriculture. Neolithic man's domestication of plants and animals eventually led to improved methods of cultivation and stock breeding and the proliferation of the crafts, which in turn eventually produced a surplus and freed some of the population to work as artisans, craftsmen, and service workers.

As human settlements increased in size, by reason of the technological advances in irrigation and cultivation, the need for improving the circulation of goods and people became ever more acute. Pre-Neolithic man leading a nomadic existence in his never-ending search for food moved largely by foot and carried his essential goods with the help of his wife and children. Neolithic man, upon achieving the domestication of animals, used them for transportation as well as for food and hides. Then came the use of draft animals in combination with a sledge equipped with runners for carrying heavier loads. The major technological achievement in the early history of transportation, however, was obviously the invention of the wheel, used first in the Tigris-Euphrates Valley about

Transportation development

3500 BC and constructed first with solid materials and only later with hubs, spokes, and rims. Wheels, to be used efficiently, required roads, and thus came road building, an art most highly developed in ancient times by the Romans. Parallel improvements were made in water transport—with rafts, dugouts, the Egyptian reed float, eventually wooden boats, and of course canals used for both navigation and irrigation.

Architectural developments

Fixed human settlement also led to great improvements in the material and the permanence of human shelters. Lewis Mumford, an architect and historian of cities, has visualized the development of the city plant as consisting of the construction of more and more complex "containers." In the Neolithic Period, the containers varied from a "hole dug out of the soil sun-dried to brick hardness," as found in Mesopotamia, to mud and other types of huts. Other Neolithic containers included stone and pottery utensils, structures such as barns and granaries, and also "collective containers" such as irrigation ditches and the villages themselves.

The increase in population size converting the village to the town and then to the city was accompanied by a great increase in the built-up area and the number of structures. Archaeologists have discovered that Megiddo in Israel covered some 3½ acres, Gurnia in Crete about 6½ acres. These were among some of the larger early cities. Much later the walled area at Mycenae contained 12 acres, and at about the same time Carchemish in Syria was built on 240 acres. Menevia in about 600 BC covered perhaps as much as 1,800 acres.

The density of structures and people within such cities was very great—partly because distances could be no greater than a person could walk, partly because the water supply had to be within carrying distance of each home, and partly because technology was too primitive for man to build many sophisticated, spacious structures far from one another. Indeed, small row houses, rather than detached houses, remained prevalent from ancient times well into the modern era. Some of the archaeological finds suggest that the population densities in ancient cities about 2000 BC ranged as high as from 76,000 to 128,000 persons per square mile. This compares with present-day densities in New York City, with 26,300 persons per square mile; San Francisco with 10,900; Frankfurt with 8,900; Tokyo with 39,700. A city like Paris, however, does have a rather high density—63,650 persons per square mile. Ancient cities, moreover, were usually walled to provide protection against enemies, and city walls, in fact, remained important structural elements down to the 18th century. Mankind did not achieve a level of technological and social organizational development to achieve cities of 100,000 or more persons until during the Greco-Roman civilization. The Greek city-state had its origin in and owed its relatively large size to the ability to acquire and dominate a hinterland by force of arms. Superior military prowess enabled the Greeks to build fortress city-states that developed economic relations with a rural service area that was physically subordinated and subjected to tribute. The same can be said of Rome and other prominent cities of antiquity. Ancient wars can in large measure be interpreted as wars between cities seeking rural hinterlands.

The example of Rome

Rome may be taken as an example of the developments achieved in the building of urban plants in the later days of antiquity. At its greatest size, in the 3rd century AD, Rome covered an area of about four square miles within its walls, with a population minimally estimated at about 800,000 persons. The original settlement of Rome was on the hills nearest the Tiber River, but as the settlement increased in size, population spread into the adjoining valleys and eventually well away from the river by means of such technological developments as aqueducts and improved roads. Moreover, at the level of the river itself, drainage and embankments permitted the use of low-lying land as well.

To provide water for the population, the Romans built aqueducts as early as 312 BC. Later aqueducts brought water from as far away as the Sabine Hills, 44 miles distant. To get the water to higher ground, the aqueducts were carried on high arches, and thence the water was distributed to individual structures by a complex system of conduits and lead pipes, which were not equalled until the present century.

In the earliest of Roman settlements, building materials consisted of wickerwork plastered with clay on a timber framework. Later developments led to timber and mud brick and, eventually, to more durable materials including stone, marble, and concrete, which went into the now famous monuments of antiquity, such as the Forum, the great public works of the Capitoline Hill, the Colosseum, the Circus Maximus, and the Pantheon. Finally, Rome serves as a good example of the walled city—its town walls serving to defend it not only during the period of its glory but also throughout the Middle Ages.

Social developments. Because usually no one village can support full-time craftsmen and other nonagricultural functionaries, such specialists normally have to wander from village to village to make their living. This must have been the case in the Neolithic Period.

The ancient city, on the other hand, required and developed more sophisticated methods of pooling and distributing surpluses of food, crafts, and other products. Forms of exchange, including money, had to be developed, which in turn required systems of recording and, therefore, the invention of writing and of numbers. The city was also characterized by large public structures, including temples for worship, granaries for sorting grain, magazines for armaments, and workshops. The rise of new administrative, security, religious, and economic functions led to more complex social organization, including upper and lower classes, with rulers, priests, military leaders, craftsmen, and peasants. Finally, the city engaged in exchange with other cities and in foreign trade in an effort to obtain new forms of products.

Ecologically, the elite—the higher clergy, government officials, aristocrats, and, in due course, the wealthier tradesmen—resided at the centre of the city near its forum or temple. Away from the centre were distributed the lower classes toward, and sometimes beyond, the safety of the city walls. Within the city separate quarters generally arose by ethnic origin or by occupational grouping. Such distinguishable quarters were often separated by lesser walls, moats, or ditches and often constituted separate, isolated worlds. This type of ecological patterning describes not only the ancient city but much of urban organization prior to the Industrial Revolution.

The extended family was the primary unit of social organization and the key to the person's social and economic position, for, with limited social mobility, kinship was a major factor in determining social and economic status. The elite household contained the members of the extended family together with domestics and workers (including slaves) related to the household's economic activity. Male dominance and age-grading tended to be the rule, with elders in the dominant power position.

Economic organization centred on specialization in product rather than specialization in process, thus guilds or their precursors were organized largely in terms of a product. Market procedures were complicated by the absence of standardization in products, weights and measures, currencies, and prices, and by extensive adulteration of products.

Technological developments. Roman technology survived the collapse of Rome, and expanded trade carried the relatively advanced technology of India and China to the West, including gunpowder, iron casting, paper and printing, silk-working machinery, and more sophisticated rigging for sailing ships. Moreover, the "barbarians" who inherited the old Roman Empire added inventions of their own, including soap, barrels and tubs, heated houses, the horseshoe, and new agricultural techniques.

Perhaps most significant in accelerating urbanization were the use of gunpowder, nonhuman sources of power, the mechanical clock, and printing.

Gunpowder helped destroy a medieval feudal order that had already been undermined by the rise of towns, the growth of trade, the toll of internecine wars, and the effects of such epidemics as the Black Death. The initial use of gunpowder was in siege artillery, which quickly reduced feudal walls and castles; the eventual addition of hand guns rendered all armoured feudal armies antiquated, and older forms of warfare and defense collapsed. The increasing use of nonhuman sources of energy—at first animal power and then water and wind—greatly increased productivity. Agriculture benefitted from improved harnesses, wheeled plows, teams of animals, and new systems of cultivation. The mill, powered by wind or water and involving such transmission mechanisms as gearing, was used mainly for grinding grain but also for moving bellows and powering hammers in the process of crushing ore and forging wrought iron. Although the sun dial, the sand glass, and the water clock can be traced to antiquity, the mechanical clock was not invented until the 14th century and proved to be a great boon to the increasingly interdependent economic and social order that required time synchronization for effective operation. Finally, the printing press greatly increased the ability of man to communicate both between and within generations and did as much to advance science and technology as it did to facilitate communication of ideas in the expanding urban world.

The physical form of medieval and Renaissance towns and cities followed the pattern of the village, spreading along a street, a crossroad, in circular patterns or in irregular shapes—though rectangular patterns tended to characterize some of the newer towns. Most streets were little more than footpaths—more a medium for communication than for transportation—and even in major cities paving was not introduced until 1184 in Paris, 1235 in Florence, and 1300 in Lübeck. As the population of the city grew, walls were often expanded, but few cities at the time exceeded a mile in length. Sometimes sites were changed as in Lübeck, and many new cities emerged with increasing population—frequently about one day's walk apart. Towns ranged in population from several hundred to perhaps 40,000 (London in the 14th century). Paris and Venice were exceptions, reaching 100,000.

Housing varied from elaborate merchant houses to crude huts and stone enclosures. Dwellings were usually two to three stories high, aligned in rows, and often with rear gardens or inner courts formed by solid blocks. Windows were small apertures with shutters, at first, and later covered with oiled cloth, paper, and glass. Heating improved from the open hearth to the fireplace and chimney. Rooms varied from the single room for the poor to differentiated rooms for specialized use by the wealthy. Space generally was at a premium. Privacy was rare and sanitation primitive.

Social developments. An increase in the size of a city often carried with it increased diversity of people. Although such heterogeneity could have resulted in conflicts between peoples of different origin, culture, ethnicity, or religion, the actual result was that the division of the city into quarters made for self-sufficiency, each quarter tending to have its own church, provision market, water supply, and social institutions. The city was, therefore, really a collection of separate quarters or neighbourhoods in which people with like interests and needs could live peacefully together.

Family and kinship

Medieval and Renaissance life was characterized by households that included not only the extended family of three or more generations and other relatives but also domestics and workers associated with the family's economic activities. Young men of the upper classes, for example, often served as waiting men in noble families, and apprentices and even journeymen lived with the master craftman's family. Household members would work together, eat together, and often sleep in the same common room arranged into dormitories.

Marriage was generally arranged by family heads, and child marriages were not infrequent in China, India, Japan, the Near East, and parts of Europe, although in child marriages the partners did not live together until adulthood. Families tended to be patriarchial; that is, the wife was subordinated to the husband, and her life was largely restricted to household duties, with few opportunities to play a role in the larger world. Children were reared to respect and obey their elders, sons often remaining under the authority of the father even after they were married. Such schooling as was available was generally limited to the upper classes and to boys.

MODERN PATTERNS OF URBANIZATION

Industrial Revolution and modernization. Just as in ancient times the growth and improvement of agriculture had produced food surpluses and thus made cities possible, so did the growth and improvement of cities in modern times produce greater division of labour and more specialization and thus make mass production in factories possible. As Adam Smith noted, the larger the size of a population, the greater the possibility of division of labour. Greater division of labour led to increased specialization. Increased specialization operated to increase productivity both because the specialist could concentrate on one relatively simple activity and because the specialized function could more easily be mechanized and accomplished through the use of nonhuman energy. It is true that this Industrial Revolution at the outset perhaps made the life of the average worker and urbanite more hundrum and impoverished, but in the long run it has led to greatly improved levels of living for the mass populations in those countries that have become industrialized.

Urban growth

Not only did cities facilitate industrialization but also, conversely, industrialization had a striking effect on the growth of cities. In the pioneer country of industrialization, England and Wales, for example, there were in 1801 only 106 cities or urban places containing 5,000 inhabitants or more—representing no more than 26 percent of the country's total population (some estimates placing the figure even lower at 10 percent). A half century later, in 1851, there were 265 urban places, constituting 45 percent of the total population. By 1891 the growth had reached 622 places, representing 68 percent of the population. By the turn of the century most of Europe had joined or was joining the processes of industrialization and urbanization. By 1920 the population of Europe (excepting the U.S.S.R.) was 32 percent urban; by 1970 it was 64 percent, with the heaviest densities in such industrial areas as the Rhineland and the English Midlands. Most significantly, whereas Europe's total population between 1920 and 1970 increased by 42 percent (from 325,000,000 to 462,000,000) its urban population jumped by 182 percent (from 104,000,000 to 293,000,000). Parallel developments of course took place in the United States: in 1800 only 6.1 percent of the population lived in urban places (defined as places of 2,500 or more); in 1970 the figure was about 73.5 percent.

Such figures contrast with the figures for countries and regions that have not yet industrialized or are only now beginnning the processes of modernization. Although the overall population densities in the underdeveloped world are generally far greater, their urban percentages are smaller. In 1970 East Asia was 30 percent urban, south Asia (from the Middle East to Southeast Asia) was 21 percent, Latin America was 56 percent, and Africa was 22 percent. The industrial nation of Japan, in comparison, was about 72 percent urban.

Communication and transportation. Urbanization and industrialization (or the factory system) thus had mutual influences. They each caused the other to spiral upward. This mutual cause-and-effect relation also applies to urbanization when twinned with other fields of development. Increased division of labour and specialization necessarily required more intercommunication of peoples in the production and distribution of goods and services. This led to great improvements in communication and transportation, which in turn permitted a larger and ever more complex order.

The developments in audiovisual communication throughout the globe have been accompanied by great improvements in interpersonal communication. Mail delivery systems made it possible for people to communicate at great distances under conditions of privacy, even though considerable time was required. Then the invention and development of the telegraph made interpersonal communication even more efficient and rapid. The invention of the telephone made interpersonal communication instantaneous, and continued improvements have made long-distance telephone communication possible not only within nations but between all parts of the world. Another important part of the story of improved communication is the accumulation of knowledge and its transmission from generation to generation—by means of the printed word, the desk calculator, and, ultimately, the modern computer. Such improvements in communication, in short, have made possible ever larger clumps of people and economic activities and therefore ever larger cities.

19th-century transportation and urban patterns

Nineteenth-century cities, when the means of transportation were relatively poor, drew dense populations tightly around the factory—within walking distance. With the advent of the horse-drawn vehicle on rails, the railroad, and the trolley car, population could spread away from the factory and the city grow ever larger. Such population dispersion as occurred, however, was relatively limited in the late 19th and early 20th centuries and extended in star-shaped fashion along the major lanes of transport—usually the commuting railroad. With the widespread use of the automobile and improvement of roads including expressways and freeways, much greater dispersion ensued. Moreover, with the introduction of expressways encircling the city, population flowed into the interstices of the earlier star-shaped urban agglomerations to fill all available residential areas with ready access to the city.

Beyond the city proper, however, the most important advances in transportation during the 19th century were first the canals and then the railroads. The development of railroads, in particular, paved the way for the great expansion and scattering of urban places and for the industrial development that accompanied it. The railroad became and remains the major means of transporting goods across land surfaces, and it was also a major means for transporting people until the automobile became popular after the 1920s and the airplane after the 1940s. On the international front, great improvements in ocean transport stimulated not only foreign trade but also international migration—mostly to cities.

In short, improvements in transportation led directly to much greater sizes of population clumps and contributed to increased productivity by improving the speed and efficiency with which supplies and people could be carried. As in the case of communication, a circular reaction was involved. Improved transportation made larger cities possible, and larger cities required better means of transportation for the circulation of people and goods.

19th-century centripetal patterns

The developing structure of urban areas: 19th century. In England, France, the United States, and other nations that experienced the Industrial Revolution relatively early, 19th-century urbanization was closely linked with industrialization. The physical structures of the cities inherited from preindustrial centuries were subjected to great modification required by the rapid growth of the factory system and the accompanying mass production. The combination of the steam engine, the belt, and the pulley set centripetal forces in motion that generated high population densities near places of work. This was especially true of the heavy industries—iron, smelting, metal products, machine building, and glass manufacture. The two most prominent features of the 19th-century industrial city were the factory and the slum.

The industrial city was characterized in physical form by rectangular blocks, generally of uniform size separated by a pattern of streets and thoroughfares, usually of uniform width. Subject to local topography, the rectangular pattern—which Mumford refers to as the nonplan—permitted, the indefinite extension of the city in all directions. As the city expanded, open lands were absorbed with little regard for areas needed for public use, including recreation. The rectangular block pattern was a boon to engineers, architects, and realty brokers, but it also created many physical problems. The streets of uniform width provided thoroughfares too broad for many residential areas and too narrow for major traffic arteries. Moreover, it was too rigid a form to adapt easily to various topographical features such as hills, valleys, rivers, lakes, and canals.

The factory introduced into the urban area unprecedented forms of pollution, fouling the atmosphere with heavy smoke containing chemical agents hazardous to both human health and surrounding agriculture. Plants were usually located on sites near water upon which they depended for steam, processing, transport, and sewerage; in consequence, rivers, lakes, and canals became open sewers with water not only unfit for human consumption or bathing but dangerous as well to fish, plants, and animals. The factory created new levels of environmental pollution, unaesthetic and hazardous to all forms of life.

The industrial cities, especially in the early part of the 19th century, contained miserable residences for the workers and their families. Housing was poorly constructed and crowded closely together—typically as tall tenements or row housing, often with little or no provision for water and sanitation. In one part of Manchester in 1843–44, for example, surveys reported only one toilet per 212 persons. Cellars—dark, dank, and unsanitary—often served as dwelling places. Provision for garbage and rubbish removal was inadequate. Windows were small and narrow and lighting inadequate. Limited space was available for gardens or children's play.

The filth and congestion bred insects and vermin that afflicted large proportions of the population. Rats, bugs, flies, and lice were the source of disease, including bubonic plague brought by rats and typhus by lice. Inadequate plumbing made typhoid widespread. In consequence, mortality, especially infant and child mortality, was inordinately high. Studies showed that city death rates greatly exceeded those in rural areas and that within cities the areas with highest densities had the highest morbidity and mortality.

Toward the end of the 19th century, however, the miserable conditions led to various forms of legislation to alleviate the condition of the working classes. Gradually the amenities of urban existence available at first only to the elite (who could not, however, escape from disease and environmental pollution) spread to the poor and persons of modest means. By the end of the 19th century the lower classes began to get the benefits of mass production reflected in their rising levels of living. Housing improved and increasingly contained piped water, sewerage, lighting, and easy access to transportation.

The developing structure of urban areas: 20th century. With improvements in transportation and communication, 20th-century technology began to set centrifugal forces in motion that operated to disperse population and economic activities across city boundaries and into the adjoining countryside. This expanding urban agglomeration transcended political units and boundaries, causing new areal concepts to be developed for describing the emerging new urban reality, as distinguished from the historical urban units. The "metropolitan area," under various national designations, came to stand for the central city together with its outlying "ring." The "urbanized area" came to be the designation for solidly built-up areas with, in general, population densities requiring residence in city block patterns—the urban concentration as seen from an airplane in which all political boundaries are obscured. "Consolidated areas" came to be used in the United States to describe contiguous metropolitan areas. Finally "megalopolis" emerged as the designation of a number of coalescing metropolitan areas.

20th-century centrifugal patterns

Continued advances in transportation and communication led not only to the dispersal of population but increasingly, also, to the decentralization of economic activities—trade, services, and production. The decentralized shopping centre diminished the dominance of the central business district for purveying many types of goods and services, and the decentralized factory, gaining the advantages of more and better space for mass production and space for automotive and truck parking, competed favourably with many inner-city industries. The central business district, nevertheless, continued to be the economic centre of the metropolitan area and dominated the metropolis with its concentration of professional and white-collar activities.

In most cases the urban physical plant—residential, in-

Urban
decay

dustrial, commercial, and governmental—was constructed hurriedly in response to rapid urbanization. Land-use
patterns and infrastructure development were largely the
product of market forces, which produced a remarkable
physical plant but which also permitted rapid obsolescence and decay as evidenced by large proportions of "substandard housing" and areas of slum. In affluent countries the automobile, which has been a major factor in the
development of the 20th-century metropolis, is now
threatening it with congestion, and new attention is being
focussed on problems of circulation within the city. Finally, problems of air and water pollution are also becoming
critical in many areas.

In the developing regions of the world—in Asia, Latin
America, and Africa—the most visible consequence of
rapid urbanization is the decadence of the urban environment. The city is characterized by a large proportion of
shanty towns and tenement slums; inadequate urban services, including poor housing, water supply, sewerage, utilities, and transport; uncontrolled land use; excessive population densities; deficient education and recreational
facilities; and inefficient commercial and marketing services. Rapid urbanization in the underdeveloped areas is
accompanied not only by a defective but also a deteriorating urban environment. It is estimated that, in Latin
America alone, some 4,000,000 or 5,000,000 families live
in urban shanty towns and slums.

With increased productivity and a growing middle class
and despite evidence of deterioration, modern housing has
been characterized overall by great advances in convenience and in safety and comfort. Since the 19th century,
space per person has greatly increased; piped water, private bathrooms and sanitary facilities, electric lighting,
central heating, and increased air conditioning have
become standard in the more affluent nations.

Urban
planning

During the 20th century, in response to physical and
other problems, governments have increasingly intervened to protect health, life, and safety. Nations in which
centralized governments exerted great control over municipal areas were quicker to respond to urban evils—nations such as England and the Scandinavian countries.
Nations with federal systems, in which state and local
governments had more autonomy, as in the United States,
were slower to respond to the need for eliminating the
evils that accompanied urban living: air and water pollution, substandard housing, slums, traffic congestion, the
"commuters' crisis," and inadequate parks and public recreational and cultural facilities. By mid-20th century,
however, programs of public housing, urban renewal, and
city planning had become almost universal among the
economically advanced nations.

The underdeveloped nations are of course aware of the
need for city and regional, as well as national, planning.
But the city planner in the underdeveloped country is
confronted with insuperable difficulties. These stem largely from low income levels; from rapid population growth,
including hordes of in-migrants from rural areas who
are ill adapted to urban living; from inadequate development services and government urban development—
all in all, from a bewildering array of needs, each of
which seems to have first priority. Although urban agglomerations of the size of Western cities are to be found,
the physical amenities associated with such in the West
have not yet developed—at least, not for the mass population. The amenities of urban existence are available
only to very small fractions of the total urban population.
It is in the impact on the already inadequate urban physical plant that the rapid rate of urbanization produces
some of its more serious consequences.

Social developments. The combination of technological and demographic developments led in the 19th century to the proliferation of cities of 1,000,000 or more
inhabitants. Prior to the 19th century, although there may
have been an occasional city in ancient China or in Japan
(Edo, the precursor of Tokyo) that reached a population
of 1,000,000, there certainly were no great number of
cities of this size. By the onset of the 19th century, however, technological and social organizational developments together with the population explosion and implo-

sion that accompanied them had reached levels that led to
the generation of a number of such great cities. According
to one estimate, by 1900 there were 10 cities of 1,000,000
or more inhabitants in the world; by 1950 there were 49
such cities.

That the city makes a difference in man's way of life
was perceived by the ancients, but especially during the
19th and early 20th centuries a number of scholars began
discussing the difference it makes and clarifying the factors involved. Twentieth-century scholars have shed further light on the impact of the city.

The effects of increasing population densities on social
life (and on individual attitudes and behaviours) can be
partly explained by reference to a hypothetical circle with
a 10-mile radius (altogether, 314 square miles). At a density of one person per square mile there are only 314
persons on the fixed land area; at a density of 25,000
(approximately the density of New York City) the size of
the population will increase to almost 8,000,000. The significance of these figures is that they indicate the magnitude of potential human interaction—that is, the maximum number of persons with whom any one person could
potentially make contact. With a density of one the maximum number of other human beings any one person
could meet is 313 (314 minus one); with a density of
25,000 the maximum number of other human beings increases to almost 8,000,000. It is to the increase in the
number of contacts that the effects of urbanization may
be traced, because the increase in contacts results in qualitative as well as quantitative changes in human interaction.

In the community of small size and low density (the
"little community," to use Robert Redfield's terminology)
people live in "primary groups" and experience "primary
contacts"—that is, human interaction is "face to face" and
encompasses virtually all spheres of activity. In the little
community interpersonal relations are intimate and often
are based on sentiment and emotion. In contrast, in the
society characterized by great size and high population
densities (the "mass society," to use Karl Mannheim's
language) people characteristically live in "secondary
groups" and have "secondary contacts"—that is, contacts
tend to be segmental—in that people interact only at that
point where their life paths intersect. It is the contact
typified by the relation between physician and patient,
lawyer and client, grocer and customer, teacher and student, or tax collector and taxpayer. In this situation human relations seldom are based on sentiment and emotion but rather on utility.

Moreover, in the mass society, behavioral heterogeneity increases not only because of size but also because of
the intermingling of persons of diverse background—diverse by culture, language, religion, ethnicity, or race.
The combination of heterogeneous and secondary contacts greatly modifies human behaviour. Thought and action tend to depend less and less on the traditional; the
influence of the folkways and mores diminishes. In ever-
larger spheres of thought and action, behaviour seems less
determined by the norms of the group. The sphere of
personal decision making is greatly extended in areas such
as the kind and degree of education, occupation or profession, residential location, choice of mate, size of family,
political affiliation, and religion.

It follows, then, that increased size and density of population, especially if accompanied by heterogeneity, diminishes the power of informal social controls. Informal
social controls, effected largely through the play of folkways and the mores, gives way to increased formal control—the control of law, police, courts, jails, regulations,
and orders. The breakdown in informal social controls is
in large measure responsible for increased personal disorganization as manifest in juvenile delinquency, crime,
prostitution, alcoholism, drug addiction, suicide, mental
disease, social unrest, and political instability. Formal
controls have by no means proved as efficacious as the
informal in regulating human behaviour.

The effect of the city on the way of life may be observed
in the adjustment problems of the newcomers. The city as
a recipient of migrants has played and continues to play a

prominent role in the modification of thought and behaviour, in subjecting people with traditional and rural backgrounds to the conditions of urban living. Most of the severe physical, social, and economic problems of the city are disproportionately manifest among newcomers and are symptomatic of the difficulties of adjustment to urban life.

It may be that, to the extent that size, density, and heterogeneity of population have changed behaviour in urban places, they represent necessary, rather than sufficient, conditions for such a transformation. For certainly much behaviour in urban places, especially in the economically underdeveloped countries, is still traditional rather than rational and, in other respects, resembles folk rather than urban characteristics. The explanation for this may lie in the difference between *potential* human interaction in the city and that actually achieved; that is, in large population clumps of high density, which are essentially an agglutination of separate and distinct noninteracting communities, human behaviour may still be largely the product of the primary group.

As a microcosm of the social whole, the family is a convenient unit through which to trace many of the influences of the city on social institutions. The family is in most societies regarded as the primary social unit: it has been a basic and largely self-sufficient economic unit, it has had primary responsibility for the socialization and education of the young, it has been a focal point for religious training and practices, it has provided for the security and protection of its members, and it has been the centre for affectional and recreational life. The family in modernized urban societies, however, has certainly been transformed: the urban family today is smaller; it is more often childless and has fewer children, if fertile; it is more mobile; it possesses comparatively little economic or social unity; it is more frequently broken by separation or divorce; and it has long since lost or shared many of its various historic functions with new, specialized urban institutions, such as the clothing store, the grocery, the restaurant, the school, the library, and systems of social security.

Social stratification

The development of the city also altered—and produced new forms of—social stratification. The rise of the commercial city greatly increased the importance of the merchants, who became an ever more powerful group. With the increasing size and power of the city, merchants displaced landlords not only in the power structure of the cities but increasingly in the power structure of larger entities, including nations as a whole. With the ascendancy of the industrial city, the industrialist, the financier, and the manager achieved positions of power arising from wealth and strategic location in the economy. The development of intellectual traditions, bolstered by the scientific revolution, provided high status to persons in intellectual and professional pursuits. To these various sources of status would be added older residual sources of social stratification based on status; that is, birth or "social" honour as well as on economic power. Contemporary urban society tends, therefore, to be stratified on three axes: power as achieved through wealth, status as achieved through birth, and prestige as achieved largely through intellectual and professional pursuits.

THE FUTURE OF URBANIZATION

Megalopolitanization. Megalopolis, as earlier suggested, is a term used to designate the coalescence of multiple metropolitan areas into a single huge clumping of people and economic activities. The term was introduced in this sense by the French geographer Jean Gottmann, who referred to the urbanized northeastern seaboard of the United States as perhaps "the cradle of a new order in the organization of inhabited space." Although maybe a new type of agglomeration, megalopolis is nevertheless undoubtedly the result of the same processes that produced urbanization; it is the logical culmination of urbanization as cities and their suburban areas continually expand, grow contiguous, and become integral parts of a continuous built-up area. Gottman's megalopolis extending from Boston to Washington, D.C., contained about 37,-

000,000 persons in 1960 in a land area comprising 53,500 square miles, about 600 miles long and 30 to 100 miles wide.

This megalopolis in the United States, and other emergent megalopolises in the world, owe their origin to (1) the economic opportunities they offered that made them areas of immigration and (2) the functions they were able to perform first in their local and regional hinterlands and later on the national and world scene. This northeastern seaboard area had the advantage of being located on the sea, thus serving as a link between Europe (and, more generally, the outside world) and inland United States: it early became the major centre for world trade between Europe and American continents; it was strategically located to be influenced by industrializing England and Europe during the 19th century and thus to become itself a locus for the industrialization of the United States; and it served as the major port of entry for immigration to the United States. Such a megalopolis also represents a "revolution in land use," in which urbanization generates an urban region, as distinct from an agricultural region (such as the Great Plains in the United States). Within megalopolis land becomes increasingly specialized for use in residence, industry, trade, and services, as well as in agricultural functions encapsulated in the area.

Other megalopolises are emergent within the United States and throughout the world: in the United States, around such areas as metropolitan Los Angeles and San Francisco, around metropolitan Dallas and Houston, around metropolitan Chicago, Milwaukee, and South Bend and other Great Lakes metro areas that could eventually consolidate the entire Great Lakes region into a major megalopolis, and in Europe in the region around London and in the Midlands, in the Greater Paris area of France, in the Ruhr industrial basin in Germany, and in The Netherlands and central Belgium. In Asia a major megalopolis is emergent in the Tokyo-Osaka complex, and in the longer run, megalopolises may well develop in China and India with their huge populations and rapidly growing governmental, commercial, and industrial cities. On the other hand, it is doubtful that European or other American areas will reach the size of the urbanized agglomeration on the northeastern seaboard of the United States—the reasons being restricted national boundaries in Europe and relatively restricted opportunity for comparable world roles in the other areas of the United States. Moreover, the complex problems of metropolitan living, which became greatly exacerbated in megalopolis —physical, personal, social, economic, and governmental problems—may conceivably lead planners to retard or prevent megalopolitan development. Should the future nevertheless bring great megalopolitan agglomerations containing 100,000,000 or more inhabitants, the northeastern seaboard in the United States will likely be the first to achieve such gargantuan size.

Suburbanization. The growth of suburbs—politically separate residential communities surrounding large cities and economically dependent upon the cities—can be traced back at least to the 19th century, when city populations were already beginning to decentralize. The 20th century has confirmed this 19th-century tendency: the "ring" outside the central city has become an increasingly larger proportion of the metropolitan demographic and economic complex.

The growth of suburbia has often been attributed to a "flight" from the city. Yet this explanation is but a half-truth, for although it is true that suburban growth in North America and parts of Europe has been mainly the product of movements out of central cities, it is also true that these central cities have until relatively recently been repopulated by in-migrants from rural and other urban areas. Furthermore, until relatively recently, newcomers to the central city have outnumbered those moving out to suburbia (only since the 1930s have some central cities begun losing populations slightly, as suburbs accelerated their growth). It is more accurate, therefore, to regard the suburb not so much as the product of a flight from the city as the result of the city ever growing and overflowing its boundaries into adjacent territory. Generally speaking,

In-
migrants

the only places that populations and economic activities can expand are in the metropolitan ring. Indeed, in some European and many Latin American and Asian cities there is little "flight" involved at all. Those who settle on the outskirts of cities—often in very high densities—are generally migrants attracted to the city but unable to find feasible inexpensive housing within it; thus they cluster around the city, usually in shanty towns and other makeshift settlements. Whereas in older American cities migrants are often drawn to the inner city containing flats and tenements abandoned by newly affluent workers and middle classes, movement in other areas of the world is generally to the urban periphery. In fact, everywhere, at least in newer cities, the tendency for in-migrants to live in the centres of cities seems to be waning.

Suburbs are thus by no means homogeneous in population type or function, and they can vary as much in socioeconomic status as do neighbourhoods within the city. Moreover, although suburbs are generally thought of as dormitory cities for persons commuting to their employment in the central city, the metropolitan ring is increasingly embracing satellite areas that are predominantly industrial or commercial.

Suburbs vary widely in the extent to which they are well planned or constitute "urban sprawl" in the economic level of their inhabitants, in their tax rates, in the quality of their educational facilities and cultural life, and in the character of their local government and public services. With increasing decentralization it can be anticipated that they will become more rather than less heterogeneous, more similar to than different from the central city, and more aware of the common needs and interests of all elements of the metropolitan area.

Regional integration. The city has always been dependent on a hinterland for its origin, its function, and its expansion. It has performed a variety of services for its surrounding area and, in turn, has been dependent upon it for sustenance. The various types of cities in this sense have thus always involved regional integration—whether they were central places performing service functions or transport cities performing services along transport routes or specialized cities (industrial, mining, commercial, political, educational, recreational, or otherwise) or relatively great cities combining some or all of these functions.

The American sociologist Otis Dudley Duncan and his colleagues have made an intensive analysis of the interrelations of metropolitan areas and regions for the United States (*Metropolis and Region*, 1960); and the English geographer Robert E. Dickerson earlier did the same for a number of countries (*City and Region: A Geographical Interpretation*, 1964). Duncan and his colleagues, for example have developed a classification of metropolitan areas in the United States that in effect, constitutes an analysis of different levels of regional integration. The classification distinguishes (1) "national metropolises," (2) urban places with "diversified manufacturing" and "metropolitan functions," (3) "regional metropolises," (4) "regional capitals," (5) urban places with "diversified manufacturing" and "few metropolitan functions," (6) "urban places with specialized manufacturing," and (7) "special cases." Although this classification has elements of hierarchy, it actually constitutes a multidimensional approach to the study of regional integration. It is probably correct to say that the potential size of individual cities or metropolitan areas depends on the size and integration of the region of which they were a part.

As the world grows increasingly interdependent and continues to shrink with rapid technological advances in communication and transportation, the integration of economic and cultural activities should become characteristic of even larger regions both within and across national boundaries. In consequence urban agglomerations will continue to increase in size toward megalopolitan dimensions.

The role of advancing technology. Continued advances in communication and transport facilities will undoubtedly permit further decentralization of population and economic activities but, undoubtedly, still within the metropolitan complex or at least within its influence. In-

stantaneous communication from anywhere to anywhere, for instance, possesses the potential for profound increases in the integrative activities of metropolitan areas on a regional, national, continental, and global basis.

Similarly, continued advances in automation and the computer can also operate to accelerate decentralization of activities within the metropolitan area and to greatly extend the dominance and influence of urban concentrations. Computer programs coupled with electronic automation will permit greater separation between central offices and production plants, since direct supervision and control can then be achieved from a distant central office, which can thus largely eliminate *intermediate* management and supervisory personnel.

Automation and computerization

The development of automation and the computer could greatly transform many present urban institutions and processes. The retail shopping facility, for example, could virtually disappear as the shopper acquires direct three-dimensional television and audio contact with warehouses containing automated distribution facilities, which could fill and package orders for home delivery. Such advances would profoundly alter not only present retail practices but also warehousing, wholesaling, jobbing, and broker practices. They could also affect the patterns and means of intracity as well as intercity transport. In theory at any rate, the possibilities for change are limited only by the imagination.

The role of population control and urban planning. Even with the most realistic success in population control, the population of this planet by the year 2000 is likely to approximate 7,000,000,000, and almost half that population (48.3 percent) is likely to be urban (residing in places of 20,000 or more). The accommodation of such an urban increase would require the construction of about 5,000 new cities of 500,000 inhabitants each.

Even with much greater success with population control than the above figures assume, it is clear that urban population will increase tremendously until the century's end. Even the economically advanced nations will be hard pressed to provide new urban amenities for the burgeoning urban population while trying to eliminate current and ongoing urban problems. In the developing nations of Asia, Latin America, and Africa, the prospect is even grimmer, for the combination of migration from rural to urban areas and high natural increase will put ever greater pressure on pathetically limited urban facilities. With what lies ahead, it is almost certain that urban planning will become increasingly necessary in both the economically advanced and the developing areas—planning that will necessarily involve not only cities but also metropolitan and regional areas and that will include not only physical layouts but also social, economic, and administrative considerations. In the decades lying ahead it is clear that urban problems will require much more attention than has been given to date.

BIBLIOGRAPHY. R.E. DICKINSON, *City and Region* (1964), a geographical interpretation of urban and regional development with comparative considerations including developments in the U.S., western Europe, Britain, France, and Germany; O.D. DUNCAN et al., *Metropolis and Region* (1960), a mid-century benchmark on metropolitan growth in the U.S. stressing structure and function and containing a classification of 50 major cities and their regional relationships; JEAN GOTTMANN, *Megalopolis* (1961), a description and analysis of the urbanization of the northeastern seaboard of the U.S. as an example of emergent megalopolis; P.K. HATT and A.J. REISS, JR. (eds.), *Cities and Society*, 2nd ed. (1957), a reader in the sociological aspects of urbanization and its impact; P.M. HAUSER (ed.), *Urbanization in Asia and the Far East* (1957), proceedings of a United Nations–UNESCO seminar on the processes and problems of urbanization together with policy considerations in Southeast Asia, *Urbanization in Latin America* (1961), proceedings of a seminar on urbanization sponsored by the UN, UNESCO, the ILO, and the Organization of American States on urbanization problems in Latin America, and ed. with L.F. SCHNORE, *The Study of Urbanization* (1965), a review and evaluation of major frameworks for research on urbanization and proposals for needed research; LEWIS MUMFORD, *The City in History* (1961), a historical review of the city from its beginnings to megalopolis with special attention to physical features and with philosophical observations and excellent illustrations; R.E. PARK, *Human Com-*

munities (1952), a pioneer sociological analysis of urbanization and its impact on the human community with early germinal suggestions for the study of human ecology; HENRI PIRENNE, *Medieval Cities* (1925), a historical treatment of the emergence of cities from the collapse of the Roman Empire through the Middle Ages with consideration of economic, social-class, and cultural developments; GIDEON SJOBERG, *The Pre-Industrial City* (1960), a comparative study of pre-industrial cities with special focus on common characteristics —demography and ecology, social class, marriage and the family, economic, political, and religious structure, communication, and education; R.E. TURNER, *The Great Cultural Traditions*, vol. 1, *The Ancient Cities* (1941), a historical synthesis of the origin of cities from Neolithic times to Greek civilization with special attention to cultural developments; UNITED NATIONS, *Urbanization: Development Policies and Planning* (1968), a review of world urbanization trends with consideration of processes of urbanization, social and economic problems and policies including attention to slums and shanty towns, and *Growth of the World's Urban and Rural Population, 1920–2000* (1969), a statistical analysis of urban and rural world population trends by continental regions and an assessment of possible future trends; RAYMOND VERNON, *Metropolis 1985* (1960), an interpretation of the results of the New York Metropolitan Region study with its implications for the future; A.F. WEBER, *The Growth of Cities in the Nineteenth Century* (1899, reprinted 1963), history and statistics of urban growth in the 19th century in the U.S., Europe, and selected Asian, African, and Latin American countries, together with comparative treatment of causes of urban growth, population structure, migration, health, and the consequences of urbanization.

(P.M.H.)

Urban Planning and Redevelopment

Urban planning and redevelopment is aimed at fulfilling social and economic objectives that go beyond the physical form and arrangement of buildings, streets, parks, utilities, and other parts of the urban environment. Urban planning takes effect largely through the operations of government and requires the application of specialized techniques of survey, analysis, forecasting, and design. It may thus be described as a social movement, as a governmental function, or as a technical profession. Each aspect has its own concepts, history, and theories. Together they fuse into the effort of modern society to shape and improve the environment within which increasing proportions of humanity spend their lives: the city.

In many countries, urban planning has been broadened to cover larger areas as the need for orderly development of the entire physical environment has been recognized. In some small countries where usable land is scarce, such planning may extend to the whole country. In Great Britain this broader approach is termed "town and country planning"; in the United States the usual term is "city and regional planning" (see also URBAN DESIGN).

URBAN PLANNING AS A SOCIAL MOVEMENT

Early history. There are examples from the earliest times of efforts to plan city development. Evidence of planning appears repeatedly in the ruins of cities in China, India, Egypt, Asia Minor, the Mediterranean world, and South and Central America. There are many signs: orderly street systems that are rectangular and sometimes radial; divisions of a city into specialized functional quarters; development of commanding central sites for palaces, temples, and what would now be called civic buildings; and advanced systems of fortifications, water supply, and drainage. Most of the evidence is in smaller cities, built in comparatively short periods as colonies. Often the central cities of ancient states grew to substantial size before they achieved governments capable of imposing controls. In Rome, for example, the evidence points to no planning prior to late applications of remedial measures.

For several centuries during the Middle Ages, there was little building of cities in Europe. There is conflicting opinion on the quality of the towns that grew up as centres of church or feudal authority, of marketing or trade. They were generally irregular in layout, with low standards of sanitation. Initially, they were probably un-

congested, providing ready access to the countryside and having house gardens and open spaces used for markets and fairs or grazing livestock. But as the urban population grew, the constriction caused by walls and fortifications led to overcrowding and to the building of houses wherever they could be fitted in. It was customary to allocate certain quarters of the cities to different nationalities, classes, or trades, as in cities of the Far East in the present day. As these groups expanded, congestion was intensified.

During the Renaissance there were conscious attempts to plan features, such as logistically practical circulation patterns and encircling fortifications, which forced overbuilding as population grew. As late as the 1860s, the radial boulevards in Paris had military as well as aesthetic purposes. The grand plan, however, probably had as its prime objective the glorification of a ruler or a state. From the 16th to the end of the 18th century, many small cities and parts of large cities were laid out and built with monumental splendour. The result may have pleased and inspired the citizens, but it rarely contributed to the health or comfort of their homes or to the efficiency of manufacturing, distribution, or marketing.

The planning concepts of the European Renaissance were transplanted to the New World; examples are Williamsburg, Virginia, and Washington, D.C. In particular, Pierre l'Enfant's plan for Washington (1791) illustrated the strength and weakness of these concepts; it was a plan ably designed to achieve monumentality and grandeur in the siting of public buildings but was in no way concerned with the efficiency of residential, commercial, or industrial development. More prophetic of the layout of U.S. cities was the rigid, gridiron plan of Philadelphia, designed by William Penn (1682), with a layout of streets and lots (plots) adaptable to rapid changes in land use but wasteful of land and inefficient for traffic. The gridiron plan travelled westward with the pioneers, since it was the simplest method of dividing surveyed territory. Its special advantage was that a new city could be planned in the eastern offices of land companies and lots sold without buyer or seller ever seeing the site.

The New England town also influenced later settlement patterns in the United States. The central common, initially a cattle pasture safe from marauding Indians, provided a focus of community life and a site for meetinghouse, tavern, smithy, and shops. It became the central square in county seats from the Alleghenies to the Pacific and remained the focus of urban activity. Also from the New England town came the tradition of the freestanding, single-family house. Set well back from the street and shaded by trees, it had an ornamental front yard and a working backyard and became the norm of American residential development. This was in contrast to the European town house, with its party wall and tiny fenced backyard.

19th century. In both Europe and the United States, the surge of industry during the 19th century was accompanied by rapid population growth, unfettered individual enterprise, great speculative profits, and remarkable lapses of community responsibility. During this era, sprawling, giant metropolitan cities developed, offering wealth and adventure, variety and change. Their slums, congestion, disorder, and ugliness provoked the beginnings of the modern housing and city-planning movements. Reacting against the slums of 19th-century industrial cities, housing reform was the first demand. Industrial slums in European and American cities were unbelievably congested, overbuilt, unsanitary, and unpleasant. The early regulatory laws enacted against these conditions set standards that improved upon the slums of the time but seemed a century later to be impossibly low. Progress was very slow, for the rent-paying ability of slum dwellers did not make it profitable to invest in better housing for them. Housing improvement as an objective, however, recurred continually. Early significant improvements in public health resulted from engineering improvements in water supply and sewerage, which were essential to the later growth of urban populations.

Toward the end of the 19th century, another effort to

Urban
design
in the
Renais-
sance

improve urban environment emerged from the recognition of the need for recreation. Parks were developed to provide visual relief and places for healthful play or relaxation. Later, playgrounds were carved out in congested areas, and facilities for games and sports were established not only for children but also for adults, whose workdays gradually shortened.

Concern for the appearance of the city had long been manifest in Europe, in the imperial tradition of court and palace and in the central plazas and great buildings of church and state. The resurgence of this tradition had a counterpart in the "city beautiful" movement in the United States following Chicago's World Columbian Exposition of 1893. This movement expressed itself widely in civic centres and boulevards, contrasting with and in protest against the surrounding disorder and ugliness.

In the course of the 19th century, a number of utopian and religious groups contributed ideas for more satisfactory urban forms, though their experimental communities met with indifferent success. The garden-city movement in England developed from the writings of the reformer Ebenezer Howard in the 1890s and was a great and continuing influence on efforts to improve the urban environment.

20th century. Early in the 20th century, during the sprawling growth of industrial cities, factories invaded residential areas, tenements crowded in among small houses, and the first skyscrapers overshadowed other buildings. To preserve property values and achieve economy and efficiency in the structure and arrangement of the city, the need was felt to sort out incompatible activities, to set some limits upon height and density, and to protect established areas from despoilment. Zoning (see below) was the result.

Conse-
quences
of
develop-
ments
in
transporta-
tion

As transportation evolved from foot and horse to street railway, underground railway or subway, elevated railroad, and automobile, the new vehicles made possible tremendous territorial urban expansion. Workers were able to live far from their jobs, and tremendously complex systems of communications developed. The new vehicles also rapidly congested the streets in the older parts of cities. By threatening strangulation, they dramatized the need to establish orderly circulation systems of new kinds.

Metropolitan growth so intensified these and other difficulties that the people living in cities—who for the first time outnumbered the rural population in many countries —began to demand an attack upon all of these problems. In response, city planning by midcentury aimed not at any single problem or reform but at the improvement of all aspects of the urban physical environment. An important concept was that all these problems were related and could not be attacked successfully in isolation. It became apparent that the planning of the urban environment could not be separated from the planning of the whole metropolitan area. This introduced issues of national planning and in many countries brought city planning into the field of planning the nation's economic and social resources as a whole.

Also at midcentury, when a coherent and unified approach to physical-development planning had finally evolved, a new urban crisis emerged with which physical planning alone could not cope. U.S. cities—especially those in the North—took in millions of black migrants, pushed off the land by changes in agricultural technology, attracted initially by wartime job opportunities. Many of them were even less equipped for urban life than the earlier European immigrants. Illiterate objects of prejudice and discrimination, they suffered severely from the reduction in low-skilled jobs caused by automation. The black ghetto in the 1960s, physically a slum, was healthier than the 19th-century slums but, in contrast to the living conditions of the middle class white majority, relatively far worse. The ghetto was the focus of unemployment, poor education, family disorganization, crime, and delinquency.

As it developed, city planning laid stress on those aspects of the urban environment that in the common interest should be improved and that required protection and

promotion through government action. Countries varied in the relative importance that they attached to these aims —some stressing the government function in promoting planning, some the role of individual enterprise, with government playing a subsidiary role as the protector of the public from the adverse effects of the actions of others.

Goals of modern urban planning. The ultimate goals had always been social, even during the period when city plans themselves related only to physical change. They had been and continued to be deeply involved with intermediate economic objectives. The expression of the goals was, of course, coloured by the culture of the society seeking them. In the United States and countries following western European traditions, the ideal urban environment would reconcile the maximum opportunity for individual choice with protection for the individual from the adverse effects of the actions of others. Of increasing weight was the goal of equality of opportunity and the redress of the grievances of disadvantaged minorities. Within this value system the physically oriented urban planning of the first half of the 20th century had evolved a set of environmental objectives that continued to be valid: (1) the orderly arrangement of parts of the city —residential, business, industrial—so that each part could perform its functions with minimum cost and conflict; (2) an efficient system of circulation within the city and to the outside world, using to the maximum advantage all modes of transportation; (3) the development of each part of the city to optimum standards, in terms of lot size, sunlight, and green space in residential areas, and parking and building spacing in business areas; (4) the provision of safe, sanitary, and comfortable housing in a variety of dwelling types to meet the needs of all families; (5) the provision of recreation, schools, and other community services of a high standard of size, location, and quality; (6) the provision of adequate and economical water supply, sewerage, utilities, and public services.

Six
objectives
of urban
planning

Even these superficially clear objectives, however, were not fully operational. They involve such terms as "adequate" and "high standard," which are relative rather than absolute, and change with new insights from experience or research (medical, psychological, social) and with new technological achievements. Inherent in the concept of city planning was the recognition that an ideal is not a fixed objective but will itself change, that the ideal city can be striven toward but never achieved. This turned the focus of planning away from the "master plan" and toward a stress upon the process and the directions of change.

By the late 1960s, hardly any major cities in the Western world had made more than token progress toward this new kind of "comprehensive" planning, involving coordination of a set of interrelated programs for directed change in physical, social, and economic conditions. Even the undertaking of this kind of planning was as yet an unfulfilled objective.

PLANNING AND GOVERNMENT

As a normal and identifiable function of government, city planning for the physical environment has been recognized in Europe and the United States since the early years of the 20th century. The year 1909 was a milestone. It saw the passage of Britain's first town planning act and, in the United States, the first national conference on city planning, the publication of Daniel Burnham's plan for Chicago, and the appointment of Chicago's Plan Commission (the first official planning agency in the U.S. was in Hartford, Connecticut, in 1907). Germany, Sweden, and other European countries also developed planning administration and law at this time.

City planning as a government function involves the coordination of all governmental activities that bear upon community growth and change, especially those that influence private development, so that they all work toward comprehensive objectives. In its early form, emphasis was on preparation of a single and authoritative plan. In time, as noted above, it was realized that the future was not precisely predictable and that the plan must be flexible. It was also realized that governmental influence on private activities must be primarily negative and that many of the decisions that resulted in significant growth and change in cities were made by private agencies, such as industries, banks, or land developers, especially in the parts of the world that permitted private economic activity. Accordingly, planning was broadened to include the measures needed to foster a realization by business and civic leaders of their stake in city development and of their opportunities to capitalize on it. In European countries, the planning powers of central as well as local government were strengthened in order that the community, through government, might take more positive action to accomplish planning objectives.

Varying approaches to the administration of planning

The place of the city-planning function in the structure of urban government has developed in different ways in different countries. On the continent of Europe, where municipal administration was strongly centralized, city planning became the sphere of an executive department with substantial authority. In Great Britain, the local planning authority was a local legislative body (the county or county borough in England and Wales, the county or burgh in Scotland), advised by a planning committee of local councillors and with a planning department to act in an executive and advisory capacity. In the United States, with its tradition of tripartite government, it was recognized that decisions of importance to community development were made both by the executive branch (mayor) and the legislative (council). Rather than impinge on the authority of either, planning was allotted to a separate commission, advisory to both, with no authority beyond the right to be consulted before any action affecting the plan was taken.

After the late 1930s there was a trend toward making city planning a staff arm of the executive, in line with a general trend toward the strengthening of executive powers. There was also, as municipal government became more complicated, a trend toward formalizing the planning of administrative operations, budgeting, and other executive functions, which led to some confusion between this kind of planning and city planning as covered in this article.

Zoning and subdivision controls. Zoning, the regulation of the use of land and buildings, the density of population, and the height, bulk, and spacing of structures, was the principal means of putting into effect a comprehensive scheme for land use. It is generally dated from the adoption of New York City's first comprehensive ordinance in 1916. Though zoning was used in Great Britain and other European countries, it was developed furthest in the United States. The first ordinances were simple regulations, intended primarily to protect existing property values and preserve light and air. As planning itself broadened its objectives and evolved its techniques during the 1930s, zoning developed into a more precise and sensitive tool. Zoning was employed more and more to give legal effect to planning policies for land use.

Parallel to the evolution of zoning in the United States was the development of subdivision controls—subjecting the initial laying out of vacant land to public regulation. It was realized, after bitter experience with suburban land speculations in the 1920s, that the interest of the owner and developer of raw land is sometimes temporary and purely financial, while the urban community must live with the results for generations afterward. Subdivision regulations in many United States cities specified that new streets conform to the overall city plan and that new lots be properly laid out for building sites. Some required the developer to give the land needed for streets, playgrounds, and school sites and to pay all or most of the cost of development of these facilities.

Zoning and subdivision control offered adequate controls over the growth of new parts of cities, where they were used by enlightened legislative bodies. It was realized, however, that they were insufficient to correct past mistakes and especially to bring about the rebuilding of the obsolete parts of cities.

Large-scale planning. In order to clear slums and to provide decent housing for slum dwellers unable to afford private housing, publicly owned and subsidized housing was developed. It was used first in Europe, especially in the 1920s, and was supplemented by cooperatives and other forms of limited-profit or publicly aided housing, particularly in Scandinavia. Public housing with federal aid became government policy in the United States in the 1930s. Most states authorized their cities to condemn and clear slums and to build public housing. In Great Britain and Europe in the 1920s and 1930s, public housing was also built in vacant suburban areas, in some cases on such a scale as to almost constitute new towns. This was a result of the recognition that all slum dwellers could not be rehoused in the same areas without repeating the slum congestion. Though such action was legal in the United States after the 1930s, it was rarely employed.

All over the Western world, in the first half of the 20th century, new towns were built, constituting a very small part of the total or urban growth but serving as experiments and as examples of what could be done. This was largely the product of England's garden-city movement, which proposed preplanned new cities, on land held by the community and limited to 30,000 population, complete with business services and employment centres and surrounded by permanent greenbelts of rural land. The initial experimental cities were undertaken in England by private initiative, motivated by a spirit of reform; Letchworth was started in the early 1900s and Welwyn Garden City in the 1920s.

Experimental new towns of the early 20th century

The concept had substantial influence in the United States. Kingsport, Tennessee, was a new city built by industrial interests. Some of the design ideas were used in suburban real-estate developments, outstanding being that of Radburn, New Jersey, which pioneered the super-block scheme as the "town for the motor age." U.S. examples, however, omitted the community-ownership feature, and almost all omitted employment centres, balanced income groups, and effective greenbelts. The federal government undertook a few large-scale housing developments for immigrant industrial workers during World Wars I and II, as make-work projects during the depression of the 1930s, and as examples of sound urban design. During the 1960s a number of private-enterprise developments at the scale of new cities were undertaken, primarily integral to expanding metropolitan areas rather than as truly independent cities. Notable were Reston, Virginia, and Columbia, Maryland, both near Washington, D.C., and the Irvine Ranch area near Los Angeles.

Also during the 1930s a number of European countries, especially France, The Netherlands, Germany, and the Soviet Union, undertook the building of new towns as governmental enterprises. Most of them (except in the Soviet Union) were residential suburbs rather than complete urban units. During the period following World War II, many European countries made strides in the regulation of new growth and in planned rebuilding of bomb-torn city centres.

After World War II, Great Britain embarked on a bold program. It reorganized the planning districts of the country; established sweeping new powers over private land use, almost nationalizing the right to develop undeveloped land; and undertook to build new towns to receive population and industry from congested great cities, which were planned for building at lower densities. By 1960, 15 new towns were under way, but the national program had suffered reverses. At first, economic exigencies interfered with the relocation of industry suggested by long-range environmental planning, and some of the controls over private land development, which appeared to impede investment and construction, had to be relaxed. Most of the new towns, nevertheless, had become centres of rapid industrial and population expansion and constituted important new work in city plan effectuation.

In countries that had sustained extensive war damage, there was much concern with planned rebuilding of obsolete areas. In the endeavour to rebuild devastated cities, several European countries, notably Britain, France, and The Netherlands, strengthened public powers to acquire land and redevelop it according to a new layout. Notable examples are Coventry in England and Rotterdam in The

Netherlands. Toward the end of the decade, many states of the United States granted urban redevelopment powers to their cities, which began to clear slums not only for public housing but also for any other public or private re-use that fitted a comprehensive plan.

Postwar
urban
redevelop-
ment
in the
United
States

By the early 1970s urban redevelopment and renewal in the United States had achieved some major successes in revitalizing the economy of central-city areas. Such programs were bitterly criticized, however, for displacing low-income families and for disregarding the network of social relationships that had meant more to these families than the squalor and danger of their physical shelter. Among the new programs evolved after the establishment of a new cabinet-level Department of Housing and Urban Development was the Model Cities program. This was an experiment, in several dozen U.S. cities, in attacking the problems of major blighted areas with massive federal financial aid. It included programs of physical improvement coordinated with social and economic upgrading through job training, school improvement, encouragement of economic enterprise, and a complete panoply of self-help and outside-help measures aimed at reducing poverty and all of its adverse concomitants.

Planning jurisdictions. Where a single municipal government included all of an urban area, tools for physical planning and effectuation seemed, in the second half of the 20th century, to be approaching adequacy. This condition, however, was exceptional. In Europe and the Americas, the metropolitan area was the typical urban form, composed of many independent municipalities, with overlapping jurisdictions of counties, school districts, and special authorities. During this period, European countries were groping toward solutions of the metropolitan planning and development problem, with some progress in Great Britain, Scandinavia, Germany (Ruhr), and The Netherlands. In the 1950s a limited metropolitan government was established for Toronto, Ontario, with planning as an integral function. As late as the early 1970s metropolitan planning efforts in the United States were still largely ineffective. Planning agencies had little voice in the decisions of not only the separate cities and suburbs but also larger public agencies, such as state highway departments, sewer and water supply authorities, and port and airport authorities. The U.S. planning movement had not yet evolved the governmental machinery for reconciling in a democratic way the conflicting interests of all of the constituents of a metropolitan area.

In Asia, the emerging industrial economies of the post-World War II period produced cities following many of the patterns of the West. These rapidly developing countries, however, are still preoccupied with political and economic problems and have made little progress in establishing an environmental planning function in city or metropolitan government effective enough to prevent the mistakes made earlier in Western cities. There are a few outstanding examples of planned new cities in such widely scattered places as India, Israel, and South America. There are also signs of increasing concern in Puerto Rico, India, Indonesia, and elsewhere for regional development programs.

BIBLIOGRAPHY. For historical background, see LEWIS MUMFORD, *The City in History* (1961), a classic work with an extensive bibliography; and ERWIN A. GUTKIND, *International History of City Development*, 5 vol. (1964–70), detailing historical developments in various geographic regions. Among the best works on modern practice are W.I. GOODMAN and ERIC C. FREUND (eds.), *Principles and Practice of Urban Planning*, 4th ed. (1968); MICHAEL P. BROOKS, *Social Planning and City Planning* (1970); KEVIN LYNCH, *Site Planning*, 2nd ed. (1971); and FREDERICK H. BAIR, JR., *Planning Cities: Selected Writings on Principles and Practice* (1970). The problems of urban planning in developing countries are well presented in CHARLES ABRAMS, *Man's Struggle for Shelter in an Urbanizing World* (1964); while JOHN FRIEDMANN and WILLIAM ALONSO (eds.), *Regional Development and Planning* (1964), examine the broader topic of the relationship between economic development, urbanization, and social change. Current information on particular national developments may be found in the following periodicals: American Institute of Planners, *Journal* (bimonthly); Town Planning Institute of Great Britain, *Journal* (10/year); University of Liverpool, *Town Planning Review* (quarterly); *Urbanistica* (Turin, quarterly); and *Urbanisme* (Paris, bimonthly).

Urmia, Lake

Lake Urmia, located in northwestern Iran, has an area that varies from 2,000 to 2,300 square miles (5,200 to 6,000 square kilometres) and is the largest lake in the Middle East. Like the Dead Sea, it is remarkable for the extreme salinity of its waters. Since 1967 it has enjoyed the status of a wetland protected region, and efforts have been made by the Iranian government to increase its wildlife. Lake Urmia (the old name for the lake as well as for the city near its western shore), has also been known since the 1930s as Daryācheh-ye ("lake") Rezā'-īyeh (the name given to the lake and the city at that time by Reza Shah Pahlavi, ruler of Iran). A third name, Daryācheh-ye Shāhī (also Persian), is derived from Jazīreh-ye Shāhī (Shāhī Island), situated in the central part of the lake.

Physiography. The lake lies in the bottom of the large central depression of the Azerbaijan region in northwestern Iran, at an elevation of 4,183 feet above sea level. The basin is surrounded by mountains in the west and north, by plateaus in the south, and by plateaus and volcanic cones in the east. The lake is about 87 miles long and 25 to 35 miles wide, with a maximum depth of 53 feet. In the south, there is a cluster of about 50 tiny islands. Jazīreh-ye Shāhī is a volcanic formation that attains an elevation of 7,182 feet; it becomes a peninsula at times of low water when its extension to the eastern shore is uncovered. The shoreline varies with the lake level; when the water is high, it extends into large salt marshes to the east and south.

Hydrography. The governing factor of Lake Urmia's hydrography is its lack of an outlet. It forms the dead end of a large drainage system that covers an area of about 20,000 square miles and is subject to great seasonal variation. The main affluents are the Talkheh Rūd (Ājī Chāī) in the northeast, which gathers the melted snows from the Sabalän and Sahand massifs, and the twin rivers Zarīneh Rūd (Jagātu Cham) and Sīmīneh Rūd (Tatavi Chāī) in the south. There are about eight other sizable rivers, mainly entering the lake from the west.

The volume of discharge of the rivers varies considerably during the year: during the spring the Talkheh Rūd and Sīmīneh Rūd may each discharge about 2,000 cubic feet per second, while the rate drops to only 130 or 60 cubic feet per second in the dry summer. This variation causes the lake itself to rise and fall, fluctuating by two to three feet.

In addition to seasonal variations, there are also longer periods of fluctuations, lasting from 12 to 20 years, with water-level fluctuations of six to nine feet. Between 1812 and 1912 at least six such long-range cycles occurred. Surface water temperature is also subject to seasonal change, varying from 28° F (−2° C) in January to 95° F (35° C) in July or August.

Because Lake Urmia's waters have no outlet, they are highly saline. The lake is one-fourth as salty as the Dead Sea, with a salt content ranging from 8 to 11 percent in the spring to 26 or 28 percent in the late autumn. The main salts are chlorine, sodium, and sulphates.

Vegetation and animal life. Organic life in the lake's waters is limited to a few salt-tolerant species. Algae, which grow into masses in flood years, provide food for brine shrimp. It is this seaweed that causes the bad smell along the shores. There are breeding populations of sheldrake, flamingo, and pelican, as well as migratory birds. Jazīreh-ye Qūyūn (also known as Qoyun Daghi Island), the easternmost of the four largest islands south of Jazīreh-ye Shāhī (Shāhī Island), supports a population of sheep and rock partridges.

Human settlement. Settlement around the lake includes the bulk of the population of both the East Azerbaijan *Ostān* (province) and the West Azerbaijan *Ostān* of Iran. The people are mainly Azeri Turks and Kurds, and there are also Persians, Nestorians, and Armenians.

Their agriculture is not dependent upon the lake but upon the sweet water from the surrounding mountains that they use for irrigation. The cities are within easy reach of the lake's shores; they include Tabriz (which has a population of about 465,000), Reẕā'īyeh (140,000), Marāgheh (60,000), and Mahābād (35,000).

Resources and navigation. The only resource of the lake is salt, but this is not exploited because of the more accessible deposits of salt domes in the hinterland. Some charcoal has been obtained from the pistachio trees that grow on the islands. The lake's mud is used for the treatment of rheumatism and skin diseases. Navigation is limited to small motor craft that provide limited cargo and passenger service between a few places on the lakeshore.

BIBLIOGRAPHY. FRIEDRICH PLATTNER, "Mehrjährige Beobachtungen über die Spiegelund Salzgehaltschwankungen des Urmiasees," *Erdkunde*, 24:134–139 (1970), contains basic observations on variations of the water level and salt content of the lake. The same author's "Über den Salzgehalt des Urmiasees," *Petermanns Mitt.*, pp. 276–278 (1955), is the first modern chemical analysis of the lake. The HYDROGRAPHIC SERVICE OF IRAN, *Hydrographic Yearbook* (annual since 1957–58), offers official data for several streams in the Urmia basin.

(H.B.)

Urodela

Salamanders, constituting the order Urodela (Caudata), together with frogs (order Anura) and caecilians (order Gymnophiona) comprise the three living groups of the class Amphibia. The relatively small and inconspicuous salamanders are important members of north temperate and some tropical animal communities. They are important as subjects of experimental studies in embryology, developmental biology, physiology, anatomy, biochemistry, genetics, and behaviour. Convenient size, low food requirements, low metabolic rate, and hardiness make them good laboratory animals.

General features. *Size range and diversity of structure.* The most typical salamanders are short-bodied, four-legged, moist-skinned vertebrates about 100 to 150 millimetres (about four to six inches) long. The tail is usually about as long as the body. There is much variation in size, and terrestrial salamanders range from 40 to nearly 350 millimetres (about 1.6 to 14 inches) in length. Some live in moist places on land but must go to water to breed. Others are completely terrestrial. Wholly aquatic salamanders attain larger sizes than do terrestrial ones, the former reaching a maximum of 180 centimetres (about six feet). Salamanders may retain gills throughout life, lose the gills but retain a spiracle (breathing pore) or gill slit, or completely metamorphose (*i.e.*, alter radically in structure and appearance) and lose both gills and gill slits. Many aquatic species resemble their terrestrial relatives in body form, but aquatic genera such as *Siren* and *Pseudobranchus* lack hindlimbs, and *Amphiuma* has an extremely elongated body, short tail, and diminutive legs; several cave-dwelling forms (*Proteus, Haideotriton, Typhlomolge*) are blind and almost without pigment.

Distribution and abundance. Salamanders are classic examples of animals with a Holarctic distribution (*i.e.*, in the north-temperate regions of both the Eastern and Western hemispheres); eight of the nine families (see below *Annotated classification*) are found almost entirely in northern regions that lie outside the tropics. Typically, they occur in moist, forested habitats, where they are often common in aquatic and terrestrial communities. Members of the family Salamandridae extend south to extreme northern Africa, the southern foothills of the Himalayas, North Vietnam, and the island of Okinawa. Some ambystomatids reach the southern margins of the Mexican Plateau, but only the lungless salamanders (plethodontids) have truly entered the tropics. One group of plethodontids, which occupies a wide variety of tropical habitats in the New World—from northern Mexico to southern Brazil and central Bolivia—contains nearly half of all recognized species of salamanders, an indication that the plethodontids have been highly successful in the tropical environment. Other areas in which salamanders have been

successful include temperate North America (Appalachian and Ozark uplands; Pacific coast areas with a moist habitat), western Europe, Japan, and China.

Natural history. *Life cycle and reproduction.* Most salamanders are terrestrial or semiterrestrial as adults, but many return to aquatic habitats to breed. Courtship, which is simple or nonexistent in hynobiids and cryptobranchids, is increasingly elaborate and prolonged in the more highly evolved families. In primitive species comprising the suborder Cryptobranchoidea, fertilization of the egg is external. The females deposit sacs or strings of eggs that may be grasped by the male, who then sheds milt (which contains the sperm) over them. Nothing is known of courtship in sirens, but they, too, may have external fertilization, for the males lack the cloacal glands that produce the spermatophore, or sperm case, in species with internal fertilization, and the females lack spermathecae—chambers inside the cloaca used for sperm storage. All other species of salamanders have more complex courtship behaviour—often differing in details between species—and internal fertilization. The male deposits from one to many spermatophores on the ground or other surface. These consist of a gelatinous base, which is produced by cloacal glands, and a so-called sperm cap at the tip. The female moves by herself or is led by the male onto the spermatophore, and she takes the sperm mass into her cloaca. Breeding often occurs in ponds, but some salamandrids and most plethodontids breed on land. Egg deposition may take place shortly after mating but in many plethodontids may be delayed for several months, the eggs being fertilized by stored sperm. Eggs are laid in masses in streams or ponds, often in the shallows near shore. In most plethodontids and in some species of other families, eggs are laid singly, in short strings, or in small groups in terrestrial sites—*e.g.*, under surface objects, in rotting logs, or underground. Some species deposit eggs in tree cavities, and tropical species may deposit them in bromeliad plants, the leaves of which are arranged so that they often hold water. Frequently, the female stays with the eggs until they hatch, a period of several weeks. The number of eggs varies greatly and is correlated with adult size. Aquatic forms deposit as many as 400 eggs; terrestrial forms, as few as five or six.

Typical salamanders undergo an aquatic larval stage that lasts for a period ranging from a few days to several years. A short period of metamorphosis usually occurs before the terrestrial phase of the life cycle begins. The newly metamorphosed salamander is usually very small, and from one to several years elapse before it achieves sexual maturity.

Some salamander species never metamorphose and thus retain most of their larval characteristics. In other species, individuals or populations may occasionally fail to metamorphose. Still other species undergo partial metamorphosis. This phenomenon, known as paedomorphosis —*i.e.*, retention of larval or juvenile features by adults— characterizes all salamanders to a degree but is particularly evident in species such as *Necturus maculosus* (mud puppy) and *Ambystoma mexicanum* (axolotl), which retain gills and other larval structures throughout life. These animals breed in what is essentially a larval state. This extreme condition, which characterizes the Proteidae, Necturidae, and Sirenidae, is also found in several species of the Plethodontidae and Ambystomatidae. In most species the permanent larval state is determined by heredity, but in some it is induced by environmental factors, such as unfavourable terrestrial conditions resulting from drought or cold. The most complete metamorphosis is found in the families Hynobiidae, Salamandridae, Ambystomatidae, and Plethodontidae.

Most species of the family Plethodontidae develop entirely on land, with no aquatic larval stage. The hatchling has either rudimentary gills that soon disappear or none at all and, in virtually all respects, is a miniature of the adult.

Females of the genus *Salamandra* (Salamandridae) may retain the fertilized eggs in the reproductive tract for a varying amount of time. The fire salamander (*Salaman-*

Fertilization

Paedomorphosis

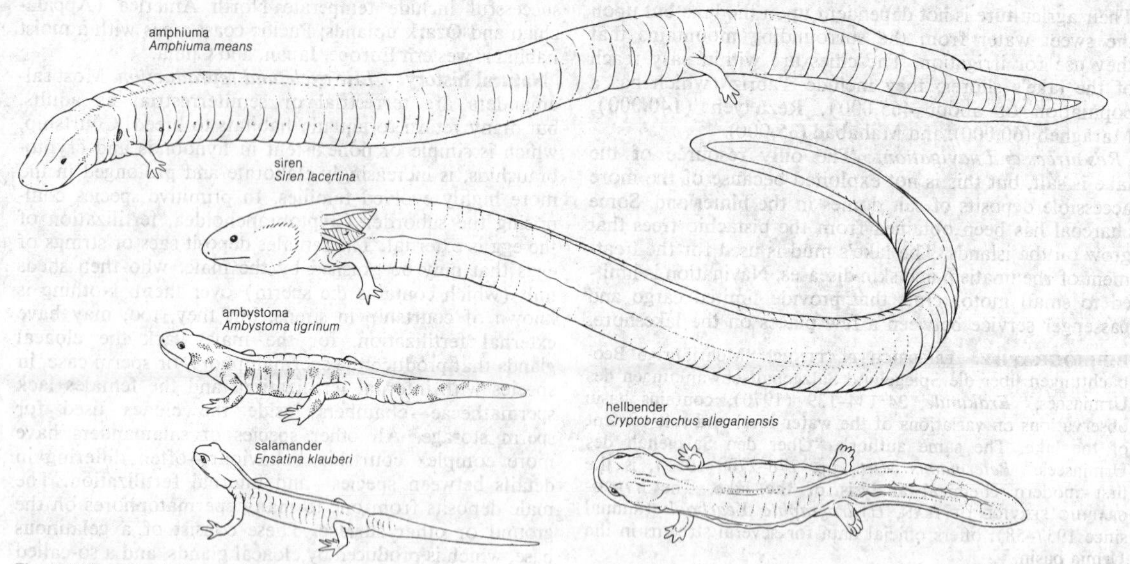

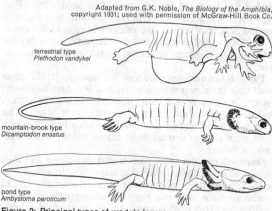

amphiuma
Amphiuma means

siren
Siren lacertina

ambystoma
Ambystoma tigrinum

salamander
Ensatina klauberi

hellbender
Cryptobranchus alleganiensis

Figure 1: Representative urodeles.

dra salamandra) deposits a relatively advanced larva in the water. In the Alpine salamander (*Salamandra atra*) and some other *Salamandra* species, fully metamorphosed individuals are born. One individual develops from the first egg in each oviduct, the tube leading from the ovary to the outside. Initially, the young salamander lives on its own yolk supply; later it eats the yolk of the other eggs, and finally it develops enlarged gills that form an intimate association with the walls of the oviduct to convey nutrients to itself. The gills are lost shortly before birth. Such salamanders are the only live-bearing members of the order.

Adapted from G.K. Noble, *The Biology of the Amphibia*, copyright 1931; used with permission of McGraw-Hill Book Co.

terrestrial type
Plethodon vandykei

mountain-brook type
Dicamptodon ensatus

pond type
Ambystoma paroticum

Figure 2: Principal types of urodele larvae.

Larval
feeding
habits

Larval salamanders are exclusively aquatic. They may occur in a variety of habitats, from temporary ponds to permanent swamps, rivers, slow-moving streams, mountain brooks, springs, and subterranean waters. In all habitats they are exclusively carnivorous, feeding primarily on aquatic invertebrates. In most salamander larvae, feeding is accomplished by a "gape and suck" method, in which the throat is expanded, or gaped, to produce a suction that draws water and prey into the opened mouth. Skin flaps around the mouth direct the water movement. The larvae are well equipped with teeth, which aid in holding and shredding prey. Pond larvae have a high fin on the upper side of the tail that extends far anteriorly (toward the head) and large gills (see Figure 2, above). Limbs are rather slow to develop. By contrast, stream larvae have a low, short tail fin, small gills, and limbs that develop early.

Metamorphosis, although a period of major reorganization, is not so dramatic as that in frogs. In the final stages, metamorphosis is usually a rapid process; it is mediated by several hormones (*i.e.*, chemical substances that serve to regulate the function of various organs) produced by the thyroid and pituitary glands. The following typically occur during metamorphosis: loss of the gills; closure of the gill slits; appearance of a tongue pad and reorganization of the gill skeleton and musculature to produce a tongue; enlargement of the mouth and eyes; development of eyelids; and major changes in the structure of the skull and skin.

Locomotion.   Locomotion is by means of limbs and by sinuous body movements. Some very elongated species of the genera *Phaeognathus*, *Batrachoseps*, *Oedipina*, and *Lineatriton* have reduced limbs and rely mainly on body movements for rapid locomotion. Species of the genus *Aneides* have arboreal (*i.e.*, tree-climbing) tendencies, and their long legs and digits, expanded toe tips, and prehensile (grasping) tails make them effective climbers. Some salamanders of the genera *Pseudoeurycea* and *Chiropterotriton*, found in the New World tropics, are similarly adapted. Others, members of the genus *Bolitoglossa*, have extensively webbed forefeet and hindfeet with indistinct digits, allowing them to move across moist leaves and other smooth surfaces.

Behaviour and ecology.   Adult salamanders are nearly all nocturnal (*i.e.*, active mainly at night) animals. They may be highly seasonal, remaining hidden underground until the breeding season, or they may emerge from hiding places on any evening when moisture and temperature are at the proper levels. Fallen logs, rocks, crevices in soil, and surface litter commonly provide daytime refuge. Home ranges of salamanders are small, often less than three or four square metres (30 to 40 square feet), and, in favourable areas, some of the smaller species can be very abundant, occasionally numbering thousands per acre.

Insects are by far the most important food of salamanders. Primitive salamanders seize their prey by a combination of jaw and tongue movements. Some members of the Salamandridae and Plethodontidae, however, have evolved highly specialized tongue protrusion mechanisms. These are especially well developed in the tropical plethodontids, many of which are arboreal. The tongue can be extended from the mouth for a considerable distance and retracted almost instantaneously, with the prey attached to the sticky tongue pad.

Most terrestrial species live near the surface of the ground, often in thick leaf litter and rock piles. Some enter subterranean retreats, sometimes by way of burrows made by mammals and invertebrates. Caves are often occupied during cold or dry periods. Climbing species live on rock faces and in crevices, in trees, on broad-leaved herbs and shrubs, and in bromeliads. Many species are semi-aquatic, frequenting streamside and spring habitats throughout their lives. The terrestrial species that have direct development have been able to free themselves entirely from reliance on standing or flowing wa-

Habitat

ter. Among one group of plethodontids, species are found in habitats ranging from true deserts and frigid Alpine areas to tropical rain forests and from sea level to elevations of more than 4,000 metres (13,000 feet).

Form and function. *Skin and external features.* The most distinctive and important feature of amphibians in general and salamanders in particular is their smooth, moist skin. This organ consists of an epidermis, or surface tissue, that is several layers thick and a rather thick dermis containing mucus and poison glands as well as pigment cells. The integument, or skin, is highly vascular and serves a major respiratory function. The poison glands of some species produce some of the most virulent toxins known. The fleshy tongue pad contains many mucus-secreting glands.

Most species are drab gray or brown; but many species, especially the more poisonous ones, are spectacularly coloured, with bright spots, blotches, or streaks on a contrasting dark background. The few integumentary specializations include keratinized (*i.e.*, infused with a tough, horny material: keratin) skins of the terrestrial stages of many salamandrids; keratinized claws in stream-dwelling hynobiids; and so-called hedonic glands (believed to stimulate sexual activity of the opposite sex) that are variously distributed in many species. Cryptobranchids have large, lateral folds of skin that serve respiratory functions.

Bones and cartilage. The rather weak skull of adults is comprised of various paired bones. These bones may fuse or be lost in different groups, and their presence and arrangement are important in classification. Much of the fusion and loss of skull bones is frequently associated with a trend toward tongue feeding. Small, double-cusped teeth line the margins of the jaw and spread over parts of the palate. They are important in holding but not chewing the prey.

Cartilage plays an important role in the urodele head, especially in supportive structures in the throat region. These are ossified (bony) to different degrees, with more cartilage in the more highly evolved groups. Species that display tongue protrusion often have flexible, cartilaginous tongue skeletons. In larvae and permanently gilled species the tongue is not developed.

The vertebrae comprising the spinal column are generalized with centrums (*i.e.*, ventral, or lower, sections connecting with the adjacent vertebrae) that are rather poorly developed. The notochord (*i.e.*, a resilient, flexible cord of specialized cells passing through the vertebral column) is usually persistent in adults. An intervertebral cartilage forms the articulation between vertebrae. If it remains cartilaginous, the vertebrae are said to be amphicoelous (biconcave, or depressed on both the anterior and posterior sides), but, if it mineralizes or ossifies, the vertebrae are termed opisthocoelous (bulged on the anterior side and depressed on the posterior side). There is one cervical vertebra with a characteristic projection called the odontoid process and two large facets for articulation with the skull. There may be from 11 (*Ambystoma talpoideum*) to 60 (*Amphiuma*) dorsal, or trunk, vertebrae, all but the last one or two usually bearing ribs. Most salamanders have from 14 to 20 trunk vertebrae. One sacral vertebra, two to four caudosacral vertebrae, and from about 20 to over 100 (*Oedipina*) caudal, or tail, vertebrae complete the column. Many plethodontids are capable of autotomizing, or dropping off, the tail, a valuable defense mechanism in the event that the tail is grasped or bitten by a predator. These salamanders have various specialized features associated with the last caudosacral and the first caudal vertebrae, between which the break usually occurs.

The limbs and girdles are similar to those of generalized vertebrates. The pectoral, or chest, girdle, supporting the forelimbs, is relatively reduced; all elements are fused and remain largely in a cartilaginous condition. An ypsiloid cartilage, used in exhalation, is present in several groups, especially ambystomatids and salamandrids. Digits and digital bones have been lost in many different groups. There are never more than four fingers, but nearly all species have five toes.

Fingers and toes

Nervous system and sense organs. The nervous system is the simplest found in any four-legged animal. The generalized brain is rather small. The relatively large cerebrum (collectively, the two large anterior lobes of the brain) is associated with the large and important olfactory and vomeronasal organs, both of which are used for smelling. The eyes, usually large and well developed, are reduced and nearly lost in some cave-dwelling species. Certain parts of the inner ear are large and well developed. Hearing mechanisms of the salamander are not fully understood. There is no middle ear cavity and no external ear. One middle ear bone rests in the structure known as the vestibular fenestra. The other bone of the middle ear rests in the posterior part of the fenestra and is joined by muscles to the pectoral girdle. The elements are variously fused or lost in different groups. The spinal cord and the peripheral nervous system—*i.e.*, the paired cranial and spinal nerves—are generalized in their structure, and there are distinct brachial and sacral plexuses, both of which are important nerve networks supplying the limbs.

Muscles and organ systems. The generalized trunk musculature shows little differentiation. The abdominal muscles are increasingly differentiated in the higher groups. The hyobranchial and branchiomeric muscles and some abdominal muscles (rectus abdominis) are highly specialized in species that use the tongue to capture prey.

The simple digestive system includes a short, nearly straight gut. The lungs are relatively simple, saclike organs in primitive groups. In stream-dwelling members of several families, the lungs are greatly reduced; they are entirely absent in all plethodontids.

The circulatory system is characterized by a highly developed vascularization of the body surface. The heart is simple, with one ventricle (*i.e.*, a chamber that pumps blood out of the heart) and two atria (chambers that receive blood from the rest of the body); separation between the two atria is not distinct in lungless forms.

The urogenital system consists of an elongated kidney with a distinct sexual segment and a posterior concentration of large renal units, which filter urine from the blood. Testes, the male sex glands, are small and compact, increasing in size with age. Ovaries of females are thin sacs. The cloaca is relatively complex in highly evolved groups with a spermatheca in females and several sets of cloacal glands in both sexes.

Gonads

Evolution and classification. *Paleontology.* Fossils have contributed little, as yet, to the understanding of salamander evolution. The earliest definitive salamander is one of unknown affinities from the Jurassic Period (about 136,000,000 to 190,000,000 years ago). Several ambystomatoid families (Prosirenidae, Scapherpetonidae, Batrachosauroididae) are known only from fossils. The relationships of urodeles to other living and fossil amphibians are unclear, but recent workers consider the three living groups to form the subclass Lissamphibia.

Distinguishing taxonomic features. The features used to establish the limits of the order and of the groups within it include: general body size and organization—*e.g.*, presence or absence of external gills, numbers and relative proportions of limbs and digits, number and arrangement of skull bones; organization of the hyobranchial apparatus (cartilage in the throat region); structure and distribution of the teeth; structure of the vertebrae and intervertebral articulations; numbers of vertebrae; number and organization of the hand and foot elements; anatomy of the pelvic girdle; anatomy of external structures, such as hedonic (sex-attractant) glands, body and tail fins, webbing of hands and feet, and cloacal glands. Distinctive also is the general way of life, whether permanently aquatic, semi-aquatic, or terrestrial.

Annotated classification. The classification below is based on that of A.H. Brame, Jr. (1967). There is as yet no widely accepted scheme for classification below the order level. The plethodontids of the New World tropics remain poorly known, taxonomically.

ORDER URODELA (OR CAUDATA)
Tailed amphibians with 2 or 4 legs; moist, usually smooth, glandular skin; the most generalized of the living amphibi-

ans not only in structure but also in way of life; about 320 species.

Suborder Cryptobranchoidea

The most primitive salamanders; external fertilization; angular bone separate from the prearticular bone in the lower jaw; 2 pairs of limbs; no external gills; aquatic, semi-aquatic, and terrestrial.

Family Hynobiidae (Asiatic salamanders)

Generalized, medium-sized (to about 250 mm, or about 10 in.), semi-aquatic and terrestrial; lacrimal and septomaxillary bones present in skull; vomerine teeth not parallel to marginal teeth; Paleocene(?) (54,000,000–65,000,000 years ago) to present; northern Asia from Ural Mountains to Japan and Taiwan; about 30 species.

Family Cryptobranchidae (giant salamanders and hellbender)

Very large, to about 180 cm (about 6 ft.), aquatic; no lacrimal or septomaxillary bones in skull; vomerine teeth parallel to marginal teeth; Oligocene (26,000,000–38,000,000 years ago) to present; Japan, China, and eastern United States; 3 species.

Suborder Sirenoidea

Mode of fertilization unknown; angular bone fused with prearticular bone in lower jaw; only anterior pair of limbs present; external gills; aquatic.

Family Sirenidae (sirens and dwarf sirens)

Small to very large, to about 100 cm (about 40 in.), predators; inhabitants of lowland waters; Late Cretaceous (65,000,000–90,000,000 years ago) to present; southeastern United States from South Carolina to Tamaulipas, Mexico; 3 species.

Suborder Salamandroidea

Fertilization internal; angular bone fused with prearticular bone in lower jaw; no septomaxillary bones in skull; tooth replacement of vomerine teeth from medial side in metamorphosed forms; 2 pairs of limbs; external gills in a few species; aquatic, semi-aquatic, and terrestrial.

Family Proteidae (olms)

Blind; lacking pigment, cave-dwelling; elongated body, length to 30 cm (about 1 ft), and slender limbs (3 fingers, 2 toes); external gills present; Pliocene (2,500,000–7,000,000 years ago) to present; 1 species, native to Yugoslavia.

Family Necturidae (mud puppies)

Small to moderately large, to 45 cm (about 1½ ft), permanently aquatic, lake and stream dwellers; eyes and skin pigmentation present; 4 fingers and 4 toes; external gills present; no fossil record; eastern North America; 5 species, of genus *Necturus*.

Family Amphiumidae (congo eels)

Large, to over 100 cm (about 40 in.); very elongated, aquatic to semi-aquatic; predaceous, with powerful jaws and teeth; limbs diminutive, 1 to 3 fingers and toes; external gills absent, but spiracle open; Late Cretaceous to present; eastern North America; 3 species, of genus *Amphiuma*.

Family Salamandridae (salamanders and newts)

Generalized form and habit; moderate size, to 32 cm (about 13 in.); limbs with 4 fingers, 4 to 5 toes; usually no external gills or spiracle; Upper Cretaceous (?) to present; Europe, North Africa; Middle East; Afghanistan to Japan, China, and North Vietnam; eastern and western North America; about 42 species.

Suborder Ambystomatoidea

Fertilization internal; angular bone fused with prearticular bone in lower jaw; septomaxillary bones present primitively in skull; tooth replacement of vomerine teeth from posterior or lateral direction; 2 pairs of limbs; external gills in some species; aquatic, semi-aquatic, or terrestrial.

Family Ambystomatidae (mole salamanders and others)

Small to moderate size, to 35 cm (about 14 in.); usually with well developed lungs; no nasolabial grooves; ypsiloid cartilage present; Paleocene to present; North America; about 33 species, including *Ambystoma*.

Family Plethodontidae (lungless salamanders)

Very small to moderate size, 4 to about 30 cm (about 1.6 to 12 in.); includes the most specialized and most terrestrial salamanders, and the only truly tropical species; lungless; nasolabial grooves present; no ypsiloid cartilage; Pliocene to present; North America, Central America, and most of South America; 2 species in Europe (Sardinia, southern France, and north central Italy); more than 200 species.

Critical appraisal. Some controversy exists concerning the classification of salamanders below the ordinal level.

Some authorities place the sirenids in a separate order, Trachystomata, while others separate the Necturidae from the Proteidae, but neither scheme has been widely accepted. Chromosomal evidence of proteidnecturid similarity has recently been presented. Close association of Ambystomatidae and Plethodontidae is now accepted, but placement of Amphiumidae remains controversial. Compare AMPHIBIA: *Annotated classification.*

BIBLIOGRAPHY. S.C. BISHOP, *Handbook of Salamanders* (1943), the only account of all the salamanders of the United States, now badly out-of-date; A.H. BRAME, JR., "A List of the World's Recent and Fossil Salamanders," *Herpeton*, 2:1–26 (1967), a taxonomic checklist of all recognized species to 1967; D.M. COCHRAN, *Living Amphibians of the World* (1961), excellent photographs, but very general text; R. CONANT, *A Field Guide to Reptiles and Amphibians of the United States and Canada East of the 100th Meridian* (1958), identifying characteristics, illustrations, and maps; E.R. DUNN, *The Salamanders of the Family Plethodontidae* (1926), a classic that retains value; R. ESTES, "Fossil Salamanders and Salamander Origins," *Am. Zool.*, 5:319–334 (1965), the most recent account in a rapidly changing area; E.T.B. FRANCIS, *The Anatomy of the Salamander* (1934), the only detailed anatomical treatment, restricted to *Salamandra;* C.J. and O.B. GOIN, *Introduction to Herpetology* (1962), an elementary textbook; G.K. NOBLE, *The Biology of the Amphibia* (1931), a classic that is out-of-date but still very useful; S.N. SALTHE, "Courtship Patterns and the Phylogeny of the Urodeles," *Copeia*, pp. 100–117 (1967), a recent summary; I.I. SCHMALHAUSEN, *The Origin of Terrestrial Vertebrates* (1968; orig. pub. in Russian, 1964), a detailed consideration of salamander morphology and evolution from an unorthodox viewpoint; R.C. STEBBINS, *A Field Guide to Western Reptiles and Amphibians* (1966), an exceptionally well illustrated guide, with maps and identifying characteristics; R. THORN, *Les Salamandres d'Europe, d'Asie et d'Afrique du Nord* (1968), an excellent, recent treatment of Old World salamanders, with maps and illustrations; V.C. TWITTY, *Of Scientists and Salamanders* (1966), a superb treatment of the life of an outstanding scientist, and of the scientific value of urodeles; D.B. WAKE, "Comparative Osteology and Evolution of the Lungless Salamanders, Family Plethodontidae," *Mem. So. Calif. Acad. Sci.*, 4:1–111 (1966), a recent account of the largest family of salamanders, with comments on other groups.

(D.B.W.)

Urticales

The flowering plant order Urticales, or nettle order, includes such important and well-known plants as the figs, breadfruit, mulberries, elms, stinging nettles, hops, and true hemp, or marihuana. Although the order is mainly tropical in distribution, many of its species are widely and abundantly dispersed in temperate regions, particularly in the Northern Hemisphere. The Urticales is distinctive morphologically and is considered to be among the more evolutionarily advanced groups of the woody flowering plants. It includes about 125 genera and about 3,100 species in four families.

GENERAL FEATURES

Size range and diversity of structure. Plants of the nettle order range from small herbaceous (nonwoody) species to large trees. The elm family (Ulmaceae) consists of shrubs and trees, including the elms (*Ulmus*) and hackberries (*Celtis*), some of which grow to 150 feet (45 metres) in height. A great diversity of mainly woody plants is found in the mulberry family (Moraceae), which contains the figs, with about 800 species. Figs are great trees of the tropical forests; some are buttressed by wide-ranging, and often finlike, spreading roots, as exemplified by *Ficus elastica*, the well-known India rubber tree. Many figs grow at first as epiphytes, or air plants, upon the branches of other trees, from seeds dropped by birds or bats. As these young plants develop, they send aerial roots down along the trunk of the supporting host tree, and in time the ever enlarging roots gradually crush the host to death. These are the so-called strangler figs, vinelike in youth but self-supporting large trees at maturity. The banyan, or Bengal fig (*F. benghalensis*), is another wide-spreading tree, an old specimen of which comes to resemble a dense grove of trees by dropping thick prop roots from its spreading branches. Some of the tree spe-

Strangler figs

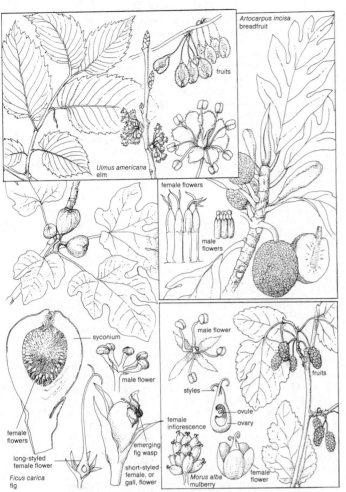

Figure 1: Representative plants of the elm and mulberry families. Upper left, family Ulmaceae. All others, Moraceae. Drawing by M. Pahl

cies bear long, sharp thorns, for which feature these plants find use as hedgerow or fencerow trees to enclose livestock or discourage trespassers (*e.g.*, *Maclura*, osage orange).

The nettle family (Urticaceae) is well-known for its stinging hairs, which can cause severe pain on contact. Although the nettle family is most abundant in the tropics, where its species are shrubby and treelike, the temperate regions of the Northern Hemisphere contain large numbers of the herbaceous nettles, seldom more than a few feet tall and often weedy looking. The hemp family (Cannabaceae) is also herbaceous: one genus (*Humulus*, hop) is a vine and the other (*Cannabis*, hemp) a tall herb.

Distribution and abundance. The species of the order Urticales are unequally divided among the genera and families. One of the two largest families of the order is the mulberry family, with more than 1,400 species in about 54 genera. Of these genera the largest are *Ficus* (more than 800 species) and *Dorstenia* (about 170 species). *Brosimum* and *Artocarpus* each contain about 50 species, which are distributed in the tropics. About 12 more genera in the mulberry family contain between ten to 25 species each. The more than 30 remaining genera have fewer than four species each, and a third of these are known by a single species each.

The nettle family also contains about 54 genera, with more than 1,400 species of mostly herbaceous or soft-wooded plants. The largest genera are *Pilea* (400 species; the tropics,) *Elatostema* (200 species; the tropics), *Boehmeria* (100 species; the tropics and northern subtropics), and *Cecropia* (100 species; tropical America). The next 20 genera, in numbers of species, all contain between ten and 50 species each; the nettles themselves (*Urtica*) comprise a group of about 50 species. There is a large group of monotypic genera, about 14 in all.

The largest genus of the elm family is *Celtis* (hackberries), with about 80 species distributed in the Northern Hemisphere and in southern Africa. The elms (*Ulmus*) consist of about 45 species, north temperate in distribution but extending as far south as the Himalayas and Indochina in Asia and to Mexico in North America. Other genera in the tropics and subtropics include *Trema*, 30 species; *Gironniera*, 15; *Ampelocera*, nine; *Parasponia*, six; and *Chaetachme*, four. The genus *Zelkova*, with seven species, is found in the eastern Mediterranean countries eastward to the Caucasus and into Asia. *Lozanella*, with two species, is native to Central and South America from Mexico to Peru and Bolivia. *Planera*, with a single species (*P. aquatica*), is native to the southern United States.

The smallest family is the hemp family (Cannabaceae), which consists of only two genera and about five species. *Humulus* (hop) occurs in north temperate regions, especially in Europe and the northeastern United States. The genus *Cannabis*, with a single species (*C. sativa*), is thought to be native to Central Asia but is now widely cultivated and has escaped from cultivation as a weed throughout much of the Northern Hemisphere (see Figure 2, below).

Economic importance. *Wood products.* Valuable timber trees include the elms, among which the cork elm, or rock elm (*Ulmus thomasi*), is considered superior because it grows to a great height before branching, thus producing long lengths of clear (knot-free) wood. The keyaki (*Zelkova acuminata*) of Japan is much appreciated for the beautiful colour and grain of its wood. Wood of the osage orange is used for railroad ties and fence posts and has been used to carve high-quality hunting bows in times past. Flexible, strong, and also durable, it has a bright orange colour that eventually turns brown.

From (female flower, stinging hair) A. Engler, *Syllabus der Pflanzenfamilien* (1964), Gebruder Borntraeger Verlag Berlin-Stuttgart; and (cystolith) A.B. Rendle, *The Classification of Flowering Plants* (1967), Cambridge University Press

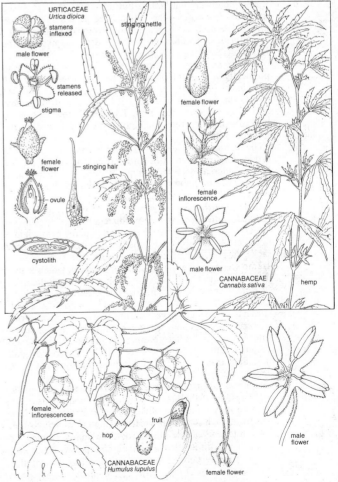

Figure 2: Representative plants of the nettle and hemp families.

Celtis occidentalis wood, sold under the name beaverwood, is used for boxes, furniture, and gift items. The wood of the African oak (*Chlorophora excelsa*), of tropical Africa, is heavy, tough, difficult to split, and resistant to termite attack. It has been used as a substitute for teak in shipbuilding and furniture making. *Chaetoptelea mexicana*, found in Mexico south of Panama, is a large tree, the wood of which is used as lumber. *Holoptelea grandis*, a tall tree of the Congo Basin, Uganda, Cameroon, and the Ivory Coast, has hard yellow wood used for house interiors and small-boat construction. *Phyllostylon brasiliensis*—San Domingo boxwood, or West Indian boxwood, of the lumber trade—is a tree ranging from the West Indies to Argentina. It produces a fine-textured, lemon-yellow, straight-grained wood valued for the high polish it will accept; stained black, it is often used as a substitute for true ebony. The wood of *Planera aquatica*, called false sandalwood, is fragrant and is used in cabinetmaking. The lightweight wood of *Chaetachme microcarpa*, a shrub of central and southern Africa, is used for the manufacture of guitars and other musical instruments.

Letterwood

Brosimum guianense, source of the expensive letterwood of the lumber trade, is a tree of the Guianas (Guyana, Surinam, and French Guiana). Its reddish-brown or brown wood, bearing black marks that resemble printed letters or hieroglyphics, is used for cabinetwork and small items such as handles, drumsticks, and violin bows. *Bosqueia angolensis*, a tree of the Congo Basin and Angola, produces yellow wood that turns pink on exposure to air; it is used in general construction and cabinetry. The wood of *Morus rubra*, the red mulberry of eastern North America, although light and not very strong, is durable and rot-resistant, qualities that make it useful in fence construction and boat building. *Brosimum paraense*, the Para breadnut tree of Brazil, produces wood called redwood or cardinal wood, used in fine furniture and fancy carpentry. Many *Ficus* species find use as lumber. *Ficus benghalensis* has wood that is durable in water. The wide, flat, finlike buttress roots of large specimens of *F. elastica*—the rubber tree grown as a houseplant—are used in tropical regions to make planks. *Ficus sycomorus*, a wood of great durability, was used by the Egyptians to make their mummy cases.

The hop and hemp. Among the most outstanding economically important plants in the Urticales is the hop (*Humulus lupulus*), the female flowers of which are used to flavour beer and to clarify it by precipitating protein materials that cause turbidity. The active principles of the hop also help prevent spoilage in beer by retarding the growth of bacteria.

The hemp, or cannabis (*Cannabis sativa*), used as a crude drug plant in Asia and Africa for centuries, has become increasingly widespread in Europe, North America, and South America since World War II. Parts of the plant are dried and offered under many names, including hashish, marihuana, pot, and grass. It is widely smoked, chewed, sniffed, or eaten to produce a mild euphoria (see NARCOTICS). The stems of the hemp plant also yield a fibre, called hemp, used mostly for rope, twine, bags, sacks, carpets, and other purposes suited to its coarseness. Hemp seeds are the source of hemp seed oil, which is used in paints, varnishes, soaps, and some edible products.

Fruits. Important fruits of the order are produced mainly by the family Moraceae. The edible fig (*Ficus carica*), cultivated since antiquity, is eaten raw, dried, preserved, or candied; when ground it serves as a substitute for tea or coffee. Numerous commercially grown varieties differ in flavour, size, colour, preserving qualities, appearance, and other features. Many other *Ficus* species also produce edible figs.

The breadfruit

An important tropical tree is the breadfruit (*Artocarpus altilis*). One of the highest yielding of food plants, a single tree may have more than 800 grapefruit-sized, seedless fruits each season. Breadfruits, high in carbohydrates, constitute one of the staple foods in many tropical regions. The fruit is filled with a starchy, pulpy, white mass that is usually cooked before eating. Closely related to the breadfruit is the jackfruit (*A. heterophyllus*), which produces fruits up to two feet long and weighing 40

pounds or more; they are not highly esteemed, however, because of their inferior flavour and seed-filled interior.

A number of lesser fruits of the order are also eaten, such as the breadnut (*Brosimum alicastrum*), mulberries (*Morus alba*, the white mulberry; *M. rubra*, the red; and *M. nigra*, the black), and hackberries (*Celtis occidentalis* and others). In addition, fruits are eaten from the following plants: *Debregeasia edulis*, a Japanese shrub that produces yellow fruits resembling strawberries; *Pourouma cecropiaefolia*, a Brazilian tree with round, fleshy berries; *Cudrania javanensis*; *Celtis selloviana* and *C. iguaneae*; *Myrianthus arborea*; and *Sahagunia strepticans*.

Fibres. Plant fibres for cloth, sacks, rope, and numerous other purposes are produced mainly by the nettle and the hemp families. The fibres of the hemp are similar to those of flax. A finer fibre is produced from the ramie, or China grass plant (*Boehmeria nivea*), also called the Chinese silk plant because its fibres make a cloth resembling silk. Ramie fibres, although eight times stronger than cotton fibres and much longer, are difficult to separate from the plant tissues. The fibres are also used to produce papers, cordage, and industrial bagging. Other plants with fibres like those of the ramie are sometimes used as substitutes for it; they include *Sarcochlamys pulcherrima* (duggal fibre) and *Pouzolzia occidentalis* (yaquilla). Olona (*Touchardia latifolia*) was formerly an important fibre plant of Hawaii, used for cloth, cordage, and especially fishnets because of its durability in water. Fibres are also obtained from the stinging nettle (*Urtica dioica*); *U. breweri*; *U. cannabina*; *Debregeasia hypoleuca*; *Villebrunea integrifolia*; and many others, including the wood nettle (*Laportea canadensis*), the fibres of which are claimed to be 50 times as strong as a cotton thread of equal diameter. Fibres extracted from the bark and aerial roots of many *Ficus* species are used locally.

Bark cloth, or tapa cloth, made from the inner bark of some trees, especially the paper mulberry (*Broussonetia papyrifera*), was once used by local populations mainly for clothing. It is still produced but now principally for religious purposes and for the tourist trade. Bark cloth is also made from the breadfruit tree, certain fig trees (*Ficus tinctoria* and others), *Pipturus albidus*, and several other genera, including *Antiaris*, *Sloetia*, and *Trema*. Paper is made from the inner bark of the paper mulberry and several other plants of the order (*e.g.*, *Streblus asper*, *Ficus religiosa*, *F. petiolaris*).

Latex products. Among the earliest sources of rubber were species of the latex-bearing family Moraceae, especially *Ficus elastica*, but the Para rubber tree (*Hevea brasiliensis*, family Euphorbiaceae) has largely displaced it. Among numerous other rubber-producing trees in the order Urticales, however, are the Mexican rubber tree (*Castilla elastica*), one of the most productive of wild rubber trees; *C. lactiflora*; *C. nicoyensis*; *C. costaricana*; *C. ulei*; *Ficus nekbudu*, the latex of which becomes red when heated; *F. gnaphalocarpa*, a source of rubberlike gutta-percha; *F. rigo*; and *F. vogeli*.

Rubber-producing trees

Latex is used in many other ways, as for birdlime, a sticky substance used to catch birds (from *Ficus anomani*, *F. glumosa*, and others); as indelible red ink (*Bosqueia angolensis*); as a red dye (*B. phoberos*); as a base for chewing gum (*Ficus platyphylla*); as a component in glue and caulking compounds (*Artocarpus altilis* and *Brosimum utile*); as a beverage (the cow tree, *Brosimum utile*); and as medicines (*F. indica* and *F. involuta*).

Other uses. Silkworms are fed almost exclusively on mulberry leaves, *Morus alba* being preferred in Western countries. In Asia, the leaves of many species of *Morus*, some *Ficus* species, and *Maclura pomifera* are also used.

Ornamental plants of the order include about 50 species of *Ficus*, among which are *F. elastica* (the India rubber plant), *F. lyrata* (fiddle-leaf fig), *F. pumila* (creeping or climbing fig), *F. benghalensis* (banyan, or Bengal fig), *Ulmus* (elms), *Celtis* (hackberries), and *Morus* (mulberries).

NATURAL HISTORY

Pollination. Most members of the order Urticales are wind-pollinated, and some species have adaptations that enhance this process. *Pilea microphylla* (Urticaceae), the artillery plant, for example, ejects its pollen in tiny explosive puffs. Many genera, particularly in the family Urticaceae, exhibit the same phenomenon. In the flower buds of the nettles (especially species of *Urtica*), the stamens (male, pollen-producing structures) are bent inward and held under tension (inflexed) in the bud. When the flower opens, the stamens are suddenly released and spring out with such violence that the anthers, or pollen sacs, are turned inside out, ejecting their pollen in a cloud. The pollen is then carried by the wind to the large, brushlike stigmas (pollen-receptive regions of the female flower parts) of other flowers. The flowers, like most wind-pollinated flowers, are inconspicuous, greenish in colour, and lack petals.

Explosive stamens

The genus *Parietaria* (Urticaceae) also has explosive stamens, but unlike most other members of the family it has bisexual flowers—flowers with functional organs of both sexes. Self-fertilization is averted by the early maturing of the pistil (female structure), a condition called protogyny. The elongated upper part of the pistil (the style) projects from the tip of the unopened bud, ready to receive pollen from other flowers that have already matured. Later, when the flower opens, the stamens are fully developed and release their pollen explosively, but the ovules of these flowers have already been fertilized, and the style has dropped off.

Some species of the Moraceae are insect-pollinated, particularly the figs. Pollination is accomplished by small wasps called fig wasps or gall wasps (*Blastophaga psenes*). In the figs, separate male and female flowers are borne in a specialized inflorescence, or flower cluster, which consists of a hollow, pear-shaped stem tip with the flowers on the inside. This structure, called a syconium, ultimately becomes a fig at maturity. The male flowers are usually arranged near the small opening at the upper end of the syconium, and the female flowers, much more numerous, line the interior. The female flowers are of two types, long-styled fertile flowers and short-styled sterile ones. The long-styled flowers eventually produce a single, small, one-seeded, hard-shelled fruit called an achene. The fig itself is actually a collection of many of these achenes surrounded by the fleshy tissue of the syconium. The short-styled flowers are called gall flowers; they do not develop fruits but are used as egg-laying sites by the gall wasps, which pollinate the other flowers in the process of egg laying. The gall flowers then become a mass of pulpy, abnormal plant tissue, the gall, on which the wasp larvae feed and in which they develop.

Pollination of the fig by wasps

The three flower cluster types—male, long-styled female, and short-styled female or gall flowers—are produced in three distinctive syconia. The first type of syconium, produced in the spring, contains male flowers and gall flowers; each of the latter may contain one of the fig wasp eggs, deposited there in the spring by wasps that had just emerged from overwintering in another type of fig. These eggs produce wingless male and winged female wasps later in the summer. The male wasp bites through the wall of a gall containing a female wasp and mates with her. On leaving the fig to search for a suitable place to lay eggs, the female wasp becomes covered with pollen from the male flowers near the small exit hole, at the tip of the fig. The second type of syconium, the true fig, bears only long-styled fertile female flowers. The female wasp, searching for egg-laying sites in summer, enters these figs and pollinates the flowers inside but does not lay eggs because the styles are too long to suit the egg-depositing anatomy of the insect. The third type of syconium, produced in the autumn, contains only short-styled gall flowers. The eggs that are laid develop in the gall flowers and produce the next year's fig wasps.

Symbiotic relationships. The close interdependence of figs and the fig wasps can be considered a form of symbiosis, or living together for mutual benefit. The fig is pollinated by the fig wasp and in return provides specialized flowers suitable for the wasp's reproductive requirements. Another kind of symbiosis, involving ants, occurs in several species of the family Urticaceae, including the trumpet tree (*Cecropia peltata*) of tropical America.

This plant has hollow stems that are inhabited by ants of the genus *Azteca*, which rush out and attack any intruder that disturbs the plant. They provide protection against leaf-cutter ants, and the plant in turn provides not only living space for the ants but also special food bodies for them on the lower side of the swollen bases of the leafstalks. As the food bodies are eaten, new ones grow to replace them. The plant also has special thin areas in the walls along the stems that make it possible for fertile female ants to burrow inside to lay their eggs. Some other *Cecropia* species, which do not harbour *Azteca* ants, are protected from leaf-cutter ants by a thick coating of wax on the stem that prevents the leaf cutters from climbing up.

About 12 genera in the family Urticaceae have stinging hairs. The principal ones include *Urtica* (50 species), *Urera* (35 species), and *Laportea* (about 25 species). In addition, *Girardinia*, *Obetia*, *Gyrotaenia*, *Parsana*, and *Hesperocnide*, all with fewer than ten species each, have stinging hairs. In some species the hairs are found on all plant parts, but in others they may be restricted to the upper surfaces of leaves, to flowers, to fruits, or to the lower surfaces of leaves along the large veins.

FORM AND FUNCTION

Vegetative characteristics. *Stinging hairs.* The stinging hairs are hollow, glandular plant hairs tipped by a sharp-pointed, glasslike terminal cell that penetrates the skin at the lightest touch, like a hypodermic needle. The brittle tip breaks off in the skin, releasing an irritant liquid into the wound. The composition of this stinging fluid is not known in all cases, but in the wood nettle of eastern North America (*Laportea canadensis*) it is formic acid, and in the tree nettle of Australia (*L. photiniphylla*) it is a mixture of toxic substances, including 5-hydroxytryptamine.

Stinging nettles, such as *Urtica dioica* and the common nettle (*U. gracilis*), which are among the more widespread stinging species in temperate regions, usually produce an initial burning sensation that may disappear within an hour or may linger as an itch for hours or even days. The tree nettle of Australia, however, produces a sting so intense that the victim may dash about wildly, screaming in pain. Deaths from the tree nettle have been reported in a few cases; irritation from contact with the plant can last for months. *Urtica holosericea*, in the western United States, has been reported to have a sting powerful enough to kill a horse.

Effect produced by stinging nettles

Although the stinging hairs cause rashes and irritation when the plant is touched, some stinging species can be used for food. The leaves of many nettle species, for example, are often boiled and eaten like spinach. The stinging juice is not poisonous and boiling renders the hairs incapable of penetrating the skin as well. Wilted plants likewise have a greatly reduced capability of stinging because the hairs lack the rigidity needed to penetrate the skin.

In addition to the stinging members of the nettle family, a few other plants in the order produce skin irritations. Contact with the fruits or leaves of the osage orange, for example, produces dermatitis in susceptible persons.

Cystoliths. Another feature characteristic of the nettle family and many members of the mulberry family is the presence of cystoliths, deposits of calcium carbonate inside enlarged epidermal (surface) cells. They are visible as dots or variously shaped marks, especially in pressed, dried leaves. Their function in the plant is unknown.

Calcium carbonate deposits occur in another form in *Chlorophora excelsa* (Moraceae), source of the iroko wood of commerce, which is very durable and practically immune to termites and wood-rotting fungi. About 3 percent of the trees carry streaks or lumps of calcium carbonate in the wood. These are called iroko stones and are hard enough to dull woodworking tools.

Fruit characteristics. The fruits of many members of the family Moraceae are multiple fruits; *i.e.*, they are formed by the fusion of several different flowers. In the mulberry this results in a small fleshy fruit that resembles a blackberry but is actually the enlarged floral axis of a

Multiple fruits of the mulberry family

whole cluster (inflorescence) of flowers, instead of the developed carpels (ovule-bearing structures) of a single flower, as in the blackberry. Among the most extreme examples of this type of fruit are the breadfruit, breadnut, jackfruit, fig, and osage orange.

The jackfruit is unusual in still another way: it is produced along the main trunk of the tree, a condition known as caulicarpy (cauliflory when considering the flowers). Such large fruits as the jackfruit could not be supported on the branches. The fig is a unique type of multiple fruit (syconium). Each "seed" in a fig is actually an individual fruit; the fig itself is the fleshy stem tip developed into a fruitlike structure.

In the family Ulmaceae the fruits are of two main types. Elms have a dry, membranous, windblown fruit called samara. In temperate regions, these fruits often mature early in the spring, before the leaves have fully expanded. The second type of fruit, found in *Celtis* and others, is a fleshy drupe, or stone-pitted fruit. These fruits are often eaten by birds and other animals, and the seeds are thereby spread.

EVOLUTION

Fossil record. One of the interesting observations to come out of the study of fossils of the earliest flowering plants, which appeared during the Cretaceous Period (from 65,000,000 to 136,000,000 years ago), is that most of them belong to plant genera living today and represent both primitive and highly evolved forms. Among the latter are many fossil members of the order Urticales, especially of the family Moraceae. It may be inferred from this that the highly evolved groups, at least, had experienced a long period of evolution and development before the great increase in flowering plants took place. So far none of this prior evolutionary history has been found in the fossil record. The earliest reliable fossils already show the differentiation of flowering plants into many distinct families.

Fossil leaves, fruits, and wood from the family Moraceae (including *Artocarpus, Morus, Artocarpidium, Ficus, Ficophyllum,* and *Ficoxylon*) are known from the Upper Cretaceous and show this group to be already firmly evolved into present-day forms. On the other hand, many fossils, particularly of leaves, have been called fig fossils with little basis for the designation except the resemblance of outline, and some records for this family

Mulberry fossils

may eventually be reassigned to other groups. The genus *Morus,* however, is well-known in the London Clay flora, a fossil deposit consisting mainly of fruits and seeds of some 500 species that lived during the Eocene Epoch (38,000,000 to 54,000,000 years ago). The late Eocene amber deposits in the Baltic region contain examples of plants belonging to the families Ulmaceae and Urticaceae. The family Moraceae is among the largest of about 18 families represented in the Wilcox flora of the early Eocene, a fossil deposit known from about 130 different localities in North America. Numerous fossils of the family Ulmaceae (including *Ulmus, Zelkova, Celtis,* and *Pteroceltis*) have been found in regions that suggest that these genera were formerly much more widely distributed than they are now. The genus *Ulmus,* for example, occurs in Eocene-age deposits in Spitsbergen and on the west coast of Greenland among other fossils that indicate a former cool temperate climate for these regions. The family Urticaceae is represented by flowers (*Forskohleanthium*) and fruits (*Urticarpum*) embedded in amber, both from the lower Eocene; fossil fragments of the genus *Urtica* date to the Pliocene (2,500,000 to 7,000,000 years ago).

Phylogeny. The fossil record has so far served mostly to show the great antiquity of several of the groups that belong to the order Urticales, but it has not revealed links with any ancestral groups. Nevertheless, some hints of the course of evolution for the order (and within the order) are reflected in the form, structure, and growth of living members. At first sight the predominantly wind-pollinated families Ulmaceae, Cannabaceae, and Urticaceae seem primitive, especially the elm family. The small, relatively simple, mostly unisexual flowers are considered

to be derived from a more complex condition rather than a primitive feature, however. This concept is supported by the presence of vestigial organs of the opposite sex in many functionally male or female flowers, indicative of a former bisexuality. Many members of the families Moraceae and Urticaceae show this feature. Based on these and other lines of evidence, the order Urticales is thought to be derived from the witch hazel order (Hamamelidales), or at least from some ancestor of that group.

Within the Urticales, the family Ulmaceae is considered to be the most primitive. The families Moraceae, Cannabaceae, and Urticaceae are more highly evolved. The Urticaceae is considered advanced over the Moraceae mainly because of its herbaceous growth habit compared to the predominantly woody habit of the mulberry family. The two families, however, are very closely related and are joined by a series of genera that are distinctly transitional. These genera (*Cecropia, Coussapoa, Poikilospermum, Musanga, Myrianthus,* and *Pourouma*) have sometimes been assigned to the Moraceae, sometimes to the Urticaceae. In the classification presented below they are considered as belonging to the Urticaceae.

CLASSIFICATION

Distinguishing taxonomic features. The order Urticales is distinguished from other orders mainly by floral characteristics. The presence of mostly unisexual (separate male and female) flowers that are wind-pollinated and produce a single seed each is a unifying feature. In the female flowers the ovary is composed of two carpels (ovule-bearing structures), but there is only one ovary chamber (locule), containing a single ovule. The male flowers have only a few stamens (pollen-bearing structures). All flowers are characteristic in having few flower parts; all lack petals.

Within the order, the family Ulmaceae is characterized by its woody habit, unequal-sided leaves, paired stipules (basal appendages to the leaves), early-appearing flowers with stamens erect in the bud, and dry, winged fruits (samaras) or fleshy, stony-pitted fruits (drupes). The family Moraceae is distinguished by its woody habit, milky sap, multiple fruits, and stipules that fall early leaving a characteristic inflated scar. The family Cannabaceae is composed of aromatic herbs with watery sap and distinctive flowers. Features characteristic of the family Urticaceae include its herbaceous or softly woody habit, stinging hairs, cystoliths, fibrous stems, and inflexed stamens that release their pollen explosively.

Recognition features for the families

Annotated classification. The following classification system is widely accepted with respect to the families presented for the order. Opinions differ, however, regarding the assignment of some genera between the families Urticaceae and Moraceae. Three small families, sometimes included in the order, are excluded here (see below *Critical appraisal*).

ORDER URTICALES

Trees, shrubs, vines, or herbs. Leaves usually simple, alternate, with stipules (basal appendages). Flowers male, female, or bisexual; regular, small, greenish; usually with 4 or 5 more or less united sepals (constituting the calyx) but lacking petals. Ovary positioned above other flower parts (superior), of 1 or 2 carpels (ovule-bearing units) but with only 1 interior chamber (locule) and 1 ovule (rarely 2), erect or pendulous. Stamens variable in number but usually few, mostly equal in number to sepals and opposite them; often inflexed in the bud. Fruit with 1 seed; at maturity a nutlet, drupe, achene, samara, or multiple. Seed with or without fleshy or oily endosperm (nutrient tissue for developing embryo). Four families, 125 genera, and about 3,100 species, with worldwide distribution.

Family Ulmaceae (elm family)

Trees or shrubs with watery sap. Leaves alternate, simple, often oblique (unequal-sided at the base), with paired stipules that fall soon after leaf buds open. Flowers bisexual (in *Ulmus*) or unisexual, solitary or usually arising in clusters (fascicles) from 1-year-old twigs. Petals absent. Sepals 4 to 8, persistent, joined into a short or long tubular calyx below. Stamens equal in number to or a few more than calyx lobes and opposite them; inserted at bottom of calyx tube; erect in the bud. Ovary superior, composed of 2 fused carpels, with usually 1 or sometimes 2 locules and 1 pendulous ovule; 2 divergent styles (narrow upper part of ovary) bearing pollen-receptive surfaces (stigmas) on inner faces. Fruit a flattened, membranous, dry, often winged samara or a slightly fleshy drupe. Seed without endosperm. Fifteen genera and about 210 species, distributed throughout the northern temperate regions of the world and abundant in tropical and subtropical regions.

Family Moraceae (mulberry family)

Trees, shrubs, or rarely herbs, with milky juice (latex). Leaves deciduous (falling) or evergreen, mostly alternate, simple, with stipules that often fall early, leaving characteristic inflated scars on the stem. Flowers male or female, very small, lacking petals, commonly with 4 separate or sometimes fused sepals (sepals sometimes reduced or absent); flowers often in dense clusters ranging from spikes, heads, and disks to crowded masses covering the insides of expanded hollow branch tips or floral axes. Male flowers with 2 to 6 (but usually 4) stamens usually equal in number to and opposite calyx lobes, reduced to 1 or 2 in some, inflexed or straight in the bud. Female flowers with ovary of 2 carpels, 1 often failing to develop; 1 locule with usually 1 pendulous ovule; usually 2 styles and stigmas. Fruit an achene or drupe, many of which often participate with enlarged calyx segments and floral axes to form a multiple fruit or syconium (a hollow enlarged stem tip with numerous flowers, and later the true fruits, on the inside, as in the fig). Seed usually with fleshy endosperm; embryo often curved. Fifty-four genera and about 1,400 species, distributed mostly in the tropics and subtropics but with a few in temperate regions.

Family Cannabaceae (hemp family)

Erect or climbing aromatic herbs with watery juice. Leaves alternate or opposite; simple with palmate (radiating from a common point) venation, or palmately compound or lobed. Stipules present, persistent. Flowers male or female on separate plants (dioecious), without petals, arising from the upper angles between the leafstalks and plant stems (axils). Male flowers in many-branched elongate clusters (panicles), each with 5 sepals and 5 stamens; anthers erect in the bud. Female flowers in dense clusters, each with large, persistent, overlapping leaflike appendages (bracts) attached just below the flowers; sepals completely joined, forming a small, membranous, smooth-edged cup closely enveloping the ovary. Ovary of 2 carpels with 1 locule and 1 pendulous, curved ovule; and a central, 2-parted style bearing 2 stigmas on inner surfaces of style branches. Fruit an achene surrounded by persistent calyx. Seed with fleshy endosperm and large curved or spirally rolled embryo. Two genera (*Cannabis* and *Humulus*) and 3 to 5 species, widely distributed in temperate parts of the Northern Hemisphere.

Family Urticaceae (nettle family)

Herbs, rarely small shrubs or small trees, or (very rarely) climbing vines, with watery sap. Stems and leaves often armed with stinging hairs; stems often fibrous; some epidermal (surface) cells usually with prominent internal crystal-like concretions (cystoliths). Leaves alternate or opposite, simple, usually with stipules. Flowers small, greenish, usually functionally male or female but with rudimentary structures of the opposite sex usually present; with 4- or 5-lobed calyx and without petals. Male flowers with stamens usually equal in number to and opposite the calyx lobes; stamens inflexed in the bud and released suddenly when flower opens, forcibly ejecting pollen. Female flowers with ovary free or enclosed by calyx; ovary composed of 1 carpel with 1 locule and 1 erect ovule. Fruit a dry achene or fleshy drupe, often enclosed by persistent calyx. Seeds mostly with oily endosperm and straight embryo. Fifty-four genera and about 1,500 species, distributed throughout the world but mostly in the tropics.

Critical appraisal. The classification system presented above is widely recognized in its broader aspects, but viewpoints concerning the details differ among authorities; for example, the inclusion in the order Urticales of the four families recognized here is a feature of practically all systems. In some, however, particularly in older systems, the two genera here recognized as the family Cannabaceae (*Cannabis* and *Humulus*) are merged into the family Moraceae. There is also considerable difference of opinion as to which family—Moraceae or Urticaceae—should contain the genera *Cecropia, Coussapoa, Poikilospermum, Musanga, Myrianthus,* and *Pourouma.* These genera have characteristics intermediate between the two families.

Three small families have sometimes been included in the order Urticales by some authorities, singly or in various combinations. These are the Rhoipteleaceae (represented only by *Rhoiptelea chiliantha* found in southwest Asia), the Barbeyaceae (represented only by *Barbeya*

oleoides, found in northeast Africa and Arabian Peninsula), and the Eucommiaceae (represented only by *Eucommia ulmoides,* found in China). The last two groups are sufficiently distinct, however, that they have been recognized as separate orders (Barbeyales and Eucommiales) in some of the most recent taxonomic systems, as is done here. The Rhoipteleaceae are generally believed to belong more properly in the walnut order (Juglandales).

Opinions are divided on the numbers of genera and species in each family, particularly the two largest. Estimates for the Moraceae range from about 1,000 to 2,300 species and from about 50 to 75 genera. The genus *Ficus* alone has been considered to contain anywhere from 800 to more than 2,000 species. Estimates for the Urticaceae range from 500 to 1,900 species. These differences reflect, in part, the growing numbers of newly described species and, in part, differences of opinion concerning the placement of genera in particular families and the validity of recognizing some genera and species at all.

BIBLIOGRAPHY. E.J.H. CORNER, "The Classification of Moraceae," *Gdns'. Bull., Singapore,* 19:187–252 (1962), and "An Introduction to the Distribution of *Ficus,*" *Reinwardtia,* 4:325–355 (1958), important papers for the advanced botanist on the classification and distribution of the mulberry family, in which the fig genus is estimated to contain about 900 species, a downward revision from earlier estimates that ranged as high as 2,000; B.M. JOHRI and R.N. KONAR, "The Floral Morphology and Embryology of *Ficus religiosa* Linn.," *Phytomorphology,* 6:97–111 (1956), a treatment of the floral structure and development of one of the fig species; H.Y.M. RAM and R. NATH, "The Morphology and Embryology of *Cannabis sativa* Linn.," *ibid.,* 14:414–429 (1964), a detailed account of the form, structure, and development of the hemp plant; A.B. RENDLE, "Urticiflorae" in *The Classification of Flowering Plants,* vol. 2, pp. 41–58 (1925, reprinted 1967), an excellent descriptive account for readers with some background in botany of the elm, mulberry, hemp, and nettle families; T. DOBZHANSKY and J. MURCA-PIRES, "Strangler Trees," *Scient. Am.,* 190:78–80 (1954), a short article for the layman that describes strangler figs and suggests how they might have evolved; H.C.D. DE WITT, "Urticales" in *De wereld der Plenten,* vol. 1 (1963; Eng. trans., *Plants of the World,* vol. 1, 1966), a descriptive account for the layman of many interesting plants in the nettle order; N.A. SATA, "A Monographic Study of the Genus *Ficus* from the Point of View of Economic Botany," *Taihoku Univ.,* vol. 32, pt. 1–2, pp. 1–104, and pt. 3–4, pp. 1–289 (1944), an extended and detailed account of the many uses to which members of the fig genus have been put.

(F.K.A.)

Uruguay

Uruguay (officially known as the República Oriental del Uruguay and locally still called the Banda Oriental, the "eastern shore" of the Uruguay River) is the smallest independent state in South America. With an area of 68,536 square miles (177,508 square kilometres), it is bounded by Brazil to the north and east, by the Atlantic Ocean to the southeast, and by the Río de la Plata to the south, while to the west the Uruguay River separates it from Argentina. In 1972 Uruguay's population was estimated to be over 2,950,000. The capital is Montevideo (which at the same time had an estimated population of more than 1,459,000).

While throughout most of the 20th century Uruguay was known for its political stability and advanced social legislation, by the early 1970s mounting economic difficulties and social unrest had thrown a pall of uncertainty over its political future. The activity of the Tupámaros, an urban guerrilla movement named after Tupac Amaru (an 18th-century Inca who rebelled against Spanish rule) that was harrassing the government in a variety of ways, seemed to many to symbolize the new and violent element that had entered Uruguay's political life. (See the city article MONTEVIDEO; for an associated physical feature, see RIO DE LA PLATA; for historical aspects, see URUGUAY, HISTORY OF.) (Ed.)

THE LANDSCAPE AND ENVIRONMENT

Relief and drainage. The eastern and southern half of Uruguay is a low hilly land, with a subsoil of weathered ancient schist (a crystalline rock) and granite, through which protrude low ridges of less weathered rocks. In central and north central Uruguay a basement of ancient schist is overlain by nearly horizontal layers of rock dating from the Permian Period (from 280,000,000 to 225,000,000 years ago) that form a low plateau. The northwestern portion is occupied by a southward extension of the Paraná Plateau of southern Brazil. This plateau is formed of horizontal beds of Triassic red sandstone (from 225,000,000 to 190,000,000 years old) of continental origin, in places faulted and capped by sheets of Triassic basalt. The plains of Uruguay are covered with deposits of sand and clay of the Pleistocene Epoch (2,500,000 to 10,000 years old) and with alluvial beds.

The northeastern part of the country consists of low rolling hills, a southward extension of the Brazilian highlands. The coastline is fringed with tidal lakes and sand dunes; the banks of the two rivers are low, unbroken stretches of level land. The northwestern section of the republic presents greater variety of relief, with occasional ridges and low plateaus, alternating with broad valleys, a southward extension of southern Brazil. None of the hills and plateaus of Uruguay exceeds 2,000 feet in elevation.

The rivers   There are no large rivers entirely within Uruguayan territory. The Río Negro, the largest stream, is navigable only in its lower part. The Uruguay River, along the border, is navigable for steamers of 14-foot draft from its mouth to Paysandú and above that point for smaller vessels to the falls at Salto, 200 miles in all. No other streams are navigable except for vessels of light draft. The Santa Lucía, Queguay Grande, and Cebollatí are the other principal watercourses.

Climate. Uruguay has a truly temperate climate, the average temperature for the summer months of January and February being about 71° F (22° C) and that of the coldest month, July, being 50° F (10° C). Frost is almost unknown along the coast. The weather of both summer and winter varies from day to day, a result of the passing of storm centres associated with cyclones (large-scale wind and pressure systems characterized by low pressure at the centre and circular wind motion). Brusque wind shifts are common, a hot northerly wind sometimes being followed immediately by the chill pampero (wind from the pampas—the vast grassy plains of Argentina) from the southwest, which brings a sudden drop in temperature. These changes give a middle latitude character to the climate of Uruguay.

There are no decided rainy and dry seasons. Maximum rainfall occurs in the autumn (April and May), rather than in the winter months, as is often supposed. Winter rains are most frequent but autumn rains are heaviest. The mean annual precipitation is about 35 inches (890 millimetres), decreasing with distance from the sea but everywhere well distributed throughout the year. In summer there are frequent thunderstorms. Fogs are common from May to October but seldom last all day on land.

Vegetation. Uruguay is mostly covered with tall, rich prairie grass. There are more trees, however, both native and introduced, than on the pampas, but these are found chiefly in narrow ribbons along the bottomlands of the watercourses. The principal species are the ombú (a scrubby plant with capacity to survive in dry areas), alder, aloe, poplar, acacia, willow, and eucalyptus. The *montes*, by which are understood plantations as well as native thickets, produce, among other useful wood, the algarrobo (carob tree) and the quebracho (a tree the wood and bark of which are used in tanning and dyeing). Indigenous palms grow in the valleys of the Sierra de San José Ignacio and, to some extent, in the departments of Lavalleja, Maldonado, and Paysandú. The myrtle, rosemary, mimosa, and the scarlet-flowered ceibo are common.

The valleys within the hills are fragrant with verbena and aromatic shrubs. The prairies are gay with the scarlet and white verbenas and other brilliant wild flowers.

Animal life. As in most of the inhabited parts of the world, the wild animals have largely disappeared. Even the rhea (the American ostrich) is now seldom seen,

---

MAP INDEX

Cities and towns

Acegúa	31·52s	54·12w
Achar	32·25s	56·10w
Agraciada	33·48s	58·15w
Aiguá	34·12s	54·45w
Algorta	32·25s	57·23w
Ansina	31·54s	55·28w
Arapey	30·58s	57·32w
Artigas	30·24s	56·28w
Atlántida	34·46s	55·45w
Baltasar Brum	30·44s	57·19w
Belén	30·47s	57·47w
Bella Unión	30·15s	57·35w
Canelones	34·32s	56·17w
Capilla de Farruco	32·53s	55·25w
Cardona	33·53s	57·23w
Cardozo	32·38s	56·21w
Carlos Reyles	33·03s	56·29w
Carmelo	34·00s	58·17w
Carmen	33·15s	56·01w
Castillos	34·12s	53·50w
Casupá	34·07s	55·39w
Cebollatí	33·16s	53·47w
Cerro Chato	33·06s	55·08w
Cerro Colorado	33·52s	55·33w
Cerro Vera	33·11s	57·28w
Chapicuy	31·39s	57·54w
Chuy	33·41s	53·27w
Colón	33·53s	54·43w
Colonia (del Sacramento)	34·28s	57·51w
Colonia Lavalleja	31·06s	57·01w
Constitución	31·05s	57·50w
Cuaró	30·37s	56·54w
Curtina	32·09s	56·07w
Dieciocho de Julio	33·41s	53·33w
Dolores	33·33s	58·13w
Durazno	33·22s	56·31w
Florencio Sánchez	33·53s	57·24w
Florida	34·06s	56·13w
Fraile Muerto	32·31s	54·32w
Francia	32·33s	56·37w
Fray Bentos	33·08s	58·18w
Fray Marcos	34·11s	55·44w
Garzón	34·36s	54·33w
General Enrique Martínez	33·12s	53·48w
Goñi	33·31s	56·24w
Greco	32·48s	57·03w
Guichón	32·21s	57·12w
Isla Patrulla	32·59s	54·35w
Ismael Cortinas	33·58s	57·06w
José Batille y Ordóñez	33·28s	55·07w
José Pedro Varela	33·27s	54·32w
Juan L. Lacaze	34·26s	57·27w
La Cruz	33·56s	56·15w
La Mariscala	34·03s	54·47w
La Paloma	34·40s	54·10w
La Paz	34·46s	56·15w
Lascano	33·40s	54·12w
Las Piedras	34·44s	56·13w
Laureles	31·22s	55·51w
Lavalleja, see Minas		
Libertad	34·38s	56·39w
Lorenzo Geyres (Queguay)	32·05s	57·55w
Maldonado	34·54s	54·57w
Melo	32·22s	54·11w
Mercedes	33·16s	58·01w
Merinos	32·24s	56·54w
Minas	34·23s	55·14w
Minas de Corrales	31·35s	55·28w
Montevideo	34·53s	56·11w
Nueva Helvecia	34·19s	57·13w
Nueva Palmira	33·53s	58·25w
Nuevo Berlín	32·59s	58·03w
Palmar	33·48s	55·59w
Palmitas	33·31s	57·49w
Pan de Azúcar	34·48s	55·14w
Pando	34·43s	55·57w
Paso del Cerro	31·29s	55·50w
Paso de los Toros	32·49s	56·31w
Paysandú	32·19s	58·05w
Piedras Coloradas	32·23s	57·36w
Piedra Sola	32·04s	56·21w
Pirarajá	33·44s	54·45w
Piriápolis	34·54s	55·17w
Plácido Rosas	32·45s	53·44w
Polanco	33·54s	55·09w
Progreso	34·40s	56·13w
Punta del Este	34·58s	54·57w
Puntas del Sauce	33·51s	57·01w
Quebracho	31·57s	57·53w
Queguay, see Lorenzo Geyres		
Retamosa	33·35s	54·44w
Río Branco	32·34s	53·25w
Rivera	30·54s	55·31w
Rocha	34·29s	54·20w
Rosario	34·19s	57·21w
Rossell y Rius	33·11s	55·42w
Salto	31·23s	57·58w
San Antonio	31·22s	57·48w
San Carlos	34·48s	54·55w
San Gregorio	32·37s	55·50w
San Javier	32·41s	58·08w
San José (de Mayo)	34·20s	56·42w
San Ramón	34·18s	55·58w
Santa Clara de Olimar	32·55s	54·58w
Santa Lucía	34·27s	56·24w
Sarandí del Yi	33·21s	55·38w
Sarandí Grande	33·44s	56·20w
Sauce	34·39s	56·04w
Solís	34·36s	55·29w
Soriano	33·24s	58·19w
Tacuarembó	31·44s	55·59w
Tala	34·21s	55·46w
Tarariras	34·17s	57·37w
Tomás Gomensoro	30·26s	57·26w
Tranqueras	31·12s	55·45w
Treinta y Tres	33·14s	54·23w
Tres Árboles	32·24s	56·43w
Trinidad	33·32s	56·54w
Valle Edén	31·50s	56·09w
Veinticinco de Mayo	34·12s	56·22w
Velázquez	34·02s	54·17w
Vergara	32·56s	53·57w
Vichadero	31·48s	54·43w
Yaguarí	31·31s	54·58w
Young	32·41s	57·38w

Physical features and points of interest

Aigúa, Arroyo del, *river*	33·38s	54·23w
Ánimas, Cerro de las, *mountain*	34·46s	55·19w
Arapey Chico, *river*	30·57s	57·30w
Arapey Grande, *river*	30·55s	57·49w
Atlantic Ocean	34·00s	52·00w
Brava, Punta, *point*	34·56s	56·10w
Castillos, Laguna de, *lake*	34·20s	53·54w
Cebollatí, *river*	33·09s	53·38w
Cerro Largo, Cuchilla, *hills*	32·44s	54·03w
Flores, Cuchilla de las, *hills*	32·51s	57·09w
Fortaleza de Santa Teresa, *national park*	33·59s	53·32w
Grande, Arroyo, *river*	33·08s	57·09w
Grande, Cuchilla, *ridge*	33·15s	55·07w
Guareim, *river*	30·12s	57·36w
Merin, Laguna, *lagoon*	33·10s	53·25w
Negra, Laguna, *lake*	34·03s	53·40w
Negro, *river*	33·24s	58·22w
Plata, Río de la, *estuary*	34·45s	57·30w
Polonio, Cabo, *cape*	34·24s	53·46w
Queguay Grande, *river*	32·09s	58·09w
Río Negro, Embalse del, *reservoir*	32·45s	56·00w
Santa Ana, Cuchilla de, *hills*	30·50s	55·35w
Santa Lucía, *river*	34·48s	56·22w
Santa María, Cabo, *cape*	34·40s	54·10w
Tacuarembó, *river*	32·25s	55·29w
Tacuarí, *river*	32·46s	53·18w
Uruguay, *river*	34·12s	58·18w
Yaguarón, *river*	32·39s	53·12w

except in a semi-domesticated state. Pumas and jaguars are found on the wooded islets and banks of the larger rivers and along the northern frontier. The fox, deer, wildcat, the capybara (or water hog), and a few small rodents nearly complete the list of native quadrupeds. A small armadillo, the mulita, is the living representative of the extinct giants, mylodon and megatherium, the fossils of which are found over the pampa.

Birdlife   There are a few specimens of the vulture, a native crow (lean, tall, and ruffed), and many partridges and quails. Parakeets are plentiful in the *montes*, and the lagoons swarm with waterfowl. The most esteemed is the *pato real*, a large duck. A characteristic sight on the prairies is that of the tiny burrowing owl sitting on top of every little eminence. Large flocks of the lapwing terutero are common; they have the habit of warning other game of the approach of danger. Of birds of bright plumage, the hummingbird and cardinal—the scarlet, the yellow, and the white—are the most attractive. White herons are frequently seen in swampy lands. The scorpion is rare, but large and venomous spiders are common.

The principal reptiles are a lizard, a tortoise, the *víbora de la cruz* (a dangerous viper, so called from marks like a cross on its head), and the rattlesnake in the department of Maldonado in the southeast and the stony lands of the Minas region nearby. The caiman (alligator) is not uncommon along the upper waters of the Uruguay River. Seals are found on small islands off the southeast coast, particularly on the Isla de Lobos.

Traditional regions.   Uruguay is one of the most coherent states in Latin America. When the country became independent in 1828, its national territory was used almost exclusively for the grazing of herds of scrubby cattle on the unfenced range, and there were few permanent settlements outside of Montevideo and Colonia del Sacramento and the villages along the Uruguay River. The grazing lands along the eastern shore of the Uruguay River constituted a kind of no-man's-land between the Portuguese in Brazil and the Spaniards in Argentina.

After independence, Uruguay received a small influx of immigrants, chiefly from Italy and Spain. This was during a time when Argentina was torn by civil strife and settlement on the pampas was not yet attractive. The newcomers entered Uruguay through Montevideo and settled in a zone along the Río de la Plata and Uruguay River. After 1852 the European immigrants to the Plata region went largely to Argentina. As a result, the agicultural zone in southern Uruguay remained static, because, unlike the situation in Argentina, livestock grazing and the cultivation of crops remained in separate geographic areas. Even as late as 1940, there was a notably sharp boundary between the pastoral region to the north and the agricultural region to the south, as at the town of Florida, only 50 miles north of the capital. After the mid-1940s, however, there was a great increase in the area devoted to agriculture. The sharp boundary between the two regions disappeared. Crops became more important than pasture as far north as Durazno, more than 100 miles north of Montevideo, and the crop zone also extended northward along the Uruguay River as far as Salto.

The grazing of animals in the pastoral region is no longer on unfenced range. Barbed wire is used throughout the interior to separate one pasture from another and to border the highways and animal driveways. Planted pasture grasses have replaced the native grasses, and the carrying capacity is high—about one animal unit per acre. There are many large ranches, or estancias, some larger than 25,000 acres, in the pastoral region. Sheep are more significant than cattle in the northwest, especially on the relatively dry, low plateaus on diabase and red sandstone. South of the Río Negro cattle are of major importance.   Cattle raising

The agricultural zone, on the other hand, has little land devoted to pasture. The chief crop is wheat, but there are also important areas of maize, flax (for linseed), oats, barley, and grapes.

Montevideo is the country's largest urban centre, and it

Elevations in metres

URUGUAY

contains the chief concentration of manufacturing. Industries were also established at Fray Bentos, Salto, and Paysandú along the Uruguay River.   (P.E.J.)

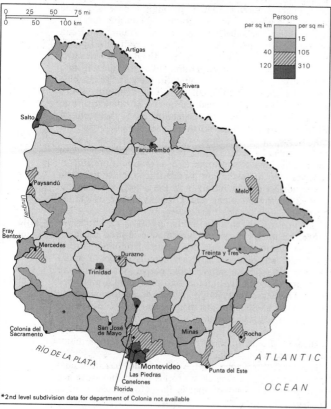

Population density of Uruguay.

PEOPLE AND POPULATION

Ethnic, linguistic, and religious groups. The people of Uruguay are predominantly white, most of them descendants of 19th- and 20th-century immigrants from Spain, Italy, and other European countries. The Indian population is almost completely extinct, and only a very small proportion of Uruguayans exhibit any noticeable Indian physical characteristics. There are few Negroes or mulattoes, probably not more than 10,000 of the former or 50,000 of the latter.

Comprehensive statistical data on religious affiliations of Uruguayans are lacking, but less satisfactory sources of information are sufficient to indicate that the large majority profess the Roman Catholic faith. Spanish is the official language and the one used in the home by an overwhelming majority of the families. In the sections along the Brazilian border, however, the language in daily use includes a large admixture of Portuguese words and phrases.

Demography. A census of population taken in 1963, the first since 1908, put the population of Uruguay at about 2,590,000. Since that time, the annual increment has amounted to about 40,000. In 1972 the official population estimate was 2,956,000. In 1963 the density of population was about 37 per square mile (14 per square kilometre). The 1963 census also furnished reliable data about the geographic distribution of Uruguay's population. The city of Montevideo contained almost half of the nation's people, with many thousands more residing nearby in the adjacent department of Canelones. The remainder of the inhabitants are concentrated in those departments that front upon the Río de la Plata, namely, Colonia, San José, and Maldonado (the chief town of which is Punta del Este), and among those adjacent to the Uruguay River, especially Soriano, Salto, and Paysandú. In addition to Montevideo, the most important cities are Salto, Paysandú, Punta del Este, Rivera, Las Piedras, Melo, Mercedes, and Minas. In 1963, 81 percent of the population was classified as urban.

Because Uruguay's birth rate has been fairly low (and stable) since 1900, the age distribution differs sharply from that of most of the other Latin American countries. In 1963 only about 28 percent of the population was less than 15 years of age, and only about 8 percent was 65 or over. This proportion of young people is only about two-thirds as high as is typically the case in Latin America, and that of the aged is almost double the percentages prevailing in most of the other countries.

Demographic age patterns

Uruguay, Area and Population				
	area		population	
	sq mi	sq km	1963 census	1972 estimate
Departments *(departmentos)*				
Artigas	4,689	12,145	53,000	...
Canelones	1,750	4,532	258,000	...
Cerro Largo	5,348	13,851	71,000	...
Colonia	2,372	6,144	105,000	...
Durazno	4,713	12,208	54,000	...
Flores	1,982	5,133	24,000	...
Florida	4,009	10,384	64,000	...
Lavalleja	3,918	10,149	66,000	...
Maldonado	1,817	4,705	61,000	...
Montevideo	198	514	1,203,000	...
Paysandú	5,446	14,106	88,000	...
Río Negro	3,721	9,637	47,000	...
Rivera	3,513	9,099	77,000	...
Rocha	4,244	10,991	55,000	...
Salto	5,544	14,359	92,000	...
San José	1,928	4,994	80,000	...
Soriano	3,442	8,914	78,000	...
Tacuarembó	6,166	15,969	77,000	...
Treinta y Tres	3,736	9,676	43,000	...
Total Uruguay	68,536	177,508*	2,596,000	2,956,000

*Area figures do not add to total given because of rounding.
Source: Official government figures.

Between 1908 and 1963, the dates of Uruguay's two most recent censuses, the growth of population averaged only 0.7 percent per annum, by far the lowest during that period for any of the Latin American countries. In all probability, however, the current rate is much higher, or about 1.4 percent per year subsequent to 1963. For the 20 Latin American countries taken together the index is about 2.8 percent per annum.

The present increase of population in Uruguay is due almost entirely to natural increase, or the difference between a birth rate of about 20 per thousand population and a death rate of 9 per thousand. Only a very low proportion of the growth of population may fairly be attributed to immigration. In this connection, however, it is notable that Uruguay's data on immigration and emigration are involved and perplexing. It was the first of the Latin American countries to legalize divorce, and by the mid-20th century Montevideo and Punta del Este had become temporary places of residence for thousands of divorce seekers from Argentina and from other populous areas in the southern part of South America.

(T.L.S./Ed.)

THE NATIONAL ECONOMY

A comparative view. The foundation of Uruguay's economy is said to have been laid in 1603, when a far-seeing governor of Paraguay, Hernando Arias de Saavedra, having observed the fertility of the empty southern pastures, shipped about 100 head of cattle and 100 horses downstream from Asunción. The animals were landed on the Uruguayan riverbank, where they were left to run wild. Later in the century, the herds were so abundant that they attracted gauchos, who crossed the Río de la Plata from Buenos Aires and began a trade in hides. The gauchos were nomads, with no desire to settle, but, gradually, merchants from Buenos Aires established themselves on the Uruguayan side of the estuary. As more cattlemen arrived, boundaries had to be fixed, and thus there came into existence the great estancias that are still characteristic of the country.

The relatively high standard of living enjoyed in and around Montevideo is closely related to the earnings

Structure
of the
economy

from pastoral and agricultural exports; prosperity is somewhat precarious because these primary products are subject to sudden fluctuations in world demand and prices. To reduce the nation's dependence on external trade, successive governments have encouraged the development of domestic industry by means of protective tariffs, import controls, exemptions of machinery from import duties, and preferential exchange rates. But, as there are no local sources of petroleum, coal, or iron and no heavy industries, Uruguay is obliged to import most of its fuel and industrial raw materials and all of its vehicles and industrial machinery. These essential supplies have to be paid for with the produce of the ranches and farms and the income derived from tourists. Uruguay is noted among Latin American countries for its highly developed social services, but these were placing an excessive burden on the country's resources.

Components of the economy. *Agriculture.* Pastoral farming is Uruguay's most important economic activity. Wool and beef are its chief products and the source of about three-fourths of its total earnings from foreign trade. All available land is in use for grazing or agriculture, and production can be increased only by improved techniques. Improvement has, in general, been slow; output has not kept pace with local demand, with the result that exports now account for only 26 percent of the total agricultural and livestock produce, compared with 46 percent in the 1930s. Government policy has generally sought to achieve national self-sufficiency in wheat. This has sometimes led to overproduction of this cereal and to a partial neglect of livestock farming, although, by contrast, wheat imports from Argentina were necessary, for example, in 1964. Other crops include corn (maize), linseed, sunflower seed, oats, barley, and rice. Fruits grown are oranges, lemons, peaches, grapes (sufficient for the local wine industry), pears, and apples.

Power and industry. The state operates a large number of public corporations. It controls electricity and the refining of imported petroleum; it manufactures alcohol and cement; it directs a meat-packing plant and the processing of fish; and it controls the railways (purchased from their British owners at the end of World War II), the principal banking institutions, and insurance.

Since the low, rolling countryside of Uruguay is not generally suited to hydroelectric development, most of the electric installations were formerly dependent on imported coal or oil; but two hydroelectric plants were built on the Río Negro.

The processing of food and other products of the land is the basic form of industry. The subsidized wool-combing industry has added to the country's exports. Consumer goods manufactured locally (mainly around Montevideo) include textiles, tires and other rubber goods, shoes, and household appliances.

Foreign trade. Wool exports in the late 1960s amounted to about 40 percent of the national total, while meat and by-products varied from 20 to 42 percent. Hides and skins were the other principal items. The chief markets were the United Kingdom, Italy, West Germany, Spain, The Netherlands, and the United States. The main imports were raw materials for industry, vehicles, machinery, and fuels. The chief suppliers of these imports were the United States, Brazil, West Germany, Argentina, and the United Kingdom. Despite import controls, the balance of trade up to the late 1960s was usually unfavourable. Uruguay was a founder-member of LAFTA (Latin American Free Trade Association), set up at Montevideo in 1960.

Banking and finance. The functions of a central bank are exercised by the state-owned Banco Central, formed in 1967. Another state bank, the Banco de la República, regulates many aspects of foreign trade and is the country's largest commercial banking organization. An admirable record of currency stability was reversed in the 1960s, when the inflationary effect of persistent budget deficits began to be felt. The rise in the cost of living index, together with the consequences of a decline in the gross domestic product as well as increasing inflation, led to social unrest and substantial emigration.

The
public
corpora-
tions

Transport and communications. In the early 1970s Uruguay possessed over 2,000 miles of railway and more than 8,000 miles of paved or surfaced highways, both systems radiating from Montevideo. The resultant competition has mainly favoured road transport, and international loans have been obtained to improve the highways, particularly those providing links with Brazil. About 775 miles of the country's inland waters are navigable. Local shipping handles only a small proportion of the country's foreign trade; in 1970 Uruguay's merchant fleet totalled about 198,000 tons. There is a hydrofoil service from Montevideo to Buenos Aires. The main airport is at Balneario Carrasco, 13 miles from Montevideo; a state airline, Primeras Líneas Uruguayas de Navegación Aérea (PLUNA), provides services within Uruguay and to neighbouring countries.

In the early 1970s the state telephone service had more than 235,000 subscribers (over four-fifths in Montevideo). Broadcasting services, including 9 television channels, are operated by state and private companies. Four cable companies provide foreign communication links; an international telex service was inaugurated in mid-1964. (I.C.Cn./G.Pe./C.P.D.)

Telephone
and broad-
casting
services

ADMINISTRATION, SOCIAL
CONDITIONS, AND CULTURAL LIFE

The structure of government. *Constitutional framework.* In 1966 a new constitution restored the presidential system of government and repudiated a *colegiado* (plural-executive) system previously in use. The president is chief of state and commander of the armed forces. The legislative branch consists of a Senate of 31 members and a Chamber of Deputies of 99, elected for four years by universal suffrage, the political parties having proportional representation.

Local government. Uruguay consists of 19 departments, each governed by a departmental council, which exercises executive functions, and by a legislative assembly; both the councils and the assemblies are elected by popular vote.

The political process. The three principal political parties are the Colorado Party (which traditionally has had an urban base), the Blanco Party (supported by the landowners), and the Frente Amplio (Broad Front), representing a coalition of Christian Democrats, Socialists, Communists, and dissident members of the two other parties. In the 1971 presidential elections, the Colorado Party received 575,000 votes, the Blanco Party 565,000, and the Frente Amplio 262,000. The radical-revolutionary Tupámaros guerrilla movement operates outside the parliamentary system.

Justice. A Supreme Court of five judges is elected for a ten-year term by the General Assembly (*i.e.*, the two houses of the legislature). The death penalty has been abolished since 1907.

The armed forces. The army, with a strength of 12,000 (1971), composed of volunteers enlisting for one or two years, comprises regiments of cavalry, engineers, infantry, artillery, and tanks. There is a small navy (about 1,800 men) and an air force (about 2,000 men) of about 200 planes. A reserve force is trained every year under a compulsory military training law.

Social conditions. *Education.* Uruguay has long been renowned for its progress in education, after reforms instituted in the late 19th century that established a system of free, compulsory, coeducational, and secular education. This progress was reflected in the high literacy rate (about 90 percent).

The Universidad de la República (founded in 1849) had an enrollment of more than 13,000 in the early 1970s. It has ten faculties, including a distinguished medical school that draws students from many South American countries. There is also a privately supported Instituto de Estudios Superiores (Institute of Higher Studies) devoted to scientific research. Vocational training is given by the Universidad del Trabajo del Uruguay, which organizes and controls a number of industrial and night schools.

Health and welfare. Since the early years of the 20th century, Uruguay has played a leading role in the de-

The 1966
constitu-
tion

Higher
education

velopment of social security. The country's comprehensive program includes extensive provisions for unemployment insurance, compensation for injuries to workmen, family allowances, and aid to the aged and indigent. With respect to problems of health and sanitation, Uruguay is among the most fortunately situated of the Latin American countries. In 1960, for example, the infant mortality rate was about 47 per thousand births, but by 1970 the rate had dropped to 43 per thousand. In 1971 there was about one physician for every 800 people. Long a South American pioneer in international cooperation, Uruguay participates in the technical assistance programs of the United States, the Organization of American States, and the United Nations.

Living and working conditions. With 1953 figured as 100, the cost of living had risen to 314 by 1960. Between 1955 and 1970, inflation increased by 9,000 percent. The strength of the trade-union movement is reflected by the number of workers—approximately 45,000—who were members of internationally affiliated trade unions in the late 1960s. A severe economic depression began in the mid-1960s and by the early 1970s had created great unrest as government officials sought, apparently unsuccessfully, to cope with the growing economic crisis.

Cultural life. Uruguay falls within the same cultural context as other Spanish-speaking American states. Interest in literature and the arts has flourished. There is a thriving press, both in Montevideo and the provinces; censorship, to which the press in many South American countries is frequently subjected, has been virtually nonexistent. Recreational facilities are provided by the sandy beaches on the coast, as well as by the wildlife resources of the interior; both have served as tourist attractions. Football is the principal sport, but basketball and horse racing are also popular. (G.I.B./Ed.)

PROSPECTS FOR THE FUTURE

Whereas Uruguayans have long prided themselves on their national slogan, *"Como Uruguay, no hay"* ("There is no country like Uruguay"), in the early 1970s Uruguay's future appeared beset by uncertainties. Continuing economic crisis, the deterioration of the party system, the emergence of the small but significant Tupámaros guerrilla movement, and the emigration of many educated Uruguayans all gave cause for concern. On the other hand, the country's strongly rooted democratic and humane traditions, its level of education, and its temperate climate were among the factors that, to some extent, offset negative factors and encouraged hopes that the country would eventually experience a return to more favourable conditions. (Ed.)

BIBLIOGRAPHY. Two general introductions to the country—its geography, history, economy, and culture—are RUSSELL H. FITZGIBBON, *Uruguay: Portrait of a Democracy* (1954); and GEORGE PENDLE, *Uruguay*, 3rd ed. (1963). See also D.C. REDDING, "The Economic Decline of Uruguay," *Inter-American Economic Affairs*, 20:55–72 (1967), a careful report on how the Uruguayan economy has been overloaded by the measures of a welfare state; and RONALD H. MCDONALD, "Electoral Politics and Uruguayan Political Decay," *ibid.*, 26:25–45 (1972), presents the argument that one of the more democratic societies of Latin America has been undermined by an organized minority. Other works of interest include CARLOS M. RAMA, *Ensayo de sociología Uruguaya* (1957) and *Las clases sociales en el Uruguay* (1960); JOHN STREET, *Artigas and the Emancipation of Uruguay* (1959); PHILIP B. TAYLOR, JR., *Government and Politics of Uruguay* (1962); MILTON I. VANGER, *José Batlle y Ordóñez of Uruguay: The Creator of His Times, 1902–1907* (1963); and MARVIN ALISKY, *Uruguay: A Contemporary Survey* (1969), a descriptive account of the economy.

(M.I.V.)

Uruguay, History of

Before the coming of the Europeans, the east bank of the Uruguay River was inhabited by a group of Indian tribes known collectively as the Charrúas. European settlers raised cattle there in the 17th century, and in 1680 the Portuguese founded a settlement at Colonia del Sacramento. With the establishment of Montevideo in 1726,

Spain began the effective occupation of the country; from 1776, it formed part of the Viceroyalty of Rio de la Plata, capital of which was at Buenos Aires. The year 1810 marked the beginning of the wars of independence in the Spanish American colonies. Buenos Aires was one of the urban centres where the independence movement was strongest; from Buenos Aires, revolutionary sentiment spread to the interior of the Rio de la Plata Viceroyalty, and also to centres of Spanish crown rule beyond the Andes. Lima and Montevideo were both bulwarks of resistance to the ideas proclaimed by the new revolutionary power groups (see further LATIN AMERICA AND THE CARIBBEAN, COLONIAL).

The struggle for national identity (1811–90). Montevideo was the site of a Spanish naval installation; in 1811 an armed insurrection led by the rural spokesman José Artigas broke out in its hinterland, the Banda Oriental del Uruguay (the east bank of the Uruguay River). Spanish authority was challenged, and unresolved colonial problems were brought to the fore. The *estancieros* (ranchers) were joined in revolt by the gauchos (cowboys), the peons, and the slaves. Artigas proposed a plan for a republican federation of the Rio de la Plata territories and a democratization of rural life based on advanced social principles.

Artigas' revolt

The Buenos Aires oligarchy, realizing how Artigas' proposals would affect them, decided to crush his growing power; their forces defeated him in 1816, ending the first manifestation of Uruguayan autonomous government. The emancipation of the Banda Oriental eventually was achieved during the period of Portuguese-Brazilian occupation (1817–28). In 1825, Juan Antonio Lavalleja and his supporters (known as the "33 *orientales*") formed an army with Argentine help and defeated the Brazilians at Ituzaingó (February 20, 1827). A preliminary peace pact with Brazil (August 27, 1828) recognized Uruguay's independence. On July 18, 1830, a constitution for the new nation was approved. Uruguay had scarcely 74,000 inhabitants; its main economic resources, livestock and land, were concentrated in the hands of a few families who had acquired economic empires in the countryside during the colonial period. The first two decades of independence were a time of testing. There were frequent uprisings in the interior, and, in the urban areas, opposing factions grew up around their leaders Fructuoso Rivera and Manuel Oribe. The colours used by each faction gave rise to the present names of Uruguay's main political parties: red, or Colorado, for Rivera's group, and white, or Blanco, for Oribe's.

The Colorados and the Blancos

Antagonism between these groups led to the civil war of 1839–51, during which the Blanco Party controlled the interior and the Colorado Party controlled Montevideo. Several foreign powers intervened—Argentina on the side of the Blancos, England and France on the side of the Colorados.

The period ended without losers or victors, and the failure to achieve national unity opened a whole new era of turbulence and uprisings, frequently involving the country in Brazilian and Argentine affairs. This led to Uruguay's participation with Brazil and Argentina in war against Paraguay (1865–70). Successive attempts at political coexistence and internal order, indispensible to Uruguay's modernization and entrance into world economics, were frustrated. Internally the caudillos, (personalist leaders) struggled for power with liberal parliamentarians known as *principistas* or "doctors." In the 1870s, control of the government passed into the hands of the military.

During the administration of Col. Lorenzo Latorre (1876–80), power was more firmly centralized: pacification of the rural areas permitted advances in stock breeding and ended the power of the caudillos. Capitalist development and internal stability continued under the governments of Gen. Máximo Santos and Gen. Máximo Tajes (1880–90).

The prosperity of the export economy (1890–1954). By the time civilian rule was restored under Julio Herrera y Obes in the 1890s, the rural economic structure had adapted itself to the demands of external markets.

Wool and dried (or jerked) beef exports rose greatly. The population, as a result of immigration from Mediterranean Europe, more than doubled during the last quarter of the 19th century, rising from 450,000 people in 1875 to about 1,000,000 in 1900. The adoption of new fiscal policies and the development of transportation and communication facilities (railroads and telegraphs) stimulated foreign loans and investment, usually of British origin.

At the beginning of the 20th century, the country was again torn by a factional dispute, based on the Blanco (or Nationalist) Party's demands for greater participation in government affairs. After a Blanco uprising and the assassination of the Colorado president, Juan Idiarte Borda, in 1897, tension between the two parties reached a climax in 1904. At this time, a year after being elected president, the Colorado leader, José Batlle y Ordóñez, was confronted by a Blanco revolt headed by Aparicio Saravia. After eight months of bloody fighting and the death of Saravia, the conflict was ended by the Peace of Aceguá. This agreement was followed by a reorganization of the political parties and marked the beginning of a long period of internal peace and orderly government for Uruguay.

The influence of Batlle y Ordóñez

From 1904 until his death in 1929, José Batlle y Ordóñez dominated the political scene. Twice president of the republic (1903–07; 1911–15), he designed reform programs that became the objectives of the modern Uruguayan state.

Administrative reforms included the creation of a Supreme Court of Justice, greater municipal autonomy, and the creation of more public services. Social reforms included the removal of public education from the control of the Roman Catholic Church, the extension of free education on the secondary and university levels, a reform of the university system, extension of the right of divorce to women, and, finally, separation of church and state in 1917.

Advanced labour legislation that was passed (the right to strike, an eight-hour workday, obligatory accident insurance) emphasized the role of the state as mediator between management and labour.

Batlle's policies discouraged foreign intervention in Uruguay's economic affairs. While North American penetration pushed on the frozen meat industry, he promoted a strong policy of nationalism, by means of several government monopolies, assuring state control of areas usually dominated by private or foreign capital (mainly British, toward which Batlle showed an open disaffection).

During World War I, the agriculturally based economy flourished with the export boom. At the same time, domestic production and consumption of manufactured goods increased, in reaction to protective tariffs in other countries and the spiralling cost of imported goods. This economic expansion was accompanied by political reform. President Batlle, fearing the power of the presidency, proposed its abolition and the substitution of a nine-member executive council. A plebiscite defeated the idea (1916), but it was partially retained in the constitution of 1917 that, while retaining the presidency, provided for the creation of a National Council of Administration made up of nine elected members. This constitutional reform, combined with the extension of suffrage rights in 1924, gave new impulse to representative government in Uruguay.

At the same time the economy entered a bad period. Exports declined with the reorganization of European markets following the war. U.S. capital was used to finance road construction, in competition with the British railway system, and U.S. business investments heralded the shift from British to U.S. economic domination. The New York stock market crash of 1929 caused a further decline in exports and a price decrease for Uruguayan goods. Complicating the situation were the Ottawa Agreements (1932), which greatly limited the accessibility of Río de la Plata meats to British markets. An austerity program was instituted in an attempt to improve the economic situation. In 1933, however, Pres. Gabriel

Terra, of the Colorado Party, proclaimed himself dictator. The constitution of 1917 was invalidated, and full power was restored to the president; this situation lasted until the middle of 1938, when Gen. Alfredo Baldomir was elected president.

With the beginning of World War II, President Baldomir kept Uruguay neutral. Many Uruguayans sympathized with the Allies, but the leader of the Blanco Party, Luis Alberto de Herrera, campaigned for strict neutrality and sought to prevent the installation of North American naval bases in the country. Other leading Blancos had definite Nazi-Fascist sympathies. Nevertheless, Uruguay, along with most of the other Latin American Republics, declared war on the Axis powers in 1945.

At the beginning of 1942 President Baldomir dissolved the Congress and prepared a new constitution. His support came not only from his own Colorado Party but also from the independent Blancos (members of the Blanco Party who, in 1933, had separated from it because of their opposition to the ideology of Herrera). The takeover of the government by Juan José Amézaga in 1943 marked a return to democratic liberalism. Once again, a war aided the Uruguayan economy. As had happened during World War I, the value of livestock products rose disproportionately, a lucrative European market opened up, and imports declined tremendously. Small industries prospered, filling the gap created by the import decline. The standard of living rose. Internal consumer markets grew; unemployment dropped; educational opportunities opened up; and labour legislation bettered the existing social security system.

Tomás Berreta, a disciple of Batlle y Ordóñez, was elected president in 1946, but his sudden death left the government in the hands of Batlle's nephew, the urban caudillo Luis Batlle Berres. The government readopted the principles of the 1917 constitution, and after reaching an agreement with the Blanco Party, created, in the constitution of 1951, the National Council of Government, which replaced the presidential office with a nine-member council.

In the early 1950s, Uruguay became a haven for anti-Peronist exiles from Argentina. They used the Uruguayan press and radio networks to win support for their cause, and had the tacit approval of the Uruguayan government. An opposition campaign and anti-Peronist committees, based in Montevideo, found support in the liberal temper of the country and were granted tacit government support. Uruguay's relations with Argentina deteriorated, reaching their lowest point just before Perón's overthrow in 1955.

Economic and political decline (1954–c. 70). The Korean War precipitated a brief economic boom, ending in 1954. Thereupon, Uruguay entered first a period of economic stagnation, then a period of recession, aggravated by the lowering of world prices on its chief exports (wools, meat, leather products) as well as by the rising price of manufactured goods. The economic deterioration resulted in labour riots, demonstrations, and general discontent among the populace.

The Blanco victory of 1958

The 1958 elections reflected this discontent. For the first time in 93 years, the Colorado Party was defeated, and the Nationalists (Blancos), promising an improvement in the economy, came to power under Martin R. Echegoyen. The change of government came at a time of tremendous inflation. In 1959, a monetary reform law was passed, providing for successive devaluations of the currency. Tension and discontent rose among all sectors of the population.

In the same year (1959), Herrera, former leader of the Blanco Party, died, and divisions within the party deepened. The Blanco government was unable to deal effectively with the crisis. Its free enterprise orientation allowed economic elite groups to import luxury items at a time when its policy was to limit imports to essential consumer goods.

The second Blanco administration (1963–66) was characterized by an even sharper disintegration of the traditional political parties, resulting in the proliferation of groups and subgroups under personalist leaders. Inflation was not halted. A 1965 bank failure staggered the monetary economy. Furthermore, the cost of living rose, affecting those income groups (mainly urban) that were least able to afford it. The inflation and production slump continued into the 1970s.

The 1966 elections returned the Colorado Party to office. Another constitutional reform restored presidential power in full. The new president, Gen. Daniel Gestido, died of a heart attack in December 1967; he was succeeded by his vice president, Jorge Pachero Areco, who in turn was followed by Juan Maria Bordaberry in 1972. Bordaberry, during a crisis caused by the widespread terrorist activities of the Tupamaro revolutionary movement, staged a coup with military backing in June 1973.

BIBLIOGRAPHY. EDUARDO ACEVEDO, *Anales historicos del Uruguay,* 2nd ed. (1933–36), a detailed description of political, economic, and administrative events covering the period 1830–1930; ROQUE FARAONE, *El Uruguay en que Vivimos, 1900–1968,* 3rd ed. (1970), an introductory manual dealing with contemporary Uruguay; R.H. FITZGIBBON, *Uruguay: Portrait of a Democracy* (1954), a study of the period immediately following World War I; S.G. HANSON, *Utopia in Uruguay* (1938), an analysis of different economic sectors affected by Batlle's reforms, covering the era 1911–30; G. LINDAHL, *Uruguay's New Path* (Eng. trans. 1962), a review of programs, finances, and economic structures from 1919–33; GEORGE PENDLE, *Uruguay,* 3rd ed. (1963), a survey of contemporary Uruguay, with particular emphasis on the birth and evolution of the welfare state; J.E. PIVEL DEVOTO and A. RANIERI DE PIVEL DEVOTO, *Historia de la República Oriental del Uruguay, 1830–1930* (1945), a didactic synthesis tracing the political processes that accompanied the formation of an independent Uruguay; JOHN STREET, *Artigas and the Emancipation of Uruguay* (1959), a concise, documented study explaining the significance of the role of Artigas; M.I. VANGER, *José Batlle y Ordoñez of Uruguay: The Creator of his Times, 1902–1907* (1963), a monographic study of the first presidency of Batlle, which also serves as one of the most lucid histories dealing with this era; ALBERTO ZUM FELDE, *Proceso histórico del Uruguay,* 4th ed. (1963), an interpretive essay that is based on now outdated sociological data, but it is still valuable.

(J.A.O.)

Usman dan Fodio

Usman dan Fodio (in Arabic ʿUthmān ibn Fūdī), often simply referred to as "Shehu" or "the Shaykh," was the most important reforming leader of Africa's Western Sudan region in the early 19th century. His importance lies partly in the new stimulus that he, as a *mujaddid,* or renewer of the faith, gave to Islām throughout the region; partly in his work as a teacher and intellectual, the focus of a network of students, author of a large corpus of writings in Arabic and Fulfulde that covered most of the Islāmic sciences and enjoyed—and still enjoy—wide circulation and influence; partly in his activities as founder of a *jamāʿa,* or Islāmic community, which became a new polity, the Sokoto caliphate, and brought the Hausa states and some neighbouring territories under a single central administration for the first time in history.

Though involved in an active life of preaching and controversy, the Shaykh was also a serious Ṣūfī who underwent mystical experiences, was familiar with *jinns* (spirits), and lived ascetically without wealth or servants.

Early years
Usman was born in 1754 at Maratta in the Hausa state of Gobir, in what is now northwest Nigeria. His father, Muhammad Fodiye, was a scholar from the Toronkawa clan, which had emigrated from Futa Toro in Senegal in about the 15th century. While still young, Usman moved south with his family to Degel, where he studied the Qurʾān with his father. Later he moved on to other scholar relatives, travelling from teacher to teacher in the traditional way and reading widely in the Islāmic sciences. One powerful intellectual and religious influence at this time was his teacher at the south Saharan city of Agadez, Jibrīl ibn ʿUmar, a radical and controversial figure whom Usman both respected and criticized and by whom he was admitted to the Qādirīyah and other Ṣūfī orders.

In about 1774–75 Usman began his active life as a teacher, and for the next 12 years combined study with peripatetic teaching and preaching in Kebbi and Gobir, followed by a further five years in Zamfara. During this latter period, though committed in principle to avoiding the courts of kings, he visited the sultan of Gobir, Bawa, from whom he won important concessions for the local Muslim community (including his own freedom to propagate Islām), and also appears to have taught the future sultan, Yunfa.

Throughout the 1780s and '90s the Shaykh's reputation was increasing, as were the size and importance of the community that looked to him for religious and political leadership. Particularly closely associated with him were his younger brother, Abdullahi, one of his first pupils, and his son, Muhammad Bello, both distinguished teachers and writers. But his own scholarly clan was slow to come over to him. Significant support seems to have come from the Hausa peasantry. Their economic and social grievances and experience of oppression under the existing dynasties stimulated millenarian hopes and led them to identify him with the Mahdī (Divinely Guided One), whose appearance was expected at that time. Though he rejected this identification, he did share and encourage their expectations.

During the 1790s, when Usman seems to have lived continuously at Degel, a division was developing between his substantial community and the Gobir ruling dynasty. In about 1797–98 Sultan Nafata, who was aware that the Shaykh had permitted his community to be armed and who no doubt feared that it was acquiring the characteristics of a state within the state, reversed the liberal policy he had adopted toward Usman 10 years earlier and issued his historic proclamation forbidding any but the Shaykh to preach, forbidding the conversion of sons from the religion of their fathers, and proscribing the use of turbans and veils.

In 1802 Yunfa succeeded Nafata as sultan, but, whatever previous ties he may have had with the Shaykh, these did not bring about any improvement in the situation. The breakdown, when it eventually occurred, turned on a confused incident in which some of the Shaykh's supporters forcibly freed Muslim prisoners taken by a Gobir military expedition. Usman, who seems to have wished to avoid a final breach, nevertheless agreed that Degel was threatened and, like the Prophet Muḥammad, whose biography, he frequently noted, had close parallels with his own, carried out a *hijrah* (migration) to Gudu, 30 miles to the northwest, in February 1804. Shortly afterward, despite his own apparent reluctance, he was elected *imām* (leader) of the community, and the new caliphate was formally established.

Elected imām

During the next five years the Shaykh's primary interests were necessarily the conduct of the *jihād* (holy war) and the organization of the caliphate. He did not himself take part in military expeditions, but appointed commanders, encouraged the army, handled diplomatic questions, and wrote widely on problems relating to the *jihād* and its theoretical justification.

On this his basic position was clear and rigorous: the Sultan of Gobir had attacked the Muslims; therefore he was an unbeliever and as such must be fought; and anyone helping an unbeliever was also an unbeliever. (This last proposition was later used to justify the conflict with Bornu.)

As regards the structure of the caliphate, the Shaykh attempted to establish an essentially simple, non-exploitative system. His views are stated in his important treatise *Bayān wujūb al-hijra* (November 1806) and elsewhere: the central bureaucracy should be limited to a loyal and honest vizier, judges, a chief of police, and a collector of taxes; local administration should be in the hands of governors (amirs), selected from the scholarly class for their learning, piety, integrity, and sense of justice.

Initially the military situation was far from favourable. Food supplies were a continuing problem; the requisitioning of local food antagonized the peasantry; increasing dependence on the great Fulani clan leaders, who alone could put substantial forces into the field, alienated the non-Fulani. At the Battle of Tsuntua in December 1804, the Shaykh's forces suffered a major defeat and were said to have lost 2,000 men, of whom 200 knew the Qur'ān by heart. But, after a successful campaign against Kebbi in the spring of 1805, they established a permanent base at Gwandu in the west. By 1805–06 the Shaykh's caliphal authority was recognized by leaders of the Muslim communities in Katsina, Kano, Daura, and Zamfara. When Alkalawa, the Gobir capital, finally fell at the fourth assault on October 1808, the main military objectives of the *jihād* had been achieved.

Return to private life

Although the *jihād* had succeeded, Usman believed the original objectives of the reforming movement had been largely lost sight of. This no doubt encouraged his withdrawal into private life. In 1809–10 Bello moved to Sokoto, making it his headquarters, and built a home for his father nearby at Sifawa, where he lived in his customary simple style, surrounded by 300 students. In 1812 the administration of the caliphate was reorganized, the Shaykh's two principal viziers, Abdullahi and Bello, taking responsibility for the western and eastern sectors, respectively. The Shaykh, though remaining formally caliph, was thus left free to return to his main preoccupations, teaching and writing. His five years at Sifawa were a productive period, to judge from the number of dated works that survive, most of them dealing with the practical problems of the community, including the series of books addressed to "the Brethren" (al-Ikhwān), arising out of the dispute with Bornu and its principal administrator and ideologist, Muḥammad al-Kanemi. At his weekly meetings on Thursday nights, he criticized aspects of the post-*jihād* caliphate (as indeed did Abdullahi and Bello), especially the tendency of the new bureaucracy and its hangers-on to become another oppressive ruling class. Around 1815 he moved to Sokoto, where Bello built him a house in the western suburbs, and where he died, aged 62, in 1817.

Serious study in English of Usman and the immense body of his writings has only recently begun. Much work remains to be done on his personal life and its relation to his public activities (his wife, 'Ā'isha, was a famous Ṣūfī, and his daughter, Asmā', a distinguished poet), on the range and quality of his scholarship, and on the various intellectual influences that were important for him, and on the relation of his movement to the whole radical and reforming tradition in the Sudan, as well as to currents of reform elsewhere. There is also much that needs to be known about the forces that stimulated the growth of the reforming movement, the extent of participation in it of various social groups at various phases of its history, and Usman's position in relation to these groups and their ideas.

BIBLIOGRAPHY. The best modern work is MURRAY LAST, *The Sokoto Caliphate* (1967), which contains a useful bibliography of the main writings of Usman and Abdullahi dan Fodio, Muḥammad Bello, and others. See also F.H. EL MASRI, "The Life of Shehu Usman dan Fodio Before the Jihād," *Journal of the Historical Society of Nigeria*, 2:435–448 (1963). Of Usman's own works, those most easily available in translation are *Wathīqat ahl al-sūdān*, trans. by A.D.H. BIVAR in *Journal of African History*, 2:235–243 (1961); *Kitāb al-farq*, trans. by M. HISKETT in *Bulletin of the School of Oriental and African Studies*, 23:558–579 (1960); and *Taʿlīm al-ikhwān*, trans. by B.G. MARTIN in *Journal of Middle Eastern Studies*, 4:50–97 (1967). Other important primary sources are M. HISKETT, "Material Relating to the State of Learning Among the Fulani Before Their Jihād," *Bulletin of the School of Oriental and African Studies*, 19:550–578 (1957), which contains a translation of Abdullahi dan Fodio's *'Idāʿ al-nusūkh;* and his *Tazyīn al-waraqāt*, ed. and trans. by M. HISKETT (1963).

(T.Ho.)

Utah

A Rocky Mountain state of the United States, Utah became the 45th member of the Union in 1896 after decades of failure to attain statehood. In its earlier history, Utah represents a unique episode in American settlement,

a story of a religious group that trekked and was driven across three-quarters of the continent in search of a "promised land." The state capital, Salt Lake City, is the world headquarters of the Church of Jesus Christ of Latter-day Saints, commonly known as Mormon, and the spiritual home of adherents throughout the world. With Mormons making up some 70 percent of the state's population of nearly 1,060,000 counted in the 1970 census, the beliefs and traditions of the Mormon Church continue to exert profound influences on many facets of the state's life and institutions.

Overview of the state

From the very beginning of settlement in 1847, the Mormon pioneers set about wresting a green land from the deserts, gradually supplementing their crops with the products of industry and the earth. The Utah of the 1970s was based on an economy in which manufacturing, tourism, and services were superimposed upon an earlier economic base of agriculture and mining. Although the state is generally conservative in political ideology, the two major parties are relatively well balanced.

Mountains, high plateaus, and deserts form most of Utah's landscapes, which show off many of the most spectacular geological phenomena on the North American continent. The state's 84,916 square miles (219,931 square kilometres) lie in the heart of the West, with Idaho to the north, Wyoming to the northeast, Colorado to the east, Arizona to the south, and Nevada to the west. At its "Four Corners," in the southeast, Utah meets Colorado, New Mexico, and Arizona at right angles, the only such meeting of states in the nation. For information on related topics, see UNITED STATES; UNITED STATES, HISTORY OF THE; NORTH AMERICA; GREAT SALT LAKE; NORTH AMERICAN DESERT; and ROCKY MOUNTAINS.

THE HISTORY OF UTAH

Prehistory and white exploration. As early as 10,000 BC, small, mobile groups of hunters and gatherers lived in caves by the great inland sea, prehistoric Lake Bonneville. This desert culture was replaced about AD 400 by the more advanced Pueblo, or Anasazi, culture, which came into Utah from the Southwest and Mexico. These Basket Makers constructed superb communal cliff apartments and raised corn, squash, and beans. They left Utah about 1250, perhaps because of an extended drought.

Early inhabitants and cultures

When white explorers and settlers came to Utah in the 18th and 19th centuries they encountered Shoshonean Indians—the Southern Paiute, Gosiute, and Ute (from whom the state takes its name)—practicing a desert culture like that of the earliest period. Some of them raised corn and pumpkins by a simple system of irrigation. Ute Indians in eastern Utah lived in a region of higher rainfall and had a better way of life. Having acquired horses from Plains Indians, their nomadic life centred around the buffalo.

After two Franciscan fathers, Francisco Atanasio Domínguez and Silvestre Vélez de Escalante, explored Utah in 1776, Utah was visited by occasional Spanish trading parties. Fur trappers and overland immigrants to California and Oregon were in the region in the 1820s and '30s. The first four of some 16 annual rendezvous between trappers and buyers were held in Utah from 1825 to 1828, indicating the early importance of the area to the industry. The "mountain men" who explored and established trading posts included James Bridger, who discovered Great Salt Lake in 1824, and Jedediah Smith, who first traversed the state from north to south and west to east in 1826–27. Explorers sent by the government included John C. Frémont, who led scientific expeditions to northern Utah in 1843 and the western Great Salt Lake area in 1845.

Mormon settlement and territorial growth. The period of settlement and territorial status is notable for the ending of the long quest (1845–47) for a Mormon homeland, wresting a civilization from an arid environment, the contest for sovereignty between Utah and the United States, and the conflict with indigenous Indians over the use of the land. Founded in Fayette, New York, in 1830, the Church of Jesus Christ of Latter-day Saints from the beginning had gathered its members together in religious, social, and economic cooperation. In Kirtland, Ohio; Jackson County, Missouri; and Nauvoo, Illinois, the Mormons had grown rapidly, but wary neighbours eventually forced their removal from each such gathering place. From Nauvoo, which the Mormons had built up from Mississippi River swampland into a prosperous community, some 16,000 Mormons escaped violent mobs in 1846 by fleeing across Iowa to Council Bluffs. When wagonloads of Mormon pioneers under the leadership of Brigham Young first entered the valley of the Great Salt Lake in 1847, they were determined to transform the arid valley land into a green and wholesome "Kingdom of God." They succeeded.

From Salt Lake City settlers were directed to colonize in all directions until they had developed a prosperous and stable economy and political structure in a territory that was originally 210,000 square miles in area, stretching from the Rockies to the Sierra Nevada and from the Columbia River in Oregon to the Gila in Arizona. Immigrant converts continued to stream into Utah from Europe and the eastern United States; they were organized into colonizing parties based upon allocations of skills and leadership abilities and sent out to build the territory. By 1860 more than 150 self-sustaining communities with 40,000 inhabitants had been established, producing crops by means of water from mountain streams carried through canals to the alluvial valley lands. Utah's place in the national scene was symbolized by the driving of the golden spike at Promontory in 1869, uniting the eastward- and westward-reaching lines of America's first transcontinental railroad.

Conflict with the Indians was held to a minimum because of the Mormon view that it was cheaper to feed than to fight them. As the presence of the colonizers became more and more ubiquitous, however, some local Indians began to raid the settlements to obtain food. The Utes were eventually placed on a reservation in the Uinta Basin, the Southern Paiutes and Shoshoni on smaller reservations, and later the lands south of the San Juan River were incorporated into a Navajo reservation.

Mormons' federal conflicts

The propensity of the Mormons to establish their own political and social system and the incompetency of federal territorial officials led to an era of conflict with the federal government. In 1857, Pres. James Buchanan, believing the Mormons to be in a state of open rebellion, ordered some 2,500 soldiers to Utah to replace Young, who had served as governor during the early years. This episode is referred to as the Utah War, although no clashes occurred. With the outbreak of the Civil War in 1861, a new camp was established east of Salt Lake City under the command of Colonel Patrick Connor. Connor openly supported his troops in prospecting for minerals and sought to "solve the Mormon problem" by initiating a miners' rush to Utah. A substantial enclave of non-Mormon miners, freighters, bankers, and businessmen was the result, and three decades of Mormon versus non-Mormon conflict characterized the political scene until Utah attained statehood in 1896.

Toward and into statehood. The Mormon settlers applied for statehood in 1849 under the name Deseret, a word from the sacred *Book of Mormon* meaning "honeybee" and signifying industry. This bid was rejected, as were the efforts of five subsequent constitutional conventions between 1856 and 1887. Before Congress and the national administration would assent to statehood for Utah, Mormon leaders were required to discontinue the church's involvement in politics through its People's Party, withdraw from an economic policy in which Mormons dealt primarily with each other, and discontinue the practice of polygamy.

After its acceptance into the union in 1896, Utah moved rapidly into the larger social, political, and economic mainstreams of the nation. The political structure changed from theocracy to a conventional democracy: non-Mormons, including three governors, were elected to important positions. The Mormon Church has been officially neutral in politics in recent decades, and the influence of economic blocs—manufacturing and mining corporations, public utilities, stockmen, educators, and

labour—has become far more important. The initial equal political division among Republicans and Democrats in the early 1890s is still reflected in the current political balance, though the state has tended to be Republican since World War II.

THE NATURAL AND HUMAN LANDSCAPE

The natural environment. *Physiographic regions.* The Colorado Plateau comprises a little over half of Utah. Relatively high in elevation, this region is cut by brilliantly coloured canyons. Utah's growing tourist industry relies upon the attraction of the region's fiery, intricately sculptured natural bridges, arches, and other masterpieces of erosion.

The western third of the state is part of the Basin and Range Province (*q.v.*), or Great Basin, a broad, flat, desert-like area with occasional mountain peaks. Great Salt Lake lies in the northeastern part of the region; to the southwest is the Great Salt Lake Desert, some 4,000 square miles, which include the Bonneville Salt Flats, famous for land speed racing. During the Pleistocene Epoch, from 2,500,000 to 10,000 years ago, the huge freshwater Lake Bonneville here covered an area as large as present Lake Michigan. The Great Salt Lake and saline Sevier Dry Lake are the remnants of evaporation.

The Middle Rockies in the northeast comprise the Uinta Mountains, the only major mountain range in the United States running in an east–west direction, and the Wasatch Range. Along the latter run the series of valleys and plateaus known as the Wasatch Front. The Wasatch Range area and the red deserts of the east and gray deserts of the west make up more than 90 percent of Utah.

Altitudes range from 13,528 feet (4,123 metres) at Kings Peak in the Uintas to about 2,000 feet in the southwestern corner of the state. The Oquirrh and Deep Creek ranges of the Great Basin are important for their deposits of copper, gold, lead, and zinc.

Climate. Utah's geographical location in relation to the mountain systems of the West, which divert much of the precipitation, makes it basically an arid state. Anomalous southwestern Utah, which has a warm, almost semitropical climate, is referred to as Utah's "Dixie." The southern part of the Colorado Plateau experiences cool, dry winters with summer precipitation and frequent thunderstorms. Northern Utah is affected by air masses from the North Pacific and continental polar air; it receives most of its precipitation in the cool season.

The state experiences four distinct seasons. Average temperatures in July range from 65° to 80° F (18° to 27° C). In winter the state average is slightly below freezing except in "Dixie." Daily temperatures vary widely: when Salt Lake City has July highs of 90° F (32° C) or above, the nights are 55° to 65° F (13° to 18° C). Relatively low humidity prevails; average precipitation is 12 inches a year, varying from less than five inches annually over the Great Salt Lake Desert to 50 inches in the Wasatch Mountains. General average snowfall received is 54 inches a year, ranging from none in the southwestern valleys to more than ten feet at ski resorts. Average growing seasons are 128 days.

Soils and waters. The desert soil that covers most of the state lacks many organic materials but contains adequate lime. Lack of adequate drainage in the Great Basin has damaged surrounding soils with saline materials and alkali salts. The richest soils are in the old Lake Bonneville area, along the delta deposits of the Wasatch Front. Most farming is done in these alluvial soils. Mountain soils provide a rich habitat for conifers and other trees.

Utah contributes to three major drainage areas, the Colorado and Columbia rivers and the Great Basin. The Colorado and its tributary, the Green, drain eastern Utah. The Upper Colorado River Storage Project includes several dams and many lakes in that area. Great Basin rivers include the Bear, Weber, Provo, Jordan, and Sevier, all of which are landlocked. All the river systems are important for their irrigation and power potential.

Vegetation and animal life. Utah's 4,000 plant species represent six climatic zones, from the semitropical Lower

Desert and mountain landscapes

Sonoran in the southwestern Virgin Valley to the Arctic on mountain peaks. In the south are found creosote bush, mesquite, cactus, yucca, and Joshua tree; the alkaline deserts are the habitat of shad scale, saltbush, and greasewood. Juniper and sagebrush grow in the foothills and mountain valleys, as do piñon pine, cedar, and native grasses for grazing. In the mountains grow pines, firs, aspen, and blue spruce. Timber covers about 15,000,000 acres, but only about one-fourth of the forest land is commercially valuable.

The mule deer is the most common of Utah's large animals since elk, bison, timber wolves, and grizzly bears have largely disappeared. Coyotes, bobcats, and lynxes are hunted. Game birds include grouse, quail, and pheasants; golden eagles, hawks, owls, and magpies are numerous. Great Salt Lake bird refuges are the home of sea gulls, blue herons, and white pelicans. Certain species of game fish are native, while others have been introduced. Reptiles and amphibians, both poisonous and nonpoisonous, are native.

Human settlement and land use. In Utah's 29 counties, 66 percent of the land is federally owned, and 7 percent is owned by the state. About 4 percent of federal land is reserved for Indian use.

The Wasatch Front, extending north–south from Ogden to Provo and including also Salt Lake City, is the main area of urban and industrial development. With a 1970 population of nearly 176,000, Salt Lake City is the political, cultural, and religious capital of Utah. Historically a trade centre, it continues to be an ideal hub for industry, commerce, and interstate transportation.

The front also has not only the largest part of the population but also the best farmland in the state. Although over 60,000 acres of cropland have been urbanized since 1958 and an urban trend continues, a rural society is still observable. Rural settlements typically have a "Mormon village" flavour, with a readily recognizable Mormon chapel or tabernacle within the town, wide streets, and a cultivated area surrounding the town itself.

Irrigation, pollution control, and conservation

Irrigation was among the first Mormon pioneer efforts in 1847, and since then irrigation and water conservation have become increasingly important. The irrigation complex in Utah as of 1970 comprised a vast number of diversion dams, multipurpose dams, storage reservoirs, canals and ditches, pipelines, and flowing wells, exclusive of the large Glen Canyon and Flaming Gorge dams. In 1969 more than 1,000,000 acres of cropland were irrigated. State boards and departments regulate water use, while the division of health maintains quality water standards under the Water Pollution Control Act of 1953.

A state air-conservation program was begun in 1967, with special attention to the Wasatch Front. Other programs of federal, state, or joint jurisdiction include watershed management and conservation, protection of wildlife resources, conservation of oil and gas reserves, and reclamation.

THE PEOPLE OF UTAH

Racial composition. In 1970, the population was about 97 percent white, mainly of northern European ancestry, with slightly more than 1 percent (11,300) Indians and less than 2 percent Oriental, blacks, and other groups. In numbers, the nonwhite population rose from 16,700 in 1960 to 27,350 in 1970, but Utah remained essentially unchanged in its small percentage of nonwhites. The population of San Juan County, however, is about one-half Indian, containing some 42 percent of Utah's Indians.

Remnant Indian cultural activities

The Navajo, famous for their wool blankets, silverwork, and turquoise jewelry, reside primarily in the Four Corners region. About 1,500 Utes live on the Uintah and Ouray Indian Reservation. Having received a large settlement from the federal government for their lands, they have built new homes with modern conveniences. Annually sponsored events include the Bear Dance in the spring, the Sun Dance in July, and the Uinta Basin Industrial Fair in August or September. About 200 Southern Paiutes, among the most depressed of the tribes, live on six small reservations in southern Utah. Except for

American Indians, nearly all of the minority racial population was in the three Wasatch Front counties of Salt Lake, Davis, and Weber.

One minority group included within the white statistics is that of about 25,000 Mexican-Americans. Increasing attention is being paid to the problems of educating and acculturating this group, many of whom are low-income workers in agriculture, mining, manufacturing, and the service trades.

Contemporary demography. The 1970 census revealed statistics in Utah that were similar to those in the country as a whole. In numbers, preschool children had declined during the 1960s, while persons over 65 increased. Birth rates and death rates declined, though the former remained well above, the latter well below, the national averages. For the most part, those counties with the highest growth rates over the decade (in the Wasatch Front) also had the highest ratio of young persons to old persons, suggesting that young people, unmarried or married, were migrating and leaving older persons in the rural counties, mainly in the central and southern portions of the state. Though Salt Lake City lost population, its surrounding county grew by 20 percent. About 70 percent of the population lived in communities of 2,500 or more, a finding conditioned somewhat by the fact that the historic pattern of Mormon life has been for people to live in compact towns or villages and to farm outlying areas. More than three-quarters of the population lived in the three front counties plus Utah County.

THE STATE'S ECONOMY

From 1847 to 1868 the Mormons, with a high degree of mutual cooperation, built a self-sufficient economy based on agriculture, handicraft, and small industry. From 1869 to 1896 this cooperative economy was supplemented by a non-Mormon enclave devoted to mining and trading. After statehood, the exportable resources of the state were exploited to an increasing extent by outside corporations and enterprisers, and the agriculture of the state turned toward such commercial crops as sugar beets, wool, and range cattle. The depressions of 1921 and 1933 were severe, but federal programs and the welfare program of the Mormon Church helped the state to recover. During World War II, several defense plants and air bases were built, and Utah had a uranium boom, followed in the late 1950s by the erection of several large plants to build rocket engines for missiles.

The state's economy emerged in the 1970s with strong diversification. The large agricultural and mining sectors were supplemented by light and heavy manufacturing, finance, transportation, and tourism. Salt Lake City is a regional centre of finance and trade, and many large enterprises have offices there. Utah workers, in the Mormon tradition, have the reputation of being industrious and well disciplined, and the productivity per man-hour is high. With the many summer and winter recreational opportunities, Utah was well above average as a desirable place to work.

Components of the economy. About 38 of Utah's more than 200 minerals are mined commercially, and in 1970 it ranked 15th nationally in mineral production. About one-fifth of the nation's new copper is produced annually in Utah, accounting for more than one-half of the value of its mineral production. Utah is the nation's largest producer of beryllium ore and ranks in the top four states as a producer of gold, silver, lead, and molybdenum. Heretofore, salt was once the only mineral extracted in quantity from the Great Salt Lake, but plants were being built in the early 1970s to extract magnesium and other minerals. When these plants are completed, Utah will have one-fourth of the nation's magnesium-production capacity.

Mineral reserves and sources of income

Utah is a major producer of coal west of the Mississippi, with estimated reserves exceeding 115,000,000,000 tons. Petroleum has replaced coal as the leading mineral fuel, however, with reserves estimated at 410,000,000 barrels. Utah is the only state producing Gilsonite, a source of road oil, paving binder, and asphalt tile. In addition to steam plants, Utah has many hydroelectric plants.

Personal income in Utah rose more than 70 percent during the 1960s and early 1970s, but per capita income was about 18 percent below the national average and 25 percent below the average of the Western states. The large size of families in Utah, together with the low wage scales and the less significant role of trade unions in the state, help to explain this disparity. When personal income is computed on a per household basis, Utah fares better in national and regional comparisons.

State and federal government employment, increasing at a faster rate than any other sector of the economy, is the largest employer in Utah. The state remains below average, however, in the proportion of personal income derived from manufacturing: in 1970 only 12 percent, compared with 20 percent nationally. Food processing, transportation equipment, nonelectrical machinery, petroleum refining, and fabricated-metal products were, in that order, the major manufacturing sectors.

Following the national trend, farm employment in Utah has declined since 1960, but farm size and productivity have increased. In 1971, Utah ranked 40th among the 50 states in total farm receipts. Almost 85 percent of Utah's farm income comes from livestock products, the remainder from field crops, fruit, and canning crops.

Utah's present broadly based tax structure appears to distribute the costs of government without discrimination against, or hardship to, any segment of the economy. Present rate structures for the various taxes are generally competitive with those of neighbouring states. The corporate-income-tax rate is lower than that of any other Western state. Legislation providing for a phase-out of the state's inventory tax and a liberal free-port tax law granting tax exemptions on goods warehoused and processed in Utah are incentives to commerce.

Transportation. Utah's transportation industry, with easy access to all national markets, is the basis for the state's development as a major distribution centre for the West. More than 3,000 miles of rails cover the state, and the Amtrak passenger system includes Ogden. Road traffic is expanding rapidly; several interstate highways supplement the state system. In addition to the major airport serving Salt Lake City, excellent feeder line facilities exist in Ogden, Logan, Provo, Cedar City, and St. George.

ADMINISTRATION AND SOCIAL CONDITIONS

Structure of government. Utah's constitution, dating from 1896, guarantees basic personal freedoms consistent with the federal Bill of Rights, prohibits sectarian control of public schools, forbids "polygamous or plural marriages," and grants equal civil, political, and religious rights, including suffrage, to both male and female citizens. Voting requirements follow national patterns, though for elections affecting tax levies a voter must have paid a property tax the previous year.

Constitutional framework of the government

Executive, legislative, and judicial branches. The governor is aided by a secretary of state, auditor, treasurer, and attorney general, while much of the administration of routine state affairs is done through more than 50 state agencies. Each of these officials serves a four-year term.

The governor has the right to veto any bill, but his decision may be overruled through repassage of that bill by a two-thirds majority of each house of the legislature. Any bill passed by the legislature and not acted upon by the governor within five days while the legislature is in session automatically becomes law. The governor, secretary of state, and the attorney general, together, form the State Board of Examiners, which reviews all official state transactions.

Legislative power is vested in the Senate and House of Representatives, as well as in the voters, who have the power to initiate legislation and to hold a referendum on all laws not passed by a two-thirds majority of both houses. After reapportionment in 1972, the legislature comprised 30 senators serving four-year terms and 75 representatives serving two-year terms.

The legislature meets annually, with regular 60-day sessions in odd-numbered years and 20-day budget sessions in even-numbered years. Special sessions may be held subject to call by the governor. Four full-time councils provide interim work on investigation and research of specific legislative and state problems, advice on budgetary matters and appropriation requests, with legal counselling and legislative accuracy, and legislative administration. In 1971, the legislature was rated by a nonpartisan committee reviewing all state legislatures as 15th in overall effectiveness, fifth in accountability to the citizenry, and eighth in being informed.

The highest judicial authority is the state Supreme Court, composed of five justices elected to ten-year terms, one every two years. Judges of the seven district courts are elected for six-year terms. There are also county and city courts and, in rural areas, justices of the peace. A juvenile court system has its own districts and judges.

Local government. The constitution requires that each county have a county-commission form of government comprising three commissioners and several other elected officials to carry out administrative, judicial, law enforcement, financial, and health, education, and welfare functions.

Forms of municipal government vary according to population. Cities with populations over 90,000—Salt Lake City only—elect a mayor and four commissioners. Cities between 15,000 and 90,000 elect a mayor and two commissioners, while smaller cities elect a mayor and five councilmen. Incorporated towns are governed by a president and four trustees. Any city commission or town council has power to appoint a city manager.

Political life. Although Utah is referred to frequently as a Republican state, in actuality no party can claim dominance. Elected officials from both parties work well together and exhibit a reasonable degree of harmony. This has been true since the early 1890s, when the normally homogeneous Mormon populace was divided into political parties by church leaders to comply with federal requirements for statehood, a remarkably even division being achieved for the 1896 election by volunteers for each party. Nearly 80 percent of the state's eligible voters cast ballots in election years, far above the national average.

The social milieu. Although minority races are little noticed and politically insignificant in Utah, the state, county, and local governments have developed programs to improve the economic and social status of Indians, Mexican-Americans, blacks, and other groups.

Public services. Health, welfare, and housing services are administered by the Department of Social Services. County health services are supervised and coordinated through the state Board of Health, which also works with school boards for child health care. Outstanding hospital systems are administered by the Mormon, Roman Catholic, and Episcopal churches.

Health, welfare, and housing

The state administers a substantial welfare program, including comprehensive old-age assistance, unemployment insurance, workmen's compensation, and other social benefits. Efforts have been made to improve and upgrade outdated labour and hazardous-occupation laws. A division of low-income housing was created within the department of community affairs in 1971 to facilitate better planning and coordination in that area. The Mormon Church also has an extensive welfare program that provides assistance to many persons per year.

Education. More than one-half of Utah's governmental expenditure is for education. In recent years Utah has had the highest proportion of its population in public schools, the highest proportion of high school graduates, and the highest medial level of school years completed of any state in the nation.

The school districts are allowed to levy local taxes to support public education; these pay for almost one-half of educational expenses, the remainder paid by the state. General public school regulations are administered by the State Board of Education, while elected local boards exercise more specific control. The U.S. Department of the Interior maintains the Intermountain Indian School in Brigham City, a secondary school for Navajo Indians of Utah and neighbouring states.

Higher education

The largest of Utah's state universities is the University of Utah, in Salt Lake City. Founded in 1850 as the University of Deseret, it enjoys a reputation for outstanding graduate and professional schools of medicine, law, and pharmacology. Utah State University, in Logan, founded in 1888 as a land-grant school, has achieved national status in the fields of agriculture, forestry, education, engineering science, and the fine arts. Brigham Young University, in Provo, is owned and operated by the Mormon Church. The largest of Utah's universities, it has a campus that is among the most beautiful in the Western states. More than 500 Indians attend the university, the largest number in any institution of higher learning in the United States.

Weber State College (1889), in Ogden, is a four-year school with rapidly expanding programs and facilities. Technical schools are located in Salt Lake City and Provo, while Westminster College (1875), in Salt Lake City, is operated by three Protestant denominations.

CULTURAL LIFE AND INSTITUTIONS

With more than two-thirds of the population adherents of the Mormon Church, that institution has a strong influence on the state's cultural life and traditions. The church is divided into "stakes," consisting of six to ten local congregations, or "wards," of about 500 members each.

Impact of Mormonism on the cultural milieu

Each stake has a "tabernacle," or stake centre, with one or more chapels and recreational and cultural facilities. Each ward, or occasionally two or three wards together, owns a chapel with a centre for collective worship, classrooms, basketball court, and dance hall. Mormon culture emphasizes close-knit family life, widespread interest in family genealogy, no consumption of alcoholic beverages and tobacco, relatively small amount of "night life," and participation in sports and personal-development programs. Other denominations also are active in cultural areas. Particularly notable is the annual three-week-long St. Marks Arts Festival, which includes music, dance, poetry reading, drama, and other creative arts.

The large number of Indians gives a unique flavour to Utah life. About 4,000 Indian children are taken into Mormon homes during the school year, putting Indian pupils into nearly every grade school classroom. They are active in sports, public speaking, and school government, and almost every block has a family with an Indian foster child. In the summer, these children return to their families.

Sports and outdoor life. Salt Lake City has professional basketball, hockey, and baseball teams, and auto racing on the Bonneville Salt Flats has gained international importance. The Mormon Church sponsors competitive team sports involving thousands of players and one of the largest basketball, softball, and golf tournaments in the nation.

Utah's nine national forests and other undeveloped areas offer great tracts of land for hunting, fishing, camping, hiking, skiing, and snowmobiling. Among the other natural attractions are five national parks (Arches, Bryce Canyon, Capitol Reef, Zion, and Canyonlands), with two more planned for the future; six national monuments (Cedar Breaks, Dinosaur, Natural Bridges, Timpanogos Cave, Rainbow Bridge, and Hovenweep); two national recreation areas (Flaming Gorge and Glen Canyon); and the Golden Spike National Historic Site. There are 43 state parks, including the Pioneer Monument State Park at Salt Lake City.

Historical institutions and celebrations. The Utah State Historical Society has an outstanding collection of manuscripts, publications, and photographs. It publishes the *Utah Historical Quarterly*, monographs, and full-volume diaries. The Daughters of Utah Pioneers and their counterpart, the National Society of the Sons of Utah Pioneers, with 1,000 branches throughout the nation, maintain monuments, preserve old landmarks, mark historical sites, collect relics and histories, establish a library of historical matter, and secure unprinted manuscripts, photographs, maps, and data to clarify the truth about Utah pioneers. Their 38-room museum depicts pioneer implements and way of life. *The Western Historical Quarterly*, official organ of the Western History Association, is published by Utah State University.

Park City and Pioneer Village in Salt Lake City are Old West towns using the original buildings and furnishings. Every county holds a fair in the autumn, highlighted by displays and competitions, concessions, and often a rodeo.

On July 24, nearly all communities hold Pioneer Day, commemorating the entrance of the Mormon pioneers into the Salt Lake Valley. It includes parades, fireworks, rodeos, orations, and colourful reminders of Utah's early settlers.

The arts. The Division of Fine Arts is a department of state government whose purpose is to promote all branches of the fine arts and to cooperate with the federal government in these matters. It sponsors the Utah Governor's Conference on the Arts, and it allocates funds advanced to the state by federal agencies to finance cultural activities.

The buildings of Utah are rarely beautiful, and few show individuality in design. The most famous buildings are the many-spired Mormon Temple and the turtle-back Mormon Tabernacle, both in Salt Lake City. The latter was built in the 1860s without nails, holds up to 10,000 persons, and has rare acoustical qualities to enrich the sounds of its world-famous organ with 10,700 pipes. Mormon temples in St. George, Manti, Provo, Ogden, and Logan reflect architectural magnificence. Homes reflect the usual sequence of styles in American domestic architecture.

Music, dance, and theatre

Among the performing arts, music is emphasized. The Mormon Tabernacle Choir, consisting of 375 persons with trained but nonprofessional voices, presents a national weekly radio and television broadcast; gives concerts in the United States and abroad; and records with a major company. The Utah Symphony Orchestra and the Salt Lake Oratorio Society are other major ensembles. Annual tourist-oriented performances include the Mormon musicals *Promised Valley*, presented for 50 performances in July and August, and *All Faces West*, presented in Ogden in July. The major universities have symphonies and choral groups performing in winter, as well as summer festivals and concerts.

The Repertory Dance Theatre, organized in 1967, is the only professional modern-dance company in the West. The University of Utah Children's Dance Theatre has performed on the East and West coasts as well as in Utah schools. The Brigham Young University folk-dance troupes, founded in 1956, have toured the United States and most parts of the world. Salt Lake City's Ballet West is ranked among the best in the nation.

Utah gained an early start in drama with the opening of the Salt Lake Theater in 1862. A replica has been constructed on the University of Utah campus, and performances are held there regularly. The Mormon Church emphasizes folk drama in its youth organization; more than 2,000 wards produce at least one play a year, many of them written locally. These culminate biennially in a large drama festival in Salt Lake City. An annual event that is gaining national fame and reputation is the Utah Shakespearean Festival, held since 1960 in Cedar City. Brigham Young University Motion Picture Productions centres on topics of Mormon Church interest.

Communications media. The state has 54 weekly newspapers, while five dailies are published in the northern cities. The most influential are the *Salt Lake Tribune* and the *Desert News*, both published in Salt Lake City. Utah has three commercial-television channels as well as educational stations at the three universities.

Prospects. Having survived over a long history of conflict, the Mormon and non-Mormon residents of Utah live in an atmosphere of harmony and goodwill. The state government is generally trusted by the people and rates high in terms of efficiency and concern. Though balanced economically, Utah still lacks the light manufacturing industry essential to further growth. Its location in the centre of the mountain West makes it a present and potentially increasing hub of transportation, commerce, and finance. Such untapped minerals as the oil shale in eastern Utah offer other portents of growth.

Cradled by stately mountain ranges and nourished by wilderness areas and recreational parks, the state enjoys a delightful and healthy environment. Less troubled and perplexed than most states, Utah will almost certainly find its population swelled by vacationers and former residents who come back to stay.

BIBLIOGRAPHY. Available introductions to Utah and its people include the Federal Writers' Project, *Utah: A Guide to the State* (1954); DONALD W. MEINIG, "The Mormon Culture Region," *Ann. Ass. Am. Geogr.*, 55:191–220 (1965); and WALLACE STEGNER, *Mormon Country* (1942). The geological history is told in J. STEWART WILLIAMS, *Geological Studies in Utah* (1948); and WILLIAM L. STOKES and EDGAR B. HEYLMUN, *Outline of the Geologic History and Stratigraphy of Utah* (1958). JESSE D. JENNINGS, "Early Man in Utah," *Utah Historical Quarterly*, 28:3–27 (1960), takes up prehistoric Indian cultures. The best history is S. GEORGE ELLSWORTH, *Utah's Heritage* (1972). A good introduction is EVERETT L. COOLEY, *Utah: A Students' Guide to Localized History* (1968). Surveys to 1900 that also describe social and economic developments include NELS ANDERSON, *Desert Saints: The Mormon Frontier in Utah* (1966); and LEONARD J. ARRINGTON, *Great Basin Kingdom: An Economic History of the Latter-day Saints, 1830–1900* (1958, paperback 1966). General histories include MILTON R. HUNTER, *Utah in Her Western Setting*, 2nd ed. (1943); and GUSTIVE O. LARSON, *An Outline History of Utah and the Mormons*, 3rd ed. (1965). A good survey of the literature on the Mormons is WILLIAM MULDER and A.R. MORTENSEN (eds.), *Among the Mormons: Historic Accounts by Contemporary Observers* (1958). The most complete history is BRIGHAM H. ROBERTS, *A Comprehensive History of the Church of Jesus Christ of Latter-day Saints: Century I*, 6 vol. (1930). One-volume histories include RAY B. WEST, JR., *Kingdom of the Saints: The Story of Brigham Young and the Mormons* (1957); and THOMAS F. O'DEA, *The Mormons* (1957), the latter by a non-Mormon. A monograph on the conflict between Mormons and non-Mormons is GUSTIVE O. LARSON, *The "Americanization" of Utah for Statehood* (1971). Utah folklore is given charming treatment in AUSTIN and ALTA FIFE, *Saints of Sage and Saddle: Folklore Among the Mormons* (1956). Utah economic activity is described in MERIN B. BRINKERHOFF and PHILLIP R. KUNZ, *Utah in Numbers: Comparisons, Trends, and Descriptions* (1969), and in the publications of the Bureau of Economic and Business Research of the University of Utah. Utah politics is treated in the UTAH FOUNDATION, *State and Local Government in Utah* (annual); FRANK H. JONAS (ed.), *Politics in the American West* (1969); and JEDON EMENHISER, *Rocky Mountain Urban Politics* (1971). Utah culture and its history is treated in JAMES L. HASELTINE, *100 Years of Utah Painting* (1966); UTAH STATE INSTITUTE OF FINE ARTS, *Report on the Fine Arts in Utah* (1968); and in articles in the *Utah Historical Quarterly*.

(L.J.A.)